Food & Beverage Market Place

Volume 3

2021
Twentieth Edition

Food & Beverage Market Place

Volume 3

Brokers

Importers & Exporters

Transportation Firms

Warehouse Companies

Wholesalers & Distributors

ALL BRAND INDEX

ALL COMPANY INDEX

Grey House Publishing

AMENIA, NY 12501

PRESIDENT: Richard Gottlieb
PUBLISHER: Leslie Mackenzie
EDITORIAL DIRECTOR: Laura Mars

PRODUCTION MANAGER: Kristen Hayes
RESEARCH ASSISTANTS: Olivia Parsonson; Sarah Reside
COMPOSITION: David Garoogian

MARKETING DIRECTOR: Jessica Moody

Grey House Publishing, Inc.
4919 Route 22
Amenia, NY 12501
518.789.8700
FAX 845.373.6390
www.greyhouse.com
e-mail: books@greyhouse.com

While every effort has been made to ensure the reliability of the information presented in this publication, Grey House Publishing neither guarantees the accuracy of the data contained herein nor assumes any responsibility for errors, omissions or discrepancies. Grey House accepts no payment for listing; inclusion in the publication of any organization, agency, institution, publication, service or individual does not imply endorsement of the editors or publisher.

Errors brought to the attention of the publisher and verified to the satisfaction of the publisher will be corrected in future editions.

Except by express prior written permission of the Copyright Proprietor no part of this work may be copied by any means of publication or communication now known or developed hereafter including, but not limited to, use in any directory or compilation or other print publication, in any information storage and retrieval system, in any other electronic device, or in any visual or audio-visual device or product.

This publication is an original and creative work, copyrighted by Grey House Publishing, Inc. and is fully protected by all applicable copyright laws, as well as by laws covering misappropriation, trade secrets and unfair competition.

Grey House has added value to the underlying factual material through one or more of the following efforts: unique and original selection; expression; arrangement; coordination; and classification.

Grey House Publishing, Inc. will defend its rights in this publication.

Copyright © 2020 Grey House Publishing, Inc.
All rights reserved
First edition published 2001
Twentieth edition published 2020
Printed in Canada

Food & beverage market place. — 20th ed. (2021) —
   3 v. ; 27.5 cm. Annual
  Includes index.
  ISSN: 1554-6334

1. Food industry and trade—United States—Directories. 2. Food industry and trade—Canada—Directories. 3. Beverage industry—United States—Directories. 4. Beverage industry—Canada—Directories. I. Grey House Publishing, Inc. II. Title: Food & beverage market place.

HD9003.T48
338-dc21

3-Volume Set   ISBN: 978-1-64265-464-6
Volume 1   ISBN: 978-1-64265-465-3
Volume 2   ISBN: 978-1-64265-466-0
Volume 3   **ISBN: 978-1-64265-467-7**

Table of Contents

VOLUME 1

Introduction
*Summary of Best Practices for Retail Food Stores, Restaurants, and
    Food Pick-Up/Delivery Services During the COVID-19 Pandemic*
The Impact of COVID-19 on Shopping Behavior

Food & Beverage Manufacturers User Guide
Food & Beverage Product Category List
Food & Beverage Product Categories
Food & Beverage Manufacturer Profiles
Brand Name Index
Ethnic Food Index
Geographic Index
Parent Company Index

VOLUME 2

Introduction
Equipment, Supplies & Services User Guide
Equipment, Supplies & Services Product Category List
Equipment, Supplies & Services Product Categories
Equipment, Supplies & Services Company Profiles
Brand Name Index
Geographic Index

VOLUME 3

Introduction	vii
Broker Companies User Guide	2
Broker Company Profiles	5
Broker Market Index	97
Brokered Product Index	105
Importers/Exporters User Guide	118
Importers/Exporters Company Profiles	121
Export Region Index	681
Import Region Index	727
Transportation Firms User Guide	738
Transportation Firm Profiles	741
Transportation Region Index	789
Transportation Type Index	793
Warehouse Companies User Guide	794
Warehouse Company Profiles	797
Warehouse Region Index	875
Warehouse Type and Service Index	879
Wholesalers/Distributors User Guide	884
Wholesalers/Distributors Company Profiles	887
Wholesale Product Type Index	1231
ALL BRANDS INDEX	1269
ALL COMPANIES INDEX	1349

Introduction

This 2021 edition of *Food & Beverage Market Place* represents the largest, most comprehensive resource of food and beverage manufacturers and service suppliers on the market today. These three volumes include over 45,000 company profiles that address all sectors of the industry—finished goods and ingredients manufacturers, equipment manufacturers, and third-party logistics providers, including transportation, warehousing, wholesalers, brokers, importers and exporters.

While the food and beverage industry generally continues to grow, the reality of the COVID-19 pandemic has presented many challenges to this truly essential industry. At the time of this writing, out of home consumption, with its high margin of profit, has been reduced nearly to a standstill for several months. Mandated quarantines have disrupted supply chains. Consumers are shifing to digital shopping and home delivery. The industry is redefining its work force and finding new ways to connect with customers.

One segment has found a silver lining in the cloud of COVID-19, and that is meal-kit companies. As consumers adapt to cooking and eating at home, meal kits, delivered to your door with conveniently packaged food and easy-to-follow recipes, have a huge appeal. Time will tell if they can sustain and build on the momentum created by the current quarantine.

Another interesting consequence of the current environment is the kinds of foods that people are eating. While certain long-standing food trends are well entrenched in our society, especially now, including natural and organic food, like those with antioxidants for healthy aging, and foods with good bacteria that promote digestive health, there is a significant uptick in online searches for cinammon roll and hot cross buns recipes, and a shortage of yeast on supermarket shelves. The growth in plant-based food is significant and, experts say, a trend that is likely to continue. While that would be a good thing, hopefully another trend—quarantine snacking—is temporary, as people start to spend less time around the house. In addition, following this Introduction in Volume 1 are two items that offer more information related to COVID-19 and the food and beverage industry: *Best Practices for Retail Food Stores, Restaurants & Food Pick Up and Delivery Services;* and *The Impact of COVID-19 on Shopping Behavior.*

Other industry trends are likely to continue, as consumers focus on foods that encourage sustainability, foods that are convenient and healthy, foods that are processed in secure and safe environments, and foods with complex world flavors.

As food and beverage consumers' needs evolve, *Food & Beverage Market Place* continues to keep pace. The research for this edition focused on ingredient, nutrition and health food manufacturers. You'll find packaging that is mindful of the environment, and processing systems that are safe and secure. Whatever slice of the market you cater to, you will find your buyers, sellers, and users in this comprehensive, three-volume reference tool containing the complete coverage our subscribers have come to expect. Our extensive indexing makes quick work of locating exactly the company, product or service you are looking for.

Data Statistics

Each of the eight chapters in *Food & Beverage Market Place* reflects a massive update effort. This 2021 edition includes hundreds of new company profiles and thousands of updates throughout the three volumes. You will find 83,214 key executives, 22,668 web sites, and 15,869 e-mails. The volumes break down as follows:

Volume 1   Food, Beverage & Ingredient Manufacturers - 14,086

Volume 2   Equipment, Supply & Service Providers - 13,465

Volume 3   Third Party Logistics
                    Brokers - 1,287
                    Importers & Exporters - 8,818
                    Transportation Firms - 707
                    Warehouse Companies - 1,044
                    Wholesalers & Distributors - 5,904

Introduction

Arrangement

The product category sections for both food and beverage products in Volume 1 and equipment and supplies in Volume 2 begin with Product Category Lists. These include over 6,000 alphabetical terms for everything from Abalone to Zinc Citrate, from Adhesive Tapes to Zipper Application Systems. Use the detailed cross-references to find the full entry in the Product Category sections that immediately follow. Here you will find up to three levels of detail, for example—*Fish & Seafood: Fish: Abalone* or *Ingredients, Flavors & Additives: Vitamins & Supplements: Zinc Citrate*—with the name, location, phone number and packaging format of companies who manufacturer/process the product you are looking for. Organic and Gluten-Free categories make it easy to locate those manufacturers who focus on these food types.

In addition to company profiles, this edition has 17 indexes, 15 chapter-specific, arranged by geographic region, product or company type, and two—All Brands and All Companies—that comprise all three volumes. See the Table of Contents for a complete list of specific indexes. Plus, chapters include User Guides that help you navigate chapter-specific data.

We are confident that this reference is the foremost research tool in the food and beverage industry. It will prove invaluable to manufacturers, buyers, specifiers, market researchers, consultants, and anyone working in food and beverage—one of the largest industries in the country.

Praise for previous editions:

> *"...This set can be used to find basic information or to track trends in a dynamic industry.... Recommended for large public or academic libraries."*

> *"...Each volume contains helpful user guides and key that describes the field of data that appear in that chapter.... This publication is essential for researchers in the food industry, and large academic and public libraries."*

—American Reference Books Annual

Online Database & Mailing Lists

Food & Beverage Market Place is also available for subscription on https://gold.greyhouse.com for even faster, easier access to this wealth of information. Subscribers can search by product category, state, sales volume, employee size, personnel name, title and much more. Plus, users can print out prospect sheets or download data into their own spreadsheet or database. This database is a must for anyone marketing a product or service to this vast industry. Visit the site, or call 800-562-2139 for a free trial.

BROKERS

User Guide
Company Profiles
Broker Market Index
Brokered Product Index

Broker Companies User Guide

The **Broker Chapter** of *Food & Beverage Market Place* includes companies that broker food and merchandise to various markets in the food and beverage industry. The descriptive listings are organized alphabetically. Following the A-Z Broker listings are two indexes: **Broker Market** that includes market terms, such as Super Market Chains and Wholesale Distributors, and **Brokered Product** that includes product terms such as Frozen Food, Dairy/Deli, and Private Label. These Indexes refer to listing numbers, not page numbers.

Below is a sample listing illustrating the kind of information that is or might be included in a Broker listing. Each numbered item of information is described in the Broker User Key on the following page.

---

1 → 243968

2 → **(HQ) L&M Company**

3 → 1342 Hartford Avenue

Johnstown, RI 02919-7193

4 → 068-923-0700

5 → 068-923-0701

6 → 800-923-0702

7 → info@lmco.com

8 → www.lmco.com

9 → Broker of groceries, frozen foods, seafood, general merchandise, dairy products and private label items.

10 → President: David Byron
CFO: Dana Williams
COO: William Thompson
Vice President: Tiffany Smith
Marketing: James Hicks
Sales: Peter Reynolds

11 → *Estimated Sales*: $1-5 Million

12 → *Number Employees*: 25

13 → *Company is also listed in the following section(s):* Manufacturer

14 → *Markets Served:* Super Market Chains, Wholesale Distributors

15 → *Primary Brands Brokered include:* Spring Street, Winter Sun, Phillips Ware

16 → *Brokered Products include*: Dairy/Deli, Frozen Food, Groceries, Private Label

Broker Companies User Key

1 → **Record Number:** Entries are listed alphabetically within each category and numbered sequentially. The entry number, rather than the page number, is used in the indexes to refer to listings.

2 → **Company Name:** Formal name of company. HQ indicates headquarter location. If names are completely capitalized, the listing will appear at the beginning of the alphabetized section.

3 → **Address:** Location or permanent address of the company. If the mailing address differs from the street address, it will appear second.

4 → **Phone Number:** The listed phone number is usually for the main office, but may also be for the sales, marketing, or public relations office as provided.

5 → **Fax Number:** This is listed when provided by the company.

6 → **Toll-Free Number:** This is listed when provided by the company.

7 → **E-Mail:** This is listed when provided, and is generally the main office e-mail.

8 → **Web Site:** This is listed when provided by the company and is also referred to as an URL address. These web sites are accessed through the Internet by typing http:// before the URL address.

9 → **Description**: This paragraph contains a brief description of the products or services that are brokered, sometimes including markets served.

10 → **Key Personnel:** Names and titles of company executives.

11 → **Estimated Sales:** This is listed when provided by the company.

12 → **Number of Employees:** Total number of employees within the company.

13 → Indicates in what other section in *Food & Beverage Market Place* this company is listed: Volume 1: Manufacturers. Volume 2: Equipment, Supplies & Services; Transportation; Warehouse; Wholesalers/Distributors. Volume 3: Brokers; Importers/Exporters.

14 → **Markets Served:** This further defines the company as serving one or more markers, such as Super Market Chains, Wholesale Distributors, Food Service Operators, etc. Companies are indexed by market.

15 → **Primary Brands Brokered include:** A list of brand names that the company brokers.

16 → **Brokered Products include**: This describes the type of product that the broker handles, such as alcoholic beverages, frozen foods, exports, ingredients, etc. Companies are indexed by product.

Food Brokers / A-Z

40000 1000 Islands River Rat Cheese
242 James St
Clayton, NY 13624-1010   315-686-2480
     Fax: 315-686-4701   800-752-1341
                support@riverratcheese.net
                www.riverratcheese.net
Distributor: NYS Cheese, Adirondack Sausage
President: Mary Scudera
1000islandsriverratcheese@gmail.com
Estimated Sales: $2,500,000
Number Employees: 10-19
Type of Packaging: Consumer, Food Service, Private Label, Bulk
Primary Brands Brokered include: River Rat Cheese
Brokered Products include:
   Confectionery, Dairy/Deli, Ingredients, Meat Products, Cheese Spreads, Maple Syrup

40001 3-D Marketing & Sales
380 Union St # 120
West Springfield, MA 01089-4123   413-731-8801
     Fax: 413-731-0142 hi3dmkt@aol.com
Broker of deli items, groceries, bakery, ingredients, meats, spices, etc. Also sell imported cheese, olives, and pasta
Owner: Thomas DE Luca
hi3dmkt@aol.com
CEO: R DeLuca
Marketing Director: J DeLuca
Estimated Sales: $2.5-5 Million
Number Employees: 1-4
Type of Packaging: Consumer, Food Service, Bulk
Markets Served:
   Food Manufacturers & Processors, Super Market Chains, Wholesale Distributors, Food Service Operators
Primary Brands Brokered include: Belgioioso; Gaspar's; Mosey/S.M.G.; Liguria; Hickory Farms; Castella Imports
Brokered Products include:
   Dairy/Deli, Groceries, Imports, Ingredients, Meat, Meat Products, Private Label, Spices, Baked Goods, Greek, Portuguese Foods

40002 A & D Sales
145 E Colt Dr
Fayetteville, AR 72703-2847   479-521-8665
                     Fax: 479-521-0841
President: Jim Stockland
jim@adchicken.com
Treasurer: Pam Stockland
Estimated Sales: $5-10 Million
Number Employees: 5-9

40003 A G Brown & Son
3500 Kempt Road
Halifax, NS B3K 4X8
Canada   902-453-0350
     Fax: 902-454-4528 agbrown@agbrown.ca
Import broker of confectionery products, general merchandise, groceries, meat products and private label items
VP: James Brown
Estimated Sales: $5.7 Million
Number Employees: 18
Type of Packaging: Consumer
Markets Served:
   Food Manufacturers & Processors, Super Market Chains, Wholesale Distributors, Food Service Operators
Primary Brands Brokered include: Avon; Graves; Snyder's; Arctic Gardens; Pastene; Ocean Fisheries
Brokered Products include:
   Confectionery, Dairy/Deli, Exports, Frozen Food, General Merchandise, Groceries, Health Food, Imports, Meat Products, Private Label, Produce, Seafood

40004 A Gazerro & Assoc
1343 Hartford Ave # 4
Suite 24
Johnston, RI 02919-7145   401-751-8850
     Fax: 401-751-8887 agazerro@aol.com
Broker of confectionery products and general merchandise
Owner/President: Andrew Gazerro
agazerro@aol.com
Marketing: Ken Murray
Sales: Jane Lucini
Estimated Sales: $8 Million
Number Employees: 1-4
Brokered Products include:
   Confectionery, General Merchandise

40005 A Labar Seafood Co
540 W Frontage Rd # 2175
Northfield, IL 60093-1224   847-441-8895
                     Fax: 847-441-8894
Owner: Anthony LA Barbera
Estimated Sales: $3-5 Million
Number Employees: 1-4

40006 A M Source Inc
261 Narragansett Park Dr
Rumford, RI 02916-1043   401-431-4080
     Fax: 401-431-0606 800-556-6254
                info@ajksales.com
Manufacturers' representative for disposable paper and plastic food service products and packaging; serving all markets
President: Arthur Kaufman
spritchard@amsourcellc.com
Controller: H John Madden
VP: Allan Kaufman
Marketing Sales Manager: Kenneth McAuliffe
Sales Exec: Scott Prichard
Estimated Sales: $20-50 Million
Number Employees: 50-99
Type of Packaging: Food Service
Markets Served:
   Super Market Chains, Wholesale Distributors, Food Service Operators
Brokered Products include:
   General Merchandise, Disposable Plastic & Paper Products

40007 A Thomas Farris & Son Inc
1310 Flagler Dr
Mamaroneck, NY 10543-4603   914-698-4705
     Fax: 914-698-2096 800-327-7471
                atfarris@aol.com
Broker of private label items, cooking sprays, household cleaners, plastic wrap and bags, etc.
President: John Farris
jfarrisjr@yahoo.com
Treasurer: Martha Farris
Estimated Sales: $1.7 Million
Number Employees: 1-4
Markets Served:
   Super Market Chains, Wholesale Distributors, Food Service Operators
Brokered Products include:
   Dairy/Deli, General Merchandise, Private Label, Cooking Sprays, Pastas, Beans, etc.

40008 A W Sisk & Son
3601 Choptank Rd
P.O. Box 70
Preston, MD 21655   410-673-7111
     Fax: 410-673-7360 sales@awsisk.com
                www.awsisk.com
Broker of general merchandise and private label items including milk and dairy related products, bread, rolls, bagels and sweet good, and vegetables.
Chief Executive Officer: Al Turner
alturn@awsisk.com
Canned Food Sales: Leon Kanner
Protein Sales: Brenan Roser
Administrative Assistant: Melissa Corbin
Year Founded: 1891
Estimated Sales: $30-40 Million
Number Employees: 5-9
Square Footage: 100000
Type of Packaging: Consumer, Food Service, Private Label
Markets Served:
   Food Manufacturers & Processors, Super Market Chains, Wholesale Distributors, Food Service Operators
Primary Brands Brokered include: Pine Cone; Pride of the Farm; Red Glo; Little Darling
Brokered Products include:
   Confectionery, Dairy/Deli, General Merchandise, Private Label

40009 A&D Sales Associates
550 Smithtown Byp
Suite: 204
Smithtown, NY 11787-5013   631-979-4000
     Fax: 631-979-4053 dbye@adsalesinc.com
Broker of groceries, produce, meat, frozen foods, seafood, general merchandise, dairy products and private label items.
President: Dave Bye
VP: Al Davis
Contact: David Bye
dbye@adsalesinc.com
Estimated Sales: Less than $20 Million
Number Employees: 4
Markets Served:
   Super Market Chains, Wholesale Distributors
Primary Brands Brokered include: A. Sturm & Sons; Aberfoyle Springs; Caruthers; Kleen Baite Labs; Senvaas Labs
Brokered Products include:
   Dairy/Deli, Frozen Food, General Merchandise, Groceries, Meat, Private Label, Produce, Seafood

40010 A.J. Seibert Company
200 York St
Louisville, KY 40203   502-582-1654
     Fax: 502-581-0469 bk@ajseibert.com
Broker of confectionery and dairy/deli products, groceries, frozen foods, meat and meat products, produce, etc.
President: M Kupper, Jr
CEO: Milton R Kupper Jr
Sales Manager: J Kallop
Contact: Aj Company
bob_kupper@yahoo.com
Branch Manager: J Mazzoni
Estimated Sales: $10-20 Million
Number Employees: 50-99
Parent Co: A.J. Seibert Company
Markets Served:
   Food Manufacturers & Processors, Super Market Chains, Wholesale Distributors, Food Service Operators
Brokered Products include:
   Confectionery, Dairy/Deli, Frozen Food, General Merchandise, Groceries, Meat, Meat Products, Private Label, Produce, Seafood, Spices

40011 A.N. Smith & Company
300 Chestnut Avenue
Suite 100A
Baltimore, MD 21211-2747   410-467-0696
     Fax: 410-467-9552 www.ansmithcompany.com
Broker of groceries and industrial ingredients including sugar, corn sweeteners, rice, tomato paste and pasta
President: Neale Smith
Treasurer: J Smith
Sales: Carol Rothman
Sales: Susan Ladner
Estimated Sales: $2.5-5 Million
Number Employees: 1-4
Square Footage: 1600
Type of Packaging: Bulk
Markets Served:
   Food Manufacturers & Processors

40012 A.R. Pellegrini & Associates
500 N Commercial St # 504
Manchester, NH 03101-1151   603-627-1600
                     Fax: 603-627-2920
Importer of Italy wines
President: Michael Pellegrini
Customer Service: Connie Miville
Administrative Director: Laurene Pellegrini
Estimated Sales: $2.5-5 Million
Number Employees: 1-4
Markets Served:
   Food Manufacturers & Processors, Super Market Chains, Wholesale Distributors, Food Service Operators
Primary Brands Brokered include: Cantina di Montefiascone: Secco (dry), Amabile (semi-Sweet), Rufus; Podere Brizio: Brunello di Montalcino, Leonensis Sant'Antimo
Brokered Products include:
   Alcoholic Beverages, Imports, Wines

40013 ABC Corp
47 Village Ct
Hazlet, NJ 07730-1535   732-888-1600
     Fax: 732-888-7520 www.google.de
Export broker of food packaging machinery worldwide
Owner: F Barakat
headoffice@abccorp.biz
Manager: Gail Sisk
Estimated Sales: $10-20 Million
Number Employees: 20-49
Markets Served:
   Food Manufacturers & Processors

Food Brokers / A-Z

40014 ABC Enterprises
66 Bells Lake Dr
Turnersville, NJ 08012　　　856-227-5555
　　　　　　　　　　Fax: 856-227-4422
Broker of poultry including chicken and turkey
President: A Messick
Contact: Alex Messick
amessick@gmail.com
Estimated Sales: $1-2.5 Million
Number Employees: 1-4
Markets Served:
　Food Manufacturers & Processors, Super Market Chains, Wholesale Distributors, Food Service Operators
Brokered Products include:
　Meat, Poultry: Chicken & Turkey

40015 ACB
3030 Bridgeway
Sausalito, CA 94965-2810　　　415-435-9768
　　　　　　　　　　Fax: 415-435-1309
Broker of confectionary products and specialty foods
President: Richard Watson
Vice President: Peter Ryce
Primary Brands Brokered include: Jason & Sons; East India Tea & Coffee; Bascom Maple Products; Venice International Foods

40016 AMT Sales & Marketing
Bloomington, IL　　　309-706-8818
　　　　　　　　　　Fax: 813-762-1378
tom@amtsalesandmarketing.net
www.amtsalesandmarketing.net
A natural/specialty food sales and marketing company.
Owner: Tom Miller
Estimated Sales: $1.9 Million
Number Employees: 12
Square Footage: 1500
Markets Served:
　Super Market Chains, Wholesale Distributors
Primary Brands Brokered include: Beaverton Foods; Hormel; Mezzetta; Fantastic Foods; Specialty Foods; Annes; Bri-Al; Bruce Foods; Twining Tea
Brokered Products include:
　Confectionery, General Merchandise, Groceries, Imports, Produce, Spices, Specialty Foods

40017 ATI
3415 S Sepulveda Blvd
Suite 610
Los Angeles, CA 90034-6060　　　310-397-9797
　　　Fax: 310-445-1411 ati@american-trading.com
　　　　　　　　　　www.american-trading.com
California-based export trading company servicing the needs of food and beverage importers worldwide in four major categories: name-brand products, generic products, private label products, and raw ingredients. All sizes and packagingstyles are available. We work closely with the US Department of Agriculture, US Department of Commerce, the California Trade and Development Agency
President/CEO: Seth Wilen
CFO: Dan Wilen
Vice President: Matthew Good
Marketing Director: Nova Gatewood
Sales Director: Mike Davis
Estimated Sales: $10-20 Million
Number Employees: 5-9
Number of Brands: 500
Number of Products: 1000
Square Footage: 10000
Type of Packaging: Consumer, Food Service, Private Label, Bulk
Markets Served:
　Food Manufacturers & Processors, Super Market Chains, Wholesale Distributors, Food Service Operators
Primary Brands Brokered include: Freshly Brand; Maxim Brand; Granja Flor Brand; Ybarra Brand; Bokumjari Brand; Jessy Brand; Mirave Brand; Paradise Brand
Brokered Products include:
　Alcoholic Beverages, Confectionery, Dairy/Deli, Exports, Frozen Food, General Merchandise, Groceries, Health Food, Imports, Ingredients, Meat, Meat Products, Private Label, Produce, Seafood, Spices

40018 Abarbanel Wine Company
247 Merrick Road
Suite 101
Lynbrook, NY 11563-2641　　　516-374-2240
　　　Fax: 516-374-2565　888-691-9463
mail@kosher-wine.com www.kosher-wine.com
Importer of kosher wines in rose, blush, dry, white, and red including Chardonnay, Merlot, Cabernet Sauvignon
President: Howard Abarbanel
Type of Packaging: Consumer
Primary Brands Brokered include: Layla Vineyards, Abarbanel Bordeaux portfolio, Byblos Semi-Dry Cabernet
Brokered Products include:
　Alcoholic Beverages, Wines

40019 Abramson & Di BenedettoMktng
19 Brigham St
Marlborough, MA 01752-3182　　　508-787-1008
　　　Fax: 508-787-1099　800-411-4388
dave@abrdib.com www.abrdib.com
Broker of food service equipment and supplies
Director/President/Principal: Mark DiBenedetto
Sales: David R. Abramson
d.abramson@abrdib.com
Estimated Sales: $1-3 Million
Number Employees: 1-4
Square Footage: 8000
Type of Packaging: Food Service
Markets Served:
　Wholesale Distributors
Brokered Products include:
　General Merchandise, Equipment & Supplies

40020 Access Partners
1250 Mountain View Circle
Azusa, CA 91702　　　626-815-4200
　　　Fax: 626-815-4300 www.accesspartners.biz
Broker of general merchandise, groceries, private label/generic items and seafood
President: John Tush
Chairman: Anthony Orfila
VP: Glenn Orfila
Secretary/Treasurer: R Colato
Sales Manager: Vince McCowin
Contact: Chrystie Aban
caban@accesspartners.biz
Director Operations: Todd Haven
Office Manager: Mary Hearn
Customer Service: Tiffany Noonan
Estimated Sales: $10-20 Million
Number Employees: 20
Square Footage: 4000
Markets Served:
　Food Manufacturers & Processors, Super Market Chains, Food Service Operators
Primary Brands Brokered include: Plastics, Inc.; Alcan Foil Products; Borden Chemical; Chicopee; National Checking; Colgate-Palmolive Company
Brokered Products include:
　General Merchandise, Groceries, Private Label, Seafood, Containers, Chef Hats, Bags, etc.

40021 Acclaim Marketing & Sales
549 Mercury Ln # A
Brea, CA 92821-4805　　　714-256-9388
　　　Fax: 714-256-9387 www.acclaimmtkg.com
Broker of dairy/deli products, frozen foods, groceries and private label items
President: Chris Leahy
cleahy@acclaimmtkg.com
Estimated Sales: $10-20 Million
Number Employees: 10-19
Markets Served:
　Super Market Chains, Wholesale Distributors
Primary Brands Brokered include: Springfield; Corporate Brand
Brokered Products include:
　Dairy/Deli, Frozen Food, Groceries, Private Label

40022 Acme Farms + Kitchen
3926 Irongate Road
Unit D
Bellingham, WA 98226
　　　　　　　　　　360-325-1903
　　　　　　　　　　800-542-8309
info@acmefarmsandkitchen.com
www.acmefarmsandkitchen.com
A local delivery service that works in partnership with local farmers, fishers, ranchers and produces to create 'Locavore Boxes' containing fresh foods, recipes and meal plans.
Contact: Maggie Stafford
maggie@acmefarmsandkitchen.com
Estimated Sales: 100 Thousand
Number Employees: 1-4
Type of Packaging: Consumer

40023 Acorn Sales Company
PO Box 491
Madison, CT 06443-0491　　　203-245-1737
　　　　　　　　　　Fax: 203-458-8877
Import broker of deli products, general merchandise, groceries, private label items and spices
President: G DeVeau
VP: P DeVeau
Number Employees: 1-4
Markets Served:
　Food Manufacturers & Processors, Super Market Chains, Wholesale Distributors, Food Service Operators
Brokered Products include:
　Dairy/Deli, General Merchandise, Groceries, Imports, Private Label, Produce, Spices

40024 Acosta Sales & Marketing Company
6600 Corporate Center Pkwy
Jacksonville, FL 32216　　　904-281-9800
　　　　　Fax: 904-281-9966 www.acosta.com
Dairy/deli products, frozen foods, general merchandise and produce.
CEO: Darian Pickett
Interim CFO: Matt Laurie
COO, Sales, North America: Ashley Taylor
COO, Marketing, Foodservice & Europe: Steve Kremser
Year Founded: 1927
Estimated Sales: $1.85 Billion
Number Employees: 37,000
Markets Served:
　Food Manufacturers & Processors, Super Market Chains, Wholesale Distributors, Food Service Operators
Primary Brands Brokered include: Bayer Healthcare; ConAgra Foods; Mortons; Sara Lee; Welch's
Brokered Products include:
　Dairy/Deli, Frozen Food, General Merchandise, Groceries, Produce

40025 Action Marketing
11503 Jones Maltsberger Rd Ste 180
San Antonio, TX 78216　　　210-493-3722
　　　Fax: 210-493-3723 actionm85@aol.com
Broker of confectionary and dairy/deli products, frozen and health foods, general merchandise, private label items, ingredients, groceries, seafood, spices, meat and meat products, etc.
Owner/President: Ray Bradley
VP: Janie Bradley
Account Executive: Rod Bradley
Estimated Sales: $1.3 Million
Number Employees: 10
Square Footage: 4800
Markets Served:
　Super Market Chains, Wholesale Distributors, Food Service Operators
Primary Brands Brokered include: North American Salt (Culligan & Carey); Foreign Candy Company; Scott LQ Gold (Touch Of Scent)
Brokered Products include:
　Confectionery, Dairy/Deli, Frozen Food, General Merchandise, Groceries, Health Food, Ingredients, Meat, Meat Products, Private Label, Seafood, Spices

40026 Action Marketing Associates
875 S Main St
Plymouth, MI 48170-2046　　　734-454-2500
　　　　　　　　　　Fax: 734-454-1300
Broker of confectionary and dairy/deli items, frozen and health foods, juices, bagged snacks, sandwiches, etc.; serving supermarket chains and wholesalers/distributors
Owner: Ed Ura
Manager: Helen De Jager
Estimated Sales: $300,000-500,000
Number Employees: 1-4
Square Footage: 17600
Markets Served:
　Super Market Chains, Wholesale Distributors
Primary Brands Brokered include: Adams U.S.A.; Little Charlies Convenience Foods; Konica

U.S.A.; Perrier Group; Smiley's Foods; Haas Baking Co.
Brokered Products include:
Confectionery, Dairy/Deli, Frozen Food, General Merchandise, Groceries, Health Food, Private Label, Juice, Bagged Snacks, Sandwiches

40027 Action Marketing Of So Ca
1550 S Anaheim Blvd # C
Anaheim, CA 92805-6218   714-535-2530
Fax: 714-491-0959
Broker of confectionery products and groceries
Partner: Bari Maxwell
maxwellb@actionsc.biz
Estimated Sales: $1-2.5 Million
Number Employees: 5-9
Markets Served:
Super Market Chains, Wholesale Distributors
Primary Brands Brokered include: Go-Lightly; Holiday Candy; Smart Ice; Impact Confections; Comfort Foods; Carrozi N.A.
Brokered Products include:
Confectionery, Groceries

40028 Action Marketing Services
3919 Southern Ave
Shreveport, LA 71106-1035   318-686-4726
Fax: 318-686-5126   bobli@aol.com
www.actfoods.com
Broker of dairy/deli products, frozen foods, groceries, meat and seafood. Serving the area of northern Louisiana
Owner/President: Robert Lindsay
Account Executive: Alice O'Neal
Estimated Sales: $3-5 Million
Number Employees: 3
Square Footage: 14400
Type of Packaging: Food Service
Markets Served:
Food Service Operators
Brokered Products include:
Confectionery, Dairy/Deli, Frozen Food, General Merchandise, Groceries, Ingredients, Meat

40029 Adtek Sales
35 Mohawk Rd
Raynham, MA 02767-5266   508-822-5822
Fax: 508-822-9673
Manufacturers' representative for flexible packaging
President: Chip Houle
Number Employees: 100-249
Markets Served:
Food Manufacturers & Processors
Brokered Products include:
General Merchandise, Flexible Packaging

40030 Advance Marketing
435 E Main Street
Suite C-2
Greenwood, IN 46143-1379   317-889-1501
Fax: 317-889-1742
Broker of dairy/deli products, frozen foods, meat and meat products and seafood
President: Russell J Dias
CEO: Randall J Dias
VP: Tod A Dias
Estimated Sales: $300,000-500,000
Number Employees: 10
Markets Served:
Super Market Chains, Wholesale Distributors
Brokered Products include:
Dairy/Deli, Meat, Meat Products, Seafood, Bakery

40031 Advance Sales & Marketing, Inc
1801 Royal Lane
Suite 1012
Dallas, TX 75229-3179   972-620-7212
Fax: 214-722-2532   cgee@advancesales.com
www.advancesales.com
Broker of dairy/deli products, frozen foods, groceries, meat and meat products, and seafood
President: Randy Gee
Marketing: Carla Gee
Contact: Harold Baldwin
hbaldwin@advancesales.com
Estimated Sales: $1-10 Million
Number Employees: 25
Type of Packaging: Food Service
Markets Served:
Food Manufacturers & Processors, Wholesale Distributors, Food Service Operators
Brokered Products include:
Dairy/Deli, Frozen Food, Groceries, Ingredients, Meat, Meat Products, Seafood, Beverages

40032 Advantage Gourmet Importers
480 Main Ave
Wallington, NJ 07057   973-777-0007
Fax: 973-591-5556   888-676-3663
crfagi@gmail.com
www.advantagegourmetimporters.com
Broker, importer and wholesaler/distributor of chestnut products including organic chestnut flour and Italian specialty foods
Owner: Nicholas Puzino
Vice President: Emile Boustani
Purchasing: V Lampariello
Estimated Sales: $2.5-5 Million
Number Employees: 1-4
Square Footage: 800
Brokered Products include:
Imports, Italian Foods & Chestnut Products

40033 Advantage Solutions
18100 Von Karman Ave
Suite 1000
Irvine, CA 92612   949-797-2900
www.advantagesolutions.net
National sales & marketing agency and foodservice brokerage with 165 offices in the United States and Canada.
CEO: Tanya Domier
tanya.domier@asmnet.com
CFO/COO: Brian Stevens
President & Chief Commercial Officer: Jill Griffin
President, Sales: Lisa Klauser
Year Founded: 1987
Estimated Sales: Over $1 Billion
Number Employees: 10000+
Markets Served:
Food Manufacturers & Processors, Super Market Chains, Wholesale Distributors, Food Service Operators
Primary Brands Brokered include: Staffers; French's Mustard; Sara Lee; Lysol; Lucky Leaf; Durkee Spices
Brokered Products include:
Dairy/Deli, Frozen Food, General Merchandise, Groceries, Produce

40034 Advantage Webco Hawaii
2840 Mokumoa St
Honolulu, HI 96819-4499   808-839-4551
Fax: 808-834-3350   www.awdhi.com
Broker of confectionery, dairy/deli products, frozen and health food, general merchandise, groceries, meat, meat products, private label items, seafood and spices
President: Greg Gomes
CEO: Jerel Reaves
djrellevant@gmail.com
Vice President: Tim Doyle
VP: Stan Markle
Estimated Sales: $20-50 Million
Number Employees: 100-249
Square Footage: 72000
Markets Served:
Food Manufacturers & Processors, Super Market Chains, Wholesale Distributors, Food Service Operators
Primary Brands Brokered include: Georgia Pacific; Campbell; M&M/Mars; Pillsbury
Brokered Products include:
Confectionery, Dairy/Deli, Frozen Food, General Merchandise, Groceries, Health Food, Meat, Meat Products, Private Label, Seafood, Spices

40035 Advertising Concepts
6 Santa Cruz
Rancho Sta Marg, CA 92688-2544   949-589-7000
Fax: 949-589-7500   www.adtouch.com
Manufacturers' representative for custom printed promotional products
Partner: Elizabeth Finn
Partner: Donald Thomas
Account Executive: Alyson Vanemburgh
Estimated Sales: Less Than $500,000
Number Employees: 1-4
Brokered Products include:
General Merchandise, Promotional Products

40036 Agri-Dairy Products
3020 Westchester Ave
Purchase, NY 10577   914-697-9580
Fax: 914-697-9586
customerservice@agridairy.com
www.agridairy.com
Dairy and food ingredients including whey and lactose, milkfat, milk powders, casein, milk proteins, cheese and butter.
President: Steven Bronfield
CEO: Frank Reeves III
CFO: Mary Ellen Storino
Year Founded: 1985
Estimated Sales: $52 Million
Number Employees: 10
Number of Products: 50+
Square Footage: 1600
Type of Packaging: Bulk
Markets Served:
Food Manufacturers & Processors, Wholesale Distributors
Brokered Products include:
Dairy/Deli, Exports, Imports, Ingredients, Private Label

40037 (HQ)Airschott Inc
PO Box 17373
Washington, DC 20041-7373   703-471-7444
Fax: 703-471-4026   sales@airschott.com
www.airschott.com
Import and export broker of seafood, alcoholic beverages, produce, etc.; warehouse providing cooler and dry storage for seafood; transportation firm providing customs brokerage, freight forwarding, domestic and international airfreight and long haul trucking
President: Robert Schott
EVP: Tony Sequeira
Marketing Director: Andrew Shotwell
Contact: Carlos Balta
carlos@airschott.com
Director Operations: Hing Buon
Estimated Sales: $20-50 Million
Number Employees: 5-9
Square Footage: 4000
Other Locations:
Airschott
Baltimore, MD Airschott
Brokered Products include:
Alcoholic Beverages, Exports, Frozen Food, Imports, Produce, Seafood

40038 Ake-Sullivan Associates
PO Box 167
Irwin, PA 15642-0167   724-864-5291
Fax: 724-864-2012
Broker of confectionery products, general merchandise, private label items and groceries
President: Tom Gaudino
Senior VP: H Ake
Number Employees: 5-9
Type of Packaging: Consumer, Bulk
Markets Served:
Super Market Chains
Brokered Products include:
Confectionery, General Merchandise, Private Label

40039 Alba Specialty Seafood Company
233 Water St
New York, NY 10038-2095   212-349-5730
Fax: 212-607-6198   sean@albaspecialty.com
Import broker of frozen foods and seafood including lobster tails, shrimp, sea bass, etc
President: Denis Moriarty
VP: Eric Kiwi
Estimated Sales: $4.2 Million
Number Employees: 17
Primary Brands Brokered include: Salimar, Regal, Kalis Bros., Tristan, Rigel Qualimar, Cape Haddie, I-C, Kold, Oceancrest, South Atlantic; Cape Capensis Fillets
Brokered Products include:
Frozen Food, Imports, Seafood

40040 Albert A Russo Inc
88 Cottage St # 1
Suite: 1
East Boston, MA 02128-2291   617-569-6995
Fax: 617-569-3791   arussoimports@comcast.net
Import broker and importer of confectionery and dairy/deli products, groceries and canned anchovies, romano cheese
CEO: Albert Russo

Food Brokers / A-Z

Estimated Sales: $5-10 Million
Number Employees: 5-9
Square Footage: 4000
Type of Packaging: Consumer, Food Service, Private Label, Bulk
Markets Served:
  Food Manufacturers & Processors, Super Market Chains, Wholesale Distributors, Food Service Operators
Primary Brands Brokered include: Cento; Daniele; Ferrara; Engraulis; BelGioioso; Bell-Carter/Lindsay; Orleans
Brokered Products include:
  Confectionery, Dairy/Deli, Groceries, Imports, Private Label, Seafood, Canned Anchovies

40041 Alexander, Koetting, Poole & Buehrle Brothers
737 Goddard Ave
Chesterfield, MO 63005   636-537-5200
  Fax: 636-537-1232 akpbbroker@aol.com
Broker of confectionery and dairy/deli products, frozen foods and general merchandise
President: J Alexander
VP: Dave Pool
Secretary: J Koetting
Estimated Sales: $10-20 Million
Number Employees: 10
Type of Packaging: Private Label
Brokered Products include:
  Confectionery, Dairy/Deli, Frozen Food, General Merchandise

40042 All Seasons Brokerage Company
PO Box 820069
Fort Worth, TX 76182   817-577-8081
  Fax: 817-428-2559
Broker of frozen foods, general merchandise, groceries, meat/meat products, private label items, produce, etc.
President: Mike Layton
VP: Layton Shirley
VP Retail Sales: Patrick O'Neal
Estimated Sales: $3 Million
Number Employees: 45
Square Footage: 7000
Markets Served:
  Super Market Chains, Wholesale Distributors
Primary Brands Brokered include: Dole; Kikkoman;
Brokered Products include:
  Groceries, Produce

40043 All-State Food Brokerage
4663 Executive Dr # 12
Columbus, OH 43220-3627   614-451-7772
  Fax: 614-451-7772 800-466-2848
  gary.davis@allstatebrokerage.com
  www.allstate.com
Broker of confectionery products and general merchandise
President: Gary Davis
gary.davis@allstatebrokerage.com
Executive VP: George Union
Estimated Sales: $10-20 Million
Number Employees: 10-19
Type of Packaging: Consumer, Private Label, Bulk
Markets Served:
  Super Market Chains, Wholesale Distributors
Brokered Products include:
  Confectionery, General Merchandise

40044 Alliance Foods
514 Earth City Expressway
Earth City, MO 63045   314-298-1933
  Fax: 314-298-1933 800-388-4158
  alliance@alliance-foods.com
  www.alliance-foods.com
A supply chain management company as an innovative provider of goods, services and solutions to both corporate and consumer customer segments in the U.S. Food Distribution, Packaging Supply and Retailing Business Sectors.
President & CEO: Jim Ericson
CFO: Craig Lynch
Contact: Candace Renda
crenda@plazaadvisors.com
Manager: Kandy Renda
Estimated Sales: $1.4 Million
Number Employees: 9
Parent Co: Alliance Foods Inc
Type of Packaging: Consumer, Private Label
Markets Served:
  Super Market Chains, Wholesale Distributors

Brokered Products include:
  Alcoholic Beverages, Confectionery, Dairy/Deli, Exports, Frozen Food, General Merchandise, Groceries, Imports, Meat, Meat Products, Private Label, Seafood, Spices

40045 (HQ)Alliance Foods Inc
605 W Chicago Rd
Coldwater, MI 49036-8400   517-278-2396
  Fax: 517-278-7936 alliance@alliance-foods.com
  www.alliance-foods.com
A supply chain management company as an innovative provider of goods, services and solutions to both corporate and consumer customer segments in the U.S. Food Distribution, Packaging Supply and Retailing Business Sectors.
President/CEO: Sal Stazzone
Chairman: Robert T Harris
rharris@alliance-food.com
CFO: Judy Rossom
Estimated Sales: $32 Million
Number Employees: 50-99
Type of Packaging: Consumer, Private Label
Markets Served:
  Super Market Chains, Wholesale Distributors
Brokered Products include:
  Alcoholic Beverages, Confectionery, Dairy/Deli, Exports, Frozen Food, General Merchandise, Groceries, Imports, Meat, Meat Products, Private Label, Seafood, Spices

40046 Allied Marketing Corp
111 Freestate Blvd # 113
Shreveport, LA 71107-6540   318-222-0311
  Fax: 318-222-0312 delston442@aol.com
Broker of dairy/deli products, frozen foods, groceries, meat and meat products, private label items, etc.
President: Dudley Elston
delston442@aol.com
Vice President: R Elston
Estimated Sales: $5-10 Million
Number Employees: 5-9
Square Footage: 4800
Markets Served:
  Food Manufacturers & Processors, Wholesale Distributors, Food Service Operators
Primary Brands Brokered include: Tony's Food Service Pizza; Plantation Foods; Cajun Chef Products; Mrs. Smith's
Brokered Products include:
  Dairy/Deli, Frozen Food, Groceries, Meat, Meat Products, Private Label, Seafood, Spices

40047 Alpha Food Marketing
10101 W 87th St
Shaawnee Mission, KS 66212-4600   913-492-7398
Broker of dairy/deli products, groceries, meat and meat products, private label items, products, etc.
Owner/Principal: Mike Miller
Estimated Sales: $1-3 Million
Number Employees: 3

40048 Alpine Summit Sales Inc
11170 E 47th Ave
Denver, CO 80239-3010   303-756-6554
  Fax: 303-756-3811 800-844-0198
  www.alpinesummit.com
Broker of fresh fruits and vegetables; Serving the Colorado area
President: Randy Brown
randy@alpinesummit.com
CFO: Karen Brown
VP: Joyce Clain
Office Manager: Debbie Haught
Estimated Sales: $1.4 Million
Number Employees: 20-49
Square Footage: 72000
Markets Served:
  Wholesale Distributors, Food Service Operators
Brokered Products include:
  Produce

40049 Alquima USA Inc
2109 Frederick St
Oakland, CA 94606   510-500-3839
Supplier of organic artisinal and wild grown herbs and citrus peel for tea companies; supplier of chia.
Markets Served:
  Wholesale Distributors
Brokered Products include:
  Ingredients, Spices

40050 Ambi-Prestigio Foods Inc
164 N Brandon Dr
Glendale Heights, IL 60139-2025   630-825-0200
  Fax: 630-825-0222 800-933-2624
  www.ambifoods.com
Import and domestic broker of dairy/deli products, frozen foods, groceries, seafood, industrial ingredients, etc.; serving food processors, wholesalers/distributors and food service operators
President: Paul Baldwin
paul_d_baldwin@notes.ntrs.com
VP: R Ledvina
Sales and Account Manager: Roger Cyrus
Key Account Sales: John Marinopoulos
Sales and Account Manager: Jeff Sonin
Estimated Sales: $1.9 Million
Number Employees: 5-9
Markets Served:
  Food Manufacturers & Processors, Wholesale Distributors, Food Service Operators
Primary Brands Brokered include: Kozy Shack; Pillar Rock; Sue Bee; Musselmans; Roland; RFF; Lindsay; Crystal Geyser; Snokist
Brokered Products include:
  Dairy/Deli, Frozen Food, Groceries, Imports, Ingredients, Seafood

40051 American Agribusiness Assistance
2916 Dartmouth Road
Alexandria, VA 22314-4822   202-429-0500
  Fax: 202-429-0525 agequip@aol.com
  www.agribusiness.org.pk
Export broker of processing and packaging equipment for baked goods, sausage, vegetables, fruits, cheese, dairy products, etc.; consultant offering plant design and equipment installation
President: James Roberts
VP: Dick Verga
Number Employees: 1-4
Markets Served:
  Food Manufacturers & Processors

40052 (HQ)American Commodity & Shipping
2102 Gallows Rd # D2
Vienna, VA 22182-3960   703-848-9422
Fax: 703-848-9424 info@americancommodity.com
  www.americancommodity.com
Import and export broker of grain, dairy, meat and vegetable oils.
Owner: Ossama Yousef
o.yousef@americancommodity.com
Owner/VP: Ossama Yousef
Number Employees: 1-4
Type of Packaging: Bulk
Brokered Products include:
  Dairy/Deli, Exports, Frozen Food, Groceries, Imports, Ingredients, Meat, Produce, Soybeans, Sugar, Edible Oils

40053 American Patriot Sales Inc
60 Central St
Norwood, MA 02062-3556   781-948-4401
  Fax: 781-948-4455 800-336-2400
  www.americanpatriotsales.com
Broker of dairy/deli products, frozen foods, spices, groceries and meat products; Serving the New England area
President: Howard Goldman
hgoldman@americanpatriotsales.com
Financial Manager: Bunny Goldman
VP: Tom Roderick
Marketing Director: Cynthia Kazanjian
Sales Representative: Joel Hempel
Estimated Sales: $10-20 Million
Number Employees: 20-49
Markets Served:
  Food Manufacturers & Processors, Super Market Chains, Wholesale Distributors, Food Service Operators
Brokered Products include:
  Dairy/Deli, Frozen Food, Groceries, Meat, Meat Products, Spices

40054 American Sales & Marketing
PO Box 95
Bahama, NC 27503   919-471-2980
  Fax: 919-471-2980
Broker, retail, wholesale, grocer of general merchandise.
Owner: Charles Roedel
Markets Served:
  Wholesale Distributors

Brokered Products include:
General Merchandise, Groceries

40055 American Trading Company
P.O.Box 6361
Silver Spring, MD 20916   301-670-6329
                        Fax: 301-942-3119
Import and export broker of dried fruits, confectionery products, health food, seafood, spices and pharmaceuticals
President: John Seiden
Estimated Sales: $2.5-5 Million
Number Employees: 1-4
Markets Served:
Food Manufacturers & Processors, Super Market Chains, Wholesale Distributors, Food Service Operators
Brokered Products include:
Confectionery, Exports, General Merchandise, Health Food, Imports, Seafood, Spices, Dried fruits

40056 (HQ)AmericanLifestyle.Com
640 Kreag Rd # 101
Pittsford, NY 14534-3737   585-381-7410
            Fax: 585-385-0935 866-230-4249
                        info@americanlifestyle.com
Export broker of vitamins and weight reduction products
Manager: Bruce Ricigliano
VP HQ Operations: Bruce Ricigliano
Director Worldwide Spanish Marketing: EvaMarie Pastrana
Director Worldwide Marketing: Nguyen Tony
Estimated Sales: $3-5 Million
Number Employees: 10-19
Square Footage: 8000
Markets Served:
Wholesale Distributors
Brokered Products include:
Exports, Vitamins, Weight Reduction Products

40057 Ames Company, Inc
PO Box 46
45 Pine Hill Road
New Ringgold, PA 17960   610-750-1032
              Fax: 413-604-0541 info@theingredientstore.com
                        www.theingredientstore.com
Vegetarian meat analogs and dry mixes
Owner: Joseph Ames, Sr.
Number Employees: 5-9
Primary Brands Brokered include: Pro Foods, Inc.
Brokered Products include:
Ingredients, Phosphates, Soy Concentrates, Etc.

40058 (HQ)Anchor Florida Marketing
1417 W Busch Blvd
Tampa, FL 33612-7601   813-932-2967
                        Fax: 813-932-4355
Broker of dairy/deli products, frozen foods, general merchandise, groceries, meat products, seafood, etc.; serving food service operators and wholesalers/distributors.
President/CEO: Jim Dougherty
Secretary/Treasurer: L Dougherty
Estimated Sales: $5-10 Million
Number Employees: 5
Markets Served:
Wholesale Distributors, Food Service Operators
Primary Brands Brokered include: All Round Foods; BCR Foods; Galaxy Foods; Harvest of the Sea; Jennie-O; Mission Foodservice; Monterey; Rotella's Bakery; Chef Paul Prudhomme; Zatarain's; Major Products; Cutler Egg Products; Ms. Desserts; Iroquis Water & First Nations Seal Oil;Boca
Brokered Products include:
Dairy/Deli, Frozen Food, General Merchandise, Groceries, Ingredients, Meat, Meat Products, Private Label, Produce, Seafood, Spices

40059 (HQ)Anchor Packaging
13515 Barrett Parkway Dr # 100
Ballwin, MO 63021-5870   314-822-7800
              Fax: 314-822-2035 800-467-3900
                        info@anchorpackaging.com
Manufacturer and exporter of plastic microwaveable packaging and container supplies including films, containers, trays, food protective and cling wrap.
President: Jeff Wolff
jeff.wolff@anchorpack.com
CFO: Steve Riek
CEO: Brad Jensen
Marketing: Michael Thaler
Sales: Frank Baumann
Public Relations: Michael Thaler
Operations: Staya Garg
Estimated Sales: $20-50 Million
Number Employees: 20-49
Type of Packaging: Food Service, Private Label
Markets Served:
Food Manufacturers & Processors, Food Service Operators
Primary Brands Brokered include: MicroRaves; The Roaster Series; The Culinary Series; Microlite; Gourmet Classics; BonFaire; DeliView; FreshView; Processor Trays; Value Line; PuritWrap; AnchorWrap; The Miler, CrystalWrap; Perforated Films; UltraWrap;
Brokered Products include:
Confectionery, Dairy/Deli, Meat, Produce

40060 Anderson Daymon Worldwide
4141 Jutland Drive
Suite 200
San Diego, CA 92117-3650   858-228-5300
              Fax: 858-228-5301 coinfo@adww.com
                        www.adww.com
Costco in house broker. Represents all categories wall to wall in Costco.
Senior Vice President: Carla Saunders
Contact: Raul Moreno
raulmoreno@adww.com
Estimated Sales: $5-10 Million
Number Employees: 204
Parent Co: Daymon Associates Worldwide
Markets Served:
Wholesale Distributors
Brokered Products include:
Confectionery, Dairy/Deli, Frozen Food, General Merchandise, Meat, Meat Products, Produce, Seafood, Spices

40061 Anthony Cea & Associates
PO Box 150
Webb, AL 36376   800-832-5343
              Fax: 800-613-4231 anthonycea@gmail.com
Import and export broker of alcoholic beverages, confectionery and dairy/deli products, frozen foods, general merchandise, groceries, etc
President: Anthony Cea
Estimated Sales: $5 Million
Number Employees: 4
Square Footage: 7500
Type of Packaging: Consumer, Food Service, Private Label, Bulk
Markets Served:
Food Manufacturers & Processors, Super Market Chains, Wholesale Distributors, Food Service Operators
Brokered Products include:
Alcoholic Beverages, Confectionery, Dairy/Deli, Exports, Frozen Food, General Merchandise, Groceries, Health Food, Imports, Ingredients, Meat Products, Private Label, Produce, Seafood, Spices

40062 Apache Brokers
43670 W Oster Dr
Maricopa, AZ 85138-2420   520-568-6392
Broker of dairy/deli products, frozen and health food, groceries, industrial ingredients, meat and meat products, seafood, spices and private label items.; serving all markets
Owner: Jim Sandner
jim@apachebrokers.com
Acct. Manager: Donna Gentile
Acct. Manager: Don Swanson
Sales/Marketing: Donna Gentile
Number Employees: 1-4
Square Footage: 4000
Markets Served:
Food Manufacturers & Processors, Super Market Chains, Wholesale Distributors, Food Service Operators
Primary Brands Brokered include: Cinch; Read Salads; Garden Burger; Peppers Unlimited, Inc.; Major San-Fran; SMG, Inc.
Brokered Products include:
Dairy/Deli, Frozen Food, Groceries, Health Food, Ingredients, Meat, Meat Products, Private Label, Seafood, Spices

40063 Apple Food Sales
117 Fort Lee Rd Ste B9
Leonia, NJ 07605   201-592-0277
              Fax: 201-585-7244 agrusa@agrusainc.com
Import broker of groceries, private label items and Italian and Spanish specialty foods; serving all markets
President/Managing Director: Jill Bush
j.bush@agrusainc.com
VP: Victor Weingast
Estimated Sales: $20 Million
Number Employees: 5
Square Footage: 2000
Markets Served:
Food Manufacturers & Processors, Super Market Chains, Wholesale Distributors, Food Service Operators
Primary Brands Brokered include: Don Peppe; Celio; Bella Italia
Brokered Products include:
Groceries, Imports, Private Label, Italian & Spanish Specialty Foods

40064 Aqua Foods
1050 W Laurel Ave
Eunice, LA 70535-3124   337-457-0111
                        Fax: 337-457-1500
Importer of catfish, tilapia, crawfish products, and alligator meat
Owner/President: Dwayne Lejeune
Office Manager: Alice Tramel
Estimated Sales: $3-5 Million
Number Employees: 4
Brokered Products include:
Seafood, Alligator Meat

40065 (HQ)Arnett Brokerage Co
4010 82nd St # 115
Suite 115
Lubbock, TX 79423-1933   806-744-1477
              Fax: 806-744-0119 www.arnettbrokerage.com
Export broker of confectionery, frozen foods, private label items, produce, seafood, dairy/deli products, general merchandise, groceries, meat and meat products, etc.
President: Mike Poteet
CEO: Jeff Poteet
poteetj@arnettbrokerage.com
VP: Mike Couch
Estimated Sales: $7 Million
Number Employees: 20-49
Square Footage: 6600
Markets Served:
Super Market Chains, Wholesale Distributors, Food Service Operators
Primary Brands Brokered include: Reynolds; Sara Lee; Dole Fresh Cut; Aurora Food; M&M/Mars; Seneca; Church & Dwight
Brokered Products include:
Dairy/Deli, Exports, Frozen Food, General Merchandise, Groceries, Ingredients, Meat, Meat Products, Private Label, Produce

40066 Arroyo Sales Company
615 Hickory Ave
Harahan, LA 70123   504-737-7336
                        Fax: 504-737-7373
Broker of groceries, meats, frozen food, dairy/deli products and produce; serving the food service market and supermarket chains
President: David Arroyo
Owner/CEO: James Arroyo
Estimated Sales: $2.4 Million
Number Employees: 18
Square Footage: 20000
Type of Packaging: Bulk
Markets Served:
Super Market Chains, Food Service Operators
Primary Brands Brokered include: Zatarain's, Inc.; Doane Products, Inc.; Longlife Dairy Products, Inc.; Armour Dairy Co.; Chocolate Group; Piknik Products Co.
Brokered Products include:
Dairy/Deli, Frozen Food, Groceries, Meat, Produce

40067 Arthur G. Meier Company/Inland Products Company
1369 Clarke Avenue Sw
Roanoke, VA 24016-4901   540-345-7793
                        Fax: 540-344-6571

Food Brokers / A-Z

Broker of confectionery products, frozen foods, general merchandise, seafood, groceries, meats, etc.; serving all markets; wholesaler/distributor of salt, cookies, compactors and balers
Owner: May M Justice
VP: J Robert Justice
Estimated Sales: $1-2.5 Million
Number Employees: 4
Markets Served:
  Food Manufacturers & Processors, Super Market Chains, Wholesale Distributors, Food Service Operators
Brokered Products include:
  Confectionery, Dairy/Deli, Frozen Food, General Merchandise, Groceries, Meat, Meat Products, Private Label, Seafood, Spices

40068 Artisanal Foods
2053 Pama Ln
Las Vegas, NV 89119   702-436-4252
info@artisanalfoods.com
www.artisanalfoods.com
Artisanal foods
Markets Served:
  Super Market Chains, Wholesale Distributors, Food Service Operators
Brokered Products include:
  Dairy/Deli, Frozen Food, General Merchandise, Groceries, Health Food, Ingredients, Meat, Meat Products

40069 Arvin Sales Company
12077 Stern Drive
Indianapolis, IN 46256   317-547-9413
Broker of frozen foods, groceries and seafood; serving food service operators, supermarket chains and wholesalers/distributors
President/CEO: Len Stange
Estimated Sales: A
Number Employees: 4
Markets Served:
  Super Market Chains, Wholesale Distributors, Food Service Operators
Primary Brands Brokered include: Icelandic; Country Skillet; Ocean Supreme Shrimp; Matlaw's
Brokered Products include:
  Frozen Food, Groceries, Seafood

40070 Asiamerica Ingredients
245 Old Hood Rd #3
Westwood, NJ 07675-3174   201-497-5993
Fax: 201-497-5994   201-497-5531
info@asiamericaingredients.com
www.asiamericaingredients.com
Processor, importer, exporter and distributor of bulk vitamins, amino acids, nutraceuticals, aromatic chemicals, food additives, herbs, mineral nutrients and pharmaceuticals.
President/Owner: Mark Zhang
CFO: Lillian Yang
Quality Control: Michelle Naomi
Sales: Cari Pandero
Contact: Elizabeth Gysbers
egysbers@asiamericaingredients.com
Purchasing: Michelle N. Riley
Estimated Sales: $5-10 Million
Number Employees: 10
Type of Packaging: Bulk

40071 Aspen Food Marketing
4500 Cherry Creek Drive S
Suite 970
Denver, CO 80246   303-320-3400
Fax: 303-320-0226
A Colorado based brokerage firm, specializing in sales and marketing to the retailers in the trading area.
President: John Olson
Estimated Sales: $30 Million
Number Employees: 14
Type of Packaging: Consumer, Food Service

40072 Associated Foodservices
600 N Bell Ave # 210
Carnegie, PA 15106-4315   412-429-1433
Fax: 412-429-9518
Broker of frozen, canned and dry foods, meats, seafood, spices, baked goods, confectionery items, etc.; serving food service operators and wholesalers/distributors
Co-President: Harvey Issenberg
Sales Director: Brian Bateman
Estimated Sales: $10-20 Million
Number Employees: 5
Type of Packaging: Food Service
Markets Served:
  Food Service Operators
Brokered Products include:
  Dairy/Deli, Frozen Food, Meat, Meat Products, Seafood, Spices

40073 Atkinson Sales Company
3653 S Inca St
Englewood, CO 80110   303-761-1898
Fax: 303-781-8035   atkrep@aol.com
Broker of general merchandise, groceries and private label/generic products; serving supermarket chains and food service operators
Owner: Robert W Atkinson Ii
VP: S Atkinson
Contact: David Atkinson
datkinson@atkinsonsales.com
Secretary: H Atkinson
Estimated Sales: $5-10 Million
Number Employees: 5
Markets Served:
  Super Market Chains, Food Service Operators
Brokered Products include:
  General Merchandise, Groceries, Private Label

40074 Atkinson-Crawford SalesCo
11999 Plano Rd # 110
Dallas, TX 75243-5419   972-234-0947
Fax: 972-234-2140   bgibbons@acsales.com
Broker of confectionery and snack products
Owner: Bruce Gibbons
Vice President: Scott Gibbons
Vice President: Rayelynn Spear
Estimated Sales: $10-20 Million
Number Employees: 10-19
Markets Served:
  Food Manufacturers & Processors, Super Market Chains, Wholesale Distributors, Food Service Operators
Primary Brands Brokered include: Brach & Brock; Arrurol; Ferrara-Pan; Topps; Hershey; Jack Links.
Brokered Products include:
  Confectionery

40075 Atlantis Smoked Foods
4126 Pleasantdale Rd
#B110
Atlanta, GA 30340-3518   770-209-0611
Fax: 770-209-0608   800-228-6480
atlantisdirect@aol.com
Importer of smoked seafood including salmon, halibut, trout, and sea bass
President: Maurice Eissner
Estimated Sales: $1.2 Million
Number Employees: 7
Square Footage: 80000
Type of Packaging: Food Service
Markets Served:
  Wholesale Distributors, Food Service Operators
Brokered Products include:
  Seafood

40076 Atlas Biscuit Co Inc
155 Pompton Ave # 207
Verona, NJ 07044-2935   973-239-8300
Fax: 973-629-5735
Food broker of bakery products
Owner: Pat Bana
pat@atlas-vista.net
President: Reginald Hitchcock
Year Founded: 1979
Estimated Sales: Less Than $500,000
Number Employees: 5-9
Brokered Products include:
  Imports, Cookies & Crackers

40077 Atlas Restaurant Supply
3329 N Shadeland Ave
Indianapolis, IN 46226-6236   317-541-1111
Fax: 317-541-1404   877-528-5275
www.atlasrestaurantsupply.com
Manufacturers' representative for bar equipment, carts, concession supplies, dishwashers, display cases, ice machines, refrigerators, can openers, steam tables, etc.; serving supermarket chains and food service operators; kitchen and interior design services
President: Thomas S Vavul
Manager: Jimmy Gravel
rickv@atlasrs.com
Estimated Sales: Below $5,000,000
Number Employees: 10-19
Markets Served:
  Super Market Chains, Food Service Operators
Primary Brands Brokered include: Oxo
Brokered Products include:
  General Merchandise, Restaurant Equipment & Supplies

40078 Automatic Packaging Systems & Conveyors Company
774 Burr Oak Dr
Westmont, IL 60559-1182   630-887-0700
Fax: 630-887-0771   800-822-0771
sales@airprocesssystems.com
www.airprocesssystems.com
Manufacturers' representative of packaging machinery including bag, bottle, carton and case handling, conveyors, detectors, filling, packing, palletizing, stretch wrapping, weighing, etc.; serving processors and wholesalers/distributors
President: Richard Matthews
Director Marketing: Heather Matthews
Components Sales: Karyn Napolitano
Packaging Director: Jay Bloom
Estimated Sales: $3-5 Million
Number Employees: 5-9
Square Footage: 40000
Parent Co: Air Process Systems & Conveyors Company
Markets Served:
  Food Manufacturers & Processors, Wholesale Distributors
Brokered Products include:
  Confectionery, General Merchandise, Ingredients, Meat, Spices, Packaging Machinery

40079 Autumn Foods
217 S Prospect Ave
Clarendon Hills, IL 60514   630-789-9981
Fax: 630-789-9982   autumnfoods@msn.com
Broker of industrial ingredients and dairy/deli and confectionery products; also, specializing in items for baking; serving food processors
Owner/President: Gwen Bilek
Estimated Sales: $3 Million
Number Employees: 1
Type of Packaging: Consumer, Food Service, Private Label, Bulk
Markets Served:
  Food Manufacturers & Processors
Brokered Products include:
  Confectionery, Dairy/Deli, Ingredients, Private Label, Spices

40080 Avatar Food Group
4121 Burns Rd
Palm Beach Gardens, FL 33410   561-694-0546
Fax: 413-702-2328
Broker of deli foods, meats, private label items and spices; serving all markets
Owner/President: Haig Berberian
Sales Director: Curt Quisenberry
General Manager: John Dougherty
Estimated Sales: $5-10 Million
Number Employees: 3
Markets Served:
  Food Manufacturers & Processors, Super Market Chains, Wholesale Distributors, Food Service Operators
Brokered Products include:
  Dairy/Deli, Frozen Food, Meat, Meat Products, Private Label

40081 Azbros Inc
7516 NW 54th St
Miami, FL 33166-4813   305-477-0142
Fax: 305-594-8692
Purchasing and exporting of bakery items, plastic ware, packaging, dry food and more
Owner/President: Peter Azan
President: Jean-Pierre Dionne
Manager: Joselle Azan
Export Manager: Joselle Jureidini
Estimated Sales: $3-5 Million
Number Employees: 1-4

40082 (HQ)B & D Sales & Marketing Inc
77 Brant Ave # 200
Clark, NJ 07066-1540   732-340-1010
Fax: 732-340-1110   www.bdsalesmarketing.com

Food brokers of dairy/deli products, frozen foods, general merchandise, groceries, meat products, etc.; serving supermarket chains and wholesalers/distributors
Owner: Andrew Tesalzo
bdsales22@aol.com
Executive VP: Walter Bycsek
Estimated Sales: $44 Million
Number Employees: 5-9
Square Footage: 2200
Markets Served:
  Super Market Chains, Wholesale Distributors
Primary Brands Brokered include: Cento Foods; Reily Foods; SunPac Ltd.; Canadaigua Wine Co.; Nutcracker
Brokered Products include:
  Dairy/Deli, Frozen Food, General Merchandise, Imports, Ingredients, Private Label

40083 B&K Agencies
202 Somerset Street
Saint John, NB E2K 2X9
Canada   506-634-8122
                           Fax: 506-634-1657
Broker of foil, foam, stretch film, cups, straws, corrugated cartons and paper products; serving all markets
President: Kent Jones
VP: Kevin Jones
Number Employees: 1-4
Type of Packaging: Food Service
Markets Served:
  Food Manufacturers & Processors, Super Market Chains, Wholesale Distributors, Food Service Operators

40084 B.C. Ritchie Company
26 Lake Trl W
Morristown, NJ 07960-6747   973-425-8930
                           Fax: 973-425-8930
Import and export broker of seafood, spices, ingredients, general mechandise, health foods, juice concentrates and dried and canned fruits and vegetables
President: Peter Desterhazy
Markets Served:
  Food Manufacturers & Processors, Wholesale Distributors
Brokered Products include:
  Exports, General Merchandise, Health Food, Imports, Ingredients, Seafood, Spices, Canned & Dried Fruits/Vegetables, Etc.

40085 (HQ)B.C. Tree Fruits Limited
1473 Water Street
Kelowna, BC V1Y 1J6
Canada   250-470-4200
           Fax: 250-762-5571 info@bctree.com
                           www.bctree.com
Exporter and importer of apples, pears, oranges, apricots, etc. Broker of plums and cherries
President: Jim Elliot
CEO: Greg Gauthier
CFO: John Bernard
VP: Glenn Cross
Director Sales: Lance McGinn
Estimated Sales: $17.8 Million
Number Employees: 39
Type of Packaging: Consumer, Food Service, Private Label
Other Locations:
  B.C. Tree Fruits Ltd.
  Toronto, ONB.C. Tree Fruits Ltd.
Markets Served:
  Food Manufacturers & Processors, Super Market Chains, Wholesale Distributors, Food Service Operators
Primary Brands Brokered include: B.C. Leaf
Brokered Products include:
  Produce, Plums, Cherries

40086 B.W. Dyer & Company
305 Society Dr Apt B3
Telluride, CO 81435   970-728-9393
           Fax: 970-728-9396 office@bwdyer.com
                           www.bwdyer.com
Import and export broker of cane and beet sugar, raisins, coconuts, spices, molasses, honey and juice concentrates including apple, strawberry and black currant; serving food processors and wholesaler/distributors
President: Chip Dyer
Sales Associate: Shirley Purdy
Estimated Sales: $5-10 Million
Number Employees: 5-9

40087 BAL Marketing
156 Mineola Blvd
Mineola, NY 11501-3977   516-248-4898
           Fax: 516-248-2063 bill@balmarketing.com
                           www.balmarketing.com
Broker of rice, canned and dried beans, wheat and rice flour, corn meal, popcorn, general merchandise, private label items
Owner/President: William Markov
CFO: Meryl Markov
Vice President: John Lintz
Contact: David Levey
dave@balmarketing.com
Estimated Sales: $3-5 Million
Type of Packaging: Food Service, Private Label
Markets Served:
  Wholesale Distributors
Brokered Products include:
  Groceries, Private Label

40088 BLV Marketing Inc
3695 N 126th St # M
Brookfield, WI 53005-2424   262-790-0900
           Fax: 262-790-1900 800-236-2582
booth@blvmarketing.com www.blvmarketing.com
Broker of confectionery products, produce, seafood, frozen foods, general merchandise, meats, etc
President: James F. Booth
Vice President of Sales: June Lamers
Business Development: Larry Vick
Key Account Sales: Dan Booth
Office Manager: Julie Kolsch
Estimated Sales: $1-2.5 Million
Number Employees: 5-9
Square Footage: 20800
Type of Packaging: Consumer, Food Service, Private Label, Bulk
Markets Served:
  Food Manufacturers & Processors, Super Market Chains, Wholesale Distributors, Food Service Operators
Primary Brands Brokered include: Barcelona Nut, McCormick; Gravy Master; Wyman Blueberries,Etc.
Brokered Products include:
  Confectionery, Dairy/Deli, Frozen Food, General Merchandise, Groceries, Health Food, Imports, Ingredients, Meat, Private Label, Produce

40089 BLV Marketing Inc
3695 N 126th St # M
Brookfield, WI 53005-2424   262-790-0900
           Fax: 262-790-1900 800-236-2582
booth@blvmarketing.com www.blvmarketing.com
Broker of confectionery products, groceries, specialty and health foods, general merchandise, produce, etc.
Owner: Jim Booth
VP Sales: June Lamers
booth@blvmarketing.com
Sales, Retail: Bruce Elliot
Office Manager: Julie Kolsch
Estimated Sales: $5-10 Million
Number Employees: 5-9
Square Footage: 20800
Markets Served:
  Food Manufacturers & Processors, Super Market Chains, Wholesale Distributors
Brokered Products include:
  Confectionery, General Merchandise, Groceries, Health Food, Private Label, Produce, Specialty Foods

40090 BSE Marketing
601 2nd Ave
New Hyde Park, NY 11040   516-326-0182
           Fax: 516-694-1234 bsemktng@aol.com
Broker of food service equipment including ovens, freezers, dishwashers, mixers, slicers, sinks, ice cube machines, fryers, griddles, ranges, broilers, microwaves, kettles, etc.; serving food service operators, supermarket chains andwholesalers/distributors
President: Mark Hessel
VP: Jeff Hessel
Sales Manager: Steve Doyle
Estimated Sales: $5-10 Million
Number Employees: 5-9
Square Footage: 19200
Parent Co: Soda Service of Long Island
Markets Served:
  Super Market Chains, Wholesale Distributors, Food Service Operators
Primary Brands Brokered include: Aero Manufacturing Co.; Alto Shaam; American Panel; Blakeslee; Panasonic; Jade Range, Inc.
Brokered Products include:
  General Merchandise, Ovens, Freezers, Sinks, Ranges

40091 Baja Foods LLC
636 W Root St
Chicago, IL 60609-2630   773-376-9030
           Fax: 773-376-9245 lisa@bajafoodsllc.com
Frozen tamales, quesadillas, chimichangas, burritos, enchiladas, taco meat and chili
Owner: Art Velasquez
donraezler@aol.com
Sales/Marketing: Jeff Rothschild
General Manager: Timothy Poisson
Purchasing Manager: Cheryl Canning
Year Founded: 2001
Estimated Sales: $10-20 Million
Number Employees: 20-49
Square Footage: 30000
Type of Packaging: Consumer, Food Service, Private Label, Bulk
Markets Served:
  Food Manufacturers & Processors
Primary Brands Brokered include: LaMarca, Tango, Chilli-O
Brokered Products include:
  Frozen Food, Meat Products, Pizza toppings

40092 Baker Brokerage Company LLC
2150 Memorial Dr Ste 214
Green Bay, WI 54303   920-494-3000
           Fax: 920-494-3013 bakerbrokerage@aol.com
Broker of confectionery and dairy/deli products, frozen foods, general merchandise, groceries, produce, etc.; serving foodserv ice operators and supermarket chains
Owner: James Baker
Sales Manager: W Baker
Estimated Sales: $5-10 Million
Number Employees: 5
Markets Served:
  Super Market Chains, Wholesale Distributors, Food Service Operators
Brokered Products include:
  Dairy/Deli, Frozen Food, Groceries, Private Label, Produce

40093 Baker Sales
206 Blanquita Way
Placentia, CA 92870   714-528-2573
           Fax: 714-961-0113 bakerroadrunner@hotmail.com
Manufacturers' representative for foodserv ice equipment including paper shortening filters and wrapping and sealing films, etc
Owner: Bill Baker
Number Employees: 1-4
Markets Served:
  Food Manufacturers & Processors, Super Market Chains, Wholesale Distributors, Food Service Operators
Primary Brands Brokered include: Carbon-Off; Metalcrest Seating; Control Seating; Hunter Filter Machines; Discovery Products
Brokered Products include:
  General Merchandise, Foodservice Equipment

40094 Baldwin & Mattson
4120 Excelsior Blvd
St Louis Park, MN 55416   952-920-5070
                           Fax: 952-920-9793
Broker of dairy/deli and private label/generic products, meat and frozen foods; serving supermarket chains
President: Jim Mattson
Estimated Sales: $20-50 Million
Number Employees: 20-49
Markets Served:
  Super Market Chains
Brokered Products include:
  Dairy/Deli, Frozen Food, Meat, Private Label

40095 Barliant & Company
319 E Van Emmon St
Yorkville, IL 60560   630-553-6992
           Fax: 630-553-6908 barliant@aol.com
                           www.barliant.com

Food Brokers / A-Z

Domestic and export broker of new and used food processing equipment including meat and poultry, as well as appraisals, liquidations, auctions and asset management programs.
Owner: Scott Swanson
Sales Manager: Kevin Chapman
Contact: Tom Baumgartner
tom@centralice.com
Estimated Sales: $1.5 Million
Number Employees: 5
Square Footage: 152000
Markets Served:
  Food Manufacturers & Processors, Food Service Operators
Brokered Products include:
  Exports, General Merchandise, Used Food Processing Equipment

40096 Barry Food Sales
809 N Bethlehem Pike
Ambler, PA 19002-2534   215-646-9771
    Fax: 215-646-9776   800-378-1548
Food Brokerage Company of fresh and frozen beef, pork, veal and lamb
Owner: Barry Katz
barry@barryfoodsales.com
Estimated Sales: Less Than $500,000
Number Employees: 1-4
Type of Packaging: Food Service, Bulk
Markets Served:
  Food Service Operators
Primary Brands Brokered include: Gold Kist Farms; Silver Springs; Don Lee Farms; House of Reeford; Horizon Snack Foods; Slam International Foods

40097 Bartlett & Co
4900 Main St # 1200
Kansas City, MO 64112-2807   816-753-6300
    Fax: 816-753-0062   800-888-6300
    rgeiger@bartlett-grain.com
    www.bartlettandco.com
Broker of food grade white and yellow corn and industrial ingredients
President/CEO: James Hebenstreit
jhebenstreit@barlettgrain.com
VP/Secretary/Treasurer: Arnold Wheeler
Manager: Dan Stanton
Estimated Sales: Over $1 Billion
Number Employees: 500-999
Square Footage: 10000
Markets Served:
  Food Manufacturers & Processors
Brokered Products include:
  Ingredients, Food Grade White & Yellow Whole Corn

40098 Bassett-Carragher Associates
287 Andrews St
Rochester, NY 14604-1105   585-254-1780
    Fax: 585-254-2154
Manufacturers' representative for food service equipment; serving wholesalers/distributors
Owner: Jeff Carragher
Owner: Fred Carragher
Inside Sales Manager: Julie Callahan
Estimated Sales: $1-3 Million
Number Employees: 5-9
Markets Served:
  Wholesale Distributors
Brokered Products include:
  General Merchandise, Foodservice Equipment

40099 Bay Brokerage Company
1776 Laurel St
San Carlos, CA 94070   650-595-1189
    Fax: 650-595-2287   www.baybrokerage.com
Broker of groceries
President/Owner: Robert Hill
President, Client Development: Brian Baldwin
Chief Information Officer: Mark Chafffin
Senior Vice President: Vilma Consuerga
General Council, Secretary: Reece Alford
Sales Director: Matt Campbell
Contact: Adam Carmon
acarmon@baybrokerageus.com
Chief Strategy Officer: Brian King
Product Line Manager: Bryan Knox
Warehouse: Lawrence Knudson
Estimated Sales: $9.8 Million
Number Employees: 48
Square Footage: 36000
Markets Served:
  Super Market Chains, Wholesale Distributors, Food Service Operators
Brokered Products include:
  Groceries

40100 Bay Pacific Marketing
20955 Foothill Boulevard
Hayward, CA 94541-1511   561-743-8001
    Fax: 510-727-0151 foodsusa@usa.com
Export and import broker of dairy/deli products, frozen foods, groceries, health food, industrial ingredients, private label items, produce, seafood, candy, etc.; serving food processors, supermarket chains andwholesalers/distributorsbakery mixes, organics, mexican foods, imported foods
President: Xin Geug
VP: Wang Weu Xou
Marketing: Xiu Ping Liang
Sales/Service: Mike Hagan
Customer Service: Linda Davis
Customer Service: Bob Schultz
Estimated Sales: $5-10 Million
Number Employees: 5-9
Square Footage: 12000
Type of Packaging: Consumer, Food Service, Private Label, Bulk
Markets Served:
  Food Manufacturers & Processors, Super Market Chains, Wholesale Distributors, Food Service Operators
Primary Brands Brokered include: Sea Witch; GoldenCrown; Juicy Magic; Harvest Classic; Dinosaur Drinks; Solar Squeeze; Traxx; Haggen; Bake Rite Cooking Products; Cliffstar Health Line; San Francisco Finest Box Chocolate Candy
Brokered Products include:
  Confectionery, Dairy/Deli, Exports, Groceries, Health Food, Imports, Ingredients, Private Label, Produce, Organics

40101 Bayha & Associates
5405 Glen Echo Ave
Gladstone, OR 97027-2603   503-657-1360
    Fax: 503-656-2149
Broker of confectionery and dairy/deli products, frozen foods, industrial ingredients, meats, grains, spices and oils
President: Neil Bayha
bayha5@msn.com
Sales: Patty Wright
Estimated Sales: $15-20 Million
Number Employees: 5
Square Footage: 3825
Markets Served:
  Food Manufacturers & Processors, Wholesale Distributors, Food Service Operators
Primary Brands Brokered include: Dole Pineapple; Dole Frozen Foods; SupHerb Farms; Ghirardelli Chocolate; CHS Sunflower; Grain Millers; Reckitt Benckiser
Brokered Products include:
  Frozen Food, Imports, Ingredients, Spices, Organics

40102 Beach Filter Products
P.O. Box 505
555 Centennial Ave
Hanover, PA 17331   717-698-1403
    Fax: 717-698-1610   800-232-2485
    sales@beachfilters.com www.beachfilters.com
Manufacturer and exporter of compressed air filters, desiccant dehumidification bags, and breather filters.
President: Wesley Jones
abuckley@beachfilters.com
Sales Manager: Lori Prickitt
Production Manager: Leslie Doll
Plant Manager/Purchasing: Leslie Doll
Estimated Sales: $500 Thousand-$1 Million
Square Footage: 16000
Type of Packaging: Consumer, Bulk
Markets Served:
  Food Manufacturers & Processors, Food Service Operators
Brokered Products include:
  General Merchandise

40103 Beck Western Brokerage
1909 S 4250 W
Salt Lake City, UT 84104-4837   801-973-6333
    Fax: 801-973-6468 inf- ut-h bb
    mchournos@beckwestern.com www.aloecorp.com
Broker of dairy, frozen and health foods, dried fruits and vegetable, extracts for health food industry, bakery and bakery ingredients
Owner/President: Mike Chournos
mchournos@beckwestern.com
Sales: Dorothy Chournos
Office Manager: Heathe Suwai
Estimated Sales: $10-15 Million
Number Employees: 1-4
Square Footage: 2400
Markets Served:
  Food Manufacturers & Processors, Wholesale Distributors, Food Service Operators
Primary Brands Brokered: Kerry Ingredients; Sunny Gem; Tree Top,Inc.; SVZ; Van Drunen Farms; Synergy Flavor
Brokered Products include:
  Confectionery, Health Food, Ingredients, Produce, Juice Concentrates, Liquid/Dry Flour

40104 Becksmith Company, Inc
12733 Ginger Dr
Jacksonville, FL 32223-1844   904-607-0777
    info@manufacturersrep.com
Broker of general merchandise, private label items, groceries, etc.; serving supermarket and drug chains, wholesalers/distributors and mass merchandisers in Florida
President: Paul Becksmith
pbecksmith@manufacturersrep.com
IT Services: John Whitehurst
Number Employees: 12
Square Footage: 10000
Markets Served:
  Super Market Chains, Wholesale Distributors
Brokered Products include:
  General Merchandise, Groceries, Private Label

40105 Bee Creek Botanicals
P.O.Box 144345
Austin, TX 78714-4345   512-926-4900
    Fax: 512-926-2345
President: Mark Blumenthal
Number Employees: 1-4

40106 Bee Jay Sales Of Florida
5245 NW 36th St # 222
Miami Springs, FL 33166-5957   305-887-3353
    Fax: 305-887-2853 71660.1273@compuserve.com
    www.beejaysales.com
Broker of groceries and canned and dried fruits and vegetable including tomatoes; serving wholesalers/distributors
President: Steve Braunstein
braunstein.s@grainger.com
VP: C Kefebvre
Estimated Sales: $5-10 Million
Number Employees: 1-4
Markets Served:
  Wholesale Distributors
Primary Brands Brokered include: Diamond A; Sacramento; Red Pack; Teresa; Stapleton; Oasis
Brokered Products include:
  Groceries, Canned/Dried Fruits & Vegetables

40107 Belcorp
1375 Kemper Meadow Dr # A
Ste A
Cincinnati, OH 45240-1650   513-825-1550
    Fax: 513-825-1896   800-555-1781
    ed@belcorpinc.com www.belcorpinc.com
Broker of packaging machinery systems, both automated and manual
Owner: Ed Kraft
ed@bellcorpinc.com
President: Larry McGovern
VP: C Kraft
Marketing Director: George Van Lieu
Estimated Sales: $6 Million
Number Employees: 1-4
Square Footage: 4800
Primary Brands Brokered include: Serpa Packaging Solutions; Premier Technology; Lambert Material Handling; Kaps-All; Cintex of America; A.M.S.

40108 (HQ)Benchmark Sales
3 Townline Cir
Rochester, NY 14623-2537   585-424-7420
    Fax: 585-295-8299
    jchisholm@benchmarksales.com
Broker of frozen foods, dairy/deli items, groceries, meat and meat products, produce, seafood, spices, etc.

President: John Narkiewicz
VP: Joe Petrin
VP Sales: Jo Eells
Contact: Mindy Wheeler
mindywheeler@benchmarksales.com
Estimated Sales: $10-20 Million
Number Employees: 3
Square Footage: 12000
Markets Served:
  Food Service Operators
Brokered Products include:
  Dairy/Deli, Frozen Food, Groceries, Meat, Meat Products, Produce, Seafood, Spices, Disposables, Equipment & Supplies

40109 Bender-Goodman Co Inc
35 Journal Sq # 925
Suite 928
Jersey City, NJ 07306-4007   201-216-9009
    Fax: 201-216-0028 www.bendergoodman.com
Broker of egg, dairy products and oil replacements
Vice President: Richard Broad
VP: R Broad
Senior VP: R Kellert
Marketing Director: R Kellert
Sales Director: R Broad
Estimated Sales: $20-50 Million
Number Employees: 5-9
Square Footage: 3000
Type of Packaging: Consumer, Bulk
Markets Served:
  Food Manufacturers & Processors, Super Market Chains, Wholesale Distributors, Food Service Operators
Primary Brands Brokered include: Papetti's; Ventura Foods; Monarch Egg; Primegg; Brown Produce; Mentone Egg
Brokered Products include:
  Dairy/Deli

40110 Benson-Mitchell
2109 1st Ave N
Fargo, ND 58102   701-237-9036
    Fax: 701-237-9069
Broker of confectionery and dairy/deli products, frozen foods, general merchandise, groceries, etc.
VP Treasurer: Dan Geraghty
VP: Charles Breneman
Contact: Dan Garidy
benmitfgo@aol.com
Estimated Sales: $2 Million
Number Employees: 14
Markets Served:
  Super Market Chains, Wholesale Distributors, Food Service Operators
Primary Brands Brokered include: Farley-Sather; Jolly Time; Rhodes; Dakota Growers
Brokered Products include:
  Confectionery, Dairy/Deli, Frozen Food, General Merchandise, Groceries, Meat, Meat Products, Private Label, Seafood, Spices

40111 Bentley Food Marketing
5555 DTC PKWY
Suite B2500
Greenwood Village, CO 80111-3066 303-741-6336
    Fax: 303-741-6446
Broker of confectionery and dairy/deli items, frozen and health foods, groceries, industrial ingredients, meat, private label and bakery items
Estimated Sales: $10-20 Million
Number Employees: 15
Square Footage: 12000
Markets Served:
  Food Manufacturers & Processors, Super Market Chains, Wholesale Distributors, Food Service Operators
Primary Brands Brokered include: Dole Dried Fruit & Nut Co.; Pompeian, Inc.; Hudson Foods; Shultz Foods; Sara Lee Baking Co.; Mott's
Brokered Products include:
  Confectionery, Dairy/Deli, Frozen Food, General Merchandise, Groceries, Health Food, Ingredients, Meat, Meat Products, Private Label

40112 Berk Enterprises
1554 Thomas Rd SE
1554 Thomas Road South East
Warren, OH 44484-5119   330-369-1192
    Fax: 330-369-6279 800-323-3547
    info@berkpaper.com www.berkpaper.com
Broker of general merchandise including insecticides, toilet bowl cleaners and paper products

Owner: Robert Berk
ap@berkpaper.com
Estimated Sales: $5 Million
Number Employees: 50-99
Type of Packaging: Consumer, Food Service, Private Label, Bulk
Markets Served:
  Food Manufacturers & Processors, Super Market Chains, Wholesale Distributors, Food Service Operators
Primary Brands Brokered include: Berkley Square; Mr. Magic; Quickill; Tidal Wave

40113 Bertran Enterprises
40 E 78th St # 6f
New York, NY 10075-1830   212-439-8361
    Fax: 212-439-8364
Import and export broker of groceries, produce and seafood; serving wholesalers/distributors
President: Salomon Moussatche
Estimated Sales: $5-10 Million
Number Employees: 5-9
Square Footage: 5200
Markets Served:
  Wholesale Distributors
Brokered Products include:
  Exports, Groceries, Imports, Produce, Seafood

40114 Best Brands
1755, boulevard Lionel-Bertrand
Boisbriand, QC J7H 1N8
Canada   450-435-0674
    Fax: 450-435-0363 800-361-7614
    p.rivard@meilleuresmarques.com
    www.meilleuresmarques.com
Import broker of groceries, confectionery products and sauces
President/General Manager: Pierre Rivard
VP, Supply Chain: Leif Ellefsen
VP, Finances-IT: Diane Bouchard
VP, Human Resources: Ginette Longchamp
VP, Marketing: Lyne Chayer
VP, Sales: Robert Comeau
Purchasing Director: Francois Blanchard
Type of Packaging: Consumer, Private Label, Bulk
Markets Served:
  Super Market Chains, Wholesale Distributors
Primary Brands Brokered include: Trebor Canada Ltd.; Chef LeLarge; Cop. Hardi; St. Lubert BBQ; Bert Helet; Van Houtte; Fine Cuisine; Loney's; Major Gourmet; Pasta Fiesta; SuWong; Atable
Brokered Products include:
  Confectionery, Groceries, Imports, Spices

40115 Best Marketing Reps
422 Gregory Ave
Weehawken, NJ 07086-5646   201-330-3303
    Fax: 201-330-3383 bestmarketing@aol.com
    www.bestmarketingreps.com
Manufacturers' representative for food service equipment and supplies including plasticware, heaters, warming carts, etc. Also furniture and furnishings including outdoor, seating, carpets, etc.
President, Principal: Manny Tehrani
manny.tehrani@bestmarketingreps.com
Sales: Teddy Tehrani
Sales: Peter Kalin
Office Manager: Kim Klima
Estimated Sales: $2 Million
Number Employees: 1-4
Markets Served:
  Wholesale Distributors, Food Service Operators
Primary Brands Brokered include: Plastics Manufacturing; Alibert; F.C.D.; Gar; Lambert; Alliance Storage Units
Brokered Products include:
  General Merchandise, Foodservice Equipment & Supplies, Etc.

40116 Beta Pure Foods
2100 Deleware Avenue
Santa Cruz, CA 95060   831-685-6565
    Fax: 831-685-6569 www.betapure.com
Organic frozen fruits and vegetables, concentrates and purees, sweeteners. Founded in 1994.
President: Loren Morr
Number Employees: 5-9
Parent Co: SunOpta
Type of Packaging: Food Service, Private Label, Bulk
Markets Served:
  Food Manufacturers & Processors

Brokered Products include:
  Frozen Food, Ingredients, Private Label

40117 (HQ)Betters International Food Corporation
60 Main St
Oakfield, NY 14125-1044   585-948-5242
    Fax: 585-948-5912
Wholesale Suppliers of Concentrates, Frozen Fruits, Frozen Vegetables and Frozen Seafood to the Food Industry
President/CEO: F Betters
CFO: P Betters
VP: B Betters
R&D: Floyd Betters
Quality Control: P Betters
Marketing: Floyd Better
Operations/Manufacturing: Becky Palmer
Production: Floyd Betters
Estimated Sales: $1.2 Million
Number Employees: 5
Type of Packaging: Consumer, Food Service, Private Label, Bulk
Markets Served:
  Food Manufacturers & Processors, Food Service Operators
Brokered Products include:
  Frozen Food, Imports, Ingredients

40118 Biltmore Trading LLC
4245 North Ryans Trail
Flagstaff, AZ 86001-1937   928-226-1900
Food broker. Founded in 2005.
Owner: Ed Herseth
tinkerbell1198@aol.com
Principal: Matt Herseth
Estimated Sales: $3-5 Million
Number Employees: 1-4

40119 (HQ)Binner Marketing & Sales
400-6 Roslyn Rd
Winnipeg, MP R3L 0G5
Canada   204-783-3177
    Fax: 204-783-6363 800-665-0160
    murrayb@binnermarketing.com
    www.binnermarketing.com
Broker of poultry, red meat, seafood, confectionery products, desserts, pasta, etc.
President/General Manager: Murray Binner
CEO: Rollie Binner
Financial/ Company Programs: Jan McCammon
Food Service Sales Manager: Brad Elkie
Regional Manager Retail Western Canada: Bryan Elkie
Estimated Sales: $5.1 Million
Number Employees: 14
Markets Served:
  Food Manufacturers & Processors, Super Market Chains, Wholesale Distributors, Food Service Operators
Brokered Products include:
  Confectionery, Groceries, Meat, Meat Products, Seafood, Pasta, Sauces, etc.

40120 Bird Marketing
4160 Medoc Dr
Kenner, LA 70065   504-468-3636
    Fax: 504-466-1881 http://birdmarketing.co.uk/
Broker of dairy/deli products, frozen foods, seafood, private label items and spices
President: George Vogel
CEO: Jay Lehmann
Managing Director: Edward Babington
Estimated Sales: $1-2.5 Million
Number Employees: 3
Type of Packaging: Food Service
Markets Served:
  Food Service Operators
Brokered Products include:
  Dairy/Deli, Exports, Frozen Food, Groceries, Spices

40121 Bireta Company
1419 S Milford Rd
Highland, MI 48357-4864   248-887-0100
    Fax: 248-887-0111 info@bireta.com
    www.bireta.com
Manufacturers' representative for food service equipment; serving wholesalers/distributors
President: Larry Bireta
Sales Representative: Jason Bireta
Contact: Joe Bireta
joe@bireta.com

Food Brokers / A-Z

Estimated Sales: $2.5-5 Million
Number Employees: 5-9
Markets Served:
   Wholesale Distributors
Primary Brands Brokered include: Middleby Marshal; Wells/Bloomfield; CTX; Wood Stone; CookTek; Tec; Ametek/NCC; TurboChef; HF Coors China Company; JR Carr; Fish Oven; Carter-Hoffmann; Fisher Faucets; Discovery Products
Brokered Products include:
   General Merchandise, Foodservice Equipment

40122 Bisek & Co Inc
4873 S Oliver Dr # 200
Suite 200
Virginia Beach, VA 23455-2700   757-460-0968
   Fax: 757-460-2185 craig@bisek.com
   www.bisek.com
Bisek & Company is a distributing agent and broker to U.S. military commissary stores worldwide and handles all brand name grocery store products including such items as confectionery, dairy/deli products, frozen foods, spicesseafood, meats and meat products, etc.
President/CEO: Craig Bisek
bisek@bisek.com
Marketing: Laurie Cust
SVP Sales: Don Stickles
Operations: Jennifer Harrell
Estimated Sales: $2.9 Million
Number Employees: 10-19
Square Footage: 5000
Type of Packaging: Consumer
Brokered Products include:
   Confectionery, Dairy/Deli, Frozen Food, General Merchandise, Groceries, Health Food, Meat, Meat Products, Seafood, Spices

40123 Bittinger Sales
281 Frederick St
Hanover, PA 17331-3614   717-637-3733
   Fax: 717-637-2242 abittinger@supernet.com
Broker of frozen vegetables and ingredients
Owner: Allen Bittinger
abittinger@supernet.com
Estimated Sales: $300,000-$500,000
Number Employees: 1-4
Markets Served:
   Food Manufacturers & Processors, Super Market Chains, Wholesale Distributors, Food Service Operators
Primary Brands Brokered include: John Copes; Bright Harvest Foods
Brokered Products include:
   Frozen Food, Private Label

40124 Bixby Food Sales
10223 S Fritz Rd
Maple City, MI 49664-9643   231-334-6660
   Fax: 231-334-6650
Broker of ingredients and frozen fruits and vegetables; serving all markets
President: Matt Bixby
Estimated Sales: Less than $500,000
Number Employees: 1-4
Markets Served:
   Food Manufacturers & Processors, Super Market Chains, Wholesale Distributors, Food Service Operators
Brokered Products include:
   Frozen Food, Ingredients, Frozen Fruits & Vegetables

40125 Blackwing Ostrich MeatsInc.
19588 Il Route 173
Antioch, IL 60002-7206   847-838-4888
   Fax: 847-838-4899 800-326-7874
   roger@blackwing.com www.blackwing.com
Organic beef, chicken, buffalo, ostrich and game meats
President/Owner: Roger Gerber
VP: Beth Kaplan
bak@blackwing.com
Estimated Sales: $12 Million
Number Employees: 26
Number of Brands: 5
Number of Products: 140
Square Footage: 32000
Type of Packaging: Consumer, Food Service, Private Label, Bulk
Markets Served:
   Super Market Chains, Wholesale Distributors, Food Service Operators
Brokered Products include:
   Meat

40126 Bloodworth & Associates
1219 SE Lafayette Street
Tualatin, OR 97062   503-939-3209
   Fax: 503-233-7605
Broker of food handling systems and private label products; serving food processors, supermarket chains and wholesalers/distributors
President: William Bloodworth
Number Employees: 1-4
Markets Served:
   Food Manufacturers & Processors, Super Market Chains, Wholesale Distributors
Primary Brands Brokered include: AD Products; Pinckney Plastics; Bently Seed Co.
Brokered Products include:
   General Merchandise, Private Label

40127 Bloomfield Bakers
10711 Bloomfield St
Los Alamitos, CA 90720-2503   562-594-4411
   Fax: 562-742-0408 800-594-4111
Cookies, cereals, crackers, bars and mixes. Founded in 1981.
President: Sam Calderon
Owner/CEO: William Ross
Research & Development Manager: Christina Lates
Quality Control Manager: Steve Huber
National Sales Manager: Russ Case
Contact: Raiza Bastidas
braiza@phonewareinc.com
COO: Gary Marx
Plant/Production Manager: Ricardo Gonzalez
Estimated Sales: $5-10 Million
Number Employees: 850
Square Footage: 300000
Type of Packaging: Private Label
Markets Served:
   Food Manufacturers & Processors, Food Service Operators
Brokered Products include:
   Dairy/Deli, Private Label

40128 Bob Rowe Sales
14899 Memorial Hwy
Miami, FL 33168   305-947-9966
   Fax: 305-947-5526
Broker of frozen foods, nondairy toppings, tea, meats, seafood, spices, etc.
President: Steve Schultz
Owner/CEO: Bob Rowe
Contact: Cheryl Dickson
cdickson@bobrowesales.com
Secretary/Treasurer: Elaine Rowe
Estimated Sales: $2.5-5 Million
Number Employees: 13
Square Footage: 30000
Markets Served:
   Wholesale Distributors, Food Service Operators
Primary Brands Brokered include: Barber Foods; Lipton; Fishery Products; Dubuque Foods; JR Simplot
Brokered Products include:
   Frozen Food, Groceries, Meat, Meat Products, Seafood, Spices, Bread Dough, Non-Dairy Toppings, Tea

40129 Bob's Seafood
8660 Olive Blvd
St Louis, MO 63132-2509   314-993-4844
   Fax: 913-451-8126 www.bobsseafoodstl.com
President: Robert Mephametham
Owner/VP: Robert Magoon
Estimated Sales: $1 Million
Number Employees: 5-9

40130 Bodie-Rickett & Associates
2189 Old Lake Cove
Memphis, TN 38119-6639   901-757-7772
   Fax: 901-757-7920 bodier6928@aol.com
Broker of groceries, confectionery products, snack foods and general merchandise
President: W Bodie
VP: G Rickett
Secretary: J Bodie
Estimated Sales: $1-2.5 Million
Number Employees: 1-4
Markets Served:
   Food Manufacturers & Processors, Super Market Chains, Wholesale Distributors, Food Service Operators
Primary Brands Brokered include: Spangler Candy Co.
Brokered Products include:
   Confectionery, General Merchandise, Groceries, Snack Foods

40131 Boehmer Sales Agency
1261 Kensington Dr
Biloxi, MS 39530-1623   228-207-0498
   Fax: 228-374-0761 800-621-8855
Broker of general merchandise and packaging products
President: Richard Boehmer
Sales Manager: Charlotte Fraisse
Secretary: Thomas Boehmer
Estimated Sales: $2.5-5 Million
Number Employees: 1-4
Markets Served:
   Food Manufacturers & Processors, Super Market Chains, Wholesale Distributors, Food Service Operators
Primary Brands Brokered include: Borden Institutional Products; Jet Plastica Industries; Alcan Foil Products, Inc.; Hamilton Plastics, Inc.; Workwell Company
Brokered Products include:
   General Merchandise, Packaging Products

40132 Booth, Schwager & Associates
2248 Sheridan Rd Ste 1
Zion, IL 60099   847-872-2245
   Fax: 847-872-5352
Broker of confectionery products, cookies, nuts, snacks, private label items, general merchandise, produce, etc.
Owner/SVP: James Booth
President/VP: Thomas Booth
CFO: Flora Booth
VP: Tim Booth
Estimated Sales: $10-20 Million
Number Employees: 5
Square Footage: 4600
Markets Served:
   Super Market Chains, Wholesale Distributors, Food Service Operators
Primary Brands Brokered include: Bob's Candies; Chocolate House; Georgia Nut Co.; Kelenbisca; Haribo of America, Inc.; F.B. Washburn
Brokered Products include:
   Confectionery, Frozen Food, General Merchandise, Groceries, Private Label, Produce, Cookies, Nuts, Snacks, Etc.

40133 Borton Brokerage Company
713 Turrentine Trl
Creve Coeur, MO 63141   314-434-2323
   Fax: 636-928-7758
Import broker of confectionery and dairy/deli items, frozen foods, groceries, meat and meat products, etc.
Owner/President: G Borton
Estimated Sales: $500,000-$1 million
Number Employees: 4
Square Footage: 10800
Markets Served:
   Food Manufacturers & Processors, Super Market Chains, Wholesale Distributors, Food Service Operators
Primary Brands Brokered include: Southern Fried Catfish; Gel-Spice; Bush Brothers; Ember Farms; Speako Foods; Colonial Beef
Brokered Products include:
   Confectionery, Dairy/Deli, Frozen Food, Groceries, Imports, Meat, Meat Products, Private Label, Produce, Seafood, Spices

40134 Bosshart Food Svc
340 Industrial Blvd
Waconia, MN 55387-1738   952-944-5610
   Fax: 952-944-5182 bosshart@visi.com
Broker of confectionery and dairy/deli products, frozen foods, groceries, industrial ingredients, meat and meat products, etc.; serving food processors and food service operators
President: B Bosshart
CEO: Bruce Bosshart
bb@bosshartfoodservice.com
Estimated Sales: Less Than $500,000
Number Employees: 1-4
Parent Co: Bosshart Food/BA Brokerage
Markets Served:
   Food Manufacturers & Processors, Food Service Operators

Primary Brands Brokered include: Bil Mar Foods; Norpac; Continental Mills; Fishking Processors; Michigan Fruit; Allen Canning
Brokered Products include:
   Confectionery, Dairy/Deli, Frozen Food, Groceries, Ingredients, Meat, Meat Products, Seafood, Spices

40135 Bottom Line Foods
15757 Pines Blvd # 302
Suite 302
Pembroke Pines, FL 33027-1207   954-843-0562
Fax: 954-843-0568
Distributor and packer, exporter for frozen foods, meats, cheese, groceries, seafood, spices, etc.
President: Rein Bos
General Manager: Brandon Koppert
Estimated Sales: $1.1 Million
Number Employees: 1-4
Square Footage: 4000
Type of Packaging: Food Service, Private Label, Bulk
Markets Served:
   Food Manufacturers & Processors, Super Market Chains, Wholesale Distributors, Food Service Operators
Primary Brands Brokered include: TopLine; IBP; Tyson
Brokered Products include:
   Dairy/Deli, Exports, Frozen Food, Groceries, Ingredients, Meat, Meat Products, Private Label, Seafood, Spices

40136 Bowerman Associates
PO Box 616
Liverpool, NY 13088   315-453-5288
Fax: 315-453-5284 info@ebowerman.com
www.ebowerman.com
Manufacturers' repesentative of food service equipment
President: Ron Bowerman
VP: Mike Johnson
Marketing Manager: Candice Ballard
Sales Representative: Stephen Homberger
Office Manager/Customer Service: Judy Tingley
Estimated Sales: $1 Million
Number Employees: 9
Markets Served:
   Wholesale Distributors
Brokered Products include:
   General Merchandise, Foodservice Equipment

40137 Brandywine Frozen Fruit
924 Oak Ridge Rd
Bryn Mawr, PA 19010   610-525-1462
Fax: 610-525-1381
Frozen fruit
Owner: Frederick Larson
Estimated Sales: $1-2.5 Million
Number Employees: 1-4
Type of Packaging: Private Label
Brokered Products include:
   Frozen Food, Private Label

40138 Bratt-Foster-Advantage Sales
306 Lakeside Rd
Syracuse, NY 13209-9729   315-488-3840
Fax: 315-488-9079 jlfoster@advanmark.com
Broker of confectionery products, frozen foods, general merchandise, groceries, produce, seafood, etc, serving the areas of Buffalo and Syracuse
President: John Foster
jlfoster@advanmark.com
VP: Stephen Barone
Estimated Sales: $4.1 Million
Number Employees: 10-19
Square Footage: 19500
Markets Served:
   Super Market Chains, Wholesale Distributors
Primary Brands Brokered include: Dole; Filippo Berio; Quickie Mfg; Jel Sert Co.
Brokered Products include:
   Confectionery, Dairy/Deli, Frozen Food, Groceries, Private Label, Produce

40139 Brennan Food Services
136 Dwight Rd
Longmeadow, MA 01106-1759   413-565-3181
brecon44@aol.com
Broker of meats, deli products, produce and baked goods; serving food service operators, wholesaler/distributors and supermarket chains; also, HACCP and SSOP services available
Owner: Jim Brennan
Co-Owner: Ann Brennan
Estimated Sales: $1-3 Million
Number Employees: 5-9
Markets Served:
   Super Market Chains, Wholesale Distributors, Food Service Operators
Brokered Products include:
   Dairy/Deli, Meat, Produce, Baked Goods, Etc.

40140 Bridge City Food Marketing
110 SE 2nd Ave
Portland, OR 97214-1001   503-239-8024
Fax: 503-236-1174
Broker of dairy/deli products, produce, seafood, spices, frozen foods, general merchandise, meats, private label items, etc.
Manager: Dan Mc Leod
Co-Owner/VP: D Wickstrom
Co-Owner/VP, Sales: P Bice
Estimated Sales: $10-20 Million
Number Employees: 5-9
Square Footage: 3200
Markets Served:
   Food Manufacturers & Processors, Super Market Chains, Wholesale Distributors, Food Service Operators
Primary Brands Brokered include: J.M. Smucker Co.; Reckitt & Colman; Tryson Co.; Pilgrim's Pride; Fishery Products International
Brokered Products include:
   Dairy/Deli, Frozen Food, General Merchandise, Meat, Meat Products, Private Label, Produce, Seafood, Spices

40141 Brierley & King Brokerage Corporation
10 Tower Office Park
Suite 100
Woburn, MA 01801-6784   781-273-4466
Fax: 781-270-6784 TedJr@BrierleyandKing.com
Broker of Confectionery, Snacks, Cookies, Novelties, Seasonal, HBC, Convenience foods and non-foods
President: Ted Brierley
tedjr@brierleyandking.com
Estimated Sales: $1.2 Million
Number Employees: 10
Markets Served:
   Super Market Chains, Wholesale Distributors, Food Service Operators
Primary Brands Brokered include: Just Born, Inc.; Ben Myerson; Van Melle, Inc.; Jaret International; Bob's; Old Dominion
Brokered Products include:
   Confectionery, General Merchandise

40142 British Confectionery Company
PO Box 188
Mount Pearl, NL A1N 2C2
Canada   709-747-2377
Fax: 709-368-3737
Manufacturers' agent of imported and domestic confectionery products
President: David Connolly
VP: Gerald Connolly
Sales Manager: Brian Kelly
Estimated Sales: $9.7 Million
Number Employees: 70
Square Footage: 156000
Primary Brands Brokered include: Leaf; Comet; Ce De Candy; Jolly Rancher; Burtons Bisuits; Lees Snow Balls
Brokered Products include:
   Confectionery, Imports

40143 Brody Food Brokerage Corporation
780 Broadway Ave Ste 2
Holbrook, NY 11741   631-244-8900
Fax: 631-244-8908
Broker of dairy/deli products, groceries, industrial ingredients, private label items, spices, etc.; serving food processors, food service operators and wholesalers/distributors
President: Philip S Brody
Estimated Sales: $1.3 Million
Number Employees: 8
Square Footage: 2000

40144 Brokerage Sales Company
1210 Boyce Ave
Towson, MD 21204   410-821-8873
Fax: 410-296-6355 w1130@aol.com
Broker of groceries; serving supermarket chains, and wholesalers/distributors
President: W Thompson
VP: S Thompson
VP: R Thompson
Estimated Sales: $300,000-500,000
Number Employees: 1-4
Markets Served:
   Food Manufacturers & Processors, Super Market Chains, Wholesale Distributors
Brokered Products include:
   Groceries

40145 Broms Brokerage
525 Tower Dr
Moore, OK 73160-6701   405-794-1561
Fax: 405-794-1596
Broker of confectionery and dairy/deli items, frozen foods, general merchandise, groceries, meat and meat products, etc.; serving all markets
Owner/President: Gerald Broms
Controller: Katie Johnson
VP: Carrie Autry
Sales Director: Teddy Thomas
Contact: Jerry Broms
g.broms@bromsbrokerage.com
Estimated Sales: B
Number Employees: 18
Markets Served:
   Food Manufacturers & Processors, Super Market Chains, Wholesale Distributors, Food Service Operators
Brokered Products include:
   Confectionery, Dairy/Deli, Frozen Food, General Merchandise, Groceries, Meat, Meat Products, Private Label

40146 Brothers International Food Corporation
1175 Lexington Ave
Rochester, NY 14606   585-343-3007
Fax: 585-343-4218
ingredients@brothersinternational.com
brothersinternational.com
Fruit ingredients
President & Co-CEO: Matt Betters
Co-CEO: Travis Betters
Estimated Sales: $6.2 Million
Number Employees: 33
Markets Served:
   Food Manufacturers & Processors
Primary Brands Brokered include: Lost Vineyards
Brokered Products include:
   Alcoholic Beverages, Frozen Food, Health Food, Imports

40147 Browning Brokerage Company
6100 W 96th Street
Suite 150
Indianapolis, IN 46278   317-344-7300
Fax: 317-344-7400 info@browninginv.com
www.browninginvestments.com
Broker of confectionery and dairy/deli products, general merchandise, private label items, health foods, meats, spices, seafood, produce, groceries, etc.; serving food service operators, supermarket chains andwholesalers/distributors
President & CEO: John F. Hirschman
VP & CFO: David S. Gabovitch
SVP of Development: Adam G. Chavers
Administrative & Marketing Associate: Erin Drake
Human Resources: Liz Hall
Dir. Of Safety & Field Operations: Jerry Harper
Estimated Sales: $10-20 Million
Number Employees: 20-49
Markets Served:
   Super Market Chains, Wholesale Distributors, Food Service Operators
Brokered Products include:
   Confectionery, Dairy/Deli, Frozen Food, General Merchandise, Groceries, Health Food, Meat, Meat Products, Private Label, Produce, Seafood, Spices

40148 Bruce Chaney & Company
5000 Track Ave
Cleveland, OH 44127   216-883-6200
Fax: 216-883-6204

Food Brokers / A-Z

Broker of frozen foods, general merchandise, groceries, industrial ingredients, private label items and seafood; serving all markets
Owner/President: James Chaney
CEO: E Chaney
VP: Chuck Chaney
Estimated Sales: $3-5 Million
Number Employees: 3
Brokered Products include:
  Confectionery, Ingredients

40149 Buckley, Thorne, Messina & McDermott
202 Twin Oaks Drive
Suite 1
Syracuse, NY 13206-1203   315-463-5621
        Fax: 315-463-5877
Broker of frozen foods, general merchandise, groceries, meat and meat products, private label items, etc.
General Manager/VP: Robert Sisson
General Manager/VP: Richard Lotano
Number Employees: 30
Square Footage: 112000
Parent Co: Buckley, Thorne, Messina & McDermott
Markets Served:
  Food Manufacturers & Processors, Super Market Chains, Wholesale Distributors, Food Service Operators
Primary Brands Brokered include: DowBrands; Lipton; Hershey; Marcal; Riviana Foods; Heluva Good Cheese
Brokered Products include:
  Confectionery, Dairy/Deli, Frozen Food, General Merchandise, Groceries, Health Food, Meat, Meat Products, Private Label, Produce, Seafood, Spices

40150 Budd Mayer Company of Jackson Inc.
785 Commerce St
Jackson, MS 39201-5618   601-355-1745
        Fax: 610-355-1745
Broker of spices, frozen food, general merchandise, meat products, groceries, dairy/deli and confectionery products, etc.; serving all markets
President: Bob Keifer
Executive VP: Gaylon Ronbinson
Executive VP: Jerry Babin
Number Employees: 10-19
Square Footage: 40000
Markets Served:
  Food Manufacturers & Processors, Super Market Chains, Wholesale Distributors, Food Service Operators
Primary Brands Brokered include: Stouffers; Sara Lee Frozen; Riceland/Chef Way; Gorton's of Gloucester; Daisy Brand; Beatrice Cheese
Brokered Products include:
  Confectionery, Dairy/Deli, Frozen Food, General Merchandise, Groceries, Meat, Meat Products, Spices

40151 Budd Mayer of Mobile
205 Government St
Mobile, AL 36602-0001   251-208-7395
  Fax: 251-208-7548 mayor@cityofmobile.org
        www.cityofmobile.org
Broker of confectionery and dairy/deli products, general merchandise, meat/meat products, dairy/deli items, etc.; serving food service operators, supermarket chains and wholesalers/distributors
Manager: Samuel L Jones
VP: G Forman
Number Employees: 5
Parent Co: Budd Mayer
Markets Served:
  Super Market Chains, Wholesale Distributors, Food Service Operators
Brokered Products include:
  Confectionery, Dairy/Deli, Frozen Food, General Merchandise, Groceries, Meat, Meat Products, Private Label, Produce, Seafood

40152 Buley Patterson Sales Company
625 Horner St
Johnstown, PA 15902   814-536-7531
  Fax: 814-539-1006 800-253-4508
Import and export broker of dairy/deli products, frozen foods, general merchandise, groceries and private label items; serving food service operators, supermarket chains and wholesaler/distributors
President: James Bruce
VP: D Bruce
Secretary: M Bruce
Estimated Sales: $5-10 Million
Number Employees: 1-4
Markets Served:
  Super Market Chains, Wholesale Distributors, Food Service Operators
Brokered Products include:
  Dairy/Deli, Exports, Frozen Food, General Merchandise, Groceries, Imports, Private Label

40153 Burdett Associates
3945 Wasatch Blvd # 321
Salt Lake City, UT 84124-2247   801-277-2356
    Fax: 801-277-2357 burdettassoc@msn.com
Broker of general merchandise and private label items; serving food processors, supermarket chains and wholesalers/distributors
Owner: Tony Burdett
CEO: Don Shepard
CFO: S Burdett
Estimated Sales: $2.5-5 Million
Number Employees: 1-4
Markets Served:
  Super Market Chains, Wholesale Distributors
Brokered Products include:
  General Merchandise, Private Label

40154 Burdette Beckmann Inc
5851 Johnson St
Hollywood, FL 33021-5635   954-983-4360
        Fax: 954-983-4405
Broker of confectionery and private label items, meat snacks and novelties
President: David Adams
dadams@bbiteam.com
Account Executive: Heath Hayes
VP: Jack Anderson
District Manager: Bill Jenkins
Estimated Sales: Less than $500,000
Number Employees: 20-49
Square Footage: 4000
Markets Served:
  Super Market Chains, Wholesale Distributors
Primary Brands Brokered include: Goetz's Candy Company; Spangler Candy Company; Beacon Sweets; Bradley Candy; Judson-Atkinson; Zeebs, Inc.
Brokered Products include:
  Confectionery, General Merchandise, Groceries, Meat Products, Private Label, Meat Snacks & Novelties

40155 Burley Brokerage
7125 Amundson Ave S
Edina, MN 55439   952-943-1970
  Fax: 952-943-1975 burleysales@burleyfoods.com
        www.burleyfoods.com
Broker of confectionery and dairy/deli products, frozen foods, industrial ingredients, meats, spices, etc
Owner: Michael Burley
GM/Sales: Janine Maurer
Sales: Bryan Buckley
Estimated Sales: $5-10 Million
Number Employees: 5-9
Markets Served:
  Food Manufacturers & Processors, Wholesale Distributors, Food Service Operators
Primary Brands Brokered include: French's Ingredients; Giorgio Foods, Inc.; KFI/OMI; The Masterson Co.; Maine Wild Blueberry Co.; Shade Foods, Inc.
Brokered Products include:
  Confectionery, Dairy/Deli, Frozen Food, Ingredients, Meat, Meat Products, Spices

40156 Bushwick Commission Company
201 Northwest Drive
Farmingdale, NY 11735   516-249-6030
  Fax: 516-249-6047 800-645-9470
        www.bushwickpotato.com
Broker of potatoes, onions, peaches, cabbage, sweet corn, broccoli, lettuce, plums, nectarines, cantaloupes and much more
Owner/President: David Gray
VP/Treasurer: Jack Hyman
VP Sales: Kenneth Gray
Contact: Joy Feesler
feeslerj@bushwickpotato.com
Estimated Sales: $2.1 Million
Number Employees: 8
Markets Served:
  Food Manufacturers & Processors, Super Market Chains, Wholesale Distributors, Food Service Operators
Brokered Products include:
  Produce

40157 Butkevich Associates
2 N Main St
Avon, MA 02322-1231   508-584-1818
  Fax: 508-583-8401 800-225-6012
        sales@butkevich.com
Manufacturers' representative for foodserv ice equipment and supplies; serving all markets in New England
Owner: Bernard Butkevich
bucky@butkevich.com
President: Mark Butkevich
Bookkeeping: Patricia Butkevich
VP: Brian Butkevich
Sales: Brian Butkevich
bucky@butkevich.com
Office Manager: Maria Wilson Sepulveda
Estimated Sales: $9 Million
Number Employees: 5-9
Square Footage: 9600
Markets Served:
  Food Manufacturers & Processors, Super Market Chains, Wholesale Distributors, Food Service Operators
Primary Brands Brokered include: Atlas Metal; Beverage Air; Bakers' Pride; Robot Coupe; Keating; Prince Castle

40158 Buzz Crown Enterprises
6349 Peters Creek Rd
Roanoke, VA 24019   540-563-2003
        Fax: 540-362-0930
Import broker of confectionery, dairy/deli products, frozen foods, general merchandise, private label items, seafood, meat and meat products; serving all markets
President: Buzz Crown
Vice President: Taylor Crown
Estimated Sales: $5-10 Million
Number Employees: 5
Square Footage: 20000
Parent Co: Buzz Crown Enterprises
Type of Packaging: Consumer, Food Service, Private Label, Bulk
Markets Served:
  Food Manufacturers & Processors, Super Market Chains, Wholesale Distributors, Food Service Operators
Brokered Products include:
  Confectionery, Dairy/Deli, Frozen Food, General Merchandise, Imports, Meat, Meat Products, Private Label, Seafood

40159 (HQ)Byrd International
30165 Wildlife Lane
Salisbury, MD 21804   410-749-7075
  Fax: 410-749-7029 Don@byrdinternational.com
        www.byrdinternational.com
Pasteurized crab meat
Owner/President: Thomas Ruark
President: Lloyd Byrd
National Sales Manager: Ron Johnson
Brokered Products include:
  Seafood

40160 Byrne & Assoc Inc
1083 Hicks Blvd # 100
Fairfield, OH 45014-2868   513-829-9117
  Fax: 513-829-1638 800-735-7928
        dennis@byrnerep.com www.byrnerep.com
Manufacturers' representative for cooking, serving and refrigeration equipment; serving wholesalers/distributors
President: Dennis Byrne
dennis@byrnerep.com
Marketing: Sharon Shields
Sales Consultant: Joe Byrne
Office Manager/Inside Sales: Neva Renners
Estimated Sales: $2.5-5 Million
Number Employees: 1-4
Markets Served:
  Wholesale Distributors
Brokered Products include:
  General Merchandise, Cooking, Serving & Refrigeration Equip.

Food Brokers / A-Z

40161 Byron A Carlson Inc
40 Radio Circle Dr # 3
Mt Kisco, NY 10549-2633   914-242-1750
          Fax: 914-242-1749 www.bacarlson.com
Broker of industrial ingredients, fruit juices, purees, concentrates, flavors, dried citrus fruits, oils and dried apple products; serving food processors
President: Bing Carlson
bcarlson@bacarlson.com
VP: Kim Carlson Touseau
Estimated Sales: $1.7 Million
Number Employees: 5-9
Markets Served:
  Food Manufacturers & Processors, Food Service Operators
Primary Brands Brokered include: Atoka Cranberries; Canandaigua Concentrates, Confoco International Ltd; Fruit Smart; Growers Co-Op; Kerry Specialty Ingredients; Northwest Naturals; RV Industries; Specialty Brands of America; Tree Top; Vita-Pakt Citrus Products
Brokered Products include:
  Confectionery, Frozen Food, Health Food, Imports, Ingredients, Fruit Juice, Concentrates, Purees

40162 (HQ)C J Irwin Co Inc
4498 Main St # 2
Suite 2
Amherst, NY 14226-3826   716-839-1015
          Fax: 716-839-0438 800-221-1273
nancy@cjirwin.com www.cjirwin.com
Broker of groceries, industrial ingredients and private label products and spices
President/CEO: Dan Irwin
dan3@cjirwin.com
VP: Nancy Irwin
Estimated Sales: $2.5-5 Million
Number Employees: 5-9
Square Footage: 700
Type of Packaging: Bulk
Markets Served:
  Food Manufacturers & Processors, Wholesale Distributors
Primary Brands Brokered include: Baker's Coconut; DeFrancesco Onion & Garlic; Monitor Sugar Company; Central Soya; Original Nut House; Papetti's Hygrade Egg Products
Brokered Products include:
  Confectionery, Dairy/Deli, General Merchandise, Groceries, Health Food, Ingredients, Private Label, Produce, Spices

40163 (HQ)C. Lloyd Johnson Company
8031 Hampton Blvd
Norfolk, VA 23505   757-423-2832
          Fax: 757-423-0645 800-446-8089
Broker of frozen foods, general merchandise and groceries
CEO: C Llyod Johnson Jr
Sales Representative/Eastern-Northern: Rosa Geroca
Contact: Carol Vangilder
cvangilder@clloydjohnson.com
Number Employees: 1-4
Markets Served:
  Food Service Operators
Primary Brands Brokered include: Mars, Inc.; Campbell's; Best Foods; Beatrice; Tropicana; Dial Corporation
Brokered Products include:
  Frozen Food, General Merchandise, Groceries

40164 C. Mascari & Associates
32823 W 12 Mile Rd
Farmington Hills, MI 48334-3304   248-488-1110
          Fax: 248-488-1438 800-446-8089
Broker of confectionery and dairy/deli items, frozen foods, general merchandise, industrial ingredients, meat and meat products, private label/generic items, etc.
President: Charles Mascari
Contact: Bill Hisle
bhisle@cmascari.com
Marketing: Ed Nault
Director Sales: Dave Thurman
Human Resource Manager: Paula Messier
Estimated Sales: $10.30 Million
Number Employees: 26
Markets Served:
  Wholesale Distributors, Food Service Operators
Brokered Products include:
  Confectionery, Dairy/Deli, Frozen Food, General Merchandise, Ingredients, Meat, Meat Products, Private Label, Seafood, Spices

40165 C.B. Powell Limited
2475 Skymark Avenue
Suite #1
Mississauga, ON L4W 4Y6
Canada   905-206-7776
          Fax: 905-625-7034 800-769-2750
                www.cbpowell.com
Full service buy & sell sales and marketing company specializing in imported consumer packaged goods.
Markets served: Mass Merchant, Gas & Convenience, Club, Food.
CEO/Chair: Tim Powell
VP Finance/Administration: Drew Macaskill
EVP: Colin Glaysher
Director Brand Development: Stan Atkinson
Director Sales: Pam Tetford
Director IT/Human Resources: Theresa Flores
Estimated Sales: $11.3 Million
Number Employees: 30
Type of Packaging: Consumer, Food Service, Private Label, Bulk
Markets Served:
  Super Market Chains
Primary Brands Brokered include: Stagg Chili; SPAM Luncheion Meat; Tabasco Brand Pepper Sauce; Patak's Indian Cuisine; Blue Diamond Almonds; Typhoo Tea; Angostura Bitters
Brokered Products include:
  Frozen Food, Imports, Ingredients, Dry Groceries, Ethnic

40166 C.H. Robinson Co.
14701 Charlson Rd
Eden Prairie, MN 55347-5076   952-683-2800
          Fax: 952-933-4747 855-229-6128
solutions@chrobinson.com www.chrobinson.com
Provides: freight transportation (TL, intermodal, ocean, and air freight), cross docking, LTL, customs brokerage, freight forwarding and trucking services, fresh produce sourcing, and information services.
CEO: Bob Biesterfeld
President, NA Surface Transportation: Mac Pinkerton
CFO: Mike Zechmeister
President, Global Freight Forwarding: Michael Short
Year Founded: 1905
Estimated Sales: $14.87 Billion
Number Employees: 15,074
Type of Packaging: Consumer, Food Service, Bulk
Brokered Products include:
  Frozen Food, Groceries, Health Food, Produce, Seafood, Beverages

40167 (HQ)C.R. Peterson Associates
355 Bodwell Street
Avon, MA 02322
          Fax: 508-238-3647 800-257-4040
                binky@crpeterson.com
Manufacturers' representative for food service equipment, furniture and silverware
President: Carl Huerth, Jr.
Contact: Roy Horan
roy@crpeterson.com
Estimated Sales: $2.2 Million
Number Employees: 13
Markets Served:
  Wholesale Distributors, Food Service Operators
Primary Brands Brokered include: Garland; MTS; Servolift; Hatco; 3-M; Admiral Craft
Brokered Products include:
  General Merchandise, Foodservice Equipment, Furniture, Etc.

40168 C.W. Shasky & Associates Ltd.
2880 Portland Drive
Oakville, ON L4K 5P2
Canada   905-829-9414
          Fax: 905-760-7715 www.shasky.com
Manufacturers' representative for foodservice, club and HMR segments
President: Michael Shasky
VP: James Shasky
Estimated Sales: $7.3 Million
Number Employees: 25
Markets Served:
  Super Market Chains, Wholesale Distributors, Food Service Operators
Brokered Products include:
  Groceries, Seafood, Spices

40169 CJ Eaton Brokerage
726 Forest Road
Glenview, IL 60025-3450   847-998-9836
                     Fax: 847-998-9837
Broker of confectionery, nuts and dried fruit
President: C Eaton
VP: M Eaton
Markets Served:
  Wholesale Distributors
Brokered Products include:
  Nuts, Dried Fruit

40170 CLVMarketing
55 Engineers Lane
Farmingdale, NY 11735-1207   631-694-7170
          Fax: 631-694-7243 sales@clvmarketing.com
                www.clvmarketing.com
Manufacturers' representative for foodservice supplies and equipment.
President: Chip Little
Contact: Gina Bush
gbush@theexperiencecorp.com
Estimated Sales: $3-5 Million
Number Employees: 5-9
Markets Served:
  Wholesale Distributors
Primary Brands Brokered include: American Metalcraft; Cambro; Crown Verity; Edlund; Grosfillex; Hall China; Homer Laughlin; Lincoln®; Mercer Tool; Server Products; Superior Products; Walco; Waring
Brokered Products include:
  General Merchandise, Foodservice Equipment, Smallwares

40171 CMT Packaging & Designs, Inc.
312 Amboy Avenue
Metuchen, NJ 08840   732-321-4029
          Fax: 732-549-3615 www.cmtpackaging.com
A custom packaging company for the food and perfume industry.
President: Priya Iyar
Vice President: Pat Archary
VP Sales: Preshal Almore
Estimated Sales: $5,000
Square Footage: 10000

40172 CS Brokers
53 River St # 12
Milford, CT 06460-3346   203-878-7788
          Fax: 203-877-6649 csbrokers@aol.com
Import and domestic broker of confectionery and specialty items, health food, spices and groceries
Owner: Cyrus Settineri
cyrus@csbrokers.com
Office Manager: Diane Palmieri
Estimated Sales: Less Than $500,000
Number Employees: 1-4
Square Footage: 1000
Markets Served:
  Super Market Chains, Wholesale Distributors, Food Service Operators
Primary Brands Brokered include: Calavita USA; Jose Cuervo; Chef Paul Prudhomme's Magic Seasonings; Koppers; Source Atlantique
Brokered Products include:
  Confectionery, Groceries, Health Food, Imports, Spices, Specialty Items

40173 (HQ)Cafe Inc
4416 Monroe Rd # A
Charlotte, NC 28205-7761   704-945-9020
                     Fax: 704-332-3233
Broker of confectionery and dairy/deli products, industrial ingredients, meats, general merchandise, seafood, spices, confectionery items, frozen foods, etc; serving all markets
Partner: Ronnie Fore
Partner: Michael Bolton
Estimated Sales: $20-50 Million
Number Employees: 5-9
Square Footage: 3750
Markets Served:
  Food Manufacturers & Processors, Super Market Chains, Wholesale Distributors, Food Service Operators
Brokered Products include:
  Confectionery, Dairy/Deli, Frozen Food, General Merchandise, Ingredients, Meat, Meat Products, Seafood, Spices

Food Brokers / A-Z

40174 Cajun Creole Products Inc
5610 Daspit Rd
New Iberia, LA 70563-8961 337-229-8464
Fax: 337-229-4814 800-946-8688
info@cajuncreole.com www.cajuncreole.com
Coffee, peanuts and seasoning
President/Manager: Joel Wallins
Secretary/Treasurer: Sandra Wallins
Estimated Sales: $300,000
Number Employees: 5-9
Type of Packaging: Consumer, Food Service, Bulk
Markets Served:
Super Market Chains, Wholesale Distributors, Food Service Operators
Primary Brands Brokered include: Hampton Farms; Flavotech; Unico
Brokered Products include:
Spices, Peanuts, Coffee

40175 California World Trade and Marketing Company
24615 Oneil Ave
Hayward, CA 94544 510-888-9393
Fax: 510-888-1482
Small organization in the grocery companies industries
Owner/President: Stan Names
stan@californiaworldtrade.com
CFO: Nancy Ostler
VP: Lucille Chan
Marketing: Alex Perez
Estimated Sales: $1-2.5 Million
Number Employees: 1-4
Type of Packaging: Food Service, Private Label
Markets Served:
Wholesale Distributors, Food Service Operators
Primary Brands Brokered include: CHE Kong Corporation; Gilt Edge Flour, Inc.; Moorehouse Foods; Riceland Foods, Inc.; Jafat/Wong Plastics
Brokered Products include:
Groceries, Imports, Private Label

40176 Caneast Foods
70 East Beaver Creek Road
Unit 204
Richmond Hill, ON L4B 3B2
Canada 905-771-7300
Fax: 905-771-6816
Import broker of frozen foods, groceries, private label items and seafood
President: Lisa McConnell
Estimated Sales: $5.99 Million
Number Employees: 19
Parent Co: T. McConnell Sales & Marketing
Markets Served:
Food Manufacturers & Processors, Super Market Chains, Wholesale Distributors, Food Service Operators
Brokered Products include:
Frozen Food, Groceries, Imports, Private Label, Seafood

40177 (HQ)Cann Brokerage Inc
210 S Reynolds Rd Ste E
Toledo, OH 43615 419-537-9058
Fax: 419-537-9058 cannbroke@aol.com
Import broker of confectionery and dairy/deli products, groceries, meat products, produce, private label items, etc.; serving food processors, supermarket chains and wholesalers/distributors
President/CEO: Kenneth Cann
Marketing/Sales: Ken Cann
Sales: Bob Wood
Office Manager: Libbey Boyk
Estimated Sales: $10-20 Million
Number Employees: 4
Square Footage: 15000
Markets Served:
Food Manufacturers & Processors, Super Market Chains, Wholesale Distributors, Food Service Operators
Brokered Products include:
Confectionery, Dairy/Deli, Groceries, Imports, Meat Products, Private Label, Produce, Spices

40178 Cardinal Brokerage
5646 Castle Glade
San Antonio, TX 78218-2305 210-732-9062
Fax: 210-732-9069
Broker of groceries
President: Charles Gomez
VP: Charles Gomez, Jr.
Regional Sales Manager: Dean Gomez
Estimated Sales: $5-10 Million
Number Employees: 5-9
Square Footage: 12800
Markets Served:
Food Service Operators
Primary Brands Brokered include: Rico's Products; Deleware Punch
Brokered Products include:
Groceries

40179 (HQ)Carlin Group
1851 Howard St.
Suite M
Elk Grove Village, IL 60007 847-871-4163
carlin-group.com
Confectionery products, general merchandise, grocery and private label items; serving supermarket chains and wholesalers/distributors
Chairman/CEO: Brad Carlin
bcarlin@carlinobrien.com
President/COO: Jeff Mahler
VP, Finance/Corporate Operations: Neil Chamness
Executive Vice President: Albert Vergilio
VP, Marketing/Analytics: Mark Metzger
Year Founded: 1962
Estimated Sales: $100+ Million
Number Employees: 300
Markets Served:
Food Manufacturers & Processors, Super Market Chains, Wholesale Distributors, Food Service Operators
Brokered Products include:
Confectionery, Dairy/Deli, Frozen Food, General Merchandise, Groceries, Health Food, Imports, Ingredients, Private Label, Spices

40180 Carlton Company
4421 Indian Creek Pkwy
Overland Park, KS 66207 855-2-5 98
Fax: 913-642-1576 800-443-2640
is@chromalox.com www.chromalox.com
Manufacturers' rep for electric heaters and controls for packaging equipment, steam tables, ovens, freezers, fryers, etc
President: Andy Gravitt
VP: Mark Stenberg
Sales Engineer: Brad Racen
Contact: Carol James
cjames@carlco.com
Estimated Sales: $1-2.5 Million
Number Employees: 5-9
Primary Brands Brokered include: Chromalox; Ameritherm; Atmosphere Furnace Company
Brokered Products include:
General Merchandise, Electric Heaters

40181 Carpenter Associates
312 Highland Road
Christiana, PA 17509-9663 717-529-3938
Fax: 717-529-3292
Broker of eggs and dairy/deli products
Owner: Don Carpenter
Number Employees: 3
Markets Served:
Wholesale Distributors
Brokered Products include:
Dairy/Deli, Eggs

40182 Carter & Klaw Foods
4029 Bradbury Dr
Marietta, GA 30062-6165 770-579-4773
Fax: 770-579-4773
Estimated Sales: $5-10 Million
Number Employees: 5-9

40183 Cascade Corp
2201 NE 201st Ave
Fairview, OR 97024-9799 503-669-6300
Fax: 503-669-6716 markw@foodguys.com
www.cascorp.com
Broker of frozen berries, fruits, juice, juice concentrates, nuts and everything under the sun
President: Mark Nyman
Senior VP: Richard S Anderson
richard.anderson@cascorp.com
Sales Manager: Mark Warner
Estimated Sales: $20-30 Million
Number Employees: 1000-4999
Type of Packaging: Bulk
Markets Served:
Food Manufacturers & Processors, Wholesale Distributors
Brokered Products include:
Imports, Ingredients

40184 Cashman-Edwards Inc
16650 N 91st St Ste 108
Scottsdale, AZ 85260 480-948-4800
Fax: 480-948-4802
Broker of confectionery, dairy/deli products, health foods, produce, groceries, bakery supplies, spices and industrial ingredients; serving all markets in Arizona and New Mexico
President: Sally Cashman
Estimated Sales: $15 Million
Number Employees: 5-9
Square Footage: 7500
Markets Served:
Food Manufacturers & Processors, Super Market Chains, Wholesale Distributors, Food Service Operators
Brokered Products include:
Confectionery, Dairy/Deli, Groceries, Health Food, Imports, Ingredients, Private Label, Produce, Spices

40185 Celright Foods
5505 Fairway Park Drive
Boynton Beach, FL 33437-1787 561-523-1122
Fax: 561-742-3898
President: Dan Cross
Brokered Products include:
Exports, Meat, Meat Products, Seafood

40186 Central Marketing Assoc
222 E William St
Delaware, OH 43015-3282 740-363-1126
Fax: 740-363-3478 800-326-8785
inforequest@centralmarketing.com
www.centralmarketing.com
Nationwide broker of fresh fruit and vegetables
President: Joyce Waroway
jwaroway@cmafoodservice.com
VP: Michael Dinovo
Estimated Sales: $5-10 Million
Number Employees: 10-19
Markets Served:
Food Manufacturers & Processors, Super Market Chains, Wholesale Distributors, Food Service Operators
Primary Brands Brokered include: Dole; Mann Packing; Sunkist; Tanimura & Antle; The Nunes Company; Pardi Produce
Brokered Products include:
Produce

40187 Central Sales & Marketing
4022 E Southport Rd
Indianapolis, IN 46237 317-786-5300
Fax: 317-786-0711 www.centralsales.net
Broker of dairy/deli products, meats and bakery items
President: D Taylor
Contact: Marsha Osborne
mosborne@centralsales.net
Estimated Sales: $2.5-5 Million
Number Employees: 10-19
Markets Served:
Super Market Chains, Wholesale Distributors
Primary Brands Brokered include: Jimmy Dean; Buddig; Plum Rose
Brokered Products include:
Dairy/Deli, Meat, Bakery Items

40188 Champon & Yung Inc
239 US Highway 22 # 5
Green Brook, NJ 08812-1916 732-968-3800
Fax: 732-968-8300 www.champonyung.com
Broker of spices, oleoresins, aromatic chemicals, etc
President: Angela Arrieta
angela@champon.com
CFO: Denise Yung
VP: Denise Yung
Public Relations: Eve O'Neil
Operations: Kathryn Gruber
Number Employees: 5-9
Brokered Products include:
Ingredients, Spices

40189 Chandler Food Sales Co
601 NW 10th St
Grand Prairie, TX 75050-5415 972-642-5700
Fax: 972-642-1997 800-926-6891

Broker of confectionery and dairy/deli products, general merchandise and groceries
President: Gary Chandler
VP: Chris Chandler
Estimated Sales: $750,000
Number Employees: 10-19
Square Footage: 10500
Markets Served:
 Super Market Chains, Wholesale Distributors
Primary Brands Brokered include: Shaffer, Clark & Company; Talk O'Texas Brands; Ghiradelli Chocolate Company; Rubschlager Baking Company; T. Marzetti Compay; Quaker Company
Brokered Products include:
 Confectionery, Dairy/Deli, General Merchandise, Groceries

40190 Chapman Fruit Co Inc
1075 S 6th Ave
Wauchula, FL 33873-3305 863-773-3161
Fax: 863-773-0443
Broker of vegetables, frozen concentrated juices, citrus drinks, dried pulp and citrus oils
Owner: Cindy Parrish
cindy@chapmanfruit.com
VP: Gloria Chapman
Estimated Sales: $10-20 Million
Number Employees: 20-49
Brokered Products include:
 Frozen Food, Produce, Citrus Drinks, Dried Pulp, etc.

40191 Chapman-Tait Brokerage, Inc.
16980 Via Tazon
Suite 285
San Diego, CA 92127-1659 858-679-9386
Fax: 951-244-4322
Broker of confectionery products, groceries, spices, general merchandise, private label items and specialty foods
President: Arnott F Tait
VP: G Thomas
Estimated Sales: $1.9 Million
Number Employees: 10
Markets Served:
 Super Market Chains, Wholesale Distributors
Brokered Products include:
 Confectionery, General Merchandise, Groceries, Private Label, Spices, Specialty Foods

40192 Charles Pace & Assoc Inc
430 Senoia Rd
Fairburn, GA 30213-1614 770-969-0488
Fax: 770-969-7277 info@pacereps.com
www.pacereps.com
Manufacturers' representative for food service equipment and supplies
Owner: Charles Pace
VP: Matt Bryant
Sales Associate: Chris Pace
paceassoc@mindspring.com
Office Manager: Cindy Sargeant
Estimated Sales: Less Than $500,000
Number Employees: 1-4
Markets Served:
 Wholesale Distributors
Primary Brands Brokered include: Middleby Marshall; Rational; Robot Coupe; Avtec; Low Temp/Colorpoint; Southbend
Brokered Products include:
 General Merchandise, Foodservice Equipment & Supplies

40193 Charles R. Bell Limited
81 Kenmount Road
St. John's, NL A1B 3P8
Canada 709-722-6700
Fax: 709-722-9408
Import broker of alcoholic beverages, confectionery and dairy/deli products, general merchandise, groceries, meat products, etc.
Secretary/Treasurer: J Conway
Number Employees: 120
Markets Served:
 Food Manufacturers & Processors, Super Market Chains, Wholesale Distributors, Food Service Operators
Primary Brands Brokered include: William Wrigley, Jr. Company; Nabisco; Philips Electronics
Brokered Products include:
 Alcoholic Beverages, Confectionery, Dairy/Deli, General Merchandise, Groceries, Imports, Meat Products, Private Label, Seafood, Spices

40194 Charles Rockel & Son
4303 Smith Rd
Cincinnati, OH 45212-4236 513-631-3009
Fax: 513-631-3083
Food brokers of dairy/deli products, frozen foods, general merchandise, groceries, industrial ingredients, etc
President: Charles Rockel
CFO: Don Rockel
Estimated Sales: $2.5-5 Million
Number Employees: 3
Markets Served:
 Food Manufacturers & Processors, Super Market Chains, Wholesale Distributors, Food Service Operators
Brokered Products include:
 Dairy/Deli, Frozen Food, Groceries, Ingredients, Private Label

40195 Charles Stube Co Inc
8116 Cazenovia Rd # 7
Manlius, NY 13104-8732 315-682-6479
Fax: 315-682-6538 kraig@stubeco.com
Domestic broker of dairy
President: Kraig Stube
kraig@stubeco.com
Estimated Sales: $1.1 Million
Number Employees: 5-9
Markets Served:
 Food Manufacturers & Processors, Wholesale Distributors
Brokered Products include:
 Dairy

40196 Charlie Brown Sales Company
640 Montezuma Ct
Walnut Creek, CA 94598 714-828-4220
Fax: 714-828-8713 cbsales@aol.com
Manufacturers' representative for food service equipment and supplies
Owner: Charlie Brown
VP, San Diego: Graff Sonsibie
Estimated Sales: $3-5 Million
Number Employees: 3
Square Footage: 12000
Markets Served:
 Wholesale Distributors
Primary Brands Brokered include: PowerSoak; SMT(Spray Master Technology); Somato; San Aire; Metcraft; Useco; Can-Tech; IMC/Teddy; Stero
Brokered Products include:
 General Merchandise, Foodservice Equipment & Supplies

40197 Chartrand Imports
328 Main St # 205
Rockland, ME 04841-3354 207-594-7300
Fax: 207-594-8098 800-473-7307
www.chartrandimports.com
Import broker of organic wine
President: Paul Chartrand
paul@chartrandimports.com
Estimated Sales: $1-3 Million
Number Employees: 1-4
Number of Brands: 50
Number of Products: 150
Type of Packaging: Consumer, Private Label
Markets Served:
 Wholesale Distributors
Brokered Products include:
 Alcoholic Beverages, Imports

40198 Chase Sales Company
320 Haddon Ave
Haddon Township, NJ 8108 856-854-6060
Fax: 856-854-2014
Import broker of dairy/deli products, frozen foods, groceries and private label items
President: Fred Chase, Jr.
Accounts Manager: Rich Chase
VP: Doug Chase
Contact: Dad Chase
dchase@chaseltd.com
Accounts Manager: Tim Chase
Estimated Sales: $10-20 Million
Number Employees: 10-19
Markets Served:
 Super Market Chains, Food Service Operators
Brokered Products include:
 Dairy/Deli, Frozen Food, Groceries, Imports, Private Label

40199 Chase-Goldenberg Associates
655 Conshohocken Rd
Conshohocken, PA 19428 610-828-7057
Fax: 610-828-7848
Broker of confectionery products, beef sticks, groceries & snacks. Markets served besides the ones listed are Convenience Stores, Vendors, Drug.
President: Christopher Chase
EVP: Patrick Rooney
Estimated Sales: $5-10 Million
Number Employees: 5
Markets Served:
 Super Market Chains, Wholesale Distributors
Primary Brands Brokered include: Just Born; Peanut Chews and Mike & Ike; Spangler; Dum-Dums; Atkinson: Chick-O-Stick; Old Wisconsin: Beef Sticks
Brokered Products include:
 Confectionery, Groceries, Meat Products, Snacks, Beef Sticks

40200 Chatila's
254 N Broadway
Salem, NH 03079-2132 603-898-5459
Fax: 603-893-1586
customercare@chatilasbakery.com
www.chatilasbakery.com
All sugar-free items. Chatila's muffins, cookies, pastries, cheesecakes, donuts, bagels, pies, breads, chocolates and ice cream. All items sweetened with Splenda and/or Melltitol, low carb, low cal, low fat, low cholestrol, notrans-fat.
President: Mohamad Chatila
cutomercare@chatilas.com
Sales: Jennifer Marks
Estimated Sales: Less Than $500,000
Number Employees: 1-4
Number of Brands: 1
Number of Products: 100+
Square Footage: 24000
Type of Packaging: Consumer, Food Service, Private Label, Bulk

40201 Chattanooga Freight Bureau
118 Lee Parkway Dr Ste 205
Chattanooga, TN 37421 423-894-4622
Fax: 423-894-4665
Transportation broker providing consultations, freight bill audit and payment services
President: Turney Thompson
Number Employees: 5-9

40202 Cheese & Dairy Products
14423 N Century Drive
Fountain Hills, AZ 85268-3172 480-837-3814
Fax: 480-837-7097 wdfranklin@aol.com
President/CEO: Walt Franklin
Estimated Sales: $3+ Million
Number Employees: 1-4
Square Footage: 4000
Type of Packaging: Consumer, Food Service, Private Label, Bulk
Markets Served:
 Food Manufacturers & Processors, Wholesale Distributors, Food Service Operators
Brokered Products include:
 Dairy/Deli

40203 Chell Brokerage Co
101 Pittston Ave # 1
Scranton, PA 18505-1150 570-344-1286
Fax: 570-346-2863 ernestchell@aol.com
Broker of dairy/deli products, produce, seafood, groceries, frozen foods, etc.
Owner: Ernest Chell, Jr.
VP: Jack Roland
Estimated Sales: $2.5-5 Million
Number Employees: 1-4
Markets Served:
 Super Market Chains, Wholesale Distributors, Food Service Operators
Primary Brands Brokered include: Compass Foods; Nolaki-America; Bertolli
Brokered Products include:
 Dairy/Deli, Frozen Food, General Merchandise, Groceries, Meat Products, Private Label, Produce, Seafood

40204 (HQ)Chernoff Sales
3308 Park Central Blvd N
Pompano Beach, FL 33064 954-972-1414
Fax: 954-972-4214 800-226-7600
sales@chernoffsales.com www.chernoffsales.com

Food Brokers / A-Z

Manufacturers' representative and wholesaler/distributor for commercial cooking and refrigeration equipment, microwave ovens, ice machines, ice cream cabinets, stainless steel sinks and tables, can openers, scales, food warmers and steamers
Principal: James Cox
Principal: Joe Andisman
Principal: Michael Turetzky
VP Sales/Marketing: Michael Turetzky
Sales: Barrie Spear
Customer Service: Tonya Smith
Estimated Sales: $15.5 Million
Number Employees: 10-19
Square Footage: 128000
Markets Served:
    Food Service Operators
Primary Brands Brokered include: Aero Manufacturing; Allied Metal Spinning; Amana; AmeriKooler; Arctic Air; BergHOFF; Beverage-Air; Dito; Edlund; Electrolux; Handy Store Fixtures; Ice-O-Matic; Imperial; Kelvinator; La Crosse; Skydyne; Stortec Systems; Roundup
Brokered Products include:
    General Merchandise, Foodservice Equipment & Supplies

40205 Chilay Corporation
1931 Rohlwing Rd Ste E
Rolling Meadows, IL 60008   847-368-1450
    Fax: 847-368-1415 www.chilaycorp.com
Import broker of dairy/deli products, frozen foods, general merchandise, groceries, private label items, meats, etc.
Chairman/CEO: Bill Castonzo
VP Service: Marty Gaggiano
Estimated Sales: $2.3 Million
Number Employees: 12
Markets Served:
    Food Manufacturers & Processors, Super Market Chains, Wholesale Distributors, Food Service Operators
Primary Brands Brokered include: ConAgra Poultry; Farmland Foods; Heartland Catfish; Churny Company
Brokered Products include:
    Dairy/Deli, Frozen Food, General Merchandise, Groceries, Imports, Meat, Meat Products, Private Label, Seafood

40206 Christian Brokerage Company/Industrial & Food
6346 Emerald Trl SE
Acworth, GA 30102   770-975-9600
    Fax: 770-975-0803
Broker serving food processors, food service operators and wholesalers/distributors
President: K Christian
Estimated Sales: Less than $500,000
Number Employees: 1-4
Markets Served:
    Food Manufacturers & Processors, Wholesale Distributors, Food Service Operators

40207 Christopher's Herb Shop
188 S Main St
Springville, UT 84663-1849   801-489-4500
    Fax: 801-489-4814 888-372-4372
    www.drchristophersherbshop.com
Food supplements manufacturer, private label items, herbs and health foods
President: David Christopher
Vice President: Ruth Christopher Bacalla
Manager: Bobbie Henderson
manager@drchristopherherbshop.com
Production Manager: James Webster
Purchasing Manager: Josh Bruni
Estimated Sales: Less Than $500,000
Number Employees: 5-9
Square Footage: 15000
Type of Packaging: Private Label
Brokered Products include:
    Health Food, Private Label

40208 Chuck Batcheller Company
27350 Southfield Rd
Lathrup Village, MI 48076   248-559-2422
    Fax: 248-559-8168
Broker of frozen foods, groceries, produce and health foods
Owner: Charles Batcheller
CEO: C Batcheller
Estimated Sales: $1-3 Million
Number Employees: 1-4

Markets Served:
    Food Manufacturers & Processors, Super Market Chains, Wholesale Distributors, Food Service Operators
Primary Brands Brokered include: National Raisin; Homa; Quality Nut Company; Oasis Date Company; Export-Import(Almonds); Gambini Farms
Brokered Products include:
    Frozen Food, Groceries, Health Food, Produce

40209 Chuckrow Sales LLC
78 Birchwood Ln
Niskayuna, NY 12309-1835   518-783-6158
    Fax: 518-783-6756 800-248-2576
Broker of dairy/deli products, frozen foods, meat and meat products, produce and seafood
President: Joseph Chuckrow
VP: Winifred Chuckrow
Estimated Sales: A
Number Employees: 1-4
Markets Served:
    Super Market Chains, Wholesale Distributors, Food Service Operators
Primary Brands Brokered include: Norwestern; Turkey Store; B.C. Rogers; Northside Packing; Jerome Foods; Citerio
Brokered Products include:
    Dairy/Deli, Frozen Food, Meat, Meat Products, Produce, Seafood

40210 Citrin-Pitoscia Company
120 Liberty Street
Bloomfield, NJ 07003-5012   973-281-9020
    Fax: 973-281-9028
Broker of confectionery products, general merchandise and health food
President: Mario Pitoscia
CEO: Arnold Citrin
VP: Anthony Cnuffo
VP Sales: Ed Demain
Estimated Sales: $1-2.5 Million
Number Employees: 20-49
Square Footage: 16000
Markets Served:
    Super Market Chains, Wholesale Distributors
Primary Brands Brokered include: Jaret International; Ricola; Dorval; NECCO; Christopher's
Brokered Products include:
    Confectionery, General Merchandise, Health Food

40211 Classic Cuisine Foods
8383 Elliott Street
Vancouver, BC V5S 2P4
Canada   604-323-2671
    Fax: 604-323-2673
johnfalcos@classiccuisinefoods.com
www.classiccuisinefoods.com
Manufacturers' representative for bagels, flat breads, cakes, pies, chiles, ice cream, pre-cooked meats, stuffed potatoes and frozen, par-baked and thaw/serve dough products, etc.; serving food service operators, supermarket chains and wholesalers/distributors
President: Christina Falcos
Director Of Sales, General Manager: John Falcos
Operations Manager: Tina Falcos
Estimated Sales: $2 Million
Number Employees: 6
Parent Co: Ameurasian Trading Corporation
Type of Packaging: Consumer, Food Service, Private Label, Bulk
Markets Served:
    Super Market Chains, Wholesale Distributors, Food Service Operators
Primary Brands Brokered include: True Soups; Upper Crust; Bennys Bagels; Nancys Specialty Foods; Stevens Roberts Originals/Classic Bakery; Oakrun Farms; Vie de France
Brokered Products include:
    Frozen Food, Health Food, Meat, Meat Products, Private Label, Bakery

40212 Clear Springs Foods Inc.
1500 E. 4424 N. Clear Lakes Rd.
PO Box 712
Buhl, ID 83316   208-543-4316
    800-635-8211
csfsales@clearsprings.com www.clearsprings.com
Fresh and frozen rainbow trout, breaded trout portions, shapes and melts.
CEO: Kurt Meyers
COO: Jeff Jermunson

Year Founded: 1991
Estimated Sales: $130 Million
Number Employees: 250-499
Number of Brands: 4
Square Footage: 7200
Type of Packaging: Consumer, Food Service, Private Label
Markets Served:
    Food Manufacturers & Processors
Primary Brands Brokered include: Clear Springs, Thousand Springs, Blue Lakes
Brokered Products include:
    Seafood

40213 (HQ)Clements Stella Marketing
53 Danes St
Patchogue, NY 11772-3834   631-758-5316
    Fax: 631-758-5947
Manufacturers' representative for heavy duty and stainless steel food service equipment including refrigerators, freezers, etc.
Partner: Thomas Clements
Partner: Michael Stella
Manager: Tom Clements
Number Employees: 1-4
Square Footage: 8000
Other Locations:
    Clements-Stella Marketing
    Westwood, NJClements-Stella Marketing
Markets Served:
    Super Market Chains, Wholesale Distributors, Food Service Operators
Primary Brands Brokered include: Eagle Group Cos.; Atlas Industries; Kolpak Industries; McCall Refrigeration
Brokered Products include:
    General Merchandise, Refrigerators, Freezers, Etc.

40214 (HQ)Clipper Mill
404 Talbert St
Daly City, CA 94014-1623   415-330-2400
    Fax: 415-330-9640 info@clippermill.com
    www.frenchfryholders.com
Manufacturer and product converter which sells and distributes its products wholesale only
General Manager: Johnny Cheung
Estimated Sales: $10-20 Million
Number Employees: 10-19
Markets Served:
    Wholesale Distributors
Primary Brands Brokered include: Ocean Harvest
Brokered Products include:
    Private Label, Kitchen Gadgets

40215 (HQ)Clofine Dairy Products Inc
1407 New Rd
P.O. Box 335
Linwood, NJ 08221   609-653-1000
    Fax: 609-653-0127 info@clofinedairy.com
    www.clofinedairy.com
Fluid and dried dairy products; proteins, cheeses, milk replacement blends, tofu and soymilk powders, vital wheat gluten, etc.
Chairman: Larry Clofine
lclofine@clofinedairy.com
President & CEO: Frederick Smith
CFO: Butch Harmon
Warehouse Coordinator: Pamela Gerety
Estimated Sales: $20-50 Million
Number Employees: 10-19
Number of Brands: 2
Number of Products: 100
Type of Packaging: Food Service, Private Label, Bulk
Other Locations:
    Midwest Officer
    Chicago, ILMidwest Officer
Markets Served:
    Food Manufacturers & Processors
Brokered Products include:
    Confectionery, Dairy/Deli, Exports, Health Food, Imports, Ingredients

40216 Clogmaster
Mobile Boutique & Fitting Truck
Costa Mesa, CA 92626   714-707-5108
    Fax: 310-657-8090 clogs@clogmaster.com
    www.clogmaster.com
Wholesaler & distributor of clogs for the food service market.
Owner: Dave Welling
Estimated Sales: Less than $500,000
Number Employees: 1-4

Food Brokers / A-Z

40217 Co-Sales De Credico
5000 Executive Pkwy # 230
San Ramon, CA 94583-4210   925-327-7311
Fax: 925-327-7311
Broker of confectionery items, dairy/deli products, frozen foods, general merchandise, groceries, health food, meat, seafood, etc.
Manager: Joseph Decredico
VP: Bob Lohman
Number Employees: 20-49
Square Footage: 44000
Markets Served:
  Super Market Chains, Wholesale Distributors
Primary Brands Brokered include: Huish Detergent Company; Langers; Florida Naturals; Authentic Specialty Foods
Brokered Products include:
  Dairy/Deli, Frozen Food, General Merchandise, Groceries, Health Food, Meat, Meat Products, Private Label, Seafood

40218 Coastal Commodities
500 Country Walk Ct
Bel Air, MD 21015-6135   410-515-1424
Fax: 410-569-2303
Industrial food, import and domestic broker of nuts including macadamias, pistachios, almonds, walnuts and pecans. Also dried fruits, industrial ingredients, confectionery products and spices
President: Scott Weatherford
sweatherford@coastalpetro.com
VP: Winifred Babiak
Estimated Sales: $1-3 Million
Number Employees: 1-4
Square Footage: 8000
Type of Packaging: Consumer, Food Service, Private Label, Bulk
Markets Served:
  Food Manufacturers & Processors, Super Market Chains, Wholesale Distributors, Food Service Operators
Primary Brands Brokered include: Paramount Farms; Kraft Food Ingredients; Klein-Berger; Carmells Pecan; C. Melchers Company; Pima Western
Brokered Products include:
  Groceries, Imports, Ingredients, Private Label, Spices

40219 Coastal Pride Co Inc
2201 Boundary St # 306
Suite #306
Beaufort, SC 29902-3881   843-522-8820
Fax: 843-522-8828   800-445-7316
www.coastalpride.com
Import broker of canned, fresh, frozen and pasteurized seafood including shrimp, soft shell crabs, scallops and oysters
President: Walter Lubkin
CFO: Tracy L Greco
tracy@coastalpride.com
VP: John Lubkin
Estimated Sales: $7 Million
Number Employees: 5-9
Square Footage: 6000
Markets Served:
  Food Manufacturers & Processors, Super Market Chains, Wholesale Distributors, Food Service Operators
Primary Brands Brokered include: Lubkin's Coastal Pride; Crystal Seas; Island; Florida Quality; Port Royal; Best; Optima; H&W
Brokered Products include:
  Frozen Food, Imports, Seafood

40220 Cobler Food Sales
1630 State St
Bettendorf, IA 52722-4990   563-445-6710
Fax: 563-388-4950   877-788-9522
Broker of frozen foods, general merchandise, groceries, meat products, private label items, seafood, etc
Owner: Dick Cobler
CFO: Karen Rank
Estimated Sales: $5-10 Million
Number Employees: 3
Square Footage: 14400
Type of Packaging: Food Service
Markets Served:
  Wholesale Distributors, Food Service Operators

Brokered Products include:
  Frozen Food, Groceries, Ingredients, Meat, Meat Products, Private Label, Produce, Seafood, Spices

40221 Cohen's Coddies Company
215 S Bethel Street
Baltimore, MD 21231-2301   410-732-0917
Fax: 410-732-0917
Broker of snack foods
President: Lloyd Cohen
Estimated Sales: $5-10 Million
Number Employees: 5-9
Brokered Products include:
  Snacks

40222 Collins Associates
430 Crompton Street
Charlotte, NC 28273-6215   704-588-8200
Fax: 704-588-8338   800-849-5348
www.usbizs.com
Manufacturers' representative for food service equipment
President: David Collins
Estimated Sales: $12 Million
Number Employees: 5
Square Footage: 5000
Markets Served:
  Food Manufacturers & Processors, Super Market Chains, Food Service Operators

40223 Colon Brothers
PO Box 363013
San Juan, PR 00936-3013   787-792-4330
Fax: 787-792-4519
Import and export broker of general merchandise
President: Jose Colon
VP: Maurice Odon
Number Employees: 5-9
Square Footage: 25000
Brokered Products include:
  Exports, General Merchandise, Imports

40224 Colony Brokerage Company
1801 N 5th St
Philadelphia, PA 19122   215-236-1700
Fax: 215-236-5926
Broker of groceries, frozen foods, meat products, private label items and seafood
President: Richard Singer
Contact: Dave Pomroy
dave.pomroy@honorfoods.com
Estimated Sales: $5.6 Million
Number Employees: 30
Markets Served:
  Wholesale Distributors, Food Service Operators
Brokered Products include:
  Frozen Food, Groceries, Meat Products, Private Label, Seafood

40225 Columbia Food MachineryInc
641 9th St NW
Salem, OR 97304-3132   503-370-7188
Fax: 503-370-4467
info@columbiafoodmachinery.com
www.columbiafoodmachinery.com
Broker of vegetable and fruit processing machinery
President: David Hendersen
daveh@columbiafoodmachinery.com
Assistant Manager: Edward Jelly, Jr.
Estimated Sales: $2.5-5 Million
Number Employees: 10-19
Square Footage: 16800
Markets Served:
  Food Manufacturers & Processors
Primary Brands Brokered include: A&K Development; BEST; Food Technology Corporation; Meyer & Garroutte; Odenberg; Olney; Reyco Systems; Sidney Manufacturing Company; VanMark Corporation
Brokered Products include:
  General Merchandise, Vegetable/Potato/Fruit Process. Equip.

40226 Commercial Kitchens Reps Inc
320 N Washington St # 118
Suite 118
Rochester, NY 14625-2316   585-249-0520
Fax: 585-249-0522 dgraf@ckreps.com
Manufacturers' representative for furniture, furnishings, dishmachines, ovens, griddles, broilers, tables, ranges, sinks, walk-in coolers and freezers, etc.; serving wholesalers/distributors
President: Bill Holmes
bholmes@ckreps.com
VP: David Bonfield
Estimated Sales: $2.5-5 Million
Number Employees: 1-4
Square Footage: 4000
Markets Served:
  Wholesale Distributors
Brokered Products include:
  General Merchandise, Griddles, Ovens, Broilers, Etc.

40227 Commodities Marketing Inc
6 Stone Tavern Dr
Clarksburg, NJ 08510   732-516-0700
Fax: 732-516-0600 weldonrice@usa.net
www.weldonfoods.com
Jasmine rice, Basmati rice, Coconut drinks, Coconut milk, Fruits, Beans, Guar gum, Fruit juices and Cashews, Almonds, Saffron (Spain) White Rice/Parboiled Rice.
President: Herbander Sahni
herbandersahni@weldonfoods.com
CEO: Gagandeep Sahni
CFO: Soena Sahni
VP: Avneet Sodhi
R&D: Manoj Hedge
Marketing: Harbinder Singh Sahni & Dee Mirchandai
Sales: Avneet Sodhi
Public Relations: Mr. Dough & Harshida Shaw
Operations: Harshida Shah
Production: Mr Nobpsaul
Plant Manager: Mr Chandej
Estimated Sales: $25 Million
Number Employees: 5-9
Number of Brands: 3
Number of Products: 6
Square Footage: 3000
Type of Packaging: Consumer, Food Service, Private Label, Bulk
Markets Served:
  Food Manufacturers & Processors, Super Market Chains, Wholesale Distributors, Food Service Operators
Primary Brands Brokered include: Weldon, Meher, Giya, Goya, Aldi, C&F Foods, Double Elephants, 7 Elephants, Royal Mount, USEC, Indian Harvest, Private Labels, Specialty
Brokered Products include:
  Exports, General Merchandise, Groceries, Imports, Ingredients, Private Label, Spices

40228 Concept Food Brokers
48 E University Dr
Arlington Hts, IL 60004   847-255-7900
Fax: 847-255-7964 www.conceptfoodbrokers.com
Broker of dairy/deli products, frozen foods, groceries, meat, meat products and private label items
President: Glen Gallas
CEO: Carl Fulkerson
EVP: Ben Schwartz
Marketing/IT Director: John Kilcullen
SVP Sales: Kurt Burton
Contact: Joyce Carla
carla.joyce@conceptfoodbrokers.com
Estimated Sales: $5-10 Million
Number Employees: 1-4
Markets Served:
  Super Market Chains, Wholesale Distributors
Primary Brands Brokered include: Giraldi Foods; Lulu's Dessert Factory; Kelsen, Inc.; National Foods; Con Agra Webber/Oldhaus; Northern Wisconsin Produce Company
Brokered Products include:
  Dairy/Deli, Frozen Food, Groceries, Meat, Meat Products, Private Label

40229 Concept Food Sales
294 W Steuben St # 6
Crafton, PA 15205-2512   412-250-2300
Fax: 412-250-2310 www.conceptfoodsales.com
Broker of dairy/deli products, private label items, frozen foods and meats
Managing Partner: Carl Dietze
Partner: Bob Sheridan
Partner: John Gallace
Sales Representative: Linda Vento
Estimated Sales: $3.20 Million
Number Employees: 20-49
Square Footage: 14000
Markets Served:
  Food Manufacturers & Processors, Wholesale Distributors, Food Service Operators

Food Brokers / A-Z

Brokered Products include:
Dairy/Deli, Frozen Food, Meat, Meat Products, Private Label

40230 Concord National
2515 Meadowpine Blvd
Unit 2
Mississauga, ON L5N 6C3
Canada 905-817-0403
www.concordnational.com
Broker of confectionery and dairy/deli items, frozen foods, general merchandise, groceries, meat products, etc.
Owner: Mike Donald
Emergency Recall Contact: Glen Berry
Estimated Sales: $14.3 Million
Number Employees: 45
Square Footage: 6000
Markets Served:
Super Market Chains, Wholesale Distributors, Food Service Operators
Primary Brands Brokered include: Tetley; Mattel; Yoplait; Old South; Arm & Hammer; Electrasol
Brokered Products include:
Confectionery, Dairy/Deli, Frozen Food, General Merchandise, Groceries, Health Food, Imports, Meat, Meat Products, Private Label, Produce, Seafood

40231 Concord National
#120, 7777-10th Street. N.E
Calgary, AB T2X 8X2
Canada 403-291-2818
Fax: 888-599-7606 www.concordnational.com
Import broker of confectionery and dairy/deli products, frozen foods, meats, seafood, private label items, general merchandise, groceries, etc.
Owner: Tim Moore
Managing Partner: Sandy Moore
Number Employees: 20-49
Markets Served:
Food Manufacturers & Processors, Super Market Chains, Wholesale Distributors, Food Service Operators
Primary Brands Brokered include: Lykes Pasco, Inc. (Old South); Colombo Dairy Foods; Milupa Company (Milupa Baby Food); Blue Water Seafoods (Bluewater Frozen Fish Products); Con Agra
Brokered Products include:
Confectionery, Dairy/Deli, Frozen Food, General Merchandise, Groceries, Imports, Meat, Meat Products, Private Label, Seafood

40232 Concord National
55 Weston Court
Dartmouth, NS B3B 1X4
Canada 902-468-8990
Fax: 902-468-2262 www.concordnational.com
Broker of confectionery and dairy/deli products, frozen foods, general merchandise, groceries, meat, etc.
Owner: Doug Reid
National President: Chris Foote
VP: Rick Whiting
Number Employees: 5
Markets Served:
Food Manufacturers & Processors, Super Market Chains, Wholesale Distributors, Food Service Operators
Brokered Products include:
Confectionery, Dairy/Deli, Frozen Food, General Merchandise, Groceries, Meat, Private Label

40233 Concord National
PO Box 3234
Regina, SK S4P 3H1
Canada 306-789-9938
Fax: 306-721-2770 www.concordnational.com
Import broker of confectionery and dairy/deli products, health and frozen foods, general merchandise, groceries, meat and meat products, produce, spices, seafood, private label items, etc.
Chairman: Mike Donald
President: Chris Foote
Manager: Cecil Petkau
Number Employees: 1-4
Markets Served:
Super Market Chains, Food Service Operators
Brokered Products include:
Confectionery, Dairy/Deli, Frozen Food, General Merchandise, Groceries, Health Food, Imports, Meat, Meat Products, Private Label, Produce, Seafood, Spices

40234 Concord National
10470 176 Street
Unit 102
Edmonton, AB T5A 0A3
Canada 780-481-8235
Fax: 780-483-4007 www.concordnational.com
Import broker of confectionery and dairy/deli products, frozen foods, general merchandise, groceries, meat, etc.
Manager: Bob Schwartz
Parent Co: Concord Sales-Prairies
Markets Served:
Super Market Chains, Food Service Operators
Brokered Products include:
Confectionery, Dairy/Deli, Frozen Food, General Merchandise, Groceries, Health Food, Imports, Meat, Meat Products, Private Label, Seafood, Spices

40235 Concord National
2750 Faithfull Avenue
Saskatoon, SK S7K 1W4
Canada 306-652-9212
Fax: 306-244-1984 www.concordnational.com
Import broker of confectionery and dairy/deli products, frozen foods, general merchandise, groceries, meat, etc.
Branch Manager: Bob Aebig
Number Employees: 1-4
Parent Co: Concord Sales-Prairies
Markets Served:
Super Market Chains, Wholesale Distributors, Food Service Operators
Brokered Products include:
Confectionery, Dairy/Deli, Frozen Food, General Merchandise, Groceries, Health Food, Imports, Meat, Meat Products, Private Label, Produce, Seafood, Spices

40236 Concord Sales-Prairies
72 Mandalay Drive
Winnipeg, MB R2P 1V8
Canada 204-774-0751
Fax: 204-774-0835 www.concordnational.com
Import and export broker of confectionery and dairy/deli products, frozen foods, general merchandise, groceries, meat, etc.
Owner: Tim Moore
Number Employees: 7
Markets Served:
Super Market Chains, Food Service Operators
Brokered Products include:
Confectionery, Dairy/Deli, Exports, Frozen Food, General Merchandise, Groceries, Health Food, Imports, Ingredients, Meat, Meat Products, Private Label, Produce, Seafood, Spices

40237 Conlin Brokerage Company
4087 Sundance Ln
Norco, CA 92860-4202 951-371-3038
Fax: 909-371-3050
billc@conlinfoodbrokerage.com
Broker of dairy/deli items, meats, including turkey and chicken, private label items, etc
Owner: Bill Conlin
President: Walter Conlin
VP: Virginia Conlin
Sales: Mike Patterson
Contact: Blake Conlin
blakeconlin@hotmail.com
Estimated Sales: $3-5 Million
Number Employees: 6
Type of Packaging: Food Service
Markets Served:
Food Manufacturers & Processors, Wholesale Distributors, Food Service Operators
Brokered Products include:
Dairy/Deli, Frozen Food, Meat, Private Label

40238 Conrad Sales Company
Poland, OH 44514 330-757-0711
Fax: 330-757-0714 800-888-0711
Broker of dairy/deli products, frozen foods, groceries, health food, industrial ingredients and meats serving all markets
Owner: Ed Conrad
Estimated Sales: $5-10 Million
Number Employees: 4
Type of Packaging: Consumer, Food Service, Private Label, Bulk
Markets Served:
Food Manufacturers & Processors, Super Market Chains, Wholesale Distributors, Food Service Operators
Brokered Products include:
Confectionery, Frozen Food, Imports, Meat, Meat Products, Private Label, Seafood, Spices

40239 Consolidated Marketers Inc
1146 Johnson Rd
Woodbridge, CT 06525-2619 203-387-2545
Fax: 203-387-4515 800-222-0514
Broker of dairy/deli products, frozen and health foods, industrial ingredients, meat and meat products, etc.
President: Gordon Cott
Executive VP: Jack Tapping
Estimated Sales: $5-10 Million
Number Employees: 1-4
Markets Served:
Food Manufacturers & Processors, Super Market Chains, Wholesale Distributors, Food Service Operators
Primary Brands Brokered include: Oasis Foods; Nozaki America; Blue Ridge; McCain; Maid-Rite; Chock Full O' Nuts
Brokered Products include:
Dairy/Deli, Frozen Food, Groceries, Health Food, Ingredients, Meat, Meat Products, Private Label, Seafood

40240 Consolidated Merchandisers
3840 Beatty Ct
Murrysville, PA 15668-1829 724-733-2300
Fax: 724-327-8176
Broker of dairy/deli items, meats, groceries, frozen foods, produce, etc.
Owner: Jim Seethaler
VP: Robert Skapinac
Estimated Sales: $1.6 Million
Number Employees: 1-4
Square Footage: 12000
Markets Served:
Super Market Chains, Wholesale Distributors, Food Service Operators
Brokered Products include:
Confectionery, Dairy/Deli, Frozen Food, Health Food, Meat, Meat Products, Private Label, Seafood

40241 Consolidated Tea Co Inc
300 Merrick Rd # 202
Lynbrook, NY 11563-2503 516-887-1144
Fax: 516-887-1643
Broker of groceries
President: Elliot Labiner
VP Sales: K Axelson
VP Operations: A Steinberger
Estimated Sales: $1.5 Million
Number Employees: 5-9
Markets Served:
Wholesale Distributors, Food Service Operators
Brokered Products include:
Groceries

40242 Constant Sales
3479 W Esplanade Avenue N
Metairie, LA 70002-1600 504-455-7616
Fax: 504-889-1730 cajunpoboy@aol.com
Broker of dairy/deli products, frozen food, meat and meat products and seafood; serving all markets in southern Louisiana
Owner: Randal Constant
Number Employees: 3
Markets Served:
Food Manufacturers & Processors, Super Market Chains, Wholesale Distributors, Food Service Operators
Primary Brands Brokered include: Beef International; Gourmet Express; Trans-Ocean Products, Inc.; Rosina Food Products; Longmont Foods; Matlaw Food Products
Brokered Products include:
Dairy/Deli, Frozen Food, Meat, Meat Products, Seafood

40243 Consumer Brands
2027 S Stewart Avenue
Springfield, MO 65804-2522 417-887-2340
Fax: 417-887-3036
Broker of dairy/deli products, meat and meat products, frozen food and seafood
Owner: Louie Addington
Number Employees: 10-19

Food Brokers / A-Z

Markets Served:
Food Manufacturers & Processors, Super Market Chains, Wholesale Distributors, Food Service Operators
Brokered Products include:
Dairy/Deli, Frozen Food, Meat, Meat Products, Seafood

40244 Consummate Marketing Company
1479 Camino Peral
Moraga, CA 94556   510-451-4470
Fax: 510-451-4471
National sales/marketing agency for olives, cooking oils and mayonnaise with olive oil
President: Art Wexler
VP: T Wexler
Marketing: Art Wexler
Sales: Art Wexler
Estimated Sales: $1-2.5 Million
Number Employees: 2
Number of Brands: 3
Type of Packaging: Consumer, Food Service, Private Label, Bulk
Markets Served:
Food Manufacturers & Processors, Super Market Chains, Wholesale Distributors, Food Service Operators
Primary Brands Brokered include: Sunera, Miss Leone's, Mayoli
Brokered Products include:
Dairy/Deli, Groceries, Health Food, Private Label

40245 Continental Food Sales Inc
600 Winslow Way E # 130
Bainbridge Isle, WA 98110-2441   206-842-7440
Fax: 206-842-7471 www.continentalfoodsales.com
Import and export broker of frozen foods and ingredients
President: Mike Barrett
mikeb@continentalfoods.com
VP: Mike Barrett
Sales: Scott Boynton
Estimated Sales: $1.6 Million
Number Employees: 5-9
Type of Packaging: Food Service, Private Label, Bulk
Markets Served:
Food Manufacturers & Processors, Food Service Operators

40246 Continental Marketing
18175 SW
100th Court
Tualatin, OR 97062   503-692-8510
Fax: 207-872-2062 info@cmsales.com
www.cmsales.com
Founder and Partner: Robert Degennaro
President and Partner: Jim Doane
Inside Sales and Marketing Coordinator: Kendall Akerman
Inside Sales Coordinator: Tawny Clark
Operations Manager: Marcy Dunn
Estimated Sales: $300,000-500,000
Number Employees: 1-4

40247 (HQ)Convenience Marketing Services
575 Round Rock West Dr # 220
Round Rock, TX 78681-5035   512-244-0700
Fax: 512-238-7944   800-256-7384
cmstexas@sbcglobal.net www.cms-texas.com
Broker of confectionery and dairy/deli products, frozen foods, groceries, meat products, etc.
President: Greg Testerman
Office Manager: Angela Leonard
Estimated Sales: $1-2.5 Million
Number Employees: 5-9
Markets Served:
Wholesale Distributors
Primary Brands Brokered include: Hoyle Products; Pine O Pine (White Cap, Inc.); Intersweet; Mr. Snacks; M-Star; Turkey Creek
Brokered Products include:
Confectionery, Dairy/Deli, Frozen Food, General Merchandise, Groceries, Meat Products, Spices

40248 Cooke Marketing Group Inc
5306 Business Pkwy # 101
Suite 101
Ringwood, IL 60072-9416   815-728-9988
Fax: 815-653-0400
Manufacturers' representative and exporter of deli and bakery products
Owner: Sue Adamavich
sue.adamavich@cookemarketinggroup.com
Number Employees: 5-9
Brokered Products include:
Dairy/Deli, Groceries, Bakery

40249 Copperwood InternationalInc
9249 S Broadway
Unit 200-238
Highland Ranch, CO 80129-5692   303-683-1234
Fax: 303-683-0933   800-411-7887
copperwoodfoods@aol.com
Broker of a wide variety of closeout, excess and discounted food items
Sales Director: Michael Casey
Estimated Sales: $5,000,000
Number Employees: 4
Number of Brands: 76
Number of Products: 127
Square Footage: 50000
Brokered Products include:
Dairy/Deli, Frozen Food, General Merchandise, Groceries, Meat, Meat Products, Private Label, Seafood, Closeouts

40250 (HQ)Core Group
14544 Central Ave
Suite 42
Chino, CA 91710   909-438-2626
win@COREgroupsales.com
www.coregroupsales.com
Broker of frozen food, private label and dairy/deli products, groceries, seafood and meat.
Chairman & CEO: John Goodman
Vice President, Finance: Jeremy Slaughter
Chief Administration Officer: Michelle Alva
Senior Vice President, Sales: DJ White
Chief Operating Officer: Travis King
Estimated Sales: $50-100 Million
Number Employees: 50-99
Brokered Products include:
Confectionery, Frozen Food, Meat, Meat Products, Private Label, Seafood

40251 Core Group
5201 W Laurel St
Tampa, FL 33607   813-282-5600
WIN@COREgroupsales.com
www.coregroupsales.com
Broker of dairy/deli products, frozen foods, groceries, meat products and seafood.
Number Employees: 50-99
Square Footage: 56000
Other Locations:
Hopco Charlotte
Charlotte, NC
Hopco Fort Lauderdale
Oakland Park, FL
Hopco Georgia
Smyrna, GA
Hopco Jacksonville
Jacksonville, FL
Hopco Orlando
Apopka, FLHopco CharlotteOakland Park
Markets Served:
Food Manufacturers & Processors, Wholesale Distributors, Food Service Operators
Brokered Products include:
Dairy/Deli, Frozen Food, Groceries, Meat Products, Seafood

40252 Costa Macaroni Manufacturing
PO Box 32308
Los Angeles, CA 90032-0308
Fax: 323-225-1667   800-433-7785
www.costapasta.com
Homemade various shapes and sizes of pastas
West Coast Sales Manager: Stephen Zoccoli
VP Foodservice Sales: Buzz Weisman
Estimated Sales: $5-10 Million
Number Employees: 20-49
Type of Packaging: Food Service, Bulk
Brokered Products include:
Pasta

40253 (HQ)Courtney Marketing Inc
301 W Deer Valley Rd # 8
Suite 8
Phoenix, AZ 85027-2117   623-434-1113
Fax: 623-434-1114   800-424-9770
info@courtneymarketing.com
www.courtneymarketing.com
Manufacturers' representative for food service equipment and supplies
Principle: David Courtney
Contract Sales: Robert Yvon
Warehouse Manager: Cory Hayduke
Estimated Sales: $10.5 Million
Number Employees: 5-9
Square Footage: 6000
Markets Served:
Super Market Chains, Wholesale Distributors, Food Service Operators
Brokered Products include:
General Merchandise, Foodservice Equipment & Supplies

40254 Cox Food Brokers
1186 Russell Street
Thunder Bay, ON P7B 5N2
Canada   807-623-3366
Fax: 804-623-6250 coxfood@baynet.net
Broker of confectionery products, frozen food, groceries, meat and meat products, seafood, etc.
President/Owner: Terrance Christiansen
Estimated Sales: B
Number Employees: 3
Square Footage: 1950
Markets Served:
Super Market Chains, Wholesale Distributors, Food Service Operators
Primary Brands Brokered include: B.C. Packers; C.P.S. Foods; Leaf Confections; General Mills; McCormick Spices; Sun Rype Juices
Brokered Products include:
Confectionery, Frozen Food, Groceries, Meat, Meat Products, Seafood, Spices

40255 Crane Sales Co
13041 W Linebaugh Ave
Tampa, FL 33626-4484   813-854-1728
Fax: 813-806-9405 info@cranesalescompany.com
www.cranesalescompany.com
Broker of confectionery products and general merchandise
President: Joe Murphy
Chairman: Herb Nelson
herb.nelson@cranesalescompany.com
CEO: Sonny Bush
VP, Retail Service Director: Anita Hans
Sales Representative: Larry Daffron
Retail Operations Manager: Nancy Rodewald
Estimated Sales: $5-10 Million
Number Employees: 5-9
Brokered Products include:
Confectionery, General Merchandise

40256 Creightons
160 Wright Avenue
Dartmouth, NS B3B 1L2
Canada   902-468-1875
Fax: 902-468-3295
Import broker of confectionery products, general merchandise, groceries, spices, private label items, industrial ingredients, meats, etc.
President: Ralph Sams
VP: Juanita Sams
Estimated Sales: $2.9 Million
Number Employees: 8
Square Footage: 92000
Markets Served:
Food Manufacturers & Processors, Super Market Chains, Wholesale Distributors, Food Service Operators
Primary Brands Brokered include: Austral; Thompsons; Degelis Charcoal; Piper Hill Coffee Beans; Harvest Time; Bertolli
Brokered Products include:
Confectionery, General Merchandise, Groceries, Imports, Ingredients, Meat, Meat Products, Private Label, Spices

40257 Cribari Vineyard Inc
4180 W Alamos Ave # 108
Suite 108
Fresno, CA 93722-3943   559-277-9000
Fax: 559-277-2420   800-277-9095
bulk@cribari.net www.sacramentalwines.com

Food Brokers / A-Z

Processor and exporter of high quality California bulk wine
CEO & CFO: John F. Cribari
Sales: Ben Cribari
Estimated Sales: $730,000
Number Employees: 1-4
Number of Brands: 7
Type of Packaging: Bulk
Markets Served:
 Food Manufacturers & Processors
Brokered Products include:
 Alcoholic Beverages

40258 Crider Brokerage Company
10920 Schuetz Rd
St Louis, CO 63146-5904
314-994-7373
Fax: 314-965-2701
Broker of confectionery and dairy/deli products, frozen foods, meat, private label items, spices, etc.
Owner: Michael Crider
Estimated Sales: $2.5-5 Million
Number Employees: 4
Markets Served:
 Food Manufacturers & Processors, Wholesale Distributors, Food Service Operators
Primary Brands Brokered include: Gilroy Foods; McCormick; Central California Packing; D.D. Williamson & Company; Cormier Rice
Brokered Products include:
 Confectionery, Dairy/Deli, Frozen Food, Ingredients, Meat, Private Label, Spices

40259 Crossmark
5100 Legacy Dr
Plano, TX 75024-3104
469-814-1000
877-699-6275
www.crossmark.com
Confectionery and dairy/deli products, frozen foods and general merchandise.
Chief Executive Officer: Chris Moye
President, Sales Agency: Jami McDermid
Chief Financial Officer: Rudy Gonzalez
Chief Transformation Officer: Lance Andersen
Year Founded: 1905
Estimated Sales: $1 Billion
Number Employees: 40,000
Markets Served:
 Food Manufacturers & Processors, Super Market Chains, Wholesale Distributors, Food Service Operators
Brokered Products include:
 Confectionery, Dairy/Deli, Frozen Food, General Merchandise

40260 Crowley Marketing AssocPark
348 Park St
Suite #106
North Reading, MA 01864-2149
978-664-6606
Fax: 978-664-2254 800-634-6667
sales@crowleymarketing.com
Manufacturers' representative for food service equipment and seating for commercial facilities
Owner: John Crowley
crowley@crowleymarketing.com
Sales Manager: Tom Rochon
Estimated Sales: $5-10 Million
Number Employees: 10-19
Markets Served:
 Super Market Chains, Food Service Operators
Primary Brands Brokered include: Randall Manufacturing; Groen; Montague; Salvajor; W.A. Brown; Auten; Carter-Hoffman; Champion; Eagle; Anets; Earthquake
Brokered Products include:
 General Merchandise, Foodservice Equipment & Supplies

40261 Crown Point
118 S Cypress St
Mullins, SC 29574-3004
843-464-8165
Fax: 843-464-8598 www.crownpt.com
Wholesaler/distributor and exporter of beans, peanuts, almonds, cashews, canned mushrooms, pizza products, popcorn, spices, tomato paste, frozen vegetables, military rations including meals and ready-to-eat, etc. Importer of mushrooms and olives
President: Kevin Gates
VP: Scott Copes
Export Sales: Virginia Harrelson
Contact: John Anderson
johna@crownpt
Estimated Sales: $3-5 Million
Number Employees: 1-4
Parent Co: Unaka Company

Type of Packaging: Consumer, Food Service, Bulk
Brokered Products include:
 Exports, Ingredients, Private Label, Produce, Spices

40262 Cruise Marketing
1054 W Sunshine St
Springfield, MO 65807
417-866-3970
Fax: 417-866-4276 800-530-5094
Broker of dairy/deli products, meat and meat products, private label and bakery items, etc.
Manager: Alan Brock
Senior VP: Alan Brock
Estimated Sales: $5-10 Million
Number Employees: 6
Square Footage: 8000
Parent Co: Cruise Marketing
Markets Served:
 Super Market Chains, Wholesale Distributors, Food Service Operators
Primary Brands Brokered include: Carl Buddig Company; Farmland Foods; Advance Brands; Cargill, Inc.; Foster Farms; Reser's Fine Foods; Maplehurst; Kings Hawaiian Bakery; MBA Poultry
Brokered Products include:
 Dairy/Deli, Meat, Meat Products, Private Label, Bakery Items

40263 Culinary Specialty Produce
1190 Route 22 West
Mountainside, NJ 07092
908-789-4700
Fax: 908-789-4702 info@culinaryproduce.com
www.culinaryproduce.com
A full-line specialty produce broker
Owner/President: Richard Leibowitz
Sales Manager: Mark Pettongel
Estimated Sales: $1-3 Million
Number Employees: 5
Type of Packaging: Consumer
Markets Served:
 Super Market Chains, Wholesale Distributors, Food Service Operators
Primary Brands Brokered include: Lettuce (Mixes), baby vegetables, herbs, potatoes, tomatoes, dry ingredients, mushrooms and tropical & exotic fruits)
Brokered Products include:
 Exports, Groceries, Imports, Ingredients, Private Label, Produce, Spices

40264 Cusick J B Co
573 E 9th Ave
Chico, CA 95926-2309
530-898-0283
Fax: 530-898-0286 phallin@jbcusick.com
www.jbcusick.com
Broker of ingredients, nuts and dried fruits
President: Pat Hallin
phallin@jbcusick.com
Sales Contact: Rogelio Ocampo
Estimated Sales: $2.5-5 Million
Number Employees: 1-4
Markets Served:
 Food Manufacturers & Processors
Brokered Products include:
 Ingredients, Nuts, Dried Fruits

40265 (HQ)Cyba-Stevens ManagementGroup
3016 19 Street NE
Suite 100
Calgary, AB T2E 6Y9
Canada
403-291-3288
Fax: 403-250-3374 info@cybastevens.com
www.cybastevens.com
Broker of confectionery and dairy/deli products, frozen foods, general merchandise and groceries
President: Kevin Colflesh
COO: John Lemoine
Estimated Sales: $22.8 Million
Number Employees: 25
Markets Served:
 Super Market Chains, Wholesale Distributors, Food Service Operators
Primary Brands Brokered include: Coca Cola; Dial; Clorox; Gerber; Georgia Pacific
Brokered Products include:
 Confectionery, Dairy/Deli, Frozen Food, General Merchandise, Groceries

40266 D&D Marketing Group, Inc.
6285 S. Mojave Rd.
Suite A
Las Vegas, NV 89120-2720
702-798-5262
Fax: 702-798-4462
Import broker of confectionery and dairy/deli products, frozen foods, general merchandise, groceries, meat products, etc.
President: Donald Kiernan
Estimated Sales: $600,000
Number Employees: 13
Square Footage: 15000
Markets Served:
 Super Market Chains
Primary Brands Brokered include: King Oscar Sardines; Jet-Puffed Marshmallows; Farley Candy
Brokered Products include:
 Confectionery, Dairy/Deli, Frozen Food, General Merchandise, Groceries, Health Food, Imports, Meat Products, Private Label, Produce, Seafood

40267 D&H Marketing, Inc
105 W Fremont St
Burgaw, NC 28425-1229
910-259-2101
Fax: 910-259-6442 888-831-2390
sales@dhmarket.com www.dhmarket.com
Regional food broker specializing in meat, poultry, seafood for customers located in the Carolinas.
President: Donnie Hinson
Sales Executive: Everett Durham
Number Employees: 21
Type of Packaging: Consumer
Brokered Products include:
 Meat, Seafood

40268 D&R Food Brokers
97 Sleepy Hollow Drive
Brick, NJ 08724-5016
732-222-7546
Fax: 732-576-8790
Import broker of confectionery products, frozen foods, general merchandise, meat products, private label items, seafood, etc.
President: J DeStefano
Secretary: S DeStefano
Estimated Sales: $300,000-500,000
Number Employees: 4
Square Footage: 1600
Markets Served:
 Super Market Chains, Wholesale Distributors, Food Service Operators
Brokered Products include:
 Confectionery, Dairy/Deli, Frozen Food, General Merchandise, Imports, Meat Products, Private Label, Seafood

40269 DBB Marketing Company
724 Oak Grove Ave Ste 110
Menlo Park, CA 94025
650-462-0770
Fax: 650-462-0780
Broker of frozen foods
Owner: Doug Clendenning
VP: Bruce Daniel
Contact: Dan Conrad
ruby@dbbmarketing.com
Estimated Sales: $5-10 Million
Number Employees: 5-9
Markets Served:
 Food Manufacturers & Processors, Super Market Chains, Wholesale Distributors
Brokered Products include:
 Frozen Food

40270 (HQ)DRC Marketing Group
4344 Lyman Dr
Hilliard, OH 43026-1243
614-577-1215
Fax: 614-367-1450 877-372-5866
info@drcmktg.com www.drcmktg
Manufacturers' representative for food service equipment
Owner: Don Cooper
Partner: Paul Gray
Founding Partner: Don Cooper
Sales Rep: Matt Burns
Office Manager/Finance: Brian Reese
donald@drcmktg.com
Estimated Sales: $2.5-5 Million
Number Employees: 5-9
Square Footage: 32800
Markets Served:
 Wholesale Distributors

Primary Brands Brokered include: Pitco; South Bend; Toastmaster; Victory; Jackson; Seco; Magic Kitchen
Brokered Products include:
General Merchandise, Foodservice Equipment

40271 DSI Food Brokerage
324 Betsy Brown Rd
Port Chester, NY 10573   914-934-1641
Fax: 914-934-1649   www.whereorg.com
Import broker of dairy/deli and confectionery items, groceries, seafood, pasta and frozen, health and specialty foods
President: Alan Glustoff
VP: David Superstein
Marketing Director: Barbara Altneu
Contact: Barbara Altneu
barbara@5spokecreamery.com
Estimated Sales: $10-20 Million
Number Employees: 10-19
Square Footage: 4000
Markets Served:
Super Market Chains, Wholesale Distributors, Food Service Operators
Brokered Products include:
Dairy/Deli, Frozen Food, Health Food, Ingredients, Private Label

40272 DVC Brokerage Company
913 High Mountain Street
Henderson, NV 89009-1000   702-739-0041
Fax: 702-566-3002
Broker of confectionery and dairy/deli products, frozen foods, general merchandise, groceries, meats, etc.
Owner: Harry Van Camp
Estimated Sales: $5-10 Million
Number Employees: 5-9
Type of Packaging: Food Service
Markets Served:
Wholesale Distributors, Food Service Operators
Primary Brands Brokered include: Bernardi; Chili Bowl; Montage; Cripple Creek Bar-B-Que; Bee Gee; Tampa Maid
Brokered Products include:
Frozen Food, Groceries, Meat Products, Seafood

40273 DW Montgomery & Company
1103 W Hibiscus Blvd
P.O. Box 177
Melbourne, FL 32901-2714   321-953-9860
Fax: 866-648-3808   800-323-7154
dwm@dwmco.com
Wholesaler/distributor and broker of industrial and grocery grade refined sugar including natural and specialty organic. Wholesaler/distributor of health foods
Owner: David Montgomery
Principal: Robert Wormley
Sales: Paul Montgomery
Contact: Andrew Montgomery
andrew@dwmco.com
Operations: David Montgomery
andrew@dwmco.com
Estimated Sales: $330,000
Number Employees: 5
Square Footage: 10428
Markets Served:
Food Manufacturers & Processors, Wholesale Distributors, Food Service Operators
Brokered Products include:
Health Food, Imports

40274 Dadant & Company
1913 E 17th St Ste 200
Santa Ana, CA 92705   714-564-8710
Fax: 714-564-0358   800-734-6220
www.dadantco.com
Broker of industrial ingredients
President: Andy Dadant
VP: Paul Dadant
Estimated Sales: $10-20 Million
Number Employees: 5-9
Square Footage: 3600
Markets Served:
Food Manufacturers & Processors
Brokered Products include:
Confectionery, Frozen Food, Ingredients

40275 Dairytown Products Ltd
49 Milk Board Road
Sussex, NB E4E 5L2
Canada   506-432-1950
Fax: 506-432-1940   800-561-5598
admin@dairytown.com   www.dairytown.com
Butter and skim milk, whole milk and buttermilk powders
CEO: Derek Roberts
Quality Assurance: Wendy Palmer
VP Sales/Marketing: George MacPhee
Operations Manager: Lynn McLaughlin
Type of Packaging: Private Label
Primary Brands Brokered include: Hershey Company; Lumsden Brothers Ltd; McCain; Continental Ingredients Canada
Brokered Products include:
Dairy/Deli, Private Label, Skim Milk Powders

40276 Dakco International
2431 60th Avenue SE
Mercer Island, WA 98040-0242   206-232-1337
Fax: 206-232-8232
Import and export broker of meat and meat products including beef, veal, pork and lamb
President: D Colasurdo
Number Employees: 5-9
Markets Served:
Food Manufacturers & Processors, Wholesale Distributors
Brokered Products include:
Exports, Imports, Meat, Meat Products, Beef, Veal, Pork, Lamb

40277 Dakota Marketing Company
6229 Juneau Lane N
Osseo, MN 55311-4165   763-559-7813
Fax: 763-559-7835
Manufacturers' representative for imported food service equipment and supplies
President: Michael Zwick
Estimated Sales: $2 Million
Number Employees: 4
Markets Served:
Wholesale Distributors, Food Service Operators
Primary Brands Brokered include: Bel-Terr China; Homer Laughlien China; Forbes Industries; Drapes 4 Show; Thunder Group; Tar-Hong Melamine
Brokered Products include:
General Merchandise, Imports, Foodservice Equipment & Supplies

40278 (HQ)Damafro, Inc
54 Rue Principale
Saint Damase, QC J0H 1J0
Canada   450-797-3301
Fax: 450-797-3507   800-363-2017
Export broker of dairy products: Brie, Camembert, Goat milk cheese, Kosher cheese, flavoured brie, etc.
President: Michel Bonnet
Chairman: Philippe Bonnet
Quality Assurance Manager: Chantal Goyette
Marketing Manager: Philippe Guerineau
VP Sales: Heiko Kastner
Controller: Denise Labrecque
Customer Service: Anick Boivin
Plant Manager: Andre Hache
Number Employees: 1-4
Other Locations:
DAMAFRO
Montreal, PQDAMAFRO
Brokered Products include:
Dairy/Deli, Exports, Brie, Camembert Cheese, Etc.

40279 Damascus Peanut Company
Highway 200 W
Damascus, GA 39841   229-725-3353
Fax: 229-725-3338
Broker of peanuts
President: James Bannon
EVP: J W Willis
Contact: Jessie Padgett
jpadgett@peanut-shellers.org
VP Operations: John Phillips
Estimated Sales: $10-20 Million
Number Employees: 50-99
Markets Served:
Food Manufacturers & Processors
Brokered Products include:
Peanuts

40280 Dambeck & Associates
851 Silvernail Rd
Pewaukee, WI 53072-5588   262-542-7005
Fax: 262-542-1610
Broker of dairy/deli products, frozen foods, general merchandise, groceries, seafood, etc.
President: Mike Dambeck
VP: Chris Dambeck
Estimated Sales: $2.6 Million
Number Employees: 13
Markets Served:
Food Manufacturers & Processors, Super Market Chains, Wholesale Distributors, Food Service Operators
Primary Brands Brokered include: Mrs. Fridays; Del Monte; Johnsonville; Shasta; Roland
Brokered Products include:
Dairy/Deli, Frozen Food, General Merchandise, Groceries, Health Food, Meat, Meat Products, Seafood

40281 Dave Roemer & Associates
540 W Frontage Rd # 3005
Northfield, IL 60093-1223   847-446-6040
Fax: 847-446-6042
daveroemercompany@msn.com
Broker of frozen foods, dairy/deli products, groceries, meat/meat products, seafood, etc.
Owner: Dave Roemer
CEO: Mary Roemer
mroemer@davidroemerphotography.com
Estimated Sales: $5-10 Million
Number Employees: 5-9
Square Footage: 2000
Type of Packaging: Food Service
Markets Served:
Food Manufacturers & Processors, Wholesale Distributors, Food Service Operators
Brokered Products include:
Confectionery, Dairy/Deli, Frozen Food, General Merchandise, Groceries, Ingredients, Meat, Seafood

40282 (HQ)Dave Swain Assoc Inc
6 Lyberty Way # 101
Suite 101
Westford, MA 01886-3642   978-392-8401
Fax: 978-425-9285   800-222-5628
sswain@daveswainassociates.com
www.swainrep.com
Manufacturers' representative for cooking equipment, coolers, freezers and refrigerated warehouses; engineering and installation services available
President: Carol Pavlik
cpavlik@swainrep.com
VP: David Swain
Sales: Nils Ahlin
Estimated Sales: $10+ Million
Number Employees: 5-9
Square Footage: 20000
Markets Served:
Food Manufacturers & Processors, Super Market Chains, Wholesale Distributors, Food Service Operators
Primary Brands Brokered include: Bally; Market Forge; Gaylord; Cuno; Continental
Brokered Products include:
Cooking Equipment, Refrigeration

40283 Davel Food Brokerage
3088 Denton Drive
Merrick, NY 11566-5113   516-868-8009
Fax: 516-868-8009
Broker of disposable paper products, seafood, groceries and private label items
President: Herbert W Kleckner
Brokered Products include:
Groceries, Private Label

40284 David E Grimes Company
P.O. Box 1198
Hollister, CA 95024   831-637-1499
Fax: 831-636-4660   831-637-1499
www.degrimes.com
Import and export broker of garlic including fresh, processed and peele and ginger
CEO: David Grimes
Estimated Sales: $2 Million
Number Employees: 1-4
Markets Served:
Super Market Chains, Wholesale Distributors, Food Service Operators
Brokered Products include:
garlic, ginger

Food Brokers / A-Z

40285 Davis & Assoc Inc
W184s8372 Challenger Dr
Muskego, WI 53150-8747   262-679-9510
Fax: 262-679-5441   888-679-9510
customerservice@davisassoc.com
www.davisassoc.com
Manufacturers' representative for food service equipment and supplies including ranges, ovens, furniture, coolers and freezers, gas hoses, smallwares, racks, cabinets, slicers, shelving, menu boards, etc
Owner/President: Bob Davis
b.davis@davisandassociates.com
VP: Debbie Davis
Estimated Sales: $1-3 Million
Number Employees: 5-9
Square Footage: 28000

40286 Davis Sales Associates
PO Box 1649
Andover, MA 01810-0028   978-470-1166
Fax: 978-470-1199
Broker of confectionery and private label/generic products and general merchandise
Chairman: Guy Munroe
President: Stephen Munroe
Estimated Sales: $2.5-5 Million
Number Employees: 1-4
Markets Served:
  Super Market Chains, Wholesale Distributors
Primary Brands Brokered include: Kendall-Futuro Company; Lactona Dental Products; Cara, Inc.; Breath Assure; Kiss Cosmetics Company
Brokered Products include:
  Confectionery, General Merchandise, Private Label

40287 Dawson Sales Co Inc
2015 Spring Rd # 275
Suite 275
Oak Brook, IL 60523-3900   630-203-8174
Fax: 630-203-8171   www.dawsonsales.com
Broker of industrial ingredients
President: Diane Dawson
Manager: Lynne Noren
lynnenoren@dawsonsales.com
Estimated Sales: B
Number Employees: 1-4
Square Footage: 7
Markets Served:
  Food Manufacturers & Processors
Brokered Products include:
  Confectionery, Dairy/Deli, General Merchandise, Ingredients, Spices, Beverages

40288 Dd Reckner Co
129 E College Ave
Westerville, OH 43081-1647   614-890-5544
Fax: 614-890-6699   800-800-3075
mike.reckner@ddreckner.com
www.ddreckner.com
Broker of frozen food, meat and meat products including canned and dry
President: Mike Reckner
mike.reckner@ddreckner.com
Vice President: Mark Reckner
Estimated Sales: $2.5-5 Million
Number Employees: 10-19
Square Footage: 24000
Markets Served:
  Wholesale Distributors, Food Service Operators
Primary Brands Brokered include: Sara Lee Bakery Company; Bil-Mar Foods; McCarty Foods; J.M. Smucker Company; Uncle Bens; Yoplait/Colombo
Brokered Products include:
  Dairy/Deli, Frozen Food, Ingredients, Meat, Meat Products

40289 DeJarnett Sales
1030 N 25th Street
Billings, MT 59101-0842   406-245-2721
Fax: 406-245-2760
Broker of frozen foods, general merchandise, groceries and private label items
Principal: Dave Allen
allend@dejarnett.com
VP: Cheryl Javid
Manager: Steve Rhoda
Estimated Sales: $1-2.5 Million
Number Employees: 1-4
Square Footage: 20000
Parent Co: Javid Enterprises

Markets Served:
  Food Manufacturers & Processors, Super Market Chains, Wholesale Distributors
Primary Brands Brokered include:
  Colgate-Palmolive; Slim Fast Foods; Bausch & Lomb; Kendall-Futuro; Oral-B; Western Family (P/L)
Brokered Products include:
  Frozen Food, General Merchandise, Groceries, Private Label

40290 DeJarnett Sales
1401 W Farmers Avenue
Amarillo, TX 79118-6134   806-372-3851
Fax: 806-372-1404
Broker of frozen foods, groceries, general merchandise and private label items
President: George Lankfordt
Vice President: Mark Griffin
Estimated Sales: $5-10 Million
Number Employees: 5-9
Markets Served:
  Super Market Chains, Wholesale Distributors
Brokered Products include:
  Frozen Food, General Merchandise, Groceries, Private Label

40291 DeMoss & Associates
15065 Lebanon Rd Ste 103
Old Hickory, TN 37138-1809
Fax: 615-851-7294   888-933-6677
Broker of dairy/deli products, frozen foods, general merchandise, groceries, ingredients, meat, etc.
President: Tom DeMoss
Middle TN Sales Associate: John Smith
Estimated Sales: $5-10 Million
Number Employees: 5-9
Type of Packaging: Food Service
Markets Served:
  Food Manufacturers & Processors, Wholesale Distributors, Food Service Operators
Brokered Products include:
  Dairy/Deli, Frozen Food, Groceries, Ingredients, Meat, Meat Products, Private Label, Seafood

40292 Dealers Choice
10 Ellsworth Rd
Larchmont, NY 10538   914-833-2070
Fax: 914-833-2073   888-381-5535
Manufacturers' representative for food service equipment including pizza ovens, refrigeration equipment, smallwares and wire racks
Owner: Joseph L Bruno
Estimated Sales: $3-5 Million
Number Employees: 1-4
Markets Served:
  Super Market Chains, Wholesale Distributors, Food Service Operators

40293 (HQ)Deibert & Associates
2977 Ygnacio Valley Road
Box #602
Walnut Creek, CA 94598   925-426-1400
Fax: 925-426-1404   www.deibertseafood.com
Import broker of seafood
President: Eric Deibert
VP: Don Harlund
Director Of Int'l Sales: Claudio Guerrero
Office Manager: Michelle Matsutani
Estimated Sales: $10-20 Million
Number Employees: 10-19
Markets Served:
  Super Market Chains, Wholesale Distributors
Primary Brands Brokered include: Ore-Cal; Iceland; Haitai;
Brokered Products include:
  Imports, Seafood

40294 Deiss Sales Co. Inc.
S. Chaparral Court
Suite 270
Anaheim, CA 92808-2282   714-974-9513
Fax: 714-974-8136   jim@deisssales.com
www.deisssales.com
Importer/exporter, wholesaler/distributor of all frozen seafood, all natural beef, poultry and other quality food products
Owner: James Deiss
Quality Control: Annabelle Wright
Estimated Sales: $10 Million
Number Employees: 6
Square Footage: 3000
Type of Packaging: Food Service, Private Label, Bulk

Other Locations:
  Northern CA
  Walnut Creek, CANorthern CA
Markets Served:
  Wholesale Distributors
Brokered Products include:
  Health Food, Seafood

40295 Delbert Craig Food Brokers
P.O.Box 967
Wilkes Barre, PA 18703   570-825-8200
Fax: 570-823-6739   800-432-8001
Broker of frozen foods, dairy/deli items, groceries, meat products and seafood
President: Gordon Williams
Estimated Sales: $10-20 Million
Number Employees: 10-19
Square Footage: 9000
Markets Served:
  Wholesale Distributors, Food Service Operators
Brokered Products include:
  Dairy/Deli, Frozen Food, Groceries, Meat Products, Seafood

40296 Dennis Sales
809 Eastern Shore Dr
Salisbury, MD 21804-5934   410-742-1585
Fax: 410-742-3789
Broker of frozen foods and ingredients
Owner: Barbara Long
President: Ryan McLaughlin
VP: Galen Gardener
Sales Director: Ellen Hitch
Contact: Brad Flem
bflem@dennissales.com
Estimated Sales: $2.2 Million
Number Employees: 10
Markets Served:
  Food Manufacturers & Processors, Super Market Chains, Wholesale Distributors, Food Service Operators
Brokered Products include:
  Frozen Food, Ingredients

40297 Di Meo-Gale Brokerage Company
457 Wilson Road
Frankfort, NY 13340   315-733-4641
Import and export broker of alcoholic beverages, confectionery, dairy/deli products, general merchandise, groceries, industrial ingredients, meats, private label items, produce, health and frozen foods, seafood, spices, etc.
President: John Bevilacqua
Estimated Sales: $1-2.5 Million
Number Employees: 1-4
Markets Served:
  Food Manufacturers & Processors, Super Market Chains, Wholesale Distributors, Food Service Operators
Brokered Products include:
  Confectionery, Dairy/Deli, Exports, Frozen Food, General Merchandise, Groceries, Health Food, Imports, Ingredients, Meat, Meat Products, Private Label, Produce, Seafood, Spices

40298 Dial Industries Inc
31 Hamlet Dr
Plainview, NY 11803-1532   516-367-2037
Fax: 718-523-4259   info@dialindustries.com
www.dialindustries.com
Manufacturers' representative of confectionery, dairy/deli and private label items, frozen foods, groceries, seafood, produce, etc
President/CEO: Stephen Mallor
CFO: Natasha Mayo
VP: Janee Mallor
VP Sales: Joanne Valentin
VP/COO: Neal Scott Mallor
Estimated Sales: $4 Million
Number Employees: 5-9
Brokered Products include:
  Confectionery, Dairy/Deli, Frozen Food, Groceries, Private Label, Produce, Seafood

40299 Diamond Chemical & Supply Co
524 S Walnut St # B
Wilmington, DE 19801-5243   302-656-7786
Fax: 302-656-3039   800-355-7786
sales@diamondchemical.com
www.diamondchemical.com
Wholesaler/distributor of paper products, commercial dishwashing and laundry chemicals, floor maintenance and janitorial equipment and insecticides

President: Susan Hartzel
susan@diamondchemical.com
CFO: Saeed Malik
VP: Richard Ventresca
Sales Manager: Gene Mirolli
Warehouse: Ryan Rynar
Estimated Sales: $5 Million
Number Employees: 20-49
Square Footage: 52000
Markets Served:
Food Manufacturers & Processors, Super Market Chains, Wholesale Distributors, Food Service Operators
Primary Brands Brokered include: Butchers; Unikem; Pirkem; Diamon Chemical Products; Rubbermaid; Fort James Paper

40300 Diaz Sales
160 Arbor Road
Lehighton, PA 18235-5203   610-377-6944
Fax: 610-377-6912
Import broker of tropical produce and seafood including frozen mahi mahi and shrimp and canned sardines, tuna and mackerel. Also agent for canning companies in Ecuador and Venezuela
President: Jose Diaz
Number Employees: 1-4
Square Footage: 2000
Markets Served:
Food Manufacturers & Processors, Wholesale Distributors, Food Service Operators
Primary Brands Brokered include: Inepaca; Seatech International; Fricomsa; Conservas Isabel; Eveba; Empacadora Bilbo S.A.
Brokered Products include:
Frozen Food, Imports, Produce, Seafood

40301 (HQ)Dick Garber Company
#202, 7900 Nova Dr.
Davie, FL 33324   954-236-0456
Fax: 954-236-0468
Cheese, meat, bakery specialties
President & CEO: Dick Garber
Chief Financial Officer: Rosalie Garber
Sales: Mark Finocchio
Estimated Sales: $5-10,000,000
Number Employees: 5-9
Type of Packaging: Private Label
Brokered Products include:
Meat, Meat Products, cheese

40302 Dino-Meat Company
PO Box 95
White House, TN 37188-0095   615-643-1022
Fax: 615-643-1022   877-557-6493
Emu meat including steaks, ground, breakfast sausage, summer sausage, hot dogs, hot links, meat balls, snack sticks and jerky. Also emu oil and emu oil products
President: Neil Williams
Type of Packaging: Consumer, Food Service
Markets Served:
Super Market Chains, Wholesale Distributors, Food Service Operators
Brokered Products include:
Health Food, Meat, Meat Products

40303 Diversifood Associates,Inc
3901 Roswell Rd # 115
Marietta, GA 30062   770-977-0420
Fax: 770-977-2557 info@diversifood.com
www.diversifood.com
Broker of frozen vegetables and fruits
President: Hollee Parker
VP: Steven Parker
Contact: Tyler Stewart
tyler@diversifood.com
Account Executive: Teri Bush
Estimated Sales: $10-20 Million
Number Employees: 5-9
Type of Packaging: Private Label, Bulk
Markets Served:
Food Manufacturers & Processors
Brokered Products include:
Frozen Food, Frozen Fruits, Vegetables

40304 (HQ)Dixie Cullen Interests
8501 East Fwy
Houston, TX 77029-1615   713-747-1101
Fax: 713-747-1422 www.dixiecullen.com
Storage of equipment and machinery export preparation of food processing equipment
President: Catherine James
catherine@dixiecullen.com
Estimated Sales: $1-2.5 Million
Number Employees: 10-19
Square Footage: 800000

40305 Dixon Marketing Inc
301 Darby Ave
PO Box 1618
Kinston, NC 28501-1694   252-522-2029
Fax: 252-527-3967
Military broker of confectionery and dairy/deli products, frozen foods, general merchandise, groceries, meat and meat products, etc.
President: D Freeman
CEO: Laura Dixon
VP Sales: Don Paddock
Estimated Sales: $10.5 Million
Number Employees: 20-49
Markets Served:
Food Service Operators
Primary Brands Brokered include: Nabisco; Planter's; Smucker's; Lifesavers; Zip Lock; Riviana
Brokered Products include:
Alcoholic Beverages, Confectionery, Dairy/Deli, Frozen Food, General Merchandise, Groceries, Imports, Meat, Meat Products, Spices

40306 Don Ford Ltd
540 W Frontage Rd Ste 3155
Northfield, IL 60093   847-441-7877
Fax: 847-441-7995
Broker of ingredients
President: Donald A Ford
Contact: Barb Anderson
banderson@csiweb.com
Estimated Sales: $1-3 Million
Number Employees: 1-4
Type of Packaging: Bulk
Markets Served:
Food Manufacturers & Processors
Brokered Products include:
Ingredients

40307 Donald R Conyer Associates
9292 Cincinnati Columbus Rd
Cincinnati, OH 542241-512   513-782-8870
Fax: 513-782-8876
Import and domestic broker of general merchandise and private label items
President/CEO: Don Conyer
Estimated Sales: $3-5 Million
Number Employees: 1-4
Markets Served:
Super Market Chains, Wholesale Distributors
Brokered Products include:
General Merchandise, Imports, Private Label

40308 Donald R Tinsman Co
5291 Devonshire Rd
Harrisburg, PA 17112-3913   717-657-5222
Fax: 717-657-5223 drtco@aol.com
Broker of private label, confectionery, produce, dairy/deli products, general merchandise, groceries, meats serving all markets
Owner/Presdient: Donald Tinsman
drtco@aol.com
VP: Jeff Tinsman
Estimated Sales: $3-5 Million
Number Employees: 5-9
Square Footage: 20000
Brokered Products include:
Confectionery, Dairy/Deli, Frozen Food, General Merchandise, Groceries, Health Food, Ingredients, Meat, Meat Products, Private Label, Produce

40309 Doug Milne Co
4595 Lexington Ave # 100
Suite: 300
Jacksonville, FL 32210-2058   904-387-6770
Fax: 904-384-8215 dmilnecomp@aol.com
Export broker of confectionery, meat and dairy/deli products, produce, private label items frozen foods, general merchandise, groceries, etc.
President: Douglas Milne
Partner: John McCorvey
VP: Jack Milne
Estimated Sales: $500,000-$1 Million
Number Employees: 5-9
Markets Served:
Super Market Chains, Wholesale Distributors
Brokered Products include:
Confectionery, Dairy/Deli, Exports, Frozen Food, General Merchandise, Groceries, Meat Products, Private Label, Produce

40310 Douglas Sales Associates
140 W. Ethel Rd.
Unit N
Piscataway, NJ 08854-5951   732-985-6770
Fax: 732-985-6615 lwagner@douglassales.com
www.douglassales.com
Broker of grocery, general merchandise, bakery, and dairy/deli
President: Kenneth Atkinson
Owner: Roni Potocco
EVP: John Pavlik
Director of Sales: Brad Atkinson
Contact: Ken Atkinson
kena@douglassales.com
Director of Administrative Services: Laura Wagner
Estimated Sales: $4.5 Million
Number Employees: 25
Square Footage: 14800
Markets Served:
Super Market Chains, Wholesale Distributors
Brokered Products include:
Confectionery, Dairy/Deli, General Merchandise, Meat Products, Private Label, Spices

40311 Dr Mauthe & Assoc
101 Camelot Dr # 3
Fond du Lac
Fond Du Lac, WI 54935-8048   920-921-1244
Fax: 920-921-2192 ktwinstead@msn.com
www.drmauthe.com
Industrial ingredient brokers
Owner: William C Mauthe
Estimated Sales: Under $500,000
Number Employees: 10-19

40312 Dreyer Marketing
3160 SE Grimes Blvd # 100
Grimes, IA 50111-5039   515-986-5957
Fax: 515-986-1411
Broker of dairy/deli products, seafood, frozen foods and meats
President: Mike Dreyer
mdreyer@dreyermktg.com
Estimated Sales: $10-20 Million
Number Employees: 10-19
Square Footage: 7200
Markets Served:
Super Market Chains
Primary Brands Brokered include: Tyson Foods; Johnsonville Sausage; Jimmy Dean Meats; Maple Leaf Farms; Buddig; Jennie-O
Brokered Products include:
Dairy/Deli, Frozen Food, Meat, Meat Products, Seafood

40313 Dunbar Brokerage DBC Ingredients
1035 Jackson Avenue
River Forest, IL 60305-1417   708-366-5300

40314 Dunbar Co
1186 Walter St
Lemont, IL 60439-3993   630-257-2900
Fax: 630-257-3434 dunbar@dunbarsystems.com
www.dunbarsystems.com
Producer of serpentine baking systems for cookies, cakes, biscuits, bread, pies, pastries, muffins and puddings.
President/Owner: Mark Dunbar
CEO/Owner: Mike Dunbar
Senior Sales Engineer: Chuck Kazen
Manager: George Dunbar
george@dunbarsystems.com
Vice President of Operations: Doug Hale
Estimated Sales: $9.7 Million
Number Employees: 10-19
Type of Packaging: Food Service
Markets Served:
Food Service Operators
Brokered Products include:
Bakery Equipment

40315 (HQ)Dunbar Sales Company, Inc
4616 Montevallo Rd
Birmingham, AL 35210   205-956-2121
Fax: 205-956-2171 www.dunbarsalesco.com
Broker of dairy/deli products, frozen foods, general merchandise, groceries, meat products, produce and seafood

Food Brokers / A-Z

President: Robert Dunbar
rcdunbar@yahoo.com
VP: Gary Stonicher
Estimated Sales: $10-20 Million
Number Employees: 10-19
Markets Served:
  Food Manufacturers & Processors, Super Market Chains, Wholesale Distributors, Food Service Operators
Brokered Products include:
  Dairy/Deli, Frozen Food, General Merchandise, Groceries, Meat Products, Produce, Seafood

40316 Dunham & Smith Agencies
8220 Elmbrook Dr
Suite 160
Dallas, TX 75247-4010   214-689-6170
                www.dunhamandsmith.com
Broker of dairy/deli products, frozen foods, general merchandise, groceries, meat and meat products, etc.
President: John Gibson
CFO: Walter Lazarcheck
VP Marketing: Shand Morga
Number Employees: 50-99
Parent Co: Eurpac Service
Markets Served:
  Food Service Operators
Brokered Products include:
  Dairy/Deli, Frozen Food, General Merchandise, Groceries, Meat, Meat Products, Seafood

40317 E A Berg & Sons Inc
75 W Century Rd # 300
Paramus, NJ 07652-1461   201-262-4139
        Fax: 201-845-8201   info@eaberg.com
Broker of confectionery items, general merchandise, groceries, health foods, private label items, etc.
Managing Director: Kim Demona
Controller: Edson Sanches
Estimated Sales: B
Number Employees: 20-49
Square Footage: 36000
Brokered Products include:
  Confectionery, General Merchandise, Groceries

40318 E K Bare & Sons Inc
252 Maple Ave
Bird In Hand, PA 17505-9703   717-397-0351
        Fax: 717-397-3919   800-233-0311
                          www.ekbare.com
Broker of potatoes
President: Robert L Horst
bob@ekbare.com
Accountant: Linda Good
Logistics Coordinator: Bradley Halladay
Sales Manager: Robert Horst
Sales Manager: Robert Hess
Office Manager: Carol Hess
bob@ekbare.com
Transportation Manager: Ragen Horst
Purchasing Manager: Richard Farneth
Estimated Sales: $1.6 Million
Number Employees: 5-9
Markets Served:
  Food Manufacturers & Processors
Brokered Products include:
  Produce

40319 (HQ)E Ruff & Assoc Inc
10823 Montgomery Rd # 4
Suite 2
Cincinnati, OH 45242-3219   513-530-0061
        Fax: 513-530-0789   800-788-8196
        office@eruffassoc.com www.eruffassoc.com
Manufacturers' representative for food service equipment, supplies and furnishings
Owner: John Hoskinson
Sales Manager: Paul Hibbitt
jhoskinson@eruffassoc.com
Office Manager: Janet Mulvey
Estimated Sales: $5-10 Million
Number Employees: 5-9
Markets Served:
  Wholesale Distributors
Brokered Products include:
  General Merchandise, Foodservice Equipment

40320 E W Carlberg Co
6400 Glenwood St # 311
Mission, KS 66202-4025   913-384-0484
                        Fax: 913-384-0486
Broker of confectionery and dairy/deli products, frozen foods, industrial ingredients and spices
President: James DE Moss
james@ewcarlberg.com
Estimated Sales: $5-10 Million
Number Employees: 1-4
Type of Packaging: Bulk
Brokered Products include:
  Frozen Food, Ingredients, Spices

40321 EFD Associate
270 Alpha Dr
Pittsburgh, PA 15238-2906   412-967-9656
        Fax: 412-967-9654 www.efdassociates.com
Independent food broker of dry goods, frozen products, center of the plate and refrigerated items covering Western Pennsylvania, West Virginia, and Ohio.
Owner: Ed Pasquale
epasquale@mandi-efd.com
CEO: Eddie DiPasquale
Marketing/Bids: Krista Bartley
Business Development Manager: Michael Grande
Estimated Sales: $100 Million
Number Employees: 50-99
Markets Served:
  Super Market Chains, Wholesale Distributors, Food Service Operators
Brokered Products include:
  Dairy/Deli, Frozen Food, Imports, Meat, Meat Products, Produce

40322 Eagle Associates
131 Plum Street
Moorestown, NJ 08057-2952   609-268-5752
                        Fax: 609-268-2777
Broker of confectionery products, general merchandise and private label items
President: Mychael Wagner
CEO: Joan Wagner
Number Employees: 5
Square Footage: 11200
Markets Served:
  Super Market Chains, Wholesale Distributors
Primary Brands Brokered include: American Pop Corn Company; Doumak Marshmallows; Diamond Brands; Blue Cross Laboratories; Konica USA, Inc.; Carter Wallace, Inc.
Brokered Products include:
  Confectionery, General Merchandise, Groceries, Private Label

40323 Eagle Marketing
11401 Valley Blvd
El Monte, CA 91731-3242   562-946-5623
                        Fax: 562-446-2319
Broker of Dry and Frozen Groceries, Deli items, Health and Natural Foods, Alcoholic Beverages, Candy, Confectionery, and General Merchandise
President/CEO: Norman Rhodes
Senior VP: Frank Boyd
Sales: Bob Moss
Estimated Sales: $7-10 Million
Number Employees: 10-19
Square Footage: 10000
Type of Packaging: Consumer
Markets Served:
  Super Market Chains, Wholesale Distributors
Primary Brands Brokered include: Mrs. Stewart's Bluing; Webster Plastic Bags; Aspen & Natures Breeze Air Fresheners; Sweets Stations Cadny; Savory Trends Dip Mix; Desert Gardens Soup; Bread & Dip Mixes; Country Kitchens Bakery; Bathroom Tissue & Paper Towels
Brokered Products include:
  Alcoholic Beverages, Dairy/Deli, Frozen Food, General Merchandise, Groceries, Health Food, Produce, Seafood, Spices, Laundry Aids, Bread, Paper Products

40324 Eastern Bag & Paper Co
200 Research Dr
Milford, CT 06460
              Fax: 203-878-0438 800-972-9622
        marketing@edpsupply.com www.ebpsupply.com
Broker of paper products, smallwares, cleaning equipment, etc.
President: Matthew Sugerman
Chief Executive Officer: Meredith Reuben
Chief Financial Officer: William O'Donnell
Chief Information Officer: Jack Jurkowski
Vice President, Supply Chain: Joe Ondriezek
Vice President, Human Resources: Joseph LoPresti
Year Founded: 1918
Estimated Sales: $50-100 Million
Number Employees: 50-99
Square Footage: 100000
Parent Co: Eastern Bag & Paper
Markets Served:
  Food Service Operators
Brokered Products include:
  General Merchandise, Smallwares, Cleaning Supplies, Etc.

40325 Eastern Sales & Marketing
2 Van Riper Rd
Montvale, NJ 07645-1838   201-307-9100
        Fax: 315-463-5877   info@esm-ny.com
Broker of confectionery and dairy/deli products, frozen foods, general merchandise, groceries, etc.
President: Tony Scudieri
CEO: Antony Ferolie
Executive VP: Ken Novak
Estimated Sales: $20,000,000
Number Employees: 100-249
Square Footage: 28000
Parent Co: Eastern Sales and Marketing
Markets Served:
  Super Market Chains, Wholesale Distributors, Food Service Operators
Brokered Products include:
  Confectionery, Dairy/Deli, Frozen Food, General Merchandise, Groceries, Meat Products, Produce

40326 Eastern Sales and Marketing
1105 Lincoln Hwy
North Versailles, PA 15137-2133   724-742-4447
        Fax: 412-824-2751   info@esm-ny.com
                          www.esm-web.com
Broker of confectionery and dairy/deli products, frozen foods, general merchandise, groceries, etc.
VP: Kevin Bradley
Number Employees: 50-99
Square Footage: 14000
Parent Co: Eastern Sales and Marketing
Markets Served:
  Super Market Chains, Wholesale Distributors, Food Service Operators
Brokered Products include:
  Confectionery, Dairy/Deli, Frozen Food, General Merchandise, Groceries, Meat Products, Produce

40327 Ebbert Sales & Marketing
701 W Ingomar Rd
Pittsburgh, PA 15237-4969   412-364-6000
                        Fax: 412-364-0297
Broker of general merchandise, groceries and private label items
President: Joseph Ebbert
VP Service: S Ebbert
Estimated Sales: $5-10 Million
Number Employees: 5-9
Markets Served:
  Super Market Chains, Wholesale Distributors
Brokered Products include:
  General Merchandise, Groceries, Private Label

40328 Ed O'Connor Associates
12026 81st Avenue
Seminole, FL 33772-4503   727-398-2895
                        Fax: 727-392-2138
Export broker of smallwares
President: Ed O'Connor
Office Manager: Judy O'Connor
Number Employees: 1-4
Markets Served:
  Wholesale Distributors, Food Service Operators
Primary Brands Brokered include: Edge Resources; Chef's Specialties; Spill Stop; Parvin; Crestware; Ex-Cell
Brokered Products include:
  Exports, General Merchandise, Smallwares

40329 Egerstrom Inc
10012 E 64th St
Raytown, MO 64133-5122   816-358-3025
        Fax: 816-737-0042   800-821-8570
                          pegerstrom@msn.com
Broker of frozen foods, general merchandise, groceries, industrial ingredients, dairy/deli and private label items
President: Paul Egerstrom
pegerstrom@msn.com
President: Tom Egerstrom
Estimated Sales: $5-10 Million
Number Employees: 1-4
Square Footage: 34000

Food Brokers / A-Z

Markets Served:
Food Manufacturers & Processors, Super Market Chains, Wholesale Distributors
Brokered Products include:
Confectionery, Groceries, Health Food, Private Label

40330 (HQ)Eiseman-Gleit Co Inc
401 E 4th St
Bridgeport, PA 19405-1815 610-278-5014
Fax: 610-278-5014
Broker of confectionery products and general merchandise
President: Carl Nelson
Owner: Brett Eisman
Contact: Chris Carper
chris@eg4star.com
Number Employees: 18
Markets Served:
Food Manufacturers & Processors, Super Market Chains, Wholesale Distributors, Food Service Operators
Brokered Products include:
Confectionery, General Merchandise, Produce

40331 Eiserloh Co Inc
5504 S Lambert St
Harahan, LA 70123-5573 504-887-8990
Fax: 504-887-8218 jtoups@eiserlohco.com
Broker serving food service operators
President: Jeffrey Toups
admin@eiserlohco.com
VP: Ed Dupui
Director: John Feliu
Estimated Sales: $20-50 Million
Number Employees: 10-19
Markets Served:
Food Service Operators

40332 Elco Fine Foods
233 Alden Road
Markham, ON L4B 1G5
Canada 905-731-7337
Fax: 905-731-2391 info@elcofinefoods.com
www.elcofinefoods.com
Distributor of premium confectionery, food and beverage products
CEO: Moe Cussen
Number Employees: 100
Square Footage: 270000

40333 Elias Shaker & Co
766 W Algonquin Rd
Arlington Hts, IL 60005-4416 847-434-0960
Fax: 847-434-0960 selling4u@eliasshaker.com
www.eliasshaker.com
Broker of confectionery products, general merchandise, groceries, health food, private label items, meat products, seafood and spices
President: Bruce Funk
bruce.funk@eliasshaker.com
Senior VP: Stanley Okragly
Field Sales Supervisor-Eastern: Don Chample
Estimated Sales: $1.80 Million
Number Employees: 20-49
Markets Served:
Super Market Chains, Wholesale Distributors
Primary Brands Brokered include: Sweet 'N Low; Helmac; Chicken of the Sea; Armour Swift-Eckrich; McCorm; Clement Pappas
Brokered Products include:
Confectionery, General Merchandise, Groceries, Health Food, Meat Products, Private Label, Seafood, Spices

40334 Elliot Horowitz & Co
675 3rd Ave
New York, NY 10017-5704 212-972-7500
Fax: 212-972-7050 ehorowitz@elliothorowitz.com
www.elliothorowitz.com
Manufacturers' representative for food service equipment and supplies including smallwares and heavy cooking and freezing equipment
Owner: Elliot Horowitz
Estimated Sales: $.5-1 million
Number Employees: 5-9
Type of Packaging: Food Service
Markets Served:
Super Market Chains, Wholesale Distributors, Food Service Operators
Brokered Products include:
General Merchandise, Foodservice Equipment & Supplies

40335 Ellis S. Fine Co., Inc.
10815 Reisterstown Rd
Owings Mills, MD 21117 410-654-5900
Fax: 410-558-6437 wbfj@hotmail.com
Import broker of dairy and deli products, general merchandise, groceries, meat and meat products, private label items, etc.
President: William Fine
VP: S Fine
VP: W Fine
Number Employees: 7
Markets Served:
Food Manufacturers & Processors, Super Market Chains, Wholesale Distributors, Food Service Operators
Brokered Products include:
Dairy/Deli, General Merchandise, Groceries, Imports, Meat, Meat Products, Private Label, Seafood, Spices

40336 Emerling International Foods
2381 Fillmore Ave
Suite 1
Buffalo, NY 14214-2197 716-833-7381
Fax: 716-833-7386 pemerling@emerfood.com
www.emerlinginternational.com
Bulk ingredients including: Fruits & Vegetables; Juice Concentrates; Herbs & Spices; Oils & Vinegars; Flavors & Colors; Honey & Molasses. Also produces pure maple syrup.
President: J Emerling
jemerling@emerfood.com
Sales: Peter Emerling
Public Relations: Jenn Burke
Year Founded: 1988
Estimated Sales: $10-20 Million
Number Employees: 20-49
Square Footage: 500000
Markets Served:
Food Manufacturers & Processors, Wholesale Distributors, Food Service Operators

40337 Encore Fruit Marketing Inc
120 W Bonita Ave
Suite 204
San Dimas, CA 91773-3035 909-394-5640
Fax: 909-394-5646 sales@encorefruit.com
Import/export manufacturers' representative of industrial ingredients, frozen fruits and vegetables, purees and juice concentrates; serving food processors, food service operators and wholesalers/distributors.
Owner & President: Greg Kaiser
Owner & CEO: Lisa Hiday-Baca
Chief Financial Officer: Kandi Ashcraft
Vice President: Erin Sill
VP, Sales: Chris Schubert
Import/Export Manager: Wes Uyemura
Year Founded: 1989
Estimated Sales: $55 Million
Number Employees: 10-19
Square Footage: 1800
Type of Packaging: Bulk
Other Locations:
Encore Fruit Marketing
Yakima, WA Encore Fruit Marketing
Markets Served:
Food Manufacturers & Processors, Wholesale Distributors, Food Service Operators
Primary Brands Brokered include: Milne; Ocean Spray; I.T.I.; Binfrut
Brokered Products include:
Exports, Frozen Food, Groceries, Imports, Ingredients, Purees, Juice Concentrates

40338 English Northwest Marketing
11937 NE Halsey St
Portland, OR 97220 503-254-7303
Fax: 503-253-4038 ENGLISHNW1@AOL.COM
Manufacturers' representative for food service equipment and supplies factory representative
President: Jeff English
CFO: Wanda English
VP: D E English
Estimated Sales: $1+ Million
Number Employees: 1-4
Square Footage: 3984
Markets Served:
Food Service Operators
Brokered Products include:
Food Service Equipment & Supplies

40339 Enterprise Food Brokers
4621 Hinckley Industrial Pkwy
Unit 1
Hinckley, OH 44233-0095 216-635-2570
Fax: 216-635-2690
Broker of frozen food, groceries, meat products, ingredients, private label items and seafood
President: Dan Diaczun
VP: C Hoell
Estimated Sales: $5-10 Million
Number Employees: 5-9
Markets Served:
Food Manufacturers & Processors, Wholesale Distributors, Food Service Operators
Brokered Products include:
Frozen Food, Groceries, Ingredients, Meat Products, Private Label, Seafood

40340 Erickson Brothers Brokerage Co
10507 165th St W # A
Lakeville, MN 55044-5716 952-736-1675
Fax: 952-736-1676
Broker of confectionery items, meat snacks, and wholesalers/distributors, Foodservice, C-Stores
Principal: Jim Scislow
jim.scislow@ericksonbrothers.net
Estimated Sales: $5-10 Million
Number Employees: 5-9
Markets Served:
Wholesale Distributors, Food Service Operators
Primary Brands Brokered include: Schwan's; Carl Buddig; Trails Best; 5HR Energy Drink; Heinz Food Service; Landshire; Palmer Candy
Brokered Products include:
Confectionery, Frozen Food, General Merchandise, Groceries, Meat Products

40341 Erlich Foods International
23679 Calabasas Road
Ste 900
Calabasas, CA 91302-1502 310-475-0777
Fax: 310-475-4619 info@erlichfoods.com
www.erlichfoods.com
Export broker of fresh and frozen poultry products
President: Reuben Erlich
VP: Jim Weston
Contact: Rocio Diaz
rocio@erlichfoods.com
Estimated Sales: $5-10 Million
Number Employees: 5-9
Primary Brands Brokered include: Sunday House; Health is Wealth; Snow Ball Foods; Sunset Farms
Brokered Products include:
Exports, Frozen Food, Poultry Products

40342 Ervan Guttman Co
8208 Blue Ash Rd
Cincinnati, OH 45236-2188 513-791-0757
Fax: 513-891-0559 800-203-9213
info@theervanguttmancompany.com
www.theervanguttmancompany.com
Candy making equipment and supplies including release papers and flavorings
Owner: Harold Guttman
harold@guttmanfam.com
Estimated Sales: Less Than $500,000
Number Employees: 1-4
Square Footage: 4000
Type of Packaging: Bulk
Markets Served:
Food Manufacturers & Processors, Food Service Operators
Brokered Products include:
Confectionery, Ingredients

40343 Esm Ferolie
2 Van Riper Rd
Montvale, NJ 07645-1838 201-307-9100
Fax: 781-314-7200 www.esmferolie.com
Broker of confectionery and dairy/deli items, frozen and health foods, groceries, meat and meat products, etc.
President: Tony Scudieri
CEO: Antony Ferolie
VP: Nick Messina
Marketing: Lorraine Nealon
Contact: Lisa Alfaiate
lalfaiate@esmferolie.com
Estimated Sales: $500,000-$1 Million
Number Employees: 5-9
Square Footage: 12000
Markets Served:
Super Market Chains, Wholesale Distributors

Food Brokers / A-Z

Brokered Products include:
Confectionery, Dairy/Deli, Frozen Food, Groceries, Health Food, Imports, Meat, Meat Products, Private Label, Produce, Seafood

40344 Esposito Brokerage
9 Ruta Dr
North Branford, CT 06471   203-484-7856
Fax: 203-484-4904
Broker of confectionery and dairy/deli products, frozen foods, general merchandise, groceries, health foods, etc
President: Anthony P Esposito
Estimated Sales: $2.5-5 Million
Number Employees: 1-4
Markets Served:
Super Market Chains, Wholesale Distributors, Food Service Operators
Primary Brands Brokered include: Mancini
Brokered Products include:
Confectionery, Dairy/Deli, Frozen Food, General Merchandise, Groceries, Health Food, Imports, Private Label

40345 Espresso Machine Experts
231 SE 102nd Ave
Portland, OR 97216-2705   503-255-9900
Fax: 503-255-9845   888-909-0002
www.espressomachineexperts.com
Wholesaler/distributor of beverage equipment including espresso. Broker of specialty foods
Owner: Scott Kellerman
scott@espressomachineexperts.com
General Manager: Bob Cox
Service Manager: Brian Conroy
Estimated Sales: $500,000-$1 Million
Number Employees: 5-9
Brokered Products include:
Groceries, Specialty Foods

40346 Essential Food Marketing
25746 Butternut Ridge Rd
North Olmsted, OH 44070   440-716-1111
Fax: 440-716-9111   800-723-7017
Import broker of confectionery products and dairy/deli products, frozen foods, general merchandise, groceries, produce, etc.
President: Edward Wiles
Estimated Sales: $1-2.5 Million
Number Employees: 1-4
Square Footage: 5600
Markets Served:
Food Manufacturers & Processors, Super Market Chains, Wholesale Distributors, Food Service Operators
Primary Brands Brokered include: Mushroom Cooperative; MGA; Creative Bakers; Altantic Spice; Italpasta Ltd.
Brokered Products include:
Confectionery, Dairy/Deli, Frozen Food, General Merchandise, Groceries, Imports, Private Label, Produce, Spices

40347 Ettinger Rosini & Associates
11114 Grader Street
Dallas, TX 75238-2403   214-343-2548
Fax: 214-343-2727   darrin@ettros.com
www.ettros.com
Manufacturers' representative for food service equipment and supplies
President: Denny Rosini
VP: Dan Scruggs
Sales Manager: Greg Rosini
Contact: Gregg Garcia
ggarcia@hondaofclearlake.com
Estimated Sales: $5-10 Million
Number Employees: 18
Square Footage: 56000
Markets Served:
Super Market Chains, Wholesale Distributors, Food Service Operators
Brokered Products include:
General Merchandise, Foodservice Equipment & Supplies

40348 Eurogulf Company
1761 Lehigh Pkwy N
Allentown, PA 18103   610-432-3232
Fax: 610-437-3333
Export broker of confections, dried milk products, peanut butter, ketchup, canned vegetables, snack foods, honey, mayonnaise, salt, pie fillings, shortenings, disposable trays, platters, paper plates, plastic cutlery and cornvegetable and soybean oil
President: Samir Moussa
Estimated Sales: $3-5 Million
Number Employees: 1-4
Primary Brands Brokered include: Stoney's; Jaber; Blaze; Blue Bird; Happy Boy
Brokered Products include:
Confectionery, Dairy/Deli, Exports, General Merchandise, Groceries, Private Label

40349 Europaeus USA
8 John Walsh Boulevard
Suite 140
Peekskill, NY 10566-5346   914-739-1900
Fax: 914-739-5229   800-992-3876
customerservice@europaeus.com
www.europaeus.com
Importer, exporter and wholesaler/distributor of hand painted ceramic tableware.
President: Daniel Salvati
Sales Director: Daniel Salvati
Contact: Michael Shaw
cdia@cdr.net
Operations Manager: Hettie Van Owen
Purchasing Agent: Daniel Salvati
Estimated Sales: $1-3 Million
Number Employees: 1-4
Square Footage: 40000
Type of Packaging: Food Service

40350 Evans & Associates
287 Andrews St
Rochester, NY 14604-1105   585-254-1780
Fax: 585-254-2154
Manufacturers' representative for food service equipment including tabletop supplies, smallwares, freezers, stoves, hoods and ranges
Owner: Jeff Carragher
Partner: William Evans
Partner: Marion Evans-Agostinelli
Estimated Sales: $1-3 Million
Number Employees: 5-9
Markets Served:
Super Market Chains, Wholesale Distributors, Food Service Operators
Primary Brands Brokered include: Victory; Champion; South Bend; Middleby Marshall; Keating; Plymold
Brokered Products include:
General Merchandise, Foodservice Equipment

40351 Evans Brokerage Company
PO Box 124
Cazenovia, NY 13035
Fax: 315-655-2962
Broker of dairy/deli items, frozen foods, general merchandise, groceries, industrial ingredients, etc.
Owner: Bradshaw Evans
Number Employees: 3
Markets Served:
Food Manufacturers & Processors, Super Market Chains, Wholesale Distributors, Food Service Operators
Brokered Products include:
Dairy/Deli, Frozen Food, General Merchandise, Groceries, Ingredients, Private Label, Produce

40352 Evers Heilig Inc
5640 Feltl Rd
Hopkins, MN 55343-7999   952-938-7494
Fax: 952-938-2035   800-682-3921
www.eversheilig.com
Broker of confectionery items, general merchandise, groceries and private label products
Principal: Ronnie Melton
VP: Mary Loujan
Estimated Sales: $5-10 Million
Number Employees: 20-49
Square Footage: 40000
Markets Served:
Food Manufacturers & Processors, Super Market Chains, Wholesale Distributors, Food Service Operators
Primary Brands Brokered include: Tootsie Rolls; American Licorice; Kellogg's; Great American; D.L. Clark; Frankford Candy
Brokered Products include:
Confectionery, General Merchandise, Groceries, Private Label

40353 Expert Customs Brokers
2595 Inkster Blvd
Winnipeg, MB R3C 2E6
Canada   204-631-1200
Fax: 204-697-9749   www.ecb.com
Food brokers; logistics services
Partner: Wayne Boiteau
Estimated Sales: $11 Million
Number Employees: 24

40354 F M Turner Co Inc
6325 Cochran Rd # 5
Unit 5
Cleveland, OH 44139-3930   216-287-5002
Fax: 440-287-5009   800-729-7545
info@fmturner.com   www.fmturner.com
Manufacturers Representative for the disposable foodservice industry
Owner: David Scott
Partner: Tom Godleswki
Northern Ohio Sales Representative: Jessica Brenneman
Office Manager: Megan Carlson
Estimated Sales: $5-10 Million
Number Employees: 5-9
Type of Packaging: Food Service
Markets Served:
Wholesale Distributors, Food Service Operators
Brokered Products include:
Disposable Products

40355 F Mc Lintocks Saloon & Dinin
750 Mattie Rd
PO Box 239
Pismo Beach, CA 93449-2059   805-773-1892
Fax: 805-773-5183   800-866-6372
fmc@mclintocks.com   www.mclintocks.com
Broker of groceries; serving supermarket chains and wholesalers/distributors
Partner: Bruce Breault
Partner: Tunny Ortali
Estimated Sales: $5-10 Million
Number Employees: 20-49
Markets Served:
Super Market Chains, Wholesale Distributors
Brokered Products include:
Groceries

40356 F. Rothman Enterprises, LLC
721 Matsonford Road
Villanova, PA 19085   610-431-4311
Fax: 610-431-1916   Service@FRothman.com
www.FRothman.com
Broker of domestic and international cheeses, meats, seafood, mushrooms, and of specialty products for the Italian, Mediterranea, pizza, deli, and retail trades.
Principal: Mike Leibowitz
Owner: Fred Rothman
Contact: Janice Kinghorn
Contact: Michael Leibowitz
mleibowitz@hotmail.com
Secretary: Janice Kinghorn
Number Employees: 1-4
Markets Served:
Food Manufacturers & Processors, Super Market Chains, Wholesale Distributors, Food Service Operators
Primary Brands Brokered include: Park Cheese/Casaro; Nasonville Dairy-Marathanae; Locatelli; Auricchio; Country Fresh Mushroom

40357 F.G. Publicover & Associates
158 Pantry Rd
Sudbury, MA 01776-1137   978-443-8628
Fax: 978-443-2438
Broker of conveyors, pot washers, carts, ranges, holding cabinets, etc.
President: Frank Publicover
VP: Veronica Publicover
Estimated Sales: $2 Million
Number Employees: 3
Square Footage: 4000
Type of Packaging: Food Service

40358 FM Carriere & Son
2909 Division St # E
Metairie, LA 70002-7039   504-454-0123
Fax: 504-454-0125   www.fmcarriereandson.com
Broker of confectionery, frozen foods, groceries, industrial ingredients, private label items and spices
Owner: Diane Carriere
VP: Robert De Paula
Estimated Sales: $3-5 Million
Number Employees: 1-4
Square Footage: 850
Markets Served:
Food Manufacturers & Processors, Wholesale Distributors

Food Brokers / A-Z

Brokered Products include:
Confectionery, Ingredients, Spices

40359 FMI Food Marketers International Ltd
11951 Nammersmith Way
Suite 233
Richmond, BC V7A 5H9
Canada
604-275-3664
Fax: 604-275-3624
Import and export broker of seafood and private label items
Partner: Harry Guenther
Partner: George Wilson
Export Manager: Bent Holme
Number Employees: 5-9
Square Footage: 6000
Markets Served:
Super Market Chains, Wholesale Distributors, Food Service Operators
Primary Brands Brokered include: St. Jean's Cannery LTD.
Brokered Products include:
Exports, Imports, Private Label, Seafood

40360 Fairley & Co Inc
8008 Castleway Dr
Indianapolis, IN 46250-1943
317-576-5335
Fax: 317-576-5339
Broker of confectionery, dairy and deli and private label items, general merchandise, groceries and meat products
President: Barry Howard
fairley@fairleyco.com
VP: John Jameson
Account Executive: R Somes
Estimated Sales: $2.5-5 Million
Number Employees: 1-4
Markets Served:
Food Manufacturers & Processors, Super Market Chains, Wholesale Distributors, Food Service Operators
Primary Brands Brokered include: Ferrara Pan; Goodmark Foods; Charms Company; Van Melle; LIC; Necco/Stark/Haviland
Brokered Products include:
Confectionery, Dairy/Deli, General Merchandise, Groceries, Meat, Meat Products, Private Label

40361 (HQ)Federated Group
3025 W Salt Creek Ln
Arlington Hts, IL 60005-1083
847-577-1200
Fax: 847-632-8302 800-234-0011
sales@fedgroup.com www.fedgroup.com
Import and export broker of confectionery and dairy/deli products, frozen foods, general merchandise, groceries, meats, seafood, etc.
Owner: Martin Gross
VP Sales/New Business: Jeff Leroy
Manager Ingles Markets: Curtis Clark
Manager Operations: Douglass Sheets
Director Labels/Packaging: Brad Stockman
Estimated Sales: $68 Million
Number Employees: 100-249
Parent Co: Federated Group
Markets Served:
Super Market Chains, Wholesale Distributors, Food Service Operators
Primary Brands Brokered include: HyTop; Prima Brite; Parade; Better Valu; Cuddle Ups; Lifemark; Effortless Entrees; Red & White
Brokered Products include:
Confectionery, Dairy/Deli, Exports, Frozen Food, General Merchandise, Groceries, Imports, Meat, Meat Products, Private Label, Produce, Seafood, Spices

40362 Feenix Brokerage LTD
6283 Johnston Rd
Albany, NY 12203-4323
518-456-7664
Fax: 518-456-0869
Broker of specialty and dairy/deli products, groceries, health foods, produce, spices, meat and meat products, private label items, etc.
President: Frank Pensabene
frank@feenix.net
Marketing Specialist: Jonathan Milks
Sales Coordinator: Judy Ogborn
Estimated Sales: $10-20 Million
Number Employees: 5-9
Square Footage: 8400

Markets Served:
Food Manufacturers & Processors, Super Market Chains, Wholesale Distributors, Food Service Operators
Brokered Products include:
Dairy/Deli, Groceries, Health Food, Meat, Meat Products, Private Label, Produce, Spices, Specialty Products

40363 Ferdinand Richards & Son
3010 W Swann Avenue
Tampa, FL 33679-0888
813-875-5562
Fax: 813-870-0530 800-842-3243
Import broker of confectionery and dairy/deli items, frozen foods, meat and meat products, general merchandise, produce, seafood, groceries, etc.
President: Willis Stoick
VP: John Richards
Estimated Sales: $880 Thousand
Number Employees: 5
Markets Served:
Food Manufacturers & Processors, Super Market Chains, Wholesale Distributors, Food Service Operators
Primary Brands Brokered include: H.J. Heinz Company; Flanagan Brothers Inc.; Kendall Refining Comapny; Col-Pak, Inc.; Timbercrest Farms Inc.; Jamaica Hell Fire
Brokered Products include:
Dairy/Deli, General Merchandise, Groceries, Meat, Meat Products, Private Label, Seafood

40364 Ferolie Esm-Metro New York
2 Van Riper Rd
Montvale, NJ 07645-1838
201-307-9100
Fax: 201-782-0878 www.esmferolie.com
Broker of confectionery and dairy/deli products, frozen foods, general merchandise, groceries, meat, etc.
President: Paul Nadel
Chairman/CEO: Lawrence Ferolie
ljferolie@froliegroup.com
VP Hbc/GM: Tony Ragazzo
VP Sales: Robert Martin
COO: Tony Scudieri
Purchasing Agent: Al Nagy
Estimated Sales: A
Number Employees: 500-999
Markets Served:
Food Manufacturers & Processors, Super Market Chains, Wholesale Distributors, Food Service Operators
Primary Brands Brokered include: Pet, Inc.; Lehn & Fink; James River/Dixie; Hershey Pasta Group; Kraft General Foods; Ferrero, USA
Brokered Products include:
Confectionery, Dairy/Deli, Frozen Food, General Merchandise, Groceries, Meat, Meat Products, Private Label, Produce, Seafood, Spices

40365 Finn Marketing Group Inc
14605 Mccormick Dr
Tampa, FL 33626-3025
813-925-1122
Fax: 813-925-1607 800-451-6755
email@finnmarketing.com
www.finnmarketing.com
Manufacturers' representative for food service equipment and supplies
Owner: Matt Ruby
matt@finnmarketing.com
VP: Ken Jennings
Estimated Sales: $2.7 Million
Number Employees: 10-19
Markets Served:
Wholesale Distributors, Food Service Operators
Primary Brands Brokered include: Blodgett; Carter-Hoffman; Magi Kitch'n; Glastender; Kolpak-McCall; Pitco; Panasonic
Brokered Products include:
General Merchandise, Foodservice Equipment & Supplies

40366 (HQ)Firing Industries Ltd
509 Glendale Avenue E
Suite 301
Niagara-On-The-Lake, ON L0S 1J0
Canada
905-688-0962
Fax: 905-688-6643 877-688-0974
firing@firing.com www.firing.com
Manufacturers' representative of food processing equipment including feeders, blenders, dryers, pulverizers, screens, centrifuges and evaporators

President: Michel Dubuc
Appliance Engineer: David Feasby
Appliance Engineer: Paul Feasby
Estimated Sales: $2 Million
Number Employees: 6
Square Footage: 12800
Other Locations:
Firing Industries
Pointe Claire, CanadaFiring Industries
Brokered Products include:
General Merchandise, Blenders, Dryers, Feeders, Etc.

40367 First Choice Sales Company
3210 N Fruit Avenue
Fresno, CA 93705
559-224-376=
Fax: 559-224-803₅
Specializing in Beef, Pork, Poultry, Cut Fruit and other quality Center of the Plate items for domestic and export Food Service Industries
President: Wayne Short
Contact: Short Kent
kent@1stchoicesales.com
Estimated Sales: $300,000-500,000
Number Employees: 1-4
Markets Served:
Wholesale Distributors, Food Service Operators
Primary Brands Brokered include: Fresno Meat Company; The Philadelphia Cheesesteak Company
Brokered Products include:
Frozen Food, Meat, Meat Products, Beef, Portion Control Steaks, etc.

40368 First Flight Foods
3120 Medlock Brg Rd Ste F200
Norcross, GA 30071
770-417-9100
Fax: 770-417-9110
Broker of confectionery, private label and dairy/deli items, meat and meat products, frozen foods, groceries, general merchandise, seafood, spices, etc.
Owner/President: Larry Mays
Owner: Jimmy Farris
VP: Rodney Mays
Estimated Sales: $3.5 Million
Number Employees: 20
Square Footage: 60000
Type of Packaging: Food Service, Private Label
Markets Served:
Food Manufacturers & Processors, Wholesale Distributors, Food Service Operators
Brokered Products include:
Confectionery, Dairy/Deli, Exports, Frozen Food, Groceries, Imports, Ingredients, Meat, Meat Products, Private Label, Produce, Seafood, Spices

40369 Fischer Group
1636 N Brian St
Orange, CA 92867-3422
714-921-2660
Fax: 714-921-2544 info@fischergroup.com
Manufacturers' representative for food service equipment
President: Brian Bolton
brianb@fishergroup.com
VP: Greg Herron
General Manager: Gene Austin
Estimated Sales: $20-50 Million
Number Employees: 20-49
Square Footage: 7500
Markets Served:
Super Market Chains, Wholesale Distributors
Food Service Operators
Primary Brands Brokered include: 3M; American Metalcraft; Barker Company; Best-Value Textiles; Blodgett; Cambro; Cooper Atkins; Dormont Mfg Co.; Fast; Forschner; FWE; GA Systems; Hamilton Beach; Hatco; Kopak; MagiKitch'n; McCall; Pitco; San Jamar; Sterno; Walco
Brokered Products include:
General Merchandise, Foodservice Equipment

40370 Five Star Packaging
613 25th Avenue NW
Birmingham, AL 35215-2233
205-856-0722
Fax: 205-853-4545
Manufacturers' representative of food service equipment
President/CEO: Randall Heaton
Number Employees: 5-9
Parent Co: C&M Finepack
Markets Served:
Wholesale Distributors, Food Service Operators

Food Brokers / A-Z

Primary Brands Brokered include: C&M Finepack; Jet Plastca; Packer Ware
Brokered Products include:
General Merchandise, Foodservice Equipment

40371 Five State Brokerage
607 E Abram St Ste 12
Arlington, TX 76010
817-265-4833
Fax: 817-265-4835
Broker of confectionery products, groceries, meats, seafood, spices, frozen foods, private label items serving all markets.
Partner: Keith Cook
Partner: Benny Sanderlin
Estimated Sales: $4 Million
Number Employees: 2
Squcre Footage: 3300
Type of Packaging: Food Service, Private Label
Markets Served:
Super Market Chains, Wholesale Distributors
Primary Brands Brokered include: Snowball, O'Steens, Matador, Rodriguez, Cream Unlimited, Pan Saver, Golden Pickles, Louisa Foods, Coleman All Natural, Naturally Fresh, Smokey Denmark
Brokered Products include:
Confectionery, Dairy/Deli, Frozen Food, Groceries, Meat, Meat Products, Private Label, Seafood

40372 Flavor Consultants
2875 Coleman St
North Las Vegas, NV 89032
702-643-4378
Fax: 702-643-4382 www.flavorconsultants.com
Manufacturers' representative and importer, exporter of flavoring ingredients.
President: Tim Wallace
tim@flavorconsultants.com
Estimated Sales: $1.1 Million
Number Employees: 6
Brokered Products include:
Ingredients, Flavors

40373 Florida Agents Inc
1444 20th St N
St Petersburg, FL 33713-5745
727-572-5200
Fax: 727-823-7766 jim@floridaagents.com
www.floridaagents.com
Manufacturers' representative for food service equipment and supplies
President: Jim Degnan
Manager: James Degnan
sales@floridaagents.com
Estimated Sales: $5-10 Million
Number Employees: 1-4
Markets Served:
Wholesale Distributors
Primary Brands Brokered include: Anets; Avtec; Bakers Pride; Bizerba; Blakeslee; Bobrick; Brown; Chill-Bite; Cres Cor; Groen; Koala Kare; Randall; Select Stainless; Sterno Group; T&S; Teknor Apex; Tomlinson; Update International; Waring; Wells/Bloomfield
Brokered Products include:
General Merchandise, Foodservice Equipment & Supplies

40374 Florida Distributing Source
14038 63rd Way N
Clearwater, FL 33760-3618
727-431-0444
Fax: 727-531-2906 800-838-1818
info@florida-distributing.com
www.florida-distributing.com
Wholesaler/distributor and broker of food service equipment
Owner/President: Kevin Eaton
CEO: Bob Eaton
bob@florida-distributing.com
Estimated Sales: $1.8 Million
Number Employees: 1-4
Primary Brands Brokered include: Sani-Serve; Cuno; Perlick
Brokered Products include:
Foodservice Equipment

40375 Flynn Sales Associates, Inc.
8680 W 96th St # 200
Overland Park, KS 66212-3333
913-383-9111
Fax: 913-383-9393 ls-flynn@swbell.net
Broker of confectionery and dairy/deli products, frozen foods, general merchandise, groceries, meat and meat products, seafood, spices, private label items, etc.
Owner: Lloyd Schaffer
VP: Chuck Vandenburg
Contact: Lloyd Schaefer
wg-flynn@swbell.net
Estimated Sales: $10-20 Million
Number Employees: 8
Square Footage: 6000
Markets Served:
Super Market Chains, Wholesale Distributors, Food Service Operators
Primary Brands Brokered include: Dubuque; Perdue Foods; Hershey Chocolate (USA); Rich/Seapak; Readi Bake; Beatrice (cheese)
Brokered Products include:
Confectionery, Dairy/Deli, Frozen Food, General Merchandise, Groceries, Meat, Meat Products, Private Label, Seafood, Spices

40376 Fold-Pak LLC
33 Powell Dr
Hazleton, PA 18201-7360
570-454-0433
Fax: 570-454-0456 800-486-0490
www.fold-pak.com
Wire handled square paper food containers, round cup style closeable food and soup containers, square closeable paper food containers (microwaveable, carry out and storage capable)
Manager: Charlie Mattson
Director of Operations: Wes Gentles
Sales Director: Jim Keitges
Corporate Credit Manager: William Moon
Plant Manager: Lee King
Number Employees: 5000-9999
Number of Brands: 16
Number of Products: 66
Square Footage: 416000
Parent Co: Rock-Tenn Company
Type of Packaging: Consumer, Food Service, Private Label
Markets Served:
Super Market Chains, Wholesale Distributors
Primary Brands Brokered include: Bio-Pak; Fold-Pak; Smart-Serv
Brokered Products include:
Paper Carry Out Food Containers

40377 Food Associates of Syracuse
2174 State Fair Blvd
Baldwinsville, NY 13027
315-635-6338
Fax: 315-635-1798
Broker of confectionery and dairy/deli products, frozen foods, general merchandise, groceries, meats, etc.
President: Nick Petrosillo
VP: Richard Thompson
Estimated Sales: $1.2 Million
Number Employees: 8
Markets Served:
Food Manufacturers & Processors, Super Market Chains, Wholesale Distributors, Food Service Operators
Primary Brands Brokered include: Giorgio Foods, Inc.; M. Polander, Inc.; Stokely, USA; Diamond/Universal Brands, Inc.; Italica/Tee Pee, Inc.
Brokered Products include:
Confectionery, Dairy/Deli, Frozen Food, General Merchandise, Groceries, Meat Products, Private Label, Produce, Seafood

40378 (HQ)Food Equipment Rep Inc
3716 SW 30th Ave
Fort Lauderdale, FL 33312-6707
954-587-9347
Fax: 954-584-7170 800-226-8389
fer@ferinc.net www.ferinc.net
Manufacturers' representative for food service equipment and supplies
Managing Partner: J Gabriel Puerto
Partner: Thomas E. Dickie
Senior Sales Associate: Daniel W. Wood
Sales Associate: Bill Peters
Sales Associates: William Trabazo
Estimated Sales: $2.5-5 Million
Number Employees: 1-4
Other Locations:
FERINC, Orlando Office
Orlando, FL
FERINC, Tampa Office
Clearwater, FL
FERINC, Daytona Office
Trails West Deland, FLFERINC, Orlando OfficeClearwater
Markets Served:
Wholesale Distributors
Primary Brands Brokered include: Alexander Industries; Cleveland; Delfield; FWE; Frymaster/Dean; Garland/US Range; Halton/Vent Master; Insinkerator; Jackson; Kysor Panel; Lincoln/MercoSavory; Lincoln/Wearever; Merrychef; Omni-Team; Royal; Varimixer
Brokered Products include:
General Merchandise, Foodservice Equipment & Supplies

40379 Food Ingredients Inc
2100 Airport Rd
Waukesha, WI 53188-2454
262-521-8118
Fax: 262-521-2085 800-448-8118
foodingil@aol.com www.foodingredientsinc.com
Broker of industrial ingredients
Owner: Al Haehle
CFO: William Rastello
Sales Representative: John Ruby
al@foodingredientsinc.com
Director of Administration: Tamma Barker
Estimated Sales: $5-10 Million
Number Employees: 20-49
Square Footage: 24000
Markets Served:
Food Manufacturers & Processors
Primary Brands Brokered include: Associated Milk Producers, Inc.; C&T/Quincy Vegetable Oil; PPG Industries; Groeb Farms; Natural Products; Colony Industries
Brokered Products include:
Ingredients

40380 Food Sales Systems
PO Box 153769
Irving, TX 75015-3769
972-721-1911
Fax: 972-554-0335 800-256-8002
Broker of general line products
President: Chuck Paradowski
VP Protein Category: Bill Bearden
Director Marketing: Amy Abell
VP Sales: Jeff Boydston
Warehouse Manager: Jim Borg
Estimated Sales: $20-50 Million
Number Employees: 30
Square Footage: 7430
Markets Served:
Wholesale Distributors, Food Service Operators
Brokered Products include:
Groceries

40381 Food Sales West
4655 W McDowell Rd Ste 110
Phoenix, AZ 85035-4145
602-246-8595
Fax: 602-249-4250 www.foodsaleswest.com
Broker of frozen foods, groceries, bakery/deli products, meat and meat products and seafood
President: David Lions
Manager: Mike McDade
Estimated Sales: $1.50 Million
Number Employees: 8
Square Footage: 4500
Parent Co: Food Sales West
Other Locations:
Food Sales West-HQ
Costa Mesa, CA
Food Sales West
Livermore, CA
Food Sales West
Fresno, CA
Food Sales West
Las Vegas, NV
Food Sales West
Portland, OR
Food Sales West
Kent, WA
Food Sales West-HQLivermore
Markets Served:
Wholesale Distributors, Food Service Operators
Primary Brands Brokered include: Awrey Bakery; French's; Icelandic; Jennie-O; Land O'Lakes; Lyons Magnus; Mars; McCormick; Nestle; Orval Kent; PPI; Simplot; Tree Top; Tyson
Brokered Products include:
Dairy/Deli, Frozen Food, Groceries, Meat, Produce, Seafood, Spices, Bakery, Juices

40382 Food Service Associates
9924 Norwalk Blvd
Santa Fe Springs, CA 90670
562-946-4599
Broker of dairy/deli products, seafood, frozen foods, groceries, meat and meat products, private label items, etc.

Estimated Sales: $50-100 Million
Number Employees: 20-49
Square Footage: 10000
Type of Packaging: Bulk
Markets Served:
  Super Market Chains, Wholesale Distributors, Food Service Operators
Primary Brands Brokered include: Charlie's Pride Meats; John Morrell; Lamb & Weston; Trident Seafoods
Brokered Products include:
  Confectionery, Dairy/Deli, Frozen Food, Groceries, Meat, Meat Products, Private Label, Seafood, Spices

40383 Food Service Connection
7676 Executive Dr
Eden Prairie, MN 55344-3677   952-895-1172
            Fax: 952-975-3658
Import broker of confectionery, dairy/deli products, groceries, industrial ingredients, meats, seafood and frozen food
Manager: Chris Melnarik
Executive VP: Norm Dyer
General Manager: Eric Stinson
Estimated Sales: $10-20 Million
Number Employees: 20
Square Footage: 15300
Parent Co: Venture Marketing
Markets Served:
  Food Manufacturers & Processors, Super Market Chains, Wholesale Distributors, Food Service Operators
Primary Brands Brokered include: Ocean Spray; Reckitt & Coleman; Uncle Ben's; J.R. Simplot, Farmland Foods; Campbell's
Brokered Products include:
  Confectionery, Dairy/Deli, Frozen Food, Groceries, Imports, Ingredients, Meat, Meat Products, Seafood

40384 Food Service Marketing of Pennsylvania
295 W Steuben St
Pittsburgh, PA 15205-2553   412-928-8600
            Fax: 412-928-9895
Broker of dairy/deli items, frozen foods and meat and meat products
President: G Allan Acrey
VP: Bill Schubert
VP Sales: Jason Thomas
Contact: Allan Acrey
allanacrey@fsmpa.com
Estimated Sales: $10-20 Million
Number Employees: 10-19
Markets Served:
  Wholesale Distributors, Food Service Operators
Brokered Products include:
  Dairy/Deli, Frozen Food, Meat, Meat Products

40385 Food Service Merchandising
6441 Ballejo Ct N
Jacksonville, FL 32210-5037   904-388-5421
            Fax: 904-388-6527
Broker of groceries, meat and meat products, private label items, seafood, dairy/deli products, frozen foods, etc
President: Jerry Hembree
VP: Charlie Maulden
Estimated Sales: $12-15 Million
Number Employees: 1-4
Square Footage: 4800
Type of Packaging: Food Service
Brokered Products include:
  Dairy/Deli, Frozen Food, Ingredients, Meat, Private Label, Spices

40386 Food Service Specialists
831 N Martway Dr
Olathe, KS 66061-7053   913-440-9596
            Fax: 913-341-7513
Broker of confectionery items, frozen foods, meat/meat products, seafood and spices
President: James Piene
CEO: Roger Eilts
Finance: Cindy Piene
VP Retail Resources: Stacy Seaba
Marketing Manager: Deidre Eilts
VP Sales: Chuck Kirby
Manager: Jim Peine
jim@fsskc.com
Product Administrator: Stan Cox

Estimated Sales: $20-50 Million
Number Employees: 20-49
Square Footage: 4500
Markets Served:
  Food Service Operators
Brokered Products include:
  Confectionery, Frozen Food, Meat, Meat Products, Seafood, Spices

40387 FoodBin Trading, Inc.
145 Willow Avenue
City of Industry, CA 91746-2047   323-724-2505
            Fax: 323-726-0934   800-327-8442
Import and export broker of frozen foods and ingredients
President: Jack Tucey
VP: William Perry
Estimated Sales: A
Number Employees: 2
Square Footage: 10000
Type of Packaging: Food Service, Bulk
Markets Served:
  Food Manufacturers & Processors
Primary Brands Brokered include: GFF Inc.; Talamo Foods; Nakano Foods
Brokered Products include:
  Exports, Frozen Food, Imports, Ingredients

40388 Foodmark Sales
30 Freneau Ave Ste 1a
Matawan, NJ 07747   732-290-9060
            Fax: 732-290-0091
Broker of dairy/deli products, frozen foods, general merchandise, groceries, meat and meat products, private label items, seafood, etc.
President: Neal Markowitz
VP: Susan Markowitz
Estimated Sales: $5-10 Million
Number Employees: 7
Markets Served:
  Super Market Chains, Wholesale Distributors
Brokered Products include:
  Dairy/Deli, Frozen Food, Meat, Private Label, Seafood, Bakery

40389 Foodsales Inc
430 E Iris Dr
Nashville, TN 37204-3108   615-292-2914
            Fax: 615-383-3735
Broker of dairy/deli products, frozen foods, general merchandise, groceries, health food, industrial ingredients, meat and meat products, etc.
President: Eric Martin
eric@foodsaleseast.com
Treasurer: Randy Sanders
Estimated Sales: $20-50 Million
Number Employees: 10-19
Markets Served:
  Super Market Chains, Food Service Operators
Brokered Products include:
  Dairy/Deli, Frozen Food, General Merchandise, Groceries, Health Food, Ingredients, Meat, Meat Products, Private Label, Seafood, Spices

40390 Foodservice Innovators
209 Glendale Dr
Clairton, PA 15025   412-922-4774
            Fax: 412-922-5204   800-458-4054
Broker of confectionery items, groceries, frozen foods, meat, spices, seafood, etc.
President: Donald Voland
CEO: Willis Voland
Primary Brands Brokered include: Nestle; Lipton; ConAgra; Barber Foods; Fishery Products International; Ken's Foods
Brokered Products include:
  Confectionery, Frozen Food, Groceries, Meat, Seafood, Spices

40391 Foodservice Marketing
741 N Wilson Rd
Columbus, OH 43204-1463   614-278-9000
            Fax: 614-278-9160   800-282-0045
Broker of dairy/deli products, frozen foods, meat and meat products, private label items, seafood and spices
Owner: Mike Dutko
General Manager: Mike Dutko
Estimated Sales: $2.5-5 Million
Number Employees: 5
Parent Co: Foodservice Marketing
Markets Served:
  Wholesale Distributors, Food Service Operators

Brokered Products include:
  Dairy/Deli, Frozen Food, Meat, Meat Products, Private Label, Seafood, Spices

40392 Foodservice Solutions & Ideas
4846 Main St
Flora, MS 39071-9515   601-879-8699
Broker of private label items, confectionery and dairy/deli products, frozen foods, groceries, meats and meat products, seafood, etc.
Owner: Baine Smith
Estimated Sales: A
Number Employees: 3
Square Footage: 51000
Markets Served:
  Food Service Operators
Brokered Products include:
  Confectionery, Dairy/Deli, Frozen Food, Groceries, Meat, Meat Products, Private Label, Seafood, Spices

40393 Foodworks International
641 Cowpath Road
Suite 204
Lansdale, PA 19446   609-688-8500
Fax: 732-783-0404 a.francois@foodworksintl.com
            www.foodworksintl.com
Imported French food specialties, cheeses and dry groceries
President: Alain Francois
Estimated Sales: Under $500,000
Number Employees: 1-4
Type of Packaging: Food Service, Private Label
Markets Served:
  Wholesale Distributors
Brokered Products include:
  Dairy/Deli, Imports

40394 Footner & Co Inc
6610 Tributary St # 300
PO Box 9973
Baltimore, MD 21224-6514   410-631-7711
            Fax: 410-631-7716 info@footner.com
            www.footner.com
Transportation broker of international freight forwarding
Owner: Roberto Gutierrez
roberto@footner.com
Manager: John Ryan
Number Employees: 10-19

40395 Forbes Frozen Foods
438 Main St
Milford, OH 45150-1128   513-576-6660
Fax: 513-576-6661 www.forbesfoods.com
Wholesaler/distributor and broker of food ingredients, fruit juice concentrates and essences, as well as frozen fruits and vegetables
President: David Winters
Estimated Sales: $2.5-5 million
Number Employees: 1-4
Brokered Products include:
  Dairy/Deli, Frozen Food, Ingredients, Meat, Produce, Seafood, Spices

40396 Forbes Hever & Wallace, Inc.
1500 Lakeside Parkway
Suite 110
Flower Mound, TX 75028-4045   972-219-8898
            Fax: 972-219-8960   800-526-1126
            www.your-rep.com
Manufacturers' representative for food service equipment and supplies
President: John Hever
shever@your-rep.com
Business Manager: Anne Forbes
Marketing/School Coordinator: Karey Clements
Sales: Donna East
Customer Serivce/Office Manager: Cheryl Williams
Inventory/Warehouse Manager: Larry Pryor
Number Employees: 5-9
Markets Served:
  Wholesale Distributors
Brokered Products include:
  General Merchandise, Foodservice Equipment & Supplies

40397 Forma Packaging, Inc.
18 Broadway Rd
Warren, NJ 07059   908-604-9500
Broker of packaging and processing machinery including conveyors and formers
President: Anthony Bruno
anthonyb@formausa.com

Food Brokers / A-Z

Number Employees: 10-19
Brokered Products include:
   General Merchandise, Conveyors, Formers

40398 Forman Group
4905 Bardstown Rd # 205
Louisville, KY 40291-1793   502-245-9728
        Fax: 502-244-6687 800-894-0702
    leonathenson@theformangroup.com
              www.formaninc.com
President: Otis Cook
otisc@papc.net
VP: Leo Nathenson
Estimated Sales: $10-20 Million
Number Employees: 10-19
Parent Co: The Forman Group
Markets Served:
   Food Service Operators

40399 Forseasons Sales
1500 West Park Drive
Suite 260
Westborough, MA 01581   508-366-7900
   Fax: 508-870-2807 bhurd@forseasons.com
            www.forseasons.com
Broker of pet food and accessories, confectionery/candy, dairy/deli products, private label items, seafood, spices, general merchandise, etc.; serving mass merchant, drug chains, dollar stores and wholesalers/distributors.
President: Willam Hurd
Contact: Hank Bazigian
hbazigian@forseasons.com
Estimated Sales: $150-200 Million
Number Employees: 20-49
Markets Served:
   Super Market Chains, Wholesale Distributors
Primary Brands Brokered include: Starkist Foods; Fort Howard Paper
Brokered Products include:
   Confectionery, Dairy/Deli, General Merchandise, Groceries, Imports, Private Label, Seafood, Spices

40400 Four Peaks, Inc.
224 Potomac St
Aurora, CO 80011   303-340-3334
       Fax: 303-340-0294 ask@4peaksinc.com
Broker of dairy/deli products, meat and seafood, mexican food and deserts.
Owner/President: Hans Schulmeyer
VP: Barney Cox
Sales Manager: D Moser
Contact: Kim Brough
kim@4peaksinc.com
Estimated Sales: $2.1 Million
Number Employees: 10
Square Footage: 36000
Markets Served:
   Food Service Operators
Primary Brands Brokered include: Pillsbury; McCormick; American Home Foods; Armour; Tyson; Rose Packing
Brokered Products include:
   Dairy/Deli, General Merchandise, Meat, Seafood

40401 Francis Musto & Co
3070 Saturn St # 201
Suite 201
Brea, CA 92821-6296   714-984-4111
        Fax: 714-984-4130 800-854-3759
             vince@francis-mustoe.com
             www.francis-mustoe.com
Broker of edible fats and oils
President: Vince Schwartz
Vice President: Bill Schlesener
Estimated Sales: $2.5-5 Million
Number Employees: 5-9
Other Locations:
   Francis-Mustoe & Company
   Bridgewater, NJFrancis-Mustoe & Company
Markets Served:
   Food Manufacturers & Processors, Food Service Operators
Primary Brands Brokered include: ADM; Cargill; AGP Processing; Honeymead Products Corporation; Plains Cooperative; Bunge Corporation
Brokered Products include:
   Ingredients, Edible Fats, Oils

40402 Frank Kinsman Assoc
397 US Route 1
Scarborough, ME 4074   207-883-4181
              Fax: 207-883-9446
Broker of dairy/deli and confectionery, groceries, general merchandise, produce, meat and meat products, private label items, frozen foods, seafood, etc.
Owner: Frank Kinsman
Sales Manager: W Duplesse
sfki@maine.rr.com
Office Manager: Arline C Gurschick
Estimated Sales: $3-5 Million
Number Employees: 10-19
Markets Served:
   Super Market Chains, Wholesale Distributors, Food Service Operators
Primary Brands Brokered include: Gilardi Foods; Apple & Eve, Inc.; Old Mother Hubbard; Stonyfield Farms; Leavitt Corporation; P.O.V. Wagner
Brokered Products include:
   Confectionery, Dairy/Deli, Frozen Food, General Merchandise, Groceries, Meat, Meat Products, Private Label, Produce, Seafood

40403 Frank M Hartley Inc
82 Village Dr
Mahwah, NJ 07430-2586   201-760-0020
        Fax: 201-760-0252 hartleywine@aol.com
Import and domestic broker of alcoholic beverages including wine and liquor from Europe, South America and California. Selling under the brands/labels of our suppliers or customer's own brands and labels.
President: Bruce Hartley
hartleywine@aol.com
Estimated Sales: $5 Million
Number Employees: 1-4
Square Footage: 450
Markets Served:
   Super Market Chains, Wholesale Distributors
Primary Brands Brokered include: Alianca, Mertes, Schenk Tresch
Brokered Products include:
   Alcoholic Beverages, Private Label

40404 Fredco Wolf
9661 Irvine Center Dr
Irvine, CA 92618-4652   949-788-7788
       Fax: 949-770-8711 office@fredcoreps.com
              www.fredcoreps.com
Manufacturers' representative for food service equipment
Owner: Ron Rubinstin
office@fredcoreps.com
Founder: Fred Rubinstein
Estimated Sales: $2.5-5 Million
Number Employees: 10-19
Markets Served:
   Wholesale Distributors
Brokered Products include:
   General Merchandise, Foodservice Equipment

40405 Freedom Food Brokers
13418 Falmouth Ave
Pickerington, OH 43147   614-833-0442
       Fax: 614-833-0484 freedombkr@aol.com
Broker of groceries, meat, confectionary and dairy/deli, frozen foods, seafood, spices, produce, etc
President: J Messer
CEO: Donald Wendel
Estimated Sales: $26 Million
Number Employees: 5-9
Square Footage: 2500
Markets Served:
   Super Market Chains, Wholesale Distributors
Brokered Products include:
   Frozen Food, Health Food, Meat, Meat Products, Produce, Seafood, Spices

40406 Freeland Bean & Grain Inc
1000 E Washington
PO Box 515
Freeland, MI 48623-8439   989-695-9131
        Fax: 989-695-5241 800-447-9131
   freeland.i@att.net www.freelandbeanandgrain.com
Manufacturer and exporter of dried beans and grains
Owner: John Hupfer
freeland.i@att.net
VP: Elenor Hupfer
Estimated Sales: $3.8 Million
Number Employees: 5-9
Type of Packaging: Bulk

40407 Freeline Organics USA
46 Colony Rd
Wetsport, CT 06880   203-557-4265
              info@freelineorganics.com
              www.freelineorganics.com
Bulk supplier of organic oils.
Owner: Peter de Kok
Owner: Theresa Stigter
Parent Co: Freeline Organic Food BV
Type of Packaging: Bulk
Brokered Products include:
   Organic oil

40408 Freeman Fruit Intl
295 E Main St # 12
Ashland, OR 97520-1848   541-552-1401
        Fax: 541-552-1402 866-670-7183
           freeman@ashlandoregon.us
Broker of organic and conventional frozen fruits and ingredients
Owner: Lincoln Freeman
lincoln@ashlandoregon.us
Estimated Sales: $7.5 Million
Number Employees: 5-9
Markets Served:
   Food Manufacturers & Processors
Brokered Products include:
   Frozen Food, Ingredients, Organic Fruits, Purees, Concentrates

40409 Freeman Signature
825, Guimond Street
Suite 200
Longueuil, QC J4G 2M7
Canada   450-651-2040
        Fax: 888-863-5106 888-641-2040
   info@freemancan.com www.freemansignature.com
Foodservice broker of dairy/deli products, general merchandise, groceries, meat products, private label items, etc.
President: Serge Labrecque
VP Finances & Administration: Charles Tanguay
IT Vice President: Paul van Doesburg
Marketing Insights Analyst: Lucka Lepage
Sales Vice-President: François Chevalier
EVP Operations: Gregory Bellas
Number Employees: 50
Markets Served:
   Super Market Chains, Wholesale Distributors, Food Service Operators
Brokered Products include:
   Dairy/Deli, General Merchandise, Groceries, Meat Products, Private Label

40410 Freiria & Company
Mercado Central Plaza
Po Box 364165
Puerto Nuevo, PR 920   787-792-4460
        Fax: 787-783-3945 888-792-0160
Import and export broker of confectionery products, frozen foods, general merchandise, corn meal, granulated garlic, dehydrated onions, paprika, adobo powder, garlic powder, apple cider and white distilled vinegar, groceries, spicesetc.
President: Enrique Freiria
CEO: F Freiria
CFO: Juan Garcia
VP: H Freiria Jr
Quality Control: Elvis Diaz
Marketing: F Freiria
Sales: Angel Rosario
Public Relations: Jose Lopez
Estimated Sales: $19.5 Millionn
Number Employees: 52
Square Footage: 120000
Parent Co: Henframar Corporation
Type of Packaging: Food Service, Private Label
Markets Served:
   Food Manufacturers & Processors, Super Market Chains, Wholesale Distributors, Food Service Operators
Primary Brands Brokered include: McCormick; Lea & Perrins; Star-Kist; La Rosa; Libby; La Choy
Brokered Products include:
   Confectionery, Exports, Frozen Food, General Merchandise, Groceries, Imports, Spices

Food Brokers / A-Z

40411 (HQ)Fromartharie Inc
85 Division Ave
P.O.Box 409
Millington, NJ 07946-1316 908-647-3386
Fax: 908-647-6590 800-899-6689
r.schinbeckler@specialitiesinc.com
www.specialitiesinc.com
Manufacturers' representative which specializes in added-value cheese and meats for the deli
Owner: Roland Schinbeckler
fromo1@aol.com
VP Sales/Marketing: Richard Kessler
Estimated Sales: $5-10 Million
Number Employees: 10-19
Markets Served:
  Wholesale Distributors, Food Service Operators
Primary Brands Brokered include: Madrange; Roth Kase; Saputo; Laura Chenel; Busseto; Beretta; Specialities Agro; Tribalat; Ermitage
Brokered Products include:
  Dairy/Deli, Meat, Meat Products, Cheeses

40412 Frozen Food Associates
3155 Frontera Way
Burlingame, CA 94010 650-652-5760
Fax: 650-652-7847
Broker of frozen foods
Owner: Arnold Loza
CEO: D Loza
Estimated Sales: $1-3 Million
Number Employees: 1-4
Number of Brands: 10
Markets Served:
  Super Market Chains, Wholesale Distributors
Primary Brands Brokered include: Big Valley, Inc.; Freezer Queen; Elena Foods; Seabrook Farms; Ateeco, Inc.; Supherb Farms
Brokered Products include:
  Frozen Food

40413 Fusion Sales Group
6514 Basile Rowe
East Syracuse, NY 13057-2942 315-488-3101
Fax: 315-488-6018 www.infusionsg.com
Export broker of dairy/deli products, frozen foods, groceries, meat and meat products, private label items, etc.
Regional President: Enzo Dentico
Vice President: Jim Robinson
jrobinson@infusionsg.com
Estimated Sales: $5-10 Million
Number Employees: 10-19
Markets Served:
  Food Manufacturers & Processors, Wholesale Distributors, Food Service Operators
Brokered Products include:
  Dairy/Deli, Exports, Frozen Food, Groceries, Meat, Meat Products, Private Label, Produce

40414 G.A. Davis Food Service
325 Sunrise Hwy Ste 1
Lindenhurst, NY 11757 516-364-0910
Fax: 516-364-0917 800-437-6322
Broker of frozen foods, dairy products and seafood
President: Gary Davis
VP Sales: Bob LoBianco
Estimated Sales: $20-50 Million
Number Employees: 20-49
Other Locations:
  G.A. Davis Food Service
  South Plains, NJG.A. Davis Food Service
Markets Served:
  Wholesale Distributors, Food Service Operators
Brokered Products include:
  Dairy/Deli, Frozen Food, Seafood

40415 GAP Food Brokers
1412 E 11 Mile Rd
Madison Heights, MI 48071 248-544-1190
Fax: 248-544-1195 gapfdbkr@bignet.net
Import broker of dairy/deli products, frozen foods, groceries, meat, meat products and seafood
President: Gerald Petty
gapfdbkr@bignet.net
VP: Donna Petty
Estimated Sales: $10-20 Million
Number Employees: 10-19
Square Footage: 8000
Markets Served:
  Food Manufacturers & Processors, Super Market Chains, Wholesale Distributors, Food Service Operators
Brokered Products include:
  Dairy/Deli, Frozen Food, Groceries, Imports, Meat, Meat Products, Seafood

40416 GCI Nutrients
1163 Chess Dr # H
Foster City, CA 94404-1119 650-376-3534
Fax: 650-697-6300 866-580-6549
mikec@gcinutrients.com www.gcinutrients.com
Processor, importer and exporter of vitamins and supplements including beta carotene, essential fatty acids, herbal products, botanical extracts, food supplements, bulk ingredients, premium raw materials for nutritional and beverage industries with over 42 years of experience
Owner: Richard Merriam
rickm@gcinutrients.com
General Manager: Mike Cronin
Controller: Fransisca Cronin
R&D: William Forgach
Marketing: Michael Sevohon
Production: Derek Cronin
Plant Manager: Mike Cronin
Purchasing Manager: Catherine Sabbah
Estimated Sales: $10 Million
Number Employees: 10-19
Number of Brands: 10
Number of Products: 300
Square Footage: 20000
Brokered Products include:
  Ingredients

40417 (HQ)GFR Worldwide
8557 154th Ave NE
Bldg K
Redmond, WA 98052-3557 425-284-3358
Fax: 425-885-5957 800-275-3654
Manufacturers' representative for food service equipment
Principal: Gerry Gilbertson
Estimated Sales: $2.5-5 Million
Number Employees: 5-9
Markets Served:
  Super Market Chains, Wholesale Distributors, Food Service Operators
Primary Brands Brokered include: Blodgett; Geneva; Pitco; Stero; Panasonic; T&S Brass; MagiKitch'n; Gemini; Stero; Salvajor; T&S Power Soak; Somat; Gates Manufacturing Company; Sani-Floor; Lakeside; Multiteria; Spring Air; TUCS Equipment; Terry
Brokered Products include:
  General Merchandise, Foodservice Equipment

40418 Gallagher Sales Corporation
715 Frederick Street
Hanover, PA 17331-5009 717-637-6594
Fax: 717-632-1976 sales@gallagherfoods.com
www.gallagherfoods.com
Broker of canned and frozen vegetables, shelf-stable commodities, private label
Co-Owner: Tim Gallagher
Estimated Sales: $5-10 Million
Number Employees: 4
Type of Packaging: Food Service
Markets Served:
  Food Service Operators
Brokered Products include:
  Confectionery, Private Label

40419 Garden Gold Foods, Inc
5700 Mariner
Tampa, FL 33609-3595 813-281-0868
Fax: 813-281-0438
Broker of general merchandise, groceries and private label items
President: Simon Dingfelder
VP: Martha Harrison
Contact: Joseph Mcdonald
dmcdonald@goldenstatefoods.com
Estimated Sales: $1 Million
Number Employees: 1-4
Type of Packaging: Consumer, Food Service
Markets Served:
  Food Manufacturers & Processors, Super Market Chains, Wholesale Distributors, Food Service Operators
Primary Brands Brokered include: Lucky Farms; Garden Gold; Sugar Rose
Brokered Products include:
  General Merchandise, Groceries, Private Label, Secondary Market

40420 Garisco Distributing
4773 Bruno Road
El Sobrante, CA 94803-3201 510-223-7252
Fax: 510-223-7360
Import and export broker of general merchandise
President: Gary Hui
Treasurer: Nicole Hui
VP: Nicole Hui
Number Employees: 1-4
Square Footage: 8000
Markets Served:
  Super Market Chains, Wholesale Distributors
Brokered Products include:
  Exports, General Merchandise, Imports

40421 Gasparini Sales Inc
917 Granger Rd
Syracuse, NY 13219-2165 315-471-1438
Fax: 315-471-8127 www.gasparinisales.com
Broker of deli meats, dairy products, imported and domestic cheese, fresh and IQF meat, english muffins, bakery and entrees.
President: Edward Gasparini
VP Deli: Susan Metz
Estimated Sales: $20,000,000
Number Employees: 5-9
Square Footage: 4000
Type of Packaging: Bulk
Markets Served:
  Food Manufacturers & Processors, Super Market Chains, Wholesale Distributors, Food Service Operators
Primary Brands Brokered include: Ambriola Company; Associated Milk Products; Bel Kaukauna USA; Angonoa Breadsticks; Chewys; Color A Cookie; Citterio Dried Meats; DiLuigi Specialty Meats; Hickory Farms; Classic Delight; Herkimer Food/Ida Mae; Gourmet Boutique
Brokered Products include:
  Dairy/Deli, Frozen Food, Imports, Meat, Meat Products, Entrees

40422 Gateway Food Service
7 Millpark Ct
Maryland Heights, MO 63043-3536 314-429-3320
Fax: 314-429-0151
Broker of confectionery products, dairy/deli items, frozen foods, meats/meat products, produce, etc.
Partner: Jim Behrends
Estimated Sales: $10-20 Million
Number Employees: 10-19
Markets Served:
  Food Manufacturers & Processors, Super Market Chains, Wholesale Distributors, Food Service Operators
Brokered Products include:
  Confectionery, Dairy/Deli, Frozen Food, Meat, Meat Products, Private Label, Produce

40423 Gehrke Co
18215 45th Ave N # A
Suite A
Minneapolis, MN 55446-4595 612-332-4497
Fax: 612-332-4130 800-488-2213
orders@gehrke.com www.gehrke.com
Broker of industrial ingredients
President: Dominic E. Fragomeni
domsr@gehrke.com
Accounting/Human Resource: Jill S. Fragomeni
VP: Kristie Pietig
Sales: Sean Bassi
Number Employees: 5-9
Parent Co: Gehrke Company
Markets Served:
  Food Manufacturers & Processors, Wholesale Distributors, Food Service Operators
Primary Brands Brokered include: Bruce Foods; Chiquita; Creative Food Ingredients; Graceland Fruit; Homel Foods; Kikkoman' McCain; Red V Industries; Sun-Maid; Treetop; Vita-Pakt; Wymans of Maine
Brokered Products include:
  Ingredients

40424 Gellman Associates
2460 General Armistead Ave Ste 217
Eagleville, PA 19403 610-630-6040
Fax: 610-630-6016
Broker of confectionery and dairy/deli products, frozen foods, meat products and private label/generic products specializing in products for vending and coffee service machines

Food Brokers / A-Z

Owner: David Gellman
Sales: Barry Gellman
Office Manager: Kate Dugan
Estimated Sales: $5-10 Million
Number Employees: 5
Square Footage: 8800
Markets Served:
 Food Manufacturers & Processors
Primary Brands Brokered include: Quaker Oats; Continental Coffee; Savannah Foods; Ocean Spray; Oscar Mayer; Everpure
Brokered Products include:
 Confectionery, Dairy/Deli, Frozen Food, Meat Products, Private Label

40425 Genesis International
34068 N 59th Place
Scottsdale, AZ 85266　　　　480-575-3002
　　　　　　　　　　　Fax: 480-575-3008
Export broker for nuts, dried fruits, canned vegetables, hot sauces, wine and beer
Owner: Sheila Brooks
Number Employees: 5-9
Square Footage: 8000
Markets Served:
 Food Manufacturers & Processors, Wholesale Distributors
Brokered Products include:
 Alcoholic Beverages, Exports, Groceries, Produce

40426 Genesis Marketing
14440 Dunbar Place
Sherman Oaks, CA 91423-4010　818-905-5254
　　　　　　　　　　　Fax: 818-905-5259
Broker of dairy/deli products, health foods and industrial ingredients
President: Albert Friedman
Number Employees: 5-9
Markets Served:
 Food Manufacturers & Processors, Super Market Chains, Wholesale Distributors, Food Service Operators
Primary Brands Brokered include: Pollio Dairies; Antonio Amato; Friendship; Bongrain; Smithfield; Carapelli; Gerhard; Gossner; Tipiak; West Point
Brokered Products include:
 Dairy/Deli, Health Food, Ingredients

40427 Genotec Nutritional
450 Commack Rd
Deer Park, NY 11729-4514　　631-254-1097
　　　　　　　　　　　Fax: 631-254-1234
Broker of vitamins and dietary food supplements including shark cartilage, and fish oil, etc.
President: George Kontonotas
CEO: Mark Meller
Estimated Sales: $2.5 Million
Number Employees: 5-9
Brokered Products include:
 Health Food, Vitamins, etc.

40428 George E. Dent Sales
3094 Niles Rd
Saint Joseph, MI 49085　　　269-428-2312
　Fax: 269-428-2956 www.georgedentsales.com
Broker of frozen fruits and vegetables
Owner: George Dent
Sales Representative: Tim Dent
Contact: Adriane Parce
adriane@georgedentsales.com
Estimated Sales: $2.5-5 Million
Number Employees: 1-4
Markets Served:
 Food Manufacturers & Processors, Super Market Chains, Wholesale Distributors, Food Service Operators
Brokered Products include:
 Frozen Food, Frozen Fruits & Vegetables

40429 George Perry & Sons Inc
164 S Grant Ave
Manteca, CA 95336-5701　　209-239-1218
　　Fax: 209-249-2425 www.perryandsons.com
Broker of produce
Owner: Arthur Perry
arthur@pioneerconcrete.com
CFO: Ron Perry
VP: Art Perry
Estimated Sales: $1.7 Million
Number Employees: 10-19
Markets Served:
 Super Market Chains, Wholesale Distributors
Brokered Products include:
 Produce, Pumpkin, Squash, Casabas & Watermelon

40430 George W. Holop Associates
PO Box 955
Madison, CT 06443-0955　　203-245-0164
　　　　　　　　　　　Fax: 203-458-8877
Broker of confectionery and bakery products, general merchandise, groceries and private label items
President: George DeVeau
VP: P DeVeau
Number Employees: 2
Markets Served:
 Food Manufacturers & Processors, Super Market Chains, Wholesale Distributors, Food Service Operators
Brokered Products include:
 Confectionery, General Merchandise, Groceries, Imports, Private Label, Bakery Products

40431 Gersony Strauss Co
171 Church St # 270
Charleston, SC 29401-3165　　843-853-7777
　　Fax: 843-853-6777 gersony@gersony.com
Export broker of vegetable oils
President: Bob Jennings
bjennings@mabc.com
VP: Lonnie James
Estimated Sales: $1-2.5 Million
Number Employees: 5-9
Square Footage: 8000
Brokered Products include:
 Exports, Vegetable Oils

40432 Gibbs & Assoc
8 N Skokie Hwy # 202
Lake Bluff, IL 60044-1750　　847-615-1256
　　　　Fax: 847-584-8843 800-634-7981
Manufacturers' representative for food service equipment and supplies
President: Terry Gibbs
Estimated Sales: $1-2.5 Million
Number Employees: 1-4
Square Footage: 14000
Markets Served:
 Food Manufacturers & Processors, Super Market Chains, Wholesale Distributors
Primary Brands Brokered include: Toastmaster; Dudson; Cres-Cor; Dito-Dean; Mainstreet Menus; Mundial
Brokered Products include:
 General Merchandise, Foodservice Equipment & Supplies

40433 Gibbs-Mccormick Inc A Ca Corp
1699 El Camino Real # 210
Millbrae, CA 94030-1273　　650-866-3757
　　　　　　　　　　　Fax: 650-692-8749
Import/export broker of confectionery, produce, seafood, groceries, ingredients, frozen foods and private label items
President: Gary Gibbs
VP: Gary Gibbs
Sales Manager: Drew Johnson
Sales Manager: Stuart Winograd
Estimated Sales: $5-10 Million
Number Employees: 1-4
Markets Served:
 Food Manufacturers & Processors, Super Market Chains, Wholesale Distributors
Brokered Products include:
 Confectionery, Exports, Frozen Food, Groceries, Imports, Ingredients, Private Label, Produce, Seafood

40434 Gilbert Foodservice Inc
4005 Stuart Andrew Blvd
Charlotte, NC 28217-1536　　704-529-1800
　　　　Fax: 704-529-0934 800-327-9281
　　　　　　　　　　　www.gilbertfoods.com
Broker of dairy/deli products, frozen foods, groceries, meat and meat products, seafood, etc
Owner/President: Gilbert Moore
gmoore@gilbertfoods.com
CFO/VP Finance: Beverly Moore
EVP/COO: Al McGarity
Sales: Jeff Humphries
Purchasing Manager: B Moore
Estimated Sales: $6.60 Million
Number Employees: 20-49
Square Footage: 30000
Brokered Products include:
 Dairy/Deli, Exports, Frozen Food, Groceries, Health Food, Imports, Meat, Meat Products, Private Label, Seafood

40435 Gillette Creamery
47 Steve's Lane
Gardiner, NY 12525
　　　　Fax: 845-419-0901 800-522-2507
　　　　　　　　　　www.gillettecreamery.com
Packaged food products, ice cream and frozen novelties, refrigerated foods and other frozen desserts
President: J.B. Gillette
Vice-President/General Manager: Rich Gillette
Type of Packaging: Consumer, Food Service, Bulk
Markets Served:
 Super Market Chains
Brokered Products include:
 Dairy/Deli, Frozen Food

40436 (HQ)Giumarra Companies
P.O. Box 861449
Los Angeles, CA 90086　　　213-627-2900
　　　Fax: 213-628-4878 www.giumarra.com
Produce marketing
Senior VP, Strategic Development: Hillary Brick
Director of Quality Control: Jim Heil
Manager: Donald Corsaro

Number Employees: 50-99
Other Locations: Giumarra Agricom

40437 Glacier Sales Inc
316 N 3rd St
PO Box 2646
Yakima, WA 98901-2341　　509-248-2866
　　　　Fax: 509-575-1438 800-541-8278
 info@glaciersales.com www.glaciersales.com
Domestic, import and export broker of frozen potato products and private label items
President: Bruce Bacon
bruce.bacon@glaciersales.com
Secretary, Treasurer: Doug Kanyer
VP: Christopher Prohaska
Marketing Manager: Kip Prohaska
Sales/CS Lead: Lana Simond
Program Director: Doug Kanyer
Estimated Sales: $4.10
Number Employees: 10-19
Type of Packaging: Consumer, Food Service, Private Label, Bulk
Markets Served:
 Food Manufacturers & Processors, Wholesale Distributors, Food Service Operators
Primary Brands Brokered include: Potato King; Potato Prince; Quincy Gold; Nor'wester; Sun Russett
Brokered Products include:
 Frozen Food

40438 Glenmoor Brokerage
8665 S 51st St # 3
Suite 3
Phoenix, AZ 85044-5742　　602-414-0060
　　　　Fax: 602-414-0061 800-315-8102
　　　　ericglenn@glenmoorbrokerage.com
　　　　　www.glenmoorbrokerage.com
Broker of confectionery and dairy/deli products, groceries, produce and spices
Owner, President: Eric Glenn
glenmooraz@wwdb.org
VP: Leland Moore
Estimated Sales: $1-3 Million
Number Employees: 1-4
Square Footage: 4000
Markets Served:
 Super Market Chains, Wholesale Distributors, Food Service Operators
Brokered Products include:
 Confectionery, Dairy/Deli, Groceries, Produce, Spices

40439 Global Citrus Resources, Inc
302 S Massachusetts Ave # 119
Lakeland, FL 33801-5091　　863-683-0071
　　　　　　　　　　　Fax: 863-683-0267
　　　　　　www.globalcitrusresources.com
Import and export broker of nonperishable foods, citrus and pineapple concentrates and tropical fruit juice purees
President: H Donovan Brown
Comptroller: Scott Brown
Sales: Steven Giddings
Estimated Sales: $3-5 Million
Number Employees: 5-9
Square Footage: 3200

Food Brokers / A-Z

Markets Served:
    Food Service Operators
Primary Brands Brokered include:
    Durand-Wayland; Chemical Dynamics; Industrial Brush; John Bean; Pacon Citrus Company of Belize; Consorcio del Gote; Agro Delta
Brokered Products include:
    Exports, Groceries, Imports, Fruit Concentrates, Purees

40440 Golden Valley Industries Inc
960 Lone Palm Ave
Modesto, CA 95351-1533   209-939-3370
    Fax: 209-957-7837
    www.goldenvalleyindustries.com
Broker of frozen foods, groceries, meat products and private label items
President & CEO: Mike Sullivan
mike@goldenvalleyindustries.com
Vice President: Michael Sullivan
Plant Manager: Victor Rubio
Estimated Sales: $10-20 Million
Number Employees: 50-99
Square Footage: 1600
Markets Served:
    Food Manufacturers & Processors, Super Market Chains, Wholesale Distributors
Brokered Products include:
    Frozen Food, Groceries, Meat Products, Private Label

40441 Golick Martins, Inc.
140 Sylvan Ave
Englewood Cliffs, NJ 7632   201-592-8800
    Fax: 201-592-9196 www.golickmartinsinc.com
Broker of confectionery and dairy/deli products, frozen foods, general merchandise, groceries, etc.
President: Manny Martins
Executive VP: Joe Lanzilli
Contact: Lamont Barrett
lamont@golickmartinsinc.com
Director Retail Operations: Henry Szczepanek
Estimated Sales: $19 Million
Number Employees: 81
Square Footage: 36000
Markets Served:
    Food Manufacturers & Processors, Super Market Chains, Wholesale Distributors, Food Service Operators
Primary Brands Brokered include: General Mills; Pastene Company; R.M. Palmer Company; Ghirardelli Chocolates; Favorite Brands International; Just Born, Inc.
Brokered Products include:
    Confectionery, Dairy/Deli, Frozen Food, General Merchandise, Groceries, Health Food, Private Label, Spices

40442 Gormick Food Brokers
48 Chestnut Hill Road
South Hadley, MA 01075-1718   413-532-3131
    Fax: 413-532-3131
Broker of confectionery and dairy/deli products, frozen foods, general merchandise, groceries, industrial ingredients, private label items, spices, etc
President: Alfred Gormick
VP: Sue Gormick
Number Employees: 2
Type of Packaging: Food Service, Private Label
Brokered Products include:
    Confectionery, Ingredients, Private Label, Seafood, Spices

40443 Gourmet Foods Intl
255 Ted Turner Dr SW
Atlanta, GA 30303-3705   404-954-7600
    Fax: 404-954-7672   800-966-6172
Full-line oils, full-line chocolate, cheese, frozen desserts, hors d'oeuvres/appetizers, full-line meat/game/pate, full-line spices, olives.
Owner: Russell Mc Call
rmccall@gfifoods.com
Marketing: Doug Jay
Number Employees: 250-499

40444 Goveco Full Service Food Brokers
PO Box 81078
Las Vegas, NV 89180-1078   702-228-8188
    Fax: 702-446-1557 govdal@aol.com
Food broker covering NV, Southern California and Arizona.
President: Linda E Gove
Estimated Sales: $5-10 Million
Number Employees: 5-9
Parent Co: Goveco Full Service Food Brokers
Type of Packaging: Consumer, Food Service, Private Label, Bulk
Markets Served:
    Food Manufacturers & Processors, Super Market Chains, Wholesale Distributors, Food Service Operators
Brokered Products include:
    Confectionery, Groceries, Health Food, Ingredients, Private Label, Produce, Seafood, Spices

40445 Grabbe-Leonard Co
13515 Lakefront Dr
Earth City, MO 63045-1416   314-298-2525
    Fax: 314-298-1995
Broker of confectionery products, groceries and private label items
Partner: J Grabbe
Partner: J Leonard
Purchasing Agent: Jill Delonge
Estimated Sales: B
Number Employees: 5-9
Markets Served:
    Super Market Chains, Wholesale Distributors, Food Service Operators
Primary Brands Brokered include: Charms; Just Born; R.M. Palmer; Chattanooga Bakery; Ferrara Pan Candy Company; Callano & Bowser
Brokered Products include:
    Confectionery, Groceries, Private Label

40446 Grant J. Hunt Company
P.O. Box 23545
Oakland, CA 94623   510-569-0304
    Fax: 510-569-2866 www.grantjhunt.com
Import broker of produce including Apples, Berries, Cherries, Citrus, Papaya, Italian Chestnuts, Rhubarb, Cranberries, Painted Pumpkins, Melons, Onions, Pears, Potatoes.
President: Salvatore Rizzo
Vice President: Maurice Portzen
Year Founded: 1934
Estimated Sales: $78 Million
Number Employees: 16
Other Locations:
    Oregon Office
    The Dalles, OR
    Washington Office
    Yakima, DCOregon OfficeYakima
Brokered Products include:
    Imports, Produce

40447 Great Atlantic Trading Company
1204 Longstreet Circle
Brentwood, TN 37027-6506   615-661-6678
    Fax: 910-575-7978   888-268-8780
    www.caviarstar.com
Fresh and frozen seafood, American and imported caviar
President: Dana Leavitt
Estimated Sales: $3.2 Million
Number Employees: 1-4
Square Footage: 5000
Parent Co: Great Atlantic Trading Company

40448 Great Southwest Sales Company
8311 81st Street
Suite P
Lubbock, TX 79423-2008   806-792-9981
    Fax: 806-792-9983
Broker of general merchandise, groceries and private label items
Owner: Art Cook
VP: Shane Cook
Estimated Sales: $2.5-5 Million
Number Employees: 1-4
Square Footage: 8000
Markets Served:
    Super Market Chains, Wholesale Distributors
Primary Brands Brokered include: Riviera Rice; Sunkist; Carnation
Brokered Products include:
    General Merchandise, Groceries, Private Label

40449 Grey Eagle Distributors
2340 Millpark Dr
Maryland Heights, MO 63043   314-429-9100
    www.greyeagle.com
Distributor of beers and malt beverages.
President & CEO: David Stokes
jpjasiek@greyeagle.com
VP, Sales & Marketing: Scott Drysdale
Chief Operating Officer: Neil Komadoski
Year Founded: 1963
Estimated Sales: $110 Million
Number Employees: 250-499
Brokered Products include:
    Alcoholic Beverages

40450 Griffin Marketing Group
#102, 1935 S. Main St
Salisbury, NC 28144   704-603-4556
    Fax: 704-603-4561   800-255-8113
    clint@griffinreps.com   www.griffinreps.com
Manufacturers' representative for food service equipment.
President: Clint Robbins
Vice President: Adam Goldenberg
Outside Sales, South Carolina: Van Smith
Estimated Sales: $0.5-1 Million
Number Employees: 11-50
Square Footage: 22000
Markets Served:
    Wholesale Distributors
Primary Brands Brokered include: Amco; Avtec; Bizerba USA; Blodgett; Blodgett Combi; Blodgett Range; FWE; FII; Groen; Hatco; In Sink Erator; KelMax; Pitco; MagiKitch'n; MagiCater; Meiko; Randall; Regal-Pinnacle Mfg.; Thermo-Kool; Turbo Chef
Brokered Products include:
    General Merchandise, Foodservice Equipment

40451 Grocery Manufacturers of America
1350 Eye (I) St NW
Washington, DC 20005   202-639-5900
    Fax: 202-639-5932 info@gmaonline.org
Food broker association
President/CEO: Pamela Bailey
CFO: Steve McCroddan
Director Marketing/Member Services: Jamie DiSimone
VP Human Resources: Carla Mitchell
Estimated Sales: $10-20 Million
Number Employees: 50-99

40452 Gulf States Food Service Marketing
3113 49th St
Metairie, LA 70001-4121   504-834-2410
    Fax: 504-834-7835
Broker of confectionery and dairy/deli products, frozen foods, meat and private label items
Owner: Al LaFaye
Estimated Sales: $5-10 Million
Number Employees: 5
Markets Served:
    Wholesale Distributors, Food Service Operators
Brokered Products include:
    Confectionery, Dairy/Deli, Frozen Food, Meat, Private Label

40453 Gurrentz International Corp
1501 Ardmore Blvd # 400
Pittsburgh, PA 15221-4451   412-351-3200
    Fax: 412-351-4051   800-245-6113
    www.gurrentz.com
Import and domestic broker of beef, lamb, pork, veal, chicken and turkey
President: Roger Gurrentz
rgurrentz@gurrentz.com
Vice President: Morton Gurrentz
Estimated Sales: $4.5 Million
Number Employees: 10-19
Other Locations:
    Buying Office
    Sydney, AustraliaBuying OfficeBuenos Aires, Argentina
Markets Served:
    Food Manufacturers & Processors, Super Market Chains, Wholesale Distributors, Food Service Operators
Brokered Products include:
    Imports, Meat, Meat Products

40454 H & G Trading LTD Inc
75 Tracey Pl
Englewood, NJ 07631-3618   201-871-3910
    Fax: 201-871-2384
Broker of canned milk, meats and sardines, general merchandise and private label items

Food Brokers / A-Z

President: L Romanach
VP: L Mendez
Estimated Sales: $5-10 Million
Number Employees: 1-4
Square Footage: 3000
Markets Served:
   Wholesale Distributors, Food Service Operators
Brokered Products include:
   Dairy/Deli, General Merchandise, Groceries, Meat, Private Label, Seafood

40455 H&T Food Marketing Company
21 Greenway S
West Hempstead, NY 11552   516-292-1484
   Fax: 516-536-1528
Broker of dairy/deli products including butter, margarine, cream cheese and packaged cheese
President: Herb Jacobs
Treasurer: Barry Jacobs
Estimated Sales: $2.5-5 Million
Number Employees: 1-4
Markets Served:
   Wholesale Distributors, Food Service Operators
Primary Brands Brokered include: Borden; Breakstone; Land O' Lakes; Swiss Valley Farms; Avonmore Cheese; Hotel Bar
Brokered Products include:
   Dairy/Deli, Groceries, Butter, Margarine, Cream Cheese, Etc.

40456 H. White Sales Company
337 Marsh Landing Loop
Oak Hill, FL 32759   609-294-3500
Broker of nutritional supplements including herbs, vitamins, etc
Owner/President: Helen Lyskowski
Estimated Sales: $500,000-1 Million
Number Employees: 1-4
Markets Served:
   Super Market Chains, Wholesale Distributors
Brokered Products include:
   Private Label, Vitamins, Herbs, Etc.

40457 H.R. Plate & Company
198 Country Club Dr
Incline Village, NV 89451-9311   775-852-0400
   Fax: 775-832-7730 info@hrplate.com
Broker of industrial ingredients, fruit products, nuts, spices, seasonings, seeds and private label items
President: James Plate
Estimated Sales: $2.5-5 Million
Number Employees: 5
Markets Served:
   Food Manufacturers & Processors, Super Market Chains, Wholesale Distributors
Brokered Products include:
   Ingredients, Private Label, Spices, Fruit Products, Nuts, Seeds, Etc.

40458 H.V. Mid State Sales Company
716 S Randolph St
Champaign, IL 61820-8314   217-351-2973
   Fax: 217-351-6079
Broker of confectionery and dairy/deli products, frozen food, general merchandise, groceries, meat and meat products, etc.
President: Tom Crain
VP: Debbie Cross
Estimated Sales: $1-2.5 Million
Number Employees: 6
Square Footage: 4000
Type of Packaging: Consumer, Food Service, Private Label, Bulk
Markets Served:
   Food Manufacturers & Processors, Super Market Chains, Wholesale Distributors, Food Service Operators
Primary Brands Brokered include: Best Maid; Goodmark Foods, Inc.; Amurol Products Company; Storck USA, L.P.; Van Melle, Inc.
Brokered Products include:
   Confectionery, Frozen Food, General Merchandise, Groceries, Health Food, Meat Products, Private Label

40459 HCB Foodservice Sales & Marketing
287 W Johnstown Rd
Gahanna, OH 43230-2732   614-475-7000
   Fax: 614-475-0325   800-955-0600
   info@kisales.com www.kisales.com
Broker of dairy/deli products, frozen foods and produce

Manager: Robert Baroni
Treasurer: R Baroni
Estimated Sales: $10-20 Million
Number Employees: 10-19
Parent Co: Chenault & Baroni
Markets Served:
   Food Manufacturers & Processors, Wholesale Distributors, Food Service Operators
Brokered Products include:
   Dairy/Deli, Frozen Food, Produce

40460 HD Marshall Ltd
91 Craig Henry Drive
Nepean, ON K2G 3S8
Canada   613-721-1289
   Fax: 613-721-9521 hdmarshall@rogers.com
Broker of dairy/deli products, frozen foods, private label items, general merchandise, groceries, etc
President: N Glube
Markets Served:
   Super Market Chains, Wholesale Distributors
Brokered Products include:
   Dairy/Deli, Frozen Food, General Merchandise, Groceries, Private Label, Spices

40461 (HQ)HGA Group
12625 E Grand River Rd
Brighton, MI 48116   810-225-7755
   Fax: 888-453-5818   800-832-6442
   info@hgagroup.com
Manufacturers' representative for food service equipment
President: Rodney Johnson
Inside Sales: Heather Archer
Contact: Matthew Buchanan
matt@hgagroup.com
Estimated Sales: $3-5 Million
Number Employees: 5-9
Other Locations:
   HGA Group
   Mount Pleasant, MI
   HGA Group
   Fishers, IN
   HGA Group
   Fort Wayne, INHGA GroupFishers
Markets Served:
   Wholesale Distributors
Brokered Products include:
   General Merchandise, Foodservice Equipment

40462 HK Marketing
5445 Oceanus Drive
Suite 106A
Huntington Beach, CA 92649-1308   714-898-1003
   Fax: 714-898-5438   800-898-0199
   info@hodaksales.com www.hodaksales.com
Manufacturers' representative for food service equipment and supplies
Principal: Rick Hodak
Principal, Owner, President: Roy Hodak
IT & Facilities Management Director: James Hadley
Sales Associate: Jeff Moore
Sales Associate: Nick Hodak
Estimated Sales: $.5-1 million
Number Employees: 1-4
Square Footage: 200000
Markets Served:
   Wholesale Distributors
Primary Brands Brokered include: Atlas Set-n-Serve; Frymaster; International Storage Systems; Market Forge; Varimixer; Woodstone
Brokered Products include:
   General Merchandise, Foodservice Equipment & Supplies

40463 Haile Resources
2650 Freewood Dr
Dallas, TX 75220-2511   214-357-1471
   Fax: 214-357-9381 debbie@haileresources.com
Broker of flavors, xanthan and other gums, yeast extracts, food grade chemicals and nutraceuticals, frozen produce, fruit juice concentrates and purees, dried fruit and industrial ingredients
President: Chris Beninate
chris@haileresources.com
EVP: Debbie Haile
Sales: Emilea Champion
Operations: Joyce Cokes
Estimated Sales: $40 Million
Number Employees: 5-9
Square Footage: 20000
Type of Packaging: Food Service, Private Label, Bulk

Markets Served:
   Food Manufacturers & Processors, Food Service Operators
Brokered Products include:
   Ingredients

40464 Halal Transactions
11636 West Center Rd
P.O. Box 4546
Omaha, NE 68104   402-572-6120
   Fax: 402-572-4020 info@halaltransactions.org
   www.halaltransactions.org
Halal meat
President: Ahmad Absy
VP: Jalot Alabsy
Estimated Sales: $.5-1 Million
Number Employees: 1-4
Markets Served:
   Wholesale Distributors, Food Service Operators
Brokered Products include:
   Meat, Halal meats, Processed foods

40465 Halling Company
PO Box 638
Novi, MI 48376-638
   Fax: 734-591-0928 hallingco@cs.com
Broker of confectionery and dairy/deli products, frozen foods, groceries, meat and meat products, produce, private label items, seafood, spices, etc.
Owner: Daniel Halling
President: Clark Spring
VP Sales: Gary Barnas
Estimated Sales: $10-20 Million
Number Employees: 15
Square Footage: 21600
Markets Served:
   Super Market Chains, Wholesale Distributors, Food Service Operators
Primary Brands Brokered include: Norpac; McCormick; Coldwater Seafood Company; Dubuque; Golden Dipt F.S.; Readi-Bake
Brokered Products include:
   Confectionery, Dairy/Deli, Frozen Food, Groceries, Meat, Meat Products, Private Label, Produce, Seafood, Spices

40466 Hanimex Company
15600 NE 8th Street
Suite B1, PMB801
Bellevue, WA 98007   425-957-9585
   Fax: 425-696-1496
Exporter/importer and marketing management
President: Herman Kwik
hanimexco@aol.com
Operations Manager: Michelle Zieroth
Type of Packaging: Consumer, Private Label, Bulk
Other Locations:
   Hanimex Indonesia
   Jakarta Pusat, IndonesiaHanimex Indonesia
Markets Served:
   Food Manufacturers & Processors, Wholesale Distributors
Primary Brands Brokered include: QUINDO
Brokered Products include:
   Exports, Groceries, Ingredients

40467 (HQ)Hanks Brokerage
1808 Monetary Ln Ste 100
Carrollton, TX 75006   972-242-1832
   Fax: 972-242-6920   800-872-7811
   sales@hanksbrokerage.com
   www.hanksbrokerage.com
Broker of two different divisions, Industrial Food Sales and Food Service Sales
President: Greg Hanks
VP: Doug Hanks
Sales Representative: Steve Cooner
Contact: Sally Arnold
sally.arnold@hanksbrokerage.com
VP Operations: Terry Sutton
Estimated Sales: $30-50 Million
Other Locations:
   San Antonio Office
   Garden Ridge, TX
   Houston Office
   Houston, TXSan Antonio OfficeHouston
Markets Served:
   Food Manufacturers & Processors, Wholesale Distributors, Food Service Operators
Brokered Products include:
   Dairy/Deli, Frozen Food, General Merchandise, Ingredients, Meat Products, Spices

Food Brokers / A-Z

40468 (HQ)Hansen Group
1770 Breckinridge Pkwy # 400
Suite 400
Duluth, GA 30096-7567   770-667-1544
    Fax: 770-667-1491   sales@thehansengroup.net
                   www.thehansengroup.net
Manufacturers' representative for food service equipment; serving wholesalers/distributors
Owner: Phil Kenny
tk@thehansengroup.net
Partner: Cris Hansen
Partner: Wayne Jones
Partner: Dave Schwefer
Inside Sales: Ashlee Myhres
Marketing/Inside Sales: Roxana Carjan
Inside/Outside Sales: Dimple Ingalls
tk@thehansengroup.net
Estimated Sales: $3-5 Million
Number Employees: 10-19
Markets Served:
    Wholesale Distributors
Brokered Products include:
    General Merchandise, Foodservice Equipment

40469 Hansid Company
148 E Longden Avenue
Arcadia, CA 91006-5244   626-574-7993
    Fax: 626-574-7415
Import/export broker of canned and dry groceries, beverages, confectionery, frozen foods, general merchandise, groceries, industrial ingredients, meat, meat products, private label items, seafood and spices; serving all markets
Owner: Shawn Tsai
VP: Sidney Tsai
VP: Hansel Tsai
Estimated Sales: $1-3 Million
Number Employees: 1-4
Parent Co: TST Group of Companies
Markets Served:
    Food Manufacturers & Processors, Super Market Chains, Wholesale Distributors, Food Service Operators
Brokered Products include:
    Alcoholic Beverages, Confectionery, Exports, Frozen Food, General Merchandise, Groceries, Imports, Ingredients, Meat, Meat Products, Private Label, Seafood, Spices, Smallwares, Flatware, Paper, Janitorial

40470 Harold J. Barrett Company
1200 Westlake Ave N
Suite 704
Seattle, WA 98109   206-284-0260
    Fax: 206-282-2494
Broker of frozen foods and produce
President: Kevin Barrett
Vice President: Leon Barrett
Office Manager: Ann Delahanty
Estimated Sales: $2.5-5 Million
Number Employees: 1-4
Markets Served:
    Food Manufacturers & Processors, Super Market Chains, Food Service Operators
Brokered Products include:
    Exports, Frozen Food, Imports, Ingredients, Private Label, Produce

40471 Harold M. Lincoln Company
2130 Madison Ave
Suite 101
Toledo, OH 43604-5135   419-255-1200
Broker of confectionery and dairy/deli products, frozen foods, general merchandise, groceries, etc. Marketing, sales planning and promotional tracking services available
President: David Lincoln
Chairman: Harold Lincoln
VP/Account Manager: John Lincoln
Estimated Sales: $20-50 Million
Number Employees: 7
Square Footage: 7000
Markets Served:
    Food Manufacturers & Processors, Super Market Chains, Wholesale Distributors, Food Service Operators
Primary Brands Brokered include: Agrilink Foods Vegetable Company; Georgia Pacific; Sugardale Foods; Dean Pickle & Specialty Company; New World Pasta Company; Jel Sert Company
Brokered Products include:
    Confectionery, Dairy/Deli, Frozen Food, General Merchandise, Groceries, Meat, Private Label, Produce, Seafood

40472 Harriet Greenland Enterprises
9425 N Meridian St # 286
Suite 286
Indianapolis, IN 46260-1308   317-251-2207
    Fax: 317-251-8098
Broker of groceries, deli products, general merchandise, produce, health foods, private label items and meats
Owner: Harriet Greenland
Estimated Sales: Less Than $500,000
Number Employees: 1-4
Markets Served:
    Food Manufacturers & Processors, Super Market Chains, Wholesale Distributors, Food Service Operators
Primary Brands Brokered include: Taiga Brands Holdings, Inc.; International Culinary Group; Rudolph Foods Company; Vidora Foods; King Nut Company
Brokered Products include:
    Dairy/Deli, General Merchandise, Groceries, Health Food, Meat, Meat Products, Private Label, Produce

40473 Harris Freeman
3110 E Miraloma Ave
Anaheim, CA 92806-1906   714-765-1190
    Fax: 714-765-1199   800-275-2378
info@harrisfreeman.com   www.harrisfreeman.com
Spices, teas and coffee
Owner/President: Anil Shah
Owner: Chirayu Borooah
Vice President: Al Paruthi
Year Founded: 1981
Estimated Sales: 20-50 Million
Number Employees: 20-49
Markets Served:
    Super Market Chains, Wholesale Distributors, Food Service Operators
Brokered Products include:
    Spices, Coffee, Tea

40474 Harry Tinseth Associates, Inc.
256 Great Rd # 8
Littleton, MA 01460-1916   978-952-4500
    Fax: 978-952-6222   htinseth@aol.com
Broker of confectionery products, private label items and general merchandise
President: Harry Tinseth
CEO: D Eustis
Estimated Sales: $1-3 Million
Number Employees: 1-4
Markets Served:
    Super Market Chains, Wholesale Distributors
Brokered Products include:
    Confectionery, General Merchandise, Private Label

40475 Hartley S. Johnson & Son
50 Beharrell St
Concord, MA 01742-2973   978-369-4190
    Fax: 978-369-7972
Import broker of confectionery and groceries
President: Ellion Johnson
Contact: Laurie Gatchell
lbgatchell@gmail.com
Estimated Sales: $5-10 Million
Number Employees: 5
Markets Served:
    Super Market Chains, Wholesale Distributors
Primary Brands Brokered include: Asher; Boston Harbour; Gimbal Brothers; Chivers; Roses; Lifeboat
Brokered Products include:
    Confectionery, Groceries, Imports

40476 Harvest Grove Inc
16 Gloucester Ct
Bordentown, NJ 08505-3120   609-291-0388
    Fax: 609-298-5461   800-545-5958
sales@harvestgrove.net   www.harvestgrove.net
Manufacturers' representative for groceries, frozen food, bakery
President: Neil Friedman
nafriedman@harvestgrove.net
VP, Retail Sales: Michael Hersh
VP Operations: Jill Friedman
Estimated Sales: $5-10 Million
Number Employees: 1-4
Number of Brands: 7
Number of Products: 100
Type of Packaging: Consumer, Food Service, Private Label, Bulk
Markets Served:
    Food Manufacturers & Processors, Super Market Chains, Wholesale Distributors
Primary Brands Brokered include: Harvest Grove Bakery; Aladdin Bakers; Horizon Snack Foods; Angels Bakery; Daisy's Bakery; Gladder's Gourmet Cookies; Exact-A-Mate; Sip'n Snak
Brokered Products include:
    Frozen Food, General Merchandise, Groceries, Health Food, Private Label, Produce

40477 Harvey-Winchell Company
1801 American Blvd E Ste 5
Minneapolis, MN 55425   952-881-7964
    Fax: 952-881-8059   harveywin@aol.com
Broker of confectionery products and salty snacks
President/Finance Executive: Don Mere
VP: Thomas Vucicevic
Estimated Sales: $4.3 Million
Number Employees: 30
Markets Served:
    Super Market Chains, Wholesale Distributors, Food Service Operators
Brokered Products include:
    Confectionery, Salty Snacks

40478 Hatch-Jennings Inc
187 Ayer Rd
Harvard, MA 01451-1102   978-456-8702
    Fax: 978-456-8067   800-225-5090
                   www.hatchjennings.com
Manufacturers' representative for food service equipment
Owner: Jerry Perkins
jerryp@hatch-jennings.com
CEO: Frederick Hatch
VP: Kenneth Jennings
Estimated Sales: $1.6 Million
Number Employees: 5-9
Markets Served:
    Super Market Chains, Wholesale Distributors, Food Service Operators
Primary Brands Brokered include: Cleveland; Crown Verity; Delfield; Frymaster; Dean; Garland; US Range; Jackson; Lincoln; Merco; Merrychef; Metro; Structural Concepts; Varimixer
Brokered Products include:
    General Merchandise, Foodservice Equipment & Supplies

40479 Hawaiian King Candies
550 Paiea St # 501
Honolulu, HI 96819-1837   808-833-0041
    Fax: 808-839-7141   800-570-1902
                   dniiro@lava.net
Macadamia nut snacks
President: David Niiro
Contact: Marvin Sialco
info@hawaiianking.com
Estimated Sales: $10-24,9,000,000
Number Employees: 50-99
Type of Packaging: Consumer, Food Service, Private Label

40480 Hawley & Assoc
614 Cepi Dr
Chesterfield, MO 63005-1221   636-537-1212
    Fax: 636-537-2916   www.hawleyandassociates.com
Broker of confectionery and dairy/deli products, frozen foods, general merchandise, meat and meat products, groceries, etc.
President: Jerry Hawley Jr
Chairman/CEO: J Hawley
Executive VP: T Hawley
Estimated Sales: $3.3 Million
Number Employees: 10-19
Square Footage: 13000
Markets Served:
    Super Market Chains, Wholesale Distributors
Primary Brands Brokered include: Clements Foods Company; Flanagan Brothers; Gilster Mary Lee; Holten Meat Company; Pompeian, Inc.; Conner
Brokered Products include:
    Confectionery, Dairy/Deli, Frozen Food, General Merchandise, Groceries, Meat, Meat Products, Private Label, Seafood

40481 Heard Brokerage Company Inc
1723 Mission Park Drive
Loganville, GA 30052-7510   770-979-2768
    Fax: 877-273-6832   800-239-1048

Food Brokers / A-Z

Broker of confectionery, dairy/deli products, spices, industrial ingredients and private label items
President: Barry Heard
Estimated Sales: $1 Million
Number Employees: 1
Markets Served:
Food Manufacturers & Processors, Food Service Operators
Brokered Products include:
Ingredients

40482 Heartland Food Brokers LTD
415 E 3rd St
Kansas City, MO 64106-1009   816-421-4777
Fax: 816-421-3554   800-383-1669
Broker of confectionery and dairy/deli products, frozen foods, groceries, meat and meat products
President: Rick Moore
VP: Blake Moore
Estimated Sales: $1.20 Million
Number Employees: 10-19
Square Footage: 24750
Type of Packaging: Food Service
Markets Served:
Food Manufacturers & Processors, Food Service Operators
Brokered Products include:
Frozen Food, Imports, Ingredients, Meat, Seafood

40483 Henry J. Hips Company
407 Executive Dr
Langhorne, PA 19047   215-504-4300
Fax: 215-504-4304
Broker of dairy/deli products, private label items, groceries, meat and meat products, produce, frozen food and seafood
President: Henry Hips
henryhips@aol.com
VP/Treasurer: Anita Hips
VP: Randy Hips
Estimated Sales: $5-10 Million
Number Employees: 3
Square Footage: 12000
Markets Served:
Food Manufacturers & Processors, Super Market Chains, Wholesale Distributors, Food Service Operators
Primary Brands Brokered include: AMPI; Barber Foods Seafood; Gold Kist; Biery Cheese; House of Raeford; Gwaltney
Brokered Products include:
Dairy/Deli, Frozen Food, Groceries, Meat, Meat Products, Private Label, Produce, Seafood

40484 Herb Barber & Sons Food
7193 E. Main Road
Westfield, NY 14787   716-326-4692
Fax: 716-326-6692   800-388-5384
herb@herb-barber-sons.com
www.herb-barber-sons.com
Broker of frozen fruits and industrial ingredients including fruit juices, purees and concentrates
President: Herbert P. Barber
CFO: Joan Barber
VP Sales: Van Barber
Office Manager: Sue Shearer
Estimated Sales: $1-3 Million
Number Employees: 1-4
Markets Served:
Food Manufacturers & Processors
Brokered Products include:
Frozen Food, Imports, Ingredients, Produce, Concentrates, Purees, Juices

40485 Herspring
15 Crow Canyon Court
#100
San Ramon, CA 94583   925-552-0220
Fax: 925-552-5205   800-871-4446
jwollenweber@herspringgibbs.com
www.herspringgibbs.com
Broker of groceries
Owner: John Wollenweber
Owner: Hardy Brunette
Office Manager: Diedre Matoza
Contact: Susan Borowczyk
sborowczyk@herspringgibbs.com
Estimated Sales: $10-20 Million
Number Employees: 10-19
Markets Served:
Super Market Chains, Wholesale Distributors, Food Service Operators

Brokered Products include:
Groceries, Meat, Private Label

40486 (HQ)Higgins & White Inc
8400 Brookfield Ave # 2
Suite 1
Brookfield, IL 60513-2096   708-526-9000
Fax: 708-526-9010   800-677-6826
bwhite@hwingredients.com
www.higginswhite.com
Manufacturers' representative for dairy/deli products, frozen foods and industrial ingredients
President: Bill White
bwhite@hwingredients.com
Executive VP: Michael Cronin
Estimated Sales: $500,000-1 Million
Number Employees: 5-9
Markets Served:
Food Manufacturers & Processors
Brokered Products include:
Dairy/Deli, Frozen Food, Ingredients

40487 Hilgenfeld Brokerage Co
9102 Cap Mountain Dr
San Antonio, TX 78255-2057   210-698-3092
Fax: 210-698-7096 shilgenfeld@satx.rr.com
www.perdue.com
Manufacturers' representative for frozen, refrigerated, and shelf stable foods and plastic utensils
Owner: Jim Hilgenfeld
jhilgenfeld@satx.rr.com
Estimated Sales: $2.5-5 Million
Number Employees: 1-4
Type of Packaging: Food Service
Markets Served:
Food Manufacturers & Processors, Wholesale Distributors, Food Service Operators
Brokered Products include:
Frozen Food, General Merchandise, Groceries, Meat, Spices, Shelf Stable Foods, Plastic Utensils

40488 Hinkle Easter Products
1600 Union Avenue
Baltimore, MD 21211-1917   410-889-1023
Fax: 410-889-0503
Broker of general merchandise including Easter egg dye
President: G Kandel
VP Marketing Services: J Kramer
VP Sales: D Joffe
Estimated Sales: $500,000-$1 Million
Number Employees: 1-4
Parent Co: Darda
Markets Served:
Super Market Chains, Wholesale Distributors, Food Service Operators
Primary Brands Brokered include: Doc Hinkle
Brokered Products include:
General Merchandise, Easter Egg Dye

40489 (HQ)Hobby Whalen Marketing
2953 S Peoria St # 100
Aurora, CO 80014-5716   303-283-0000
Fax: 303-283-1000
Broker of dairy/deli products, frozen foods, meats, produce, seafood and spices and general merchandise
President: Dave Loomis
dloomi@hobbywhalen.com
President: J R Hobby
CFO: Linda Hobby
Executive VP: Richard Whalen
VP Sales/Marketing: Richard Whalen
Director Sales: Rich Chirco
Plant Manager: Tom Lefever
Estimated Sales: $4.2 Million
Number Employees: 10-19
Square Footage: 38000
Markets Served:
Wholesale Distributors, Food Service Operators
Brokered Products include:
Dairy/Deli, Frozen Food, General Merchandise, Meat, Meat Products, Produce, Seafood, Spices

40490 (HQ)Hockenberg Newburgh
1400 NW 100th St
Clive, IA 50325-6734   515-222-0100
Fax: 515-222-0111 hniowa@hockenberg.net
www.hnsales.com
Confectionery and dairy/deli products, general merchandise, groceries, meat and meat products, frozen food, bakery products, food service, etc.

President: Ronald Feder
CFO: Mark Merfeld
mark.merfeld@hockenberg.net
Estimated Sales: $24.9 Million
Number Employees: 50-99
Square Footage: 13500
Other Locations:
Hockenberg Newburgh Foodservice
Fargo, ND
Hockenberg Newburgh Foodservice
Eden Prairie, MN
Hockenberg Newburgh Foodservice
Omaha, NEHockenberg Newburgh
FoodserviceEden Prairie
Markets Served:
Super Market Chains, Wholesale Distributors, Food Service Operators
Brokered Products include:
Confectionery, Dairy/Deli, Frozen Food, General Merchandise, Groceries, Meat, Meat Products, Private Label, Seafood, Spices

40491 Hockenberg Newburgh
7576 Market Place Dr
Eden Prairie, MN 55344-3636   952-942-9494
Fax: 952-942-9493 hnminnesota@hockenberg.net
www.hnsales.com
Broker of confectionery and dairy/deli products, frozen foods, general merchandise, groceries, meat and meat products, etc.
Vice President: Doug Jensen
doug.jensen@hockenberg.net
VP: D Vanderploeg
VP: Doug Jensen
Estimated Sales: $10-20 Million
Number Employees: 20-49
Type of Packaging: Bulk
Markets Served:
Food Manufacturers & Processors, Super Market Chains, Wholesale Distributors, Food Service Operators
Primary Brands Brokered include: Tony's Pizza; La Canasta Mexican
Brokered Products include:
Confectionery, Dairy/Deli, Frozen Food, General Merchandise, Groceries, Meat, Meat Products, Private Label, Seafood

40492 Hockenberg-Newburgh Sales
9358 G Ct
Omaha, NE 68127-1229   402-592-3901
Fax: 402-592-4115 hnnebraska@hockenberg.net
www.hnsales.com
Broker of dairy/deli products, general merchandise, groceries, produce and meat/meat products
President: Ronald Feder
CFO: Mark Merfeld
VP: Barbara Conitz
Marketing/Sales: Jodi Whited
Sales Manager: Al Gomez
Estimated Sales: $10-20 Million
Number Employees: 10-19
Parent Co: Hockenberg Newburgh
Other Locations:
Hockenberg Newburgh, HQ
Des Moines, IA
Hockenberg Newburgh
Eden Prairie, MN
Hockenberg Newburgh
Fargo, NDHockenberg Newburgh, HQEden Prairie
Markets Served:
Food Manufacturers & Processors, Wholesale Distributors, Food Service Operators
Brokered Products include:
Dairy/Deli, General Merchandise, Groceries, Meat, Meat Products, Produce

40493 Hollar & Greene
230 Cabbage Row
P.O. Box 3500
Boone, NC 28607
     800-222-1077
info@hollarandgreene.com
www.hollarandgreene.com
Import and export broker of produce.
Sales: Jeff Greene
Estimated Sales: $20-50 Million
Number Employees: 50-99
Square Footage: 40000
Markets Served:
Wholesale Distributors
Brokered Products include:
Exports, Imports, Produce

Food Brokers / A-Z

40494 Homeplace Food Group
100 Creekside Dr
Georgetown, KY 40324
502-863-0563
502-863-0563
hfraleyjr@aol.com
Broker of private label items; serving retail food chains and food service operators
President: Henry Fraley
Estimated Sales: Less than $500,000
Number Employees: 1-4
Markets Served:
　Food Manufacturers & Processors, Food Service Operators
Brokered Products include:
　Confectionery, Frozen Food, General Merchandise, Groceries, Imports, Private Label

40495 Housewaresdirect Inc
20 Myles Standish Rd
Weston, MA 02493-2124
877-438-4932
Fax: 877-438-4932　877-438-4932
dspencer@gourmetbusiness.com
Cooking implements/housewares, magazines
Marketing: David Spencer
Number Employees: 1-4

40496 Howell Associates
55 Acorn Ponds Dr
Roslyn, NY 11576-2817
516-829-2330
Fax: 516-829-2334　howell18@aol.com
Import and export broker of confectionery and dairy/deli products, frozen foods, groceries, industrial ingredients, meats, etc. Servicing food services & canadian products
President: Howard Duchin
howell18@aol.com
VP: William Jaffee
Public Relations: Irene Lumia
Estimated Sales: $12 Million
Number Employees: 1-4
Type of Packaging: Consumer, Food Service, Private Label
Markets Served:
　Wholesale Distributors, Food Service Operators
Brokered Products include:
　Frozen Food, Groceries, Ingredients, Private Label, Spices, cleaning supplies

40497 Hoyt
8969 Brecksville Rd Ste 5
Cleveland, OH 44141
440-526-9500
Fax: 440-526-5247　800-669-9508
hoytinc@hoytinc.com
Broker of industrial ingredients and produce; serving food processors in Ohio, Indiana, Michigan, western Pennsylvania, and northern Kentucky
President/CEO: Lawrence Hoyt
VP: Dolores Hoyt
Contact: Dolores Hoyt
dhoyt@hoytinc.com
Estimated Sales: $5-10 Million
Number Employees: 5-9
Markets Served:
　Food Manufacturers & Processors
Primary Brands Brokered include: Del Monte; KFI/Bakers; Nabisco; Rogers; Diamond Walnuts; Aromes de Bretagne
Brokered Products include:
　Ingredients, Produce

40498 Hugh T. Gilmore Company
180 Main Street
Avoca, PA 18641-0126
570-457-7451
Fax: 570-457-0981
Broker of confectionery and dairy/deli products, frozen foods, health foods, groceries, etc.
President: Hugh Gilmore
General Manager: T Gilmore
Estimated Sales: $10-20 Million
Number Employees: 1-4
Markets Served:
　Super Market Chains, Wholesale Distributors, Food Service Operators
Brokered Products include:
　Confectionery, Dairy/Deli, Frozen Food, General Merchandise, Groceries, Health Food, Meat Products, Private Label, Produce, Seafood

40499 Hundley Brokerage Company
613 North River Drive
PO Box 838
Marion, IN 46952-0838
765-662-0027
Fax: 765-662-0028
Broker of groceries and private label items
President: D Hundley
Secretary: L Hundley
Estimated Sales: $2.5-5 Million
Number Employees: 1-4
Markets Served:
　Food Manufacturers & Processors, Super Market Chains, Wholesale Distributors, Food Service Operators
Brokered Products include:
　Groceries, Private Label

40500 Hunter Walton & Co Inc
120 Circle Dr N
Piscataway, NJ 08854-3703
732-805-0808
Fax: 732-805-0282　hunterwalton@earthlink.com
www.hunterwalton.com
Distributor and manufacturer of dairy products and food oils. Continuous and batch churn butter, domestic natural and processed cheese, dry cheese, milk powders and custom blends, margarine and shortenings (vegetable and animal)
President: Glenn Grimshaw
hunterwalton@earthlink.net
CEO: Peter Love
Sales Director: Gary Behie
Estimated Sales: $18 Million
Number Employees: 10-19
Type of Packaging: Consumer, Food Service, Private Label, Bulk
Markets Served:
　Food Manufacturers & Processors, Super Market Chains, Wholesale Distributors, Food Service Operators
Brokered Products include:
　Dairy/Deli, Ingredients

40501 Huron Food Sales
4441 Timberlane Dr
Kalamazoo, MI 49008
269-344-6800
Fax: 269-344-0185
Import and export broker of frozen foods and produce
President: John Franzblau
Estimated Sales: $2.5-5 Million
Number Employees: 1-4
Brokered Products include:
　Exports, Frozen Food, Imports, Produce, Fruits & Vegetables

40502 Hynes Bond Ellison
PO Box 152046
Tampa, FL 33684-2046
813-623-1735
Fax: 813-623-5714
Broker of confectionery products and general merchandise
President: Robert Bond
Sales Manager: Bob Rohl
General Manager: Michael Wasp
Estimated Sales: $10-20 Million
Number Employees: 10-19
Parent Co: Hynes Sales
Markets Served:
　Super Market Chains
Brokered Products include:
　Confectionery, General Merchandise

40503 Hynes Bond Ellison
8936 Western Way
Suite 190
Jacksonville, FL 32256-8396
904-772-0218
Fax: 904-772-0877
Broker of general merchandise
President: Robert Bond
VP: D McCarthy
Sales Manager: Bob Rohl
General Manager: Michael Wasp
Estimated Sales: $5-10 Million
Number Employees: 5-9
Markets Served:
　Super Market Chains
Brokered Products include:
　General Merchandise

40504 ISB Sales Company
1322 Edna St SE
Grand Rapids, MI 49507
616-243-5222
Fax: 616-243-9793
Broker of confectionery and dairy/deli products and frozen foods
President: L Steele
CFO: H Hicks
Vice President: Rick Kearney
Sales Director: J Czonka
Operations Manager: Rick Kearney
Estimated Sales: $10-20 Million
Number Employees: 10-19
Square Footage: 14400
Markets Served:
　Super Market Chains, Wholesale Distributors
Primary Brands Brokered include: AC Humko; Campbell; J.W. Allen; Kellogg's; ConAgra; Meurer
Brokered Products include:
　Confectionery, Dairy/Deli, Frozen Food

40505 ISC of Indiana
3220 S Arlington Ave # F
Indianapolis, IN 46203-5713
317-352-8765
Fax: 317-352-8780　iscind@aol.com
Broker of spices, seafood, meat/meat products, groceries, dairy/deli items, etc.
Owner: Ron McBride
VP Sales: Mike Pershing
Estimated Sales: $20-50 Million
Number Employees: 20-49
Markets Served:
　Wholesale Distributors, Food Service Operators
Primary Brands Brokered include: Pillsbury; Marzetti; Universal Foods; Cargill; BilMar; Knouse Foods
Brokered Products include:
　Dairy/Deli, Frozen Food, Groceries, Meat, Meat Products, Seafood, Spices

40506 ISSCO
10 Pony Circle
Roslyn Heights, NY 11577-1959
516-621-7320
Broker of private label items, confectionery and dairy/deli products, frozen foods and coffee brewing equipment
President: Ivor Summer
Marketing: T Allison
Sales Manager: Anita Grossberg
Number Employees: 2
Square Footage: 800
Markets Served:
　Super Market Chains, Wholesale Distributors, Food Service Operators
Brokered Products include:
　Confectionery, Groceries, Private Label, bakery coffee brewing equipment

40507 ITA Inc
4635 Fruitland Ave
Vernon, CA 90058-3213
323-587-0909
Fax: 323-586-0909　info@itafoods.com
www.itafoods.com
Import and export broker of coffee, meat and meat products, mayonnaise, jellies, preserves, canned goods, oils, potato chips and dairy/deli items including cheese, butter, yogurt, etc.
President: Robert Korol
Estimated Sales: $2.5-5 Million
Number Employees: 10-19
Square Footage: 8000
Markets Served:
　Super Market Chains, Wholesale Distributors
Primary Brands Brokered include: Crawford Foods; Sun World; Midwest Biscuit Company; Avalon Beverage; Stroh Brewery Company
Brokered Products include:
　Dairy/Deli, Exports, Imports, Meat, Meat Products, Coffee, Oils, Butter, Yogurt, Etc.

40508 ITOCHU International, Inc
335 Madison Ave
New York, NY 10017
212-818-8000
Fax: 212-818-8282　www.itochu.com
Import and export broker of frozen foods and meats, sugar, coffee, cocoa
President/CEO: Yasuyuki Harada
CFO & SVP: Mamora Seki
SVP & CAO: Shiro Hayashi
SVP & General Counsel: Eric Laptook
Contact: Christopher Banks
banksc@itochu.com
COO/Division Companies Operation: Akira Yokota
Parent Co: ITOCHU Corporation
Other Locations:
　ITOCHU International
　New York, NY
　ITOCHU International
　Washington, DC
　ITOCHU International
　Houston, TX
　ITOCHU International
　Schaumburg, IL
　ITOCHU International
　West Lake Village, CA

Food Brokers / A-Z

ITOCHU International
San Francisco, CA
ITOCHU InternationalWashington
Markets Served:
  Super Market Chains, Food Service Operators
Brokered Products include:
  Frozen Food, Meat

40509 Iceberg Seafood Inc
74 Main St
Sag Harbor, NY 11963-3006 631-725-1100
  Fax: 631-725-6048
Import broker and wholesaler/distributor of frozen shellfish and Alaskan/Canadian fish items
President: John Geoffroy
icebergsea@gmail.com
Sales Manager: Charlie Hillen
Purchasing: Eugene Alper
Estimated Sales: $1-2.5 Million
Number Employees: 1-4
Square Footage: 8000
Markets Served:
  Food Manufacturers & Processors, Super Market Chains, Wholesale Distributors, Food Service Operators
Primary Brands Brokered include: 49th Star; Arctic Royal; Seawest
Brokered Products include:
  Frozen Food, Imports, Seafood

40510 Imark of Pennsylvania
925 Pennsylvania Blvd
Langhorne, PA 19053-7815 215-322-9200
  Fax: 215-322-9388 sales@imarkpa.com
Broker of dairy/deli products, industrial ingredients, meat, meat products, private label items, beverages, confectionery, frozen foods and dry goods
Partner: David Kramer
Partner: Richard Davidov
Partner: Joel Kramer
VP: Louis Kramer
Marketing Director: Keith Nagler
Sales Director: Robert Angler
Estimated Sales: $20-50 Million
Number Employees: 1-4
Square Footage: 12000
Parent Co: Mar-Dru
Markets Served:
  Food Manufacturers & Processors, Super Market Chains, Wholesale Distributors, Food Service Operators
Primary Brands Brokered include: Orval Kent; Uncle Ben's; Tropicana; Chinet; Pillsbury; Vie De France
Brokered Products include:
  Confectionery, Dairy/Deli, Frozen Food, Ingredients, Meat, Meat Products, Private Label, Dry Goods, Beverages

40511 Imperal Freight Broker
2287 NW 102nd Pl
Doral, FL 33172-2523 305-592-6910
  Fax: 305-593-1781 sales@imperialfreight.com
  www.imperialfreight.com
Transportation firm providing freight forwarding and customs clearance of goods for the food industry in Florida
President: Ralph Delarosa
ralph.delarosa@imperialfreight.com
Number Employees: 10-19

40512 Imperial Dade
255 Route 1 & 9
Jersey City, NJ 07306 201-437-7440
  Fax: 201-437-7442 contact@imperialdade.com
  www.imperialdade.com
Wholesaler/distributor of paper and plastic products, disposables, janitorial supplies and film for produce and meat.
Chief Executive Officer: Robert Tillis
Office Manager: Ella Raiden
eraiden@dadepaper.com
Sales Director: Richard Beck
General Manager: Chuck Howard
Assistant General Manager: Tere Martin
Operations Manager: Randy Goins
Year Founded: 1935
Estimated Sales: $100+ Million
Number Employees: 2000
Parent Co: Venco
Type of Packaging: Consumer, Food Service, Private Label, Bulk
Markets Served:
  Food Manufacturers & Processors, Super Market Chains, Wholesale Distributors, Food Service Operators

40513 Imperial Florida Sales
1832 Harden Blvd
Lakeland, FL 33803-1833 863-687-2386
  Fax: 863-683-3190 jacimp@aol.com
Broker of confectionery and dairy/deli products, frozen foods, general merchandise, groceries, produce, etc.
President: Ann G Varasse
jacimp@aol.com
President: Ann Varasse
CFO: Keith Dodds
Vice President: Tina Dodds
Estimated Sales: $5-10 Million
Number Employees: 1-4
Markets Served:
  Super Market Chains
Brokered Products include:
  Confectionery, Dairy/Deli, General Merchandise

40514 Imperial Frozen Foods Co
189 Sunrise Hwy # 205
Suite 205
Rockville Centre, NY 11570-4723 516-763-4800
  Fax: 516-487-0607 800-645-6569
  jonw@imperialfrozenfoods.com
  www.imperialfrozenfoods.com
Broker of frozen fruits including apples, blackberries, blueberries, cherries, etc.
President/Owner: Peter Skolnick
Director Sales Industrial/Retail: Jon Waxman
Number Employees: 1-4
Other Locations:
  Imperial Frozen Foods
  Monterey, CAImperial Frozen Foods
Markets Served:
  Food Manufacturers & Processors, Wholesale Distributors, Food Service Operators
Primary Brands Brokered include: Sun-Vale (Sliced sweetened strawberries)
Brokered Products include:
  Frozen Food, Frozen Berries, Purees, Concentrates

40515 Imperial House Sales
50 boul cremazie o bureau 700
Montreal, QC H2P 2T4
Canada 514-381-8815
  Fax: 514-381-0844
Broker of confectionery and private label items
President: Michael Korenberg
Estimated Sales: $6.5 Million
Number Employees: 20
Parent Co: Prestige Sales
Markets Served:
  Food Manufacturers & Processors
Brokered Products include:
  Confectionery, Private Label

40516 Imperial Trading
9583 Indigo Creek Boulevard
Murrells Inlet, SC 29576-8626 843-215-3835
  Fax: 843-215-3836
Wholesaler/distributor of frozen foods, groceries, meats and seafood
Chairman: Ted Petroff
President: Shirley Petroff
VP: Michael Petroff
Estimated Sales: $8 Million
Number Employees: 5-9
Brokered Products include:
  Meat, Meat Products

40517 Ingredient Exchange Co
401 N Lindbergh Blvd # 315
St Louis, MO 63141-7839 314-872-8850
  Fax: 314-872-7550 info@ingexchange.com
Importer of cheese, dairy ingredients; buyer of salvage and surplus; jobber of frozen foods, spices, concentrates and sweetners
President: Jerry Behimer
Manager: Chris Heupel
cheupeo@ingexchange.com
Estimated Sales: $15-20 Million
Number Employees: 1-4
Markets Served:
  Food Manufacturers & Processors, Wholesale Distributors
Primary Brands Brokered include: McCormick
Brokered Products include:
  Dairy/Deli, Exports, Frozen Food, Imports, Ingredients, Meat Products, Spices

40518 Ingredient Inc
1130 W Lake Cook Rd
Suite 320
Buffalo Grove, IL 60089-1986 847-419-9595
  Fax: 847-419-9547 sales@ingredientsinc.com
  www.ingredientsinc.com
Supplies specialty ingredients to the food/beverage, nutraceutical and pharmaceutical industries in North America.
President: James Stewart
Chief Executive Officer, Owner: Debbie Stew
Contact: Glenn Bluemer
gbluemer@ingredientsinc.com
Estimated Sales: $5-10 Million
Number Employees: 5-9
Parent Co: J. Stewart & Company
Type of Packaging: Bulk
Markets Served:
  Food Manufacturers & Processors, Wholesale Distributors
Brokered Products include:
  Frozen Food, General Merchandise, Health Food, Ingredients, Meat, Produce, Beverage, Vegetarian

40519 Ingredient Innovations
313 NW North Shore Dr
Kansas City, MO 64151-1455 816-587-1426
  Fax: 816-587-4167
  roxanne@ingredientinnovations.com
  www.ingredientinnovations.com
Natural dairy, chemical, fruit and meat flavors and colors; cereal ingredients
President: Roxanne Armstrong
roxanne@ingredientinnovations.com
Estimated Sales: $1-3 Million
Number Employees: 1-4
Markets Served:
  Food Manufacturers & Processors
Brokered Products include:
  Ingredients

40520 Insulated Structures/PBGroup
369 Lexington Ave Rm 1201
New York, NY 10017-6527
  Fax: 845-425-2519 800-887-2635
Manufacturers' representative and wholesaler/distributor of food service equipment. Design, installation and service for refrigerated buildings also available
President: Kevin Lewis
VP: Veronica Yacono
Number Employees: 5-9
Other Locations:
  Insulated Structures-West
  Novato, CAInsulated Structures-West
Markets Served:
  Food Manufacturers & Processors, Wholesale Distributors
Primary Brands Brokered include: Insulated Structures; Anthony Manufacturing; National Conveyor; Triton Refrigeration
Brokered Products include:
  General Merchandise, Foodservice Equipment

40521 Integra Marketing Inc
15613 Blackburn Ave
Norwalk, CA 90650-6848 562-229-0404
  Fax: 562-229-0999
  LAURA@integra-marketing.com
  www.integra-marketing.com
Manufacturers' representative for food service equipment and supplies
Marketing: Amanda Smith
Inside Sales: Blanca Fernandez
Manager: Julie Bevis
julie@integra-marketing.com
Operations Manager: Laura Villalpando
Estimated Sales: $10-20 Million
Number Employees: 10-19
Square Footage: 35200
Markets Served:
  Wholesale Distributors
Primary Brands Brokered include: Victory; Kool Star; Perlick; Univex; APW Wyott; Baker's Pride; Doughpro; Royal; T&S Brass; SaniServ; RDT Refrigeration; Gemini Air Systems; John Boos; Winston; Titan Shelving; Mundial; Win-Holt; Leading Edge; Shat-R-Shield; Crestware; Electrolux

Food Brokers / A-Z

Brokered Products include:
General Merchandise, Foodservice Equipment & Supplies

40522 Integrity Marketing
1000 N Rand Rd # 123
Wauconda, IL 60084-1199   863-644-0200
Fax: 863-644-2772   800-406-6417
sherry@seminarvalue.com   www.seminarvalue.com
President: Cindy Tabert
Estimated Sales: $5-10 Million
Number Employees: 5-9

40523 Inter-American Products
1240 State Ave
Cincinnati, OH 45204   513-762-4900
Fax: 513-244-3668   800-645-2233
edi@inter-americanfoods.com
www.interamericanproducts.com
Gelatins and puddings, nuts, powdered beverages, natural processed cheese, tea, extracts, peanut butter, coffee, soy sauce, steak and Worcestershire sauce, coconut, syrup, salad dressing, mayonnaise, preserves, jellies andbeverages.
Senior Marketing Manager: Jeff Pahl
Contact: Sergio Balegno
sbalegno@interamericanproducts.com
Technical Director: Terry Shamblin
Estimated Sales: Under $500,000
Number Employees: 5-9
Parent Co: Kroger Company
Markets Served:
Food Manufacturers & Processors, Super Market Chains, Wholesale Distributors, Food Service Operators
Brokered Products include:
Alcoholic Beverages, Confectionery, Dairy/Deli, Exports, Frozen Food, General Merchandise, Groceries, Health Food, Ingredients, Spices

40524 Interep Company
4312 Loire Dr Apt A
Kenner, LA 70065   504-466-6343
Fax: 504-468-8291
Export broker of canned, dry and nonperishable goods
Owner: Marysol Lombana
Import Manager: Sandra Lombana
Estimated Sales: $2.5-5 Million
Number Employees: 1-4
Brokered Products include:
Exports, Groceries, Canned, Dry & Non-Perishable Goods

40525 Intermountain Food Brokerage
1106 S 29th St W
Suite B
Billings, MT 59102-7481   406-259-8822
Fax: 406-259-8821   800-253-4088
Broker of dairy/deli products, frozen foods, general merchandise, groceries, meats and seafood
Owner/President: Gregory Oliphant
Estimated Sales: $20 Million
Number Employees: 8
Square Footage: 3000
Markets Served:
Food Manufacturers & Processors, Super Market Chains, Wholesale Distributors, Food Service Operators
Primary Brands Brokered include: Campbells; Nalley's; Schwans; Hormel; Land O' Lakes; Specialty Brands
Brokered Products include:
Dairy/Deli, Frozen Food, General Merchandise, Groceries, Ingredients, Meat, Meat Products, Private Label, Seafood

40526 International Coffee Corporation
300 Magazine Street
New Orleans, LA 70190   504-586-8700
Fax: 504-523-3301   800-535-9100
www.iccnola.com
Coffee traders and brokers
President: Matt Madary
VP: Bill Madary
Sales manager: Jude Toepfer
Contact: Brian Bolerjack
brian@iccnola.com
Estimated Sales: $1-2.5 Million
Number Employees: 10-19
Markets Served:
Super Market Chains, Wholesale Distributors, Food Service Operators
Brokered Products include:
Imports, Coffee

40527 International Gourmet Products
6030 Bethelview Rd # 203
Cumming, GA 30040-8022   770-887-0807
Fax: 770-887-0708   800-486-4717
igpinc@igpinc.net   www.igpinc.net
Import and export broker of dairy/deli items, meat, meat products and seafood
President: Frank Simpson
VP Sales: Ron Simpson
Estimated Sales: $5-10 Million
Number Employees: 5-9
Markets Served:
Food Manufacturers & Processors, Super Market Chains, Wholesale Distributors, Food Service Operators
Primary Brands Brokered include: Alessi Bakery; Anco Fine Cheese; Atkins Elegant Desserts; Barilla; Bertolli; BC-USA; Hatfield Quality Meats; Suncrest Farms; Swaggerty Sausage;
Brokered Products include:
Dairy/Deli, Exports, Imports, Meat, Meat Products, Seafood

40528 (HQ)International Pacific Sales
22111 Fraserwood Way
Richmond, BC V6W 1J5
Canada   604-273-7035
Fax: 604-273-6720   800-525-5155
laura@intlpac.com
www.internationalpacificsales.com
Broker of confectionery products, frozen foods, groceries and seafood
President: Laura Driscoll
CEO: Michael Driscoll
Finance Director: Lalindra Anthony
Number Employees: 20-49
Other Locations:
Calgary Office
Calgary, AlbertaCalgary OfficeSaskatchewan
Markets Served:
Food Service Operators
Brokered Products include:
Confectionery, Frozen Food, Groceries, Seafood

40529 International Pacific Seafood
1219 John Reed Court
City of Industry, CA 91745-2405   626-369-4000
Fax: 626-444-3843
Import and export broker of seafood
President: Gearoid Tooe
VP: R Decorpo
Sales Manager: Jerry Tores
Contact: Sarah Chan
sarah.chan@pacificaseafood.com
Owner: Vincent Decorpo
Estimated Sales: $5-10 Million
Number Employees: 10-19
Square Footage: 35200
Markets Served:
Food Manufacturers & Processors, Super Market Chains, Wholesale Distributors, Food Service Operators
Primary Brands Brokered include: Pacifica; Samband
Brokered Products include:
Exports, Imports, Seafood

40530 International Sales & Brokerage Company
235 Clent Road
Great Neck, NY 11021-4906   516-466-3335
Fax: 516-466-0254
Import broker of confectionery and meat products, private label items, general merchandise, dairy/deli products, health and beauty aids, etc.
President: Neil Esposito
VP: Rose Esposito
Retail Sales: Andrew Esposito
Sales Manager: Neil Esposito
Number Employees: 4
Square Footage: 2000
Markets Served:
Food Manufacturers & Processors, Super Market Chains, Wholesale Distributors, Food Service Operators
Primary Brands Brokered include: Marco Polo; Atlanta; Celebrity; Martel; Paradise; Sandt's; Nutcracker; Beatiful Denmark; Jacobsen's; Homestyle; Express
Brokered Products include:
Confectionery, Dairy/Deli, General Merchandise, Groceries, Imports, Meat Products, Private Label, Spices

40531 Interpack NW Frozen Food
355 Ericksen Ave NE # 422
Bainbridge Isle, WA 98110-1889   206-842-9464
Fax: 206-842-5119   sales@interpacknw.com
interpacknw.com
Broker of frozen fruit and juice concentrates
Sales Manager: Thomas Greene
Estimated Sales: $1-3 Million
Number Employees: 7
Type of Packaging: Food Service, Private Label, Bulk
Markets Served:
Food Manufacturers & Processors, Wholesale Distributors, Food Service Operators
Brokered Products include:
Confectionery, Dairy/Deli, Frozen Food, Ingredients, Private Label

40532 (HQ)Interpex
600 Cleveland Street
Suite 920
Clearwater, FL 33755-4160   813-831-0291
Fax: 707-221-2118   interpex@usa.net
Import/export broker of groceries, seafood, produce and private label items
President: Tony Tanner
VP: Narunat Tanner
Director: John Pierterse
Number Employees: 10-19
Square Footage: 3600
Other Locations:
Interpex USA Ltd.
Bangkok, ThailandInterpex USA Ltd.
Primary Brands Brokered include: Kejo; Five Star; Black Jack; Uuka-Uuka
Brokered Products include:
Exports, Groceries, Imports, Private Label, Produce, Seafood

40533 Intershell Seafood Corp
9 Blackburn Dr
Gloucester, MA 01930-2237   978-281-2523
Fax: 978-283-1303   info@intershell.biz
www.intershell.biz
Shellfish
President: Yibing Gao
yibing@intershell.biz
Chairman: Monte Rome
Accounting: Linda Amaral
Research & Development: Shannon Blakeley
Quality Control: Eric Strong
Sales: Chrisopher J Blankenbaker
Plant Manager: Eric Strong
Purchasing Manager: Monte Rome
Estimated Sales: $5 Million
Number Employees: 50-99
Type of Packaging: Bulk
Brokered Products include:
Frozen Food, Seafood, Sushi

40534 Intersouth Foodservice Group
320 Kershaw Industrial Blvd
Montgomery, AL 36117-5546   334-277-4708
Fax: 334-244-9151   800-239-3663
Broker of dairy/deli products, groceries, industrial ingredients, meat and meat products, frozen foods, seafood, etc.
President: Ted Norton
CFO: Becky Norton
VP Administrative Services: Lynn Allen
VP Customer Service: Betsy Yates
Estimated Sales: $10-20 Million
Number Employees: 10-19
Square Footage: 9000
Markets Served:
Food Manufacturers & Processors, Wholesale Distributors, Food Service Operators
Primary Brands Brokered include: Simplot; Pillsbury; Americas Catch; Icelandic; Hormel; Keebler
Brokered Products include:
Confectionery, Dairy/Deli, Frozen Food, Groceries, Ingredients, Meat, Meat Products, Seafood

40535 Interstate Food Brokers
3123 Walnut Hill Road
Metamora, MI 48455-8953   810-797-2172
Fax: 810-797-2173   pad2@centurytel.net
Broker of dairy/deli products, frozen foods, meats, spices and private label items, etc.

Food Brokers / A-Z

President: Philip Dimercurio
CEO: Patricia Dimercurio
Number Employees: 5-9
Markets Served:
  Super Market Chains, Wholesale Distributors, Food Service Operators
Primary Brands Brokered include: Penobscot; Virgil's Root Beer; Green Giant/Aunt Nellie's; Seneca; KAJLB Frozen Foods; Montana Silver Springs
Brokered Products include:
  Dairy/Deli, Frozen Food, Meat Products, Private Label, Spices, Imported Root Beer

40536 Interwest Ingredient Sales
2995 S West Temple
Suite C
Saltlake City, UT 84114   801-978-0700
        Fax: 801-978-0762 800-329-9328
        kayi@interwestingredient.com
        www.interwestingredient.com
Broker of ingredients
Owner: Vaughn Johnson
Estimated Sales: $5-10 Million
Number Employees: 5-9
Square Footage: 14000
Markets Served:
  Food Manufacturers & Processors, Wholesale Distributors
Primary Brands Brokered include: Williams Food; HP Schmid; Sun Diamond Growers; Morningstar; Kraft Bakers Division; Houston's Peanuts; Barry/Callebaut; Chiquita; Blue Diamond Almonds; Young Pecan Company; Agway
Brokered Products include:
  Ingredients

40537 Intralinks Inc
150 E 42nd St # 8
New York, NY 10017-5626   212-543-7700
        Fax: 212-543-7978 www.intralinks.com
Import and export broker of biscuits, snack foods, confectionery products, groceries, industrial ingredients and nuts
President: Josef Ducat
Executive VP: Bill Conklin
bconklin@intralinks.com
Estimated Sales: $20-50 Million
Number Employees: 100-249
Square Footage: 700
Markets Served:
  Wholesale Distributors
Brokered Products include:
  Confectionery, Exports, Groceries, Imports, Ingredients, Nuts, Biscuits, Snacks

40538 Inverso Johnson LLC
4901 Benner St
Philadelphia, PA 19135   215-338-6315
        Fax: 215-338-4737 ncinv1@comcast.net
Manufacturers' representative for food service equipment and furniture
Owner: Marie Johnson
Estimated Sales: $1-2.5 Million
Number Employees: 1-4
Markets Served:
  Super Market Chains, Wholesale Distributors, Food Service Operators
Primary Brands Brokered include: CapKold; Color Point; Keating; WA Brown; Southbend; Powered Aire; MTS; GAR; Plymold; JAB Designs; Kettler International; Midwest Folding Products
Brokered Products include:
  General Merchandise, Foodservice Equipment & Furniture

40539 J Carroll & Assoc
419 Friday Rd
Pittsburgh, PA 15209-2113   412-821-8960
        Fax: 412-928-9682 www.leepercompanies.com
Broker of candy and cookies
Owner: Wally Eylinowski
Estimated Sales: $2.5-5 Million
Number Employees: 5-9
Parent Co: Williams & Drake
Markets Served:
  Super Market Chains, Food Service Operators
Primary Brands Brokered include: Tootsie Rolls; Goetze's Caramel Creams; Ferarra Pan Candy; Golden Valley; King Bee; Riccola
Brokered Products include:
  Confectionery, Cookies

40540 J Cipelli Merchants
21 St. Clair Ave East
Suite 304
Toronto, ON M4T 1L9
Canada   416-924-9886
        Fax: 416-924-4776 agrifoods@jcipelli.com
Agri-food importer/broker of bolk commodities such as wines, fruit juice concentrates, fruit purees, tomatoe products, dehydrated fruits and vegetables, gherkins
President: Joseph Cipelli
Estimated Sales: $1.7 Million
Number Employees: 5
Type of Packaging: Bulk
Markets Served:
  Food Manufacturers & Processors

40541 J M Sales
300 Mount Lebanon Blvd # 207a
Pittsburgh, PA 15234-1507   412-341-4949
        Fax: 412-341-4950 800-966-2209
Broker of general merchandise including paper and plastic bags and sacks, film, gloves, deli-wrap, can liners, etc.
President: John Macurak
jmacurak@jmsales.org
Estimated Sales: $5-10 Million
Number Employees: 5-9
Square Footage: 3600

40542 J N Rhodes Co Inc
309 Laurelwood Rd
Suite 18
Santa Clara, CA 95054-2313   408-727-1890
        Fax: 408-727-7536 jnrhodes@flash.net
Broker of dairy/deli products, frozen foods, meats, seafood, spices and private label items
Owner: R Farahani
VP: Jim Rhodes
Estimated Sales: $2.5-5 Million
Number Employees: 1-4
Markets Served:
  Food Manufacturers & Processors, Super Market Chains, Wholesale Distributors, Food Service Operators
Primary Brands Brokered include: Chef America Hot Pockets; Great Foods; Baumer Foods, Inc.; J.S.L.; Gehi's Guerhsey Farms, Inc.
Brokered Products include:
  Dairy/Deli, Frozen Food, Groceries, Meat Products, Private Label, Seafood, Spices

40543 J R Kelly Co
703 S Bluff Rd
Collinsville, IL 62234-1339   618-344-2910
        Fax: 618-344-2297 888-344-4392
        info@jrkelly.com www.jrkelly.com
Export and domestic broker of horseradish roots, spices and produce
President: Dennis Diekemper
dennis.diekemper@jrkelly.com
Estimated Sales: $4 Million
Number Employees: 1-4
Square Footage: 64000
Type of Packaging: Bulk
Markets Served:
  Food Manufacturers & Processors, Super Market Chains, Wholesale Distributors
Brokered Products include:
  Horseradish Roots

40544 J T Gibbons Inc
600 Elmwood Park Blvd # 2
New Orleans, LA 70123-3310   504-831-9907
        Fax: 504-837-5516
Wholesaler/distributor and export and import broker of frozen foods, groceries, industrial ingredients and private label items
President: Richard Keeney
rkeeney@gibbonsinc.com
CFO: Arthur Schott
Purchasing: Tammy Ducote
Estimated Sales: Less Than $500,000
Number Employees: 1-4
Square Footage: 60000
Type of Packaging: Consumer, Food Service, Private Label
Markets Served:
  Super Market Chains, Wholesale Distributors, Food Service Operators
Primary Brands Brokered include: Lucky Leaf; Musselman; Kingsway; Super Fresh
Brokered Products include:
  Exports, Groceries, Private Label

40545 J&D Transportation
2608 S 24th St # E-D
Council Bluffs, IA 51501-6981   712-328-7235
        Fax: 712-325-1182
Owner: Lana Beer
Estimated Sales: $300,000-500,000
Number Employees: 1-4

40546 J&J Brokerage
1005 S Ward Street
Geneva, AL 36340-7425   334-684-9289
        Fax: 334-684-9289
Broker of meat and meat products, deli/dairy products and seafood
President: Jim Rudd
VP: Melba Rudd
Estimated Sales: $1-2.5 Million
Number Employees: 1-4
Markets Served:
  Super Market Chains, Wholesale Distributors, Food Service Operators
Primary Brands Brokered include: Southern Pride Catfish; Beaver Street Fisheries; Certified Deli Masters; El Jay Poultry; Thorn Apple Valley; Gulf Marketing
Brokered Products include:
  Dairy/Deli, Meat, Meat Products, Seafood

40547 J&S Food Brokerage
P.O.Box 6856
Edison, NJ 08818-6856   732-225-4770
        Fax: 732-225-4730 jsfoodbkg@aol.com
Import broker of canned fruit, vegetables, tomatoes, juices, tuna, frozen foods, shelled nuts, nut oils, etc.
President: Jeff Kramer
j.kramer@jsfoodbrokerage.com
CEO: Sandy Fishman
Estimated Sales: $5-10 Million
Number Employees: 5-9
Type of Packaging: Consumer, Food Service
Markets Served:
  Food Service Operators
Primary Brands Brokered include: Libby; Redpack; Perfection; Sacramento; Seneca; Florida Gold
Brokered Products include:
  Frozen Food, Groceries, Imports, Ingredients, Private Label, Seafood, Shelled Nuts, Nut Oils, Juices, Etc.

40548 J. Maganas Sales Company
8 Stonehenge Ln
Malvern, PA 19355   610-647-7950
        Fax: 610-647-2689
Broker of general merchandise and groceries
Owner: John Maganas
Estimated Sales: $1-2.5 Million
Number Employees: 1-4
Markets Served:
  Super Market Chains, Wholesale Distributors
Brokered Products include:
  Groceries

40549 J.E. Julian & Associates
3080 Beller Drive
Darien, IL 60561-1765   630-985-0863
Broker of meat and meat products and private label/generic products
President: J Julian
Number Employees: 1-4
Markets Served:
  Food Manufacturers & Processors, Super Market Chains, Wholesale Distributors, Food Service Operators
Brokered Products include:
  Meat, Meat Products, Private Label

40550 J.F. Benz Company
253 E North Broadway Street
Columbus, OH 43214-4144   614-262-8777
Import broker of general merchandise, groceries, private label brands, industrial ingredients, spices, confectionery products and frozen foods
Owner: Joe Benz
VP Food Service: Judith Grabske
VP/Sales Manager: Joy Benz
Markets Served:
  Food Manufacturers & Processors, Super Market Chains, Wholesale Distributors, Food Service Operators
Brokered Products include:
  Confectionery, Frozen Food, General Merchandise, Groceries, Imports, Ingredients, Private Label, Spices

40551 J.F. Kelly
150 River Road
Bldg A, Unit I
Montville, NJ 07045 973-299-9100
Fax: 973-299-0161 rich@jfkelly.com
www.jfkelly.com
Broker/Manufacturers' representative specializing in ingredients
President: Michael Kelly
Founder: James Kelly
Office Manager/Customer Service: BJ Mistick
VP Sales: Richard Knors
Sales Associate: James Fiorella
Estimated Sales: B
Number Employees: 5
Square Footage: 1800
Markets Served:
 Food Service Operators
Brokered Products include:
 Confectionery, Frozen Food, Groceries, Ingredients, Meat Products, Spices

40552 (HQ)J.H. Bridgins & Associates
PO Box 98
Richfield, WI 53076-0098 262-628-8722
Fax: 262-628-5110 800-558-8722
Manufacturers' representative for food service equipment including smallwares, ovens, freezers, furniture, etc.
President: Paul Riley
Treasurer: Anne Riley
Number Employees: 5-9
Other Locations:
 J.H. Bridgins & Associates
 Temple Hills, MDJ.H. Bridgins & Associates
Markets Served:
 Wholesale Distributors
Brokered Products include:
 General Merchandise, Foodservice Equipment & Supplies

40553 J.L. Epstein & Son
676 Westwood Ave
River Vale, NJ 07675-6307 201-722-1200
Fax: 201-722-0930
Broker of meat and meat products
Manager: Fred Epstein
Estimated Sales: $5-10 Million
Number Employees: 1-4
Markets Served:
 Food Manufacturers & Processors, Super Market Chains, Wholesale Distributors, Food Service Operators
Brokered Products include:
 Meat, Meat Products

40554 J.M. Swank Company
520 W Penn St
North Liberty, IA 52317-9775 319-626-3683
Fax: 319-626-3662 800-567-9265
www.jmswank.com
Ingredient blending, label and special palletizing, inventory management, quality control and freight consolidation
President: Taylor Strubell
VP: Ron Pardekooper
Contact: George Nulty
george.nulty@conagrafoods.com
Estimated Sales: $29.5 Million
Number Employees: 175
Parent Co: Conagra Brands
Markets Served:
 Food Manufacturers & Processors
Brokered Products include:
 Confectionery, Ingredients

40555 J.W. Harrison & Son
7490 Conowingo Ave # A
Jessup, MD 20794 410-799-5858
Fax: 410-799-0224
Broker of produce
Owner: Bill Harrison
CEO: T Harrison
Estimated Sales: $1-2.5 Million
Number Employees: 1-4
Markets Served:
 Super Market Chains, Wholesale Distributors, Food Service Operators
Brokered Products include:
 Produce

40556 J.W. Kuehn Company
1504 Cliff Rd E
Burnsville, MN 55337-1415 952-890-4881
Fax: 952-890-1484 jwk4881@aol.com
Broker of general merchandise including portable mixing systems, tanks, bins and vats, mixing vessle lifts and dumps, conveyors, rotary airlocks, diverters, valves, etc.
President: Jo Ann Le Clair
Sales Director: John Moeller
Estimated Sales: $2.5-5 Million
Number Employees: 1-4
Markets Served:
 Food Manufacturers & Processors
Primary Brands Brokered include: Cambelt; Custom Metalcraft; Snyder Industries; Pulsair Systems; Nippon Magnetics; General Resource
Brokered Products include:
 General Merchandise, Containers, Tanks, Mixing Systems, Etc.

40557 JABEX Associates, LLC
PO Box 10664
Bedford, NH 03110-0664 800-377-7987
Fax: 800-381-0413 www.mafsi.org/jabex/
Broker of wire mesh conveyor belting and wire forms including metal baskets, screens and racks, cooking computers, timers and electronic controllers for food processing applications
President: Richard Bellerose
Primary Brands Brokered include: Archer Wire International; American Wire; National Controls Corporation; Wire Mesh Products, Inc.
Brokered Products include:
 General Merchandise, Wire Forms, Cooking Computers, Etc.

40558 JL Stemp Marketing Agents
316 Kimberly Court
Sanford, FL 32771-9708 407-330-2540
Fax: 407-330-9402 jlstemp@aol.com
Broker of general merchandise, confectionery and dairy/deli products, health food, industrial ingredients, dessert items, etc
Owner: Jim Stempkowski
CEO: Helen Stempkowski
Sales: Chyris Sherman
Number Employees: 5-9
Square Footage: 7200
Type of Packaging: Food Service
Markets Served:
 Food Manufacturers & Processors, Super Market Chains, Wholesale Distributors, Food Service Operators
Brokered Products include:
 Confectionery, Exports, General Merchandise, Ingredients, Spices

40559 JM Overton Sales & Marketing
P.O. Box 567
Stoughton, MA 02072 781-344-8200
Fax: 781-821-1124
Import broker of confectionery and dairy/deli products, frozen food, produce, groceries, health food, etc
Founder: John Overton Sr.
Vice President: Matt Overton
Retail Sales Manager: L Pike
Sales Manager: JM Overton Jr
Account Manager: Michelle Overton
Estimated Sales: $5-10 Million
Number Employees: 5

40560 JML Sales Co
2733 Columbia Ave
Lancaster, PA 17603-4115 717-392-5767
Fax: 717-392-0943
Wholesaler/distributor and broker of frozen foods
President: Jeff Lawrence
Estimated Sales: $1-2.5 Million
Number Employees: 1-4
Markets Served:
 Food Manufacturers & Processors, Super Market Chains, Wholesale Distributors, Food Service Operators
Brokered Products include:
 Frozen Food

40561 JP Bissonnette
CP 2085
Noranda, QC J9X 5A5
Canada
 819-762-3204
Fax: 819-762-2239
Broker of alcoholic beverages, dairy/deli products, general merchandise, groceries, pet food, private label/generic items, etc.
President: M Lambert
Number Employees: 1-4
Markets Served:
 Super Market Chains, Wholesale Distributors
Primary Brands Brokered include: First Brand; Effet Marketing; McCormick Spice; Vincor International; A. Lassonde, Inc.; Ferrero Canada Ltee.
Brokered Products include:
 Alcoholic Beverages, Dairy/Deli, Frozen Food, General Merchandise, Groceries, Private Label, Spices

40562 JP Carroll Company
40 Sconset Circle
Sandwich, MA 02563-2675 508-420-2092
Fax: 508-420-2092
Broker of frozen foods, groceries, private label items and produce; serving food processors, supermarket chains and wholesalers/distributors
President: Joseph Carroll
Markets Served:
 Food Manufacturers & Processors, Super Market Chains, Wholesale Distributors
Brokered Products include:
 Frozen Food, Groceries, Private Label, Produce

40563 JVS Group
4288 Nutmeg Rd
Gilmer, TX 75644-3799 903-725-3713
Fax: 903-725-7017 jimsmith@jvsgroupinc.com
www.jvsgroupinc.com
Broker serving food service operators in Puerto Rico
Owner: Jim Smith
jimsmith@jvsgroupinc.com
VP: Daniel Vergel
Estimated Sales: Less Than $500,000
Number Employees: 5-9
Markets Served:
 Food Service Operators

40564 Jack Curren & Associates
6520 N Mustang Road
Yukon, OK 73099-1105 405-350-1327
Fax: 405-843-4772
Broker of confectionery and dairy/deli products, meat and meat products and produce
President: J Curren
VP: A Curren
Estimated Sales: $2.5-5 Million
Number Employees: 10-19
Markets Served:
 Food Manufacturers & Processors, Wholesale Distributors, Food Service Operators
Primary Brands Brokered include: Ocean Spray; Sara Lee; Lipton; Van Den Bergh
Brokered Products include:
 Confectionery, Dairy/Deli, Frozen Food, Meat, Meat Products, Seafood

40565 Jacobsen-Clahan & Company
18110 Vassar Court
Sonoma, CA 95476-4158 707-935-3793
Fax: 707-996-2068
Broker of private label items and groceries, including canned salmon and yams
President: Henry Jacobsen
Estimated Sales: $1-2.5 Million
Number Employees: 1-4
Markets Served:
 Food Manufacturers & Processors, Super Market Chains, Wholesale Distributors
Primary Brands Brokered include: Wards Cove Packing Company; Bruce Foods
Brokered Products include:
 Groceries, Private Label

40566 (HQ)Jam Group of Company
4200 Chino Hills Parkway
Suite 375
Chino Hills, CA 91709-5825 213-627-9194
Fax: 213-627-9312
Export broker of sugar, wheat, rice, powdered milk, soybeans, butter, oils, etc. Importer of frozen fish
President: Javed Matin
VP: Bill Schnack
Number Employees: 10-19
Square Footage: 12800
Brokered Products include:
 Exports, Groceries, Ingredients, General Commodities

Food Brokers / A-Z

40567 James W Valleau & Company
608 S Washington St Ste 201
Naperville, IL 60540   630-355-2806
        Fax: 630-355-8526   800-454-2806
Import and export broker of frozen fruits, vegetables and juice concentrates
President: Jim Valleau
Secretary: Mildred Larou
Estimated Sales: $3 Million
Number Employees: 1-4
Square Footage: 1600
Markets Served:
    Food Manufacturers & Processors
Brokered Products include:
    Frozen Food, Juice Concentrates

40568 Jay Mark Group LTD
175 Lively Blvd
Elk Grove Vlg, IL 60007-1620   847-545-1918
    Fax: 857-545-1932   847-545-1918
    info@jaymark.net   www.jaymark.net
Manufacturers' representative for food service equipment
Owner: Jim Heffernan
dheffernan@jaymark.net
Estimated Sales: $2.5-5 Million
Number Employees: 5-9
Square Footage: 8800
Markets Served:
    Super Market Chains, Wholesale Distributors
Primary Brands Brokered include: Advance Tabco; Atlas Industries; Blodgett; Continental; Despense-Rite; Hatco; LaCrosse; MagiKitch'n; Master-Bilt; Pitco Frialator; Waymar; Connect It; Teknor Apex; Tucker/Burnguard; Zurn Plumbing Products
Brokered Products include:
    General Merchandise, Foodservice Equipment

40569 Jeb Plastics
3519 Silverside Rd Ste 106
Wilmington, DE 19810   302-479-9223
        Fax: 302-479-9227   800-556-2247
        www.jebplastics.com
Wholesaler/distributor/broker of poly bags, vinyl bags, heat sealers and packaging supplies
Owner: Sherri Lindner
Estimated Sales: Below $500,000
Number Employees: 1-4
Square Footage: 4000

40570 Jeram Associates
3059 Hayfield Lane
Baldwinsville, NY 13027-1625   315-635-1544
        Fax: 315-635-3676   888-848-5842
Broker of dairy/deli products, spices, water coolers, coffee brewing equipment and cappuccino and beverage dispensers
Owner: Robert Jeram
Secretary/Treasurer: Shirley Rode
Sales: Edward Walsh
Estimated Sales: $2.5-5 Million
Number Employees: 1-4
Markets Served:
    Super Market Chains, Wholesale Distributors, Food Service Operators
Primary Brands Brokered include: Wilbur Curtis; Rockline Filters; Lockwood; Cordley Temprite; Pinnacle Foods; Food Trading Corporation of America
Brokered Products include:
    Dairy/Deli, General Merchandise, Spices, Coffee Brewing Equipment, Etc.

40571 Jewell/Barksdale Associates
5440 Saint Charles Rd Ste 203
Berkeley, IL 60163   708-547-7570
        Fax: 708-547-7577
Broker of ingredients
Partner: J Summers
Partner: J Welter
Sales Director: L Anfuso
Estimated Sales: $20-50 Million
Number Employees: 3
Type of Packaging: Bulk
Markets Served:
    Food Manufacturers & Processors, Wholesale Distributors
Brokered Products include:
    Ingredients

40572 Jilasco Food Exports
1415 2nd Avenue
Unit 2005
Seattle, WA 98101-2072   206-684-9433
        Fax: 206-233-9440
Export broker of frozen foods, groceries, meat and meat products, seafood, spices, frying equipment, general merchandise, etc.
President: Eduardo Bicierro
Vice President: Luisa Bicierro
Operations Manager: Bernard Corsles
Number Employees: 1-4
Square Footage: 2200
Parent Co: Jilasco LLC
Type of Packaging: Food Service, Private Label, Bulk
Markets Served:
    Food Service Operators
Primary Brands Brokered include: J.R. Simplot Company; Mitsui & Company (USA), Inc.; Aviko USA, LLC; Anchor Products; Tones Products; Price Costco
Brokered Products include:
    Dairy/Deli, Exports, Frozen Food, General Merchandise, Groceries, Imports, Meat, Meat Products, Seafood, Spices, Frying Equipment, Etc.

40573 Jim Pless & Company
PO Box 30719
Tampa, FL 33630-3719   954-584-7882
        Fax: 954-584-0845
Broker of confectionery and dairy/deli products, frozen foods, meat products and private label items
President: Bud Taylor
Estimated Sales: $10-20 Million
Number Employees: 10-19
Parent Co: Jim Pless & Company
Markets Served:
    Food Manufacturers & Processors, Wholesale Distributors, Food Service Operators
Brokered Products include:
    Confectionery, Dairy/Deli, Frozen Food, Meat Products, Private Label

40574 Jodawnco
P.O.Box 3028
Escondido, CA 92033   760-741-6046
        Fax: 760-741-7491
Import broker of industrial ingredients including sorbic acid, potassium sorbate, CMC and calcium chloride
President: Peter Dooley
VP: John Rogers
Number Employees: 1-4
Square Footage: 6400
Markets Served:
    Food Manufacturers & Processors, Wholesale Distributors
Primary Brands Brokered include: Daicell Chemical Industries; Nippo Gohsei
Brokered Products include:
    Imports, Ingredients, Sorbic Acid, Potassium Sorbate, Etc.

40575 John H Thier Co
5725 Dragon Way # 100
Cincinnati, OH 45227-4519   513-527-4545
        Fax: 513-527-4210 thierco@aol.com
        www.thierco.com
Broker of confectionery and dairy/deli products, spices and industrial ingredients
Owner: John H Thier
thierco@aol.com
Sales Manager: G Hehman
Office Manager: Cooki Thier
Estimated Sales: $2.5-5 Million
Number Employees: 1-4
Markets Served:
    Food Manufacturers & Processors, Wholesale Distributors, Food Service Operators
Brokered Products include:
    Confectionery, Dairy/Deli, Ingredients, Spices

40576 John H. Elton
11821 Queens Blvd Ste 203
Flushing, NY 11375   718-520-8900
        Fax: 718-261-2538 info@jhelton.com
        www.jhelton.com
Import and domestic broker of spices, nuts, seeds, herbs, dehydrated vegetables, beans, botanicals and essential oils
President: Ron Elton
VP: John Elton
Contact: Jeffrey Stern
jeffs@jhelton.com
Office Manager: Maria Gonzalez
Trader: Rob Schlomann
Estimated Sales: $5-10 Million
Number Employees: 7
Square Footage: 4800
Markets Served:
    Food Manufacturers & Processors, Super Market Chains, Wholesale Distributors, Food Service Operators
Brokered Products include:
    Imports, Ingredients, Produce, Spices, Seeds, Herbs, Oils, Botanicals, Etc.

40577 John J Wollack Co Inc
15052 Springdale St # K
Suite K
Huntington Beach, CA 92649-1162   714-890-5980
        Fax: 714-890-5983
Broker of dairy/deli products, cheeses, general merchandise, groceries, meat and meat products, ingredients, seafood, frozen foods, etc
President: Thomas Keyes
Sales: George Mullin
Manager: Joanne Mesta
Estimated Sales: $1-2.5 Million
Number Employees: 5-9
Type of Packaging: Consumer, Food Service, Private Label, Bulk
Markets Served:
    Food Manufacturers & Processors, Super Market Chains, Wholesale Distributors, Food Service Operators
Primary Brands Brokered include: Singleton Seafood / Sunflower Farms
Brokered Products include:
    Dairy/Deli, Frozen Food, Imports, Private Label, Seafood

40578 John L. Pieri & Sons
4242 Ridge Lea Rd # 3a
Amherst, NY 14226-1051   716-835-6575
        Fax: 716-835-6577
Broker of dairy/deli products, groceries, meat and meat products, private label items, seafood and spices
President: F Pieri
Sales Manager: J Pieri
Estimated Sales: $2.5-5 Million
Number Employees: 1-4
Type of Packaging: Consumer, Food Service, Private Label, Bulk
Markets Served:
    Wholesale Distributors
Primary Brands Brokered include: Patricia Cudahy; Victoria Packing; Fox River; Atlantic Spice; Sahari Food Products
Brokered Products include:
    Dairy/Deli, Groceries, Meat, Meat Products, Seafood, Spices

40579 John Mangum Company
PO Box 17067
San Antonio, TX 78217-0067   210-824-9585
        Fax: 210-828-9747
Broker of dairy/deli products, frozen foods, general merchandise, groceries, meats, private label items and seafood
President: Jim Hood
Account Manager: Baltazar Gonzales
Food Service Sales Manager: Carl West
Markets Served:
    Super Market Chains, Wholesale Distributors, Food Service Operators
Brokered Products include:
    Dairy/Deli, Frozen Food, General Merchandise, Groceries, Meat Products, Private Label, Seafood

40580 (HQ)Johnny Bee Sales
3700 Havana St # 208
Unite 208
Denver, CO 80239-3242   314-231-5074
        Fax: 303-433-3290   877-835-0122
        www.ignitefoodservice.com
Manufacturers' representative for food service equipment and supplies
CEO: Carl Kisner
Territory Manager: Steve Commins
Marketing Director: Dave Kisner
Office Manager: Olivia Booth

Estimated Sales: $1-2.5 Million
Number Employees: 1-4
Other Locations:
  Johnny Bee Sales Co.
  Scottsdale, AZJohnny Bee Sales Co.
Markets Served:
  Wholesale Distributors
Primary Brands Brokered include: American Permanent Ware; American Wyott; Jade Range; Blickman; Carroll Chair; Classico Seating
Brokered Products include:
  General Merchandise, Foodservice Equipment & Supplies

40581 (HQ)Johnson Commercial Agents
1408 Northland Dr # 406
Suite 406
St Paul, MN 55120-1013   651-686-8499
      Fax: 651-686-7670   800-676-8488
      info@jdpinc.com www.jdpinc.com
Manufacturers' representative for water filtration/treatment systems and food service equipment and supplies
CEO: Thomas Johnson
CFO: Paul Johnson
VP: Paul Johnson
Sales Manager: Scott McBeath
Warehouse Manager: Mike Sumner
Estimated Sales: $5-10 Million
Number Employees: 5-9
Markets Served:
  Wholesale Distributors
Primary Brands Brokered include: Groen; Randell; Avtec; Montague; Perlick; Wells
Brokered Products include:
  General Merchandise, Foodservice Equipment & Supplies, Etc.

40582 Johnson Holmes & Assoc Inc
913 9th St # A
West Des Moines, IA 50265-3681   515-223-1317
      Fax: 515-223-1951
Broker of confectionery items and groceries
President: Paul Johnson
pjohnson-holmes@msn.com
Sales Manager: Terry Thomas
Estimated Sales: $1-2.5 Million
Number Employees: 5-9
Markets Served:
  Super Market Chains, Wholesale Distributors, Food Service Operators
Primary Brands Brokered include: Pearson Candy Company; Charms Company; Beer Nuts, Inc.; Golden Valley Farms; Garnetto's Market; Ferrarra Paw Candy Company
Brokered Products include:
  Confectionery, Groceries

40583 Johnson O'Hare Co
1 Progress Rd
Billerica, MA 01821-5731   978-663-9000
      Fax: 978-262-2000 info@johare.com
      www.johare.com
Broker of confectionery and dairy/deli goods, frozen food, general merchandise, groceries, etc.
President/COO: John Saidnawey
Chairman/CEO: Chip O'Hare
cohare@johare.com
EVP Regional Director Produce: Tom Casey
VP Business Development: Bobbie O'Hare
EVP/Sales Manager: Gerry Castignetti
SVP Corporate Retail Operations: Carl Annese
Number Employees: 100-249
Markets Served:
  Food Manufacturers & Processors, Super Market Chains, Wholesale Distributors, Food Service Operators
Primary Brands Brokered include: French Products; Woolite Products; Airwick Brand; Softsoap Products; 4C Foods; Berio Olive Oil; Melitta Coffee; Colgate
Brokered Products include:
  Confectionery, Dairy/Deli, Frozen Food, General Merchandise, Groceries, Meat Products, Private Label, Produce

40584 Johnson, Arlyn & Associates
1339 E Hanover St
Springfield, MO 65804-4232   417-886-3367
      Fax: 417-886-4859
Broker of frozen foods and meat and meat products including turkey, etc.
Owner: Rex Johnson
Number Employees: 1-4
Type of Packaging: Bulk
Markets Served:
  Food Manufacturers & Processors, Wholesale Distributors
Primary Brands Brokered include: ConAgra; Cargill; Norbest; Sunday House Foods; Hudson Food
Brokered Products include:
  Exports, Poultry

40585 Jon Morris & Company
275 Turnpike St Ste 100
Canton, MA 02021   781-278-8940
      Fax: 781-502-6549   800-537-0023
      www.morris-co.com
Manufacturers' representative to the in-store supermarket bakery industry
President: Henry Deegan
CFO: Jim Fabrizio
VP: Brian Gerraughty
Sales: Paul Trocki
Contact: Colum Moraghan
cmoraghan@aol.com
Estimated Sales: $1-3 Million
Number Employees: 20-49
Type of Packaging: Consumer
Markets Served:
  Super Market Chains
Brokered Products include:
  bakery

40586 Jones Neitzel Co
12850 Spurling Dr # 114
Suite 114
Dallas, TX 75230-1278   214-526-2876
      Fax: 214-522-0091 www.jonesneitzel.com
Broker of dairy/deli products, private label items, general merchandise, groceries, produce, frozen food, etc.
Partner: Jim Neitzel
jneitzel@jonesneitzel.com
Partner: Brad McCauley
Partner: Robert Baker
Estimated Sales: $1.8 Million
Number Employees: 10-19
Markets Served:
  Food Manufacturers & Processors, Super Market Chains, Wholesale Distributors, Food Service Operators
Brokered Products include:
  Dairy/Deli, Frozen Food, General Merchandise, Groceries, Health Food, Meat, Private Label, Produce, Seafood

40587 Jones-McCormick & Associates
229 E Kingston Ave
Charlotte, NC 28203-4743   704-344-1101
      Fax: 704-344-1764
Manufacturers' representative for food service equipment
President: J Brooke Jones
Partner: Robert McCormick
Estimated Sales: $500,000-1 Million
Number Employees: 10-19
Markets Served:
  Super Market Chains, Wholesale Distributors, Food Service Operators
Primary Brands Brokered include: W.A. Brown & Sons; Delfield; Cambro Manufacturing; Edlund; Merco; Prince Castle
Brokered Products include:
  General Merchandise, Foodservice Equipment

40588 Jos Iorio Company
5820 Main St
Williamsville, NY 14221-5776   716-204-0200
      Fax: 716-204-1200
Manufacturers' representative for groceries, confectionery and dairy/deli products, frozen foods, spices, general merchandise, seafood, private label items, produce, meats, health food, etc. and non foods
President: Joseph Iorio
VP: Nancy Wojtkowiak
Production Manager: Amy Bradford
Estimated Sales: $2.5-5 Million
Number Employees: 5-9
Markets Served:
  Super Market Chains, Wholesale Distributors, Food Service Operators
Brokered Products include:
  Confectionery, Dairy/Deli, Frozen Food, General Merchandise, Groceries, Health Food, Imports, Ingredients, Meat Products, Private Label, Produce, Spices

40589 Jose M Perez-Pages
PO Box 714
Mayaguez, PR 00681-0714   787-833-4677
      Fax: 787-831-4677 josemperezpages@prtc.net
Broker of dairy/deli products, frozen foods, groceries, meats, produce, etc.
President: Jose M Perez-Pages
VP: J Perez-Fernandez
Number Employees: 1-4
Markets Served:
  Super Market Chains
Brokered Products include:
  Confectionery

40590 Joseph Caragol
29 S Central Ave
Valley Stream, NY 11580-5431   516-568-1497
      Fax: 516-568-2125   800-635-4999
Import broker of olives, anchovies, mackerel in olive oil, Spanish tuna in brine/oil, olive oil, apricots, artichokes, red peppers, etc.
President: Joseph Caragol
Sales Director: Kara Gallagher
Operations Manager: Kim Horan
Estimated Sales: $2.5-5 Million
Number Employees: 1-4
Square Footage: 6000
Type of Packaging: Consumer, Food Service, Private Label
Markets Served:
  Food Manufacturers & Processors, Super Market Chains, Wholesale Distributors, Food Service Operators
Primary Brands Brokered include: Rezumar; Borges; Conva; Confrusa; Puig; Alisa; La Soledad; Alcachofas; Tomates
Brokered Products include:
  General Merchandise, Groceries, Imports, Ingredients, Private Label, Seafood, Spices

40591 Joseph P. Sullivan & Company
50 Barnum Rd
Ayer, MA 01432   978-772-3321
      Fax: 978-772-7809   800-370-2700
      sales@jpsullivan.com www.jpsullivan.com
Domestic and export broker of apples
Partner: Russ Sullivan
Partner: Ed O'Neil
Contact: Edward O'Neill
eoneil@jpsullivan.com
Estimated Sales: $5-10 Million
Number Employees: 10-19
Primary Brands Brokered include: Yankee
Brokered Products include:
  Exports, Produce, Apples

40592 (HQ)Joseph W Ciatti Co
1101 5th Ave # 170
San Rafael, CA 94901-2903   415-458-5150
      Fax: 415-458-5160 reception@ciatti.com
      www.ciatti.com
Import/export broker of grapes, bulk wine, grape juice, concentrates, alcohol and spirits
President: Greg Livengood
reception@ciatti.com
Estimated Sales: $20-50 Million
Number Employees: 20-49
Other Locations:
  Joseph W. Ciatti Co.
  MendozaJoseph W. Ciatti Co.

40593 Joseph W Nath Co
207 S State Rd
Upper Darby, PA 19082-3533   610-352-3533
      Fax: 610-352-5127   800-611-4877
Broker of frozen and dry pastas, meats, seafood, cookies, desserts, specialty drinks, etc.
President: Donald J Nath
Partner: Susan Nath-Conolly
Partner: Joe Nath, Jr.
Estimated Sales: $10-20 Million
Number Employees: 10-19
Square Footage: 3600
Markets Served:
  Food Manufacturers & Processors, Super Market Chains, Wholesale Distributors, Food Service Operators
Brokered Products include:
  Frozen Food, Groceries, Meat, Seafood, Frozen & Dry Pasta, Sauces, Etc.

Food Brokers / A-Z

40594 Joylin Food Equipment Corporation
51 Chestnut Ln
Woodbury, NY 11797-1918
Fax: 516-742-2123 800-456-9546
joylin1961@aol.com
Manufacturers' representative for food service equipment
President: Rich Kirsner
Marketing Director: Tom Pitts
Sales Director: M Kohn
Operations Manager: Tom DiRusso
Purchasing Manager: Yvette Western
Estimated Sales: $20-50 Million
Number Employees: 21
Number of Brands: 16
Square Footage: 12000
Markets Served:
  Super Market Chains, Wholesale Distributors, Food Service Operators
Primary Brands Brokered include: Amana; Champion; Duke; Groen; Victory Refrigeration; Vollrath; Avtec; Berkel; Corule; Carter Hoffmann; Thermokool; Coldzone; Traycon; Woodstone; Uveco; Follett; Prince Castle; Imperial
Brokered Products include:
  General Merchandise, Foodservice Equipment

40595 Jpo/Dow Inc
305 Canal St
Lemont, IL 60439-3603 630-257-0001
Fax: 630-257-0005 800-800-5761
www.apex-reps.com
Manufacturers' representative for Janitorial/Sanitary Supply, Foodservice Disposables, Safety/Industrial
President: Nadia Fry
nadia@apex-reps.com
VP: Craig Miller
Marketing Coordinator: Monica Merkel
Sales: Marybeth Flynn
Estimated Sales: $1-2.5 Million
Number Employees: 5-9
Square Footage: 24000
Markets Served:
  Food Service Operators
Brokered Products include:
  General Merchandise, Jan/San, Foodservice Disposables

40596 Jso Associates Inc
17 Maple Dr # 1
Great Neck, NY 11021-2000 516-773-0000
Fax: 516-773-0193 800-421-0404
jaredort@jsoinc.com www.jsoassociates.com
Industrial sales agent specializing in the sale of fruit, fruit purees, juice concentrate, vegetables and various other food products to the manufactuing trade.
President: Barbara Dejose
barbara@jsoinc.com
CEO: Jerry Sunshine
Sales: Jared Ort
Purchasing Manager: Joel Ort
Estimated Sales: $1.7 Million
Number Employees: 10-19
Square Footage: 12000
Type of Packaging: Bulk
Markets Served:
  Food Manufacturers & Processors, Super Market Chains, Wholesale Distributors
Brokered Products include:
  Frozen Food, Groceries, Imports, Produce, Frozen Fruits, Juices & Vegetables

40597 Jubilee Sales of Carolina
5 Cunningham Rd
Taylors, SC 29687-4126 864-268-9377
Fax: 864-292-2426
Import, export and domestic broker of confectionery and dairy/deli products, frozen foods, general merchandise, groceries, etc.
President: Michael Fortner
Estimated Sales: $10-20 Million
Number Employees: 10-19
Markets Served:
  Super Market Chains, Wholesale Distributors, Food Service Operators
Primary Brands Brokered include: Yoo Hoo; Newman's Own
Brokered Products include:
  Confectionery, Dairy/Deli, Exports, Frozen Food, General Merchandise, Groceries, Imports, Private Label

40598 Juhl Brokerage
5436 F St
Omaha, NE 68117 402-733-8500
Fax: 402-733-8200 nesales@juhlbrokerage.com
Broker of dairy/deli products, frozen foods, general merchandise and meat
Manager: Jim McKain
Contact: Rebecca Kirk
r.kirk@juhlbrokerage.com
Manager: John Chvatal
Estimated Sales: $5-10 Million
Number Employees: 5
Parent Co: Juhl Brokerage
Markets Served:
  Food Manufacturers & Processors, Wholesale Distributors, Food Service Operators
Primary Brands Brokered include: Butcher Boy; Fred's; Pierce; Awrey; Supreme; Portion; Pac
Brokered Products include:
  Dairy/Deli, Frozen Food, General Merchandise, Meat

40599 Juhl Brokerage
1701 1st Ave N
Fargo, ND 58102-4280 701-293-5851
Fax: 701-232-4183
Broker of dairy/deli items, groceries, meat and meat products, seafood, produce, spices, health foods, general merchandise, etc.
President: Tom Smith
VP: Jerry Jernberg
Estimated Sales: $5-10 Million
Number Employees: 5
Square Footage: 20000
Parent Co: Juhl Brokerage
Markets Served:
  Super Market Chains, Wholesale Distributors, Food Service Operators
Primary Brands Brokered include: Lamb-Weston; IFP; Nabisco; Pillsbury/McGlynn's; Kelloggs; Oscar Mayer
Brokered Products include:
  Confectionery, Dairy/Deli, Frozen Food, General Merchandise, Groceries, Health Food, Meat, Meat Products, Produce, Seafood, Spices

40600 Julito Ramirez Corporation
PO Box 364166
San Juan, PR 00936-4166 787-782-6252
Fax: 787-782-6694 teremdr@hotmail.com
Broker of general merchandise, groceries and private label items
CEO: Julito Ramirez Sr
VP: Maria T Ramirez
Operations: Edwin Lopez
Number Employees: 10-19
Square Footage: 24000
Primary Brands Brokered include: Red Wing; Torbitt & Castleman; Presto Products; Cliffstar Corp.; Huish Detergents

40601 Julius Levy Company
33 Patriot Hill Drive
Basking Ridge, NJ 07920-4210 908-470-0300
Fax: 908-470-0301
Broker of confectionery and dairy/deli products, groceries, industrial ingredients, private label items and seafood
President: Norman Lapidus
VP: Jody Dicker
General Manager: Myrna Lapidus
Number Employees: 10-19
Markets Served:
  Food Manufacturers & Processors, Super Market Chains, Wholesale Distributors, Food Service Operators
Brokered Products include:
  Confectionery, Dairy/Deli, Groceries, Ingredients, Private Label, Seafood

40602 Julius M. Dean Company
7 Carriage Lane
Kennebunk, ME 04043-7427 207-967-2752
Fax: 207-985-2160
Broker of confectionery products, frozen foods, general merchandise, groceries, meat products, private label items, etc.
President: Julius Dean
Secretary: R Dean
Number Employees: 3
Markets Served:
  Food Manufacturers & Processors, Super Market Chains, Wholesale Distributors

Primary Brands Brokered include: Floral Affairs, Inc.; Basket-Ease; Freedom Foods
Brokered Products include:
  Confectionery, Frozen Food, General Merchandise, Groceries, Meat Products, Private Label, Produce

40603 Juncker Associates
11 Parker St
Gloucester, MA 01930-3025 978-281-4555
Fax: 978-281-0867
President: Dennis Digregorio
dennis@junckerassociates.com
Estimated Sales: Less Than $500,000
Number Employees: 1-4

40604 K J Plastics Inc
415 N Broad St
Lansdale, PA 19446-2413 215-361-8222
Fax: 215-361-1929 www.kjplastics.net
Distributor/broker of recycled plastic scrap.
President: Kimberly Bergen
kimberlybergen@kjplastics.net
Number Employees: 1-4

40605 K L Keller Imports
5332 College Ave
Suite 201
Oakland, CA 94618-2805 510-839-7890
Fax: 510-839-7895 orders@klkeller.com
www.klkeller.com
Olive, nut and, truffle oils; vinegar; condiments; herbs; spices; sea salts, and confections.
Owner: Kitty Keller
Sales: Lauren Zaira
Number Employees: 1-4

40606 K&K Truck Brokers
1810 Webster Street
Hudson, WI 54016-0341 715-386-8833
Fax: 715-386-8834 800-826-7113
Transportation broker providing reefers, vans and flats with sides/tarps. ICC licensed and bonded cargo insured
President: H Pommerening
VP: S Pommerening
Estimated Sales: $300,000-500,000
Number Employees: 1-4
Square Footage: 2800

40607 K&S Sales
P.O.Box 219
Sultana, CA 93666-0219 559-595-1976
Broker of nectarines, peaches, plums, and apricots
Estimated Sales: $1-3 Million
Number Employees: 1-4

40608 KBRW
8375 SW Beaverton Hillsdale Highway
Suite D
Portland, OR 97225-2252 323-526-1394
Fax: 323-526-1395
Manufacturers' representative for food service equipment
Office Manager: Jori Polentas
Estimated Sales: $2.5-5 Million
Number Employees: 1-4
Markets Served:
  Wholesale Distributors
Primary Brands Brokered include: EPCO; Holman; Wilbur Curtis; Katch All; Continental; Rockline
Brokered Products include:
  General Merchandise, Foodservice Equipment

40609 KDH Sales
33 Bedford St Ste 12
Lexington, MA 02420 781-863-0373
Fax: 781-863-0767
Broker of confectionery and private label products, frozen foods, general merchandise, groceries and produce
President: K Hintlian
Account Manager: H Dowd
Estimated Sales: $1-2.5 Million
Number Employees: 1-4
Markets Served:
  Super Market Chains, Wholesale Distributors
Brokered Products include:
  Confectionery, Frozen Food, General Merchandise, Groceries, Private Label, Produce

Food Brokers / A-Z

40610 (HQ)KH McClure & Company
456 Glenbrook Rd
Stamford, CT 06906-1800   203-969-1615
   Fax: 203-327-3462
Exporter and broker of hard candies and chocolates
Owner: Harard Goerin
CEO: Linda Shippee
CFO: Debbie Kuter
Estimated Sales: $5-10 Million
Number Employees: 10-19
Square Footage: 8000
Type of Packaging: Consumer, Bulk
Markets Served:
   Wholesale Distributors
Brokered Products include:
   Confectionery, Exports

40611 KIKO Foods Inc
2628 Lexington Ave
Kenner, LA 70062-5369   504-466-2090
   Fax: 504-467-2863 www.kikofoods.com
Broker of dairy/deli products, frozen foods, groceries, meat and meat products and seafood
President/CEO: Max Burnell
CFO: Ferrel Gioe
SVP Research & Development: Enrique Cerda
acastian@kikofoods.com
Contact: Castian Ashley
acastian@kikofoods.com
Purchasing: Shane Jordan
Estimated Sales: $4.70 Million
Number Employees: 50-99
Markets Served:
   Wholesale Distributors, Food Service Operators
Brokered Products include:
   Dairy/Deli, Frozen Food, Groceries, Meat, Meat Products, Seafood

40612 Kahler-Senders Inc
523 SE 9th Ave
Portland, OR 97214-2233   503-236-7363
   Fax: 503-239-8040
ksgoregon@kahler-senders.com
www.kahler-senders.com
Import broker of confectionery items and general merchandise
President: Walt Freed
VP: Nathan Wood
Estimated Sales: $9.4 Million
Number Employees: 10-19
Markets Served:
   Super Market Chains, Wholesale Distributors
Primary Brands Brokered include: American Licorice Company; Spangler Candy Company; Fleer Corporation; Andre Prost, Inc.; Herman Goelitz Company; F&F Laboratories
Brokered Products include:
   Confectionery, Health Food

40613 Kandy King Confections
7061 Sunset Drive
Mentor on the Lake, OH 44060-2947 440-951-5155
   Fax: 440-951-9219
Broker of confectionery products, general merchandise, groceries and private label items
President: Darrell McGroarty
Estimated Sales: $2.5-5 Million
Number Employees: 5-9
Markets Served:
   Super Market Chains, Wholesale Distributors, Food Service Operators
Primary Brands Brokered include: King Nut Company; Stauffer Biscuit; Heritage Wafers; Comet Confectionery
Brokered Products include:
   Confectionery, General Merchandise, Groceries, Private Label, Nuts, Candy, Snacks, Etc.

40614 Kappert/Hyzer Company
9427 F Street
Omaha, NE 68127-1215   402-597-6895
   Fax: 402-597-0740
Broker of dairy/deli products, frozen foods, general merchandise, groceries, meats, etc.
President: J Kappert
Number Employees: 10-19
Square Footage: 16000
Markets Served:
   Super Market Chains, Wholesale Distributors
Primary Brands Brokered include: International Home Food; Comstock Michigan Fruit; Fort James; Kitchens of Sara Lee; Tenneco Packaging; Continental Mills
Brokered Products include:
   Dairy/Deli, Frozen Food, General Merchandise, Groceries, Meat, Meat Products, Private Label, Seafood, Spices

40615 Karoun Dairies Inc
13023 Arroyo St
San Fernando, CA 91340   818-767-7000
   Fax: 818-767-7024 888-767-0778
contact@karouncheese.com
www.karouncheese.com
Cheese and cultured dairy products.
President & Chairman: Ara Baghdassarian
CFO: Tsolak Khatcherian
COO: Rostom Baghdassarian
Year Founded: 1990
Estimated Sales: $62.5 Million
Number of Brands: 6
Parent Co: Parmalat Canada
Type of Packaging: Consumer, Food Service
Primary Brands Brokered include: California Premium, Stella, California Gold
Brokered Products include:
   Dairy/Deli

40616 Kathryn's Food Service Brokers
107 Oak St
Greenville, SC 29611-4121   864-295-2658
   Fax: 864-295-2659 888-295-2659
Broker of deli items, frozen foods, meats, private label items, etc.
Owner: J B Smith
Owner: E Young
Partner: J B Smith
Estimated Sales: $1-2.5 Million
Number Employees: 6
Square Footage: 2496
Markets Served:
   Food Manufacturers & Processors, Wholesale Distributors, Food Service Operators
Primary Brands Brokered include: Jenkins Foods; Swaggerty Sausage Company; Orangeburg Farms; 12 Baskets, Inc.; Sugar Creek, Inc.; Braselton
Brokered Products include:
   Dairy/Deli, Frozen Food, Groceries, Meat, Meat Products, Private Label

40617 Kaufholz & Company
14 E Stratford Avenue
Lansdowne, PA 19050-2042   610-622-0170
   Fax: 610-622-0171
Buyers and sellers of off-grade, damaged and surplus ingredients including sodium benzoate, citric acid, guar gum and corn syrup, flour, fruit juice concentrates and sugar
President: Ford Kaufholz
Number Employees: 1-4
Brokered Products include:
   Off-grade, Damaged, Surplus, Chemicals

40618 Kay's Foods
705 N 7th Ave
Phoenix, AZ 85007   602-252-8911
   Fax: 602-252-6515
Wholesaler/distributor and broker of specialty foods including meat, fish, cheese and confectionery products
Owner: Bill Kay
Estimated Sales: $5-10 Million
Number Employees: 10-19
Brokered Products include:
   Confectionery, Dairy/Deli, Meat, Seafood

40619 Kayco
72 New Hook Rd
Bayonne, NJ 07002   718-369-4600
customercare@kayco.com
kayco.com
Kosher, all natural, gluten free, vegan, and fair trade products; also specializes in grape juice.
President: Ilan Ron
CEO: Mordy Herzog
Financial Manager: Dov Levi
Executive Vice President: Harold Weiss
Year Founded: 1948
Estimated Sales: $86 Million
Number Employees: 500-999
Number of Brands: 76
Type of Packaging: Consumer, Food Service, Bulk
Markets Served:
   Food Manufacturers & Processors
Primary Brands Brokered include: 778; Absolutely Gluten Free; Alprose; Bartneure; Bauer; Bazooka; Beetology; Beigel Beigel; Blanchard & Blanchard; Blends By Orly; Bloch's Best; Carmel; Chosen Bean; Classic Cooking; Crispy O's; David's Kosher Salt; Dorot; Dr. Praegers; Knorr; Lays;+60
Brokered Products include:
   Alcoholic Beverages, Confectionery, Dairy/Deli, Exports, Frozen Food, Groceries, Health Food, Ingredients, Spices, Preserves

40620 Kdm Foodsales Inc
30 S Valley Rd # 307
Suite 307
Paoli, PA 19301-1476   610-644-8800
   Fax: 610-296-8868
customerservice@kdmfoodsales.com
www.kdmfoodsales.com
Broker of industrial ingredients, commodities and bakeware
President: John G. Devlin
Co-Owner: William Kalkbrenner
Executive VP/Sales & Marketing: Debra Kalkbrenner Diener
Certified Public Accountant: Carlo Silvesti
Customer Service, Sample Support: Michelle Srolls
Estimated Sales: B
Number Employees: 1-4
Square Footage: 9000
Type of Packaging: Bulk
Brokered Products include:
   Ingredients, Spices

40621 Kedem
72 New Hook Rd
Bayonne, NJ 07002   718-369-4600
customercare@kayco.com
www.kayco.com
Kosher, gluten free and all natural products. Kosher grape juice, non-alcoholic wines, jams and, cooking products and biscuits.
President: Ilan Ron
CEO: Mordy Herzog
Financial Manager: Dov Levi
Executive Vice President: Harold Weiss
Year Founded: 1948
Estimated Sales: $50-90 Million
Number of Brands: 23
Parent Co: Kayco
Type of Packaging: Consumer
Markets Served:
   Food Manufacturers & Processors
Primary Brands Brokered include: 778; Absolutely Gluten Free; Bartenura; Beigel Beigel; David's Kosher Salt; Elit; Fox's Ubet; Gefen; Harrison's Sweet Shoppe; Jane's Crazy Mixed Up Seasonings; Jeff Nathan Creations; Kedem; Kedem Fresh; Knorr; Lays; Lipton; Manhattan Chocolates;+6
Brokered Products include:
   Alcoholic Beverages, Confectionery, Dairy/Deli, Exports, Frozen Food, Groceries, Health Food, Ingredients, Spices, Preserves

40622 Keeth & Associates
531 W 18th St
Edmond, OK 73013-3631   405-330-2000
   Fax: 405-330-2026 800-324-6767
Broker of confectionery and dairy/deli products, frozen foods, canned goods, meat and meat products, groceries, private label items, general merchandise, seafood, etc.
President/CEO: Robert Hill
VP: Judi Shortt
Marketing: Cara Brophy
Contact: Nancy Huckle
nancy@hunterandsage.com
COO: Greg Delaney
Estimated Sales: $3.2 Million
Number Employees: 13
Square Footage: 18000
Markets Served:
   Super Market Chains, Wholesale Distributors, Food Service Operators
Primary Brands Brokered include: Campbell Soup Company; Quaker Oats; Orval Kent; Beatrice; Reynolds Aluminum; Doskocil/Wilson
Brokered Products include:
   Confectionery, Dairy/Deli, Frozen Food, General Merchandise, Groceries, Meat, Meat Products, Private Label, Seafood, Canned Goods, etc.

Food Brokers / A-Z

40623 Kelley-Clarke
2233 Presidents Drive
West Valley City, UT 84120-7240 801-972-4484
Fax: 801-906-4195
Broker of confectionery and dairy/deli products, frozen foods, general merchandise, groceries, etc.
President: R Aldrich
Senior VP: S Allen
Number Employees: 50-99
Square Footage: 40000
Parent Co: Kelley-Clarke
Markets Served:
Food Manufacturers & Processors, Super Market Chains, Wholesale Distributors, Food Service Operators
Primary Brands Brokered include: Ore-Ida; Weight Watchers; Schering Plough; Clairol; Pillsbury; Colgate
Brokered Products include:
Confectionery, Dairy/Deli, Frozen Food, General Merchandise, Groceries, Meat, Private Label, Produce, Seafood

40624 Kelley-Clarke
PO Box 79019
Seattle, WA 98119-7919 206-622-2581
Fax: 206-682-0424
Export broker and wholesaler/distributor of frozen salmon, Dungeness crab meat and tiny Pacific shrimp
Manager: Todd Raasch
Estimated Sales: $5-10 Million
Number Employees: 10-19
Parent Co: Kelley-Clarke
Brokered Products include:
Exports, Frozen Food, Seafood

40625 Kelly Associates/Food Brokers
1208 Horseshoe Pike
Downingtown, PA 19335-1153 610-269-7441
Fax: 610-269-6137
Broker of dairy/deli products, groceries, private label items and spices
CEO: D Kelly
CFO: C Kelly
Estimated Sales: $5-10 Million
Number Employees: 6
Type of Packaging: Consumer, Food Service
Markets Served:
Super Market Chains, Food Service Operators
Brokered Products include:
Dairy/Deli, Groceries, Private Label, Spices

40626 (HQ)Kelly Flour Company
1208 N Swift Rd
Addison, IL 60101-6104 630-678-5300
Fax: 630-678-5311
Dry milk replacers and dry egg extenders
Manager: Dan Hoberg
Executive VP: Donald Kelly, Jr.
Plant Manager: Samuel Vergara
Estimated Sales: $3-5 Million
Number Employees: 20-49
Square Footage: 60
Type of Packaging: Food Service, Private Label
Markets Served:
Food Manufacturers & Processors, Food Service Operators
Brokered Products include:
Ingredients

40627 Kelly/Mincks Northwest Agents
9617 Crystal Lake Drive
Woodinville, WA 98077-9501 425-806-0100
Fax: 425-806-3872 www.mafsi.org/kelly-mincks/
Manufacturers' representative for food service equipment including supplies and furniture
Principal: James Mincks
Principal: David Mincks
Principal: Bill Kelly
Estimated Sales: $2.5-5 Million
Number Employees: 1-4
Markets Served:
Wholesale Distributors
Primary Brands Brokered include: Hamilton Beach; Lincoln Foodservice; Robot Coupe; Apache Mat; Rubbermaid; Tablecraft
Brokered Products include:
General Merchandise, Foodservice Equipment

40628 Kemper Food Brokers
1820 NW 3rd St
Oklahoma City, OK 73106-2813 405-236-5550
Fax: 405-236-4244
Broker of confectionery and dairy/deli products, frozen foods, private label items, meat and meat products, general merchandise, etc.
President: Charles Kemper
Estimated Sales: $3 Million
Number Employees: 5
Square Footage: 32000
Markets Served:
Food Manufacturers & Processors, Wholesale Distributors, Food Service Operators
Primary Brands Brokered include: Gilster; Mary Lee; Quaker; Shultz
Brokered Products include:
Confectionery, Dairy/Deli, Frozen Food, General Merchandise, Meat, Meat Products, Private Label

40629 Kennett Roepke Gavilan
15335 Calle Enrique
Suite 201
Morgan Hill, CA 95037-5622 408-779-1773
Fax: 408-778-2105
Broker of dairy products, frozen foods, groceries, meats, produce and seafood
President: Alex Kennett
CEO: Peter Roepke
Number Employees: 10-19
Square Footage: 10000

40630 Kenney Sales
8425 Oakleigh Rd
Baltimore, MD 21234 410-661-4242
Fax: 410-882-6015 800-661-4245
kenney@kenneysales.com
Import and domestic broker of frozen foods, dairy/deli products, general merchandise, groceries, meat and meat products, etc.
President: Melvin Kenney Jr
sandy.o@kenneysales.com
Executive VP: Patti Kenney
Estimated Sales: $10-20 Million
Number Employees: 5-9
Square Footage: 8000
Markets Served:
Super Market Chains, Wholesale Distributors
Brokered Products include:
Alcoholic Beverages, Confectionery, Dairy/Deli, Frozen Food, General Merchandise, Groceries, Imports, Meat, Meat Products, Private Label, Produce, Seafood, Spices

40631 Kenny's Candy & Confections
Perham, MN 56573
kennyscandy.com
Fruit snacks, gummies, licorice and popcorn
Founder: Ken Nelson Year Founded: 1987
Type of Packaging: Private Label

40632 Key Carlin O'Brien, LLC
11011 Smetana Rd
Minnetonka, MN 55343-4726 952-979-1531
Fax: 952-979-1547 www.key-sales.com
Broker of confectionery and dairy/deli products, frozen and health foods, general merchandise, groceries, etc.
President: Ray Fowler
CEO: Brad Carlin
EVP: Bud Lowell
COO: Jeff Mahler
Estimated Sales: $20-50 Million
Number Employees: 20-49
Parent Co: Carlin O'Brien, Inc.
Primary Brands Brokered include: Leaf, Inc.; Goodmark Foods; Very Fine Products; Favorite Brands; Ken Davis Products; Fisher Nut
Brokered Products include:
Confectionery, Dairy/Deli, Frozen Food, General Merchandise, Groceries, Health Food, Ingredients, Private Label, Produce

40633 Key Impact Sales & Systems Inc
95 Connecticut Dr # D
Burlington, NJ 08016-4180 609-265-8300
Fax: 609-267-6662 800-955-0600
info@kisales.com www.kisales.com
Broker of dairy/deli products, frozen foods, meats and meat products, private label brands, seafood, etc.
President: Randy Wieland
Chief Executive Officer: Dan Cassidy
Chief Financial Officer: Kathleen Mooy
Chief Information Officer: Neil Johnson
EVP, Client Management: Rob Monroe
SVP, Segment Sales: Butch Cassidy
Chief Marketing Officer: Brenda Lotesta
SVP, Region Presidents East: Joe Hargadon
SVP, Region Presidents West: Chuck Paradowski
Estimated Sales: $36 Million
Number Employees: 500-999
Square Footage: 11000
Markets Served:
Food Manufacturers & Processors, Wholesale Distributors, Food Service Operators
Primary Brands Brokered include: Tyson; Pillsbury Bakery USA; McCain; Uncle Ben's; Norpac; Jac Pac
Brokered Products include:
Dairy/Deli, Frozen Food, Meat, Meat Products, Private Label, Seafood, Spices

40634 Key Sales & Marketing
306 Erie Ave
Morton, IL 61550-9600 309-284-0558
Fax: 309-284-0559 csamuelson@keysales.com
Broker of confectionery and dairy/deli products, frozen foods, general merchandise, groceries, health food, etc
President: Craig Samuelson
Estimated Sales: $15 Million
Number Employees: 10-19
Square Footage: 4000
Markets Served:
Super Market Chains, Wholesale Distributors
Brokered Products include:
Dairy/Deli, Frozen Food, Groceries, Meat, Produce, Seafood

40635 Key Sales Group
1834 Walden Office Square
Suite 100
Schaumburg, IL 60173 847-397-7400
Fax: 847-397-7401
Broker of confectionery and dairy/deli products, frozen foods, general merchandise, groceries, meats, private label items, produce, seafood and spices
President: Douglas Piggott
Contact: Doug Piggot
doug.piggot@keysales.com
Estimated Sales: A
Number Employees: 3
Markets Served:
Food Manufacturers & Processors, Super Market Chains, Wholesale Distributors, Food Service Operators
Primary Brands Brokered include: Clabber Girl Baking Powder; Old Family Recipe; Chadalee Farms; Welden Farms; Lady Dianne; Thomson Berry Farms
Brokered Products include:
Confectionery, Dairy/Deli, Frozen Food, General Merchandise, Groceries, Meat, Meat Products, Private Label, Produce, Seafood, Spices

40636 KeyImpact Sales & Systems, Inc.
1400 Lake Dr W
Chanhassen, MN 55317 952-227-3199
Fax: 952-227-3198 info@kisales.com
www.kisales.com
Broker of dairy and deli items, frozen foods, groceries, meat and meat products and seafood
President and Chief Executive Officer: Dan Cassidy
Senior VP: Shawn McAllister
Chief Financial Officer: Kathleen Mooy
EVP Client Management: Rob Monroe
Chief Marketing Officer: Brenda Lotesta
Customer Service Manager: Diane Syhre
Estimated Sales: $5-10 Million
Number Employees: 5-9
Square Footage: 28800
Markets Served:
Wholesale Distributors, Food Service Operators
Primary Brands Brokered include: Tyson; Stouffers; Van Der Berch; Ore-Ida; Jerome Foods
Brokered Products include:
Dairy/Deli, Frozen Food, Groceries, Meat, Meat Products, Seafood

40637 Kidd Enterprises
2602 Towne House Drive NE
Cedar Rapids, IA 52402-2233 319-393-5938

Food Brokers / A-Z

Broker of dairy/deli products, frozen foods, groceries and seafood
President: R Kidd
Sales Manager: Don Davis
Number Employees: 1-4
Parent Co: Kidd Enterprises
Markets Served:
  Super Market Chains, Wholesale Distributors
Brokered Products include:
  Dairy/Deli, Frozen Food, Groceries, Seafood

40638 Kiefer's
9760 N Ash Ave
Kansas City, MO 64157-9742   816-436-7877
  Fax: 816-761-0677 800-561-5432
  kiefersnax@aol.com
Broker of confectionery items, meat products and snack foods
Owner: Deborah Keefer
Partner: Ann Kiefer
Partner: Cathy Sturm
Estimated Sales: $500,000-$1 Million
Number Employees: 1-4
Markets Served:
  Food Manufacturers & Processors, Super Market Chains, Wholesale Distributors, Food Service Operators
Primary Brands Brokered include: Honey Creek; IPSI Meat Snacks; Pretzels, Inc.; Palmer Candy; Trophy Nuts; Jack Line Snack Foods
Brokered Products include:
  Confectionery, Meat Products, Snack Foods

40639 Kinder-Smith Company
4112 North Ave
Cincinnati, OH 45236   513-891-0522
Broker of dairy/deli products, frozen foods, general merchandise, groceries, private label items and spices
Owner: James W Kinder Sr
Executive VP/COO: Barbara Lewis
Estimated Sales: $1-3 Million
Number Employees: 4
Markets Served:
  Food Manufacturers & Processors, Super Market Chains, Wholesale Distributors, Food Service Operators
Brokered Products include:
  Dairy/Deli, Frozen Food, General Merchandise, Groceries, Private Label, Spices

40640 King Food Service
7810 42nd St W
Rock Island, IL 61201-7319   309-787-4488
  Fax: 309-787-4501 www.kingfoodservice.com
Seafood, poultry & meat
President: Matthew Cutkomp
CEO/CFO: Mike Cutkomp
Director of Sales & Marketing: Kelly McDonald
VP Operations: Chad Gaul
Estimated Sales: $24 Million
Number Employees: 10-19
Number of Products: 1500

40641 King Midas Seafood Enterprises
309 N Lake St Ste 200
Mundelein, IL 60060   847-680-6500
  Fax: 847-680-6407
President: Richard Wells
Estimated Sales: $1-3 Million
Number Employees: 1-4

40642 King Sales & Engineering Co
9 Jules Dr
Novato, CA 94947-2015   415-892-7961
  Fax: 415-892-3642 david@kingpac.com
  www.kingpac.com
Manufacturers' representative for packaging machinery and conveyor systems
President: David Rossman
Contact: Chip Barcus
chip@kingpac.com
Estimated Sales: $2.5-5 Million
Number Employees: 1-4
Square Footage: 16000
Brokered Products include:
  General Merchandise, Packaging Machinery, Conveying Systems

40643 Kingery & Assoc
1347 IL Highway 1
Carmi, IL 62821-4929   618-382-3347
  Fax: 618-382-3611 888-844-1665
  www.grocerytraders.com
Grocery, meat, produce and HBC
President: Ron Kingery
VP: Woodie Pontey
President: Ron Kingery
Public Relations: Bob Estes
Operations: Steve Kemer
IT: Tammy Sisco
tsisco@yourclearwave.com
Estimated Sales: $10-20 Million
Number Employees: 5-9
Square Footage: 33300
Type of Packaging: Consumer, Food Service, Private Label, Bulk
Markets Served:
  Super Market Chains, Wholesale Distributors, Food Service Operators
Brokered Products include:
  Confectionery, Dairy/Deli, Frozen Food, General Merchandise, Groceries, Ingredients, Meat, Meat Products, Private Label, Produce, Spices

40644 Kings Seafood Co
3185 Airway Ave
Suite H
Costa Mesa, CA 92626-4601   714-432-0400
  Fax: 714-432-0111 800-269-8425
  samking@kingsseafood.com
  www.kingsseafood.com
Seafood
Owner: Steve Rhee
CEO: Sam King
sking@kingssseafood.com
CFO: Roger Doan
Estimated Sales: $5 Million
Number Employees: 20-49
Square Footage: 60000
Type of Packaging: Food Service

40645 Kingsbrook Foods
PO Box 255493
Sacramento, CA 95865   916-979-7341
  www.kingsbrook.com
Broker of produce and produce products specializing in tomato paste, tomato products, and fruit concentrates
Number Employees: 6
Square Footage: 8000
Type of Packaging: Bulk
Markets Served:
  Food Manufacturers & Processors
Brokered Products include:
  Tomato Paste, Products, Peppers, Etc.

40646 Kinnetic Food Sales
36888 View Ridge Drive
Elizabeth, CO 80107   303-646-4191
Food ingredients and marketing.
President: Ray Kinn
Operations: Jeannie Speer
Number Employees: 2
Number of Brands: 6
Number of Products: 30
Square Footage: 320
Type of Packaging: Consumer, Food Service, Bulk

40647 Kirkbride & Associates
153 Center St
Brewster, MA 02631-1132   508-896-7210
  Fax: 508-896-9298 kirkbri@banet.net
Manufacturer's representative for commercial dishwashing equipment, waste disposal systems and water heating equipment-s/s fabrication-conveyors
Owner: Pete Kirkbride
Estimated Sales: Less than $500,000
Number Employees: 1-4
Parent Co: Kirkbride Industries
Markets Served:
  Super Market Chains, Food Service Operators

40648 Kirstein Brokerage Company
1 Odell Plz
Yonkers, NY 10701-1402   914-377-0169
  Fax: 914-377-0428
Broker of dairy/deli products, frozen food, seafood, groceries, meat, spices, etc.
President: Bruce Kirstein
Senior VP: James Orkin
Sales Manager: Rob Silverman
Number Employees: 25
Square Footage: 21600
Markets Served:
  Food Manufacturers & Processors, Super Market Chains, Wholesale Distributors, Food Service Operators
Primary Brands Brokered include: Pillsbury; J.M. Smuckers; McCain's; Sweet Street; Viking Seafood; Tyson Foods
Brokered Products include:
  Dairy/Deli, Frozen Food, General Merchandise, Groceries, Meat, Meat Products, Seafood, Spices

40649 (HQ)Klass Ingredients Inc
3885 N Buffalo St
Orchard Park, NY 14127-1839   716-662-2056
  Fax: 716-662-0285 patb@klassingredients.com
  www.klassingredients.com
Broker of industrial ingredients including sweeteners, dried and frozen fruits and vegetables, cocoa/chocolate and fruit juice concentrates and citrus products
President: Patrick Backman
patb@klassingredients.com
Administration Manager: Penny Russo
Estimated Sales: $5-10 Million
Number Employees: 5-9
Square Footage: 14400
Type of Packaging: Bulk
Markets Served:
  Food Manufacturers & Processors
Primary Brands Brokered include: ADM; Diamond Walnut; Ocean Spray; Imperial Holly; Sunsweet; Vita Pakt
Brokered Products include:
  Ingredients, Sweeteners, Cocoa, Nut Meats, Etc.

40650 Klensch Cheese Company
529 S Jefferson St
Ste 10
Green Bay, WI 54301-4125   920-437-8554
  Fax: 920-437-9375 800-621-1349
  donovanbud@aol.com
Broker of cheese including cheddar, colby, monterey, mozzarella, ricotta, romano, provolone, muenster, brick, swiss, havarti, string cheese and organics
Partner: Patricia Klensch
Partner: Jwalter Donovan
Estimated Sales: $300,000-500,000
Number Employees: 1-4
Type of Packaging: Consumer, Food Service, Private Label, Bulk
Markets Served:
  Food Manufacturers & Processors, Super Market Chains, Wholesale Distributors, Food Service Operators
Brokered Products include:
  Dairy/Deli, Private Label

40651 Klinger & Speros Food Brokers
2045 S Arlington Hts Rd # 114
Arlington Hts, IL 60005-4151   847-956-8300
  Fax: 847-956-8301
Import broker of dairy/deli products, frozen foods, groceries, industrial ingredients, meat and meat products, etc.
VP: Mike Klinger
Office Manager: Kay Klinger
Estimated Sales: $5-10 Million
Number Employees: 1-4
Square Footage: 10400
Markets Served:
  Food Manufacturers & Processors, Super Market Chains, Wholesale Distributors, Food Service Operators
Primary Brands Brokered include: C&F Foods; Imperial Holly; Plochman; Star Fine Foods; America's Catch; Eldorado Seafood
Brokered Products include:
  Dairy/Deli, Frozen Food, Groceries, Imports, Ingredients, Meat, Meat Products, Seafood

40652 Klondike Foods
14804-119th Avenue
Edmonton, AB T5L 2P2
Canada   780-451-6677
  Fax: 780-451-7733 info@klondikefoods.com
  www.klondikefoods.com/
Wholesaler/distributor and import broker of confectionery and dairy/deli products, frozen foods, general merchandise, groceries, private label items, etc. Warehouse providing dry storage for cheese and dry food products alsoavailable
President: Jacob Trach
CEO: Wayne Slosky
CFO: Neville Crawford
Office Manager: Charmaine Slosky

Food Brokers / A-Z

Number Employees: 5
Square Footage: 24000
Parent Co: Klondike Foods Import Export Division
Markets Served:
   Food Manufacturers & Processors, Super Market Chains, Wholesale Distributors, Food Service Operators
Primary Brands Brokered include: Heritage Foods Cheemo Products; European Egg Noodle-Pasta Time Products; Klondike Foods Import/Export; Summerland Sweets; Alpha Polybag Corporation; Joe's Bagelry
Brokered Products include:
   Confectionery, Frozen Food, General Merchandise, Groceries, Health Food, Imports, Private Label

40653 Knutsen Coffees
1448 Pine St Ste 209
San Francisco, CA 94109   415-922-9570
   Fax: 415-922-1045   800-231-7764
   kcltd@pacbell.net
Import and broker of raw coffee beans
President: Erna Knutsen
erna@knutsencoffees.com
CFO: John Rapinchuk
Estimated Sales: $2 Million
Number Employees: 1-4
Type of Packaging: Bulk
Markets Served:
   Food Manufacturers & Processors
Brokered Products include:
   Imports, Raw Coffee Beans

40654 (HQ)Koch & Assoc
505 Freyer Dr NE
Marietta, GA 30060-1409   770-218-8911
   Fax: 770-218-8914 www.kochfoodbroker.com
Broker of confectionery and dairy/deli products, frozen foods, general merchandise, produce and groceries
CEO: Tom Koch
kochassoc@bellsouth.net
Retail Sales Manager: Lindsay Koch
Estimated Sales: $10-20 Million
Number Employees: 5-9
Square Footage: 4000
Other Locations:
   Koch & Associates
   Irondale, ALKoch & Associates
Markets Served:
   Super Market Chains, Wholesale Distributors
Primary Brands Brokered include: Edwards; Tampico; Texas Pete; Mrs. Cubbison's; Crown Prince; Gold Eagle
Brokered Products include:
   Confectionery, Dairy/Deli, Frozen Food, General Merchandise, Groceries, Produce

40655 Koehler Borden & Assoc
7600 Freedom Ave NW
North Canton, OH 44720-6904   330-497-1151
   Fax: 330-497-9966   800-356-1151
   tomb@koehlerborden.com
   www.koehlerborden.com
Manufacturers' representative for food service equipment
Owner: Matt Perry
mattp@koehlerborden.com
Office Assistant: Jean Wasson
Office Assistant: Laura Turner
Director, Business Development: Tom Borden
Sales: John Dishman
mattp@koehlerborden.com
Customer Service: Shelly Borden
Estimated Sales: $5-10 Million
Number Employees: 10-19
Markets Served:
   Super Market Chains, Wholesale Distributors, Food Service Operators
Brokered Products include:
   Smallwares, Equipment, Seating

40656 Korth Marketing
84 N. Bridge Street
P.O. Box 398
Markesan, WI 53946-0398   920-398-2510
   Fax: 920-398-2768   800-962-7815
Domestic, import and export broker of confectionery, frozen foods, groceries, industrial ingredients, meat products, seafood, etc.
President: C. Ken Werth
Account Executive: J Werth
Account Executive: A Werth

Number Employees: 1-4
Square Footage: 2000
Type of Packaging: Consumer, Food Service, Private Label, Bulk
Markets Served:
   Food Manufacturers & Processors, Super Market Chains, Wholesale Distributors, Food Service Operators
Brokered Products include:
   Confectionery, Exports, Frozen Food, Groceries, Imports, Ingredients, Private Label

40657 Kramer Brokerage Co
148 Linden St # 202
Wellesley, MA 02482-7916   781-235-4746
   Fax: 781-235-2207 kramerbrok@aol.com
Broker of baking and confectionery products including flour and sugar
Owner: Gerald Kramer
kramerbrok@aol.com
Estimated Sales: $5-10 Million
Number Employees: 5-9
Markets Served:
   Food Manufacturers & Processors, Super Market Chains, Food Service Operators
Brokered Products include:
   Confectionery, Groceries, Ingredients

40658 Krass-Joseph
401 Hackensack Ave
Floor: 3
Hackensack, NJ 07601-6405   201-488-6500
   Fax: 201-488-6525 artapples@aol.com
Broker of produce including apples, pears, cherries, asparagus and citrus
President: Harold Chubinsky
Sales Manager: Matthew Chubinsky
Office Manager: Jennifer Chubinsky
Estimated Sales: $1.8 Million
Number Employees: 7
Square Footage: 4200
Markets Served:
   Super Market Chains, Wholesale Distributors
Brokered Products include:
   Imports, Produce, Apples, Pears, Cherries, Etc.

40659 Kurtz Food Brokers
1028 Peach Street
San Luis Obispo, CA 93401   805-543-3727
   Fax: 866-633-2140   800-696-7423
   kevin@kurtz.net www.kurtzfoodbrokers.com
Broker of confectionery products, industrial ingredients, rice, rice crackers, raisins, nuts, etc.
President: Ed Kurtz
Diretor Sales/Marketing: Kevin Magon
Sales Coordinator: Vicki Crawford
Contact: Nicole Ansbro
nicole@kurtzinc.net
Estimated Sales: A
Number Employees: 3
Square Footage: 1500
Markets Served:
   Food Manufacturers & Processors, Wholesale Distributors, Food Service Operators
Primary Brands Brokered include: Farmers' Rice Cooperative; Riceland Foods; Sweet Dried Fruit; Guerra Walnut Company; Sesmark Foods; Del Ray Packing Company, TH Foods; Hamilton Ranches
Brokered Products include:
   Confectionery, Ingredients, Rice, Raisins, Nuts, Etc.

40660 L H Gamble Co LTD
3615 Harding Ave # 502
Honolulu, HI 96816-3757   808-735-8199
   Fax: 808-737-2835
Broker of food service equipment
Owner: Ray Barry
raybarry@lhgamble.com
Estimated Sales: $20-50 Million
Number Employees: 20-49
Markets Served:
   Super Market Chains, Wholesale Distributors, Food Service Operators
Primary Brands Brokered include: American Home Foods; Borden Foodservice; General Mills; Hormel Foods; Nestle Brands; Morningstar Group
Brokered Products include:
   General Merchandise, Foodservice Equipment

40661 L&S Sales Company
1600 School Street #102
Moraga, CA 94556   925-376-9720
   Fax: 925-376-1976 info@lns-sales.com
   lns-sales.com
Broker of confectionery products, frozen foods, general merchandise, groceries, baked goods, beverages, produce, meat products, etc
President: Stuart Scherr
CEO: Nancy Scherr
CFO: Darryl Scherr
VP: David Scherr
Founder: Alvin Low
Founder: Phillip Schwartz
Sales Associate: Phil Backstrom
Estimated Sales: $5-10 Million
Number Employees: 6
Square Footage: 2400
Type of Packaging: Consumer, Private Label, Bulk
Markets Served:
   Super Market Chains, Wholesale Distributors
Brokered Products include:
   Confectionery, Dairy/Deli, Exports, Frozen Food, General Merchandise, Meat, Meat Products, Private Label

40662 LA Teste Services
PO Box 3014
Conroe, TX 77305-3014   936-441-0134
   Fax: 936-441-0188
   lateste@falconexportservices.com
   www.falconexportservices.com
Export broker of frozen foods, meats, groceries, general merchandise, health food, spices, private label items, etc.
Chairman/President/Founder: Luis Teste
Manager: Luis Teste, Jr.
VP: Pam Teste
Estimated Sales: $5-10 Million
Number Employees: 10-19
Square Footage: 80000
Markets Served:
   Super Market Chains, Wholesale Distributors, Food Service Operators
Brokered Products include:
   Exports, Frozen Food, General Merchandise, Groceries, Health Food, Meat, Meat Products, Private Label, Spices

40663 LAD Foodservice Sales
66 Franklin Street
Suite 200
Oakland, CA 94607-3726   510-839-9293
   Fax: 510-465-2809
Broker of dairy/deli products, frozen foods, meat and meat products and groceries
President: Paul DeVincenzi
VP Sales: Barry Knizek
Operations Manager: Marge Harwood
Estimated Sales: $20-50 Million
Number Employees: 20-49
Square Footage: 7500
Markets Served:
   Wholesale Distributors, Food Service Operators
Primary Brands Brokered include: Anchor Food Products; ConAgra Foodservice; Jennie-O-Foods; Keebler; Pillsbury Bakeries & Foodservice, Inc.; Hillshire
Brokered Products include:
   Dairy/Deli, Frozen Food, Groceries, Meat, Meat Products

40664 LBM Sales, LLC
8770 Transit Rd
Suite 4
East Amherst, NY 14051
   Fax: 315-510-4119 cs@lbmsales.com
   www.lbmsales.com
Broker of confectionery products, general merchandise and snacks
Estimated Sales: $2.5-5 Million
Number Employees: 1-4
Square Footage: 16000
Markets Served:
   Super Market Chains, Wholesale Distributors, Food Service Operators
Primary Brands Brokered include: Tootsie Roll; R.M. Palmer Company; Beer Nuts, Inc.; Just Born (Hershey Broker Div.); Van Melle; Charms
Brokered Products include:
   Confectionery, General Merchandise

Food Brokers / A-Z

40665 LIN-PAK, LLC.
110 Sanderson Ave.
PO Box 88
Swanton, OH 43558   419-826-9977
Fax: 800-878-2897   800-524-4845
jrlinpak@gmail.com www.linpak.com
Export broker of foil laminate pouch material for food products, labeling equipment and labels including pressure sensitive and lithograph
President: Doug Smith
VP: Douglas Smith
Contact: John Redfox
jrlinpak@gmail.com
Estimated Sales: $500,000-$1 Million
Number Employees: 5-9
Type of Packaging: Private Label
Brokered Products include:
  Exports, General Merchandise, Labels, Labeling Equipment, Etc.

40666 LMGO International Inc
1590 Ponce de Leon Avenue
San Juan, PR 00926-1802   787-724-1697
Fax: 787-721-5332
Manufacturer Representative of dairy/deli items, frozen food, groceries, industrial ingredients, meat and meat products, produce, private label items, seafood, etc
President: Eduardo Martinez
CEO: F Ojeda
VP: Pedro Martinez
Sales: Alberto Arango
Number Employees: 7
Square Footage: 4400
Type of Packaging: Consumer, Food Service, Private Label, Bulk
Markets Served:
  Food Manufacturers & Processors, Super Market Chains, Wholesale Distributors, Food Service Operators
Primary Brands Brokered include: Private Labels
Brokered Products include:
  Exports, Frozen Food, General Merchandise, Groceries, Imports, Ingredients, Meat, Meat Products, Private Label, Produce, Seafood

40667 LMS Associate
2205 W Division St # A9
Suite A-9
Arlington, TX 76012-3623   817-548-7575
Fax: 817-548-0500   800-725-7377
www.lmsassociates.com
Manufacturers' representative for food service equipment including ovens, mixers, bakeware, faucets, ovens, ranges, slicers, health care equipment, heat and hold cabinets etc.
President: Dan Lang
CEO, South Texas & Houston Territory: Steve Langston
steve@lmsassociates.com
CFO: Kimberly Wandrey
Estimated Sales: $1-2.5 Million
Number Employees: 1-4
Markets Served:
  Wholesale Distributors
Primary Brands Brokered include: Chicago Faucet; Holman Cooking; Hot Food Boxes; Market Forge; Master Disposers; Normandie Racks
Brokered Products include:
  General Merchandise, Foodservice Equipment

40668 LT's Brokerage
P.O.Box 415
Broken Arrow, OK 74013-0415   918-251-2044
Transportation broker for refrigerated and frozen foods, as well as dry. All types of equipment
President: Lyle Tracy
Number Employees: 5-9

40669 Lactalis American GroupInc
2376 S Park Ave
Buffalo, NY 14220
877-522-8254
www.lactalisamericangroup.com
Processor, exporter and importer of cheeses including Brie, Swiss, Roquefort, feta, edam, Gouda, mozzarella, ricotta, fontina, Asiago, shredded/grated, Parmesan and romano, as well as snack and spreadable cheese.
CEO: Thierry Clement
SVP & Chief Legal Officer: Pierre Lorieau
Marketing Director: Karine Blake
VP of Sales: Yann Connan
Year Founded: 1992
Estimated Sales: $415 Million
Number Employees: 1,600
Number of Brands: 10
Square Footage: 16231
Parent Co: Groupe Lactalis
Type of Packaging: Consumer, Food Service, Private Label

40670 Laetitia Vineyard & Winery
453 Laetitia Vineyard Dr
Arroyo Grande, CA 93420-9701   805-481-1772
Fax: 805-481-6920   888-809-8463
info@laetitiawine.com www.laetitiawine.com
Wine
President & Head Winemaker: Eric Hickey
HR Executive: Jan Wilkinson
jan@laetitiawine.com
Marketing Coordinator: Jackie Ross
Division Sales Manager: Tabitha Alger
Operations: Dave Hickey
President & Head Winemaker: Eric Hickey
Estimated Sales: Below $5 Million
Number Employees: 50-99

40671 Lake & Lake Inc
44 Bristol St # 3
Canandaigua, NY 14424-1690   585-394-2277
Fax: 585-394-2013
Export broker of industrial ingredients, produce, dried oats, rye, barley and buckwheat
Owner: Bob Kiesewetter
Sales: George Smith
lakeandlake@frontiernet.net
Estimated Sales: $1-2.5 Million
Number Employees: 1-4
Type of Packaging: Bulk
Markets Served:
  Food Manufacturers & Processors, Wholesale Distributors
Brokered Products include:
  Exports, Ingredients, Dried Beans, Oats, Barley, Rye, Etc.

40672 Lake Michigan Growers
2576 E 132nd Street
Grant, MI 49327-9355   616-784-6551
Fax: 616-784-6554
Broker of produce
Owner: Walt Vanderwall
Estimated Sales: $1-2.5 Million
Number Employees: 1-4
Type of Packaging: Consumer, Food Service, Private Label, Bulk
Markets Served:
  Super Market Chains, Wholesale Distributors, Food Service Operators
Primary Brands Brokered include: Lake Michigan Growers
Brokered Products include:
  Produce

40673 Lakeside Food Sales Inc
175 E Hawthorn Pkwy # 300
Suite 300
Vernon Hills, IL 60061-1467   847-808-8686
Fax: 847-808-8645   800-808-6745
www.lakesidefoodsales.com
Broker of frozen and canned fruits, juice concentrates and tomatoes including paste, diced and crushed
Owner/CEO: Todd Chroman
tchroman@lakesidefoodsales.com
Vice President: Scott Winer
VP Regional Sales / Quality Dept. MGR.: Eric Nelson
Vice President-Sales Division: Tony Dacks
Number Employees: 10-19
Square Footage: 10000
Markets Served:
  Food Manufacturers & Processors, Wholesale Distributors, Food Service Operators
Brokered Products include:
  Frozen Food, Groceries, Juice Concentrates, Tomato Products

40674 Lamborn & Company
PO Box 31
Cos Cob, CT 06807-0031   203-661-9181
Fax: 203-972-7736
Domestic import broker of industrial ingredients including sugar, salt and corn sweeteners
President: Leon Salerno
Estimated Sales: $3-5 Million
Number Employees: 1-4
Markets Served:
  Food Manufacturers & Processors, Wholesale Distributors
Primary Brands Brokered include: Jack Frost; Florida Crystals; Pioneer; Potrero; United Salt Company; Sunlight
Brokered Products include:
  Imports, Ingredients, Sugar, Salt, Corn Sweeteners

40675 Lampson & Tew
2700 E 82nd St
Minneapolis, MN 55425   952-854-1545
Fax: 952-854-8749
Broker of dairy/deli items, frozen foods, meats, seafood, spices and private label products
President: Robert Tunning
Food Service President: R Tunning
CFO: Kusila Wijesetua
Vice President: Randy Fleck
Sales Director: Janice Rost
Contact: Julie Muilenburg
jam39@hotmail.com
Operations Manager: Lisa Spiege
Estimated Sales: $10-20 Million
Number Employees: 15
Markets Served:
  Food Manufacturers & Processors, Food Service Operators
Brokered Products include:
  Dairy/Deli, Frozen Food, Ingredients, Meat, Meat Products, Private Label, Seafood, Spices

40676 Lancaster Packing Company
7615 Lancaster Avenue
PO Box 465
Myerstown, PA 17067   717-397-9727
Fax: 717-397-7744   www.jakeandamos.com
Pennsylvania Dutch-style pickles, preserves, relishes, syrups, pickled vegetables and fruits, chow chow and fruit butters packed in glass canning jars
President: David Doolittle
CEO: Sue Doolittle
Estimated Sales: $5-10 Million
Number Employees: 5-9
Square Footage: 40000
Type of Packaging: Consumer, Private Label

40677 Lance Agencies
892 Ross Road
North Vancouver, BC V7K 1C5
Canada   604-987-6136
Fax: 604-980-9188
Broker of industrial ingredients and spices
President: Lance Pilot
Number Employees: 1-4
Markets Served:
  Food Manufacturers & Processors, Food Service Operators
Brokered Products include:
  Ingredients, Spices

40678 Landers Ag Resources
422 Cedar View Road
Hudson, WI 54016-8053   715-381-9640
Broker of produce specializing in contracting onions for food service and processors
President: Rett Landers
Type of Packaging: Food Service, Bulk
Markets Served:
  Food Manufacturers & Processors, Super Market Chains, Wholesale Distributors, Food Service Operators
Brokered Products include:
  Ingredients, Produce, Spices

40679 Landmark Foods
5340 Legacy Dr # 205
Plano, TX 75024-3146   469-298-4700
Fax: 972-980-8741
Domestic and export broker of poultry and seafood
President: Michael Loehr
Manager: Rod Stevenson
rod.stevenson@yahoo.com
Number Employees: 10-19
Markets Served:
  Food Manufacturers & Processors, Super Market Chains, Wholesale Distributors, Food Service Operators
Brokered Products include:
  Exports, Seafood, Poultry

Food Brokers / A-Z

40680 Lane Marketing Group LLC
582 Bellerive Rd # 4a
#4A
Annapolis, MD 21409-4611   410-757-0293
    Fax: 410-757-0293 dlane@lanegroup.com
    www.lanegroup.com
Manufacturers' representative for food service equipment including cook/chill, refrigeration, ventilation, food processing and shelving
Owner: Danny Lane
Sales Representative: Steve Houcck
Sales Representative: Robert Enzor
dlane@lanegroup.com
Estimated Sales: $500,000-$1 Million
Number Employees: 5-9
Primary Brands Brokered include: Garland; Cleveland; Robot Coupe; W.A. Brown & Son; Frymaster; Ventmaster; Delfield; Everpure; Dormont
Brokered Products include:
    General Merchandise, Foodservice Equipment, Shelving, etc.

40681 Larry Fox & Co
PO Box 729
Valley Stream, NY 11582-0729   516-791-7929
    Fax: 516-791-1022   800-397-7923
Ellen@larryfox.com www.thebuttonmanswife.com
Manufacturer's representative concentrating on advertising specialties such as decals, pencils, marking, writing pens, buttons, and embroidered uniform emblems
CEO: Ellen Ingber
CEO: Larry Fox
larry@larryfox.com
Estimated Sales: $.5-1 million
Number Employees: 5-9
Markets Served:
    Food Manufacturers & Processors, Super Market Chains, Wholesale Distributors, Food Service Operators

40682 LeMire Sales
6413 Cambridge St
Minneapolis, MN 55426   952-472-3220
Broker of dairy/deli products, frozen foods, meats, private label items and seafood
President: Jerry LeMire
Treasurer: George LeMire
VP: Susan Cullen
Estimated Sales: $2.5-5 Million
Number Employees: 1-4
Square Footage: 4800
Markets Served:
    Food Manufacturers & Processors, Super Market Chains, Wholesale Distributors, Food Service Operators
Primary Brands Brokered include: Simmon's; OK Processors; Maple Leaf Farms; ConAgra Industrial; Royal Quality Foods; Honeysuckle White Deli Products
Brokered Products include:
    Dairy/Deli, Frozen Food, Meat, Meat Products, Private Label, Seafood

40683 Leblanc Foodservice Marketing
1121 Orion Ave
Metairie, LA 70005-1525   504-832-9903
    Fax: 504-832-9983
Broker of groceries, private label items, industrial ingredients, frozen foods and meat products
Owner: Andrew Leblanc
Estimated Sales: $1-2.5 Million
Number Employees: 1-4
Markets Served:
    Food Service Operators
Primary Brands Brokered include: Agrilink Foods; Chicken of the Sea; Kerry Ingredients; Papa Jim's Boneless; Golden Dipt Foodservice; Charles Dennery
Brokered Products include:
    Frozen Food, Groceries, Ingredients, Meat Products, Private Label

40684 Legion Export & Import Company
479 Washington St
New York, NY 10013-1325   212-925-4627
    Fax: 212-925-4627
Importer and exporter of flavoring extracts, food preservatives and essential oils
President: Libery Raho
Treasurer: Peter Raho
Estimated Sales: $500,000-$1 Million
Number Employees: 20-49
Square Footage: 44000

40685 Lehigh Food Sales Inc
2374 Seipstown Rd # 208
Fogelsville, PA 18051-2200   610-285-2039
    Fax: 610-285-4562 www.profruit.com
Importer of strawberries, broker of frozen foods
President: Terry Muth
tmuth@lehighfoods.com
Estimated Sales: $3-5 Million
Number Employees: 20-49
Markets Served:
    Food Manufacturers & Processors, Super Market Chains, Wholesale Distributors, Food Service Operators
Brokered Products include:
    Frozen Food

40686 Lehmann Brokerage Co
481b John R Junkin Dr
Suite: B
Natchez, MS 39120-3825   601-442-2744
    Fax: 601-442-4573
Broker of confectionery and dairy/deli products, frozen foods, groceries, meat and meat products, private label items, spices, etc. Also operates Lehmann Cash & Carry, a full line wholesaler of food and paper products.
President: Jay Lehmann
lehmanbrokerage@att.net
Estimated Sales: Less Than $500,000
Number Employees: 1-4
Square Footage: 6000
Type of Packaging: Consumer, Food Service, Private Label
Markets Served:
    Food Manufacturers & Processors, Wholesale Distributors, Food Service Operators
Brokered Products include:
    Confectionery, Frozen Food, Groceries, Ingredients, Meat, Meat Products, Seafood, Spices

40687 Lemmons Company
4300 Beltway Drive
Addison, TX 75001-3703   972-233-5028
    Fax: 972-386-7000 lemmons@lemmonsco.com
Broker of dairy/deli products, frozen foods, groceries, meat, meat products, spices and poultry
President: Larry Lemmons
Estimated Sales: $5.1-7.1 Million
Number Employees: 21-30
Square Footage: 34000
Type of Packaging: Food Service
Markets Served:
    Wholesale Distributors, Food Service Operators
Primary Brands Brokered include: Tyson Foods; Mrs. Smith; Schawn's Foodservice; Imperial Sugar; Pillsbury Foods; South Pride Catfish Company
Brokered Products include:
    Dairy/Deli, Frozen Food, Groceries, Meat, Seafood, Spices, Poultry

40688 Len Miller & Associates
100 Stone Hill Rd
Springfield, NJ 07081-2115   973-379-2121
    Fax: 973-564-5069
Manufacturers' representative for food service and tabletop supplies including glassware, china and flatware
VP: Michael Friedman
Number Employees: 1-4
Markets Served:
    Wholesale Distributors
Primary Brands Brokered include: Cardinal International; Royal Doulton; Walco Flatware; Forbes Ind.; Hollowick
Brokered Products include:
    General Merchandise, Foodservice & Tabletop Supplies

40689 Leonard H Sisitzky Sales Inc
244 W Cummings Park
Woburn, MA 01801-6346   781-935-1601
    Fax: 781-935-6378
Import broker of confectionery products, groceries, private label items and general merchandise
Owner: Leonard H Sisitzky
VP: Leonard Sisitzky
Marketing Director: Diane Giangrande
Sales Director: Greg Pugh
lhsinc@sisitzkysales.com
Estimated Sales: $5-10 Million
Number Employees: 10-19
Square Footage: 7200
Markets Served:
    Food Manufacturers & Processors, Super Market Chains, Wholesale Distributors, Food Service Operators
Primary Brands Brokered include: R.M. Palmer Company; Necco; Foreing Candy Company; The Tops Company; Storck USA; Lindt Sprungli; Guxlian USA
Brokered Products include:
    Confectionery, General Merchandise, Groceries, Imports, Meat Products, Private Label

40690 Leopold & Diner Associates
5775 E Stapleton Dr N
Ste 200
Denver, CO 80216-6417   303-333-9222
    Fax: 303-399-2645
Broker of general merchandise and groceries
President: Ed Diner
Secretary: J Diner
Estimated Sales: $2.5-5 Million
Number Employees: 2
Brokered Products include:
    General Merchandise, Groceries

40691 Lever Associates
440 Overlook Drive
Monroe, CT 06468   203-261-2202
    Fax: 203-261-2202
Broker of dairy/deli products, frozen foods, groceries, meats, private label items, etc
President: Dick Lever
CFO: J Lever
Estimated Sales: $5-10 Million
Number Employees: 6
Type of Packaging: Consumer, Food Service, Private Label, Bulk
Markets Served:
    Food Manufacturers & Processors, Wholesale Distributors, Food Service Operators
Brokered Products include:
    Dairy/Deli, Frozen Food, Groceries, Imports, Meat, Meat Products, Private Label, Seafood, Spices

40692 Lewin Group
4801 W Peterson Ave # 200
Chicago, IL 60646-5725   773-202-1300
    Fax: 773-472-1435
President: Benjamin Lewin
Estimated Sales: $3-5 Million
Number Employees: 20-49

40693 Lifewise Ingredients
3540 N 126 St
Suite D
Brookfield, IL 53005   262-788-9141
    Fax: 262-788-9143 info@lifewise1.com
    www.lifewise1.com
Processor and exporter of healthy food ingredients including monosodium glutamate replacements, flavor enhancers, and flavor maskers
Founder: Richard Share
Sales Director: Richard Share
Contact: Dean Antczak
dantczak@lifewise1.com
Lab Manager: Millie Galey
General Manager: Carol Bender
Estimated Sales: Below $5 Million
Number Employees: 5-9
Square Footage: 14000
Markets Served:
    Food Manufacturers & Processors
Primary Brands Brokered include: Ingredients
Brokered Products include:
    Ingredients

40694 Lilburn Gulf
127 Arcado Rd SW
Lilburn, GA 30047-2904   770-381-7997
    Fax: 770-381-9428 www.gulfoil.com
Broker of dairy/deli products, seafood, frozen foods, meat and meat products
Owner: Parag Patel
Partner: D Hudalla
Partner: Rick Franklin
Estimated Sales: $500,000-$1 Million
Number Employees: 1-4
Markets Served:
    Food Manufacturers & Processors, Wholesale Distributors, Food Service Operators

Primary Brands Brokered include: Ocean Spray; Mrs. Smith's Foodservice; Ken's Foods; David's Cookies; Perdue Farms; Reily Foods
Brokered Products include:
Dairy/Deli, Frozen Food, Meat, Meat Products, Seafood

40695 Linwood-Welch Marketing
8014 Santa Fe Dr
Overland Park, KS 66204-3624   913-385-3000
Fax: 913-385-5333   888-291-6417
welchfood@aol.com www.linwoodwelch.com
Broker of industrial ingredients, groceries, meat and meat products, private label items, frozen foods, etc
President: Jeffrey Welch
welchfood@aol.com
Estimated Sales: $10-20 Million
Number Employees: 10-19
Type of Packaging: Consumer, Food Service, Private Label, Bulk
Markets Served:
Food Manufacturers & Processors, Wholesale Distributors, Food Service Operators
Primary Brands Brokered include: Linwood Farms
Brokered Products include:
Dairy/Deli, Frozen Food, Groceries, Imports, Ingredients, Meat, Meat Products, Private Label

40696 Lisberg-Voegeli Hanson
N50w13740 Overview Drive
Menomonee Falls, WI 53051-7062   262-781-3450
Fax: 262-781-1073 hlvfb@execpc.com
Broker of dairy/deli products, frozen foods, general merchandise, meat and meat products, groceries, etc.
President: Ron Hanson
CEO: Ken Voegeli
CFO: Richard Lisberg
Number Employees: 20-49
Markets Served:
Food Manufacturers & Processors, Super Market Chains, Wholesale Distributors, Food Service Operators
Primary Brands Brokered include: McCain Citrus
Brokered Products include:
Dairy/Deli, Frozen Food, General Merchandise, Groceries, Meat, Meat Products, Private Label, Produce

40697 Littler Brokerage Co Inc
1399 Clairmont Rd
Decatur, GA 30033-5311   404-633-1231
Fax: 404-633-2300
Broker of dairy/deli products, frozen foods, seafood, industrial ingredients, general merchandise, meat products, etc.
President: Janet Littler
VP: Tom Littler
Number Employees: 5-9
Markets Served:
Food Manufacturers & Processors, Wholesale Distributors, Food Service Operators
Brokered Products include:
Dairy/Deli, Frozen Food, General Merchandise, Groceries, Ingredients, Meat Products, Private Label, Seafood

40698 Littman & Associates
6547 Cliff Ridge Lane
Cincinnati, OH 45213-1049   513-351-8806
Import and export broker of meat and meat products, seafood and private label items
President: M Littman
Number Employees: 5-9
Markets Served:
Food Manufacturers & Processors, Super Market Chains, Wholesale Distributors, Food Service Operators
Brokered Products include:
Exports, Imports, Meat, Meat Products, Private Label, Seafood

40699 Lloyd A Gray Co Inc
5132 Shawland Rd
Jacksonville, FL 32254-1651   904-786-2080
Fax: 904-786-1007 www.lagwarehouse.biz
Broker of general merchandise and groceries, with a warehouse providing dry storage
President/Owner: Tom Watkins
info@lagwarehouse.biz
Estimated Sales: $500,000-$1 million
Number Employees: 5-9
Square Footage: 100000
Other Locations:
Dry: 22,000 Sq Ft, Cool: 30,000 SF
Jacksonville, FL Dry: 22,000 Sq Ft, Cool: 30,000 SF
Markets Served:
Super Market Chains, Wholesale Distributors, Food Service Operators
Brokered Products include:
General Merchandise, Groceries

40700 Lloyd Hollander Company
7260 Washington Avenue S
Minneapolis, MN 55444   952-829-5500
Fax: 952-829-9664
Manufacturers' representative for food service equipment and supplies
President: Tim Prener
Number Employees: 1-4
Markets Served:
Wholesale Distributors
Brokered Products include:
General Merchandise, Foodservice Equipment & Supplies

40701 Loar & Young Inc
1603 Oregon Pike
Lancaster, PA 17601-4335   717-293-8055
Fax: 717-293-8960   800-327-0490
Broker of industrial ingredients, general merchandise and private label/generic products; serving all markets
President: David Young
david@loar-young.com
VP: Don Siglin
VP: Eva Young
Office Manager: Robyn Powers
Sales Representative: Nikol Parmer
Estimated Sales: $1-2.5 Million
Number Employees: 5-9
Markets Served:
Food Manufacturers & Processors, Super Market Chains, Wholesale Distributors, Food Service Operators
Primary Brands Brokered include: Good Food, Inc.; Dutch Gold Honey, Inc.; Tree Top, Inc./Guernsey Bel Industrial Div.; Lawrence Foods, Inc.; QA Products; Quality Ingredients
Brokered Products include:
Ingredients, Private Label, Spices

40702 Lobel Food Brokers
15 Warehouse Row
Albany, NY 12205-5744   518-453-1744
Fax: 518-438-6208   800-456-6264
Broker of dairy/deli products, frozen foods, groceries and private label items
Principle: Charlie Carroll
charlie@lobels.com
Estimated Sales: $230
Number Employees: 3
Parent Co: Lobel Food Brokers
Markets Served:
Super Market Chains, Wholesale Distributors, Food Service Operators
Brokered Products include:
Dairy/Deli, Frozen Food, Groceries, Private Label

40703 Lomac & May Associates
17 Walker Way
Albany, NY 12205-4945   518-452-7041
Fax: 518-452-2826
Broker of confectionery and deli foods, frozen foods, perishables, meat, seafood, etc.; serving all markets
Owner: Robert Mc Dermott
CEO: Bob McDermott
Director Sales East: Maryellen Arsenault
Contact: Caren Braiman
braimanc@lomacassociates.com
Estimated Sales: $10-20 Million
Number Employees: 7
Other Locations:
Lomac & May Associates
Syracuse, NY
Lomac & May Associates
Buffalo, NY Lomac & May Associates Buffalo
Markets Served:
Food Manufacturers & Processors, Super Market Chains, Wholesale Distributors, Food Service Operators
Primary Brands Brokered include: Chloe Foods; Give & Go; Conroy Foods; Hanover Foods; Hansel'n Gretel; Par-Way Tryson Company; Sun Rich Fruit; Rich's Foods; Phillips Seafood; Tribe Rite Foods
Brokered Products include:
Confectionery, Dairy/Deli, Frozen Food, Ingredients, Meat Products, Private Label, Produce, Seafood

40704 Loman Brown
PO Box 510
Richfield, OH 44210   330-659-9391
Fax: 330-659-4478 inquiries@lomanbrown.com
www.lomanbrown.com
Broker of industrial ingredients
President: Loman Brown
Office Manager: Mardie Motz
Marketing Director: Laura Hunt
Sales Associate: Shad Gregg
Estimated Sales: $15-20 Million
Number Employees: 5
Square Footage: 1200
Parent Co: Midwest Ingredients
Type of Packaging: Bulk
Markets Served:
Food Manufacturers & Processors, Super Market Chains, Wholesale Distributors, Food Service Operators
Brokered Products include:
Frozen Food, Ingredients, Spices

40705 Long & Littleton
3835 Presidential Pkwy Ste 140
Atlanta, GA 30340   770-986-4166
Fax: 770-986-4167
Manufacturers' representative for food service equipment
President: William Long
VP: Michael Littleton
Estimated Sales: $500,000-$1 Million
Number Employees: 5-9
Markets Served:
Wholesale Distributors
Primary Brands Brokered include: Wells Manufacturing; Bloomfield; Dito Dean; World Dryer; Wittco Mfg.; Fleetwood
Brokered Products include:
General Merchandise, Foodservice Equipment

40706 Loretta Foods
4090 Ridgeway Drive Unit #14
Mississauga, ON L5L 5X5
Canada   905-820-1515
Fax: 905-820-1818
Import and export broker of general merchandise, groceries, private label/generic items, seafood and spices
President: John Penny
General Manager: J Pannozzo
Number Employees: 75
Parent Co: Loretta Foods
Markets Served:
Food Manufacturers & Processors, Food Service Operators
Primary Brands Brokered include: Aliments Orca Foods; Les Ventes Mike David Ltee; Bruce Dobson Sales; In Zone Brands; Norshore Sales; Boakes & Associates
Brokered Products include:
Exports, General Merchandise, Groceries, Imports, Private Label, Seafood, Spices

40707 Lorey & Lorey
PO Box 30719
Tampa, FL 33630-3719   813-908-6186
Fax: 704-442-1270   800-849-8020
Broker of dairy/deli products, canned goods, frozen foods, industrial ingredients, private label items, meat and meat products, seafood, etc.
President: Jeff Lorey
Vice President: Beth Lorey
Estimated Sales: $5-10 Million
Number Employees: 13
Square Footage: 4800
Type of Packaging: Food Service
Markets Served:
Food Manufacturers & Processors, Super Market Chains, Wholesale Distributors, Food Service Operators
Primary Brands Brokered include: Smithfield, Perdue, Frionor, Barilla, Veryfine
Brokered Products include:
Confectionery, Dairy/Deli, Frozen Food, General Merchandise, Ingredients, Meat, Meat Products, Private Label, Seafood

Food Brokers / A-Z

40708 Los Angeles Chemical Company
4545 Ardine St
South Gate, CA 90280   323-562-9500
                          Fax: 323-773-0909
Broker of industrial ingredients
President: David Miller
VP: Ron Espalin
Estimated Sales: $40-50 Million
Number Employees: 100-249
Square Footage: 15000
Markets Served:
   Food Manufacturers & Processors
Brokered Products include:
   Ingredients

40709 Lotto International
PO Box 4447
McAllen, TX 78502-4447   956-682-0333
          Fax: 956-631-1131 888-682-0333
Import and export broker of fresh produce including mangos, peaches, grapes, cantaloupes, nectarines, limes, apples, pears, plums, onions, celery and tomatoes
President: Rafael Chacra
Estimated Sales: $300,000-500,000
Number Employees: 1-4
Square Footage: 220000
Markets Served:
   Wholesale Distributors
Primary Brands Brokered include: Lotto International
Brokered Products include:
   Exports, Imports, Produce, Tomatoes, Mangos, Celery, Plums, etc.

40710 Louis F. Leeper Company/Cleveland
5145 Brecksville Rd
Building 201
Richfield, OH 44286-9163   330-523-1100
   Fax: 330-523-1101 www.leepercompanies.com
Broker of confectionery and dairy/deli products, frozen foods, general merchandise, groceries, seafood, spices, produce, meats, etc. Serving northeast Ohio, western Pennsylvania and West Virginia
Prin: Louis Leeper
lleeper@asmnet.com
Finance: Maria Latina
VP: James Kenzie
Director Marketing: Tom Craig
Number Employees: 4
Square Footage: 14600
Markets Served:
   Super Market Chains, Wholesale Distributors
Primary Brands Brokered include: Clorox; Ore-Ida; Motts; Glad; Kraft Foods; Welch's
Brokered Products include:
   Confectionery, Dairy/Deli, Frozen Food, Groceries, Health Food, Meat, Meat Products, Produce, Beauty Aids

40711 Lowe & Associates
1722 Lampman Drive
Billings, MT 59102-7465   406-655-4911
                           Fax: 406-656-8088
Broker of spices, seafood, produce, private label items, meat, meat products, etc.
President Food Service: J Lowe
VP Food Service: R Houston
Bakery Specialist: Clayton Kuntz
Estimated Sales: $10-20 Million
Number Employees: 4
Square Footage: 36000
Markets Served:
   Food Manufacturers & Processors, Wholesale Distributors, Food Service Operators
Primary Brands Brokered include: Tyson; J.R. Simplot; Stouffer's; Reynolds; Ocean Spray; Bunge
Brokered Products include:
   Confectionery, Dairy/Deli, Frozen Food, Meat, Meat Products, Private Label, Produce, Seafood, Spices

40712 Ludwig Mueller Co Inc
366 N Broadway # 204
Jericho, NY 11753-2000   516-394-8181
                          Fax: 516-394-8190
Importer and exporter of spices, seeds, herbs, tomato powder, oleoresins, dried fruits and nuts
President: Jalina Beck
jbeck@houlihanlawrence.com
President: Gilbert Oliver
Estimated Sales: $300,000-500,000
Number Employees: 10-19
Square Footage: 12000
Type of Packaging: Bulk
Markets Served:
   Food Manufacturers & Processors, Wholesale Distributors

40713 Luke Soules Southwest
PO Box 773657
Houston, TX 77215-3657   713-435-3000
                          Fax: 713-435-3050
Import broker of confectionery and dairy/deli items, groceries, frozen foods, private label products, etc.
President: G Trippie
Executive VP: K Falkner
Estimated Sales: $5-10 Million
Number Employees: 100-249
Markets Served:
   Food Manufacturers & Processors, Super Market Chains, Wholesale Distributors, Food Service Operators
Brokered Products include:
   Confectionery, Dairy/Deli, Frozen Food, General Merchandise, Groceries, Imports, Meat, Meat Products, Private Label, Seafood

40714 Lund-Iorio Inc
29122 Rancho Viejo Rd # 115
Suite 115
San Juan Cpstrno, CA 92675-1020 949-443-4855
      Fax: 949-443-4856 sales@lund-iorio.com
                          www.lund-iorio.com
Manufacturers' representative for food service equipment
Owner: Greg Iorio
sales@lund-iorio.com
Inside Sales Manager: Debbie Weiland
Estimated Sales: $10-20 Million
Number Employees: 10-19
Square Footage: 4000
Markets Served:
   Wholesale Distributors
Primary Brands Brokered include: Barmaid; Beverage-Air; Lincoln Foodservice Products; Star Manufacturing; Sun Coast Industries; Pronto Products
Brokered Products include:
   General Merchandise, Foodservice Equipment

40715 (HQ)Luxco Inc
5050 Kemper Ave
St Louis, MO 63139-1106   314-772-2626
         Fax: 314-772-6021 contactus@luxco.com
                           www.luxco.com
Manufacturer, bottler, importer and exporter of quality destilled spirits and wines.
Chairman/CEO: Donn Lux
President/COO: David Bratcher
VP Finance/CFO: Steve Soucy
Chief Marketing Officer: Steve Einig
Director, Corporate R&D: John Rempe
EVP Sales: Dan Streepy
Contact: Tina Aebi
t.aebi@luxco.com
Warehouse Manager: Douglas Finkeldey
Estimated Sales: $23.8 Million
Number Employees: 1-4
Square Footage: 200000
Type of Packaging: Private Label
Primary Brands Brokered include: Arrow, Barbella, Caffe Lolita, El Mayor, Everclear, Ezra Brooks, Juarez, Pearl, Purple Passion, Rebel Yell, Saint Brendan's, Salvadore's, Salvadore's 100%, Tvarscki, Yago Sant'Gria
Brokered Products include:
   Alcoholic Beverages, Private Label

40716 M Arkans & Son
1001 Easton Road
Apt 406
Willow Grove, PA 19090-2041   215-947-2626
                              Fax: 215-947-5899
Broker of groceries and private label items
President: Florence Arkans
Consultant: Marvin Arkans
Sales: Steven Arkans
Estimated Sales: Less than $500,000
Number Employees: 3
Type of Packaging: Private Label, Bulk
Markets Served:
   Food Manufacturers & Processors, Super Market Chains

40717 M Fellinger Co
1315 W College Ave # 203
Suite 203
State College, PA 16801-2776   814-234-1400
                               Fax: 814-867-0723
Broker of groceries, spaghetti sauce
Owner: Mike Fellinger
Estimated Sales: A
Number Employees: 10-19
Type of Packaging: Consumer, Food Service
Markets Served:
   Super Market Chains, Food Service Operators
Brokered Products include:
   Groceries, Imports, Meat

40718 M K Food Svc Equipment Inc
4700 Pine St
Philadelphia, PA 19143-1810   215-471-4700
          Fax: 215-471-8916   800-654-0505
Manufacturers' representative for food service equipment
President: Mark Kurm
markkurm@mkfoodservice.com
Number Employees: 5-9
Markets Served:
   Wholesale Distributors
Primary Brands Brokered include: American Metalcraft; Cooper; Cambro; Mars Air Doors; Wilbur Curtis; Corning
Brokered Products include:
   General Merchandise, Foodservice Equipment

40719 M&W Associates
20 Frederick Dr
Saratoga Springs, NY 12866-5933 518-587-3486
          Fax: 716-675-0390 sho4speed@aol.com
Manufacturers' representative for food service equipment and supplies
Owner: Tom Wishart
Contact: Mary Wishart
mary.wishart@lcecorp.com
Estimated Sales: Less than $500,000
Number Employees: 1-4
Markets Served:
   Wholesale Distributors
Primary Brands Brokered include: Blodgett; J.H. Henkles; Bianco Brothers; Thermohauser; Chicago Faucet; Star Manufacturing Company
Brokered Products include:
   General Merchandise, Foodservice Equipment & Supplies

40720 M. Pencar Associates
13775 Geranium Avenue
Flushing, NY 11355-4130   718-939-7031
         Fax: 718-359-5782 800-788-5781
Broker of general merchandise including light bulbs and counterfeit money detectors; serving food processors and supermarket chains
President: Mark Pencar
Markets Served:
   Food Manufacturers & Processors, Super Market Chains
Primary Brands Brokered include: Chromalux; Lumichrome; Cash Scan & Counterfighter
Brokered Products include:
   General Merchandise, Counterfeit Money Detectors, Etc.

40721 M. Soffer Company
115 Tulip Rd
Southampton, PA 18966   215-322-8880
                         Fax: 215-322-8881
Broker of dairy/deli and private label items, frozen and canned foods, industrial ingredients, seafood, spices and groceries
President: Stanley Soffer
Estimated Sales: $1-2.5 Million
Number Employees: 1-4
Markets Served:
   Food Manufacturers & Processors, Super Market Chains, Wholesale Distributors, Food Service Operators
Brokered Products include:
   Dairy/Deli, Frozen Food, Groceries, Private Label, Seafood, Spices

40722 M.E. Dilanian Company
PO Box 920359
Needham, MA 02492-0004   781-449-4633
                          Fax: 781-449-3960
Broker and wholesaler/distributor of dairy/deli and confectionery products, frozen food, groceries and private label items

Food Brokers / A-Z

President: D Dilanian
Chairman: M Dilanian
Estimated Sales: $5-10 Million
Number Employees: 5-9
Markets Served:
  Super Market Chains, Wholesale Distributors, Food Service Operators
Brokered Products include:
  Confectionery, Dairy/Deli, Frozen Food, Groceries, Meat, Meat Products, Private Label

40723 M.E. Strauss Brokerage Company
5695 Ashbriar Ave
Memphis, TN 38120   901-761-1920
Fax: 901-761-1923 straussb@accessus.net
Import and export broker of poultry, meat, meat products and seafood; serving all markets
President: A Ronald Wilk
Exporter: Marla Wilk
Estimated Sales: $500,000-$1 Million
Number Employees: 1-4
Square Footage: 1200
Markets Served:
  Food Manufacturers & Processors, Super Market Chains, Wholesale Distributors, Food Service Operators
Brokered Products include:
  Exports, Imports, Meat, Meat Products, Seafood, Poultry

40724 M.J. Borelli & Company
2200 Powell St Ste 850
Emeryville, CA 94608   510-420-8700
Fax: 510-428-9186
Import and export broker of meat products including beef, pork and poultry
President: Michael Conway
Controller: John Brusseau
VP: Liz Brusseau
Estimated Sales: $2.5-5 Million
Number Employees: 5-9
Markets Served:
  Wholesale Distributors
Brokered Products include:
  Exports, Imports, Meat Products

40725 MAV Sales Co
176 Nia Frontier Term # 5
Buffalo, NY 14206-3078   716-822-2711
Fax: 716-822-2759
Import broker of confectionery and dairy/deli products, frozen foods, general merchandise, groceries and private label items
Owner: Lance Volitze
mavsales1@aol.com
VP: D Veolitze
Estimated Sales: $2.5-5 Million
Number Employees: 1-4
Markets Served:
  Food Manufacturers & Processors, Super Market Chains, Wholesale Distributors, Food Service Operators
Brokered Products include:
  Confectionery, Dairy/Deli, Frozen Food, General Merchandise, Groceries, Imports, Private Label

40726 MLE Marketing
2651 Coolidge Road
East Lansing, MI 48823-6360   734-428-8352
Fax: 734-428-7387
Broker of beef, lamb and pork
President: Thomas Reed
Number Employees: 20-49
Parent Co: Southern States Cooperative
Brokered Products include:
  Meat

40727 MLG Enterprises Ltd.
PO Box 52568
Mississauga, ON L5J 4S6
Canada   905-696-6947
Fax: 905-696-6955
office-mgr@mlgfoodingredients.com
www.mlgfoodingredients.com
Processor and distributor of specialty food ingredients
President: Terry McCann
Sales Manager: Patrick McCann
Estimated Sales: $10 Million
Number Employees: 10
Square Footage: 44000
Type of Packaging: Food Service, Private Label, Bulk

Brokered Products include:
  Health Food, Imports, Ingredients

40728 Machine Brokers
6070 Bridle Path Lane
Parker, CO 80134-5222   610-459-4697
Fax: 610-459-3751

40729 Maddan & Co Inc
601 Montgomery St # 655
San Francisco, CA 94111-2662   415-421-5777
Fax: 415-421-2031 maddancomp@aol.com
www.maddanco.com
Broker of groceries, private label items and produce
President: Melissa Cook
mcook@maddanco.com
VP: Lynn Maddan
VP Sales: Michael Maddan Jr
Operations: Patricia Maddan
Estimated Sales: $10-20 Million
Number Employees: 10-19
Markets Served:
  Super Market Chains, Wholesale Distributors
Brokered Products include:
  Groceries, Private Label, Produce

40730 Madden & Assoc
1 Billings Rd # 3
Suite 3
Quincy, MA 02171-2456   617-328-5656
info@mgs49.com
Broker of general merchandise, meats, spices, specialty foods, private label items, etc.
President: Ken Madden
krm@madden-associates.com
Financial Manager: Diane Frohnapfel
Principal/Business Dev Manager: Brian Riccio
Estimated Sales: D
Number Employees: 5-9
Markets Served:
  Food Service Operators
Primary Brands Brokered include: Victoria Packaging; Magla Products; Catalina Industries; Zebra Pen; OWD, Inc.; Brimms
Brokered Products include:
  Frozen Food, General Merchandise, Health Food, Imports, Meat, Meat Products, Private Label, Spices, Specialty Foods

40731 Magic Valley Truck Brokers Inc
2906 S Featherly Way
Boise, ID 83709-2985   208-375-5677
Fax: 208-377-0956 800-635-3053
wes@magicvalleytruckbrokers.com
www.magicvalleytruckbrokers.com
Transportation broker providing reefer, vans and flatbed loads for fresh produce and frozen foods, and other products
Owner: Wes Blazer
wes@magicvalleytruckbrokers.com
Vice President: Debbie Blaser
Number Employees: 5-9
Markets Served:
  Food Manufacturers & Processors, Super Market Chains, Wholesale Distributors, Food Service Operators
Brokered Products include:
  Dairy/Deli, Frozen Food, General Merchandise, Groceries, Meat, Produce

40732 Main Street Marketing
2317 Main St
Tucker, GA 30084-4471   770-491-1122
Fax: 770-491-3005
www.mainstreet-naturalsales.com
Broker of confectionery and dairy/deli products, frozen foods, general merchandise, groceries, spices, etc.
President: R Mayer
CEO: L Mayer
VP: D Mayer
Estimated Sales: $5-10 Million
Number Employees: 5-9
Markets Served:
  Super Market Chains, Wholesale Distributors, Food Service Operators
Brokered Products include:
  Confectionery, Dairy/Deli, Frozen Food, General Merchandise, Groceries, Health Food, Meat, Meat Products, Private Label, Produce, Spices, Specialty Foods

40733 Maine Sea Harvest
PO Box 717
Newcastle, ME 04553-0717   207-563-2340
Fax: 207-563-2345
President: Mary Nagel

40734 Maine Sea International
PO Box 1350
Portland, ME 04104-1350   207-780-0149
Fax: 407-886-1516

40735 Major Marketing Service
44 West Main
Spokane, WA 99201   509-458-2667
www.mainmarket.coop
Import and export broker of confectionery and dairy/deli products, frozen foods, general merchandise, groceries, etc.
President: Michael Wallach
VP: George Scott
Estimated Sales: $10-20 Million
Number Employees: 10-19
Square Footage: 18000
Markets Served:
  Food Manufacturers & Processors, Super Market Chains, Wholesale Distributors, Food Service Operators
Primary Brands Brokered include: Lipton Company; ADM; Amalgumated Sugar; Huish Detergents; Ragu; CI Seafoods
Brokered Products include:
  Confectionery, Dairy/Deli, Exports, Frozen Food, General Merchandise, Groceries, Imports, Meat, Meat Products, Private Label, Produce, Seafood, Spices

40736 Mako Services
4297 Buford Dr
Suite 2A
Buford, GA 30518-3400   770-932-3292
Fax: 770-932-3290
Full line seafood, meats
Owner: Joe Connor
Estimated Sales: $10-20 Million
Number Employees: 10-19

40737 Maloney Veitch Associates
PO Box 5909
Clearwater, FL 33758-5909   727-442-3038
Fax: 727-447-4973 800-886-3038
Manufacturers' representative for food service equipment and supplies
President: Tom Maloney
Number Employees: 5-9
Markets Served:
  Super Market Chains, Wholesale Distributors
Primary Brands Brokered include: Cambro; Duke; Holman; In-Sink-Erator; Market Forge; Polar Ware; Drackett Professionals
Brokered Products include:
  General Merchandise, Foodservice Equipment & Supplies

40738 Mancini & Groesbeck
164 E 3900 S
Salt Lake City, UT 84107-1529   801-266-4453
Fax: 801-265-9847
Broker of confectionery and dairy/deli products, frozen foods, general merchandise, groceries, etc.
Contact: Jay Agoado
agoado@mancini-slc.com
Estimated Sales: $22 Million
Number Employees: 145
Parent Co: Mancini & Groesbeck
Markets Served:
  Super Market Chains, Wholesale Distributors, Food Service Operators
Brokered Products include:
  Confectionery, Dairy/Deli, Frozen Food, General Merchandise, Groceries, Meat Products, Private Label

40739 Mancini Packing Co
3500 Mancini Pl
Zolfo Springs, FL 33890-4710   863-735-2000
Fax: 863-735-1172 800-741-1778
rmancini@mancinifoods.com
www.mancinifoods.com
Peppers and olive oil
Chairman/President: Frank Mancini
fmancini@mancinifoods.com
VP: Alan Mancini
Estimated Sales: $11 Million
Number Employees: 50-99

Food Brokers / A-Z

Type of Packaging: Consumer, Food Service, Private Label, Bulk
Brokered Products include:
General Merchandise, Groceries, Ingredients

40740 Mancini Sales & Marketing
2110 Overland Ave # 104a
Billings, MT 59102-6440   406-652-5581
     Fax: 406-652-4989   www.mancini-slc.com
Broker of dry grocery products, meat and meat products, pet food, frozen foods, etc.
Manager: Monte Waite
mwaite@mgimontana.com
VP: P Groesbeck
Sales Manager: M Hofferber
Estimated Sales: $10-20 Million
Number Employees: 1-4
Square Footage: 18000
Markets Served:
Super Market Chains, Wholesale Distributors, Food Service Operators
Primary Brands Brokered include: Borden; Nestle Frozen/Refrigerated; Heinz USA; Quaker Diversified; American Home Foods; First Brands
Brokered Products include:
Confectionery, Dairy/Deli, Frozen Food, General Merchandise, Groceries, Meat, Meat Products, Private Label, Spices

40741 Manuel's Mexican-American Fine Foods
2007 S 300 W
Salt Lake City, UT 84115-1808   801-484-1431
     Fax: 801-484-1440   800-748-5072
Tortilla chips, taco shells, corn tortilla, tostada shells and pre-cut tortillas
President: Orlando Torres
VP: Mike Torres
VP/Sales Exec: Paul Torres
Estimated Sales: Below $5 Million
Number Employees: 40
Type of Packaging: Consumer, Food Service, Private Label, Bulk
Markets Served:
Food Manufacturers & Processors, Super Market Chains, Wholesale Distributors, Food Service Operators
Brokered Products include:
Private Label

40742 Manzo Food Brokers
13290 N.W. 25 Street
Miami, FL 33182-1509   305-406-2747
     Fax: 305-406-2630 sales@manzofood.com
               www.manzofood.com
Import broker of dairy/deli products, frozen foods, general merchandise, groceries, meat products, produce, etc.
Founder: Rino Manzo
VP Sales: Sergio Boni
Office Manager: Alice Barry
Estimated Sales: $5-10 Million
Number Employees: 5
Markets Served:
Food Manufacturers & Processors, Super Market Chains, Wholesale Distributors, Food Service Operators
Brokered Products include:
Dairy/Deli, Frozen Food, General Merchandise, Groceries, Imports, Ingredients, Meat Products, Private Label, Produce, Spices

40743 Marathon Marketing
314 Roma Jean Parkway
Streamwood, IL 60107-2933   630-736-0703
     Fax: 630-736-9661
Broker of specialty/natural foods, confectionery and dairy/deli products, groceries, frozen foods and private label items
President: Larry Lavaty
VP Sales: Mike Orlando
Estimated Sales: $5-10 Million
Number Employees: 5-9
Square Footage: 9600
Primary Brands Brokered include: Hain Food Group; Red Oval Farms; Celestial Seasonings; Auburn Farms; Chambord; St. Dalfour
Brokered Products include:
Confectionery, Dairy/Deli, Frozen Food, Groceries, Private Label, Specialty/Natural Foods

40744 Marbran USA
200 S 10th St Ste 1104
McAllen, TX 78501   956-630-2941
     Fax: 956-984-0487   www.marbran.com
Import and export broker of frozen foods, fruits and vegetables
President: Danilo Lyons
Contact: Alicia Cardenas
acardenas@marbran.com.mx
Estimated Sales: $20-50 Million
Number Employees: 10-19
Markets Served:
Food Manufacturers & Processors, Super Market Chains, Wholesale Distributors, Food Service Operators
Brokered Products include:
Frozen Food, Produce

40745 Marchetti Co
3091 Mayfield Rd # 310
Suite No. 310
Cleveland, OH 44118-1732   216-321-4162
     Fax: 216-321-1946 www.scopertaimporting.com
Import broker of European wine
President: Kathleen Flynn
kathy@tmarchettico.com
CEO: Bridget Assing
Vice President of Sales: Kathleen Flynn
Business Development and marketing: Tim Hallet
Marketing & Direct Import Management: Sue Bauman
Sales: Justin Marchetti
Operations Manager: Bridget Assing Marok
Number Employees: 5-9
Type of Packaging: Private Label
Markets Served:
Wholesale Distributors
Brokered Products include:
Alcoholic Beverages, Imports, Private Label, European, Japanese & American Wines

40746 Marino Marketing Group
12 Baer Cir
East Haven, CT 06512-4166   203-469-7196
                 Fax: 203-469-7196
Import and export broker of dairy/deli items, frozen foods, general merchandise, groceries, private label items, baked goods, etc.
Owner: Dave Marino
frank.marinogroup@marinogrp.com
CEO: Robert Testa
CFO: Sam Schlinder
Estimated Sales: $1-3 Million
Number Employees: 1-4
Square Footage: 8000
Markets Served:
Food Manufacturers & Processors, Super Market Chains, Wholesale Distributors, Food Service Operators
Primary Brands Brokered include: Paramount; Golden Glow; Pechter's; Cartier Distillers; Meyers; Neumans
Brokered Products include:
Confectionery, Dairy/Deli, Exports, Frozen Food, General Merchandise, Groceries, Imports, Private Label, Spices, Baked Goods, etc.

40747 Marjo & Associates
15956 Alameda Dr
Bowie, MD 20716-1332   301-249-1515
     Fax: 301-390-9195
Broker of frozen food, dairy/deli products, seafood, meat and meat products
Owner: Marjorie Ligelis
VP Administration: Mary Maulk
Retail Supervisor: Chery Golden
Estimated Sales: $5-10 Million
Number Employees: 1-4
Square Footage: 17000
Markets Served:
Food Manufacturers & Processors, Super Market Chains, Wholesale Distributors, Food Service Operators
Primary Brands Brokered include: Mrs. D's Gourmet Cookies; D.H.B. Brand Cheese; Rapello of California; Rite Foods; V.W. Joyner Red Eye Hams; Vega Products, Inc.
Brokered Products include:
Dairy/Deli, Frozen Food, Meat, Meat Products, Seafood

40748 Mark's International Seafood Brokers
PO Box 602
Fairhaven, MA 02719-0602   508-992-2115
     Fax: 508-991-2072
President: Mark Wright
Estimated Sales: $10-20 Million
Number Employees: 20-49

40749 Market Pro International
5320 E Paradise Lane
Scottsdale, AZ 85254-1132   602-482-3144
     Fax: 602-493-9739   mktproint@aol.com
Import, export and domestic broker of snacks, pet foods, beverages, pastas, meats, mexican food products, private label, seasonings, etc.
President: A Colon
Type of Packaging: Consumer, Food Service, Private Label, Bulk
Markets Served:
Super Market Chains, Food Service Operators
Brokered Products include:
Confectionery, Exports, Frozen Food, Groceries, Imports, Ingredients, Meat, Private Label, Seafood, Spices, Pasta, Snack Foods, Beverages, etc.

40750 Market Smart
5180 Cameron Street
Suite 2
Las Vegas, NV 89118-4906   702-873-6363
     Fax: 702-873-4440
Broker of confectionery and dairy/deli products, frozen foods, grocery products, meats/meat products, produce, etc.
President: Rick Wyum
CEO: William O'Connell
CFO: Diane Lloyd
Sales Manager: Danielle Farrar
Administrative Services: Lois Fletcher
Estimated Sales: $10-20 Million
Number Employees: 22
Markets Served:
Super Market Chains, Wholesale Distributors, Food Service Operators
Brokered Products include:
Confectionery, Dairy/Deli, Frozen Food, Groceries, Meat, Meat Products, Produce

40751 Market West Company
610 Garrison Street
Suite W
Lakewood, CO 80215-5882   303-233-2113
     Fax: 303-238-1336
Broker of dairy/deli and bakery products, produce, meat and meat products, frozen foods and seafood
President: B Bradley
VP: P Bradley
VP: P Cahill
Estimated Sales: $10-20 Million
Number Employees: 10-19
Square Footage: 10500
Markets Served:
Food Manufacturers & Processors, Super Market Chains, Wholesale Distributors, Food Service Operators
Primary Brands Brokered include: Jennie-o Turkey Products; Reser's Foods; Cooks Family Foods; Ruiz Mexican Foods; Dubuque Foods; Gilardi's Foods
Brokered Products include:
Dairy/Deli, Frozen Food, Meat, Meat Products, Produce, Seafood, Bakery Products

40752 Marketing Agents South
848 Centre St
Ridgeland, MS 39157   601-956-4661
              sales@masouth.com
              www.masouth.com
Manufacturers' representative for food service equipment and supplies
President: Bob Rowan
Year Founded: 1960
Square Footage: 1400
Markets Served:
Wholesale Distributors
Primary Brands Brokered include: Alto-Shaam; American Panel; CookTek; Follett; Groen; IMC/Teddy; Meiko; Metro; Power Soak; Randell; Robot Coupe; Southbend; Turbo Chef; ARC-Cardinal; E-Control Systems; T & S Brass; Mars Air Door; Terry Water Filters

Brokered Products include:
General Merchandise, Foodservice Equipment & Supplies

40753 Marketing Development Associates
2669 Myrtle Avenue
Suite 115
Long Beach, CA 90755-2744   562-492-9556
Fax: 562-492-9510   800-330-7456
mdabroad@aol.com
Manufacturers' representative for fooodservice equipment and supplies
President: Robert Broad
VP: Matthew Broad
Estimated Sales: $2.5-5 Million
Number Employees: 1-4

40754 Marketing Management Inc
4717 Fletcher Ave
Fort Worth, TX 76107-6826   817-731-4176
Fax: 817-732-5610   800-433-2004
sales@mmibrands.com   www.mmibrands.com
Retail & merchadising marketing, brand development, quality assurance, consumer research, consumer response, procurement, inventory management, category development, package design, information technology, networking and e-commercemulti media and more
President: Randy Hurr
CEO: Herb Pease Jr
VP, CFO: Donna Smith
Vice President: Ed Mieskoski
R&D: Bill Bradshaw
VP, Market Solutions: Steve Thomas
Sales: Bill Bradshaw
Public Relations: Joni Grulke
Operations: H Pease Jr
Estimated Sales: $10-20 Million
Number Employees: 50-99
Square Footage: 130000
Markets Served:
Food Manufacturers & Processors, Super Market Chains, Wholesale Distributors
Brokered Products include:
Confectionery, Dairy/Deli, Exports, Frozen Food, General Merchandise, Groceries, Health Food, Imports, Meat, Meat Products, Private Label, Produce, Seafood, Spices

40755 Marmelstein Associates
PO Box 1268
Jackson, NJ 08527-0262   732-363-5626
Fax: 732-905-6570
Broker of confectionery and deli/deli products, frozen foods, general merchandise, dariy, groceries, industrial ingredients, etc
President: S Marmelstein
VP/Secretary/Treasurer: L Marmelstein
VP: H Marmelstein
Estimated Sales: $2.5-5 Million
Number Employees: 1-4
Square Footage: 12000
Type of Packaging: Private Label
Markets Served:
Super Market Chains, Wholesale Distributors
Brokered Products include:
Dairy/Deli, Groceries, Imports, Private Label, Seafood, Spices

40756 Marshall Associates
51 Eastern Ave
Essex, MA 01929-1301   978-768-0055
Fax: 978-762-8928   800-322-9758
marshall@gis.net
Manufacturers' representative for food service equipment including dishwashers, tables, shelves, faucets and walk-in refrigerators
Owner: Carley Chicklo
carley.chicklo@gmail.com
VP: Kenneth Lanler
Estimated Sales: $2.5-5 Million
Number Employees: 1-4
Square Footage: 3600
Markets Served:
Wholesale Distributors
Primary Brands Brokered include: Amco; Advanced Tavco; Jackson Products; Caddy Corporation; T.S. Brass & Bronze; Star Manufacturing; Penn Refrigeration
Brokered Products include:
General Merchandise, Foodservice Equipment

40757 Marshall Sales Co
PO Box 495
Castle Rock, CO 80104-0495   303-660-1781
Fax: 410-749-9960
sam@marshallsalescompany.com
Broker, importer and exporter of industrial foods focusing on fruits, vegetables and ingredients, fresh and processed
Manager: Kathy Williams
VP: Paul Capucille
Marketing Director: Paul Capucille
Sales Director: Dave Krester
Office Manager: Kathy Williams
Estimated Sales: Less Than $500,000
Number Employees: 1-4
Type of Packaging: Consumer, Food Service, Private Label, Bulk
Markets Served:
Food Manufacturers & Processors
Brokered Products include:
Exports, Frozen Food, Imports, Ingredients, Private Label, Produce

40758 Martin Preferred Foods
5566 Red Bird Center Dr
Dallas, TX 75237-1931   214-442-5987
Fax: 214-442-5988   800-356-7390
www.martinpreferredfoods.com
Broker of meat, meat products and poultry
President: Kathy Mancini
Office Manager: David Pruitt
Estimated Sales: $2.5-5 Million
Number Employees: 20-49
Markets Served:
Food Manufacturers & Processors, Wholesale Distributors, Food Service Operators
Brokered Products include:
Dairy/Deli, Frozen Food, Meat, Meat Products

40759 Marty Scanlon BrokerageCo
1222 Hope Hollow Rd
Carnegie, PA 15106-3637   412-279-5322
Fax: 412-279-5327
Broker of dairy/deli products, frozen foods, groceries, meats and seafood
President: Michael Scanlon
Sales Manager: Michael Scanlon
Estimated Sales: $1-3 Million
Number Employees: 1-4
Markets Served:
Food Manufacturers & Processors, Wholesale Distributors, Food Service Operators
Brokered Products include:
Dairy/Deli, Frozen Food, Groceries, Meat, Seafood

40760 Marubeni America Corp.
375 Lexington Ave.
New York, NY 10017   212-450-0100
Fax: 212-450-0700   www.marubeniamerica.com
Marubeni exports grains, meat, sugar and other foodstuffs to Asia.
President/CEO: Fumiya Kokubu
Year Founded: 1951
Estimated Sales: $273,000
Parent Co: Marubeni Corporation

40761 Massey-Fair Industrial Southwest
1035 Nicholson Rd Ste 200
Garland, TX 75042   972-494-3330
Fax: 972-494-3344   800-282-3101
Broker of industrial ingredients
President: Randy Cimorelli
CEO: Tim Cambias
CFO: Phil Ammons
VP Sales: Don Malone
VP of Sales: Kyle Dallape
Sales Representative: Mike Lockwood
VP of Manufacturing: Ken Atkins
VP of Procurement: Michael Ahlfeld
Estimated Sales: $10-20 Million
Number Employees: 1-4
Square Footage: 6000
Parent Co: Massey Fair Industrial
Markets Served:
Food Manufacturers & Processors

40762 Master Marketing South
1400 English Street NW
Atlanta, GA 30318-5557   404-872-8135
Fax: 404-872-0471   800-678-6569
Manufacturers' representative for food service equipment
President: Jerry Hennebaul
VP/General Manager: Walt Hennebaul
Contact: Jennifer Hedlund
jenniferhedlund@wafflehouse.com
General Manager: Tyler Proud
Estimated Sales: $5-10 Million
Number Employees: 10-19
Markets Served:
Wholesale Distributors
Primary Brands Brokered include: Alto-Shaam; American Panel; Blickman; Dormont; Ember-Glo; Epco
Brokered Products include:
General Merchandise

40763 Master Marketing Sunlow, Inc.
1400 English Street NW
Atlanta, GA 30318   404-872-8135
Fax: 404-872-0471   800-678-6569
www.master-marketing.com
Broker of food service equipment including ovens, grills, refrigerators, ventilators, etc.
Contact: Jennifer Hedlund
jenniferhedlund@wafflehouse.com
Estimated Sales: $2.5-5 Million
Number Employees: 10-19
Markets Served:
Food Service Operators
Primary Brands Brokered include: American Wyatt; Imperial; Hodges Shelving
Brokered Products include:
General Merchandise, Foodservice Equipment

40764 Master Sales & Marketing
PO Bos 103
Springfield, NJ 07041   973-912-9312
Fax: 973-912-0982
Distributors of grocery products
President: Steven Shtafman
Vice President: Dotti Shtafman
Estimated Sales: $1-2.5 Million
Number Employees: 1-4
Markets Served:
Super Market Chains, Wholesale Distributors, Food Service Operators
Primary Brands Brokered include: Jel-Sert Company Fla-Vor-Ice; Daily Juice Products; U.S. Mills, Inc.; Seafare Foods; Comstock-Michigan Fruit
Brokered Products include:
Confectionery, Dairy/Deli, General Merchandise, Groceries, Health Food, Imports, Meat, Private Label, Produce, Spices

40765 Mathews Associates
2 Greenwood Road
Wilbraham, MA 01095-1628   413-596-9419
Fax: 413-596-9419
Broker of industrial ingredients, confectionery, dairy products, paper goodsand packaging
Owner: Joseph R Mathews
CEO: Rena M Matthews
Number Employees: 1-4
Type of Packaging: Food Service
Markets Served:
Food Manufacturers & Processors, Food Service Operators
Brokered Products include:
Confectionery, Dairy/Deli, Ingredients, Packaging Supplies

40766 Matrix Group Inc.
16 Yantecaw Ave
Bloomfield, NJ 07003   973-338-5638
Fax: 973-338-0164   info@m8trix.com
www.m8trix.com
Consulting to natural foods maraketplace; master broker
President: Ray Wolfson
rwolfson@m8trix.com
VP: Irene Sherman
Sales: Ray Wolfson
rwolfson@m8trix.com
Estimated Sales: $2.5-5 Million
Number Employees: 5
Number of Brands: 3-6
Type of Packaging: Consumer
Markets Served:
Super Market Chains, Wholesale Distributors
Brokered Products include:
Dairy/Deli, Frozen Food, Groceries

Food Brokers / A-Z

40767 Max Pratt Company
421 E Mulberry St
Sherman, TX 75090 903-893-7315
 Fax: 903-893-4851
Manufacturers' representative for commercial cooking equipment, dishwashers and slicers
Owner: Max Pratt
Sales Director: Gary Pratt
Estimated Sales: $1-3 Million
Number Employees: 5-9
Markets Served:
 Super Market Chains, Wholesale Distributors
Primary Brands Brokered include: Imperial Commercial Cooking Equipment; Jackson Machine; Articemp; Nemco; Fleetwood Slicers; Franklin Machine Products
Brokered Products include:
 General Merchandise, Cooking Equipment, Dishwashers, Etc.

40768 Mc Crary & Assoc
327 Dahlonega St # 1004
Cumming, GA 30040-8210 770-887-5757
 Fax: 770-887-0035
Frozen foods, produce, cod, perch, shrimp, pollock
President: Charles Mc Crary
clmccrary@att.net
Estimated Sales: $3-5 Million
Number Employees: 1-4

40769 Mc Namara Assoc Inc
903 Sneath Ln # 126
San Bruno, CA 94066-2407 650-872-2525
 Fax: 650-873-3703 800-995-0430
 mcna@mindspring.com
Broker of dairy/deli products, frozen foods, groceries, industrial ingredients, private label items and produce
President: Neil Mc Namara
mcna@mindspring.com
Estimated Sales: $1-3 Million
Number Employees: 1-4
Square Footage: 2400
Type of Packaging: Consumer, Food Service, Private Label, Bulk
Markets Served:
 Food Manufacturers & Processors, Super Market Chains, Wholesale Distributors, Food Service Operators
Primary Brands Brokered include: American Fine Foods; Gray & Company; Manzana Products Company, Inc.; Maui Pineapple Company; California Custom Canners; Valley Sun Dried, Inc.
Brokered Products include:
 Groceries, Imports, Ingredients, Private Label, Produce, Spices

40770 McArdle
PO Box 5467
Diamond Bar, CA 91765-7467 909-860-3434
 Fax: 909-860-3475 mcardleinc@aol.com
Broker of food, confectionery, snacks merchandise to include pre paid telephone products to all classes of trade
Owner: Mark Mc Ardle
Estimated Sales: $5-10 Million
Number Employees: 1-4
Markets Served:
 Super Market Chains, Wholesale Distributors, Food Service Operators
Brokered Products include:
 Confectionery, General Merchandise

40771 McCarty Brokerage Company
1635 NE Loop 410
Suite: 502
San Antonio, TX 78209-1618 210-826-8400
 Fax: 210-826-1303
Broker of frozen, canned and dehydrated fruits and vegetables, groceries and industrial ingredients
President: O McCarty
CEO: W McCarty
Estimated Sales: $10-20 Million
Number Employees: 15
Square Footage: 2400
Type of Packaging: Food Service, Bulk
Markets Served:
 Food Manufacturers & Processors, Food Service Operators
Brokered Products include:
 Frozen Food, Groceries, Imports, Ingredients, Spices

40772 McClement Sales Company
1s280 Summit Avenue
Oakbrook Terrace, IL 60181-3984 630-789-4340
 Fax: 630-789-2623
Broker of food ingredients including tomato paste, dairy flavors and dried fruits
President: Elex McClement
Sales: Jeanne Kessler
Sales: Ken Billings
Estimated Sales: $5-10 Million
Number Employees: 5-9
Square Footage: 14000
Markets Served:
 Food Manufacturers & Processors, Wholesale Distributors
Primary Brands Brokered include: Crain Walnuts; Kalustyan Spices; Morningstar Packing; Joseph Adams Corporation; Level Valley Dairy; Pilgrim Farms
Brokered Products include:
 Ingredients, Spices, Tomato Paste, Dairy Flavors, etc.

40773 McCormick Brokerage Company
696 Concord Rd SE
Smyrna, GA 30082 770-435-8812
 Fax: 770-435-8806
Broker of confectionery and dairy/deli products, frozen foods, general merchandise, meats and private label items
Owner: Gary Mc Cormick
Estimated Sales: $10-20 Million
Number Employees: 15
Markets Served:
 Super Market Chains, Wholesale Distributors, Food Service Operators
Brokered Products include:
 Confectionery, Dairy/Deli, Frozen Food, General Merchandise, Meat, Meat Products, Private Label

40774 McGovern & Whitten
278 Franklin Rd # 294
Brentwood, TN 37027-3208 615-370-1311
 Fax: 615-370-1317
Manfacturers' representative of food service equipment and supplies
President: Mike Whitten
VP: Mike Whitten
Estimated Sales: $1-3 Million
Number Employees: 5-9
Markets Served:
 Wholesale Distributors
Primary Brands Brokered include: Dean Delfield; Thermokool; General Slicing; Hatco; Rankin Deleet; Middleby Marshall/CTX
Brokered Products include:
 General Merchandise, Foodservice Equipment & Supplies

40775 Meadows Brokerage Company
2414 Hartford Hwy
Dothan, AL 36305-4915 334-793-1117
 Fax: 334-671-8351
Broker of frozen foods, general merchandise and groceries
Owner: Michael Duncan
VP: D Meadows
Estimated Sales: $500,000-$1 million
Number Employees: 7
Markets Served:
 Super Market Chains, Wholesale Distributors, Food Service Operators
Primary Brands Brokered include: Fisherman Net Sardines; Swan; Sani-Cat-Litter; Precious Diapers; United Salt; Norwegian Sardines
Brokered Products include:
 Frozen Food, General Merchandise, Groceries

40776 Measured Sales & Marketing
4449 Walnut Woods Drive
West Bloomfield, MI 48323-2779 248-682-8437
 Fax: 248-682-8437 jrdrauer@aol.com
Broker of general merchandise, confectionery and private label items, groceries, health food, etc.
General Manager: John Drauer
Estimated Sales: $3-5 Million
Number Employees: 1-4
Square Footage: 4000
Markets Served:
 Food Manufacturers & Processors, Super Market Chains, Wholesale Distributors, Food Service Operators
Primary Brands Brokered include: Ontario Foods; KSM Nutritionals, Inteplast; Helmac Products
Brokered Products include:
 Confectionery, General Merchandise, Groceries, Health Food, Private Label, Produce

40777 Menu Planners
1310 Mac Dr
Stow, OH 44224-1311
 Fax: 330-528-3280 mplanners@aol.com
Broker of bakery and dairy/deli products, frozen food, groceries, meats, produce, etc.
Owner: Rich Teolis
VP Sales/Marketing: M Rogoff
Food Service Sales: G Sladek
Estimated Sales: $5-10 Million
Number Employees: 6
Markets Served:
 Food Manufacturers & Processors, Super Market Chains, Wholesale Distributors, Food Service Operators
Brokered Products include:
 Dairy/Deli, Frozen Food, Groceries, Meat, Meat Products, Produce, Seafood, Bakery Goods

40778 Mercantum Corp
225 Broadway # 3700
New York, NY 10007-3044 212-233-0412
 Fax: 212-233-0506 sales@mercant.com
 www.mercant.com
Import/export broker of frozen and aseptic fruit purees and concentrates including apple, pineapple, mango, etc. Also tomatoes, tomato paste, sun dried tomatoes, banana flakes, etc.
Owner: Joe Christovao
joec@mercant.com
VP: Marie Christovao
Estimated Sales: $2.5-5 Million
Number Employees: 5-9
Square Footage: 12000
Markets Served:
 Food Manufacturers & Processors, Wholesale Distributors, Food Service Operators
Primary Brands Brokered include: Doe Joe; Tre Sorelle; Fruveg
Brokered Products include:
 Exports, Frozen Food, Health Food, Imports, Ingredients, Produce, Purees, Concentrates, Tomatoes, etc.

40779 Meridian Products
13217 Cambridge St
Santa Fe Springs, CA 90670 562-921-6800
 Fax: 562-921-6580 800-845-1416
Import and export broker of seafood
President: Rick Martin
Executive VP: Fred Vincent
Estimated Sales: $3-5 Million
Number Employees: 20-49
Parent Co: ConAgra/Meridian
Other Locations:
 Meridian Products
 Miami Lakes, FL Meridian Products
Markets Served:
 Food Manufacturers & Processors, Super Market Chains, Wholesale Distributors, Food Service Operators
Primary Brands Brokered include: Kroger's
Brokered Products include:
 Exports, Imports, Seafood

40780 Meridian Trading Co
1136 Pearl Street
Boulder, CO 80302 303-442-8683
 Fax: 303-379-5199 info@meridiantrading.com
 www.meridiantrading.com
Distribution of herbal products which includes extracts, teas, spices and medicinal herbs
President: David Black
Contact: Jesse Canizio
jesse@meridiantrading.com
Estimated Sales: $5 Million
Number Employees: 1-4
Primary Brands Brokered include: Herbal Tea Companies, Breweries
Brokered Products include:
 Spices, Herbs

40781 Merit Sales Corporation
25820 Southfield Road
Southfield, MI 48075-1800 248-569-3634
 Fax: 248-569-3040 888-586-3748
 sales@meritsalescorp.com
 www.meritsalescorp.com

Food Brokers / A-Z

Broker of confectionery and dairy/deli products, frozen foods, general merchandise, groceries, health food, etc.
President: Larence Willenborg
VP Specialty Foods: Abe Cohen
VP HBC/General Merchandise: Marvin Billet
Contact: Larry Willenborg
tracy@wenkegreenhouses.com
Estimated Sales: $5-10 Million
Number Employees: 5
Square Footage: 4800
Markets Served:
   Food Manufacturers & Processors, Super Market Chains, Wholesale Distributors, Food Service Operators
Primary Brands Brokered include: Vigo Importing; Woeber Mustard Manufacturing Company; Kalua Corporation; Hatfield Meats; Cooper Farms Turkey
Brokered Products include:
   Confectionery, Dairy/Deli, Frozen Food, General Merchandise, Groceries, Health Food, Ingredients, Meat, Meat Products, Private Label, Spices

40782 Michael R Fish & Co
593 Brookstone Ct
Copley, OH 44321-1262   330-666-2442
   Fax: 330-666-4176 home.earthlink.net/~mrfco/
Broker of general merchandise and private label items
President: Michael Fish
VP: Bob Fish
VP: Judy Fish
Estimated Sales: $2.5-5 Million
Number Employees: 1-4
Markets Served:
   Super Market Chains, Wholesale Distributors
Primary Brands Brokered include: Dickinson; Kiss Products; Lumiscope; Precision; Roberts
Brokered Products include:
   General Merchandise, Private Label

40783 Michael Raymond Desserts Inc
15986 NW 49th Ave
Hialeah, FL 33014-6309   305-624-9994
   Fax: 305-626-9011
Broker, wholesaler, and distributor of desserts and bakery products including cakes, pies, and cheesecakes
President: Howard Schwartz
drdessert@bellsouth.net
Director Purchasing/Plant Manager: Debbi Cian
Estimated Sales: $5-10 Million
Number Employees: 10-19
Square Footage: 20000
Type of Packaging: Food Service, Private Label
Brokered Products include:
   Confectionery, Dairy/Deli, Frozen Food, Produce

40784 Mickelson & Associates
3300 Montreal Industrial Way
Tucker, GA 30084-5251   770-938-0250
   Fax: 770-908-0590
Broker of meat and meat products, general merchandise and groceries including condiments and sauces
President: W Mickelson
Vice President: M Mickelson
Number Employees: 5
Square Footage: 20000
Markets Served:
   Food Manufacturers & Processors, Super Market Chains, Wholesale Distributors, Food Service Operators
Primary Brands Brokered include: Cajun Chef; Forrester/Diamond; Friedmont Beef
Brokered Products include:
   Groceries, Meat, Meat Products, Condiments, Sauces, Plasticware

40785 Micosa Inc
3415 N Kennicott Ave # C
Arlington Hts, IL 60004-7819   847-632-1200
   Fax: 847-632-1217 www.micosafoods.com
Import broker of seafood and meats including pork and poultry
President: J Goldman
Commodity Sales Manager: B Anderson
VP/Sales Manager: J Cchudik
Estimated Sales: $2.5-5 Million
Number Employees: 5-9
Markets Served:
   Super Market Chains, Food Service Operators

Brokered Products include:
   Imports, Meat, Meat Products, Seafood

40786 Mid-America Marketing Inc
9675 Hamilton Rd # 400
Suite 400
Eden Prairie, MN 55344-3400   952-935-4404
   Fax: 952-935-4947
   www.midamericamarketinginc.com
Broker and liquidators of food, general merchandise, HBA, toys, hardware, cosmetics, etc.
Owner: Danielle Shaffer
CFO: Anita Kingery
Sales Director: Brian Allen
dani.wagner.511@gmail.com
Estimated Sales: $3-5 Million
Number Employees: 5-9

40787 Mid-American Brokerage of St. Louis
11738 Administration Dr
St Louis, MO 63146-3406   314-872-9520
   Fax: 314-567-1041
Broker of dairy/deli products, frozen foods, general merchandise, groceries, meat and meat products, etc.
President: C Evola
Estimated Sales: $2.5-5 Million
Number Employees: 10-19
Markets Served:
   Food Manufacturers & Processors, Super Market Chains, Wholesale Distributors, Food Service Operators
Brokered Products include:
   Dairy/Deli, Frozen Food, General Merchandise, Groceries, Meat, Meat Products, Produce, Seafood

40788 Mid-Continent Sales
15200 E Girard Avenue
Suite 2075
Aurora, CO 80014-0002   303-695-4275
   Fax: 303-695-0970
Wholesaler/distributor of spices. Broker of dairy/deli products, frozen foods, general merchandise, groceries, industrial ingredients, spices, etc.
President: R Kinn
CEO: J Loyacono
Estimated Sales: Less than $500,000
Number Employees: 1-4
Square Footage: 5600
Markets Served:
   Food Manufacturers & Processors, Super Market Chains, Wholesale Distributors, Food Service Operators
Brokered Products include:
   Dairy/Deli, Frozen Food, General Merchandise, Groceries, Ingredients, Private Label, Spices

40789 Mid-State Food Brokers
7489 Henry Clay Blvd
Liverpool, NY 13088   315-451-2080
   Fax: 315-451-6653 hlapatra@midstatefood.com
Broker of dairy/deli products, frozen foods, groceries, meat and meat products, spices, seafood, etc.
President: Harold F. La Patra
Vice President: Craig Mueller
Marketing Manager: Rich Mastin Jr.
Office Manager: Leanne Caswell
Estimated Sales: $5-10 Million
Number Employees: 25
Markets Served:
   Food Service Operators
Brokered Products include:
   Dairy/Deli, Frozen Food, Groceries, Meat, Meat Products, Private Label, Seafood, Spices

40790 Mid-West Associates
2892 N Reynolds Rd # E
Toledo, OH 43615-2000   419-531-9300
   Fax: 419-531-9057 mwabobg@aol.com
Manufacturers' representative for food service equipment; serving wholesalers/distributors
President: Bob Gatchel
Vice President: Michael Lacoursiere
Estimated Sales: Less than $500,000
Number Employees: 1-4
Parent Co: MW Group
Markets Served:
   Wholesale Distributors, Food Service Operators
Brokered Products include:
   General Merchandise, Imports, Supplies

40791 Mid-West Sales Agency
5335 N Tacoma Ave Ste 17b
Indianapolis, IN 46220   317-722-1622
   Fax: 317-722-1644
Import broker of dairy/deli products, baked goods, general merchandise, groceries, industrial ingredients, private label items, etc
President: Ollie Davis
Sales Manager: J Davis
Estimated Sales: $3-5 Million
Number Employees: 4
Square Footage: 4800
Type of Packaging: Private Label
Markets Served:
   Food Manufacturers & Processors, Super Market Chains, Wholesale Distributors, Food Service Operators
Brokered Products include:
   Confectionery, Dairy/Deli, General Merchandise, Groceries, Ingredients, Private Label

40792 Midland Marketing Co-Op Inc
219 E 9th St
Hays, KS 67601-4415   785-628-3221
   Fax: 785-628-3222   800-841-6228
   corporate@midlandmarketing.org
   www.midlandmarketing.org
Broker of private label items including dry, packaged and frozen foods, dairy/deli and paper, laundry and cleaning products
General Manager: Vance Westhusin
Manager: Lee Niblock
lee@midlandmarketing.org
Office Manager: Randy Schoenthaler
Estimated Sales: $500,000-$1 Million
Number Employees: 50-99
Type of Packaging: Private Label
Markets Served:
   Super Market Chains
Brokered Products include:
   Confectionery, Dairy/Deli, Frozen Food, Groceries, Private Label, Spices

40793 Midlantic Sweetener Co
3526 Centre Cir
Fort Mill, SC 29715-9732   803-548-3877
   Fax: 803-548-3536 www.atlanticingredients.com
Broker of industrial ingredients and private label items
CEO: Philip Gentlesk, Sr.
VP/CFO: Philip Gentlesk, Jr.
Estimated Sales: $10-20 Million
Number Employees: 5-9
Parent Co: Atlantic Sweetener Company
Markets Served:
   Food Manufacturers & Processors, Wholesale Distributors, Food Service Operators
Primary Brands Brokered include: Savannah Sugar; ADM; Barry Callebout; GS Dunn & Company
Brokered Products include:
   Confectionery, Ingredients, Meat, Meat Products, Private Label, Spices, Sweeteners

40794 Midstates Marketing Inc
2771 104th St # B
Urbandale, IA 50322-3883   515-246-8829
   Fax: 515-246-8837
   marke@midstates-marketing.com
   www.midstates-marketing.com
Broker of spices, seafood, produce, private label items, meats, general merchandise, etc.
Manager: John Withers
johnw@midstates-marketing.com
VP: Elworth Mark
Sales Manager: Randy Rowen
Estimated Sales: $10-20 Million
Number Employees: 1-4
Square Footage: 8100
Markets Served:
   Food Service Operators
Primary Brands Brokered include: Dole Foods; Minute Maid Company; Pitt Plastic; Swift & Company
Brokered Products include:
   Confectionery, Dairy/Deli, Frozen Food, General Merchandise, Meat, Meat Products, Private Label, Produce, Seafood, Spices

40795 Midwest Frozen Foods, Inc.
2185 Leeward Ln
Hanover Park, IL 60133-6026   630-784-0123
   Fax: 630-784-0424   866-784-0123

Food Brokers / A-Z

Midwest Frozen Foods provides in house and private label frozen fruits and vegetables to the retail, food services and industrial manufacturing sectors.
President: Zafar Iqbal
VP: Athar Siddiq
Operations: Rob Linchesky
Production: Jose Manjarrez
Estimated Sales: $5 Million
Number Employees: 18
Number of Brands: 2
Number of Products: 100+
Square Footage: 20000
Type of Packaging: Food Service, Private Label, Bulk

40796 Midwest Ingredient Sales
7116 Benton Court
Des Moines, IA 50322-4727   515-727-8044
            Fax: 515-727-8046 daveraife@aol.com
Broker of industrial ingredients, meat products, spices
Partner: David Raife
Partner: Don Catus
Office Manager: Ann Raife
Estimated Sales: $1-2.5 Million
Number Employees: 1-4
Square Footage: 3600
Markets Served:
   Food Manufacturers & Processors
Primary Brands Brokered include: Ocean Spray Cranberries; Diamond Walnut Growers; Baker's Chocolate & Coconut; Chiquita Brands; Tree Top; Oscar Mayer Ingredients
Brokered Products include:
   Ingredients

40797 Midwest Ingredients Inc
103 W Main St
PO Box 186
Princeville, IL 61559-7511   309-385-1035
   Fax: 309-385-1036 www.midwestingredients.com
Midwest Ingredients has purchased excess and close coded food products and ingredients across the continental United States since 1994. The inventory is sold with any restrictions the manufacturer requires. We work with retail orinstitutional packaging and also bulk pack products.
CFO: Ruthi Coats
ruthi@midwestingredients.com
Estimated Sales: Above $5 Million
Number Employees: 5-9
Markets Served:
   Food Manufacturers & Processors, Super Market Chains, Wholesale Distributors, Food Service Operators
Brokered Products include:
   Confectionery, Dairy/Deli, Exports, Frozen Food, General Merchandise, Groceries, Health Food, Imports, Ingredients, Meat, Meat Products, Private Label, Produce, Seafood, Spices, any food inventory that is close coded

40798 Midwest Juice
3993 Roger B Chaffee Mem SE #F
Suite F
Grand Rapids, MI 49548-3404   616-774-6832
      Fax: 616-774-0373   877-265-8243
info@midwestjuice.com www.midwestjuice.com
Beverages, coffee dispensers, aseptic portion cups
President: Mike Luhn
Owner: Noel Luhn
Number Employees: 5-9
Type of Packaging: Food Service, Private Label, Bulk
Markets Served:
   Food Service Operators
Brokered Products include:
   Beverages

40799 Milky Whey Inc
910 Brooks St # 203
Suite 203
Missoula, MT 59801-5784   406-542-7373
      Fax: 406-542-7377   800-379-6455
dairy@themilkywhey.com
www.themilkywhey.com
Whey proteins and dry dairy ingredients including nonfat dry milk, whole milk, whey powder, butter, buttermilk powder, caseinates, lactose, nondairy creamers, whey protein concentrates and isolates, and cheese powders

President: Curt Pijanowski
curt@themilkywhey.com
CFO: Steve Schmidt
Vice President: Dan Finch
Operations Manager: Carla Messerly
Reception: Tony Cavanaugh
Estimated Sales: $1.2 Million
Number Employees: 10-19
Type of Packaging: Consumer, Private Label, Bulk
Markets Served:
   Food Manufacturers & Processors, Wholesale Distributors, Food Service Operators
Brokered Products include:
   Confectionery, Dairy/Deli, Exports, Frozen Food, Health Food, Ingredients, Meat Products, Private Label, Seafood, Spices

40800 Miller & Smith Foods
5770 Hurontario Street
Suite 505
Mississauga, ON L5R 3G5
Canada
                905-501-8383
         Fax: 905-501-8388
Import and export broker of industrial ingredients and frozen foods including canned goods and concentrates
President: R Asada
Sales (Frozen Fruit): T Spina
Sales (Concentrates): C Calaghan
Number Employees: 12
Square Footage: 14000
Markets Served:
   Food Manufacturers & Processors, Wholesale Distributors, Food Service Operators
Primary Brands Brokered include: Mayfield Farms; Oxford; Abbotsford; Biggar's; Iroquois Cranberry Growers; Morning Star
Brokered Products include:
   Exports, Frozen Food, Imports, Ingredients, Canned Goods & Concentrates

40801 Miller & Stryker Assoc Inc
613 N Edgewood Ave
Wood Dale, IL 60191-2605   630-766-0077
      Fax: 630-766-8777   800-301-1431
millerstryker@msn.com www.cadco-ltd.com
Manufacturers' representative for food service equipment and supplies
Owner: Peter Stryker
pstryker@millerandstryker.com
Estimated Sales: $1-2.5 Million
Number Employees: 5-9
Markets Served:
   Wholesale Distributors
Primary Brands Brokered include: AMCO; Blodgett; Champion; Candle Corporation; American Metalcraft; T & S Brass
Brokered Products include:
   General Merchandise, Foodservice Equipment & Supplies

40802 Miller's Market
600 N Ohio Street
Salina, KS 67401-2408   785-823-1629
         Fax: 785-825-9231
Import and export broker of fruit, confectionery, general merchandise, groceries, health and frozen food, private label items, seafood and spices
President: J Miller
Estimated Sales: Less than $500,000
Number Employees: 1-4
Square Footage: 1200000
Markets Served:
   Food Manufacturers & Processors, Super Market Chains, Wholesale Distributors, Food Service Operators
Primary Brands Brokered include: Earth Quake of San Francisco; Lanzar
Brokered Products include:
   Confectionery, Exports, Frozen Food, General Merchandise, Groceries, Health Food, Imports, Private Label, Produce, Seafood, Spices

40803 Miller, Stabler & Smith
P.O.Box 361198
Birmingham, AL 35236-1198
         Fax: 205-979-0599
Broker of confectionery, dairy/deli products, general merchandise, frozen foods, private label items, produce and groceries
Owner: Kevin Miller
CEO: R Kevin Miller
CFO: L Ron Stabler

Estimated Sales: $5-10 Million
Number Employees: 5-9
Type of Packaging: Consumer
Markets Served:
   Super Market Chains, Wholesale Distributors, Food Service Operators
Primary Brands Brokered include: Hershey; American Candy Company; The Fonda Group
Brokered Products include:
   Confectionery, Dairy/Deli, Frozen Food, General Merchandise, Groceries, Private Label, Produce

40804 Miltenberg & Samton Inc.
2 Hollyhock Road
Wilton, CT 06897   203-834-0002
   Fax: 203-834-1002 miltsam@miltsam.com
               www.miltsam.com
Import and export broker of confectionery processing equipment, high speed wrapping machines and ingredients for chewing gum bases
Chief Business Advisor: Ronald Kehle
VP of Sales and Logisics: Edward J. Strycharz
Contact: Frank Franze
ffranze@miltsam.com
General Manager: Frank Franze
Estimated Sales: $2.5-5 Million
Number Employees: 5-9
Primary Brands Brokered include:
   Theegarten-Pactec; Goodyear; P. Prat; Extrufood B.V.; ProForm S.A.
Brokered Products include:
   Exports, General Merchandise, Imports, Ingredients, Confectionery Processing Equipment

40805 Mirandas' Sales & Merchandising
16 Blair Lane
Buffalo, NY 14224-3611   716-675-8976
         Fax: 716-675-8976
Import broker of confectionery products, frozen foods, general merchandise, seafood, groceries and private label items
President: Carmen Miranda
Managing Partner: Ralph Miranda
Number Employees: 1-4
Square Footage: 4800
Markets Served:
   Super Market Chains, Wholesale Distributors
Primary Brands Brokered include: Shirley Foods (Frozen tortillas); Strohmeyer & Arpe
Brokered Products include:
   Frozen Food

40806 Mirkovich & Assoc Inc
1064 N Garfield St
Lombard, IL 60148-1336   630-792-0080
      Fax: 630-792-9914   800-733-5238
pat@mirkovich.com www.mirkovich.com
Manufacturers' representative for food service equipment and supplies
President: Edward Chisholm
edward@mirkovich.com
Office Manager: Kate Gagliano
Number Employees: 5-9
Square Footage: 20000
Markets Served:
   Food Manufacturers & Processors, Super Market Chains, Wholesale Distributors, Food Service Operators
Primary Brands Brokered include: McCall Reach-Ins; Bloomfield; Hamilton Beach; Robot Coup; 3-M; Kol Pak Walk-Ins; Edlund; Holman
Brokered Products include:
   General Merchandise, Foodservice Equipment & Supplies

40807 Mitchel Beck Company
PO Box 81
Scarsdale, NY 10583-0081   914-725-1150
      Fax: 914-725-1246 mitbeck@aol.com
Import broker of nuts and dried fruits
President: Gary Cochrane
Estimated Sales: $2.5-5 Million
Number Employees: 1-4
Markets Served:
   Food Manufacturers & Processors, Wholesale Distributors
Brokered Products include:
   Groceries, Imports, Nuts & Dried Fruits

Food Brokers / A-Z

40808 (HQ)Mitchell & Co Inc
601 Scott St
Little Rock, AR 72201-4536   501-372-2321
                                 Fax: 501-376-8634
www.mitchellandcompanyinc.com
Broker of confectionery products, frozen foods, general merchandise, meats and private label items
President: Dana Durney
dana@mitchco1.com
Chief Operating Officer: Dana Mitchell Durney
Estimated Sales: $5-10 Million
Number Employees: 5-9
Markets Served:
   Super Market Chains, Wholesale Distributors, Food Service Operators
Brokered Products include:
   Confectionery, Dairy/Deli, Frozen Food, Meat, Private Label, Seafood

40809 Mitchell Agencies
93 Glencoe Dr
Mount Pearl, NL A1N 4S7
Canada   709-368-8336
                                 Fax: 709-747-3428
Broker of confectionery products, general merchandise, groceries, meat products and seafood
President: G Osmond
Sales Manager: D Reid
Markets Served:
   Food Manufacturers & Processors, Super Market Chains, Wholesale Distributors, Food Service Operators
Primary Brands Brokered include: Ocean Spray; Welch's; Mott's; Mennon; Q Tips; Colgate
Brokered Products include:
   Confectionery, General Merchandise, Groceries, Meat Products, Seafood

40810 Mitchell of Mississippi
212 Avalon Cir
Brandon, MS 39047   601-992-3303
                                 Fax: 601-992-4879
Broker of confectionery and dairy/deli products, frozen and health foods, general merchandise and meats, etc.
President: Glenn Mitchell
Estimated Sales: $10-20 Million
Number Employees: 10-19
Square Footage: 3900
Markets Served:
   Food Manufacturers & Processors, Super Market Chains, Wholesale Distributors, Food Service Operators
Primary Brands Brokered include: McCarty Foods; Carnation Company Frozen; Chef America; Orval Kent; Bryan Foods; Ocean Spray Cranberries
Brokered Products include:
   Confectionery, Dairy/Deli, Frozen Food, General Merchandise, Health Food, Meat, Meat Products, Private Label, Seafood

40811 Moneuse Sales Agency
200 Blue Lake Drive
Longwood, FL 32779-3504   407-862-4313
   Fax: 407-788-8281 paulsr@moneusesales.com
                                www.moneusesales.com
Manufacturers' representative for food service equipment and supplies
Owner, Founder: Paul Moneuse
Founder: Chris Moneuse
chris@moneusesales.com
Founder: Dennis DeMatos
Estimated Sales: $300,000-500,000
Number Employees: 1-4
Markets Served:
   Food Manufacturers & Processors, Super Market Chains, Wholesale Distributors, Food Service Operators
Primary Brands Brokered include: Caddy Corporation; Champion; Wilder; Baxter; Oliver Products; Master Disposers; Acme
Brokered Products include:
   General Merchandise, Foodservice Equipment & Supplies

40812 Monterey Food Ingredients
574 Cortes St # B
Monterey, CA 93940-3244   831-375-9543
   Fax: 831-375-3989 aliciaMFI@sbcglobal.net
Broker of frozen foods and ingredients
Owner: Alicia Hammond
VP: Tracy Hammond
Estimated Sales: $13 Million
Number Employees: 1-4
Markets Served:
   Food Manufacturers & Processors
Brokered Products include:
   Frozen Food, Ingredients

40813 Moody Dunbar Inc
2000 Waters Edge Dr # 21
Johnson City, TN 37604-8312   423-952-0100
                                 Fax: 423-952-0289
customerservice@moodydunbar.com
www.moodydunbar.com
Processor of bell peppers, pimientos and sweet potatoes, products are certified Kosher
CEO: Stanley Dunbar
CFO: Christy Dunbar
R&D/Quality Assurance Manager: Katie Rohrbacher Nixa
Vice President of Sales & Marketing: Ed Simerly
Estimated Sales: $37,000,000
Number Employees: 20-49
Number of Brands: 11
Type of Packaging: Consumer, Food Service, Private Label
Other Locations:
   Saticoy Foods Corporation
   Santa Paula, CA
   Dunbar Foods Corporation
   Dunn, NCSaticoy Foods CorporationDunn
Markets Served:
   Food Manufacturers & Processors, Super Market Chains, Wholesale Distributors
Brokered Products include:
   Groceries, Private Label, Canned Goods

40814 Mooney International
21 Pancoast Road
Waretown, NJ 08758-2650   609-693-9602
   Fax: 201-239-9191 jmooney182@aol.com
Import and export broker of industrial food ingredients. vegetables, gherkins, pepperonchini, olives, capers, marashcino cherries, pickles, peppers, canned vegetables and fruit, essential oils, absolutes, extracts: herbal, spicebotanical. fruit products: tropical juice concentrates. growing mediums for orchids and gesneriads: New Zealand sphagum Moss
CEO: Joan B Mooney
VP: Charles Mooney
Operations: Charles G Mooney
Estimated Sales: $1-1.5 Million
Number Employees: 3
Type of Packaging: Bulk
Markets Served:
   Food Manufacturers & Processors, Wholesale Distributors, Food Service Operators
Brokered Products include:
   Imports, Ingredients, Private Label

40815 Mordhorst Automation
90 Nolan Court
Suite 38
Markham, ON L3R 4L9
Canada   905-477-1347
   Fax: 905-477-9547 hmordhorst@mordhorst.com
Domestic and import broker of packaging and processing equipment including mixers, granulators, homogenizers, mobile lifters, blister and horizontal pouch machines, fillers, closers, tray formers, cartoners and robotic palletizers
President: Harald Mordhorst
Number Employees: 4

40816 Morgan Sampson USA
11155 Dana Cir
Cypress, CA 90630-5133   714-894-0646
   Fax: 714-897-8284 hq@morgansampsonusa.com
Broker of general merchandise and groceries
President: Chip Carter
VP: Tom Paalman
Number Employees: 10-19
Markets Served:
   Wholesale Distributors
Primary Brands Brokered include: Del Monte; Specialty Brands; Very Fine; Hain Foods; Ralston; Estee; Brita; Sunbeam; Mirro; Coleman; Cold-Eeze
Brokered Products include:
   General Merchandise, Groceries

40817 Morley Sales Co
119 N 2nd St
Geneva, IL 60134-2226   630-845-8750
                                 Fax: 630-845-8749
Import and export broker of seafood, frozen foods, dairy/deli products, groceries and private label items
Secretary/Treasurer: Gary Slavik
Manager: Jessica Weaver
Contact: Al Mazulis
al@morleysales.com
Estimated Sales: $1.9 Million
Number Employees: 1-4
Square Footage: 1000
Markets Served:
   Food Manufacturers & Processors, Super Market Chains, Wholesale Distributors, Food Service Operators
Primary Brands Brokered include: North Star; Idaho's Best; Southern Belle; Comeau Seafoods; Fishbrook; Sea Garden
Brokered Products include:
   Dairy/Deli, Exports, Frozen Food, Groceries, Imports, Private Label, Seafood

40818 Morton & Associates
7478 SW Coho Ct
Tualatin, OR 97062-9277   503-691-1331
                                 Fax: 503-691-0707
morton@foodservice-brokers.com
Import broker of dairy/deli, frozen foods, groceries, meat, meat products, private label brands, etc.
President: Donald Morton Sr
Treasurer: Willetta Morton
Contact: Trevor Bellmore
trevor@foodservice-brokers.com
Estimated Sales: $6.60 Million
Number Employees: 37
Markets Served:
   Food Manufacturers & Processors, Wholesale Distributors
Brokered Products include:
   Dairy/Deli, Frozen Food, Groceries, Imports, Meat, Meat Products, Private Label, Produce, Seafood

40819 Morton F Schweitzer Sales
5582 Pocusset Street
Pittsburgh, PA 15217-1913   412-521-3674
                                 Fax: 412-421-2595
Broker of confectionery and meat products, spices, produce, health food, general merchandise, etc
President: M Schweitzer
CEO: Laura Petrini
Number Employees: 1-4
Markets Served:
   Super Market Chains, Wholesale Distributors, Food Service Operators
Brokered Products include:
   Confectionery, Health Food, Imports, Ingredients, Private Label, Produce

40820 Mosher Products Inc
4318 Hayes Ave
Cheyenne, WY 82001-2349   307-632-1492
   Fax: 307-632-1492 info@wheatandgrain.com
                                 www.wheatandgrain.com
Organic grain
President: Leonard O Mosher
leonard@wheatandgrain.com
Estimated Sales: Below $5 Million
Number Employees: 20-49
Square Footage: 240000
Other Locations:
   Bushnell, NE
Brokered Products include:
   Health Food, Ingredients, Organic

40821 Moten Company
13789 Dearborn Street
Corona, CA 92880-4207   909-481-2812
   Fax: 909-948-7189 themotencompany@aol.com
President: Dale Moten
Vice President: Kari Moten
Public Relations: Brittni Motron
Estimated Sales: $100,000
Number Employees: 3
Number of Brands: 4
Number of Products: 50
Square Footage: 8000
Type of Packaging: Consumer, Private Label
Primary Brands Brokered include: Harvest Farms, Brook Street Baking, 20th Century Foods, Seafood Dimensions
Brokered Products include:
   Dairy/Deli, Frozen Food, Meat, Meat Products, Seafood

Food Brokers / A-Z

40822 Mountain Creek Marketing
6565 S Dayton St # 2000
Suite 2000
Greenwood Vlg, CO 80111-6185   303-741-6336
                Fax: 303-741-6446 www.mtn-creek.com
Owner: Theresa Compton
tcompton@mtn-creek.com
Fresh Food Tech and Grocery Support: Sandy Tucker
Business Manager: Theresa Compton
Number Employees: 5-9

40823 Mountain Sales & Svc Inc
6759 E 50th Ave
Commerce City, CO 80022-4618   303-289-5558
          Fax: 303-286-7054 800-847-2557
                    www.mtnsales.com
Wholesaler/distributor and manufacturers' representative for water filter systems, beer systems and parts, cooking equipment, microwave ovens, soft serve equipment, refrigerators and freezers including walk-in and ice making equipment
General Manager: Rick Muckler
rmuckler@mtnsales.com
Estimated Sales: $10-20 Million
Number Employees: 20-49
Square Footage: 24000
Brokered Products include:
    General Merchandise, Water Filters, Beer Systems, etc.

40824 Mueller Yurgae
1055 SE 28th St
Grimes, IA 50111-4958   515-986-0492
        Fax: 515-986-0492 www.pantryful.com
Broker of confectionery products, general merchandise, groceries, meat, dairy/deli products and private label items
President: Phillip Yurgae
Marketing: Rosie Yurgae
VP Sales: Jeff Yurgae
Estimated Sales: $28.70 Million
Number Employees: 5-9
Square Footage: 17500
Markets Served:
    Super Market Chains, Wholesale Distributors, Food Service Operators
Primary Brands Brokered include: Malt-O-Meal Cereals; Favorite Brands; Bow Wow-Tuffy Dog Food; Amurol Products; Tropicana; Keebler
Brokered Products include:
    Confectionery, Dairy/Deli, General Merchandise, Groceries, Meat Products, Private Label

40825 Multy-Grain Foods
2227 Oakwood Lane
Atco, NJ 08004-1468   856-753-3335
    Fax: 856-753-3336 multygrainfoods@aol.com
Manufacturers' representative for imported and exported products including confectionery and dairy/deli products, general merchandise, groceries, industrial ingredients, meat products, etc
President: William Neilson
Number Employees: 20-49
Square Footage: 300000
Markets Served:
    Food Manufacturers & Processors
Brokered Products include:
    Frozen Food, Vegetarian

40826 Munchies
1714 Colburn Street
Honolulu, HI 96819-3243   808-841-6641
            Fax: 808-848-8861
Wholesaler/distributor of baked goods, general merchandise, private label items, seafood, dried fruits, nuts, beef jerky, pork jerky, flavored and sweet popcorn, jams, jellies, tea, coffee, chocolates, gummy candies, chips and Hawaiian snacks
President: Tracy Yokouchi Ng
VP: June Otake
Estimated Sales: $1-3 Million
Number Employees: 10-19
Number of Products: 400
Square Footage: 14000
Parent Co: Ari Group Hawaii USA
Markets Served:
    Super Market Chains, Wholesale Distributors
Brokered Products include:
    Confectionery, Private Label, Seafood, Spices

40827 Munn Marketing Group
4845 Keller Springs Rd
Addison, TX 75001-5912   972-732-0057
                Fax: 972-248-2161
Manufacturers' representative for food service equipment and supplies
President: Lewis Munn
CFO: Marla Munn
VP: Zach Munn
Estimated Sales: $15-20 Million
Number Employees: 5-9
Square Footage: 20000
Markets Served:
    Super Market Chains, Wholesale Distributors, Food Service Operators
Primary Brands Brokered include: Baxter Ovens; Ember-Glo; Epco; General Slicing/Red Goat Disposers; Hatco; Flame Guard
Brokered Products include:
    Equipment

40828 Murray Industrial Food Sales Inc
Parkway Plaza
8839 Long Street
Lenexa, KS 66215-3523   913-492-1771
        Fax: 913-492-2498 800-338-4074
            service@murrayfoodsales.com
            www.murrayfoodsales.com
Broker of Ingredients
President: Rick Murray
VP Outside Sales: Mike DeRienzo
Estimated Sales: $5-10 Million
Number Employees: 5
Type of Packaging: Bulk
Markets Served:
    Food Manufacturers & Processors
Brokered Products include:
    Ingredients

40829 N Star Seafood LLC
2213 NW 30th Pl # 7a
Pompano Beach, FL 33069-1026   954-984-0006
        Fax: 954-984-5912   800-631-8524
Manager: Doug Boadway
dougboadway@northstarseafood.com
Number Employees: 20-49

40830 N.H. Cohen & Associates
519 Malabar Drive
Pittsburgh, PA 15239-2525   412-374-9600
        Fax: 412-374-9700 richcandyman@aol.com
Broker of confectionery items, frozen foods, general merchandise, groceries, etc.
Owner: Rich Cohen
Owner: N Cohen
Estimated Sales: $500,000-$1 Million
Number Employees: 1-4
Markets Served:
    Super Market Chains, Wholesale Distributors
Primary Brands Brokered include: Trolli Philadelphia
Brokered Products include:
    Confectionery, Frozen Food, General Merchandise, Groceries

40831 (HQ)NEMA Associates
2500 S 17th Street
1st Floor
Philadelphia, PA 19145-4515   215-334-5223
        Fax: 215-334-5244 nemaphilly@aol.com
Manufacturers' representative of heavy duty food service equipment including ovens, walk-in freezers, conveyors, heaters and commercial ventilation equipment
Sales/Marketing Manager: Michael Stempkowski
Sales Representative: Bradley Carr
Sales Representative: Frank Taylor
Number Employees: 5-9
Other Locations:
    North East Marketing Associat
    Drums, PA North East Marketing Associat
Markets Served:
    Wholesale Distributors, Food Service Operators
Primary Brands Brokered include: Thermo-Kool; Perfection; Lang; Wittco; Gemini; Lo-Temp
Brokered Products include:
    General Merchandise, Heavy Duty Foodservice Equipment

40832 (HQ)Nagy Associates
375 Sylvan Ave # 39
Englewood Cliffs, NJ 07632-0071   201-567-8590
                Fax: 201-567-5447
Local and Import and export broker of foods, private label, groceries and seafood
President: Alber Nagy
VP: A H Nagy
Estimated Sales: $2-2.5 Million
Number Employees: 1
Type of Packaging: Consumer, Food Service, Private Label
Other Locations:
    Nagy Associates
    Englewood Cliffs, NJ Nagy Associates
Markets Served:
    Super Market Chains, Wholesale Distributors, Food Service Operators
Primary Brands Brokered include: Private Label; House Brand
Brokered Products include:
    Groceries, Seafood

40833 Naman Marketing
9870 Pineview Avenue
Theodore, AL 36582-7403   251-438-2617
                Fax: 251-433-5032
President: George Naman

40834 Nanni-Marketal
125 Gagnon
Suite 202
Montreal, QC H4N 1T1
Canada   514-389-2553
            Fax: 514-389-6654
Import and export broker of dairy/deli products, frozen foods, dry pasta, canned tomatoes and tomato paste, margarine and edible oils
President: Andre Ledere
Partner: Marcel Charbonneau
VP: P Nanni
Number Employees: 1-4
Markets Served:
    Super Market Chains, Wholesale Distributors
Brokered Products include:
    Dairy/Deli, Exports, Frozen Food, Groceries, Imports, Pasta, Canned Tomatoes & Paste, etc.

40835 Napoleon Co.
310 120th Ave NE
#A203
Bellevue, WA 98005-3013   425-455-3776
        Fax: 425-454-3142 info@napoleon-co.com
                www.napoleon-co.com
Specialty foods importer/broker
President: Joe Magnano
joe@napoleon-co.com
VP: Roger Thorson
Estimated Sales: $17-20 Million
Number Employees: 10-19
Number of Brands: 5
Number of Products: 100
Type of Packaging: Consumer, Food Service, Private Label, Bulk
Markets Served:
    Super Market Chains, Wholesale Distributors
Brokered Products include:
    Groceries, Health Food, Ethnic

40836 Nash Wright Brokerage
5007 Carriage Dr # G2
Roanoke, VA 24018-2228   540-989-1218
                Fax: 540-989-1217
Broker of dairy/deli products, frozen foods, groceries, seafood, spices, private label items, meats, etc
CEO: Nash Wright
CFO: Lou Bohon
VP: David Wright
Sales: David Wright
Public Relations: Dan Wright
Purchasing Director: Lou Bohon
Estimated Sales: $2.5-5 Million
Number Employees: 4
Square Footage: 3200
Markets Served:
    Food Manufacturers & Processors, Super Market Chains, Wholesale Distributors, Food Service Operators
Primary Brands Brokered include: Beef International; Fisher
Brokered Products include:
    Frozen Food, Health Food, Ingredients, Meat, Meat Products, Private Label, Seafood, Spices

Food Brokers / A-Z

40837 Natco Worldwide Representative
23004 Frisca Dr
Santa Clarita, CA 91354-2225 661-296-8778
Fax: 661-296-8778 npatow@aol.com
www.natcoglobal.com
Importer, Exporter of canned seafood, Broker for frozen seafood
Owner: Natalia Patow
npatow@aol.com
Estimated Sales: $2.5-$5 Million
Number Employees: 5-9
Square Footage: 12000
Type of Packaging: Consumer, Private Label

40838 National Brokerage Network
32081 Via Flores
Suite 300
San Juan Capistrano, CA 92675-3867 949-661-1254
Fax: 949-661-1254
Export broker of private label items and seafood
VP: Daniel Robinson
Number Employees: 20-49
Square Footage: 260000
Markets Served:
  Super Market Chains, Wholesale Distributors, Food Service Operators
Brokered Products include:
  General Merchandise, Imports, Private Label, Spices

40839 National Carriers Inc
3925 Carbon Rd
Irving, TX 75038
800-835-2097
ekentner@nationalcarriers.com
www.nationalcarriers.com
Transportation broker providing long and short haul trucking
President: Jim Franck
VP Sales: Loren Bridge
Year Founded: 1968
Estimated Sales: $100-$500 Million
Number Employees: 100-249
Parent Co: Farmland Industries

40840 National Commodity Sales
105 Stoneforest Dr
Woodstock, GA 30189-2554 770-928-9288
Fax: 770-928-0103
Broker of private label, frozen foods, groceries and general merchandise
Manager: Diana Kay
VP Sales/Marketing: W Hammond
Executive VP: B Rushton
Marketing Manager: Brad Rushton
Sales Manager: Howell Hammond
Manager: Lee Glenn
lee.glenn@ncsgroup.com
Estimated Sales: $5-10 Million
Number Employees: 5-9
Markets Served:
  Super Market Chains, Food Service Operators
Brokered Products include:
  Frozen Food, General Merchandise, Groceries, Imports, Private Label, Seafood

40841 National Food Group
46820 Magellan Dr # A
Novi, MI 48377-2454 248-669-3000
Fax: 734-453-1800 888-824-0700
info@nationalfoodgroup.com
www.nationalfoodgroup.com
Broker of USDA commodities including frozen, dried and canned fruits, turkey, ground beef and pork, chicken, powdered eggs, etc.
President: Sean H Zecman
CFO: Scott Kamen
VP, General Manager: Tracey Komata
Vice President: Jim Murton
Contact: Kristine Buyers
buyerskristine@nationalfoodgroup.com
Estimated Sales: Less Than $500,000
Number Employees: 1-4
Square Footage: 40000
Markets Served:
  Food Manufacturers & Processors, Wholesale Distributors, Food Service Operators
Brokered Products include:
  Dairy/Deli, Frozen Food, Groceries, Ingredients, Meat, Meat Products, Canned & Dried Fruits, Beef, Pork, Etc.

40842 National Food Sales
6 Mackey Ct
Landenberg, PA 19350 610-869-4650
Fax: 610-869-4657 800-762-4517
www.nationalfoodsales.net
Broker of meat, deli items, seafood and frozen foods
President: William Hinderer
VP: Debbie Hinderer
Marketing: Audrey Cespuglio
Sales: Bob Kuhn
Contact: Deb Hinderer
debh@nationalfoodsales.net
Estimated Sales: $10-20 Million
Number Employees: 10-19
Square Footage: 1400
Markets Served:
  Food Manufacturers & Processors, Super Market Chains, Wholesale Distributors, Food Service Operators
Primary Brands Brokered include: Jennie-O; Patrick Cudahy; Rosina Food Products; Pinnacle; Gol-pak; Oven-Poppers
Brokered Products include:
  Dairy/Deli, Frozen Food, Meat, Meat Products, Seafood

40843 (HQ)National Food Sales
150 Calapooia St SW # B
Albany, OR 97321-2281 541-924-2744
Fax: 541-924-2745
Broker of private label items, industrial ingredients and frozen foods
President: Jim Decker
CFO: Valerie Decker
Public Relations: Tabitha Miller
Estimated Sales: $2.5-5 Million
Number Employees: 1-4
Type of Packaging: Consumer, Food Service, Private Label, Bulk
Other Locations:
  National Food Sales
  Salem, ORNational Food Sales
Markets Served:
  Food Manufacturers & Processors, Food Service Operators
Brokered Products include:
  Frozen Food, Imports, Ingredients, Private Label

40844 National Foodservice Marketing
632 W Summit Avenue
Charlotte, NC 28203-4353 800-762-3002
Fax: 704-896-0086
Broker of confectionery and dairy/deli products, frozen foods, groceries, meats, etc.
Managing Partner: Frank Fields
Managing Partner: Milburn Morris
Sales Director: Tory Moore
Number Employees: 10-19
Square Footage: 8000
Markets Served:
  Wholesale Distributors, Food Service Operators
Primary Brands Brokered include: Sara Lee Refrigerated Foods; Carolina Pride; Domino Sugar; Schwatrz Pickle; Zartic; Tampa Maid
Brokered Products include:
  Confectionery, Dairy/Deli, Frozen Food, Groceries, Meat, Meat Products, Seafood, Spices

40845 National Fruit & Essences
11023 Mill Creek Way #703
Ft. Myers, FL 33913
239-225-6111
Fax: 239-225-6112
nationalfruitessences@yahoo.com
Purchases, sells and distributes fruit juice concentrates, essential oils, essences, and natural colors.
President: Kathleen Medore
Sales: Victor Medore & Joleen Medore
Estimated Sales: $2 Million
Number Employees: 3
Other Locations:
  Fort Myers, FL

40846 National Heritage SalesCompany
1515 W Chester Pike # D2
West Chester, PA 19382-7783 610-692-2092
Fax: 610-692-2863 ussales@axs2000.net
Broker of dairy/deli items, frozen foods, general merchandise, groceries, meat/meat products, private label items, etc

Manager: Theron Male
CEO: C G Gallagher
CFO: R Gallagher
Marketing: P G Gallagher
Contact: R Gallagher
r@consultpsych.com
Estimated Sales: $5-10 Million
Number Employees: 1-4
Markets Served:
  Super Market Chains, Wholesale Distributors, Food Service Operators
Brokered Products include:
  Dairy/Deli, Frozen Food, Groceries, Meat, Meat Products, Private Label, Produce, Seafood

40847 National Retail Marketing Network Inc.
60 East 42nd Street
Suite 2226
New York, NY 10165 212-922-1610
Fax: 212-658-9156 teleib8137@gmail.com
Organic/natural, sugar-free, spirits, frozen desserts, hors d'oeuvres/appetizers, marinades, popcorn.
Marketing: Thomas Leib

40848 National Sign Corporation
1255 Westlake Ave N
Seattle, WA 98109-3531 206-282-0700
Fax: 206-285-3091 info@nationalsigncorp.com
www.nationalsigncorp.com
Manufacturing, installation and servicing of interior and exterior signage, including ADA signs.
President: Timothy Zamberlin
Estimated Sales: $5-10 Million
Number Employees: 35
Square Footage: 60000
Markets Served:
  Food Manufacturers & Processors, Super Market Chains, Wholesale Distributors, Food Service Operators

40849 (HQ)Nature's Products Inc
1301 Sawgrass Corporate Pkwy
Sunrise, FL 33323-2813 954-233-3300
Fax: 954-233-3301 800-752-7873
info@natures-products.com
Manufacturer and supplier of raw materials specializing in gelatin, flavors, active pharmaceuticals, botanicals and pharmaceutical additives. Providing import/export services, warehousing and freight forwarding to and from the UnitedStates and worldwide
President: Jose Minski
josem@npi-gmi.com
Number Employees: 100-249
Type of Packaging: Private Label, Bulk
Markets Served:
  Food Manufacturers & Processors, Wholesale Distributors
Primary Brands Brokered include: Curt Georgi Flavors
Brokered Products include:
  Confectionery, Exports, Health Food, Imports, Ingredients

40850 Nelson Cheese Factory
S237 State Road 35 S
Nelson, WI 54756 715-673-4725
Fax: 715-673-4218
nelsoncheesefactory@gmail.com
www.nelsoncheese.com
Broker and importer of Wisconsin and imported cheeses, as well as wines and a selection of breads, scones and cookies.
Owner: Edward Greenheck
nelsoncheesefactory@gmail.com
Estimated Sales: Less Than $500,000
Number Employees: 5-9
Type of Packaging: Consumer, Food Service
Other Locations:
  Nelson Cheese Factory-Eau Claire
  Eau Claire, WI
  Nelson Cheese Factory-Rochester
  Rochester, MNNelson Cheese Factory-Eau ClaireRochester
Brokered Products include:
  Alcoholic Beverages, Dairy/Deli, Groceries, Health Food, Imports

40851 Nesco Brokerage Company
4343 Lindbergh Dr
Addison, TX 75001 972-239-3451
Fax: 972-934-8520

Food Brokers / A-Z

Import and export broker of dairy/deli products, frozen foods, general merchandise, groceries, meats and private label items
Owner: J Neese
CEO: Harrel Neese
jbneese@yahoo.com
Sales Manager: Brandt Neese
Estimated Sales: $3-5 Million
Number Employees: 1-4
Square Footage: 4000
Type of Packaging: Food Service
Markets Served:
  Food Manufacturers & Processors, Wholesale Distributors, Food Service Operators
Brokered Products include:
  Confectionery, Dairy/Deli, Exports, Frozen Food, General Merchandise, Groceries, Ingredients, Meat, Private Label, Seafood

40852 Network Sales, Inc
8965 92 Avenue
Fort Saskatchewan, AB T8L 1A3
Canada 780-998-4946
Fax: 780-998-5491
Broker of alcoholic beverages, confectionery and dairy/deli products, frozen foods, general merchandise, groceries, etc. Network Sales covers British Columbia, Alberta, Sask, and Manitoba.
President: Dale Gaehring
Secretary: Carol Gaehring
Estimated Sales: B
Number Employees: 8
Square Footage: 2000
Parent Co: Network Sales
Type of Packaging: Consumer, Food Service, Private Label, Bulk
Markets Served:
  Super Market Chains, Wholesale Distributors, Food Service Operators
Brokered Products include:
  Alcoholic Beverages, Confectionery, Frozen Food, General Merchandise, Groceries, Health Food, Meat, Private Label, Seafood, Spices

40853 New Horizons
525 Aero Drive
Buffalo, NY 14225-1405 716-633-2193
Fax: 716-633-9890 800-245-2018
Broker of dairy/deli products, frozen foods, meats, seafood, spices, etc.
President: W Knittel
Secretary/Treasurer: S Knittel
VP: M Seward
Estimated Sales: $5-10 Million
Number Employees: 5-9
Square Footage: 14000
Markets Served:
  Super Market Chains, Wholesale Distributors, Food Service Operators
Primary Brands Brokered include: Simplot; Sea Legs; Barber Foods; Clorox; John Morrell Foodservice; Kerry Ingredients
Brokered Products include:
  Dairy/Deli, Frozen Food, Meat, Meat Products, Seafood, Spices

40854 New Organics
600 Lawnwood Road
Kenwood, CA 95452 734-677-5570
Fax: 707-833-0105
Organic ingredient supplier-grains, sweetners, oils, soy powders
President: Jethren Phillips
Manager: Mathew Keegan
Estimated Sales: $17.5 Million
Number Employees: 74
Number of Brands: 3
Number of Products: 100
Square Footage: 25000
Type of Packaging: Bulk
Other Locations:
  American Health & Nutrition
  Eaton Rapids, MIAmerican Health & Nutrition
Markets Served:
  Food Manufacturers & Processors, Wholesale Distributors
Brokered Products include:
  Exports, Health Food, Imports, Ingredients, Organic Products

40855 Next Phase Enterprises
4020 N 20th St
Suite 305
Phoenix, AZ 85016
nextphase-enterprises.com
National mass merchandiser, wholesale club and supermarket brokers of frozen, refrigerated, fresh deli, produce, dry grocery, bakery haroline and sundries categories.
Founder & CEO: Mike Parker
Year Founded: 1995
Estimated Sales: $200 Million
Number Employees: 70
Type of Packaging: Consumer, Private Label
Markets Served:
  Super Market Chains, Wholesale Distributors
Brokered Products include:
  Confectionery, Dairy/Deli, Frozen Food, Groceries, Meat, Meat Products, Private Label, Produce, Seafood, hardlines

40856 Nicholas & Co Inc
5520 W Harold Gatty Dr
Salt Lake City, UT 84116 801-531-1100
800-873-3663
custservice@nicholasandco.com
www.nicholasandco.com
Wholesaler/distributor of seafood, groceries, meats, produce, dairy products, frozen foods, baked goods, equipment and fixtures, general merchandise and private label items.
President & CEO: Peter Mouskondis
peter.mouskkondis@nicholasandco.com
Co-CEO: Nicole Mouskondis
Year Founded: 1939
Estimated Sales: $50-100 Million
Number Employees: 500-999
Square Footage: 175000
Type of Packaging: Consumer, Food Service, Private Label, Bulk
Brokered Products include:
  Confectionery, Dairy/Deli, Frozen Food, General Merchandise, Groceries, Health Food, Ingredients, Meat, Meat Products, Private Label, Produce, Seafood, Spices

40857 Nikol Foods
85 Webster St
Pawtucket, RI 02861 401-724-7810
Fax: 401-725-0891
Wholesaler/distributor and broker of specialty and nonperishable items including pasta, cookies and coffee
Owner: Michael Silva
VP: Bill Gianetti
Estimated Sales: $20-50 Million
Number Employees: 20-49
Brokered Products include:
  Groceries, Cookies, Pasta & Coffee

40858 Nikola's Foods
8301 Grand Ave S
#110
Bloomington, MN 55420 952-229-4183
Fax: 952-253-5995 888-645-6527
sales@nikolasbakery.com www.nikolasbakery.com
A manufacturing and baking company that offers a full line of bakery products including muffins, cakes, dessert breads, cookies, croissants and macaroons; produces gluten free, organic and kosher products.
Director of Development and Innovation: Michael Itskovich
Contact: Gregory Noah
gnoah@nikolasbakery.com
Estimated Sales: $3.5 Million
Number Employees: 12
Type of Packaging: Consumer, Food Service

40859 Nippon Food Company
1426 Minnesota St
San Francisco, CA 94107 415-648-1444
Fax: 415-648-1486
Broker of Oriental food products including soy sauce, roasted eel and udon noodles
Manager: Richard Ito
Estimated Sales: $2.5-5 Million
Number Employees: 1-4
Markets Served:
  Super Market Chains, Wholesale Distributors, Food Service Operators
Primary Brands Brokered include: Choyce Unagi; Nanka; Cheristar; Kikkoman
Brokered Products include:
  Groceries, Seafood, Soy Sauce, Roated Eel, etc.

40860 Nobert Marketing
5250 Mendenhall Park Pl
Memphis, TN 38115-5904 901-795-6711
Fax: 901-363-9363
Import broker of confectionery and dairy/deli products, frozen foods, general merchandise, meat and meat products, etc.
President/CEO: Johnny Smith
CFO: Doug Nobert
Contact: Donald Nobert
donald@nobertmarketing.com
Estimated Sales: $10-20 Million
Number Employees: 10-19
Square Footage: 15000
Markets Served:
  Food Manufacturers & Processors, Super Market Chains, Wholesale Distributors, Food Service Operators
Primary Brands Brokered include: JR Simplot; Quaker; Uncle Ben's; Reckitt & Colman; Coldwater Seafood Corporation; T.J. Lipton Company
Brokered Products include:
  Confectionery, Dairy/Deli, Frozen Food, General Merchandise, Imports, Ingredients, Meat, Meat Products, Private Label, Produce, Seafood, Spices, Commercial Cleaning Products

40861 Noble Foods
P.O.Box 11282
Albany, NY 12211-282
Fax: 518-458-2709
Import broker of meat products, dairy/deli items, frozen foods, groceries and domestic product overruns
President: Frank Stramiello
Estimated Sales: $300,000-500,000
Number Employees: 1-4
Markets Served:
  Food Manufacturers & Processors, Super Market Chains, Wholesale Distributors, Food Service Operators
Brokered Products include:
  Dairy/Deli, Frozen Food, Groceries, Imports, Meat Products, Overruns

40862 Noble House Trading Company
PO Box 36
Woodland, CA 95776-0036 530-668-5916
Fax: 530-668-4635 noblehouse@saber.net
Broker of ingredients, instant rice, wild rice, and brown rice
Co-Owner: Harold Noble
Co-Owner: Patricia Noble
Number Employees: 1-4
Square Footage: 3600
Type of Packaging: Bulk
Markets Served:
  Food Manufacturers & Processors
Primary Brands Brokered include: Nor-Cal; AC Humko; Northland; Cenex
Brokered Products include:
  Ingredients

40863 (HQ)Nomura & Co
40 Broderick Rd
Burlingame, CA 94010-2202 650-692-5457
Fax: 650-692-8297 www.kokuhorice.com
Broker of milled California rice and private label items
President: George Okamoto
CEO: G Okamoto
CFO: Polly Okamoto
Estimated Sales: $5-10 Million
Number Employees: 5-9
Square Footage: 4800
Other Locations:
  Nomura & Company
  Glenn, CANomura & Company
Markets Served:
  Super Market Chains, Wholesale Distributors
Primary Brands Brokered include: Kokuho Rose Rice
Brokered Products include:
  Private Label, Milled California Rice

40864 Noon International
3840 Blackhawk Rd # 100
Danville, CA 94506-4649 925-736-6696
Fax: 925-736-6177 info@noon-intl.com
Importer and exporter of fruits and vegetables

President: Lillian Noon
lnoon@noon-intl.com
Manager: Betty Johnson
Estimated Sales: $10-20 Million
Number Employees: 10-19
Type of Packaging: Bulk
Markets Served:
  Super Market Chains, Wholesale Distributors
Brokered Products include:
  Exports, Frozen Food, Groceries, Produce

40865 Norman Brokerage Co
7407 Melrose Ave
St Louis, MO 63130-1719   314-727-3399
          Fax: 419-735-9657   800-264-3399
Broker of industrial ingredients, nuts, frozen and dried fruit, produce, seeds, spices, cheese sauces, confectionery products, baked goods, snack foods, dips, spreads, health foods, etc.
President: Tom Norman
VP Sales: Rick Seppala
Specialty Sales: Jane Lautric
Estimated Sales: Less Than $500,000
Number Employees: 1-4
Markets Served:
  Wholesale Distributors
Brokered Products include:
  Confectionery, Frozen Food, Groceries, Health Food, Imports, Ingredients, Produce, Spices

40866 Norman Hecht
835 Queens Road
Vineland, NJ 08361-6029   856-691-9427
      Fax: 856-692-1326 storman@snip.net
President: Norman Hecht
Type of Packaging: Food Service
Markets Served:
  Food Manufacturers & Processors, Super Market Chains, Wholesale Distributors, Food Service Operators
Brokered Products include:
  Dairy/Deli, Groceries, Imports, Meat Products, Spices

40867 North Bay Seafood
PO Box 832
Agoura Hills, CA 91376-0832   818-889-8316
          Fax: 818-889-4860
Owner: Howard Gordon

40868 North Bay Trading Co
13904 E US Highway 2
Brule, WI 54820-9038   715-372-5031
          800-348-0164
borg@cheqnet.net www.northbaytrading.com
Organic and Canadian wild rice, heirloom beans, dehydrated vegetables, dry soup mixes
Owner: Greggar Isaksen
greggar@northbaytrading.com
Estimated Sales: $160,000
Number Employees: 5-9
Number of Brands: 2
Number of Products: 6
Type of Packaging: Consumer, Food Service, Bulk
Markets Served:
  Super Market Chains, Wholesale Distributors, Food Service Operators
Brokered Products include:
  Health Food

40869 North Eastern Sales Solutions
27 Curve St
Needham, MA 2492   781-444-7604
          Fax: 781-444-7607
alan@northeasternsalessolutions.com
Broker of confectionery and dairy/deli products, general merchandise, private label items, produce, etc.
Owner: Frank D'Orlando
Estimated Sales: A
Number Employees: 3
Square Footage: 14400
Primary Brands Brokered include: Twin Mountain; Guzzlers; Swell; Lil Drug Store; Dum Dums; Teens Drinks
Brokered Products include:
  Confectionery, Dairy/Deli, Frozen Food, General Merchandise, Groceries, Private Label, Produce

40870 North Star Agency
7348 Ohms Ln
Minneapolis, MN 55439-2330   763-545-1400
      Fax: 763-545-7158   800-328-4827
          sales@northstaragency.com
          www.northstaragency.com
Manufacturers' representative for food service equipment and supplies
President: Jim Froelich
sales@northstaragency.com
Estimated Sales: $1-2.5 Million
Number Employees: 1-4
Markets Served:
  Super Market Chains, Food Service Operators

40871 Northeast Calamari Inc
13 Forest St
Gloucester, MA 01930-2807   978-281-6553
          Fax: 978-281-2656
President: Maria Maniaci
Estimated Sales: Less Than $500,000
Number Employees: 1-4

40872 Northeast Retail Services
PO Box 682
Natick, MA 01760-0007   508-893-0660
          Fax: 508-893-6000
Broker of groceries, private label items and general merchandise
President: Chip Fagan
Office Manager: Paula Gately
VP Operations: Brian Locapo
Number Employees: 20-49
Square Footage: 2800
Markets Served:
  Super Market Chains, Wholesale Distributors
Primary Brands Brokered include: Leshner Company; Ossipee Mountain Land Company; Valley Forge Flag Company; Hoover Company; Carolina Glove Company; Glove Specialties
Brokered Products include:
  General Merchandise, Groceries, Private Label

40873 Northeastern Enterprises
422 Main St
Stoneham, MA 02180-2606   781-438-6868
          Fax: 781-438-9045
Broker of dairy/deli products, frozen foods, meats and seafood
President: Vincent Serino
Account Executive: Anthony Serino
Estimated Sales: $5-10 Million
Number Employees: 5-9
Square Footage: 14000
Markets Served:
  Food Manufacturers & Processors, Super Market Chains, Wholesale Distributors
Brokered Products include:
  Dairy/Deli, Frozen Food, Meat, Meat Products, Seafood

40874 Northland Express Transport
11288 US-31
Grand Haven, MI 49417-9665   616-846-8450
      Fax: 616-846-5300   800-748-0550
          ewiers@northlandexpresstransport.com
          www.northlandexpresstransport.com
Transportation broker providing long haul and short haul trucking
Owner: Richard Brolick
President, CEO: Todd Bustard
VP, Finance: Edward Wiers
Sales Director: Michelle Voss
General Manager: Matt Nease
Number Employees: 20-49
Parent Co: Spectral Enter
Markets Served:
  Food Manufacturers & Processors, Super Market Chains, Wholesale Distributors
Brokered Products include:
  Dairy/Deli, Frozen Food, General Merchandise, Groceries, Health Food, Meat, Private Label, Produce, Seafood

40875 Northland Organic Foods Corporation
495 Portland Ave
Saint Paul, MN 55102   651-221-0070
          Fax: 651-221-0856
Leading organic food brokerage company. Specializes in the production and exportation of premium-quality, non-genetically modified, organic soybean, wheat, corn, rice and other cereal grains as well as certified organic commodities such as oils, meals and flour
Owner: Peter Shortridge
Estimated Sales: $1-3 Million
Number Employees: 5-9

40876 Northumberland Dairy
256 Lawlor Lane
Miramichi, NB E1V 3M3
Canada   506-627-7720
          800-501-1150
info@northumberlanddairy.ca
www.northumberlanddairy.ca
Dairy products including milk and cream; wholesaler/distributor of bottled water, ice cream, ice milk mix, fruit drinks and butter; serving the food service market
Director, Sales & Marketing: Paul Chiasson
Year Founded: 1942
Estimated Sales: $50 Million
Number Employees: 273
Number of Brands: 5
Square Footage: 79416
Parent Co: Agropur Dairy Co-Operative
Type of Packaging: Consumer, Food Service, Private Label
Brokered Products include:
  Dairy/Deli, Frozen Food

40877 Northwestern Foods
1260 Grey Fox Road
Arden Hills, MN 55112   651-644-8060
      Fax: 651-644-8248   800-236-4937
          northwestern.n2ocompanies.com
Mixes including cocoa, cake, pancake, cappuccino, iced tea, power drinks and pizza dough
President: Kurt Kiaser
CEO: Bob Schafer
Vice President: Mimie Pollard
Sales Manager: Bob Freemore
Contact: Linda Petersen
lpetersen@n2ocompanies.com
Purchasing Manager: Nadine Vandeventer
Estimated Sales: $10-20 Million
Number Employees: 20-49
Square Footage: 48000
Type of Packaging: Consumer, Food Service, Private Label, Bulk
Markets Served:
  Food Manufacturers & Processors, Super Market Chains, Food Service Operators
Primary Brands Brokered include: Gourmet Awards
Brokered Products include:
  Ingredients

40878 Nova Seafood
P.O.Box 350
Portland, ME 04112-0350   207-774-6324
      Fax: 207-774-6385 www.novaseafood.com
Canadian seafood: Fresh Whole and Fresh Fillet Products-Cod, Haddock, Hake, Cusk, Catfish, Pollock, Flounder, Dabs, Grey Sole, Yellowtail, Salmon, Monk, Monk Tail, Halibut; Specialty Items: Clams, Maine Shrimp, Swordfish, Scallops(Dry Sea), Tuna Loin, C/K Lobster Meat, Crab Meat
President: Angelo Ciocca
Sales: Ernie Salamone
Estimated Sales: $20-50 Million
Number Employees: 20-49
Brokered Products include:
  Imports, Seafood

40879 Nu-Lane Cargo Services
Po Box 7360
Visalia, CA 93290
      Fax: 559-625-9700   800-310-6506
Company moves refrigerated truck loads from the shipper to consignee.
Sales Rep.: Steve Brasiel

40880 O'Brien & Associates Brokerage Company
618 Cepi Dr
Suite: A
Chesterfield, MO 63005   636-532-7070
      Fax: 636-532-2367 tobrien@stlobrien.com
          www.stlobrien.com

Food Brokers / A-Z

Broker of dairy/deli products, general merchandise, groceries, meats, frozen foods, private label items, seafood, spices, produce, etc.
Owner/Principle: Louis O'Brien
Financial Officer: Timothy J. O'Brien
Sales Manager: Patricia O'Brien
Merchandising: Fred Kurtz
Estimated Sales: $5.40 Million
Number Employees: 25
Markets Served:
   Food Manufacturers & Processors, Super Market Chains, Wholesale Distributors, Food Service Operators
Primary Brands Brokered include: ConAgra; Georgia Pacific; Sun Diamondl Fresh Express; USA Detergents; T. Marzetti Company
Brokered Products include:
   Dairy/Deli, Frozen Food, General Merchandise, Groceries, Meat, Private Label, Produce, Seafood, Spices

40881 O'Hanlon Group
313 N Gay St
Knoxville, TN 37917-7529   865-546-6735
    Fax: 865-546-6804   800-697-6735
    www.ohginc.com
Manufacturers' representative for general merchandise including lighting fixtures, modular wiring and poles
President: Jack O'Hanlon
johanlon@ohginc.com
Estimated Sales: Less Than $500,000
Number Employees: 1-4
Markets Served:
   Food Manufacturers & Processors, Super Market Chains, Wholesale Distributors, Food Service Operators
Primary Brands Brokered include: Prescolite; Peerless; Sterner; Tivoli; Visa; GE
Brokered Products include:
   General Merchandise, Lighting Fixtures, Wiring, Poles, etc.

40882 O'Neill Marketing Agents
29 Third St
Suite 203
New City, NY 10956-4929   845-638-9306
    Fax: 845-638-9031 www.oneillreps.com
Manufacturers' representative for food service equipment and supplies including smallwares, china, chairs, butane stoves and fuel, shelving, food slicers, under bar, etc.
President, Principal: James O'Neill
Principal: Dave Smith
VP: William O'Neill
Sales Manager: Gary Emory
Sales Agent: Harry King
Contact: Carol Amato
carol@oneillreps.com
Office Manager: Carol Amato
Estimated Sales: $300,000-500,000
Number Employees: 1-4
Square Footage: 4800
Markets Served:
   Wholesale Distributors
Primary Brands Brokered include: Admiral Craft; Alston; Ex-Cell Metal Products; Iwatani; Falcon Hodges; Krowne Metal Corporation
Brokered Products include:
   Foodservice Equipment & Supplies

40883 O.R. Elder
58 W 40th St
Floor: 151
New York, NY 10018-2658   212-695-2724
    Fax: 212-643-9894
Broker of alcoholic beverages and general merchandise; serving food service operators
President: Robert Elder
Estimated Sales: B
Number Employees: 5
Markets Served:
   Food Service Operators
Brokered Products include:
   Alcoholic Beverages, General Merchandise

40884 Oak Farms Dairy
2711 N Haskell Ave
Suite 3400
Dallas, TX 75204
     800-303-3400
    www.oakfarmsdairy.com
Wholesaler/distributor/broker of dairy products.
Accounting Manager: Betty Renteria
Sales Director: Eric Eves
Sanitation Lead: Brenda Davis
Year Founded: 1908
Estimated Sales: $100-500 Million
Number Employees: 200-499

40885 Oak Leaf Sales Co
801 S Hamlin Ave
Park Ridge, IL 60068-4315   847-692-3253
    Fax: 847-692-6137 oakleafsales@aol.com
Broker of general merchandise, groceries, private label items, seafood, spices, etc
Owner: Richard B Spatafora
VP: Bob Henriksen
Sales: Carrie Lynch
Estimated Sales: Less Than $500,000
Number Employees: 1-4
Square Footage: 4800
Type of Packaging: Consumer, Private Label
Markets Served:
   Super Market Chains, Wholesale Distributors
Brokered Products include:
   Dairy/Deli, General Merchandise, Groceries, Private Label, Spices

40886 Occidental Foods International, LLC
4 Middlebury Blvd
Suite 3, Aspen Business Park
Randolph, NJ 07869   973-970-9220
    Fax: 973-970-9222 info@occidentalfoods.com
    www.occidentalfoods.com
Representatives and importers of bulk spices and seeds, including paprika; pure mancha saffron; chilies dried, crushed and ground; turmeric; granulated garlic and garlic powder; cardamom; annatto, allspice and sesame seeds
President: Scott Hall
Chief Financial Officer: Denise Hall
Estimated Sales: $4.9 Million
Type of Packaging: Food Service, Bulk
Markets Served:
   Food Manufacturers & Processors, Wholesale Distributors
Brokered Products include:
   Ingredients, Spices, herbs, edible seeds, spice oleoresins

40887 Oekerman Sales
PO Box 100
Oceanside, OR 97134-0100   503-842-4044
    Fax: 503-842-7215   877-842-4044
    specialtysales@pacific.com
Import broker of frozen foods, groceries, health food, meat and meat products, spices, general merchandise items, etc
Owner: V Oekerman
Number Employees: 1-4
Type of Packaging: Consumer, Food Service, Private Label, Bulk
Markets Served:
   Food Manufacturers & Processors, Super Market Chains, Wholesale Distributors, Food Service Operators
Primary Brands Brokered include: Roland, Texmati, Fall River Wild Rice, Big Valley Buffalo
Brokered Products include:
   Confectionery, Dairy/Deli, Exports, Frozen Food, General Merchandise, Groceries, Health Food, Imports, Ingredients, Meat, Meat Products, Private Label, Seafood, Spices

40888 Ohm Design
26 Court St
Brooklyn, NY 11242-0103   718-254-0900
    Fax: 718-254-0806   888-646-6030
Merger and acquisition-RPA seeking food and beverage manufacturers for sale in the United States-$5 million to 500 million annual sales
President: Matthew Becker
CEO: T English
Estimated Sales: $300,000-500,000
Markets Served:
   Food Manufacturers & Processors, Super Market Chains, Wholesale Distributors, Food Service Operators
Primary Brands Brokered include: Beyond Food

40889 Oley Distributing Company
PO Box 4660
Fort Worth, TX 76164-0660   817-625-8251
    Fax: 817-626-7269
President: Patricia O'Neal
VP: Phil O'Neal, Jr.
General Manager: Bill Smith
Estimated Sales: $5-10 Million
Square Footage: 225000

40890 Omni Food Inc
2001 3rd Ave N
Bessemer, AL 35020-4913   205-426-6650
    www.omnifoodsinc.com
Wholesaler/distributor of general line items; rack jobber services available
President: Arnold Shiland
stuartshiland@bellsouth.net
Estimated Sales: $5-10 Million
Number Employees: 1-4
Square Footage: 220000
Type of Packaging: Consumer, Food Service, Private Label, Bulk
Markets Served:
   Super Market Chains
Primary Brands Brokered include: Major company brands
Brokered Products include:
   Frozen Food, Ingredients, Produce

40891 Orca Foods
720 Notre Dame Street
Repentigny, QC J6A 2X3
Canada   450-654-9099
    Fax: 450-654-9093   877-701-6722
Import and export broker of bakery and pastry products including private label
CEO: Gene Gosselin
Vice President: Louise Gosselin
Number Employees: 10-19
Type of Packaging: Private Label
Markets Served:
   Food Manufacturers & Processors, Super Market Chains, Wholesale Distributors, Food Service Operators
Primary Brands Brokered include: Manor; IGA; Metro; Provigo; Chef's Choice; Buon Gusto; Port Normandie; Loretta Foods; Dipardo Packing
Brokered Products include:
   Exports, Groceries, Imports, Private Label, Seafood, Spices, Tomatoes & Salmon

40892 Orchard Paper
PO Box 16141
Saint Louis, MO 63105-0841   573-754-6700
    Fax: 636-993-8049
Broker of metallized foils, corrugated and chipboard boxes, mailing tubes and plastic bags
President: Edgar Orchard
Estimated Sales: $1-2.5 Million
Number Employees: 1-4
Primary Brands Brokered include: Orco Lok; Alubec
Brokered Products include:
   General Merchandise, Metallized Foil, Boxes, Tubes & Bags

40893 Osage Food Products Inc
120 W Main St # 200
Washington, MO 63090-2121   636-390-9477
    Fax: 636-390-9485 sales@osagefood.com
    www.osagefood.com
Osage is a multi-dimensional company supplying ingredients and food products. Our ingredients for manufacturing. Our packaged goods division supplies national brands and private label products for food service and retail. Our specialtyproducts division works with manufacturers, marketing residual ingredients and finished goods that are needed to sell
President: William Dickinson
Estimated Sales: $2.5-5,000,000
Number Employees: 5-9
Type of Packaging: Consumer, Food Service, Private Label, Bulk
Markets Served:
   Wholesale Distributors, Food Service Operators
Brokered Products include:
   Confectionery, Frozen Food, Groceries, Ingredients, Meat, Private Label, Produce, Seafood, Spices

40894 Osborn Food Sales Company
3925 California Ave
Long Beach, CA 90807-3511   562-422-2203
    Fax: 562-423-5338

Food Brokers / A-Z

Broker of frozen fruits and vegetables, fruit juice concentrates and seafood
President: Bill Osborn
Estimated Sales: $500,000-$1 Million
Number Employees: 1-4
Markets Served:
  Food Manufacturers & Processors, Super Market Chains, Food Service Operators
Brokered Products include:
  Frozen Food, Seafood, Fruit Juice Concentrates

40895 Outback Sales
2555 W Le Moyne St # F-1
Melrose Park, IL 60160-1830 708-345-9000
  Fax: 708-345-9005
Owner: Alan Davidson
Estimated Sales: Less Than $500,000
Number Employees: 1-4

40896 Overseas Service Corp
1100 Northpoint Pkwy # 200
West Palm Beach, FL 33407-1983 561-683-4090
  Fax: 561-689-6427 www.overseasservice.com
Broker of dairy/deli items, frozen foods, general merchandise, meat and meat products, produce and seafood
President: Paul Hogan
CEO: Francis Hogan
CFO: Rebecca Thompson
VP: Mark Shaffer
VP Sales: Roy Hardwick
Estimated Sales: $18.5 Million
Number Employees: 20-49
Brokered Products include:
  Dairy/Deli, Frozen Food, General Merchandise, Meat, Meat Products, Produce, Seafood

40897 PLT Health Solutions Inc
119 Headquarters Plz
Morristown, NJ 07960-6834 973-984-0900
  Fax: 973-984-5666 www.plthomas.com
Extracts for food, supplements and cosmeceuticals.
President & CEO: Paul Flowerman
Executive Vice President: Seth Flowerman
Contact: Jenson Chang
jensonchang@hotmail.com
Number Employees: 50-99

40898 PacNorth Group
3615 W Valley Hwy N
Auburn, WA 98001-2441 253-333-8044
  Fax: 253-333-8045 www.pacnorth.com
Manufacturers' representative for disposable food service supplies including take-out containers, can liners, pizza boxes, specialty food bags, gloves, aprons, trays, plastic dinnerware, etc.
President: David Herron
VP: Manuel Arias
Special Projects: Luanne Arias
Financial Manager: Deborah Elsbree
Marketing Coordinator: Liann Holt
Contact: Luanne Arias
l.arias@pacnorth.com
Estimated Sales: $5-10 Million
Number Employees: 10-19
Square Footage: 60000
Markets Served:
  Food Manufacturers & Processors, Super Market Chains, Wholesale Distributors, Food Service Operators
Brokered Products include:
  General Merchandise, Disposable Pizza Boxes, Gloves, etc.

40899 Pace Target Brokerage
716 Clayton Rd
Williamstown, NJ 08094-3530 856-629-2551
  Fax: 856-629-8546 800-257-7303
  www.pacetarget.com
Broker of confectionery and deli products, groceries, baked goods and private label items
President/CEO: Joseph Pace Jr
Chief Financial Officer: Nicholas D. Pace
Vice President of Sales: Joseph J. Pace III
Estimated Sales: $2.5-5 Million
Number Employees: 20-49
Square Footage: 24000
Markets Served:
  Food Manufacturers & Processors, Super Market Chains, Wholesale Distributors
Primary Brands Brokered include: President Baking Company; Austin Foods Company; Hazelwood Farms; Townsend Culinary; Ripon Foods, Inc.; Ginsburg Bagels
Brokered Products include:
  Confectionery, Dairy/Deli, Groceries, Private Label, Baked Goods

40900 Pacific Ingredient Exchange
7960 Soquel Dr # B383
Aptos, CA 95003-3999 831-685-6535
  Fax: 831-685-6540 pie@pacificingredient.com
  www.pacificingredient.com
Industrial ingredients and imported/domestic dried fruits, frozen fruits, and concentrates
President: Richard Branson
CFO: Shelly Branson
Sales: Jon Meyers
Estimated Sales: $3-5 Million
Number Employees: 1-4
Square Footage: 4800
Type of Packaging: Bulk
Markets Served:
  Food Manufacturers & Processors
Brokered Products include:
  Ingredients

40901 Pacific Salmon Company
21630 98th Ave W
Edmonds, WA 98020-3923 425-774-1315
  Fax: 425-774-6856
Black cod, halibut, salmon, shark, smelt, squid, kosher foods and fish patties
Owner: John Mc Callum
Contact: James Chapa
johnmccallum@msn.com
Estimated Sales: $5-10 Million
Number Employees: 10 to 19
Brokered Products include:
  Frozen Food, Seafood

40902 Pacific Shrimp Co
2422 S Canal St
Chicago, IL 60616-2224 312-326-0803
  Fax: 312-326-2728
President: Hyman Moy
Estimated Sales: $5-10 Million
Number Employees: 5-9

40903 Pacific Trading CompanyInternational
PO Box 3593
Mission Viejo, CA 92690-1593 949-240-4626
  Fax: 949-240-5931 patraco@earthlink.net
Import/export broker of wine, fruit, coffee, fresh and canned vegetables, olive oil, preserves, canned seafood, nuts, fish meal flour, etc.
Director: Alberto Dona
hobbyclub@earthlink.net
Number Employees: 5-9
Square Footage: 12000
Markets Served:
  Food Manufacturers & Processors, Super Market Chains, Wholesale Distributors, Food Service Operators
Primary Brands Brokered include: Covadona; Robinson Crusoe; Arizu/Luigi Bosca; Romapor
Brokered Products include:
  Alcoholic Beverages, Exports, Groceries, Imports, Produce, Seafood, Preserves, Coffee, Olive Oil, etc.

40904 Palms & Co
515 Lake St S # 203
6421 Lake Washington Blvd NE, 408
Kirkland, WA 98033-6441 425-828-6774
  Fax: 425-827-5528 food@peterpalms.com
  www.twocupsofjoy.com
Export management company of grains, meats, rabbit meat, canned foods, wines. EMC services in Eastern Europe, China, Russia for US manufacturers-canned boneless wholechicken; purchasing agent-nitric fertilizer-russian export
President: Peter Palms
CEO: Pyotr Joannevicn
CFO: Alexander Wislobokov
VP: Alexander Goldenberg
Research & Development: Alex Repin
Marketing: Yakon Soblev
Public Relations: Anke Van Waal
Estimated Sales: $20-50 Million
Number Employees: 1-4
Number of Brands: 200
Number of Products: 1500
Type of Packaging: Consumer, Food Service, Private Label, Bulk

40905 Pankow Associates Inc
5214 Main St # 100
Skokie, IL 60077-2173 847-679-7010
  Fax: 847-679-0079 info@pankowassoc.com
  www.pankowassoc.com
Broker of snack foods, health & beauty care products, general merchandise and groceries
President/Chief Executive Officer: Allen Hirschfield
CFO: Laurence Salasche
Vice President, National Accounts: Dave Zande
Director, Technology Support: Jeff Meltzer
Marketing Manager: Dave Zande
Vice President, Sales: Henry Gehrisch
Vice President, Finance/Human Resources: Laurence Salasche
Administrative Services Manager: Donna Zeman
Chain Support Manager: Sue Butler
Estimated Sales: $5 Million
Number Employees: 20-49
Square Footage: 12000
Type of Packaging: Private Label
Markets Served:
  Super Market Chains, Wholesale Distributors, Food Service Operators
Primary Brands Brokered include: Apple & Eve; DeWafelbakkers' Milnot; Ralston Foods; JM Smucker; Star Snacks; Tree Top Juices; World Harbor/Angostura
Brokered Products include:
  General Merchandise, Health Food, Private Label, Health Beauty Care Products

40906 Paradise Food Brokers
4001 E Topeka Dr
Phoenix, AZ 85050 602-494-8260
  Fax: 602-494-8259
Broker of groceries and seafood
President: W Gordon
VP: T Gordon
Estimated Sales: $2.5-5 Million
Number Employees: 1-4
Markets Served:
  Super Market Chains, Wholesale Distributors
Primary Brands Brokered include: Crown Prince/Ocean Prince

40907 Paris Paper Box Company
33 Teed Drive
Randolph, MA 02368-4201 781-961-3378
  Fax: 781-986-2656
Broker of packaging products
President: Lawrence Nigrosh
Estimated Sales: $1-3 Million
Number Employees: 1-4
Square Footage: 28800
Brokered Products include:
  General Merchandise, Packaging Products

40908 Parker's Wine Brokerage
16101 Maple Park Drive
Suite 4
Maple Heights, OH 44137 216-475-4173
  Fax: 216-472-8990 winebrokaergae@yahoo.com
Import and export food and beverage
President: Michael Parker
Marketing Director: Carolyn Williams
Sales Director: Maud Wilson
Estimated Sales: $500,000
Number Employees: 4
Square Footage: 10000
Type of Packaging: Food Service, Private Label, Bulk

40909 Parks Brokerage Company
PO Box 6037
Moore, OK 73153-0037 405-793-7093
  Fax: 405-799-6619
Broker of dairy/deli, bakery and meat products including cheese
President: William Parks
VP: David Parks
Sales Manager: Mike Wigley
Estimated Sales: $1-2.5 Million
Number Employees: 1-4
Markets Served:
  Super Market Chains, Wholesale Distributors
Primary Brands Brokered include: Lactalis, Belgioioso, Vans Oriental, Hickory Farms, Snack Factory, Sparrer Sausage Company, Fillo Factory, Huxtable's Kitchen, Rubschlager Baking Corporation, Bryant Preserving Company
Brokered Products include:
  Dairy/Deli, Frozen Food, Meat, Meat Products

Food Brokers / A-Z

40910 Patman Foods Inc
704 Torrance Blvd
Redondo Beach, CA 90277-3442   310-540-3015
                                Fax: 310-540-4466
Broker of meat products and seafood
President: Pat Patman
p_patman@patmanmeatgroup.com
Sr. VP: Don Patman
VP/General Manager Retail Sales: Phil Baron
VP Operations: Mike Pogue
VP Technical Services: Karen Gorrell
Estimated Sales: $20-50 Million
Number Employees: 20-49
Markets Served:
  Super Market Chains, Food Service Operators
Primary Brands Brokered include: Jennie-O-Turkey; Dutch Quality House; Jac Pac; Gold Star; Omalia Steak; Viking Seafoods
Brokered Products include:
  Meat Products, Seafood

40911 Patman Meat Group
704 Torrance Blvd
Redondo Beach, CA 90277   310-540-8995
  Fax: 310-540-4466 info@patmanmeatgroup.com
                    www.patmanmeatgroup.com
Broker of dairy/deli products, frozen foods, general merchandise, meat, meat products and seafood
President: Patrick Patman
Contact: Iris Alvarado
iris@patmanmeatgroup.com
Markets Served:
  Super Market Chains, Wholesale Distributors
Primary Brands Brokered include: Dutch Quality House; Request Foods; Ssi Foods, Tridnt Foods, John Morrell Foods
Brokered Products include:
  Dairy/Deli, Frozen Food, General Merchandise, Meat, Meat Products, Seafood

40912 Patterson Co Inc
425 Huehl Rd # 17
Northbrook, IL 60062-2322   847-714-1200
                                 Fax: 847-714-1275
Broker of confectionery, meat and private label items, frozen food, general merchandise and groceries
Manager: Jim Patterson
jimpattersonjr@pattersonco.com
CEO: M Patterson
CFO: P Patterson
Estimated Sales: $10-20 Million
Number Employees: 10-19
Markets Served:
  Super Market Chains, Wholesale Distributors
Brokered Products include:
  Confectionery, Frozen Food, Groceries

40913 Paul Esposito Inc
6-12 N Union Ave # 8
Cranford, NJ 07016-2182   908-709-1399
                      paulespo1@verizon.net
Import broker of confectionery and dairy/deli products, spices, groceries, private label items, dried fruits and nuts, bakers supplies
Owner: Mary Esposito
m.esposito@paulesposito.org
Secretary/Treasurer: M Esposito
Vice President: R Esposito
Estimated Sales: $1-2.5 Million
Number Employees: 1-4
Markets Served:
  Food Manufacturers & Processors, Super Market Chains, Wholesale Distributors, Food Service Operators
Primary Brands Brokered include: Mariani Packing Company
Brokered Products include:
  Confectionery, Exports, General Merchandise, Imports, Ingredients, Produce, Spices, Dried Fruit & Nuts

40914 Paul G Nester & Son Co Inc
259 Claremont Ave
Tamaqua, PA 18252-4302   570-668-1282
                                 Fax: 570-668-4525
Broker of grocery and dairy/deli products, frozen foods, meats, private label items, produce, etc.
President: Jan Gabriel
CEO: Gary Larkin
Estimated Sales: $10-20 Million
Number Employees: 5-9
Type of Packaging: Consumer, Private Label
Markets Served:
  Super Market Chains, Wholesale Distributors
Brokered Products include:
  Confectionery, Dairy/Deli, Frozen Food, Groceries, Meat, Private Label, Produce, Baked Goods

40915 (HQ)Paul Inman Associates
30095 Northwestern Highway
Farmington Hills, MI 48334   248-626-8300
                                 Fax: 248-626-7893
Broker of confectionery products, frozen foods, general merchandise, groceries and private label items
President/CEO: Ron Fairchild
Executive VP/COO: Charlie Pountney
Number Employees: 300
Markets Served:
  Food Manufacturers & Processors, Super Market Chains, Wholesale Distributors, Food Service Operators
Primary Brands Brokered include: Tropicana; Ocean Spray; Reckitt & Colman; International Home Foods; Hershey Chocolate; Beatrice Cheese
Brokered Products include:
  Confectionery, Frozen Food, General Merchandise, Groceries, Private Label

40916 Peak Corporation
7 Calle Tabonuuco
203
San Juan, PR 00920   787-792-7750
          Fax: 787-792-7292 carloss@tld.net
Import broker of frozen foods, general merchandise, groceries and private label items
President/General Manager: C Garcia
Chairman: M Montalvo
Number Employees: 5-9
Markets Served:
  Super Market Chains, Wholesale Distributors, Food Service Operators
Primary Brands Brokered include: Senoret Chemical; Heinz; Scott's Liquid Gold; Neoteric; Halouer Foods; Alfin Del North
Brokered Products include:
  Frozen Food, General Merchandise, Groceries, Imports, Private Label

40917 Pennickers Food Distribution
5 Charles Street
Winnipeg, MB R2W 3Z9
Canada   204-586-9694
                                 Fax: 204-586-9696
Import broker of confectionery products, frozen foods, groceries, general merchandise, seafood, private label items, etc.
President/General Manager: D Graham
Sales Manager Retail: G Graham
Sales Manager Food Service: J Graham
Number Employees: 5
Square Footage: 27200
Markets Served:
  Food Manufacturers & Processors, Super Market Chains, Wholesale Distributors, Food Service Operators
Brokered Products include:
  Confectionery, Frozen Food, General Merchandise, Groceries, Imports, Private Label, Seafood

40918 Peter Blease Sales
688 Youngs Hill Rd
Easton, PA 18040   610-253-4800
          Fax: 610-253-8486 peterb@enter.net
Broker of frozen foods and groceries. Supplier of closeout food items
Owner: Peter Blease
Estimated Sales: $1-3 Million
Number Employees: 1-4
Markets Served:
  Super Market Chains, Wholesale Distributors
Brokered Products include:
  Frozen Food, Groceries, IQF Foods; Closeouts, Surplus, Salvage

40919 Peter Johansky Studio
152 W 25th St
New York, NY 10001-7402   212-242-7013
                          peter@johansky.com
                          www.johansky.com
Total food ingredient source with technical support. Dry, canned, refrigerated and frozen ingredients
Owner: Peter Johansky
pjohansky@michaelhowardstudios.com
Estimated Sales: Less Than $500,000
Number Employees: 1-4
Square Footage: 202800
Type of Packaging: Bulk
Markets Served:
  Food Manufacturers & Processors

40920 Peters & Fair
2520 Trent Dr
Marietta, GA 30066-5734   770-977-8970
                                 Fax: 770-973-6104
Import broker of confectionery and dairy/deli items, meats, produce, seafood, etc.
Owner: Larry Lieber
llieber@mindspring.com
Estimated Sales: $.5-1 million
Number Employees: 1-4
Markets Served:
  Food Manufacturers & Processors, Super Market Chains, Wholesale Distributors, Food Service Operators
Primary Brands Brokered include: Beef International; Country Farm Quail; Rema Foods; Patrick Cudahy; Magic Seasoning Blends; Paris Delights
Brokered Products include:
  Confectionery, Dairy/Deli, Imports, Meat, Meat Products, Produce, Seafood, Spices

40921 Peters & Peters Manufacturer's Agents
8737 Dunwoody Pl # 5
Atlanta, GA 30350-6203   770-992-0656
                                 Fax: 770-992-0635
Manufacturers' representative for food service equipment and supplies
Principal: G Peters
Marketing Agent: Gerhard Kleinen
Marketing Agent: Bryant Curley
Estimated Sales: $2.5-5 Million
Number Employees: 1-4
Markets Served:
  Wholesale Distributors
Primary Brands Brokered include: Baker's Aid; Servolift Eastern; Somat Company; Vent Master; Stero; Yorkraft
Brokered Products include:
  General Merchandise, Foodservice Equipment & Supplies

40922 Phillips Sales Co
875 Waimanu St # 535
Honolulu, HI 96813-5266   808-591-2441
          Fax: 808-591-2943 888-591-2441
                          www.phillipstoyota.com
Import broker of frozen seafood
President: Dick Phillips
dick.phillipssales.hawaii@hawaiiantel.net
General Manager: Rick McCaunaghy
Vice President: Martha Phillips
Estimated Sales: $5-10 Million
Number Employees: 5-9
Square Footage: 8800
Markets Served:
  Food Manufacturers & Processors, Super Market Chains, Wholesale Distributors, Food Service Operators
Primary Brands Brokered include: PSC
Brokered Products include:
  Frozen Food, Imports, Seafood

40923 Phoenix Food Sales
1052 NE 210th Terrace
Miami, FL 33179-2062   305-651-3733
                                 Fax: 305-652-7667
Export broker of frozen foods, grocery items, meats, meat products, seafood and spices
CEO: Carmela Delmonico
Vice President: Gerald Delmonico
Sales Director: Anthony Fortuna
Estimated Sales: $2.5-5 Million
Number Employees: 1-4
Markets Served:
  Super Market Chains, Wholesale Distributors, Food Service Operators
Brokered Products include:
  Exports, Frozen Food, Groceries, Meat, Meat Products, Seafood, Spices

Food Brokers / A-Z

40924 Phoenix Foods Inc
723 Cowan St
Nashville, TN 37207-5621   615-742-4989
Fax: 615-742-3864   800-624-3268
Roylee@phoenixfoods.com
www.phoenixfoods.com
Broker of confectionery and private label items, frozen foods, general merchandise, groceries, etc.
President: Roy Lee Maguire
HR Executive: Dawn Davis
ddavis@phoenixfoods.com
Quality Assurance: Jay Pugh
Purchasing: Jennifer Glancy
Estimated Sales: $5-10 Million
Number Employees: 50-99
Square Footage: 4000
Markets Served:
    Food Manufacturers & Processors, Super Market Chains, Wholesale Distributors
Primary Brands Brokered include: Bake Line Products; Compass Foods; Comstock Michigan Fruit; Kleen Brite; The Red Wing Company
Brokered Products include:
    Confectionery, Frozen Food, General Merchandise, Groceries, Private Label

40925 Pierce Cartwright Company
1205 East International Airport Road
Suite 204
Anchorage, AK 99518   907-563-3032
Fax: 907-562-3473   garyc@pc.ak.net
www.piercecartwright.com
Broker of confectionery and dairy/deli products, frozen food, general merchandise, seafood, groceries and meats
President/CEO: Gary Cartwright
VP/Foodservice Dept Mgr: Pam Christy
Deli Department Mgr/Foodservice Sales: Gail Hubble
Distributor Manager: David Sisk
Confection Department Manager: Vicky Kelly
Estimated Sales: $3.1 Million
Number Employees: 19
Square Footage: 7500
Markets Served:
    Food Manufacturers & Processors, Super Market Chains, Wholesale Distributors, Food Service Operators
Primary Brands Brokered include: AdvancePierre Foods; Bel/Kaukauna U.S.A.; Dawn Food Products; E S Foods; Farmland Foods; Foster Farms; Galaxy Desserts; Iserino's; Kerry; Longhorn BBQ; Maple Leaf Farms; MegaMex; Michael's Foods; Nestle; Schwan's; Simplot Foods; Trident Foods
Brokered Products include:
    Confectionery, Dairy/Deli, Frozen Food, General Merchandise, Groceries, Meat, Meat Products, Seafood

40926 Pinski Portugal & Associate
1933 Broadway
Suite 322
Los Angeles, CA 90007   213-763-5722
Fax: 213-763-5747   866-402-3663
www.pinski-portugal.com
Broker of confectionery and private label items, spices and gourmet/specialty foods including pastas, vinegars, oils, sauces, nuts, dry mixes, etc.
President: Lynn Portugal
VP: Lisa Portugal
Contact: Fiorella Rodriguez
fiorella.rodriguez@pinski-portugal.com
Estimated Sales: B
Number Employees: 3
Markets Served:
    Wholesale Distributors, Food Service Operators
Primary Brands Brokered include: Yohay Baking; Nunes Farm; McStevens
Brokered Products include:
    Confectionery, Private Label, Spices, Gourmet/Specialty Foods

40927 Pioneer Food Brokers
4301 Stuart Andrew Blvd Ste P
Charlotte, NC 28217-1587
Fax: 704-523-9424
Broker of confectionery products, frozen foods, general merchandise, groceries and private label items
President: Bernie Ellinghaus
Chairman: W Kinncaid
Sr. VP: Rex Nelson
Estimated Sales: $2.5-5 Million
Number Employees: 5-9
Markets Served:
    Super Market Chains, Wholesale Distributors
Brokered Products include:
    Confectionery, Frozen Food, General Merchandise, Groceries, Private Label

40928 Pioneer Food Service
8933 Roebuck Boulevard
Birmingham, AL 35206-1572   205-681-9677
Fax: 205-681-9290
Broker of dairy/deli products, frozen foods, meats and meat products and seafood
President: W Lemons
Estimated Sales: $2.5-5 Million
Number Employees: 1-4
Type of Packaging: Food Service, Private Label
Markets Served:
    Wholesale Distributors, Food Service Operators
Brokered Products include:
    Dairy/Deli, Frozen Food, Groceries, Meat, Meat Products, Seafood, Spices

40929 Pioneer Marketing International
188 Westhill Drive
Los Gatos, CA 95032-5032   408-356-4990
Fax: 408-356-2795   www.pioneer.com
Corn, soybeans, alfalfa, canola, wheat, sunflowers; marketing, sales and product promotion
Partner: Russ Tritomo
Director Sales: Ed DeSoto
Estimated Sales: $1-5 Million
Number Employees: 4
Markets Served:
    Food Manufacturers & Processors, Super Market Chains, Wholesale Distributors
Brokered Products include:
    Confectionery, Exports, Imports, Private Label, Snack Foods

40930 Plastic Industrial Products
8619 Oak St
New Orleans, LA 70118-1221   504-861-1500
Fax: 504-865-1525   www.tarpbuilder.com
Broker of industrial ingredients
President: John E Beaumont
jbeau@bellsouth.net
VP: John Beaumont, Jr.
Sales Exec: John Beaumont
Estimated Sales: $5-10 Million
Number Employees: 20-49
Brokered Products include:
    Ingredients

40931 Plum & Assoc Inc
15441 Knoll Trail Dr # 200
Dallas, TX 75248-7067   972-386-0196
Fax: 972-386-0199   sales@plumandassociates.com
A Texas based family run company representing food manufacturers and industrial food producers in the Southwest.
Owner: Brooke Harold
brooke@plumgroupfoods.com
CEO: Brooke Plum Herold
Vice President: Rick Herold
Number Employees: 1-4
Number of Brands: 20
Number of Products: 1000
Parent Co: Plum & Associates
Type of Packaging: Bulk
Primary Brands Brokered include: Basic American Foods, DSM Savory, Ingomar, Jardox, Kikkoman, Lakeside foods, McCain/Jon-Lin, Mgp Ingredients, Pacific Farms, Rembrandt Eggs, Roland Foods, Seenergy Foods, Solae, Santa Fe Ingredients, York Pecans
Brokered Products include:
    Industrial

40932 Polish Folklore Import Co
2428 Rose St
Franklin Park, IL 60131-3323   847-288-0708
Fax: 847-288-0816   pfimport@aol.com
www.polishfolklore.com
Import broker of confectionery products including jams and preserves. Wholesaler/distributor of specialty food products
President: Bogumila Mielski
pfimport@aol.com
Vice President: Christopher Bogacz
Sales Director: Marta Sliwa
Estimated Sales: $2.5-5 Million
Number Employees: 5-9
Markets Served:
    Super Market Chains, Wholesale Distributors
Brokered Products include:
    Confectionery, Imports, Jams & Preserves

40933 Posternak Bauer Associates
479 White Plains Road
Eastchester, NY 10709   914-793-9000
Fax: 914-793-9209   INFO@PBAREP.COM
www.pbarep.com
Manufacturers' representative for food service equipment
Partner: Michael R. Posternak
Partner: Steve Bauer
IT/Office Manager: Herb Rembert, Jr.
Estimated Sales: $2.5-5 Million
Number Employees: 10-19
Markets Served:
    Wholesale Distributors
Primary Brands Brokered include: Traulsen; Vulcan; Lincoln Foodservice; Inter Metro; Randall Manufacturing; World Crisa; APW/Wyatt
Brokered Products include:
    General Merchandise, Foodservice Equipment

40934 Poteet Seafood Co
107 Speedy Tostensen Blvd
Brunswick, GA 31520-3149   912-264-5340
Fax: 912-267-9695
Seafood
Owner: Speedy Tostensen
poteetseafood@bellsouth.net
Estimated Sales: $350,000
Number Employees: 1-4

40935 Powell May International
2475 Skymark Avenue
Unit 1
Mississauga, ON L4W 4Y6
Canada   905-625-9301
Fax: 905-625-7034
lfurtado@powellmay.cbpowell.com
www.powellmay.com
Import broker of seafood, private label items and industrial ingredients
CEO: Tim Powell
Vice President: Johan Petersen
VP Sales: Ray Lalonde
Sales Manager: Pam Bentley
Number Employees: 5-9
Markets Served:
    Food Manufacturers & Processors, Wholesale Distributors, Food Service Operators
Primary Brands Brokered include: Sun-Maid Growers of California; Diamond Walnuts of California; Japan Foods Canada; D.D. Williamson Caramel; Sun Sweet Growers; McIlhenng Corporation
Brokered Products include:
    Imports, Ingredients, Private Label, Seafood, Spices

40936 Preferred Brokerage Company
2819 Richmond Dr NE
Albuquerque, NM 87107-1918   505-842-5996
Fax: 505-842-1449
Import and export broker of dairy/deli products, frozen and health foods, meats, seafood, spices, general merchandise, groceries, industrial ingredients, etc.
President: V Schroeder
Vice President: P Schroeder
Sales Director: Daryl Strader
Contact: Betty Maestas
bmaestas@kisales.com
Estimated Sales: $5-10 Million
Number Employees: 5-9
Square Footage: 13200
Type of Packaging: Food Service, Private Label, Bulk
Markets Served:
    Food Manufacturers & Processors, Super Market Chains, Wholesale Distributors, Food Service Operators
Primary Brands Brokered include: Quaker Oats Company; Sugar Foods Corporation; John Morrell; Lipton; Specialty Brands; Pillsbury
Brokered Products include:
    Confectionery, Dairy/Deli, Exports, Frozen Food, Groceries, Health Food, Ingredients, Meat, Meat Products, Private Label, Produce, Seafood, Spices, Beverages

Food Brokers / A-Z

40937 Preisco Jentash
91 Glacier Street
Coquitlam, BC V3K 5Z1
Canada   604-941-8502
Fax: 604-941-8509
Broker of dairy/deli products, frozen foods, groceries, meat and meat products, nonalcoholic beverages, private label, seafood and general merchandise.
President: Jim Zalusky
Partner: Terry Johnston
CEO: Steve Cowan
Senior VP/CFO: Brian McBride
VP Retail: Rick Lawrence
Key Account Executive: Richard Greville
Marketing Manager: Ken Nielsen
Marketing Manager: Nicky Ahmed
Operations Manager: Ken Blatherwick
VP Purchasing/Food Service: Sue Williams
Number Employees: 50-99
Square Footage: 400000
Markets Served:
   Food Manufacturers & Processors, Super Market Chains, Wholesale Distributors, Food Service Operators
Primary Brands Brokered include: Polaris Water; Bunge Foods; Oscar's Syrups; Kikkoman; Mission/Dionne's; Camp Maple Syrup
Brokered Products include:
   Dairy/Deli, Frozen Food, General Merchandise, Groceries, Meat, Meat Products, Private Label, Seafood, Non-Alcoholic Beverages

40938 Premier
2109 SE J St
Bentonville, AR 72712-3860   479-271-6000
Fax: 479-271-6006   800-376-1353
josh@prconcepts.com   www.prconcepts.com
Export broker of confectionery and dairy/deli products, frozen and health foods, general merchandise, seafood, produce, meat products, private label items, groceries, etc.
President/CEO: Thomas Korn
CEO: Darren Horton
Estimated Sales: $20-50 Million
Number Employees: 20-49
Square Footage: 16000

40939 Premier Food Marketing
6 Way Rd # 309
Middlefield, CT 06455-1080   860-349-7040
Fax: 860-349-7041   800-864-2748
Broker of dairy/deli items and baked goods
President: Robert Goodman
VP: Dave Grennnan
VP: Joseph Holovach
Estimated Sales: $.5-1 million
Number Employees: 5-9
Square Footage: 12000
Markets Served:
   Food Manufacturers & Processors, Super Market Chains, Wholesale Distributors, Food Service Operators
Primary Brands Brokered include: Heinz Bakery Products; Sara Lee; Dawn Food Products; T. Marzetti; Pasta Warehouse; Fleischer (Bagels)
Brokered Products include:
   Dairy/Deli, Baked Goods

40940 Premier Food Service Sales
1021 W Harimaw Court
Metairie, LA 70001-6231   504-833-4605
Fax: 504-833-4608
Broker of dairy/deli products, frozen foods, groceries, industrial ingredients, meat and meat products, etc.
Owner: Frank Taormina, Jr.
Co-Owner: John Prieur, Jr.
Estimated Sales: $5-10 Million
Number Employees: 5-9
Square Footage: 12000
Markets Served:
   Food Manufacturers & Processors, Super Market Chains, Wholesale Distributors, Food Service Operators
Brokered Products include:
   Dairy/Deli, Frozen Food, Groceries, Ingredients, Meat, Meat Products, Seafood, Spices, Baked Goods

40941 Premier Marketing
166 S River Road
Suite 202
Bedford, NH 03110-6928   603-621-5155
Fax: 603-766-5755   800-544-2481
Manufacturers' representative for food service equipment and supplies including china and glassware
President: Greg Skorich
Estimated Sales: $.5-1 million
Number Employees: 1-4
Markets Served:
   Wholesale Distributors
Primary Brands Brokered include: Cambro; Lincoln; Homer Lauglin; Amana Commercial Cooking; American Metalcraft
Brokered Products include:
   General Merchandise, China, Glassware, etc.

40942 Premium Seafood Co
157 E 57th St # 18a
F.D.R. Station
New York, NY 10022-2115   212-750-5377
Fax: 212-308-0223   premiumsfd@aol.com
www.premiumseafood.com
Broker of seafood
Owner: Patti Sirkus
premiumseafood@premiumseafood.com
VP: Patti Sirkus
Estimated Sales: $1-2.5 Million
Number Employees: 1-4
Markets Served:
   Food Manufacturers & Processors, Super Market Chains, Wholesale Distributors, Food Service Operators
Primary Brands Brokered include: Sirkiss Pride
Brokered Products include:
   Frozen Food, Seafood

40943 Prestige Marketing
5150 Palm Valley Rd Ste 102
Ponte Vedra Beach, FL 32082   904-280-0565
Fax: 904-280-2014   meatsrus@bellsouth.net
Broker of frozen foods, meat and meat products, seafood and dairy/deli items
Owner: J Cheek
CFO: S Cheek
Sales Manager: Chris Cheek
Estimated Sales: $10-20 Million
Number Employees: 5-9
Square Footage: 12000
Markets Served:
   Super Market Chains
Primary Brands Brokered include: Boston (lamb); Chicago (veal); Cumberland Gap; Maverick Ranch (beef); Rosen (lamb); Rose Packing Company
Brokered Products include:
   Dairy/Deli, Frozen Food, Imports, Meat, Meat Products, Private Label, Seafood

40944 Prestige Sales
50 Boul Cremazie O Bureau 700
Montreal, QC H2P 2T4
Canada   514-381-8815
Fax: 514-381-0844
Broker of confectionery products, frozen foods, general merchandise, groceries, private label items, etc.
President: Michael Korenberg
Chairman: L Pedvis
Executive VP: Natalie Toussaint
Number Employees: 26
Markets Served:
   Super Market Chains, Wholesale Distributors, Food Service Operators
Brokered Products include:
   Confectionery, Frozen Food, General Merchandise, Groceries, Health Food, Private Label

40945 Prestige Sales & Marketing
45 Eisenhower Drive
Paramus, NJ 07652-1452   201-368-1400
Fax: 201-368-8882
Broker of frozen foods, general merchandise, grocery products, meats, etc.
President: Rob Monroe
VP Administration: Susie Higgins
VP: Ted Zack
Marketing Specialist: Carloe Hemmes
Sales Manager: Robert Allen
Director Food Sales: Jim McManus
Estimated Sales: $20-50 Million
Number Employees: 20-49
Square Footage: 8000
Markets Served:
   Food Manufacturers & Processors, Super Market Chains, Wholesale Distributors, Food Service Operators
Primary Brands Brokered include: Sara Lee; Reynolds Metals; Anchor; Rich Products; Dubuque; Chicopee
Brokered Products include:
   Confectionery, Dairy/Deli, Frozen Food, General Merchandise, Groceries, Meat, Meat Products, Private Label, Produce, Seafood, Disposables

40946 Pro Line Marketing Inc
5942 Las Positas Rd
Livermore, CA 94551-7804   925-456-7990
Fax: 925-456-7991   www.prolinereps.com
Manufacturers' representative for general merchandise and food service equipment including ovens, ranges, fryers, steamers, kettles, warmers, refrigerators, etc.
Partner: Casey McLaughlin
VP: Malcolm Cerri
Sales: Casey McLaughlin
Office Manager and Service: Sue Lambert Cerri
Estimated Sales: $500,000-$1 Million
Number Employees: 5-9
Square Footage: 6400
Markets Served:
   Wholesale Distributors
Primary Brands Brokered include: Cleveland; Garland; Frymaster; U.S. Range; Vent Master; Federal
Brokered Products include:
   General Merchandise, Ovens, Ranges, Fryers, Steamers, etc.

40947 Pro Pacific Agents
8802 122nd Ave NE
Kirkland, WA 98033-5828   425-827-7279
Fax: 425-828-0464   800-490-6511
sales@pro-pacific.com   www.pro-pacific.com
Manufacturers' representative for food service equipment
Owner: Robin Oury
robin@pro-pacific.com
Partner: Mike Walker
Principal: Larry Jaeck
Sales Representative: Rick Burby
robin@pro-pacific.com
Office Manager: June Vellat
Estimated Sales: $1-2.5 Million
Number Employees: 5-9
Square Footage: 8400
Markets Served:
   Wholesale Distributors
Primary Brands Brokered include: Supreme Metal; Amco; Plymold Seating; Avtec; Norlake; Alto Shaam
Brokered Products include:
   General Merchandise, Foodservice Equipment

40948 Pro Reps W
3191 Airport Loop Dr # C
Costa Mesa, CA 92626-3404   510-654-2544
Fax: 714-662-7866   800-820-1073
sales@proreps.com
Manufacturers' representative for food service equipment and supplies
Owner: Steve Mc Kay
Principal: Kevin Westley
Principal: Dave Rall
Marketing, Inside Sales and Support: Sharon Stephens
Inside Sales: Jill Hamblin
Contact: Susaneun Choung
echoung@proreps.com
Accounting and Human Resources Manager: Sam Chung
Number Employees: 10-19
Markets Served:
   Wholesale Distributors
Primary Brands Brokered include: Berkel; Wells Manufacturing; Randell Manufacturing Company; Fisher; Prince Castle; Lakeside/Aris
Brokered Products include:
   General Merchandise, Foodservice Equipment & Supplies

40949 Pro-Quip Corporation
2117 Hillshire Cir
Suite 102
Bartlett, TN 38133-6014   901-766-9375
Fax: 901-766-9384   800-866-7767
jimkerwick@foodserviceequipment.com
www.foodserviceequipment.com
Manufacturers' representative for food service equipment

Food Brokers / A-Z

Co-Owner: Andy Andrews
Co-Owner: Jim Kerwick
Co-Owner: Clay Compton
Sales Director: Carey Bowen
Contact: Donna Bryan
donnabryan@foodserviceequipment.com
Office Assistant: Vicki French
Estimated Sales: $3-5 Million
Number Employees: 1-4
Markets Served:
  Wholesale Distributors
Primary Brands Brokered include: Alvey Washing; Cleveland Range; Globe Food Equipment; Greenheck Fan; APW/Wyott; Vanguard Technology, Inc.
Brokered Products include:
  General Merchandise, Foodservice Equipment

40950 Proactive Sales & Marketing
1800 W Hawthorne Ln # B
West Chicago, IL 60185-1863   630-293-5400
        Fax: 630-876-3860 tmb30@aol.com
Broker of dairy/deli products, frozen foods, groceries, meats, private label items, etc.
President: Steve Diebold
Estimated Sales: $5-10 Million
Number Employees: 1-4
Primary Brands Brokered include: Webber Farms, Inc.; Dutch Quality House/Wayne Farms; Carolina Turkeys; Vincent Gordano Corporation; Gangi Brothers Packing Company
Brokered Products include:
  Dairy/Deli, Frozen Food, Groceries, Meat, Meat Products, Private Label, Seafood

40951 Processors Co-Op
1110 Powers Pl
Alpharetta, GA 30009-8389   770-664-1516
                                 Fax: 770-636-3006
Seafood, meats, poultry
President, CEO: Alan Brown
alanjr@cutyourfoodcost.com
Director of Marketing: Terrie Bradley
Operations Manager: Robert Bragg
Director of Purchasing: Bill Larsen
Estimated Sales: $10-20 Million
Number Employees: 10-19

40952 Professional Food Service
1204 Durrett Lane
Louisville, KY 40213-2026   502-367-1404
                                 Fax: 502-367-0003
Broker of dairy/deli products, frozen foods, meat and meat products, private label items, seafood and spices
President: Nancy Bean
Vice President: J Bean
Estimated Sales: $10-20 Million
Number Employees: 10-19
Markets Served:
  Wholesale Distributors, Food Service Operators
Primary Brands Brokered include: Quaker; Ocean Spray; Redi-Bake; Bernardi
Brokered Products include:
  Dairy/Deli, Frozen Food, Meat, Meat Products, Private Label, Seafood, Spices

40953 Professional Manufacturers' Representatives
6079 Oakbrook Pkwy
Norcross, GA 30093-1701   770-441-3100
        Fax: 770-449-6834 800-836-2716
        pmroffice@pmreps.com www.pmreps.com
Manufacturers' representative for food service equipment and supplies
Owner: Shannon Steward
Principle: Mike Hensley
Principle: Shannon Steward
Vice President, Principle: Tom Bernhard
Inside Sales: Michael Moore
Sales, Georgia: Lisa Bashline
Inside Sales: Michelle Black
Contact: Tom Bernhard
bernhard@pmreps.com
Estimated Sales: $1-2.5 Million
Number Employees: 10-19
Markets Served:
  Wholesale Distributors
Primary Brands Brokered include: Amco; Avtec; Blodgett-Combi; Duke Manufacturing; In-Sink-Erator; Magi Kitch

Brokered Products include:
  General Merchandise, Foodservice Equipment & Supplies

40954 Professional Reps of Arizona
23005 North 15th Avenue
Suite 104
Phoenix, AZ 85027-6308   602-995-8922
        Fax: 602-864-1754 877-995-8922
        brian@professionalreps.com
Manufacturers' representative for food service equipment and supplies
Owner: Bob Toloskiewich
CEO: Robert Toloskiewich
Estimated Sales: $2.5-5 Million
Number Employees: 1-4
Markets Served:
  Super Market Chains, Wholesale Distributors, Food Service Operators
Primary Brands Brokered include: American Metalcraft; Delfield; Eagle; Harco Corporation; Metal Masters/Eagle; Borden China
Brokered Products include:
  General Merchandise, Foodservice Equipment & Supplies

40955 Progressive Brokerage Co Inc
1900 Veterans Memorial Blvd
Metairie, LA 70005-2655   504-835-6407
                                 Fax: 504-838-0115
Broker of confectionery, meats, dairy/deli products, frozen foods, general merchandise, private label items, groceries, produce, etc.
President: Neal Rome
Estimated Sales: $10-20 Million
Number Employees: 20-49
Markets Served:
  Super Market Chains, Wholesale Distributors, Food Service Operators
Brokered Products include:
  Confectionery, Dairy/Deli, Frozen Food, General Merchandise, Groceries, Meat, Private Label, Produce

40956 Progressive Food Service Broker
PO Box 918
Bryant, AR 72089-0918   501-847-3952
                                 Fax: 501-847-8701
Broker of dairy/deli, frozen foods, meat/meat products, groceries, private label items, seafood, etc.
President: Larry Turner
Estimated Sales: $10-20 Million
Number Employees: 10-19
Markets Served:
  Wholesale Distributors, Food Service Operators
Brokered Products include:
  Dairy/Deli, Frozen Food, Groceries, Meat, Meat Products, Private Label, Seafood

40957 Progressive Marketing Systems
8026 Vantage Dr
San Antonio, TX 78230-4733   210-525-9171
                                 Fax: 210-525-9910
Import broker of confectionery products, general merchandise, groceries, meats, private label items, etc.
President: Anthony Cruise
Estimated Sales: $1-2.5 Million
Number Employees: 1-4
Markets Served:
  Super Market Chains, Wholesale Distributors, Food Service Operators
Brokered Products include:
  Confectionery, General Merchandise, Groceries, Imports, Meat Products, Private Label

40958 Progressive Sales & Marketing
11 N Westfield St
Feeding Hills, MA 01030-1600   413-786-7768
        Fax: 413-789-0958 info@progressive-1.com
                         www.progressive-1.com
Broker of dairy/deli products, groceries, frozen foods and private label items
Owner: Joe Davis
jdavis@progressive-1.com
Managing Partner: Bob Godfrey
Key Account Sales, Business Manager: Bob Godfrey
Key Account Sales, Business Manager: Les Tye
jdavis@progressive-1.com
Estimated Sales: $2.5-5 Million
Number Employees: 10-19
Type of Packaging: Private Label

Markets Served:
  Super Market Chains, Wholesale Distributors, Food Service Operators
Brokered Products include:
  Dairy/Deli, Frozen Food, General Merchandise, Groceries, Private Label, Produce

40959 Promesa
PO Box 1309
Weslaco, TX 78599-1309   956-969-2769
        Fax: 956-968-2788 800-824-8524
                         promesa@flash.net
Import broker of frozen fruits including Mexican strawberries, IQF diced mangos, guava and mango purees, etc.
President: Juan Barreto
Secretary/Treasurer: Cleofas De Luna
Sales Director: Guillermo Barreto
Estimated Sales: $1-3 Million
Number Employees: 1-4
Markets Served:
  Food Manufacturers & Processors, Super Market Chains, Wholesale Distributors, Food Service Operators
Brokered Products include:
  Frozen Food, Imports, Mango & Guava Purees, etc.

40960 Providence Bay Fish Co
189 Briarwood Dr
Wakefield, RI 02879-2834   401-789-0900
        Fax: 401-789-5002 mvincent@providencebay.com
                         www.providencebay.com
Broker of frozen seafood including lobster, scallops, monkfish, dogfish, herring, mackerel, squid, shrimp, etc.
Managing Director: Martin Vincent
mvincent@providencebay.com
Estimated Sales: $1-2.5 Million
Number Employees: 1-4
Brokered Products include:
  Frozen Food, Seafood

40961 Providence Brokerage
5666 Mount Berry Ln
Norcross, GA 30092   770-446-2273
                                 Fax: 770-446-9214
Broker of general merchandise, snack foods and confectionery items
President: Frank Garrett
frank.garrett@providencegroup.com
Estimated Sales: $300,000-500,000
Number Employees: 1-4
Markets Served:
  Super Market Chains, Wholesale Distributors
Primary Brands Brokered include: American Candy Company; American Licorice; Silverado Foods; Impact Confections; Ben Myerson
Brokered Products include:
  Confectionery, General Merchandise, Snack Foods

40962 Provincial
205-4700 Rue De La Savone
Montreal, QC H4P 1T7
Canada   514-733-8663
                                 Fax: 514-733-8840
Import and export broker of alcoholic beverages, confectionery products, frozen foods, general merchandise, groceries, etc.
President: Pierre Drouin
Chairman: Ken Kouri
VP Finance: Raymond Francoeur
VP Sales: Jean Smith
VP Sales: Denys Beaudry
VP Sales: Robert Broduer
Number Employees: 96
Markets Served:
  Super Market Chains, Wholesale Distributors, Food Service Operators
Primary Brands Brokered include: Better Brands; Canadian Fishing; Minute Maid; Slim Fast; Newman's Own; VanMelle
Brokered Products include:
  Alcoholic Beverages, Confectionery, Exports, Frozen Food, General Merchandise, Groceries, Imports, Private Label

40963 Purcell & Madden Associates
93 Schumacher Drive
New Hyde Park, NY 11040-3644   516-873-1749
        Fax: 516-873-6256 purmadinc@aol.com
Manufacturers' representative of foodsevice equipment

Food Brokers / A-Z

President: Mike Purcell
Number Employees: 5-9
Markets Served:
  Wholesale Distributors
Primary Brands Brokered include: Crimsco; Dito Dean Food Prep; Everpure; Lakeside Manufacturing; Server Products; Nu-Vu Foodservice System; Scotsman Ice Systems
Brokered Products include:
  General Merchandise, Foodservice Equipment

40964 Pure Sales
660 Baker St
Suite 367
Costa Mesa, CA 92626-4470   714-540-5455
            Fax: 714-540-5974 puresales@aol.com
Export broker of organically grown ingredients
President: James Silver
puresales@aol.com
Estimated Sales: $2.5 Million
Number Employees: 1-4
Type of Packaging: Private Label, Bulk
Markets Served:
  Food Manufacturers & Processors
Brokered Products include:
  Exports, Health Food, Ingredients, Organically Grown Ingredients

40965 Quality Brokerage Company
3548 Marie St
Orangeburg, SC 29118   803-531-1503
            Fax: 803-534-0280
Broker of dairy/deli products, spices, frozen foods, meat and meat products, seafood, etc.
President: Wayne Davis
VP: W Davis
Contact: Sue Pace
space@qualitybrokerageinc.com
Estimated Sales: $20-50 Million
Number Employees: 5-9
Square Footage: 5000
Markets Served:
  Food Manufacturers & Processors, Wholesale Distributors, Food Service Operators
Brokered Products include:
  Dairy/Deli, Frozen Food, Meat, Meat Products, Seafood, Spices

40966 Quality Food Company
25 Bath Street
Providence, RI 2908   401-421-5668
            Fax: 401-421-8570 877-233-3462
            info@qualityfoodcompany.com
            www.qualitybeefcompany.com
Ground beef and seafood
Secretary: William Catauro
billcatauro@qualityfoodcompany.com
Vice President: Vincent Catauro, III
Sales: Gary Flynn
Purchasing: Mark Engelhardt
Year Founded: 1931
Estimated Sales: $10-20 Million
Number Employees: 20-49
Type of Packaging: Food Service
Markets Served:
  Food Service Operators
Brokered Products include:
  Meat, Meat Products, Ground Beef

40967 Quality Rep Source
287 Andrews St
Rochester, NY 14604   585-924-9440
            Fax: 585-924-1445   800-388-1718
            qrs@frontiernet.net
Manufacturer's representative of food service equipment including cooking, holding, transportation and refrigeration equipment
Owner: Carl Dalo
Owner: Ray Ward
Estimated Sales: $5-10 Million
Number Employees: 5-9
Brokered Products include:
  General Merchandise, Foodservice Equipment

40968 (HQ)Quality Sales & Marketing, Inc.
P.O.Box 680757
Charlotte, NC 28216-0013   704-599-4773
            Fax: 704-599-6118   800-968-5808
Broker serving supermarket chains and food service operators

President/Partner: Wayne Davis
CEO: Frank Price
VP: Stan Ashley
VP Sales/Partner: Stan Ashley
Contact: Bob Chinn
b.chinn@qsmcarolinas.com
Estimated Sales: $20-50 Million
Number Employees: 50-99
Square Footage: 16000
Other Locations:
  Quality Sales & Marketing
  Orangeburg, SC Quality Sales & Marketing
Markets Served:
  Super Market Chains, Food Service Operators

40969 Quality Sales & Marketing
696 Concord Rd SE
Suite A
Smyrna, GA 30082-2629   770-435-8812
            Fax: 770-435-8806
Broker of dairy/deli products, frozen foods, groceries, meat and meat products, general merchandise, private label/generic items, etc.
President: Joseph Shay
Treasurer: John Flintom
VP: Wayne Davis
Estimated Sales: $3.90 Million
Number Employees: 19
Square Footage: 25500
Markets Served:
  Food Manufacturers & Processors, Wholesale Distributors, Food Service Operators
Primary Brands Brokered include: Schwan's Foodservice (Red Baron Pizza, Little Charles, Minh); Curtis Burns Foods; Gold Kist, Inc.; ASE Foodservice (Healthy Choice, Armour, Eckrich); Handgards, Inc.; State Fair Foods
Brokered Products include:
  Dairy/Deli, Frozen Food, General Merchandise, Groceries, Meat, Meat Products, Private Label, Seafood, Non-Foods, Disposables

40970 R G Sellers Co
3185 Elbee Rd
Moraine, OH 45439-1919   937-299-1545
            Fax: 937-299-2527
Broker of dairy/deli products, frozen foods, groceries, meats, private label items, etc.
Owner: Doug Sellers
rgsellers@aol.com
CEO: D Sellers
CFO: T Sellers
Estimated Sales: $20-50 Million
Number Employees: 20-49
Square Footage: 10000
Markets Served:
  Super Market Chains, Wholesale Distributors
Primary Brands Brokered include: Rich's; Wilson Meat; Pillsbury; Cargill Poultry; Parco Foods; Kellogg's
Brokered Products include:
  Dairy/Deli, Frozen Food, Groceries, Meat, Meat Products, Private Label, Seafood, Baked Goods

40971 R H Moulton Company
7 Burton Road
Burlington, MA 01803-3117   781-272-6070
            Fax: 781-273-1254
Broker of frozen foods, bakery flour and pie fillings
President: R Moulton
CEO: J Moulton
Number Employees: 1-4
Markets Served:
  Food Manufacturers & Processors, Wholesale Distributors
Brokered Products include:
  Ingredients, Private Label, Produce

40972 R J Bickert & Associates
10205 Main St
Clarence, NY 14031-2011   716-759-8876
            Fax: 716-759-2823 rbickert@msn.com
Broker of confectionery and dairy/deli products, groceries, meat and meat products, frozen foods, private label items, seafood, spices, etc.; serving supermarket chains, wholesalers/distributors and food processors
President: Roger Bickert
VP: Nora Drogi
Sales: Chris Campbell
Operations Manager: Becky Bickert
Estimated Sales: $5-10 Million
Number Employees: 10-19
Square Footage: 12000

Type of Packaging: Consumer, Food Service, Bulk
Markets Served:
  Super Market Chains, Wholesale Distributors
Brokered Products include:
  Confectionery, Groceries, Health Food, Meat Products, Private Label, Spices

40973 R&F Cocoa Services
102 Bishop St
Staten Island, NY 10306-2108   718-667-8266
            Fax: 718-667-8265
Broker of chocolate liquor and cocoa products including beans, butter and powder
President: Frank Hopkins
Estimated Sales: $5-10 Million
Number Employees: 7
Markets Served:
  Food Manufacturers & Processors, Wholesale Distributors
Brokered Products include:
  Confectionery, Ingredients, Cocoa Products

40974 R. Becker Marketing & Sales
62 Lepage Court
North York, ON M3J 1Z9
Canada   416-740-2966
            Fax: 416-740-9890
Import and export broker of frozen foods, dairy/deli products, seafood, private label items, spices, produce, industrial ingredients, health foods and groceries
President: Rose Becker
Number Employees: 10-19
Markets Served:
  Food Manufacturers & Processors, Super Market Chains, Wholesale Distributors, Food Service Operators
Primary Brands Brokered include: Swiftsure Seafood; Schwan's Foodservice; Give & Go Prepared Foods; Hubbert's Industries
Brokered Products include:
  Dairy/Deli, Exports, Frozen Food, Groceries, Health Food, Imports, Ingredients, Private Label, Produce, Seafood, Spices

40975 R.F. Cannon Company
21 Cardinal Drive
Williamsville, NY 14221-3429   716-634-5033
            Fax: 716-634-5961
Broker of dairy/deli items, frozen foods, groceries, meat and meat products, produce, seafood, private label items, etc.
President: R Cannon, Sr.
VP: R Cannon, Jr.
Number Employees: 5-9
Markets Served:
  Super Market Chains, Wholesale Distributors, Food Service Operators
Brokered Products include:
  Dairy/Deli, Frozen Food, Groceries, Meat, Meat Products, Private Label, Produce, Seafood

40976 R.J.K. Sales
3000 Hudson St
Baltimore, MD 21224-4949   443-398-0430
            Fax: 443-418-5358 www.rjksalesinc.com
Estimated Sales: $3-5 Million
Number Employees: 10-19

40977 R.W. Berkeley & Associates
PO Box 1059
Whittier, CA 90609-1059   562-944-2615
            Fax: 562-941-2628
Broker of general merchandise and private label items
Owner: Robert Berkeley
General Manager: M Berkeley
Sales: E Johnson
Number Employees: 5
Square Footage: 8000
Markets Served:
  Food Manufacturers & Processors, Super Market Chains, Wholesale Distributors, Food Service Operators
Primary Brands Brokered include: Practical Products, Inc.; American Cleaning Supply, Inc.; New York Lighter Corporation; Babies Best, Inc.; Whit Corporation
Brokered Products include:
  General Merchandise, Private Label

Food Brokers / A-Z

40978 RH Sulker Sales
4220 Steeles Avenue W
Woodbridge, ON L4L 3S8
Canada
905-856-2808
Fax: 905-856-5653
Broker of frozen foods, groceries, general merchandise and private label items. Computerized warehousing and invoicing services available
President: R Sulker
VP: R Klacza
Number Employees: 10-19
Square Footage: 13600
Type of Packaging: Food Service, Private Label
Markets Served:
 Food Manufacturers & Processors, Super Market Chains, Wholesale Distributors, Food Service Operators
Brokered Products include:
 Confectionery, Groceries, Imports, Ingredients, Private Label

40979 RIC, Inc
P.O.Boc 125
Riverside, IL 60546-0125
312-909-5077
Fax: 756-583-6305 800-561-1039
ricincmarketing@aol.com
Since 1974, selling high volume consumable products to all classes of trade in the USA.
President: Charles Jinrich
CFO: Rose Nesvacil
VP: John Bialek
Marketing: Rebecca Wood
Sales: Gordon Kingdon
Public Relations: Georgia Jindrich
Estimated Sales: $6 Million
Number Employees: 6
Number of Brands: 15
Parent Co: RIC, Inc

40980 RMCI Foodservice
4000 Homewood Rd
Memphis, TN 38118-6150
901-794-5555
Fax: 901-794-5580
Broker of confectionery and dairy/deli products, frozen foods, general merchandise, groceries, health foods, etc.
Owner: Danny Robinson
VP: K Robinson
Branch Manager: Richard McCain
Estimated Sales: $3-5 Million
Number Employees: 1-4
Square Footage: 22000
Markets Served:
 Food Manufacturers & Processors, Super Market Chains, Wholesale Distributors, Food Service Operators
Primary Brands Brokered include: Tropicana; Gold Kist; Readi Bake; McCormicks; Armour Swift Eckrich; Michael Foods
Brokered Products include:
 Confectionery, Dairy/Deli, Frozen Food, General Merchandise, Groceries, Health Food, Meat, Meat Products, Private Label, Seafood, Spices

40981 Rabe Sales Corp
80 Rolling Green Ln
Elma, NY 14059-9217
716-652-6650
Fax: 716-652-4278
Broker of confectionery products, general merchandise, groceries and private label items
President: J Leumer
Estimated Sales: Less Than $500,000
Number Employees: 1-4
Markets Served:
 Super Market Chains, Wholesale Distributors
Brokered Products include:
 General Merchandise, Private Label

40982 Rainbow
98-715 Kuahao Pl
Pearl City, HI 96782-3114
808-487-6455
Fax: 808-487-0888
President: John Schile
CEO: William Prideaux
CFO: John Pantenburly
Contact: Colleen Cambra
c.cambra@rsmhawaii.net
Estimated Sales: $20-50 Million
Number Employees: 20-49

40983 Rainbow Sales & Marketing
888 N Nimitz Hwy
Honolulu, HI 96817-6517
808-487-6455
Fax: 808-487-0888 info@rsmhawaii.com
www.rsmhawaii.net
We focus in growth and have the understanding to know what needs to be done.
President: Gary Hanagami
CEO: William Prideaux
Controller: Larry Kimata
VP: Dorothy Prideaux
VP Sales/Quality Control: Natalie Uchida
Estimated Sales: $4.40 Million
Number Employees: 20-49
Markets Served:
 Food Manufacturers & Processors, Super Market Chains, Wholesale Distributors, Food Service Operators
Primary Brands Brokered include: Brown Cow/Storeyfield; C&H; Chicken of the Sea; Daisy; Dannon; Heinz/Escalono/Diane's Desserts; Farmer John; Kellogg's FAFH; Nestle's Professional
Brokered Products include:
 Confectionery, Dairy/Deli, Frozen Food, General Merchandise, Groceries, Ingredients, Meat, Meat Products, Private Label, Produce

40984 Raleigh W. Johnson & Company
9525 Katy Freeway
Suite 475
Houston, TX 77024
713-623-6360
Fax: 713-623-6359 sales@raleighjohnson.com
www.raleighjohnson.com
Manufacturers' representative for food service equipment and supplies
President: David Johnson
Estimated Sales: $1-2.5 Million
Number Employees: 1-4
Markets Served:
 Wholesale Distributors
Primary Brands Brokered include: APW/Wyott; Blodgett Oven Company; Cleveland; Follett Corporation; Pitco Frialator; Sunkist Growers
Brokered Products include:
 General Merchandise, Foodservice Equipment & Supplies

40985 Rancho Sales & Marketing
41831 McAlby Ct # A
Murrieta, CA 92562-7037
951-694-5225
Fax: 909-600-8385
Broker of general merchandise, groceries and private label items
Co-Partner: W Jody Graves
Co-Partner: Mike Krone
Estimated Sales: $2.5-5 Million
Number Employees: 1-4
Markets Served:
 Super Market Chains, Wholesale Distributors
Primary Brands Brokered include: Hoover; Dopaco; Western Commerce; Galderma Labs; Suburbanite/Butler; Oralabs
Brokered Products include:
 General Merchandise, Groceries, Private Label

40986 Randag & Assoc Inc
187 S Lawndale Ave
Elmhurst, IL 60126-3523
630-530-2830
Fax: 630-530-2834 Info@RandagInc.com
Contract packager of confectionery products, frozen foods, health foods, industrial ingredients and spices
President: John Randag
info@randaginc.com
VP: Nancy Randag
Purchasing Director: Jennifer Randag
Estimated Sales: Less Than $500,000
Number Employees: 1-4
Number of Products: 30
Type of Packaging: Consumer, Food Service, Bulk
Markets Served:
 Food Manufacturers & Processors, Food Service Operators
Brokered Products include:
 Confectionery, Health Food, Ingredients, Spices

40987 Rast Produce Co
1316 W Center Ave
Visalia, CA 93291-5804
559-738-5445
Fax: 559-635-4988 rastproco@aol.com
www.rastproduce.com
Marketer and buying broker for table grapes, tree fruit, and fresh produce
Owner: Jack Rast
jack@rastproduce.com
Number Employees: 1-4
Brokered Products include:
 Produce

40988 Ratcliff Food Brokers
5401 Cordova St Ste 102
Anchorage, AK 99518
907-562-1020
Fax: 907-562-1076
Broker of confectionery and dairy/deli products, frozen foods, groceries, health food, meats, private label items, seafood and spices
President: Edward Ratcliff
Estimated Sales: $2.5-5 Million
Number Employees: 5-9
Type of Packaging: Food Service, Bulk
Markets Served:
 Super Market Chains, Wholesale Distributors, Food Service Operators
Brokered Products include:
 Confectionery, Dairy/Deli, Frozen Food, Groceries, Health Food, Meat, Meat Products, Private Label, Seafood, Spices

40989 Ray Cosgrove Brokerage Company
PO Box 281
Saddle River, NJ 07458-0281
201-825-0979
Fax: 201-327-8588
Import and export broker and wholesaler/distributor of seafood, private label items, frozen foods, groceries and health food
President: Ray Cosgrove
Number Employees: 20-49
Type of Packaging: Food Service, Private Label
Brokered Products include:
 Seafood

40990 Ray's Pride Brokerage Company
PO Box 3490
Bessemer, AL 35023-0490
334-365-2181
Fax: 334-361-1608
Broker of spices, seafood, private label and dairy/deli items, frozen foods, meat and meat products, groceries, etc.
President: Bill Ray
VP: Ken Dabbs
Estimated Sales: $5-10 Million
Number Employees: 10-19
Markets Served:
 Wholesale Distributors, Food Service Operators
Primary Brands Brokered include: Castleberry's Foods; McCormick Company; National Fruit Portion Pac, Inc.; Bush Brothers; H.B. Hunter; Tri Valley Growers
Brokered Products include:
 Dairy/Deli, Frozen Food, Groceries, Meat, Meat Products, Private Label, Seafood, Spices

40991 Real Food Marketing
711 W Camino Real Ave # 204
Arcadia, CA 91007-9326
626-445-3818
Fax: 626-445-4452 mike@realfoodmarketing.com
www.realfoodmarketing.com
Import and export broker of frozen foods, industrial ingredients, fruit juice concentrates and purees
Owner: Michael Real
mike@realfoodmarketing.com
Estimated Sales: $3-5 Million
Number Employees: 1-4
Type of Packaging: Bulk
Brokered Products include:
 Ingredients

40992 (HQ)Reede International Seafood Corporation
PO Box 199
Roslyn Heights, NY 11577-0199
516-365-0265
Fax: 516-365-2956
Import and export broker of seafood, private label items and frozen foods
President: Stephen Reede
VP: Rose Reede
Sales/Marketing: Glenn Rosenblatt
Public Relations: Mariann Kuznetz
Estimated Sales: $15-20 Million
Number Employees: 5
Number of Brands: 5
Number of Products: 30
Square Footage: 4000
Type of Packaging: Consumer, Food Service, Private Label, Bulk

Food Brokers / A-Z

Markets Served:
Food Manufacturers & Processors, Wholesale Distributors, Food Service Operators
Primary Brands Brokered include: Sea-Reed; Pacific Andes; Andes; Andes Pride
Brokered Products include:
Exports, Frozen Food, Imports, Private Label, Seafood

40993 (HQ)Reese Brokerage Co
2820 Bransford Ave
Nashville, TN 37204-3102   615-269-3456
   Fax: 615-269-9348 dreese@reesegroupinc.com
              www.reesegroupinc.com
Broker of produce, spices, private label items, meat and meat products, groceries, confectionery, frozen foods, general merchandise, etc.
President: Darrell Reese
CFO: Rhonda Holmes
Account Executive: Ryan Reese
Estimated Sales: $47 Million
Number Employees: 20-49
Square Footage: 10000
Markets Served:
Food Manufacturers & Processors, Super Market Chains, Wholesale Distributors
Primary Brands Brokered include: Bush Brothers; Playtex; Dean Food Company; McCormick Spice Company; Ralston; Tri-Valley (Libby);
Brokered Products include:
Confectionery, Dairy/Deli, Frozen Food, General Merchandise, Groceries, Meat, Meat Products, Private Label, Produce, Spices

40994 (HQ)Reichenbach & Associates
730 Old Kitchawan Road N
Ossining, NY 10562   914-941-1717
   Fax: 914-941-1744 info@tri-statemarketing.com
              www.tri-statemarketing.com
Broker of confectionery and dairy/deli products, frozen foods, spices, groceries, meat products, etc.
President: Herbert Reichenbach
EVP: Pat Ianaconi
Marketing Director: Keith Nagler
Sales Manager: Roger Hill
Estimated Sales: $6.5 Million
Number Employees: 30
Markets Served:
Food Manufacturers & Processors, Super Market Chains, Wholesale Distributors, Food Service Operators
Primary Brands Brokered include: Perdue Farms, Inc.; Nichirei Foods America; Fishery Products International, Inc.; Nestle Brands Foodservice Company; Readi-Bake, Inc.; Wm. H. Leahy Associates, Inc.
Brokered Products include:
Confectionery, Dairy/Deli, Frozen Food, Groceries, Meat Products, Private Label, Seafood, Spices

40995 Reliable Mercantile Company
21 Kensett Road
Manhasset, NY 11030-2105   516-365-7808
              Fax: 516-365-7808
Importer and wholesaler/distributor of spices
President: M Abrahamian
Brokered Products include:
Nuts, Dried Fruits & Pulses

40996 Rene Rivet
960 Industrial Boulevard
Terrebonne, CA H7L 4R9
Canada   450-621-3362
   Fax: 450-621-3392 800-465-9241
              info@renerivet.com
Import and export broker of dairy/deli products and industrial ingredients including dehydrated fruits, pure vanilla extracts, caramel color and cocoa products
President: Michel Langlois
VP: Marie-Claude Langlois
Director Sales: Manon Gilliard
Number Employees: 10-19
Markets Served:
Food Manufacturers & Processors, Wholesale Distributors, Food Service Operators
Brokered Products include:
Confectionery, Dairy/Deli, Imports, Ingredients

40997 Rep Source
5500 SW Longspur Ln
Palm City, FL 34990-8829   772-463-7674
   Fax: 772-463-7675 800-860-1666
              www.repsource.us
Manufacturers' representative for food service equipment
Owner, President: James Robinson
james@repsource.us
VP: Justin Throneburg
Customer Service/Office Manager: Carolun Predgen
Estimated Sales: $1-2.5 Million
Number Employees: 1-4
Markets Served:
Super Market Chains, Wholesale Distributors, Food Service Operators
Primary Brands Brokered include: Corning; Snap-Drape; Tara Linen; Pelouze Scale; Mainstreet Menu; Adcraft
Brokered Products include:
General Merchandise, Foodservice Equipment

40998 Res-Q Network
16933 Parthenia St # 200
Northridge, CA 91343-4564   818-891-7811
   Fax: 818-892-6576 877-219-8169
              support@tripinsurance.com
              www.tripinsurance.com
Broker of bottle clips, telephone handset covers, portable misting systems, etc. Also training and services for environmental and occupational health and safety available
Owner: Paul Golstein
Estimated Sales: $1-3 Million
Number Employees: 10-19
Markets Served:
Food Manufacturers & Processors, Wholesale Distributors, Food Service Operators
Primary Brands Brokered include: Ecowater; Tropical Mist; Safe-T-Quake; Gookinaid; Universal
Brokered Products include:
General Merchandise, Health & Safety Equipment

40999 Resource One
1024 Executive Parkway Dr
Creve Coeur, MO 63141   314-628-0880
   Fax: 314-628-0990 www.resource-1.com
Broker of frozen foods, dairy products, ice cream, meats, groceries and private label items.
Chairman/CEO: Ed Cuccio
President/Managing Partner: Kevin Holden
Executive Vice President: Michael Klein
VP, Business Development: Bill Wolfe
Marketing Director: Jenell Derstine
SVP, Sales: Mark Kotcher
Year Founded: 1987
Estimated Sales: $350 Million
Number Employees: 20-49
Markets Served:
Super Market Chains, Wholesale Distributors
Brokered Products include:
Confectionery, Dairy/Deli, Frozen Food, General Merchandise, Groceries, Imports, Meat, Meat Products, Private Label, Seafood, Spices, Ice Cream

41000 Restaurant Equipment Professionals
3750 Oakcliff Rd
Atlanta, GA 30340-3405   770-662-8027
   Fax: 770-662-8028 800-235-3263
Manufacturers' representative for food service equipment
Co Owner: Barry Ford
Co Owner: Andy Sparks
Sales: Glen Denton
Estimated Sales: $1-2.5 Million
Number Employees: 1-4

41001 Reuven International
1881 Yonge Street
Suite 201
Toronto, ON M4S 3C4
Canada   416-929-1496
   Fax: 416-929-1499 info@reuven.com
              www.reuven.com
Broker of frozen foods and chicken
General Manager: Maureen Cullen
Number Employees: 5
Markets Served:
Food Manufacturers & Processors

Brokered Products include:
Frozen Food, Meat, Chicken

41002 Rheuark/F.S.I. Sales
5809 Reeds Rd
Shawnee Mission, KS 66202   913-432-9500
   Fax: 913-432-9565 800-394-9456
              info@rheuarkfsi.com acosta.com
Broker of confectionery and dairy/deli products, frozen foods, general merchandise, industrial ingredients, meat and meat products, seafood, etc.
President & CEO: Robert Hill
VP: Paul Fournier
Contact: Paul Fournier
fournier@rheuarkfsi.com
COO: Greg Delaney
Estimated Sales: $10-20 Million
Number Employees: 10-19
Square Footage: 8000
Markets Served:
Food Manufacturers & Processors, Wholesale Distributors, Food Service Operators
Primary Brands Brokered include: Lamb Weston; Ocean Spray; Rich Products; Allen Canning Company; Specialty Brands; Iceland Seafood
Brokered Products include:
Confectionery, Dairy/Deli, Frozen Food, General Merchandise, Groceries, Ingredients, Meat, Meat Products, Produce, Seafood, Prepared Salads, Baked Goods, etc.

41003 Rich Audette Associates
20022 E Santiago Canyon Road
Orange, CA 92869-1632   714-288-2700
              Fax: 714-288-2700
Broker of general merchandise
President: Richard Audette
CEO: Audrey Audette
Number Employees: 5
Markets Served:
Super Market Chains, Wholesale Distributors
Primary Brands Brokered include: Stanly Knitting Mills, Inc.; R. Audette Headwear; Convenience Kits International; C.R. Murray Manufacturing Company; Roylal Trend; GSC
Brokered Products include:
General Merchandise

41004 Richardson Petkovsek & Associates
10711 Red Run Blvd Ste 115
Owings Mills, MD 21117   410-998-9811
              Fax: 410-998-9269
Broker of frozen foods, general merchandise, groceries, meat and meat products, produce, seafood, etc.
President: Bob Petkovsek
Office Manager: Pam LaMacchia
Sales Manager: Dave Barnett
dbarnett@rpainc.net
Estimated Sales: $20-50 Million
Number Employees: 20-49
Square Footage: 4500
Markets Served:
Wholesale Distributors, Food Service Operators
Primary Brands Brokered include: Anchor Foods; Casa Di Bertacchi; Lamb Weston; Rich Products; Wampler; Very Fine
Brokered Products include:
Frozen Food, General Merchandise, Groceries, Meat, Meat Products, Private Label, Produce, Seafood

41005 Richs Sales Company
3500 NW Boca Raton Boulevard
Suite 611
Boca Raton, FL 33431-5853   954-481-1993
Broker of frozen foods, meat, meat products and seafood
President: Rich Harnist
VP/Secretary: D Harnist
Estimated Sales: $2.5-5 Million
Number Employees: 1-4
Type of Packaging: Bulk
Markets Served:
Food Manufacturers & Processors, Wholesale Distributors, Food Service Operators
Primary Brands Brokered include: Maple Leaf Farms; Berry Veal; Plantation Turkey; Foodcomm International; Chiapetti (Lamb & veal)
Brokered Products include:
Frozen Food, Meat, Meat Products, Seafood

Food Brokers / A-Z

41006 Ringland Associates
28911 Lathrup Blvd
Lathrup Village, MI 48076-2830   248-559-4840
Fax: 248-557-4272
Broker of general merchandise, groceries, meat products and private label items
President: John Minnich
VP: J Minnich
Estimated Sales: $5-10 Million
Number Employees: 7
Markets Served:
Super Market Chains, Wholesale Distributors, Food Service Operators
Brokered Products include:
General Merchandise, Groceries, Meat Products, Private Label

41007 Riteway Co
1225 Pleasant Hill Rd
Lawrenceville, GA 30044-3003   678-380-5060
Fax: 678-380-5065 dbennett@ritewayga.com
www.ritewayga.com
Broker of dairy/deli products, frozen foods, general merchandise, groceries, meats and private label items, etc.
VP: Dick Bennett
dickbennett@ritewayga.com
Marketing Director: Phyllis Sanders
Sales Director: Larry Williams
Purchasing Manager: Phyllis Sanders
Estimated Sales: $12-18 Million
Number Employees: 5-9
Square Footage: 3300
Parent Co: Riteway Company
Markets Served:
Wholesale Distributors
Primary Brands Brokered include: Maruchan; Stokley USA; WolfGang Puck Food Company; Carolina Products
Brokered Products include:
Confectionery, Dairy/Deli, Frozen Food, General Merchandise, Groceries, Health Food, Meat, Private Label, Seafood

41008 Ritt-Beyer Inc
9900 S Franklin Dr
Franklin, WI 53132-8846   414-421-9505
Fax: 414-421-6484 sales@rbwinc.com
www.rbwinc.com
Broker of candy and snack foods
President: R Beyer
Estimated Sales: $5-10 Million
Number Employees: 20-49
Markets Served:
Super Market Chains, Wholesale Distributors
Brokered Products include:
Confectionery, Snack Foods

41009 River City Sales & Marketing
11700 Congo Ferndale Rd
Alexander, AR 72002-7007   501-316-3663
Fax: 501-794-0605
Owner: Vick Pannell
vickpannell@vickpannell.com
Estimated Sales: $1-5 Million
Number Employees: 1-4

41010 Rizwitsch Sales
11240 Cornell Park Dr # 100
Suite 100
Blue Ash, OH 45242-1800   513-563-1222
Fax: 513-563-4886 800-308-8655
www.rizwitsch.com
Broker of frozen foods, meats and seafood
President: John Rizzo
Estimated Sales: $10-20 Million
Number Employees: 10-19
Square Footage: 3400
Markets Served:
Food Manufacturers & Processors, Super Market Chains, Wholesale Distributors, Food Service Operators
Brokered Products include:
Frozen Food, Meat, Seafood

41011 Rizwitsch Sales
7100 Huntley Rd # 101
Columbus, OH 43229-1076   614-431-2505
Fax: 614-431-0609 www.rizwitsch.com
Broker of meats, baked goods, dairy/deli products, frozen food and seafood
Manager: Jim Gerbec
jgerbec@rizwitsch.com
Sales Manager: John McGann
Estimated Sales: $2.5-5 Million
Number Employees: 1-4
Square Footage: 6800
Parent Co: Rizwitsch Sales
Markets Served:
Super Market Chains, Wholesale Distributors, Food Service Operators
Primary Brands Brokered include: Orval Kent Foods; Heinz; Pillsbury; Bridgford; Domino Sugar; Lamb Weston
Brokered Products include:
Dairy/Deli, Frozen Food, Meat, Seafood, Baked Goods

41012 Robbins Sales Co
95 Froehlich Farm Blvd
Woodbury, NY 11797-2930   516-364-7200
Fax: 516-921-8488 ptroyal@aol.com
Import broker of groceries, private label items, seafood and spices
President: Jeffrey Zwecker
jzwecker@robbinssales.com
VP: S Zwecker
Secretary: Carolyn Salzwedel
Number Employees: 1-4
Type of Packaging: Food Service, Private Label
Markets Served:
Super Market Chains, Wholesale Distributors, Food Service Operators
Primary Brands Brokered include: Premium
Brokered Products include:
Groceries, Imports, Private Label, Seafood

41013 Robert A. Haines Companies
8410 Market Place Ln
Suite: A
Cincinnati, OH 45242-5352   513-793-9350
Fax: 513-794-3342
Broker of confectionery products, general merchandise, private label items, etc.
President: R Haines
VP: J Buck
Estimated Sales: $1-3 Million
Number Employees: 4
Markets Served:
Super Market Chains, Wholesale Distributors
Primary Brands Brokered include: Ovaltine
Brokered Products include:
Confectionery, General Merchandise, Private Label, Seafood, Rice, Sauerkraut

41014 Robert Chapter Company
845 W Westwood Drive
Glenwood, IL 60425-1325   708-754-2761
Fax: 708-754-2769
President: Robert Chapter

41015 Robert Emig & Associates
2519 Niagara Falls Blvd
Amherst, NY 14228-3527   716-691-4444
Fax: 716-691-4446
Manufacturers' representative for food service equipment including tabletop items, smallwares, linens, dishwashing machines and pizza ovens
Owner: Robert Seibert
VP: Robert Emig Jr
Secretary/Treasurer: Suellen Emig
Estimated Sales: $1-2.5 Million
Number Employees: 1-4
Type of Packaging: Bulk

41016 Robert W. Hayman Inc
109 N Water Street
Edgartown, MA 2539   508-627-9415
Import broker of shrimp and squid
President: Robert Hayman Jr
Treasurer: Elizabeth Hayman
Estimated Sales: B
Number Employees: 6
Markets Served:
Super Market Chains, Wholesale Distributors, Food Service Operators
Brokered Products include:
Imports, Seafood, Shrimp, Squid

41017 Rocky Mountain Motel
1204 9th St
Rock Springs, WY 82901-5419   307-362-3443
Fax: 307-382-5250
Web design, marketing, public relations, promotions and desktop publishing and design
Owner: Celete Disano
Senior VP: Rebecca Reihman
Group VP: Jerry Stone
Estimated Sales: Less Than $500,000
Number Employees: 1-4
Parent Co: Kelley-Clarke
Markets Served:
Super Market Chains, Wholesale Distributors
Brokered Products include:
Confectionery, Dairy/Deli, Frozen Food, General Merchandise, Groceries, Health Food, Meat, Meat Products, Private Label, Produce, Seafood, Spices

41018 Rodon Foods
7783 S Allen St
Midvale, UT 84047-7227   801-566-0616
Fax: 801-566-6931 rodonfoods@cs.com
Broker of dairy/deli products, frozen foods, meat and private label items
Manager: Scott Rasmussen
scott-rasmussen@rodonfoods.com
VP: Scott Rasmussen
Retail Sales Manager: Kevin Beal
Food Service Sales Manager: Dick Wright
Estimated Sales: $10-20 Million
Number Employees: 10-19
Square Footage: 30000
Markets Served:
Food Manufacturers & Processors, Super Market Chains, Wholesale Distributors, Food Service Operators
Brokered Products include:
Dairy/Deli, Frozen Food, Meat, Meat Products, Private Label

41019 Roehl Corp
33 S Main St
Oconomowoc, WI 53066-5218   262-569-3000
Fax: 262-569-3019 www.sourcewurx.com
Export and import broker of frozen foods, groceries, private label items, etc.
President: Peter Roehl
proehl@roehl.org
Estimated Sales: $10-20 Million
Number Employees: 10-19
Markets Served:
Food Manufacturers & Processors, Super Market Chains, Wholesale Distributors, Food Service Operators
Brokered Products include:
Exports, Frozen Food, Groceries, Imports, Private Label

41020 Roger J. Wood Company
2200 Market St # A
Camp Hill, PA 17011-4643   717-737-1068
Fax: 717-737-4641
Broker of general merchandise, produce, groceries and confectionery and private label items
Owner: Allison Wood
Estimated Sales: $300,000-500,000
Number Employees: 1-4
Markets Served:
Super Market Chains, Wholesale Distributors, Food Service Operators
Primary Brands Brokered include: RV Industries; Eastern Tea; Royal Oak; Street Enterprises
Brokered Products include:
Confectionery, General Merchandise, Groceries, Private Label, Produce

41021 (HQ)Roller & Associates
3625 Woodland Park Ave N
Seattle, WA 98103   206-547-3555
Fax: 206-547-8630 800-736-7249
customerservice@rollerassoc.com
Manufacturers' representative for food service equipment
President: Mike Roller
Vice President: Mike Roller
Estimated Sales: $2.5-5 Million
Number Employees: 10-19
Other Locations:
Roller & Associates
Vancouver, WA Roller & Associates
Markets Served:
Wholesale Distributors
Primary Brands Brokered include: Classico; Seco; Buffalo China; Inter Metro; Star Manufacturing; Onieda Foodservice
Brokered Products include:
General Merchandise, Foodservice Equipment

Food Brokers / A-Z

41022 Roos-Mohan
375 Northgate Dr
Warrendale, PA 15086   724-933-6091
Fax: 724-933-6095 swolff@wolffgroupinc.com
Broker of frozen foods, meat, seafood, private label items, etc.
Controller: Gerry Sheehy
Estimated Sales: $3.60 Million
Number Employees: 19
Markets Served:
  Food Manufacturers & Processors, Super Market Chains, Wholesale Distributors, Food Service Operators
Primary Brands Brokered include: Pillsbury; Pierre; Pet, Inc.; Jac Pac; Frionor; Northern Star
Brokered Products include:
  Dairy/Deli, Frozen Food, Groceries, Meat, Private Label, Seafood

41023 Roosevelt Dairy Trade, Inc
2 W Market Street
Suite 400
Westchester, PA 19382   610-692-1866
Fax: 610-692-5733 www.rooseveltdairy.com
Whey powders, whole milk powder, casein/caseinates, whey protein concentrate, butter, lactose, buttermilk powder, nonfat dry milk, brewer's yeast, permeate, fluid products
President: Thomas Roosevelt
Estimated Sales: $40 Million
Number Employees: 6
Type of Packaging: Bulk
Markets Served:
  Food Manufacturers & Processors, Wholesale Distributors
Brokered Products include:
  Dairy/Deli, Exports, Ingredients

41024 Rosenfeld & Gigante
112 Denton Avenue
New Hyde Park, NY 11040   516-328-9040
Fax: 516-328-8126 www.rgfinefoods.com
Broker of groceries and private label items; serving all markets in NY and NJ
President: Herbert Rosenfeld
Office Manager: Linda Pernicano
VP: Joseph Gigante
Contact: Jon Gigante
gigante516@optonline.net
Estimated Sales: $1 Million
Number Employees: 5
Square Footage: 1800
Markets Served:
  Food Manufacturers & Processors, Wholesale Distributors, Food Service Operators
Primary Brands Brokered include: Stanislaus Food Products Company; Musco Olive Company; P.M. Sales LLC
Brokered Products include:
  Groceries, Imports, Private Label

41025 Rosett Brokerage Company
PO Box 700307
San Antonio, TX 78270-0307   210-826-8059
Fax: 210-826-1371
Broker of frozen foods and groceries
President: Bill Hockersmith
VP: Danny Pierce
Number Employees: 10-19
Markets Served:
  Food Service Operators
Primary Brands Brokered include: Quaker; Gatorade
Brokered Products include:
  Frozen Food, Groceries

41026 Ross Empire State Brokers
6501 Basile Rowe
Suite:C
Manlius, NY 13104   315-234-6430
Fax: 315-682-2654
Broker of confectionery products, beverages, groceries, private label brands and snack foods
Chairman: R Ross
President: D Falkowitz
Estimated Sales: $10-20 Million
Number Employees: 10-19
Markets Served:
  Super Market Chains, Wholesale Distributors, Food Service Operators
Primary Brands Brokered include: Storck USA; Fleer Corporation; Ferrara Pan Candy; Hunt Wesson Foods; Necco; American Licorice Company
Brokered Products include:
  Confectionery, Groceries, Private Label, Beverages, Snack Foods

41027 Roughstock Distillery
81211 Gallatin Road
Suite A
Bozeman, MT 59718   406-551-6409
Fax: 406-443-0092
Broker of vodka, gin, bourbon
Owner: Bob Lemm
Marketing Director: David Lemm
Contact: Kari Schultz
kari@montanawhiskey.com
Operations Manager: Michelle Lemm
Plant Manager: Craig Hagen
Estimated Sales: $5 Million
Number Employees: 10-19
Type of Packaging: Private Label
Brokered Products include:
  Alcoholic Beverages, Private Label

41028 Roxy Trading Inc
389 N Humane Way
Pomona, CA 91768-3345   626-610-1388
Fax: 626-610-1339 info@roxytrading.com
www.roxytrading.com
Importer and distributor of Asian specialty food products.
President: Elvis Sae-Tang
General Manager: Paulette Ho
Business Development Manager: Benjamin Sae-Tang
Estimated Sales: $8 Million
Number Employees: 20-49
Number of Brands: 28
Square Footage: 45000
Type of Packaging: Consumer
Other Locations:
  Roxy Trading-Northern California
  Union City, CARoxy Trading-Northern CaliforniaScarborough, ON, Canada

41029 Royal Wine Corp
63 Lefante Dr
Bayonne, NJ 07002-5024   718-384-2400
Fax: 718-388-8444 info@royalwines.com
www.royalwine.com
Manufacturer, importer and distributer of premium kosher wines, spirits and liquors. Affiliate of Kedem Food Products International.
President: David Herzog
CEO: Mordy Herzog
Chief Financial Officer: Sheldon Ginsberg
Executive Vice President: Sheldon Ginsberg
SVP: Phillip Herzog
Executive Vice President of Sales: Nathan Herzog
Estimated Sales: $49.5 Million
Number Employees: 200
Number of Brands: 61
Square Footage: 184000
Parent Co: KayCo
Type of Packaging: Consumer, Food Service
Markets Served:
  Food Manufacturers & Processors
Brokered Products include:
  Alcoholic Beverages, Exports, Imports

41030 Rubenstein Seafood Sales
6210 Campbell Rd Ste 210
Dallas, TX 75248   972-380-8288
Fax: 972-380-8404 shrimpdepot@msn.com
www.shrimpsales.com
Broker and sales agent of frozen seafoods
Dallas Operator: Barry Rubenstein
Dallas Operator: Jason Rubenstein
Austin Operator: Adam Rubenstein
Sales: Marvin Rubenstein
Sales: Adam Rubenstein
Estimated Sales: $5-10 Million
Number Employees: 5-9
Markets Served:
  Food Manufacturers & Processors, Super Market Chains, Wholesale Distributors, Food Service Operators
Brokered Products include:
  Seafood

41031 Rudolph Brady, Inc
127 S Brighton Pl
Arlington Hts, IL 60004   847-870-7020
Fax: 847-870-7676
Broker of frozen foods, groceries, health foods, industrial ingredients, dried fruits and spices.

President: James Hopwood
Estimated Sales: A
Number Employees: 3
Type of Packaging: Consumer, Food Service, Bulk
Markets Served:
  Food Manufacturers & Processors, Super Market Chains, Wholesale Distributors, Food Service Operators
Primary Brands Brokered include: Great Lakes; Nonpareil; Tree Top; Peloian Packing; Zoria Farms, Inc.; Sunny Lee Foods
Brokered Products include:
  Frozen Food, Groceries, Health Food, Imports, Ingredients, Spices, Dried Fruits

41032 S B Davis Co
2695 Elmridge Dr NW # A
PO Box 141576
Grand Rapids, MI 49534-1302   616-791-9400
Fax: 616-791-0212   800-253-3891
Broker of fresh produce
President: Steve Davis
Estimated Sales: $2.5-5 Million
Number Employees: 5-9
Brokered Products include:
  Produce

41033 S Kamberg & Co LTD
445 Northern Blvd # 25
Great Neck, NY 11021-4804   516-482-4141
Fax: 516-482-4147 www.skamberg.com
Supplier of Corn Meal, Dairy Products, Fats, Flour, Fruits, Honey, Nut Meats, Seeds, Sprinkles/Chocolate and Tomoato Products.
President: Doreen Tiseo
dtiseo@skamberg.com
CEO: Mark Kamberg
Sales Manager: Mark Glickman
Estimated Sales: $5-10 Million
Number Employees: 5-9

41034 S&K Sales Company
300 Main St
Stamford, CT 06901-3033   203-973-0730
Fax: 203-973-0757 info@sksales.com
www.sksales.com
Broker of alcoholic beverages, confectionery products, frozen food, groceries, general merchandise, meats, etc.
President: Richard T. Ray
Chairman of the Board: Robin D. Ray
Vice President Finance: Steve Jones
Vice President: Katherine M. Hines
Vice President of International Sales: John Eakin
Contact: Barbara Biehl
b.biehl@sksales.com
Estimated Sales: $2.5-5 Million
Number Employees: 1-4
Markets Served:
  Super Market Chains, Food Service Operators
Brokered Products include:
  Alcoholic Beverages, Confectionery, Frozen Food, General Merchandise, Groceries, Meat Products, Spices

41035 (HQ)S. Kamberg & Company
445 Northern Blvd
Great Neck, NY 11021   516-482-4141
Fax: 516-482-4147 info@skamberg.com
www.skamberg.com
Broker of quality ingredients, confectionery and dairy/deli products, groceries, private label items and spices
Founder/President: Stephen Kamberg
CEO: Mark Kamberg
Sales Manager: Mark Glickman
Type of Packaging: Bulk
Markets Served:
  Food Manufacturers & Processors, Super Market Chains, Wholesale Distributors, Food Service Operators
Brokered Products include:
  Confectionery, Dairy/Deli, Groceries, Ingredients, Private Label, Produce, Spices

41036 S.A.K.S. Foods International
4052 Augusta Court
Bloomfield Hills, MI 48302-1702   248-594-5924
Fax: 248-594-5951
President: Sheldon Falkauff
VP/Treasurer: Marshall Davis
Estimated Sales: $5-10 Million
Number Employees: 1-4

Food Brokers / A-Z

41037 SCS Sales Company
410 Clearview Ave Ste D
Feasterville Trevose, PA 19053 215-357-0805
Fax: 215-357-8352 scssell@bellatlantic.net
Broker of confectionery items, general merchandise, groceries, meats, private label items, beverages, etc
Partner: Robert Camelier
Sales: Al Miacti
Estimated Sales: $5-10 Million
Number Employees: 11
Square Footage: 6000
Markets Served:
  Super Market Chains, Wholesale Distributors
Brokered Products include:
  Confectionery, General Merchandise, Groceries

41038 SFS Marketing
2630 Lexington Avenue
Kenner, LA 70062-5369 800-272-2161
Fax: 504-467-0530
Broker of soap, detergent and portion-packed food service sanitation systems
General Manager: Chuck Ainsworth
Field Training Coordinator: Mike Tilton
Regional Manager: Kyle Cunningham
Markets Served:
  Food Service Operators
Primary Brands Brokered include: SFS Pac
Brokered Products include:
  General Merchandise, Soap, Detergent, Sanitation Systems

41039 SGS International Rice Inc
6 Stone Tavern Dr
Millstone Twp, NJ 08510-1733 732-603-5077
Fax: 732-603-5037 weldonrice@optonline.com
www.sgsgroup.us.com
Jasmine rice, basmati rice, coconut milk, coconut juice, canned and dried fruits, beans, spices, fruit juices, nuts and raisins, tuna, cashew, seasame seeds-packer in put labels
President: Maria Gorfain
mariagorfain@weldonfoods.com
CEO: Surinder Sahni
CFO: Soena Sahni
VP: Gagan Sahni
Research & Development: Avneet Sodhi
Marketing: Harbinder Sahni
Manager: Dee Mirchandani
Production: Manoj Hedge
Purchasing: Harbinder Sahnl
Estimated Sales: $10 Million
Number Employees: 5-9
Square Footage: 1200
Type of Packaging: Consumer, Food Service, Private Label, Bulk
Markets Served:
  Super Market Chains
Brokered Products include:
  Exports, Groceries, Imports, Private Label

41040 SHA Services
252 N Grand Street
Cobleskill, NY 12043-4122 716-988-5026
Fax: 716-988-5003
Import and export broker of alcoholic beverages, confectionery and dairy/deli products, frozen foods, general merchandise, groceries, etc. finance broker
Owner: Samuel Austin
Number Employees: 1-4
Markets Served:
  Food Manufacturers & Processors, Super Market Chains, Wholesale Distributors, Food Service Operators
Brokered Products include:
  Alcoholic Beverages, Confectionery, Dairy/Deli, Exports, Frozen Food, General Merchandise, Groceries, Health Food, Imports, Ingredients, Meat, Meat Products, Private Label, Produce, Seafood, Spices

41041 SJE Marketing Corporation
PO Box 30
Sugar Loaf, NY 10981-0030 845-469-4840
Fax: 845-469-2977
Import and domestic broker of general merchandise, groceries, health foods, industrial ingredients, private label items and produce
President: Spencer Effron
Markets Served:
  Food Manufacturers & Processors, Super Market Chains, Wholesale Distributors

Primary Brands Brokered include: Calavo; Amport; Garry; Claxton; Clarke Dried Fruits Ltd.; Kalashian Packing Company
Brokered Products include:
  Dairy/Deli, Groceries, Health Food, Imports, Private Label

41042 SJH Enterprises
2415 Parview Rd Ste 4
Middleton, WI 53562 608-831-3001
Fax: 608-831-3001 888-745-3845
Broker of organic grains and natural colors and flavors
Manager: Hank Zimmerman
Estimated Sales: $170,000
Number Employees: 1-4
Type of Packaging: Consumer, Food Service, Private Label, Bulk
Markets Served:
  Food Manufacturers & Processors
Primary Brands Brokered include: Upland Kitchens; Food Innovations
Brokered Products include:
  Frozen Food, Ingredients, Meat Products, Private Label, Spices, Natural Colors

41043 STI International
PO Box 7257
San Carlos, CA 94070-7257 650-592-8320
Fax: 650-592-8320
Wholesaler/distributor and exporter of canned meat, fruit, juices and vegetables including tomatoes. Wholesaler/distributor of private label items and health food
President: Todd Stewart
Number Employees: 1-4
Type of Packaging: Consumer, Food Service, Private Label, Bulk
Brokered Products include:
  Exports, Groceries, Private Label

41044 SWMCO Multi Products
20 Taurus Drive
Novato, CA 94947-1922 207-934-9287
Fax: 207-934-6288
Broker-Food Products
President: Elinor Strandburg
Type of Packaging: Consumer, Food Service

41045 Sabal Marketing
120 W Pineview St
Altamonte Springs, FL 32714 407-788-9391
Fax: 407-862-7520 sealane@sealanemkg.com
Broker of general merchandise, groceries, health food and private label items
President: Charles E Lane
Number Employees: 5-9
Markets Served:
  Super Market Chains, Wholesale Distributors, Food Service Operators
Brokered Products include:
  General Merchandise, Groceries, Health Food, Private Label

41046 Sabbers & Assoc Inc
466 Old Hook Rd # 24c
Emerson, NJ 07630-1368 201-262-5959
Fax: 201-262-8765 sabbers@sabbers.com
Broker of dairy/deli products, frozen foods, private label items and general merchandise including coffee equipment
Owner: Jerry Sabbers
sabbers@sabbers.com
CEO: A Sabbers
Vice President: Joe Sabbers
Estimated Sales: $5-10 Million
Number Employees: 5-9
Markets Served:
  Food Manufacturers & Processors, Super Market Chains, Food Service Operators
Brokered Products include:
  Dairy/Deli, Frozen Food, General Merchandise, Private Label, Coffee Equipment

41047 Sachem Co
1033 South Blvd # 243
Suite 243
Oak Park, IL 60302-2882 708-848-4303
Fax: 708-848-4278 laurie@sachemco.com
Broker of dairy/deli products, frozen foods, general merchandise, seafood, groceries, meat and meat products, etc.
Owner: Paul Sachem
paul@sachemco.com

Estimated Sales: $5-10 Million
Number Employees: 20-49
Markets Served:
  Food Manufacturers & Processors, Super Market Chains, Wholesale Distributors, Food Service Operators
Brokered Products include:
  Confectionery, Dairy/Deli, Frozen Food, General Merchandise, Groceries, Meat, Meat Products, Private Label, Seafood

41048 Saggese Brothers
143 Route 59
Hillburn, NY 10931 914-730-3088
Fax: 914-273-1750 saggese@mindstring.com
Import broker of peppers, tomato products, olive oil
President: Edward Saggese
Number Employees: 6
Brokered Products include:
  Groceries, Imports, Produce, Peppers, Olive Oil, Etc.

41049 Salad Oils Intl Corp
5070 W Harrison St
Chicago, IL 60644-5141 773-261-0500
Fax: 773-261-7555 saladoilcori@earthlink.net
www.saladoils.net
Import and export broker of private label items including cottonseed, corn, olive and soybean oils
Owner: R Paris
CEO: Frank Paris
VP: John Pacente
Estimated Sales: $1-2.5 Million
Number Employees: 5-9
Square Footage: 56000
Type of Packaging: Consumer, Food Service, Private Label, Bulk
Markets Served:
  Food Manufacturers & Processors, Super Market Chains, Wholesale Distributors, Food Service Operators
Brokered Products include:
  Imports, Private Label, Corn, Olive, Cottonseed & Soy Bean Oils

41050 Sales
PO Box 1535
Hendersonville, TN 37077-1535 615-824-9736
Fax: 615-824-9736
Import broker of general merchandise and private label items
President: Lynn Scott
Estimated Sales: Less than $500,000
Number Employees: 1-4
Markets Served:
  Super Market Chains, Food Service Operators
Brokered Products include:
  General Merchandise, Imports, Private Label

41051 Sales & Marketing Dev
33 Timberline
Irvine, CA 92604-3033 949-552-0405
Fax: 949-552-0406 800-319-8906
smdtrading@aol.com www.smdtrading.com
Importer and exporter of disposable food service products including: chef hats, dollies, glasscovers, coasters, baking cups, cups, plates, dual-ovenable trays, microwavable bowls, containers and trays, aluminum containers & rolls, foodservices film and wraps, airlaid and paper napkins, placemats and traycovers
CEO: Kathryn Gillespie
CFO: John Gillespie
VP: John Gillespie
Estimated Sales: $3-5 Million
Number Employees: 1-4
Type of Packaging: Consumer, Food Service, Private Label, Bulk
Markets Served:
  Food Service Operators
Primary Brands Brokered include: SKP; Premier
Brokered Products include:
  General Merchandise, Groceries, Canned Foods, Bags, Aluminum Foil, Etc.

41052 Sales Corporation of Alaska
1300 East 5th Avenue
Anchorage, AK 99501 907-522-3057
Fax: 907-344-7932 800-250-6883
www.aksales.com
Broker of confectionery, meatsm, dairy/deli products, groceries, general merchandise, frozen food, etc.

Food Brokers / A-Z

President: Robert Galosich
Secretary/Treasurer: P Cohen
VP: R Henderson
Estimated Sales: $10-20 Million
Number Employees: 7
Markets Served:
  Food Manufacturers & Processors, Super Market Chains, Wholesale Distributors, Food Service Operators
Primary Brands Brokered include: Nalley; Old El Paso; Helene Curtis; Leaf; O'bag Oberto; Keebler Company
Brokered Products include:
  Confectionery, Dairy/Deli, Frozen Food, General Merchandise, Groceries, Meat Products, Private Label, Seafood, Spices

41053 Sales Marketing Svc LLC
211 S Main St
Bentonville, AR 72712-5962   479-271-8333
    Fax: 479-271-8879 StanKesslerSMS@aol.com
    www.salesmarketingservices.com
Import and export broker of confectionery products, general merchandise, groceries, meats, private label items, etc.
President: Stanley Kessler
Marketing Manager: Russ Pilcher
Operations Manager: Sue Cain
Estimated Sales: Less Than $500,000
Number Employees: 1-4
Square Footage: 14000
Markets Served:
  Food Manufacturers & Processors, Super Market Chains, Wholesale Distributors, Food Service Operators
Primary Brands Brokered include: Melita; Lodge Manufacturing; Precisionaire; Rheem, IN-SINK-ERATOR
Brokered Products include:
  Confectionery, Exports, General Merchandise, Groceries, Imports, Meat, Private Label

41054 Sales Results
1192 Clubview Blvd S
Columbus, OH 43235   614-885-4127
    Fax: 614-885-2621
Import broker of private label items, meat and meat products, seafood, spices, groceries, etc
Owner: P Malenky
CEO: S Malenky
Estimated Sales: $1-3 Million
Number Employees: 1-4
Markets Served:
  Super Market Chains, Wholesale Distributors, Food Service Operators
Primary Brands Brokered include: Power Max; Kroger Bakery
Brokered Products include:
  Confectionery, Frozen Food, Groceries, Health Food, Imports, Ingredients, Private Label, Seafood

41055 Sales Specialties
401 Substation Road
Venice, FL 34285-6077   941-485-1989
    Fax: 941-485-9156
Broker of display items including clips to hold food displays in place
Owner: Dee Deaterly
President: L Deaterly
Number Employees: 40
Markets Served:
  Super Market Chains, Wholesale Distributors
Brokered Products include:
  General Merchandise, Display Items

41056 Salmans & Assoc
1126 W Chestnut St
Chicago, IL 60642-4111   312-226-1820
    Fax: 312-226-6806 sales@salmans.com
Cheese
President: Van Salmans
van@salmans.com
Estimated Sales: $650,000
Number Employees: 5-9

41057 San Francisco Reps
25025 Viking St
Hayward, CA 94545-2768   510-887-2220
    Fax: 510-785-1100 info@sanfranciscoreps.com
    www.sanfranciscoreps.com
Manufacturers' repesentative for food service equipment

Partner: Bill Schmitz
sfreps@pacbell.net
Sales: Sharon Castanera
Sales: Liz Bruno
Sales: Valerie Abend
Inside Sales: Liz Bruno
Estimated Sales: $5-10 Million
Number Employees: 5-9
Square Footage: 32000
Markets Served:
  Wholesale Distributors
Brokered Products include:
  General Merchandise, Foodservice Equipment

41058 San Francisco Wine Exchange
943 Howard
San Francisco, CA 94103   415-546-0484
    Fax: 415-243-0636 www.sfwe.com
Broker of wines
President/Owner: Hugh Thacher
General Manager/Executive VP: Diego Lo Prete
National Sales Manager: Phil Nugent
Estimated Sales: $5-10 Million
Number Employees: 5-9
Markets Served:
  Wholesale Distributors
Primary Brands Brokered include: Foppiano; Fox Mountain; Riverside Farm; David Bruce Winery; Navarro Vineyards; Quady Winery; Mills Reef; Whitehaven; Oak Knoll
Brokered Products include:
  Alcoholic Beverages

41059 Sana Foods
PO Box 10818
Bainbridge Island, WA 98110-0818   206-842-4741
Food Brokers
President: Tina Nelson
VP: Paul Lang
Sales Manager: Bill Poulos

41060 Sanco Food Brokerage
8275 E 250 S
Zionsville, IN 46077   317-769-5080
    Fax: 317-769-5081 sancofb@aol.com
Broker of frozen foods, meats, private label items, etc.
President: James Sanford
Vice President: Karla Sandford
Estimated Sales: $2.5-5 Million
Number Employees: 1-4
Square Footage: 7200
Brokered Products include:
  Imports, Ingredients, Meat, Meat Products, Private Label, Crusts

41061 (HQ)Santucci Associates
1010 Millcreek Dr
Po Box 326
Feastervl Trvs, PA 19053-7321   215-676-2300
    Fax: 215-355-0986 mainbox@santucci.prserv.net
Broker of confectionery and dairy/deli products, general merchandise, groceries, health food, nuts, dried fruits, industrial ingredients, etc.
President/Owner: Anthony Santucci
Treasurer: Gerald Santucci
VP: Stephen Santucci
VP: Stephen Deleo
Sales: Marilyn Kaptik
Estimated Sales: $3.40 Million
Number Employees: 20
Type of Packaging: Consumer, Food Service, Bulk
Markets Served:
  Food Manufacturers & Processors, Super Market Chains, Wholesale Distributors, Food Service Operators
Primary Brands Brokered include: Twinings Teas; Red Oval Stoned Wheat Thins; Romanoff Caviars; Toblerone Chocolate; First Colony Coffee
Brokered Products include:
  Confectionery, Dairy/Deli, General Merchandise, Groceries, Health Food, Ingredients, Produce, Spices, Nuts, Dried Fruits

41062 Sanyo Corporation of America
500 Fifth Ave.
Suite 3620
New York, NY 10110   212-221-7890
    Fax: 212-221-7828 hohata@sanyocorp.com
Importer of packaging films including PVA barrier, plain and metallized nylon, FDA grade polyester, polypropylene and PE

Contact: Jun Aoki
jaoki@sanyocorp.com
Manager Plastics: Naruhiro Kiyota
Estimated Sales: $10-20 Million
Number Employees: 13
Parent Co: Sanyo Trading Company

41063 Saratoga Food Safety
771 W Crossroads Pkwy
Bolingbrook, IL 60490   708-562-4484
    Fax: 708-562-8811   800-451-0407
info@saratogafs.com www.saratogafs.com
Cleaning and sanitation chemical solutions, service & equipment
VP: Wade McGeorge
R&D: Keith Seyfried
Quality Control: Alnoor Lakhani
Sales: Sonya Jackson
Contact: Kelly Tabor
ktabor@saratogafs.com
Operations: Jim Bejna
Purchasing Manager: Ron Batzer
Estimated Sales: $9 Million
Number Employees: 20
Number of Brands: 1
Number of Products: 200
Square Footage: 20000
Type of Packaging: Private Label, Bulk
Markets Served:
  Food Manufacturers & Processors
Primary Brands Brokered include: X
Brokered Products include:
  Private Label, x

41064 Sargent's Trucking
64 Main St
Mars Hill, ME 04758   207-429-8106
    Fax: 207-429-9739   800-444-9753
Info@sargenttrucking.com
President: Bruce Sargent
Contact: Lana Danko
lana.danko@sargenttrucking.com
Estimated Sales: $5-10 Million
Number Employees: 20-49

41065 Saugy Inc.
9 Sachemor Rd
Cranston, RI 02920-4514   401-640-1879
    Fax: 401-383-9374   866-467-2849
saugy@cox.net www.saugys.com
Frankfurters
President & CEO: Mary O'Brien
Estimated Sales: $900,000
Number Employees: 3
Type of Packaging: Consumer, Food Service, Private Label, Bulk
Markets Served:
  Super Market Chains, Wholesale Distributors, Food Service Operators

41066 Saverino & Assoc
538 Randy Rd
Carol Stream, IL 60188-2134   630-653-9333
    Fax: 630-653-2390   800-242-6036
sav538@aol.com www.teamsaverino.com
Broker of dairy/deli and confectionery products, private label items, frozen foods, meat and produce
Owner: Frank Saverino
franksr@teamsaverino.com
VP: Frank Saverino Jr
Estimated Sales: $20-50 Million
Number Employees: 20-49
Markets Served:
  Food Manufacturers & Processors, Super Market Chains, Wholesale Distributors, Food Service Operators
Brokered Products include:
  Confectionery, Dairy/Deli, Frozen Food, Meat, Private Label, Produce

41067 Scavuzzo Sales & Marketing
225 3rd St W
Milan, IL 61264   309-787-4656
Broker of dairy/deli products, frozen foods, general merchandise, groceries, private label items, produce, etc.
President: Frank Scavuzzo
Estimated Sales: $5-10 Million
Number Employees: 4
Markets Served:
  Food Manufacturers & Processors, Super Market Chains, Wholesale Distributors, Food Service Operators

Brokered Products include:
Dairy/Deli, Frozen Food, General Merchandise, Groceries, Private Label, Produce, Seafood, Spices

41068 (HQ)Schaper Company
892 County Road 956
Iuka, MS 38852-8523 662-841-2242
Fax: 662-841-0302 800-647-2537
President: Kenneth Schaper
Secretary/Treasurer: Linda Morgan
Vice President: Phil Vandevander
Estimated Sales: $20-50 Million
Number Employees: 10-19
Type of Packaging: Food Service, Bulk
Markets Served:
Super Market Chains, Wholesale Distributors
Brokered Products include:
Meat

41069 Schare & Associates
350 E Penn St
Long Beach, NY 11561-4332 516-482-4628
Fax: 516-482-4698 877-859-4861
keith@juicedeals.com juicedeals.com
Broker of fruit juice concentrates, frozen fruits, purees, essences, flavors and bases and natural colors
Owner: Keith Schare
Contact: Tom Egelandsdal
tom@juicedeals.com
Estimated Sales: $1-3 Million
Number Employees: 1-4
Markets Served:
Food Manufacturers & Processors
Brokered Products include:
Exports, Frozen Food, Imports, Ingredients, Meat

41070 Scheidegger Trading Co Inc
351 California St # 1400
San Francisco, CA 94104-2429 415-397-3837
Fax: 415-397-8916 www.stcsf.com
President: Bjorn Scheidegger
Vice President: Mary T Murphy
stc@stcsf.com
Estimated Sales: $20-50 Million
Number Employees: 10-19

41071 Schiff Food Products CoInc
994 Riverview Dr
Totowa, NJ 07512-1129 973-237-1990
Fax: 973-237-1999 sales@schifffood.com
www.schifffoods.com
Manufacturer, importer and exporter of spices, seeds, herbs and dehydrated vegetables
President: David Deutscher
david.deutscher@schiffs.com
Estimated Sales: $15 Million
Number Employees: 20-49
Square Footage: 600000
Type of Packaging: Consumer, Private Label
Markets Served:
Food Manufacturers & Processors, Super Market Chains, Wholesale Distributors, Food Service Operators
Brokered Products include:
Spices

41072 Schraad & Associates
5125 N Santa Fe Ave
P.O. Box 18495
Oklahoma City, OK 73118-7509 405-528-3327
Fax: 405-557-0622 jim.dinger@schraadinc.com
www.schraadinc.com
Broker of confectionary, deli, general merchandise, frozen foods, general merchandise, spices, produce, groceries, bakery items, meats, seafood, etc.
President & CEO: Bill Schraad Jr.
billjr.schraad@schraadinc.com
Chief Financial Officer: Nancy Schraad
VP, Division Manager Oklahoma: Jim Dinger
Estimated Sales: $12 Million
Number Employees: 41
Square Footage: 17000
Markets Served:
Food Manufacturers & Processors, Super Market Chains, Wholesale Distributors, Food Service Operators
Primary Brands Brokered include: Chef America; Allen Canning; Austin Quality Foods; Luigino's; Jel Sert; Maruchan
Brokered Products include:
Confectionery, Dairy/Deli, Frozen Food, General Merchandise, Groceries, Meat Products, Private Label, Produce, Seafood, Spices

41073 Schreiber Foods Inc.
400 N. Washington St.
Green Bay, WI 54301 920-437-7601
Fax: 920-437-1617 contact@schreiberfoods.com
www.schreiberfoods.com
Dairy products such as cheese, yogurt, milk, milk powders and more.
President/CEO: Ron Dunford
SVP/CFO: Matt Mueller
SVP, U.S. Operations: Tony Nowak
SVP, Information Services: Tom Andreoli
SVP, Quality & Innovation: Vinith Poduval
SVP & Chief Commercial Officer: Trevor Farrell
Year Founded: 1945
Estimated Sales: Over $1 Billion
Number Employees: 8,000
Type of Packaging: Consumer, Food Service, Private Label, Bulk
Other Locations:
Tempe, AZ
Gainesville, GA
Carthage, MO
Clinton, MO
Monett, MO
Mt Vernon, MOGainesville
Markets Served:
Food Manufacturers & Processors, Food Service Operators
Brokered Products include:
Dairy/Deli, Ingredients

41074 Schurman's Wisconsin Cheese Country
1401 Hwy 23 North
Dodgeville, WI 53533 608-935-5741
Fax: 608-794-2194
dodgeville@schurmanscheese.com
www.schurmanscheese.com
Broker of health foods, natural cheeses, packaging and private label items
President: Lorraine Schurman
CEO: Jim Morgan
CFO: Jim Morgan
R&D: John Schurman
Quality Control: Jim Morgan
Estimated Sales: $10-20 Million
Number Employees: 20-49
Type of Packaging: Private Label
Markets Served:
Wholesale Distributors
Brokered Products include:
Dairy/Deli, General Merchandise, Health Food, Private Label, Natural Cheeses, Packaging

41075 Scooter Bay Seafood Sales Company
739 Roosevelt Rd
Glen Ellyn, IL 60137-5877 630-545-2383
Fax: 630-545-9770 www.scooterbay.com
President: Scott Shoub
Estimated Sales: $5-10 Million
Number Employees: 10-19

41076 Scott & Associates
2454 N McMullen Booth Rd # 205
Clearwater, FL 33759-1300 727-726-1677
Fax: 727-799-2110
Wholesaler/distributor and broker of equipment for the food industry
Manager: Cindy Mollett
Estimated Sales: $.5-1 million
Number Employees: 10-19
Markets Served:
Super Market Chains, Wholesale Distributors
Brokered Products include:
General Merchandise, Food Industry Equipment

41077 Seaboard Foods
9000 W. 67th St.
Suite 200
Shawnee Mission, KS 66202
  800-262-7907
info@seaboardfoods.com seaboardfoods.com
Fresh, frozen and processed pork products.
President/CEO: Darwin Sand
Vice President, Marketing: Tom Blumhardt
Vice President, Plant Operations: Marty Hast
Year Founded: 1995
Estimated Sales: $38.8 Million
Number Employees: 4,986
Number of Brands: 5
Parent Co: Seaboard Corporation
Type of Packaging: Consumer, Food Service, Private Label, Bulk
Other Locations:
Processing Plant
Guymon, OKMount Dora Farms Management
Houston, TXDaily's Premium Meats Bacon Plant
Salt Lake City, UT
Daily's Premium Meats Bacon Plant
Missoula, MT
Processing PlantReynosa, MEXICO
Markets Served:
Food Manufacturers & Processors, Super Market Chains, Wholesale Distributors, Food Service Operators
Primary Brands Brokered include: Triumph Foods
Brokered Products include:
Meat, Meat Products, Private Label

41078 Seachase Foods
1726 Ridge Road
Suite 106
Homewood, IL 60430-1846 708-481-7321
Fax: 708-481-7320
President: Mel Jones
Estimated Sales: $3-5 Million
Number Employees: 1-4

41079 Seafood Dimensions Brokerage
320 Fielding Rd
Versailles, KY 40383-1499 859-873-2255
Fax: 859-873-2290
CEO: Bob Barnes
Estimated Sales: $.5-1 million
Number Employees: 5-9

41080 Seafood Hawaii Inc
875 Waimanu St # 634
Suite 634
Honolulu, HI 96813-5265 808-597-1971
Fax: 808-538-1973
Seafood
President: Jed J Inouye
Estimated Sales: $5-10 Million
Number Employees: 20-49

41081 Seafood International
1051 Old Henderson Hwy
Henderson, LA 70517-7805 337-228-7568
Fax: 337-228-7573 www.seafoodfromnorway.com
Seafood
Owner: Roy Robert
seafoodintl@cox-internet.com
Estimated Sales: $3,300,000
Number Employees: 5-9

41082 Seafood Sales
PO Box 353
Syosset, NY 11791-0353 516-496-8377
Fax: 516-496-8519 lamboo2@aol.com
Import and export broker of pasta, freeze dried items and frozen seafood including shrimp
President: Ajay Dhawan
VP: Rachna Dhawan
Sales: Nancy Frey
Estimated Sales: $1-3 Million
Number Employees: 1-4
Square Footage: 1400
Markets Served:
Food Manufacturers & Processors, Super Market Chains, Wholesale Distributors, Food Service Operators
Primary Brands Brokered include: Ace; Ravi; Haroon; Castle Rock; Seasnow; Crown
Brokered Products include:
Exports, Frozen Food, Imports, Seafood, Pasta, Freeze Dried Foods

41083 Seamark Corporation
63 Main Street
Gloucester, MA 01930-5722 978-283-4476
Fax: 978-281-6490
Estimated Sales: $300,000-500,000
Number Employees: 1-4

41084 Select Sales & Marketing Inc
116 Jay Street
Belle Chasse, LA 70037-1220 504-392-8848
Fax: 504-392-8821 selectsm@aol.com
Manufacturers' representative for general merchandise and private label items

Food Brokers / A-Z

President/CEO: Ronald Thibodaux
VP: Renee Marie
Sales: Ron Bruner
Contact: Ron Thibodaux
rthibodaux@select-smg.com
Estimated Sales: $10-20 Million
Number Employees: 13
Square Footage: 4000
Markets Served:
   Super Market Chains, Wholesale Distributors
Brokered Products include:
   General Merchandise, Private Label

41085 Sell Group
8601 F Street
Omaha, NE 68127-1604   402-339-8886
   Fax: 402-339-2433
Broker of confectionery and dairy/deli products, general merchandise, frozen foods, groceries, produce, spices, etc.; serving supermarket chains and wholesalers/distributors
VP: Rick Vance
Estimated Sales: $20-50 Million
Number Employees: 20-49
Markets Served:
   Super Market Chains, Wholesale Distributors
Brokered Products include:
   Confectionery, Dairy/Deli, Frozen Food, General Merchandise, Groceries, Produce, Spices

41086 Service Group
98-1787 Kaahumanu St # D
Aiea, HI 96701-1821   808-454-1524
   Fax: 808-455-1984 servicegr@aol.com
Broker of frozen foods, groceries, seafood, spices, general merchandise, private label items, etc.
President: Paul Matsuda
VP: Brenda Furtado
Estimated Sales: $5-10 Million
Number Employees: 20-49
Markets Served:
   Super Market Chains, Food Service Operators
Brokered Products include:
   Frozen Food, General Merchandise, Groceries, Private Label, Seafood, Spices

41087 Sesame King Foods
1958 Port Edward Place
Newport Beach, CA 92660-6614   714-217-0390
Manufacturers' representative for imported and exported sauces including soy, teriyaki and barbecue. Also iced tea and coffee, soft drinks, Japanese noodles, vinegar and sesame oil
Account Executive: Wayne Lin
Sales Manager: Mark Lin
Parent Co: Shin Chen Oil Corporation
Primary Brands Brokered include: Sesame King
Brokered Products include:
   Groceries, Sauces, Sesame Oil, Vinegar, Etc.

41088 Sessions & Associates
PO Box 20465
Houston, TX 77225-0465   281-376-9998
   Fax: 281-251-7172
Broker of confectionery and dairy/deli products, frozen food, general merchandise, groceries, health food, etc.
CEO: Leon Sessions
Director Food Services: Gene Beck
Director Retail: Daryl Wilson
Estimated Sales: $2.5-5 Million
Number Employees: 1-4
Square Footage: 4800
Markets Served:
   Food Manufacturers & Processors, Super Market Chains, Wholesale Distributors, Food Service Operators
Primary Brands Brokered include: Gel Spice; Bud's Best Cookies; Precision Foods, Inc.; Rex Pure Foods; Holsum Foods; Strout Plastic
Brokered Products include:
   Confectionery, Dairy/Deli, Frozen Food, General Merchandise, Groceries, Health Food, Meat, Meat Products, Private Label, Seafood, Spices, Snack Foods

41089 Settables Inc
408 E 4th St # 102
Bridgeport, PA 19405-1823   610-277-8400
   Fax: 610-277-8448 office@settables.com
Manufacturers' representative for food service equipment and supplies incuding smallwares, glassware, china flatware, linens, table skirting, menu covers, etc.

Owner: Barry Trevor
Estimated Sales: $5+ Million
Number Employees: 1-4
Markets Served:
   Wholesale Distributors
Primary Brands Brokered include: Cardinal International; Snap-Drape International; Risch; Winco; Infinity Hospitality Products; Thermos; Cooktek; Chefs Choice
Brokered Products include:
   General Merchandise, Foodservice Equipment & Supplies

41090 Shamrock Seafood
PO Box 1458
Gloucester, MA 01931-1458   978-281-6465
   Fax: 978-281-7069
President: John O'Toole

41091 Shields Brokerage
9720 W 115th Street
Overland Park, KS 66210-2921   913-338-3301
   Fax: 913-338-1352
Broker of general merchandise
President: Rae Ann Thompson
Markets Served:
   Super Market Chains, Wholesale Distributors
Brokered Products include:
   General Merchandise

41092 Shore Distribution Resources
18 Manitoba Way
Marlboro, NJ 07746-1219   732-972-1297
   Fax: 732-972-7669 800-876-9727
   shordist@aol.com
Wholesaler/distributor of packaging materials and equipment including plastic containers, polyester film, cellophane and polypropylene; also, carry out platters, bowls, disposable thermometers and food safety products
President: Elaine Shore
CEO: Harvey Shore
shordist@aol.com
Sales: Harvey Shore
Operations: Scott Shore
Estimated Sales: $1-2.5 Million
Number Employees: 5-9
Square Footage: 12000
Type of Packaging: Food Service
Markets Served:
   Food Manufacturers & Processors, Super Market Chains, Wholesale Distributors, Food Service Operators
Brokered Products include:
   Ingredients

41093 Shrimp Tex Distributors
34431 Island Estates St
San Benito, TX 78586-6658   956-361-2432
   Fax: 956-361-3043 800-227-4746
Domestic and import broker/packer of frozen shrimp
President: Ron Penny
VP: Lorraine Penny
Estimated Sales: $1-2.5 Million
Number Employees: 1-4
Square Footage: 4000
Markets Served:
   Food Manufacturers & Processors, Super Market Chains, Wholesale Distributors, Food Service Operators
Primary Brands Brokered include: Sea Choice; Texas Treasure; Golden Gulf; Gulf King; Monas; Wonder
Brokered Products include:
   Frozen Food, Imports, Seafood, Frozen Shrimp

41094 Sid Alpers Organic Sales Company
PO Box 242
New Milford, NJ 07646-0242   201-265-3695
   Fax: 201-265-3819
Import and export broker of cereal/breakfast products, grains, flours, kosher foods and syrups
CEO: Sid Alpers
VP: H Alpers
Number Employees: 10
Markets Served:
   Super Market Chains, Wholesale Distributors, Food Service Operators
Primary Brands Brokered include: Grey Owl Rice; Shesh Dried Fruits; Adirondak Maple Syrup
Brokered Products include:
   Confectionery, Dairy/Deli, Exports, Groceries, Health Food, Imports, Produce, Spices

41095 Sid Green Frozen Foods
7833 N 7th Street
Phoenix, AZ 85020-4132   602-943-4687
   Fax: 602-944-4497
Wholesaler/distributor of seafood and frozen foods
President: Ronald Green
Secretary/Treasurer: Shirley Green
Vice President: Barry Green
Estimated Sales: $3-5 Million
Number Employees: 1-4
Square Footage: 36000
Markets Served:
   Wholesale Distributors
Brokered Products include:
   Seafood

41096 Siegerr, Ken
P.O.Box 400
Worth, IL 60482-0400   708-233-9700
   Fax: 708-233-9757
President: Jim Barakat
Estimated Sales: $300,000-500,000
Number Employees: 1-4

41097 (HQ)Sinco
750 Pleasant Street
Belmont, MA 2478   617-484-8212
   Fax: 617-484-2279 sales@sinco-inc.com
   www.sinco-inc.com
Import and export broker of confectionery and dairy/deli products, frozen foods, general merchandise, groceries, health food, meat and meat products, industrial ingredients, private label items, etc.
President: Robert Snyder
VP: Paul Dembling
Contact: Dave Carney
dcarney@sincoinc.com
Estimated Sales: $10-20 Million
Number Employees: 20-49
Square Footage: 12000
Markets Served:
   Food Manufacturers & Processors, Super Market Chains, Wholesale Distributors, Food Service Operators
Primary Brands Brokered include: Pacific Seas; Pataya; Filippo Riccio; Andrea; Recipe; Harry; Marifano
Brokered Products include:
   Confectionery, Dairy/Deli, Exports, Frozen Food, General Merchandise, Groceries, Health Food, Imports, Ingredients, Meat, Meat Products, Private Label

41098 Singer Lee & Associates
7263 Lansdowne Ave
St Louis, MO 63119-3421   314-644-5565
   Fax: 314-644-0870 dlee@singerlee.com
Broker of confectionery products
Owner: Doug Lee
Estimated Sales: $10-$20 Million
Number Employees: 10-19
Brokered Products include:
   Confectionery

41099 (HQ)Skidmore Sales & Distributing Company
9889 Cincinnati Dayton Rd
West Chester, OH 45069-3825   513-755-4200
   Fax: 513-759-4270 800-468-7543
   stevejackson@skidmore-sales.com
   www.skidmore-sales.com
Wholesaler/distributor of industrial ingredients, including fruit powder
President/CEO: Doug Skidmore
Chairman: Gerard Skidmore
CFO: Steppi Frey
Information Technology Manager: Dennis Meyers
VP Sales/Marketing: Steve Jackson
VP Supply Chain: Jack Buecker
Estimated Sales: $8.0 Million
Number Employees: 36
Square Footage: 450000
Other Locations:
   Skidmore Sales & Distributing
   Hunt Valley, MD Skidmore Sales & Distributing

41100 Slagle & Associates
3027 New Hall Rd
Greenbrier, TN 37073-6200   615-672-4397
   Fax: 615-672-0703
Broker of frozen food, groceries and meat/meat products
President: Tom Slagle

Estimated Sales: $160
Number Employees: 1
Markets Served:
 Wholesale Distributors, Food Service Operators
Brokered Products include:
 Frozen Food, Groceries, Meat, Meat Products

41101 Slattery Marketing Corporation
33 Clinton Road
Suite 201
West Caldwell, NJ 7006   973-882-8060
                           Fax: 973-882-8062
Broker of groceries and private label items; serving supermarkets chains and wholesalers/distributors
President/CEO: Michael Slattery
Executive VP/COO: Edward Kubarewicz
SVP: Vincent McMahon
VP, Sales: Anthony Paranzino
Contact: Daniel Kubarewicz
dkubarewicz@slatterymarketing.com
Estimated Sales: $10-20 Million
Number Employees: 10-19
Square Footage: 10000
Type of Packaging: Private Label
Markets Served:
 Super Market Chains, Wholesale Distributors
Primary Brands Brokered include: Ruby Kist; King Cole; Kadem; C&F Beans; Orchard Park; Shultz
Brokered Products include:
 Groceries, Private Label

41102 Slaybaugh & Associates
60 South Trooper Rd.
Norristown, PA 19403-3076   610-539-5135
                              Fax: 610-539-8931
craigs@slaybaughassociates.com
www.slaybaughassociates.com
Broker of canned fruits and vegetables, dairy/deli products, industrial ingredients, frozen foods, groceries and general merchandise
President: David Slaybaugh
Treasurer: Fred Slaybaugh
Sales Manager: Craig Slaybaugh
Estimated Sales: $5-10 Million
Number Employees: 5
Markets Served:
 Food Service Operators
Brokered Products include:
 Dairy/Deli, Frozen Food, General Merchandise, Groceries, Ingredients, Canned Fruits & Vegetables

41103 Sloan Sales Inc
1 Pleasure Island Rd # 1a
Wakefield, MA 01880-1229   781-245-7500
                             Fax: 781-246-2561 sam@sloansales.com
Import broker of confectionery and dairy/deli products, frozen foods, health foods, private label items, etc.
President: Sam Sloan
sam@sloansales.com
Treasurer: M Sloan
Estimated Sales: $10-20 Million
Number Employees: 10-19
Markets Served:
 Food Manufacturers & Processors, Super Market Chains, Wholesale Distributors, Food Service Operators
Brokered Products include:
 Confectionery, Dairy/Deli, Frozen Food, Groceries, Health Food, Imports, Ingredients, Private Label, Produce, Seafood, Spices

41104 Smart Cycling, Inc.
1882 Johns Dr
Glenview, IL 60025-1657   847-998-0200
                            Fax: 847-998-8059
Broker of dairy/deli products, frozen foods, general merchandise, goceries, meat products, spices, etc
Owner: Steve Thordarson
CEO/Owner: WL Stickney III
VP: M Kawala
Number Employees: 10-19
Markets Served:
 Wholesale Distributors, Food Service Operators
Brokered Products include:
 Confectionery, Dairy/Deli, Frozen Food, General Merchandise, Groceries, Health Food, Imports, Ingredients, Meat, Meat Products, Private Label, Produce, Seafood, Spices

41105 Smigiel Marketing & Sales Ltd.
2 S York Rd
Bensenville, IL 60106-2179   630-350-8600
Broker of confectionery products, general merchandise, groceries, seafood, spices, private label items, etc.
Owner: R Smigiel
Office Manager: J Paetsch
Sales Manager: J Mazza
Estimated Sales: $5-10 Million
Number Employees: 5-9
Square Footage: 4000
Markets Served:
 Super Market Chains, Wholesale Distributors
Primary Brands Brokered include: Gakkity Ind.; Durable Alum; Mobil Oil; Trident Seafood; Maryland Plastics; Sunshine Ind.
Brokered Products include:
 Confectionery, General Merchandise, Groceries, Private Label, Seafood, Spices

41106 Snax Sales Company
PO Box 273
Louisville, CO 80027-0273   262-782-4196
                              Fax: 262-782-7376
Broker of confectionery products, general merchandise and private label items
Owner: Tron Horn
Number Employees: 3
Markets Served:
 Wholesale Distributors
Brokered Products include:
 Confectionery, Imports, Private Label

41107 Solo Cup Company
150 Spouth Saunders Rd.
Lake Forest, IL 60045
                              info@solocup.com
                              www.solocup.com
Single-use cups, plates, cutlery, take-out contaiers.
CEO, Dart Container Corporation: Jim Lammers
Year Founded: 1936
Estimated Sales: $1.6 Billion
Number Employees: 6,400
Parent Co: Dart Container Corporation
Type of Packaging: Consumer, Food Service, Private Label, Bulk
Brokered Products include:
 General Merchandise

41108 Soudronic Limited
465 N State Rd # 2
Briarcliff Manor, NY 10510-1458   914-941-4808
                                    Fax: 914-941-5144 www.soudronic.com
Imported and export broker of general merchandise including can-making equipment and leak testers
President: Urs Keller
urs.keller@soudronic.com
VP Engineering: H Fankhauser
Estimated Sales: $20-50 Million
Number Employees: 20-49
Primary Brands Brokered include: Bauer & Kunzi; Bonfiglioli; Karges-Hammer; Oscam; Sabatier; Soudronic
Brokered Products include:
 General Merchandise, Can-Making Equipment, Etc.

41109 South Cape Seafood
1084 Main St
Chatham, MA 02633   508-945-1223
                      Fax: 508-945-4911
President: Mark Bulman

41110 South East Sales
1913 W Cary St # B
Richmond, VA 23220-5372   804-282-5061
                            Fax: 804-282-8845 main@southeastsales.us
                            www.southeastsales.us
Broker of spices and industrial ingredients
President: Michael E Crowder
Operations: Laura Streat
Estimated Sales: $3-5 Million
Number Employees: 5-9
Square Footage: 5600
Markets Served:
 Food Manufacturers & Processors, Food Service Operators
Primary Brands Brokered include: ADM; Cutler; Industrial Commodities; Domino; Idaho Pacific; Red Arrow, E-Com, Groeb Farms
Brokered Products include:
 Ingredients, Spices

41111 South Group Marketing
2511 Winford Ave
Nashville, TN 37211   615-244-2728
                       Fax: 615-242-4368
Broker of dairy/deli products, frozen foods, meat and meat products, seafood, spices, etc.
President: Tim Helton
Office Manager: Brigitte Kinley
Sales Manager: Mike Martin
Estimated Sales: $10-20 Million
Number Employees: 5-9
Markets Served:
 Food Manufacturers & Processors, Wholesale Distributors, Food Service Operators
Primary Brands Brokered include: Hormel Foods; Jennie-O Foods; Cargill Poultry; Russer Foods; Granny's Kitchen; Mrs. Crockett's Kitchens
Brokered Products include:
 Dairy/Deli, Frozen Food, Meat, Meat Products, Seafood, Spices, Bakery Products

41112 Southeastern Manufacturer's
3020 Amwiler Rd
Atlanta, GA 30360-2813   770-246-0111
                           Fax: 770-246-0544 877-264-7362
Manufacturers' representative for food service equipment and supplies
Owner, President: Pete Caberilli
pcabrelli@semareps.com
Sales: Barry Ford
General Manager: Richard Filitor
Estimated Sales: $5-10 Million
Number Employees: 5-9
Square Footage: 8000
Markets Served:
 Wholesale Distributors
Primary Brands Brokered include: Berkel; Edlund Company; Beverage Air; Champion Industries; CresCor; Prince Castle; Advance Tabco; Bally Refr. Boxes; T&S Brass
Brokered Products include:
 General Merchandise, Foodservice Equipment

41113 Southeastern Paper Group Inc
50 Old Blackstock Rd
Spartanburg, SC 29301-5571   864-574-0440
                               Fax: 864-576-3828 800-858-7230
sepaper@sepapergroup.com www.sepg.com
Import broker of produce, groceries, meats, dairy/deli items and general merchandise including pallet wrap, material handling equipment, labels, bar code printers, laser scanners, etc.; serving all markets
President: Lewis Miller
COO: Will Green
wgreen@sepapergroup.com
CFO: Jim Heatherly
VP: Linda Garner
Director Marketing: Tammy Thompson
VP Sales: Greg Rizzi
Operations Manager: Kristie Graffagnino
Estimated Sales: $20 Million
Number Employees: 50-99
Square Footage: 16000
Markets Served:
 Food Manufacturers & Processors, Super Market Chains, Wholesale Distributors, Food Service Operators
Primary Brands Brokered include: Mobil; Borden; Sealed Air
Brokered Products include:
 Dairy/Deli, General Merchandise, Groceries, Imports, Meat Products, Private Label, Produce

41114 Southern Commodities Inc
214 Whitney St
Eatonton, GA 31024-5734   706-484-2201
                            Fax: 229-985-1329
Manufacturers' representative for raisins, apricots and shelled nuts including pecans, walnuts, almonds, cashews, hazelnuts, peanuts, etc.
President: C Allen
Estimated Sales: Less Than $500,000
Number Employees: 1-4
Brokered Products include:
 Groceries, Pecans, Walnuts, Raisins, Etc.

41115 Southern Seafood Connection
PO Box 9187
Houma, LA 70361-9187   410-968-3366
                         Fax: 410-968-1429
President: Greg Loney

Food Brokers / A-Z

41116 Specialty Equipment Sales Co
5705 Valley Belt Rd
Brooklyn Heights, OH 44131-1421   216-661-6286
Fax: 216-898-9999   800-222-0558
www.sesco.biz
Manufacturers' representative for food service equipment
Vice President: Ed Ahern
eda@sesco.biz
Partner: Jim Reitano
Vice President of Business developments: Steve Wright
VP Operations: Mark Kapinski
Purchasing: Jim Ania
Estimated Sales: $10-20 Million
Number Employees: 20-49
Markets Served:
   Wholesale Distributors
Primary Brands Brokered include: Amana; Silver Kin; ThermoKool; Exellence; Magikitchen; Nieco
Brokered Products include:
   General Merchandise, Foodservice Equipment

41117 Specialty Partners
970 Raymond Avenue
Suite G-30
Saint Paul, MN 55114-1146   651-645-8193
Fax: 651-646-5138
Import broker of confectionery and dairy/deli products, groceries, health food, private label items, specialty foods, etc.
Director Brokerage Operations: Dave Tauscher
Account Executive: Walt Pawlyshyn
Account Executive: David Peterson
Number Employees: 10
Square Footage: 16000
Markets Served:
   Super Market Chains, Wholesale Distributors
Primary Brands Brokered include: Vigo Importing; Hain Food Group; Mott's USA; Nestle Specialty; Belgioioso Cheese; Health Valley
Brokered Products include:
   Confectionery, Dairy/Deli, Groceries, Health Food, Imports, Private Label, Spices, Specialty Foods

41118 Specialty Sales & Marketing
809 S Westover Boulevard
Albany, GA 31707-4953   229-439-1418
Fax: 229-439-1418
Broker of confectionery and dairy/deli items, frozen foods, general merchandise, groceries and private label brands
Branch Manager: Lee Merritt
Estimated Sales: Less than $500,000
Number Employees: 1-4
Parent Co: Budd Mayer
Markets Served:
   Food Manufacturers & Processors, Super Market Chains, Wholesale Distributors, Food Service Operators
Brokered Products include:
   Confectionery, Dairy/Deli, Frozen Food, General Merchandise, Groceries, Private Label

41119 Spectrum Foodservice Associates
8 Halfmoon Executive Park Dr
Clifton Park, NY 12065   518-373-3810
Fax: 513-348-0637   800-724-1775
www.foodservicebroker.com
Broker of dairy/deli and dry grocery products, frozen foods, meat and meat products, private label items, etc.
Chairman: Ed Evers
President/COO: Glenn Oliver
Sales Manager: David Merchant
Estimated Sales: $10-20 Million
Number Employees: 10-19
Square Footage: 47400
Parent Co: Spectrum Foodservice Associates
Markets Served:
   Super Market Chains, Wholesale Distributors, Food Service Operators
Primary Brands Brokered include: Wampler; Lipton; Mrs. Smith's; Uncle Bens; Campbells; Specialty Brands
Brokered Products include:
   Dairy/Deli, Frozen Food, Groceries, Meat, Meat Products, Private Label, Seafood, Spices

41120 Spectrum Foodservices
202 Twin Oaks Drive
Syracuse, NY 13206-1203   315-463-8259
Fax: 315-463-4807
Broker and manufacturers' representative for dairy/deli products, frozen foods, meats, private label items, seafood and spices
President: Ed Evers
Senior VP: Glenn Oliver
VP Buffalo/Rochester Office: Clarence Houk
Estimated Sales: $2.5-5 Million
Number Employees: 1-4
Square Footage: 8000
Markets Served:
   Wholesale Distributors, Food Service Operators
Brokered Products include:
   Dairy/Deli, Frozen Food, Meat, Meat Products, Private Label, Seafood, Spices

41121 Spence Wells Assoc
34 Central Ave
Needham, MA 02494-2914   781-449-1040
Fax: 781-455-8592   bspenceco@aol.com
www.spencewells.com
Manufacturers' representative for smallwares; also, trays, salad bar equipment, pots, pans, dish racks, etc.
President: Robert Spence
bspenceco@aol.com
Estimated Sales: $2.5-5 Million
Number Employees: 1-4
Markets Served:
   Wholesale Distributors
Brokered Products include:
   General Merchandise, Smallwares, Trays, Pots, Pans, Etc.

41122 Spencer & Assoc
11630 SE 40th Ave # B
Suite B
Portland, OR 97222-6195   503-659-2611
Fax: 503-659-8688   888-976-9890
mikes@spencerinc.com
Broker of confectionery and dairy/deli products, frozen foods, general merchandise, groceries, meat and produce
President: Mike Spencer
mikes@spencerinc.com
Chief Executive Officer: John Spencer
Chief Financial Officer: Carole Spencer
Sales: Lynette Duane
Sales: Chris Merris
Estimated Sales: $5-10 Million
Number Employees: 1-4
Square Footage: 4000
Type of Packaging: Consumer, Food Service, Private Label, Bulk
Markets Served:
   Food Manufacturers & Processors, Super Market Chains, Wholesale Distributors, Food Service Operators
Brokered Products include:
   Dairy/Deli, Frozen Food, General Merchandise, Groceries, Health Food, Ingredients, Meat, Private Label, Spices

41123 Spice Rack Extracts
30 Garfield Place
Hempstead, NY 11550-6206   516-481-7312
Fax: 516-481-5417
Import and export broker of fruit juice concentrates, essential oils, fragrances, flavors and spices
President: Pamela A Ringgold
CEO: Rodney O Johnson
Number Employees: 1-4

41124 Spurry & Associates
8615 Commerce Street
Suite 5
Easton, MD 21601-7421   410-820-7100
Fax: 410-820-7123   c.spurry@dmw.com
Manufacturers' representative for food service equipment
President/Principal: Chris F. Spurry
Associate: Michael B. Witty
Associate: Jamie Curren
Contact: Sherrie Davis
sherrie@spurry.net
Office Manager: Sherrie Davis
Estimated Sales: $2.5-5 Million
Number Employees: 5-9
Markets Served:
   Wholesale Distributors
Primary Brands Brokered include: Travlsen; Champion; American Panel; Color Point; Market Forge; FWE
Brokered Products include:
   General Merchandise, Foodservice Equipment

41125 Squier Associates
14650 Rothgeb Dr # H
Rockville, MD 20850-5386   301-762-3710
Fax: 301-762-2303   www.squierinc.com
Manufacturers' representative for food service equipment and supplies
President: Alan Squier
alansquier@squierinc.com
VP: Bill Squier
Sales: Michelle McConnell
Sales: Chris Mulholland
Sales: Bob Barrett
Customer Service: Jennifer Mullennex
Office Manager: Brenda Ritchie
Estimated Sales: Less Than $500,000
Number Employees: 5-9
Markets Served:
   Wholesale Distributors
Brokered Products include:
   General Merchandise, Foodservice Equipment & Supplies

41126 St Charles Trading Inc
650 N Raddant Rd
Batavia, IL 60510-4207   630-377-0608
Fax: 630-406-1936
customerservice@stcharlestrading.com
Food ingredient distributor
President/VP Sales: Al Cicanci
CEO: William Manns
williammanns@stcharlestrading.com
Quality Assurance Officer: Dana Capes
Director of Operation: Janet Matthews
Estimated Sales: $15,000,000
Number Employees: 20-49
Square Footage: 40000
Markets Served:
   Food Manufacturers & Processors, Super Market Chains, Wholesale Distributors
Brokered Products include:
   Confectionery, Dairy/Deli, Exports, General Merchandise, Ingredients, Meat, Private Label, Spices

41127 St Charles Trading Inc
650 N Raddant Rd
Batavia, IL 60510-4207   630-377-0608
Fax: 630-406-1936
customerservice@stcharlestrading.com
Distributor, importer/exporter of food ingredients, specializing in beans and seeds; oar products; batters, coatins & breadcrumbs; dairy, potato, wheat, corn and protein products; cocoa and chcolate; dehydrated onion and garlic; spices; food chemicals and sweeteners; dehydrated vegetables and fruits; and rice.
CEO: William Manns
williammanns@stcharlestrading.com
Executive Vice President: Dave Nolan
Director, Manufacturing & Quality Contro: Andrew Rumshas
Vice President of Operations: Janet Matthews
Purchasing Manager: Novita Rahim
Estimated Sales: $64.4 Million
Number Employees: 20-49
Number of Brands: 49
Type of Packaging: Bulk

41128 St. Ours & Company
1571 Commercial St
East Weymouth, MA 02189-3015   781-331-8520
Fax: 781-331-8628   email@saintours.com
www.saintours.com
Processor of frozen shellfish, including lobster, crab, dehydrated clam and seafood broths; wholesaler and distributor of seafood and specialty foods.
President: Fred St. Ours
Marketing Manager: Sharon St. Ours
Sales: John Christian
Director of Manufacturing: Richard St. Ours
Estimated Sales: $3-5 Million
Number Employees: 5-9
Type of Packaging: Consumer, Food Service, Bulk
Markets Served:
   Food Manufacturers & Processors, Super Market Chains, Wholesale Distributors, Food Service Operators

Food Brokers / A-Z

41129 Starliper & Associates
2570 New Schuylkill Rd
P.O. Box 389
Parker Ford, PA 19457-389　　　610-363-5688
　Fax: 610-363-6746　eric@starliperassociates.com
　　　　　　www.starliperassociates.com
Manufacturers' representative for food service equipment
President, Owner: Eric Starliper
Outside Sales: Dave Basch
Contact: David Basch
dave@starliperassociates.com
Customer Service: Sue Phipps
Estimated Sales: $1-2.5 Million
Number Employees: 5-9
Markets Served:
　Wholesale Distributors
Primary Brands Brokered include: Cres Cor; Delfield; Flo-Aire; Gates Manufacturing; Globe; Jackson
Brokered Products include:
　General Merchandise, Foodservice Equipment

41130 Statewide Brokerage Company
2231 E Enterprise Pkwy
Twinsburg, OH 44087　　　330-963-5999
　Fax: 330-487-5629
Import broker of confectionery products, frozen foods, general merchandise, groceries and private label items
President: R King
Sales Manager: E King
Office Manager: Alicia Dean
Estimated Sales: $1-2.5 Million
Number Employees: 6
Square Footage: 6000
Markets Served:
　Food Manufacturers & Processors, Super Market Chains, Wholesale Distributors, Food Service Operators
Primary Brands Brokered include: American Candy; Kellogg; Brown & Haley Company; Capital Cookies; Clover Hill Bakeries; Sunshine Biscuit
Brokered Products include:
　Confectionery, Frozen Food, General Merchandise, Groceries, Imports, Private Label

41131 Stern Ingredients
338 W Oakdale Ave
Chicago, IL 60657　　　773-472-0825
　Fax: 773-472-0545　www.sterningredients.com
Fruit and confection products
President: Joni Stern
Administrative Assistant: Anna Mora
Sales Manager: Jeff Faller
Estimated Sales: $2.5-5 Million
Number Employees: 1-4

41132 Stern International Consultants
E9-212 Gladwin Crescent
Ottawa, ON K1B 5N1
Canada　　　613-733-8237
　Fax: 613-733-6161
Import and broker of dairy/deli products, frozen food, general merchandise, groceries, etc. Consultant providing market studies. Warehouse providing dry and cooler storage. Transportation firm providing local trucking fulfillment
President: Richard Stern
CEO: Doris Stern
CFO: Rene Melancon
Number Employees: 3
Square Footage: 20000
Markets Served:
　Super Market Chains, Wholesale Distributors, Food Service Operators
Brokered Products include:
　Confectionery, Frozen Food, General Merchandise, Groceries, Meat

41133 Stevens & Associates
2 Wilkens Drive
Plainville, MA 02762-2274　　　508-699-4790
　Fax: 617-332-7989　www.bubbleking.com
Manufacturers' representative for smallwares, tabletops and light equipment
Owner: Steven Silverman
Owner/VP: Steve Campbell
Estimated Sales: $15 Million
Number Employees: 1-4
Square Footage: 3000
Type of Packaging: Food Service

Markets Served:
　Food Manufacturers & Processors, Super Market Chains, Wholesale Distributors, Food Service Operators
Primary Brands Brokered include: World Crisa; Aero Manufacturing; Le-Jo Enterprises; Gaychrome; Normandie; Golden West Sales; Johnson & Rose Corporation
Brokered Products include:
　General Merchandise, Smallware, Tabletops Lighting Equipment

41134 Stiefel Associates
3125 Pine Tree Road
Suite C
Lansing, MI 48911　　　517-393-3019
　Fax: 517-393-3023　800-860-4887
info@stiefelrep.com　www.stiefelrep.com
Manufacturers' representative for food service equipment
President, Principal: Philip Stiefel
Principal: Cheryl Bowker
Treasurer, Principal: Bill Stiefel
VP, Principal: John Stiefel
Marketing & Data Processing: Nicole Koepke
Contact: Jodi Cartwright
jodi@stiefelrep.com
Office Manager, Customer Service, Data P: Megan Bodell
Estimated Sales: $1-3 Million
Number Employees: 5-9
Square Footage: 4000
Markets Served:
　Food Manufacturers & Processors, Super Market Chains, Wholesale Distributors, Food Service Operators
Primary Brands Brokered include: APW/Wyott; Cres-Cor; Continental Refrigeration; Boldgett/Maytag Foodservice; Duke Manufaturing; Jackson Dishmachines.
Brokered Products include:
　General Merchandise, Foodservice Equipment

41135 Stockdale & Reagan
14 Jewel Drive
Wilmington, MA 01887-3361　　　978-658-6446
　Fax: 978-658-7117　800-458-4089
Broker of confectionery products, frozen foods and groceries
Owner: C Reagan
CEO: James Reagan
CFO: Charles Reagan
Estimated Sales: $300,000-500,000
Number Employees: 5-9
Markets Served:
　Super Market Chains, Wholesale Distributors
Brokered Products include:
　Confectionery, Dairy/Deli, Groceries, Private Label, Produce

41136 Stockett Associates
2515 Wilson Road
White Hall, MD 21161-9476　　　410-343-1331
　Fax: 410-343-1147　800-540-8617
rtstockett@aol.com
Manufacturers' representative for ice machines, water filtration systems, ovens, baking equipment and juice and beverage dispensers
President: Randy Stockett
Number Employees: 1-4
Markets Served:
　Wholesale Distributors
Primary Brands Brokered include: Booth; Crystal Tips; Cuno, Inc.; Karma, Inc.; Summit; New View Foodservice Systems
Brokered Products include:
　General Merchandise, Foodservice Equipment

41137 Stone Crabs Inc
11 Washington Ave
Miami Beach, FL 33139-7395　　　305-534-8788
　Fax: 305-532-2704　800-260-2722
Fresh and frozen stone crabs, whole lobsters and lobster tails
President: Stephen Sawitz
alopez@stonecrabsinc.com
CFO: Marc Fine
Marketing Director: Tracie Gordon
Operations Manager: James McClendon
Facilities: Alex Lopez
Plant Manager: Ron Pressley
Estimated Sales: $10-20 Million
Number Employees: 20-49
Type of Packaging: Consumer, Food Service

Brokered Products include:
　Seafood

41138 Strong & Associates
19717 62nd Ave S Ste F106
Kent, WA 98032　　　253-872-2090
　Fax: 253-395-0529
Broker of confectionery products and snack foods
President: Rick Bolton
CEO: John Strong
Vice President: Bruce Taggart
Contact: Rick Bolten
rbolten@cpastrong.com
Estimated Sales: $10-20 Million
Number Employees: 1-4
Markets Served:
　Super Market Chains, Wholesale Distributors, Food Service Operators
Primary Brands Brokered include: Blue Diamond; Tootsie Roll; Coronets; Ferriro USA; Goetzes
Brokered Products include:
　Confectionery, Snack Foods

41139 Stroup Ingredients Resources
6030 Bethelview Rd # 301
Suite 301
Cumming, GA 30040-8023　　　770-205-8281
　Fax: 770-205-7227　www.stroupingredients.com
Broker of confectionery, dairy/deli products, salad dressings, sauces, baked goods, industrial ingredients, etc.
President/Owner: Robert Stroup, CPMR
Territory Manager: AnneMarie Huber
VP of Sales and Business Development: Nathan Roberts
Customer Service: Diane Watson
Operations Manager: Rodney Hudson
Estimated Sales: $5-10 Million
Number Employees: 5-9
Square Footage: 8000
Markets Served:
　Food Manufacturers & Processors, Wholesale Distributors
Primary Brands Brokered include: Honey Tree, Inc.; Nikken Foods; French's Ingredients; Dole Packaged Foods; Morning Star Packing Company; Wan Ja Shan
Brokered Products include:
　Confectionery, Dairy/Deli, Frozen Food, Groceries, Ingredients, Spices, Salad Dressings, Sauces, Baked Goods

41140 Sturdivant Company
6279 East Slauson Ave
Suite: 107
Cty of Commerce, CA 90040-3900　　　323-269-8322
　Fax: 323-269-5651　800-869-8322
Broker of grocery products, food service product dairy/deli products, frozen foods, general merchandise, products serving all markets
President: John Sturdivant
VP: Dick Tjaden
Contact: Priscilla Mendia
priscilla@sturdivantco.com
Square Footage: 18000
Markets Served:
　Food Manufacturers & Processors, Super Market Chains, Wholesale Distributors, Food Service Operators
Primary Brands Brokered include: TNT; California Girl; Crestwood; Golden Tip; Ful-Flav-R; Gourmet House; Pennant/White Swan; Maria; Cal Maid; MPK; San Benito, Old California and Oregon Trail; Flavr Pac; Stapleton; Triple H; Toma-Tek Old California
Brokered Products include:
　Frozen Food, Groceries, Imports, Private Label

41141 Sturgill Food Brokerage
5015 Roberts Rd
Hilliard, OH 43026-9630　　　614-876-5191
Broker of dairy/deli products, frozen foods, industrial ingredients, meats and meat products, produce, seafood, etc.
President: James Sturgill
Number Employees: 1-4
Markets Served:
　Food Manufacturers & Processors, Super Market Chains, Wholesale Distributors, Food Service Operators
Brokered Products include:
　Dairy/Deli, Frozen Food, Ingredients, Meat, Meat Products, Private Label, Produce, Seafood

Food Brokers / A-Z

41142 Sullivan & Fitzgerald Food Brokers
513 W Mount Pleasant Ave Ste 200
Livingston, NJ 07039   973-994-3800
Fax: 973-994-4311 sullfitz@verizon.net
Importer broker of fresh and frozen seafood including shrimp, scallops, trout, salmon, sole, turbot and flounder
President: Eugene Sullivan
CEO: Gene Sullivan Jr
Estimated Sales: $3-5 Million
Number Employees: 5-9
Square Footage: 8000
Type of Packaging: Consumer, Food Service, Private Label, Bulk
Markets Served:
Food Manufacturers & Processors, Super Market Chains, Wholesale Distributors, Food Service Operators
Primary Brands Brokered include: Cold River; Salmo America; Jubilee; Country Skillet; Maple Leaf Foods International; King & Prince
Brokered Products include:
Frozen Food, Seafood

41143 Summit Brokerage
4011 SE International Way #601
Milwaukie, OR 97222-8858   503-654-7501
Fax: 503-654-7372   800-283-3022
Broker of confectionery and dairy/deli products, frozen foods, meat and meat products and private label items
President: Bonnie Freistone
Estimated Sales: $2.5-5 Million
Number Employees: 20-49
Markets Served:
Food Service Operators
Primary Brands Brokered include: Alden Merrell; AIPC; ASE Foodservice; Belgioioso; Chinet; Moody Dunbar; Raskas; P&C Bakeries; Sun Rich; Tillamook
Brokered Products include:
Confectionery, Dairy/Deli, Frozen Food, Meat, Meat Products, Private Label

41144 Summit FS LTD
N22W22931 Nancys Court
suite 2
Waukesha, WI 53186-1300   262-513-9235
Fax: 262-513-9235   800-884-9894
Broker of confectionery and dairy/deli products, groceries, frozen foods, health food, meat and meat products, seafood, etc.
President: Tim Yahle
Estimated Sales: $3.0 Million
Number Employees: 23
Square Footage: 12600
Type of Packaging: Bulk
Markets Served:
Food Manufacturers & Processors, Super Market Chains, Wholesale Distributors, Food Service Operators
Primary Brands Brokered include: Norpac; Borden Pasta; Culinary Foods; Rich Products; Dole Packaged Foods
Brokered Products include:
Confectionery, Dairy/Deli, Frozen Food, Groceries, Health Food, Meat, Meat Products, Private Label, Seafood, Spices

41145 Sun Food Service Brokerage
11266 SE 21st Avenue
Suite 104
Portland, OR 97222-7776   503-654-6351
Fax: 503-654-1986   800-598-4528
Broker of canned and frozen foods, meats and groceries
President: Rich Lenardson
Number Employees: 1-4
Square Footage: 5200
Markets Served:
Wholesale Distributors
Primary Brands Brokered include: Ghirardelli Chocolate Company; Gulf Pacific; Red Hot Chicago; Nielsen Citrus; Pompeian, Inc.; Wei-chaun
Brokered Products include:
Dairy/Deli, Frozen Food, Groceries, Ingredients, Meat, Spices, Canned Foods

41146 Sun Marketing Agents Inc
2032 Talley Rd # 3
Suite #3
Leesburg, FL 34748-3486   813-956-0069
Fax: 352-365-6147   800-716-2900
sunmarkinc@aol.com
www.sunmarketingagents.com
Manufacturers' representative for food service equipment including gas/electrical cooking, refrigeration, walk-in coolers/freezers, warewashing, material handling, storage products, waste disposal and sanitation
President, Founder: Rich Abernethy
Owner: Patrick Giannini
VP, Stockholder: John English
Regional Sales Representative: Jim DeMara
Office Manager: Holly Giannini
General Manager, Stockholder: Bob Rademacher
Estimated Sales: $2.5-5 Million
Number Employees: 5-9
Square Footage: 12000
Markets Served:
Food Manufacturers & Processors, Super Market Chains, Wholesale Distributors, Food Service Operators
Primary Brands Brokered include: Intermetro Industries; American Panel Corporation; The Montague Company; The Stero Company; Randell Manufacturing; ColdZone
Brokered Products include:
General Merchandise, Foodservice Equipment

41147 Sun Rich Fresh Foods USA Inc
515 E Rincon St
Corona, CA 92879-1391   951-735-3800
Fax: 951-735-3322   800-735-3801
customerservice@sun-rich.com www.sunrich.com
Fresh cut fruit
Vice President: Roxanne Emmerling
roxannee@sun-rich.com
EVP/CFO: Neville Israel
Vice President of Supply Chain: Jeff Pitchford
Quality Assurance Technician: Daysi Aleman
Sales/Marketing Coordinator: Lisa Ten Heggeler
Vice President of Sales and Marketing: Cam Haygarth
HR Manager: Sylvia Del Rio
roxannee@sun-rich.com
VP Operations: Dan O'Connell
Senior Production Manager: Javier Lopez
Number Employees: 100-249
Square Footage: 66000
Type of Packaging: Consumer, Food Service
Other Locations:
Vancouver, Canada Los Angeles, CA
Toronto, Canada Reading, PA Los Angeles

41148 (HQ)Sundown Foods USA, Inc.
10891 Business Dr
Fontana, CA 92337   909-606-2800
Fax: 909-606-2700 sundfoods@aol.com
www.sundownfoods.com
Import and export broker of industrial ingredients, frozen foods, groceries, private label items and seafood; serving all markets
President: Jeff Wartell
Quality Assurance Manager: Diane Boese
Sales: David Martell
david@sundownfoods.com
Plant Manager: Mary Salcido
Estimated Sales: $4 Million
Number Employees: 20-49
Other Locations:
Berelson Export Corp.
Chino, CA Berelson Export Corp.
Markets Served:
Food Manufacturers & Processors, Super Market Chains, Wholesale Distributors, Food Service Operators
Primary Brands Brokered include: Sundown (fresh roasted tomatoes)
Brokered Products include:
Exports, Frozen Food, Groceries, Imports, Ingredients, Private Label, Seafood

41149 Sunwest Sales Co
17731 Irvine Blvd # 108
Ste #108
Tustin, CA 92780-3235   714-368-9808
Fax: 714-368-9809 peteh@sunwestsales.com
www.sunwestsales.com
Broker of confectionery products, grocery products, health food and spices
Owner: Mike Horne
jhorne@sunwestsales.com
Account Executive: Jeffrey Horne
Vice President: Jeff Horne
VP: Pete Horne
VP of Marketing: Warren Burgess
SVP of Sales: Pete Horne
Estimated Sales: $10-20 Million
Number Employees: 10-19
Markets Served:
Super Market Chains, Wholesale Distributors
Primary Brands Brokered include: Buitoni; Perugina; Weetalix; Grainfield's; Colarita Zatarains
Brokered Products include:
Confectionery, Groceries, Health Food, Spices

41150 Super Sale Brokerage Company
PO Box 7523
Little Rock, AR 72217-7523   501-664-6233
Fax: 501-225-6308
Broker of confectionery products, frozen foods, groceries, general merchandise, meats, Mexican foods, cookies, etc.
Owner: Dan Schwartz
Secretary/Treasurer: Rose Schwartz
Number Employees: 1-4
Markets Served:
Food Manufacturers & Processors, Super Market Chains, Wholesale Distributors, Food Service Operators
Primary Brands Brokered include: Intersweet, Inc.; Glazed Fruit; Nuts In Shel-Angires Company; Diet Tea Lacile Beau Company; Specks; Snack Cookies
Brokered Products include:
Confectionery, Dairy/Deli, Frozen Food, General Merchandise, Groceries, Health Food, Meat, Private Label, Seafood, Spices, Mexican Foods, Cookies

41151 Superior Food Brokers
2000 Linwood Ave # 2v
Fort Lee, NJ 07024-3002   201-592-6667
Fax: 201-592-1252   877-592-6667
Broker of confectionery and dairy/deli products, frozen foods, groceries, meat and meat products, etc.
President: Peter Hans
Director Sales/Marketing: Sheryl Hans
Estimated Sales: $5-10 Million
Number Employees: 5-9

41152 Supermarket Representatives
20 E Sunrise Hwy # 300
Valley Stream, NY 11581-1257   516-872-8840
Fax: 516-872-0231   800-645-3520
Broker of general merchandise
President: D Lipskin
CEO: A Fried
CFO: J Bellsey
Vice President: S Lipskin
Estimated Sales: $30 Million
Number Employees: 10-19
Square Footage: 3000
Markets Served:
Super Market Chains, Wholesale Distributors, Food Service Operators
Primary Brands Brokered include: Regalware, Inc.; Arrow Plastics; Hartin International; Bacova Guild; Dayspring Enterprises; Avon Glove Company
Brokered Products include:
General Merchandise

41153 (HQ)Supreme Foods
8755 Keele Street
Concord, ON L4K2N1
Canada   905-738-4204
Wholesaler/distributor and import broker of kosher foods, confectionery, frozen foods, general merchandise, natural foods, specialty foods, groceries, meats, spices, etc.
President: J Simon
Secretary/Treasurer: P Bonder
Vice President: R Simon
Number Employees: 50
Square Footage: 220000
Markets Served:
Food Manufacturers & Processors, Super Market Chains, Wholesale Distributors, Food Service Operators
Primary Brands Brokered include: Streits; Croyden House; Ceres; Carrs; Vitasoy; Glaceau

Brokered Products include:
Confectionery, Dairy/Deli, Frozen Food, General Merchandise, Groceries, Imports, Meat Products, Private Label, Spices

41154 Supreme Foodservice Sales
17520 Von Karman Avenue
Irvine, CA 92614-6208 949-261-6696
Fax: 949-261-6749 www.supremefoodservice.com
Broker of confectionery and dairy/deli products, frozen foods, meat/meat products, private label/generic items and produce
President: W Waldo
Estimated Sales: $5-10 Million
Number Employees: 20-49
Markets Served:
Food Manufacturers & Processors, Wholesale Distributors, Food Service Operators
Brokered Products include:
Confectionery, Dairy/Deli, Frozen Food, Meat, Meat Products, Private Label, Produce

41155 Sutton International
1933 Davis St # 260
San Leandro, CA 94577-1264 510-635-8761
Fax: 510-635-8762
Broker of snack products, frozen foods, general merchandise and health foods
President: Charles Davis
charles@eaglefrizzell.com
General Manager: Ned Prochnow
Estimated Sales: $1-2.5 Million
Number Employees: 5-9
Square Footage: 40000
Type of Packaging: Consumer, Food Service
Primary Brands Brokered include: Military Vending
Brokered Products include:
Frozen Food, General Merchandise, Groceries, Health Food, Snacks

41156 Swiss American International
1059 E Gartner Rd
Naperville, IL 60540 630-778-7245
Fax: 630-778-7246
Wholesaler/distributor and export broker of natural brewed tea concentrates and industrial ingredients
President: Richard L Hutter
VP: George Kienberger
Estimated Sales: $1-2.5 Million
Number Employees: 1-4
Square Footage: 2400
Type of Packaging: Consumer, Food Service

41157 Symons-Bodtker Associates
35 Pamaron Way Ste B
Novato, CA 94949 415-883-2567
Fax: 415-883-2572
Manufacturers' representative for food service equipment
President: Erik Bodtker
ispanel@yahoo.com
Estimated Sales: $1-2.5 Million
Number Employees: 1-4
Markets Served:
Wholesale Distributors
Primary Brands Brokered include: Econo Max; McCray; Nexel; Omni Temp; Master-Bilt; Oscartielle Delicases
Brokered Products include:
General Merchandise, Foodservice Equipment

41158 (HQ)T C Jacoby & Co
1716 Hidden Creek Ct # 200
St Louis, MO 63131-1889 314-821-4456
Fax: 314-821-3251 800-325-9556
rod@jacoby.com www.jacoby.com
Import/export broker of milk replacers and ingredients, cheese, ice cream blends, whey, proteins, casein, caseinates, nonfat dry and whole milk, etc.
President: Ted Jacoby Jr
rod@jacoby.com
VP Cheese Sales: Ted Jacoby
Sales: Rod Jacoby
Office Manager: Shelby Leadford
rod@jacoby.com
Estimated Sales: $10-20 Million
Number Employees: 20-49
Other Locations:
Jacoby, T.C., & Company
Col. del ValleJacoby, T.C., & Company
Primary Brands Brokered include: Nulat; TCJ; Alpari
Brokered Products include:
Dairy/Deli, Exports, Imports, Ingredients, Cheese, Milk, Ice Cream Blends, Etc.

41159 T. McConnell Sales & Marketing
14 Oxford Street
Richmond Hill, ON L4C 4L5
Canada 905-771-7300
Fax: 905-771-7304
Import and export broker of dairy/deli products, frozen foods, groceries, meat and meat products, private label items, seafood, etc.
President: Graham McConnell
VP Corporate Brands: Andrew Wallace
Number Employees: 10-19
Markets Served:
Food Manufacturers & Processors, Super Market Chains, Wholesale Distributors, Food Service Operators
Brokered Products include:
Dairy/Deli, Exports, Frozen Food, Groceries, Imports, Meat, Meat Products, Private Label, Seafood

41160 T.F.S. & Associates
3002 Woodbridge Drive
Anniston, AL 36207-6980 256-236-0007
Broker of groceries and private label items
Owner: John Feeney
Markets Served:
Super Market Chains, Wholesale Distributors, Food Service Operators
Brokered Products include:
Groceries, Private Label

41161 T.J. Hines & Company
321 Via El Cuadro
Santa Barbara, CA 93111-2750 805-692-9907
Fax: 805-692-9938
Broker of seafood
President: Tom Hines
Estimated Sales: $500,000-$1 Million
Number Employees: 1-4
Markets Served:
Food Manufacturers & Processors, Super Market Chains, Wholesale Distributors
Primary Brands Brokered include: Sea Sure; San Miguel; Ablone
Brokered Products include:
Seafood

41162 T.W. Wilson & Son
2715 Westwood Dr
Nashville, TN 37204-2711 615-256-1234
Fax: 615-298-5255
Broker of confectionery and dairy/deli products, frozen foods, general merchandise, groceries, meat and meat products, etc.
Partner: Steven Wilson
Partner: Tandy Wilson
VP Sales: Alan Gordon
Estimated Sales: $7.90 Million
Number Employees: 55
Markets Served:
Food Manufacturers & Processors, Super Market Chains, Wholesale Distributors, Food Service Operators
Brokered Products include:
Confectionery, Dairy/Deli, Frozen Food, General Merchandise, Groceries, Meat, Meat Products, Private Label, Produce

41163 TMC Foods
3402 Acorn Street
Suite 1
Williamsburg, VA 23188-1014 757-253-2080
Fax: 757-253-2079 800-486-0073
Broker of fresh and frozen seafood, prepared entrees, meat and meat products, IQF stuffed pasta, Italian foods, etc.
President: Chris Meehan
CFO: Ted Moreland
Sales: Jason Jenderson
Number Employees: 5
Square Footage: 12000
Brokered Products include:
Frozen Food, Private Label, Seafood

41164 (HQ)TOPS Markets
P.O.Box 1027
Buffalo, NY 14240-1027 716-635-5000
Fax: 716-635-5102 800-522-2522
www.topsmarkets.com
An international group of food retail and food service companies that operate under their own brands
President/CEO: Anthony Schiano
EVP, Finance/CFO: Rick Herring
CEO: Frank Curci
Contact: Tara Abbatoy
tabbatoy@topsmarkets.com
Estimated Sales: $3-5 Million
Number Employees: 5,000-9,999
Parent Co: WFI Acquisition, Inc
Type of Packaging: Food Service
Other Locations:
Nu-Lane Cargo Services
Marion, INNu-Lane Cargo Services

41165 TRFG Inc
300 E Auburn Ave
Springfield, OH 45505-4703 937-322-2040
Fax: 937-322-2254
Sales and sales management; representing a wide range of packaged goods like confections, salted snacks, natural foods
President: Jeff Kreidenweis
jkreidenweis@aol.com
Estimated Sales: $3-5 Million
Number Employees: 1-4
Type of Packaging: Food Service, Private Label
Markets Served:
Food Service Operators
Brokered Products include:
Confectionery, Private Label

41166 Taormina Sales Company
1 Dewolf Rd Ste 208
Old Tappan, NJ 07675 201-297-0600
Fax: 201-297-0007
Import broker of groceries, industrial ingredients, private label items, specialty products, canned vegetables, etc.
CEO: Anna Gannon
CFO: Jim Cosentino
Sales: Joe Fragola
Sales: Peter Ferrari
Sales Director: Helena Dane
Number Employees: 10-19
Square Footage: 9200
Type of Packaging: Consumer, Food Service, Private Label, Bulk
Markets Served:
Food Manufacturers & Processors, Wholesale Distributors, Food Service Operators
Primary Brands Brokered include: Umbria Olii; Nestle; Granos La Macarena, S.A.; Acetifico Marcello; DelMonte; Intermex
Brokered Products include:
Groceries, Imports, Ingredients, Meat Products, Private Label, Canned Vegetables, Etc.

41167 Team Northwest
4105 SE International Way
Suite: 50
Portland, OR 97222 503-659-6722
Fax: 503-659-5514
Broker of dairy/deli products, frozen foods and groceries
President: Tom McAvoy
VP: Ron Olsen
Estimated Sales: $29.6 Million
Number Employees: 75
Markets Served:
Super Market Chains, Food Service Operators
Brokered Products include:
Dairy/Deli, Frozen Food, Groceries

41168 Team Northwest
10305 E Montgomery Dr
Spokane Valley, WA 99206 509-922-3236
Fax: 509-922-3237
Broker of confectionery and dairy/deli products, frozen foods, general merchandise, groceries, meat, etc.
Manager: Joe Cooney
Estimated Sales: $10-20 Million
Number Employees: 10-19
Markets Served:
Super Market Chains, Wholesale Distributors
Brokered Products include:
Confectionery, Dairy/Deli, Frozen Food, General Merchandise, Groceries, Meat, Private Label, Produce

Food Brokers / A-Z

41169 Teasley & Assoc
617 N Harbor Blvd
La Habra, CA 90631-4023 562-697-0989
Fax: 562-691-7889 teasley@gte.net
www.teasleyandassociates.com
Broker of disposables, foods items, aluminum, film, containers, trays, ovenable and microwaveable packaging, guest checks, doilies, bags, straws and cutlery
Owner: Victoria Teasley
teasley@gte.net
Estimated Sales: $10-20 Million
Number Employees: 10-19
Markets Served:
 Food Manufacturers & Processors, Super Market Chains, Wholesale Distributors, Food Service Operators
Brokered Products include:
 General Merchandise, Groceries, Disposables, Aluminum, Film, Etc.

41170 Technical Food Sales Inc
1050 Mehring Way
Cincinnati, OH 45203-1832 513-621-0544
Fax: 513-345-2222 800-622-1050
service@techfood.com www.techfood.com
Total food ingredients source with technical support. Dry, canned, refrigerated and frozen ingredients
President: Jane Makstell
jmakstell@techfood.com
Regional Sales Manager: Lloyd Makstell
Regional Sales Manager: Nadine Whitsett
Estimated Sales: $25-50 Million
Number Employees: 5-9
Square Footage: 200000
Type of Packaging: Bulk
Markets Served:
 Food Manufacturers & Processors
Brokered Products include:
 Ingredients

41171 Technical Sales Associates
16w361 S Frontage Road
Suite 127
Burr Ridge, IL 60527 630-789-6220
Fax: 630-789-6227 800-789-6227
wbecht@aol.com
Import broker of industrial ingredients, meat products and spices. Marketing and technical assistance on food ingredients available
President: W Becht
Office Manager: S Hoskins
Estimated Sales: $5-10 Million
Number Employees: 5-9
Square Footage: 3600
Markets Served:
 Food Manufacturers & Processors, Super Market Chains
Primary Brands Brokered include: Oscar Mayer Ingredients; Cumberland Packing; D.D. Williamson; DMV/USA; Gist Brocades; Haas Foods
Brokered Products include:
 Imports, Ingredients, Meat Products, Spices

41172 Tees & Persse Brokerage Acosta Sales And Marketing Company, Inc
100 Dewdney Ave
Suite 1
Regina, SK SRN 0E5
Canada 306-525-1211
Broker of confectionery and dairy/deli products, frozen foods, general merchandise, groceries, meat products, seafood and spices
President: Doug Lawrence
VP Sales: Bruce Cribbs
Sales Manager: D Krezanski
Parent Co: Cribbs Company
Markets Served:
 Food Manufacturers & Processors, Super Market Chains, Wholesale Distributors, Food Service Operators
Primary Brands Brokered include: Rich Products; Quaker Oats Company; McCormick Canada, Inc.; Trophy Foods
Brokered Products include:
 Confectionery, Dairy/Deli, Frozen Food, General Merchandise, Groceries, Meat Products, Seafood, Spices

41173 Tees & Persse Brokerage
1299 56 Street
Delta, BC V4L 2A6
Canada 604-520-6002
Fax: 604-520-6898
Broker of confectionery products, meat, dairy/deli, frozen foods, general merchandise, groceries, health food, seafood, etc.
President/CEO: Doug Lawrence
Director Food Service Sales: Bruce Cribbs
Director Grocery Sales: Stuart Hartt
Number Employees: 50-99
Markets Served:
 Super Market Chains, Wholesale Distributors, Food Service Operators
Primary Brands Brokered include: Clorox; Lee Foods; Church & Dwight; Blistex Ltd.; Benevia; Oetker
Brokered Products include:
 Confectionery, Dairy/Deli, Frozen Food, General Merchandise, Groceries, Health Food, Meat, Private Label, Seafood, Spices

41174 Tepper & Assoc
5330 Central Ave
St Petersburg, FL 33707-6130 727-322-1212
Fax: 727-322-1313 info@tepperreps.com
www.tepperreps.com
Manufacturers' representative for food service equipment and supplies
President: Randy Tepper
rtepper@tepperreps.com
Vice President: Thomas Whitmill
Outside Sales and End-User Market: George Engilis
Inside Customer Service: Bonny Brennan
Estimated Sales: $2.5-5 Million
Number Employees: 1-4
Markets Served:
 Wholesale Distributors
Primary Brands Brokered include: Thomas Whitmill; Ember Glo; Chicago Metallic; Brewmatic; Emjac-Kool Company; Gemini
Brokered Products include:
 General Merchandise, Foodservice Equipment & Supplies

41175 Terra Nova Brokers
PO Box 21219
St. John's, NL A1A 5B2
Canada 709-754-2840
Fax: 709-753-8935
Broker of dairy/deli items, frozen foods, general merchandise, confectionery, seafood, spices, groceries and produce
President: Stephen Winter
Number Employees: 20-49
Markets Served:
 Super Market Chains, Food Service Operators
Primary Brands Brokered include: Mars; Snickers; Betty Crocker; Ocean Spray; Uncle Ben's; Pillsbury; Bayer
Brokered Products include:
 Confectionery, Dairy/Deli, Frozen Food, General Merchandise, Groceries, Produce, Seafood, Spices

41176 Texas Foods
1280 Cheers St
Brownsville, TX 78521-4432 956-838-1345
Fax: 956-350-4277 800-848-2487
Export broker of industrial ingredients and nutritional supplements
President: Roberto Ramirez Jr
Estimated Sales: Less than $500,000
Number Employees: 1-4
Markets Served:
 Food Manufacturers & Processors, Food Service Operators
Brokered Products include:
 Exports, Ingredients

41177 The Cherry Company Ltd.
4461 Malaai St
Honolulu, HI 96818 808-422-6555
Fax: 808-422-6721 www.cherryco.com
Wholesale distributor and importer of Japanese foods and restaurant supplies
Chairman: Noritoshi Kanai
President: Kosei Yamamoto
Vice President: Takateru Kishii
Sales Manager: Wesley Sakamoto
Contact: Rorie Mitsui
mitsui@cherryco.com
Accounting Manager: Rorie Mitsui
Warehouse Manager: Shane Riveral
Estimated Sales: $15 Million
Number Employees: 25
Square Footage: 25514
Parent Co: Mutual Trading Company Inc
Type of Packaging: Consumer, Food Service, Private Label
Markets Served:
 Super Market Chains, Wholesale Distributors, Food Service Operators
Primary Brands Brokered include: Yamasa, Salonpas, Orion Beer, Koshihikari Echigo Beer, Takara Sake, Kagomi, Yamaki, Kingisushi
Brokered Products include:
 Alcoholic Beverages, Confectionery, Dairy/Deli, General Merchandise, Groceries, Health Food, Ingredients, Meat Products, Private Label, Seafood, Spices

41178 The Thurber Company
1110 Lake Cook Road
Suite 270
Buffalo Grove, IL 60089 847-541-3663
Fax: 847-541-3684 800-833-6637
www.thurberco.com
Broker of industrial ingredients. Contract packaging of dry and liquid products available
Principal: Craig Thurber
CEO: Scott Thurber
Inside Sales: Diane Smith
Contact: Kurt Schroeder
craigthurber@thurberco.com
Officer Manager: Diane Groth
Estimated Sales: $2.5-5 Million
Number Employees: 1-4
Square Footage: 3200
Type of Packaging: Private Label, Bulk
Markets Served:
 Food Manufacturers & Processors, Wholesale Distributors, Food Service Operators
Primary Brands Brokered include: All American Foods; American Lecithin Company; Avatar Corporation; Columbus Foods Company; Feaster Foods; Food Ingredients; Hampton Farms; Klassic Coconut; Ottens Flavors; Superior Nut Company; Tulkoff Food Products
Brokered Products include:
 Confectionery, Dairy/Deli, Frozen Food, General Merchandise, Health Food, Ingredients, Meat, Private Label, Produce, Spices, Beverages

41179 Thomas Food Brokers
37475 Schoolcraft Road
Livonia, MI 48150-1007 734-443-6719
Fax: 248-443-6898
Import broker of dairy/deli items, frozen foods, groceries, meat and meat products, private label items and spices
President: Robert Thomas
Account Representative: Jeff Thomas
Sales Manager: Jim Gomulka
Estimated Sales: $2.5-5 Million
Number Employees: 1-4
Type of Packaging: Food Service, Private Label
Markets Served:
 Super Market Chains, Wholesale Distributors
Primary Brands Brokered include: Deer; Kanimi; Bellezza; Prima; Tieco; Pel Freez
Brokered Products include:
 Dairy/Deli, Frozen Food, Imports, Ingredients, Private Label, Spices

41180 Thomas Vaccaro Inc
300 Middle Rd
Hammonton, NJ 08037-8905 609-561-1909
Fax: 609-561-1978
Broker of fresh fruits and vegetables
President: William Vaccaro
thomasvaccaro@comcast.net
Estimated Sales: $1-2.5 Million
Number Employees: 1-4
Markets Served:
 Super Market Chains, Food Service Operators
Brokered Products include:
 Produce

41181 (HQ)Thomas, Large & Singer
15 Allstate Parkway
Suite 500
Markham, ON L3R 5B4
Canada 905-754-3500
   Fax: 905-754-3501 www.thomaslargesinger.com
Broker of confectionery and dairy/deli products, frozen foods, general merchandise, groceries, etc.
President & Chief Executive Officer: Peter Singer
Chief Financial Officer: Peter Wagner
Estimated Sales: $21 Million
Number Employees: 65
Square Footage: 160000
Type of Packaging: Private Label
Markets Served:
   Food Manufacturers & Processors, Super Market Chains, Wholesale Distributors, Food Service Operators
Primary Brands Brokered include: Swanson; Eagle; Added Touch; Rich's; Tropicana; Tetley
Brokered Products include:
   Confectionery, Dairy/Deli, Frozen Food, General Merchandise, Groceries, Imports, Ingredients, Private Label, Produce, Seafood, Spices

41182 (HQ)Thomson-Leeds Company
450 Park Avenue S
2nd Floor
New York, NY 10016-7320 914-428-7255
   Fax: 914-428-7047 800-535-9361
Manufacturer, importer and exporter of displays, fixtures, package designs and point of purchase merchandising materials. Broker of specialty displays
President: Vince Esposito
CEO: Douglas Leeds
Director Marketing: Peter Weiller
Estimated Sales: $2.5-5 Million
Number Employees: 50-99
Square Footage: 80000
Markets Served:
   Food Manufacturers & Processors, Super Market Chains, Food Service Operators
Brokered Products include:
   General Merchandise, Specialty Displays

41183 Thormann Associates
950 Watertown St Ste 12
West Newton, MA 02465 617-332-0918
   Fax: 617-965-7169
Manufacturers' representative for food service equipment and general merchandise including scales, racks, filters, convection ovens, folding tables, cake pans, oven mitts, chef's hats, aprons, etc
Owner: Michael Thormann
Estimated Sales: $.5-1 million
Number Employees: 2
Square Footage: 1400
Markets Served:
   Super Market Chains, Wholesale Distributors, Food Service Operators
Brokered Products include:
   General Merchandise, Food Service Equipment

41184 Tilkin & Cagen Inc
1805 Spruce St
Highland Park, IL 60035-2150 847-579-9001
   Fax: 847-579-9006 steve@tilkinsales.com
Broker of material handling and recycling containers, waste receptacles and emergency lighting signs
Partner: Steve Tilkin
steve@tilkinsales.com
Vice President: Lori Tilkin
Number Employees: 1-4
Markets Served:
   Wholesale Distributors
Brokered Products include:
   General Merchandise, Waste Receptacles, Etc.

41185 Tisdale Food Ingredients
304 S Tennessee St
Mckinney, TX 75069-5620 972-542-8222
   Fax: 972-542-9222
   bo@tisdalefoodingredients.com
   www.tisdalefoodingredients.com
Manufacturer' representative for industrial ingredients and spices
Owner: William Tisdale
Vice President: Bo Tisdale
Marketing Manager: Kathy Tisdale
Inside Sales Manager: Sharon Sandling
tizzy@tisdalefoodingredients.com
Estimated Sales: $2.5-5 Million
Number Employees: 1-4
Type of Packaging: Bulk
Markets Served:
   Food Manufacturers & Processors
Brokered Products include:
   Spices

41186 Tobiason Potato Co Inc
216 Gateway Dr
Grand Forks, ND 58203-2425 701-772-1712
   Fax: 701-772-7734
Export broker of seed potatoes for growers in the United States and overseas
President: Brian Baglien
brianbaglien@outlook.com
Estimated Sales: $1-2.5 Million
Number Employees: 1-4
Markets Served:
   Food Manufacturers & Processors, Super Market Chains, Wholesale Distributors, Food Service Operators
Primary Brands Brokered include: Toby's Brand
Brokered Products include:
   Produce, Potatoes

41187 Todd Brokerage Company
3815 N Santa Fe Avenue
Suite 104
Oklahoma City, OK 73118-8524 405-525-2366
Broker of confectionery and dairy/deli products, frozen foods, general merchandise, groceries, meat/meat products, etc.
President: T Todd
Secretary/Treasurer: V Todd
Sales Manager: N Breedlove
Estimated Sales: $5-10 Million
Number Employees: 5-9
Square Footage: 32400

41188 Toho America Corporation
9751 Ikena Cir
Honolulu, HI 96821 808-395-5885
   Fax: 808-395-5242
Fish and seafood broker
President: Toyoki Higashishiba

41189 Tom Quinn & Associates
P.O.Box 1226
Mandeville, LA 70470-1226 985-626-5371
   Fax: 985-626-5861 800-828-3005
Broker of industrial ingredients, spices and general merchandise
Owner: Tom Quinn
Office Manager: Stefani Sollberger
Estimated Sales: $1-2.5 Million
Number Employees: 1-4
Square Footage: 10400
Markets Served:
   Food Manufacturers & Processors
Primary Brands Brokered include: Empire Foods; McCormick; Brown & Haley; Tomatek; Supherb Farms; Minnesota Corn Processors
Brokered Products include:
   General Merchandise, Ingredients, Spices

41190 Top O' The Table
420 Westdale Avenue
Westerville, OH 43082-8724 614-899-9500
   Fax: 614-899-9797 800-341-2488
   custservice@topothetable.com
Manufacturers' representative for food service supplies
Regional VP: Kevin Jennings
Territory Manager: Jessica Nagel
Territory Manager: Melissa Greenwald
VP, General Manager: Steve Castle
Marketing Analyst: Amy Mampieri
Sales Coordinator: Marie Gibbs
Contact: Tisha Baisden
tishb@zinkfsg.com
Director, Culinary Operations: David Ash
Estimated Sales: $5-10 Million
Number Employees: 5-9
Square Footage: 26000
Markets Served:
   Food Manufacturers & Processors, Super Market Chains, Wholesale Distributors, Food Service Operators
Primary Brands Brokered include: Anchor Hocking; Carlisle; Dito Dean; Edlund; Iwatani; Zeroll; Vertex China; Mundial
Brokered Products include:
   General Merchandise, Foodservice Supplies

41191 Torter Corporation
P.O.Box 367
Montville, NJ 07045 973-299-2811
   Fax: 973-299-0252 800-867-8371
Importer of frozen fruits and juice concentrates; broker of ingredients
President: Joseph Torter
VP Sales: Thomas Torter
Estimated Sales: $5-10 Million
Number Employees: 5-9
Type of Packaging: Bulk
Markets Served:
   Food Manufacturers & Processors
Brokered Products include:
   Ingredients

41192 Toteco Packaging Co
13353 NE Bel Red Rd # 202
Suite 202
Bellevue, WA 98005-2329 425-641-0356
   Fax: 425-641-7148 www.toteco.com
Manufacturer's representative for general merchandise including laminated bulk bins, etc.
Head: Cliff Mikkelsen
cmik@toteco.com
Marketing: Bonnie Mickelson
Sales, Services: Pite Mikkelsen
Customer Service and Operations: Sue Walker
Estimated Sales: $3-5 Million
Number Employees: 1-4
Brokered Products include:
   General Merchandise, Laminated Bulk Bins, Etc.

41193 Tower Intercontinental Group
19 Spear Rd
Ramsey, NJ 07446-1235 201-327-2228
   Fax: 201-327-2275
Import and export broker of groceries, private label items, industrial ingredients and seafood
President: T Albertsen
Secretary: E Albertsen
Estimated Sales: $300,000-500,000
Number Employees: 1-4
Markets Served:
   Food Manufacturers & Processors, Food Service Operators
Brokered Products include:
   Exports, Groceries, Imports, Ingredients, Private Label, Seafood

41194 Tr International Trading Co
600 Stewart St # 1801
Suite 1801
Seattle, WA 98101-1258 206-505-3500
   Fax: 206-505-3501 800-761-7717
   info@trichemicals.com www.chemblend.net
Broker of industrial ingredients including propylene glycol, citric and fumaric acids, starch, methyl salicylate and vitamins
President: Anthony M Ridnell
CFO: Jeffrey Wright
Regional Manager: Joe Riverman
Systems Manager: Brian Gorzoch
Director of Marketing: Jennifer Calvery
Vice President of Sales: John P. Godina
Contact: Jason Anderson
jason.anderson@tritrading.com
Operations Manager: Michelle Connor
Estimated Sales: $10-20 Million
Number Employees: 1-4
Square Footage: 3500
Markets Served:
   Food Manufacturers & Processors
Brokered Products include:
   Ingredients

41195 Trading Corporation of America
9521 Jefferson Davis Highway
Richmond, VA 23237 804-275-7848
   Fax: 804-271-0327 800-446-7255
   www.chesterfieldtrading.com
Broker of frozen foods and produce
President: Bennie Thomas
General Manager: Ben Cale
VP, Sales: Charlie Bell
Estimated Sales: $1-2.5 Million
Number Employees: 1-4
Markets Served:
   Food Manufacturers & Processors
Brokered Products include:
   Frozen Food, Produce

Food Brokers / A-Z

41196 Transatlantic Foods
PO Box 286677
New York, NY 10128   212-330-8286
Fax: 646-607-9555 info@transatlanticfoods.com
Fresh, frozen, dried and processed wild and exotic mushrooms, as well as select specialty food products.
Contact: Francois Baumont
francoisbaumont@transatlanticfoods.com

41197 Transit Trading Corporation
196-198 West Broadway
New York, NY 10013   212-925-1020
Fax: 212-925-1629 ttcspices@aol.com
Importer of seeds including anise, caraway, celery, dill, cumin, fenugreek, fennel, poppy, sesame and coriander; also, beans, couscous, allspice, basil, oregano, paprika, parsley flakes, rosemary, thyme, cardamon, dillweed, peppermarjoram, etc.
Estimated Sales: $5 Million
Number Employees: 20-49
Type of Packaging: Bulk

41198 Trend Marketing Services
5440 Bay Center Drive
Tampa, FL 33609-3414   813-286-1920
Fax: 813-287-8391 trend@trend-marketing.net
Broker serving the food industry
Owner: Jim Quisenberry
Area Manager: Jim Lenhart
Estimated Sales: $1-2.5 Million
Number Employees: 10-19
Parent Co: Trend Marketing Service

41199 Tri-State Logistics Inc
3156 Spring Valley Road
Dubuque, IA 52001-1531   563-690-0926
Fax: 775-417-6709 866-331-7660
Freight/transportation brokerage services specializing in refrigerated truck movements-frozen & refrigerated foods
President: Evan Fleisher
VP: Randy Sirk
Markets Served:
  Food Manufacturers & Processors, Super Market Chains, Wholesale Distributors, Food Service Operators
Brokered Products include:
  Confectionery, Dairy/Deli, Exports, Frozen Food, General Merchandise, Groceries, Health Food, Imports, Ingredients, Meat, Meat Products, Private Label, Produce, Seafood, Spices

41200 Triad Brokers Inc
1025 Willowbrook Dr
Greensboro, NC 27403-2059   336-852-8581
Fax: 336-852-3145
Broker of industrial ingredients
President: C Kennedy
Secretary/Treasurer: E Kennedy
Estimated Sales: Less Than $500,000
Number Employees: 1-4
Markets Served:
  Food Manufacturers & Processors, Wholesale Distributors, Food Service Operators
Brokered Products include:
  Ingredients

41201 Triangle Sales
5000 Old Buncombe Rd # 17
Greenville, SC 29617-8208   864-246-8837
Fax: 864-246-5440 www.trianglesalescorp.com
Broker of canned goods, nuts, bleach, popcorn, peppers, portion control items, mushrooms, sugar, shortening, cherries, toppings and fountain syrup, honey
Partner: Robert Nix
Estimated Sales: $6 Million
Number Employees: 1-4
Number of Brands: 17
Number of Products: 20
Square Footage: 4800
Markets Served:
  Food Service Operators
Primary Brands Brokered include: Seneca, Azar, Austin, Idaho Pacific, Plastech, Sue Bee, Premium, Stickney, Poore
Brokered Products include:
  Groceries

41202 Try-Angle Food Brokers Inc
17 Accord Park Dr # 202
Norwell, MA 02061-1629   781-871-6969
Fax: 781-871-7974 sales@try-angle.com
www.newenglandfoodbrokers.net
Broker of meat, poultry, seafood
President: Ed Arseneau
earseneau@tegramedical.com
CEO: Mike Naticchioni
Marketing Manager: Al Walker
Estimated Sales: $20-50 Million
Number Employees: 20-49
Square Footage: 4500
Markets Served:
  Food Manufacturers & Processors, Super Market Chains, Wholesale Distributors
Primary Brands Brokered include: BallPark; Amy Foods; Carl Buddig; Hansel n' Gretel; Jimmy Dean; Liguria; Maple Leaf Farms; Mosey's; Nathan's; Purdue; Trans-Ocean
Brokered Products include:
  Meat, Poultry

41203 Tucker Sales
1519 Continental Ave
Bismarck, ND 58504   701-223-9246
Fax: 701-223-4313
Broker of confectionery and dairy/deli products, frozen foods, general merchandise, groceries, meat, etc.
Food Service President: Pat Koch
Retail President: Steve Ely
steve@tucker-sales.com
Partner: Tyler Speidel
Technology: Kevin James
Estimated Sales: $3.6 Million
Number Employees: 20
Markets Served:
  Food Manufacturers & Processors, Super Market Chains, Wholesale Distributors, Food Service Operators
Brokered Products include:
  Confectionery, Dairy/Deli, Frozen Food, General Merchandise, Groceries, Meat, Private Label, Produce

41204 Tufts Ranch
27260 State Highway 128
Winters, CA 95694-9066   530-795-4144
Fax: 530-795-3844
Grower and packer of apricots, prunes, kiwifruit and persimmons. Broker of walnuts and almonds
General Manager: Stan Tufts
Office Manager: Brad Graf
Estimated Sales: $5-10 Million
Number Employees: 50 to 99
Brokered Products include:
  Groceries, Walnuts, Almonds

41205 Tulip Group Inc
79 Shepard Rd
Hartford, CT 06110
Fax: 860-521-2021 800-718-6198
Broker of seafood
President: Diva Dhanan
VP Sales: Amit Chakraborty
Number Employees: 3
Type of Packaging: Food Service, Private Label
Brokered Products include:
  Seafood, Spices

41206 Twin City Food Brokers
119 E 19th St
N Little Rock, AR 72114-2914   501-771-2242
Fax: 501-771-0305
www.twincityfoodbrokerage.com
Broker of dairy/deli products, frozen foods, groceries, meat and meat products, private label items, etc.
Co-Owner: Bill Warren
Co-Owner: Joan Warren
Estimated Sales: $5-10 Million
Number Employees: 10-19
Square Footage: 8800
Markets Served:
  Food Manufacturers & Processors, Super Market Chains, Wholesale Distributors, Food Service Operators
Primary Brands Brokered include: Campbell's Soup; Foster Farms; Reser Fine Foods; John Morrell; Signature Foods; Total Ultimate Foods
Brokered Products include:
  Dairy/Deli, Frozen Food, Groceries, Meat, Meat Products, Private Label, Produce, Seafood, Spices

41207 Two Guys Spice Company
2404 Dennis Street
Jacksonville, FL 32204-1712   949-248-1269
Fax: 904-791-9330 800-874-5656
www.twoguysgrilling.net
Broker and wholesaler/distributor of dehydrated onions, garlic and vegetables; also, spices and industrial ingredients
President: Michael Simmons
Vice President: Guy Simmons
Estimated Sales: $2.4 Million
Number Employees: 1-4
Number of Brands: 1
Number of Products: 500
Square Footage: 20800
Type of Packaging: Food Service, Private Label, Bulk
Markets Served:
  Food Manufacturers & Processors, Wholesale Distributors, Food Service Operators
Primary Brands Brokered include: Basic Vegetable Products; Newlywed's Foods; Texas Pete's Hot Sauce & Spice Company
Brokered Products include:
  Ingredients, Spices

41208 UBC Marketing
PO Box 6308
Saginaw, MI 48608-6308   517-793-9907
Broker of dairy/deli products, frozen foods, groceries, general merchandise, meat products, pet food, etc.
Corporate VP/General Manager: Michael Schofield
Sales Manager: John Steck
Meat Manager: Dave McIntosh
Square Footage: 16000
Markets Served:
  Food Manufacturers & Processors, Super Market Chains, Wholesale Distributors, Food Service Operators
Primary Brands Brokered include: Mobil Chemical Company; Bil Mar Foods; Comstock Michigan Fruit; Thornapple Valley; Crown Prince
Brokered Products include:
  Dairy/Deli, Frozen Food, General Merchandise, Groceries, Meat Products, Private Label, Produce, Seafood, Spices

41209 US Distilled Products Co
1607 12th St S
Princeton, MN 55371-2311   763-389-4903
Fax: 763-389-2549 info@usdp.com
www.usdp.com
Alcoholic beverages
President: Bradley P Johnson
CFO: Pat Pelzer
Production Manager: Kevin Issendorf
Purchasing Manager: Todd Rhode
Year Founded: 1981
Estimated Sales: $20-30 Million
Number Employees: 250-499
Square Footage: 250000
Markets Served:
  Wholesale Distributors
Brokered Products include:
  Alcoholic Beverages

41210 (HQ)US Food Products
1084 Queen Anne Rd
Teaneck, NJ 07666-3508   201-833-8100
Fax: 201-833-1920 edsbeef@aol.com
www.usfoodproducts.com
Broker, wholesaler and exporter of all categories of frozen-chilled and dry food
President/CEO: Edward W Holland
edsbeef@aol.com
CFO: Chona Canillas
Estimated Sales: $20-50 Million
Number Employees: 20-49
Number of Brands: 50
Number of Products: 5000
Square Footage: 25000
Type of Packaging: Food Service
Markets Served:
  Wholesale Distributors, Food Service Operators
Brokered Products include:
  Alcoholic Beverages, Confectionery, Dairy/Deli, Exports, Frozen Food, General Merchandise, Groceries, Health Food, Imports, Ingredients, Meat, Meat Products, Private Label, Produce, Seafood, Spices

Food Brokers / A-Z

41211 Union Standard Equipment Company
801 E 141st Street
Bronx, NY 10454-1917
718-585-0200
800-237-8873
sales@unionmachinery.com
www.unionmachinery.com
Broker of used and rebuilt packaging and food processing machinery including mixers, tanks, kettles, grinders, pumps, heat exchangers, etc.
Vice President: Andy Greenberg
Contact: David Feinne
david@unionmachinery.com
Estimated Sales: $10-20 Million
Number Employees: 20-49
Square Footage: 530000
Parent Co: National Equipment Corporation
Markets Served:
  Food Manufacturers & Processors
Brokered Products include:
  General Merchandise, Packaging, Food Processing Machinery

41212 United Brands
7548 Jewella Ave
Shreveport, LA 71108-4705
318-687-3400
Fax: 318-687-3487 866-900-8740
info@unitedbrandsinc.net
Import and export broker of confectionery and dairy/deli products, frozen foods, general merchandise, groceries, meat and meat products, etc.; serving food service operators, supermarket chains and wholesalers/distributors
Owner: Bill Gordon
VP: Ann Gordon
Sales Manager: James Thomas
bjeffgordon@aol.com
Estimated Sales: $1.2 Million
Number Employees: 10-19
Markets Served:
  Super Market Chains, Wholesale Distributors, Food Service Operators
Brokered Products include:
  Confectionery, Dairy/Deli, Exports, Frozen Food, General Merchandise, Groceries, Imports, Meat, Meat Products, Private Label, Produce, Seafood, Spices

41213 United Brokers Company
6210 NE 92nd Dr Ste 101
Portland, OR 97220
503-251-9936
Fax: 503-251-9939
Export broker of onions
Co-Owner: Scott Hawkins
scott@unitedbusinessbrokers.com
Estimated Sales: $2.5-5 Million
Number Employees: 5-9
Markets Served:
  Super Market Chains, Wholesale Distributors, Food Service Operators
Brokered Products include:
  Exports, Produce, Onions

41214 United Foodservice Sales
517 Deering St
Irondale, AL 35210-2041
205-244-1000
Fax: 205-244-1001
Broker of confectionery and dairy/deli products, frozen foods, general merchandise, meat and meat products, etc.
President: Bill Prewitt
Vice President: Linda Prewitt
Estimated Sales: $20-50 Million
Number Employees: 10-19
Square Footage: 8800
Markets Served:
  Super Market Chains, Wholesale Distributors, Food Service Operators
Brokered Products include:
  Confectionery, Dairy/Deli, Frozen Food, General Merchandise, Groceries, Meat, Meat Products, Private Label, Seafood

41215 United International Indstrs
104 Mullach Ct # 1008
Suite 1008
Wentzville, MO 63385-4858
636-327-5910
Fax: 636-327-5904 800-292-3509
tcarlisle@uinternational.com
www.uinternational.com
Wholesaler/distributor of whey, dry milk, casein, processed and imitation cheese and cheese powders, butter, etc
Chief Executive Officer: M Jane Carlisle
CFO: James Dolson
VP: Thomas Carlisle Jr
Sales: Kris Jenkins
Estimated Sales: $6-$10 Million
Number Employees: 10-19
Markets Served:
  Food Manufacturers & Processors, Wholesale Distributors, Food Service Operators
Brokered Products include:
  Confectionery, Dairy/Deli, Exports, Frozen Food, Groceries, Imports, Ingredients, Meat, Meat Products, Private Label, Seafood, Spices, Concentrates

41216 United Restaurant Specialties
1694 Moss Dr
Snellville, GA 30078-2741
770-454-9229
Fax: 770-457-5879
Broker/manufacturers' representative for cooking, baking and restaurant equipment, coolers and freezers, meal delivery, etc.
President: Steve Anthony
Estimated Sales: $1-2.5 Million
Number Employees: 1-4
Markets Served:
  Food Service Operators
Brokered Products include:
  General Merchandise

41217 Univar USA
17411 NE Union Hill Rd
Redmond, WA 98052-3375
425-889-3400
855-888-8648
www.univarusa.com
Distributor of specialty and basic food ingredients and chemicals used in the food manufacturing industry.
Director, Food Ingredients: Austin Nichols
Product Management: Denise McLaughlin
Number Employees: 10-19

41218 Universal Marketing
5501-7b Avenue
Delta, Bc, CA V4M 1S7
Canada
604-943-9029
Fax: 604-943-9012 skarse@dccnet.com
Food equipment rep/agency manufacturers' representative for imported, exported and domestic general merchandise including parts, doors, racks, fittings, dinnerware, napery, glass washers, gas hoses, commercial faucets, greasetrap/interepetors, heavy duty gas ranges, fryers, broilers and more
President/Owner: Sandy R Karse
CEO: Joanne Karse
Estimated Sales: $500,000
Number Employees: 1-4
Square Footage: 4000

41219 V-Tech Ingredients
2001 W Garfield Street
Seattle, WA 98119-3119
206-282-8821
Brokerage firm for various food products including spice, restuarants etc
Owner: Zir Zisriggi
Estimated Sales: $1-3 Million
Number Employees: 1-4

41220 (HQ)V.M. Calderon
4040 Red Rock Ln
Sarasota, FL 34231
941-366-3708
Fax: 941-951-6529 888-654-8365
vmcalderon@aol.com
Wholesaler/distrubutor, import broker and contract packager of brined vegetables, black and green olives, pepperoncini, cherries, capers, onions and pickles
President: Victor Calderon
Estimated Sales: $1-3 Million
Number Employees: 1-4
Square Footage: 7200
Type of Packaging: Consumer, Food Service, Private Label, Bulk
Markets Served:
  Super Market Chains, Wholesale Distributors, Food Service Operators
Primary Brands Brokered include: Goddess Gourmet; South Shore
Brokered Products include:
  Groceries, Imports, Private Label

41221 VP Northeast
Ste 8
100 Waverly St
Ashland, MA 01721-1773
508-987-7171
Fax: 508-987-7070 800-852-3823
Manufacturers' representative for food service supplies and equipment including fryers, coffee servers, menu boards, smallwares, char broilers, ventilation and warewashing systems, display cases, matting, steamers, etc.
President: Tom Vajcovec
CEO/Co-Owner: Debra Vajcovec
Equipment Division Manager: Michael Gavin
Supply Division Manager: Peter Wnukowski
Office Manager/Inside Sales: JoAnn Thorstenson
Customer Service: Carolyn Cass
Estimated Sales: $10-20 Million
Number Employees: 10-19
Markets Served:
  Wholesale Distributors
Primary Brands Brokered include: Bloomfield Industries; Server Brothers; Table Craft Products; Edlund; Mainstreet Menu Systems; Dito Dean Food Prep
Brokered Products include:
  General Merchandise, Fryers, Coffee Servers, Steamers, Etc.

41222 Vader & Landgraf
1047 10th Ave SE
Minneapolis, MN 55414-1312
612-331-1251
Fax: 612-331-1846 800-852-0447
cs@vaderandlandgraf.com
www.vaderandlandgraf.com
Manufacturers' representative for food service equipment and supplies
President, Principal: Dennis Mc Guire
dmcguire@vaderandlandgraf.com
Principal: Paul Slack
Sales and Estimating: Garrett Zimmerman
Manager: Dennis Mc Guire
dmcguire@vaderandlandgraf.com
Office Manager: Karen Sekevitch
Estimated Sales: $1-2.5 Million
Number Employees: 5-9
Markets Served:
  Wholesale Distributors
Primary Brands Brokered include: Amco; Cleveland Range; Cres-Cor; Delfield; Service Ideas; Wolf Range
Brokered Products include:
  General Merchandise, Foodservice Equipment & Supplies

41223 Van Kam, G. Trading Company
4920 De Maisonneuve W
Montreal, QC H3H 1L1
Canada
514-481-0247
Fax: 514-483-6563 info@gvankam.com
Import and export broker of dairy/deli, industrial ingredients and health food; serving food processors and wholesalers/distributors
President: George Kampouris
Estimated Sales: $10 Million
Number Employees: 1-4
Markets Served:
  Food Manufacturers & Processors, Wholesale Distributors
Brokered Products include:
  Dairy/Deli, Exports, Health Food, Imports, Ingredients

41224 Van Reed Sales Company
PO Box 367
Spring House, PA 19477-0367
215-646-2247
Fax: 215-646-2058
Broker of dairy/deli and private label products, groceries, price marking and bar coding labels and applicators; serving all markets
President: C Van Reed
Area Manager: K Van Reed
Area Manager: M Van Reed
Estimated Sales: $5-10 Million
Number Employees: 7
Square Footage: 12000
Markets Served:
  Food Manufacturers & Processors, Super Market Chains, Wholesale Distributors, Food Service Operators
Primary Brands Brokered include: Dispense All; Laidlaw; South/Win
Brokered Products include:
  Dairy/Deli, General Merchandise, Groceries,

91

Food Brokers / A-Z

Private Label, Price Marking, Bar Coding Applicators

41225 Van Rex Gourmet Foods
5260 Stonehaven Drive
Yorba Linda, CA 92887-2629 714-970-8602
Food broker, distributor of gourmet food and bakery ingredients to restaurants, hotels and bakeries
Sales Manager: Rich Hall

41226 Virginia Fruit Sales Service
PO Box 2785
Winchester, VA 22604 540-662-4302
Fax: 540-667-8599
Export broker of produce
Owner: Gilbert Sine
Estimated Sales: Less than $500,000
Number Employees: 1-4
Markets Served:
Super Market Chains, Wholesale Distributors, Food Service Operators
Brokered Products include:
Produce

41227 Vivion Inc
929 Bransten Rd
San Carlos, CA 94070-4073 650-595-3600
Fax: 650-595-2094 800-479-0997
www.vivioninc.com
Broker and distributor of food ingredients.
Founder: Edward Poleselli
President: Michael Poleselli
mpoleselli@vivioninc.com
General Manager: Patrick Rhodes
Estimated Sales: $28 Million
Number Employees: 10-19
Other Locations:
Branch/Warehouse
Vernon, CA
Branch/
Portland, OR
Branch
Ogden, UT
Branch
Phoenix/Warehouse, AZ
Warehouse
Salt Lake City, UT
Warehouse
San Carlos, CA
Branch/WarehousePortland
Markets Served:
Wholesale Distributors
Brokered Products include:
Health Food, Ingredients

41228 W.B. Marketing Group
5515 Pearl Road
Parma, OH 44129-2526 440-842-2800
Fax: 440-842-2833 800-366-7520
www.wbmarketing.com
Manufacturers' representative for food service equipment
Partner: Douglas Wank
Partner: Barry Wank
Partner: Stan Brickner
Sales Representative: Dan Dubin
Contact: Chris Cheap
chrisc@wbmarket.net
Number Employees: 5-9
Markets Served:
Wholesale Distributors
Brokered Products include:
General Merchandise, Foodservice Equipment

41229 W.H. Escott Company
95 Alexander Avenue
Winnipeg, MB R3B 2Y8
Canada 204-942-5127
Fax: 204-943-5320 800-463-1907
info@whescott.com www.whescott.com
Broker of confectionery products, general merchandise, groceries, meat products, private label items, seafood, etc. Re-packing services available for cereals, etc.
President: Ray Prokopchuk
Marketing Manager: Ed Neufeld
Logistics: Don Kiely
Director Packaging: Darren Turner
Estimated Sales: $2.5 Million
Number Employees: 25
Markets Served:
Super Market Chains, Wholesale Distributors, Food Service Operators

Brokered Products include:
Confectionery, General Merchandise, Groceries, Meat Products, Private Label, Seafood, Spices

41230 W.H. Moseley Co.
4090 W State St
Suite 1
Boise, ID 83703 208-342-2621
Fax: 208-336-1611 www.whmoseley.com
Importer and exporter of frozen, dehydrated and fresh potatoes. Broker of frozen foods
President: Bill Moseley
VP/Sales: Tom Reeb
Estimated Sales: $5-10 Million
Number Employees: 1-4
Markets Served:
Super Market Chains, Wholesale Distributors, Food Service Operators
Primary Brands Brokered include: Lamb-Weston
Brokered Products include:
Exports, Frozen Food, Private Label, potato flak

41231 W.H. Schilbe Citrus Brokerage / Citriservices
821 NE 36th Ter # 7
Ocala, FL 34470-1033 352-624-2111
Fax: 352-624-2384
Broker of frozen juice concentrates
President: Paul Schilbe
Estimated Sales: $3-5 Million
Number Employees: 1-4
Square Footage: 3800
Parent Co: Citriservices
Type of Packaging: Bulk
Markets Served:
Food Manufacturers & Processors
Brokered Products include:
Ingredients

41232 W.H. Sullivan & Associates
24 Claypit Hill Road
Wayland, MA 01778-2003 781-235-1414
Fax: 781-235-1595
Broker of dairy/deli products, frozen foods, general merchandise, produce, groceries, private label items, etc.
President: William Sullivan Jr
Number Employees: 5
Brokered Products include:
Confectionery, Dairy/Deli, Frozen Food, Groceries, Private Label, Produce

41233 WENS Brokerage
2724 Kahoaloha Ln Apt 1205
Honolulu, HI 96826 808-524-9367
Fax: 808-536-1292
Broker of dairy/deli products, frozen foods, groceries, meats, poultry products and seafood
President: Edward Tengan
VP: Joy Mnaiia
Estimated Sales: $300,000-500,000
Number Employees: 1-4
Markets Served:
Food Manufacturers & Processors, Super Market Chains, Wholesale Distributors, Food Service Operators
Brokered Products include:
Dairy/Deli, Frozen Food, Groceries, Health Food, Ingredients, Meat, Meat Products, Private Label, Seafood

41234 WJ Pence Company
W227n880 Westmound Dr # E
Waukesha, WI 53186-7000 262-524-6300
Fax: 262-524-6310
Broker of dairy/deli and meat products, frozen foods, groceries, produce, seafood, private label items, etc
President: John Pence
VP: Dale Kresse
Contact: Dale Kresse
dkresse@wjpence.com
Estimated Sales: $20-50 Million
Number Employees: 20-49
Square Footage: 6000
Type of Packaging: Consumer, Private Label
Markets Served:
Super Market Chains, Wholesale Distributors
Brokered Products include:
Dairy/Deli, Frozen Food, Groceries, Imports, Meat, Meat Products, Private Label, Produce, Seafood

41235 WMK Marketing
PO Box 915
Indian Rocks Beach, FL 33785-0915 727-595-6054
Fax: 727-596-5141
Domestic and import broker of citrus products
President: Bill Kane
Number Employees: 1-4
Markets Served:
Food Manufacturers & Processors, Wholesale Distributors
Brokered Products include:
Imports, Produce, Citrus Products

41236 WTD Associates
70 Three Mile Stretch Rd
Ellisville, MS 39437 601-426-6325
Fax: 601-649-4406 800-821-2597
Manufacturers' representative for food service equipment and supplies
President: Wally Damlouji
Estimated Sales: $3-5 Million
Number Employees: 5-9
Markets Served:
Wholesale Distributors
Primary Brands Brokered include: Beverage Air; Cres Cor; Advance Tabco; Jackson MSC; Univex; Tablecraft
Brokered Products include:
General Merchandise, Foodservice Equipment & Supplies

41237 Wallin Group Inc
5820 River Oaks Rd S
New Orleans, LA 70123-2155 504-733-3344
Fax: 504-733-0854 800-695-5017
www.wallingroup.com
Manufacturers' representative for food service equipment and supplies
Owner: James Landry
jlandry@wallingroup.com
Principal Owner: Cliff Ordoyne
Inside Sales Support: Jeanne Landry
jlandry@wallingroup.com
Outside Sales: Larry Delahoussaye
Office Manager: Stephanie Wray
Estimated Sales: $2.5-5 Million
Number Employees: 5-9
Markets Served:
Wholesale Distributors
Brokered Products include:
General Merchandise, Foodservice Equipment & Supplies

41238 Wallis & Barcinski
2060 N Collins Blvd # 105
Richardson, TX 75080-2657 972-238-1556
Fax: 972-470-0713 wallisb@flash.net
www.wallisandbarcinski.com
Broker of industrial ingredients
Sales Mgr.: Lisa Whitner
Office Manager: Christina Rodriguez
Estimated Sales: $3-5 Million
Number Employees: 1-4
Markets Served:
Food Manufacturers & Processors, Wholesale Distributors, Food Service Operators
Primary Brands Brokered include: McCormick Company; Papetti Egg Company; ADM; Century Foods; Sunshine Biscuit
Brokered Products include:
Ingredients

41239 Ward Hughes Co
10203 Plano Rd
Suite 116
Dallas, TX 75238 214-349-5581
Fax: 214-349-6623
david.hughes@wardhughesco.com
www.wardhughesco.com
Broker of bakery dairy/deli items, frozen foods, groceries and industrial ingredients and packaging.
Owner: David Hughes
david.hughes@wardhughesco.com
Year Founded: 1967
Estimated Sales: $20-30 Million
Number Employees: 1-4
Markets Served:
Food Manufacturers & Processors, Super Market Chains
Brokered Products include:
Dairy/Deli, Frozen Food, Ingredients

Food Brokers / A-Z

41240 Waterway Foods Intl
157 Follins Ln
St Simons Island, GA 31522-4266 912-634-0240
Fax: 912-634-6011
President: William Dart
Estimated Sales: $1-3 Million
Number Employees: 1-4

41241 Watson & Associates
936 N Amelia Ave
San Dimas, CA 91773-1401 909-305-9630
Fax: 909-305-9631
Export broker of dairy/deli products, frozen foods, meats, private label items, seafood, etc.
Owner: Robert Watson
Contact: Rick Seiier
seiier@watson-associates.com
Business Manager: Robert Eggert
Estimated Sales: $10-20 Million
Number Employees: 20-49
Square Footage: 15000
Parent Co: Food Service Sales
Markets Served:
  Food Manufacturers & Processors, Super Market Chains, Wholesale Distributors, Food Service Operators
Primary Brands Brokered include: Dean Foods; Tropicana; Hershey; Taco Bell; Domino Sugar; Ruiz
Brokered Products include:
  Dairy/Deli, Exports, Frozen Food, Ingredients, Meat, Meat Products, Private Label, Seafood

41242 (HQ)Waypoint
5211 Militia Hill Rd
Plymouth Meeting, PA 19462-1216 610-825-5700
Fax: 610-825-6912 800-732-4266
Broker of meat and meat products, produce, seafood, spices, groceries, industrial ingredients, etc.
President: Eric Hanson
eric.hanson@asm.com
CFO: Carl Sorzano
Executive VP: Mark Hanson
Sales Manager: Ed Ward
Estimated Sales: $14.1 Million
Number Employees: 50-99
Square Footage: 14200
Other Locations:
  Grant Hanson Associates
  Yonkers, NY Grant Hanson Associates
Markets Served:
  Food Manufacturers & Processors, Super Market Chains, Wholesale Distributors, Food Service Operators
Brokered Products include:
  Dairy/Deli, Frozen Food, General Merchandise, Groceries, Ingredients, Meat, Meat Products, Produce, Seafood, Spices

41243 Webco General Partnership
3998 Fair Ridge Drive
Fairfax, VA 22033-2907 703-293-3699
Fax: 703-383-5391
Broker of confectionery products, frozen foods, general merchandise, meat and meat products
President: Joe Olding
Chairman/CEO: Roy Thomas
CFO: Tim Ivey
VP Business Development: Lori Stillman
VP Marketing: Joe Giacco
President Operations: Rick Thomas
VP Exchange Operations: John Catlett
Estimated Sales: G
Number Employees: 50-99
Markets Served:
  Food Service Operators
Brokered Products include:
  Confectionery, Frozen Food, General Merchandise, Meat, Meat Products

41244 Webeco Foods, Inc
P.O.Box 228764
8225 NW 80th St
Miami, FL 33166-2160 305-639-2147
Fax: 305-639-6052 888-635-1188
Import, export broker of cheese. Wholesaler/distributor of dairy products, meats including cheese and private label items
President: Luis Teijeiro
luis@webecofoods.com
VP/Treasurer: Jose Teijeiro
Logistics Manager: Kim Gobie
Marketing Specialist: Filena Hernandez
DSD Sales Manager: Manny Fernandez
Warehouse Manager: Rafael Rodriguez
Buyer: Mercy de la Torre
Estimated Sales: $10-20 Million
Number Employees: 20-49
Square Footage: 62000
Markets Served:
  Food Manufacturers & Processors, Super Market Chains, Wholesale Distributors
Primary Brands Brokered include: El Hollandes®; Gayo Azul®; Hollandammer®; Northern Star®; Dutch Morning®
Brokered Products include:
  Dairy/Deli, Exports, Imports, Meat, Cheese

41245 Wehrfritz & Associates
PO Box 6618
Big Bear Lake, CA 92315-6618 909-584-7667
Fax: 909-584-7669
Import broker of general merchandise, groceries, private label products, seafood, etc
President: Alex Wehrfritz
CEO: Rita Wehrfritz
CFO: T Hughes
Estimated Sales: $4 Million
Number Employees: 5-9
Square Footage: 1600
Type of Packaging: Food Service, Private Label
Markets Served:
  Food Manufacturers & Processors, Super Market Chains, Wholesale Distributors, Food Service Operators
Primary Brands Brokered include: Mirage Foods; Brookman & Sons Products; Goodwin Company; Mulsen Trading Company, Miami Spice; Poumodori Brothers
Brokered Products include:
  General Merchandise, Groceries, Private Label, Seafood

41246 Welch Holme & Clark Co
7 Avenue L
Newark, NJ 07105-3805 973-465-1200
Fax: 973-465-3486 www.welch-holme-clark.com
Sells and distributes: refined, USP/NF, crude and kosher vegetable oils.
President: William Dugan
bill@whcsales.com
Estimated Sales: $10-20 Million
Number Employees: 10-19
Type of Packaging: Bulk

41247 Welltep International Inc
138 Palm Coast Pkwy NE # 192
Palm Coast, FL 32137-8241 386-437-7545
Fax: 386-437-7546
Broker of grocery related products
President: Luis Lopez
Estimated Sales: $1-3 Million
Number Employees: 1-4

41248 Wendlandt Brokerage Company
622 Pedernales St
Austin, TX 78702 512-477-1311
Fax: 512-473-2017
Import broker of groceries, private label products, spices and general merchandise
President: T Wendlandt
Vice President: G Wendlandt
Estimated Sales: $2.5-5 Million
Number Employees: 1-4
Square Footage: 64000
Markets Served:
  Food Manufacturers & Processors, Wholesale Distributors, Food Service Operators
Brokered Products include:
  General Merchandise, Groceries, Imports, Private Label, Spices

41249 Wesco Food Brokerage
PO Box 68236
Portland, OR 97268-0236 503-654-5401
Fax: 503-654-5404
Broker of dairy/deli and private label/generic products, frozen food and groceries
Manager: Jerry Coates
Vice President: B Landing
Estimated Sales: $2.5-5 Million
Number Employees: 1-4
Markets Served:
  Food Manufacturers & Processors, Super Market Chains, Wholesale Distributors, Food Service Operators
Brokered Products include:
  Dairy/Deli, Frozen Food, Groceries, Private Label

41250 Wesnic Services Inc
6000 Bowdendale Ave
Jacksonville, FL 32216-6008 904-733-8444
Fax: 904-733-3736 800-874-8558
www.wesnic.com
Broker of general merchandise including wood, steel and aluminum benches, fiberglass planters and trash receptacles, table tops and bases, umbrellas, chairs, booths, etc.
President: Bob Hines
r.d.hines@att.net
Director Sales/Marketing: Bill Gilbert
Estimated Sales: $5-10 Million
Number Employees: 5-9
Square Footage: 13200
Parent Co: Hines III
Brokered Products include:
  General Merchandise, Benches, Chairs, Booths, Etc.

41251 (HQ)Westcon Foods
P.O.Box 255493
Sacramento, CA 95865-5493 916-979-7341
Fax: 916-979-7347 info@westconfoods.com
www.westconfoods.com
Broker of industrial tomato products
President: Garry Warren
Estimated Sales: $5-10 Million
Number Employees: 5-9
Type of Packaging: Bulk
Markets Served:
  Food Manufacturers & Processors
Brokered Products include:
  Tomato Products

41252 Western Manufacturers Agents
6900 SW Sandburg Street
Portland, OR 97223-8039 503-968-1849
Fax: 503-620-0100 800-943-8847
Manufacturers' representative for food service equipment
President: John Schallberger
CEO: Kevin Clouser
CFO: Carlos Botero
Number Employees: 10-19
Square Footage: 60000
Markets Served:
  Wholesale Distributors
Primary Brands Brokered include: Toastmaster; Doughpro; Tomlinson
Brokered Products include:
  General Merchandise, Foodservice Equipment

41253 Westex
11420 James Watt Dr
El Paso, TX 79936-6409 915-595-4792
Fax: 915-595-4796
Broker of frozen foods, general merchandise and groceries
Manager: Javier Porras
Manager: Edward Habe
Estimated Sales: $5-10 Million
Number Employees: 50-99
Parent Co: Westexico Sales Company
Markets Served:
  Super Market Chains, Wholesale Distributors
Brokered Products include:
  Frozen Food, General Merchandise, Groceries

41254 Whitby Co
1909 Ala Wai Blvd # 1104
Honolulu, HI 96815-1804 808-941-0981
Fax: 808-944-8292
Broker of snacks, confectionery products and groceries
Owner: Mark Reisert
sellsellsell@hawaii.rr.com
Sales Manager: Hans Reisert
Estimated Sales: $1-2.5 Million
Number Employees: 5-9
Square Footage: 40000
Markets Served:
  Food Manufacturers & Processors, Super Market Chains, Wholesale Distributors, Food Service Operators

Food Brokers / A-Z

Brokered Products include:
  Confectionery, Groceries, Snack Foods

41255 (HQ)Wick's Pies Inc
217 SE Greenville Ave
PO Box 268
Winchester, IN 47394-1714 765-584-8401
  Fax: 765-584-3700 800-642-5880
  www.wickspies.com
Frozen pies and pie shells
President: Mike Wickersham
wickspies@wickspies.com
VP: Clark Loney
Quality Control: Sue Bone
Marketing/Sales: Marsha Welch
Purchasing: Steve Burge
Estimated Sales: $9 Million
Number Employees: 50-99
Square Footage: 80000
Type of Packaging: Consumer, Food Service
Markets Served:
  Food Manufacturers & Processors
Primary Brands Brokered include: Wicks
Brokered Products include:
  Pies, Pie shells

41256 Wieber-McLain Company
4077 E Galbraith Road
Suite 104
Cincinnati, OH 45236-2323 513-796-1340
Broker of frozen foods, general merchandise, groceries, industrial ingredients, private label items and spices
Partner: R Wieber
Partner: W McLain
Number Employees: 1-4
Square Footage: 24
Markets Served:
  Food Manufacturers & Processors, Super Market Chains, Wholesale Distributors, Food Service Operators
Brokered Products include:
  Frozen Food, General Merchandise, Groceries, Ingredients, Private Label, Spices

41257 William B. Steedman & Sons
396 Foundry St
Athens, GA 30601-2621 706-543-1525
  Fax: 706-208-9040
Broker of fresh and frozen meat products
Owner/Manager: J Steedman
Estimated Sales: $2.5-5 Million
Number Employees: 1-4
Square Footage: 16000
Markets Served:
  Food Manufacturers & Processors, Super Market Chains, Wholesale Distributors, Food Service Operators
Primary Brands Brokered include: Emge Packing Company; Colorado Boxed Beef Company; Indiana Packers
Brokered Products include:
  Frozen Food, Meat Products

41258 William Bernstein Company
155 W 72nd St Rm 301
New York, NY 10023 212-799-3200
  Fax: 212-799-3209
Importer and exporter of gums/incense including frankincense, olibanum, myrrh, benzoin and shellac, apricot kernels, tonka beans and camphor tablets
Owner: E Bernstein
Contact: Daisy Renigan
wbernsteinco@aol.com
Operations: Daisy Renigan
Estimated Sales: $1-3 Million
Number Employees: 1-4
Markets Served:
  Food Manufacturers & Processors
Brokered Products include:
  Ingredients, Spices

41259 William Hyman Jr Associates
609 Lakeside Park
Southampton, PA 18966-4000 215-942-0565
  Fax: 215-942-0560 800-533-8595
Manufacturers' representative for general merchandise including walk-in freezers, cooking and beverage equipment
President: Bill Hyman
Public Relations: Marci Hyman
Estimated Sales: $1-2.5 Million
Number Employees: 1-4

Markets Served:
  Super Market Chains, Wholesale Distributors, Food Service Operators

41260 William M. Dunne & Associates Ltd
10 Director Court
Suite 300
Woodbridge, ON L4L 7E8
Canada 905-856-5240
  Fax: 905-856-5241 800-417-8207
  mcrosby@wmdassoc.com
Import broker of confectionery and dairy/deli products, frozen foods, general merchandise, groceries, meat/meat products, etc.
President: Bob Brema
EVP Finance/Administration: Michael Crosby
Markets Served:
  Food Manufacturers & Processors, Super Market Chains, Wholesale Distributors, Food Service Operators
Brokered Products include:
  Confectionery, Dairy/Deli, Exports, Frozen Food, General Merchandise, Groceries, Imports, Meat Products, Private Label, Produce, Seafood, Spices

41261 Williams Brokerage Company
2427 5th Ave N
St Petersburg, FL 33713-7007 727-328-8533
Broker of confectionery products, general merchandise, groceries, private label items and spices
Owner: Brian Williams
Estimated Sales: $500,000-$1 million
Number Employees: 1-4
Markets Served:
  Super Market Chains, Wholesale Distributors, Food Service Operators
Brokered Products include:
  Confectionery, General Merchandise, Groceries, Private Label, Spices

41262 Williams Resource & Associates
1200 California Street
Suite 255
Redlands, CA 92374 909-748-7671
  Fax: 909-748-7621
Dairy products for industrial food processors, milk powder, butter, cheese
CEO: H. G. Richard Williams
Operations Manager: Breanna Lucier
Estimated Sales: $2.5-5 Million
Number Employees: 1-4
Type of Packaging: Food Service, Bulk

41263 Willing Group
222 Saint Johns Avenue
Yonkers, NY 10704-2717 914-964-5800
  Fax: 914-964-5293 cgctradingintl@aol.com
President: Louis J Goldstein
CEO: Carmela P Goldstein
CFO: Peter L Gallucci
Estimated Sales: $10-20 Million
Number Employees: 20
Square Footage: 15000
Type of Packaging: Consumer, Food Service, Private Label, Bulk
Markets Served:
  Food Manufacturers & Processors, Super Market Chains, Wholesale Distributors, Food Service Operators
Brokered Products include:
  Confectionery, Exports, General Merchandise, Groceries, Health Food, Imports, Ingredients, Private Label, Spices

41264 Wilson Food Brokers
280 Spindrift Drive
Williamsville, NY 14221-7807 716-631-3671
  Fax: 716-631-2244
Broker of dairy/deli and confectionery products, frozen foods, private label items and seafood
President: Judith Wilson
Vice President: Janice McIntyre
Number Employees: 10-19
Markets Served:
  Super Market Chains, Wholesale Distributors, Food Service Operators
Primary Brands Brokered include: Malt-O-Meal Cereal; Kodak Film; Crown-Prince; Matlaws
Brokered Products include:
  Confectionery, Dairy/Deli, Frozen Food, Groceries, Private Label, Seafood

41265 Wiltsie & Company
15240 Merriman Rd
Livonia, MI 48154 734-525-2500
  Fax: 734-525-3939
Import broker of confectionery and private label items, dairy/deli and frozen foods, produce, general merchandise, groceries and spices
Owner: Bill Wiltsie Sr
CFO: David Wiltsie
Contact: David Wiltsie
d.wiltsie@wiltsie.com
Estimated Sales: $10-20 Million
Number Employees: 5-9
Type of Packaging: Consumer, Food Service, Bulk
Markets Served:
  Super Market Chains, Wholesale Distributors, Food Service Operators
Brokered Products include:
  Confectionery, Frozen Food, General Merchandise, Groceries, Health Food, Imports

41266 (HQ)Winmix/Natural Care Products
7466 Cape Girardeau Street
Englewood, FL 34224-8004 941-475-7432
  Fax: 941-475-7432
Processor and exporter of soft serve ice cream and sorbets, meat analogs, fruit juice and beverage bases, low-fat replacers and nonfat mixes. Importer of juice and coffee bases.
Board of Directors: Winsor Eveland
Owner: Martha Efird
Estimated Sales: $100000
Number Employees: 2
Number of Products: 350
Square Footage: 8000
Type of Packaging: Consumer, Food Service, Private Label, Bulk
Markets Served:
  Food Manufacturers & Processors, Super Market Chains, Wholesale Distributors, Food Service Operators
Primary Brands Brokered include: SoyFlax 500; Winmix; Natural Care Products
Brokered Products include:
  Dairy/Deli, Exports, Frozen Food, Health Food, Imports, Ingredients, Private Label

41267 Winpac
PO Box 1269
Honolulu, HI 96807-1269 808-927-6317
  Fax: 808-521-0766 winpacinc@aol.com
Import broker of general merchandise
President: Richard Wyrgatsch
Estimated Sales: $2.5-5 Million
Number Employees: 1-4
Markets Served:
  Super Market Chains, Food Service Operators
Brokered Products include:
  General Merchandise, Imports

41268 Wisconsin Cheese Group
105 3rd St
Monroe, WI 53566-1028 608-325-2012
  Fax: 608-329-2381 800-332-6518
customerservice@wisconsincheesegroup.com
  www.wisconsincheesegroup.com
Broker or cheeses, chorizos and desserts focusing on the brands El Viajero, La Morenita and Reynaldo's.
CEO: Douglas Reed
Manager: Travis Stauffacher
tstauffacher@wisconsincheesegroup.com
Estimated Sales: $32.4 Million
Number Employees: 50-99
Number of Brands: 3
Primary Brands Brokered include: El Viajero, La Morenita, Reynaldo's
Brokered Products include:
  Dairy/Deli, Cheese Products, Desserts

41269 Wishbone Utensil Tableware Line
15 Paramount Pkwy
Wheat Ridge, CO 80215-6615 303-238-8088
  Fax: 253-595-7673 866-266-5928
Forever replaces chopsticks. One piece tong, skewer & ergonomic utensil. Child safe. Dishwasher friendly. Assisted living compatible. Solution for the chopstick challenged. Popular among hotel/resorts, restaurateur and occupationalhealth. Ten motif-friendly colors. FDA approved. Stylish, durable, reusable, fun. Sanitized and individually wrapped. Gourmet quality Feng Shui tableware
CEO: R Farlan Krieger Sr

Estimated Sales: Under $300,000
Number Employees: 9
Number of Brands: 4
Number of Products: 8
Square Footage: 50000
Parent Co: RF Krieger, LLC
Type of Packaging: Consumer, Food Service, Private Label, Bulk
Markets Served:
  Wholesale Distributors, Food Service Operators
Primary Brands Brokered include: Wishbone Utensil
Brokered Products include:
  Exports, Private Label

41270 Woollard Company
523 W Old Northwest Hwy
Barrington, IL 60010   847-382-7771
          Fax: 847-382-7676 800-523-4779
               woollard@megsinet.net
Broker of nuts and nut meats including pistachios, soy, almonds, cashews, pecans, filberts, walnuts, macadamias, pea, Brazil nuts, dried and glace fruits, sunflower seeds, spices, etc.
President: Lawrence Woollard
Estimated Sales: $1-2.5 Million
Number Employees: 1-4
Brokered Products include:
  Spices, Pistachios, Almonds, Cashews, Etc.

41271 Woolsey & Assoc Inc
N8w22520 Johnson Dr # K
Waukesha, WI 53186-1668
          262-436-0102
          Fax: 262-436-0109 800-383-2524
               www.woolseyassociates.com
Manufacturers' representative for general merchandise including food service equipment and supplies
Owner: Kim Woolsey
Office Manager: Gwyn Loveless
VP: Kim Woolsey
Outside Sales: Renee Cull
Estimated Sales: $1-3 Million
Number Employees: 5-9
Markets Served:
  Wholesale Distributors
Primary Brands Brokered include: Atlas/Precision; Berkel; Greenheck Ventilation; American Metalcraft; Cambro Manufacturing; Candle Corp.
Brokered Products include:
  General Merchandise, Foodservice Equipment & Supplies

41272 World Wide Safe Brokers
112 Cromwell Court
Woodbury, NJ 08096   856-863-1225
          Fax: 856-845-2266 800-593-2893
               info@worldwidesafebrokers.com
               www.worldwidesafebrokers.com
Fire safes, electronic safes, gun safes, safe deposit boxes, hotel room safes, insulated files, burglary safe, vaults, vault doors, in-floor safes, depository safes, custom designed and manufactured safes.
President: Edward Dornisch
VP: Mildred Dornisch
Estimated Sales: $.5-1 million
Number Employees: 3
Square Footage: 16000
Markets Served:
  Food Manufacturers & Processors, Super Market Chains, Wholesale Distributors, Food Service Operators
Brokered Products include:
  Safes-Security Containers

41273 Worldwide Express Inc
70 Jansen Ave # 202
Essington, PA 19029-1541   610-521-5450
          Fax: 610-521-5740 info@worldwideexpress.com
               www.worldwideexpress.com
Transportation broker providing freight forwarding, customs house and express package services
President: Al Hendri
  ahendri@wwex.com
Number Employees: 5-9
Parent Co: Worldwide Express

41274 Wrap-It Packaging
PO Box 750250
Dayton, OH 45475-0250   937-438-8075
          Fax: 937-438-8629

Manufacturers' representative for packaging, filling, tamper evident, laser coding and testing equipment including metal detectors, check weighers, x-ray, plus rotationally molded plastic containers and hoppers. Manufacturersrepresentative
President: Leif Jacobsen
VP: Anna-May Jacobsen
Estimated Sales: $3-5 Million
Number Employees: 5-9
Markets Served:
  Food Manufacturers & Processors, Super Market Chains, Wholesale Distributors, Food Service Operators
Brokered Products include:
  Alcoholic Beverages, Confectionery, Dairy/Deli, Frozen Food, General Merchandise, Health Food, Ingredients, Meat, Meat Products, Private Label, Produce, Seafood, Spices

41275 Wyman Foorman
480 Boulevard Way
Suite #1
Oakland, CA 9461C   510-601-7540
          Fax: 510-601-7541 info@wymanfoorman.com
Broker of industrial ingredients, nuts, dried eggs, dried meat and corn syrup, cereal ingredients, etc.
President: Robert A Adams
Number Employees: 250-499
Markets Served:
  Food Manufacturers & Processors
Primary Brands Brokered include: US Soy; Oregon Spice; G.S. Dunn; Nikken Foods; Red V; GMI Products; Kellogg's; ECOM
Brokered Products include:
  Ingredients, Meat Products, Dried Eggs, Nuts, Corn Syrup, Etc.

41276 Yankee Marketers
5 Birch Rd
P.O. Box 370
Middleton, MA 01949-2261   978-777-9181
          Fax: 978-777-5823 800-343-8272
               headquarters@yankeemarketers.com
Broker of confectionery and dairy/deli products, groceries, meat and meat products, general merchandise, private label items, frozen foods, seafood and spices
Chairman: J Robert Johnson
President: Brad Johnson
Vice President, Sales: Julie Gordon
Estimated Sales: $75 Million
Number Employees: 10-19
Square Footage: 6000
Type of Packaging: Consumer, Food Service, Private Label, Bulk
Markets Served:
  Food Manufacturers & Processors, Wholesale Distributors, Food Service Operators
Brokered Products include:
  Confectionery, Dairy/Deli, Frozen Food, General Merchandise, Groceries, Health Food, Imports, Ingredients, Meat, Meat Products, Produce, Seafood, Spices

41277 Yates Sales Associates
89 Locust Lane
Upper Saddle River, NJ 07458-2231   201-327-6990
Import broker of confectionery products, groceries, health food, spices and seafood
President: J Yates
CEO: S Yates
Number Employees: 2
Square Footage: 2800
Markets Served:
  Super Market Chains, Wholesale Distributors
Brokered Products include:
  Confectionery, Groceries, Health Food, Imports, Seafood, Spices

41278 Yeager & Associates
79158 Buff Bay Court
Bermuda Dunes, CA 92203-1567   760-345-7404
          Fax: 760-345-8816 pjyeager@gmail.com
Experts in developing new products using chicken, beef and pork for private labels. We have the ability to cook your meat/poultry product to final specification for further processing or packaging for retail sales. We haverepresentation in all major retail markets and food service.
President: Paula Yeager
VP: Robert Carian
Quality Control: Jason Carian
Sales: Paula Yeager
Sales: Lauren Hagadorn

Estimated Sales: $6 Million
Number Employees: 5
Square Footage: 16000
Parent Co: P&R Sales, Inc.
Type of Packaging: Consumer, Food Service, Private Label, Bulk
Markets Served:
  Food Manufacturers & Processors, Super Market Chains, Wholesale Distributors
Primary Brands Brokered include: Kings Delight; Far West; Robert Corian Enterprises
Brokered Products include:
  Imports, Meat, Meat Products, Private Label

41279 York Cheese
461 W Fullerton Ave
Elmhurst, IL 60126   630-941-3320
          Fax: 630-941-0686
Broker of cheese, dairy/deli products, frozen foods, seafood, meats and private label items
Co-Owner: Michael Petermann
Co-Owner: William Amos
Estimated Sales: $10-20 Million
Number Employees: 20-49
Markets Served:
  Food Manufacturers & Processors, Super Market Chains, Wholesale Distributors, Food Service Operators
Primary Brands Brokered include: Norseland; Bongrain Cheese, USA; MD Food; Volpi; Stefano's; Willowbrook Foods
Brokered Products include:
  Dairy/Deli, Frozen Food, General Merchandise, Groceries, Imports, Meat Products, Private Label, Seafood

41280 York Hospitality & Gaming
1611-A South Melrose Ave.
Suite 292
Vista, CA 92081   760-727-3055
          Fax: 760-727-3056 csharpell@yorkhg.com
               www.yorkhg.com
Manufacturers' representative for furnishings, tabletop supplies and smallwares
President/CEO: Tom York
VP/CFO: Helen York
Estimated Sales: $1-3 Million
Number Employees: 5-9
Square Footage: 9600
Markets Served:
  Wholesale Distributors, Food Service Operators
Primary Brands Brokered include: Libbey; Syracuse; Grasser Chair Company; World Tableware; Snap-Drape; Service Ideas
Brokered Products include:
  General Merchandise, Tabletop Supplies, Smallwares, Etc.

41281 York Sutch & Assoc
26863 Calle Hermosa
Capistrano Beach, CA 92624-1635   949-661-9229
          Fax: 949-661-2973 800-325-7349
               ysabrokers.com
Import broker of nuts, seeds, dairy/deli and confectionery products, chocolate and dry fruit
President: York Sutch
  ysasutch@aol.com
Vice President of Finance: Shelley Sutch
VP Sales: Mark Rush
Estimated Sales: $500,000-$1 Million
Number Employees: 10-19
Square Footage: 8000
Markets Served:
  Food Manufacturers & Processors, Wholesale Distributors
Brokered Products include:
  Confectionery, Dairy/Deli, Health Food, Imports, Nuts, Seeds, Dry Fruit

41282 Young-Block Associates
243 Schooner Cir
Neptune, NJ 07753   201-461-3333
          Fax: 201-461-3233
          CustomerService@YoungBlockAssociates.com
               www.youngblockassociates.com
Manufacturers' representative for food service equipment and supplies including ovens, ranges, broilers, display cases, dishwashers, reach-in and walk-in refrigerators, etc.
President: Hal Block
  halb@youngblockassociates.com
CEO: Philip Young
Vice President: Douglas Block

Food Brokers / A-Z

Estimated Sales: $5-10 Million
Number Employees: 5-9
Markets Served:
  Super Market Chains, Food Service Operators
Primary Brands Brokered include: South Bend Range; Holmaw; Refcon; Stero; Wilder; Greenheck; Norlake
Brokered Products include:
  General Merchandise, Reach-In & Walk-In Refrigerators, Etc.

41283 Z&A Vending
23743 Research Drive
Farmington Hills, MI 48335   248-474-1700
    Fax: 248-474-5743 info@atozvend.com
Manufacturers' representative for steel gumball, candy and snack vending machines
President: Terry Zink
Estimated Sales: $500,000-$1 Million
Number Employees: 5-9
Square Footage: 3200
Primary Brands Brokered include: RouteMaster
Brokered Products include:
  General Merchandise, Quarter Snack Vending Machines

41284 Zambito Produce Sales
736 White Horse Pike
West Collingswood, NJ 08107-1722   856-546-0700
    Fax: 856-546-7828 cfzambito@aol.com
Domestic, import and export broker of produce including apples, vegetables, potatoes and onions
President: Charles Zambito
Estimated Sales: $1-2.5 Million
Number Employees: 1-4
Markets Served:
  Wholesale Distributors
Primary Brands Brokered include: Blue Jay; California Citrus; Johnston Farms; Greyhound; Elba; Riveridge
Brokered Products include:
  Exports, Imports, Produce, Apples, Vegetables, Potatoes, Onions

41285 Zanichelli & Associates
8241 Tim Tam Trl
Evergreen, CO 80439-6339   303-674-9060
    Fax: 303-670-2735 charlietza@aol.com
Import broker of confectionery and dairy/deli products, general merchandise, groceries, olive oil, nuts, produce, seafood, ingredients and meat and meat products
Sales Manager: Charles Zanichelli
Sales: Jan Cleveland
Office Manager: Sharon Trenkle
Number Employees: 1-4
Square Footage: 3600
Markets Served:
  Food Manufacturers & Processors, Super Market Chains, Wholesale Distributors, Food Service Operators
Primary Brands Brokered include: Mitsui Foods; Azari Nut Company; Anco Foods; Napoleon; Arthur Schuman, Inc.; Daniele
Brokered Products include:
  Confectionery, Dairy/Deli, General Merchandise, Groceries, Imports, Ingredients, Meat, Meat Products, Produce, Seafood, Nuts, Olive Oil, Etc.

41286 Zink Marketing
420 Westdale Ave
Westerville, OH 43082-8728   614-899-9500
    Fax: 614-899-9797 800-492-7400
        info@zinkmarketing.com
Manufacturers' representative for food service supplies and equipment
Owner: Jim Zink
info@zinkmarketing.com
Estimated Sales: $10-20 Million
Number Employees: 20-49
Markets Served:
  Wholesale Distributors
Primary Brands Brokered include: Kolpak; McCall; Tonka; Prince Castle; Tomlinson; Keating
Brokered Products include:
  General Merchandise, Foodservice Supplies & Equipment

41287 Zonner
100 Spear St # 320
San Francisco, CA 94105-1523   415-227-9960
    Fax: 415-227-9965 chris@zonnerinc.com
Broker of industrial ingredients, meats and spices
President: Christopher Tatum
Estimated Sales: $5-10 Million
Number Employees: 5-9
Square Footage: 4000
Markets Served:
  Food Manufacturers & Processors
Primary Brands Brokered include: Gilroy Foods; Delmonte Corporation; Anthony Foods; ADM Cocoa; Sun Garden Packing; Paramount Farms
Brokered Products include:
  Ingredients, Meat Products, Spices

Broker Market / Food Manufacturing & Processing

Food Manufacturing & Processing

3-D Marketing & Sales, 40001
A G Brown & Son, 40003
A W Sisk & Son, 40008
A.J. Seibert Company, 40010
A.N. Smith & Company, 40011
A.R. Pellegrini & Associates, 40012
ABC Corp, 40013
ABC Enterprises, 40014
Access Partners, 40020
Acorn Sales Company, 40023
Acosta Sales & Marketing Company, 40024
Adtek Sales, 40029
Advance Sales & Marketing, Inc, 40031
Advantage Solutions, 40033
Advantage Webco Hawaii, 40034
Agri-Dairy Products, 40036
Albert A Russo Inc, 40040
Allied Marketing Corp, 40046
Ambi-Prestigio Foods Inc, 40050
American Agribusiness Assistance, 40051
American Patriot Sales Inc, 40053
American Trading Company, 40055
Anchor Packaging, 40059
Anthony Cea & Associates, 40061
Apache Brokers, 40062
Apple Food Sales, 40063
Arthur G. Meier Company/Inland Products Company, 40067
ATI, 40017
Atkinson-Crawford Sales Co, 40074
Automatic Packaging Systems & Conveyors Company, 40078
Autumn Foods, 40079
Avatar Food Group, 40080
B&K Agencies, 40083
B.C. Ritchie Company, 40084
B.C. Tree Fruits Limited, 40085
B.W. Dyer & Company, 40086
Baja Foods LLC, 40091
Baker Sales, 40093
Barliant & Company, 40095
Bartlett & Co, 40097
Bay Pacific Marketing, 40100
Bayha & Associates, 40101
Beach Filter Products, 40102
Beck Western Brokerage, 40103
Bender-Goodman Co Inc, 40109
Bentley Food Marketing, 40111
Berk Enterprises, 40112
Beta Pure Foods, 40116
Betters International Food Corporation, 40117
Binner Marketing & Sales, 40119
Bittinger Sales, 40123
Bixby Food Sales, 40124
Bloodworth & Associates, 40126
Bloomfield Bakers, 40127
BLV Marketing Inc, 40088, 40089
Bodie-Rickett & Associates, 40130
Boehmer Sales Agency, 40131
Borton Brokerage Company, 40133
Bosshart Food Svc, 40134
Bottom Line Foods, 40135
Bridge City Food Marketing, 40140
Brokerage Sales Company, 40144
Broms Brokerage, 40145
Brothers International Food Corporation, 40146
Buckley, Thorne, Messina & McDermott, 40149
Budd Mayer Company of Jackson Inc., 40150
Burley Brokerage, 40155
Bushwick Commission Company, 40156
Butkevich Associates, 40157
Buzz Crown Enterprises, 40158
Byron A Carlson Inc, 40161
C J Irwin Co Inc, 40162
Cafe Inc, 40173
Caneast Foods, 40176

Cann Brokerage Inc, 40177
Carlin Group, 40179
Cascade Corp, 40183
Cashman-Edwards Inc, 40184
Central Marketing Assoc, 40186
Charles R. Bell Limited, 40193
Charles Rockel & Son, 40194
Charles Stube Co Inc, 40195
Cheese & Dairy Products, 40202
Chilay Corporation, 40205
Christian Brokerage Company/Industrial & Food, 40206
Chuck Batcheller Company, 40208
Clear Springs Foods Inc., 40212
Clofine Dairy Products Inc, 40215
Coastal Commodities, 40218
Coastal Pride Co Inc, 40219
Collins Associates, 40222
Columbia Food Machinery Inc, 40225
Commodities Marketing Inc, 40227
Concept Food Sales, 40229
Concord National, 40231, 40232
Conlin Brokerage Company, 40237
Conrad Sales Company, 40238
Consolidated Marketers Inc, 40239
Constant Sales, 40242
Consumer Brands, 40243
Consummate Marketing Company, 40244
Continental Food Sales Inc, 40245
Core Group, 40251
Creightons, 40256
Cribari Vineyard Inc, 40257
Crider Brokerage Company, 40258
Crossmark, 40259
Cusick J B Co, 40264
Dadant & Company, 40274
Dakco International, 40276
Damascus Peanut Company, 40279
Dambeck & Associates, 40280
Dave Roemer & Associates, 40281
Dave Swain Assoc Inc, 40282
Dawson Sales Co Inc, 40287
DBB Marketing Company, 40269
DeJarnett Sales, 40289
DeMoss & Associates, 40291
Dennis Sales, 40296
Di Meo-Gale Brokerage Company, 40297
Diamond Chemical & Supply Co, 40299
Diaz Sales, 40300
Diversifood Associates, Inc, 40303
Don Ford Ltd, 40306
Dunbar Sales Company, Inc, 40315
DW Montgomery & Company, 40273
E K Bare & Sons Inc, 40318
Egerstrom Inc, 40329
Eiseman-Gleit Co Inc, 40330
Ellis S. Fine Co., Inc., 40335
Emerling International Foods, 40336
Encore Fruit Marketing Inc, 40337
Enterprise Food Brokers, 40339
Ervan Guttman Co, 40342
Essential Food Marketing, 40346
Evans Brokerage Company, 40351
Evers Heilig Inc, 40352
F. Rothman Enterprises, LLC, 40356
Fairley & Co Inc, 40360
Feenix Brokerage LTD, 40362
Ferdinand Richards & Son, 40363
Ferolie Esm-Metro New York, 40364
First Flight Foods, 40368
FM Carriere & Son, 40358
Food Associates of Syracuse, 40377
Food Ingredients Inc, 40379
Food Service Connection, 40383
FoodBin Trading, Inc., 40387
Francis Musto & Co, 40401
Freeman Fruit Intl, 40408
Freiria & Company, 40410
Fusion Sales Group, 40413
GAP Food Brokers, 40415
Garden Gold Foods, Inc, 40419
Gasparini Sales Inc, 40421
Gateway Food Service, 40422
Gehrke Co, 40423
Gellman Associates, 40424

Genesis International, 40425
Genesis Marketing, 40426
George E. Dent Sales, 40428
George W. Holop Associates, 40430
Gibbs & Assoc, 40432
Gibbs-Mccormick Inc A Ca Corp, 40433
Glacier Sales Inc, 40437
Golden Valley Industries Inc, 40440
Golick Martins, Inc., 40441
Goveco Full Service Food Brokers, 40444
Gurrentz International Corp, 40453
H.R. Plate & Company, 40457
H.V. Mid State Sales Company, 40458
Haile Resources, 40463
Hanimex Corporation, 40466
Hanks Brokerage, 40467
Hansid Company, 40469
Harold J. Barrett Company, 40470
Harold H. Lincoln Company, 40471
Harriet Greenland Enterprises, 40472
Harvest Grove Inc, 40476
HCB Foodservice Sales & Marketing, 40459
Heard Brokerage Company Inc, 40481
Heartland Food Brokers LTD, 40482
Henry J. Hips Company, 40483
Herb Barber & Sons Food, 40484
Higgins & White Inc, 40486
Hilgenfeld Brokerage Co, 40487
Hockenberg Newburgh, 40491
Hockenberg-Newburgh Sales, 40492
Homeplace Food Group, 40494
Hoyt, 40497
Hundley Brokerage Company, 40499
Hunter Walton & Co Inc, 40500
Iceberg Seafood Inc, 40509
Imark of Pennsylvania, 40510
Imperial Dade, 40512
Imperial Frozen Foods Co, 40514
Imperial House Sales, 40515
Ingredient Exchange Co, 40517
Ingredient Inc, 40518
Ingredient Innovations, 40519
Insulated Structures/PB Group, 40520
Inter-American Products, 40523
Intermountain Food Brokerage, 40525
International Gourmet Products, 40527
International Pacific Seafood, 40529
International Sales & Brokerage Company, 40530
Interpack NW Frozen Food, 40531
Intersouth Foodservice Group, 40534
Interwest Ingredient Sales, 40536
J Cipelli Merchants, 40540
J N Rhodes Co Inc, 40542
J R Kelly Co, 40543
J.E. Julian & Associates, 40549
J.F. Benz Company, 40550
J.L. Epstein & Son, 40553
J.M. Swank Company, 40554
J.W. Kuehn Company, 40556
Jack Curren & Associates, 40564
Jacobsen-Clahan & Company, 40565
James W Valleau & Company, 40567
Jewell/Barksdale Associates, 40571
Jim Pless & Company, 40573
JL Stemp Marketing Agents, 40558
JML Sales Co, 40560
Jodawnco, 40574
John E Thier Co, 40575
John H. Elton, 40576
John J Wollack Co Inc, 40577
Johnson O'Hare Co, 40583
Johnson, Arlyn & Associates, 40584
Jones Neitzel Co, 40586
Joseph Caragol, 40590
Joseph W Nath Co, 40593
JP Carroll Company, 40562
Jso Associates Inc, 40596
Juhl Brokerage, 40598
Julius Levy Company, 40601
Julius M. Dean Company, 40602
Kathryn's Food Service Brokers, 40616
Kayco, 40619

Kedem, 40621
Kelley-Clarke, 40623
Kelly Flour Company, 40626
Kemper Food Brokers, 40628
Key Impact Sales & Systems Inc, 40633
Key Sales Group, 40635
Kiefer's, 40638
Kinder-Smith Company, 40639
Kingsbrook Foods, 40645
Kirstein Brokerage Company, 40648
Klass Ingredients Inc, 40649
Klensch Cheese Company, 40650
Klinger & Speros Food Brokers, 40651
Klondike Foods, 40652
Knutsen Coffees, 40653
Korth Marketing, 40656
Kramer Brokerage Co, 40657
Kurtz Food Brokers, 40659
Lake & Lake Inc, 40671
Lakeside Food Sales Inc, 40673
Lamborn & Company, 40674
Lampson & Tew, 40675
Lance Agencies, 40677
Landers Ag Resources, 40678
Landmark Foods, 40679
Larry Fox & Co, 40681
Lehigh Food Sales Inc, 40685
Lehmann Brokerage Co, 40686
LeMire Sales, 40682
Leonard H Sisitzky Sales Inc, 40689
Lever Associates, 40691
Lifewise Ingredients, 40693
Lilburn Gulf, 40694
Linwood-Welch Marketing, 40695
Lisberg-Voegeli Hanson, 40696
Littler Brokerage Co Inc, 40697
Littman & Associates, 40698
LMGO International Inc, 40666
Loar & Young Inc, 40701
Lomac & May Associates, 40703
Loman Brown, 40704
Loretta Foods, 40706
Lorey & Lorey, 40707
Los Angeles Chemical Company, 40708
Lowe & Associates, 40711
Ludwig Mueller Co Inc, 40712
Luke Soules Southwest, 40713
M Arkans & Son, 40716
M. Pencar Associates, 40720
M. Soffer Company, 40721
M.E. Strauss Brokerage Company, 40723
Magic Valley Truck Brokers Inc, 40731
Major Marketing Service, 40735
Manuel's Mexican-American Fine Foods, 40741
Manzo Food Brokers, 40742
Marbran USA, 40744
Marino Marketing Group, 40746
Marjo & Associates, 40747
Market West Company, 40751
Marketing Management Inc, 40754
Marshall Sales Co, 40757
Martin Preferred Foods, 40758
Marty Scanlon Brokerage Co, 40759
Massey-Fair Industrial Southwest, 40761
Mathews Associates, 40765
MAV Sales Co, 40725
Mc Namara Assoc Inc, 40769
McCarty Brokerage Company, 40771
McClement Sales Company, 40772
Measured Sales & Marketing, 40776
Menu Planners, 40777
Mercantum Corp, 40778
Meridian Products, 40779
Merit Sales Corporation, 40781
Mickelson & Associates, 40784
Mid-American Brokerage of St. Louis, 40787
Mid-Continent Sales, 40788
Mid-West Sales Agency, 40791
Midlantic Sweetener Co, 40793
Midwest Ingredient Sales, 40796
Midwest Ingredients Inc, 40797
Milky Whey Inc, 40799
Miller & Smith Foods, 40800

97

Broker Market / Food Service Operators

Miller's Market, 40802
Mirkovich & Assoc Inc, 40806
Mitchel Beck Company, 40807
Mitchell Agencies, 40809
Mitchell of Mississippi, 40810
Moneuse Sales Agency, 40811
Monterey Food Ingredients, 40812
Moody Dunbar Inc, 40813
Mooney International, 40814
Morley Sales Co, 40817
Morton & Associates, 40818
Multy-Grain Foods, 40825
Murray Industrial Food Sales Inc, 40828
Nash Wright Brokerage, 40836
National Food Group, 40841
National Food Sales, 40842, 40843
National Sign Corporation, 40848
Nature's Products Inc, 40849
Nesco Brokerage Company, 40851
New Organics, 40854
Nobert Marketing, 40860
Noble Foods, 40861
Noble House Trading Company, 40862
Norman Hecht, 40866
Northeastern Enterprises, 40873
Northland Express Transport, 40874
Northwestern Foods, 40877
O'Brien & Associates Brokerage Company, 40880
O'Hanlon Group, 40881
Occidental Foods International, LLC, 40886
Oekerman Sales, 40887
Ohm Design, 40888
Orca Foods, 40891
Osborn Food Sales Company, 40894
Pace Target Brokerage, 40899
Pacific Ingredient Exchange, 40900
Pacific Trading Company International, 40903
PacNorth Group, 40898
Paul Esposito Inc, 40913
Paul Inman Associates, 40915
Pennickers Food Distribution, 40917
Peter Johansky Studio, 40919
Peters & Fair, 40920
Phillips Sales Co, 40922
Phoenix Foods Inc, 40924
Pierce Cartwright Company, 40925
Pioneer Marketing International, 40929
Powell May International, 40935
Preferred Brokerage Company, 40936
Preisco Jentash, 40937
Premier Food Marketing, 40939
Premier Food Service Sales, 40940
Premium Seafood Co, 40942
Prestige Sales & Marketing, 40945
Promesa, 40959
Pure Sales, 40964
Quality Brokerage Company, 40965
Quality Sales & Marketing, 40969
R H Moulton Company, 40971
R&F Cocoa Services, 40973
R. Becker Marketing & Sales, 40974
R.W. Berkeley & Associates, 40977
Rainbow Sales & Marketing, 40983
Randag & Assoc Inc, 40986
Reede International Seafood Corporation, 40992
Reese Brokerage Co, 40993
Reichenbach & Associates, 40994
Rene Rivet, 40996
Res-Q Network, 40998
Reuven International, 41001
RH Sulker Sales, 41002
Rheuark/F.S.I. Sales, 41002
Richs Sales Company, 41005
Rizwitsch Sales, 41010
RMCI Foodservice, 40980
Rodon Foods, 41018
Roehl Corp, 41019
Roos-Mohan, 41022
Roosevelt Dairy Trade, Inc, 41023
Rosenfeld & Gigante, 41024
Royal Wine Corp, 41029

Rubenstein Seafood Sales, 41030
Rudolph Brady, Inc, 41031
S. Kamberg & Company, 41035
Sabbers & Assoc Inc, 41046
Sachem Co, 41047
Salad Oils Intl Corp, 41049
Sales Corporation of Alaska, 41052
Sales Marketing Svc LLC, 41053
Santucci Associates, 41061
Saratoga Food Safety, 41063
Saverino & Assoc, 41066
Scavuzzo Sales & Marketing, 41067
Schare & Associates, 41069
Schiff Food Products Co Inc, 41071
Schraad & Associates, 41072
Schreiber Foods Inc., 41073
Seaboard Foods, 41077
Seafood Sales, 41082
Sessions & Associates, 41088
SHA Services, 41040
Shore Distribution Resources, 41092
Shrimp Tex Distributors, 41093
Sinco, 41097
SJE Marketing Corporation, 41041
SJH Enterprises, 41042
Sloan Sales Inc, 41103
South East Sales, 41110
South Group Marketing, 41111
Southeastern Paper Group Inc, 41113
Specialty Sales & Marketing, 41118
Spencer & Assoc, 41122
St Charles Trading Inc, 41126
St. Ours & Company, 41128
Statewide Brokerage Company, 41130
Stevens & Associates, 41133
Stiefel Associates, 41134
Stroup Ingredients Resources, 41139
Sturdivant Company, 41140
Sturgill Food Brokerage, 41141
Sullivan & Fitzgerald Food Brokers, 41142
Summit FS LTD, 41144
Sun Marketing Agents Inc, 41146
Sundown Foods USA, Inc., 41148
Super Sale Brokerage Company, 41150
Supreme Foods, 41153
Supreme Foodservice Sales, 41154
T. McConnell Sales & Marketing, 41159
T.J. Hines & Company, 41161
T.W. Wilson & Son, 41162
Taormina Sales Company, 41166
Teasley & Assoc, 41169
Technical Food Sales Inc, 41170
Technical Sales Associates, 41171
Tees & Persse Brokerage Acosta Sales And Marketing Company, Inc, 41172
Texas Foods, 41176
The Thurber Company, 41178
Thomas, Large & Singer, 41181
Thomson-Leeds Company, 41182
Tisdale Food Ingredients, 41185
Tobiason Potato Co Inc, 41186
Tom Quinn & Associates, 41189
Top O' The Table, 41190
Torter Corporation, 41191
Tower Intercontinental Group, 41193
Tr International Trading Co, 41194
Trading Corporation of America, 41195
Tri-State Logistics Inc, 41199
Triad Brokers Inc, 41200
Try-Angle Food Brokers Inc, 41202
Tucker Sales, 41203
Twin City Food Brokers, 41206
Two Guys Spice Company, 41207
UBC Marketing, 41208
Union Standard Equipment Company, 41211
United International Indstrs, 41215
Van Kam, G. Trading Company, 41223
Van Reed Sales Company, 41224
W.H. Schilbe Citrus Brokerage / Citriservices, 41231
Wallis & Barcinski, 41238
Ward Hughes Co, 41239
Watson & Associates, 41241

Waypoint, 41242
Webeco Foods, Inc, 41244
Wehrfritz & Associates, 41245
Wendlandt Brokerage Company, 41248
WENS Brokerage, 41233
Wesco Food Brokerage, 41249
Westcon Foods, 41251
Whitby Co, 41254
Wick's Pies Inc, 41255
Wieber-McLain Company, 41256
William B. Steedman & Sons, 41257
William Bernstein Company, 41258
William M. Dunne & Associates Ltd, 41260
Willing Group, 41263
Winmix/Natural Care Products, 41266
WMK Marketing, 41235
World Wide Safe Brokers, 41272
Wrap-It Packaging, 41274
Wyman Foorman, 41275
Yankee Marketers, 41276
Yeager & Associates, 41278
York Cheese, 41279
York Sutch & Assoc, 41281
Zanichelli & Associates, 41285
Zonner, 41287

Food Service Operators

3-D Marketing & Sales, 40001
A G Brown & Son, 40003
A M Source Inc, 40006
A Thomas Farris & Son Inc, 40007
A W Sisk & Son, 40008
A.J. Seibert Company, 40010
A.R. Pellegrini & Associates, 40012
ABC Enterprises, 40014
Access Partners, 40020
Acorn Sales Company, 40023
Acosta Sales & Marketing Company, 40024
Action Marketing, 40025
Action Marketing Services, 40028
Advance Sales & Marketing, Inc, 40031
Advantage Solutions, 40033
Advantage Webco Hawaii, 40034
Albert A Russo Inc, 40040
Allied Marketing Corp, 40046
Alpine Summit Sales Inc, 40048
Ambi-Prestigio Foods Inc, 40050
American Patriot Sales Inc, 40053
American Trading Company, 40055
Anchor Florida Marketing, 40058
Anchor Packaging, 40059
Anthony Cea & Associates, 40061
Apache Brokers, 40062
Apple Food Sales, 40063
Arnett Brokerage Co, 40065
Arroyo Sales Company, 40066
Arthur G. Meier Company/Inland Products Company, 40067
Artisanal Foods, 40068
Arvin Sales Company, 40069
Associated Foodservices, 40072
ATI, 40017
Atkinson Sales Company, 40073
Atkinson-Crawford Sales Co, 40074
Atlantis Smoked Foods, 40075
Atlas Restaurant Supply, 40077
Avatar Food Group, 40080
B&K Agencies, 40083
B.C. Tree Fruits Limited, 40085
Baker Brokerage Company LLC, 40092
Baker Sales, 40093
Barliant & Company, 40095
Barry Food Sales, 40096
Bay Brokerage Company, 40099
Bay Pacific Marketing, 40100
Bayha & Associates, 40101
Beach Filter Products, 40102
Beck Western Brokerage, 40103
Benchmark Sales, 40108
Bender-Goodman Co Inc, 40109
Benson-Mitchell, 40110
Bentley Food Marketing, 40111

Berk Enterprises, 40112
Best Marketing Reps, 40115
Betters International Food Corporation, 40117
Binner Marketing & Sales, 40119
Bird Marketing, 40120
Bittinger Sales, 40123
Bixby Food Sales, 40124
Blackwing Ostrich Meats Inc., 40125
Bloomfield Bakers, 40127
BLV Marketing Inc, 40088
Bob Rowe Sales, 40128
Bodie-Rickett & Associates, 40130
Boehmer Sales Agency, 40131
Booth, Schwager & Associates, 40132
Borton Brokerage Company, 40133
Bosshart Food Svc, 40134
Bottom Line Foods, 40135
Brennan Food Services, 40139
Bridge City Food Marketing, 40140
Brierley & King Brokerage Corporation, 40141
Broms Brokerage, 40145
Browning Brokerage Company, 40147
BSE Marketing, 40090
Buckley, Thorne, Messina & McDermott, 40149
Budd Mayer Company of Jackson Inc., 40150
Budd Mayer of Mobile, 40151
Buley Patterson Sales Company, 40152
Burley Brokerage, 40155
Bushwick Commission Company, 40156
Butkevich Associates, 40157
Buzz Crown Enterprises, 40158
Byron A Carlson Inc, 40161
C. Lloyd Johnson Company, 40163
C. Mascari & Associates, 40164
C.R. Peterson Associates, 40167
C.W. Shasky & Associates Ltd., 40168
Cafe Inc, 40173
Cajun Creole Products Inc, 40174
California World Trade and Marketing Company, 40175
Caneast Foods, 40176
Cann Brokerage Inc, 40177
Cardinal Brokerage, 40178
Carlin Group, 40179
Cashman-Edwards Inc, 40184
Central Marketing Assoc, 40186
Charles R. Bell Limited, 40193
Charles Rockel & Son, 40194
Chase Sales Company, 40198
Cheese & Dairy Products, 40202
Chell Brokerage Co, 40203
Chernoff Sales, 40204
Chilay Corporation, 40205
Christian Brokerage Company/Industrial & Food, 40206
Chuck Batcheller Company, 40208
Chuckrow Sales LLC, 40209
Classic Cuisine Foods, 40211
Clements Stella Marketing, 40213
Clogmaster, 40216
Coastal Commodities, 40218
Coastal Pride Co Inc, 40219
Cobler Food Sales, 40220
Collins Associates, 40222
Colony Brokerage Company, 40224
Commodities Marketing Inc, 40227
Concept Food Sales, 40229
Concord National, 40230, 40231, 40232, 40233, 40234, 40235
Concord Sales-Prairies, 40236
Conlin Brokerage Company, 40237
Conrad Sales Company, 40238
Consolidated Marketers Inc, 40239
Consolidated Merchandisers, 40240
Consolidated Tea Co Inc, 40241
Constant Sales, 40242
Consumer Brands, 40243
Consummate Marketing Company, 40244
Continental Food Sales Inc, 40245
Core Group, 40251
Courtney Marketing Inc, 40253

Broker Market / Food Service Operators

Cox Food Brokers, 40254
Creightons, 40256
Crider Brokerage Company, 40258
Crossmark, 40259
Crowley Marketing Assoc Park, 40260
Cruise Marketing, 40262
CS Brokers, 40172
Culinary Specialty Produce, 40263
Cyba-Stevens Management Group, 40265
D&R Food Brokers, 40268
Dakota Marketing Company, 40277
Dambeck & Associates, 40280
Dave Roemer & Associates, 40281
Dave Swain Assoc Inc, 40282
David E Grimes Company, 40284
Dd Reckner Co, 40288
Dealers Choice, 40292
Delbert Craig Food Brokers, 40295
DeMoss & Associates, 40291
Dennis Sales, 40296
Di Meo-Gale Brokerage Company, 40297
Diamond Chemical & Supply Co, 40299
Diaz Sales, 40300
Dino-Meat Company, 40302
Dixon Marketing Inc, 40305
DSI Food Brokerage, 40271
Dunbar Co, 40314
Dunbar Sales Company, Inc, 40315
Dunham & Smith Agencies, 40316
DVC Brokerage Company, 40272
DW Montgomery & Company, 40273
Eastern Bag & Paper Co, 40324
Eastern Sales & Marketing, 40325
Eastern Sales and Marketing, 40326
Ed O'Connor Associates, 40328
EFD Associate, 40321
Eiseman-Gleit Co Inc, 40330
Eiserloh Co Inc, 40331
Elliot Horowitz & Co, 40334
Ellis S. Fine Co., Inc., 40335
Emerling International Foods, 40336
Encore Fruit Marketing Inc, 40337
English Northwest Marketing, 40338
Enterprise Food Brokers, 40339
Erickson Brothers Brokerage Co, 40340
Ervan Guttman Co, 40342
Esposito Brokerage, 40344
Essential Food Marketing, 40346
Ettinger Rosini & Associates, 40347
Evans & Associates, 40350
Evans Brokerage Company, 40351
Evers Heilig Inc, 40352
F M Turner Co Inc, 40354
F. Rothman Enterprises, LLC, 40356
Fairley & Co Inc, 40360
Federated Group, 40361
Feenix Brokerage LTD, 40362
Ferdinand Richards & Son, 40363
Ferolie Esm-Metro New York, 40364
Finn Marketing Group Inc, 40365
First Choice Sales Company, 40367
First Flight Foods, 40368
Fischer Group, 40369
Five Star Packaging, 40370
Flynn Sales Associates, Inc., 40375
FMI Food Marketers International Ltd, 40359
Food Associates of Syracuse, 40377
Food Sales Systems, 40380
Food Sales West, 40381
Food Service Associates, 40382
Food Service Connection, 40383
Food Service Marketing of Pennsylvania, 40384
Food Service Specialists, 40386
Foodsales Inc, 40389
Foodservice Marketing, 40391
Foodservice Solutions & Ideas, 40392
Forman Group, 40398
Four Peaks, Inc., 40400
Francis Musto & Co, 40401
Frank Kinsman Assoc, 40402
Freeman Signature, 40409
Freiria & Company, 40410
Fromartharie Inc, 40411

Fusion Sales Group, 40413
G.A. Davis Food Service, 40414
Gallagher Sales Corporation, 40418
GAP Food Brokers, 40415
Garden Gold Foods, Inc, 40419
Gasparini Sales Inc, 40421
Gateway Food Service, 40422
Gehrke Co, 40423
Genesis Marketing, 40426
George E. Dent Sales, 40428
George W. Holop Associates, 40430
GFR Worldwide, 40417
Glacier Sales Inc, 40437
Glenmoor Brokerage, 40438
Global Citrus Resources, Inc, 40439
Golick Martins, Inc., 40441
Goveco Full Service Food Brokers, 40444
Grabbe-Leonard Co, 40445
Gulf States Food Service Marketing, 40452
Gurrentz International Corp, 40453
H & G Trading LTD Inc, 40454
H&T Food Marketing Company, 40455
H.V. Mid State Sales Company, 40458
Haile Resources, 40463
Halal Transactions, 40464
Halling Company, 40465
Hanks Brokerage, 40467
Hansid Company, 40469
Harold J. Barrett Company, 40470
Harold M. Lincoln Company, 40471
Harriet Greenland Enterprises, 40472
Harris Freeman, 40473
Harvey-Winchell Company, 40477
Hatch-Jennings Inc, 40478
HCB Foodservice Sales & Marketing, 40459
Heard Brokerage Company Inc, 40481
Heartland Food Brokers LTD, 40482
Henry J. Hips Company, 40483
Herspring, 40485
Hilgenfeld Brokerage Co, 40487
Hinkle Easter Products, 40488
Hobby Whalen Marketing, 40489
Hockenberg Newburgh, 40490, 40491
Hockenberg-Newburgh Sales, 40492
Homeplace Food Group, 40494
Howell Associates, 40496
Hugh T. Gilmore Company, 40498
Hundley Brokerage Company, 40499
Hunter Walton & Co Inc, 40500
Iceberg Seafood Inc, 40509
Imark of Pennsylvania, 40510
Imperial Dade, 40512
Imperial Frozen Foods Co, 40514
Inter-American Products, 40523
Intermountain Food Brokerage, 40525
International Coffee Corporation, 40526
International Gourmet Products, 40527
International Pacific Sales, 40528
International Pacific Seafood, 40529
International Sales & Brokerage Company, 40530
Interpack NW Frozen Food, 40531
Intersouth Foodservice Group, 40534
Interstate Food Brokers, 40535
Inverso Johnson LLC, 40538
ISC of Indiana, 40505
ISSCO, 40506
ITOCHU International, Inc, 40508
J Carroll & Assoc, 40539
J N Rhodes Co Inc, 40542
J T Gibbons Inc, 40544
J&J Brokerage, 40546
J&S Food Brokerage, 40547
J.E. Julian & Associates, 40549
J.F. Benz Company, 40550
J.F. Kelly, 40551
J.L. Epstein & Son, 40553
J.W. Harrison & Son, 40555
Jack Curren & Associates, 40564
Jeram Associates, 40570
Jilasco Food Exports, 40572
Jim Pless & Company, 40573

JL Stemp Marketing Agents, 40558
JML Sales Co, 40560
John H Thier Co, 40575
John H. Elton, 40576
John J Wollack Co Inc, 40577
John Mangum Company, 40579
Johnson Holmes & Assoc Inc, 40582
Johnson O'Hare Co, 40583
Jones Neitzel Co, 40586
Jones-McCormick & Associates, 40587
Jos Iorio Company, 40588
Joseph Caragol, 40590
Joseph W Nath Co, 40593
Joylin Food Equipment Corporation, 40594
Jpo/Dow Inc, 40595
Jubilee Sales of Carolina, 40597
Juhl Brokerage, 40598, 40599
Julius Levy Company, 40601
JVS Group, 40563
Kandy King Confections, 40613
Kathryn's Food Service Brokers, 40616
Keeth & Associates, 40622
Kelley-Clarke, 40623
Kelly Associates/Food Brokers, 40625
Kelly Flour Company, 40626
Kemper Food Brokers, 40628
Key Impact Sales & Systems Inc, 40633
Key Sales Group, 40635
KeyImpact Sales & Systems, Inc., 40636
Kiefer's, 40638
KIKO Foods Inc, 40611
Kinder-Smith Company, 40639
Kingery & Assoc, 40643
Kirkbride & Associates, 40647
Kirstein Brokerage Company, 40648
Klensch Cheese Company, 40650
Klinger & Speros Food Brokers, 40651
Klondike Foods, 40652
Koehler Borden & Assoc, 40655
Korth Marketing, 40656
Kramer Brokerage Co, 40657
Kurtz Food Brokers, 40659
L H Gamble Co LTD, 40660
LA Teste Services, 40662
LAD Foodservice Sales, 40663
Lake Michigan Growers, 40672
Lakeside Food Sales Inc, 40673
Lampson & Tew, 40675
Lance Agencies, 40677
Landers Ag Resources, 40678
Landmark Foods, 40679
Larry Fox & Co, 40681
LBM Sales, LLC, 40664
Leblanc Foodservice Marketing, 40683
Lehigh Food Sales Inc, 40685
Lehmann Brokerage Co, 40686
LeMire Sales, 40682
Lemmons Company, 40687
Leonard H Sisitzky Sales Inc, 40689
Lever Associates, 40691
Lilburn Gulf, 40694
Linwood-Welch Marketing, 40695
Lisberg-Voegeli Hanson, 40696
Littler Brokerage Co Inc, 40697
Littman & Associates, 40698
Lloyd A Gray Co Inc, 40699
LMGO International Inc, 40666
Loar & Young Inc, 40701
Lobel Food Brokers, 40702
Lomac & May Associates, 40703
Loman Brown, 40704
Loretta Foods, 40706
Lorey & Lorey, 40707
Lowe & Associates, 40711
Luke Soules Southwest, 40713
M Fellinger Co, 40717
M. Soffer Company, 40721
M.E. Dilanian Company, 40722
M.E. Strauss Brokerage Company, 40723
Madden & Assoc, 40730
Magic Valley Truck Brokers Inc, 40731
Main Street Marketing, 40732
Major Marketing Service, 40735
Mancini & Groesbeck, 40738

Mancini Sales & Marketing, 40740
Manuel's Mexican-American Fine Foods, 40741
Manzo Food Brokers, 40742
Marbran USA, 40744
Marino Marketing Group, 40746
Marjo & Associates, 40747
Market Pro International, 40749
Market Smart, 40750
Market West Company, 40751
Martin Preferred Foods, 40758
Marty Scanlon Brokerage Co, 40759
Master Marketing Sunlow, Inc., 40763
Master Sales & Marketing, 40764
Mathews Associates, 40765
MAV Sales Co, 40725
Mc Namara Assoc Inc, 40769
McArdle, 40770
McCarty Brokerage Company, 40771
McCormick Brokerage Company, 40773
Meadows Brokerage Company, 40775
Measured Sales & Marketing, 40776
Menu Planners, 40777
Mercantum Company, 40778
Meridian Products, 40779
Merit Sales Corporation, 40781
Mickelson & Associates, 40784
Micosa Inc, 40785
Mid-American Brokerage of St. Louis, 40787
Mid-Continent Sales, 40788
Mid-State Food Brokers, 40789
Mid-West Associates, 40790
Mid-West Sales Agency, 40791
Midlantic Sweetener Co, 40793
Midstates Marketing Inc, 40794
Midwest Ingredients Inc, 40797
Midwest Juice, 40798
Milky Whey Inc, 40799
Miller & Smith Foods, 40800
Miller's Market, 40802
Miller, Stabler & Smith, 40803
Mirkovich & Assoc Inc, 40806
Mitchell & Co Inc, 40808
Mitchell Agencies, 40809
Mitchell of Mississippi, 40810
Moneuse Sales Agency, 40811
Mooney International, 40814
Morley Sales Co, 40817
Morton F Schweitzer Sales, 40819
Mueller Yurgae, 40824
Munn Marketing Group, 40827
Nagy Associates, 40832
Nash Wright Brokerage, 40836
National Brokerage Network, 40838
National Commodity Sales, 40840
National Food Group, 40841
National Food Sales, 40842, 40843
National Foodservice Marketing, 40844
National Heritage Sales Company, 40846
National Sign Corporation, 40848
NEMA Associates, 40831
Nesco Brokerage Company, 40851
Network Sales, Inc, 40852
New Horizons, 40853
Nippon Food Company, 40859
Nobert Marketing, 40860
Noble Foods, 40861
Norman Hecht, 40866
North Bay Trading Co, 40868
North Star Agency, 40870
Northwestern Foods, 40877
O'Brien & Associates Brokerage Company, 40880
O'Hanlon Group, 40881
O.R. Elder, 40883
Oekerman Sales, 40887
Ohm Design, 40888
Orca Foods, 40891
Osage Food Products Inc, 40893
Osborn Food Sales Company, 40894
Pacific Trading Company International, 40903
PacNorth Group, 40898
Pankow Associates Inc, 40905

Broker Market / Supermarket Chains

Patman Foods Inc, 40910
Paul Esposito Inc, 40913
Paul Inman Associates, 40915
Peak Corporation, 40916
Pennickers Food Distribution, 40917
Peters & Fair, 40920
Phillips Sales Co, 40922
Phoenix Food Sales, 40923
Pierce Cartwright Company, 40925
Pinski Portugal & Associate, 40926
Pioneer Food Service, 40928
Powell May International, 40935
Preferred Brokerage Company, 40936
Preisco Jentash, 40937
Premier Food Marketing, 40939
Premier Food Service Sales, 40940
Premium Seafood Co, 40942
Prestige Sales, 40944
Prestige Sales & Marketing, 40945
Professional Food Service, 40952
Professional Reps of Arizona, 40954
Progressive Brokerage Co Inc, 40955
Progressive Food Service Broker, 40956
Progressive Marketing Systems, 40957
Progressive Sales & Marketing, 40958
Promesa, 40959
Provincial, 40962
Quality Brokerage Company, 40965
Quality Food Company, 40966
Quality Sales & Marketing, Inc., 40968
Quality Sales & Marketing, 40969
R. Becker Marketing & Sales, 40974
R.F. Cannon Company, 40975
R.W. Berkeley & Associates, 40977
Rainbow Sales & Marketing, 40983
Randag & Assoc Inc, 40986
Ratcliff Food Brokers, 40988
Ray's Pride Brokerage Company, 40990
Reede International Seafood Corporation, 40992
Reichenbach & Associates, 40994
Rene Rivet, 40996
Rep Source, 40997
Res-Q Network, 40998
RH Sulker Sales, 40978
Rheuark/F.S.I. Sales, 41002
Richardson Petkovsek & Associates, 41004
Richs Sales Company, 41005
Ringland Associates, 41006
Rizwitsch Sales, 41010, 41011
RMCI Foodservice, 40980
Robbins Sales Co, 41012
Robert W. Hayman Inc, 41016
Rodon Foods, 41018
Roehl Corp, 41019
Roger J. Wood Company, 41020
Roos-Mohan, 41022
Rosenfeld & Gigante, 41024
Rosett Brokerage Company, 41025
Ross Empire State Brokers, 41026
Rubenstein Seafood Sales, 41030
Rudolph Brady, Inc, 41031
S&K Sales Company, 41034
S. Kamberg & Company, 41035
Sabal Marketing, 41045
Sabbers & Assoc Inc, 41046
Sachem Co, 41047
Salad Oils Intl Corp, 41049
Sales, 41050
Sales & Marketing Dev, 41051
Sales Corporation of Alaska, 41052
Sales Marketing Svc LLC, 41053
Sales Results, 41054
Santucci Associates, 41061
Saugy Inc., 41065
Saverino & Assoc, 41066
Scavuzzo Sales & Marketing, 41067
Schiff Food Products Co Inc, 41071
Schraad & Associates, 41072
Schreiber Foods Inc., 41073
Seaboard Foods, 41077
Seafood Sales, 41082
Service Group, 41086
Sessions & Associates, 41088
SFS Marketing, 41038
SHA Services, 41040
Shore Distribution Resources, 41092
Shrimp Tex Distributors, 41093
Sid Alpers Organic Sales Company, 41094
Sinco, 41097
Slagle & Associates, 41100
Slaybaugh & Associates, 41102
Sloan Sales Inc, 41103
Smart Cycling, Inc., 41104
South East Sales, 41110
South Group Marketing, 41111
Southeastern Paper Group Inc, 41113
Specialty Sales & Marketing, 41118
Spectrum Foodservice Associates, 41119
Spectrum Foodservices, 41120
Spencer & Assoc, 41122
St. Ours & Company, 41128
Statewide Brokerage Company, 41130
Stern International Consultants, 41132
Stevens & Associates, 41133
Stiefel Associates, 41134
Strong & Associates, 41138
Sturdivant Company, 41140
Sturgill Food Brokerage, 41141
Sullivan & Fitzgerald Food Brokers, 41142
Summit Brokerage, 41143
Summit FS LTD, 41144
Sun Marketing Agents Inc, 41146
Sundown Foods USA, Inc., 41148
Super Sale Brokerage Company, 41150
Supermarket Representatives, 41152
Supreme Foods, 41153
Supreme Foodservice Sales, 41154
T. McConnell Sales & Marketing, 41159
T.F.S. & Associates, 41160
T.W. Wilson & Son, 41162
Taormina Sales Company, 41166
Team Northwest, 41167
Teasley & Assoc, 41169
Tees & Persse Brokerage Acosta Sales And Marketing Company, Inc, 41172
Tees & Persse Brokerage, 41173
Terra Nova Brokers, 41175
Texas Foods, 41176
The Cherry Company Ltd., 41177
The Thurber Company, 41178
Thomas Vaccaro Inc, 41180
Thomas, Large & Singer, 41181
Thomson-Leeds Company, 41182
Thormann Associates, 41183
Tobiason Potato Co Inc, 41186
Top O' The Table, 41190
Tower Intercontinental Group, 41193
TRFG Inc, 41165
Tri-State Logistics Inc, 41199
Triad Brokers Inc, 41200
Triangle Sales, 41201
Tucker Sales, 41203
Twin City Food Brokers, 41206
Two Guys Spice Company, 41207
UBC Marketing, 41208
United Brands, 41212
United Brokers Company, 41213
United Foodservice Sales, 41214
United International Indstrs, 41215
United Restaurant Specialties, 41216
US Food Products, 41210
V.M. Calderon, 41220
Van Reed Sales Company, 41224
Virginia Fruit Sales Service, 41226
W.H. Escott Company, 41229
W.H. Moseley Co., 41230
Wallis & Barcinski, 41238
Watson & Associates, 41241
Waypoint, 41242
Webco General Partnership, 41243
Wehrfritz & Associates, 41245
Wendlandt Brokerage Company, 41248
WENS Brokerage, 41233
Wesco Food Brokerage, 41249
Whitby Co, 41254
Wieber-McLain Company, 41256
William B. Steedman & Sons, 41257
William Hyman Jr Associates, 41259
William M. Dunne & Associates Ltd, 41260
Williams Brokerage Company, 41261
Willing Group, 41263
Wilson Food Brokers, 41264
Wiltsie & Company, 41265
Winmix/Natural Care Products, 41266
Winpac, 41267
Wishbone Utensil Tableware Line, 41269
World Wide Safe Brokers, 41272
Wrap-It Packaging, 41274
Yankee Marketers, 41276
York Cheese, 41279
York Hospitality & Gaming, 41280
Young-Block Associates, 41282
Zanichelli & Associates, 41285

Supermarket Chains

3-D Marketing & Sales, 40001
A G Brown & Son, 40003
A M Source Inc, 40006
A Thomas Farris & Son Inc, 40007
A W Sisk & Son, 40008
A&D Sales Associates, 40009
A.J. Seibert Company, 40010
A.R. Pellegrini & Associates, 40012
ABC Enterprises, 40014
Access Partners, 40020
Acclaim Marketing & Sales, 40021
Acorn Sales Company, 40023
Acosta Sales & Marketing Company, 40024
Action Marketing, 40025
Action Marketing Associates, 40026
Action Marketing Of So Ca, 40027
Advance Marketing, 40030
Advantage Solutions, 40033
Advantage Webco Hawaii, 40034
Ake-Sullivan Associates, 40038
Albert A Russo Inc, 40040
All Seasons Brokerage Company, 40042
All-State Food Brokerage, 40043
Alliance Foods, 40044
Alliance Foods Inc, 40045
American Patriot Sales Inc, 40053
American Trading Company, 40055
AMT Sales & Marketing, 40016
Anthony Cea & Associates, 40061
Apache Brokers, 40062
Apple Food Sales, 40063
Arnett Brokerage Co, 40065
Arroyo Sales Company, 40066
Arthur G. Meier Company/Inland Products Company, 40067
Artisanal Foods, 40068
Arvin Sales Company, 40069
ATI, 40017
Atkinson Sales Company, 40073
Atkinson-Crawford Sales Co, 40074
Atlas Restaurant Supply, 40077
Avatar Food Group, 40080
B & D Sales & Marketing Inc, 40082
B&K Agencies, 40083
B.C. Tree Fruits Limited, 40085
Baker Brokerage Company LLC, 40092
Baker Sales, 40093
Baldwin & Mattson, 40094
Bay Brokerage Company, 40099
Bay Pacific Marketing, 40100
Becksmith Company, Inc, 40104
Bender-Goodman Co Inc, 40109
Benson-Mitchell, 40110
Bentley Food Marketing, 40111
Berk Enterprises, 40112
Best Brands, 40114
Binner Marketing & Sales, 40119
Bittinger Sales, 40123
Bixby Food Sales, 40124
Blackwing Ostrich Meats Inc., 40125
Bloodworth & Associates, 40126
BLV Marketing Inc, 40088, 40089
Bodie-Rickett & Associates, 40130
Boehmer Sales Agency, 40131
Booth, Schwager & Associates, 40132
Borton Brokerage Company, 40133
Bottom Line Foods, 40135
Bratt-Foster-Advantage Sales, 40138
Brennan Food Services, 40139
Bridge City Food Marketing, 40140
Brierley & King Brokerage Corporation, 40141
Brokerage Sales Company, 40144
Broms Brokerage, 40145
Browning Brokerage Company, 40147
BSE Marketing, 40090
Buckley, Thorne, Messina & McDermott, 40149
Budd Mayer Company of Jackson Inc., 40150
Budd Mayer of Mobile, 40151
Buley Patterson Sales Company, 40152
Burdett Associates, 40153
Burdette Beckmann Inc, 40154
Bushwick Commission Company, 40156
Butkevich Associates, 40157
Buzz Crown Enterprises, 40158
C.B. Powell Limited, 40165
C.W. Shasky & Associates Ltd., 40168
Cafe Inc, 40173
Cajun Creole Products Inc, 40174
Caneast Foods, 40176
Cann Brokerage Inc, 40177
Carlin Group, 40179
Cashman-Edwards Inc, 40184
Central Marketing Assoc, 40186
Central Sales & Marketing, 40187
Chandler Food Sales Co, 40189
Chapman-Tait Brokerage, Inc., 40191
Charles R. Bell Limited, 40193
Charles Rockel & Son, 40194
Chase Sales Company, 40198
Chase-Goldenberg Associates, 40199
Chell Brokerage Co, 40203
Chilay Corporation, 40205
Chuck Batcheller Company, 40208
Chuckrow Sales LLC, 40209
Citrin-Pitoscia Company, 40210
Classic Cuisine Foods, 40211
Clements Stella Marketing, 40213
Co-Sales De Credico, 40217
Coastal Commodities, 40218
Coastal Pride Co Inc, 40219
Collins Associates, 40222
Commodities Marketing Inc, 40227
Concept Food Brokers, 40228
Concord National, 40230, 40231, 40232, 40233, 40234, 40235
Concord Sales-Prairies, 40236
Conrad Sales Company, 40238
Consolidated Marketers Inc, 40239
Consolidated Merchandisers, 40240
Constant Sales, 40242
Consumer Brands, 40243
Consummate Marketing Company, 40244
Courtney Marketing Inc, 40253
Cox Food Brokers, 40254
Creightons, 40256
Crossmark, 40259
Crowley Marketing Assoc Park, 40260
Cruise Marketing, 40262
CS Brokers, 40172
Culinary Specialty Produce, 40263
Cyba-Stevens Management Group, 40265
D&D Marketing Group, Inc., 40266
D&R Food Brokers, 40268
Dambeck & Associates, 40280
Dave Swain Assoc Inc, 40282
David E Grimes Company, 40284
Davis Sales Associates, 40286
DBB Marketing Company, 40269
Dealers Choice, 40292
Deibert & Associates, 40293
DeJarnett Sales, 40289, 40290
Dennis Sales, 40296
Di Meo-Gale Brokerage Company, 40297
Diamond Chemical & Supply Co, 40299
Dino-Meat Company, 40302

Broker Market / Supermarket Chains

Donald R Conyer Associates, 40307
Doug Milne Co, 40309
Douglas Sales Associates, 40310
Dreyer Marketing, 40312
DSI Food Brokerage, 40271
Dunbar Sales Company, Inc, 40315
Eagle Associates, 40322
Eagle Marketing, 40323
Eastern Sales & Marketing, 40325
Eastern Sales and Marketing, 40326
Ebbert Sales & Marketing, 40327
EFD Associate, 40321
Egerstrom Inc, 40329
Eiseman-Gleit Co Inc, 40330
Elias Shaker & Co, 40333
Elliot Horowitz & Co, 40334
Ellis S. Fine Co., Inc., 40335
Esm Ferolie, 40343
Esposito Brokerage, 40344
Essential Food Marketing, 40346
Ettinger Rosini & Associates, 40347
Evans & Associates, 40350
Evans Brokerage Company, 40351
Evers Heilig Inc, 40352
F Mc Lintocks Saloon & Dinin, 40355
F. Rothman Enterprises, LLC, 40356
Fairley & Co Inc, 40360
Federated Group, 40361
Feenix Brokerage LTD, 40362
Ferdinand Richards & Son, 40363
Ferolie Esm-Metro New York, 40364
Fischer Group, 40369
Five State Brokerage, 40371
Flynn Sales Associates, Inc., 40375
FMI Food Marketers International Ltd, 40359
Fold-Pak LLC, 40376
Food Associates of Syracuse, 40377
Food Service Associates, 40382
Food Service Connection, 40383
Foodmark Sales, 40388
Foodsales Inc, 40389
Forseasons Sales, 40399
Frank Kinsman Assoc, 40402
Frank M Hartley Co, 40403
Freedom Food Brokers, 40405
Freeman Signature, 40409
Freiria & Company, 40410
Frozen Food Associates, 40412
GAP Food Brokers, 40415
Garden Gold Foods, Inc, 40419
Garisco Distributing, 40420
Gasparini Sales Inc, 40421
Gateway Food Service, 40422
Genesis Marketing, 40426
George E. Dent Sales, 40428
George Perry & Sons Inc, 40429
George W. Holop Associates, 40430
GFR Worldwide, 40417
Gibbs & Assoc, 40432
Gibbs-Mccormick Inc A Ca Corp, 40433
Gillette Creamery, 40435
Glenmoor Brokerage, 40438
Golden Valley Industries Inc, 40440
Golick Martins, Inc., 40441
Goveco Full Service Food Brokers, 40444
Grabbe-Leonard Co, 40445
Great Southwest Sales Company, 40448
Gurrentz International Corp, 40453
H. White Sales Company, 40456
H.R. Plate & Company, 40457
H.V. Mid State Sales Company, 40458
Halling Company, 40465
Hansid Company, 40469
Harold J. Barrett Company, 40470
Harold M. Lincoln Company, 40471
Harriet Greenland Enterprises, 40472
Harris Freeman, 40473
Harry Tinseth Associates, Inc., 40474
Hartley S. Johnson & Son, 40475
Harvest Grove Inc, 40476
Harvey-Winchell Company, 40477
Hatch-Jennings Inc, 40478
Hawley & Assoc, 40480

HD Marshall Ltd, 40460
Henry J. Hips Company, 40483
Herspring, 40485
Hinkle Easter Products, 40488
Hockenberg Newburgh, 40490, 40491
Hugh T. Gilmore Company, 40498
Hundley Brokerage Company, 40499
Hunter Walton & Co Inc, 40500
Hynes Bond Ellison, 40502, 40503
Iceberg Seafood Inc, 40509
Imark of Pennsylvania, 40510
Imperial Dade, 40512
Imperial Florida Sales, 40513
Inter-American Products, 40523
Intermountain Food Brokerage, 40525
International Coffee Corporation, 40526
International Gourmet Products, 40527
International Pacific Seafood, 40529
International Sales & Brokerage Company, 40530
Interstate Food Brokers, 40535
Inverso Johnson LLC, 40538
ISB Sales Company, 40504
ISSCO, 40506
ITA Inc, 40507
ITOCHU International, Inc, 40508
J Carroll & Assoc, 40539
J N Rhodes Co Inc, 40542
J R Kelly Co, 40543
J T Gibbons Inc, 40544
J&J Brokerage, 40546
J. Maganas Sales Company, 40548
J.E. Julian & Associates, 40549
J.F. Benz Company, 40550
J.L. Epstein & Son, 40553
J.W. Harrison & Son, 40555
Jacobsen-Clahan & Company, 40565
Jay Mark Group LTD, 40568
Jeram Associates, 40570
JL Stemp Marketing Agents, 40558
JML Sales Co, 40560
John H. Elton, 40576
John J Wollack Co Inc, 40577
John Mangum Company, 40579
Johnson Holmes & Assoc Inc, 40582
Johnson O'Hare Co, 40583
Jon Morris & Company, 40585
Jones Neitzel Co, 40586
Jones-McCormick & Associates, 40587
Jos Iorio Company, 40588
Jose M Perez-Pages, 40589
Joseph Caragol, 40590
Joseph W Nath Co, 40593
Joylin Food Equipment Corporation, 40594
JP Bissonnette, 40561
JP Carroll Company, 40562
Jso Associates Inc, 40596
Jubilee Sales of Carolina, 40597
Juhl Brokerage, 40599
Julius Levy Company, 40601
Julius M. Dean Company, 40602
Kahler-Senders Inc, 40612
Kandy King Confections, 40613
Kappert/Hyzer Company, 40614
KDH Sales, 40609
Keeth & Associates, 40622
Kelley-Clarke, 40623
Kelly Associates/Food Brokers, 40625
Kenney Sales, 40630
Key Sales & Marketing, 40634
Key Sales Group, 40635
Kidd Enterprises, 40637
Kiefer's, 40638
Kinder-Smith Company, 40639
Kingery & Assoc, 40643
Kirkbride & Associates, 40647
Kirstein Brokerage Company, 40648
Klensch Cheese Company, 40650
Klinger & Speros Food Brokers, 40651
Klondike Foods, 40652
Koch & Assoc, 40654
Koehler Borden & Assoc, 40655
Korth Marketing, 40656
Kramer Brokerage Co, 40657

Krass-Joseph, 40658
L H Gamble Co LTD, 40660
L&S Sales Company, 40661
LA Teste Services, 40662
Lake Michigan Growers, 40672
Landers Ag Resources, 40678
Landmark Foods, 40679
Larry Fox & Co, 40681
LBM Sales, LLC, 40664
Lehigh Food Sales Inc, 40685
LeMire Sales, 40682
Leonard H Sisitzky Sales Inc, 40689
Lisberg-Voegeli Hanson, 40696
Littman & Associates, 40698
Lloyd A Gray Co Inc, 40699
LMGO International Inc, 40666
Loar & Young Inc, 40701
Lobel Food Brokers, 40702
Lomac & May Associates, 40703
Loman Brown, 40704
Lorey & Lorey, 40707
Louis F. Leeper Company/Cleveland, 40710
Luke Soules Southwest, 40713
M Arkans & Son, 40716
M Fellinger Co, 40717
M. Pencar Associates, 40720
M. Soffer Company, 40721
M.E. Dilanian Company, 40722
M.E. Strauss Brokerage Company, 40723
Maddan & Co Inc, 40729
Magic Valley Truck Brokers Inc, 40731
Main Street Marketing, 40732
Major Marketing Service, 40735
Maloney Veitch Associates, 40737
Mancini & Groesbeck, 40738
Mancini Sales & Marketing, 40740
Manuel's Mexican-American Fine Foods, 40741
Manzo Food Brokers, 40742
Marbran USA, 40744
Marino Marketing Group, 40746
Marjo & Associates, 40747
Market Pro International, 40749
Market Smart, 40750
Market West Company, 40751
Marketing Management Inc, 40754
Marmelstein Associates, 40755
Master Sales & Marketing, 40764
Matrix Group Inc., 40766
MAV Sales Co, 40725
Max Pratt Company, 40767
Mc Namara Assoc Inc, 40769
McArdle, 40770
McCormick Brokerage Company, 40773
Meadows Brokerage Company, 40775
Measured Sales & Marketing, 40776
Menu Planners, 40777
Meridian Products, 40779
Merit Sales Corporation, 40781
Michael R Fish & Co, 40782
Mickelson & Associates, 40784
Micosa Inc, 40785
Mid-American Brokerage of St. Louis, 40787
Mid-Continent Sales, 40788
Mid-West Sales Agency, 40791
Midland Marketing Co-Op Inc, 40792
Midwest Ingredients Inc, 40797
Miller's Market, 40802
Miller, Stabler & Smith, 40803
Mirandas' Sales & Merchandising, 40805
Mirkovich & Assoc Inc, 40806
Mitchell & Co Inc, 40808
Mitchell Agencies, 40809
Mitchell of Mississippi, 40810
Moneuse Sales Agency, 40811
Moody Dunbar Inc, 40813
Morley Sales Co, 40817
Morton F Schweitzer Sales, 40819
Mueller Yurgae, 40824
Munchies, 40826
Munn Marketing Group, 40827
N.H. Cohen & Associates, 40830
Nagy Associates, 40832

Nanni-Marketal, 40834
Napoleon Co., 40835
Nash Wright Brokerage, 40836
National Brokerage Network, 40838
National Commodity Sales, 40840
National Food Sales, 40842
National Heritage Sales Company, 40846
National Sign Corporation, 40848
Network Sales, Inc, 40852
New Horizons, 40853
Next Phase Enterprises, 40855
Nippon Food Company, 40859
Nobert Marketing, 40860
Noble Foods, 40861
Nomura & Co, 40863
Noon International, 40864
Norman Hecht, 40866
North Bay Trading Co, 40868
North Star Agency, 40870
Northeast Retail Services, 40872
Northeastern Enterprises, 40873
Northland Express Transport, 40874
Northwestern Foods, 40877
O'Brien & Associates Brokerage Company, 40880
O'Hanlon Group, 40881
Oak Leaf Sales Co, 40885
Oekerman Sales, 40887
Ohm Design, 40888
Omni Food Inc, 40890
Orca Foods, 40891
Osborn Food Sales Company, 40894
Pace Target Brokerage, 40899
Pacific Trading Company International, 40903
PacNorth Group, 40898
Pankow Associates Inc, 40905
Paradise Food Brokers, 40906
Parks Brokerage Company, 40909
Patman Foods Inc, 40910
Patman Meat Group, 40911
Patterson Co Inc, 40912
Paul Esposito Inc, 40913
Paul G Nester & Son Co Inc, 40914
Paul Inman Associates, 40915
Peak Corporation, 40916
Pennickers Food Distribution, 40917
Peter Blease Sales, 40918
Peters & Fair, 40920
Phillips Sales Co, 40922
Phoenix Food Sales, 40923
Phoenix Foods Inc, 40924
Pierce Cartwright Company, 40925
Pioneer Food Brokers, 40927
Pioneer Marketing International, 40929
Polish Folklore Import Co, 40932
Preferred Brokerage Company, 40936
Preisco Jentash, 40937
Premier Food Marketing, 40939
Premier Food Service Sales, 40940
Premium Seafood Co, 40942
Prestige Marketing, 40943
Prestige Sales, 40944
Prestige Sales & Marketing, 40945
Professional Reps of Arizona, 40954
Progressive Brokerage Co Inc, 40955
Progressive Marketing Systems, 40957
Progressive Sales & Marketing, 40958
Promesa, 40959
Providence Brokerage, 40961
Provincial, 40962
Quality Sales & Marketing, Inc., 40968
R G Sellers Co, 40970
R J Bickert & Associates, 40972
R. Becker Marketing & Sales, 40974
R.F. Cannon Company, 40975
R.W. Berkeley & Associates, 40977
Rabe Sales Corp, 40981
Rainbow Sales & Marketing, 40983
Rancho Sales & Marketing, 40985
Ratcliff Food Brokers, 40988
Reese Brokerage Co, 40993
Reichenbach & Associates, 40994
Rep Source, 40997
Resource One, 40999

Broker Market / Wholesale Distributors

RH Sulker Sales, 40978
Rich Audette Associates, 41003
Ringland Associates, 41006
Ritt-Beyer Inc, 41008
Rizwitsch Sales, 41010, 41011
RMCI Foodservice, 40980
Robbins Sales Co, 41012
Robert A. Haines Companies, 41013
Robert W. Hayman Inc, 41016
Rocky Mountain Motel, 41017
Rodon Foods, 41018
Roehl Corp, 41019
Roger J. Wood Company, 41020
Roos-Mohan, 41022
Ross Empire State Brokers, 41026
Rubenstein Seafood Sales, 41030
Rudolph Brady, Inc, 41031
S&K Sales Company, 41034
S. Kamberg & Company, 41035
Sabal Marketing, 41045
Sabbers & Assoc Inc, 41046
Sachem Co, 41047
Salad Oils Intl Corp, 41049
Sales, 41050
Sales Corporation of Alaska, 41052
Sales Marketing Svc LLC, 41053
Sales Results, 41054
Sales Specialties, 41055
Santucci Associates, 41061
Saugy Inc., 41065
Saverino & Assoc, 41066
Scavuzzo Sales & Marketing, 41067
Schaper Company, 41068
Schiff Food Products Co Inc, 41071
Schraad & Associates, 41072
Scott & Associates, 41076
SCS Sales Company, 41037
Seaboard Foods, 41077
Seafood Sales, 41082
Select Sales & Marketing Inc, 41084
Sell Group, 41085
Service Group, 41086
Sessions & Associates, 41088
SGS International Rice Inc, 41039
SHA Services, 41040
Shields Brokerage, 41091
Shore Distribution Resources, 41092
Shrimp Tex Distributors, 41093
Sid Alpers Organic Sales Company, 41094
Sinco, 41097
SJE Marketing Corporation, 41041
Slattery Marketing Corporation, 41101
Sloan Sales Inc, 41103
Smigiel Marketing & Sales Ltd., 41105
Southeastern Paper Group Inc, 41113
Specialty Partners, 41117
Specialty Sales & Marketing, 41118
Spectrum Foodservice Associates, 41119
Spencer & Assoc, 41122
St Charles Trading Inc, 41126
St. Ours & Company, 41128
Statewide Brokerage Company, 41130
Stern International Consultants, 41132
Stevens & Associates, 41133
Stiefel Associates, 41134
Stockdale & Reagan, 41135
Strong & Associates, 41138
Sturdivant Company, 41140
Sturgill Food Brokerage, 41141
Sullivan & Fitzgerald Food Brokers, 41142
Summit FS LTD, 41144
Sun Marketing Agents Inc, 41146
Sundown Foods USA, Inc., 41148
Sunwest Sales Co, 41149
Super Sale Brokerage Company, 41150
Supermarket Representatives, 41152
Supreme Foods, 41153
T. McConnell Sales & Marketing, 41159
T.F.S. & Associates, 41160
T.J. Hines & Company, 41161
T.W. Wilson & Son, 41162
Team Northwest, 41167, 41168
Teasley & Assoc, 41169

Technical Sales Associates, 41171
Tees & Persse Brokerage Acosta Sales And Marketing Company, Inc, 41172
Tees & Persse Brokerage, 41173
Terra Nova Brokers, 41175
The Cherry Company Ltd., 41177
Thomas Food Brokers, 41179
Thomas Vaccaro Inc, 41180
Thomas, Large & Singer, 41181
Thomson-Leeds Company, 41182
Thormann Associates, 41183
Tobiason Potato Co Inc, 41186
Top O' The Table, 41190
Tri-State Logistics Inc, 41199
Try-Angle Food Brokers Inc, 41202
Tucker Sales, 41203
Twin City Food Brokers, 41206
UBC Marketing, 41208
United Brands, 41212
United Brokers Company, 41213
United Foodservice Sales, 41214
V.M. Calderon, 41220
Van Reed Sales Company, 41224
Virginia Fruit Sales Service, 41226
W.H. Escott Company, 41229
W.H. Moseley Co., 41230
Ward Hughes Co, 41239
Watson & Associates, 41241
Waypoint, 41242
Webeco Foods, Inc, 41244
Wehrfritz & Associates, 41245
WENS Brokerage, 41233
Wesco Food Brokerage, 41249
Westex, 41253
Whitby Co, 41254
Wieber-McLain Company, 41256
William B. Steedman & Sons, 41257
William Hyman Jr Associates, 41259
William M. Dunne & Associates Ltd, 41260
Williams Brokerage Company, 41261
Willing Group, 41263
Wilson Food Brokers, 41264
Wiltsie & Company, 41265
Winmix/Natural Care Products, 41266
Winpac, 41267
WJ Pence Company, 41234
World Wide Safe Brokers, 41272
Wrap-It Packaging, 41274
Yates Sales Associates, 41277
Yeager & Associates, 41278
York Cheese, 41279
Young-Block Associates, 41282
Zanichelli & Associates, 41285

Wholesale Distributors

3-D Marketing & Sales, 40001
A G Brown & Son, 40003
A M Source Inc, 40006
A Thomas Farris & Son Inc, 40007
A W Sisk & Son, 40008
A&D Sales Associates, 40009
A.J. Seibert Company, 40010
A.R. Pellegrini & Associates, 40012
ABC Enterprises, 40014
Abramson & Di Benedetto Mktng, 40019
Acclaim Marketing & Sales, 40021
Acorn Sales Company, 40023
Acosta Sales & Marketing Company, 40024
Action Marketing, 40025
Action Marketing Associates, 40026
Action Marketing Of So Ca, 40027
Advance Marketing, 40030
Advance Sales & Marketing, Inc, 40031
Advantage Solutions, 40033
Advantage Webco Hawaii, 40034
Agri-Dairy Products, 40036
Albert A Russo Inc, 40040
All Seasons Brokerage Company, 40042
All-State Food Brokerage, 40043
Alliance Foods, 40044
Alliance Foods Inc, 40045
Allied Marketing Corp, 40046

Alpine Summit Sales Inc, 40048
Alquima USA Inc, 40049
Ambi-Prestigio Foods Inc, 40050
American Patriot Sales Inc, 40053
American Sales & Marketing, 40054
American Trading Company, 40055
AmericanLifestyle.Com, 40056
AMT Sales & Marketing, 40016
Anchor Florida Marketing, 40058
Anderson Daymon Worldwide, 40060
Anthony Cea & Associates, 40061
Apache Brokers, 40062
Apple Food Sales, 40063
Arnett Brokerage Co, 40065
Arthur G. Meier Company/Inland Products Company, 40067
Artisanal Foods, 40068
Arvin Sales Company, 40069
ATI, 40017
Atkinson-Crawford Sales Co, 40074
Atlantis Smoked Foods, 40075
Automatic Packaging Systems & Conveyors Company, 40078
Avatar Food Group, 40080
B & D Sales & Marketing Inc, 40082
B&K Agencies, 40083
B.C. Ritchie Company, 40084
B.C. Tree Fruits Limited, 40085
B.W. Dyer & Company, 40086
Baker Brokerage Company LLC, 40092
Baker Sales, 40093
BAL Marketing, 40087
Bassett-Carragher Associates, 40098
Bay Brokerage Company, 40099
Bay Pacific Marketing, 40100
Bayha & Associates, 40101
Beck Western Brokerage, 40103
Becksmith Company, Inc, 40104
Bee Jay Sales Of Florida, 40106
Bender-Goodman Co Inc, 40109
Benson-Mitchell, 40110
Bentley Food Marketing, 40111
Berk Enterprises, 40112
Bertran Enterprises, 40113
Best Brands, 40114
Best Marketing Reps, 40115
Binner Marketing & Sales, 40119
Bireta Company, 40121
Bittinger Sales, 40123
Bixby Food Sales, 40124
Blackwing Ostrich Meats Inc., 40125
Bloodworth & Associates, 40126
BLV Marketing Inc, 40088, 40089
Bob Rowe Sales, 40128
Bodie-Rickett & Associates, 40130
Boehmer Sales Agency, 40131
Booth, Schwager & Associates, 40132
Borton Brokerage Company, 40133
Bottom Line Foods, 40135
Bowerman Associates, 40136
Bratt-Foster-Advantage Sales, 40138
Brennan Food Services, 40139
Bridge City Food Marketing, 40140
Brierley & King Brokerage Corporation, 40141
Brokerage Sales Company, 40144
Broms Brokerage, 40145
Browning Brokerage Company, 40147
BSE Marketing, 40090
Buckley, Thorne, Messina & McDermott, 40149
Budd Mayer Company of Jackson Inc., 40150
Budd Mayer of Mobile, 40151
Buley Patterson Sales Company, 40152
Burdett Associates, 40153
Burdette Beckmann Inc, 40154
Burley Brokerage, 40155
Bushwick Commission Company, 40156
Butkevich Associates, 40157
Buzz Crown Enterprises, 40158
Byrne & Assoc Inc, 40160
C J Irwin Co Inc, 40162
C. Mascari & Associates, 40164
C.R. Peterson Associates, 40167

C.W. Shasky & Associates Ltd., 40168
Cafe Inc, 40173
Cajun Creole Products Inc, 40174
California World Trade and Marketing Company, 40175
Caneast Foods, 40176
Cann Brokerage Inc, 40177
Carlin Group, 40179
Carpenter Associates, 40181
Cascade Corp, 40183
Cashman-Edwards Inc, 40184
Central Marketing Assoc, 40186
Central Sales & Marketing, 40187
Chandler Food Sales Co, 40189
Chapman-Tait Brokerage, Inc., 40191
Charles Pace & Assoc Inc, 40192
Charles R. Bell Limited, 40193
Charles Rockel & Son, 40194
Charles Stube Co Inc, 40195
Charlie Brown Sales Company, 40196
Chartrand Imports, 40197
Chase-Goldenberg Associates, 40199
Cheese & Dairy Products, 40202
Chell Brokerage Co, 40203
Chilay Corporation, 40205
Christian Brokerage Company/Industrial & Food, 40206
Chuck Batcheller Company, 40208
Chuckrow Sales LLC, 40209
Citrin-Pitoscia Company, 40210
CJ Eaton Brokerage, 40169
Classic Cuisine Foods, 40211
Clements Stella Marketing, 40213
Clipper Mill, 40214
CLVMarketing, 40170
Co-Sales De Credico, 40217
Coastal Commodities, 40218
Coastal Pride Co Inc, 40219
Cobler Food Sales, 40220
Colony Brokerage Company, 40224
Commercial Kitchens Reps Inc, 40226
Commodities Marketing Inc, 40227
Concept Food Brokers, 40228
Concept Food Sales, 40229
Concord National, 40230, 40231, 40232, 40235
Conlin Brokerage Company, 40237
Conrad Sales Company, 40238
Consolidated Marketers Inc, 40239
Consolidated Merchandisers, 40240
Consolidated Tea Co Inc, 40241
Constant Sales, 40242
Consumer Brands, 40243
Consummate Marketing Company, 40244
Convenience Marketing Services, 40247
Core Group, 40251
Courtney Marketing Inc, 40253
Cox Food Brokers, 40254
Creightons, 40256
Crider Brokerage Company, 40258
Crossmark, 40259
Cruise Marketing, 40262
CS Brokers, 40172
Culinary Specialty Produce, 40263
Cyba-Stevens Management Group, 40265
D&R Food Brokers, 40268
Dakco International, 40276
Dakota Marketing Company, 40277
Dambeck & Associates, 40280
Dave Roemer & Associates, 40281
Dave Swain Assoc Inc, 40282
David E Grimes Company, 40284
Davis Sales Associates, 40286
DBB Marketing Company, 40269
Dd Reckner Co, 40288
Dealers Choice, 40292
Deibert & Associates, 40293
Deiss Sales Co. Inc., 40294
DeJarnett Sales, 40289, 40290
Delbert Craig Food Brokers, 40295
DeMoss & Associates, 40291
Dennis Sales, 40296
Di Meo-Gale Brokerage Company, 40297
Diamond Chemical & Supply Co, 40299
Diaz Sales, 40300

Broker Market / Wholesale Distributors

Dino-Meat Company, 40302
Donald R Conyer Associates, 40307
Doug Milne Co, 40309
Douglas Sales Associates, 40310
DRC Marketing Group, 40270
DSI Food Brokerage, 40271
Dunbar Sales Company, Inc, 40315
DVC Brokerage Company, 40272
DW Montgomery & Company, 40273
E Ruff & Assoc Inc, 40319
Eagle Associates, 40322
Eagle Marketing, 40323
Eastern Sales & Marketing, 40325
Eastern Sales and Marketing, 40326
Ebbert Sales & Marketing, 40327
Ed O'Connor Associates, 40328
EFD Associate, 40321
Egerstrom Inc, 40329
Eiseman-Gleit Co Inc, 40330
Elias Shaker & Co, 40333
Elliot Horowitz & Co, 40334
Ellis S. Fine Co., Inc., 40335
Emerling International Foods, 40336
Encore Fruit Marketing Inc, 40337
Enterprise Food Brokers, 40339
Erickson Brothers Brokerage Co, 40340
Esm Ferolie, 40343
Esposito Brokerage, 40344
Essential Food Marketing, 40346
Ettinger Rosini & Associates, 40347
Evans & Associates, 40350
Evans Brokerage Company, 40351
Evers Heilig Inc, 40352
F M Turner Co Inc, 40354
F Mc Lintocks Saloon & Dinin, 40355
F. Rothman Enterprises, LLC, 40356
Fairley & Co Inc, 40360
Federated Group, 40361
Feenix Brokerage LTD, 40362
Ferdinand Richards & Son, 40363
Ferolie Esm-Metro New York, 40364
Finn Marketing Group Inc, 40365
First Choice Sales Company, 40367
First Flight Foods, 40368
Fischer Group, 40369
Five Star Packaging, 40370
Five State Brokerage, 40371
Florida Agents Inc, 40373
Flynn Sales Associates, Inc., 40375
FM Carriere & Son, 40358
FMI Food Marketers International Ltd, 40359
Fold-Pak LLC, 40376
Food Associates of Syracuse, 40377
Food Equipment Rep Inc, 40378
Food Sales Systems, 40380
Food Sales West, 40381
Food Service Associates, 40382
Food Service Connection, 40383
Food Service Marketing of Pennsylvania, 40384
Foodmark Sales, 40388
Foodservice Marketing, 40391
Foodworks International, 40393
Forbes Hever & Wallace, Inc., 40396
Forseasons Sales, 40399
Frank Kinsman Assoc, 40402
Frank M Hartley Inc, 40403
Fredco Wolf, 40404
Freedom Food Brokers, 40405
Freeman Signature, 40409
Freiria & Company, 40410
Fromartharie Inc, 40411
Frozen Food Associates, 40412
Fusion Sales Group, 40413
G.A. Davis Food Service, 40414
GAP Food Brokers, 40415
Garden Gold Foods, Inc, 40419
Garisco Distributing, 40420
Gasparini Sales Inc, 40421
Gateway Food Service, 40422
Gehrke Co, 40423
Genesis International, 40425
Genesis Marketing, 40426
George E. Dent Sales, 40428
George Perry & Sons Inc, 40429
George W. Holop Associates, 40430
GFR Worldwide, 40417
Gibbs & Assoc, 40432
Gibbs-Mccormick Inc A Ca Corp, 40433
Glacier Sales Inc, 40437
Glenmoor Brokerage, 40438
Golden Valley Industries Inc, 40440
Golick Martins, Inc., 40441
Goveco Full Service Food Brokers, 40444
Grabbe-Leonard Co, 40445
Great Southwest Sales Company, 40448
Griffin Marketing Group, 40450
Gulf States Food Service Marketing, 40452
Gurrentz International Corp, 40453
H & G Trading LTD Inc, 40454
H&T Food Marketing Company, 40455
H. White Sales Company, 40456
H.R. Plate & Company, 40457
H.V. Mid State Sales Company, 40458
Halal Transactions, 40464
Halling Company, 40465
Hanimex Company, 40466
Hanks Brokerage, 40467
Hansen Group, 40468
Hansid Company, 40469
Harold M. Lincoln Company, 40471
Harriet Greenland Enterprises, 40472
Harris Freeman, 40473
Harry Tinseth Associates, Inc., 40474
Hartley S. Johnson & Son, 40475
Harvest Grove Inc, 40476
Harvey-Winchell Company, 40477
Hatch-Jennings Inc, 40478
Hawley & Assoc, 40480
HCB Foodservice Sales & Marketing, 40459
HD Marshall Ltd, 40460
Henry J. Hips Company, 40483
Herspring, 40485
HGA Group, 40461
Hilgenfeld Brokerage Co, 40487
Hinkle Easter Products, 40488
HK Marketing, 40462
Hobby Whalen Marketing, 40489
Hockenberg Newburgh, 40490, 40491
Hockenberg-Newburgh Sales, 40492
Hollar & Greene, 40493
Howell Associates, 40496
Hugh T. Gilmore Company, 40498
Hundley Brokerage Company, 40499
Hunter Walton & Co Inc, 40500
Iceberg Seafood Inc, 40509
Imark of Pennsylvania, 40510
Imperial Dade, 40512
Imperial Frozen Foods Co, 40514
Ingredient Exchange Co, 40517
Ingredient Inc, 40518
Insulated Structures/PB Group, 40520
Integra Marketing Inc, 40521
Inter-American Products, 40523
Intermountain Food Brokerage, 40525
International Coffee Corporation, 40526
International Gourmet Products, 40527
International Pacific Seafood, 40529
International Sales & Brokerage Company, 40530
Interpack NW Frozen Food, 40531
Intersouth Foodservice Group, 40534
Interstate Food Brokers, 40535
Interwest Ingredient Sales, 40536
Intralinks Inc, 40537
Inverso Johnson LLC, 40538
ISB Sales Company, 40504
ISC of Indiana, 40505
ISSCO, 40506
ITA Inc, 40507
J N Rhodes Co Inc, 40542
J R Kelly Co, 40543
J T Gibbons Inc, 40544
J&J Brokerage, 40546
J. Maganas Sales Company, 40548
J.E. Julian & Associates, 40549
J.F. Benz Company, 40550
J.H. Bridgins & Associates, 40552
J.L. Epstein & Son, 40553
J.W. Harrison & Son, 40555
Jack Curren & Associates, 40564
Jacobsen-Clahan & Company, 40565
Jay Mark Group LTD, 40568
Jeram Associates, 40570
Jewell/Barksdale Associates, 40571
Jim Pless & Company, 40573
JL Stemp Marketing Agents, 40558
JML Sales Co, 40560
Jodawnco, 40574
John H Thier Co, 40575
John H. Elton, 40576
John J Wollack Co Inc, 40577
John L. Pieri & Sons, 40578
John Mangum Company, 40579
Johnny Bee Sales, 40580
Johnson Commercial Agents, 40581
Johnson Holmes & Assoc Inc, 40582
Johnson O'Hare Co, 40583
Johnson, Arlyn & Associates, 40584
Jones Neitzel Co, 40586
Jones-McCormick & Associates, 40587
Jos Iorio Company, 40588
Joseph Caragol, 40590
Joseph W Nath Co, 40593
Joylin Food Equipment Corporation, 40594
JP Bissonnette, 40561
JP Carroll Company, 40562
Jso Associates Inc, 40596
Jubilee Sales of Carolina, 40597
Juhl Brokerage, 40598, 40599
Julius Levy Company, 40601
Julius M. Dean Company, 40602
Kahler-Senders Inc, 40612
Kandy King Confections, 40613
Kappert/Hyzer Company, 40614
Kathryn's Food Service Brokers, 40616
KBRW, 40608
KDH Sales, 40609
Keeth & Associates, 40622
Kelley-Clarke, 40623
Kelly/Mincks Northwest Agents, 40627
Kemper Food Brokers, 40628
Kenney Sales, 40630
Key Impact Sales & Systems Inc, 40633
Key Sales & Marketing, 40634
Key Sales Group, 40635
KeyImpact Sales & Systems, Inc., 40636
KH McClure & Company, 40610
Kidd Enterprises, 40637
Kiefer's, 40638
KIKO Foods Inc, 40611
Kinder-Smith Company, 40639
Kingery & Assoc, 40643
Kirstein Brokerage Company, 40648
Klensch Cheese Company, 40650
Klinger & Speros Food Brokers, 40651
Klondike Foods, 40652
Koch & Assoc, 40654
Koehler Borden & Assoc, 40655
Korth Marketing, 40656
Krass-Joseph, 40658
Kurtz Food Brokers, 40659
L H Gamble Co LTD, 40660
L&S Sales Company, 40661
LA Teste Services, 40662
LAD Foodservice Sales, 40663
Lake & Lake Inc, 40671
Lake Michigan Growers, 40672
Lakeside Food Sales Inc, 40673
Lamborn & Company, 40674
Landers Ag Resources, 40678
Landmark Foods, 40679
Larry Fox & Co, 40681
LBM Sales, LLC, 40664
Lehigh Food Sales Inc, 40685
Lehmann Brokerage Co, 40686
LeMire Sales, 40682
Lemmons Company, 40687
Len Miller & Associates, 40688
Leonard H Sisitzky Sales Inc, 40689
Lever Associates, 40691
Lilburn Gulf, 40694
Linwood-Welch Marketing, 40695
Lisberg-Voegeli Hanson, 40696
Littler Brokerage Co Inc, 40697
Littman & Associates, 40698
Lloyd A Gray Co Inc, 40699
Lloyd Hollander Company, 40700
LMGO International Inc, 40666
LMS Associate, 40667
Loar & Young Inc, 40701
Lobel Food Brokers, 40702
Lomac & May Associates, 40703
Loman Brown, 40704
Long & Littleton, 40705
Lorey & Lorey, 40707
Lotto International, 40709
Louis F. Leeper Company/Cleveland, 40710
Lowe & Associates, 40711
Ludwig Mueller Co Inc, 40712
Luke Soules Southwest, 40713
Lund-Iorio Inc, 40714
M K Food Svc Equipment Inc, 40718
M&W Associates, 40719
M. Soffer Company, 40721
M.E. Dilanian Company, 40722
M.E. Strauss Brokerage Company, 40723
M.J. Borelli & Company, 40724
Maddan & Co Inc, 40729
Magic Valley Truck Brokers Inc, 40731
Main Street Marketing, 40732
Major Marketing Service, 40735
Maloney Veitch Associates, 40737
Mancini & Groesbeck, 40738
Mancini Sales & Marketing, 40740
Manuel's Mexican-American Fine Foods, 40741
Manzo Food Brokers, 40742
Marbran USA, 40744
Marchetti Co, 40745
Marino Marketing Group, 40746
Marjo & Associates, 40747
Market Smart, 40750
Market West Company, 40751
Marketing Agents South, 40752
Marketing Management Inc, 40754
Marmelstein Associates, 40755
Marshall Associates, 40756
Martin Preferred Foods, 40758
Marty Scanlon Brokerage Co, 40759
Master Marketing South, 40762
Master Sales & Marketing, 40764
Matrix Group Inc., 40766
MAV Sales Co, 40725
Max Pratt Company, 40767
Mc Namara Assoc Inc, 40769
McArdle, 40770
McClement Sales Company, 40772
McCormick Brokerage Company, 40773
McGovern & Whitten, 40774
Meadows Brokerage Company, 40775
Measured Sales & Marketing, 40776
Menu Planners, 40777
Mercantum Corp, 40778
Meridian Products, 40779
Merit Sales Corporation, 40781
Michael R Fish & Co, 40782
Mickelson & Associates, 40784
Mid-American Brokerage of St. Louis, 40787
Mid-Continent Sales, 40788
Mid-West Associates, 40790
Mid-West Sales Agency, 40791
Midlantic Sweetener Co, 40793
Midwest Ingredients Inc, 40797
Milky Whey Inc, 40799
Miller & Smith Foods, 40800
Miller & Stryker Assoc Inc, 40801
Miller's Market, 40802
Miller, Stabler & Smith, 40803
Mirandas' Sales & Merchandising, 40805
Mirkovich & Assoc Inc, 40806
Mitchel Beck Company, 40807
Mitchell & Co Inc, 40808

103

Broker Market / Wholesale Distributors

Mitchell Agencies, 40809
Mitchell of Mississippi, 40810
Moneuse Sales Agency, 40811
Moody Dunbar Inc, 40813
Mooney International, 40814
Morgan Sampson USA, 40816
Morley Sales Co, 40817
Morton & Associates, 40818
Morton F Schweitzer Sales, 40819
Mueller Yurgae, 40824
Munchies, 40826
Munn Marketing Group, 40827
N.H. Cohen & Associates, 40830
Nagy Associates, 40832
Nanni-Marketal, 40834
Napoleon Co., 40835
Nash Wright Brokerage, 40836
National Brokerage Network, 40838
National Food Group, 40841
National Food Sales, 40842
National Foodservice Marketing, 40844
National Heritage Sales Company, 40846
National Sign Corporation, 40848
Nature's Products Inc, 40849
NEMA Associates, 40831
Nesco Brokerage Company, 40851
Network Sales, Inc, 40852
New Horizons, 40853
New Organics, 40854
Next Phase Enterprises, 40855
Nippon Food Company, 40859
Nobert Marketing, 40860
Noble Foods, 40861
Nomura & Co, 40863
Noon International, 40864
Norman Brokerage Co, 40865
Norman Hecht, 40866
North Bay Trading Co, 40868
Northeast Retail Services, 40872
Northeastern Enterprises, 40873
Northland Express Transport, 40874
O'Brien & Associates Brokerage Company, 40880
O'Hanlon Group, 40881
O'Neill Marketing Agents, 40882
Oak Leaf Sales Co, 40885
Occidental Foods International, LLC, 40886
Oekerman Sales, 40887
Ohm Design, 40888
Orca Foods, 40891
Osage Food Products Inc, 40893
Pace Target Brokerage, 40899
Pacific Trading Company International, 40903
PacNorth Group, 40898
Pankow Associates Inc, 40905
Paradise Food Brokers, 40906
Parks Brokerage Company, 40909
Patman Meat Group, 40911
Patterson Co Inc, 40912
Paul Esposito Inc, 40913
Paul G Nester & Son Co Inc, 40914
Paul Inman Associates, 40915
Peak Corporation, 40916
Pennickers Food Distribution, 40917
Peter Blease Sales, 40918
Peters & Fair, 40920
Peters & Peters Manufacturer's Agents, 40921
Phillips Sales Co, 40922
Phoenix Food Sales, 40923
Phoenix Foods Inc, 40924
Pierce Cartwright Company, 40925
Pinski Portugal & Associate, 40926
Pioneer Food Brokers, 40927
Pioneer Food Service, 40928
Pioneer Marketing International, 40929
Polish Folklore Import Co, 40932
Posternak Bauer Associates, 40933
Powell May International, 40935
Preferred Brokerage Company, 40936
Preisco Jentash, 40937
Premier Food Marketing, 40939
Premier Food Service Sales, 40940
Premier Marketing, 40941
Premium Seafood Co, 40942
Prestige Sales, 40944
Prestige Sales & Marketing, 40945
Pro Line Marketing Inc, 40946
Pro Pacific Agents, 40947
Pro Reps W, 40948
Pro-Quip Corporation, 40949
Professional Food Service, 40952
Professional Manufacturers' Representatives, 40953
Professional Reps of Arizona, 40954
Progressive Brokerage Co Inc, 40955
Progressive Food Service Broker, 40956
Progressive Marketing Systems, 40957
Progressive Sales & Marketing, 40958
Promesa, 40959
Providence Brokerage, 40961
Provincial, 40962
Purcell & Madden Associates, 40963
Quality Brokerage Company, 40965
Quality Sales & Marketing, 40969
R G Sellers Co, 40970
R H Moulton Company, 40971
R J Bickert & Associates, 40972
R&F Cocoa Services, 40973
R. Becker Marketing & Sales, 40974
R.F. Cannon Company, 40975
R.W. Berkeley & Associates, 40977
Rabe Sales Corp, 40981
Rainbow Sales & Marketing, 40983
Raleigh W. Johnson & Company, 40984
Rancho Sales & Marketing, 40985
Ratcliff Food Brokers, 40988
Ray's Pride Brokerage Company, 40990
Reede International Seafood Corporation, 40992
Reese Brokerage Co, 40993
Reichenbach & Associates, 40994
Rene Rivet, 40996
Rep Source, 40997
Res-Q Network, 40998
Resource One, 40999
RH Sulker Sales, 40978
Rheuark/F.S.I. Sales, 41002
Rich Audette Associates, 41003
Richardson Petkovsek & Associates, 41004
Richs Sales Company, 41005
Ringland Associates, 41006
Riteway Co, 41007
Ritt-Beyer Inc, 41008
Rizwitsch Sales, 41010, 41011
RMCI Foodservice, 40980
Robbins Sales Co, 41012
Robert A. Haines Companies, 41013
Robert W. Hayman Inc, 41016
Rocky Mountain Motel, 41017
Rodon Foods, 41018
Roehl Corp, 41019
Roger J. Wood Company, 41020
Roller & Associates, 41021
Roos-Mohan, 41022
Roosevelt Dairy Trade, Inc, 41023
Rosenfeld & Gigante, 41024
Ross Empire State Brokers, 41026
Rubenstein Seafood Sales, 41030
Rudolph Brady, Inc, 41031
S. Kamberg & Company, 41035
Sabal Marketing, 41045
Sachem Co, 41047
Salad Oils Intl Corp, 41049
Sales Corporation of Alaska, 41052
Sales Marketing Svc LLC, 41053
Sales Results, 41054
Sales Specialties, 41055
San Francisco Reps, 41057
San Francisco Wine Exchange, 41058
Santucci Associates, 41061
Saugy Inc., 41065
Saverino & Assoc, 41066
Scavuzzo Sales & Marketing, 41067
Schaper Company, 41068
Schiff Food Products Co Inc, 41071
Schraad & Associates, 41072
Schurman's Wisconsin Cheese Country, 41074
Scott & Associates, 41076
SCS Sales Company, 41037
Seaboard Foods, 41077
Seafood Sales, 41082
Select Sales & Marketing Inc, 41084
Sell Group, 41085
Sessions & Associates, 41088
Settables Inc, 41089
SHA Services, 41040
Shields Brokerage, 41091
Shore Distribution Resources, 41092
Shrimp Tex Distributors, 41093
Sid Alpers Organic Sales Company, 41094
Sid Green Frozen Foods, 41095
Sinco, 41097
SJE Marketing Corporation, 41041
Slagle & Associates, 41100
Slattery Marketing Corporation, 41101
Sloan Sales Inc, 41103
Smart Cycling, Inc., 41104
Smigiel Marketing & Sales Ltd., 41105
Snax Sales Company, 41106
South Group Marketing, 41111
Southeastern Manufacturer's, 41112
Southeastern Paper Group Inc, 41113
Specialty Equipment Sales Co, 41116
Specialty Partners, 41117
Specialty Sales & Marketing, 41118
Spectrum Foodservice Associates, 41119
Spectrum Foodservices, 41120
Spence Wells Assoc, 41121
Spencer & Assoc, 41122
Spurry & Associates, 41124
Squier Associates, 41125
St Charles Trading Inc, 41126
St. Ours & Company, 41128
Starliper & Associates, 41129
Statewide Brokerage Company, 41130
Stern International Consultants, 41132
Stevens & Associates, 41133
Stiefel Associates, 41134
Stockdale & Reagan, 41135
Stockett Associates, 41136
Strong & Associates, 41138
Stroup Ingredients Resources, 41139
Sturdivant Company, 41140
Sturgill Food Brokerage, 41141
Sullivan & Fitzgerald Food Brokers, 41142
Summit FS LTD, 41144
Sun Food Service Brokerage, 41145
Sun Marketing Agents Inc, 41146
Sundown Foods USA, Inc., 41148
Sunwest Sales Co, 41149
Super Sale Brokerage Company, 41150
Supermarket Representatives, 41152
Supreme Foods, 41153
Supreme Foodservice Sales, 41154
Symons-Bodtker Associates, 41157
T. McConnell Sales & Marketing, 41159
T.F.S. & Associates, 41160
T.J. Hines & Company, 41161
T.W. Wilson & Son, 41162
Taormina Sales Company, 41166
Team Northwest, 41168
Teasley & Assoc, 41169
Tees & Persse Brokerage Acosta Sales And Marketing Company, Inc, 41172
Tees & Persse Brokerage, 41173
Tepper & Assoc, 41174
The Cherry Company Ltd., 41177
The Thurber Company, 41178
Thomas Food Brokers, 41179
Thomas, Large & Singer, 41181
Thormann Associates, 41183
Tilkin & Cagen Inc, 41184
Tobiason Potato Co Inc, 41186
Top O' The Table, 41190
Tri-State Logistics Inc, 41199
Triad Brokers Inc, 41200
Try-Angle Food Brokers Inc, 41202
Tucker Sales, 41203
Twin City Food Brokers, 41206
Two Guys Spice Company, 41207
UBC Marketing, 41208
United Brands, 41212
United Brokers Company, 41213
United Foodservice Sales, 41214
United International Indstrs, 41215
US Distilled Products Co, 41209
US Food Products, 41210
V.M. Calderon, 41220
Vader & Landgraf, 41222
Van Kam, G Trading Company, 41223
Van Reed Sales Company, 41224
Virginia Fruit Sales Service, 41226
Vivion Inc, 41227
VP Northeast, 41221
W.B. Marketing Group, 41228
W.H. Escott Company, 41229
W.H. Moseley Co., 41230
Wallin Group Inc, 41237
Wallis & Barcinski, 41238
Watson & Associates, 41241
Waypoint, 41242
Webeco Foods, Inc, 41244
Wehrfritz & Associates, 41245
Wendlandt Brokerage Company, 41248
WENS Brokerage, 41233
Wesco Food Brokerage, 41249
Western Manufacturers Agents, 41252
Westex, 41253
Whitby Co, 41254
Wieber-McLain Company, 41256
William B. Steedman & Sons, 41257
William Hyman Jr Associates, 41259
William M. Dunne & Associates Ltd, 41260
Williams Brokerage Company, 41261
Willing Group, 41263
Wilson Food Brokers, 41264
Wiltsie & Company, 41265
Winmix/Natural Care Products, 41266
Wishbone Utensil Tableware Line, 41269
WJ Pence Company, 41234
WMK Marketing, 41235
Woolsey & Assoc Inc, 41271
World Wide Safe Brokers, 41272
Wrap-It Packaging, 41274
WTD Associates, 41236
Yankee Marketers, 41276
Yates Sales Associates, 41277
Yeager & Associates, 41278
York Cheese, 41279
York Hospitality & Gaming, 41280
York Sutch & Assoc, 41281
Zambito Produce Sales, 41284
Zanichelli & Associates, 41285
Zink Marketing, 41286

Brokered Product / Alcoholic Beverages

Alcoholic Beverages

A.R. Pellegrini & Associates, 40012
Abarbanel Wine Company, 40018
Airschott Inc, 40037
Alliance Foods, 40044
Alliance Foods Inc, 40045
Anthony Cea & Associates, 40061
ATI, 40017
Brothers International Food Corporation, 40146
Charles R. Bell Limited, 40193
Chartrand Imports, 40197
Cribari Vineyard Inc, 40257
Dixon Marketing Inc, 40305
Eagle Marketing, 40323
Frank M Hartley Inc, 40403
Genesis International, 40425
Grey Eagle Distributors, 40449
Hansid Company, 40469
Inter-American Products, 40523
JP Bissonnette, 40561
Kayco, 40619
Kedem, 40621
Kenney Sales, 40630
Luxco Inc, 40715
Marchetti Co, 40745
Nelson Cheese Factory, 40850
Network Sales, Inc, 40852
O.R. Elder, 40883
Pacific Trading Company International, 40903
Provincial, 40962
Roughstock Distillery, 41027
Royal Wine Corp, 41029
S&K Sales Company, 41034
San Francisco Wine Exchange, 41058
SHA Services, 41040
The Cherry Company Ltd., 41177
US Distilled Products Co, 41209
US Food Products, 41210
Wrap-It Packaging, 41274

Confectionery

1000 Islands River Rat Cheese, 40000
A G Brown & Son, 40003
A Gazerro & Assoc, 40004
A W Sisk & Son, 40008
A.J. Seibert Company, 40010
Action Marketing, 40025
Action Marketing Associates, 40026
Action Marketing Of So Ca, 40027
Action Marketing Services, 40028
Advantage Webco Hawaii, 40034
Ake-Sullivan Associates, 40038
Albert A Russo Inc, 40040
Alexander, Koetting, Poole & Buehrle Brothers, 40041
All-State Food Brokerage, 40043
Alliance Foods, 40044
Alliance Foods Inc, 40045
American Trading Company, 40055
AMT Sales & Marketing, 40016
Anchor Packaging, 40059
Anderson Daymon Worldwide, 40060
Anthony Cea & Associates, 40061
Arthur G. Meier Company/Inland Products Company, 40067
ATI, 40017
Atkinson-Crawford Sales Co, 40074
Automatic Packaging Systems & Conveyors Company, 40078
Autumn Foods, 40079
Bay Pacific Marketing, 40100
Beck Western Brokerage, 40103
Benson-Mitchell, 40110
Bentley Food Marketing, 40111
Best Brands, 40114
Binner Marketing & Sales, 40119
Bisek & Co Inc, 40122
BLV Marketing Inc, 40088, 40089
Bodie-Rickett & Associates, 40130
Booth, Schwager & Associates, 40132
Borton Brokerage Company, 40133
Bosshart Food Svc, 40134
Bratt-Foster-Advantage Sales, 40138
Brierley & King Brokerage Corporation, 40141
British Confectionery Company, 40142
Broms Brokerage, 40145
Browning Brokerage Company, 40147
Bruce Chaney & Company, 40148
Buckley, Thorne, Messina & McDermott, 40149
Budd Mayer Company of Jackson Inc., 40150
Budd Mayer of Mobile, 40151
Burdette Beckmann Inc, 40154
Burley Brokerage, 40155
Buzz Crown Enterprises, 40158
Byron A Carlson Inc, 40161
C J Irwin Co Inc, 40162
C. Mascari & Associates, 40164
Cafe Inc, 40173
Cann Brokerage Inc, 40177
Carlin Group, 40179
Cashman-Edwards Inc, 40184
Chandler Food Sales Co, 40189
Chapman-Tait Brokerage, Inc., 40191
Charles R. Bell Limited, 40193
Chase-Goldenberg Associates, 40199
Citrin-Pitoscia Company, 40210
Clofine Dairy Products Inc, 40215
Concord National, 40230, 40231, 40232, 40233, 40234, 40235
Concord Sales-Prairies, 40236
Conrad Sales Company, 40238
Consolidated Merchandisers, 40240
Convenience Marketing Services, 40247
Core Group, 40250
Cox Food Brokers, 40254
Crane Sales Co, 40255
Creightons, 40256
Crider Brokerage Company, 40258
Crossmark, 40259
CS Brokers, 40172
Cyba-Stevens Management Group, 40265
D&D Marketing Group, Inc., 40266
D&R Food Brokers, 40268
Dadant & Company, 40274
Dave Roemer & Associates, 40281
Davis Sales Associates, 40286
Dawson Sales Co Inc, 40287
Di Meo-Gale Brokerage Company, 40297
Dial Industries Inc, 40298
Dixon Marketing Inc, 40305
Donald R Tinsman Co, 40308
Doug Milne Co, 40309
Douglas Sales Associates, 40310
E A Berg & Sons Inc, 40317
Eagle Associates, 40322
Eastern Sales & Marketing, 40325
Eastern Sales and Marketing, 40326
Egerstrom Inc, 40329
Eiseman-Gleit Co Inc, 40330
Elias Shaker & Co, 40333
Erickson Brothers Brokerage Co, 40340
Ervan Guttman Co, 40342
Esm Ferolie, 40343
Esposito Brokerage, 40344
Essential Food Marketing, 40346
Eurogulf Company, 40348
Evers Heilig Inc, 40352
Fairley & Co Inc, 40360
Federated Group, 40361
Ferolie Esm-Metro New York, 40364
First Flight Foods, 40368
Five State Brokerage, 40371
Flynn Sales Associates, Inc., 40375
FM Carriere & Son, 40358
Food Associates of Syracuse, 40377
Food Service Associates, 40382
Food Service Connection, 40383
Food Service Specialists, 40386
Foodservice Innovators, 40390
Foodservice Solutions & Ideas, 40392
Forseasons Sales, 40399
Frank Kinsman Assoc, 40402
Freiria & Company, 40410
Gallagher Sales Corporation, 40418
Gateway Food Service, 40422
Gellman Associates, 40424
George W. Holop Associates, 40430
Gibbs-Mccormick Inc A Ca Corp, 40433
Glenmoor Brokerage, 40438
Golick Martins, Inc., 40441
Gormick Food Brokers, 40442
Goveco Full Service Food Brokers, 40452
Grabbe-Leonard Co, 40445
Gulf States Food Service Marketing, 40452
H.V. Mid State Sales Company, 40458
Halling Company, 40465
Hansid Company, 40469
Harold M. Lincoln Company, 40471
Harry Tinseth Associates, Inc., 40474
Hartley S. Johnson & Son, 40475
Harvey-Winchell Company, 40477
Hawley & Assoc, 40480
Hockenberg Newburgh, 40490, 40491
Homeplace Food Group, 40494
Hugh T. Gilmore Company, 40498
Hynes Bond Ellison, 40502
Imark of Pennsylvania, 40510
Imperial Florida Sales, 40513
Imperial House Sales, 40515
Inter-American Products, 40523
International Pacific Sales, 40528
International Sales & Brokerage Company, 40530
Interpack NW Frozen Food, 40531
Intersouth Foodservice Group, 40534
Intralinks Inc, 40537
ISB Sales Company, 40504
ISSCO, 40506
J Carroll & Assoc, 40539
J.F. Benz Company, 40550
J.F. Kelly, 40551
J.M. Swank Company, 40554
Jack Curren & Associates, 40564
Jim Pless & Company, 40573
JL Stemp Marketing Agents, 40558
John H Thier Co, 40575
Johnson Holmes & Assoc Inc, 40582
Johnson O'Hare Co, 40583
Jos Iorio Company, 40588
Jose M Perez-Pages, 40589
Jubilee Sales of Carolina, 40597
Juhl Brokerage, 40599
Julius Levy Company, 40601
Julius M. Dean Company, 40602
Kahler-Senders Inc, 40612
Kandy King Confections, 40613
Kay's Foods, 40618
Kayco, 40619
KDH Sales, 40609
Kedem, 40621
Keeth & Associates, 40622
Kelley-Clarke, 40623
Kemper Food Brokers, 40628
Kenney Sales, 40630
Key Carlin O'Brien, LLC, 40632
Key Sales Group, 40635
KH McClure & Company, 40610
Kiefer's, 40638
Kingery & Assoc, 40643
Klondike Foods, 40652
Koch & Assoc, 40654
Korth Marketing, 40656
Kramer Brokerage Co, 40657
Kurtz Food Brokers, 40659
L&S Sales Company, 40661
LBM Sales, LLC, 40664
Lehmann Brokerage Co, 40686
Leonard H Sisitzky Sales Inc, 40689
Lomac & May Associates, 40703
Lorey & Lorey, 40707
Louis F. Leeper Company/Cleveland, 40710
Lowe & Associates, 40711
Luke Soules Southwest, 40713
M.E. Dilanian Company, 40722
Main Street Marketing, 40732
Major Marketing Service, 40735
Mancini & Groesbeck, 40738
Mancini Sales & Marketing, 40740
Marathon Marketing, 40743
Marino Marketing Group, 40746
Market Pro International, 40749
Market Smart, 40750
Marketing Management Inc, 40754
Master Sales & Marketing, 40764
Mathews Associates, 40765
MAV Sales Co, 40725
McArdle, 40770
McCormick Brokerage Company, 40773
Measured Sales & Marketing, 40776
Merit Sales Corporation, 40781
Michael Raymond Desserts Inc, 40783
Mid-West Sales Agency, 40791
Midland Marketing Co-Op Inc, 40792
Midlantic Sweetener Co, 40793
Midstates Marketing Inc, 40794
Midwest Ingredients Inc, 40797
Milky Whey Inc, 40799
Miller's Market, 40802
Miller, Stabler & Smith, 40803
Mitchell & Co Inc, 40808
Mitchell Agencies, 40809
Mitchell of Mississippi, 40810
Morton F Schweitzer Sales, 40819
Mueller Yurgae, 40824
Munchies, 40826
N.H. Cohen & Associates, 40830
National Foodservice Marketing, 40844
Nature's Products Inc, 40849
Nesco Brokerage Company, 40851
Network Sales, Inc, 40852
Next Phase Enterprises, 40855
Nicholas & Co Inc, 40856
Nobert Marketing, 40860
Norman Brokerage Co, 40865
North Eastern Sales Solutions, 40869
Oekerman Sales, 40887
Osage Food Products Inc, 40893
Pace Target Brokerage, 40899
Patterson Co Inc, 40912
Paul Esposito Inc, 40913
Paul G Nester & Son Co Inc, 40914
Paul Inman Associates, 40915
Pennickers Food Distribution, 40917
Peters & Fair, 40920
Phoenix Foods, 40924
Pierce Cartwright Company, 40925
Pinski Portugal & Associate, 40926
Pioneer Food Brokers, 40927
Pioneer Marketing International, 40929
Polish Folklore Import Co, 40932
Preferred Brokerage Company, 40936
Prestige Sales, 40944
Prestige Sales & Marketing, 40945
Progressive Brokerage Co Inc, 40955
Progressive Marketing Systems, 40957
Providence Brokerage, 40961
Provincial, 40962
R J Bickert & Associates, 40972
R&F Cocoa Services, 40973
Rainbow Sales & Marketing, 40983
Randag & Assoc Inc, 40986
Ratcliff Food Brokers, 40988
Reese Brokerage Co, 40993
Reichenbach & Associates, 40994
Rene Rivet, 40996
Resource One, 40999
RH Sulker Sales, 40978
Rheuark/F.S.I. Sales, 41002
Riteway Co, 41007
Ritt-Beyer Inc, 41008
RMCI Foodservice, 40980
Robert A. Haines Companies, 41013
Rocky Mountain Motel, 41017
Roger J. Wood Company, 41020
Ross Empire State Brokers, 41026
S&K Sales Company, 41034
S. Kamberg & Company, 41035
Sachem Co, 41047
Sales Corporation of Alaska, 41052
Sales Marketing Svc LLC, 41053
Sales Results, 41054

105

Brokered Product / Dairy/Deli

Santucci Associates, 41061
Saverino & Assoc, 41066
Schraad & Associates, 41072
SCS Sales Company, 41037
Sell Group, 41085
Sessions & Associates, 41088
SHA Services, 41040
Sid Alpers Organic Sales Company, 41094
Sinco, 41097
Singer Lee & Associates, 41098
Sloan Sales Inc, 41103
Smart Cycling, Inc., 41104
Smigiel Marketing & Sales Ltd., 41105
Snax Sales Company, 41106
Specialty Partners, 41117
Specialty Sales & Marketing, 41118
St Charles Trading Inc, 41126
Statewide Brokerage Company, 41130
Stern International Consultants, 41132
Stockdale & Reagan, 41135
Strong & Associates, 41138
Stroup Ingredients Resources, 41139
Summit Brokerage, 41143
Summit FS LTD, 41144
Sunwest Sales Co, 41149
Super Sale Brokerage Company, 41150
Supreme Foods, 41153
Supreme Foodservice Sales, 41154
T.W. Wilson & Son, 41162
Team Northwest, 41168
Tees & Persse Brokerage Acosta Sales And Marketing Company, Inc, 41172
Tees & Persse Brokerage, 41173
Terra Nova Brokers, 41175
The Cherry Company Ltd., 41177
The Thurber Company, 41178
Thomas, Large & Singer, 41181
TRFG Inc, 41165
Tri-State Logistics Inc, 41199
Tucker Sales, 41203
United Brands, 41212
United Foodservice Sales, 41214
United International Indstrs, 41215
US Food Products, 41210
W.H. Escott Company, 41229
W.H. Sullivan & Associates, 41232
Webco General Partnership, 41243
Whitby Co, 41254
William M. Dunne & Associates Ltd, 41260
Williams Brokerage Company, 41261
Willing Group, 41263
Wilson Food Brokers, 41264
Wiltsie & Company, 41265
Wrap-It Packaging, 41274
Yankee Marketers, 41276
Yates Sales Associates, 41277
York Sutch & Assoc, 41281
Zanichelli & Associates, 41285

Dairy/Deli

1000 Islands River Rat Cheese, 40000
3-D Marketing & Sales, 40001
A G Brown & Son, 40003
A Thomas Farris & Son Inc, 40007
A W Sisk & Son, 40008
A&D Sales Associates, 40009
A.J. Seibert Company, 40010
Acclaim Marketing & Sales, 40021
Acorn Sales Company, 40023
Acosta Sales & Marketing Company, 40024
Action Marketing, 40025
Action Marketing Associates, 40026
Action Marketing Services, 40028
Advance Marketing, 40030
Advance Sales & Marketing, Inc, 40031
Advantage Solutions, 40033
Advantage Webco Hawaii, 40034
Agri-Dairy Products, 40036
Albert A Russo Inc, 40040
Alexander, Koetting, Poole & Buehrle Brothers, 40041
Alliance Foods, 40044
Alliance Foods Inc, 40045
Allied Marketing Corp, 40046
Ambi-Prestigio Foods Inc, 40050
American Commodity & Shipping, 40052
American Patriot Sales Inc, 40053
Anchor Florida Marketing, 40058
Anchor Packaging, 40059
Anderson Daymon Worldwide, 40060
Anthony Cea & Associates, 40061
Apache Brokers, 40062
Arnett Brokerage Co, 40065
Arroyo Sales Company, 40066
Arthur G. Meier Company/Inland Products Company, 40067
Artisanal Foods, 40068
Associated Foodservices, 40072
ATI, 40017
Autumn Foods, 40079
Avatar Food Group, 40080
B & D Sales & Marketing Inc, 40082
Baker Brokerage Company LLC, 40092
Baldwin & Mattson, 40094
Bay Pacific Marketing, 40100
Benchmark Sales, 40108
Bender-Goodman Co Inc, 40109
Benson-Mitchell, 40110
Bentley Food Marketing, 40111
Bird Marketing, 40120
Bisek & Co, 40122
Bloomfield Bakers, 40127
BLV Marketing Inc, 40088
Borton Brokerage Company, 40133
Bosshart Food Svc, 40134
Bottom Line Foods, 40135
Bratt-Foster-Advantage Sales, 40138
Brennan Food Services, 40139
Bridge City Food Marketing, 40140
Broms Brokerage, 40145
Browning Brokerage Company, 40147
Buckley, Thorne, Messina & McDermott, 40149
Budd Mayer Company of Jackson Inc., 40150
Budd Mayer of Mobile, 40151
Buley Patterson Sales Company, 40152
Burley Brokerage, 40155
Buzz Crown Enterprises, 40158
C J Irwin Co Inc, 40162
C. Mascari & Associates, 40164
Cafe Inc, 40173
Cann Brokerage Inc, 40177
Carlin Group, 40179
Carpenter Associates, 40181
Cashman-Edwards Inc, 40184
Central Sales & Marketing, 40187
Chandler Food Sales Co, 40189
Charles R. Bell Limited, 40193
Charles Rockel & Son, 40194
Chase Sales Company, 40198
Cheese & Dairy Products, 40202
Chell Brokerage Co, 40203
Chilay Corporation, 40205
Chuckrow Sales LLC, 40209
Clofine Dairy Products Inc, 40215
Co-Sales De Credico, 40217
Concept Food Brokers, 40228
Concept Food Sales, 40229
Concord National, 40230, 40231, 40232, 40233, 40234, 40235
Concord Sales-Prairies, 40236
Conlin Brokerage Company, 40237
Consolidated Marketers Inc, 40239
Consolidated Merchandisers, 40240
Constant Sales, 40242
Consumer Brands, 40243
Consummate Marketing Company, 40244
Convenience Marketing Services, 40247
Cooke Marketing Group Inc, 40248
Copperwood InternationalInc, 40249
Core Group, 40251
Crider Brokerage Company, 40258
Crossmark, 40259
Cruise Marketing, 40262
Cyba-Stevens Management Group, 40265
D&D Marketing Group, Inc., 40266
D&R Food Brokers, 40268
Dairytown Products Ltd, 40275
Damafro, Inc, 40278
Dambeck & Associates, 40280
Dave Roemer & Associates, 40281
Dawson Sales Co Inc, 40287
Dd Reckner Co, 40288
Delbert Craig Food Brokers, 40295
DeMoss & Associates, 40291
Di Meo-Gale Brokerage Company, 40297
Dial Industries Inc, 40298
Dixon Marketing Inc, 40305
Donald R Tinsman Co, 40308
Doug Milne Co, 40309
Douglas Sales Associates, 40310
Dreyer Marketing, 40312
DSI Food Brokerage, 40271
Dunbar Sales Company, Inc, 40315
Dunham & Smith Agencies, 40316
Eagle Marketing, 40323
Eastern Sales & Marketing, 40325
Eastern Sales and Marketing, 40326
EFD Associate, 40321
Ellis S. Fine Co., Inc., 40335
Esm Ferolie, 40343
Esposito Brokerage, 40344
Essential Food Marketing, 40346
Eurogulf Company, 40348
Evans Brokerage Company, 40351
Fairley & Co Inc, 40360
Federated Group, 40361
Feenix Brokerage LTD, 40362
Ferdinand Richards & Son, 40363
Ferolie Esm-Metro New York, 40364
First Flight Foods, 40368
Five State Brokerage, 40371
Flynn Sales Associates, Inc., 40375
Food Associates of Syracuse, 40377
Food Sales West, 40381
Food Service Associates, 40382
Food Service Connection, 40383
Food Service Marketing of Pennsylvania, 40384
Food Service Merchandising, 40385
Foodmark Sales, 40388
Foodsales Inc, 40389
Foodservice Marketing, 40391
Foodservice Solutions & Ideas, 40392
Foodworks International, 40393
Forbes Frozen Foods, 40395
Forseasons Sales, 40399
Four Peaks, Inc., 40400
Frank Kinsman Assoc, 40402
Freeman Signature, 40409
Fromartharie Inc, 40411
Fusion Sales Group, 40413
G.A. Davis Food Service, 40414
GAP Food Brokers, 40415
Gasparini Sales Inc, 40421
Gateway Food Service, 40422
Gellman Associates, 40424
Genesis Marketing, 40426
Gilbert Foodservice Inc, 40434
Gillette Creamery, 40435
Glenmoor Brokerage, 40438
Golick Martins, Inc., 40441
Gulf States Food Service Marketing, 40452
H & G Trading LTD Inc, 40454
H&T Food Marketing Company, 40455
Halling Company, 40465
Hanks Brokerage, 40467
Harold M. Lincoln Company, 40471
Harriet Greenland Enterprises, 40472
Hawley & Assoc, 40480
HCB Foodservice Sales & Marketing, 40459
HD Marshall Ltd, 40460
Henry J. Hips Company, 40483
Higgins & White Inc, 40486
Hobby Whalen Marketing, 40489
Hockenberg Newburgh, 40490, 40491
Hockenberg-Newburgh Sales, 40492
Hugh T. Gilmore Company, 40498
Hunter Walton & Co Inc, 40500
Imark of Pennsylvania, 40510
Imperial Florida Sales, 40513
Ingredient Exchange Co, 40517
Inter-American Products, 40523
Intermountain Food Brokerage, 40525
International Gourmet Products, 40527
International Sales & Brokerage Company, 40530
Interpack NW Frozen Food, 40531
Intersouth Foodservice Group, 40534
Interstate Food Brokers, 40535
ISB Sales Company, 40504
ISC of Indiana, 40505
ITA Inc, 40507
J N Rhodes Co Inc, 40542
J&J Brokerage, 40546
Jack Curren & Associates, 40564
Jeram Associates, 40570
Jilasco Food Exports, 40572
Jim Pless & Company, 40573
John H Thier Co, 40575
John J Wollack Co Inc, 40577
John L. Pieri & Sons, 40578
John Mangum Company, 40579
Johnson O'Hare Co, 40583
Jones Neitzel Co, 40586
Jos Iorio Company, 40588
JP Bissonnette, 40561
Jubilee Sales of Carolina, 40597
Juhl Brokerage, 40598, 40599
Julius Levy Company, 40601
Kappert/Hyzer Company, 40614
Karoun Dairies Inc, 40615
Kathryn's Food Service Brokers, 40616
Kay's Foods, 40618
Kayco, 40619
Kedem, 40621
Keeth & Associates, 40622
Kelley-Clarke, 40623
Kelly Associates/Food Brokers, 40625
Kemper Food Brokers, 40628
Kenney Sales, 40630
Key Carlin O'Brien, LLC, 40632
Key Impact Sales & Systems Inc, 40633
Key Sales & Marketing, 40634
Key Sales Group, 40635
KeyImpact Sales & Systems, Inc., 40636
Kidd Enterprises, 40637
KIKO Foods Inc, 40611
Kinder-Smith Company, 40639
Kingery & Associates, 40643
Kirstein Brokerage Company, 40648
Klensch Cheese Company, 40650
Klinger & Speros Food Brokers, 40651
Koch & Assoc, 40654
L&S Sales Company, 40661
LAD Foodservice Sales, 40663
Lampson & Tew, 40675
LeMire Sales, 40682
Lemmons Company, 40687
Lever Associates, 40691
Lilburn Gulf, 40694
Linwood-Welch Marketing, 40695
Lisberg-Voegeli Hanson, 40696
Littler Brokerage Co Inc, 40697
Lobel Food Brokers, 40702
Lomac & May Associates, 40703
Lorey & Lorey, 40707
Louis F. Leeper Company/Cleveland, 40710
Lowe & Associates, 40711
Luke Soules Southwest, 40713
M. Soffer Company, 40721
M.E. Dilanian Company, 40722
Magic Valley Truck Brokers Inc, 40731
Main Street Marketing, 40732
Major Marketing Service, 40735
Mancini & Groesbeck, 40738
Mancini Sales & Marketing, 40740
Manzo Food Brokers, 40742
Marathon Marketing, 40743
Marino Marketing Group, 40746
Marjo & Associates, 40747
Market Smart, 40750

Brokered Product / Exports

Market West Company, 40751
Marketing Management Inc, 40754
Marmelstein Associates, 40755
Martin Preferred Foods, 40758
Marty Scanlon Brokerage Co, 40759
Master Sales & Marketing, 40764
Mathews Associates, 40765
Matrix Group Inc., 40766
MAV Sales Co, 40725
McCormick Brokerage Company, 40773
Menu Planners, 40777
Merit Sales Corporation, 40781
Michael Raymond Desserts Inc, 40783
Mid-American Brokerage of St. Louis, 40787
Mid-Continent Sales, 40788
Mid-State Food Brokers, 40789
Mid-West Sales Agency, 40791
Midland Marketing Co-Op Inc, 40792
Midstates Marketing Inc, 40794
Midwest Ingredients Inc, 40797
Milky Whey Inc, 40799
Miller, Stabler & Smith, 40803
Mitchell & Co Inc, 40808
Mitchell of Mississippi, 40810
Morley Sales Co, 40817
Morton & Associates, 40818
Moten Company, 40821
Mueller Yurgae, 40822
Nanni-Marketal, 40834
National Food Group, 40841
National Food Sales, 40842
National Foodservice Marketing, 40844
National Heritage Sales Company, 40846
Nelson Cheese Factory, 40850
Nesco Brokerage Company, 40851
New Horizons, 40853
Next Phase Enterprises, 40855
Nicholas & Co Inc, 40856
Nobert Marketing, 40860
Noble Foods, 40861
Norman Hecht, 40866
North Eastern Sales Solutions, 40869
Northeastern Enterprises, 40873
Northland Express Transport, 40874
Northumberland Dairy, 40876
O'Brien & Associates Brokerage Company, 40880
Oak Leaf Sales Co, 40885
Oekerman Sales, 40887
Overseas Service Corp, 40896
Pace Target Brokerage, 40899
Parks Brokerage Company, 40909
Patman Meat Group, 40911
Paul G Nester & Son Co Inc, 40914
Peters & Fair, 40920
Pierce Cartwright Company, 40925
Pioneer Food Service, 40928
Preferred Brokerage Company, 40936
Preisco Jentash, 40937
Premier Food Marketing, 40939
Premier Food Service Sales, 40940
Prestige Marketing, 40943
Prestige Sales & Marketing, 40945
Proactive Sales & Marketing, 40950
Professional Food Service, 40952
Progressive Brokerage Co Inc, 40955
Progressive Food Service Broker, 40956
Progressive Sales & Marketing, 40958
Quality Brokerage Company, 40965
Quality Sales & Marketing, 40969
R G Sellers Co, 40970
R. Becker Marketing & Sales, 40974
R.F. Cannon Company, 40975
Rainbow Sales & Marketing, 40983
Ratcliff Food Brokers, 40988
Ray's Pride Brokerage Company, 40990
Reese Brokerage Co, 40993
Reichenbach & Associates, 40994
Rene Rivet, 40996
Resource One, 40999
Rheuark/F.S.I. Sales, 41002
Riteway Co, 41007
Rizwitsch Sales, 41011
RMCI Foodservice, 40980

Rocky Mountain Motel, 41017
Rodon Foods, 41018
Roos-Mohan, 41022
Roosevelt Dairy Trade, Inc, 41023
S. Kamberg & Company, 41035
Sabbers & Assoc Inc, 41046
Sachem Co, 41047
Sales Corporation of Alaska, 41052
Santucci Associates, 41061
Saverino & Assoc, 41066
Scavuzzo Sales & Marketing, 41067
Schraad & Associates, 41072
Schreiber Foods Inc., 41073
Schurman's Wisconsin Cheese Country, 41074
Sell Group, 41085
Sessions & Associates, 41088
SHA Services, 41040
Sid Alpers Organic Sales Company, 41094
Sinco, 41097
SJE Marketing Corporation, 41041
Slaybaugh & Associates, 41102
Sloan Sales Inc, 41103
Smart Cycling, Inc., 41104
South Group Marketing, 41111
Southeastern Paper Group Inc, 41113
Specialty Partners, 41117
Specialty Sales & Marketing, 41118
Spectrum Foodservice Associates, 41119
Spectrum Foodservices, 41120
Spencer & Assoc, 41122
St Charles Trading Inc, 41126
Stockdale & Reagan, 41135
Stroup Ingredients Resources, 41139
Sturgill Food Brokerage, 41141
Summit Brokerage, 41143
Summit FS LTD, 41144
Sun Food Service Brokerage, 41145
Super Sale Brokerage Company, 41150
Supreme Foods, 41153
Supreme Foodservice Sales, 41154
T C Jacoby & Co, 41158
T. McConnell Sales & Marketing, 41159
T.W. Wilson & Son, 41162
Team Northwest, 41167, 41168
Tees & Persse Brokerage Acosta Sales And Marketing Company, Inc, 41172
Tees & Persse Brokerage, 41173
Terra Nova Brokers, 41175
The Cherry Company Ltd., 41177
The Thurber Company, 41178
Thomas Food Brokers, 41179
Thomas, Large & Singer, 41181
Tri-State Logistics Inc, 41199
Tucker Sales, 41203
Twin City Food Brokers, 41206
UBC Marketing, 41208
United Brands, 41212
United Foodservice Sales, 41214
United International Indstrs, 41215
US Food Products, 41210
Van Kam, G. Trading Company, 41223
Van Reed Sales Company, 41224
W.H. Sullivan & Associates, 41232
Ward Hughes Co, 41239
Watson & Associates, 41241
Waypoint, 41242
Webeco Foods, Inc, 41244
WENS Brokerage, 41233
Wesco Food Brokerage, 41249
William M. Dunne & Associates Ltd, 41260
Wilson Food Brokers, 41264
Winmix/Natural Care Products, 41266
Wisconsin Cheese Group, 41268
WJ Pence Company, 41234
Wrap-It Packaging, 41274
Yankee Marketers, 41276
York Cheese, 41279
York Sutch & Associates, 41281
Zanichelli & Associates, 41285

Exports

A G Brown & Son, 40003
ABC Corp, 40013
Agri-Dairy Products, 40036
Airschott Inc, 40037
Alliance Foods, 40044
Alliance Foods Inc, 40045
American Commodity & Shipping, 40052
American Trading Company, 40055
AmericanLifestyle.Com, 40056
Anthony Cea & Associates, 40061
Arnett Brokerage Co, 40065
ATI, 40017
B.C. Ritchie Company, 40084
B.W. Dyer & Company, 40086
Barliant & Company, 40095
Bay Pacific Marketing, 40100
Bertran Enterprises, 40113
Bird Marketing, 40120
Bottom Line Foods, 40135
Buley Patterson Sales Company, 40152
Celright Foods, 40185
Clofine Dairy Products Inc, 40215
Colon Brothers, 40223
Commodities Marketing Inc, 40227
Concord Sales-Prairies, 40236
Crown Point, 40261
Culinary Specialty Produce, 40263
Dakco International, 40276
Damafro, Inc, 40278
Di Meo-Gale Brokerage Company, 40297
Doug Milne Co, 40309
Ed O'Connor Associates, 40328
Encore Fruit Marketing Inc, 40337
Erlich Foods International, 40341
Eurogulf Company, 40348
Federated Group, 40361
First Flight Foods, 40368
FMI Food Marketers International Ltd, 40359
FoodBin Trading, Inc., 40387
Freiria & Company, 40410
Fusion Sales Group, 40413
Garisco Distributing, 40420
Genesis International, 40425
Gersony Strauss Co, 40431
Gibbs-Mccormick Inc A Ca Corp, 40433
Gilbert Foodservice Inc, 40434
Global Citrus Resources, Inc, 40439
Hanimex Company, 40466
Hansid Company, 40469
Harold J. Barrett Company, 40470
Hollar & Greene, 40493
Huron Food Sales, 40501
Ingredient Exchange Co, 40517
Inter-American Products, 40523
Interep Company, 40524
International Gourmet Products, 40527
International Pacific Seafood, 40529
Interpex, 40532
Intralinks Inc, 40537
ITA Inc, 40507
J T Gibbons Inc, 40544
Jam Group of Company, 40566
Jilasco Food Exports, 40572
JL Stemp Marketing Agents, 40558
Johnson, Arlyn & Associates, 40584
Joseph P. Sullivan & Company, 40591
Jubilee Sales of Carolina, 40597
Kayco, 40619
Kedem, 40621
Kelley-Clarke, 40624
KH McClure & Company, 40610
Korth Marketing, 40656
L&S Sales Company, 40661
LA Teste Services, 40662
Lake & Lake Inc, 40671
Landmark Foods, 40679
LIN-PAK, LLC., 40665
Littman & Associates, 40698
LMGO International Inc, 40666
Loretta Foods, 40706
Lotto International, 40709
M.E. Strauss Brokerage Company, 40723

M.J. Borelli & Company, 40724
Major Marketing Service, 40735
Marino Marketing Group, 40746
Market Pro International, 40749
Marketing Management Inc, 40754
Marshall Sales Co, 40757
Mercantum Corp, 40778
Meridian Products, 40779
Midwest Ingredients Inc, 40797
Milky Whey Inc, 40799
Miller & Smith Foods, 40800
Miller's Market, 40802
Miltenberg & Samton Inc., 40804
Morley Sales Co, 40817
Nanni-Marketal, 40834
Nature's Products Inc, 40849
Nesco Brokerage Company, 40851
New Organics, 40854
Noon International, 40864
Oekerman Sales, 40887
Orca Foods, 40891
Pacific Trading Company International, 40903
Paul Esposito Inc, 40913
Phoenix Food Sales, 40923
Pioneer Marketing International, 40929
Preferred Brokerage Company, 40936
Provincial, 40962
Pure Sales, 40964
R. Becker Marketing & Sales, 40974
Reede International Seafood Corporation, 40992
Roehl Corp, 41019
Roosevelt Dairy Trade, Inc, 41023
Royal Wine Corp, 41029
Sales Marketing Svc LLC, 41053
Schare & Associates, 41069
Seafood Sales, 41082
SGS International Rice Inc, 41039
SHA Services, 41040
Sid Alpers Organic Sales Company, 41094
Sinco, 41097
St Charles Trading Inc, 41126
STI International, 41043
Sundown Foods USA, Inc., 41148
T C Jacoby & Co, 41158
T. McConnell Sales & Marketing, 41159
Texas Foods, 41176
Tower Intercontinental Group, 41193
Tri-State Logistics Inc, 41199
United Brands, 41212
United Brokers Company, 41213
United International Indstrs, 41215
US Food Products, 41210
Van Kam, G. Trading Company, 41223
W.H. Moseley Co., 41230
Watson & Associates, 41241
Webeco Foods, Inc, 41244
William M. Dunne & Associates Ltd, 41260
Willing Group, 41263
Winmix/Natural Care Products, 41266
Wishbone Utensil Tableware Line, 41269
Zambito Produce Sales, 41284

Frozen Food

A G Brown & Son, 40003
A&D Sales Associates, 40009
A.J. Seibert Company, 40010
Acclaim Marketing & Sales, 40021
Acosta Sales & Marketing Company, 40024
Action Marketing, 40025
Action Marketing Associates, 40026
Action Marketing Services, 40028
Advance Sales & Marketing, Inc, 40031
Advantage Solutions, 40033
Advantage Webco Hawaii, 40034
Airschott Inc, 40037
Alba Specialty Seafood Company, 40039
Alexander, Koetting, Poole & Buehrle Brothers, 40041
Alliance Foods, 40044

Brokered Product / Frozen Food

Alliance Foods Inc, 40045
Allied Marketing Corp, 40046
Ambi-Prestigio Foods Inc, 40050
American Commodity & Shipping, 40052
American Patriot Sales Inc, 40053
Anchor Florida Marketing, 40058
Anderson Daymon Worldwide, 40060
Anthony Cea & Associates, 40061
Apache Brokers, 40062
Arnett Brokerage Co, 40065
Arroyo Sales Company, 40066
Arthur G. Meier Company/Inland Products Company, 40067
Artisanal Foods, 40068
Arvin Sales Company, 40069
Associated Foodservices, 40072
ATI, 40149
Avatar Food Group, 40080
B & D Sales & Marketing Inc, 40082
Baja Foods LLC, 40091
Baker Brokerage Company LLC, 40092
Baldwin & Mattson, 40094
Bayha & Associates, 40101
Benchmark Sales, 40108
Benson-Mitchell, 40110
Bentley Food Marketing, 40111
Beta Pure Foods, 40116
Betters International Food Corporation, 40117
Bird Marketing, 40120
Bisek & Co Inc, 40122
Bittinger Sales, 40123
Bixby Food Sales, 40124
BLV Marketing Inc, 40088
Bob Rowe Sales, 40128
Booth, Schwager & Associates, 40132
Borton Brokerage Company, 40133
Bosshart Food Svc, 40134
Bottom Line Foods, 40135
Brandywine Frozen Fruit, 40137
Bratt-Foster-Advantage Sales, 40138
Bridge City Food Marketing, 40140
Broms Brokerage, 40145
Brothers International Food Corporation, 40146
Browning Brokerage Company, 40147
Buckley, Thorne, Messina & McDermott, 40149
Budd Mayer Company of Jackson Inc., 40150
Budd Mayer of Mobile, 40151
Buley Patterson Sales Company, 40152
Burley Brokerage, 40155
Buzz Crown Enterprises, 40158
Byron A Carlson Inc, 40161
C. Lloyd Johnson Company, 40163
C. Mascari & Associates, 40164
C.B. Powell Limited, 40165
C.H. Robinson Co., 40166
Cafe Inc, 40173
Caneast Foods, 40176
Carlin Group, 40179
Chapman Fruit Co Inc, 40190
Charles Rockel & Son, 40194
Chase Sales Company, 40198
Chell Brokerage Co, 40203
Chilay Corporation, 40205
Chuck Batcheller Company, 40208
Chuckrow Sales LLC, 40209
Classic Cuisine Foods, 40211
Co-Sales De Credico, 40217
Coastal Pride Co Inc, 40219
Cobler Food Sales, 40220
Colony Brokerage Company, 40224
Concept Food Brokers, 40228
Concept Food Sales, 40229
Concord National, 40230, 40231, 40232, 40233, 40234, 40235
Concord Sales-Prairies, 40236
Conlin Brokerage Company, 40237
Conrad Sales Company, 40238
Consolidated Marketers Inc, 40239
Consolidated Merchandisers, 40240
Constant Sales, 40242
Consumer Brands, 40243

Convenience Marketing Services, 40247
Copperwood International Inc, 40249
Core Group, 40250, 40251
Cox Food Brokers, 40254
Crider Brokerage Company, 40258
Crossmark, 40259
Cyba-Stevens Management Group, 40265
D&D Marketing Group, Inc., 40266
D&R Food Brokers, 40268
Dadant & Company, 40274
Dambeck & Associates, 40280
Dave Roemer & Associates, 40281
DBB Marketing Company, 40269
Dd Reckner Co, 40288
DeJarnett Sales, 40289, 40290
Delbert Craig Food Brokers, 40295
DeMoss & Associates, 40291
Dennis Sales, 40296
Di Meo-Gale Brokerage Company, 40297
Dial Industries Inc, 40298
Diaz Sales, 40300
Diversifood Associates, Inc, 40303
Dixon Marketing Inc, 40305
Donald R Tinsman Co, 40308
Doug Milne Co, 40309
Dreyer Marketing, 40312
DSI Food Brokerage, 40271
Dunbar Sales Company, Inc, 40315
Dunham & Smith Agencies, 40316
DVC Brokerage Company, 40272
E W Carlberg Co, 40320
Eagle Marketing, 40323
Eastern Sales & Marketing, 40325
Eastern Sales and Marketing, 40326
EFD Associate, 40321
Encore Fruit Marketing Inc, 40337
Enterprise Food Brokers, 40339
Erickson Brothers Brokerage Co, 40340
Erlich Foods International, 40341
Esm Ferolie, 40343
Esposito Brokerage, 40344
Essential Food Marketing, 40346
Evans Brokerage Company, 40351
Federated Group, 40361
Ferolie Esm-Metro New York, 40364
First Choice Sales Company, 40367
First Flight Foods, 40368
Five State Brokerage, 40371
Flynn Sales Associates, Inc., 40375
Food Associates of Syracuse, 40377
Food Sales West, 40381
Food Service Associates, 40382
Food Service Connection, 40383
Food Service Marketing of Pennsylvania, 40384
Food Service Merchandising, 40385
Food Service Specialists, 40386
FoodBin Trading, Inc., 40387
Foodmark Sales, 40388
Foodsales Inc, 40389
Foodservice Innovators, 40390
Foodservice Marketing, 40391
Foodservice Solutions & Ideas, 40392
Forbes Frozen Foods, 40395
Frank Kinsman Assoc, 40402
Freedom Food Brokers, 40405
Freeman Fruit Intl, 40408
Freiria & Company, 40410
Frozen Food Associates, 40412
Fusion Sales Group, 40413
G.A. Davis Food Service, 40414
GAP Food Brokers, 40415
Gasparini Sales Inc, 40421
Gateway Food Service, 40422
Gellman Associates, 40424
George E. Dent Sales, 40428
Gibbs-Mccormick Inc A Ca Corp, 40433
Gilbert Foodservice Inc, 40434
Gillette Creamery, 40435
Glacier Sales Inc, 40437
Golden Valley Industries Inc, 40440
Golick Martins, Inc., 40441
Gulf States Food Service Marketing, 40452
H.V. Mid State Sales Company, 40458

Halling Company, 40465
Hanks Brokerage, 40467
Hansid Company, 40469
Harold J. Barrett Company, 40470
Harold M. Lincoln Company, 40471
Harvest Grove Inc, 40476
Hawley & Assoc, 40480
HCB Foodservice Sales & Marketing, 40459
HD Marshall Ltd, 40460
Heartland Food Brokers LTD, 40482
Henry J. Hips Company, 40483
Herb Barber & Sons Food, 40484
Higgins & White Inc, 40486
Hilgenfeld Brokerage Co, 40487
Hobby Whalen Marketing, 40489
Hockenberg Newburgh, 40490, 40491
Homeplace Food Group, 40494
Howell Associates, 40496
Hugh T. Gilmore Company, 40498
Huron Food Sales, 40501
Iceberg Seafood Inc, 40509
Imark of Pennsylvania, 40510
Imperial Frozen Foods Co, 40514
Ingredient Exchange Co, 40517
Ingredient Inc, 40518
Inter-American Products, 40523
Intermountain Food Brokerage, 40525
International Pacific Sales, 40528
Interpack NW Frozen Food, 40531
Intershell Seafood Corp, 40533
Intersouth Foodservice Group, 40534
Interstate Food Brokers, 40535
ISB Sales Company, 40504
ISC of Indiana, 40505
ITOCHU International, Inc, 40508
J N Rhodes Co Inc, 40542
J&S Food Brokerage, 40547
J.F. Benz Company, 40550
J.F. Kelly, 40551
Jack Curren & Associates, 40564
James W Valleau & Company, 40567
Jilasco Food Exports, 40572
Jim Pless & Company, 40573
JML Sales Co, 40560
John J Wollack Co Inc, 40577
John Mangum Company, 40579
Johnson O'Hare Co, 40583
Jones Neitzel Co, 40586
Jos Iorio Company, 40588
Joseph W Nath Co, 40593
JP Bissonnette, 40561
JP Carroll Company, 40562
Jso Associates Inc, 40596
Jubilee Sales of Carolina, 40597
Juhl Brokerage, 40598, 40599
Julius M. Dean Company, 40602
Kappert/Hyzer Company, 40614
Kathryn's Food Service Brokers, 40616
Kayco, 40619
KDH Sales, 40609
Kedem, 40621
Keeth & Associates, 40622
Kelley-Clarke, 40623, 40624
Kemper Food Brokers, 40628
Kenney Sales, 40630
Key Carlin O'Brien, LLC, 40632
Key Impact Sales & Systems Inc, 40633
Key Sales & Marketing, 40634
Key Sales Group, 40635
KeyImpact Sales & Systems, Inc., 40636
Kidd Enterprises, 40637
KIKO Foods Inc, 40611
Kinder-Smith Company, 40639
Kingery & Assoc, 40643
Kirstein Brokerage Company, 40648
Klinger & Speros Food Brokers, 40651
Klondike Foods, 40652
Koch & Assoc, 40654
Korth Marketing, 40656
L&S Sales Company, 40661
LA Teste Services, 40662
LAD Foodservice Sales, 40663
Lakeside Food Sales Inc, 40673
Lampson & Tew, 40675

Leblanc Foodservice Marketing, 40683
Lehigh Food Sales Inc, 40685
Lehmann Brokerage Co, 40686
LeMire Sales, 40682
Lemmons Company, 40687
Lever Associates, 40691
Lilburn Gulf, 40694
Linwood-Welch Marketing, 40695
Lisberg-Voegeli Hanson, 40696
Littler Brokerage Co Inc, 40697
LMGO International Inc, 40666
Lobel Food Brokers, 40702
Lomac & May Associates, 40703
Loman Brown, 40704
Lorey & Lorey, 40707
Louis F. Leeper Company/Cleveland, 40710
Lowe & Associates, 40711
Luke Soules Southwest, 40713
M. Soffer Company, 40721
M.E. Dilanian Company, 40722
Madden & Assoc, 40730
Magic Valley Truck Brokers Inc, 40731
Main Street Marketing, 40732
Major Marketing Service, 40735
Mancini & Groesbeck, 40738
Mancini Sales & Marketing, 40740
Manzo Food Brokers, 40742
Marathon Marketing, 40743
Marbran USA, 40744
Marino Marketing Group, 40746
Marjo & Associates, 40747
Market Pro International, 40749
Market Smart, 40750
Market West Company, 40751
Marketing Management Inc, 40754
Marshall Sales Co, 40757
Martin Preferred Foods, 40758
Marty Scanlon Brokerage Co, 40759
Matrix Group Inc., 40766
MAV Sales Co, 40725
McCarty Brokerage Company, 40771
McCormick Brokerage Company, 40773
Meadows Brokerage Company, 40775
Menu Planners, 40777
Mercantum Corp, 40778
Merit Sales Corporation, 40781
Michael Raymond Desserts Inc, 40783
Mid-American Brokerage of St. Louis, 40787
Mid-Continent Sales, 40788
Mid-State Food Brokers, 40789
Midland Marketing Co-Op Inc, 40792
Midstates Marketing Inc, 40794
Midwest Ingredients Inc, 40797
Milky Whey Inc, 40799
Miller & Smith Foods, 40800
Miller's Market, 40802
Miller, Stabler & Smith, 40803
Mirandas' Sales & Merchandising, 40805
Mitchell & Co Inc, 40808
Mitchell of Mississippi, 40810
Monterey Food Ingredients, 40812
Morley Sales Co, 40817
Morton & Associates, 40818
Moten Company, 40821
Multy-Grain Foods, 40825
N.H. Cohen & Associates, 40830
Nanni-Marketal, 40834
Nash Wright Brokerage, 40836
National Commodity Sales, 40840
National Food Group, 40841
National Food Sales, 40842, 40843
National Foodservice Marketing, 40844
National Heritage Sales Company, 40846
Nesco Brokerage Company, 40851
Network Sales, Inc, 40852
New Horizons, 40853
Next Phase Enterprises, 40855
Nicholas & Co Inc, 40856
Nobert Marketing, 40860
Noble Foods, 40861
Noon International, 40864
Norman Brokerage Co, 40865
North Eastern Sales Solutions, 40869

Brokered Product / General Merchandise

Northeastern Enterprises, 40873
Northland Express Transport, 40874
Northumberland Dairy, 40876
O'Brien & Associates Brokerage Company, 40880
Oekerman Sales, 40887
Omni Food Inc, 40890
Osage Food Products Inc, 40893
Osborn Food Sales Company, 40894
Overseas Service Corp, 40896
Pacific Salmon Company, 40901
Parks Brokerage Company, 40909
Patman Meat Group, 40911
Patterson Co Inc, 40912
Paul G Nester & Son Co Inc, 40914
Paul Inman Associates, 40915
Peak Corporation, 40916
Pennickers Food Distribution, 40917
Peter Blease Sales, 40918
Phillips Sales Co, 40922
Phoenix Food Sales, 40923
Phoenix Foods Inc, 40924
Pierce Cartwright Company, 40925
Pioneer Food Brokers, 40927
Pioneer Food Service, 40928
Preferred Brokerage Company, 40936
Preisco Jentash, 40937
Premier Food Service Sales, 40940
Premium Seafood Co, 40942
Prestige Marketing, 40943
Prestige Sales, 40944
Prestige Sales & Marketing, 40945
Proactive Sales & Marketing, 40950
Professional Food Service, 40952
Progressive Brokerage Co Inc, 40955
Progressive Food Service Broker, 40956
Progressive Sales & Marketing, 40958
Promesa, 40959
Providence Bay Fish Co, 40960
Provincial, 40962
Quality Brokerage Company, 40965
Quality Sales & Marketing, 40969
R G Sellers Co, 40970
R. Becker Marketing & Sales, 40974
R.F. Cannon Company, 40975
Rainbow Sales & Marketing, 40983
Ratcliff Food Brokers, 40988
Ray's Pride Brokerage Company, 40990
Reede International Seafood Corporation, 40992
Reese Brokerage Co, 40993
Reichenbach & Associates, 40994
Resource One, 40999
Reuven International, 41001
Rheuark/F.S.I. Sales, 41002
Richardson Petkovsek & Associates, 41004
Richs Sales Company, 41005
Riteway Co, 41007
Rizwitsch Sales, 41010, 41011
RMCI Foodservice, 40980
Rocky Mountain Motel, 41017
Rodon Foods, 41018
Roehl Corp, 41019
Roos-Mohan, 41022
Rosett Brokerage Company, 41025
Rudolph Brady, Inc, 41031
S&K Sales Company, 41034
Sabbers & Assoc Inc, 41046
Sachem Co, 41047
Sales Corporation of Alaska, 41052
Sales Results, 41054
Saverino & Assoc, 41066
Scavuzzo Sales & Marketing, 41067
Schare & Associates, 41069
Schraad & Associates, 41072
Seafood Sales, 41082
Sell Group, 41085
Service Group, 41086
Sessions & Associates, 41088
SHA Services, 41040
Shrimp Tex Distributors, 41093
Sinco, 41097
SJH Enterprises, 41042
Slagle & Associates, 41100
Slaybaugh & Associates, 41102
Sloan Sales Inc, 41103
Smart Cycling, Inc., 41104
South Group Marketing, 41111
Specialty Sales & Marketing, 41118
Spectrum Foodservice Associates, 41119
Spectrum Foodservices, 41120
Spencer & Assoc, 41122
Statewide Brokerage Company, 41130
Stern International Consultants, 41132
Stroup Ingredients Resources, 41139
Sturdivant Company, 41140
Sturgill Food Brokerage, 41141
Sullivan & Fitzgerald Food Brokers, 41142
Summit Brokerage, 41143
Summit FS LTD, 41144
Sun Food Service Brokerage, 41145
Sundown Foods USA, Inc., 41148
Super Sale Brokerage Company, 41150
Supreme Foods, 41153
Supreme Foodservice Sales, 41154
Sutton International, 41155
T. McConnell Sales & Marketing, 41159
T.W. Wilson & Son, 41162
Team Northwest, 41167, 41168
Tees & Persse Brokerage Acosta Sales And Marketing Company, Inc, 41172
Tees & Persse Brokerage, 41173
Terra Nova Brokers, 41175
The Thurber Company, 41178
Thomas Food Brokers, 41179
Thomas, Large & Singer, 41181
TMC Foods, 41163
Trading Corporation of America, 41195
Tri-State Logistics Inc, 41199
Tucker Sales, 41203
Twin City Food Brokers, 41206
UBC Marketing, 41208
United Brands, 41212
United Foodservice Sales, 41214
United International Indstrs, 41215
US Food Products, 41210
W.H. Moseley Co., 41230
W.H. Sullivan & Associates, 41232
Ward Hughes Co, 41239
Watson & Associates, 41241
Waypoint, 41242
Webco General Partnership, 41243
WENS Brokerage, 41233
Wesco Food Brokerage, 41249
Westex, 41253
Wieber-McLain Company, 41256
William B. Steedman & Sons, 41257
William M. Dunne & Associates Ltd, 41260
Wilson Food Brokers, 41264
Wiltsie & Company, 41265
Winmix/Natural Care Products, 41266
WJ Pence Company, 41234
Wrap-It Packaging, 41274
Yankee Marketers, 41276
York Cheese, 41279

General Merchandise

A G Brown & Son, 40003
A Gazerro & Assoc, 40004
A M Source Inc, 40006
A Thomas Farris & Son Inc, 40007
A W Sisk & Son, 40008
A&D Sales Associates, 40009
A.J. Seibert Company, 40010
Abramson & Di Benedetto Mktng, 40019
Access Partners, 40020
Acorn Sales Company, 40023
Acosta Sales & Marketing Company, 40024
Action Marketing, 40025
Action Marketing Associates, 40026
Action Marketing Services, 40028
Adtek Sales, 40029
Advantage Solutions, 40033
Advantage Webco Hawaii, 40034
Advertising Concepts, 40035
Ake-Sullivan Associates, 40038
Alexander, Koetting, Poole & Buehrle Brothers, 40041
All-State Food Brokerage, 40043
Alliance Foods, 40044
Alliance Foods Inc, 40045
American Sales & Marketing, 40054
American Trading Company, 40055
AMT Sales & Marketing, 40016
Anchor Florida Marketing, 40058
Anderson Daymon Worldwide, 40060
Anthony Cea & Associates, 40061
Arnett Brokerage Co, 40065
Arthur G. Meier Company/Inland Products Company, 40067
Artisana Foods, 40068
ATI, 40017
Atkinson Sales Company, 40073
Atlas Restaurant Supply, 40077
Automatic Packaging Systems & Conveyors Company, 40078
B & D Sales & Marketing Inc, 40082
B.C. Ritchie Company, 40084
Baker Sales, 40093
Barliant & Company, 40095
Bassett-Carragher Associates, 40098
Beach Filter Products, 40102
Becksmith Company, Inc, 40104
Benson-Mitchell, 40110
Bentley Food Marketing, 40111
Best Marketing Reps, 40115
Bireta Company, 40121
Bisek & Co Inc, 40122
Bloodworth & Associates, 40126
BLV Marketing Inc, 40088, 40089
Bodie-Rickett & Associates, 40130
Boehmer Sales Agency, 40131
Booth, Schwager & Associates, 40132
Bowerman Associates, 40136
Bridge City Food Marketing, 40140
Brierley & King Brokerage Corporation, 40141
Broms Brokerage, 40145
Browning Brokerage Company, 40147
BSE Marketing, 40090
Buckley, Thorne, Messina & McDermott, 40149
Budd Mayer Company of Jackson Inc., 40150
Budd Mayer of Mobile, 40151
Buley Patterson Sales Company, 40152
Burdett Associates, 40153
Burdette Beckmann Inc, 40154
Buzz Crown Enterprises, 40158
Byrne & Assoc Inc, 40160
C J Irwin Co Inc, 40162
C. Lloyd Johnson Company, 40163
C. Mascari & Associates, 40164
C.R. Peterson Associates, 40167
Cafe Inc, 40173
Carlin Group, 40179
Carlton Company, 40180
Chandler Food Sales Co, 40189
Chapman-Tait Brokerage, Inc., 40191
Charles Pace & Assoc Inc, 40192
Charles R. Bell Limited, 40193
Charlie Brown Sales Company, 40196
Chell Brokerage Co, 40203
Chernoff Sales, 40204
Chilay Corporation, 40205
Citrin-Pitoscia Company, 40210
Clements Stella Marketing, 40213
CLVMarketing, 40170
Co-Sales De Credico, 40217
Colon Brothers, 40223
Columbia Food Machinery Inc, 40225
Commercial Kitchens Reps Inc, 40226
Commodities Marketing Inc, 40227
Concord National, 40230, 40231, 40232, 40233, 40234, 40235
Concord Sales-Prairies, 40236
Convenience Marketing Services, 40247
Copperwood InternationalInc, 40249
Courtney Marketing Inc, 40253
Crane Sales Co, 40255
Creightons, 40256
Crossmark, 40259
Crowley Marketing Assoc Park, 40260
Cyba-Stevens Management Group, 40265
D&D Marketing Group, Inc., 40266
D&R Food Brokers, 40268
Dakota Marketing Company, 40277
Dambeck & Associates, 40280
Dave Roemer & Associates, 40281
Davis Sales Associates, 40286
Dawson Sales Co Inc, 40287
DeJarnett Sales, 40289, 40290
Di Meo-Gale Brokerage Company, 40297
Dixon Marketing Inc, 40305
Donald R Conyer Associates, 40307
Donald R Tinsman Co, 40308
Doug Milne Co, 40309
Douglas Sales Associates, 40310
DRC Marketing Group, 40270
Dunbar Sales Company, Inc, 40315
Dunham & Smith Agencies, 40316
E A Berg & Sons Inc, 40317
E Ruff & Assoc Inc, 40319
Eagle Associates, 40322
Eagle Marketing, 40323
Eastern Bag & Paper Co, 40324
Eastern Sales & Marketing, 40325
Eastern Sales and Marketing, 40326
Ebbert Sales & Marketing, 40327
Ed O'Connor Associates, 40328
Eiseman-Gleit Co Inc, 40330
Elias Shaker & Co, 40333
Elliot Horowitz & Co, 40334
Ellis S. Fine Co., Inc., 40335
Erickson Brothers Brokerage Co, 40340
Esposito Brokerage, 40344
Essential Food Marketing, 40346
Ettinger Rosini & Associates, 40347
Eurogulf Company, 40348
Evans & Associates, 40350
Evans Brokerage Company, 40351
Evers Heilig Inc, 40352
Fairley & Co Inc, 40360
Federated Group, 40361
Ferdinand Richards & Son, 40363
Ferolie Esm-Metro New York, 40364
Finn Marketing Group Inc, 40365
Firing Industries Ltd, 40366
Fischer Group, 40369
Five Star Packaging, 40370
Florida Agents Inc, 40373
Flynn Sales Associates, Inc., 40375
Food Associates of Syracuse, 40377
Food Equipment Rep Inc, 40378
Foodsales Inc, 40389
Forbes Hever & Wallace, Inc., 40396
Forma Packaging, Inc., 40397
Forseasons Sales, 40399
Four Peaks, Inc., 40400
Frank Kinsman Assoc, 40402
Fredco Wolf, 40404
Freeman Signature, 40409
Freiria & Company, 40410
Garden Gold Foods, Inc, 40419
Garisco Distributing, 40420
George W. Holop Associates, 40430
GFR Worldwide, 40417
Gibbs & Assoc, 40432
Golick Martins, Inc., 40441
Great Southwest Sales Company, 40448
Griffin Marketing Group, 40450
H & G Trading LTD Inc, 40454
H.V. Mid State Sales Company, 40458
Hanks Brokerage, 40467
Hansen Group, 40468
Hansid Company, 40469
Harold M. Lincoln Company, 40471
Harriet Greenland Enterprises, 40472
Harry Tinseth Associates, Inc., 40474
Harvest Grove Inc, 40476
Hatch-Jennings Inc, 40478
Hawley & Assoc, 40480
HD Marshall Ltd, 40460
HGA Group, 40461
Hilgenfeld Brokerage Co, 40487

Brokered Product / Groceries

Hinkle Easter Products, 40488
HK Marketing, 40462
Hobby Whalen Marketing, 40489
Hockenberg Newburgh, 40490, 40491
Hockenberg-Newburgh Sales, 40492
Homeplace Food Group, 40494
Hugh T. Gilmore Company, 40498
Hynes Bond Ellison, 40502, 40503
Imperial Florida Sales, 40513
Ingredient Inc, 40518
Insulated Structures/PB Group, 40520
Integra Marketing Inc, 40521
Inter-American Products, 40523
Intermountain Food Brokerage, 40525
International Sales & Brokerage Company, 40530
Inverso Johnson LLC, 40538
J.F. Benz Company, 40550
J.H. Bridgins & Associates, 40552
J.W. Kuehn Company, 40556
JABEX Associates, LLC, 40557
Jay Mark Group LTD, 40568
Jeram Associates, 40570
Jilasco Food Exports, 40572
JL Stemp Marketing Agents, 40558
John Mangum Company, 40579
Johnny Bee Sales, 40580
Johnson Commercial Agents, 40581
Johnson O'Hare Co, 40583
Jones Neitzel Co, 40586
Jones-McCormick & Associates, 40587
Jos Iorio Company, 40588
Joseph Caragol, 40590
Joylin Food Equipment Corporation, 40594
JP Bissonnette, 40561
Jpo/Dow Inc, 40595
Jubilee Sales of Carolina, 40597
Juhl Brokerage, 40598, 40599
Julius M. Dean Company, 40602
Kandy King Confections, 40613
Kappert/Hyzer Company, 40614
KBRW, 40608
KDH Sales, 40609
Keeth & Associates, 40622
Kelley-Clarke, 40623
Kelly/Mincks Northwest Agents, 40627
Kemper Food Brokers, 40628
Kenney Sales, 40630
Key Carlin O'Brien, LLC, 40632
Key Sales Group, 40635
Kinder-Smith Company, 40639
King Sales & Engineering Co, 40642
Kingery & Assoc, 40643
Kirstein Brokerage Company, 40648
Klondike Foods, 40652
Koch & Assoc, 40654
L H Gamble Co LTD, 40660
L&S Sales Company, 40661
LA Teste Services, 40662
Lane Marketing Group LLC, 40680
LBM Sales, LLC, 40664
Len Miller & Associates, 40688
Leonard H Sisitzky Sales Inc, 40689
Leopold & Diner Associates, 40690
LIN-PAK, LLC., 40665
Lisberg-Voegeli Hanson, 40696
Littler Brokerage Company, 40697
Lloyd A Gray Co Inc, 40699
Lloyd Hollander Company, 40700
LMGO International Inc, 40666
LMS Associate, 40667
Long & Littleton, 40705
Loretta Foods, 40706
Lorey & Lorey, 40707
Luke Soules Southwest, 40713
Lund-Iorio Inc, 40714
M K Food Svc Equipment Inc, 40718
M&W Associates, 40719
M. Pencar Associates, 40720
Madden & Assoc, 40730
Magic Valley Truck Brokers Inc, 40731
Main Street Marketing, 40732
Major Marketing Service, 40735
Maloney Veitch Associates, 40737

Mancini & Groesbeck, 40738
Mancini Packing Co, 40739
Mancini Sales & Marketing, 40740
Manzo Food Brokers, 40742
Marino Marketing Group, 40746
Marketing Agents South, 40752
Marketing Management Inc, 40754
Marshall Associates, 40756
Master Marketing South, 40762
Master Marketing Sunlow, Inc., 40763
Master Sales & Marketing, 40764
MAV Sales Co, 40725
Max Pratt Company, 40767
McArdle, 40770
McCormick Brokerage Company, 40773
McGovern & Whitten, 40774
Meadows Brokerage Company, 40775
Measured Sales & Marketing, 40776
Merit Sales Corporation, 40781
Michael R Fish & Co, 40782
Mid-American Brokerage of St. Louis, 40787
Mid-Continent Sales, 40788
Mid-West Associates, 40790
Mid-West Sales Agency, 40791
Midstates Marketing Inc, 40794
Midwest Ingredients Inc, 40797
Miller & Stryker Assoc Inc, 40801
Miller's Market, 40802
Miller, Stabler & Smith, 40803
Miltenberg & Samton Inc., 40804
Mirkovich & Assoc Inc, 40806
Mitchell Agencies, 40809
Mitchell of Mississippi, 40810
Moneuse Sales Agency, 40811
Morgan Sampson USA, 40816
Mountain Sales & Svc Inc, 40823
Mueller Yurgae, 40824
N.H. Cohen & Associates, 40830
National Brokerage Network, 40838
National Commodity Sales, 40840
NEMA Associates, 40831
Nesco Brokerage Company, 40851
Network Sales, Inc, 40852
Nicholas & Co Inc, 40856
Nobert Marketing, 40860
North Eastern Sales Solutions, 40869
Northeast Retail Services, 40872
Northland Express Transport, 40874
O'Brien & Associates Brokerage Company, 40880
O'Hanlon Group, 40881
O.R. Elder, 40883
Oak Leaf Sales Co, 40885
Oekerman Sales, 40887
Orchard Paper, 40892
Overseas Service Corp, 40896
PacNorth Group, 40898
Pankow Associates Inc, 40905
Paris Paper Box Company, 40907
Patman Meat Group, 40911
Paul Esposito Inc, 40913
Paul Inman Associates, 40915
Peak Corporation, 40916
Pennickers Food Distribution, 40917
Peters & Peters Manufacturer's Agents, 40921
Phoenix Foods Inc, 40924
Pierce Cartwright Company, 40925
Pioneer Food Brokers, 40927
Posternak Bauer Associates, 40933
Preisco Jentash, 40937
Premier Marketing, 40941
Prestige Sales, 40944
Prestige Sales & Marketing, 40945
Pro Line Marketing Inc, 40946
Pro Pacific Agents, 40947
Pro Reps W, 40948
Pro-Quip Corporation, 40949
Professional Manufacturers' Representatives, 40953
Professional Reps of Arizona, 40954
Progressive Brokerage Co Inc, 40955
Progressive Marketing Systems, 40957
Progressive Sales & Marketing, 40958

Providence Brokerage, 40961
Provincial, 40962
Purcell & Madden Associates, 40963
Quality Rep Source, 40967
Quality Sales & Marketing, 40969
R.W. Berkeley & Associates, 40977
Rabe Sales Corp, 40981
Rainbow Sales & Marketing, 40983
Raleigh W. Johnson & Company, 40984
Rancho Sales & Marketing, 40985
Reese Brokerage Co, 40993
Rep Source, 40997
Res-Q Network, 40998
Resource One, 40999
Rheuark/F.S.I. Sales, 41002
Rich Audette Associates, 41003
Richardson Petkovsek & Associates, 41004
Ringland Associates, 41006
Riteway Co, 41007
Robert A. Haines Companies, 41013
Rocky Mountain Motel, 41017
Roger J. Wood Company, 41020
Roller & Associates, 41021
RMCI Foodservice, 40980
S&K Sales Company, 41034
Sabal Marketing, 41045
Sabbers & Assoc Inc, 41046
Sachem Co, 41047
Sales, 41050
Sales & Marketing Dev, 41051
Sales Corporation of Alaska, 41052
Sales Marketing Svc LLC, 41053
Sales Specialties, 41055
San Francisco Reps, 41057
Santucci Associates, 41061
Scavuzzo Sales & Marketing, 41067
Schraad & Associates, 41072
Schurman's Wisconsin Cheese Country, 41074
Scott & Associates, 41076
SCS Sales Company, 41037
Select Sales & Marketing Inc, 41084
Sell Group, 41085
Service Group, 41086
Sessions & Associates, 41088
Settables Inc, 41089
SFS Marketing, 41038
SHA Services, 41040
Shields Brokerage, 41091
Sinco, 41097
Slaybaugh & Associates, 41102
Smart Cycling, Inc., 41104
Smigiel Marketing & Sales Ltd., 41105
Solo Cup Company, 41107
Soudronic Limited, 41108
Southeastern Manufacturer's, 41112
Southeastern Paper Group Inc, 41113
Specialty Equipment Sales Co, 41116
Specialty Sales & Marketing, 41118
Spence Wells Assoc, 41121
Spencer & Assoc, 41122
Spurry & Associates, 41124
Squier Associates, 41125
St Charles Trading Inc, 41126
Starliper & Associates, 41129
Statewide Brokerage Company, 41130
Stern International Consultants, 41132
Stevens & Associates, 41133
Stiefel Associates, 41134
Stockett Associates, 41136
Sun Marketing Agents Inc, 41146
Super Sale Brokerage Company, 41150
Supermarket Representatives, 41152
Supreme Foods, 41153
Sutton International, 41155
Symons-Bodtker Associates, 41157
T.W. Wilson & Son, 41162
Team Northwest, 41168
Teasley & Associates, 41169
Tees & Persse Brokerage Acosta Sales And Marketing Company, Inc, 41172
Tees & Persse Brokerage, 41173
Tepper & Assoc, 41174
Terra Nova Brokers, 41175

The Cherry Company Ltd., 41177
The Thurber Company, 41178
Thomas, Large & Singer, 41181
Thomson-Leeds Company, 41182
Thormann Associates, 41183
Tilkin & Cagen Inc, 41184
Tom Quinn & Associates, 41189
Top O' The Table, 41190
Toteco Packaging Co, 41192
Tri-State Logistics Inc, 41199
Tucker Sales, 41203
UBC Marketing, 41208
Union Standard Equipment Company, 41211
United Brands, 41212
United Foodservice Sales, 41214
United Restaurant Specialties, 41216
US Food Products, 41210
Vader & Landgraf, 41222
Van Reed Sales Company, 41224
VP Northeast, 41221
W.B. Marketing Group, 41228
W.H. Escott Company, 41229
Wallin Group Inc, 41237
Waypoint, 41242
Webco General Partnership, 41243
Wehrfritz & Associates, 41245
Wendlandt Brokerage Company, 41248
Wesnic Services Inc, 41250
Western Manufacturers Agents, 41252
Westex, 41253
Wieber-McLain Company, 41256
William M. Dunne & Associates Ltd, 41260
Williams Brokerage Company, 41261
Willing Group, 41263
Wiltsie & Company, 41265
Winpac, 41267
Woolsey & Assoc Inc, 41271
Wrap-It Packaging, 41274
WTD Associates, 41236
Yankee Marketers, 41276
York Cheese, 41279
York Hospitality & Gaming, 41280
Young-Block Associates, 41282
Z&A Vending, 41283
Zanichelli & Associates, 41285
Zink Marketing, 41286

Groceries

3-D Marketing & Sales, 40001
A G Brown & Son, 40003
A&D Sales Associates, 40009
A.J. Seibert Company, 40010
Access Partners, 40020
Acclaim Marketing & Sales, 40021
Acorn Sales Company, 40023
Acosta Sales & Marketing Company, 40024
Action Marketing, 40025
Action Marketing Associates, 40026
Action Marketing Of So Ca, 40027
Action Marketing Services, 40028
Advance Sales & Marketing, Inc, 40031
Advantage Solutions, 40033
Advantage Webco Hawaii, 40034
Albert A Russo Inc, 40040
All Seasons Brokerage Company, 40042
Alliance Foods, 40044
Alliance Foods Inc, 40045
Allied Marketing Corp, 40046
Ambi-Prestigio Foods Inc, 40050
American Commodity & Shipping, 40052
American Patriot Sales Inc, 40053
American Sales & Marketing, 40054
AMT Sales & Marketing, 40016
Anchor Florida Marketing, 40058
Anthony Cea & Associates, 40061
Apache Brokers, 40062
Apple Food Sales, 40063
Arnett Brokerage Co, 40065
Arroyo Sales Company, 40066
Arthur G. Meier Company/Inland Products Company, 40067

Brokered Product / Groceries

Artisanal Foods, 40068
Arvin Sales Company, 40069
ATI, 40017
Atkinson Sales Company, 40073
Baker Brokerage Company LLC, 40092
BAL Marketing, 40087
Bay Brokerage Company, 40099
Bay Pacific Marketing, 40100
Becksmith Company, Inc, 40104
Bee Jay Sales Of Florida, 40106
Benchmark Sales, 40108
Benson-Mitchell, 40110
Bentley Food Marketing, 40111
Bertran Enterprises, 40113
Best Brands, 40114
Binner Marketing & Sales, 40119
Bird Marketing, 40120
Bisek & Co Inc, 40122
BLV Marketing Inc, 40088, 40089
Bob Rowe Sales, 40128
Bodie-Rickett & Associates, 40130
Booth, Schwager & Associates, 40132
Borton Brokerage Company, 40133
Bosshart Food Svc, 40134
Bottom Line Foods, 40135
Bratt-Foster-Advantage Sales, 40138
Brokerage Sales Company, 40144
Broms Brokerage, 40145
Browning Brokerage Company, 40147
Buckley, Thorne, Messina & McDermott, 40149
Budd Mayer Company of Jackson Inc., 40150
Budd Mayer of Mobile, 40151
Buley Patterson Sales Company, 40152
Burdette Beckmann Inc, 40154
C J Irwin Co Inc, 40162
C. Lloyd Johnson Company, 40163
C.H. Robinson Co., 40166
C.W. Shasky & Associates Ltd., 40168
California World Trade and Marketing Company, 40175
Caneast Foods, 40176
Cann Brokerage Inc, 40177
Cardinal Brokerage, 40178
Carlin Group, 40179
Cashman-Edwards Inc, 40184
Chandler Food Sales Co, 40189
Chapman-Tait Brokerage, Inc., 40191
Charles R. Bell Limited, 40193
Charles Rockel & Son, 40194
Chase Sales Company, 40198
Chase-Goldenberg Associates, 40199
Chell Brokerage Co, 40203
Chilay Corporation, 40205
Chuck Batcheller Company, 40208
Co-Sales De Credico, 40217
Coastal Commodities, 40218
Cobler Food Sales, 40220
Colony Brokerage Company, 40224
Commodities Marketing Inc, 40227
Concept Food Brokers, 40228
Concord National, 40230, 40231, 40232, 40233, 40234, 40235
Concord Sales-Prairies, 40236
Consolidated Marketers Inc, 40239
Consolidated Tea Co Inc, 40241
Consummate Marketing Company, 40244
Convenience Marketing Services, 40247
Cooke Marketing Group Inc, 40248
Copperwood InternationalInc, 40249
Core Group, 40251
Cox Food Brokers, 40254
Creightons, 40256
CS Brokers, 40172
Culinary Specialty Produce, 40263
Cyba-Stevens Management Group, 40265
D&D Marketing Group, Inc., 40266
Dambeck & Associates, 40280
Dave Roemer & Associates, 40281
Davel Food Brokerage, 40283
DeJarnett Sales, 40289, 40290
Delbert Craig Food Brokers, 40295
DeMoss & Associates, 40291
Di Meo-Gale Brokerage Company, 40297

Dial Industries Inc, 40298
Dixon Marketing Inc, 40305
Donald R Tinsman Co, 40308
Doug Milne Co, 40309
Dunbar Sales Company, Inc, 40315
Dunham & Smith Agencies, 40316
DVC Brokerage Company, 40272
E A Berg & Sons Inc, 40317
Eagle Associates, 40322
Eagle Marketing, 40323
Eastern Sales & Marketing, 40325
Eastern Sales and Marketing, 40326
Ebbert Sales & Marketing, 40327
Egerstrom Inc, 40329
Elias Shaker & Co, 40333
Ellis S. Fine Co., Inc., 40335
Encore Fruit Marketing Inc, 40337
Enterprise Food Brokers, 40339
Erickson Brothers Brokerage Co, 40340
Esm Ferolie, 40343
Esposito Brokerage, 40344
Espresso Machine Experts, 40345
Essential Food Marketing, 40346
Eurogulf Company, 40348
Evans Brokerage Company, 40351
Evers Heilig Inc, 40352
F Mc Lintocks Saloon & Dinin, 40355
Fairley & Co Inc, 40360
Federated Group, 40361
Feenix Brokerage LTD, 40362
Ferdinand Richards & Son, 40363
Ferolie Esm-Metro New York, 40364
First Flight Foods, 40368
Five State Brokerage, 40371
Flynn Sales Associates, Inc., 40375
Food Associates of Syracuse, 40377
Food Sales Systems, 40380
Food Sales West, 40381
Food Service Associates, 40382
Food Service Connection, 40383
Foodsales Inc, 40389
Foodservice Innovators, 40390
Foodservice Solutions & Ideas, 40392
Forseasons Sales, 40399
Frank Kinsman Assoc, 40402
Freeman Signature, 40409
Freiria & Company, 40410
Fusion Sales Group, 40413
GAP Food Brokers, 40415
Garden Gold Foods, Inc, 40419
Genesis International, 40425
George W. Holop Associates, 40430
Gibbs-Mccormick Inc A Ca Corp, 40433
Gilbert Foodservice Inc, 40434
Glenmoor Brokerage, 40438
Global Citrus Resources, Inc, 40439
Golden Valley Industries Inc, 40440
Golick Martins, Inc., 40441
Goveco Full Service Food Brokers, 40444
Grabbe-Leonard Co, 40445
Great Southwest Sales Company, 40448
H & G Trading LTD Inc, 40454
H&T Food Marketing Company, 40455
H.V. Mid State Sales Company, 40458
Halling Company, 40465
Hanimex Company, 40466
Hansid Company, 40469
Harold M. Lincoln Company, 40471
Harriet Greenland Enterprises, 40472
Hartley S. Johnson & Son, 40475
Harvest Grove Inc, 40476
Hawley & Assoc, 40480
HD Marshall Ltd, 40460
Henry J. Hips Company, 40483
Herspring, 40485
Hilgenfeld Brokerage Co, 40487
Hockenberg Newburgh, 40490, 40491
Hockenberg-Newburgh Sales, 40492
Homeplace Food Group, 40494
Howell Associates, 40496
Hugh T. Gilmore Company, 40498
Hundley Brokerage Company, 40499
Inter-American Products, 40523
Interep Company, 40524

Intermountain Food Brokerage, 40525
International Pacific Sales, 40528
International Sales & Brokerage Company, 40530
Interpex, 40532
Intersouth Foodservice Group, 40534
Intralinks Inc, 40537
ISC of Indiana, 40505
ISSCO, 40506
J N Rhodes Co Inc, 40542
J T Gibbons Inc, 40544
J&S Food Brokerage, 40547
J. Maganas Sales Company, 40548
J.F. Benz Company, 40550
J.F. Kelly, 40551
Jacobsen-Clahan & Company, 40565
Jam Group of Company, 40566
Jilasco Food Exports, 40572
John L. Pieri & Sons, 40578
John Mangum Company, 40579
Johnson Holmes & Assoc Inc, 40582
Johnson O'Hare Co, 40583
Jones Neitzel Co, 40586
Jos Iorio Company, 40588
Joseph Caragol, 40590
Joseph W Nath Co, 40593
JP Bissonnette, 40561
JP Carroll Company, 40562
Jso Associates Inc, 40596
Jubilee Sales of Carolina, 40597
Juhl Brokerage, 40599
Julius Levy Company, 40601
Julius M. Dean Company, 40602
Kandy King Confections, 40613
Kappert/Hyzer Company, 40614
Kathryn's Food Service Brokers, 40616
Kayco, 40619
KDH Sales, 40609
Kedem, 40621
Keeth & Associates, 40622
Kelley-Clarke, 40623
Kelly Associates/Food Brokers, 40625
Kenney Sales, 40630
Key Carlin O'Brien, LLC, 40632
Key Sales & Marketing, 40634
Key Sales Group, 40635
KeyImpact Sales & Systems, Inc., 40636
Kidd Enterprises, 40637
KIKO Foods Inc, 40611
Kinder-Smith Company, 40639
Kingery & Assoc, 40643
Kirstein Brokerage Company, 40648
Klinger & Speros Food Brokers, 40651
Klondike Foods, 40652
Koch & Assoc, 40654
Korth Marketing, 40656
Kramer Brokerage Co, 40657
LA Teste Services, 40662
LAD Foodservice Sales, 40663
Lakeside Food Sales Inc, 40673
Leblanc Foodservice Marketing, 40683
Lehmann Brokerage Co, 40686
Lemmons Company, 40687
Leonard H Sisitzky Sales Inc, 40689
Leopold & Diner Associates, 40690
Lever Associates, 40691
Linwood-Welch Marketing, 40695
Lisberg-Voegeli Hanson, 40696
Littler Brokerage Co Inc, 40697
Lloyd A Gray Co Inc, 40699
LMGO International Inc, 40666
Lobel Food Brokers, 40702
Loretta Foods, 40706
Louis F. Leeper Company/Cleveland, 40710
Luke Soules Southwest, 40713
M Fellinger Co, 40717
M. Soffer Company, 40721
M.E. Dilanian Company, 40722
Maddan & Co Inc, 40729
Magic Valley Truck Brokers Inc, 40731
Main Street Marketing, 40732
Major Marketing Service, 40735
Mancini & Groesbeck, 40738
Mancini Packing Co, 40739

Mancini Sales & Marketing, 40740
Manzo Food Brokers, 40742
Marathon Marketing, 40743
Marino Marketing Group, 40746
Market Pro International, 40749
Market Smart, 40750
Marketing Management Inc, 40754
Marmelstein Associates, 40755
Marty Scanlon Brokerage Co, 40759
Master Sales & Marketing, 40764
Matrix Group Inc., 40766
MAV Sales Co, 40725
Mc Namara Assoc Inc, 40769
McCarty Brokerage Company, 40771
Meadows Brokerage Company, 40775
Measured Sales & Marketing, 40776
Menu Planners, 40777
Merit Sales Corporation, 40781
Mickelson & Associates, 40784
Mid-American Brokerage of St. Louis, 40787
Mid-Continent Sales, 40788
Mid-State Food Brokers, 40789
Mid-West Sales Agency, 40791
Midland Marketing Co-Op Inc, 40792
Midwest Ingredients Inc, 40797
Miller's Market, 40802
Miller, Stabler & Smith, 40803
Mitchel Beck Company, 40807
Mitchell Agencies, 40809
Moody Dunbar Inc, 40813
Morgan Sampson USA, 40816
Morley Sales Co, 40817
Morton & Associates, 40818
Mueller Yurgae, 40824
N.H. Cohen & Associates, 40830
Nagy Associates, 40832
Nanni-Marketal, 40834
Napoleon Co., 40835
National Commodity Sales, 40840
National Food Group, 40841
National Foodservice Marketing, 40844
National Heritage Sales Company, 40846
Nelson Cheese Factory, 40850
Nesco Brokerage Company, 40851
Network Sales, Inc, 40852
Next Phase Enterprises, 40855
Nicholas & Co Inc, 40856
Nikol Foods, 40857
Nippon Food Company, 40859
Noble Foods, 40861
Noon International, 40864
Norman Brokerage Co, 40865
Norman Hecht, 40866
North Eastern Sales Solutions, 40869
Northeast Retail Services, 40872
Northland Express Transport, 40874
O'Brien & Associates Brokerage Company, 40880
Oak Leaf Sales Co, 40885
Oekerman Sales, 40887
Orca Foods, 40891
Osage Food Products Inc, 40893
Pace Target Brokerage, 40899
Pacific Trading Company International, 40903
Patterson Co Inc, 40912
Paul G Nester & Son Co Inc, 40914
Paul Inman Associates, 40915
Peak Corporation, 40916
Pennickers Food Distribution, 40917
Peter Blease Sales, 40918
Phoenix Food Sales, 40923
Phoenix Foods Inc, 40924
Pierce Cartwright Company, 40925
Pioneer Food Brokers, 40927
Pioneer Food Service, 40928
Preferred Brokerage Company, 40936
Preisco Jentash, 40937
Premier Food Service Sales, 40940
Prestige Sales, 40944
Prestige Sales & Marketing, 40945
Proactive Sales & Marketing, 40950
Progressive Brokerage Co Inc, 40955
Progressive Food Service Broker, 40956

Brokered Product / Health Food

Progressive Marketing Systems, 40957
Progressive Sales & Marketing, 40958
Provincial, 40962
Quality Sales & Marketing, 40969
R G Sellers Co, 40970
R J Bickert & Associates, 40972
R. Becker Marketing & Sales, 40974
R.F. Cannon Company, 40975
Rainbow Sales & Marketing, 40983
Rancho Sales & Marketing, 40985
Ratcliff Food Brokers, 40988
Ray's Pride Brokerage Company, 40990
Reese Brokerage Co, 40993
Reichenbach & Associates, 40994
Resource One, 40999
RH Sulker Sales, 40978
Rheuark/F.S.I. Sales, 41002
Richardson Petkovsek & Associates, 41004
Ringland Associates, 41006
Riteway Co, 41007
RMCI Foodservice, 40980
Robbins Sales Co, 41012
Rocky Mountain Motel, 41017
Roehl Corp, 41019
Roger J. Wood Company, 41020
Roos-Mohan, 41022
Rosenfeld & Gigante, 41024
Rosett Brokerage Company, 41025
Ross Empire State Brokers, 41026
Rudolph Brady, Inc, 41031
S&K Sales Company, 41034
S. Kamberg & Company, 41035
Sabal Marketing, 41045
Sachem Co, 41047
Saggese Brothers, 41048
Sales & Marketing Dev, 41051
Sales Corporation of Alaska, 41052
Sales Marketing Svc LLC, 41053
Sales Results, 41054
Santucci Associates, 41061
Scavuzzo Sales & Marketing, 41067
Schraad & Associates, 41072
SCS Sales Company, 41037
Sell Group, 41085
Service Group, 41086
Sesame King Foods, 41087
Sessions & Associates, 41088
SGS International Rice Inc, 41039
SHA Services, 41040
Sid Alpers Organic Sales Company, 41094
Sinco, 41097
SJE Marketing Corporation, 41041
Slagle & Associates, 41100
Slattery Marketing Corporation, 41101
Slaybaugh & Associates, 41102
Sloan Sales Inc, 41103
Smart Cycling, Inc., 41104
Smigiel Marketing & Sales Ltd, 41105
Southeastern Paper Group Inc, 41113
Southern Commodities Inc, 41114
Specialty Partners, 41117
Specialty Sales & Marketing, 41118
Spectrum Foodservice Associates, 41119
Spencer & Assoc, 41122
Statewide Brokerage Company, 41130
Stern International Consultants, 41132
STI International, 41043
Stockdale & Reagan, 41135
Stroup Ingredients Resources, 41139
Sturdivant Company, 41140
Summit FS LTD, 41144
Sun Food Service Brokerage, 41145
Sundown Foods USA, Inc., 41148
Sunwest Sales Co, 41149
Super Sale Brokerage Company, 41150
Supreme Foods, 41153
Sutton International, 41155
T. McConnell Sales & Marketing, 41159
T.F.S. & Associates, 41160
T.W. Wilson & Son, 41162
Taormina Sales Company, 41166
Team Northwest, 41167, 41168
Teasley & Assoc, 41169

Tees & Persse Brokerage Acosta Sales And Marketing Company, Inc, 41172
Tees & Persse Brokerage, 41173
Terra Nova Brokers, 41175
The Cherry Company Ltd., 41177
Thomas, Large & Singer, 41181
Tower Intercontinental Group, 41193
Tri-State Logistics Inc, 41199
Triangle Sales, 41201
Tucker Sales, 41203
Tufts Ranch, 41204
Twin City Food Brokers, 41206
UBC Marketing, 41208
United Brands, 41212
United Foodservice Sales, 41214
United International Indstrs, 41215
US Food Products, 41210
V.M. Calderon, 41220
Van Reed Sales Company, 41224
W.H. Escott Company, 41229
W.H. Sullivan & Associates, 41232
Waypoint, 41242
Wehrfritz & Associates, 41245
Wendlandt Brokerage Company, 41248
WENS Brokerage, 41233
Wesco Food Brokerage, 41249
Westex, 41253
Whitby Co, 41254
Wieber-McLain Company, 41256
William M. Dunne & Associates Ltd, 41260
Williams Brokerage Company, 41261
Willing Group, 41263
Wilson Food Brokers, 41264
Wiltsie & Company, 41265
WJ Pence Company, 41234
Yankee Marketers, 41276
Yates Sales Associates, 41277
York Cheese, 41279
Zanichelli & Associates, 41285

Health Food

A G Brown & Son, 40003
Action Marketing, 40025
Action Marketing Associates, 40026
Advantage Webco Hawaii, 40034
American Trading Company, 40055
Anthony Cea & Associates, 40061
Apache Brokers, 40062
Artisanal Foods, 40068
ATI, 40017
B.C. Ritchie Company, 40084
Bay Pacific Marketing, 40100
Beck Western Brokerage, 40103
Bentley Food Marketing, 40111
Bisek & Co Inc, 40122
BLV Marketing Inc, 40088, 40089
Brothers International Food Corporation, 40146
Browning Brokerage Company, 40147
Buckley, Thorne, Messina & McDermott, 40149
Byron A Carlson Inc, 40161
C J Irwin Co Inc, 40162
C.H. Robinson Co., 40166
Carlin Group, 40179
Cashman-Edwards Inc, 40184
Christopher's Herb Shop, 40207
Chuck Batcheller Company, 40208
Citrin-Pitoscia Company, 40210
Classic Cuisine Foods, 40211
Clofine Dairy Products Inc, 40215
Co-Sales De Credico, 40217
Concord National, 40230, 40233, 40234, 40235
Concord Sales-Prairies, 40236
Consolidated Marketers Inc, 40239
Consolidated Merchandisers, 40240
Consummate Marketing Company, 40244
CS Brokers, 40172
D&D Marketing Group, Inc., 40266
Dambeck & Associates, 40280
Deiss Sales Co. Inc., 40294
Di Meo-Gale Brokerage Company, 40297

Dino-Meat Company, 40302
Donald R Tinsman Co, 40308
DSI Food Brokerage, 40271
DW Montgomery & Company, 40273
Eagle Marketing, 40323
Egerstrom Inc, 40329
Elias Shaker & Co, 40333
Esm Ferolie, 40343
Esposito Brokerage, 40344
Feenix Brokerage LTD, 40362
Foodsales Inc, 40389
Freedom Food Brokers, 40405
Genesis Marketing, 40426
Genotec Nutritional, 40427
Gilbert Foodservice Inc, 40434
Golick Martins, Inc., 40441
Goveco Full Service Food Brokers, 40444
H.V. Mid State Sales Company, 40458
Harriet Greenland Enterprises, 40472
Harvest Grove Inc, 40476
Hugh T. Gilmore Company, 40498
Ingredient Inc, 40518
Inter-American Products, 40523
Jones Neitzel Co, 40586
Jos Iorio Company, 40588
Juhl Brokerage, 40599
Kahler-Senders Inc, 40612
Kayco, 40619
Kedem, 40621
Key Carlin O'Brien, LLC, 40632
Klondike Foods, 40652
LA Teste Services, 40662
Louis F. Leeper Company/Cleveland, 40710
Madden & Assoc, 40730
Main Street Marketing, 40732
Marketing Management Inc, 40754
Master Sales & Marketing, 40764
Measured Sales & Marketing, 40776
Mercantum Corp, 40778
Merit Sales Corporation, 40781
Midwest Ingredients Inc, 40797
Milky Whey Inc, 40799
Miller's Market, 40802
Mitchell of Mississippi, 40810
MLG Enterprises Ltd., 40727
Morton F Schweitzer Sales, 40819
Mosher Products Inc, 40820
Napoleon Co., 40835
Nash Wright Brokerage, 40836
Nature's Products Inc, 40849
Nelson Cheese Factory, 40850
Network Sales, Inc, 40852
New Organics, 40854
Nicholas & Co Inc, 40856
Norman Brokerage Co, 40865
North Bay Trading Co, 40868
Northland Express Transport, 40874
Oekerman Sales, 40887
Pankow Associates Inc, 40905
Preferred Brokerage Company, 40936
Prestige Sales, 40944
Pure Sales, 40964
R J Bickert & Associates, 40972
R. Becker Marketing & Sales, 40974
Randag & Assoc Inc, 40986
Ratcliff Food Brokers, 40988
Riteway Co, 41007
RMCI Foodservice, 40980
Rocky Mountain Motel, 41017
Rudolph Brady, Inc, 41031
Sabal Marketing, 41045
Sales Results, 41054
Santucci Associates, 41061
Schurman's Wisconsin Cheese Country, 41074
Sessions & Associates, 41088
SHA Services, 41040
Sid Alpers Organic Sales Company, 41094
Sinco, 41097
SJE Marketing Corporation, 41041
Sloan Sales Inc, 41103
Smart Cycling, Inc., 41104

Specialty Partners, 41117
Spencer & Assoc, 41122
Summit FS LTD, 41144
Sunwest Sales Co, 41149
Super Sale Brokerage Company, 41150
Sutton International, 41155
Tees & Persse Brokerage, 41173
The Cherry Company Ltd., 41177
The Thurber Company, 41178
Tri-State Logistics Inc, 41199
US Food Products, 41210
Van Kam, G Trading Company, 41223
Vivion Inc, 41227
WENS Brokerage, 41233
Willing Group, 41263
Wiltsie & Company, 41265
Winmix/Natural Care Products, 41266
Wrap-It Packaging, 41274
Yankee Marketers, 41276
Yates Sales Associates, 41277
York Sutch & Assoc, 41281

Imports

3-D Marketing & Sales, 40001
A G Brown & Son, 40003
A.R. Pellegrini & Associates, 40012
Acorn Sales Company, 40023
Advantage Gourmet Importers, 40032
Agri-Dairy Products, 40036
Airschott Inc, 40037
Alba Specialty Seafood Company, 40039
Albert A Russo Inc, 40040
Alliance Foods, 40044
Alliance Foods Inc, 40045
Ambi-Prestigio Foods Inc, 40050
American Commodity & Shipping, 40052
American Trading Company, 40055
AMT Sales & Marketing, 40016
Anthony Cea & Associates, 40061
Apple Food Sales, 40063
ATI, 40017
Atlas Biscuit Co Inc, 40076
B & D Sales & Marketing Inc, 40082
B.C. Ritchie Company, 40084
B.W. Dyer & Company, 40086
Bay Pacific Marketing, 40100
Bayha & Associates, 40101
Bertran Enterprises, 40113
Best Brands, 40114
Betters International Food Corporation, 40117
BLV Marketing Inc, 40088
Borton Brokerage Company, 40133
British Confectionery Company, 40142
Brothers International Food Corporation, 40146
Buley Patterson Sales Company, 40152
Buzz Crown Enterprises, 40158
Byron A Carlson Inc, 40161
C.B. Powell Limited, 40165
California World Trade and Marketing Company, 40175
Caneast Foods, 40176
Cann Brokerage Inc, 40177
Carlin Group, 40179
Cascade Corp, 40183
Cashman-Edwards Inc, 40184
Charles R. Bell Limited, 40193
Chartrand Imports, 40197
Chase Sales Company, 40198
Chilay Corporation, 40205
Clofine Dairy Products Inc, 40215
Coastal Commodities, 40218
Coastal Pride Co Inc, 40219
Colon Brothers, 40223
Commodities Marketing Inc, 40227
Concord National, 40230, 40231, 40233, 40234, 40235
Concord Sales-Prairies, 40236
Conrad Sales Company, 40238
Creightons, 40256
CS Brokers, 40172
Culinary Specialty Produce, 40263
D&D Marketing Group, Inc., 40266

Brokered Product / Ingredients

D&R Food Brokers, 40268
Dakco International, 40276
Dakota Marketing Company, 40277
Deibert & Associates, 40293
Di Meo-Gale Brokerage Company, 40297
Diaz Sales, 40300
Dixon Marketing Inc, 40305
Donald R Conyer Associates, 40307
DW Montgomery & Company, 40273
EFD Associate, 40321
Ellis S. Fine Co., Inc., 40335
Encore Fruit Marketing Inc, 40337
Esm Ferolie, 40343
Esposito Brokerage, 40344
Essential Food Marketing, 40346
Federated Group, 40361
First Flight Foods, 40368
FMI Food Marketers International Ltd, 40359
Food Service Connection, 40383
FoodBin Trading, Inc., 40387
Foodworks International, 40393
Forseasons Sales, 40399
Freiria & Company, 40410
GAP Food Brokers, 40415
Garisco Distributing, 40420
Gasparini Sales Inc, 40421
George W. Holop Associates, 40430
Gibbs-Mccormick Inc A Ca Corp, 40433
Gilbert Foodservice Inc, 40434
Global Citrus Resources, Inc, 40439
Grant J. Hunt Company, 40446
Gurrentz International Corp, 40453
Hansid Company, 40469
Harold J. Barrett Company, 40470
Hartley S. Johnson & Son, 40475
Heartland Food Brokers LTD, 40482
Herb Barber & Sons Food, 40484
Hollar & Greene, 40493
Homeplace Food Group, 40494
Huron Food Sales, 40501
Iceberg Seafood Inc, 40509
Ingredient Exchange Co, 40517
International Coffee Corporation, 40526
International Gourmet Products, 40527
International Pacific Seafood, 40529
International Sales & Brokerage Company, 40530
Interpex, 40532
Intralinks Inc, 40537
ITA Inc, 40507
J&S Food Brokerage, 40547
J.F. Benz Company, 40550
Jilasco Food Exports, 40572
Jodawnco, 40574
John H. Elton, 40576
John J Wollack Co Inc, 40577
Jos Iorio Company, 40588
Joseph Caragol, 40590
Jso Associates Inc, 40596
Jubilee Sales of Carolina, 40597
Kenney Sales, 40630
Klinger & Speros Food Brokers, 40651
Klondike Foods, 40652
Knutsen Coffees, 40653
Korth Marketing, 40656
Krass-Joseph, 40658
Lamborn & Company, 40674
Leonard H Sisitzky Sales Inc, 40689
Lever Associates, 40691
Linwood-Welch Marketing, 40695
Littman & Associates, 40698
LMGO International Inc, 40666
Loretta Foods, 40706
Lotto International, 40709
Luke Soules Southwest, 40713
M Fellinger Co, 40717
M.E. Strauss Brokerage Company, 40723
M.J. Borelli & Company, 40724
Madden & Assoc, 40730
Major Marketing Service, 40735
Manzo Food Brokers, 40742
Marchetti Co, 40745
Marino Marketing Group, 40746
Market Pro International, 40749

Marketing Management Inc, 40754
Marmelstein Associates, 40755
Marshall Sales Co, 40757
Master Sales & Marketing, 40764
MAV Sales Co, 40725
Mc Namara Assoc Inc, 40769
McCarty Brokerage Company, 40771
Mercantum Corp, 40778
Meridian Products, 40779
Micosa Inc, 40785
Mid-West Associates, 40790
Midwest Ingredients Inc, 40797
Miller & Smith Foods, 40800
Miller's Market, 40802
Miltenberg & Samton Inc., 40804
Mitchel Beck Company, 40807
MLG Enterprises Ltd., 40727
Mooney International, 40814
Morley Sales Co, 40817
Morton & Associates, 40818
Morton F Schweitzer Sales, 40819
Nanni-Marketal, 40834
National Brokerage Network, 40838
National Commodity Sales, 40840
National Food Sales, 40843
Nature's Products Inc, 40849
Nelson Cheese Factory, 40850
New Organics, 40854
Nobert Marketing, 40860
Noble Foods, 40861
Norman Brokerage Co, 40865
Norman Hecht, 40866
Nova Seafood, 40878
Oekerman Sales, 40887
Orca Foods, 40891
Pacific Trading Company International, 40903
Paul Esposito Inc, 40913
Peak Corporation, 40916
Pennickers Food Distribution, 40917
Peters & Fair, 40920
Phillips Sales Co, 40922
Pioneer Marketing International, 40929
Polish Folklore Import Co, 40932
Powell May International, 40935
Prestige Marketing, 40943
Progressive Marketing Systems, 40957
Promesa, 40959
Provincial, 40962
R. Becker Marketing & Sales, 40974
Reede International Seafood Corporation, 40992
Rene Rivet, 40996
Resource One, 40999
RH Sulker Sales, 40978
Robbins Sales Co, 41012
Robert W. Hayman Inc, 41016
Roehl Corp, 41019
Rosenfeld & Gigante, 41024
Royal Wine Corp, 41029
Rudolph Brady, Inc, 41031
Saggese Brothers, 41048
Salad Oils Intl Corp, 41049
Sales, 41050
Sales Marketing Svc LLC, 41053
Sales Results, 41054
Sanco Food Brokerage, 41060
Schare & Associates, 41069
Seafood Sales, 41082
SGS International Rice Inc, 41039
SHA Services, 41040
Shrimp Tex Distributors, 41093
Sid Alpers Organic Sales Company, 41094
Sinco, 41097
SJE Marketing Corporation, 41041
Sloan Sales Inc, 41103
Smart Cycling, Inc., 41104
Snax Sales Company, 41106
Southeastern Paper Group Inc, 41113
Specialty Partners, 41117
Statewide Brokerage Company, 41130
Sturdivant Company, 41140
Sundown Foods USA, Inc., 41148
Supreme Foods, 41153

T C Jacoby & Co, 41158
T. McConnell Sales & Marketing, 41159
Taormina Sales Company, 41166
Technical Sales Associates, 41171
Thomas Food Brokers, 41179
Thomas, Large & Singer, 41181
Tower Intercontinental Group, 41193
Tri-State Logistics Inc, 41199
United Brands, 41212
United International Indstrs, 41215
US Food Products, 41210
V.M. Calderon, 41220
Van Kam, G Trading Company, 41223
Webeco Foods, Inc, 41244
Wendlandt Brokerage Company, 41248
William M. Dunne & Associates Ltd, 41260
Willing Group, 41263
Wiltsie & Company, 41265
Winmix/Natural Care Products, 41266
Winpac, 41267
WJ Pence Company, 41234
WMK Marketing, 41235
Yankee Marketers, 41276
Yates Sales Associates, 41277
Yeager & Associates, 41278
York Cheese, 41279
York Sutch & Assoc, 41281
Zambito Produce Sales, 41284
Zanichelli & Associates, 41285

Ingredients

1000 Islands River Rat Cheese, 40000
3-D Marketing & Sales, 40001
Action Marketing, 40025
Action Marketing Services, 40028
Advance Sales & Marketing, Inc, 40031
Agri-Dairy Products, 40036
Alquima USA Inc, 40049
Ambi-Prestigio Foods Inc, 40050
American Commodity & Shipping, 40052
Ames Company, Inc, 40057
Anchor Florida Marketing, 40058
Anthony Cea & Associates, 40061
Apache Brokers, 40062
Arnett Brokerage Co, 40065
Artisanal Foods, 40068
ATI, 40017
Automatic Packaging Systems & Conveyors Company, 40078
Autumn Foods, 40079
B & D Sales & Marketing Inc, 40082
B.C. Ritchie Company, 40084
Bartlett & Co, 40097
Bay Pacific Marketing, 40100
Bayha & Associates, 40101
Beck Western Brokerage, 40103
Bentley Food Marketing, 40111
Beta Pure Foods, 40116
Betters International Food Corporation, 40117
Bixby Food Sales, 40124
BLV Marketing Inc, 40088
Bosshart Food Svc, 40134
Bottom Line Foods, 40135
Bruce Chaney & Company, 40148
Burley Brokerage, 40155
Byron A Carlson Inc, 40161
C J Irwin Co Inc, 40162
C. Mascari & Associates, 40164
C.B. Powell Limited, 40165
Cafe Inc, 40173
Carlin Group, 40179
Cascade Corp, 40183
Cashman-Edwards Inc, 40184
Champon & Yung Inc, 40188
Charles Rockel & Son, 40194
Clofine Dairy Products Inc, 40215
Coastal Commodities, 40218
Cobler Food Sales, 40220
Commodities Marketing Inc, 40227
Concord Sales-Prairies, 40236
Consolidated Marketers Inc, 40239
Creightons, 40256

Crider Brokerage Company, 40258
Crown Point, 40261
Culinary Specialty Produce, 40263
Cusick J B Co, 40264
Dadant & Company, 40274
Dave Roemer & Associates, 40281
Dawson Sales Co Inc, 40287
Dd Reckner Co, 40288
DeMoss & Associates, 40291
Dennis Sales, 40296
Di Meo-Gale Brokerage Company, 40297
Don Ford Ltd, 40306
Donald R Tinsman Co, 40308
DSI Food Brokerage, 40271
E W Carlberg Co, 40320
Encore Fruit Marketing Inc, 40337
Enterprise Food Brokers, 40339
Ervan Guttman Co, 40342
Evans Brokerage Company, 40351
First Flight Foods, 40368
Flavor Consultants, 40372
FM Carriere & Son, 40358
Food Ingredients Inc, 40379
Food Service Connection, 40383
Food Service Merchandising, 40385
FoodBin Trading Inc., 40387
Foodsales Inc, 40389
Forbes Frozen Foods, 40395
Francis Musto & Co, 40401
Freeman Fruit Intl, 40408
GCI Nutrients, 40416
Gehrke Co, 40423
Genesis Marketing, 40426
Gibbs-Mccormick Inc A Ca Corp, 40433
Gormick Food Brokers, 40442
Goveco Full Service Food Brokers, 40444
H.R. Plate & Company, 40457
Haile Resources, 40463
Hanimex Company, 40466
Hanks Brokerage, 40467
Hansid Company, 40469
Harold J. Barrett Company, 40470
Heard Brokerage Company Inc, 40481
Heartland Food Brokers LTD, 40482
Herb Barber & Sons Food, 40484
Higgins & White Inc, 40486
Howell Associates, 40496
Hoyt, 40497
Hunter Walton & Co Inc, 40500
Imark of Pennsylvania, 40510
Ingredient Exchange Co, 40517
Ingredient Inc, 40518
Ingredient Innovations, 40519
Inter-American Products, 40523
Intermountain Food Brokerage, 40525
Interpack NW Frozen Food, 40531
Intersouth Foodservice Group, 40534
Interwest Ingredient Sales, 40536
Intralinks Inc, 40537
J&S Food Brokerage, 40547
J.F. Benz Company, 40550
J.F. Kelly, 40551
J.M. Swank Company, 40554
Jam Group of Company, 40566
Jewell/Barksdale Associates, 40571
JL Stemp Marketing Agents, 40558
Jodawnco, 40574
John H Thier Co, 40575
John H. Elton, 40576
Jos Iorio Company, 40588
Joseph Caragol, 40590
Julius Levy Company, 40601
Kayco, 40619
Kdm Foodsales Inc, 40620
Kedem, 40621
Kelly Flour Company, 40626
Key Carlin O'Brien, LLC, 40632
Kingery & Assoc, 40643
Klass Ingredients Inc, 40649
Klinger & Speros Food Brokers, 40651
Korth Marketing, 40656
Kramer Brokerage Co, 40657
Kurtz Food Brokers, 40659
Lake & Lake Inc, 40671

113

Brokered Product / Meat

Lamborn & Company, 40674
Lampson & Tew, 40675
Lance Agencies, 40677
Landers Ag Resources, 40678
Leblanc Foodservice Marketing, 40683
Lehmann Brokerage Co, 40686
Lifewise Ingredients, 40693
Linwood-Welch Marketing, 40695
Littler Brokerage Co Inc, 40697
LMGO International, 40666
Loar & Young Inc, 40701
Lomac & May Associates, 40703
Loman Brown, 40704
Lorey & Lorey, 40707
Los Angeles Chemical Company, 40708
Mancini Packing Co, 40739
Manzo Food Brokers, 40742
Market Pro International, 40749
Marshall Sales Co, 40757
Mathews Associates, 40765
Mc Namara Assoc Inc, 40769
McCarty Brokerage Company, 40771
McClement Sales Company, 40772
Mercantum Corp, 40778
Merit Sales Corporation, 40781
Mid-Continent Sales, 40788
Mid-West Sales Agency, 40791
Midlantic Sweetener Co, 40793
Midwest Ingredient Sales, 40796
Midwest Ingredients Inc, 40797
Milky Whey Inc, 40799
Miller & Smith Foods, 40800
Miltenberg & Samton Inc., 40804
MLG Enterprises Ltd., 40727
Monterey Food Ingredients, 40812
Mooney International, 40814
Morton F Schweitzer Sales, 40819
Mosher Products Inc, 40820
Murray Industrial Food Sales Inc, 40828
Nash Wright Brokerage, 40836
National Food Group, 40841
National Food Sales, 40843
Nature's Products Inc, 40849
Nesco Brokerage Company, 40851
New Organics, 40854
Nicholas & Co Inc, 40856
Nobert Marketing, 40860
Noble House Trading Company, 40862
Norman Brokerage Co, 40865
Northwestern Foods, 40877
Occidental Foods International, LLC, 40886
Oekerman Sales, 40887
Omni Food Inc, 40890
Osage Food Products Inc, 40893
Pacific Ingredient Exchange, 40900
Paul Esposito Inc, 40913
Plastic Industrial Products, 40930
Powell May International, 40935
Preferred Brokerage Company, 40936
Premier Food Service Sales, 40940
Pure Sales, 40964
R H Moultor Company, 40971
R&F Cocoa Services, 40973
R. Becker Marketing & Sales, 40974
Rainbow Sales & Marketing, 40983
Randag & Assoc Inc, 40986
Real Food Marketing, 40991
Rene Rivet, 40996
RH Sulker Sales, 40978
Rheuark/F.S.I. Sales, 41002
Roosevelt Dairy Trade, Inc, 41023
Rudolph Brady, Inc, 41031
S. Kamberg & Company, 41035
Sales Results, 41054
Sanco Food Brokerage, 41060
Santucci Associates, 41061
Schare & Associates, 41069
Schreiber Foods Inc., 41073
SHA Services, 41040
Shore Distribution Resources, 41092
Sinco, 41097
SJH Enterprises, 41042
Slaybaugh & Associates, 41102
Sloan Sales Inc, 41103
Smart Cycling, Inc., 41104
South East Sales, 41110
Spencer & Assoc, 41122
St Charles Trading Inc, 41126
Stroup Ingredients Resources, 41139
Sturgill Food Brokerage, 41141
Sun Food Service Brokerage, 41145
Sundown Foods USA, Inc., 41148
T C Jacoby & Co, 41158
Taormina Sales Company, 41166
Technical Food Sales Inc, 41170
Technical Sales Associates, 41171
Texas Foods, 41176
The Cherry Company Ltd., 41177
The Thurber Company, 41178
Thomas Food Brokers, 41179
Thomas, Large & Singer, 41181
Tom Quinn & Associates, 41189
Torter Corporation, 41191
Tower Intercontinental Group, 41193
Tr International Trading Co, 41194
Tri-State Logistics Inc, 41199
Triad Brokers Inc, 41200
Two Guys Spice Company, 41207
United International Indstrs, 41215
US Food Products, 41210
Van Kam, G. Trading Company, 41223
Vivion Inc, 41227
W.H. Schilbe Citrus Brokerage / Citriservices, 41231
Wallis & Barcinski, 41238
Ward Hughes Co, 41239
Watson & Associates, 41241
Waypoint, 41242
WENS Brokerage, 41233
Wieber-McLain Company, 41256
William Bernstein Company, 41258
Willing Group, 41263
Winmix/Natural Care Products, 41266
Wrap-It Packaging, 41274
Wyman Foorman, 41275
Yankee Marketers, 41276
Zanichelli & Associates, 41285
Zonner, 41287

Meat

3-D Marketing & Sales, 40001
A&D Sales Associates, 40009
A.J. Seibert Company, 40010
ABC Enterprises, 40014
Action Marketing, 40025
Action Marketing Services, 40028
Advance Marketing, 40030
Advance Sales & Marketing, Inc, 40031
Advantage Webco Hawaii, 40034
Alliance Foods, 40044
Alliance Foods Inc, 40045
Allied Marketing Corp, 40046
American Commodity & Shipping, 40052
American Patriot Sales Inc, 40053
Anchor Florida Marketing, 40058
Anchor Packaging, 40059
Anderson Daymon Worldwide, 40060
Apache Brokers, 40062
Arnett Brokerage Co, 40065
Arroyo Sales Company, 40066
Arthur G. Meier Company/Inland Products Company, 40067
Artisanal Foods, 40068
Associated Foodservices, 40072
ATI, 40017
Automatic Packaging Systems & Conveyors Company, 40078
Avatar Food Group, 40080
Baldwin & Mattson, 40094
Benchmark Foods, 40108
Benson-Mitchell, 40110
Bentley Food Marketing, 40111
Binner Marketing & Sales, 40119
Bisek & Co Inc, 40122
Blackwing Ostrich Meats Inc., 40125
BLV Marketing Inc, 40088
Bob Rowe Sales, 40128
Borton Brokerage Company, 40133
Bosshart Food Svc, 40134
Bottom Line Foods, 40135
Brennan Food Services, 40139
Bridge City Food Marketing, 40140
Broms Brokerage, 40145
Browning Brokerage Company, 40147
Buckley, Thorne, Messina & McDermott, 40149
Budd Mayer Company of Jackson Inc., 40150
Budd Mayer of Mobile, 40151
Burley Brokerage, 40155
Buzz Crown Enterprises, 40158
C. Mascari & Associates, 40164
Cafe Inc, 40173
Celright Foods, 40185
Central Sales & Marketing, 40187
Chilay Corporation, 40205
Chuckrow Sales LLC, 40209
Classic Cuisine Foods, 40211
Co-Sales De Credico, 40217
Cobler Food Sales, 40220
Concept Food Brokers, 40228
Concept Food Sales, 40229
Concord National, 40231, 40232, 40233, 40234, 40235
Concord Sales-Prairies, 40236
Conlin Brokerage Company, 40237
Conrad Sales Company, 40238
Consolidated Marketers Inc, 40239
Consolidated Merchandisers, 40240
Constant Sales, 40242
Consumer Brands, 40243
Copperwood International Inc, 40249
Core Group, 40250
Cox Food Brokers, 40254
Creightons, 40256
Crider Brokerage Company, 40258
Cruise Marketing, 40262
D&H Marketing, Inc, 40267
Dakco International, 40276
Dambeck & Associates, 40280
Dave Roemer & Associates, 40281
Dd Reckner Co, 40288
DeMoss & Associates, 40291
Di Meo-Gale Brokerage Company, 40297
Dick Garber Company, 40301
Dino-Meat Company, 40302
Dixon Marketing Inc, 40305
Donald R Tinsman Co, 40308
Dreyer Marketing, 40312
Dunham & Smith Agencies, 40316
EFD Associate, 40321
Ellis S. Fine Co., Inc., 40335
Esm Ferolie, 40343
Fairley & Co Inc, 40360
Federated Group, 40361
Feenix Brokerage LTD, 40362
Ferdinand Richards & Son, 40363
Ferolie Esm-Metro New York, 40364
First Choice Sales Company, 40367
First Flight Foods, 40368
Five State Brokerage, 40371
Flynn Sales Associates, Inc., 40375
Food Sales West, 40381
Food Service Associates, 40382
Food Service Connection, 40383
Food Service Marketing of Pennsylvania, 40384
Food Service Merchandising, 40385
Food Service Specialists, 40386
Foodmark Sales, 40388
Foodsales Inc, 40389
Foodservice Innovators, 40390
Foodservice Marketing, 40391
Foodservice Solutions & Ideas, 40392
Forbes Frozen Foods, 40395
Four Peaks, Inc., 40400
Frank Kinsman Assoc, 40402
Freedom Food Brokers, 40405
Fromarthurie Inc, 40411
Fusion Sales Group, 40413
GAP Food Brokers, 40415
Gasparini Sales Inc, 40421
Gateway Food Service, 40422
Gilbert Foodservice Inc, 40434
Gulf States Food Service Marketing, 40452
Gurrentz International Corp, 40453
H & G Trading LTD Inc, 40454
Halal Transactions, 40464
Halling Company, 40465
Hansid Company, 40469
Harold M. Lincoln Company, 40471
Harriet Greenland Enterprises, 40472
Hawley & Assoc, 40480
Heartland Food Brokers LTD, 40482
Henry J. Hips Company, 40483
Herspring, 40485
Hilgenfeld Brokerage Co, 40487
Hobby Whalen Marketing, 40489
Hockenberg Newburgh, 40490, 40491
Hockenberg-Newburgh Sales, 40492
Imark of Pennsylvania, 40510
Imperial Trading, 40516
Ingredient Inc, 40518
Intermountain Food Brokerage, 40525
International Gourmet Products, 40527
Intersouth Foodservice Group, 40534
ISC of Indiana, 40505
ITA Inc, 40507
ITOCHU International, Inc, 40508
J&J Brokerage, 40546
J.E. Julian & Associates, 40549
J.L. Epstein & Son, 40553
Jack Curren & Associates, 40564
Jilasco Food Exports, 40572
John L. Pieri & Sons, 40578
Jones Neitzel Co, 40586
Joseph W Nath Co, 40593
Juhl Brokerage, 40598, 40599
Kappert/Hyzer Company, 40614
Kathryn's Food Service Brokers, 40616
Kay's Foods, 40618
Keeth & Associates, 40622
Kelley-Clarke, 40623
Kemper Food Brokers, 40628
Kenney Sales, 40630
Key Impact Sales & Systems Inc, 40633
Key Sales & Marketing, 40634
Key Sales Group, 40635
KeyImpact Sales & Systems, Inc., 40636
KIKO Foods Inc, 40611
Kingery & Assoc, 40643
Kirstein Brokerage Company, 40648
Klinger & Speros Food Brokers, 40651
L&S Sales Company, 40661
LA Teste Services, 40662
LAD Foodservice Sales, 40663
Lampson & Tew, 40675
Lehmann Brokerage Co, 40686
LeMire Sales, 40682
Lemmons Company, 40687
Lever Associates, 40691
Lilburn Gulf, 40694
Linwood-Welch Marketing, 40695
Lisberg-Voegeli Hanson, 40696
Littman & Associates, 40698
LMGO International Inc, 40666
Lorey & Lorey, 40707
Louis F. Leeper Company/Cleveland, 40710
Lowe & Associates, 40711
Luke Soules Southwest, 40713
M Fellinger Co, 40717
M.E. Dilanian Company, 40722
M.E. Strauss Brokerage Company, 40723
Madden & Assoc, 40730
Magic Valley Truck Brokers Inc, 40731
Main Street Marketing, 40732
Major Marketing Service, 40735
Mancini Sales & Marketing, 40740
Marjo & Associates, 40747
Market Pro International, 40749
Market Smart, 40750
Market West Company, 40751
Marketing Management Inc, 40754
Martin Preferred Foods, 40758
Marty Scanlon Brokerage Co, 40759
Master Sales & Marketing, 40764

Brokered Product / Meat Products

McCormick Brokerage Company, 40773
Menu Planners, 40777
Merit Sales Corporation, 40781
Mickelson & Associates, 40784
Micosa Inc, 40785
Mid-American Brokerage of St. Louis, 40787
Mid-State Food Brokers, 40789
Midlantic Sweetener Co, 40793
Midstates Marketing Inc, 40794
Midwest Ingredients Inc, 40797
Mitchell & Co Inc, 40808
Mitchell of Mississippi, 40810
MLE Marketing, 40726
Morton & Associates, 40818
Moten Company, 40821
Nash Wright Brokerage, 40836
National Food Group, 40841
National Food Sales, 40842
National Foodservice Marketing, 40844
National Heritage Sales Company, 40846
Nesco Brokerage Company, 40851
Network Sales, Inc, 40852
New Horizons, 40853
Next Phase Enterprises, 40855
Nicholas & Co Inc, 40856
Nobert Marketing, 40860
Northeastern Enterprises, 40873
Northland Express Transport, 40874
O'Brien & Associates Brokerage Company, 40880
Oekerman Sales, 40887
Osage Food Products Inc, 40893
Overseas Service Corp, 40896
Parks Brokerage Company, 40909
Patman Meat Group, 40911
Paul G Nester & Son Co Inc, 40914
Peters & Fair, 40920
Phoenix Food Sales, 40923
Pierce Cartwright Company, 40925
Pioneer Food Service, 40928
Preferred Brokerage Company, 40936
Preisco Jentash, 40937
Premier Food Service Sales, 40940
Prestige Marketing, 40943
Prestige Sales & Marketing, 40945
Proactive Sales & Marketing, 40950
Professional Food Service, 40952
Progressive Brokerage Co Inc, 40955
Progressive Food Service Broker, 40956
Quality Brokerage Company, 40965
Quality Food Company, 40966
Quality Sales & Marketing, 40969
R G Sellers Co, 40970
R.F. Cannon Company, 40975
Rainbow Sales & Marketing, 40983
Ratcliff Food Brokers, 40988
Ray's Pride Brokerage Company, 40990
Reese Brokerage Co, 40993
Resource One, 40999
Reuven International, 41001
Rheuark/F.S.I. Sales, 41002
Richardson Petkovsek & Associates, 41004
Richs Sales Company, 41005
Riteway Co, 41007
Rizwitsch Sales, 41010, 41011
RMCI Foodservice, 40980
Rocky Mountain Motel, 41017
Rodon Foods, 41018
Roos-Mohan, 41022
Sachem Co, 41047
Sales Marketing Svc LLC, 41053
Sanco Food Brokerage, 41060
Saverino & Assoc, 41066
Schaper Company, 41068
Schare & Associates, 41069
Seaboard Foods, 41077
Sessions & Associates, 41088
SHA Services, 41040
Sinco, 41097
Slagle & Associates, 41100
Smart Cycling, Inc., 41104
South Group Marketing, 41111
Spectrum Foodservice Associates, 41119
Spectrum Foodservices, 41120
Spencer & Assoc, 41122
St Charles Trading Inc, 41126
Stern International Consultants, 41132
Sturgill Food Brokerage, 41141
Summit Brokerage, 41143
Summit FS LTD, 41144
Sun Food Service Brokerage, 41145
Super Sale Brokerage Company, 41150
Supreme Foodservice Sales, 41154
T. McConnell Sales & Marketing, 41159
T.W. Wilson & Son, 41162
Team Northwest, 41168
Tees & Persse Brokerage, 41173
The Thurber Company, 41178
Tri-State Logistics Inc, 41199
Try-Angle Food Brokers Inc, 41202
Tucker Sales, 41203
Twin City Food Brokers, 41206
United Brands, 41212
United Foodservice Sales, 41214
United International Indstrs, 41215
US Food Products, 41210
Watson & Associates, 41241
Waypoint, 41242
Webco General Partnership, 41243
Webeco Foods, Inc, 41244
WENS Brokerage, 41233
WJ Pence Company, 41234
Wrap-It Packaging, 41274
Yankee Marketers, 41276
Yeager & Associates, 41278
Zanichelli & Associates, 41285

Meat Products

1000 Islands River Rat Cheese, 40000
3-D Marketing & Sales, 40001
A G Brown & Son, 40003
A.J. Seibert Company, 40010
Action Marketing, 40025
Advance Marketing, 40030
Advance Sales & Marketing, Inc, 40031
Advantage Webco Hawaii, 40034
Alliance Foods, 40044
Alliance Foods Inc, 40045
Allied Marketing Corp, 40046
American Patriot Sales Inc, 40053
Anchor Florida Marketing, 40058
Anderson Daymon Worldwide, 40060
Anthony Cea & Associates, 40061
Apache Brokers, 40062
Arnett Brokerage Co, 40065
Arthur G. Meier Company/Inland Products Company, 40067
Artisanal Foods, 40068
Associated Foodservices, 40072
ATI, 40017
Avatar Food Group, 40080
Baja Foods LLC, 40091
Benchmark Sales, 40108
Benson-Mitchell, 40110
Bentley Food Marketing, 40111
Binner Marketing & Sales, 40119
Bisek & Co Inc, 40122
Bob Rowe Sales, 40128
Borton Brokerage Company, 40133
Bosshart Food Svc, 40134
Bottom Line Foods, 40135
Bridge City Food Marketing, 40140
Broms Brokerage, 40145
Browning Brokerage Company, 40147
Buckley, Thorne, Messina & McDermott, 40149
Budd Mayer Company of Jackson Inc., 40150
Budd Mayer of Mobile, 40151
Burdette Beckmann Inc, 40154
Burley Brokerage, 40155
Buzz Crown Enterprises, 40158
C. Mascari & Associates, 40164
Cafe Inc, 40173
Cann Brokerage Inc, 40177
Celright Foods, 40185
Charles R. Bell Limited, 40193
Chase-Goldenberg Associates, 40199
Chell Brokerage Co, 40203
Chilay Corporation, 40205
Chuckrow Sales LLC, 40209
Classic Cuisine Foods, 40211
Co-Sales De Credico, 40217
Cobler Food Sales, 40220
Colony Brokerage Company, 40224
Concept Food Brokers, 40228
Concept Food Sales, 40229
Concord National, 40230, 40231, 40233, 40234, 40235
Concord Sales-Prairies, 40236
Conrad Sales Company, 40238
Consolidated Marketers Inc, 40239
Consolidated Merchandisers, 40240
Constant Sales, 40242
Consumer Brands, 40243
Convenience Marketing Services, 40247
Copperwood InternationalInc, 40249
Core Group, 40250, 40251
Cox Food Brokers, 40254
Creightons, 40256
Cruise Marketing, 40262
D&D Marketing Group, Inc., 40266
D&R Food Brokers, 40268
Dakco International, 40276
Dambeck & Associates, 40280
Dd Reckner Co, 40288
Delbert Craig Food Brokers, 40295
DeMoss & Associates, 40291
Di Meo-Gale Brokerage Company, 40297
Dick Garber Company, 40301
Dino-Meat Company, 40302
Dixon Marketing Inc, 40305
Donald R Tinsman Co, 40308
Doug Milne Co, 40309
Douglas Sales Associates, 40310
Dreyer Marketing, 40312
Dunbar Sales Company, Inc, 40315
Dunham & Smith Agencies, 40316
DVC Brokerage Company, 40272
Eastern Sales & Marketing, 40325
Eastern Sales and Marketing, 40326
EFD Associate, 40321
Elias Shaker & Co, 40333
Ellis S. Fine Co., Inc., 40335
Enterprise Food Brokers, 40339
Erickson Brothers Brokerage Co, 40340
Esm Ferolie, 40343
Fairley & Co Inc, 40360
Federated Group, 40361
Feenix Brokerage LTD, 40362
Ferdinand Richards & Son, 40363
Ferolie Esm-Metro New York, 40364
First Choice Sales Company, 40367
First Flight Foods, 40368
Five State Brokerage, 40371
Flynn Sales Associates, Inc., 40375
Food Associates of Syracuse, 40377
Food Service Associates, 40382
Food Service Connection, 40383
Food Service Marketing of Pennsylvania, 40384
Food Service Specialists, 40386
Foodsales Inc, 40389
Foodservice Marketing, 40391
Foodservice Solutions & Ideas, 40392
Frank Kinsman Assoc, 40402
Freedom Food Brokers, 40405
Freeman Signature, 40409
Fromartharie Inc, 40411
Fusion Sales Group, 40413
GAP Food Brokers, 40415
Gasparini Sales Inc, 40421
Gateway Food Service, 40422
Gellman Associates, 40424
Gilbert Foodservice Inc, 40434
Golden Valley Industries Inc, 40440
Gurrentz International Corp, 40453
H.V. Mid State Sales Company, 40458
Halling Company, 40465
Hanks Brokerage, 40467
Hansid Company, 40469
Harriet Greenland Enterprises, 40472
Hawley & Assoc, 40480
Henry J. Hips Company, 40483
Hobby Whalen Marketing, 40489
Hockenberg Newburgh, 40490, 40491
Hockenberg-Newburgh Sales, 40492
Hugh T. Gilmore Company, 40498
Imark of Pennsylvania, 40510
Imperial Trading, 40516
Ingredient Exchange Co, 40517
Intermountain Food Brokerage, 40525
International Gourmet Products, 40527
International Sales & Brokerage Company, 40530
Intersouth Foodservice Group, 40534
Interstate Food Brokers, 40535
ISC of Indiana, 40505
ITA Inc, 40507
J N Rhodes Co Inc, 40542
J&J Brokerage, 40546
J.E. Julian & Associates, 40549
J.F. Kelly, 40551
J.L. Epstein & Son, 40553
Jack Curren & Associates, 40564
Jilasco Food Exports, 40572
Jim Pless & Company, 40573
John L. Pieri & Sons, 40578
John Mangum Company, 40579
Johnson O'Hare Co, 40583
Jos Iorio Company, 40588
Juhl Brokerage, 40599
Julius M. Dean Company, 40602
Kappert/Hyzer Company, 40614
Kathryn's Food Service Brokers, 40616
Keeth & Associates, 40622
Kemper Food Brokers, 40628
Kenney Sales, 40630
Key Impact Sales & Systems Inc, 40633
Key Sales Group, 40635
KeyImpact Sales & Systems, Inc., 40636
Kiefer's, 40638
KIKO Foods Inc, 40611
Kingery & Assoc, 40643
Kirstein Brokerage Company, 40648
Klinger & Speros Food Brokers, 40651
L&S Sales Company, 40661
LA Teste Services, 40662
LAD Foodservice Sales, 40663
Lampson & Tew, 40675
Leblanc Foodservice Marketing, 40683
Lehmann Brokerage Co, 40686
LeMire Sales, 40682
Leonard H Sisitzky Sales Inc, 40689
Lever Associates, 40691
Lilburn Gulf, 40694
Linwood-Welch Marketing, 40695
Lisberg-Voegeli Hanson, 40696
Littler Brokerage Co Inc, 40697
Littman & Associates, 40698
LMGO International Inc, 40666
Lomac & May Associates, 40703
Lorey & Lorey, 40707
Louis F. Leeper Company/Cleveland, 40710
Lowe & Associates, 40711
Luke Soules Southwest, 40713
M.E. Dilanian Company, 40722
M.E. Strauss Brokerage Company, 40723
M.J. Borelli & Company, 40724
Madden & Assoc, 40730
Main Street Marketing, 40732
Major Marketing Service, 40735
Mancini & Groesbeck, 40738
Mancini Sales & Marketing, 40740
Manzo Food Brokers, 40742
Marjo & Associates, 40747
Market Smart, 40750
Market West Company, 40751
Marketing Management Inc, 40754
Martin Preferred Foods, 40758
McCormick Brokerage Company, 40773
Menu Planners, 40777
Merit Sales Corporation, 40781
Mickelson & Associates, 40784
Micosa Inc, 40785

115

Brokered Product / Private Label

Mid-American Brokerage of St. Louis, 40787
Mid-State Food Brokers, 40789
Midlantic Sweetener Co, 40793
Midstates Marketing Inc, 40794
Midwest Ingredients Inc, 40797
Milky Whey Inc, 40799
Mitchell Agencies, 40809
Mitchell of Mississippi, 40810
Morton & Associates, 40818
Moten Company, 40821
Mueller Yurgae, 40824
Nash Wright Brokerage, 40836
National Food Group, 40841
National Food Sales, 40842
National Foodservice Marketing, 40844
National Heritage Sales Company, 40846
New Horizons, 40853
Next Phase Enterprises, 40855
Nicholas & Co Inc, 40856
Nobert Marketing, 40860
Noble Foods, 40861
Norman Hecht, 40866
Northeastern Enterprises, 40873
Oekerman Sales, 40887
Overseas Service Corp, 40896
Parks Brokerage Company, 40909
Patman Foods Inc, 40910
Patman Meat Group, 40911
Peters & Fair, 40920
Phoenix Food Sales, 40923
Pierce Cartwright Company, 40925
Pioneer Food Service, 40928
Preferred Brokerage Company, 40936
Preisco Jentash, 40937
Premier Food Service Sales, 40940
Prestige Marketing, 40943
Prestige Sales & Marketing, 40945
Proactive Sales & Marketing, 40950
Professional Food Service, 40952
Progressive Food Service Broker, 40956
Progressive Marketing Systems, 40957
Quality Brokerage Company, 40965
Quality Food Company, 40966
Quality Sales & Marketing, 40969
R G Sellers Co, 40970
R J Bickert & Associates, 40972
R.F. Cannon Company, 40975
Rainbow Sales & Marketing, 40983
Ratcliff Food Brokers, 40988
Ray's Pride Brokerage Company, 40990
Reese Brokerage Co, 40993
Reichenbach & Associates, 40994
Resource One, 40999
Rheuark/F.S.I. Sales, 41002
Richardson Petkovsek & Associates, 41004
Richs Sales Company, 41005
Ringland Associates, 41006
RMCI Foodservice, 40980
Rocky Mountain Motel, 41017
Rodon Foods, 41018
S&K Sales Company, 41034
Sachem Co, 41047
Sales Corporation of Alaska, 41052
Sanco Food Brokerage, 41060
Schraad & Associates, 41072
Seaboard Foods, 41077
Sessions & Associates, 41088
SHA Services, 41040
Sinco, 41097
SJH Enterprises, 41042
Slagle & Associates, 41100
Smart Cycling, Inc., 41104
South Group Marketing, 41111
Southeastern Paper Group Inc, 41113
Spectrum Foodservice Associates, 41119
Spectrum Foodservices, 41120
Sturgill Food Brokerage, 41141
Summit Brokerage, 41143
Summit FS LTD, 41144
Supreme Foods, 41153
Supreme Foodservice Sales, 41154
T. McConnell Sales & Marketing, 41159
T.W. Wilson & Son, 41162
Taormina Sales Company, 41166
Technical Sales Associates, 41171
Tees & Persse Brokerage Acosta Sales And Marketing Company, Inc, 41172
The Cherry Company Ltd., 41177
Tri-State Logistics Inc, 41199
Twin City Food Brokers, 41206
UBC Marketing, 41208
United Brands, 41212
United Foodservice Sales, 41214
United International Indstrs, 41215
US Food Products, 41210
W.H. Escott Company, 41229
Watson & Associates, 41241
Waypoint, 41242
Webco General Partnership, 41243
WENS Brokerage, 41233
William B. Steedman & Sons, 41257
William M. Dunne & Associates Ltd, 41260
WJ Pence Company, 41234
Wrap-It Packaging, 41274
Wyman Foorman, 41275
Yankee Marketers, 41276
Yeager & Associates, 41278
York Cheese, 41279
Zanichelli & Associates, 41285
Zonner, 41287

Private Label

3-D Marketing & Sales, 40001
A G Brown & Son, 40003
A Thomas Farris & Son Inc, 40007
A W Sisk & Son, 40008
A&D Sales Associates, 40009
A.J. Seibert Company, 40010
Access Partners, 40020
Acclaim Marketing & Sales, 40021
Acorn Sales Company, 40023
Action Marketing, 40025
Action Marketing Associates, 40026
Advantage Webco Hawaii, 40034
Agri-Dairy Products, 40036
Ake-Sullivan Associates, 40038
Albert A Russo Inc, 40040
Alliance Foods, 40044
Alliance Foods Inc, 40045
Allied Marketing Corp, 40046
Anchor Florida Marketing, 40058
Anthony Cea & Associates, 40061
Apache Brokers, 40062
Apple Food Sales, 40063
Arnett Brokerage Co, 40065
Arthur G. Meier Company/Inland Products Company, 40067
ATI, 40017
Atkinson Sales Company, 40073
Autumn Foods, 40079
Avatar Food Group, 40080
B & D Sales & Marketing Inc, 40082
Baker Brokerage Company LLC, 40092
BAL Marketing, 40087
Baldwin & Mattson, 40094
Bay Pacific Marketing, 40100
Becksmith Company, Inc, 40104
Benson-Mitchell, 40110
Bentley Food Marketing, 40111
Beta Pure Foods, 40116
Bittinger Sales, 40123
Bloodworth & Associates, 40126
Bloomfield Bakers, 40127
BLV Marketing Inc, 40088, 40089
Booth, Schwager & Associates, 40132
Borton Brokerage Company, 40133
Bottom Line Foods, 40135
Brandywine Frozen Fruit, 40137
Bratt-Foster-Advantage Sales, 40138
Bridge City Food Marketing, 40140
Broms Brokerage, 40145
Browning Brokerage Company, 40147
Buckley, Thorne, Messina & McDermott, 40149
Budd Mayer of Mobile, 40151
Buley Patterson Sales Company, 40152
Burdett Associates, 40153
Burdette Beckmann Inc, 40154
Buzz Crown Enterprises, 40158
C J Irwin Co Inc, 40162
C. Mascari & Associates, 40164
California World Trade and Marketing Company, 40175
Caneast Foods, 40176
Cann Brokerage Inc, 40177
Carlin Group, 40179
Cashman-Edwards Inc, 40184
Chapman-Tait Brokerage, Inc., 40191
Charles R. Bell Limited, 40193
Charles Rockel & Son, 40194
Chase Sales Company, 40198
Chell Brokerage Co, 40203
Chilay Corporation, 40205
Christopher's Herb Shop, 40207
Classic Cuisine Foods, 40211
Clipper Mill, 40214
Co-Sales De Credico, 40217
Coastal Commodities, 40218
Cobler Food Sales, 40220
Colony Brokerage Company, 40224
Commodities Marketing Inc, 40227
Concept Food Brokers, 40228
Concept Food Sales, 40229
Concord National, 40230, 40231, 40232, 40233, 40234, 40235
Concord Sales-Prairies, 40236
Conlin Brokerage Company, 40237
Conrad Sales Company, 40238
Consolidated Marketers Inc, 40239
Consolidated Merchandisers, 40240
Consummate Marketing Company, 40244
Copperwood International Inc, 40249
Core Group, 40250
Creightons, 40256
Crider Brokerage Company, 40258
Crown Point, 40261
Cruise Marketing, 40262
Culinary Specialty Produce, 40263
D&D Marketing Group, Inc., 40266
D&R Food Brokers, 40268
Dairytown Products Ltd, 40275
Davel Food Brokerage, 40283
Davis Sales Associates, 40286
DeJarnett Sales, 40289, 40290
DeMoss & Associates, 40291
Di Meo-Gale Brokerage Company, 40297
Dial Industries Inc, 40298
Donald R Conyer Associates, 40307
Donald R Tinsman Co, 40308
Doug Milne Co, 40309
Douglas Sales Associates, 40310
DSI Food Brokerage, 40271
Eagle Associates, 40322
Ebbert Sales & Marketing, 40327
Egerstrom Inc, 40329
Elias Shaker & Co, 40333
Ellis S. Fine Co., Inc., 40335
Enterprise Food Brokers, 40339
Esm Ferolie, 40343
Esposito Brokerage, 40344
Essential Food Marketing, 40346
Eurogulf Company, 40348
Evans Brokerage Company, 40351
Evers Heilig Inc, 40352
Fairley & Co Inc, 40360
Federated Group, 40361
Feenix Brokerage LTD, 40362
Ferdinand Richards & Son, 40363
Ferolie Esm-Metro New York, 40364
First Flight Foods, 40368
Five State Brokerage, 40371
Flynn Sales Associates, Inc., 40375
FMI Food Marketers International Ltd, 40359
Food Associates of Syracuse, 40377
Food Service Associates, 40382
Food Service Merchandising, 40385
Foodmark Sales, 40388
Foodsales Inc, 40389
Foodservice Marketing, 40391
Foodservice Solutions & Ideas, 40392
Forseasons Sales, 40399
Frank Kinsman Assoc, 40402
Frank M Hartley Inc, 40403
Freeman Signature, 40409
Fusion Sales Group, 40413
Gallagher Sales Corporation, 40418
Garden Gold Foods, Inc, 40419
Gateway Food Service, 40422
Gellman Associates, 40424
George W. Holop Associates, 40430
Gibbs-Mccormick Inc A Ca Corp, 40433
Gilbert Foodservice Inc, 40434
Golden Valley Industries Inc, 40440
Golick Martins, Inc., 40441
Gormick Food Brokers, 40442
Goveco Full Service Food Brokers, 40444
Grabbe-Leonard Co, 40445
Great Southwest Sales Company, 40448
Gulf States Food Service Marketing, 40452
H & G Trading LTD Inc, 40454
H. White Sales Company, 40456
H.R. Plate & Company, 40457
H.V. Mid State Sales Company, 40458
Halling Company, 40465
Hansid Company, 40469
Harold J. Barrett Company, 40470
Harold M. Lincoln Company, 40471
Harriet Greenland Enterprises, 40472
Harry Tinseth Associates, Inc., 40474
Harvest Grove Inc, 40476
Hawley & Assoc, 40480
HD Marshall Ltd, 40460
Henry J. Hips Company, 40483
Herspring, 40485
Hockenberg Newburgh, 40490, 40491
Homeplace Food Group, 40494
Howell Associates, 40496
Hugh T. Gilmore Company, 40498
Hundley Brokerage Company, 40499
Imark of Pennsylvania, 40510
Imperial House Sales, 40515
Intermountain Food Brokerage, 40525
International Sales & Brokerage Company, 40530
Interpack NW Frozen Food, 40531
Interpex, 40532
Interstate Food Brokers, 40535
ISSCO, 40506
J N Rhodes Co Inc, 40542
J T Gibbons Inc, 40544
J&S Food Brokerage, 40547
J.E. Julian & Associates, 40549
J.F. Benz Company, 40550
Jacobsen-Clahan & Company, 40565
Jim Pless & Company, 40573
John J Wollack Co Inc, 40577
John Mangum Company, 40579
Johnson O'Hare Co, 40583
Jones Neitzel Co, 40586
Jos Iorio Company, 40588
Joseph Caragol, 40590
JP Bissonnette, 40561
JP Carroll Company, 40562
Jubilee Sales of Carolina, 40597
Julius Levy Company, 40601
Julius M. Dean Company, 40602
Kandy King Confections, 40613
Kappert/Hyzer Company, 40614
Kathryn's Food Service Brokers, 40616
KDH Sales, 40609
Keeth & Associates, 40622
Kelley-Clarke, 40623
Kelly Associates/Food Brokers, 40625
Kemper Food Brokers, 40628
Kenney Sales, 40630
Key Carlin O'Brien, LLC, 40632
Key Impact Sales & Systems Inc, 40633
Key Sales Group, 40635
Kinder-Smith Company, 40639
Kingery & Assoc, 40643
Klensch Cheese Company, 40650
Klondike Foods, 40652
Korth Marketing, 40656

Brokered Product / Produce

L&S Sales Company, 40661
LA Teste Services, 40662
Lampson & Tew, 40675
Leblanc Foodservice Marketing, 40683
LeMire Sales, 40682
Leonard H Sisitzky Sales Inc, 40689
Lever Associates, 40691
Linwood-Welch Marketing, 40695
Lisberg-Voegeli Hanson, 40696
Littler Brokerage Co Inc, 40697
Littman & Associates, 40698
LMGO International Inc, 40666
Loar & Young Inc, 40701
Lobel Food Brokers, 40702
Lomac & May Associates, 40703
Loretta Foods, 40706
Lorey & Lorey, 40707
Lowe & Associates, 40711
Luke Soules Southwest, 40713
Luxco Inc, 40715
M. Soffer Company, 40721
M.E. Dilanian Company, 40722
Maddan & Co Inc, 40729
Madden & Assoc, 40730
Main Street Marketing, 40732
Major Marketing Service, 40735
Mancini & Groesbeck, 40738
Mancini Sales & Marketing, 40740
Manuel's Mexican-American Fine Foods, 40741
Manzo Food Brokers, 40742
Marathon Marketing, 40743
Marchetti Co, 40745
Marino Marketing Group, 40746
Market Pro International, 40749
Marketing Management Inc, 40754
Marmelstein Associates, 40755
Marshall Sales Co, 40757
Master Sales & Marketing, 40764
MAV Sales Co, 40725
Mc Namara Assoc Inc, 40769
McCormick Brokerage Company, 40773
Measured Sales & Marketing, 40776
Merit Sales Corporation, 40781
Michael R Fish & Co, 40782
Mid-Continent Sales, 40788
Mid-State Food Brokers, 40789
Mid-West Sales Agency, 40791
Midland Marketing Co-Op Inc, 40792
Midlantic Sweetener Co, 40793
Midstates Marketing Inc, 40794
Midwest Ingredients Inc, 40797
Milky Whey Inc, 40799
Miller's Market, 40802
Miller, Stabler & Smith, 40803
Mitchell & Co Inc, 40808
Mitchell of Mississippi, 40810
Moody Dunbar Inc, 40813
Mooney International, 40814
Morley Sales Co, 40817
Morton & Associates, 40818
Morton F Schweitzer Sales, 40819
Mueller Yurgae, 40824
Munchies, 40826
Nash Wright Brokerage, 40836
National Brokerage Network, 40838
National Commodity Sales, 40840
National Food Sales, 40843
National Heritage Sales Company, 40846
Nesco Brokerage Company, 40851
Network Sales, Inc, 40852
Next Phase Enterprises, 40855
Nicholas & Co Inc, 40856
Nobert Marketing, 40860
Nomura & Co, 40863
North Eastern Sales Solutions, 40869
Northeast Retail Services, 40872
Northland Express Transport, 40874
O'Brien & Associates Brokerage Company, 40880
Oak Leaf Sales Co, 40885
Oekerman Sales, 40887
Orca Foods, 40891
Osage Food Products Inc, 40893
Pace Target Brokerage, 40899

Pankow Associates Inc, 40905
Paul G Nester & Son Co Inc, 40914
Paul Inman Associates, 40915
Peak Corporation, 40916
Pennickers Food Distribution, 40917
Phoenix Foods Inc, 40924
Pinski Portugal & Associate, 40926
Pioneer Food Brokers, 40927
Pioneer Marketing International, 40929
Powell May International, 40935
Preferred Brokerage Company, 40936
Preisco Jentash, 40937
Prestige Marketing, 40943
Prestige Sales, 40944
Prestige Sales & Marketing, 40945
Proactive Sales & Marketing, 40950
Professional Food Service, 40952
Progressive Brokerage Co Inc, 40955
Progressive Food Service Broker, 40956
Progressive Marketing Systems, 40957
Progressive Sales & Marketing, 40958
Provincial, 40962
Quality Sales & Marketing, 40969
R G Sellers Co, 40970
R H Moulton Company, 40971
R J Bickert & Associates, 40972
R. Becker Marketing & Sales, 40974
R.F. Cannon Company, 40975
R.W. Berkeley & Associates, 40977
Rabe Sales Corp, 40981
Rainbow Sales & Marketing, 40983
Rancho Sales & Marketing, 40985
Ratcliff Food Brokers, 40988
Ray's Pride Brokerage Company, 40990
Reede International Seafood Corporation, 40992
Reese Brokerage Co, 40993
Reichenbach & Associates, 40994
Resource One, 40999
RH Sulker Sales, 40978
Richardson Petkovsek & Associates, 41004
Ringland Associates, 41006
Riteway Co, 41007
RMCI Foodservice, 40980
Robbins Sales Co, 41012
Robert A. Haines Companies, 41013
Rocky Mountain Motel, 41017
Rodon Foods, 41018
Roehl Corp, 41019
Roger J. Wood Company, 41020
Roos-Mohan, 41022
Rosenfeld & Gigante, 41024
Ross Empire State Brokers, 41026
Roughstock Distillery, 41027
S. Kamberg & Company, 41035
Sabal Marketing, 41045
Sabbers & Assoc Inc, 41046
Sachem Co, 41047
Salad Oils Intl Corp, 41049
Sales, 41050
Sales Corporation of Alaska, 41052
Sales Marketing Svc LLC, 41053
Sales Results, 41054
Sanco Food Brokerage, 41060
Saratoga Food Safety, 41063
Saverino & Assoc, 41066
Scavuzzo Sales & Marketing, 41067
Schraad & Associates, 41072
Schurman's Wisconsin Cheese Country, 41074
Seaboard Foods, 41077
Select Sales & Marketing Inc, 41084
Service Group, 41086
Sessions & Associates, 41088
SGS International Rice Inc, 41039
SHA Services, 41040
Sinco, 41097
SJE Marketing Corporation, 41041
SJH Enterprises, 41042
Slattery Marketing Corporation, 41101
Sloan Sales Inc, 41103
Smart Cycling, Inc., 41104
Smigiel Marketing & Sales Ltd., 41105
Snax Sales Company, 41106

Southeastern Paper Group Inc, 41113
Specialty Partners, 41117
Specialty Sales & Marketing, 41118
Spectrum Foodservice Associates, 41119
Spectrum Foodservices, 41120
Spencer & Assoc, 41122
St Charles Trading Inc, 41126
Statewide Brokerage Company, 41130
STI International, 41043
Stockdale & Reagan, 41135
Sturdivant Company, 41140
Sturgill Food Brokerage, 41141
Summit Brokerage, 41143
Summit FS LTD, 41144
Sundown Foods USA, Inc., 41148
Super Sale Brokerage Company, 41150
Supreme Foods, 41153
Supreme Foodservice Sales, 41154
T. McConnell Sales & Marketing, 41159
T.F.S. & Associates, 41160
T.W. Wilson & Son, 41162
Taormina Sales Company, 41166
Team Northwest, 41168
Tees & Persse Brokerage, 41173
The Cherry Company Ltd., 41177
The Thurber Company, 41178
Thomas Food Brokers, 41179
Thomas, Large & Singer, 41181
TMC Foods, 41163
Tower Intercontinental Group, 41193
TRFG Inc, 41165
Tri-State Logistics Inc, 41199
Tucker Sales, 41203
Twin City Food Brokers, 41206
UBC Marketing, 41208
United Brands, 41212
United Foodservice Sales, 41214
United International Indstrs, 41215
US Food Products, 41210
V.M. Calderon, 41220
Van Reed Sales Company, 41224
W.H. Escott Company, 41229
W.H. Moseley Co., 41230
W.H. Sullivan & Associates, 41232
Watson & Associates, 41241
Wehrfritz & Associates, 41245
Wendlandt Brokerage Company, 41248
WENS Brokerage, 41233
Wesco Food Brokerage, 41249
Wieber-McLain Company, 41256
William M. Dunne & Associates Ltd, 41260
Williams Brokerage Company, 41261
Willing Group, 41263
Wilson Food Brokers, 41264
Winmix/Natural Care Products, 41266
Wishbone Utensil Tableware Line, 41269
WJ Pence Company, 41234
Wrap-It Packaging, 41274
Yeager & Associates, 41278
York Cheese, 41279

Produce

A G Brown & Son, 40003
A&D Sales Associates, 40009
A.J. Seibert Company, 40010
Acorn Sales Company, 40023
Acosta Sales & Marketing Company, 40024
Advantage Solutions, 40033
Airschott Inc, 40037
All Seasons Brokerage Company, 40042
Alpine Summit Sales Inc, 40048
American Commodity & Shipping, 40052
AMT Sales & Marketing, 40016
Anchor Florida Marketing, 40058
Anchor Packaging, 40059
Anderson Daymon Worldwide, 40060
Anthony Cea & Associates, 40061
Arnett Brokerage Co, 40065
Arroyo Sales Company, 40066
ATI, 40017
B.C. Tree Fruits Limited, 40085
B.W. Dyer & Company, 40086

Baker Brokerage Company LLC, 40092
Bay Pacific Marketing, 40100
Beck Western Brokerage, 40103
Benchmark Sales, 40108
Bertran Enterprises, 40113
BLV Marketing Inc, 40088, 40089
Booth, Schwager & Associates, 40132
Borton Brokerage Company, 40133
Bratt-Foster-Advantage Sales, 40138
Brennan Food Services, 40139
Bridge City Food Marketing, 40140
Browning Brokerage Company, 40147
Buckley, Thorne, Messina & McDermott, 40149
Budd Mayer of Mobile, 40151
Bushwick Commission Company, 40156
C J Irwin Co Inc, 40162
C.H. Robinson Co., 40166
Cann Brokerage Inc, 40177
Cashman-Edwards Inc, 40184
Central Marketing Assoc, 40186
Chapman Fruit Co Inc, 40190
Chell Brokerage Co, 40203
Chuck Batcheller Company, 40208
Chuckrow Sales LLC, 40209
Cobler Food Sales, 40220
Concord National, 40230, 40233, 40235
Concord Sales-Prairies, 40236
Crown Point, 40261
Culinary Specialty Produce, 40263
D&D Marketing Group, Inc., 40266
Di Meo-Gale Brokerage Company, 40297
Dial Industries Inc, 40298
Diaz Sales, 40300
Donald R Tinsman Co, 40308
Doug Milne Co, 40309
Dunbar Sales Company, Inc, 40315
E K Bare & Sons Inc, 40318
Eagle Marketing, 40323
Eastern Sales & Marketing, 40325
Eastern Sales and Marketing, 40326
EFD Associate, 40321
Eiseman-Gleit Co Inc, 40330
Esm Ferolie, 40343
Essential Food Marketing, 40346
Evans Brokerage Company, 40351
Federated Group, 40361
Feenix Brokerage LTD, 40362
Ferolie Esm-Metro New York, 40364
First Flight Foods, 40368
Food Associates of Syracuse, 40377
Food Sales West, 40381
Forbes Frozen Foods, 40395
Frank Kinsman Assoc, 40402
Freedom Food Brokers, 40405
Fusion Sales Group, 40413
Gateway Food Service, 40422
Genesis International, 40425
George Perry & Sons Inc, 40429
Gibbs-Mccormick Inc A Ca Corp, 40433
Glenmoor Brokerage, 40438
Goveco Full Service Food Brokers, 40444
Grant J. Hunt Company, 40446
Halling Company, 40465
Harold J. Barrett Company, 40470
Harold M. Lincoln Company, 40471
Harriet Greenland Enterprises, 40472
Harvest Grove Inc, 40476
HCB Foodservice Sales & Marketing, 40459
Henry J. Hips Company, 40483
Herb Barber & Sons Food, 40484
Hobby Whalen Marketing, 40489
Hockenberg-Newburgh Sales, 40492
Hollar & Greene, 40493
Hoyt, 40497
Hugh T. Gilmore Company, 40498
Huron Food Sales, 40501
Ingredient Inc, 40518
Interpex, 40532
J.W. Harrison & Son, 40555
John H. Elton, 40576
Johnson O'Hare Co, 40583
Jones Neitzel Co, 40586

117

Brokered Product / Seafood

Jos Iorio Company, 40588
Joseph P. Sullivan & Company, 40591
JP Carroll Company, 40562
Jso Associates Inc, 40596
Juhl Brokerage, 40599
Julius M. Dean Company, 40602
KDH Sales, 40609
Kelley-Clarke, 40623
Kenney Sales, 40630
Key Carlin O'Brien, LLC, 40632
Key Sales & Marketing, 40634
Key Sales Group, 40635
Kingery & Assoc, 40643
Koch & Assoc, 40654
Krass-Joseph, 40658
Lake Michigan Growers, 40672
Landers Ag Resources, 40678
Lisberg-Voegeli Hanson, 40696
LMGO International Inc, 40666
Lomac & May Associates, 40703
Lotto International, 40709
Louis F. Leeper Company/Cleveland, 40710
Lowe & Associates, 40711
Maddan & Co Inc, 40729
Magic Valley Truck Brokers Inc, 40731
Main Street Marketing, 40732
Major Marketing Service, 40735
Manzo Food Brokers, 40742
Marbran USA, 40744
Market Smart, 40750
Market West Company, 40751
Marketing Management Inc, 40754
Marshall Sales Co, 40757
Master Sales & Marketing, 40764
Mc Namara Assoc Inc, 40769
Measured Sales & Marketing, 40776
Menu Planners, 40777
Mercantum Corp, 40778
Michael Raymond Desserts Inc, 40783
Mid-American Brokerage of St. Louis, 40787
Midstates Marketing Inc, 40794
Midwest Ingredients Inc, 40797
Miller's Market, 40802
Miller, Stabler & Smith, 40803
Morton & Associates, 40818
Morton F Schweitzer Sales, 40819
National Heritage Sales Company, 40846
Next Phase Enterprises, 40855
Nicholas & Co Inc, 40856
Nobert Marketing, 40860
Noon International, 40864
Norman Brokerage Co, 40865
North Eastern Sales Solutions, 40869
Northland Express Transport, 40874
O'Brien & Associates Brokerage Company, 40880
Omni Food Inc, 40890
Osage Food Products Inc, 40893
Overseas Service Corp, 40896
Pacific Trading Company International, 40903
Paul Esposito Inc, 40913
Paul G Nester & Son Co Inc, 40914
Peters & Fair, 40920
Preferred Brokerage Company, 40936
Prestige Sales & Marketing, 40945
Progressive Brokerage Co Inc, 40955
Progressive Sales & Marketing, 40958
R H Moulton Company, 40971
R. Becker Marketing & Sales, 40974
R.F. Cannon Company, 40975
Rainbow Sales & Marketing, 40983
Rast Produce Co, 40987
Reese Brokerage Co, 40993
Rheuark/F.S.I. Sales, 41002
Richardson Petkovsek & Associates, 41004
Rocky Mountain Motel, 41017
Roger J. Wood Company, 41020
S B Davis Co, 41032
S. Kamberg & Company, 41035
Saggese Brothers, 41048
Santucci Associates, 41061

Saverino & Assoc, 41066
Scavuzzo Sales & Marketing, 41067
Schraad & Associates, 41072
Sell Group, 41085
SHA Services, 41040
Sid Alpers Organic Sales Company, 41094
Sloan Sales Inc, 41103
Smart Cycling, Inc., 41104
Southeastern Paper Group Inc, 41113
Stockdale & Reagan, 41135
Sturgill Food Brokerage, 41141
Supreme Foodservice Sales, 41154
T.W. Wilson & Son, 41162
Team Northwest, 41168
Terra Nova Brokers, 41175
The Thurber Company, 41178
Thomas Vaccaro Inc, 41180
Thomas, Large & Singer, 41181
Tobiason Potato Co Inc, 41186
Trading Corporation of America, 41195
Tri-State Logistics Inc, 41199
Tucker Sales, 41203
Twin City Food Brokers, 41206
UBC Marketing, 41208
United Brands, 41212
United Brokers Company, 41213
US Food Products, 41210
Virginia Fruit Sales Service, 41226
W.H. Sullivan & Associates, 41232
Waypoint, 41242
William M. Dunne & Associates Ltd, 41260
WJ Pence Company, 41234
WMK Marketing, 41235
Wrap-It Packaging, 41274
Yankee Marketers, 41276
Zambito Produce Sales, 41284
Zanichelli & Associates, 41285

Seafood

A G Brown & Son, 40003
A&D Sales Associates, 40009
A.J. Seibert Company, 40010
Access Partners, 40020
Action Marketing, 40025
Advance Marketing, 40030
Advance Sales & Marketing, Inc, 40031
Advantage Webco Hawaii, 40034
Airschott Inc, 40037
Alba Specialty Seafood Company, 40039
Albert A Russo Inc, 40040
Alliance Foods, 40044
Alliance Foods Inc, 40045
Allied Marketing Corp, 40046
Ambi-Prestigio Foods Inc, 40050
American Trading Company, 40055
Anchor Florida Marketing, 40058
Anderson Daymon Worldwide, 40060
Anthony Cea & Associates, 40061
Apache Brokers, 40062
Aqua Foods, 40064
Arthur G. Meier Company/Inland Products Company, 40067
Arvin Sales Company, 40069
Associated Foodservices, 40072
ATI, 40017
Atlantis Smoked Foods, 40075
B.C. Ritchie Company, 40084
Benchmark Sales, 40108
Benson-Mitchell, 40110
Bertran Enterprises, 40113
Binner Marketing & Sales, 40119
Bisek & Co Inc, 40122
Bob Rowe Sales, 40128
Borton Brokerage Company, 40133
Bosshart Food Svc, 40134
Bottom Line Foods, 40135
Bridge City Food Marketing, 40140
Browning Brokerage Company, 40147
Buckley, Thorne, Messina & McDermott, 40149
Budd Mayer of Mobile, 40151
Buzz Crown Enterprises, 40158

Byrd International, 40159
C. Mascari & Associates, 40164
C.H. Robinson Co., 40166
C.W. Shasky & Associates Ltd., 40168
Cafe Inc, 40173
Caneast Foods, 40176
Celright Foods, 40185
Charles R. Bell Limited, 40193
Chell Brokerage Co, 40203
Chilay Corporation, 40205
Chuckrow Sales LLC, 40209
Clear Springs Foods Inc., 40212
Co-Sales De Credico, 40217
Coastal Pride Co Inc, 40219
Cobler Food Sales, 40220
Colony Brokerage Company, 40224
Concord National, 40230, 40231, 40233, 40234, 40235
Concord Sales-Prairies, 40236
Conrad Sales Company, 40238
Consolidated Marketers Inc, 40239
Consolidated Merchandisers, 40240
Constant Sales, 40242
Consumer Brands, 40243
Copperwood InternationalInc, 40249
Core Group, 40250, 40251
Cox Food Brokers, 40254
D&D Marketing Group, Inc., 40266
D&H Marketing, Inc, 40267
D&R Food Brokers, 40268
Dambeck & Associates, 40280
Dave Roemer & Associates, 40281
Deibert & Associates, 40293
Deiss Sales Co. Inc., 40294
Delbert Craig Food Brokers, 40295
DeMoss & Associates, 40291
Di Meo-Gale Brokerage Company, 40297
Dial Industries Inc, 40298
Diaz Sales, 40300
Dreyer Marketing, 40312
Dunbar Sales Company, Inc, 40315
Dunham & Smith Agencies, 40316
DVC Brokerage Company, 40272
Eagle Marketing, 40323
Elias Shaker & Co, 40333
Ellis S. Fine Co., Inc., 40335
Enterprise Food Brokers, 40339
Esm Ferolie, 40343
Federated Group, 40361
Ferdinand Richards & Son, 40363
Ferolie Esm-Metro New York, 40364
First Flight Foods, 40368
Five State Brokerage, 40371
Flynn Sales Associates, Inc., 40375
FMI Food Marketers International Ltd, 40359
Food Associates of Syracuse, 40377
Food Sales West, 40381
Food Service Associates, 40382
Food Service Connection, 40383
Food Service Specialists, 40386
Foodmark Sales, 40388
Foodsales Inc, 40389
Foodservice Innovators, 40390
Foodservice Marketing, 40391
Foodservice Solutions & Ideas, 40392
Forbes Frozen Foods, 40395
Forseasons Sales, 40399
Four Peaks, Inc., 40400
Frank Kinsman Assoc, 40402
Freedom Food Brokers, 40405
G.A. Davis Food Service, 40414
GAP Food Brokers, 40415
Gibbs-Mccormick Inc A Ca Corp, 40433
Gilbert Foodservice Inc, 40434
Gormick Food Brokers, 40442
Goveco Full Service Food Brokers, 40444
H & G Trading LTD Inc, 40454
Halling Company, 40465
Hansid Company, 40469
Harold M. Lincoln Company, 40471
Hawley & Assoc, 40480
Heartland Food Brokers LTD, 40482
Henry J. Hips Company, 40483

Hobby Whalen Marketing, 40489
Hockenberg Newburgh, 40490, 40491
Hugh T. Gilmore Company, 40498
Iceberg Seafood Inc, 40509
Intermountain Food Brokerage, 40525
International Gourmet Products, 40527
International Pacific Sales, 40528
International Pacific Seafood, 40529
Interpex, 40532
Intershell Seafood Corp, 40533
Intersouth Foodservice Group, 40534
ISC of Indiana, 40505
J N Rhodes Co Inc, 40542
J&J Brokerage, 40546
J&S Food Brokerage, 40547
Jack Curren & Associates, 40564
Jilasco Food Exports, 40572
John J Wollack Co Inc, 40577
John L. Pieri & Sons, 40578
John Mangum Company, 40579
Jones Neitzel Co, 40586
Joseph Caragol, 40590
Joseph W Nath Co, 40593
Juhl Brokerage, 40599
Julius Levy Company, 40601
Kappert/Hyzer Company, 40614
Kay's Foods, 40618
Keeth & Associates, 40622
Kelley-Clarke, 40623, 40624
Kenney Sales, 40630
Key Impact Sales & Systems Inc, 40633
Key Sales & Marketing, 40634
Key Sales Group, 40635
KeyImpact Sales & Systems, Inc., 40636
Kidd Enterprises, 40637
KIKO Foods Inc, 40611
Kirstein Brokerage Company, 40648
Klinger & Speros Food Brokers, 40651
Lampson & Tew, 40675
Landmark Foods, 40679
Lehmann Brokerage Co, 40686
LeMire Sales, 40682
Lemmons Company, 40687
Lever Associates, 40691
Lilburn Gulf, 40694
Littler Brokerage Co Inc, 40697
Littman & Associates, 40698
LMGO International Inc, 40666
Lomac & May Associates, 40703
Loretta Foods, 40706
Lorey & Lorey, 40707
Lowe & Associates, 40711
Luke Soules Southwest, 40713
M. Soffer Company, 40721
M.E. Strauss Brokerage Company, 40723
Major Marketing Service, 40735
Marjo & Associates, 40747
Market Pro International, 40749
Market West Company, 40751
Marketing Management Inc, 40754
Marmelstein Associates, 40755
Marty Scanlon Brokerage Co, 40759
Menu Planners, 40777
Meridian Products, 40779
Micosa Inc, 40785
Mid-American Brokerage of St. Louis, 40787
Mid-State Food Brokers, 40789
Midstates Marketing Inc, 40794
Midwest Ingredients Inc, 40797
Milky Whey Inc, 40799
Miller's Market, 40802
Mitchell & Co Inc, 40808
Mitchell Agencies, 40809
Mitchell of Mississippi, 40810
Morley Sales Co, 40817
Morton & Associates, 40818
Moten Company, 40821
Munchies, 40826
Nagy Associates, 40832
Nash Wright Brokerage, 40836
National Commodity Sales, 40840
National Food Sales, 40842
National Foodservice Marketing, 40844
National Heritage Sales Company, 40846

Brokered Product / Spices

Nesco Brokerage Company, 40851
Network Sales, Inc, 40852
New Horizons, 40853
Next Phase Enterprises, 40855
Nicholas & Co Inc, 40856
Nippon Food Company, 40859
Nobert Marketing, 40860
Northeastern Enterprises, 40873
Northland Express Transport, 40874
Nova Seafood, 40878
O'Brien & Associates Brokerage Company, 40880
Oekerman Sales, 40887
Orca Foods, 40891
Osage Food Products Inc, 40893
Osborn Food Sales Company, 40894
Overseas Service Corp, 40896
Pacific Salmon Company, 40901
Pacific Trading Company International, 40903
Patman Foods Inc, 40910
Patman Meat Group, 40911
Pennickers Food Distribution, 40917
Peters & Fair, 40920
Phillips Sales Co, 40922
Phoenix Food Sales, 40923
Pierce Cartwright Company, 40925
Pioneer Food Service, 40928
Powell May International, 40935
Preferred Brokerage Company, 40936
Preisco Jentash, 40937
Premier Food Service Sales, 40940
Premium Seafood Co, 40942
Prestige Marketing, 40943
Prestige Sales & Marketing, 40945
Proactive Sales & Marketing, 40950
Professional Food Service, 40952
Progressive Food Service Broker, 40956
Providence Bay Fish Co, 40960
Quality Brokerage Company, 40965
Quality Sales & Marketing, 40969
R G Sellers Co, 40970
R. Becker Marketing & Sales, 40974
R.F. Cannon Company, 40975
Ratcliff Food Brokers, 40988
Ray Cosgrove Brokerage Company, 40989
Ray's Pride Brokerage Company, 40990
Reede International Seafood Corporation, 40992
Reichenbach & Associates, 40994
Resource One, 40999
Rheuark/F.S.I. Sales, 41002
Richardson Petkovsek & Associates, 41004
Richs Sales Company, 41005
Riteway Co, 41007
Rizwitsch Sales, 41010, 41011
RMCI Foodservice, 40980
Robbins Sales Co, 41012
Robert A. Haines Companies, 41013
Robert W. Hayman Inc, 41016
Rocky Mountain Motel, 41017
Roos-Mohan, 41022
Rubenstein Seafood Sales, 41030
Sachem Co, 41047
Sales Corporation of Alaska, 41052
Sales Results, 41054
Scavuzzo Sales & Marketing, 41067
Schraad & Associates, 41072
Seafood Sales, 41082
Service Group, 41086
Sessions & Associates, 41088
SHA Services, 41040
Shrimp Tex Distributors, 41093
Sid Green Frozen Foods, 41095
Sloan Sales Inc, 41103
Smart Cycling, Inc., 41104
Smigiel Marketing & Sales Ltd, 41105
South Group Marketing, 41111
Spectrum Foodservice Associates, 41119
Spectrum Foodservices, 41120
Stone Crabs Inc, 41137
Sturgill Food Brokerage, 41141

Sullivan & Fitzgerald Food Brokers, 41142
Summit FS LTD, 41144
Sundown Foods USA, Inc., 41148
Super Sale Brokerage Company, 41150
T. McConnell Sales & Marketing, 41159
T.J. Hines & Company, 41161
Tees & Persse Brokerage Acosta Sales And Marketing Company, Inc, 41172
Tees & Persse Brokerage, 41173
Terra Nova Brokers, 41175
The Cherry Company Ltd., 41177
Thomas, Large & Singer, 41181
TMC Foods, 41163
Tower Intercontinental Group, 41193
Tri-State Logistics Inc, 41199
Tulip Group Inc, 41205
Twin City Food Brokers, 41206
UBC Marketing, 41208
United Brands, 41212
United Foodservice Sales, 41214
United International Indstrs, 41215
US Food Products, 41210
W.H. Escott Company, 41229
Watson & Associates, 41241
Waypoint, 41242
Wehrfritz & Associates, 41245
WENS Brokerage, 41233
William M. Dunne & Associates Ltd, 41260
Wilson Food Brokers, 41264
WJ Pence Company, 41234
Wrap-It Packaging, 41274
Yankee Marketers, 41276
Yates Sales Associates, 41277
York Cheese, 41279
Zanichelli & Associates, 41285

Spices

3-D Marketing & Sales, 40001
A.J. Seibert Company, 40010
Acorn Sales Company, 40023
Action Marketing, 40025
Advantage Webco Hawaii, 40034
Alliance Foods, 40044
Alliance Foods Inc, 40045
Allied Marketing Corp, 40046
Alquima USA Inc, 40049
American Patriot Sales Inc, 40053
American Trading Company, 40055
AMT Sales & Marketing, 40016
Anchor Florida Marketing, 40058
Anderson Daymon Worldwide, 40060
Anthony Cea & Associates, 40061
Apache Brokers, 40062
Arthur G. Meier Company/Inland Products Company, 40067
Associated Foodservices, 40072
ATI, 40017
Automatic Packaging Systems & Conveyors Company, 40078
Autumn Foods, 40079
B.C. Ritchie Company, 40084
B.W. Dyer & Company, 40086
Bayha & Associates, 40101
Benchmark Sales, 40108
Benson-Mitchell, 40110
Best Brands, 40114
Bird Marketing, 40120
Bisek & Co Inc, 40122
Bob Rowe Sales, 40128
Borton Brokerage Company, 40133
Bosshart Food Svc, 40134
Bottom Line Foods, 40135
Bridge City Food Marketing, 40140
Browning Brokerage Company, 40147
Buckley, Thorne, Messina & McDermott, 40149
Budd Mayer Company of Jackson Inc., 40150
Burley Brokerage, 40155
C J Irwin Co Inc, 40162
C. Mascari & Associates, 40164
C.W. Shasky & Associates Ltd., 40168

Cafe Inc, 40173
Cajun Creole Products Inc, 40174
Cann Brokerage Inc, 40177
Carlin Group, 40179
Cashman-Edwards Inc, 40184
Champon & Yung Inc, 40188
Chapman-Tait Brokerage, Inc., 40191
Charles R. Bell Limited, 40193
Coastal Commodities, 40218
Cobler Food Sales, 40220
Commodities Marketing Inc, 40227
Concord National, 40233, 40234, 40235
Concord Sales-Prairies, 40236
Conrad Sales Company, 40238
Convenience Marketing Services, 40247
Cox Food Brokers, 40254
Creightons, 40256
Crider Brokerage Company, 40258
Crown Point, 40261
CS Brokers, 40172
Culinary Specialty Produce, 40263
Dawson Sales Co Inc, 40287
Di Meo-Gale Brokerage Company, 40297
Dixon Marketing Inc, 40305
Douglas Sales Associates, 40310
E W Carlberg Co, 40320
Eagle Marketing, 40323
Elias Shaker & Co, 40333
Ellis S. Fine Co., Inc., 40335
Essential Food Marketing, 40346
Federated Group, 40361
Feenix Brokerage LTD, 40362
Ferolie Esm-Metro New York, 40364
First Flight Foods, 40368
Flynn Sales Associates, Inc., 40375
FM Carriere & Son, 40358
Food Sales West, 40381
Food Service Associates, 40382
Food Service Merchandising, 40385
Food Service Specialists, 40386
Foodsales Inc, 40389
Foodservice Innovators, 40390
Foodservice Marketing, 40391
Foodservice Solutions & Ideas, 40392
Forbes Frozen Foods, 40395
Forseasons Sales, 40399
Freedom Food Brokers, 40405
Freiria & Company, 40410
Glenmoor Brokerage, 40438
Golick Martins, Inc., 40441
Gormick Food Brokers, 40442
Goveco Full Service Food Brokers, 40444
H.R. Plate & Company, 40457
Halling Company, 40465
Hanks Brokerage, 40467
Hansid Company, 40469
Harris Freeman, 40473
HD Marshall Ltd, 40460
Hilgenfeld Brokerage Co, 40487
Hobby Whalen Marketing, 40489
Hockenberg Newburgh, 40490
Howell Associates, 40496
Ingredient Exchange Co, 40517
Inter-American Products, 40523
International Sales & Brokerage Company, 40530
Interstate Food Brokers, 40535
ISC of Indiana, 40505
J N Rhodes Co Inc, 40542
J.F. Benz Company, 40550
J.F. Kelly, 40551
Jeram Associates, 40570
Jilasco Food Exports, 40572
JL Stemp Marketing Agents, 40558
John H Thier Co, 40575
John H. Elton, 40576
John L. Pieri & Sons, 40578
Jos Iorio Company, 40588
Joseph Caragol, 40590
JP Bissonnette, 40561
Juhl Brokerage, 40599
Kappert/Hyzer Company, 40614
Kayco, 40619
Kdm Foodsales Inc, 40620

Kedem, 40621
Kelly Associates/Food Brokers, 40625
Kenney Sales, 40630
Key Impact Sales & Systems Inc, 40633
Key Sales Group, 40635
Kinder-Smith Company, 40639
Kingery & Assoc, 40643
Kirstein Brokerage Company, 40648
LA Teste Services, 40662
Lampson & Tew, 40675
Lance Agencies, 40677
Landers Ag Resources, 40678
Lehmann Brokerage Co, 40686
Lemmons Company, 40687
Lever Associates, 40691
Loar & Young Inc, 40701
Loman Brown, 40704
Loretta Foods, 40706
Lowe & Associates, 40711
M. Soffer Company, 40721
Madden & Assoc, 40730
Main Street Marketing, 40732
Major Marketing Service, 40735
Mancini Sales & Marketing, 40740
Manzo Food Brokers, 40742
Marino Marketing Group, 40746
Market Pro International, 40749
Marketing Management Inc, 40754
Marmelstein Associates, 40755
Master Sales & Marketing, 40764
Mc Namara Assoc Inc, 40769
McCarty Brokerage Company, 40771
McClement Sales Company, 40772
Meridian Trading Co, 40780
Merit Sales Corporation, 40781
Mid-Continent Sales, 40788
Mid-State Food Brokers, 40789
Midland Marketing Co-Op Inc, 40792
Midlantic Sweetener Co, 40793
Midstates Marketing Inc, 40794
Midwest Ingredients Inc, 40797
Milky Whey Inc, 40799
Miller's Market, 40802
Munchies, 40826
Nash Wright Brokerage, 40836
National Brokerage Network, 40838
National Foodservice Marketing, 40844
Network Sales, Inc, 40852
New Horizons, 40853
Nicholas & Co Inc, 40856
Nobert Marketing, 40860
Norman Brokerage Co, 40865
Norman Hecht, 40866
O'Brien & Associates Brokerage Company, 40880
Oak Leaf Sales Co, 40885
Occidental Foods International, LLC, 40886
Oekerman Sales, 40887
Orca Foods, 40891
Osage Food Products Inc, 40893
Paul Esposito Inc, 40913
Peters & Fair, 40920
Phoenix Food Sales, 40923
Pinski Portugal & Associate, 40926
Pioneer Food Service, 40928
Powell May International, 40935
Preferred Brokerage Company, 40936
Premier Food Service Sales, 40940
Professional Food Service, 40952
Quality Brokerage Company, 40965
R J Bickert & Associates, 40972
R. Becker Marketing & Sales, 40974
Randag & Assoc Inc, 40986
Ratcliff Food Brokers, 40988
Ray's Pride Brokerage Company, 40990
Reese Brokerage Co, 40993
Reichenbach & Associates, 40994
Resource One, 40999
RMCI Foodservice, 40980
Rocky Mountain Motel, 41017
Rudolph Brady, Inc, 41031
S&K Sales Company, 41034
S. Kamberg & Company, 41035
Sales Corporation of Alaska, 41052

119

Brokered Product / Spices

Santucci Associates, 41061
Scavuzzo Sales & Marketing, 41067
Schiff Food Products Co Inc, 41071
Schraad & Associates, 41072
Sell Group, 41085
Service Group, 41086
Sessions & Associates, 41088
SHA Services, 41040
Sid Alpers Organic Sales Company, 41094
SJH Enterprises, 41042
Sloan Sales Inc, 41103
Smart Cycling, Inc., 41104
Smigiel Marketing & Sales Ltd., 41105
South East Sales, 41110
South Group Marketing, 41111
Specialty Partners, 41117
Spectrum Foodservice Associates, 41119
Spectrum Foodservices, 41120
Spencer & Assoc, 41122
St Charles Trading Inc, 41126
Stroup Ingredients Resources, 41139
Summit FS LTD, 41144
Sun Food Service Brokerage, 41145
Sunwest Sales Co, 41149
Super Sale Brokerage Company, 41150
Supreme Foods, 41153
Technical Sales Associates, 41171
Tees & Persse Brokerage Acosta Sales And Marketing Company, Inc, 41172
Tees & Persse Brokerage, 41173
Terra Nova Brokers, 41175
The Cherry Company Ltd., 41177
The Thurber Company, 41178
Thomas Food Brokers, 41179
Thomas, Large & Singer, 41181
Tisdale Food Ingredients, 41185
Tom Quinn & Associates, 41189
Tri-State Logistics Inc, 41199
Tulip Group Inc, 41205
Twin City Food Brokers, 41206
Two Guys Spice Company, 41207
UBC Marketing, 41208
United Brands, 41212
United International Indstrs, 41215
US Food Products, 41210
W.H. Escott Company, 41229
Waypoint, 41242
Wendlandt Brokerage Company, 41248
Wieber-McLain Company, 41256
William Bernstein Company, 41258
William M. Dunne & Associates Ltd, 41260
Williams Brokerage Company, 41261
Willing Group, 41263
Woollard Company, 41270
Wrap-It Packaging, 41274
Yankee Marketers, 41276
Yates Sales Associates, 41277
Zonner, 41287

IMPORTERS/EXPORTERS

User Guide
Company Profiles
Export Region Index
Import Region Index

Importers/Exporters User Guide

The **Importers/Exporters Chapter** of *Food & Beverage Market Place* includes companies that import to or export from the food and beverage industry market, worldwide. The descriptive listings are organized alphabetically. Following the A-Z Importer/Exporter listings are two indexes: **Export Region** with region terms, indicating where the company exports to; and **Import Region** with terms, indicating where the company imports from. These Indexes refer to listing numbers, not page numbers.

Below is a sample listing illustrating the kind of information that is or might be included in an Importer/Exporter listing. Each numbered item of information is described in the Importer/Exporters User Key on the following page.

---

1 → 300004

2 → **(HQ) M&J Foods Corporation**

3 → 1272 Willow Avenue

Sun Valley, CA 91352-1121

4 → 023-698-4444

5 → 023-698-4443

6 → 888-698-4445

7 → info@M&Jfoods.com

8 → www.M&Jfoods.com

9 → Importer and exporter of carbonated beverages, nutritional shakes, ice tea mixes and powders; also manufacturer of carbonating equipment.

10 → President: Joshua Tyson
CFO: Tim Allen
COO: Lori Simmons
Vice President: Tonya Wicks
Marketing: Victor Johnson
Sales: Timothy Shaw

11 → *Estimated Sales*: $10-20 Million

12 → *Parent Co.:* M. Shaw Corporation

13 → *Number Employees*: 160

14 → *Company is also listed in the following section(s):* Equipment, Supplies and Services

15 → *Brands Exported:* Healthy Servin' Shakes

16 → *Regions Exported to:* Mexico, Canada, Asia

17 → *Percentage of Business in Exporting:* 10

18 → *Brands Imported:* Tasty Tea

19 → *Regions Imported from:* Asia, United Kingdom

20 → *Percentage of Business in Importing:* 15

Importers/Exporters User Key

1 → **Record Number:** Entries are listed alphabetically within each category and numbered sequentially. The entry number, rather than the page number, is used in the indexes to refer to listings.

2 → **Company Name:** Formal name of company. HQ indicates headquarter location. If names are completely capitalized, the listing will appear at the beginning of the alphabetized section.

3 → **Address:** Location or permanent address of the company. If the mailing address differs from the street address, it will appear second.

4 → **Phone Number:** The listed phone number is usually for the main office, but may also be for the sales, marketing, or public relations office as provided.

5 → **Fax Number:** This is listed when provided by the company.

6 → **Toll-Free Number:** This is listed when provided by the company.

7 → **E-Mail:** This is listed when provided, and is generally the main office e-mail.

8 → **Web Site:** This is listed when provided by the company and is also referred to as an URL address. These web sites are accessed through the Internet by typing http:// before the URL address.

9 → **Description**: This paragraph contains a brief description of the products the company imports or exports, sometimes including markets served.

10 → **Key Personnel:** Names and titles of company executives.

11 → **Estimated Sales:** This is listed when provided by the company.

12 → **Parent Co.:** If the listing is a division of another company, that parent is listed here.

13 → **Number of Employees:** Total number of employees within the company.

14 → Indicates in what other section in *Food & Beverage Market Place* this company is listed: Volume 1: Manufacturers. Volume 2: Equipment, Supplies & Services; Transportation; Warehouse; Wholesalers/Distributors. Volume 3: Brokers; Importers/Exporters.

15 → **Brands Exported:** Listing of Brand Names that are exported.

16 → **Regions Exported to:** Listing of states, regions or countries that company exports to. Companies are indexed by Export Region.

17 → **Percentage of Business in Exporting**: Total percentage of business in exporting.

18 → **Brands Imported**: Listing of Brand Names that are imported.

19 → **Regions Imported from**: Listing of states, regions or countries that company imports from.

20 → **Percentage of Business in Importing**: Total percentage of business in importing. Companies are indexed by Import Region.

Importers & Exporters / A-Z

41471 21st Century Products, Inc.
2692 Gravel Dr
Bldg 5
Fort Worth, TX 76118-6976 817-284-8299
Fax: 817-284-4844
Processor and exporter of vitamins; also, mineral and weight loss drinks
President: Greg Harris
Vice President: Dixon Ray
National Sales Director: Richard Fabose
Estimated Sales: $100,000
Number Employees: 2
Type of Packaging: Consumer, Food Service, Private Label, Bulk
Regions Exported to: Worldwide

41472 3V Company
110 Bridge Street
Brooklyn, NY 11201 718-858-7333
Fax: 718-858-7371 3v.co
Fruit-based beverage products.
CEO: Eren Spring
Contact: Hershy Gombo
hgombo@3v.co
Number of Brands: 3
Type of Packaging: Consumer, Food Service, Private Label, Bulk
Brands Exported: 3-V
Regions Exported to: Central America, South America, Europe, Asia, Middle East
Regions Imported from: Central America, South America, Europe, Asia, Middle East

41473 4C Foods Corp
580 Fountain Ave
Brooklyn, NY 11208-6002 718-272-4242
Fax: 718-272-2899 inthekitchen@4c.com
www.4c.com
Iced tea, soft drink mix; imported cheese; bread crumbs and soup mix.
Founder and President: John Celauro
sally@4c.com
SVP Operations: Wayne Celauro
Number Employees: 100-249
Square Footage: 420000
Type of Packaging: Food Service, Private Label

41474 (HQ)4M Fruit Distribution
34 Market St
Suite 18
Everett, MA 02149 617-387-7575
Fax: 617-387-7272 maria@4mfruit.com
4mfruit.com
Importer and distributor of produce, including apples, appricots, berries, cherries, cantalopes, figs, grapefruit, grapes, kiwi, lemons, mixed melons, pears, oranges, peaches, plums, pomegranates, quince, tangelos, tangerineswatermelon, nectarines, and more.
President & Principal: Mark DeFrancesco
mark@4mfruit.com
Officer Manager: Maria DeFrancesco *Year Founded:* 1996
Type of Packaging: Consumer, Food Service
Regions Imported from: Central America, South America
Percentage of Business in Importing: 90

41475 8estiny Plastics
31981 Dove Canyon Dr
Trabuco Canyon, CA 92679-1985 949-709-1985
Fax: 949-766-9459
Square Footage: 5

41476 A & B Process Systems Corp
201 S Wisconsin Ave
P.O. Box 86
Stratford, WI 54484 715-687-4332
Fax: 715-687-3225 888-258-2789
www.abprocess.com
Manufacturer and exporter of ASME U stamps, process systems, tanks, vessels and custom components.
Chairman/Co-Founder: Ajay Hilgemann
Chief Executive Officer: Paul Kinate
pkinate@abprocess.com
Sales & Marketing Manager: Andrea Wiese
Health & Safety Manager: Bill Thompson
Year Founded: 1973
Estimated Sales: $120 Million
Number Employees: 50-99
Square Footage: 175000
Type of Packaging: Food Service, Bulk
Regions Exported to: Central America, South America, Europe

Percentage of Business in Exporting: 5

41477 A B Co Of Wisconsin
6525 W Proesel Ave
Lincolnwood, IL 60712-3918 847-933-9767
Fax: 847-933-9764 abcompanyinc@yahoo.com
www.abcoimport.com
Spirits, wine, full-line oils, chocolate bars, cheese, pate, jams, jellies.
Owner: Alex Burekovic
abcompanyinc@yahoo.com
Number Employees: 10-19

41478 A C Horn & Co Sheet Metal
1269 Majesty Dr
Dallas, TX 75247-3917 214-630-3311
Fax: 214-905-1365 800-657-6155
www.achornco.com
Food processing, packaging, and material handling equipment.
President: Doug Horn
CEO: Ricardo Pounds
rpounds@achornmfg.com
Vice President: Mark Ritter
Research/Development: Paul Lima
Quality Control: Paul Lima
Director Marketing/Sales: Mark Ritter
Public Relations: Michael Horn, Jr
Plant/Production Manager: Tommy Galloway
Purchasing: Elizabeth Durban
Estimated Sales: $10-20 Million
Number Employees: 50-99
Square Footage: 240000
Parent Co: A.C. Horn & Company
Regions Exported to: Central America, South America, Europe, Asia, Middle East

41479 A G Brown & Son
3500 Kempt Road
Halifax, NS B3K 4X8
Canada 902-453-0350
Fax: 902-454-4528 agbrown@agbrown.ca
Import broker of confectionery products, general merchandise, groceries, meat products and private label items
VP: James Brown
Estimated Sales: $5.7 Million
Number Employees: 18
Type of Packaging: Consumer

41480 A G Russell Knives
2900 S 26th St
Rogers, AR 72758-8571 479-631-0130
Fax: 479-631-8734 800-255-9034
ag@agrussell.com www.agrussell.com
Manufacturer and exporter of household knives
Owner: A G Russell
goldie@agrussell.com
CFO: Michael Donnovan
Sales Exec: Goldie Russell
Estimated Sales: $20-50 Million
Number Employees: 20-49
Regions Exported to: Central America, Europe, Asia

41481 A Gift Basket by Carmela
64 Magnolia Cir
Longmeadow, MA 01106 413-746-1400
Fax: 413-746-1441
Customized gift baskets; importer of plum tomatoes, olive oil, balsamic vinegar, coffee, cookies, cakes, artichokes and gourmet foods from Italy
President: Carmela Denille
Estimated Sales: Less than $500,000
Number Employees: 1-4
Square Footage: 32800
Brands Imported: Daniele
Regions Imported from: Europe
Percentage of Business in Importing: 50

41482 (HQ)A J Antunes & Co
180 Kehoe Blvd
Carol Stream, IL 60188-1814 630-784-1000
Fax: 630-784-1650 800-253-2991
scott.march@antunes.com
Manufacturer and exporter of stainless steel food service equipment for restaurants and concession operations including tables and serving equipment in addition to filtration products that remove particulates, bacteria, and virusesfrom water.

President: Glenn Bullock
CEO: Juan Arzate
juan.arzate@ajantunes.com
CFO: Bill Nelson
Executive VP: William Hickey
Director New Business Development: Scott March
VP Sales/Marketing: Tom Krisch
Estimated Sales: $ 50 - 100 Million
Number Employees: 100-249
Type of Packaging: Food Service
Brands Exported: Roundup; Antunes Control
Regions Exported to: Worldwide
Percentage of Business in Exporting: 20

41483 A La Carte
5610 W Bloomingdale Ave
Chicago, IL 60639-4110 773-237-3000
Fax: 773-237-3075 800-722-2370
service@alacarteline.com
Custom promotional products including hard candy and popcorn in decorative tins, jars, boxes, etc.
President: Michael Shulkin
CEO: Adam Robins
Sales Director: James Janowski
Purchasing: Marly Robins
Estimated Sales: $ 10 - 20 Million
Number Employees: 50-99
Parent Co: David Scott Industries
Type of Packaging: Food Service, Private Label, Bulk
Regions Exported to: Central America, Canada
Percentage of Business in Exporting: 1

41484 A Legacy Food Svc
12683 Corral Pl
Santa Fe Springs, CA 90670-4748 562-320-3100
Fax: 888-604-1066 800-848-4440
info@alegacy.com www.alegacy.com
Manufacturer and exporter of top-of-range aluminum cookware. Also, restaurant supplies and equipment
President: Brett Gross
Sales Director: Eric Gross
Manager: Eric Gross
egross@alegacy.com
Estimated Sales: $ 1 - 5 Million
Number Employees: 5-9
Square Footage: 320000
Other Locations:
 Leonard, Harold, & Co.
 Chicago, ILLeonard, Harold, & Co.
Brands Exported: Eagleware; Haleu
Regions Exported to: Central America, South America, Europe, Asia, Middle East, Australia

41485 A T Ferrell Co Inc
1440 S Adams St
Bluffton, IN 46714-9793 260-824-3400
Fax: 260-824-5463 800-248-8318
www.atferrell.com
Manufacturer and exporter of automatic electric feed mills, augers, pneumatic feed conveyors and aluminum beverage can crushers
President: Steve Stuller
bsstuller@atferrell.com
Estimated Sales: $ 1-2.5 Million
Number Employees: 50-99
Number of Brands: 2
Brands Exported: Modern Mill
Regions Exported to: Canada
Percentage of Business in Exporting: 20

41486 A T Ferrell Co Inc
1440 S Adams St
Bluffton, IN 46714-9793 260-824-3400
Fax: 260-824-5463 800-248-8318
info@atferrell.com www.atferrell.com
Manufacturer and exporter of grain and seed cleaners and separators, hammer and roller mills, grain and feed coolers and vibrator and air conveyors
President: Steve Stuller
bsstuller@atferrell.com
CFO: Roger Stackhouse
Vice President: Phillip Petrakos
Research & Development: Dan Johnson
Sales Director: John Hay
Plant Manager: Howard Vaughn
Purchasing Manager: Brian Dynes
Estimated Sales: $ 5 - 10 Million
Number Employees: 50-99
Square Footage: 100000
Other Locations:
 Clipper Separation Technologies
 Bluffton, IN

Ferrell-Ross Division
Amarillo, TXClipper Separation TechnologiesAmarillo
Brands Exported: Clipper; Ferrell Ross Roller Mills; Mix-Mill; Farmatic Hammer Mills
Regions Exported to: Worldwide
Percentage of Business in Exporting: 20

41487 A Taste for Life
11025 Carolina Place Pkwy
Pineville, NC 28134   908-591-1507
ataste4life@gmail.com
www.ataste.net
Gourmet Spanish foods

41488 A&A International
131 Medhurst Drive
Ottawa, ON K2G 4J9
Canada   613-228-3521
Fax: 613-228-9405
Processor, importer and exporter of milk powder, margarine, flour and meats
President: Hussein Al Saleh
VP: Shahira Al Saleh
Number Employees: 6
Regions Exported to: South America, Europe, Asia, Middle East, Africa
Percentage of Business in Exporting: 25
Regions Imported from: South America, Europe, Asia, Middle East, Africa
Percentage of Business in Importing: 75

41489 A&A Line & Wire Corporation
5118 Grand Ave Ste 10
Flushing, NY 11378   718-456-2657
Fax: 718-366-8284 800-886-2657
jlach@aalinewire.com
Manufacturer, importer and exporter of rope, twine and doormats, also sausage and pastella twine
President: Wally Greenburg
Treasurer: F Lach
Contact: Robert Giragosian
rgiragosian@aalinewire.com
Estimated Sales: Below $ 5 Million
Number Employees: 10-19
Square Footage: 32000
Parent Co: Long Island Import Center
Brands Exported: Crown
Regions Exported to: Canada, Caribbean
Regions Imported from: Worldwide
Percentage of Business in Importing: 15

41490 A&A Marine & Drydock Company
10417 Front Line
PO Box 547
Blenheim, ON N0P 1A0
Canada   519-676-2030
Fax: 519-676-4343 www.aamarine.ca
Frozen perch and pickerel.
President: George Anderson
Vice President: Sherry Anderson
Estimated Sales: $3.5 Million
Number Employees: 25
Type of Packaging: Consumer, Food Service
Regions Exported to: USA
Percentage of Business in Exporting: 80

41491 A&B Safe Corporation
114 Delsea Dr S
Glassboro, NJ 08028   856-863-1186
Fax: 856-863-1208 800-253-1267
info@a-bsafecorp.com www.a-bsafecorp.com
Manufacturer, importer and exporter of depository, burglary and insulated safes and chests; also, insulated filing cabinets, safes and locks
President: Edward Dornisch
Sales Director: Edward C Dornisch
Operations Manager: Mildred Dornisch
Estimated Sales: $ .5 - 1 million
Number Employees: 1-4
Number of Brands: 20
Square Footage: 10000
Regions Exported to: Central America, South America, Europe, Asia, Middle East
Percentage of Business in Exporting: 20
Regions Imported from: Europe, Asia
Percentage of Business in Importing: 60

41492 A&C Quinlin Fisheries
1220 Highway 330
Centreville, NS B0W 2G0
Canada   902-745-2742
Fax: 902-745-1788
Salted fish and seafood.
President: Aaron Quinlin
Estimated Sales: $5-10 Million
Number Employees: 20
Type of Packaging: Consumer, Food Service
Brands Exported: Chelsea
Percentage of Business in Exporting: 75

41493 A&D Weighing
1756 Automation Pkwy
San Jose, CA 95131-1873   408-263-5333
Fax: 408-263-0119 800-726-3364
scales@andweighing.com www.andonline.com
Manufacturer and exporter of balances, scales and indicators
President: Paul Huber
President, Chief Executive Officer: Teruhisa Moriya
CEO: Peru Moriya
Marketing Communications Coordinator: Regina Starzyk
Director Sales: Dan Ashton
dashton@andweighing.com
Estimated Sales: $ 20-50 Million
Number Employees: 20-49
Square Footage: 3000
Regions Exported to: Central America, South America, Canada, Latin America, Mexico
Percentage of Business in Exporting: 15

41494 A&H Seafood Market
4960 Bethesda Ave
Bethesda, MD 20814   301-986-9692
Fax: 301-986-5555
Owner: Santi Zabaleta
Sales Manager: Kalimar Maia
Contact: Herminio Martinez
martinez@anhmarket.com
Estimated Sales: $ .5 - 1 million
Number Employees: 1-4

41495 A&J Mixing International
8-2345 Wyecroft Road
Oakville, ON L6L 6L8
Canada   905-827-7288
Fax: 905-827-5045 800-668-3470
lyndon@ajmixing.com www.ajmixing.com
Manufacturer and exporter of food dry ingredient mixers, mixing sytems, vacuum coaters, dryers and continuous mixers.
President: A Flower
Sales: Lyndon Flower
Estimated Sales: $2.5 Million
Square Footage: 5000
Other Locations:
Sycamore, IL
Brands Exported: Phlauer™
Regions Exported to: Central America, South America, Europe
Percentage of Business in Exporting: 75

41496 A&L Laboratories
1001 Glenwood Ave
Minneapolis, MN 55405   612-374-9141
Fax: 612-374-5426 800-225-3832
Detergents and sanitizers
President: Guy Pochard
VP: Gabreiele Wittenburg
Contact: Roger Beers
beers@aandl-labs.com
Estimated Sales: $20-50 Million
Number Employees: 20-49
Regions Exported to: Central America, South America, Europe
Percentage of Business in Exporting: 9

41497 A&M Industries
3610 North Cliff Avenue
Sioux Falls, SD 57104   605-332-4877
Fax: 605-338-6015 800-888-2615
amindustries@amindustries.com
www.amindustries.com
Manufacturer and exporter of rebuilt packaging, food processing and confectionery machinery, carton over-wrappers and specialty tooling
Owner: Richard Miller
Estimated Sales: Below $ 5 Million
Number Employees: 1-4
Square Footage: 20000
Type of Packaging: Consumer, Food Service, Private Label
Regions Exported to: Central America, South America, Asia
Percentage of Business in Exporting: 15

41498 A&M Process Equipment
487 Westney Rd.
S., Unit #1
Ajax, ON L1S 6W7
Canada   905-619-8001
Fax: 905-619-8816
Food processing equipment including powder mixing and size reduction; exporter of ribbon, conical and twin shell blenders
President: John Lang
Number Employees: 4
Square Footage: 8000
Brands Exported: A&M
Regions Exported to: USA
Percentage of Business in Exporting: 30

41499 A&M Thermometer Corporation
17 Piney Park Road
Asheville, NC 28806-1727   828-251-9092
Fax: 828-254-5611 800-685-9211
Manufacturer and exporter of glass thermometers
President: M Pflaumbaum
R&D: Armin Pflaumbaum
Marketing: Kathy Toomey
Production: Armin Pflaumbaum
Purchasing Director: M Pflaumbaum
Estimated Sales: $2.5-5 Million
Number Employees: 10-19
Type of Packaging: Private Label, Bulk
Regions Exported to: Central America, South America, Europe, Asia, Middle East

41500 A-1 Booth Manufacturing
375 S 250 E
Burley, ID 83318-3718   208-678-2877
Fax: 800-952-3285 800-820-3285
sales@a1booth.com www.a1booth.com
Manufacturer and exporter of tables, chairs and seats
President: Robert Silcock
Estimated Sales: $1-2.5 Million
Number Employees: 5-9
Type of Packaging: Food Service
Regions Exported to: Worldwide

41501 A-1 Refrigeration Co
1720 E Monticello Ct
Ontario, CA 91761-7740   909-930-9910
Fax: 909-930-9026 800-669-4423
custserv@a1flakeice.com www.a1flakeice.com
Ice machines.
Plant Manager: Tony Gallinucci
Estimated Sales: Less Than $500,000
Number Employees: 1-4
Number of Products: 10
Brands Exported: A-1 Flake Ice Machines
Regions Exported to: Central America, South America, Asia, South Pacific
Percentage of Business in Exporting: 50

41502 A-A1 Aaction Bag
5601 Logan St
Denver, CO 80216-1301   303-297-9955
Fax: 303-297-9960 800-783-1224
searichcorp@aol.com www.centralbag.com
Manufacturer and exporter of bags including plastic, burlap and cotton; also, plastic film; importer of burlap and woven polypropylene bags
President: Esther Seaman
Partner: Elly Zussman
elly@centralbag.com
VP: Lewis Bradford
Sales Director: Morton Seaman
Estimated Sales: $ 500,000 - $ 1 Million
Number Employees: 10-19
Square Footage: 48000
Parent Co: Sea-Rich Corporation
Type of Packaging: Bulk
Regions Exported to: Central America, Canada
Regions Imported from: South America, Asia

41503 A-B-C Packaging MachineCorp
811 Live Oak St
Tarpon Springs, FL 34689-4199   727-937-5144
Fax: 727-938-1239 800-237-5975
sales@abcpackaging.com www.abcpackaging.com
Manufacturer and exporter of packaging machinery
President: Donald G Reichert
Director Sales/Marketing: Bryan Sinicrope
Estimated Sales: $10-20 Million
Number Employees: 50-99
Square Footage: 200000
Regions Exported to: Central America, South America, Asia

Importers & Exporters / A-Z

41504 A-L-L Magnetics Inc
2831 E Via Martens
Anaheim, CA 92806-1751   714-632-1754
      Fax: 714-632-1757 800-262-4638
   sales@allmagnetics.com www.allmagnetics.com
Manufacturer, exporter and importer of magnets used for holding, separating and water treatment
President: John Nellessen
john@allmagnetics.com
CFO: John Nellessen
Sales: Rosemary Kute
Estimated Sales: Below $ 5 Million
Number Employees: 10-19
Square Footage: 80000
Brands Exported: The Magnet Source
Percentage of Business in Exporting: 10
Brands Imported: The Magnet Source
Percentage of Business in Importing: 15

41505 A-Z Factory Supply
10512 United Pkwy
Schiller Park, IL 60176-1716   847-261-0620
   Fax: 800-233-4512 800-323-4511
      sales@azsupply.com www.azsupply.com
Manufacturer and exporter of material handling and storage equipment, shelving, carts, shelf trucks, boxes, bins, hoppers, corrugated steel containers, conveyors, lifts, hoists, etc
Manager: Henry Bolden
henry@azsupply.com
VP: R Hannesson
Sales Manager: B Spurling
Estimated Sales: Below $5,000,000
Number Employees: 10-19
Regions Exported to: Central America, Canada, Caribbean, Mexico
Percentage of Business in Exporting: 10

41506 A. Gagliano Co Inc
300 N Jefferson St # 1
PO Box 511382
Milwaukee, WI 53202-5920   414-272-1515
      Fax: 414-272-7215 800-272-1516
         info@agagliano.com
Fresh fruits and vegetables
Owner: Anthony Gagliano
tony@agagliano.com
Owner: Nick Gagliano
Owner: Mike Gagliano
Warehouse Manager: Rick Alsum
Estimated Sales: $20 Million
Number Employees: 50-99
Number of Brands: 1
Number of Products: 500
Square Footage: 200000
Type of Packaging: Consumer, Food Service, Private Label, Bulk
Regions Imported from: Worldwide
Percentage of Business in Importing: 20

41507 A. Smith Bowman Distillery
1 Bowman Dr
Fredericksburg, VA 22408   540-373-4555
      Fax: 540-371-2236 www.asmithbowman.com
Bourbon, scotch, rum, tequila, whiskey, gin and vodka
President/CEO: John Adams Jr
CFO/COO: Kent Broussard
VP Production and Distiller: Joseph Dangler
Estimated Sales: $20-50 Million
Number Employees: 20-49
Number of Brands: 2
Number of Products: 9
Percentage of Business in Exporting: 80

41508 A. Suarez & Company
PO Box 364054
San Juan, PR 00936-4054   787-782-6117
      Fax: 787-782-6047 asuarez@icepr.com
Importer and exporter of oil, rice, canned sardines, tableware and packaging products
President: Julio Suarez
VP: Antonio Suarez
Number Employees: 5-9
Square Footage: 40000
Regions Exported to: Caribbean, Latin America
Percentage of Business in Exporting: 80
Regions Imported from: Europe, Canada

41509 A.B. Sealer, Inc.
N 7212 Farwell Road
PO Box 635
Beaver Dam, WI 53916-0635   920-885-9299
      Fax: 920-885-0288 877-885-9299
      sales@absealer.com www.absealer.com
Manufacturer and exporter of packaging machinery including portable case erectors and sealers and custom equipment systems
Owner: Lou Stikowsky
CEO: Russell Quandt
Estimated Sales: $1-2.5 Million
Number Employees: 50-99
Regions Exported to: Worldwide

41510 A.C. Legg
6330 Highway 31
PO Box 709
Calera, AL 35040-5131   205-324-3451
      Fax: 205-324-5971 800-422-5344
      sales@aclegg.com www.aclegg.com
Processor of custom-blended seasonings for meat, poultry, seafood and snack foods.
President/CEO: James Purvis
jpurvis@aclegg.com
EVP: Charles Purvis
EVP: Sandra Purvis
Year Founded: 1923
Estimated Sales: $20-50 Million
Number Employees: 100-249
Number of Brands: 1
Square Footage: 131000
Type of Packaging: Food Service, Private Label, Bulk
Brands Exported: Legg's Old Plantation
Regions Exported to: Central America, South America
Percentage of Business in Exporting: 5

41511 A.D. Joslin Manufacturing Company
33 Artic St
Manistee, MI 49660   231-723-2908
      Fax: 231-723-2908 www.manistee.com/joslin
Manufacturer and exporter of handheld and electric seal embossing machinery, dating machinery, steel code marking stamps, ticket validators and handheld case numbering machines
General Manager: Norman Ware
Office Manager: Carol Westberg
Estimated Sales: $ 3 - 5 Million
Number Employees: 10-19
Parent Co: Cosco Industries
Regions Exported to: Worldwide
Percentage of Business in Exporting: 30

41512 A.F. Coffee Products
2419 Smallman Street
Pittsburgh, PA 15222-4675   412-261-0160
      Fax: 412-261-0898 www.fuentecoffee.com

41513 A.J. Trucco
343-344 NYC Terminal Market
Bronx, NY 10474   718-893-3060
      Fax: 718-617-9884 866-258-7822
   info@truccodirect.com www.truccodirect.com
Importer of garlic, figs, dates, cannellini beans, lupini beans and chestnuts, including fresh, dried and frozen
President: Salvatore Vacca
Estimated Sales: $ 10 - 20 Million
Number Employees: 10-19
Type of Packaging: Consumer, Bulk
Brands Imported: Cavalier; Indian; Liberty; Seca; Cangianiello; Montanaro
Regions Imported from: Europe
Percentage of Business in Importing: 100

41514 A.K. Robins
4100 Pistorio Road
Baltimore, MD 21229-5509   410-247-4000
      Fax: 410-247-9165 800-486-9656
Manufacturer and exporter of cleaners, conveyors, cookers, cutters, exhausters, extractors, etc.; also, CAD engineering and design and USDA services available
Sales Manager: Steve Ward
Operations Manager: Ken Vogel
Number Employees: 50
Regions Exported to: Worldwide

41515 A.L. Duck Jr Inc
26231 River Run Trail
Zuni, VA 23898-3215   757-562-2387
Smoked sausage
President: Brenda Redd
Estimated Sales: $1-2.5 Million
Number Employees: 5-9
Type of Packaging: Consumer, Food Service

41516 A.M. Manufacturing
14151 Irving Ave
Dolton, IL 60419   708-841-0959
      Fax: 708-841-0975 800-342-6744
         www.ammfg.com
Baking equipment
Owner: Claudia Kunis
Co-owner: Holly Rentner
Contact: Wojciechows Mentz
wojo2424@aol.com
Estimated Sales: $ 5 - 10 Million
Number Employees: 20-49
Square Footage: 28000

41517 A.O. Smith Water Products Company
600 E John Carpenter Fwy # 200
Irving, TX 75062-3985   972-792-4371
      Fax: 972-719-5967 800-527-1953
   techctr@hotwater.com www.hotwater.com
Manufacturer and exporter of tank-type water heaters and boilers and booster heaters
Chairman, Chief Executive Officer: Paul Jones
Vice President, Controller: Daniel Kempken
President, Chief Operating Officer: Ajita Rajendra
Project Manager: Will Harris
Number Employees: 50-99
Square Footage: 4000000
Parent Co: A.O. Smith Corporation
Regions Exported to: Worldwide
Percentage of Business in Exporting: 15

41518 A.R. Pellegrini & Associates
500 N Commercial St # 504
Manchester, NH 03101-1151   603-627-1600
         Fax: 603-627-2920
Importer of Italy wines
President: Michael Pellegrini
Customer Service: Connie Miville
Administrative Director: Laurene Pellegrini
Estimated Sales: $2.5-5 Million
Number Employees: 1-4

41519 A/R Packaging Corporation
PO Box 466
Brookfield, WI 53008-0466   262-549-1500
      Fax: 262-549-3711 800-414-0125
   wiorders@spectrumcorporation.com
         www.arpackaging.com
Contract packager and exporter of specialty lubricants; wholesaler/distributor of industrial lubricants
Chairman: Alan Baumann
Executive Vice President: Craig Baumann
VP Sales: Bruce Davidson
Contact: Brian Leach
bleach@spectrumcorporation.com
Plant Manager: Greg Wrobbel
Estimated Sales: $1-2.5 Million
Number Employees: 20-49
Square Footage: 200000
Type of Packaging: Private Label
Regions Exported to: South America, Asia
Percentage of Business in Exporting: 10

41520 A1 Tablecloth Co
450 Huyler St # 102
South Hackensack, NJ 07606-1563   201-727-4364
      Fax: 201-727-8988 800-727-8987
   a1@a1tablecloth.com www.a1tablecloth.com
Manufacturer and exporter of tablecloths, napkins, table skirting, chair covers and drapes
Owner: Robert Fox
Contact: Pearle Adam
ap@a-1tablecloth.com
Estimated Sales: $ 10 - 50,000,000
Number Employees: 1-4
Regions Exported to: Worldwide

41521 AAK
2520 7th Street Rd
Louisville, KY 40208-1029   502-636-1321
      Fax: 502-636-3904 800-622-3055
         www.aak.com

Shortenings including flaked, creamy liquid and votated; also, soybean and cottonseed oils; as well as identity preserved oils for GMO-free market.
President/CEO: Timothy Helson
Regional Sales Manager: Jason Glaser
Operations Manager: Sam Marrillia
Estimated Sales: $11.6 Million
Number Employees: 100-249
Square Footage: 200000
Parent Co: AAK USA Inc.
Type of Packaging: Food Service, Bulk
Brands Exported: Golden Foods; Golden Brands
Regions Exported to: Europe, Middle East
Percentage of Business in Exporting: 5

41522 AAMD
7342 Tomwood Dr
Liverpool, NY 13090-3747   315-451-0951
          Fax: 315-451-8740 800-887-4167
Manufacturer, importer and exporter of packaging machinery including tamper evident sealing equipment, closure lining equipment, assembly machines, metal closure threaders, tamper evident cap slitting machines, etc.; also, consulting services available
VP Sales/Marketing: Eugene Orr
Estimated Sales: $ 1 - 3 Million
Number Employees: 1-4
Square Footage: 52000
Regions Exported to: Worldwide
Percentage of Business in Exporting: 12
Regions Imported from: Europe
Percentage of Business in Importing: 12

41523 AANTEC
3116 N Pointer Rd
Appleton, WI 54911   920-830-9723
          Fax: 920-830-9840
Packaging equipment; case packers, palletizers, tray packers/formers, case erectors/sealers, napkin folders, towel and tissue interfolders, tissue rewinders, napkin wrappers and bundlers, roll wrappers, conveyors, grip per elevators and lowerators, high-speed case-packers
President: Robert Schuh
VP: Corben Hoffman
Sales: Jeffrey Aissen
Public Relations: Julia Kirsch
Operations: Paul Tassoul
Estimated Sales: $ 5 - 10 Million
Number Employees: 10-19
Type of Packaging: Consumer, Food Service, Private Label, Bulk
Brands Exported: All-Involvo, TMC, Schneider, PackAir, Bretting, AANTEC
Regions Exported to: Europe
Percentage of Business in Exporting: 10
Brands Imported: TMC, Involvo
Regions Imported from: Europe
Percentage of Business in Importing: 50

41524 AB InBev
One Busch Pl.
St. Louis, MO 63118   314-577-7427
          www.ab-inbev.com
Beer, malt liquor, ales, lagers, and non-alcoholic brews.
Zone President, North America: Michel Dukeris
CEO: Carlos Brito
Chief Financial/Solutions Officer: Felipe Dutra
Chief Marketing Officer: Pedro Earp
Chief Sales Officer: Ricardo Tadeu
Year Founded: 2008
Estimated Sales: $56.6 Billion
Number Employees: 182,915
Number of Brands: 500+
Type of Packaging: Consumer, Food Service, Bulk
Other Locations:
  Brewery
  Baldwinsville, NY
  Brewery
  Cartersville, GA
  Brewery
  Columbus, OH
  Brewery
  Fairfield, CA
  Brewery
  Fort Collins, CO
  Brewery
  Houston, TX
  Brewery Cartersville
Brands Exported: Budweiser; Bud Light; Michelob
Regions Exported to: Worldwide
Percentage of Business in Exporting: 22
Brands Imported: Azteca; Rio Cristal; Kirin

Regions Imported from: South America, Asia, Canada, Mexico

41525 ABB
North American Headquarters
305 Gregson Dr
Cary, NC 27511   440-585-7804
          Fax: 919-666-1377 800-435-7365
contact.center@us.abb.com new.abb.com
Manufacturer and exporter of presses and drives for high-pressure food processing equipment for pasteurization and sterilization, generators, control systems, drives, motors, instrumentation and metering.
CEO: Peter Voser
Managing Director, U.S.: Maryrose Sylvester
CFO, U.S.: Michael Gray
Year Founded: 1891
Estimated Sales: $27.9 Billion
Number Employees: 147,000
Parent Co: ABB Group
Regions Exported to: Worldwide

41526 ABC Coffee & Pasta
9063 San Fernando Rd
Sun Valley, CA 91352-1412   818-252-1414
          Fax: 818-252-7771
Importer of pasta making machinery and espresso/cappuccino and coffee machines and carts
Owner: David Fines
Estimated Sales: $ 1 - 3 Million
Number Employees: 10-19
Square Footage: 24000
Brands Imported: Gaggia; La Parmigiana
Regions Imported from: Europe
Percentage of Business in Importing: 100

41527 ABCO Industries Limited
PO Box 1120
Lunenburg, NS B0J 2C0
Canada   902-634-8821
          Fax: 902-634-8583 866-634-8821
          www.abco.ca
Manufacturer and exporter of aluminum and stainless steel food processing equipment including steam blanchers evaporative coolers
President: John Meisner
CEO: J Eisenhauer
Marketing Director: Graham Gerhardt
Sales Director: Dan Croft
Number Employees: 50-99
Square Footage: 120000
Regions Exported to: South America, Europe, Asia, Mexico, Australia
Percentage of Business in Exporting: 25

41528 ABCO Laboratories Inc
2450 S Watney Way
Fairfield, CA 94533-6730   707-432-2200
          Fax: 707-432-2240 800-678-2226
          www.abcolabs.com
Nutraceutical products-liquids, tablets, capsules, powder blends. Foods-spices, dry blends, seasonings, functional food blends.
President: David Baron
Founder: Allen Baron
abaron@abcolabs.com
R&D: Dr Muhammed Al-Nasassrah
Quality Control: Rich Hale
Marketing: Greg Northam
Sales: Victoria Gonzales
Operations: Richard Snowden
Plant Manager: Dick Snowden
Purchasing Director: Carl Falcone
Number Employees: 100-249
Number of Brands: 10
Number of Products: 5000
Square Footage: 800000
Type of Packaging: Consumer, Food Service, Private Label, Bulk

41529 ABI Limited
8900 Keele Street, Unit 1
Concord, ON L4K 2N2
Canada   905-738-6070
          Fax: 905-738-6085 800-297-8666
          info@abiltd.com
ABI Ltd. manufacturers automated food processing equipment with the emphasis on performance, durability, reliability and simplicity in maintenance.
President: Alex Kuperman
Marketing: Regine Kuperman
Production VP: Mike Kuperman
Number Employees: 20
Square Footage: 60000

Brands Exported: ABI Ltd.
Regions Exported to: Europe
Percentage of Business in Exporting: 65

41530 ABJ/Sanitaire Corporation
9333 N 49th St
Milwaukee, WI 53223-1472   414-365-2200
          Fax: 414-365-2210 www.sanitaire.com
Manufacturer and exporter of anaerobic wastewater systems including sequencing batch reactors
President: Tom Pokovsky
CFO: Tom Thompson
Finance Executive: Scott Tysen
R&D: Joe Krall
Marketing: Laurie Besch
Manager Sales/Marketing: Roger Byrne
Public Relations: Laurie Besch
Customer Service Manager: Ken George
Production: Loras Lux
Purchasing: Loras Lux
Estimated Sales: $50 Million
Number Employees: 100-249
Square Footage: 7000
Brands Exported: Abj - Iceas

41531 ABM Marking
2799 S Belt W
Belleville, IL 62226-6777   618-277-3773
          Fax: 618-277-3782 800-626-9012
          abmmarking@aol.com www.abmmarking.com
Manufacturer and exporter of ink jet printers and coding inks for porous and nonporous surfaces including coated, plastic and polyethylene; importer of tape dispensers and machines
Owner: Al Merchiori
Sales Manager: Alberto Merchiori
abmmarking@aol.com
Operations: Roger Schaefer
Estimated Sales: $ 3 - 5 Million
Number Employees: 5-9
Square Footage: 24000
Brands Exported: ABM; Safemark Inks
Regions Exported to: Central America, South America, Europe, Asia
Brands Imported: Cyklop - Stayer
Regions Imported from: Europe

41532 ABO Industries
13620 Lindamere Ln
San Diego, CA 92128   858-566-9750
          Fax: 858-566-9590
Manufacturer, exporter and importer of industrial progressive cavity, peristaltic, gear, metering and air operated diaphragm pumps
President: Joseph Schulman
VP: Ming Li
Estimated Sales: $ 1 - 5 Million
Number Employees: 5-9
Square Footage: 5000
Brands Exported: Delasco; Kracht; Sera; PCM; Blagdon
Regions Exported to: Central America, South America
Percentage of Business in Exporting: 20
Brands Imported: Delasco; Kracht; Sera; PCM; Blagdon
Regions Imported from: Europe
Percentage of Business in Importing: 40

41533 ACCO Systems
12755 E 9 Mile Rd
Warren, MI 48089   845-456-2236
          Fax: 586-758-1901 800-342-2226
          www.accosystems.co.uk
Manufacturer and exporter of material handling systems and equipment
President: Anthony Gore
Director Sales/Marketing: Mark Murray
Contact: Glenn Clannell
gclannell@andek.com
Number Employees: 250-499
Parent Co: Durr GmbH
Regions Exported to: South America, Europe, Canada, Latin America, Mexico

41534 ACH Food Co Inc
One Parkview Plz
5th Floor
Oakbrook Terrace, IL 60181   630-586-3740
          Fax: 630-954-6661 www.achfood.com
ACH's spice and seasonings brands, oils and shortenings, canola, vegetable, olive, and mixed blends.

Vice President & General Manager: Robert Soth
Chief Executive Officer: Imad Bazzi
EVP & Chief Financial Officer: Steve Zaruba
Vice President, Human Resources: Sarah Blankenship
sblankenship@achfood.com
Year Founded: 1868
Estimated Sales: $20-50 Million
Number Employees: 1000-4999
Square Footage: 768000
Type of Packaging: Consumer, Food Service, Private Label
Brands Exported: Sunola
Regions Exported to: Europe, Middle East
Percentage of Business in Exporting: 5
Regions Imported from: Europe
Percentage of Business in Importing: 1

41535 ACLAUSA Inc
509 Thomson Park Dr
Cranberry Twp, PA 16066-6425   724-776-0099
                   Fax: 724-776-0477
Manufacturer and exporter of material handling equipment including rollers, tires, wheels, bumpers and seals
President: Andy Mc Intyre
andym@aclausa.com
Estimated Sales: $1-2.5 Million
Number Employees: 1-4
Parent Co: ACLA
Regions Exported to: Central America, South America

41536 ACMA/GD
501 Southlake Blvd
Richmond, VA 23236-3078   804-794-6688
      Fax: 804-379-2199   800-525-2735
paul.smith@gidi.it   www.acmavolpak.com
Manufacturer, importer and exporter of liquid filling machinery and vertical and horizontal form/fill/seal equipment
CEO: Guiseppe Venturi
Marketing: Glen Coater
Estimated Sales: Below $ 500,000
Number Employees: 250-499
Square Footage: 800000
Regions Exported to: Worldwide
Brands Imported: Volpak

41537 ACO
501 SW 19th St
Moore, OK 73160-5427   405-794-7662
     Fax: 405-236-4014   www.mcdonalds.com
Manufacturer and exporter of material handling boxes, trays and racks
Founder: Ray Kroc
Estimated Sales: $1-2.5 Million
Number Employees: 10-19

41538 ACTS
7600 Glover Road
Langley, BC V2Y 1Y1
Canada   604-513-2044
       Fax: 604-899-0318   acts@twu.ca
           www.acts.twu.ca
Exporter of soybeans and honey; importer of olives and olive oil
President: Essam Dohair
General Manager: Muhammad Adherr
Number Employees: 5-9
Square Footage: 4400
Regions Exported to: Middle East
Percentage of Business in Exporting: 40
Regions Imported from: Europe
Percentage of Business in Importing: 60

41539 ADCO Manufacturing Inc
2170 Academy Ave
Sanger, CA 93657-3795   559-875-5563
       Fax: 559-875-7665   sales@adcomfg.com
           www.adcomfg.com
Manufacturer and exporter of packaging machinery for cartons
President: Frank Hoffman
CEO: Kate King
kking@adcomfg.com
VP Marketing: Scott Reed
VP Sales: Paul Kessock
Human Resources Manager: Maureen Say
Operations/Plant Manager: Dale Kingen
Purchasing Director: Juanita Johnson
Estimated Sales: $24 Million
Number Employees: 100-249
Square Footage: 76000

Type of Packaging: Consumer, Food Service, Private Label
Regions Exported to: Central America, South America, Europe, Asia, Middle East
Percentage of Business in Exporting: 100

41540 ADH Health Products Inc
215 N Route 303
Congers, NY 10920-1726   845-268-0027
       Fax: 845-268-2988   info@adhhealth.com
           www.adhhealth.com
All-natural vitamins, minerals, botanicals and high-quality health supplements.
President: Balu Advani
Chairman/CEO: Balram Advani
CFO: Navin Advani
VP/Vice Chairman/Human Resource Director: Maya Advani
COO: Ashwin Advani
VP Production: Arun Deshpande
Estimated Sales: $12.6 Million
Number Employees: 50-99
Square Footage: 100000
Type of Packaging: Private Label
Brands Exported: Prenatabs; Vita Kids; GeriVita; Gineroid; Ginko Biloba, Dorphynol DLPA; Dorphynol DLPA with SOD; Albutamin
Regions Exported to: Europe, Asia, Middle East
Percentage of Business in Exporting: 10

41541 ADI Systems
370 Wilsey Rd
Fredericton, NB E3B 6E9
Canada   506-452-7307
       Fax: 506-452-7308   800-561-2831
     systems@adi.ca   www.adisystemsinc.com
Wastewater treatment and water reuse.
President: Graham Brown
CFO: Hazen Hawker

41542 ADM Wild Flavors & Specialty
1261 Pacific Ave
Erlanger, KY 41018-1260   859-342-3600
       Fax: 859-342-3610   info@wildflavors.com
           www.wildflavors.com
Processor and exporter of flavors, colors and other ingredients for food and beverage
President: Kody Gibson
kcgibson@sbts.edu
Marketing Manager: Oliver Hodapp
Estimated Sales: $5-10 Million
Number Employees: 1000-4999
Parent Co: Archer Daniels Midland Company
Type of Packaging: Food Service, Private Label
Regions Exported to: Worldwide

41543 ADSI Inc
22971 State Road 78
Durant, OK 74701-1130   580-924-4461
       Fax: 580-924-7375   adsi@adsiinc.com
           www.adsiinc.com
Manufacturer & exporter of commercial egg breaking machinery, egg washing & sanitizing machines.
President, Sales, & Operations: Mike Maynard
VP, Sales, Production & Plant Mgr.: Steve Maynard
Estimated Sales: Below $ 5 Million
Number Employees: 10-19
Type of Packaging: Food Service
Brands Exported: Centri-Matic III; Egg Valet
Regions Exported to: Worldwide
Percentage of Business in Exporting: 30

41544 AEP Colloids
6299 Route 9N
Hadley, NY 12835   518-696-9900
       Fax: 518-696-9997   800-848-0658
           www.aepcolloids.com
Supplier and manufacturer of gums including agar agar, guar, karaya, locust bean, tragacanth, carrageenan and psyllium husk.
Quality Manager: Drew Tomis
Contact: Adam Strouse
a.strouse@aepcolloids.com
Year Founded: 1966
Number Employees: 5-9
Square Footage: 40000
Parent Co: Sarcom Inc
Type of Packaging: Bulk
Regions Exported to: South America, Europe, Asia
Percentage of Business in Exporting: 5
Regions Imported from: Europe, Asia
Percentage of Business in Importing: 90

41545 AEP Industries Inc
1970 Excel Dr
Mankato, MN 56001-5903   507-386-4420
       Fax: 507-388-4420   800-999-2374
           www.aepinc.com
Manufacturer and exporter of disposable gloves, aprons, bibs, table covers, specialty bags and films including cling, polyethylene, stretch and shrink
President: Jenny Pherson
Research & Development: Thea Ellingson
Marketing Director: Mike Sauer
Sales Director: Ken Christensen
Operations/Purchasing: Mike Ellis
Estimated Sales: $ 20 - 50 Million
Number Employees: 100-249
Parent Co: Atlantis Plastics
Type of Packaging: Consumer, Food Service, Bulk
Other Locations:
    Mankato-Institutional Operations
    Mankato, MN Mankato-Institutional Operations

41546 AEW Thurne
1148 Ensell Road
Lake Zurich, IL 60047-1539   847-726-8000
       Fax: 847-726-1600   800-239-7297
  chicago@aewdelford.com   www.aewdelford.com
Manufacturer and exporter of high-speed bandsaws and automated portion control slicing systems
President: Chris Mason
Chief Operating Officer, Chief Executive: Sigsteinn Gretarsson
Regional Sales Manager: David Bertelsen
Estimated Sales: $300,000-500,000
Number Employees: 9
Square Footage: 32000
Brands Exported: AEW Delford
Percentage of Business in Exporting: 50

41547 AFF International
1265 Kennestone Circle
Marietta, GA 30066-6037   770-427-8177
       Fax: 770-427-0964   800-241-7764
Processor and exporter of aromatic flavors and fragrances
President/Owner: Richard Neill
Estimated Sales: $10-20 Million
Number Employees: 20-49
Type of Packaging: Bulk
Regions Exported to: Worldwide
Percentage of Business in Exporting: 15

41548 AFL Industries
1751 W 10th St
West Palm Beach, FL 33404-6431   561-844-5200
       Fax: 561-844-5246   800-807-2709
           www.rwlwater.com
Manufacturer and exporter of oil and water separators for wastewater treatment systems
CEO: Tom Bieneman
CEO: Thomas Bieneman
tbieneman@aflindustries.com
Sales Manager: Ray Lopez
Administrative VP: Beverly Willcox
Estimated Sales: $ 1 - 2.5 Million
Number Employees: 10-19
Square Footage: 80000
Regions Exported to: Worldwide
Percentage of Business in Exporting: 10

41549 AFT Advanced Fiber Technologies
72 Queen Street
Sherbrooke, QC J1M 2C3
Canada   819-562-4754
       Fax: 819-562-6064   800-668-7273
  info@aikawagroup.com   www.aft-global.com
Manufacturer, importer and exporter of custom made screen and extraction plates
President: Roch Leblanc
CFO: Norman Pogdin
R&D: Robert Gooding
Quality Control: Serge Turcotte
Sales Manager: Jean Marc Brousseau
Number Employees: 175
Square Footage: 436560
Parent Co: CAE
Regions Exported to: Central America, South America, Latin America, Mexico
Percentage of Business in Exporting: 70
Percentage of Business in Importing: 10

Importers & Exporters / A-Z

41550 AFire Inc.
9711 Valley Boulevard
Suite B
Rosemead, CA 91770
Fax: 847-859-2728 877-234-7315
marlenachang@afireinc.com www.afireinc.com
Seller natural grilling products, patio furniture. Manufacturer of grilling natural planks, gluten free rubs, and KOKO charcoal that is made from coconut shells.
CEO: Marlena Chang
CFO: Ben Chang
Director of Sales: Marlena Chang
Estimated Sales: $100,000
Number Employees: 5
Square Footage: 150
Type of Packaging: Food Service, Private Label

41551 AG Processing Inc
12700 W Dodge Rd
Omaha, NE 68154-2154   402-496-7809
Fax: 402-492-7721 800-247-1345
info@agp.com www.agp.com
Emulsifiers, lecithin, vegetable fats, soybean flours, soy proteins and oils including vegetable, almond, amaranth, avocado, canola, coconut, corn, cottonseed, grape seed, lemon, olive, palm, peanut, and safflower.
Chairman: Brad Davis
CEO: J Keith Spackler
CFO/Group VP: Scott Simmelink
Senior VP: Mark Craigmile
mcraigmile@agp.com
VP: Matt Caswell
SVP, HR: Duke Vair
SVP, Operations: Mark Craigmile
Estimated Sales: Over $1 Billion
Number Employees: 1000-4999
Parent Co: AGP
Other Locations:
  AG Processing Plant
  Eagle Grove, IA
  AG Processing Plant
  Emmetsburg, IA
  AG Processing Plant
  Manning, IA
  AG Processing Plant
  Mason City, IA
  AG Processing Plant
  Sergeant Bluff, IA
  AG Processing Plant
  Sheldon, IA
  AG Processing PlantEmmetsburg

41552 AGC
10129 Piper Ln
Bristow, VA 20136-1418   703-257-1660
Fax: 703-330-7940 800-825-8820
info@agcengineering.com
www.agcheattransfer.com
Manufacturer and exporter sanitary plate heat exchangers and replacement parts
President: Tamika Carter
cartert@agc.org
Director, Research & Development: George Tholl
Director, Sales & Marketing: John C. Bohn
Office Manager - Western Factory: Jill Davis
Estimated Sales: $3-$5 Million
Number Employees: 20-49
Square Footage: 160000
Type of Packaging: Bulk
Regions Exported to: Worldwide

41553 AHD International, LLC
3340 Peachtree Rd NE
Suite 1685
Atlanta, GA 30326-1143   404-233-4022
Fax: 404-233-4041 info@ahdintl.com
www.ahdintl.com
Contract manufacturer of vitamins and nutritional products; Importer and exporter of nutritional raw materials and oils
President: John Alkire
Estimated Sales: $ 10 - 20 Million
Number Employees: 10-19
Type of Packaging: Bulk
Regions Exported to: Central America, South America, Europe
Regions Imported from: South America, Europe, Asia

41554 AIDP Inc
19535 E Walnut Dr S
City Of Industry, CA 91748-2318 909-718-0124
Fax: 626-964-6739 866-262-6699
customercare@aidp.com www.aidp.com
Wholesaler/distributor, importer and exporter of vitamins, specialty chemicals and herbal extracts
President: Edward Lee
edward.lee@aidp.com
SVP: Dave Dannenhold
Director Business Development: Katherine Lund
VP, Business Development: Kathy Lund
Estimated Sales: $ 1 - 3 Million
Number Employees: 20-49
Type of Packaging: Bulk
Brands Exported: Long Jax; Longjax™; Quikesan™; Tea Thea™; Kolla2®
Regions Exported to: South America, Europe, Asia
Regions Imported from: Europe, Asia

41555 AJ Trucco, Inc
343-344 New York City
Terminal Market
Bronx, NY 10474   718-893-3060
Fax: 718-617-9884 info@truccodirect.com
www.truccodirect.com
Importer, Distributor and Wholesaler of Chestnuts, Kiwi, Tomatoes, Garlic, Grapes, Figs and Clementines, Hazelnuts, Dried Fruits and Nuts
President: Salvatore Vacca
Partner: Nick Pacia
Estimated Sales: $ 10 - 20 Million
Number Employees: 4

41556 AKC Commodities Inc
1086 Stelton Rd
Piscataway, NJ 08854-5201   732-339-0071
Fax: 732-339-0073 800-252-1716
info@akccommodities.com
Importer, exporter and wholesaler/distributor of dried fruits, nuts, spices, beans, basmati rice, seeds, apricots, cashews, dates, pistachio, raisins, organic product and cranberries
Owner: Azam Kadeer
VP: Azam Kadeer
Marketing: Kyas Nazir
Number Employees: 5-9
Type of Packaging: Food Service
Regions Exported to: Europe, Canada
Brands Imported: Indus River; Laziz; Arya; Sawara
Regions Imported from: Asia, Middle East

41557 AL Systems
385 Franklin Ave
Suite C
Rockaway, NJ 07866   973-586-8500
Fax: 973-586-8865 888-960-8324
Manufacturer and exporter of automated control systems and software
President: Paul Lightfoot
Contact: Hilary Galt
hilary@cardiomedicalproducts.com
Director Operations: Gary Oriani
Director of Product Management: Gary Clemens
Estimated Sales: $ 1 - 5 Million
Number Employees: 20-49
Regions Exported to: Mexico
Percentage of Business in Exporting: 1

41558 (HQ)ALCO Designs
407 E Redondo Beach Blvd
Gardena, CA 90248   310-353-2300
Fax: 310-353-2301 800-228-2346
www.alcodesigns.com
Manufacturer and exporter of water treatment systems including outdoor fogging and standard and reverse osmosis misting, fogging and humidification
President: Samuel Cohen
Owner: Sam Cohen
CFO: Sam Cohen
VP: Issac Cohen
Marketing: Dick Wardlaw
Administrator: Liz Luna
Estimated Sales: $ 3 - 5 Million
Number Employees: 20-49
Square Footage: 5000
Other Locations:
  Vege Mist
  Tucker, GAVege Mist
Regions Exported to: Central America, South America, Europe
Percentage of Business in Exporting: 30

41559 ALP Lighting & Ceiling Products
6965 Airport Highway Ln
Pennsauken, NJ 08109   856-663-0095
Fax: 856-661-0870 800-633-7732
www.alplighting.com
Manufacturer, importer and exporter of lighting fixtures including louvers, lens, fluorescent fixture diffusers and components
VP: Steven Dix
Contact: William Foley
b.foley@alplighting.com
Estimated Sales: $ 1 - 5,000,000
Number Employees: 100-249
Square Footage: 120000
Regions Exported to: Worldwide
Brands Imported: Toshiba
Regions Imported from: Japan

41560 (HQ)ALPI Food Preparation Equipment
511 Piercey Road
Bolton, ON L7E 5B8
Canada   905-951-1067
Fax: 905-951-1608 800-928-2574
www.alpiinc.com
Manufacturer, exporter and importer of stainless steel convection/steam ovens, pasta cookers, pizza equipment, exhaust hoods, etc; consultant specializing in restaurant equipment design services
President: Pier Luigi Odorico
VP: Gian Paolo O'Dorico
National Sales Manager: Nazareno Cavallaro
Number Employees: 2
Square Footage: 28000
Type of Packaging: Food Service
Other Locations:
  ALPI Food Preparation Equipme
  Fort Lauderdale, FLALPI Food Preparation Equipme
Regions Exported to: Africa
Regions Imported from: Italy

41561 AM Todd Co
1717 Douglas Ave
Kalamazoo, MI 49007   269-343-2603
Fax: 269-343-3399 www.wildflavors.com
Processor and exporter of natural flavor extracts including alfalfa, black walnut hulls, wild cherry bark, dandelion, spice, oleoresins, xanthan gum, agar agar, fruit aromas (essences), essential oils, ethyl vanillin, papain, coffeeechinacea and ginseng
Director, Business Development: Matt Redd
Estimated Sales: $50-100 Million
Number Employees: 50-99
Square Footage: 95000
Parent Co: Wild Flavours
Type of Packaging: Bulk
Regions Exported to: Europe, Asia

41562 AM-Mac
311 US Highway 46 # C
Fairfield, NJ 07004-2419   973-575-7567
Fax: 973-575-1956 800-829-2018
ammac1@aol.com www.am-mac.com
Manufacturer and exporter of meat and bread slicers, mixers, vegetable cutters and meat grinders; wholesaler/distributor of food handling and storage equipment, wire shelving and ovens
President: Judith Spritzer
ammac1@aol.com
Vice President: Jon Spritzer
Estimated Sales: $10-20,000,000
Number Employees: 10-19
Brands Exported: Arimex; Lan Elec
Regions Exported to: Worldwide

41563 AME Nutrition
545 Metro Place S
Suite 100
Dublin, OH 43017   614-766-3638
sales@amenutrition.com
www.amenutrition.com
Plant- and dairy-based ingredients manufacturer
Director of Sales & Marketing: Bill Brickson

41564 AMETEK Inc
1100 Cassatt Rd
PO Box 1764
Berwyn, PA 19312-1177   610-647-2121
Fax: 215-323-9337 www.ametek.com
CEO: David A Zapico
david.zapico@ametek.com
VP: Tim Croal

Estimated Sales: Over $1 Billion
Number Employees: 10000+

41565 AMETEK National Controls Corp
1725 Western Dr
West Chicago, IL 60185-1877 630-231-5900
Fax: 630-231-1377 800-323-5293
webmaster@ametek.com www.ametekncc.com
Manufacturer and exporter of cooking computers, electronic timers and thermometers
COO: Tim Croal
tim.croal@ametek.com
VP: Tim Croal
General Manager: Nick Hoilds
Sales/Marketing Executive: John Meggesin
Sales Manager: Gerald Brown
Purchasing Manager: Cathy Porch
Number Employees: 20-49
Parent Co: Ametek
Regions Exported to: Worldwide
Percentage of Business in Exporting: 2

41566 AMF Bakery Systems Corp
2115 W Laburnum Ave
Richmond, VA 23227-4315 804-355-7961
Fax: 804-355-1074 800-225-3771
service-us@amfbakery.com www.amfbakery.com
Manufacturer and exporter of bakery and packaging equipment
President: Ken Newsome
CFO: Margaret Shaia
Director Product Marketing: Larry Gore
Sales Director: Richard MacArthur
Number Employees: 100-249
Square Footage: 400000
Parent Co: Bakery Holding
Type of Packaging: Consumer, Food Service, Private Label, Bulk
Other Locations:
  AMF Bakery Systems
  Sherbrooke, QuebecAMF Bakery Systems
Brands Exported: AMF
Regions Exported to: Central America, South America, Europe, Asia, Middle East, Worldwide
Percentage of Business in Exporting: 60

41567 AMF CANADA
1025 Cabana Street
Sherbrooke, QC J1K 2M4
Canada 819-563-3111
Fax: 819-821-2832 800-255-3869
mbissonnette@amfcanada.com
www.amfbakery.com
Manufacturer and exporter of mixers, ovens, troughs, trough elevators, fermentation rooms, dividers, rounders, moulders, panners, final proofers, slicers and baggers for the baking industry
CFO: Manon Bissonnette
Vice President Sales & Marketing: Jason Ward
Research & Development: Alain Lemieux
Director of Sales & Marketing: Larry Gore
Public Relations: Marie-Eve Raqieot
Operations Manager: Claude La Jeunesse
Production Manager: Danny Morin
Purchasing Manager: Jean-Pierre Rosa
Number Employees: 180
Square Footage: 500000

41568 AMI
PO Box 70520
Richmond, CA 94807-0520 510-234-5050
Fax: 510-234-5055 800-942-7466
www.amiincorporated.com
Manufacturer and exporter of food service serving carts, portable bars, mirror display products, cooking carts, maitre d' desks, etc
President: Kent Brown
CEO: Josh Yarrington
Sales: Lois Kitiuk
Plant Manager: Dang Nuygen
Number Employees: 10-19
Square Footage: 32000
Brands Exported: Arion
Regions Exported to: Central America, South America, Europe, Asia, Middle East, Canada
Percentage of Business in Exporting: 20

41569 AMSECO
228 E. Star of India Lane
236
Carson, CA 90746-1418 310-538-4670
Fax: 310-538-9932 800-421-1096
Manufacturer and exporter of burglar and fire alarms, closed circuit televisions, annunciator systems and security equipment
President: Yukata Odawara
VP Sales: Tom Galvez
Advertising Manager: Sergio Galvez
Estimated Sales: $10-20 Million
Number Employees: 10-19
Parent Co: AMSECO
Regions Exported to: Worldwide
Percentage of Business in Exporting: 30

41570 AMSOIL Inc
925 Tower Ave
Superior, WI 54880-1582 715-392-7101
Fax: 715-392-5225 www.amsoil.com
Manufacturer and exporter of lubricating oils and greases, vitamins and filters including air and water
President: Albert Amatuzio
aamatuzio@amsoil.com
COO: Alan Amatuzio
Estimated Sales: G
Number Employees: 100-249
Regions Exported to: Central America, South America, Europe, Asia, Middle East

41571 AMT Labs Inc
680 N 700 W
North Salt Lake, UT 84054-2733 801-294-3126
Fax: 801-299-0220 customercare@amtlabs.net
Processor and exporter of food supplements including mineral supplements, amino acid chelates, ascorbates, citrates, etc.
President: Bing Fang
President: Layne Hadley
Chairman: Dr Sen-Maw Fang PhD
VP/Research & Development: Dr. Oliver Fang MD
VP Manufacturing: Todd Rasmussen
Estimated Sales: $8.2 Million
Number Employees: 50-99
Square Footage: 400000
Type of Packaging: Private Label, Bulk
Regions Exported to: Worldwide
Percentage of Business in Exporting: 20

41572 ANDRITZ Inc
35 Sherman St
Muncy, PA 17756-1227 704-943-4343
www.andritz.com
Manufacturer and exporter of size reduction, screening, mixing, pelleting, material handling, conveyor, cereal cooking, dehydration, grading, barley, blending, milling, crushing, grinding, separating and storage equipment
President: Timothy J Ryan
timothy.ryan@andritz.com
Estimated Sales: $ 90 Million
Number Employees: 500-999
Square Footage: 400000
Parent Co: Andritz Maschinenfabrik AG

41573 (HQ)ANVER Corporation
36 Parmenter Rd
Hudson, MA 1749 978-568-0221
Fax: 978-568-1570 800-654-3500
rfq13@anver.com www.anver.com
Manufacturer and exporter of FDA approved vacuum lifting equipment and parts including components, pumps and cups
President: Frank Vernooy
Contact: Anver Anderson
anver@anver.com
Estimated Sales: $ 10 - 20 Million
Number Employees: 50-99
Square Footage: 120000
Regions Exported to: Worldwide
Percentage of Business in Exporting: 25
Regions Imported from: Europe, Asia

41574 AOI Tea Company
16651 Gothard Street
Unit M
Huntington Beach, CA 92647 714-841-2716
877-264-0877
consumer@AOItea.com www.aoitea.com
Matcha green tea
Madam President: Ayano Honda
Contact: Andrew Ge
age@aoimatcha.com
Regions Exported to: North America

41575 (HQ)AP Dataweigh Inc
2730 Northgate Ct
Cumming, GA 30041-6482 678-679-8000
Fax: 678-679-8001 877-409-2562
www.checkweigh.com
Manufacturer and exporter of check weighers, in-motion conveyor scales and checkweighers.
President: Myrna Stanczak
myrnastanczak@apdataweigh.com
Operations Manager: Scott Gibson
Estimated Sales: $1 Million
Number Employees: 10-19
Number of Brands: 2
Number of Products: 14
Brands Exported: Drummaster; AP In-Motion Checkweigh
Regions Exported to: South America, Europe
Regions Imported from: Europe, Asia
Percentage of Business in Importing: 1

41576 APC Inc
2425 SE Oak Tree Ct
Ankeny, IA 50021-7199 515-289-7600
Fax: 515-289-4360 800-369-2672
www.functionalproteins.com
Manufacturer of dairy replacer for bakery, confectionery and beverage applications.
CEO: Ryan Black
rblack@proliant.com
Number Employees: 50-99
Parent Co: Lauridsen Group
Other Locations:
  U.S. Office
  Ankeny, IAProduction
  Melrose, MNU.S. OfficeEl Marqu,s, Quer,taro

41577 API Heat Transfer Inc
2777 Walden Ave # 1
Buffalo, NY 14225-4788 716-684-6700
Fax: 716-684-2155 877-274-4328
sales@apiheattransfer.com
www.apiheattransfer.com
Manufacturer and exporter of thermal processing equipment and systems including plate heat exchangers, pasteurizers, evaporators, sterilizers and de-alcoholization systems
President: Joseph Cordosi
CEO: Mike Laisure
mlaisure@apiheattransfer.com
CFO: Jeff Lennox
Quality Control: Barry Kent
R&D: David Sijas
Marketing Director: Gary Trumpfheller
General Manager: David Parrott
Estimated Sales: $ 50 - 100 Million
Number Employees: 500-999
Regions Exported to: Central America, Canada, Carribean, Mexico
Percentage of Business in Exporting: 20
Regions Imported from: Europe

41578 APM
1500 Hillcrest Rd
Norcross, GA 30093-2617 770-921-6300
Fax: 770-925-7801 800-226-5557
www.apminc.org
Wholesaler/distributor and importer of mesh bags, pallet netting, bulk containers and pressure sensitive labels
Owner: James Sabourin
Sales Manager: Joel Corner
Estimated Sales: $5-10 Million
Number Employees: 10-19
Parent Co: NNZ Beheer
Regions Exported to: Worldwide
Percentage of Business in Exporting: 80

41579 APN Inc
921 Industry Rd
Caledonia, MN 55921-1838 507-725-3392
Fax: 507-725-2073
Batch control systems, filtration equipment, piping, fittings and tubing
President: Richard Bever
rbever@apn-inc.net
Vice President: Neil Goetzinger
Estimated Sales: $2.5-5 000,000
Number Employees: 20-49

41580 APV Americas
611 Sugar Creek Road
Delavan, WI 53115 847-678-4300
Fax: 800-252-5012 800-252-5200
apvproducts.us@apv.com www.apv.com

Manufacturer and exporter of automation, process systems, heat exchangers, dryers, evaporizers, membrane filtration systems, tanks, mixers, blenders, evaporators, etc.; spray drying available
Marketing Director: Richard Johnston
Project Sales Manager: Enrique Hinojosa
Contact: Dick Powner
dick.powner@apv.com
Estimated Sales: $ 1 - 5 Million
Number Employees: 50-100
Square Footage: 1800000
Parent Co: Invensys
Regions Exported to: Worldwide
Percentage of Business in Exporting: 10

41581 APV Baker
1200 W Ash St
Goldsboro, NC 27530 919-736-4309
Fax: 919-735-5275 www.apvbaker.com
Manufacturer and exporter of baking equipment: conveyors, ovens and mixers
VP Sales Bakery Machinery: Ricahrd Kirkland
Contact: Cindi Congdon
cindi.congdon@apv.com
Estimated Sales: $ 50-100 Million
Number Employees: 2800

41582 (HQ)APW Wyott Food Service Equipment Company
1938 Wyott Dr
Cheyenne, WY 82007-2102 307-634-5801
Fax: 307-637-8071 800-527-2100
www.apwwyott.com
Manufacturer and exporter of hardware, stainless steel kitchen pans, bun toasters, hot plates, food wells, broiling grills, dish dispensers and commercial food warming equipment
President: Lawrence Rosenbloom
Director National Accounts: Bruce Deckard
VP: Jim Humphrey
VP Marketing: Jeff King
Estimated Sales: $20-50 Million
Number Employees: 100-249
Type of Packaging: Food Service
Other Locations:
  APW/WYOTT Food Service Equipment
  New Rochelle, NYAPW/WYOTT Food Service Equipment

41583 ASCENT Technics Corporation
PO Box 981
Brick, NJ 08723-0981 732-279-0144
Fax: 732-255-3152 800-774-7077
Manufacturer and exporter of pressure sensitive label applicators including automatic, semi-automatic and handheld, also; labels and packaging systems
President: Ched Greenhill
Estimated Sales: Below $ 5 Million
Number Employees: 15
Number of Products: 6
Square Footage: 20000
Brands Exported: Air-Ply Systems; Touchless Vacu-Jet; S.M.A.R.T Labelers
Regions Exported to: Central America, South America, Europe, Australia
Percentage of Business in Exporting: 10

41584 ASI Data Myte
2800 Campus Dr # 60
Plymouth, MN 55441-2669 763-553-1040
Fax: 763-553-1041 800-455-4359
info@asidatamyte.com www.asidatamyte.com
Manufacturer and exporter of packaging and quality control software
Chairman: Joel Ronning
President: Rick Bump
rickbump@asidatamyte.com
Global Financial Controller: Dave Nelson
CTO & VP Engineering: Raj Chauhan
R&D: Cecil Nelson
Quality Control: Douglas Stohr
VP Global Marketing: Mary Braunwarth
VP Sales: Rudiger Laabs
Customer Manager: Mike McCalley
Sr. Director, Global Operations: John Cullinane
Number Employees: 50-99
Brands Exported: Data Metrics Software; Inspect Software
Regions Exported to: Central America, South America, Europe, Asia, Middle East, Mexico, Australia
Percentage of Business in Exporting: 10

41585 ASI Electronics Inc
13006 Cricket Hollow Ln
Cypress, TX 77429-2262 281-373-3835
Fax: 281-256-1406 800-231-6066
www.asielectronics.com
Manufacturer, exporter and importer of process controllers including level, weight and gate
Owner: William Jackson
Vice President: Alice Jackson
Sales: Bill Jackson
bjackson54@aol.com
Estimated Sales: $150,000
Number Employees: 1-4
Square Footage: 1000
Type of Packaging: Food Service, Bulk
Brands Exported: Kasiweigh
Regions Exported to: Canada
Percentage of Business in Exporting: 10

41586 (HQ)ASI International Inc
10 Shawnee Dr # M
Suite B5
Watchung, NJ 07069-5803 908-753-4448
Fax: 908-753-1917 sales@info-asi.net
www.info-asi.net
Importer and distributor of bulk raw material ingredients to the nutritional, food, beverage and cosmetic industries.
Owner: Joseph Campis
joseph@info-asi.net
VP: Joseph Campis
Operations: John Wyckoff
Number Employees: 1-4
Type of Packaging: Bulk
Other Locations:
  Padre Warehouse - California
  Anaheim, CA
  Arco Warehouse - New Jersey
  Passaic, NJPadre Warehouse - CaliforniaPassaic

41587 ASI/Restaurant Manager
1734 Elton Rd Ste 219
Silver Spring, MD 20903 800-356-6037
Fax: 301-445-6104 800-356-6037
sales@actionsystems.com
The most compreneive and user-friendly POS system available. Improve service, reduce labor costs and makes faster, more informed decisions to boost your bottom line with powerful backoffice tracking. Choose the traditional touchscreen POS or give your servers the Write-On Handheld for the ultimate in imporved tableside service.
Owner: Smiley Shu
VP: Lisa Wilson
Sales/Marketing Director: Craig Bednarovsky
Contact: Rm Asi
asi.rm@rmpos.com
Estimated Sales: $1-3 Million
Number Employees: 10-19
Square Footage: 12000
Type of Packaging: Food Service
Brands Exported: Restaurant Manager
Regions Exported to: Central America, South America, Europe, Asia, Middle East
Percentage of Business in Exporting: 10

41588 ATD-American Co
135 Greenwood Ave
Wyncote, PA 19095-1396 215-576-1000
Fax: 215-576-1827 800-523-2300
american@atd.com www.atdamerican.com
Furniture, steel shelving, cabinets, bins, table linens and chef aprons; exporter of furniture, linens and food service equipment
President: Janet Wischnia
janet@atd.com
VP: S Zaslow
VP: A Zaslow
R&D: Eric Wischnia
Estimated Sales: $ 65Million
Number Employees: 100-249
Regions Exported to: Central America, Canada, Caribbean, Latin America

41589 ATI
3415 S Sepulveda Blvd
Suite 610
Los Angeles, CA 90034-6060 310-397-9777
Fax: 310-445-1411 ati@american-trading.com
www.american-trading.com
California-based export trading company servicing the needs of food and beverage importers worldwide in four major categories: name-brand products, generic products, private label products, and raw ingredients. All sizes and packagingstyles are available. We work closely with the US Department of Agriculture, US Department of Commerce, the California Trade and Development Agency
President/CEO: Seth Wilen
CFO: Dan Wilen
Vice President: Matthew Good
Marketing Director: Nova Gatewood
Sales Director: Mike Davis
Estimated Sales: $10-20 Million
Number Employees: 5-9
Number of Brands: 500
Number of Products: 1000
Square Footage: 10000
Type of Packaging: Consumer, Food Service, Private Label, Bulk
Brands Exported: A&W; Welch's; Sunkist; Royal Islands; Ocean Spray; Sara Lee; Hormel; 7-UP; Pepsi; Sunny Delight; Dr. Pepper; John Marren; Con Agra; Land O' Lakes; Ventura; Tyson
Regions Exported to: Central America, South America, Europe, Asia, Middle East, Worldwide

41590 ATM Corporation
2450 S Commerce Dr
New Berlin, WI 53151 414-453-1100
Fax: 262-786-5074 800-511-2096
atm@execpc.com
Manufacturer and exporter of testing sieves and particle size measurement equipment
President: James Lang
VP: Stephen Kohl
VP of Marketing: Tony Romano
Contact: Eduardo Bolognesi
e.bolognesi@advantechmfg.com
Estimated Sales: $5-10,000,000
Number Employees: 20-49
Regions Exported to: Worldwide
Percentage of Business in Exporting: 15

41591 ATOFINA Chemicals
2000 Market St
Philadelphia, PA 19103-3231 215-419-7000
Fax: 215-419-7591 800-225-7788
bill.pernice@atofina.com
Manufacturer, importer and exporter of cleaning equipment and supplies including liquid chlorine and caustic soda
President: Doug Sharp
CFO: Larry Hartnett
R&D: Louis Hegedus
Contact: Francois Girin
francois.girin@atofina.com
Number Employees: 500-999
Regions Exported to: Worldwide
Regions Imported from: Worldwide

41592 ATS Rheosystems
231 Crosswicks Rd # 7
Bordentown, NJ 08505-2602 609-298-2522
Fax: 609-298-2795 www.atsrheosystems.com
www.cannoninstrument.com
A comprehensive analytical instrumentation, rheological consulting and materials testing, technical support and services company. Rheometer and viscometer design, viscometers and viscosity measurements, research level rheometers andrheology measurements, capillary rheometers, dynamic shear rheometers for asphalt testing, and dynamic mechanical thermal analysis. Other materials characterization techniques are also available, including thermal analysis, surface tension, andcontact angle.
President/CEO: Steven Colo
Manager: Louise Colo
lc@atsrheosystems.com
Estimated Sales: Less Than $500,000
Number Employees: 1-4

41593 AUTEC
20695 S Western Ave Ste 101
Torrance, CA 90501 310-212-6070
Fax: 310-212-5867 www.audio-technica.co.jp
Contact: Lucas Furst
tomo@autec-usa.com
Estimated Sales: $ .5 - 1 million
Number Employees: 1-4

Importers & Exporters / A-Z

41594 AV Olsson Trading Company
2001 West Main St
Suite 215
Stamford, CT 06902 203-969-2090
Fax: 203-969-2098 877-929-3999
ken@avolsson.com www.avolsson.com
Bulk cheeses, herring, cookies and crackers, unbleached paper products imported from Scandinavia
President/CEO: Kenneth Olsson
CFO: Danielle Ferrandi
Quality Control: Kenneth Olsson
Marketing: Terry Mandelkow
Sales: Terry Mandelkow
Public Relations: Tracey Tarver
Operations: Heather Smith
Purchasing: Kenneth Olsson
Estimated Sales: $ 1 - 3 Million
Number Employees: 5-9
Number of Brands: 8
Type of Packaging: Private Label, Bulk
Brands Imported: Scandic; Skansen; Beyong Gourmet; Goteborg's; Swedish Kitchen; Saetre; Gille; Saetre; Leksands
Regions Imported from: Europe
Percentage of Business in Importing: 100

41595 AZO Food
4445 Malone Road
P.O.Box 181070
Memphis, TN 38181-1070 901-794-9480
Fax: 901-794-9934 info@azo.com
www.azo-inc.com
Pneumatic and automated handling equipment and systems for ingredients; also, mixers, hoppers, bins, batching and mixing controls and process control and weighing systems
President: Robert Moore
CFO: Jack Kerwin
Executive VP: Jim Cavender
Sales Manager: Kevin Pecha
Contact: Karl-Heinz Bubbach
bkh@azo.de
Estimated Sales: $ 10 - 20 Million
Number Employees: 50-99

41596 Aabbitt Adhesives
2403 N Oakley Ave
Chicago, IL 60647-2093 773-227-2700
Fax: 773-227-2103 800-222-2488
info@aabbitt.com www.aabbitt.com
Manufacturer and exporter of hot melt and water based labeling adhesives, casein-based ice proof label glue and resin emulsion systems
President: Benjamin Sarmas
ben@aabbitt.com
VP: Daniel Sarmas
Sales Manager: Greg Sarmas
General Manager/VP Sales: David Sarmas
Purchasing Director: Donna Hendrickson
Estimated Sales: $20-50 Million
Number Employees: 5-9
Square Footage: 150000
Brands Exported: Adhesives
Regions Exported to: Central America, South America, Europe, Asia, Middle East

41597 (HQ)Aaburco Inc
17745 Atwater Ln
Grass Valley, CA 95949-7416 530-268-2734
Fax: 530-273-9312 800-533-7437
support@piemaster.com www.piemaster.com
Manufacturer, exporter and wholesaler/distributor of food processing equipment including manually operated, semi-automatic and electro-pneumatic machines and dough rollers for calzones, empanadas and pierogies
President: Edward Downs
aaburco@piemaster.com
CFO: F Burgard
Estimated Sales: Less Than $500,000
Number Employees: 1-4
Square Footage: 40000
Type of Packaging: Consumer, Food Service
Brands Exported: Piemaster
Regions Exported to: Worldwide
Percentage of Business in Exporting: 75

41598 Aak USA Inc
131 Marsh St
Newark, NJ 07114 973-344-1300
betterwithaak@aak.com
www.aak.com
Processor and importer of cocoa butter substitutes and oils including coconut, cottonseed, palm, soybean, sunflower, vegetable, etc.; exporter of lauric oil products
President, USA & North Latin America: Octavio Diaz de Leon
VP, Operations: Frank Miller
Estimated Sales: $50-100 Million
Number Employees: 50-99
Parent Co: AAK AB
Type of Packaging: Bulk
Other Locations:
AAK USA Inc - Port Newark Plant
Port Newark, NJ
AAK USA K1/K2 - Lousiville Plant
Louisville, KY
AAK Foodservice, USA
Hillside, NJ
AAK USA Richmond Corp.
Richmond, CAAAK USA Inc - Port Newark PlantLouisville
Regions Exported to: South America, Canada, Mexico
Regions Imported from: Asia

41599 Aaladin Industries Inc
32584 477th Ave
Elk Point, SD 57025-6700 605-356-3325
Fax: 605-356-2330 800-356-3325
info@aaladin.com www.aaladin.com
Manufacturer and exporter of portable, stationary pressure and aqueous parts washers
President of Systems: Pat Wingen
pwingen@aaladin.com
Purchasing Manager: Don Klunder
Estimated Sales: $ 10-20 Million
Number Employees: 50-99
Square Footage: 450000
Regions Exported to: Worldwide
Percentage of Business in Exporting: 5

41600 Aaron Equipment Co Div Areco
735 E Green St
P.O. Box 80
Bensenville, IL 60106-2549 630-350-2200
Fax: 630-350-9047 sales@aaronequipment.com
www.aaronequipment.com
Provider of new, used and reconditioned process equipment and asset management services to the chemical, plastics, pharmaceutical, food, mining and related industries.
President: Jerrold V Cohen
Vice President of Business Development: Bruce Baird
Estimated Sales: $20-50 Million
Number Employees: 5-9
Square Footage: 250000
Regions Exported to: Worldwide
Percentage of Business in Exporting: 30

41601 Abalon Precision Manufacturing Corporation
1040 Home Street
Bronx, NY 10459 718-589-5682
Fax: 718-589-0300 800-888-2225
info@abalonmfg.com
Manufacturer and exporter of fryer tanks, display store racks and metal fabricated rack parts
President: Norman Orent
Estimated Sales: $2.5 Million
Number Employees: 25
Square Footage: 160000
Parent Co: Abalon Precision Manufacturing Corporation

41602 Abanaki Corp
17387 Munn Rd
Chagrin Falls, OH 44023-5400 440-543-7400
Fax: 440-543-7404 800-358-7546
skimmers@abanaki.com www.abanaki.com
Manufacturer and exporter of oil and grease skimming equipment including portable models and multi-belt systems
President/Owner: Tom Hobson
tom@abanaki.com
Estimated Sales: $ 1 - 2.5 Million
Number Employees: 10-19
Square Footage: 20000
Brands Exported: Abanaki Concentrators; Abanaki Mighty Minn; Abanaki Oil Grabber; Abanaki Petro Extractor; Abanaki Tote-Its; Grease Grabber; Mighty Mini; Oil Concentrator; Oil Grabber Multi-Belt
Regions Exported to: Worldwide

41603 Abarbanel Wine Company
247 Merrick Road
Suite 101
Lynbrook, NY 11563-2641 516-374-2240
Fax: 516-374-2565 888-691-9463
mail@kosher-wine.com www.kosher-wine.com
Importer of kosher wines in rose, blush, dry, white, and red including Chardonnay, Merlot, Cabernet Sauvignon
President: Howard Abarbanel
Type of Packaging: Consumer
Brands Imported: Abarbanel, Dalton, Mouton Cadet, Beckett's Flat
Regions Imported from: Central America, France
Percentage of Business in Importing: 100

41604 Abbeon Cal Inc
123 Gray Ave
Santa Barbara, CA 93101-1895 805-966-0810
Fax: 805-966-7659 800-922-0977
abbeoncal@abbeon.com www.abbeon.
Manufacturer, exporter and importer of temperature, humidity and moisture measurement instruments and plastic cutting, bending & welding tools.
President: Alice Wertheim
CEO: Mark Tubbs
mtubbs@abbeon.com
CFO: Karen Barros
VP: Mara Hassenbein
Quality Control: Robyn Ramirez
Mktg/Sales/Pub Relations/Operations: Bob Brunsman
Estimated Sales: $ 2.5 - 5 Million
Number Employees: 5-9
Square Footage: 40000
Percentage of Business in Exporting: 2
Brands Imported: Lufft
Regions Imported from: Europe
Percentage of Business in Importing: 50

41605 Abbotsford Growers Ltd.
31825 Marshall Road
Abbotsford, BC V2T 5Z8
Canada 604-864-0022
Fax: 604-864-0020 info@abbotsfordgrowers.com
www.abbotsfordgrowers.com
Raspberry & blueberry packer; frozen purees; and pasteurized and aseptic purees.
General Manager: Colin Hutchinson
Quality Assurance Supervisor: Dan Sigfusson
Sales/Plant/Production: Stephen Evans
Estimated Sales: $10-24 Million
Number Employees: 250
Square Footage: 100000
Type of Packaging: Bulk
Regions Exported to: Europe, Asia, Australia
Percentage of Business in Exporting: 70

41606 Abbott & Cobb Inc
4151 E Street Rd
Feasterville, PA 19053-4995 215-245-6666
Fax: 215-245-9043 800-345-7333
acseed@abbottcobb.com www.abbottcobb.com
Breeder, producer and marketer of vegetable seeds, specifically corn, peppers, pumpkins, beans, squash and cucumbers.
Owner: Art Abbott
aandcseeds@aol.com
VP of Sales & Product Management: Luther McLaugglin
Vice President of Public Relations: Harriett Ryan
Senior Vice President of Operations: Bob Rumer
Estimated Sales: $38.7 Million
Number Employees: 20-49
Type of Packaging: Private Label, Bulk
Other Locations:
Nogales, AZ
West Palm Beach, FL
Caldwell, ID
Los Mochis, MexicoWest Palm Beach
Regions Exported to: Central America, South America, Europe, Mexico
Regions Imported from: Central America, South America, Europe, Mexico

41607 Abco International
163 Kenwood Ave
Oneida, NY 13421 631-427-9000
Fax: 631-427-9001 888-263-7195
www.oneida.com
Manufacturer and exporter of dinnerware, flatware, glassware, hollowware and ovenware
Manager: Bill Grannis
Managing Director: Peter Kranes

Importers & Exporters / A-Z

Estimated Sales: Below $500,000
Number Employees: 10-19
Parent Co: Delco Tableware International
Type of Packaging: Food Service
Regions Exported to: Worldwide

41608 Abco Products
6800 NW 36th Ave
Miami, FL 33147-6504   305-694-9465
    Fax: 305-694-0451   888-694-2226
Manufacturer and exporter of mops, brooms, brushes and dust control treatment systems
President: Mark Gray
m.gray@jea.com
VP of Sales: Jonathan Clark
Quality Control Manager: Bill Scheler
VP Sales/Marketing: Christopher Meaney
Customer Service Coordinator: Tiff Vereen
Estimated Sales: Below $500,000
Number Employees: 20-49
Type of Packaging: Food Service
Regions Exported to: Worldwide

41609 Abel Manufacturing Co
1100 N Mayflower Dr
Appleton, WI 54913-9656   920-734-4443
    Fax: 920-734-1084 sales@abel-usa.com
    www.abelusa.com
Manufacturer and exporter of material handling equipment and batch weighing and bulk storage systems
President: Donald Abel
abel@abelusa.com
Estimated Sales: $5 - 10 Million
Number Employees: 10-19
Type of Packaging: Bulk
Regions Exported to: Central America, South America, Europe, Asia, Middle East

41610 Abimar Foods Inc
5425 N 1st St
Abilene, TX 79603-6424   325-691-5425
    Fax: 325-691-5471
    salesinquiry@abimarfoods.com
Bakery products including cookies and crackers.
Chief Executive Officer: Patricia Canal
pcanal@abimarfoods.com
Director, Business Development: Rafael Henao
Director, Operations: Brandon Heiser
Plant Manager: Luis Felipe Velasquez Lopez
Director, Procurement: Mauricio Perez
Estimated Sales: $29 Million
Number Employees: 100-249
Number of Brands: 4
Parent Co: Grupo Empresarial Nutresa
Type of Packaging: Consumer
Regions Exported to: Central America, Mexico, Caribbean

41611 Abimco USA, Inc.
43 Hampshire Dr
Mendham, NJ 07945   973-543-7393
    Fax: 973-543-2948
Fruit juice concentrates; importer and exporter of dried and frozen fruits and vegetables; Importer of juice concentrates, honey and tomato paste; exporter of fresh mushrooms
President: Paulette Krelman
General Manager: Arthur Kupperman
Number Employees: 1-4
Type of Packaging: Bulk
Regions Exported to: Europe
Percentage of Business in Exporting: 25
Regions Imported from: South America, Europe, Asia, Mexico

41612 Able Sales Company
Centro Distribucin Del Norte Edificio 1
Carr. 869 Bo. Palmas
Catano, PR 00962   787-620-4141
    Fax: 787-620-4100 info@ablesales.com
    www.ablesales.com
Import, wholesale and distribution of raw material for food and pharmaceutical industries, including sugar flour, salt, juice concentrates. Warehousing and logistic services.
President: Luis Silva
Chairman of the Board: Alvaro Silva
CFO/Treaurer: Jose Rodriguez
Estimated Sales: $16 Million
Number Employees: 120
Square Footage: 75000
Parent Co: Able Sales Company
Type of Packaging: Consumer, Food Service, Private Label, Bulk
Regions Exported to: Caribbean
Percentage of Business in Exporting: 10
Regions Imported from: Central America, South America, Asia
Percentage of Business in Importing: 90

41613 Abond Plastic Corporation
10050 Chemin Cote de Liesse
Lachine, QC H8T 1A3
Canada   514-636-7979
    Fax: 514-273-3155   800-886-7947
    info@abondcorp.com
Manufacturer and importer of tablecloths, oven mitts, place mats and vinyl bags
Sales Manager: R Katz
Estimated Sales: Below $500,000
Number Employees: 20

41614 Abraham of North America
21217 Seevetal
Lincoln Park, NJ 07035   973-686-3700
    Fax: 973-686-0709 info.de@bellfoodgroup.com
Prosciutto
President/CEO: Claas Abraham
Estimated Sales: $3 Million
Number Employees: 5

41615 Absorbco
68 Anderson Road
Walterboro, SC 29488
    Fax: 843-538-8678   888-335-6439
    www.absorbco.com
Manufacturer and exporter of disposable wipers
VP: Scott Brown
Director Marketing: Randy Schubert
Number Employees: 107
Type of Packaging: Consumer, Food Service, Private Label, Bulk
Regions Exported to: Central America, South America, Middle East

41616 Abuelita Mexican Foods
9209 Enterprise Ct
Manassas Park, VA 20111-4809   703-369-0232
    Fax: 703-369-0875 office@abuelita.com
    www.abuelita.com
Corn tortillas and corn tortilla chips.
President: Eugene Suarez
General Manager: Peggy Suarez
Sales Director: Steve Dill
Estimated Sales: $4.7 Million
Number Employees: 1-4
Number of Brands: 3
Number of Products: 45
Square Footage: 106000
Brands Exported: Abuelita
Regions Exported to: Central America
Percentage of Business in Exporting: 1

41617 Abunda Life
208 3rd Ave
Asbury Park, NJ 07712-6097   732-775-9338
    Fax: 732-502-0899
Natural health products including vitamins, goat milk powder, fiber supplements, herbal spices, herbal teas, rice bran syrups and sweeteners including: banana, grape, pineapple and orange.
Founder: Dr Robert Sorge
Estimated Sales: $300,000-500,000
Number Employees: 10-19
Square Footage: 16800
Type of Packaging: Consumer, Private Label
Regions Exported to: Asia, Africa
Percentage of Business in Exporting: 10

41618 Acadian Seaplants
30 Brown Avenue
Dartmouth, NS B3B 1X8
Canada   902-468-2840
    Fax: 902-468-3474   800-575-9100
    info@acadian.ca www.acadianseaplants.com
Seaweed based products for food, biochemical, agricultural, and agrichemical markets.
Director of Sales: Robert Sperdakes
Account Manager: Linda Linquist
Year Founded: 1981
Estimated Sales: $20 Million
Number Employees: 300
Type of Packaging: Private Label, Bulk
Regions Exported to: Worldwide
Percentage of Business in Exporting: 98

41619 Acatris USA
3300 Edinborough Way
Suite 712
Edina, MN 55435-5963   952-920-7700
    Fax: 952-920-7704 www.acatris.com
Blended dough conditioners, antioxidant solutions, release agents and lubricants; wholesaler/distributor of soy flour, vitamin/mineral blends and oils including soybean and canola
President: Laurent Leduc
Manager: Joni Johnson
Sales Manager: Cherie Jones
Estimated Sales: $5-10 Million
Number Employees: 20-49
Number of Brands: 15
Square Footage: 64000
Parent Co: Royal Schouten Group
Type of Packaging: Bulk
Regions Exported to: Canada
Percentage of Business in Exporting: 12
Regions Imported from: Canada
Percentage of Business in Importing: 60

41620 Access Solutions
8705 Unicorn Dr Ste C302
Knoxville, TN 37923   865-531-0971
    Fax: 865-531-3547 www.accesssolutionsinc.com
Manufacturer and exporter of advertising specialties and forms; also, embroidery available
Owner: Randy Philipps
Estimated Sales: Below $5,000,000
Number Employees: 10-19
Regions Exported to: Worldwide

41621 Accraply/Trine
3070 Mainway
Units 16-19
Burlington Ontario, ON L7M 3X1
Canada   905-336-8880
    Fax: 905-335-5988   800-387-6742
    sales@accraply.com www.accraply.com
Supplier of product identification and decorating systems, offering pressure sensitive labeling systems, stand-alone label applicators, print and apply labeling systems, trine roll-fed labeling systems, shrink sleeve applicators andRFID solutions.
Manager: Peter Nicholson
Vice President: Rob Leonard
Sales Director: Stuart Moss
Operations Manager: Peter Nicholson
Number Employees: 100-249
Number of Brands: 5
Square Footage: 88000
Parent Co: Barry-Wehmiller Companies Inc

41622 Accu Temp Products Inc
8415 Clinton Park Dr
Fort Wayne, IN 46825-3197   260-490-5870
    Fax: 260-493-0318   800-210-5907
    sswogger@accutemp.net www.accutemp.net
Manufacturer and exporter of vacuum steam cookers and flat top grills and griddles.
President/CEO: Scott Swogger
sswogger@accutemp.com
CFO: Dave Ogram
Research & Development: Dean Stanley
Estimated Sales: $20 Million
Number Employees: 50-99
Square Footage: 45000

41623 Accu-Sort Systems
511 School House Rd
Telford, PA 18969
    Fax: 215-996-8249   800-227-2633
    info@accusort.com www.accusort.com
Manufacturer and exporter of bar code scanners, CCD cameras, RFID solutions, integrated solutions, and data collection systems for material handling applications
President: Bob Joyce
CFO: Greg Banning
Marketing: Mark Verheyden
Sales: Don De Lash
Contact: Melissa Barsuhn
melissa.barsuhn@accusort.com
Production: John Broderick
Estimated Sales: $50-100 Million
Type of Packaging: Bulk
Regions Exported to: Worldwide

Importers & Exporters / A-Z

41624 Accuflex Industrial Hose LTD
36663 Van Born Rd # 300
Romulus, MI 48174-4160   734-713-4100
   Fax: 734-713-4190 sales@accuflex.com
               www.accuflex.com
Manufacturer, exporter and importer of food and beverage pressure and vacuum hoses and tubing; NSF, FDA and USDA approved
President: Les Kraska
Estimated Sales: $ 5 - 10 Million
Number Employees: 10-19
Brands Exported: Bev-flex; Bevlex; Bev-Seal
Regions Exported to: Central America, South America, Europe, Asia
Percentage of Business in Exporting: 10

41625 Accurate Ingredients Inc
125 Schmitt Blvd
Farmingdale, NY 11735-1403   516-496-2500
       Fax: 516-496-2516 info@acing.net
Ingredients
President: Dan Saber
Vice President of Sales: Vince Pasquale
Sales, Vice President of Operations: Rich Hamerschlag
Estimated Sales: $15.6 Million
Number Employees: 20-49
Type of Packaging: Consumer, Food Service, Bulk
Other Locations:
   Accurate Ingredients
   Santa Ana, CAAccurate Ingredients

41626 Accutek Packaging Equipment
1399 Specialty Dr
Vista, CA 92081-8521   760-734-4177
   Fax: 760-734-4188 800-989-1828
           sales@accutekpackaging.com
Manufacturer of turnkey packaging solutions.
President: Edward Chocholek
ed@accutekpackagingequipment.com
VP: Darren Chocholek
Estimated Sales: $3-5 Million
Number Employees: 50-99
Square Footage: 80000
Brands Exported: Accucap; Accucapper; Accuvac; Auto Pinch-25; Auto Pinch-50; Auto-Mini; Handle Capper; Mini-Pinch; Mini-Six; Pinch-25
Regions Exported to: Central America, South America, Europe, Asia, Middle East
Percentage of Business in Exporting: 30

41627 Ace Co Precision Mfg
4419 S Federal Way
Boise, ID 83716-5528   208-343-7712
   Fax: 208-343-1237 800-359-7012
   info@aceco.com www.aceco.com
Manufacturer and exporter of industrial knives and water knife assemblies; also, custom cutting assemblies available
President: Sheng Vang
svang@acecosemicon.com
CFO: Sid Sullivan
VP: William Moynihan
Sales/Marketing: Joe Jensen
Technical Support: Larry Rupe
Estimated Sales: $ 10 - 20,000,000
Number Employees: 50-99
Brands Exported: Strapslicer System
Regions Exported to: Worldwide

41628 Ace Development
31194 State Highway 51
Bruneau, ID 83604-5076   208-845-2487
   Fax: 208-845-2274 copakarobert@hotmail.com
Aquaculture fisheries.
President: Robert Williams
Year Founded: 1984
Estimated Sales: $800,000
Number Employees: 1-4
Brands Exported: Tilapia
Regions Exported to: Canada
Percentage of Business in Exporting: 100

41629 Ace Engineering Company
10200 Jacksboro Hwy
Fort Worth, TX 76135   817-237-7700
   Fax: 817-237-2777 800-431-4223
      tchapman@aceworldcompanies.com
            www.aceworldcompanies.com
Manufacturer and exporter of hoists, load blocks and end trucks

President: John Watson
CFO: Mike Harris
Vice President: Rick Reeves
Contact: Ellen Bellamy
ellen.bellamy@aceworldcompanies.com
Estimated Sales: $ 20 - 50 Million
Number Employees: 50-99
Regions Exported to: Worldwide

41630 Ace Manufacturing & Parts Co
300 Ramsey Dr
Sullivan, MO 63080-1456   573-468-4181
    Fax: 573-468-1711 800-325-6138
     acesrmv@pacbell.net www.ace-mfg.com
Manufacturer and exporter of wire containers and decks, shelving and racks:cantilever, pallet, drive-in and push-back; also, repair services available
President: Richard Vartanian
HR Executive: Tina Cook
tcook@ace-mfg.com
Estimated Sales: $2.5-5 Million
Number Employees: 50-99
Square Footage: 92000

41631 Ace Specialty Mfg Co Inc
9616 Valley Blvd
Rosemead, CA 91770-1510   626-444-3867
         Fax: 626-444-6395
Manufacturer and exporter of can ejectors.
President: Karl Anderson
Secretary/Treasurer: Keith Anderson
Estimated Sales: Less Than $500,000
Number Employees: 1-4
Square Footage: 12000
Brands Exported: Ace
Regions Exported to: Central America, South America, Europe, Asia
Percentage of Business in Exporting: 5

41632 Ace Technical Plastics Inc
150 Park Ave
East Hartford, CT 06108-4011   860-278-2444
   Fax: 860-525-7000 www.acetechnicalplastics.com
Manufacturer, importer and exporter of packaging materials including skin, blister, shrink, trays, etc
President: Robert Pomerantz
Estimated Sales: Below $ 5 Million
Number Employees: 5-9
Square Footage: 24000
Regions Exported to: Worldwide
Percentage of Business in Exporting: 8
Regions Imported from: Worldwide
Percentage of Business in Importing: 18

41633 Acesur North America
2700 Westchester Ave
Suite 105
Purchase, NY 10577-2554   914-925-0450
      Fax: 914-925-0458 info@acesur.com
                www.acesur.com
Olive oil and other specialty Spanish products
USA Director: Antonio Rubiales

41634 Aceto Corporation
4 Tri Harbor Court
Port Washington, NY 11050   516-627-6000
       Fax: 516-627-6093 aceto@aceto.com
                www.aceto.com
Importer and exporter of specialty chemicals including antioxidants, acidulants, thickeners, stabilizers and cellulose ethers.
Chairman: Albert Eilender
President & Chief Executive Officer: William Kennally, III
SVP/General Counsel/Corporate Secretary: Steven Rogers
SVP & Chief Accounting Officer: Frances Scally
Chief Operating Officer: Walter Kaczmarek III
Year Founded: 1947
Estimated Sales: $2 Million
Regions Exported to: Central America, South America, Europe, Asia, Middle East
Percentage of Business in Exporting: 10
Regions Imported from: Europe, Asia
Percentage of Business in Importing: 90

41635 Acharice Specialties
PO Box 690
Greenville, MS 38702-0690   800-432-4901
          Fax: 901-381-3287
Rice and grain products

President/CEO: Jack Stratol
Research & Development: Bill Land
Sales/Marketing: Nelson Wurth
Operations/Production: Mike Well
Plant Manager: Pat Roy
Number Employees: 500-999
Type of Packaging: Private Label
Brands Exported: United States Of America & International Markets.

41636 Achilles USA
1407 80th St SW
Everett, WA 98203-6295   425-353-7000
   Fax: 425-348-6683 www.achillesusa.com
Manufacturer and exporter of flexible and semi-rigid polyvinyl chloride film and sheeting
President: Hillary Askins
askins@achillesgroup.com
Vice President, Finance: Jestin Fought
Research & Development Manager: Bach Nguyen
Human Resources Manager/Safety Manager: Mike Burrows
Quality Systems Manager: James Knosp
VP, Manufacturing Sales/Operations: Chad Turner
Estimated Sales: $ 34 Million
Number Employees: 50-99
Square Footage: 14910
Parent Co: Achilles Corporation
Type of Packaging: Bulk

41637 Acme Engineering & Mfg Corp
1820 N York St
Muskogee, OK 74403-1451   918-682-7791
   Fax: 918-682-0134 marketing@acmefan.com
               www.acmefan.com
Manufacturer and exporter of kitchen ventilation systems and fans.
EVP, Sales & Marketing: Doug Yamashita
Year Founded: 1938
Estimated Sales: $50-100 Million
Number Employees: 500-999
Square Footage: 500000
Other Locations:
   Acme Engineering & Manufacture
   Fort Smith, ARAcme Engineering & Manufacture
Brands Exported: Centrimaster; Mastervent
Regions Exported to: Central America, South America, Asia, Middle East, Latin America, Canada, Mexico, Caribbean
Percentage of Business in Exporting: 10

41638 Acme Import Co Inc
408 Bloomfield Ave # D
Montclair, NJ 07042-3573   973-783-5001
   Fax: 973-783-5004 800-747-0332
       customerservice@acmeimport.com
             www.acmeimport.com
European cookies, snacks and confectionery.
President/CEO: Jerrold Einhorn
jeinhorn@acmeimport.com
Manager: Laura Begley
Estimated Sales: $3.5 Million
Number Employees: 1-4

41639 Acme Pizza & Bakery Equipment
7039 E Slauson Ave
Commerce, CA 90040   323-722-7900
           Fax: 323-726-4700
Ovens and dough rollers
President: Mario Labatt
Marketing Director: Jeff Elliott
Number Employees: 150

41640 Acme Scale Co
1801 Adams Ave
PO Box 1922
San Leandro, CA 94577-1069   510-638-5040
   Fax: 510-638-5619 888-638-5040
               www.acmescales.com
Manufacturer, importer and exporter of scales including butchers', counting, portable, portion control, warehouse, educational and laboratory
Owner: Lou Buran
CFO: Lou Buran
VP: Lou Buran
Quality Control: Ron Widgren
Sales Manager: Barbara Byrd
Manager: Jerry Anderson
janderson@acmescale.com
Estimated Sales: Below $ 5 Million
Number Employees: 20-49
Square Footage: 52000
Parent Co: Buran & Reed

Importers & Exporters / A-Z

Other Locations:
  Acme Scale Co.
  Santa Fe Springs, CAAcme Scale Co.
Regions Exported to: Central America, Europe, Asia
Percentage of Business in Exporting: 30
Regions Imported from: Europe, Middle East
Percentage of Business in Importing: 10

41641 Acme Smoked Fish Corporation
30-56 Gem Street
Brooklyn, NY 11222   718-383-8585
       Fax: 718-383-9115 www.acmesmokedfish.com
Processor and importer of smoked fish and herring.
President: Eric Caslow
CFO: Eduardo Carlajasa
EVP: Robert Caslow
Director of Sales: Buzz Billik
VP of Operations: Davis Caslow
Year Founded: 1901
Estimated Sales: $20-50 Million
Number Employees: 100-249
Regions Imported from: South America
Percentage of Business in Importing: 15

41642 Acme Sponge & Chamois Co Inc
855 Pine St
Tarpon Springs, FL 34689-5902   727-937-3222
       Fax: 727-942-3064 sales@acmesponge.com
              www.acmespongeandchamoisonline.com
Manufacturer, distributor and exporter of chamois and natural sponges
President: James Cantonis
CEO: George Cantonis
gcantonis@acmesponge.com
VP of Sales/Marketing: Steve Heller
Sales Manager: Nancy Troio
Estimated Sales: $ 5-10 Million
Number Employees: 50-99
Square Footage: 200000
Type of Packaging: Consumer, Food Service, Private Label, Bulk
Brands Exported: Thenatural; Tanners Select; Careware; Aqua
Regions Exported to: Worldwide
Percentage of Business in Exporting: 10

41643 Acme Steak & Seafood
31 Bissell Ave
Youngstown, OH 44505-2707   330-270-8000
       Fax: 330-270-8006 800-686-2263
       support@acmesteak.com www.acmesteak.com
Fresh produce, seafood, sausage, hamburgers and portion controlled meat.
Owner/President: Michael Mike
mike@acmesteak.com
Year Founded: 1947
Estimated Sales: $2.40 Million
Number Employees: 10-19
Square Footage: 68000
Type of Packaging: Consumer, Food Service, Private Label
Percentage of Business in Importing: 3

41644 Aco Container Systems
794 McKay Road
Pickering, ON L1W 2Y4
Canada'
       Fax: 905-683-2969   905-683-8222
                           800-542-9942
       custserv@acotainers.com www.acotainers.com
Manufacturer and exporter of polyethylene tanks including full draining, transportable and semi-bulk; also, custom fabricator of liquid dispensing systems
President and CFO: Stefan Assmann
Order Desk: Kevin Wentzell
Quality Control: Dave Marsden
General Manager: Stephan Assman
Plant Manager: Mike Banas
Number Employees: 30
Square Footage: 50000

41645 Acorsa USA Inc
3531 Sw 13th St
Miami, FL 33145   305-361-7200
       Fax: 305-361-7639 www.agrofoods.com
Importer of Kosher olives.

41646 Acorto
1287 120th Ave NE
Bellevue, WA 98005   425-453-2800
       Fax: 425-453-2167 800-995-9019
       contactus@concordiacoffee.com
              www.concordiacoffee.com
Manufacturer and exporter of fully automatic espresso, cappuccino and latte machines
President: David Isett
CFO: Ann Dimond
VP: Mike McLaughlin
Sales Director: Robin Mooney
Contact: Tony Grossi
tgrossi@acorto.com
VP, Operation: Wayne Stearns
Estimated Sales: $10-20 Million
Number Employees: 20-49
Square Footage: 32000
Brands Exported: Acorto
Regions Exported to: Central America, South America, Europe, Asia, Middle East, Worldwide
Percentage of Business in Exporting: 20

41647 Acp Inc
225 49th Avenue Dr SW
Cedar Rapids, IA 52404-4772   319-368-8120
       Fax: 319-622-8589 319-368-8198
       commercialservice@acpsolutions.com
              www.acpsolutions.com
Manufacturer and exporter of commercial microwave and combination ovens.
Cio/Cto: Steve Gimse
sgimse@acp.com
Marketing Communications Manager: Wendy Roltgen
Estimated Sales: $ 1 - 5 Million
Number Employees: 10-19
Square Footage: 7200000
Parent Co: Maytag Corporation
Type of Packaging: Food Service
Regions Exported to: Central America, South America, Europe, Asia, Middle East

41648 Acra Electric Corporation
P. O. Box 9889
Tulsa, OK 74157   918-224-6755
       Fax: 918-224-6866 800-223-4328
              www.acraelectric.com
Manufacturer and exporter of electric heating elements for soup pots, food warmers, dispensers, popcorn machines and coffee brewing equipment; also, drum and pail heaters
President: Robert Browne
Sales Director: Gary Marschke
Estimated Sales: $ 10 - 20 Million
Number Employees: 85
Brands Exported: Acrawatt
Regions Exported to: Europe, Middle East
Percentage of Business in Exporting: 10

41649 (HQ)Acraloc Corp
113 Flint Rd
Oak Ridge, TN 37830-7033   865-483-1368
       Fax: 865-483-3500 acraloc@comcast.net
              www.acraloc.com
Manufacturer and exporter of food processing equipment, vacuum packaging equipment, robotic saws, fixtures, etc
President: George Andre
CFO: Kent Park
R&D: Scott Andre
Quality Control: David Dyer
Director Corporate Development: Scott Andre
VP Engineering: Harry Ailey
Estimated Sales: $ 5 - 10 Million
Number Employees: 50-99
Square Footage: 100000
Regions Exported to: Central America, South America, Europe, Asia, Middle East
Percentage of Business in Exporting: 40

41650 (HQ)Acrison Inc
20 Empire Blvd
Moonachie, NJ 07074-1382   201-440-8301
       Fax: 201-440-4939 800-422-4266
       informail@acrison.com www.acrison.com
Manufacturer and exporter of metering equipment, hoppers, blenders and microprocessor controls and control systems.
President: Sam Berry
normajean.loftus@pearson.com
Marketing/Sales: John Shaw
Estimated Sales: $ 50 - 100 Million
Number Employees: 100-249
Square Footage: 130000
Other Locations:
  Acrison
  Manchester, EnglandAcrison
Brands Exported: ccrison; Acri Lok; Batch Lok; MD-II; MD-II-2000
Regions Exported to: Worldwide
Percentage of Business in Exporting: 35

41651 Acromag Inc.
30765 S Wixom Rd
P.O. Box 437
Wixom, MI 48393-2417   248-624-1541
       Fax: 248-624-9234 sales@acromag.com
              www.acromag.com
Manufactures measurement and control instrumentation, signal conditioning products, network I/O modules, VMEbus, PCI, and CompactPCI Bus Boards as well as industry pack and PMC mezzanine modules
President: David Wolfe
Quality Control: Chuck Smith
Marketing: Robert Greenfield
Sales Director: Donald Lupo
Contact: Debbie Baron
dbaron@acromag.com
Plant Manager: Bret Stephenson
Purchasing Agent: Reg Crawford
Estimated Sales: $10-20 Million
Number Employees: 50-99
Brands Exported: Acromag
Regions Exported to: Worldwide
Percentage of Business in Exporting: 22

41652 Acta Health Products
380 N Pastoria Avenue
Sunnyvale, CA 94085-4108   408-732-6830
       Fax: 408-732-0208 www.actaproducts.com
Processor and exporter of vitamins, minerals, herbal extracts and other dietary supplements; importer of raw materials
President: David Chang
david.chang@actaproducts.com
VP: K Y Chang
Director Quality Control: Michael Chang
Director Marketing/Sales: Cal Bewicke
Director Purchasing: Leo Liu
Estimated Sales: $3 Million
Number Employees: 30
Square Footage: 124000
Type of Packaging: Private Label, Bulk
Regions Exported to: Central America, Europe, Asia, Middle East
Regions Imported from: Europe, Asia

41653 Action Engineering
4373 Lilburn Industrial Way
P.O. Box 505
Liburn, GA 30047   770-717-1000
       Fax: 770-717-3000 800-228-4668
              www.actionengineering.com
Manufacturer and exporter of oil skimmers, separators, wastewater equipment, corn bins, mixers, heavy-duty, low-profile dollies and flexible tank liners
President: Amos Broughton
CFO: Patricia Broughton
Estimated Sales: $ .5 - 1 million
Number Employees: 5-9
Number of Brands: 3
Brands Exported: Hi-Rise LLS; Hunter Oil Skimmer; Tred-Ties; Adjustable Railroad Crossties; Pump Strainers, Oil/Water Separators, Freshwater/Beire Skimo

41654 Action Lighting
310 Ice Pond Rd
Bozeman, MT 59715-5380   406-586-5105
       Fax: 406-585-3078 800-248-0076
              action@actionlighting.com
              www.actionlighting.com
Manufacturer and exporter of lighting for restaurants, bars, casinos, etc
Owner: Jeff Buckley
jeff@actionlighting.com
CFO: Hubert Reid
General Manager: Robert Stone
Sales & Marketing: Allan Kottwitz
Manager: Dan Corthes
Estimated Sales: $ 5 - 10,000,000
Number Employees: 10-19
Type of Packaging: Food Service
Regions Exported to: Mexico, Canada

41655 Action Packaging Automation
15 Oscar Dr
P.O.Box 190
Roosevelt, NJ 08555-7010   609-448-9210
       Fax: 609-448-8116 800-241-2724
       sales@apaiusa.com www.apaiusa.com

Importers & Exporters / A-Z

Manufacturer, exporter and importer of automatic packaging machinery for recloseable pouches including counters, scales and support equipment, high speed counting systems, blister packaging machines
Owner: John Wojnicki
Marketing Administrative Assistant: Robin Carroll
Sales Manager: John Wojnicki
Office Manager: Robin Carroll
robin.carroll@apai-usa.com
Estimated Sales: $2.5-5 Million
Number Employees: 20-49
Brands Exported: Autocard; Autopouch; Flat-Pak
Brands Imported: Fuji; Koch Maschinenbau; Deltapack; Van Nobelen

41656 Action Technology
1150 First Avenue
Suite 500
Prussia, PA 19406   217-935-8311
Fax: 217-935-9132   Info@tekni-plex.com
www.tekni-plex.com
Manufacturer and exporter of extruded tubing for beverage dispensing and food handling, extruded coffee stirrers, cheese spreader applicators, sticks and tubing for frozen foods, etc
Sales Manager: Frank Lofrano
Plant Manager: Jason Gribbins
Number Employees: 100-249
Square Footage: 240000
Parent Co: Tekni-Plex
Other Locations:
    Action Technology
    City of Industry, CAAction Technology
Regions Exported to: Worldwide
Percentage of Business in Exporting: 10

41657 Actionpac Scales Automation
1300 Yarnell Pl
Oxnard, CA 93033-2457   805-486-5754
Fax: 805-487-0719   800-394-0154
info@actionpacscales.com
www.actionpacscales.com
Manufacturer and exporter of packaging machinery including automated bag filling; also, weighing machinery
President: John Dishion
john@actionpacscales.com
Sales & Services Manager: Johnathan Cantalupo
Sales Assistant: Jennifer Taylor
Purchasing Manager: Justin Pence
Estimated Sales: $500,000-$1 Million
Number Employees: 20-49
Square Footage: 8000
Brands Exported: Actionpac
Regions Exported to: Worldwide
Percentage of Business in Exporting: 5

41658 Actron
PO Box 572244
Tarzana, CA 91357-2244   818-654-9744
Fax: 818-654-9788   800-866-8887
flymaster@actroninc.com
Manufacturer and exporter of flying-insect control systems and washable and decorative insect light and glue traps
Director Marketing: Abe Thomas
Estimated Sales: Below $ 500,000
Brands Exported: Gardner; ILT; EFK
Regions Exported to: Central America, South America, Europe, Asia, Middle East, Latin America, Mexico, Australia
Percentage of Business in Exporting: 80

41659 Acumen Data Systems Inc
2223 Westfield St
West Springfield, MA 01089-2000   413-737-4800
Fax: 413-737-5544   888-816-0933
info@acumendatasystems.com
Manufacturer and exporter of computer software for bakery management including order, production, formulation, delivery, billing, etc
Owner: Edward W Squires
edward.squires@acumendatasystems.com
VP: Dan Coffey
Estimated Sales: $ 2.5 - 5,000,000
Number Employees: 10-19
Brands Exported: Clockview; Laborview; Inview; Proview; Opmview
Regions Exported to: Worldwide
Percentage of Business in Exporting: 15

41660 Acutemp
2900 Dryden Rd
Moraine, OH 45439-1618   937-242-6768
Fax: 937-312-1277   866-312-0114
www.csafeglobal.com
President: Pam Koglman
pkoglman@ganleyauto.com
Number Employees: 20-49

41661 Ad Art Litho.
3133 Chester Ave
Cleveland, OH 44114   216-696-1460
Fax: 216-696-1463   800-875-6368
Menus and menu covers; also, printing and silk screening available
President: Felicia West
CFO: Felicia West
Director Operations: Felicia West
Estimated Sales: $ 1 - 2,500,000
Number Employees: 10

41662 Adagio Teas
141 Lanza Ave Bldg 18d
Garfield, NJ 07026   973-253-7400
cynthia@adagio.com
www.adagioxl.com
Teas (black, flavored, oolong, white, green, herbal, roobios and decaf) teaware, bags, tins and iced
President: Michael Cramer
Contact: Charles Cain
charles@adagio.com
Estimated Sales: $1.2 Million
Number Employees: 8

41663 Adamatic
814 44th St NW Ste 103
Auburn, WA 98001   206-322-5474
Fax: 206-322-5425   800-578-2547
info@adamatic.com   www.adamatic.com
Manufacturer and exporter of bakers' equipment including ovens and machinery; also, refrigerators
General manager and Controller: Michael Hartnett
R&D: Walter Kopp
Quality Control: Michael Liberatore
Contact: Scott Ummel
scottu@belshaw-adamatic.com
General Manager: John Muldowney
Estimated Sales: $ 10 - 20 Million
Number Employees: 55
Parent Co: PMI Food Equipment Group
Type of Packaging: Consumer, Food Service
Regions Exported to: Worldwide

41664 Adamation
7039 E Slauson Ave
Commerce, CA 90040-3620   323-722-7900
Fax: 323-726-4700   800-383-8800
www.adamationinc.com
Manufacturer and exporter of dish washing and silver burnishing machinery, tray conveyors and food waste shredder disposal systems
Owner: Jeff Branstein
CEO: Hubert Perry, Jr.
CFO: Joe Braver
Operations Manager: John Onu
Plant Manager: Cliff Bergland
Purchasing Manager: Mike Schulng
Estimated Sales: $5 Million
Number Employees: 50-99
Square Footage: 84000
Parent Co: Winbro Group
Brands Exported: Adamation
Regions Exported to: Europe, Asia, Australia
Percentage of Business in Exporting: 8

41665 Adamba Imports Intl
585 Meserole St
Brooklyn, NY 11237-1119   718-628-9700
Fax: 718-628-0920   www.adamba.com
Importer of fresh and dehydrated vegetables, mushrooms, preserves, jams, fruits in syrup, fish products, candy, snacks, chocolates, seasoning, soup, juice concentrates, oils, essence and alcoholic beverages
President: Adam M Bak
adam@adamba.com
VP: Gino Palazzolo
VP: Danuta Tamiolakis
Estimated Sales: $2.5-5 Million
Number Employees: 20-49
Brands Imported: Adamba; Goldwasser; Jarzebiak; Krupnik; Luksusowa; Polish Naturals; Starka; Vavel; Wedel; Wisniak; Wisniak Luksusowy; Wisniowka; Zytnia
Regions Imported from: Europe

Percentage of Business in Importing: 100

41666 Adams & Brooks Inc
1915 S Hoover St
Los Angeles, CA 90007-1322   213-749-3226
Fax: 213-746-7614   info@adams-brooks.com
Bagged candy including: chocolate cups, candy bars, lollypops, novelty, nut, caramel and taffy. Also vending, fund raising and theatre packaging.
President: John Brooks
Cmo: Steve Misinger
steve.misingerbrooks@adams-brooks.com
VP of Marketing & Product Development: Cindy Brooks
Estimated Sales: $10-20 Million
Number Employees: 100-249
Type of Packaging: Consumer, Private Label, Bulk
Brands Exported: Dino Pops; Unicorn Pops; P-Nuttles; Coffee Rio; Fairtime; Cup-O-Good
Regions Exported to: Europe, Asia, Middle East, Australia, Canada, Mexico
Percentage of Business in Exporting: 5

41667 Adams Fisheries Ltd
617 Bear Point Rd
Shag Harbour, NS B0T 1W0
Canada   902-723-2435
Fax: 902-723-2325
Salted cod, pollack and haddock and live lobster
President: Donald Adams
Estimated Sales: $3.2 Million
Number Employees: 8
Square Footage: 34000
Regions Exported to: Caribbean
Percentage of Business in Exporting: 85
Regions Imported from: Europe
Percentage of Business in Importing: 90

41668 Adams Vegetable Oils Inc
P.O. Box 956
Arbuckle, CA 95912   530-668-2005
Fax: 530-476-2315   info@adamsgrp.com
www.adamsvegetableoils.com
Vegetable oils, grain and seeds.
Sales Manager: David Hoffsten
Estimated Sales: $100+ Million
Number Employees: 50-99
Square Footage: 5889
Type of Packaging: Bulk
Regions Exported to: Japan.

41669 Adcom Worldwide
P.O. Box 3627
Bellevue, WA 98009   425-462-1094
800-843-4784
www.adcomworldwide.com
Transportation services include air freight forwarding and long and short haul trucking of general line items. An import/export service with no specific brands of food products.
Contact: David Britnell
dbritnell@adcomworldwide.com
Number Employees: 10-19

41670 Adex Medical Inc
6101 Quail Valley Ct # D
Riverside, CA 92507-0764   951-653-9122
Fax: 951-653-9133   800-873-4776
info@adexmed.com   www.adexmed.com
Manufacturer, wholesaler/distributor, importer and exporter of disposable apparel including gloves, goggles, aprons, hair nets, caps, masks, shoe covers, etc.; also, towels, industrial safety products, emergency preparednessproducts
President/CEO: Michael Ghafouri
mmg@adexmed.com
Estimated Sales: $5 Million
Number Employees: 20-49
Number of Brands: 3
Number of Products: 200
Square Footage: 44000
Type of Packaging: Consumer, Food Service, Private Label
Regions Exported to: South America, Europe
Percentage of Business in Exporting: 10
Regions Imported from: Asia
Percentage of Business in Importing: 40

41671 Adhesive Applications
41 Oneil St
Easthampton, MA 01027-1103   413-527-7120
Fax: 413-527-7249   800-356-3572
Manufacturer and exporter of pressure sensitive foam cloth adhesive tapes

Importers & Exporters / A-Z

President: Michael Schaefer
mschaefer@stikiiproducts.com
Sales Manager: David Premo
Sales Specialist: Judette Savino
Estimated Sales: $ 10 - 20 Million
Number Employees: 20-49
Parent Co: October Company
Regions Exported to: Worldwide

41672 Adhesive Technologies Inc
3 Merrill Industrial Dr
Hampton, NH 03842-1995   603-929-5300
   Fax: 603-926-1780   800-458-3486
   marketing@adhesivetech.com
   www.adhesivetech.com
Manufacturer, importer and exporter of application-based systems: hot melts, sprays, solids, 2-part reactives and a wide range of applicators (glue guns) from craft to industrial.
Chief Executive Officer, Founder: Peter Melendy
pmelendy@adhesivetech.com
Marketing Director: Laura Scaccia
VP Sales: John Starer
Public Relations: Laura Scaccia
Estimated Sales: $20-50 Million
Number Employees: 20-49
Brands Exported: Crafty; Ad-Tech
Regions Exported to: Central America, South America, Europe, Asia, Middle East
Percentage of Business in Exporting: 10
Regions Imported from: Asia
Percentage of Business in Importing: 10

41673 Admatch Corporation
36 W 25th St
Fl 8
New York, NY 10010   212-696-2600
   Fax: 212-696-0620   800-777-9909
   ask@admatch.com   www.admatch.com
Manufacturer, exporter and importer of wood and paper matches with custom printed boxes and books, wood toothpicks, paper napkins, place mats, coasters and tissues
President: Mark Nackman
Sales Manager: Agatha Laura
Contact: King Chau
king@admatch.com
Estimated Sales: $10-20 Million
Number Employees: 10-19
Type of Packaging: Consumer, Food Service, Private Label, Bulk
Brands Exported: Admatch
Regions Exported to: Central America, Asia, Mexico, Canada
Regions Imported from: Europe, Asia

41674 Admiral Craft
940 S Oyster Bay Rd
Hicksville, NY 11801-3518   516-433-2291
   Fax: 516-433-4453   info@admiralcraft.com
   www.admiralcraft.com
Importer and wholesaler/distributor of food service utensils includinng pails, scoops, funnels, pans, spatulas, etc.; also, containers, ingredient bins, processing drums, pumps and tanks; serving the food service market
President: Victor Caglioti
victor.caglioti@admiralcraft.com
VP of Finance: Robert Vogel
Executive VP: Rick Powers
Director Marketing: Kerri Frino
VP Procurement/Material Handling: Michael Lazco
Estimated Sales: $20-30 Million
Number Employees: 20-49
Square Footage: 120000
Regions Imported from: Asia
Percentage of Business in Importing: 80

41675 Adobe Creek Packing Co Inc
4825 Loasa Dr
Kelseyville, CA 95451   707-279-4204
   Fax: 707-279-0366   shirleyacp@sbcglobal.net
Bartlett pears
President/Grower: Kenneth Barr
Controller: Shirley Campbell
Shipping Manager: Floyd Saderlund
Office Manager: Margot Hoyt
Estimated Sales: $2.7 Million
Number Employees: 250-499
Type of Packaging: Consumer, Food Service, Bulk
Regions Exported to: Canada, Mexico

41676 (HQ)Adolf's Meats & Sausage Kitchen
35 New Britain Ave
Hartford, CT 06106-3306   860-522-1588
Meats
President: Joseph Gorski
joegorski@live.com
Estimated Sales: Less Than $500,000
Number Employees: 1-4
Type of Packaging: Consumer, Food Service, Bulk
Other Locations:
   Adolf's Meat & Sausage
   Norwalk, CTAdolf's Meat & Sausage
Regions Imported from: Europe
Percentage of Business in Importing: 30

41677 Adonis Health Products
810 E 1650th Rd
Baldwin City, KS 66006   785-594-2791
Wholesaler/distributor, importer and exporter of vitamins, etc
Owner: Mike Hiebert
CEO: Sue Nanninga
CFO: Linda Lynn
Estimated Sales: $300,000-500,000
Number Employees: 1-4
Square Footage: 40000
Type of Packaging: Bulk
Brands Exported: Adonis; Universal
Regions Exported to: South America, Europe
Percentage of Business in Exporting: 38
Regions Imported from: South America
Percentage of Business in Importing: 40

41678 Adpro
30500 Solon Industrial Pkwy
Solon, OH 44139-4330   440-542-1111
   www.ad-pro.net
Manufacturer and importer of boxes including folding, set-up and corrugated; shrink packaging available; also, designer of sales promotion and marketing materials
VP: Stephen Lebby
Estimated Sales: $2.5-5 Million
Number Employees: 20-49
Square Footage: 130000
Parent Co: ADPRO
Regions Imported from: Worldwide
Percentage of Business in Importing: 10

41679 Adria Imports
47-00 Northern Blvd
Long Island City, NY 11101   718-326-4610
   Fax: 718-326-4601   www.adriaimports.com
Pickles, Peppers, Tomato Products, Caponata, Eggplant, Zucchini, Vegetable Spread (Ajvar), Cabbage, Vegeta (seasoning), Mustard, Horseradish, Sauerkraut, Garlic & Onions, Mushrooms, Beets, Fuit in Syrups, Toast, Noodles, Soup, TeaMineral Water, Ice Tea, Juices and Nectars, Coffee, Syrup, Candies, Chocolate Bars, Boxed Chocolates, Preserves, Wafers, Biscuit & Cookies, Crackers, Sardines, Mackerel, Grains, Honey, Pate
Presdident: Jon Ardeljan
Manager: Aneta Onuc
Estimated Sales: $1.5 Million
Number Employees: 10

41680 Adrienne's Gourmet Foods
849 Ward Dr
Santa Barbara, CA 93111   805-964-6848
   Fax: 805-964-8698   800-937-7010
Organic and kosher cookies, crackers and high protein pastas.
President: John O'Donnell
Vice President: Adrienne O'Donnell
Contact: Sarah Guiginano
sarah@adriennes.com
Estimated Sales: $5-10 Million
Number Employees: 20-49
Type of Packaging: Consumer, Food Service, Private Label, Bulk
Brands Exported: Lavosh Hawaii; Appeteasers; Courtney's; Darcia's; Papadini Pasta
Regions Exported to: Europe, Asia, Canada, Caribbean, Mexico
Percentage of Business in Exporting: 10
Regions Imported from: Europe
Percentage of Business in Importing: 20

41681 Adro International Inc
1142 E 5th St
Brooklyn, NY 11230-3336   718-252-0119
   Fax: 718-258-5258
Owner: Bill Kraus
Vice President: Lili Kraus
Estimated Sales: $ 1 - 3 Million
Number Employees: 1-4

41682 Advance Energy Technologies
1 Solar Dr
Halfmoon, NY 12065-3402   518-371-2140
   Fax: 518-371-0737   800-724-0198
   sales@advanceet.com   www.advanceet.com
Manufacturer and exporter of walk-in coolers and freezers, refrigerated warehouses, foam injected insulated panels, clean rooms and environmental chambers.
President: Timothy Carlo
sales@advanceet.com
General Manager: Dan Carlo
Estimated Sales: $10-20 Million
Number Employees: 20-49
Square Footage: 60000
Type of Packaging: Bulk
Regions Exported to: Worldwide
Percentage of Business in Exporting: 10

41683 Advance Fittings Corp
218 W Centralia St
Elkhorn, WI 53121-1606   262-723-6699
   Fax: 262-723-6643   advance@genevaonline.com
Manufacturer, importer and exporter of filtration equipment, fittings, clamps, tanks, sampling devices, tube and pipe supports, tubes and valves; also, custom fabrications available
President: Edward W Mentzer
ementzer@advancefittingscorp.com
VP: Roger Klemp
Marketing/Sales: Jeffery Klemp
VP of Sales: Peter Mentzer
Estimated Sales: $5-10 Million
Number Employees: 20-49
Regions Exported to: Worldwide
Percentage of Business in Exporting: 3
Regions Imported from: Europe
Percentage of Business in Importing: 20

41684 Advance Pierre Foods
9987 Carver Rd.
Suite 500
Cincinnati, OH 45242
   800-969-2747
   www.advancepierre.com
Packaged sandwiches, fully cooked chicken and beef products, Philly-style steak, breaded beef, pork and poultry, and bakery products.
President/CEO: John Simons
CFO: Michael Sims
Year Founded: 1946
Estimated Sales: $600 Million
Number Employees: 4,000+
Number of Brands: 10
Parent Co: Tyson Foods
Type of Packaging: Consumer, Food Service, Private Label
Other Locations:
   Advance Food Company
   Caryville, TN
   Advance Food Company
   Scanton, PA
   Advance Food Company - Sales
   Oklahoma City, OKAdvance Food CompanyScanton
Brands Exported: 2000 Products made from beef, pork, poultry, lamb and veal, and bakery products
Regions Exported to: Canada, Mexico, Germany, Japan and the Caribbean
Percentage of Business in Exporting: 8

41685 Advance Storage Products
7341 Lincoln Way
Garden Grove, CA 92841-1428   714-902-9000
   Fax: 714-902-9001   888-478-7422
   asp@advstore.com
   www.advancestorageproducts.com
Technology-driven company dedicated to developing the most efficient and economical solution to our customers' material storage needs. State-of-the-art engineering-providing turnkey systems. In business over 40 years

President: John Krummell
asp@advstore.com
CFO: Rick Callow
R&D: T J Imholte
Marketing/Public Relations: Judy Pugh
Sales Director: Adel Santner
Operations Manager: T Imholte
Purchasing Manager: Lisa Ramirez
Estimated Sales: $ 20 - 50 Million
Number Employees: 20-49
Regions Exported to: Central America, South America, Caribbean, Mexico
Percentage of Business in Exporting: 10
Regions Imported from: Mexico

41686 Advance Technology Corp
79 N Franklin Tpke
Suite 103
Ramsey, NJ 07446-2035   201-934-7127
     Fax: 201-236-1891 sales@vetstar.com
                       www.vetstar.com
Manufacturer and exporter of laboratory information management system software
President: John Cummins
Sales Manager: Susan Cummins
IT: Eileen Costello
eeaston@vetstar.com
Number Employees: 10-19
Brands Exported: Vetstar; V-Lims
Regions Exported to: Worldwide

41687 Advanced Control Technologies
6805 Hillsdale Ct
Indianapolis, IN 46250-2039   317-806-2750
     Fax: 317-806-2770   800-886-2281
                     info@act-solutions.com
Manufacturer and exporter of HVAC controls
President: Gary Colip
gcolip@act-solutions.com
Estimated Sales: $5-10,000,000
Number Employees: 10-19
Regions Exported to: Worldwide
Percentage of Business in Exporting: 2

41688 Advanced Detection Systems
4740 W Electric Ave
Milwaukee, WI 53219-1626   414-672-0553
     Fax: 414-672-5354 dsmith@adsdetection.com
                    www.adsdetection.com
Manufacturer and exporter of electronic metal detectors with reject devices, conveyors and pipeline systems; also, washdown severe-duty models
CFO: Matt Nagel
mnagel@adsdetection.com
Human Resources: Sue Medbed
Sales Manager: Dave Smith
Production Manager: Chuck Morgan
Estimated Sales: $10-20,000,000
Number Employees: 50-99
Parent Co: Venturedyne
Regions Exported to: Central America, South America, Europe, Asia, Middle East

41689 Advanced Equipment
2104 Front St # Frnt
Cuyahoga Falls, OH 44221-3261   330-922-0123
     Fax: 330-922-4200   800-589-3420
           advancedequipment@sbcglobal.net
                      www.coldtreats.com
Importer of spiral, contact belt and I.Q.F. vegetable freezers
Owner: Tom Treptow
Sales Manager: Mike Barber
Estimated Sales: $20-50 Million
Number Employees: 1-4
Square Footage: 3000
Regions Imported from: Worldwide

41690 Advanced Equipment
2411 Vauxhall Place
Richmond, BC V6V 1Z5
Canada   604-276-8989
     Fax: 604-276-8962 info@advancedfreezer.com
                   www.advancedfreezer.com
Manufacturer and exporter of freezers
President: Peter Pao
Purchasing Agent: Thomas Leung
Estimated Sales: Below $5 Million
Number Employees: 40
Square Footage: 80000
Regions Exported to: Europe, Asia, USA, Latin America
Percentage of Business in Exporting: 95

41691 Advanced Food Systems
21 Roosevelt Ave
Somerset, NJ 08873-5030   732-873-6776
     Fax: 732-873-4177   800-787-3067
         info@afsnj.com   www.afsnj.com
Customized ingredient systems for meat and poultry products, frozen foods, sauces and marinades, and more.
President: Yongkeun Joh
arun.abraham@acegroup.com
CFO: Pamela Cooper
EVP: Warren Love
Sales Executive: Chris Kelly
Operations Director: Bob Lijana
Purchasing Director: Mike Walker
Estimated Sales: $6.5 Million
Number Employees: 50-99
Square Footage: 107200
Brands Exported: Actoloid; Actobind; Actogel; Sealtite; SeasonRite
Regions Exported to: Central America, Europe
Percentage of Business in Exporting: 10
Regions Imported from: South America, Europe, Asia
Percentage of Business in Importing: 10

41692 Advanced Ingredients, Inc.
401 N 3rd St
Suite 400
Minneapolis, MN 55401
     Fax: 763-201-5820   888-238-4647
              info@advancedingredients.com
              www.advancedingredients.com
Specialty ingredients
President: Fred Greenland
Estimated Sales: $ 1 - 3 Million
Number Employees: 5-9
Brands Exported: EnergySmart; Fruitrim, Moisturlok, FruitSaver, BakeSmart & Energy Source.
Regions Exported to: Europe, Asia, Canada, Australia, New Zealand

41693 (HQ)Advanced Instruments Inc
2 Technology Way # 1
Norwood, MA 02062-2630   781-320-9000
     Fax: 781-320-8181   800-225-4034
     info@aicompanies.com   www.aicompanies.com
Manufacturer and exporter of clinical, industrial laboratory and food and dairy quality control equipment.
CEO: John Coughlin
CFO: Jim Noris
jimn@aicompanies.com
Marketing Manager: Kristen Vuotto
Sales: John Ryder
Plant Manager: Mike Graham
Estimated Sales: $10-20 Million
Number Employees: 50-99
Number of Brands: 4
Number of Products: 6
Square Footage: 80000
Other Locations:
     Advanced Instruments
     Bethesda, MDAdvanced Instruments
Brands Exported: Advanced; Fiske; Spiral Biotech

41694 Advanced Insulation Concepts
8055 Production Dr
Florence, KY 41042-3094   859-342-8550
     Fax: 859-342-5445   800-826-3100
                     info@aicinsulate.com
        www.advancedinsulationconcepts.com
Manufacturer and exporter of insulated panels and doors for refrigerated and other atmosphere-controlled rooms including horizontal sliding, bi-parting, vertical lift and swing. Also insulated fire wall panels
President: W Burton Lloyd
VP: Michael Lloyd
Sales: Michael Lloyd
Estimated Sales: $6-10 Million
Number Employees: 30
Square Footage: 124000
Brands Exported: Isowall; Regent; Insulrock
Regions Exported to: South America
Percentage of Business in Exporting: 5

41695 (HQ)Advanced Labelworx Inc
1006 Larson Dr
Oak Ridge, TN 37830-8013   864-224-2122
     Fax: 865-813-9918
           marketing@advancedlabelworx.com
                 www.advancedlabelworx.com
Manufacturer and exporter of pressure sensitive paper labels and tapes
President: Lana Sellers
CFO: Clyde Duncan
HR Executive: Dan Piper
dpiper@advancedlabelworx.com
Quality Control: Gabrina Kelly
Number Employees: 50-99
Square Footage: 120000
Type of Packaging: Bulk
Brands Exported: Johnson & Johnson; Kimberly Clark; GE; Eaton Corp.; Square D
Regions Exported to: Central America, South America, Europe, Mexico, Canada

41696 Advanced Spice & Trading
1808 Monetary Ln Ste 100
Carrollton, TX 75006   972-242-8580
     Fax: 972-242-6920   800-872-7811
                  sales@advancedspice.com
                   www.advancedspice.com
Spices and ingredients
President: Douglas Hank
CEO: Greg Hank
greg@advancedspice.com
Estimated Sales: $2.3 Million
Number Employees: 15
Square Footage: 268800
Type of Packaging: Consumer, Food Service, Private Label, Bulk

41697 Advantage Gourmet Importers
480 Main Ave
Wallington, NJ 07057   973-777-0007
     Fax: 973-591-5556   888-676-3663
                       crfagi@gmail.com
       www.advantagegourmetimporters.com
Broker, importer and wholesaler/distributor of chestnut products including organic chestnut flour and Italian specialty foods
Owner: Nicholas Puzino
Vice President: Emile Boustani
Purchasing: V Lampariello
Estimated Sales: $2.5-5 Million
Number Employees: 1-4
Square Footage: 800
Regions Imported from: Europe

41698 Advantage Puck Technologies
1 Plastics Rd # 6
Corry, PA 16407-8538   814-664-4810
     Fax: 814-663-6081 sales@advantagepuck.com
                      www.advantagepuck.com
Manufacturer and exporter of plastic product carriers for assembly line filling
President: Kurt Sieber
Estimated Sales: $1-2.5 Million
Number Employees: 1-4
Regions Exported to: Worldwide
Percentage of Business in Exporting: 30

41699 Advantus Corp.
12276 San Jose Blvd
Building 618
Jacksonville, FL 32223   904-482-0091
     Fax: 904-482-0099 www.mcgillinc.com
Manufacturer and exporter of coin changers
President: Wayne Schwartzman
R&D: Becky McDaniel
VP Sales: Jim Booth
Estimated Sales: $ 5 - 10 Million
Number Employees: 10-19
Square Footage: 260000

41700 Adventure Foods
481 Banjo Lane
Whittier, NC 28789-7999   828-497-4113
     Fax: 828-497-7529
        CustomerService@adventurefoods.com
                    www.adventurefoods.com
Freeze-dried; dehydrated; shelf stable foods and instant food; food storage programs; health food markets; baking mixes, bulk spices and ingredients; specialty foods and special packing for vegetarian, diabetics, gluten intolerance andother food or health restrictions.
President: Jean Spangenberg
jean@adventurefoods.com
CEO: Sam Spangenberg
Number Employees: 5-9
Parent Co: Jean's Garden Greats
Type of Packaging: Consumer, Food Service, Private Label, Bulk
Brands Exported: BakePacker; Adventure Foods

Importers & Exporters / A-Z

Regions Exported to: Asia, Middle East, Canada
Percentage of Business in Exporting: 1

41701 Aeration Industries Intl LLC
4100 Peavey Rd
Chaska, MN 55318-2353   952-448-6789
    Fax: 952-448-7293   800-328-8287
aii@aireo2.com www.aireo2.com
Manufactures waste water treatment systems & equipment, including the dual-process Triton aerator and mixer to provide solutions for challenging wastewater needs.
President: Daniel Durda
aii@aireo2.com
VP: Brian Cohen
Estimated Sales: $10-20 Million
Number Employees: 20-49
Square Footage: 500000
Brands Exported: Aire-02 Aspirator; Aire-02 Turbo; Aire-02 Microfloat; Aire-02 275 Series Aspirato

41702 Aero Manufacturing Co
310 Allwood Rd
PO Box 1250
Clifton, NJ 07012-1786   973-473-5300
    Fax: 973-473-3794   800-631-8378
sales@aeromfg.com www.aeromfg.com
Stainless steel sinks, dishtables, cabinets, shelving, and custom fabrication.
President/CEO: Wayne Phillips
kkreiss@aeromfg.com
Sales Exec: Ken Kreiss
Number Employees: 50-99
Square Footage: 600000
Regions Exported to: Central America, South America, Asia, Middle East
Percentage of Business in Exporting: 5

41703 AeroFreeze, Inc.
2551 Viking Way
Richmond, BC, BC V6V 1N4
Canada   604-278-4118
    Fax: 604-278-4847 www.aerofreeze.com
Manufacturers of freezers, chillers and air cooling products.

41704 Aeromat Plastics Inc
801 Cliff Rd E # 104
Suite 104
Burnsville, MN 55337-1534   952-890-4697
    Fax: 952-890-1814   888-286-8729
www.aero-mat.com
Manufacturer and exporter of plastic proofer trays and machined plastic parts
President: Bruce Dahlke
bruce@aeromatplastics.com
Estimated Sales: $2.5 Million
Number Employees: 10-19
Square Footage: 34000
Regions Exported to: South America, Europe, Asia
Percentage of Business in Exporting: 1

41705 Aeromix Systems
7135 Madison Ave W
Minneapolis, MN 55427   763-746-8400
    Fax: 763-746-8408   800-879-3677
www.aeromix.com
Water and wastewater treatment equipment for the municipal, industrial and freshwater markets. Also offers a line of eco-friendly equipment that is completely powered by solar energy
President and CEO: Henry J. Charrabe
Contact: Limor Amar
lamar@nirosoft.com
Operations: Peter Gross
Estimated Sales: $ 5-10 Million
Number Employees: 25
Brands Exported: Tornado; Zephyr; Hurricane; Monsoon; Twister; Diffusers
Regions Exported to: Central America, South America, Europe, Asia, Middle East
Percentage of Business in Exporting: 25

41706 Aerovent Co
5959 Trenton Ln N
Minneapolis, MN 55442-3237   763-551-7500
    Fax: 763-551-7501 aerovent_sales@aerovent.com
www.tcf.com
Manufacturer and exporter of fans

President: Charles Barry
CEO: Chuck Barry
cbarry@tcf.com
CFO: Julie Dale
VP Sales: Dave Laclerc
Estimated Sales: $ 50 - 75 Million
Number Employees: 100-249
Parent Co: Twin City Fan Company
Brands Exported: Axipal; Axiad II; Axico
Regions Exported to: Worldwide

41707 Aerowerks
6625 millcreek drive
Mississauga, ON L5M 5M4
Canada   905-363-6999
    Fax: 905-363-6998   888-774-1616
aman@aero-werks.com www.aero-werks.com
Manufacturer and exporter of conveyors
President: Balbir Singh
Sales Manager: Aman Singh
Number Employees: 35
Parent Co: Aerotool
Regions Exported to: USA
Percentage of Business in Exporting: 40

41708 Aervoid By Diebel Manufacturing
6505 Oakton Street
Morton Grove, IL 60053-2730   847-879-1150
    Fax: 847-879-1153 sales@aervoid.com
aervoid.com
Estimated Sales: $ 10 - 20 Million
Number Employees: 50-99

41709 (HQ)Afec Commodities
10214 Caddo Trail
Magnolia, TX 77354-4007   713-897-0078
    Fax: 713-897-0086 afec@acihouston.com
Importer of pine nuts and seeds, including sesame and pumpkin
President: Teun Baas
Number Employees: 20-49
Square Footage: 26000
Type of Packaging: Bulk
Other Locations:
    Afec Commodities
    ManaguaAfec Commodities
Regions Imported from: Asia
Percentage of Business in Importing: 100

41710 Affiliated Resource Inc
3839 N Western Ave
Chicago, IL 60618-3733   773-509-9300
    Fax: 773-509-9929   800-366-9336
info@4ledsigns.com www.forledsigns.com
Manufacturer, wholesaler/distributor of indoor and outdoor electronic signs
President: Stephen Stillman
stephen@yledsigns.com
National Sales Manager: Rick Markle
Regional Sales Manager: Pam Zayas
Estimated Sales: $ 1 - 3 Million
Number Employees: 1-4
Square Footage: 4000

41711 Affiliated Rice Milling
715 N. 2nd St.
Alvin, TX 77511-3674   281-331-6176
    Fax: 281-585-0336
Rice and rice flour.
Manager: Johnny Dunham
VP, Operations: Johnny Dunham
Estimated Sales: $20-50 Million
Number Employees: 1-10
Square Footage: 130000
Parent Co: Rice Belt Warehouse
Regions Exported to: Central America, Middle East
Percentage of Business in Exporting: 87

41712 Ag-Pak
8416 State Street
PO Box 304
Gasport, NY 14067   716-772-2651
    Fax: 716-772-2555 info@agpak.com
www.agpak.com
Manufacturer and exporter of produce weighers and bag fillers
President: Andy Currie
VP, Technical Support: Joe Gabree
Sales Manager: Greg Lureman
Plant Manager/ Engineering: Warren Farewell
Estimated Sales: Below $ 5 Million
Number Employees: 10-19

41713 Age International Inc
229 W Main St # 202
Suite 202
Frankfort, KY 40601-1879   502-223-9874
    Fax: 502-223-9877 www.blantonsbourbon.com
Wholesaler/distributor and exporter of liquor, including bourbon
President: Yutaka Takano
Cio/Cto: Justin Williams
jwilliams@ageintl.com
CFO: Nancy Fulks
Treasurer: Nancy Fulks
Marketing/Sales: John Polo
Number Employees: 5-9
Parent Co: Buffalo Trace Distillery
Brands Exported: Blanton's Single Barrel Bourbon
Regions Exported to: Worldwide

41714 Agger Fish Corp
63 Flushing Ave # 313
Brooklyn, NY 11205-1081   718-855-1717
    Fax: 718-855-4545 marcagger@gmail.com
www.aggerfish.com
Monkfish, fluke, monkfish liver and shark fins, bones and cartilage for food supplements and ingredients.
President: Marc Agger
marcagger@gmail.com
Estimated Sales: $500,000-$1 Million
Number Employees: 500-999
Square Footage: 12000
Type of Packaging: Bulk
Regions Exported to: Europe, Asia
Regions Imported from: Central America, South America, Europe

41715 Agostoni Chocolate USA
8616 La Tijera Blvd
Suite 512
Los Angeles, CA 90045   213-261-0057
    Fax: 310-670-0596
epirotte@agostonichocolate.com
www.agostonichocolate.com
Fair trade,functional (antioxidants), kosher, organic/natural, cocoa/baking chocolate, chocolate bars, full-line chocolate, other chocolate.
Contact: Bruno Montesano
bmontesano@agostonichocolate.com

41716 AgraWest Foods
PO Box 760
Souris
Prince Edward Island, NS C0A 2B0
Canada   902-687-1400
    Fax: 902-687-1401   877-687-1400
agrawest@agrawest.com www.agrawest.com
Dehydrated potato granules
President/CEO: Wally Browning
VP Finance: Baden Burt
VP/GM: John Schodde
Quality Assurance Manager: Kendra Deagle
Sales Manager: Mary Croucher
Production Manager: Jamie Trainor
Parent Co: Idaho Pacific Corporation
Type of Packaging: Food Service, Bulk
Regions Exported to: Worldwide

41717 Agrana Fruit US Inc
6850 Southpointe Pkwy
Cleveland, OH 44141-3260   440-546-1199
    Fax: 440-546-0038   800-477-3788
www.agrana.us
Sugar; starch; and processed fruits.
President/CEO: Johann Marihart
Board Member: Fritz Gattermeyer
Estimated Sales: $10-20 Million
Number Employees: 50-99
Parent Co: SIAS MPA
Type of Packaging: Food Service, Private Label, Bulk
Regions Exported to: Worldwide
Percentage of Business in Exporting: 15

41718 Agrexco USA
15012 132nd Ave
Jamaica, NY 11434   718-481-8700
    Fax: 718-481-8710 amoso@agrexco.com
Fruits including dried dates, grapefruits and oranges, vegetables, herbs, and flowers.

President: Yoram Shalev
CFO/VP, Quality Control: Jack Aschkeigi
Produce Sales Manager: Joseph Benjuya
Contact: Abelardo Zeron
abelardoz@agrexco.com
Estimated Sales: $20-50 Million
Number Employees: 20-49

41719 **Agri-Dairy Products**
3020 Westchester Ave
Purchase, NY 10577   914-697-9580
                    Fax: 914-697-9586
customerservice@agridairy.com
www.agridairy.com
Dairy and food ingredients including whey and lactose, milkfat, milk powders, casein, milk proteins, cheese and butter.
President: Steven Bronfield
CEO: Frank Reeves III
CFO: Mary Ellen Storino
Year Founded: 1985
Estimated Sales: $52 Million
Number Employees: 10
Number of Products: 50+
Square Footage: 1600
Type of Packaging: Bulk
Regions Exported to: Central America, South America, Asia, Middle East
Regions Imported from: Central America, South America, Europe

41720 **Agri-Food Export GroupQuebec-Canada**
1971 Leonard De Vinci
Ste-Julie, QC J3E 1Y9
Canada   450-461-6266
Fax: 450-461-6255 nicolasmoisan@groupexport.ca
                    www.groupexport.ca
Agency/trade organization

41721 **Agri-Mark Inc**
958 Riverdale St
West Springfield, MA 01089-4621   978-552-5500
Fax: 978-552-5587 information@agrimark.net
                    www.agrimark.net
whey and Dairy products including butter and nonfat, skim and condensed milk; exporter of butter powder.
President/CEO: Richard Stammer
SVP: Robert Wellington
VP/Marketing: John Burke
Communications Director: Douglas DiMento
Plant Manager: Gary Carlow
Year Founded: 1919
Estimated Sales: $20-50 Million
Number Employees: 50-99
Type of Packaging: Private Label, Bulk
Other Locations:
  Agri-Mark Manufacturing Plant
  West Springfield, MA
  Agri-Mark Manufacturing Plant
  Middlebury, VT
  Agri-Mark Manufacturing Plant
  Cabot, VT
  Agri-Mark Manufacturing Plant
  Chateaugay, NYAgri-Mark Manufacturing
  PlantMiddlebury
Brands Exported: Agri-Mark
Regions Exported to: Europe, Asia, Middle East, Caribbean, Mexico
Percentage of Business in Exporting: 2

41722 **Agricor Inc**
1626 S Joaquin Dr
Marion, IN 46953-9633   765-662-0606
       Fax: 765-662-7189 www.grainmillers.com
Whole grain ingredients
President: Steve Wickes
IT: Bill Cramer
bill.cramer@grainmillers.com
Year Founded: 1983
Number Employees: 20-49
Type of Packaging: Bulk
Brands Exported: Agricor
Regions Exported to: Central America, South America, Asia, Middle East, Mexico, Canada, Caribbean

41723 **(HQ)Agricore United**
1600 Utica Avenue South
Suite 350
St Louis Park, MN 55416   952-460-7450
                    Fax: 952-460-7404 877-509-5865
Wheat; barley; oats; 3-grain and instant cereals; pancake mix; organic flour and herb food bars and beans.
President/CEO: Mayo Schmidt
CFO: Rex McLennan
COO-Grain: Fran Malecha
Parent Co: Agricore United Int'l.
Type of Packaging: Consumer, Food Service, Bulk
Other Locations:
  ManitobaSaskatchewanAlbertaBritish
  ColumbiaSaskatchewan
Brands Exported: Alberta
Regions Exported to: Worldwide

41724 **Agriculture Ohio Dept**
8995 E Main St
Reynoldsburg, OH 43068-3342   614-466-5550
            Fax: 614-728-2622 www.agri.ohio.gov
Manager: Robert Boggs
Estimated Sales: Less Than $500,000
Number Employees: 5-9

41725 **Agro Foods, Inc.**
3531 SW 13th St
Miami, FL 33145   786-552-9006
            Fax: 305-361-7639 www.agrofoods.com
Spanish olives
Manager: Isa Knight
Estimated Sales: $1-2.5 Million
Number Employees: 5-9
Square Footage: 526000
Parent Co: Agro Aceitunera SA
Type of Packaging: Consumer, Food Service, Private Label, Bulk
Regions Exported to: Europe
Percentage of Business in Exporting: 1
Regions Imported from: Europe
Percentage of Business in Importing: 99

41726 **AgroCepia**
9703 Dixie Highway
Suite 3
Miami, FL 33156   305-704-3488
            Fax: 305-666-6930 www.agrocepia.cl
Low moisture colored apple flakes and nuggets, evaporated apple dices, grinds, rings and wedges, low moisture powders, dehydrated tomato, green bell pepper, red bell pepper and jalapeno pepper dices and granules
Sales Director: Mike Zobel
Contact: George Bartels
gbartels@acusallc.com
Estimated Sales: $ 3 - 5 Million
Number Employees: 1-4

41727 **(HQ)Agrocan**
176 Benjamin Hudon
Ville St Laurent, QC H4N 1H8
Canada   514-272-2512
      Fax: 514-270-6370 877-247-6226
info@agrocanfoods.com www.agrocanfoods.com
Manufacturer and exporter of fruit, olives, oil, vegetables and miscellaneous products
President: John Karellis
Number Employees: 3
Type of Packaging: Private Label
Other Locations:
  Agrocan
  Aeginion, N. PieriasAgrocán
Regions Exported to: Europe, Middle East, Australia, Latin America, USA
Percentage of Business in Exporting: 90

41728 **(HQ)Agropur**
510 Rue Principale
Granby, QC J2G 7G2
Canada   450-375-1991
         Fax: 450-375-7160 800-363-5686
         jarollan@agropur.com www.agropur.com
Dairy products
Chairman: Jacques Cartier
CEO: Claude Menard
Secretary: Andre Gauthier
Director, Dairy Ingredient Sales: Kevin Thomson
Number Employees: 650
Parent Co: Agropur MSI, LLC
Type of Packaging: Consumer, Food Service
Other Locations:
  Agropur Coop. Agro-Alimentair
  Markham, ONAgropur Coop. Agro-Alimentair
Regions Exported to: South America, Europe, Asia, USA
Regions Imported from: Europe

41729 **Agrusa**
PO Box 267
117 Fort Lee Road
Leonia, NJ 07605-7244   201-592-5950
         Fax: 201-585-7244 agrusa@agrusainc.com
                    www.agritalia.com
Italian foods, including: pasta, olive oil, balsamic vinegar, tomatoes, risotto, rice and frozen pizza.
President: Jill Bush
Number Employees: 5
Square Footage: 8000
Type of Packaging: Consumer, Food Service, Private Label, Bulk
Brands Imported: Celio, Remo; Tosca; Don Peppe; Sapore Di Napoli; Chirico; Lilla; Bella Italia
Regions Imported from: Europe
Percentage of Business in Importing: 90

41730 **Agtron Inc**
9395 Double R Blvd
Reno, NV 89521-5919   775-850-4600
            Fax: 775-850-4611 agtron@aol.com
                    www.agtron.net
Manufacturer and exporter of spectrophotometers used in the food industry to measure the degree of roasted, baked or fried goods or color grading of most food products.
President: Carl Staub
agtron@aol.com
CEO: Mike Rowley
CFO: Mike Rowley
Sales/Marketing: Kim Franke
Estimated Sales: $ 1 - 2.5 Million
Number Employees: 5-9
Square Footage: 80000
Regions Exported to: Worldwide
Percentage of Business in Exporting: 35

41731 **Agvest**
7589 First Pl Ste 2
Cleveland, OH 44146   216-464-3737
           Fax: 440-735-1680 www.agvest.com
Frozen apples, elderberries, bilberries; sugar infused blueberries, cranberries and cherries; and fruit flakes and powders.
President/CEO: Barry Schneider
CFO: Steve Hamilton
Contact: Bob Newman
bob@agvest.com
Estimated Sales: $1-2.5 Million
Number Employees: 5-9
Type of Packaging: Food Service
Regions Exported to: Europe, Asia
Percentage of Business in Exporting: 2

41732 **Ahmad Tea**
P.O.Box 876
Deer Park, TX 77536   281-478-0957
         Fax: 281-479-0521 800-637-7704
         info@ahmadteausa.com www.ahmadtea.com
Tea and tea gift producer
Marketing: Karim Afshar
Contact: Ali Afshar
ali@ahmadtea.com

41733 **Aidi International Hotels of America**
1050-17th Street NW
Suite 600
Washington, DC 20036-   202-331-9299
         Fax: 202-478-0367 sales@royalregencyhotels.com
                    www.royalregencyhotels.com
Engineering and marketing consultant specializing in construction, management, decoration and operations in overseas hotels; wholesaler/distributor and exporter of equipment, furniture and food
President: Ghassane Aidi
Chairman: Adnan Aidi
VP: Samia Aidi
Number Employees: 200
Square Footage: 28000
Parent Co: Aidi Group
Regions Exported to: Europe, Middle East, Russia
Percentage of Business in Exporting: 60

41734 **Air Logic Power Systems**
1745 S. 38th Street
Suite 100
Milwaukee, WI 53215   414-671-3332
         Fax: 414-671-6645 800-325-8717
         info@alpsleak.com www.alpsleak.com
On-line leak detection equipment for the plastic container manufacturing industry.

Importers & Exporters / A-Z

President: Roger Tambling
Sales Manager: Scott Heins
Contact: Pierre Aterianus
pierrea@alpsleak.com
Estimated Sales: $5-10 Million
Number Employees: 20-49
Square Footage: 80000
Brands Exported: ALPS Total Quality Systems

41735 Air Quality Engineering
7140 Northland Dr N
Minneapolis, MN 55428-1520 888-883-3273
  Fax: 763-531-9900 800-328-0787
  info@air-quality-eng.com
  www.air-quality-eng.com
Manufacturer and exporter of electronic and media air cleaners, parts and accessories
President & CEO: Heidi Oas
VP, Sales: Ira Golden
Estimated Sales: $ 5 - 10 Million
Number Employees: 50-75
Square Footage: 142800
Brands Exported: Smokemaster; Miracle Air, Mist Buster
Regions Exported to: Central America, South America, Europe, Asia, Middle East
Percentage of Business in Exporting: 8

41736 (HQ)Air Savers Inc
4400 Lawndale Ave
Lyons, IL 60534-1726 708-447-4646
  Fax: 708-447-6259 888-447-4643
  www.air-savers.com
Wholesaler/distributor and exporter of air cleaning equipment; serving the food service market
President/CEO: Mark Olson
Estimated Sales: $5-10 Million
Number Employees: 10-19
Square Footage: 12000
Other Locations:
  Air Savers
  Lyons, ILAir Savers
Brands Exported: It's All About Clean Air; Honeywell; Trion; Smokemaster; Smokeeter; Friedrich
Regions Exported to: Worldwide

41737 (HQ)Air-Scent International
290 Alpha Drive RIDC Industrial Park
Pittsburgh, PA 15238 412-252-2000
  Fax: 412-252-1010 800-247-0770
  info@airscent.com www.airscent.com
Manufacturer and exporter of air fresheners, sanitizers and odor control systems including aerosol dispensers and refills; also, aerosol insecticides
President: Arnold Zlotnik
Estimated Sales: Below $5 Million
Number Employees: 50-99
Square Footage: 160000
Brands Exported: Air-Scent
Regions Exported to: Europe, Asia
Percentage of Business in Exporting: 10

41738 Airfloat LLC
2230 N Brush College Rd
Decatur, IL 62526-5522 217-423-6001
  Fax: 217-422-1049 800-888-0018
  sales@alignprod.com
Manufacturer and exporter of lift, tilt and turn tables
President: Jason Stoecker
Marketing Manager: Kara Demarjian
Estimated Sales: $10-20 Million
Number Employees: 20-49
Regions Exported to: Worldwide

41739 (HQ)Airmaster Fan Co
1300 Falahee Rd # 5
Jackson, MI 49203-3548 517-764-2300
  Fax: 517-764-3838 800-255-3084
  sales@airmasterfan.com www.airmasterfan.com
Industrial and commercial fans, stainless steel fan guards, aluminum air circulator blades and explosion proof fans
President: Richard Stone
CEO: Robert Lazebrick
CFO: Ronald Johnson
Marketing: Maryann Talbot
Director Of Sales: Mike Pignataro
Product Manager: Mike Hemer
Estimated Sales: $10-20 Million
Number Employees: 20-49
Square Footage: 1500000

41740 Airomat Corp
2916 Engle Rd
Fort Wayne, IN 46809-1198 260-747-7408
  Fax: 260-747-7409 800-348-4905
  airomat@airomat.com
Manufacturer and exporter of safety and fatigue relief matting
President: Joanne K Feasel
VP: Jody Feasel
Marketing/Sales: Claudia Logan
Operations Manager: Pam Peters
Plant Manager: John Solga
Estimated Sales: $ 1 - 3,000,000
Number Employees: 5-9
Square Footage: 6000
Regions Exported to: South America, Japan, Mexico

41741 (HQ)Airosol Co Inc
1101 Illinois St
Neodesha, KS 66757-1475 620-325-2666
  Fax: 620-325-2602 800-633-9576
  www.airosol.com
Manufacturer and exporter of insecticides and counter cleaners
President: Carl G Stratemeier
Marketing Specialist: Jim Leiker
VP Sales/Marketing: Don Gillen
Contact: Tim Bell
tbell@airosol.com
Estimated Sales: $20-50 Million
Number Employees: 10-19
Square Footage: 80000
Regions Exported to: Worldwide
Percentage of Business in Exporting: 5

41742 Airsan Corp
4554 W Woolworth Ave
Milwaukee, WI 53218-1497 414-353-5800
  Fax: 414-353-8402 800-558-5494
Manufacturer and exporter of filters including air and restaurant grease extractor
Owner: Randy Perry
Quality Control: Kurt Gleisner
VP Sales: Kurt Glaisner
randyperry@airsan.com
Estimated Sales: $5-10 Million
Number Employees: 10-19
Type of Packaging: Food Service
Regions Exported to: South America, Europe, Middle East, Worldwide
Percentage of Business in Exporting: 5

41743 Aiya America Inc
2807 Oregon Ct
Unit D-5
Torrance, CA 90503-2635 310-212-1395
  Fax: 310-212-1386 info@aiya-america.com
  www.aiya-america.com
Wholesaler and distributor of matcha green tea and premium leaf teas used in many types of food and beverage applications.
Sales Assistant/Customer Service: Daniel Coniglio
daniel@aiya-america.com

41744 (HQ)Ajinomoto Foods North America, Inc.
4200 Concours St.
Suite 100
Ontario, CA 91764 909-477-4700
  Fax: 919-477-4600 www.ajinomotofoods.com
Specializes in frozen ethnic dishes, such as Italian, Mexican and Asian including lasagna, meat balls, ravioli, spaghetti sauce, potstickers, spring rolls, and burritos.
President/CEO: Takaaki Nishii
President, North America: Bernard Kreilmann
Year Founded: 1909
Estimated Sales: $670 Million
Number Employees: 2,500+
Number of Brands: 14
Parent Co: Ajinomoto Co., Inc.
Type of Packaging: Consumer, Food Service
Other Locations:
  Amino Acid Technologies
  Raleigh, NC
  Wellness & Sports Nutrition
  Raleigh, NC
  Food Ingredients
  Itasca, ILAjinomoto Heartland, Inc.
  Chicago, IL
  Ajinomoto Althea, Inc.
  San Diego, CA
  Amino Acid TechnologiesRaleigh

Regions Exported to: Asia, Canada
Percentage of Business in Exporting: 25
Regions Imported from: Asia, Canada
Percentage of Business in Importing: 5

41745 Ajinomoto Frozen Foods USA, Inc.
4200 Concours Street
Suite 100
Ontario, CA 91764
  866-536-8008
  www.ajifrozenusa.com
Asian ingredients and prepared foods.
Parent Co: Ajinomoto Co., Inc.
Type of Packaging: Consumer, Food Service, Private Label
Other Locations:
  Los Angeles, CA
  Portland, OR
  Honolulu, HIPortland
Brands Exported: Ajinomoto
Regions Exported to: Asia, Canada
Percentage of Business in Exporting: 25
Brands Imported: Ajinomoto
Regions Imported from: Asia, Canada
Percentage of Business in Importing: 5

41746 Ajinomoto Heartland Inc
8430 W Bryn Mawr Ave
Suite 650
Chicago, IL 60631-3421 773-380-7000
  Fax: 773-380-7006 www.lysine.com
Feed-grade amino acids
President: Daniel Bercovici
Number Employees: 10-19
Parent Co: Ajinomoto Co., Inc.
Type of Packaging: Bulk
Regions Exported to: South America
Regions Imported from: Europe

41747 Akay USA LLC
500 Hartle St
Suite E
Sayreville, NJ 08872-2770 732-254-7177
  akayusallc@gmail.com
  www.akay-group.com
Paprika and other spices.
Senior Vice President of Sales USA: Rajive Joseph
Manager: Balu Maliakel
balu.maliakel@akay-group.com
Number Employees: 1-4
Parent Co: Akay Group

41748 Akzo Nobel Functional Chemicals
P.O. Box 40350
Denver, CO 80201-0350 303-937-7482
  Fax: 303-936-3989 800-662-8170
  www.akzonoble.com
Importer of sodium carboxy methyl and cellulose gum
Manager: Jim Schmitt
Sales: Marianne Law
Estimated Sales: $500,000-$1 Million
Number Employees: 1-4
Parent Co: Akzo Nobel
Type of Packaging: Bulk
Brands Imported: Akucell
Regions Imported from: Holland
Percentage of Business in Importing: 100

41749 Al Gelato Bornay
9133 Belden Ave
Franklin Park, IL 60131-3505 847-455-5355
  Fax: 847-455-7553 algelatochicago@gmail.com
  www.algelatochicago.com
Ice cream, sorbet, spumoni, natural fruit sorbets, and frozen desserts.
President: Paula DiNardo
pdinardo@laibensebornay.com
Estimated Sales: Less Than $500,000
Number Employees: 5-9
Square Footage: 20000
Type of Packaging: Food Service, Private Label, Bulk
Brands Exported: al Gelato
Regions Exported to: South America
Brands Imported: La Bornay
Regions Imported from: Europe

41750 (HQ)Al Pete Meats
2100 E Willard St
Muncie, IN 47302-3737 765-288-8817
  Fax: 765-281-2759 www.petespride.net

Frozen portion control foods; including corn dogs, breaded meat and cheese, raw and cooked breaded mushrooms and cauliflower; Exporter of frozen portion controlled breaded meat products.
President: Arlin Mann
CEO: John Hartmeyer
Purchasing Manager: Paul Whitechair
Estimated Sales: $10-20 Million
Number Employees: 20-49
Square Footage: 450000
Type of Packaging: Consumer, Food Service, Private Label
Other Locations:
  Manufacturing Facility
  Muncie, IN
  Manufacturing Facility
  Fairbury, ILManufacturing FacilityFairbury
Regions Exported to: Canada

41751 Al Safa Halal
100 Church St
8th Floor
New York City, NY 10007
   800-268-8147
connect@alsafafoods.com www.alsafahalal.com
Processor and exporter of halal processed foods including pizza, beef burgers, chicken nuggets, fish sticks.
President: David Muller
VP: Steve Hahn
Number Employees: 10-19
Number of Brands: 40
Parent Co: Engro Foods Canada Ltd.
Type of Packaging: Consumer, Food Service
Other Locations:
  Al Safa Halal
  Cambridge, OntarioAl Safa Halal
Brands Exported: Al Safa Halal
Regions Exported to: Central America

41752 Al-Rite Fruits & SyrupsCo
18524 NE 2nd Ave
Miami, FL 33179-4427   305-652-2540
  Fax: 305-652-4478 www.al-rite.com
Processor and exporter of kosher products including isotonic iced tea, fountain and slush beverage, ice cream and nondairy bases. Also fudge and chocolate syrups, toppings, frozen cocktail/bar mixes and extracts and flavors forbeverages and desserts
Manager: Alfredo Faubel
Vice President: Cliff Spring
cspring@al-rite.com
Estimated Sales: $5-10 Million
Number Employees: 10-19
Type of Packaging: Consumer, Food Service, Private Label, Bulk
Brands Exported: Tropical; Al-Rite; Iso-Sport
Regions Exported to: Central America, South America, Caribbean
Percentage of Business in Exporting: 15

41753 Alabama Bag Co Inc
230 Broadway Ave
Talladega, AL 35160-3659   256-362-4921
  Fax: 256-362-1801 800-888-4921
  www.alabamabag.com
Manufacturer and exporter of food bags, twine, uniforms, aprons, butcher frocks, disposable wipers, stockinettes, elastic netting, knit gloves, ham tubings, shrouds, money bags, courier bags, transit bags, locking bags and coin andcurrency bags, Poly money bags, coin wrappers, bill straps, tags, security seals.
President: Larkin Coker
wc@alabamabag.com
Number Employees: 10-19
Brands Exported: US Bag
Regions Exported to: Central America, South America, Europe, Worldwide

41754 Alacer Corp
Carlisle, PA 17013
   888-425-2362
  www.emergenc.com
Dietary supplements, mineral ascorbates, vitamins and distilled water.
President: Ron Fugate
Vice President: Bruce Sweyd
Year Founded: 1978
Estimated Sales: $20-50 Million
Number Employees: 50-99
Square Footage: 57000
Type of Packaging: Consumer
Brands Exported: E-mer'gen-C
Regions Exported to: Europe, Canada
Percentage of Business in Exporting: 5

41755 Aladdin Bakers
240 25th St
Brooklyn, NY 11232-1338   718-499-1818
  Fax: 718-788-5174 kasindorf@aladdinbakers.com
  www.aladdinbakers.com
Sandwich wraps and gourmet flour tortillas; pita; panini and specialty breads; bagels; bread sticks; toast; croutons; and flatbreads.
President: Joseph Ayoub
ayoub@aladdinbakers.com
CFO/GM: Donald Guzzi
Quality Control Director: Javier Vasquez
VP Sales/Marketing: Paul Kasindorf
Human Resources Director: Barbara Adams
COO/Plant Manager: Arkadi Karachun
Production Manager: Ed Curran
Year Founded: 1972
Estimated Sales: $20-50 Million
Number Employees: 100-249
Square Footage: 9774
Type of Packaging: Consumer, Food Service, Private Label, Bulk
Regions Exported to: Worldwide
Percentage of Business in Exporting: 10

41756 Aladdin Temp-Rite, LLC
250 East Main Street
Hendersonville, TN 37075-2521   615-537-3600
  Fax: 615-537-3634 800-888-8018
  info@aladdin-atr.com www.aladdintemprite.com
Manufacturer and exporter of serving and heating equipment
President: Martin A. Rothshchild
VP Marketing: Marty Rothchild
VP Sales: Steve Avery
Contact: Kimmie Biggs
kbiggs@aladdin-atr.com
Estimated Sales: $300,000-500,000
Number Employees: 1-4
Parent Co: ENOCIS
Type of Packaging: Food Service
Brands Exported: Isul-Plus; Temp Rite Excel II

41757 Alar Engineering Corp
9651 196th St
Mokena, IL 60448-9307   708-479-6100
  Fax: 708-479-9059 info@alarcorp.com
  www.alarcorp.com
Manufacturer and exporter of water pollution control equipment including filters for dewatering sludges, clarifiers, separators, carbon columns, drum compactors and holding tanks
President: Paula Jackfert
paulaj@alarcorp.com
CEO: Vickey Hassen
Estimated Sales: $5-10 Million
Number Employees: 20-49
Square Footage: 78000

41758 Alarm Controls Corp
19 Brandywine Dr
Deer Park, NY 11729-5721   631-586-4220
  Fax: 631-586-6500 800-645-5538
  info@alarmcontrols.com www.alarmcontrols.com
Manufacturer and exporter of electronic burglar and smoke alarm systems and timers
President: Howard Berger
info@alarmcontrols.com
Sales Manager: John Benedetto
Estimated Sales: $5-10 Million
Number Employees: 10-19

41759 Alaska Ocean Trading
4101 Westland Cir
Anchorage, AK 99517-1430   907-243-4399
  Fax: 907-243-4399
Fish and seafood
CFO: Roger Park
Estimated Sales: Under $500,000
Number Employees: 1-4

41760 Alaska Sausage & Seafood
2914 Arctic Blvd
Anchorage, AK 99503-3811   907-562-3636
  Fax: 907-562-7343 800-798-3636
  aks@ak.net www.alaskasausage.com
Sausage, processed meats and smoked fish; exporter of smoked salmon
President: Herbert Eckmann
Secretary/Treasurer: Eva Eckmann
Quality Control Manager: Martin Eckmann
IT: Amanda Ingram
aks@ak.net
Estimated Sales: $10-20 Million
Number Employees: 20-49
Square Footage: 30000
Type of Packaging: Consumer, Food Service, Private Label, Bulk
Regions Exported to: Central America, Europe
Percentage of Business in Exporting: 5

41761 Alaska Smokehouse
21616 87th Ave SE
Woodinville, WA 98072-8017   360-668-9404
  Fax: 360-668-1005 800-422-0852
  service@alaskasmokehouse.com
  www.alaskasmokehouse.com
Smoked salmon, spreads, jerky, cookies, fruit purees and coffee.
President/CEO: Jack Praino
customerservice@alaskasmokehouse.com
SVP: Tiffany Andriesen
Estimated Sales: $1.5 Million
Number Employees: 20-49
Square Footage: 60000
Type of Packaging: Consumer, Private Label
Brands Exported: Alaska Smokehouse
Regions Exported to: Worldwide
Percentage of Business in Exporting: 10

41762 Alaskan Gourmet Seafoods
1020 International Airport Road
Anchorage, AK 99518
  Fax: 907-563-2592 800-288-3740
  www.akgourmet.com
Frozen and canned smoked halibut and salmon.
President: Paul Schilling
Estimated Sales: $5-10 Million
Number Employees: 18
Square Footage: 40000
Brands Exported: Alaskan Gourmet
Regions Exported to: South America, Europe, Asia
Percentage of Business in Exporting: 10

41763 Alati-Caserta Desserts
277 Rue Dante
Montr,al, QC H2S 1K3
Canada   514-271-3013
  Fax: 514-277-5860 877-377-5680
  info@alaticaserta.com www.alaticaserta.com
Desserts including almond cakes, cannoli ricotta and chocolate mousse.
President: Vittorio Caldarone
Co-Owner: Marco Caldarone
Estimated Sales: $243,000
Number Employees: 6
Type of Packaging: Food Service
Regions Exported to: USA

41764 Alba Specialty Seafood Company
233 Water St
New York, NY 10038-2095   212-349-5730
  Fax: 212-607-6198 sean@albaspecialty.com
Import broker of frozen foods and seafood including lobster tails, shrimp, sea bass, etc
President: Denis Moriarty
VP: Eric Kiwi
Estimated Sales: $4.2 Million
Number Employees: 17

41765 Albert A Russo Inc
88 Cottage St # 1
Suite: 1
East Boston, MA 02128-2291   617-569-6995
  Fax: 617-569-3791 arussoimports@comcast.net
Import broker and importer of confectionery and dairy/deli products, groceries and canned anchovies, romano cheese
CEO: Albert Russo
Estimated Sales: $5-10 Million
Number Employees: 5-9
Square Footage: 4000
Type of Packaging: Consumer, Food Service, Private Label, Bulk
Brands Imported: Engraulis; Almar; Joseph Russo
Regions Imported from: South America, Europe
Percentage of Business in Importing: 50

Importers & Exporters / A-Z

41766 Albert Uster Imports Inc
9211 Gaither Rd
Gaithersburg, MD 20877-1419   301-963-5074
Fax: 301-948-2601   800-231-8154
info@auiswiss.com
Wholesaler/distributor and importer of European chocolates, cookies, hors d'oeuvres, soups/soup bases, mixes, flavors, dehydrated fruits, cereals, liqueur concentrates, pistachios, glazes, knives, molds, etc.
President: Albert Uster
CEO: Philipp Braun
CEO: Philipp Braun
Branch Manager: Lisa Barrantes
Sales Coordinator: Joanna Peschin
Estimated Sales: $20-50 Million
Number Employees: 20-49
Brands Imported: Carma; Laderach; Flachsmann; Hug; Hugli; Bambasei; Vanini; Bio-Familia
Regions Imported from: Europe
Percentage of Business in Importing: 95

41767 Albion Machine & Tool Co
1001 Industrial Blvd
Albion, MI 49224-8551   517-629-9135
Fax: 517-629-6888
customercentral@casterconcepts.com
www.albionmachine.com
Manufacturer and exporter of specialty and reworked food processing equipment; repair services available
President: Robert Herwarth
CEO/Chairman: William Stoffer
wstoffer@albionmachine.com
VP: James Herwarth
Estimated Sales: $ 3 - 5 Million
Number Employees: 10-19
Regions Exported to: Central America, South America, Europe, Asia
Percentage of Business in Exporting: 5

41768 Alca Trading Co.
5301 Blue Lagoon Dr
Suite 570
Miami, FL 33126   305-265-8331
www.alcatradingcorp.com
Banana juices and mango purees.
Contact: Andrea Cordova
andrea@alcatradingcorp.com

41769 Alchemie USA Inc.
790 S Main
Suite 2C
Southington, CT 06489   860-621-2470
Fax: 860-621-9570 psavla@alchemieusa.com
www.alchemieusa.com
Wholesaler/distributor and importer of vitamin supplements including melatonin, ranitidine and niacin
President/CEO: Pete Savla
VP: Bhame Savla
Estimated Sales: $ 3 - 5 Million
Number Employees: 1-4
Type of Packaging: Bulk
Brands Imported: Niacin; Niacinamide
Regions Imported from: Asia

41770 Alcoa - Massena Operations
45 County Route 42
P.O. Box 5278
Massena, NY 13662
www.alcoa.com
Rod, billet, sow.
Number Employees: 480
Regions Exported to: Worldwide
Percentage of Business in Exporting: 50

41771 Alconox Inc
30 Glenn St # 309
Suite 309
White Plains, NY 10603-3252   914-437-7585
Fax: 914-948-4088 cleaning@alconox.com
www.alconox.biz
Manufacturer and exporter of USDA approved detergents for critical cleaning applications including food preparation surfaces
President: Stewart Katz
skatz@alconox.com
CFO: Elliot Lebowitz
CEO: Elliot M Lebowitz
General Manager: Malcolm McLaughlin
Estimated Sales: $ 3 - 5 Million
Number Employees: 5-9
Type of Packaging: Food Service
Brands Exported: Alconox; Liqui-Nox; Terg-A-Zyme; Alcojet; Citranox; Det-O-Jet; Detergent 8; Alco Tabs
Regions Exported to: Europe, Asia, Middle East, Canada

41772 Alderfer Inc
382 Main St
PO Box 2
Harleysville, PA 19438-2310   215-256-8818
Fax: 215-256-6120   800-341-1121
www.alderfermeats.com
Pork, beef and turkey products
President/CEO: Jim Van Stone
jvanstone@alderfermeats.com
CFO: Sandy Sloyer
Marketing Manager: Samantha Alderfer
Sales Executive: Chet Dudzinski
Human Resources Manager: Janise Stauffer
Plant Manager: Brent Shoemaker
Purchasing Manager: Ray Ganser
Estimated Sales: $12 Million
Number Employees: 50-99
Number of Brands: 1
Number of Products: 300
Square Footage: 60000
Type of Packaging: Consumer, Food Service, Private Label, Bulk
Brands Exported: Alderfer
Regions Exported to: Asia, Middle East, Canada
Percentage of Business in Exporting: 3

41773 Alexander Machinery
P.O.Box 6446
Spartanburg, SC 29304   864-963-3624
Fax: 864-963-7018 alexcoair@aol.com
Manufacturer and exporter of pneumatic coalescer filters and system drainage equipment
President: Martin Cornelson
VP: W Spearman
Pneumatic Systems Design: Cliff Troutman
Estimated Sales: $20-50 Million
Number Employees: 20-49
Square Footage: 400000
Brands Exported: Alexco
Regions Exported to: South America, Europe
Percentage of Business in Exporting: 18

41774 Alfa Cappuccino Import LTD
231 Millway Avenue
Unit 7
Concord, ON L4K 3T7
Canada   905-660-2750
Fax: 905-660-2755   800-764-2532
info@expresso.com www.espresso.com
Importer of cappuccino machines
President: Ross Cammalleri
Number Employees: 10
Brands Imported: Gaggia Espresso Machines; Ionia Coffee; Slush Machines
Regions Imported from: Italy
Percentage of Business in Importing: 100

41775 Alfa Chem
2 Harbor Way
Kings Point, NY 11024-2117   516-504-0059
Fax: 516-504-0039   800-375-6869
alfachem@gmail.com www.alfachem1.com
Provides raw materials to industries such as manufacturing, repackaging, research, pharmaceutical, food and cosmetics, as well as Universities and Hospitals.
President: Alfred Khalily
alfredkhalily@yahoo.com
Estimated Sales: $2.5 000,000
Number Employees: 1-4
Number of Products: 300
Square Footage: 7500
Type of Packaging: Private Label, Bulk
Brands Exported: Private Label
Brands Imported: Private Label
Regions Imported from: Central America, South America, Europe, Asia

41776 Alfa International Corp
4 Kaysal Ct # 1
Armonk, NY 10504-1309   914-273-2222
Fax: 914-273-3666   800-327-2532
www.alfaco.com
Wholesaler/distributor, importer and exporter of replacement parts for food processing equipment including mixers, slicers, bandsaws, cutters, graters/shredders, etc.; also, aprons, gloves, metal mesh, blades and small food choppersand cheese graters
President: Roger Madigan
rmadigan@alfaco.com
Controller: Joseph Valerio
R&D: Eric Stull
Quality Control: Jose Quintero
Marketing Director: Christar Cambriello
Sales Director: Charles Boccia
Public Relations: Jolita Meskauskaite
Operations: David Tate
Production: Ted Sumaski
Plant Manager: Greg Hintze
Purchasing Agent: Michael Henry
Estimated Sales: $5-10 Million
Number Employees: 10-19
Square Footage: 80000
Type of Packaging: Food Service
Brands Exported: G&B; L&W; Krefft, Schermer, ARI, Jelco
Regions Exported to: Central America, South America, Europe, Middle East
Percentage of Business in Exporting: 10
Brands Imported: Yu Yung, Krefft, Schermer Fama Cheese Grater, Jelco Soup & Food Warmers
Regions Imported from: Europe, Asia

41777 Alfa Laval Ashbrook Simon-Hartley
10470 Deer Trail Dr
Houston, TX 77038   713-934-3160
ashbrook.sales@alfalaval.com
Manufacturer and exporter of liquid solid separation equipment (presses) and thickeners
Project Manager: Carl Boyd
Estimated Sales: $20-50 Million
Number Employees: 250-499
Parent Co: Alfa Laval Inc
Regions Exported to: Worldwide

41778 Alfa Laval Inc
5400 International Trade Dr
Richmond, VA 23231
Fax: 804-236-3276   866-253-2528
customerservice.usa@alfalaval.com
www.alfalaval.us
Manufacturer and exporter of centrifuges including liquid/liquid and liquid/solid separators for edible oil, fish, meat, starch, protein, grain, yeast, wine, beer, coffee and sugar processing.
President & CEO: Tom Erixon
CFO: Jan Allde
Corporate Social Responsibility: Catarina Paulson
Senior VP, Communications: Peter Torstensson
Corporate General Counsel: Emma Adlerton
Executive VP, Global Sales & Service: Joakim Vilson
President, Operations: Mikael Tyden
Year Founded: 1883
Estimated Sales: $28 Billion
Number Employees: 17,000
Parent Co: Alfa Laval AB
Regions Exported to: Central America, South America, Europe, Asia, Middle East, Australia

41779 Alfa Systems Inc
522 Boulevard
Westfield, NJ 07090-3208   908-654-0255
Fax: 908-654-0256 www.alfasystems.biz
Manufacturer and exporter of custom automation equipment and packaging systems including tamper evident packaging, print registration systems, sealer mounted shrink tunnels, fragile product automatic infeeders, random product bar codescanning, etc
Owner: Steve Williams
Vice President: Chuck Holata
Estimated Sales: $1.25 Million
Number Employees: 10-19
Square Footage: 6000
Regions Exported to: Central America, Europe, Latin America,Mexico
Percentage of Business in Exporting: 5

41780 Alfonso Gourmet Pasta
2211 NW 30th Pl
Pompano Beach, FL 33069-1026   954-960-1010
Fax: 954-974-2773   800-370-7278
customerservice@alfonsogourmetpasta.com

Ravioli and prepared foods including fresh, frozen and processed.
President: Joseph Delfavero
jdelfavero@ppg.com
Estimated Sales: $2.5 Million
Number Employees: 5-9
Square Footage: 48000
Type of Packaging: Food Service
Regions Exported to: Worldwide
Percentage of Business in Exporting: 10

41781 Alfred L. Wolff, Inc.
1440 Renaissance Drive
Park Ridge, IL 60068   847-759-8888
    Fax: 312-265-9888 www.alwolff.com
Importer of dehydrated vegetables, herbs, honey and other bee products including royal jelly, bee pollen and propolis; also, gum arabic, acidulating agents and nutritional fiber
General Manager: Magnus von Buddenbrock
Estimated Sales: $5 Million
Number Employees: 3
Parent Co: Alfred L. Wolff GmbH
Type of Packaging: Bulk
Brands Imported: ALW Selection; Quick Gum; Quick Fiber; Quick Coat; Quick Acid; Quick Polish; Quick Lac; Finest Honey Selection; Finest Honey Organic
Regions Imported from: Central America, South America, Europe, Asia
Percentage of Business in Importing: 100

41782 Algene Marking Equipment Company
P.O. Box 410
Garfield, NJ 7026   973-478-9041
    Fax: 973-473-3847
Manufacturer, importer and exporter of marking and printing equipment, coders, hand marking tools, air feed systems and indenters.
President: Milton Mann
VP/Production: Garry Mann
Plant Manager: Garry Mann
Estimated Sales: $1-1.5 Million
Number Employees: 5-9
Number of Brands: 19
Number of Products: 15
Square Footage: 10000
Regions Exported to: Worldwide
Percentage of Business in Exporting: 13
Regions Imported from: Asia, Australia
Percentage of Business in Importing: 6

41783 Alger Creations
P.O.Box 800604
Miami, FL 32380   954-454-3272
    Fax: 954-239-5773 luisa@algercreations.com
Manufacturer and exporter of plastic bags, advertising specialties, displays and exhibits; importer of inflatable displays.
President: Alvin Brenner
Sales/Marketing: Ogden Farray
Contact: Luisa Maichel
luisa@algercreations.com
Estimated Sales: $2.5-5 Million
Number Employees: 20-49
Number of Brands: 1
Number of Products: 100
Square Footage: 40000
Type of Packaging: Private Label
Regions Exported to: Worldwide
Regions Imported from: Asia
Percentage of Business in Importing: 90

41784 Algood Food Co
7401 Trade Port Dr
Louisville, KY 40258-1896   502-637-3631
    Fax: 502-637-1502 bmcdonald@algoodfood.com
    www.algoodfood.com
Processor and exporter of peanut butter, jams, jellies and preserves
President: Nicolas Melhuish
CEO: Cecil Barnett
VP & CFO: Kathleen Powell
Vice President: Gillian Barnett
Sales Manager: Ashley Keeney
Operations Executive: Dan Schmidt
Production Manager: Danny Ludwig
Number Employees: 100-249
Square Footage: 400000
Brands Exported: Algood; Cap'n Kid
Regions Exported to: Europe, Asia, Middle East, Canada, Caribbean, Mexico

Percentage of Business in Exporting: 5

41785 (HQ)Ali Group
P.O.Box 4149
Winston Salem, NC 27115-4149   336-661-1556
    Fax: 336-661-1979 800-532-8591
    champion@championindustries.com
    www.championindustries.com
Manufacturer and exporter of dishwashers, dish tables, manual and powered glass washers, pot and pan washers and waste disposal systems
President: Dexter Laughlin
CFO: Christian Miller
CEO: Hank Holt
Estimated Sales: $ 20 - 50 Million
Number Employees: 100-249
Brands Exported: Champion; Coldelite; Moyer Diebel
Regions Exported to: Worldwide

41786 Alimentaire Whyte's Inc
1540 Rue Des Patriotes
Laval, QC H7L 2N6
Canada
    866-420-9520
    customer.service@whytes.ca www.whytes.ca
Sauces, cherries, olives, condiments, relish, cooking oils, and table syrup
Year Founded: 1892
Estimated Sales: $32.35 Million
Number Employees: 325
Square Footage: 250000
Brands Exported: Trans Alpine; Via Italia; Mrs. Whytes; Coronation
Regions Exported to: USA
Regions Imported from: South America, Europe, Asia
Percentage of Business in Importing: 30

41787 Aline Heat Seal Corporation
13700 South Broadway
Los Angeles, CA 90061   310-715-6600
    Fax: 310-715-6606 888-285-3917
    alineinfo@sorbentsystems.com www.alinesys.com
Manufacturer and exporter of packaging machinery including shrink wrap, bundling, tube, bag and blister sealing and custom heat sealers for plastic films
President: Charles Schapira
Controller: Susanna Cano
VP: John Rydgren
Marketing and Sales: Charles Schapira
Customer Service: Pat Almanza
Plant Supervisor: Domingo Ayala
Estimated Sales: $ 5 - 10 Million
Number Employees: 10-19
Square Footage: 20000
Regions Exported to: Worldwide

41788 Aliotti Wholesale Fish Company
2 Wharf II
PO Box 3325
Monterey, CA 93940   408-722-4597
    Fax: 408-722-3456
Processor and exporter of frozen squid
President/Purchasing Manager: Joe Aliotii
Estimated Sales: $2.7 Million
Number Employees: 8
Type of Packaging: Food Service
Regions Exported to: Worldwide
Percentage of Business in Exporting: 60

41789 Aliseo Foods
PO Box 29868
Austin, TX 78755   512-207-0064
    Fax: 512-551-0038
Blood orange juice, olive oil, cheese, wine, coffee, honey, chocolate and sauces
Marketing: Stefania Rigo

41790 Alkar Rapid Pak
932 Development Dr
Lodi, WI 53555-1300   608-592-3211
    Fax: 608-592-4039 marketing@alkar.com
    www.alkar.com
Manufacturer and exporter of chillers including air blast, brine and glycol; also, smokehouses and continuous cook/chill systems.
President: Magdy Albert
Estimated Sales: $50-100 Million
Number Employees: 20-49
Square Footage: 80000
Regions Exported to: Central America, South America, Europe, Asia, Middle East

41791 Alkazone/Better Health Lab
200 S Newman St
Hackensack, NJ 07601-3124   201-880-7966
    Fax: 201-880-7967 800-810-1888
    contactus@alkazone.com www.alkazone.com
Manufacturer and exporter of antioxidant water and alkaline mineral supplement and water ionizers.
President: Robert Kim
Estimated Sales: $5-10 Million
Number Employees: 8
Square Footage: 80000
Type of Packaging: Consumer
Brands Exported: Alkazone
Regions Exported to: Worldwide
Percentage of Business in Exporting: 5

41792 Alkota Cleaning SystemsInc
105 Broad St
PO Box 288
Alcester, SD 57001-2120   605-934-2222
    Fax: 605-934-1808 800-255-6823
    info@alkota.com www.alkota.com
Manufacturer and exporter of high-pressure washers and parts, steam cleaners, water reclaim units and waste water/oil separators
President: Gary Scott
CEO: Jeff Burros
burrosjeff@spellcapital.com
CEO: Joseph Bjorkman
Head of Engineering: Roger Walz
Marketing Manager: Jim Scott
VP Sales: Jeff Burros
Estimated Sales: $10-20 Million
Number Employees: 50-99
Square Footage: 50000
Brands Exported: Alkota
Regions Exported to: Central America, South America, Europe, Asia, Middle East
Percentage of Business in Exporting: 5

41793 All A Cart Custom Mfg
2001 Courtright Rd
Columbus, OH 43232-4216   614-443-5544
    Fax: 614-443-4248 800-695-2278
    jjmorris@allacart.com
Manufacturer and exporter of vending carts, kiosks, trucks, mobile kitchens, catering vehicles and trailers
Owner: Jeff Morris
jjmorris@allacart.com
Estimated Sales: $ 5 - 10 Million
Number Employees: 20-49
Square Footage: 120000
Brands Exported: All A Cart
Regions Exported to: Central America, South America, Europe, Asia, Middle East
Percentage of Business in Exporting: 10

41794 All American Container
9330 NW 110th Ave
Miami, FL 33178   305-887-0797
    Fax: 305-888-4133 sales@americancontainers.com
    www.allamericancontainers.com
Supplier of glass, plastic bottles and jars, can, pumps, sprayers and atomizers.
President: Remedios Diaz-Oliver
sales@americancontainers.com
Chief Executive Officer: Fausto Diaz-Oliver
Estimated Sales: $120 Million
Number Employees: 100-249
Square Footage: 100000
Other Locations:
    All American Containers
    Tampa, FLAll American Containers
Regions Exported to: Central America, South America, Europe, Asia, Middle East
Percentage of Business in Exporting: 30
Regions Imported from: South America, Asia
Percentage of Business in Importing: 3

41795 All American Seasonings
10600 E 54th Ave
Suite B
Denver, CO 80239-2132   303-623-2320
    Fax: 303-623-1920
    www.allamericanseasonings.com
Baking mixes for bread, cakes, other pasteries; assorted seasoned snacks including: chips, popcorn, nuts, & pretzels; sauces; variety of hot and cold beverages, energy drinks, and mixers.
Chairman: Andy Rodriguez
Director Of Quality Assurance: Mary Davis
Marketing Director: Joseph Gallagher

Importers & Exporters / A-Z

Year Founded: 1968
Estimated Sales: $12 Million
Number Employees: 20-49
Square Footage: 70000
Type of Packaging: Consumer, Food Service, Private Label, Bulk
Regions Exported to: Central America
Percentage of Business in Exporting: 1

41796 All Fill Inc
418 Creamery Way
Exton, PA 19341-2536   610-524-1918
     Fax: 610-524-7346   866-255-4455
     info@all-fill.com www.all-fill.com
Manufacturer and exporter of auger and Liouis filling and check weighing machinery
President/CEO: Ryan Edginton
ryane@allfill.com
CFO: Bill Egan
Executive VP/General Manager: Raymond Arra Jr
VP of Sales & Marketing: Kyle Edginton
Regional Sales Manager: Raymond Arra
All-Fill Operations Manager: Rick Brennecke
Purchasing Manager: Nick Dienno
Estimated Sales: $ 10-20 Million
Number Employees: 20-49
Square Footage: 110000
Regions Exported to: Central America, South America, Europe, Asia, Australia
Percentage of Business in Exporting: 15

41797 All Foils Inc
16100 Imperial Pkwy
Strongsville, OH 44149-0600   440-572-3645
     Fax: 440-378-0161   800-521-0054
     www.allfoils.com
Manufacturer and exporter of aluminum, foil and sheet gauges; importer of aluminum and copper; also, printing and laminating services available
President: Robert B Papp
rpapp@allfoils.com
Estimated Sales: $20-50 Million
Number Employees: 50-99
Square Footage: 140000
Regions Exported to: Central America, Europe, Middle East

41798 All Packaging MachineryCorp
90 13th Ave # 11
Unit 11
Ronkonkoma, NY 11779-6818   631-588-7310
     Fax: 631-467-4690   800-637-8808
     sales@apmpackaging.com
     www.allpackagingmachinery.com
Manufacturer and exporter of packaging machinery and parts
President: Daniel Wood
Corp Comms: Lynn Miranda
lynn@allpackagingmachinery.com
Marketing/Sales: Lynn Miranda
Plant Manager: Dan Wood
Number Employees: 20-49
Square Footage: 80000
Parent Co: All Packaging Machinery & Supplies Corporation
Brands Exported: APM
Regions Exported to: Worldwide
Percentage of Business in Exporting: 3

41799 All QA Products
63 Mcadenville Rd
Belmont, NC 28012-2434   704-829-6600
     Fax: 704-829-6602   800-845-8818
     sales@allqa.com www.allqa.com
Wholesaler/distributor and importer of thermometers; also, HAACP plans and training materials available
Owner: Janet Cox
sales@allqa.com
Number Employees: 1-4

41800 All Round Foods Bakery Prod
437 Railroad Ave
Westbury, NY 11590-4314   516-338-1888
     Fax: 516-338-5151   800-428-8802
     www.allroundfoods.com
Processor and exporter of frozen doughnuts including plain, glazed, sugar, cinnamon, jelly, etc.
Owner: Glen Wolther
glen@allroundfoods.com
VP, Sales (Central): John Brahm
Executive VP: Robert Glasser
VP, Sales/Marketing (South): Greg Hanson
Purchasing: Steven Finkelstein
Estimated Sales: $ 3 - 5 Million
Number Employees: 10-19
Square Footage: 336000
Type of Packaging: Food Service

41801 All Seasonings Ingredients Inc
1043 Freedom Dr
Oneida, NY 13421-7108   315-361-1066
     Fax: 315-361-1048   800-255-7748
     bfarnach@allseasonings.com
     www.allseasonings.com
Custom blended spices and seasonings
President: Cheryl Ano
cano@allseasonings.com
Controller: Steven Tornabene
VP: Brendan Farnach
Manager/Director: Darby Smith
Estimated Sales: Less than $500,000
Number Employees: 1-4
Square Footage: 199504
Type of Packaging: Consumer, Food Service, Private Label, Bulk

41802 All Star Carts & Vehicles
1565 5th Industrial Ct # B
Bay Shore, NY 11706-3434   631-666-5581
     Fax: 631-666-1319   800-831-3166
     info@allstarcarts.com www.allstarcarts.com
Quality carts, kiosks, trailers and trucks for the food service and general merchandise industries
President: Stephen Kronrad
info@allstarcarts.com
Sales Director: Mark Weiner
VP: Robert Kronrad
Sales Executive: Michael Clark
Estimated Sales: $ 5 - 10 Million
Number Employees: 20-49
Square Footage: 50000
Regions Exported to: Worldwide
Percentage of Business in Exporting: 30

41803 All-Clad METALCRAFTERS LLC
424 Morganza Rd
Canonsburg, PA 15317-5716   724-745-8300
     Fax: 724-746-5035   800-255-2523
     www.all-clad.com
Manufacturer and exporter of stainless steel, aluminum and copper cookware and utensils.
CEO: Peter Cameron
Manager: Hideyuki Nishizawa
hnishizawa@tubecityims.com
Estimated Sales: $ 20-50 Million
Number Employees: 100-249
Parent Co: Clad Metals

41804 Allan Bros. Inc.
31 Allan Rd.
Naches, WA 98937   509-653-2625
     info@allanbrosfruit.com
     www.allanbrosfruit.com
Apples, apple juice, and cherries.
CEO: Miles Kohl
Year Founded: 1951
Number Employees: 200-500
Type of Packaging: Private Label
Brands Exported: Allan Bros. Fruit

41805 Allann Brothers Coffee Roasters
1852 Fescue St SE
Albany, OR 97322-7075   541-812-8013
     Fax: 541-812-8010   800-926-6886
     sales@allannbroscoffee.com
Coffee and teas
Owner: Allan Stuart
Sales Director: Michael Harris
info@allannbroscoffee.com
Estimated Sales: Less than $500,000
Number Employees: 10-19
Type of Packaging: Consumer, Food Service, Private Label, Bulk

41806 Alldrin Brothers
P.O.Box 10
Ballico, CA 95303-0010   209-667-1600
     Fax: 209-667-0463 www.almondcafe.com
Processor and exporter of almonds.
President: Gary Alldrin
Purchasing Manager: Gary Alldrin
Estimated Sales: $1-2.5 Million
Number Employees: 50-99
Type of Packaging: Bulk
Regions Exported to: Worldwide
Percentage of Business in Exporting: 95

41807 Alleghany's Fish Farm
2755 Route 281
Saint Philemon, QC G0R 4A0
Canada   418-469-2823
     Fax: 418-469-2872
Live trout eggs
GM: Yves Boulanger
Estimated Sales: $1-5 Million
Number Employees: 22
Type of Packaging: Consumer, Food Service
Regions Exported to: France, Germany

41808 Allegheny Bradford Corp
P.O. Box 200
Bradford, PA 16701   814-362-2590
     Fax: 814-362-2574   800-542-0650
     sales@alleghenybradford.com
     www.alleghenybradford.com
Manufacturer and exporter of sanitary stainless steel heat exchangers, filter housings, tanks, pressure vessels, manifolds and modular process systems; custom fabrication available
President & CEO: Dan McCune
dmccune@alleghenybradford.com
Estimated Sales: $ 50 - 100 Million
Number Employees: 50-99
Square Footage: 40000
Regions Exported to: South America, Europe, Canada, Caribbean
Percentage of Business in Exporting: 15

41809 Allegro Coffee Co
12799 Claude Ct
Suite B
Thornton, CO 80241-3828   303-444-4844
     Fax: 303-920-5468   800-666-4869
     www.allegrocoffee.com
Roasted specialty coffees; importer of green coffee beans.
President/General Manager: Jeff Teter
jeff_teter@allegro-coffee.com
CFO: Clarence Peterson
VP: David Kubena
Marketing Director: Tara Cross
Sales Director: Glenda Chamberlain
Human Resources Director: Mimi Fins
Plant Operations Manager: Alejandro Rodolfo
Marketing/Purchasing Manager: Susan Drexel
Estimated Sales: $10 Million
Number Employees: 50-99
Square Footage: 50000
Parent Co: Whole Foods Market
Regions Imported from: Central America, South America, Africa

41810 Allegro Fine Foods Inc
1595 Highway 218 Byp
PO Box 1262
Paris, TN 38242-6632   731-642-6113
     Fax: 731-642-6116 info@allegromarinade.com
     www.allegromarinade.com
Meat and vegetable marinades
President: John Fuqua
john@allegromarinade.com
VP: Thomas Harrison
Quality Assurance Manager: Marti Jones
Marketing Manager: Tim Phifer
VP Operations: Stan Nelms
Purchasing: Melanie Mathis
Estimated Sales: $3 Million
Number Employees: 50-99
Square Footage: 80000
Type of Packaging: Consumer, Food Service, Private Label, Bulk

41811 Allemagnia Imports Inc
10731 Forest St
Santa Fe Springs, CA 90670-3927   562-941-7225
     Fax: 562-941-4704
Wholesaler/distributor of baking products, candies, potato products, pickles, mustards, chocolates, cookies, cheeses, etc.; importer of pickles, red and white cabbage, mustards, canned vegetables and fruits, fish, dextrose productsjams, noodles, ketchup
President: Helmut Graef
allemania1@juno.com
Estimated Sales: $ 3 - 5 Million
Number Employees: 1-4
Square Footage: 21200
Type of Packaging: Consumer
Brands Imported: Kuhne; Hengstenberg
Regions Imported from: Europe
Percentage of Business in Importing: 95

41812 Allen Gauge & Tool Co
421 N Braddock Ave
Pittsburgh, PA 15208-2514 412-241-6410
Fax: 412-242-8877 info@allengauges.com
www.allengauges.com
Manufacturer and exporter of sausage linking machinery and other meat processing equipment
Owner: Charles Allen
Manager: C Moekle
Number Employees: 10-19
Parent Co: Allen Gauge & Tool Company

41813 (HQ)Allen Harim Foods LLC
126 N Shipley St
Seaford, DE 19973-3100 302-629-9136
Fax: 302-629-5081 877-397-9191
info@allenharimllc.com www.allenharimllc.com
Poultry products including frozen parts and whole birds; exporter of frozen poultry items
CEO: Steve Evans
Chairman: Warren Allen
CFO: Brian Hildreth
Director of Planning, IT and QA: Allen Harim
Director of Sales and Marketing: Dr.Key Lee
VP Human Resources: Tracy Morris
VP Live Operations: Gary Gladys
Production Coordinator: Karlyn Lemon
Purchasing Director: Gary Lacher
Number Employees: 1000-4999
Type of Packaging: Consumer, Food Service, Private Label, Bulk
Other Locations:
  Allen Family Foods
  Delmar, DE
  Allen Family Foods
  Hurlock, MD
  Allen Family Foods
  Linkwood, MDAllen FoodsHurlock
Regions Exported to: Europe, Asia, Middle East
Percentage of Business in Exporting: 6

41814 Allen Industries
11351 49th St N
Clearwater, FL 33762-4808 727-573-3076
Fax: 727-572-4815 800-677-3076
www.allenindustries.com
President: David Allen
david.allen@allenindustries.com
Estimated Sales: $ 10 - 20 Million
Number Employees: 50-99

41815 Allen Signs Co
2408 Chapman Hwy
Knoxville, TN 37920-1910 865-579-1683
Fax: 865-579-0356 800-844-3524
www.allensign.com
Manufacturer and exporter of advertising specialties, flags, pennants, banners, electric signs, lighting and flag poles, etc.; also, sign painting services available
Owner: Tom Allen
tom@allensign.com
CFO: Tom Allen
Public Relations: Scott Marshall
Operations Manager: Benjamin Booker
Plant Manager: Andrew Asbury
Estimated Sales: Below $5,000,000
Number Employees: 10-19
Square Footage: 7500
Regions Exported to: Worldwide

41816 Allendale Cork Company
4 Walnut St
Rye, NY 10579 914-921-2787
Fax: 914-967-9605 800-816-2675
Manufacturer and exporter of wine and tapered cork stoppers and champagne corks; importer of cork
President: Dale Balun
Vice President: Ken Queen
Contact: Ken Queen
ken12564@aol.com
Estimated Sales: $1-2,500,000
Number Employees: 10-19
Regions Exported to: Worldwide
Percentage of Business in Exporting: 10
Regions Imported from: Portugal
Percentage of Business in Importing: 100

41817 Alliance Industrial Corp
208 Tomahawk Industrial Park
Lynchburg, VA 24502-4153 434-239-2642
Fax: 434-239-5692 800-368-3556
www.allianceindustrial.com
Designer and manufacturer of conveying systems, material handling machinery, and controls. Spiral Conveyers for bulk and case, Depalletisers, Elevators, and Lowerators for can, bottle and case, rinsers, case switches, bulk case, andair conveyer systems and much more.
President: Bob Abbott
babbott@allianceindustrial.com
Marketing/Sales: David Loyd
Sales Manager: Wayne Walker
Purhasing: Todd Farrar
Estimated Sales: $ 20-50 Million
Number Employees: 100-249
Square Footage: 80000
Regions Exported to: Central America, South America, Canada
Percentage of Business in Exporting: 20

41818 Alliance Rubber Co
210 Carpenter Dam Rd
Hot Springs, AR 71901-8219 501-262-2700
Fax: 501-262-5268 800-626-5940
sales@alliance-rubber.com www.rubberband.com
Manufacturer and exporter of imprinted rubber bands for brand identification, logos, produce, etc.; also, UPC imprinted tape for produce
Owner: Lance Gyldenege
Marketing Manager: Jason Risa
Sales Manager: Rachel Atkinson
lance_gyldenege@msn.com
Operations Manager: Brandon Hughes
Estimated Sales: $ 50 - 100 Million
Number Employees: 100-249
Number of Brands: 10
Number of Products: 4500
Square Footage: 160000
Type of Packaging: Consumer, Food Service, Private Label, Bulk
Regions Exported to: Central America, South America, Europe, Asia, Middle East
Percentage of Business in Exporting: 5

41819 (HQ)Allied Custom Gypsum Company
1550 Double Drive
Norman, OK 73069-8288
Fax: 405-366-9515 800-624-5963
customerservice@alliedcustomgypsum.com
www.alliedcustomgypsum.com
Food
Manager & CFO: Tracy Shirley
Executive VP: Dan Northcutt
VP Operations: Kris Kinder
Estimated Sales: $1-5 Million
Number Employees: 10-19
Number of Products: 1
Square Footage: 200000
Parent Co: Harrison Gypsum
Type of Packaging: Food Service

41820 (HQ)Allied Engineering
94 Riverside Drive
North Vancouver, BC V7H 2M6
Canada 604-929-1214
Fax: 604-929-5184 877-929-1214
sales@alliedboilers.com www.alliedboilers.com
Manufacturers of gas and electric boilers, tankless coils and electric boosters.
President: George Gilbert
Quality Control: Brad Gilbert
Marketing Director: Garry Epstein
Sales Director: T Weaver
Operations Manager: Urbano Pandin
Plant Manager: Howard Larlee
Purchasing Manager: Harry Bowker
Number Employees: 60
Square Footage: 340000
Regions Exported to: Europe

41821 Allied Glove Corporation
433 E Stewart St
Milwaukee, WI 53207 414-481-0900
Fax: 414-481-0700 800-558-9263
Manufacturer, importer and exporter of safety products and disposable wear for food handlers including industrial gloves and X-ray protective materials
Manager: Sarah Cunningham
VP: Ray Sroka
Plant Manager: Dan Sroka
Estimated Sales: $ 1 - 3 Million
Number Employees: 10-19
Square Footage: 300000
Brands Exported: Security; Superguard; White Hawk
Regions Exported to: Central America, South America, Europe, Middle East, Canada, Mexico, Latin America
Percentage of Business in Exporting: 10
Regions Imported from: Central America, South America, Europe, Asia, Latin America
Percentage of Business in Importing: 30

41822 (HQ)Allied International Corp
22570 Markey Ct # 108
Sterling, VA 20166-6915 703-444-5515
Fax: 703-444-6493 800-626-2623
allied@alliedint.com www.aicit.com
Wholesaler/distributor and importer of candy, chocolate, cookies, crackers, teas, coffee, preserves, dill pickles, gum, pasta, honey, oils, cereals, dried fruits etc. and exporter
President: Chad Akhavan
Chairman: Kelly Akhavan
CFO: Willy Gloriouso
CEO: Kelly Ackland
Quality Control: Heather Vincent
Marketing Director: Asad Kasini
Sales Director: Bob Kinothe
Public Relations: Paul Akhavan
Purchasing Manager: Chad Akhavan
Estimated Sales: $10-20 Million
Number Employees: 10-19
Number of Brands: 10
Square Footage: 200000
Type of Packaging: Consumer, Food Service, Private Label
Brands Exported: Forrelli; Bon Sante; Swan; InstCafe
Regions Exported to: Europe, Australia
Percentage of Business in Exporting: 5
Brands Imported: Forrelli; Bon Sante; Swan; InstCafe; Sunrise Valley; Smith & Johnson; Holly
Regions Imported from: Central America, South America, Europe, Middle East, Egypt
Percentage of Business in Importing: 95

41823 Allied International Corp
22570 Markey Ct # 108
Suite 108
Sterling, VA 20166-6915 703-444-5515
Fax: 703-444-6493 allied@alliedint.com
www.aicit.com
Preserves, cookies, Italian puff pastries, Gummi Bears, bulk and packaged candy, tea, coffee, dill pickles, crackers, cereals, chocolate bars, travel tins, nuts, sardines, olive oil, chocolate peanuts, boxed chocolate
President: Kelly Akhavan
CEO: Chad Akhavan
CFO: Shaun Akhavan
CEO: Kelly Ackland
Research & Development: Harrison Akhavan
Estimated Sales: $500,000-$1 Million
Number Employees: 10-19
Number of Brands: 12
Number of Products: 350
Type of Packaging: Private Label

41824 Allied Liquid Coffee Company
3540 Agricultural Center Drive
Saint Augustine, FL 32092 904-823-9106
Fax: 904-823-9024 lci@liquidcoffee.com
Owner: Andres Gaviria

41825 Allied Metal Spinning
1290 Viele Ave
Bronx, NY 10474-7133 718-893-3300
Fax: 718-589-5780 800-615-2266
www.alliedmetalusa.com
Woks, cake rings, pizza screens, trays, cutters and bakery, pizza and chinese cooking utensils; also, pans including cake, pie, pizza, black nonstick, anodized, sheet extenders, etc. Importer of 2000 items to complement manufacturedline
Owner: Arlene Saunders
alliedsteam@aol.com
Plant Manager: Carlos Heredia
Purchasing Manager: Arlene Saunders
Number Employees: 20-49
Type of Packaging: Food Service, Private Label, Bulk

Importers & Exporters / A-Z

41826 Allied Old English Inc
100 Markley St
Port Reading, NJ 07064-1897   732-602-8955
   Fax: 732-636-2538   info@alliedoldenglish.com
              www.alliedoldenglish.com
Processor and exporter of Oriental prepared foods including noodles and sauces; also, pancake syrup, molasses, salad dressings, jams, jellies, preserves, salsa and barbecue sauce
President: Brian Dean
COO: Sean Colon
scolon@alliedoldenglish.com
Director of Purchasing: Beverley Gould
Estimated Sales: $8 Million
Number Employees: 50-99
Square Footage: 2000
Type of Packaging: Consumer, Food Service, Private Label, Bulk

41827 Allied Wine Corporation
70 Berme Rd
Ellenville, NY 12428   845-796-4160
   Fax: 845-796-4161   800-796-4100
l.goldman@alliedwine.com www.alliedwine.com
Kosher wines and spirits
Manager: David Fieldman
VP: Herman Schwartz
Estimated Sales: $500,000-$1 Million
Number Employees: 1-4
Type of Packaging: Food Service, Private Label
Brands Exported: Armon
Regions Exported to: Europe
Percentage of Business in Importing: 15

41828 Alloy Hardfacing & Engineering
20425 Johnson Memorial Dr
Jordan, MN 55352-9518   952-492-5569
   Fax: 952-492-3100   800-328-8408
          juliek@alloyhardfacing.net
          www.alloyhardfacing.com
Manufacturer and exporter of primary waste water equipment, CIP-option pumps, heat exchangers and custom cooking vessels
President: Mark Aulik
paulr@alloyhardfacing.net
Sales Director: Paul Rothenberger
Estimated Sales: $5-10 Million
Number Employees: 20-49
Regions Exported to: Central America, South America, Europe, Asia
Percentage of Business in Exporting: 10

41829 Alloyd Brands
1401 Pleasant St
Dekalb, IL 60115-2663   815-756-8452
   Fax: 815-756-5187   800-756-7639
      info@alloyd.com www.tegrant.com
Formerly SCA Consumer Packaging, manufacturers of light-gauge custom thermoformed retail packaging.
President: Ron Leach
Vice President of Business Development: Prakash Mahesh
Marketing: Rob VanGilse
Contact: Joy Butzke
jbutzke@alloyd.com
Estimated Sales: $ 20 - 50 Million
Number Employees: 1-4
Type of Packaging: Bulk
Regions Exported to: Worldwide

41830 (HQ)Allstrong Restaurant Eqpt Inc
1839 Durfee Ave
South El Monte, CA 91733-3708   626-448-7878
   Fax: 626-448-7838   800-933-8913
              www.allstrong.com
Manufacturer and exporter of Chinese woks, exhaust systems and stainless steel work and steam tables
President: Yuancansing Situ
Manager: Yuan Situ
yuan.situ@allstronginc.com
General Manager: Ken Situ
Estimated Sales: Less than $ 500,000
Number Employees: 20-49
Other Locations:
   Allstrong Restaurant Equipmen
   Alhambra, CAAllstrong Restaurant Equipmen
Regions Exported to: Central America

41831 Almex USA Inc
6925 Aragon Cir # 11
Buena Park, CA 90620-1184   714-739-0303
   Fax: 714-739-0404   800-528-0557
      info@almexusa.com www.almexusa.com
Importer of farm-raised fresh Atlantic salmon
Owner: Scott Sterling
ssterling@palamida.com
Operations Manager: Jeffrey Carmen
Estimated Sales: $5-10 Million
Number Employees: 20-49
Parent Co: Salmones Multiexport SA

41832 Alnor Oil Co Inc
70 E Sunrise Hwy
Suite 418
Valley Stream, NY 11581   516-561-6146
                 877-561-6146
              www.alnoroil.com
Wholesaler/distributor of domestic and imported vegetable oils.
President: Marjorie Klayman
marge@alnoroil.com
Vice President & Treasurer: Gordon Kaplan
Vice President & Secretary: Nancy Kaplan
Sales: Joan Bassi
Year Founded: 1968
Estimated Sales: $20-50 Million
Square Footage: 3750
Regions Imported from: South America, Asia, Middle East
Percentage of Business in Importing: 50

41833 Aloe Farms Inc
3102 Wilson Rd
Harlingen, TX 78552-5011   956-425-1289
   Fax: 956-425-3390   800-262-6771
   info@aloeverafarms.com www.aloeverafarms.com
Aloe vera juice, gel and capsules.
President: Mark Berry
VP: Elvia Berry
Estimated Sales: Less Than $500,000
Number Employees: 1-4
Square Footage: 4224
Type of Packaging: Consumer, Private Label, Bulk
Brands Exported: Aloe Farms
Regions Exported to: Europe, Asia
Percentage of Business in Exporting: 10

41834 Aloe Laboratories
5821 E Harrison Ave
Harlingen, TX 78550-1811   956-428-8416
   Fax: 956-428-8482   800-258-5380
   lrodriguez@aloelabs.com www.aloelabs.com
Organic and conventional aloe vera gel, juice, concentrates and powder.
President: Luis Rodriguez
lrodriguez@aolelabs.com
CEO: Hide Aragaki
Operations and Logistics: Mike Hernandez
Estimated Sales: $3-5 Million
Number Employees: 50-99
Square Footage: 160000
Parent Co: Aloe Farms, Inc.
Brands Exported: Aloe Burst
Regions Exported to: Asia, Australia
Percentage of Business in Exporting: 10

41835 Aloe'Ha Drink Products
1908 Augusta Drive
Apt 2
Houston, TX 77057-3717   713-978-6359
   Fax: 713-978-6858   www.aloeha.com
Carbonated fruit drinks including rasberry, kiwi-strawberry, peach, lemon-lime, etc.
Operations Manager: Doyle Gaskamp
Number Employees: 5
Type of Packaging: Consumer, Food Service
Regions Exported to: Worldwide

41836 Aloecorp, Inc.
3005 1st Ave
Seattle, WA 98121   360-486-7415
                 800-458-2563
              www.aloecorp.com
Aloe vera and other aloe ingredients.
CEO: KS Yoon
Vice President, Chief Scientific Officer: Ken Jones
Quality Unit & Scientific Reg. Affairs: Ramiro Gallegos
Sales Representative: Julia Foo
Customer Service Manager: Norma Garza
Director of Operations: Juan Saldana
Number Employees: 5-9
Other Locations:
   Hainan Aloecorp Co. Ltd
   Shanghai, ChinaHainan Aloecorp Co. Ltd

41837 Aloha Distillers
5 Sand Island Access Rd
Unit 118
Honolulu, HI 96819-2222   808-841-5787
   Fax: 808-847-2903   alohadistillersinc@yahoo.com
Processor and exporter of liqueurs including coffee, chocolate-coconut and chi-chi
President/Purchasing Manager: Dave Fazendin
alohadistillersinc@yahoo.com
Marketing: Ann Fazendin
Estimated Sales: $1-2.5 Million
Number Employees: 1-4
Number of Brands: 1
Number of Products: 1
Type of Packaging: Consumer
Regions Exported to: Worldwide

41838 Alouette Cheese USA
400 S Custer Ave
New Holland, PA 17557
                 800-322-2743
      customer.service@alouettecheese.com
              www.alouettecheese.com
French cheese
President & CEO: Dominique Huth
Director, Research & Development: Steve Schalow
Year Founded: 1974
Estimated Sales: $100 Million
Number Employees: 200-500
Brands Imported: Le Bon Dip Alouette©, Le Petite Fromage Alouette©, Fine Cheese Importers, Ile de France©, Saint-Agur©, Saint-Andre©, Supreme©, Chaume©, Saint-Albray©, Etorki© and Fol Epi©
Regions Imported from: France

41839 Alouf Plastics
4 Glenshaw St
Orangeburg, NY 10962-1207   845-512-8864
   Fax: 845-365-2294   800-394-2247
      ron.s@alufplastics.com www.alufplastics.com
Plastic and polyethylene bags
President: Reuven Rosenberg
Estimated Sales: $ 20 - 50 Million
Number Employees: 10-19
Parent Co: API Industries
Brands Exported: Commander
Regions Exported to: Worldwide

41840 Alpha MOS America
7502 Connelley Drive
Suite 110
Hanover, MD 21076-1075   410-553-9736
   Fax: 410-553-9771   800-257-4249
              www.alpha-mos.com
Importer of inspection and analysis instrumentation and systems including electronic nose for testing shelf life, spoilage & mishandling.
CEO: Jean-Paul Ansel
General Manager: Andrew Cowell
Estimated Sales: $1-2.5 Million
Number Employees: 5-9
Parent Co: Alpha MOS Sa
Brands Imported: The Fox System
Regions Imported from: France
Percentage of Business in Importing: 100

41841 Alpha Packaging
1555 Page Industrial Blvd
St Louis, MO 63132-1309   314-427-4300
   Fax: 314-427-5445   800-421-4772
              www.alphap.com
Manufacturer and exporter of jars, bottles and caps
CEO: David Spence
ds@alphaplastic.com
CFO: Jim Flower
VP: Dan Creston
R&D: Robert Wilson
Quality Control: Shane Vorden
Sales: Paul Bonastia
Operations Manager: Roy Allen
Plant Manager: Darren Viernes
Estimated Sales: $20-50 Million
Number Employees: 100-249
Square Footage: 210000
Regions Exported to: Europe, Asia, Canada
Percentage of Business in Exporting: 10

Importers & Exporters / A-Z

41842 Alpha ProTech
60 Centurian Drive
Suite 112
Markham, ON L3R 9R2
Canada   905-479-0654
Fax: 905-479-9732 jsandler@alphaprotech.com
www.alphaprotech.com
President: Al Millar
CEO: Sheldon Hoffman
CFO: Lloyd Hoffman
SVP: Danny Montgomery

41843 Alpine Gloves
41093 County Center Dr
Temecula, CA 92591   951-296-2521
Fax: 951-296-2541 800-888-4669
www.alpinegloves.com
Importer and wholesaler/distributor of protective clothing including disposable gloves, aprons and caps; serving the food service market
President/CEO: Patrick Schmidt
Estimated Sales: $ 5 - 10 Million
Number Employees: 10-19
Square Footage: 160000
Type of Packaging: Consumer, Food Service, Private Label, Bulk

41844 Alsum Farms & Produce
N9083 County Road E
Cambria, WI 53923-9668   920-348-5127
Fax: 920-348-5174 800-236-5127
www.alsum.com
Potatoes and onions; fresh fruits and vegetables.
President & CEO: Larry Alsum
CEO: Randy Fischer
randy.fischer@alsum.com
National Sales & Marketing Manager: Heidi Alsum-Randall
Year Founded: 1972
Number Employees: 100-249
Number of Brands: 4
Number of Products: 300
Type of Packaging: Consumer, Food Service, Private Label, Bulk
Regions Exported to: Central America, Canada
Percentage of Business in Exporting: 1
Regions Imported from: Central America, Canada
Percentage of Business in Importing: 2

41845 Altech Packaging Company
330 Himrod St
Brooklyn, NY 11237   718-386-8800
Fax: 718-366-2398 800-362-2247
mitchell@altechpackaging.com
www.altechpackaging.com
Wholesaler/distributor, importer of shrink, skin, blister, sealing, stretch, bag closing, heat sealing and vacuum packaging systems; also, packaging materials including bags, films, boxes, labels, display board and vacuumpouches
President: Mitchell Lomazow
chicoman57@aol.com
Estimated Sales: $4 Million
Number Employees: 10-19
Number of Brands: 50
Number of Products: 300
Square Footage: 180000
Type of Packaging: Food Service, Private Label, Bulk
Regions Exported to: Worldwide
Percentage of Business in Exporting: 5
Regions Imported from: Canada
Percentage of Business in Importing: 30

41846 Altek Co
245 E Elm St
Torrington, CT 06790-5059   860-482-7626
Fax: 860-496-7113 info@altekcompany.com
www.altekcompany.com
Manufacturer and exporter of can testing equipment; also, food and beverage can and bottle testing services available
President: Stephen Altschuler
steve@altekcompany.com
Marketing: Brian Mazurkivich
Office Manager: David Altschuler
Estimated Sales: $ 10-20,000,000
Number Employees: 100-249
Square Footage: 46000
Regions Exported to: Worldwide
Percentage of Business in Exporting: 10

41847 Alternative Health & Herbs
425 Jackson St SE
Albany, OR 97321   541-791-8400
Fax: 541-791-8401 800-345-4152
healthinfo@healthherbs.com
www.healthherbs.com
Liquid herbal formulations; herbal teas and vitamins.
Owner: Bishop Truman Berst
Estimated Sales: Less than $500,000
Number Employees: 1-4
Square Footage: 12000
Type of Packaging: Consumer, Private Label, Bulk
Regions Exported to: Central America, South America, Europe, Asia, Canada
Percentage of Business in Exporting: 30
Regions Imported from: Central America, South America, Asia, Middle East
Percentage of Business in Importing: 20

41848 Altira Inc
3225 NW 112th St
Miami, FL 33167-3330   305-687-8074
Fax: 305-688-8029 sales@altira.com
www.altira.com
Manufacturer and exporter of blow molded plastic bottles; also, silk screening, pressure sensitive labeling and hot stamping available
President: Ramon Poo
Vice President: Concepcion Alonso
alonso@altira.com
General Manager: Art Hammel
Estimated Sales: $10-20 Million
Number Employees: 100-249
Percentage of Business in Exporting: 5

41849 Altman Industries
699 Altman Road
Gray, GA 31032-3431   478-986-3116
Fax: 478-986-1699
Manufacturer and exporter of processing machinery for peppers, citrus fruits, cabbage, cauliflower, carrots, celery, etc
President: James E Altman
OFC Administrator: Jeri Hastings
Secretary: Gwen Jones
Estimated Sales: Below $5 Million
Number Employees: 10
Square Footage: 40000
Regions Exported to: Central America, South America, Europe, South Africa, Mexico
Percentage of Business in Exporting: 15

41850 Alto-Shaam
W164n9221 Water St
P.O. Box 450
Menomonee Falls, WI 53052   262-251-7067
800-329-8744
www.alto-shaam.com
Warming ovens, low temperature cook and holding equipment, hot deli display cases, smokers, combination oven/steamers, quick chillers, fryers and convection ovens.
President: Steve Maahs
stevem@alto-shaam.com
Director, Finance: Kevin Noonan
Vice President, Marketing: John Muldowney
Year Founded: 1950
Estimated Sales: $29 Million
Number Employees: 250-499
Number of Brands: 3
Number of Products: 200
Square Footage: 350000
Type of Packaging: Food Service
Brands Exported: Halo Heat; Quickchiller; Combitherm
Regions Exported to: Central America, South America, Europe, Asia, Middle East
Percentage of Business in Exporting: 30

41851 Aluma Shield
725 Summerhill Drive
Deland, FL 32724-2024   386-626-6789
877-638-3266
Manufacturer and exporter of cold storage panels and doors
President: John Peters
Sales Director: Allen Rockafellow
Estimated Sales: $20-50 Million
Number Employees: 10

41852 Alumaworks
16850-112 Collins Avenue #185
Sunny Isle Beach, FL 33160   305-635-6100
Fax: 866-790-2153 800-277-7267
rod@alumaworks.com www.alumaworks.com
Manufacturer and exporter of aluminum bakeware and cookware including frying, sauce, saute, cake and pizza pans, stock pots, deep fryers, pasta cookers, roasters, steamers, etc
President: Rod Haber
Sales Manager: Rod Haber
Number Employees: 14
Square Footage: 40000
Regions Exported to: Worldwide
Percentage of Business in Exporting: 10

41853 Alumin-Nu Corporation
PO Box 24359
Lyndhurst, OH 44124   216-421-2116
Fax: 216-791-8018 800-899-7097
www.aluminnu.com
Cleaners for drains, septics, ponds, lakes, fish, bird bath cleaner, aluminum and vinyl doors, window, gutters, siding and boats.
President/Purchasing Director: Howard Kaufman
aluminnu@aol.com
Plant Manager: Charles Moon
Number Employees: 3
Number of Products: 11
Square Footage: 30000
Type of Packaging: Consumer, Private Label, Bulk
Brands Exported: Nice N Easy; Dispoz-All; Power
Regions Exported to: Central America, South America, Europe, Canada
Percentage of Business in Exporting: 5

41854 Alvarado Street Bakery
2225 S McDowell Blvd.
Petaluma, CA 94954-5661   707-789-6700
Fax: 707-283-0350
info@alvaradostreetbakery.com
www.alvaradostreetbakery.com
Organic goods including sprouted wheat bread, kosher bagels, tortillas and whole grain and oil-free granola; exporter of frozen organic wheat bread and kosher bagels.
CEO: Bryan Long
Sales Director: Jim Canterbury
Purchasing: Jamie Mitchell
Year Founded: 1979
Estimated Sales: $23 Million
Number Employees: 100-249
Number of Brands: 2
Number of Products: 27
Square Footage: 75000
Type of Packaging: Consumer, Private Label
Brands Exported: Alvarado Street Bakery
Regions Exported to: Europe, Asia, Canada
Percentage of Business in Exporting: 10

41855 Amano Enzyme USA Company, Ltd
1415 Madeline Ln
Elgin, IL 60124   847-649-0101
Fax: 847-649-0205 800-446-7652
sales@amanoenzymeusa.com
Non-animal and non-GMO enzymes for the dietary supplement, nutraceutical, food, diagnostic and pharmaceutical industries.
President: Motoyuki Amano
VP Science/Technology: James Jolly
Contact: Kumiko Paik
kpaik@amanoenzymeusa.com
Estimated Sales: $15 Million
Number Employees: 440
Square Footage: 50000
Parent Co: Amano Enzyme
Regions Exported to: Central America, South America, Latin America, Canada, Mexico, Caribbean
Percentage of Business in Exporting: 10
Regions Imported from: Asia

41856 Amarillo Mop & Broom Company
801 S Fillmore
Suite 205
Amarillo, TX 79101   806-372-8596
Fax: 806-379-8724 800-955-8596
Mop manufacturer
President: E Bryan
VP: Sue Ann Bryan

Importers & Exporters / A-Z

Estimated Sales: $2.5-5 Million
Number Employees: 10-19
Square Footage: 96000
Type of Packaging: Private Label, Bulk

41857 Amark Packaging Systems
4717 E. 119th Street
PO Box 9824
Kansas City, MO 64134   816-965-9000
Fax: 816-965-9003 amarkpkg@sprintmail.com
www.amarkpackaging.com
Manufacturer, exporter of conveyors, bag closers, sewing machines, heat sealers, scales, and pinch closers; custom fabrications available.
Owner: Bob Mc Cullough
Plant Manager: Jack Groblebe
Estimated Sales: $2.5-5 Million
Number Employees: 10
Number of Products: 15
Square Footage: 80000
Brands Exported: Dura-Pak
Regions Exported to: Central America, Asia, Middle East
Percentage of Business in Exporting: 2
Brands Imported: Simionato
Regions Imported from: Europe
Percentage of Business in Importing: 15

41858 Amazon Trading, Ltd.
257 Siri Dhamma Mawatha
Colombo, 10
Sri Lanka
www.amazontea.biz
Loose leaf teas and tea bags.
Owner: Gamini Jayaweera
CEO: Suranga Herath
Square Footage: 80000

41859 Ambassador Fine Foods
16625 Saticoy St
Van Nuys, CA 91406   818-787-2000
Fax: 818-778-6464 www.ambassadorfoods.com
Wholesaler/distributor and importer of baking ingredients including flour, decorative elements and colorings
Owner: Cory Vestal
VP: Kathy Schreiber
Contact: Peter Seeger
peter.seeger@qzina.com
Office Manager: Victoria Morfin
Estimated Sales: $10-20 Million
Number Employees: 20-49

41860 Ambassador Fine Foods
441 Clifton Blvd.
Clifton, NJ 07013-1834   973-815-1300
Fax: 973-815-0052   800-272-8694
Importer of bakers' and confectioners' supplies including almond and gum paste, sauces, fillings, glazes, shells, chocolate cups, dough and fruit jams; also, frozen cakes
Manager: John Abatemarco
General Manager: Arthur Kretchman
Estimated Sales: $2.5-5 Million
Number Employees: 5-9
Parent Co: Ambassador Fine Foods
Type of Packaging: Food Service, Bulk
Brands Imported: Sweet Inspiration; Cresco Italian
Regions Imported from: Europe
Percentage of Business in Importing: 100

41861 Amber Glo
4140 W Victoria St
Chicago, IL 60646-6727   773-604-8700
Fax: 773-604-4070   866-705-0515
info@emberglo.com www.emberglo.com
Manufacturer and exporter of commercial cooking equipment including gas broilers and steam cookers
President: Teryl A Stanger
Marketing Director: J Kelderhouse
National Sales Manager: Karen Trice
Contact: Joseph Hrabovecky
karent@emberglo.com
Estimated Sales: $3,000,000
Number Employees: 100-249
Number of Brands: 1
Square Footage: 320000
Parent Co: Midco International
Type of Packaging: Food Service
Brands Exported: Ember-Glo
Regions Exported to: Europe, Middle East, Australia
Percentage of Business in Exporting: 10

41862 Ambriola Co
7 Patton Dr
West Caldwell, NJ 07006-6404   973-228-3600
Fax: 201-434-5505   800-962-8224
info@ambriola.com www.ambriola.com
Importer of cheeses
President: Mary Anna Ajemian
CEO: Phil Marfuggi
Estimated Sales: $10-20 Million
Number Employees: 5-9
Brands Imported: Locatelli; Pinna
Regions Imported from: Europe
Percentage of Business in Importing: 100

41863 Amco Metals Indl
461 S 7th Ave
City Of Industry, CA 91746-3119   626-855-2550
Fax: 626-855-2551 info@amcocorporation.com
www.amcocorporation.com
Manufacturer and exporter of racks, utensils, carts, dollies, trucks, mobile storage equipment, shelving, etc
Owner: Fank Ko
amcocorporation@aol.com
Sales Director: Dennis Dominic
Estimated Sales: $ 20-50 Million
Number Employees: 10-19
Square Footage: 240000
Parent Co: Leggett & Platt Storage Products Group
Regions Exported to: Worldwide
Percentage of Business in Exporting: 5

41864 Amende & Schultz Co
1017 Fremont Ave
South Pasadena, CA 91030-3224   323-682-3806
Fax: 626-799-7572
Importer and wholesaler/distributor of fish including lobster, scallops, scampi, etc; serving the food service market
President: Terry Schultz
Vice President: Bruce Beagle
Estimated Sales: $ 5 - 10 Million
Number Employees: 5-9
Percentage of Business in Importing: 50

41865 Ameri Candy
3618 Saint Germaine Ct
Louisville, KY 40207-3722   502-583-1776
Fax: 502-583-1776 omar@americandybar.com
www.americandybar.com
Chocolates
Owner: Omar Patum
omar@americandybar.com
Estimated Sales: Less than $500,000
Number Employees: 1-4
Type of Packaging: Consumer, Private Label, Bulk
Brands Exported: AmeriCandy; Asher
Regions Exported to: Worldwide
Percentage of Business in Exporting: 25

41866 Ameri-Kal Inc
5405 Centime Drive
Suite 400
Wichita Falls, TX 76305-5271   940-322-5400
Nutritional supplements, vitamins, minerals, herbal formulations, sports nutrition products, herb flavored grapeseed oil, capsules, tablets, bulk powder, liquids, soft gel, etc.
Director: Djoko Soejoto
CEO: Tom Soejoto
Director/Of Marketing: Ron Soejoto
Contact: Keith Mccray
keith@ameri-kal.com
Number Employees: 18
Square Footage: 142000
Type of Packaging: Private Label, Bulk
Regions Exported to: Asia, Canada
Percentage of Business in Exporting: 25

41867 America's Classic Foods
1298 Warren Rd
Cambria, CA 93428-4642   805-927-0745
Fax: 805-927-2280 webmail@amcf.com
www.amcf.com
Powdered ice cream mix, ice cream freezers, processor and exporter of mixes including ice cream, baking, doughnut, etc.
President: Monty Rice
mgr@amcf.com
Estimated Sales: $1 Million
Number Employees: 1-4
Square Footage: 120000
Type of Packaging: Food Service, Private Label, Bulk

Brands Exported: America's Classic Foods; Mommy's Choice; Mommy's Helper; Empower; American Creamery
Regions Exported to: Central America, South America, Europe, Asia, Middle East
Percentage of Business in Exporting: 70
Brands Imported: Spaceman
Regions Imported from: Asia

41868 American Agrotrading
P.O.Box Am
P.O. Box 1141
Carmel, CA 93921   831-625-5603
831-622-0936
www.agrotrade.com
Raw, processed, gourmet and specialty food products. Dried bananas, dried apples, pears, prunes, peaches and raisins; almonds, walnuts, pistachios and hazelnuts
General Manager: Eugene Andruchowicz
VP: Eugene Andruchowicz
Estimated Sales: $2.5-5 Million
Number Employees: 1-4
Type of Packaging: Bulk
Regions Imported from: Eduador, Argentina, Chile

41869 American Bag & Burlap Company
36 Arlington St
Chelsea, MA 2150   617-884-7600
Fax: 617-437-7917 info@cormanbag.com
www.cormanbag.com
Manufacturer and importer of bags including burlap, paper and plastic; also, weighing, filling and closing machinery
President: Elliot Corman
VP: Barry Corman
VP: Julie Corman
Estimated Sales: $ 12 Million
Number Employees: 10-19
Square Footage: 50000
Type of Packaging: Private Label
Regions Imported from: South America, Europe, Asia
Percentage of Business in Importing: 30

41870 American Botanicals
24750 Highway Ff
Eolia, MO 63344   573-485-2300
Fax: 573-485-3801   800-684-6070
info@americanbotanicals.com
www.americanbotanicals.com
American herbs.
President: Allen Lockard
ambotncls@aol.com
Quality Control: Denise Kunzweiler
Operations: Chris Zumwalt
Milling Production: Ron Kunzweiler
Purchasing Agent: Tom Duncan
Purchasing Agent: Gennie Martinez
Estimated Sales: $12 Million
Number Employees: 20-49
Number of Products: 200
Square Footage: 35000
Type of Packaging: Bulk
Regions Exported to: Europe, Asia
Percentage of Business in Exporting: 50

41871 American Brush Company
3150 NW 31st Avenue
Suite 3
Portland, OR 97210   503-234-5064
Fax: 503-234-1270   800-826-8492
info@americanbrush.com
www.americanbrush.com
Manufacturer and exporter of industrial and commercial brooms and brushes
President: Laddie M. Wirth, Sr.
CEO: John S. Martin
Vice President: Janine M. Wirth
Contact: Gladys Doern
gladys@americanbrush.com
Estimated Sales: $2.5-5 Million
Number Employees: 10-19
Square Footage: 40000
Regions Exported to: Central America, Europe, Asia
Percentage of Business in Exporting: 15

41872 American Chalkis Intl. Food Corp.
20120 Paseo Del Prado Ste A
Walnut, CA 91789   562-232-4105
Fax: 562-232-4106 info@chalkistomato.us
Tomato products & tomato paste, apricot puree, pomegranate, apple & grape concentrates.

41873 (HQ)American Commodity & Shipping
2102 Gallows Rd # D2
Vienna, VA 22182-3960   703-848-9422
Fax: 703-848-9424 info@americancommodity.com
www.americancommodity.com
Import and export broker of grain, dairy, meat and vegetable oils.
Owner: Ossama Yousef
o.yousef@americancommodity.com
Owner/VP: Ossama Yousef
Number Employees: 1-4
Type of Packaging: Bulk
Regions Exported to: Middle East, North Africa

41874 American Containers Inc
2526 Western Ave
Plymouth, IN 46563-1050   574-936-4068
Fax: 574-936-4036 info@acontainers.com
www.acontainers.com
Manufacturer and exporter of corrugated boxes
Owner: Leonard D Isban
misban@acontainers.com
CFO: Steve Tubes
Estimated Sales: $ 5 - 10 Million
Number Employees: 50-99
Regions Exported to: Worldwide

41875 American Coolair Corp
3604 Mayflower St
Jacksonville, FL 32205-5378   904-389-3646
Fax: 904-387-3449 info@coolair.com
www.coolair.com
Manufacturer and exporter of ventilation fans and systems
President: Harry M Graves Jr
VP: Neal Taylor
Marketing/Sales Manager: Mark Fales
Estimated Sales: $ 20 - 50 Million
Number Employees: 100-249
Square Footage: 110000
Regions Exported to: Worldwide

41876 American Culinary Garden
3508 E Division St
Springfield, MO 65802-2499   417-799-1410
Fax: 417-831-9933 888-831-2433
Balsamic vinegar and soy sauce and also dessert glazes and burgundy soy marinade.
Manager/Sales Director: Gary Anderson
Vice President: Judy Sipe
Order Desk: Lisa Clifford
Estimated Sales: $2.5-5 Million
Number Employees: 1
Type of Packaging: Consumer, Food Service
Regions Exported to: Canada
Percentage of Business in Exporting: 5

41877 American Design Studios
6353 Corte Del Abeto Ste A106
Carlsbad, CA 92011   760-438-8880
Fax: 760-438-8488 800-899-7104
Manufacturer and importer of shirts with names and logos
President: Robert Peritz
Marketing Director: Judy Morrill
Contact: Mike Srtingfellow
mike@mss.net
Estimated Sales: $ 10-20 Million
Number Employees: 10-19
Regions Imported from: Asia

41878 American Eagle Food Machinery
3557 S Halsted St
Chicago, IL 60609   773-376-0800
Fax: 773-376-2010 888-390-0800
Info@AmericanEagleMachine.com
www.americaneaglemachine.com
Manufacturer, importer and exporter of bakery machinery including mixers, bread slicers and grinders-meat tenderizer, dough sheets, dough roller, dividers of rounders and dough molders.
Owner: Spencer Yang
Contact: Didicher Grace
grace@ameagle.biz

Estimated Sales: $1-2,500,000
Number Employees: 10-19
Brands Exported: American Eagle
Regions Exported to: Central America, South America, Canada, Caribbean, Mexico
Regions Imported from: Asia

41879 American European Systems
5456 Louie Lane
Reno, NV 89510-7061   775-852-1114
Fax: 775-852-1163 info@aes-sorma.com
www.aes-sorma.com
Importer and wholesaler/distributor of cutting, peeling, bagging and weighing equipment
President: Robert Sapeta
Sales/Marketing Executive: Don Bergin
Estimated Sales: $ 3 - 5 Million
Number Employees: 5-9
Square Footage: 32000
Regions Exported to: South America, Canada, Mexico
Percentage of Business in Exporting: 15
Brands Imported: Fam; Finis; Spang; Sorma
Regions Imported from: Europe
Percentage of Business in Importing: 100

41880 American Excelsior Co
850 Avenue H E
Arlington, TX 76011-7720   817-385-3500
Fax: 817-649-7816 800-777-7645
www.americanexcelsior.com
Manufacturer, custom molder and exporter of foam packaging products including inserts, contours, protectors, pads, liners and fillers
President, Chief Executive Officer: Terry A. Sadowski
tsadowski@americanexcelsior.com
VP, CFO: Todd A. Eblen
Vice President of Sales and Marketing: Ken Starrett
Vice President of Operations: Kevin Stew
Estimated Sales: $ 5-10 Million
Number Employees: 50-99

41881 (HQ)American Extrusion Intl
498 Prairie Hill Rd
South Beloit, IL 61080-2563   815-624-6616
Fax: 815-624-6628 rickw@americanextrusion.com
www.americanextrusion.info
Supplier and exporter of direct expansion extruders and auxiliary equipment including forced air ovens, fryers, seasoning systems, wear parts, reel cutters, mixers, tumblers and conveyors
President: Richard J Warner
rickw@americanextrusion.com
R&D: Dr. Samir El-Shatter
Director of Sales: Rick Warner
Sales Director: Rick Warner
General Manager: Daniel Thompson
Estimated Sales: $.5-$1 million
Number Employees: 50-99
Square Footage: 54000
Other Locations:
    American Extrusion Internatio
    South Beloit, ILAmerican Extrusion Internatio
Brands Exported: American Extrusion International
Regions Exported to: Worldwide
Percentage of Business in Exporting: 95

41882 American Fine Food Corporation
3600 NW 114th Ave
Doral, FL 33178-1842   305-392-5000
Fax: 305-392-5400
Groceries
President: Sam Amoudi
Marketing/Export Manager: Fadi Ladki
Estimated Sales: $5-10 Million
Number Employees: 5-9

41883 American Fire SprinklerServices, Inc
16221 NW 57th Ave
Hialeah, FL 33014-6709   305-628-0100
Fax: 305-628-3556 Sprinklerheads@bellsouth.net
www.americanfiresprinklers.com
Manufacturer and exporter of sprinkler systems
Owner: Anisa Oweiss
Contact: Omar Oweiss
sprinklerheads@bellsouth.net
Operations Director: Ken Oweis
Estimated Sales: $2.5-5 Million
Number Employees: 10-19
Type of Packaging: Consumer, Food Service
Regions Exported to: Bahamas

Percentage of Business in Exporting: 5

41884 American Flag & Banner Co Inc
28 S Main St
Clawson, MI 48017-2088   248-288-3010
Fax: 248-288-5630 800-892-5168
flagsetc@aol.com
Manufacturer and exporter of flags, pennants and banners
President: William S Miles
flagsetc@aol.com
Sales Manager: Michelle Angle
Estimated Sales: Less Than $500,000
Number Employees: 1-4

41885 American Food & AG Exporter
P.O.Box 810391
Boca Raton, FL 33481-0391   561-994-1188
Fax: 561-994-1610
exporter@phoenixmedianet.com
Publisher: Ken Whitacre
Estimated Sales: $ 10 - 20 Million
Number Employees: 20-49

41886 American Food Equipment
1301 N Miami Ave
Miami, FL 33136-2815   305-377-8991
Fax: 305-358-4328
michael@americanfoodequipment.com
www.americanfoodequipment.com
Manufacturer and supplier of restaurant equipment such as coolers, freezers, and ice machines
Founder: Robert Green
President/Owner: Michael Clements
americanfoodequipment@gmail.com
Estimated Sales: $460,000
Number Employees: 5-9
Square Footage: 28000
Parent Co: American Grinding And Equipment Company.
Type of Packaging: Consumer, Private Label, Bulk
Regions Exported to: Worldwide
Percentage of Business in Exporting: 85
Regions Imported from: Latin America

41887 American Food Equipment Company
21040 Forbes Ave
Hayward, CA 94545-1116   510-783-0255
Fax: 510-783-0409 amfec@amfec.com
www.amfec.com
Manufacturer and exporter of mixers, dumpers, belt and screw conveyors, vacuum stuffers, tumblers and massagers
President: Michael Botto
Quality Control: Melvin Hauss
Contact: Leticia Alexandre
lalexandre@amfec.com
Controller: Simone Manos
Plant Manager: Ron Balthasar
Estimated Sales: $ 5 - 10 Million
Number Employees: 20-49
Square Footage: 80000
Regions Exported to: Worldwide
Percentage of Business in Exporting: 20

41888 American Food Traders
10661 N Kendall Dr Ste 206A
Miami, FL 33176   305-273-7090
Fax: 305-670-6468 www.americanfoodtraders.com
Wholesaler/distributor, importer and exporter of corned beef, peanut butter, juices, foam, plastic and paper disposable goods and sodas
President: Freddy Olcese
Number Employees: 1-4
Type of Packaging: Consumer, Food Service, Private Label, Bulk
Brands Exported: Happy Kids; Fruit Blasters; Super Toro
Regions Exported to: Central America, South America, Caribbean
Percentage of Business in Exporting: 85
Brands Imported: Happy Kids; Fruit Blasters; Super Toro; Toro
Regions Imported from: Central America, South America, Asia
Percentage of Business in Importing: 15

41889 American Foods Group LLC
500 S. Washington St.
Green Bay, WI 54301-4219
    800-345-0293
info@AmericanFoodsGroup.com
www.americanfoodsgroup.com

Beef products.
President/COO: Steven Van Lannen
Chairman/CEO: Tom Rosen
CFO: David Jagodzinske
Executive Vice President: Jeff Jones
Year Founded: 2005
Estimated Sales: $225.5 Million
Number Employees: 4,500
Square Footage: 60000
Parent Co: Rosen's Diversified, Inc.
Type of Packaging: Consumer, Food Service
Other Locations:
　Mitchell, SD
　Sharonville, OHSharonville
Regions Exported to: South America, Europe, Worldwide

41890 American Glass Research
615 Whitestown Rd
Butler, PA 16001-8703　　724-482-2163
　　Fax: 724-482-2767　agrsales@agrintl.com
　　　　　　www.agrintl.com
Quality Assurance & Process Control Systems for the Packaging Industry
CEO: Henry Dimmick Jr
Marketing: David Dineff
Operations: Robert Cowden
Estimated Sales: $ 20 - 50 Million
Number Employees: 100-249
Square Footage: 100000
Regions Exported to: Central America, South America, Europe, Asia, Middle East
Percentage of Business in Exporting: 60

41891 American Hotel RegisterCo
100 S Milwaukee Ave
Vernon Hills, IL 60061-4035
　　Fax: 800-688-9108　800-323-5686
　　　orderdpt@americanhotel.com
　　　www.americanhotel.com
Wholesaler/distributor, importer and exporter of food preparation equipment for hotels/motels, restaurant chains, medical facilities and government and airline food service operators.
Chairman: James F Leahy, Jr.
Vice Chairman: Tom Leahy
President & CEO: Angela Koromopilas
akorompilas@americanhotel.com
Year Founded: 1865
Estimated Sales: $50-100 Million
Number Employees: 500-999
Square Footage: 250000
Type of Packaging: Food Service
Regions Exported to: Central America, South America, Middle East, Latin America, Canada, Caribbean,Mexico
Percentage of Business in Exporting: 5
Regions Imported from: Asia
Percentage of Business in Importing: 5

41892 American Housewares
755 E 134th St
Bronx, NY 10454-3419　　718-665-9500
　　　　Fax: 718-292-0830
　　sales@americanhousewaresmfg.com
　　www.americanhousewaresmfg.com
Manufacturer and exporter of kitchen utensils and equipment including strainers, colanders, basting spoons, forks, pancake turners, mashers, fry baskets, splatter screens, roast racks, kitchen tools and gadgets
Owner: Paul Mayer
strainer4@juno.com
COO: Irving Spiegel
Estimated Sales: $5-10 Million
Number Employees: 50-99
Regions Exported to: Central America, South America, Europe
Percentage of Business in Exporting: 5

41893 American Identity
1520 Albany Pl SE
Orange City, IA 51041　　712-737-4925
　　Fax: 712-737-2408　800-369-2277
Manufacturer, importer and exporter of promotional items including caps, jackets, uniforms, etc
Manager: Larry Sanson
Marketing Manager: Greg Ebel
Contact: Paul Awtry
paul.awtry@americanid.com
Estimated Sales: $50-100 Million
Number Employees: 250-499
Parent Co: American Marketing Industry
Regions Exported to: Worldwide
Brands Imported: Swingster
Regions Imported from: Worldwide
Percentage of Business in Importing: 20

41894 American Importing Co.
550 Kasota Ave SE
Minneapolis, MN 55414
　　　　　　　　855-273-0466
　　　　　www.amportfoods.com
Snack foods including trail mixes, dried fruits and sunflower seeds.
President: Jeff Vogel
Contact: Kim Ewanika
kim@amportfoods.com
Parent Co: Flagstone Foods
Type of Packaging: Consumer, Private Label, Bulk
Regions Exported to: Central America, South America, Europe, Asia, Middle East
Percentage of Business in Exporting: 10
Regions Imported from: Central America, South America, Asia, Middle East
Percentage of Business in Importing: 50

41895 American Instants Inc
117 Bartley Flanders Rd
Flanders, NJ 07836　　973-584-8811
　　sales@americaninstants.com
　　www.americaninstants.com
Instant coffees and teas, cappuccino, granita, chai, fresh brew tea, hot chocolate, drink mixes and liquid coffee extract
President: Martin Wagner
CEO: Christopher Roche
rshipe@americaninstants.com
Director, R&D: Kristin Truglio
Estimated Sales: $30 Million
Number Employees: 50-99
Square Footage: 72000
Type of Packaging: Food Service, Private Label

41896 (HQ)American Italian Pasta Company
1000 Italian Way
Excelsior Springs, MO 64024
　　　　　　　　877-328-7278
　　　　　www.makesameal.com
Dry pasta
President, TreeHouse Foods: Dennis Riordan
CEO, TreeHouse Foods: Sam Reed
Parent Co: TreeHouse Private Brands, Inc.
Type of Packaging: Consumer, Food Service, Private Label, Bulk
Other Locations:
　Columbia, SC
　Kenosha, WIKenosha

41897 American Key Food Products Inc
1 Reuten Dr
Closter, NJ 07624-2115　　201-767-8022
　　Fax: 201-767-9124　877-263-7539
　contactus@akfponline.com　www.akfponline.com
Bulk quantity starches, spices and ingredients.
Manager: Luis Mansueto
VP: Ivan Sarda
Sales: Mel Festejo
Manager: Foss Carter
cfoss@akfponline.com
Operations: Edwin Pacia
Purchasing: Connie Ponce de Leon
Number Employees: 1-4
Type of Packaging: Bulk
Brands Imported: Emsland Starke Potato Starches, King Lion, Rose
Regions Imported from: Central America, South America, Europe, Asia, Middle East
Percentage of Business in Importing: 75

41898 American LEWA
132 Hopping Brook Road
Holliston, MA 01746　　508-429-7403
　　Fax: 508-429-8615　888-539-2123
　　　　　　www.lewa.com
Manufacturer and exporter of precision metering and mixing pumps and systems for blending and proportioning all liquids; also, seal-less controlled volume pumps for process services and moderate high pressures
President/Owner: Mike Meraji
Contact: Larry Bell
houston@amlewa.com
Purchasing Director: Charlie Riordan
Number of Brands: 1
Number of Products: 4
Parent Co: OTT Holding Internationa GmbH
Brands Exported: American LEWA
Regions Exported to: South America, USA, Canada

41899 (HQ)American Labelmark Co
5724 N Pulaski Rd
Chicago, IL 60646-6797　　773-478-0900
　　Fax: 773-478-6054　800-621-5808
　　sales@labelmaster.com　www.labelmaster.com
Manufacturer and exporter of signs including indoor, outdoor, painted and silk screened for restaurants, food manufacturers, etc
President: Alan Schoen
CFO: Ed Kaplan
VP/Marketing: Marilyn Paprocki
Estimated Sales: $30-50 Million
Number Employees: 100-249
Type of Packaging: Food Service

41900 American Laboratories
4410 South 102nd Street
Omaha, NE 68127　　402-339-2494
　　　　　　Fax: 402-339-0801
　　sales@americanlaboratories.com
　　www.americanlaboratories.com
Pancreatin and pepsin enzymes
President: Kenny Soejoto
Chairman/CEO: Jeff Jackson
Senior Vice President: Rod Schake
Vice President of Administration: Janet Giwoyna
Vice President of Quality Assurance: Thomas Langdon
Vice President of Sales: Bret Wyant
Contact: Dan Aase
d.aase@americanlaboratories.com
Vice President of Production: Mark Schufeldt
Purchasing Manager: Tom Hall
Number Employees: 50-99
Number of Products: 960
Type of Packaging: Bulk
Regions Exported to: Central America, South America, Europe, Asia, Middle East
Percentage of Business in Exporting: 25
Regions Imported from: South America, Asia
Percentage of Business in Importing: 10

41901 American Lecithin Company
115 Hurley Road
Unit 2B
Oxford, CT 06478　　203-262-7100
　　Fax: 203-262-7101　800-364-4416
　　　　www.americanlecithin.com
Lecithin products and specialty phospholipids; importer of lecithin
President: Randall Zigmont
Contact: Dianne Bukowski
customerService@americanLecithin.Com
Year Founded: 1928
Estimated Sales: $ .5 - 1 million
Number Employees: 6
Square Footage: 28000
Parent Co: The Lipod Group
Type of Packaging: Consumer, Bulk
Brands Exported: Alcolec
Regions Exported to: South America, Europe
Percentage of Business in Exporting: 10
Regions Imported from: Europe
Percentage of Business in Importing: 30

41902 American Lifts
P.O. Box 1058
Guthrie, OK 73044　　405-282-5200
　　Fax: 405-282-8105　877-360-6777
　　sales@autoquip.com　www.americanlifts.com
Manufacturer, importer and exporter of lifts including hydraulic scissor and stainless steel; also, hydraulic tilters, and pallet trucks
Manager: Clay Brinson
Estimated Sales: $ 10 - 20 Million
Number Employees: 50-99
Square Footage: 140000
Parent Co: Columbs McKinnon Corporation
Regions Exported to: Central America, South America, Europe, Australia, Canada, Caribbean, Mexico
Percentage of Business in Exporting: 10
Regions Imported from: Asia, Canada
Percentage of Business in Importing: 5

41903 American Louver Co
7700 Austin Ave
Skokie, IL 60077-2603　　847-470-3300
　　Fax: 847-470-0420　800-772-0355

Manufacturer and exporter of fluorescent lighting louvers, acrylic mirror sheets, handheld shopping baskets and convex security mirrors
President: Mark Comella
mcomella@plasticade.com
Chairman the Board: Walter Glass
VP: Barry Peterson
CFO: Lucy Polk
Marketing Manager: Butch Cavello
Estimated Sales: $ 20 - 50 Million
Number Employees: 50-99
Regions Exported to: Central America, Europe, Asia
Percentage of Business in Exporting: 10

41904 American Manufacturing-Engrng
4600 W 160th St
Cleveland, OH 44135-2630   440-899-9400
    Fax: 440-899-9401 800-822-9402
    info@ameco-usa.com www.ameco-usa.com
Steel and stainless steel fabricated beverage and liquid distribution/fillers, steam pressure vessels and mixer components; exporter of stainless and regular steel manufactured products
President and CEO: Michael Perkins
Sales/Marketing Manager: Fred Swanson
Sales Engineer: Tom Miller
Estimated Sales: $500,000-$1 Million
Number Employees: 20-49
Square Footage: 200000
Regions Exported to: Central America, South America, Middle East
Percentage of Business in Exporting: 10

41905 American Marketing International
112 Nod Road
Suite 11
Clinton, CT 06413   860-669-4100
    Fax: 860-669-4200 info@amimail.net
    www.amicontract.com
Exporter of commercial kitchen equipment
Owner, President: Victor Mc Grady
Managing Director, India: K.N. Dattatraya
CFO: Debbie Fetherson
Vice President: John Kozub
Senior Sales Coordinator: Carol Vaillancourt
Chain Accounts Manager: John Kozub
Estimated Sales: $ .5 - 1 million
Number Employees: 5-9
Square Footage: 8000

41906 American Material Handling Inc
9013 Highway 165
PO Box 17878
N Little Rock, AR 72117-9728   501-375-6611
    Fax: 501-375-8931 800-482-5801
    sales@amermaterial.com www.amermaterial.com
Wholesaler/distributor and exporter of material handling systems; also, design consultant
Owner: Jackie Lackie
General Manager: Jay Carman
VP of Marketing: Albert Redding
Sales Manager: Adam Dickens
Manager: Adam Dickens
adam.dickens@amermaterial.com
Estimated Sales: $5-10 Million
Number Employees: 10-19
Square Footage: 80000
Parent Co: Cetrum Industries
Regions Exported to: Canada, Latin America
Percentage of Business in Exporting: 10

41907 American Metalcraft Inc
3708 River Rd
Suite 800
Franklin Park, IL 60131-2158   708-345-1177
    Fax: 708-345-5758 info@amnow.com
    www.amnow.com
Manufacturer, importer, exporter and wholesaler/distributor of stainless steel restaurant/bar tabletop supplies, funnels, pizza trays and food covers; serving the food service market
President: David Kahn
davidk@amnow.com
Sales Manager: Richard Packer
Estimated Sales: $10-20 Million
Number Employees: 50-99
Square Footage: 240000
Type of Packaging: Food Service
Regions Exported to: Central America, South America, Europe, Asia, Middle East
Percentage of Business in Exporting: 10

Regions Imported from: Asia
Percentage of Business in Importing: 10

41908 American National Rubber
P.O. Box 878
Ceredo, WV 25507-6396   304-453-1311
    Fax: 304-453-2347 www.anro.com
Manufacturer and exporter of sponge rubber including gaskets and seals
Sales Manager: Ed Littlehales
Estimated Sales: $ 20-50 Million
Number Employees: 250-500
Regions Exported to: Europe, Canada

41909 American Natural & Organic
4180 Business Center Dr
Fremont, CA 94538-6354   510-440-1044
    info@organicspices.com
    www.organicspices.com
Natural and organic spices
CEO & President: John Chansari
Contact: Clara Bonner
clara@organicspices.com
Estimated Sales: $1.2 Million
Number Employees: 5-9
Type of Packaging: Bulk

41910 American Packaging Machinery
2550 S Eastwood Dr
Woodstock, IL 60098-9112   815-337-8580
    Fax: 815-337-8583 888-755-2705
    sales@apm-machinery.com
    www.americanpackaging-machinery.com
High speed servo controlled shrink wrapping systems and high speed shrink bundling equipment
Owner: Tadiya Peric
apmmachinery@aol.com
Estimated Sales: $ 10 - 20 000,000
Number Employees: 10-19
Type of Packaging: Bulk
Regions Exported to: Worldwide
Percentage of Business in Exporting: 2

41911 American Panel Corp
5800 SE 78th St
Ocala, FL 34472-3412   352-245-7055
    Fax: 352-245-0726 800-327-3015
    sales@americanpanel.com
    www.americanpanel.com
Manufacturer and exporter of walk-in coolers and freezers, blast chillers, refrigerated warehouses and refrigeration systems
President: Danny E Duncan
danny@americanpanel.com
CEO: Marvin Duncan
VP: Harmon Lewis
Sales Manager: Kevin Graham
Sales Associate: Jenn Duncan
Estimated Sales: $ 20 - 50 Million
Number Employees: 100-249
Square Footage: 100000
Type of Packaging: Food Service
Regions Exported to: Worldwide
Percentage of Business in Exporting: 5

41912 American Pasien Co
109 Elbow Ln
Burlington, NJ 08016-4123   609-387-3130
    Fax: 609-387-7204 info@109elbow.com
    www.amcocustomdrying.biz
Functional protein ingredients and protein polymers for edible applications
CEO: Jamil Ahmed
jamilahmed@americancasein.com
CEO: Dennis Bobker
CFO: Jack Pipala
Account Manager: Jane Macey
Sales Manager: Cliff Lang
Human Resources Manager/IT Manager: Ellen Iuliucci
Facilities Manager: Chris Lockard
Estimated Sales: $5.8 Million
Number Employees: 20-49
Square Footage: 120000
Type of Packaging: Bulk
Regions Exported to: Asia, Latin America
Percentage of Business in Exporting: 10

41913 American Pop Corn Co
1 Fun Pl
P.O. Box 178
Sioux City, IA 51102   712-239-1232
    Fax: 712-239-1268 henry@jollytime-export.com
    www.jollytime.com

Various flavours of microwavable and pre-popped popcorn.
President: Jeff Naslund
naslund@americanpopdigital.com
Chairman: Carlton Smith
VP, Production: Greg Hoffman
Year Founded: 1914
Estimated Sales: $30.60 Million
Number Employees: 185
Type of Packaging: Consumer, Bulk
Brands Exported: Jolly Time Pop Corn
Regions Exported to: Worldwide

41914 American Production Co Inc
2734 Spring St
Redwood City, CA 94063-3524   650-368-5334
    Fax: 650-368-4547 www.americanproduction.com
Manufacturer and exporter of commercial and industrial stainless steel insulated food and beverage containers and thermal dispensers
Owner: Owen Conley
info@americanproduction.com
Estimated Sales: $2.5-5 Million
Number Employees: 5-9
Parent Co: Tilley Manufacturing Company
Regions Exported to: Canada

41915 American Range
13592 Desmond St
Pacoima, CA 91331-2315   818-897-0808
    Fax: 818-897-1670 888-753-9898
    info@americanrange.com
    www.americanrange.com
Manufacturer and exporter of commercial cooking equipment including exhaust hoods, ranges, ovens, hot plates, open burners, stock pot stoves, broilers, griddles, woks, cheese melters, chicken rotisseries, etc
President: Courtney Cochran
courtney.cochran@fetzer.com
Quality Control: Cristie Merriot
Estimated Sales: $ 10 - 20 Million
Number Employees: 100-249
Square Footage: 70000
Brands Exported: American Range
Regions Exported to: Central America, South America, Europe, Asia, Middle East
Percentage of Business in Exporting: 10

41916 American Renolit Corp LA
6900 Elm St
Commerce, CA 90040-2625   323-721-2720
    Fax: 323-725-6466 www.renolit.com
Manufacturer and exporter of plastic materials including PVC films, compounds and roll stock for packaging and devices requiring food grade applications
President: Rich Sterndahl
rich.sterndahl@renolit.com
Finance Executive: Laurie Dunbar
VP Sales: Mark Stern
Estimated Sales: $10-20 Million
Number Employees: 100-249
Square Footage: 170000
Regions Exported to: Worldwide
Percentage of Business in Exporting: 25

41917 American Roland Food Corporation
71 W 23rd St
New York, NY 10010-4102   212-741-8290
      800-221-4030
    salessupport@rolandfood.com
    www.rolandfood.com
Importer and exporter of vegetables, seafood, condiments, olive oil and specialty foods; wholesaler/distributor of general line items, canned fruit, seafood and specialty food; serving the food service market.
CEO: Charles Scheidt
Marketing Director: Joanne Scheidt
Contact: Tyrus Brailey
tyrus.r.brailey@jpmorgan.com
Estimated Sales: $ .5 - 1 million
Number Employees: 50-99
Type of Packaging: Consumer, Food Service, Bulk
Brands Exported: Roland; Consul
Regions Exported to: Central America, South America, Caribbean, Latin America, Mexico, Canada
Brands Imported: Roland; Costamar; Don Bruno; Consul
Regions Imported from: Worldwide
Percentage of Business in Importing: 99

Importers & Exporters / A-Z

41918 American Sales & Marketing
PO Box 95
Bahama, NC 27503   919-471-2980
                      Fax: 919-471-2980
Broker, retail, wholesale, grocer of general merchandise.
Owner: Charles Roedel

41919 American Seafood Imports Inc.
560 Sylvan Ave
Suite 1010
Englewood Cliffs, NJ 07632-3124   201-568-2525
          Fax: 201-568-7737   800-989-3939
          charlie@americanseafoodimports.com
          www.americanseafoodimports.com
Frozen seafood
Partner: Charlie Goldstein
cherlie@americanseafoodimports.com
Partner: George Lemery
Partner: Brian Lemery
Estimated Sales: $ 20 - 50 Million
Number Employees: 10-19
Type of Packaging: Consumer, Food Service, Private Label, Bulk
Regions Exported to: Central America, Europe, Middle East
Percentage of Business in Exporting: 15
Brands Imported: Capt's Catch; Sea Jewel; Mayflower
Regions Imported from: Central America, South America, Asia, Middle East
Percentage of Business in Importing: 75

41920 American Seafoods
Market Place Tower
2025 First Ave, Suite 900
Seattle, WA 98121   206-448-0300
          www.americanseafoods.com
Seafood, including Alaska pollock, Pacific Hake, Yellowfin sole, and Pacific cod.
Chief Executive Officer: Mikel Durham
President: Inge Andreassen
Chief Financial Officer: Kevin McMenimen
EVP, Product & Business Development: Scott McNair
scott.mcnair@americanseafoods.com
Estimated Sales: $430 Million
Number Employees: 1000+
Type of Packaging: Bulk
Other Locations:
   Seattle, WA
   Dutch Harbor, AK
   New Bedford, MA
   Greensboro, ALDutch Harbor
Regions Exported to: Worldwide
Percentage of Business in Exporting: 60

41921 (HQ)American Solving Inc.
6519 Eastland Rd
Unit 5
Brook Park, OH 44142-1347   440-234-7373
         Fax: 440-234-9112   440-234-2285
         sales@solvinginc.com www.solvinginc.com
Manufacturer, importer and exporter of pneumatic load-handling solutions
President: Andre Alho
andre.alho@solving.com
General Manager: Orley Aten
General Manager: Stanley Aten
Production Manager: Doug Eckert
Estimated Sales: $ 3 - 5 Million
Number Employees: 5-9
Square Footage: 12000
Brands Exported: Solving; American Solving
Regions Exported to: South America, Canada
Percentage of Business in Exporting: 30
Brands Imported: Solving, Aerdon
Regions Imported from: South America, Canada
Percentage of Business in Importing: 40

41922 American Specialty Coffee & Culinary
1360 Union Hill Road
Suite E
Alpharetta, GA 30004   770-754-0092
        Fax: 770-754-0093   800-472-5282
Wholesaler/distributor and importer of food service equipment including espresso/cappuccino machines, coffee grinders, granita machines, deli showcases, pasta machinery, pasta cookers, wood-fired pizza ovens and water filtrationsystems; also, espresso coffee
President: Ron Sciortino
r.sciortino@americanspecialtycoffee.com
Estimated Sales: 1-5 Million
Number Employees: 5-9
Square Footage: 20000
Parent Co: ASCC
Brands Imported: La Cimbali
Regions Imported from: Europe
Percentage of Business in Importing: 75

41923 American Star Cork Company
33-53 62nd Street
P.O. Box 770449
Woodside, NY 11377   718-335-3000
         Fax: 718-335-3037   800-338-3581
         www.amstarcork.com
Manufacturer, exporter and importer of cork and cork products
President: Thomas Petrosino
amstarcork@gmail.com
Estimated Sales: $ .5 - 1 million
Number Employees: 1-4
Regions Exported to: Worldwide
Regions Imported from: Portugal

41924 American Store Fixtures
7700 Austin Avenue
Skokie, IL 60077-2603
                          Fax: 847-966-8074
Manufacturer and exporter of shopping baskets, security mirrors
CEO: Geoff Glass
CFO: Lucy Polk
Quality Control: Carol Salas
Marketing: Donna Kelner
Sales Manager: Debi Greenberg
Public Relations: Donna Kelner
Operations: Carol Salas
Plant Manager: Carol Salas
Estimated Sales: $ 1 - 5 Million
Number Employees: 100-250
Square Footage: 480000
Parent Co: American Louver
Regions Exported to: Central America, Europe, Asia, Middle East, Australia
Percentage of Business in Exporting: 10

41925 American Tartaric Products
1865 Palmer Ave
Larchmont, NY 10538   914-834-1881
        Fax: 914-834-4611 atp@americantartaric.com
        www.americantartaric.com
Tartaric acid, cream of tartar and baking powder
President: Emilio Zanin
Vice President: Luca Zanin
Estimated Sales: $5-10 Million
Number Employees: 27
Other Locations:
   American Tartaric Products
   Windsor, CAAmerican Tartaric Products

41926 American Time & Signal Co
140 3rd St
PO Box 707
Dassel, MN 55325-4511   320-275-2101
       Fax: 320-275-2603   800-328-8996
       theclockexperts@atsclock.com
       www.american-time.com
Manufacturer and exporter of food preparation timers and clocks
President: Dieter Pape
dpape@atsclock.com
Estimated Sales: $10-20 Million
Number Employees: 50-99
Square Footage: 80000
Brands Exported: James Remind-O-Timer
Regions Exported to: Central America, South America, Europe, Asia, Middle East

41927 American Trading Company
866 Americas Rm 901
New York, NY 10001   212-685-0081
         Fax: 212-937-6839   800-275-0106
Wholesaler/distributor, importer and exporter of linens and uniforms
President/CEO: Henry Salem
Purchasing: Henry Salem
Estimated Sales: $1 Million
Number Employees: 10
Square Footage: 40000
Type of Packaging: Bulk
Brands Exported: Textiles, Tablecloth - Placemats - Napkins
Regions Exported to: Central America
Brands Imported: American Chinese
Regions Imported from: South America, Europe, Asia, Middle East
Percentage of Business in Importing: 60

41928 American Ultraviolet Co
212 S Mount Zion Rd
Lebanon, IN 46052-9479   765-483-9514
          Fax: 765-483-9525   800-288-9288
          www.americanultraviolet.com
Manufacturer and exporter of germicidal ultraviolet air and water systems for air and water sterilization
President: Meredith C Stines
mstines@auvco.com
Estimated Sales: $ 10 - 20 Million
Number Employees: 100-249
Number of Brands: 4
Square Footage: 70000
Type of Packaging: Food Service
Regions Exported to: Central America, South America, Europe, Asia, Middle East
Percentage of Business in Exporting: 20

41929 American Water Broom
3565 Mccall Pl
Doraville, GA 30340-2801   770-451-2000
         Fax: 770-455-4478   800-241-6565
         info@waterbrooms.com www.waterbrooms.com
Manufacturer and exporter of commercial and residential high pressure water brooms
Vice President: Archie Merlin
amerlin@waterbrooms.com
VP: Beverly Roberts
Number Employees: 5-9
Brands Exported: American Water Brooms
Regions Exported to: Central America, South America, Europe, Asia, Middle East, Mexico, Canada, Latin America, Caribbean
Percentage of Business in Exporting: 2

41930 American Wax Co Inc
3930 Review Ave
PO Box 1943
Long Island City, NY 11101-2020   718-361-4820
                    Fax: 718-482-9366
          solutions@cleaning-solutions.com
                  www.heathsprings.net
Manufacturer and exporter of detergents, deodorants, disinfectants, germicides, floor polish and soap
President: Michelle Devito
michelled@cleaning-solutions.com
Vice President: Ronald Ingber
Sales Manager: Allen Winik
Purchasing Manager: Ron Ingber
Estimated Sales: $ 2.5 - 5 Million
Number Employees: 20-49
Square Footage: 124000
Regions Exported to: South America, Europe, Asia, Middle East, Canada, Caribbean, Australia
Percentage of Business in Exporting: 5

41931 (HQ)Americana Art China Company
PO Box 310
Sebring, OH 44672   330-938-6133
         Fax: 330-938-9546   800-233-6133
         amerimug@sbcglobal.net
Custom decorator of ceramic and glassware.
President/CEO: James Puckett
Research & Development: Lisa Cox
Manager of Quality Control: Wendy Davidson
Marketing Director: Jim Puckett
Operations: Jim Puckett
Estimated Sales: $1-3 Million
Number Employees: 32
Number of Products: 126
Square Footage: 80000
Type of Packaging: Private Label, Bulk
Other Locations:
   Americana Art China Co.
   Sebring, OHAmericana Art China Co.
Regions Exported to: Europe, Middle East
Percentage of Business in Exporting: 10
Regions Imported from: Asia
Percentage of Business in Importing: 80

41932 Americana Marketing
840 Tourmaline Dr
Newbury Park, CA 91320   805-499-0451
         Fax: 805-499-4668   800-742-7520
         fdi@follmerdevelopment.com
         www.follmerdevelopment.com
Aerosol nonstick cooking, baking and flavor sprays

President/CEO: Garrett Follmer
fdi@follmerdevelopment.com
Sales/Marketing VP: David McKenzie
Number Employees: 50-99
Type of Packaging: Consumer, Food Service, Private Label
Brands Exported: Pure & Simple
Regions Exported to: Asia, Canada, Mexico
Percentage of Business in Exporting: 10

41933 Americo
601 E Barton Ave
West Memphis, AR 72301-2011   870-735-4848
          Fax: 870-735-4129 800-626-2350
Laminated and vinyl table covers; also, upholstery fabrics
President: Ed Straub
ed@americo-inc.com
Chairman of the Board: Wallace Dunbar
Sales Director: Jerry Van Houten
Estimated Sales: $1-2.5 Million
Number Employees: 20-49

41934 Ameriglobe LLC
153 S Long St
Lafayette, LA 70506-3019   337-234-3211
          Fax: 337-234-3213
marlener@ameriglobe-fibc.com
www.ameriglobe-fibc.com
Bulk bags and weigh/fill stations; also, bulk bag refurbishing services available
President: Daniel R Schnaars
dans@ameriglobe-fibc.com
CFO: Randy Girourard
Marketing Director: Blaine Beck
Sales Director: Marlene Rodrigue
Estimated Sales: $50-100 Million
Number Employees: 50-99

41935 Ameripak Packaging Equipment
2001 County Line Rd
Warrington, PA 18976-2486   215-343-1530
          Fax: 215-343-5293 www.opschuman.com
Packaging equipment including horizontal wrappers, filled tray sealers, rigid box and thermoforming; rebuilt equipment available; importer of thermoforming equipment; exporter of rigid box machinery and horizontal wrappers
President: William T Schuman
schumanwt@opschuman.com
VP Marketing/Sales: Phil Kelly
Estimated Sales: $5-10 Million
Number Employees: 20-49
Number of Products: 5
Square Footage: 240000
Parent Co: SKS Equipment Company
Brands Exported: AmeriPak
Regions Exported to: Central America, Europe, Asia, Canada, Caribbean, Mexico
Percentage of Business in Exporting: 10
Brands Imported: Illig
Regions Imported from: Europe
Percentage of Business in Importing: 10

41936 Ameristamp/Sign-A-Rama
1300 N Royal Ave
Evansville, IN 47715-7808   812-477-7763
          Fax: 812-477-7898 800-543-6693
websales@SignsOverAmerica.com
www.signsoveramerica.com
Manufacturer and exporter of marking devices, including rubber stamps
Owner: Walter Valiant
walter@signsoveramerica.com
VP of Public Relations: Grant Valiant
Estimated Sales: $ 1-2.5 Million
Number Employees: 10-19
Square Footage: 6000
Type of Packaging: Consumer, Food Service, Bulk
Regions Exported to: Canada
Percentage of Business in Exporting: 1

41937 Amerivacs
1518 Lancaster Point Way
San Diego, CA 92154-7700   619-498-8227
          Fax: 619-498-8222 info@amerivacs.com
www.amerivacs.com
Clean room compatible chamber and retractable nozzle vacuum sealers with gas purge for all heat sealable bags, including all ESD bags by using quiet, nonparticle generating, maintenance-free compressed air-driven vacuum pumps. Standardimpulse sealers also available. One week trial period. Custom designs upon request. One year limited warranty. Made in the USA
President: Peter Tadlock
petertadlock@amerivacs.com
Estimated Sales: $ 1 - 2.5 Million
Number Employees: 1-4
Number of Brands: 1
Number of Products: 8
Square Footage: 8000
Brands Exported: Amerivacs
Regions Exported to: Worldwide
Percentage of Business in Exporting: 10

41938 Amerol Chemical Corporation
71 Carolyn Blvd
Farmingdale, NY 11735   631-694-4700
          Fax: 631-694-9177
Synthetic and natural antioxidants and mixed tocopherols.
President: C J Monteleone
CEO: D Sartorio
CFO: A Diaz
R&D: Y Liang
Marketing: S Jean Charles
Operations: F Monteleone
Production: D Ghiglieri
Purchasing Director: D Raleigh
Estimated Sales: $300,000-500,000
Number Employees: 1-4
Square Footage: 46000
Type of Packaging: Private Label, Bulk
Brands Exported: Amerol Antioxidants

41939 Ames Company, Inc
PO Box 46
45 Pine Hill Road
New Ringgold, PA 17960   610-750-1032
          Fax: 413-604-0541 info@theingredientstore.com
www.theingredientstore.com
Vegetarian meat analogs and dry mixes
Owner: Joseph Ames, Sr.
Number Employees: 5-9
Percentage of Business in Exporting: 50
Regions Imported from: Europe

41940 Ames International Inc
4401 Industry Dr E
Bldg. A
Fife, WA 98424-1832   253-946-4779
          Fax: 253-926-4127 888-469-2637
questions@emilyschocolates.com
www.emilyschocolates.com
Nut products, gourmet chocolates and cookies
President: George Paulose
gpaulose@amesinternational.com
VP: Susan Paulose
Marketing: Amy Paulose
Estimated Sales: $5-10 Million
Number Employees: 50-99
Square Footage: 220000
Type of Packaging: Private Label, Bulk
Regions Exported to: Asia
Percentage of Business in Exporting: 75

41941 Amest Food
Stony Point, NY 10980   718-360-0886
          info@amest.com
www.amest.com
Estonian chocolate, marzipan and dark rye bread

41942 Ametco Manufacturing Corp
4326 Hamann Pkwy
Willoughby, OH 44094-5626   440-951-4300
          Fax: 440-951-2542 800-321-7042
ametco@ametco.com www.ametco.com
Iron and steel security fencing; also, perforated plastics and expanded, perforated, heavy weld and bar metal gratings
President: Greg Mitrovich
ametco@ametco.com
Sales Manager: Ludwig Weber
Estimated Sales: $5-10,000,000
Number Employees: 20-49
Regions Imported from: Italy
Percentage of Business in Importing: 10

41943 Ametek
900 E Clymer Ave
Sellersville, PA 18960-2628   215-257-6531
    Fax: 215-257-4711 chatillon.fl-lar@ametek.com
www.usgauge.com
Manufacturer and exporter of pressure and temperature gauges
Manager: Joe Karpov
Sales Manager: Amil Demicco
Estimated Sales: $ 1 - 5 Million
Number Employees: 500-999
Parent Co: Ametek
Regions Exported to: Worldwide
Percentage of Business in Exporting: 25

41944 Amick Farms LLC
2079 Batesburg Hwy.
Batesburg, SC 29006   803-532-1400
          Fax: 803-532-1491 800-926-4257
www.amickfarms.com
Chicken products.
Chief Executive Officer: Ben Harrison
bharrison@amickfarms.com
Vice President, Sales & Marketing: Steve Kernen
Year Founded: 1941
Estimated Sales: $100-499 Million
Number Employees: 1000-4999
Number of Brands: 2
Square Footage: 10992
Parent Co: OSI Industries, LLC
Type of Packaging: Consumer, Food Service, Private Label, Bulk
Other Locations:
  Hurlock, MD
Regions Exported to: Worldwide

41945 Amida Food Corp
17531 Railroad St # L
City Of Industry, CA 91748-1106   626-581-0889
          Fax: 626-965-8780 www.amidafoodusa.com
Owner: K Chen
Estimated Sales: $ 10 - 20 Million
Number Employees: 10-19

41946 Amigos Canning Company
4669 Highway 90 W
San Antonio, TX 78237   210-798-5360
          www.amigosfoods.com
Mexican foods, including refried beans, dips, sauces, peppers, and taco shells.
Manager: Clint McNew
Controller: Ivan Kerr
ikerr@amigosfoods.com
Sales Contact: Heather McNew
Plant Manager: Carlos Menchaca
Year Founded: 1925
Estimated Sales: $11.5 Million
Number Employees: 90
Square Footage: 39000
Parent Co: Durrset Amigos
Type of Packaging: Consumer, Private Label
Brands Exported: Amigos
Regions Exported to: Europe, Middle East, Canada, Mexico
Percentage of Business in Exporting: 5

41947 Amira Foods
1315 E Saint Andrew Place
Suite D
Santa Ana, CA 92705   714-966-2153
          Fax: 714-966-2154 amirafoods@amirafoods.com
www.amirafoods.com
Rice
Marketing: Alireza Yazdi

41948 Amity Packing Co Inc
4220 S Kildare Ave
Chicago, IL 60632-3930   773-475-9398
          Fax: 312-942-0413 800-837-0270
byanz@amitypacking.com www.amitypacking.com
Fresh and frozen pork and beef products.
President: Richard T Samuel
Vice President: Matt Buol
VP Sales/Marketing: Tom Laplant
Contact: Ray Green
rgreen@amitypacking.com
Operations Manager: Jim Stamm
Estimated Sales: $110,000
Number Employees: 10-19
Square Footage: 11224

Importers & Exporters / A-Z

41949 Ammeraal Beltech Inc
750 Saint Louis Ave
Skokie, IL 60076-4033
847-673-6720
Fax: 847-673-6373   800-323-4170
info@ammeraalbeltechusa.com
www.ammeraal-beltech.com
Manufacturer, importer and exporter of belts for packaging machinery and the processing of cookies, crackers, confectionery items, bread, rolls, meat and poultry
President: Jeffrey W Nank
Vice President: Jim Ekedahl
Estimated Sales: $ 20-50 Million
Number Employees: 50-99
Square Footage: 55000
Parent Co: Verseidag
Brands Exported: Polytek; Burtek; Rapptex; Rapplon
Regions Exported to: Central America, South America, Europe, Canada, Caribbean, Latin America, Mexico
Percentage of Business in Exporting: 10
Regions Imported from: Europe
Percentage of Business in Importing: 20

41950 Ammirati Inc
500 Fifth Ave
Pelham, NY 10803-1206
914-738-2500
Fax: 914-738-2503   800-441-8101
www.ammiraticoffee.com
Importer and wholesaler/distributor of espresso machines; serving the food service market. La Cimbali espresso machines and La Vazza premium coffees
Owner: T J Taratetta
info@ammiraticoffee.com
Estimated Sales: $2.5-5 Million
Number Employees: 20-49
Type of Packaging: Food Service
Regions Imported from: Italy

41951 Amoretti
451 Lombard St
Oxnard, CA 93030-5143
805-983-2903
Fax: 818-718-0204   800-266-7388
www.amoretti.com
Nut flour, paste and butter
Founder, CEO: Jack Barsoumian
info@amoretti.com
Marketing President: Maral Barsoumian
Manufacturing President: Ara Barsoumian
Year Founded: 1989
Estimated Sales: $20+ Million
Number Employees: 20-49
Type of Packaging: Food Service, Bulk
Brands Exported: Amoretti; Capriccio
Regions Exported to: Worldwide

41952 Ampak
4580 E 71st St
Cleveland, OH 44125
216-341-2022
Fax: 216-341-2163   800-342-6329
custserv@ampakco.com
www.heatsealco.com/about-ampak
Manufacturer and exporter of packaging machinery including bag/cup wrapping, skin and die cutting
Southeast Equipment Sales Manager: Dan Barnes
Customer Service: Troy Roberts
General Manager: Les Szakallas
Estimated Sales: $5-10 Million
Number Employees: 20-49
Square Footage: 80000
Parent Co: Heat Sealing Equipment Manufacturing Company
Brands Exported: Ampak; Maxima; Shipmate; Master; Rotocut
Regions Exported to: Worldwide
Percentage of Business in Exporting: 10

41953 Ampak Seafoods Corporation
315 Whitney Ave
New Haven, CT 06511-3715
203-786-5121
Fax: 203-786-5120
Importer and wholesaler/distributor of pasteurized crabmeat; serving the food service market
CEO: Barry White
Estimated Sales: $2.5-5 Million
Number Employees: 1-4
Square Footage: 2000
Type of Packaging: Consumer, Food Service, Private Label
Brands Imported: LongWharf
Regions Imported from: Asia
Percentage of Business in Importing: 100

41954 Ampco Pumps Co Inc
2045 W Mill Rd
Milwaukee, WI 53209-3444
414-540-1597
Fax: 414-643-4452   800-737-8671
ampcocs@ampcopumps.com
www.ampcopumps.com
Manufacturer and exporter of pumps including centrifugal, sanitary, wastewater and water
Owner: Mike Nicholson
CFO: Loori Neisner
R&D: Loori Neisner
Quality Control: Oori Neisner
Midwestern Regional Manager: Matt Schultz
mnicholson@ampcopumps.com
Estimated Sales: $ 1 - 2.5 Million
Number Employees: 10-19
Regions Exported to: Worldwide
Percentage of Business in Exporting: 5

41955 Amphora International
20622 Canada Rd
Lake Forest, CA 92630
949-609-0600
888-380-4808
amphorafoods.com
Olive oil, organic dried fruit, condiments and spices
Number of Brands: 1
Number of Products: 19
Type of Packaging: Consumer
Regions Imported from: Europe

41956 Ample Industries
4000 Commerce Center Dr
Franklin, OH 45005
937-746-9700
Fax: 937-746-2234   888-818-9700
Carry-out containers, food trays, french fry and pizza boxes and hot dog clam shells; exporter of pizza boxes
Vice President Of Sales: David Ernst
Contact: Ty Gardner
tgardner@huhtamaki.com
General Manager: Robert Fairchild, Jr.
Plant Manager: Bill Bausmith
Estimated Sales: $50 Million
Number Employees: 100-249
Square Footage: 110000
Regions Exported to: Canada, Mexico
Percentage of Business in Exporting: 1

41957 Amrita Snacks
Hartsdale, NY 10530
888-728-7779
www.amritahealthfoods.com
Plant-based, vegan, all-natural protein bars, protein snack bites and energy bars in various flavors
Founder/CEO: Arshad Bahl
Number of Brands: 1
Number of Products: 21
Type of Packaging: Consumer, Private Label
Brands Exported: Amrita
Regions Exported to: USA, Canada

41958 Amsterdam Printing & Litho Inc
166 Wallins Corners Rd
Amsterdam, NY 12010-1817
518-842-6000
Fax: 518-843-5204   800-203-9917
cs@amsterdamprinting.com
www.amsterdamprinting.com
Writing instruments including fine point, felt tip and ball point pens; also, advertising specialties including calendars, mugs, etc.; importer of roller ball pens
President: Robert Rosenthal
HR Executive: Donna Graham
dgraham@banyanincentives.com
Sales/Marketing: Jim Zuzzolo
Purchasing Manager: David Laemle
Estimated Sales: $10-20 Million
Number Employees: 500-999
Square Footage: 52000
Regions Imported from: Worldwide
Percentage of Business in Importing: 32

41959 Amtab Manufacturing Corp
652 N Highland Ave
Aurora, IL 60506-2940
630-301-7600
Fax: 312-421-3448   800-878-2257
info@amtab.com   www.amtab.com
Manufacturer and exporter of folding banquet tables
Owner: Greg Hanusiak
g_hanusiak@amtab.com
CEO: Chris Cornier
VP: Greg Hanusiak
Estimated Sales: $ 5-10 Million
Number Employees: 20-49
Square Footage: 70000
Type of Packaging: Food Service, Private Label
Regions Exported to: Europe, Middle East, Canada
Percentage of Business in Exporting: 10

41960 Amtekco
1205 Refugee Rd
Columbus, OH 43207-2114
614-228-6590
Fax: 614-737-8017   800-336-4677
www.amtekco.com
Manufacturer and exporter of stainless steel tables, commercial sinks, wood cabinets, fixtures, table tops, bars and back bars.
President/Owner: Bruce Wasserstrom
brucewasserstrom@amtekco.com
CFO: Robert Hudgins
Research & Development: Roger Henry
Sales Manager: Nancy Green
Public Relations: Adena Bogdan
Plant Manager: Ron Fishking
Purchasing Manager: Hans Woschkolup
Estimated Sales: $18-20 Million
Number Employees: 100-249
Square Footage: 400000
Type of Packaging: Bulk
Regions Exported to: Worldwide

41961 Amtrade Inc.
303 5th Ave
Suite 1303
New York, NY 10016
212-725-0679
Fax: 212-725-0718   800-446-3538
tejensen@aol.com   www.amtradefood.com
Instant mixes, spices, curries, ready to eat and frozen foods
President/Owner: Tejen Sen
Estimated Sales: $6 Million
Number Employees: 8

41962 Amy's Kitchen Inc
2330 Northpoint Pkwy
Santa Rosa, CA 95407
707-781-6600
www.amys.com
Frozen organic meals and entrees; also canned soups and bottled pasta sauces.
Co-Owner: Andy Berliner
Co-Owner: Rachel Berliner
EVP: Jack Chipman
Director, Contract Manufacturing: Norma Mery
Estimated Sales: $92.3 Million
Number of Brands: 1
Number of Products: 146
Square Footage: 100000
Type of Packaging: Consumer, Food Service
Brands Exported: Amy's
Regions Exported to: Europe, Asia, Canada
Percentage of Business in Exporting: 5

41963 AnaCon Foods Company
1145 Main St
PO Box 651
Atchison, KS 66002
913-367-2885
Fax: 913-367-1794   800-328-0291
anacon@journey.com
Processor and exporter of simulated nut and fruit particulates and analogs
Executive Director: Tom Miller
VP Sales/Marketing: Jane Hallas
Director Operations: Marvin Mikkelson
Estimated Sales: $2.5-5 Million
Number Employees: 20-49

41964 Anabol Naturals
1550 Mansfield St
Santa Cruz, CA 95062-1720
831-479-1403
Fax: 831-479-1406   800-426-2265
www.anabolnaturals.com
Sports nutrition supplements
President: Roger Prince
anabol@cruzio.com
Estimated Sales: $500,000-$1 Million
Number Employees: 5-9
Square Footage: 20000
Brands Exported: Anabol Naturals
Regions Exported to: South America, Europe, Asia, Middle East
Percentage of Business in Exporting: 10

41965 Analite
24 Newtown Plz
Plainview, NY 11803-4506
516-752-1818
Fax: 516-752-0554   800-229-3357

Manufacturer and exporter of relative humidity and temperature probes, controllers and transmitters
President: Morris Wasser
Vice President: Julius Levin
Estimated Sales: $2.5-5 Million
Number Employees: 10-19
Square Footage: 15200
Brands Exported: Humitran-C; Humitran-T; Humitran-DP; Humitran
Regions Exported to: Central America, South America, Europe, Asia, Canada
Percentage of Business in Exporting: 20

41966 Analytical Development
65 Cavender Run
Dahlonega, GA 30533   770-237-2330
Fax: 770-237-2332
Manufacturer and exporter of hand-held portable luminometers
President: Ed Nemec
Estimated Sales: $500,000-$1 Million
Number Employees: 1-4
Brands Exported: Inspector
Regions Exported to: Worldwide
Percentage of Business in Exporting: 25

41967 Analytical Measurements
22 Mountain View Drive
Chester, NJ 07930
800-635-5580
phmeter@verizon.net
www.analyticalmeasurements.com
Manufacturer/supplier of pH and ORP instrumentation, probes, and other related materials
President: W Richard Adey
Contact: Frank G Paully
frank@analyticalmeasurements.com
Estimated Sales: 500,000
Number Employees: 3
Square Footage: 2000
Regions Exported to: Europe, Middle East
Percentage of Business in Exporting: 15

41968 Anchor Brewing Company
1705 Mariposa St
San Francisco, CA 94107   415-863-8350
Fax: 415-552-7094 info@anchorbrewing.com
www.anchorbrewing.com
Beer and ale
Marketing, Communications & Events: Teagan Thompson
VP Sales: Martin Geraghty
VP Logistics: Alfredo Mialma
Year Founded: 1896
Estimated Sales: $20-50 Million
Number Employees: 50-99
Parent Co: Sapporo Holdings
Type of Packaging: Consumer, Private Label
Regions Exported to: Europe, Asia

41969 Anchor Crane & Hoist Service Company
455 Aldine Bender Road
Houston, TX 77060   281-405-9048
Fax: 281-448-7500 800-835-2223
anchor@anchorcrane.com
www.proservanchor.com
Manufacturer and exporter of overhead crane systems
Manager: Greg Salinas
Contact: Tommy Cochran
cochran@proservanchor.com
Purchasing Manager: Bob Steward
Number Employees: 100-249
Parent Co: RPC
Regions Exported to: Worldwide

41970 Anchor Hocking Operating Co
519 N Pierce Ave
Lancaster, OH 43130-2969   740-681-6275
Fax: 740-681-6040 800-562-7511
consumerar@anchorhocking.com
www.anchorhocking.com
Manufacturer and exporter of glass tabletop products including beverageware, stemware, dinnerware, ovenware and floral and table accessories
President: J David Reed
CEO: Mark Eichorn
Vice President Sales & Marketing: Jackie Sokol
Contact: Ben Baird
bb322801@ohiou.edu
Vice President Of Operations: Margaret Homers
Estimated Sales: Less Than $500,000
Number Employees: 1-4
Parent Co: Newell Rubbermaid
Other Locations:
  Anchor Hocking Glass Co.
  Richmond Hill, ONAnchor Hocking Glass Co.
Regions Exported to: Worldwide
Percentage of Business in Exporting: 10

41971 (HQ)Anchor Packaging
13515 Barrett Parkway Dr # 100
Ballwin, MO 63021-5870   314-822-7800
Fax: 314-822-2035 800-467-3900
info@anchorpackaging.com
www.anchorpackaging.com
Manufacturer and exporter of plastic microwaveable packaging and container supplies including films, containers, trays, food protective and cling wrap.
President: Jeff Wolff
jeff.wolff@anchorpack.com
CFO: Steve Riek
CEO: Brad Jensen
Marketing: Michael Thaler
Sales: Frank Baumann
Public Relations: Michael Thaler
Operations: Staya Garg
Estimated Sales: $ 20 - 50 Million
Number Employees: 20-49
Type of Packaging: Food Service, Private Label
Brands Exported: Fresh View; MicroLite; Culinary Classics; Gourmet Classics; MicroRaves; Purity Wrap; Anchor Wrap; Crystal Wrap; Bonfaire
Regions Exported to: Central America, South America, Europe, Asia, Middle East

41972 Andco Environmental Processes
415 Commerce Dr
Amherst, NY 14228   716-691-2100
Fax: 716-691-2880 andco@localnet.com
www.localnet.com/~buffalo/customer/andco/andco.htm
Manufacturer and exporter of waste and ground water pollution elimination systems
Sales Manager: Jack Reich
Chief Process Engineer: Michael Laschinger
Estimated Sales: less than $ 500,000
Number Employees: 5-9
Square Footage: 44000
Regions Exported to: Worldwide
Percentage of Business in Exporting: 10

41973 Andersen 2000
2011 Commerce Dr N
Peachtree City, GA 30269   770-486-2000
Fax: 770-487-5066 800-241-5424
Manufacturer and exporter of air pollution control systems for odor control, spray dryer dust and visible aerosol.
President/CEO: Jack Brady
CFO: Randall Morgan
CEO: Randall Morgan
Marketing/Sales: Tom Van Remmen
Contact: Randall Morgan
r.morgan@verantis.com
Purchasing Manager: Doug Topley
Number Employees: 50-99
Square Footage: 60000
Parent Co: Crown Andersen
Other Locations:
  Andersen 2000
  SevenumAndersen 2000
Regions Exported to: Central America, South America, Europe, Asia, Middle East
Percentage of Business in Exporting: 80

41974 Anderson Dahlen Inc
6850 Sunwood Dr NW
Ramsey, MN 55303-3601   763-852-4700
Fax: 763-852-4795 877-205-0239
sales@andersondahlen.com
www.andersondahlen.com
President: Thomas Knoll
thomasknoll@andersondahlen.com
Estimated Sales: $ 20 - 50 Million
Number Employees: 100-249

41975 Anderson Erickson Dairy
2420 E University Ave
Des Moines, IA 50317   515-265-2521
www.aedairy.com
Milks, orange juice, lemonade, yogurt, cottage cheese, dips, sour cream, eggnog, buttermilk and creams, and ice cream mix.
President: Miriam Erickson Brown
Chief Financial Officer: Warren Erickson
Director of Marketing: Kim Peter
Year Founded: 1930
Estimated Sales: $44.40 Million
Number Employees: 250-499
Square Footage: 190000
Type of Packaging: Food Service
Other Locations:
  Kansas City, KS
Regions Exported to: Worldwide

41976 Anderson Erickson Dairy
5431 Speaker Rd
Kansas City, KS 66106   913-621-4801
www.aedairy.com
Milks, orange juice, lemonade, yogurt, cottage cheese, dips, sour cream, eggnog, buttermilk and creams, and ice cream mix.
President: Miriam Erickson Brown
Year Founded: 1930
Estimated Sales: $20-50 Million
Number Employees: 250-499
Type of Packaging: Food Service
Regions Exported to: Worldwide

41977 Anderson International Corp
4545 Boyce Pkwy
Stow, OH 44224-1770   216-641-1112
Fax: 216-641-0709 800-336-4730
www.expeller.info
Manufacturer and exporter of screw press machinery for the continuous extraction of vegetable oils and animal fats
President: Len Trocano
lenny.trocano@andersonintl.com
CFO: Kathleen O'Hearn
VP: Vincent Vavpot
Marketing: Vincent Vavpot
Sales: Bruce Brown
Plant Manager: Dave Botson
Estimated Sales: $ 10 - 20 Million
Number Employees: 50-99
Brands Exported: Expeller; Solvex Expander; Hivex Expander; Dox Expander
Regions Exported to: Central America, South America, Europe, Asia, Middle East
Percentage of Business in Exporting: 60

41978 Anderson Machine Sales
1066 Harvard Pl
P.O. Box 220
Fort Lee, NJ 07024-1630
Fax: 201-641-7952 amscapper@aol.com
Manufacturer and exporter of single spindle and rotary capping machines, pump placers and crimpers, conveyors and accumulating tables
Manager: Howard Cunningham
Estimated Sales: $ 2.5-5,000,000
Number Employees: 1-4
Parent Co: Anderson Machine Systems
Regions Exported to: Worldwide
Percentage of Business in Exporting: 10

41979 Anderson Seafood
4780 E Bryson St
Anaheim, CA 92807-1901   714-777-7100
Fax: 714-777-7116
contactus@andersonseafoods.com
www.shopandersonseafoods.com
Fresh and frozen seafood
President: Dennis Anderson
CFO: Alberto Andrade
Vice President: Todd Anderson
VP, Procurement, Sales & Operations: Carl Oliphant
Year Founded: 1979
Number Employees: 20-49
Type of Packaging: Consumer, Food Service

41980 Anderson Tool & Engineering Company
P.O.Box 1158
Anderson, IN 46015-1158   765-643-6691
Fax: 765-643-5022
Manufacturer and exporter of packaging, automation and material handling equipment; also, electrical design and assembly services available
President: Ted Fiock
Sales/Marketing Manager: David Keller
Operations Manager: Tom Tuterow
Purchasing Manager: Ron King
Estimated Sales: $ 10 - 20 Million
Number Employees: 100-249
Square Footage: 85000

Importers & Exporters / A-Z

Regions Exported to: Worldwide
Percentage of Business in Exporting: 15

41981 Anderson-Crane Company
1213-19 Harmon Pl
Minneapolis, MN 55403   612-332-0331
Fax: 612-332-0384 800-314-2747
minneapolis@anderson-crane.com
www.anderson-crane.com
Manufacturers of stainless steel screw conveyors @ screw feeders to food grade specs.
President: Bob Crane
Director Of Sales: Rob Crane
Contact: Steven Johnson
steven.johnson@screw-conveyor.com
Estimated Sales: $10-20 Million
Number Employees: 20-49
Square Footage: 60000
Regions Exported to: Central America, South America, Europe, Asia
Percentage of Business in Exporting: 5

41982 Anderson-Negele
156 Auriesville Rd
Fultonville, NY 12072   518-922-5315
Fax: 518-922-8997 800-833-0081
info@anderson-negele.com
www.anderson-negele.com
sensors for food and life sciences.
General Manager: Parker Burke
Sr. Product and Marketing Manager: Paul Wagner
Director of Sales: Joe Gamradt
Estimated Sales: $50-60 Million
Number Employees: 100-249
Parent Co: Fortive Corporation

41983 Andex Corp
69 Deep Rock Rd
Rochester, NY 14624-3575   585-328-3790
Fax: 585-328-3792
Manufacturer and exporter of paper coffee filters
President: Andrew Cherre
andexcorp@aol.com
Estimated Sales: $1-2 Million
Number Employees: 20-49
Square Footage: 40000
Type of Packaging: Food Service, Private Label, Bulk
Brands Exported: Gourmay; Tru Brew
Regions Exported to: Puerto Rico
Percentage of Business in Exporting: 10

41984 Andrew Peller Limited
697 S. Service Rd.
Grimsby, ON L3M 4E8
Canada   905-643-4131
Fax: 905-643-4944 info@andrewpeller.com
www.andrewpeller.com
Wines.
President: Randy Powell
Chairman/CEO: John Peller
Executive VP, IT/CFO: Steve Attridge
Executive VP, Marketing: Shawn MacLeod
Executive VP, National Sales: Erin Rooney
Executive VP, Human Resources: Sara Presutto
Executive VP, Operations: Brendan Wall
Year Founded: 1927
Estimated Sales: $363.8 Million
Number Employees: 1,198
Number of Brands: 10
Square Footage: 89782
Type of Packaging: Consumer, Food Service, Bulk
Regions Exported to: Asia, Carribean, Worldwide

41985 Andros Foods North America
10119 Old Valley Pike
Mount Jackson, VA 22842   540-217-4100
844-426-3767
sales@androsna.com www.androsna.com
Fruit based food and beverages, confectionary, preserves, frozen desserts
CEO/COO: Terry Stoehr
Estimated Sales: $52.3 Million
Number Employees: 500-999
Parent Co: Andros Group

41986 Anetsberger
P.O. Box 501
Concord, NH 06062   603-225-6684
Fax: 603-225-8472
ANETS - Gas & Electric Fryers, Filter Systems, Chrome Grills, Pasta Cookers

President: Paul Angrick
VP: Steve Spittle
VP Sales/Marketing: Bonnie Bolster
Contact: Tracy Doer
tdoer@anets.com
Estimated Sales: $10-20 Million
Number Employees: 50-99
Parent Co: Middleby Corp
Regions Exported to: Europe, Middle East

41987 Anglo American Trading
P.O. Box 97
Harvey, LA 70059-0097   504-341-5631
Fax: 504-341-5635
Manager: Dennis Skrmetta
CEO: Eric Skrmetta

41988 Angry Orchard Cider Company, LLC
2241 Albany Post Rd.
Walden, NY 12586
888-845-3311
www.angryorchard.com
Apple, pear and ros, hard ciders
Head Producer: Ryan Burk
Number of Brands: 1
Number of Products: 6
Type of Packaging: Consumer, Private Label
Brands Exported: Angry Orchard
Regions Exported to: USA, Canada

41989 (HQ)Anguil Environmental Systems
8855 N 55th St
Milwaukee, WI 53223   414-365-6400
Fax: 414-365-6410 800-488-0230
sales@anguil.com www.anguil.com
Manufacturer and exporter of air pollution abatement and oxidation systems
President: Gene Anguil
CEO: Gene Anugil
Vice President: Chris Anguil
Marketing Director: Kevin Summ
Contact: Mathew Andrews
mathew.andrews@anguil.com
Estimated Sales: $20-25 Million
Number Employees: 50-99
Square Footage: 25000
Regions Exported to: Central America, South America, Europe, Asia, Canada, Mexico
Percentage of Business in Exporting: 25

41990 Anhydro Inc
20000 Governors Dr Ste 301
Olympia Fields, IL 60461   708-747-7000
Fax: 708-755-8815 anhydroinc@anhydro.com
www.anhydro.com
Manufacturer and exporter of food drying equipment including spray, tower, flash, fluid bed and ring; also, consulting, design and engineering services available
President: Guy Lonergan
Contact: Dawn Braddy
d.braddy@anhydro.com
Number Employees: 20-49
Square Footage: 80000
Parent Co: Drytec
Regions Exported to: Central America, South America, Europe, Asia, Middle East
Percentage of Business in Exporting: 20

41991 Animal Pak
3 Terminal Rd
New Brunswick, NJ 08901-3615   732-545-3130
Fax: 732-509-0458 800-872-0101
info@animalpak.com www.animalpak.com
Vitamins, supplements, and powdered proteins
President: Clyde Rockoff
VP Marketing: Michael Rockoff
VP Sales: Tim Tantum
VP Operations: Bob Glucken
Plant Manager: Dave Mitchell
Estimated Sales: $35.1 Million
Number Employees: 100-249
Square Footage: 100000
Parent Co: Universal Nutrition
Regions Exported to: Central America, South America, Europe, Asia, Middle East

41992 Anita's Mexican Foods Corporation
1390 West 4th Street
San Bernardino, CA 92408   909-884-8706

Mexican foods including tortilla chips and taco and tostada shells, plus organic snacks, chips and popcorn
President: Jose Gomez
Contact: Mark Schneeberger
mark.schneeberger@anitasmexicanfood.com
Plant Manager: Frank Coser
Estimated Sales: $20-50 Million
Number Employees: 100-249
Square Footage: 30000
Parent Co: La Reina
Type of Packaging: Consumer, Food Service, Private Label, Bulk
Regions Exported to: Worldwide
Percentage of Business in Exporting: 25

41993 Anjo's Imports
PO Box 4031
Cerritos, CA 90703-4031   562-865-9544
Fax: 562-865-9544 anjosimports@earthlink.net
www.anjosimports.com
Importer of specialty Jamaican sauces including hot and regular pepper; also, savory and payaya jams and jellies
President: Valerie Webster
Marketing Director: Lloyd Webster
Number Employees: 1-4
Square Footage: 1600
Brands Imported: Island Treasure; Juliana; Jamaica Best; Nel's; Nel's Hell Hot
Regions Imported from: Caribbean
Percentage of Business in Importing: 100

41994 Ankeny Lake Wild Rice
9594 Sidney Rd S
PO Box 3667
Salem, OR 97306-9448   503-363-3241
Fax: 503-371-9080 800-555-5380
ankenylakes_st.maries@yahoo.com
www.wildriceonline.com
Certified organic wild rice and nonorganic and wild rice blends
Owner: Larry Payne
paynels@netzero.com
Co-Owner: Sharon Jenkins-Payne
Estimated Sales: $500,000
Number Employees: 1-4
Square Footage: 12000
Type of Packaging: Consumer, Food Service, Private Label, Bulk
Brands Imported: Canadian Lake
Regions Imported from: Canada
Percentage of Business in Importing: 20

41995 Ann Arbor Computer
34375 W 12 Mile Road
Farmington Hills, MI 48331-3375   248-553-1000
Fax: 248-553-1228 800-526-9322
info@jerviswebb.com
Manufacturer and exporter of computer software inventory control systems for warehouses and distribution centers; also, complete integrated control systems for material handling and factory automation
President & CEO: Brian Stewart
Sr. Vice President & CFO: John Doychich
Vice President Sales And Marketing: Bruce Buscher
Sales Manager: Art Fleischer
Vice President Of Operations: Lon McAllister
Number Employees: 80
Square Footage: 148000
Parent Co: Jervis B. Webb Company
Brands Exported: PC/AIM; Basis
Regions Exported to: Worldwide
Percentage of Business in Exporting: 10

41996 Annie's Frozen Yogurt
5200 W 74th St # A
Suite A
Minneapolis, MN 55439-2223   952-835-2110
800-969-9648
www.anniesyogurt.com
Soft serve equipment for frozen yogurt.
President: Lawrence Cerf
ldcerf@aol.com
Number Employees: 10-19
Regions Exported to: Mexico

41997 Annie's Naturals
1610 5th St
Berkeley, CA 94710-1715   510-558-7500
Fax: 802-456-8865 800-434-1234
www.annies.com

Dressings and vinaigrettes, BBQ sauces, marinades and Worcestershire sauce.
Owner/Production Development: Annie Christopher
Owner/Sales/Marketing: Peter Backman
Number Employees: 10-19
Type of Packaging: Consumer, Food Service, Private Label
Brands Exported: Annie's Naturals
Regions Exported to: Europe

41998 Anritsu Industrial Solutions
1001 Cambridge Dr
Elk Grove Vlg, IL 60007-2453 847-419-9729
Fax: 847-419-8266
Food inspection equipment.
President: Erik Brainard
ebrainard@us.anritsu-industry.com
Number Employees: 20-49
Regions Exported to: Central America, South America, North America

41999 Anton Caratan & Son
PO Box 2797
1625 Road 160
Bakersfield, CA 93303-2797 661-725-2575
Fax: 661-725-5829
Table grapes
President: Anton Caratan
Sales Manager: George Ann Caratan
Estimated Sales: $10-20 Million
Number Employees: 250-499
Type of Packaging: Consumer
Regions Exported to: Worldwide

42000 Antone's Import Company
2424 Dunstan Road
Suite 100
Houston, TX 77005-2569 713-521-2883
Fax: 713-521-1973
Wholesaler/distributor of imported specialty foods
Owner: Kay Nader
CEO: Randolph Clendenen
Manager: Laura Armstrong
Contact: Forrest Coppock
forrest@txmusicgroup.com
Estimated Sales: $20-50 Million
Number Employees: 2

42001 Antoni Ravioli Co
879 N Broadway
North Massapequa, NY 11758-2353 516-799-0350
Fax: 516-799-0357 800-783-0350
www.antoniravioli.com
Ravioli, stuffed shells and manicotti, tortellini, cavatelli and gnocchi, fresh pasta, also gluten free products.
President: Gene Saucci
philrino@msn.com
Estimated Sales: $1.5 Million
Number Employees: 10-19
Square Footage: 12000
Type of Packaging: Food Service, Private Label, Bulk

42002 Apac Chemical Corporation
150 N Santa Anita Ave
Suite 850
Arcadia, CA 91006 626-203-0066
Fax: 626-203-0067 866-849-2722
sales@apacchemical.com www.apacchemical.com
Potassium sorbate and sorbic acid
President: Sun Chang
Vice President: Tom Kusaka
Account Executive: Sergio Scarcella
Account Executive: Dave Plowman
Estimated Sales: $4 Million
Number Employees: 7

42003 (HQ)Apache Stainless Equipment
200 Industrial Dr
Beaver Dam, WI 53916-1136 920-356-9900
Fax: 920-887-0206 800-444-0398
info@apachestainless.com
www.apachestainless.com
Manufacturer and exporter of stainless steel food processing machinery including sanitary and ASME pressure vessels, tanks, blenders, mixers, conveyors, sanitary lifts, stuffers, dumpers and paced boning systems
President and R&D: D Foulkes
CAO: Fern Core
fcore@apachestainless.com
CFO: D Seifert
VP: W Lynn
Quality Control: Jerome Scharrer
Plant Manager: Duane Crouse
Estimated Sales: $ 5 - 10 Million
Number Employees: 100-249
Square Footage: 200000
Other Locations:
  Apache Stainless Equipment Co
  Beloit, WIApache Stainless Equipment Co
Brands Exported: Mepaco
Regions Exported to: Worldwide
Percentage of Business in Exporting: 10

42004 Apex Fountain Sales Inc
1140 N American St
Philadelphia, PA 19123-1514 215-627-4526
Fax: 215-627-7877 800-523-4586
www.apexfountains.com
Manufacturer and exporter of champagne fountains, chafing dishes, punch bowls, candelabra and food stands
President: Abe Weinberg
info@apexfountains.com
Manager: Jody Clemente
Estimated Sales: $1-2.5 Million
Number Employees: 5-9
Regions Exported to: South America, Europe

42005 Apex Machine Company
3000 NE 12th Ter
Oakland Park, FL 33334-4497 954-566-1572
Fax: 954-563-2844 email@apexmachine.com
www.apexmachine.com
Manufacturer and exporter, designs and engineers customized part handling and printing-packaging solutions for 3D products.
President: Todd Coningsby
CEO & Chairman: A. Robert Coningsby
toddc@apexmachine.com
Corp. Controller: Chris Bardelang
National Sales Manager: Russell Coningsby
Engineering Manager: Greg Coningsby
Director Production-Purchasing: Arthur Jordan
Estimated Sales: $5-10 Million
Number Employees: 50-99
Other Locations:
  Capex Corporation
  Fort Lauderdale, FL
  Desco Machine Company
  Twinsburg, OHCapex CorporationTwinsburg
Regions Exported to: Europe, Worldwide
Regions Imported from: Asia

42006 Apex Packing & Rubber Co
1855 New Hwy # D
Farmingdale, NY 11735-1599 631-420-8150
Fax: 631-756-9639 800-645-9110
info@apexgaskets.com
Manufacturer and exporter of sanitary replacement parts for the dairy, food, beverage and pharmaceutical industries
President: Ralph Oppenheim
ralph@apexgaskets.com
General Manager: Larry Hodes
Purchasing Agent: Leon Davidson
Estimated Sales: $2.5-5,000,000
Number Employees: 5-9
Brands Exported: Apex
Regions Exported to: Worldwide
Percentage of Business in Exporting: 20

42007 Apogee Translite Inc
593 Acorn St # B
Deer Park, NY 11729-3613 631-254-6975
Fax: 631-254-3860 www.apogeetranslite.com
Manufacturer and exporter of lighting fixtures for food processing range hoods, hose down and wet locations
President: Richard Nicolai
President: Mike Shada
Estimated Sales: $ 10 - 20,000,000
Number Employees: 20-49
Square Footage: 38000
Other Locations:
  Apogee Lighting Group
  Riverdale, ILApogee Lighting Group
Regions Exported to: Worldwide
Percentage of Business in Exporting: 5

42008 Appennino USA
39-12 Street
Long Island City, NY 11101 917-373-3544
Fax: 212-223-0966 sara@appenninoft.it
www.appenninofunghietartufi.it
Importer of fresh Mushrooms & Truffles.

42009 Apple & Eve LLC
2 Seaview Blvd # 100
3rd Floor
Port Washington, NY 11050-4634 516-621-1122
Fax: 516-621-2164 800-969-8018
info@appleandeve.com www.appleandeve.com
Natural juices and juice blends; importer of fruit concentrates
Founder/CEO: Gordon Crane
gordon@appleandeve.com
CFO: Paul Bevilacqua
VP: Joan Segal
VP Innovation & Development: Ken Gootkind
Director of Marketing/Advertising: Jeff Damiano
VP Sales/Marketing: Cary Crane
Operations Executive: Tyron Charles
Plant Manager: John Donlon
Purchasing Manager: Mary Ellen Brothers
Estimated Sales: $15.1 Million
Number Employees: 50-99
Number of Products: 100+
Square Footage: 42000
Type of Packaging: Consumer
Regions Exported to: Asia, Middle East
Regions Imported from: South America, Europe

42010 Apple Acres
4633 Cherry Valley Turnpike
La Fayette, NY 13084 603-893-8596
Fax: 315-677-5143 sam@appleacres.com
www.appleacres.com
Apples
CEO: Walter Blackler
Co-Owner: Bob Rigdon
Estimated Sales: $10 Million
Number Employees: 20-49
Square Footage: 128000
Type of Packaging: Consumer
Regions Exported to: Central America, Europe
Percentage of Business in Exporting: 25

42011 Appleton Produce Company
1408 Weiser River Road
PO Box 110
Weiser, ID 83672 208-414-3352
Fax: 208-414-1862 onions@appletonproduce.com
Onions
President: C. Robert Woods
President/Owner: Steve Woods
Marketing/Sales Manager: Steve Walker
Purchasing Manager: Dave Price
Estimated Sales: $12 Million
Number Employees: 50
Type of Packaging: Consumer, Food Service, Private Label, Bulk
Regions Exported to: Central America, Asia, Pacific Rim, Canada

42012 Applewood Orchards Inc
2998 Rodesiler Hwy
Deerfield, MI 49238-9789 517-447-3002
Fax: 517-447-3006 800-447-3854
jim@applewoodapples.com
www.applewoodapples.com
Apples
Owner: James Swindeman
james@applewoodapples.com
Vice President: Steve Swindeman
VP: Scott Swindeman
Estimated Sales: $5-10 Million
Number Employees: 20-49
Type of Packaging: Consumer
Regions Exported to: Worldwide

42013 Applewood Winery
82 Four Corners Rd.
Warwick, NY 10990 845-988-9292
info@applewoodwinery.com
www.applewoodwinery.com
Merlot, Cabernet, Riesling, Chardonnay, Red wine blends, fruit-flavoured wine, hard cider
Owner: Jonathan Hull
Year Founded: 1993
Number of Brands: 2
Number of Products: 21
Type of Packaging: Consumer, Private Label

Importers & Exporters / A-Z

Brands Exported: Applewood Winery, Naked Flock
Regions Exported to: USA

42014 Applied Chemical Technology
4350 Helton Dr
Florence, AL 35630 256-760-9600
Fax: 256-760-9638 800-228-3217
act@appliedchemical.com
www.appliedchemical.com
Manufacturer and exporter of fluid beds, feeders and granulators. Development and engineering of processing plants available
President: A Ray Shirley
CFO: Ginger Lewey
VP: Curtis Lewey
Quality Control: Curtis Lewey
Marketing: Alan Nix
Contact: Craig Arnett
carnett@appliedchemical.com
Purchasing Manager: Roger Kilburn
Estimated Sales: Below $ 5 Million
Number Employees: 50
Square Footage: 70000
Regions Exported to: Central America, South America, Europe, Middle East, Latin America, Canada
Percentage of Business in Exporting: 45

42015 Applied Industrial TechInc
1 Applied Plz
Cleveland, OH 44115-2519 216-426-4000
Fax: 216-426-4845 www.applied.com
Wholesaler/distributor and exporter of electric motors, belting, packing and power transmission equipment for food processing machinery
Branch Operations Manager: Ronnie Moore
Branch Manager: Matt Loe
Estimated Sales: Over $1 Billion
Number Employees: 5000-9999

42016 Applied Robotics Inc
648 Saratoga Rd
Schenectady, NY 12302-5837 518-384-1000
Fax: 518-384-1200 800-309-3475
info@arobotics.com www.appliedrobotics.com
ARI is a leading provider of automation end-of-arm connectivity solutions designed to bring greater speed and flexibility to automation-based processes.
CEO: Michael F Quinn
mquinn@appliedrobotics.com
CEO: Tom Petronis
CFO: Paul Cullen
CEO: Thomas J Petronis
Research & Development: Clay Cooper
Quality Control: Mike Gallo
Marketing Director: Joanne Brown
Public Relations: Joanne Brown
Production Manager: Bob Butterfield
Plant Manager: John Sezfilippi
Estimated Sales: $ 10-20,000,000
Number Employees: 20-49
Square Footage: 18000
Regions Exported to: Central America, South America, Europe, Asia

42017 Applied Thermal Technologies
906 Boardwalk Ste B
San Marcos, CA 92069-4071 760-744-5083
Fax: 442-744-5031 800-736-5083
Manufacturer and exporter of water chilling systems for batch cooling, food, confectionery and dairy products.
President: Kimberly Howard
khoward@appliedthermaltech.com
Plant Manager: Dale Anderson
Estimated Sales: $500,000-$1 Million
Number Employees: 1-4
Square Footage: 10000
Brands Exported: Hydro-Miser
Regions Exported to: Worldwide
Percentage of Business in Exporting: 10

42018 Aqua Foods
1050 W Laurel Ave
Eunice, LA 70535-3124 337-457-0111
Fax: 337-457-1500
Importer of catfish, tilapia, crawfish products, and alligator meat
Owner/President: Dwayne Lejeune
Office Manager: Alice Tramel
Estimated Sales: $ 3 - 5 Million
Number Employees: 4

42019 (HQ)Aqua Measure
9567 Arrow Rte # E
Suite E
Rancho Cucamonga, CA 91730-4550 909-941-7776
Fax: 909-941-6444 800-966-4788
sales@aquameasure.com www.finnagroup.com
Manufacturer and exporter of moisture meters and systems for measuring moisture content in solids for the food processing industry
Owner: John Lundrstrom
Sales: Gabriel Cote Jr
Contact: Steven Brunasso
sbrunasso@aquameasure.com
Estimated Sales: $2.5-5 Million
Number Employees: 5-9
Other Locations:
Aqua Measure InstrumentCo.
La Verne, CAAqua Measure InstrumentCo.
Brands Exported: Moisture Meters
Regions Exported to: Central America, South America, Europe, Asia, Middle East

42020 Aqua Star
2025 1st Ave # 200
Seattle, WA 98121-2115 206-448-5400
Fax: 206-448-2818 800-232-6280
www.aquastar.com
Importer of fresh and frozen seafood including shrimp, salmon and crab
Owner: Mike Girton
mgirton@aquastar.com
Estimated Sales: $27 Million
Number Employees: 50-99
Type of Packaging: Consumer, Food Service
Regions Imported from: Worldwide

42021 Aqua-Aerobic Systems Inc
6306 N Alpine Rd
Loves Park, IL 61111-4396 815-639-9803
Fax: 815-654-2508 800-940-5008
solutions@aqua-aerobic.com
www.aqua-aerobic.com
Manufacturer and exporter of water and wastewater treatment systems for both municipal and industrial market, including direct drive aerators, down draft mixers and sequencing batch reactors; also, shallow bed, gravity sand and clothmedia filtration equipment
President: Robert J Wimmer
rwimmer@aqua-aerobic.com
R&D: Lloyd Johnson
VP Marketing: Deb Lavelle
VP Sales: Steven Schupbach
VP International Sales: Sharon DeDoncker
Operations: Rick Reiland
Estimated Sales: $20-50 Million
Number Employees: 100-249
Square Footage: 100000
Brands Exported: Aqua-Jet Aerator; Aqua SBR; Aqua DDM Mixer
Regions Exported to: Australia, Canada, Latin America, Mexico
Percentage of Business in Exporting: 15

42022 Aquatech
6221 Petersburg St
Anchorage, AK 99507-2006 907-563-1387
Fax: 907-563-1852 877-938-2722
www.crabfactory.com
Live, fresh and frozen Alaskan king crab.
Partner: Miki Ballard
Partner: Lamar Ballard
aquatech@ak.net
General Manager: Sarah Ballard
Estimated Sales: $ 3 - 5 Million
Number Employees: 5-9

42023 Aquathin Corporation
950 South Andrews Avenue
Pompano Beach, FL 33069 954-781-7777
Fax: 954-781-7336 800-462-7634
info@aquathin.com www.aquathin.com
Manufacturer and exporter of water purification systems including reverse osmosis, softening and filtration
President: Alfred Lipshultz
Estimated Sales: $ 5 -14 Million
Number Employees: 20-49
Square Footage: 130000
Brands Exported: Aqualite, Aquathin, Country Hutch, Lead Out, Megachar, Platinum 90, Sodia Lite, Soft N Clean, Yes, Aqua Shield.
Regions Exported to: Worldwide
Percentage of Business in Exporting: 63

42024 Aquionics Inc
1455 Jamike Ave # 100
Suite 100
Erlanger, KY 41018-3147 859-341-0710
Fax: 859-341-0350 800-925-0440
sales@aquionics.com www.aquionics.com
Manufacturer and exporter of ultraviolet disinfection equipment
President: Oliver Lawal
oliver.law@aquionics.com
Manager: Rica Williams
Food/Beverage Sales Manager: Ralph Lopez
Number Employees: 20-49
Square Footage: 60000
Parent Co: Halma
Brands Exported: Aquionics

42025 Aralia Olive Oils
1105 Massachusetts Avenue
Suite 2E
Cambridge, MA 02138 617-354-8556
Fax: 617-249-1855 877-585-9510
www.araliaoliveoils.com
Olive Oils
President: Emmanuel Daskalakis
Number Employees: 2

42026 Arbee Transparent Inc
1450 Pratt Blvd
Elk Grove Vlg, IL 60007-5713 847-593-0400
Fax: 847-593-0291 800-642-2247
www.arbee.com
A supplier of Plastic Bags
President: Bob Harris
bagplastic@aol.com
Estimated Sales: $20-50 Million
Number Employees: 100-249
Square Footage: 25000

42027 Archie Moore's
15 Factory Ln
Milford, CT 06460-3306 203-876-5088
Fax: 203-876-0525
Manufacturer and exporter of buffalo wing sauce and flavored potato chips
President: Todd Ressler
tressler@archiemoores.com
Estimated Sales: $ .5 - 1 million
Number Employees: 20-49
Square Footage: 10000
Parent Co: Archie Moore's Bar & Restaurant
Type of Packaging: Consumer, Food Service, Private Label, Bulk
Brands Exported: Archie Moore's
Regions Exported to: Central America, Canada, Mexico, Curacao

42028 Architecture Plus Intl Inc
2709 N Rocky Point Dr # 201
Rocky Point, FL 33607-5562 813-281-9299
Fax: 813-281-9292 info@apiplus.com
www.apiplus.com
Manufacturer and exporter of aseptic packaging equipment and components, over and shrink wrappers and case packers, stackers and unstackers
President: Jean-Louis Limousin
CEO: Juan Romero
VP Sales: Keith Wennik
Number Employees: 50-99
Regions Exported to: Central America, South America, Europe, Asia, Canada, Mexico

42029 Archon Industries Inc
357 Spook Rock Rd
Suffern, NY 10901-5314 845-368-3600
Fax: 845-368-3040 800-554-1394
sales@archonind.com www.shoparchonind.com
Manufacturer, importer and exporter of washdown stations, sanitary fittings and ball, butterfly, gage and sanitary valves
CEO: Mario Faustini
Sales Manager: Linda Kyriakos
Engineering Manager: Konrad Mayer
Estimated Sales: $ 5 - 10 Million
Number Employees: 5-9
Brands Exported: Archon Washdown Stations
Regions Exported to: Worldwide
Percentage of Business in Exporting: 50
Brands Imported: Zimmerlin; Boyer; Kieslemann; Hake
Regions Imported from: Worldwide

Importers & Exporters / A-Z

42030 Archon Vitamin Corp
3775 Park Ave
Suite 1
Edison, NJ 08820-2566 973-371-1700
Fax: 973-371-1277 800-848-0089
purchasing@archonvitamin.com
www.archonvitamin.com
Vitamins, minerals, herbs, and other nutritionals.
President: Tom Pugsley
tpugsley@archonvitamin.com
VP Products Division: Paul Stevens
Quality Assurance Manager: Susan Jackson
Sales Manager: Rick McNall
Operations Executive: Jose Camaano
Purchasing Director: Tracy Daniiel
Estimated Sales: $ 5 - 10 Million
Number Employees: 50-99
Number of Brands: 1
Square Footage: 200000
Type of Packaging: Consumer, Private Label, Bulk
Brands Exported: Bionutrient
Percentage of Business in Exporting: 10

42031 Arcobaleno Pasta Machines
160 Greenfield Rd
Lancaster, PA 17601-5815 717-394-1402
800-875-7096
www.arcobalenollc.com
Pasta machinery and bakery processing lines, continuous and general purpose mixers, pasta preparation machinery, dough cutters and sheeters, pasteurizers, etc; exporter of calzone and pizza lines, ravioli machines and dough sheeters
President: Antonio Adiletta
info@arcobalenollc.com
VP, Marketing & Sales: Maja Adijetta
Number Employees: 10-19
Square Footage: 80000
Brands Exported: Pasta Machines
Regions Exported to: USA, Australia
Percentage of Business in Exporting: 98

42032 Arctic Air
6440 City West Pkwy Ste 2
Eden Prairie, MN 55344 952-941-2270
Fax: 952-941-3066 800-853-3508
info@arcticairco.com www.arcticairco.com
Manufacturer and exporter of refrigerators including reach-in and NSF approved chest freezers.
Owner: Walter Broich Sr
wbroich@arcticairco.com
Estimated Sales: $10-20 Million
Number Employees: 4
Square Footage: 10000
Parent Co: Broich Enterprises
Brands Exported: Arctic Air
Regions Exported to: Worldwide
Percentage of Business in Exporting: 2

42033 Arctic Industries
9731 NW 114th Way
Medley, FL 33178 305-883-5581
Fax: 305-883-4651 800-325-0123
rio@arcticwalk-ins.com www.arcticwalk-ins.com
Manufacturer and exporter of walk-in coolers, freezers and cold storage facilities, as well as step-in freezers and coolers.
President: Donald Goodstein
Vice President: Barbara Bowman
Sales Director: Rio Giardinieri
Contact: Gary Albright
galbright@arcticwalkins.com
Office Manager: Barbara Bowman
Estimated Sales: $ 5 - 100 Million
Number Employees: 100-249
Square Footage: 50000
Brands Exported: Arctic; Penguin
Regions Exported to: Central America, South America, Europe, Asia, Middle East
Percentage of Business in Exporting: 10

42034 Arctic Star Distributing
412 W 53rd Ave
Anchorage, AK 99518 907-563-3454
Fax: 907-562-3548
Wholesaler/distributor, importer and exporter of snack foods, general merchandise, beverages, etc.; serving the food service market in Alaska and Washington; also, rack jobber services available
President/CEO: Jim Baumann
Sales Manager: Bob Capeletti
General Manager: George Derr
Estimated Sales: $ 5 - 10 Million
Number Employees: 5-9
Square Footage: 50000
Parent Co: Arctic Star Distribution
Type of Packaging: Food Service

42035 Arde Inc
875 Washington Ave
Carlstadt, NJ 07072-3001 201-784-9880
Fax: 201-784-9710 800-909-6070
abmix@ardeinc.com www.ardeinc.com
Manufacturer and exporter of mixing equipment systems used to disperse gums and stabilizers to prepare emulsions
Manager: Sue Belaus
Sales/Engineering Manager: Roy Scott
Public Relations: Cindy Roehling
Purchasing: Tom Stephens
Estimated Sales: $5 Million
Number Employees: 50-99
Square Footage: 280000
Parent Co: Arde, Inc.
Regions Exported to: Central America, South America, Europe, Asia, Middle East, All
Percentage of Business in Exporting: 15

42036 Arde Inc
875 Washington Ave
Carlstadt, NJ 07072-3001 201-784-9880
Fax: 201-784-9710 800-909-6070
ABmix@Ardeinc.com www.ardeinc.com
Mixing equipment for beverage, sauces, preserves
Manager: Roy Scott
Manager: Kirk Sneddon
Estimated Sales: $ 2.5 - 5 000,000
Number Employees: 50-99
Square Footage: 20000

42037 Arden Companies
30400 Telegraph Road
Southfield, MI 48025 248-415-8500
Fax: 248-415-8520 www.ardencompanies.com
Manufacturer and exporter of aprons, chef coats, baker's mits, handle holders, cleaners, outdoor pads and cushions, grill covers, pot holders and oven mitts
President: Robert Sachs
CFO: John Connell
Sales/Marketing: William Sachs
Estimated Sales: $20-50 Million
Number Employees: 50-99
Square Footage: 675000
Type of Packaging: Consumer, Food Service
Regions Exported to: Central America, Europe, Asia
Percentage of Business in Exporting: 7

42038 Argo & Company
182 Ezell Street
P.O. Box 2747
Spartanburg, SC 29304 864-583-9766
Fax: 864-585-5056 argosheen@bellsouth.net
Manufacturer and exporter of cleaning supplies including cotton pads, rug mops and carpet/upholstery chemicals and machines
President: Anne Sanders
Estimated Sales: $ 10-20 Million
Number Employees: 20-49
Square Footage: 200000
Brands Exported: Argosheen Carpet Cleaner; Argomops; Argonaut Machines; Argo Carpet Pads
Regions Exported to: Europe, Asia, Australia
Percentage of Business in Exporting: 15

42039 Argo Century, Inc.
840 Edgewood Ave
Suite 202
Jacksonville, FL 32205 704-525-6180
Fax: 704-525-6280 800-446-7108
info@tontonsauce.com www.tontonsauce.com
Ginger dressing, teriyaki sauce and vinaigrettes.
President: Yoshi Shioda
Estimated Sales: $ 1 - 3 Million
Number Employees: 1-4
Type of Packaging: Consumer

42040 Arguimbau & Co
4 Davenport Ave # 1
P.O. Box 632
Greenwich, CT 06830-7167 203-661-7080
Fax: 203-661-6019 www.arguimbau-co.com
Importer and exporter of olives, olive oil, capers and peppers
Owner: Vincent Arguimbau
vincent@arguimbau-co.com
Estimated Sales: $2.5-5 Million
Number Employees: 1-4
Regions Exported to: Europe, Canada, Latin America
Regions Imported from: Spain, Morocco, Greece, Turkey
Percentage of Business in Importing: 100

42041 Ari Industries Inc
381 S Ari Ct
Addison, IL 60101-4353 630-953-9100
Fax: 630-953-0590 800-237-6725
sales@ariindustries.com www.ariindustries.com
Manufacturer and exporter of temperature sensors and electric heaters
President: Dan Malcolm
brandi.crouch@lmco.com
VP Sales/Marketing: Dan Malcolm
Public Relations: Darlene Sosnowski
Operations: John Mulvey
Estimated Sales: $5-10 Million
Number Employees: 50-99
Square Footage: 56000

42042 Ariel Vineyards
860 Napa Valley Corporate Way
Suite C
Napa, CA 94558-6281 707-258-8050
Fax: 707-258-8052 800-456-9472
info@arielvineyards.com www.arielvineyards.com
Nonalcoholic wine
Manager: Craig Rosser
info@jlohr.com
VP Operations: Jeff Meier
Estimated Sales: $5-10 Million
Number Employees: 1-4
Square Footage: 256000
Parent Co: J. Lohr Vineyards & Wines
Brands Exported: Ariel
Regions Exported to: Central America, Europe, Asia, Middle East
Percentage of Business in Exporting: 18

42043 Arise & Shine Herbal Products
P.O.Box 400
Medford, OR 97501 541-282-0891
Fax: 541-773-8866 800-688-2444
www.ariseandshine.com
Digestive aids and herbal supplements.
Founder: Dr. Richard Anderson
CEO: Avona L'Carttier
Contact: Denise Shannon
dshannon@ariseandshine.com
Regions Exported to: Worldwide
Percentage of Business in Exporting: 5

42044 Arista Industries Inc
557 Danbury Rd
Wilton, CT 06897-2218 203-761-1009
Fax: 203-761-4980 800-255-6457
info@aristaindustries.com
www.aristaindustries.com
Oils, frozen shrimp, lobster tails and octopus. Importer of octopus, shrimp, squid, lobster tails, oils and surimi products.
President: Alan Weitzer
CEO: Charles Hillyer
Chairman: Stephen Weitzer
steve@aristaindustries.com
Estimated Sales: $2.5-5 Million
Number Employees: 20-49
Type of Packaging: Consumer, Food Service
Regions Exported to: Central America, South America, Europe, Asia
Brands Imported: Sea Devils
Regions Imported from: Central America, South America, Asia

42045 Arizona Cowboy
3010 N 24th St
Phoenix, AZ 85016-7816 602-278-1427
Fax: 602-484-9482 800-529-8627
www.ameliocenterprises.com
Salsa, jellies, hot sauces, tortilla chips, honey, candy and nuts.
Owner/President: Amelio Casciato
Estimated Sales: $500,000-1 Million
Number Employees: 5-9
Square Footage: 6600
Type of Packaging: Consumer, Food Service, Private Label

Importers & Exporters / A-Z

42046 Arizona Dairy Ingredient
1221 West Gila Bend Highway
Casa Grande, AZ 85222 520-374-2603
glindsey@eriefoods.com
www.eriefoods.com
Manufacture of dry blending, extrusion, milling, grinding and pouch packaging machines.
President: David Reisenbigler
Estimated Sales: $80,000
Number Employees: 2
Square Footage: 400000
Parent Co: Erie Foods, Inc.

42047 Arizona Instrument LLC
3375 N Delaware St
Chandler, AZ 85225-1134 602-470-1414
Fax: 602-281-1745 800-528-7411
sales@azic.com www.azic.com
An ISO 9001:200 registered company that designs, manufactures, and markets Computrac precision moisture, solids, and ash analyzers and Jerome toxic gas analyzers.
President: George Hays
ghays@azic.com
Research & Development: Tom Hatfield
Quality Control: Blaine Nelson
Marketing: Shari Houtler
Operations Manager: Ben Brown
Estimated Sales: $10 Million
Number Employees: 50-99
Number of Brands: 4
Number of Products: 13
Regions Exported to: Central America, South America, Europe, Asia, Middle East

42048 Arizona Natural Products
12815 N Cave Creek Rd
Phoenix, AZ 85022-5834 602-997-6098
Fax: 602-288-8331 800-255-2823
info@arizonanatural.com www.arizonanatural.com
Herbal and vitamin supplements.
President/CEO: Michael Hanna
Contact: Ranna Hanna
rhanna@arizonanatural.com
Estimated Sales: Less Than $500,000
Number Employees: 5-9
Square Footage: 40000
Brands Exported: Arizona Natural; Allirich
Regions Exported to: South America, Europe, Australia
Percentage of Business in Exporting: 30

42049 Arkansas Glass Container Corp
516 W Johnson Ave
Jonesboro, AR 72401-1994 870-932-0168
Fax: 870-268-6217 800-533-4527
agcsalesdept@agcc.com www.agcc.com
Manufacturer and exporter of glass jars and bottles
CEO: Luann Sutton
lsutton@agcc.com
CEO: Anthony M Ramplex
VP Sales: Melton Harrison
VP Operations: Joel Sharp
Estimated Sales: $ 30 - 50 Million
Number Employees: 1-4
Square Footage: 450000

42050 Arkfeld Mfg & Distributing Co
1230 W Monroe Ave
Norfolk, NE 68701-6664 402-371-9430
Fax: 402-371-5137 800-533-0676
arkfeldm@ncfcomm.com
Manufacturer, distributor and exporter of custom metal fabricated poultry scales, livestock dial scales and feed/grain hopper dial scales, custom automatic watering systems and security and frozen product storage cabinets.
President: Robert Arkfeld
CEO: Janet Arkfeld
CFO: Anthony Arkfeld
Sales Director: Janet Arkfeld
Sales: Robert Arkfeld
Number Employees: 10-19
Square Footage: 5000
Brands Exported: Arkfeld Instant Way
Regions Exported to: Central America, South America, Europe, Canada
Percentage of Business in Exporting: 10

42051 Arla Foods Inc
675 Rivermede Road
Concord, ON L4K 2G9
Canada
905-669-9393
Fax: 905-669-5614 www.arlafoods.com
Cheese
President: Andrew Simpson
Estimated Sales: $19 Million
Number Employees: 120
Square Footage: 200000
Type of Packaging: Consumer, Food Service, Private Label, Bulk
Regions Imported from: South America, Europe, Latin America
Percentage of Business in Importing: 40

42052 (HQ)Armaly Brands
1900 Easy St
Commerce Twp, MI 48390-3220 248-669-2100
Fax: 248-669-3505 800-772-1222
orderdesk207@armalybrands.com
www.armalybrands.com
Manufacturer and exporter of sponges, scrubbers, cotton cheesecloth and scouring pads
Owner: John Armaly
jwarmaly@armalybrands.com
VP: Gilbert Armaly
Estimated Sales: $ 1 - 5 Million
Number Employees: 20-49
Square Footage: 400
Type of Packaging: Consumer, Food Service, Private Label, Bulk
Brands Exported: Estracell; Scourlite; Auto Show
Regions Exported to: Central America, South America, Asia, Middle East
Percentage of Business in Exporting: 5

42053 Armanino Foods of Distinction
30588 San Antonio St
Hayward, CA 94544-7102 510-441-9300
Fax: 510-441-0101 800-255-8888
customerservice@armanino.biz
Exporter of Italian foods including sauces, pasta, meatballs and bread. Importer of Italian cheeses.
CEO: Edmond Pera
Estimated Sales: F
Number Employees: 20-49
Square Footage: 24000
Type of Packaging: Consumer, Food Service
Regions Exported to: Worldwide
Percentage of Business in Exporting: 5
Regions Imported from: Italy

42054 Armbrust Paper Tubes Inc
6255 S Harlem Ave # D
Chicago, IL 60638-3990 773-586-3232
Fax: 773-586-8997 tubesrus@corecomm.net
www.tubesrus.com
Manufacturer and exporter of packaging products including paper tubes, cores, cans and push-ups for frozen sherbet, gyros, etc.; also, containers for dry goods
President: Bernard Armbrust
bernard@tubesrus.com
VP: Chris Armbrust
Marketing: Bill Constable
Sales: Marc Armbrust
Secretary: Dorothee Johnstone
Plant Manager: Mike Johnstone
Estimated Sales: $5-10 Million
Number Employees: 20-49
Square Footage: 170000
Type of Packaging: Food Service, Private Label
Regions Exported to: Canada, Caribbean, Mexico
Percentage of Business in Exporting: 2

42055 Armeno Coffee Roasters LTD
75 Otis St
Northborough, MA 01532-2412 508-393-2821
Fax: 508-393-2818 beans@armeno.com
www.armeno.com
Coffee roaster
Owner: Chuck Koffman
beans@armeno.com
Co-Owner: John Parks
Estimated Sales: Under $1 Million
Number Employees: 1-4
Square Footage: 20000
Type of Packaging: Consumer, Private Label

42056 Armstrong Hot Water
221 Armstrong Blvd
Three Rivers, MI 49093-2374 269-279-3602
Fax: 269-279-3150 www.armstrong-intl.com
Manufacturer and exporter of hose stations and thermostatic mixing valves
President: David Armstrong
General Manager/Sales/Marketing Exec.: Paul Knight
Purchasing Agent: Steven Shutes
Number Employees: 20-49
Parent Co: Armstrong International
Brands Exported: Rada; Steamix
Regions Exported to: Worldwide

42057 Arnabal International, Inc.
13459 Savanna
Tustin, CA 92782 714-665-9477
Fax: 714-665-9477 armen@arnabal.com
www.arnabal.com
Oils and vinegars
Owner: Nairy Balian
Co-Owner: Jeff Stratton
Estimated Sales: $ .5 - 1 million
Number Employees: 1-4

42058 Arnold Equipment Co
24400 Highpoint Rd # 5
Cleveland, OH 44122-6027 216-831-8485
Fax: 216-831-8414 800-642-1824
www.arnoldeqp.com
Wholesaler/distributor and exporter of blenders, ovens, agitators, filters, dryers, packaging plastic granulators, centrifuges, pumps, evaporators, condensers, kettles, homogenizers and material handling and laboratory testingequipment, etc
CEO: Jon Arnold
CFO: Seth Arnold
Estimated Sales: Less Than $500,000
Number Employees: 1-4
Square Footage: 120000
Regions Exported to: Europe, Asia, Middle East, Africa, Latin America, Caribbean, Australia
Percentage of Business in Exporting: 10

42059 Arnold's Meat Food Products
274 Heyward Street
Brooklyn, NY 11209 718-963-1400
Fax: 718-963-2303 800-633-7023
www.arnolds-sausage.com
Smoked sausage, scrapple, chorizos, kielbasa and bacon.
President: Sheldon Dosik
michelle_shao@colpal.com
VP: Jason Judd
Year Founded: 1967
Estimated Sales: $3.6 Million
Number Employees: 25
Square Footage: 33940
Type of Packaging: Consumer, Food Service, Private Label, Bulk

42060 Aroma Vera
5310 Beethoven St
Los Angeles, CA 90066-7015 310-204-3392
Fax: 310-306-5873 800-669-9514
cservice@aromavera.com
Processor, importer and exporter of essential oils
President: Marcel Lavabre
CEO: Klee Irwin
Estimated Sales: $59,000
Number Employees: 1
Square Footage: 200000
Brands Exported: Aroma Vera
Regions Exported to: Central America, South America, Europe, Asia
Percentage of Business in Exporting: 20
Brands Imported: Silver
Regions Imported from: South America, Europe, Asia

42061 Aroma-Life
16161 Ventura Boulevard
Encino, CA 91436-2522 818-905-7761
Fax: 818-905-0292 mzwan@aol.com
Almond and macadamia oils
President: Moshe Zwang
CEO: Diana Zwang
Estimated Sales: $300,000-500,000
Number Employees: 1-4
Number of Brands: 18
Number of Products: 16
Square Footage: 110000
Type of Packaging: Private Label, Bulk
Brands Exported: Aroma-Life
Regions Exported to: Europe, Asia, Middle East
Percentage of Business in Exporting: 50
Regions Imported from: South America, Europe, Asia, Middle East, Africa
Percentage of Business in Importing: 30

Importers & Exporters / A-Z

42062 Aromachem
599 Johnson Ave
Brooklyn, NY 11237 718-497-4664
Fax: 718-821-2193
Flavors, essential oils and fragrances
President: M Edwards
CEO: Leona Levine
Estimated Sales: $3 Million
Number Employees: 30
Square Footage: 100000
Type of Packaging: Bulk
Regions Exported to: South America, Europe, Asia, Mexico
Percentage of Business in Exporting: 20
Regions Imported from: South America, Europe, Asia, Canada
Percentage of Business in Importing: 10

42063 Aromatech USA
5770 Hoffner Avenue
Suite 103
Orlando, FL 32822 407-277-5727
Fax: 407-277-5725 americas@aromatech.fr
www.aromatech.fr/en/f.usa.htm
Flavorings for beverages, candies, baking, snacks and pastries.
Regions Exported to: South America, Europe, Asia, North America

42064 Aromi D' Italia
5 North Calhoun Street
Baltimore, MD 21223-1814 443-703-4001
Fax: 443-703-2194 877-435-2869
Contact: Hannah Follis
hfollis@aromibeauty.com
Estimated Sales: $ .5 - 1 million
Number Employees: 5-9

42065 Aromor Flavors & Fragrances
560 Sylvan Ave # 2030
Englewood Cliffs, NJ 07632-3165 201-503-1662
Fax: 201-503-1663 866-425-1600
Flavors and fragrances
Manager: Carol Feldman
cfeldman@aromor-usa.com
General Manager: Gary Romans
Number Employees: 1-4
Regions Imported from: Israel
Percentage of Business in Importing: 50

42066 (HQ)Arpac LP
9511 River St
Schiller Park, IL 60176-1019 847-678-9034
Fax: 847-671-7006 info@arpac.com
www.arpac.com
One stop shop packaging solutions. Manufacture shrink bundles, multipackers, horizontal shrin wrappers, corrugated tray and case erectors, box formers, corrugated board try and case packers, pallet stretch wrappers and pallet stretchhooders.
President: Michael Levy
Marketing Manager: Greg Levy
VP Sales: Gary Ehmka
Contact: Stephen Archer
sarcher@arpac.com
Estimated Sales: $ 10 - 50 Million
Number Employees: 5-9
Square Footage: 260000
Regions Exported to: Central America, South America, Europe, Asia, Middle East
Percentage of Business in Exporting: 10

42067 Arrow Chemical Inc
41 W Putnam Ave
Third Floor
Greenwich, CT 06830-5300 203-769-1740
Fax: 203-769-1741
Wholesaler/distributor and importer of preservatives
Owner: Roger Trief
Estimated Sales: $ 1 - 3 Million
Number Employees: 10-19
Square Footage: 4000
Type of Packaging: Bulk
Regions Imported from: Europe, Asia
Percentage of Business in Importing: 90

42068 Arrow Plastic Mfg Co
701 E Devon Ave
Elk Grove Vlg, IL 60007-6700 847-595-9000
Fax: 847-595-9122 info@arrowplastic.com
www.arrowplastic.com
Manufacturer and exporter of plastic cutting boards
President: Robert Kleckauskas
rkleck@arrowplastic.com
Estimated Sales: $20-50 Million
Number Employees: 100-249
Type of Packaging: Food Service
Regions Exported to: Worldwide

42069 Arrow Tank Co
16 Barnett Pl
Buffalo, NY 14215-3898 716-893-7200
Fax: 716-893-0693 sales@arrowtankco.com
www.arrowtankco.com
Manufacturer, exporter of wood tanks and tank hoops
President: William H Wehr
sales@arrowtankco.com
Operations: W H Wehr
Plant Manager: R Willis
Estimated Sales: $1-3,000,000
Number Employees: 5-9
Square Footage: 25000
Brands Exported: Arrow Tanks
Regions Exported to: Central America, South America, Europe, Middle East
Percentage of Business in Exporting: 50

42070 Arrowac Fisheries
Fisherman's Commerce Building
4039 21st Ave W, Suite 200
Seattle, WA 98199-1252 206-282-5655
Fax: 206-282-9329 info@arrowac-merco.com
www.arrowac-merco.com
Fresh and frozen seafood.
President: Frank Mercker
Vice President: Waltraut Yanagisawa
Estimated Sales: $25 Million
Number of Brands: 3
Number of Products: 15
Square Footage: 2000
Type of Packaging: Consumer, Food Service, Private Label, Bulk
Brands Exported: Arrow; Merco; Ocean Dawn
Regions Exported to: Worldwide
Percentage of Business in Exporting: 60
Regions Imported from: Europe, Asia, Mexico, Latin America
Percentage of Business in Importing: 25

42071 Art Printing Company
244 Bartley Drive
Toronto, ON M4A 1G1
Canada 416-751-9111
Fax: 416-751-8967 800-361-8113
artginou@artprinting.com www.artprinting.com
Prints place mates, try liners and coupons since 1932
President & CEO: Jim Ginou
Sales Director: Jonathan Ginou

42072 Art Wire Works Co
6711 S Leclaire Ave
Chicago, IL 60638-6417 708-458-3993
Fax: 708-458-3008 dcollignon@artwireworks.com
www.artwireworks.com
Manufacturer and exporter of display racks, point of purchase displays, back room trays and hand carts
President: David Collignon
dcollignon@artwireworks.com
CFO: Ksenia Nalysnyk
R&D/Quality Control: Danny Tomasevich
Sales: Gayle Blakeslee
Plant Manager: Wally Kaim
Purchasing: Gayle Blakeslee
Estimated Sales: $5 Million
Number Employees: 20-49
Square Footage: 80000

42073 Art-Phyl Creations
16250 NW 8th Avenue
Hialeah, FL 33014-6415 305-624-2333
Fax: 305-621-4093 800-327-8318
info@art-phyl.com
Manufacturer and exporter of store display fixtures, peghooks, merchandising aids, point of purchase displays, etc.
President: Arthur Hochman
CEO: S Gwinn
CFO: C Pomerantz
Sales: William Rodriguez
Estimated Sales: $ 5 - 10 Million
Number Employees: 20-49
Number of Products: 400
Square Footage: 200000
Regions Exported to: Worldwide
Percentage of Business in Exporting: 10

42074 Artemis International
3711 Vanguard Dr # A
Fort Wayne, IN 46809-3301 260-436-6899
Fax: 260-478-6900
info@artemis-international.com
www.artemis-international.com
Importer of fruit, juice concentrates, fibers and colors
Manager: Leslie Gallo
Sales/Marketing Assistant: Amber Hamilton
Estimated Sales: Less Than $500,000
Number Employees: 1-4
Brands Imported: Rubini
Regions Imported from: Italy
Percentage of Business in Importing: 100

42075 Artex International
1405 Walnut St
Highland, IL 62249 618-654-2113
Fax: 618-654-0200
Manufacturer and exporter of table linens including covers, skirts, napkins and place mats, restaurant design, linen processing, trade show listing, linen presentations
Manager: Mike Kirchoff
Estimated Sales: $50-100 Million
Number Employees: 50-99
Regions Exported to: Worldwide
Percentage of Business in Exporting: 1

42076 Arthur G Russell Co Inc
750 Clark Ave
P.O. Box 237
Bristol, CT 06010-4065 860-583-4109
Fax: 860-583-0686 agr@arthurgrussell.com
www.arthurgrussell.com
Manufacturer and exporter of automated packaging, counting, inspecting and assembling equipment for food and disposable manufacturers; custom design services available
President: Robert J Ensminger
robert.ensminger@arthurgrussell.com
Applications Engr.: John Picoli
Vice President Sales & Marketing: William Mis
Human Resources Manager: Shelly Bove
robert.ensminger@arthurgrussell.com
Operations Manager: Craig Churchill
Estimated Sales: $ 10-20 Million
Number Employees: 100-249
Square Footage: 166000
Regions Exported to: Worldwide
Percentage of Business in Exporting: 25

42077 Artisan Industries
73 Pond St
Waltham, MA 02451-4594 781-893-6800
Fax: 781-647-0143 info@artisanind.com
www.artisanind.com
Equipment to purify, concentrate, deodorize or recover/remove solvents or fatty acids
President: Andrew Donevan
SVP/General Manager: Perry Alasti
Director Marketing/Sales: Richard Giberti
Contact: Louis Decker
lou@dectechassociates.com
Pilot Plant Services: Robert DiLoreto
Estimated Sales: $ 5-10 Million
Number Employees: 100

42078 Artisanal Pantry
70 Pine St
New Canaan, CT 06840 877-478-9422
info@artisanalpantry.net
artisanalpantry.net
Artisanal foods

42079 Artiste Flavor
35 Franklin Tpke
Waldwick, NJ 07463 201-447-1311
Ingredients, flavors, colors and additives
President: Joseph Raimondo
Contact: Tracy Hennig
thennig@artiste.us.com
Estimated Sales: $500,000- 1 Million
Number Employees: 5-9
Type of Packaging: Consumer

42080 Artkraft Strauss LLC
1776 Broadway # 1810
New York, NY 10019-2017 212-265-5156
Fax: 212-265-5262 info@artkraft.com
www.artkraft.com
Manufacturer and exporter of advertising signs

Importers & Exporters / A-Z

President: Tama Starr
CFO: Neil Vonknoblauch
Vice President Design & Engineering: Robert Jackowitz
VP Sales: Bob Neuberger
Manager: Amy Hu
alexandra.labrie@mercer.com
Estimated Sales: $ 10 - 20 Million
Number Employees: 5-9
Type of Packaging: Consumer, Food Service, Bulk
Regions Exported to: Worldwide

42081 Ashlock Co
855 Montague St
P.O. Box 1676
San Leandro, CA 94577-4327   510-351-0560
  Fax: 510-357-0329   info@ashlockco.com
  www.ashlockco.com
Manufacturer and exporter of pitters for dates, prunes, cherries and olives. Also olive slicers
President: Tom Rettagliata
info@ashlockco.com
CFO: Sheryl Sullivan
R & D: Jeff Davis
Marketing Director: Alan Stender
Office Manager: S Sullivan
info@ashlockco.com
Manager, Operations: Jeff Davis
Estimated Sales: $5-10 Million
Number Employees: 10-19
Square Footage: 24800
Parent Co: Vistan Corporation
Regions Exported to: South America, Europe, Middle East, Australia
Percentage of Business in Exporting: 7

42082 Ashworth Bros Inc
450 Armour Dl
Winchester, VA 22601-3459   540-662-3494
  Fax: 540-662-3150   800-682-4594
ashworth@ashworth.com www.ashworth.com
Manufacturer and exporter of conveyor belts
President: Keith Almryde
keith.almryde@ashworth.com
VP: Joe Lackner
Quality Control: Jonathan Lasecki
Commercial Support Manager: Kenneth King
Sales: Marty Tabaka
Estimated Sales: $ 20 - 50 Million
Number Employees: 100-249
Regions Exported to: Worldwide

42083 Asia Etc. LLC
2566 Shallowford Rd
Suite 104
Atlanta, GA 30345   404-728-0632
  Fax: 404-320-9390 www.asia-etc.com
Marketing company specializing in Asian products
President & CEO: Nick Johnson
Executive Vice President: Ken Ishii
Operations: Nagendra Ingnam
Other Locations:
  San Francisco, CA
  Los Angeles, CALos Angeles

42084 Asiago PDO & Speck AltoAdige PGI
26 West 23rd Street
6th Floor
New York, NY 10010   646-624-2885
  Fax: 646-624-2893
Cheese, cured meats i.e. prosciutto/bacon.
Marketing: Flavio Innocenzi

42085 Asiamerica Ingredients
245 Old Hood Rd #3
Westwood, NJ 07675-3174   201-497-5993
  Fax: 201-497-5994   201-497-5531
info@asiamericaingredients.com
www.asiamericaingredients.com
Processor, importer, exporter and distributor of bulk vitamins, amino acids, nutraceuticals, aromatic chemicals, food additives, herbs, mineral nutrients and pharmaceuticals.
President/Owner: Mark Zhang
CFO: Lillian Yang
Quality Control: Michelle Naomi
Sales: Cari Pandero
Contact: Elizabeth Gysbers
egysbers@asiamericaingredients.com
Purchasing: Michelle N. Riley
Estimated Sales: $5-10 Million
Number Employees: 10
Type of Packaging: Bulk

42086 Aspen Mulling Company Inc.
C/O World Pantry Company
1192 Illinois Street
San Francisco, CA 94107   800-622-7736
  Fax: 970-925-5408   866-972-6879
aspenspices@worldpantry.com
www.aspenspices.com
Manufacturer and exporter of mulling spices
Manager: Leo Varade
Marketing: David Kallen
Estimated Sales: Under $5 Million
Number Employees: 5-9
Type of Packaging: Consumer, Food Service
Regions Exported to: Europe, Canada
Percentage of Business in Exporting: 10

42087 Assembled Products Corp
112 E Linden St
Rogers, AR 72756-6035   479-636-5776
  Fax: 479-636-5776   800-548-3373
techservice@assembledproducts.com
www.assembledproducts.com
Manufacturer and exporter of electric shopping carts for supermarkets and high pressure spray cleaning systems
President: Lori Barlar
lorib@martcart.com
Sr. VP Sales/Marketing: Steve Scroggine
Estimated Sales: $ 5-10 Million
Number Employees: 100-249
Square Footage: 256000
Parent Co: Assembled Products Corporation
Brands Exported: Spray Master Technologies
Regions Exported to: Central America, South America, Europe, Asia, Middle East, Canada
Percentage of Business in Exporting: 3

42088 Assembly Technology & Test
12841 Stark Rd
Livonia, MI 48150-1525   734-522-1900
  Fax: 734-522-9344
Designer and manufacturer of software for material handling implementation and electrified monorail systems for ingredient transport
Founder: Klaus Woerner
VP: James Diedrich
VP Sales/Marketing: Jim Anderson
Contact: Daniel Haubert
dhaubert@assembly-testww.com
Estimated Sales: $50-100 Million
Number Employees: 100-249
Square Footage: 200000
Parent Co: DT Industries
Brands Exported: Material Handling
Regions Exported to: Central America, South America, Europe, Asia, Worldwide

42089 Associated Fruit Company
3721 Colver Rd
Phoenix, OR 97535-9705   541-535-1787
  Fax: 541-535-6936
Manufacturer and exporter of fresh fruit including plums and pears
President: David Lowry
Purchasing: Scott Martinez
delrae.erickson@exchangebank.com
Estimated Sales: $1-2.5 Million
Number Employees: 6
Type of Packaging: Bulk
Regions Exported to: Worldwide

42090 Associated Packaging Equipment Corporation
70 Gibson Drive
Units 5 & 6
Markham, ON L3R 2Z3
Canada   905-475-6647
  Fax: 905-479-9752
Manufacturer and exporter of roll fed labeling machinery
President: M Malthouse
Controller: Kenneth Bick
Sales Director: Klaus See
Plant Manager: John Malthouse
Purchasing Manager: R Manoharan
Estimated Sales: $ 1 Million
Number Employees: 15
Square Footage: 24000
Type of Packaging: Food Service, Private Label
Regions Exported to: Worldwide
Percentage of Business in Exporting: 98

42091 Associated Products Inc
1901 William Flynn Hwy
P.O. Box 8
Glenshaw, PA 15116-1742   412-486-2255
  Fax: 412-486-7710   800-243-5689
Manufacturer and exporter of air fresheners, deodorants and deodorizers; importer of essential oils and aromatic chemicals
President: Ralph Simons
mrsimon@sani-air.com
CFO: Harlan Simons
Estimated Sales: $2.5-5 Million
Number Employees: 20-49
Number of Products: 100
Square Footage: 360000
Type of Packaging: Consumer, Private Label, Bulk
Regions Exported to: Worldwide
Regions Imported from: Worldwide

42092 Astor Chocolate Corp
651 New Hampshire Ave
Lakewood, NJ 08701-5452   732-901-1001
  Fax: 732-901-1003 info@astorchocolate.com
  www.astorchocolate.com
Manufacturer, importer and exporter of chocolate including fund raising, foiled novelties, bars, truffles, mints, shells and boxed.
President: Teri Aboud
teri.aboud@gmail.com
President: David Grunhut
CFO: Nat Vernaci
Sales Director: Howard Cubberly
Human Resource Executive: Arie Lax
Purchasing Manager: Karen Garrison
Estimated Sales: $25,000
Number Employees: 50-99
Square Footage: 66162
Type of Packaging: Consumer, Food Service, Private Label, Bulk
Regions Exported to: South America, Asia, Middle East, Canada, Caribbean
Percentage of Business in Exporting: 5
Regions Imported from: Europe
Percentage of Business in Importing: 50

42093 Astoria General Espresso
7912 Industrial Village Rd
Greensboro, NC 27409   336-393-0224
  Fax: 336-393-0295 info@geec.com
  www.usa.astoria.com
Manufacturer, importer and exporter of espresso and cappuccino machines, coffee grinders, espresso equipment accessories and sandwich grills
Owner: Roberto Daltio
CEO: Umberto Terreni
Accounting/Office Manager: Linda Sizemore
Sales & Marketing: Courtney Baber
Managing/Sales Director: Scott Gordon
Technical Support Specialist: Jimmy Wardell
Number Employees: 5-9
Number of Brands: 2
Number of Products: 36
Square Footage: 50000
Parent Co: CMA
Type of Packaging: Private Label
Brands Exported: Grillmaster; Astoria
Regions Exported to: Worldwide, Caribbean Area
Percentage of Business in Exporting: 10
Brands Imported: Grillmaster; Astoria
Regions Imported from: Europe, Caribbean Area
Percentage of Business in Importing: 90

42094 (HQ)Astra Manufacturing Inc
21520 Blythe St # A
Canoga Park, CA 91304-6609   818-340-1800
  Fax: 818-340-5830   877-340-1800
sales@astramfr.com www.astramfr.com
Manufacturer and exporter of espresso and cappuccino equipment including coffee grinders
President: Richard Hourizadeh
richard@astramfr.com
Estimated Sales: $3 Million
Number Employees: 5-9
Square Footage: 40000
Type of Packaging: Food Service
Brands Exported: Astra
Regions Exported to: Worldwide
Percentage of Business in Exporting: 20

Importers & Exporters / A-Z

42095 Astral Extracts
50 Eileen Way
Unit 6
Syosset, NY 11791-5313   516-496-2505
Fax: 516-496-4248 info@astralextracts.com
www.astralextracts.com
Processor, wholesaler, distributor, importer and exporter of fruit juice concentrates, essential oils and citrus products
President: Cynthia Astrack
info@astralextracts.com
General Manager: Joan Pace
Estimated Sales: $5-10 Million
Number Employees: 5-9
Square Footage: 30000
Type of Packaging: Food Service, Private Label, Bulk
Regions Exported to: South America, Europe, Asia, Canada, Mexico
Percentage of Business in Exporting: 20
Regions Imported from: South America, Europe, Asia, Worldwide
Percentage of Business in Importing: 20

42096 Astro Pure Water
1441 SW 1st Way
Deerfield Beach, FL 33441-6753   954-422-8966
Fax: 954-422-8966
Manufacturer and exporter of water purifiers and filters
President and CFO: Roger Stefl
VP Sales: Mary Munn
Office Manager: Miki Kaye
Estimated Sales: Below $ 5 Million
Number Employees: 10-19
Number of Brands: 1
Number of Products: 39
Square Footage: 6000
Type of Packaging: Consumer, Food Service, Private Label, Bulk
Regions Exported to: Europe

42097 At Last Naturals Inc
401 Columbus Ave # 2
Valhalla, NY 10595-1375   914-747-3599
Fax: 914-747-3791 800-527-8123
www.alast.com
Manufacturer and exporter of laxative tea and natural herbal health products.
Vice President: Fred Rosen
fred@alast.com
Estimated Sales: $ 1 - 3 Million
Number Employees: 1-4
Square Footage: 148000
Type of Packaging: Consumer
Regions Exported to: Central America, South America, Europe, Asia, Middle East
Percentage of Business in Exporting: 5

42098 At-Your-Svc Software Inc
450 Bronxville Rd
Bronxville, NY 10708-1133   914-337-9030
Fax: 914-337-9031 888-325-6937
sales@costguard.com www.costguard.com
Develops Cost Guard restaurant and foodservice software
President: Matthew Starobin
CEO: Pamela Terr
Contact: Mathew Starobin
matt@costguard.com
Estimated Sales: $2.5-5 Million
Number Employees: 5-9
Regions Exported to: Worldwide
Percentage of Business in Exporting: 10

42099 Atalanta Corporation
1 Atalanta Plz
Elizabeth, NJ 07206   908-351-8000
Fax: 908-555-8000 www.atalantacorp.com
Multi-national food importer specializing in meat, cheese, groceries, fruit, juice concentrates and fish products from around the world.
Chairman & Owner: George Gellert
Executive Vice President: Robert Gellert
Year Founded: 1945
Estimated Sales: $385 Million
Number Employees: 150
Other Locations:
Atalanta Corporation
Dawsonville, GA
Atalanta Corporation
Lexington, MA
Atalanta Corporation
Bartlett, IL
Atalanta Corporation
Arlington, TX
Atalanta Corporation
Kingwood, TX
Atalanta Corporation
Rockford, MI
Atalanta CorporationLexington

42100 Athea Laboratories
7855 N Faulkner Rd
Milwaukee, WI 53224   414-354-6417
Fax: 414-354-9219 800-743-6417
info@athea.com www.athea.com
Manufacturer and exporter of chemical specialties including ground and sewer maintenance chemicals, insecticides, aerosol, liquid and waterless hand cleaners and lotion; packager of aerosol and other products
President: Steve Hipp
VP Technical: Pete Martin
National Sales Manager: Ron Lloyd
Contact: Zech Ashba
zech.ashba@athea.com
Estimated Sales: $20-50 Million
Number Employees: 10
Parent Co: Share Company
Regions Exported to: Central America, Europe, Asia, Middle East
Percentage of Business in Exporting: 15

42101 Athena Controls Inc
5145 Campus Dr # 1
Plymouth Meeting, PA 19462-1195   610-828-2490
Fax: 610-828-7084 800-782-6776
sales@athenacontrols.com
www.athenacontrols.com
Manufacturer and exporter of temperature, power and process controls
Manager: Bob Schlegel
Sales/Marketing: Jennifer Klinedinst
Manager: C Bill
bc@athenacontrols.com
Estimated Sales: $10-20 Million
Number Employees: 50-99
Parent Co: Inductotherm Industries
Other Locations:
Athena Controls
Plymouth Meeting, PAAthena Controls
Regions Exported to: Worldwide

42102 Athenee Imports Distributors
515 Peninsula Blvd
Hempstead, NY 11550-5422   718-793-4805
Fax: 516-505-4876 info@atheneeimporters.com
www.atheneeimporters.com
Importer of wines and beer
Owner: Giota Englisis
VP: Giota Englisis
Estimated Sales: $5-10 Million
Number Employees: 10-19
Brands Imported: Aphrodite; Othelle; Keo Ouzo; Alkion; Thisbe; Bellapais; St. John Commandaria; St. Panteleimon; V.S.O.P. Brandy; Domaine D'ahera; Keo Beer
Regions Imported from: Cyprus , Greece
Percentage of Business in Importing: 100

42103 Atkins Elegant Desserts
11852 Allisonville Rd
Fishers, IN 46038-2312   317-570-1850
Fax: 317-773-3766 800-887-8808
Frozen cheesecakes, pies, cakes and pastries.
Manager: Debbie Llewellyn
CEO: Tom Atkins Jr
CFO: Tom Atkins
R&D: Darrell Bell
Quality Control: John Parent
Canadian National Manager: Wayne Barefoot
VP Sales & Marketing: Bob Barry
National Accounts Manager: Lisa Atkins Miller
Operations: Bill Beglin
Production: Jeff Fascko
Plant Manager: Terry Graves
Purchasing: Denise Miller
Estimated Sales: $12-13 Million
Number Employees: 50-99
Square Footage: 70000
Type of Packaging: Consumer, Food Service, Private Label
Brands Exported: Frozen Desserts; Cheesecakes; Cakes
Regions Exported to: Europe, Asia, Canada, Carribean

42104 Atkins Ginseng Farms
RR 1
PO Box 1125
Waterford, ON N0E 1Y0
Canada   519-443-7236
Fax: 519-443-4565 800-265-0239
Manufacturer, importer and exporter of ginseng products including capsules, also grower of american ginseng
Owner/President: Micheal Atkins
Estimated Sales: $20-50 Million
Number Employees: 5-9
Square Footage: 6000
Type of Packaging: Consumer, Private Label, Bulk
Regions Exported to: Europe
Percentage of Business in Exporting: 20
Regions Imported from: Asia
Percentage of Business in Importing: 20

42105 Atkins Temptec
6911 NW 22nd St Ste B
Gainesville, FL 32653   352-378-5555
Fax: 352-378-5550 www.cooperatkins.com
Chief Marketing Officer: Michael Carpenter
International Sales Manager: Ron Alonzo
Estimated Sales: $ 20 - 50 Million
Number Employees: 50-99
Parent Co: Cooper Instrument Corporation

42106 Atlanta SharpTech
403 Westpark Ct Ste 130
P.O. Box 11000
Peachtree City, GA 30269-3577
Fax: 404-752-9034 800-462-7297
Manufacturer and exporter of meat and bone cutting equipment including bandsaw blades, grinder plates, grinder knives, handsaw frames and handsaw blades
CEO: Tom Orelup
Estimated Sales: $20-50 Million
Number Employees: 100-249
Brands Exported: One Way; Swift Tooth; Double Cut; Powermate Kam-Lok
Regions Exported to: Central America, South America, Europe, Asia, Middle East
Percentage of Business in Exporting: 25

42107 Atlantic Aqua Farms
918 Brush Wharf Rd
Orwell Cove, PE C0A 2E0
Canada   902-651-2563
Fax: 902-651-2513 terry@canadiancove.pe.ca
www.canadiancove.com
Manufacturer and exporter of fresh mussels, oysters and clams-hardshell
GM: Brian Fortune
Number Employees: 50
Type of Packaging: Consumer, Food Service, Private Label, Bulk
Brands Exported: Canadian Cove
Regions Exported to: U.S.

42108 Atlantic Blueberry
7201 Weymouth Rd # A
Hammonton, NJ 08037-3414   609-561-8600
Fax: 609-561-5033 staff@atlanticblueberry.com
www.atlanticblueberry.com
Processor and exporter of fresh and frozen blueberries
President/CEO: Arthur Galletta
Harvest Crew Supervisor: Paul Galletta
Food Safety, Security, and Defense, QC: John Galletta
Sales: Art Galletta
General Inquiries, Press Inquiries: Denny Doyle
Operations: Robert Galletta
Year Founded: 1935
Estimated Sales: $5-10 Million
Number Employees: 10-19
Number of Brands: 1
Number of Products: 1
Square Footage: 320000
Type of Packaging: Private Label
Brands Exported: Atlantic Blueberry Co Private
Regions Exported to: South America, Europe

42109 (HQ)Atlantic Capes Fisheries
985 Ocean Dr
Cape May, NJ 08204-1855   609-884-3000
Fax: 609-884-3261 info@atlanticcapes.com
www.atlanticcapes.com
Fresh and frozen scallops, fish, clams, mackerel, squid and monkfish; importer of scallops; exporter of fresh and frozen scallops, squid, butterfish and mackerel

Importers & Exporters / A-Z

President: Daniel Cohen
dcohen@atlanticcapesfisheries.com
VP, Sales/Marketing: Jeff Bolton
VP, Operations: David Shaw
Estimated Sales: $15 Million
Number Employees: 20-49
Square Footage: 40000
Other Locations:
 ACF Production Facility
 Point Pleasant Beach, NJ
 ACF Sales/Marketing Office
 New Bedford, MAACF Production FacilityNew Bedford
Regions Exported to: Worldwide
Percentage of Business in Exporting: 30
Regions Imported from: Asia

42110 Atlantic Chemicals Trading
116 N Maryland Ave # 210
Glendale, CA 91206-4270   818-246-0077
    Fax: 617-292-0073   usa@act.de
    www.act.de
Manufacturer and distributor of flavors such as peppermint & menthol, sweeteners, acidifiers and preservatives. Food additives and preservatives
General Manager: Jaklin Minasian
Number Employees: 5-9
Regions Exported to: Europe, Asia, USA

42111 Atlantic Coast CrushersInc
128 Market St
Kenilworth, NJ 07033-2026   908-259-9292
   Fax: 908-259-9280   info@gocrushers.com
    www.gocrushers.com
Owner: Jack Paddock
paddockj@gocrushers.com
Estimated Sales: $ 3 - 5 Million
Number Employees: 5-9

42112 Atlantic Fish Specialties
17 Walker Drive
Charlottetown, PE C1A 8S5
Canada   902-894-7005
   Fax: 902-566-3546   macneill@cookeaqua.com
    www.cookeaqua.com
Manufacturer and exporter of smoked salmon, mackerel and trout
President: Glenn Cooke
General Manager: Doug Galen
Number Employees: 40
Type of Packaging: Consumer, Food Service, Private Label, Bulk
Regions Exported to: USA

42113 Atlantic International Products
1301 Broad St
Po Box 4429
Utica, NY 13501-1605   315-738-4370
   Fax: 315-738-7855   888-724-4837
    joel@aipi.net   www.aipi.net
Coffee, full-line oils, full-line vinegar, cheese, pasta (dry), full-line meat/game/pate, olives, other vegetables/fruit.
Sales Exec: Joel Mc Intyre
Number Employees: 20-49

42114 Atlantic Meat Company
2600 Louisville Rd
Savannah, GA 31415   912-964-8511
    Fax: 912-964-6831
Fresh and frozen ground beef, including hamburger patties
President/CEO: Lee Javetz
Purchasing Agent: Marc Javetz
Estimated Sales: $20-50 Million
Number Employees: 50
Square Footage: 30000
Type of Packaging: Consumer, Food Service, Private Label, Bulk

42115 Atlantic Mussel Growers Corporation
PO Box 70
Pointe Pleasant Road
Murray Harbour, PE C0A 1R0
Canada   902-962-3089
   Fax: 902-962-3741   800-838-3106
Manufacturer and exporter of fresh mussels
Executive Manager: John Sullivan
Business Manager: Rollie McInnis
Operations Manager: Marjorie Henderson
Number Employees: 25
Type of Packaging: Consumer, Private Label, Bulk
Regions Exported to: U.S.

42116 Atlantic Rubber Products
3065 Cranberry Hwy 13
East Wareham, MA 02538-1325   508-291-1211
   Fax: 508-291-1123   800-695-0446
Manufacturer, importer and exporter of rubber safety flooring for kitchens, bars and entrance ways
Owner: John Donahue
Sales Director: Susan Boyens
Contact: Susan Donahue
donahue@atlanticrubber.com
General Manager: Jerry Donahue
Estimated Sales: $ 5-10 Million
Number Employees: 10-19
Number of Products: 85
Square Footage: 56000
Type of Packaging: Consumer, Food Service, Bulk
Regions Exported to: Central America, South America, Europe, Asia, Caribbean, Latin America, Mexico, Africa
Percentage of Business in Exporting: 5
Percentage of Business in Importing: 40

42117 Atlantic Seafood Direct
12 A Portland Fish Pier
PO Box 682
Portland, ME 04104
    800-774-6025
Seafood fresh and frozen
President: Jerry Knecht
VP/General Manager: Mike Norton

42118 Atlantic Ultraviolet Corp
375 Marcus Blvd
Hauppauge, NY 11788-2026   631-273-0500
   Fax: 631-273-0771   866-958-9085
   sales@ultravioletuv.com   www.ultraviolet.com
Manufacturer and exporter of ultraviolet sterilization products for air, water and surfaces
CEO: Hilary Boehme
CFO: Arlene Metzroth
VP: Thomas Dituro Sr.
Director of Marketing: Ann Wysocki
Estimated Sales: $ 10 - 20 Million
Number Employees: 20-49
Square Footage: 50000
Brands Exported: Nutripure; Sanitaire; Hygeaire; Sanitron; Mighty-Pure; Minipure; Tank Master; Magnum; Megatron
Regions Exported to: Central America, South America, Europe, Asia, Middle East
Percentage of Business in Exporting: 40

42119 Atlantic Veal & Lamb Inc
275 Morgan Ave
Brooklyn, NY 11211
    800-222-8325
  info@atlanticveal.com   www.atlanticveal.com
Processor and exporter of individually vacuumed frozen veal including portion controlled, hand sliced, leg cutlets, roasts and cubed.
Chief Executive Officer: Phillip Peerless
ppeerless@atlanticveal.com
Chairman: Marty Weiner
CFO: Joe Saccardi
VP: Martin Weiner
Lamb Sales Director: Dan Salmon
National Sales Director: John Ricci
Customer Service Manager: Mario Vigorito
Chief Operating Officer: Shawn Peerless
Estimated Sales: $20-50 Million
Number Employees: 100-249
Type of Packaging: Consumer, Food Service
Regions Exported to: Europe, Asia, Middle East
Percentage of Business in Exporting: 10

42120 Atlantis Industries Inc
1 Park St
Milton, DE 19968-1108   302-684-8542
   Fax: 302-684-3367   contact@atlantisusa.com
    www.atlantisusa.com
Manufacturer and exporter of injection molded plastic tumblers, dessert dishes, bowls, salad bowls and mugs
President: Kenneth Orr
kenneth@atlantisusa.com
VP: Ken Orr
Sales: Judie Brasure
Estimated Sales: $ 2.5-5 Million
Number Employees: 20-49
Square Footage: 56000
Brands Exported: Sparkle-Lite
Regions Exported to: Worldwide
Percentage of Business in Exporting: 3

42121 Atlantis Plastics Linear Film
PO Box 9769
Tulsa, OK 74157-0769   918-446-1651
   Fax: 918-227-2454   800-324-9727
    paul.saari@atlantisplastics.com
Manufacturer and exporter of polyethylene stretch film
Manager: Randy Goodman
CFO: Paul G Saari
VP Sales: John Buchan
Estimated Sales: $10-20 Million
Number Employees: 100-249
Parent Co: Atlantis Films
Regions Exported to: Central America, Europe, Asia
Percentage of Business in Exporting: 5

42122 Atlantis Smoked Foods
4126 Pleasantdale Rd
#B110
Atlanta, GA 30340-3518   770-209-0611
   Fax: 770-209-0608   800-228-6480
    atlantisdirect@aol.com
Importer of smoked seafood including salmon, halibut, trout, and sea bass
President: Maurice Eissner
Estimated Sales: $1.2 Million
Number Employees: 7
Square Footage: 80000
Type of Packaging: Food Service
Brands Imported: Imperial, Fjord Superior
Regions Imported from: South America, Europe
Percentage of Business in Importing: 55

42123 Atlantix Commodities
5110 12th Ave
Brooklyn, NY 11219   718-256-1000
   Fax: 718-256-2743   877-595-1155
   info@atlantixco.com   www.atlantixco.com
Importer of nuts and dried fruit.
CEO: Bentzy Klein

42124 Atlapac Trading Inc
2240 Garfield Ave
Commerce, CA 90040-1808   323-278-1936
   Fax: 323-726-3452   800-254-2472
   atlapac@aol.com   www.atlapactrading.com
Importer of canned and fresh specialty foods
Owner: Vicki Chekel
CFO: T Knoll
Sales Manager: D Torrington
vicki@atlapactrading.com
Estimated Sales: $10-20 Million
Number Employees: 20-49
Square Footage: 100000
Brands Imported: California Girl
Percentage of Business in Importing: 100

42125 Atlas Match Company
45 Leadale Avenue
Toronto, ON M4G 3E9
Canada   416-929-8147
   Fax: 416-961-3275   888-285-2783
   nmackay11@rogers.com   www.atlasmatch.com
Manufacturer, importer and exporter of custom designed wooden and book matches; also, reusable board coasters and cocktail and dinner napkins.
President: N Mackay
CFO: Sohan Kansal
Sales: W Teltz
Operations: Esther Tarahdmi
Number Employees: 5-9
Number of Brands: 2
Number of Products: 5
Square Footage: 8000
Type of Packaging: Food Service, Private Label, Bulk
Brands Exported: Atlas
Regions Exported to: Central America, South America, USA
Percentage of Business in Exporting: 60
Regions Imported from: USA
Percentage of Business in Importing: 20

42126 Atlas Match Corporation
1801 S Airport Cir
Euless, TX 76040   817-354-7474
   Fax: 817-354-7478   800-628-2426
   custserv@atlasmatch.com   www.atlasmatch.com
Manufacturer, exporter and importer of matchbooks, box matches, scratchbooks and scratchpads
President: David Bradley
COO: Doug Lamb

Estimated Sales: $10-20 Million
Number Employees: 50-99
Square Footage: 130000
Regions Exported to: Europe
Percentage of Business in Exporting: 2
Regions Imported from: Asia

42127 (HQ)Atlas Minerals & Chemicals Inc
1227 Valley Rd
P.O. Box 38
Mertztown, PA 19539-8827   610-682-7171
    Fax: 610-682-9200   800-523-8269
    sales@atlasmin.com   www.atlasmin.com
Manufacturer and exporter of construction materials including floor plates, drains and coatings and corrosion prevention; also, tanks for processing and storage
President: Francis X Hanson
fhanson@atlasmin.com
Marketing: Scott Gallagher
Sales: Steve Abernathy
Number Employees: 50-99
Type of Packaging: Food Service, Private Label
Regions Exported to: Worldwide

42128 (HQ)Atlas Pacific Engineering
1 Atlas Ave
P.O. Box 500
Pueblo, CO 81001-4833   719-948-3040
    Fax: 719-948-3058   sales@atlaspacific.com
Manufacturer and exporter of decidious fruit and vegetable processing equipment including pitters, slicers, peelers, washers, cutters, sorters and scrubbers
President: Erik Teranchi
CFO: Don Freeman
VP Marketing: Robb Morris
Manager: Tom Ogrodny
tomo@atlaspacific.com
Estimated Sales: $20-50 Million
Number Employees: 100-249
Square Footage: 175000
Parent Co: Gulftech
Regions Exported to: Central America, South America, Europe, Asia, Middle East, Australia
Percentage of Business in Exporting: 40

42129 Atlas Packaging Inc
13165 NW 38th Ave
Opa Locka, FL 33054-4530   305-688-5096
    Fax: 305-685-0843   800-662-0630
    randy@atlaspackaginginc.com
    www.atlaspackaginginc.com
Designer and manufacturer of all types of packaging, litho laminated boxes and displays. Also provides promotional items such as standers and casecards.
President: Penny Kroker
penny@flhosp.org
Sales Manager: Randy Macias
Estimated Sales: $ 5-10 Million
Number Employees: 50-99
Square Footage: 112000
Regions Exported to: Central America, South America, Caribbean
Percentage of Business in Exporting: 5

42130 Atoka Cranberries, Inc.
3025 Route 218
Manseau, Quebec, QC G0X 1V0
Canada   819-356-2001
    Fax: 819-356-2111   infoatoka@atoka.qc.ca
Grower and processor of fresh and dried cranberries, and cranberry juice concentrate for industrial applications. Founded in 1984.
President: Mark Bieler
Regions Exported to: Europe, Asia, North America

42131 (HQ)Atrium Biotech
1405 Boul
Quebec, QC G1P 4P5
Canada   418-652-1116
    Fax: 866-628-6661
Processor, importer and exporter of shark cartilage, nutritional supplements and powders. Developers and marketing of value added ingredients
President: Richard Bordeleau
CEO: Luc Dupont
Vice President/CFO: Jocelyn Harvey
Development: Serge Yelle
Sales: Johan Aerts
Purchasing: Rene Augstburger

Estimated Sales: $1.5 Million
Number Employees: 20
Number of Brands: 3
Number of Products: 20
Square Footage: 400000
Brands Exported: Cartilade
Regions Exported to: South America, Europe, Asia, Middle East, Australia
Percentage of Business in Exporting: 30
Regions Imported from: Central America

42132 (HQ)Attias Oven Corp
926 3rd Ave
Brooklyn, NY 11232-2002   347-619-0314
    Fax: 212-979-1423   800-928-8427
    info@attiasco.com   www.attiasco.com
Manufacturer and exporter of pizza ovens, rotisseries, mixers, slicers, ice makers, refrigerators, freezers, dishwashers, toasters, blenders, sheeters, dividers and rounders
President: Simon Attias
Estimated Sales: $ 3 - 5 Million
Number Employees: 5-9
Regions Exported to: Middle East, Russia
Percentage of Business in Exporting: 5

42133 Atwater Block Brewing Company
237 Joseph Campau St
Detroit, MI 48207   313-877-9205
    Fax: 313-877-9241   atwater@atwaterbeer.com
    www.atwaterbeer.com
German-style lager, ale and beer; importer of malt and hops
President: Mark Rieth
Contact: Chelsea Iadipaolo
chelsea@atwaterbeer.com
Estimated Sales: $ .5 - 1 million
Number Employees: 10-19
Square Footage: 80000
Type of Packaging: Consumer, Food Service, Private Label
Regions Imported from: Europe
Percentage of Business in Importing: 10

42134 Atwater Foods
10182 Roosevelt Hwy
Route 18
Lyndonville Orleans, NY 14098-9785   585-765-2639
    Fax: 585-765-9443   www.shorelinefruit.com
Manufacturer, exporter and wholesaler of many kinds of dried fruit, including apples, cherries, cranberries, blueberries and strawberries. Star-K Kosher. Our customer service support is responsive to timelines and responsible forkeeping everything on track
Manager: Randy Atwater
Quality Control: Chris Fraser
Sales/Marketing: Jim Palmer
Contact: Fred Freeman
fred@atwaterfoods.com
Plant Manager: Steve Mohr
Purchasing Manager: Pat Glidden
Estimated Sales: 15-20 Million
Number Employees: 50-99
Number of Products: 50+
Square Footage: 180000
Type of Packaging: Private Label, Bulk
Regions Exported to: Europe, Canada
Percentage of Business in Exporting: 25

42135 (HQ)Audion Automation
1533 Crescent Dr # 102
Carrollton, TX 75006-3642   972-389-0777
    Fax: 972-389-0790   info@clamcopackaging.com
    www.audionltd.com
Manufacturer and exporter of flexible packaging machinery including bag opening, filling and heat sealing; also, shrink packaging
President: Mark Goldman
markg@paçaids.com
CFO: David Johnson
Vice President Marketing & Sales: Dennis McGrath
Sales Manager: Bob Sorrentino
Operations Manager: David Bibb
Estimated Sales: $ 20 - 50 Million
Number Employees: 20-49
Square Footage: 56000
Brands Exported: Titan; Sergeant
Regions Exported to: Central America, South America, Europe, Asia
Percentage of Business in Exporting: 15

42136 Auger Fab
418 Creamery Way
Exton, PA 19341-2500   610-524-3350
    Fax: 610-363-2821   800-334-1529
    info@auger-fab.com   www.augerfabrication.com
Manufacturer and exporter of stainless steel and plastic liquid and powder filling equipment including replacement augers and funnels
President: Erick Edginton
ericke@augerfab.com
CFO: Bill Egan
Regional Sales Manager: Allen Stewart
VP, Sales & Marketing: Kyle Edginton
Operations Manager: Rick Brennecke
Estimated Sales: $ 10-20 Million
Number Employees: 100-249
Square Footage: 100000
Regions Exported to: Worldwide
Percentage of Business in Exporting: 15

42137 August Thomsen Corp
36 Sea Cliff Ave
Glen Cove, NY 11542-3699   516-676-7100
    Fax: 516-676-7108   800-645-7170
    www.atecousa.com
Manufacturer, importer and exporter of pastry tubes, pastry bags and other baking utensils
President: Jeffrey Schneider
jeff@atecousa.com
VP: Douglas Schneider
Estimated Sales: $ 10 - 20 Million
Number Employees: 20-49
Brands Exported: Ateco
Regions Exported to: Central America, South America, Europe, Asia
Percentage of Business in Exporting: 25
Brands Imported: Ateco
Regions Imported from: Europe, Asia
Percentage of Business in Importing: 40

42138 Aunt Sally's Praline Shops
750 Saint Charles Ave
New Orleans, LA 70130-3714   504-522-2126
    Fax: 504-944-5925   800-642-7257
    service@auntsallys.com   www.auntsallys.com
New Orleans style creamy praline candies in four flavors, and other specialty food items.
Manager: Bethany Gex
CEO: Frank Simoncioni
Sales: Becky Hebert
Sales: Cherie Cunningham
Director Of Operations: Karl Schmidt
Estimated Sales: $5 Million+
Number Employees: 20-49
Square Footage: 20000
Type of Packaging: Consumer, Food Service, Private Label, Bulk

42139 Auromere Inc
2621 W Highway 12
Lodi, CA 95242-9200   209-339-3710
    Fax: 209-339-3715   800-735-4691
    info@auromere.com   www.auromere.com
Wholesaler/distributor, importer and exporter of supplements and jams, also deals with natural body care
President: Dakshina Vanzetti
dakshina@auromere.com
VP: Vishnu Eschner
Estimated Sales: Less Than $500,000
Number Employees: 1-4
Square Footage: 28000
Type of Packaging: Consumer
Brands Exported: Auromere; Chandrika; Herbomineral
Regions Exported to: Europe, Canada
Brands Imported: Auromere; Chandrika; Herbomineral; Ayurvedic
Regions Imported from: Asia

42140 Aurora Design Associates, Inc.
1308 South 1700 East
Suite 203
Salt Lake City, UT 84108   801-588-0111
    Fax: 801-588-0333
Manufacturer and exporter of servers and ice buckets for wine, water and champagne
President: Rob Norton
Contact: Robert Norton
robnorton1@att.net
Advertising Manager: Rick Daynes
Estimated Sales: Less than $500,000
Number Employees: 1-4

Number of Products: 6
Square Footage: 14000
Brands Exported: Aurora Design Servers
Regions Exported to: Europe
Brands Imported: Aurora Design Servers
Regions Imported from: Asia

42141 Aurora Packing Co Inc
125 S Grant St
North Aurora, IL 60542-1603 630-897-0551
Fax: 630-897-0647 www.aurorabeef.com
Processor and exporter of beef. Meat packing plant founded in 1939.
CFO: Don Tanis
dtanis@aurorapacking.com
VP: Marvin Doty
Estimated Sales: $41 Million
Number Employees: 100-249
Number of Brands: 1
Type of Packaging: Consumer, Food Service, Private Label
Regions Exported to: Asia

42142 Aust & Hachmann
1751 Richardson Street
Suite 4303
Montreal, Quebec, CN H3K 1G0
Canada 514-482-4615
Fax: 514-482-6183
Importer and wholesaler/distributor of vanilla beans and vanilla by-products
Director: David Van Der Walde
Fin.: Diane Lotosky
Sales Director: Patricia Raymond
Regions Imported from: Europe, Asia, India
Percentage of Business in Importing: 100

42143 Austrade
3309 Northlake Blvd
Suite 201
Palm Beach Gardens, FL 33403 561-586-7145
Fax: 561-585-7164 info@austradeinc.com
www.austradeinc.com
Importer, wholesaler of non-GMO and organic ingredients
President: Gary Bartl
Finance Director: Schantl Joseph
VP: Stephen Barti
Vice President Business Development: Robert Rice
VP Operations: Josef Schantl
Estimated Sales: $380,000
Number Employees: 1-4
Square Footage: 8000
Parent Co: GBI Bartl Intertrading
Type of Packaging: Private Label, Bulk
Regions Exported to: Central America, South America, Canada, Mexico
Percentage of Business in Exporting: 20
Brands Imported: Agrana, Dena
Regions Imported from: Europe, Asia, Latin America
Percentage of Business in Importing: 100

42144 Autio Co
93750 Autio Loop
Astoria, OR 97103-8400 503-458-6191
Fax: 503-458-6409 800-483-8884
office@autioco.com www.autioco.com
Manufacturer and exporter of grinders and pumps
President: Marvin Autio
marvin.autio@autioco.com
Office Manager: Marilyn Anderson
Estimated Sales: $ 1 - 3 Million
Number Employees: 10-19
Regions Exported to: Central America, Europe, Asia, Canada

42145 Auto Labe
3101 Industrial Avenue
Suite 2
Fort Pierce, FL 34946 772-465-4441
Fax: 772-465-5177 800-634-5376
info@autolabe.com www.autolabe.com
Manufacturer and exporter of labeling equipment for fruits and vegetables, bottles, cans, boxes, cartons, bar coding, etc
President: Robert Smith
Marketing/Sales: Bob Peterson
Public Relations: Roy Shepherd
Production/Plant Manager: Dean Stauffer
Estimated Sales: $10-20 Million
Number Employees: 50-99
Square Footage: 50000
Parent Co: Booth Manufacturing Company

Regions Exported to: Central America, South America, Mexico

42146 Autobar Systems
1800 Bloomsbury Ave
Asbury Park, NJ 07712-3975 732-922-3355
Fax: 732-922-2221 autobarcorp@aol.com
Manufacturer and exporter of alcoholic beverage dispensers and control equipment for bars, convention centers and restaurants
CEO: Donald Ullery
Estimated Sales: Below $ 5 Million
Number Employees: 5-9
Square Footage: 8000
Brands Exported: Autobar
Regions Exported to: Central America, Europe, Middle East, Canada, Latin America, Mexico
Percentage of Business in Exporting: 10

42147 Autocon Mixing Systems
2360 Vallejo St
St Helena, CA 94574-2432 707-963-3998
Fax: 707-963-3978 800-225-6192
tom@theosten.com www.autoconsystems.com
Manufacturer and exporter of continuous solid/liquid feeders and dry blending processing systems
President: Thomas Haas
info@autoconsystems.com
Estimated Sales: $ 5 - 10 Million
Number Employees: 20-49
Square Footage: 10000
Brands Exported: Osio Mixer
Regions Imported from: South America, Europe, Asia

42148 Autofry
10 Forbes Rd
Northborough, MA 01532-2501 508-460-9800
Fax: 508-393-5750 800-348-2976
www.autofry.com
Deep fryers
Mktg. Manager: Heather Guerriero
Regional Sales Manager: Laird Hansberger
Sales Manager: Gary Santos
Estimated Sales: Less Than $500,000
Number Employees: 1-4

42149 Automated Business Products
50 Clinton Pl # 1
Hackensack, NJ 07601-4562 201-489-1440
Fax: 201-489-9443 800-334-1440
Manufacturer, importer and exporter of money processing and handling systems, packagers, sorters, counters and automatic wrappers; also, food stamp counters, endorsers and microencoders
President: Robert J Mahalik
bmahalik@aol.com
Estimated Sales: $1-2,500,000
Number Employees: 10-19
Regions Exported to: Worldwide
Percentage of Business in Exporting: 30
Regions Imported from: Japan
Percentage of Business in Importing: 10

42150 Automated Flexible Conveyors
55 Walman Ave
Clifton, NJ 07011-3416 973-340-1414
Fax: 973-340-8216 800-694-7271
www.afcsolutions.com
Spiral and volumetric feeders, cartridge type bag dump stations and bulk bag unloading equipment; exporter of spiral feeders
President: Kevin Devaney
kfdevaney@aol.com
Vice President: Grace Faria
Estimated Sales: Below $5 Million
Number Employees: 5-9
Square Footage: 88000
Regions Exported to: Central America, South America, Europe, Asia, Middle East, Australia
Percentage of Business in Exporting: 10

42151 Automated Food Systems
1000 Lofland Dr
Waxahachie, TX 75165-6200 469-517-0470
Fax: 469-517-0476 sales@afstexas.com
www.afstexas.com
Manufacturer, exporter and importer of production systems for corn dogs, kebabs, skewering, sausage sticking and funnel cakes. Fryers, mixers, pumps; special design

President: Robert Walser
robin@afstexas.com
CFO: Tina Walser
Marketing Director/Sales: Chris Consalus
Marketing Coordinator: Robin Seeton
Production Manager: Jerry Reidel
Plant Manager: Charles Stone
Purchasing Manager: Robert Walser
Estimated Sales: $2.5-5 Million
Number Employees: 10-19
Square Footage: 48000
Brands Exported: Automated Food Systems, Inc.
Regions Exported to: Central America, Europe, Asia, Middle East, Africa, Australia, Canada
Percentage of Business in Exporting: 20
Brands Imported: Spikomat
Regions Imported from: Germany

42152 Automatic Bar Controls Inc
790 Eubanks Dr
Vacaville, CA 95688-9470 707-448-5151
Fax: 707-448-1521 800-722-6738
sales@wunderbar.com
Portable bars and dispensers including soft drink, liquor, juice, wine, beer and condiment; importer of beer dispensers; exporter of liquor, soft drink and condiment dispensers
President: Rick Martindale
rick.martindale@wunderbar.com
Sales/Marketing: Brent Baker
Purchasing Agent: Tim Schroeder
Estimated Sales: $ 50 - 100 Million
Number Employees: 100-249
Square Footage: 70000
Brands Exported: Wunder-Bar
Regions Exported to: Central America, South America, Europe, Asia, Middle East, Canada, Caribbean, Latin America, Mexico
Percentage of Business in Exporting: 25
Brands Imported: Celli-Codefesca
Regions Imported from: Australia, Canada, Europe
Percentage of Business in Importing: 2

42153 Automatic Handling Int
360 LA Voy Rd
Erie, MI 48133-9436 734-847-0633
Fax: 734-847-1823 info@automatichandling.com
www.automatichandling.com
Manufacturer and exporter of conveyors and conveyor systems, platforms, walkways and stairs; also, custom fabrication and custom stainless steel machinery available
President: Daniel Pienta
dan.pienta@automatichandling.com
Operations Manager: Dennis Barutha
Estimated Sales: $1.5,000,000
Number Employees: 100-249
Square Footage: 66000
Parent Co: Automatic Handling
Regions Exported to: Worldwide

42154 Automatic Products
PO Drawer 719
Williston, SC 29853 803-266-8891
Fax: 803-266-5150 800-523-8363
www.automaticproducts.com
Manufacturer and exporter of hot beverage vending machinery
President: Alan J Suitor
Sales Manager: Len McElhaney
Regions Exported to: Worldwide
Percentage of Business in Exporting: 50

42155 Automatic Products/Crane
165 Bridgepoint Dr
South St Paul, MN 55075-2500 651-288-2975
Fax: 651-224-5559 www.automaticproducts.com
Manufacturer and exporter of vending machinery including candy, pastry, snacks, coffee, hot drinks, ice cream and refrigerated/frozen foods
President: Robert J Sutter
CFO: Scott Edgergon
VP Marketing: James Radant
Quality Control: Randy Denver
Estimated Sales: Less Than $500,000
Number Employees: 1-4
Regions Exported to: Central America, South America, Europe, Asia, Middle East
Percentage of Business in Exporting: 15

42156 Automatic Specialties Inc
422 Northboro Road Central # 2
Marlborough, MA 01752-1895   508-481-2370
              Fax: 508-485-6276 800-445-2370
sales@auspin.com www.automaticspecialties.com
Manufacturer and exporter of wire racks and baskets, stainless steel fry baskets, trays and food machinery parts
President: Wilfred Moineau
Vice President: Bill Moineau
Marketing/Sales: Jay Graham
Public Relations: Jay Graham
Estimated Sales: $ 3 - 5 Million
Number Employees: 20-49
Square Footage: 60000
Brands Exported: Guardian Angel II; Wafios; Can Ready; Quick - Fill
Regions Exported to: Central America, South America, Europe, Asia, Middle East, Worldwide
Percentage of Business in Exporting: 20

42157 Automatic Timing & Controls
8019 Ohio Riv
8019 Ohio River Blvd.
Newell, WV 26050   304-387-1200
       Fax: 304-387-1212 800-727-5646
customerRFQ@marshbellofram.com
www.marshbellofram.com
Manufacturer and exporter of controls including temperature, counters, timers and photoelectric sensors
President: Arnold Siemer
Cmo: Dwight Nafziger
dnafziger@marshbellofram.com
CFO: Roger Bailey
R&D: Tom Villano
Production Manager: J Tornetta
Production: E Allgyer
Estimated Sales: $ 10 - 20 Million
Number Employees: 50-99
Square Footage: 120000
Parent Co: Desco Corporation
Regions Exported to: Central America, Europe, Asia, Canada, Mexico
Percentage of Business in Exporting: 10

42158 Automation Ideas Inc
9945 Greenland Ave NE
Rockford, MI 49341-9338   616-874-4041
       Fax: 616-874-3454 877-254-3327
jerry@automationideas.com
www.automationideas.com
Equipment for the water bottling, dairy and food processing industries.
President: Jerry Bott
jerry@automationideas.com
Vice President: Mick Donahue
Sales, Midwest Region: Dave Westra
Operations Manager: Justin Bott
Parts orders / Purchasing / Logistics: Brandon Totten
Number Employees: 20-49

42159 Autoprod
807 W Kimberly Rd
Davenport, IA 52806   563-391-1100
                      Fax: 563-391-0017
Manufacturer and exporter of packaging machinery for filling and closing pre-formed metallic, paper and plastic containers
President: Paul Desocio
CEO: Barry Shoulders
R & D: Hans Koule
Vice President Marketing & Sales: Tom Riggins
Sales: Barb Peeters
Trade Show Coordinator/Marketing: Mary Baltzell
Plant Manager: Larry Loftus
Purchasing Manager: Harvey Cassell
Number Employees: 50-99
Parent Co: IWKA Company
Type of Packaging: Consumer, Food Service, Private Label
Brands Exported: Fast-Pack; Versa-Pack; SLH
Regions Exported to: Worldwide
Percentage of Business in Exporting: 50

42160 Autoquip Corp
1058 W Industrial Rd
Guthrie, OK 73044-6046   405-282-5200
       Fax: 405-282-8105 877-360-6777
dcrabtree@autoquip.com www.autoquip.com
Manufacturer and exporter of material handling equipment including scissor lifts, turntables and tilters
President: Joe Robillard
jrobillard@autoquip.com
Plant Manager: Chris Curning
Manager, Marketing & Sales: Louis Coleman
Sales: Donnie Crabtree
Operations Director: Chris Kuehni
Engineering Director: Mike Adel
Supervisor, Parts & Services: Mike Calvert
Estimated Sales: $ 10 - 20 Million
Number Employees: 100-249
Parent Co: Autoquip Corporation
Regions Exported to: Worldwide

42161 Autotron
195 W Ryan Rd
Oak Creek, WI 53154-4400   414-764-7500
       Fax: 414-764-4298 800-527-7500
info@elwood.com www.elwood.com
Manufacturer and exporter of industrial photoelectric controls
President: Robert Larsen
Vice President/CFO: Terry Levin
Vice President: David Johnson
Quality Manager: John Hoeppner
Estimated Sales: $ 5 - 10 Million
Number Employees: 20-49
Square Footage: 60000
Regions Exported to: Central America, South America, Europe, Asia, Middle East
Percentage of Business in Exporting: 1

42162 Avalon Manufacturer
509 Bateman Cir
Corona, CA 92880-2012   951-340-0280
                      Fax: 951-340-0283 800-876-3040
info@avalonmfg.com www.avalonmfg.com
Manufacturer and exporter of fryers, glazers and stainless steel (aluminum) proof boxes
Owner: Troy Enger
troy@avalonmfg.com
VP: Troy Enger
Estimated Sales: $2.5-5 Million
Number Employees: 10-19
Square Footage: 80000
Regions Exported to: Central America, Middle East
Percentage of Business in Exporting: 10

42163 Avanti Products Inc
10880 NW 30th St
Doral, FL 33172-2189   305-592-7834
       Fax: 305-591-3629 800-323-5029
info@avantiproducts.com
www.avantiproducts.com
Importer of microwaves, freezers, compact refrigerators, wine coolers, gas ranges, mini kitchens, laundry products, water dispensers and vaccum cleaners
Owner: Frank E Mackle
Sales Rep: Randy Sizemore
Estimated Sales: $20-50 Million
Number Employees: 50-99
Parent Co: Mackle Company
Regions Imported from: Worldwide

42164 Avatar Corp
500 Central Ave
University Park, IL 60484-3147   708-534-5511
       Fax: 708-534-0123 800-255-3181
inquiries@avatarcorp.com www.avatarcorp.com
Manufacture, refine and supply raw materials and ingredients for the food, drug and personal care industries.
Owner: Kari Boykin
k.boykin@avatarholdings.com
President: Michael Shamie
VP Marketing: David Darwin
Chief Operating Officer: Phil Ternes
Plant Manager: Kent Taylor
Purchasing: Kristina Gutyan
Year Founded: 1982
Estimated Sales: $9 Million
Number Employees: 10-19
Square Footage: 80000
Type of Packaging: Private Label, Bulk
Regions Imported from: Central America, South America

42165 Avebe America Inc.
101 Interchange Plaza
Suite 101
Cranbury, NJ 08512   609-865-8981
                         www.avebe.com
Starch specialties for texture, protein enrichment, stability and appearance.
Estimated Sales: $20-50 Million
Number Employees: 20-49
Parent Co: AVEBE Group

42166 Avery Dennison Corporation
207 N Goode Avenue
Suite 500
Glendale, CA 91203-1301   626-304-2000
                         www.averydennison.com
Manufacturer and exporter of pressure sensitive labels.
Chairman/President/CEO: Mitch Butier
SVP/Chief Financial Officer: Greg Lovins
SVP/Chief Human Resources Officer: Anne Hill
SVP/General Counsel/Secretary: Susan Miller
VP/General Manager, Retail Branding: Deon Stander
VP/Global Operations/Supply Chain: Kamran Kian
Year Founded: 1935
Estimated Sales: $7.5 Billion
Number Employees: 30,000
Other Locations:
   Avery Research Center (AEM)
   Irwindale, CA
   Business Media
   Buffalo, NY
   Corporate
   Framingham, MA
   Corporate Int'l Manufacturing
   Covina, CA
   Corporate Office at Brea
   Brea, CA
   Corporate Office at Framingham
   Framingham, MA
   Avery Research Center (AEM)Buffalo

42167 Avery Weigh-Tronix
1000 Armstrong Dr
Fairmont, MN 56031-1439   507-238-4461
       Fax: 507-238-4195 877-368-2039
usinfo@awtxglobal.com
www.averyweigh-tronix.com
Manufacturer and exporter of industrial scales.
Estimated Sales: $533 Million
Number Employees: 5,500
Square Footage: 330000
Parent Co: Illinois Tool Works Inc.
Brands Exported: Avery Weigh-Tronix; GSE; Salter Brecknell
Regions Exported to: Central America, South America, Europe, Asia, Middle East

42168 Avery Weigh-Tronix LLC
1000 Armstrong Dr
Fairmont, MN 56031-1439   507-238-4461
       Fax: 507-238-4195 800-368-2039
usinfo@awtxglobal.com
www.averyweigh-tronix.com
Manufacturer, importer and exporter of point-of-sale interface scales that link to cash registers and computers; also, portion control scales
Cmo: Peggy Trimble
peggi.trimble@weigh-tronix.com
VP: Peggy Trimble
Worldwide Marketing Director: P Trimble
Sales Director: D Cone
Number Employees: 250-499
Square Footage: 130000
Parent Co: Weigh-Tronix
Other Locations:
   Weigh-Tronix
   Tonbridge, KentWeigh-Tronix
Brands Exported: NCI
Regions Exported to: Worldwide
Percentage of Business in Exporting: 2
Regions Imported from: Asia
Percentage of Business in Importing: 15

42169 Avestin
2450 Don Reid Drive
Ottawa, ON K1H 1E1
Canada   613-736-0019
       Fax: 613-736-8086 888-283-7846
avestin@avestin.com
Manufacturer and exporter of high pressure homogenizers, filters, extruders and liposome extruders
President: Mark Ruzbie
Vice President: Hilde Linder
Marketing Manager: Sophie Sommerer
Number Employees: 10
Brands Exported: Emulsiflex; Liposofast
Regions Exported to: Central America, South America, Europe, Asia, Middle East, USA
Percentage of Business in Exporting: 95

Importers & Exporters / A-Z

42170 Avo-King Internatl
2050 W Chapman Ave
Suite 210
Orange, CA 92868-2649 714-937-1551
Fax: 714-937-1974 800-286-5464
info@avo-king.com www.avo-king.com
Processor and importer of frozen guacamole and avocado pulp
Owner: Guido Doddoli
Controller: Francisco Philibert
commets@avo-king.com
Vice President: Pablo Doddoli
Estimated Sales: $2.5 Million
Number Employees: 1-4
Parent Co: Doddoli Hermanos Group

42171 Avoca
PO Box 129
841 Avoca Road
Merry Hill, NC 27957 252-482-2133
Fax: 252-482-8622 www.avocainc.com
Manufacturer and exporter of flavors and fragrances
President: David Peele
Director/ Business Development: Richard Maier
COO: Danny White
Research & Development: Richard Teague
Marketing Director: Shannon Sloan
Plan. Manager: Danny White
Number Employees: 50-99
Regions Exported to: Europe

42172 Avon Tape
79 Florence St Apt 310s
Chestnut Hill, MA 2467 508-584-8273
Manufacturer and exporter of pressure-sensitive tapes
President: Howard Shuman
Estimated Sales: $5-10 Million
Number Employees: 50-99
Regions Exported to: Worldwide
Percentage of Business in Exporting: 75

42173 Aw Sheepscot Holding CoInc
8809 Industrial Dr
Franksville, WI 53126-9337 262-884-9800
Fax: 262-884-9810 800-850-6110
sales@aw-lake.com www.awcompany.com
Manufacturer and distributor of flow control products including positive displacement flow meters, turbine flow meters, electronic sensors, flow computers, on-line optical sensors and signal conditioners.
President: Roger Tambling
Contact: Greg Baldwin
gbaldwin@aw-lake.com
Estimated Sales: $ 5 - 10 Million
Number Employees: 1-4
Square Footage: 60000
Brands Exported: FluidScan; EMAG; ProScan; FluidPro
Regions Exported to: Worldwide
Percentage of Business in Exporting: 15

42174 Award Baking Intl
206 State Ave S
New Germany, MN 55367-9521 952-353-2533
Fax: 952-353-8066 800-333-3523
awardbaking@oblaten.com www.oblaten.com
Biscottis and all natural specialty baked goods.
Owner: Tim Kraft
tkraft@oblaten.com
Co-Owner: Ken Barron
Marketing: Rhonda Kossack
Year Founded: 1948
Estimated Sales: $1-2.5 Million
Number Employees: 20-49
Square Footage: 40000
Parent Co: Kenny B's Cookie

42175 Awe Sum Organics
123 Locust St
Santa Cruz, CA 95060 831-462-2244
info@awesumorganics.com
www.awesumorganics.com
Organic apples, grapes, citrus, pears, kiwis, and blueberries
General Manager: Matt Landi
Financial Controller: Michael Meschi
Sales Coordinator: Sara Pettit
Year Founded: 1985
Number Employees: 20-49
Regions Imported from: Central America, South America, Europe, Oceania

42176 Awmco Inc
11560 184th Pl
Orland Park, IL 60467-4904 708-478-6032
Fax: 708-478-6041 awmco@aol.com
www.awmcoinc.com
Manufacturer and exporter of baking decks and cooking stones for pizza, pretzel and bagel ovens
President: Mark O'Toole
Manager: Mark Otoole
Estimated Sales: $2 Million
Number Employees: 5-9
Number of Brands: 4
Number of Products: 12
Square Footage: 72000
Type of Packaging: Food Service
Brands Exported: Fribrament; Oven Stone

42177 Axelrod, Norman N
445 E 86th St
New York, NY 10028-6433 212-369-2885
www.axelrodassociates.com
Manufacturer and exporter of optical sensing and vision systems for automated quality and process control systems for food processing and packaging. Consultant, market studies on optical sensing and control technologies
President: Norman N Axelrod, Phd
Manager of Systems Integration: C Chang
Manager Software Development: R Rolle
Estimated Sales: Less Than $500,000
Number Employees: 1-4
Regions Exported to: Europe, Canada

42178 Axelsson & Johnson Fish Company
PO Box 180
933 Ocean Drive
Cape May, NJ 08204-0180 609-884-8426
Fax: 609-898-0221 ajfish@bellatlantic.net
www.jerseyseafood.nj.gov
Exporter and importer of fresh seafood
Manager: Andrew Axelsson
Estimated Sales: $5-10 Million
Number Employees: 10-19

42179 Axiflow Technologies, Inc.
1955 Vaughn Road
Suite 103
Kennesaw, GA 30144 770-795-1195
Fax: 770-795-1342 www.axiflowtechnologies.com
Pumps, blenders and food processing machines for the food & beverage industries.
Regions Exported to: North America

42180 Axiohm USA
2411 N Oak Street
Suite 203 C
Myrtle Beach, SC 29577 843-443-3155
Fax: 888-505-9555 namsales@Axiohm.com
www.axiohm.com
Manufacturer and exporter of magnetic strip card readers and thermal laser receipt printers
President and CEO: Lindsey Allen
Director Marketing/Communications: Mark Basla
Number Employees: 60
Regions Exported to: Worldwide

42181 Ayush Herbs Inc
2239 152nd Ave NE
Redmond, WA 98052-5519 425-637-1400
Fax: 425-451-2670 800-925-1371
customerservice@ayush.com www.ayush.com
Wholesaler/distributor of general line items and health food including herbal and Ayurvedic extracts, standarized powder, raw herbs/spices, essential oils and Ayurvedic, herbal and green teas; importer and exporter of herbs
President: Shailinder Sodhi
shailinder@ayush.com
Sales Manager: Tarlok Kumar
Estimated Sales: $500,000-$1 Million
Number Employees: 5-9
Square Footage: 20000
Type of Packaging: Consumer, Bulk
Regions Exported to: Europe, Asia, Italy, Switzerland, Germany
Percentage of Business in Exporting: 25
Regions Imported from: Asia, India, Fiji
Percentage of Business in Importing: 60

42182 Azbros Inc
7516 NW 54th St
Miami, FL 33166-4813 305-477-0142
Fax: 305-594-8692
Purchasing and exporting of bakery items, plastic ware, packaging, dry food and more
Owner/President: Peter Azan
President: Jean-Pierre Dionne
Manager: Joselle Azan
Export Manager: Joselle Jureidini
Estimated Sales: $ 3 - 5 Million
Number Employees: 1-4

42183 Aztec Grill
PO Box 820037
Dallas, TX 75382 214-343-1897
Fax: 214-341-9996 800-346-8114
www.aztecgrill.com
Manufacturer and exporter of wood burning grills and rotisseries
Contact: Dennis Whiting
dennis@aztecgrill.com
Estimated Sales: $ 1 - 5 Million
Number Employees: 2
Square Footage: 16000
Type of Packaging: Food Service
Regions Exported to: Europe, Mexico
Percentage of Business in Exporting: 2

42184 Aztecas Design
P.O.Box 1189
Spring Valley, CA 91979 719-471-4189
Fax: 619-579-3891 877-729-8322
dina@aztecadesign.com www.aztecadesign.com
Owner: John Grabowski
Owner: Gabriela Grabowski
Estimated Sales: $ .5 - 1 million
Number Employees: 5-9

42185 (HQ)Azuma Foods Intl Inc USA
20201 Mack St
Hayward, CA 94545-1224 510-782-1112
Fax: 510-782-1188 www.azumafoods.com
Processor, exporter and importer of frozen seafood, caviar and ready-made sushi
President/CEO: Takahiro Tamura
Chairman: Toshinobu Azuma
Estimated Sales: $5-10 Million
Number Employees: 50-99
Other Locations:
  New York Branch
  East Rutherford, NJ
  Hawaii Sales Office
  Honolulu, HI
  West Coast American Division Sales
  Novato, CA
  East Coast American Division Sales
  Boston, MANew York BranchHonolulu
Regions Exported to: Worldwide
Percentage of Business in Exporting: 30
Regions Imported from: Worldwide
Percentage of Business in Importing: 50

42186 Azumex Corp.
9295 Siempre Viva Rdza
Suite A-B
San Diego, CA 92154 619-710-8855
619-207-0877
info@azumexsugar.com www.azumexsugar.com
Importer of cane sugar.
Contact: Noelle Campbell
ncampbell@azumexsugar.com
Regions Imported from: Mexico

42187 Azz/R-A-L
8500 Hansen Rd
Houston, TX 77075 713-943-0340
Fax: 713-943-8354 www.azz.com
Lighting fixtures for the food service industry.
Regions Exported to: Central America, North America, Worldwide

42188 (HQ)B & P Process Equipment
1000 Hess Ave
Saginaw, MI 48601-3729 989-757-1300
Fax: 989-757-1301 sales@bpprocess.com
www.bpprocess.com
Manufacturer and exporter of food processing machinery and equipment including automatic scales, sifters, etc

President: Alan Martin
alan@sandrofilm.com
R&D: Doug Hillman
Executive: Joe Flynn
CFO: Allen Martin
Estimated Sales: $ 20 - 50 Million
Number Employees: 50-99
Regions Exported to: Worldwide

42189 B G Smith & Sons Oyster Co
787 Oakley Ln
Sharps, VA 22548   804-394-2721
     Fax: 804-394-2741 877-483-8279
Manufacturer and exporter of fresh and frozen oysters; processor and packager of ice
President/CEO: B Smith
Estimated Sales: $2.5-5 Million
Number Employees: 10-19
Number of Brands: 3
Number of Products: 1
Square Footage: 400000
Type of Packaging: Consumer, Food Service, Private Label
Brands Exported: Chesapeake Pride; Perch Creek
Regions Exported to: Canada
Percentage of Business in Exporting: 10

42190 B H Bunn Co
2730 Drane Field Rd
Lakeland, FL 33811-1325   863-647-1555
    Fax: 863-686-2866 800-222-2866
    info@bunntyco.com www.bunntyco.com
Bunn tying machines for poultry, pork and beef
Owner: John R Bunn
jbunn@bunntyco.com
Estimated Sales: $ 3 - 5 Million
Number Employees: 10-19
Square Footage: 68000
Brands Exported: Bunn Tying Machines
Regions Exported to: Central America, South America, Europe, Middle East

42191 B T Engineering Inc
29 Bala Ave # 209
Bala Cynwyd, PA 19004-3269   610-664-9500
    Fax: 610-664-0317 bte123123@aol.com
    www.btengineering.com
Automated sanitary liquid food processing equipment and control systems including clean-in-place pipeline systems, pasteurizers and volumetric filling machines; exporter of skidded food systems; design services available
President/CEO: William Willard
CFO: Thomas Berger Sr
Secretary/Treasurer: Thomas Berger
Manager: W Willard
wilwillard@aol.com
Estimated Sales: $ 1-2.5 Million
Number Employees: 1-4
Square Footage: 5000
Type of Packaging: Food Service
Percentage of Business in Exporting: 5
Brands Imported: Alfa Laval; Lumaco
Regions Imported from: Europe
Percentage of Business in Importing: 20

42192 B W Cooney & Associates
28 Simpson Road
Bolton, Ontario, ON L7E 1G9
Canada   905-857-7880
    Fax: 905-857-7883 info@bwcooney.com
    www.bwcooney.ca
Shrink wrapping and tray stretch machines, flow wrappers, verticle form fill & seal systems, packaging film and retail food trays.
President: Brian Cooney
Number Employees: 2

42193 B&D Food Corporation
575 Madison Ave
Suite 1006
New York, NY 10022-8511   212-937-8456
     Fax: 212-412-9034
Roasted, ground coffee; chocolate beverages and cappuccinos; and spray dried agglomerated soluble coffee and powdered tea.
Chief Executive Officer/Board Directors: Yaron Arbell
Chief Financial Officer/Board Directors: Yossi Haras
Number Employees: 1-4
Type of Packaging: Food Service

42194 B. Terfloth & Company
229 Peachtree Street NE
Suite 1125, International Tower
Atlanta, GA 30303-1625   404-524-2204
     Fax: 404-524-8194
     worldmerchant@terflothusa.com
     www.terfloth.com
Meats, poultry, frozen goods, dry goods, canned goods, paper goods, produce, cheese
President: Boerries Terfloth
Executive VP: Raymond Evans
Type of Packaging: Consumer, Food Service, Private Label, Bulk
Regions Exported to: Central America, South America, Europe, West Indies
Brands Imported: Grace; Tradwinds; Fray Bentos; Buffet and Bar
Regions Imported from: Central America, South America, Europe, Far West

42195 B. Terfloth & Company
229 Peachtree Street NE
Suite 1125, International Tower
Atlanta, GA 30303-2808   404-524-2204
     Fax: 404-524-8194
     worldmerchant@terflothusa.com
     www.terfloth.com
Importer and exporter of frozen, canned, dried and pickled foods, oils, fats and fresh fruits and vegetables
Executive VP: Raymond Evans
VP: Carlton Myco
Number Employees: 10-19
Brands Exported: Grace; Eastson
Regions Exported to: Central America, South America, Caribbean
Percentage of Business in Exporting: 85
Regions Imported from: Central America, South America
Percentage of Business in Importing: 15

42196 B.A.G. Corporation
11510 Data Dr
Suite 170
Richardson, TX 75081   800-331-9200
    Fax: 214-340-4598 800-331-9200
    www.bagcorp.com
Manufacturer and exporter of the Super Sack container, a woven polypropylene FIBC for shipping, handling, and storing dry-flowable and fluid products
President: Karl Reimers
Estimated Sales: $5-10 Million
Number Employees: 20-49
Type of Packaging: Food Service, Bulk
Regions Exported to: Worldwide

42197 (HQ)B.C. Tree Fruits Limited
1473 Water Street
Kelowna, BC V1Y 1J6
Canada   250-470-4200
    Fax: 250-762-5571 info@bctree.com
    www.bctree.com
Exporter and importer of apples, pears, oranges, apricots, etc. Broker of plums and cherries
President: Jim Elliot
CEO: Greg Gauthier
CFO: John Bernard
VP: Glenn Cross
Director Sales: Lance McGinn
Estimated Sales: $17.8 Million
Number Employees: 39
Type of Packaging: Consumer, Food Service, Private Label
Other Locations:
    B.C. Tree Fruits Ltd.
    Toronto, ONB.C. Tree Fruits Ltd.
Regions Exported to: Central America, South America, Europe, Asia, Worldwide
Percentage of Business in Exporting: 35
Percentage of Business in Importing: 1

42198 B.M. Lawrence & Company
601 Montgomery St
Suite 1115
San Francisco, CA 94111-2614   415-981-2926
     Fax: 415-981-2926 info@bmlawrence.com
Wholesaler/Processor and distributor of soft drinks, nonalcoholic beer, canned fruits, vegetables, juices and fish
President: B Lawrence
Purchasing Agent: Hugh Ditzler
info@bmlawrence.com
Estimated Sales: $5-10 Million
Number Employees: 5-9
Square Footage: 8000
Brands Exported: California Farms; U.S. Cola
Regions Exported to: Asia, Middle East
Percentage of Business in Exporting: 90

42199 B/R Sales Company
31308 Via Colinas Ste 109
Westlake Village, CA 91362   818-597-5727
     Fax: 818-705-2935 brsclsout@aol.com
Exporter and wholesaler/distributor of closeout items including meats, fruit, vegetables, beverages, entrees, condiments, dry goods and frozen foods
President: Darrell Garnett
Estimated Sales: $2.5-5 Million
Number Employees: 1-4
Type of Packaging: Consumer, Food Service, Private Label, Bulk

42200 BAKERY.COM
48 N Ayer St
Harvard, IL 60033-2803   815-943-8730
    Fax: 815-943-7942 877-622-5379
    sales@bakery.com www.bakery.com
Bakery.com is a unique family owned and operated company providing quality and services to the bakery and food related industries. Focused on customer service through knowledge and experience, we are prepared to offer practicalsolutions and the best value for equipment, ingredients, and packaging available
President: John Stricker
john@bakery.com
Sales & Business Development: John Stricker
Equipment: Tony Stricker
Ingredients & Commodities: Kurt Stricker
Estimated Sales: Less Than $500,000
Number Employees: 1-4

42201 BBCA USA
20825 E Rocky Point Ln
Walnut, CA 91789-4029
     Fax: 626-581-3543 bbca1688@aol.com
Wholesaler/distributor, importer and exporter of citric acid, lactic acid; additive for food industry, potasium citrate, sodium citrate, calcium citrate
President: Walter Wang
Chairman: Kelvie Wen
Vice President: Wei Yang
Estimated Sales: $ 3 - 5 Million
Number Employees: 1-4
Square Footage: 60000
Parent Co: BBCA Biochemical Group
Regions Exported to: Asia
Regions Imported from: Asia

42202 BBQ Pits by Klose
1355 Judiway Street #B
Houston, TX 77018-6005   713-686-8720
     Fax: 713-686-8793 800-487-7487
     www.bbqpits.com
Manufacturer, importer and exporter of barbecue equipment including grills and smokers; also, catering trailers; wood, charcoal and gas fired.
President: David Klose
Sales: Dana Harlow
Contact: Carla Hadley
carla.hadley@bbqpits.com
Estimated Sales: $1-3 Million
Number Employees: 10-19
Number of Products: 500
Square Footage: 24000
Type of Packaging: Consumer, Food Service, Bulk
Brands Exported: Klose BBQ Pits
Regions Exported to: Worldwide
Percentage of Business in Exporting: 40
Regions Imported from: Worldwide
Percentage of Business in Importing: 20

42203 BCS International
47-15 33rd Street
Long Island City, NY 11101   718-392-3355
     Fax: 718-392-2072 www.bcsroyal.com
Cookies, crackers,, sugar-free, tea, non-alcoholic beverages, water, chips, nuts.
Contact: Dan Choi
dan.choi@bcsroyal.com

42204 BEI
1375 Kalamazoo St
South Haven, MI 49090   269-637-8541
     Fax: 269-637-4233 800-364-7425

Importers & Exporters / A-Z

Manufacturer and exporter of berry harvesters and packing equipment
President: William De Witt Jr
Vice President: Butch Greiffendorf
Contact: Rodney Tolbert
rtolbert@beiintl.com
Manager: J Greiffendorf
Estimated Sales: $5-10 Million
Number Employees: 20-49
Square Footage: 48000

42205 BEUMER Corp
800 Apgar Dr
Somerset, NJ 8873 732-893-2800
 Fax: 732-563-0905 usa@beumer.com
  www.beumer.com
Manufacturer, importer and exporter of material handling equipment including automatic palletizing systems and automatic shrink and stretch hood unitizing systems
President: Matthias Erdsmannadoerf
matthias.erdsmannadoerf@beumer.com
VP: Hanno Behm
Number Employees: 20-49
Square Footage: 10400
Parent Co: Beumer Maschinenfabrik GmbH & Company KG
Regions Exported to: Central America, South America, Canada, Caribbean, Latin America, Mexico
Regions Imported from: Europe

42206 BEVCO
9354-194th Street Surrey
Canada, BC V4N 4E9
Canada 604-888-1455
 Fax: 604-888-2887 800-663-0090
 info@bevco.net www.bevco.net
Manufacturer and exporter of material handling and distribution equipment including accumulators, conveyors, conveyor systems, depalletizers and elevators; also, warmers and bottle rinsers
President: Brian Fortier
CEO: D Hargrove
CFO: Dianne Hargrove
Sales/Marketing Executive: Murray Kendrick
Estimated Sales: $ 5 - 10 Million
Number Employees: 45
Square Footage: 80000
Regions Exported to: Central America, South America, Asia, Middle East, Canada, Mexico, Australia, Caribbean
Percentage of Business in Exporting: 90

42207 BEX Inc
836 Phoenix Dr
Ann Arbor, MI 48108-2221 734-464-8282
 Fax: 734-389-0470 sales@bex.com
  www.bex.com
Manufacture of spray nozzles and accessories for parts cleaning, rinsing and food processing.
Number Employees: 5-9
Regions Exported to: Europe, North America

42208 BFM Equipment Sales
209 Steel Road
P.O. Box 117
Fall River, WI 53932-0117 920-484-3341
 Fax: 920-484-3077 info@bfmequip.com
  www.bfmequip.com
Manufacturer, importer, exporter and wholesaler/distributor of food processing machinery, can end cleaners and dryers, replacement parts and supplies
Owner: Richard Bindley
Executive Manager: Russell Quandt
Contact: Leann Vick
lvick@bfmequip.com
Estimated Sales: Below $ 5 Million
Number Employees: 1-4
Square Footage: 40000
Brands Exported: Badger
Regions Exported to: Central America, South America
Percentage of Business in Exporting: 1
Regions Imported from: Europe

42209 BKI Worldwide
2812 Grandview Dr
Simpsonville, SC 29680-6217 864-963-3471
 Fax: 864-963-5316 800-927-6887
 customerservice@bkideas.com www.bkideas.com
Manufacturer and exporter of rotisseries, ovens, fryers, deli cases, ventless hood systems and food warmers

President: Randy A Karns
Controller: Reggy Skelton
COO: Dave Korcsmaros
Quality Control Manager: Wade Pitts
Operations Manager: Reed Walpole
Production Manager: Reed Walpole
Purchasing Manager: Wade Pitts
Number Employees: 100-249
Parent Co: Standex International Corporation

42210 BLH Electronics
75 Shawmut Rd
Canton, MA 02021 781-821-2000
 Fax: 781-828-1451 sales@blh.com
  www.blh.com
Manufacturer and exporter of process weighing and web tension systems, strain gauges and load systems/instruments
President: Robert E Murphy
Vice President: William Sheehan
Research & Development: David Scanlon
Sales Director: Art Koehler
Facilities Manager: Alan Sandman
Estimated Sales: $50-100 Million
Number Employees: 1-4
Square Footage: 55000
Parent Co: Spectra-Physics AB
Other Locations:
 BLH Electronics
 Toronto, ON BLH Electronics
Brands Exported: BLH
Regions Exported to: Worldwide
Percentage of Business in Exporting: 20

42211 BMT Commodity Corporation
950 3rd Ave
10th Floor
New York, NY 10022 212-302-4200
 Fax: 212-302-0007 bmt@bmtny.com
  www.bmtny.com
Importer and wholesaler/distributor of fruit purees and pastes, dehydrated foods, tomato powders, health foods, dried fruit, sun dried tomatoes, honey, garlic, etc.; serving the foodservice and retail markets.
President: Robert Ganz
Executive Vice President: Edward Siel
Year Founded: 1922
Estimated Sales: $30-60 Million
Number Employees: 20-49
Parent Co: A/T Products Corporation
Type of Packaging: Consumer, Bulk
Regions Exported to: Europe
Brands Imported: Delca Brand; A/T Product Brand
Regions Imported from: South America, Europe, Asia, Middle East, North America
Percentage of Business in Importing: 90

42212 BNW Industries
7930 N 700 E
Tippecanoe, IN 46570-9613 574-353-7855
 Fax: 574-353-8152 sales@norristhermal.com
Manufacturer and exporter of coolers and dehydrators; manufacturer of balance/single weave wire belts
Founder/President: Dan Norris
dnorris@bnwindustries.com
Vice President Sales: Aaron Norris
Purchasing Manager: Troy Eaton
Estimated Sales: $1-3 Million
Number Employees: 10-19
Square Footage: 52000
Parent Co: Lee Norris Construction & Grain Company
Brands Exported: Belt-O-Matic
Regions Exported to: Worldwide
Percentage of Business in Exporting: 50

42213 BVL Controls
661, The Pit
Bois-Des-Filion, QC J6Z 4T2
Canada 450-965-0502
 Fax: 450-965-8751 866-285-2668
 info@bvlcontrols.com www.bvlcontrols.com
Manufacturer, importer and exporter of portion control and cooling equipment and supplies for beer, wine, soft drinks and liquors
President: Alvin Guerette
Controller: Josee Merchand
Vice President: Gilles Guerette
Estimated Sales: $1-3 Million
Number Employees: 10-19
Square Footage: 48000
Brands Exported: BVL; True Measure; Oberdorfer

Regions Exported to: Central America, Europe, Canada
Percentage of Business in Exporting: 40
Regions Imported from: Central America, Europe
Percentage of Business in Importing: 15

42214 (HQ)BW Container Systems
1305 Lakeview Dr
Romeoville, IL 60446-3900 630-759-6800
 Fax: 630-759-2299 sales@fleetinc.com
  www.bwcontainersystems.com
Manufacturer and exporter of magnetic and specialized food handling and processing equipment including conveyors, capping, sealing, seaming, canning and food packing
Chairman of the Board: Robert H Chapman
CEO: Phil Ostapowicz
postapowicz@fgwa.com
CFO: David Brown
CEO: Phil Ostapowicz
VP Sales: Neil McConnellogue
Estimated Sales: $ 20 - 50 Million
Number Employees: 100-249
Square Footage: 200000
Parent Co: Barry-Wehmiller
Other Locations:
 Fleetwood Systems
 Orlando, FL Fleetwood Systems
Regions Exported to: Central America, South America, Europe, Asia, Middle East
Percentage of Business in Exporting: 50

42215 BWI, Inc.
5711 Corsa Ave
Westlake Village, CA 818-991-6644
 Fax: 818-991-8829 info@bwi-imports.com
  bwi-imports.com
Baked goods; confectionery; chips; condiments; soups, stews and beans; soft drinks; and tea.
CEO: Kerry Bamberger
Year Founded: 1987
Number Employees: 51-200
Brands Imported: Cadbury; Fitzpatrick's; Pudding Lane; Soreen; Mrs. Darlington's; Jolly Good; Welsh Hills Bakery; Ribena; The London Tea Company; HP Sauce; Guiness; Green's; and more.
Regions Imported from: Central America
Percentage of Business in Importing: 100

42216 Baader-Linco
2955 Fairfax Trfy
Kansas City, KS 66115-1317 913-621-3366
 Fax: 913-621-1729 800-288-3434
  www.baader.com
Designer, manufacturer and distributors of poultry and fish processing equipment.
President: Andy Miller
andy.miller@baaderna.com
Controller: Shaun Nicolas
Corporate Accounts/Sales Manager - US: Gehrig Chandler
Estimated Sales: $15.10 Million
Number Employees: 100-249
Square Footage: 13209
Parent Co: Baader Food Processing Machinery
Regions Exported to: North America

42217 Babco International, Inc
911 S Tyndall
Tucson, AZ 85719 520-628-7596
 Fax: 520-628-9622 contactus@babcotucson.com
  www.babcotucson.com
Glassware, china, skirting, linen and silverware
Owner: Patrick Brodecky
patrick.brodecky@babcotucson.com
Marketing/Customer Service Director: Betsy Marco
Estimated Sales: $2.5-5 Million
Number Employees: 5-9

42218 Babcock & Wilcox Power Generation Group
20 S Van Buren Ave
Barberton, OH 44203-0351 330-753-4511
 Fax: 330-860-1886 800-222-2625
 slmccaulley@babcock.com www.babcock.com
Manufacturer and exporter of steam generation boilers and auxiliary equipment

Importers & Exporters / A-Z

President, COO: J. Randall Data
Senior Vice President, General Counsel,: James D. Canafax
SVP, CFO: Anthony S. Colatrella
SVP, Chief Administrative Officer: Kairus K. Tarapore
R&D Director: Stan Vecci
Manager Advertising: Phil Stillitano
Contact: Mel Albrecht
malbrecht@babcock.com
Director of Operation: Alan Nethery
Number Employees: 1,000-4,999
Parent Co: McDermott International
Regions Exported to: Worldwide
Percentage of Business in Exporting: 60

42219 Babcock Co
36 Delaware Ave
Bath, NY 14810-1607   607-776-3341
    Fax: 607-776-7483 www.babcock.com
Manufacturer and exporter of small wooden crates
President: Marc Mc Connell
Sales/Marketing Executive: A Cranmer
Manager: Mike Bishop
Estimated Sales: $2.5-5 Million
Number Employees: 10-19
Square Footage: 154000

42220 Babe Farms Inc
1485 N Blosser Rd
Santa Maria, CA 93458-2043   805-925-4144
    Fax: 805-922-3950 800-648-6772
        customerservice@babefarms.com
        www.babefarms.com
Specialty and baby produce items, including peeled carrots and root vegetables
Founder: Will Souza
CEO: Judy Lundberg
judy@babefarms.com
Finance Manager: Carrie Jordan
Operations: Jeff Lundberg
Year Founded: 1986
Estimated Sales: $7 Million
Number Employees: 100-249
Type of Packaging: Food Service, Private Label
Regions Exported to: Japan, Hong Kong
Regions Imported from: Mexico

42221 Baby Mum-Mum

Richmond, BC V6V 1M8
Canada
        mummums.com
Baby rice snacks
Year Founded: 1947
Parent Co: National Importers

42222 Bacardi Canada, Inc.
3250 Bloor St. W
East Tower, Suite 1050
Toronto, ON M8X 2X9
Canada   905-451-6100
    Fax: 905-451-6753 www.bacardi.com
Rum, vodka, scotch, gin, vermouth, carbonated low proof beverages, liqueurs
General Manager: Blair MacNeil
Estimated Sales: 250-499
Number Employees: 100
Parent Co: Bacardi Limited
Type of Packaging: Consumer, Food Service
Brands Imported: Martini & Rossi; Benedictine; B&B; Sacco; China Martini; Gaston de Lagrange
Regions Imported from: Europe

42223 Bacardi USA Inc
2701 S Le Jeune Rd
Suite 400
Coral Gables, FL 33134-5809   305-573-8511
    Fax: 305-573-0756 800-222-2734
        hrbmusa@bacardi.com
        www.bacardilimited.com/us/en
Tropical drink flavored coolers, rum, vodka, prepared mixed drinks
President: Pete Carr
CEO: Mahesh Madhavan
Estimated Sales: $650 Million
Number Employees: 250-499
Parent Co: Bacardi International
Type of Packaging: Consumer, Food Service

42224 Bacchus Wine Cellars
14027 Memorial Drive #228
Houston, TX 77079-9826   281-496-4495
    Fax: 284-496-5855 800-487-8812
        bacchuswinecellars.com
Manufacturer, importer and exporter of temperature and humidity controlled wine cellars, cabinets and storage equipment
President: Pierre Guinaudeau
Estimated Sales: Less than $500,000
Number Employees: 75
Square Footage: 40000
Brands Exported: Le Cellier; Provintech
Regions Exported to: Europe, Asia, Middle East
Brands Imported: Provintech
Regions Imported from: South America
Percentage of Business in Importing: 10

42225 Bachman Company
801 Hill Avenue
Wyamissing, PA 19610   610-320-7800
    Fax: 610-320-7897 800-523-8253
        www.bachmanco.com
Pretzels, jax, tortilla chips, popcorn, potato chips, party mix and onion rings.
President: Scott Carpenter
CEO: Joanne Millisock
Director: Marcia Welch
Sales: Andy Kapusta
Director of Human Resources: Deanna Williams
VP Manufacturing/Operations: Mark Miller
VP Manufacturing: Daniel Meyers
Purchasing Director: Lisa George
Estimated Sales: $10-20 Million
Number Employees: 350
Square Footage: 40000
Type of Packaging: Consumer, Food Service

42226 Backerhaus Veit Limited
70 Whitmore Road
Woodbridge, ON L4L 7Z4
Canada   905-850-9229
    Fax: 905-850-9292 info@backerhausveit.com
        www.backerhausveit.com
Artisan bread manufacturer
Sales & Marketing: Tobia Donath
Type of Packaging: Consumer, Food Service, Private Label, Bulk
Brands Exported: Backerhaus Veit Bread

42227 Bacon America
255 Rue Rocheleau
Drummondville, QC J2C 7G2
Canada   819-475-3030
    Fax: 819-475-4164
Bacon
President: Marcel Heroux
Estimated Sales: $ 5-10 Million
Number Employees: 500-999
Parent Co: J.M. Schneider
Type of Packaging: Consumer, Food Service, Private Label
Regions Exported to: Worldwide
Regions Imported from: U.S.A.

42228 Bad Seed Cider Company, LLC
43 Baileys Gap Rd.
Highland, NY 12528   845-236-0956
        info@badseedhardcider.com
        www.badseedhardcider.com
Hard dry ciders
Co-Owner/Partner: Albert Wilkilow
Co-Owner/Partner: Devin Britton
Co-Owner/Partner: Bram Kincheloe
Year Founded: 2011
Number of Brands: 1
Number of Products: 4
Type of Packaging: Consumer, Private Label
Brands Exported: Bad Seed
Regions Exported to: USA

42229 Badger Meter Inc
4545 W Brown Deer Rd
P.O. Box 245036
Milwaukee, WI 53224
    800-876-3837
        www.badgermeter.com
Manufacturer and exporter of water meters and flowmeters.

President: Richard Meeusen
SVP & Chief Operating Officer: Kenneth Bockhorst
SVP, Finance/CFO/Treasurer: Richard Johnson
Vice President, Engineering: Fred Begale
VP/General Counsel/Secretary: Williams R.A. Bergum
VP, Business Development: Gregory Gomez
VP, Sales & Marketing: Kimberly Stoll
Vice President, Controller: Beverly L.P. Smiley
Vice President, Manufacturing: Raymond Serdynski
Vice President, Human Resources: Trina Jashinsky
Vice President, International Operations: Horst Gras
Year Founded: 1905
Estimated Sales: $100-500 Million
Number Employees: 1000-4999
Regions Exported to: Central America, South America, Europe, Middle East

42230 Badia Spices Inc.
PO Box 226497
Doral, FL 33322-4697   305-629-8000
        877-629-8000
        info@badiaspices.com www.badiaspices.com
Herbs, spices and seasonings including garlic, buboric, jalapeno, lindo and taco flavoring.
President: Joseph Badia
info@badia-spices.com
Year Founded: 1967
Estimated Sales: $100 Million
Number Employees: 100-249
Number of Brands: 1
Square Footage: 100000
Type of Packaging: Consumer, Food Service, Private Label, Bulk
Regions Exported to: Worldwide
Percentage of Business in Exporting: 35

42231 Bag Company
1650 Airport Rd NW
Suite 104
Kennesaw, GA 30144-7039   770-422-4187
    Fax: 800-417-7273 800-533-1931
        www.bagco.com
Manufacturer and exporter of polyethylene and polypropylene bags; importer of plastic bags.
Director of Marketing: Katherine Remick
Estimated Sales: $13 Million
Number Employees: 10-19
Type of Packaging: Consumer
Brands Exported: Zippit®, Specimen Buggs, Kangaroo® Pouch Bag
Regions Exported to: Worldwide

42232 Bagcraft Papercon
3900 W 43rd St
Chicago, IL 60632-3490   773-254-8000
    Fax: 773-254-8204 800-621-8468
        www.bagcraft.com
Manufacturer and exporter of foil, film, paper, window and coffee bags and tin-tie
Vice President: Chuck Hathaway
chathaway@pkdy.com
Vice President, General Manager: Dan Vice
Director of Marketing: Barak Bright
Vice President of Sales: Chuck Hathaway
Customer Service Manager: Fredia Hess
chathaway@pkdy.com
Vice President - Operations: Grady Wetherington
Number Employees: 250-499
Square Footage: 1860000
Parent Co: Packaging Dynamics
Brands Exported: Dubl-Wax; Dubl-Fresh; Cameo; Dubl-View
Regions Exported to: Central America, South America, Europe, Middle East, Australia

42233 Bahlsen GmbH & Co. Kg
1335 North Fairfax Avenue
Suite 6
West Hollywood, CA 90046   323-850-7093
    Fax: 323-850-6693 bahlsenusa@sbcglobal.net
        www.bahlsen.com
Bread/biscuits, cookies, other baked goods, other candy.

42234 Baja Foods LLC
636 W Root St
Chicago, IL 60609-2630   773-376-9030
    Fax: 773-376-9245 lisa@bajafoodsllc.com
Frozen tamales, quesadillas, chimichangas, burritos, enchiladas, taco meat and chili

Importers & Exporters / A-Z

Owner: Art Velasquez
don:aezler@aol.com
Sales/Marketing: Jeff Rothschild
General Manager: Timothy Poisson
Purchasing Manager: Cheryl Canning
Year Founded: 2001
Estimated Sales: $ 10 - 20 Million
Number Employees: 20-49
Square Footage: 30000
Type of Packaging: Consumer, Food Service, Private Label, Bulk
Regions Exported to: Canada
Percentage of Business in Exporting: 1

42235 BakeMark Canada
2345 Francis-Hughes Avenue
Laval, QC H7S 1N5
Canada 450-667-8888
Fax: 450-667-3342 800-361-4998
www.bakemarkcanada.com
Processor and exporter of bakers' and confectioners' supplies including fondants, cocoa chips and pieces, apricot and strawberry glazes, rainbow and chocolate sprinkles and fruit pie fillings
President: Larry Sullivan
Contact: Stephanie Corrente
Year Founded: 1915
Number Employees: 10-19
Square Footage: 280000
Parent Co: CSM Bakery Supplies North America
Type of Packaging: Food Service, Private Label

42236 BakeMark Ingredients Canada
2480 Viking Way
Richmond, BC V6V 1N2
Canada 604-303-1700
Fax: 604-270-8002 800-665-9441
www.yourbakemark.com
Baked goods, breads, baking mixes, cookies, pie filling, icing, frozen fruit
President: Larry Sullivan
Vice President: Michael Armstrong
Marketing: David Lopez
Sales Manager: Jeff Bligh
General Manager: Rick Barnes
Manufacturing: Ellen Tsang
Estimated Sales: $23 Million
Number Employees: 160
Number of Brands: 12
Number of Products: 2000
Type of Packaging: Private Label, Bulk
Brands Exported: Bakemark
Regions Exported to: South America
Brands Imported: Caravan, Brill, Marguerite, Bib Ulmer Spatz, Diamalt, Meistermarken, DeGoede, dreiDoppel
Regions Imported from: South America, Europe

42237 (HQ)BakeMark USA
7351 Crider Ave
Pico Rivera, CA 90660-3705 562-949-1054
Fax: 562-948-5506 866-232-8575
information@bakemark.com
www.yourbakemark.com
Baking mixes, fillings, icings, glazes, and bakery supplies
President & CEO: Gary Schmidt
CFO: Refugio Reynoso
VP Sales & Marketing: Rick Bennett
Estimated Sales: $ 20 - 50 Million
Number Employees: 20-49

42238 Baker Hughes
17021 Aldine Westfield
Houston, TX 77073
www.bakerhughes.com
Manufacturer and exporter of centrifuges and filters for liquid/solid separations.
Chairman & CEO: Lorenzo Simonelli
CFO: Brian Worell
EVP, Turbomachinery & Process Solutions: Rod Christie
Chief Marketing & Technology Officer: Derek Mathieson
Year Founded: 1907
Estimated Sales: $22.8 Billion
Number Employees: 67,000
Regions Exported to: Central America, South America, Europe, Asia, Middle East
Percentage of Business in Exporting: 25

42239 Baker Perkins Inc
3223 Kraft Ave SE
Grand Rapids, MI 49512-2063 616-785-7500
Fax: 616-784-0973 800-458-2560
eriknadig@invensys.com www.bakerperkins.com
Manufacturer, importer and exporter of food processing equipment including bakers and confectioners, mixing, forming, baking and product handling equipment
Vice President: Paul Abbott
paul.abbott@bakerperkinsgroup.com
VP: John Lucas
R&D: Mark Glover
Marketing: Erik Nagig
VP Sales: Paul Abbott
Manager Process Optimization: Dan Smith
Number Employees: 50-99
Square Footage: 240000
Parent Co: APV plc

42240 Baker Produce
212 W Railroad Avenue
PO Box 6757
Kennewick, WA 99336 509-586-6174
Fax: 509-582-3694 800-624-7553
pquinn@bakerproduce.com
www.bakerproduce.com
Apples, onions, potatoes
Sales Manager: Pam Quinn
Sales Representative: Savannah Dean
Shipping Clerk: Kiley Dean
Number Employees: 250-499
Type of Packaging: Consumer, Food Service, Bulk

42241 Baker's Coconut
100 Deforest Ave
East Hanover, NJ 07936 901-381-6636
Fax: 901-381-6524 855-535-5648
www.mondelezinternational.com
Coconut concentrate
Contact: Mary Taylor
Number Employees: 100-249
Parent Co: Kraft Foods
Type of Packaging: Bulk
Brands Exported: Baker's Coconut; Oscar Mayer; Kraft
Regions Exported to: Worldwide
Percentage of Business in Exporting: 25

42242 Baker's Point Fisheries
33 Bakers Point Rd East
Oyster Pond Jeddore, NS B0J 1W0
Canada 902-845-2347
Fax: 902-845-2770 janette@bakerspoint.ca
Fresh and frozen haddock, cod, pollack, hake and cusk
Co-Owner: Janette Faulkner
Co-Owner: Wyman Baker
Number Employees: 50-99
Type of Packaging: Bulk
Regions Exported to: USA
Percentage of Business in Exporting: 50

42243 Bakers Choice Products
4 Railroad Avenue Ext
Railroad Avenue Ext.
Beacon Falls, CT 6403 203-720-1000
Fax: 203-720-1004
Manufacturer, importer and exporter of sanitary food containers and cups for candy, cookie and baking; also, hot dog trays
Estimated Sales: $ 1 - 5 Million
Number Employees: 50-99
Square Footage: 120000
Parent Co: Reynolds Metals Company
Regions Exported to: Canada
Regions Imported from: Europe, Canada

42244 Bakers Pride Oven Company
145 Huguenot St Ste Mz1
New Rochelle, NY 10801 914-576-0745
Fax: 914-576-0605 800-431-2745
sales@bakerspride.com www.bakerspride.com
Manufacturer and exporter of char-broilers and pizza and counter top ovens
President: Hylton Jonas
VP: Tom Marston
Technical Writer: Daniel J Rivera
Quality Manager: Jim Ponnwitz
Estimated Sales: $ 20-50 Million
Number Employees: 100-249
Parent Co: APW/WYOTT Food Service Equipment
Regions Exported to: Central America, South America, Europe, Asia, Middle East

42245 Bakery Systems
7246 Beach Dr SW 1
Ocean Isle Beach, NC 28469 910-575-2253
Fax: 910-575-5057 800-526-2253
Importer, exporter and wholesaler/distributor of bakery equipment nd supplies
President: Hayden O'Neil
patzcuaro@juno.com
Sales Manager: Lee Wagner
Estimated Sales: $2.5 Million
Number Employees: 5-9
Square Footage: 2000

42246 Bakery Things
7142 East Condor Street
Commerce, CA 90040 323-888-0008
Fax: 323-888-0003 800-242-4KGP
Importer, exporter and wholesaler/distributor of ginseng, herb teas, processed bean, portable gas range, etc
President: Chung Sup Song
CEO: Soon Song
VP: Thomas Lee
Marketing Director: Steve Ham
Sales Director: Kristin Kim
Estimated Sales: $5 Million
Number Employees: 5-9
Number of Brands: 80
Number of Products: 30
Square Footage: 20000
Brands Exported: Midcom; IMX
Regions Exported to: Asia
Brands Imported: Taeguk; KGP; Longlite; Daedoo
Regions Imported from: Asia

42247 Bakon Yeast
33415 N 64th Place
Scottsdale, AZ 85266-7363 480-595-9370
Fax: 480-595-9371 bakonyeast@aol.com
bakonyeast.samsbiz.com
Vegetable derived bacon flavored seasonings and hickory smoked torula yeast
President: Phyll Ray
VP: Larry Ray
Plant Manager: Rebecca Schaefer
Year Founded: 1933
Estimated Sales: $600,000
Number Employees: 2-4
Square Footage: 40000
Parent Co: Bakon Yeast
Type of Packaging: Consumer, Food Service, Bulk
Brands Exported: Bakon Yeast
Regions Exported to: Europe, Australia, New Zealand
Percentage of Business in Exporting: 25

42248 Bal Seal Engineering Inc
19650 Pauling
Foothill Ranch, CA 92610-2610 949-460-2100
Fax: 949-460-2300 800-366-1006
sales@balseal.com www.balseal.com
Manufacturer and exporter of spring loaded PTFE seals
President: Rob Sjostedt
CEO: Rick Dawson
rdawson@balseal.com
Sales Director: Michael Anderson
Estimated Sales: $ 20 - 50 Million
Number Employees: 250-499
Regions Exported to: Central America, South America, Europe, Asia
Percentage of Business in Exporting: 30

42249 Bal/Foster Glass Container Company
1 Glass Pl
Port Allegany, PA 16743-1154 814-642-2521
Fax: 814-642-3204 www.sgcontainers.com
Manufacturer and exporter of glass bottles and jars
Plant Manager: Ed Stewart
Estimated Sales: $ 1 - 5 Million
Number Employees: 250-499

42250 Balboa Dessert Co Inc
1760 E Wilshire Ave
Santa Ana, CA 92705-4615 714-972-4972
Fax: 714-972-0605 800-974-9699
customerservice@balboadessert.com
Processor and exporter of desserts including frozen cakes, cheesecakes and tortes, gourmet baked goods, wholesale and retail

Owner: Anna Ochoa
aochoa@balboadessert.com
Owner: Brett Pollack
Vice President: Dan Hamilton
Year Founded: 1987
Estimated Sales: $4 Million
Number Employees: 5-9
Square Footage: 72000
Type of Packaging: Food Service
Regions Exported to: Worldwide

42251 Baldewein Company
9109 Belden Avenue
Lake Forrest, IL 60045   847-455-1686
Fax: 847-455-1706 800-424-5544
info@baldeweinco.com www.baldeweinco.com
Manufacturer and exporter of food processing equipment including sanitary fittings, pumps, valves, hose assemblies, brushes, steelware and steam and water mixers
President: Valentin R Baldewein Jr
Sales: Tina Sanders
Treasurer: Val Baldwewin
Estimated Sales: Below $5 Million
Number Employees: 10
Square Footage: 40000
Regions Exported to: South America, Asia, Caribbean, Mexico
Percentage of Business in Exporting: 5

42252 Baldor Electric Co
5711 Rs Boreham Jr St
P.O. Box 2400
Fort Smith, AR 72901-8394   479-646-4711
Fax: 479-648-5792 www.baldor.com
Marketers, designers and manufacturers of industrial electric motors, mechanical power transmission products, drive and generators, specializing in products for the food and pharmaceutical industries. A member of the ABB group since2011.
CEO: Ronald Tucker
rtucker@baldor.com
VP, Finance and Corporate Secretary: Larry Johnston
EVP: Edward Ralston
VP, Channel Management: Chris Keyser
VP Marketing: Tracy Long
Vice President, Sales: Randy Colip
COO, Baldor Operations: Wayne Thurman
Estimated Sales: Over $1 Billion
Number Employees: 5000-9999
Square Footage: 4000000
Regions Exported to: Central America, South America, Europe, Asia, Middle East, Australia
Percentage of Business in Exporting: 25

42253 Baldor Specialty Foods Inc
155 Food Center Dr # 1
Bronx, NY 10474-7136   718-860-9100
Fax: 718-328-9944 www.baldorfood.com
Fresh dairy, imported and domestic cheeses, specialties such as foie gras, pates, cured meats, truffle products, Balsamic vinegar, extra virgin olive oil, and a full like of pastry products.
CEO: Kevin Murphy
Number Employees: 1-4

42254 Ballantine Produce Company
P.O.Box 756
10550 S Button Willeen Ave
Reedley, CA 93654-4400   559-875-2583
Fax: 559-637-2159
Manufacturer and processor of over 200 varieties of plums, peaches, nectarines, pluots, white flesh, apricots, grapes, Asian pears, quince, pomegranates, persimmons and apples.
President: Virgil Rasmussen
Partner: Herbert Kaprielian
CFO: Richard Graham
Manufacturing Executive: Ron Fraughenheim
Year Founded: 1919
Estimated Sales: $10-20 Million
Number Employees: 1-4
Type of Packaging: Consumer, Food Service
Other Locations:
  Reedley Sales Office
  Reedley, CAReedley Sales Office
Brands Exported: Ballentine
Regions Exported to: Worldwide
Regions Imported from: Chile
Percentage of Business in Importing: 10

42255 (HQ)Ballantyne Food Service Equipment
4350 McKinley St
Omaha, NE 68112   402-453-4444
Fax: 402-453-7238 800-424-1215
www.ballantyne-omaha.com
Manufacturer and exporter of commercial restaurant equipment including electric pressure and gas pressure fryers, gourmet grills, cook and hold barbecue ovens, smokers and rotisseries
President/CEO: John Wilmers
Senior VP: Ray Boegner
VP: Michael Nulty
Estimated Sales: $ 1 - 5 Million
Number Employees: 100-249
Square Footage: 400000
Parent Co: Ballantyne of Omaha
Type of Packaging: Food Service, Private Label
Brands Exported: Flavor-Crisp
Regions Exported to: Central America, South America, Europe, Asia, Middle East
Percentage of Business in Exporting: 30

42256 Ballas Egg Products Corp
40 N 2nd St
Zanesville, OH 43701-3446   740-453-0386
Fax: 740-453-0491 www.ballasegg.com
Frozen, dried and liquid egg products.
President: Craig Ballas
Estimated Sales: $10 Million
Number Employees: 50-99
Type of Packaging: Consumer, Bulk
Brands Exported: Ballas Dried-Frozen-Liquid Egg Products
Regions Exported to: Central America, South America, Europe, Asia, Middle East

42257 (HQ)Bally Block Co
30 S 7th St
30 South Seventh Street
Bally, PA 19503-9665   610-845-7511
Fax: 610-845-7726 bbc@ballyblock.com
www.butcherblock.com
Manufacturer and exporter of cutting benches, blocks, tables and boards
President: James Reichart
Vice President of Sales and Marketing: Joe Barbercheck
Vice President Sales & Marketing: Pat Stanley
Vice President, Production: Emmet Wood
Estimated Sales: $ 5-10 Million
Number Employees: 50-99
Square Footage: 500000
Regions Exported to: Europe, Asia, Middle East
Percentage of Business in Exporting: 5

42258 Bally Refrigerated Boxes Inc
135 Little Nine Rd
Morehead City, NC 28557-8483   252-240-2829
Fax: 252-240-0384 800-242-2559
ballysales@ballyrefboxes.com
www.ballyrefboxes.com
Walk-in cooler and freezers, refrigerated buildings, modular structures, blast chillers and refrigeration for the foodservice and scientific industries.
President: Michael Coyle
cm@ballyrefboxes.com
Sales Manager: William Strompf
Plant Manager: Alan Summers
Purchasing Manager: William Stomps
Estimated Sales: $ 20-50 Million
Number Employees: 250-499
Parent Co: United Refrigeration
Type of Packaging: Food Service
Other Locations:
  Bally Refrigerated Boxes
  King of Prussia, PABally Refrigerated Boxes
Regions Exported to: Central America, South America, Europe, Asia, Middle East, Caribbean

42259 Balsu
1160 Kane Concourse
Suite 100A
Bay Harbour Islands, FL 33154   305-993-5045
Fax: 305-993-5047 balsu@balsusa.com
www.balsusa.com
Hazelnuts
President/CHR: H. Zapsu
Director/Sales And Marketing: Sezen Donmezer
Sales Director: Karim Azzaoui
kazzaoui@aol.com
Year Founded: 1980
Estimated Sales: A
Number Employees: 1-4
Type of Packaging: Bulk
Regions Imported from: Turkey
Percentage of Business in Importing: 100

42260 Baltic Linen Co Inc
1999 Marcus Ave
Lake Success, NY 11040   516-791-4500
Fax: 516-792-2124 800-422-5842
info@balticlinen.com www.balticlinen.com
Supplier of bed and bath linens for the hospitality, cruise, retail and healthcare service industries.
Chief Executive Officer: Frank Greenberg
fgreenberg@balticlinen.com
Year Founded: 1936
Estimated Sales: $50-100 Million
Number Employees: 50-99

42261 Baltimore Aircoil Co
7600 Dorsey Run Rd
Jessup, MD 20794-9328   410-799-1300
Fax: 410-799-6416 info@baltimoreaircoil.com
www.baltimoreaircoil.com
Manufacturer and marketer of heat transfer and ice thermal storage products that conserve resources and respect the environment.
President: Steve Duerwachter
Contact: Glenn Babcock
amy@aafame.ccsend.com
Estimated Sales: $17 Million
Number Employees: 20-49
Parent Co: Amsted Industries
Regions Exported to: Central America, South America, Europe, Asia, Middle East

42262 Balzac Brothers & Co Inc
11 Fulton St
Charleston, SC 29401-1920   843-723-8020
Fax: 843-723-0242
Importer of coffee
President: Richard Balzac
richardf@balzac.net
Treasurer: John Balzac
Estimated Sales: $500,000-$1 Million
Number Employees: 5-9
Regions Imported from: Central America, South America, Asia, Caribbean, Mexico, Latin America

42263 Bama Fish Atlanta
3113 Main Street
East Point, GA 30344-4802   404-765-9896
Fax: 404-765-9874
Fresh and frozen fish

42264 Bama Foods LTD
5377 E 66th St N
Tulsa, OK 74117-1813   918-592-0778
Fax: 918-732-2902 800-756-2262
www.bama.com
Frozen baked goods including cookies, pies and biscuits; dough, pastry and crumb crust pie shells
CEO: Matt Alley
alley@bama.com
Chief Executive Officer: Paula A. Marshall
Chief Financial Officer - US Operations: Rocky Moore
Executive Vice President: William L. Chew
Vice President of Research and Developme: Joe McDilda
QC Manager: Maurice Lawry
Director Brand Sales: Gary Wilson
Vice President of Operations: Kevin C. Wilson
Number Employees: 100-249
Type of Packaging: Consumer, Food Service
Brands Exported: Bama

42265 Bama Sea Products Inc
756 28th St S
St Petersburg, FL 33712-1907   727-327-3474
Fax: 727-322-0580 www.bamasea.com
Wholesaler/distributor and exporter of frozen fish and seafood; warehouse providing cooler and freezer storage for frozen food items
Owner: Hillary Hubble-Flinn
Director Quality Control: Fred Stengard
Marketing & Product Development: Dottie Stephens Guy
VP Sales: Jon Philbrick
hillary.hubbleflinn@leememorial.org
VP of Operations and Plant GM: John Jackson
VP Purchasing: Adam Zewen
Estimated Sales: $2.5-5 Million
Number Employees: 100-249
Square Footage: 360000

Importers & Exporters / A-Z

Brands Exported: American Freezers
Regions Exported to: Europe, Asia
Percentage of Business in Exporting: 5

42266 Banfi Vintners
1111 Cedar Swamp Rd
Old Brookville, NY 11545-2109 516-626-9200
Fax: 516-626-9218 800-645-6511
banfiwines@gmail.com www.banfiwines.com
Wine
Principal: James Mariani
President & CEO: Cristina Mariani-May
Marketing Director: Gary Clayton
VP Public Relations: Lars Leicht
Estimated Sales: $34 Million
Number Employees: 50-99

42267 Banner Chemical Co
111 Hill St
Orange, NJ 07050-3901 973-676-0105
Fax: 973-676-4564 info@bannerchemical.com
www.bannerchemical.com
Cleaning products and sanitary maintenance chemicals including glass cleaners, floor cleaners, wates and strippers, kitchen and bathroom cleaners, disinfectants and many other chemicals for food service and industry.
President: Stanley Reichel
bannerchem@aol.com
VP: David Herman
Estimated Sales: $ 2.5 - 5 Million
Number Employees: 5-9
Regions Exported to: Europe, Mexico
Percentage of Business in Exporting: 5
Regions Imported from: Middle East
Percentage of Business in Importing: 10

42268 Banner Equipment Co
1370 Bungalow Rd
Morris, IL 60450-8929 815-941-9600
Fax: 815-941-9700 800-621-4625
internetsales@bannerbeer.com
www.bannerbeer.com
Manufacturer and exporter of draft beer tapping and dispensing equipment
President: Jim Groh
jgroh@bannerbeer.com
VP: Michael Tannhauser
Estimated Sales: $ 10 - 20 Million
Number Employees: 20-49
Square Footage: 80000
Regions Exported to: South America, Europe, Worldwide
Percentage of Business in Exporting: 10
Brands Imported: Homark, Alumasc
Regions Imported from: Europe, Canada

42269 Banner Pharmacaps
4100 Mendenhall Oaks Pkwy
Suite 301
High Point, NC 27265 336-812-7003
Fax: 336-812-7030 800-526-6993
www.patheon.com
Vitamins
President/CEO: Roger Gordon
CFO: Damien Reynolds
Global VP/R&D/Operations: Aqeel Fatmi
kevin.cogdell@wellsfargo.com
Contact: Kevin Cogdell
kevin.cogdell@wellsfargo.com
Global VP/Commercial Operations: Timothy Doran
Parent Co: Sobel-Holland
Other Locations:
Banner Pharmacaps
Chatsworth, CABanner PharmacapsAlberta, Canada

42270 Bar Keepers Friend Cleanser
5240 Walt Pl
Indianapolis, IN 46254-5795 317-636-7760
Fax: 317-264-2192 800-433-5818
www.barkeepersfriend.com
Manufacturer and exporter of powdered and liquid cleansers for the removal of rust, lime, stains and mildew; also, polishes, bathroom and toilet bowl cleaners
President: Nick Childers
nchilders@barkeepersfriend.com
VP Sales: Tony Patterson
Estimated Sales: $ 20 - 50 Million
Number Employees: 20-49
Square Footage: 30000
Parent Co: SerVaas
Type of Packaging: Consumer, Private Label

Brands Exported: Bar Keepers Friend; Shiny Sinks; Power House; Copper Glo; Just 'N Time
Regions Exported to: Central America, South America, Europe, Asia, Middle East, Caribbean, Canada
Percentage of Business in Exporting: 10

42271 Bar Maid Corp
2950 NW 22nd Ter
Pompano Beach, FL 33069-1045 954-960-1468
Fax: 954-960-1647 info@barmaidwashers.com
www.barmaidwashers.com
Manufacturer and exporter of portable, submersible and upright electric glass and muffin pan washers; also, low-sud detergents and sanitizers
President: George E Shepherd
CEO: Diane Michaud
diane@barmaidwashers.com
Marketing Director: Tammie Rice
Estimated Sales: Below $ 5 Million
Number Employees: 10-19
Number of Brands: 2
Square Footage: 16000
Brands Exported: Bar Maid
Regions Exported to: Worldwide
Percentage of Business in Exporting: 25

42272 Bar-Maid Corp
362 Midland Ave # 1
Garfield, NJ 07026-1736 973-478-7070
Fax: 973-478-2106 800-227-6243
www.bar-maid.com
Refrigerators, minibars and freezers.
President: George Steele
CEO: James Steele
Vice President: John Steele
Marketing Director: Ken Lasini
Sales Director: K Zanda
Public Relations: Mike Castle
Estimated Sales: $50-100 Million
Number Employees: 50-99
Square Footage: 80000

42273 Barbara's Bakery
20802 Kensington Blvd
Lakeville, MN 55044
800-343-0590
www.barbaras.com
Organic and natural cereals, crackers, cookies, bars, puffs and chips.
President: Barabara Jaffe
Research & Development Manager: Deborah Flindall
Vice President, Marketing: Kent Spalding
Year Founded: 1971
Estimated Sales: $20-50 Million
Number Employees: 175
Square Footage: 102500
Type of Packaging: Consumer, Private Label
Other Locations:
Barbara's Bakery
Sacramento, CABarbara's Bakery
Brands Exported: Barbara's; Nature's Choice

42274 Barbeque Wood Flavors Enterprises
141 Lyons Road
Ennis, TX 75119 972-875-8391
Fax: 972-875-8872
Manufacturer and exporter of wood firelogs
President and CEO: George C Wartsbaugh
Sales Manager: Charles Wartsbaugh
Estimated Sales: $ 5 - 10 Million
Number Employees: 10
Square Footage: 92000
Parent Co: Stephen Weber Production Company
Regions Exported to: Canada

42275 Barber Foods
PO Box 219
Kings Mountain, NC 28086
877-447-3279
www.barberfoods.com
Frozen chicken: stuffed breasts
Year Founded: 1955
Estimated Sales: $ 3 - 5 Million
Square Footage: 600000
Parent Co: Advance Pierre Foods
Type of Packaging: Consumer, Food Service
Other Locations:
Barber Foods Production Plant
Portland, MEBarber Foods Production Plant
Regions Exported to: Canada

42276 Barber's Farm Distillery LLC
3609 NY-30
Middleburgh, NY 12122
www.1857spirits.com
Gluten-free, farm-to-bottle vodka
President/General Manager: Dorcas Roehrs
Head Distiller: Elias Barber
Marketing/Sales Director: Larry Friedberg
Number of Brands: 1
Number of Products: 1
Type of Packaging: Consumer, Private Label
Brands Exported: 1857 Spirits
Regions Exported to: USA

42277 Bardo Abrasives
1666 Summerfield St
Ridgewood, NY 11385 718-456-6400
Fax: 718-366-2104 www.bardoabrasives.com
Manufacturer and exporter of blending, finishing and buffing wheels for food processing equipment
President: Edwin F Doyle
VP: Ted Wood
Estimated Sales: $ 20 - 50 Million
Number Employees: 100-249
Square Footage: 90000
Parent Co: Barker Brothers
Brands Exported: Bardo Flex
Regions Exported to: Europe, Asia
Percentage of Business in Exporting: 15

42278 Barhyte Specialty Foods Inc
912 Airport Rd
Pendleton, OR 97801-4589 541-276-0259
Fax: 503-691-8918 800-227-4983
chris@mustardpeople.com www.barhyte.com
Mustards
Owner: Brad Hill
Secretary/Treasurer: Irene Barhyte
Director Sales Marketing: Chris Barhyte
chris@barhyte.com
Public Relation President: Kelly M. Mooney
Year Founded: 1982
Estimated Sales: $2.5-5,000,000
Number Employees: 5-9
Percentage of Business in Exporting: 5
Regions Imported from: Asia

42279 Bari Italian Foods
3875 Bengert St
Orlando, FL 32808-4659 407-298-0560
Fax: 407-293-2032 www.bellissimofoods.com
Wholesaler/distributor and importer of Italian foods; serving the food service market
President: Joe Paparella
Contact: Anthony Paparella
anthony@bellissimofoods.com
Estimated Sales: $20-50 Million
Number Employees: 50-99
Parent Co: Bellissimo Foods
Type of Packaging: Food Service

42280 Barilla USA
885 Sunset Ridge Road
Northbrook, IL 60062 847-405-7500
Fax: 847-405-7505 800-922-7455
www.barilla.com
Pastas and pasta sauces.
President: Jean-Pierre Comte
VP Marketing: Melissa Tendick
Contact: Carroll Alba
alba.carroll@barilla.com
Logistics Customer Manager: Pasquale DeChiara
Number Employees: 100-249
Number of Brands: 3
Type of Packaging: Food Service
Regions Imported from: Europe

42281 Barker Company
703 Franklin St
P.O. Box 478
Keosauqua, IA 52565 319-293-3777
Fax: 319-293-3776 sales@bakercompany.com
www.barkercompany.com
Manufacturer and importer of refrigerated, hot and dry display cases
President: Pat Mahon
Contact: Amanda Brauns
amanda.brauns@barkercompany.com
Estimated Sales: $ 10 - 20,000,000
Number Employees: 250-499
Square Footage: 84000
Regions Imported from: Europe, Canada, Mexico

Importers & Exporters / A-Z

42282 Barlean's Fisheries
3660 Slater Rd
Ferndale, WA 98248-9518   360-384-0325
Fax: 360-384-1746 bfmain@barleansfishery.com
www.barleansfishery.com
Organic flaxseed oil, fish oil
Owner/President: Cindy Smith
Vice President: Ronan Smith
Marketing Director: Andreas Koch
Manager: Yehya Ahmed
yahmed@barleans.com
Year Founded: 1972
Number Employees: 10-19
Brands Exported: Highest Lignan Flax Oil; Essential Woman; Omega Man, Forti-Flax; Fresh Catch Fish Oil
Regions Exported to: Europe, Asia, Australia, Canada
Percentage of Business in Exporting: 10
Regions Imported from: Canada
Percentage of Business in Importing: 10

42283 Barliant & Company
319 E Van Emmon St
Yorkville, IL 60560   630-553-6992
Fax: 630-553-6908 barliant@aol.com
www.barliant.com
Domestic and export broker of new and used food processing equipment including meat and poultry, as well as appraisals, liquidations, auctions and asset management programs.
Owner: Scott Swanson
Sales Manager: Kevin Chapman
Contact: Tom Baumgartner
tom@centralice.com
Estimated Sales: $1.5 Million
Number Employees: 5
Square Footage: 152000
Regions Exported to: Central America, South America, Europe, Asia, Canada, Mexico

42284 Barn Furniture Mart
6206 Sepulveda Blvd
Van Nuys, CA 91411-1110   818-785-4253
Fax: 818-785-4564 888-302-2276
www.barnfurnituremart.com
Manufacturer and exporter of chairs, barstools, bars, tables and booths; custom designing services available
Owner: Leon Tuberman
manya3@aol.com
VP: Leon Tuberman
Number Employees: 20-49
Square Footage: 840000
Regions Exported to: Worldwide

42285 Barrette Outdoor Living
7830 Freeway Cir
Cleveland, OH 44130-6307   440-891-0790
Fax: 440-891-5267 800-336-2383
www.barretteoutdoorliving.com
Manufacturer and exporter of structural foam products, regular and tote trays, pallets, carts, plant displays, produce tables, lattice panels, plastic trellises, plastic arbors and plastic fencing
President: Karin Golan
karin.golan@us.ebarrette.com
CFO: Nick Kokotovich
Vice President: William Goslin
Marketing Director: Ron Smith
Sales Director: John Payne
Product Manager: Mark Sprague
Purchasing Manager: Steve Armstrong
Number Employees: 1000-4999
Square Footage: 1400000
Brands Exported: Powershelf; Tuffrit
Regions Exported to: Central America, South America, Europe, Asia, Middle East, Australia
Percentage of Business in Exporting: 5

42286 Barrie House Gourmet Coffee
4 Warehouse Lane
Elmsford, NY 10523   914-233-1561
800-876-2233
www.barriehouse.com
Coffees, teas, accessories and equipment
President: Paul Goldstein
CEO: Craig M James
CFO/COO: George Ercolino
Quality/R&D Director: Zurab Jacobi
VP Sales & Customer Service: Kathleen Collins
Contact: Edward Goldstein
egoldstein@barriehouse.com
Year Founded: 1934
Estimated Sales: $20-50 Million
Number Employees: 20-49
Number of Products: 200
Type of Packaging: Food Service, Private Label, Bulk
Brands Exported: Barrie House Gourmet Coffee
Regions Exported to: Asia, Caribbean
Percentage of Business in Exporting: 75

42287 Barrows Tea Company
PO Box 40278
New Bedford, MA 02744-0003   774-488-8684
Fax: 508-990-2760 800-832-5024
www.barrowstea.com
Teas
President: Sam Barrows
Estimated Sales: $1-2.5 Million
Number Employees: 1-4
Number of Brands: 1
Number of Products: 15
Type of Packaging: Consumer, Food Service
Regions Imported from: Europe, Asia

42288 Barry Food Sales
809 N Bethlehem Pike
Ambler, PA 19002-2534   215-646-9771
Fax: 215-646-9776 800-378-1548
Food Brokerage Company of fresh and frozen beef, pork, veal and lamb
Owner: Barry Katz
barry@barryfoodsales.com
Estimated Sales: Less Than $500,000
Number Employees: 1-4
Type of Packaging: Food Service, Bulk

42289 Barry Group
415 Griffin Dr
Corner Brook, NL A2H 3E9
Canada   709-785-7387
bgi@barrygroupinc.com
www.barrygroupinc.com
Frozen fish and seafood; grenadier fillets; fish oil.
Founder & CEO: Bill Barry
VP, Sales: Kevin Baldwin
Year Founded: 1854
Estimated Sales: $283.03 Million
Number Employees: 3,000
Parent Co: Westfish International
Type of Packaging: Consumer, Food Service, Private Label, Bulk
Brands Exported: Seafreez; Ocean Leader
Regions Exported to: Europe, Asia, Caribbean
Percentage of Business in Exporting: 98
Regions Imported from: Europe, Asia

42290 Bartek Ingredients, Inc.
421 Seaman Street
Stoney Creek, ON L8E 3J4
Canada   905-662-1127
Fax: 905-662-8849 800-263-4165
sales@bartek.ca www.bartek.ca
Acidulants
Chief Executive Officer: Raffaele Brancato
Vice President: David Tapajna
Vice President: Jason Perry
Year Founded: 1978
Estimated Sales: $40 Million
Number Employees: 80
Square Footage: 40000
Regions Exported to: Worldwide
Percentage of Business in Exporting: 95

42291 Barton Beers
55 E Monroe St Ste 1700
Chicago, IL 60603   312-346-9200
www.bartonbeers.com
Processor, importer and exporter of beer
President: William Hackett
CEO: Andy Berk
CEO: Alexander Berke
Marketing Director: Tom McNichols
Sales Director: Martin Birkel
Number Employees: 100-249
Number of Brands: 10
Number of Products: 18
Parent Co: Constellations Brands
Type of Packaging: Consumer
Other Locations:
  Stevens Point Brewery
  Stevens Point, WI Stevens Point Brewery
Brands Imported: Corona Extra/Light; Coronita; Negra Modelo; Modelo Especial; Pacifico; Peroni; Tsingtao; St. Pauli Girl Dark; St. Pauli Girl; Double Diamond Ale; Tetley's
Regions Imported from: Europe, Asia, Mexico
Percentage of Business in Importing: 95

42292 Barwell Food Sales
Suite 202
London, ON N6A 2S2
Canada   519-645-1070
Fax: 519-645-7249 veggies@bartlettfarms.com
www.bartlettfarms.com
Importer and wholesaler/distributor of frozen fruits and vegetables; serving supermarket chains and the food service market
Owner/President: Donald Bartlett

42293 Bascom Family Farms Inc
74 Cotton Mill Hl # A106
Brattleboro, VT 05301-8603   802-254-5529
Fax: 802-257-8111 888-266-6271
sales@bascomfamilyfarms.com
www.maplesource.com
Pure maple syrup and sugar; organic and kosher varieties available
President: Bruce Bascom
Director of Sales and Marketing: Arnold Coombs
Estimated Sales: $ .5 - 1 million
Number Employees: 10-19
Number of Brands: 3
Type of Packaging: Consumer, Food Service, Private Label, Bulk
Brands Exported: Coombs Vermont Gourmet
Regions Exported to: Worldwide
Percentage of Business in Exporting: 15
Regions Imported from: Canada

42294 Bascom Food Products
36 E 13th St
Paterson, NJ 07524   973-569-1558
Fax: 973-684-6544 basfood@aol.com
Importer of gourmet and specialty foods
President: John Fressie
Research & Development: Guadalupe Fernandez
Sales Director: Brian Egan
Estimated Sales: $5-10 Million
Number Employees: 5-9
Square Footage: 600000
Type of Packaging: Consumer, Food Service, Private Label, Bulk
Brands Imported: Gemini; Coco Lopex; Bascom
Regions Imported from: Central America, South America, Europe, Asia, Middle East
Percentage of Business in Importing: 90

42295 Basic American Foods
2185 N California Blvd
Suite 215
Walnut Creek, CA 94596-3566   925-472-4000
Fax: 925-472-4360 www.baf.com
Mashed potatoes, hashbrowns & cut potatoes, potato casseroles, and beans & chili
President & CEO: Loren Kimura
lkimura@baf.com
CFO: John Argent
Brand Manager: Hans Kohte
Development Manager: Gary Eversoll
Production Supervisor: Leon Mortensen
Marketing Manager: Jane Foreman
Director, Ingredient Sales: Daniela Boyd
Senior Manager Media Relations: Pat Burke
VP Supply Chain Operations: Mark Klompien
Project Manager: Jerome Bullock
Purchasing: Chris Gentry
Number Employees: 100-249
Square Footage: 13814
Type of Packaging: Consumer, Food Service, Private Label, Bulk
Regions Exported to: Central America, South America, Europe, Asia, Middle East

42296 Basic Food Flavors
3950 E Craig Rd
North Las Vegas, NV 89030-7504   702-643-0043
Fax: 702-643-6149 info@basicfoodflavors.com
www.basicfoodflavors.com
Industrial ingredients, including hydrolyzed vegetable proteins, processed flavors, soy sauce and soy bases

Importers & Exporters / A-Z

President & CFO: Cathy Staley
cstaley@staleyinc.com
Vice President: Bill Robertson
Lab Manager; R&D: Randy Pierce
Quality Assurance Manager: Geetika Duggal
Customer Service: Cathy Hooper
Director of Sales & Marketing: Dave Wood
Operations Director: Phil Price
Estimated Sales: $10 Million
Number Employees: 50-99
Square Footage: 60000
Type of Packaging: Food Service, Bulk
Regions Exported to: Central America, South America, Europe, Asia, Middle East

42297 Basic Food Intl Inc
901 S Federal Hwy
Suite 202
Fort Lauderdale, FL 33316   954-467-1700
          Fax: 954-764-5110 info@basicfood.com
                            www.basicfood.com
Importer, exporter and wholesaler/distributor of produce, dairy products, frozen meats, poultry, fish, groceries, oils, etc.
Owner: John Bauer
Year Founded: 1968
Estimated Sales: $20-50 Million
Number Employees: 20-49
Square Footage: 20000
Type of Packaging: Food Service, Private Label, Bulk
Brands Exported: Marea Premium Seafood
Regions Exported to: Central America, South America, Europe, Asia, Middle East
Percentage of Business in Exporting: 55
Brands Imported: Global
Regions Imported from: Central America, South America, Asia
Percentage of Business in Importing: 45

42298 (HQ)Basic Leasing Corporation
12a Port Kearny
Kearny, NJ 07032-4612   973-817-7373
Consultant specializing in the design of industrial kitchens; exporter of ice makers, dishwashers, etc.; importer of ice machines; wholesaler/distributor of equipment and fixtures and frozen drink machines and coffee machines
President: Harold Weber
VP: Johnathan Weber
Estimated Sales: $20-50 Million
Number Employees: 50-99
Square Footage: 28500
Regions Imported from: Europe, Asia
Percentage of Business in Importing: 3

42299 Basketfull
276 5th Ave Rm 201
New York, NY 10001   212-686-2175
          Fax: 212-255-9019 800-645-4438
Gourmet food and fruit and gift baskets
President: Nancy Forest
Estimated Sales: Less than $500,000
Number Employees: 5-9
Regions Exported to: Africa

42300 Batavia Wine Cellars
235 N Bloomfield Road
Canandaigua, NY 14424-1059   585-396-7600
          Fax: 585-396-7833
Wines
President: Ned Cooper
Ceo/Vice President: Tim Richenberg
Contact: Marty Bognanno
marty.bognanno@cwine.com
Number Employees: 100-249
Parent Co: Canandaigua Wine Company
Type of Packaging: Consumer, Food Service, Private Label, Bulk
Brands Exported: Vintner's Choice
Regions Exported to: South America, Europe, Asia

42301 Batching Systems
50 Jibsail Dr
Prince Frederick, MD 20678-3467   410-414-8111
          Fax: 410-414-8121 800-311-0851
                           info@batchingsystems.com
                           www.batchingsystems.com
Manufacturer and exporter of optical part counting, scanning, filling and batching machines.
Owner: Don Wooldridge
Marketing: Raven Easton
Sales: David Wooldridge
sales@batchingsystems.com

Estimated Sales: $10-20 Million
Number Employees: 20-49
Brands Exported: Batchmaster; Bagmaster
Regions Exported to: Europe, Canada, Mexico
Percentage of Business in Exporting: 12

42302 Battaglia Distributing Corp
2500 S Ashland Ave
Chicago, IL 60608   312-738-1111
                           www.battagliafoods.com
Italian mozzarella, sausage, extra virgin olive oil, and wine.
President: Frank Battaglia
fbattaglia@battaglia.com
Year Founded: 1902
Estimated Sales: $100-500 Million
Number Employees: 50-200
Type of Packaging: Private Label
Regions Imported from: Europe
Percentage of Business in Importing: 100

42303 Baublys Control Laser
2419 Lake Orange Dr
Orlando, FL 32837   407-926-3500
          Fax: 407-926-3590 866-612-8619
          clcsales@controllaser.com www.controllaser.com
Fully integrated lasers and mechanical coding, marking, engraving, deep engraving, and 3D engraving systems and solution for the aerospace, automotive, coining and jewerly, consumer/commercial, electronic, medical, mold and diepackaging, tooling and trophy and awards industries. Our Laser Markink Systems are available: 10 Watt, 25 Watt, 50 Watt and CO2 with wigh power Nd:YAD and Nd:YLF lamp and diode pumped infrared, Green, UV and Deep UV systems.
President: Steve Graham
CEO: Antoine Dominic
Marketing Director: Monica Correal
Contact: Michele Fencik
mfencik@controllaser.com
Number Employees: 50-99
Number of Products: 20
Square Footage: 104000
Parent Co: Excel Technology
Brands Exported: InstaMark Signature; InstaMark Script; InstaMark Stylus
Regions Exported to: Worldwide
Percentage of Business in Exporting: 16

42304 Bauducco Foods Inc.
1705 NW 133 Ave
Suite 101
Miami, FL 33182   305-477-9270
          Fax: 305-477-4703 sales@bauduccofoods.com
                           www.bauducco.com
Panettone, wafers, cookies, crackers and bars
President/General Manager: Stefano Mozzi
Manager: Fred Rodrigues
Contact: Alfredo Rivera
alfredor@bauduccofoods.com
Year Founded: 2004
Estimated Sales: $5 Million
Number Employees: 1-4
Regions Exported to: Central America, Caribbean, Canada, Mexico
Regions Imported from: South America

42305 Baumer Foods Inc
2424 Edenborn Ave
Suite 510
Metairie, LA 70001   504-482-5761
                           www.baumerfoods.com
Sauces, including hot sauce, steak sauce, worcestershire, oriental and wing sauce.
Regional Sales Manager: Kevin Eber
Vice President, Exports: Marwan Kabbani
Year Founded: 1923
Estimated Sales: $39.9 Million
Number Employees: 100-249
Number of Brands: 1
Number of Products: 11
Square Footage: 120000
Type of Packaging: Consumer, Food Service, Private Label
Brands Exported: Crystal
Regions Exported to: Central America, South America, Europe, Asia, Middle East

42306 Baur Tape & Label Co
130 Lombrano St
San Antonio, TX 78207-1832   210-738-3000
          Fax: 210-738-0070 877-738-3222
          baurlabel@swbell.net www.baurlabel.com

Manufacturer and exporter of shipping and metal labels
President: Leonard Humble
baurlabel@swbell.net
Sales Manager: Peter Humble
Estimated Sales: $1-2.5 Million
Number Employees: 5-9
Square Footage: 8000
Type of Packaging: Consumer, Food Service, Private Label, Bulk
Regions Exported to: Central America, Mexico
Percentage of Business in Exporting: 1

42307 Bauscher Inc
10900 World Trade Blvd
Raleigh, NC 27617-4202   919-844-2801
          Fax: 919-844-7669 888-840-4333
          info@bauscherinc.com www.bauscherhepp.com
Wholesaler/distributor and importer of china and flatware, serving the food service market
President: Jeffery Heany
jeffery@bauscherinc.com
Number Employees: 5-9

42308 Baxter Manufacturing Inc
19220 State Route 162 E
Orting, WA 98360-9236   360-893-5554
          Fax: 360-893-6836 800-777-2828
                           www.baxtermfg.com
Manufacturer and exporter of bakery and deli equipment including rack and revolving ovens, proof boxes, fryers, inventory supply items, ingredient bins, molders and dividers
Design/Marketing Manager: Laura Barrentine
Manager: Gabrielle Devault
gabrielle.devault@baxtermfg.com
Estimated Sales: $1 - 5 Million
Number Employees: 100-249
Square Footage: 228000
Parent Co: Hobart Corporation
Brands Exported: Baxter

42309 Baxter Manufacturing Inc
19220 State Route 162 E
Orting, WA 98360-9236   360-893-5554
          Fax: 360-893-6836 800-777-2828
                           www.baxtermfg.com
Manufacturer and designer of quality bakery and foodservice equipment
President: John McDonough
Manager: Gabrielle Devault
gabrielle.devault@baxtermfg.com
Number Employees: 100-249

42310 Bay Valley Foods
1390 Pullman Dr.
El Paso, TX 79936
                             800-236-1119
                           www.bayvalleyfoods.com
Pickles, powder, syrups & sauces, aseptic, liquid creamer, refrigerated dressing & egg substitutes, soup, broth & gravy, infant foods, salsa, salad dressings, marinades & barbecue sauces, fruit spreads & sauces, salad dressingsmarinades and mayonnaise.
President/CEO: Steve Oakland
CFO: Matthew Foulston
Executive VP/General Counsel: Thomas O'Neill
Year Founded: 1862
Estimated Sales: $116.3 Million
Number Employees: 1,000
Square Footage: 50000
Parent Co: TreeHouse Foods, Inc.
Type of Packaging: Consumer, Food Service, Private Label, Bulk
Brands Exported: Non-Dairy Creamers & Flavor Charm
Regions Exported to: Worldwide

42311 Bayard Kurth Company
19321 Mount Elliott St
Detroit, MI 48234-2724   313-891-0800
          Fax: 313-891-8966
Manufacturer and exporter of advertising displays, decalcomanias and packaging materials
President: Bayard Kurth Jr
VP: Bayard Kurth
Estimated Sales: $5-10 Million
Number Employees: 5-9
Type of Packaging: Consumer, Food Service, Bulk
Regions Exported to: Worldwide
Percentage of Business in Exporting: 3

Importers & Exporters / A-Z

42312 Baycliff Co Inc
608 South Ave.
Garwood, NJ 07027   212-772-6078
    Fax: 212-472-8980   866-772-7569
           www.sushichef.com
Rice vinegar, soy sauce, soy salad dressing, teriyaki sauce, rice, rice cracker mix, green tea, and soups
President: Helen Tandler
ht@sushichef.com
VP: Alan Johnson
Estimated Sales: $20-50 Million
Number Employees: 20-49
Type of Packaging: Consumer, Food Service
Brands Exported: Sushi Chef
Regions Exported to: Central America, South America, Europe, Middle East, Australia, Canada, Caribbean, Mexico, Latin America
Regions Imported from: Asia

42313 Bayhead Products Corp.
173 Crosby Rd
Dover, NH 03820-4356   603-742-3000
    Fax: 603-743-4701   800-229-4323
         sales@bayheadproducts.com
         www.bayheadproducts.com
Plastic and steel industrial items, tilt and box trucks, self-dumping hoppers, pallet containers, barrels, boxes, containment trays, totes, cases, tanks, steel racks and carts; exporter of tilt trucks and boxes
President: Elissa Moore
sales@bayheadproducts.com
Estimated Sales: $1.9 Million
Number Employees: 20-49
Square Footage: 50000
Type of Packaging: Bulk
Regions Exported to: Canada, Mexico

42314 Bayou Food Distributors
949 Industry Rd
Kenner, LA 70062-6848   504-469-1745
    Fax: 504-469-1852   800-516-8283
         bayoufoods@hughes.net
Fillet fish, crabs, shrimp; frozen foods, such as beef, pork, poultry and seafood
CEO: Arthur Mitchell
bayoufoods@hughes.net
Estimated Sales: $5-10 Million
Number Employees: 5-9
Square Footage: 54400
Type of Packaging: Food Service
Regions Imported from: Central America, South America
Percentage of Business in Importing: 5

42315 Bayside Motion Group
27 Seaview Boulevard
Port Washington, NY 11050-4610   516-484-5482
    Fax: 516-484-5496   800-305-4555
         www.baysideinfo.com
Manufacturer and exporter of environmentally sealed gear heads
Marketing Coordinator: Paul Gallagher
Estimated Sales: $ 5 - 10 Million
Number Employees: 150

42316 Bazzini Holdings LLC
1035 Mill Rd
Allentown, PA 18106-3101   610-366-1606
    Fax: 610-366-1606 www.bazzininuts.com
Nuts, mixes, bars and pistachios
Owner/President: Rocco Damato
COO: Richard Toltzis
VP of Marketing: Carrie Madigan
Manager: Jen Bowman
jbowman@cherrydalefarms.com
Number Employees: 1-4
Square Footage: 200000
Other Locations:
    Allentown, PA
Regions Exported to: Middle East
Percentage of Business in Exporting: 1
Regions Imported from: South America, Europe, Asia, Middle East, Latin America

42317 Be & Sco
1623 N San Marcos
San Antonio, TX 78201-6436   210-734-5124
    Fax: 210-737-3925   800-683-0928
         sales@bescomfg.com www.minom.com
Manufacturer and exporter of flour tortilla and tamale equipment and grills
President: Robert Escamilla
robert@bescomfg.com
VP: Rosie Ecamilla
Estimated Sales: $2.5-5 Million
Number Employees: 20-49
Square Footage: 120000
Regions Exported to: Central America, South America, Europe, Asia, Middle East
Percentage of Business in Exporting: 20

42318 Beach Filter Products
P.O. Box 505
555 Centennial Ave
Hanover, PA 17331   717-698-1403
    Fax: 717-698-1610   800-232-2485
         sales@beachfilters.com www.beachfilters.com
Manufacturer and exporter of compressed air filters, desiccant dehumidification bags, and breather filters.
President: Wesley Jones
abuckley@beachfilters.com
Sales Manager: Lori Prickitt
Production Manager: Leslie Doll
Plant Manager/Purchasing: Leslie Doll
Estimated Sales: $500 Thousand - $1 Million
Square Footage: 16000
Type of Packaging: Consumer, Bulk
Regions Exported to: Central America, South America, Europe, Asia, Middle East, Africa
Regions Imported from: Central America, South America, Europe, Asia, Middle East, Africa

42319 Beam Industries
1700 W 2nd St
Webster City, IA 50595   515-832-4620
    Fax: 515-832-6659   800-369-2326
         lars.hybel@beamvac.com www.beamvac.com
Manufacturer and exporter of central vacuum cleaner systems and parts
President: Russell S Minick
CFO: Dave Thompson
Commercial Sales Manager: Bill Smith
Contact: Joel Fritz
joelfritz@beamsind.com
Estimated Sales: $20-50 Million
Number Employees: 100-249
Square Footage: 100000
Regions Exported to: Worldwide

42320 Beam Suntory
222 W. Merchandise Mart Plaza
Suite 1600
Chicago, IL 60654   312-964-6999
         www.beamsuntory.com
Alcohol, including cognac, bourbon and bourbon mixes, whisky, rum, and tequila.
President/CEO: Albert Baladi
President, Brands: Jessica Spence
Senior VP/CFO: Marc Andre Tousignant
Senior VP/General Counsel: Todd Bloomquist
Senior VP/Chief Human Resources Officer: Paula Erickson
EVP/Chief Supply Chain Officer: David Hunter
Year Founded: 2014
Estimated Sales: $3.1 Billion
Number Employees: 4,800
Number of Brands: 50+
Square Footage: 50000
Parent Co: Suntory Holdings
Type of Packaging: Consumer, Food Service
Other Locations:
    Jim Beam Brands Co.
    Geyserville, CAJim Beam Brands Co.

42321 Bean Machines
18619 Middlefield Rd
Sonoma, CA 95476-1998   707-996-0706
    Fax: 707-996-0704
Manufacturer and exporter of soybean processing equipment used to produce soy milk, tofu, yogurt, etc.; importer of multiple filter centrifuges
President: W Rogers
CEO: S Fiering
Estimated Sales: $350,000
Number Employees: 6
Square Footage: 5600
Type of Packaging: Food Service
Regions Exported to: Central America, South America, Europe, Asia
Brands Imported: Kawanishi
Regions Imported from: Asia

42322 Bear Creek Country Kitchens
325 W 600 S
Heber City, UT 84032-2230   516-333-9326
    Fax: 435-654-5449   800-516-7286
         www.bearcreekcountrykitchens.com
Soup and pasta mixes
Owner: Donald White
President/CEO: Kevin Ruda
CFO: Al Van Leeuwen
Director R&D: Brian Brinkerhoff
VP Sales/Marketing: Stephen White
VP Operations: Kevin Kowalski
Purchasing Manager: Mark Hartman
Estimated Sales: $40 Million
Number Employees: 100-249
Square Footage: 180000
Parent Co: American Capital Strategies
Type of Packaging: Consumer, Food Service
Brands Exported: Bear Creek Country Kitchens
Regions Exported to: Asia, Middle East, Canada

42323 Bear Creek Operations
PO Box 9000
Medford, OR 97501-0303   541-779-5080
    Fax: 541-864-2926 jroberts@bco.com
Importer and wholesaler/distributor of apples, pears and stonefruit; wholesaler/distributor of groceries, meats, produce, dairy and bakery products and seafood; exporter of fresh pears; mail order fruit gift packs available
CEO: Nancy Tait
CFO: Jane Emkes
Sr VP: John Roberts
Quality Control VP: Perry Higgins
Contact: Tiffany Swartz
tswartz@bco.com
Operations: Lawna Wyatt
Estimated Sales: $ 1 - 3 Million
Number Employees: 1,000-4,999
Square Footage: 1000000
Parent Co: Bear Creek Corporation
Type of Packaging: Bulk
Brands Exported: Bear Creek
Regions Exported to: Europe
Percentage of Business in Exporting: 1
Brands Imported: Enza Multiple Brands Used To Supply Fruit Gift Requirements For Harry And Davis
Regions Imported from: South America, New Zealand, South Africa
Percentage of Business in Importing: 25

42324 Bear Stewart Corp
1025 N Damen Avenue
Chicago, IL 60622   773-276-0400
    Fax: 773-276-3512   800-697-2327
         info@bearstewart.com www.bearstewart.com
Fillings, jams, jellies, and premade mixes for bakers and confectioners.
VP of Sales: Michael Hoffman
COO: Jason Brooks
Year Founded: 1966
Estimated Sales: $5-10 Million
Number Employees: 1-4
Square Footage: 200000
Type of Packaging: Food Service, Bulk
Regions Exported to: Central America, Europe, Middle East
Percentage of Business in Exporting: 5

42325 Beatrice Bakery Co
201 S 5th St
Beatrice, NE 68310-4408   402-223-2358
    Fax: 402-223-4465   800-228-4030
         www.beatricebakery.com
Dessert cakes, fruit cakes, and liqueur-filled cakes
President: Greg Leech
greg@beatricebakery.com
Quality Control/Production Manager: Robin Dickinson
Sales Manager: Connie Warnsing
Public Relations: Brooklyn Soft
Estimated Sales: $ 5 -10 Million
Number Employees: 20-49
Number of Brands: 10
Number of Products: 125
Square Footage: 200000
Type of Packaging: Private Label
Brands Exported: Grandma's; Ye Olde English
Regions Exported to: Europe, Canada
Percentage of Business in Exporting: 1

42326 Beaufurn
5269 US Highway 158
Advance, NC 27006-6905   336-941-3446
    Fax: 336-941-3568   888-766-7706
         info@beaufurn.com www.beaufurn.com
Manufacturer, importer and exporter of chairs and tables

Importers & Exporters / A-Z

President/CEO: Bill Bongaerts
bill@beaufurn.com
CFO: Monique De Proost
Sales: Lou Ann Bogulski
Public Relations: Janet Stanford
Estimated Sales: $3-4 Million
Number Employees: 20-49
Regions Exported to: Central America, South America
Regions Imported from: South America, Europe, Asia
Percentage of Business in Importing: 90

42327 Beaumont Products
1560 Big Shanty Dr NW
Kennesaw, GA 30144-7040   770-514-7400
Fax: 770-514-7400   800-451-7096
cnatu31927@aol.com
www.beaumontproducts.com
Fruit and vegetable wash, citrus based and glycerine hand soaps, air fresheners and cleaners
Owner: Robert Rice
Vice President: Mark Woods
mwoods@beaumontproducts.com
Public Relations: Wat Bagley
Office Manager: Peggy Dunne
Estimated Sales: $10-20 Million
Number Employees: 20-49
Number of Brands: 5
Number of Products: 20
Square Footage: 52000
Parent Co: Beaumont Products, Inc.
Type of Packaging: Consumer, Private Label
Brands Exported: Clearly Natural Soaps
Regions Exported to: Europe, Asia, Australia, Canada
Percentage of Business in Exporting: 2

42328 Beaumont Rice Mills
1800 Pecos Street
Beaumont, TX 77701   409-832-2521
lbroussard@gtbizclass.com
www.bmtricemills.com
Rice
President: Louis Broussard
lbroussard@gtbizclass.com
Vice President: Ben Broussard
Secretary: Sheryl Graham
Assistant Secretary/Treasurer: Brenda Cook
Estimated Sales: $17.5 Million
Number Employees: 50-99
Type of Packaging: Consumer
Regions Exported to: Worldwide

42329 Beaver Street Fisheries
1741 W. Beaver St.
Jacksonville, FL 32209   800-252-5661
800-874-6426
www.beaverstreetfisheries.com
Lobster tail, clams, oysters, shrimp, crab, mussels, swai fillets, tilapia fillets, breaded fish, imitation crab, smoked salmon, frog legs, crawfish, conch, squid & calamari and octopus & scallops. Also manufactures beef, pork, poultry and lamb.
President: Alfred Frisch
CFO: Jeff Edwards
Executive Vice President: Mark Frisch
Director, Marketing: Bluzette Carline
Year Founded: 1950
Estimated Sales: $442.8 Million
Number Employees: 250-499
Number of Brands: 5
Square Footage: 300000
Type of Packaging: Consumer, Food Service, Private Label, Bulk
Regions Exported to: Central America, Canada, Caribbean
Brands Imported: Island Queen; Sea Best; Franco; Our Island
Regions Imported from: Central America, South America, Europe, Asia, Middle East, Canada, Mexico, Caribbean
Percentage of Business in Importing: 75

42330 Beaverton Foods Inc
7100 NE Century Boulevard
Hillsboro, OR 97124   503-646-8138
800-223-8076
www.beavertonfoods.com
Horseradish, mustard, garlic and sauces.
Founder: Rose Biggi
CEO: Domonic Biggi
Business/Customer Service Manager: Roger Klingsporn
Estimated Sales: $10-20 Million
Number Employees: 50-99
Number of Brands: 6
Number of Products: 150
Square Footage: 65000
Type of Packaging: Consumer, Food Service, Private Label, Bulk
Brands Exported: Beaver; Inglehoffer
Regions Exported to: Central America, South America, Europe, Canada
Percentage of Business in Exporting: 9

42331 Beayl Weiner/Pak
610 Palisades Drive
Pacific Palisades, CA 90272-2849   310-454-1354
Fax: 310-459-6545 weinerb@aol.com
Manufacturer and importer of flexible packaging materials including printed and laminated roll stock, bags and pouches
Owner: Jeanne Weiner
Number Employees: 95
Square Footage: 200000
Type of Packaging: Food Service, Private Label, Bulk
Regions Imported from: Asia
Percentage of Business in Importing: 3

42332 Beck Flavors
1301 Mattec Drive
Loveland, OH 45140   314-878-7522
Fax: 513-889-1268 beckflavors.net
Bakery, beverage, coffee, tea, and dairy flavors
General Manager: Joe Willoughby
Contact: Darienne Bils
dbils@beckflavors.net
Type of Packaging: Bulk
Other Locations:
  Ardsley, NY
  Bakersfield, CA
  Lakeland, FL
  New Century, KS Bakersfield
Regions Exported to: Central America, South America, Europe, Asia
Percentage of Business in Exporting: 20

42333 Becker Brothers Graphite Co
39 Legion St
Maywood, IL 60153-2321   708-410-0700
Fax: 708-410-0701 sales@beckergraphite.com
www.beckergraphite.com
Self-lubricating and heat resistant graphite bushings, bearings, seals, rings and plates
President: Cheryl Ivanovich
sales@beckergraphite.com
Sales: Linda Egelhart
Customer Service: Linda Egelhart
Director Operations: Pedro Espinoza
Plant Manager: Pedro Espinoza
Estimated Sales: $ 2.5-5,000,000
Number Employees: 5-9
Square Footage: 20000
Regions Exported to: Europe, Middle East
Percentage of Business in Exporting: 1

42334 Becker Foods
15136 Goldenwest Cir
Westminster, CA 92683-5235   714-891-9474
www.beckerfoods.com
Custom processor and packager of; fresh and frozen poultry, beef, pork, lamb, veal, cheese products, and more
President: Stan Becker
stan@beckerfoods.com
Vice President: Dian Vendel
Number Employees: 5-9
Type of Packaging: Food Service, Private Label

42335 Becton Dickinson & Co.
1 Becton Dr.
Franklin Lakes, NJ 07417-1880   201-847-6800
Fax: 201-847-6475 www.bd.com
Diagnostic tests and instruments for microbiology.
President/COO: Thomas Polen
Executive Chairman: Vincent Forlenza
vincent_forlenza@bd.com
Executive VP/CFO/CAO: Christopher Reidy
Executive VP/General Counsel: Samrat Khichi
Executive VP/Chief Quality Officer: Davide Shan
Executive VP/Chief Marketing Officer: Tony Ezell
EVP/Chief Human Resources Officer: Betty Larson
Year Founded: 1897
Estimated Sales: $17.2 Billion
Number Employees: 70,000+

42336 Bede Inc
PO Box 8263
Haledon, NJ 07508-0263   973-956-2900
Fax: 973-956-0600   866-239-6565
bedeinc@aol.com
Processor and exporter of instant hot cereals including peanut porridge, banana, plantain, etc.; also, peanut-based health beverage mixes
President: Jasseth Cummings
CFO: Gloria Johnson
Buyer: Sam Cummings
Quality Control: King H
Estimated Sales: $2.5-5,000,000
Number Employees: 1-4
Brands Exported: Cream of Peanut; Peanut Porridge Mix; Banana Porridge

42337 Bedemco Inc
3 Barker Ave Ste 325
White Plains, NY 10601   914-683-1119
Fax: 914-683-1482 info@bedemco.com
www.bedemco.com
Organic dried fruit, dried vegetables, nuts and seeds.
President: Elazar Demeshulam
Vice President: Roy Demeshulam
Quality Control Manager: Natalie Levy
Marketing Director: Emily Cantor
Sales: Murray Feinblatt
Contact: Roni Detoledo
roni@bedemco.com
Production Manager: Robert Haas
Estimated Sales: $ 3 - 5 Million
Number Employees: 1-4
Type of Packaging: Food Service, Private Label, Bulk
Brands Exported: Bedemco
Regions Exported to: Europe, Middle East, Worldwide
Percentage of Business in Exporting: 10
Brands Imported: Bedemco
Regions Imported from: Central America, South America, Asia, Middle East, Worldwide
Percentage of Business in Importing: 90

42338 Bedessee Imports
2350 Midland Avenue
Scarborough, ON M1S 1P8
Canada   416-292-2400
www.bedessee.com
Importer, exporter and wholesaler/distributor of East/West Indian and Latin American foods including noodles, dried peas and beans, flour, coconut and mustard oils, meats, canned fish and spices
President: Lionel Bedessee
VP: Vernan Bedessee
VP: Rayman Bedessee
Number Employees: 10-19
Square Footage: 100000
Type of Packaging: Consumer, Food Service
Percentage of Business in Exporting: 20
Percentage of Business in Importing: 60

42339 Bedford Enterprises Inc
1940 W Betteravia Rd
Santa Maria, CA 93455-5926   805-922-4977
Fax: 805-928-7241   800-242-8884
bedfordscrap@gmail.com www.beibedford.com
Manufacturer and exporter of stainless platforms, hand railing, stair treads, ladders and decking; wholesaler/distributor of fiberglass gratings; installation services available
Vice President: Hugh Bedford
bedford@tcsn.net
VP: David Thomas
Estimated Sales: $ 1-2.5 Million
Number Employees: 10-19
Brands Exported: Bestdeck; Bestread
Regions Exported to: Central America, South America, Europe, Asia, Middle East
Percentage of Business in Exporting: 15

42340 Bedford Industries
1659 Rowe Ave
P.O. Box 39
Worthington, MN 56187   507-376-4136
Fax: 507-376-6742   800-533-5314
www.bedfordind.com
Manufacturer and exporter of identification ties and tags, twist ties, recloseable twist ties, and ElasitTag® Products.
President: Kim Milbrandt
CEO: Bob Ludlow
Marketing Director: Deb Houseman
Sales Director: Martin Rickers

Importers & Exporters / A-Z

Estimated Sales: $ 20 - 50 Million
Number Employees: 100-249
Square Footage: 84000

42341 Bedoukian Research Inc
21 Finance Dr
Danbury, CT 06810-4133   203-830-4000
Fax: 203-830-4010   800-424-9300
customerservice@bedoukian.com
www.bedoukian.com
Flavors and aromas.
President: Robert Bedoukian
robert@bedoukian.com
Regulatory and Technical Services: Joseph Bania
Year Founded: 1972
Estimated Sales: $10-24 Million
Number Employees: 50-99

42342 Bee International
2311 Boswell Rd
Suite 1
Chula Vista, CA 91914-3512   619-710-1800
Fax: 619-710-1822   800-421-6465
info@beeinc.com   www.beeinc.com
Manufacturer and importer of Easter, Valentine, Halloween, Christmas and novelty candy items
Owner/CEO: Louis Block
louisblock@beeinc.com
Quality Assurance Manager: Martin Quezada
VP Operations: Charles Block
Estimated Sales: $18 Million
Number Employees: 20-49
Square Footage: 165000
Type of Packaging: Consumer
Regions Imported from: Asia

42343 Beehive Botanicals
16297 W Nursery Rd
Hayward, WI 54843-7138   715-634-4274
Fax: 715-634-3523   800-233-4483
www.beehivebotanicals.com
Processor and exporter of health supplements derived from honey, propolis, pollen and royal jelly; also, sugar-free propolis chewing gum.
President/CEO: Linda Graham
linda.graham@beehivebotanicals.com
Quality Control Manager: Denise Gregory
Purchasing Manager: Lisa Johnson
Year Founded: 1972
Estimated Sales: $6.5 Million
Number Employees: 20-49
Square Footage: 24000
Brands Exported: Honey Silk; Beehive Botanicals
Regions Exported to: Europe, Asia, Middle East
Percentage of Business in Exporting: 35

42344 Beehive/Provisur Technologies
9100 191st Street
Mokena, IL 60448   708-479-3500
Fax: 708-479-3598   www.provisur.com
Food processing equipment.
Regions Exported to: Worldwide

42345 Beemak-IDL Display
16711 Knott Ave
La Mirada, CA 90638-6013   714-367-5580
Fax: 310-764-0330   800-421-4393
info@beemak.com   www.beemak-idl.com
Manufacturer and exporter of displays and holders for recipe cards, brochures and pamphlets
President: Robert Gray
robert@warden.com
CEO: Thomas Quinn
Finance Executive: Christy Harp
Manager Sales: Julia Alty
Estimated Sales: $ 10 - 20 Million
Number Employees: 50-99
Square Footage: 72000
Parent Co: Jordon Industries
Brands Exported: Beemak
Regions Exported to: Central America
Percentage of Business in Exporting: 5

42346 Beer Import Co
2536 Springfield Ave
Vauxhall, NJ 07088-1016   908-686-0800
Fax: 908-686-0609
Importer and wholesaler/distributor of European beer
Marketing Manager: Doug Oley
Estimated Sales: $ 20 - 50 Million
Number Employees: 1-4
Regions Imported from: Europe

42347 Beer Magic Devices
20 Railway Street
Hamilton, ON L8R 2R3
Canada   905-522-3081
Fax: 905-527-1957
Manufacturer, wholesaler/distributor and importer of portion control dispensing machines for beer, wine and liquor
President: Fred Palermo
Number Employees: 4
Regions Imported from: Canada

42348 Beetroot Delights
72 Spruceside Crescent
Foothill, ON L0S 1E1
Canada   888-842-3387
Fax: 905-892-1080
Manufacturer and exporter of beetroot condiments including cherry beet pepper and ginger beet jelly, spiced beet ketchup and beet relish. Founded in 1985.
President: Grace Lallemand
Number Employees: 3
Square Footage: 3200
Type of Packaging: Consumer, Food Service
Regions Exported to: USA, Canada
Percentage of Business in Exporting: 15

42349 Behnke Lubricants/JAX
W134 N 5373 Campbell Dr
Menomonee Falls, WI 53051   262-781-8850
Fax: 262-781-3906   800-782-8850
info@jax.com   www.jax.com
Manufacturer and exporter of food grade and high temperature synthetic lubricants
President: Eric Peter
Manager Central Region: Carter Anderson
Manager Western Region: Mitch Clark
Estimated Sales: $ 10-20 Million
Number Employees: 20-49
Parent Co: JAX
Brands Exported: JAX
Regions Exported to: Worldwide
Percentage of Business in Exporting: 3

42350 Behrens Manufacturing LLC
1250 E Sanborn St
Winona, MN 55987   507-454-4664
Fax: 507-452-2106
customerservice@behrensmfg.com
www.behrensmfg.com
Steel and metal containers.
President: Keith Dau Schmidt
CEO: Steve Tuscic
Year Founded: 1911
Estimated Sales: $10-20 Million
Number Employees: 50-99
Number of Brands: 1
Type of Packaging: Bulk

42351 Bel Brands USA
30 S. Wacker Dr.
Suite 3000
Chicago, IL 60606-7413   312-462-1500
Fax: 847-879-1999   www.belbrandsusa.com
Nacho sauce, salsa and cheeses.
CEO: Bill Graham
Vice President, Human Resources: Kerri Gollias
Vice President, Marketing: Shannon Maher
Year Founded: 1865
Estimated Sales: $103 Million
Number Employees: 250-499
Number of Brands: 7
Square Footage: 130000
Type of Packaging: Consumer, Food Service, Bulk
Other Locations:
  Bel Brands USA
  Little Chute, WI
  Bel Brands USA
  Leitchfield, KY
  Bel Brands USA
  Brookings, SD Bel Brands USA Leitchfield
Regions Imported from: Europe
Percentage of Business in Importing: 2

42352 Bel Canto Foods LLC
1300 Viele Ave
Bronx, NY 10474-7134   718-497-3888
Fax: 718-497-3799   800-597-2151
belcantofoods@chefswarehouse.com
Specialty foods

President: Christopher Pappas
Executive VP: Steve Kass
skass@belcantofoods.com
Sales Director: Angela Zambelli
VP Operations, Purchasing: Alan Butzbach
Estimated Sales: $5-10 Million
Number Employees: 100-249
Square Footage: 340
Type of Packaging: Private Label

42353 (HQ)Bel-Art Products
661 State Route 23
Wayne, NJ 07470-6814   973-694-0500
Fax: 973-694-7199   800-423-5278
www.belart.com
Manufacturer and exporter of plastic laboratory supplies including sterile and nonsterile sampling devices and magnetic stirring bars; also, laboratory cleaning products
President: David Landsberger
CEO: William Downs
Estimated Sales: $ 10 - 20 Million
Number Employees: 100-249
Square Footage: 160000
Type of Packaging: Consumer, Private Label, Bulk
Other Locations:
  Bel-Art Products
  Pequannock, NJ Bel-Art Products
Brands Exported: Clavies; Cleanware; Scienceware; Spinbar, Sterileware
Regions Exported to: Central America, South America, Europe, Asia, Middle East, Australia

42354 Belgium's Chocolate Source
66 Central Street
Suite 7
Wellesley, MA 02482   781-283-5787
Fax: 781-237-1787   877-426-8543
sales@belgiumschocolatesource.com
www.belgiumschocolatesource.com
Importer/distributor of belgian chocolates
Marketing: Christopher Van Riet
Contact: Christophe Riet
nirvanachocolates@gmail.com

42355 Belgravia Imports
275 Highpoint Ave
Portsmouth, RI 02871   401-683-3323
Fax: 401-683-2717   800-848-1127
belgravia@belgraviaimports.com
www.belgraviaimports.com
Organic and natural gourmet foods.
President: Ronald Dick
Contact: Vinny Constanza
vin-warehouse@belgraviaimports.com
Year Founded: 1937
Estimated Sales: $1-2.5 Million
Number Employees: 5-9

42356 Bell & Evans
154 W Main St
Fredericksburg, PA 17026   717-865-6626
info@bellandevans.com
www.bellandevans.com
Processor and exporter of fresh chicken, chicken nuggets, sausages, burgers, and diced IQF chicken breast
President: Scott Sechler
CFO: Dan Chirico
Year Founded: 1894
Estimated Sales: Over $1 Billion
Number Employees: 500-999
Number of Brands: 2
Square Footage: 180000
Regions Exported to: Asia
Percentage of Business in Exporting: 5

42357 Bell Amore Imports Inc
300 W Elizabeth Ave
Linden, NJ 07036-4274   908-862-1968
Fax: 908-862-1968   www.bellamoreimports.com
Importer of cookies, confectionery, bread sticks, panettone, baby cookies, wafers, toast, tiramisu, snacks, basket items, gift boxes, and many others baked good products; chocolate, croissants, lady fingers, torrone, sugar free products
President: Sam Conti
sam@bellamoreimports.com
Estimated Sales: $1-2.5 Million
Number Employees: 1-4
Square Footage: 80000
Type of Packaging: Consumer, Food Service, Private Label, Bulk

181

Brands Imported: Bell'amore; Panettone; Ciabor; Castello; Dolcital; Belli; Bisconova; Colussi; Vecchio Formo; Sgambaro; Bonomi; Fida; Nord Dolciara; Aurora; Tonon; Verona; Appendino; Bianco; Forno
Regions Imported from: South America
Percentage of Business in Importing: 100

42358 Bell Flavors & Fragrances
500 Academy Dr
Northbrook, IL 60062-2497   847-291-8300
Fax: 847-291-1217   info@bellff.com
www.bellff.com
Manufacturer and exporter of natural and artificial flavoring extracts for food and beverages; also, spice compounds.
President: Jim Heinz
jheinz@bellff.com
Director of Marketing: Kelli Heinz
Year Founded: 1912
Estimated Sales: $39 Million
Number Employees: 50-99
Square Footage: 100000
Type of Packaging: Consumer, Food Service

42359 Bell'Amore Imports
300 W Elizabeth Ave
Linden, NJ 07036   908-862-5000
Fax: 908-862-1968 bellamoreimports.com
Baked goods and confectionary products.
President: Sam Conti   *Year Founded:* 1989
Regions Imported from: Europe
Percentage of Business in Importing: 100

42360 (HQ)Bell-Mark Corporation
331 Changebridge Road
PO Box 2007
Pine Brook, NJ 7058   973-882-0202
Fax: 973-808-4616 info@bell-mark.com
www.bell-mark.com
Manufacturer and exporter of innovative coding and printing systems to the packaging and converting markets
President: John Marozzi
CFO: James Pontrella
VP: Tom Pugh
Marketing: Glenn Breslauer
Sales: Bob Batesko
Contact: Doug Buch
dbuch@bell-mark.com
Plant Manager: Dale Miller
Purchasing: Lou Ciccone
Estimated Sales: $16-20 Million
Number Employees: 50-99
Number of Brands: 5
Number of Products: 30
Square Footage: 90000
Brands Exported: Inteljet; Flex Print; Easy Print
Regions Exported to: Central America, South America, Europe, Asia, Middle East

42361 Bella Coola Fisheries
3133 188 St
Surrey, BC V3S 9V5
Canada   604-541-0339
Fax: 604-541-0370
Processor and exporter of fresh and frozen herring roe and salmon
General Manager: Frank Taylor
Number Employees: 10-19
Type of Packaging: Consumer, Food Service, Private Label, Bulk
Regions Exported to: Worldwide

42362 Bella Sun Luci
1220 Fortress St
Chico, CA 95973-9029   530-899-2661
Fax: 530-899-7746   mooneyfarm@aol.com
www.bellasunluci.com
Sun dried tomatoes, pesto, risotto, olive oil, BBQ marinade and tomato sauces.
Owner: Maryellen Mooney
Partner/Production: Stephen Mooney
Quality Assurance Manager: Jett Uribe
Sales/Marketing: Lisa Mooney
Business Management: Tammy Goss
Estimated Sales: $30 Million
Number Employees: 20-49
Square Footage: 100000
Type of Packaging: Consumer, Food Service, Private Label, Bulk
Brands Exported: Bella Sun Luci
Regions Exported to: South America, Europe, Canada

Percentage of Business in Exporting: 5

42363 Belle River Enterprises
12 Waterview Lane
Belle River, PE C0A 1B0
Canada   902-962-2248
Fax: 902-962-4276
Processor and exporter of rock crab combo and minced crab, cocktail claws and salad meat and lobsters. Founded in 1982.
General Manager: Howard Hancock
Vice President: Dean Hancock
Estimated Sales: $1-5 Million
Number Employees: 75
Square Footage: 32000
Percentage of Business in Exporting: 60

42364 Belleharvest Sales Inc
11900 Fisk Road
Belding, MI 48809-9413
800-452-7753
sales@belleharvest.com www.belleharvest.com
Manufacturer, wholesaler/distributor, exporter, and packer of fresh apples.
President/CEO: Mike Rothwell
bellehar@iserv.net
Controller: Tony Kramer
Director of Marketing: Chris Sandwick
Director of Field Operations: Tony Blattner
Plant Manager: Brad Pitsch
Number Employees: 50-99
Parent Co: Belding Fruit Storage
Type of Packaging: Private Label, Bulk
Regions Exported to: Central America, South America, Europe, Carribean
Percentage of Business in Exporting: 70

42365 Bells Foods International
3213 Waconda Rd NE
Gervais, OR 97026   503-390-1425
Fax: 503-390-9526 info@bellfoodsintl.com
www.bellfoodsintl.com
A food processor, manufacturer specialized in co-packing
President: Craig Bell
CFO: Paul Leipzig
Marketing Director: Cody Bell
VP Sales: Doug Zibell
Plant Manager: Monica Guzman
Estimated Sales: $65,000
Number Employees: 20-49
Parent Co: Bell Farms
Type of Packaging: Consumer, Food Service, Private Label, Bulk
Regions Exported to: Asia, Middle East, Latin America
Percentage of Business in Exporting: 35

42366 Belly Treats, Inc.
210-200 Wellington St W
Toronto, ON M5V 3C7
Canada   416-418-3285
Fax: 905-479-4135 www.bellytreats.com
Candies and nuts
Owner/Sales & Marketing: George Tsioros
Estimated Sales: $1 Million
Number of Products: 500+
Type of Packaging: Bulk
Regions Exported to: Worldwide
Regions Imported from: Worldwide

42367 Belmont Chemicals
50 Mount Prospect Ave
Clifton, NJ 07013-1900   973-777-2225
Fax: 973-777-6384   800-722-5070
Processor and exporter of vitamins, nutritional and protein supplements, herbs and amino acids
Owner/President: Paul Egyes
Sales Manager: Paul Egyes
Public Relations: Mary Apuzzo
Estimated Sales: $4.5 Million
Number Employees: 4
Number of Products: 50
Square Footage: 4000
Type of Packaging: Bulk

42368 Belshaw Adamatic Bakery Group
814 44th St NW # 103
Suite 103
Auburn, WA 98001-1754   206-322-5474
Fax: 206-322-5425   800-578-2547
info@belshaw.com www.belshaw-adamatic.com

Machinery and production solutions for donut producers in every retail and wholesale category. Doughnut systems fryers, glazers, and icers; also pancake and batter depositers; and piston filler depositers. One-hundred percent dedicated to the donut and to donut-makers worldwide.
President: Roger Faw
roger_faw@belshaw.com
CFO: William Yee
Marketing Coordinator: Mike Baxter
Sales: John DeMarre
Estimated Sales: $ 20 - 50 Million
Number Employees: 100-249
Square Footage: 120000
Parent Co: Welbilt Corporation
Type of Packaging: Food Service
Regions Exported to: Central America, South America, Europe, Asia, Middle East, Africa
Percentage of Business in Exporting: 40

42369 Belson Outdoors Inc
111 N River Rd
North Aurora, IL 60542-1324   630-264-2396
Fax: 630-897-0573   800-323-5664
sales@belson.com www.belson.com
Manufacturer and distributor of the finest outdoor cooking equipment available. Don't be misled, insist on certified (ul, csa, nsf) safe equipment. product line includes gas and charcoal grills, pig roasters, steam tables, trailerpits, smokers and more.
Manager: John Hauptman
hj@belson.com
Number Employees: 20-49

42370 (HQ)Belt Technologies Inc
11 Bowles Rd
Agawam, MA 01001-3812   413-786-9922
Fax: 413-789-2786 www.belttechnologies.com
Manufacturer and exporter of pulleys and metal belts used for conveyors, power transmissions, etc.; importer of backed belts
President: Alan Wosky
Quality Control: John Robertson
Sales Manager: Timothy Potrikus
Human Resources: Cindy Gadbois
Estimated Sales: Below $5 Million
Number Employees: 20-49
Square Footage: 46000
Other Locations:
   Belt Technologies
   Durham CityBelt Technologies
Regions Exported to: Worldwide
Percentage of Business in Exporting: 15
Regions Imported from: Europe

42371 Beltram Foodservice Group
6800 N Florida Ave
Tampa, FL 33604-5558   813-239-1136
Fax: 813-238-6673   800-940-1136
bfgtampa@beltram.com www.beltram.com
Wholesaler/distributor of food service supplies and equipment; serving the food service market
President: Dan Beltram
dan@beltram.com
CFO: Hal Herdman
VP: Allen Cope
VP: Kathy McCain
Purchasing Manager: John Zloch
Estimated Sales: $ 20 - 50 Million
Number Employees: 50-99
Parent Co: Beltram Foodservice Group
Regions Exported to: Central America, South America, Europe, Asia, Middle East

42372 Belukus Marketing
3304 Longmire Dr
College Station, TX 77845-5812   979-680-8530
Importer of European beer
President: Brad Batson
b.batson@belukus.net
CFO: Chuck Robertson
Vice President: Ken Goodman
Number Employees: 5-9
Brands Imported: Young's; Belhaven; Chimay; Duvel; Maredsous; De Kininck
Regions Imported from: Europe
Percentage of Business in Importing: 100

42373 Belxport
74 Farmington Chase Crescent
Farmington, CT 06032-3135   860-677-9611
Fax: 860-677-9611   855-573-9976
belxport@aol.com
Importer and exporter of mineral water

President: Sava Belanian
CEO: Bonnie Stare
CFO: Mark Belanian
Number Employees: 1-4
Square Footage: 2400
Brands Exported: Emperor
Regions Exported to: Europe
Percentage of Business in Exporting: 20
Brands Imported: Emperor
Regions Imported from: Europe
Percentage of Business in Importing: 80

42374 Bematek Systems Inc
96 Swampscott Rd # 7
Salem, MA 01970-7004   978-744-5816
     Fax: 978-922-7801   877-236-2835
     bematek@bematek.com www.bematek.com
Manufacturer and exporter of food processing equipment including in-line mixers, colloid mills, homogenizers, grinders and dispersers; also, laboratory testing machinery for wet mixing and size reduction, continuous or batch
President: David Ekstrom
bematek@bematek.com
Technical Director: Stephen Masucci
Administration: Denise Raimo
Sales Manager: Lindsey Humphrey
Estimated Sales: $ 1 - 3 Million
Number Employees: 1-4
Square Footage: 8600
Brands Exported: Bematek; Speco; Colby
Regions Exported to: Central America, South America, Europe, Asia
Percentage of Business in Exporting: 10

42375 Ben-Bud Growers Inc.
9210 Glades Rd
Boca Raton, FL 33434   561-347-3120
     Fax: 561-347-3101 www.ben-bud.com
Processor and importer of vegetables.
President: Ben Litowich
Quality Control Manager: Robert Graham
Sales Manager: Andrew Wilson
Year Founded: 1910
Estimated Sales: $20-50 Million
Number Employees: 10-19
Type of Packaging: Consumer, Bulk
Regions Imported from: Central America, South America
Percentage of Business in Importing: 15

42376 Benko Products
5350 Evergreen Pkwy
Sheffield Vlg, OH 44054-2446   440-934-2180
     Fax: 440-934-4052 info@benkoproducts.com
     www.benkoproducts.com
Manufacturer or revolutionary ergonomic beverage cart that eliminates the need to bend when loading and unloading.
President: John Benko
jbenko@benkoproducts.com
VP: Robert Benko
Sales/Marketing Manager: Laurie Benko
Estimated Sales: $10 Million
Number Employees: 50-99
Square Footage: 70000
Regions Exported to: Worldwide
Percentage of Business in Exporting: 10

42377 Benner China & Glassware Inc
5329 Powers Ave
Jacksonville, FL 32207-8084   904-733-4620
     Fax: 904-733-4622
Manufacturer, importer and exporter of glassware and china
Vice President: Scott Miles
smiles@odyseyfl.com
VP: Marie Wang
General Manager: Edward Mills
Estimated Sales: $ 5-10 Million
Number Employees: 20-49
Square Footage: 100000
Parent Co: Jacksonville Ginter Box Company
Regions Exported to: Canada, Bermuda
Regions Imported from: Europe, Asia

42378 Bentan Corporation
4555 196th Pl
Flushing, NY 11358   718-281-1978
     Fax: 718-793-2527 coffeemix@aol.com
     members.aol.com/coffemix/default.htm
Importer and wholesaler/distributor of instant beverages, biscuits, cookies, coffee, ginger tea, cereal, etc
Manager: Richard Tan
rtan@bentan.com
Estimated Sales: $5-10 Million
Number Employees: 5-9
Brands Imported: Coffeemix
Regions Imported from: Malaysia

42379 Bentley Instruments Inc
4004 Peavey Rd
Chaska, MN 55318-2344   952-448-7600
     Fax: 952-368-3355 info@bentleyinstruments.com
     www.bentleyus.com
Manufacturer and exporter of milk analyzers and control systems
President: Bent Lyder
blyder@bentleyinstruments.com
Estimated Sales: $2.5-$5 Million
Number Employees: 10-19
Square Footage: 38000
Type of Packaging: Food Service, Bulk
Regions Exported to: Worldwide
Percentage of Business in Exporting: 75

42380 Berberian Nut Company
6100 Wilson Landing Rd.
Chico, CA 95973-8902   530-981-4900
     Fax: 209-465-6008 www.berberiannut.com
Chandler, Howard, Tulare, and Hartley walnuts
Principal: Pete Turner
Quality Assurance Supervisor: Yesica Salcido
Marketing Manager: Ken Wagner
General Manager: Terry Turner
Plant Manager: Ren Fairbanks
Estimated Sales: $20-50 Million
Number Employees: 50-99
Type of Packaging: Consumer, Food Service, Private Label, Bulk
Regions Exported to: Worldwide

42381 Berg Chilling Systems
51 Nantucket Blvd.
Toronto, ON, ON M1P 2N5
Canada   416-755-2221
     Fax: 416-755-3874 bergsales@berg-group.com
     www.berg-group.com
Manufacturer and exporter of industrial cooling equipment, fluid recirculation, cold storage and pumping systems, ice machines, chillers and cooling towers
Chairman/CEO: Lorne Berggren
VP Sales: Stephanie Goudie
Estimated Sales: $ 20-50 Million
Number Employees: 100-249
Square Footage: 75000
Brands Exported: Berg
Regions Exported to: Worldwide
Percentage of Business in Exporting: 68

42382 Berg Chilling Systems
51 Nantucket Blvd.
Toronto, ON M1P 2N5
Canada   416-755-2221
     Fax: 416-755-3874 bergsales@berg-group.com
     www.berg-group.com
Manufacturer and exporter of process cooling equipment, large ice-making machines, freeze dryers, turnkey food processing/refrigeration systems and brine chillers for meat
VP: S Goudie
Estimated Sales: $ 1-2.5 Million
Number Employees: 1-4
Parent Co: Berg Chilling Systems
Regions Exported to: Central America, Europe, Asia, Middle East, Caribbean, Mexico
Percentage of Business in Exporting: 45

42383 Berg Co
2160 Industrial Dr
Monona, WI 53713-4805   608-221-4281
     Fax: 608-221-1416 sales@berg-controls.com
     www.bergliquorcontrols.com
Liquor dispensers, beer equipment and beverage dispensing systems
Estimated Sales: $2.5-5 Million
Number Employees: 10-19
Parent Co: DEC International
Brands Exported: All-Bottle; Laser; Infinity; Tap-1
Regions Exported to: Central America, Europe, Asia, Middle East
Percentage of Business in Exporting: 30

42384 Berghoff Brewery
1730 W Superior St # 3w
Chicago, IL 60622-5639   608-358-4992
     Fax: 608-325-3198 www.berghoffbeer.com
Beer and malt liquor in kegs, bottles and cans
President/Plant Manager: Gary Olson
CEO: Harry Cumberbatch
Director of Brewing/Quality Control: Kris Kalav
Production Manager: Dick Tschanz
Estimated Sales: $10 Million
Number Employees: 20-49
Regions Exported to: Canada (Manitoba, Calgary and Saskatchewan), Japan

42385 Bericap North America, Inc.
835 Syscon Court
CDN-Burlington, ON L7L 6C5
Canada   905-634-2248
     Fax: 905-634-7780 info.na@bericap.com
     www.bericap.com
Manufacturer, importer and exporter of tamper-evident pourer closures, capsules for bottled liquids and flat top dispensing closures
President: Scott Ambrose
Number Employees: 10
Square Footage: 58000
Parent Co: Rical SA
Regions Exported to: South America, Europe, Middle East, USA, Caribbean
Percentage of Business in Exporting: 35
Regions Imported from: Europe
Percentage of Business in Importing: 20

42386 Bering Sea Fisheries
4413 83rd Avenue SE
Snohomish, WA 98290-5204   425-334-1498
Processor and exporter of frozen salmon. Founded in 1961.
President: H William Bodey
Vice President: Russell Bodey
Estimated Sales: $780,000
Number Employees: 10
Type of Packaging: Private Label
Regions Exported to: Japan
Percentage of Business in Exporting: 100

42387 Berje
5 Lawrence St Ste 10
Bloomfield, NJ 07003   973-748-8980
     Fax: 973-680-9618 berje@berjeinc.com
     www.berjeinc.com
Importer, exporter and wholesaler/distributor of essential oils and aromatic chemicals for teas and fusion flavored juices
President: Kim Bleimann
VP: Marc Parrilli
Executive VP: Barry Dowles
Contact: Charlene Burkett
ombud@idoa.in.gov
Estimated Sales: $20-50 Million
Number Employees: 50-99
Square Footage: 180000
Regions Exported to: Worldwide
Percentage of Business in Exporting: 27
Regions Imported from: Worldwide
Percentage of Business in Importing: 60

42388 Berkshire Dairy
1258 Penn Ave
Wyomissing, PA 19610-2147   610-378-9999
     Fax: 610-378-4975   877-696-6455
info@berkshiredairy.com www.berkshiredairy.com
Manufacturer, importer and exporter of analog extenders, dehydrated dairy products, powders, cheese, creamers, lactose, milk and whey, whole milk powder, Anhydreos milkfat butter, nonfat dry milk, permeate
President & CEO: Dale Mills
dmills@berkshiredairy.com
Sales Director: Steve Cinesi
Estimated Sales: $2.7 Million
Number Employees: 10-19
Parent Co: Dairy Farmers of America, Inc.
Type of Packaging: Private Label, Bulk
Regions Exported to: Central America, South America, Asia, Middle East
Regions Imported from: Middle East, New Zealand, Australia
Percentage of Business in Importing: 10

Importers & Exporters / A-Z

42389 Berlekamp Plastics Inc
2587 County Road 99
Fremont, OH 43420-9316   419-334-4481
Fax: 419-334-9094   sales@berlekamp.com
www.berlekamp.com
Manufacturer and exporter of plastic signs and badges
President: Kenneth Berlekamp, Jr., CAS
Manager: Ken Berlekamp
ken@berlekamp.com
Estimated Sales: $1-2.5 Million
Number Employees: 20-49
Regions Exported to: Worldwide

42390 Berlin Foundry & Mach Co
489 Goebel St
P.O. Box 127
Berlin, NH 03570-2338   603-752-4550
Fax: 603-752-2798   htardiff@berlinfoundry.com
www.berlinfoundry.com
Manufacturer and exporter of wrapping and packaging machines for paper towels and toilet tissue.
Owner: Gary Hamel
Sales/Plant Manager: Gary Hamel
Manager: Helene Tardiff
foundry2@verizon.net
Operations: Gary Hamel
Estimated Sales: $1.5 Million
Number Employees: 10-19
Square Footage: 60000
Regions Exported to: South America, Europe, Canada
Percentage of Business in Exporting: 5

42391 Bermar America
42 Lloyd Ave # A
Malvern, PA 19355-3000   610-889-4900
Fax: 610-889-0289   888-289-5838
info@bermaramerica.com
www.bermaramerica.com
Manufacturer and importer of vacuum and pressure seal wine preservation systems
Owner: Aline Bouilland
alineb@bermaramerica.com
Estimated Sales: Less Than $500,000
Number Employees: 1-4
Brands Imported: Bermar
Regions Imported from: Germany
Percentage of Business in Importing: 25

42392 Bernal Technology
2960 Technology Dr
Rochester Hills, MI 48309-3588   248-299-3600
Fax: 248-299-3601   800-237-6251
sales@bernalinc.com   www.bernalinc.info
Manufacturer and exporter of die cutting and packaging machines for cereal, coffee, snack foods, etc
President: Luigi Pessarelli
CFO: Kelly Lang
lang@bernalinc.com
Director: Rey Hsu, Ph. D.
Vice President Sales & Marketing: Mark Voorhees
Sales Manager: Steven Leigh
Plant Manager: Frank Penksa
Estimated Sales: $20 Million
Number Employees: 20-49
Square Footage: 45000
Regions Exported to: Central America, South America, Europe, Asia

42393 Bernard Food IndustriesInc
P.O. Box 1497
Evanston, IL 60204
Fax: 847-869-5315   800-323-3663
www.bernardfoods.com
Dessert toppings, soup bases, drinks and baking ingredients.
President & CEO: Steve Bernard
VP, Sales & Operations: Lou Haan
Year Founded: 1947
Estimated Sales: $20-50 Million
Number Employees: 50-99
Square Footage: 60000
Type of Packaging: Consumer, Food Service, Private Label, Bulk
Regions Exported to: Worldwide
Percentage of Business in Exporting: 5

42394 Berner International Corp
111 Progress Ave
New Castle, PA 16101-7601   724-652-7106
Fax: 724-652-0682   800-245-4455
sales@berner.com   www.berner.com
Berner International Corp. has established itself as the leading manufacturer of air doors for insect and climate control and cooler/freezer applications. Berner also has its own line of patio heaters, arctic seal doors, strip doorsand bakery rack covers.
Owner: Georgia Berner
gberner@berner.com
Sales Manager: Michael Coscarelli
Estimated Sales: $10-20 Million
Number Employees: 50-99
Square Footage: 100000
Type of Packaging: Food Service
Brands Exported: Berner; Flystop; Aristocrat; Posi-Flow; Zaphyr; Maxair; Aura; In-Ceiling Mount; Artic Seal
Regions Exported to: Worldwide
Percentage of Business in Exporting: 7

42395 (HQ)Berns Co
1250 W 17th St
Long Beach, CA 90813-1391   562-436-1074
Fax: 562-436-1074   800-421-3773
Gary@thebernscompany.com
www.thebernscompany.com
Wholesaler/distributor, importer and exporter of pallet trucks and forkliftparts
Owner: Steve Berns
Sales/Marketing Executive: Steve Berns
bernsco@aol.com
Estimated Sales: $5 Million
Number Employees: 20-49
Square Footage: 80000
Brands Exported: Clark; Hyster; CAT; Toyota; Nissan; BT; Bishamon
Regions Exported to: Central America, South America, Europe
Brands Imported: BT; Bishamon

42396 Berry Global
P.O. Box 959
Evansville, IN 47706-0959   812-424-2904
800-343-1295
www.berryglobal.com
Manufacturer and exporter of injection molded plastic containers and lids; also, container fillers.
Chairman & CEO: Tom Salmon
Chief Financial Officer: Mark Miles
SVP & Strategic Corp. Development: Brett Bauer
EVP & Chief Information Officer: Debbie Garrison
EVP, Operations: Rodgers Greenawalt
EVP/Chief Legal Officer/Secretary: Jason Greene
EVP, Human Resources: Ed Stratton
Year Founded: 1967
Estimated Sales: $13 Billion
Number Employees: 48,000
Other Locations:
Berry Plastics
Henderson, NV Berry Plastics
Regions Exported to: Canada, Mexico
Percentage of Business in Exporting: 4

42397 Bert Manufacturing
1276 Pit Rd # 3
Unit 3
Gardnerville, NV 89460-8723   775-265-3900
Fax: 775-265-3939   bertmfg2@aol.com
www.bertmanufacturing.com
Manufacturer and exporter of chucks and rolls for food processing machinery
Owner: Dennis Bertucci
bertmfg2@aol.com
Sales: Brian Bertucci
Technical Director: Paul Coleman
Engineering & Programming: Luis Martinez
Estimated Sales: Less Than $500,000
Number Employees: 1-4
Type of Packaging: Bulk
Regions Exported to: Worldwide
Percentage of Business in Exporting: 50

42398 (HQ)Bertek Systems Inc
133 Bryce Blvd
Fairfax, VT 05454-5491   802-752-3170
Fax: 802-868-3872   800-367-0210
www.berteksystems.com
Manufacturer and exporter of data processing and pressure sensitive labels
Owner: Sam Peters
Sales and Marketing Director: Peter Kvam
0: Ken Whitcomb
MIS Systems Manager: Mike Saunders
Sales/Marketing Manager: Peter Kvam
Sales Representative: Danielle Ryea
HR/Ex Assistant: Amy Kimball
General Manager: Barney Kijeh
Account Executive: Debbie Chadwick
Estimated Sales: $ 10 - 20 Million
Number Employees: 100-249
Regions Exported to: Worldwide
Percentage of Business in Exporting: 20

42399 Bertels Can Company
1300 Brass Mill Road
Belcamp, MD 21017   410-272-0090
sales@independentcan.com
www.independentcan.com
Manufacturer of specialty metal cans and lithography
President: Rick Huether
Director Of Sales: Neil DeFrancisco
Plant Manager: Frank Sorokach
Estimated Sales: $ 20 - 50 Million
Number Employees: 20-49
Square Footage: 60000
Parent Co: Independent Can Company

42400 Berti Produce Co
1960 Jerrold Ave
San Francisco, CA 94124-1603   415-824-0112
Fax: 415-824-4516
Importer and distributor of Asian produce
CEO: Raymond Mah
CEO: Raymond Mah
Estimated Sales: $2.5-5 Million
Number Employees: 5-9
Regions Imported from: Asia

42401 Bessamaire Sales Inc
10145 Philipp Pkwy # B
Unit B
Streetsboro, OH 44241-4706   330-650-5001
Fax: 440-439-1625   800-321-5992
bill@bessamaire.com   www.bessamaire.com
Manufacturer and exporter of indirect heating equipment for gas/oil, make-up air heating and summer evaporative cooling units.
Owner: Bill Sullivan
Marketing Director: Joseph Marg
Product Manager: Mark McGinty
Contact: Joseph Marg
marg@bessamaire.com
Estimated Sales: Less Than $500,000
Number Employees: 1-4
Number of Brands: 1
Number of Products: 9
Square Footage: 100000
Type of Packaging: Food Service
Brands Exported: Bessam-Aire
Regions Exported to: Central America, South America, Asia, Middle East
Percentage of Business in Exporting: 22

42402 Best
1071 Industrial Pkwy N
Brunswick, OH 44212   330-273-1277
Fax: 330-225-8740   800-827-9237
sales@bestvibes.com   www.bestvibes.com
Manufacturer and exporter of pneumatic and electric vibrators, bulk bag unloaders, bulk bag loaders, conveyors, tables, screeners and dry process systems.
President: Ed Verbos
VP of Engineering: Tim Conway
Marketing: S Fitzpatrick
Sales Manager: R Breudigam
Estimated Sales: $1-2,500,000
Number Employees: 10-19
Number of Products: 100+
Square Footage: 30000
Type of Packaging: Bulk

42403 Best & Donovan
5570 Creek Rd
Blue Ash, OH 45242-4004   513-791-9180
Fax: 513-791-0925   800-553-2378
info@bestanddonovan.com
www.bestanddonovan.com
Manufacturer and exporter of portable power meat saws, skinners, hock cutters, dehiders and dehorners

Owner: Scott Andre
info@bestanddonovan.com
Finance Executive: Ken Park
VP: Scott Andre
Estimated Sales: $ 5 - 10 Million
Number Employees: 20-49
Square Footage: 110000
Brands Exported: Best & Donovan
Regions Exported to: Central America, South America, Europe, Asia, Middle East
Percentage of Business in Exporting: 35

42404 Best Brands Home Products
20 W 33rd St # 5
New York, NY 10001-3305 212-684-7456
Fax: 212-684-7630 www.bestbrands.com
Manufacturer and importer of towels, tablecloths, place mats, pot holders, linen goods, display racks, vinyl & fabric table cloths and place mats, oven and barbecue mitts, barbecue aprons and vinyl coasters, all bath towel products
President: Jack Albert
CEO: Jack Kassin
jacksr@bestbrands.com
Vice President: Rodnie Gindi
Marketing Director: Cari Bennett
Sales Director: Rodnie Gindi
Secretary: David Meyer
Estimated Sales: $25 Million+
Number Employees: 20-49
Type of Packaging: Consumer, Private Label
Regions Exported to: Central America
Brands Imported: Cannon; Julie Ingleman
Regions Imported from: Worldwide

42405 Best Buy Uniforms
500 E 8th Ave
Homestead, PA 15120-1904 412-461-4600
Fax: 412-461-4016 800-345-1924
customer-service@bestbuyuniforms.com
www.bestbuyuniforms.com
Manufacturer, wholesaler/distributor and importer of image apparel uniforms; also, custom T-shirts, table cloths, napkins and work uniforms; serving the food service market
Owner: David Frischman
davidf@bestbuyuniforms.com
CEO: Lester Frischman
Estimated Sales: $ 1 - 5 Million
Number Employees: 5-9
Square Footage: 24000
Type of Packaging: Food Service
Regions Imported from: Asia
Percentage of Business in Importing: 5

42406 Best Cheese Corporation
2700 Westchester Avenue
Suite 309,
Purchase, NY 10577 914-241-2300
Fax: 914-241-8989 info@bestcheeseusa.com
www.bestcheeseusa.com
Importer of specialty and commodity cheeses from Holland and England
President: Henk Engelkes
Marketing: Steven Margarites
Estimated Sales: $ .5 - 1 million
Number Employees: 5-9

42407 Best Chicago Meat
4649 W Armitage Ave
Chicago, IL 60639
www.bestchicagomeat.com
Meat products including frozen hamburger patties, sausages, spare ribs, chitterlings, bacon, ham, breakfast links, chicken nuggets, rib tips and kosher hot dogs
CFO: Paul Dwyer
Regional Sales Manager: Edward Allaway
Estimated Sales: $20-50 Million
Number Employees: 20-49
Number of Brands: 4
Square Footage: 20000
Parent Co: Beavers Holdings
Type of Packaging: Consumer, Food Service
Brands Imported: Majesty
Regions Imported from: Europe
Percentage of Business in Importing: 2

42408 Best Cooking Pulses, Inc.
110 10th St NE
Portage la Prairie, MB R1N 1B5
Canada 204-857-4451
margaret@bestcookingpulses.com
www.bestcookingpulses.com
Peas, chickpea, lentil and bean flours and pea fiber. Certified Kosher, Halal, Conventional or Certified-Organic, free of all major allergens, and gluten free.
President: Trudy Heal
Director, Sales & Marketing: Jennifer Evancio
General Manager: Mike Gallais
Estimated Sales: $11.25 Million
Number Employees: 23
Type of Packaging: Bulk
Regions Exported to: South America, Europe

42409 Best Diversified Products
107 Flint Street
Jonesboro, AR 72401-6717 870-935-0970
Fax: 870-935-3661 800-327-9209
www.bestconveyors.com
Manufacturer and exporter of conveyors including flexible, expandable, skatewheel and roller
President: James E Markley
Sales/Marketing Director: Charlie Appleby
Contact: Roger Haynes
rogerhaynes@bestconv.com
Estimated Sales: $20-50 Million
Number Employees: 100-249
Regions Exported to: Canada

42410 Best Foods
700 Sylvan Ave
Englewood Cliffs, NJ 07632 201-894-4000
Fax: 201-894-2186 www.bestfoods.com
Best Foods manufactures the best-selling mayonnaise in the United States. East of the Rockies, Best Foods is known as Hellman's.
President, Unilever Foods: Amanda Sourry
Contact: Cordell Price
cordell.price@unilever.com
Number Employees: 44,000
Number of Products: 13
Parent Co: Unilever
Type of Packaging: Consumer, Food Service

42411 Best Provision Co Inc
2401 Morris Ave.
Union, NJ 07083 973-242-5000
Fax: 973-648-0041 800-631-4466
info@bestprovision.com www.bestprovision.com
Corned beef, roast beef, frankfurters, pastrami and bacon
President: Floyd Jason
fjayson@bestprovision.com
Co-Owner: Kevin Karp
Co-Owner: Richard Dolinko
Human Resource Director: Clara Mendez
Year Founded: 1938
Estimated Sales: $35 Million
Number Employees: 100-249
Square Footage: 65000
Type of Packaging: Consumer, Food Service
Regions Exported to: Bermuda
Percentage of Business in Exporting: 2

42412 Best Value Textiles
7240 Cross Park Drive
North Charleston, SC 29418 262-723-6133
Fax: 843-767-0494 800-858-8589
customercare@chefrevival.com
www.chefrevival.com
Manufacturer, importer and exporter of chef/crew apparel and tools. Flame retardant items including gloves, table linens, aprons, uniforms and oven mitts
Manager: Alex Onda
CFO: Tone Long
R&D: Elizabeth Weiler
Marketing: Rob Johnson
Sales: Claude Brewer
Production: Arturo Gomez
Purchasing Director: Elizabeth Weiler
Estimated Sales: $15 Million
Number Employees: 20-49
Square Footage: 85000
Parent Co: The Coleman Group
Type of Packaging: Food Service
Brands Exported: Gold Lion; Thermo Protect; Bestguard
Regions Exported to: Canada
Percentage of Business in Exporting: 10
Brands Imported: Best-Tex; Best-Guard; Gold Lion; Ulta-Mitt; Thermo Guard
Regions Imported from: Central America, Asia, Middle East
Percentage of Business in Importing: 60

42413 Bestech Inc
442 S Dixie Hwy E
Pompano Beach, FL 33060-6910 954-785-4550
Fax: 954-785-4678 800-977-2378
bestek@aol.com
Manufacturer and exporter of water purification systems and vending machines
President: Gary Barr
bestek@aol.com
Director Sales: Gary Barr
Estimated Sales: $1-2.5 Million
Number Employees: 5-9
Square Footage: 20000
Regions Exported to: Worldwide
Percentage of Business in Exporting: 40

42414 Beta Screen Corp
707 Commercial Ave # A
Carlstadt, NJ 07072-2685 201-939-2400
Fax: 201-939-7656 800-272-7336
info@betascreen.com www.betascreen.com
Manufacturer and exporter of vinyl doors for automatic kitchen dining room access
President: Arnold Serchuk
info@betascreen.com
Public Relations Director: Stu Serchuk
Estimated Sales: $ 3 - 5 Million
Number Employees: 5-9
Parent Co: Beta Industries
Type of Packaging: Food Service
Brands Exported: Betadoor
Regions Exported to: Central America, South America, Europe, Asia, Middle East
Percentage of Business in Exporting: 25

42415 Bete Fog Nozzle Inc
50 Greenfield St
Greenfield, MA 01301-1378 413-772-0846
Fax: 413-772-6729 800-235-0049
sales@bete.com www.bete.com
Manufacturer and exporter of nozzles for food and dairy processing and spray drying nozzles for food processing
President: Matthew Bete
mbete@bete.com
CEO: Lincoln Soule
Owner: David Bete
Research & Development: Dan Delesdernier
Quality Control: Tom Bassett
Sales Director: Susan Cole
Public Relations: Heidi Arnold
Estimated Sales: $ 15 Million
Number Employees: 100-249
Square Footage: 108000
Brands Exported: ScrubMate; MaxiPass; Twist & Day
Regions Exported to: South America, Europe, Asia, Middle East, Australia
Percentage of Business in Exporting: 30

42416 Bethel Engineering & Equipment Inc
13830 McBeth Road
P.O.Box 67
New Hampshire, OH 45870 419-568-1100
Fax: 419-568-1807 800-889-6129
info@bethelengr.com www.bethelengr.com
Manufacturer and exporter of ovens, washers and spray booths
Owner: David Whitaker
Director Sales/Marketing: Tom Shield
Estimated Sales: $ 5 - 10 Million
Number Employees: 20-49
Parent Co: Finishing Systems Holdings
Regions Exported to: Worldwide
Percentage of Business in Exporting: 10

42417 Bettcher Industries Inc
6801 State Route 60
Wakeman, OH 44889-8509 440-965-4422
Fax: 440-965-4900 440-321-8763
sales@bettcher.com www.bettcher.com
Optimex® breading machine and power knife

President: Don Esch
Chairman and Chief Executive Officer: Laurence A. Bettcher
tclark@mobilityworks.com
Chief Financial Officer: Tim McNeil
Research/Development: Ed Steele
Quality Control: Mike Casteel
VP/Marketing: Paul Pirozzola
Public Relations: Wayne Daggett
Plant Manager: David Mears
Purchasing Director: Ed Gross
Number Employees: 100-249
Type of Packaging: Food Service
Brands Exported: Bettcher
Regions Exported to: Central America, South America, Europe, Middle East
Percentage of Business in Exporting: 45

42418 Bette's Oceanview Diner
1807 4th St
Berkeley, CA 94710-1910   510-644-3230
   Fax: 510-644-3209 bettesdiner@worldpantry.com
Manufacturer and exporter of pancake mixes including buttermilk, oatmeal and buckwheat; also, scone mixes including raisin, cranberry and lemon currant
Owner: Bette Kroening
Number Employees: 20-49
Type of Packaging: Consumer, Food Service
Regions Exported to: Europe, Asia
Percentage of Business in Exporting: 1

42419 Better Living Products
208 Harvard Drive
Princeton, TX 75407   972-736-6691
   Fax: 903-298-0014 zetawize@yahoo.com
   www.betterlivingusa.com
Processor, importer of kava kava powder, aloe vera juice and herbs. Founded in 1996.
Founder: Don Ansley
COO: Ed Carter
Estimated Sales: Less than $500,000
Number Employees: 1-4
Parent Co: Zeta Wize LLC Company
Regions Exported to: Worldwide
Regions Imported from: Asia
Percentage of Business in Importing: 10

42420 Better Made Snack Foods
10148 Gratiot Ave
Detroit, MI 48213   313-925-4774
   Fax: 313-925-6028 800-332-2394
   info@bettermadesnackfoods.com
   www.bettermadesnackfoods.com
Potato chips, popcorn, crunchy chips, pretzels, pork rinds, tortilla chips, beef jerky, chocolate covered potato chips and pretzels, salsas and cheese dips.
President: David Jones
Year Founded: 1930
Estimated Sales: $62 Million
Number Employees: 100-249
Type of Packaging: Consumer, Food Service
Regions Exported to: Canada

42421 Better Packages
4 Hershey Dr
Ansonia, CT 06401   203-926-3700
   800-237-9151
   info@betterpackages.com
   www.betterpackages.com
Carton-sealing systems and packaging solutions
President & CEO: Philip White
Vice President Sales & Marketing: Jeffrey Deacon
Director Research & Development: Allen Crowe
Marketing Director: Lynn Padell
Director of Sales: Marc Schaible
Operations Director: Paul Kromberg
Number Employees: 100-249
Regions Exported to: Europe, Asia, Canada

42422 Betty Lou's
750 SE Booth Bend Rd
PO Box 537
McMinnville, OR 97128   503-434-5205
   Fax: 503-472-8643 800-242-5205
   www.bettylousinc.com
Processor and exporter of oil and, low-fat oven baked apple butter, low-fat and wheat-free fruit bars and fat-free cookies, snack foods and candies, protein bars. Founded in 1978.
Owner: Betty Carrier
VP Sales: John Sizemore

Estimated Sales: $2.5-5 Million
Number Employees: 20-49
Square Footage: 36000
Type of Packaging: Consumer, Private Label
Regions Exported to: Canada
Percentage of Business in Exporting: 5

42423 (HQ)Beverage Air
3779 Champion Blvd
Winston Salem, NC 27105-2667   336-245-6400
   Fax: 336-245-6453 800-845-9800
   sales@bevair.com www.beverage-air.com
Manufacturer and exporter of commercial beverage coolers and food service refrigeration equipment
President: Philippo Berti
CEO: Filippo Berti
fberti@bevair.com
National Sales Manager: Bill Stowik
VP Sales/Marketing: Jack McDonald
National Service Manager: Loran Tucker
Estimated Sales: $1 - 5 Million
Number Employees: 500-999
Square Footage: 2000000
Parent Co: Specialty Equipment Companies
Type of Packaging: Food Service
Other Locations:
   Beverage-Air
   Honea Path, SCBeverage-Air
Brands Exported: Marketeer; Beverage Air
Regions Exported to: Worldwide
Percentage of Business in Exporting: 20

42424 Beverage Capital Corporation
2209 Sulphur Spring Rd
Baltimore, MD 21227-2933   410-242-7404
   Fax: 410-247-2977
   bevcapsales@beveragecapital.com
Bottled and canned soft and juice drinks and juice; also, seltzer water; contract packaging available
Chairman: Harold Honickman
Controller: John Schmitj
Treasurer: Walter Wilkinson
Vice President: Rick Smith
Contact: Florence Stewart
fstewart@capitol-beverage.com
Purchasing Agent: Kim Quinn
Estimated Sales: $28 Million
Number Employees: 350
Square Footage: 365000
Type of Packaging: Consumer, Private Label
Other Locations:
   Whitehead Court Manufacturing
   Baltimore, MD
   30th Street Manufacturing
   Baltimore, MDWhitehead Court ManufacturingBaltimore
Regions Exported to: Central America, South America

42425 Beverage Express
4580 Fieldgate Rd
Oceanside, CA 92056   760-941-9114
   800-923-8372
   www.beverageexpress.com
Wholesaler/distributor and exporter of post mix and Italian soda syrups, coffee and juice concentrates; also, portable carbonating appliances
Co-Owner: Gordon Mirrett
Co-Owner: Charlene Mirrett
Estimated Sales: Less than $500,000
Number Employees: 1-4
Square Footage: 2000
Type of Packaging: Consumer
Regions Exported to: Canada
Percentage of Business in Exporting: 20

42426 Beverly International
1768 Industrial Rd
Cold Spring, KY 41076-8610   859-781-3474
   Fax: 859-781-7590 800-781-3475
   www.beverlyinternational.net
Manufacturer and exporter of multiple vitamin and mineral packs; also, protein powders. Founded in 1967.
Owner: Roger Riedinger
Owner: Sandy Riedinger
sandyr@beverlyinternational.net
Estimated Sales: Less Than $500,000
Number Employees: 5-9
Type of Packaging: Consumer, Food Service, Private Label
Regions Exported to: South America, Europe, Asia, Middle East
Percentage of Business in Exporting: 20

42427 Bevinco
210-515 Consumers Road
Toronto, ON M2J 4Z2
Canada   416-490-6266
   Fax: 416-490-6899 info@bevinco.com
   www.bevinco.com

42428 Bevles Company
729 3rd Ave
Dallas, TX 75230-2098   214-421-7366
   Fax: 214-565-0976 800-441-1601
   info@apwyott.com www.apwyott.com
Manufacturer and exporter of kitchen equipment including heated holding, transport and storage cabinets, low temperature roast and hold ovens, proofing cabinets and racks
President: Hylcon Jonas
CFO: Don Wall
Quality Control: Jim Austin
Marketing Assistant: Martha Patino
VP of Sales/Marketing: John Kossler
Estimated Sales: $20 - 50 Million
Number Employees: 100-249
Square Footage: 45000
Regions Exported to: Central America, South America, Asia, Middle East
Percentage of Business in Exporting: 10

42429 Bewley Irish Imports
1130 Greenhill Rd
West Chester, PA 19380-4005   610-696-2682
   Fax: 610-344-7618 888-239-5397
   info@bewleyirishimports.com
   www.bewleyirishimports.com
Importer of Irish specialties
Owner: Bruce Flamm
info@bewleyirishimports.com
Sales/Marketing: Alison Watkins
Estimated Sales: $500,000-$1 Million
Number Employees: 1-4
Number of Brands: 15
Number of Products: 162
Square Footage: 14400
Type of Packaging: Food Service, Private Label
Brands Imported: Bewleys; Jacobs; Lakeshore Foods; McCanns Oatmeal; Barry's & Lyons; Morleys Preserves; Mileeven; Goodalls; Irish Village Foods
Regions Imported from: Europe
Percentage of Business in Importing: 80

42430 Biagio's Banquets
4242 N Central Ave
Chicago, IL 60634-1810   773-736-9009
   Fax: 773-587-3011 800-392-2837
   rperrye@aol.com www.suparossa.com
Processor and exporter of pasta, breaded appetizers and pizza including deep dish, thin crust, pan and self-rising. Founded in 1977.
President: Samuel Cirrincione
Sales Director: Michelle Rubino
Contact: Peter Lesniak
peter@suparossa.com
General Manager: Tom Cirrincione
Estimated Sales: $10-20 Million
Number Employees: 50-99
Square Footage: 60000
Regions Exported to: Asia
Percentage of Business in Exporting: 12

42431 Bianchi Winery
3380 Branch Rd
Paso Robles, CA 93446-8314   805-226-9922
   Fax: 805-226-8230 info@bianchiwine.com
   www.bianchiwine.com
Manufacturer and exporter of red and white wines. Founded in 2001.
Owner: Glenn A Bianchi
gl@bianchiwine.com
Principal: Al Smart
CFO: Mike Gardnier
Vice President: Albert Paul
Operations: Edward Ortease
Manager/Winemaster: Tom Lane
Estimated Sales: $5 Million
Number Employees: 5-9
Number of Brands: 3
Number of Products: 20
Type of Packaging: Consumer, Food Service, Bulk
Brands Exported: Bianchi Vineyards
Regions Exported to: Europe, Asia
Percentage of Business in Exporting: 5

Importers & Exporters / A-Z

42432 Biazzo Dairy Products Inc
1145 Edgewater Ave
Ridgefield, NJ 07657-2102   201-941-6800
Fax: 201-941-4151 info@biazzo.com
www.biazzo.com
Fresh, chunk and shredded mozzarella, ricotta and string cheese.
President: Sergio Espinoza
sergio.espinoza@schreiberfoods.com
Vice President: John Iapichino, Jr.
Food Safety & Quality Assurance Manager: Sanya Bici
Director of Sales: Steven Cilento
Estimated Sales: $ 20 - 50 Million
Number Employees: 50-99
Square Footage: 58000
Type of Packaging: Consumer, Food Service, Private Label, Bulk
Regions Exported to: Central America, Europe
Percentage of Business in Exporting: 1

42433 Bien Padre Foods Inc
1459 Railroad St
Eureka, CA 95501-2147   707-442-4585
Fax: 707-269-2140 www.bienpadre.com
Manufacturer and exporter of tortilla chips, corn and flour tortillas and salsas. Founded in 1974.
President/Owner: Benito Lim
stevebpf@gmail.com
Sales Exec: Steve Frenz
Estimated Sales: $1-2.5 Million
Number Employees: 20-49
Square Footage: 56000
Type of Packaging: Consumer, Food Service, Private Label, Bulk

42434 Bijol & Spices Inc
2154 NW 22nd Ct
Miami, FL 33142-7346   305-634-9030
Fax: 305-634-7454 888-245-6570
info@bijol.com www.bijol.com
Contract packager and exporter of spices and herbs. Founded in 1991.
President: Ida Borges
Vice President: Diego Borges
Estimated Sales: $2.5-5 Million
Number Employees: 5-9
Type of Packaging: Consumer
Regions Exported to: Columbia,Canada
Percentage of Business in Exporting: 10

42435 Bijur Lubricating Corporation
2250 Perimeter Park Dr.
Suite 120
Morrisville, NC 27560   919-465-4448
Fax: 919-465-0516 800-631-0168
info@bijurlube.com www.bijur.com
Manufacturer, exporter and importer of automatic lubricating equipment and fluid dispensers
CEO: Thomas Arndt
Marketing Communications Manager: Peter Sweeney
Sales: Kevin Ryan
Estimated Sales: $ 10 - 20 Million
Number Employees: 20-49
Square Footage: 160000
Parent Co: Vesper Corporation
Regions Exported to: Central America, South America, Europe, Asia
Regions Imported from: Europe, Asia

42436 Bilt-Rite Conveyors
735 Industrial Loop Road
New London, WI 54961-3530   920-982-6600
Fax: 920-982-7750 www.bilt-rite.com
Manufacturer and exporter of stainless steel conveyors including belt, tabletop, chain and wire mesh
Owner: Jeffrey Bellig
R&D: Orlando Rojas
Contact: T Ramesh
trramesh@bilt.ae
Estimated Sales: $ 5 - 10 Million
Number Employees: 20-49
Parent Co: Titan Industies, Inc.
Regions Exported to: Central America, South America, Europe, Middle East
Percentage of Business in Exporting: 10

42437 Bindi-Dessert Service,Inc
405 Minnisink Rd
Totowa, NJ 07512   973-812-8118
Fax: 973-812-5020 info@bindiusa.com
www.bindiusa.com
Importer and exporter of Italian cakes, sorbets and semifredes
President: Attillio Bindi
VP: Giacomo Berretta
Contact: Daniel Adami
adami@bindiusa.com
Estimated Sales: $20-50 Million
Number Employees: 100-249
Parent Co: SIPA
Type of Packaging: Consumer, Food Service
Regions Exported to: Bermuda
Percentage of Business in Exporting: 1
Regions Imported from: Italy
Percentage of Business in Importing: 99

42438 Biner Ellison PackagingSysts
2685 S Melrose Dr
Vista, CA 92081-8783   760-598-6500
Fax: 760-598-7600 800-733-8162
sales@binerellison.com www.accutekcapping.com
Manufacturer and exporter of bottle labeling, conveying, liquid filling and capping machinery and integrated packaging systems
President: Tom Ellison Jr
Contact: Timothy Hussman
timothy@newportmeat.com
Operations: Jeff Schwarz
Estimated Sales: $2.5-5 Million
Number Employees: 10-19
Regions Exported to: Central America, South America

42439 Binks Industries Inc
1997a Aucutt Rd
Montgomery, IL 60538-1135   630-801-1100
Fax: 630-801-0819 info@binksindustries.com
www.binksindustries.com
Manufacturer and exporter of pin hole detection equipment
President: Carolyn Calkins
binksinc@binksindustries.com
Estimated Sales: Less Than $500,000
Number Employees: 1-4
Square Footage: 12000
Brands Exported: Binks Industries
Regions Exported to: Central America, South America, Asia, Middle East
Percentage of Business in Exporting: 40
Regions Imported from: Europe, Asia, Middle East
Percentage of Business in Importing: 50

42440 Binney & Smith
P.O.Box 431
Easton, PA 18044-0431   610-253-6271
Fax: 610-250-5768 www.binney-smith.com
CEO: Mark J Schwab
Number Employees: 1,000-4,999

42441 Bio Cide Intl Inc
2845 Broce Dr # A
Norman, OK 73072-2448   405-329-5556
Fax: 405-329-2681 800-323-1398
www.bio-cide.com
Manufacturer and exporter of chlorine dioxide based products for sanitization, disinfection, deodorization and water treatment
CEO: B C Danner
Sales Director: Damon Dickinson
Contact: Mark Cochran
mcochran@bio-cide.com
Chairman: B Danner
Estimated Sales: $1-2.5 Million
Number Employees: 20-49
Square Footage: 80000
Brands Exported: Purogene; Sanogene; Oxine
Regions Exported to: Europe, Asia, Canada, Mexico
Percentage of Business in Exporting: 40

42442 Bio Zapp Laboratories
PO Box 20127
Sarasota, FL 34276   941-922-9199
Fax: 210-805-9196 biozapp@biozapp.com
www.biozapp.com
Manufacturer and exporter of odor elimination systems, degreasers, glass ans surface cleaners
Founder: Miky Gershenson
miky@biozapp.com
Director Operations: Denise Novick
Estimated Sales: $5,000,000
Number Employees: 5-9
Number of Products: 20
Type of Packaging: Consumer, Food Service, Private Label, Bulk
Regions Exported to: Worldwide
Percentage of Business in Exporting: 25

42443 Bio-Foods
104 Bloomfield Avenue
Pine Brook, NJ 07058   973-808-5856
Fax: 973-396-2999 bobkoetzner@aol.com
www.biofoodsltd.com
Manufacturer and exporter of nutrients and spices.
President: Bharat Patel
Vice President: Robert Koetzner
Number Employees: 5-9
Square Footage: 36000
Type of Packaging: Bulk
Regions Exported to: Europe, Asia
Percentage of Business in Exporting: 10

42444 BioAmber
3850 Annapolis Ln N
Suite 180
Plymouth, MN 55447   763-253-4480
kristine.weigal@bio-amber.com
Succinic acid, BDO, plasticizers, polymers and C6 chemicals
President & CEO: Jean-Francois HUC
CTO: Jim Millis
CFO: Andrew Ashworth
Executive VP: Mike Hartmann
Chief Commercial Officer: Babette Pettersen
Contact: Marie Beaumont
marie.beaumont@bio-amber.com
Chief Operations Officer: Fabrice Orecchioni
Estimated Sales: $560 Thousand
Number Employees: 74
Regions Exported to: Europe, Asia, Australia

42445 BioExx Specialty Proteins
33 Fraser Ave
Suite G11
Toronto, ON M6K 3J9
Canada   416-588-4442
Fax: 416-588-1999 www.bioexx.com
Oil and high-value proteins from Canola.
CEO & Director: Chris Schnarr
CFO: Greg Furyk
EVP: Samah Garringer
VP Operations: Clinton Smith
Regions Exported to: Europe, United States

42446 Bioclimatic Air Systems LLC
600 Delran Pkwy # D
Delran, NJ 08075-1255   856-764-4300
Fax: 856-764-4301 800-962-5594
mail@bioclimatic.com www.bioclimatic.com
Manufacturer and exporter of air purification systems
President: Michele Bottino
mbottino@bioclimatic.com
Estimated Sales: Below $ 5 Million
Number Employees: 20-49
Brands Exported: Aeromat; Aerotec
Regions Exported to: Europe, Asia
Percentage of Business in Exporting: 10

42447 (HQ)Biocontrol Systems Inc
12822 SE 32nd St
Bellevue, WA 98005-4340   425-603-1123
Fax: 425-603-0070 800-245-0113
bcs_us@biocontrolsys.com
www.biocontrolsys.com
Manufacturer and exporter of diagnostic microbiology test kits and equipment
President: Phillip Feldsine
CEO: Khyati Shah
shahkhyati123@gmail.com
R&D: David Kerr
Sr. Vice President: Carolyn Feldsine
Quality Control: Julia Terry
Director Marketing: Maritta Ko
Marketing Assistant: Jennifer Hawton
Estimated Sales: $ 3 - 5 Million
Number Employees: 50-99
Other Locations:
  Biocontrol Systems
  Westbrook, MEBiocontrol Systems
Regions Exported to: South America, Europe, Asia, Canada, Mexico, Caribbean

42448 Biolog Inc
21124 Cabot Blvd
Hayward, CA 94545-1130   510-785-2585
Fax: 415-782-4639 800-284-4949
csorders@biolog.com www.biolog.com

Importers & Exporters / A-Z

Manufacturer and exporter of microbiological identification products
President/CEO & CSO: Barry R Bochner
bbochner@biolog.com
Vice President Of Finance/CFO: Edwin R Fineman
Vice President Of Operations: Doug E Rife
Number Employees: 20-49
Brands Exported: MicroLog; Rainbow Agar
Regions Exported to: Worldwide
Percentage of Business in Exporting: 60

42449 Biomerieux Inc
100 Rodolphe St
Durham, NC 27712-9402   919-620-2000
          Fax: 800-968-9494 800-682-2666
                    www.biomerieux-usa.com
Manufacturer and exporter of food processing equipment including aseptic, bacterial detection and microbiological
Chairman: Jean Luc Belingard
CEO: Alexandre Merieux
CFO: Brian Armstrong
R&D: Brian Daniel
Quality Control: Katie Foushee
VP Sales: Harry Schrick
CVP, Human Resources & Communications: Michel Baugenault
Estimated Sales: $ 5 - 10,000,000
Number Employees: 500-999
Parent Co: Azko Nobel
Regions Exported to: Worldwide

42450 Bionova Produce
PO Box 1586
Nogales, AZ 85628   520-281-2612
          Fax: 520-761-3311
Importer and exporter of organic and fresh produce including watermelons, cantaloupes, honeydew, cherry and Roma tomatoes, squash, beans, cucumbers, grapes, eggplants and bell peppers including green, red and orange
President: Fidel Hoyos
CFO: Carlos Barraza
Sales Manager: Danny Stoller
Estimated Sales: $1-2.5 Million
Number Employees: 20-49
Brands Exported: Showcase; Master's Touch
Regions Exported to: Worldwide
Regions Imported from: Mexico

42451 Biotest Diagnostics Corporation
400 Commons Way
Rockaway, NJ 07866-2030   973-625-1300
          Fax: 973-625-9454 800-522-0090
Manufacturer and exporter of environmental monitoring products
President: William Wiess
Quality Control: Lara Soltis
Marketing Director: Carol Julich
Contact: Angelene Atwal
angelene_atwal@bio-rad.com
Production Manager: Dan Behler
Estimated Sales: $ 10 - 20 Million
Number Employees: 20-49
Parent Co: Biotest AG
Type of Packaging: Bulk
Regions Exported to: Worldwide

42452 Biothane Corporation
2500 Broadway
Camden, NJ 08104   856-541-3500
          Fax: 856-541-3366 sales@biothane.com
                    www.biothane.com
Manufacturer and exporter of anaerobic biological waste water treatment systems
President: Robert Sax
VP: Jay Murphy
VP Marketing/Sales: Denise Johnston
Contact: William Donnell
b.odonnell@biothane.com
Estimated Sales: $ 3 - 5 Million
Number Employees: 30
Square Footage: 80000
Parent Co: Joseph Oat Corporation
Regions Exported to: Canada

42453 Birch Street Seafoods
31 Birch St
Digby, NS B0V 1A0
Canada   902-245-6551
          Fax: 902-245-6554
Processor and exporter of fresh and frozen salted groundfish

Vice President: William Cottreau
Contact: Janice Oliver
Plant Manager: Alan Frankland
Estimated Sales: $500,000 - 1 Million
Number Employees: 25
Type of Packaging: Consumer, Food Service, Private Label, Bulk
Regions Exported to: USA

42454 Birchwood Foods Inc
3111 152nd Ave
PO Box 639
Kenosha, WI 53144-7630   262-859-2272
          Fax: 262-859-2078 800-541-1685
bwinfo@bwfoods.com www.bwfoods.com
Manufactuer and exporter of cryogenically frozen and vacuum-packed fresh ground beef in bulk and patties; importer of boneless beef
President, CEO & Director: Dennis Vignieri
CEO: Cindy Anderson
canderson@bwfoods.com
CFO & Director: Jerry King
VP HR & Safety: Phyllis Murray
Quality Assurance Supervisor: Cathy Miller
VP Sales & Marketing: Wayne Wehking
EVP Operations & Procurement: John Ruffolo
Product Manager: Doug Ladd
Manager of Purchasing: Alex Savaglio
Estimated Sales: $2.76 Million
Number Employees: 500-999
Square Footage: 240000
Type of Packaging: Consumer, Food Service, Private Label, Bulk
Other Locations:
    Frankfort Manufacturing Facility
    Frankfort, IN
    Columbus Manufacturing Facility
    Columbus, OH
    Atlanta Manufacturing Facility
    Atlanta, GA Frankfort Manufacturing
    FacilityColumbus
Regions Exported to: Europe, Asia, Middle East, Caribbean
Percentage of Business in Exporting: 5
Regions Imported from: South America, Australia, New Zealand
Percentage of Business in Importing: 20

42455 Birdsong Corp.
612 Madison Ave.
PO Box 1400
Suffolk, VA 23434-1400   757-539-3456
          Fax: 757-539-7360 www.birdsongpeanuts.com
Raw peanuts.
President: Jeff Johnson
CEO: George Birdsong
gbirdsong@birdsong-peanuts.com
CFO: Stephen Huber
Year Founded: 1914
Estimated Sales: $50.50 Million
Number Employees: 500-999
Square Footage: 10000
Type of Packaging: Food Service
Other Locations:
    Birdsong Corp.
    Gorman, TXBirdsong Corp.
Regions Exported to: Central America, South America, Europe, Asia, Middle East

42456 Birkholm's Solvang Bakery
460 Alisal Rd
Solvang, CA 93463-2726   805-688-8188
          Fax: 805-686-4407 www.birkholmsbakery.com
Processor and exporter of bread, cake and Danish tarts
President: Susan Halme
susan@solvangbakery.com
General manager: Melissa Redell
Estimated Sales: Less Than $500,000
Number Employees: 5-9
Type of Packaging: Consumer, Food Service
Regions Exported to: Worldwide

42457 (HQ)Birko Corporation
19950 West 161st Street
Olathe, KS 66062   913-764-0321
          Fax: 913-764-0779 800-444-8360
djohnson@birkocorp.com www.birkocorp.com
Manufactures 250 cleaning, sanitation and production chemicals, and specialized chemical delivery equipment for HACCP meat, poultry and food plants.

President: Mike Gangel
CEO: Mike Swanson
VP, Business Development: Kelly Green
Research/Development VP: Terry MacAninch
VP sales: Philip Snellen
Customer Service: Rosey Hohendorf
Estimated Sales: $9 Million
Number Employees: 20-49
Other Locations:
    Birko Distribution Center
    Atlanta, GA
    Birko Distribution Center
    Boise, ID
    Birko Distribution Center
    Louisville, KY
    Birko Distribution Center
    Modesto, CA
    Birko Distribution Center
    Philadelphia, PA
    Birko Distribution Center
    Phoenix, AZ
    Birko Distribution CenterBoise
Regions Exported to: Central America, South America

42458 Biro Manufacturing Co
1114 W Main St
Lakeside Marblhd, OH 43440-2099   419-798-4451
          Fax: 419-798-9106 sales@birosaw.com
                    www.birosaw.com
Manufacturer and exporter of meat cutting and processing equipment including grinders and mixer grinders, vacuum tumblers, tenderizers, horizontal slicing machines, cutters, meat mixers and industrial power saws; also, frozen foodflakers
President: Theresa Bahm
tbahm@birosaw.com
VP of Sales & Marketing: D.L (Skip) Muir
Sales Manager: David Dursbacky
Estimated Sales: $ 5 - 10 Million
Number Employees: 50-99
Type of Packaging: Bulk
Brands Exported: Biro
Regions Exported to: Central America, South America, Europe, Asia, Middle East, China, Australia

42459 Biscotti & Co.
145-157 St John Street
White Plains, NY EC1V 4PW   914-682-2165
          Fax: 914-328-4276
Bulk and wrapped shelf stable biscotti and gourmet cookies
President: Gary Spirer
Marketing Director: Jerry O'Donnell
Sales Director: Debbie Rittberg
General Manager: Jerry O'Donnell
Number Employees: 10-19
Square Footage: 36000
Type of Packaging: Consumer, Bulk
Regions Exported to: Canada, Carribean, Latin America, Mexico

42460 Bishamon Industry Corp
5651 E Francis St
Ontario, CA 91761-3601   909-390-7093
          Fax: 909-390-0060 800-358-8833
info@bishamon.com www.bishamon.com
Scissor and skid lifts, pallet trucks and manual levelers/positioners and mobile loading docks; exporter of pallet levelers/positioners; importer of pallet jacks
President: Wataru Sugiura
wsugiura@bishamon.com
Quality Control: Margie Giordano
VP Sales/Marketing: Robert Clark
Sales Manager: Steve O'Connell
Estimated Sales: $10-20 Million
Number Employees: 20-49
Square Footage: 260000
Brands Exported: Bishamon; Ez-Loaders
Regions Exported to: Central America, South America, Europe, Asia, Middle East
Percentage of Business in Exporting: 5
Brands Imported: Bishamon
Regions Imported from: Asia
Percentage of Business in Importing: 25

42461 Bissett Produce Company
P.O.Box 279
1436 North NC Hwy 581
Spring Hope, NC 27882-0279   252-478-4158
          Fax: 252-478-7798 800-849-5073
Bissettproducecompanyinc@msn.com

Grower, packer and exporter of sweet potatoes, pickling cucumbers and banana and specialty peppers and seedless watermelons. Founded in 2001.
Manager: Don Sparks
Finance Executive: Dan Bissett
Vice President: Lee Bissett
Sales Director: Don Sparks
Contact: Dan Bissett
bissettproducecompanyinc@msn.com
Estimated Sales: $2.5-5 Million
Number Employees: 20
Square Footage: 240000
Type of Packaging: Consumer, Food Service, Private Label, Bulk
Brands Exported: Bissett's; Rue's Choice
Regions Exported to: Europe, Canada
Percentage of Business in Exporting: 20

42462 Bissinger's HandcraftedChocolatier
1600 North Broadway
St. Louis, MO 63102 314-615-2400
www.bissingers.com
Fine chocolates and caramels.
CEO: Tim Fogerty
Estimated Sales: $6000000
Number Employees: 5-9
Type of Packaging: Consumer, Bulk

42463 Bittersweet Pastries
385 Chestnut St
Norwood, NJ 07648-2001 201-768-7005
Fax: 973-882-6998 800-217-2938
Desserts including tarts, layer cakes, and flourless chocolate truffle cakes. Also sold frozen and dessert bars. Founded in 1984.
President: Bob Trier
Vice President: Louis Florencia
info@bittersweetpastries.com
Estimated Sales: $1-5 Million
Number Employees: 20-49
Square Footage: 18000
Parent Co: Fairfield Gourmet Foods Corporation
Type of Packaging: Food Service
Brands Exported: Bittersweet Pastries
Regions Exported to: Bermuda
Percentage of Business in Exporting: 1

42464 Blachere Group
210 Holabird Ave
Winsted, CT 06098-1747 860-738-1100
Fax: 860-738-1103 800-641-4808
eva@blachere.com www.blachere.com
Wholesaler/distributor and importer of stainless steel and French silverplated flatware, earthenware, hollowware and china; serving the food service market
President: Eva Blachere
eva@blachere.com
Vice President: Jean Paul Blachere
Estimated Sales: Less than $500,000
Number Employees: 1-4
Brands Imported: Chambly; Luneville; Europ Felix; GDA Limoges; Blacnere Flatware
Regions Imported from: Europe

42465 (HQ)Black Brothers
501 9th Ave
PO Box 401
Mendota, IL 61342-1927 815-539-7451
Fax: 815-538-2451 800-252-2568
www.blackbros.com
Manufacturer and exporter of gluing, coating and laminating machines for packaging of food products
President: Matthew Carroll
CFO: Jeff Simonton
Director Sales/Service: Walter Weiland
Sales: Todd Phalen
IT: Jeffrey Simonton
rburkhart@reimersinc.com
Estimated Sales: $10-20 Million
Number Employees: 50-99
Other Locations:
 Black Brothers Co.
 Warsaw, INBlack Brothers Co.
Brands Exported: Black
Regions Exported to: Worldwide
Percentage of Business in Exporting: 15

42466 Black's Products of HighPoint
2800 Westchester Drive
High Point, NC 27262-8039 336-886-5011
Fax: 336-886-4734 blacks@highpoint.net
www.blacksfurniture.com
Manufacturer and exporter of leather and restaurant furniture polishes
Estimated Sales: $ 1 - 5 Million
Number Employees: 20-49
Square Footage: 40000
Brands Exported: Black's
Regions Exported to: South America, Asia, Canada
Percentage of Business in Exporting: 10

42467 Blackhawk Molding Co Inc
120 W Interstate Rd
Addison, IL 60101 630-458-2100
Fax: 630-543-3904 www.blackhawkmolding.com
Manufacturer and exporter of Tamper-Evident closures for the dairy, juice, and bottled water industires.
Human Resources Director: Roberto Castro
Director of Operations: Jeff Davis
Plastics Engineer: Robert Komperda
Automation Engineer: Andrew Dreasler
Year Founded: 1949
Estimated Sales: $100-500 Million
Number Employees: 100-249
Type of Packaging: Consumer, Food Service, Private Label, Bulk
Brands Exported: Blackhawk
Regions Exported to: Central America, South America, Europe, Asia, Middle East
Percentage of Business in Exporting: 33

42468 Blair's Sauces & Snacks
188 Bay Ave
PO Box 363
Highlands, NJ 07732-1624 732-872-0755
Fax: 732-872-2035 800-982-5247
www.extremefood.com
Manufacturer of hot sauces, BBQ rubs and snacks.
Owner: Blair Lazar
Number of Brands: 1
Type of Packaging: Consumer
Brands Exported: Blair's
Regions Exported to: Central America, South America, Europe, Asia, Australia, New Zealand, Canada

42469 Blakeslee, Inc.
1228 Capital Drive
Addison, IL 60101 630-532-5021
Fax: 630-532-5020 blakeslee@blakesleeinc.com
www.blakesleeinc.com
Manufacturer and exporter of dishwashers, dishwasher racks, mixers, grinders, peelers and slicers
President: Pirjo Stafseth
CFO: Gary Stafseth
Executive VP: Chirs Berg
Marketing/Sales: Pirjo Stafsethh
Contact: Blakeslee Glass
blakeslee@hfse.com
Plant Manager: Gary Berg
Purchasing Manager: Ron Pentis
Square Footage: 400000
Parent Co: Blako
Regions Exported to: Worldwide
Percentage of Business in Exporting: 5

42470 Blancett
8635 Washington Ave
Racine, WI 53406-3738 262-639-6770
Fax: 262-417-1155 800-235-1638
info@blancett.com www.blancett.com
Manufacturer and exporter of 3-A sanitary liquid turbine flow meters
President: John Erskine
pascualespinoza@blancett.com
Sales: Pascual Espinoza
Purchasing Manager: Chuck Tucker
Estimated Sales: $ 3 - 5 Million
Number Employees: 100-249
Square Footage: 40000
Parent Co: Racine Federated
Type of Packaging: Bulk
Regions Exported to: Worldwide
Percentage of Business in Exporting: 3

42471 Blanche P. Field, LLC
1 Design Center Pl
Boston, MA 02210 617-423-0715
Fax: 617-330-6876 800-895-0714
www.blanchefield.com
Manufacturer and exporter of custom lamp shades
President: Stephen G W Walk
CEO: Mitchell Massey
Estimated Sales: $2.5-5 Million
Number Employees: 20-49

Regions Exported to: Worldwide

42472 Blanver USA
1515 S Federal Hwy
Suite 204
Boca Raton, FL 33432-7404 561-416-5513
Fax: 561-416-5563 tesau@blanver.com
www.blanver.com.br
Purified cellulose excipients, gums and gels used to increase fiber content, improve texture, stabilize and thicken food products.
President: Sergio Frangioni
Founder: Valdemir Passos
Contact: Scott Geary
scott.geary@blanver.com
Operations Manager: Rehanna Birbal
Estimated Sales: $1.3 Million
Parent Co: Blanver
Type of Packaging: Bulk
Regions Exported to: South America, Asia, Canada, Mexico, Australia, Africa

42473 Blau Oyster Co Inc
11321 Blue Heron Rd
Bow, WA 98232-9326 360-766-6171
Fax: 360-766-6115 www.blauoyster.com
Processor and exporter of oysters. Founded in 1933.
President: Paul E Blau
blauoysterco@gmail.com
Marketing Manager: Pete Nordlund
Director of Operations: Paul Blau
Estimated Sales: $2.5-5 Million
Number Employees: 10-19
Type of Packaging: Consumer, Food Service, Private Label, Bulk
Regions Exported to: Canada
Percentage of Business in Exporting: 15

42474 Blaze Products Corp
1101 Isaac Shelby Dr
Shelbyville, KY 40065-8171 502-633-0650
Fax: 502-633-0685 blazesales@blazeproducts.com
www.blazeproducts.com
Manufacture chafing dish fuel
COO: Cindy Foster
Number Employees: 1-4
Brands Exported: Blaze Chafing Dish Fuel
Regions Exported to: Central America, South America, Europe, Asia, Middle East

42475 Blend Pak Inc
10039 High Grove Rd
PO Box 458
Bloomfield, KY 40008-7178 502-252-8000
Fax: 502-252-8001 salesinfo@blendpak.com
www.blendpak.com
Manufactures batter, breaders, marinades, seasoning blends, specialty mixes, and custom blended dry formulas. Founded in 1990.
CEO/Human Resources Director: Dan Sutherland
dan@blendpak.com
EVP: Sue Sutherland
R&D: Linda Mikels
Quality Control: Rob Elkin
Operations: Dave Montgomery
Plant Manager: Matt Elder
Estimated Sales: $10 Million
Number Employees: 20-49
Square Footage: 44000
Type of Packaging: Food Service, Private Label, Bulk
Regions Exported to: Europe
Percentage of Business in Exporting: 1

42476 Blendtec
1206 S 1680 W
Orem, UT 84058 801-222-0888
Fax: 801-224-7150 800-748-5400
www.blendtec.com
Exporter of commercial blenders.
CEO & Chairman: Tom Dickson
Year Founded: 1976
Estimated Sales: $50-100 Million
Number Employees: 100-249
Parent Co: K-Tec

42477 Blessed Herbs
109 Barre Plains Rd
Oakham, MA 01068 508-882-3839
Fax: 508-882-3755 800-489-4372
info@blessedherbs.com www.blessedherbs.com

Importers & Exporters / A-Z

Manufacturer, importer and exporter of organic and wildcrafted dried herbs, extracts, formulas and tablets; also, echinacea angustifolia root; exporter and importer of dried herbs and colon cleansers.
Co-Founder: Michael Volchok
Co-Founder: Martha Volchok
CEO: Scott Leonard
Marketing Director: Shalom Volchok
Contact: Alicia Rocco
alicia@blessedherbs.com
Estimated Sales: $500,000-$1 Million
Number Employees: 14
Square Footage: 24000
Type of Packaging: Consumer, Bulk
Regions Exported to: Europe
Percentage of Business in Exporting: 25
Regions Imported from: South America, Europe
Percentage of Business in Importing: 25

42478 Blodgett Co
10840 Seaboard Loop
Houston, TX 77099-3401 281-933-6195
Fax: 281-933-6196 info@theblodgettcompany.com
www.theblodgettcompany.com
Manufacturer and exporter of packaging equipment including scales, controls and vertical form/fill/seal, packaging machines
President: Amber Blodgett
ablodgett@theblodgettcompany.com
CFO and R&D: Bradley Blodgett
Purchasing Agent: Pete Duncan
Estimated Sales: $ 1 - 2.5 Million
Number Employees: 1-4
Square Footage: 11000
Brands Exported: Omni Packaging Machines; Weight Miser Scales
Regions Exported to: Worldwide
Percentage of Business in Exporting: 52

42479 Blodgett Corp
44 Lakeside Ave
Burlington, VT 05401-5242 802-658-6600
Fax: 802-864-0183 800-331-5842
literature@blodgett.com www.blodgett.com
Manufacturer and exporter of steamer ovens
President: Mark Pumphret
dreyn2@maytag.com
VP of Marketing: Des Hague
VP of Sales: Jeff Cook
Number Employees: 100-249
Parent Co: Maytag Corporation
Regions Exported to: Worldwide

42480 (HQ)Blodgett Oven Co
44 Lakeside Ave
Burlington, VT 05401-5274 802-860-3700
Fax: 802-864-0183 800-331-5842
literature@blodgett.com www.blodgett.com
Manufacturer and exporter of ovens including convection, range, deck, pizza and conveyor; also, steamers, fryers, kettles, grills, mobile food carts, charbroilers, catering equipment and filtering systems
President: Gary Mick
CFO: Gary Mick
IT Executive: Sarah Home
sarah@copelandfurniture.com
Director Corporate Communications: Ann Williams
IT Executive: Sarah Home
sarah@copelandfurniture.com
Number Employees: 100-249
Parent Co: Maytag Corporation
Regions Exported to: Worldwide
Percentage of Business in Exporting: 15

42481 (HQ)Blommer Chocolate Co
600 W Kinzie St
Chicago, IL 60654-5585 312-226-7700
Fax: 312-226-4141 800-621-1606
www.blommer.com
Processor and exporter of chocolate ingredients for the bakery, dairy and confectionery industries including milk and dark chocolate, confectioner and pastel coatings, cookie drops, chocolate liquor, cocoa butter, cocoa powder, icecream ingredients, etc. Founded in 1939.
President: Peter Blommer
Founder, Chairman & CEO: Henry Blommer
CFO: Jack S Larsen
jack@blommer.com
Vice President: Rich Blommer
Manager of Quality Assurance: Radka Kacena
Marketing & Purchasing Manager: Leanna Hicks
Sales Support: Chief Marketing Officer Kidd
VP of Operations: Rich Blommer
Plant Mnaager: Joe Chwala
Purchasing Manager: Faye Garcia
Estimated Sales: $38.4 Million
Number Employees: 1-4
Square Footage: 340000
Type of Packaging: Bulk
Other Locations:
Union City, CA
East Greenville, PA
Campbellford, ONEast Greenville
Regions Exported to: Worldwide
Percentage of Business in Exporting: 15

42482 Blossom Farm Products
545 State Rt 17
Suite 2003
Ridgewood, NJ 07450 201-493-2626
Fax: 201-493-2666 800-729-1818
Processor, importer and exporter of dairy products including milk powders, dry blends, whey, caseinates, lactose, butter fats, etc.
President: Paul Podell
Manager: Kathy Oviedo
VP: Marcia Podell
Operations Manager: Kathy Oviedo
Number Employees: 5-9
Type of Packaging: Consumer, Food Service, Bulk
Regions Exported to: Central America, South America, Asia
Percentage of Business in Exporting: 50
Regions Imported from: South America, Europe
Percentage of Business in Importing: 50

42483 Blower Application Co Inc
N114w19125 Clinton Dr
PO Box 279
Germantown, WI 53022-3013 262-255-5580
Fax: 262-255-3446 800-959-0880
sales@bloapco.com www.bloapco.com
Manufacturer and exporter of waste disposal systems and equipment shredders
President: John Stanislowski
bac@bloapco.com
Sales Director: Ric Johnson
Estimated Sales: $ 5 - 10 Million
Number Employees: 20-49
Square Footage: 80000
Brands Exported: Blo ApCo
Regions Exported to: Worldwide
Percentage of Business in Exporting: 25

42484 BluMetric EnvironmentalInc.
3108 Carp Road
P.O. Box 430
Ottawa, ON K0A 1L0
Canada 613-839-3053
Fax: 613-839-5376 info@blumetric.ca
www.blumetric.ca
Manufacturer and exporter of food processing equipment including membrane and whey processing and brine systems; also, filtration equipment and water and waste water treatment systems.
President, Water: Dan L. Scroggins
CEO: Roger M. Woeller
Chief Financial Officer: Ian Malone, B.A. Hons.
Reaserch/Development: Sam Ali
Sales/Marketing: Gary Black
Director Process Development: Greg Choryhanna
Number Employees: 15
Square Footage: 34000
Type of Packaging: Bulk
Regions Exported to: Central America, South America, Asia, Mexico, Caribbean, India
Percentage of Business in Exporting: 60

42485 Blue Crab Bay
29368 Atlantic Dr.
Melfa, VA 23410 757-787-3602
Fax: 757-787-3430 800-221-2722
sales@bluecrabbay.com www.bluecrabbay.com
Wholesaler & retailer of bloody mary mixers, seafood soups, seasonings, snacks, crab meat; also salt, mustard, and marinade, stoneware. Founded in 1985.
President: Pamela Barefoot
pam@baybeyond.net
VP Finance: Dawn Brasure
Marketing Director: Kelly Drummond
Sales Manager: Victoria DiLeo
Chief Operating Officer: Paul Driscoll
Purchasing: Linda Nyborg
Estimated Sales: $1-3 Million
Number Employees: 22
Square Footage: 86000
Parent Co: Bay Beyond, Inc.
Type of Packaging: Consumer
Regions Exported to: Europe, Asia, Canada, Australia
Percentage of Business in Exporting: 3

42486 Blue Cross Laboratories
20950 Centre Pointe Pkwy
Santa Clarita, CA 91350
bmahler@bc-labs.com
www.bc-labs.com
Cleaning products including air fresheners, nonchlorine bleach, anti-bacterial liquid soap, health and beauty care products.
President: Darrell Mahler
Formulation Development & Q.A.: Jagdish Koshti
Estimated Sales: $28 Million
Number Employees: 50-99
Number of Products: 150
Square Footage: 150000
Type of Packaging: Consumer, Private Label
Other Locations:
Blue Cross Laboratories
Phoenix, ARBlue Cross Laboratories
Regions Exported to: Central America, South America, Asia, Middle East
Percentage of Business in Exporting: 6
Regions Imported from: Asia, Canada
Percentage of Business in Importing: 8

42487 Blue Diamond Growers
1802 C St.
Sacramento, CA 95811
 800-987-2329
www.bluediamond.com
Processor, grower and exporter of almonds, macadamians, pistachios and hazelnuts. Two thousand almond products in many cuts, styles, sizes and shapes for use in confectionery, bakery, dairy and processed foods. In house R/D for customproducts.
President/Chief Executive Officer: Mark Jansen
Chairman of The Board: Clinton Shick
CFO: Dean LaVallee
Vice Chairman: Dale Van Groningen
Quality Assurance Lab Manager: Steven Phillips
Director, Marketing: Al Greenlee
Manager, Communications: Cassandra Keyse
Manager, Operations: Bruce Lisch
Manager, Product Development: Mike Stoddard
Senior Vice President, Procurement: David Hills
Year Founded: 1910
Estimated Sales: $709 Million
Number Employees: 1,100
Type of Packaging: Consumer, Food Service, Private Label, Bulk

42488 Blue Feather Products Inc
165 Reiten Dr
Ashland, OR 97520-9020 541-482-5268
Fax: 541-482-2338 800-472-2487
www.blue-feather.com
Manufacturer, importer and exporter of synthetic chamois, magnetic picture frames and refrigerator magnets
Vice President: John R King
johninashland@charter.net
VP: John King
Marketing Manager: Ashley Black
Office Manager: Lisa Gentle
Estimated Sales: Less Than $500,000
Number Employees: 1-4
Square Footage: 8000
Type of Packaging: Consumer
Regions Exported to: Europe, Canada
Percentage of Business in Exporting: 8
Regions Imported from: Europe
Percentage of Business in Importing: 4

Importers & Exporters / A-Z

42489 Blue Giant Equipment Corporation
85 Heart Lake Road South
Brampton, ON L6W 3K2
Canada   905-457-3900
Fax: 905-457-2313 800-668-7078
sales@bluegiant.com www.bluegiant.com
Manufacturer and exporter of loading dock equipment, vehicle restraints, dock lifts, lift tables and industrial trucks and the Blue Genius Tech Control Panels
Chairman: Bill Kostenko
Director of Sales and Marketing: Steve Greco
VP of Sales/Marketing: Jeff Miller
Estimated Sales: $ 35 Million
Number Employees: 100-250
Square Footage: 85000
Brands Exported: Blue Giant; Rol - Lift
Regions Exported to: Central America, South America, Europe, Asia, Middle East
Percentage of Business in Exporting: 15
Brands Imported: Voyager
Regions Imported from: Europe, Asia
Percentage of Business in Importing: 5

42490 Blue Harvest Foods
86 Macarthur Dr
New Bedford, MA 02740-7214 508-993-5700
Fax: 508-991-5133 www.blueharvestfisheries.com
Fresh and frozen scallops including bay and sea and fillets including flounder, cod, yellow tail and haddock; importer of cod fish and scallops; exporter of scallops
President: Albert J Santos
al@scallops-fillets.com
CEO: Linda Wisniewski
Treasurer/Vice President: Carmine Romano
Sales Manager: Patrick Moriarty
Manager: Albert Santos
al@scallops-fillets.com
Estimated Sales: $10-20 Million
Number Employees: 20-49
Square Footage: 60000
Type of Packaging: Consumer, Food Service, Private Label, Bulk
Brands Exported: Hygrade
Regions Exported to: Europe, Asia
Percentage of Business in Exporting: 20
Regions Imported from: South America, Asia, Canada, Latin America, Mexico
Percentage of Business in Importing: 20

42491 Blue Mountain Enterprise Inc
4000 Commerce Dr
Kinston, NC 28504-7906 252-522-1544
Fax: 252-522-2599 800-522-1544
Savory flavors for the food industry, also contract manufacturing and packaging
President: William Baugher
labs@bluemountainsflavors.com
Manager of Scientific Affairs: Jonathan Baugher
Corporate Secretay/Treasurer: Teresa Baugher
Research/Development: William Recktenwald
Quality Control: Margaret Jones
Customer Service: Maureen Suggs
Operations Manager: Laura Key
Production: Perry Price, Jr
Estimated Sales: $4 Million
Number Employees: 10-19
Number of Products: 150
Square Footage: 67775
Parent Co: Blue Mountain Enterprises
Type of Packaging: Bulk
Brands Exported: Blue Mountain Flavors
Regions Exported to: Asia, Canada

42492 (HQ)Blue Pacific Flavors & Fragrances
1354 Marion Ct
City of Industry, CA 91745 626-934-0099
www.bluepacificflavors.com
Basic manufacturer of natural flavors, extracts, essences and functional ingredients to the beverage, dairy, confectionery, baking and pharmaceutical industries. Founded in 1992.
President: Donald Wilkes
Contact: Kelly Anderson
kelly.anderson@cgtech.com
Estimated Sales: $ 5 - 9 Million
Number Employees: 20-49
Number of Brands: 5
Square Footage: 40000
Type of Packaging: Food Service, Private Label, Bulk
Other Locations:
Blue Pacific Asia
MalaysiaBlue Pacific AsiaBeijing, China
Brands Exported: Blue Pacific
Regions Exported to: South America, Asia
Percentage of Business in Exporting: 30

42493 Blue Planet Foods
9104 Apison Pike
PO Box 2178
Collegedale, TN 37315 423-396-3145
Fax: 423-396-3402 877-396-3145
sales@blueplanetfoods.net
Grain based products, granola, nutrition and granola bar components, bread bases and nutritional fillers; exporter of granola products
President: Russell McKee
Human Resources Director: Wayne White
Director of Operations: Deris Bagli
Production Manager: Cliff Myers
Plant Manager: Frank Park
Parent Co: McKee Foods Corporation
Type of Packaging: Consumer, Food Service, Private Label, Bulk
Regions Exported to: Canada

42494 Blue Ribbon Fish Co
800 Food Center Dr # 67
Unit 67
Bronx, NY 10474-0041 718-620-8580
www.blueribbonfish.com
Importer and wholesaler/distributor of seafood; serving the food service market
Partner/VP: Bob Samuels
Estimated Sales: $2.5-5 Million
Number Employees: 5-9
Regions Imported from: South America

42495 Blue Ridge Converting
100 Fairview Road
Asheville, NC 28803 828-274-2100
Fax: 828-274-0000 800-438-3893
Manufacturer, importer and exporter of disposable and waterproof clothing and nonwoven wipers
CEO: Thomas Snell
Vice President: Daniel Neal
VP Sales: Daniel Neal
Purchasing: Jo Curtis
Estimated Sales: $2 Million
Number Employees: 24
Square Footage: 480000
Regions Exported to: South America, Europe
Percentage of Business in Exporting: 25
Regions Imported from: Worldwide
Percentage of Business in Importing: 10

42496 Blue Sky Beverage Company
550 Monica Circle
Suite 201
Corona, CA 92880 505-995-9761
Fax: 505-982-4004 800-426-7367
info@drinkbluesky.com www.drinkbluesky.com
Manufacturer and exporter of natural and energy sodas; also sparkling and artesian drinking water
Chairman/CEO: Rodney Sacks
President/COO/CFO: Hilton Schlosberg
Estimated Sales: $48,000
Brands Exported: Blue Sky
Regions Exported to: Central America, Europe, Asia, Canada
Percentage of Business in Exporting: 8

42497 Blue Star Food Products
3000 NW 109th Ave
Doral, FL 33172 305-836-6858
info@bluestarfoods.com
www.bluestarfoods.com
Seafood
Executive Chairman & CSO: John Keeler
jkeeler@bluestarfoods.com
Estimated Sales: $50-100 Million
Number Employees: 20-49
Number of Brands: 4
Regions Exported to: Europe, Asia
Regions Imported from: Asia

42498 Bluebird Manufacturing
6670 St. Patrick
Montreal, QC H8N 1V2
Canada 514-762-2505
800-406-2505
admin@bluebird.ca www.bluebird.ca
Manufacturer, exporter and importer of metal cookware including pots, pans, fry baskets, etc; also, custom services available
President: Harvey Engelberg
Brands Exported: Bluebird
Brands Imported: Bron; Gobel; Tellier
Regions Imported from: Europe, Asia
Percentage of Business in Importing: 20

42499 Bluff Manufacturing Inc
1400 Everman Pkwy # 156
Suite 156
Fort Worth, TX 76140-5034 817-293-3018
Fax: 817-293-7570 800-433-2212
jae@bluffmanufacturing.com
www.bluffmanufacturing.com
Manufacturers exporter of dockboards, dock plates and edge-of-dock levelers
President: Phillip Amrozowicz
phillip@bluffmanufacturing.com
Director, Financing & Accounting: Bruce Parker
VP, Marketing: Amy Hamilton
Estimated Sales: $10-20 Million
Number Employees: 5-9
Regions Exported to: Central America, South America, Europe
Percentage of Business in Exporting: 1

42500 Bluffton Slaw Cutter Company
331 N Main St Ste 1
Bluffton, OH 45817 419-358-9840
Fax: 419-358-9840 www.blufftonslawcutter.com
Manufacturer and exporter of lid removers, cheese shredders, apple slicers and slaw cutters
President and CFO: Paul King
VP: T King
Quality Control: Louis Stier
Marketing Director: L King
Estimated Sales: Below $ 5 Million
Number Employees: 1-4
Square Footage: 2400
Regions Exported to: Asia, Canada
Percentage of Business in Exporting: 10

42501 Blundell Seafoods
11351 River Road
Richmond, BC V6X 1Z6
Canada 604-270-3300
Fax: 604-270-6513 info@blundellseafoods.com
www.blundellseafoods.com
Fresh and frozen seafood including clams, oysters, exotic fish, fin fish, freshwater fish, crustaceans, caviar
President: Ian Tak Yen Law
Vice President: Jeremy Kwun Hon Law
VP Sales: Rick Ogilvie
Manager: Bill Leung
Estimated Sales: $30 Million
Number Employees: 75
Type of Packaging: Consumer, Food Service, Private Label, Bulk
Regions Exported to: Worldwide
Percentage of Business in Exporting: 50

42502 Bmh Equipment Inc
1217 Blumenfeld Dr
P.O. Box 162109
Sacramento, CA 95815-3903 916-922-8828
Fax: 916-922-8820 800-350-8828
www.bmhe.com
Distributor/exporter of custom material handling equipment, hand trucks, casters, conveyor systems, dollies, pallet jacks and racks, aluminum ramps, dock boards, shelving and work tables; design and engineering for nonstandard materialhandling problems
President: Jack Alexander
jackalex@bmhequipment.com
VP: Jerry Berg
Conveyor Specialist: Richard Wales
Estimated Sales: $2.5-5 Million
Number Employees: 10-19
Square Footage: 20800
Regions Exported to: Worldwide

42503 Boardman Molded Products Inc
1110 Thalia Ave
Youngstown, OH 44512-1825 330-788-2401
Fax: 330-788-9665 800-233-4575
tbobonick@spacelinks1.com
www.boardmanmolded.com
Safety mats and flooring

Importers & Exporters / A-Z

Owner: Ron Kessler
Controller: Jim Bowser
QA Manager: Jeff Westlake
VP Marketing: Dan Kessler
VP of Sales: Tom Bobonick
rkessler@spacelinks1.com
Plant Manager: George Lolakis
Estimated Sales: $ 20 - 50 Million
Number Employees: 100-249
Regions Exported to: Worldwide
Percentage of Business in Exporting: 5

42504 Bob Gedan & Associates
6980 SW 10th St
Plantation, FL 33317-4241   954-792-3724
        Fax: 954-792-3724 rlg1035@aol.com
Owner: Robert Gedan
Estimated Sales: $ .5 - 1 million
Number Employees: 1-4

42505 Bob Gordon & Associates
940 Linden Avenue
Oak Park, IL 60302-1349   708-524-9611
Processor and importer of green and black olives, maraschino cherries, pickled onions, pickled mushrooms and Greek pepperoncini. Founded in 1976.
President: Roberta Seefeldt
Vice President: Aaron Seefeldt
VP of Sales: Marcel Seefeldt
Controller: James Gosling
Estimated Sales: $1.2 Million
Number Employees: 10
Type of Packaging: Food Service, Private Label, Bulk
Regions Imported from: South America, Europe
Percentage of Business in Importing: 60

42506 Boca Bagelworks
8177 Glades Rd # 1
Boca Raton, FL 33434-4063   561-852-8992
        Fax: 561-852-5798 info@bagelworks.com
                www.bagelworks.com
Owned and operated by H&L Restaurants. Processor and exporter of bagels
Owner: Paul Herman
VP: Steven Goldstein
Estimated Sales: $500,000 appx.
Number Employees: 20-49
Regions Exported to: Worldwide

42507 Boca Bons East
5190 Lake Worth Road
Greenacres, FL 33463   954-346-0494
        Fax: 954-346-0497 800-314-2835
Manufacturer and exporter of a certified kosher chocolate that is a combination of a truffle, fudge, and a brownie.
President: Susan Kanter
Sales Executive: Robin Kula
Estimated Sales: $1-3 Million
Number Employees: 10-19
Square Footage: 10000
Type of Packaging: Consumer, Food Service, Private Label, Bulk
Brands Exported: Boca Bons
Regions Exported to: Europe, Asia, Canada
Percentage of Business in Exporting: 10

42508 Body Breakthrough Inc
561 Acorn St # I
St Unit I
Deer Park, NY 11729-3600   631-243-2443
        Fax: 631-243-2464 800-924-3343
                www.bodybreakthrough.com
Processor and exporter of teas including herbal, dietary and antioxidant; also, weight loss aids
President: Cori Lichter
Executive Director: Glenn Lichter
Estimated Sales: Under $800,000
Number Employees: 5-9
Square Footage: 10000
Type of Packaging: Consumer, Private Label
Brands Exported: Anti Oxidant Edge; Dailyedge; Dieter's Edge Tabs; Trim Maxx; Trim Maxx Burners
Regions Exported to: Central America, South America, Europe, Middle East

42509 Boehringer Mfg. Co. Inc.
6500 Highway 9
Unit F
Felton, CA 95018   831-704-7732
        Fax: 831-704-7731 800-630-8665
Manufacturer and exporter of burlap sack needles, block scrapers, dough cutters, boning, meat hooks, and specialty blades; custom plastic injection moldings; also bbq tools and accessories
Secretary: Mark Fowles
Estimated Sales: $ 300-500,000
Number Employees: 5-9
Number of Products: 50
Square Footage: 2500
Parent Co: Boehringer Manufacturing Company
Type of Packaging: Consumer, Private Label
Regions Exported to: Central America, South America, Europe, Australia, Canada, Mexico, Latin America
Percentage of Business in Exporting: 25
Regions Imported from: Europe, Asia
Percentage of Business in Importing: 10

42510 Bohn & Dawson
3500 Tree Court Industrial Blv
St Louis, MO 63122-6685   636-225-5011
        Fax: 636-825-6111 800-225-5011
                www.bohnanddawson.com
Manufacturer and exporter of metal fabricators, tubular parts and assemblies; also, tool and die services available
President: Steven L Hurster
Engineer: J Koopman
VP: R Wiele
CFO: Steve Leibach
Quality Control: Mike Schneider
Estimated Sales: $ 20 - 50 Million
Number Employees: 10-19
Regions Exported to: Worldwide
Percentage of Business in Exporting: 5

42511 Boisset Family Estates
849 Zinfandel Ln
St Helena, CA 94574-1645   707-963-6900
                800-878-1123
info@boisset.com www.boissetfamilyestates.com
Wine
President: Jean-Charles Boisset
Controller: Phillip Marquand
VP: Alain Leonnet
Marketing Manager: Lisa Heisinger
Director of Consumer Marketing: Michelle Sitton
Estimated Sales: $7.8 Million
Number Employees: 5-9
Parent Co: LaFamille des Grands Vins

42512 Bolner's Fiesta Spices
426 Menchaca St
San Antonio, TX 78207
                info@fiestaspices.com
                www.fiestaspices.com
Processor and importer of dehydrated vegetables, liquid extracts and spices, herbs and seasonings, including: bay leaves, cinnamon, cloves, cumin, sage, nutmeg, oregano, paprika, onion salt, anise, caraway, garlic, celery and mustardseeds, black pepper.
Founder: Clifton Bolner
Plant Manager: James Morris
Estimated Sales: Under $1 Million
Number Employees: 100-249
Type of Packaging: Consumer, Food Service, Private Label, Bulk
Regions Imported from: Central America, Asia, Middle East
Percentage of Business in Importing: 70

42513 Bolzoni Auramo
17635 Hoffman Way
Homewood, IL 60430-2186   708-957-8809
        Fax: 708-957-8832 800-358-5438
                sales.us@bolzoni-auramo.com
                www.bolzoni-auramo.it
Manufacturer, importer and exporter of lift truck attachments
Vice President: Ad Artuso
eartuso@bolzoni-auramo.com
VP: Ad Artuso
VP Sales: Ronnie Keene
VP Operations: Ed Artuso
Plant Manager: Jose Cardonas
Purchasing Manager: Brian Cummings
Estimated Sales: $20 Million
Number Employees: 20-49
Square Footage: 14700
Parent Co: Bolzoni SPA
Brands Exported: Bolzoni
Regions Exported to: Central America, South America, Canada
Percentage of Business in Exporting: 10

Brands Imported: Bolzoni
Regions Imported from: Europe
Percentage of Business in Importing: 50

42514 Bolzoni Auramo
17635 Hoffman Way
Homewood, IL 60430-2186   708-957-8809
        Fax: 708-957-8832 800-358-5438
                sales.us@bolzoni-auramo.com
                www.bolzoni-auramo.it
Manufacturer and exporter of lift truck attachments
President: Roberto Scotti
Vice President: Ad Artuso
eartuso@bolzoni-auramo.com
General Manager: Dick Fennessey
Estimated Sales: $5-10 Million
Number Employees: 20-49
Parent Co: Auramo O.Y.
Regions Exported to: Worldwide

42515 Bon Appetit International
3737 Savannah Loop
Oviedo, FL 32765-9204   407-366-4973
        Fax: 407-359-8861 800-473-3513
info@bonappetit-int.com www.bonappetit-int.com
Wholesaler/distributor and importer of smoked, marinated and frozen portion control salmon; exporter of countertop display cases and smoked salmon
President: Mick Chandler
VP: Marcelle Simon
Number Employees: 1-4
Parent Co: Trade Europe
Type of Packaging: Consumer, Food Service
Regions Exported to: Central America, South America, Canada, Europe, Latin America
Percentage of Business in Exporting: 20
Regions Imported from: Europe

42516 Bon Chef
205 State Route 94
Lafayette, NJ 07848-4617   973-383-8848
        Fax: 973-383-1827 800-331-0177
                info@bonchef.com www.bonchef.com
Food presentation items. Products include chafing dishes, coffee urns, sandstone servingware, buffet bars, custom counter-tops and more.
President: Salvatore Torre
Vice President: Anthony Lo Grippo
Director of Sales Administration: Amy Passafaro
Estimated Sales: $2.5-5 Million
Number Employees: 20-49

42517 Bon Secour Fisheries Inc
17449 County Road 49 S
Bon Secour, AL 36511   251-949-7411
        Fax: 251-949-6478
bonsec@bonsecourfisheries.com
                www.bonsecourfisheries.com
Fresh and frozen flounder, whiting, snapper, shrimp, oysters, scallops, crawfish, snow, soft shell and king crab, lobster, cod, catfish, tuna, grouper, pollock, shark, mahi, talapia, etc.; also, alligator meat.
CFO: Melani Parker
Vice President: Chris Nelson
Director, Sales: Leon Russell
Procurement Manager: Robert Eckerle
Year Founded: 1896
Estimated Sales: $25.10 Million
Number Employees: 100-249
Square Footage: 60000
Type of Packaging: Consumer, Food Service, Bulk
Brands Exported: Nelson Brand

42518 Bonduelle North America
540 Chemin Des Patriotes
Saint-denis-sur-richelieu
Quebec, ON J0H 1K0
Canada   450-787-3411
        Fax: 450-787-3537 www.familytradition.com
Manufacturer and importer of frozen fruits and vegetables; exporter of canned corn and IQF vegetables
President/CEO: John Omstead
Number Employees: 100-249
Square Footage: 1284000
Type of Packaging: Consumer, Food Service
Other Locations:
    Family Tradition Foods
    Tecumseh, Ontario Family Tradition Foods
Regions Exported to: South America, Europe, Asia, Latin America, USA
Regions Imported from: Europe, Asia, USA

Importers & Exporters / A-Z

42519 (HQ)Bonneau Company
3334 South Tech Boulevard
Miamisburg, OH 45342   937-886-9100
Fax: 937-886-9300   800-394-0678
www.bonneaucompany.com
Manufacturer, importer and exporter of commercial and industrial dyes including paraffin, microcrystalline waxes and blends
President: Timothy Muldoon
VP/Technical Director: Paul Guinn
Estimated Sales: $ 5 - 10 Million
Number Employees: 1-4
Square Footage: 60000
Brands Exported: Bonne Dye; Bonn Trace
Regions Exported to: Europe, Canada
Percentage of Business in Exporting: 10
Regions Imported from: Asia
Percentage of Business in Importing: 15

42520 Bonnot Co
1301 Home Ave
Akron, OH 44310-2654   330-896-6544
Fax: 330-896-0822 info@thebonnotco.com
www.thebonnotco.com
Manufacturer and exporter of extruders for food, chemicals, ceramics, catalysts, etc
President: George Bain
CFO: Becky Goulden
VP: John Negrelli
Engineering Manager: Kurt Houk
General Manager: George W. Bain
Contact: Vince Damicone
damicone@thebonnotco.com
Controller: Becky Bouldon
Estimated Sales: $ 2.5 - 5 Million
Number Employees: 10-19
Square Footage: 160000
Brands Exported: Bonnot
Regions Exported to: Central America, South America, Europe, Asia, Middle East
Percentage of Business in Exporting: 30

42521 Boricua Empaque
S Puerta De Tierra
P.O. Box 9021741
San Juan, PR 00902-1741   787-723-5366
Fax: 787-722-3567 bempaque@spiderlink.net
Wholesaler/distributor and importer of biscuits, cookies, groceries, canned seafood and general merchandise including bags and dinnerware
President/Chairman: J Llanos-Pinera
Treasurer/Secretary: A Llanos
Number Employees: 20-49
Square Footage: 120000
Type of Packaging: Consumer
Brands Imported: Noel; Colortex; Selva
Regions Imported from: South America, Asia, Latin America, Mexico
Percentage of Business in Importing: 80

42522 Bormioli Rocco Hotel Products
22601 Davis Drive
Sterling, VA 20164   800-296-7508
Fax: 703-787-6645   800-296-7508
info@fortessa.com www.fortessa.com
High-end tableware, glassware and metalware
Number Employees: 170

42523 Borroughs Corp
3002 N Burdick St
Kalamazoo, MI 49004-3483   269-342-0161
Fax: 269-342-4161   800-748-0227
www.borroughs.com
Manufacturer and exporter of industrial and commercial steel shelving, checkout counters and office filing units
President: Timothy Tyler
ttyler@borroughs.com
Sales: Rick Stear
Estimated Sales: $20-50 Million
Number Employees: 250-499
Square Footage: 450000
Brands Exported: Series 90
Regions Exported to: Central America, Middle East, Canada, Caribbean, Mexico
Percentage of Business in Exporting: 5

42524 Bos Smoked Fish Inc
1175 Patullo Avenue
Woodstock, ON N4S 7W3
Canada   519-537-5000
Fax: 519-537-5522 info@bossmokedfish.com
www.bossmokedfish.com
Smoked fish
President: Rein Bos
Sales: Chris Bruines
Sales: Kirk VanderSpek
Plant Manager: Pieter Bos
Estimated Sales: $6 Million
Number Employees: 15
Type of Packaging: Consumer, Food Service, Private Label, Bulk
Regions Exported to: Europe

42525 Bosch Packaging Technology
869 S Knowles Ave
New Richmond, WI 54017-1745   715-246-6511
Fax: 715-246-6539 sales@doboy.com
www.boschpackaging.com
Manufacturer and exporter of carton and tray forming and sealing machines, horizontal wrappers and bag closing machines
President: William Heilhecker
CFO: Julie Foss
Sales: Mike Wilcox
Director Sales: John Bowerman
Director Operations: Mark Hanson
Estimated Sales: $ 30 - 50 Million
Number Employees: 100-249
Parent Co: SIG
Regions Exported to: Central America, South America, Europe, Asia, Middle East, Canada, Mexico, Latin America
Percentage of Business in Exporting: 5

42526 Boskovich Farms Inc
711 Diaz Ave
PO Box 1352
Oxnard, CA 93030-7247   805-487-2299
Fax: 805-487-5189
feedback@boskovichfarms.com
www.boskovichfarms.com
Bok choy, artichokes, cilantro, endive, cebollitas, brussels sprouts, onions, lettuce, celery, carrots, cabbages, bell peppers, apples, radishes, spinach, beets, asparagus, kale, leeks, napa, parsley, radish, strawberries and sugarpeas.
President: Philip Boskovich
Co-CEO: Joseph Boskovich
Co-CEO: George Boskovich
lmartinez@boskovichfarms.com
CFO: Lynn Grayson
Sales Manager: Russ Widerburg
Human Resources Manager: Martha Mayorga
Estimated Sales: Over $1 Billion
Number Employees: 1000-4999
Type of Packaging: Consumer, Food Service
Other Locations:
  Transwest Cooling
  Yuma, AZ
  Growers Street Cooling
  Salinas, CA
  Shipping Distribution
  Oxnard, CATranswest CoolingSalinas
Regions Exported to: Canada

42527 Boss Manufacturing Co
1221 Page St
Kewanee, IL 61443-2159   309-852-2131
Fax: 309-852-0848   800-447-4581
custserv@bossgloves.com
Manufacturer, importer and exporter of gloves, boots, protective clothing and aprons
CEO: Louis Graziado
lgraziado@bossgloves.com
VP Sales/Marketing: Brian Wise
Sales Manager: Gerry Stockelman
Purchasing Manager: Summer Cohen
Estimated Sales: $ 40 Million
Number Employees: 50-99
Parent Co: Boss Holdings
Type of Packaging: Consumer, Food Service, Private Label, Bulk
Other Locations:
  Boss Manufacturing Co.
  Concord, ONBoss Manufacturing Co.
Brands Exported: Boss
Regions Exported to: Europe, Canada
Percentage of Business in Exporting: 5
Brands Imported: Boss
Regions Imported from: Asia, Mexico
Percentage of Business in Importing: 90

42528 Boston Beer Co Inc.
1 Design Center Pl.
Suite 850
Boston, MA 02210   617-368-5000
Fax: 617-368-5500   888-661-2337
www.bostonbeer.com
Beer.
President/CEO: David Burwick
Chairman/Founder: C. James Koch
CFO/Treasurer: Frank Smalla
VP, Brewing: David Grinnell
Chief Sales Manager: John Geist
Year Founded: 1984
Estimated Sales: $921 Million
Number Employees: 1000-4999
Number of Brands: 5
Square Footage: 33500
Type of Packaging: Consumer, Food Service
Regions Exported to: Worldwide
Percentage of Business in Exporting: 1

42529 Boston Chowda
30 River St
Haverhill, MA 01832-5402   978-478-0500
Fax: 978-478-3588   800-992-0054
info@bostonchowda.com www.bostonchowda.com
Frozen soups and chowders
President: Richard Lamattina
Director: Paul Cassidy
Director: John Leroy
Director: Alan Katz
Manager: Michael Lamattina
Year Founded: 1987
Estimated Sales: Less Than $500,000
Number Employees: 5-9
Square Footage: 13000
Percentage of Business in Exporting: 5

42530 (HQ)Boston Retail
400 Riverside Ave
Medford, MA 02155-4949   781-395-2656
Fax: 781-395-0155   800-225-1633
info@bostonretail.com www.bostonretail.com
Manufacturer and exporter of space frame systems, damage control products, bumper guards, fixtures and display products
President & CEO: Russell Rubin
rrubin@bostonretail.com
CFO & Vice President: Victor Martin
Estimated Sales: $ 20 - 50 Million
Number Employees: 50-99
Other Locations:
  Boston Retail Products
  Youngstown, OHBoston Retail Products
Regions Exported to: Central America, South America, Europe, Asia, Middle East

42531 Boston Sausage & Provision
7 Wells Avenue
Newton Center, MA 02459   508-647-0558
Wholesaler/distributor and exporter of eggs, seafood, fresh and frozen beef, poultry and pork; importer of beef
President/CEO: Arthur Weiss
arthur@bostonagrex.com
VP: Joe Valdivia
Manager International Sales: J Cochran
Estimated Sales: $20-50 Million
Number Employees: 12
Square Footage: 2000
Regions Exported to: Europe, Caribbean
Percentage of Business in Exporting: 70
Regions Imported from: Central America
Percentage of Business in Importing: 15

42532 Boston Seafarms
119 Marlborough Street
Boston, MA 2116   617-784-4777
Fax: 800-692-9907 bostonseafarms@gmail.com
www.bostonseafarm.com
Processor, wholesaler/distributor, importer and exporter of seafood including fish and shellfish
President/CEO: Adam Weinberg
bostonseafarms@gmail.com
Estimated Sales: $12-13,000,000
Number Employees: 5
Square Footage: 36000
Regions Exported to: Worldwide
Percentage of Business in Exporting: 30
Regions Imported from: Central America, South America, Latin America , Mexico

42533 Boston's Best Coffee Roasters
43 Norfolk Ave
South Easton, MA 02375-1190   508-238-8393
Fax: 508-238-6835   800-898-8393
sales@bostonsbestcoffee.com
www.bostonsbestcoffee.com
Coffee, mixers and filters

President: Jacqueline Dovner
CEO: Stephen Fortune
Director of Fundraising Sales: Erin Woodard
Contact: Mary Burke
marymb@bostonsbestcoffee.com
Production Manager: Rocky Raposa
Estimated Sales: Less Than $500,000
Number Employees: 5-9
Square Footage: 5692
Type of Packaging: Consumer, Food Service, Private Label, Bulk
Brands Exported: Interstate; Boston's Best
Regions Exported to: Asia, Middle East, Worldwide
Percentage of Business in Exporting: 20
Regions Imported from: Central America, South America, Europe, Mexico
Percentage of Business in Importing: 75

42534 Botanical Products
34725 Bogart Dr
Springville, CA 93265-9602
559-539-3432
Fax: 559-539-2058
Processor and exporter of tablets, capsules, extracts and powders made from yucca and melatonin
President: Gordon Bean
VP: Joyce Bean
Estimated Sales: $1-2.5 Million
Number Employees: 1-4
Square Footage: 4000
Type of Packaging: Consumer
Brands Exported: Desert Pride
Regions Exported to: Europe, Asia, Worldwide
Percentage of Business in Exporting: 5

42535 Botsford Fisheries
Po Box 1093
Cap Pele, NB E4N 3B3
Canada
506-577-4327
Fax: 506-577-2846 info@botsfordfisheries.com
www.botsfordfisheries.com
Processor and exporter of fresh and smoked herring
President: William LeBlanc
Export Sales Manager: Janice Ryan
Plant Manager: Clement LeBlanc
Estimated Sales: $2,500,000
Number Employees: 50-99
Square Footage: 80000
Type of Packaging: Consumer, Food Service, Private Label, Bulk
Brands Exported: Canadian Star; Botsford; Deli-Mare
Regions Exported to: Europe, Middle East, Caribbean, Worldwide
Percentage of Business in Exporting: 100

42536 Bouchard Family Farm
3 Strip Rd
Fort Kent, ME 04743-1550
207-834-3237
Fax: 207-834-7422 800-239-3237
bouchard@ployes.com www.ployes.com
Processor and exporter of buckwheat pancake mixes and flour
Owner: Joseph Bouchard
bouchard@ployes.com
Director: Jane Crawford
Treasurer: Aldan Bouchard
Sales/Marketing Executive: Elaine Mininger
Estimated Sales: Under $200,000
Number Employees: 5-9
Square Footage: 110000
Type of Packaging: Consumer, Food Service
Brands Exported: Bouchard Family Farm
Regions Exported to: Worldwide
Percentage of Business in Exporting: 3

42537 Boundary Fish Company
225 Sigurdson Ave
Blaine, WA 98230-4004
360-332-6715
Fax: 360-332-8785 arnold@boundaryfish.com
www.boundaryfish.com
Dungeness crab, pacific salmon, halibut, black cod, dogfish.
President: Arnold Yuki
Estimated Sales: $ 20 - 50 Million
Number Employees: 20-49
Type of Packaging: Consumer, Food Service
Regions Exported to: Worldwide

42538 Bouras Mop Manufacturing Company
1330 Dolman Street
Saint Louis, MO 63104-2908
314-241-5800
Fax: 314-241-9759 800-634-9153
virgil.bouras@sbcgobal.net
Manufacturer and exporter of corn brooms and brushes, mop heads, deck mops, dust mops and applicators
President: Virgil Bouras
R & D: James Bouras
Estimated Sales: Below $5 Million
Number Employees: 10
Square Footage: 200000
Regions Exported to: Worldwide

42539 Bowers Process Equipment
487 Lorne Avenue E
Stratford, ON N5A 6T3
Canada
519-271-4757
Fax: 519-271-1092 800-567-3223
mail1@clemmersteelcraft.ca www.steelcraft.ca
Manufacturer and exporter of agitators, blenders, bins, kettles, tube fillers, portable air-driven mixers and dairy equipment; also, tanks including mixing
President: Keith Zehr
Chief Executive Officer: Paul Summers
Quality Control: Roy Langford
Marketing: Chris Wyatt
Division Manager, Engineered Products Di: Darcy Vanneste
Operations Manager: Jayson Barlow
Number Employees: 150
Square Footage: 640000
Parent Co: Clemmer Steelcraft Technologies Inc.
Brands Exported: Bowers
Regions Exported to: Worldwide
Percentage of Business in Exporting: 40

42540 Bowman Hollis Mfg Corp
2925 Old Steele Creek Rd
Charlotte, NC 28208-6726
704-374-1500
Fax: 704-333-5520 888-269-2358
sbroadwell@bowmanhollis.com
www.bowmanhollis.com
A full service industrial distributor specializing in industrial belting of all types.
President: Tom Bowman
tbowman@bowmanhollis.com
Marketing/Sales: Steve Broadwell
Sales: Rick Siler
Production Manager: Tom Bowman
Estimated Sales: $5-10 Million
Number Employees: 20-49
Regions Exported to: Central America, South America, Canada, Mexico
Percentage of Business in Exporting: 10

42541 Boxerbrand
423 W Broadway # 202
Boston, MA 02127-2266
617-269-8244
Fax: 617-464-4401 800-253-2772
info@boxerbrand.com www.boxerbrand.com
Owner: David Salk
info@boxerbrand.com
Estimated Sales: $ 3 - 5 Million
Number Employees: 20-49

42542 (HQ)Boxes.com
184 S Livingston Avenue
Suite 9
Livingston, NJ 07039
201-646-9050
Fax: 201-646-0990 www.boxes.com
Manufacturer and exporter of paper folding boxes, point of purchase displays and cardboard inserts
Estimated Sales: $ 1 - 5 Million
Number Employees: 19
Square Footage: 100000
Type of Packaging: Consumer, Food Service, Private Label
Regions Exported to: Central America, South America, Europe, Asia, Middle East
Percentage of Business in Exporting: 25

42543 Boyajian LLC
144 Will Dr
Canton, MA 02021-3704
781-828-9966
Fax: 781-828-9922 800-965-0665
customerservice@boyajianinc.com
www.boyajianinc.com
Vinegars, infused oils and natural flavorings.
Owner/President: John Boyajian
jboyajian@boyajianinc.com
Director of Marketing: Amy Alberti
Human Resources Manager: Zovig Kanarian
General Manager: Zanig Kanarian
Estimated Sales: $1 Million
Number Employees: 10-19
Square Footage: 40000
Type of Packaging: Consumer, Food Service, Private Label, Bulk
Percentage of Business in Importing: 25

42544 Boyd Lighting Company
30 Liberty Ship Way
Suite 3150
Sausalito, CA 94965
415-778-4300
Fax: 415-778-4319 info@boydlighting.com
www.boydlighting.com
Manufacturer, exporter and importer of decorative and architectural interior lighting; designing services available
President: John Sweet Jr
CEO: Jay Sweet
Design Director: Doyle Crosby
Director of Marketing: Erin Geiszler
Sales Manager: Jane Culligan
Estimated Sales: $ 10 - 20 Million
Number Employees: 50-99
Square Footage: 80000
Parent Co: Boyd Lighting Company
Other Locations:
 Boyd Lighting Co.
 Colorado Springs, COBoyd Lighting Co.
Regions Exported to: Central America, Europe, Asia, Middle East, Canada, Caribbean, Latin America, Mexico
Percentage of Business in Exporting: 10
Regions Imported from: Europe, Asia
Percentage of Business in Importing: 5

42545 (HQ)Boyd's Coffee Co
Portland, OR 97230
800-735-2878
customerservicena@farmerbros.com
www.boydscoffeestore.com
Coffees, teas, cocoa, hot and frozen beverages
Senior Sales Manager: Gabriel Dominguez
VP of Manufacturing: Mitch Karstadt
Estimated Sales: $49 Million
Number Employees: 250-499
Number of Brands: 7
Parent Co: Farmer Bros Co
Type of Packaging: Food Service
Other Locations:
 Boyd's Coffee Company
 Coeur D Alene, IDBoyd's Coffee Company
Brands Exported: Boyd's

42546 Bradford A Ducon Company
N25 W23040 Paul Road
Pewaukee, WI 53072-2537
Fax: 800-789-4046 800-789-1718
info@bradfordfittings.com
www.bradfordfittings.com
Manufacturer and importer of stainless steel sanitary fittings, clamps, valves, machined castings and forgings
Quality Control: Bruce Anderson
Marketing: William Duyser
Sales: Jeff Casillo
Operations: Sally Besgrove
Number Employees: 5-9
Square Footage: 40000
Parent Co: Dixon Valve & Coupling
Regions Imported from: Europe, Asia
Percentage of Business in Importing: 90

42547 (HQ)Bradford Soap Works Inc
200 Providence St
West Warwick, RI 02893-2511
401-821-2141
Fax: 401-821-1660 info@bradfordsoap.com
www.bradfordsoap.com
Manufacturer and exporter of cake soap and industrial detergents
CEO: John H Howland
jhowland@bradfordsoap.com
CEO: John H Howland
VP Sales: Ed Windsor
Estimated Sales: $20-50 Million
Number Employees: 250-499
Type of Packaging: Private Label

Importers & Exporters / A-Z

42548 Bradley Lifting
1030 Elm St
York, PA 17403-2597   717-848-3121
    Fax: 717-843-7102 www.bradleylifting.com
Manufacturer and exporter of material handling equipment including slab and ingot tongs, plate and sheet lifters and coil and paper roll grabs
President: Tom Thole
info@bradleylifting.com
CFO: Winfred Bradley
Estimated Sales: $ 5 - 10 Million
Number Employees: 20-49
Parent Co: Xtek, Inc.
Regions Exported to: Worldwide
Percentage of Business in Exporting: 5

42549 Bradman Lake Inc
3050 Southcross Blvd
Rock Hill, SC 29730-9055   803-366-3688
    Fax: 704-588-3302 usa@bradmanlake.com
                www.bradman-lake.com
Specializes in the design and manufacture of packaging machinery
Manager: Steve Irwin
Marketing Director: Mervat El RaFei
Sales Director: Nick Bishop
Plant Manager: Sam Hunnicutt
Estimated Sales: Less Than $500,000
Number Employees: 1-4
Parent Co: Bradman Lake Ltd
Type of Packaging: Bulk
Other Locations:
    Bradman Lake Group
        Charlotte, NCBradman Lake Group
Regions Exported to: Central America, South America, Europe, Asia, Middle East

42550 Brady Enterprises Inc
167 Moore Rd
East Weymouth, MA 02189-2332   781-337-5000
    Fax: 781-337-9338 www.bradyenterprises.com
Manufacturer and exporter of cocktail, powdered drink, stuffing and meatloaf mixes and seasonings; importer of seasoning; also, spray drying and dish detergent
President: Kevin Maguire
Chairman/CEO: John Brady
CFO: Mary Gudalawicz
Director QC/R&D: Mike Waytowich
Director Sales/Marketing: Desi Gould
Human Resources: Jack Brady Jr.
Estimated Sales: $11.60 Million
Number Employees: 100-249
Number of Brands: 3
Number of Products: 16
Type of Packaging: Consumer, Food Service
Regions Exported to: Worldwide
Percentage of Business in Exporting: 2
Regions Imported from: Europe

42551 Bragard Professional Uniforms
201 E 42nd St # 1805
New York, NY 10017-5710   212-759-0202
    Fax: 212-353-0318 800-488-2433
        customersupport@bragardusa.com
                www.bragardusa.com
Manufacturer, importer and exporter of uniforms and special clothing including aprons, linens, chef's hats and coats, footwear, cloth towels, etc.; complete embroidery services available
CEO: Lu Aranzamendez
lua@bragardusa.com
Vice President: Peter Isom
Chief Operating Officer: Benjamin Bragard
Estimated Sales: $1-2.5 Million
Number Employees: 1-4
Parent Co: Bragard SA
Regions Exported to: Canada, Brazil, Mexico
Regions Imported from: France
Percentage of Business in Importing: 75

42552 Bragard Uniforms
30-30 47th Avenue 4th Floo
Long Island City, NY 10001   212-982-8031
    Fax: 212-353-0318 800-488-2433
        customersupport@bragardusa.com
                www.bragardusa.com

42553 (HQ)Brakebush Brothers
N4993 6th Dr
Westfield, WI 53964
                    800-933-2121
                www.brakebush.com
Frozen chicken.
Research & Development Director: Jon Brakebush
Quality Assurance Manager: Donna Halbach
Marketing Manager: Steve Ross
Sales & Marketing Director: Scott Sanders
ssanders@brakebush.com
Production Manager: Steve Deery
VP, Purchasing: Chris Brakebush
Year Founded: 1925
Estimated Sales: $33.5 Million
Number Employees: 500-999
Number of Products: 200+
Square Footage: 500000
Type of Packaging: Consumer, Food Service
Regions Exported to: Worldwide

42554 Bran & Luebbe
1234 Remington Rd
Schaumburg, IL 60173-4812   847-882-8116
    Fax: 847-882-2319 www.pumpsandprocess.com
Manufacturer and exporter of metering pumps, food blending systems and analyzers for determination of protein, fat, moisture and other parameters in food products
President: Robert Arcaro
Marketing Coordinator: Kelly Breitlando
Director Sales: Jim Hunson
Estimated Sales: $ 20-50 Million
Number Employees: 50-99
Square Footage: 36000
Parent Co: Bran & Luebbe GmbH
Regions Exported to: Mexico

42555 Brandmeyer Popcorn Co
3785 NE 70th Ave
Ankeny, IA 50021-9734   515-262-3243
    Fax: 866-631-6276 800-568-8276
                www.lottapop.com
Processor and exporter of popcorn including gift boxes and specialty items
Owner: Arlie Brandmeyer
arlie@lottapop.com
Estimated Sales: $110,000
Number Employees: 1-4
Regions Exported to: South America, Europe, Asia, Caribbean
Percentage of Business in Exporting: 25

42556 Brands of Britain
2410 Camino Ramon
Suite 265
San Ramon, CA 94583   925-806-9400
    Fax: 925-806-9450 800-646-6974
        info@brandsofbritain.com
                www.brandsofbritain.com
Coffee and tea, soups, chutney, natural bars, water, fever-tree mixes
President: Mark Rajeski
Marketing: Mark Rajeski
Contact: Jamie Bresnahan
jamie@brandsofbritain.com
Estimated Sales: $4.5 Million
Number Employees: 8

42557 Brandt Farms Inc
6040 Avenue 430
P.O. Box 852
Reedley, CA 93654-9008   559-638-6961
    Fax: 559-638-6964 www.brandtfarms.com
Peaches, nectarines, plums.
President: Wayne Brandt
CEO: Eleanor Brandt
COO: Jack Brandt
Sales Exec: Dave Maddux
Public Relations: Dave Maddox
davemaddux@treeripe.com
Estimated Sales: $20 Million
Number Employees: 100-249
Square Footage: 60000
Brands Exported: Brandt; Crystal R-Best
Regions Exported to: Central America, South America, Europe, Asia

42558 Branford Vibrator Company
3600 Cougar Drive
Peru, IL 61354-9336   815-224-1200
    Fax: 815-224-1241 800-262-2106
                www.cougarindustries.com
Manufacturer and exporter of pneumatic and electric vibrators
President: D Pedritti
Manager: T Zagorski
Estimated Sales: $20-50 Million
Number Employees: 50
Parent Co: Cougar Industries
Regions Exported to: Europe, Canada
Percentage of Business in Exporting: 5

42559 Branson Ultrasonics Corp
41 Eagle Rd # 1
P.O. Box 1961
Danbury, CT 06810-4179   203-796-0400
    Fax: 203-796-0450 www.emersonindustrial.com
The industry leader in the design, development, manufacture, and marketing of plastics joining, precision cleaning, ultrasonic processing, and ultrasonic metal welding equipment.
President: Ed M Boone
eboone@bransonultrasonics.com
VP Finance: Robert Tibbets
VP/General Manager-North America: Richard Gehrin
VP Sales: Rodger Martin
VP Operations: Anthony Prioreschi
Number Employees: 1000-4999
Regions Exported to: Worldwide

42560 Brass Smith
5125 Race Court
Denver, CO 80216   303-331-8777
    Fax: 303-331-8444 800-662-9595
                www.zguard.com
Manufacturer and exporter of sneeze guards, hot merchandising display cases, railing systems, crowd control posts, menu stands, etc
Human Resources: Dave Carr
Marketing: Wayne Sirmons
Regional Sales Manager: Benny Martinez
Contact: Michael Ackerman
mackerman@bsidesigns.com
Estimated Sales: $5-10 Million
Number Employees: 50-99
Square Footage: 400000
Parent Co: BSI
Regions Exported to: Worldwide

42561 Brasserie Brasel Brewery
8477 Rue Cordner
Lasalle, QC H8N 2X2
Canada   514-365-5050
    Fax: 514-365-2954 800-463-2728
Processor and exporter of lager beers
President: Marcel Jagermann
Managing Director: Stan Jagermann
Number Employees: 10-19
Square Footage: 24000
Type of Packaging: Consumer, Food Service, Private Label
Brands Exported: Hopps Brau; Hopps Aux Pommes; Brasal Light; Brasal Special Amber; Brasal Bock
Regions Exported to: Europe, USA
Percentage of Business in Exporting: 10
Brands Imported: Clausthaler
Regions Imported from: Europe
Percentage of Business in Importing: 10

42562 Bratt-Foster-Advantage Sales
306 Lakeside Rd
Syracuse, NY 13209-9729   315-488-3840
    Fax: 315-488-9079 jlfoster@advanmark.com
Broker of confectionery products, frozen foods, general merchandise, groceries, produce, seafood, etc, serving the areas of Buffalo and Syracuse
President: John Foster
jlfoster@advanmark.com
VP: Stephen Barone
Estimated Sales: $4.1 Million
Number Employees: 10-19
Square Footage: 19500
Brands Imported: M.W. Polar Foods
Regions Imported from: Europe, Asia

42563 Braun Brush Co
43 Albertson Ave
Albertson, NY 11507-2198   516-741-6000
    Fax: 516-741-6299 800-645-4111
                sales@brush.com
Manufacturer, importer and exporter of sanitary cleaning brushes used for baking, confectionery processing, etc
President: Lance Cheney
lance@brush.com
Business Development Director: Peter Lassen
Customer Service: Jerilyn Leis
Accounting: Joan Egidio
Estimated Sales: $2 Million
Number Employees: 20-49

Importers & Exporters / A-Z

Square Footage: 28000
Parent Co: Braun Industries
Type of Packaging: Consumer, Food Service, Private Label, Bulk

42564 Braun Brush Co
43 Albertson Ave
Albertson, NY 11507-2198 516-741-6000
Fax: 516-741-6299 800-645-4111
sales@brush.com
Manufacturer, importer and exporter of USDA standard and custom designed brushes
President: Lance Cheney
lance@brush.com
President: Max Cheney
Director of Business Development: Peter Lassen
Customer Service: Jerilyn Leis
Accounting: Joan Egidio
Estimated Sales: $2.5-5 Million
Number Employees: 20-49
Square Footage: 28000
Regions Exported to: Central America, South America, Europe, Asia
Percentage of Business in Exporting: 5
Regions Imported from: South America, Asia
Percentage of Business in Importing: 1

42565 Bravo Systems International
7347 Atoll Ave
North Hollywood, CA 91605 818-982-7286
Fax: 818-982-7396 800-333-2728
sales@bravo-systems.com
www.bravo-systems.com
Importer of restaurant equipment including espresso and capuccino machines, fresh pasta machines, wood-fired pizza ovens, and toaster grills
Owner: Augusto Bisani
Estimated Sales: $ 3 - 5 Million
Number Employees: 10-19

42566 Brazos Legends
9087 Knight Rd
Houston, TX 77054-4305 713-795-0266
Fax: 713-795-5534 800-882-6253
sbailey@texastamale.com www.texastamale.com
Gourmet food products
President: J Boles
CEO: Shirley Bailey
sbailey@texastamali.com
Sales Director: Shirley Bailey
Operations Manager: Shirley Bailey
Plant Manager: Ana Flores
Estimated Sales: $3-5,000,000
Number Employees: 10-19
Number of Brands: 5
Number of Products: 125
Square Footage: 25000
Type of Packaging: Consumer, Food Service, Private Label, Bulk

42567 Breakwater Fisheries
14 O'Briens Hill
St John's, NL A1B 4G4
Canada 709-754-1999
Fax: 709-754-9712
Processor and exporter of frozen snow crab, capelin, turbot, cod, mackerel, herring, squid and shrimp; importer of frozen squid
President/CEO: Randy Barnes
General Manager/Co-Owner: Lemuel White
Vice President: Ken White
Estimated Sales: $10-20 Million
Number Employees: 500
Number of Brands: 1
Square Footage: 75000
Brands Exported: Breakwater
Regions Exported to: Europe, Asia
Percentage of Business in Exporting: 97
Regions Imported from: South America, Australia
Percentage of Business in Importing: 3

42568 Brechbuhler Scales
1414 Scales St SW
Canton, OH 44706 330-453-2424
Fax: 330-453-5322 www.brechbuhler.com
Manufacturer and exporter of scales including dormant, flour, warehouse, portable, etc
Contact: Mike Ambs
mambs@bscales.com
Manager: Roger Doerr
Branch Manager: Rick Spradling
Estimated Sales: $1-2.5 Million
Number Employees: 160
Parent Co: Brechbuhler Scales

Type of Packaging: Bulk

42569 Brechteen
30060 23 Mile Rd
Chesterfield, MI 48047-5718 586-949-2240
Manufacturer and importer of packaging materials including plastic, cellulose, collagen and fibrous; manufacturer of stuffing equipment
VP of Sales: Roger Allen
Number Employees: 100-249
Brands Imported: Betan; Optan; Tripan; Viscofan; NCC; Coffi
Regions Imported from: Europe
Percentage of Business in Importing: 95

42570 Brecoflex Co LLC
222 Industrial Way W
Eatontown, NJ 07724-2206 732-460-9500
Fax: 732-542-6725 888-463-1400
www.brecoflex.com
Manufacturer, and exporter of polyurethane, USDA and FDA approved timing belts, pulleys, and accessories
President: Bernie Fulleman
VP: Rudolf Schoendienst
Research & Development: Johnathan Weir
Quality Control: Dararith Son
Marketing Director: Joy Guigo
Estimated Sales: $ 2.5 - 5,000,000
Number Employees: 1-4
Regions Exported to: Central America, South America, Canada

42571 Breddo Likwifier
1230 Taney N.
Kansas City, MO 64116 816-561-9050
Fax: 816-561-7778 800-669-4092
don.wolfe@corbion.com www.breddo.com
Manufacturer and exporter of high shear blender with scraped surface heat transfer
President: Ron Ashton
Sales: Don Wolfe
dwolfe@caravaningredients.com
Estimated Sales: $ 5 Million
Number Employees: 10-19
Parent Co: American Ingredients Company
Regions Exported to: Central America, South America, Europe, Asia, Middle East
Percentage of Business in Exporting: 2

42572 Bremner Biscuit Company
4600 Joliet St
Denver, CO 80239-2922 303-371-8180
Fax: 303-371-8185 866-972-6879
bremner@worldpantry.com
www.bremnerbiscuitco.com
Processor and exporter of gourmet, snack and oyster crackers
Manager: Neil Bremner
Contact: Bryan Dare
bdare@darefoods.com
Estimated Sales: $5-10 Million
Number Employees: 20-49
Square Footage: 126000
Parent Co: Dare Foods
Type of Packaging: Consumer, Food Service, Private Label, Bulk
Brands Exported: Bremner
Regions Exported to: Canada
Percentage of Business in Exporting: 1

42573 (HQ)Brenner Tank LLC
450 Arlington Ave
Fond Du Lac, WI 54935-5571 920-922-5020
Fax: 920-922-3303 800-558-9750
sales@brennertank.com www.brennertank.com
Manufacturer, importer and exporter of stainless steel tank transports and intermodal tank containers
President: Bruce D Yakley
byakley@brennertank.com
Sales Manager: Thomas Ballon
Estimated Sales: $20-50 Million
Number Employees: 100-249
Square Footage: 300000
Parent Co: Wabash National Corp.

42574 Brenton Engineering Co
4750 County Road 13 NE
Alexandria, MN 56308-8022 320-852-7705
Fax: 320-852-7621 800-535-2730
bec@becmail.com
www.roboticpackagingsystems.com
Manufacturer and exporter of case packers, handling, robotics, and shrink wrappers

President: Jeff Bigger
Sales: Scott Leuschke
Marketing Director: Karen Kielmeyer
Vice President Sales: Troy Snader
Estimated Sales: $20-50 Million
Number Employees: 100-249
Parent Co: ProMach
Brands Exported: Brenton
Regions Exported to: South America, Europe, Asia
Percentage of Business in Exporting: 10

42575 Brewmatic Company
P.O.Box 2959
Torrance, CA 90509 310-787-5444
Fax: 310-787-5412 800-421-6860
Manufacturer and exporter of thermal coffee servers, commercial and domestic drip brewing equipment and accessories; importer of espresso machines
Manager: Ed Esteban
Research & Development: Traian Zaionciuc
Quality Control: Ron Mann
Marketing Director: Eddison Esteban
Sales Director: Cindi Watson Kramer
Plant Manager: John Galvin
Purchasing Manager: Frank Cherry
Number Employees: 50-99
Square Footage: 300000
Parent Co: Farmer Brothers Company
Type of Packaging: Food Service, Private Label
Other Locations:
  Brewmatic Company
  St. Louis, MOBrewmatic Company
Brands Exported: Brewmatic
Regions Exported to: Central America, South America, Europe, Asia
Percentage of Business in Exporting: 40
Brands Imported: Carimali
Regions Imported from: Europe, Asia

42576 (HQ)Brewster Dairy Inc
800 Wabash Ave S
Brewster, OH 44613 330-767-3492
Fax: 330-767-3386 800-874-8874
www.brewstercheese.com
All natural swiss cheese.
Owner & CEO: Fritz Lehman
VP & Chief Financial Officer: Emil Alecusan
VP Sales & Marketing: James Straughn
Manager National Sales: Mike Walpole
flehman@brewstercheese.com
Plant Manager/Production Development: John Scott
Year Founded: 1965
Estimated Sales: $28.4 Million
Number Employees: 100-249
Square Footage: 78914
Type of Packaging: Consumer, Food Service, Private Label, Bulk
Other Locations:
  Stockton Cheese, Inc.
  Stockton, IL
  Brewster West LLC
  Rupert, IDStockton Cheese, Inc.Rupert
Regions Exported to: Canada

42577 Bri Al
300 Broadacres Dr
Bloomfield, NJ 07003-3153 973-338-0300
Fax: 973-338-0382 www.worldfiner.com
Bri-Al is a specialty importer of products that include bread mixes, condiments, spices, oils and vinegars, cookies, crackers, preserves, spreads and pasta.
Number Employees: 10-19
Parent Co: World Finer Foods

42578 Brick Brewery
400 Bimgemans Centre Drive
Kitchener, ON N2B 3X9
Canada 519-742-2732
Fax: 519-742-9874 800-505-8971
info@waterloobrewing.com
www.waterloobrewing.com
Light and dark lagers, ales, coolers, ciders, craft beers.
Chairman: Peter Schwartz
President/CEO: George Croft
CFO: David J Birch
Director Brewing, Quality and Logistics: Bill Henry
VP Marketing: Norm Pickering
VP Sales: Craig Prentice
Chief Operating Officer: Russell Tabata
Year Founded: 1984
Estimated Sales: $20-50 Million

Number Employees: 20-49
Square Footage: 45000
Type of Packaging: Consumer
Brands Exported: Brick Premium, Brick Red Baron

42579 Bridge Machine Company
614 Kennedy Street
Palmyra, NJ 8065   856-829-1800
Fax: 856-786-8147   877-754-1800
sales@bridgeonline.com   www.bridgeonline.com
Designs and manufactures a complete line of food processing equipment such as patty formers, tenderizers, dumpers/meat tubs, hand tenderizers, cutlet flatteners, meatball formers, macerators, spreading conveyors, dicers and stripcutters
President: Terry Bridge
Contact: David Hicks
david.hicks@bridgeonline.com
Estimated Sales: $ 10 - 20 Million
Number Employees: 50-99
Square Footage: 28000
Regions Exported to: Worldwide
Percentage of Business in Exporting: 15

42580 (HQ)Brinkmann Corporation
4215 McEwen Rd
Dallas, TX 75244   972-387-4939
800-468-5252
Manufacturer and exporter of smokers and cookers; also, lighting including portable emergency, flashlights, lanterns, electronic flashers and electronic assemblies
President: Jon Brinkmann
VP: Erma Eddins
Contact: Brad Adams
badams@thebrinkmanncorp.com
Estimated Sales: $20-50 Million
Number Employees: 100-249

42581 Brisk Coffee Co
402 N 22nd St
Tampa, FL 33605-6086   813-248-6264
Fax: 813-248-2947   800-899-5282
customer@briskcoffee.com   www.briskcoffee.com
Processor and exporter of roasted coffee; also, leasing of coffee equipment available
President/CEO: Richard Perez
VP/COO: Denise Reddick
dreddick@briskcoffee.com
Finance Executive: Julie Beck
Vice President: Mary Perez
VP, Quality Control & Manufacturing: Randy Gonzalez
VP Production: Randall Gonzalez
Estimated Sales: $2.9 Million
Number Employees: 20-49
Square Footage: 40000
Type of Packaging: Food Service
Percentage of Business in Exporting: 80

42582 Brisker Dry Food Crisper
PO Box 7000
Oldsmar, FL 34677   813-854-5231
Fax: 800-854-3069   800-356-9080
Manufacturer and exporter of essential kitchen countertop storage appliances designed to keep crackers, chips, cereals, etc. free of humidity
CEO: Anita Rybicki
Estimated Sales: $ 1 - 5 Million
Number Employees: 7
Number of Brands: 1
Number of Products: 1
Square Footage: 48000
Type of Packaging: Consumer, Food Service
Brands Exported: Brisker
Regions Exported to: Central America, South America
Percentage of Business in Exporting: 1

42583 British Aisles
1634 Greenland Road
Greenland, NH 03840   603-431-5075
Fax: 603-431-5079   800-520-UKOK
sales@britishaisles.com   www.britishaisles.com
Wholesaler/distributor and importer of biscuits, jams, apple juice, condiments, mustards, cereals, tea and chocolate; wholesaler/distributor of health, specialty and private label items
President: Stephanie Pressinger
Co-Founder: Denise Pressinger
Co-Founder: Gerry Pressinger
VP: Gerald Pressinger
Estimated Sales: $1-2.5 Million
Number Employees: 5-9
Square Footage: 40000
Brands Imported: Thursday Cottage; Taylor's Original 1830 Mustard; English Country Chandler; Dorset Cereal; Cole's Traditional Bakery; St. James Tea; Berry Bros & Rudd; DJ Miles & Co.; Picnic Fayre
Regions Imported from: United Kingdom
Percentage of Business in Importing: 90

42584 British Depot
2650 N University Dr
Sunrise, FL 33322-2433   954-746-4469
Fax: 561-243-3138   www.britishdepotonline.com
Importer of British food
President/CEO: Lawrence Miller
Estimated Sales: Less than $500,000
Number Employees: 1-4
Regions Imported from: Europe
Percentage of Business in Importing: 100

42585 British Shoppe LLC
809 N Mills Ave
Orlando, FL 32803-4021   407-898-1634
Fax: 203-245-3477   888-965-1700
gourmet@thebritishshoppe.com
www.thebritishshoppe.com
Importer and wholesaler/distributor of tea and tea accessories
Owner: John Hanson
VP: Fern Grace
Estimated Sales: Less Than $500,000
Number Employees: 1-4
Square Footage: 20000
Brands Imported: Rather Jolly Tea
Regions Imported from: Europe

42586 British Wholesale Imports
5711 Corsa Ave
Westlake Village, CA 91362-4001   818-991-6644
Fax: 818-991-8829   info@bwi-imports.com
www.bwi-imports.com
Importer and wholesaler/distributor of equipment and fixtures, general merchandise, groceries, provisions/meats and specialty and frozen foods and English tea
Owner: Kerry Bamberger
kerry@bwi-imports.com
VP: Susan Wells
Business Development Manager: Jim Owens
Marketing: James Schreiber
HR/ Customer Service Manager: Sue Harwood
Estimated Sales: $10-20 Million
Number Employees: 20-49
Regions Imported from: England

42587 Broadleaf Venison USA Inc
5600 S Alameda St
Vernon, CA 90058-3428   323-826-9890
Fax: 323-826-9830   800-336-3844
support@broadleafgame.com
www.broadleafgame.com
Specialty and exotic meats; Wagyu Beef, Buffalo, Cervena Venison, kurobuta Pork
Owner: Mark Mitchell
broadleaf@broadleafgame.com
CEO: Pat McGowan
CFO: Ara Temuryan
Vice President: Annie Mitchell
Sales Director: Nathan Cooney
broadleaf@broadleafgame.com
Operations Manager: Pierre La Breton
Production Manager: Randy Eves
Plant Manager: Jose Madera
Purchasing Manager: Edward Townsend
Estimated Sales: $20-30 Million
Number Employees: 50-99
Square Footage: 56000
Type of Packaging: Consumer, Food Service
Brands Exported: Broadleaf; Greg Norman Signature Wagyu Premium Beef
Regions Exported to: Central America, South America
Percentage of Business in Exporting: 4
Brands Imported: Broadleaf Cervena
Regions Imported from: New Zealand, Australia
Percentage of Business in Importing: 60

42588 Broaster Co LLC
2855 Cranston Rd
Beloit, WI 53511-3991   608-365-0193
Fax: 608-363-7957   800-365-8278
broaster@broaster.com
www.genuinebroasterchicken.com
Manufacturer and exporter of gas and electric pressure fryers, ventless fryers, warmers, broilers and rotisseries
President: Richard Schrank
rschrank@broaster.com
Vice President: Tracy Choppi
Marketing Director: Mark Markwardt
Sales Director: Randy McKinney
Plant Manager: Gene Halley
Purchasing Manager: Lee Blehinger
Number Employees: 50-99
Brands Exported: Broaster™; Genuine Broaster Chicken™
Regions Exported to: Central America, South America, Europe, Asia, Middle East
Percentage of Business in Exporting: 20

42589 Brock Seed Company
75 Richwood Rd
Finley, TN 38030-3051   731-286-2430
Fax: 760-353-1693
Manufacturer and exporter of asparagus and asparagus seed
Owner: Clark Brock
Manager: Don Brock
Estimated Sales: $210,000
Number Employees: 3
Type of Packaging: Consumer, Food Service, Private Label

42590 Brogdex Company
1441 W 2nd St
Pomona, CA 91766   909-622-1021
Fax: 909-629-4564
Manufacturer and exporter of cleaners and chemicals for use in film/wax coatings for fresh fruits and vegetables; exporter of fruit and vegetable processing and handling equipment
President: Kirk Bannerman
Vice President: Greg Appel
Contact: Linda Smith
lindas@paceint.com
Number Employees: 50-99
Brands Exported: Britex
Regions Exported to: Central America, South America, Asia, Middle East, Mexico, Canada, Latin America
Percentage of Business in Exporting: 10

42591 Brolite Products Inc
1900 S Park Ave
Streamwood, IL 60107-2944   630-830-0340
Fax: 630-830-0356   888-276-5483
info@bakewithbrolite.com
www.bakewithbrolite.com
Flavors, stabilizers, yeast foods, dough accelerators and conditioners, egg yolk and whole egg substitutes and fudge, English muffin and bread bases; exporter of white and rye sour dough flavors
President: David Delghingaro
d.delghingaro@broliteproducts.com
R&D: Daniel Garcia
Marketing/Sales VP: Tom MacDonald
Plant Manager: Mike Koziol
Estimated Sales: $15 Million
Number Employees: 50-99
Square Footage: 108000
Type of Packaging: Bulk
Regions Exported to: Asia, Australia

42592 Brom Food Group
5595 Cote De Liesse
St. Laurent, QC H4M 1V2
Canada   514-744-5152
Fax: 514-744-8195
Processor, importer and exporter of frozen foods and frozen and fresh pierogies including cheese, potato/onion, beef and chicken
Director Marketing: Tom Luczak
Director Operations: Bruce Luczak, M.B.A.
Square Footage: 36000
Type of Packaging: Consumer, Food Service, Private Label, Bulk
Brands Exported: Ogi's
Regions Exported to: USA
Percentage of Business in Exporting: 10
Percentage of Business in Importing: 35

Importers & Exporters / A-Z

42593 Brookfield Farm
24 Hulst Rd.
Amherst, MA 01002 413-253-7991
info@brookfieldfarm.org
www.brookfieldfarm.org
Fresh and frozen pork and beef
President/Ceo: Frank Swan
President/Ceo: Dennis Gleason
Manager: Abbe Vredenburg
abbe@brookfieldfarm.org
Estimated Sales: Less Than $500,000
Number Employees: 500-999
Type of Packaging: Consumer, Food Service

42594 Brooklace
P.O.Box 2038
Oshkosh, WI 54903-2038
Fax: 203-937-4583 800-572-4552
www.brooklace.com
Manufacturer and exporter of paper, foil, glassine and grease-proof doilies, place mats, tray covers, baking cups, cake decorating triangles and hot dog trays
President: Charles Foster
VP of Sales: Brian Schofield
VP of Manufacturing: James Stryker
Estimated Sales: $ 30 - 50 Million
Number Employees: 50-99
Square Footage: 50000
Parent Co: Hoffmaster
Brands Exported: Brooklace
Regions Exported to: Worldwide
Percentage of Business in Exporting: 25

42595 Brooklyn Cider House
1100 Flushing Ave.
Brooklyn, NY 11237 347-295-0308
www.brooklyncidershouse.com
Hard dry craft ciders
Founder/Co-Owner: Peter Yi
Founder/Co-Owner: Susan Yi
Year Founded: 2014
Number of Brands: 1
Number of Products: 5
Type of Packaging: Consumer, Private Label
Brands Exported: Brooklyn Cider House
Regions Exported to: USA

42596 (HQ)Brooklyn Sugar Company
920 E 149th St
Bronx, NY 10455 718-401-1212
Fax: 718-401-3111 800-711-2237
solarwiz@aol.com
Wholesaler/distributor, exporter and importer of sugar and rice products; serving the food service market
Owner/President: Mel Glickman
VP: Mark Glickman
VP: Eric Glickman
Contact: Barbara Glickman
barbara@brooklynsugar.com
Estimated Sales: $20-50 Million
Number Employees: 20-49
Square Footage: 15000
Parent Co: Powerhouse Logistics, Inc.
Type of Packaging: Consumer, Food Service, Private Label, Bulk
Other Locations:
Brooklyn Sugar Co.
Bronx, NYBrooklyn Sugar Co.

42597 Brooks Instrument LLC
407 W Vine St
Hatfield, PA 19440-3000 215-362-3500
Fax: 215-362-3745 888-554-3569
brooksam@brooksinstrument.com
www.brooksinstrument.com
Manufacturer and exporter of measurement instrumentation for gas and liquid flow
President: Jim Dale
Cmo: Jim Hollis
jim.hollis@emersonprocess.com
CFO: Joe Doeters
Quality Control: Kevin Gallagher
R & D: Steve Glaudel
Marketing: T Hannigan
Sales: R Fravel
Number Employees: 100-249
Parent Co: Emerson Electric Company
Regions Exported to: Central America, South America, Europe, Asia, Middle East, Worldwide
Percentage of Business in Exporting: 40
Regions Imported from: Central America, Europe

42598 Brooks Tropicals Inc
18400 SW 256th St
Homestead, FL 33031-1892 305-247-3544
Fax: 305-242-7393 800-327-4833
maryo@brookstropicals.com
Grower, packer and shipper of papayas, avocados, starfruit, limes, passion fruit, mangos, guavas, uglyfruit and other tropical produce.
President: Pal Brooks
CEO: Greg Smith
Year Founded: 1928
Number Employees: 100-249
Type of Packaging: Bulk
Brands Imported: Caribbean Red & Caribbean Sunrise Papayas, Uniq Fruit Limes, Mangos, Key Limes, Coconuts, Malanga, Yams, Yuca, Ginger, Alse, Bomato, Chayote
Regions Imported from: Central America, South America
Percentage of Business in Importing: 60

42599 Brookside Foods
3899 Mt. Lehman Road
Abbotsford, BC V4X 2N1
Canada 604-607-6650
Fax: 604-607-7046 800-468-1714
info@brooksidefoods.com
www.brooksidefoods.com
Base concentrates, fruit fillings, custom ice cream inclusions, confectionery coatings, and paned and deposited chocolate confections, etc. Importer of cocoa butter, cocoal powder, chocolate liquer, etc. Exporter of real fruit chipschocolate, panned and deposited chocolate confections, etc. Custom dry blending and private labeling.
President: Kenneth Shaver
Director Sales: Alan Whitteker
Estimated Sales: $26.5 Million
Number Employees: 150
Parent Co: Brookside Foods
Type of Packaging: Consumer, Private Label, Bulk
Regions Exported to: Worldwide
Percentage of Business in Exporting: 20
Regions Imported from: Worldwide

42600 Brotherhood Winery
100 Brotherhood Plaza Dr
P.O.Box 190
Washingtonville, NY 10992-2279 845-496-3661
Fax: 845-496-8720
contact@brotherhood-winery.net
www.brotherhood-winery.com
wines.
President: Hernan Donoso
Co-Owner: Cesar Baeza
Vice President: Philip Dunsmore
Commercial Assistant, Marketing & Sales: Ren,e Schweizer
Production Manager: Mark Daigle
Plant Manager: Carol Tepper
Estimated Sales: $10 Million
Number Employees: 50
Type of Packaging: Consumer, Food Service, Private Label, Bulk
Regions Exported to: Europe, Asia
Regions Imported from: South America

42601 Brothers International Food Corporation
1175 Lexington Ave
Rochester, NY 14606 585-343-3007
Fax: 585-343-4218
ingredients@brothersinternational.com
brothersinternational.com
Fruit ingredients
President & Co-CEO: Matt Betters
Co-CEO: Travis Betters
Estimated Sales: $6.2 Million
Number Employees: 33
Brands Imported: Lost Vineyards
Regions Imported from: South America, Asia

42602 Brothers Metal Products
1780 E McFadden Ave #117
Santa Ana, CA 92705-4648 714-972-3008
Fax: 714-632-5032
Manufacturer and exporter of vegetable slicers and dryers; also, wash tank conveyors and packaging and receiving tables
President: Gregory Siegmann
Estimated Sales: $600,000
Number Employees: 4
Square Footage: 22000

Type of Packaging: Food Service
Brands Exported: LeGrow
Regions Exported to: Central America, Asia, Middle East, Canada
Percentage of Business in Exporting: 2

42603 Brower
609 Main Street
P.O. Box 2000
Houghton, IA 52631 319-469-4141
Fax: 319-469-4402 800-553-1791
sales@hawkeyesteel.com www.hawkeyesteel.com
Manufacturer and exporter of poultry processing equipment including scalders, pickers, eviscerating equipment and related accessories. Specialize in small and medium plants.
President: Tom Wenstrand
VP Sales: Cindy Wellman
Estimated Sales: $ 10 - 20 Million
Number Employees: 50-99
Square Footage: 400000
Parent Co: Hawkeye Steel Products
Type of Packaging: Consumer
Brands Exported: Batch Pik; Brower; Super Pik; Super Scald
Regions Exported to: Central America, South America, Europe, Asia, Middle East
Percentage of Business in Exporting: 35

42604 Brown & Haley
3500 20th St E
Suite C
Fife, WA 98424
800-426-8400
sweets@brown-haley.com www.brown-haley.com
Manufacturer and exporter of confectionery items including Almond Roca.
President & COO: John Melin
jmelin@brown-haley.com
CFO: Clarence Guimond
Year Founded: 1914
Estimated Sales: $86.9 Million
Number of Brands: 3
Type of Packaging: Consumer, Private Label, Bulk
Brands Exported: Almond Roca Buttercrunch; Belgian Cremes; Mountain Bar; Zingos
Regions Exported to: Central America, South America, Europe, Asia, Middle East

42605 (HQ)Brown Fired Heater
300 Huron St
Elyria, OH 44035-4829 440-323-3291
Fax: 440-323-5734 www.enerconsystems.com
Manufacturer and exporter of process temperature control systems, fluid heat systems and incinerators
President: David Hoecke
dhoecke@enerconsystemsinc.com
Vice President: John Somodi
Estimated Sales: $3 Million
Number Employees: 10-19
Square Footage: 100000
Brands Exported: Super-Trol; Consertherm; Ventomatic; Brown Fired Heater
Regions Exported to: Central America, South America, Asia
Percentage of Business in Exporting: 20

42606 Brown International Corp LLC
333 Avenue M NW
Winter Haven, FL 33881-2405 863-299-2111
Fax: 863-294-2688 info@brown-intl.com
www.brown-intl.com
Manufacturer and exporter of fruit and vegetable processing equipment including extractors, pulpers, finishers, dewaterers, sizers and processing lines
President: Scott Alexander
COO: Pete Devito
pete.d@brown-intl.com
VP: Ann Williams
Sales: Jim Sheppard
Operations: Bryce Adolph
Purchasing: Bruce Strong
Estimated Sales: $20-50 Million
Number Employees: 50-99
Number of Brands: 1
Number of Products: 85
Square Footage: 70000
Brands Exported: Brown
Regions Exported to: Central America, South America, Europe, Asia, Middle East
Percentage of Business in Exporting: 30

Importers & Exporters / A-Z

42607 Brown Machine LLC
330 N Ross St
Beaverton, MI 48612   989-435-7741
Fax: 989-435-2821   877-702-4142
brownmachinegroup.com
Thermoforming machinery
Vice President, Operations & COO: Brian Keeley
Estimated Sales: $42 Million
Number Employees: 100-249
Number of Brands: 1
Square Footage: 140000
Brands Exported: Brown
Regions Exported to: Central America, South America, Europe, Asia, Middle East
Percentage of Business in Exporting: 25

42608 Brown Manufacturing Company
125 New St Ste A
Decatur, GA 30030   404-378-8311
Fax: 404-378-8311   www.bottleopener.com
Manufacturer and exporter of stationary bottle openers; custom imprinting available.
President: David Brim
Number Employees: 1-4
Square Footage: 5000
Brands Exported: Starr
Regions Exported to: Worldwide
Percentage of Business in Exporting: 48

42609 Brown Produce Company
Route 37
Farina, IL 62838   618-245-3301
Fax: 618-245-3552
Eggs and egg products including frozen, liquid, whites, whole and yolk
President: Larry Seger
Vice President: Larry Pemberton
Plant Supervisor: Larry Jahraus
Estimated Sales: $10-20 Million
Number Employees: 50-99
Square Footage: 20000000
Type of Packaging: Consumer, Bulk
Regions Exported to: Canada, Japan, Spain
Percentage of Business in Exporting: 2

42610 Brown's Sign & Screen Printing
8299 Hazelbrand Road NE
Covington, GA 30014-3406   770-786-2257
Fax: 770-784-1324   800-540-3107
Manufacturer and exporter of flags, pennants, banners, signs and advertising specialties; screen printing and lettering services available
President: Mike Brown
Estimated Sales: Less than $500,000
Number Employees: 4
Regions Exported to: Worldwide

42611 Brown-Forman Corp
850 Dixie Hwy.
Louisville, KY 40210   502-585-1100
Fax: 502-774-6633   brown-forman@b-f.com
www.brown-forman.com
Wine, tequila, champagne, whiskey, vodka, scotch, and liqueurs.
Chairman: Garvin Brown
President/CEO: Lawson Whiting
Executive VP/CFO: Jane Morreau
Executive VP/General Counsel/Secretary: Matthew Hamel
Senior VP/Chief Production Officer: Alejandro Alvarez
Year Founded: 1870
Estimated Sales: $3.8 Billion
Number Employees: 4,600
Number of Brands: 18
Type of Packaging: Consumer
Other Locations:
  Atlanta, GA
  Baltimore, MD
  Braintree, MA
  Coral Gables, FL
  Dallas, TX
  Hauppauge, NYBaltimore
Brands Exported: Jack Daniel's, Sonoma-Cutrer
Regions Exported to: Central America, South America, Europe, Asia, Middle East, Australia
Percentage of Business in Exporting: 53
Brands Imported: El Jimador, Finlandia, Chambord
Regions Imported from: South America, Europe

42612 Bruce Coffee Svc Plan USA
77 Weston St
PO Box 987
Hartford, CT 06120-1593   860-527-7253
Fax: 860-524-9130   800-227-6638
info@baronetcoffee.com www.baronetcoffee.com
Manufacturer and importer of coffee.
President: Bruce Goldsmith
Estimated Sales: $10-20 Million
Number Employees: 10-19
Number of Brands: 1
Type of Packaging: Consumer, Food Service, Private Label

42613 Brucia Plant Extracts
3855 Dividend Dr
Shingle Springs, CA 95682   530-676-2774
Fax: 530-676-0574   brucia@naturex.com
www.naturex.com
Antioxidants, colors, herbs & spices oleoresins and essential oils, and botanical extracts for the food, flavor and nutraceutical industries
CEO: Thierry Lambert
Group Marketing Director: Antoine Dauby
Sales: David Yuengniaux
Plant Manager: Chris Young
Purchasing Manager: Romain Bayzelon
Estimated Sales: $45 Million
Number Employees: 20-49
Number of Brands: 10
Number of Products: 400
Square Footage: 85000
Parent Co: Naturex
Type of Packaging: Bulk
Regions Exported to: Europe, Asia, Middle East, Australia
Regions Imported from: South America, Europe, Asia, Middle East

42614 Brulin & Company
2920 Dr Andrew J Brown Ave
Indianapolis, IN 46205   317-923-3211
Fax: 317-925-4596   800-776-7149
www.brulin.com
Manufacturer and exporter of sanitation products including disinfectants, hand care, food sanitation and floor care chemicals. ISO 9002 certified
President: Charles Pollnow
VP Sales/Marketing: Michael Falkowski
Marketing Coordinator: Janet Cleary Salisbury
Marketing Manager (Commerical Products): Garry Thornley
Estimated Sales: $10-20 Million
Number Employees: 100-249
Brands Exported: Brulin
Regions Exported to: Worldwide
Percentage of Business in Exporting: 10

42615 Brum's Dairy
631 Bruham Ave
Pembroke, ON K8A 4Z8
Canada   613-735-2325
Fax: 613-735-2068   www.ic.gc.ca
Process and distribute fresh dairy products as well as fresh juice
President: Stanley W. Brum
Manager: D.A. Fleury
Vice President: Barry D. Brum
Estimated Sales: $12.7 Million
Number Employees: 46
Square Footage: 40000
Type of Packaging: Consumer, Private Label
Brands Imported: Citrus International
Regions Imported from: USA

42616 Brush Research Mfg Co Inc
4642 Floral Dr
Los Angeles, CA 90022-1288   323-261-6162
Fax: 323-268-6587   info@brushresearch.com
Manufacturer and exporter of conveyor brushes.
President: Tara Rands
sales@brushresearch.com
VP: Robert Fowlie
General Manager: Don Didier
Estimated Sales: $5-10 Million
Number Employees: 50-99
Square Footage: 300000
Regions Exported to: Worldwide
Percentage of Business in Exporting: 27

42617 Brute Fabricators
PO Box 1621
Castroville, TX 78009-1621   210-648-2370
Fax: 210-648-5811   800-777-2788
www.bruterack.com
Manufacturer and exporter of heavy structural steel pallet racks including drive-in, drive-thru and cantilever drive-in
President: Fred Siebrecht
CEO: Brandie Siebrecht
CFO: Ben Cogdell
Number Employees: 20
Square Footage: 81000
Parent Co: Brute Fabricators
Regions Exported to: Worldwide
Percentage of Business in Exporting: 10

42618 Bry-Air Inc
10793 E State Route 37
Sunbury, OH 43074-9311   740-965-2974
Fax: 740-965-5470   877-379-2479
info@bry-air.com   www.bry-air.com
Manufacturers of industrial dehumidifiers.
President/CEO: Mel Meyers
bryair1@bry-air.com
Executive VP: Doug Howery
Quality Control: Rick Frenier
Plant Manager: Ron Busch
Purchasing Director: Debra Kemmer
Estimated Sales: $5-10 Million
Number Employees: 20-49
Brands Exported: Bry-Air
Regions Exported to: Central America, South America, Asia, Canada
Percentage of Business in Exporting: 25

42619 Bryan Boilers
783 Chili Ave
Peru, IN 46970   765-473-6651
Fax: 765-473-3074   inquires@bryansteam.com
www.bryanboilers.com
Manufacturer and exporter of boilers, blow down separators, boiler feed systems and de-aerators
President: Tom May
CEO: Dale Bowman
Sales/Marketing Manager: Dick Holmquist
Estimated Sales: G
Number Employees: 250-499
Parent Co: Bryan Steam LLC
Regions Exported to: Worldwide

42620 Bryant Products Inc
W1388 Elmwood Ave
Ixonia, WI 53036-9437   920-206-6920
Fax: 920-206-6929   800-825-3874
www.bryantpro.com
Manufacturer and exporter of tensioning devices for conveyors, straight and tapered rollers, machine grade conveyor pulleys
President: Fred Thimmel
Vice President: Dave Roessler
dave@bryantpro.com
Purchasing: Jody Mack
Estimated Sales: $20-50 Million
Number Employees: 20-49
Square Footage: 50000
Brands Exported: Telescoper
Regions Exported to: Central America, South America, Europe, Australia, Canada, Mexico
Percentage of Business in Exporting: 2

42621 Bubbies Homemade Ice Cream
99-1267 Waiua Pl # B
Aiea, HI 96701-5642   808-487-7218
Fax: 808-484-5800
bubbiesicecream@hawaii.rr.com
www.bubbiesicecream.com
Mocha ice cream
President: Keith Robbins
bubbiesicecream@hawaii.rr.com
CFO: Sandra Robbins
VP: Gertrude Robbins
Quality Control: Jayci Robbins
Marketing/Sales Director: Rick Wiser
National Sales Manager: Wayne Shervey
Public Relations: Jo Lacar
Estimated Sales: $2,9,000,000
Number Employees: 5-9
Square Footage: 18000
Type of Packaging: Bulk
Brands Exported: Bubbies Ice Cream
Regions Exported to: Asia

Importers & Exporters / A-Z

42622 Buck Knives
660 S Lochsa St
Post Falls, ID 83854-5200   208-262-0500
Fax: 208-262-0738   800-326-2825
www.buckknives.com
Manufacturer and exporter of fish fillet knives and cutlery.
Chairman: Charles Buck
CEO: Cj Buck
chuckbuck@buckknives.com
VP Sales/Marketing: Rob Morgan
Estimated Sales: $20-50 Million
Number Employees: 100-249
Square Footage: 200000
Brands Exported: Buck
Regions Exported to: Central America, South America, Europe, Asia, Middle East
Percentage of Business in Exporting: 18

42623 Buckeye International
2700 Wagner Pl
Maryland Heights, MO 63043-3400   314-291-1900
Fax: 314-298-2850
www.buckeyeinternational.com
Manufacturer and exporter of cleaning chemicals including hand soap and floor polish for restaurants
President: Kristopher Kosup
Cio/Cto: Noel Haden
nhaden@buckeyeinternational.com
Estimated Sales: $20-50 Million
Number Employees: 100-249
Type of Packaging: Food Service, Bulk
Regions Exported to: Worldwide

42624 Buckhead Beef
4500 Wickersham Dr
Atlanta, GA 30337-5122   404-355-4400
Fax: 404-355-4541   800-888-5578
hf@buckheadbeef.com   www.buckheadbeef.com
Fresh and frozen specialty cut meat products including beef, veal, lamb and pork
Founder/CEO: Howard Halpern
President: Chad Stine
CFO: Paul Mooring
frcstypauly@yahoo.com
Vice President: Andrew Malcolm
Director of Marketing: Rick Morris
Vice President of Sales: Beverly Ham
Human Resources Executive: Sue Kozbiel
Manager: Chris Aloia
Director of Production: Raymond Morehouse
Director of Purchasing: Jason Lees
Number Employees: 500-999
Type of Packaging: Food Service

42625 Buckhorn Canada
8028 Torbram Road
Brampton, ON L6T 3T2
Canada   905-791-6500
Fax: 905-791-9942   800-461-7579
sales@buckhorncanada.com
www.buckhorninc.com/
Manufacturer, importer and exporter of reusable plastic pallets and boxes for storage, processing, dipping and freezing
Sales Manager: Tim Walsh
Number Employees: 20
Square Footage: 180000
Parent Co: Myers Industries
Regions Exported to: Central America, South America
Percentage of Business in Exporting: 10
Regions Imported from: Europe
Percentage of Business in Importing: 50

42626 (HQ)Buckhorn Inc
55 W Techne Center Dr # A
Milford, OH 45150-9779   513-831-4402
Fax: 513-831-5474   800-543-4454
sales@buckhorninc.com   www.buckhorninc.com
Manufacturer and exporter of reusable plastic packaging systems, including plastic totes, bulk boxes, containers, trays & pallets for shipping & in-process use.
President: R. David Banyard
CEO: R. David Banyard
Dir. Engineering & Product Development: Jack Fillmore
Director of Sales: Lane Pence
Director of Human Resources: Lorraine Gibbs
Parent Co: Meyers Industries Inc.
Brands Exported: Nestier
Regions Exported to: Worldwide
Percentage of Business in Exporting: 5

Brands Imported: Nestier

42627 Buddy Squirrel LLC
1801 E Bolivar Ave
St Francis, WI 53235-5317   414-483-4500
Fax: 414-483-4137   800-972-2658
www.buddysquirrel.com
Processor, exporter and packer of candy including regular and sugar-free boxed, chocolates, brittles, toffees, holiday, mints, molded novelties, etc.; also, nuts, nut mixes and gourmet popcorn
President: Margaret Gile
margaretg@qcbs.com
Number Employees: 100-249
Number of Brands: 2
Number of Products: 2000
Square Footage: 120000
Parent Co: Quality Candy Shoppes
Type of Packaging: Consumer, Food Service, Private Label, Bulk
Regions Exported to: Canada

42628 Budget Blinds Inc
1927 N Glassell St
Orange, CA 92865-4313   714-637-2100
Fax: 714-637-1400   800-800-9250
corporateoffice@budgetblinds.com
www.budgetblinds.com
Manufacturer and exporter of decorative items including centerpieces, candleabras, vases, candlesticks, etc
CEO: John Akins
centralbirmingham@budgetblinds.com
Executive VP: Mark Frankel
Office Manager: Cindy Mason
Number Employees: 1-4
Square Footage: 60000
Brands Exported: Franklinware; Band-It; Finesse; Garden Romance
Regions Exported to: South America, Europe, Middle East, Canada, Mexico
Percentage of Business in Exporting: 10

42629 Buena Vista Historic Tstng Rm
18000 Old Winery Rd
PO Box 1842
Sonoma, CA 95476-4840   707-996-4438
Fax: 707-252-0392   800-926-1266
info@buenavistawinery.com
www.buenavistawinery.com
Manufacturer, importer and exporter of wine and also, importer of champagne
President/CEO: Harry Parsley
CFO/VP: Peter Kasper
Human Resources: Dorothy Kines
Site Manager: Starla Perez
Estimated Sales: $5-10 Million
Number Employees: 20-49
Square Footage: 240000
Type of Packaging: Consumer, Private Label
Brands Exported: Buena Vista Carneros
Regions Exported to: Europe, Asia
Percentage of Business in Exporting: 8
Brands Imported: Maison Thorin; Champagne Bricout; Viala
Regions Imported from: Europe
Percentage of Business in Importing: 1

42630 (HQ)Buffalo Technologies Corporation
750 E Ferry Street
Buffalo, NY 14211-1106   716-895-2100
Fax: 716-895-8263   800-332-2419
sales@buflovak.com   www.btcorp.com
Manufacturer and exporter of food dryers, flaking drums, material handling and lifting equipment, coolers, evaporators, heat exchangers, conveyors, mills, etc
CEO/Chairman: Theodore Dann
Product Manager: Todd Murray
Production Manager: Patrick Scanlon
Estimated Sales: $ 10-20 Million
Number Employees: 2
Square Footage: 500000
Regions Exported to: Central America, South America, Europe, Asia
Percentage of Business in Exporting: 60

42631 Buffalo Trace Distillery
113 Great Buffalo Trce
Frankfort, KY 40601   502-696-5978
800-654-8471
info@buffalotrace.com
www.buffalotracedistillery.com
Bourbon and rum; importer of wine.
Marketing Services Director: Meredith Moody
Public Relations & Events Manager: Amy Preske
Year Founded: 1771
Estimated Sales: $29.3 Million
Number Employees: 100-249
Type of Packaging: Bulk
Regions Exported to: South America, Europe, Asia, Canada
Regions Imported from: Europe
Percentage of Business in Importing: 10

42632 Buffalo Wire Works Co Inc
1165 Clinton St
Buffalo, NY 14206-2825   716-821-7866
Fax: 716-826-8271   800-828-7028
info@buffalowire.com   www.buffalowire.com
Buffalo Wire Works offers screening media for industrial and food processing, including circular screens, taped edge, hooked panel and rolled goods for all major OEM's
CEO: Joseph Abramo
jabramo@buffalowire.com
CFO: George Ulrich
VP of Technology: Erich Steadman
R&D: Zach Hall
Quality Control: Rick Zimmer
Marketing: Melissa Kenneweg
Executive VP of Sales: Dominic Nasso
Customer Service: Beth Dajka
Operations: Kevin Shoemaker
Production: Terrie Battaglia
Plant Manager: Kevin Shoemaker
Purchasing Director: Tom Duriak
Estimated Sales: $ 10 - 20 Million
Number Employees: 100-249
Type of Packaging: Food Service
Regions Exported to: Central America, South America, Asia

42633 Bulk Pack
1025 N 9th St
Monroe, LA 71201   318-387-3260
Fax: 318-387-6362   800-498-4215
sales@bulk-pack.com   www.bulk-pack.com
Manufacturer and exporter of bulk containers including flexible and intermediate
President: Peter Anderson
Quality Control: Jane Burden
VP Marketing/Sales: Peter Anderson
Sales: Ron Shemwell
Estimated Sales: $ 1 - 3 Million
Number Employees: 5-9
Square Footage: 90000
Type of Packaging: Bulk
Brands Imported: Turkey
Regions Imported from: Europe
Percentage of Business in Importing: 25

42634 (HQ)Bulk Sak Intl Inc
103 Industrial Dr
Malvern, AR 72104-2009   501-332-8745
Fax: 501-332-8438   bags@bulksak.com
www.bulksak.com
Bulk shipping containers; importer and exporter of bulk bags
President: Grant Patterson
gpatterson@bulksak.com
VP: Grant Patterson
Vice President/Sales: David Whitt
Plant Manager: Mike Nissen
Estimated Sales: $8,000,000
Number Employees: 50-99
Square Footage: 48500
Type of Packaging: Bulk
Other Locations:
   Bulk Sak
   Memphis, TN Bulk Sak
Regions Imported from: Asia
Percentage of Business in Importing: 50

42635 Bull and Barrel Brewpub
988 Rte. 22
Brewster, NY 10509   845-278-2855
www.bullandbarrelbrewpub.com
IPAs and fruit-flavored Ales
Co-Owner: Rick Cipriani
Co-Owner: Wendy Wulkan
Number of Brands: 1
Number of Products: 6
Type of Packaging: Consumer, Private Label
Brands Exported: Bull and Barrel
Regions Exported to: USA

Importers & Exporters / A-Z

42636 Bullet Guard Corporation
3963 Commerce Dr W
West Sacramento, CA 95691   916-373-0402
          Fax: 916-373-0208 800-233-5632
          Sheila@bulletguardmail.com
          www.bulletguard.com
Manufacturer and exporter of drive-through and walk-up windows including bullet resistant; also, interior counter enclosures; installation and custom fabrication available
President: Karlin Lynch
CFO: Marcia Lynch
Vice President: Ken Lynch
Production Manager: Kevin Lynch
Marketing Director: Jeannine Ricci
Sales Manager: Sheila Lynch
Estimated Sales: $ 3 - 5 Million
Number Employees: 25
Square Footage: 30000
Regions Exported to: Central America, South America, Europe, Asia, Worldwide

42637 Bunge Canada
2190 S. Service Road West
Oakville, ON L6L 5N1
Canada   905-825-7900
          www.bungenorthamerica.com
Oil seeds, protein meals and edible oil products.
Director, Bulk Oil Sales: Steve Caloren

42638 Bunge North America Inc.
1391 Timberlake Manor Pkwy.
Chesterfield, MO 63017   314-292-2000
          www.bungenorthamerica.com
Grain originator, processor and exporter.
CEO: Gregory Heckman
CFO: Luciano Salvatierra
Year Founded: 1918
Estimated Sales: $3.6 Billion
Parent Co: Bunge Limited
Type of Packaging: Consumer, Food Service, Private Label, Bulk
Regions Exported to: Worldwide

42639 Bunker Foods Corp.
79 Madison Ave
2nd Floor
New York, NY 10016   646-738-4020
          info@bunkerfoodscorp.com
Importer of sunflower and chia seeds; as well as beans, chickpeas, corn, peanuts and other products.
President: Nicolas Lartitigoyen
Parent Co: Bunker Foods
Type of Packaging: Consumer, Food Service, Private Label
Regions Imported from: South America
Percentage of Business in Importing: 100

42640 (HQ)Bunn-O-Matic Corp
1400 Adlai Stevenson Dr
Springfield, IL 62703-4291   217-529-6601
          Fax: 217-585-7699 800-352-2866
          www.bunnautomatic.com
Manufacturer and exporter of coffee brewers, decanters, grinders and warmers as well as coffee and iced tea filters, hot water systems, iced tea brewers, water filtration systems, and hot powdered and frozen drink systems
President/CEO: Arthur Bunn
CFO: Gene Wilken
R&D: Robert Kobylarz
Quality Control: Kurt Powell
Sales: John Kielb
Public Relations: Melinda McDonald
Production: John Vanderveldt
Plant Manager: Doug Schwartz
Purchasing Director: John Essig
Estimated Sales: $ 10 - 20 Million
Number Employees: 500-999
Other Locations:
  Bunn-O-Matic Corporation
  Cerritos, CABunn-O-Matic Corporation
Regions Exported to: Central America, South America, Europe, Asia, Worldwide
Percentage of Business in Exporting: 10

42641 Buonitalia
75 9th Ave
New York, NY 10011   212-633-9090
          Fax: 212-633-9717 info@buonitalia.com
          www.buonitalia.com
Gourmet Italian foods including pasta, rice, mushrooms, truffles, flour, jams, oils, cheeses, vinegar, fruit mustard, cookies, biscuits and sweets
Owner: Mimmo Majiulo
Contact: Stacey Bonilla
staceybonilla@buonitalia.com
Manager: Scandt Zyleg
Bookkeeper: Yaribeth Dalmonte
Estimated Sales: $3.8 Million
Number Employees: 20-49
Square Footage: 20000
Parent Co: Misono Food
Type of Packaging: Consumer, Food Service, Private Label, Bulk
Regions Imported from: Europe, Italy
Percentage of Business in Importing: 80

42642 Burgess Enterprises, Inc
1000 SW 34th St
Bldg W2 Suite A
Renton, WA 98057   206-763-0255
          Fax: 206-763-8039 800-927-3286
          marketing@burgessenterprises.net
          www.burgessenterprises.net
Carts and kiosks; importer and exporter of espresso machines
President/CEO: Robert S Burgess
CFO: Don Paschal
Sales: Robert Connor
Contact: Bob Connor
bconnor@burgessenterprises.net
Estimated Sales: Below $2.5 Million
Number Employees: 5-9
Number of Brands: 4
Number of Products: 12
Brands Imported: La Spazial Espresso Machines and Nuova Simonelli Espresso Machines
Percentage of Business in Importing: 40

42643 Burgess Mfg. - Oklahoma
1250 Roundhouse Rd
P.O. Box 237
Guthrie, OK 73044-4700   405-282-1913
          Fax: 405-282-7132 800-804-1913
          bmfg@sbcglobal.net www.burgesspallets.com
Manufacturer and exporter of pallets, boxes, crating and lumber; wholesaler/distributor of lumber, plywood, stretch film, plastic pallets, chipboard and plastic components
Plant Manager: Lee Williams
Estimated Sales: $ 3 Million
Number Employees: 20-49
Square Footage: 42000
Regions Exported to: Central America, South America, Australia, New Zealand, Mexico
Percentage of Business in Exporting: 2

42644 Burke Brands
521 NE 189th St
Miami, FL 33179-3909   305-249-5628
          Fax: 305-651-6018 877-436-7225
          info@cafedonpablo.com www.cafedonpablo.com
Fine specialty coffee and gourmet food products.
President: Darron Burke
Vice President: Eliana Burke
Director of International Sales & Market: Thomas Stout
VP Sales: Carl Fiadini
Contact: Brian Vaughn
bvaughn@burkebrands.com
General Manager: Michele Fera
Production: Gladys Menjura
Estimated Sales: $1.8 Million
Number Employees: 19
Number of Brands: 4
Number of Products: 27
Square Footage: 10000
Type of Packaging: Consumer, Food Service, Private Label, Bulk
Other Locations:
  Burke Brands
  N Miami Beach, FLBurke Brands

42645 Burke Corp
1516 S D Ave
PO Box 209
Nevada, IA 50201-2708   515-382-3575
          Fax: 515-382-2834 800-654-1152
          sales_info@burkecorp.com www.burkecorp.com
Sausages and other prepared meats

President: William Burke Jr.
CFO: Marcy Hansen
SVP: David Weber
VP Research and Development: Casey Frye
Process and Quality Control Manager: Jim Chittenden
Marketing Director: Liz Hertz
VP Sales/Marketing: Doug Cooprider
Director: Scott Licht
VP Purchasing: Thomas Burke
Estimated Sales: $28.9 Million
Number Employees: 250-499
Type of Packaging: Food Service, Private Label, Bulk
Brands Exported: Premoro®; Tezzata®; MagniFoods®; Burke; NaturaSelect™
Regions Exported to: Central America, Asia

42646 Burling Instrument Inc
16 River Rd
P.O. Box 298
Chatham, NJ 07928-1988   973-635-9481
          Fax: 973-635-9530 800-635-2526
          www.burlinginstruments.com
Manufacturer and exporter of temperature controls, limits and sensors; importer of thermostats
President: Bruce Freed
bfreed@burlinginstruments.com
Sr. VP: Roger Nation
VP of Sales: Michael Wetterer
Estimated Sales: $2.5-5 Million
Number Employees: 10-19
Square Footage: 44000
Brands Exported: Jumo
Regions Exported to: Europe
Percentage of Business in Exporting: 2
Brands Imported: Jumo
Regions Imported from: Europe
Percentage of Business in Importing: 5

42647 Burlodge USA Inc
3760 Industrial Dr
P.O.Box 4088
Winston Salem, NC 27105-2637   336-776-1010
          Fax: 336-776-1090 877-738-4376
          info@burlodgeusa.com www.burlodgeusa.com
President: Neil Kirven
pschick@burlodgeusa.com
Sales Exec: Paul Schick
Number Employees: 5-9

42648 Burnett Bros Engineering
20 Magnolia Via
Anaheim, CA 92801-1034   714-526-2448
          Fax: 714-526-4961 info@burnettbros.com
          www.burnettbros.com
Manufacturers and importers of machinery including bunch and shrink wrappers, carton overwrappers, colloid, roll-fed labelers for water, soft drink and milk bottles. Also produce wrapper for cauliflower, cabbage, iceberg lettuceetc
President: Malcolm Burnett
mfburnett@aol.com
Sales VP: Malcolm Burnett
Estimated Sales: Less Than $500,000
Number Employees: 1-4
Brands Imported: Burnley Packaging Machinery; Associated Packaging Equipment; Newrap; G.C. Hurrell; Sung Hung Machinery

42649 (HQ)Burnette Foods
701 US-31
Elk Rapids, MI 49629   231-264-8116
          Fax: 231-264-9597 info@burnettefoods.com
          www.burnettefoods.com
Canned fruits and vegetables including cherries, apples, plumbs, kidney beans, asparagus, green beans and potatoes.
Owner/President: Teresa Amato
CEO: John Pelizzari
CFO: Jennifer Sherman
Quality Manager/Sales Executive: Jennifer Boyer
Operations Manager: Dave Schroderus
Production Manager: Eric Rockafellow
Plant Manager: Gary Wilson
Estimated Sales: $40-$50 Million
Number Employees: 50-99
Square Footage: 12066
Type of Packaging: Consumer, Food Service
Other Locations:
  Burnette Foods Plant
  East Jordan, MI
  Burnette Foods Plant
  Hartford, MIBurnette Foods PlantHartford

Importers & Exporters / A-Z

Regions Exported to: Worldwide

42650 Burrows Paper Corp
501 W Main St # 1
Little Falls, NY 13365-1899   315-823-2300
        Fax: 315-823-0867 800-272-7122
papersales@burline.com www.burrowspaper.com
Integrated paper manufacturer with operations in the US and Europe.
President/CEO: R W Burrows
Corporate Secretary: Margaret Goldman
Corporate VP: Michael Lengvarsky
VP/General Manager: Hai Ninh
Vice President, Sales: Duane Judd
Estimated Sales: $20-50 Million
Number Employees: 1000-4999
Square Footage: 120000
Type of Packaging: Food Service
Regions Exported to: Asia, Canada
Percentage of Business in Exporting: 3

42651 Bush Brothers ProvisionCo
1931 N Dixie Hwy
West Palm Beach, FL 33407-6084   561-832-6666
        Fax: 561-832-1460 800-327-1345
orders@bush-brothers.com
www.bush-brothers.com
Processor and exporter of fresh and frozen portion cut beef, veal, lamb, pork and poultry; wholesaler/distributor of dairy products; serving the food service market.
President: Harry Bush
sales@bushb-brothers.com
Vice President: Billy Bush
Sales Manager: Doug Bush
Operations Manager: John Bush
Estimated Sales: $13.3 Million
Number Employees: 20-49
Square Footage: 10000
Type of Packaging: Consumer, Food Service, Private Label, Bulk
Regions Exported to: Caribbean
Percentage of Business in Exporting: 10

42652 Bush Refrigeration Inc
1700 Admiral Wilson Blvd # A
Pennsauken, NJ 08109-3990   856-963-1801
        Fax: 856-361-2772 800-220-2874
info@bushrefrigeration.com
www.bushrefrigeration.com
Manufacturer and exporter of walk-in, display and storage coolers and freezers. Refrigerated deli and bakery display cases. Prep tables and under the counter prep tables.
Owner: Alex Bush
abush@bushrefrigeration.com
Estimated Sales: $2.5-5 Million
Number Employees: 20-49
Regions Exported to: Worldwide

42653 Bushman Equipment Inc
W133n4960 Campbell Dr
Menomonee Falls, WI 53051-7056   262-790-4200
        Fax: 262-790-4202 800-338-7810
www.bushman.com
Manufacturer and exporter of material handling equipment including cranes, hooks, coil, sheet and pallet lifters, beams, spreaders, blocks and tongs
President: Ralph Deger
custinfo@bushman.com
Sales Manager: Chuck Nettesheim
Estimated Sales: $20-50 Million
Number Employees: 20-49
Brands Exported: Bushman
Regions Exported to: Central America, South America, Mexico

42654 Busse/SJI Corp
124 N Columbus St
Randolph, WI 53956-1204   920-326-3131
        Fax: 920-326-3134 800-882-4995
inquiry@arrowheadsystems.com
www.arrowheadsystems.com
Manufacturer and exporter of palletizers and depalletizers for glass, can and plastic beverage containers; also, retort crate loading and unloading
President: Thomas Young
tyoung@arrowheadsystems.com
Marketing Director: Nick Osterholt
Sales Manager: Dan Erdman
General Manager: George Vroom
Number Employees: 50-99
Parent Co: Arrowhead Systems

Other Locations:
Busse
Shelton, CT Busse
Regions Exported to: Central America, South America, Europe, Asia, Middle East
Percentage of Business in Exporting: 30

42655 Butter Buds Food Ingredients
2330 Chicory Rd
Racine, WI 53403-4113   262-598-9900
        Fax: 262-598-9999 800-426-1119
bbfi@bbuds.com www.bbuds.com
Processor and exporter of cholesterol-free butter flavored oils and sprays; also, natural dairy concentrates including butter, cheese and cream.
CEO: Jonh Buhler
Director of Business Development: Tom Buhler
Director of Administration: Jan Schmaus
General Manager: Bill Buhler
Estimated Sales: $5-10 Million
Number Employees: 50
Square Footage: 10000
Type of Packaging: Consumer, Food Service, Private Label, Bulk
Regions Exported to: Worldwide
Percentage of Business in Exporting: 25

42656 Buzzards Bay Trading Company
PO Box 600
Fairhaven, MA 02719-0600   508-996-0242
        Fax: 508-996-2421
Fresh and frozen seafood

42657 Bylada Foods
140 W Commercial Ave
Moonachie, NJ 07074-1703   201-933-7474
        Fax: 201-933-1530 www.chefgustofoods.com
Frozen pizza and pizza bagels including regular and bite-size; exporter of pizza bagels
Vice President: Eric Silverman
eric@byladafoods.com
VP: Eric Silbeerman
Office Manager: Fay Campisi
Production Manager: Dan D'Amico
Estimated Sales: $5-10 Million
Number Employees: 10-19
Square Footage: 38000
Type of Packaging: Consumer, Food Service, Private Label
Brands Exported: Bocconcino
Regions Exported to: Canada
Percentage of Business in Exporting: 10

42658 (HQ)Byrd International
30165 Wildlife Lane
Salisbury, MD 21804   410-749-7075
        Fax: 410-749-7029 Don@byrdinternational.com
www.byrdinternational.com
Pasteurized crab meat
Owner/President: Thomas Ruark
President: Lloyd Byrd
National Sales Manager: Ron Johnson
Regions Imported from: South East Asia

42659 Byrnes & Kiefer Company
131 Kline Avenue
Callery, PA 16024   724-538-5200
contactus@bkcompany.com
www.bkcompany.com
Bakery products, including baking supplies, fillings and icings, and read-to-eat baked goods, such as brownies, cookies, and pastries.
Year Founded: 1902
Estimated Sales: $10-20 Million
Number Employees: 20-49
Square Footage: 60000
Type of Packaging: Food Service, Private Label
Brands Exported: Chefmaster
Regions Exported to: Central America, South America, Europe
Percentage of Business in Exporting: 15

42660 C & D Valve Mfg Co
201 NW 67th St
Oklahoma City, OK 73116-8247   405-843-5621
        Fax: 405-840-0443 800-654-9233
www.cdvalve.com
Manufacturer and exporter of valves for refrigeration equipment
President: Brad Denning
bdenning@cdvalve.com
Estimated Sales: $ 5 - 10 Million
Number Employees: 20-49

42661 C & E Canners Inc
1249 Mays Landing Rd
PO Box 229
Hammonton, NJ 08037-2816   609-561-1078
        Fax: 609-567-2776
Processor, exporter and canner of sauces and ketchup
President: Robert Cappuccio
r.cappuccio@chi-rho.com
Corporate Secretary: Joseph Cappuccio
COO: David Cappuccio
Director Manufacturing: Stephen Cappuccio
Estimated Sales: $1.3 Million
Number Employees: 20-49
Square Footage: 320000
Type of Packaging: Consumer
Regions Exported to: Caribbean
Percentage of Business in Exporting: 2

42662 (HQ)C & F Foods Inc
15620 E Valley Blvd
City Of Industry, CA 91744-3926   626-723-1000
        Fax: 626-723-1212 mmendoza@cnf-foods.com
www.cnf-foods.com
Dried beans, lentils, popcorn, peas and rice
President & CEO: Luis Faura
CFO: Alex Tran
VP Sales & Marketing: Paul Cromidas
Sr. Director of Operations: Mark Mendoza
Year Founded: 1975
Estimated Sales: $32.6 Million
Number Employees: 100-249
Type of Packaging: Consumer, Food Service, Private Label
Other Locations:
C&F Foods
Hansen, ID
C&F Foods
Sikeston, MO
C&F Foods
Manvel, ND
C&F Food
Raleigh, NC C&F Foods Sikeston
Regions Exported to: Worldwide

42663 C & K Machine Co
56 Jackson St # 1
Holyoke, MA 01040-5582   413-536-8122
        Fax: 413-532-9819 email@ckmachine.com
www.ckmachine.com
Manufacturer and exporter of nonshrink, conforming wrapping machines for cookies, candies and sandwiches; also, bakery slicing machines and gum and candy cartoners
President: James Tallon
jjtallon@hge.net
Sales/Marketing: James Tallon
Estimated Sales: $1-3 Million
Number Employees: 1-4
Square Footage: 24000
Brands Exported: Wrap King; Redington
Regions Exported to: Worldwide
Percentage of Business in Exporting: 35

42664 C C Pollen
3627 E Indian School Rd # 209
Phoenix, AZ 85018-5134   602-957-0096
        Fax: 602-381-3130 800-875-0096
beemail1@ccpollen.com www.beepollen.com
Bee pollen and beehive products
President: Bruce Brown
Estimated Sales: $7 Million
Number Employees: 10-19
Number of Brands: 7
Type of Packaging: Consumer, Food Service, Private Label, Bulk
Brands Exported: High Desert; Pollenergy; Presidents Lunch; First Lady's Lunch; 24-Hour Royal Jelly
Regions Exported to: Europe, Asia, Middle East, Canada

42665 C E Elantech Inc
170 Oberlin Ave N # 5
Suite 5
Lakewood, NJ 08701-4548   732-370-5559
        Fax: 732-370-3888 888-232-4676
sales@ceelantech.com www.ceelantech.com
Importer of nitrogen/protein analyzers
President: Richard Hancock
rick@ceelantech.com
Estimated Sales: $2.5-5 Million
Number Employees: 5-9
Square Footage: 14400

Regions Exported to: Europe
Percentage of Business in Exporting: 100
Brands Imported: CE Instruments
Regions Imported from: Italy
Percentage of Business in Importing: 100

42666 C E Rogers Co
1895 Frontage Rd
PO Box 118
Mora, MN 55051-7133   320-679-2172
Fax: 320-679-2180   800-279-8081
cerogers@cerogers.com www.cerogers.com
Manufacturer, exporter and importer of free-standing multi-effect and waste water evaporators, horizontal and vertical spray dryers and related heating and cooling equipment; installation service available
President/Sales: Howard Rogers
hrogers@cerogers.com
Chief Engineer: Steven Degeest
Parts: Carol Dutton
Estimated Sales: $ 5-10 Million
Number Employees: 20-49
Square Footage: 8000
Parent Co: CFR Group
Brands Exported: C.E. Rogers Co.
Regions Exported to: Worldwide
Percentage of Business in Exporting: 40
Regions Imported from: Worldwide
Percentage of Business in Importing: 50

42667 C E Zuercher
7415 Saint Louis Ave
Skokie, IL 60076-4031   847-324-0400
Fax: 847-324-0396 web@zuercher.biz
www.zuercher.biz
Specialty cheeses and specialty foods.
Contact: Althea Allen
aallen@zuercher.biz
Number Employees: 10-19

42668 C F Gollott & Son Seafood
9357 Central Ave
PO Box 1191
Diberville, MS 39540-5301   228-392-2747
Fax: 228-392-3701 cfgollot@gmail.com
www.gollottseafood.com
Frozen shrimp
Co-Owner: Brian Gollott
Co-Owner: Armond Gollott
Co-Owner: Dale Gollott
Co-Owner: Nicky Gollott
Plant Operations: Todd Gollott
Estimated Sales: $20-50 Million
Number Employees: 50-99
Square Footage: 7800
Type of Packaging: Consumer, Food Service, Private Label
Regions Imported from: South America
Percentage of Business in Importing: 10

42669 C H Babb Co Inc
445 Paramount Dr
Raynham, MA 02767-5178   508-977-0600
Fax: 508-977-1985 sales@chbabb.com
www.tunnelovens.com
Manufacturer and exporter of automated final proofers, tunnel ovens, cooling conveyors and complete systems for pizza, bagels, breads and rolls, pastries, pies, etc
President: Charles Foran
cforan@babbco.com
Sales Representative: William Foran
Number Employees: 20-49
Square Footage: 150000
Brands Exported: Babbco
Regions Exported to: Worldwide
Percentage of Business in Exporting: 35

42670 C Nelson Mfg Co
265 N Lake Winds Pkwy
Oak Harbor, OH 43449-9012   419-898-3305
Fax: 419-898-4098   800-922-7339
nelsonoh@aol.com
Manufacturer and exporter of refrigerated pushcarts and ice cream storage cabinets
Owner: Kelley Smith
Sr. Engineer: Paul Cox
Sales Manager: Tammy Almendinger
nelsonoh@aol.com
Account Manager: Tammy Almendinger
Purchasing: Paul Zylka
Estimated Sales: $10-20 Million
Number Employees: 20-49
Square Footage: 40000

42671 C P Industries
560 N 500 W
Salt Lake City, UT 84116-3429   801-521-0313
Fax: 801-539-0510   800-453-4931
info@cpindustries.net
Manufacturer and exporter of industrial and household cleaners, ice melters and detergents
Owner: Ann Lieber
ann@cpindustries.net
National Detergent Manager: Ted Olsen
Estimated Sales: $ 10 - 20 Million
Number Employees: 20-49
Square Footage: 500000
Type of Packaging: Consumer, Food Service, Private Label, Bulk
Brands Exported: CP Industries
Regions Exported to: South America, Europe, Asia
Percentage of Business in Exporting: 5

42672 C P Vegetable Oil
601 SW 21st Terrace
Suite 1
Fort Lauderdale, FL 33312-2278
Canada   954-584-0420
Fax: 905-792-9461   800-398-7154
info@cpvusa.com www.cpvegoil.com
Vegetable oils
Ceo: Christian Pellerin
Manager: Giuseppe Vinci
gvinci@cpvusa.com
Number Employees: 10-19
Type of Packaging: Food Service, Bulk

42673 C Pacific Foods Inc
13503 Pumice St
Norwalk, CA 90650-5250   562-802-2199
Fax: 562-802-3022 www.cpacificfoods.com
Wholesaler/distributor, importer and exporter of canned goods, seafood and food ingredients, paper products and specialty food; serving the food service market; also, warehouse for canned goods, specialty Asian cuisine
President: Eric Chan
Sales Manager: Ed Chan
Manager: Ed Chan
Operations Manager: Alice Shih
Estimated Sales: $1-2.5 Million
Number Employees: 10-19
Square Footage: 200000
Type of Packaging: Food Service
Brands Imported: Jack Pot; Sunpak; Sunrise
Regions Imported from: Europe, Asia
Percentage of Business in Importing: 65

42674 C R Daniels Inc
3451 Ellicott Center Dr
Ellicott City, MD 21043-4191   410-461-2100
Fax: 410-461-2987   800-933-2638
info@crdaniels.com www.crdaniels.com
Manufacturer and exporter of conveyor belting, trucks and plastic totes, carts, hampers and tubs; importer of cotton duck
President: Gary Abel
CEO: Gary V Abel
Vice President: Vic Keeler
Quality Control: J Singh
Estimated Sales: $ 20 - 50 Million
Number Employees: 100-249
Square Footage: 250000
Brands Exported: Dandux
Regions Exported to: Central America, South America, Canada
Percentage of Business in Exporting: 5
Regions Imported from: Asia
Percentage of Business in Importing: 8

42675 C R Mfg
10240 Deer Park Rd
Waverly, NE 68462-1416   402-786-2000
Fax: 402-786-2096   877-789-5844
lisag@pmc-group.com
Manufacturer and exporter of plastic pour spouts, scoops, spreaders, spatulas, funnels, knives, spoons, bowls, pitchers, corkscrews, tongs, etc
General Manager: Daryl Chapelle
Quality Control: Ace Dettinger
Vice President: Mary Gaber
mary.gaber@pmc-group.com
Estimated Sales: $ 5 - 10 Million
Number Employees: 100-249

42676 C W Cole & Co
2560 Rosemead Blvd
South El Monte, CA 91733-1593   626-443-2473
Fax: 626-443-9253 info@colelighting.com
www.colelighting.com
Custom lighting fixtures for cooking hoods, walk-in coolers and salad bar/pie cases; also, refrigerator door light switches
President: Stephen W Cole
scole@colelighting.com
Co-Owner: Donald Cole
Sales Manager: Sam Serrano
Sales Engineer: Kevin Brummett
Engineering & Design: Dan Wilkins
Plant Manager: Gustavo Castillo
Purchasing Manager: Jim Cotney
Estimated Sales: $5 Million
Number Employees: 20-49
Square Footage: 50000
Regions Exported to: Asia, Canada, Caribbean
Percentage of Business in Exporting: 1

42677 C&H Store Equipment Company
2530 S Broadway
Los Angeles, CA 90007   213-748-7165
Fax: 213-749-6135   800-648-4979
Manufacturer, wholesaler/distributor and exporter of store fixtures, office furniture, showcases, and metal shelving
CEO: Cheon Kim
Estimated Sales: $ 2.5-5,000,000
Number Employees: 10-19
Regions Exported to: Worldwide

42678 C&P Additives
950 Peninsula Corp Cir
Suite 3018
Boca Raton, FL 33487   561-995-7071
Fax: 561-995-7075   877-857-2623
office@cp-additives.com www.cp-additives.com
Seasonings and enzymes
Type of Packaging: Private Label, Bulk
Regions Exported to: South America, Europe, Asia, Canada, Mexico, Africa

42679 C&T Refinery
PO Box 9300
Minneapolis, MN 55440   804-287-1340
Fax: 804-285-9168   800-227-4455
www.cargill.com
Processor and exporter of vegetable oil
President: C Sauer
VP: Robert Holden
Parent Co: C.F. Sauer Company
Type of Packaging: Consumer, Food Service, Private Label, Bulk
Regions Exported to: Europe, Canada

42680 C. Cretors & Company
3243 N California Ave
Chicago, IL 60618   773-588-1690
Fax: 773-588-2171   800-228-1885
info@creators.com www.cretors.com
Manufacturer and exporter of popcorn machines and cotton candy equipment and supplies
President: Andrew Cretors
CFO: Dan Williams
Quality Control: Walter Karzak
Marketing Manager: Beth Cretors
Product Manager: John Concannon
Estimated Sales: $ 10 - 20 Million
Number Employees: 100-249
Square Footage: 106000
Brands Exported: Cretors; Flo-Thru
Regions Exported to: Central America, South America, Europe, Asia, Middle East
Percentage of Business in Exporting: 40

42681 C. Gould Seafoods
PO Box 14566
Scottsdale, AZ 85267-4566   480-314-9250
Fax: 480-314-9240
Seafood
President: Carla Gould
Owner: Carlos Garcia
Secretary/Treasurer: Helen Sambrano
Vice President: Robert Llewellyn
Estimated Sales: $550,000
Number Employees: 4

Importers & Exporters / A-Z

42682 C.B. Powell Limited
2475 Skymark Avenue
Suite #1
Mississauga, ON L4W 4Y6
Canada   905-206-7776
    Fax: 905-625-7034 800-769-2750
                www.cbpowell.com
Full service buy & sell sales and marketing company specializing in imported consumer packaged goods. Markets served: Mass Merchant, Gas & Convenience, Club, Food.
CEO/Chair: Tim Powell
VP Finance/Administration: Drew Macaskill
EVP: Colin Glaysher
Director Brand Development: Stan Atkinson
Director Sales: Pam Tetford
Director IT/Human Resources: Theresa Flores
Estimated Sales: $11.3 Million
Number Employees: 30
Type of Packaging: Consumer, Food Service, Private Label, Bulk

42683 C.E. Fish Company
69 Roque Bluffs Road
Jonesboro, ME 4648   207-434-2631
           Fax: 207-434-6940
Soft-shelled and steamer clams
President: Barbara Fish
Treasurer: Marge Fish
Vice President: Ralph Fish
Estimated Sales: $83,000
Number Employees: 5-9
Square Footage: 10500
Type of Packaging: Consumer
Regions Exported to: Asia

42684 C.H. Robinson Co.
14701 Charlson Rd
Eden Prairie, MN 55347-5076   952-683-2800
    Fax: 952-933-4747 855-229-6128
   solutions@chrobinson.com www.chrobinson.com
Provides: freight transportation (TL, intermodal, ocean, and air freight), cross docking, LTL, customs brokerage, freight forwarding and trucking services, fresh produce sourcing, and information services.
CEO: Bob Biesterfeld
President, NA Surface Transportation: Mac Pinkerton
CFO: Mike Zechmeister
President, Global Freight Forwarding: Michael Short
Year Founded: 1905
Estimated Sales: $14.87 Billion
Number Employees: 15,074
Type of Packaging: Consumer, Food Service, Bulk

42685 C.L. Deveau & Son
PO Box 1
Salmon River, NS B0W 2Y0
Canada   902-649-2812
          Fax: 902-649-2812
Salted fish and frozen herring roe
President: Irvan Paul Deveau
Number Employees: 10-19
Type of Packaging: Consumer, Food Service, Private Label, Bulk
Regions Exported to: Worldwide

42686 C.M. Goettsche & Company, Inc.
106 Allen Road
Basking Ridge, NJ 07920   908-580-9100
   Fax: 908-580-9300 sales@strohmeyer.com
                www.strohmeyer.com
Importer of bulk honey. Also a supplier of private label canned vegetables and fruit
President: Charles Kocot
charles.kocot@strohmeyer.com
Parent Co: Strohmeyer & Arpe Company
Type of Packaging: Bulk
Regions Exported to: Europe
Percentage of Business in Exporting: 10

42687 CAI International
Steuart Tower
1 Market Plaza, Suite 900
San Francisco, CA 94105   415-788-0100
       Fax: 415-788-3430 www.capps.com
Wholesaler/distributor, importer and exporter of groceries, wine, beer, sherry and port.
President & CEO: Victor Garza
VP, Information Technology: Matthew Easton
Chief Financial Officer: Timothy Page
VP, Finance & Corporate Controller: David Morris
SVP, Global Marketing: Daniel Hallahan
SVP, Logistics Sales & Marketing: Jason Miller
VP, Operations & Human Resources: Camille Cutino
Estimated Sales: $174 Million
Number Employees: 91
Type of Packaging: Consumer, Food Service
Regions Exported to: South America, Asia
Percentage of Business in Exporting: 5
Regions Imported from: South America, Europe, Asia, South Africa
Percentage of Business in Importing: 75

42688 CBORD Group Inc
61 Brown Rd
Ithaca, NY 14850-1247   607-257-2410
    Fax: 607-257-1902 800-982-4643
         sales@cbord.com www.cbord.com
Manufacturer and exporter of computer software that generates LTC food service, tickets, nourishment labels, production tallies, recipes, inventory, nutritional analysis, etc
President: Max Steinhardt
mxs@cbord.com
Vice President of Client Support and Edu: Nancy Sullivan
Vice President of Human Resources: Lisa Patz
Executive Vice President: Bruce Lane
Director of Development, Odyssey Systems: Shane Boyer
VP, Marketing: Cindy McCall
VP, Sales: Read Winkelman
Director of Contract Administration: Chris Curkendall
Senior Director, Service Operations: Jodi Denman
Estimated Sales: Below $5 Million
Number Employees: 250-499
Parent Co: GeriMenu
Brands Exported: GeriMenu
Regions Exported to: Canada

42689 CCL Container
105 Gordon Baker Rd
Suite 500
Toronto, ON M2H 3P8
Canada   416-756-8500
             ccl@cclind.com
             www.cclind.com
Manufacturer and exporter of aluminum aerosol cans and tubes
President & CEO: Geoffrey Martin
Executive Chairman: Donald Lang
Vice President, General Manager: Andy Iseli
Sales Manager: Joe Meldrew
Senior Vice President of Corporate Commu: Janis Wade
Estimated Sales: $1 - 5 Million
Regions Exported to: Central America, Europe

42690 CCS Stone, Inc.
9-11 Caeser Place
Moonachie, NJ 07074-1702   201-933-1515
    Fax: 201-933-5744 800-227-7785
     info@ccsstone.com www.ccsstone.com
Manufacturer and importer of restaurant and bar furniture including chairs, barstools, marble and granite tabletops and bases
President: Donald Mitnick
Controller: Corey Mitnick
VP: John Mitnick
Purchasing Manager: Michael Rivkin
Estimated Sales: $5-10 Million
Number Employees: 20-49
Square Footage: 200000
Regions Exported to: Caribbean, Canada, Mexico
Percentage of Business in Exporting: 10
Regions Imported from: Central America, South America, Europe, Asia, Canada
Percentage of Business in Importing: 90

42691 CCi Scale Company
PO Box 1767
Clovis, CA 93613   559-325-7900
    Fax: 888-693-2792 800-900-0224
      sales@cciscale.com www.cciscale.com
Manufacturer and importer of mechanical, electronic digital, portable, portion control, receiving, counting and battery operated scales
CEO: Tom Bouton
Sales Manager: Terri McGinn
Estimated Sales: Below $5 Million
Number Employees: 1-4
Brands Imported: CCI
Regions Imported from: Asia

42692 CDI Service & Mfg Inc
2181 34th Way
Largo, FL 33771-3952   727-536-2207
       Fax: 727-536-2208 www.cdimfg.com
Manufacturer and exporter of booths, tables and bars; also, custom design services available.
President: David Goudy
VP: Deborah Goudy
Sales Director: David Goudy
Estimated Sales: Less than $900,000
Number Employees: 5-9
Square Footage: 15200
Type of Packaging: Food Service, Private Label
Regions Exported to: Worldwide
Percentage of Business in Exporting: 5

42693 CEA Instrument Inc
160 Tillman St # 2
Suite 1
Westwood, NJ 07675-2624   201-967-5660
    Fax: 201-967-8450 888-893-9640
      ceainstr@aol.com www.ceainstr.com
Manufacturer, importer and exporter of monitors for toxic and combustible gas and oxygen levels
Manager: Steven Adelman
ceainstr@aol.com
Vice President: Steve Adelman
General Manager: Martin Adelman
Estimated Sales: $2-3 Million
Number Employees: 5-9
Number of Brands: 4
Number of Products: 18
Square Footage: 8000
Brands Exported: Gas Baron; Gas Baron 2; CEA 266; Series U; MD-16
Regions Exported to: Worldwide
Percentage of Business in Exporting: 10
Brands Imported: Riken Keiki; Bionics; GMI; Gas Data; Crowcon
Regions Imported from: Europe, Asia
Percentage of Business in Importing: 60

42694 CEM Corporation
3100 Smith Farm Rd
Matthews, NC 28104-5044   704-821-7015
    Fax: 704-821-7894 800-726-3331
         info@cem.com www.cem.com
Manufacturer and exporter of microwave instruments for moisture/solids, protein and fat analysis; also, digestion and solvent extraction systems and muffle furnaces.
Owner: Michael Collins
Senior Research & Development Scientist: Alicia Stell
Marketing Manager: Keller Barnhardt
Director of North American Sales: Bobbie McManus
Director of Manufacturing: Cathy McDonald
Estimated Sales: $20 - 30 Million
Number Employees: 100-249
Square Footage: 60000
Brands Exported: MAS-7000; FAS-9001; Star Systems; Mars 5; Smart Systems
Regions Exported to: Worldwide
Percentage of Business in Exporting: 45

42695 CHLU International
P.O. Box 10027
Toronto, ON M2M 4K3
Canada   416-250-7098
Research and development of innovative nutraceutical ingredients
President: Richard Lu
Number of Brands: 7
Number of Products: 25
Square Footage: 15000
Type of Packaging: Bulk

42696 CHS Inc.
5500 Cenex Dr.
Inver Grove Hts., MN 55077   651-355-6000
                           800-328-6539
                www.chsinc.com
Agriculture, energy, transportation and business services company, with food products through subsidiary Ventura Foods.
President/CEO: Jay Debertin
Executive VP/CFO: Olivia Nelligan
Executive VP/General Counsel: Jim Zappa

204

Estimated Sales: $32.6 Billion
Number Employees: 10000+
Type of Packaging: Consumer, Food Service, Private Label, Bulk
Regions Exported to: Central America, Caribbean
Percentage of Business in Exporting: 5

42697 CHS Sunflower
220 Clement Ave
Grandin, ND 58038-4017   701-484-5313
Fax: 701-484-5657 sunflower@chsinc.com
www.chssunflower.com
Sunflower kernels, in-shell sunflower, flax, millet, buckwheat, pumpkin seeds, and soybean.
President/CEO: James Krogh
james.krogh@chsinc.com
Research & Development: Joel Schaefer
Sales Director: Wes Dick
Sales Director: Bruce Fjelde
Plant Superintendent: Arvid Terry
Controller: Chuck Schmidt
Number Employees: 100-249
Parent Co: CHS, Inc.
Type of Packaging: Consumer, Food Service, Private Label, Bulk
Regions Exported to: Europe, Asia, Middle East

42698 CHS Sunprairie
1800 13th St SE
Minot, ND 58701-6061
Canada   701-852-1429
Fax: 701-852-2755   800-556-6807
Organic flour, pancake mixes and hot breakfast cereals; exporter of hot organic breakfast cereals, bars and herbal supplements
Member: Peggy Lesueur-Brymer
Broker Sales Manager: Pat Maloney
Sales Coordinator: Sarah Sanders
Manager: Brad Haugeberg
brad.haugeberg@chsinc.com
Operations Manager: Curt Currie
Estimated Sales: $17,500,000
Number Employees: 20-49
Type of Packaging: Consumer, Food Service
Brands Exported: Prairie Sun
Regions Exported to: USA
Percentage of Business in Exporting: 10

42699 CJ America
3530 Wilshire Blvd.,
Suite 1220
Los Angeles, CA 90010   213-427-5566
Fax: 213-427-7878 www.cjamerica.com
Manufactuerer of amino acids, flavor enhancers and sweeteners.
President: Joonmo Suh
Vice President: Stephen Chang
Food Ingredients Sales Manager: Cecilia Kim
Product Manager: Chris Lee
Purchasing Agent: Jane Cho
Estimated Sales: $ .5 - 1 million
Number Employees: 10
Square Footage: 31304
Parent Co: Cheiljedang
Type of Packaging: Consumer, Food Service, Private Label, Bulk
Regions Exported to: Asia
Brands Imported: MSG, Nucleotide
Regions Imported from: Asia

42700 CJ Omni
4591 Firestone Blvd
South Gate, CA 90280   323-567-8171
Korean foods; specialize in mini wontons and korean sauces
President: James Chae
Estimated Sales: $ 3.5 Million
Number Employees: 50
Regions Imported from: Asia

42701 CJI Group LTD
4759 Hammermill Rd
Tucker, GA 30084-6611   770-934-4474
Fax: 770-934-7376 www.cjigroupltd.com
Packaging and packaging materials for processed foods, baked goods and dairy products
President: Charles Jing
cjigroup@yahoo.com
Estimated Sales: $ 3 - 5 Million
Number Employees: 5-9

42702 CK Products
310 Racquet Dr
Fort Wayne, IN 46825-4229   260-484-2517
Fax: 260-484-2510   888-484-2517
mail@ckproducts.com www.ckproducts.com
Wholesaler/distributor, importer and exporter of chocolate and chocolate coatings; also, candy making, bakery and cake decorating supplies
President: Orlie Brand
Contact: Steve Burdick
steve.burdick@ckproducts.com
Estimated Sales: $2.5-5 Million
Number Employees: 50-99
Square Footage: 220000
Regions Imported from: Europe, Asia, South Africa
Percentage of Business in Importing: 10

42703 CL&D Graphics
1101 Wests 2nd Street
Oconomowoc, WI 53066-0644
Fax: 262-569-4075   800-777-1114
marketing@cldgraphics.com
www.cldgraphics.com
Manufacturer and exporter of pressure sensitive labels and unsupported opp film
President: Mike Dowling
CFO: Scott Demski
Quality Control: Patrick Dillon
R&D: Greg McLain
Sales Manager: Ned Price
Estimated Sales: $ 20 - 50 Million
Number Employees: 100-249
Type of Packaging: Bulk
Regions Exported to: Worldwide

42704 CMT
P.O.Box 297
Hamilton, MA 01936   978-768-2555
Fax: 978-768-2525 cmtinc@tiac.net
Manufacturer and exporter of temperature and humidity monitors, alarms and controls sustems for climate sensitive goods such as wine and cigars.
President: David C De Sieye
Estimated Sales: $500,000-$1 Million
Number Employees: 1-4
Number of Products: 50
Square Footage: 8000
Regions Exported to: Worldwide
Percentage of Business in Exporting: 10

42705 CNS Confectionery Products
33 Hook Rd
Bayonne, NJ 07002-5006   201-823-1400
Fax: 201-823-2452   888-823-4330
sales@cnscoinc.com www.cnscoinc.com
Importer, processor and national distributor of sweetened, toasted and desiccated coconut as well as other sweet, dry baking ingredients. Certified kosher.
Owner: Eva Deutsch
e.deutsch@cnscoinc.com
CFO: Irene Fishman
VP Sales: Miriam Gross
e.deutsch@cnscoinc.com
Chief, Production/Purchasing: Eva Deutsch
Estimated Sales: $1-2.5 Million
Number Employees: 10-19
Type of Packaging: Private Label

42706 COVERIS
501 Williams St
Tomah, WI 54660-1454   608-372-2153
Fax: 608-372-5702 www.coveris.com
Manufacturer and exporter of polyethylene film and bags
Quality Control: Don Bergum
President: Stan Bikulege
Sales Manager: Bruce Baker
Plant Manager: Terry Smith
Estimated Sales: $ 20 - 50 Million
Number Employees: 250-499
Parent Co: Union Camp Corporation
Type of Packaging: Consumer, Bulk
Regions Exported to: Worldwide

42707 CP Kelco
Cumberland Center II
3100 Cumberland Blvd, Suite 600
Atlanta, GA 30339   678-247-7300
800-535-2687
www.cpkelco.com
Texturizing and stabilizing ingredients.
President & CEO: Dieder Viala
Year Founded: 1929
Estimated Sales: $370.5 Million
Number Employees: 2,200
Number of Brands: 10
Number of Products: 24
Parent Co: J.M. Huber Company
Other Locations:
CP Kelco Production Plant
Okmulgee, OK
CP Kelco Production Plant
San Diego, CACP Kelco Production PlantSan Diego
Brands Exported: Keltrol, Kelcogel, Simplesse, Genu, Genu Gum, Genutine, Genulacta, Genuvisco, Slendid, Kelgum, Simplesse
Regions Exported to: Central America, South America, Europe, Asia, Middle East, Worldwide
Percentage of Business in Exporting: 40

42708 CPM Century Extrusion
2412 W Aero Park Ct
Traverse City, MI 49686-9102   231-947-6400
Fax: 231-947-8400 sales@centuryextrusion.com
www.centuryextrusion.com
Manufacturer & supplier of extruders and extrusion parts.
President: Bob Urtel
urtelb@centuryextrusion.com
General Manager: Charlie Spearing
Number Employees: 50-99
Parent Co: CPM Extrusion Group
Regions Exported to: Central America, South America, Europe, Asia, North America

42709 CPM Roskamp Champion
2975 Airline Cir
Waterloo, IA 50703-9631   319-232-8444
Fax: 319-236-0481   800-366-2563
www.cpm.net
Manufacturer and exporter of particle sizing equipment including roller and hammer mills, flakers, crushers, pallet mills, coolers and crumblers for food processing; also, testing/lab facility available
President: Ted Waitman
CEO: Heath Hartwig
CFO: Doug Ostrich
Research & Development: Ron Fuller
Marketing Director: Scott Anderson
Sales Director: Linda Kruckenberg
Manager: J Manning
julie.manning@cpm.net
Operations Manager: Jim Hughes
Plant Manager: Terry Tackenberg
Purchasing Manager: Stuart Downs
Estimated Sales: $20 Million
Number Employees: 50-99
Square Footage: 50000
Parent Co: California Pellet Mill
Brands Exported: Roskamp; Champion
Regions Exported to: Worldwide
Percentage of Business in Exporting: 35

42710 (HQ)CPM Wolverine Proctor LLC
121 Proctor Ln
Lexington, NC 27292-7630   336-248-5181
Fax: 336-248-5118 www.wolverineproctor.com
Manufacturer and exporter of energy efficient equipment including conveyor dryers, roasters, toasters, coolers, ovens and the JETZONE fluidized dryers, puffers and toasters for the processing of fruits, vegetables, nuts, bakery, snackfoods, meat, poultry, pet foods, etc. Also offers batch drying equipment including tray, truck and laboratory dryers. Fully equipped Tech Centers available for demonstration purposes and development of new products and processes.
CEO: Steven Chilenski
CFO: Mark Brown
VP: Paul E Smith
Sales: Terry Midden
Estimated Sales: $15-25 Million
Number Employees: 50-99
Square Footage: 60000
Brands Exported: JETZONE, Proctor
Regions Exported to: Worldwide
Percentage of Business in Exporting: 40

42711 CROPP Cooperative
One Organic Way
La Farge, WI 54639
Fax: 608-625-2600   888-444-6455
contact.us@organicvalley.coop www.farmers.coop

Importers & Exporters / A-Z

Organic products including dried and fresh cheeses, eggs, yogurt, milk and butter; also, organic vegetables and certified organic pork, beef and chicken; importer of certified organic bananas.
CEO: Robert Kirchoff
Project Advisor: Mike Bedessem
Executive VP, Marketing: Lewis Goldstein
Year Founded: 1988
Estimated Sales: $1.157 Billion
Number Employees: 932
Number of Brands: 2
Square Footage: 10000
Type of Packaging: Consumer, Food Service, Private Label, Bulk
Brands Exported: Organic Valley
Regions Exported to: Europe, Asia
Percentage of Business in Exporting: 1
Regions Imported from: South America
Percentage of Business in Importing: 1

42712 CSC Scientific Co Inc
2799 Merrilee Dr # B
Fairfax, VA 22031-4419   703-564-4306
    Fax: 703-280-5142   800-621-4778
    www.cscscientific.com
Manufacturer and exporter of sieves and laboratory analyzers to measure water, moisture, filtration equipment, solids, surface tension, particle size and consistency; also, calibration services available
President: Al Gatenby
agatenby@cscscientific.com
Vice President: Tim Comwell
Marketing Director: Wendy Liu
Operations Manager: Theresa Andreoni
Estimated Sales: $ 2.5 - 5 Million
Number Employees: 20-49
Regions Exported to: Central America, South America, Europe, Asia, Middle East
Brands Imported: Kem; Endicotts
Regions Imported from: Europe, Asia

42713 (HQ)CSC Worldwide
4401 Equity Dr
Columbus, OH 43228-3856   614-850-1460
    Fax: 614-850-0741   800-848-3573
Manufacturer, designer and exporter of refrigerated and heated display cases; also store fixtures
CEO: Carl J Aschinger Jr
Marketing: Jennier Bobbitt
Contact: Carl Aschinger
c.aschingerjr@cscworldwide.com
Estimated Sales: $ 20-50 Million
Number Employees: 100-249
Regions Exported to: Central America, Europe, Asia, Canada, Caribbean, Latin America, Mexico
Percentage of Business in Exporting: 7

42714 CSS International Corp
2061 E Glenwood Ave
PO Box 19560
Philadelphia, PA 19124-5674   215-533-6110
    Fax: 215-288-8030   800-278-8107
    sales@cssintl.com
Manufacturer and exporter of container handling equipment and packaging machinery
Vice President: Eugene Fijalkowski
gene@cssintl.com
Vice President: Albert Andrew
VP Productions: Gene Fijalkowski
Number Employees: 20-49
Parent Co: CSS International Corporation
Type of Packaging: Consumer, Food Service, Private Label
Regions Exported to: Central America, South America, Europe, Asia, Middle East

42715 CTC Manufacturing
416 Meridian Road SE
Suite B12
Calgary, AB T2A 1X2
Canada   403-235-2428
    Fax: 403-272-9558   800-668-7677
Lollypops
President: G Paul Allen
Sales Manager: David Skultety
Plant Manager: Malcolm Steel
Number Employees: 10-19
Square Footage: 6900
Parent Co: Candy Tree Company
Type of Packaging: Consumer, Food Service, Private Label
Brands Exported: The Candy Tree
Regions Exported to: USA

Percentage of Business in Exporting: 40

42716 CTK Plastics
1815 Stadacona Street W.
Moose Jaw, SK S6H 7K8
Canada   306-693-7075
    Fax: 306-693-9944   800-667-8847
Plastic bottles and sheeting; importer of resin and bottling equipment; exporter of plastic bottles and rigid sheeting
President: Dennis Wastle
Sales/Marketing: Dennis Wastle
General Manager: Brian McGuigan
Supervisor: Bernice Larose
Number Employees: 10
Square Footage: 120000
Parent Co: CTK Developments
Regions Exported to: USA
Percentage of Business in Exporting: 25
Regions Imported from: U.S.A.
Percentage of Business in Importing: 25

42717 CUTCO Corp
1116 E State St
Olean, NY 14760-3814   716-372-3111
    Fax: 716-790-7160   www.cutco.com
Manufacturer and exporter of knives, forks and spoons
President: Brent Driscoll
CEO: James E Stitt
jstitt@alcas.com
President: James Stitt
Executive Vice President of Eastern Regi: Amar Dave
President, Chief Operating Officer: John Whelpley
Estimated Sales: H
Number Employees: 1000-4999
Parent Co: Alcas-Cutco Corporation
Type of Packaging: Consumer
Regions Exported to: Worldwide

42718 CVP Systems Inc
2518 Wisconsin Ave
Downers Grove, IL 60515-4230   630-852-1190
    Fax: 630-852-1386   800-422-4720
    sales@cvpsystems.com   www.cvpsystems.com
Manufacturer and exporter of cost effective, bags and packaging machinery including microbial reduction units, wrap around label systems and vacuum and modified atmosphere systems
President: Wesley Bork
VP: L Mykleby
Estimated Sales: $ 10 - 20 Million
Number Employees: 20-49
Type of Packaging: Consumer, Food Service, Private Label, Bulk
Brands Exported: CVP Fresh Vac
Regions Exported to: Central America, South America, Europe, Asia, Middle East
Percentage of Business in Exporting: 25

42719 Cabo Rojo Enterprises
3301 Combate
Boqueron, PR 622   787-254-0015
    Fax: 787-254-2048
Processor and importer of salt
President: Jeffrey Padilla Montero
Treasurer: Edwin Almodovar
Secretary: Lourdes Collado
Estimated Sales: $380,000
Number Employees: 5
Type of Packaging: Consumer
Regions Imported from: Central America

42720 Cabot Corp
2 Seaport Ln # 1300
Boston, MA 02210-2019   617-345-0100
    Fax: 617-342-6312   www.cabot-corp.com
Manufacturer and exporter of treated and untreated fumed silica
President/CEO: Patrick Prevost
CEO: Sean D Keohane
sean_keohane@cabot-corp.com
Executive Vice President/CFO: Eduardo Cordeiro
Vice President: James Belmont
Vice President, Research & Development: Yakov Kutsovsky
National Sales Manager: James Litrun
Vice President, Operations: James Turner
Estimated Sales: Over $1 Billion
Number Employees: 1000-4999
Parent Co: Cabot Corporation
Brands Exported: Cab-O-Sil

Regions Exported to: Central America, South America, Europe, Asia

42721 Cabot Creamery Co-Op
193 Home Farm Way
Waitsfield, VT 05673-7512   802-496-1200
    Fax: 802-371-1200   888-792-2268
    info@cabotcheese.com   www.cabotcheese.com
Cheese and other dairy products
President/CEO: Rich Stammer
Master Cheddar Maker: Marcel Gravel
CFO: Margaret Bertolino
Senior VP: David Hill
david.hill@cabotcheese.com
Director of Q/C: May Leach
Senior VP of Marketing: Roberta Macdonald
Sales & Marketing Manager: Sara Wing
Public Relations Manager: Bob Schiers
VP of Operations: Dick Gilangworthy
Plant Manager: Chris Pearl
Purchasing Manager: Kathleen McDonnell
Estimated Sales: $300 Million
Number Employees: 50-99
Square Footage: 450000
Parent Co: Agri-Mark
Type of Packaging: Consumer, Food Service, Private Label, Bulk
Brands Exported: Cabot
Regions Exported to: Europe

42722 Cache Box
2009 14th Street N
Suite 415
Arlington, VA 22201-2514   703-276-2500
    Fax: 703-276-2504   800-603-4834
Manufacturer and exporter of touchscreen turn-key point of sale systems
CEO: Lorenzo Salhi
VP Engineering: Murali Nagaraj
CTO: Dilip Ranade
VP, Technical Marketing: Shaloo Shalini
Contact: John Groff
john@cachebox.com
COO: John Groff
Estimated Sales: $5-10 Million
Number Employees: 20-49

42723 (HQ)Cacique
800 Royal Oaks Dr
Suite 200
Monrovia, CA 91017   626-961-3399
    Fax: 626-369-8083   800-521-6987
    www.caciqueinc.com
Processor and exporter of mozzarella and fresco cheeses, beef chorizo, pork choriso, soy choriso, mexican cremes, yogurts and beverages.
President: Gilbert Decardenas
Manager: Margarita Hodge
Estimated Sales: $ 50-100 Million
Number Employees: 325
Number of Brands: 5
Square Footage: 200000
Other Locations:
    Cacique
    Cedar City, UTCacique

42724 (HQ)Cadco Inc
145 Colebrook River Rd
Winsted, CT 06098-2203   860-738-2500
    Fax: 860-738-9772   info@cadco-ltd.com
    www.cadco-ltd.com
Wholesaler/distributor, exporter and marketer of convection ovens, buffet ranges, waffle irons, juicers, toasters, can openers, soup kettles and cordless stick mixers; serving the food service market
President: Mike Shanahan
mike@cadco-ltd.com
Chairman: Neil Gerhardt
Finance & HR: Patricia Warner
Quality Control: Marc Faulkner
Marketing Director: Erin Shanahan
Sales/Culinary Manager: Christopher Kasik
Customer Service: Lisa Smith
Estimated Sales: $5-10 Million
Number Employees: 5-9
Square Footage: 120000
Other Locations:
    Cadco Ltd.
    Winsted, CTCadco Ltd.

Importers & Exporters / A-Z

42725 Caddy Corporation of America
509 Sharptown Road
Bridgeport, NJ 08014-0345   856-467-4222
Fax: 856-467-5511 mbodine@caddycorp.com
www.caddycorp.com
Manufacturer and exporter of food service equipment including conveyors, transport/delivery carts, kitchen ventilation hoods and utility distribution systems
President: Harry Schmidt
CEO: Craig Cohen
CFO: John McNamee
VP of Corporate Services: Al Scuderi
Vice President, Sales: Phil Bailis
National Sales Manager: Donald Morrison
Engineering Manager: Brad Wallace
Purchasing: Robin Corma
Estimated Sales: $5-10 Million
Number Employees: 50-99
Square Footage: 288000
Regions Exported to: Worldwide

42726 Cadie Products Corp
151 E 11th St
Paterson, NJ 07524-1228   973-278-8300
Fax: 973-278-0303 www.cadieproducts.com
Manufacturer and exporter of cloths including dusting, polishing, cheese, pastry and sponge; also, cooking parchment, microwave cooking bags, seat covers, salad bags, ice cube bags, hamburger (patty) bags, and non-stick oven liner
President: Edwin Meyers
CFO: Bob Appelbaum
Vice President: Kenny Meyers
Estimated Sales: $ 20 - 50 Million
Number Employees: 20-49
Square Footage: 35000
Type of Packaging: Consumer, Private Label, Bulk
Regions Exported to: South America, Europe, Asia
Percentage of Business in Exporting: 45
Regions Imported from: South America, Europe, Asia
Percentage of Business in Importing: 25

42727 Cafe Altura
760 East Santa Maria Street
Santa Paula, CA 93060   805-933-3027
Fax: 805-933-9367 800-526-8328
www.cafealtura.com
Processor, importer and exporter of organic coffee
President: Chris Shepard
Sales Manager: Elizabeth Blatz
Estimated Sales: $2.5-5 Million
Number Employees: 5-9
Square Footage: 4000
Parent Co: Clean Foods
Regions Exported to: Asia, Canada, Australia
Percentage of Business in Exporting: 5
Brands Imported: Cafe Altura Organic Coffee
Regions Imported from: Mexico

42728 Cafe Du Monde Coffee Stand
1039 Decatur St
New Orleans, LA 70116-3309   504-581-2914
Fax: 504-587-0847 800-772-2927
office@cafedumonde.com www.cafedumonde.com
Processor and exporter of beignet doughnut mix, coffee and roasted chicory for coffee flavoring
CFO: J Roman
burt@cafedumonde.com
Manager: Burt Benrud
burt@cafedumonde.com
Manager: Robert Maher
Estimated Sales: $500,000 appx.
Number Employees: 10-19
Square Footage: 30000
Other Locations:
 Cafe Du Monde-French Market
 New Orleans, LA
 Cafe Du Monde-Riverwalk Marketplace
 New Orleans, LA
 Care Du Monde-New Orleans Centre
 New Orleans, LA
 Cafe Du Monde-Oakwood Mall
 Gretna, LA
 Cafe Du Monde-Lakeside Mall
 Metairie, LA
 Cafe Du Monde-Esplanade Mall
 Kenner, LA
 Cafe Du Monde-French MarketNew Orleans
Brands Exported: Cafe Du Monde
Regions Exported to: Asia

42729 Cafe Moak
509 E Division Street
Rockford, MI 49341-1342   616-866-7625
Fax: 616-866-6422
Bread sticks, subs, pizzas and coffee; importer of coffee
Owner: Sal Russo
Administrative Assistant: Becky Fate
Brands Imported: Moak
Regions Imported from: Italy

42730 Cafejo
3423 West Fordham Ave
Santa Ana, CA 92704-4422   714-432-8800
Fax: 714-432-8802 info@cafejo.com
www.aquabrew.com
Owner: Patrick Rolfes
Estimated Sales: $ 3 - 5 Million
Number Employees: 20-49

42731 Caffe Luca Coffee Roaste
1025 Industry Drive
Seattle, WA 98188   206-466-5579
Fax: 206-575-0537 800-728-9116
info@caffeluca.com www.caffeluca.com
Processor, exporter and importer of espresso and blended coffee; also, custom roasting available
Owner: Carol Dema
caroldema@caffeluca.com
Estimated Sales: $380,000
Number Employees: 5
Square Footage: 4000
Type of Packaging: Consumer, Food Service
Brands Exported: Caffe Luca; Casa Luca; Leonardo; Gregorio
Regions Exported to: Asia, Canada
Percentage of Business in Exporting: 30
Regions Imported from: Central America, South America, Mexico, Latin America, North Africa
Percentage of Business in Importing: 10

42732 Cajun Boy's Louisiana Products
136 Austin Dr
Church Point, LA 70525   337-207-2391
Fax: 225-357-6888 800-880-9575
datcajunboysco@aol.com
datcajunboysco.com/products
Seasoned beans, blended seasonings and mixes.
Owner/President: Gerald Hicks
Number Employees: 1-4
Type of Packaging: Consumer
Brands Exported: Cajun Boy's Louisiana Products
Regions Exported to: Mexico, Canada, Australia
Percentage of Business in Exporting: 10

42733 Cajun Creole Products Inc
5610 Daspit Rd
New Iberia, LA 70563-8961   337-229-8464
Fax: 337-229-4814 800-946-8688
info@cajuncreole.com www.cajuncreole.com
Coffee, peanuts and seasoning
President/Manager: Joel Wallins
Secretary/Treasurer: Sandra Wallins
Estimated Sales: $300,000
Number Employees: 5-9
Type of Packaging: Consumer, Food Service, Bulk
Brands Exported: Cajun Creole

42734 Cajun Original Foods Inc
704 Avenue D
New Iberia, LA 70560-0527   337-367-1344
Fax: 337-364-4968 www.cajunoriginal.com
Processor and exporter of liquid injectable marinades for poultry and red meats, and dry seasonings
President/CEO: Dennis Higginbotham
cajunoriginal@bellsouth.net
Estimated Sales: $1-2.5 Million
Number Employees: 10-19
Square Footage: 54400
Type of Packaging: Consumer, Bulk
Brands Exported: Cajun Aujus; Cajun Injector; Cajun Poultry Marinade; Cajunshake
Regions Imported from: Asia
Percentage of Business in Importing: 15

42735 Cal Controls
1675 Delany Road
Gurnee, IL 60031
Fax: 847-782-5223 800-866-6659
NA@West-CS.com www.cal-controls.com
Manufacturer and exporter of temperature and machine controllers for packaging and processing equipment
Sales Manager: Dave Chylstek
Estimated Sales: $15 Million
Number Employees: 21
Regions Exported to: Central America, South America
Percentage of Business in Exporting: 5

42736 Cal Harvest Marketing Inc
8700 Fargo Ave
Hanford, CA 93230-9771   559-582-4494
Fax: 559-582-0683 www.calharvest.com
Fresh fruits and vegetables
President: John Fagundes IV
johnf2006@hughes.net
Purchasing: John Fagundes
Estimated Sales: $2 Million
Number Employees: 5-9
Type of Packaging: Consumer, Private Label, Bulk
Brands Exported: Cal-King
Regions Exported to: Central America, South America, Asia
Regions Imported from: New Zealand

42737 Cal India Foods Inc
13591 Yorba Ave
Chino, CA 91710-5071   909-613-1660
Fax: 909-613-1663
www.systemicenzymetherapy.com
Fruit juices, purees and concentrates
President: Vic Rathi
info@4enzymes.com
Quality Control: Vilas Amin
Purchasing Agent: Priscilla Ferreri
Estimated Sales: $5-7 Million
Number Employees: 20-49
Square Footage: 24000
Parent Co: Specialty Enzymes and Biochemicals Company
Type of Packaging: Bulk

42738 Cal Trading Company
1731 Adriand Rd
Suite 2
Burlingame, CA 94010-2101   650-697-4615
Fax: 650-692-1049
Importer/Exporter of coffees and decaffeinated coffees
Regions Exported to: Worldwide
Percentage of Business in Exporting: 50
Regions Imported from: Central America, South America, Asia, Middle East
Percentage of Business in Importing: 50

42739 Cal-Grown Nut Company
8616 E. Whitmore
Hughson, CA 95326-0069   209-883-4081
Fax: 209-883-0305 www.californiagrown.com
Processor and exporter of almonds
President: Frank Assali
frankassali@californiagrown.com
Vice President: Marie Assali
Office Manager: Linda Thomas
Estimated Sales: $ .5 - 1 million
Number Employees: 5-9
Regions Exported to: Worldwide
Percentage of Business in Exporting: 95

42740 Cal-Maine Foods Inc.
3320 Woodrow Wilson Dr.
Jackson, MS 39209   601-948-6813
Fax: 601-969-0905 ir@cmfoods.com
www.calmainefoods.com
Shell eggs.
CEO/Chairman: Adolphus Baker
abaker@cmfoods.com
Chairman Emeritus: Fred Adams
VP/CFO/Treasurer/Secretary/Director: Max Bowman
Vice President/General Counsel: Rob Holladay
VP Sales: Jeff Hardin
VP, Controller: Mike Castleberry
President/COO/Director: Sherman Miller
Year Founded: 1969
Estimated Sales: $1.037 Billion
Number Employees: 1000-4999
Number of Brands: 3
Type of Packaging: Food Service, Private Label, Bulk

42741 Cal-Mil Plastic Products Inc
4079 Calle Platino
Oceanside, CA 92056-5805   760-630-5100
Fax: 760-630-5010 800-321-9069
www.calmil.com

Importers & Exporters / A-Z

Manufacturer, exporter and importer of acrylic counter top cabinets, mirrored displays, crocks, platters, risers, bowls, pedestals, tables, domes, etc. for the catering and banquet industries.
President: Barney Callahan
bcallahan@calmil.com
Marketing Director: Mike Juneman
Sales Director: Mike Juneman
Estimated Sales: $10-20 Million
Number Employees: 20-49
Number of Products: 1460
Type of Packaging: Bulk
Brands Exported: Cal-Mil
Regions Exported to: Central America, Europe, Asia
Percentage of Business in Exporting: 20
Regions Imported from: Asia

42742 Cal-Tex Citrus Juice LP
402 Yale St
Houston, TX 77007-2530   713-869-3471
Fax: 713-869-3277 800-231-0133
gary.van.liew@cal-texjuice.com
www.cal-texjuice.com
Fresh and frozen concentrate citrus juices
CEO: Ronald Peterson
Quality Control: Alvaro Falquez
National Sales Manager: Vicki White
Operations: Danny Teague
Purchasing: Kory Mason
Estimated Sales: $40 Million
Number Employees: 100-249
Number of Brands: 3
Number of Products: 63
Parent Co: Country Pure Foods
Type of Packaging: Consumer, Food Service, Private Label
Regions Imported from: Central America, Europe
Percentage of Business in Importing: 40

42743 Calavo Growers
1141A Cummings Rd
Santa Paula, CA 93060   805-525-1245
Fax: 805-921-3232 www.calavo.com
Growers and processors of pineapples, papayas, and avocados; Manufacturer of; salsa and corn chips
Chairman/President/CEO: Lecil Cole
lecilc@calavo.com
CEO: Robin Osterhues
COO/CFO/Corporate Secretary: Arthur Bruno
VP/Fresh Sales & Marketing: Rob Wedin
Quality Assurance Manager: Diane Valine
Vice President, Sales & Marketing: Alan Ahmer
Fresh Operations: Mike Browne
Plant Manager: Brett Viera
Purchasing Agent: Bruce Spurrell
Estimated Sales: $ 551 Million
Number Employees: 1000-4999
Type of Packaging: Consumer, Food Service, Bulk
Other Locations:
  Temecula Packinghouse
  Temecula, CA
  Santa Paula Packinghouse
  Santa Paula, CA
  Calavo Processing Plant
  Santa Paula, CATemecula PackinghouseSanta Paula

42744 Calbee America Inc
2600 Maxwell Way
Fairfield, CA 94534-1915   707-427-2500
Fax: 707-428-2900
Processor and exporter of potato chips
President/Ceo: Masanori Yasunaga
Vice President: Doug Warner
Manager Sales and Marketing: Takashi Katsunoi
VP Human Resources: Yoshi Ishiquro
IT Executive: Masa Suito
msaito@calbeeamerica.com
Estimated Sales: $15 Million
Number Employees: 100-249
Regions Exported to: Japan, Hong Kong

42745 Caldic USA Inc
2425 Alft Ln
Elgin, IL 60124-7864
    847-468-0001
customerservice@caldic.us
Sourcing, R&D, processing, warehousing and distribution of ingredients.
Owner: Bob Leonard
bleonard@nealanders.com
Number Employees: 10-19
Parent Co: Caldic

42746 Caldwell Group
5055 26th Avenue
Rockford, IL 61109   815-229-5667
Fax: 815-229-5686 800-628-4263
contact@caldwellinc.com www.caldwellinc.com
Manufacturer and exporter of crane lifting attachments
Owner: Howard Will
VP: William McLeod
Estimated Sales: $ 5-10 Million
Number Employees: 50-99
Regions Exported to: Canada

42747 Calgrain Corporation
P.O.Box 2501
875 Sansome Street
San Francisco, CA 94126-2501   415-788-6320
Fax: 415-788-1827 calgrain@pacbell.net
Exporter of dairy products, animal feed, bird seed, pulses
President: Kumar Dass
Estimated Sales: $2.5-5 Million
Number Employees: 5-9
Regions Exported to: Asia
Percentage of Business in Exporting: 100

42748 California Agriculture & Foodstuff
6220 Stanford Ranch Rd
Suite 200
Rocklin, CA 95765-4428   916-899-6183
Fax: 916-889-6184 nature-expo.com
Nuts and dried fruit
President: D Ajami
president@Californiafoodstuff.com
Managing Director/Partner: M Safaie
Type of Packaging: Food Service, Bulk

42749 California Cereal Products
1267 14th St
Oakland, CA 94607-2246   510-452-4500
Fax: 510-452-4545 californiacereal.com
Gluten-free cereal ingredients, including rice, cereal and flour products.
President: Mark Graham
Co-Founder/Chairman/CEO: Robert Sterling Savely
Accounting: Richard O'Connor
Estimated Sales: $13.9 Million
Number Employees: 75
Square Footage: 600000
Type of Packaging: Consumer, Private Label, Bulk
Other Locations:
  Manufacturing Facility
  Macon, GAManufacturing Facility
Brands Exported: CCP
Regions Exported to: Central America, Asia
Percentage of Business in Exporting: 5
Regions Imported from: Central America, South America, Asia
Percentage of Business in Importing: 5

42750 California Custom Foods
2325 Moore Ave
Fullerton, CA 92833-2510   714-870-0490
Fax: 714-870-5609 gilbertj@vanlaw.com
www.vanlaw.com
Processor and exporter of refrigerated and shelf stable salad dressings, pancake syrup, syrup concentrates, flavorings, extracts, colorings, ice cream toppings and barbecue and teriyaki sauces; importer of romano and parmesan cheeseolive oil and balsamic vinegar
Owner: Matthew Jones
jonesm@vanlaw.com
Director of Quality Assurance: Anna Tran
VP Sales/Marketing: John Gilbert
jonesm@vanlaw.com
Estimated Sales: $ .5 - 1 million
Number Employees: 100-249
Square Footage: 520000
Type of Packaging: Consumer, Food Service, Private Label
Regions Exported to: Worldwide
Percentage of Business in Exporting: 10
Regions Imported from: Worldwide
Percentage of Business in Importing: 10

42751 California Custom Fruits
15800 Tapia St
Baldwin Park, CA 91706-2178   626-736-4130
Fax: 626-736-4145 877-558-0056
info@ccff.com www.ccff.com
Fruit products and flavors

Owner: Monica Ahuero
President: Mike Mulhausen
CFO: Jim Fragnoli
Marketing Manager: Christine Long
Director Operations: Jack Miller
Production Manager: Eric Nielsen
Director of Flavor Development: Phillip Barone
Purchasing Director: Phyllis Ferguson
Estimated Sales: $20-35 Million
Number Employees: 100-249
Square Footage: 33000
Type of Packaging: Bulk
Brands Exported: CCFF, B2B, Private Label
Regions Exported to: Asia, Canada, Mexico
Percentage of Business in Exporting: 7

42752 California Dairies Inc.
2000 N. Plaza Dr.
Visalia, CA 93291   559-625-2200
Fax: 559-625-5433 info@californiadairies.com
www.californiadairies.com
Dairy products.
Chairman: Simon Vander Woude
President/CEO: Brad Anderson
Year Founded: 1999
Estimated Sales: Over $1 Billion
Number Employees: 500-999
Type of Packaging: Consumer, Food Service, Bulk
Other Locations:
  Artesia, CA
  Fresno, CA
  Los Banos, CA
  Tipton, CA
  Turlock, CAFresno
Brands Exported: Challenge Dairy Products, DairyAmerica
Regions Exported to: 40 countries worldwide

42753 California Independent Almond Growers
13000 Newport Road
Merced, CA 95303-9704   209-667-4855
Fax: 209-667-4854
Growers, packers, processors and shippers worldwide. California grown whole natural almonds direct from the source. State-of-the-art equipment
President: Karen Barstow
Estimated Sales: $2.5-5 Million
Number Employees: 50-99
Square Footage: 60000
Type of Packaging: Consumer, Food Service, Private Label, Bulk
Brands Exported: California Independent Brand
Regions Exported to: Worldwide

42754 California Natural Products
1250 Lathrop Rd
Lathrop, CA 95330-9709   209-858-2525
Fax: 209-858-4076 marci.howe@cnp.com
www.cnp.com
Organic food ingredients, rice and soy beverages, nutritional drinks, soups, broths, teas and wine.
President: Robert Hatch
CEO/Owner: Pat Mitchell
patm@californianatural.com
Vice President of Finance: Gene Guelfo
Vice President: Kevin Haslebacher
Vice President of R&D: Khalid Shammet
Quality Regulatory: Connie Gutierrez
Technical Sales Manager: John Ashby
Director of Human Resources: Skip Lindstrom
Operations Manager: Emil Skaria
Purchasing Manager: Chirs Mifsud
Estimated Sales: $42 Million
Number Employees: 250-499
Type of Packaging: Private Label
Regions Exported to: Europe, Asia
Percentage of Business in Exporting: 3

42755 California Oils Corp
1145 Harbour Way S
Richmond, CA 94804-3618   510-233-7660
Fax: 510-233-1329 800-225-6457
www.caloils.com
Vegetable oils and meal; exporter of corn and safflower oils
CEO: Sihira Ito
Controller: Masako Hirose
Vice President/Sales Executive: Joevic Fabregas
Sales and Marketing Manager: Karol Sop
Number Employees: 20-49
Parent Co: Mitsubishi

Importers & Exporters / A-Z

42756 California Olive Oil Council
801 Camelia St # D
Suite D
Berkeley, CA 94710-1459　510-524-4523
　　Fax: 510-898-1530　888-718-9830
　　oliveoil@cooc.com　www.cooc.com
Processor and exporter of oils including garlic, sesame, peanut, olive, canola, mineral, soybean, citrus, infused, organic, cold pressed and unrefined; also, balsamic vinegar and cooking wines; importer of kosher certified soy sauce
Owner: Claudia Siniawski
Vice President: Robert Mandia
CFO: Dave Lofgren
VP Sales/Marketing: Mark Moffitt
Contact: Alison Altomari
alison@cooc.com
Executive Director: Patricia Darragh
Estimated Sales: $420,980
Number Employees: 5-9
Square Footage: 76000
Parent Co: East Coast Olive Corporation
Type of Packaging: Consumer, Food Service, Private Label, Bulk
Regions Exported to: Europe, Asia
Percentage of Business in Exporting: 10
Regions Imported from: Central America, South America, Europe, Asia
Percentage of Business in Importing: 90

42757 California Saw & Knife Works
721 Brannan St
San Francisco, CA 94103-4927　415-861-0644
　　Fax: 415-861-0406　888-729-6533
　　calsaw@calsaw.com　www.calsaw.com
Manufacturer and exporter of machine knives and circular saws for food processing equipment
President: Warren Bird
wbird@calsaw.com
CFO: Mike Weber
Vice President: Benson Joseph
VP Production: S Bird
Estimated Sales: $5-10 Million
Number Employees: 10-19
Square Footage: 36000
Regions Exported to: Worldwide

42758 California World Trade and Marketing Company
24615 Oneil Ave
Hayward, CA 94544　510-888-9393
　　Fax: 510-888-1482
Small organization in the grocery companies industries.
Owner/President: Stan Names
stan@californiaworldtrade.com
CFO: Nancy Ostler
VP: Lucille Chan
Marketing: Alex Perez
Estimated Sales: $1-2.5 Million
Number Employees: 1-4
Type of Packaging: Food Service, Private Label
Regions Exported to: Central America, Asia
Regions Imported from: Central America, Asia

42759 Calio Groves
58 Calvert Court
Piedmont, CA 94611　707-402-4700
　　Fax: 707-402-4747　800-865-4836
Olive oil and extra virgin olive oil; importer of olive oil
President: Brendan Frasier
VP Production & Farming: Bob Singletary
Estimated Sales: $20-50 Million
Number Employees: 20-49
Parent Co: NVK Realty
Type of Packaging: Consumer, Food Service, Private Label, Bulk
Regions Imported from: Italy , Spain
Percentage of Business in Importing: 2

42760 Calkins & Burke
#800-1500 Georgia St
Vancouver, BC V6G 2Z6
Canada　604-669-3741
　　Fax: 604-699-9732　800-669-7992
　　www.calbur.com
Fresh and frozen halibut, salmon and crab
President: David Calkins
Secretary: Micheal Calkins
VP: Micheal Kolinn
Head of Marketing: Ken Jonn
Estimated Sales: $11.95
Number Employees: 60
Type of Packaging: Consumer, Food Service, Private Label
Regions Exported to: USA

42761 Calmar
501 South 5th Street
Richmond, VA 23219-0501　804-444-1000
Manufacturer and exporter of plastic pump dispensers
President: James Buzzard
Chairman/Chief Executive Officer: John Luke
Chief Financial Officer: Mark Rajkowski
Senior Vice President: Linda Schreiner
General Counsel/Secretary: Wendell Willkie
Vice President, Strategy & Marketing: Todd Fister
Communications: Donna Owens Cox
Supply Chain: Nik Hiremath
Estimated Sales: $ 50 - 100 Million
Number Employees: 200
Type of Packaging: Bulk
Regions Exported to: Worldwide

42762 Caloritech
1420 West Main Street
P.O. Box 146
Greensburg, IN 47240　812-663-4141
　　Fax: 812-663-4202　800-473-2403
　　info@ccithermal.com　www.caloritech.com
Manufacturer and exporter of components for electrical cooking equipment, air heating immersion and clamp-on radiant equipment
President: Harold Roozen
VP Sales/Marketing: Bob Pender
Number Employees: 200
Square Footage: 440000
Parent Co: CCI Thermal Technologies
Regions Exported to: Worldwide
Percentage of Business in Exporting: 10

42763 Calpro Ingredients
1787 Pomona Road
Corona, CA 951-735-59　909-493-4890
　　Fax: 909-493-4845　www.calprofoods.com
Whey protein concentrates
President: Garry Johns
Operations: Carole Northup
Number Employees: 5-9
Square Footage: 6000
Parent Co: Golden Cheese Company of California
Type of Packaging: Bulk
Brands Exported: Calpro
Regions Exported to: Europe, Asia, Mexico

42764 Cam Spray
520 Brooks Rd
Iowa Falls, IA 50126-8005　641-648-5011
　　Fax: 641-648-5013　800-648-5011
　　sales@camspray.com　www.camspray.com
Manufacturer and exporter of high pressure washers; importer of pumps
Manager: Jim Gillestie
CFO: Jim Gillispie
Estimated Sales: $5-10 Million
Number Employees: 20-49
Square Footage: 150000
Parent Co: Campbell Supplies
Brands Exported: Cam Spray
Regions Exported to: Worldwide
Percentage of Business in Exporting: 16
Regions Imported from: Italy

42765 (HQ)Cambridge Intl. Inc.
105 Goodwill Rd
PO Box 399
Cambridge, MD 21613-2980　410-228-3000
　　Fax: 410-221-1100　800-638-9560
　　info@cambridge-intl.com
　　www.cambridge-intl.com
Manufacturer and Exporter of conveyor belting, filters, vibration screens and filter leaves
Manager: Jody Padelko
CEO: Tracy Tyler
ttyler@cambridge-intl.com
International Sales Manager: Bart Shellabarger
Belt Sales Manager: Larry Windsor
Director of Sales: Larry Windsor
Customer Service Manager: Breanne Hemphill
Estimated Sales: $300,000-500,000
Number Employees: 250-499

42766 (HQ)Cambridge Viscosity, Inc.
101 Station Lndg
Medford, MA 02155-5134　781-393-6500
　　Fax: 781-393-6515　800-554-4639
　　info@cambridgeviscosity.com
　　www.cambridgeapplied.com
Manufacturer and exporter of viscometers
President: Robert Kasameyer
Marketing Manager: Art MacNeill
Contact: Victoria Benea
beneavictoria@paclp.com
Director Engineering: Dan Airey
Estimated Sales: $ 1 - 2.5 Million
Number Employees: 20-49
Brands Exported: Cambridge Applied Systems
Regions Exported to: Central America, South America, Europe, Asia, Middle East, Australia
Percentage of Business in Exporting: 30

42767 Cambro Manufacturing Co
5801 Skylab Rd
Huntington Beach, CA 92647-2056　714-848-1555
　　800-833-3003
　　webmaster@cambro.com　www.cambro.com
Food service equipment and supplies including bus boxes, insulated food carriers, carts and beverage containers, plastic insert pans, fiberglass trays and polyethylene boxes.
President: Argyle Campbell
acampbell@cambro.com
Chief Financial Officer: David Capestro
Year Founded: 1951
Estimated Sales: $74 Million
Number Employees: 250-499
Type of Packaging: Food Service
Other Locations:
　Warehouse
　Brampton, CanadaManufacturing Facility
　Mebane, NCWarehouseStuttgart, Germany
Brands Exported: Cambro
Regions Exported to: Central America, South America, Europe, Asia, Middle East, Worldwide

42768 Camellia Beans
5401 Toler Street
Harahan, LA 70183　504-733-8480
　　Fax: 504-733-8155　info@camelliabeans.com
　　www.camelliabrand.com
Dried beans, peas and lentils
Partner: Ken Hayward
Partner: Connely Hayward
Estimated Sales: $10-20 Million
Number Employees: 20-49
Type of Packaging: Consumer, Food Service, Bulk
Regions Exported to: Worldwide
Percentage of Business in Exporting: 10

42769 Cameo China
1938 Chico Ave
South El Monte, CA 91733-2946　626-652-0828
　　Fax: 626-652-0832　www.cameochina.com
President: David Hou
Manager: Dheepa Ramanujam
dheepa@krea.in
Estimated Sales: $ 10 - 20 Million
Number Employees: 5-9

42770 Camerican International
45 Eisenhower Dr
Paramus, NJ 07652　201-587-0101
　　info@camerican.com
　　www.camerican.com
Importer of cheese, dried and canned fruits, tomato paste, honey, canned meats and fish and fruit beverage concentrates including apple, cherry, berry, pineapple, guava, lemon and pear; exporter of fruit beverage concentrates andcanned fish.
Chief Executive Officer: Larry Abramson
labr@atalanta1.com
Year Founded: 1916
Estimated Sales: $1.1 Billion
Number Employees: 50-99
Parent Co: Gellert Global Group
Regions Imported from: South America, Europe, Asia, Middle East
Percentage of Business in Importing: 98

42771 Cameron Birch Syrup & Confections
951 Hermon Road
Suite 6
Wasilla, AK 99654-7379　907-373-6275
　　Fax: 907-373-6274　800-962-4724
Birch syrup, marinades, salad dressing and candy

Importers & Exporters / A-Z

President: Marlene Cameron
Number Employees: 1-4
Square Footage: 2500
Type of Packaging: Consumer, Food Service, Private Label, Bulk
Brands Exported: Cameron's
Regions Exported to: Europe, Canada
Percentage of Business in Exporting: 50

42772 Cameron Intl. Corp.
Park Towers South
Houston, TX   281-285-4376
www.slb.com/companies/cameron
Manufacturer and exporter of oil-free centrifugal compressors.
CEO, Schlumberger: Olivier Le Peuch
VP. Finance: Jeff Altamari
Year Founded: 1920
Estimated Sales: $9.8 Billion
Number Employees: 23,412
Parent Co: Schlumberger Limited
Regions Exported to: Worldwide
Percentage of Business in Exporting: 60

42773 Camerons Brewing Co.
1165 Invicta Drive
Oakville, ON L6H 4M1
Canada   905-849-8282
Fax: 905-849-5578 info@cameronsbrewing.com
www.cameronsbrewing.com
Manufacturer and exporter of micro brewing equipment
President: Gary Deathe
Number Employees: 17
Regions Exported to: Worldwide

42774 Campagana Winery
10950 West Road
Redwood Valley, CA 95470-9741   707-485-1221
Fax: 707-485-1225 www.winesandromance.com
Winery
Chairman: Joseph Campagna
CEO: Tony Coturri
CFO/COO: George Pruden
Marketing Director: Paul White
Sales Director: Paul White
Production Manager: Nic Coturri
Estimated Sales: $3,000,000
Number Employees: 8
Type of Packaging: Private Label
Brands Exported: Gabrielli
Regions Exported to: Asia
Percentage of Business in Exporting: 10

42775 Campbell Soup Co.
1 Campbell Pl.
Camden, NJ 08103-1701   856-342-4800
Fax: 856-342-3878 800-257-8443
www.campbellsoupcompany.com
Soups, snacks, beverages and simple meals.
President/CEO: Mark Clouse
Executive VP/CFO: Mick Beekhuizen
Executive VP/General Counsel: Adam Ciongoli
Executive VP, Global R&D: Craig Slavtcheff
Executive VP, Global Supply Chain: Bob Furbee
Year Founded: 1869
Estimated Sales: Over $1 Billion
Number Employees: 18,000
Number of Brands: 21
Type of Packaging: Consumer, Food Service, Bulk
Other Locations:
Toronto, CanadaCorporate Headquarters
Camden, NJ
Pepperidge Farm Headquarters
Norwalk, CT
Bolthouse Farms Headquarters
Bakersfield, CA
Norre Snede, DenmarkSelangor, MalaysiaCamden
Brands Exported: Campbell's, Pace, Prego, Swanson, V8, Pepperidge Farm, StockPot
Regions Exported to: Central America, South America, Canada
Brands Imported: Erasco, Liebig, Royco, D&L, Heisse Tasse, Arnott's
Regions Imported from: Central America, South America, Europe, Asia, Australia

42776 Campus Collection, Inc.
PO Box 2904
Tuscaloosa, AL 35403   205-758-0678
Fax: 205-758-4848 800-289-8744
sales@campuscollection.net
www.campuscollection.net

Manufacturer and exporter of printed and embroidered T-shirts, hats
President: Chet Goldstein
Contact: Chris Ballard
chris@campuscollection.net
Regions Exported to: Antilles Islands
Percentage of Business in Exporting: 5

42777 Can & Bottle Systems, Inc.
2525 SE Stubb St
Milwaukie, OR 97222-7323   503-236-9010
Fax: 503-232-8453 866-302-2636
www.canandbottle.com
Manufacturer, sales and service and exporter of reverse vending machines and systems for beverage container redemption and recycling. Can, plastic and glass beverage container crushers/recyclers
President: Bill Janner
Number Employees: 20-49
Number of Products: 15
Square Footage: 40000
Brands Exported: CanDo
Regions Exported to: Europe, Middle East, Canada

42778 Can Lines Engineering Inc
9839 Downey Norwalk Rd
P.O. Box 7039
Downey, CA 90241-7039   562-861-2996
www.canlines.com
Can and bottle handling conveyors.
President: Keenan Koplien
Director, Mechanical Engineering: Steve Lusa
Director, Operations: Darwin Smock
Year Founded: 1960
Estimated Sales: $20 Million
Number Employees: 10-19
Square Footage: 40000
Regions Exported to: Central America, South America, Europe, Asia
Percentage of Business in Exporting: 20

42779 Canada Bread Co, Ltd
10 Four Seasons Place
Etobicoke, ON M9B 6H7
Canada   416-622-2040
    800-465-5515
www.canadabread.com
Baked goods, snacks and bread company.
President: Joseph McCarthy
Year Founded: 1911
Estimated Sales: $1.3 Billion
Number Employees: 4,175
Number of Brands: 7
Number of Products: 1K+
Parent Co: Grupo Bimbo
Type of Packaging: Consumer, Food Service, Private Label, Bulk
Brands Exported: Olivieri; Rachel's Top-It
Regions Exported to: USA
Percentage of Business in Exporting: 40

42780 Canada Cutlery Inc.
1964 Notion Road
Pickering, ON L1V 2G3
Canada   905-683-8480
Fax: 905-683-9184 800-698-8277
www.canadacutlery.com
Food service cutlery
Owner, President: Peter Huebner, HAAC
VP & Marketing Director: Mary Louise Huebner
Estimated Sales: $1-3 Million
Number Employees: 5-9
Square Footage: 20000
Type of Packaging: Consumer, Food Service, Private Label, Bulk
Brands Exported: Superior Culinary Master
Regions Exported to: USA
Brands Imported: Superior Culinary Master
Regions Imported from: Europe, Asia, USA

42781 Canadian Display Systems
60 Corstate Ave
Concord, ON L4K 4X2
Canada   905-265-7888
Fax: 905-265-7692 800-895-5862
cds1@on.aibn.com
www.canadiandisplaysystems.com
Display coolers
President: Gary Sohi
Number Employees: 15

42782 Canadian Fish Exporters
134 Rumford Ave # 202
Suite 202
Auburndale, MA 02466-1377   617-916-0900
Fax: 617-926-8214 800-225-4215
cfe@cfeboston.com www.cfeboston.com
Saltfish including bacalao, pollock, hake, cusk, haddock, herring, mackerel and cod; importer of Italian cheeses and canned tomatoes
CEO: Robert Metafora
CFO/Treasurer: Janelle Calamari
VP: James Scannell
Estimated Sales: $ 10 - 20 Million
Number Employees: 10-19
Type of Packaging: Consumer, Private Label, Bulk
Brands Exported: Cristobal; BacalaRico; Buena Ventura
Regions Exported to: Central America, South America, Caribbean
Brands Imported: Rossella; Buena Ventura; BacalaRico; Cristobal
Regions Imported from: Asia, Canada

42783 Canadian Food ExportersAssociation
885 Don Mills Road
Suite 301
Toronto, ON M3C 1V9
Canada   416-445-3747
Fax: 416-510-8024 info@cfea.com
www.cfea.com
Cookies, other baked goods, cheese, cured meats i.e. prociutto/bacon, agency/trade organization
Marketing: Susan Powell

42784 Canadian Mist Distillers
202 MacDonald Road
Collingwood, ON L9Y 4J2
Canada   705-445-4690
Fax: 705-445-7948 www.canadianmist.com
Processor and exporter of whiskey
Officer: Pat Sullivan
Manager Admin./Commodities: Steve Sly
Manager Production: Don Jaques
Plant Manager: Harold Ferguson
Estimated Sales: $24.4 Million
Number Employees: 35
Square Footage: 1000000
Parent Co: Brown-Forman Corporation
Type of Packaging: Consumer, Food Service
Brands Exported: Canadian Mist
Regions Exported to: USA
Percentage of Business in Exporting: 95

42785 Canarm, Ltd.
2157 Parkedale Avenue
PO Box 367
Brockville, ON K6V 5V6
Canada   613-342-5424
Fax: 800-263-4598 info@canarm.ca
www.canarm.com
Manufacturer and importer of ceiling fans
President: James A. Cooper
Vice President - HVAC & Agri Products: Doug Matthews
Marketing Manager: John McBride
Sales Manager: Tim Sutton
Director Operations: Steven Read
Number Employees: 30
Type of Packaging: Consumer, Food Service, Private Label
Brands Imported: Four Seasons; Pleasantaire
Regions Imported from: Asia

42786 Candle Lamp Company
1880 Compton Avenue
Ste. 101
Corona, CA 92881   951-682-9600
Fax: 951-784-5801 877-526-7748
www.candlelamp.com
Chafing dish and lamp fuel; also, table lamps for the restaurant/hotel industry
President: Daniel Stoner
VP: L Murlin
Marketing Services: J Van Osdel
Contact: Karina Garcia
kgarcia@sternocandlelamp.com
Estimated Sales: $ 10 - 20 Million
Number Employees: 100-249

Importers & Exporters / A-Z

42787 Candy & Company/Peck's Products Company
4100 West 76th Street
Chicago, IL 60652
800-837-9189
daleyinternational.com/
Manufacturer and exporter of industrial disinfectant cleaners, janitorial supplies, sanitizers, laundry supplies and specialty cleaning chemicals
President: Joh Daley
Sales Manager: Joann Stoskoph
Estimated Sales: $ 1 - 5 Million
Number Employees: 1-4
Square Footage: 160000
Parent Co: J.F. Daley International
Regions Exported to: Asia, Middle East, Canada, Mexico
Percentage of Business in Exporting: 10

42788 (HQ)Candy Flowers
9286 Mercantile Drive
Mentor, OH 44060-4525
440-974-1333
Fax: 440-974-1338
Chocolate and candy flowers, chocolate covered pretzels, coffee spoons and cookies and theme wrapped chocolate bars; exporter of candy flowers; importer of chocolates
President: Joanne Henry
Marketing: Anthony Henry
Estimated Sales: $5-10,000,000
Number Employees: 20-49
Square Footage: 42000
Type of Packaging: Food Service
Brands Exported: Sweet Blossoms; Spoon Full of Flavors; Sweet & Salty; O Choco's; Theme Bars; Candy Flowers
Regions Exported to: Worldwide
Percentage of Business in Exporting: 5
Brands Imported: Bruyeree Le Chocolatier
Percentage of Business in Importing: 1

42789 Candy Manufacturing Co
5633 W Howard St
Niles, IL 60714-4011
847-588-2639
Fax: 847-588-0055 info@candycontrols.com
www.candycontrols.com
Manufacturer and exporter of industrial timing controls including differentials, positioners, cam switches, timing hubs, and web handling systems
President: Robert Hendershot
Quality Control: Al Rosenow
Sales Director: Jacob Ninan
Estimated Sales: Below $ 5 Million
Number Employees: 5-9
Square Footage: 60000
Regions Exported to: Central America, South America, Europe, Asia
Percentage of Business in Exporting: 5

42790 Candy Mountain Sweets & Treats
1484 Atlanta Industrial Dr NW
Suite A
Atlanta, GA 30331-1031
404-505-7332
Fax: 404-696-4003 800-621-1954
www.tootarts.com
Sugar free candy
President & CEO: Armand Hammer
VP Purchasing: Bob Davis
VP Sales: Al Silva
Estimated Sales: $20-50 Million
Number Employees: 50-99
Regions Exported to: Worldwide

42791 Candy Tech LLC
151 Morth Hastings Lane
Buffalo Grove, IL 60089
847-229-1011
Fax: 847-229-1211 sweetsales@candytech.com
www.candytech.com
Manufacturer, importer and distributor of candy
CEO: David Babiarz
Square Footage: 400000
Type of Packaging: Food Service, Private Label, Bulk
Brands Imported: Nestle; Baron; Fruit Chews Txt Message
Regions Imported from: Central America, South America, Europe, Asia
Percentage of Business in Importing: 98

42792 Canelake's Candy
414 Chestnut St
Virginia, MN 55792-2526
218-741-1557
Fax: 218-741-1557 888-928-8889
Processor and exporter of candies and chocolates; importer of nuts
President: James Cina
candy@canelakes.com
Estimated Sales: Less Than $500,000
Number Employees: 5-9
Square Footage: 6000
Type of Packaging: Consumer
Regions Exported to: Canada

42793 Cangel
60 Paton Road
Toronto, ON M6H 1R8
Canada
416-532-5111
Fax: 416-532-6231 800-267-4795
Manufacturer and exporter of food, hydrolyzed and technical gelatins
President: Richard Manka
Number Employees: 2
Square Footage: 160000
Type of Packaging: Bulk

42794 Cannoli Factory
75 Wyandanch Ave
Wyandanch, NY 11798-4441
631-643-2700
Fax: 631-643-2777 sales@cannolifactory.com
www.cannolifactory.com
Processor and exporter of Italian and New York style cheesecake, tiramisu, lobster tail pastries and cannoli products including chocolate covered shells, cream and tarts
Owner: Michael Zucaro
Contact: John Edwards
johne@cannolifactory.com
Estimated Sales: $4 Million
Number Employees: 50-99
Type of Packaging: Food Service
Regions Exported to: Canada
Percentage of Business in Exporting: 1

42795 Cantech Industries Inc
2222 Eddie Williams Rd
Johnson City, TN 37601-2871
423-926-9748
Fax: 423-928-0311 800-654-3947
cii@cttgroup.com www.cantechtn.com
Manufacturer and exporter of pressure sensitive tapes including duct, masking, box sealing, filament, double-coated, and electrical for industrial, automotive and retail markets
President: L Cohen
CFO: H Cohen
Research & Development: H Matsuura
VP Marketing/Sales: Ronald Jacobs
VP Sales: P Cohen
Plant Manager: Mark Patton
Estimated Sales: $50 Million
Number Employees: 50-99
Number of Brands: 2
Number of Products: 70
Square Footage: 100000
Parent Co: Canadian Technical Tape
Type of Packaging: Consumer, Food Service, Private Label, Bulk
Brands Exported: Clipper; Cantech
Regions Exported to: Central America, South America, Europe, Asia, Middle East, Worldwide
Percentage of Business in Exporting: 20

42796 Capay Canyon Ranch
P.O.Box 508
Esparto, CA 95627-0508
530-662-2372
Fax: 530-662-2306 capaycanyonranch.com
Processor and exporter of almonds, walnuts and grapes, and inshell chandler walnuts.
Sales Director: Leslie Barth
Contact: Stan Barth
stan@capaycanyon.com
Plant Operations: Todd Barth
Estimated Sales: $1 - 2,499 Million
Number Employees: 4
Number of Brands: 2
Number of Products: 8
Square Footage: 10000
Type of Packaging: Bulk
Brands Exported: Capay Canyon Ranch; Zanonk Brand
Regions Exported to: Europe, Asia, Middle East
Percentage of Business in Exporting: 70
Brands Imported: Capay Canyon Ranch

42797 Cape Cod Potato Chips
100 Breeds Hill Rd
Hyannis, MA 02601-1886
508-775-3358
Fax: 508-775-2808 800-438-1880
www.capecodchips.com
Popcorn including white cheddar cheese, natural and butter; also, kettle-cooked potato chips
President: Margaret Wicklund
Chief Executive Officer: Roger Gray
Sr Vice President: Dan Collins
Vice President: Chuck Fisher
Estimated Sales: $20-50 Million
Number Employees: 100-249
Square Footage: 30000
Parent Co: Snyder's Lance
Type of Packaging: Consumer
Regions Exported to: Central America, Europe

42798 (HQ)Capital Plastics
15060 Madison Rd
Middlefield, OH 44062-9450
440-632-5800
Fax: 440-632-0012 collector@capitalplastics.com
www.capitalplastics.com
Manufacturer and exporter of custom plastic displays for acrylic cutting boards, clip boards, plaques and trophies
President: Lyle Schwartz
Estimated Sales: $ 2.5 - 5 Million
Number Employees: 10-19
Regions Exported to: Worldwide

42799 Capitol Foods
PO Box 751541
Memphis, TN 38175-1541
662-781-9021
Fax: 662-781-0697
Canned vegetables, diced peaches, mixed fruits and edible oils; exporter of canned vegetables; wholesaler/distributor of bakery, dairy and grocery products, soups and bases, produce, syrups, oils, pasta, meats; serving the food servicemarkets
President: Kenneth Porter
CFO: Phillip Duncan
Number Employees: 134
Square Footage: 20000
Type of Packaging: Consumer, Food Service
Brands Exported: Capitol Foods
Regions Exported to: Caribbean
Percentage of Business in Exporting: 1

42800 Capitol Hardware, Inc.
402 N Main Street
P.O. Box 70
Middlebury, IN 46540-2573
800-327-6083
Fax: 800-544-4054
Manufacturer and exporter of retail store fixtures, peripheral display hardware and electric lighting fixtures
President: Joe Shelby
capitolhardware@leggett.com
Senior Vice President: David DeSonier
Executive Vice President of Sales: Joel Katterhagen
Executive Vice President of Operations: Ron McComas
Estimated Sales: $ 2.5-5 Million
Number Employees: 20-49
Square Footage: 1000000
Parent Co: Leggett & Platt Store Fixtures Group
Brands Exported: Capitol Hardware
Regions Exported to: Canada, Caribbean
Percentage of Business in Exporting: 1

42801 Capmatic, Ltd.
12180 Boul. Albert-Hudon
Monreal North, QC H1G 3K7
Canada
514-332-0062
Fax: 514-322-0063 info@capmatic.com
www.capmatic.com
Manufacturer and exporter of packaging machinery and bottling equipment
President: Charles Lacasse
CFO: Nicole Murray
President: Alioscia Bassani
Sales Director: Christian Normandin
Number Employees: 20
Regions Exported to: Central America, South America, Europe, Asia, Middle East, Africa, Mexico

42802 Cappo Drinks
15011 Badillo St.
Baldwin Park, CA 91706
626-813-1006
sales@cappodrinks.com
www.cappodrinks.com
Manufacturer and exporter of smoothie mixes.

Importers & Exporters / A-Z

CEO: Scott Berberian
Contact: Ara Berberian
aberberian@cappodrinks.com
Regions Exported to: Worldwide

42803 Cappola Foods
25 Lappage Ct
Toronto, ON M3J 3M3
Canada　　　　　　　　　416-633-0389
　　Fax: 416-787-1535　sales@cappolafood.com
　　　　　　　　www.cappolafood.com
Processor and exporter of Italian flavored ices
Owner: Dom Cappola
Type of Packaging: Consumer, Food Service
Regions Exported to: Worldwide
Percentage of Business in Exporting: 35

42804 Cappuccino Express Company
1718 Waukegan Rd
Glenview, IL 60025　　　　　847-361-9776
　　Fax: 847-824-7103　800-824-8041
Wholesaler/distributor and importer of fully automatic espresso and cappuccino machines
CEO: Jim Morton
Estimated Sales: $ .5 - 1 million
Number Employees: 1-4
Regions Imported from: Italy

42805 Capri Bagel & Pizza Corporation
215 Moore St
Brooklyn, NY 11206-3745　　　718-497-4431
　　　　　　　　Fax: 718-497-7567
Manufacturer and exporter of pizza, pizza bagels and mini pizzas
President: Adrian Cooper
Plant Manager: Ikey Tuachi
Estimated Sales: $500,000-$1,000,000
Number Employees: 20-49
Square Footage: 31000
Type of Packaging: Consumer, Food Service, Private Label

42806 Capriccio
10021 1/2 Canoga Avenue
Chatsworth, CA 91311-0981　　818-718-7620
　　　　　　　　Fax: 818-718-0204
Manufacturer and exporter of food ingredients
CEO: Jack Barsoumian
Estimated Sales: $500,000-$1,000,000
Number Employees: 1-4
Type of Packaging: Food Service
Brands Exported: Capriccio, Baristella
Regions Exported to: Worldwide

42807 Captain Alex Seafoods
8874 N Milwaukee Ave
Niles, IL 60714-1752　　　　847-803-8833
 Fax: 847-803-9854　www.fishandseafoodniles.com
Seafood
President/Secretary: Alex Malidis
Vice President: Matthew Mallidis
Office Manager: Ilir Veliu
Estimated Sales: $530,000
Number Employees: 5-9

42808 Captiva Limited Inc
45 Us Highway 206 Ste 104
Augusta, NJ 7822　　　　　973-579-7883
　　　　　　　　Fax: 973-579-2509
Processor and exporter of bottled water including still, carbonated and flavored; also, sports/health drinks
Owner: Don Destefano
VP: Mary Ann Bell
Estimated Sales: $ 3 - 5 Million
Number Employees: 1-4
Square Footage: 6000
Type of Packaging: Consumer, Food Service, Private Label, Bulk
Brands Exported: Nature's Mist; Pro-Life

42809 Capway Conveyor Systems Inc
725 Vogelsong Rd
York, PA 17404-1765　　　　717-843-0003
　　Fax: 717-843-1654　877-222-7929
　　sales@capwayusa.com　www.capwayusa.com
Manufacturer and exporter of bakery and food processing equipment including depanners, proofers, coolers, pan storage systems, conveyors, etc
President: Frank Achterberg
fachterberg@capwayusa.com
General Manager: Frank Achterberg
Estimated Sales: $5-10 Million
Number Employees: 20-49

Square Footage: 72000
Parent Co: Capway Systems
Regions Exported to: South America, Europe, Canada, Mexico

42810 Carando Technologies Inc
345 N Harrison St
Stockton, CA 95203-2801　　　209-948-6500
　　Fax: 209-948-6757　sales@carando.net
　　　　　　　　www.carando.net
Manufacturer and exporter of container production machinery
President: Sid Schuetz
CFO: Laura Keir
lkeir@carando.net
Sales Coordinator: Laura Keir
Estimated Sales: $5-10 Million
Number Employees: 10-19

42811 Caraustar Industries, Inc.
3900 Comanche Drive
Archdale, NC 27263-3158　　　770-948-3101
　　　　　　　　　　　800-223-1373
　　info@caraustar.com　www.caraustar.com
Manufacturer and exporter of composite cans, tubes, metal ends and injection molded plastic products used for packaging wet and dry, hot fill and frozen products
Marketing Director: Andrew McGowan
Type of Packaging: Consumer, Food Service
Regions Exported to: Central America, South America, Europe, Asia

42812 Caravan Packaging Inc
6427 Eastland Rd
Brookpark, OH 44142-1305　　440-243-4100
　　Fax: 440-243-4383　info@caravanpackaging.com
　　　　　　　　www.caravanpackaging.com
Manufacturer and exporter of wooden boxes and custom packaging
President: Fred Hitti
fred@caravanpackaging.com
Estimated Sales: $500,000-$1 Million
Number Employees: 1-4
Type of Packaging: Food Service, Bulk
Regions Exported to: Worldwide
Percentage of Business in Exporting: 75

42813 Caravell
3978 N Panam Expy
San Antonio, TX 78219-2205　　210-222-1936
　　Fax: 888-829-1726　888-829-7445
　　　　　　　　caravellus@aol.com
Importer of freezers and coolers
Sales Manager: John Dillree
Number Employees: 1-4
Square Footage: 20000
Parent Co: Caravell A/S
Brands Imported: Caravell
Regions Imported from: Canada, Mexico.
Percentage of Business in Importing: 100

42814 Carbis Inc
1430 W Darlington St
Florence, SC 29501-2124　　　843-669-6668
　　Fax: 843-662-1536　800-948-7750
　　　　　　　　sales@carbissolutions.com
Stainless steel products, including loading racks, arms, stairs, platforms and handrails
President: Sam Cramer
sam.cramer@carbissolutions.com
Marketing Director: Rob Cooksey
General Manager: Ron Bennett
Number Employees: 250-499
Square Footage: 1200000
Regions Exported to: Canada

42815 Cardinal Meat Specialists
155 Hedgedale Road
Brampton, ON L6T 5P3
Canada　　　　　　　　　905-459-4436
　　Fax: 905-459-8099　800-363-1439
　　　　　　　　www.cardinalmeats.com
Hamburger patties and steaks
President: Brent Cator
Estimated Sales: $5-10 Million
Number Employees: 35
Type of Packaging: Food Service
Regions Exported to: USA

42816 Cardinal Packaging Prod LLC
300 Exchange Dr # A
Suite A
Crystal Lake, IL 60014-6290　　815-444-6000
　　Fax: 815-444-6379　866-216-4942
　　info@cardinalpack.com　www.cardinalpack.com
Manufacturer and exporter of set-up paper boxes, specialty folding cartons, incorporating domicut platforms, etc. Also hot leaf (foil) stamping
President: Bob Colletti
b.colletti@cardinalpkgproducts.com
Sales: Steve Overlee
Estimated Sales: Less Than $500,000
Number Employees: 1-4
Regions Exported to: Europe
Percentage of Business in Exporting: 15

42817 Cardinal Rubber & Seal Inc
1545 Brownlee Ave SE
Roanoke, VA 24014-2609　　　540-982-0091
　　Fax: 540-982-6750　800-542-5737
　　　　　　　　sales@cardinalrubber.com
　　　　　　　　www.cardinalrubber.com
Manufacturer and exporter of rubber seals, gaskets, O-rings, hoses, etc.
CEO: Loren Bruffey, Sr.
Vice President: Pat Lawhorn
Inside Sales: Pat Worley
Purchasing: Connie Dowdy
Estimated Sales: $10-20 Million
Number Employees: 20-49

42818 Cardinal Scale Mfg Co
203 E Daugherty St
P.O. Box 151
Webb City, MO 64870-1929　　417-673-4631
　　Fax: 417-673-5001　800-441-4237
　　cardinal@cardet.com　www.cardinalscale.com
Manufacturer and exporter of scales
Owner: Brock Dawson
bdawson@detecto.com
CEO: W Perry
CFO: Charles Nasters
Vice President: Herbert Harwood
Estimated Sales: $ 50 - 100 Million
Number Employees: 500-999
Square Footage: 400000
Regions Exported to: Worldwide
Percentage of Business in Exporting: 10

42819 (HQ)Care Controls, Inc.
PO Box 12014
Mill Creek, WA 98082　　　　425-745-1252
　　Fax: 425-745-8934　800-593-6050
　　info@carecontrols.com　www.carecontrols.com
Manufacturer and exporter of on-line inspection systems including check weighers, vacuum and pressure detectors, etc
President: Ray Pynsky
Marketing: Rob Laroche
Contact: Brenda Ballard
brenda@carecontrols.com
Brands Exported: Canalyzer; Quantum
Regions Exported to: Worldwide
Percentage of Business in Exporting: 25

42820 Caremoli USA
23959 580th Ave
Ames, IA 50010-9390　　　　515-233-1255
　　Fax: 515-233-2933　www.caremoligroup.com
Ingredients of naturally processed grains, flours and fibers
President: Andrea Caremoli
a.caremoli@caremoli-usa.com
Quality Manager: Bethany Christensen
VP Sales/Marketing: Devin Miller
Sales Manager, North & South America: Carolina Calvert
Estimated Sales: $24 Million
Number Employees: 20-49

42821 (HQ)Cargill Inc.
P.O. Box 9300
Minneapolis, MN 55440-9300
　　　　　　　　　　　800-227-4455
　　　　　　　　www.cargill.com
Stores, trades, processes and distributes grains, oilseeds, vegetable oils and meals; raises livestock and produces animal feed; produces food ingredients such as starches, glucose syrups, oils and fats.

Chairman/CEO: David MacLennan
CFO: David Dines
Chief Compliance Officer/General Counsel: Anna Richo
Cheif Human Resources Officer: LeighAnne Baker
Business Operations & Supply Chain: Ruth Kimmelshue
Year Founded: 1865
Estimated Sales: $114.6 Billion
Number Employees: 166,000
Type of Packaging: Bulk

42822 Cargill Kitchen Solutions Inc.
15407 McGinty Rd. W.
Wayzata, MN 55391
833-535-5205
CustomerService_Protein@Cargill.com
www.sunnyfresh.com
Eggs and breakfast products for foodservice operatos, convenience stores, chain restaurants, healthcare foodservice facilities, and schools.
Parent Co: Cargill Inc.
Type of Packaging: Bulk

42823 Carhoff Company
13404 Saint Clair Ave
Cleveland, OH 44110   216-541-4835
            Fax: 216-541-4022
Manufacturer and exporter of silicone and chemically treated cleansing tissues
V.P.: Jim Lauer
Estimated Sales: $5-10 Million
Number Employees: 10-19
Regions Exported to: Worldwide

42824 Caribbean Food DelightsInc
117 Route 303 # B
Suite B
Tappan, NY 10983-2136   845-398-3000
            Fax: 845-398-2316
info@caribbeanfooddelights.com
www.caribbeanfooddelights.com
Manufacturer and exporter of Jamaican baked goods including breads, fruit cakes and buns; also, beef, chicken and vegetable patties, jerk chicken, sausage, curried goat, rice, peas, etc
President/CEO: Vincent HoSang
CEO: Vincent Hosang
Estimated Sales: $10-20 Million
Number Employees: 50-99
Square Footage: 120000
Parent Co: Royal Caribbean Bakery
Type of Packaging: Consumer, Food Service, Private Label, Bulk

42825 Caribbean Produce Exchange
4th St Bldg. D, Mrcado Cntl
P.O. Box 11990
San Juan, PR 00920-1990   787-793-0750
    Fax: 787-792-2617   888-783-2754
Wholesaler/distributor, exporter and importer of fresh fruits and vegetables
President: Gualberto Rodriguez
VP: Luis Rodriquez
VP: Marta Zanvela
Accounts Payable: Ivtte Rivera
Purchasing Coordinator: Felix Martinez
Purchasing Director: Manny Garcia
Number Employees: 100-249
Square Footage: 240000
Regions Exported to: Caribbean
Percentage of Business in Exporting: 10
Brands Imported: Dole; Foxy; Ready Pac; Caprex
Regions Imported from: Worldwide
Percentage of Business in Importing: 90

42826 Carillon Company
500 Frank W Burr Boulevard
Teaneck, NJ 07666-6804   201-836-7799
Alcoholic beverages
President: Michel Roux
Estimated Sales: $100-500 Million
Number Employees: 20-49
Parent Co: Diageo United Distillers and Vinters

42827 Caristrap International
1760 Fortin Boulevard
Laval, QC H7S 1N8
Canada   450-667-4700
    Fax: 450-663-1520   800-361-9466
info@caristrap.com   www.caristrap.com
Manufacturer and exporter of polyester cord strapping

President: Audrey Karass
Operations: Gerry Elis
Plant Manager: Norm Stevenson
Number Employees: 150
Regions Exported to: Central America, South America, Europe, Asia
Percentage of Business in Exporting: 60

42828 Carl Brandt Inc
55 Walls Dr
Suite 303
Fairfield, CT 06824-5163   203-256-8133
    Fax: 203-256-8135   800-275-4326
ssettineri@carlbrandt.com   www.carlbrandt.com
Importer of cookies, cake including ladyfingers, rye and pumpernickel bread, chocolate, marzipan, tea and diabetic products
President: Henry Witte
Controller: Brenda Adriani
Marketing/Sales: Susanne Settineri
Contact: April Sellers
april.sellers@carlbrandt.com
Estimated Sales: $5-10 Million
Number Employees: 5-9
Square Footage: 48000
Parent Co: Carl Brandt GmbH
Type of Packaging: Consumer
Brands Imported: Brandt; Feodora; Niederegger; Onno Behrends; Mestemacher; Norda; Messmer; SchneeKoppe; Kuchenmeister; Dreher
Regions Imported from: Europe
Percentage of Business in Importing: 100

42829 (HQ)Carle & Montanari-O P M
625 Hutton St # 107
Raleigh, NC 27606-6321   919-664-7401
    Fax: 919-664-7407   www.cm-opm.com
Importer and wholesaler/distributor of confectionery equipment and supplies including molding plants, wrapping equipment, pans, etc.; serving processors only
President: Moreno Roncato
Estimated Sales: $1-2.5 Million
Number Employees: 1-4
Square Footage: 40000
Regions Exported to: Central America, South America, Europe, Asia, Middle East
Brands Imported: C&M Spa; Lehmann
Regions Imported from: Europe
Percentage of Business in Importing: 100

42830 Carleton Helical Technologies
30 S Sand Rd
Doylestown, PA 18901-5123   215-230-8900
    Fax: 215-230-8033   sales@feedscrew.com
www.carletonhelical.com
Container handling products and systems including timing screws, invertors, inline air rinsers, carton twisters, etc
President: Nick Carleton
ncarleton@feedscrew.com
Operations Manager: Connie McDermott
Production Manager: Mike Anrein
Production: Mark McDermott
Purchasing Manager: Edward Amrein
Estimated Sales: $ 2 - 3 Million
Number Employees: 10-19
Number of Brands: 5
Number of Products: 1
Square Footage: 52000
Regions Exported to: Central America, South America, Canada, Latin America, Mexico

42831 Carleton Technologies Inc
10 Cobham Dr
Orchard Park, NY 14127-4195   716-662-0006
    Fax: 716-662-0747   info@carltech.com
www.cobham.com
Manufacturer and exporter of testing equipment for flexible package seal integrity and strength
President/CEO: Paddy Cawdery
Cmo: Stuart Buckley
stuart.buckley@cobham.com
Estimated Sales: $20-50 Million
Number Employees: 100-249
Square Footage: 93000
Parent Co: FR Group PLC
Regions Exported to: Europe, Asia
Percentage of Business in Exporting: 10

42832 Carlin Manufacturing
466 West Fallbrook Avenue
Suite 106
Fresno, CA 93711   559-276-0123
    Fax: 559-222-1538   888-212-0801
info@carlinmfg.com   www.carlinmfg.com
Manufacturer and exporter of custom mobile kitchens, military field kitchens and specialty vehicles.
Owner: Kevin Carlin
Sales/FMP/CEO: Bob Farrar
Contact: Robin Goldbeck
goldbeck@carlinmfg.com
Estimated Sales: $5-10 Million
Number Employees: 10-19
Number of Brands: 1
Square Footage: 74000
Brands Exported: Carlin
Regions Exported to: Central America, South America, Europe, Asia, Middle East
Percentage of Business in Exporting: 50

42833 Carlisle Food Svc Products Inc
4711 E Hefner Rd
Oklahoma City, OK 73131   405-475-5600
    Fax: 800-872-4701   800-654-8210
customerservice@carlislefsp.com
www.carlislefsp.com
Dishware, tabletop accessories, coffee and tea supplies, buffet service, food bars and accessories, food service trays, bar supplies, catering equipment, kitchen accessories, storage and handling and cleaning tools.
President: Trent Freiberg
trentfreiberg@carlislefsp.com
Chief Financial Officer: Carolyn Ford
Vice President: Todd Manor
Vice President of Sales: Jim Calamito
Year Founded: 1946
Estimated Sales: $238.8 Million
Number Employees: 250-499
Number of Brands: 100
Number of Products: 1600
Square Footage: 150000
Type of Packaging: Food Service
Other Locations:
  Central Distribution Center
  Oklahoma City, OK
  Western Distribution Center
  Reno, NV
  Eastern Distribution Center
  Charlotte, NCCentral Distribution CenterReno
Brands Exported: Stack-All; Durus; King Line; Epicare; Encore; AbeyPellet; OptiClean; Optimizer; Maximize; Cabernet; Crystalism; DallasWare; Lexington; Designer Display; Clutter Busters
Regions Exported to: Central America, South America, Europe, Asia, Middle East

42834 Carlisle Sanitary Mntnc Prods
4711 E Hefner Rd
PO Box 53006
Oklahoma City, OK 73131-6114   405-475-5600
    Fax: 405-475-5607   800-654-8210
www.carlislefsp.com
Manufacturer and exporter of custom-designed brushes including floor scrub, clean-up, fryers, nylon paddle scraper, grill, grease, glass and washing
CEO: Ruth Marciniec
ruthmarciniec@carlislefsp.com
Director Sales/Marketing: Christopher Meaney
General Manager: Robert Daley, Jr.
Estimated Sales: $200,000
Number Employees: 6
Square Footage: 16652
Type of Packaging: Food Service, Bulk
Brands Exported: Broiler Master; Galaxy; Hercules; Hi-Lo; Long Reach; Meteor; Venus
Regions Exported to: Central America, South America, Europe, Asia, Middle East
Percentage of Business in Exporting: 4

42835 Carlota Foods International
9821 Summerwood Circle
Apt 2923
Dallas, TX 75243-7749   214-340-5416
    Fax: 214-340-5330   carlotafoods@hotmail.com
Importer and exporter of canned, dried and frozen fruits, vegetables, confectionery, cookies, juices, jams, condiments, spices, ingredients, sauces, etc
President: Alfonso Izcoa
Number Employees: 1-4
Square Footage: 3200
Type of Packaging: Consumer, Bulk

Importers & Exporters / A-Z

Regions Exported to: Worldwide
Percentage of Business in Exporting: 20
Regions Imported from: Central America, South America, Latin America, Mexico
Percentage of Business in Importing: 60

42836 Carlson Products
4601 N Tyler Rd
P.O. Box 429
Maize, KS 67101-8734   316-722-0265
Fax: 316-721-0158   800-234-1069
sales@carlsonproducts.com
www.carlsonproducts.com
Manufacturer and exporter of lightweight double-acting aluminum impact and sliding aluminum cooler and freezer doors; also pizza pans
President: Austin Peterson
austin@carlsonproducts.com
Sales Manager: Rich Dreiling
Estimated Sales: $5-10 Million
Number Employees: 50-99
Square Footage: 100000
Parent Co: Jay Ca
Regions Exported to: Central America, South America, Europe, Canada, Mexico
Percentage of Business in Exporting: 5

42837 Carnes Company
PO Box 930040
Verona, WI 53593   608-845-6411
Fax: 608-845-6470 carnes@carnes.com
www.carnes.com
Carnes Company is a manufacturer of commercial HVAC equipment. Its product line offering includes registers, grilles, diffusers. terminal units, ventilation equipment, louvers, penthouses, fire and smoke dampers, steam humidifiers andenergy recovering ventilators. Carnes has been a supplier of HVAC equipment since 1939.
VP, Sales & Marketing: David Stankevich
dstankevich@carnes.com
Estimated Sales: $50-100 Million
Number Employees: 11-50
Square Footage: 93000
Regions Exported to: Worldwide
Percentage of Business in Exporting: 25

42838 (HQ)Carolina Beverage Corp
1413 Jake Alexander Blvd S
Salisbury, NC 28146-8359   704-633-4550
Fax: 704-633-7491 custserv@cheerwine.com
www.cheerwine.com
Syrups and beverage concentrates; exporter of soft drinks and concentrates; wholesaler/distributor of soft drinks and water
President: Clift Ritchie
critchie@carolinabottlingcompanyinc.com
CFO: Tommy Page
CIO: Bill Barten
VP Operations: David Swaim
Estimated Sales: $10-20 Million
Number Employees: 20-49
Square Footage: 75000
Parent Co: Cheerwine & Diet Cheerwine
Type of Packaging: Consumer
Other Locations:
 Carolina Beverage Corp.
 Hickory, NC
 Carolina Beverage Corp.
 Greenville, SCCarolina Beverage Corp.Greenville
Brands Exported: Cheerwine

42839 Carolina Canners Inc
300 Highway 1 S
P.O. Box 1628
Cheraw, SC 29520   843-537-5281
Fax: 843-537-6743
amity.albridge@carolinacanners.com
www.carolinacanners.com
Wholesaler/distributor of beverages and fountain syrups.
President: Mark Avent
Chief Executive Officer: Jeff Stevens
Chief Financial Officer: Frank Cobia
Vice President: Lee Teeter
Secretary: Maughan Hull
Chief Information Officer: Tim Geddings
VP, Sales & Marketing: Sterling Whitley
VP, Human Resources: Jerry Tucker
VP, Manufacturing: David Rhine
Estimated Sales: $33.7 Million
Number Employees: 100-249
Brands Exported: Pepsi Cola

42840 Carolina Knife
224 Mulvaney St
Asheville, NC 28803-1499   828-253-6796
Fax: 828-258-0693   800-520-5030
info@cknife.com
Manufacturer and exporter of machine knives
President: Walter Ashbrook
wally@cknife.com
Sales Manager: Paul Turner
Technical Rep.: Bart Loudermilk
Estimated Sales: $2.5-5 Million
Number Employees: 20-49
Square Footage: 12000
Parent Co: Hamilton Industrial Knife & Machine
Regions Exported to: Central America, Canada
Percentage of Business in Exporting: 10

42841 Carolina Mop
819 Whitehall Road
Anderson, SC 29625-2119   864-225-8351
Fax: 864-225-1917   800-845-9725
www.carolinamop.com
Manufacturer, importer and exporter of dust mops, wet mops, brooms and broom handles
President: Pam Ritter
Estimated Sales: $ 5 - 10 Million
Number Employees: 20-49
Square Footage: 100000
Regions Exported to: Caribbean, Mexico
Percentage of Business in Exporting: 1
Regions Imported from: Canada
Percentage of Business in Importing: 3

42842 Carolina Pride Foods
1 Packer Ave.
Greenwood, SC 29646   864-229-5611
Fax: 864-229-0541 www.carolinapride.com
Fresh pork and bacon, smoked meats and processed luncheon meats including deli loaves and bologna; exporter of skinned jowls, pork kidneys, liver and stomachs, flat belly skins, etc.
President: Michael Cox
CFO: Mark Litts
Year Founded: 1920
Estimated Sales: $185 Million
Number Employees: 500-999
Number of Brands: 1
Square Footage: 250000
Type of Packaging: Consumer, Food Service, Private Label, Bulk
Regions Exported to: Asia, Middle East, Latin America, Mexico
Percentage of Business in Exporting: 8

42843 Carolina Treet
Po Box 1017
Wilmington, NC 28402   910-762-1950
Fax: 910-762-1438   800-616-6344
info@carolinatreet.com www.carolinatreet.com
Processor and importer of barbecue sauce, condiments, syrups, brewed tea, bar mixes and beverage concentrates
President: Joe King
Vice President: Lenwood King
General Manager: Allen Finberg
Estimated Sales: $1.4 Million
Number Employees: 13
Number of Brands: 5
Number of Products: 20
Square Footage: 80000
Type of Packaging: Consumer, Food Service, Private Label, Bulk
Regions Imported from: Worldwide

42844 Carothers Olive Oil
P.O. Box 3307
Flint, MI 48502   810-235-2055
Importer and exporter of Spanish olive oil
Manager: Marie Killein
Estimated Sales: Under $300,000
Number Employees: 1-4
Type of Packaging: Private Label
Brands Exported: Carothers
Regions Exported to: Canada
Percentage of Business in Exporting: 2
Regions Imported from: Europe
Percentage of Business in Importing: 98

42845 Carpenter Emergency Lighting
2 Marlen Drive
Hamilton, NJ 08691   609-689-3090
Fax: 609-689-3091   888-884-2270
sales@carpenterlighting.com
www.carpenterlighting.com
Manufacturer and exporter of emergency lighting equipment, emergency exit, portable and rechargeable lights
President: Avinash Diwan
National Sales Manager: Philip Salvatore
Contact: Evi Nash
info@carpenterlighting.com

42846 Carpigiani Corporation of America
3760 Industrial Drive
Winston Salem, NC 27105   336-661-9893
Fax: 336-661-9895   800-648-4389
info@carpigiani-usa.com www.carpigiani-usa.com
Manufacturer, importer and exporter of self serve frozen dessert and drink machines, whip cream dispensers and batch ice cream freezers
VP: Randy Karns
General Manager: Jim Hall
Sales Manager: Jim Marmion
Operations Manager: Bill Van Hine
National Sales Manager: Jerry Hoefer
Estimated Sales: $ 5-10 Million
Number Employees: 10-19
Square Footage: 80000
Parent Co: Carpigiani Viaemilia
Type of Packaging: Food Service
Other Locations:
 Coldelite Corp. of America
 BolognaColdelite Corp. of America
Brands Exported: Coldelite
Regions Exported to: Central America, South America
Percentage of Business in Exporting: 15
Regions Imported from: Europe

42847 Carrageenan Company
200 E 61st St Apt 27a
New York, NY 10065-8580
Fax: 714-850-9865
sales@carrageenancompany.com
Processor, importer and exporter of gum and hydrocolloide blends; also, custom blending of carrageenan products for dairy, meat and poultry
President: Vincent Zaragoza
Executive Director: Javier Zaragoza
Marketing Director: Yolanda Zaragoza
Sales Director: Carla Gonzales
Public Relations: Cristina Gonzales
Managing Director: Vincente Zaragoza
Estimated Sales: Below $5 Million
Number Employees: 5-9
Type of Packaging: Private Label
Regions Exported to: Central America, South America, Europe, Asia, Canada, Australia
Percentage of Business in Exporting: 25

42848 Carrie's Chocolates
9216-63 Avenue
Edmonton, AB T6E 0G3
Canada   780-435-7900
     877-778-2462
Processor and exporter of handmade novelty and gift chocolates, promotional bars, and wedding candy
Owner: Carrie MacKenzie
Number Employees: 2
Square Footage: 1800
Type of Packaging: Consumer, Food Service, Private Label, Bulk
Regions Exported to: USA
Percentage of Business in Exporting: 15

42849 Carrier Corp
1 Carrier Pl
Farmington, CT 06032-2562
     800-227-7437
www.carrier.com
Manufacturer and exporter of refrigerating units for delivery trucks, marine containers and commercial refrigeration equipment.
President & CEO: Dave Gitlin
Executive VP & CFO: Tim McLevish
VP & Chief Legal Officer: Kevin O'Connor
VP, Communications & Marketing: Mary Milmoe
VP, Operations: Rishi Grover
Year Founded: 1902
Estimated Sales: $12.5 Billion
Number Employees: 55,000
Regions Exported to: Worldwide

42850 (HQ)Carrier Vibrating EquipInc
3400 Fern Valley Rd
Louisville, KY 40213-3554 502-969-3171
Fax: 502-969-3172 cve@carriervibrating.com
www.carriervibrating.com
Manufacturer and exporter of custom designed screening conveyor systems and feeders, bin dischargers, stainless steel dairy dryers, coolers and bulk handling vibrating equipment
CEO: Brian M Trudel
CEO: Brian M Trudel
Sales Manager: Steve Baker
Estimated Sales: $ 30 Million
Number Employees: 100-249
Square Footage: 185000
Other Locations:
  Carrier Europe
  Nivelles, BelgiumCarrier Europe
Regions Exported to: South America, Europe, Asia
Percentage of Business in Exporting: 30

42851 Carriere Foods Inc
540 Chemin Des Patriotes
Saint-Denis-Sur-Richelie, QC J0H 1K0
Canada 450-787-3411
Fax: 450-787-3537 marketing@carrierefoods.com
www.bonduelle.ca
Manufacturer and exporter of frozen and canned vegetables and fruits including peas, waxed beans, chick peas, green beans, asparagus and corn, dried beans, blueberries, cranberries, rasberries, rhubarb, strawberries, soups and sauces;importer of asparagus, carrots and spinach
President: Marcel Ostiguy
Number Employees: 250-499
Type of Packaging: Consumer, Private Label
Brands Exported: Artic Gardens; Snyder; Paula; Carriere; Manon
Regions Exported to: Europe, USA, Caribbean
Regions Imported from: Europe, Middle East, USA

42852 Carroll Co
2900 W Kingsley Rd
Garland, TX 75041-2378 972-278-1304
Fax: 972-840-0678 800-527-5722
info@carrollco.com www.carrollconverting.com
Manufacturer and exporter of soap, cleaners, disinfectants and germicides
President: Kyle Ogden
CEO: Frank Antonacci
fantonacci@carrollco.com
VP Technical: Ron Cramer
VP Sales: Craig Neely
Estimated Sales: $20-50 Million
Number Employees: 500-999
Square Footage: 220000
Regions Exported to: Worldwide
Percentage of Business in Exporting: 2

42853 Carroll Manufacturing International
23 Vreeland Rd
Florham Park, NJ 07932-1510 973-966-6000
Fax: 973-966-0315 800-444-9696
info@carrollmi.com www.carrollmi.com
Manufacturer and exporter of exhaust systems, fire protection equipment, heat reclaim units and utility distribution systems
Chairman of the Board: Barry J Carroll
VP Sales: Richard Moon
Contact: Bill Burrus
info@carrollmi.com
General Manager: Byron Read
Estimated Sales: $ 10 - 15 Million
Number Employees: 10-19
Square Footage: 150000
Parent Co: Carroll International Corporation
Regions Exported to: Worldwide
Percentage of Business in Exporting: 10

42854 Carron Net Co Inc
1623 17th St
PO Box 177
Two Rivers, WI 54241-2995 920-793-2217
Fax: 920-793-2122 800-558-7768
sales@carronnet.com www.carronnet.com
Manufacturer and exporter of hardware and netting for racks and conveyors
President/CEO: Bill Kiel Jr
bkieljr@carronnet.com
EVP/ CFO: Troy Christiansen
VP: Donald Schweiger
Estimated Sales: $5-10 Million
Number Employees: 20-49

Type of Packaging: Bulk
Regions Exported to: Worldwide
Percentage of Business in Exporting: 2

42855 Carry-All Canvas Bag Co.
1983 Coney Island Ave
Brooklyn, NY 11223-2328 718-375-4230
Fax: 718-375-4230 888-425-5224
sales@carryallbag.com www.carryallbag.com
Advertising specialties, bags and aprons; importer of tote bags; logo imprinting services available
Owner: Mitchel Kraut
Estimated Sales: $400,000
Regions Imported from: India
Percentage of Business in Importing: 3

42856 Carson Manufacturing Company
PO Box 750338
Petaluma, CA 94975-0338 707-778-3141
Fax: 707-778-8691 800-423-2380
sales@carsonmanufacturing.com
www.carsonmfg.com
Manufacturer and exporter of vinyl aprons
President: Curtis Lang
Number Employees: 10-19
Type of Packaging: Private Label, Bulk
Regions Exported to: Worldwide
Percentage of Business in Exporting: 2

42857 Carter Products
2871 Northridge Dr NW
Grand Rapids, MI 49544-9109 616-647-3380
Fax: 616-647-3387 888-622-7837
sales@carterproducts.com
www.carterproducts.com
Manufacturer and exporter of guide line and inspection lights; also, bandsaw guides, wheels and tires
President: Peter Perez
perez@carterproducts.com
VP: Terry Camp
Marketing Director: Kip Walworth
Operations Manager: Jeff Folkert
Purchasing Manager: Char Mooney
Estimated Sales: $ 3 - 5 Million
Number Employees: 20-49
Square Footage: 30000
Brands Exported: Laser; Laser Diode; Carter; Guidall; Micro-Precision; Inspecto-Light; Flip-Pod
Regions Exported to: Worldwide

42858 Carter-Day International Inc
500 73rd Ave NE # 100
Minneapolis, MN 55432-3271 763-571-1000
Fax: 763-571-3012 bulldog@carterday.com
www.carterday.com
Manufacturer and exporter of grain cleaning and sizing equipment
President: Paul Ernst
HR Executive: Tim Ryan
bulldog@carterday.com
Director International Agribusiness: Matthew Ernst
Estimated Sales: $ 10 - 20 Million
Number Employees: 100-249
Regions Exported to: Worldwide
Percentage of Business in Exporting: 50

42859 Carter-Hoffmann LLC
1551 Mccormick Blvd
Mundelein, IL 60060-4491 847-362-5500
Fax: 847-367-8981 800-323-9793
sales@carter-hoffmann.com
www.carter-hoffmann.com
Manufacturer and exporter of stainless steel food carts including refrigerator, banquet and heated holding/transport
President: Bob Fortmann
jfagan@carter-hoffman.com
CFO: Jim Fagan
CEO: Robert Fortman
Research & Development: Jim Minard
Marketing Director: Kim Aaron
Sales Director: Mark Anderson
IT Executive: Jim Fagan
Production Manager: John Bartoski
Purchasing Manager: Vince Unger
Estimated Sales: $20-25 Million
Number Employees: 100-249
Number of Products: 300+
Brands Exported: Carter Hoffmann
Regions Exported to: Worldwide

42860 Carts Food Equipment
113 8th St
Brooklyn, NY 11215-3115 718-788-5540
Fax: 718-788-4962 www.cartsfoodeqp.com
Sinks, reach-in and underbar refrigerators and marble top pizza and stainless steel work tables; exporter of mobile food vending carts
Owner: David Nadler
dave@cartsfoodeqp.com
CFO: Florence Rosenberg
VP: Dave Nadler
Estimated Sales: $2.5-5 Million
Number Employees: 10-19
Square Footage: 120000
Brands Exported: Carts Unlimited

42861 Carts Of Colorado Inc
5420 S Quebec St # 204
Suite 204
Greenwood Vlg, CO 80111-1902 303-329-0101
Fax: 303-329-6577 800-227-8634
carts@cartsofcolorado.com
www.cartsofcolorado.com
Manufacturer and exporter of mobile food carts, kiosks, and modular systems
President: Dan Gallery
dgallery@cartsofcolorado.com
Accountant: Bill Sheakin
Research & Development: Craig Green
Quality Control Manager: Jeff Clonk
Sales Director: John Gallery
Operations Manager: Jim Covey
Purchasing Manager: Deborah Gallery
Estimated Sales: $ 500,000 - $ 1 Million
Number Employees: 10-19
Number of Brands: 4
Number of Products: 10
Square Footage: 240000

42862 Casa Amador
810 Texas Ave
El Paso, TX 79901 915-533-7861
Fax: 915-533-8585 866-323-9649
casa-amador@sbcglobal.net
Importer and distributor of pinatas and other mexican handcrafts
President/COO: Ann Pearson
Estimated Sales: $500,000-$1 Million
Number Employees: 1-4
Square Footage: 26240
Regions Imported from: Mexico

42863 Casa Di Lisio Products Inc
486 Lexington Ave # 3
Mt Kisco, NY 10549-2779 914-666-5021
Fax: 914-666-7209 800-247-4199
info@casadilisio.com www.casadilisio.com
Frozen Italian sauces including walnut and sun dried tomato pesto, clam, marinara, puttanesca, basil pesto, cilantro pesto provencal,alfredo and roasted red peppers pest
Owner: Linda DiLisio
ldilisio@kitchencooked.net
VP: Lucy DiLisio
Year Founded: 1973
Estimated Sales: $ 20 - 50 Million
Number Employees: 50-99
Number of Brands: 1
Number of Products: 25
Square Footage: 4000
Type of Packaging: Consumer, Food Service, Private Label, Bulk
Brands Exported: Casa DiLisio
Regions Exported to: Central America, Middle East
Percentage of Business in Exporting: 10

42864 Casa Herrera
2655 Pine St
Pomona, CA 91767-2115 909-392-3930
Fax: 909-392-0231 800-624-3916
rudyh@casaherrera.com www.casaherrera.com
Manufacturer and exporter of tortilla and corn chip machinery including cookers, millers, sheeters, bakers, coolers, dividers, pressers, seasoners, etc
President: Michael Herrera
michaelh@casaherrera.com
CEO: Ron Meade
VP Sales: Christopher Herrera
Manager: Susana Herrera
Estimated Sales: $20-50 Million
Number Employees: 100-249
Square Footage: 100000
Regions Exported to: Worldwide

Importers & Exporters / A-Z

Percentage of Business in Exporting: 25

42865 Casa Pons USA
66 Palmer Ave
Suite 32
Bronxville, NY 10708   914-337-9872
Fax: 914-337-9874 866-766-7872
info@casaponsusa.net www.casaponsusa.net
Importer of olive oils, vinegars, olives, olive pate, capers, caperberries, piquillo pimientos, saffron, rice, etc
Executive Director: John Horne
Marketing: Jordi Nolla
Contact: Millie Gonzalez
mgonzalez@casaponsusa.net
Estimated Sales: $2.5-5 Million
Number Employees: 1-4
Type of Packaging: Consumer, Food Service
Other Locations:
  Euroaliment S.L.
  Rosello, SpainEuroaliment S.L.
Brands Imported: Mas Portell; Romulo; Pons
Regions Imported from: Europe

42866 (HQ)Casa Visco
819 Kings Rd
Schenectady, NY 12303-2627   518-377-8814
Fax: 518-377-8269 888-607-2823
www.casavisco.com
Kosher products including spaghetti and barbecue sauces, salsa and mustard; exporter of spaghetti sauce
Owner: Joe Viscusi
info@casavisco.com
VP: Michael Viscusi
Sales & Marketing: Adine Gallo
Production Manager: Michael Viscusi, Jr.
Estimated Sales: $1-2.5 Million
Number Employees: 5-9
Square Footage: 100000
Parent Co: Casa Visco Finer Food
Type of Packaging: Consumer, Food Service, Private Label, Bulk
Brands Exported: Casa Visco
Regions Exported to: Middle East
Percentage of Business in Exporting: 15

42867 Cascade Mountain Winery
835 Cascade Road
Amenia, NY 12501   845-373-9021
Fax: 845-373-7869 info@cascademt.com
www.cascademt.com
Processor and exporter of dry and semi-dry and nonsweet table wines
Owner: William Wathmore
CEO: Margaret Wetmore
Estimated Sales: $ 3 - 5 Million
Number Employees: 5-9
Number of Products: 8
Square Footage: 24000
Type of Packaging: Consumer
Regions Exported to: Asia

42868 Cascadian Farm Inc
719 Metcalf St
Sedro Woolley, WA 98284-1456   360-855-0542
Fax: 360-855-0444 www.cascadianfarm.com
Processor, importer, manufacturer and marketer of frozen organic foods including fruits, vegetables and juice concentrates; also pickles and fruit spreads.
President: Maria Morgan
CEO: Steve Sanger
Estimated Sales: $10-20 Million
Number Employees: 50-99
Square Footage: 28930
Parent Co: Small Planet Foods
Type of Packaging: Consumer, Food Service, Bulk
Other Locations:
  Cascadian Farm
  Napa, CACascadian Farm
Regions Exported to: Worldwide
Percentage of Business in Exporting: 10
Brands Imported: Muir Glen; Cascadian Farm
Regions Imported from: Central America, Canada

42869 Casella Lighting
10183 Croydon Way # C
Suite C
Sacramento, CA 95827-2103   916-363-2888
Fax: 888-489-9543 Info@CasellaLighting.com
www.casellalighting.com
Manufacturer and exporter of portable floor and table lamps, wall sconces, chandeliers and solid brass fixtures
Owner: Chuck Bird
chuck@casellalighting.com
Buyer: Margig Yaka
Office Manager: Ronda Simi
Estimated Sales: $5-10 Million
Number Employees: 5-9
Square Footage: 120000
Type of Packaging: Food Service
Brands Exported: Casella; Grag Studios
Regions Exported to: Central America, South America, Europe, Asia, Middle East
Percentage of Business in Exporting: 15

42870 Casey Fisheries
PO Box 86
Digby, NS B0V 1A0
Canada   902-245-5801
Fax: 902-245-5552 info@caseyfisheries.com
www.caseyfisheries.com
Processor and exporter of fresh and frozen scallops and salmon
President: Joseph Casey
Plant Manager: Duncan Casey
Estimated Sales: $1.6 Million
Number Employees: 15
Type of Packaging: Consumer, Food Service, Private Label, Bulk
Regions Exported to: USA

42871 Casey's Seafood Inc
807 Jefferson Ave
Newport News, VA 23607-6117   757-928-1979
Fax: 757-928-0257 www.caseysseafood.com
Canned and frozen blue crab meat; also, heat and serve gourmet crab cakes and deviled crabs and crawfish cakes
Owner: Jim Casey
jim@caseysseafood.com
Marketing Director: Mike Casey
Estimated Sales: $3 Million
Number Employees: 50-99
Square Footage: 40000
Type of Packaging: Consumer, Food Service
Regions Exported to: Worldwide
Percentage of Business in Exporting: 10

42872 Cash Register Sales
4851 White Bear Pkwy
St Paul, MN 55110-3325   651-294-2700
Fax: 651-294-2900 800-333-4949
moreinfo@crs-usa.com www.crs-usa.com
Wholesaler/distributor and importer of cash registers, calculators and small business machines; serving the food service market
President: David Sanders
Controller: Bill Oas
Direct Sales: James R. Sanders
Contact: Annette Borrelli
aborrelli@mmm.com
Estimated Sales: $10-20 Million
Number Employees: 1-4
Type of Packaging: Consumer, Food Service
Regions Imported from: Asia
Percentage of Business in Importing: 90

42873 Caspian Trading Company
3321 W. Gary Drive
P.O.Box 400
Tempe, AZ 85280   480-967-3454
Fax: 480-967-3482 800-227-7426
info@caspiantrading.net www.caspiantrading.net
Wholesaler, importer and exporter of fresh, frozen, dried and canned seafood
President: Mohammad Bozorgnia
CFO: Bruce Kochanck
VP: S Mehrostami
Estimated Sales: $1-2.5 Million
Number Employees: 1-4
Square Footage: 2000
Type of Packaging: Bulk
Brands Exported: Caspian
Regions Exported to: Europe, Asia, Middle East
Regions Imported from: Central America, Asia, Middle East

42874 Casso Guerra & Company
215 Regal Drive
Suite 527
Laredo, TX 78041-2336   956-725-9185
cassoguerra@surfus.net
Wholesaler/distributor, importer and exporter of general line items, equipment and produce; serving the food service market
President: A Casso, Sr.
Estimated Sales: $20-50 Million
Number Employees: 20-49
Regions Exported to: Mexico
Regions Imported from: Mexico

42875 Casso-Solar Corporation
506 Airport Executive Park
P.O. Box 163
Nanuet, NY 10954   845-354-2010
Fax: 845-547-0328 800-988-4455
sales@cassosolartechnologies.com
www.cassosolar.com
Manufacturer and exporter of dryers, ovens, and electric and gas conveyor systems
President: Doug Canfield
VP Finance: Harry Lyons
Quality Control Manager: Alex Mankiewicz
VP Sales/Marketing: Frank Lu
Plant Manager: Jan Michalski
Purchasing Manager: John Moles
Estimated Sales: $10 Million
Number Employees: 20-49
Number of Products: 100
Square Footage: 50000
Brands Exported: Solar Infrared Heater
Regions Exported to: Central America, South America, Europe, Asia, Middle East
Percentage of Business in Exporting: 15

42876 (HQ)Castle Cheese
2850 Perry Hwy
Slippery Rock, PA 16057   724-368-3022
Fax: 724-368-9456 800-252-4373
Processor and exporter of cheese foods including substitutes, imitation and natural blends
President: George Myrter
Purchasing Manager: Michelle Sabol
Estimated Sales: $370,000
Number Employees: 2
Square Footage: 13112
Type of Packaging: Consumer, Food Service, Private Label, Bulk
Other Locations:
  Castle Cheese
  Vernon, BCCastle Cheese
Regions Exported to: Asia, Canada, Mexico
Percentage of Business in Exporting: 20

42877 Cat Pumps
1681 94th Ln NE
Minneapolis, MN 55449-4372   763-780-5440
Fax: 763-780-2958 techsupport@catpumps.com
www.catpumps.com
Manufacturer and exporter of pumps including high-pressure, positive displacement, piston and plunger, stainless steel, hightemp, custom designed power units, submersible and end-suction centrifugal
CEO: William Bruggeman
CEO: William Bruggeman
Marketing Director: Darla Jean Thompson
Sales: Scott Stelzner
Estimated Sales: $50-100 Million
Number Employees: 100-249
Square Footage: 130000
Brands Exported: CAT PUMPS
Regions Exported to: Central America, South America, Europe, Asia, Middle East

42878 Catalyst International
1285 101st Street
Lemont, IL 60439   630-972-9800
Fax: 630-972-9876 800-236-4600
info@cdcsupply.com www.cdcsupply.com
Manufacturer and exporter of computer software for warehouse management
President: J Scott Pearson
CEO: Mitchell Radar
CFO: Tim Ward
Office Manager: Laurie Goodwin
VP, Business Development: Thomas Geza Varga
Controller: Mike Grecco
Marketing Coordinator: Wendy Erwin
Director Of Sales: Bryan Gaines
VP Operations: James H Martin
Number Employees: 70
Type of Packaging: Bulk
Regions Exported to: Worldwide

42879 Catch Up Logistics
5711 Friendship Ave
Pittsburgh, PA 15206-3616   412-441-9512
Fax: 412-441-9517 catchup@bellatlantic.net
www.catchuplogistics.com

Processor and exporter of plain and kosher frozen pizza; also, Italian specialties including pasta
Owner: Ronald Pasekoff
ronald.pasekoff@catchuplogistics.com
COO: Donald Paskoff
Estimated Sales: $2.5-5 Million
Number Employees: 5-9
Type of Packaging: Consumer, Food Service, Private Label, Bulk

42880 Cates Addis Company
2640 McIver Road
Parkton, NC 28371   910-858-3439
           Fax: 910-858-3074 800-423-1883
Grower of fresh vegetables for pre-prepared salads and food services.
President: Curtiss Cates
Estimated Sales: $3-5 Million
Number Employees: 7
Type of Packaging: Bulk
Regions Exported to: Europe, Asia, Canada
Percentage of Business in Exporting: 1

42881 Catfish Wholesale
P.O.Box 759
Abbeville, LA 70511   337-643-6700
           Fax: 337-643-1396 800-334-7292
Processor and distributor of catfish, garfish, crawfish, shrimp, crabs, flounder and trout
President: James Rich
Sales Executive: Shab Calahan
Sales Manager: David Lowery
Estimated Sales: $2.5 Million
Number Employees: 60
Number of Brands: 1
Square Footage: 32000
Type of Packaging: Consumer, Food Service, Private Label, Bulk
Regions Exported to: Worldwide

42882 Catskill Brewery
672 Old Rte. 17
Livingston Manor, NY 12758   845-439-1232
                  info@catskillbrewery.com
                  www.catskillbrewery.com
IPA, Pilsner, Lager, Stout and sour beer
Founder: Ramsay Adams
Number of Brands: 1
Number of Products: 14
Type of Packaging: Consumer, Private Label
Brands Exported: Catskill Brewery
Regions Exported to: USA

42883 Catskill Craftsmen Inc
15 W End Ave
Stamford, NY 12167-1296   607-652-7321
   Fax: 607-652-7293 info@catskillcraftsmen.com
                  www.catskillcraftsmen.com
Manufacturer and exporter of butcher block tables, cutting boards, solid maple housewares and kitchen furniture and work counters
President: Duncan Axtel
catskill@telenet.net
Vice President: Kenneth Smith
Quality Control: John Locastro
VP Sales: Dick Carpenter
Purchasing Manager: Hank Cioccari
Estimated Sales: $ 5 - 10 Million
Number Employees: 50-99
Number of Products: 17
Square Footage: 208000
Type of Packaging: Consumer, Food Service, Private Label
Regions Exported to: Central America, South America, Europe, Asia
Regions Imported from: Asia

42884 Catskill Mountain Specialties
1411 Route 212
Saugerties, NY 12477-3040   845-246-0900
           Fax: 845-246-5313 800-311-3473
                  www.newworldhomecooking.com
Condiments including roasted habanero, chipotle, barbecue, Jamaican jerk, etc.; importer of hot peppers, spices, etc.; also, co-packer of acidified foods
Owner: Liz Corrado
VP: Edward Palluth
Number Employees: 1-4
Square Footage: 8000
Type of Packaging: Consumer, Food Service, Private Label, Bulk
Regions Imported from: Central America, Caribbean
Percentage of Business in Importing: 28

42885 Cattle Boyz Foods
Suite 314, #14
900 Village Lane
Okotoks, Alberta,, CA T1S 1Z6
Canada   403-995-2279
           Fax: 403-995-2056 888-662-9366
           sales@cattleboyz.com www.CattleBoyZ.com
Manufacturer and exporter of unique latchtop bottle containing versatile gourmet sauces for barbecuing, marinades, glaze for all meats and seafoods. Available in 17 and 35 oz. sizes
Managing Partner/Owner: Karen Hope
Managing Partner: Joe Ternes
Quality Control: Roxanne Quest
Sales: Karen Hope
Number Employees: 1-4
Number of Brands: 1
Number of Products: 4
Type of Packaging: Consumer, Food Service, Private Label, Bulk
Brands Exported: Cattle Boyz
Regions Exported to: USA

42886 Catty Inc
6111 White Oaks Rd
Harvard, IL 60033-8307   815-943-2288
   Fax: 815-943-4473 plawther@cattycorp.com
                  www.cattycorp.com
Manufacturer and exporter of flexible packaging including foil, foil/paper, poly structures, margarine and candy wraps and lidding
President: Vincent Jefferson
vince.jefferson@comcast.net
CFO: Bill Schmiederer
Marketing and Sales Coordinator: Kristen Dahm
Sales Manager: Sheri Morelli
Operations Manager: Chuck DiPietro
Vice President, Engineering: Ron Klint
Number Employees: 50-99
Square Footage: 270000
Regions Exported to: Central America
Percentage of Business in Exporting: 100

42887 Caudill Seed Co Inc
1402 W Main St
Louisville, KY 40203-1328   502-583-4402
           Fax: 502-583-4405 800-626-5357
                  hf@caudillseed.com
Distributor of seeds and supplies
President: Dan Caudill
dcaudill@caudillseed.com
CFO: Iris Mudd
Vice President: Edgar Caudill
Branch Manager: Eugene Stratton
Sales Director: Jack Donahoe
Year Founded: 1947
Estimated Sales: $20 Million
Number Employees: 20-49
Number of Brands: 5
Number of Products: 400
Square Footage: 275000
Type of Packaging: Private Label, Bulk
Regions Imported from: Central America, South America, Asia

42888 Cavallini Coffee & Tea
2324 Shorecrest Dr
Dallas, TX 75235-1804   214-353-0328
   Fax: 214-353-0074 info@cavallinicoffee.com
                  www.cavallinicoffee.com
Importer of granita and espresso machines, tea, coffee roasters and sandwich grills
President: Bonnie Itzig
bitzig@cavallinicoffee.com
Estimated Sales: Less Than $500,000
Number Employees: 5-9
Parent Co: Globex
Type of Packaging: Food Service
Brands Imported: Astra; Ugolini; Solobar
Regions Imported from: Europe, Canada , Italy
Percentage of Business in Importing: 100

42889 Caviar & Caviar LLC
5527 N Nob Hill Rd
Sunrise, FL 33351-4708   954-746-4423
           Fax: 954-745-4423 188-542-8427
                  sales@caviarmerchant.com
                  www.sasaniancaviar.com
Other condiments, balsamic vinegar, caviar, smoked seafood, honey, jams, foodservice, private label.
Owner: Michael Jalileyan
jalileyan@gmail.com
Marketing: Michael Jalileyan
Number Employees: 5-9

42890 Cawley Co
1544 N 8th St
PO Box 2110
Manitowoc, WI 54220-1902   920-686-7000
           Fax: 920-686-7080 800-822-9539
           info@cawleyco.com www.thecawleyco.com
Manufacturer and exporter of engravable badges, plates, plaques and awards; also, electronic personalization systems for do-it-yourself engraving
President/CEO: Jim Peterson
CFO: Jerry Harris
HR Executive: Jean Slaby
jeans@thecawleyco.com
R & D: Jim Peterson
Quality Control: Paul Mueller
Marketing Director: Molly Peterson
Public Relations: Molly Peterson
Operations/Productions Manager: Paul Mueller
Plant Manager: Diane Fogltanz
Estimated Sales: Below $5 Million
Number Employees: 100-249
Square Footage: 112000
Parent Co: Contemporary
Regions Exported to: Worldwide
Percentage of Business in Exporting: 20

42891 Cawy Bottling Co
2440 NW 21st Ter
Miami, FL 33142-7182   305-634-2291
           Fax: 305-634-2291 877-917-2299
                  cawy@cawy.net www.cawy.net
Soft drinks
CEO/VP/Public Relations: Vincent Cossio
Quality Control: Ramon Mesa
Sales Director: Harris Padron
Operations Manager: Mayra Alfonsin
Production Manager: Carlos Garcia
Estimated Sales: $10-20 Million
Number Employees: 20-49
Square Footage: 120000
Type of Packaging: Consumer, Food Service
Brands Exported: Cawy
Regions Exported to: Central America, South America, Europe, Caribbean
Percentage of Business in Exporting: 15

42892 Cayne Industrial Sales Corp
429 Bruckner Blvd
Bronx, NY 10455-5007   718-993-5800
                  Fax: 718-402-9465
Manufacturer and exporter of industrial racks, handling equipment and food lockers including custom plastic.
President: Steven Cayne
Manager: Hank Cayne
hankcayne@aol.com
Estimated Sales: Less Than $500,000
Number Employees: 1-4
Square Footage: 20000
Regions Exported to: Worldwide

42893 Ccw Products
5861 Tennyson St
Arvada, CO 80003-6902   303-427-9663
           Fax: 303-427-1608 vickie.h@ccwproducts.com
                  www.ccwproducts.com
Manufacturer and exporter of clear wide-mouth plastic containers used for food packaging and point-of-purchase displays
President: David Teneyck
CEO: Mort Saffer
Sales Manager: Donald Johnston
Contact: Mirza Beg
beg@ccwproducts.com
Operations Manager: Roger Lamb
Estimated Sales: Less Than $500,000
Number Employees: 1-4
Number of Products: 300+
Square Footage: 160000
Type of Packaging: Consumer, Food Service, Private Label, Bulk

42894 Cedar Lake Foods
5333 Quarter Line Rd
Cedar Lake, MI 48812   989-427-5143
           Fax: 989-427-5392 800-246-5039
                  www.cedarlakefoods.com
Processor and exporter of canned and frozen vegetable protein entrees including meat analogs; also, dry soy milk and vegetarian foods

President: Alejo Pizzaro
Contact: Cheri Graves
Production Manager: John Sias
Plant Manager: John Sias
Purchasing Manager: Ann Britten
Estimated Sales: $5-9.9 Million
Number Employees: 20-49
Type of Packaging: Consumer, Food Service, Private Label, Bulk
Brands Exported: Cedar Lake; MGM Brands
Regions Exported to: Central America, South America, Asia, Canada, Mexico, Caribbean
Percentage of Business in Exporting: 30

42895 Cedarvale Food Products
11 Wiltshire Avenue
Toronto, ON M6N 2V7
Canada   416-656-3330
Fax: 416-656-6803 lounsbury@lounsbury.ca
Mustard and sauces including horseradish, cocktail, mint and tartar; importer of tomato paste
VP: David Higgins
Manager Export Sales/Marketing: Tim Higgins
General Manager: Gil Marks
Estimated Sales: $487,000
Number Employees: 12
Square Footage: 60000
Parent Co: Lounsbury Foods
Type of Packaging: Consumer, Food Service, Private Label, Bulk

42896 Ceilcote Air Pollution Control
7251 Engle Rd
Suite 300
Middleburg Hts, OH 44130   440-243-0700
Fax: 440-243-9854 800-554-8673
1us@verantis.com www.verantis.com
Manufacturer and exporter of air pollution control equipment including fans, tower packing, blowers, mist eliminators, resin systems and ionizing wet scrubbers, turn key systems, emergency vapor spill equipment
President: Larry Hein
CEO: Lars Buttkus
Sales: John Tonkewicz
Engineering Director: Nat Dickinson
Number Employees: 20-49
Square Footage: 100000
Regions Exported to: Worldwide
Percentage of Business in Exporting: 20

42897 Ceilidh Fisherman's Cooperative
158 Main St
Port Hood, NS B0E 2W0
Canada   902-787-2666
Fax: 902-787-2388 www.ceilidhlobster.ca
Processor and exporter of salted cod, live lobster and crab.
General Manager: Bernie MacDonald
Year Founded: 1985
Estimated Sales: $6 Million
Number Employees: 35
Type of Packaging: Consumer, Food Service, Private Label, Bulk
Regions Exported to: Japan
Percentage of Business in Exporting: 25

42898 Celite Corporation
2500 San Miguelito Rd
Lompoc, CA 93436   805-736-1221
Fax: 805-736-1222 info@worldminerals.com
www.worldminerals.com
Manufacturer and exporter of diatomite filter aids and functional fillers; also, absorbents, synthetic calcium silicate and mineral fillers
CEO: John Oskam
Contact: George Christoferson
christoferong@worldminerals.com
Estimated Sales: $5 - 10 Million
Number Employees: 250-499
Brands Exported: Celite; Hysorb; Micro-Cel; Super Floss; Kenite
Regions Imported from: Central America, South America, Europe, Asia, Middle East

42899 Cellofoam North America
1917 Rockdale Industrial Blvd
PO Box 406
Conyers, GA 30012   770-483-4491
Fax: 770-929-3608 800-241-3634
info@cellofoam.com www.cellofoam.com
Manufacturer and exporter of expanded polystyrene foam insulation
President: Steve Gardner
VP Sales/Marketing: Cliff Hanson
Estimated Sales: $10-20 Million
Number Employees: 100-249
Brands Exported: Cello Foam; Permaspan; Permafloat
Regions Exported to: Central America, South America, Caribbean, Mexico, Canada
Percentage of Business in Exporting: 10

42900 Cellox Corp
1200 Industrial St
Reedsburg, WI 53959-2154   608-524-2316
Fax: 608-524-2362 sales@cellox.com
www.cellox.com
Manufacturer and exporter of packaging supplies and plastic molding for advertising displays
President: Craig Hutchison
Estimated Sales: $10 - 20 Million
Number Employees: 50-99
Regions Exported to: Canada

42901 (HQ)Cellucap Manufacturing Co
4626 N 15th St
Philadelphia, PA 19140-1197   215-324-1541
Fax: 215-324-1290 800-523-3814
sales@cellucap.com www.cellucap.com
Personal protective apparel with a full range of headwear, disposable apparel, aprons and gloves
President: Jane Harris
cellucap@aol.com
Executive VP: Mark Davis
VP Sales: John Twamley
VP Sales: Nancy Lozoff
Operations Manager: David Richman
Estimated Sales: $2.5-5 Million
Number Employees: 20-49
Type of Packaging: Food Service
Regions Exported to: Worldwide

42902 (HQ)Centennial Food Corporation
4412 Manilla Rd
Calgary, AB T2G 4A7
Canada   403-214-0044
Fax: 403-214-1656
www.centennialfoodservice.com
Processor and exporter of fresh and frozen meat products including spiced and formed ground beef, beef patties, battered and breaded steaks and cutlets, vacuum sealed and aged beef cuts, bacon wrapped scallops and marinated short ribs; importer of beef and seafood
Chairman: Ron Kovitz
CEO/President: J Kalef
VP/General Manager: Nashir Vasanji
Number Employees: 250-499
Type of Packaging: Consumer, Food Service, Private Label, Bulk
Other Locations:
  Centennial Food Corp.
  Calgary, ABCentennial Food Corp.
Brands Exported: Centennial; Canadian Gourmet; Mastercut
Regions Exported to: Asia, USA
Percentage of Business in Exporting: 15
Regions Imported from: Asia, USA
Percentage of Business in Importing: 10

42903 Centent Co
3879 S Main St
Santa Ana, CA 92707-5787   714-979-6491
Fax: 714-979-4241 info@centent.com
www.centent.com
Manufacturer and exporter of industrial controls for factory automation including computer guided multiple axis positioning systems
President: August Freimanis
august.freimanis@centent.com
Estimated Sales: $2.5-5 Million
Number Employees: 10-19

42904 Centflor Manufacturing Co
545 W 45th St # L1
New York, NY 10036-3490   212-246-8307
Fax: 212-262-9717 www.mcmahonmed.com
Processor and exporter of essential oils and aromatic chemicals
President: Robert Beller
robjbeller@gmail.com
General Manager: Gloria Rose
Estimated Sales: $1.5 Million
Number Employees: 5-9
Square Footage: 48000
Regions Exported to: Worldwide

42905 (HQ)Central Coast Seafood
5495 Traffic Way
Atascadero, CA 93422-4246   805-462-3474
Fax: 805-466-6613 800-273-4741
www.ccseafood.com
Wholesaler/distributor and exporter of fresh seafood; serving the food service market in California
CEO: Giovanni Comin
VP Sales/Marketing: Nancy Osorio
Estimated Sales: $5.9 Million
Number Employees: 5-9
Square Footage: 40000
Other Locations:
  Central Coast Seafoods
  Morro Bay, CACentral Coast Seafoods

42906 Central Decal
6901 High Grove Blvd
Burr Ridge, IL 60527-7583   630-325-9892
Fax: 630-325-9878 800-869-7654
info@centraldecal.com www.centraldecal.com
Manufacturer and exporter of flexible nameplates, pressure sensitive labels and decals
President: Bob Keflin
bkeflin@centraldecal.com
CFO: Jennifer Loconte
VP: Robert Kaplan
Sales Manager: George Labine
Estimated Sales: $10 - 20 Million
Number Employees: 50-99
Square Footage: 60000
Regions Exported to: Canada, Mexico
Percentage of Business in Exporting: 5

42907 Central Fabricators Inc
408 Poplar St
Cincinnati, OH 45214-2481   513-621-1240
Fax: 513-621-1243 800-909-8265
esales@centralfabricators.com
www.centralfabricators.com
Manufacturer and exporter of stainless and carbon steel pressure vessels, heat exchangers, storage tanks, condensers, cookers, evaporators and kettles; also, other alloys available
President: Mike Lewis
mlewis@centralfabricators.com
CEO: Dave Angner
CFO: Dan Meade
Vice President: Tim Maly
Operations Manager: Troy Black
Estimated Sales: $3 - 5 Million
Number Employees: 10-19
Square Footage: 40000
Regions Exported to: Central America, South America
Percentage of Business in Exporting: 1

42908 Central Package & Display
3901 85th Ave N
Minneapolis, MN 55443-1907   763-425-7444
Fax: 763-425-7917
customerservice@centralcontainer.com
www.centralpackage.com
Manufacturer and wholesaler/distributor of corrugated boxes, cushion packaging, flexible films, litho labels and static control products
President: James E Haglund
CEO: Mike Haglund
mhaglund@centralpackage.com
Sales: Steve Braun
VP Sales/Marketing: Steve Braun
General Manager: Jerry Condon
Estimated Sales: $10-20 Million
Number Employees: 100-249
Square Footage: 300000

42909 Central Seaway Company, Inc.
650 Dundee
Suite 180
Northbrook, IL 60062   224-723-5800
Fax: 847-446-9410 800-323-1815
www.censea.com
Importer of frozen seafood including catfish, oysters, octopus, shrimp, lobster tails, squid, snapper, crayfish and abalone; also, frogs' legs
President: Lee Feigon
VP Marketing: Nate Torch
Sales: Dave Bennett
Contact: Mike Cape
m.cape@censea.com
VP Purchasing: Jeff Stern

Estimated Sales: $10-20 Million
Number Employees: 10-19
Brands Imported: Censea; Brolos; Eiland Urk; Sydney Traulers; Lucky 7; Sea Smap; Monana; Sandford

42910 (HQ)Century Blends LLC
11110 Pepper Rd # A
Hunt Valley, MD 21031-1204   410-771-6606
   Fax: 410-771-6608 jwaynewheeler@sun-ripe.com
Processor and exporter of bakery and confectionary supplies and mixes including dry bar, salad dressings and sauces
Owner: J Wayne Wheeler
Production Manager: Tim Wheeler
Estimated Sales: $1,000,000
Number Employees: 5-9
Type of Packaging: Food Service, Bulk
Brands Exported: Sun-Ripe
Regions Exported to: Europe, Canada, Caribbean
Percentage of Business in Exporting: 10

42911 Century Chemical Corp
28790 County Road 20
Elkhart, IN 46517-1125   574-293-9521
   Fax: 574-522-5723 800-348-3505
   sales@centurychemical.com
Manufacturer and exporter of industrial and household deodorants and sanitizers; also, nontoxic anti-freeze
President: Edward A Fetters
edfetters@centurychemical.com
Office Manager: Bobbi Holdeman
Plant Manager: David Eller
Estimated Sales: $ 1-2.5 Million
Number Employees: 5-9

42912 Century Foods Intl LLC
400 Century Ct
Sparta, WI 54656-2468   608-269-1900
   Fax: 608-269-1910 800-269-1901
   www.centuryfoods.com
Century Foods International is a manufacturer of nutritional powders and ready-to-drink beverages under private label and contract manufacturing agreements for food, sports, health and nutritional supplement industries. Other servicesprovided include agglomeration, blending and instantizing, research and development, analytical testing, and packaging from bulk to consumer size.
President: Tom Miskowski
VP R&D: Julie Wagner
VP Sales/Marketing: Gene Quast
VP Operations: Wade Nolte
Number Employees: 250-499
Square Footage: 1680000
Parent Co: Hormel Foods Corporation
Type of Packaging: Private Label, Bulk
Brands Exported: CenPrem

42913 Century Glove Corp
145 John Bankston Dr
Summerville, GA 30747-5124   706-857-6444
   Fax: 706-857-6446 www.centuryglove.com
Manufacturer and importer of cotton work and uniform gloves
Manager: Mary Seiler
Sales: Mary Seiler
Estimated Sales: less than $ 500,000
Number Employees: 20-49

42914 Century Industries Inc
299 Prather Ln
Sellersburg, IN 47172-1739   812-246-3371
   Fax: 812-246-5446 800-248-3371
   info@centuryindustries.com
   www.centuryindustries.com
Manufacturer and exporter of mobile concession trailers and kitchens
President: Robert Uhl
robertuhl@centuryindustries.com
VP: John Uhl
Sales Manager: Matt Gilland
Estimated Sales: $5-10 Million
Number Employees: 20-49
Type of Packaging: Food Service
Regions Exported to: Central America, South America, Europe, Asia, Middle East

42915 Ceramica De Espana
7700 NW 54th St
Doral, FL 33166-4106   305-597-9161
   Fax: 305-597-9161
Manufacturer and importer of ceramic tableware, vases and candlesticks, bathroom, table top, cookware, table accessories, pottery, garden pottery
President: Monica Ruiz
Estimated Sales: $5-10 Million
Number Employees: 5-9
Type of Packaging: Consumer, Food Service

42916 (HQ)Cereal Food Processors Inc
2001 Shawnee Mission Pkwy #110
Mission Woods, KS 66205-2097   913-890-6300
   Fax: 913-890-6382 info@cerealfood.com
Manufacturer and exporter of flour.
President: J. Breck Barton
Executive VP: Mark L Dobbins
m.dobbins@cerealfoods.com
Year Founded: 1972
Estimated Sales: $20-50 Million
Number Employees: 20-49
Type of Packaging: Consumer
Other Locations:
   Cereal Food Processors Plant
   Los Angeles, CA
   Cereal Food Processors Plant
   Kansas City, MO
   Cereal Food Processors Plant
   McPherson, KS
   Cereal Food Processors Plant
   Billings, MT
   Cereal Food Processors Plant
   Great Falls, MT
   Cereal Food Processors Plant
   Cleveland, OH
   Cereal Food Processors PlantKansas City
Regions Exported to: Worldwide

42917 Chad Co Inc
19950 W 161st St # A
Olathe, KS 66062-2717   913-764-0321
   Fax: 913-764-0779 800-444-8360
Manufacturer and exporter of automated washing and pasteurizing equipment for meat slaughtering operations
President: Mike Gangel
mike@chadcompany.com
Estimated Sales: Below $ 5 Million
Number Employees: 10-19
Square Footage: 10400
Brands Exported: Chad Company
Regions Exported to: South America, Europe
Percentage of Business in Exporting: 10

42918 Challenge Dairy Products, Inc.
6701 Donion Way
Dublin, CA 94568   877-883-2479
   Fax: 925-551-7591 800-733-2479
   consumerinfo@challengedairy.com
   www.challengedairy.com
Processor and exporter of butter and dehydrated milk; wholesaler/distributor of butter and frozen foods.
President, CEO: Irv Holmes
Controller: Geoffrey Uy
SR VP Retail & Foodservice: Tim Anderson
EDI Coordinator: Michael Jenkins
Office Manager: Daisrea Smith
Estimated Sales: $500 Thousand
Number Employees: 175
Number of Brands: 2
Square Footage: 8500
Type of Packaging: Consumer, Food Service, Private Label, Bulk
Brands Exported: Challenge; Danish Creamery
Regions Exported to: Worldwide
Percentage of Business in Exporting: 20

42919 Champion Chemical Co
8319 Greenleaf Ave
Whittier, CA 90602-2998   562-945-1456
   800-621-7868
   service@championchemical.com
   www.cleanthatpot.com
Manufacturer and exporter of carbon and grease removers
Owner: Andrew Ellis
service@championchemical.com
Estimated Sales: $ 1 - 5 Million
Number Employees: 10-19
Square Footage: 72000
Brands Exported: Sokoff; Dip-R-Spray; Swash; Surf-Kleen
Regions Exported to: Asia
Percentage of Business in Exporting: 15

42920 Champion Industries Inc
3765 Champion Blvd
Winston Salem, NC 27105-2667   336-661-1556
   Fax: 336-661-1979 800-532-8591
   info@championindustries.com
   www.championindustries.com
Manufacturer and exporter of commercial dishwashers, pot and pan washers and waste disposal systems
Owner: Luciano Berti
Chairman of the Board: Luciano Berti
CEO: Hank Holt
CFO: Christa Miller
R & D: Perry Money
Director Sales: Pete Michailo
Advertising Manager: Patrick Elworth
lberti@championindustries.com
Purchasing Manager: Donna Mealka
Estimated Sales: $20-50 Million
Number Employees: 100-249
Square Footage: 130000
Parent Co: Comenda-Alispa
Type of Packaging: Food Service
Brands Exported: Moyer Diebel
Regions Exported to: Worldwide
Percentage of Business in Exporting: 15

42921 Champion Nutrition Inc
1301 Sawgrass Corporate Pkwy
Sunrise, FL 33323-2813   954-233-3300
   Fax: 925-689-0821 800-225-4831
   www.champion-nutrition.com
Processor and exporter of sports nutrition supplements
Owner: Malcolm Borg
VP Finance: Jannie Motta
Industry Contact: Christy Olson
Estimated Sales: Less Than $500,000
Number Employees: 1-4
Square Footage: 18188
Brands Exported: Revenge; Metabolol; Heavyweight Gainer 900; Met-Max; Oxi Pro Metabolol; Muscle Nitro
Regions Exported to: Worldwide
Percentage of Business in Exporting: 5

42922 Champion Plastics
220 Clifton Blvd
Clifton, NJ 07011
   Fax: 800-526-1238 800-526-1230
   sales@championplastics.com
   www.championplastics.com
Manufacturer and exporter of polyethylene bags and films.
Founding Partner: John Callaghan
Year Founded: 1972
Estimated Sales: $20-30 Million
Number Employees: 100-249
Square Footage: 96000
Parent Co: X-L Plastics
Regions Exported to: Worldwide
Percentage of Business in Exporting: 10

42923 (HQ)Champion Trading Corporation
P.O.Box 227
Marlboro, NJ 07746   732-780-4200
   Fax: 732-780-9839 info@champtrading.com
   www.champtrading.com
Manufacturer and exporter of used and rebuilt processing and packaging machinery
Principal: David Matthews
Co-Owner: James Matthew
Co-Owner: Michael Matthews
Contact: Adrienne Schere
schere@champtrading.com
Plant Manager: S Bassett
Estimated Sales: $1-2,500,000
Number Employees: 5-9
Square Footage: 50000
Regions Exported to: Worldwide
Percentage of Business in Exporting: 10

42924 (HQ)Chaney Instrument Co
965 S Wells St
P.O. Box 70
Lake Geneva, WI 53147-2468   262-248-4449
   Fax: 262-248-8707 800-777-0565
   info@chaney-inst.com www.acurite.com
Manufacturer and exporter of digital and analog kitchen thermometers, timers and clocks
President: Valerie Wilson
v.wilson@laonastatebank.com
National Sales Manager Food Service: Allan Ahrens

Number Employees: 100-249
Square Footage: 95000
Type of Packaging: Consumer, Food Service, Private Label, Bulk
Other Locations:
 Chaney Instruments
 Lake Geneva, WIChaney Instruments
Brands Exported: Acu-Rite; Chaney Instruments

42925 Channel Fish Processing
88 Commercial St
Gloucester, MA 01930-5096   978-283-4121
 Fax: 978-283-5948 800-457-0054
 t.zaffiro@channelfish.com
Processor and exporter of frozen catfish, cod, halibut, herring, smelt, squid, shrimp, scallops and whiting; portion-controlled breaded and prepared seafood
President: Frank Cefalo
Sales Manager: Joe Bertolino
Contact: Jim Cross
jcross@channelfish.com
Operations Manager: James Stuart
Estimated Sales: $4.20 Million
Number Employees: 20-49
Square Footage: 160000
Type of Packaging: Consumer, Food Service
Brands Exported: North Atlantic
Regions Exported to: Europe, Middle East
Percentage of Business in Exporting: 5
Regions Imported from: Worldwide
Percentage of Business in Importing: 10

42926 Chantland Company, The
PO Box 69
Humboldt, IA 50548   515-332-4040
 Fax: 515-332-4923 info@chantlandpulley.com
 www.chantlandpulley.com
Manufacturer and exporter of belt conveyors, bag filling equipment and bag palletizers
CEO: Donald Sosnoski
Year Founded: 1943
Estimated Sales: $33 Million
Number Employees: 200
Square Footage: 140000

42927 Chapman Manufacturing Co Inc
481 W Main St
Avon, MA 02322-1695   508-587-7592
 Fax: 508-587-7592 info@chapmanco.com
 www.chapmanco.com
Manufacturer and exporter of lamps and lighting fixtures, encompasses table and floor lamps, chandeliers, sconces, accent furniture and decorative accessories. Authentic reproductions, traditional adaptations and transitional andoriginal contemporary designs
President: Richard Amaral
ramaral@chapmanco.com
Estimated Sales: $10-20 Million
Number Employees: 50-99

42928 Charcuterie LaTour Eiffel
1020, boul. MichŠle-Bohec
Blainville, QC J7C 5E2
Canada   418-687-2840
 Fax: 418-688-9558 800-361-0001
 www.toureiffel.ca
Processor and exporter of fresh and frozen pork
Marketing Director: Francois Couture
Parent Co: McCain Foods USA
Type of Packaging: Bulk
Regions Exported to: Caribbean
Percentage of Business in Exporting: 5

42929 Charles Beck Machine Corporation
400 W Church Road
King of Prussia, PA 19406-3185   610-265-0500
 Fax: 610-265-5627 beckmachine@verizon.net
 www.beckmachine.com
Manufacturer and exporter of set-up box lidders and rotary shear sheet cutters
President: Arthur Beck
Manager Parts/Service: Robert Pickell
Estimated Sales: Below $5 Million
Number Employees: 10
Regions Exported to: Worldwide
Percentage of Business in Exporting: 40

42930 Charles Beseler Company
2018 W Main St
P.O. Box 431
Stroudsburg, PA 18360   570-517-0400
 Fax: 800-966-4515 800-237-3537
 www.beselershrinkpackaging.com
Manufacturer and exporter of shrink wrap machinery.
Estimated Sales: $100-500 Million
Regions Exported to: Central America, South America
Percentage of Business in Exporting: 2

42931 Charles E. Roberts Company
539 Fairmont Rd
Wyckoff, NJ 07481-1318   973-345-3035
 Fax: 973-345-8516 800-227-2684
Manufacturer and exporter of embossed ribbon for awards, badges, prizes, contests, emblems, fairs and conventions
Owner/President: Bernard Gallant
Estimated Sales: $5-10 Million
Number Employees: 10-19
Square Footage: 28000
Regions Exported to: Europe, Canada
Percentage of Business in Exporting: 10

42932 Charles H Baldwin & Sons
1 Center St
P.O.Box 372
West Stockbridge, MA 01266-9502   413-232-7785
 Fax: 413-232-0114 www.baldwinextracts.com
Flavoring extracts and flavors, maple table syrup and supplier of baking supplies.
Owner: Jackie Moffatt
jackie@baldwinextracts.com
Estimated Sales: $500,000-$1 Million
Number Employees: 1-4
Regions Exported to: Worldwide
Percentage of Business in Exporting: 10

42933 Charles Mayer Studios
105 E Market St
Suite 114
Akron, OH 44308-2037   330-535-6121
 Fax: 330-434-2016
Manufacturer, exporter and importer of hotel and restaurant menu boards, white liquid chalk boards, bulletin boards, easels, trade show displays and today's specials boards, custom tables
Owner: Jeffrey Mayer
Executive VP: M Barton
Estimated Sales: $1-3 Million
Number Employees: 20-49
Square Footage: 210000
Type of Packaging: Food Service
Brands Exported: Mayer Hook N' Loop
Regions Exported to: Central America, South America, Europe, Australia, Canada, Carribean, Mexico
Percentage of Business in Exporting: 7
Percentage of Business in Importing: 1

42934 (HQ)Charles Ross & Son Co
710 Old Willets Path
Hauppauge, NY 11788-4193   631-234-0500
 Fax: 631-234-0691 800-243-7677
 mail@mixers.com www.mixers.com
Manufacturer, importer and exporter of mixing, blending and dispersion equipment
President: Richard Ross
rross@mixers.com
Executive VP: Bogard Lagman
Estimated Sales: $20-50 Million
Number Employees: 100-249
Square Footage: 150000
Other Locations:
 Ross, Charles, & Son Co.
 Savannah, GARoss, Charles, & Son Co.
Brands Exported: Ross
Regions Exported to: Central America, South America, Europe, Asia, Middle East

42935 Charlie's Pride
2650 Leonis Boulevard
Vernon, CA 90058
 Fax: 323-587-7317 877-866-0992
 www.charliespride.com
Prepared meats manufacturer founded in 1969.

Co-CEO: Jim Dickman
Co-CEO: Robert Dickman
CFO: Ted Murphy
VP, Sales: Peter Goldsberry
Plant Manager: Krystal Valle
Purchasing Manager: Yahaira Martinez
Number Employees: 140
Square Footage: 60000
Type of Packaging: Consumer, Food Service, Private Label, Bulk
Regions Exported to: Guam
Percentage of Business in Exporting: 1

42936 Charm Sciences Inc
659 Andover St
Lawrence, MA 01843-1032   978-687-9200
 Fax: 978-687-9216 info@charm.com
 www.charm.com
Manufacturer and exporter of food safety diagnostic instruments for antibiotic, aflatoxin and pesticide residues, ATP sanitation/hygiene, pasteurization efficiency and doneness in meat products
President: Dr Stanley Charm
VP Sales: Gerard Ruth
Contact: Rami Abraham
r.abraham@charm.com
Estimated Sales: Less Than $500,000
Number Employees: 1-4
Regions Exported to: Worldwide

42937 (HQ)Charmel Enterprises
638 Lindero Canyon Rd # 363
Oak Park, CA 91377   818-991-8760
 Fax: 818-889-6305 charmelent@aol.com
Dealer/wholesaler of foodservice equipment
President: Frank Abundis
CEO: Michael Bulmer
CFO: Irwin Parker
Sales: Frank Abundis
Contact: Martin Shea
martin_shea@wellsfargo.com
Estimated Sales: $1 Million
Number Employees: 4
Square Footage: 2000
Type of Packaging: Food Service
Brands Imported: Libbey, World Tableware Inc, Update International, Wing Inc
Regions Imported from: South America, Europe, Asia
Percentage of Business in Importing: 50

42938 (HQ)Chart Industries Inc
1 Infinity Corporate Ctr # 300
Cleveland, OH 44125-5370   440-753-1490
 Fax: 440-753-1491 800-247-4446
 mary.nelson@chart-ind.com
 www.chartindustries.com
Manufacturer and exporter of CO2 storage tanks used for carbonation in soda dispensing machines
President: John Wikstrom
CEO: William C Johnson
william.johnson@chart-ind.com
VP: Eric M Rottier
Marketing Director: Mary Nelson
Sales Director: Dick Mich
Estimated Sales: $20-50 Million
Number Employees: 1000-4999
Type of Packaging: Food Service
Regions Exported to: Worldwide

42939 Chas Boggini Co.
733 Bread & Milk Street
Coventry, CT 06238   860-742-2652
 Fax: 860-742-7903 glen@bogginicola.com
 www.bogginicola.com
Manufacturer and exporter of flavoring extracts
President: Glen Boggini
VP: David Boggini
Estimated Sales: $5-10 Million
Number Employees: 5-9
Type of Packaging: Consumer
Regions Exported to: Canada

42940 Chase Industries Inc
10021 Commerce Park Dr
West Chester, OH 45246-1333   513-860-5565
 Fax: 513-860-0933 800-543-4455
 www.chasedoors.com

Chase Industries, Inc. manufactures a full line of manual and semi-automatic L-Sealers, Shrink Tunnels, and Bar Sealers as well as fully automatic Sleeve Wrappers, Bundlers, Blister Sealers, Clam Shell Sealers, Curing Systems andFormfill equipment. Our goal as a manufacturer, is to provide top performance and top quality to the customer in as many combinations of size and options as possible. We like to work closely with our distributors and their customers for the bestpossible standards
CEO: Robert W Muir
bmuir@chaseind.com
CEO: Elizabeth Braslow
CEO: Jim Braslow
R&D: James Braslow
Purchasing: Jose Garcia
Estimated Sales: $ 5 - 10 Million
Number Employees: 250-499
Number of Brands: 10
Square Footage: 30000
Brands Exported: Chase; CII; Ultra Blister
Regions Exported to: Central America, South America, Europe, Asia, Middle East
Percentage of Business in Exporting: 30

42941 (HQ)Chase-Doors
10021 Commerce Park Dr
Cincinnati, OH 45246 513-860-5565
Fax: 513-245-7045 800-543-4455
www.chasedoors.com
Manufacturer and exporter of vinyl and roll up doors, fire and insulated doors, door operators and air curtains
CEO: Dan O'Connor
CFO: Drew Bachman
CEO: Robert W Muir
R&D: Rory Falato
Marketing: Rory Falato
General Manager: Carl Johnson
Plant Manager: Rick Schweitzer
Purchasing Director: Diane Wells
Estimated Sales: $ 20 - 50 Million
Number Employees: 100-249
Number of Brands: 10
Number of Products: 35
Other Locations:
    Chase-Durus
    Memphis, TNChase-Durus
Regions Exported to: Central America, South America, Europe, Asia, Middle East

42942 Chase-Logeman Corp
303 Friendship Dr
Greensboro, NC 27409-9332 336-665-0754
Fax: 336-665-0723 info@chaselogeman.com
Manufacturer and exporter of liquid filling, plugging and screw capping machinery, tray loaders and unloaders, conveyors, unscramblers, rotary tables, accumulators and monoblocks; also, custom designing available
President: Alan Gillespie
alang@chaselogeman.com
Vice President: Joel Slazyk
Quality Control: Louis Stier
Plant Manager: Lew Stier
Estimated Sales: $ 1 Million
Number Employees: 10-19
Square Footage: 36000
Regions Exported to: Central America, South America, Asia, Middle East, Latin America, Australia
Percentage of Business in Exporting: 10

42943 Chases Lobster Pound
7935 Hwy 6
PO Box 1
Port Howe, NS B0K 1K0
Canada 902-243-2408
Fax: 902-243-3334 www.chaseslobsterltd.ca
Processor and exporter of fresh and frozen lobster
Owner/Manager: Earl Chase
Number Employees: 10-19
Type of Packaging: Consumer, Food Service, Private Label, Bulk
Regions Exported to: Europe, USA
Percentage of Business in Exporting: 70

42944 Chaucer Foods, Inc. USA
2238 Yew St
Forest Grove, OR 97116
www.chaucergroup.co.uk
Manufacturers freeze dried ingredients and specialty bread products.
CEO: Andy Ducker
Number Employees: 5-9
Parent Co: Chaucer Foods Ltd

42945 Checker Bag Co
10655 Midwest Industrial Blvd
St Louis, MO 63132-1281 314-423-3131
Fax: 314-423-1329 800-489-3130
www.checkerbag.com
Manufacturer, importer and exporter of polyethylene, polypropylene and cellophane bags including bakery, confection and gourmet
President: Robert Freund
VP: Al Stix
Number Employees: 20-49
Regions Exported to: Canada
Percentage of Business in Exporting: 5
Percentage of Business in Importing: 10

42946 Checker Machine
2701 Nevada Ave N
Minneapolis, MN 55427-2879 763-544-5000
Fax: 763-544-1272 888-800-5001
cm@checkermachine.com
Spiral conveyors, ovens and freezers
President: Steve Lipinski
CFO: John Ackerman
Vice President: Steve Lipinski
Sales/Marketing Manager: Don Hockman
Production Manager: Brad Schmitt
Plant Manager: Steve Lipinski
Estimated Sales: $ 5 - 10 Million
Number Employees: 50-99
Square Footage: 400000
Parent Co: Checker Machine
Brands Exported: Stein/Checker
Regions Exported to: Worldwide
Percentage of Business in Exporting: 25

42947 Cheese Merchants of America
248 Tubeway Dr
Carol Stream, IL 60188 630-768-0317
Fax: 630-221-0584 johnp@cheesemerchants.com
www.cheesemerchants.com
Processors of custom blends of Italian cheeses, converters of hard Italian cheeses to grated, shredded, and shaved.
EVP/Managing Partner: Robert Greco
Director Purchasing/Quality Assurance: Paul DelleGrazie
Central Regional Sales Manager: Mark Lewis
EVP Sales: Jim Smart
Contact: Brian Barrett
brianb@cheesemerchants.com
Estimated Sales: $19.3 Million
Number Employees: 90
Square Footage: 105000
Type of Packaging: Consumer, Food Service, Bulk
Regions Imported from: Europe

42948 Cheeseland, Inc.
P.O. Box 22230
Seattle, WA 98122-0230 206-709-1220
cheeselandinc.com
Dutch cheese and cheese products
Owner & Founder: Jan Kos
Number Employees: 6
Brands Imported: Balarina Goat; Delft Blue; DoubleCream Gooda; Dutch Girl Goat; Dutch Vintage; Edam Balls; Honeybee Goat; Kokos; Leyden; Mustard Seeds Gooda; Peppercorns Gooda; and more.
Regions Imported from: Central America
Percentage of Business in Importing: 50

42949 Chef America
9601 Canoga Ave
Chatsworth, CA 91311 818-718-8111
www.chefamerica.com
Prepared frozen foods including stuffed sandwiches and croissants, pizza snacks and waffles
CEO: Paul Merage
CFO: Glenn Lee
VP: Larry Johnson
Research & Development: Phil Mason
V P Finance: Glenn Lee
Contact: John Mccarthy
john.mccarthy@us.nestle.com
Purchasing Director: George Turner
Purchasing Manager: Russ Shroyer
Plant Manager: Mike Crawford
Number Employees: 500-999
Type of Packaging: Consumer, Food Service

42950 Chef Hans' Gourmet Foods
310 Walnut St
Monroe, LA 71201-6712 318-322-2334
Fax: 318-322-2340 800-890-4267
ckorrodi@bayou.com
www.chefhansgourmetfoods.com
Processor and exporter of soup bases, batter, spices, seafood, breading, seasonings, wild rice pilaf, rice, desserts, bran, jambalaya, gumbo, etouffee, etc.
President: Hans Korrodi
ckorrodi@bayou.com
Estimated Sales: $1-2.5 Million
Number Employees: 1-4
Square Footage: 88000
Brands Exported: Chef Hans
Regions Exported to: Central America, Europe
Percentage of Business in Exporting: 5

42951 Chef Merito Inc
7915 Sepulveda Blvd
Van Nuys, CA 91405-1032 818-787-0100
Fax: 818-787-5900 800-637-4861
info@chefmerito.com www.chefmerito.com
Processor, importer and exporter of dried spices, seasonings, seasoned rice, batters, breading mixes, soups and sauces
President/CEO: Plinio Garcia, Jr
Project Manager: Sara Nicholson
Estimated Sales: $10-20 Million
Number Employees: 50-99
Number of Brands: 4
Square Footage: 30000
Type of Packaging: Consumer, Food Service, Bulk
Brands Exported: Chef Merito; Pikos Pikosos; Sabrosito Peppers
Regions Exported to: Europe
Percentage of Business in Exporting: 5
Regions Imported from: Central America, South America, Europe, Asia
Percentage of Business in Importing: 10

42952 Chef Revival
7240 Cross Park Drive
North Charleston, SC 29418 800-858-8589
Fax: 843-767-0494 800-248-9826
www.chefrevival.com
Manufacturer, importer and exporter of traditional and contemporary chef uniforms including jackets,aprons,pants, hats,clogs,as well as a full line of ladies and chilrens clothing.
President: Jerry Rosenblum
VP: Kim dela Villefromoy
Marketing Director: Kelly Gloor
Sales: Jack Kramer
Contact: Rob Johnson
rob@chefrevival.com
Production: Louis Nardella
Plant Manager: Paul Brady
Number Employees: 20
Square Footage: 16000
Type of Packaging: Consumer, Food Service
Brands Exported: Chef Revival; Knife & Steel; Checkerboard
Regions Exported to: Central America, South America, Europe, Asia
Regions Imported from: Central America, Europe, Asia

42953 Chef Specialties
411 W Water St
Smethport, PA 16749-1199 814-887-5652
Fax: 814-887-2021 800-440-2433
info@chefspecialties.com
www.chefspecialties.com
Manufacturer, exporter and importer of metal and wood kitchen specialties including peppermills, spice mills, salad bowls and cutting boards
Owner: Jack Pierotti
Sales: Mike Wagner
info@chefspecialties.com
Estimated Sales: $500,000-$1 Million
Number Employees: 5-9
Square Footage: 50000
Type of Packaging: Consumer, Food Service, Private Label, Bulk
Regions Exported to: Central America, South America, Europe, Asia, Canada, Caribbean, Mexico
Percentage of Business in Exporting: 5
Regions Imported from: Asia
Percentage of Business in Importing: 20

221

Importers & Exporters / A-Z

42954 Chef Works
12325 Kerran St # A
Poway, CA 92064-6801   858-643-5600
  Fax: 858-643-5624   800-372-6621
  www.chefwork.com
Manufacturer and supplier of Chef's coats, aprons, shirts, slacks and footwear
Estimated Sales: Less Than $500,000
Number Employees: 1-4

42955 Chef's Choice Mesquite Charcoal
1729 Ocean Oaks Rd
PO Box 707
Carpinteria, CA 93014-0707   805-684-8284
  Fax: 805-684-8284
Manufacturer and importer of mesquite charcoal
Owner: Bill Lord
Number of Products: 2
Type of Packaging: Food Service
Regions Imported from: Mexico

42956 Chef's Choice by EdgeCraft
825 Southwood Rd
Avondale, PA 19311-9765   610-268-0500
  Fax: 610-268-3545
President: Samuel Weiner
Estimated Sales: $ 20 - 50 Million
Number Employees: 100-249

42957 Chefwear
2300 W Windsor Ct # C
Addison, IL 60101-1491   312-427-6700
  Fax: 630-396-8337   800-568-2433
  info@chefwear.com   www.chefwear.com
Manufacturer and exporter of culinary apparel and accessories
President: Rochelle Huppin Fleck
CEO: Gary Fleck
Vice President: Carol Mueller
carol.mueller@chefwear.com
VP Sales/Marketing: Carol Mueller
Sales Director: Glenn Woerz
General Manager: Rob James
Estimated Sales: Less than $500,000
Number Employees: 50-99
Square Footage: 24000
Brands Exported: Chef-R-Alls; Chefwear; Pint Size Duds
Regions Exported to: Central America, South America, Europe, Asia, Middle East, Australia, Canada, Mexico
Percentage of Business in Exporting: 4

42958 Chelan Fresh Marketing
PO Box 669
Chelan, WA 98816   509-682-2591
  Fax: 509-682-4620   www.chelanfresh.com
Apples, pears and cherries from Washington state.
Domestic Sales Manager: Daniel Gebbers
General Manager: Tom Riggan
Type of Packaging: Consumer, Bulk

42959 Chelten House Products
607 Heron Dr
Swedesboro, NJ 08085
  info@cheltenhouse.com
  www.cheltenhouse.com
Organic and all-natural dressings, sauces, marinades, salsa and ketchup. QAI certified and OU approved.
President & COO: Jason Dabrow
Chairman & CEO: Steve Dabrow
CFO: Ken Pawloski
VP, Business Development: David Elchynski
VP, Operations: Jeff Skirvin
Estimated Sales: $40 Million
Number Employees: 50-99
Number of Brands: 3
Square Footage: 150000
Type of Packaging: Consumer, Food Service, Private Label
Brands Exported: Chelten House
Regions Exported to: Europe, Canada

42960 Chem-Tainer Industries Inc
361 Neptune Ave
West Babylon, NY 11704-5800   631-661-8300
  Fax: 631-661-8209   800-275-2436
  sales@chemtainer.com   www.chemtainer.com
Manufacturer and exporter of plastic tanks and containers
President: James Glen
VP Marketing: Tony Lamb
Contact: Joan Flaxman
joanflaxman@chem-tainer.com
Estimated Sales: $5-10 Million
Number Employees: 1-4
Square Footage: 1000000
Regions Exported to: Central America, South America, Europe
Percentage of Business in Exporting: 5

42961 Chem-Tainer Industries Inc
361 Neptune Ave
West Babylon, NY 11704-5800   631-661-8300
  Fax: 631-661-8209   800-938-8896
  sales@chemtainer.com   www.chemtainer.com
Manufacturer and exporter of plastic tanks, containers and material handling equipment
President: James Glen
Executive VP: A Lamb
Contact: Joan Flaxman
joanflaxman@chem-tainer.com
Estimated Sales: $5-10,000,000
Number Employees: 1-4
Square Footage: 40000
Parent Co: Chem-Trainer Industries
Regions Exported to: Worldwide
Percentage of Business in Exporting: 5

42962 ChemTreat, Inc.
4461 Cox Rd
Glen Allen, VA 23060-3331   804-935-2000
  Fax: 804-965-0154   800-648-4579
  cs_orders@chemtreat.com   www.chemtreat.com
Manufacturer and exporter of water treatment chemicals for boilers and cooler, cooker and waste water treatment and clarification systems
Contact: Roy Arnett
arnett@chemtreat.com
Manager, Food Industry Marketing: David Anthony
Dierctor Food Industry Division: Dennis Martin
Purchasing Manager: Steve Hemmis
Estimated Sales: $300,000-500,000
Number Employees: 1-4
Regions Exported to: Central America, South America, Canada, Caribbean, Latin America, Mexico
Percentage of Business in Exporting: 2

42963 Chemclean Corp
13045 180th St
Jamaica, NY 11434-4194   718-525-4500
  Fax: 718-481-6470   800-538-2436
  info@chemclean.com   www.chemclean.com
Manufacturer and exporter of industrial cleaners, degreasers, disinfectants, and deodorizers
President: Alberto Bodhert
alberto@chemclean.com
CEO: Frank Bass
Manager: S Emil Johnsen
Estimated Sales: $20-50 Million
Number Employees: 20-49
Square Footage: 20000
Regions Exported to: South America, Europe, Asia, Latin America

42964 Chemdet Inc
730 Commerce Center Dr # D
Sebastian, FL 32958-3128   772-388-2755
  Fax: 772-388-8813   800-645-1510
  info@chemdet.com   www.chemdet.com
Manufacturer and exporter of stainless steel tank washers
President: Phillip Joachim
Estimated Sales: $2.5-5 Million
Number Employees: 10-19
Regions Exported to: Central America, South America, Canada, Latin America, Mexico
Percentage of Business in Exporting: 5

42965 Chemex Division/International Housewares Corporation
11 Veterans Drive
Chicopee, MA 1022   413-499-2370
  Fax: 413-443-3546   800-243-6399
  www.chemexcoffeemaker.com
Manufacturer, importer and exporter of drip coffee makers and filters
President: Eliza Grassy
Estimated Sales: $ 1 - 3 Million
Number Employees: 5-9
Type of Packaging: Consumer
Brands Exported: Chemex
Regions Exported to: Asia
Percentage of Business in Exporting: 10
Percentage of Business in Importing: 1

42966 Chemicolloid Laboratories, Inc.
P.O.Box 251
New Hyde Park, NY 11040-0251   516-747-2666
  Fax: 516-747-4888
  customersupport@colloidmill.com
  www.colloidmill.com
Manufacturer and exporter of colloid mills used in applications to process materials being dispersed, suspended, emulsified, homogenized or comminuted, and process equipment.
VP: Robert Best
Marketing: Susan Okeefe
Sales Director: George Ryder
Purchasing: Steve Best
Estimated Sales: $ 3 - 5 Million
Number Employees: 20-49
Square Footage: 144000
Brands Exported: Charlotte Colloid Mills
Regions Exported to: Central America, South America, Europe, Asia, Middle East
Regions Imported from: Central America, South America, Europe, Asia, Middle East

42967 Chemifax
11641 Pike St
Santa Fe Springs, CA 90670   562-908-0405
  Fax: 562-908-0077   800-527-5722
  info@carrollco.com   www.carrollco.com
Manufacturer and exporter of cleaning products including floor waxes, finishes, detergents, soaps and chemical specialties
Manager: Mohammed Nilchian
Sales Manager: Mike Greene
Contact: Eddie Ayala
eayala@carrollco.com
Sales Manager: Mike Meller
Estimated Sales: $ 20 - 50 Million
Number Employees: 50-99
Square Footage: 80000
Parent Co: Carroll Company
Regions Exported to: Asia, Mexico
Percentage of Business in Exporting: 10

42968 (HQ)Chemindustrial Systems Inc
W 53 N 560 Highl & Dr
Cedarburg, WI 53012   262-375-8570
  Fax: 262-375-8559   info@chemindustrial.com
  www.chemindustrial.com
Manufacturers of pH control, neutralizing process systems and hydrocyclones.
CEO: Michael Lloyd
mlloyd@chemindustrial.com
Sales Manager: Michael Lloyd
Estimated Sales: $5-10 Million
Number Employees: 10-19
Square Footage: 6000

42969 Cher-Make Sausage Co
2915 Calumet Avenue
Manitowoc, WI 54220
  Fax: 920-683-5990   800-242-7679
  www.cher-make.com
Processor and exporter of kippered beef, sausage and meat snacks; importer of frozen meat.
Founder: Art Chermak
Director Finance/Vp Fin: Lawrence Franke
VP of Operations: Chuck Hoefner
Plant Manager: Chuck Hoefner
Purchasing Manager: Jim Coulson
Estimated Sales: $10-20 Million
Number Employees: 100-249
Square Footage: 80000
Type of Packaging: Consumer, Private Label
Regions Exported to: Mexico
Percentage of Business in Exporting: 1
Regions Imported from: Europe
Percentage of Business in Importing: 1

42970 Cherbogue Fisheries
98 Cliff St
Yarmouth, NS B5A 4B3
Canada   902-742-9157
  Fax: 902-742-7708
Processor and exporter of fresh and frozen seafood
President/ Founder: Alfred Le Blanc
VP: Alfred LeBlanc
Number Employees: 20-49
Type of Packaging: Bulk
Regions Exported to: Worldwide

Importers & Exporters / A-Z

42971 Cherith Valley Gardens
4009 Eloop 820 South
Suite B
Fort Worth, TX 76119 817-466-0600
Fax: 817-446-0602 800-610-9813
terriw@cherithvalley.com
Processor, importer and exporter of gourmet pickles, pickled vegetables, salsas, jellies, fruit toppings, peppers, relishes and hors d'oeuvres
President: Alan Werner
Public Relations: Terri Werner
Operations Manager: Christa Werner
Estimated Sales: $ 5 - 10 Million
Number Employees: 10-19
Square Footage: 24000
Type of Packaging: Consumer, Food Service
Regions Exported to: Europe
Percentage of Business in Exporting: 5
Regions Imported from: Central America
Percentage of Business in Importing: 5

42972 Cherokee Trading Co
951 Peek St NW
PO Box 1508
Conyers, GA 30012-4447 770-922-9600
Fax: 770-483-3047 sales@cherokeetrading.com
www.cherokeetrading.com
Sales and exporter of turkey and chicken
President: Jim Baker
jbaker@cherokeetrading.com
Sales Director: Michael Carter
Operations Manager: Wendy Cowan
Estimated Sales: Less Than $500,000
Number Employees: 5-9
Type of Packaging: Consumer, Bulk
Regions Exported to: Central America, South America, Europe, Asia
Percentage of Business in Exporting: 95

42973 Cherry Central Cooperative, Inc.
1771 N. US Highway 31 S.
Traverse City, MI 49684 231-946-1860
Fax: 231-941-4167 info@cherrycentral.com
www.cherrycentral.com
Red tart cherries, apples and blueberries and also a major supplier of cranberries, strawberries, pomegranate arils and asparagus. Supplier to major manufacturers for dried, frozen, canned and custom products.
President/CEO: Steve Eisler
Director, Food Service: David Barger
Retail National Sales Manager: Vince Higgs
Director, Private/Custom Label: Frank Wolff
Year Founded: 1973
Estimated Sales: $154 Million
Number Employees: 100-249
Square Footage: 15500
Type of Packaging: Consumer, Food Service, Private Label, Bulk
Brands Exported: Cherry Central, Grand Traverse
Regions Exported to: Europe, Asia
Percentage of Business in Exporting: 15

42974 Cherry's Industrial Eqpt Corp
600 Morse Ave
Elk Grove Vlg, IL 60007-5102 847-364-0200
Fax: 800-350-8454 800-350-0011
sales@cherrysind.com www.cherrysind.com
Manufacturer and exporter of aluminum shipping containers and pallet transfer machines, inverters and retrievers; importer of pallet inverters
President: David Novak
david@cherrysind.com
National Accounts Manager: James Woods
Estimated Sales: $500,000-$750,000
Number Employees: 10-19
Square Footage: 60000
Regions Exported to: Asia
Regions Imported from: UK

42975 Chesapeake Spice Company
4613 Mercedes Dr
Belcamp, MD 21017-1224 410-272-6100
Fax: 410-273-2122 www.chesapeakespice.com
Processor and importers of spices and seasonings, including anise, cumin, sage, sage oil, black pepper, paprika, cinnamon, saffron, thyme and ginger.
President: Larry Lessans
Vice President: David Lessans
Estimated Sales: $5-10 Million
Number Employees: 20-49
Square Footage: 200000
Type of Packaging: Bulk
Other Locations:
  Chesapeake Spice Company - Reno
  Reno, NVChesapeake Spice Company - Reno
Regions Imported from: Central America, South America, Europe, Asia, Middle East, Canada, Caribbean, Latin America, Mexico

42976 Chester Hoist
PO Box 449
Lisbon, OH 44432 330-424-7248
Fax: 330-424-3126 800-424-7248
www.chesterhoist.com
Manufacturer and importer of hoists including manual chain, worm-drive and electrical low headroom; exporter of manual and electric chain hoists
Manager: Bob Burkey
Quality Control: Bob Eusanio
Sales Rep.: Chris Reynolds
Application Engineer: Vince Anderson
Product Manager: Joe Runyon
Estimated Sales: $10-20 Million
Number Employees: 50-99
Parent Co: Columbus McKinnon Corporation
Brands Exported: Chester Hoist
Regions Exported to: Worldwide
Percentage of Business in Exporting: 10
Regions Imported from: Worldwide
Percentage of Business in Importing: 10

42977 Chester Inc Information
555 Eastport Centre Dr
Valparaiso, IN 46383-2911 219-465-7555
Fax: 219-462-2652 800-778-1131
clark@chesterinc.com www.chesterinc.com
Processor and exporter of popcorn
Chairman/CEO: Peter Peuquet
President: Larry Holt
EVP: Leonard Clark
Contact: James Chester
jchester@chestertech.com
Estimated Sales: $5-10 Million
Number Employees: 5-9
Type of Packaging: Consumer, Private Label
Other Locations:
  Francesville, IN
  Gary, IN
  Troy, MIGary
Regions Exported to: Worldwide
Percentage of Business in Exporting: 10

42978 Chester Plastics
Highway 3
P.O. Box 460
Chester, NS B0J 1J0
Canada 902-275-3522
Fax: 902-275-5002
Manufacturer and exporter of rigid plastic packaging and thermoformed plastic bottles; importer of plastic sheeting
President: George Nemskeri
General Manger: John Babiak
Marketing Manager: Ed Baker
General Manager: Michael Johnston
Number Employees: 90
Square Footage: 108000
Percentage of Business in Exporting: 30
Regions Imported from: Europe

42979 Chester's International, LLC
2020 Cahaba Rd
Suite 325
Mountain Brook, AL 35223-1179 205-949-4690
Fax: 205-298-0332 800-288-1555
info@chestersinternational.com
www.chestersinternational.com
Manufacturer and exporter of fried chicken products including breading mixes, seasonings, packaging supplies, deep fryers, fry kettles, marinades, warmers, breading tables, etc
President: Blue Akers
bluea@chestersinternational.com
CFO: Wade King
Director of Operations: Jamees Venable
Estimated Sales: $5.9 Million
Number Employees: 5-9

42980 (HQ)Chester-Jensen Co., Inc.
345 Tilghman St
Chester, PA 19013-3432 610-876-6276
Fax: 610-876-0485 800-685-3750
htxchng@chester-jensen.com
www.chester-jensen.com
stainless steel food processing equipment, including sanitary chillers, ice builders (thermal storage), batch mixing processors, plate heat exchangers & cook-chill equipment.
President: Richard Miller
CEO: Steven Miller
Sales Director: Robert Skoog
Estimated Sales: $10-20 Million
Square Footage: 76000
Type of Packaging: Consumer, Food Service, Private Label, Bulk
Other Locations:
  Chester-Jensen Company
  Cattaraugus, NYChester-Jensen Company
Regions Exported to: Worldwide
Regions Imported from: Worldwide

42981 Chestnut Identity Appare, Inc.
2001 River Road
P.O. Box 253
Brookdale, CA 95007-0253
800-336-8977
sales@chestnutid.com www.chestnutid.com
Industrial clothing, footwear, caps and accessories

42982 Chex Finer Foods Inc
71 Hampden Rd # 100
Mansfield, MA 02048-1807 508-226-0660
Fax: 508-226-7060 800-227-8114
info@chexfoods.com www.chexfoods.com
Processor and importer of gourmet foods including biscuits, confectionery items, specialties, etc
President: David Isenberg
Controller: Donald Robillard
Purchasing: Dan Powers
Estimated Sales: $10-20 Million
Number Employees: 20-49
Type of Packaging: Consumer
Regions Imported from: Worldwide

42983 Chia Corp USA
Turnberry Plaza
Suite 801
Miami, FL 33180 305-330-5485
www.chiacorp.com
Importer of chia seeds.
Parent Co: Chia International Corporation
Other Locations:
  Warehouse
  Vernon, CAWarehouse
Regions Imported from: South America
Percentage of Business in Importing: 100

42984 Chia I Foods Company
P.O.Box 670
La Puente, CA 91747-670
Fax: 626-401-9519
Wholesaler/distributor and importer of sliced, diced and granulated dehydrated fruits including pineapple, papaya, mango and coconut; also, crystallized ginger, dried red chili peppers, etc.; rack jobber services available; serving thefood service market
President: Ann Huang
VP: Steve Huang
Estimated Sales: $1-2.5 Million
Number Employees: 10-19
Square Footage: 36000
Type of Packaging: Bulk
Regions Imported from: Asia
Percentage of Business in Importing: 100

42985 Chicago 58 Food Products
135 Haist Ave
Woodbridge, ON L4L 5V6
Canada 416-603-4244
Fax: 905-265-0566
chicago58foodproducts@bellnet.ca
Meat products including beef, pastrami, smoked salami, frankfurters; also, herring, condiments and cheese; importer of beef cuts
President and Production Manager: Mosho Ami
Secretary and Sales Director: Ted Bernholtz
VP: Shane Reiken
Estimated Sales: $6.8 Million
Number Employees: 12
Square Footage: 60000
Type of Packaging: Consumer, Food Service, Private Label, Bulk
Percentage of Business in Exporting: 5
Percentage of Business in Importing: 5

Importers & Exporters / A-Z

42986 Chicago Food Corporation
5800 N Pulaski Rd
Chicago, IL 60646 773-478-0007
Fax: 773-478-0084 chcgofood@aol.com
www.chicagofood.com
Wholesaler/distributor and exporter of produce, frozen items, seafood and Oriental foods; importer of frozen seafood
Owner: Kipyo Hong
Contact: Ki Hong
k_hong@chicagofood.com
Estimated Sales: $20-50 Million
Number Employees: 10-19
Type of Packaging: Private Label, Bulk
Regions Imported from: South America, Asia, Canada
Percentage of Business in Importing: 30

42987 Chicago Importing Company
1250 Davis Road
Elgin, IL 60123 847-289-0180
Fax: 847-289-0183 800-828-7983
sales@chicagoimporting.com
www.chicagoimporting.com
Fine food and confectionery specialties
President/Owner: Lars Berntson
Contact: Jack Berntson
jack@chicagoimporting.com
Estimated Sales: $7 Million
Number Employees: 19

42988 Chicago Meat Authority Inc
1120 W 47th Pl
Chicago, IL 60609 773-254-3811
Fax: 773-254-5851 800-383-3811
info@chicagomeat.com www.chicagomeat.com
Pork and pork products as well as beef and beef products.
Founder/Owner/President: Jordan Dorfman
jdorfman@chicagomeat.com
Quality Control Manager: Charles Clayton
Year Founded: 1990
Estimated Sales: $29.7 Million
Number Employees: 250
Square Footage: 50000
Type of Packaging: Consumer, Food Service, Private Label, Bulk
Regions Exported to: Worldwide

42989 Chicago Scale & Slicer Company
2359 Rose St
Franklin Park, IL 60131-3504 847-455-3400
Fax: 847-455-3450
Manufacturer, importer and exporter of hand operated and electric slicers; also, grinders and knives
Owner: Eugene Dee
Estimated Sales: $ 1 - 5 Million
Number Employees: 10 to 19
Square Footage: 28000
Parent Co: Lawndale Corporation
Regions Exported to: Central America
Percentage of Business in Exporting: 5
Regions Imported from: Europe

42990 Chicago Stainless Eqpt Inc
1280 SW 34th St
Palm City, FL 34990-3308 772-781-1441
Fax: 772-781-1488 800-927-8575
www.chicagostainless.com
Since 1937, manufacturer of high quality sanitary pressure gauges, homogenizer gauges and digital thermometers
Manager: Jerry Williamson
VP of Marketing: Mark Mistarz
Sales Director: Jerry Williamson
Manager: John Kalousek
john@chicagostainless.com
Estimated Sales: $2.5-5 Million
Number Employees: 10-19

42991 Chickasaw Trading Company
PO Box 1418
Denver City, TX 79323 806-592-3515
Fax: 806-592-3460 800-848-3515
Processor and exporter of lean beef jerky and smoked turkey breast strips
Co-Owner: Linda Kay
Co-Owner: Joe Kay
Number Employees: 1-4
Square Footage: 10000
Type of Packaging: Private Label
Regions Exported to: Worldwide
Percentage of Business in Exporting: 5

42992 Chicken Of The Sea
2150 E. Grand Ave.
El Segundo, CA 90245 844-267-8862
www.chickenofthesea.com
Tuna, salmon, shrimp, crab, oysters, clams, mackerel and sardines.
CEO, Chicken of the Sea International: Valentin Ramirez
Year Founded: 1917
Estimated Sales: $600 Million
Number Employees: 1000-4999
Parent Co: Thai Union Group
Type of Packaging: Consumer, Food Service, Private Label

42993 Chico Nut Company
2020 Esplanade
Chico, CA 95926 530-891-1493
Fax: 530-893-5381 almonds@chiconut.com
Processor, exporter and packer of almonds
Owner: Peter D Peterson
Contact: Cheri Azevedo
azevedoc@chiconut.com
Estimated Sales: $ 3 - 5 Million
Number Employees: 20-49
Type of Packaging: Bulk
Brands Exported: Chico
Regions Exported to: South America, Europe, Asia
Percentage of Business in Exporting: 50

42994 Chief Industries
PO Box 848
Kearney, NE 68848-0848 308-237-3186
Fax: 308-237-2650 800-359-8833
agri@chiefind.com www.chiefind.com
Manufacturer and exporter of grain drying and handling equipment; also, bins
President: Roger Townsend
Research & Development: Jim Moffit
Sales Director: Ed Benson
Plant Manager: Duene McCann
Purchasing Manager: Rob Morris
Estimated Sales: $20-50 Million
Number Employees: 100-249
Number of Brands: 3
Number of Products: 12
Square Footage: 90000
Parent Co: Chief Industries
Type of Packaging: Bulk
Regions Exported to: Worldwide

42995 Chief Wenatchee
1705 N Miller St
Wenatchee, WA 98801-1585 509-662-5197
Fax: 509-662-9415
Grower and exporter of apples, cherries and pears
President: Brian Birsall
Operations Manager: Skip Coonfield
Number Employees: 250 to 499
Type of Packaging: Bulk
Brands Exported: Chief Supreme; Chief Chelan; Chief Wenatchee; Wenatchee Gold
Regions Exported to: Central America, South America, Europe, Asia, Middle East
Percentage of Business in Exporting: 40

42996 Chil-Con Products
PO Box 1385
Brantford, ON N3T 5T6
Canada 519-759-3010
Fax: 519-759-1611 800-263-0086
www.henrytech.com
Manufacturer and exporter of pressure vessels, oil separators, condensers, process cooling heat exchangers, direct expansion and flooded chillers
General Manager: Scott Rahmel
President, Chief Executive Officer: Michael Giordano
Business Manager: Harry Stewart
Plant Manager: Myron Harasym
Number Employees: 95
Square Footage: 400000
Parent Co: Valve, Henry, Company
Regions Exported to: Worldwide
Percentage of Business in Exporting: 80

42997 Chile Guy
168 Calle Don Francisco
Bernalillo, NM 87004-6519 505-867-4251
Fax: 505-867-4252 800-869-9218
www.thechileguy.com
Wholesaler/distributor, importer and exporter of exotic dried chiles including whole and powdered
Owner: Mark Sanchez
mark@thechileguy.com
Office Manager: Pam Harris
Estimated Sales: $5-10 Million
Number Employees: 5-9
Parent Co: Direct Marketing de Santa Fe
Type of Packaging: Bulk
Regions Exported to: Worldwide
Percentage of Business in Exporting: 10
Regions Imported from: Worldwide

42998 Chilean Seafood Exchange
5000 Godfrey Rd
Coral Springs, FL 33067-4148 954-255-7848
Fax: 954-255-7925 info@csx.org
Importer and exporter of seafood including salmon, trout, king dip, mussels, seabass and whiting
President: Sebastien Gros
Marketing Director: Jean-Sebastien Gros
Estimated Sales: $ 3 - 5 Million
Number Employees: 5-9
Type of Packaging: Consumer, Food Service, Private Label, Bulk
Brands Exported: Cryofresh; Simply Fresh Seafood; Golden Salmon
Regions Exported to: Europe, Carribean
Percentage of Business in Exporting: 5
Brands Imported: Cryofresh; Golden Salmon
Regions Imported from: Worldwide
Percentage of Business in Importing: 95

42999 Chill & Moore
3221 May Street
Fort Worth, TX 76110-4124 505-769-2649
Fax: 505-762-0571 800-676-3055
Frozen ices
Sales Manager (Food Service): Bob Moore
Sales Manager (Retail): Jay Jackson
Type of Packaging: Consumer, Food Service
Regions Exported to: Europe, Mexico
Percentage of Business in Exporting: 4

43000 Chillers Solutions
101 Alexander Ave # 3
Pompton Plains, NJ 07444-1854 973-835-2800
Fax: 973-835-3222 800-526-5201
www.edwards-eng.com
Manufacturer and exporter of heating/cooling equipment and products, control components, hydronic heating/cooling systems and vapor recovery units for pollution and process control; also, packaged industrial chillers
President: R Waldrop
VP Engineering: G Passaro
Manager: Aaron Herl
aherl@frhsd.com
Plant Manager: Jose Mercedes
Estimated Sales: $ 40 Million
Number Employees: 50-99

43001 China Lenox Incorporated
1414 Radcliffe Street
Bristol, PA 19007-5413 267-525-7800
www.lenox.com
Manufacturer and exporter of fine china dinnerware and giftware
Contact: Nea Ahern
nea_ahern@msn.com
Human Resources Manager: Jim Haddix
Estimated Sales: $ 91 Million
Number Employees: 1,500
Square Footage: 9774
Parent Co: Brown-Foreman
Type of Packaging: Food Service
Regions Exported to: Worldwide

43002 China Mist Brands
7435 E Tierra Buena Ln
Scottsdale, AZ 85260-1608 480-998-8807
Fax: 480-443-8384 800-242-8807
info@chinamist.com www.organichotteas.com
China mist and leaves pure teas
President: Rommie Flammer
rommie@chinamist.com
CEO: John Martinson
President/CEO/Finance Executive: Rommie Flammer
Marketing Coordinator: Kiley Biggins
Director of Retail Sales: Ed Baird
Human Resource Manager: Wade McKesson
rommie@chinamist.com
Plant Manager: Kevin McCullough

Estimated Sales: $3.8 Million
Number Employees: 20-49
Square Footage: 70000
Brands Exported: China Mist; Frenzy Herbal; Green Star; Leaves Pure Teas
Regions Exported to: Central America, Asia

43003 China Pharmaceutical Enterprises
8323 Ohara Court
Baton Rouge, LA 70806-6513   225-924-1423
   Fax: 225-924-4154   800-345-1658
Processor and importer of ascorbic acid, caffeine anhydrous and vitamin B-12
Office Manager: Susan Giska
Type of Packaging: Bulk
Regions Imported from: China
Percentage of Business in Importing: 100

43004 China Products
1043 Oyster Bay Rd # 2
East Norwich, NY 11732-1063
   Fax: 516-935-3959
Importer of tea, coffee, honey, nuts and seeds
President: Ronald Phipps
Vice President: Pam Phipps
Estimated Sales: $5-10 Million
Number Employees: 5-9
Type of Packaging: Bulk
Regions Imported from: Asia, Latin America
Percentage of Business in Importing: 100

43005 (HQ)Chincoteague Seafood CoInc
7056 Forest Grove Rd
PO Box 88
Parsonsburg, MD 21849-2096   443-260-4800
   Fax: 443-260-4900 gourmetsoups@hotmail.com
     www.chincoteagueseafood.com
Processor and distributor of gourmet specialty seafood items: canned and frozen products including fried clams, stuffed clams, New England/Manhattan clam chowders, corn chowder, lobster/clam/shrimp/lobster and cheddar bisques, cream ofcrab/vegetable crab/crab and cheddar soups, white/red clam sauces, chopped clams, clam juice
Owner: Leonard Rubin
lrubin60@aol.com
CEO: Bernard Rubin
CFO: Toby Rubin
Estimated Sales: $1-2.5 Million
Number Employees: 5-9
Number of Brands: 4
Number of Products: 25
Square Footage: 24000
Type of Packaging: Consumer, Food Service, Private Label, Bulk
Brands Exported: CapeCod; Chincoteague; Capt'n Ed's
Regions Exported to: Europe, Canada
Percentage of Business in Exporting: 1

43006 Chipmaker Tooling Supply
7352 Whittier Ave
Whittier, CA 90602-1131   562-698-5840
   Fax: 562-698-5646   800-659-5840
chipmakerca@yahoo.com www.chip-makers.com
A major supplier of machines and parts to the food industry.
Manager: Patty Rivera
Contact: Stephen Smith
chipmakerca@yahoo.com
Office Manager/Purchasing Agent: Laura Kurbel
Estimated Sales: $ 3 - 5 Million
Number Employees: 1-4
Square Footage: 48000
Regions Exported to: Europe, Asia, Australia
Percentage of Business in Exporting: 5

43007 Chipurnoi Inc
3 Cemetery Hill Rd
P.O. Box 1708
Sharon, CT 06069-2073   860-364-0870
   Fax: 860-364-5982   800-982-9002
     www.checkmatescandy.com
Importer and wholesaler/distributor of confectionery products and specialty foods
President: Laurence Chipurnoi
lchipurnoi@chipurnoi.com
General Manager: J Schmidt
Estimated Sales: $ 3 - 5 Million
Number Employees: 5-9
Brands Imported: Chips; Puntini
Regions Imported from: South America, Europe

43008 Chiquita Brands LLC.
DCOTA Office Center
1855 Griffin Rd., Suite C-346
Fort Lauderdale, FL 33004-2275   954-924-5700
     www.chiquita.com
Fruit and vegetable grower and producer of fresh and prepared food products.
President: Carlos Lopez Flores
VP: Chris Dugan
Year Founded: 1899
Estimated Sales: $3 Billion
Number Employees: 20,000
Number of Brands: 3
Parent Co: Cutrale-Safra
Type of Packaging: Consumer, Food Service, Private Label, Bulk
Regions Exported to: Worldwide
Regions Imported from: Central America

43009 Chlorinators Inc
1044 SE Dixie Cutoff Rd
Stuart, FL 34994-3436   772-288-4854
   Fax: 772-287-3238   800-327-9761
     regal@regalchlorinators.com
     www.regalchlorinators.com
Manufacturer and exporter of gas chlorinators, waste water treatment systems, sulphonators, dual cylinder scales, chlorine gas detectors, flow pacing control valves and vacuum monitors
President: Diane Haskett
Vice President: Chris Myers
Marketing Manager: Jill Majka
Operations Manager: John Hentz
Estimated Sales: $ 3 - 5 Million
Number Employees: 20-49
Square Footage: 20000
Brands Exported: Regal

43010 Chock Full O'Nuts
     888-246-2598
     www.chockfullonuts.com
Regular and decaffeinated, ground, instant, and flavoured coffees
Estimated Sales: $67,000
Square Footage: 8984
Parent Co: Massimo Zanetti Beverage
Type of Packaging: Consumer, Food Service, Private Label
Other Locations:
   Chock Full O'Nuts Corp.
   Brooklyn, NYChock Full O'Nuts Corp.

43011 Chocolat Belge Heyez
16 Ch De La Rabastaliere E
St-Lazare-De-Bellechasse, QC J3V 2A5
Canada   450-653-5616
   Fax: 450-653-1445
Processor and importer of chocolates
Chairman: Bernard Falmagne
VP: Marc Voyer
Treasurer: Dominique Tran
Secretary: Claude Leblanc
Administrator: Sharmila Amin
Estimated Sales: $371,000
Number Employees: 6
Square Footage: 16000
Type of Packaging: Consumer, Private Label

43012 Chocolate Concepts
114 S Prospect Ave
Hartville, OH 44632-8906   330-877-3322
   Fax: 330-877-1100 cc@dmpweb.net
Manufacturer, importer and exporter of chocolate equipment including tempering tanks, measuring pumps, vibrating tables, cooling conveying tunnels, coin machines and kettles; manufacturer and exporter of plastic standard and custommolds
Owner: Scott Huckestein
shuckestein@dmpweb.net
Estimated Sales: $ 1 - 2.5 Million
Number Employees: 5-9
Number of Products: 55
Square Footage: 120000
Parent Co: LCF
Brands Exported: Chocolate Concepts
Regions Exported to: Central America, South America, Europe, Asia
Brands Imported: APT
Regions Imported from: Europe

43013 Chocolate House
4121 South 35th Street
Milwaukee, WI 53221   414-281-7803
   Fax: 414-423-2484   800-236-2022
Manufacturer and exporter of chocolate
Manager: Irene Hyducki
Executive Vice President: Gary Winder
Estimated Sales: $10-20 Million
Number Employees: 50-99
Type of Packaging: Consumer
Regions Exported to: Canada
Percentage of Business in Exporting: 2

43014 Chocolate Stars USA
333 Fairfield Rd
Fairfield, NJ 07004-1961   973-461-2434
     www.chocolatestars.com
Chocolate bars, truffles, cookies
Marketing Manager: Carolina Gavet

43015 Chocolate Street of Hartville
114 South Prospect Avenue
Hartville, OH 44632-1010   330-877-1999
   Fax: 330-877-1100   888-853-5904
     www.discoverhartville.com
Custom chocolate products including 3-D corporate logos, bars and personalized gold foil wrapped coins; also, private label available; exporter of chocolate processing equipment including cooling tunnels, vibration tables, measuringpumps, etc
General Manager: Robert Barton
Estimated Sales: $ 10 - 20 Million
Number Employees: 20-49
Square Footage: 26000
Type of Packaging: Consumer, Food Service, Private Label, Bulk
Regions Exported to: Europe
Percentage of Business in Exporting: 3

43016 Chocolaterie Bernard Callebaut
133 1st Street SE
Calgary, AB T2G 5L1
Canada   403-265-5777
   Fax: 403-265-7738   800-661-8367
     www.bernardcallebaut.com
Processor and exporter of quality chocolates and chocolate products, including spreads, sauces and ice cream bars
President/CEO: Bernard Callebaut
Number Employees: 20-49
Type of Packaging: Consumer, Private Label
Regions Exported to: USA
Percentage of Business in Exporting: 30

43017 Chocolates a La Carte
24836 Avenue Rockefeller
Valencia, CA 91355   661-257-3700
   Fax: 661-257-4999   800-818-2462
orders@candymaker.com www.candymaker.com
Processor, importer and exporter of chocolate designs for desserts, amenities and gifts including pianos, swans, sea shells, etc
President: Rena Pocrass
CEO/VP: Richard Pocrass
VP Finance and Administration: Michael Pocrass
Marketing Manager: Diane Rudman
Contact: Tony Aguirre
taguirre@candymaker.com
EVP/Head of Operations: Frank Geukens
Estimated Sales: $26 Million
Number Employees: 165
Square Footage: 110000
Type of Packaging: Food Service
Regions Exported to: Europe, Asia, Australia
Percentage of Business in Exporting: 15
Regions Imported from: Europe
Percentage of Business in Importing: 20

43018 Choctaw Maid Farms
Old Highway 15 N
Jackson, MS 39209   601-683-4000
   Fax: 601-298-5497
Processor, importer and exporter of fresh and frozen chicken parts
Owner: Tammy Etheridge
Purchasing Agent: Ruthie Harper
Number Employees: 250-499
Type of Packaging: Bulk

Importers & Exporters / A-Z

43019 Choice Organic Teas
600 S Brandon St
Seattle, WA 98108-2240   206-525-0051
Fax: 206-523-9750   866-972-6879
choiceorganicteas@worldpantry.com
www.choiceorganicteas.com
Processor and exporter of organic teas including black, green and herbal
Founder: Blake Rankin
Estimated Sales: $1-$2.5 Million
Number Employees: 20-49
Parent Co: Granum Inc
Type of Packaging: Consumer, Food Service, Private Label, Bulk
Brands Exported: Choice
Regions Exported to: Europe, Asia, Canada

43020 Choklit Molds LTD
23 Carrington St
Lincoln, RI 02865-1702   401-725-7377
Fax: 401-724-7776   800-777-6653
www.choklitmolds.com
Manufacturer and exporter of reusable plastic chocolate molds. Wholesaler of packaging supplies for the candy retail.
President: Lea Goyette
CEO: Richard Goyette
VP/Treasurer: Lea Goyette
Contact: Richard Oyette
choklitmolds@cox.net
Plant Manager: Chris Mottram
Purchasing: Kelly Mottram
Number Employees: 1-4
Square Footage: 20000
Type of Packaging: Bulk
Regions Exported to: Europe, Canada
Percentage of Business in Exporting: 2

43021 Chong Imports
838 Grant Ave # 2
San Francisco, CA 94108-1718   415-982-1432
Fax: 415-982-4896
Importer and exporter of porcelain kitchenware
Owner: Stephen Tom
Manager: Bill Tom
Estimated Sales: Less Than $500,000
Number Employees: 5-9
Parent Co: National Exporters Company
Regions Exported to: Asia
Percentage of Business in Exporting: 30
Regions Imported from: Asia
Percentage of Business in Importing: 70

43022 Chooljian Bros Packing Co
3192 S Indianola Avenue
PO Box 395
Sanger, CA 93657   559-875-5501
Fax: 559-875-1582
k.elliott@chooljianbrothers.com
www.chooljianbrothers.com
Processor and exporter of raisins; also, custom packaging services
President: Michael Chooljian
mchooljian@chooljianbrothers.com
Estimated Sales: $500,000
Number Employees: 50-99
Parent Co: Chooljian Brothers Packing Company
Type of Packaging: Consumer, Food Service, Private Label, Bulk
Brands Exported: Chooljian; Prize
Regions Exported to: Central America, South America, Europe, Asia, Middle East

43023 Choyce Produce
3140 Ualena St
Suite 206
Honolulu, HI 96819-1965   808-839-1502
President: Edmund Choy
Contact: Annette Forness
aforness@choycehi.com
Estimated Sales: $ 5 - 10 Million
Number Employees: 5-9

43024 (HQ)Christianson Systems Inc
20421 15th St SE
PO Box 138
Blomkest, MN 56216-9706   320-995-6141
Fax: 320-995-6145   800-328-8896
info@christianson.com   www.onyxrp.com
Manufacturer and exporter of pneumatic conveyors and ship and barge unloaders
President: Jim Gerhardt
jger@christianson.com
Marketing Manager: Barbara Gilberts
Sales: Tim Flaan
Estimated Sales: $5-10 Million
Number Employees: 50-99
Square Footage: 170000
Brands Exported: Vac-U-Vator; Handlair; Chem-Vac; Push-Pac; SuperTower; SuperPortable

43025 Christopher Ranch LLC
305 Bloomfield Ave.
Gilroy, CA 95020   408-847-1100
Fax: 408-847-5488   Info@christopherranch.com
www.christopherranch.com
Garlic. Varieties include fresh peeled, fresh roasted, whole fresh, chopped and crushed in oil, chopped and minced in water, pickled garlic, elephant garlic, fresh ginger, fresh shallots, specialty onions, sun dried tomatoes, cherriespeeled specialty onions, horseradish, sweet corn, organic, and dried chiles.
President/CEO: Bill Christopher
Year Founded: 1956
Estimated Sales: $135 Million
Number Employees: 1000-4999
Square Footage: 220000
Type of Packaging: Consumer, Food Service, Bulk

43026 Christy Industries Inc
1812 Bath Ave # 1
Brooklyn, NY 11214-4690   718-236-0211
Fax: 718-259-3294   800-472-2078
www.christy-ind.com
Manufacturer and exporter of fire and burglar alarms; wholesaler/distributor of intercoms and television equipment including security and closed circuit
President: Statz Cheryl
s.cheryl@alarmdistributor.com
Estimated Sales: $ 1 - 3 Million
Number Employees: 5-9
Square Footage: 6000
Regions Exported to: Worldwide
Percentage of Business in Exporting: 5

43027 Christy Machine Co
118 Birchard Ave
P.O. Box 32
Fremont, OH 43420-3008   419-332-6451
Fax: 419-332-8800   888-332-6451
www.christymachine.com
Manufacturer and exporter of conveyers; also, filling, icing and glazing machinery
President: Randy L Fielding
cmc1@cros.net
Estimated Sales: $ 1 - 2.5 Million
Number Employees: 10-19
Regions Exported to: Worldwide

43028 Christy Wild Blueberry Farms
1167 Southhampton Road
Amherst, NS B4H 3Y4
Canada   902-667-3013
Fax: 902-667-0350   chrisgaklis@comcast.net
christywildblueberryfarms.com/
Processor and exporter of IQF wild blueberries
President: Chris Gaklis
Estimated Sales: $1.95 Million
Number Employees: 15
Parent Co: International Food Trade
Brands Exported: Blue Boy
Regions Exported to: Europe, USA, Canada
Percentage of Business in Exporting: 30

43029 Chromalox Inc
103 Gamma Dr # 2
Pittsburgh, PA 15238-2981   412-967-3800
Fax: 412-967-3938   800-443-2640
www.chromalox.com
Manufacturer and exporter of electric heating elements for commercial cooking equipment
Managing Director: Steve Valentino
CEO: Anthony Deane
deanea@dmipartners.com
Chief Financial Officer/Secretary: Edward Cumberledge
Vice President: Peter Ranalli
Vice President, Engineering: Roger Ormsby
Quality Manager: Jack Foster
Marketing Manager: Paul Skidmore
Senior Vice President, Sales: John Halloran
Facilities Manager: Roger Iverson
Procurement Manager: Kristina McCann
Estimated Sales: $ 161 Million
Number Employees: 100-249
Square Footage: 20259
Parent Co: Emerson Electric Company
Regions Exported to: Worldwide

43030 Chuppa Knife Manufacturing
133 N Conalco Drive
Jackson, TN 38301   731-424-1212
Fax: 731-424-8937   chuppak@aol.com
Manufacturer and exporter of stainless steel and aluminum handle cutlery
President: Elmer Rausch
Estimated Sales: $ 1 - 2.5 Million
Number Employees: 8
Number of Products: 350
Type of Packaging: Consumer, Food Service, Private Label
Brands Exported: Chuppa
Regions Exported to: Worldwide
Percentage of Business in Exporting: 10

43031 Church & Dwight Co., Inc.
Princeton South Corporate Center
500 Charles Ewing Boulevard
Ewing, NJ 08628   609-806-1200
800-833-9532
www.churchdwight.com
Personal care, household cleaning, fabric care, and health and well-being products for the consumer market. Manufacturer of Arm & Hammer brand sodium bicarbonate (baking soda), and other leavening products for the baking industry.
Chairman/President/CEO: Matthew Farrell
Executive VP/CFO: Rick Dierker
Executive VP/General Counsel/Secretary: Patrick de Maynadier
Executive V, Global R&D: Carlos Linares
Executive VP/CMO: Britta Bomhard
Executive VP, U.S. Sales: Paul Wood
Executive VP, Global Operations: Rick Spann
Year Founded: 1846
Estimated Sales: $4.15 Billion
Number Employees: 4,700
Number of Brands: 34
Type of Packaging: Consumer, Food Service, Bulk
Brands Exported: ARM & HAMMER
Regions Exported to: Europe, Asia, Middle East, Canada, Caribbean, Mexico, UK
Percentage of Business in Exporting: 15
Regions Imported from: Europe
Percentage of Business in Importing: 15

43032 Ciao Imports
2805 N Commerce Pkwy
Miramar, FL 33025-3956   954-437-7849
Fax: 866-353-8866   866-249-0400
jw@ciaoimports.com   www.ciaoimports.com
Authentic, premium quality specialty foods from Italy and around the world.
Manager: Nancy Mesa
Marketing Contact: John Woram
Manager: Lilly Catter
info@ciaoimports.com
Number Employees: 5-9
Number of Brands: 25
Other Locations:
Metro NY Warehouse
Newark, NJ
Florida Warehouse
Miramar, FLMetro NY WarehouseMiramar

43033 Cibao Meat Products Inc
630 Saint Anns Ave
Bronx, NY 10455-1404   718-993-5072
Fax: 718-993-5638   info@cibaomeat.com
www.cibaomeat.com
Processor and exporter of Spanish sausage and salami.
President: Lutzi Vieluf
CEO: Heinz Vielus
Estimated Sales: $5-10 Million
Number Employees: 50-99
Type of Packaging: Food Service, Bulk
Regions Exported to: Central America

43034 Cin-Made Packaging Group
3150 Clinton Ct
Norcross, GA 30071   770-476-9088
Fax: 513-541-5945   800-264-7494
info@cin-made.com
Manufacturer and exporter of paper composite cans and tubes for specialty markets including wine and spirits, fancy foods and teas.

Importers & Exporters / A-Z

Manager: Hartmut Geisselbrecht
CFO: John Ewalt
Quality Control: Erik Frey
Marketing Director: Hartmut Geisselbrecht
Sales Manager: Janet Pickerell
Plant Manager: Eric Frey
Purchasing Manager: Phyllis Dietrich
Estimated Sales: $10-20 Million
Number Employees: 20-49
Type of Packaging: Consumer, Private Label
Regions Exported to: Worldwide
Percentage of Business in Exporting: 1

43035 Cincinnati Industrial Machry
4600 N Mason Montgomery Rd
Mason, OH 45040-9176   513-923-5600
    Fax: 513-769-0697 800-677-0076
    sales@cinind.com www.thearmorgroup.com
Manufacturer and exporter of baking ovens and can washing equipment; also turnkey finishing systems and cleaning/drying/curing systems
Owner: Frank Ahaus
fahaus@cinind.com
Marketing Director: Liz Chamberlain
Public Relations: Liz Chamberlain
Operations Manager: Joe Bohlen
Estimated Sales: $ 20 - 25 Million
Number Employees: 250-499
Square Footage: 317000
Regions Exported to: Central America, South America, Europe, Asia, Middle East
Percentage of Business in Exporting: 50

43036 Cincinnati Preserving Co
3015 E Kemper Rd
Cincinnati, OH 45241-1514   513-771-2000
    Fax: 513-771-8381 800-222-9966
    www.clearbrookfarms.com
Fruit preserves ,jams,jellies,canned fruit,pie fillings,fruit pie mixes.
Owner/CFO: Andrew Liscow
VP: Dan Cohen
Contact: Joe Heinrich
joe@clearbrookfarms.com
Estimated Sales: 1.8 Million
Number Employees: 18
Square Footage: 120000
Parent Co: Cincinatti Preserving Company
Type of Packaging: Consumer
Regions Exported to: Asia, Canada

43037 Cinelli Esperia
380 Chrislea Road
Woodbridge, ON L4L 8A8
Canada
        905-856-1820
    albert@cinelli.com
    www.gcinelli-esperia.com
Manufacturer and exporter of spiral mixers, bagel and roll machinery, steam proofers, baguette and bread molders, automatic bun dividers, rounders, sheeters, etc.; importer of coffee machines and revolving rack and convection ovens
President: Guido Cinnelli
Sales/Marketing Manager: Albert Cinelli
Number Employees: 50
Square Footage: 160000
Regions Exported to: Worldwide

43038 Cinnabar Specialty Foods Inc
1134 Haining St # C
Prescott, AZ 86305-1693   928-778-3687
    Fax: 928-778-4289 866-293-6433
    info@cinnabarfoods.com www.cinnabarfoods.com
Processor and exporter of sauces including ethnic and barbecue; also, fruit chutneys, dry spice blends, Caribbean salsa, kashmiri marinade, rice mixes, soup enhancers, etc
Owner: Alana Morrison
sales@cinnabarfoods.com
Vice President: Ted Schleicher
Estimated Sales: $1-4.9 Million
Number Employees: 1-4
Square Footage: 4000
Type of Packaging: Consumer, Food Service, Private Label, Bulk
Brands Exported: Cinnabar Specialty Foods
Regions Exported to: Worldwide
Percentage of Business in Exporting: 5

43039 Cintex of America
283 E Lies Rd
Carol Stream, IL 60188   630-588-0900
    Fax: 425-962-4600 800-424-6839
    www.centex.com

Manufacturer and exporter of metal detection check weighing equipment, x-ray inspection systems and vision systems
President: Anthony Divito
CEO: Simon Armstrong
CFO: Richard Harwood Smith
Marketing: Dan Izzard
Sales: Dan Izzaro
Production: Jeff Hoffman
Plant Manager: Jeff Hoffman
Purchasing: Sandy Sell
Estimated Sales: $10-20 Million
Number Employees: 50-99
Number of Brands: 10
Number of Products: 4
Square Footage: 60000
Regions Exported to: Central America, South America, Europe, Asia, Middle East, Australia

43040 Cipriani
30271 Tomas
Rancho Sta Marg, CA 92688-2123   949-589-3978
    Fax: 949-589-3979 www.ciprianicorp.com
Manufacturer, distributor and importer of hygienic stainless steel valves
President: Maria Carlo
mg@ciprianicorp.com
CEO: Robert Moreno
Vice President: Maria Grazia Cipriani
Marketing/Sales VP: Carlo Cipriani
Sales Manager: Chris P Winsek
Estimated Sales: $1,000,000
Number Employees: 5-9
Square Footage: 6000
Brands Imported: Tassalini
Regions Imported from: Europe
Percentage of Business in Importing: 98

43041 Cipriani's Spaghetti & Sauce Company
1025 West End Avenue
Chicago Heights, IL 60411-2742   708-755-6212
    Fax: 708-755-6272
Processor and exporter of pasta including angel hair, vermicelli, linguine, fettuccine, lasagna, spinach, etc.; also, pasta sauces
President/Purchasing Manager: Annette Johnson
Executive VP: Arthur Petrarca
Estimated Sales: $5-10 Million
Number Employees: 10-19
Square Footage: 43572
Type of Packaging: Consumer, Food Service, Private Label, Bulk
Brands Exported: Cipriani's
Regions Exported to: Asia
Percentage of Business in Exporting: 10

43042 Circle Valley Produce LLC
1370 Burgess St
Idaho Falls, ID 83402-1825   208-524-2628
    Fax: 208-524-2630 www.idahopotato.com
Processor and exporter of potatoes
President: Kent Cornelison
Communications: Kirk Hart
Purchasing: Dave Owens
Estimated Sales: $8.8 Million
Number Employees: 50-99
Type of Packaging: Consumer, Bulk

43043 Circuits & Systems Inc
59 2nd St
East Rockaway, NY 11518-1236   516-593-4607
    Fax: 516-593-4607 800-645-4301
    sales@arlynscales.com www.arlynscales.com
Manufacturer and exporter of electronic scales
President: Arnold Gordon
a.gordon@chaverware.com
Estimated Sales: Below $5 Million
Number Employees: 20-49
Square Footage: 20000
Brands Exported: Circuits & Systems, Inc.
Regions Exported to: Central America, South America

43044 Ciro Foods
PO Box 44096
Pittsburgh, PA 15205-0296   412-771-9018
    Fax: 412-771-9018 cirofoods@usa.net
Roasted red pepper spread, Italian salsa, sauces including pizza, barbecue and cooking and hot honey mustard; wholesaler/distributor of hot pepper sauce; serving the food service market; importer of vinegar; exporter of hot honeymustard

President: Robert Pasquarelli
VP: Josephine Proto
Marketing Executive: Armand Pasquarelli
Number Employees: 20
Type of Packaging: Consumer, Food Service, Private Label
Brands Exported: Raffaele's, Ciro
Regions Exported to: South America, Caribbean, Canada
Percentage of Business in Exporting: 5
Regions Imported from: Europe, Canada

43045 Cisco Brewers
5 Bartlett Farm Rd
Nantucket, MA 02554-4341   508-325-5929
    Fax: 508-325-5209 tracy@ciscobrewers.com
    www.ciscobrewers.com
Producer of ale and lager beers
Owner: Randy Hudson
randy@ciscobrewers.com
CEO: Jay Harman
Web And Social Media Manager: Kristen V Hull
randy@ciscobrewers.com
Estimated Sales: $600,000
Number Employees: 1-4
Square Footage: 12800
Type of Packaging: Consumer
Regions Exported to: Europe

43046 (HQ)Citadelle Maple Syrup Producers' Cooperative
2100 St-Laurent, CP 310
Plessisville, QC G6L 2Y8
Canada
        819-362-3241
    Fax: 819-362-2830 citadelle@citadelle.coop
    www.citadelle.coop
Processor and exporter of fruit spreads, honey, pure maple syrup and maple sugar.
CEO: Martin Plante
Director Financial Services & Treasurer: Patrick Fleurent, CPA, CMA
Dir. of Corporate Affairs & Secretary: Jean-Marie Chouinard
Director of Marketing: Sylvie Chapron
Princial Sales Director: Stephane Vachon, M.Sc.
Human Resources Director: Richard Cote
Director Operations & Quality: Remi Fortin, ing. MBA
Number Employees: 150
Square Footage: 360000
Type of Packaging: Consumer, Food Service, Private Label, Bulk
Other Locations:
    La Guadeloupe Facility
    Guadeloupe, QC
    Restigouche Brand Inc
    Saint-Quentin, NB
    Facility & Distribution Centre
    Plessisville, QC
    Tertiary Transformation Facility
    Plessisville, QC
    Cranberry Transformation Facility
    Aston-Jonction, QCLa Guadeloupe
    FacilitySaint-Quentin
Brands Exported: Citadelle; Camp; Maple Gold; Cleary's; O'Canada
Regions Exported to: Europe, Asia, Australia, USA
Percentage of Business in Exporting: 86

43047 Citra-Tech
2 Prespas Street
Lefkosia, CY 33811
    info@citra-tech.com
    www.citra-tech.com
Manufacturer and exporter of fruit handling and processing machinery; consultant specializing in the design and construction of fresh and citrus fruit processing facilities
President: P M Irby
VP: P Irby, Jr.
Number Employees: 25
Square Footage: 8000
Regions Exported to: Worldwide
Percentage of Business in Exporting: 90

43048 Citrico
155 Revere Dr # 1
Northbrook, IL 60062-1558   847-835-4368
    Fax: 847-945-7405 800-445-2171
    www.creativeimpactgroup.com
An independent manufacturer of citrus products for the food, beverage, pharmaceutical and nutraceutical industries.

Owner: Joanne Brooks
VP Technical Sales: Robert Vieregg
Sales: Timothy Grano
Contact: Todd Heinz
th@citico.com
Estimated Sales: $4.8 Million
Number Employees: 10-19
Number of Brands: 20
Parent Co: Citrico International
Brands Imported: Citrico Pectin
Regions Imported from: Central America, South America, Mexico, Worldwide
Percentage of Business in Importing: 50

43049 Citrosuco North AmericaInc
5937 State Road 60 E
Lake Wales, FL 33898-9279   863-696-7400
    Fax: 863-696-1303   800-356-4592
citrosuco@citrosuco.com.br   www.citrosuco.com
Orange juice and concentrates; importer of frozen orange and apple concentrates and not from concentrate orange juice; exporter of frozen orange juice concentrates and not from concentrate orange juice
President: Nick Emanuel
CEO: Kathy Baker
kbaker@citrosuco.com
CFO: Dennis Helms
Sales Manager: Michael DuBrul
Plant Manager: Jim Bolden
Purchasing Manager: Gary Brundage
Estimated Sales: Less Than $500,000
Number Employees: 1-4
Square Footage: 38200
Parent Co: Citrosuco
Type of Packaging: Bulk
Regions Exported to: Europe, Asia
Percentage of Business in Exporting: 25
Regions Imported from: South America
Percentage of Business in Importing: 50

43050 Citrus Service
120 S Dillard St
Winter Garden, FL 34787   407-656-4999
    Fax: 407-656-4999   beroper@iag.net
Manufacturer and exporter of frozen organic citrus juices and frozen juice concentrates
President: Bert Roper
CEO: Charles Roper
Estimated Sales: $4 Million
Number Employees: 20-49
Square Footage: 42000
Type of Packaging: Bulk
Regions Exported to: Europe, Asia
Percentage of Business in Exporting: 20

43051 Citrus and Allied Essences
3000 Marcus Ave, Ste 3e11
New Hyde Park, NY 11042   516-354-1200
    Fax: 516-354-1502   www.citrusandallied.com
Supplier of essential oils, oleoresins, aromatic chemicals and specialty flavor ingredients.
President/CEO/Owner: Richard Pisano Jr.
Executive Vice President: Stephen Pisano
Sales Manager: Ann Heller
Contact: Jodi Adams
jadams@citrusandallied.com
Director Purchasing: Rob Haedrich
Number Employees: 100+
Type of Packaging: Food Service, Bulk

43052 Citterio USA
2008 State Route 940
Freeland, PA 18224-3256   570-636-3171
    Fax: 570-636-1267   800-435-8888
sales@citteriousa.com   www.citteriousa.com
Processor and importer of Italian Speciality deli meat products
President/COO: Osvaldo Vanucci
CEO: Michelle Basista
mbasista@citteriousa.com
CEO: Nick Dei Tos
VP Sales: Joseph Petruce
VP Manufacturing: Michael Zieminski
Estimated Sales: $5-10 Million
Number Employees: 100-249
Parent Co: Giuseppe Citterio Spa
Type of Packaging: Consumer, Food Service, Private Label, Bulk
Regions Imported from: Europe

43053 City Brewing Company
925 S 3rd St
La Crosse, WI 54601   608-785-4200
    inquiries@citybrewery.com
    www.citybrewery.com
Manufacturer/processor of beer for major and private label brands.
VP & Chief Financial Officer: Gregory Inda
Director, Supply Chain: Jeff Glynn
Year Founded: 1939
Estimated Sales: $38 Million
Number Employees: 400
Type of Packaging: Consumer
Other Locations:
   Latrobe, PA
   Memphis, TNMemphis
Regions Exported to: Worldwide

43054 City Foods Inc
4230 S Racine Ave
Chicago, IL 60609-2526   773-523-1566
    Fax: 773-523-1414   info@beasbest.com
    www.beasbest.com
Processor, importer and exporter of frozen beef products including corned beef brisket, short ribs, corned, sliced, roast beef, pastrami, and beef bacon
President: Kenneth Kohn
CEO: John Campbell
john@beasbest.com
Information Technology Manager: Chris Humberg
Sales Manager: Scott Weiss
Director Of Purchasing: John Campbell
Estimated Sales: $48 Million
Number Employees: 50-99
Number of Brands: 3
Square Footage: 43000
Type of Packaging: Consumer, Food Service, Private Label, Bulk
Brands Exported: Pride of Chicago; Silver Label; Bea's Best; Chef's Pride; City Food's Salted Beet
Regions Exported to: Central America, South America, Middle East
Percentage of Business in Exporting: 3

43055 City Grafx
243 Grimes Street
Suite D
Eugene, OR 97402   541-345-1101
    Fax: 541-345-1942   800-258-2489
    www.citygrafx.com
Manufacturer and exporter of tabletop signs, table numbers, specialty merchandising boards, custom signs, menu boards and dimensional graphics
President: Jeff Phoenix
j.phoenix@citygrafx.com
VP: Mary Phoenix
Estimated Sales: Below $ 5 Million
Number Employees: 1-4
Square Footage: 16000
Regions Exported to: Canada, Caribbean, Mexico
Percentage of Business in Exporting: 1

43056 Clabber Girl Corporation
900 Wabash Ave
Terre Haute, IN 47807-3208   812-232-9446
    Fax: 812-232-2397   www.clabbergirl.com
Manufacturer of baking powder, baking soda, dessert mixes and corn starch for retail, food service and industrial customers.
National Sales Manager: Mark Rice
Type of Packaging: Consumer, Food Service, Private Label, Bulk
Brands Exported: Clabber Girl
Regions Exported to: Central America, Asia, Middle East, Canada, Africa, Caribbean, Mexico, Latin America
Percentage of Business in Exporting: 12

43057 Clamco Corporation
775 Berea Industrial Parkway
Berea, OH 44017   216-267-1911
    Fax: 216-267-8713   www.clamcocorp.com
Manufacturer and exporter of shrink packaging machinery and bag sealers

Owner: Serge Bergun
CEO: Mark Goldman
VP: Dennis McGrath
R&D: Rob Patton
Marketing: Dennis McGrath
Sales Director: Bruce Howell
Contact: Sandy Waite
swaite@clamcocorp.com
General Manager: Larry Boyles
Purchasing: Bob Snyder
Estimated Sales: $ 5-10 Million
Number Employees: 40
Square Footage: 48000
Parent Co: PAC Machinery Group
Type of Packaging: Consumer, Food Service, Private Label, Bulk
Regions Exported to: Worldwide
Percentage of Business in Exporting: 25

43058 Clamp Swing Pricing Co Inc
8386 Capwell Dr
Oakland, CA 94621-2114   510-567-1600
    Fax: 510-567-1830   800-227-7615
cspinfo@clampswing.com   www.clampswing.com
Manufacturer and exporter of pricing tags, sign holders, display hooks, hand trucks, handheld plastic shopping baskets, etc.
President: Trageser Ed
ed@clampswing.com
Sales/Marketing Executive: Kamran Faizi
Purchasing Manager: Ron Coffman
Estimated Sales: $ 3 - 5 Million
Number Employees: 20-49
Regions Exported to: Central America, South America
Percentage of Business in Exporting: 1

43059 Clarendon Flavor Engineering
2500 Stanley Gault Parkway
Louisville, KY 40223   502-634-9215
    Fax: 502-634-1438   www.clarendonflavors.com
Manufactures natural and artificial flavors to food and beverage industry. Specializes in natural soft drinks, juice added and flavored sparkling waters
President: Richard Rigney
Estimated Sales: $5-10 Million
Number Employees: 6
Square Footage: 80000
Type of Packaging: Bulk
Regions Exported to: South America, Europe, Asia, Canada
Percentage of Business in Exporting: 5

43060 (HQ)Claridge Products & Equipment
601 US 32
Harrison, AR 72602
    Fax: 870-743-1908   orders@claridgeproducts.com
    www.claridgeproducts.com
Manufacturer and exporter of menu signs and boards, display cases and cabinets, easels, chalkboards, markerboards, etc.; importer of raw materials
President: Helen Clavey
CFO: Leslie Eddings
VP: Paul Clavey
Purchasing Director: John Wilson
Number Employees: 250-499
Square Footage: 300000
Other Locations:
   Claridge Products & Equipment
   Mamaroneck, NY
   Claridge Products & Equipment
   Palatine, IL
   South Central Claridge
   Farmers Branch, TX
   Claridge Products & Equipment
   San Leandro, CAClaridge Products & EquipmentPalatine

43061 Clark-Cooper Division Magnatrol Valve Corporation
855 Industrial Highway
Unit 4
Cinnaminson, NJ 08077   856-829-4580
    Fax: 856-829-7303   techsupport@clarkcooper.com
    www.clarkcooper.com
Metering pumps and valves; exporter of pumps and skid systems

Manager: Brian White
CEO: Brian Hagan
CFO: Kevin Hagan
Contact: John Bush
johnb@clarkcooper.com
Plant Manager: John Chando
Estimated Sales: $ 3 - 5 Million
Number Employees: 10-19
Square Footage: 32000
Regions Exported to: South America, Asia
Percentage of Business in Exporting: 10

43062 Clarke American Sanders
14600 21st Ave N
Minneapolis, MN 55447-4617 336-372-8080
800-253-0367
info@clarkeus.com www.americansanders.com
Floor maintenance equipment such as floor polishers, floor sanders, carpet extractors and vacuum cleaners
CEO: Mark Hefty
CFO: Niels Olsen
R&D: Tom Benton
Marketing: Rob Godlewski
Sales: John Castaldo
Estimated Sales: $10-20 Million
Number Employees: 300
Number of Products: 150
Square Footage: 500000
Parent Co: Incentive Group

43063 Clarkson Grain Co Inc
320 E South St
P.O. Box 80
Cerro Gordo, IL 61818-4035 217-763-2861
Fax: 217-763-2111 800-252-1638
www.clarksongrain.com
Wholesaler/distributor and exporter of organic, raw and cleaned food grade white and yellow corn and soybeans. Also exporter of organic, nongmo, conrentional food grade corns and soybeans
President: Lynn Clarkson
lynn.clarkson@clarksongrain.com
VP/General Manager: Dick Widmer
VP Specialty Crop: Jim Traub
Estimated Sales: $20-50 Million
Number Employees: 10-19
Brands Exported: Mas Maiz; Fresh Pure Green;
Regions Exported to: South America, Europe, Asia, Canada, Latin America, Mexico
Percentage of Business in Exporting: 35

43064 Clarkson Scottish Bakery
1715 Lakeshore Road West
Mississauga, ON L5J 1J4
Canada 905-823-1500
Scottish baked goods including pies, pastries and breads; importer of Scottish and English meats, candies and chocolates
Proprietor: Catherine Whitelaw
Number Employees: 1-4
Square Footage: 1800
Brands Imported: Nestle; Lee's; Cadbury
Regions Imported from: Europe
Percentage of Business in Importing: 50

43065 Classic Flavors & Fragrances
878 W End Ave Apt 12b
New York, NY 10025 212-777-0004
Fax: 212-353-0404 cffi125@aol.com
Manufacturer, importer and exporter of flavors, essential oils, aromatics, etc
CEO: George Ivolin
Estimated Sales: $2.5-5 Million
Number Employees: 5-9
Square Footage: 3600
Type of Packaging: Bulk
Regions Exported to: Central America, South America, Europe, Asia, Middle East, Africa, Australia
Percentage of Business in Exporting: 25
Regions Imported from: Central America, South America, Europe, Asia, Middle East, Africa, Australia
Percentage of Business in Importing: 20

43066 (HQ)Classic Tea
649 Innsbruck Court
Libertyville, IL 60048-1845 630-680-9934
Processor, importer and exporter of ceylon (black) tea, liquid tea syrup and iced tea concentrates
Managing Director: Thomas Rielly
Director: F Court Bailey
Number Employees: 20-49
Square Footage: 80000
Type of Packaging: Consumer, Food Service, Private Label, Bulk
Other Locations:
    Classic Tea Ltd.
    Chicago, IL Classic Tea Ltd.
Brands Exported: Ceylon Classic
Regions Exported to: Central America, South America, Europe, Asia, Middle East, Canada, Caribbean, Mexico
Percentage of Business in Exporting: 18
Regions Imported from: Asia
Percentage of Business in Importing: 50

43067 Classico Seating
801 N Clay St
Peru, IN 46970-1068 765-473-6691
Fax: 800-242-9787 800-968-6655
Manufacturer and exporter of metal chairs, barstools, dinettes, tables and table bases
President: Kim Regan
CFO: Hank Richardson
Estimated Sales: $ 20 - 50 Million
Number Employees: 100-249
Square Footage: 125000
Type of Packaging: Consumer, Food Service
Brands Exported: Classico Seating
Regions Exported to: Central America, South America, Europe, Asia, Middle East
Percentage of Business in Exporting: 8

43068 Clawson Machine Co Inc
12 Cork Hill Rd
Franklin, NJ 07416-1304 973-827-8209
Fax: 973-827-4613 800-828-4088
eclipse@nac.net www.clawsonmachine.com
Cole slaw cutters and ice crushers and shavers for sno-cones; exporter of ice crushers, ice shavers and slaw cutters
Owner: Charles Fletcher
Customer Service: Diane Olsen
eclipse@nac.net
Estimated Sales: $ 10 - 20 Million
Number Employees: 20-49
Square Footage: 20000
Parent Co: Technology General Corporation
Type of Packaging: Food Service
Brands Exported: HQ-S, PC 2000, CM-30, CM-48, RE-1, RE-2. RE-SBK
Regions Exported to: Central America, South America, Europe, Asia, Middle East, Canada
Percentage of Business in Exporting: 15

43069 Claxton Bakery Inc
203 W Main St
PO Box 367
Claxton, GA 30417-1705 912-739-3097
Fax: 912-739-3097 800-841-4211
service@claxtonfruitcake.com
www.claxtonfruitcake.com
Established in 1910. Manufacturer and exporter of fruit cake, pecans, candies, and dressings.
Vice President: Paul Parker
ppgolf912@bellsouth.net
Estimated Sales: $20-50 Million
Number Employees: 100-249
Type of Packaging: Consumer

43070 Clayton & Lambert Manufacturing
3813 West Highway 146
Buckner, KY 40010 502-222-1411
Fax: 502-222-1415 800-626-5819
info@claytonlambert.com
www.claytonlambert.com
Manufacturer and exporter of galvanized and stainless steel tanks for storage
President: John Lambert
Estimated Sales: $ 2.5-5 Million
Number Employees: 10-19
Square Footage: 700000
Regions Exported to: Canada
Percentage of Business in Exporting: 5

43071 Clayton Corp.
866 Horan Dr
Fenton, MO 63026-2416 636-349-5333
Fax: 636-349-5335 800-729-8220
rberger@claytoncorp.com www.claytoncorp.com
Aerosol Valves, Actuators, Dispensing Systems, Covers, Barrier Packaging and assorted plastic moulded parts
President & CEO: Barry Baker
bakerb@claycorp.com
Director of Sales: Ric Berger
Number Employees: 100-249
Type of Packaging: Bulk
Regions Exported to: South America, Europe, Asia, Middle East

43072 Clayton Industries
17477 Hurley St
City Of Industry, CA 91744-5106 626-435-1200
Fax: 626-435-0180 800-423-4585
sales@claytonindustries.com
www.claytonindustries.com
Manufacturer and exporter of steam generators
President: Boyd Calvin
boyd.calvin@claytonind.com
Chairman: William N
CFO: Boyd Calvin
Quality Control: Jess Alvear
Sales: Marsha Ashley
Plant Manager: Robin Pope
Purchasing Director: Maria Serna
Estimated Sales: $20-50 Million
Number Employees: 500-999
Brands Exported: Clayton
Regions Exported to: Central America, South America, Europe, Asia, Middle East

43073 Clean Water Systems
2322 Marina Dr
PO Box 146
Klamath Falls, OR 97601-9110 541-882-9993
Fax: 541-882-9994 866-273-9993
info@cleanwatersysintl.com
www.cleanwatersysintl.com
Manufacturer and exporter of solid state ballasts, UV sensing, monitor and control system, ultraviolet water, and waste water treatment systems and air ozone units
President/CEO: Charles Romary
Estimated Sales: Less Than $500,000
Number Employees: 1-4
Square Footage: 6000
Parent Co: C G Romary & Son
Type of Packaging: Private Label
Brands Exported: CWS
Regions Exported to: Central America, South America, Europe, Asia, Middle East, Australia, New Zealand
Percentage of Business in Exporting: 30

43074 Clean Water Technology
151 W 135th St
Los Angeles, CA 90061-1645 310-380-4658
Fax: 310-380-4658 info@cleanwatertech.com
www.cleanwatertech.com
Wastewater treatment systems
VP: Linda Englander Mills
Manager: Joanna Parra
jparra@cleanwatertech.com
Number Employees: 10-19
Parent Co: The Marvin Group
Regions Exported to: Central America, South America, Europe, Asia, North America
Percentage of Business in Exporting: 10
Percentage of Business in Importing: 10

43075 Clear Springs Foods Inc.
1500 E. 4424 N. Clear Lakes Rd.
PO Box 712
Buhl, ID 83316 208-543-4316
800-635-8211
csfsales@clearsprings.com www.clearsprings.com
Fresh and frozen rainbow trout, breaded trout portions, shapes and melts.
CEO: Kurt Meyers
COO: Jeff Jermunson
Year Founded: 1991
Estimated Sales: $130 Million
Number Employees: 250-499
Number of Brands: 4
Square Footage: 7200
Type of Packaging: Consumer, Food Service, Private Label
Regions Exported to: Canada

Importers & Exporters / A-Z

43076 Clearly Canadian Beverage Corporation
220 Viceroy Rd
Units 11/12
Vanghan, ON L4K 3CA
Canada 905-761-0597
Fax: 607-742-5301 866-414-2326
www.clearly.ca
Processor and exporter of water including sparkling fruit, carbonated mineral and artesian
President: David Reingold
CEO: Roy Hessel
CFO: Craig Lennox
Director of Business Intelligence & FP&A: Ibrahim Kamar
Director, Human Resources: Nancy Savard
COO: Nancy Morison
Estimated Sales: $10.62million
Number Employees: 20
Type of Packaging: Consumer, Food Service
Regions Exported to: Worldwide

43077 Clearwater Fine Foods
757 Bedford Highway
Bedford, NS B4A 3Z7
Canada 902-443-0550
Fax: 902-443-8367 www.clearwater.ca
Processor and exporter of frozen shrimp, lobster, scallops, crabs and clams
Chairman: Colin MacDonald
CEO: Ian Smith
Number Employees: 100-249
Type of Packaging: Consumer, Food Service
Regions Exported to: Asia
Percentage of Business in Exporting: 50

43078 Clearwater Packaging Inc
615 Grand Central St # B
Clearwater, FL 33756-3438 727-442-2596
Fax: 727-447-3587 800-299-2596
www.clearwaterpackaging.com
Manufacturer and exporter of packaging machinery
President: Jon Hoover
sales@clearwaterpackaging.com
Estimated Sales: $ 5 - 10 Million
Number Employees: 20-49

43079 Clearwater Paper Corporation
Suite 1100
Spokane, WA 99201 509-344-5900
877-847-7831
www.clearwaterpaper.com
Manufacturer and exporter of paper packaging products
President/CEO: Linda Massman
Chief Financial Officer/SVP: John Hertz
SVP/General Counsel/Corporate Secretary: Michael Gadd
SVP, Human Resources: Jackson Lynch
Facility Manager: Rick Tucker
Vice President, Procurement: Terry Borden
Estimated Sales: $ 1.87 Billion
Number Employees: 3,860
Parent Co: Bell Fibre Company
Type of Packaging: Consumer, Bulk
Regions Exported to: Worldwide

43080 Cleaver-Brooks Inc
221 Law St
Thomasville, GA 31792 229-226-3024
800-250-5583
info@cleaverbrooks.com cleaverbrooks.com
Manufacturer and exporter of packaged steam and hot water boilers; applications include food processing, packaging, sterilization, heating/ventilation/air conditioning, etc.
President & CEO: Bart Aitken
President, Boiler Systems: Earle Pfefferkorn
Chief Financial Officer: Jimmy Sprouse
SVP, Sales & Marketing: Paul Anderson
Chairman Emeritus: P. Welch Goggins, Jr.
Year Founded: 1929
Estimated Sales: $100-500 Million
Number Employees: 1,400
Brands Exported: Cleaver-Brooks
Regions Exported to: Central America, South America, Asia, Middle East, Canada, Caribbean, Latin America, Mexico

43081 Cleland Manufacturing Company
2125 Argonne Dr NE
Columbia Heights, MN 55421-1317 763-571-4606
Fax: 763-571-4606
clealandmanufacturing@tcq.net
Manufacturer and exporter of grain/seed cleaners and spiral separators
President: Robert Maxton
Quality Control: George Maxton
VP: Mary Maxton
Contact: Bob Maxton
glen@agmercury.com
Estimated Sales: Less than $ 500,000
Number Employees: 2
Square Footage: 6000
Brands Exported: Expert Line
Regions Exported to: Worldwide
Percentage of Business in Exporting: 60

43082 (HQ)Cleland Sales Corp
11051 Via El Mercado
Los Alamitos, CA 90720-2878 562-598-6616
Fax: 562-598-3858
sales@blizzardbeersystems.com
www.blizzardbeersystems.com
Manufacturer, importer and exporter of automatic refill devices, beer chillers and beverage and dry powder dispensers.
President: Arlene Cleland
Vice President: Jimmy Cleland
Sales Director: Mike Pollock
Manager: Kevin Wesley
kevin@clelandsales.com
Estimated Sales: $ 1 - 3 Million
Number Employees: 5-9
Square Footage: 40000
Type of Packaging: Food Service
Other Locations:
 Cleland Sales Corp.
 Los Alamitos, CACleland Sales Corp.
Brands Exported: Dove; Star Line; Auto-mix
Regions Exported to: Worldwide
Percentage of Business in Exporting: 8
Brands Imported: Cafe Bar
Regions Imported from: Worldwide
Percentage of Business in Importing: 2

43083 (HQ)Clements Foods Co
6601 N Harvey Pl
Oklahoma City, OK 73116 405-842-3308
Fax: 405-843-6894 800-654-8355
clementsfoodscompany.com
Apple butter, preserves, jellies, salad dressings, pie fillings, mayonnaise, mustard, sauces, syrups, vinegar, peanut butter and imitation vanilla; exporter of salad dressings and mustards
President: Edward Clements
Executive Vice President: Robert Clements
Year Founded: 1952
Estimated Sales: $61 Million
Number Employees: 100-249
Number of Brands: 8
Square Footage: 150000
Type of Packaging: Consumer, Food Service, Private Label
Other Locations:
 Clements Foods Company
 Lewisville, TXClements Foods Company
Brands Exported: Garden Club
Regions Exported to: Central America, South America, Europe, Middle East, Latin America, Mexico
Percentage of Business in Exporting: 1

43084 Cleveland Menu Printing
1441 E 17th St
Cleveland, OH 44114-2012 216-241-5256
Fax: 216-241-5696 800-356-6368
web_sales@clevelandmenu.com
www.clevelandmenu.com
Manfacturer and exporter of menus and menu boards, covers, holders and displays
Owner: Thomas Ramella
tramella@clevelandmenuprinting.com
Estimated Sales: $2.5-5 Million
Number Employees: 20-49
Regions Exported to: Worldwide
Percentage of Business in Exporting: 5

43085 Cleveland Metal Stamping Company
1231 W Bagley Rd #1
Berea, OH 44017-2942 440-234-0010
Fax: 440-234-8050
Manufacturer and exporter of bottle openers, burner bowls for gas ranges and metal shelf extenders; also, barbecue utensils including spatulas and forks.
Manager: Frank Ghinga
CFO: Dorina Ghinga
VP: Pascu Ghinga
Estimated Sales: $ 1 - 3 Million
Number Employees: 50 to 99
Number of Products: 200
Square Footage: 86000
Type of Packaging: Private Label, Bulk

43086 Cleveland Range
1333 E 179th St
Cleveland, OH 44110 216-481-4900
Fax: 216-481-3782 800-338-2204
www.clevelandrange.com
Manufacturer and exporter of steam cooking equipment including convection steamers, kettles, skillets, combi-ovens and cook-chill systems
President: Rick Cutler
rcutler@clevelandrange.com
Estimated Sales: $ 48 Million
Number Employees: 100-249
Square Footage: 150000
Parent Co: The Manitowoc Company, Inc.
Type of Packaging: Food Service
Brands Exported: Steamcraft; Combicraft; Spectrum
Regions Exported to: Worldwide

43087 (HQ)Cleveland Specialties Co
6612 Miami Trails Dr
Loveland, OH 45140-8044 513-677-9787
Fax: 513-683-4132
Plastic closures, plastic shrink film, milk carton handles and polycoated paperboard products including folding boxes and cartons; importer of packaging products
President: Nancy Hartmann
Vice President: James Downing
Estimated Sales: Less Than $500,000
Number Employees: 1-4
Type of Packaging: Consumer, Food Service, Private Label, Bulk

43088 Cleveland Wire Cloth & Mfg Co
3573 E 78th St
Cleveland, OH 44105-1596 216-341-1832
Fax: 216-341-1876 800-321-3234
cleveland@wirecloth.com www.wirecloth.com
Manufacturer, importer and exporter of woven wire cloth and wire cloth products.
President: C Crone
CFO: Joe Sarasa
VP Marketing: Larry Schrader
Estimated Sales: $ 5 - 10 Million
Number Employees: 20-49
Square Footage: 200000
Regions Exported to: Worldwide
Percentage of Business in Exporting: 5
Regions Imported from: Worldwide
Percentage of Business in Importing: 20

43089 Cleveland-Eastern Mixers
4 Heritage Park Rd
Clinton, CT 06413-1836 860-669-1199
Fax: 860-669-7461 800-243-1188
Manufacturer and exporter of industrial fluid mixers
President: James Donkin
Sales Director: Sean Donkin
Estimated Sales: $10 Million
Number Employees: 20-49
Number of Brands: 30
Number of Products: 2
Square Footage: 50000
Parent Co: EMI Inc Technology Group

43090 Clextral USA
14450 Carlson Cir
Tampa, FL 33626 813-854-4434
Fax: 813-855-2269 www.clextral.com
Manufacturer and exporter of food processing machinery including twin screw extruders.
President: Jose Coelho
Sales Manager, North America: Justin Montgomery
Contact: Alice Albaret
aalbaret@clextral.com
Pilot Plant Manager: Julie Probst
Estimated Sales: Below $ 5 Million
Number Employees: 10-19
Parent Co: Clextral
Brands Exported: Clextral

Regions Exported to: Central America, South America
Percentage of Business in Exporting: 25

43091 Climate Master Inc
7300 SW 44th St
Oklahoma City, OK 73179-4307   405-745-6000
Fax: 405-745-6058   877-436-0263
cyperry@climatemaster.com
www.climatemaster.com
Manufacturer and exporter of heat pumps, air conditioners, filters and controls
President: Daniel Ellis
CEO: Dan Ellis
dellis@climatemaster.com
Estimated Sales: H
Number Employees: 250-499
Parent Co: LSB Corporation
Regions Exported to: Worldwide

43092 Climax Packaging Machinery
25 Standen Dr
Hamilton, OH 45015-2209   513-874-1664
Fax: 513-874-3375 info@climaxpackaging.com
www.climaxpackaging.com
Manufacturer and exporter of uncasing and case packing equipment, bottle conveyors, lane dividers, tray stackers and carton and flap openers
President: William George
Marketing/Sales: Jack Bunce
Manager: Nick Jody
njody@climaxpackaging.com
Purchasing: Barb Ruthwell
Estimated Sales: $ 5 - 10 Million
Number Employees: 20-49
Square Footage: 40000
Parent Co: GL Industries
Brands Exported: Climax
Regions Exported to: Central America, South America, Europe, Asia, Middle East, Canada
Percentage of Business in Exporting: 25

43093 Clipper Belt Lacer Company
1995 Oak Industrial Dr NE
Grand Rapids, MI 49505   616-459-3196
Fax: 616-459-4976 info@flexco.com
www.flexco.com
Manufacturer and exporter of mechanical belt fastening systems for conveyors
Manager: Nancy Ayres
CFO: Lee Merys
Marketing Specialist: Beth Miller
Estimated Sales: $10-20 Million
Number Employees: 50-99
Square Footage: 304000
Parent Co: Flexco - Grand Rapids
Regions Exported to: Central America, South America, Europe, Asia, Middle East
Percentage of Business in Exporting: 15

43094 Clipper Seafood
209 NE 95th St # 2
Miami Shores, FL 33138-2745   305-759-5400
Fax: 305-759-5050 clipperseafood@aol.com
Importer and wholesaler/distributor of frozen fish including mahi mahi, wahoo, tuna, shark, marlin, alaskan pollock, whiting and swordfish
President: Olga Serrano
VP: Estaban Serrano
Estimated Sales: $1-2.5 Million
Number Employees: 1-4
Brands Imported: Transmarina
Regions Imported from: South America, Asia

43095 (HQ)Clofine Dairy Products Inc
1407 New Rd
P.O. Box 335
Linwood, NJ 08221   609-653-1000
Fax: 609-653-0127 info@clofinedairy.com
www.clofinedairy.com
Fluid and dried dairy products; proteins, cheeses, milk replacement blends, tofu and soymilk powders, vital wheat gluten, etc.
Chairman: Larry Clofine
lclofine@clofinedairy.com
President & CEO: Frederick Smith
CFO: Butch Harmon
Warehouse Coordinator: Pamela Gerety
Estimated Sales: $20-50 Million
Number Employees: 10-19
Number of Brands: 2
Number of Products: 100
Type of Packaging: Food Service, Private Label, Bulk
Other Locations:
    Midwest Officer
    Chicago, ILMidwest Officer
Brands Exported: Soyfine, Soy Products - Fine Mix & Milk Replacement Blends
Regions Exported to: South America, Asia, Middle East, Russia
Percentage of Business in Exporting: 10
Regions Imported from: Asia
Percentage of Business in Importing: 7

43096 Clos Du Val Co LTD
5330 Silverado Trl
Napa, CA 94558-9410   707-261-5200
Fax: 707-252-6125 cdv@closduval.com
www.closduval.com
Producer and exporter of wines
President: Steve Tamburelli
COO: Lazaro Cardenas
lazaro.cardenas@dgs.ca.gov
Director of Operations: Jon-Mark Chappellet
Estimated Sales: $5.2 Million
Number Employees: 50-99
Square Footage: 128000
Regions Exported to: Europe, Asia, Canada, Caribbean, Australia
Percentage of Business in Exporting: 30

43097 Cloud Inc
4855 Morabito Pl
San Luis Obispo, CA 93401-8748   805-549-8093
Fax: 805-549-0131   800-234-5650
mkemp@cloudinc.com www.cloudinc.com
Manufacturer and exporter of rotary tank cleaning machines
Owner: Brian Buell
Product and Marketing Manager: Mike Kemp
Regional Sales Manager: Lee LaFond
brian@cloudinc.com
Division Manager: Greg Boege
Job Shop Division Mgr.: Richard Riggs
Manufacturing Mngr.: Brad Erickson
Estimated Sales: Less Than $500,000
Number Employees: 1-4
Regions Exported to: Worldwide
Percentage of Business in Exporting: 50

43098 Cloud Nine
216 W. Second Street
Claremont, CA 91711   909-624-3147
Fax: 909-624-3951 cloudninepaper@hotmail.com
www.cloudninepaper.com
Processor and exporter of hard candy, organic breath mints, caramel popcorn and natural, gourmet, dairy, nondairy, low-fat and organic chocolate bars
President: Josh Taylor
CFO: Lana Nguyen
Marketing Director: Robert Wagg
Sales Director: Sharon Desser
Director Operations: Andrew Spector
Number Employees: 10-19
Square Footage: 8000
Type of Packaging: Consumer, Private Label
Brands Exported: Cloud Nine; Tropical Source; Peakeasy
Regions Exported to: Europe, Middle East

43099 (HQ)Cloverdale Foods
3015 34th St NW
Mandan, ND 58554
    800-669-9511
www.cloverdalefoods.com
Manufacturer and wholesaler/distributor of meat products including hickory smoked franks, bacon, ham and sausages, along with other quality pork products.
President & CEO: Scott Russell

Estimated Sales: $49 Million
Number Employees: 250-499
Number of Brands: 2
Square Footage: 61000
Type of Packaging: Consumer, Food Service, Private Label, Bulk
Other Locations:
    Cloverdale Foods Plant
    Minot, NDCloverdale Foods Plant
Brands Exported: Cloverdale
Regions Exported to: Asia
Percentage of Business in Exporting: 2

43100 Cloverhill Bakery-Vend Corporation
2035 N Narragansett Ave
Chicago, IL 60639-3842   773-745-9800
Fax: 773-745-1647 www.cloverhill.com
Processor and exporter of sweet goods, doughnuts, cakes, muffins, danishes and cinnamon rolls.
President: William Gee
Executive VP: Edward Gee
Quality Control: Dan Gee
VP Sales: Robert Gee
Production Manager: Joe Perez
Year Founded: 1961
Estimated Sales: $20-50 Million
Number Employees: 100-249
Square Footage: 140000
Parent Co: Hostess
Type of Packaging: Consumer, Food Service

43101 Clown Global Brands
3184 Doolittle Dr
Northbrook, IL 60062-2409   847-498-4696
Fax: 847-564-9076   800-323-5778
info@clown-gysin.com
www.clownglobalbrands.com
Producer and importer of marshmallows, snack foods, breadsticks, toasted onion bits, sesame dots, confectionery, and caramel apple dip items; importer of toasted onion bits and breadsticks
President: Herb Horn
Contact: Martin Haver
mhaver@clownglobalbrands.com
Estimated Sales: $7-10 Million
Number Employees: 5-9
Number of Brands: 2
Square Footage: 8000
Parent Co: Food Network
Type of Packaging: Food Service
Regions Imported from: Europe
Percentage of Business in Importing: 10

43102 Cma Dishmachines
12700 Knott St
Garden Grove, CA 92841-3904   714-898-8781
Fax: 71- 89- 214   800-854-6417
sales@cmadishmachines.com
Manufacturer, importer and exporter of commercial dishmachines, glasswashers and dishtables
President: David Crane
Vice President: Mike Belleville
mike.belleville@cmadishmachines.com
Marketing Director: Matt Swift
Sales Assistant: Kimberly Feldstein
Plant Manager: Mike Belleville
Number Employees: 50-99
Square Footage: 135000
Parent Co: S.C. Johnson & Son
Regions Exported to: Worldwide
Percentage of Business in Exporting: 10
Regions Imported from: Worldwide
Percentage of Business in Importing: 10

43103 Co-Rect Products Inc
7105 Medicine Lake Rd
Golden Valley, MN 55427-3675   763-542-9200
Fax: 763-542-9205   800-328-5702
customerservice@co-rectproducts.com
www.co-rectproducts.com
Bar and restaurant supplies; serving the food service market
President & CEO: Michael Pierce
Vice President: Steve Ess
Sales Manager: Bryan Mattson
Accounts Representative: Brian Mattson
Purchasing: Rose Bruhn
Estimated Sales: $10-20 Million
Number Employees: 20-49
Number of Brands: 20
Square Footage: 60000
Type of Packaging: Food Service, Private Label, Bulk
Regions Exported to: Central America, South America, Europe, Asia, Middle East

43104 Coast Scientific
P.O. Box 185
Rancho Santa Fe, CA 92067
Fax: 800-791-8999   800-445-1544
www.medcosupplies.com
Manufacturer and exporter of adhesive mats, aprons, polyethylene bags, bouffant caps, carts, shelving, latex and vinyl gloves, convection ovens and disposable wipers

Importers & Exporters / A-Z

Manager: Alex Sardarian
Director Operations: Stacy Camp
Estimated Sales: $2.5-5 Million
Number Employees: 10-19
Regions Exported to: Worldwide
Percentage of Business in Exporting: 20

43105 Coast Seafoods Company
14711 NE 29th Pl Ste 111
Bellevue, WA 98007   425-702-8800
    Fax: 425-702-0400   800-423-2303
info@coastseafoods.com www.coastseafoods.com
Processor and exporter of fresh oysters and clams
President: John Petrie
CFO: Kay Christopher
Contact: Sharon Adams
sharon@cni.org
Manager: Jim Donaldson
Estimated Sales: $2.5-5 Million
Number Employees: 1-4
Parent Co: Coast Seafoods Company
Type of Packaging: Consumer, Food Service
Regions Exported to: Worldwide

43106 Coastal Seafoods
39 Acre Ln
Ridgefield, CT 06877-5501   203-431-0453
    Fax: 203-438-7099
Seafood
President: Robert Iseley
CFO/Secretary: Linda Iseley
Operations: Manuel Reyes
Estimated Sales: $2.5-5 Million
Number Employees: 10-19
Square Footage: 5000
Type of Packaging: Food Service, Private Label
Brands Imported: Coastal Seafoods.
Regions Imported from: South America

43107 Coastside Lobster Company
PO Box 151
Stonington, ME 04681-0151   207-367-2297
    Fax: 207-367-5929
Lobster
President: Peter Collin
Purchsing Director: Karen Rains
Number Employees: 5-9

43108 Coating Place Inc
200 Paoli St
Verona, WI 53593-8702   608-845-9521
    Fax: 608-845-9526 info@encap.com
    www.coatingplace.com
Contract manufacturer specializing in wurster fluid bed coating services for encapsulation of solid particulate materials such as powders, grenules, crystals and capsules
President: Tim Breuning
tbreuning@encap.com
R&D: Charles Frey
Quality Control: Scott Young
Purchasing Director: Kurt Schmidt
Estimated Sales: $10-20 Million
Number Employees: 100-249
Square Footage: 220000
Type of Packaging: Bulk
Regions Exported to: Europe, Middle East, Canada
Percentage of Business in Exporting: 5

43109 Cobatco
1327 NE Adams St
Peoria, IL 61603   309-676-2663
    Fax: 309-676-2667   800-426-2282
    info@cobatco.com www.cobatco.com
Manufacturer and exporter of specialty baking equipment for waffles, waffle cones, doughnuts, edible shells, etc.; also, mixes including vanilla and chocolate waffle cone, regular and multigrain waffle and vanilla and chocolatedoughnut
President: Donald Stephens
Contact: Brett Crosthwaite
bcrosthwaite@cobatco.com
Estimated Sales: $ 2.5-5 Million
Number Employees: 10-19
Square Footage: 240000
Type of Packaging: Food Service
Brands Exported: Cobatco
Regions Exported to: Worldwide
Percentage of Business in Exporting: 25

43110 Cober Electronics, Inc.
151 Woodward Ave
Norwalk, CT 06854-4721   203-855-8755
    Fax: 203-855-7511   800-709-5948
    sales@cober.com www.cober.com
Manufacturer and exporter of batch and continuous conveyorized microwave ovens for the food scientist and production floor; also, laboratory and pilot plant services, process development and engineering design
CEO: Bernard Krieger
bern@cober.com
President: Martin Yonnone
VP Engineering: Martin Yonnone
Estimated Sales: $30-50 Million
Number Employees: 20-49
Square Footage: 39000
Regions Exported to: Worldwide
Percentage of Business in Exporting: 20

43111 (HQ)Coburn Company
P.O.Box 147
Whitewater, WI 53190-0147   262-473-2822
    Fax: 262-473-3522   800-776-7042
    www.coburn.com
Manufacturer and exporter of dairy equipment including milking and sanitation
President: Jim Coburn
Finance: Jason Alexander
Marketing: Ginny Coburn
Sales: Joe Coburn
Operations: Thayer Coburn
Export Manager: Jack Kolo
Purchasing: Jim Coburn
Estimated Sales: $5-10 Million
Number Employees: 20-49
Type of Packaging: Bulk
Regions Exported to: Central America, South America, Europe, Asia, Middle East
Regions Imported from: Europe, Asia

43112 (HQ)Coby's Cookies
17 Vickers Rd
Toronto, ON M9B 1C1
Canada   416-633-1567
    Fax: 416-633-9812
Processor and exporter of frozen cookie dough, muffin and brownie batter; also, retail pack rice crispy squares and brownies
President: Michael Topolinkski
Executive VP: Jay Punwasee
Estimated Sales: $9.3 Million
Number Employees: 150
Square Footage: 60000
Type of Packaging: Consumer, Food Service, Private Label
Other Locations:
    Coby's Cookies
    Downsview, ONCoby's Cookies
Brands Exported: Coby's Cookies, Inc.; Saratoga; Just Great Bakers, Inc.
Regions Exported to: USA
Percentage of Business in Exporting: 15

43113 Coca-Cola European Partners
Pemberton House
Bakers Road
Uxbridge, Middx, UB8 1EZ
UK
    800-418-4223
    comms@ccep.com www.cocacolaep.com
Coca-Cola brands products.
Chairman: Sol Daurella
CEO: Damian Gammell
CFO: Nik Jhangiani
Chief Public Affairs Officer: Lauren Sayeski
Estimated Sales: $10.9 Billion
Number Employees: 23,300
Number of Brands: 44
Type of Packaging: Consumer, Food Service, Bulk

43114 Coco Lopez Inc
3401 SW 160th Ave # 350
Miramar, FL 33027-6306   954-450-3111
    Fax: 954-450-3111   800-341-2242
    customerservice@cocolopez.com
    www.cocolopez.com
Canned fruits and vegetables, preserves, jams and jellie. Also manufacturer of cream of coconut, coconut milk, and coconut juice.
President: Leonardo Vargas
VP: Gisela Sanchez
Manager: Nicole Bennett
nbennett@kaplanuniversity.edu
Estimated Sales: $1,888,884
Number Employees: 10-19
Brands Exported: Coco Lopez
Regions Exported to: Worldwide
Regions Imported from: Dominican Republic, Latin America

43115 Codema
11790 Troy Ln N
Maple Grove, MN 55369   763-428-2266
    Fax: 763-428-4411 info@codemallc.com
Manufacturer, importer and exporter of processing equipment; packaging systems. Also have reconditioned and used equipment.
President: Heinz Baecker
h.baecker@codemallc.com
VP: Steve Parker
VP sales: Larry Yarger
VP Engineering: Rick Gilles
Estimated Sales: $1-2.5 Million
Number Employees: 5-9
Square Footage: 70000
Regions Exported to: Worldwide
Percentage of Business in Exporting: 45
Regions Imported from: Europe, Asia
Percentage of Business in Importing: 7

43116 Coffee Bean Intl
9120 NE Alderwood Rd
Portland, OR 97220-1366   503-227-4490
    Fax: 503-225-9604   800-877-0474
    info@coffeebeanintl.com www.coffeebeanintl.com
Roasted coffee, tea, cocoa, syrups, and confectionary products; manufacturer of coffee equipment, importer of coffee beans and teas.
President & CEO: Patrick Criteser
pcriteser@coffeebeanintl.com
VP Product Development & Training: Bruce Mullins
Creative Director: Audrey Crespo
Vice President of Marketing: Joe Prewett
Vice President of Sales: Rich Sermone
Manager of Internet Marketing: Vickie Grimes
Operations Executive: Les McDonald
Roastmaster: Paul Thornton
Purchasing Manager: Mark Peldyak
Estimated Sales: $ 29.3 Million
Number Employees: 100-249
Square Footage: 500000
Parent Co: Farmer Brothers Company
Type of Packaging: Consumer, Food Service, Private Label, Bulk
Regions Imported from: Worldwide

43117 Coffee Brothers Inc
1204 Via Roma
Colton, CA 92324-3909   909-370-1100
    Fax: 909-370-1101   888-443-5282
    info@coffeebrothers.com www.coffeebrothers.com
Coffee and espresso; importer and wholesaler/distributor of espresso machines
Owner: Cal Amodemo
cal@coffeebrothers.com
General Manager: Max Amodeo
Estimated Sales: $2.5-5 Million
Number Employees: 1-4
Square Footage: 44000
Type of Packaging: Private Label, Bulk
Regions Imported from: Europe
Percentage of Business in Importing: 50

43118 Coffee Exchange
207 Wickenden St Uppr
Providence, RI 02903-4348   401-273-1198
    Fax: 401-273-4440   877-263-3334
    info@thecoffeeexchange.com
    www.thecoffeeexchange.com
Processor and importer of regular and decaffeinated whole bean organic coffee; gift baskets available
Owner: Charles Fishbein
charlie@mailordercoffee.com
CEO: Susan Wood
Cafe Manager: Tania Montenegro
Estimated Sales: $1-2.5 Million
Number Employees: 20-49
Regions Imported from: Asia, Africa, Latin America
Percentage of Business in Importing: 25

Importers & Exporters / A-Z

43119 Coffee Express RoastingCo
47722 Clipper St
Plymouth, MI 48170-2437   734-459-4900
Fax: 734-459-5511   800-466-9000
info@coffeeexpressco.com
www.coffeeexpressco.com
Wholesaler roaster of specialty coffees; distributors of associated products.
President: Tom Isaia
Office Manager: Joyce Novak
Contact: Genevieve Boss
g.boss@coffeeexpressco.com
Production: Scott Novak
Estimated Sales: Less Than $500,000
Number Employees: 1-4
Number of Brands: 8
Number of Products: 20
Square Footage: 32000
Type of Packaging: Consumer, Food Service, Private Label, Bulk
Brands Imported: Rancilio Macchine per Caffe; Jamaican Wallenford Blue Mountain; Jamaican Baronhall Estate
Regions Imported from: Central America, Europe
Percentage of Business in Importing: 10

43120 Coffee Inns
3617 E La Salle St
Phoenix, AZ 85040   602-438-8286
Fax: 602-437-2270   800-528-0552
Owner: John Bergmann
john.bergmann@2mfg.com
Estimated Sales: $ 20 - 50 Million
Number Employees: 100-249

43121 Coffeeco
10134 Colvin Run Rd Ste D
Great Falls, VA 22066   703-757-7936
Fax: 703-757-7953
Importer of coffee
Partner: Debra Zeh
Estimated Sales: $300,000-500,000
Number Employees: 1-4
Brands Imported: Coffeeco Ltd.
Regions Imported from: Central America
Percentage of Business in Importing: 100

43122 Colavita USA
1 Runyons Ln
Edison, NJ 08817-2219   732-404-8300
Fax: 732-287-9401   888-265-2848
usa@colavita.com www.colavita.com
Grains and oils including; extra virgin olive oil, vinegar, pasta, sauces, gnocchi, polenta, rice, marinated vegetables, and gift baskets and foodservice bulk supply
President: Sophia Aspromatis
sophiaa@colavita.com
CEO: Giovanni Colavita
VP Quality Control: Anthony Profaci
VP of Sales: Tom Marrone
VP Sales & Marketing: John Profaci
Director of Marketing: Nicole Jeannette
Plant Manager: Les Horowitz
VP Purchasing: Robert Profaci
Estimated Sales: $15 Million
Number Employees: 50-99

43123 Colchester Foods
17 Schwartz Rd
Bozrah, CT 6334   860-886-2445
Fax: 860-886-1138   860-243-0469
Processor and exporter of brown and white eggs
VP: Kevin O'Brien
Number Employees: 20-49
Parent Co: Kofkoff Egg Farm
Type of Packaging: Consumer, Food Service, Private Label
Regions Exported to: Hong Kong
Percentage of Business in Exporting: 5

43124 Cold Chain Technologies
29 Everett St
Holliston, MA 1746   508-429-1395
Fax: 508-429-9056   800-370-8566
info@coldchaintech.com www.coldchaintech.com
Manufacturer and exporter of insulated shipping containers and refrigerant packs for perishable food shipments
President: Larry Gordon
VP, General Manager: Bob Bohne
R&D Manager: Richard Formato
VP Sales/Marketing: TJ Rizzo
Contact: Paul Anderson
panderson@coldchaintech.com
Number Employees: 100-249
Square Footage: 80000
Type of Packaging: Food Service, Private Label, Bulk
Regions Exported to: Europe
Percentage of Business in Exporting: 1

43125 Cold Hollow Cider Mill
3600 Waterbury-Stowe Rd
PO Box 420
Waterbury Center, VT 05677-8020   802-244-8771
Fax: 802-244-7212   800-327-7537
info@coldhollow.com www.coldhollow.com
Apple products including cider, cider jelly, butters, syrup, sauce, preserves and juices; exporter of cider jelly; wholesaler/distributor of health and specialty foods, general merchandise, private label items and produce
Owner: Paul Brown
Vice President: Gayle Brown
Estimated Sales: $ 5 - 10 Million
Number Employees: 20-49
Square Footage: 40000
Type of Packaging: Consumer, Food Service, Bulk
Regions Exported to: Asia

43126 Cold Jet, LLC
455 Wards Corner
Loveland, OH 45140   513-831-3211
Fax: 513-831-1209   800-337-9423
service@coldjet.com www.coldjet.com
Manufacturer and exporter of dry ice cleaning solutions and dry ice production equipment.
President & CEO: Gene Cooke III
Vice President of Global Marketing: Christian Rogiers
Sr. Vice President of Sales: Brian Allen
Human Resources Manager: Jennifer Ellspermann
Chief Operating Officer: Scott Gatje
Estimated Sales: $1-2.5 Million
Number Employees: 1-4
Regions Exported to: Worldwide

43127 ColdZone
8101 E Kaiser Blvd Ste 110
Anaheim, CA 92808-2661
Fax: 714-529-8503
Manufacturer and exporter of refrigeration equipment including remote racks and fluid coolers
President: Jim Grob
VP: Ken Falk
National Sales Manager: R Echols
Contact: Sherry Rister
sherry.rister@htpgusa.com
Product Manager: R Dotson
Estimated Sales: $ 20 - 50 Million
Number Employees: 100-249
Square Footage: 260000
Parent Co: Ardco
Type of Packaging: Food Service
Regions Exported to: Central America, South America
Percentage of Business in Exporting: 5

43128 Coldmatic Refrigeration
8500 Keel Street
Concord, ON L4K 2A6
Canada   905-326-7600
Fax: 905-326-7601 mark@summitproducts.com
www.coldmatic.com
Manufacturer and exporter of automatic and manual doors including cold storage, double acting, plastic and refrigerator
President: Mark Galea
CFO: Stafford Mass
VP: Rex Palmatier
Marketing Director: Dan Gregero
Sales Manager- Ontario & Eastern Canada: Mike Robbie
Plant Manager: Derrick Lee
Estimated Sales: $ 1 - 3 Million
Number Employees: 5-9
Parent Co: Coldmatic Refrigeration
Regions Exported to: Central America, South America, Asia, Middle East
Percentage of Business in Exporting: 10

43129 Coldstream Products Corporation
10 McCool Crescent
P.O. Box 878
Crossfield, AB T0M 0S0
Canada   403-946-4097
Fax: 403-946-0148   888-946-4097
Manufacturer and exporter of coolers, freezers and display cases
President: George Zafir
VP: Trevor Rees
VP Marketing: Trevor Rees
Director of Sales: Ken Savard
Operations: Rick Lewis
Purchasing: Les Lewis
Number Employees: 100-249
Number of Brands: s
Number of Products: 75
Square Footage: 1000000
Parent Co: Coldmatic Group of Companies
Brands Exported: Cold Stream

43130 Coleman Manufacturing Co Inc
48 Waters Ave
Everett, MA 02149-2099   617-389-0380
Fax: 617-389-0769 www.coleman.com/home
Manufacturer and exporter of hand cleaners
President: Richard Coleman
dickcoleman@coleman.com
Estimated Sales: $ 1 - 2.5 Million
Number Employees: 5-9
Square Footage: 40000

43131 (HQ)Coleman Natural
PO Box 768
Kings Mountain, NC 28086   303-468-2920
Fax: 303-277-9263   800-442-8666
info@colemannatural.com
www.colemannatural.com
Premium natural and organic poultry, pork, and prepared foods. No antibiotics or growth hormones, 100% vegetarian diets and no animal byproducts.
Ceo: Mark McKay
Vice President Of Marketing: Gudjon Olafsson
Vice President Of National Sales: Hans Liebl
Vice President Of Operations: Bart Vittori
Plant Manager: George Lofink
Purchasing Manager: Kevin Rafferty
Estimated Sales: $1 million
Number Employees: 2,300
Square Footage: 50000
Type of Packaging: Food Service
Brands Exported: Coleman Natural Beef
Regions Exported to: Central America, Asia

43132 Colgate-Palmolive Professional Products Group
895 Don Mills Rd
North York, ON M3C 1W3
Canada
    800-468-6502
Manufacturer and exporter of cleaning supplies
Chairman, President & CEO: Ian Cook
Estimated Sales: $100-500 Million
Number Employees: 1,000-4,999
Type of Packaging: Food Service

43133 Colin Ingram
P.O.Box 146
Comptche, CA 95427-0146   707-937-1824
Fax: 707-937-5834
Manufacturer, importer and exporter of essential oils
President: John Weir
bill.lechtner@petco.com
Estimated Sales: $2.5-5 Million
Number Employees: 1-4
Type of Packaging: Consumer, Food Service, Private Label, Bulk
Regions Exported to: Worldwide
Regions Imported from: Worldwide

43134 Collin Street Bakery

Corsicana, TX 75110
    800-267-4657
www.collinstreet.com
Pecan cakes, coffees, cheesecake, cookies, cakes, pecan pies, breads, muffins and candies
Chief Marketing Officer: Hayden Crawford
Plant Manager: Debbie Watson
Purchasing Manager: Marcia Longo
Year Founded: 1896
Estimated Sales: $20-50 Million

Importers & Exporters / A-Z

Number Employees: 600
Square Footage: 125000
Type of Packaging: Consumer

43135 Collins & Aikman
1212 7th St SW
Canton, OH 44707 330-253-3826
Fax: 330-456-0849 800-321-0244
www.collinsaikman.com
Manufacturer and exporter of rubber and vinyl matting
Quality Control: Chris Carpenter
CEO: Mike Geaghan
Contact: Michelle Petruska
michellepetruska@devry.edu
VP Merchandising: Scot Landeis
Production Manager: Gary Taylor
Plant Manager: Todd Weber
Estimated Sales: $ .5 - 1 million
Number Employees: 20-49
Type of Packaging: Food Service
Regions Exported to: Worldwide

43136 Collins International
273 Nagog Hill Rd
Acton, MA 1720 978-263-0727
Fax: 978-263-5057 www.collinsinternational.com
Importer of English and Scottish ale; also, Irish pork products including back and spare ribs
Owner: Steve Lin
seasonal@collinsinternational.com
Number Employees: 1-4
Brands Imported: Old Speckled Hen; Belhaven
Regions Imported from: Europe

43137 Coloma Frozen Foods Inc
4145 Coloma Rd
Coloma, MI 49038-8967 269-944-1421
Fax: 269-944-3291 800-642-2723
www.colomafrozen.com
Frozen fruits, vegetables, juices and juice concentrates.
President: Brad Wendzel
CFO: Doug Singleton
Estimated Sales: $25 Million
Number Employees: 50-99
Type of Packaging: Food Service, Bulk
Regions Exported to: Europe, Canada
Percentage of Business in Exporting: 5
Percentage of Business in Importing: 1

43138 Colombian Coffee Federation
140 E 57th St # 2
New York, NY 10022-2765 212-421-8300
Fax: 212-758-3816 www.cafedecolombia.com
Green coffee trading
President: Juan Orduz
jeorduz@juanvaldez.com
Marketing Director: Mary Petitt
Operations Manager: Miguel Salazar
Estimated Sales: $1-2.5 Million
Number Employees: 10-19

43139 Colombina Candy Company
5200 Blue Lagoon Drive
Suite 220
Miami, FL 33126 786-265-1920
Fax: 305-599-9009 www.colombina.com
Importer of gourmet sugar candy
Contact: Nancy Alvarez
nalvarez@colombina.com
Manager: Jacobo Tovar
Estimated Sales: Less than $500,000
Number Employees: 1-4
Parent Co: Colombina Candy Company
Type of Packaging: Consumer
Regions Imported from: Colombia
Percentage of Business in Importing: 100

43140 Colombo Importing US IncEmma & Casa Italia
3700 Steeles Avenue W
Suite 702
Woodbridge, ON L4L 8K8
Canada 905-850-9010
Fax: 905-850-2874
gvarricchione@jkoverweel.com
Imports and distributes Italian, Dutch, English Danish, Spanish, Australian, Argentinean, American, German, Swiss and Canadian cheese products. Also carries olive oil, vinegar, coffee, marinated vegetables, biscuits, hazlenut spreadfish, cocoa, and water. Tomatoes, pasta and rice products and cured meat products from Europe.

President: Arthur Pelliccione Sr
Vice President: Arthur Pelliccione Jr
Estimated Sales: $948,000
Number Employees: 3

43141 Colonial Coffee Roasters Inc
3250 NW 60th St
Miami, FL 33142-2125 305-638-0885
Fax: 305-634-2538 info@colonialcoffee.com
Importer and wholesaler/distributor of coffee and espresso machinery including coffee roasters
Owner: Rafael Acevedo
main@colonialcoffee.com
CEO: Ava Acevedo
Number Employees: 10-19
Square Footage: 60000
Parent Co: Colonial Coffee Roasters
Brands Exported: Bezzera; Gind Rossi
Regions Exported to: Central America, South America
Percentage of Business in Exporting: 50
Brands Imported: Bezzera; Espresso; Cappuccino Machines
Regions Imported from: Europe

43142 Color Box
623 S G St
Richmond, IN 47374 765-966-7588
Fax: 765-962-5584 www.gp.com
Manufacturer and exporter of paper boxes and cartons
Manager: Jeff Pobanz
VP Sales: Frank Mazzei
Contact: Michael Adams
madams@cskcorp.com
VP Manufacturing: Mike Roark
Estimated Sales: $ 20-50 Million
Number Employees: 250-499
Parent Co: Georgia Pacific
Type of Packaging: Consumer, Bulk
Regions Exported to: Canada, Mexico
Percentage of Business in Exporting: 2

43143 Color-Ons
1700 S Eisenhower Ave
Mason City, IA 50401-1539 641-424-1511
Fax: 641-423-7843 cq@mach3ww.com
www.color-ons.com
Owner: George Sammis
sammis@mach3ww.com
Number Employees: 20-49

43144 Colorado Nut Co
2 Kalamath St
Denver, CO 80223-1550 303-733-7311
800-876-1625
sales@coloradonutco.com
www.coloradonutco.com
Manufactures and Imports candies, chocolates, unique trail mixes, snack mixes, dried fruits and gift baskets for any occasion. Also roast nuts on site. Also offer products with private labeling and customized logos for a variety of specialized events.
Owner: Mark Goodman
mgoodman@coloradonutco.com
Owner: Roger Renaud
Estimated Sales: Less Than $500,000
Number Employees: 5-9
Type of Packaging: Consumer, Private Label

43145 Colorcon Inc
275 Ruth Rd
Harleysville, PA 19438-1952 215-256-7700
Fax: 215-661-2626 www.colorcon.com
Custom dispersed colorant systems, natural colorants, pearlescent color systems, barrier coatings, glazes, FD&C certified pigments, color blends and monogramming and nontoxic printing inks for food packaging applications; exporter of food colorants, coatings, inks, etc.
CEO: William Motzer
wmotzer@colorcon.com
Senior Business Manager - Naturals/Food: Lou Palermo
Business Manager - Food/Confectionary: John Jaworski
Estimated Sales: $50-100 Million
Number Employees: 250-499
Parent Co: Berwind Pharmaceutical Services
Type of Packaging: Bulk
Other Locations:
 NA Headquarters
 Westport, PA
 Colorcon No-Tox Products

 Chalfont, PA
 Colorcon, Inc.
 Irvine, CA
 Colorcon, Inc.
 Indianapolis, IN
 Colorcon, Inc.
 Stoughton, WI
 Colorcon P.R., Inc.
 Humacao, PR
 NA HeadquartersChalfont
Regions Exported to: Worldwide
Percentage of Business in Exporting: 5

43146 Colson Caster Corp
3700 Airport Rd
Jonesboro, AR 72401-4463 870-932-4501
Fax: 870-932-1446 800-643-5515
info1@colsoncaster.com www.colsoncaster.com
Manufacturer and exporter of casters, wheels and bumpers
President: Don Laux
dlaux@colsoncaster.com
CEO: Jim Blankenship
Chairman the Board: Robert Pritzker
VP: Bill Blackley
Marketing: Cary Gillespie
Estimated Sales: $ 50 - 100 Million
Number Employees: 100-249

43147 Columbia Food Laboratories
36740 E. Historic Columbia River Hwy.
PO Box 353
Corbett, OR 97019 503-695-2287
Fax: 503-695-5187 info@columbiafoodlab.com
www.columbiafoodlab.com
Analytical laboratory providing nutritional, food chemistry pesticide and herbicide residue analysis
President: Lee Gion
VP: Colin Campbell
Estimated Sales: $500,000-$1 Million
Number Employees: 5-9
Square Footage: 16000

43148 Columbia Labeling Machinery
1580 Dale Ave
PO Box 5290
Benton City, WA 99320
Fax: 509-588-5080 888-791-9590
sales@rippedsheets.com www.columbialabel.com
Manufacturer and exporter of automatic and semi-automatic labeling machines and supplies; also, bar code printing and labeling equipment
President: Raymond MacNeill
Sales: Catherine Bryson
Estimated Sales: $1-2.5 Million
Number Employees: 4
Square Footage: 100000
Brands Exported: Columbia Labeling Machinery
Regions Exported to: Central America, South America, Canada, Mexico
Percentage of Business in Exporting: 5

43149 Columbia Lighting
701 Millennium Blvd.
Greenville, SC 29607 864-678-1000
Fax: 864-678-1740
www.hubbell.com/columbialighting/en
Lighting fixtures including electric and fluorescent.
Chairman/President/CEO: David Nord
Senior VP/CFO: William Sperry
Year Founded: 1897
Estimated Sales: $100-500 Million
Number Employees: 500-999
Number of Brands: 1
Square Footage: 680000
Parent Co: Hubbell Lighting
Brands Exported: Columbia
Regions Exported to: Canada, Mexico
Percentage of Business in Exporting: 2

43150 Columbian TecTank
2101 S 21st St
Parsons, KS 67357 620-421-0200
Fax: 620-421-9122 800-421-2788
www.columbiantectank.com
Manufacturer and exporter of bolted and welded carbon steel, stainless steel and aluminum storage tanks and silos
Contact: Robert Baker
rwbaker@columbiantectank.com
Plant Manager: Steve Allen
Estimated Sales: $ 20 - 50 Million
Number Employees: 100-249
Brands Exported: Columbian TecTank; Aquastore; SealWeld; Harvestore

Importers & Exporters / A-Z

Regions Exported to: Central America, South America, Europe, Asia, Middle East

43151 Columbus Instruments
950 N Hague Ave
Columbus, OH 43204-2121 614-279-9607
Fax: 614-276-0529 800-669-5011
sales@colinst.com www.colinst.com
Manufacturer and exporter of respirometers for measuring the sterility, bacterial and fungal growth, biodegradation and oxidation of fats; also, calorimeters, precision gas mixers and air dryers
President: Jan A Czekajewski
Manager: Frank Pence
frank.pence@service.colinst.com
Estimated Sales: $ 2.5 - 5 Million
Number Employees: 20-49
Square Footage: 40000
Regions Exported to: Central America, South America, Europe, Asia, Middle East
Percentage of Business in Exporting: 50

43152 Columbus McKinnon Corporation
205 Crosspoint Pkwy.
Getzville, NY 14068 716-689-5400
800-888-0985
www.cmworks.com
Chains, hoists, forgings, lift tables, jib arms, manipulators and conveyors.
Chairman: Richard Fleming
President/CEO: Mark Morelli
Vice President, Finance/CFO: Gregory Rustowicz
Vice President, Information Services: Mark Paradowski
Year Founded: 1875
Estimated Sales: $597 Million
Number Employees: 3,328
Regions Exported to: Worldwide

43153 Comark Instruments
P.O.Box 9029
Everett, WA 98206-9029 360-435-5571
Fax: 360-403-4243 800-555-6658
sales@comarkusa.com global.bayliner.com
Supplier of electronic measurement instruments inculding food and industrial thermometers, thermocouples, temperature probes, data loggers, data management systems and timers plus humidity and pressure instruments.
President: Jeff Behan
Marketing Manager: Alan Mellinger
National Sales Manager: Bob Bader
Estimated Sales: $5-10 Million
Number Employees: 1,000-4,999
Number of Brands: 1
Number of Products: 200
Parent Co: Brunsik Corporation
Type of Packaging: Food Service
Brands Exported: KM; Comark
Regions Exported to: Central America, South America
Percentage of Business in Exporting: 5
Brands Imported: KM Kanemay; Comark
Regions Imported from: Europe, Asia
Percentage of Business in Importing: 100

43154 Comasec Safety, Inc.
8 Niblick Road
Enfield, CT 06082 860-749-0506
Fax: 860-741-0881 800-333-0219
Manufacturer and importer of gloves including PVC/nitrile, knit lined latex, plastic, cotton/mesh lined, heavy unlined rubber; exporter of knit lined latex gloves
General Manager: P Gelinas
Tecnical Manager: Joe Krocheski
Estimated Sales: $ 5-10 Million
Number Employees: 10-19
Regions Exported to: Europe
Regions Imported from: Europe

43155 Combi Packaging Systems LLC
5365 E Center Dr NE
PO Box 9326
Canton, OH 44721-3734 330-456-9333
Fax: 330-456-4644 866-472-5236
sales@combi.com www.combi.com
30 year manufacturer of case erectors, case packers and case sealers, robotic pick and place pakcers with integrated case erectors; ergonomic hand packaging stations and drop packers with integrated case erectors.

President/CEO: John Fisher
jfisher@combi.com
CFO: Barb Karch
Research & Development: Bill Mitchell
Marketing Director: Sue Lewis
Sales Director: Mark Freidly
Plant Manager: Brian Miller
Estimated Sales: $10-20 Million
Number Employees: 100-249
Square Footage: 270000
Brands Exported: Combi America
Regions Exported to: Central America, South America
Percentage of Business in Exporting: 2
Brands Imported: Carmarme
Regions Imported from: Europe
Percentage of Business in Importing: 3

43156 Comeau's Seafoods
60 Saulnierville Rd
Saulnierville, NS B0W 2Z0
Canada
902-769-2101
info@comeausea.com
www.comeauseafoods.com
Fresh, frozen and processed seafoods, herring, smoked salmon.
President & CEO: Noel Despres
Vice President & General Manager: Kim d'Entremont
Estimated Sales: $50-100 Million
Number Employees: 375
Type of Packaging: Consumer, Food Service, Private Label, Bulk
Regions Exported to: Worldwide
Percentage of Business in Exporting: 50

43157 Command Communications
14510 E Fremont Ave
Centennial, CO 80112-4233 304-839-4051
Fax: 303-792-0899 800-288-3491
Manufacturer and exporter of wireless, staff, guest, hostess and waitress paging systems. Also communication products designed to reduce the number of phone lines— saving monthly phone line expenses
President/CEO: Craig Hibbard
chibbard@commandcom.com
VP Operations: Mary Larson
Director of Communications/Online Mkting: Michael Rose
National Accounts Sales Manager: Charla Martin
Estimated Sales: $ 3 - 5 Million
Number Employees: 10-19
Number of Products: 10
Type of Packaging: Consumer, Food Service, Private Label, Bulk
Brands Exported: PrivatePage; GuestPage; ASAP; ComSwitch; StaffPage
Regions Exported to: Worldwide
Percentage of Business in Exporting: 30

43158 Command Electronics Inc
15670 Morris Industrial Dr
Schoolcraft, MI 49087-9628 269-679-4011
Fax: 269-679-5410
info@commandelectronics.com
www.commandelectronics.com
Manufacturer and exporter of fluorescent and incandescent lighting
President: Cary Campagna
Vice President: Dan Campagna
Estimated Sales: $ 1 - 5 Million
Number Employees: 10-19
Square Footage: 52000

43159 (HQ)Commencement Bay Corrugated
13414 142nd Ave E
Orting, WA 98360-9560 253-845-3100
Fax: 253-445-0772 www.cbcbox.com
Manufacturer and exporter of corrugated paper boxes
Manager: Paul Winber
Sales Coordinator: James Kressler
Manager: Steve Mc Donald
mcdonald@cbcbox.com
General Manager: Joe McQuade
Plant Manager: Randy Snow
Estimated Sales: $ 20 - 50 Million
Number Employees: 100-249
Square Footage: 130000
Regions Exported to: Canada
Percentage of Business in Exporting: 2

43160 Commercial Creamery Co
159 S Cedar St
Spokane, WA 99201 509-747-4131
sales@cheesepowder.com
www.cheesepowder.com
Dried cheese and yogurt powders; processor and exporter of snack seasoning and spray dried dairy flavors
Owner/VP Sales & Marketing: Megan Boell
mboell@cheesepowder.com
Year Founded: 1908
Estimated Sales: $28 Million
Number Employees: 5-9
Regions Exported to: Asia, Middle East

43161 (HQ)Commercial Dehydrator Systems
256 Bethel Dr
Eugene, OR 97402-2504 541-688-5282
Fax: 541-688-5989 800-369-4283
darryl@dryer.com www.dehydrator.com
Berry crate washers, insect sterilization chambers, roasters, cookers and dryers including continuous belt, bin and tray; exporter of dryers/roasters and sorting/grading belting.
President: David Stone
marketing@dryer.com
Vice President: David Stone
National Sales Manager: Darryl Hastings
Field Representative: Darryl Hastings
Estimated Sales: $1-2.5 Million
Number Employees: 50-99
Square Footage: 54000
Regions Exported to: Central America, South America, Asia, Canada, Mexico
Percentage of Business in Exporting: 25

43162 (HQ)Commercial Furniture Group Inc
810 W Highway 25 70
Newport, TN 37821-8044 423-623-0031
Fax: 423-587-8872 800-873-3252
www.commercialfurnituregroup.com
Manufacturer and exporter of chairs, benches, booths and tables
Manager: Bob Branstetter
CFO: Neal Restivo
Marketing Specialist: Teri Winters
IT: Stefanie Thompson
sthompson@commercialfurniture.com
Number Employees: 1000-4999
Type of Packaging: Food Service
Brands Exported: Falcon; Howe; Johnson
Regions Exported to: Central America, South America, Europe, Asia, Middle East, Worldwide
Regions Imported from: Europe, Asia

43163 Commercial Lighting Design
43 S Dudley St
Memphis, TN 38104 901-774-5771
Fax: 901-946-2478 800-774-5799
www.lumalier.com
Manufacturer and exporter of lighting fixtures
President: Charles Dunn
CEO: Charles Dunn, Sr.
VP: Charles Dunn, Jr.
Estimated Sales: $1-2,500,000
Number Employees: 10-19
Regions Exported to: Worldwide

43164 Commercial Manufacturing
2432 S Railroad Ave
Fresno, CA 93706-5187 559-237-1855
Fax: 559-266-5149 info@commercialmfg.com
www.commercialmfg.com
Manufacturer and exporter of bin handling systems, conveyors, bucket elevators, air dryers, coolers and cleaners, washers, centrifuges, food pumps, graders and mix and blend systems
President: Larry Hagopian
info@commercialmfg.com
Sales Manager: Jack Kraemer
Sales Engineer: Jim MacKenzie
Sales Engineer: Bob Peschel
Estimated Sales: $ 10-20 Million
Number Employees: 50-99
Regions Exported to: Worldwide
Percentage of Business in Exporting: 20

Importers & Exporters / A-Z

43165 Commercial Refrigeration Service, Inc.
2501 West Behrend Drive
Suite 39
Phoenix, AZ 85027-4148   623-869-8881
          Fax: 623-869-8882 www.comrefsvc.com
Manufacturer and exporter of beverage dispensers
Contact: Sandra Forsythe
s.forsythe@crhinc.com
Estimated Sales: $ 1 - 5 Million
Number Employees: 100-250
Square Footage: 240000
Type of Packaging: Food Service
Brands Exported: Jet Spray
Regions Exported to: Worldwide
Percentage of Business in Exporting: 50

43166 Commissariat Imports
PO Box 643025
Los Angeles, CA 90064-0271   310-475-5628
          Fax: 310-475-8246 info@bombaybrand.com
Processor, importer and exporter of indian chutneys, pickles, curry powder and pastes including curry, biryani, ginger, garlic and tandoori; certified kosher available
President/CEO: Parvez Commissariat
VP: Aban Commissariat
Estimated Sales: Over $500,000
Number Employees: 2
Type of Packaging: Food Service, Private Label
Brands Exported: Bombay
Percentage of Business in Exporting: 10
Brands Imported: Bombay
Regions Imported from: Asia
Percentage of Business in Importing: 60

43167 Commodities Marketing Inc
6 Stone Tavern Dr
Clarksburg, NJ 08510   732-516-0700
          Fax: 732-516-0600 weldonrice@usa.net
                    www.weldonfoods.com
Jasmine rice, Basmati rice, Coconut drinks, Coconut milk, Fruits, Beans, Guar gum, Fruit juices and Cashews, Almonds, Saffron (Spain) White Rice/Parboiled Rice.
President: Herbander Sahni
herbandersahni@weldonfoods.com
CEO: Gagandeep Sahni
CFO: Soena Sahni
VP: Avneet Sodhi
R&D: Manoj Hedge
Marketing: Harbinder Singh Sahni & Dee Mirchandai
Sales: Avneet Sodhi
Public Relations: Mr. Dough & Harshida Shaw
Operations: Harshida Shah
Production: Mr Nobpsaul
Plant Manager: Mr Chandej
Estimated Sales: $25 Million
Number Employees: 5-9
Number of Brands: 3
Number of Products: 6
Square Footage: 3000
Type of Packaging: Consumer, Food Service, Private Label, Bulk
Brands Exported: Weldon; Meher
Regions Exported to: Europe, Middle East
Percentage of Business in Exporting: 5
Brands Imported: Weldon - Meher; Private Labels
Regions Imported from: Europe, Asia
Percentage of Business in Importing: 98

43168 Commodity Traders International
101 E. Main Street
P.O. Box 6
Trilla, IL 62469-0006   217-235-4322
          Fax: 217-235-3246 sales@commoditytraders.biz
                    www.commoditytraders.biz
Manufacturer and exporter of new and used milling, grain handling and seed processing machinery
Executive Trustee: Charles Stodden
Regions Exported to: Canada, Mexico

43169 Common Folk Farm
PO Box 141
Naples, ME 04055-0141   207-787-2764
          Fax: 207-787-3894
Processor and exporter of herbal teas, seasonings and culinary mixes
Owner: Betz Golon
Owner: Dale Golon
Type of Packaging: Consumer, Private Label, Bulk
Regions Exported to: Worldwide

Percentage of Business in Exporting: 10

43170 Community Coffee Co.
3332 Partridge Ln.
Building A
Baton Rouge, LA 70809   800-884-5282
          Fax: 800-643-8199
customerservice@communitycoffee.com
                    www.communitycoffee.com
Coffee and tea; importer of green coffee; and wholesaler/distributor of coffee creamer.
President/CEO: David Belanger
dbelanger@communitycoffee.com
Chairman: Matthew Saurage
CFO: Annette Vaccaro
Year Founded: 1919
Estimated Sales: $195 Million
Number Employees: 1000-4999
Type of Packaging: Consumer, Food Service, Private Label, Bulk
Regions Imported from: Central America, South America

43171 Comobar LLC
174 NE 24th Street
Miami, FL 33137
                    305-438-1254
                    info@comobar.com
                    www.comobar.com
Cappuccino and espresso coffees and machines
Manager/Owner: Paolo Cometto
Sales & Marketing: Cheri Steen
Contact: Michele Cometto
m.cometto@comobar.com
Estimated Sales: $ 5 - 10 Million
Number Employees: 10-19
Type of Packaging: Private Label
Regions Exported to: Europe

43172 Compacker Systems LLC
9104 N Zenith Ave
P.O. Box 2026
Davenport, IA 52806-6432   563-391-2751
          Fax: 563-391-8598
Manufacturer and exporter of case packing and sealing equipment including case erectors, wrap-around and top and bottom sealers, traymakers, etc
President: Keith Tucker
CEO: John Curtis
compacker@compacker.com
Quality Control: Jane Bower
Marketing Manager: Michael Bower
General Manager: Keith Tucker
Estimated Sales: $5-10 Million
Number Employees: 10-19
Square Footage: 80000
Regions Exported to: Asia, Canada
Percentage of Business in Exporting: 20

43173 Compact Industries Inc
3945 Ohio Ave
St Charles, IL 60174-5467   630-513-9600
          Fax: 630-513-9655 801-513-4262
                    www.compactind.com
Private label and contract packager: dry product packaging, in-house blending, formulating
President/CEO: Michael Brown
CFO: Steve Zaruba
VP Sales: Gary Johnson
Estimated Sales: $9 Million
Number Employees: 100-249
Square Footage: 300000
Type of Packaging: Consumer, Food Service, Private Label, Bulk
Brands Exported: Casa Verde; John Foster Green; Los Portales
Regions Exported to: Europe, Far East
Percentage of Business in Exporting: 5
Regions Imported from: South America, Europe, Columbia, Brazil, Mexico, Holland
Percentage of Business in Importing: 20

43174 Compactors Inc
71 Lighthouse Rd # 221
Hilton Head Isle, SC 29928-7297   843-363-5077
          Fax: 843-686-3290 800-423-4003
                    info@compactorsinc.com
Manufacturer and exporter of can and bottle crushers, trash compactors and densifiers
President: Mike Pierson
mike@compactorsinc.com
VP: Bill Phillips
Estimated Sales: Below $5 Million
Number Employees: 1-4

Square Footage: 8000
Parent Company: Hilton Head SC
Brands Exported: Can Saver II; Pac Crusher I; Densifier; Compactors; Glass Crushers
Regions Exported to: Central America, South America, Europe, Asia, Middle East, Worldwide
Percentage of Business in Exporting: 20

43175 Compania De Comercio
159 Ave Carlos Chardon
San Juan, PR 00918-1712   787-294-0101
          Fax: 787-782-5699
                    www.comercioyexportacion.com
Water, salad dressing, other candy, cheese, exotic meats, marinades, nuts, honey.
Number Employees: 10-19

43176 (HQ)Complete Packaging & Shipping
83 Bennington Ave
Freeport, NY 11520-3913   516-546-2100
          Fax: 516-546-0717 877-269-3236
                    johnc@completepackage.com
                    www.completesupplyusa.com
Corrugated boxes; exporter and importer of tapes, cartons, stretch film, impulse sealers and plastic strapping materials. 3000 box sizes in stock
Owner: Jeffery Berkowitz
Director Of Sales: Tom DiGiacomo
Estimated Sales: $ 10-20 Million
Number Employees: 10-19
Regions Exported to: Worldwide
Percentage of Business in Exporting: 30
Regions Imported from: Canada
Percentage of Business in Importing: 5

43177 Compliance Control Inc
1595 Cabin Branch Dr
Hyattsville, MD 20785-3816   301-773-6485
          Fax: 301-773-4044 800-810-4000
info@hygenius.com www.tempgenius.com
Manufacturer and exporter of handwashing verification systems
President: Neil Segal
nsegal@compliancecontrolinc.com
Executive VP: Bill Karlin
Estimated Sales: $2.5-5 Million
Number Employees: 20-49
Type of Packaging: Food Service, Private Label
Brands Exported: Hygenius
Regions Exported to: Worldvide
Percentage of Business in Exporting: 3

43178 (HQ)Component Hardware Group Inc
1890 Swarthmore Ave
Lakewood, NJ 08701-4530   323-888-9395
          Fax: 732-363-9864 800-526-3694
Manufacturer, importer and exporter of food service equipment including beverage preparation and serving products, dispensers, faucets, spray washers, water stations, tables including legs and bases, drains, grease filters, castersetc
President: Alfred Klein
VP Marketing: William Matthaei
VP Sales: Pat Campbell
Contact: Steve Bruno
sbruno@chgusa.com
Estimated Sales: Less Than $500,000
Number Employees: 1-4
Square Footage: 96000
Brands Exported: Encore
Regions Exported to: Worldwide
Percentage of Business in Exporting: 25
Regions Imported from: Europe, Asia, Canada
Percentage of Business in Importing: 20

43179 Composition Materials Co Inc
249 Pepes Farm Rd
Milford, CT 06460-3671   203-874-6500
          Fax: 203-874-6505 800-262-7763
                    info@compomat.com www.compomat.com
Plastic Blasting Media, a distributor of a multitude of filers and extenders, supplier of Walnut Shell grits and flours, and importer of birch wood flour from Sweden.
President: Alan Nudelman
nudelman@compomat.com
Chairman: Theodore Diamond
Sales Representative: Steven D. Essex
Product Operations Manager: David M. Elster

Importers & Exporters / A-Z

Estimated Sales: $2.5-5 Million
Number Employees: 10-19
Square Footage: 30000
Regions Exported to: Central America, South America, Europe, Asia, Middle East, South Africa
Percentage of Business in Exporting: 20
Regions Imported from: Sweden

43180 Compris Technologies
2651 Satellite Blvd
Duluth, GA 30096-5810   770-418-4616
Fax: 770-795-3333   800-615-3301
www.compristech.com
Manufacturer and exporter of computer software including point of sale, labor, inventory, scheduling, executive information and cash management
President: Alaa Pasha
Vice President, Development: Eric Kobres
Area VP Sales: Ron Small
Contact: Mills Bronson
brown.james@ncr.com
Estimated Sales: $ 5 - 10 Million
Number Employees: 100-249
Regions Exported to: Europe, Asia, Middle East, Latin America, Canada
Percentage of Business in Exporting: 30

43181 Computer Controlled Machines
1 Magnuson Ave
Pueblo, CO 81001-4889   719-948-9500
Fax: 719-948-9540 sales@magnusoncorp.com
www.magnusoncorp.com
Manufacturer and exporter of vegetable processing equipment for sweet corn, green beans and peas
Owner: Bob Smith
VP/General Manager: Craig Furlo
Estimated Sales: $ 5 - 10 Million
Number Employees: 20-49
Parent Co: Atlas-Pacific Engineering
Regions Exported to: Worldwide

43182 (HQ)Computerized Machinery Systs
11733 95th Ave N
Maple Grove, MN 55369-5551   763-493-0099
Fax: 763-493-0093 sales@cmsitechnologies.com
www.labelmart.com
Manufacturer and exporter of pressure sensitive labels; wholesaler/distributor and exporter of barcode printers, label scanners and applicators
Owner: Kate Jackson
Sales: Eric Sorensen
kate@labelmart.com
Estimated Sales: Below $ 5 Million
Number Employees: 20-49
Regions Exported to: Canada
Percentage of Business in Exporting: 5

43183 Computrition
19808 Nordhoff Pl
Chatsworth, CA 91311   818-701-5544
Fax: 818-701-1702   800-222-4488
info@computrition.com www.computrition.com
Offers completely integrated food service and nutrition care management software systems for operations of all size. Software features include diet order, recipe, menu and inventory management, online order entry and nutrient analysis
President: Luros Luros-Elson RD
CEO: Scott Saklad
R&D: Joseph Bibbo
Manager, Marketing: Marty Yadrick, RD
Sales: Scott Saklad
Contact: Bindu Amin
bamin@computrition.com
Operations: Kim Goldberg
Estimated Sales: $20-50 Million
Number Employees: 50-99
Square Footage: 17000
Type of Packaging: Food Service
Regions Exported to: Canada

43184 (HQ)Computype Inc
2285 County Road C W
St Paul, MN 55113-2567   651-633-0633
Fax: 651-633-5580   800-328-0852
www.computype.com
Manufacturer and exporter of bar code labels, printers and applicators

President: R Huntsinger
CEO: Sonia Artola
soniaartola@hotmail.com
VP: J Ammann
CEO: William Roche
Estimated Sales: $20-50 Million
Number Employees: 100-249
Other Locations:
  Computype
  Concord, NH Computype
Regions Exported to: Central America, South America, Europe, Asia, Middle East
Percentage of Business in Exporting: 25

43185 Comstock Castle Stove Co
119 W Washington St
Quincy, IL 62301-3860   410-829-4199
Fax: 217-223-0007   800-637-9188
sales@castlestove.com www.castlestove.com
Manufacturer, importer and exporter of cooking equipment including gas broilers, deep fat fryers, ovens, griddles, ranges, hot plates, etc
Vice President: Tim Spake
tspake@comstockcastlestoveco.com
Vice President: Timothy Spake
Marketing/Sales: Curtis Spake
Purchasing Manager: Bob Speckhart
Estimated Sales: $5-10 Million
Number Employees: 20-49
Square Footage: 170000
Type of Packaging: Food Service, Private Label
Brands Exported: Castle; Economy
Regions Exported to: Central America, South America, Asia, Middle East, Canada, Caribbean, Latin America, Mexico
Percentage of Business in Exporting: 15
Regions Imported from: Asia, Mexico
Percentage of Business in Importing: 1

43186 Comtec Industries
10210 Werch Dr
Suite 204
Woodridge, IL 60517   630-759-9000
Fax: 630-759-9009
feedback@comtecindustriesltd.com
www.comtecindustriesltd.com
Baking equipment and supplies including dough formers for pot pies, hors d'oeuvres and top/bottom crusts; also, dies and tooling for pies, tarts, cheesecakes, etc.; exporter of dough presses
President: James Reilly
Contact: Dolores Reilly
dreilly@comtecindustriesltd.com
Estimated Sales: $ 1 - 3 Million
Number Employees: 10
Square Footage: 8000
Regions Exported to: South America, Europe, Asia, Middle East
Percentage of Business in Exporting: 25

43187 Comus Restaurant Systems
9667 Fleetwood Court
Frederick, MD 21701   301-698-6208
Manufacturer and exporter of point of sale and full back office software
Marketing: Fred Ihrer
Estimated Sales: $ 2.5-5 Million
Number Employees: 10
Square Footage: 4000
Parent Co: Comus Software
Regions Exported to: Canada
Percentage of Business in Exporting: 5

43188 Con Agra Snack Foods
2301 Washington St
Hamburg, IA 51640-1835   712-382-2202
Fax: 712-382-1357   800-831-5818
www.vogelpopcorn.com
Processor and exporter of popcorn and popping oils; importer of popcorn and popcorn seeds.
President/CEO: Sean Connolly
Estimated Sales: $20-50 Million
Number Employees: 50-99
Number of Brands: 2
Parent Co: ConAgra Foods
Type of Packaging: Consumer, Food Service, Private Label, Bulk
Brands Exported: Act II, Vogel
Regions Exported to: Central America, South America, Europe, Asia, Middle East
Percentage of Business in Exporting: 15
Brands Imported: Vogel Argentina
Regions Imported from: South America
Percentage of Business in Importing: 5

43189 Con-tech/Conservation Technology
2783 Shermer Rd
Northbrook, IL 60062-7708   847-559-5505
Fax: 847-559-5505   800-728-0312
www.con-techlighting.com
Manufacturer, importer and exporter of lighting products and industrial fans
President: John Ranshaw
Secretary: Sandy Grossman
VP: John Ranshow
Sales/Marketing Executive: Olga Draqunsky
Contact: Sally Baybutt
sbaybutt@con-techlighting.com
Purchasing Agent: Larry Sabatino
Estimated Sales: $20-50 Million
Number Employees: 20-49
Square Footage: 36000
Regions Exported to: Central America, South America
Percentage of Business in Exporting: 5
Regions Imported from: Europe, Asia

43190 ConSup North America
170 Beaverbrook Rd
Unit 2
Lincoln Park, NJ 07035-1441   973-628-7330
Fax: 973-628-2919 customerservice@consup.us
www.consupna.com
Importer of German food brands
Owner: Martin Moog
m.moog@consup.us
Marketing: Russ Harlock
Estimated Sales: $ 5-10 Million
Number Employees: 5-9

43191 (HQ)Conagra Brands Inc
222 W. Merchandise Mart Plaza
Chicago, IL 60654   312-549-5000
   877-266-2472
www.conagrafoods.com
Consumer brands.
President & CEO: Sean Connolly
Executive VP/CFO: David Marberger
Executive Vice President: Colleen Batcheler
Executive VP/Co-COO: Tom McGough
Estimated Sales: $11 Billion
Number Employees: 18,000
Number of Brands: 70
Type of Packaging: Consumer, Food Service, Bulk

43192 Conagra Foodservice
222 W. Merchandise Mart Plaza
Suite 1300
Chicago, IL 60654   312-549-5000
   877-266-2472
www.conagrabrands.com
Supplies restaurants, retailers, commercial customers and other foodservice suppliers.
President/CEO: Sean Connolly
Executive VP/CFO: David Marberger
Executive VP/General Counsel: Colleen Batcheler
Executive VP/Co-COO: Tom McGough
Estimated Sales: K
Number Employees: 10,000+
Number of Brands: 70
Square Footage: 11042
Parent Co: Conagra Brands
Type of Packaging: Consumer, Food Service, Bulk
Other Locations:
  ConAgra Headquarters
  Kennewick, WA
  ConAgra Headquarters
  Naperville, IL
  Sales Office
  Anaheim, CA
  Sales Office
  Mesa, AR
  Sales Office
  San Antonio, TX
  Sales Office
  Plano, TX
  ConAgra Headquarters Naperville
Regions Exported to: Worldwide

43193 Conax Buffalo Technologies
2300 Walden Ave
Buffalo, NY 14225-4779   716-684-4500
Fax: 716-684-7433   800-223-2389
conax@conaxtechnologies.com
www.conaxbuffalo.com
Manufacturer and exporter of measurement systems including temperature sensors, sealing devices and fiber optic systems

237

Importers & Exporters / A-Z

President: Robert Fox
Marketing Director: Richard Paluch
Director of Sales and Marketing: Michael Valachos
Purchasing: Joe Kelly
Estimated Sales: $10-20 Million
Number Employees: 50-99
Square Footage: 186000
Regions Exported to: South America, Europe, Asia, Middle East

43194 Conca D'Oro Importers
72-02 51st Avenue
Woodside, NY 11377   718-446-0800
   Fax: 718-424-3300 psalvia@concadoro.com
                      concadorofood.com
Importer and wholesaler/distributor of Italian and specialty gourmet foods including pasta, olive oil, coffee, tomatoes and confectionery products
President: Paul Salvia
Secretary: Ciro Salvia
Marketing: Paolo Salvia
Contact: Ciro Salvia
agriturismo@concadoro.com
Estimated Sales: $20-50 Million
Number Employees: 20-49
Square Footage: 20000
Brands Imported: Ciro; Labbate; ZiCaffe; Iposea; Nokahbo; Ciccorese; Paget; Bella di Cerignola
Regions Imported from: Europe
Percentage of Business in Importing: 60

43195 Concannon Vineyard
4590 Tesla Rd
Livermore, CA 94550-9002   925-456-2505
     Fax: 925-583-1160   800-258-9866
            info@concannonvineyard.com
            www.concannonvineyard.com
Processor and exporter of bottled wines; grower of grapes
CFO: Jim Page
Estimated Sales: $1.6 Million
Number Employees: 50-99
Square Footage: 29912
Parent Co: Wine Group
Type of Packaging: Consumer, Private Label
Brands Exported: Concannon Vineyard
Regions Exported to: Central America, South America, Europe, Asia, Middle East, Australia, Caribbean, Mexico
Percentage of Business in Exporting: 15

43196 Conchita Foods Inc
9115 NW 105th Way
Medley, FL 33178-1221   305-888-9703
     Fax: 305-888-1020 www.conchita-foods.com
Wholesaler/distributor and importer of beans, fruits, vegetable oils, olives, pimientos, rice, etc
President: Sixto Ferro
Estimated Sales: $20-50 Million
Number Employees: 50-99
Regions Imported from: South America

43197 Conductive Containers Inc
4500 Quebec Ave N
Minneapolis, MN 55428-4915   763-537-2090
     Fax: 763-537-1738   800-327-2329
            info@corstat.com www.corstat.com
Manufacturer and exporter of containers including conductive fiberboard, corrugated, chipboard and plastic
President: Brad Ahlm
VP: Paul Granning
VP Operations/R&D: Robert Marlovits
Estimated Sales: $ 1-2.5 Million
Number Employees: 50-99
Square Footage: 100000
Regions Exported to: Europe, Canada, Mexico, Caribbean, Latin America

43198 Conflex, Inc.
W130 N10751 Washington Drive
Germantown, WI 53022   262-512-2665
     Fax: 262-512-1665   800-225-4296
            info@conflex.com www.conflex.com
Manufacturer and exporter of shrink wrapping equipment
President: Bill Morrissey
CEO: Joe Morrissey
CFO: Jim Benton
Research & Development: Mark Kubisiak
Tech Services: Kevin Thomas
Product Manager: Joe Morrissey
Purchasing Manager: Bill Morrissey, Jr.

Number Employees: 20-49
Square Footage: 320000
Type of Packaging: Consumer, Food Service, Bulk
Regions Exported to: South America, Worldwide
Percentage of Business in Exporting: 10

43199 Conflow Technologies, Inc.
18 Regan Road
Units 28 & 29
Brampton, ON L7A 1C2
Canada   905-840-6800
     Fax: 905-840-6799   800-275-9887
            sales@conflow.ca www.conflow.ca
Manufacturer and importer of food processing machinery including certified milk reception and loadout systems, in-plant sanitary flow meters and calibration services and batch and blend control systems; also, transport custody dispensing systems
President: Gary Collins
CFO: Anna Lynn Wiebe
Vice President: Gerry Camirand
Research & Development: Anna Lynn
Quality Control: Gerry Camirand
Number Employees: 7
Square Footage: 5400
Regions Imported from: Europe

43200 Conimar Corp
1724 NE 22nd Ave
Ocala, FL 34470-4702   352-732-3262
     Fax: 352-732-6888   800-874-9735
            corp@conimar.com www.conimar.com
Beverage coaster, flexible cutting mats and bamboo cutting boards
Owner: Terry Crawford
CFO: Eric Robinson
VP: Ron Dampier
Marketing: Terry Putty
Estimated Sales: $10-15 Million
Number Employees: 50-99
Square Footage: 140000
Type of Packaging: Private Label
Regions Exported to: Central America, South America, Asia
Percentage of Business in Exporting: 10
Regions Imported from: Asia
Percentage of Business in Importing: 5

43201 Connecticut Laminating Co Inc
162 James St
New Haven, CT 06513-3845   203-787-2184
     Fax: 203-787-4073   800-753-9119
            info@ctlaminating.com www.ctlaminating.com
Manufacturer and exporter of plastic laminated advertising signs, place mats, tags, menus and cards
President: Henry Snow
henry@ctlaminating.com
VP: Steve Snow
Estimated Sales: $10 Million+
Number Employees: 100-249
Square Footage: 110000
Regions Exported to: Central America, South America, Europe, Middle East
Percentage of Business in Exporting: 5

43202 (HQ)Connection Chemical LP
126 S State St # 200
Suite 200
Newtown, PA 18940-3524   215-497-3063
            www.connectionchemical.com
Wholesaler/distributor and importer of acidulants and humectants/solvents including citric acid, sodium citrate, glycerine and sodium benzoate
President & CEO: Frank Farish
CFO: Martin L. Pagliughi
Vice President - Eastern Region: Samuel J. McGinness
VP Sales Northeast Region: Steve Brewster
Contact: Frank Alari
falari@connectionchemical.com
Number Employees: 5-9
Square Footage: 120000
Regions Imported from: South America, Europe, Asia
Percentage of Business in Importing: 80

43203 Connell International Company
200 Connell Drive
Berkeley Heights, NJ 07922-2805   908-673-3700
     Fax: 908-673-3800 www.connellco.com
Importer and exporter of packaging equipment and materials and ingredients for the dairy, poultry, meat, bottling, brewing and food industries

President: Grover Connell
Executive VP: George Alayeto
Contact: Dick Armocido
armocido@connellco.com
Estimated Sales: $20-50 Million
Number Employees: 100-249
Regions Exported to: Worldwide
Regions Imported from: Worldwide

43204 Conquest International LLC
1108 SW 8th St
Plainville, KS 67663-3106   785-434-2483
     Fax: 785-434-2736 conquest@ruraltel.net
            www.enviroliteconquestusa.com
Water treatment and purification systems. Turn-key bottled water plants and water stores.
President: Ned Colburn
CFO: Jeffrey Van Dyke
Estimated Sales: A
Number Employees: 1-4
Square Footage: 40000
Regions Exported to: Central America, South America, Europe, Asia, Middle East, Canada, Mexico, Caribbean, Africa
Percentage of Business in Exporting: 50
Percentage of Business in Importing: 50

43205 Consolidated Baling Machine Company
P.O.Box 6922
Jacksonville, FL 32236-6922   904-358-3812
     Fax: 904-358-7013   800-231-9286
            sales@intl-baler.com www.intl-baler.com
Manufacturer and exporter of balers, compactors and drum crushers/packers
President: William Nielsen
CEO: Roger Griffin
Sales Manager: Jerry Wise
Estimated Sales: F
Number Employees: 50-99
Square Footage: 8000
Parent Co: Waste Technology Corporation
Regions Exported to: Central America, South America, Europe, Asia, Middle East, Australia

43206 Consolidated Can Co
15725 Illinois Ave
Paramount, CA 90723-4112   562-634-5245
     Fax: 562-634-8689   888-793-2199
                  www.consolidatedcan.com
Manufacturer and exporter of tin cans; also, tops, bottoms, plugs and caps for containers
Owner: Doug Lampson
consilidatedcan@aol.com
CFO: Doug Lampson
Estimated Sales: $ 1 - 2.5 Million
Number Employees: 1-4
Square Footage: 6000
Type of Packaging: Bulk
Regions Exported to: Canada

43207 Consolidated Commercial Controls
200 International Way
Winsted, CT 6098   860-738-7112
     Fax: 860-738-7140   800-227-1511
            CustServ@AllPointsFPS.com
                  www.allpointsfps.com
Manufacturer and exporter of commercial cooking and refrigeration equipment parts; importer of cast iron parts and supplies.
CEO: John Hanby
CFO: Dan Cox
Vice President: Azie Kahn
Research & Development: Azie Kahn
Marketing Director: John McDermott
Sales Director: Phil Wisehart
Contact: Rick Hernandez
rhernandez@allpointsfps.com
Purchasing Manager: Linda Feichtl
Estimated Sales: $15-20 Million
Number Employees: 20-49
Square Footage: 90000
Type of Packaging: Food Service
Brands Exported: All American Food Equipment Spare Parts
Regions Exported to: Central America, South America, Europe, Asia, Middle East
Percentage of Business in Exporting: 25
Brands Imported: Cast Iron Parts
Regions Imported from: South America, Asia
Percentage of Business in Importing: 20

Importers & Exporters / A-Z

43208 Consolidated CommericalControls
8130 River Dr
Morton Grove, IL 60053-2637 847-966-9700
Fax: 847-966-9701 www.ccc-parts.net
Manufacturer and exporter of commerical cooking and refrigerated equipment parts, importer of cast iron parts
President: Erwin Shakin
CFO: Wayne Woodworth
General Manager: Azie Khan
Marketing: John McDermott
Sales: Pat Pope
Contact: Khan Azie
akhan@ccc-parts.com
Purchasing Director: Gary Shakin
Estimated Sales: $15-20 Million
Square Footage: 45000
Type of Packaging: Food Service
Brands Exported: All American Food Equipment Spare Parts
Regions Exported to: Central America, Europe, Asia, Middle East
Brands Imported: Cast Iron Parts

43209 (HQ)Consolidated Container Co LLC
3101 Towercreek Pkwy SE # 300
Suite 300
Atlanta, GA 30339-3256 678-742-4600
Fax: 678-742-4750 888-831-2184
www.ccclllc.com
Manufacturer and exporter of blow molded plastic bottles
President/Director/CEO: Jeffrey Greene
jeffrey.greene@ccclllc.com
Vice President, Human Resources: Bradley Newman
Estimated Sales: $ 237 Million
Number Employees: 1000-4999
Square Footage: 16000
Parent Co: Bain Capital, LLC
Regions Exported to: Asia
Percentage of Business in Exporting: 6

43210 Consolidated Label Company
925 Florida Central Pkwy
Longwood, FL 32750 407-339-2626
Fax: 407-331-1711 800-475-2235
liz@consolidatedlabel.com
www.consolidatedlabel.com
Manufacturer and exporter of pressure sensitive labels and tags
President: Joel Carmany
National Sales Manager: Beau Bowman
Plant Manager: Dick St Hilaire
Estimated Sales: $ 20-50 Million
Number Employees: 50-99
Square Footage: 35000
Type of Packaging: Private Label, Bulk
Regions Exported to: Central America, South America
Percentage of Business in Exporting: 5

43211 Consolidated Thread Mills, Inc.
P.O. Box 1107
Fall River, MA 02722 508-672-0032
Fax: 508-674-3773
www.consolidatedthreadmills.com
Manufacturer and exporter of bounded and waxed industrial twine including nylon, polyester, rayon and cotton
Owner: Colleen Pacheco
Estimated Sales: $ 1 - 5 Million
Number Employees: 5-9

43212 Constantia Colmar
92 County Line Rd
Colmar, PA 18915-9606 215-997-6222
Fax: 215-997-3976
Manufacturer and exporter of foil, juice and yogurt lids, butter wrappers, etc
CEO: Jerry Decker
jerryd@hnpack.com
CEO: Jerry Decker
Estimated Sales: $ 50-100 Million
Number Employees: 50-99
Parent Co: H&N Packaging
Type of Packaging: Bulk
Regions Exported to: Worldwide

43213 Constar International
41605 Ann Arbor Road
Plymouth, MI 48170 734-455-3600
info@plastipak.com
Plastic containers and bottles for soft drinks, mustard, edible oils, wine and liquors
President: Mike Hoffman
CFO: Bill Rymer
R&D: Don Deual
Production: Craig Renton
Estimated Sales: $ 2.5 - 5 Million
Number Employees: 20
Parent Co: Crown Cork & Seal
Regions Exported to: Central America, South America, Europe
Percentage of Business in Exporting: 8

43214 Constellation Brands Inc
207 High Point Dr.
Suite 100
Victor, NY 14564 585-678-7100
888-724-2169
www.cbrands.com
Beer, champagne, table, sparkling and kosher wines, Scotch whiskey, spirits, etc.
Executive Chair: Robert Sands
robert.sands@cbrands.com
President/CEO: Bill Newlands
CFO: Garth Hankinson
Executive Vice Chair: Richard Sands
Chief Marketing Officer: Jim Sabia
Chief Human Resources Officer: Thomas Kane
Estimated Sales: $7.3 Billion
Number Employees: 10,000
Number of Brands: 100+
Type of Packaging: Consumer
Other Locations: Constellation Brands
Regions Exported to: Central America, South America, Europe, Asia

43215 Containair Packaging Corporation
37 E 6th St
Paterson, NJ 7524 973-523-1800
Fax: 973-523-1818 888-276-6500
Manufacturer and exporter of semi-bulk containers for food ingredients; also, slotted cartons and graphic displays available
CEO/President: Lawrence Taylor
VP: Paul Davis
Plant Manager: Ken Kutner
Estimated Sales: $2.5-5 Million
Number Employees: 20-49
Square Footage: 94000
Brands Exported: K-Box
Regions Exported to: South America, Europe
Percentage of Business in Exporting: 5

43216 Container Machinery Corporation
1060 Broadway
Albany, NY 12204 518-694-3310
Fax: 608-719-8380 www.cmc-kuhnke.com
High speed notching presses; exporter of seam quality inspection and measuring systems; importer of can making machinery
Managing Director: Thomas Duve
VP: Alex Grossjohann
Technical Service Manager: Markus Kellner
Marketing Manager: Aura Marcks
Sales Manager Southeast Asia: Ning Qian
Customer Service Manager: Jose Rodriguez
Vice President, Managing Director: Alex Grossjohann
Estimated Sales: $ 1 - 3 Million
Number Employees: 5-9
Square Footage: 60000
Brands Exported: SEAM Products
Regions Exported to: Central America, South America, Europe, Asia, Middle East, Australia
Percentage of Business in Exporting: 15
Brands Imported: Bibra; NSM; Bertil Ohlsson; Sanyu; Lanico; Tecnomachinery; Krupp; SIG; Manfred Kohnve Measurement Systems
Regions Imported from: Central America, Europe, Asia
Percentage of Business in Importing: 20

43217 Container Supply Co
12571 Western Ave
Garden Grove, CA 92841-4012 562-594-9370
Fax: 714-892-3824
tbertoglio@containersupplycompany.com
www.containersupplycompany.com
Manufacturer and exporter of tin cans and plastic pails and containers
Owner: Robert Hurtt
cscmaster@aol.com
Quality Control: C Bonnet
Regional Sales Manager: T Carlson
Director Sales: Tony Bertoglio
Export Sales: F Ceja
Estimated Sales: $ 20 - 50 Million
Number Employees: 100-249
Square Footage: 160000
Regions Exported to: Central America, South America, Canada, Mexico

43218 Contech Enterprises Inc
314 Straight Ave SW
Grand Rapids, MI 49504-6439 616-818-1520
Fax: 616-459-4140 800-767-8658
Manufacturer and exporter of pesticide-free insect trapping adhesives
President and CEO: Mark Grambart
VP of Sales and Marketing: Allen Spigelman
VP of Sales and Marketing: Allen Spigelman
Contact: John Borden
john.borden@contech-inc.com
VP of Operations: Bill Jones
Estimated Sales: $ 2.5 - 5 Million
Number Employees: 5-9
Square Footage: 80000
Type of Packaging: Private Label
Brands Exported: Tanglefoot
Regions Exported to: Central America, South America, Europe, Asia, Middle East, Australia

43219 Contemporary Product Inc
273 Hein Dr
Garner, NC 27529-7221 919-779-4228
Fax: 919-779-9734
Manufacturer and importer of award plaques and shields, trophies and cup bases
VP: David Hamilton
Manager: Joan Squillini
Manager: Joan Squillini
Estimated Sales: $ 1 - 5 Million
Number Employees: 1-4
Regions Imported from: Europe

43220 (HQ)Contico Container
15510 Blackburn Ave
Norwalk, CA 90650 562-921-9967
Fax: 562-926-4979 www.contico.com
Manufacturer and exporter of polyethylene containers
Engineering-R&D: Michael Angelo
Contact: Nick Man
nickm@conticospraychem.com
Estimated Sales: $ 20 - 50 Million
Number Employees: 100-249
Parent Co: Contico International

43221 Continental Cart by Kullman Industries
1 Kullman Corporate Campus Dr
Lebanon, NJ 08833-2163 908-236-0220
Fax: 908-236-0848 888-882-2278
Manufacturer and exporter of carts and kiosks; also, modular construction for diners, schools and correctional facilities
President: Amy Marks
CEO: Avi Telyas
Vice President of Operations: Michael Hathaway
Vice President of Production: Bobby Pohlman
Estimated Sales: $ 50 - 60 Million
Number Employees: 250-499

43222 Continental Commercial Products
305 Rock Industrial Park Dr.
Bridgeton, MO 63044 314-656-4301
Fax: 800-327-5492 800-325-1051
janics@contico.com
www.continentalcommercialproducts.com
Wastebaskets, recycle collection and trash receptacles, utility carts, liners, mopping equipment, squeegees, trigger sprayers, caution signs, plastic shelves, food service products and mobile equipment
President: Mike Boland
VP: Jim Dunn
Contact: Gary Anton
ganton@continentalcommercialproducts.com
Number Employees: 250-499
Square Footage: 12000000
Parent Co: Katy Industries

239

Importers & Exporters / A-Z

43223 Continental Equipment Corporation
P.O.Box 18662
6103 N. 76th Street
Milwaukee, WI 53218   414-463-0500
        Fax: 414-463-3199 www.ceceq.com
Manufacturer and exporter of custom washing machinery
President: Will Leistikow
Manager: Mark Kelso
VP Sales: Doug Piszczek
Engineer: Brennen Cullen
Estimated Sales: $ 3-5 Million
Number Employees: 20-49
Square Footage: 60000
Brands Exported: Aqueous
Regions Exported to: Central America, South America, Asia, Middle East
Percentage of Business in Exporting: 10

43224 Continental Girbau Inc
2500 State Road 44
Oshkosh, WI 54904-8914   920-231-8222
        Fax: 920-231-4666 800-256-1073
                www.cgilaundry.com
Manufacturer and exporter of commercial and industrial laundry equipment
President: Mike Floyd
mike.floyd@continentalgirbau.org
VP Sales & Customer Service: Joel T Jorgensen
Director Human Resources: Kelly Zabel
Number Employees: 20-49
Parent Co: Girbau S.A.
Brands Exported: Pro-Series; L-Series
Brands Imported: Pro-Series; L-Series

43225 Continental Grain Company
787 5th Ave
15th Fl
New York, NY 10153-0015   212-207-5100
                information@conti.com
                www.continentalgrain.com
Grain, poultry, pork, beef, animal feed, aquaculture, and flour milling.
Directeur General: Charles Fribourg
Chairman & CEO: Paul J. Fribourg
CFO: Frank Baier
General Counsel: Michael Mayberry
Executive Vice President: David Tanner
COO: Robert Golden
Estimated Sales: $2.5 Billion
Number Employees: 11,000
Type of Packaging: Consumer, Bulk
Regions Exported to: Worldwide
Percentage of Business in Exporting: 100

43226 Continental Identification
140 E Averill
Sparta, MI 49345   616-887-7341
        Fax: 616-887-0154 800-247-2499
                cipinfo@continentalid.com
                www.continentalid.com
Manufacturer and exporter of counter mats, screen printed decals and cooler doors danglers
President: James Clay
Contact: John Begerow
jbegerow@continentalid.com
Operations Manager: Dave Clay
Estimated Sales: $ 10 - 20 Million
Number Employees: 100-249
Parent Co: Celia Corporation
Regions Exported to: Worldwide
Percentage of Business in Exporting: 5

43227 Continental Marketing
18 Lithgow St
Winslow, ME 04901   207-872-4938
        Fax: 207-872-2062
Exporter and wholesaler/distributor of closeout food items from overstocks, package changes, buy backs, downgrades, etc.; serving the food service market
CEO: Charles Ladd
Estimated Sales: $2 Milion
Number Employees: 1-4
Square Footage: 100000
Type of Packaging: Food Service
Regions Exported to: Central America, South America, Europe
Percentage of Business in Exporting: 15
Regions Imported from: Central America, Europe, Middle East
Percentage of Business in Importing: 10

43228 Continental Mills Inc
18100 Andover Park W
Tukwila, WA 98188-4703   206-816-7000
        Fax: 253-872-7954 www.continentalmills.com
Manufacturer and exporter of baking products including dry flour mixes. Continental Mills has acquired the Pillsbury foodservice small package dry mix business from Best Brands Corporation
President: John Heily
CEO: John M Heily
jheily@continentalmills.com
CFO: Michael Castle
Vice President: Bob Wallach
Research & Development: Dan Donahue
Quality Control: Christy Johnson
Marketing Director: Steve Donley
Sales Director: Steve Giuditta
Public Relations: Clyde Walker
Operations Manager: Mark Harris
Production Manager: Mike Meredith
Year Founded: 1932
Estimated Sales: $43.2 Million
Number Employees: 100-249
Number of Brands: 10
Square Footage: 300000
Parent Co: Pillsbury Food Service
Type of Packaging: Consumer, Food Service, Private Label, Bulk
Brands Exported: Krusteaz, Private Label
Regions Exported to: Worldwide
Percentage of Business in Exporting: 3

43229 Continental Seasoning
1700 Palisade Ave
Teaneck, NJ 07666   201-837-6111
        Fax: 201-837-9248 800-631-1564
Processor, importer and exporter of sauces, spices, seasonings and food additives
President: Pete Federer
CFO: Jeffrey Bovit
Vice President: Edward Levine
Quality Control: Marty Haas
VP Production: Ann Davis
Plant Manager: Steve Wagner
Estimated Sales: $5 Million
Number Employees: 50
Square Footage: 80000
Type of Packaging: Food Service, Private Label, Bulk
Regions Exported to: Central America, South America, Europe, Caribbean
Percentage of Business in Exporting: 5
Regions Imported from: Central America, South America, Europe, Asia, Middle East, Australia
Percentage of Business in Importing: 10

43230 Continental-Fremont
Airport Industrial Park 1685 S. County
PO Box 489
Tiffin, OH 44883   419-448-4045
        Fax: 419-448-4048
Manufacturer and exporter of carbon and stainless steel storage tanks, plating, bins, hoppers, and silos; sanitary and metal fabrication services available
President: C William Harple
CFO: Melissa Hoover
Quality Control: Ron Ranson
Marketing/Sales: Don Harple
Operations Manager: Ron Ransom
Estimated Sales: Below $ 5 Million
Number Employees: 20-49
Square Footage: 100000

43231 Contour Packaging
637 W Rockland St
Philadelphia, PA 19120   215-457-1600
        Fax: 215-457-5040
Manufacturer and exporter of stand-up pouches and blow molded plastic bottles and containers; also, screen printing and hot foil stamping services available
President: Stephen D Mannino
Sales Engineer: Mark Rysak
Estimated Sales: $10-20 Million
Number Employees: 50-99

43232 Contract & Leisure
20 Nassau Street
Suite 237
Princeton, NJ 08542-4505   609-860-6700
        Fax: 609-860-6701
Wholesaler/distributor and importer of stacking plastic chairs and tables for indoor and outdoor use and cantilevered umbrellas; exporter of cantilevered umbrellas
Manager: Jack Dessailly
Number Employees: 1-4
Type of Packaging: Food Service
Brands Exported: Collet Parasol
Regions Exported to: South America
Percentage of Business in Exporting: 10
Brands Imported: Stamp; Collet Parasol; Sartaki; Tango; Mambo
Regions Imported from: Europe
Percentage of Business in Importing: 90

43233 Contrex Inc
8900 Zachary Ln N
Maple Grove, MN 55369-4018   763-424-7800
        Fax: 763-424-8734 info@contrexinc.com
                www.contrexinc.com
Manufacturer and exporter of electronic controls including universal motor speed, universal motor synchronizing, rotary die/knife synchronizing, cut-to-length/indexing and digital DC motor
President: Gary C Hansen
VP: Glen Gauvin
Estimated Sales: $5-10 Million
Number Employees: 10-19
Regions Exported to: Europe, Canada, Latin America
Percentage of Business in Exporting: 5

43234 Control & Metering
6500 Kestrel Road
Mississauga, ON L5T 1Z6
Canada   905-795-9696
        Fax: 905-795-9654 800-736-5739
                sales@candm.ca
Manufacturer and exporter of dry material handling equipment including bulk bag dischargers, fillers and controls
President: Chris Gadula
COO: Don Mackrill
Marketing Manager: Don Mackrill
Operationa Manager: Carmine Cacciarro
Number Employees: 15
Regions Exported to: Central America, Europe, Asia
Percentage of Business in Exporting: 5

43235 Control Beverage
PO Box 578
Adelanto, CA 92301-0578   330-549-5376
        Fax: 330-549-9851
Manufacturer and exporter of drink dispensers including liquor and soft drink; also, portable bars
President: P Beeghly
VP/Division Manager: Glenn Lewis
Sales Director: Kenneth Wogberg
Manager Technical Services: Dan Pershing
Purchasing Manager: Glenn Lewis
Estimated Sales: $1-3 Million
Number Employees: 6
Square Footage: 10000
Parent Co: International Carbonic
Regions Exported to: Central America, Canada, Mexico
Percentage of Business in Exporting: 10

43236 Control Chief Holdings Inc
200 Williams St
Bradford, PA 16701-1411   814-362-6811
        Fax: 814-368-4133 sales@controlchief.com
                www.controlchief.com
Wireless industrial remote control manufacturer
President: Doug Bell
CEO: Greg Caggiano
gcaggiano@controlchief.com
CFO: David Dedionisio
R&D: David Higgs
Quality Control: Christine Foster
Marketing Director: Allison Ambrose
Sales: Brian Landries
Operations: Paul McCord
Production: Jack Zelina
Purchasing Director: Dan Johnston
Estimated Sales: $ 10 - 20 Million
Number Employees: 20-49

43237 Control Concepts Inc.
18760 Lake Dr E
Chanhassen, MN 55317-9384   952-474-6200
        Fax: 952-474-6070 800-765-2799
                www.ccipower.com

Manufacturer and exporter of electric temperature process controls. Not to be confused with Control Concepts, Inc. located in Putnam, CT.
President: Gary Gretenhuis
CEO: Stan Kintigh
CEO: Stanley S Kintigh
Director Sales Support: William Rovick
Contact: Lynn Abraham
lynn@controlconcepts.net
Operations Manager: Don Christomer
Production Manager: Linh Nguyen
Number Employees: 20
Square Footage: 28000

43238 Control Instruments Corp
25 Law Dr # 1
Fairfield, NJ 07004-3295   973-575-9114
Fax: 973-575-0013 info@controlinstruments.com
www.controlinstruments.com
Manufacturer and exporter of hazardous gas detection systems
CEO: Chris Schaeffer
cschaeffer@controlinstruments.com
CEO: Chris Schaeffer
Marketing Manager: Patty Gardner
Sales Director: Debra Woods
Estimated Sales: $ 5-10 Million
Number Employees: 50-99
Type of Packaging: Private Label
Regions Exported to: Central America, South America, Europe

43239 Control Module
89 Phoenix Ave
Enfield, CT 6082   860-745-2433
Fax: 860-741-6064 800-722-6654
info@controlmod.com www.controlmod.com
Manufacturer and exporter of bar code data collection equipment including label printers, laser scanners, data collection terminals and cluster buffers
President: James Bianco
VP: John Fahy
VP Marketing/Sales: James Bianco
Contact: Denise Batalha
dbatalha@controlmod.com
Estimated Sales: $10-20 Million
Number Employees: 50-99
Square Footage: 80000
Brands Exported: Control Module
Regions Exported to: Worldwide
Percentage of Business in Exporting: 20

43240 Control Pak Intl
11494 Delmar Dr # 100
Suite #100
Fenton, MI 48430-9018   810-735-2800
Fax: 734-761-2880 info@controlpak.com
www.controlpak.com
Manufacturer and exporter of energy management control systems for temperature, humidity and HVAC applications
Owner: Tim Glinke
Office Manager: Julie Bodziak
Engineer: Len Poma
Estimated Sales: Less Than $500,000
Number Employees: 5-9
Regions Exported to: Worldwide
Percentage of Business in Exporting: 25

43241 Control Products Inc
1724 Lake Dr W
Chanhassen, MN 55317-8580   952-448-2217
Fax: 952-448-1606 800-947-9098
www.protectedhome.com
Digital electronic temperature, humidity and pressure controls including timers, alarms, indicators and controllers; also, custom design available
President: Chris Berghoff
VP Operations: Paul Carlson
IT Executive: John Abbott
jabbott@controlproductsinc.com
Director Foodservice Industry: Jerry Brown
Marketing Manager: Mark Bjornstad
National Sales Manager: Greg Colvin
IT Executive: John Abbott
jabbott@controlproductsinc.com
Estimated Sales: $ 20 - 50 Million
Number Employees: 100-249

43242 Convay Systems
9800 Bren Road East
Suite 300
Minnetonka, MN 55343
Canada   905-279-9970
Fax: 888-329-1099 800-334-1099
Manufacturer and exporter of washing and drying systems, pasteurizers, coolers, warmers and dry trash removal systems for the food, beverage and dairy industries
President: Roger Potts
Controller: Carol Ruggiero
Engineering Manager: Michael Voss
Number Employees: 18
Square Footage: 28000
Regions Exported to: Central America, South America, Asia, Middle East, USA
Percentage of Business in Exporting: 65

43243 Convectronics
111 Neck Rd
Ward Hill Industrial Park
Haverhill, MA 01835-8027   978-374-7714
Fax: 978-374-7794 800-633-0166
info@convectronics.com www.convectronics.com
Manufacturer and exporter of electric air heaters and thermocouples
President: Philip G Aberizk Jr
VP/Quality Control: Steve Becker
sbecker@connectronics.com
R&D: Bryce Budrow
Sales: Leslie Woodfall
Estimated Sales: Below $ 5 Million
Number Employees: 10-19
Square Footage: 40000
Regions Exported to: Central America, Europe
Percentage of Business in Exporting: 5

43244 Convergent Label Technology
620 S Ware Blvd
Tampa, FL 33619   813-621-8128
Fax: 813-620-1206 800-252-6111
Manufacturer and exporter of weigh price labeling equipment and labels
President: Graham Lloyd
Marketing Director: Paula Nelson
Sales/Marketing: Chris Walker
Contact: Nancy Solman
n_solman@discovery-academy.org
Purchasing Manager: Steve Halbrook
Estimated Sales: $60 Million
Number Employees: 100-249
Square Footage: 166000
Type of Packaging: Food Service
Regions Exported to: South America

43245 Conveyance Technologies LLC
24803 Detroit Rd
Cleveland, OH 44145   440-899-7440
Fax: 440-835-3107 800-701-2278
billwalzer@conveyancecart.com
www.conveyancecart.com
Manufacturer, importer and exporter of material handling products including mobile loading docks, stocking systems, hydraulic lifts, nestable warehouse carts, stocking carts, conveyors, pallet carriers and platform trucks
President: William Walzer
Sales Manager: Sam Aquino
Estimated Sales: $ 1 - 2 Million
Number Employees: 20-49
Square Footage: 220000
Brands Exported: Roll-A-Bench
Regions Exported to: Canada
Percentage of Business in Exporting: 1
Regions Imported from: Canada
Percentage of Business in Importing: 1

43246 Conveyor Accessories
7013 High Grove Blvd
Burr Ridge, IL 60527-7593   630-655-4205
Fax: 630-655-4209 800-323-7093
cai@conveyoraccessories.com
www.conveyoraccessories.com
Manufacturer and exporter of conveyor belt fasteners, tools and accessories
President: Thomas Richardson
sales@conveyoraccessories.com
Estimated Sales: $10-20 Million
Number Employees: 20-49
Square Footage: 60000
Brands Exported: Steelgrip; Staplegrip; Riv - Nail; Flexfrip
Regions Exported to: Central America, South America, Europe, Asia, Middle East, Worldwide
Percentage of Business in Exporting: 30

43247 Conveyor Components Co
130 Seltzer Road
Croswell, MI 48422-9180   810-679-4211
Fax: 810-679-4510 800-233-3233
info@conveyorcomponents.com
www.conveyorcomponents.com
Quality engineered conveyor accessories including emergency stop switches & pull cords, compact stop controls, belt mi-alignment switches, tripper position switches, bucket elevator alignment switches, damaged belt detectors, bulkmaterial flow switches, motion controls and zero speed switches, aeration pads, level controls including rotating paddles and tilt switches, skirtboard clamps, a rotary brush style belt cleaner as well as a wide variety of other conveyor beltcleaners.
President/CEO: Clint Stimpson
General Manager: Barb Stimpson
Sales Manager: Rich Washkevich
Purchasing Coordinator: Sandy VanBrande
Estimated Sales: $5-10 Million
Number Employees: 50-99
Square Footage: 80000

43248 Conveyor Components Co
130 Seltzer Rd
Croswell, MI 48422-9180   810-679-4211
Fax: 810-679-4510 800-552-3337
info@cotterman.com
www.conveyorcomponents.com
Manufacturer and exporter of rolling safety and fixed ladders including powder-coated and aluminum; also, portable elevating work platforms
President/CEO: C Stimpson
CFO: B Stimpson
Research & Development: J Kerr
Sales Manager: David Taylor
Manufacturing Manager: Robert Stimpson
Production Manager: L Higgins
Purchasing Manager: G Smith
Estimated Sales: $20-50 Million
Number Employees: 50-99
Square Footage: 60000
Parent Co: Material Control

43249 Conveyor Dynamics Corp
7000 W Geneva Dr
St Peters, MO 63376-5712   636-279-1111
Fax: 636-279-1121
info@conveyordynamicscorp.com
www.conveyordynamicscorp.com
Manufacturer and exporter of vibratory processing machinery for bulk and material handling applications
President: Michael Didion
info@conveyordynamicscorp.com
Engineer: Scott Milsark
Estimated Sales: $ 500,000 - $ 1,000,000
Number Employees: 1-4
Square Footage: 72000
Regions Exported to: Europe, Mexico

43250 Convoy
PO Box 8589
Canton, OH 44711   330-453-8163
Fax: 330-453-8181 800-899-1583
Manufacturer and exporter of plastic collapsible containers and plastic tote boxes
President: Phillip Dannemiller
National Sales Manager: Daren Newman
Estimated Sales: $ 2.5 - 5 Million
Number Employees: 10-19
Type of Packaging: Bulk
Regions Exported to: Worldwide

43251 Conway Import Co Inc
11051 Addison Street
Franklin Park, IL 60131
        800-323-8801
info@conwaydressings.com
www.conwaydressings.com
High quality salad dressing and sauce pods for the finest hoels, airlines, cruiselines, and restaurants.
Owner/Vice President, Operations: Gregg Heineman
conwaydressings@mindspring.com
Founder: Albert Heineman
VP Marketing & Sales: Robert Burns
Number Employees: 50-99
Number of Products: 370+
Square Footage: 240000

Importers & Exporters / A-Z

Type of Packaging: Food Service, Private Label, Bulk
Regions Exported to: Europe, Bermuda, Canada, Mexico, Virgin Islands

43252 Conwed Global Netting Sltns
530 Gregory Ave NE
Roanoke, VA 24016-2129   540-981-0879
Fax: 540-345-8421 800-368-3610
www.conwedplastics.com
Manufacturer and exporter of bags including vented plastic netting, onion netting, mesh linings and netting pallet wrap for fruits, vegetables and meats; also, fruit and vegetable juice filter support cartridges
President: Lawrance Ptaschek
Sales Manager: Michael Woldanski
Controller: Del Ramsey
Plant Manager: Charlie Boxler
Estimated Sales: $ 10 - 20 Million
Number Employees: 50-99
Parent Co: Siemens Corporation
Brands Exported: Polynet
Regions Exported to: Worldwide
Percentage of Business in Exporting: 10

43253 Cook & Beals Inc
221 S 7th St
Loup City, NE 68853-8041   308-745-0154
Fax: 308-745-0154 www.cooknbeals.com
Manufacturer and exporter of honey processing equipment including rotary knife uncappers, spin float honey-wax separators, heat exchange units, honey pumps, wax melters, etc
President: Patrick Kuehl
info@cooknbeals.com
Secretary: Carol Kuehl
VP: Lawrence Kuehl
Estimated Sales: $1-2.5 Million
Number Employees: 5-9
Regions Exported to: Europe, Canada
Percentage of Business in Exporting: 5

43254 CookTek
156 N. Jefferson Street
Suite 300
Chicago, IL 60661-1436   312-563-9600
Fax: 312-432-6220 888-266-5835
www.cooktek.com
Manufacturer and exporter of induction cooking systems
President: Robert Wolters
Quality Control: Robbe Gibb
Marketing Director: Tricia Cleary
Contact: Steven Lopez
slopez@cooktek.com
Estimated Sales: $ .5 - 1 million
Number Employees: 1-4
Number of Brands: 1
Number of Products: 5
Square Footage: 100000
Parent Co: Wolters Group International
Brands Exported: Cooktek
Regions Exported to: Central America, South America, Europe, Asia, Middle East, Worldwide
Percentage of Business in Exporting: 30

43255 Cooke Marketing Group Inc
5306 Business Pkwy # 101
Suite 101
Ringwood, IL 60072-9416   815-728-9988
Fax: 815-653-0400
Manufacturers' representative and exporter of deli and bakery products
Owner: Sue Adamavich
sue.adamavich@cookemarketinggroup.com
Number Employees: 5-9
Percentage of Business in Exporting: 5

43256 Cookie Tree Bakeries
4010 W Advantage Circle
Salt Lake City, UT 84104   801-268-2253
www.cookietree.com
Frozen gourmet cookies and cookie dough; also, fat-free available.
Purchasing: Wayne Davis
Year Founded: 1981
Estimated Sales: $20-50 Million
Type of Packaging: Consumer, Food Service, Private Label, Bulk
Brands Exported: Cookietree Bakeries
Regions Exported to: Central America, Europe, Asia, Middle East, Australia

43257 Cookies United
141 Freeman Ave
Islip, NY 11751-1428   631-581-4000
Fax: 631-581-4510 info@cookiesunited.com
Manufacturer and national marketer of branded and private label baked goods.
President: Joseph Vitarelli
joseph@silverlakecookie.com
Number Employees: 250-499
Type of Packaging: Consumer, Food Service, Private Label, Bulk

43258 Cooking Systems International
76 Pelican Ln
Redwood City, CA 94065   650-556-6222
Fax: 203-377-8187 info@mysck.com
www.sck.com
Manufacturer and exporter of rethermalizing units for cook chill, sous vide, precooked and frozen food
Chairman: B Koether
Executive VP: Scott Wakeman
VP Sales/Marketing: George Koether
Part Time Controller: Scott C Kennedy
Estimated Sales: $ 10 - 20 Million
Number Employees: 25
Square Footage: 80000
Type of Packaging: Food Service
Regions Exported to: Europe, Asia, South Africa
Percentage of Business in Exporting: 10

43259 Cool Care
4020 Thor Drive
Boynton Beach, FL 33426-8407   561-364-5711
Fax: 561-364-5766 www.coolcarehvac.com
Manufacturer, importer and exporter of ripening rooms for produce with cold storage and controlled atmosphere; also, vacuum coolers, ice injectors, etc.; installation services available
President: Mike Bianco
Director Sales: Ron Roberts
Engineering Manager: Bob Windecker
Number Employees: 20-49
Square Footage: 100000
Parent Co: Dole Food Company
Regions Exported to: Central America, South America, Europe, Asia, Middle East, Canada, Caribbean, Mexico, Latin America, Bahamas, Russia
Percentage of Business in Exporting: 25
Regions Imported from: Europe
Percentage of Business in Importing: 5

43260 Cooling Products Inc
500 N Pecan Ave
Broken Arrow, OK 74012-2333   918-251-8588
Fax: 918-251-8837 coolprod@gorilla.net
Manufacturer and exporter of heat exchangers, radiators, finned tubes and condensers
Manager: Steve Chalmers
schalmers@coolprod.com
Production: Harold Gordon
Sales Manager: Stephen Chalmers
Estimated Sales: $ 20 - 50 Million
Number Employees: 50-99
Regions Exported to: Worldwide
Percentage of Business in Exporting: 20

43261 Cooling Technology Inc
1800 Orr Industrial Ct
Charlotte, NC 28213-6342   704-596-4109
Fax: 704-597-8697 800-872-1448
info@coolingtechnology.com
www.coolingtechnology.com
Manufacturer and exporter of temperature controllers, chillers and evaporative cooling and pumping systems.
Owner: Chrystel Baker
Marketing Director: Chris Fore
Director of Sales and Marketing: Laura Walker
cbaker@coolingtech.gd
Operations Manager: Sheetal Desai
Estimated Sales: $3-5 Million
Number Employees: 20-49
Number of Products: 20
Square Footage: 40000

43262 Cooper Instrument Corporation
P.O. Box 450
Middlefield, CT 06455-0450   860-349-3473
Fax: 860-349-8994 800-835-5011
sbennett@cooperinstrument.com
www.cooper-atkins.com
CEO: Carol P Wallace
Director of Marketing: Cherylann Hunt
Estimated Sales: $ 1 - 5 Million
Number Employees: 100-249

43263 Cooperheat/MQS
P.O.Box 123
Alvin, TX 77512-0123   281-331-6154
Fax: 281-331-4107 800-526-4233
cooperheat-mqs@2isi.com
Manufacturer and exporter of heat treating equipment, accesories and services, heat tracing equipment and services; also, induction equipment and nondestructive testing
President: Kenneth Tholan
VP Sales: Charels Silver
VP International Sales: Jim Campbell
Number Employees: 20-49
Square Footage: 160000
Parent Co: International Industrial Services
Brands Exported: Versatrace; Eagle
Regions Exported to: Central America, South America
Percentage of Business in Exporting: 5

43264 Copper Brite
PO Box 50610
Santa Barbara, CA 93150-0610   805-565-1566
Fax: 805-565-1394
Manufacturer and exporter of insecticides and wood rot fungicides; also, cleaner and polish for copper, brass and stainless steel
President/ CEO: Alan D. Brite
CFO: Alan Brite
Executive VP: Terry Brite
R&D: Alan Brite
Quality Control: Terry Brite
Estimated Sales: $ 2.5 - 5 Million
Number Employees: 1-4
Brands Exported: Roach Prufe
Regions Exported to: Canada, Australia

43265 Cora Italian Specialties
9630 Joliet Rd
Countryside, IL 60525-4138   708-482-4660
Fax: 708-482-4663 800-696-2672
info@corainc.com www.corainc.com
Monin syrups, Oregon chai, Guitiard and Ghirardelli chocolates, Mocafe, Jet tea etc
President: John Cora
jcora@corainc.com
Sales: Paul Rekstad
Estimated Sales: 1.80 Million
Number Employees: 10-19
Square Footage: 60000
Type of Packaging: Food Service
Brands Imported: Sirman; La Spaziale; Mazzer; Cunill; Elektra

43266 Corbin Foods-Edibowls
P.O.Box 28139
Santa Ana, CA 92799-8139   714-966-6695
Fax: 949-640-0279 800-695-5655
www.edibowls.com
Processor and exporter of edible bowls for salads, desserts and tarts; club packs available
Manager: R J Hill
Estimated Sales: $5-10 Million
Number Employees: 5-9
Square Footage: 400000
Type of Packaging: Consumer, Food Service, Bulk
Brands Exported: Edibowls
Regions Exported to: Europe

43267 Corby Distilleries
225 King Street West
Suite 1100
Toronto, ON M5V 3M2
Canada
   416-479-2400
Fax: 416-369-9809 800-367-9079
corbyweb@adsw.com www.corby.ca
Whiskey, Scotch whiskey, Irish whiskey, bourbon, rum, gin, vodka, tequila, cognac and brandy.
President/CEO: Patrick O'Driscoll
VP/CFO: Thierry Pourchet
VP Marketing: Jeff Agdern
VP Sales: Andy Alexander
VP SP/Customer Service: Chris Chan
VP Production: Jim Stanski
Number Employees: 100-249
Number of Brands: 45
Parent Co: Allied Lyons
Type of Packaging: Consumer, Food Service
Regions Imported from: Central America, South America, Europe

43268 Corby Hall
3 Emery Ave
Randolph, NJ 07869-1308   973-366-8300
Fax: 973-366-9833 info@corbyhall.com
www.corbyhall.com
Manufacturer and exporter of stainless steel and silver plated flatware and hollowware; importer of flatware
Vice President: Bill Adams
bill.adams@hollowick.com
CFO: Alan Millward
Vice President: Adrian Millward
Quality Control: Andrew Millward
VP Marketing: Andrew Millward
Estimated Sales: $ 500,000 - $ 1 Million
Number Employees: 5-9
Square Footage: 30000
Type of Packaging: Food Service
Brands Exported: Corby Hall
Regions Exported to: Worldwide
Percentage of Business in Exporting: 20
Brands Imported: Corby Hall
Regions Imported from: Europe

43269 Cordon Bleu International
8383 Rue J Rene Ouimet
Anjou, QC H1J 2P8
Canada   514-352-3000
Fax: 514-352-3226 800-363-1182
info@cordonbleu.ca www.cordonbleu.ca
Processor and exporter of pickled food products, sauces, gravies, chicken broth, meat pates, beef and chicken entrees and red kidney beans in tomato sauce.
Director Advertising/Promotions: Michelle Guibord
Director Sales: Jacques LeGare
Purchasing: Kristen Gerard
Number Employees: 100-249
Parent Co: J-R Ouimet
Type of Packaging: Consumer, Private Label
Brands Exported: Cordon Bleu
Regions Exported to: USA
Percentage of Business in Exporting: 10

43270 Core Products Co
401 Industrial Park
PO Box 669
Canton, TX 75103-2817   903-567-1341
Fax: 903-567-1346 800-825-2673
www.coreproductsco.com
Manufacturer and exporter of odor control agents, carpet and upholstery cleaning products, stain and rust removers, degreasers and cleaners for tub, tile, glass, chrome and stainless steel
President: Brent Crawford
core@coreproductsco.com
CFO: Debbie Crawford
VP: Debbie Crawford
Sales Manager: Brian Hawkins
Estimated Sales: $500,000-$1 Million
Number Employees: 10-19
Square Footage: 80000
Regions Exported to: Central America, Europe

43271 Corenco
3275 Dutton Ave
Santa Rosa, CA 95407-7891   707-824-9868
Fax: 707-528-3197 888-267-3626
ngorsuch@corenco.com www.corenco.biz
Manufactures size reduction equipment for the food processing industry.
President/CEO: Chris Cory
ccory@corenco.biz
Corporate Secretary/Accounting: Saraj Cory
VP/COO: Jeff Boheim
Inside Machinery Sales: Neil Gorsuch
Production Manager: Matt Young
Estimated Sales: $1-2.5 Million
Number Employees: 5-9
Number of Brands: 1
Number of Products: 14
Square Footage: 14000
Brands Exported: Corenco
Regions Exported to: Central America, South America, Europe, Asia, Middle East
Percentage of Business in Exporting: 20

43272 (HQ)Corfu Foods Inc
755 Thomas Dr
Bensenville, IL 60106-1624   630-595-2510
Fax: 630-595-3884 info@corfufoods.com
www.corfufoods.com
Processor and exporter of pita bread, honey mustard sauce and beef and chicken gyro products including cones, patties, deli kits, sauce and loaves; importer of cheese, olives and stuffed grape leaves.
President: Vasilios Memmos
vmemmos@corfufoods.com
VP: Sophie Maroulis
Purchasing Agent: Ron Fallot
Estimated Sales: $ 10 - 20 Million
Number Employees: 50-99
Square Footage: 140000
Other Locations:
   Corfu Foods
   Long Island City, NYCorfu Foods
Regions Exported to: Canada
Percentage of Business in Exporting: 25
Regions Imported from: Greece

43273 Coriell Associates
149 Coriell Avenue
Fanwood, NJ 07023-1611   908-889-5537
Fax: 908-889-5535
Importer and distributor of specialty confections, gourmet candies and semi-liquid and paste coffee concentrates; also, new product development consulting and sourcing of ingredients for the food trade
President: Jane Chuffo
Director: Tony Chuffo
Number Employees: 1-4
Square Footage: 24000
Type of Packaging: Food Service, Private Label, Bulk
Regions Imported from: Europe

43274 Corim Industries Inc
1112 Industrial Pkwy
Brick, NJ 08724-2508   732-840-1640
Fax: 732-840-1608 800-942-4201
sales@corimindustries.com
www.corimindustries.com
Manufacturer, wholesaler and exporter of gourmet coffees, custom printed sugar packets, instant cappuccino, chai, and soluble milk for vending machines, custom blending and supplies, and also custom branding for private labelsuppliers.
President: Nathan Teren
nathan.teren@marinemax.com
CEO: Sam Teren
Treasurer/Controller: Nathan Teren
Estimated Sales: $2.1 Million
Number Employees: 20-49
Square Footage: 41672
Type of Packaging: Consumer, Food Service, Private Label, Bulk

43275 Cork Specialties
1454 NW 78th Ave #305
Miami, FL 33126   305-477-1506
Fax: 305-591-0593 corkspec@aol.com
Manufacturer, importer and exporter of corks and plastic top stoppers
President: Rafael Figueroa
VP: Orlando Barranco
Estimated Sales: Below $ 5 Million
Number Employees: 5-9
Regions Exported to: Central America, Europe, Asia, Caribbean, Australia
Regions Imported from: Europe

43276 Cormier Rice Milling CoInc
501 W 3rd St
De Witt, AR 72042-2500   870-946-3561
Fax: 870-946-3029 www.cormierrice.com
Processor and exporter of long and medium grain, milled, brown and organic brown rice
Owner: Robert Ellis
robert@cormierrice.com
Vice President: Julie Simpson
VP: J Ferguson
Estimated Sales: $10-20 Million
Number Employees: 10-19
Type of Packaging: Consumer, Food Service, Private Label, Bulk

43277 Cornelius
2421 15th SW
Mason City, IA 50401   641-424-3601
     800-238-3600
www.cornelius.com
Manufacturer and exporter of ice makers and dispensers.
Year Founded: 1931
Estimated Sales: $100-$500 Million
Number Employees: 4,500
Type of Packaging: Food Service
Regions Exported to: Worldwide

43278 Cornelius Inc.
101 Broadway St. W
Osseo, MN 55369   763-488-8200
Fax: 763-488-4298 800-238-3600
publications@cornelius.com
www.cornelius-usa.com
Beverage dispensing and ice making equipment.
President: Tim Hubbard
Year Founded: 1931
Estimated Sales: $241.8 Million
Number Employees: 4,500+
Number of Brands: 4
Number of Products: 6
Parent Co: Marmon Beverage Technologies Inc.
Type of Packaging: Food Service
Other Locations:
   IMI Cornelius
   Norwood, MAIMI Cornelius
Regions Exported to: Central America, South America, Europe, Asia, Middle East
Percentage of Business in Exporting: 30

43279 Cornell Machine Co
45 Brown Ave
Springfield, NJ 07081-2992   973-379-6860
Fax: 973-379-6854 info@cornellmachine.com
www.cornellversator.com
Manufacturer and exporter of food processing equipment including homogenizers, emulsifiers, mixers, oxygen removers, deaerators and defoaming equipment
President: Martin Huska
Contact: Alan Huska
ajhuska@cornellmachine.com
Estimated Sales: $1-2.5 Million
Number Employees: 5-9
Brands Exported: Cornell Versator
Regions Exported to: Central America, South America, Europe, Asia

43280 Cornell Pump Company
P.O.Box 6334
Portland, OR 97228-6334   503-653-0330
Fax: 503-653-0338 info@cornellpump.com
www.cornellpump.com
Manufacturer, importer and exporter of pumps for food product handling, hot oil circulation, refrigeration and waste handling
President: Jeff Markham
Marketing: Brenda Case
Number Employees: 100-249
Parent Co: Roper Industries

43281 Corona College Heights
8000 Lincoln Ave
Riverside, CA 92504-4343   951-351-7880
Fax: 951-689-5115 www.cchcitrus.org
Processor and exporter of oranges, lemons and grapefruit.
Director: Thomas Chao
Vice President, Field Operations: Ruben Gutierrez
Export Sales Manager: Jessica Chavez
Plant Manager: Brad Tilden
Estimated Sales: $ 35 Million
Number Employees: 100-249
Square Footage: 180000
Type of Packaging: Consumer, Bulk
Regions Exported to: Asia
Percentage of Business in Exporting: 40

43282 Coronet Chandelier Originals
12 Grand Blvd # 16
Brentwood, NY 11717-5195   631-273-1177
Fax: 631-273-1247
Manufacturer and exporter of custom chandeliers; importer of chandelier crystals, wrought iron tables, wall solders, pendents
President: Irwin Goldberg
Estimated Sales: $ 1 - 3 Million
Number Employees: 10-19
Square Footage: 60000
Regions Imported from: Europe, Asia

43283 Corp Somat
165 Independence Ct
Lancaster, PA 17601-5838   717-392-6714
Fax: 717-291-0877 800-237-6628
www.somatcompany.com
Manufacturer and exporter of waste pulping and dewatering systems for processing and reduction of food service wastes

Importers & Exporters / A-Z

Manager: Scott Witmer
R&D: Steve Eno
Marketing: Lin Sensenig
Food Service Equipment Sales: Herman Williams
Contact: Dolores Alexander
dalexander@somat.com
Production: Barry Alexander
Plant Manager: Rich Zimmerman
Number Employees: 5-9
Square Footage: 78000
Brands Exported: Somat

43284 Corrin Produce Sales
23667 E Dinuba Ave
Dinuba, CA 93618   559-596-0517
    Fax: 559-638-8508
Grower and exporter of fresh fruit including peaches, plums, nectarines and table grapes; also, raisins
President: Harold Seitz
CFO: Robert Greiner
Manager: Lisa Macedo
Estimated Sales: $400,000
Number Employees: 5
Type of Packaging: Bulk

43285 Corson Manufacturing Company
20 Michigan Street
24
Lockport, NY 14094-2628   716-434-8871
    Fax: 716-434-8801
Paper boxes for cereal, snacks, cookies, etc
CEO: Anthony Gioia
Estimated Sales: $ 3 - 5 Million
Number Employees: 230
Regions Exported to: Canada

43286 Corson Rubber Products Inc
105 Smith St
Clover, SC 29710-1333   803-222-7779
    Fax: 803-222-9022 info@corsonrubber.com
    www.corsonrubber.com
Color coded sanitation was FDA compliant knobby mats.
President: Denis Garvey
Plant Manager: Terry Wallace
Estimated Sales: $9-15 Million
Number Employees: 10-19
Type of Packaging: Consumer, Food Service, Private Label, Bulk
Regions Exported to: Central America, South America, Europe, Asia
Percentage of Business in Exporting: 10

43287 Cosa Xentaur Corp
84 Horseblock Rd # F
Yaphank, NY 11980-9742   631-345-3434
    Fax: 201-767-6804 cosa@cosaic.com
    www.cosa-instrument.com
Importer and wholesaler/distributor of protein and moisture analyzers
President: Christopher Mueller
Contact: Bryan Flanagan
b.flanagan@cosaxentaur.com
Estimated Sales: $5-10 Million
Number Employees: 20-49
Brands Imported: Elementar; KF; Rapid N

43288 Cosco Home & Office Products
2525 State St
Columbus, IN 47201
    Fax: 636-745-1005   800-628-8321
    customer.service@coscoproducts.com
    www.coscoproducts.com
Manufacturer and exporter of home and office furniture.
President: Troy Franks
tfranks@coscoproducts.com
Year Founded: 1939
Estimated Sales: $100-500 Million
Number Employees: 1000-4999
Parent Co: Dorel Home Furnishings
Type of Packaging: Food Service
Regions Exported to: Worldwide

43289 Cosgrove Enterprises Inc
14300 NW 77th Ct
Miami Lakes, FL 33016-1534   305-820-5600
    Fax: 305-623-6935   800-888-3396
    orders@e-cosgrove.com
    www.cosgroveenterprises.com
Manufacturer, exporter and importer of cleaning equipment and janitorial supplies including brooms, brushes and paper products
President: Robert Cosgrove
robert@cosgroveenterprises.com
Quality Control: Louides Cohen
VP: Randy Shelton
Estimated Sales: $ 500,000 - $ 1 Million
Number Employees: 20-49
Square Footage: 220000
Regions Exported to: Central America, South America, Caribbean
Percentage of Business in Exporting: 20
Regions Imported from: Central America, South America

43290 Cosmo Food Products
200 Callegari Dr
P.O. Box 256
West Haven, CT 06516-6234   203-933-9323
    Fax: 203-937-7283   800-942-6766
    claudano@cosmosfoods.com
    www.cosmosfoods.com
Processor, packer and importer of olives, artichokes, capers, peppers, marinated mushrooms and roasted peppers; also, sun-dried tomatoes, hot cherry peppers, pepperoncini and garlic.
President: Cosmo Laudano
claudano@cosmosfoods.com
VP: Lisa Laudano
Sales Manager: Mario Laudano
Production: Peter Merola
Estimated Sales: $5-10 Million
Number Employees: 20-49
Number of Products: 39
Square Footage: 90000
Type of Packaging: Consumer, Food Service, Private Label, Bulk
Brands Imported: Cosmo's
Regions Imported from: Greece, Spain, Morocco, Turkey
Percentage of Business in Importing: 20

43291 Cosmopolitan Wine Agents
680 Raymur Avenue
Vancouver, BC V6A 2R1
Canada   604-254-4214
    Fax: 604-254-6377
Importer of Italian wines
Owner: Gustav Panz
Number Employees: 1-4
Brands Imported: Bosco Nestore
Regions Imported from: Europe

43292 Coss Engineering Sales Company
3943 S Creek Drive
Ts
Rochester Hills, MI 48306-4729   248-370-0707
    Fax: 248-370-9211   800-446-1365
Manufacturer and exporter of pneumatic conveying systems, surge hoppers and storage silos
CEO and President: Carter Coss
Estimated Sales: Less than $500,000
Number Employees: 4
Regions Exported to: South America, Asia, Middle East, Canada
Percentage of Business in Exporting: 20

43293 Costa Broom Works
3606 E 4th Ave
Tampa, FL 33605-5835   813-385-1722
    Fax: 813-247-6060
Brooms, mops, mop heads and brushes; importer of related products for cleaning
Owner: Frank J Costa
Estimated Sales: $ 1-2.5 Million
Number Employees: 20-30
Type of Packaging: Food Service, Bulk

43294 Costa Deano's Gourmet Foods
PO Box 6367
Canton, OH 44706-0367   330-453-1555
    Fax: 330-453-9766   800-337-2823
Processor and exporter of gourmet pasta sauces
President: Dean Bacopoulos
VP: Bill Bacopoulos
Number Employees: 5-9
Square Footage: 60000
Parent Co: Costa Deano's Enterprises
Type of Packaging: Consumer, Food Service, Private Label, Bulk
Brands Exported: Costa Deano's
Regions Exported to: Europe, Asia, Middle East
Percentage of Business in Exporting: 5

43295 Costco Wholesale Corporation
P.O. Box 34331
999 Lake Drive
Issaquah, WA 98027   425-313-8100
    800-955-2292
    www.costco.com
Wholesaler/distributor/grocery store manufacturing and selling general merchandise, general line items, meats, confectionery, frozen foods, baked goods, produce, beer, wine, etc.
Chairman: Hamilton James
Chief Executive Officer: W. Craig Jelinek
VP/Chief Financial Officer: Richard Galanti
Chief Information Officer: Paul Moulton
Year Founded: 1976
Estimated Sales: $152.7 Billion
Number Employees: 254,000
Type of Packaging: Consumer, Food Service, Private Label, Bulk
Other Locations:
    Manufacturing Facility - Dairy
    Seattle, WA
    Manufacturing Facility - Meats
    Hillsboro, ORManufacturing Facility - DairyHillsboro
Brands Exported: Private Label
Regions Exported to: Central America, South America, Europe, Asia, Middle East, Worldwide

43296 (HQ)Cotton Goods Mfg Co
259 N California Ave
Chicago, IL 60612-1903   773-265-0088
    Fax: 773-265-0096 cotton2@earthlink.net
    www.cottongoodsmfg.com
Manufacturer and exporter of table skirts and linens
President/CEO: Edward Lewis
cotton2@earthlink.net
Sales Manager: Kevin Higgins
Estimated Sales: $ 3 - 5 Million
Number Employees: 10-19
Square Footage: 20000
Brands Exported: Fite Rite; Bar-L; See Saw; Grip Clips
Regions Exported to: Central America, South America, Europe, Asia, Middle East
Regions Imported from: Europe

43297 Cottura Commerciale
2900 Rowena Avenue
Los Angeles, CA 90039-2042   323-662-2112
    Fax: 323-662-4149 cottura@msn.com
Importer of dinnerware
President: Jim Zimmerman
Wholesale Coordinator: Robin Rogers
Number Employees: 20-49
Brands Imported: Cottura
Regions Imported from: Italy
Percentage of Business in Importing: 100

43298 Couch & Philippi
10680 Fern Ave
PO Box A
Stanton, CA 90680-2600   714-527-2261
    Fax: 714-827-2077   800-854-3360
    sales@couchandphilippi.com
Designing and producing innovative products for restaurants and beverage copmanies nationwide.
President: Steve Ellsworth
sellsworth@primus-group.com
Estimated Sales: $ 5 - 10 Million
Number Employees: 50-99
Regions Exported to: Worldwide

43299 Coulter Giufre & Co Inc
8579 Lakeport Rd
Chittenango, NY 13037-9577   315-687-6510
    Fax: 315-687-6637
Processor and exporter of produce including onions and turf grass
Owner: Chris Coulter
Estimated Sales: $ 3 - 5 Million
Number Employees: 5-9
Regions Exported to: Central America, Europe
Percentage of Business in Exporting: 25

43300 Council of International Restaurant Brokers
PO Box 9296
Greensboro, NC 27429-0296   866-247-2123
    Fax: 866-247-2329

244

Importers & Exporters / A-Z

43301 Country Butcher Shop
286 Mcallister Church Rd
Carlisle, PA 17015-9504
717-249-4691
Fax: 573-769-4652 800-272-9223
www.countrybutchershopinc.com
Processor and distributor of lamb, beef and pork.
Owner: Mary Finkenbinder
finkenbinder@socket.net
Estimated Sales: $10-20 Million
Number Employees: 5-9
Type of Packaging: Private Label
Regions Exported to: Worldwide

43302 Country Home Creations Inc
5132 Richfield Rd
Flint, MI 48506-2121
810-244-7348
Fax: 810-244-5348 800-457-3477
chcdips@countryhomecreations.com
Processor and exporter of mixes including cheesecake, cookie, dip and soup.
Owner: Shirley Kautman Jones
chcdips@countryhomecreations.com
Estimated Sales: $-5 Million
Number Employees: 20-49
Square Footage: 40000
Type of Packaging: Consumer, Private Label

43303 Country Pure Foods Inc
58 West Rd
Ellington, CT 06029
877-995-8423
info@juice4u.com www.juice4u.com
Fruit drinks, bottled spring water and juices including apple, orange, grape and pineapple.
Number Employees: 100-249
Square Footage: 51266
Type of Packaging: Consumer, Food Service, Private Label
Regions Exported to: Canada
Percentage of Business in Exporting: 5

43304 Country Save Products Corp
19704 60th Ave NE
Arlington, WA 98223-4736
360-435-9868
Fax: 360-435-0896 info@countrysave.com
www.countrysave.com
Manufacturer and exporter of phosphate-free laundry detergent and dishwashing powder; also, chlorine-free powdered bleach
President: Kris Anderson
krisa@countrysave.com
Estimated Sales: $2.5-5 Million
Number Employees: 5-9
Brands Exported: Country Save
Regions Exported to: Central America, Asia, Canada
Percentage of Business in Exporting: 15

43305 Country Smoked Meats
510 Napolean Road
Bowling Green, OH 43402-0171
419-353-0783
Fax: 419-352-7330 800-321-4766
Processor and exporter of chunked, sliced and deli style Canadian bacon, smoked sausage, pork loins, hocks, turkey parts and ham, pepperoni, bratwurst, kielbasa, chorizos, egg and muffin sandwiches, fresh link sausage and freshboneless pork loins and ten
National Sales Manager: Bruce Schroeder
Estimated Sales: $2.5-5 Million
Number Employees: 20-49
Square Footage: 84000
Type of Packaging: Consumer, Food Service, Private Label, Bulk
Brands Exported: Country Smoked Meats; Cholula Brand
Regions Exported to: Central America, South America, Asia
Percentage of Business in Exporting: 10

43306 Couprie Fenton
4282 Belair Frontage Rd
Suite 5
Augusta, GA 30909
706-650-7017
Fax: 706-868-1534
Crab, conch, crabmeat, dogfish, full line seafood, halibut, lobster, lobster meat
Manager: Yves Latremouille
Estimated Sales: $ .5 - 1 million
Number Employees: 1-4

43307 Courtright Companies
26749 S. Governors Hwy.
Monee, IL 60449-8095
708-534-8400
Fax: 708-534-9140 sales@right-tape.com
www.right-tape.com
Manufacturer & exporter of reusable shipping containers, Teflon tapes, shellac adhesives, tensilized polypropylene and stretch film
Owner: Patricia Schoenbeck
Sales Director: Ted Bachand
Purchasing Manager: Ted Bachand
Estimated Sales: $3-5 Million
Number Employees: 6
Square Footage: 40000
Type of Packaging: Food Service, Private Label
Regions Exported to: Europe, Asia, Middle East
Percentage of Business in Exporting: 5

43308 Cousins D&N
1129 Northern Blvd # 305
Manhasset, NY 11030-3022
516-869-5700
Fax: 516-869-5600
Exporter of frozen poultry, beef and pork; also, chicken and pork hot dogs, alcoholic beverages, game meats, rice and soups
President: David Eluashvili
CEO: Nathan Tsitlishvili
VP: Isaac Koren
Estimated Sales: $5-10 Million
Number Employees: 10-19
Square Footage: 10000
Brands Exported: Amcous; Tyson; Perdue; Allen's; IBP
Regions Exported to: Russia
Percentage of Business in Exporting: 100

43309 Couture Farms
30650 Quebec Ave
Kettleman City, CA 93239
559-386-9865
Fax: 559-386-4365
Processor and importer of asparagus, pistachios and mixed melons
Co-Partner: Steve Couture
Co-Partner: Christina Couture
stcou@aol.com
Partner: Chris Couture
stcou@aol.com
Estimated Sales: $2.2 Million
Number Employees: 20-49
Square Footage: 8640
Type of Packaging: Consumer, Food Service, Private Label, Bulk
Brands Exported: ""C""
Regions Exported to: South America, Europe, Asia
Percentage of Business in Exporting: 40
Regions Imported from: Central America, South America, Caribbean, Mexico
Percentage of Business in Importing: 50

43310 Cove Four
195 E Merrick Rd
Freeport, NY 11520-4012
516-379-4232
Fax: 516-379-4563 www.covefour.com
Wire products including corkscrews and custom; also, forming available
President: Barry Jaffe
erikcovefour@aol.com
VP Marketing: Bill Freedman
Sales Exec: Erik Christopher
Estimated Sales: $ 10 - 20 Million
Number Employees: 50-99
Regions Exported to: Worldwide
Percentage of Business in Exporting: 25

43311 Cover The World
755 Il Route 83 # 219
Bensenville, IL 60106-1267
630-616-0010
Fax: 630-616-0655
Meats and meat products
President: Steve Lee
CEO/Operations Manager: Helen Lee
Estimated Sales: $11.9 Million
Number Employees: 1-4

43312 Cowan Costumes
108 S Caddo St
Cleburne, TX 76031-5503
817-641-3126
Fax: 817-641-3149 info@cowancostumes.com
www.cowancostumes.com
Owner: Karen Cowan
kcowan@cowancostumes.com
Estimated Sales: $ 1 - 3 Million
Number Employees: 10-19

43313 (HQ)Cozzini LLC
4300 W Bryn Mawr Ave
Chicago, IL 60646-5943
773-478-9700
Fax: 773-478-8689 sales@cozzini.com
www.rapidpaktec.com
Manufacturer and exporter of meat processing equipment and blades
President: Peter J Samson
psamson@cozzini.com
VP: Oscar Cozzini
R&D: Greg Grady
Quality Control: Mario Lucchesi
Catalog Sales Technical Assistance: Pete Pierazzi
Estimated Sales: $20 Million
Number Employees: 100-249
Square Footage: 65000
Other Locations:
 Cozzini
 SoucyCozzini
Brands Exported: Cozzini
Regions Exported to: Worldwide
Percentage of Business in Exporting: 40

43314 Cozzoli Machine Co
50 Schoolhouse Rd
Somerset, NJ 08873-1289
732-564-0400
Fax: 732-564-0444 www.cozzoli.com
Designs and manufactures integrated precision packaging systems solutions.
President: Frank Cozzoli
General Manager: Fred Hart
Controller: Michael Shanker
Marketing Director: Crystal Basiluk
Sales: Bruce Teeling
Purchasing Manager: Steve Turkus
Estimated Sales: $10-20 Million
Number Employees: 5-9
Number of Brands: 2
Number of Products: 200
Square Footage: 180000
Parent Co: Cozzoli Machine Company
Type of Packaging: Food Service
Regions Exported to: Central America, South America, Europe, Asia, Middle East

43315 Craft Distillers
108 W Clay St
Ukiah, CA 95482-5420
707-468-7899
Fax: 707-462-8103 800-782-8145
Distiller and exporter of brandy and specialty spirits
President: Ansley J Coale Jr
VP,CFO: Denise Niderost
Estimated Sales: $1-2,500,000
Number Employees: 5-9
Square Footage: 40000
Type of Packaging: Consumer, Private Label
Brands Imported: Maison; Surrenne; Cognacs
Regions Imported from: Europe
Percentage of Business in Importing: 20

43316 Crain Ranch
10660 Bryne Ave
Los Molinos, CA 96055-9560
530-527-1077
Fax: 530-529-4143 billcrain@crainranch.com
www.crainranch.com
Processor, grower and exporter of walnuts in the shell.
Owner: Charles R Crain
charles@crainranch.com
Business Office: Kerry Crain
Production: Hal Crain
Estimated Sales: $300,000-500,000
Number Employees: 10-19
Square Footage: 320000
Type of Packaging: Consumer, Private Label, Bulk
Brands Exported: Crain Ranch
Regions Exported to: Worldwide
Percentage of Business in Exporting: 80

43317 Cramer Company
105 Nutmeg Rd S
South Windsor, CT 6074
877-684-6464
Fax: 860-610-0897
customer-service@mhrhodes.com
Manufacturer and exporter of motors and timers for process control systems
President: Kenneth Mac Cormac
VP: Wayne Taylor
Director Operations: Frank Darmig
Estimated Sales: $ 3 - 5 Million
Number Employees: 5-9
Square Footage: 220000
Parent Co: Owosso Corporation
Type of Packaging: Bulk

Importers & Exporters / A-Z

Regions Exported to: Europe, Asia
Percentage of Business in Exporting: 10

43318 Cramer Products
381 Park Ave S
New York, NY 10016-8806 212-645-2368
Fax: 212-242-6799 www.abpaonline.org
Manufacturer and exporter of temperature controlled storage units, humidors, wire and wood storage racks and cooling panels for wine and cheese
President: Richard Rothschild
Treasurer: Valerie Tomaselli
Vice President: Nancy Hall
Estimated Sales: Less than $500,000
Number Employees: 1-4

43319 Crandall Filling Machinery
80 Gruner Rd
Buffalo, NY 14227-1007 716-897-3486
Fax: 716-897-3488 800-280-8551
cai@conveyoraccessories.com www.crandall.com
Manufacturer and exporter of filling, packaging and closing machinery
Owner: Scott Reed
Technician: Scott Reed
VP sales: Charles Wood
dave@crandall.com
Estimated Sales: $ 1 - 3 Million
Number Employees: 1-4
Square Footage: 16000
Brands Exported: Crandall Filling Machinery
Regions Exported to: Worldwide
Percentage of Business in Exporting: 35

43320 Crane & Crane Inc
100 Crane Orchard Rd
PO Box 277
Brewster, WA 98812 509-689-3447
Fax: 509-689-2214
Grower and exporter of apples
President: Meg Spellman
meg@craneandcrane.com
Secretary/Treasurer: Margaret Crane
Vice President: Robert Reimmer
Estimated Sales: $ 930,000
Number Employees: 100-249
Square Footage: 196000
Type of Packaging: Consumer, Food Service, Private Label, Bulk
Regions Exported to: Central America, South America, Europe, Asia, Middle East, Tahiti
Percentage of Business in Exporting: 50

43321 Crane Composites Inc
23525 W Eames St
Channahon, IL 60410-3220 815-467-8600
Fax: 815-467-8666 800-435-0080
sales@cranecomposites.com
www.cranecomposites.com
Fiber-reinforced composite materials.
President: Thomas Jeff Craney
Cmo: Cleve Madlock
cmadlock@cranecomposites.com
VP of Building Products: Kelly Erdmann
Eastern Regional Sales Manager: Kevin Bellinger
Western Regional Sales Manager: Chris Schamer
Number Employees: 100-249

43322 Crane Environmental
2650 Eisenhower Ave Ste 100a
Norristown, PA 19403 610-631-7700
Fax: 610-631-6800 800-633-7435
www.cranenv.com
Manufacturer and exporter of water treatment equipment including reverse osmosis, demineralizers, softeners, filters, CB pumps, deaerators and steam specialty items
Manager: Russ Burke
Marketing Manager: Russell Burke
Purchasing Agent: Sandra Bisci
Estimated Sales: $ 20-30 Million
Number Employees: 1-4
Square Footage: 100000
Parent Co: Crane Company
Regions Exported to: Central America, South America, Europe, Asia, Middle East, Canada
Percentage of Business in Exporting: 25

43323 Crane Pumps & Systems
420 Third St
Piqua, OH 45356 937-778-8947
Fax: 937-773-7157 cranepumps@cranepumps.com
www.cranepumps.com
Manufacturer and exporter of pumps for the agricultural and food processing industries.
Year Founded: 1946
Estimated Sales: $100-$500 Million
Number Employees: 250-499
Square Footage: 400000
Parent Co: Crane Pumps & Systems
Brands Exported: Midland; Weinman

43324 Crc Industries Inc
885 Louis Dr
Warminster, PA 18974-2869 301-843-5226
Fax: 215-674-2196 800-556-5074
kcantwell@crcindustries.com
www.crc-industries.com
Manufacturer and exporter of cleaners, degreasers, lubricants, corrosion inhibitors, hand cleaners, adhesives and sealants; also, cleaning compound dispensers
President & Chief Executive Officer: Dennis Conlon
Contact: Tony Arends
tony.arends@unisys.com
Estimated Sales: $ 91 Million
Number Employees: 10-19
Regions Exported to: Worldwide

43325 Crea Fill Fibers Corp
10200 Worton Rd
Chestertown, MD 21620-3545 410-810-0779
Fax: 410-810-0793 800-832-4662
fiber@creafill.com www.creafill.com
Processor and exporter of powdered cellulose and pure vegetable fibers
President: Paolo Fezzi
pfezzi@creafill.com
Sales Associate: Sara Emgland
Estimated Sales: $5.5 Million
Number Employees: 20-49
Type of Packaging: Bulk
Regions Exported to: Worldwide

43326 Creative Automation
61 Willet St Ste 3b
Passaic, NJ 7055 973-778-0061
Fax: 973-614-8336
Manufacturer and exporter of automatic feeders, bar code verification equipment, turnkey systems, leaflet inserters and outserters, vertical, form, fill and seal equipment
President: John Calabrese
jcalabrese@creative-auto.com
CEO: John Bartlo
VP: John Calabrese
Estimated Sales: $1-2.5 Million
Number Employees: 1-4
Regions Exported to: South America, Europe
Percentage of Business in Exporting: 5

43327 Creative Coatings Corporation
28 Charron Avenue
1165
Nashua, NH 03063-1783 603-889-8040
Fax: 603-889-3780 800-229-1957
flocking@aol.com
Packaging materials including laminated vinyls, metallized barrier and pressure sensitive films, etc.; importer of bakery and confectionery mixers and homogenizers
CEO: Robert Borowski
Customer Service Manager: Barbara Landry
Number Employees: 5
Square Footage: 20000
Brands Imported: Hansa
Regions Imported from: Europe
Percentage of Business in Importing: 50

43328 Creative Cookie
8673 Commerce Dr
Suite 7
Easton, MD 21601 410-819-0091
Fax: 410-819-0255 800-451-4005
www.creativecookieetc.com
Manufacturer and exporter of themed fortune cookies and candy boxes
Owner: Marty Schwartz
Vice President: Joan Schwartz
General Manager: Martin Schwartz
Estimated Sales: Less than $500,000
Number Employees: 1-4
Number of Products: 80
Type of Packaging: Consumer, Food Service, Private Label, Bulk
Regions Exported to: Europe, Canada, Australia

43329 Creative Essentials
2155 5th Ave
Ronkonkoma, NY 11779-6908 631-467-8370
Fax: 631-467-4255 800-355-5891
sales@menudesigns.com
Manufacturer and exporter of menu covers, acrylic stands, placemats, recipe holders, menus and check presenters
President: Allen Fischer
Sales Manager: Jonathan Sunshine
Sales: Karen Chalson
Number Employees: 20-49
Square Footage: 64000
Regions Exported to: Worldwide

43330 Creative Foam Corp
300 N Alloy Dr
Fenton, MI 48430-2649 810-629-4149
Fax: 810-629-7368 www.creativefoam.com
Manufacturer and exporter of packaging and material handling systems
President: David Swallow
daswallow@creativefoam.com
Sales Manager: David Rosser
Estimated Sales: $ 20 - 50 Million
Number Employees: 100-249
Type of Packaging: Bulk
Regions Exported to: Worldwide

43331 Creative Forming
PO Box 128
Ripon, WI 54971-0128 920-748-7285
Fax: 920-748-9466 www.creativeforming.com
Manufacturer and exporter of thermoformed plastic trays
President: Glen Yurjevich
General Manager: John Beard
Estimated Sales: $ 20 - 50 Million
Number Employees: 100-249
Parent Co: Wellman
Type of Packaging: Consumer, Food Service, Bulk
Regions Exported to: Worldwide

43332 Creative Impressions
7697 9th St
Buena Park, CA 90621-2898 714-521-4441
Fax: 714-522-2733 800-524-5278
email@emenucovers.com
Clear and soft plastic menu covers in 30 colors and textures; also, inserts available
President: Marc Abbott
email@emenucovers.com
Estimated Sales: $5-10 Million
Number Employees: 20-49

43333 Creative Packaging Corporation
700 Corporate Grove Dr
Buffalo Grove, IL 60089 847-459-1001
Fax: 847-325-3919
Manufacturer and exporter of dispensing closures
President: John Weeks
CFO: Mike Farreoo
Quality Control: Samantha Gibson
VP Sales/Marketing: Jeff Teth
Corporate Manager: Robert Giles
Estimated Sales: $50-75 Million
Number Employees: 10
Square Footage: 1100000
Parent Co: Courtesy Corporation
Regions Exported to: Worldwide
Percentage of Business in Exporting: 15

43334 Creative Techniques
2441 N Opdyke Rd
Auburn Hills, MI 48326 248-373-3050
Fax: 248-373-3458 800-473-0284
www.creativetechniques.com
Manufacturer and exporter of packaging and material handling products
President: Richard Yeakey
Sales Manager: Stanley Shore
Contact: Joe Banfield
banfieldj@creativetechniques.com
Estimated Sales: $20-50 Million
Number Employees: 100-249
Regions Exported to: Worldwide
Percentage of Business in Exporting: 3

43335 Creative Works
96 Kings Hwy
Brooklyn, NY 11214-1510 718-234-5031
Fax: 718-234-7673 800-216-8182
info@creativeworksusa.com
www.creativeworksusa.com

Importers & Exporters / A-Z

Importer and distributor of floral baskets, glass vases, tin containers and gift supplies
Contact: Catherine Yang
creativeworksusa@hotmail.com
Number Employees: 1-4

43336 Creature Comforts Toys
3909 Witmer Road
Unit 1007
Niagara Falls, NY 14305   888-228-5001
Fax: 888-228-4888   800-667-2327
sales@creaturecomfortstoys.com
creaturecomfortstoys.com

43337 Creegan Animation Company
508 Washington St
Steubenville, OH 43952-2140   740-283-3708
Fax: 740-283-4117
Manufacturer and exporter of animations, costume characters and audio-animatronics
Owner: George Creegan
Contact: Sandy Baumgard
sandy.baumgard@creegans.com
Estimated Sales: $ 1 - 5 Million
Number Employees: 20-49
Regions Exported to: Worldwide
Percentage of Business in Exporting: 25

43338 Cres Cor
5925 Heisley Rd
Mentor, OH 44060-1833   440-350-1100
Fax: 440-350-7267   877-273-7267
www.crescor.com
A complete line of quality mobile food service equipment including hot cabinets, utility cabinets and racks, banquet cabinets, dish dollies, ovens and more. Since 1936...There is no equal.
President: Clifford D Baggott
cbaggott@crescor.com
VP: Rio DeGennaro
Director of Engineering: Heather Stewart
Sales/Marketing Director: Michael Capretta
Number Employees: 100-249
Brands Exported: CresCor
Regions Exported to: Central America, South America, Asia, Middle East, Canada, Caribbean, Latin America, Mexico
Percentage of Business in Exporting: 10

43339 Cres Cor
5925 Heisley Rd
Mentor, OH 44060-1833   440-350-1100
Fax: 440-350-7267   877-273-7267
www.crescor.com
Mobile foodservice equipment including heated cabinets, utility cabinets and racks, banquet cabinets, dish dollies, ovens and more.
President/CEO: Clifford Baggott
cbaggott@crescor.com
VP: Rio DeGennaro
Director: Heather Stewart
Sales/Marketing Director: Michael Capretta
Number Employees: 100-249

43340 Crescent Duck Farm
10 Edagr Ave
PO Box 500
Aquebogue LI, NY 11931-0500   631-722-8000
www.crescentduck.com
Processor and exporter of fresh and frozen duck. Founded in 1908.
President: Douglas Corwin
Controller: Janet Corwin Wedel
Maintenance Engineer and Manager: Jeffrey Corwin
Plant Manager: Arnold Tilton
Estimated Sales: $ 7 Million
Number Employees: 50-99
Type of Packaging: Consumer, Food Service
Brands Exported: White Pekin; Crescent; Peconic Bay

43341 Cresco Food Technologies
717 2nd Ave SE
Cresco, IA 52136-1703   563-547-4241
Fax: 563-547-4504   cft@iowatelecom.net
www.aveka.com
Nutraceutical and food processing facility.
Manager: John Anderson
john_@iowatelecom.net
Number Employees: 50-99
Parent Co: Aveka, Inc.

43342 Crespac Incorporated
5032 N Royal Atlanta Drive
Tucker, GA 30084   770-938-1900
Fax: 770-939-4900   800-438-1900
info@crespac.com
Disposable thermoformed food trays and containers; exporter of produce and food containers
CEO: Jeff Moon
Estimated Sales: $5-10 Million
Number Employees: 50-99
Square Footage: 400000
Regions Exported to: Central America, South America, Canada, Caribbean, Latin America, Mexico
Percentage of Business in Exporting: 15

43343 Cresset Chemical Company
One Cresset Center
PO Box 367
Weston, OH 43569   419-669-2041
Fax: 419-669-2200   800-367-2020
cresset@cresset.com   www.cresset.com
Manufacturer and exporter of hand cleaners, release agents and admixtures
President: Mike Baty
CFO: Roger Davis
Vice President: Mike Baty
Quality Control: Rick Reynolds
Inside Sales Representative: Shanelle Scott
Estimated Sales: Below $5 Million
Number Employees: 10
Regions Exported to: Central America, South America, Europe, Asia, Middle East
Percentage of Business in Exporting: 5

43344 Cresthill Industries
196 Ashburton Ave
Yonkers, NY 10701-4001   914-965-9510
Fax: 914-965-9534   www.whereorg.com
Manufacturer and exporter of bag closures
President: Christopher Rie
Treasurer: J Rie
Contact: Rhoda Needelman
rhoda@cresthillindustries.com
Estimated Sales: $ 10-20 Million
Number Employees: 50-99
Parent Co: Cresthill Industries
Regions Exported to: Worldwide

43345 Crestware
520 N Redwood Rd
PO Box 540210
North Salt Lake, UT 84054-2747   801-292-0656
Fax: 801-295-5732   800-345-0513
sales@crestware.com   www.crestware.com
Manufacturer and importer of china, flatware, steamtable pans, chafers, pots, pans, smallwares, thermometers and scales
President: Hal Harrison
Vice President: Julie Jackson
jjackson@crestware.com
VP Marketing: Stephen Jordan
VP Operations: Greg Harrison
Estimated Sales: $ 10 - 20 Million
Number Employees: 10-19
Square Footage: 160000
Regions Exported to: Central America, South America, Asia, Canada, Caribbean, Latin America, Mexico
Percentage of Business in Exporting: 1
Brands Imported: Crestware
Regions Imported from: Europe, Asia, Mexico
Percentage of Business in Importing: 85

43346 Crevettes Du Nord
139 Rue De La Reine
C.P. 6380
Gaspe, QC G4X 2R8
Canada   418-368-1414
Fax: 418-368-1812   gesco@globetrotter.qc.ca
Processor and exporter of fresh and frozen shrimp
President: Amedee La Pierre
Number Employees: 50-99
Type of Packaging: Bulk
Regions Exported to: Europe, USA
Percentage of Business in Exporting: 75

43347 Cribari Vineyard Inc
4180 W Alamos Ave # 108
Suite 108
Fresno, CA 93722-3943   559-277-9000
Fax: 559-277-2420   800-277-9095
bulk@cribari.net   www.sacramentalwines.com
Processor and exporter of high quality California bulk wine
CEO & CFO: John F. Cribari
Sales: Ben Cribari
Estimated Sales: $730,000
Number Employees: 1-4
Number of Brands: 7
Type of Packaging: Bulk
Regions Exported to: Europe, Asia, Caribbean, Canada
Percentage of Business in Exporting: 30

43348 Criders Poultry
1 Plant Avenue
PO Box 398
Stillmore, GA 30464-0398   912-562-4435
Fax: 912-562-4168   800-342-3851
info@criderinc.com   www.cridercorp.com
Fresh, frozen, canned and further processed chicken
Owner/CEO: William Crider Jr
CFO: Max Harrell
Research & Development: Phil Hudspeth
Quality Control: Stan Wallen
Operations: Lee Thompkins
Plant Manager: Kenneth Houghton
Purchasing: Ritchie Young
Estimated Sales: $ 20 - 50 Million
Number Employees: 400
Type of Packaging: Food Service, Private Label, Bulk
Regions Exported to: Worldwide

43349 Crispy Lite
10 Sunnen Drive
St. Louis, MO 63143-3800   775-689-5700
Fax: 314-781-5445   888-356-5362
clientcare@wellsbloomfield.com
www.wellsbloomfield.com
Manufacturer and exporter of display cases, filters, pressure fryers, fans, hoods and food warmers
Vice President, Sales/Marketing, Wells-B: Paul Angrick
VP Sales/Marketing: David Moore
Mngr.: D Joseph Lambert
Number Employees: 250-499
Square Footage: 248000
Parent Co: Wells Bloomfield Company
Type of Packaging: Food Service
Regions Exported to: Worldwide

43350 Critelli Olive Oil
2445 South Watney Way, Ste D
Fairfield, CA 94533-6721   707-426-3400
Fax: 707-426-3423   800-865-4836
www.critelli.com
Manufacturer of organic olive oil and dipping oil. Importer of culinary oil, Balsamic, Varietal Wine, and flavored vinegars from around the world.
Director Food Service: Mike Brossier
Director Of Operations: Brian Witbracht
Type of Packaging: Food Service, Private Label

43351 Critzas Industries Inc
4041 Park Ave Frnt
St Louis, MO 63110-2391   314-773-8510
Fax: 314-773-4837   800-537-1418
goop@earthlink.net   www.goophandcleaner.com
Manufacturer and exporter of premium waterless hand cleaner.
President/Treasurer: John Critzas
Contact: Gerald Pogue
critzas@aol.com
Estimated Sales: $10-20 Million
Number Employees: 10-19
Square Footage: 120000
Brands Exported: Goop
Regions Exported to: Central America, South America, Europe, Asia, Middle East

43352 Crockett Honey
1040 W Alameda Dr
Tempe, AZ 85282-3332   480-731-3936
Fax: 480-731-3938   800-291-3969
bnipper@crocketthoney.com
www.crocketthoney.com
Processor and exporter of honey
Owner: Brian Nipper
Secretary: Linda Nipper
VP: Brian Nipper
Estimated Sales: $5-10 Million
Number Employees: 5-9
Square Footage: 48000
Type of Packaging: Consumer, Food Service, Bulk
Regions Exported to: Asia

Importers & Exporters / A-Z

Percentage of Business in Exporting: 10

43353 Croda Inc
300 Columbus Cir # A
Edison, NJ 08837-3907   732-417-0800
    Fax: 732-417-0804 marketing-usa@croda.com
                                www.crodausa.com
Super refined marine and plant oils, proteins, and peptides for nutraceuticals, functional foods and dietary supplements.
President: Sandra Breene
Vice President: Esther Horowitz
ehorowitz@itsadeal.ie
Estimated Sales: $20-50 Million
Number Employees: 100-249
Square Footage: 45000
Parent Co: Croda International P/C
Regions Exported to: Worldwide

43354 Croll Reynolds Inc
6 Campus Dr # 5
Suite 1
Parsippany, NJ 07054-4406   908-232-4200
                        Fax: 908-232-2146
Manufacturer and exporter of food processing machinery including combined evactor/condenser/liquid ring vacuum, vapor recovery and vacuum cooling systems and ejectors
Vice President: Philip Reynolds
preynolds@croll.com
CEO: Samuel W. Croll
CEO: Samuel W Croll Iii
Division Manager: Henry Hage
Plant Manager: Ellis Production/Shipping
Estimated Sales: $ 5 - 10 Million
Number Employees: 20-49
Regions Exported to: Central America, South America, Europe, Asia, Middle East
Percentage of Business in Exporting: 20

43355 Crookston Bean
1600 S Main St
Crookston, MN 56716-2445   218-281-2567
       Fax: 218-281-2567 www.eteamz.com
Processor and exporter of dried edible beans
President: Paul Biermaier
paul.biermaier@crookston.mn.us
Manager: Dave Seaver
Estimated Sales: $10-20 Million
Number Employees: 5-9
Type of Packaging: Private Label, Bulk
Regions Exported to: Worldwide
Percentage of Business in Exporting: 50

43356 Crosby Molasses Company
327 Rothesay Avenue
Saint John, NB E2J 2C3
Canada   506-634-7515
        Fax: 506-634-1724 800-561-2206
       feedback@crosbys.com www.crosbys.com
Molasses, corn syrup, and glucose for co-manufactured retail and food service.
President: James Crosby
Senior Vice President: Lorne Goodman
Director of Sales & Marketing: William Crosby
VP of Operations: Jeanette Howley
Estimated Sales: $7.8 Million
Number Employees: 60
Type of Packaging: Consumer, Food Service, Private Label, Bulk
Regions Exported to: Asia, USA
Regions Imported from: Caribbean

43357 Crossings Fine Foods
123 W Service Rd
Champlain, NY 12919   508-755-5860
        Fax: 508-755-6548 800-209-6141
              contact@crossingsfinefoods.com
Importer and distributor of french specialty foods
Vice-President, Founder: Bureau Crook
Marketing, Sales Coordinator: Regnault Justine
Vice-President, Sales Marketing: Libbrecht Nicolas
Contact: Francoise Crook
francoise@crossingsfrenchfood.com
Estimated Sales: $ 5 - 10 Million
Number Employees: 5-9

43358 Crouse-Hinds
1201 Wolf St
Syracuse, NY 13208
            Fax: 315-477-5179 866-764-5454
            crousecustomerctr@eaton.com
www.cooperindustries.com/content/public/en/crouse-hinds.html

Manufacturer and exporter of outdoor and emergency lighting
President/Owner: Scott Hearn
Estimated Sales: $135 Million
Number Employees: 1,300
Parent Co: Eaton

43359 Crouzet Corporation
3237 Commander Drive
Carrollton, TX 75006-2506   972-620-7713
        Fax: 972-250-3865 800-677-5311
                              www.crouzet.com
Manufacturer and exporter of OEM products for packaging and processing equipment: timers, proximity sensors, counters, control relays, solid state relays and temperature controllers
President: Gerald Vincent
VP Marketing: Phillipe Dubois
Contact: Rosemary Martinez
martinezr@us.crouzet.com
Estimated Sales: $20-50 Million
Number Employees: 100-249
Parent Co: Crouzet
Regions Exported to: Canada

43360 Crowley Sales & Export Co
303j Salinas Rd
Royal Oaks, CA 95076-5252   831-722-8192
        Fax: 831-722-8194 ugro@crowleysales.com
                           www.crowleysales.com
Exporter of cherries, strawberries, blueberries, kiwifruit, citrus fruits, asparagus, bell peppers and lettuce
Manager: Charles Ukestad
Vice President: Sean Crowley
Office Manager: Jenny Nevarez
Estimated Sales: $5-10 Million
Number Employees: 1-4
Brands Exported: Shortcake; Sweet Kiss
Regions Exported to: South America, Europe, Asia
Percentage of Business in Exporting: 80

43361 Crown Battery Mfg
1445 Majestic Dr
Fremont, OH 43420-9190   419-334-7181
        Fax: 419-334-7416 800-487-2879
                           www.crownbattery.com
Manufacturer and exporter of industrial batteries used in lift trucks and food service equipment
President: Hal Hawk
Senior VP: Bill Bessire
bbessire@crownbattery.com
Director Marketing: Mark Kelley
Estimated Sales: $ 20 - 50 Million
Number Employees: 250-499
Square Footage: 200000
Brands Exported: Crown
Regions Exported to: Worldwide
Percentage of Business in Exporting: 10

43362 Crown Candy Corp
4145 Mead Rd
Macon, GA 31206   478-781-4911
                                  800-241-3529
       info@crowncandy.com www.crowncandy.com
Processor and exporter of confectionery products including brittles, chocolate, coconut, peanut and pecan candies and fudge.
CEO: James Weatherford
jweatherford@crowncandy.com
Estimated Sales: $10-24.9 Million
Number Employees: 100-249
Type of Packaging: Consumer, Private Label, Bulk
Regions Exported to: Canada

43363 Crown Closures Machinery
1765 W Fair Ave
Lancaster, OH 43130-2325   740-681-6593
        Fax: 740-681-6527 sheila.heath@crowncork.com
                             www.crowncork.com
Capping/sealing equipment since 1913. Formerly known as Anchor Hocking Packaging. Member of Crown Cork and Seal family of corporations. Precision CNC machining capabilities. Machine building and rebuilding
CAO: Amanda Marutz
amanda.marutz@crowncork.com
Operations Manager: Sheila Heath
Plant Manager: Ed Schott
Purchasing Manager: Greg Henwood
Estimated Sales: Below $ 5 Million
Number Employees: 20-49
Square Footage: 192000
Parent Co: Crown Cork & Seal

Regions Exported to: Asia, Canada, Mexico

43364 Crown Controls Inc.
2316 Crown Point Executive Drive
Charlotte, NC 28227   704-841-1622
        Fax: 704-841-1655 800-541-7874
               crowncontrols@windstream.net
                            www.crowncontrols.com
Manufacturer and exporter of level controls and open channel flow meters; also, food processing equipment
President: Charles Stevens
Number Employees: 20-49
Regions Exported to: South America, Europe, Asia
Percentage of Business in Exporting: 10

43365 Crown Custom Metal Spinning
1-176 Creditstone Road
Concord, ON L4K 4H7
Canada   416-243-0112
        Fax: 416-243-0112 800-750-1924
       sales@crowncookware.ca www.crowncookware.ca
Manufacturer and exporter of bakery racks and aluminum cookware including stockpots and cake and pizza pans; importer of stainless steel mixing bowls
President: David P Vella
CFO: Franco Mazzuca
Customer Service: Carmen D'Cruze
Administrator: Gilda Leib
Number Employees: 10
Square Footage: 80000
Type of Packaging: Consumer, Food Service, Bulk
Regions Exported to: South America, Europe, USA
Percentage of Business in Exporting: 5
Regions Imported from: Europe, India

43366 Crown Equipment Corp.
44 S. Washington St.
New Bremen, OH 45869   419-629-2311
        Fax: 419-629-2900 www.crown.com
Lift trucks.
Chairman/Chief Executive Officer: James Dicke
President: James Dicke
VP: Keith Sinram
Senior Vice President: James Mozer
Senior Vice President: Timothy Quellhorst
Senior Vice President: John Tate
Vice President, Sales: Christopher Rahe
Vice President, Engineering: Steven Dues
Vice President, Design: Michael Gallagher
Vice President, Manufacturing Operations: David Beddow
Year Founded: 1945
Estimated Sales: $3.48 Billion
Number Employees: 16,100
Regions Exported to: Worldwide

43367 Crown Foods International
500 S County Farm Rd # 100
Wheaton, IL 60187-2415   630-462-1600
                        Fax: 630-462-1636
Importer and exporter of frozen vegetables including corn, peas, beans, broccoli, etc.; also, frozen fruits, fruit concentrates and purees
Manager: Joe Zahour
VP: Jefferey Eckert
Director Operations: Humbero Pagan
Estimated Sales: $ 3 - 5 Million
Number Employees: 10-19
Square Footage: 12000
Type of Packaging: Consumer, Food Service, Private Label, Bulk
Brands Exported: Crown Classic
Regions Exported to: Central America, South America, Europe, South Africa
Percentage of Business in Exporting: 50
Regions Imported from: Central America, South America, Europe, North Africa
Percentage of Business in Importing: 50

43368 Crown Holdings, Inc.
770 Township Line Rd.
Yardley, PA 19067   215-698-5100
                                  ir@crowncork.com
                                www.crowncork.com
Bottle caps, can tops, crowns and cans including tin, beer and ale; also, bottling machinery
Chairman: John Conway
President/CEO: Timothy Donahue
Senior VP/CFO: Thomas Kelly
VP/Treasurer: Kevin Clothier
Executive VP/COO: Gerard Gifford

Year Founded: 1892
Estimated Sales: $11.7 Billion
Number Employees: 33,000
Type of Packaging: Consumer, Food Service, Private Label, Bulk
Other Locations:
  Crown Cork & Seal Co.
  Apopka, FLCrown Cork & Seal Co.
Regions Exported to: Worldwide

43369 (HQ)Crown Iron Works Company
2500 County Road C W # A
Roseville, MN 55113-2523 651-639-8900
 Fax: 651-639-8051 888-703-7500
sales@crowniron.com www.crowniron.com
Manufacturer and exporter of oil extractors, oil/fat processing systems and dryer/cooler systems.
Product Sales Manager: Richard Ozer
General Manager: Bill Antilla
Estimated Sales: $ 1 - 5 Million
Number Employees: 50-99
Brands Exported: Crown; Wurster & Sanger
Regions Exported to: Central America, South America, Europe, Asia, Middle East, Mexico
Percentage of Business in Exporting: 60

43370 Crown Metal Manufacturing Company
765 South State
Route 83
Elmhurst, IL 60126-4228 630-279-9800
 Fax: 630-279-9807 ca-sales@crownmetal.com
 www.crownmetal.com
Manufacturer and exporter of store fixtures including wall standards, brackets, showcase hardware and sign holders
Manager: Mike Volosin
Operations Manager: Mike Volosin
Estimated Sales: Less than $500,000
Number Employees: 1-4
Parent Co: Crown Metal
Regions Exported to: Worldwide

43371 (HQ)Crown Metal Mfg Co
8768 Hellman Ave
Rancho Cucamonga, CA 91730-4418 909-291-8585
 Fax: 909-291-8587 ca-sales@crownmetal.com
 www.crownmetal.com
Manufacturer and exporter of metal store fixtures, pegboard equipment and sign holders
Manager: Mike Volosin
Vice President: Glenn Dalglerish
Research & Development: Steve Varon
Sales Director: Scott Durham
Manager: Chris Montoya
cmontoya@crownmetal.com
Production Manager: Wayne Baker
Estimated Sales: Less Than $500,000
Number Employees: 1-4
Number of Brands: 8
Number of Products: 500
Square Footage: 340000
Type of Packaging: Bulk
Other Locations:
  Crown Metal Manufacturing Co.
  Rancho Cucamonga, CACrown Metal Manufacturing Co.
Regions Exported to: Worldwide
Percentage of Business in Exporting: 2

43372 (HQ)Crown Packing Company
5 Foster Road
Salinas, CA 93908-9339 831-424-2067
 Fax: 831-424-7812
Grower and packer of lettuce, celery and cauliflower; exporter of lettuce and celery
President: Chris Bunn
Sales Manager: Rob Steitz
Sales: Tonya Tempalski
Estimated Sales: $ 3 - 5 Million
Number Employees: 2
Type of Packaging: Consumer, Food Service, Private Label, Bulk
Brands Exported: Bunny
Regions Exported to: Asia
Percentage of Business in Exporting: 5

43373 Crown Point
118 S Cypress St
Mullins, SC 29574-3004 843-464-8165
 Fax: 843-464-8598 www.crownpt.com
Wholesaler/distributor and exporter of beans, peanuts, almonds, cashews, canned mushrooms, pizza products, popcorn, spices, tomato paste, frozen vegetables, military rations including meals and ready-to-eat, etc. Importer of mushroomsand olives
President: Kevin Gates
VP: Scott Copes
Export Sales: Virginia Harrelson
Contact: John Anderson
johna@crownpt.com
Estimated Sales: $ 3 - 5 Million
Number Employees: 1-4
Parent Co: Unaka Company
Type of Packaging: Consumer, Food Service, Bulk
Brands Exported: Crown Point

43374 Crown Processing Company
10754 Artesia Blvd
Cerritos, CA 90703-2650 562-865-0293
Processor, importer and exporter of citrus rinds including graded, sliced, cooked, canned, made into marmalade. Founded in 1960.
President: John Bowen
Estimated Sales: $5-10 Million
Number Employees: 20-49
Square Footage: 108000
Type of Packaging: Food Service
Brands Exported: Crown
Regions Exported to: Asia, Japan, Canada
Percentage of Business in Exporting: 25
Brands Imported: Crown
Regions Imported from: Canada

43375 Crown Products
P.O.Box 6558
Metairie, LA 70009 504-837-5342
 Fax: 504-831-1219 USA@crown-products.com
 www.crown-products.com
Exporter of popcorn, sunflower seeds, mayonnaise, peanut butter, canned corn and nondairy coffee creamer
President: Kee Lee
VP: Jeffrey Teague
Estimated Sales: $5-10 Million
Number Employees: 5-9

43376 Crown Tonka Walk-Ins
15600 37th Ave N # 100
Minneapolis, MN 55446-3204 763-541-1410
 Fax: 763-541-1563 800-523-7337
sales@crowntonka.com www.crowntonka.com
Manufacturer and exporter of walk-in coolers and freezers
President: Mike Kahler
mikek@crowntonka.com
Senior Vice President Sales & Marketing: Greg Sullens
Estimated Sales: $5-10 Million
Number Employees: 50-99
Type of Packaging: Consumer, Food Service
Regions Exported to: Worldwide
Percentage of Business in Exporting: 2

43377 Crown Verity
37 Adams Boulevard
Brantford, ON N3S 7V8
Canada 519-751-1800
 Fax: 519-751-1802 888-505-7240
info@crownverity.com www.crownverity.com
Manufacturer and exporter of stainless steel barbecues
President: William Verity
Founder: Bill Verity
CFO: Tracy McIngrrey
Quality Control: Allan Frennett
R & D: William Verity
Sales Manager: John Foulger
Number Employees: 10
Square Footage: 48000
Regions Exported to: Caribbean, USA
Percentage of Business in Exporting: 30

43378 Crownlite Manufacturing Corporation
1546 Ocean Ave
Bohemia, NY 11716-1916 631-589-9100
 Fax: 631-589-4584
Manufacturer and exporter of fluorescent and HID lighting fixtures and supplies; specializing in supermarket lighting
President: William Siegel
Sales Executive: Lois Carbonaro
Sales Manager: C Longo
Estimated Sales: $ 5 - 10 Million
Number Employees: 50 to 99

43379 Crs Inc
4851 White Bear Pkwy
St Paul, MN 55110-3325 651-294-2940
 Fax: 651-294-2900 moreinfo@crs-usa.com
 www.crs-usa.com
Importer and distributor of POS scanners, touch terminals, displays, scales, monitors and printers
President: Matt Haley
mhaley@crs.org
Vice President/Finance: Bill Oas
Vice President, Marketing: Bruce Mann
Advertising Manager: Tim Harris
mhaley@crs.org
Product Development Manager: Loren Foley
Estimated Sales: $ 20 - 50 Million
Number Employees: 50-99

43380 Cruvinet Winebar Co LLC
610 S Rock Blvd # 115
Sparks, NV 89431-8118 775-827-4044
 Fax: 800-873-7894 800-278-8463
info@cruvinetsys.com www.cruvinetsys.com
Manufacturer, importer and exporter of wine dispensing/preserving systems, nitrogen-based preserving systems and wine storage cases; also, service, repair and preventative maintenance for all makes and models of wine dispensing andcellaring systems
President/CEO: Matt Kuchnis
Vice President: Jennifer Kuchnis
Director of Sales: Matt Kuehnis
Production: Matt Kuehnis
Estimated Sales: Less Than $500,000
Number Employees: 1-4
Square Footage: 19960
Brands Exported: Petite Sommelier; Cruvinet; Estate; Le Grand Cruvinet, Le Cruvinet, Ultra Cruvinet, Le Grand Cruvinet Mubile; Le Grand Cruvinet Premier; Cruvinet Collector Series
Regions Exported to: Central America, South America, Europe, Asia, Middle East, Canada, Caribbean, Mexico
Percentage of Business in Exporting: 35

43381 Cryochem
PO Box 20268
St Simons Island, GA 31522-8268 912-262-0033
 Fax: 912-262-9990 800-237-4001
sales@cryochem.com www.cryochem.com
Manufacturer and exporter of cryogenic freezing and chilling equipment including single and tri-deck freezers, immersion and batch cabinets; also, custom-designed systems
Marketing Manager: Bryan Smith
General Manager: Frank Grillo
Estimated Sales: $ 1 - 5 Million
Number Employees: 18
Square Footage: 120000
Parent Co: Cryogenic Industries
Regions Exported to: Central America, South America, Europe, Asia, Middle East, Canada
Percentage of Business in Exporting: 60

43382 Crystal Creamery
529 Kansas Ave
Modesto, CA 95351 209-576-3400
  866-225-4821
 crystalcreamery.com
Milk.
President & CEO: Martin Devine
CFO: Bonnie Chan
VP, Human Resources: Walter Mendez
VP, Manufacturing: Hugo Andrade
Year Founded: 1901
Estimated Sales: $160 Million
Number Employees: 500-999
Type of Packaging: Consumer, Food Service, Private Label, Bulk
Other Locations:
  Crystal Cream & Butter Co.
  Sacramento, CACrystal Cream & Butter Co.
Regions Exported to: Central America, Asia, Mexico

43383 Crystal Creative Products
PO Box 450
Middletown, OH 45042 513-423-0731
 Fax: 513-423-0516 800-776-6762
Manufacturer, importer and exporter of tissue including wrapping and industrial

Importers & Exporters / A-Z

President: James Akers
Vice President: John Crider
Sales Director: Ed Miller
Purchasing Manager: Randy Clark
Estimated Sales: $ 20-50 Million
Number Employees: 100-249
Regions Exported to: Worldwide
Regions Imported from: Worldwide

43384 Crystal Food Import Corporation
245 Sumner St
Boston, MA 02128   617-569-7500
                        Fax: 617-561-0397
Importer and distribuor of Italian cheeses

43385 Crystal Food Import Corporation
19 Ward St
Somerville, MA 2143   781-599-0202
            Fax: 781-592-2424 800-225-3573
Wholesaler/distributor and importer of specialty cheeses including romano, parmesan, mozzarella, etc.; also, olive oil, crackers, sauces and breads
President: John Ciano
Controller: Bill Martin
Marketing Manager: Stephanie Ciano
Contact: William Burke
wburke@crystalfoodimport.com
Estimated Sales: $10-20 Million
Number Employees: 50-99
Square Footage: 32000
Brands Imported: L'Arc de Triomphe; Notre Dame; Triomphe Creme; Doumo Di Milano; Gelmini; Crown Jewel; Grinzing; Arnoldi; Peck; Olio Carli; Greisinger; Plaza Mayor; Cerignola Bells; Croccantina
Regions Imported from: Europe, Canada
Percentage of Business in Importing: 80

43386 (HQ)Crystal Lake Farms
1200 E Roller Ave
Decatur, AR 72722   479-752-8274
                            800-382-4425
Processor and exporter of chicken
Manager: Daryl Hopkins
Vice President: Lisa Garrett
lisa@crystallakefarms.com
Sr Director, Commodity Sales: Bruce Bayley
VP Human Resources: Janet Wilkerson
Sr VP, Development: Dennis Martin
Estimated Sales: $500,000-$1 Million
Number Employees: 1000-4999
Type of Packaging: Food Service, Private Label, Bulk
Other Locations:
    Crystal Lake
    North Kansas City, MOCrystal Lake
Brands Exported: Crystal Lake
Regions Exported to: Europe, Middle East
Percentage of Business in Exporting: 7

43387 Crystal Lake Mfg Inc
2225 Highway 14 W
Autaugaville, AL 36003-2541 334-365-3342
            Fax: 334-365-3332 800-633-8720
            customerservice@crystallakemfg.com
            www.homeworkclean.com
Manufacturer and exporter of brooms, mops and handles
President: James Pearson
james.pearson@crystallakemfg.com
Chairman: Theresa Dunn
Chairman the Board: Theresa Dunn
Sales Director: Ron Poole
Estimated Sales: $ 10 - 20 Million
Number Employees: 100-249
Square Footage: 406000
Type of Packaging: Consumer, Food Service, Private Label, Bulk
Regions Exported to: Middle East
Percentage of Business in Exporting: 3

43388 Crystal Star Herbal Nutrition
1542 N Sanborn Rd
Salinas, CA 93905-4760   831-422-7500
            Fax: 800-260-4349 www.crystalstar.com
Processor, importer and exporter of herbal extracts, capsules, teas, powdered drink mixes and sports nutrition products
Manager: Julie Lu
Founder: Linda Page PhD
VP Sales: Scott Seabaugh
VP Operations: Glenn Korando
Estimated Sales: Less than $500,000
Number Employees: 1-4

Square Footage: 40000
Parent Co: Jones Products International
Type of Packaging: Consumer, Bulk
Brands Exported: Crystal Star Herbal Nutrition
Regions Exported to: Europe, Middle East, Caribbean, Canada, Mexico
Percentage of Business in Exporting: 5

43389 Crystal-Flex Packaging Corporation
10 Oxford Road
Rockville Centre, NY 11570-2122   770-218-3556
            Fax: 732-967-9839 888-246-7325
            sales@crystalflex.com www.crystalflex.com
Manufacturer and exporter of polyethylene bags, plastic and barrier film, food packaging, pouches and laminations
President: Lesley Craig Litt
Number Employees: 6
Regions Exported to: Worldwide
Percentage of Business in Exporting: 10

43390 Crystal-Vision Packaging Systems
23870 Hawthorne Blvd
Torrance, CA 90505-5908   310-373-6057
            Fax: 310-373-6157 800-331-3240
            don@crystalvisionpkg.com
            www.crystalvisionpkg.com
Shrink film; printed shrink labels; dry food weigh/fill machines; packaging machines and bag sealers; food bags; & printed stand-up food bags.
President/CEO/CFO: Donald Hilmer
Quality Control: Emilio Diaz
Sales: Karl Behrens
Contact: Mark Bayless
mbayless@drbayless.com
General Manager: Jeff Hilmer
Purchasing: Bernie Johnson
Estimated Sales: $5 Million
Number Employees: 11
Square Footage: 60000
Parent Co: AID Corporation
Brands Exported: MultiVac; Crystal Vision; AIE
Regions Exported to: Asia
Percentage of Business in Exporting: 10
Regions Imported from: Europe, Asia
Percentage of Business in Importing: 40

43391 Cube Plastics
190 Maplecrete Road
Concord, Ontario, ON L4K 2B6
Canada   905-669-8669
            Fax: 905-669-8646 877-260-2823
Microwavable food containers in a variety of sizes.
Regions Exported to: Worldwide

43392 Cuisine de France
350 S Northwest Hwy Ste 302
Park Ridge, IL 60068   847-692-1916
                        Fax: 847-318-0087
Contact: Jason Beck
jason.beck@cuisinedefrance.com
Estimated Sales: $ 1 - 3 Million
Number Employees: 20-49

43393 Culinary Collective
12407-B Mukilteo Speedway
Suite 245
Lynnwood, WA 98087   425-398-9761
            Fax: 425-398-9765 info@culinarycollective.com
                        www.culinarycollective.com
Spanish and Peru foods
Co-Founder: Betsy Power
Co-Founder: Pere Selles
Sales Manager: Marion Sproul
Estimated Sales: $ 3 - 5 Million
Number Employees: 5-9
Regions Imported from: From Spain and Peru

43394 (HQ)Culinary Depot
2 Melnick Dr.
Monsey, NY 10952
            Fax: 845-352-2700 888-845-8200
            customerservice@culinarydepot.biz
                        www.culinarydepotinc.com
Kitchen and restaurant equipment, janitorial supplies, restaurant furniture and food storage and transport materials
Founder/President: Sholem Potash
CEO: Michael Lichter
Regions Exported to: USA

43395 Culinary Institute Lenotre
7070 Allensby St
Houston, TX 77022-4322   713-692-0077
            Fax: 713-692-7399 888-536-6873
Processor, importer and exporter of frozen strudel, muffins, cakes, cookies, danish, etc
Owner: Alain Lenotre
alenotre@culinaryinstitute.edu
VP: Marie Le Notre
Estimated Sales: $2 Million
Number Employees: 50-99
Square Footage: 120000
Type of Packaging: Private Label
Regions Exported to: Latin America
Regions Imported from: Europe
Percentage of Business in Importing: 5

43396 Culinary Masters Corporation
69 Brandywine Trl
Suite 109
Alpharetta, GA 30005   770-667-1688
            Fax: 770-667-1682 800-261-5261
                        www.culinarymasters.com
Wholesaler/distributor and importer of specialty foods, baked goods, equipment and tools; serving the food service market; exporter of spices, blends and specialty equipment
Master Chef/President: Helmut Holzer
Controller: Beth Ann Jackson
Vice President: Sara Jane Holzer
Sales: Michelle Brayley
Estimated Sales: $ 3 - 5 Million
Number Employees: 5-9
Square Footage: 16000
Type of Packaging: Food Service, Private Label
Brands Exported: Masters Blends; Culinary Masters
Regions Exported to: Europe, Caribbean
Percentage of Business in Exporting: 10
Regions Imported from: Europe
Percentage of Business in Importing: 90

43397 Culinary Specialties
1231 Linda Vista Dr
San Marcos, CA 92078-3809   760-744-8220
            Fax: 760-744-1486 info@culinaryspecialties.net
                        www.culinaryspecialties.net
Importer and wholesaler/distributor mousse and sponge cake mixes, pastry shells, couvertures, chocolate cups, pastes, compounds, marmalades, glazes and flavorings; wholesaler/distributor of frozen foods, general merchandise, generalline items, etc
President: Christian Schragner
cschragner@culinaryspecialties.net
VP: Tom Solomon
National Sales Manager: Vishka Rosenblum
Production Manager: Francois Resch
Director of Purchasing: Dwayne Ferris
Estimated Sales: $1-2.5 Million
Number Employees: 20-49
Square Footage: 300000
Regions Imported from: Europe

43398 Culligan Company
1 Culligan Parkway
Northbrook, IL 60062-6287   847-205-6000
            Fax: 847-205-6030 800-527-8637
            feedback@culligan.com www.culligan.com
Manufacturer and exporter of commercial/industrial water softeners, filters, deionizers, dealkalizers and reverse osmosis units
President: Tim Tousignant
Sales Director: Doug Dickinson
Contact: Nisha Aggarwal
naggarwal@culligan.com
Estimated Sales: $ 35 - 40 Million
Number Employees: 250-500
Square Footage: 120000
Regions Exported to: Central America, South America, Europe, Asia, Middle East
Percentage of Business in Exporting: 20

43399 Culligan International Company
9399 West Higgins Road
Rosemont, IL 60018   847-430-2800
            Fax: 847-430-1524 866-775-0260
                        www.culligan.com
Contact: Beth Abrams
beth.abrams@culligan.com
Number Employees: 1,000-4,999

Importers & Exporters / A-Z

43400 Culture Systems Inc
3224 N Home St
Mishawaka, IN 46545-4436 574-258-0602
Fax: 574-258-1136 info@culturesystemsinc.com
www.culturesystemsinc.com
Processor, exporter and wholesaler/distributor of dairy ingredients; also, researcher for the food industry
President: David Kim
dhyungkim@aol.com
Estimated Sales: $1-2.5 Million
Number Employees: 10-19
Square Footage: 16000
Regions Exported to: Asia

43401 Culver Duck Farms Inc
12215 County Road 10
PO Box 910
Middlebury, IN 46540-9694 574-825-9537
Fax: 574-825-2613 800-825-9225
info@culverduck.com www.culverduck.com
Duck, chicken and sausage products.
President: John Metzger
Year Founded: 1858
Estimated Sales: $20-50 Million
Number Employees: 100-249
Square Footage: 30000
Type of Packaging: Food Service
Brands Exported: Five Generation
Regions Exported to: Central America, Middle East

43402 Cumberland Dairy
899 Landis Ave
Rosenhayn, NJ 08352 856-451-1300
Fax: 856-451-1332 800-257-8484
sales@cumberlanddairy.com
www.cumberlanddairy.com
Ice cream mixes, juices, soy products and milk including whole, skim, 1% and 2%; processor of ice cream
President: Carmine Catalana
CFO: Stan Fronczkowski
Director of Research & Development: John Contino
Director of Quality: Richard Grigsby
VP Sales: David A Catalana
VP Operations: Frank Catalana
Year Founded: 1932
Estimated Sales: $20-50 Million
Number Employees: 100-249
Type of Packaging: Consumer, Food Service, Private Label, Bulk
Regions Exported to: Central America, Canada, Caribbean, Mexico
Percentage of Business in Exporting: 10

43403 Cumberland Packing Corp
2 Cumberland St
Brooklyn, NY 11205
info@cpack.com
cpack.com
Artificial sweeteners and butter flavor spreads.
Chairman: Marvin Eisenstadt
Year Founded: 1946
Estimated Sales: $100-500 Million
Number Employees: 250-499
Type of Packaging: Consumer
Regions Exported to: Worldwide

43404 Cummings
PO Box 23194
Nashville, TN 37202-3194 615-673-8999
Fax: 615-782-6699
stacey.hawke@cummingssigns.com
Manufacturer and exporter of electric signs and marquees
President: Stephen R Kerr
Sr VP: Bruce Cornett
Contact: T Cummings
t.cummings@thesign.com
Executive VP National Accounts: Jerry Morrison
Estimated Sales: $20-50 Million
Number Employees: 50-99
Square Footage: 175000
Regions Exported to: Europe
Percentage of Business in Exporting: 2

43405 Cummins Allison Corp
852 Feehanville Dr
Mt Prospect, IL 60056-6001 847-759-6207
Fax: 847-299-4940 inquire@cumminsallison.com
www.cumminsallison.com
CEO: William Jones
Contact: Navin Abraham
abrahamn@cumminsallison.com
Number Employees: 1-4

43406 Cup Pac Packaging Inc
777 Progressive Ln
South Beloit, IL 61080-2618 815-624-7060
Fax: 815-624-8170 877-347-9725
info@cuppac.com www.cuppac.com
Manufacturer and exporter of machinery for filling, tamper-evident sealing, lidding and code dating plastic cups; contract packaging available
President: Dennis James
Vice President: Jim Philipp
VP Sales: Russell James
Estimated Sales: $4 Million
Number Employees: 20-49
Square Footage: 68000
Type of Packaging: Consumer, Food Service, Private Label, Bulk
Regions Exported to: Central America, South America, Europe, Asia, Middle East
Percentage of Business in Exporting: 40

43407 (HQ)Cupper's Coffee Company
1502C 3rd Avenu South
Lethbridge, AB T1J 0K8
Canada 403-380-4555
Fax: 403-328-8004 cuppercoffee@gmil.com
Importer and exporter of coffee
President: Al Anctil
Number Employees: 20-49
Regions Exported to: Europe, USA
Percentage of Business in Exporting: 10
Regions Imported from: Africa, Latin America, U.S.A.
Percentage of Business in Importing: 10

43408 Curly's Foods Inc
5201 Eden Ave # 181
Suite 370
Edina, MN 55436-2449 612-920-3400
Fax: 612-920-9889 www.curlys.com
Beef including roast, corned, barbecued and cooked and frozen ribs.
President: John Pauley
Vice President: Ken Fineberg
Manager, R&D: Brian Quandt
Estimated Sales: $22 Million
Number Employees: 500-999
Number of Brands: 1
Square Footage: 100000
Parent Co: John Morrell/Smithfield Foods
Type of Packaging: Consumer, Food Service, Private Label, Bulk

43409 Currie Machinery Co
1150 Walsh Ave
Santa Clara, CA 95050-2647 408-727-0422
Fax: 408-727-8892 currieco@aol.com
www.curriepalletizers.com
Manufacturer and exporter of material handling equipment including automatic palletizers, case elevators, beverage pallet stackers and powered discharge conveyors; also, dispensers including pallet, slip and tier sheet
President: Bradley Patrick
b.patrick@curriepalletizers.com
Marketing Director: Gerry Haase
Estimated Sales: $5-10 Million
Number Employees: 1-4
Square Footage: 160000
Brands Exported: Currie
Regions Exported to: South America, Europe, Asia, Middle East, Australia, Canada, Mexico, Africa
Percentage of Business in Exporting: 20

43410 Curry King Corporation
34 West Prospect St
Waldwick, NJ 07463 201-652-6228
Fax: 201-447-3291 800-287-7987
info@curryking.com www.curryking.com
Processor and importer of curry, balti and tandoori sauce; also, mango chutney; exporter of curry sauce
President: Lall Kwatra
lall@addesign.net
Vice President: Pamela Kwatra
Estimated Sales: Under $500,000
Number Employees: 3
Square Footage: 10000
Type of Packaging: Food Service, Private Label, Bulk
Regions Exported to: Europe, Middle East, Canada, Mexico, Caribbean, United Kingdom
Percentage of Business in Exporting: 10
Regions Imported from: Worldwide
Percentage of Business in Importing: 15

43411 Curtis Packaging
44 Berkshire Rd
Sandy Hook, CT 06482-1499 203-426-5861
Fax: 203-426-2684 www.curtispackaging.com
Manufacturer and exporter of folding paper boxes; also, hot stamping and UV coating available
Chairman, President & CEO: Donald Droppo
Estimated Sales: $35 Million
Number Employees: 100-249
Square Footage: 150000
Regions Exported to: Worldwide
Percentage of Business in Exporting: 1

43412 Curtis Ward Company
3722 28th Street
Long Island City, NY 11101-2629 718-478-4900
Fax: 718-478-1030
Wholesaler/distributor and exporter of general merchandise including commercial refrigerators, air conditioners and cooking equipment; serving the food service market
President: Jay Pachtman
Vice President: Stuart Ellison
Estimated Sales: $1-2.5 Million
Number Employees: 1-4
Square Footage: 24000
Regions Exported to: Worldwide
Percentage of Business in Exporting: 2

43413 Curwood Specialty Films
2200 Badger Ave
PO Box 2968
Oshkosh, WI 54904-9118 920-303-7300
Fax: 920-303-7309 800-544-4672
curwood@bemis.com www.curwood.com
Supplier of films, trays, lids and other packaging materials for the food and beverage industries.
Founder: Howard Curler
Founder: Bob Woods
Contact: Tom Bordona
tsbordona@bemis.com
Estimated Sales: Less Than $500,000
Number Employees: 5-9
Regions Exported to: Worldwide

43414 Custom Culinary Inc.
1000 E. State Pkwy.
Suite 1
Schaumberg, IL 60173-4569 866-878-3827
800-621-8827
www.customculinary.com
Gravy mixes, soup bases, soup mixes and sauce & gravy concentrates.
Regional Manager: Tom Nemanich
Vice President Operations: David Love
Year Founded: 1945
Estimated Sales: $100 Million
Number Employees: 100-249
Number of Brands: 3
Square Footage: 75000
Parent Co: Griffith Laboratories, Inc.
Type of Packaging: Food Service, Bulk
Brands Exported: Gold Label

43415 Custom Diamond Intl.
895 Munck Avenue
Laval, QC H7S 1A9
Canada 450-668-0330
Fax: 450-662-1326 800-326-5926
Smokers, ovens, combi-oven systems, food transport systems, heated and refrigerated stainless steel tables, counters, carts, dollies, feeding systems, etc.; exporter of food service equipment including ovens, prison food carts, andrethermalization food systems
President/CEO: Ron Diamond
CFO: D Bucci
Vice President: Allan Weber
R&D: Jason B
Marketing: Alex Malikian
Sales/Public Relations: Nick V
Production/Plant Manager: Paul Nesi
Plant Manager: H Diamond
Purchasing: George D
Square Footage: 204000
Type of Packaging: Bulk
Brands Exported: Brute

Importers & Exporters / A-Z

43416 (HQ)Custom Food Machinery
1881 E Market Street
Stockton, CA 95205-5673   209-463-4343
Fax: 209-463-3831
Rebuilder, importer and exporter of machinery including canning, beverage and beer bottling, fruit and vegetable, processing, filling, sterilization, can closing, packaging, cartoning, etc
President: Ron McNiel Sr
VP Sales/Advertising (Inventory): Richard Gomez-Stockton
VP Operations: Ron McNiel, Jr.
Estimated Sales: $ 10 - 20 Million
Number Employees: 50-99
Other Locations:
   Custom Food Machinery
   Sampron NakornpathomCustom Food Machinery
Regions Exported to: Worldwide
Percentage of Business in Exporting: 70
Regions Imported from: Asia, Mexico
Percentage of Business in Importing: 1

43417 Custom Metal Design Inc
921 W Oakland Ave
Oakland, FL 34760-8855   407-656-7771
Fax: 407-656-6230   800-334-1777
sales@custommetaldesigns.com
www.custommetaldesigns.com
Manufacturer and exporter of material handling equipment including conveyors and systems, depalletizers, elevators, accumulators and bagging equipment and supplies
President: Dennis Bankowitz
dennis@custommetaldesigns.com
Estimated Sales: $10-20 Million
Number Employees: 20-49
Type of Packaging: Bulk

43418 Custom Packaging Inc
1003 Commerce Rd
Richmond, VA 23224-7007   804-232-3299
Fax: 804-232-6230 www.custompack.com
Manufacturer and exporter of corrugated boxes and point of purchase displays
President: Ed Beadels
custompackaging@verizon.net
VP: Jackie Cowden
VP Sales: Gary West
Estimated Sales: $20-50 Million
Number Employees: 10-19
Regions Exported to: Canada

43419 Custom Poly Packaging
3216 Congressional Pkwy
Fort Wayne, IN 46808-4417   260-483-4008
Fax: 260-484-5166   800-548-6603
info@custompoly.com www.custompoly.com
Polyethylene, polypropylene, trash, shopping and laboratory bags; importer of sample bags
Owner: Michael Carpenter
info@custompoly.com
Estimated Sales: $2.5-5,000,000
Number Employees: 10-19
Square Footage: 13000
Brands Imported: Nopa
Regions Imported from: Canada
Percentage of Business in Importing: 2

43420 Custom Rubber Stamp Co
326 5th St NE
Crosby, MN 56441-1513   218-545-4977
Fax: 866-485-9205   888-606-4579
orders@crstamp.com www.crstamp.com
Manufacturer, exporter and importer of custom rubber stamps, self-inking and pre-inked stamps, embossers, engraved plastic signs, name tags and inks
President: James Grimes
Co-Owner: Jean Grimes
Employee: Paula Steigauf
Estimated Sales: Less Than $500,000
Number Employees: 1-4
Square Footage: 4000
Regions Exported to: Europe
Percentage of Business in Exporting: 1
Brands Imported: Trodat
Regions Imported from: Europe
Percentage of Business in Importing: 2

43421 Custom Sales & Svc Inc
275 S 2nd Rd
Hammonton, NJ 08037-8445   609-561-6900
Fax: 609-567-9318   800-257-7855
info@foodcart.com
Manufacturer and exporter of mobile food equipment including trucks, trailers, vans and cart systems
CEO: William Sikora
VP Sales/Marketing: Lynda Sikora
IT: Jay Celona
jay.celona@foodcart.com
Estimated Sales: $5-10 Million
Number Employees: 100-249
Square Footage: 140000
Regions Exported to: Worldwide
Percentage of Business in Exporting: 4

43422 Custom Source LLC
36 Harlow St
Worcester, MA 01605   508-304-7330
Fax: 508-656-8771 customsourcellc.com
European confections
Owner: Lewis Finkelstein
contact@customsourcellc.com
Year Founded: 2015
Estimated Sales: Less than $500,000
Number Employees: 3
Brands Imported: Paris Caramels; Gavottes; Chocolat Bonnat; P,cou Confections; St Michel
Regions Imported from: Central America
Percentage of Business in Importing: 100

43423 (HQ)Custom Stamp Company
37449 Regal Blue Trail
Anza, CA 92539-8806   323-292-0753
Fax: 323-292-0754
Manufacturer and exporter of pressure sensitive labels, rubber stamps, name plates, stencils, daters, marking products, metal tags and serial numbering on metal
President: Jack Coleman
Sales Manager: Steve Glass
Number Employees: 8
Square Footage: 7200
Type of Packaging: Food Service
Brands Exported: Custom; Cosco; Garvey; Dymo; Roovers; Melind; JRS
Regions Exported to: Central America
Percentage of Business in Exporting: 15

43424 Customized Equipment SE
4186 Railroad Ave
Tucker, GA 30084-4484   770-934-9300
Fax: 770-934-0610
Manufacturer and exporter of packaging machinery including automatic and semi-automatic baggers and sealers; also, random and fixed size carton taping machinery
President: Kermit Cooper
Sales Director: Bruce Cooper
Estimated Sales: $ 1 - 5 Million
Number Employees: 10 to 19
Square Footage: 40000
Regions Exported to: Central America, South America

43425 Cutie Pie Corp
443 W 400 N
Salt Lake City, UT 84103-1227   801-533-9550
Fax: 801-355-8021   800-453-4575
www.getcutiepie.com
Processor and exporter of frozen fruit snack pies
Principal: Bob Sharp
CFO: Lee Rucker
Director: Lee Wacker
Manager: Williams Arroyo
arroyo@horizonsnackfoods.com
Estimated Sales: Under $500,000
Number Employees: 50-99
Type of Packaging: Consumer, Food Service

43426 Cutler Industries
8300 Austin Avenue
Morton Grove, IL 60053-3209   847-965-3700
Fax: 847-965-8585   800-458-5593
Manufacturer and exporter of revolving tray, rack and utility ovens and under counter proofers
Director Marketing Support: Kathleen Casey
Estimated Sales: $ 1 - 5 Million
Number Employees: 50-99
Square Footage: 340000
Regions Exported to: Asia, Middle East, Canada, Latin America
Percentage of Business in Exporting: 16

43427 Cutrite Company
PO Box 851
Fremont, OH 43420-0851   419-332-1380
Fax: 419-334-2383   800-928-8748
sales@arius-eickert.com
Manufacturer and exporter of cooking knives, poultry shears and meat processing specialty tools and utensils
Sales Manager: Ramon Eickert
General Manager: Becky Smith
Estimated Sales: $ 3-5 Million
Number Employees: 20-50
Square Footage: 100000
Parent Co: A. Eickert Company
Brands Exported: Cutrite
Regions Exported to: Central America, South America, Europe, Worldwide
Percentage of Business in Exporting: 20
Regions Imported from: Europe
Percentage of Business in Importing: 2

43428 Cyanotech Corp
73-4460 Queen Kaahumanu
Suite 102
Kailua Kona, HI 96740-2637   808-326-1353
Fax: 808-329-4533   800-395-1353
info@cyanotech.com www.cyanotech.com
Cyanotech Corporation, the world's leader in microalgae technology, produces high-value natural products from microalgae, and is the world's largest commercial producer of natural astaxanthin from microalgae. Products include HawaiiamSpirulina Pacifica, a nutrient-rich dietary supplement; BioAstin, a natural astaxanthin, a powerful antioxidant with expanding applications as a human nutraceutical
CEO: Gerald R Cysewski
gcysewski@cyanotech.com
VP Sales/Marketing: Robert Capelli
Sales Manager: Jeane Vinson
Estimated Sales: F
Number Employees: 100-249
Number of Brands: 3
Number of Products: 2
Square Footage: 1306800
Parent Co: Cyanotech Corporation
Type of Packaging: Consumer, Private Label, Bulk
Brands Exported: Spirulina Pacifica & NatuRose; BioAstin
Regions Exported to: South America, Europe, Asia, Worldwide
Percentage of Business in Exporting: 55

43429 Cybros
P.O.Box 851
Waukesha, WI 53187-0851   262-547-1821
Fax: 262-547-8946   800-876-2253
Fine breads, rolls, cookies and other products
Owner: Debbie Brooks
General Manager: Paul Geboy
Estimated Sales: $2.5-5 Million
Number Employees: 10-19
Square Footage: 32000
Brands Imported: Dimpflmier
Regions Imported from: Canada
Percentage of Business in Importing: 4

43430 Cyclamen Collection
2140 Livingston St
Oakland, CA 94606   510-434-7620
Fax: 510-434-7624 CYCLAMENCOLL@aol.com
www.cyclamencollection.com
Manufacturer and exporter of dinnerware, serveware, bakeware and vitrified stoneware, pitchers, vases, and lamps
Owner: Julie Sanders
julie.sanders@cyclamencollection.com
Sales: Julie Sanders
julie.sanders@cyclamencollection.com
Estimated Sales: $500,000-$1,000,000
Number Employees: 5-9
Number of Products: 200+
Type of Packaging: Bulk
Regions Exported to: Worldwide
Percentage of Business in Exporting: 10

43431 Cyclonaire Corp
2922 N Division Ave
P.O.Box 366
York, NE 68467-9775   402-362-2000
Fax: 402-362-2001   800-445-0730
sales@cyclonaire.com www.cyclonaire.com
Manufacturer and exporter of pneumatic conveying equipment and accessories

President: Dan Reckner
dreckner@ddreckner.com
CEO: Don Baker
VP: Scott Schmidt
Sales: Joe Morris
Plant Manager: Deryl Kliewer
Purchasing: Sheila Miller
Estimated Sales: $ 10 - 20 Million
Number Employees: 20-49
Square Footage: 80000
Brands Exported: Cyclonaire
Regions Exported to: Central America, South America, Europe, Asia
Percentage of Business in Exporting: 25

43432 Cyclone Enterprises Inc
146 Knobcrest Dr
Houston, TX 77060-1213 281-872-0087
Fax: 281-872-7645 www.cyclone-ent.com
Processor and importer of Mexican food including hot sauce and peppers. Distributors of dry, canned, processed and frozen grocery items including juices, drinks, dairy products, meats, cheeses, deli products, specialty foods, herbs&spices, candy and snac
Owner: Mike Germany
Sales: Jim Petree
mgermany@cyclone-ent.com
Customer Support: Dora Mendoza
General Information: Martha Gibbs
Purchasing: Lam Townsend
Estimated Sales: $2.5-5 Million
Number Employees: 100-249
Type of Packaging: Consumer, Food Service, Private Label
Regions Imported from: Mexico
Percentage of Business in Importing: 80

43433 Cyrk
14224 167th Avenue
Monroe, WA 98272
Fax: 800-545-8840 800-426-3125
Manufacturer and exporter of advertising novelties including screen printed promotional materials
Sales Manager: Steve Paradiso
Contact: Kathy Heineman
kheineman@cyrk.com
Estimated Sales: $ 40 Million
Number Employees: 250-500
Type of Packaging: Food Service
Regions Exported to: Worldwide

43434 Cyro Industries/Degussa
P.O.Box 677
Parsippany, NJ 07054-0677 973-541-8000
Fax: 973-541-8445 800-631-5384
cyro@degussa.com www.cyro.com
Manufacturer and exporter of molding and extrusion compounds for food bins and displays
President: Thomas Bates
Marketing Director: Cynthia Zey
Public Relations: Gail Wood
Number Employees: 500-999
Parent Co: Cytec Industries/Rohm GmbH
Brands Exported: ACRYLITE® Acrylic Polymers, CYROLITE® and XT® Polymer Acrylic Based Multipolymer Compounds, ACRYLITE® Acrylic Sheet

43435 D & L Manufacturing
1818 S 71st St
Milwaukee, WI 53214 414-256-8160
Fax: 414-476-0564 sales@kempsmith-dl.com
www.kempsmith-dl.com
Manufacturer and exporter of machinery including file folder, paper converting, cutting, creasing, folding carton, folding and glueing, laminating, printing, embossing and rotary die cutting
President: Brett Burris
CEO: Robert Burris
Sales Director: Judy Lewis
Estimated Sales: $10-20 Million
Number Employees: 20-49
Square Footage: 116000
Brands Exported: Web Fed Carton Cutters
Regions Exported to: Central America, South America, Europe, Asia
Percentage of Business in Exporting: 40

43436 D & S Mfg
14 Sword St # 4
Auburn, MA 01501-2170 508-799-7812
Fax: 508-753-3468
Knives; also, screens for granulators and choppers

President: Graham Scarsbrook
Contact: Robert Johnson
dsmanufacturing@aol.com
Estimated Sales: $ 1 - 2.5 Million
Number Employees: 10-19
Parent Co: L. Hardy

43437 D & W Fine Pack
800 Ela Rd
Lake Zurich, IL 60047-2340 847-438-2171
Fax: 847-438-0369 800-323-0422
www.dwfinepack.com
Manufacturer and exporter of metal baking pans for muffins, cupcakes, breads, baguettes, pizza, pies, buns and rolls; also, aluminum foil containers, plastic domes, plastic containers, and plastic clamshells
President & CEO: Dave Randall
Cio/Cto: Mike Jenkins
CFO, VP Finance: Tom Nickele
VP, CIO: Michael Casula
VP Sales Grocery & Processor: Rick Barton
SVP Operations: Jay DuBois
Number Employees: 100-249
Square Footage: 1200000
Type of Packaging: Consumer, Food Service, Private Label, Bulk
Brands Exported: Bakalon; Bake King; Chicago Metallic; Sure Bake; Sure Bake And Glaze
Regions Exported to: Worldwide
Percentage of Business in Exporting: 10

43438 D D Bean & Sons Co
207 Peterborough St
Jaffrey, NH 03452-5868 603-532-8311
Fax: 603-532-6001 800-326-8311
info@ddbean.com www.ddbean.com
Manufacturer and exporter of matchbooks
President: D Bean
CEO: Delcie D Bean
dbean@ddbean.com
VP: Peter Leach
Manager: Terry Fecto
Estimated Sales: $ 20-50 Million
Number Employees: 50-99
Square Footage: 100000
Type of Packaging: Food Service, Private Label
Regions Exported to: Central America, South America, Europe, Middle East
Percentage of Business in Exporting: 1

43439 D D Williamson & Co Inc
1901 Payne St
Louisville, KY 40206-1902 502-895-2438
Fax: 502-895-7381
Global manufacturer of natural colour for the food and beverage industries with facilities in Africa, Asia, Europe and North and South America.
Chairman & CEO: Ted Nixon
Type of Packaging: Bulk
Regions Exported to: Central America, South America, Europe, Asia, Middle East; Worldwide

43440 D R Technology Inc
73 South St
Freehold, NJ 07728-2317 732-780-4664
Fax: 732-780-1545 sales@DRTechnologyInc.com
www.drtechnologyinc.com
Manufacturer and exporter of wet scrubbers used to control atmospheric emissions in food manufacturing plants
President: Richard Schwartz
CEO: Doris Schwartz
drtinfo@aol.com
Marketing Director: Debra Kruggen
Estimated Sales: $ .5 - 1 million
Number Employees: 5-9
Square Footage: 5000
Regions Exported to: Central America, South America, Europe, Asia, Middle East
Percentage of Business in Exporting: 10

43441 D Steengrafe Co Inc
1726 Main St
Pleasant Valley, NY 12569-5611 845-635-4067
Fax: 845-635-4239
Manufacturer and importer of beeswax, botanicals, kola nuts and nut powder, quassia chips, dried ginger and spices
VP: Margot Nordenholt
m_nordenholt@yahoo.com
VP: Carl Schmidt
Estimated Sales: $5 Million
Number Employees: 1-4

Type of Packaging: Bulk
Regions Imported from: West Africa, Caribbean Islands
Percentage of Business in Importing: 100

43442 D Waybret & Sons Fisheries
3 Clam Point
Shelburne, NS B0T 1W0
Canada 902-745-3477
Fax: 902-745-2112
Manufacturer and exporter of fresh and salted haddock, cod, halibut and hake; also, fresh lobster
President/Co-Owner: Dewey Waybret
Manager/Co-Owner: Cecil Waybret
Number Employees: 50
Type of Packaging: Bulk
Regions Exported to: USA , Bermuda
Percentage of Business in Exporting: 75

43443 D'Ac Lighting
420 Railroad Way
PO BOX 262
Mamaroneck, NY 10543-2257 914-698-5959
Fax: 914-698-6061 www.daclighting.com
Manufacturer and importer of lighting fixtures including electric and flourescent
President: Robert N Haidinger
Customer Service: Peggy Guglielmo
General Manager: Moshe Toledo
Estimated Sales: $ 1-2.5 Million
Number Employees: 50-99
Square Footage: 100000
Regions Imported from: Spain , Italy

43444 D'Arrigo Brothers Company of New York, Inc
315 Hunts Point Terminal Market
Bronx, NY 10474 718-991-5900
Fax: 718-960-0544 gdarrigo@darrigony.com
www.darrigony.com
Wholesale/Distributor of produce.
President & Buyer Western Veg: Paul D'Arrigo
CFO: David Bub
Director of Marketing: Gabriela D'Arrigo
VP, Sales & Fruit Buyer: Michael D'Arrigo
Corp. Sales/Deliveries/Drop Shipments: Steve Grandquist
Human Resources/Facilities Manager: Joe Schneider
Year Founded: 1948
Estimated Sales: $71 Million
Number Employees: 100-249
Square Footage: 75000

43445 D'Light Lighting Company
533 W Windsor Road
Glendale, CA 91204-1812 818-956-5656
Fax: 818-956-5657 ben@dlights.com
www.dlights.com
Estimated Sales: $ 1 - 3 Million
Number Employees: 5-9

43446 D'Lights
533 West Windsor Road
Glendale, CA 91204 818-956-5656
Fax: 818-956-2157 slsmgr@dlights.com
www.dlights.com
Manufacturer and exporter of lighting fixtures and food warmers
President: Kent Erle Sokolow
General Manager: Steve Sink
Estimated Sales: Below $5 Million
Number Employees: 10
Regions Exported to: Worldwide

43447 D.A. Colongeli & Sons
16 Pomeroy Street
Cortland, NY 13045-2241 607-753-0888
Fax: 607-756-2997 800-322-7687
Established in 1970; purveyors of fine foods.
President: Donald Colongeli
Number Employees: 1
Square Footage: 4000
Type of Packaging: Food Service

43448 D.F. International
4821 Chino Ave
Chino, CA 91710 909-613-9424
Fax: 909-613-9013 dfi9488@hotmail.com
www.dfindustries.com
Importer and exporter of natural honey, royal jelly, propolis, bee's wax, spearmint oil and aroma materials including menthol; import and wholesale of crawfish tail meat

Importers & Exporters / A-Z

President: Jeffrey Dong
Vice President: John Dong
Estimated Sales: $ .5 - 1 million
Number Employees: 3
Square Footage: 4400
Type of Packaging: Bulk
Regions Exported to: Asia
Brands Imported: Bulk Honey and Bee Products
Regions Imported from: Central America, South America, Asia

43449 DAB-A-DO Delicacies
PO Box 692
Isle of Palms, SC 29451-0692   843-832-4668

43450 DB Kenney Fisheries
301 Water Street
PO Box 1210
Westport, NS B0V 1H0
Canada   902-839-2023
    Fax: 902-839-2070
    dbkenney@dbkenneyfisheries.com
    www.dbkenneyfisheries.com
Manufacturer and exporter of scallops, lobster, cod and haddock
President: Daniel Kenney Jr
Controller: Steven Lombard
Sales Manager: Dave Titus
Operations manager: Glenn Wadman
Number Employees: 50-99
Type of Packaging: Bulk
Regions Exported to: USA

43451 (HQ)DBE Inc
310 Rayette Road
Concord, ON L4K 2G5
Canada   905-738-0353
    Fax: 905-738-7585   800-461-5313
    www.dbe-vsi.com
Manufacturer, importer and exporter of seafood equipment including commercial fish/lobster tanks, electrical fish sealers, customized seafood tanks
President: Fima Dreff
Marketing Director: Lesya Sklyarenko
Sales Director: Joe Albis
Public Relations: Lesya Sklyarenko
Plant Manager: Jean-Pierre Paquette
Estimated Sales: $ 10 - 20 Million
Number Employees: 15
Number of Brands: 6
Square Footage: 100000
Other Locations:
    DBE Food Equipment
    KyivDBE Food Equipment
Regions Exported to: Central America, South America, Middle East
Percentage of Business in Exporting: 50
Regions Imported from: Europe
Percentage of Business in Importing: 30

43452 (HQ)DCL Solutions LLC
4201 Torresdale Ave
Philadelphia, PA 19124-4701   215-743-4201
    Fax: 215-288-0847   800-426-1127
    sales@dclsolutions.com www.big3packaging.com
Manufacturer and exporter of floor finishes, strippers, oven/grill cleaners, hand soaps, degreasers and portion control water soluble packets
Owner: Steve Seneca
sseneca@pakit.com
CFO: Bill Harry
VP: Bill Paris
Estimated Sales: $ 5 - 10 Million
Number Employees: 50-99
Square Footage: 120000
Regions Exported to: Central America, South America, Europe, Asia, Middle East
Percentage of Business in Exporting: 10

43453 DFG Foods, LLC
111 North Canal Street
Suite 1111
Chicago, IL 60606-7218   312-279-1327
    Fax: 312-650-4501
Estimated Sales: $ 5 - 10 Million
Number Employees: 5-9

43454 DFI Organics Inc.
711 Bay Area Blvd
Suite 321
Webster, TX 77598
    888-970-9993
    sales@dfiorganics.com us.dfiorganics.com
Importer & exporter of organic food and feed ingredients.
Founder/CEO: Paul Magnotto
Commerical Director: Dennis Minnaard
Chief Commerical Officer: Richard Bellas
Parent Co: Doens Food Ingredients

43455 DH/Sureflow
402 SE 31st Avenue
Portland, OR 97214-1929   503-236-9263
    Fax: 503-236-9264   800-654-2548
    sureflow@dhsales.com
Manufacturer and exporter of drain cleaning machinery and power snakes
Owner and President: Doug Hemenway
VP: Geoff Hemenway
Number Employees: 3
Square Footage: 10000
Brands Exported: Sureflow
Regions Exported to: Worldwide
Percentage of Business in Exporting: 5

43456 DIC International
35 Waterview Blvd Ste 100
Parsippany, NJ 07054-1270
    Fax: 201-836-4962
    www.dic.co.jp/eng/products/pps/global.html
Manufacturer, importer and exporter of a natural nontoxic chlorophyll colorant
President: Shintaro Asada
CFO: Yuzi Koike
Marketing Manager: Y Akiyama
Contact: Christine Medordi
christine@dica.com
Number Employees: 20-49
Parent Co: Dainippou Ink & Chemicals
Regions Exported to: Central America, Canada, Latin America, Mexico
Regions Imported from: Asia
Percentage of Business in Importing: 85

43457 DLX Industries
1609 Roote 202
Pomona, NY 10970-2902   845-517-2200
    www.dlxonline.com
Manufacturer and exporter of vinyl-imprinted advertising specialties and promotional items
Estimated Sales: $78,000
Number Employees: 2
Number of Products: 120
Square Footage: 12804
Parent Co: DLX
Regions Exported to: Worldwide
Percentage of Business in Exporting: 1

43458 DMC-David ManufacturingCompany
1600 12th Street NE
Mason City, IA 50401-2543   641-424-7010
    Fax: 641-424-7017
Manufacturer and exporter of grain-handling equipment including cleaners and dryers; also, moisture sensing devices for flowing or moving material
CEO and President: Wes Cagle
Sales/Marketing Manager: Jim Balk
Estimated Sales: $20-50 Million
Number Employees: 100-249
Square Footage: 157000
Regions Exported to: South America, Europe, Asia, Canada
Percentage of Business in Exporting: 10

43459 DNE World Fruit Sales
1900 N Old Dixie Hwy
Fort Pierce, FL 34946
    Fax: 772-465-1181   800-327-6676
    www.dneworld.com
Grower, packer, marketer, and importer of citrus fruit including navel oranges, clementines, lemons and limes; exporter of grapefruit, oranges, tangerines and juice.
Senior Director, Sales: Mark Hanks
Sales: Kevin Carroll
Year Founded: 1914
Estimated Sales: $20-50 Million
Number Employees: 50-99
Parent Co: Wonderful Packing LLC
Type of Packaging: Consumer, Food Service, Private Label, Bulk
Brands Exported: Indian River Pride; Ocean Spray
Regions Exported to: Central America, South America, Europe, Asia, Middle East, Worldwide, Australia, Canada, Caribbean
Percentage of Business in Exporting: 35

Brands Imported: Riversun
Regions Imported from: South America, Europe, Australia, Caribbean
Percentage of Business in Importing: 15

43460 DPI Midwest
6800 Santa Fe Dr
Suite E
Hodgkins, IL 60525   708-698-5701
    Fax: 708-588-1326 www.dpispecialtyfoods.com
Distributor of specialty perishable foods from around the world, all natural and all organic, 6,000 items carried.
Chief Executive Officer: Mike Rodrigue
President, Chief Commercial Officer: Russ Blake
Chief Financial Officer: Conor Crowley
VP, Information Technology: Nadia Rosseels
VP, Human Resouces: Kristen Flynn
Chief Operating Officer: Jeff Steiner
Number Employees: 50-99
Parent Co: DPI Specialty Foods
Type of Packaging: Food Service, Private Label
Other Locations:
    DPI Corporate
    Wilmette, IL
    DPI Rock Mountain
    Henderson, CO
    DPI Northwest
    Tualatin, OR
    DPI West
    Ontario, CA
    DPI Southwest
    Albuquerque, NM
    DPI Arizona
    Mesa, AZ
    DPI CorporateHenderson

43461 DSM Fortitech Premixes
2105 Technology Dr
Schenectady, NY 12308-1151
    info@dsm.com
    www.dsm.com
Vitamin and mineral pre mixes, amino acids, nucleotides, nutraceuticals and herbs
VP & CFO: Brian Wilcox
SEVP & Chief Scientific Officer: Ram Chaudhari
Senior QC Specialist: Cindy Grimm
International Project Manager: Dominic Kwiatkowski
Director, Human Resources: Joanne Murphy
Director, Manufacturing: Ed Webster
Purchasing Manager, North America: Thomas Morba
Estimated Sales: K
Number Employees: 10,000+
Square Footage: 68000
Parent Co: DSM
Type of Packaging: Food Service
Other Locations:
    Fortitech
    EuropeFortitechSouth America
Regions Exported to: Central America, South America, Europe, Asia
Percentage of Business in Exporting: 25
Regions Imported from: Central America, South America, Europe, Asia

43462 DSW Converting Knives
1504 8th Avenue N
Birmingham, AL 35203   205-322-2021
    Fax: 205-322-2576
Manufacturer and exporter of machine knives
President: Chris Mc Ilvaine
Estimated Sales: Below $ 5 Million
Number Employees: 10-19
Type of Packaging: Bulk
Regions Exported to: Worldwide

43463 (HQ)DT Industrials
949 S McCord Rd
Holland, OH 43528   567-703-8550
    Fax: 419-866-4656 sales@dtindustrials.com
    dtindustrials-lubricants.com
Food grade oils and greases
Sales & Marketing: Erica Jaspers
Regions Exported to: Worldwide
Percentage of Business in Exporting: 5

43464 DWL Industries Company
65 Industrial Road
Lodi, NJ 07644   973-916-9958
    Fax: 973-916-9959   888-946-2682
    cs@wincous.com www.wincodwl.com

Wholesaler/distributor, importer and exporter of knives, utensils and tableware; serving the food service market
President: David Li
Officer: Jieyui Ding
VP Sales: Steve Chang
Contact: Steven Chu
1and1admin@wincous.com
Number Employees: 15
Square Footage: 40000
Regions Exported to: Central America, South America, Europe, Canada, Caribbean, Latin America
Percentage of Business in Exporting: 5
Brands Imported: Winco
Regions Imported from: Central America, South America, Europe, Korea, China, Canada, Caribbean, Latin America
Percentage of Business in Importing: 5

43465 Dacam Corporation
PO Box 310
Madison Heights, VA 24572-0310   434-929-4001
   Fax: 434-847-4487 www.dacammachinery.com
Manufacturer and exporter of packaging machinery
President: Ed Tolle
Sales And Marketing: Dean Hargis
Director Engineering: David Vaughan
Estimated Sales: $ 2.5-5 Million
Number Employees: 20-49
Square Footage: 80000
Brands Exported: DACAM
Regions Exported to: Central America, South America, Europe
Percentage of Business in Exporting: 10

43466 Dade Engineering
15150 Nighthawk Drive
Tampa, FL 33625   813-264-2273
   Fax: 813-343-8117 800-321-2112
   richard@starsouth.us www.daeco.net
Manufacturer and exporter of walk-in coolers and freezers and cold storage doors
President: Joanne Goodstein
Estimated Sales: $ 5 - 10 Million
Number Employees: 10-19
Square Footage: 80000
Brands Exported: Daeco
Regions Exported to: Worldwide
Percentage of Business in Exporting: 10

43467 Dahl-Tech Inc
5805 Saint Croix Trl N
Stillwater, MN 55082-6593   651-439-2946
   Fax: 651-439-2976 800-626-5812
   daltechinc@qwestoffice.net
   www.dahltechplastics.com
Custom blew molding company and manufacturer of plastic containers, devices, and hollow structures for the food packaging, chemical, automotive, agricultural, healthcare, recreational, and household products industries.
President: Bob Dahlke
bob.dahlke@dahltechplastics.com
Sales: Nichole Blekum
Plant Manager: Brian Hell
Estimated Sales: $5 Million
Number Employees: 50-99
Square Footage: 128000
Type of Packaging: Consumer, Food Service, Private Label, Bulk
Regions Exported to: Canada
Percentage of Business in Exporting: 2

43468 Daily Printing Inc
2333 Niagara Ln N
Plymouth, MN 55447-4712   763-475-2333
   Fax: 763-449-6320 800-622-6596
   info@dailyprinting.com www.dailyprinting.com
Manufacturer and exporter of size reduction equipment for grinding, deagglomerating and pulverizing feeds, foods, spices, etc
President: Pete Jacobson
pjacobson@dailyprinting.com
CFO: Ken Rein
EVP: Don Bergeron
VP of Sales and Marketing: Tom Moe
Estimated Sales: $ 10 - 20 Million
Number Employees: 50-99
Square Footage: 200000
Regions Exported to: Central America, South America, Europe, Asia, Middle East

43469 Daimaru New York Corporation
1114 Avenue of the Americas
Room 2600
New York, NY 10036-7703   212-730-7138
   Fax: 212-840-7645
Importer and exporter of frozen and marinated meat and meat products and agricultural products
VP: Shiro Kazino
Estimated Sales: $1-2.5 Million
Number Employees: 1-4
Parent Co: Daimaru

43470 (HQ)Dairy Conveyor Corp
38 Mount Ebo Rd S
Brewster, NY 10509-4005   845-278-7878
   Fax: 845-278-7305 info@dairyconveyor.com
   www.dairyconveyor.com
Manufacturer and exporter of material handling equipment for dairies and ice cream plants
President: Karl Kleinschrod
CEO: Karl Kleinsahrod
Southeast Regional Sales Manager: Greg Reid
Eastern Regional Sales Manager: Tony Gomez
Estimated Sales: $12 Million
Number Employees: 100-249
Square Footage: 24000
Regions Exported to: Central America, South America

43471 (HQ)Dairy Fresh Foods Inc
21405 Trolley Industrial Dr
Taylor, MI 48180-1811   313-299-0735
   Fax: 313-295-6950
Beverages, cheeses, deli foods and frozen foods; importer of cheese and meats including corned beef and ham; exporter of cheese
Co-President: Alan Must
amust@dairyfreshfoods.com
Co-President: Joel Must
Number Employees: 100-249
Square Footage: 800000
Type of Packaging: Consumer, Food Service, Bulk
Brands Exported: Dairy Fresh
Regions Exported to: Canada
Percentage of Business in Exporting: 10
Regions Imported from: Central America, South America, Europe, Asia
Percentage of Business in Importing: 20

43472 Dairy Specialties
8536 Cartney Ct
Dublin, OH 43017   614-764-1216
   Fax: 614-855-3114 dsibrown@aol.com
Exporter, importer and wholesaler/distributor of milk proteins, flavor producing enzymes and dried dairy ingredients
President: David Brown
d.brown@dsm.com
CEO: V Brown
Estimated Sales: $2 Million
Number Employees: 1-4
Square Footage: 6000
Type of Packaging: Bulk
Brands Exported: DSI; Milei
Regions Exported to: Central America, South America, Europe, Canada
Percentage of Business in Exporting: 50
Brands Imported: Milei; DSI
Regions Imported from: Europe
Percentage of Business in Importing: 90

43473 Dairy State Foods Inc
6035 N Baker Rd
Milwaukee, WI 53209-3701   414-228-1240
   Fax: 414-228-9747 800-435-4499
   sales@dairystatefoods.com
   www.dairystatefoods.com
Manufacturer and exporter of juvenile cookies and animal, oyster crackers, also contract packaging available
President: Larry Rabin
rabin@dairystatefoods.com
Estimated Sales: $1-2.5 Million
Number Employees: 20-49
Square Footage: 120000
Type of Packaging: Consumer, Food Service, Private Label
Brands Exported: Toy Bus Animal Crackers
Regions Exported to: Worldwide

43474 (HQ)Dairy-Mix Inc
3020 46th Ave N
St Petersburg, FL 33714-3863   727-525-6101
   Fax: 727-522-0769 800-955-6101
   ecoryn@dairymix.com www.dairymix.com
Manufacturer and exporter of ice cream, ice milk and milk shake mixes, frozen dessert
President: Edward Coryn
ecoryn@dairymix.com
Corporate VP: John Coryn
Sales/Marketing: Mike Costello
Plant Manager: Jerry Maine
Estimated Sales: $8 Million
Number Employees: 10-19
Type of Packaging: Food Service, Bulk
Regions Exported to: Central America
Percentage of Business in Exporting: 1

43475 DairyAmerica
4974 E Clinton Way
Suite C-121
Fresno, CA 93727   559-251-0992
   Fax: 559-251-1078 800-722-3110
   webmaster@dairyamerica.com
   www.dairyamerica.com
Manufacturer and exporter of milk including low heat, medium heat, high heat, whole and dry buttermilk
President/SVP: Keith Gomes
CEO: Hoyt Huffman
Controller: Jean McAbee
CEO: Rich Lewis
Director Sales/Marketing: Dan Block
International Sales: Steve Gulley
Contact: Craig Alexander
acraig@dairyamerica.com
Operations Manager: Frances Zapanta
Estimated Sales: $1-2,500,000
Number Employees: 20-49
Type of Packaging: Bulk
Other Locations:
   Manufacturing Plant
   Los Banos, CA
   Manufacturing Facility
   Turlock, CA
   Manufacturing Facility
   Visalia, CA
   Manufacturing Facility
   Artesia, CA
   Manufacturing Facility
   Bactavia, NY Manufacturing Plant Turlock
Brands Exported: DairyAmerica, Inc.
Regions Exported to: Central America, South America, Asia, Middle East, Africa, Caribbean
Percentage of Business in Exporting: 30

43476 DairyChem Inc.
9120 Technology Ln
Fishers, IN 46038-2839   317-849-8400
   Fax: 317-849-8213 cservice@dairychem.com
   www.dairychem.com
Manufacturer and exporter of natural dairy flavors including butter, cream, buttermilk, sour cream, cream cheese, cultured dairy, yogurt, milk, starter distillate and starter flavors.
Owner: Grant Church
VP: Diana Church
Sales Manager: Travis McMahan
gchurch@dairychem.com
Operations Manager/Purchasing: Paul Hampton
Estimated Sales: $1 Million
Number Employees: 10-19
Square Footage: 33400
Type of Packaging: Private Label, Bulk
Regions Exported to: Central America, Europe, Asia
Percentage of Business in Exporting: 30

43477 Dairygold
140 Commerce Way
Totowa, NJ 07512-1158   201-604-1516
   Fax: 201-604-1523 800-386-7577
Importer of dairy products, cheese, loin cut lean bacon, sausage (bangers) and pork ribs
Regional Sales Manager: Jeremy Burne
Regional Sales Manager: Claire Donovan
Number Employees: 5-9
Square Footage: 8100
Parent Co: Dairy Gold Cooperative
Type of Packaging: Consumer, Food Service, Private Label, Bulk
Brands Imported: Shannon Tradtional; Galtec; Horlick's Farmhouse; Bally Cashel
Regions Imported from: Europe

Importers & Exporters / A-Z

43478 Dairyland USA Corp
1300 Viele Ave
Bronx, NY 10474-7134   626-465-4200
                          Fax: 718-378-2234
Wholesaler/distributor and importer of groceries, tomatoes, cheeses, olive oil and butter; serving the food service market
President: Christopher Pappas
VP/Treasurer: Dean Facatselis
VP/Secretary: John Pappas
Contact: Brian Adair
brianadair@chefswarehouse.com
Estimated Sales: $20-50 Million
Number Employees: 1-4
Brands Imported: Monini; Spoleto; Teo; Valrhona Chocolate, Decceis Pasta
Regions Imported from: South America, Europe
Percentage of Business in Importing: 20

43479 Daisy Brand
12750 Merit Dr.
Suite 600
Dallas, TX 75251
                          877-292-9830
                          www.daisybrand.com
Sour cream and cottage cheese.
President: David Sokolsky
Director, Human Resources: Julie King
Year Founded: 1917
Estimated Sales: $171 Million
Number Employees: 300
Square Footage: 12000
Type of Packaging: Consumer, Food Service, Private Label, Bulk
Regions Exported to: Europe, Asia, Mexico

43480 Dakota Specialty Milling, Inc.
4014 15th Ave N
Fargo, ND 58102-2833
                          844-633-2746
              sales@dakotaspecialtymilling.com
              www.dakotaspecialtymilling.com
Producer of grain-based mixes and ingredients.
President: Peter Matthaei
Vice President of Sales & Marketing: Brian Andrews
Senior Director of Sales: Richard Karnemaat
Manager of Customer Logistics: Bernadine King
Director of Milling Operations: Brian Sorenson
bsorenson@dakotaspecialtymilling.com
Director of Technical Services: Bob Meyer
VP of Engineering & Manufacturing: Daryl Bashor
Estimated Sales: $15,000,000
Number Employees: 50-99
Type of Packaging: Consumer, Food Service, Private Label, Bulk
Regions Exported to: Asia, Canada, Mexico
Percentage of Business in Exporting: 3

43481 Dal-Don Produce
PO Box 29
Oldsmar, FL 34677-0029   352-394-2161
                          Fax: 352-394-0517 800-874-9059
Importer, exporter and wholesaler/distributor of watermelons
Regions Exported to: Canada, Caribbean
Percentage of Business in Exporting: 1
Regions Imported from: Central America, Mexico
Percentage of Business in Importing: 5

43482 Dalemark Industries
575 Prospect St
Bldg. 211
Lakewood, NJ 08701-5040   732-367-3100
         Fax: 732-367-7031 sales@dalemark.com
                           www.dalemark.com
Manufacturer and exporter of coding, imprinting and labeling equipment
President: Michael Delli Gatti
CFO: Kathy Scalzo
Research & Development: Thurman Becker
Marketing: Maria Rau
Sales: Maria Rau
Purchasing: Maria Rau
Estimated Sales: $1 Million
Number Employees: 10-19
Number of Brands: 15
Number of Products: 25
Square Footage: 24000
Type of Packaging: Food Service
Regions Exported to: Europe, Asia
Regions Imported from: Europe, Asia
Percentage of Business in Importing: 100

43483 Daley Brothers ltd.
215 Water Street, Suite 301
St John's, NL A1C 6C9
Canada   709-364-8844
                          Fax: 709-364-7216
Manufacturer and exporter of fresh and frozen seafood
President: Terry Daley
CEO: Steve Hoskins
Sales Manager: Rosemary Buckingham
Number Employees: 20-49
Type of Packaging: Bulk
Regions Exported to: Worldwide

43484 Dallas Group of America Inc
374 US Highway 22
Whitehouse, NJ 08888-9800 908-534-7800
          Fax: 908-534-0084 800-367-4188
                            info@dallasgrp.com
Magnesium silicate, frying oil purifiers, filter aids and absorbents; exporter of magnesium silicate
Owner: Bob Dallas Sr
Estimated Sales: $ 10-20,000,000
Number Employees: 20-49
Type of Packaging: Food Service, Bulk
Brands Exported: Magnesol; Dalsorb
Regions Exported to: Worldwide

43485 (HQ)Dalmatian Bay Wine Company
1384 E 40th St
Cleveland, OH 44103-1102 216-391-1717
                          Fax: 216-391-6315
Wholesaler/distributor and importer of wine, coffee, specialty foods, groceries, general merchandise and private label items
President: Barry Martinis
VP: Tina Martinis
Sales Manager: Pete Milicevic
Estimated Sales: USD $8,016,000
Number Employees: 10-19
Square Footage: 40000

43486 (HQ)Damafro, Inc
54 Rue Principale
Saint Damase, QC J0H 1J0
Canada   450-797-3301
            Fax: 450-797-3507 800-363-2017
Export broker of dairy products: Brie, Camembert, Goat milk cheese, Kosher cheese, flavoured brie, etc.
President: Michel Bonnet
Chairman: Philippe Bonnet
Quality Assurance Manager: Chantal Goyette
Marketing Manager: Philippe Guerineau
VP Sales: Heiko Kastner
Controller: Denise Labrecque
Customer Service: Anick Boivin
Plant Manager: Andre Hache
Number Employees: 1-4
Other Locations:
   DAMAFRO
   Montreal, PQDAMAFRO

43487 Damas Corporation
1977 N Olden Avenue Ext
Suite 289
Trenton, NJ 08618-2112   609-695-9121
                          Fax: 609-695-9225
Manufacturer and exporter of washing and drying equipment for laboratory glassware, trays, tote bins, tubs, pallets and carts
President: David M Smith
Engineer: Dave Smith
Estimated Sales: $1-2,500,000
Number Employees: 5-9
Regions Exported to: Central America, Caribbean
Percentage of Business in Exporting: 1

43488 Damp Rid
W.M. Barr
P.O. Box 1879
Memphis, TN 38101-6948   407-851-6230
          Fax: 407-851-6246 888-326-7743
                            www.damprid.com
Manufacturer and exporter of mildew preventatives, moisture absorbers and odor eliminators
President: Darien Jalka
CFO: Ken Lasseter
Quality Control: Oliver Cunanan
Sales Director: Darin Galka
Purchasing Manager: Roy Rosado
Estimated Sales: $5-10 Million
Number Employees: 10
Square Footage: 288000
Parent Co: Tetra Technologies Incorporated
Type of Packaging: Consumer
Brands Exported: Damp Rid; Fresh-All; Magic Disk
Regions Exported to: Central America, South America, Asia, Middle East, Australia, Carribean
Percentage of Business in Exporting: 5

43489 Damrow Company
894 S Military Rd
Fond Du Lac, WI 54935   920-922-1500
          Fax: 920-922-1502 800-236-1501
Dairy and food processing equipment including cheese making, automated control systems, process and storage tanks, evaporators, CIP systems and process piping; exporter of cheese making equipment
Manager: Gary Ring
Sales Director: Mark Steffens
Operations: Todd Martin
Estimated Sales: $ 10 - 20 Million
Number Employees: 5-9
Square Footage: 300000
Parent Co: Carlisle Process Systems

43490 Dan-D Foods Ltd
11760 Machrina Way
Richmond, BC V7A 4V1
Canada   604-274-3263
          Fax: 604-274-3268 800-633-4788
                            www.dan-d-pak.com
Fine food importer, manufacturer and distributor of cashews, dried fruits, rice crackers, snack foods, spices etc. from around the world.
Chairman/President/CEO/Founder: Dan On
Number Employees: 500
Type of Packaging: Food Service, Bulk

43491 Dana-Lu Imports
280 N Midland Ave Ste 414
Saddle Brook, NJ 07663   201-791-2244
                          Fax: 201-791-2288
Importer and wholesaler/distributor of CMA espresso machines and grinders
President: Dana Rafferty
Sales: Maryann Tomko
Sales: Elaine Molnar
Number Employees: 10-19
Square Footage: 70000
Brands Imported: Linea Scanno; Rancilio; Solis; Rotel
Regions Imported from: Europe

43492 (HQ)Danafilms Inc
5 Otis St
Westborough, MA 01581-3311 508-366-8884
          Fax: 508-898-0106 www.danafilms.com
Manufacturer and exporter of polyethylene films for packaging.
President: Sherman Olson
solson@danafilms.com
VP Sales: Bob Simoncini
Marketing Director: Steve Crimmin
Sales Manager: Steve Crimmin
General Manager: Alan Simoncini
Purchasing Manager: Alan Simoncini
Estimated Sales: $20-30 Million
Number Employees: 50-99
Square Footage: 40000
Type of Packaging: Consumer, Food Service, Private Label, Bulk
Other Locations:
   Danafilms
   Hopedale, MADanafilms
Regions Exported to: Central America, Caribbean
Percentage of Business in Exporting: 1

43493 Danbury Plastics
239 Castleberry Industrial Dr
Cumming, GA 30040-9051   678-455-7391
         Fax: 203-790-6801 info@danburyplastics.com
                           www.danburyplastics.com
Manufacturer, importer and exporter of compression and injection molded bottle caps as well as linings and gaskets
President: Michael Da Cruz
Quality Control: Diana Cepada
Sales: Donna Dyke
Plant Manager: Rocco Grosse

Estimated Sales: $2.5-5 Million
Number Employees: 10-19
Square Footage: 18000
Type of Packaging: Consumer, Private Label
Regions Exported to: Europe, Middle East
Percentage of Business in Exporting: 5
Regions Imported from: Europe
Percentage of Business in Importing: 3

43494 Dangold Inc
13843 78th Rd
Flushing, NY 11367-3241   718-591-5286
   Fax: 718-591-5193   www.dangoldinc.com
Snacks, cookies, crackers, wafers, chocolates, biscuits
President: Dan Gross
Estimated Sales: Less Than $500,000
Number Employees: 1-4

43495 Daniele Inc
105 Davis Dr
Pascoag, RI 02859-3507   401-568-6228
   Fax: 401-568-4788   800-451-2535
   www.danielefoods.com
Manufacturer of dry-cured delicacies and other gourmet Italian products.
Co-Owner: Stefano Dukcevich
Co-Owner: Davide Dukcevich
Number Employees: 50-99
Regions Exported to: South America, Asia, Canada

43496 Daniele International
49 Cadwell Dr
Springfield, MA 01104-1703   413-731-8805
   Fax: 413-731-8904
Importer of Italian foods including anchovies, pasta, olive oil, balsamic vinegar, cookies, plum tomatoes, candies; manufacturer of gift baskets for corporate accounts
President: Frank Daniele
Estimated Sales: $ 3 - 5 Million
Number Employees: 5-9
Brands Imported: Daniele; Carmela; Domenico
Regions Imported from: Europe
Percentage of Business in Importing: 100

43497 Dannon Yo Cream
5858 NE 87th Ave
Portland, OR 97220
   800-962-7326
   info@yocream.com   www.yocream.com
Frozen dessert, snacks and beverages
CFO: W. Douglas Caudell
Estimated Sales: $70 Million
Number Employees: 100-249
Number of Brands: 4
Parent Co: The Dannon Company
Type of Packaging: Consumer, Food Service, Private Label, Bulk
Percentage of Business in Exporting: 5

43498 Daprano & Co
1930 Center Park Dr # A
Charlotte, NC 28217-2918   704-927-0590
   Fax: 704-927-0591   877-365-2337
   sales@daprano.com   www.sidari.us
Importer of Italian confections
Owner: Mick Sidari
sales@daprano.com
Estimated Sales: $ 5 - 10 Million
Number Employees: 5-9
Regions Imported from: Europe, Asia
Percentage of Business in Importing: 100

43499 Darcor Casters
7 Staffordshire Place
Toronto, ON M8W 1T1
Canada   416-255-8563
   Fax: 416-251-6117   800-387-7206
   casters@darcor.com   www.darcor.com
Manufacturer and exporter of casters and wheels
President: Rob Hilborn
Controller: Dan Watson
Engineering Manager: Adrian Steenson
Director of Marketing: Kirk Tobias
Number Employees: 75
Square Footage: 320000
Parent Co: Darcor Casters
Brands Exported: Darcor
Regions Exported to: Worldwide
Percentage of Business in Exporting: 5

43500 Dare Foods
3750 N. Blackstock Rd
Spartanburg, SC 29303   781-639-1808
   Fax: 781-639-2286   800-668-3273
   www.darefoods.com
Cookies, candies and crackers; also, ground cookie ingredients
National Sales Manager: Neil S Voutt
Number Employees: 60
Type of Packaging: Bulk
Regions Exported to: Worldwide

43501 Darik Enterprises Inc
1999 Marcus Ave # 212
New Hyde Park, NY 11042-1021   516-355-7400
   Fax: 516-775-1507   www.shrimppeople.com
Importer of frozen shrimp
Contact: Bob Mctammany
bob@shrimppeople.com
Estimated Sales: $ 3 - 5 Million
Number Employees: 5-9
Square Footage: 80000
Brands Imported: Pearl Island; Julie; Diamond; Marian Sea; Capi Baidal; Sea Breeze; Vagabundo; AAA; Locket
Regions Imported from: Central America, South America, Asia
Percentage of Business in Importing: 100

43502 Darisil
15 Campbell Avenue
Suffern, NY 10901-6301   845-357-2740
   Fax: 845-357-1966
Wholesaler/distributor and exporter of grain, rice, dairy products, dry beans, peas, potatoes, poultry, etc
President: Joseph Silver
VP: William Stewart
VP: Richard Silver
Estimated Sales: Less than $500,000
Number Employees: 1-4
Square Footage: 20000
Brands Exported: Beauty Queen; Atlas
Regions Exported to: Central America, South America, Europe, Asia, Middle East, Africa
Percentage of Business in Exporting: 75

43503 Dark Tickle Company
75 Main St.
PO Box 160
St Lunaire-Griquet, NL A0K 2X0
Canada   709-623-2354
   Fax: 709-623-2354   www.darktickle.com
Wild berry jams, toppings, beverage concentrate, relish and vinegars
President: Stephen Knudsen
Number Employees: 5-9
Square Footage: 5000
Type of Packaging: Consumer
Brands Exported: Dark Tickle
Regions Exported to: Europe, Asia, Canada
Percentage of Business in Exporting: 5

43504 Darnell-Rose Inc
17915 Railroad St
City Of Industry, CA 91748-1113   626-912-1688
   Fax: 626-912-3765   800-327-6355
   www.casters.com
Manufacturer and exporter of casters and wheels, including stainless steel models and other mobility products
President: Brent Bargar
bbargar@casters.com
Research & Development: Bob Siegried
Quality Control: Phil Mazzolini
Marketing Director: Brent Bargar
Sales Director: Bob Siegried
Operations Manager: Richard Martinez
Purchasing Manager: Robbie McCullah
Estimated Sales: $10-20 Million
Number Employees: 50-99
Square Footage: 170000
Type of Packaging: Food Service, Bulk
Regions Exported to: Central America, Europe, Asia, Middle East
Percentage of Business in Exporting: 10

43505 Dart Container Corp.
500 Hogsback Rd.
Mason, MI 48854
   Fax: 517-676-3883   800-248-5960
   sales@dart.biz   www.dartcontainer.com
Disposable tabletop supplies including foam cups, containers and lids, plastic cups and lids, fusion cups, foam plastic dinnerware, foam hinged lid containers, clear containers, portion containers and lids, and plastic cutlery.
President: Jim Lammers
Executive VP/CFO: Christine Waltz
Executive VP, Sales: Robert Novak
Year Founded: 1960
Estimated Sales: Over $1 Billion
Number Employees: 15,000
Number of Brands: 37
Brands Exported: Dart
Regions Exported to: Central America, South America, Europe, Asia, Middle East, Caribbean, Latin America, Mexico

43506 Dashco
17 Westpark Drive
Gloucester, ON K1B 3G6
Canada   613-834-6825
   Fax: 613-834-6826
Manufacturer and exporter of degradable plastic carry-out/check-out bags
President: Dave Paul
Number Employees: 2
Brands Exported: Dashco
Regions Exported to: Worldwide
Percentage of Business in Exporting: 50

43507 (HQ)Datapaq
187 Ballardvale St
Wilmington, MA 01887-1082   978-988-9000
   Fax: 978-988-0666   800-326-5270
   websales@datapaq.com   www.datapaq.com
Monitors the temperature profiles of a food product as it passes through continuous cook, bake, chill, freeze, and fry processes. A Datapaq system is comprised of four major components: a data logger, a protective thermal barrier toprotect the logger, thermocouple probes, and easy-to-use software to analyze and store temperature data collected during a process. Detailed graphical information gives a complete picture of the continuous process
President: Michael E White
Marketing Director: Kathleen Higgins
Sales Director: Bill Adaschik
Contact: D Abbrat
abbrat@datapaq.com
Estimated Sales: $5-10 Million
Number Employees: 10-19
Square Footage: 19200
Other Locations:
   Datapaq
   CambridgeDatapaq
Brands Exported: Datapaq
Regions Exported to: Central America, South America

43508 Davenport Machine
301 Second St
PO Box 6635
Rock Island, IL 61201   309-786-1500
   Fax: 309-786-0771
Manufacturer and exporter of rotary dryers and coolers, foundry equipment and continuous dewatering presses
President: R Nixon Jr
General Sales Manager: Lauren Reimer
Chief Engineer: R Bateman
Estimated Sales: $ 5-10 Million
Number Employees: 20-50
Square Footage: 172000
Parent Co: Middle States Corporation
Brands Exported: Davenport
Regions Exported to: Central America, South America, Europe, Asia
Percentage of Business in Exporting: 15

43509 David Food Processing Equipment, Inc.
52 Carrier Drive
Unit 14
Rexdale, ON M9W 5R1
Canada   416-675-5566
   Fax: 416-675-7431   800-461-3058
   info@davidfoodprocessing.com
   www.davidfoodprocessing.com
Wholesaler/distributor and importer of food processing equipment including meat slicers, patty machines, sausage stuffers, etc
President: W Butcher
Number Employees: 5-9
Square Footage: 22400

Brands Imported: Hollymatic; Henkovac; Talsa; Globe; Old Hickory

43510 David's Cookies
11 Cliffside Dr
Cedar Grove, NJ 07009
800-500-2800
custserv@davidscookies.com
www.davidscookies.com
Thaw and serve tarts, layer cakes and single serve desserts, cookies, cookie dough, scones, crumbcake, rugalach, butter cookies, brownies and mini-muffins
President: Ari Margulies
Vice President: Michael Zuckerman
Year Founded: 1979
Estimated Sales: $90 Million+
Number Employees: 350
Number of Brands: 2
Square Footage: 160000
Parent Co: Fairfield Gourmet Foods Corp.
Type of Packaging: Consumer, Food Service
Brands Exported: David's Cookies
Regions Exported to: Worldwide
Percentage of Business in Exporting: 5

43511 David's Goodbatter
PO Box 102
Bausman, PA 17504-0102   717-872-0652
                Fax: 717-872-8152
Processor, packager and exporter of organic pancakes and baking mixes, pasta, couscous, Irish oatmeal, dried beans, bean blends and gluten-free and wheat-free foods; importer of maple candies and syrup; also, custom packaging and private labeling available
Owner: Jane David
Estimated Sales: $1-2.5 Million appx.
Number Employees: 1-4
Square Footage: 52000
Type of Packaging: Consumer, Food Service, Private Label, Bulk
Brands Exported: David's Goodbatter; Gabriel & Rose
Regions Exported to: Canada
Percentage of Business in Exporting: 15
Brands Imported: Jakemans Maple Products
Regions Imported from: Europe, Canada
Percentage of Business in Importing: 2

43512 Davidson's Organics
PO Box 11214
Reno, NV 89510-1214   775-356-1690
        Fax: 775-356-3713 800-882-5888
                www.davidsonstea.com
Teas, herbs, cocoa, spices, and accessories for the specialty trade and retail use
Estimated Sales: $5-10 Million
Number Employees: 10-19
Square Footage: 50000
Brands Exported: Davidson's
Regions Exported to: Canada
Percentage of Business in Exporting: 2
Regions Imported from: Asia
Percentage of Business in Importing: 10

43513 Davis & Small Decor
1888 Clements Ferry Rd
Charleston, SC 29492   843-881-8990
        Fax: 800-227-7398 800-849-5082
                orders@dsdecor.com
Manufacturer and exporter of decorative wall items for restaurants
President: Thomas M Davis
Estimated Sales: $3 - 5 Million
Number Employees: 20-49
Regions Exported to: Worldwide

43514 Davis Strait Fisheries
71 McQuade Lake Crescent
Halifax, NS B3S 1C4
Canada   902-450-5115
    Fax: 902-450-5006 john@davisstrait.com
Seafood products such as northern shrimp, scallops, clams, cod, haddock, and pollack fish
President: Grant Stonehouse
Marketing Director: John Andrews
Operations Manager: Grant Stonehouse
Year Founded: 1991
Estimated Sales: $32 Million
Number Employees: 82
Type of Packaging: Bulk
Brands Exported: Fisher King; Davis Strait
Regions Exported to: Europe, Asia, USA

Percentage of Business in Exporting: 66
Regions Imported from: Europe, Asia, U.S.A.
Percentage of Business in Importing: 22

43515 Davis Trade & Commodities
515 S. Flower Street
36th Floor
Los Angeles, CA 90071   323-595-5317
          Fax: 323-389-0501 info@dtcint.com
                  www.dtcint.com
International traders of US origin agricultural and food products.
Owner: William Davis
Estimated Sales: $ 4 Million
Number Employees: 10-19
Number of Products: 30
Type of Packaging: Food Service, Private Label, Bulk
Brands Exported: Wheat; Soybeans; Sorghum; Barley; Fruits; Vegetables; Grains; Oilseeds; Nuts And Sweeteners
Regions Exported to: Central America, South America, Europe, Asia, Middle East, North American
Brands Imported: Food By-Products
Regions Imported from: Central America, South America, Asia

43516 Davlynne International
3383 E Layton Ave Stop 3
Cudahy, WI 53110   414-481-1011
        Fax: 414-481-3155 800-558-5208
Manufacturer and exporter of strip curtains and doors, custom cart covers and enclosures
President: Kristin Larson
CEO: Randall Larson
Marketing Director: Krista Larson
Estimated Sales: $ 2.5-5 Million
Number Employees: 7
Square Footage: 13000
Regions Exported to: Middle East, Canada, Mexico
Percentage of Business in Exporting: 5

43517 Davron Technologies Inc
4563 Pinnacle Ln
Chattanooga, TN 37415-3811   423-870-1888
      Fax: 423-870-1108 sales@davrontech.com
                www.davrontech.com
Manufacturer and exporter of all types of custom process equipment including, but not limited to, ovens, conveying systems, washing systems and frying systems
President: Ronald Speicher
Director Sales/Marketing: Jimmy Evans
Contact: Bobby Bishop
bbishop@davrontech.com
Equipment Design Manager: David Craft
Estimated Sales: $ 10 - 20 Million
Number Employees: 50-99
Regions Exported to: Brazil, Spain, Mexico, Puerto Rico

43518 Dawes Hill Honey Company
12 S State St
Po Box 429
Nunda, NY 14517   585-468-2535
        Fax: 585-468-5995 888-800-8075
                info@onceagainnutbutter.com
                www.onceagainnutbutter.com
Honey, royal jelly and fruit honey cream spread
Owner: Sandi Alexander
Comptroller: Sandra Alexander
Purchasing Agent: Lloyd Kirwan
Estimated Sales: $10-20 Million
Number Employees: 10-19
Square Footage: 40000
Parent Co: Once Again Nut Butter
Type of Packaging: Consumer, Private Label, Bulk
Brands Exported: Dawes Hill
Regions Exported to: Asia, Canada
Percentage of Business in Exporting: 15
Regions Imported from: Central America, South America, Canada
Percentage of Business in Importing: 25

43519 Day & Ross Transportation Group
398 Main Street
Hartland, NB E7P 1C6
Canada   506-375-4401
                 800-561-0013
custservice@dayandrossinc.ca www.dayross.com

National transportation with 40 terminals across 10 Canadian provinces; Provides LTL, TL, temperature-controlled, specialized transportation, flatbed, and cross-border services
President, Day & Ross Freight: Doug Tingley
President/CEO: Bill Doherty
VP Pricing & Administration: Tony Crann
SVP Sales & Marketing: Bruce Morin
Director Human Resources: Janet Fidgen
VP Linehaul Operations: Frank MacIntyre
VP Terminals: Shawn Browne
Number Employees: 1000-4999
Parent Co: McCain Foods Ltd.
Regions Exported to: Worldwide
Percentage of Business in Exporting: 75

43520 Day Spring Enterprises
45 Benbro Dr
Cheektowaga, NY 14225-4805   716-685-4340
        Fax: 716-685-0810 800-879-7677
                www.rainbowpops.com
Hard candy and lollypops; also, seasonal items available
President: Linda Zangerie
Sales Manager: Jeff Baran
Plant Manager: George Sparks
Estimated Sales: $50,000
Number Employees: 1
Square Footage: 32000
Type of Packaging: Consumer, Food Service, Private Label, Bulk
Regions Exported to: Europe, Canada
Percentage of Business in Exporting: 20

43521 Daydots
1801 Riverbend West Dr
Fort Worth, TX 76118   817-590-4500
        Fax: 817-590-4501 800-321-3687
                sales@daydots.com www.daydots.com
A goal of making the world a safer place to eat. Daydots offers more than 4,000 products and services including original day of the week food safety labels. Produce and distribute products for food rotation, temperature control; cross-contamination prevention; personal hygiene and sanitation and cleaning, employee safety and food safety education.
President/Owner: Mark Smith
Marketing: Paul McGinnis
Sales: Laura Manatis
Contact: Shawn Blazuir
shawnb@daydots.com
Operations: Chad Logan
Number Employees: 50-99
Number of Products: 4000
Square Footage: 200000
Type of Packaging: Food Service, Private Label
Brands Exported: Daydots
Regions Exported to: Europe
Percentage of Business in Exporting: 2

43522 Daymark Safety Systems
12830 S Dixie Hwy
Bowling Green, OH 43402-9697   419-353-2458
        Fax: 419-354-0514 corgan@daymarklabel.com
                www.daymarksafety.com
Manufacturer, importer and exporter of dissolve-a-way food labels, coding, dating and marking equipment, label applicators and food rotation systems
VP/General Manager: Jeff Palmer
jpalmer@daymarsafety.com
Estimated Sales: $ 1 - 3 Million
Number Employees: 5-9
Square Footage: 172000
Parent Co: CMC Group
Brands Exported: Dissolve-A-Way®; DayMark®
Regions Exported to: Central America, South America, Europe, Australia

43523 Daymark Safety Systems
12830 S Dixie Hwy
Bowling Green, OH 43402-9697   419-353-2458
                                   800-847-0101
                www.daymarksafety.com
President: Jeff Palmer
jpalmer@daymarsafety.com
Estimated Sales: $ 1 - 3 Million
Number Employees: 5-9

43524 Daystar Desserts LLC
10440 Leadbetter Rd
Ashland, VA 23005-3415   804-550-7660
                Fax: 804-550-7662
Manager: John Fernandez

Estimated Sales: $ 5 - 10 Million
Number Employees: 100-249

43525 Dayton Bag & Burlap Co
322 Davis Ave
Dayton, OH 45403-2900   937-258-8000
         Fax: 937-258-0029 800-543-3400
         info1@daybag.com www.daybag.com
Manufacturer and exporter of bags including burlap, feed, grain, greaseproof, paper, paper lined, plastic and polypropylene for shipping commodities
President: Samuel Lumby
slumby@daybag.com
VP Marketing: Sue Spiegel
Industrial Sales Manager: Sue Spiegel
Customer Service: Delilah Oda
Estimated Sales: $ 1 - 3 Million
Number Employees: 100-249
Square Footage: 150000
Type of Packaging: Bulk
Regions Exported to: Worldwide

43526 De Boer Food Importers
P.O.Box 953846
Lake Mary, FL 32795-3846
         Fax: 407-322-1815 800-762-9660
                           www.deboerfood.com
Importer of Holland toast, rye bread, crackers, biscuits, cookies, spreads, mustard and peppermint
President: Evert De Boer
Estimated Sales: $ 1 - 3 Million
Number Employees: 5-9
Brands Imported: Van der Muilen; Hellema; Jaka; BZZ; Marne; Fortuin
Regions Imported from: Holland
Percentage of Business in Importing: 100

43527 De Bruyn Produce Company
709 NW 12th Ter
Ponpano Beach, FL 33069-2041   954-788-6707
         Fax: 954-788-6340 800-733-9177
Onions an carrots
President: Margret DeBruyn
CEO: Mike Diaz
EVP: Ralph Diaz
Sales/Marketing: Betty Aquire
Operations Manager: Kevin Hubbard
Type of Packaging: Consumer, Food Service
Other Locations:
  Cooling And Manufacturing Plant
  Byron Center, MI
  Carrot Manufacturing Plant
  Weslaco, TX
  Onion Manufacturing Plant
  Farmersville, TX
  Vegetable Cooling Plant
  Tifton, GA
  Spanish Onion Manufacturing
  Ontario, ORCooling And Manufacturing
  PlantWeslaco
Regions Exported to: Worldwide

43528 De Choix Specialty Foods Company
5825 52nd Avenue
Woodside, NY 11377-7402   718-507-8080
         Fax: 718-335-9150 800-332-4649
                           dechoix@dechoix.com
Wholesaler/distributor and importer of specialty cheeses, chocolates, vanilla, vinegar, spices, mustards, smoked fish, dried fruits, herring, coffees, teas, grains, salami, prosciutto, preserves, fruit purees, olives, olive oilcaviar, nuts and pate
President: Gene Kaplan
CEO: Henry Kaplan
Executive VP: Bob Bruno
Number Employees: 20-49
Square Footage: 142000
Brands Imported: Callebaut; Amazon; San Pietro; Brezzi; Nielsen Massey; Pidy; Sicoly; Ticino; Campagne; Castellino; De Zaan; Fabbri; La Gentile; Cruzilles; Primolio; Lanfranco; Beaufor; Biassac
Regions Imported from: Europe, Asia, Canada
Percentage of Business in Importing: 80

43529 De Coty Coffee Co
1920 Austin St
San Angelo, TX 76903-8704   325-655-5607
         Fax: 325-655-6837 800-588-8001
         eric@decoty.com www.decoty.com
Importer, Roaster, & Distributor of coffe. Manufacturer of coffee, tea, spices & seasonings.
CEO/President: Michael Agan
agan@decoty.com
Sales/Marketing: Bryan Baker
Operations: Ronnie Wallace
Production Manager: Eric Fischer
Purchasing: Teresa Rocha
Estimated Sales: $12 Million
Number Employees: 50-99
Square Footage: 50000
Type of Packaging: Food Service, Private Label, Bulk
Regions Imported from: Worldwide
Percentage of Business in Importing: 80

43530 De Laval
11100 N Congress Ave
Kansas City, MO 64153-1222   816-891-7700
                      Fax: 816-891-1606
                 www.delavalcleaningsolutions.com
Manufacturer and suppliers of cleaning and sanitizing products for the dairy, food, and beverage processing industies.
Number Employees: 100-249
Regions Exported to: North America

43531 De Leone Corp
1258 SW Lake Rd
Redmond, OR 97756-8611   541-504-3311
         Fax: 541-504-8411 sam@deleone.com
                            www.cascadelabel.com
Manufacturer and exporter of pressure sensitive and custom labels; wholesaler/distributor of label dispensers
President: Samuel A DE Leone
steve@deleone.com
General Manager: David Hawes
Sales Director: Diana Jibiden
Estimated Sales: $5-10 Million
Number Employees: 20-49
Regions Exported to: Worldwide
Percentage of Business in Exporting: 10

43532 De Medici Imports
One Atlantic Plaza
Elizabeth, NJ 07206   908-372-0965
         Fax: 908-372-0960 info@demedici.com
                            www.demedici.com
Oils, teas, rice, pastas, olives, vinegars, sea salts, chocolates, condiments, dulce de leche
Ceo: George Gellert
Cfo: Bernard Lillis
Marketing: Steve Kaufman
Contact: Robert Gellert
robert.gellert@demedici.com
Number Employees: 7

43533 De Ster Corporation
225 Peachtree Street
Suite 400
Atlanta, GA 30303-1727   404-659-9100
         Fax: 404-659-5116 800-237-8270
         info@dester.com www.dester.com
Manufacturer, importer and exporter of disposable and reusable trays, plates, flatware, containers, cups and cutlery
Executive VP: Gerrit de Kiewit
Director Marketing/Development: John Squire
Senior VP Sales: Dan Whitehead
Estimated Sales: $ 5-10 Million
Number Employees: 150-200
Square Footage: 640000
Parent Co: De Ster Holding BV
Type of Packaging: Consumer, Food Service, Private Label, Bulk
Regions Exported to: Central America, South America, Europe, Canada, Mexico, Caribbean, Latin America
Percentage of Business in Exporting: 25
Regions Imported from: Europe, Asia
Percentage of Business in Importing: 18

43534 DeLallo Foods
1 DeLallo Way
Mount Pleasant, PA 15666
                           877-355-2556
                           www.delallo.com
Organic pasta, sauces and olive oil
VP: Anthony DiPietro
Operations: Jeff Latimer

43535 DeLima Coffee
7546 Morgan Rd
Liverpool, NY 13090   315-457-3725
         Fax: 315-457-3730 800-962-8864
         info@delimacoffee.com www.delimacoffee.com
Coffee
Principle: Paul Lima
President: Michael Garlick
CFO: Steve Zaremba
Vice President Sales: Donald Hughes
dhughes@delimacoffee.com
VP Human Resources: Peter Sansone
Purchasing Agent: Lisa Priest
Type of Packaging: Consumer, Food Service

43536 DeMedici Imports
1 Atalanta Plaza
Elizabeth, NY 7206   908-372-0965
         Fax: 908-372-0960 info@demedici.com
                            www.demedici.com
Gourmet specialty foods
President: Paul Farber
Estimated Sales: $1-2.5 Million
Number Employees: 1-4
Parent Co: DeMedici Imports

43537 DeVries Imports
16700 Schoenborn Street
North Hills, CA 91343-6108   818-893-6906
                      Fax: 818-893-9446
Wholesaler/distributor and importer of specialty foods and confectionery products including candy and chocolates; also, basket supplies including wrap, bows, etc
President/Owner: Hugh DeVries
VP/Owner: Louise DeVries
Estimated Sales: $2.5-5 Million
Number Employees: 10-19
Square Footage: 52000
Type of Packaging: Consumer, Private Label
Brands Imported: Lindt; Tobler; Ferraro; Carr's, Twining, Ghirardelli
Regions Imported from: Europe, Asia

43538 Dealers Food Products Co
23800 Commerce Park # D
Cleveland, OH 44122-5828   216-292-6666
         Fax: 216-292-4600 www.dealersfoods.com
Wholesaler/distributor, exporter and importer of milk powders, cheese powders, flavors, snack food seasonings, industrial ingredients, candy canes, lollypops, caramels, energy candy, cough drops, wrapped hard candy and dehydratedpotato products
President: Bob Glaser
bob@dealersfoods.com
Export Manager: Dennis Krall
Estimated Sales: $2.5-5 Million
Number Employees: 1-4
Square Footage: 8000
Type of Packaging: Consumer, Food Service, Private Label, Bulk
Regions Exported to: Central America, South America, Europe, Asia, Middle East
Percentage of Business in Exporting: 75

43539 Dean Industries
14501 S Broadway
Gardena, CA 90248   310-353-5000
         Fax: 310-327-3343 800-995-1210
                            salesmkt@frymaster.com
Manufacturer and exporter of fryer baskets and deep fat fryers
Owner: Jimmy Dean
General Manager: Al Cote
Estimated Sales: $300,000-500,000
Number Employees: 1-4
Parent Co: ENODIS
Percentage of Business in Exporting: 10

43540 Dearborn Mid-West Conveyor Co
8245 Nieman Rd # 123
Overland Park, KS 66214-1509   913-384-9950
                      Fax: 913-261-2470
Manufacturer and exporter of material handling systems including conveyors, palletizers and palletizing systems
President, CEO: Tony Rosati
Executive VP: Sudy Ohra
sudyv@dmwcc.com
Manager of Sales: Gerry Cohen
Number Employees: 20-49

Importers & Exporters / A-Z

43541 Debaudringhien Inc.
1724 Hollybrook Avenue
Po Box 551103
Gastonia, NC 28054-1318   704-671-2436
  Fax: 704-671-2615 wim@debaudringhien.com
Contact: Wim Debaudringhien
wim@debaudringhien.com

43542 Deboer Food Importers
PO Box 953846
Lake Mary, FL 32795-3846
  Fax: 407-322-1815 800-762-9660
Importers of biscuits, chocolates, cookies and mustards
President: Evert De Boer
Estimated Sales: $5-9.9 Million
Number Employees: 5-9
Type of Packaging: Private Label

43543 Decartes Systems Group
120 Randall Drive
Waterloo, ON N2V 1C6
Canada   519-746-8110
  Fax: 519-747-0082 info@descartes.com
    www.descartes.com
Computer accounting systems for the dairy, beverage and food industries
Executive Vice President of Information: Raimond Diederik
Regional Manager: Rick Spencer
Estimated Sales: $ 1 - 5 Million
Type of Packaging: Bulk
Regions Exported to: USA, Europe
Percentage of Business in Exporting: 70

43544 Decko Products Inc
2105 Superior St
Sandusky, OH 44870-1891   419-626-5757
  Fax: 419-626-3135 800-537-6143
    shumphrey@decko.com www.decko.com
Edible cake and candy decorations and packaged rings, gels
President: F William Niggemyer
Marketing Director: Sara Humphrey
Estimated Sales: $10 Million
Number Employees: 50-99
Square Footage: 105000
Type of Packaging: Private Label
Brands Exported: Private Label
Regions Exported to: Europe

43545 Dedert Corporation
20000 Governors Dr # 3
Olympia Fields, IL 60461-1034   708-747-7000
  Fax: 708-755-8815 info@dedert.com
    www.anhydro.com
Manufacturer and exporter of evaporators, filters, centrifuges and liquid/solid separation equipment; importer of filters, liquid/solid separation equipment and centrifuges
President: Guy Lonergan
Marketing Director: John Ruhl
Contact: Pat Baumgartner
p.baumgartner@dedert.com
Estimated Sales: $20-50 Million
Number Employees: 20-49
Brands Exported: Dedert
Regions Exported to: Worldwide
Percentage of Business in Exporting: 30
Brands Imported: Vetter; Gouda; Reineveld
Regions Imported from: Europe
Percentage of Business in Importing: 10

43546 Deep Creek Custom Packing
Mile 137 Sterling Highway
PO Box 39752
Ninilchik, AK 99639   907-567-3395
  Fax: 907-567-3579 800-764-0078
    dccp@ptialaska.net
Alaska smoked salmon, halibut, canned giftpacks, custom processing and gourmet seafood
CEO: Jeff Berger
Plant Manager: Chris Baobo
Estimated Sales: $7 Million
Number Employees: 20-49
Square Footage: 24000
Brands Exported: Deep Creek Custom Packing, Inc.
Regions Exported to: Asia
Percentage of Business in Exporting: 90

43547 Deep Foods Inc
1090 Springfield Rd
Suite 1
Union, NJ 07083-8147   908-810-7500
  Fax: 908-810-8482 www.deepfoods.com
Indian foods such as snacks, frozen meals, ice creams and others.
Vice President: Pravin Amin
deepfoods@aol.com
VP Marketing: Archit Amin
Sales Director: Chintam Trivedi
Estimated Sales: $5-10 Million
Number Employees: 50-99
Square Footage: 120000
Type of Packaging: Consumer, Food Service, Bulk
Other Locations:
  Deep Foods
  Mississagua, CANADA, ONDeep Foods
Regions Imported from: Asia
Percentage of Business in Importing: 30

43548 Deep River Snacks
PO Box 1127
Deep River, CT 06417   860-434-7347
  Fax: 860-434-7512 info@deepriversnacks.com
    www.deepriversnacks.com
Chips and popcorn
President: James Goldberg
info@deepriversnacks.com
Estimated Sales: $2 Million
Number Employees: 5-9

43549 Deep Sea Fisheries
3900 Railway Ave
Everett, WA 98201-3840   425-388-0255
  Fax: 425-742-8699 sales@deepseafisheries.com
    www.deepseafisheries.com
Black cod, Pacific cod, bottomfish, king crab, snow crab
President: John Boggs
johnboggs@deepseafisheries.com
Sales Director: Julie Ruopp
Operations Manager: Mary Boggs
Number Employees: 10-19

43550 Deep Sea Products
1735 NW 79th Avenue
Doral, FL 33126-1112   305-594-3816
  Fax: 305-594-9705
Wholesaler/distributor and importer of shrimp
President: Robert Daglio, Jr.
Estimated Sales: $500,000-$1 Million
Number Employees: 1-4
Brands Imported: El Salvador Pride; Supper Club
Regions Imported from: Central America
Percentage of Business in Importing: 100

43551 (HQ)Deerland Probiotics & Enzymes
3800 Cobb International Blvd.
Kennesaw, GA 30152
  Fax: 770-919-1194 800-697-8179
    www.deerland.com
Manufacturer and exporter of digestive enzymes and nutritional supplements
Chief Executive Officer: Scott Ravech
VP, Science & Technology: John Deaton
Director, Innovation & Education: John Davidson
Director, Quality Assurance & Control: Maggie Leroux
VP, Marketing & Strategy: Sam Michini
Estimated Sales: $ 20 - 50 Million
Number Employees: 50-99
Type of Packaging: Private Label, Bulk

43552 Deerland Probiotics & Enzymes
15366 US Highway 160
Forsyth, MO 65653-8107
      800-825-8545
    www.deerland.com
Manufacturer and exporter of digestive enzymes and nutritional supplements
Type of Packaging: Private Label, Bulk

43553 (HQ)Defranco Co
1000 Lawrence St
Los Angeles, CA 90021-1620   213-627-8575
  Fax: 213-627-9837 800-992-3992
Defrancomp@aol.com www.defrancoandsons.com
We are a family owned business that offers fresh produce and nuts.
Manager: Paul De Franco
CEO: Paul DeFranco
CFO: Jerry De Franco
VP: Gerald DeFranco
R&D: Salvatore DeFranco
Estimated Sales: $15 Million
Number Employees: 20-49
Square Footage: 150000
Type of Packaging: Consumer, Food Service, Private Label, Bulk
Brands Exported: Sunripe - DeFranco
Regions Exported to: Central America, South America, Europe, Asia, Middle East, Mexico
Percentage of Business in Exporting: 20
Regions Imported from: Central America, South America, Europe, Middle East

43554 Dehyco Company
1000 Kansas Street
Memphis, TN 38106-1925   901-774-3322
  Fax: 901-774-2076
Manufacturer and exporter of hammer mills, custom grinders, pulverizers, separators and packaging machinery
President: Mike Broussard
VP: Albert Harris, Jr.
Estimated Sales: $10-20 Million
Number Employees: 20-49

43555 Dehydrates Inc
1251 Peninsula Blvd
Hewlett, NY 11557-1223   516-295-3700
  Fax: 516-295-3777 800-983-4443
    dehydrates123@hotmail.com
    www.dehydratesinc.com
Dehydrated fruits, vegetables and herbs
President: Steven Reich
Marketing: Gail Whiteford
Public Relations: Lori Zahler
Estimated Sales: $1.5 Million
Number Employees: 1-4
Square Footage: 80000
Type of Packaging: Food Service, Private Label, Bulk
Brands Imported: Deco
Regions Imported from: South America, Europe, Middle East
Percentage of Business in Importing: 50

43556 Deiss Sales Co. Inc.
S. Chaparral Court
Suite 270
Anaheim, CA 92808-2282   714-974-9513
  Fax: 714-974-8136 jim@deisssales.com
    www.deisssales.com
Importer/exporter, wholesaler/distributor of all frozen seafood, all natural beef, poultry and other quality food products
Owner: James Deiss
Quality Control: Annabelle Wright
Estimated Sales: $10 Million
Number Employees: 6
Square Footage: 3000
Type of Packaging: Food Service, Private Label, Bulk
Other Locations:
  Northern CA
  Walnut Creek, CANorthern CA
Regions Exported to: Central America, South America, Europe
Regions Imported from: Central America, South America, Europe

43557 Deko International Company
4283 Shoreline Dr
Earth City, MO 63045-1209   314-298-0910
  Fax: 314-298-0081 dekointl@aol.com
    www.dekointl.com
Distributor of products and ingredients for the food service industry.
President/CEO: Peter Dekointl
Vice President: Nung Kuo
Sales Coordinator: Jennifer Suen
Customer Service: Johnny Liu
Vice President of Operations: Art Chung
Purchasing Manager: Sarah Zhang
Number Employees: 10-19
Type of Packaging: Food Service
Other Locations:
  Rancho Cucamonga, CA
  Clifton, NJ
  Norcross, GAClifton

Importers & Exporters / A-Z

43558 Del Monte Foods Inc.
3003 Oak Rd.
Walnut Creek, CA 94598
www.delmonte.com
Canned fruits and vegetables. Not affiliated with Del Monte Fresh Produce.
President & CEO: Gregory Longstreet
CFO: Gene Allen
General Counsel/Chief Compliance Officer: William Sawyers
Chief Marketing Officer: Bibie Wu
Contact: Gerald Abele
gerald.abele@delmontefoods.com
Year Founded: 1886
Estimated Sales: $3.8 Billion
Number Employees: 7,800
Number of Brands: 7
Parent Co: Del Monte Pacific, Ltd.
Type of Packaging: Consumer, Food Service, Private Label
Other Locations:
 Del Monte Foods
 Cambria, WIDel Monte Foods
Regions Exported to: Worldwide
Percentage of Business in Exporting: 4

43559 (HQ)Del Monte Fresh Produce Inc.
PO Box 149222
Coral Gables, FL 33114-9222 305-520-8400
Fax: 305-567-0320 800-950-3683
contact-us-executive-office@freshdelmonte.com
www.freshdelmonte.com
Fresh and fresh-cut fruit and vegetables.
President/COO: Youssef Zakharia
Chairman/CEO: Mohammad Abu-Ghazaleh
mabughazaleh@freshdelmonte.com
Senior VP/CFO: Eduardo Bezerra
Senior VP/General Counsel/Secretary: Marlene Gordon
Senior VP, North America Operations: Annunciata Cerioli
Year Founded: 1886
Estimated Sales: $3.9 Billion
Number Employees: 45,000
Number of Brands: 11
Type of Packaging: Consumer, Food Service
Other Locations:
 Del Monte Fresh Plant
 Forest Park, GA
 Del Monte Fresh Plant
 Kankakee, IL
 Del Monte Fresh Plant
 Jessup, MD
 Del Monte Fresh Plant
 Kansas City, MO
 Del Monte Fresh Plant
 Bloomfield, NJ
 Del Monte Fresh Plant
 Mappsville, VA
 Del Monte Fresh PlantKankakee
Regions Exported to: Worldwide

43560 Del Rey Packing
5287 S Del Rey Ave
P.O. Box 160
Del Rey, CA 93616 559-888-2031
Fax: 559-888-2715
gchooljian@delreypacking.com
www.delreypacking.com
Manufacturer and exporter of raisins.
President: Gerald Chooljian
gchooljian@delreypacking.com
Vice President: Kathy Merlo
Estimated Sales: $20-50 Million
Number Employees: 50-99
Number of Brands: 2
Type of Packaging: Consumer, Food Service, Private Label, Bulk
Regions Exported to: Central America, South America, Europe, Asia, Middle East
Percentage of Business in Exporting: 35

43561 Del Rio Nut Company
15391 Vinewood Circle
P.O. Box 396
Livingston, CA 95334 209-394-7945
Fax: 209-394-7955 david@delrionut.com
www.delrionut.com
Natural almonds
President/ Marketing Director: David Arakelian
Contact: Barret Arakelian
arakelianbarret@delrionut.com
Operations Manager: Mona Menezes
Estimated Sales: $ 3 - 5 Million
Number Employees: 20-49
Square Footage: 36000
Type of Packaging: Consumer, Food Service, Private Label, Bulk
Brands Exported: Del Rio; Private Labels
Regions Exported to: Europe, Asia, Middle East
Percentage of Business in Exporting: 65

43562 Delavan Spray Technologies
2730 W Tyvola Rd # 600
Charlotte, NC 28217-4578 704-423-7000
Fax: 704-423-4098 www.goodrich.com
Manufacturer, importer and exporter of spray nozzles and accessories including flat spray, straight stream, hollow and solid cone, etc
President: Ray Davis
Division Controller: Carolin Kirsch
CEO: Marshall O Larsen
Contact: Tom Barrow
tom.barrow@utas.utc.com
Executive Vice President of Operation: Jerry Witowski
Estimated Sales: $5-10 Million
Number Employees: 10,000
Parent Co: Coltec Industries
Brands Exported: SDX
Regions Exported to: Worldwide
Percentage of Business in Exporting: 28
Regions Imported from: England
Percentage of Business in Importing: 13

43563 Delavan-Delta
11 Rado Drive
Naugatuck, CT 06770-2220 203-720-5610
Fax: 203-720-5616
Manufacturer and exporter of level controls
Sales/Marketing Manager: Dean Cheramie
Number Employees: 65
Parent Co: Coltec Industries
Regions Exported to: Worldwide

43564 Delavau LLC
10101 Roosevelt Blvd
Philadelphia, PA 19154 215-671-1400
sales@delavau.com
www.delavau.com
Contract packager for the pharmaceutical, food and nutritional industries.
Chief Executive Officer: John Burrows
VP & General Manager, Food Division: Jeff Billig
Applications Research/Technical Service: Matt Patrick
Sales Manager: Rick Diamond
Year Founded: 1847
Estimated Sales: $34 Million
Number Employees: 350
Square Footage: 20000
Type of Packaging: Consumer, Bulk
Regions Exported to: Central America, South America, Europe, Asia, Canada
Percentage of Business in Exporting: 30
Regions Imported from: Europe, Asia

43565 Delaware Department of Agriculture
99 Kings Hwy
Dover, DE 19901 302-739-4271
Fax: 302-697-6287 www.delawarebeef.org
President: Richard Wilkins
VP: Doug Lowe

43566 Delfield Co
980 S Isabella Rd
Mt Pleasant, MI 48858 989-773-7981
Fax: 800-669-0619 800-733-8821
www.delfield.com
Manufacturer and exporter of freezers and cabinets, display cases, cafeteria/restaurant serving counters, dispensers, ventilation systems, commercial refrigerators, mobile cafeteria systems, salad bars, pizza tables and stationary andmobile hot tables.
Year Founded: 1949
Estimated Sales: $100-500 Million
Number Employees: 500-999
Parent Co: The Manitowoc Company
Regions Exported to: Canada, Caribbean, Latin America, Mexico
Percentage of Business in Exporting: 4

43567 Delfin Design & Mfg
23301 Antonio Pkwy
Rancho Sta Marg, CA 92688-2664 949-888-4644
Fax: 949-888-4626 800-354-7919
john@delfinfs.com www.delfinfs.com
Manufacturer and exporter of plastic displayware including crocks, bowls, platters, trays, domes and covers
President: John Rief
john@delfinff.com
VP Sales: Gary Mazzone
Estimated Sales: $ 2.5-5,000,000
Number Employees: 20-49
Square Footage: 25000
Regions Exported to: Worldwide
Percentage of Business in Exporting: 2

43568 Delgrosso Foods Inc.
632 Sauce Factory Drive
Tipton, PA 16684 814-684-5880
Fax: 814-684-3943 800-521-5880
michaeld@delgrossofoods.com
www.delgrossofoods.com
Manufacturer and importer of traditional spaghetti sauce, pizza sauce, salsa, sloppy joe sauce, country garden spaghetti sauce and meatballs.
President: James Del Grosso
R&D: Sean Etters
Quality Control: Fredrick Del Grosso
Marketing: Michael Del Grosso
Sales Manager: Robert DelGrosso
Public Relations: Sean Albright
Manager: Joseph Del Grosso
Estimated Sales: $10-20 Million
Number Employees: 50-99
Square Footage: 315000
Type of Packaging: Consumer, Food Service
Regions Imported from: Canada
Percentage of Business in Importing: 2

43569 (HQ)Delicato Family Vineyards
455 Devlin Rd
Suite 201
Napa, CA 94558 707-265-1700
Fax: 707-253-1471 intlmrktg@dfvwines.com
www.delicatofamilyvineyards.com
Wines.
President & CEO: Chris Indelicato
SVP, Operations: Jay Indelicato
VP, Exclusive Brands & Innovation: Jim Ferguson
Regional Accounts Manager: Adam Basala
abasala@dfvwines.com
Year Founded: 1924
Estimated Sales: $29.5 Million
Number Employees: 250-499
Square Footage: 12000
Type of Packaging: Consumer, Food Service, Private Label, Bulk
Brands Exported: Delicato; Dore
Regions Exported to: Europe, Asia
Percentage of Business in Exporting: 1

43570 Delicious Desserts
785 5th Ave
Brooklyn, NY 11232-1750 718-680-1156
Fax: 718-369-6665
Italian desserts including spumoni, tartufo, tortoni, tiramisu, cannolis and cakes; importer of fruit sorbet and Italian cakes
President: Joe Fusceo
Contact: D Lisa
lisa@deliciousdesserts.net
Estimated Sales: Less Than $500,000
Number Employees: 1-4
Square Footage: 8000
Type of Packaging: Private Label
Brands Imported: La Ibense Bornay; Pasticuria Torino
Regions Imported from: Europe
Percentage of Business in Importing: 50

43571 Delizia Olive Oil Company
1991 Dennison St
Oakland, CA 94606-5225 510-535-6833
Fax: 510-532-2837 www.evoliveoil.com
Owner: Mike Bradley
Contact: Veronica Bradley
v.bradley@evoliveoil.com
Estimated Sales: $ 20 - 50 Million
Number Employees: 20-49

Importers & Exporters / A-Z

43572 (HQ)Delmonaco Winery & Vineyards
600 Lance Dr
Baxter, TN 38544-3530   931-858-1177
barbara@delmonacowinery.com
www.delmonacowinery.com
Wines
President/Winemaker: David Delmonaco
david@delmonacowinery.com
Vice President: Barbara Delmonaco
Estimated Sales: $3 Million
Number Employees: 1-4
Type of Packaging: Bulk
Brands Exported: Delmonico's
Regions Exported to: Central America, South America
Percentage of Business in Exporting: 20

43573 Delta Catfish Products
602 E Lee St
PO Box 99
Eudora, AR 71640   870-355-4192
Fax: 714-778-0998
Catfish
President/CEO: Thomas Marshall

43574 Delta International
1754 Carr Rd # 216
Calexico, CA 92231-9509   760-357-4678
Fax: 760-357-4686 www.deltausmex.com
Exporter of dairy products including milk, yogurt and cottage and cream cheeses; also, parts for dairy packaging machinery; importer of plastic containers for milk, juice and beverages
President: Carlos Fuentes
cfuentes@deltausmex.com
Manager: Alfredo Dipp
Estimated Sales: $ 1 - 3 Million
Number Employees: 5-9
Square Footage: 40000
Type of Packaging: Private Label
Regions Exported to: Mexico
Percentage of Business in Exporting: 90
Regions Imported from: Mexico
Percentage of Business in Importing: 10

43575 Delta Machine & Maufacturing
137 Teal St
St Rose, LA 70087-4022   504-949-8304
Fax: 504-467-0071 debra@deltamachinemfg.com
Manufacturer and exporter of bakery equipment including trough elevators
President/Owner: Dale Kessler
CEO: Andrew Kessler, Jr.
CFO: Debra Kessler
Estimated Sales: Below $ 1 Million
Number Employees: 1-4
Regions Exported to: South America, Europe, Asia, Middle East, Mexico
Percentage of Business in Exporting: 20

43576 Delta Pure Filtration Corp
11011 Richardson Rd
Ashland, VA 23005-3418   804-798-2888
Fax: 804-798-3923 800-785-9450
tfurbee@deltapure.com www.deltapure.net
Manufacturer and exporter of active carbon cartridge filters for water, juice, vegetable oil, etc
President: Todd Furbee
tfurbee@deltapure.com
Operations Manager: Frank Williams
Number Employees: 20-49
Square Footage: 36000
Type of Packaging: Bulk
Brands Exported: Delta Pure
Regions Exported to: Central America, South America, Asia, Middle East

43577 Delta Wire And Mfg.
29 Delta Drive
Harrow, ON N0R 1G0
Canada
                    519-738-3514
Fax: 519-738-3468 800-221-3794
contact@deltawire.com www.deltawire.com
Manufacturer and exporter of welded wire mesh products including pallet racks and containers
President: Geoffrey Scully
CFO: Geoffrey Scully
National Sales Manager: Larry Cunningham
Estimated Sales: $ 10 - 20 Million
Number Employees: 10-19
Regions Exported to: Canada, Mexico

43578 DeltaTrak
P.O.Box 398
Pleasanton, CA 94566   925-249-2250
Fax: 925-249-2251 800-962-6776
salesinfo@deltatrak.com www.deltatrak.com
DeltaTrak, Inc. is a leading innovator of cold chain management and temperature monitoring solutions. DeltaTrak offers a wide range of temperature and humidity data loggers and wireless systems. DeltaTrak develops and manufactures highquality portable test instruments that monitor/record temperature and humidity. DeltaTrak's comprehensive cold chain management systems also include professional digital probe and infrared thermometers.
Quality Assurance Manager: Tony Trapolino
VP Marketing & Business Development: Ray Carson
Director, Operations: Rick Delgado
Estimated Sales: $8,000,000
Number Employees: 250
Number of Brands: 20
Number of Products: 80+
Type of Packaging: Food Service, Private Label, Bulk
Regions Exported to: Central America, South America, Europe, Asia, Middle East, Australia
Percentage of Business in Exporting: 20

43579 Delux Manufacturing Co
4650 Airport Rd
PO Box 1027
Kearney, NE 68847-3761   308-237-2274
Fax: 308-234-3765 800-658-3240
info@deluxmfg.com www.deluxmfg.com
Manufacturer and exporter of grain dryers
President: Eric D Michel
eric.dm@deluxmfg.com
VP/Sales Manager: Bob Schultz
Estimated Sales: $2.5-5 Million
Number Employees: 20-49
Square Footage: 144000

43580 Deluxe Equipment Company
P.O.Box 11390
4414 28th St. West
Bradenton, FL 34207   941-753-3184
Fax: 941-753-4529 800-367-8931
deluxe@gte.net www.deluxeovens.com
Manufacturer and exporter of ovens, proofers, warmers.
President: Gib Smith
CFO: Sandra Smith
VP/Sales: Russ D'Aiuto
Estimated Sales: $2.5-5 Million
Number Employees: 10-19
Square Footage: 50000
Brands Exported: Deluxe, Convect A Ray
Regions Exported to: Central America, South America, Asia
Percentage of Business in Exporting: 2

43581 (HQ)Dema Engineering Co
10020 Big Bend Rd
St Louis, MO 63122-6457   314-966-3533
Fax: 314-965-8319 800-325-3362
sales@demaeng.com
Manufacturer and exporter of warewash, laundry and liquid soap dispensers including injectors, proportioning detergent feeders, rinse pumps and foamers
President: Jonathan Deutsch
jonathand@demaeng.com
VP, Marketing: Dan Gillespie
SVP, Global Sales: Ron Dickerson
Purchasing Manager: David Deutsch
Estimated Sales: $ 10-20 Million
Number Employees: 20-49
Square Footage: 56000
Other Locations:
    Dema Engineering Co.
    Gerald, MODema Engineering Co.
Regions Exported to: Worldwide
Percentage of Business in Exporting: 15

43582 Demaco
4645 Metropolitan Ave
Ridgewood, NY 11385
                    Fax: 718-417-9264 www.demaco.nl/en/
Manufacturer and exporter of pasta equipment
President: Leonard Defrancisci
VP: John Deluca
Mngr: Amy Casaburri
Estimated Sales: $10-20 Million
Number Employees: 20-49
Parent Co: Howden Food Equipment
Regions Exported to: Central America, South America, Europe, Middle East, Eastern Europe
Percentage of Business in Exporting: 30

43583 Demag Cranes & Components Corp
29201 Aurora Rd
Cleveland, OH 44139-1895   440-248-2400
Fax: 440-248-3086 www.demagcranes.us
Manufacturer and exporter of cranes and hoists
President: John Paxton
Corp Comms: Dan Konstantinovsk
Administrative Assistant: Maureen Tilly
Estimated Sales: H
Number Employees: 250-499
Parent Co: Demag Material Handling
Regions Exported to: Worldwide

43584 Dempster Systems
PO Box 1388
Toccoa, GA 30577-1424   706-886-2327
Fax: 706-886-0088
Manufacturer and exporter of refuse handling systems
President: John Boonstra
Estimated Sales: $20-50 Million
Number Employees: 100-249
Parent Co: Technology
Type of Packaging: Consumer, Food Service, Bulk
Regions Exported to: Worldwide

43585 Dependable Distributors
1301 Union Ave
Pennsauken, NJ 08110   856-665-1762
Fax: 856-488-6332
Importer and exporter of cocoa beans; also, warehouse providing storage for cocoa beans
Owner: Harvey Weiner
VP: Harvey Weiner
Contact: Richard Petrone
p.richard@taggroup.net
Estimated Sales: $2.5-5 Million
Number Employees: 20 to 49
Square Footage: 560000
Percentage of Business in Exporting: 10
Percentage of Business in Importing: 90

43586 Dependable Machine, Inc.
308 S. 14th St. - Coeur
d'Alene, ID 83814   973-239-7800
Fax: 973-239-7855 866-967-0146
dmi-cnc.com
Manufacturer, importer and exporter of screen and pad printing equipment, printing inks and accessories
President: Thomas Skeels
VP: Brett Skeels
Estimated Sales: $ 2.5 - 5 Million
Number Employees: 10-19
Square Footage: 40000
Brands Exported: Dependable
Regions Exported to: Central America, South America
Percentage of Business in Exporting: 20
Brands Imported: Moss
Regions Imported from: South America, Europe
Percentage of Business in Importing: 40

43587 Derco Foods Intl
2670 W Shaw Ln # 101
Fresno, CA 93711-2772   559-435-2664
Fax: 559-435-8520 derco@dercofoods.com
www.dercofoods.com
Dried fruits, nuts, specialty foods, pineapple, mushrooms, canned fruit, caned fruit, beans and popcorn
President: Leon Dermenjian
leon@dercofoods.com
Quality Control: Debbie McMillan
VP Sales/Purchasing: Ago Dermanjian
Sales/Marketing: Jeff Margarian
Estimated Sales: $20-50 Million
Number Employees: 10-19
Square Footage: 6000
Brands Exported: Derco
Regions Exported to: Worldwide
Brands Imported: Derco
Regions Imported from: South America, Asia, Middle East
Percentage of Business in Importing: 10

Importers & Exporters / A-Z

43588 Desco USA
9620 Joliet Rd
Countryside, IL 60525 708-588-1099
Fax: 708-588-1097 info@descousa.com
www.descousa.com
US sales for Desco pasta cookers
Owner: John Cora
Estimated Sales: $ 1 - 3 Million
Number Employees: 1-4
Parent Co: Desco SRL
Brands Imported: Desco
Regions Imported from: Europe
Percentage of Business in Importing: 100

43589 Descon EDM
54 W Main St
PO Box 189
Brocton, NY 14716 716-792-9300
Fax: 716-792-9363 us.kompass.com/
Manufacturer and exporter of material handling equipment including vibrating and belt conveyors, graders, etc
CEO: David Beehler
R&D: Christopher Beehler
General Manager: C Beehler
Estimated Sales: Below $ 5 Million
Number Employees: 1-4
Square Footage: 20000
Regions Exported to: Europe
Percentage of Business in Exporting: 40

43590 Desert King International
7024 Manya Cir
San Diego, CA 92154-4711 619-429-5222
Fax: 619-429-5001 800-982-2235
info@desertking.com www.desertking.com
Quillaja and yucca extracts for root beer and oil flavors
President: Paul Hiley
philey@desertking.com
VP: Joel Powers
Regional Sales Manager: Raymond Kramer
Estimated Sales: $3-5 Million
Number Employees: 10-19
Square Footage: 60000
Type of Packaging: Private Label, Bulk
Brands Exported: Foamation
Regions Exported to: South America, Europe, Asia, Australia
Percentage of Business in Exporting: 45

43591 Deshazo Crane Company
P.O.Box 1450
Alabaster, AL 35007-2062 205-664-2006
Fax: 205-664-3668 www.deshazo.com
Manufacturer and exporter of cranes including overhead bridge, gantry and semi-gantry
CEO: Guy K Mitchell Jr
Estimated Sales: $ 20-50 Million
Number Employees: 100-249
Type of Packaging: Bulk
Regions Exported to: Worldwide

43592 Design Packaging Company
100 Hazel Ave
Glencoe, IL 60022-1731 773-486-8100
Fax: 773-486-2160 800-321-7659
Polypropylene and polyethylene bags and sheets; importer of polyethylene and polyproplyne bags; exporter of polyethylene sleeves and bags
President: Myron Horvitz
CFO: Greg Horvitz
VP: Randy Block
Sales Representative: Greg Horvitz
Contact: Conrad Capulong
conrad.capulong@designpackaging.net
Purchasing Agent: Randy Block
Estimated Sales: $ 5 - 10 Million
Number Employees: 20-49
Square Footage: 80000
Regions Exported to: Canada
Percentage of Business in Exporting: 1
Regions Imported from: Asia
Percentage of Business in Importing: 20

43593 Design Technology Corporation
26 Mason Street
Lexington, MA 02421 781-862-5107
Fax: 303-440-5127 800-597-7063
Manufacturer and exporter of material handling equipment, food processing machinery and process control systems
President: Marvin Menzin
Estimated Sales: $1-2,500,000
Number Employees: 4
Regions Exported to: Europe, North America
Percentage of Business in Exporting: 10

43594 Design-Mark Industries
3 Kendrick Rd
Wareham, MA 02571-1093 508-295-9591
Fax: 508-295-6752 800-451-3275
sales@design-mark.com www.design-mark.com
Manufacturer and exporter of labels, nameplates and membrane switch panels
President: Carl Burquist
Cmo: Denise Shurtleff
denise@design-mark.com
Quality Control: Jim Brawders
Operations: Jon Winzler
Marketing Director: Denise Shurtley
Estimated Sales: $ 14 Million
Number Employees: 50-99
Square Footage: 40000
Type of Packaging: Bulk

43595 Designed Nutritional Products
1199 South 1480 West
Orem, UT 84058-4907 801-224-4518
Fax: 801-434-8270 info@designednutritional.com
www.designednutritional.com
Dietary supplements including organic germanium, saw palmetto extracts, ascorbigen, melatonin and indole-3-carbinol; exporter of melatonin, gramine, bisindolylmethane and glycogen
President: David Parish
Marketing: Omar Filippelli
Contact: Gus Diaz
customerservice@designednutritional.com
Purchasing Director: Craig Hansen
Estimated Sales: $10-20 Million
Number Employees: 5-9
Square Footage: 10000
Type of Packaging: Bulk
Regions Exported to: South America, Asia

43596 Desserts by David Glass
400 Chapel Road
Unit 2d Bissell Commons
South Windsor, CT 6074 860-462-7520
Fax: 860-242-4408
Desserts including chocolate truffle cake, cheesecake and chocolate mousse balls
President: David Glass
Estimated Sales: $10-20 Million
Number Employees: 20-49
Square Footage: 20000
Type of Packaging: Consumer, Food Service
Regions Exported to: Europe, Canada
Percentage of Business in Exporting: 10

43597 Destileria Serralles Inc
P.O. Box 198
Mercedita, PR 00715-0198 787-840-1000
Fax: 787-840-1155
Rum, vodka, gin, cordials and wine; importer of scotch; exporter of rum; wholesaler/distributor of general merchandise
President & CEO: Felix Serralles, Jr.
Chief Financial Officer: Jorge Vazquez
Product Quality Director: Roberto Pantoja
Chief Marketing Officer: Gabriela Ripepi
State Manager: Vanessa Gehl
Human Resources Director: Daniel Beautista
Estimated Sales: $28.5 Million
Number Employees: 370
Square Footage: 18777
Type of Packaging: Consumer, Private Label, Bulk
Brands Exported: Don-Q-Lemon, Palo Viejo Rum.
Regions Exported to: Worldwide
Percentage of Business in Exporting: 5
Brands Imported: Cutty Sark; Jim Beam; Louis Roederer; Perfut Joiet
Regions Imported from: Europe
Percentage of Business in Importing: 20

43598 Detecto Scale Co
203 E Daugherty St
Webb City, MO 64870-1929 417-673-4631
Fax: 417-673-5001 800-641-2008
detecto@cardet.com www.detecto.com
Manufacturer and exporter of scales including portion control, top loading, price computing, bench, platform, counter, pre-packaging, hanging and receiving
President: David Perry
Chief Financial Officer: Elise Crume
Vice President: Larry Hicks
Research And Development: Tony Herrin
Quality Control: Ginger Harper
Marketing Director: Jonathan Sabo
Sales Exec: Brock Dawson
Advertising Manager: Jonathan Sabo
brockdawson@detecto.com
Estimated Sales: $ 50 - 60 Million
Number Employees: 10-19
Square Footage: 400000
Parent Co: Cardinal Scale Manufacturing Company
Type of Packaging: Food Service
Brands Exported: Detecto; Cardinal
Regions Exported to: Central America, South America, Europe, Asia, Middle East
Percentage of Business in Exporting: 18

43599 Detecto Scale Co
203 E Daugherty St
Webb City, MO 64870-1929 417-673-4631
Fax: 417-673-5001 800-641-2008
detecto@cardet.com www.detecto.com
Weighing scales
President: David H Perry
brockdawson@detecto.com
Chief Financial Officer: Elise Crume
Vice President: Larry Hicks
Research/Development: Tony Herrin
Quality Control: Ginger Harper
Marketing: Jonathan Sabo
Sales Exec: Brock Dawson
Operations/Production: Matt Stovern
Estimated Sales: $45 Million
Number Employees: 10-19
Square Footage: 350000
Parent Co: Cardinal Scale Manufacturing Company

43600 Detroit Forming
19100 W 8 Mile Rd
Southfield, MI 48075-5792 248-440-1317
Fax: 248-352-0445 sales@detroitforming.net
www.detroitforming.com
Manufacturer and exporter of plastic food trays for meat, produce, ice cream and cookies
President: Leigh Rodney
leigh.rodney@detroitforming.net
National Sales Manager: Ken Sherry
Estimated Sales: $ 10 - 20 Million
Number Employees: 100-249
Type of Packaging: Food Service
Regions Exported to: Canada

43601 Detroit Quality Brush Mfg Co
32165 Schoolcraft Rd
Livonia, MI 48150-1833 734-525-5660
Fax: 734-525-0437 800-722-3037
sales@dqb.com www.dqb.com
Manufacturer and exporter of brooms and brushes
Owner: Donald Weinbaum
don@gqb.com
Manufacturing Manager: Mike Lindemoth
Estimated Sales: $2.5-5 Million
Number Employees: 50-99
Square Footage: 200000
Parent Co: Erco Housewares
Type of Packaging: Consumer, Food Service, Private Label, Bulk

43602 Devansoy Farms
206 W 7th St
PO Box 885
Carroll, IA 51401-2317 712-792-9665
Fax: 712-792-2712 800-747-8605
info@devansoy.com www.devansoy.com
Powdered and liquid soy milk and soy flours;. Organic and parve available
President: Elmer Schettler
eschettler@devansoy.com
VP/Sales & Mktg: Montgomery Kilburn
VP/Operations: Deb Wycoff
Estimated Sales: $510,000
Number Employees: 1-4
Number of Products: 8
Type of Packaging: Food Service, Private Label, Bulk

43603 (HQ)Dewied International Inc
5010 Interstate 10 E
San Antonio, TX 78219-3352 210-661-6161
Fax: 210-662-6112 800-992-5600
www.dewied.com

263

Importers & Exporters / A-Z

Natural and synthetic sausage casings specializing in hog, sheep and beef casings
President: Phil Bohlender
philb@dewiedint.com
VP Sales: George Burt
Estimated Sales: $10-20 Million
Number Employees: 50-99
Brands Exported: Dewied Real; Dewied Select; Synthe
Regions Exported to: Worldwide
Percentage of Business in Exporting: 25
Regions Imported from: South America, Europe, Asia, Middle East, Australia
Percentage of Business in Importing: 15

43604 Dexter Russell Inc
44 River St
Southbridge, MA 01550-1834 508-765-0201
 Fax: 508-764-2897 800-343-6042
 sales@dexter1818.com www.dexter1818.com
Manufacturer and exporter of knives, turners and spatulas
President: Alan Peppel
apeppel@dexter1818.com
Sales: Kevin Clark
Estimated Sales: $10 - 20 Million
Number Employees: 250-499
Brands Exported: Connoisseur; Dexter Russell; Russell Green River; Russell International; Sani-Safe; Sofgrip; L-Lo
Regions Exported to: Worldwide

43605 Di Lusso & Be Bop Baskote LLC
1950 SW Badger Ave
Suite 105
Redmond, OR 97756 541-388-8164
 Fax: 541-389-6185 888-545-7487
 orders@be-bop.net www.be-bop.net
Biscotti and specialty roasted coffees
Owner: Bob Golden
bgolden@dilusso.com
Roastmaster: Dona Houtz
Vice President: M Lee
Sales Representative: Abbie Keenan
Estimated Sales: $ 20 - 50 Million
Number Employees: 50-99
Square Footage: 6000
Type of Packaging: Consumer, Food Service
Regions Imported from: Central America, Latin America, Mexico

43606 (HQ)Di Mare Fresh Inc
4529 Diplomacy Rd
Fort Worth, TX 76155-2621 817-385-3000
 Fax: 817-385-3015 www.dimarefresh.com
Growers, packers and distributors of fresh fruits and vegetables.
President: Paul DiMare
CFO: Cheryl Taylor
cheryl.taylor@dimarefresh.com
Year Founded: 1930
Number Employees: 50-99
Type of Packaging: Consumer, Food Service, Private Label, Bulk
Regions Exported to: Central America, Europe, Asia, Australia
Percentage of Business in Exporting: 20
Regions Imported from: Central America, South America, Mexico
Percentage of Business in Importing: 30

43607 DiLeo Brothers
23 Commercial Street
Waterbury, CT 06702-1002 203-759-3600
 Fax: 203-759-3606 800-441-4762
Wholesaler/distributor and exporter of sugar, butter, cheese, tea, groceries, meats, private label items, dairy products, frozen foods, general merchandise, etc.; serving independent retailers; rack jobber services available
President: J DiLeo J.
CEO: J C Lord
VP: John Dileo
Marketing: Christine Dileo
Operations: Rich Bellemarc
Estimated Sales: $14 Million
Number Employees: 20-49
Number of Products: 8500
Square Footage: 170000
Brands Exported: Arizona; SoBe; Slim Jims; Mississippi Mud; Midnight Dragon; Crazy Horse; Czecho Slovian; Bissell Household Products; Ever Fresh Juices
Regions Exported to: Worldwide

Percentage of Business in Exporting: 50

43608 Diab International
611 Live Oak Drive
McLean, VA 22101-1562 703-917-9440
 Fax: 703-917-9422 www.diabfoods.com
Export, Marketing, Logistics Planning
President: Yousef Diab
VP: Isahm Diab
Estimated Sales: $1 Million
Number Employees: 4
Number of Brands: 4
Number of Products: 20
Type of Packaging: Consumer, Food Service, Private Label, Bulk
Regions Exported to: Europe
Percentage of Business in Exporting: 100

43609 Diablo Chemical
216 Court Dale Ave
Kingston, PA 18704
 Fax: 570-288-1227 800-548-1384
 diablochemicalco@aol.com
Manufacturer and exporter of soaps, detergent and oven cleaners
President: Ernest Clamar
VP, Sales & Marketing: E.J. Clamar

Estimated Sales: $2.8 Million
Number Employees: 1-4
Regions Exported to: Worldwide
Percentage of Business in Exporting: 20

43610 Diageo Canada Inc.
401 The West Mall
Suite 800
Toronto, ON M9C 5P8
Canada 416-626-2000
 Fax: 416-626-2688 www.diageo.com
Processor and exporter of gin and wine
President/Board Member: John Kennedy
Head of Corporate Communications: Rowan Pearman
Parent Co: Grand Metropolitan
Type of Packaging: Consumer, Food Service
Regions Exported to: Worldwide

43611 Diamond Automation
23550 Haggerty Rd
Farmington Hills, MI 48335 248-426-9394
 Fax: 248-476-0849 www.diamondsystems.com
Manufacturer and exporter of automated packaging equipment; also, egg production and processing equipment
President: Michel Defenbau
Estimated Sales: $ 20 - 50 Million
Number Employees: 1-4
Regions Exported to: Worldwide

43612 (HQ)Diamond Bakery Co LTD
756 Moowaa St
Honolulu, HI 96817-4405 808-847-3551
 Fax: 808-847-7482 www.diamondbakery.com
Crackers and cookies, including all natural crackers.
President: Gary Yoshioka
Manager: Katy Leung
kleung@diamondbakery.com
Year Founded: 1921
Estimated Sales: Less Than $500,000
Number Employees: 5-9
Number of Products: 50+
Square Footage: 50500
Type of Packaging: Consumer, Food Service, Private Label, Bulk
Brands Exported: Diamond, King David
Regions Exported to: Asia, Japan, US, South Pacific
Percentage of Business in Exporting: 1

43613 Diamond Chain
402 Kentucky Ave
Indianapolis, IN 46225-1174 317-635-8422
 Fax: 317-633-2243 800-872-4246
 custsvc@diamondchain.com
 www.diamondchain.com
Manufacturer and exporter of transmission chains and chain drives

President: Mike Fwiderski
VP Operations: Jerry Randich
CFO: Sheeley Faback
Quality Control: Joe Fossard
VP Sales/Marketing: Douglas Bademoch
Contact: Kristen Abbott
kabbott@diamondchain.com
VP Operations: Pat Taylor
Purchasing Manager: Barbara Heacock
Number Employees: 1-4
Parent Co: Amsted Industries

43614 Diamond Chemical Co Inc
Union Ave & Dubois St
East Rutherford, NJ 7073 201-935-4300
 Fax: 201-935-6997 800-654-7627
 sales@diamondchem.com www.diamondchem.com
Manufacturer and exporter of detergents and cleaners for meat and poultry plants; also, laundry detergent and bleach
President: Harold Diamond
hdiamond@diamondchem.com
CFO: R Diamond
Estimated Sales: $ 20 - 50 Million
Number Employees: 100-249
Square Footage: 137000
Brands Exported: Diamond
Regions Exported to: Worldwide

43615 Diamond Crystal Brands Inc
3000 Tremont Rd
Savannah, GA 31405
  800-654-5115
 www.dcbrands.com
Low-sodium mixes including soup, milk shake, ice cream, sauce, sugar-free dessert and fruit drink; also, instant breakfast beverages, cookies, nutritional chocolate bars and portion packed condiments including jelly, mustard, etc.
President & CEO: Tony Muscato
Director, Information Technology: Arlete Bacon
Year Founded: 1966
Estimated Sales: $45.2 Million
Number Employees: 250-499
Number of Brands: 12
Square Footage: 1200000
Parent Co: Peak Rock Capital of Austin
Type of Packaging: Food Service, Private Label
Other Locations:
 Diamond Crystal Specialty Foo
 Aurora, ONDiamond Crystal Specialty Foo
Brands Exported: Diamond Crystal
Regions Exported to: Canada

43616 Diamond Foods
2200 Delaware Avenue
Santa Cruz, CA 95060 831-457-3200
 Fax: 831-460-9407 www.emeraldnuts.com
Processor and exporter of gummys, jelly beans, gels, yogurt, chocolate confections and sugar-free and natural candies; also, dried fruit, banana chips and snack and trail mixes
Cfo: Dennis Barrow
Vice President: Dennis Daniels
Estimated Sales: $1-2.5 Million
Number Employees: 100-249
Square Footage: 600000
Type of Packaging: Consumer, Food Service, Private Label, Bulk
Regions Exported to: Central America, South America, Asia, Canada, Latin America, Mexico
Percentage of Business in Exporting: 4

43617 Diamond Fruit Growers
3515 Chevron Dr
Hood River, OR 97044 541-354-5300
 Fax: 541-354-5394 www.diamondfruit.com
Cooperative grower, packer, shipper and exporter of apples, pears and cherries.
President & CEO: David Garcia
Controller: Linda Gray
Field Representative: Grady Leiblein
Food Safety Coordinator: Corey Yasui
VP, Operations: Bob Wymore
VP, Raw Product: Chad Wimmers
Purchasing Coordinator: Wes Bailey
Year Founded: 1913
Estimated Sales: $20-50 Million
Number Employees: 100-249
Type of Packaging: Bulk
Brands Exported: Diamond
Regions Exported to: Central America, South America, Europe, Asia, Middle East, Canada, Caribbean, Latin America, Mexico

Importers & Exporters / A-Z

43618 Diamond Machining Technology
85 Hayes Memorial Dr # 1
Marlborough, MA 01752-1892   508-481-5944
            Fax: 508-485-3924 800-666-4368
            www.dmtsharp.com
Manufacturer and exporter of knife sharpeners
President: Christine Miller
Chairman: Elizabeth Powell
R&D: Stan Watson
Sales Manager: George Pettee
Manager: Kris Byron
dmtcustomercare@dmtsharp.com
Estimated Sales: $ 1 - 2.5 Million
Number Employees: 1-4
Square Footage: 40000
Regions Exported to: Worldwide
Percentage of Business in Exporting: 30

43619 Diamond Nutrition
2219 Lee Ave
South El Monte, CA 91733-2509   626-279-6999
            Fax: 626-279-1699
Wholesaler/distributor, importer and exporter of health food and general line items including fish oil and lecithin
President: George Liu
Estimated Sales: $96,000
Number Employees: 1-4
Regions Exported to: Asia
Percentage of Business in Importing: 90

43620 (HQ)Diamond Packaging
111 Commerce Dr
Rochester, NY 14623-3503   585-334-8030
            Fax: 585-334-9141 800-333-4079
            sales@diamondpkg.com
            www.diamondpackaging.com
Folding carton manufacturing and contract packaging services
President/Owner: Kirsten Werner
CEO/Owner: Karla Fichter
kfichter@diamondpkg.com
CFO: Keith Robinson
CEO: Karla Fichter
Research & Development: Dave Ziemba
Quality Control: Heidi Ingersol
Director of Marketing: Dennis Bacchetta
Director of Business Development: Sue Julien
Director of Business Development: Dave Semrau
Plant Manager: Dan Gurbacki
Estimated Sales: $ 20 - 50 Million
Number Employees: 100-249
Square Footage: 90000
Type of Packaging: Consumer, Private Label
Other Locations:
  Diamond Packaging Company
  Rochester, NYDiamond Packaging Company

43621 Diamond Wipes Intl Inc
4651 Schaefer Ave
Chino, CA 91710-5542   909-230-9888
            Fax: 909-230-9885 800-454-1077
            info@diamondwipes.com
            www.diamondwipes.com
Manufacturer and exporter of pre-moistened paper towels
Founder, Owner & President: Eve Yen
eyen@diamondwipes.com
R&D: Map Taing
Quality Control: Anthony Castro
Marketing: Anthony Reyes
Estimated Sales: $ 5 - 10 Million
Number Employees: 50-99
Square Footage: 15000
Brands Exported: Diamond Wipes
Regions Exported to: Central America, Europe, Middle East, Canada, Mexico
Percentage of Business in Exporting: 10

43622 Diazteca Inc
993 E Frontage Rd
Rio Rico, AZ 85648-6234   520-761-4621
            Fax: 520-281-1024 www.diazteca.com
Processor and distributor of Mexican fresh mangos, fresh hot peppers, granulated cane sugar, refrigerated and frozen lean beef, frozen shrimp, frozen IQF fruits and vegetables, aseptic fruit purees and other food products.
Owner/President: Ismael Diaz
Vice President: Roderigo Diaz
Estimated Sales: Less Than $500,000
Number Employees: 5-9

Type of Packaging: Consumer, Private Label, Bulk
Regions Exported to: Africa

43623 Dickerson & Quinn
4000 Executive Parkway
Suite 160
San Ramon, CA 94583-4314   925-904-5300
            Fax: 925-256-8880
Wholesaler/distributor and exporter of confectionery items, meats, private label items, groceries and general merchandise; serving the food service market
President: D Dickerson
VP: R Quinn
Estimated Sales: $20-50 Million
Number Employees: 5-9
Regions Exported to: Pacific Rim

43624 Dickey Manufacturing Company
3632 Stem Avenue
St Charles, IL 60174   630-584-2918
            Fax: 630-584-0261 info@securityseals.com
            www.securityseals.com
Manufacturer and exporter of security and tamper proof seals for containers, rail cars, trucks, etc.; also, locking devices
Manager: Terry Mauger
Sales: Dan Bemis
General Manager: Terry Mauger
Estimated Sales: Below $5,000,000
Number Employees: 20-49
Square Footage: 80000
Regions Exported to: Worldwide
Percentage of Business in Exporting: 50

43625 Dickson Brothers
8170 E 46th St
Tulsa, OK 74145-4821   918-628-1285
            Fax: 918-665-8326
Wholesaler/distributor, importer and exporter of water treatment systems including purification, reverse osmosis and ultra violet applications; also, portable systems
President: John Hambrick
Vice President: Jay Hambrick
jayhambrick@hfinctul.com
Sales: Jim Mangette
Estimated Sales: $2.5-5 Million
Number Employees: 5-9
Square Footage: 20000

43626 Die Cut Specialties Inc
12543 Rhode Island Ave
Savage, MN 55378-1136   952-890-7590
            Fax: 952-890-7590
Manufacturer and exporter of packaging materials and bulk boxes for sugar, cocoa etc
President: Robert Jones
Plant Manager: Mike Jones
Estimated Sales: $ 500,000-$ 1 Million
Number Employees: 10-19
Square Footage: 20000
Type of Packaging: Bulk
Regions Exported to: Asia

43627 Dieffenbach's Potato Chips
51 Host Rd
Womelsdorf, PA 19567-9421   610-589-2385
            Fax: 610-589-2866 www.dieffenbachs.com
Dieffenbach's Old Fashioned Potato Chips; Uglies Kettle-Cooked Chips, which are made from potatoes that do not adhere to USDA cosmetic regulations for produce
President & CEO: Nevin Dieffenbach
VP, Business Development: Dwight Zimmerman
Chief Operating Officer: Michael Marlowe
Estimated Sales: $ 5 - 10 Million
Number Employees: 10-19
Number of Brands: 2
Type of Packaging: Consumer, Private Label
Other Locations:
  Factory Outlet Store
  Womelsdorf, PAFactory Outlet Store
Brands Exported: Dieffenbach's, Uglies
Regions Exported to: USA

43628 Diehl Food Ingredients
136 Fox Run Dr
Defiance, OH 43512   419-782-5010
            Fax: 419-783-4319 800-251-3033
Lactose free beverages, powdered fat, coffee creamers and whip topping bases.

President: Charles Nicolais
CFO: Darren Lane
CEO: Peter Diehl
Research & Development: Joan Hasselman
Quality Control: Kelly Roach
Marketing Director: Dennis Reid
Sales Director: Jim Holdrieth
Number Employees: 100-249
Parent Co: Diehl
Type of Packaging: Consumer, Food Service, Bulk

43629 Dietzco
6 Bigelow St
Hudson, MA 01749-2697   508-481-4000
            Fax: 508-481-4004 www.entwistleco.com
Spiral winding equipment for production of composite, paper and fiber cans; exporter of paper converting equipment
President: H Corkin
CEO: V Robinson
VP: R J Heidel
Estimated Sales: G
Number Employees: 100-249
Square Footage: 200000
Parent Co: Entwistle Company
Brands Exported:
Regions Exported to: Central America, South America, Europe, Asia

43630 Dillanos Coffee Roasters
1607 45th St E
Sumner, WA 98390-2202   253-826-1807
            Fax: 253-826-1827 800-234-5282
            www.dillanos.com
Coffee
Owner: Chris Heyer
chrish@dillanos.com
CFO: Rand Hill
Estimated Sales: $3 Million
Number Employees: 50-99
Type of Packaging: Food Service
Brands Imported: White coffee
Regions Imported from: Central America, Asia
Percentage of Business in Importing: 100

43631 Dimpflmeier Bakery
26-36 Advance Road
Toronto, ON M8Z 2T4
Canada   416-236-2701
            Fax: 416-239-5370 800-268-2421
            orders@dimpflmeierbakery.com
            www.dimpflmeierbakery.com
German-style breads including rye, pumpernickel, sourdough and monastery; also, rolls and buns
President: Alfonse Dimpflmier
Number Employees: 170
Type of Packaging: Consumer, Food Service
Regions Exported to: USA

43632 Dings Co Magnetic Group
4740 W Electric Ave
Milwaukee, WI 53219-1626   414-672-7830
            Fax: 414-672-5354 magnets@dingsco.com
            www.dingsmagnets.com
Manufacturer and exporter of magnetic separators for the removal of ferrous metal contaminants from free-flowing powders and granular materials
President: Harold Bolstad
CEO: Brian Nahey
Manager: Gene Poker
Estimated Sales: $10-20 Million
Number Employees: 50-99
Regions Exported to: Central America, South America

43633 Dipal Enterprises
44 Stelton Road
Piscataway, NJ 08854-2600   908-754-1444
            Fax: 908-754-8484
Import and export

43634 Dipasa USA Inc
6600 Ruben Torres Sr Blvd # B
Brownsville, TX 78526-6954   956-831-4072
            Fax: 956-831-5893 info@dipasausa.com
            www.dipasausa.com
Tahini and sesame seeds, raisins, oil, flour and candy; wholesaler/distributor of onion and cheese breadsticks, baked snacks, halvah and confectionery items, natural colors, oleoresins

Importers & Exporters / A-Z

Vice President: Garry Lowder
garrylowder@dipasausa.com
Vice President: Garry Lowder
garrylowder@dipasausa.com
Vice President, Marketing: Garry Lowder
Estimated Sales: $8 Million
Number Employees: 10-19
Number of Brands: 2
Number of Products: 10
Square Footage: 80000
Type of Packaging: Consumer, Food Service, Private Label, Bulk
Brands Exported: Dipasa; Biladi; De Fontain; Sesamin
Regions Exported to: South America
Brands Imported: Dipasa; De Fontain; Sesamin
Regions Imported from: Central America, South America, Europe, Asia, Middle East, Mexico
Percentage of Business in Importing: 90

43635 Dipix Technologies
1051 Baxter Road
Ottawa, ON K2C 3P2
Canada 613-596-4942
Fax: 613-249-7341 info@dipix.com
www.dipix.com
Manufacturer and exporter of two dimensional and three dimensional vision inspection systems for the detection of defects in the color, size and shape of baked goods
President: Anton Kitai
Chairman And Acting CEO: Don Gibbs
VP Engineering: Andy Peters
VP Marketing/Sales: John Lawrence
Director of Sales: Geoff Evans
Chief Operating Officer: Peter Wakeman
Square Footage: 60000
Brands Exported: L800; QualiVision
Regions Exported to: South America, Europe, Asia, USA
Percentage of Business in Exporting: 85

43636 Dipwell Co
106 Industrial Dr
Northampton, MA 01060-2327 413-587-4673
Fax: 413-587-4609 rinse@dipwell.com
www.dipwell.com
Manufacturer and exporter of food processing equipment including creamery, ice cream, mashed potatoes, butter, sour cream, cole slaw and peas; also, stainless steel running water wells to keep scoops sanitary
Owner: Tom Baird
rinse@dipwell.com
President: Lynn Perry-Alstadt
VP: Fred Perry, Jr.
Estimated Sales: Less Than $500,000
Number Employees: 1-4
Square Footage: 5000
Type of Packaging: Food Service
Brands Exported: Dipwell
Regions Exported to: Canada
Percentage of Business in Exporting: 5

43637 Direct Fire Technical
45 Bounty Road W
Benbrook, TX 76132-1043 817-568-8778
Fax: 817-568-8784 888-920-2468
Manufacturer and exporter of industrial hot water heaters and steam generators
President: J Baker
VP: Jack Nichols
Estimated Sales: $1-2,500,000
Number Employees: 20-49
Regions Exported to: Worldwide

43638 Discovery Products Corporation
13619 Mukilteo Speedway # 1180
Lynnwood, WA 98087-1626 425-267-9577
Fax: 425-267-9156
President: Dennis A Clark
Vice President of Sales and Marketing: David Muir
Estimated Sales: $300,000-500,000
Number Employees: 1-4

43639 Dishaka Imports
11300 S Sam Houston Pkwy W
Houston, TX 77031-2350 832-831-3456
Fax: 713-988-2905 888-424-4724
www.zafaranirice.com
Importer and wholesaler/distributor of bismati rice, snacks, beverages - fruit juices, biscuits and cookies
Owner: Kawal Oberoi

Estimated Sales: $20 Million
Number Employees: 5-9
Square Footage: 100000
Type of Packaging: Consumer, Food Service, Private Label, Bulk
Brands Exported: Zafarani, Chirag, Mangola
Regions Exported to: South America
Percentage of Business in Exporting: 10
Brands Imported: Brookeband, Lipton, Ashoka, Golden Temple India Chef
Regions Imported from: Central America, Europe, Asia, Middle East
Percentage of Business in Importing: 90

43640 Dismat Corporation
336 N Westwood Ave
Toledo, OH 43607 419-531-8963
Fax: 419-531-8965
Powdered soup mixes and seasonings
President: John Donofrio
mckayssoupmix@bex.net
Operations VP: Sandra Lee Jones
Estimated Sales: $1-$2 Million
Number Employees: 5-9
Number of Brands: 1
Number of Products: 3
Square Footage: 48000
Type of Packaging: Consumer, Bulk
Regions Exported to: Canada

43641 Dispense Rite
2205 Carlson Dr
Northbrook, IL 60062 847-753-9595
Fax: 847-753-9648 800-772-2877
sales@dispense-rite.com www.dispense-rite.com
Dispensing equipment for the foodservice industry
President: Robert Gapp
R&D: Robert Riley
Quality Control: Don Hitchcock
VP Marketing/Sales: Ronald Klein
Contact: Donald Hitchcock
dhitchcock@dispense-rite.com
Plant Manager: Don Hitchcok
Purchasing Agent: Robert Gapp
Estimated Sales: $ 3 - 5,000,000
Number Employees: 20-49
Number of Brands: 1
Number of Products: 250
Parent Co: Diversified Metal Products
Brands Exported: Dispense Rite
Regions Exported to: Worldwide

43642 Display Studios Inc
5420 Kansas Ave
Kansas City, KS 66106-1143 913-754-8900
Fax: 913-754-8901 800-648-8479
www.displaystudios.com
Manufacturer and exporter of displays and exhibits
President: John Mc Coy
jmccoy@displaystudios.com
Estimated Sales: $ 2.5 - 5 Million
Number Employees: 20-49
Regions Exported to: Worldwide
Percentage of Business in Exporting: 3

43643 Display Tray
5475 Royalmount Avenue
Mont-Royal, QC H4P 1J3
Canada 514-735-2988
Fax: 514-735-8933 800-782-8861
displaytray@hotmail.com
Manufacturer and exporter of high impact styrene food display and market trays; also, plastic proof and bagel boards
President: Gail Cantor
CEO: Simy Oliel
Sales: Yoel Acoca
Number Employees: 4
Square Footage: 8000

43644 Distaview Corp
121 E Wooster St # 201
Bowling Green, OH 43402-2920 419-353-6080
Fax: 419-353-6080 800-795-9970
sales@distaview.com
Manufacturer and exporter of liquid and material process controllers
President: Rick Kramer
rkramer@distaview.com
Estimated Sales: Less Than $500,000
Number Employees: 5-9
Square Footage: 27200
Brands Exported: LiquaVision/Twoview 2Point

43645 Distinguished Products
347 E 53rd St # Ld
New York, NY 10022-4974 212-564-1883
Fax: 212-629-0955 800-445-6041
mail@dpionlineinc.com www.dpionlineinc.com
Owner: Paul Navarro
distpinc@aol.com
Number Employees: 1-4

43646 Distribution Results
900 Moe Dr
Akron, OH 44310-2519 330-633-0727
Fax: 330-633-0728 800-737-9671
sales@icsponge.com www.icsponge.com
Manufacturer, importer and exporter of cellulose sponges for the bakery, dairy and candy industries
Owner: Larry Rowlands
VP: Larry Rowlands
Research & Development: Jeff Shaffer
Quality Control: Carol Schaffer
Sales: Sherwood Shoemaker
Contact: Dotty Barrett
dotty@icsponge.com
Operations: Dotty Barrott
Estimated Sales: $1 Million
Number Employees: 10-19
Square Footage: 60000
Parent Co: Distribution Results
Brands Imported: Spontex

43647 Dito Dean Food Prep
10200 David Taylor Drive
Charlotte, NC 28262 916-652-5824
Fax: 704-547-7401 866-449-4200
dito-foodservice@electrolux.com
professional.electroluxusa.com
Manufacturer and exporter of blenders, cheese shredding and cubing equipment, cutters, slicers, food and vegetable processors, salad dryers and verticle cutters and mixers
President: Gary Probert
Estimated Sales: $1-2.5 Million
Number Employees: 5-9
Parent Co: WCI
Type of Packaging: Food Service
Regions Exported to: Canada
Percentage of Business in Exporting: 2

43648 Ditting USA
1000 Air Way
Glendale, CA 91201-3030 818-247-9479
Fax: 818-247-9722 800-835-5992
info@ditting.com www.ditting.com
Manufacturer, importer and exporter of commercial coffee grinders
President: Albert Bezjian
nancy@ditting.com
CEO: Nancy Wideman
CFO: Mike Hatun
Estimated Sales: Below $ 5 Million
Number Employees: 5-9
Number of Brands: 1
Square Footage: 16000
Brands Imported: Ditting
Regions Imported from: Europe
Percentage of Business in Importing: 100

43649 Diversified Capping Equipment
8030 Broadstone Road
Perrysburg, OH 43551-4856 419-666-2566
Fax: 419-666-0275
Manufacturer and exporter of closure application machines, cap sorters and cap conveying equipment
VP: Jack Weber
Engineering Manager: John Louy
Estimated Sales: $ 2.5-5 Million
Number Employees: 10-19
Square Footage: 128000
Brands Exported: Diversified
Regions Exported to: Worldwide
Percentage of Business in Exporting: 20

43650 Diversified Lighting Diffusers Inc
175-B Liberty St
Copiague, NY 11726 631-842-0099
Fax: 631-980-7668 800-234-5464
info@receilit.com www.1800ceiling.com
Manufacturer and distributor of fluorescent safety sleeves and vapor-tight lenses; also, custom fabrication of acrylic and lexan diffusers
CEO: Joe Broser
COO: Colleen Baum

Estimated Sales: $ 1 - 3 Million
Number Employees: 5-9
Square Footage: 100000
Regions Exported to: Worldwide

43651 Diversified Metal Engineering
54 Hilstrom Ave.
PO Box 553
Charlottetown, PE C1E 2C6
Canada 902-628-6900
Fax: 902-628-1313 info@dmeinternational.com
Manufacturer and exporter of washers, cookers, conveyors, graders and coolers for fish; also, brewery and dairy tanks, potato and vegetable shapers, turnkey microbrewery systems, portion packing equipment and piping systems andconveyors for dairy products, pressure vessels, complete skid systems and tanks.
President: Peter Toombs
VP Marketing/Sales: Barry MacLeod
Marketing Director: Kelly Lantz
Director of Sales and Marketing: David Campbell
Production Manager: Blair MacKinnon
Purchasing Manager: Ralph MacDonald
Estimated Sales: $7 Million
Number Employees: 50-99
Square Footage: 80000
Regions Exported to: Worldwide
Percentage of Business in Exporting: 80

43652 Dixie Canner Machine Shop
326 Commerce Blvd
Athens, GA 30606-0824 706-549-0592
Fax: 706-549-0137 sales@dixiecanner.com
www.dixiecanner.net
Manufacturer and exporter of low-volume canning equipment including seamers, retorts, exhausters and vacuum closers; also, blanchers, pulpers/finishers and lye peelers
President: B Gentry
Chairman: W Stapleton Sr
VP Manufacturing: J Campbell
VP Sales: Parrish Stapleton
Contact: Bill Gentry
bill@dixiecanner.com
Estimated Sales: $1-2.5 Million
Number Employees: 5-9
Square Footage: 24000
Regions Exported to: Worldwide
Percentage of Business in Exporting: 30

43653 Dixie Egg Co
5139 Edgewood Ct
Jacksonville, FL 32254-3601 904-783-0950
Fax: 904-786-6227 800-394-3447
kjkeggs@aol.com www.dixieegg.com
Fresh shell eggs
President: Jacques Klempf
CEO: Edward Klempf
sshimoda@dixieegg.com
Controller: Paul Stevenson
IT: Steve Slayter
Feed/Production Manager: Dennis Hughes
Number Employees: 250-499
Parent Co: Foodonics International
Type of Packaging: Consumer, Bulk
Regions Exported to: Central America
Percentage of Business in Exporting: 50

43654 Dixie Flag Mfg Co
1930 N Interstate 35
San Antonio, TX 78208-1925 210-227-5039
Fax: 210-227-5920 800-356-4085
dixieflg@dixieflag.com www.dixieflag.com
Manufacturer and exporter of flags, street net banners and pennants
President: Henry P Van Deputte Jr
pete@dixieflag.com
VP: Sally Van de Putte
VP: Glenda Krueger
Estimated Sales: $ 5 - 10 Million
Number Employees: 20-49
Regions Exported to: Europe

43655 Dixie USA
P.O. Box 1969
Tomball, TX 77377 832-616-3366
Fax: 832-201-0765 800-233-3668
info@dixieusa.com www.dixiediner.com
Meat analogs, tofu, soy products and low carb products; exporter of soy
President: Brenda K. Oswalt
Chairman, Founder: Bob Beeley
EVP: Jim Oswalt

Estimated Sales: $5-10 Million
Number Employees: 20-49
Square Footage: 120000
Type of Packaging: Consumer, Food Service, Private Label, Bulk
Percentage of Business in Exporting: 20

43656 Do-It Corp
1201 Blue Star Hwy
PO Box 592
South Haven, MI 49090-9784 269-639-2600
Fax: 269-637-7223 800-426-4822
sales@do-it.com www.do-it.com
Manufacturer, importer and exporter of self-adhesive plastic hangers and hang tabs; also, contract packaging available
President: Mark Mc Clendon
sales@do-it.com
Director Marketing: John Deschaine
VP Sales: Chuck Miller
Estimated Sales: $5-10 Million
Number Employees: 50-99
Square Footage: 80000
Regions Exported to: Worldwide
Percentage of Business in Exporting: 15

43657 Doering Machines Inc
2121 Newcomb Ave
San Francisco, CA 94124-1300 415-526-2131
Fax: 415-526-2136 sales@doeringmachines.com
www.doeringmachines.com
Manufacturer and exporter of pumping, extruding, portioning, metering, cartoning and wrapping systems for high viscosity products including dough, butter, cheese and polymers
President: Richard Doering
richard.doering@doeringmachines.com
CEO: Tim Doering
Estimated Sales: $ 2.5-5 Million
Number Employees: 5-9
Square Footage: 60000
Regions Exported to: Europe, Middle East
Percentage of Business in Exporting: 25

43658 Dolco Packaging Co
2110 Patterson St
Decatur, IN 46733-1892 260-728-2161
Fax: 260-728-9958 www.tekni-plex.com
Manufacturer and exporter of polystyrene foam packaging
CEO: Steve Harvey
steve.harvey@tekni-plex.com
Vice President: Norm Patterson
Quality Control: Doug Keller
Marketing Director: Phil Laughlin
Public Relations: Amy Geradoj
Production Manager: Jeff Brown
Plant Manager: Roger Lichtle
Purchasing Manager: Terry Alberson
Estimated Sales: $20-50 Million
Number Employees: 100-249
Parent Co: Tekni Plex
Type of Packaging: Food Service

43659 Dole Food Company, Inc.
PO Box 5700
Thousand Oaks, CA 91359-5700
800-356-3111
www.dole.com
Fresh fruit, vegetables, prepared foods and salads.
Chairman: David Murdock
President/CEO: Johan Linden
Vice President/CFO: Johan Malmqvist
President, Dole Fresh Vegetables: Michael Solomon
Year Founded: 1851
Estimated Sales: $4.5 Billion
Number Employees: 59,000
Type of Packaging: Consumer, Food Service, Private Label, Bulk
Other Locations:
Dole Manufacturing Facility
(9) ArizonaDole Manufacturing Facility(11) California

43660 (HQ)Dole Refrigerating Co
1420 Higgs Rd
Lewisburg, TN 37091-4402 931-359-6211
Fax: 931-359-8664 800-251-8990
sales@doleref.com www.kencoplastics.com
Manufacturer and exporter of truck refrigeration units including eutectic plate and blower; also, quick freeze plates for food processing, double contact quick freezing freezers and fiberglass coolers

President: John Cook
johnjr@doleref.com
CFO: Joe Mulliniks
Sales Manager: Bobby Dunnivant
Chief Engineer: Rod Hardy
Estimated Sales: $ 20 - 50 Million
Number Employees: 50-99
Square Footage: 55000
Regions Exported to: Worldwide
Percentage of Business in Exporting: 25

43661 Dolphin Natural Chocolates
1975 Woodview Avenue
Cambria, CA 93428-5168 805-927-7103
Fax: 831-722-0318 800-236-5744
Sugar and dairy-free chocolates; also, chocolate dipped apricots, papaya and pineapple
Owner: Henry McKowen
Estimated Sales: $2.5-5 Million
Number Employees: 5-9
Square Footage: 4000
Type of Packaging: Consumer
Regions Exported to: Canada
Percentage of Business in Exporting: 5

43662 DomainMarket
9812 Falls Road Ste.
Suite 290
Potomac, MD 20854 973-366-7500
Fax: 973-366-7453 888-694-6735
contact@DomainMarket.com
Manufacturer and exporter of converting equipment for food packaging
CEO: John Wilkes
Estimated Sales: $ 10-20 Million
Number Employees: 50-99

43663 Dominex
P.O.Box 5069
St Augustine, FL 32085 904-810-2132
Fax: 904-810-9852 sales@dominexeggplant.com
www.dominexeggplant.com
Eggplant cutlets and appetizers; including peeled, breaded, battered, deep fried and IQF. All natural fully cooked breaded in italian crumbs, eggplant appetizers and cutlets
President: John McGarvey
Director- Sales and Marketing: Miranda Chalke
chalke@dominexeggplant.com
Estimated Sales: 10-19
Number Employees: 50-99
Number of Brands: 10
Number of Products: 145
Type of Packaging: Food Service, Private Label, Bulk
Regions Exported to: Europe, Middle East

43664 Dona Yiya Foods
P.O.Box 1623
San Sebastian, PR 00685 787-896-4007
Fax: 787-280-1430 jd@donayiya.com
www.donayiya.com
Manufacturer, exporter and importer of spices and seasonings including garlic in oil or water, soffritto, condiments and tropical candies
President: Javier Quinones
Plant Manager: Luis Denis
Estimated Sales: $3.1 Million
Number Employees: 12
Number of Brands: 2
Number of Products: 23
Square Footage: 40000
Type of Packaging: Consumer, Food Service, Private Label, Bulk
Regions Exported to: North America
Percentage of Business in Exporting: 80
Regions Imported from: Latin , North America
Percentage of Business in Importing: 5

43665 (HQ)Donahower & Company
15615 S Keeler Ter
Olathe, KS 66062-3509 913-829-2650
Fax: 913-829-5494
Manufacturer and exporter of conveyors including package handling, flat top chain and material handling; also, lidding and capping machinery and bottle rotators
President: Carol Brooks
Vice President: Ken Koelzer
Estimated Sales: $1-2.5 Million
Number Employees: 5-9
Square Footage: 10000

Importers & Exporters / A-Z

43666 Donaldson Co Inc
1400 W 94th St
Bloomington, MN 55431   952-887-3131
www.donaldson.com
Manufacturer, importer and exporter of dust control and filtration equipment.
Chairman, President & CEO: Tod Carpenter
tod.carpenter@donaldson.com
Senior VP & CFO: Scott Robinson
Year Founded: 1915
Estimated Sales: $2.85 Billion
Number Employees: 11,700
Brands Exported: DCE Dalamatic; Siloair; Maxcell
Regions Exported to: Worldwide
Percentage of Business in Exporting: 15
Regions Imported from: Worldwide
Percentage of Business in Importing: 10

43667 Dong Us I
2590 Main St
Irvine, CA 92614-6227   949-251-1768
Fax: 949-251-8865   888-580-0088
info@dongyu.us www.dongyu.us
Manufacturer and distributor of L-Carnitine products, amino acids, vitamins, sweeteners, sports nutrition ingredients, food and beverage ingredients
Manager: Weili Zhang
Number Employees: 10-19
Square Footage: 40000
Regions Exported to: Europe, Canada, Mexico

43668 Donoco Industries
P.O. Box 3208
Huntington Beach, CA 92605   714-893-7889
Fax: 714-897-7968   888-822-8763
info@encoreplastics.com www.encoreplastics.com
Manufacturer and exporter of plastic mugs and tumblers
President: Richard Harvey
Estimated Sales: $ 5 - 10 Million
Number Employees: 25
Regions Exported to: Worldwide
Percentage of Business in Exporting: 20

43669 Doosan Industrial Vehicle America Corp
2475 Mill Center Parkway
Suite 400
Buford, GA 30518   678-745-2200
Fax: 678-745-2250 www.doosanlift.com
Manufacturer, importer and exporter of industrial trucks.
VP & CEO: Tony Jones
National Sales Director: Jeff Powell
Year Founded: 1962
Estimated Sales: $7 Billion
Number Employees: 7,728
Square Footage: 150000
Parent Co: Doosan Group
Regions Exported to: Canada
Brands Imported: Daewoo
Regions Imported from: Asia
Percentage of Business in Importing: 100

43670 Dopaco
492 Sovereign Court
London, ON N6M 1B2
Canada   519-659-9940
Fax: 519-659-3465
Manufacturer and supplier of hot & cold cups, take out containers, fry cartons, food trays and pizza boxes.

43671 Doran Scales Inc
1315 Paramount Pkwy
Batavia, IL 60510-1460   630-879-1200
Fax: 630-879-0073   800-365-0084
sales@doranscales.com www.doranscales.com
Stainless steel washdown safe scales.
President: Mark Podl
markp@doranscales.com
Chairman/CEO: William Podl
CEO: William Podl
Marketing Coordinator: Mark Anderson
Applications Engineer: Mark Podl
Estimated Sales: $ 5 - 10 Million
Number Employees: 20-49
Square Footage: 80000
Brands Exported: Doran
Regions Exported to: Central America, South America, Europe, Asia, Middle East, Canada, Latin America, Mexico

Percentage of Business in Exporting: 10

43672 (HQ)Dorina So-Good Inc
17400 Jefferson St
Union, IL 60180-9705   815-923-2144
Fax: 815-923-2151
Manufacturer and exporter of shelf stable barbecue beef and pork; also, mustard, sauces, salsa, salad dressings, chip dips, olive salad and cheesespreads
President: Tim Young
CEO: Darwin Young
Estimated Sales: $.5-1 Million
Number Employees: 20-49
Square Footage: 24000
Type of Packaging: Consumer, Food Service, Private Label, Bulk
Brands Exported: Bar-B-Q Delight
Regions Exported to: Worldwide

43673 Dorset Fisheries
215 Water St
Suite 302
St Josephs, NL A1C 6C9
Canada   709-739-7147
Fax: 709-739-0586
Manufacturer and exporter of fresh lobster and cod
President: Derick Philpott
Estimated Sales: $5 Million
Number Employees: 30
Type of Packaging: Bulk
Regions Exported to: Worldwide
Percentage of Business in Exporting: 80

43674 Dorton Incorporated
3436 N Kennicott Ave
Arlington Hts, IL 60004-7814   847-577-8600
Fax: 847-392-6212   800-299-8600
www.dortongroup.com
President: Ed Collins
CFO: Al Nowak
VP: Marie Collins
R&D: Milt Lynn
Marketing: Micki Bagnuolo
Sales: Micki Bagnuolo
Public Relations: Ed Collins
Operations Manager: Michelle Gilbert
Production: M Levinberg
Purchasing: Cindy Byrne
Number Employees: 10-19
Number of Brands: 2
Number of Products: 12
Square Footage: 15200
Type of Packaging: Food Service
Brands Exported: Dorton
Regions Exported to: Central America, South America
Percentage of Business in Exporting: 5
Brands Imported: Sammic; Tellier; Lacor; Eurast
Regions Imported from: Europe
Percentage of Business in Importing: 50

43675 Dorval Trading Co LTD
55 Old Turnpike Rd
Suite 106
Nanuet, NY 10954-2449   845-624-3031
Fax: 845-624-8137   800-367-8252
info@dorvaltrading.com
Importer of candy including, licorice, lollipops, mints, sourballs, hard and filled, caramels, chocolates, gift items, gift boxes and gum.
President: Roberta Cappel
rcappel@dorvaltrading.com
Sales/Marketing Manager: Lance Reiter
Estimated Sales: $ 10 - 20 Million
Number Employees: 10-19
Square Footage: 4000
Type of Packaging: Consumer, Private Label, Bulk
Brands Imported: Dorval™; Droste™; Top Pops™; King™; Sour Power™ Rendez vous™; Flavigny Elite™

43676 Dot-It Food Safety Products
2011 E Randol Mill Rd
Arlington, TX 76011   817-275-7714
Fax: 817-275-0122   800-642-3687
Labels and tags
Manager: Ben Nicholson
Director Sales: Robert Galan
General Manager: Sonya Peterson
Estimated Sales: $ 1 - 3 Million
Number Employees: 5-9
Square Footage: 72000
Parent Co: Craftmark Label Graphics

43677 Double Wrap Cup & Container
728 W Jackson Blvd
Ste 1002
Chicago, IL 60661   312-337-0072
Fax: 847-777-0586
High quality, low cost insulated wrap for paper coffee cups.
CEO: Ted Alpert
VP: Ted Alpert
Marketing Director: Ted Alpert
Sales Director: Ted Alpert
Public Relations: Ted Alpert
Operations Manager: Ted Alpert
Estimated Sales: $ 3 - 5 Million
Number Employees: 10-19
Type of Packaging: Food Service
Brands Exported: Comfort Grip Wrap
Regions Exported to: Central America, South America, Europe, Asia, Middle East

43678 Doucette Industries
20 Leigh Dr
York, PA 17406-8474   717-718-8944
Fax: 717-845-2864   800-445-7511
info@doucetteindustries.com
www.doucetteindustries.com
Manufacturer and exporter of suction line and vented double wall heat exchangers, CO2 Vaporizers, coaxial coils, counterflow condensers and vibration absorbers for air conditioning, refrigeration and hydronic applications
President: John Lebo
johnl@doucetteindustries.com
Number Employees: 20-49
Brands Exported: AC; CADS; SLHE NSY Series Heat Exchangers
Regions Exported to: Worldwide
Percentage of Business in Exporting: 10

43679 Douglas Homs Corporation
295 Old County Road
Suite 12
San Carlos, CA 94070-6240   650-592-1616
Fax: 650-592-1619   800-592-1616
Wholesaler/distributor and importer of scales
President: J Nielsen
Number Employees: 1-4
Regions Imported from: Europe, Asia
Percentage of Business in Importing: 100

43680 Douglas Machines Corp.
4500 110th Ave North
Clearwater, FL 33762   727-461-3477
Fax: 727-449-0029   800-331-6870
info@dougmac.com www.dougmac.com
Automated industrial and commercial washing and sanitizing equipment
President/Owner: Dave Ward
VP, Finance: Susan Mader
Marketing Manager: Darcel Schouler
Sales Manager: Kevin Quinn
Operations Manager: Dale Breedlove
Estimated Sales: $5-10 Million
Number Employees: 50-99
Number of Brands: 3
Number of Products: 40
Square Footage: 50000
Brands Exported: Douglas
Regions Exported to: South America, Europe, Asia, Canada, Mexico
Percentage of Business in Exporting: 5

43681 Dove Screen Printing Co
18 Salem Rd
Royston, GA 30662-7406   706-245-4975
Fax: 706-245-7500 www.dovescreenprinting.com
Manufacturer and exporter of advertising specialties, signs and restaurant aprons; importer of caps and coffee mugs
Owner: Ronny Dove
ronnydove@aol.com
Estimated Sales: Less Than $500,000
Number Employees: 1-4
Regions Exported to: Worldwide
Brands Imported: Nissin; K.C. Caps
Regions Imported from: Asia

43682 Dover Chemical Corp
3676 Davis Rd NW
Dover, OH 44622-9771   330-343-7711
Fax: 330-364-1579   800-321-8805
www.doverchem.com
Manufacturer and exporter of bleaches, muratic acids and antioxidants

President: Kevin Burke
burke@cranechempharma.com
CFO: Mike Caffrey
Quality Control: Dave Schlarb
Quality Issues: Carol Churilla
Marketing Coordinator: Wendy Finch
US Sales Manager: Chad McGlothlin
Purchasing Agent: Robert Ren
Number Employees: 100-249
Parent Co: ICC Industries
Regions Exported to: Worldwide
Percentage of Business in Exporting: 20

43683 Dover Parkersburg
PO Box 610
Follansbee, WV 26037-610
Fax: 304-485-3214
Manufacturer and importer of tinware including baking pans, garbage cans, buckets, tubs, wringers and mopping equipment
Sales: Donna Burns
Director Operations: William Cusack, Jr.
Estimated Sales: $10-20 Million
Number Employees: 50-99
Parent Co: Louis Berkman
Type of Packaging: Bulk

43684 Dovex Export Co
1705 N Miller St
Wenatchee, WA 98801-1585   509-662-8062
Fax: 509-662-7066 richr@dovex.com
www.dovex.com
Exporter of fresh apples, pears, cherries, plums, carrots, melons, grapes, peaches, garlic and nectarines
Export Dir.: Todd George
Export Dir.: Richard H Roberts, Jr.
Export Dir.: Mauro Felizia
VP: Jay Fulbright
Estimated Sales: $20-50 Million
Number Employees: 250-499
Type of Packaging: Private Label, Bulk
Brands Exported: Dovex; A-Plus; Grand Chelan; Mad River
Regions Exported to: Central America, South America, Europe, Asia, Middle East
Percentage of Business in Exporting: 100

43685 Dow Distribution
524 Ohohia St
Honolulu, HI 96819-1934   808-836-3511
Fax: 808-833-3634
Fish and seafood
President: Craig Mitchell
cmitch@hawaii.rr.com
Estimated Sales: $ 10 - 20 Million
Number Employees: 10-19

43686 Dow Industries
271 Ballardvale St
Wilmington, MA 01887-1081   978-658-8200
Fax: 978-658-2307 800-776-1201
sales@dowindustries.com www.smythco.com
Manufacturer and exporter of pressure sensitive labels and automatic labeling equipment
President: Walter Dow
CEO: Andy Farquharson
CFO: John Morrison
Quality Control: Scott Boucher
Senior VP: Bill Donovan
Operations Manager: D Apgar
Estimated Sales: $20 Million
Number Employees: 50-99
Square Footage: 64000
Type of Packaging: Consumer, Private Label
Regions Exported to: Central America
Percentage of Business in Exporting: 4

43687 Dow Packaging
2211 H.H. Dow Way
Midland, MI 48674   989-636-1000
Fax: 989-382-1456 800-331-6451
www.dow.com
Processor and exporter of ethylene oxide/ethylene glycol, coating materials, industrial performance chemicals, polyolefin resins and compounds, solvents intermediates and monomers, UCAR emulsion systems, specialty polymers andproducts.
Chairman & CEO: Andrew Liveris
President & COO: James Fitterling
Vice Chairman & CFO: Howard Underleider
EVP & General Counsel: Charles Kalil
Controller/VP of Controllers & Tax: Ron Edmonds
Year Founded: 1917
Number Employees: 2,300
Parent Co: The Dow Chemical Company
Type of Packaging: Bulk
Regions Exported to: Worldwide
Percentage of Business in Exporting: 30

43688 Downs Crane & Hoist Co Inc
8827 Juniper St
Los Angeles, CA 90002-1899   323-589-6061
Fax: 323-589-6066 800-748-5994
sales@downscrane.com www.downscrane.com
Manufacturer and exporter of lifting devices including grabs, tongs, spreaders, manipulators, hooks, cranes and crane wheels and assemblies
President: John W Downs Jr
Number Employees: 5-9
Type of Packaging: Bulk
Brands Exported: Grabmaster
Regions Exported to: Canada, Mexico
Percentage of Business in Exporting: 5

43689 Doyon
Canada
800-265-2600
www.mieldoyon.com
Beeswax and honey; exporter of honey; importer of pollen
President: Paul Doyon
CEO: David Sugarman
Number Employees: 15
Square Footage: 60000
Parent Co: McCormick & Co.
Type of Packaging: Consumer, Food Service, Bulk
Regions Exported to: Europe, Asia
Percentage of Business in Exporting: 5
Regions Imported from: Europe
Percentage of Business in Importing: 5

43690 Doyon Equipment
1255 Rue Principale
Liniere, QC G0M 1J0
Canada   418-685-3431
Fax: 418-685-3948 800-463-4273
sales@nu-vu.com www.doyon.qc.ca
Baking equipment
President: Karl Doyon
Research & Development: Pierre Poirier
Marketing Director: Jennifer Letourneau
Regional Sales Director: John Herbert
Regional Sales Director: Jim Markee
Estimated Sales: $10-20 Million
Number Employees: 20
Brands Exported: Doyon; Jet Air
Regions Exported to: Worldwide
Percentage of Business in Exporting: 75

43691 Dr Konstantin Frank's Vinifera
9749 Middle Rd
Hammondsport, NY 14840-9612   800-320-0735
Fax: 607-868-4888 800-320-0735
info@drfrankwines.com www.drfrankwines.com
Manufacturer and exporter of table wine and champagne
President: Fred Frank
VP & Vineyard Manager: Eric Volz
Consulting Winemaker & Regional Sales Ma: Barbara Frank
Contact: Peter Bell
pbell@spidergraphics.com
Estimated Sales: $ 5 - 10 Million
Number Employees: 5-9
Type of Packaging: Consumer
Brands Exported: Dr. Konstantin Frank; Chateau Frank
Regions Exported to: Asia, Canada
Percentage of Business in Exporting: 10

43692 Dr. Christopher's Herbal Supplements
155 W 2050 N
Spanish Fork, UT 84660   801-453-1406
Fax: 801-794-6801 800-453-1406
www.drchristopher.com
Supplements and herbal formulas
Sales/Marketing: Troy Fukumitsu
Contact: Robert Scott
rscott@drchristopher.com
Estimated Sales: $20-50 Million
Number Employees: 20-49
Type of Packaging: Consumer, Private Label, Bulk
Regions Exported to: Worldwide

43693 Dr. John's Candies
2201 Oak Industrial Dr NE
Grand Rapids, MI 49505   616-454-3707
Fax: 616-459-3378 888-375-6462
www.drjohns.com
Wholesaler/distributor of sugar-free candy including lollipops, sour balls, taffy, caramels, toffee, mints, etc
President/CEO: Debra Bruinsma
Estimated Sales: $500,000
Number Employees: 1-4
Number of Brands: 1
Number of Products: 10
Square Footage: 20000
Type of Packaging: Consumer, Private Label, Bulk
Brands Exported: All Sugar-Free Candies
Regions Exported to: Central America, South America, Europe, Canada

43694 Dr. Paul Lohmann Inc.
1757-10 Veterans Memorial Hwy
Islandia, NY 11749   631-851-8810
Fax: 631-851-8815
Specialty mineral salts

43695 Draco Natural Products Inc
539 Parrott St
San Jose, CA 95112-4121   408-287-7871
Fax: 408-287-8838 info@dracoherbs.com
www.draconatural.com
Wholesales herbal extracts
CEO: Jerry Wu
Sales: Ed Schack
Estimated Sales: $3 Million
Number Employees: 10-19

43696 Dragnet Fisheries
4141 B St
Anchorage, AK 99503-5940   907-276-4551
Fax: 907-274-3617
Fresh and frozen herring, black cod, halibut and salmon
President: Jay Cherrier
Estimated Sales: Less than $500,000
Number Employees: 1-4
Type of Packaging: Consumer, Food Service

43697 Drake Co
1401 Greengrass Dr
Houston, TX 77008-5005   713-869-9121
Fax: 713-869-3512 800-299-5644
Manufacturer and exporter of corrugated boxes and lithographic displays
CEO: John Carrico
CFO: Shelley Golden
sgolden@drakecompany.com
Sales/Service Manager: Kevin Fiedler
Estimated Sales: $ 1 - 5 Million
Number Employees: 100-249
Regions Exported to: Central America, Europe, Canada
Percentage of Business in Exporting: 5

43698 Drake Corp
154 Tices Ln
East Brunswick, NJ 08816   732-254-1530
Fax: 732-254-3509 info@drakecorp.com
Owner: Ramano Discacciati
ramano@drakecorp.com
Estimated Sales: $ 1 - 3 Million
Number Employees: 5-9

43699 Draper Valley Farms
1000 Jason Ln
Mt Vernon, WA 98273-2490   360-748-9466
Fax: 360-424-1666 800-562-2012
www.drapervalleyfarms.com
Free range chicken
Vice President: Jeff Power
CFO: Richard Koplowitz
VP & General Manager: Bob Wolfe
Sales & Marketing Manager: Vicki Knutson
Human Resources Manager: Colleen Helgeson
Plant Manager: John Michalak
Head of Purchasing: Jody Dethman
Number Employees: 250-499
Square Footage: 131196
Type of Packaging: Consumer, Food Service
Regions Exported to: Worldwide

Importers & Exporters / A-Z

43700 Drapes 4 Show
12811 Foothill Blvd
Sylmar, CA 91342-5316 818-838-0852
Fax: 818-222-7469 800-525-7469
staff@drapes.com www.drapes.com
Tabletop accessories including napkins, table skirting and table linens
CEO: Karen Honigberg
Customer Service: Kathryn Pereyra
Estimated Sales: Below $5 Million
Number Employees: 20-49
Square Footage: 12800

43701 Dreaco Products
172 Reaser Court
Elyria, OH 44035-6285 440-366-7600
Fax: 440-365-5858 800-368-3267
Manufacturer and exporter of exhaust hoods and fans; also, make-up air fans
Owner and President: Robert Gargasz
Sales/Marketing Executive: Karen Kauk
Purchasing Agent: Michael Gargasz
Estimated Sales: $2.5-5 Million
Number Employees: 20-49
Square Footage: 100000
Regions Exported to: Worldwide

43702 (HQ)Dream Confectioners LTD
540 Cedar Ln
Teaneck, NJ 07666-1742 201-836-9000
Fax: 201-836-9015
Manufacturer and exporter of pretzels
President: Joseph Podolski
Estimated Sales: $2.5-5 Million
Number Employees: 1-4
Type of Packaging: Consumer, Private Label, Bulk
Brands Exported: Great Pretzels
Regions Exported to: Central America, South America, Europe, Canada, Caribbean
Percentage of Business in Exporting: 5

43703 Drehmann Paving & Flooring Company
847 Bethel Ave
Pennsauken, NJ 08110-2605 856-486-0202
Fax: 856-486-0808 800-523-3800
Manufacturer and exporter of brick floor coatings, plates and drains; installation services available
President: William Varra
VP: J Kline, Jr.
Executive VP: Horace Furman
Research & Development: M Bojesuk
Quality Control: S Furman
Contact: J Kline
kklinejr@drehmann.com
Estimated Sales: $5,000,000
Number Employees: 75-100
Number of Brands: 1
Number of Products: 10
Square Footage: 36000
Type of Packaging: Private Label
Regions Exported to: South America, Europe, Worldwide, Phillipines
Percentage of Business in Exporting: 10
Regions Imported from: Europe
Percentage of Business in Importing: 3

43704 Dresco Belting Co Inc
122 East St
PO Box 890026
East Weymouth, MA 02189-2198 781-335-1350
Fax: 781-340-0500 sales@drescobelt.com
www.drescobelt.com
Manufacturer and exporter of conveyor and transmission belting
Owner: James Dresser
jim.dresser@drescobelt.com
VP, Manufacturing & Technology: James G. Dresser
VP, Sales: Norman K. Dresser
Estimated Sales: $1-2.5 Million
Number Employees: 1-4
Square Footage: 40000
Brands Exported: Dresco
Regions Exported to: Central America, South America, Asia, Middle East, Africa
Percentage of Business in Exporting: 10

43705 Dreumex USA
3445 Board Rd
York, PA 17406-8409 717-767-6881
Fax: 717-767-6888 800-233-9382
dreumex@dreumex.com www.dreumex.com
Manufacturer and exporter of waterless gel and lotion hand cleaners and liquid soap; also, hand and multi-purpose wipes, dispensing systems, and car/truck wash
President/CEO: Jim Strickler
Research & Development: Gail Shermeyer
Quality Control: Gail Shermeyer
Marketing Director: Karen Hansen
Sales Director: Jim Strickler
Contact: Craig Bennett
c.bennett@dreumex.com
Operations Manager: Jeff Strickler
Production Manager: Jim Mitzel
Plant Manager: Jim Mitzel
Purchasing Manager: Bob Keyser
Estimated Sales: $ 5 - 10 Million
Number Employees: 20-49
Number of Brands: 13
Number of Products: 13
Square Footage: 160000
Type of Packaging: Private Label
Brands Exported: Grime Grabber; Citrus Lotion; Gent-L-Kleen; Power Wipes; Advantage; Zapper; Premium Blue; GLK-SS

43706 Dri Mark Products
15 Harbor Park Dr
Port Washington, NY 11050 516-484-6200
Fax: 516-484-6279 800-645-9118
www.drimark.com
Manufacturer and exporter of pens including nylon, felt and plastic tip, ball point, roller ball and counterfeit detector; also, watercolor and permanent markers, highlighters and drawing sets
President: Charles Reichmann
CFO: Cathy Owens
VP Sales: Mark Dobbs
Purchasing Manager: Mickey Cirrani
Estimated Sales: $ 20 - 50 Million
Number Employees: 100-249
Square Footage: 70000
Regions Exported to: Central America, South America, Europe, Middle East
Percentage of Business in Exporting: 10

43707 Driall Inc
1144 E 800 N
Attica, IN 47918-8027 765-295-2255
Fax: 317-272-1097
Manufacturer and exporter of grain dryers and air curtain destructors for controlled open residue burning
Manager: Dave Scott
Estimated Sales: Less Than $500,000
Number Employees: 1-4
Type of Packaging: Food Service, Bulk
Regions Exported to: Worldwide
Percentage of Business in Exporting: 40

43708 Driscoll Strawberry Assoc Inc
345 Westridge Dr
Watsonville, CA 95076-4169 831-424-0506
Fax: 831-761-1090 www.driscolls.com
Grower of premium berries.
Chairman & CEO: Miles Reiter
Manager: J M Reiter
jm.reiter@driscolls.com
Number Employees: 50-99
Regions Exported to: Central America, South America, Europe, Asia, Middle East
Percentage of Business in Exporting: 10

43709 Droubi's Imports
2721 Hillcroft Street
Houston, TX 77057-5003 713-334-1829
Fax: 713-988-9506
Manufacturer, importer and wholesaler/distributor of tea and coffee
President: A Droubi
VP: Sharon Droubi
Estimated Sales: $1-2.5 Million
Number Employees: 20-49
Square Footage: 48000
Parent Co: Droubi's Bakery & Delicatessen

43710 Drum Rock Specialty Co Inc
44 Fullerton Rd
Warwick, RI 02886-1422 401-737-5165
Fax: 401-737-5060
marketing@drumrockproducts.com
www.drumrockproducts.com
Manufacturer and exporter of fritter breading and batter mixes for vegetables, seafood and poultry; also, custom dry blending and mixing and private labeling services available
President: Stephen Hinger
Sales Manager: Paul Skorupa
Estimated Sales: $1-2.5 Million
Number Employees: 5-9
Type of Packaging: Food Service, Private Label, Bulk
Regions Exported to: Canada
Percentage of Business in Exporting: 1

43711 Drum-Mates Inc.
PO Box 636
Lumberton, NJ 08048-0636 609-261-1033
Fax: 609-261-1034 800-621-3786
info@drummates.com www.drummates.com
Manufacturer and supplier of sanitary duty drum and IBC heaters, mixers, pumps, hand dispensing nozzles, bung equipment, fittings, global ThreadConverters and adapters.
Technical Sales: David Marcmann
Estimated Sales: $ 1 - 5 Million
Number Employees: 20
Square Footage: 100000
Brands Exported: Drum-Mates
Regions Exported to: Worldwide
Percentage of Business in Exporting: 5
Percentage of Business in Importing: 5

43712 Dry Creek Vineyard
3770 Lambert Bridge Rd
Healdsburg, CA 95448-9713 707-433-1000
Fax: 707-433-5329 800-864-9463
dcv@drycreekvineyard.com
www.drycreekvineyard.com
Wines
President: Lynda Abbott
traceyrathjen@cabainc.com
CFO: Dru Cochran
VP: Don Wallace
Consumer Manager: Michael Longerbeam
traceyrathjen@cabainc.com
Estimated Sales: $10-20 Million
Number Employees: 20-49
Type of Packaging: Consumer, Food Service
Brands Exported: Dry Creek Vineyard Wine
Regions Exported to: Europe, Asia, Canada, Caribbean, New Zealand
Percentage of Business in Exporting: 10

43713 DuPont Nutrition & Biosciences
4 New Century Pkwy
New Century, KS 66031 913-764-8100
www.food.dupont.com
Ingredients for baking, bars, beverages, confectionery, culinary, diary, frozen desserts, fruit applications, meat alternatives, meat/poultry/seafood, oils and fats, and pet food
President, Nutrition & Biosciences: Mathhias Heinzel
Estimated Sales: $4.4 Billion
Number Employees: 10,000
Parent Co: DuPont
Type of Packaging: Consumer, Bulk
Other Locations:
Central Soya Company - Processing Decatur, IN
Central Soya Company - Processing Gibson City, IL
Central Soya Company - Processing Marion, OH
Central Soya Company - Grain Plant Indianapolis, IN
Central Soya Company - Processing Bellevue, OH
Central Soya Company - Grain Plant Cincinnati, OH
Central Soya Company - ProcessingGibson City
Regions Exported to: Central America, South America, Europe, Asia, Middle East, Worldwide
Regions Imported from: Europe

43714 Dualite Sales & Svc Inc
1 Dualite Ln
Williamsburg, OH 45176-1121 513-724-7100
Fax: 513-724-9029 dualite@dualite.com
www.dualite.com
National account sign manufacturer

President: Frank W Schube
fschube@dualite.com
Executive VP Administration: E Lynn Webb
R&D: Pat Seggerson
National Sales Manager: Robert Stephany
Plant Manager: Jerry Hinnenkamp
Purchasing: Greg Hoffer
Estimated Sales: $35-50 Million
Number Employees: 250-499
Square Footage: 600000
Parent Co: Dualite

43715 Ducktrap River Of Maine
57 Little River Dr
Belfast, ME 04915-6035   207-338-6280
Fax: 207-338-6288   800-434-8727
ducktrap.sales@marineharvest.com
www.ducktrap.com
Pate and smoked seafood including trout fillets, Atlantic salmon, peppered and herb mackerel, mussels, scallops and shrimp
CEO: Alf-Helge Aarskog
General Manager: Don Cynewski
Estimated Sales: $20-50 Million
Number Employees: 100-249
Square Footage: 25000
Type of Packaging: Consumer, Food Service, Bulk
Regions Imported from: Central America, South America, Europe, Asia, Canada, Latin America

43716 Dudson USA Inc
5604 Departure Dr
Raleigh, NC 27616-1841   919-877-0200
Fax: 919-877-0300   800-438-3766
usasales@dudson.com
Importer and wholesaler/distributor of dinnerware including china; serving the food service market
President: Elmer Carr
VP: Lorraine Delois
VP Marketing/Sales: Joel DeNoble
VP Corporate Accounts: Maire-Anne Bassil
Manager: Steve Abourisk
Estimated Sales: $1-2.5 Million
Number Employees: 10-19
Square Footage: 180000
Parent Co: Dudson Company
Type of Packaging: Food Service
Regions Imported from: United Kingdom

43717 Duke Manufacturing Co
2305 N Broadway
St Louis, MO 63102-1420   314-231-1130
Fax: 314-231-5074   800-735-3853
www.dukemfg.com
Manufacturer and exporter of ingredient bins, cabinets, sneeze guards, conveyors, counters, filters, freezers, ovens, steam tables, pans, racks, coolers, kiosks, fire extinguishing systems, sinks, carts, etc
President: Jack Hake
jhake@dukemfg.com
CFO: Larry Reader
Quality Control: Art Lamley
Estimated Sales: $20-50 Million
Number Employees: 100-249
Square Footage: 300000
Regions Exported to: Central America, Canada
Percentage of Business in Exporting: 2

43718 Dulcette Technologies
2 Hicks Street
Lindenhurst, NY 11757   631-752-8700
Fax: 631-752-8117 sales@dulcettetech.com
Sweeteners, nutraceuticals & antioxidants
CEO: M Blum
Quality Control: M Samuels
Marketing: E Saltsberg
Sales: Luke Verdet
Estimated Sales: $500,000-1 Million
Number Employees: 7

43719 Dunbar Manufacturing Co
390 N Gilbert St
South Elgin, IL 60177-1398   847-741-6394
Fax: 847-741-6394
www.dunbarmanufacturing.com
Manufacturer and exporter of caramel and regular popcorn equipment including mixers, tumblers, poppers and sprayers
President: Ray Goode Jr
rgoode4@gmail.com
Estimated Sales: Less than $500,000
Number Employees: 1-4
Number of Products: 40
Square Footage: 12000
Regions Exported to: Central America, South America, Europe, Asia, Middle East
Percentage of Business in Exporting: 20

43720 Dundee Groves
28421 US Highway 27
PO Box 829
Dundee, FL 33838   863-439-2284
Fax: 863-439-5049   800-294-2266
info@dundeegroves.com
www.davidsonofdundee.com
Fresh citrus fruit including; oranges, ruby red grapefruits, all natural citrus candies, coconut patties, citrus marmalades, citrus jellies, butters and orange blossom honey. Gift baskets available
President: Glen Davidson
CEO: Susan Davidson
Estimated Sales: $6 Million
Number Employees: 100-249
Number of Brands: 1
Number of Products: 112
Square Footage: 450000
Type of Packaging: Consumer, Private Label
Brands Exported: Flordia Citrus Candy; Flordia Marmalade & Jelly; Davidson of Dundee
Regions Exported to: Central America, South America, Europe
Regions Imported from: Central America, Europe

43721 Dungeness Development Associates
12969 74th PL. NE
Kirkland, WA 98034   425-823-0770
Fax: 425-823-5049
Producer and importer of Dungeness Crab and Pacific Tiny Shrip
Owner: Joel Van Ornun
Contact: Tena Boggs
tenab@dungenessassoc.com
Plant Manager: Mel Corbitt
Estimated Sales: $ 5 - 10 Million
Number Employees: 20-49

43722 Dunhill Food Equipment Corporation
PO Box 496
Armonk, NY 10504   718-625-4006
Fax: 718-625-0155   800-847-4206
sales@dunhill-esquire.net
Manufacturer and exporter of cafeteria and kitchen equipment including cashier stands, serving counters, sinks, refrigerated display cases and tables
President: Geoffrey Thaw
VP: Larry Dubow
Estimated Sales: $ 5-10 Million
Number Employees: 10-19
Square Footage: 100000
Parent Co: Esquire Mechanical Group
Type of Packaging: Food Service
Brands Exported: Dunhill
Regions Exported to: Middle East, Caribbean
Percentage of Business in Exporting: 5

43723 Dunkley International Inc
1910 Lake St
Kalamazoo, MI 49001-3274   269-343-5583
Fax: 269-343-5614   800-666-1264
Manufacturer and exporter of pitters, de-stemmers and electronic sorters, inspection systems and conveyors
President: Richard L Bogard
Manager: Nick Hatzinikolis
nhatzinikolis@dunkleyinyl.com
General Manager: Ernest Kenneway
Plant Manager: Rob Prange
Estimated Sales: $ 1 - 3 Million
Number Employees: 10-19
Square Footage: 120000
Parent Co: Cherry Central
Regions Exported to: South America, Europe, Asia, Middle East, Canada, Latin America, Australia
Percentage of Business in Exporting: 25

43724 Duplex Mill & Mfg Co
415 Sigler St
Springfield, OH 45506-1144   937-325-5555
Fax: 937-325-0859 www.dmmc.com
Diverter valves and mixing, blending, conveying, elevating, size reduction and slide gate machinery; exporter of mixers, conveyors and hammer mills

CEO: Eric Wise
eww@dmmc.com
Sales Manager: Eric Wise
Production Manager: Eric Brickson
Plant Manager: Eric Brickson
Estimated Sales: $2-3 Million
Number Employees: 10-19
Square Footage: 320000
Brands Exported: Kelly Duplex
Regions Exported to: Worldwide

43725 Dupps Co
548 N Cherry St
Germantown, OH 45327-1185   937-855-0623
Fax: 937-855-6554 info@dupps.com
www.dupps.com
Manufacturer and exporter of process equipment and protein waste recovery systems including cookers and dryers; also, computerized control and information systems, screw presses, conveyor systems, high viscosity material pumps and sizereduction equipment
President: John A Dupps Jr
VP: Frank Dupps
frank.dupps@dupps.com
Quality Control: Tim Seebach
Marketing Manager: Rich Hollmeyer
Estimated Sales: $20-50 Million
Number Employees: 100-249
Square Footage: 120000
Regions Exported to: Worldwide

43726 Dur-Able Aluminum Corporation
1555 Barrington Rd
Hoffman Estates, IL 60169-1019   847-843-1100
Fax: 847-843-0764
Manufacturer and exporter of aluminum foil bakeware including pans, plates, trays and cooking and baking utensils
Estimated Sales: $ 20-50 Million
Number Employees: 1-4
Type of Packaging: Food Service, Bulk
Regions Exported to: Worldwide

43727 Dura Electric Lamp Company
64 E Bigelow Street
Newark, NJ 07114-1699   973-624-0014
Fax: 973-624-3945
Manufacturer and exporter of incandescent and fluorescent lamps and starters
President: Lawrence Portnow
General Manager: A Gross
Estimated Sales: $2.5-5 Million
Number Employees: 5-9
Square Footage: 80000
Regions Exported to: Scandinavia
Percentage of Business in Exporting: 3

43728 Dura-Flex
95 Goodwin St
East Hartford, CT 06108-1146   860-528-9838
Fax: 860-528-2802   877-251-5418
contact_us@dur-a-flex.com www.dur-a-flex.com
Commercial and seamless industrial flooring systems and wall coatings and polymer components - epoxies, urethanes and methyl methacrylates (MMA) plus premium colored quartz aggregates.
CEO: Robert Smith
roberts@dur-a-flex.com
Marketing: Mark Paggioli
Number Employees: 50-99
Square Footage: 260000
Regions Exported to: Central America, South America, Europe, Asia, Middle East
Percentage of Business in Exporting: 5

43729 Dura-Ware By Carlisle
PO Box 53006
Oklahoma City, OK 73152   405-475-5600
Fax: 405-475-5607   800-654-8210
Number Employees: 250-499

43730 (HQ)Dura-Ware Company of America
PO Box 53006
Oklahoma City, OK 73152-3006   405-475-5600
Fax: 405-475-5607   800-664-3872
customerservice@carlislefsp.com
www.carlislefsp.com
Manufacturer, importer and exporter of commercial cookware and servingware including stock pots, frying pans, sauce pans, pasta cookers, chafers, etc
President: David Shannon
VP Sales: David Wasserman

Importers & Exporters / A-Z

Estimated Sales: $ 20 - 50 Million
Number Employees: 50-99
Square Footage: 70000
Brands Exported: Dura-Ware
Regions Exported to: Central America, South America, Europe, Asia, Middle East, Mexico, Caribbean, Canada, Latin America
Percentage of Business in Exporting: 5
Regions Imported from: Central America, Europe, Asia
Percentage of Business in Importing: 20

43731 Durable Engravers
521 S County Line Rd
Franklin Park, IL 60131   630-766-6420
Fax: 630-766-0219   800-869-9565
www.durable-tech.com
Manufacturer and exporter of steel and brass codes, logo blocks and holders for the food and pharmaceutical industries.
CEO: Gary Berenger
g.berenger@durable-tech.com
VP: Jim Maybach
Estimated Sales: $ 1-2.5 Million
Number Employees: 20-49
Square Footage: 20000
Type of Packaging: Food Service, Bulk
Regions Exported to: Europe, Canada

43732 Durable Packaging
750 Northgate Pkwy
Wheeling, IL 60090-2660   847-541-4400
Fax: 847-541-8360   sales@durablepackaging.com
www.durablepackaging.com
President: Michael Rabin
rabin@durablepackaging.com
Number Employees: 500-999

43733 Duralite Inc
15 School St
Riverton, CT 06065-1013   860-379-3113
Fax: 860-379-5879   888-432-8797
sales@duralite.com   www.duralite.com
Manufacturer and exporter of quartz tubes for heating/cooking equipment with element enclosed is tube or wrapped around tube, also heating elements (electric) heating and cooking, coiled or not
Owner: Mark Jessen
markj@duralite.com
CEO: Elliott Jessen
Chairman: Elliot Jessen
Sales Director: Barbara Asselin
markj@duralite.com
Estimated Sales: $1 Million+
Number Employees: 10-19
Square Footage: 15000
Regions Exported to: Central America, South America, Europe
Percentage of Business in Exporting: 2

43734 Duramitt North America
429 W Ohio St
Chicago, IL 60654   312-616-8888
Fax: 312-616-8951
Estimated Sales: $ 5 - 10 Million
Number Employees: 5-9

43735 (HQ)Durand-Wayland Inc
101 Durand Rd
Lagrange, GA 30241-2501   706-882-8161
Fax: 706-882-0052   800-241-2308
sales@durand-wayland.com
www.durand-wayland.com
Manufacturer and exporter of fruit processing and packing machinery including conveyors, cleaners, sizers, sorters, blemish graders and sprayers
President: Brooks Lee
brooksl@durand-wayland.com
VP Sales: Ray Perry
Marketing Director: Ashley Scott
Sales Manager: Suzanne Bryan
Purchasing Manager: Savral Patel
Number Employees: 100-249
Other Locations:
  Durand-Wayland
  Reedley, CADurand-Wayland

43736 (HQ)Durango-Georgia Paper
4301 Anchor Plaza Parkway
Suite 360
Tampa, FL 33634   813-286-2718
Fax: 912-576-0713
Manufacturer and exporter of bleached boards for folding cartons; also, grease resistant decorative paper plates and lightweight cups, bleached and natural kraft paper
VP Marketing: Joseph Meighan
Estimated Sales: $ 1 - 5 Million
Parent Co: Corporation Durango.

43737 Durastill Export Inc
86 Reservoir Park Dr
Rockland, MA 02370-1062   781-878-5577
Fax: 781-878-2224   800-449-5260
sales@durastill.com   www.durastill.com
Manufacturer and exporter of water distillation systems
Owner: M Anthony
Director Sales: Horace Mansfield
Sales: Jeff Thompson
Estimated Sales: Less Than $500,000
Number Employees: 1-4
Parent Co: Master Pitching Machine Company
Regions Exported to: Worldwide
Percentage of Business in Exporting: 40

43738 Durham Manufacturing Co
201 Main St
Durham, CT 06422-2108   860-349-3427
Fax: 860-349-8572   800-243-3744
info@durhammfg.com   www.durhammfg.com
Manufacturer and exporter of pallet rack and industrial duty steel shelving
President: Paul H Frick Jr
Sales/Marketing Administrative Manager: David Massie
Estimated Sales: $2.5-5 Million
Number Employees: 100-249

43739 Durham Ranch
1330 Capital Blvd
Suite A
Reno, NV 89502   775-322-4073
800-444-5687
sales@sierrameat.com   durhamranch.com
Wholesaler/distributor of beef, pork, lamb and veal; importer of venison; exporter of venison and buffalo.
President: John Flocchini
Year Founded: 1965
Estimated Sales: $20-50 Million
Number Employees: 50-99
Percentage of Business in Importing: 5

43740 Durkan Hospitality
P.O.Box 12069
Calhoun, GA 30703   706-629-7721
800-241-4494
mohawkind@mohawkind.com
www.mohawkind.com
Manager: Donnie Smith
Number Employees: 250-499

43741 Durkee-Mower
2 Empire Street
Lynn, MA 01902   781-593-8007
www.marshmallowfluff.com
Manufacturer and exporter of marshmallow creme
Estimated Sales: $ 5 - 10 Million
Number Employees: 24
Square Footage: 140000
Type of Packaging: Consumer, Food Service
Brands Exported: Marshmallow Fluff
Regions Exported to: Europe, Middle East, Australia

43742 (HQ)Dutch Gold Honey Inc
2220 Dutch Gold Dr
Lancaster, PA 17601   717-393-1716
Fax: 717-393-8687   800-338-0587
info@dutchgoldhoney.com
www.dutchgoldhoney.com
Honey and honey products
VP Finance & Administration: Charles Schatzman
Operations Manager: Jody Gable
Year Founded: 1946
Estimated Sales: $20-50 Million
Number Employees: 20-49
Number of Brands: 5
Square Footage: 100000
Type of Packaging: Consumer, Food Service, Private Label, Bulk
Other Locations:
  Dutch Gold Honey
  Littleton, NHDutch Gold Honey
Regions Exported to: Middle East
Regions Imported from: South America, Canada

43743 Dutchess Bakers' Machinery Co
302 Grand Ave
Superior, WI 54880-1243   715-394-2387
Fax: 715-394-6199   800-777-4498
www.dutchessbakers.com
Dutchess Bakers' Machinery Company has been manufacturing high quality dough dividers and dough divider rounders for the foodservice industry since 1886! We are the originator and most respected & recognized name in the world for this kind of equipment; also offers the bun & bagel slicer.
President: Kent Phillips
Marketing Director: Tony Marino
Plant Manager: John Skandel
Estimated Sales: $ 3 - 5 Million
Number Employees: 20-49
Square Footage: 120000
Parent Co: Superior-Lidgerwood-Mundy Corporation
Brands Exported: Dutchess
Regions Exported to: Worldwide
Percentage of Business in Exporting: 10

43744 Dutro Co
675 N 600 W # 2
Logan, UT 84321-3197   435-752-3921
Fax: 435-752-6360   866-388-7660
contact@dutro.com   www.dutro.com
Manufacturer and exporter of carts, dollies and trucks
President: Josh Adams
j.adams@dutro.com
CEO: William Dutro
Estimated Sales: $17,483,702
Number Employees: 50-99
Number of Products: 16
Regions Exported to: Worldwide
Percentage of Business in Exporting: 5

43745 Dwyer Instruments Inc
102 Indiana Highway 212
Michigan City, IN 46360-1956   219-879-8000
Fax: 219-872-9057   800-872-3141
info@dwyer-inst.com   www.dwyer-inst.com
Manufacturer and exporter of HVAC instruments including air filter gauges, thermostats, air velocity transmitters, temperature and process controllers and mercury switches
President: Steve Clark
CFO: Tom Dhaeze
Quality Control: Don Goad
Manager: Dave Lange
dlange@love-controls.com
Purchasing Manager: Dave Pilarski
Estimated Sales: $ 50 - 100 Million
Number Employees: 250-499
Regions Exported to: Worldwide

43746 Dyco
50 Naus Way
Bloomsburg, PA 17815-8784   570-752-2757
Fax: 570-752-7366   800-545-3926
sales@dyco-inc.com   www.dyco-inc.com
Manufacturer and exporter of material handling equipment including case conveyors, car conveyors, diverter gates, fittings, and can rinsers
President: David M Rauscher
VP Sales/Marketing: David Rauscher, Jr.
Manager: Lewis Abram
labram@dyco-inc.com
Office Manager: Lea Ann O'Quinn
Estimated Sales: $ 2.5-5 Million
Number Employees: 50-99
Square Footage: 10000
Regions Exported to: South America, Mexico, Canada
Percentage of Business in Exporting: 10

43747 Dyna Tabs LLC
1933 E 12th St
Brooklyn, NY 11229-2703   718-376-6084
sales@dynatabs.com
www.dynatabs.com
Health, wellness, beauty products including oral edible strips, aloe vera drinking gel and passion punch.
Executive Director: Harold Baum
hbaum@dynatabs.com
CFO: Setty Baum
Estimated Sales: $830,000
Number Employees: 10-19
Parent Co: Baum International, Inc
Type of Packaging: Consumer, Private Label

Importers & Exporters / A-Z

43748 Dyna-Veyor Inc
10 Hudson St
Newark, NJ 07103-2804   973-484-1119
Fax: 973-484-7790 800-326-5009
dynaveyor@aol.com www.dyna-veyor.com
Manufacturer and exporter of plastic conveyor chain belting, sprockets, idlers and corner tracks for the food processing, beverage, canning, pharmaceutical, packaging and container industries
Owner: Tony Ayre
dynaveyor@aol.com
Estimated Sales: $5-10 Million
Number Employees: 10-19
Brands Exported: Dyna-Veyor
Regions Exported to: Central America, South America, Europe, Asia, Middle East, Caribbean
Percentage of Business in Exporting: 15

43749 Dynamic Air Inc
1125 Willow Lake Blvd
St Paul, MN 55110-5193   651-484-2900
Fax: 651-484-7015 info@dynamicair.com
www.dynamicair.com
Pneumatic conveying of bulk solids for the processing industries.
President: James Steele
james.steele@dynamicair.com
National Sales Manager: Tom Acheson
Estimated Sales: $20-50 Million
Number Employees: 100-249
Regions Exported to: Central America, South America, Europe, Asia

43750 Dynamic Cooking Systems
5900 Skylab Rd
Huntington Beach, CA 92647-2061   714-372-7000
Fax: 714-372-7096 800-433-8466
info@dcsappliances.com www.dcsappliances.com
Manufacturer and exporter of ranges, broilers, counter equipment, drop-in-cook tops, wall and convection ovens, ventilation hoods, outdoor barbecues and patio heaters
President: Mike Goadby
President: Michael Markowich
VP: Randy Rummel
CFO: Jeff Elder
Quality Control: Chillie Waiemas
Marketing Manager: Scott Davies
Contact: Vince Barott
vince.barott@fisherpaykel.com
Estimated Sales: $ 5 - 10 Million
Number Employees: 500-999
Square Footage: 66000
Regions Exported to: Europe, Middle East

43751 Dynamic Packaging
5725 International Pkwy
Minneapolis, MN 55428-3079   763-535-8669
Fax: 763-535-8768 800-878-9380
www.dynamicpkg.com
Printed and laminated flexible packaging films, roll stock and bags including simplex style and wicketed side-weld polyethylene; importer of polypropylene and polyester packaging films
Owner: George Butgusaim
VP Sales: James Pater, Jr.
VP Production: Thoams Guerity
Contact: Cindy Carr
ccarr@packaging-specialties.com
Estimated Sales: $1-2.5 Million
Number Employees: 10-19
Square Footage: 80000
Regions Imported from: South America, Asia
Percentage of Business in Importing: 10

43752 Dynapro International
451 N Main St
Kaysville, UT 84037-1114   801-621-1413
Fax: 801-621-8258 800-877-1413
sales@dynaprointernational.com
www.dynaprointernational.com
Manufacturer and exporter of vitamins and herbal supplements
Owner: Bailey Hall
sales@dynaprointernational.com
Marketing Director: Gary Hoffman
Estimated Sales: Less Than $500,000
Number Employees: 5-9
Square Footage: 15600
Regions Exported to: Europe, Canada

43753 Dynaric Inc
5740 Bayside Rd
Virginia Beach, VA 23455-3004   757-460-3725
Fax: 757-363-8016 800-526-0827
gd@d-y-c.com www.dynaric.com
Manufacturer and exporter of strapping machinery and nonmetallic strapping
President: Joseph Martinez
CEO: Mike Moses
CFO: John Guzdus
Plant Manager: Vernon Wilson
Assistant Marketing Manager: Brian Cosgrove
Manager: Dennis Fuller
dennisf@dynaric.com
Plant Manager: Dennis Fuller
Number Employees: 100-249
Square Footage: 200000
Type of Packaging: Consumer, Food Service, Private Label, Bulk
Brands Exported: Dynaric; Strapping Products; Strapping Systems
Regions Exported to: Central America, South America, Caribbean, Mexico, Latin America
Percentage of Business in Exporting: 10

43754 (HQ)Dynynstyl
855 NW 17th Avenue
Suite A
Delray Beach, FL 33445-2520   561-547-5585
Fax: 561-547-0993 800-774-7895
Manufacturer and exporter of china, flatware, hollowware, chafing dishes, trays, buffetware, etc.; also, polishers, burnishers, silver cleaners and canned fuel for chafing dishes, etc.; silver and stainless steel repair servicesavailable
CEO: Dennis Paul
Vice President: Debra Cosner
Estimated Sales: $ 1 - 5 Million
Number Employees: 10
Regions Exported to: Worldwide
Percentage of Business in Exporting: 65
Regions Imported from: South America, Asia

43755 E & E Process Instrumentation
4-40 North Rivermede Road
Concord, Ontario, ON L4K 2H3318
Canada   905-669-4857
Fax: 905-669-2158 info@eeprocess.com
www.eeprocess.com
Manufacturer, importer and exporter of thermometers, hygrometers and hydrometers. Instruments for quality control and research and development. Nist certification of test instruments for FDA & USDA compliance
President: Todd Teichert
Estimated Sales: $1-2.5 Million
Number Employees: 5-9
Square Footage: 16000
Parent Co: E & E Process Instrumentation
Brands Exported: Brooklyn
Regions Exported to: Central America, South America, Asia, Middle East
Regions Imported from: Europe

43756 (HQ)E & J Gallo Winery
600 Yosemite Blvd.
Modesto, CA 95354-2760
     877-687-9463
www.gallo.com
Wines, brandy and sparkling wine.
Chief Marketing Officer: Stephanie Gallo
Year Founded: 1933
Estimated Sales: Over $1 Billion
Number Employees: 5000-9999
Type of Packaging: Consumer, Food Service
Other Locations:
  E&J Gallo Winery
  Mississauga, ON
  E&J Gallo Winery
  Fresno, CA
  E&J Gallo Winery
  Livingston, CAE&J Gallo WineryFresno
Brands Exported: California Wine
Brands Imported: Ecco Domani, Gallo Family Vineyards Sonoma Reserve

43757 E F Bavis & Assoc Inc
201 Grandin Rd
Maineville, OH 45039-9762   513-677-0500
Fax: 513-677-0552 info@bavis.com
www.bavis.com
Manufacturer and exporter of drive-thru and vertical conveyor systems including transaction cash drawers
President: William Sieber
wps@bavis.com
R&D: Mike Brown
Director Marketing/Sales: Terry Roberts
Estimated Sales: $ 5 - 10 Million
Number Employees: 20-49
Number of Products: 2
Type of Packaging: Food Service
Regions Exported to: South America, Middle East, Australia

43758 E Waldo Ward & Son Marmalades
273 E Highland Ave
Sierra Madre, CA 91024-2014   626-355-1218
Fax: 626-355-5292 800-355-9273
service@waldoward.com www.waldoward.com
Manufacturer and importer of gourmet foods including olives, preserves, jellies, marmalades, brandied fruits and sauces including meat, relish and seafood cocktail; exporter of marmalades. Services, private labeling and anufacturing tolarge and small companies. Also offers consulting services
Owner: Richard Ward
richard@waldoward.com
VP: Jeffrey Ward
Estimated Sales: $810,000
Number Employees: 10-19
Number of Brands: 2
Number of Products: 150
Square Footage: 40000
Type of Packaging: Consumer, Private Label
Regions Exported to: Asia
Percentage of Business in Exporting: 10
Regions Imported from: Europe
Percentage of Business in Importing: 10

43759 E-Cooler
4320 S. Knox Avenue
Chicago, IL 80632   773-284-9975
Fax: 773-284-9973 866-955-3266
www.e-cooler.com
Supplier of corrugated boxes and custom designed boxes for the meat, seafood and produce industries.
Regions Exported to: Europe, North America

43760 E-Fish-Ent Fish Company
1941 Goodridge Road
Sooke, BC V0S 0C6
Canada   250-642-4007
Fax: 250-642-4057 www.e-fish-ent.ca
Manufacturer and exporter of smoked salmon in retort pouch; meat products in pouch, stews, chili, curry.
President: Bryan Mooney
VP: Linda Mooney
Number Employees: 4
Square Footage: 32000
Type of Packaging: Private Label

43761 E-J Industries Inc
1275 S Campbell Ave
Chicago, IL 60608-1013   312-226-5023
Fax: 312-226-5976 www.e-jindustries.com
Manufacturers of contract commercial seating and cabinetry for the hospitality industry.
Vice President: Bill Colles
bcolles@ejindus.com
CEO/CFO: Keith Weitzman
VP: Keith Weitzman
Quality Control: W Nowak
Estimated Sales: $7 Million
Number Employees: 50-99
Square Footage: 240000
Regions Exported to: Central America, South America, Europe, Asia, Middle East

43762 E-Lite Technologies
2285 Reservoir Ave
Trumbull, CT 06611   203-371-2070
Fax: 203-371-2078 877-520-3951
Manufacturer and exporter of electroluminescent lamps
President: Mark Appelberg
President: Mark Appleberg
VP/COO: Mark Appelberg
Contact: Paul Burge
pburge@elitetechnologies.uk.com
Office Manager: Judith Sepelak
Estimated Sales: Below $ 5,000,000
Number Employees: 10-19
Brands Exported: Flatlite
Regions Exported to: Worldwide
Percentage of Business in Exporting: 50

Importers & Exporters / A-Z

43763 E-Z Edge Inc
6119 Adams St
West New York, NJ 07093-1505   201-295-1171
            Fax: 201-295-1115 800-232-4470
            order@e-zedge.com www.e-zedge.com
Manufacturer, exporter and importer of food processing equipment including shears, knives and grinders for meat, fish and poultry; importer of stainless steel fish shears, bowl cutter knives and cutlery
Owner: Michael Maffei
ezedgeusa@aol.com
VP: Michael Maffei
Manager: Paul Povinelli
Estimated Sales: Less Than $500,000
Number Employees: 1-4
Square Footage: 15000
Brands Exported: Steffens
Regions Exported to: South America, Mexico
Percentage of Business in Exporting: 5
Brands Imported: Finney; Steffens; Gresser
Regions Imported from: Europe
Percentage of Business in Importing: 45

43764 E-Z Lift Conveyors
2000 S Cherokee St
Denver, CO 80223-3917   303-733-5642
    Fax: 303-733-5642 800-821-9966
            ez@ezliftconveyors.com
            www.ezliftconveyors.com
Manufacturer and exporter of lightweight conveyors for beans, fruits, nuts and vegetables including troughing belt, belt bucket, bottom dump car unloader and floor-to-floor
President: Kenneth B Drost
Estimated Sales: $1-2.5 Million
Number Employees: 10-19
Square Footage: 20000
Regions Exported to: Canada, Mexico

43765 E. Boyd & Associates
P.O. Box 99189
Raleigh, NC 27624-9189   919-846-8000
    Fax: 919-846-8197 www.eboyd.com
Exporter of frozen fruits, vegetables, berries, pork and poultry
President: Elbert Boyd
CEO: Ty Baker
CFO: Jerry Boyd
Executive Assistant: Brenda Kindall
Estimated Sales: $20-50 Million
Number Employees: 10-19
Square Footage: 18000

43766 E. Gagnon & Fils
405 Rte 102
St Therese-De-Gaspe, QC G0C 3B0
Canada   418-385-3011
    Fax: 418-385-3021
Manufacturer and exporter of frozen snow crabs, crab
President: Roger Gagnon
Estimated Sales: $2.3 Million
Number Employees: 5
Type of Packaging: Food Service
Regions Exported to: Worldwide
Percentage of Business in Exporting: 95

43767 E.D. Smith Foods Ltd
8 Burford Rd
Hamilton, ON L8E 5B1
Canada   905-573-1207
            inquiry@edsmith.com
            www.edsmith.com
Manufacturer and exporter of jams, ketchup, pie fillings, barbecue and pasta sauces, fruit toppings, salsas and syrups
President/CEO: Michael Burrows
VP Finance: David Smith
VP Operations: Dorothy Pethick
Type of Packaging: Consumer, Food Service, Private Label, Bulk

43768 E.F. Lane & Son
744 Kevin Ct
Oakland, CA 94621   510-569-8980
    Fax: 510-569-0240
Manufacturer and exporter of honey and peanut products
Manager: Phyllis Tut
Estimated Sales: $500,000-$1 Million
Number Employees: 1-4
Type of Packaging: Consumer, Food Service, Private Label, Bulk
Regions Exported to: Worldwide

43769 (HQ)E.L. Nickell Company
385 Centreville St
Constantine, MI 49042   269-435-2475
            Fax: 616-435-8216
Manufacturer and exporter of pressure vessels and heat exchangers
President: Brian Hicks
Sales Manager: Roger Bainbridge
Estimated Sales: $5-10 Million
Number Employees: 20-49
Square Footage: 60000
Regions Exported to: Canada
Percentage of Business in Exporting: 1

43770 (HQ)E.W. Knauss & Son
625 East Broad Street
Quakertown, PA 18951-1713   215-536-4220
    Fax: 215-536-1129 800-648-4220
            www.knaussfoods.com
Sliced dried beef products including beefsticks, beef jerky, hot sausage and pickled meat products.
CEO: Robert Longacre
VP Sales: William Carter
Estimated Sales: $20-50 Million
Number Employees: 50-99
Number of Brands: 2
Square Footage: 100000
Type of Packaging: Consumer, Food Service, Private Label, Bulk
Brands Exported: Knauss
Regions Exported to: Canada, Caribbean
Percentage of Business in Exporting: 3

43771 EB Eddy Paper
P.O. Box 5003
Port Huron, MI 48061-5003   810-982-0191
    Fax: 810-982-4057 www.domtar.com
Manufacturer and exporter of packaging and specialty coated papers
Vice President: Mark Ushpol
Marketing Manager: Rob Belanger
Contact: John Beecroft
johnbeecroft@domtar.com
Production Manager: David Rushton
Estimated Sales: $ 30 - 50 Million
Number Employees: 20-49
Parent Co: Domtar
Regions Exported to: Worldwide

43772 EDA International Corp
4907 SW 75th Ave
Miami, FL 33155-4440   305-669-1894
    Fax: 305-669-1797 edaintl@aol.com
            www.edainternational.com
Exporter of steam kettles, convection ovens, steam cookers, gas cooking ranges, ice cream cabinets and freezers, butcher blocks, cutting boards and stainless steel tables, food service components, ovens, countertop cooking equipment
President: Edward DE Aguiar
Estimated Sales: $5-10 Million
Number Employees: 5-9
Brands Exported: U.S. Range; C. Nelson; Continental Refrigerator; John Boos & Co.; APW; Bakers Pride; Bevles; Component Hardware; SeniServ; Earthstone; Cookshack; Prolon
Regions Exported to: Central America, South America, Asia, Middle East
Percentage of Business in Exporting: 100

43773 EDCO Food Products Inc
2815 Packerland Dr # 23
Suite #23
Hobart, WI 54313-6182   920-499-7651
    Fax: 920-499-8023 800-255-3768
            james@edcofood.com www.edcofood.biz
Importer and exporter of industrial ingredients, produce, spices and peppers including chile, jalapeno, cayenne and cascabella
President: James Manning
accounting@edcofood.com
VP: Ed Manning
Business Development: David J. Sinkula
Estimated Sales: $ 3 - 5 Million
Number Employees: 5-9
Type of Packaging: Food Service, Bulk
Regions Imported from: Mexico

43774 EDCO Food Products Inc
2815 Packerland Dr # 23
P.O. Box 12511
Hobart, WI 54313-6182   920-499-7651
    Fax: 920-499-8023 800-255-3768
            sales@edcofood.biz www.edcofood.biz
Processor and importer of peppers including jalapeno, serrano, sport and cascabella; also, cauliflower buttons, chipotle powder and pickled vegetables
President: James Manning
accounting@edcofood.com
VP: Edward Manning
VP: Sylvia Roman
Business Development: David J. Sinkula
Customer Service & Logistics: James Gumtow
Estimated Sales: $ 3 - 5 Million
Number Employees: 5-9
Square Footage: 64000
Type of Packaging: Food Service, Private Label, Bulk
Regions Imported from: Central America, Mexico

43775 EFCO Importers
PO Box 741
Foxcroft Square, PA 19046   215-885-8597
            Fax: 215-885-4584
Importer of liquor, wine and beer
President: Martin Friedland
m.friedland@faganmusic.com
Assistant to the President: Loretta Krauss
Estimated Sales: $1-2.5 Million
Number Employees: 5-9
Brands Imported: Pitu Brazilian Cachaca; Broyhan Beer; Glide Pilsener Beer; St. Feuillien Ales; Meteor Beers

43776 EFG Food Solutions
3040 Remico SW
Grandville, MI 49418   616-261-5416
            Fax: 616-261-5426
Importer and distributor of high quality imported and domestic specialty foods.

43777 EGS Electrical Group
7770 Frontage Rd
Skokie, IL 60077   847-679-7800
            Fax: 847-268-6011
Manufacturer and exporter of electrical products including controls, switches and lighting fixtures
President: Eric Meyer
CFO: Michael Bryant
Quality Control: L Engler
Marketing Communication Manager: Michelle Miller
Contact: Peter Strong
pstrong@egseg.com
Estimated Sales: $ 20 - 50 Million
Number Employees: 100-249
Parent Co: EGS Electrical Group
Regions Exported to: Worldwide

43778 EGW Bradbury Enterprises
479 US Highway 1
PO Box 129
Bridgewater, ME 04735-0129   207-429-8141
    Fax: 207-429-8188 800-332-6021
            info@bradburybarrel.com
            www.bradburybarrel.com
Manufacturer and exporter of tongue and groove white cedar barrels, tubs and barrelcraft and wooden display fixtures; also, custom wooden displays, fixtures and accessories
President/CEO: Adelle Bradbury
Sales/Marketing Manager: Wayne Bradbury
Office Manager: Jennifer Griffin
Estimated Sales: $5-10 Million
Number Employees: 20-49
Regions Exported to: Central America, Europe, Middle East, Canada, Mexico
Percentage of Business in Exporting: 2

43779 EIT
532 W Lake St
Elmhurst, IL 60126-1408   630-279-3400
    Fax: 630-279-3420 eitpromo@aol.com
Manufacturer and exporter of flags and promotional products
Owner: Mark Tober
CFO: Lucille Tobor
VP: Mark Tobor
Quality Control: Beth Pirc
Chairman of the Board: Earl Tobor

Estimated Sales: Below $ 5 Million
Number Employees: 5 to 9
Square Footage: 32000
Regions Exported to: Worldwide

43780 EKATO Corporation
700 C Lake St
St Ramsey, NJ 07436 201-825-4684
Fax: 201-825-9776 jerry.baresich@ekato.com
Manufacturer and exporter of industrial mixers and agitators for fluids and solids
President: Paul Dwelle
Sales Director: Michael Starer
Estimated Sales: $ 5-10,000,000
Number Employees: 10-19
Parent Co: EKATO Ruhr Und Mischtechnik-GmbH
Regions Exported to: Worldwide

43781 ELF Machinery
1555 S State Road 39
La Porte, IN 46350-6301 219-325-3060
Fax: 219-324-2884 800-328-0466
www.elfmachines.com
Manufacturer and exporter of liquid packaging equipment including fillers, cappers, labelers, induction sealers, coders, bottle cleaners, unscramblers, conveyors, turntables, etc
President: Thomas Ake Reed
CEO: Ron Sarto
International Sales Manager: Eric Thorgren
Number Employees: 100-249
Square Footage: 320000
Type of Packaging: Food Service
Regions Exported to: Worldwide
Percentage of Business in Exporting: 40

43782 EMCO
170 Monarch Ln
Miamisburg, OH 45342 661-294-9966
Fax: 937-865-6605 800-722-3626
www.emcolabels.com
Manufacturer and exporter of code labelers and printers for price marking and UPC/EAN code printing
President: Robert H Hay
Sales Manager: Morris Bargorch
Estimated Sales: $5-10 Million
Number Employees: 10
Regions Exported to: Central America, South America, Europe, Middle East

43783 EMU Americas, LLC
360 Fairfield Ave Ste 300
Bridgeport, CT 06604 203-384-8573
Fax: 203-384-8691 info@emuamericas.com
Manager: Jennifer Francis
Contact: Dan Cordova
dan@emuamericas.com
Estimated Sales: $ 1 - 3 Million
Number Employees: 5-9

43784 ENM Co
5617 N Northwest Hwy
Chicago, IL 60646-6177 773-775-8400
Fax: 773-775-5968 enmco@aol.com
www.enmco.com
Manufacturer and exporter of counting and number devices and hour meters; also, mechanical, electro-mechanical and electronic digital counters
Owner: Nicholas Polydoris
npolydoris@enmco.com
Sales Manager: Dale Hall
Sales Manager: Lee Bryant
Sales Engineer: Megan Fitzgerald
Estimated Sales: $ 20 - 50 Million
Number Employees: 50-99
Regions Exported to: Europe, Asia

43785 EP International
9850 N. 73rd St. #2086
Suite 2086
Scottsdale, AZ 85258 480-991-3206
Fax: 490-991-3207 www.beanexporter.com
Exporter of agriculture products (beans, peas, lentils and seeds)
CEO: William Kim
VP: James Park
Sales: Edward Kim
Operations: Carol Kim
Estimated Sales: $6 Million
Number Employees: 4
Type of Packaging: Bulk
Brands Exported: Clipper; Rumba; Jack Rabbit; Wheeler
Regions Exported to: Central America, South America, Europe, Asia
Percentage of Business in Exporting: 100

43786 EPCO
P.O.Box 20428
Murfreesboro, TN 37129-0428 615-893-8432
Fax: 615-890-3196 800-251-3398
www.useco.com
Manufacturer and exporter of food service equipment including bun racks, heater/proofer cabinets, banquet carts, can racks and air curtain refrigerators
Controller: Philip Keller
VP/General Manager: Thomas Taylor
VP Sales/Marketing: James Jean
Number Employees: 10-19
Square Footage: 400000
Parent Co: Standex International Corporation
Type of Packaging: Food Service
Brands Exported: Epco
Regions Exported to: Worldwide

43787 ERC Parts Inc
4001 Cobb International Blvd N
Kennesaw, GA 30152-4374 770-984-0276
Fax: 770-951-1875 800-241-6880
marketing@erconline.com www.erconline.com
Drive-thru displays, recording devices and timers and battery chargers; importer of cash register parts; exporter of point of sale systems, parts and software; wholesaler/distributor of VAR products; serving the food service market
Owner: Chuck Rollins
cerollins@erconline.com
CFO: Stuart Dobson
Vice President: Charles Barnes
Research & Development: Timothy Adams
Marketing Director: Bryon Finkel
Parts/Manufacturing Division: Eric Hart
Purchasing Manager: Rob Haight
Estimated Sales: $ 1 - 2.5 Million
Number Employees: 50-99
Square Footage: 180000
Other Locations:
  ERC Parts
  Louisville, KY
  ERC Parts
  Lexington, KY
  ERC Parts
  Cleveland, OH
  ERC Parts
  Las Vegas, NV
  ERC Parts
  Baltimore, MD
  ERC Parts
  Greensboro, NC
  ERC PartsLexington
Regions Exported to: South America, Canada, Carribean, Mexico
Percentage of Business in Exporting: 5
Regions Imported from: Japan
Percentage of Business in Importing: 25

43788 ERO/Goodrich Forest Products
19255 SW 65th Ave # 110
Tualatin, OR 97062-9717 503-885-9414
Fax: 503-625-5825 800-458-5545
Manufacturer and exporter of plywood shipping containers and pallets
Manager: Elizabeth Brashear
Sales Manager: Harry Nelson
Estimated Sales: $ 1 - 5 Million
Number Employees: 16
Type of Packaging: Bulk
Regions Exported to: Central America, South America, Europe, Asia
Percentage of Business in Exporting: 35

43789 ESD Waste2water Inc
495 Oak Rd
Ocala, FL 34472-3005 352-680-9134
Fax: 352-867-1320 800-277-3279
info@waste2water.com www.waste2water.com
Manufacturer and exporter of water treatment equipment
Manager: Kevin Hawkins
Estimated Sales: $2.5-5 Million
Number Employees: 20-49
Square Footage: 100000
Parent Co: Zentox
Regions Exported to: Worldwide
Percentage of Business in Exporting: 5

43790 ESS Technologies
3160 State St
Blacksburg, VA 24060-6603 540-961-5716
Fax: 540-961-5721 info@esstechnologies.com
www.esstechnologies.com
Supplier of packaging equipment including overwrapping and bundling; shrinkwrapping, stretch banding, automatic cartoning and case packing; candy wrapping equipment; filling and packaging equipment; turnkey lines and integrationservices.
President: Kevin Browne
Vice President: Linda Browne
Director, Global Business Development: Walter Langosch
Estimated Sales: $1-2.5 Million
Regions Exported to: Canada, Mexico
Percentage of Business in Exporting: 10

43791 ET International Technologies
3705 Kipling Street
Suite 103
Wheat Ridge, CO 80033 303-854-9087
Fax: 303-722-7379 855-412-5726
Manufacturer and exporter of hot tapping machines for the HVAC/R and piping industries
President: Greg Apple
Regions Exported to: Worldwide
Percentage of Business in Exporting: 10

43792 EVAPCO Inc
5151 Allendale Ln
Taneytown, MD 21787-2155 410-876-3782
Fax: 410-756-6450 marketing@evapco.com
www.evapco.com
Manufacturer and exporter of industrial refrigeration equipment including evaporative condensers, cooling towers, evaporators, vessels, valves, recirculator packages, rooftop hygienic air systems, and closed circuit coolers
President: Bill Bartley
bbartley@evapco.com
CFO: Harold Walsh
VP: Joseph Mondato
VP Marketing/Sales: Dave Rule
Number Employees: 5-9
Square Footage: 360000
Brands Exported: ATC; PMCB; LSCB; NTL; NTS; NTW; UBC; UBT; VLR; HLR; NTX; NTC; AT; ICT; SST; SCT
Regions Exported to: Central America, South America, Europe, Asia

43793 (HQ)Eagle Coffee Co Inc
1027 Hillen St
Baltimore, MD 21202-4132 410-685-5893
Fax: 410-528-0369 contactus@eaglecoffee.com
www.eaglecoffee.com
Restaurant and gourmet coffees, coffee machines and grinders and coffee beans; serving the food service market
Owner: Nick Constantine
eaglecoffee@aol.com
Controller: Tom Brooks
VP: Jacqueline Parris
Estimated Sales: $1.6 Million
Number Employees: 10-19
Square Footage: 120000
Type of Packaging: Food Service, Private Label
Other Locations:
  Eagle Coffee Co.
  Baltimore, MDEagle Coffee Co.

43794 Eagle Foodservice Equipment
100 Industrial Blvd
Clayton, DE 19938 302-653-3000
Fax: 302-653-2065 800-441-8440
answers@eaglegrp.com www.eaglegrp.com
Manufacturer and exporter of wire, solid and polymer shelving, work tables, sinks, handsinks, countertop equipment, underbar equipment, bun pans, as well as custom fabricated items
Owner: Larry N McAllister
Sales Director: Linda Donavon
Number Employees: 250-499
Type of Packaging: Food Service
Regions Exported to: Worldwide

43795 Eagle Group
100 Industrial Blvd
Clayton, DE 19938-8903 302-653-3000
Fax: 302-653-2065 800-441-8440
customerservice@eaglegrp.com

Importers & Exporters / A-Z

Manufacturer and exporter of stainless steel food service equipment including shelving, sinks, tables, cookers, warmers and bar equipment
Owner: Larry Mccallister
Sales: Linda Donavon
lmccallister@eaglegroup.com
Estimated Sales: $ 50 - 75 Million
Number Employees: 250-499
Parent Co: Eagle Group
Brands Exported: Panco; Lifestore
Regions Exported to: Worldwide

43796 Eagle Home Products
1 Arnold Dr # 1
Huntington, NY 11743-3981   631-673-3500
Fax: 631-673-6700 www.eaglehomeproducts.com
Manufacturer, importer and exporter of cleaning aids and rubber gloves
Owner: Robert Chemtob
rchemtob@eaglehomeproducts.com
Vice President: Andre Chemtob
Estimated Sales: $ 5-10 Million
Number Employees: 20-49
Square Footage: 200000
Brands Exported: Eagle; Diamond Brite; Denta-Brite
Regions Exported to: Central America, South America, Europe, Middle East
Percentage of Business in Exporting: 10
Regions Imported from: Asia, Latin America, Mexico
Percentage of Business in Importing: 60

43797 Eagle Products Company
P.O.Box 431601
Houston, TX 77243-1601   713-690-1161
Fax: 713-690-7661 info@eaglechair.com
www.eaglechair.com
Quality manufacturer and exporter of booths, chairs, bar stools, tabletops and bases
Executive Director: Maximillian Yurgulich
CEO: Natalia Jurcic-Koc
CFO: Nathalai Kac
Contact: Max Yuglich
max@eaglechair.com
Director of Operations: Max Yuglich
Estimated Sales: $ 5 - 10 Million
Number Employees: 10-19
Square Footage: 80000
Parent Co: Eagle Chair
Type of Packaging: Food Service
Regions Exported to: Central America, South America, Europe, Asia, Middle East, Canada, Mexico, Latin America
Percentage of Business in Exporting: 10

43798 Eagleware Manufacturing
2835 E Ana Street
Compton, CA 90221-5601   310-604-0404
Fax: 310-604-1748
Manufacturer and exporter of cookware
President: Jesse Gross
Vice President: Brett Gross
Estimated Sales: Below $5,000,000
Number Employees: 10
Square Footage: 140000
Parent Co: Harold Leonard & Company
Regions Exported to: Worldwide

43799 Earth Saver
20725 NE 16th Ave # A17
Miami, FL 33179-2132   305-493-3940
Fax: 305-493-3943 info@earth-saver.com
www.earth-saver.com
High-quality, reusable shopping bags for grocery stores and boutiques. Product is made of eco-friendly, biodegradable materials..
President: Doug Bailey
doug@earth-savers.com
VP: Carlos Kovalsky
VP Sales: Juan Benito
Estimated Sales: Less Than $ 5 Million
Number Employees: 5-9
Number of Brands: 2
Square Footage: 5000
Type of Packaging: Private Label, Bulk
Brands Exported: Earth-Saver
Regions Exported to: Central America, South America, Europe
Percentage of Business in Exporting: 20
Brands Imported: Earth-Saver
Regions Imported from: South America, Asia
Percentage of Business in Importing: 80

43800 Earth Science
475 N Sheridan St
Corona, CA 92880   951-371-7565
Fax: 909-371-0509
Vitamin C products
President: Kristine Schoenauer
VP: Michael Rutledge
Contract Sales Manager: Diane Smart
Contact: Sergio Aguirre
saguirre@cosmedxscience.com
Number Employees: 100-249
Square Footage: 160000
Type of Packaging: Consumer, Bulk

43801 Earthstone Oven
6717 San Fernando Rd
Glendale, CA 91201-1704   818-553-1134
Fax: 818-553-1133 800-840-4915
earthstone@earthlink.net
www.cookingwithfirebook.com
Number Employees: 10-19

43802 Earthstone Wood-Fire Ovens
6717 San Fernando Rd
Glendale, CA 91201-1704   818-553-1134
Fax: 818-553-1133 800-840-4915
info@earthstoneovens.com
www.earthstoneovens.com
Manufacturer/exporter of wood and gas fire ovens including pre-assembled, commercial kit and residential; also, wood fire training available
Principal: Maurice Yotnegparian
Principal: Jean-Paul Yotnegparian
Estimated Sales: $ 3 - 5 Million
Number Employees: 15
Square Footage: 60000
Brands Exported: Earthstone

43803 East Bay International
2434 Research Drive
Livermore, CA 94550-3850   925-373-9547
Fax: 925-373-1989 800-982-6167
wdrenik@eastbayusa.com
Importer of coconut milk powder; exporter of restaurant equipment and supplies to international franchises. Also offers consulting services
President: William Drenik
Estimated Sales: $5-10 Million
Number Employees: 10-19
Square Footage: 80000
Regions Exported to: South America, Europe, Asia, Middle East
Percentage of Business in Exporting: 90
Brands Imported: Emma
Regions Imported from: Asia
Percentage of Business in Importing: 10

43804 East Coast Sea Port Corporation
338 Northern Boulevard
Great Neck, NY 11021-4808   516-487-0353
Fax: 516-487-9522
Importer and exporter of confectionery products and seafood including crabs, lobster, shrimp and scallops; exporter of coffee creamers, orange juice, gelatin desserts, fruit juice powders and cocktail mixes
President: Philip Levine
CEO: Fredrick Sternau
Sales Manager: Paul Topper
Estimated Sales: $10-20 Million
Number Employees: 5-9
Square Footage: 1200
Brands Exported: East Port; Sun Country; Sea Spray
Regions Exported to: Europe, Asia
Percentage of Business in Exporting: 5
Regions Imported from: Worldwide

43805 East Coast Seafood Inc
448 Boston St
PO Box 790
Topsfield, MA 01983-1216   781-593-1737
Fax: 781-593-9583 www.eastcoastseafood.com
Importer, exporter and wholesaler/distributor of live lobster, fresh skatewings, dogfish, monk tails, etc.; serving the food service market
President: Michael Tourkistas
CFO: James Bouras
VP: Spiros Tourkakis
Estimated Sales: $10-20 Million
Number Employees: 10-19
Square Footage: 120000
Parent Co: American Holdco
Type of Packaging: Food Service
Regions Exported to: Europe, Asia

Percentage of Business in Exporting: 50
Regions Imported from: South America, Europe, Canada
Percentage of Business in Importing: 10

43806 Easterday Fluid Technologies
4343 S Kansas Ave
Saint Francis, WI 53235   414-482-4488
Fax: 414-482-3720
Supplies the food processing industry thermal sensitive coding links. Manufactures thermal sensitive, solid color, and UV jet inks for noncontact jet printers for tough, reliable product codes on retorted food containers and pasteurization processes of the beer and beverage industry
President: Max Baum
Director Operations: Lee Robbins
National/International Services Manager: Paul Oetlinger
Estimated Sales: $1-3 Million
Number Employees: 5-9
Square Footage: 12000
Regions Exported to: Central America, South America, Europe
Percentage of Business in Exporting: 30

43807 Eastern Energy LightingSystems
PO Box 1543
Greenwood Lake, NY 10925-1543   914-674-0093
Fax: 914-674-0433 800-794-0083
Wholesaler/distributor and exporter of lighting fixtures
President: Ted Siebert
VP: Lance Edwards
Estimated Sales: $5-10 Million
Number Employees: 10-19
Square Footage: 8000

43808 (HQ)Eastern Fish Company
Glennpointe Centre East
300 Frank W Burr Blvd Ste 30
Teaneck, NJ 07666   201-801-0800
Fax: 201-801-0802 800-526-9066
www.easternfish.com
Manufacturer and importer of farm raised shrimp and other seafood, bay and sea scallops, lobster, king crab legs and claws, snow crab clusters, yellow fin tuna
Founder: Bill Bloom
President: Eric Bloom
Secretary: Charna Bloom
Vice President: Lee Bloom
Estimated Sales: $6.7 Million
Number Employees: 30
Square Footage: 18000
Type of Packaging: Private Label
Other Locations:
  Norwestern Sales Office
  Kingston, WA
  Western Sales Office
  Anaheim, CA
  Northeastern Sales Office
  Gloucester, MA
  Southeastern Sales Office
  Coral Springs, FLNorwestern Sales OfficeAnaheim
Regions Exported to: Europe, US, Canada, Japan, Tawian, China

43809 Eastern Machine
80 Turnpike Dr # 2
Middlebury, CT 06762-1830   203-598-0066
Fax: 203-598-0068
Manufacturer and exporter of capping machinery for metal and plastic screw and snap caps; also, cap tighteners, fitment applicators and trigger sprayers
President: David Baker
Number Employees: 5-9
Square Footage: 20000
Regions Exported to: Central America, South America, Middle East, Australia
Percentage of Business in Exporting: 25

43810 Eastern Overseas Marketing
One West Ames Court
Suite 202
Plainview, NY 11803   516-576-3800
Fax: 516-576-3810
Importer of fresh fish and seafood including tuna, swordfish, snapper, grouper, mahi mahi, marlin, mackerel and shrimp; exporter of dry beans, peas, peanuts, rice, fresh garlic, chilled apples, pears, grapes and carrots

43810 (continued)

President: J Cohen
Contact: Susan Gold
s.gold@dma.com
Number Employees: 1-4
Square Footage: 4000

43811 Eastern Sea Products

11 Addison Avenue
Scoudouc, NB E4P 3N3
Canada   506-532-6111
    Fax: 506-532-9111   800-565-6364
    maurice@easternsea.ca
Manufacturer and exporter of salted and smoked seafood: herring, mackerel, salmon
President: Maurice Allain
Director: Joanne Allain
Estimated Sales: $1.3 Million
Number Employees: 10
Number of Brands: 2
Number of Products: 10
Square Footage: 48000
Type of Packaging: Consumer, Private Label
Brands Exported: Seapro; Cape Royal
Regions Exported to: USA, Caribbean, Europe
Percentage of Business in Exporting: 90

43812 Eastern Tabletops

445 Park Ave
Brooklyn, NY 11205-2735   718-522-4142
    Fax: 718-522-4155   sales@easterntabletop.com
    www.easterntabletop.com
President: Dina Weberman
Estimated Sales: $ 10 - 20 Million
Number Employees: 5-9

43813 Eastern Tea Corp

1 Engelhard Dr
Monroe Twp, NJ 08831-3722   609-860-1100
    Fax: 609-860-1105   800-221-0865
    www.bromleytea.com
Manufacturer, importer and exporter of packaged and loose tea; also, tea bags and tapioca
President: Paul Barbakoff
paul@bromleytea.com
Vice President: Ira Barbakoff
VP of Manufacturing: Glenn Barbakoff
Estimated Sales: $5-10 Million
Number Employees: 50-99
Square Footage: 360000
Type of Packaging: Consumer, Food Service, Private Label
Brands Imported: Bromley; Island; Chin Chu; Buckingham Select
Regions Imported from: Central America, South America, Europe, Asia, Latin America
Percentage of Business in Importing: 90

43814 Eastimpex

500 Selby Street
San Francisco, CA 94124-1122   415-282-2000
    Fax: 415-282-1020
Wholesaler/distributor, importer and exporter of groceries including short-grain rice, oyster sauce and bamboo shoots
President: Don Chan
Number Employees: 20-49
Square Footage: 440000

43815 Eastland Food Corp

9475 Gerwig Ln # N
Columbia, MD 21046-2885   410-381-8126
    Fax: 410-381-2079   800-645-0769
    marketing@eastlandfood.com
RTD- ready to drink (coffee, tea, concentrates, powders), rice, ethnic sauces (soy,curry, etc.).
President: Michael Chen
michael@eastlandfood.com
Marketing: Pook Sirvicha
Number Employees: 50-99

43816 Eastman Chemical Co

200 S Wilcox Dr
Kingsport, TN 37660-5147   423-229-2000
    Fax: 423-229-2145   800-327-8626
    eastman1@eastman.com   www.eastman.com
Chemical, fibers and plastics that are used in the packaging and health and wellness industries as well as many other industries.
CEO: Mark J. Costa
Sr Vice President & CFO: Curt Espeland
Senior VP: Godefroy Motte
gmotte@eastman.com
Chief Operating Officer: Ronald C. Lindsay
Estimated Sales: Over $1 Billion
Number Employees: 10000+
Square Footage: 4640000
Brands Exported: Tenox; Eastman; Eastapak; MXSTEN
Regions Exported to: Worldwide
Percentage of Business in Exporting: 25

43817 Eatec Corporation

1900 Powell St
Suite 230
Emeryville, CA 94608   510-594-9011
    Fax: 510-549-1959   877-374-4783
    info@agilysys.com   www.agilysys.com
A provider of enterprise back-office software and services for the foodservice and hospitality industries. EatecNetX, Eatec's proven software solution, is recognized as a state-of-the-art foodservice management system that iscentralizzed, scalable, web-centric and user-friendly for food and beverage operators of every variety.
Contact: Scot Benbow
s.benbow@eatec.com
Manager: Jeff Gebhardt
Estimated Sales: $ 5 - 10 Million
Number Employees: 20-49
Brands Exported: EatecNetX
Regions Exported to: Europe, Asia, Canada, Australia, Puerto Rico
Percentage of Business in Exporting: 20

43818 Eatem Foods Co

1829 Gallagher Dr
Vineland, NJ 08360-1548   856-692-1663
    Fax: 856-692-0847   800-683-2836
    sales@eatemfoods.com   www.eatemfoods.com
Food base manufacturing; supplier of savory flavor systems, flavor concentrates, broth concentrates and seasoning bases.
Vice President: Gerrie Bouchard
gerriebouchard@gmail.com
Chief Technical Officer: John Randazzi
Chief Financial Officer: Danine Freeman
Vice President, Treasurer: Mario Riviello
Director, R&D: Bill Cawley
Marketing Manager: Gerrie Bouchard
Vice President, Sales: Don Witherspoon
Director of Operations: Jerry Santo
Estimated Sales: $14 Million
Number Employees: 50-99
Square Footage: 12916
Type of Packaging: Consumer, Food Service, Bulk
Brands Exported: Eatem
Regions Exported to: Worldwide

43819 (HQ)Eaton Corporation

1000 Eaton Blvd
Beachwood, OH 44122
    800-386-1911
    www.eaton.com
Manufacturer and exporter of emergency, indoor and outdoor lighting
Chairman & CEO: Craig Arnold
Vice Chairman & CFO: Richard Fearon
Executive VP & General Counsel: April Miller Boise
Executive VP, Supply Chain Management: Rogerico Branco
Estimated Sales: $21.4 Billion
Number Employees: 97,000
Regions Exported to: Central America, South America, Europe, Asia, Middle East

43820 Eaton Filtration, LLC

44 Apple Street
Tinton Falls, NJ 07724   732-212-4700
    Fax: 952-906-3706   800-859-9212
    www.filtration.eaton.com
Manufacturer and exporter of fluid filters and strainers
Chairman & CEO: Craig Arnold
President & COO, Industrial Sector: Heath Monesmith
Vice Chairman & CFO: Richard H. Fearon
Number Employees: 50-99
Parent Co: Eaton Corporation
Brands Exported: Ronningen-Petter
Regions Exported to: Worldwide
Percentage of Business in Exporting: 35

43821 Eaton Manufacturing Co

1201 Holly St
Houston, TX 77007-6241   713-223-2331
    Fax: 713-223-2342   800-328-6610
    www.eatonmfg.com
Manufacturer and exporter of labels, laminated films, cash control envelopes and bags including polyethylene, polypropylene and ice
President: Tom B Eaton Jr
General Manager: Joe Williams
Estimated Sales: $5-10 Million
Number Employees: 20-49
Square Footage: 100000
Regions Exported to: Canada, Mexico
Percentage of Business in Exporting: 5

43822 Ebonex Corporation

2380 S. Wabash Street
Melvindale, MI 48122   313-388-0060
    Fax: 313-388-6495   ebonex@flash.net
    www.ebonex.com
Wholesaler/distributor and importer of ammonium carbonate
President: Michelle Toenniges
Pres.: Michael Szczepanik
Tech. Dir.: Michele Toenngies
Estimated Sales: $2.5-5 Million
Number Employees: 10-19
Square Footage: 32000
Regions Imported from: Europe

43823 Ecce Panis Inc

3 Brick Plant Rd
East Brunswick, NJ 08816   732-254-1770
Exporter of bread for bakeries and restaurants.
Engineering Manager: Joseph Haun
Estimated Sales: $100-500 Million
Number Employees: 50-200

43824 Eckels Bilt

7700 Harwell St
Fort Worth, TX 76108-1806   817-246-4555
    Fax: 817-246-7139   800-343-9020
    info@eckelsbilt.com   www.eckelsbilt.com
Manufacturer and exporter of conveyor belt automatic tracking systems
President: John Mic Kunas
johnm@eckelsbilt.com
Sales Manager: Tony Keeton
Estimated Sales: $5-10 Million
Number Employees: 10-19
Square Footage: 15000
Brands Exported: True Tracker
Regions Exported to: Central America, Europe
Percentage of Business in Exporting: 5

43825 (HQ)Eckhart Corporation

7110 Redwood Blvd Ste A
Novato, CA 94945   415-898-9528
    Fax: 415-898-1917   800-200-4201
    info@eckhartcorp.com   www.eckhartcorp.com
Manufacturer and exporter of vitamins, food supplements and diet aids
President: Deepak Chopra
VP/Latin America: Arnoldo Rosas
Estimated Sales: $500,000-1 Million
Number Employees: 8
Square Footage: 640000
Type of Packaging: Consumer, Food Service, Private Label, Bulk
Brands Exported: Nature's Edge; Staywell; Kinder Vites; Stanogen
Regions Exported to: Central America, South America, Europe, Asia, Middle East
Percentage of Business in Exporting: 25
Regions Imported from: Central America, South America, Europe, Asia, Middle East
Percentage of Business in Importing: 10

43826 Ecklund-Harrison Technologies

11000 Metro Pkwy # 40
Fort Myers, FL 33966-1245   239-936-6032
    Fax: 239-936-6327   www.ecklund-harrison.com
Manufacturer and exporter of heat penetration equipment and pasteurization monitor computers
President: Daneil Highbaugh
kathy@ecklund-harrison.com
Estimated Sales: $500,000
Number Employees: 1-4

Importers & Exporters / A-Z

43827 Eckroat Seed Company
1106 Martin Luther King Avenue
Oklahoma City, OK 73117   405-427-2484
          Fax: 405-427-7174 800-331-7333
                         www.eckroatseed.com
Manufacturer, importer and exporter of mung beans
President: Robert Eckroat
VP: Don Eckroat
Estimated Sales: $5-10 Million
Number Employees: 10-19
Square Footage: 400000
Type of Packaging: Consumer, Food Service, Private Label, Bulk
Brands Exported: Eckroat's Green Dragon
Regions Exported to: Asia, Canada
Percentage of Business in Exporting: 10

43828 Eclipse Innovative Thermal Solutions
5040 Enterprise Blvd
Toledo, OH 43612   419-729-9726
          Fax: 419-729-9705 800-662-3966
                         sales@exothermics.com
Industrial air-to-air heat exchangers and heat recovery equipment; exporter of industrial heat exchangers
Manager: Paul Wilde
R&D: Bob Shaffer
Contact: Sheryl Holbrook
sholbrook@eclipsenet.com
Number Employees: 20-49
Square Footage: 70000
Parent Co: Eclipse
Regions Exported to: Worldwide
Percentage of Business in Exporting: 12

43829 Eclipse Systems Inc
943 Hanson Ct
Milpitas, CA 95035-3166   408-263-2201
              Fax: 408-559-2252
Manufacturer and exporter of mixers including electric and pneumatic drive
Owner: Jerry Grose
CFO: Helen Fletcher
Sales Director: Diane Olsen
jerrygrose@eclipsesystems.com
Estimated Sales: $20-50 Million
Number Employees: 1-4
Square Footage: 30000
Parent Co: Technology General Corporation
Brands Exported: Pneumix
Regions Exported to: South America, Europe, Asia, Middle East, Phillipines, Mexico, Argentina, Canada
Percentage of Business in Exporting: 2

43830 Eco Wine & Spirits
3235 N San Fernando Road
Los Angeles, CA 90065-1443   323-257-9055
          Fax: 323-257-6997 ecows@aol.com
Importer and wholesaler/distributor of wine, beer and spirits
President: Vahan Plovzian
VP: Harry Apikian
Estimated Sales: $1 Million
Number Employees: 5-9
Square Footage: 20000
Type of Packaging: Consumer
Brands Imported: Brandy, Staraya Moskva, Kotayk Beer, Arinian Wines, Caribbean Rum.
Regions Imported from: South America, Russia, Caribbean, Armenia
Percentage of Business in Importing: 100

43831 Eco-Air Products
7466 Carroll Rd # 101
San Diego, CA 92121-2356   858-271-8111
          Fax: 858-578-3816 800-284-8111
                         pcurrie@shoreline.com
Manufacturer and exporter of air, rangehood and grease filters
President: Wesley Measamer
CFO: John Hodson
Vice President of Division: Charlie Kwiatkowski
Manager: Robert Jaquay
Quality Control: Bill Stevens
VP Marketing: Bill O'Brien
Director of Sales: Bill Cawley
Senior Vice President of Operations: Kirk Dominick
Estimated Sales: $30-50 Million
Number Employees: 20-49
Square Footage: 110000
Brands Exported: Eco-Air Products, Inc.
Regions Exported to: Central America, South America, Europe, Asia, Middle East
Percentage of Business in Exporting: 25

43832 Eco-Bag Products
23-25 Spring St, #302
Ossining, NY 10562   914-944-4556
          Fax: 914-271-4867 800-720-2247
          sales@ecobags.com www.eco-bags.com
Manufacturer, importer and exporter of natural and organic cotton bags including shopping and promotional tote, lunch and produce; printing services available
President: Sharon Rowe
Marketing: Ellen Ornato
PR & Communications: Rob Bradey
Estimated Sales: Below $ 5 Million
Number Employees: 1-4
Type of Packaging: Consumer, Food Service, Bulk
Brands Exported: Eco-Bags®
Regions Exported to: Worldwide
Percentage of Business in Exporting: 5
Regions Imported from: India
Percentage of Business in Importing: 60

43833 EcoNatural Solutions
997 Dixon Rd
Boulder, CO 80302   303-357-5682
          Fax: 303-358-4111 sales@stclaires.com
                         www.stclaires.com
Manufacturer and exporter of organic sweets
CEO: Debra St Claire
d.stclaire@stclaires.com
Estimated Sales: $2.5-5 Million
Number Employees: 5-9
Type of Packaging: Consumer
Regions Exported to: Canada, Mexico
Percentage of Business in Exporting: 5

43834 Ecodyne Water Treatment, LLC
1270 Frontenac Rd
Naperville, IL 60563   630-961-5043
          Fax: 630-671-8846 800-228-9326
Manufacturer and exporter of water treatment equipment including softeners, filters and reverse osmosis systems
President: Patrick O'Neill
Finance Executive: Todd Mc Gee
Research & Development: Wayne Simpson
Quality Control: Mark Thenhaus
Sales Director: Patrick O'Neill
Public Relations: Patrick O'Neill
Operations Manager: Mark Thenhaus
Production Manager: Mark Thenhaus
Plant Manager: Mark Thenhaus
Purchasing Manager: Mark Thenhaus
Estimated Sales: $ 5 - 10,000,000
Number Employees: 20-49
Square Footage: 50000
Brands Exported: Ecodyne; Red Line
Regions Exported to: Central America, South America, Europe, Asia, Middle East

43835 Ecolo Odor Control Systems Worldwide
59 Penn Drive
North York, ON M9L 2A6
Canada   416-740-3900
          Fax: 416-740-3800 800-667-6355
                         info@ecolo.com www.ecolo.com
Manufacturer and exporter of odor control systems and air solutions to deodorize washrooms, garbage rooms, transfer stations, waste water treatment plants, etc
President: Calvin Sager
Vice President: Ian Howard
Marketing Director: Cindy Pickard
Director Manufacturing: John Linthwaite
Number Employees: 20
Square Footage: 60000
Parent Co: Sager Industries
Brands Exported: Ecolo; Air Solution
Regions Exported to: Worldwide
Percentage of Business in Exporting: 75

43836 Ecological Labs Inc
13 Hendrickson Ave
Lynbrook, NY 11563-1201   516-823-3441
          Fax: 516-379-3632 800-645-2976
          info@propump.com www.microbelift.com
Live bacterial cultures
President: Barry Richter
barryrichter@microbelist.com
Estimated Sales: $5-10 Million
Number Employees: 10-19
Type of Packaging: Bulk

43837 Ecological Technologies
PO Box 4733
Boynton Beach, FL 33424   561-585-8196
              Fax: 561-547-0993
Wholesaler/distributor and exporter of waste water treatment systems; serving the food service market
President: Dennis Paul
Estimated Sales: $1-2.5 Million
Number Employees: 10-19
Parent Co: DynynStyl
Brands Exported: PolySolv; BioClean; PRS System; Odor Eliminator; EcoSolv; FilmFree
Regions Exported to: Worldwide
Percentage of Business in Exporting: 80

43838 Econo Frost Night Covers
PO Box 40
Shawnigan Lake, BC V0R 2W0
Canada   250-743-1222
          Fax: 250-743-1221 800-519-1222
          info@econofrost.com www.mgvinc.com
Manufacturer, importer and exporter of color corrected lighting and night covers for refrigerated display cases
President: Mark Granfar
Marketing: Samantha Criddle
International Sales Director: Carlos Paniagua
Product Development: Trevor Brien
Number Employees: 20-49
Number of Products: 1
Square Footage: 6000
Parent Co: MGV Inc
Type of Packaging: Food Service
Regions Exported to: Worldwide
Regions Imported from: Worldwide

43839 Econocorp Inc
72 Pacella Park Dr
Randolph, MA 02368-1791   781-986-7500
          Fax: 781-986-1553 www.econocorp.com
Manufacturer and exporter of carton sealing machinery
President: Wayne Goldberg
wayne@econocorp.com
Quality Control: Richard Norton
VP: Mark Jacobson
Estimated Sales: $ 10 - 20 Million
Number Employees: 50-99
Square Footage: 42000
Brands Exported: Econoseal Cartoning Machines
Regions Exported to: Worldwide
Percentage of Business in Exporting: 40

43840 Econofrost Night Covers
Box 40
Shawnigan Lake, BC V0R 2W0
Canada   250-743-1222
          Fax: 250-743-1221 800-519-1222
          info@econofrost.com www.econofrost.com
Night covers for the refrigerated display cases in supermarkets.
President: Mark Granfar
Marketing: Lyn Rose
Sales: Trevor Brien
Sales: Scott Werhun
Sales: Jamie Farr
International Sales: Carlos Paniagua
Number Employees: 15
Number of Brands: 2
Square Footage: 3000
Type of Packaging: Private Label
Brands Exported: Econofrost
Regions Exported to: Central America, South America, Europe, Asia, North America
Percentage of Business in Exporting: 90

43841 Economy Folding Box Corporation
2601 S La Salle St
Chicago, IL 60616   312-225-2000
          Fax: 312-225-3082 800-771-1053
Manufacturer and exporter of paper boxes
President: Michael M Mitchel
CEO: Clifford Moos
guizhou@yahoo.com
VP/Treasurer: Michael Mitchel
Purchasing Officer: Marie Hernandez
Sales Manager: Joseph Moos

Estimated Sales: $ 10 - 20 Million
Number Employees: 50-99
Square Footage: 330000
Type of Packaging: Consumer, Food Service, Private Label
Regions Exported to: Central America, Canada, Caribbean
Percentage of Business in Exporting: 5

43842 Economy Label Sales Company
515 Carswell Ave
Daytona Beach, FL 32117-4411 386-253-4741
Fax: 386-238-0775
Manufacturer and exporter of flexible plastic and vinyl labels including pressure sensitive, plain, hot-stamped and printed
Estimated Sales: $5-10 Million
Number Employees: 50-99
Parent Co: Meadow USA

43843 Economy Novelty & Printing Co
407 Park Ave S # 26a
Suite 26A
New York, NY 10016-8420 212-481-3022
Fax: 212-481-4514 info@thinkideas.com
www.thinkideas.com
Manufacturer and importer of advertising specialties including badges, medals, decals and ribbons
President: Robert Becker
einfo@thinkideas.com
VP: Warren Becker
Estimated Sales: Less Than $500,000
Number Employees: 1-4
Square Footage: 2000
Parent Co: Economy Novelty
Regions Imported from: Asia
Percentage of Business in Importing: 20

43844 Economy Paper & Restaurant Co
180 Broad St
Clifton, NJ 07013-1299 973-279-5500
Fax: 973-279-4140 sales@economysupply.com
www.economysupply.com
Soaps, degreasers and custom fabricated equipment; wholesaler/distributor and exporter of food service equipment, disposables, janitorial supplies, smallwares, glassware, flatware and china; installation and consulting available
President: L J Konzelman
CFO: Susan Majors
VP: Micheal Konzelman
R&D: Alex Nasarone
Public Relations: Susan Majors
Purchasing: Kevin Konzelman
Estimated Sales: $ 3 - 5 Million
Number Employees: 10-19
Square Footage: 50000
Type of Packaging: Food Service
Brands Exported: Hobart; Vulcan; Traulsen; Cleveland; Oneida; Libby; Frymaster; Delfielo; True; Beverage Air; Garland; Usrange; Wof; Globe; Pitco; Eagle; Kolpak; Aenn; Harford
Regions Exported to: Central America, South America, Europe, Asia
Percentage of Business in Exporting: 20
Brands Imported: WMF, Miscela D'Oro
Regions Imported from: Europe

43845 Economy Tent Intl
2995 NW 75th St
Miami, FL 33147-5943 305-694-1234
Fax: 305-835-7098 800-438-3226
sales@economytent.com www.mmicreateweb.com
Supplier and exporter of party tents for the food service industry
Owner: Hal Lapping
hlapping@economytent.com
VP Marketing: Hal Lapping
Estimated Sales: $ 1 - 2.5 Million
Number Employees: 20-49
Type of Packaging: Food Service
Regions Exported to: Caribbean

43846 (HQ)Ecoval Dairy Trade
Takenhofplein 6
1st Floor
Nijmegen, 6538 SZ
Netherlands
www.ecoval.com
Wholesaler/distributor, importer and exporter of dairy products including nonfat dry milk, whey powder, butter, oil, buttermilk powder and cheese; serving the food service market

President: Donald Street
Director Sales: Carolyn Spack
Number Employees: 20-49
Square Footage: 12000
Parent Co: Louis Dreyfus Commodities Suisse S.A.
Type of Packaging: Food Service
Other Locations:
  M.E. Franks
  Stillwater, MNM.E. Franks
Brands Exported: Melfran
Regions Exported to: Central America, South America, Europe, Asia, Middle East
Percentage of Business in Exporting: 60
Regions Imported from: Europe
Percentage of Business in Importing: 1

43847 Ecs Warehouse
2381 Fillmore Ave
Buffalo, NY 14214-2129 716-833-7380
Fax: 716-833-7386 pemerling@emerfood.com
www.ecswarehouse.com
A warehouse that understands your needs. Frozen, dry, refrigerated warehouse on Canadian border, within 500 miles of 70% of the entire Canadian population and 55% of the entire USA population. Services include: pick & pack, crossdocking, express service, repacking, distribution, TL & LTL, rail, consolidation, salvage, quick access to NYC, Boston, D.C., Cleveland, Buffalo, Toronto, Rockland, Syracuse, Detroit and Cincinnati. If you have special product needs, call us.
CEO: Peter Emerling
pemerling@emerfood.com
Number Employees: 10-19
Square Footage: 500000
Type of Packaging: Bulk

43848 Ecuadorian Rainforest LLC
25 Main St
Building 6
Belleville, NJ 07109 973-759-2002
Fax: 973-759-3002 info@intotherainforest.com
www.intotherainforest.com
Wholsaler of bulk raw materials; nutraceutical ingredient supplier.
Owner: Marlene Siegel
Vice President: Steve Siegel

43849 Eda's Sugar Free
4900 N 20th St
Philadelphia, PA 19144-2402 215-324-3412
Fax: 888-626-7785 brianberry44@gmail.com
www.edassugarfree.com
Manufacturer, processor and exporter of sugar free hard candies.
Owner: Mike Bernert
mbernert@edassugarfree.com
Estimated Sales: Less Than $500,000
Number Employees: 1-4
Number of Brands: 1
Number of Products: 28
Square Footage: 80000
Type of Packaging: Consumer, Food Service, Private Label, Bulk
Brands Exported: Eda's
Regions Exported to: Central America, South America, Europe
Percentage of Business in Exporting: 5
Brands Imported: Eda Sugarfree Candy

43850 Eden
PO Box 544
Utica, OH 43080-0544 740-745-2745
Fax: 740-745-2748 800-831-9505
Importer, exporter and wholesaler/distributor of natural food supplements
President: Deborah Ruyan
Estimated Sales: $500,000-$1 Million
Number Employees: 5-9
Square Footage: 100000
Brands Exported: Swedish Supreme; Swedish Pollenique; AB Cernelle Supplements
Regions Exported to: Central America, South America, Europe, Asia
Brands Imported: Cernilton; Pollitabs; Ventrux; Cervital; Napolen Gold; Cerni-Queen
Regions Imported from: Europe

43851 Eden Foods Inc
701 Tecumseh Rd
Clinton, MI 49236-9599 517-456-7424
Fax: 517-456-6075 888-424-3336
info@edenfoods.com

Established in 1969. Natural and organic foods including pasta, soymilk, green tea, beans, tomatoes, spaghetti sauce, etc
President/CEO: Michael Potter
CEO: Manuela Della
manueladella@hfhs.org
CFO: Jay Hughes
Vice President: Jim Fox
Quality Control: Jon Solomon
VP Marketing & Sales: Sue Becker
VP Operations: William Swaney
Estimated Sales: $20-50 Million
Number Employees: 100-249
Type of Packaging: Food Service
Brands Exported: Edensoy; EdenBlend; Edensoy Extra
Regions Imported from: Japan

43852 Ederback Corporation
505 South Maple Road
Ann Arbor, MI 48103 734-665-8877
Fax: 734-665-9099 800-422-2558
info@eberbachlabtools.com
www.eberbachlabtools.com
Manufacturer and exporter of laboratory equipment including shakers, mixers, homogenizers and blenders
President: Ralph Boehnke Jr
Estimated Sales: $ 3 - 5 Million
Number Employees: 10-19
Regions Exported to: Worldwide
Percentage of Business in Exporting: 5

43853 Edgar A Weber & Co
549 Palwaukee Dr
Wheeling, IL 60090-6049 847-215-1980
Fax: 847-215-2073 800-558-9078
info@weberflavors.com
www.weberflavors.com
Manufacturer and exporter of flavoring extracts for wine, liquor, baked goods and ice cream
Owner: Pam Grossman
pamg@weberflavors.com
CFO: Judith Turyna
Marketing Manager: Roger Passaglia
Plant Manager: Mike Sciore
Purchasing: Carol Myers
Estimated Sales: $3 Million
Number Employees: 50-99
Square Footage: 20000
Regions Exported to: Worldwide

43854 Edge Manufacturing
1120 Mason Cir S
Pevely, MO 63070-1637 636-224-0004
Fax: 636-479-3710 sales@edgemfg.com
Knife sharpeners and sharpening tools, grinders and blades.
President: John Wightman
jwightman@edgemfg.com
Number Employees: 100-249
Regions Exported to: Central America, South America, Europe, Asia, North America, Worldwide

43855 Edge Resources
1 Menfi Way
Unit 20
Hopedale, MA 01747-1542 508-634-8214
Fax: 508-634-9888 888-849-0998
info@edgeresources.com www.edgeresources.com
Manufacturer and importer of food service equipment and supplies; consultant specializing in marketing and sales services
President/CEO: Frank Curty
Estimated Sales: $500,000-$1 Million
Number Employees: 5-9
Square Footage: 16000
Brands Imported: ICEL; Firm Grip
Regions Imported from: Worldwide
Percentage of Business in Importing: 95

43856 Edgecraft Corp
825 Southwood Rd
Avondale, PA 19311-9765 610-268-0500
Fax: 610-268-3545 800-342-3255
val.gleason@edgecraft.com www.chefschoice.com
Manufacturer and exporter of manual and power driven sharpeners slicer and cutlery
President: Samuel Weiner
samuel.weiner@edgecraft.com
CEO: Daniel Friel Sr
Estimated Sales: G
Number Employees: 100-249
Brands Exported: Chef's Choice

Importers & Exporters / A-Z

Regions Exported to: Central America, South America, Europe, Asia, Middle East

43857 Edhard Corp
279 Blau Rd
Hackettstown, NJ 07840-5221   908-850-8444
Fax: 908-850-8445 888-334-2731
meter@edhard.com www.edhard.com
Bakers' equipment and supplies including plastic injection molds and dies
President: Ed Bars
ed@edhard.com
CFO: Joe Englert
Sales Manager: Nancy Neri
Estimated Sales: $ 2.5 - 5 Million
Number Employees: 20-49

43858 Edison Price Lighting
4150 22nd St
Long Island City, NY 11101-4815   718-685-0700
Fax: 718-786-8530 jlattanzio@epl.com
www.epl.com
Manufacturer and exporter of architectural, energy efficient, recessed and surface mounted lighting fixtures
President: Emma Price
eprice@epl.com
Finance: MaryAnna Romano
R&D: Richard J. Shaver
Sales/Marketing: Joel Seigel
Sales Service: Joanie Lattanzio
Customer Service: Stephanie Smith
Administration: James D. Vizzini
purchasing/operations: George H. Closs
Number Employees: 100-249
Brands Exported: Bablux; Duplux; Simplux; Multipurpose; Sight Line; Artima; Anglux; Triples
Regions Exported to: Central America, South America, Asia, Middle East
Percentage of Business in Exporting: 20

43859 Edl Packaging Engineers
1260 Parkview Rd
Green Bay, WI 54304-5619   920-336-7744
Fax: 920-336-8585 sales@edlpackaging.com
www.edlpackaging.com
Manufacturer and exporter of shrink and stretch bundling machinery
President: Ken Carter
sales@edlpackaging.com
Director Of Sales: Larry D Cozine
Product Manager/Bagged Product: Jariath Harkin
Estimated Sales: $ 5 - 10,000,000
Number Employees: 50-99
Number of Products: 4
Square Footage: 50000
Parent Co: EDL UK
Type of Packaging: Consumer, Food Service, Private Label, Bulk
Regions Exported to: South America

43860 (HQ)Edlong Corporation
225 Scott St
Elk Grove Village, IL 60007-1299   847-631-6700
info@edlong.com
www.edlong.com
Cheese, butter, milk & cream, cultured, sweet and functional flavors. Concentrated dairy flavors.
President & CEO: Laurette Rondenet
CFO: David Starr
Vice President, Global R&D: Laura Enriquez
Vice President, Operations: Ken Mack
Square Footage: 360000
Type of Packaging: Food Service, Private Label, Bulk
Other Locations:
 Edlong Dairy Flavors
 SuffolkEdlong Dairy FlavorsUnited Kingdom
Brands Exported: Edlong Brand Flavors
Regions Exported to: Central America, South America, Europe, Asia, Middle East, Worldwide
Percentage of Business in Exporting: 20

43861 Edlund Co
159 Industrial Pkwy
Burlington, VT 05401-5494   802-862-9661
Fax: 802-862-4822 800-772-2126
scrane@edlundco.com www.edlundco.com
Develops and manufactures operator-oriented stainless steel equipment for the food service industry product line of which includes can crushers; manual, electric and air-powered can openers; high speed industrial systems; mechanicaland digital portion control scales; mechanical and digital receiving scales; knife sharpeners; knife racks; and tongs.
President: Willett S Foster Iv
Cmo: Peter Nordell
pnordell@edlundco.com
Vice President: Peter Nordell
Vice President of Sales and Marketing: David Sebastianelli
Estimated Sales: $ 10-25 Million
Number Employees: 100-249
Regions Exported to: Worldwide

43862 Edmeyer
315 27th Ave NE
Minneapolis, MN 55418-2715   651-450-1210
Fax: 651-450-0003 www.edmeyerinc.com
Manufacturer and exporter of casers, conveyors, case packers and palletizers
President: Larry Smith
VP: Jerry Kisch
Sales Manager: Greg Reid
Estimated Sales: $ 20-50 Million
Number Employees: 20-49
Square Footage: 12000

43863 Edmonton Potato Growers
12220 - 170 Street
Edmonton, AB T5V 1L7
Canada   780-447-1860
Fax: 780-447-1899 admin@epg.ab.ca
www.epg.ab.ca
Manufacturer and exmporter of potatoes including table, seed and processed, onions
President: Wayne Groot
VP: Ernie Van Boom
Sales: Darcy Olson
General Manager: Bob Jensen
Estimated Sales: $13 Million
Number Employees: 23
Type of Packaging: Consumer, Food Service, Bulk
Regions Exported to: USA, Mexico
Percentage of Business in Exporting: 33

43864 Edoko Food Importers
1335 Kebet Way
Port Coquitlam, BC V3C 6G1
Canada   604-944-7332
Fax: 604-944-8557 info@edokofood.ca
www.edokofood.ca
Importer/Distributor of specialty European confectionery food products
President: Neal Letourneau
VP Sales: Brian Woods
Business Manager: Don Cullen
Plant Manager: Bill Hughes
Number Employees: 35
Square Footage: 96000
Regions Imported from: South America, Europe, Asia

43865 (HQ)Edom Labs Inc
100 E Jefryn Blvd
Suite M
Deer Park, NY 11729-5729   631-586-2266
Fax: 631-586-2385 800-723-3366
info@edomlaboratories.com
www.edomlaboratories.com
Vitamins and dietary supplements
Owner: Eric Pollack
Estimated Sales: Less Than $500,000
Number Employees: 1-4
Type of Packaging: Consumer, Private Label, Bulk
Brands Exported: Edom Laboratories; Edom Pet Products Animal Care Division
Regions Exported to: Central America, South America, Europe, Asia, Middle East

43866 Edson Packaging Machinery
215 Hempstead Drive
Hamilton, ON L8W 2E6
Canada   905-385-3201
Fax: 905-385-8775 800-493-3766
value@edson.com www.edson.com
Manufacturer and exporter of robotic top load packers, packaging machinery including case openers, robotic palletizers, stretch bundlers, sealers and automatic packers
CEO: Robert Hattin
Vice President, General Manager: Gary Evans
Engineering Manager: Bob Krouse
Quality Control: Bob Krause
Account Manager: Scott Killins
Estimated Sales: $10 Million
Number Employees: 70
Number of Brands: 5
Square Footage: 96600
Type of Packaging: Consumer, Food Service
Brands Exported: Edson
Regions Exported to: Central America, Europe, Asia, Middle East, USA, Mexico, Australia
Percentage of Business in Exporting: 70

43867 Educational Institute of the American Hotel & Lodging Assoc.
2113 N High St
Lansing, MI 48906   517-372-8800
Fax: 517-372-5141 800-344-3320
VP: George Glazer
Contact: Scott Anderson
sanderson@ei-ahla.org
Estimated Sales: $ 3 - 5 Million
Number Employees: 20-49

43868 Edward & Sons Trading Co
4420 Via Real
Suite C
Carpinteria, CA 93013-1635   805-684-8500
Fax: 805-684-8220 www.edwardandsons.com
Manufacturer, importer and exporter of natural, organic and specialty foods: condiments, confectionery products, crackers, vegetarian soup mixes, snack foods, canned organic vegetables, vegetarian bouillon cubes, cake decorationsorganic coconut milk
President: Joel Dee
edwardsons@aol.com
Vice President: Alison Cox
Estimated Sales: $1 Million
Number Employees: 10-19
Type of Packaging: Consumer, Food Service, Private Label
Regions Imported from: South America, Europe, Asia

43869 Efco Importers
PO Box 741
Foxcroft Square, PA 19046   215-885-8597
Fax: 215-885-4584 888-234-9210
efcoimport@aol.com
Beer, wine, liquor and specialty foods
President/CEO: Martin Friedland
m.friedland@faganmusic.com
Estimated Sales: $1-2.5 Million
Number Employees: 5-9
Type of Packaging: Private Label

43870 Eide Industries Inc
16215 Piuma Ave
Cerritos, CA 90703-1528   562-402-8335
Fax: 562-924-2233 800-422-6827
info@eideindustries.com www.eideindustries.com
Manufacturer and exporter of commercial awnings, canopies, tension structures and custom fabric covers
President: Luis Barragan
barraganl@gmail.com
VP Manufacturing/ Chairman: Jesse Borrego
Secretary/VP Marketing: Joe Belli
VP Sales & Marketing: Dan Neill
Human Resources: Lourdes Jordan
Production Coordinator: Ignacio Pellegrin
Chairman/VP Manufacturing: Jesse Borrego
Estimated Sales: $8 Million
Number Employees: 50-99
Square Footage: 82000

43871 Einson Freeman
200 Robin Road
Paramus, NJ 7652   201-221-2800
Fax: 201-226-9262 info@cafsnj.org
www.cafsnj.org
Manufacturer and exporter of point of purchase displays, exhibits and sales promotion items
President & CEO: Jerrold B. Binney
Treasurer & CFO: Joanne Mandry
EVP & Chief Development Officer: Elizabeth Mason
Senior Project Manager: Jeff Shapiro
Estimated Sales: $ 10 - 20 Million
Number Employees: 50-99
Parent Co: WPP Group PLC

Importers & Exporters / A-Z

43872 Eirich Machines
4033 Ryan Rd
Gurnee, IL 60031-1255   847-336-2444
Fax: 847-336-0914 eirich@eirichusa.com
www.eirich.com/en/eirich-machines
Manufacturer and exporter of high speed, ribbon, paddle, plow and fluidized zone mixers, finishers, bag dump work stations, viscous pumps, blenders and hoppers
Co-President: Paul Eirich
VP Sales: Richard Zak
Estimated Sales: $10-20 Million
Number Employees: 100-249
Square Footage: 150000
Parent Co: Maschinenfabrik G. Eirich GmbH
Regions Exported to: Central America, South America, Caribbean, Mexico
Percentage of Business in Exporting: 10

43873 Eisenmann Corp USA
150 E Dartmoor Dr
Crystal Lake, IL 60014-8710   815-455-4100
Fax: 815-455-1018 www.eisenmann.com
Manufacturer and exporter of turnkey material handling systems including electrified monorail systems and belt, power, chain, overhead chain and free conveyors; system design services available
VP: Craig Benner
Manager: Jeff Wehner
info@eisenmann.com
General Manager (General Industry): R Trenn
Estimated Sales: $50-100 Million
Number Employees: 20-49
Square Footage: 300
Parent Co: Eisenmann Corporation
Type of Packaging: Bulk
Regions Exported to: Worldwide

43874 El Charro Mexican Food Ind
1711 S Virginia Ave
Roswell, NM 88203-1829   575-622-8590
Fax: 575-622-8590 ectortilla@yahoo.com
Manufacturer and exporter of chili sauce and tortilla chips
Owner: Micheal Trujillo
Owner: Mireya Trujillo
Estimated Sales: $5-10 Million
Number Employees: 10-19
Type of Packaging: Consumer, Food Service, Private Label, Bulk
Brands Exported: La Pablanita; El Charro
Regions Exported to: Central America, Europe

43875 El Dorado Packaging Inc
204 Prescolite Dr
El Dorado, AR 71730-6677   870-862-4977
Fax: 870-862-8520 www.eldoradobag.com
Manufacturer and exporter of paper bags
President: Louis Hall
CEO: Louis T Hall Iii
Estimated Sales: $ 20 - 50 Million
Number Employees: 100-249
Type of Packaging: Consumer
Regions Exported to: Worldwide

43876 El Milagro
3050 W 26th St
Chicago, IL 60623-4130   773-579-6120
www.el-milagro.com
Corn and flour tortilla manufacturer in the Midwest.
President: Raphael Lopez
Contact: Phil Crookham
pcrookham@el-milagro.com
Year Founded: 1942
Estimated Sales: Less Than $500,000
Number Employees: 5-9
Type of Packaging: Consumer, Food Service
Regions Exported to: Canada

43877 El Peto Products
65 Saltsman Drive
Cambridge, ON N3H 4R7
Canada
   519-650-4614
Fax: 519-650-5692 800-387-4064
info@elpeto.com www.elpeto.com
Manufacturer and exporter of wheat, gluten and milk-free products including bake mixes, breads, muffins, cakes, buns, pies, cookies, frozen doughs and batters, pastas, soups and specialty flours
President: Elisabeth Riesen
VP: Peter Riesen
Estimated Sales: $3 Million
Number Employees: 18
Number of Brands: 3
Square Footage: 18000
Type of Packaging: Consumer, Food Service, Bulk
Regions Exported to: USA, South Africa
Percentage of Business in Exporting: 5
Regions Imported from: Europe

43878 El Rey Cooked Meats
6190 Bermuda Dr
St Louis, MO 63135-3298   314-521-3113
dryan@elreycookedmeats.com
www.elreycookedmeats.com
Manufacturer and exporter of frozen foods including chili, tamales, roast and barbecued beef, taco meat and pork; also, barbecue sauce
Owner: Joseph Frisella
elreyfoods@aol.com
VP, Sales: Don Ryan
Estimated Sales: $10-20 Million
Number Employees: 5-9
Square Footage: 6000
Type of Packaging: Consumer, Food Service

43879 El Toro Food Products
504 El Rio Street
Watsonville, CA 95076-3540   831-728-9266
Fax: 831-688-8766
Manufacture of canned salsas varieties including sauces and vegetables
President: Richard Thomas
Estimated Sales: $5-10 Million
Number Employees: 5-9
Number of Brands: 6
Number of Products: 10
Square Footage: 24000
Type of Packaging: Food Service, Private Label, Bulk
Regions Exported to: Canada

43880 Elan Vanilla Co
268 Doremus Ave
Newark, NJ 07105-4879   973-344-8014
Fax: 973-344-5880 www.elanvanilla.com
Organic kosher certified vanilla extract, flavoring and synthetic and natural aromatic chemicals
President: Jocelyn Manship
jmanship@elan-chemical.com
Quality Control Manager: Phil Kapp
VP Sales: David Pimentel
Director of Customer Service: Marilyn Santiago
Estimated Sales: $20-50 Million
Number Employees: 50-99
Type of Packaging: Bulk
Regions Exported to: Worldwide
Percentage of Business in Exporting: 10

43881 Elberta Crate & Box Company
231 W Main Street
Suite 207
Carpentersville, IL 60110-1769   847-426-3491
Fax: 847-426-3520 888-672-9260
Manufacturer and exporter of wirebound boxes, crates and expendable pallets
CEO: Ramsay Simmons
Sales Director: Walter Eschenbach
Public Relations: Todd Mills
Estimated Sales: $ 1 - 5 Million
Number Employees: 1-4
Parent Co: Elberta Crate & Box Company
Type of Packaging: Food Service, Bulk
Regions Exported to: South America, Europe, Asia

43882 Elco Fine Foods
7660 Winston Street
Burnaby, BC V5A 4N2
Canada
   604-944-2505
Fax: 604-944-2569
Wholesaler/distributor and importer of Dutch and European cookies, crackers, rusk, honey and candy cake, sauces, jams, dressings, confectionary, smoked herring, soup and soup concentrates and other gourmet food items.
Branch Manager: Fred van Rijswijk
Number Employees: 5-9
Square Footage: 36000
Parent Co: Holtzheuser Brothers
Brands Imported: Honig; Tantos; Verkade; Balla; Brink; Hille; Mistic; Conimex; Venco; San Esu; Good For You; Dan'T's
Regions Imported from: Central America, Europe, Asia
Percentage of Business in Importing: 90

43883 Elco Fine Foods
233 Alden Road
Markham, OT L3R 3W6
Canada   905-474-2400
Fax: 905-474-2499 800-421-ELCO
info@elcofinefoods.com www.elcocanada.com
Importer and wholesaler/distributor of international specialty food products including confectionery items and cheeses; also, general merchandise and health foods; serving the food service market
Sales Manager: Brian Wright
Number Employees: 10-19
Parent Co: Elco Fine Foods
Type of Packaging: Consumer, Food Service, Private Label, Bulk
Regions Imported from: Worldwide
Percentage of Business in Importing: 95

43884 Eldorado Coffee Distributors
5675 49th St
Flushing, NY 11378-2012   718-418-4100
Fax: 718-418-4500 800-635-2566
www.eldoradocoffee.com
Established in 1980. Manufacturer and roaster of coffee.
Founder: Segunda Martin
eldoradon1@aol.com
VP: Juan Martin
VP of Sales: Albert Valdes
Estimated Sales: $20-50 Million
Number Employees: 20-49
Type of Packaging: Consumer, Food Service, Private Label
Regions Exported to: Europe, Asia
Percentage of Business in Exporting: 3

43885 Eleanor's Best LLC
PO Box 9
Garrison, NY 10524   646-296-6870
info@eleanorsbest.com
www.eleanorsbest.com
Handmade, vegan, gluten free jams and marmalades, maple syrup, wildflower honey
Founder/Owner: Jennifer Mercurio
Year Founded: 2013
Number Employees: 10
Number of Brands: 1
Number of Products: 16
Type of Packaging: Consumer, Private Label
Brands Exported: Eleanor's Best
Regions Exported to: USA

43886 Electric Contract Furniture
450 Fashion Ave # 2710
Suite 2701
New York, NY 10123-2710   212-967-5504
Fax: 212-760-8823 888-311-6272
eclecticinc@aol.com www.eclecticcontract.com
Tables, chairs, booths and barstools
Owner: Junior Ferma
junior@eclecticcontract.com
Estimated Sales: Less than $500,000
Number Employees: 1-4

43887 Electro Freeze
2116 8th Ave
East Moline, IL 61244   309-755-4553
Fax: 309-755-9858 sales@electrofreeze.com
www.hcduke.com
Manufacturer, importer and exporter of soft serve ice cream, slush, shake and frozen yogurt equipment
Marketing: Joe Clark
Contact: Shane Allen
sallen@electrofreeze.com
Estimated Sales: $ 20 - 50 Million
Number Employees: 100-249
Square Footage: 115000
Parent Co: H.C. Duke & Son
Brands Exported: Electro Freeze
Regions Exported to: Central America, South America, Europe, Asia, Middle East, Africa
Regions Imported from: Worldwide

43888 Electro Lift Inc
204 Sargeant Ave
Clifton, NJ 07013-1932   973-471-0204
Fax: 973-471-2814 info2@electrolift.com
www.electrolift.com
Manufacturer and exporter of hoists for monorail, dual rail, hatchway or base-mounted applications
Owner: Deborah Rechtschaffer
debbie@electrolift.com
Estimated Sales: $ 5 - 10 Million
Number Employees: 20-49

281

Type of Packaging: Bulk

43889 (HQ)Electrodex
4554 19th St Ct E
Bradenton, FL 34203 941-753-5663
 Fax: 941-753-7049 800-362-1972
Manufacturer and exporter of lighting fixtures
President: Mike Guritz
Sales Manager: Warren Dalton
Estimated Sales: $2.5-5 Million
Number Employees: 10-19
Type of Packaging: Food Service
Regions Exported to: Worldwide

43890 Electronic Weighing Systems
664 Fisherman Street
Opa Locka, FL 33054 305-685-8067
 Fax: 305-685-2440
Manufacturer and exporter of electronic scales for receiving, counter, heavy duty, warehouse and crane scale
VP: Victor Perez, Jr.
Estimated Sales: $ 2.5-5 Million
Number Employees: 7
Square Footage: 84000
Brands Exported: EWS
Regions Exported to: Worldwide
Percentage of Business in Exporting: 60

43891 Elena's
2650 Paldan
Auburn Hills, MI 48326 248-373-1100
 Fax: 248-373-1120 800-723-5362
 info@elenas.com www.elenas.com
Manufacturer and exporter of pasta, pasta sauce and pasta salad
President: Elena Houlihan
VP Finance: Caroline Moose
VP Operations: John Houlihan
Estimated Sales: $2.5-5 Million
Number Employees: 20-49
Parent Co: Houlihan's Culinary Traditions
Type of Packaging: Food Service, Private Label, Bulk

43892 (HQ)Eliason Corp
9229 Shaver Rd
Portage, MI 49024-6799 269-327-7003
 Fax: 269-327-7006 800-828-3655
 doors@eliasoncorp.com
Manufacturer and exporter of swing doors and night covers for open refrigerated cases and freezers.
Owner: Edwanda Eliason
CEO: Doug Morrison
dmking851027@gmail.com
Marketing Director: Michael Woolsey
Estimated Sales: $ 5 - 10 Million
Number Employees: 50-99
Square Footage: 350000
Other Locations:
 Eliason Corporation
 Woodland, CAEliason Corporation
Brands Exported: Eliason; Easy Swing Doors; Econo-Cover
Regions Exported to: South America, Europe, Asia
Percentage of Business in Exporting: 3

43893 Elite Forming Design Solutions
15 Commerce Ct SE
Rome, GA 30161-6848 706-232-3021
 Fax: 706-232-3121 info@eliteforming.com
  www.eliteforming.com
Manufacturer and supplier of OEM plates and parts.
Owner: Jim Mauer
Number Employees: 10-19
Regions Exported to: North America, USA

43894 Elite Naturel USA
44 Mound St
Lindenhurst, NY 11757 631-567-8844
 Fax: 631-567-8079 info@elitenaturel.com
  www.elitenaturel.com
100% certified pure organic and natural fruit juice and seed extract
National Sales and Operations Manager: Ali Suman

43895 Elite Spice Inc
7151 Montevideo Rd
Jessup, MD 20794-9308 410-796-1900
 Fax: 410-379-6933 800-232-3531
 jbrandt@elitespice.com www.elitespice.com
Spice, seasoning, capsicum, oil & oleoresin, and dehydrated vegetable producer.

President & CEO: Isaac Samuel
CFO/Human Resources Director: Debbie Ingle
R&D Director: Leslie Krause
Quality Control Directory: Dave Anthony
Marketing Executive: Kathy Lyons
VP, Sales: Paul Kurpe
VP/Plant Manager: George Mayer
Purchasing Manager: Margie Schneidman
Year Founded: 1988
Estimated Sales: $20-50 Million
Number Employees: 100-249
Square Footage: 11000
Type of Packaging: Private Label
Regions Imported from: Central America, Europe, Asia, Middle East, Africa

43896 Elki
2215 Merrill Creek Pkwy
Everett, WA 98203-5853 425-261-1002
 Fax: 425-261-1001 gnorde@elki.com
Preserves, crackers, pesto, asian sauces, bruschettas/tapenades, gourmet dips, gourmet mixes, gift boxed candy, skandi snaps, chutneys and simmer sauces
Owner: Elizabeth Lie
CFO: Clay Lundgren
VP: Ruth Lie
Marketing: Giovanna Norde
Regional Sales Manager: Erin These
elie@elki.com
Number Employees: 5-9

43897 Ellehammer Industries
20146 100 A Avenue
Langley, BC V1M 3G2
Canada 604-882-9326
 Fax: 604-882-9703
Manufacturer and exporter of plastic bags and film
Quality Control: Jack Tucker
Plant Manager: Ralph Schnitzer
Number Employees: 50
Regions Exported to: USA

43898 Ellenco
4419 41st Street
Brentwood, MD 20722-1515 301-927-4370
 Fax: 301-927-4376
Manufacturer and exporter of fire alarm systems
VP: Bob Harding
Estimated Sales: $ 1 - 5 Million
Number Employees: 20-50

43899 Ellett Industries
1575 Kingsway Avenue
Port Coquitlam, BC V3C 4E5
Canada 604-941-8211
 Fax: 604-941-6854
Manufacturer and exporter of fabricated alloy metal, tanks, stills, heat exchangers, vessels, stainless steel and titanium pipes and fittings
President/CEO: J Ellett
Vice President: Bob Gill
Sales Director: L Osberg
Production Manager: David Clift
Purchasing Manager: Don Young
Estimated Sales: $ 20 Million
Number Employees: 100-250
Square Footage: 120000
Regions Exported to: USA
Percentage of Business in Exporting: 54

43900 Ellingers Agatized WoodInc
923 S 21st St
Sheboygan, WI 53081-4702 920-457-7746
 Fax: 920-457-2972 888-287-8906
 jenny@ellingerswoodproducts.com
  www.agatized.com
Manufacturer and exporter of wood bowls, bar trays, cutting boards and wood bowl gift sets.
President: Joyce Neese
jennye@bytehead.com
Sales Director: Jennifer Stafford
Estimated Sales: $800,000
Number Employees: 10-19
Number of Products: 35
Square Footage: 25000
Type of Packaging: Consumer, Food Service
Brands Exported: Agatized Wood
Regions Exported to: Asia
Percentage of Business in Exporting: 40

43901 Elliot Lee
445 Central Ave Unit 100
Cedarhurst, NY 11516 516-569-9595
 Fax: 516-569-8088 sales@misterpromotion.com
  www.misterpromotion.com
Manufacturer, importer and wholesaler/distributor of advertising specialties including sign holders, awards, badges, bags, cups, pens and plaques
President/CFO: Victor Deutsch
CFO: Elliot Deutsch
Marketing Director: Elliot Deutsch
Estimated Sales: Below $ 5 Million
Number Employees: 5-9
Regions Imported from: South America, Europe, Asia
Percentage of Business in Importing: 5

43902 Elliott Manufacturing Co Inc
2664 S Cherry Ave
Fresno, CA 93706-5494 559-233-6235
 Fax: 559-233-9833 elliottmfg@elliott-mfg.com
  www.elliott-mfg.com
Manufacturer and exporter of date and raisin processing machinery and olive, date and prune pitters; also, packaging machinery including erectors, sealers, cartoners and case packers
President, Chief Executive Officer: Terry Aluisi
National Sales Manager: John Rea
Estimated Sales: $1-5 Million
Number Employees: 20-49
Square Footage: 120000
Brands Exported: OEM
Regions Exported to: Central America, South America, Europe, Asia, Middle East
Percentage of Business in Exporting: 10

43903 Elliott-Williams Company
3500 E 20th St
Indianapolis, IN 46218 317-635-1660
 Fax: 317-453-1977 800-428-9303
Manufacturer and exporter of blast chillers, walk-in coolers, freezers and refrigerators; also, pre-fabricated refrigerated warehouses
Owner: Stuart Mc Keehan
CFO: R Scott
Contact: Michael Elliott
mark.m.elliott@williams.com
Purchasing Manager: K McCoy
Estimated Sales: $20-50 Million
Number Employees: 100-249
Square Footage: 100000
Regions Exported to: Worldwide
Percentage of Business in Exporting: 10

43904 Ellison Milling Company
PO Box 400
Lethbridge, AB T1J 3Z2
Canada 403-328-6622
 Fax: 403-327-3772
Durum Semolina, Hard and Soft Wheat Flours
President: Michael Greer
Quality Control: Paolo Santangelo
Marketing Director: Bob Grebinsky
Plant Manager: B McConnell
Number Employees: 65
Parent Co: Parrish & Heimbecker
Type of Packaging: Food Service, Private Label, Bulk
Brands Exported: Alberta; Dream Cake; Royal Pastry; Durum Semolina
Regions Exported to: South America, Asia, USA

43905 Elmar Worldwide
200 Gould Avenue
P.O.Box 245
Depew, NY 14043-0245 716-681-5650
 Fax: 716-681-4660 800-433-3562
 elmar@elmarworldwide.com
  www.elmarworldwide.com
Manufacturer, exporter and designer of rotary valve piston fillers, multi-flex particulate fillers, vacuum syrupers and monoblock systems; also, re-manufacturing, R&D, computer/electronic line control systems, product testing andflush-in place systems
President: Mark Dahlquist
CEO: Martin Jolden, Jr.
CFO: Linda Gregorio
Sales: Tom Depczynski
Estimated Sales: $ 10 - 20 Million
Number Employees: 50-99
Brands Exported: Elmar
Regions Exported to: Central America, South America, Europe, Asia, Middle East
Percentage of Business in Exporting: 40

Importers & Exporters / A-Z

43906 Elmer Chocolate®
401 N 5th St
Ponchatoula, LA 70454
985-386-6166
800-843-9537
www.elmerchocolate.com
Only one Elmer Chocolate product can be purchased year-round, which is Gold Brick Topping, also manufactures Christmas, Valentine's and Easter chocolates.
Chairman & CEO: Robert Nelson
Safety Manager: Jeffrey Bell
Year Founded: 1914
Estimated Sales: $26.7 Million
Number Employees: 300
Square Footage: 250000
Type of Packaging: Consumer
Regions Exported to: Worldwide

43907 Elmer Hansen Produce Inc
471 S Milwaukee Ave
Moses Lake, WA 98837-2788
509-765-8895
Fax: 509-765-6708
Packer and exporter of onions
President: Amy Hansen
Vice President: Alex Hansen
Sales Director: Guy Hansen
Estimated Sales: $ 10 - 20 Million
Number Employees: 1-4
Square Footage: 102000
Type of Packaging: Food Service, Private Label
Brands Exported: Pride of the West; Northwest
Regions Exported to: Central America, Europe, Asia, Canada, Mexico
Percentage of Business in Exporting: 15

43908 Elmo Rietschle - A Gardner Denver Product
1800 Gardner Expressway
Qunicy, IL 62305
217-222-5400
Fax: 217-228-8243
Compressors and pumps for the beverage and food production industries.
President & CEO: Barry Pennypacker
Chairman Board Of Directors: Frank Hansen
frank.hansen@garnerdenver.com
Regions Exported to: USA, Worldwide

43909 Elmwood Sensors
500 Narragansett Park Dr
Pawtucket, RI 00861
401-727-1300
Fax: 401-728-5390 800-356-9663
linda.lundgren@invensys.com
www.elmwoodsensors.com
Manufacturer and exporter of thermostats and controls
VP/General Manager: Steven Fof
Estimated Sales: $ 50-100 Million
Number Employees: 100-250
Square Footage: 160000
Parent Co: Fasco
Regions Exported to: Worldwide

43910 Elo Touch Systems
301 Constitution Dr
Menlo Park, CA 94025-1110
650-361-4800
Fax: 650-361-4721 800-557-1458
eloinfo@elotouch.com www.elotouch.com
Manufacturer and exporter of operator interfaces and point of sale systems
General Manager: Mark Mendenhall
Chief Executive Officer: Craig Witsoe
CFO: Roxi Wen
Vice President, Chief Technical Officer: Bruno Thuillier
VP, Corporate Development: Sharon Segev
VP, Global Quality: Anita Chang
Manager of Marketing: Fumiko Sasaki
Vice President of Global Sales: Sean Miller
Contact: Thuillier Bruno
bruno.thuillier@elotouch.com
Vice President of Operations: Mike Moran
Number Employees: 500-999
Parent Co: Amp
Type of Packaging: Food Service

43911 Elopak Americas
46962 Liberty Dr
Wixom, MI 48393
248-486-4600
www.elopak.com
Cartons, aseptic and plastic pouches, form/fill/seal systems and packaging equipment for paper and plastic; importer of filling machinery.
Director, National Accounts, Americas: Julia Viter

Year Founded: 1906
Estimated Sales: $13 Billion
Number Employees: 2,800
Square Footage: 175000
Parent Co: Ferd Groups
Brands Exported: Pure-Pak
Regions Exported to: Worldwide
Brands Imported: Shikoku
Regions Imported from: Europe, Asia, Middle East, Mexico, Canada

43912 Elwell Parker
4200 Casteel Drive
Coraopolis, PA 15108
216-432-0638
Fax: 216-881-7555 800-272-9953
nick@elwellparker.com www.elwellparker.com
Manufacturer and exporter of material handling equipment including rider style, electric fork and platform trucks
Sales and Marketing: Nick Marshall
VP Sales/Marketing: Jeff Leggett
Manager Sales/Parts/Service/Support: Curt Roupe
Estimated Sales: $ 3 - 5 Million
Number Employees: 5-9
Regions Exported to: Worldwide
Percentage of Business in Exporting: 20

43913 Elwood International Inc
89 Hudson St
Copiague, NY 11726-1505
631-842-6600
Fax: 631-842-6603 info@elwoodintl.com
Manufacturer and exporter of regular and dietetic portion controlled condiments including dressings, jellies, mayonnaise, mustard, ketchup, peanut butter, table syrups, private label and contract packaging
President: Stuart Roll
Vice President: Richard Roll
IT: Anna Marx
anna@elwoodintl.com
Estimated Sales: $2.90 Million
Number Employees: 10-19
Number of Brands: 3
Number of Products: 40
Square Footage: 92000
Type of Packaging: Consumer, Food Service, Private Label, Bulk
Regions Exported to: Worldwide
Percentage of Business in Exporting: 1
Regions Imported from: Worldwide
Percentage of Business in Importing: 1

43914 Elwood Safety Company
2180 Elmwood Ave
Buffalo, NY 14216
716-308-0573
Fax: 716-874-2110 866-326-6060
leslie@elwoodsafety.com www.elwoodsafety.com
Manufacturer and exporter of protective clothing including aprons, coveralls, sweatbands, lab coats and flame retardant clothing; also, voltage testers, food and beverage coolers and filtration systems
VP/ Sr. Sales Representative: Leslie Meyers
Estimated Sales: $ 1 - 5 Million
Number Employees: 10-19
Square Footage: 30000
Regions Exported to: Worldwide
Percentage of Business in Exporting: 20

43915 Embassy Flavours Ltd.
5 Intermodal Drive
Unit 1
Brampton, ON L6T 5V9
Canada
905-789-3200
Fax: 905-789-3201 800-334-3371
info@embassyflavours.com
www.embassyflavours.com
Manufacturer and exporter of extracts, flavors, colors, essential oils, bases and mixes including cake, pastry and bread. Certifications include BRC, Canadian Celiac Association, Kosher and Halal. Facility is peanut free.
President: Martino Brambilla
R&D: Anne Klingerman
National Sales/Marketing Manager: Mike Taras
Estimated Sales: $1.7 Million
Number Employees: 38
Square Footage: 57600
Type of Packaging: Consumer, Food Service, Private Label, Bulk
Regions Exported to: Worldwide
Percentage of Business in Exporting: 10

43916 Emblem & Badge
123 Dyer Street
Suite 2
Providence, RI 02903-3907
401-365-1265
Fax: 401-365-1263 800-875-5444
sales@recognition.com www.recognition.com
Manufacturer, importer and exporter of plaques, trophies, advertising novelties, name badges, desk sets, glassware, custom awards, etc
President: David Resnik
Vice President: Mike Hersherits
Sales: RI Johnston
Contact: Dinna Finnegan
dinna@recognition.com
Number Employees: 50-99
Square Footage: 100000
Type of Packaging: Bulk
Brands Exported: Emblem & Badge
Regions Exported to: Europe, Asia, Middle East, Canada, Caribbean, Latin America
Percentage of Business in Exporting: 2
Regions Imported from: Europe, Asia
Percentage of Business in Importing: 1

43917 Emc Solutions
302 S Ash St
Celina, OH 45822-2210
419-586-2388
Fax: 419-586-3311 sales@emcconveyor.com
www.emcconveyor.com
Stainless steel and painted overhead trolley conveyors.
Owner: Jeffrey Hazel
econo-mfg@bright.net
Estimated Sales: Less Than $500,000
Number Employees: 1-4
Square Footage: 20000
Type of Packaging: Food Service
Regions Exported to: Central America, South America, Canada, Mexico
Percentage of Business in Exporting: 15

43918 Emerald City Closets Inc
301 - 30th St. NE, #106
Auburn, WA 98002
425-497-8808
Fax: 425-497-8311 800-925-1521
www.emeraldcc.com
Manufacturer, importer and exporter of induction ranges and ovens
Owner: John Pearson
johnp@emeraldcc.com
Purchasing Manager: Winston Chiu
Estimated Sales: $2.5-5 Million
Number Employees: 1-4
Square Footage: 30000
Type of Packaging: Food Service, Private Label
Brands Exported: Fuji Electric
Regions Exported to: Central America, Europe, Asia
Percentage of Business in Exporting: 10
Brands Imported: Fuji Electric
Regions Imported from: Asia
Percentage of Business in Importing: 20

43919 Emerald Kalama Chemical, LLC
1296 Third Street, N.W.
Kalama, WA 98625
360-673-2550
Fax: 360-673-3564 800-223-0035
kalama@emeraldmaterials.com
www.emeraldmaterials.com/epm/kalama
Manufacturer and exporter of specialty chemicals including benzaldehyde, cinnamic aldehyde, benzyl benzoate, benzyl alcohol, benzylacetate, potassium benzoate, benzoic acid and sodium benzoate
President: Edward T. Gotch
Sr. Vice President, Finance: Daniel Emmett
Vice President Operations and HS&E: Brian A. Denison
Number Employees: 175
Parent Co: Emerald Performance Materials
Regions Exported to: Central America, South America, Europe, Asia
Percentage of Business in Exporting: 25

43920 Emerald Performance Materials
2020 Front St
Cuyahoga Falls, OH 44221-3257
330-916-6700
Fax: 330-916-6734
corporate@emeraldmaterials.com
www.emeraldmaterials.com
Produces and markets technologically advanced speciality chemicals for a broad range of food and industrial applications

283

Importers & Exporters / A-Z

President: Carrington Don
carrington.don@winwholesale.com
VP/CFO: Candace Wagner
Number Employees: 500-999

43921 Emerling International Foods
2381 Fillmore Ave
Suite 1
Buffalo, NY 14214-2197   716-833-7381
   Fax: 716-833-7386 pemerling@emerfood.com
          www.emerlinginternational.com
Bulk ingredients including: Fruits & Vegetables; Juice Concentrates; Herbs & Spices; Oils & Vinegars; Flavors & Colors; Honey & Molasses. Also produces pure maple syrup.
President: J Emerling
jemerling@emerfood.com
Sales: Peter Emerling
Public Relations: Jenn Burke
Year Founded: 1988
Estimated Sales: $10-20 Million
Number Employees: 20-49
Square Footage: 500000
Regions Exported to: Central America, South America, Europe, Asia, Canada
Percentage of Business in Exporting: 15
Regions Imported from: Central America, South America, Europe, Asia, Canada
Percentage of Business in Importing: 15

43922 Emerson Process Management
7070 Winchester Cir
Boulder, CO 80301-3506   303-527-5200
   Fax: 303-530-8459   800-522-6277
   flowcustomercare.americas@emerson.com
          www2.emersonprocess.com
Measurement and process controls for the food and beverage industry, as well as solutions for water and wastewater treatments.
Business Leader: Steven Sonnenberg
Number Employees: 500-999

43923 Emery Smith Fisheries Limited
5309 Hwy 3
Shag Harbour, NS B0W 3B0
Canada   902-723-2115
   Fax: 902-723-2372
Manufacturer and exporter of salt fish
President: Emery Smith
Estimated Sales: $12 Million
Number Employees: 25
Type of Packaging: Bulk
Regions Exported to: Worldwide
Percentage of Business in Exporting: 100

43924 Emery Thompson Company
15350 Flight Path Dr
Brooksville, FL 34604   718-588-7300
   Fax: 352-796-0720   813-862-2776
          steve@emerythompson.com
          www.emerythompson.com
Contact: Connie Dominguez
connie@emerythompson.com

43925 Emery Thompson Machine &Supply Company
15350 Flight Path Drive
Brooksville, FL 34604-6861   718-588-7300
   Fax: 352-796-0720
   STEVE@EMERYTHOMPSON.COM
          www.emerythompson.com
Manufacturer, importer and exporter of ice cream, Italian ice, frozen lemonade and frozen custard making machinery.
President: Steve Thompson
CEO: Ted Thompson
Estimated Sales: $2.5-5 Million
Number Employees: 20-49
Square Footage: 180000
Regions Exported to: Worldwide
Percentage of Business in Exporting: 47
Regions Imported from: Mexico
Percentage of Business in Importing: 10

43926 Emery Winslow Scale Co
73 Cogwheel Ln # A
Seymour, CT 06483-3930   203-881-9333
   Fax: 203-881-9477   www.emerywinslow.com
Industrial scale manufacturer
Owner/CEO: Walter Young
CEO: Rudi Baisch
emeryscale@aol.com
CFO/President: Bill Fischer
VP/Marketing: Rudi Baisch
Research & Development: Sam Sagarsee
Sales: David Young
Operations Manager: Bill Rosser
Plant Manager: Jim Evinger
Purchasing Manager: Jonathan Young
Estimated Sales: $20 Million+
Number Employees: 20-49
Number of Brands: 3
Square Footage: 120000
Other Locations:
   Pennsylvania Scale Company
   Lancaster, PAPennsylvania Scale Company
Brands Exported: Emery Winslow; Pennsylvania Scale
Regions Exported to: Central America, South America, Asia, Middle East, Canada
Percentage of Business in Exporting: 5

43927 Emkay Trading Corporation
250 Clearbrook Road
PO Box 504
Elmsford, NY 10523   914-592-9000
   Fax: 914-347-3616 hkpilot@aol.com
Manufacturer and distributor of cheese including cream, bakers, neuchatel, lite, tvorog (Russian style soft cheese) and quark, also, bulk cream, custom fluid diary blends, bulk skim, sour cream, bulk cultured buttermilk and condensedskim milk
Owner: Howard Kravitz
tlindquistturner@limitedbrands.com
Vice President: Ruth Kravitz
Estimated Sales: $2 Million
Number Employees: 30
Square Footage: 800000
Type of Packaging: Consumer, Food Service, Private Label, Bulk
Regions Exported to: Worldwide

43928 Emmy's Organics
629 West Buffalo St
Ithaca, NY 14850   855-463-6697
          info@emmysorganics.com
          emmysorganics.com
Buckwheat-based cereals
Co-Founder: Ian Gaffney
Co-Founder: Samantha Abrams
Regions Exported to: Canada, Mexico

43929 Empire International
1351 East Chief Privado
Ontario, CA 91761   909-923-8588
   Fax: 909-947-6888
   customerservice@empire-international.com
          www.empire-international.com

43930 Empire Screen Printing Inc
N5206 Marco Rd
Onalaska, WI 54650-8818   608-783-3301
   Fax: 608-783-3306   www.empirescreen.com
Empire is a leader in the latest printing processes including flexographic, screen & digital printing, as well as doming. Empire is a supplier to the appliance, retail, food, and beverage industries. Products include retail signagepackage labels, and marketing support items.
President: Johns Freismuth
CEO: James Brush
jamesbr@empirescreen.com
Vice President: James Schwinefus
Research & Development: Keith Cole
Quality Control: Steve Johnson
Marketing Director: Douglas Billings
Sales Director: Kathleen Cuellar
Public Relations: Douglas Billings
Operations Manager: John Johnsonth
Plant Manager: Lee Vieth
Purchasing Manager: Lori Taube
Estimated Sales: $25 Million
Number Employees: 250-499
Number of Brands: 2
Square Footage: 150000
Type of Packaging: Food Service, Private Label

43931 Empire Spice Mills
908 William Avenue
Winnipeg, NB R3E 0Z8
Canada   204-786-1594
   Fax: 204-783-2847
Flavoring extracts and whole ground and blended spices, herbs and seeds, seasonings
President: Don Ramage
Estimated Sales: $1 Million
Number Employees: 10
Square Footage: 64000
Type of Packaging: Consumer, Food Service, Private Label, Bulk
Regions Imported from: South America, Europe, Asia, Middle East
Percentage of Business in Importing: 80

43932 Empire Tea Svc
1965 St James Pl
Columbus, IN 47201-2805   812-375-1937
   Fax: 812-376-7382   800-790-0246
   sales@empiretea.com   www.empiretea.com
Importer of tea in tins, black tea, green tea, herb tea bulk tea, tea bags in wood boxes and various forms of packing
President: Lalith Guy Paranavitana
info@empiretea.com
Plant Manager: Cheryl Paranavitana
Estimated Sales: $250,000
Number Employees: 1-4
Number of Brands: 3
Number of Products: 27
Square Footage: 8000
Type of Packaging: Consumer, Food Service, Private Label, Bulk
Brands Imported: Unicom; Guy's Tea; Tea Temptations
Regions Imported from: Asia
Percentage of Business in Importing: 70

43933 (HQ)Empresas La Famosa
PO Box 51968
Toa Baja, PR 00950-1968   787-251-0060
          Fax: 787-251-2270
Fruit juices, coconut, cream & milk, beans and tomato willow
President: Jose Corripio
Purchasing Supervisor: Carmen Menes
Estimated Sales: $5.6 Million
Number Employees: 61
Square Footage: 960000
Regions Exported to: US, Canada, Virgin Islands

43934 Empress Chocolate Company
5518 Avenue N
Brooklyn, NY 11234   718-951-2251
   Fax: 718-951-2254   800-793-3809
Manufacturer and exporter of custom and stock molded chocolate novelties, cream filled chocolates, truffles and gift boxes
President: Jack Grunhut
VP: Ernest Grunhut
Sales Director: Jerry Sumner
Estimated Sales: $3 Million
Number Employees: 35
Square Footage: 80000
Parent Co: Ernex Corporation
Type of Packaging: Consumer, Private Label
Brands Exported: Empress; Ernex
Regions Exported to: South America, Europe, Middle East
Percentage of Business in Exporting: 5

43935 Emtrol
425 E Berlin Rd
York, PA 17408-8810   717-846-4000
   Fax: 717-846-3624   800-634-4927
   cgales@emtrol.com   www.weldonmachinetool.com
Manufacturer, importer and exporter of material handling equipment and controls, plant automation equipment and custom warehouse/inventory software
President: George Sipe
Executive VP: Matthew Anater
VP Sales/Marketing: Nicholas Selch
Estimated Sales: $20-50 Million
Number Employees: 50-99
Square Footage: 52000
Regions Exported to: Asia, Latin America
Percentage of Business in Exporting: 5
Regions Imported from: Europe

43936 Emuamericas
1799 Pennsylvania St
4th Floor
Denver, CO 80203   303-733-3385
   Fax: 303-733-3384   800-726-0368
   info@emuamericas.com   www.emuamericas.com

Wholesaler/distributor and importer of indoor and outdoor chairs and tables; serving the food service market
President: Benjamin Fromgaglia
Brands Imported: Emu Furniture
Regions Imported from: Europe

43937 Encore Fruit Marketing Inc
120 W Bonita Ave
Suite 204
San Dimas, CA 91773-3035   909-394-5640
Fax: 909-394-5646   sales@encorefruit.com
www.encorefruit.com
Import/export manufacturers' representative of industrial ingredients, frozen fruits and vegetables, purees and juice concentrates; serving food processors, food service operators and wholesalers/distributors.
Owner & President: Greg Kaiser
Owner & CEO: Lisa Hiday-Baca
Chief Financial Officer: Kandi Ashcraft
Vice President: Erin Sill
VP, Sales: Chris Schubert
Import/Export Manager: Wes Uyemura
Year Founded: 1989
Estimated Sales: $55 Million
Number Employees: 10-19
Square Footage: 1800
Type of Packaging: Bulk
Other Locations:
   Encore Fruit Marketing
   Yakima, WA Encore Fruit Marketing
Regions Exported to: Central America
Percentage of Business in Exporting: 50
Regions Imported from: Central America
Percentage of Business in Importing: 50

43938 Encore Plastics
P.O. Box 3208
Huntington Beach, CA 92605   714-893-7889
Fax: 714-897-7968   888-822-8763
info@encoreplastics.com www.encoreplastics.com
Manufacturer and exporter of beverageware and plastic stemware
President: Richard Harvey
Quality Control: David Martin
VP: Donald Okada
Contact: Donald Okada
dokada@encoreplastics.com
Estimated Sales: $500,000-$1 Million
Number Employees: 10
Parent Co: Donoco Industries
Regions Exported to: Worldwide

43939 Encore Specialty Foods LLC
350 Lincoln St
Suite 1107
Hingham, MA 02043-1579   781-749-7491
Fax: 866-216-7772   www.encorefoods.com
Crackers, full-line condiments, mustards, nut-oils, olive oil, hor d'oeuvres/appetizers, rice, olives.
Owner: Ron Johnson
ronjohnson@encorefoods.com
Marketing: Jeremy Johnson
Number Employees: 5-9

43940 Endico Potatoes Inc
160 N Macquesten Pkwy
Mt Vernon, NY 10550-1099   914-664-1151
Fax: 914-664-9267   www.endicopotatoes.com
Frozen potato, vegetable, chicken and appetizer products.
CEO: Mike Edwards
Manager: Mike Acocella
michael.roff@gmail.com
Estimated Sales: $860,000
Number Employees: 20-49
Square Footage: 240000
Type of Packaging: Consumer, Food Service

43941 (HQ)Ener-G Foods
5960 1st Ave S
Seattle, WA 98108-3248   206-767-3928
Fax: 206-764-3398   800-331-5222
samiii@ener-g.com
Manufacturer and exporter of wheat free and gluten free, dairy free, nut free; bread, hamburger buns, cereals, cookies, pasta, mixes, etc.; also allergy-free foods; importer of gluten-free pasta and starches, Medical and diet foods and low protein foods for PKU.
President: Sam Wylde III
cje@ener-g.com
Marketing/Sales: Jerry Colburn
Sales Exec: Jerry Colburn
Production Manager: Roger Traynor
Purchasing Manager: Sabina Milovic
Estimated Sales: $10 Milion
Number Employees: 20-49
Number of Brands: 2
Number of Products: 200
Square Footage: 40000
Type of Packaging: Consumer, Food Service, Private Label
Brands Exported: Ener-G Foods
Regions Exported to: Central America, South America, Europe, Asia, Canada, Latin America
Percentage of Business in Exporting: 30
Regions Imported from: Central America, Asia, Middle East, Canada
Percentage of Business in Importing: 20

43942 (HQ)Energen Products Inc
14631 Best Ave
Norwalk, CA 90650-5258   562-926-5522
Fax: 562-921-0039   800-423-8837
Manufacturer and exporter of vitamins, wheat germ oil and brewers' yeast
President: Joseph Bensler
energen@ix.netcom.com
Estimated Sales: $3 Million
Number Employees: 20-49
Number of Brands: 13
Number of Products: 250
Square Footage: 300000
Type of Packaging: Food Service, Private Label
Brands Exported: American Dietary
Regions Exported to: Central America, Asia, Middle East
Percentage of Business in Exporting: 10

43943 Energy Beverage Company
518 50th Ave
Long Island City, NY 11101-5712   718-392-9330
Fax: 718-392-9301   800-545-1002
Energy drinks
Owner: Bruce Burwick
Estimated Sales: $ 3 - 5 Million
Number Employees: 5-9

43944 Energy Sciences Inc
42 Industrial Way # 1
Wilmington, MA 01887-3471   978-658-3731
Fax: 978-694-9046   www.ebeam.com
Manufacturer and exporter of electron beam processing machinery used for drying and curing packaging materials, printed foil, etc
President: Tsuneo Kobayashi
Manager: Harvey Clough
Accounts: Sharon Lagos
Chief Operating Officer: Ed Maguire
Estimated Sales: $ 7 Million
Number Employees: 50-99
Square Footage: 52000
Parent Co: Iwasaki Electric
Regions Exported to: Worldwide

43945 Energymaster
105 Liberty St
Walled Lake, MI 48390   248-624-6900
Fax: 248-624-6975   www.energymasterusa.com
Manufacturer and exporter of energy conservation equipment for heating and cooling, summer/winter ventilation and make-up air
President: Erik Hall
Estimated Sales: $ 2.5 - 5 Million
Number Employees: 10-19
Square Footage: 3600
Type of Packaging: Consumer, Food Service
Brands Exported: EnergyMaster; SeasonMaster; TuffDuct
Regions Exported to: Worldwide
Percentage of Business in Exporting: 7

43946 Engineered Plastics Inc
211 Chase St
PO Box 227
Gibsonville, NC 27249-2877   336-449-4121
Fax: 336-449-6352   800-711-1740
engplas@triad.rr.com www.engplas.com
Illuminated buffet and ice sculpture display equipment, acrylic serving bowls and trays and specialty display items
President: Dwight M Davidson
engplas@triad.rr.com
Sales Manager: Robert Ratliff
Food Service Manager: W Mottinger
Estimated Sales: $ 2.5-5 Million
Number Employees: 20-49
Square Footage: 150000

43947 Engineered Products Corp
355 Woodruff Rd # 204
Greenville, SC 29607-3494   864-234-4888
Fax: 864-234-4860   800-868-0145
sales@engprod.com www.engprod.com
Manufacturer and exporter of pallet storage racks, gravity flow storage systems and conveyors; also, turnkey warehouse engineering services available
Manager: David Shupe
Sales/Marketing Executive: Charles Rouse
Manager: Andre Butler
asbutler@epco.com
Purchasing Agent: Allen Griffith
Estimated Sales: $ 5-10 Million
Number Employees: 100-249
Square Footage: 400000
Parent Co: Gower
Regions Exported to: Central America, South America, Europe, Asia, Middle East
Percentage of Business in Exporting: 20

43948 Engineered Products Group
P.O. Box 8050
Madison, WI 53708   608-222-3484
Fax: 608-222-9314   800-626-3111
www.boumatic.com
Manufacturer and exporter of heat transfer equipment, jacketed shells, troughs, baffles and tanks, plates for fluid bed coolers and heaters, process vessels and storage and mixing tanks; also, carbon steel, stainless stell, titanium and other alloys available
Owner: John Kotts
Sales: R Albrecht
Estimated Sales: $1-2.5 Million
Number Employees: 250-499
Parent Co: DEC International
Regions Exported to: Mexico, Canada
Percentage of Business in Exporting: 10

43949 Engineered Security System Inc
1 Indian Ln
Towaco, NJ 07082-1015   973-257-0555
Fax: 973-257-0550   800-742-1263
info@engineeredsecurity.com
www.engineeredsecurity.com
Manufacturer and exporter of computer based security systems; closed circuit TV monitoring available
Owner: David George
dgeorge@engineeredsecurity.com
Estimated Sales: $20-50 Million
Number Employees: 50-99
Square Footage: 8500
Regions Exported to: Central America, South America, Europe, Middle East
Percentage of Business in Exporting: 10

43950 English Bay Batter Us Inc
2241 Citygate Dr
Columbus, OH 43219-3564   614-471-9994
Fax: 614-890-9992   800-253-6844
www.englishbaycookies.com
Frozen batter and baked goods
Manager: Dan Rudd
Estimated Sales: $ 5 - 10 Million
Number Employees: 20-49
Parent Co: English Bay Batter
Type of Packaging: Consumer, Food Service, Private Label, Bulk

43951 Engraving Services Co.
818 Port Road
Woodville South, SA 05011
engrave@engravingservices.com.au
www.engravingservices.com.au
Manufacturer and exporter of labels, nameplates, decals and engraved plastic and electric signs
Sales/Marketing Director: Peter Vasic
Production Manager: Jamie Smale
Estimated Sales: $5-10 Million
Number Employees: 50-99
Type of Packaging: Bulk
Regions Exported to: Worldwide

Importers & Exporters / A-Z

43952 Enjoy Foods International
10601 Beech Ave
Fontana, CA 92337   909-823-2228
Fax: 909-355-1573 info@EnjoyBeefJerky.com
www.enjoybeefjerky.com
Manufacturer and exporter of beef and turkey jerky and meat snacks; exporter of steak kabobs
Chairman: Waleed Saab
VP Mohamad Kabab
Marketing/Sales: Pierre Taylor
Contact: Walter Dorrouh
waleed@enjoybeefjerky.com
Plant Manager: Dennis Quinzon
Estimated Sales: $6.3 Million
Number Employees: 40
Square Footage: 40584
Type of Packaging: Consumer
Regions Exported to: Asia, Canada

43953 Ennio International
1005 N. Commons Drive
Aurora, IL 60504-4100   630-851-5808
Fax: 630-851-7744 www.enniousa.com
Manufacturer and supplier of high quality netting and casings for the meat and poultry industries.
Director Of Sales: Ralph Schuster
Contact: Ennio Hand
ennio.hand@enniousa.com
Regions Exported to: Central America, South America, Europe, Australia, New Zealand, North America, USA And Western Europe

43954 Enrick Co
150 E 1st St
PO Box 37
Zumbrota, MN 55992-1552   507-732-5215
Fax: 507-625-6570 rollorkari@yahoo.com
www.enrickco.com
Manufacturer and exporter of hand trucks, dollies and carts
Owner: Vince Small
Estimated Sales: $ 1-2.5 Million
Number Employees: 5-9

43955 Ensemble Beverages
600 S Court Street
Suite 460
Montgomery, AL 36104-4106   334-324-7719
Manufacturer, importer and exporter of beverages including carbonated, sports drinks, nutritional shakes, iced tea and powders
President: James Harris
CFO: Cornelius Blanding, Jr
Number Employees: 10-19
Regions Exported to: Europe, Asia, Middle East, Africa, Australia , Latin America
Percentage of Business in Exporting: 5
Percentage of Business in Importing: 20

43956 Ensinger Inc
365 Meadowlands Blvd
Washington, PA 15301-8900   724-746-6050
Fax: 724-746-9078 800-243-3221
sales@ensinger-ind.com www.ensinger-inc.com
Manufacturer and exporter of plastic packaging materials
President: Frank Bavaro
fbavaro@ensinger-inc.com
Director Sales/Marketing: Bruce Dickinson
Technical Director: Ken Schwartz
Estimated Sales: $ 10 - 20 Million
Number Employees: 20-49
Parent Co: Dana Her Corporation
Type of Packaging: Bulk
Regions Exported to: Canada

43957 Enstrom Candies, Inc.
701 Colorado Ave
Grand Junction, CO 81501
Fax: 970-683-1011 800-367-8766
www.enstrom.com
Manufacturing and sales of confectionery products, including Almond Toffee, Truffles, Chocolates, Brittles, Fudges.
Owner: Doug Simons
Secretary/Treasurer & VP, Marketing: Jamee Simons
Quality Control Manager: Ginny Ansbaugh
National Sales Director: Bob Jackson
Contact Center Manager: Wendy Hanway
wendy@enstrom.com
Chief Technology Officer: Daniel Lively
Manufacturing Director: Doug Tuttle
Buyer: Diana Wilsey
Year Founded: 1929
Estimated Sales: $25 Million
Number Employees: 107
Number of Brands: 1
Square Footage: 19360
Type of Packaging: Consumer
Other Locations:
  Enstrom Candies
  Denver, COEnstrom Candies
Regions Exported to: Worldwide
Percentage of Business in Exporting: 1

43958 Entech Systems Corp
607 Maria St
Kenner, LA 70062-7400   504-469-6541
Fax: 504-465-9192 800-783-6561
entech@msn.com www.entech.cc
Manufacturer and exporter of automatic ULV insect fogging systems for killing crawling and flying insects; also, semi-automatic and portable systems, sanitation audits and insecticides
President: Robert Drude
robert.drudge@entech.cc
Corporate Secretary: Gail Stumpf
Purchasing Manager: Marcus Curtis
Estimated Sales: Below $ 5 Million
Number Employees: 5-9
Square Footage: 16000
Percentage of Business in Exporting: 10

43959 Enterprise Company
616 S Santa Fe
Santa Ana, CA 92705   714-835-0541
Fax: 714-543-2856
Manufacturer and exporter of baling presses
President: Orval Gould
VP: Albert Gould
Marketing Director: John Gould
Contact: Dan Scott
dan@enterpriseco.com
Estimated Sales: $2.5-5 Million
Number Employees: 50-99
Type of Packaging: Bulk
Regions Exported to: Central America, South America, Asia, Middle East
Percentage of Business in Exporting: 25

43960 Enterprises Pates et Croutes
14 Rue De Montgolfier
Boucherville, QC J4B 7Y4
Canada   450-655-7790
Fax: 450-655-8037 800-265-7790
patesetcroutes.com
Manufacturer and exporter of frozen pie dough and shells; processor of baked muffins,bakery products,pastry products,and food product machinery.
President: Francine Benoit
Estimated Sales: 3.8 Million
Number Employees: 40
Type of Packaging: Consumer, Food Service
Regions Exported to: USA
Percentage of Business in Exporting: 2

43961 Enting Water Conditioning Inc
3211 Dryden Rd Frnt
Moraine, OH 45439-1400   937-456-5151
Fax: 937-294-5485 800-735-5100
sales@enting.com www.enting.com
Manufacturer and exporter of water treatment systems including softeners, reverse osmosis, cartridge filters and ultra-violet purifiers
President: Mel Entingh
President/COO: Dan Entingh
info@enting.com
Estimated Sales: $5-10 Million
Number Employees: 10-19
Square Footage: 86800
Brands Exported: Enting
Regions Exported to: South America, Europe, Middle East

43962 Enviro-Clear Co
152 Cregar Rd
High Bridge, NJ 08829-1003 908-638-5507
Fax: 908-638-4636 info@enviro-clear.com
www.enviro-clear.com
Manufacturer and exporter of clarifiers and belt and pressure filters and separators
President: Joe Muldowney
sales@enviro-clear.com
VP Marketing: Cindy Meyer
Sales: James Grau
Estimated Sales: $ 3 - 5 Million
Number Employees: 5-9
Square Footage: 40000
Brands Exported: Enviro-Clear
Regions Exported to: Central America, South America, Europe, Asia, Middle East, Far East, Africa

43963 Environmental Products Company
197 Poplar Place #3
North Aurora, IL 60542-8191 630-892-2414
Fax: 630-892-2467 800-677-8479
Manufacturer and exporter of polyvinyl chloride strip doors, heat recycling fans and welding screens
Manager: Kurt Pfoutz
kpfoutz@hotmail.com
Office Manager: Kurt Pfoutz
Estimated Sales: $ 5 - 10 Million
Number Employees: 10 to 19
Square Footage: 30000
Parent Co: Material Control
Regions Exported to: Central America, South America, Europe
Percentage of Business in Exporting: 5

43964 Enzamar
10060 London Avenue
Montreal, QC H1H 4H1
Canada   514-323-6068
Fax: 514-323-1989
Wholesaler/distributor, importer and exporter of gourmet Italian beverages, desserts, chocolates, cakes and Canadian spring water; serving the food service market; also, private label available
President: Enza Cappadoro
Vice President: Marilena Cappadoro
Director: Franco Cappadoro
Estimated Sales: $1-3 Million
Number Employees: 5-9
Type of Packaging: Consumer, Food Service
Brands Exported: Seibella; Brio
Regions Exported to: USA
Percentage of Business in Exporting: 30
Percentage of Business in Importing: 16

43965 Enzyme Development Corporation
505 Eighth Avenue
Suite 500
New York, NY 10018   212-736-1580
Fax: 212-279-0056
info@enzymedevelopment.com
www.enzymedevelopment.com
Manufacturer, importer and exporter of industrial and specialty enzymes.
Technical Sales Representative: Christina Barsa
Contact: Bobby Gau
bobby.gau@scinopharm.com
Type of Packaging: Bulk
Regions Exported to: South America, Asia, Canada, Mexico
Percentage of Business in Exporting: 10
Regions Imported from: Europe, Asia, Africa
Percentage of Business in Importing: 80

43966 Epcon Industrial Systems
17777 I-45 South
Conroe, TX 77385   936-273-3300
Fax: 936-273-4600 800-447-7872
sales@epconlp.com www.epconlp.com
Manufacturer and exporter of air pollution control systems for enclosures, odor control systems and oxidizers; also, general bake ovens
President and R&D: Aziz Jamaluddin
CFO: Sunny Naidu
Quality Control: Mike Paddie
Sales Engineer: Brad Morello
Engineer Designer: Nedzad Hadzajlic
Estimated Sales: $ 5 - 10 Million
Number Employees: 50-99
Square Footage: 400000
Regions Exported to: Worldwide
Percentage of Business in Exporting: 35

43967 Epi De France Bakery
1749 Tullie Circle NE
Atlanta, GA 30329   404-325-1016
Fax: 404-325-0735 800-325-1014
bdoan@epibreads.com www.epibreads.com
Fresh and frozen bread, hoagies, table breads, baguettes, buns and rolls, sliced loaves, and ciabattas.
President: Nic Mulliez
CEO: Hugh Sullins
Sales Manager: B Doan

Estimated Sales: $20-50 Million
Square Footage: 42500
Type of Packaging: Consumer, Food Service, Private Label, Bulk
Regions Exported to: Canada, Caribbean
Percentage of Business in Exporting: 5
Regions Imported from: Europe, Canada
Percentage of Business in Importing: 5

43968 Epic
280 Madison Ave Rm 1210
New York, NY 10016 212-308-7039
Fax: 212-308-7266
Wholesaler/distributor, importer and exporter of refractometers and polarimeters
President: Peter Letica
CEO: Florence Dan
CFO: Anna Volovik
Estimated Sales: $750,000
Number Employees: 3
Square Footage: 6000
Brands Exported: B&S
Brands Imported: B&S (Refraction Meters) (Polarimeters)

43969 Epicure Foods Corporation
1 Atalanta Plz Ste 2
Po Box 6628
Elizabeth, NJ 07206 908-527-8080
Fax: 908-527-8441 800-746-6660
www.epicurefoodscorp.com
Imports and distributes gourmet cheeses and cheeses complements
President/Owner: Damir Drezga
VP: Jennifer Drezga
Marketing: Matthew Kevill
Estimated Sales: $1.6 Million
Number Employees: 9

43970 Epicurean Food & Beverages
2299 Perimeter Park Dr
Suite 240
Atlanta, GA 30341 770-457-0300
Fax: 770-457-0330 info@epicureanbeverages.com
www.epicureanbeverages.com
French sparkling beverages and spring water
Owner: Marc Ducloz
Number Employees: 5-9

43971 Epsen Hillmer Graphics Co
13748 F St
Omaha, NE 68137-1166 402-342-7000
Fax: 402-342-9284 800-328-9940
www.ehg.net
Manufacturer and exporter of labels including pressure sensitive, glue applied litho, in-mold and PET beverage
President: Tom Hillmer
thillmer@ehg.net
VP Opers.: Thomas Hillmer
VP Sales/Marketing: R Craig Cunran
VP Operations: Thomas Hillmer
Estimated Sales: $ .5 - 1 million
Number Employees: 50-99
Regions Exported to: Central America

43972 Equipex Limited
765 Westminster St
Providence, RI 02903-4018 401-273-3300
Fax: 401-273-3328 800-649-7885
sales@equipex.com www.equipex.com
Manufacturer and exporter of ovens and restaurant equipment
President: Loretta Clark
lorettac@equipex.com
VP: Val Ginzburg
Sales/Marketing Division: Irina Mirsky-Zayas
Operations: Loretta Fortier
Estimated Sales: $2.5-5,000,000
Number Employees: 1-4
Brands Exported: Sodir
Regions Exported to: Central America, South America, Canada
Percentage of Business in Exporting: 10

43973 Equipment Distributor Div
1307 11th St SE
Jamestown, ND 58401-5909 701-252-3333
Fax: 701-252-3339
Wholesaler/distributor and exporter of high pressure cleaning equipment, meat grinders, slicers and choppers; serving the food service market
Owner: Paul Tahran
equipdis@daktel.com
General Manager: Dave Tahran
Estimated Sales: $500,000-$1 Million
Number Employees: 1-4
Type of Packaging: Food Service, Bulk
Regions Exported to: Canada

43974 Equipment Specialists Inc
9489 Hawkins Dr
Manassas, VA 20109-3907 703-361-2227
Fax: 703-361-4965
www.equipmentspecialistsinc.com
Manufacturer and exporter of new and used food processing and packaging equipment
Owner: Allan Tousha
CEO: Beverly Gordon
Vice President: Jeremy Gordon
Sales Director: Mariano Montealegre
allan@esitrucks.com
Operations Manager: Jose Macy
Plant Manager: Reinaldo Mendoza
Purchasing Manager: Eric Ball
Estimated Sales: $10-20 Million
Number Employees: 10-19
Square Footage: 300000
Type of Packaging: Food Service
Regions Exported to: Central America, South America, Asia, Middle East
Percentage of Business in Exporting: 85

43975 (HQ)Erba Food Products
2 Metro Tech Ctr. Ste 2000
Brooklyn, NY 11201-3838 718-272-7700
Fax: 718-272-7711
Manufacturer, importer and exporter of kosher foods including vegetables, juices, coffee, spices, seasonings, baked goods, fruits, condiments, fish, nuts, oils, etc
Manager: Heeren Patel
VP of Marketing: Abraham Perkowski
Sales: Jen O'Connor
Number Employees: 10-19
Type of Packaging: Consumer, Food Service
Regions Exported to: South America, Europe, Canada, Mexico

43976 Erell Manufacturing Co
2678 Coyle Ave
Elk Grove Vlg, IL 60007-6404 847-427-3000
Fax: 847-663-9970 800-622-6334
Plastic aprons; exporter and manufacturer of vinyl industrial and promotional products
President: Randy Silton
randy@erell.com
Estimated Sales: $ 1-2.5 Million
Number Employees: 10-19
Square Footage: 34000
Regions Exported to: Central America
Percentage of Business in Exporting: 2

43977 Erickson Industries
717 Saint Croix St
River Falls, WI 54022 715-426-9700
Fax: 715-426-9701 800-729-9941
Manufacturer and exporter of refrigerators, freezers, walk-in coolers and pre-fabricated cooling and freezing warehouses; also, manufacturer of tubular towers and planter grids
Owner: Paul Erickson
Sales: Debbie Huppert
Sales Engineering: Joel Johnson
Advertising Manager: H Walsh
Estimated Sales: $1-2.5 Million
Number Employees: 1-4
Square Footage: 80000
Brands Exported: Chill-Air; Kool-Rite; Erickson
Regions Exported to: Central America, South America, Asia, Middle East, Canada, Mexico, Caribbean
Percentage of Business in Exporting: 14

43978 (HQ)Erie Foods Intl Inc
401 7th Ave
PO Box 648
Erie, IL 61250 309-659-2233
Fax: 309-659-2822 glindsey@eriefoods.com
www.eriefoods.com
Co-dried and concentrated milk proteins; also sodium, calcium, combination and acid-stable caseinates and dairy blends; importer of milk proteins
President/CEO: David Reisenbigler
dreisenbigler@eriefoods.com
CFO: Mark Delaney
COO: Jim Klein
Technical Services Manager: Craig Air
Quality Manager: Rene Perla
Purchasing Manager: Jake VanDeWostine
Process Development Manager: Jim Jacoby
Purchasing Manager: Shawn Larson
Estimated Sales: $1-2.5 Million
Number Employees: 10-19
Square Footage: 120000
Parent Co: Erie Foods International Inc
Type of Packaging: Bulk
Other Locations:
 Erie Foods International
 Beenleigh QLDErie Foods International
Regions Exported to: Europe, Asia
Regions Imported from: Asia, Pacific Rim, India
Percentage of Business in Importing: 89

43979 Eriez Magnetics
4700 W 23rd St
Erie, PA 16506
Fax: 814-838-4960 800-346-4946
eriez@eriez.com www.eriez.com
Manufacturer and exporter of vibratory feeders and conveyors, magnetic separators, metal detectors, vibratory and material-sizing screeners, lifting magnets and magnetic conveyors.
Chairman: R Merwin
President/CEO: Tim Shuttleworth
Treasurer: M Mandel
Quality Control: J Snyder
Marketing: K Jones
VP Sales/Marketing: C Ingram
VP Operations: M Mankosa
Plant Manager: J Kiehl
Estimated Sales: $ 50 - 100 Million
Number Employees: 250-499
Square Footage: 110000
Brands Exported: E-Z Tec; Hi-Vi; MetAlarm
Regions Exported to: Central America, South America, Europe, Asia, Middle East
Percentage of Business in Exporting: 30

43980 Erlab, Inc
388 Newburyport Turnpike
Rowley, MA 01969 978-948-2216
Fax: 978-948-3354 800-964-4434
captairsales@erlab.com www.erlab.com
Wholesaler/distributor and exporter of ductless filtering fume hoods, filtering storage cabinets, laminar flow hoods, balance enclosures and PCR workstations
Owner: George Hallatt
Marketing Director: Karen Ardinger
Product Specialist: Vicki Willett
Contact: Josh Bartholomew
jbartholomew@erlab.com
General Manager: Stephan Hauville
Production Manager: Brian Scanlon
Plant Manager: Jan Griffin
Estimated Sales: $2.5-5 Million
Number Employees: 10-19
Square Footage: 60320
Regions Exported to: Canada
Percentage of Business in Exporting: 10

43981 Ermanco
6870 Grand Haven Rd
Norton Shores, MI 49456 231-798-4547
Fax: 231-798-8322 info@ermanco.com
www.ermanco.com
Manufacturer and exporter of conveyors including belt/live roller, lineshaft driven, belt driven and sortation; also, turnkey systems
President: Leon Kirschner
Quality Control: Bob Dorgan
VP of Marketing: Lee Schomberg
VP of Sales: Gordon Hellberg
Contact: Tom Bergy
tombergy@ermanco.com
Estimated Sales: $ 30 - 50 Million
Number Employees: 100-249
Square Footage: 100000
Parent Co: Paragon Technologies
Brands Exported: Xenorol; Xenopressure; Accurol; EWX100; NBS Sortation Systems
Regions Exported to: South America, Europe, Asia, South Africa, Canada, Australia
Percentage of Business in Exporting: 5

Importers & Exporters / A-Z

43982 Ertelalsop
132 Flatbush Ave
Kingston, NY 12401-2202   845-331-4552
      Fax: 845-339-1063 800-553-7835
sales@ertelalsop.com www.ertelalsop.com
Manufacturer and exporter of filtration equipment, filter media and mixers for liquids; also, glass crushing equipment
President: George Quigley
VP: George Quigley
Marketing Manager Food & Beverage: Mike Kelly
VP Sales/Marketing: William Kearney
Estimated Sales: $ 5 - 10 Million
Number Employees: 50-99
Regions Exported to: Worldwide
Percentage of Business in Exporting: 40

43983 Erwyn Products Inc
200 Campus Dr # C
Morganville, NJ 07751-2101   732-972-1440
      Fax: 732-972-1263 800-331-9208
steve@erwyn.com www.erwyn.com
Manufacturer, importer and exporter of waste paper baskets and ice buckets
President: Randy Grant
randy.grant@erwyn.com
Estimated Sales: $ 10 - 20 Million
Number Employees: 20-49
Regions Exported to: Central America, Europe, Asia, Middle East, Canada, Caribbean
Regions Imported from: Asia

43984 Escalade Limited
37 W Shore Rd # 2
Huntington, NY 11743-7206   631-659-3373
      Fax: 631-659-3376 latitudeltd@aol.com
      www.latitudeltdusa.com
Ingredients and additives, including anti-oxidants, preservatives, sweeteners and minerals
President: Lourel Mandel
VP: Dedi Avner
Contact: Dedi Avner
escalade@bezeqint.net
Estimated Sales: $500,000- 1 Million
Number Employees: 8

43985 Esha Research
4747 Skyline Rd S # 100
Suite 100
Salem, OR 97306-5700   503-540-7518
      Fax: 503-585-5543 800-659-3742
      info@esha.com www.esha.com
Software for formulation development and nutrition labeling; exporter of nutritional labeling software
CEO: Craig Bennett
c@esha.com
CEO: Robert Geltz
Vice President: David Hands
Sales Director: Scott Hadsall
Estimated Sales: $2 Million
Number Employees: 20-49
Number of Brands: 6
Number of Products: 6
Square Footage: 1000
Brands Exported: Genesis R&D
Regions Exported to: Worldwide

43986 Espresso Coffee MachineCo
3709 1st Avenue
Burnaby, BC V5C 3V6
Canada   604-291-6363
      Fax: 604-291-6302 800-971-8833
Wholesaler/distributor and importer of Italian espresso and cappuccino machines; serving the food service market
Sales Manager: Tim Mercier
Number Employees: 10-19
Type of Packaging: Food Service
Regions Imported from: Italy

43987 Espresso Specialists
4544 Leary Way NW
Seattle, WA 98107   206-784-9563
      Fax: 206-784-9582 800-367-0235
Importer of commercial espresso machines and grinders
President: Pat Loraas
VP Sales/Marketing: Joe Monaghan
Contact: Marga Gyger
gygerm@esiespresso.com
Estimated Sales: $2.5-5 Million
Number Employees: 20-49
Brands Imported: La Marzocco; Rio; Franke
Regions Imported from: Europe

Percentage of Business in Importing: 100

43988 Espro Manufacturing
2800 Ayers Avenue
Vernon, CA 90058   323-415-8544
      Fax: 323-268-4060
Manufacturer and packager of food ingredients, including custom dry powder blends.
Contact: Blas Tiangson
blas.tiangson@kp.org

43989 Esquire Mechanical Corp.
PO Box 496
Armonk, NY 10504   718-625-4006
      Fax: 718-625-0155 800-847-4206
      sales@dunhill-esquire.net
      www.dunhill-esquire.com
Manufacturer and exporter of cafeteria and kitchen equipment including cashier stands, serving counters, sinks, refrigerated display cases, tables and bbq and rotisserie machines.
President: Geoffrey Thaw
Estimated Sales: $ 1 - 5 Million
Number Employees: 10-19
Square Footage: 240000
Parent Co: Dunhill Food Equipment
Type of Packaging: Food Service
Brands Exported: Esquire
Regions Exported to: Central America, South America
Percentage of Business in Exporting: 5

43990 Esselte Meto
1200t American Road
Morris Plains, NJ 07950-2453   973-359-0947
      Fax: 201-455-7492 800-645-3290
Manufacturer and exporter of handheld labeling and merchandising systems, thermal and laser bar code printers and supplies, tags and labels
President: Travis Howe
VP Marketing: Bob Cantono
VP Sales: Bob Evans
Estimated Sales: $300,000-500,000
Number Employees: 50-99
Square Footage: 270000
Parent Co: Esselte AB
Type of Packaging: Consumer, Private Label
Brands Exported: Meto; Primark
Regions Exported to: Central America, South America, Europe, Asia
Percentage of Business in Exporting: 5

43991 Essential Industries Inc
28391 Essential Rd
Merton, WI 53056   262-538-1122
      Fax: 262-538-1354 800-551-9679
      sales@essind.com www.essind.com
Manufacturer and exporter of household and industrial hand, glass and window cleaners, liquid and powder dishwashing compounds and soap, detergents and floor polish
President: Michael Wheeler
mwheeler@essind.com
Chief Executive Officer: Jim Coddington
Controller: Carol Sanchez
Senior Vice President: Nick Contos
Quality & Safety Regional Manager: Maureen Smith
Vice President, Sales & Marketing: Ed Zgrabik
Vice President, Operations: Thomas Gitzlaff
Production Manager: Brandon Coulter
Director, Purchasing: Kathleen Leemon
Estimated Sales: $ 15 Million
Number Employees: 50-99
Square Footage: 110000
Type of Packaging: Private Label, Bulk
Brands Exported: Superbase
Regions Exported to: South America, Europe, Asia, Canada, Mexico, Australia
Percentage of Business in Exporting: 5

43992 Essential Products of America
6710 Benjamin Road
Suite 700
Tampa, FL 33634-4314   813-886-9698
      Fax: 813-886-9661 800-822-9698
Manufacturer, importer and exporter of essential oils
President: Michael Alexander
Estimated Sales: $2.5-5 Million
Number Employees: 5
Square Footage: 4800
Type of Packaging: Consumer, Private Label, Bulk
Brands Exported: Whole Spectrum
Regions Exported to: Asia
Percentage of Business in Exporting: 25

Regions Imported from: Central America, South America, Europe, Asia, Middle East
Percentage of Business in Importing: 80

43993 Essiac Canada International
164 Richmond Rd
Ottawa, ON K1Z 6W2
Canada   514-695-2299
      888-900-2299
      www.essiaccanadainternational.com
Manufacturer and exporter of herbal dietary supplements
President: Terrence Maloney
Estimated Sales: $975,000
Number Employees: 6
Number of Brands: 2
Number of Products: 2
Parent Co: Essiac Canada International
Type of Packaging: Consumer, Food Service
Brands Exported: Essiac; Phytaid
Regions Exported to: Central America, South America, Europe, Asia, Middle East

43994 Esteem Products
1800 136th Pl NE
Ste 5
Bellevue, WA 98005   425-562-1281
      Fax: 425-562-1284 800-255-7631
      customerservice@esteemproducts.com
      www.esteemproducts.com
Manufacturer, wholesaler/distributor and exporter of nutritional supplements and specialty vitamins. All combination formulas for consumer simplicity
CEO/President: John Sheaffer
VP: Linda Sheaffer
Marketing: Amy Braisford
Contact: Chana Madsen
chana@esteemproducts.com
Estimated Sales: $500,000-$1 Million
Number Employees: 5-9
Square Footage: 20000
Brands Exported: Golden Life; Shark Plus; Esteem Plus
Regions Exported to: Central America, Asia, Canada
Percentage of Business in Exporting: 15

43995 Eternal Marketing Group
2003 Pewaukee Road
Suite 5
Waukesha, WI 53188-2469   262-549-1705
      Fax: 262-549-1555 877-854-5494
      info@eternalwater.com www.eternalwater.com
Wholesaler/distributor and importer of bottled water; serving the food service market
President: Jim Klein
Number Employees: 5-9
Type of Packaging: Consumer, Food Service
Brands Imported: Eternal Spring
Regions Imported from: New Zealand

43996 (HQ)Ettlinger Corp
175 Olde Half Day Rd # 247
Lincolnshire, IL 60069-3063   847-564-5020
      Fax: 847-564-0802
Cereal grains, barley & wheat, reduced lactose whey
President: Peter Ettlinger
peter@ettlingercorp.com
Estimated Sales: $1-2.5 Million
Number Employees: 5-9
Type of Packaging: Food Service, Bulk
Regions Imported from: Asia
Percentage of Business in Importing: 25

43997 Ettore
2100 N Loop Rd
Alameda, CA 94502-8010   510-748-4130
      Fax: 510-638-0928 info@ettore.com
Manufacturer and exporter of window and floor squeegees and window washing equipment
Chairman of the Board: Michael Smahlik
michael.smahlik@ettore.com
VP Sales/Marketing: Patrick Murphy
National Sales Manager: Herman Miron
Estimated Sales: $ 1 - 2.5 Million
Number Employees: 50-99
Type of Packaging: Consumer, Food Service, Bulk
Brands Exported: Ettore
Regions Exported to: Central America, South America, Europe, Asia, Middle East
Percentage of Business in Exporting: 15

Importers & Exporters / A-Z

43998 Euclid Coffee Co
17230 S Waterloo Rd
Cleveland, OH 44110-3811   216-481-3330
                Fax: 216-383-7269
Wholesaler/distributor, exporter and importer of coffees and teas; wholesaler/distributor of groceries
President: James Repak
james.repak@euclidcoffee.com
Vice President: Andrew Repak
Estimated Sales: $5-10 Million
Number Employees: 10-19
Type of Packaging: Consumer, Food Service
Regions Exported to: Central America, South America, Asia
Regions Imported from: Central America, South America

43999 Eureka Company
807 N Main St
Bloomington, IL 61701   309-828-2367
        Fax: 309-823-5335   800-282-2886
kathy.luedke@eureka.com www.eureka.com
Manufacturer and exporter of commercial vacuums including canisters, uprights, home cleaning, built-ins and rechargeable
President: John Case
CEO: Jan Wolansky
VP Advertising: Don Johnson
Quality Control: Steve Knuth
Contact: Bruce Gold
bruce.gold@electrolux.com
Number Employees: 250-499
Parent Co: White Consolidated Industries
Type of Packaging: Consumer

44000 Eurex International
4 Brower Ave # 1
Woodmere, NY 11598-1798   516-295-5300
        Fax: 516-295-5169 www.eurexchange.com
Exporter of frozen meat and poultry
CEO: Jerry Shapiro
eurex2@aol.com
Vice President: Nancy Shapiro
Estimated Sales: $2.5-5 Million
Number Employees: 1-4
Square Footage: 5200
Brands Exported: All Major Brands
Regions Exported to: South America, Europe, Asia, Middle East, Worldwide
Percentage of Business in Exporting: 99

44001 Euro American Brands
95 Route 17 South
Suite 314
Paramus, NJ 07652   201-368-2624
                Fax: 201-368-2512
lwette@euroamericanbrands.com
www.euroamericanbrands.com
Importer of water, cookies, jams, pickles, sauerkraut, crackers and holiday items
Owner: Dite Van Clief
Marketing: Linda Wette
Contact: Rhonda Azevedo
razevedo@euroamericanbrands.com
Estimated Sales: $5-10 Million
Number Employees: 5-9
Type of Packaging: Consumer, Bulk
Brands Imported: Balshen; Vandych; Albgold; Zorbiger; Appel; Bismark; Gundersheim; Frenzel; Sarotti; Ritter Sport
Regions Imported from: Worldwide
Percentage of Business in Importing: 80

44002 Euro Mart/Stolzle Cberglas
7219 Investment Dr
North Charleston, SC 29418-8304   843-767-1994
        Fax: 843-767-5953   877-786-5953
info@stolzle-usa.com www.stolzle-usa.com
Wholesaler/distributor and importer of china, porcelain dishes, crystal stemware and glassware, in addition to being a European (German) manufacturer of fine lead-free crystal for the food service and retail market.
President: Ed Artildello
VP: Jay Aule
Estimated Sales: $5-10 Million
Number Employees: 5-9
Square Footage: 60000
Regions Imported from: Austria, Switzerland

44003 Euro Source Gourmet
220 Little Falls Road
Unit 2
Cedar Grove, NJ 07009-1255   973-857-6000
        Fax: 973-857-8862 tjvambass@aol.com
Gourmet foods
Owner: Thomas Calvaruso
Sales: Janka Delatte

44004 Euro USA
44901 Falcon Pl
Suite 104
Sterling, VA 20166-9531   703-450-0090
        Fax: 703-435-5272   800-899-5616
www.eurousa.com
Importer and distributor of fine foods and seafoods
CEO: Terry Comer
comer@eurousa.net
Marketing: Mike Clark
Number Employees: 20-49

44005 Euro USA Inc
4481 Johnston Pkwy
Cleveland, OH 44128-2952   216-714-0500
        Fax: 216-714-0550   800-999-5939
www.eurousa.com
Importer and distributor of fine foods and seafoods
Marketing: Mike Clark
Manager: Joseph O'Donnell
joseph.odonnell@eurousa.net
Number Employees: 50-99

44006 Euro-Bake
1927 4th Ave S
Saint Petersburg, FL 33712   727-823-1113
        Fax: 727-823-1201   800-806-3900
info@eurobake.com www.eurobake.com
Wholesaler/distributor, exporter and importer of frozen par-baked bread, rolls, danishes; also, ready-baked pretzels, desserts and cakes
President: Harty Gerhard
mike@eurobake.com
Marketing Director: Ralph Hoffman
Purchasing Manager: Mike Gerhard
Estimated Sales: $10-20 Million
Number Employees: 50-99
Square Footage: 25000
Type of Packaging: Food Service, Private Label, Bulk
Brands Exported: Euro-Bake
Regions Exported to: Caribbean
Regions Imported from: Germany

44007 Euro-Excellence
8559 Dalton
Mont-Royal, QC H4T 1V5
Canada   450-632-9440
        Fax: 450-600-5528   800-461-3876
info@euro-excellence.ca www.euro-excellence.ca
Wholesaler/distributor and importer of produce and genereal line items including candy, jam and cookies; serving the food service market
President: Andre Clemence
Controller: Sandra Romann
Purchasing Agent: Ibanne Puchuluteguy
Number Employees: 10-19
Square Footage: 12000
Type of Packaging: Consumer
Brands Imported: Cote D'Or; Vichy Hollywood; Barnier; Doucet, Comel; Poppies; Abtex; Meli; Biscuiterie De L'Abbaye
Regions Imported from: Europe
Percentage of Business in Importing: 90

44008 EuroBrew Inc.
58 Union St
Ashland, MA 01721   508-881-9900
        Fax: 508-881-9919 www.eurobrews.com
Gourmet import
President: Dominique Levesque
CEO: Pascal Benichou
a.bhat@grainger.com

44009 Euroam Importers Inc
1302 S 293rd Pl
Auburn, WA 98003-3756   253-839-5240
        Fax: 253-839-4171   888-839-2702
euroaminc1@aol.com
Coffee
President: Vito Rizzo
euroaminc1@aol.com
VP: Anita Goransson
Estimated Sales: $270,000
Number Employees: 1-4

Number of Brands: 10
Number of Products: 20
Square Footage: 7200
Parent Co: Euro Am Imports
Brands Imported: Zoega Swedish Coffee
Regions Imported from: Europe, Asia

44010 Eurobubblies
58 Union Street
Ashland, MA 01721   508-881-9900
                800-273-0750
christian@eurobubblies.com
www.eurobubblies.com
Beverage and food products from Europe
President: Pascal Benichou
Estimated Sales: Under $500,000
Number Employees: 5-9
Type of Packaging: Consumer, Food Service, Private Label, Bulk
Brands Imported: Efferve; Alpenrose; Siracuse; Bel Normande; Dupont D'Isigny; Wychwood; St. Peter's; Black Sheep
Regions Imported from: Europe
Percentage of Business in Importing: 100

44011 Eurodib
PO Box 1798
1320 State Route 9
Champlain, NY 12919   450-641-8700
        Fax: 451-641-8705   888-956-6866
shaun@eurodib.com www.eurodib.com
Importer of citrus and centrifugal juicers, dispensers, coffee grinders, blenders, vegetable cutters, grills, mandolines, cookware, and dishwashers
President: Jean Yves Dumaine
VP: Shaun McDonald
Marketing: Shaun McDonald
Contact: Shaun Mcdonald
jydumaine@eurodib.com
Purchasing Manager: Robert Perrier
Number Employees: 14
Number of Brands: 15
Number of Products: 500
Square Footage: 176000
Brands Exported: Santos; Mauviei; Bron Coucke; Tellier; Deglou; Krampouz; Lamber; Tournus; Sirman; Saint-Romain; Combrichon
Brands Imported: Santos; Mauviei; Bron Coucke; Tellier; Krampouz; Lamber; Tournus; Sirman; Saint-Romain; Combrichon
Regions Imported from: Europe
Percentage of Business in Importing: 50

44012 Eurofood Distributors
PO Box 1381
Newport, RI 02840-0997   401-841-8238
                Fax: 401-841-8239
Importer and wholesaler/distributor of frozen desserts including ice cream

44013 Europaeus USA
8 John Walsh Boulevard
Suite 140
Peekskill, NY 10566-5346   914-739-1900
        Fax: 914-739-5229   800-992-3876
customerservice@europaeus.com
www.europaeus.com
Importer, exporter and wholesaler/distributor of hand painted ceramic tableware.
President: Daniel Salvati
Sales Director: Daniel Salvati
Contact: Michael Shaw
cdia@cdr.net
Operations Manager: Hettie Van Owen
Purchasing Agent: Daniel Salvati
Estimated Sales: $1 - 3 Million
Number Employees: 1-4
Square Footage: 40000
Type of Packaging: Food Service
Brands Exported: Piral; Royale; Varm
Brands Imported: Piral; Royale; Varm
Regions Imported from: South America
Percentage of Business in Importing: 90

44014 Europe's Finest Imports
733 Springtown Rd
Tillson, NY 12486   845-658-9258
                Fax: 845-658-8489
Food and non food products
President: Franziska Bornemann
f.bornemann@europesfinestimports.com
Estimated Sales: $2.5-5 Million
Number Employees: 5-9
Type of Packaging: Private Label

Importers & Exporters / A-Z

44015 European Foods
6 Farmhouse Lane
P O Box 14842
Panmure, AK NZ
Canada   649-551-7410
          Fax: 649-551-7411 info@europeanfood.co.nz
Importer and wholesaler/distributor of European jams, preserves and cheeses
President: Oliver Pokrandt
VP: George Pokrandt
Number Employees: 5-9
Regions Imported from: Europe

44016 European Hotel & Restaurant Imports
343 Horner Avenue
Etobicoke, ON M8W 1Z6
Canada   416-253-9449
          Fax: 416-253-9552
Wholesaler/distributor and importer of food service supplies and equipment including fixtures; serving the food service market
President: John Rainbow
Secretary: Gary Crawford
Number Employees: 10-19

44017 European Imports
2475 N Elston Ave
Chicago, IL 60647   773-227-0600
          Fax: 773-227-6775   800-323-3464
          info@eiltd.com   www.eiltd.com
Importer and wholesaler/distributor of olive oil, cheeses, gourmet foods and pastry products
President: Seymour Binstein
VP: Glenn Binstein
VP: Jeff Binstein
Marketing: Trish Pohanka
Contact: Caryn Burgess
caryn@askttt.com
Estimated Sales: $20-50 Million
Number Employees: 100-249
Regions Imported from: Europe
Percentage of Business in Importing: 65

44018 European Roasterie
250 W Bradshaw St
Le Center, MN 56057-1121   507-357-2272
          Fax: 507-357-4478   888-588-5282
                    www.euroroast.com
Coffees and teas
President/CEO: Timothy Tulloch
timothy@euroroast.com
Sales: Cindy Dorzinski
Operations: Thomas Dotray
Estimated Sales: $20-50 Million
Number Employees: 20-49
Type of Packaging: Private Label

44019 Eutek Systems
2925 NW Aloclek Dr
Hillsboro, OR 97124-7523   503-601-0843
          Fax: 503-615-2906
Manufacturer and exporter of wastewater reclamation and reuse equipment; also, grit removers
Operations: Steve Tansley
Contact: Mohamed Abu
mabu@hydro-int.com
Estimated Sales: Less Than $500,000
Number Employees: 1-4

44020 Evans Food Group LTD
4118 S Halsted St
Chicago, IL 60609-2693   773-254-7400
          Fax: 773-254-7791   866-254-7400
                    www.evansfood.com
Manufacturer and exporter of rendered pork rinds.
Chairman/CEO: Jose Luis Prado
Purchasing: Ed McKenna
Estimated Sales: $20-50 Million
Number Employees: 100-249
Number of Brands: 4
Square Footage: 104000
Type of Packaging: Consumer, Private Label
Brands Exported: Evans
Regions Exported to: Central America, South America
Percentage of Business in Exporting: 10

44021 Evaporator Dryer Technologies
1805 Ridgeway St
Hammond, WI 54015-5044   715-796-2313
          Fax: 715-796-2378 info@evapdryertech.com
                    www.evapdryertech.com
Engineering and supply of custom evaporators and spray drying systems, heat recovery, dust collection, and exclusive sanitary designed components: liquid-activated, retractable CIP spray nozzles and systems, fire suppression systemssanitary, heavy-duty manways and inspection ports
Owner: Peter Jensen
info@evapdryertech.com
Purchasing: Jeff Derrick
Estimated Sales: $3-10 Million
Number Employees: 10-19
Square Footage: 13000
Other Locations:
     Stainless Steel Machining Division
     Fond du Lac, WIStainless Steel Machining Division
Regions Exported to: Central America, South America, Europe, Asia

44022 Eve Sales Corp
945 Close Ave
Bronx, NY 10473   718-589-6800
          Fax: 718-617-6717 executiveoffice@evesales.com
Juice; instant coffee; tea; concentrates and powders; BBQ sauce; marinades; seasonings; and chips
Vice President: Stuart Gale
Year Founded: 1965
Estimated Sales: $299531
Number Employees: 13
Type of Packaging: Private Label
Brands Imported: Baba Roots; Big Bamboo; Carita; Cydrax; Home Choice; Island Vibes; Kelly's; LASCO; Mabel's; Ovaltine; Peardrax; Pickapeppa; Pure; San Marcos; Seaside; St. Mary's; Trew Brew; & more
Percentage of Business in Importing: 50

44023 Event Equipment Sales
9000 67th St
Hodgkins, IL 60525-7606   708-352-0662
          Fax: 708-352-8267   800-337-0093
                    sales@eventequipment.com
                    www.eventequipment.com
Wholesaler/distributor of equipment and fixtures and general merchandise including tables, grills, china, wood folding chairs, etc
Owner: Mary Shipper
sales@eventequipment.com
CEO: Douglas Crowe
VP, Sales: Roberta Decillo
sales@eventequipment.com
Number Employees: 5-9

44024 Ever Fresh Fruit Co
35855 SE Kelso Rd
PO Box 1177
Boring, OR 97009-7064   503-668-8026
          Fax: 503-668-5823   800-239-8026
                    www.everfreshfruit.com
Apples
Owner: Brittany Beem
brittany@everfreshfruit.com
VP: LeAnn Miller
Estimated Sales: $10-20 Million
Number Employees: 50-99
Type of Packaging: Consumer, Food Service, Private Label
Regions Imported from: Worldwide
Percentage of Business in Importing: 10

44025 (HQ)Everbrite LLC
4949 S. 110th St.
Greenfield, WI 53228   414-529-3500
                    800-558-3888
          sales@everbrite.com www.everbrite.com
Signs and displays including indoor, outdoor, neon, electric and menu boards.
Vice President, Sales/Marketing: Jay Jensen
Year Founded: 1927
Estimated Sales: $74.8 Million
Number Employees: 500-999
Square Footage: 1000000
Type of Packaging: Food Service
Regions Exported to: Central America, South America, Europe, Asia, Latin America, Mexico
Percentage of Business in Exporting: 5

44026 Everedy Automation
345 Renninger Rd
Frederick, PA 19435   610-754-1775
          Fax: 610-754-1108
Manufacturer and exporter of bakery machinery for batter, scaling, cake cutting, icing, splitting, slicing, cake sandwich, pie, custard and fruit filling and meringue/cream topping; also, raisin cleaning and stemming equipmentavailable.
President: Irv Fisher
Sales Director: Irv Fisher
Number Employees: 2
Square Footage: 31200
Regions Exported to: Central America, South America, Europe
Percentage of Business in Exporting: 5

44027 Everfresh Beverages
6600 E 9 Mile Rd
Warren, MI 48091-2673   586-755-9500
          Fax: 586-755-9587   800-323-3416
                    www.everfreshjuice.com
Manufacturer and exporter of soft drinks and fruit juices including orange and grape
President/CEO: Stan Sheridan
Telecommunications: Ray Laurinaitis
Operations: Dave Piontkowski
Plant Manager: Matt Filipovitch
Purchasing Director: Walter Koziara
Number Employees: 50-99
Square Footage: 500000
Parent Co: National Beverages Corporation
Type of Packaging: Consumer, Private Label

44028 Everfresh Food Corporation
501 Huron Blvd SE
Minneapolis, MN 55414   612-331-6393
          Fax: 612-331-1172 george_edgar@yahoo.com
Chow mein noodles and vanilla including pure and imitation; importer of bamboo shoots and water chestnuts including whole and sliced
VP: Rita Sorsveen
Estimated Sales: $5-10 Million
Number Employees: 10-19
Type of Packaging: Consumer, Food Service, Private Label, Bulk
Regions Imported from: China

44029 Evergreen Manufacturing
6159 28th Street SE
Suite 9
Grand Rapids, MI 49546-6968   616-977-0939
          Fax: 616-977-0878 www.napkinbands.com

44030 Evergreen Packaging
5350 Poplar Ave
Suite 600
Memphis, TN 38119   901-821-5350
                    evergreenpackaging.com
Gable top packaging equipment and gable top cartons.
President & CEO: John Rooney
Estimated Sales: $5.5 Billion
Number Employees: 3,800
Square Footage: 40000
Type of Packaging: Consumer, Food Service
Regions Exported to: Central America, South America, Europe, Asia, Middle East, Worldwide
Percentage of Business in Exporting: 49

44031 Everpure, LLC
1040 Muirfield Drive
Hanover Park, IL 60133   630-307-3000
          Fax: 630-307-3030 info@everpure.com
                    www.everpure.com
Manufacturer and exporter of water filters
Contact: Peter Gorr
gorr@everpure.com
Estimated Sales: $ 35 - 40 Million
Number Employees: 1-4
Parent Co: Culligan International Company
Regions Exported to: Central America, South America, Europe, Asia, Middle East, Australia
Percentage of Business in Exporting: 30

44032 Everson District
280 New Ludlow Rd
Chicopee, MA 01020-4468   413-533-9261
          Fax: 413-536-4564 bob@treasuretreats.com
Wholesaler/distributor, importer and contract packager of candy
President: Robert Everson
robert@treasuretreats.com
Director of Sales: Tami Sharrow-Gero
Office Manager: Diana Gaouette
Production Supervisor: Steve Harris

Estimated Sales: $7 Million
Number Employees: 20-49
Square Footage: 80000
Type of Packaging: Private Label

44033 Evonik Corporation North America
299 Jefferson Rd
Parsippany, NJ 07054   973-929-8000
corporate.evonik.us
Precipitated and fumed silica used to improve the flow properties of food products, prevent caking, transfer liquids into free-flowing powders, improve dispersability, and function as processing aids in spray drying and millingapplications.
President, North America Region: John Rolando
Estimated Sales: $3.5 Billion
Number Employees: 4,800
Parent Co: Evonik Industries AG
Other Locations:
 Production/Health & Nutrition
  Blair, NE
 Production/Inorganic Materials
  Clavert City, KY
 Production/R&D
  Chester, PA
 Production/Coatings & Additives
  Deer Park, TX
 Production/Performance Polymers
  Fortier, LA
 Production/Advanced Intermediates
  Galena, KS
 Production/Health & NutritionClavert City
Regions Exported to: South America, Europe, Asia, Africa, Canada, Mexico

44034 Ex Drinks
1879 Whitney Mesa Dr
Henderson, NV 89014   702-949-6555
Fax: 702-949-6556 866-753-4929
hq@exdrinks.com
Energy drinks and vitamin water
Headquarters Manager: Natasha Platin
Senior Director of Business Development: Clark Wright
Director of Strategic Planning: Kristen Hirtz
Marketing: Travis Arnesen
Contact: Travis Arnesen
tarnesen@exdrinks.com
Estimated Sales: $500,000- 1 Million
Number Employees: 5-9

44035 Ex-Cell KAISER LLC
11240 Melrose Ave
Franklin Park, IL 60131-1332   847-451-0451
Fax: 847-451-0458 service@ex-cell.com
www.ex-cell.com
Manufacturer and exporter of metal check order rails, long handle dust pans, handheld dust pans, waste receptacles, bus tub and water carts, bar speed rails, bottlecap catchers, mobile coat racks, condiment trays, luggage racks, andluggage carriers
Owner: Tom Berg
tom@processdisplays.com
Managing Member: Janet Kaiser
Vice President/General Manager: Jeffrey Speizman
Human Resources/Purchasing: Elaine Abba
Estimated Sales: $ 8 Million
Number Employees: 100-249
Square Footage: 70000
Brands Exported: Ex-Cell
Regions Exported to: Central America, Caribbean, Latin America, Mexico, Israel
Percentage of Business in Exporting: 15

44036 Exact Target
141 W Green Meadows Drive
Suite 3
Greenfield, IN 46140-3082   317-467-4486

44037 Exaxol Chemical Corp
14325 60th St N
Clearwater, FL 33760-2708   727-524-7732
Fax: 727-532-8221 800-739-2965
info@exaxol.com www.exaxol.com
Manufacturer and exporter of food quality control laboratory chemicals
Owner: Joe Papa
Estimated Sales: $ 1 - 2,500,000
Number Employees: 1-4
Regions Exported to: South America, Europe, Caribbean
Percentage of Business in Exporting: 10

44038 Excalibur Miretti Group LLC
285 Eldridge Rd
Fairfield, NJ 07004-2508   973-808-8399
Fax: 973-808-8398 sales@exequipment.com
www.exequipment.com
Explosion-proof forklifts, electric and forklift trucks, exporter of forklifts
President: Angelo Miretti
Number Employees: 20-49
Square Footage: 88000
Regions Exported to: Europe, Asia, Middle East
Percentage of Business in Exporting: 5

44039 Excalibur Seasoning
1800 Riverway Dr
Pekin, IL 61554-9307   309-347-1221
Fax: 309-347-9086 800-444-2169
sales@excaliburseasoning.com
www.excaliburseasoning.com
Seasoning
President: Jay Hall
CEO: Blake Taylor
btaylor@lumc.edu
Estimated Sales: $ 5 - 10 Million
Number Employees: 50-99

44040 Exceldor Cooperative
5700 Rue J.B.Michaud
Bureau 500
Levis, QC G6V 0B1
Canada   418-830-5600
info@exceldor.com
www.exceldor.ca
Manufacturer and exporter of fresh and frozen chicken.
President & CEO: René Proulx
VP, Operations: ☐É☐ric Cadoret
VP, Finance: Christian Jacques
VP, Quality Assurance & R&D: Geneviève Arsenault
VP, Communications & Marketing: Isabelle Drouin
VP, Sales: Luc Gagnon
VP, Human Resources: Clémence Drouin
SVP, Chicken Division: Joël Cormier
SVP, Turkey Division: Anthony Tavares
Year Founded: 1945
Estimated Sales: $229 Million
Number Employees: 1400
Square Footage: 7502
Type of Packaging: Consumer, Private Label, Bulk
Regions Exported to: Worldwide
Percentage of Business in Exporting: 5

44041 Excellence Commercial Products
1750 N University Dr
Pompano Beach, FL 33071-8903   954-752-0010
Fax: 954-752-0080 800-441-4014
howard@stajac.com www.stajac.com
Wholesaler/distributor, importer and exporter of coolers, freezers and ice cream cabinets
President: Howard Noskowicz
Quality Control: Catherina Derr
Number Employees: 1-4
Parent Co: Stajac Industries
Brands Exported: Excellence Commercial Products
Regions Exported to: Central America, South America, Canada, Latin America, Caribbean, Mexico
Percentage of Business in Exporting: 10
Brands Imported: Excellence Commercial Products
Regions Imported from: Europe, Asia

44042 Excello Machine Co Inc
236 Stevens St SW
Grand Rapids, MI 49507-1566   616-949-1861
Fax: 616-949-2810 800-678-2409
sales@excellomachineco.com
www.excellomachineco.com
Wholesaler/distributor and exporter of folding carton equipment for box marking of cake mix, cereal, etc.; also, printing machinery repairing and rebuilding available
President: Mark Cassis
excellomac@aol.com
Purchasing Agent: Ronald Meschke
Estimated Sales: $500,000-$1 Million
Number Employees: 1-4
Square Footage: 19400
Regions Exported to: Worldwide
Percentage of Business in Exporting: 20

44043 Exel
509 Lee Ave
Lincolnton, NC 28092-2522   704-735-6535
Fax: 704-735-4899 www.excelhandling.com
Manufacturer and exporter of industrial hand, flat deck, order picking and specially fabricated trucks. Also, material handling carts, dollies, pin trucks, and yarn and beam transports
President/CEO: Charles Eurey
ceurey@excelcontainer.com
VP Administration/Sales: Jim Eurey
Estimated Sales: $20-50 Million
Number Employees: 10-19
Square Footage: 65000
Regions Exported to: Central America, South America, Europe, Canada, Caribbean, Mexico
Percentage of Business in Exporting: 5

44044 Exeter Ivanhoe Citrus Assn
901 Rocky Hill Dr
Exeter, CA 93221   559-592-3141
Fax: 559-592-5936 torr@exetercitrus.com
Packer of citrus fruit including oranges
General Manager: Terry Orr
Controller: Mike Hulsey
Sales: Joe Little
Jlittle@exetercitrus.com
Estimated Sales: $20-50 Million
Number Employees: 50-99
Type of Packaging: Consumer, Food Service, Private Label, Bulk
Brands Exported: Skyrocket; Moon Rocket; Space Rocket; Cascade of Gold
Regions Exported to: Worldwide
Percentage of Business in Exporting: 35

44045 Exeter Produce
215 Thames Road West
Exeter, ON N0M 1S3
Canada   519-235-0141
info@exeterproduce.com
exeterproduce.com
Grower, packer and shipper of beans, peppers, lettuce, cabbage and other hydroponic and field produce.
President: Leonard Veri
Director: James Veri
Director: Michael Veri *Year Founded:* 1951
Type of Packaging: Bulk
Regions Exported to: Europe, USA, Caribbean
Percentage of Business in Exporting: 70
Regions Imported from: USA
Percentage of Business in Importing: 2

44046 Exhausto
PO Box 720651
Atlanta, GA 30358-2651   770-587-3238
Fax: 770-587-4731 800-255-2923
steenh@exhausto.com www.exhausto.com
Manufacturer, importer and exporter of kitchen exhaust/grease fans
President: Steen Hagensen
Marketing Director: Kelly Johnson
Sales Director: Mark Sylvia
Purchasing Manager: Joan Chenier
Estimated Sales: $ 40 Million
Number Employees: 100
Number of Brands: 1
Square Footage: 18000
Parent Co: Exhausto A/S
Type of Packaging: Bulk
Regions Exported to: Central America
Percentage of Business in Exporting: 1
Regions Imported from: Denmark
Percentage of Business in Importing: 99

44047 Exhibitron Co
505 SE H St
Grants Pass, OR 97526-3262   541-471-7400
Fax: 541-471-7200 800-437-4571
info@exhibitroncorp.com
www.exhibitroncorp.com
Screen printing commercial signage, and decor products and garments, aisle markers for grocery and retail stores; also, general fabrication and screen printing available
Owner: Ken Northrup
exhibitron@uci.net
CEO: Kenneth Northup
Vice President: Marlene King
Estimated Sales: Less Than $500,000
Number Employees: 1-4
Square Footage: 13000
Regions Exported to: Asia, Canada

Importers & Exporters / A-Z

Percentage of Business in Exporting: 10

44048 Eximcan Canada
481 University Avenue
Suite 301
Toronto, ON M5G 259
Canada   416-979-7967
Fax: 416-979-8866 export@eximcan.com
eximcan.com
Beans; seeds; dairy products; rice; salt; juice; spices; oil; sparkling wine; dry fruits and nuts.
CEO: Mike Mehta
Import Export Coordinator: Roxana Fotouhi
Year Founded: 1992
Number Employees: 11-50
Regions Exported to: Central America, Europe, Asia
Regions Imported from: Central America, South America, Europe, Asia, Middle East

44049 (HQ)Eximco Manufacturing Company
5311 N Kedzie Ave
Chicago, IL 60625-4711   773-463-1470
Fax: 773-583-5131
Fluorescent lighting fixtures, light bulbs, energy-saving lighting, alkaline batteries and fluorescent ballasts; importer and exporter of lamps
President: R Ramsden
General Manager: John Perell
Estimated Sales: $2.5-5 Million
Number Employees: 20-49
Square Footage: 40000
Other Locations:
Eximco Manufacturing Co.
Chicago, ILEximco Manufacturing Co.
Regions Exported to: Central America, South America, Europe, Asia
Percentage of Business in Exporting: 15
Regions Imported from: Central America, South America, Europe, Asia
Percentage of Business in Importing: 10

44050 Expo Displays
3401 Mary Taylor Rd
Birmingham, AL 35235-3234   205-439-8284
Fax: 205-439-8201 800-367-3976
www.expodisplays.com
Manufacturer and exporter of portable and modular displays and exhibits for tradeshow exhibition and marketplace display
Owner: Jeff Colton
jeff@expodisplays.com
CEO: Jeff Culton
VP: Jay Burkette
Marketing: Sara Mathews
Public Relations: Jay Burkette
Estimated Sales: $ 10 - 20 Million
Number Employees: 50-99
Square Footage: 60000

44051 Export Contract Corporation
PO Box 382
Vienna, VA 22183-0382   904-384-3964
Fax: 703-242-1685
Exporter of food service equipment including slicing machines, meat grinders and bone saws, rotisseries and mobile food equipment
President/General Manager: K Taylor
Marketing Manager: D Taylor
Estimated Sales: Less than $500,000
Number Employees: 1-4
Type of Packaging: Food Service
Regions Exported to: Central America, South America, Europe, Asia, Middle East
Percentage of Business in Exporting: 100

44052 Expresso Supply
1123 NW 51st St
Seattle, WA 98107-5126   206-782-6670
Fax: 206-789-8221 info@espressosupply.com
www.brewaway.com
Owner: Laura Sommers
l.sommers@espressosupply.com
Estimated Sales: $ .5 - 1 million
Number Employees: 20-49

44053 Expro Manufacturing
2800 Ayers Avenue
Vernon, CA 90058   323-415-8544
Fax: 323-268-4060
Manufacturer and packager of food ingredients, including custom dry powder blends

President: Peter Ernster
CEO: Douglas Kantner
R&D: Greg Rowland
VP Sales: Michele Mullen
Contact: Daniel Diaz
ddiaz@expromfg.com
Purchasing: James Ernster
Number Employees: 20

44054 Extrutech Plastics Inc
5902 W Custer St
Manitowoc, WI 54220-9790   920-684-2065
Fax: 920-684-4344 888-818-0118
info@epiplastics.com www.epiplastics.com
Plastic panels that are lightweight and easy to install. Panels can be used both indoors and out for dairy barns, foodplants, car washes and will not rust, peel, rot or corrode and are very easy to clean.
President/CEO/CFO: Greg Sheehy
Research/Development: Mike Sheehy
Quality Control: Ashley Shulz
Marketing: Greg Sheehy
Sales Representative: Scott Charles
Senior Project Engineer: Chuck Grozis
Estimated Sales: $10 Million
Number Employees: 5-9
Regions Exported to: USA, Worldwide

44055 F & A Dairy Products Inc
212 State Road 35 S
Dresser, WI 54009   715-755-3485
Fax: 715-755-3480 800-657-8582
info@fadairy.com www.fadairy.com
Cheese including mozzarella, provolone, romano and parmesan; importer of pecorino romano
President: Chuck Engdahl
chuck@fadairy.net
Controller: Clyde Loch
CFO: Jay Benusa
QC: Ralph Ramos
Sales: Chris Slavek
Sales: Renzo Sciortino
Human Resources: Carl Gutierrez
VP Wisconsin Operations: Mike Breault
VP New Mexico Operations: Bob Snyder
Estimated Sales: $10-24.9 Million
Number Employees: 50-99
Type of Packaging: Food Service
Other Locations:
F&A Dairy Products
Las Cruces, NMF&A Dairy Products
Regions Imported from: Europe
Percentage of Business in Importing: 1

44056 F & A Fabricating Inc
104 Arbor St
Battle Creek, MI 49015-3068   269-965-8371
Fax: 269-965-8371 www.fa-fabricating.com
Manufacturer and exporter of stainless steel fabricated products including belt conveyors
President: Hiep Nguyen
Estimated Sales: $ 2.5-5 Million
Number Employees: 20-49
Type of Packaging: Food Service, Bulk
Regions Exported to: Worldwide
Percentage of Business in Exporting: 10

44057 (HQ)F B Washburn Candy Corp
137 Perkins Ave
P.O. Box 3277
Brockton, MA 02302-3891   508-588-0820
Fax: 508-588-2205 www.fbwashburncandy.com
Manufactured and distributor of hard candies, specializing in ribbon candies; offer rebagging, private label and wrapping services.
President: James Gilson
jamesgilson@fbwashburncandy.com
Treasurer: Douglas Gilson
Estimated Sales: $10 Million
Number Employees: 20-49
Number of Brands: 2
Square Footage: 150000
Type of Packaging: Consumer, Private Label
Regions Exported to: Canada

44058 F B Wright Co
9999 Mercier St
Dearborn, MI 48120-1410   313-843-8250
Fax: 313-843-8450 fbw401@aol.com
www.fbwright.com
Wholesaler/distributor and exporter of gloves including plastic and rubber

President: Jack Doer
CEO: Jack Doerr
fbw401@aol.com
CEO: Wj Reno
Estimated Sales: $20-50 Million
Number Employees: 50-99
Brands Exported: Granet; Pioneer
Regions Exported to: Worldwide

44059 F C Bloxom & Co
2250 Occidental Ave S
Seattle, WA 98134-1414   206-624-1000
Fax: 206-682-1435
Wholesaler/distributor, importer and exporter of produce
Owner: Robert Bloxom
robertb@fcbloxom.com
Estimated Sales: $10-20 Million
Number Employees: 20-49

44060 F C C
700 NE Highway 99w
Mcminnville, OR 97128-2711   503-472-2157
Fax: 503-472-3821
Milk, butter and powdered milk
President: Dan Bansen
CEO: Michael Anderson
manderson@farmerscoop.org
Estimated Sales: $4.9 Million
Number Employees: 5-9
Square Footage: 224000
Type of Packaging: Consumer, Food Service, Bulk
Regions Exported to: Worldwide

44061 F H Overseas Export Inc
551 Village Dr
Edison, NJ 08817-2637   732-985-1040
Fax: 732-985-9142 abuhael@gmail.com
Exporter of electric water coolers, walk-in freezers, cold storage rooms, ice machines, polycarbonate water bottles, refrigerator motors and compressors
Owner: F Husni
Estimated Sales: $1-2.5 Million
Number Employees: 1-4
Square Footage: 1600
Brands Exported: A.O. Smith; Tecumseh; Aem Products; Mars
Regions Exported to: Middle East

44062 (HQ)F I L T E C-Inspection Systems
3100 Fujita St
Torrance, CA 90505-4007   310-325-5633
Fax: 310-530-1000 888-434-5832
www.filtec.com
Manufacturer and exporter of automatic inspection systems for empty bottles, cases, missing caps, labels, filler/seamer monitors and packaging line detectors
President/Chief Executive Officer: Steve Calhoun
Managing Director: Reginaldo Pereira
Chief Financial Officer: Dan Leo
Manager, Research & Development: Kendall Hudson
Vice President, Sales & Marketing: Joanie Natisin
Chief Operating Officer: Bob Catalanotti
Purchasing Agent: Bill Herich
Estimated Sales: $ 44 Million
Number Employees: 250-499
Square Footage: 155000
Type of Packaging: Food Service
Other Locations:
Industrial Dynamics Co.Ltd.
Hamburg 30, WestIndustrial Dynamics Co.Ltd.
Regions Exported to: Central America, South America, Europe, Asia, Middle East
Percentage of Business in Exporting: 73

44063 F N Sheppard & Co
1261 Jamike Ave
P. O. Box 18520
Erlanger, KY 41018-3115   859-525-2358
Fax: 859-525-8467 800-733-5773
beltinfo@fnsheppard.com www.fnsheppard.com
Manufacturer and exporter of industrial belting for packaging including custom, flat, surreys and power transmission; also, design assistance, custom fabrication, field service, splicing tools and equipment available

CEO: James E. Reilly
Vice President: Frank Klaene
R&D: Tim Reilly
Quality Control: Bob Black
Marketing Director: Flint Coltharp
Sales Director: Wayne Siemer
Manufacturing Executive: Dan Martin
Plant Manager: Jim Reilly, Jr.
Purchasing Manager: Jack Fassel
Estimated Sales: $ 10 - 20 Million
Number Employees: 50-99
Square Footage: 40000
Regions Exported to: Europe
Percentage of Business in Exporting: 5

44064 F N Smith Corp
1200 S 2nd St
P.O. Box 179
Oregon, IL 61061-2330 815-732-2171
Fax: 815-732-6173 fnsmith@fnsmithcorp.com
www.fnsmithcorp.com
Bins, conveyors, packaging and extrusion equipment, knives, cartoning equipment and forming rolls for flaking/forming food; exporter of oat hullers and grain steamers
President: Ed Smith
CEO: Fred Smith
fnsmith@fnsmithcorp.com
CFO: Fred Smith
VP: Edward Smith
Estimated Sales: $2.5-5 Million
Number Employees: 20-49
Square Footage: 70000
Regions Exported to: Central America, South America, Europe
Percentage of Business in Exporting: 3

44065 F&Y Enterprises
1205 Karl Ct
Suite 115
Wauconda, IL 60084-1090 847-526-0620
Manufacturer and exporter of hickory smoked meat snacks including sausage sticks and beef jerky
President: Frank Vitek
VP: Bonnie Vitek
Estimated Sales: $2 Million
Number Employees: 40
Parent Co: F&Y Enterprises
Type of Packaging: Consumer, Food Service, Private Label
Brands Exported: Texas Brand
Regions Exported to: Europe, Asia, Canada
Percentage of Business in Exporting: 2

44066 F.B. Pease Company
1450 E Henrietta Road
Rochester, NY 14623-3184 585-475-1870
Fax: 716-475-9621
Paring, coring, slicing and conveying machinery for apples, kiwifruit, potatoes, squash and eggplant; exporter of apple parers, corers and slicers
Chairman: Warren Pease
President: Dudley Pease
Export Manager: Vivian Bubel
Estimated Sales: $2.5-5 Million
Number Employees: 19
Square Footage: 88000
Parent Co: Pease Development Company
Regions Exported to: Worldwide
Percentage of Business in Exporting: 30

44067 F.H. Taussig Company
111 Brook St
Scarsdale, NY 10583-5143 914-472-6464
Fax: 914-472-1846
Importer and exporter of tartaric and amino acids, cream of tartar, cod liver and fish oils, botanicals and nutrients for the pharmaceutical and health food industries
Pres.: Henry Weingartner
V.P.: Marilyn Weingartner
Estimated Sales: $ 3 - 5 Million
Number Employees: 1-4
Square Footage: 4000
Parent Co: Henry Weingartner & Company
Regions Exported to: Central America, Europe
Percentage of Business in Exporting: 10
Regions Imported from: South America, Europe, Asia
Percentage of Business in Importing: 90

44068 F.M. Corporation
1360 SW 32nd Way
Deerfield Beach, FL 33442-8110 954-570-9860
Fax: 954-570-9865
Manufacturer and exporter of kitchen ventilation equipment including oven hoods
Plant Manager: Twayn Katz
Estimated Sales: $ 1 - 5,000,000
Number Employees: 20-50
Parent Co: Hood Depot
Type of Packaging: Food Service
Regions Exported to: Worldwide
Percentage of Business in Exporting: 15

44069 F.P. Smith Wire Cloth Company
11700 W Grand Avenue
Northlake, IL 60164-1373 708-562-3344
Fax: 800-310-8999 800-323-6842
Manufacturer and exporter of woven and welded wire cloth
VP of Manufacturing: John Crupper
VP Sales: Ted Kapp
VP Manufacturing: Dr. John Crupper
Estimated Sales: $2.5-5 Million
Number Employees: 500
Square Footage: 114000
Regions Exported to: Worldwide
Percentage of Business in Exporting: 20

44070 FAGE USA Dairy Ind Inc
1 Opportunity Dr
Johnstown Industrial Park
Johnstown, NY 12095 518-762-5912
Fax: 518-762-5918 866-962-5912
usa.fage
Greek yogurt and feta cheese
Manager: Antonios Maridakis
Vice President: Ioannis Ravanis
info@fageusa.com
Number Employees: 250-499
Type of Packaging: Consumer

44071 FCD Tabletops
812 Snediker Ave
Brooklyn, NY 11207 718-649-1002
Fax: 800-938-0818 800-822-5399
Manufacturer and exporter of table, bar and counter tops
Sales Manager: Eric Grossman
VP Sales: Peter Stagg
Estimated Sales: $ 5-10,000,000
Number Employees: 20-49
Square Footage: 35000
Regions Exported to: Canada, Caribbean, Mexico
Percentage of Business in Exporting: 10

44072 FDC Corporation
PO Box 208
Williamsburg, VA 23187-0208 757-221-0900
Fax: 757-220-2483
Importer of meat and meat products, canned tuna and juices; exporter of canned vegetables
VP: Herbert Toms
Number Employees: 20-49
Regions Exported to: Europe, Middle East
Percentage of Business in Exporting: 5
Regions Imported from: South America, Asia
Percentage of Business in Importing: 70

44073 FDI Inc
5440 Saint Charles Rd
Suite 201
Berkeley, IL 60163-1231 708-544-1880
Fax: 708-544-4117 info@fdiusa.net
www.fdiusa.net
Canned and frozen foods; uses freeze-drying to preserve herbs, fruits, vegetables, spices, meat, pasta and fish
President: Joseph Lucas
National Sales Manager: Barbara Laffey
Manager: Terry Bliudzius
info@fdiusa.net
Estimated Sales: $1.3 Million
Number Employees: 10-19
Parent Co: Groneweg Group
Type of Packaging: Consumer

44074 FECO/MOCO
1745 Overland Avenue
Warren, OH 44483 330-372-8511
Fax: 330-372-8608 800-547-1527
www.ajaxtocco.com
Custom designing and manufacturing industrial ovens and thermal processing equipment Engineering and design capabilities include the unique ability to combine heat-processing and curing technologies with material handling and conveying methods
President: Dave Ekers
Project Manager Conveyors: Jim Hercik
Project Manager Ovens: Alan Semetana
Purchasing Manager: Jack Specker
Estimated Sales: $10-20 Million
Number Employees: 10
Square Footage: 240000
Parent Co: Park Ohio Company
Regions Exported to: Central America, South America, Europe, Asia, Middle East

44075 FEI Inc
934 S 5th Ave
Mansfield, TX 76063-2794 817-473-3344
Fax: 817-473-3124 800-346-5908
sales@feiconveyors.com
Manufacturer and exporter of sanitary and anti-corrosive conveyors including gravity, powered and stainless steel skate wheels; also, conveyor components
President: Duane Murray
duane@feiconveyors.com
VP: David Murray
Estimated Sales: $ 5-10 Million
Number Employees: 20-49
Square Footage: 68000
Regions Exported to: Central America, Canada, Mexico
Percentage of Business in Exporting: 3

44076 FFI Corporation
P.O. Box 20
1004 East Illinois Street
Assumption, IL 62510 217-226-5100
Manufacturer and exporter of continuous flow commercial and industrial grain dryers
Estimated Sales: $ 50-100 Million
Number Employees: 250-499
Regions Exported to: Worldwide

44077 FIB-R-DOR
10021 Commerce Park Dr.
P.O.Box 13268
Cincinnati, OH 45246 501-758-9494
Fax: 501-758-9496 800-342-7367
fibrdor@fibrdor.com www.fibrdor.com
Manufacturer and exporter of fiberglass doors, etc.
President: Jason Dileo
Marketing Director: Wes Lacewell
Sales Director: Mike Ferrell
Estimated Sales: $2.5 Million
Number Employees: 10-19
Number of Products: 3
Square Footage: 50000
Parent Co: Advance Fiberglass
Type of Packaging: Bulk
Brands Exported: Fib-R-Dor
Regions Exported to: Central America, Canada
Percentage of Business in Exporting: 5

44078 (HQ)FLEXcon Company
1 FLEXcon Industrial Park
Spencer, MA 01562-2642 508-885-8200
Fax: 508-885-8400 www.flexcon.com
Pressure sensitive film and adhesive products
President & CEO: Neil McDonough
CEO: Neil McDonough
Number Employees: 1,000-4,999
Regions Exported to: Worldwide

44079 FPEC Corporation
13623 Pumice St
Santa Fe Springs, CA 90670-5105 562-802-3727
Fax: 562-802-8621 salescal@fpec.com
www.fpec.com
Manufacturer and exporter of food processing equipment including blenders, conveyors and vacuum tumblers
President: Alan Davison
Contact: Laura Flynn
flynnl@fpec.com
Plant Manager: Dwayne Lee
Estimated Sales: $ 5 - 10 Million
Number Employees: 20-49
Square Footage: 212000
Brands Exported: FPEC
Regions Exported to: Central America, South America, Asia
Percentage of Business in Exporting: 10

Importers & Exporters / A-Z

Brands Imported: LIMA Sepenatols
Regions Imported from: Europe

44080 FRC Environmental
1635 Oakbrook Dr
Gainesville, GA 30507 770-534-3681
Fax: 770-535-1887
Manufacturer and exporter of stainless steel waste water treatment equipment and systems
President: Lonnie Finley
Estimated Sales: $2,600,000
Number Employees: 25
Square Footage: 72000
Type of Packaging: Bulk
Regions Exported to: Worldwide
Percentage of Business in Exporting: 25

44081 FRC Systems International
1770 Ridgefield Drive
Roswell, GA 30075 770-534-3681
Fax: 770-992-2289 info@FRCsystems.com
www.frcsystems.com
Water and wastewater treatment systems for the dairy, poultry, meat & seafood processing industries.
Regions Exported to: Central America, South America, Europe, North America, USA

44082 FSD International
2451 Cumberland Parkway
Suite 3443
Atlanta, GA 30339 710-988-8801
Fax: 710-988-8804 jkirschbaum@fsdintl.com
www.fsdintl.com
Kosher, organic/natural, flour, rice, ethnic sauces (soy, curry, etc.), olives, foodservice, private label.
Marketing: Jeff Kirschbaum
Contact: Pang Chiang
pangyc@fsdintl.com

44083 FX-Lab Company
725 Lehigh Avenue
Union, NJ 07083-7642 908-810-1212
Fax: 908-810-1630
Manufacturer and exporter of beneficial bacterial cleaning compounds and liquefiers for septic tanks and cesspools
President: George Weinik
Number Employees: 5
Square Footage: 4800
Brands Exported: FX 4
Regions Exported to: Europe, Middle East, Canada
Percentage of Business in Exporting: 3

44084 Fa Lu Cioli
553 Lehigh Ave
Union, NJ 07083-7976 908-258-8651
Manufacturer of a variety of meats.
Number Employees: 1-4
Regions Exported to: North America

44085 Faber Foods and Aeronautics
1153 Evergreen Parkway
Suite M105
Evergreen, CO 80439-9501 800-237-3255
Fax: 303-670-0971
Low-fat muesli cereal including strawberry/banana, cranberry/apricot, papaya/peach, blueberry/peach, raspberry/apple, etc.; also, custom blend cereals; exporter of extruded crisp rice, edible seeds, canned oats dried fruit raisins andnuts
President: Maria Faber
Estimated Sales: $300,000-500,000
Number Employees: 10-19
Square Footage: 40000
Type of Packaging: Consumer, Food Service, Private Label, Bulk
Regions Exported to: Worldwide
Percentage of Business in Exporting: 30

44086 Fabohio Inc
521 E 7th St
Uhrichsville, OH 44683-1613 740-922-4233
Fax: 740-922-4785 www.fabohio.com
Manufacturer and exporter of protective clothing and products including drum liners, meat cutters' aprons and smocks and shoe covers. Also custom fabrication available.
President: Don Coy
dcoy@fabohio.com
CEO: Kurt Shelley
CFO: Kurt Shelley
Purchasing Manager: Dennis Sautters

Estimated Sales: $1-3 Million
Number Employees: 20-49
Square Footage: 50000
Regions Exported to: Europe, Asia
Percentage of Business in Exporting: 2

44087 Fabreeka International
696 W Amity Rd
Boise, ID 83705-5401 208-342-4681
Fax: 208-343-8043 800-423-4469
www.beltservice.com
Manufacturer and exporter of lightweight custom conveyor belting including food grade, food grade incline, special profile, harvester, PVC and polyurethane
Branch Manager: Bob Holda
General manager: Toby Grindstaff
Division Manager: Toby Grindstaff
Assistant Division Manager: Mitz Pellicciotta
Estimated Sales: Below $ 5 Million
Number Employees: 10-19
Square Footage: 400000
Parent Co: Fabreeka International
Other Locations:
  Fabreeka International
  Oakville, ONFabreeka International
Regions Exported to: Central America, South America, Europe, Asia, Middle East
Percentage of Business in Exporting: 30

44088 Fabricated Components Inc
2018 W Main St
PO Box 431
Stroudsburg, PA 18360 570-421-4110
Fax: 570-421-2553 800-233-8163
info@fabricatedcomponents.com
www.fabricatedcomponents.com
Manufacturer and exporter of pallets, dollies, carts, cabinetry and containers
President: Bob Deinarowicz
Estimated Sales: $2.5-5 Million
Number Employees: 20-49
Square Footage: 200000
Type of Packaging: Private Label
Regions Exported to: Asia, Mexico, Latin America
Percentage of Business in Exporting: 30

44089 Fabricon Products Inc
1721 W Pleasant St
River Rouge, MI 48218-1099 313-841-8200
Fax: 313-841-4819 bdinda@fabriconproducts.com
www.fabriconproducts.com
Manufacturer, importer and exporter of flexible packaging materials including printed waxed and coated paper, films, frozen/novelty food packaging and wrapping, preformed paper bags and film laminated pouches; also, package designservices available
President: Bruce Dinda
bdinda@fabriconproducts.com
CFO: Roland David
Sales Director: Bruce L Dinda
Customer Service: Becky Smith
Production Manager: Mike Aslanian
Plant Manager: John Kuzawinski
Purchasing Manager: Colleen Loweifer
Estimated Sales: $9 Million
Number Employees: 50-99
Square Footage: 302000
Type of Packaging: Consumer, Food Service, Private Label, Bulk
Regions Exported to: Central America, Canada
Percentage of Business in Exporting: 3
Regions Imported from: Europe, Canada, Mexico
Percentage of Business in Importing: 5

44090 Fabriko
P.O.Box 67
Altavista, VA 24517-0067 434-369-1170
Fax: 434-369-1169 888-203-8098
afbriko@voyager.net www.fabriko.com
Manufacturer and importer of barbecue and waist aprons, coolers and bags including lunch, grocery and shopping
Owner: Ranata Allbeck
Sales Manager: Jerry Fischer
Estimated Sales: $ 3 - 5 Million
Number Employees: 10-19
Regions Imported from: Philippines, China , Mexico
Percentage of Business in Importing: 30

44091 Fabwright Inc
13912 Enterprise Dr
Garden Grove, CA 92843-4021 714-554-5544
Fax: 714-554-5545 800-854-6464
Manufacturer and exporter of custom stainless steel kitchen equipment fabrication; complete line of commercial food waste disposers
Owner: Della Williams
della@fabwrightinc.com
Vice President: J Wright
Purchasing Manager: D Yeardley
Number Employees: 10-19
Type of Packaging: Food Service
Regions Exported to: South America, Europe, Middle East, Canada, Japan
Percentage of Business in Exporting: 1

44092 Faciltec Corporation
73 S Riverside Dr
Elgin, IL 60120-6425 847-931-9500
Fax: 847-931-9629 800-284-8273
Manufacturer and exporter of a rooftop grease containment system for food service and industrial markets; also, cleaning services available
Executive VP: Christopher Barry
National Sales/Service Manager: Patrick Molloy
Estimated Sales: $ 1 - 5 Million
Number Employees: 50-99
Square Footage: 104000
Type of Packaging: Food Service
Brands Exported: Grease Guard; G2 Grease Guard XD; G2 Grease Guard XHD
Regions Exported to: Europe, Canada, Mexico
Percentage of Business in Exporting: 5

44093 Fair Publishing House
15 Schauss Ave
PO Box 350
Norwalk, OH 44857-1851 419-668-3746
Fax: 419-663-3247 orders@fairsupplies.com
www.fairpublishing.com
Manufacturer and exporter of award ribbons, tickets and signs including advertising
President: Kevin Doyle
kevin@fairsupplies.com
Sales Director: Charles Doyle
Production Manager: Kenneth Kosie
Estimated Sales: $ 3 - 5 Million
Number Employees: 20-49
Square Footage: 50000
Parent Co: Rotary Printing Company
Other Locations:
  Fair Publishing House
  Norwalk, OHFair Publishing House
Regions Exported to: Canada
Percentage of Business in Exporting: 1

44094 Fairbanks Scales
821 Locust St
Kansas City, MO 64106-1925 816-471-0231
Fax: 816-471-0241 800-451-4107
www.fairbanks.com
Manufacturer and exporter of stainless steel hostile environment scales including bench, unirail, omnicells, digital indicators, bench and portable scales, and bar code dataprinter
President: Richard Norden
rnorden@fairbanks.com
Chairman: F.A. Norden
Chief Financial Officer: Steve Wurtzler
Vice President, Engineering: Tom Luke
Quality Assurance Manager: Craig Schnepf
Vice President, Sales & Marketing: Bob Jozwiak
Director, Product Development: Derrick Mashaney
Plant Manager: Wayne Gaboriault
Purchasing Manager: Keith George
Estimated Sales: $ 81 Million
Number Employees: 20-49
Square Footage: 12000
Parent Co: Fancor, Inc.
Regions Exported to: Central America, South America, Europe, Asia, Middle East

44095 Fairborn USA Inc
205 Broadview St
Upper Sandusky, OH 43351-9628 419-294-4987
Fax: 419-294-4980 800-262-1188
info@fairbornusa.com www.fairbornusa.com
Manufacturer and exporter of truck and rail loading dock enclosures
President: Mark Dillon
dillonm@fairbornusa.com
General Manager: Mark Dillon
Number Employees: 100-249

Importers & Exporters / A-Z

44096 Fairchild Industrial Products
3920 Westpoint Blvd
Winston Salem, NC 27103-6727   336-659-3400
         Fax: 336-659-9323   800-334-8422
sales@fairchildproducts.com www.soldousa.com
Manufacturer and exporter of industrial controls including electro-pneumatic transducers and pneumatic pressure regulators; also, mechanical power transmission equipment including differential and draw transmissions
President: Mark Cuthbert
CEO: Bryan Buono
bryan.buono@rotork.com
Director, Finance: David C. Velten
VP Industrial Controls: Thomas McNichol
Quality Control: Greg Argrabright
R&D: Andy Askew
Director of Sales: Claudio Borges
VP Power Transportation Equipment: Jack Dunivant
Estimated Sales: $ 10 - 20 Million
Number Employees: 100-249
Square Footage: 176000
Brands Exported: Fairchild
Regions Exported to: Worldwide
Percentage of Business in Exporting: 30

44097 Fairco Foods
518 Gravier St
New Orleans, LA 70130   337-981-4071
         Fax: 337-524-6931   www.faircoinc.com
Exporter of confectionery products, snack foods, dried fruits, nuts, shrimp, cake mixes, aluminum foil and cereals
President: Edgar Bourg
Estimated Sales: $5-10 Million
Number Employees: 5-9
Brands Exported: Excellence; Fairco; Pepper King
Regions Exported to: Worldwide
Percentage of Business in Exporting: 100

44098 Fairfield Line Inc
605 W Stone Ave
PO Box 500
Fairfield, IA 52556-2223   641-472-3191
         Fax: 641-472-3194   800-247-3383
         www.fairfieldlineinc.com
Manufacturer, importer and exporter of work gloves including cotton, leather, leather-palm, coated and string knits
President: Nicole Vivacqua
nvivacqua@fairfieldline.com
VP: Larry Sheffler
Sales Manager: Larry Ray Sheffler
Estimated Sales: $ 5 - 10 Million
Number Employees: 20-49
Parent Co: Fairfield Line
Regions Exported to: Central America, South America, Middle East
Percentage of Business in Exporting: 15
Regions Imported from: Asia, Middle East
Percentage of Business in Importing: 40

44099 Fairhaven Cooperative Flour Mill
1115 Railroad Ave
Bellingham, WA 98225-5007   360-757-9947
         Fax: 360-734-9947   fairhavenflour@q.com
         www.fairhavenflour.com
Manufacturer and exporter of flour including whole grain, wheat, rye, corn, buckwheat, rice, etc
Manager: Bill Distler
Estimated Sales: $1-2.5 Million
Number Employees: 1-4
Type of Packaging: Consumer, Bulk
Regions Exported to: Canada

44100 Falco Technologies
1245 Rue Industrielle
La Prairie, QC J5R 2E4
Canada   450-444-0566
         Fax: 450-444-2227   www.falcotechnologies.com
Manufacturer and exporter of stainless steel food processing equipment including silos, hoppers, mixing kettles, wine storage units, brewery machinery, dairy processing equipment and custom fabrication turn key solutions to simple and complex problems - from tank installation to complete process
Co-President: Bertrand Blanchette
Co-President: Marc Regnaud
Quality Control: Andre Pichette
Marketing/Sales: Nicolas Courchesne
Vice President of Sales and Marketing: Stephane Audy
Production/Plant Manager: Jonathan Gingras
Purchasing: Susan Hynes
Estimated Sales: $10 Million
Number Employees: 75
Square Footage: 130000
Parent Co: Falco

44101 Falcon Rice Mill Inc
600 S Avenue D
PO Box 771
Crowley, LA 70526-5606   337-783-3825
         Fax: 337-783-1568   800-738-7423
         www.falconrice.com
Long and medium grain rice, jasmine rice, popcorn rice.
President: Mona Trahan
CFO: Robert Trahan
VP, Sales: Charles Trahan
General Manager: Tom Dew
Estimated Sales: $20-50 Million
Number Employees: 20-49
Number of Brands: 6
Type of Packaging: Consumer, Food Service, Private Label, Bulk
Regions Exported to: Central America, Mexico, Caribbean

44102 Falcon Trading Intl Corp
4606 Fairfield Rd
East Fairfield, VT 05448-4917   802-849-2021
         Fax: 877-790-7901   falconti@together.net
         www.falconti
Wholesaler/distributor, importer and exporter of herbs, spices, oils, proteins, vitamins, amino acids, enzymes, fibers, gelatin capsules, desiccants and alcohol
President: Robert Adams
radams@together.net
Number Employees: 1-4
Type of Packaging: Bulk
Regions Exported to: Worldwide
Percentage of Business in Exporting: 10
Regions Imported from: Worldwide
Percentage of Business in Importing: 10

44103 Fall River Wild Rice
41577 Osprey Road
Fall River Mills, CA 96028   530-336-5222
         Fax: 530-336-5265   800-626-4366
         www.frwr.com
Wild rice
General Manager: Walt Oiler
Estimated Sales: $420,000
Number Employees: 4
Square Footage: 56000

44104 Fallas Automation Inc.
7000 Imperial Dr
Waco, TX 76712-6816   254-772-9524
         Fax: 254-751-1242   sales@fallasautomation.com
         www.fallasautomation.com
Automatic packaging machinery
President: Dave Fallas
dfallas@fallasautomation.com
Vice President: Mark McAninch
Sales Manager: Chris Calebrese
Spare Parts Manager: Curtis Gross
Estimated Sales: $ 10 - 20 Million
Number Employees: 50+
Square Footage: 130000
Type of Packaging: Consumer, Food Service, Private Label, Bulk
Brands Exported: Fallas
Regions Exported to: Europe, Asia, Canada
Percentage of Business in Exporting: 5

44105 Fallwood Corp
75 S Broadway
Suite 494
White Plains, NY 10601-4413   914-304-4065
         Fax: 914-304-4063   ana@fallwoodcorp.com
         www.fallwoodcorp.com
Manufacturer and supplier of all natural nutraceutical ingredients and raw materials. All glanulars - Bovine and Porcine Enzymes
President/CEO: Jorge Millan
Vice President: Graciela Rocchia
Sales: Wayne Battenfield
Manager: Anne-Marie Rodriguez
anna@fallwoodcorp.com
Adminstration: Anne Marie Rodriguez
Estimated Sales: Under $500,000
Number Employees: 1-4
Parent Co: Loboratorio Opoterapico Argentino

44106 Famarco Limited
1381 Air Rail Ave
Virginia Beach, VA 23455-3301   757-460-3573
         Fax: 757-460-2621
Raw material importer and processor for spice, botanicals and carob
President: Bruce Martin
bruce@famarco.com
VP: Ken Hartfelder
Quality Control: Darrick Bargher
Marketing: Mark Herrick
Plant Manager: James O'Neil
Estimated Sales: $10 Million
Number Employees: 20-49
Square Footage: 80000
Parent Co: B&K International
Type of Packaging: Private Label, Bulk
Brands Exported: "Virginia Roast" Carob Powder
Regions Exported to: Europe, Asia
Regions Imported from: Europe, Asia

44107 Famco Automatic SausageLinkers
P. O. Box 8647
Pittsburgh, PA 15221   412-241-6410
         Fax: 412-242-8877   info@famcousa.com
         www.famcousa.com
Linking machines for sausage and frankfurter production
President: Charles Allen
Vice President: R. Robert Allen
Sales: Dick Carson
Regions Exported to: USA, Worldwide

44108 Family Tree Farms
41646 Road 62
Reedley, CA 93654-9124   559-591-8394
         Fax: 559-595-7795   866-352-8671
         www.familytreefarms.com
Plumcots, white peaches and nectarines, donut peaches and nectarines, yellow peaches and nectarines, apricots, apriums, plums, blueberries, cherries, satsumas
President: David Jackson
djackson@familytreefarms.com
CFO: Dan Clenney
Executive Director of Global Development: Gerome Raco
Director of Research & Development: Eric Wuhl
Quality Control: Mary Ortiz
Director of Marketing: Don Goforth
Estimated Sales: $ 20 - 50 Million
Number Employees: 250-499

44109 Fancy Heat
370 Adams Street
376
Newark, NJ 07114-2902   973-589-1450
         Fax: 973-589-5786   www.fancyheat.com
Contact: Joseph Diasparra
joseph@fancyheat.com
Estimated Sales: $ 20 - 50 Million
Number Employees: 20-49

44110 Fantastic World Foods
313 Iron Horse Way
Providence, RI 02908
         www.fantasticfoods.com
Vegetarian convenience foods including soups and rice; importer of rice.
Estimated Sales: $20-50 Million
Number Employees: 30
Square Footage: 150000
Type of Packaging: Consumer
Regions Imported from: Europe, Asia, Middle East
Percentage of Business in Importing: 5

44111 Fantasy Chocolates
2045 High Ridge Rd
Boynton Beach, FL 33426-8713   561-276-9007
         Fax: 561-265-0027   800-804-4962
         fantasychocolate@aol.com
         www.williamsandbennett.com

295

Importers & Exporters / A-Z

Manufacturer and exporter of chocolate novelties and gourmet pretzels including chocolate, keylime, chocolate pizza, caramel and chocolate apple
President: Becky Gardner
Contact: Bill Gardner
b.gardner@williamsandbennett.com
Products: Bill Gardner
Estimated Sales: $1.2,000,000
Number Employees: 1-4
Type of Packaging: Consumer, Private Label, Bulk
Regions Exported to: Asia, Canada, Caribbean
Percentage of Business in Exporting: 2

44112 Fantis Foods Inc
60 Triangle Blvd
Carlstadt, NJ 07072-2701 201-933-6200
Fax: 201-933-8797 info@fantisfoods.com
Olive oil, olives, cheese, seafood, gourmet, pasta, mineral water, cookies and baked goods, gyros, frozen pastries, herbs and spices, confectionary, bean and rice, drinks
President: George Makris
fantisfoods@aol.com
VP/CFO: Jerry Makris
VP/Manager: Steve Makris
Sales Executive/Sales Manager: Bill Paelekanos
Estimated Sales: $6 Million
Number Employees: 20-49
Square Footage: 210000
Type of Packaging: Consumer
Brands Imported: Fantis
Regions Imported from: Europe
Percentage of Business in Importing: 75

44113 Far West Meats
7759 Victoria Ave
PO Box 248
Highland, CA 92346-5637 909-864-1990
Fax: 909-864-0554
Processor and exporter of meat products including smoked sausage, knockwurst, bologna, salami, bratwurst, frankfurters, kielbasa, beef, pork and smoked pork and turkey parts
Owner: Tom Serrato
raemica@pacbell.net
President: Michael Serrato
CFO/Vice President: Wade Snyder
Estimated Sales: $13 Million
Number Employees: 50-99
Square Footage: 50000
Type of Packaging: Consumer, Private Label, Bulk
Brands Exported: Far West Meats; IBP; John Morrell; Excel
Regions Exported to: Asia, Mexico, Samoa
Percentage of Business in Exporting: 10

44114 Faraday
805 S Maumee St
Tecumseh, MI 49286-2053 517-423-2111
Fax: 517-423-2320 www.faraday.com
Manufacturer and exporter of fire alarm systems
Manager: Tim Wertz
Contact: Hugo Hortiz
hugo@faradaybikes.com
Estimated Sales: $ 20 - 50 Million
Number Employees: 100-249
Parent Co: Cerberus Pryotronics
Regions Exported to: Worldwide

44115 Farm 2 Market
Pier 45 Shed B
San Francisco, CA 94118
Fax: 866-821-9598 800-447-2967
www.farm-2-market.com
Seafood including farm raised shrimp, freshwater prawns, scallops, crawfish and oysters; importer of Australian crawfish and freshwater prawns
President: Marshall Schnider
Estimated Sales: $3-5 Million
Number Employees: 10-19
Type of Packaging: Consumer, Food Service
Regions Imported from: Asia, Australia
Percentage of Business in Importing: 15

44116 Farm Pak Products Inc
7840 Old Bailey Hwy
Spring Hope, NC 27882 252-459-3101
Fax: 252-459-9020 800-367-2799
sales@farmpak.com www.farmpak.com
Produce including sweet potatoes.
Vice President: Johnny Barnes
International Sales Manager: Jose "Pepe" Calderon
Packing House Supervisor: Frank Salinas

Year Founded: 1969
Estimated Sales: $20-50 Million
Number Employees: 100-249
Type of Packaging: Consumer, Bulk

44117 Farmers Rice Milling Co
3211 Highway 397 S
Lake Charles, LA 70615 337-433-5205
Fax: 337-433-1735 sales@FRMCO.com
www.frmco.com
Processor and grower of rice
General Manager: Philip Bertrand
CEO: Jamie Warshaw
jamiew@frmco.com
By-Product Sales: Jerry Sonnier
Year Founded: 1917
Number Employees: 50-99
Parent Co: The Powell Group
Type of Packaging: Consumer, Food Service
Regions Exported to: Worldwide

44118 Farmington Foods Inc
7419 West Franklin St
Forest Park, IL 60130-1016 708-771-3600
Fax: 708-771-4140 800-609-3276
info@farmingtonfoods.com
www.farmingtonfoods.com
Pork chops, boneless pork, baby back ribs, St. Louis-style spareribs, pre-packaged kabobs made with beef, chicken and pork, frenched pork racks, and seasoned port tenderloins and roasts
President: Tony Dijohn
tony.dijohn@farmingtonfoods.com
CFO: Albert LaValle
Quality Assurance: Marnie Adamski
Sales Manager: Tony DiJohn
Plant Manager/Director Operations: Dan Bernkopf
Warehouse Manager: Ram McKee
Estimated Sales: $30 Million
Number Employees: 100-249
Square Footage: 55000
Regions Exported to: South America, Europe, Asia, Canada, Mexico

44119 Fas-Co Coders
422 Thornton Rd # 103
Lithia Springs, GA 30122-1581 770-739-7798
Fax: 480-545-1998 800-478-0685
Manufacturer and exporter of coding and marking equipment
Owner: Victor Er
CFO: Roger Van Steenkiste
VP: Dan Piercy
Quality Control: Ty Martin
Estimated Sales: $6,000,000
Number Employees: 20-49
Square Footage: 30000
Regions Exported to: Worldwide
Percentage of Business in Exporting: 40

44120 Fast Industries
1850 NW 49th St
Fort Lauderdale, FL 33309-3304 954-776-0066
Fax: 954-776-5387 800-775-5345
Manufacturer and exporter of label placement systems, sign holders and merchandising aids; also, cleaning supplies including stain, laundry, rust and odor removers
President: Jacob Fast
Market Manager: Mike Brinkman
Estimated Sales: $ 10 - 15 Million
Number Employees: 100 to 249
Square Footage: 190000
Brands Exported: Carpet Gun; One Drop; Rust Gun; Smoking Gun; Stain Gun; Frontrunner; EZ View; Sell Strip, One Spray
Regions Exported to: Central America, South America, Europe, Asia, Australia
Percentage of Business in Exporting: 5

44121 Fast Pak Trading Inc
70 Outwater Lane
Suite 2
Garfield, NJ 07026-3854 973-925-1111
Fax: 973-926-1117 info@fastpakstore.com
www.fastpakstore.com
Imports European foods
Co-Owner: Ivanco Ivanovski
Co-Owner: Kiro Ivanovski
Contact: Michael Lippart
mike@fastpakstore.com
Estimated Sales: $2.5 Million
Number Employees: 8

44122 Favorite Foods
6934 Greenwood Street
Burnaby, BC V5A 1X8
Canada 604-420-5100
Fax: 604-420-9116 www.favoritefoods.com
Manufacturer and exporter of sauces including light and dark soy, oyster, teriyaki, marinade, barbecue, black bean, stir fry, Szechuan spicy hot and plum
President: Chris Barstow
VP of Sales: Chris Langella
Sr. Marketing Manager: Pearl Lyman
Chief Operating Officer: John Libby
Category Managers/Purchasing: Steve Gerasimchik
Estimated Sales: $1 - 5 million
Number Employees: 24
Square Footage: 70000
Type of Packaging: Consumer, Food Service, Private Label, Bulk
Brands Exported: Golden Dragon
Regions Exported to: USA
Percentage of Business in Exporting: 1

44123 Fawema Packaging Machinery
1701 Desoto Road
Palmetto, FL 34221-3066 941-351-9597
Fax: 941-351-4673 www.fawema.com
Manufacturer, importer and exporter of bag packaging systems including formers, fillers and closers; also, control modules, checkweighers and hot melt glue applicators
Customer Service Manager: Frank Potvin
Estimated Sales: $1-2.5 Million
Number Employees: 1-4
Square Footage: 20000
Parent Co: Fawema Maschinenfabrik GmbH
Brands Exported: Allen Bradley; Electro Cam; Nordson; Hi-Speed; Emerson
Regions Exported to: Europe
Percentage of Business in Exporting: 5
Brands Imported: Fawema; Kettner
Regions Imported from: Europe
Percentage of Business in Importing: 95

44124 Fax Foods
1205 Activity Dr
Vista, CA 92081-8510 760-599-6030
Fax: 760-599-6040
Manufacturer and exporter of plastic food replica.
Owner: Judy Preston
Square Footage: 60000
Parent Co: Fax Plastics
Type of Packaging: Food Service
Regions Exported to: Central America, South America, Europe, Asia, Middle East, Antartica
Percentage of Business in Exporting: 10

44125 Fay Paper Products
124 Washington St # 101
Foxboro, MA 02035-1368 781-769-4620
Fax: 781-769-8522 800-765-4620
Manufacturer and exporter of cash register rolls and stationery items
President: Gregory Steele
VP: Peter Steele
Estimated Sales: $5-10 Million
Number Employees: 20-49
Regions Exported to: Canada

44126 Feather Duster Corporation
10 Park St
Amsterdam, NY 12010-4214 518-842-3690
Fax: 518-842-3754 800-967-8659
Manufacturer, importer and exporter of dusters including ostrich feather and wool; also, applicator pads
President and CFO: Neil Stravitz
Quality Control: Susan Spagnola
Plant Manager: Susan Spagnola
Estimated Sales: Below $ 5 Million
Number Employees: 5-9
Square Footage: 20000
Regions Exported to: Australia
Percentage of Business in Exporting: 1
Regions Imported from: South America, Asia, Middle East, Canada
Percentage of Business in Importing: 10

44127 Feature Foods
30 Finley Rd.
Brampton, ON L6T 1A9
Canada 905-452-7741
Fax: 905-452-9210 info@featurefoods.com
www.featurefoods.com

Manufacturer and exporter of pickled eggs and herring; also, herb horseradish
President: Lorne Krongold
Number Employees: 20-49
Type of Packaging: Consumer
Regions Exported to: USA

44128 Federal Heath Sign Co LLC
3609 Ocean Ranch Blvd # 204
Suite #204
Oceanside, CA 92056-8601   760-901-7447
   Fax: 760-727-2279   800-527-9495
marketing@federalheath.com
www.federalheath.com
Manufacturer and exporter of custom interior and exterior signs including plastic and metal; also, installation and maintenance available
CEO: Kevin Stotmeister
kstotmeister@fedsign.com
Account Executive: Randy Cearlock
Estimated Sales: $1-2.5 Million
Number Employees: 100-249
Square Footage: 300000
Parent Co: Federal Signal Corporation
Regions Exported to: Worldwide
Percentage of Business in Exporting: 4

44129 Federal Industries
215 Federal Ave
Belleville, WI 53508-9201   608-424-3331
   Fax: 608-424-3234   800-356-4206
geninfo@federalind.com   www.federalind.com
Refrigerated and nonrefrigerated display cases for bakery and deli products
National Sales Manager (Food Service): Bill Rice
Plant Manager: Gary Hamburg
Estimated Sales: $20-50 Million
Number Employees: 50-99
Parent Co: Standex International Corporation

44130 Federal Machine Corp
8040 University Blvd
Clive, IA 50325-1118   515-274-1555
   Fax: 515-274-9256   800-247-2446
www.vending.com
Manufacturer and exporter of vending machines for snacks, candy, pastries, milk, canned drinks, gum, mints, hot beverages, frozen foods and ice cream; also machine parts (full line vending equipment manufacturing company).
President: Todd Wiggins
twiggins@wittern.com
CFO: Ray Lantz
CEO: F A Wittern Jr
Sales: Gary Bahr
Director Operations: Gary Bahr
Estimated Sales: $5-10 Million
Number Employees: 5-9
Number of Brands: 10
Number of Products: 20
Square Footage: 1400000
Type of Packaging: Food Service, Private Label

44131 Federation-Southern Cprtvs
2769 Church St
Atlanta, GA 30344-3258   404-765-0991
   Fax: 404-765-9178   fsc@federation.coop
www.federationsoutherncoop.com
Manufacturer and exporter of fresh vegetables
Chairman: Shirley Williams Blakely
Vice Chair: Daniel Bustamante
Secretary: Satina James
Treasurer: Carrie Fulghum
Estimated Sales: $500,000-$1 Million
Number Employees: 20-49
Type of Packaging: Consumer, Bulk

44132 Fee Brothers
453 Portland Ave
Rochester, NY 14605-1597   585-544-9530
   Fax: 585-544-9530   800-961-3337
info@feebrothers.com   www.feebrothers.com
Manufacturer and exporter of cocktail mixes including whiskey sour, daiquiri, margarita, pina colada, etc.; also, slush bases, bitters, nonalcoholic cordials, tea and juice concentrates, grenadine, coffee flavoring syrups, maraschino cherries, olives, cocktail
President: John Fee
CEO: Ellen Fee
Treasurer: Joe Fee
Estimated Sales: $1 Million
Number Employees: 10-19
Number of Brands: 1
Number of Products: 90
Square Footage: 96000
Type of Packaging: Food Service, Private Label, Bulk
Brands Exported: Fee Brothers
Regions Exported to: Europe, Canada, Caribbean
Percentage of Business in Exporting: 2

44133 Felbro Food Products
5700 W Adams Blvd
Los Angeles, CA 90016   323-936-5266
   Fax: 323-936-5946   www.felbro.com
Manufacturer, importer and exporter of fountain syrups, sno cone syrups, dessert toppings, fillings, puddings, sauces, dressings and drink bases for shakes, punches and slushies.
CEO: Mike Feldmar
CFO: Brian Seigel
Business Development Manager: Jim DeBiase
COO: Daniel Feldmar
Year Founded: 1946
Estimated Sales: $20-50 Million
Number Employees: 20-49
Number of Brands: 4
Square Footage: 80000
Type of Packaging: Consumer, Food Service, Private Label, Bulk
Regions Exported to: South America, Europe, Asia, Middle East
Percentage of Business in Exporting: 10
Regions Imported from: Central America, Europe, Asia, Latin America, Mexico
Percentage of Business in Importing: 10

44134 Felco Packaging Specialist
4001 E Baltimore St
Baltimore, MD 21224-1544   410-675-2664
   Fax: 410-276-2367   800-673-8488
Manufacturer, importer and exporter of corrugated boxes, tapes, burlap, canvas, pallets, paper products and bags
President: Jeffrey Feldman
jeff@felcoinc.com
Controller: Sherry Feldman
Estimated Sales: $ 5 - 10 Million
Number Employees: 10-19
Square Footage: 150000
Regions Imported from: Asia
Percentage of Business in Importing: 20

44135 (HQ)Feldmeier Equipment Inc
6800 Townline Rd
Syracuse, NY 13211-1325   315-454-8608
   Fax: 315-454-3701   sstanks@feldmeier.com
www.feldmeier.com
Manufacturer and exporter of heat exchangers, pasteurizers, stainless steel tanks, processing vessels, strainers, and stainless steel ice builders
President: John Feldmeier
CEO: Robert Feldmeier
CFO: Margaret Feldmeier
VP: Robert Feldmeier
Estimated Sales: $40 Million
Number Employees: 100-249
Other Locations:
   Feldmeier Equipment
   Little Falls, NY
   Feldmeier Equipment
   Reno, NV
   Feldmeier Equipment
   Cedar Falls, IAFeldmeier EquipmentReno
Brands Exported: Triple-Tubes

44136 Felins USA Inc
8306 W Parkland Ct
Milwaukee, WI 53223-3832   414-355-7747
   Fax: 414-355-7559   800-343-5667
sales@felins.com   www.felins.com
Manufacturer, importer and exporter of manual and automatic bundling, tying, wrapping, strapping and banding equipment; also, automated banding systems for multi-packing food products
Manager: Bruce Bartelt
Owner: James Chisholm
CFO: Ron Kuzia
Marketing: Peter Chapman
Sales: Mark Meyer
Public Relations: Neal Donding
Production: Bruce Lanham
Estimated Sales: $8.5 Million
Number Employees: 20-49
Square Footage: 50000
Brands Exported: Pak-Tyer; Loop Plus; JD-240; JD-150; Flex Strap; Bundling Machinery
Regions Exported to: Central America, South America, Europe, Asia, Middle East
Brands Imported: ATS-US2000 Series; JD Series; MS-420 Banding Machines
Regions Imported from: Central America, Europe, Asia

44137 Felix Storch Inc
770 Garrison Ave
Bronx, NY 10474-5603   718-328-8101
   Fax: 718-842-3093   800-932-4267
sales@summitappliance.com
www.summitappliance.com
Manufacturer, importer and exporter of beer taps, wine coolers, ice cream freezers and beverage merchandisers, minibars and coolers
President: Floria Lee
lee.floria@gmail.com
Vice President of Marketing: Steve Ross
R&D: Phil Yacht
Quality Control: Jeff Musnikow
Sales Director: Stephen Ross
Vice President: Paul Storch
Estimated Sales: $ 25 Million
Number Employees: 100-249
Square Footage: 140000
Parent Co: Felix Storch
Brands Exported: Summit
Regions Exported to: South America
Percentage of Business in Exporting: 5
Regions Imported from: Worldwide
Percentage of Business in Importing: 70

44138 Fenner Drives
311 W Stiegel St
Manheim, PA 17545-1747   717-665-2421
   Fax: 717-665-2649   800-243-3374
info@fennerdrives.com
Industrial transmission conveyor belts
President: Debbie Adler
d.adler@phillyjcc.com
CEO: Nick Hobson
Marketing Director: Robin Palmer
Sales Director: Craig Harris
Estimated Sales: $50+ Million
Number Employees: 100-249
Type of Packaging: Private Label, Bulk

44139 Fenton Art Glass Company
700 Elizabeth St
Williamstown, WV 26187   304-375-6122
   Fax: 304-375-7833   800-933-6766
askfenton@fentonartglass.com
www.fentonartglass.com
Manufacturer and exporter of decorative glassware and lamps
President: George Fenton
CFO: Stan Van Lanqingham
VP: Tom Fenton
R&D: Nancy Fenton
Quality Control: Tom Bobbitt
Sales VP: Scott Fenton
Public Relations: Terry Nutter
Purchasing Director: Mike Fenton
Estimated Sales: $25-30 Million
Number Employees: 250-499
Type of Packaging: Consumer, Bulk
Regions Exported to: Europe, Canada, Australia
Percentage of Business in Exporting: 2

44140 Fermin Usa
375 County Ave
Secaucus
New York, NJ 07094   201-293-4757
   Fax: 866-474-3280   www.ferminiberico.com
Pork products
Marketing: Santiago Martin

44141 Fernandez Chili Co
8267 County Road 10 S
Alamosa, CO 81101-9176   719-589-6043
   Fax: 719-587-0485
Manufacturer and importer of chili and taco sauces, spices and prepared chili mixes; also, Mexican corn products
Vice President: Blair Fernandez
VP: Blair Fernandez
Estimated Sales: $5-10 Million
Number Employees: 5-9
Square Footage: 45000
Type of Packaging: Consumer, Food Service, Bulk
Regions Imported from: Central America, Asia
Percentage of Business in Importing: 20

Importers & Exporters / A-Z

44142 Fernholtz Engineering
15471 Victory Boulevard
Van Nuys, CA 91406-6241   818-785-5800
                    Fax: 818-785-8406
Manufacturer and exporter of mills, sifting and screening machinery, wet and dry magnetic separators, mixers, blenders and agitators
President: Vivian Fernholtz
VP: Frank Fernholtz
Estimated Sales: $500,000-$1 Million
Number Employees: 1-4
Regions Exported to: Central America, South America, Europe, Asia, Middle East
Percentage of Business in Exporting: 70

44143 Ferntrade Corporation
1010 S 3rd St
San Jose, CA 95112   408-971-0997
        Fax: 408-286-1866 fcgferntrade@aol.com
Wholesaler/distributor and importer of Oriental specialty foods; exporter of canned fruits, vegetables and groceries, for American food products; also an importer for Philippine food products
President: Fernando Guevarra
CFO: Maria Guevarra
Marketing Director: Ramon Guevarra
Estimated Sales: $8 Million
Number Employees: 5-9
Square Footage: 40000
Type of Packaging: Consumer, Food Service, Private Label, Bulk
Regions Exported to: Asia
Percentage of Business in Exporting: 5
Brands Imported: Anahaw
Regions Imported from: Asia
Percentage of Business in Importing: 90

44144 Ferrara Bakery & Cafe
195 Grand St
b/w Mulberry & Mott St
New York, NY 10013-3717   212-226-6150
    Fax: 212-226-0667 information@ferraranyc.com
            www.ferraranyc.com
Manufacturer and importer of confectionery products including candies, novelties, Italian and seasonal products; also, syrups, coffee and baked goods
Owner: Ernest Lepore
ernestl@ferraracafe.com
Owner/CEO: Peter Lepore
Estimated Sales: $5-10 Million
Number Employees: 100-249
Type of Packaging: Consumer, Private Label
Regions Imported from: Europe

44145 Ferrara Candy Co Inc
404 W Harrison St
Suite 650
Chicago, IL 60607
                        800-323-1768
talktous@ferrarausa.com www.ferrarausa.com
Candy including butterscotch, caramels, chocolate, jelly beans, hard, licorice, lollypops, mints, marshmallows, nougats, etc.
CEO: Todd Siwak
CFO: Maurizio Ficarra
VP, Business Development: Willy Pfenning
Chief Customer Officer: Mike Sayles
COO: Michael Murray
Estimated Sales: $50 Million
Number Employees: 500-999
Number of Brands: 18
Square Footage: 365000
Parent Co: Catterton Management Company
Type of Packaging: Food Service, Private Label, Bulk
Other Locations:
   Farley's & Sathers - Distribution
    Chattanooga, TN
   Farley's & Sathers - Manufacturing
    Des Plaines, IL
   Farley's & Sathers - Manufacturing
    Reynosa, MXFarley's & Sathers -
    DistributionDes Plaines
Brands Exported: Brach's
Regions Exported to: Worldwide

44146 Ferrell-Ross
PO Box 50669
Amarillo, TX 79159   806-359-9051
        Fax: 806-359-9064 800-299-9051
        info@ferrellross.com www.ferrellross.com
Manufacturer and exporter of grinding and flaking mills for breakfast cereals, spices and snack foods; also, grain and cereal blenders, grain and seed cleaning machinery
President: David Ibach
Vice President: Philip Petrakos
Sales Director: Clay Gerber
Estimated Sales: $10 - 20 Million
Number Employees: 10
Square Footage: 50000
Parent Co: Bluffton Agri Industrial Corporation
Other Locations:
   Ferrell-Ross
    Bluffton, IN Ferrell-Ross
Brands Exported: Mix Mill; Farmatic; Ferrell-Ross; Clipper
Regions Exported to: Central America, South America, Europe, Asia, Middle East, Worldwide

44147 Ferrer Corporation
415 Calle San Claudio
San Juan, PR 00926-4206   787-761-5151
                    Fax: 787-755-0450
Manufacturer and exporter of interior and exterior signs including electric, metal, neon and plastic
President: Juan Ferrer Davila
Controller: Jose Vazquez
Sales Manager: Enid Cintron
Number Employees: 50
Square Footage: 80000
Brands Exported: Rotulos Ferrer
Regions Exported to: Caribbean
Percentage of Business in Exporting: 10

44148 Ferris Organic Farms
3565 Onondaga Rd
Eaton Rapids, MI 48827-9608   517-628-2506
        Fax: 517-628-8257 800-628-8736
        ferrisorganicfarm@gmail.com
        www.ferrisorganicfarm.com
Manufacturer, grower and exporter of organic beans including black, soy, black turtle and pinto; also, grains including wheat and barley; wholesaler/distributor of organic natural foods
Co-Owner: Richard Ferris
ferrisorganicfarm@excite.com
Estimated Sales: $1-2.5 Million
Number Employees: 1-4
Square Footage: 14000
Type of Packaging: Bulk
Regions Exported to: Europe, Asia
Percentage of Business in Exporting: 30

44149 Ferro Corporation
6060 Parkland Blvd
Suite 250
Mayfield Heights, OH 44124   216-875-5600
        Fax: 216-875-5627 www.ferro.com
Manufacturer and exporter of printing inks, labels and label supplies.
Chairman/President/CEO: Peter Thomas
VP/Chief Financial Officer: Ben Schlater
VP/General Counsel/Secretary: Mark Duesenberg
VP/Human Resources: Pepe Tortajada
Year Founded: 1919
Estimated Sales: $1,075 Million
Number Employees: 4,846
Parent Co: Ferro Corporation
Regions Exported to: Worldwide
Percentage of Business in Exporting: 30

44150 Ferroclad Fishery
Mamainse Pt
Batchawana Bay, ON P0S 1A0
Canada   705-882-2295
        Fax: 705-882-2297
Manufacturer, importer and exporter of herring, trout, whitefish and caviar
Owner: Gary Symons
Number Employees: 20-49
Parent Co: Presteve Foods Limited
Type of Packaging: Consumer, Food Service
Regions Exported to: Europe
Regions Imported from: Europe
Percentage of Business in Importing: 50

44151 Festive Foods
389 Edwin Dr # 100
Virginia Beach, VA 23462-4548   757-490-9186
        Fax: 757-490-9494 www.festivefoods.com
Sauces including spicy and extra spicy
President: Bobby Cannon
bcannon@festivefoods.com
Purchasing: Robert Buchanan
Estimated Sales: $.5 - 1,000,000
Number Employees: 1-4
Type of Packaging: Consumer
Regions Exported to: Europe
Percentage of Business in Exporting: 5

44152 Fetco
600 Rose Rd
Lake Zurich, IL 60047-1560   847-719-3000
        Fax: 847-719-3001 800-338-2699
        info@fetco.com www.fetco.com
Manufacturer, importer and exporter of food service equipment including coffee carts, tea brewing equipment servers, commissary systems and coffee and tea equipment
President: Zbigniew Lassota
zlassota@fetco.com
CFO: Zeel Lasoda
VP: Christopher Nowak
VP of Marketing and Sales: Richard Baggett
Estimated Sales: $10 - 20 Million
Number Employees: 100-249

44153 Fetzer Vineyards
12901 Old River Rd
Hopland, CA 95449-9813   707-744-1250
        Fax: 707-744-7605 800-846-8637
        Fernando.Avalos@fetzer.com www.fetzer.com
Manufacturer and exporter of table wines, barrels and corks
Head Operations: Pat Voss
Manager: Tim Nall
Director Winemaking: Dennis Martin
Estimated Sales: $19.2 Million
Number Employees: 250-499
Parent Co: Brown-Forman Corporation
Type of Packaging: Consumer, Food Service, Private Label, Bulk
Brands Exported: Fetzer; Bel Arbors; Bon Terra
Regions Exported to: Worldwide
Percentage of Business in Exporting: 50

44154 Fiber Does
1470 N 4th Street
San Jose, CA 95112-4715   408-453-5533
                    Fax: 408-453-9303
Manufacturer and exporter of fiber optic lighted signs including indoor, outdoor and window display
CEO: Song Lee
Sales/Customer Service Manager: Rick Perez
Estimated Sales: $3,000,000
Number Employees: 20-50
Percentage of Business in Exporting: 15

44155 Fibre Converters Inc
1 Industrial Park Dr
PO Box 130
Constantine, MI 49042-8735   269-279-1700
        jamey.southland@fibreconverters.com
        www.fibreconverters.com
Manufacturer and exporter of die cut slip sheets for replacement of pallets as well as special laminated or solid fibre paperboard
Owner: Jim Stuck
st@net-link.net
Chairman: David T Stuck
Operations Manager: Stephen Reed
Estimated Sales: $25 Million
Number Employees: 50-99
Square Footage: 160000
Brands Exported: Fibre-Pul; Fico; Valdor

44156 Fibre Leather Manufacturing Company
686 Belleville Avenue
New Bedford, MA 02745-6093   508-997-4557
        Fax: 508-997-7268 800-358-6012
Manufacturer and exporter of latex-impregnated and coated paper for box coverings; also, base stock for pressure sensitive tapes and jean label stock.
President: Daniel Finger
fibreleather@earthlink.net
VP: Louis Finger
Production Manager: Ellen Hull
Shipping Manager: Charles Hull
Estimated Sales: $10-20 Million
Number Employees: 50-99
Square Footage: 400000
Regions Exported to: Europe, Asia, Middle East, Canada
Percentage of Business in Exporting: 25

Importers & Exporters / A-Z

44157 (HQ)Fiebing Co
421 S 2nd St
Milwaukee, WI 53204-1612   414-271-5011
    Fax: 414-271-3769 800-558-1033
    custserv@fiebing.com www.fiebing.com
Manufacturer and exporter of soap and waterproofers
President: Richard Chase
jchase@fiebing.com
R&D: Mansur Abul
VP: Dennis Kendall
Estimated Sales: $ 10 - 20 Million
Number Employees: 5-9
Square Footage: 140000

44158 Fieldbrook Foods Corp.
1 Ice Cream Dr.
P.O. Box 1318
Dunkirk, NY 14048   716-366-5400
    Fax: 716-366-3588 800-333-0805
    www.fieldbrookfoods.com
Ice cream, frozen yogurt, sherbert and sorbet, sandwiches, ice cream/fudge bars, ice pops, juice and fruit bars, cones, cups, sorbet bars, etc.
President/Chief Executive Officer: Robin Galloway
Chief Financial Officer: Derek Kamholz
Senior VP, Sales & Marketing: James Masood
COO: Mark McLenithan
Vice President, Purchasing: Robert Griewisch
Year Founded: 2001
Estimated Sales: $101 Million
Number Employees: 250-499
Number of Brands: 3
Square Footage: 280000
Type of Packaging: Consumer, Food Service, Private Label, Bulk
Other Locations:
    Fieldbrook Farms
    Columbus, GAFieldbrook Farms
Regions Exported to: Europe, Canada, Caribbean
Percentage of Business in Exporting: 10

44159 Fiesta Farms
200 Christie St.
Toronto, ON M6G 3B6
Canada   416-537-1235
    Fax: 416-537-1244 www.fiestafarms.ca
Onions including red, yellow and white
President: Garry Bybee
Secretary: Tamara Bybee
VP: Marc Bybee
Estimated Sales: $ 10 - 20 Million
Number Employees: 20-49
Type of Packaging: Consumer, Food Service, Private Label, Bulk
Regions Exported to: Central America, Asia

44160 Fiesta Gourmet of Tejas
42 Oak Villa Road
Canyon Lake, TX 78133-3102   210-212-5233
    Fax: 210-212-5240 800-585-8250
Manufacturer and exporter of Texas-made wines, chiles, salsas, sauces, jellies, oils, coffees and teas; custom-made gift baskets available
Owner: Maricela Smith
Estimated Sales: Less than $500,000
Number Employees: 1-4
Square Footage: 4000
Parent Co: Fiesta Gourmet del Sol
Type of Packaging: Consumer, Food Service, Private Label
Regions Exported to: Worldwide

44161 Fig Garden Packing Inc
5545 W Dakota Ave
Fresno, CA 93722-9749   559-271-9000
    Fax: 559-271-1332
Manufacturer, exporter and packer of dried and diced figs and fig paste including regular and crushed seed
President: Michael Jura
Partner: Lisa Jura
lisa@figgardenpacking.com
Marketing Executive: Bert Zigenman
Estimated Sales: $1.3 Million
Number Employees: 50-99
Square Footage: 9646
Regions Exported to: Worldwide
Percentage of Business in Exporting: 5

44162 Figaro Company
3601 Executive Blvd
Mesquite, TX 75149   972-288-3587
    Fax: 972-288-1887
Manufacturer and exporter of hickory liquid smoke, mesquite liquid smoke, fajita marinade, brisket cooking sauce
Owner: J K Mc Kenney
CEO: Dave McCormack
Sales: Dave McCormack
Public Relations: Linda Willett
Operations: Anita Watson
Production: C Platero
Number Employees: 10-19
Number of Products: 6
Square Footage: 42000
Type of Packaging: Consumer, Food Service, Private Label
Regions Exported to: Europe, Asia

44163 Filler Specialties
440 100th Ave
Zeeland, MI 49464-2061   616-772-9235
    Fax: 616-772-4544 filler@filler-specialties.com
    www.filler-specialties.com
Manufacturer and exporter of capping and closing equipment, conveyor systems and fillers and filling equipment
President: Ron Slagh
rslagh@filler-specialties.com
Sales Manager: Jim Grant
Estimated Sales: $5-10,000,000
Number Employees: 10-19
Regions Exported to: Central America, South America, Asia, Middle East

44164 Filling Equipment Co Inc
1539 130th St
Flushing, NY 11356-2481   718-445-2111
    Fax: 718-463-6034 800-247-5071
    filling@fillingequipment.com
    www.fillingequipment.com
Manufacturer and exporter of packaging equipment, tables, conveyors, automatic cap tighteners, etc
President: Robert Hampton
Sales: G Hite
Sales: J Popper
Estimated Sales: $1-2.5 Million
Number Employees: 10-19
Regions Exported to: Europe, Asia, Middle East, North America, Caribbean, Latin America, Africa
Percentage of Business in Exporting: 5

44165 Fillit
18105 Trans Canada Highway
Kirkland, QC H9J 3Z4
Canada   514-694-2390
    Fax: 514-694-6552 rzajko@kalishdti.com
Manufacturer and exporter of conveying, filling, capping and counting equipment
President/Owner: ý
Production Manager: Richard Zajko
Number Employees: 100-249
Regions Exported to: Worldwide
Percentage of Business in Exporting: 30

44166 Fillmore Piru Citrus
357 N Main St
P.O. Box 350
Piru, CA 93040   805-521-1781
    Fax: 805-521-0990 www.fillmorepirucitrus.com
Oranges, lemons and avocados
President: Brett Kirkpatrick
brett@fpcitrus.com
CFO: Christina Morris
Sales Manager: Lupita Fernandez
VP, Operations: Tim Shugrue
Grower Relations: Samuel Orozco
Plant Supervisor: Antonio Martinez
Year Founded: 1897
Estimated Sales: $20-50 Million
Number Employees: 50-99
Type of Packaging: Consumer, Food Service
Regions Exported to: Europe, Asia, Middle East, Canada, Mexico
Percentage of Business in Exporting: 65

44167 Fillo Factory, The
Northvale, NJ 07647   201-439-1036
    Fax: 201-385-0012 800-653-4556
    ronrex@bellatlantic.net www.fillofactory.com
Gourmet appetizers, baklava, strudel, pastries and fillo dough; importer of dough
President: Ron Rexroth
VP Marketing: Tony Falletta
Contact: Tim Bennett
t.bennett@fillofactory.com
Estimated Sales: $1-3 Million
Number Employees: 60
Square Footage: 12000
Type of Packaging: Consumer, Food Service, Private Label, Bulk
Brands Imported: Lilas
Regions Imported from: Canada
Percentage of Business in Importing: 5

44168 Filmco Inc
1450 S Chillicothe Rd
Aurora, OH 44202-9264   330-562-6111
    Fax: 330-562-2740 800-545-8457
    www.linpac.com
Manufacturer and exporter of PVC film
President: Rolland Castellanos
Customer Service: Marianne Martone
General Manager: Richard Pohland
Purchasing Manager: Susan Burkholder
Estimated Sales: $20-50 Million
Number Employees: 50-99
Parent Co: Linpac Plastics Inc.

44169 Filtercorp
9805 NE 116th St
Kirkland, WA 98034-4245   425-820-4850
    Fax: 425-820-2816 www.filtercorp.com
President: Robin Bernard
Contact: Hal Bancroft
hbancroft@aol.com

44170 (HQ)Filtercorp
2585 S Sarah Street
Fresno, CA 93706-5034   559-495-3140
    Fax: 559-495-3145 800-473-4526
    www.filtercorp.com
Manufacturer, importer and exporter of nonwoven cellulose fiber filter pads used for cooking fats and oils
President: Don Eskes
sales@filtercorp.com
Estimated Sales: $500,000-$1 Million
Number Employees: 4
Square Footage: 24000
Brands Exported: Supersorb Carbon Pads
Regions Exported to: South America, Europe
Regions Imported from: Europe

44171 Filtrine Manufacturing
15 Kit St
Keene, NH 03431-5911   603-352-5500
    Fax: 603-352-0330 800-930-3367
    www.filtrine.com
Water filtration systems and ingredient water coolers for baked goods, confections, brewing, etc
Chairman: John Hansel
President: Peter Hansel
Sales: Philip Tussing
IT: David Hansel
dhansel@filtrine.com
Estimated Sales: $ 10 - 20 Million
Number Employees: 50-99
Square Footage: 500000
Brands Exported: Filtrine; Steri-Flo; Taste Master; Larco
Regions Exported to: Worldwide
Percentage of Business in Exporting: 30

44172 Finca La Tacitac/o Falla Imports
101 8th Avenue
Estell Manor, NJ 08319-1707   609-476-4106
    Fax: 609-476-0412
Importer of Coffee
President: Roderick Falla
Parent Co: Falla Imports

44173 Finding Home Farms
140 Eatontown Rd.
Middletown, NY 10940   845-355-4335
    www.findinghomefarms.com
Organic maple syrup, waffle and pancake mix, maple mustard and maple candy
Founder/Co-Owner: Laura Putnam
Founder/Co-Owner: Dana Putnam
Year Founded: 2013
Number of Brands: 1
Number of Products: 5
Type of Packaging: Consumer, Private Label
Brands Exported: Finding Home Farms
Regions Exported to: USA

Importers & Exporters / A-Z

44174 Fine Chemicals
211 Randolph Ave
Avenel, NJ 07001-2402   732-382-2100
Fax: 732-499-7799
Importer of citric and ascorbic acid, sodium erythorbate, food phosphate, food benzoate; exporter of crude sulphate turpentine
President: Art Dhom
Manager Fine Chemicals: Bob Conlan
Number Employees: 20-49
Square Footage: 14000
Parent Co: Amalgamated Metal Corporation
Type of Packaging: Bulk
Regions Exported to: Europe
Percentage of Business in Exporting: 15

44175 Fine Cocoa Products
224 48th St
Brooklyn, NY 11220-1012   201-244-9210
Fax: 201-244-8555 info@cocoasupply.com
www.cocoasupply.com
Importers and distributors of conventional, organic, and kosher cocoa and other ingredients. Some of their products include Cocoa Powders, Cacao Nibs & Beans, Cocoa Butter, Cocoa Liquor/Mass, Chocolate Couvertures and more.
Estimated Sales: Less Than $500,000
Number Employees: 2 - 10
Type of Packaging: Consumer, Food Service, Private Label, Bulk
Regions Exported to: Central America
Regions Imported from: Ecuador

44176 Fine Foods Australia
5419 Hollywood Boulevard
C 133
Los Angeles, CA 90027   323-375-1777
Fax: 323-309-2208 info@finefoodsaustralia.com
Imports specialty foods from Australia
Estimated Sales: $500,000
Number Employees: 2
Number of Brands: 10
Number of Products: 49
Type of Packaging: Consumer

44177 Finest Call
810 Progress Blvd
New Albany, IN 47150   812-944-3585
finestcallinfo@abmcocktails.com
www.finestcall.com
Alcoholic and nonalcoholic cocktail mixes.
Estimated Sales: $20-50 Million
Number Employees: 50-99
Square Footage: 110000
Type of Packaging: Consumer, Food Service, Private Label
Other Locations:
American Beverage Marketers
Overland Park, KS American Beverage Marketers
Brands Exported: Big Jim's; Coco Real; Master of Mixes; Barmaster

44178 Finest Foods
355 Food Center Dr # B260
Bronx, NY 10474-7000   718-893-5410
Fax: 718-893-6645
Wholesaler/distributor and importer of produce including fruits and vegetables
Buyer: Aaron Bertell
Estimated Sales: $ 20 - 50 Million
Number Employees: 50-99
Regions Imported from: Central America, South America, Asia

44179 Finlay Extracts & Ingredients USA, Inc.
23 Vreeland Road
Suite 201
Florham Park, NJ 07932-1510   973-539-8030
Fax: 973-539-4816   800-288-6272
infoUSA@finlays.net www.finlayusa.com
Bleding facility for tea and tea products.
Chief Executive Officer: Dushanth Ratwatte
HR Director, Extracts & Ingredients: Tamie Hutchins
Vice President, R&D: Catherine Robinson
NJ Contact: Steve Olyha
Estimated Sales: $ 10-20 000,000
Number Employees: 5-9
Parent Co: Finlays
Type of Packaging: Bulk
Other Locations:
Manufacturing Facilty
Lincoln, RI Manufacturing Facilty

44180 Fiori Bruna Pasta Products
5340 NW 163rd St
Miami Lakes, FL 33014-6228   305-705-2534
Fax: 305-621-4997 info@fioribruna.com
www.fioribruna.com
Manufacturer and exporter of frozen cheese tortellini, ravioli, cavatelli and potato gnocchi; also, dry egg fettuccine and linguine
President: Romano Fiori
fiori@bellsouth.net
VP Sales/Co-Founder: Cesare Bruna
Estimated Sales: $2.5-5 Million
Number Employees: 10-19
Square Footage: 20000
Type of Packaging: Consumer, Food Service, Private Label, Bulk
Regions Exported to: Caribbean
Percentage of Business in Exporting: 5

44181 Fiorucci Foods USA Inc
1800 Ruffin Mill Rd
S Chesterfield, VA 23834-5910   804-520-8392
Fax: 804-520-7180   800-524-7775
marketing@cfg-america.com
www.fioruccifoods.com
Manufacturer and exporter of Italian speciality meats including prosciutto, salami, regional specialty meats, pre-sliced, diced, small salamis, pepperoni, balsamic vinegar
President/CEO: Claudio Colmignoli
CEO: Chris Maze
Finance Executive: Mark Morrison
Quality Assurance Manager: Richard Wilson
Marketing: Keith Amrhein
VP Sales/Marketing: John Jack
Human Resources Manager: Carey Tillett
VP Operations: Oliviero Colmignoli
Plant Manager: Mark Bragalone
Purchasing Manager: Jennifer Erdelyi
Estimated Sales: $10-20 Million
Number Employees: 1-4
Square Footage: 280000
Parent Co: Cesare Fiorucci
Type of Packaging: Consumer, Food Service, Private Label, Bulk
Regions Exported to: South America, Asia
Percentage of Business in Exporting: 45
Brands Imported: Fiorucci
Regions Imported from: Europe

44182 (HQ)Firematic Sprinkler Devices
900 Boston Turnpike
Shrewsbury, MA 1545   508-845-2121
Fax: 508-842-3523   800-225-7288
Manufacturer and exporter of fire protection devices and control valves
Sales Manager: Greta Heath
Estimated Sales: $10-20 Million
Number Employees: 20-49

44183 Firestone Farms
18400 N Highway 99 W
Dayton, OR 97114-7225   503-864-2672
Fax: 503-864-2816 www.seattlechinesepost.com
Wholesaler/distributor and exporter of hazelnuts
Owner: Joan Firestone
ffarms@nwlink.com
VP: Joan Firestone
Estimated Sales: Less Than $500,000
Number Employees: 1-4
Regions Exported to: Worldwide

44184 Firl Industries Inc
321 W Scott St
Fond Du Lac, WI 54937-2121   920-921-6942
Fax: 920-921-7329   800-558-4890
info@firlindustries.com www.firlindustries.com
Manufacturer and exporter of doors and accessories including vinyl strip-traffic.
President: John M Buser
Estimated Sales: Less Than $500,000
Number Employees: 10-19

44185 First Choice Sales Company
3210 N Fruit Avenue
Fresno, CA 93705   559-224-3764
Fax: 559-224-8038
Specializing in Beef, Pork, Poultry, Cut Fruit and other quality Center of the Plate items for domestic and export Food Service Industries
President: Wayne Short
Contact: Short Kent
kent@1stchoicesales.com

Estimated Sales: $300,000-500,000
Number Employees: 1-4

44186 (HQ)First Colony Coffee & Tea Company
204 W 22nd Street
Po Box 11005
Norfolk, VA 23517-2231   757-622-2224
Fax: 757-623-2391   800-446-8555
Processor, importer and exporter of teas and coffees including varietal, blends and flavored
President/CEO: Bruce Grembowitz
Marketing Director: Julie Anderson
National Sales Director: Joyce Jordan
Contact: John Bergsten
john.bergsten@orbitalatk.com
Production Manager: Justin Goodman
Estimated Sales: $13 Million
Number Employees: 80
Square Footage: 94000
Type of Packaging: Consumer, Food Service, Private Label, Bulk
Regions Exported to: Central America, South America, Europe, Asia, Middle East, Australia, Canada
Percentage of Business in Exporting: 10
Regions Imported from: Central America, South America, Asia, Middle East
Percentage of Business in Importing: 90

44187 First District Association
101 S. Swift Ave.
Litchfield, MN 55355   320-693-3236
info@firstdistrict.com
www.firstdistrict.com
Dairy products including lactose blends and mixes, specialty cheeses, cream, wheys, whey protein concentrates and milk powders.
President/CEO: Clinton Fall
cfall@firstdistrict.com
Director, Quality Assurance: Dawn Raymond
Director, Sales/Marketing: Glenn Kaping
Director, Operations: Doug Anderson
Year Founded: 1894
Estimated Sales: $476.6 Million
Number Employees: 100-249
Square Footage: 100000
Brands Exported: Fieldgate
Regions Exported to: South America, Europe, Asia
Percentage of Business in Exporting: 10

44188 Fischbein LLC
151 Walker Rd
Statesville, NC 28625-2535   704-838-4600
Fax: 704-872-3303 sales@fischbein.com
www.fischbein.com
Manufacturer and exporter of bag closing equipment including bag closing, sealing and flexible material handling
President: Craig Blaske
cblaske@fischbein.com
VP Of Sales/Marketing: Lee Thompson
Manager: Mike Hersey
VP Sales/Marketing: Sean O'Flynn
Sales Development Manager: Tom Conroy
Operations Manager: Lynn McDonald
Purchasing Manager: Curt Poppe
Estimated Sales: $ 5,000,000
Number Employees: 100-249
Number of Brands: 3
Number of Products: 21
Square Footage: 56000
Parent Co: AXIA
Brands Exported: Fischbein; Fischbein/Saxon
Regions Exported to: Worldwide
Percentage of Business in Exporting: 60

44189 Fish Oven & Equipment Co
120 Kent Ave
PO Box 875
Wauconda, IL 60084-2441   847-526-8686
Fax: 847-526-7447   877-526-8720
info@fishoven.com www.fishoven.com
Manufacturer and exporter of mechanical revolving tray, rotating rack, and woodburning ovens for baking, roasting, supermarket, food service and institutions.
President: James M Campbell III
j.campbell@browardschools.com
Sales Manager: Sandra Bradley
Estimated Sales: $2.5-5 Million
Number Employees: 20-49

Square Footage: 160000
Parent Co: Campbell International
Regions Exported to: Central America, South America, Europe, Asia, Middle East
Percentage of Business in Exporting: 10

44190 Fisher Honey Co
1 Belle Ave # 21
Lewistown, PA 17044-2433   717-242-4373
Fax: 717-242-3978 fisherhoney@fisherhoney.com
www.fisherhoney.com
Manufacturer and exporter of honey, beeswax, beekeepers supplies, containers, glass, metal and plastic
Owner: Scott Fisher
fisherhoney@fisherhoney.com
Plant Supervisor: Scott Fisher
Estimated Sales: $1-2 Million
Number Employees: 1-4
Square Footage: 40000
Type of Packaging: Consumer, Food Service, Private Label, Bulk
Regions Exported to: Middle East
Percentage of Business in Exporting: 40

44191 Fisher Manufacturing Company
1900 South O Street
PO Box 60
Tulare, CA 93274   559-685-5200
Fax: 800-832-8238   800-421-6162
info1@fisher-mfg.com www.fisher-mfg.com
Manufacturer and exporter of stainless steel faucets, spray washers and water stations
President: Ray Fisher Jr
Quality Control: Delbert Poole
CFO: Rudy Fernandes
Contact: Michael Emoff
michael.emoff@outtathebox.com
Estimated Sales: $ 10 - 20 Million
Number Employees: 50-99
Type of Packaging: Food Service
Regions Exported to: Worldwide

44192 Fisher Scientific Company
2000 Park Lane Dr
Pittsburgh, PA 15275-1104   412-490-8300
Fax: 412-490-8759 www.fishersci.com
Manufacturer and exporter of food grade laboratory chemicals
Contact: Lawrence Crooks
larry.cook@fishersci.com
Estimated Sales: $ 50-100 Million
Number Employees: 500-999
Parent Co: Fisher Scientific International

44193 Fishers Investment
8950 Rossash Road
Cincinnati, OH 45236-1210   513-731-3400
Fax: 513-731-8113   800-833-5916
Manufacturer and exporter of cleaning equipment and supplies including glass cleaners, hand soap, dishwashing and washing compounds
Number Employees: 10
Type of Packaging: Food Service, Private Label
Regions Exported to: Worldwide

44194 Fishmore
1231 East New Haven Avenue
PO Box 24018
Melbourne, FL 32901   321-723-4751
Fax: 321-726-0939
Manufacturer, exporter and importer of custom fish processing equipment including automatic scaling, heading and gutting machines, glazers, conveyors, cutting tables etc
President: Al Sebastian
VP: Tim Cojocari
Estimated Sales: $300,000-500,000
Number Employees: 4
Square Footage: 12000
Brands Exported: Simor
Regions Exported to: South America, Europe, Asia
Percentage of Business in Exporting: 40
Regions Imported from: USA
Percentage of Business in Importing: 3

44195 Fiskars Consumer Products
PO Box 320
Baldwinsville, NY 13027-0320   315-635-5911
Fax: 315-635-1089 www.fiskars.com
President: Ray Carrock
Number Employees: 250-499

44196 Fitec International Inc
3525 Ridge Meadow Pkwy # 200
Suite 200
Memphis, TN 38115-4081   901-366-9144
Fax: 901-366-9446   800-332-6387
www.castnets.com
Manufacturer, importer and exporter of cotton and nylon mesh bags; also, netting, twine and rope
President: Mark Hall
hall@castnets.com
Sales: Mark Hall
Estimated Sales: $ 5 - 10 Million
Number Employees: 5-9
Type of Packaging: Bulk
Regions Exported to: Central America, South America, Europe, Asia
Percentage of Business in Exporting: 25
Regions Imported from: Central America, South America, Asia
Percentage of Business in Importing: 75

44197 Fitzpatrick Brothers
10700 88th Ave
Pleasant Prairie, WI 53158   773-722-3100
Fax: 773-722-5133   800-233-8064
boconnor@oldsfitz.com
Manufacturer and exporter of scouring powders, cleansers and detergents
General Manager/VP: Odie Ramien
VP: William O'Connor
VP: Tim McAvoy
Plant Manager: Vic Luburich
Estimated Sales: $ .5 - 1 million
Number Employees: 1-4
Parent Co: Olds Products Company
Regions Exported to: Europe

44198 Fitzpatrick Co
832 N Industrial Dr
Elmhurst, IL 60126-1179   630-592-4425
Fax: 630-530-0832 info@fitzmill.com
www.fitzmill.com
Manufacturer and exporter of grinder and hammer mills, fluid bed dryers, roll compactors and continuous mixers
President: Scott Patterson
Quality Control: Jose Molimar
CFO: Gary Minta
R&D: Scott Waemmnerstrun
Director Development/Marketing: Scott Wennerstrum
Manager, Sales: Tom Kendrick
Plant Manager: Al Cedno
Estimated Sales: $ 20 - 50 Million
Number Employees: 100-249
Square Footage: 150000
Regions Exported to: Worldwide
Percentage of Business in Exporting: 35

44199 Fixtur World
1555 Interstate Dr
Cookeville, TN 38501-4124   931-528-7259
Fax: 931-528-9214   800-634-9887
www.fixturworld.com
Manufacturer and exporter of wooden and stainless steel furniture including stands, benches, booths, chairs, cushions, pads, counters/tabletops and hot food tables; custom fabrications available
President: Randy Dyer
rdyer@fixturworld.com
Sales Director: Bobby Hull
General Manager: Al Paker
Estimated Sales: $ 10-20 Million
Number Employees: 100-249
Square Footage: 240000
Regions Exported to: Canada, Mexico
Percentage of Business in Exporting: 2

44200 Fizzle Flat Farm, L.L.C.
18773 E 1600th Avenue
Yale, IL 62448   618-793-2060
Fax: 618-793-2060 mcmanges@fizzleflatfarm.com
www.fizzleflatfarm.com
Organic popcorn and food grade certified organic grains including white, yellow and blue corn, wheat, soybeans, buckwheat. Grass fed beef raised on certified organic pastures (pasture-raised).
Owner/Manager: Marvin Manges
Owner/Manager: Lori Wells
Estimated Sales: $1-3 Million
Number Employees: 4
Square Footage: 8750
Type of Packaging: Bulk
Regions Exported to: Worldwide

Percentage of Business in Exporting: 50

44201 Flaghouse
601 Us Highway 46 W
Department 9009
Hasbrouck Hts, NJ 07604   201-288-7600
Fax: 201-288-7887   800-793-7900
info@flaghouse.com www.flaghouse.com
Wholesaler/distributor and exporter of office furniture, cabinets, tables and chairs
President: George Cramel
Contact: Janet Alston
jalston@flaghouse.com
Estimated Sales: $20-50 Million
Number Employees: 100-249
Regions Exported to: Worldwide
Percentage of Business in Exporting: 5

44202 Flakice Corporation
6920 Seaway Blvd
Everett, WA 98203   425-347-6100
Fax: 425-446-5116   800-654-4630
www.fluke.com
Manufacturer and exporter of fluid chillers and industrial ice machines
President: Antoine Hajjar
Vice President: Robert Butler
Chairman: William Adelman
Number Employees: 25
Square Footage: 50000
Brands Exported: Instant-Ice; Liquid Freeze; Flakice
Regions Exported to: Central America, South America, Europe, Asia, Middle East, Africa, Canada, Latin America
Percentage of Business in Exporting: 25

44203 Flame Gard
1890 Swarthmore Avenue
PO Box 2020
Lakewood, NJ 08701   800-526-3694
Fax: 732-364-8110 sales@flamegard.com
www.flamegard.com
Manufacturer and exporter of UL classified and commercial grease extracting filters, baffles for kitchen exhaust hoods and grease containment products
President: Lawrence Capalbo
CFO: Gary Barros
VP: Gary Barros
Estimated Sales: Below $5 Million
Number Employees: 20-49
Square Footage: 48000
Parent Co: Component Hardware Group, Inc.
Brands Exported: Flame Gard
Percentage of Business in Exporting: 15

44204 Flamingo Flats
100 Talbot St
PO Box 441
St Michaels, MD 21663   410-745-2053
Fax: 410-745-2402   800-468-8841
bigbird@flamingoflats.com
www.flamingoflats.com
Wholesaler/distributor and importer of garlic, mustards, olives, olive oils, hot sauces, peppers and vinegar; also, specialty Caribbean, Cajun, Southwest, Indian and Oriental products
Owner/President: Robert Deppe
bigbird@flamingoflats.com
Estimated Sales: Less than $500,000
Number Employees: 1-4
Square Footage: 3200
Regions Imported from: Central America, South America, Europe, Asia, Middle East, Jamaica, Grenada, Virgin Islands, Caribbean, Costa Rica
Percentage of Business in Importing: 25

44205 Flamingo Food Service Products
3095 E 11th Ave
Hialeah, FL 33013   305-691-4641
Fax: 305-696-7342   800-432-8269
info@flamingopaper.com
www.flamingopaper.com
Manufacturer and exporter of paper napkins
President: Tonny Arias
Operations Manager: Evelyn Hernandez
Estimated Sales: $ 1 - 5 Million
Number Employees: 10-19
Type of Packaging: Consumer, Food Service
Brands Exported: Logo Napkins; Coaster
Regions Exported to: South America, Europe, Middle East
Brands Imported: Naptidi

Importers & Exporters / A-Z

44206 Flanigan Farms
9522 Jefferson Blvd
PO Box 347
Culver City, CA 90232   310-836-8437
Fax: 310-838-0743   800-525-0228
www.flaniganfarms.com
Nut mixes and dried organic persimmons
Owner: Patsy Flanigan
Operations: C Flanigan
Estimated Sales: $3 Million
Number Employees: 10-19
Number of Products: 42
Square Footage: 24000
Type of Packaging: Consumer, Food Service, Private Label
Regions Exported to: Asia
Percentage of Business in Exporting: 1

44207 Flat Plate Inc
2161 Pennsylvania Ave
York, PA 17404-1793   717-767-9060
Fax: 717-767-9160   888-854-2500
www.flatplate.com
Manufacturer and exporter of brazed plate heat exchangers
President: Steven Wand
CEO: Charles Schmidt
CFO: Mike Losties
Quality Control: Brian Emery
R&D: Brian Emery
Marketing Head: Steve Wand
Estimated Sales: Less Than $500,000
Number Employees: 1-4
Regions Exported to: Worldwide
Percentage of Business in Exporting: 10

44208 Flavor Consultants
2875 Coleman St
North Las Vegas, NV 89032   702-643-4378
Fax: 702-643-4382 www.flavorconsultants.com
Manufacturers' representative and importer, exporter of flavoring ingredients.
President: Tim Wallace
tim@flavorconsultants.com
Estimated Sales: $1.1 Million
Number Employees: 6
Regions Imported from: Europe, Asia, Middle East, Australia, Latin America

44209 Flavor Dynamics Two
640 Montrose Ave
South Plainfield, NJ 07080-2602   908-822-8855
Fax: 908-822-8547   888-271-8424
customercare@flavordynamics.com
Food and beverage flavors
President: Dolf DeRovira
R&D Director: Norma Schwarz
Estimated Sales: 20.5 Million
Number Employees: 20-49
Square Footage: 29000
Type of Packaging: Food Service, Private Label, Bulk
Other Locations:
   Flavor Dynamics
   Glenview, IL
   Flavor Dynamics
   Corona Del Mar, CA
   Flavor Dynamics
   Cape Charles, VAFlavor DynamicsCorona Del Mar
Regions Exported to: Central America, South America, Europe, Asia, Middle East, Canada
Percentage of Business in Exporting: 10
Regions Imported from: Europe

44210 Flavor House, Inc.
9516 Commerce Way
Adelanto, CA 92301-3947   760-246-9131
Fax: 760-246-8431 flavorhouseinc.com
Manufacturer and exporter of flavor concentrates including meat, poultry and seafood; also, hydrolyzed vegetable proteins and liquid and dry soy sauce.
Estimated Sales: $4 Million
Number Employees: 20-49
Square Footage: 84000
Type of Packaging: Bulk
Regions Exported to: Canada
Percentage of Business in Exporting: 12

44211 (HQ)Flavor Sciences Inc
652 Nuway Cir
Lenoir, NC 28645-3646   828-758-2525
Fax: 828-758-2424   800-535-2867
information@flavorsciences.com
Natural and artificial flavors and essential oils; exporter of natural and artificial flavors and extracts
President: Roger Kiley
rogerkiley@gmail.com
Vice President: Joyce Kiley
Estimated Sales: $ 3 - 5 Million
Number Employees: 5-9
Regions Exported to: Central America, Europe, Middle East
Percentage of Business in Exporting: 18

44212 Flavor Systems Intl.
10139 Commerce Park Dr
Cincinnati, OH 45246   513-870-4900
Fax: 513-870-4909   800-498-2783
info@flavorsystems.com
Custom flavorings and specialty food systems
President: William Wasz
Owner: Bob Bahoshy
VP: William Baker
R&D: Angie Lantman
Quality Control: Alan Baker
Contact: Bill Baker
bill.baker@flavorsystems.com
Plant Manager: Rick Messinger
Purchasing: Roger Sage
Estimated Sales: $20 Million
Number Employees: 55
Square Footage: 25000
Type of Packaging: Bulk
Brands Exported: Bar Pro

44213 Flavor Wear
28425 Cole Grade Road
Valley Center, CA 92082-6572   760-749-1332
Fax: 760-749-6164   800-647-8372
www.flavorwear.com
Manufacturer and exporter of uniform accessories including ties, vests, hair accessories, hats, suspenders, bows, shirts and aprons
President: Lawrence Schleif
Owner/CEO: Martin Anthony
Vice President: Annie Smith
Estimated Sales: $2 Million
Number Employees: 23
Number of Brands: 2
Number of Products: 50
Square Footage: 40000
Parent Co: Anthony Enterprises
Type of Packaging: Food Service, Private Label
Brands Exported: Flavor Wear; Flavor Touch; Flavor Weave
Regions Exported to: Central America, South America, Europe, Asia, Middle East, Worldwide
Percentage of Business in Exporting: 35

44214 Flavor-Crisp of America
P.O.Box 488
Fort Calhoun, NE 68023-0488   402-453-4444
Fax: 402-453-7238   800-262-5016
www.flavor-crisp.com
Wholesaler/distributor and exporter of food service equipment including fryers, smokers, rotisseries and accessories; serving the food service market
Owner: Brad French
flavorcrisp@gmail.com
Executive VP Sales: Ray Boegner
VP Sales: Michael Nulty
Estimated Sales: $20-50 Million
Number Employees: 50-99
Square Footage: 280
Parent Co: Ballantyne of Omaha
Type of Packaging: Food Service

44215 Flavorchem Corp
1525 Brook Dr
Downers Grove, IL 60515-1024   630-932-8100
Fax: 630-932-4626   800-435-2867
www.flavorchem.com
Manufacturer and exporter of flavorings and food colorings; processor of pure vanilla extract; importer of fine chemicals and essential oils.
President: Ken Malinowski
kmalinowski@flavorchem.com
Year Founded: 1971
Number Employees: 100-249
Square Footage: 215000
Type of Packaging: Consumer, Food Service, Private Label, Bulk
Other Locations:
   Headquarters
   Downers Grove, IL
   Flavorchem West
   San Clemente, CAHeadquartersSan Clemente
Brands Exported: Flavorchem
Regions Exported to: Worldwide
Percentage of Business in Exporting: 5
Regions Imported from: Worldwide
Percentage of Business in Importing: 15

44216 Flavorganics
268 Doremus Ave
Newark, NJ 07105-4875   973-344-8014
Fax: 973-344-1948   866-972-6879
flavorganics@worldpantry.com
www.flavorganics.com
Organic extracts including vanilla, almond, peppermint, lemon and orange
President: Jocelyn Manship
Contact: Jenny Fagundes
jenny@ecsalesco.com
Estimated Sales: $ 20 - 50 Million
Number Employees: 50-99
Parent Co: Elan
Type of Packaging: Private Label, Bulk
Regions Exported to: Worldwide

44217 (HQ)Flavormatic Industries
230 All Angels Hill Rd
Wappingers Falls, NY 12590   845-297-9100
Fax: 845-297-2881 sales@flavormatic.com
www.flavormatic.com
Manufacturer, importer and exporter of flavors, fragrances and essential oils
President: Judith Back
Executive VP: Ronald Black
Sales: Frank Wells
Operation Manager: Richard Febles
Estimated Sales: $2.5 Million
Number Employees: 20-49
Square Footage: 63000
Type of Packaging: Bulk
Other Locations: Flavormatic Industries
Regions Exported to: Central America, Europe, Asia
Percentage of Business in Exporting: 20
Regions Imported from: South America, Europe, Asia, Middle East

44218 Flavouressence Products
1-6750 Davand Drive
Mississauga, ON L5T 2L8
Canada   905-795-0318
Fax: 905-795-0317   866-209-7778
backbaytrading.com
Beverage syrups, juices, bar mixes and slush; exporter of juices, bar mixes and beverage syrups
President/CEO: Mark Weber
CFO: Brain Ferry
Marketing: Bob Graham
Sales: Jolene Davies
Plant Manager: David Milner
Estimated Sales: $5 Million
Number Employees: 5-9
Square Footage: 21000
Type of Packaging: Food Service, Private Label, Bulk
Regions Exported to: South America, USA
Percentage of Business in Exporting: 15

44219 Fleet Wood Goldco Wyard
10615 Beaver Dam Rd
Cockeysville, MD 21030-2204   410-785-1934
Fax: 410-785-2909 service@fgwa.com
www.barrywehmiller.com
Manufacturer and exporter of mechanical conveyors and low pressure accumulating conveying and blending systems; also, package line engineering and integration of systems
President: Tom Spangenberg
VP: John Molite
R&D: Tom Spangenberg
Marketing: Dee Yakel
Sales: Michael Tymowezak
Contact: Don Powell
dpowell@bwcontainersystems.com
Operations: Bob Jones
Estimated Sales: $30 Million
Number Employees: 20-49
Square Footage: 50000
Type of Packaging: Consumer, Food Service, Private Label, Bulk

44220 FleetwoodGoldcoWyard
1305 Lakeview Dr
Romeoville, IL 60446   630-759-6800
Fax: 630-759-2299 www.fgwa.com

Manufacturer and exporter of depalletizers, brewery pasteurizers, warmers, coolers, complete turnkeys, conveyors and rinsers; also, engineering and installation services available
President: David Brown
CEO: Phil Ostapowicz
R&D: Neil McConnellogue
Chairman of the Board: Robert Chapman
General Sales Manager: Richard Witte
Contact: Ronald Burns
rburns@bwcontainersystems.com
Number Employees: 100-249
Square Footage: 200000
Parent Co: Barry-Wehmiller Co.
Regions Exported to: Worldwide
Percentage of Business in Exporting: 25

44221 Fleig Commodities
657 Sussex Drive
Janesville, WI 53546-1915   608-754-6457
                              Fax: 608-754-2899
Wholesaler/distributor and exporter of Wisconsin cheese
President: Michael Fleig
Number Employees: 1-4
Type of Packaging: Consumer, Food Service, Private Label, Bulk
Regions Exported to: Worldwide
Percentage of Business in Exporting: 25

44222 Fleischer's Bagels
1688 N Wayneport Rd
Macedon, NY 14502-8765   315-986-9999
    Fax: 315-986-7200 mark@fleischersbagels.com
Fresh, frozen and refrigerated bagels
President: Robert Drago
SVP Operations/CFO: Keith Bleier
Quality Assurance Manager: George Sparks
VP Sales/Marketing: Robert Pim
Contact: Marc Fleischer
mfleischer@fleischersbagels.com
Production Manager: Mike O'Hara
Estimated Sales: $6 Million
Number Employees: 135
Square Footage: 85370
Type of Packaging: Consumer, Food Service, Private Label, Bulk
Brands Exported: Fleischer's Bagels
Regions Exported to: Asia, Middle East, Worldwide
Percentage of Business in Exporting: 5

44223 Fleischmann's Yeast
Chesterfield, MO 63017
                                   800-777-4959
info@fleischmannsyeast.com
                              www.breadworld.com
Active and inactive yeasts, vinegars, leaveners and mold inhibitors; also, technical consulting for bakeries available
Estimated Sales: $50-100 Million
Number Employees: 74
Number of Brands: 1
Parent Co: Garfield Weston Foundation
Type of Packaging: Food Service, Bulk
Regions Exported to: Worldwide

44224 Fletcher's Fine Foods
502 Boundary Blvd
Auburn, WA 98001-6503
Canada   253-735-0800
                              www.fletchers.com
Manufacturer and exporter of pork and by-products
President/CEO: Fred Knoedler
President: Michael Lattifi
Manager: Ed Clark
clark@fletchers.com
Number Employees: 100-249
Parent Co: Fletcher's Fine Foods
Type of Packaging: Food Service, Bulk
Regions Exported to: Worldwide
Percentage of Business in Exporting: 30

44225 Fleur De Lait Foods Inc
400 S Custer Ave
New Holland, PA 17557-9220   717-355-8580
          Fax: 717-355-8561 800-322-2743
              alouetteculinary@savenciacheeseusa.com
                  www.savenciafoodserviceusa.com
Cheese manufacturer
President & CEO: Dominique Huth
National Sales: Larry Rosenberg

44226 Fleurchem Inc
33 Sprague Ave
Middletown, NY 10940-5128   845-341-2100
          Fax: 845-341-2121 info@fleurchem.com
                              www.fleurchem.com
Natural and synthetic flavoring agents and fragrances including acidulants, anethole, citronellal, eucalyptol, furfural, geraniol, heptanal, methyl actetate, etc
CEO: Charles Barton
cbarton@fleurchem.com
CEO: George Gluck
CFO: Sara Gluck
CEO: Rochele Gluck
Quality Control: Brian Merdler
VP Marketing: Jack Snicolo
Operations Manager: Louis Mercun
Production: Larry Costa
Purchasing Manager: Angie Roman
Estimated Sales: $10-20 Million
Number Employees: 20-49
Square Footage: 400000
Type of Packaging: Private Label, Bulk
Regions Exported to: Europe, Asia, Middle East
Percentage of Business in Exporting: 10
Regions Imported from: Central America, South America, Europe, Asia, Middle East
Percentage of Business in Importing: 25

44227 Flex Products
640 Dell Rd # 1
Carlstadt, NJ 07072-2202   201-933-3030
          Fax: 201-933-2396 800-526-6273
                              www.flex-products.com
Manufacturer and exporter of plastic extruded tube containers, closures and caps
President: Ed Friedhoff
Vice President: Bill Rooney
Sales Director: Darby Rosa
Plant Manager: Chris Smolar
Estimated Sales: $ 5-10 Million
Number Employees: 10-19
Square Footage: 130000
Regions Exported to: Central America, South America, Europe, Asia, Middle East, Mexico
Percentage of Business in Exporting: 5

44228 Flex-Hose Co Inc
6801 Crossbow Dr
East Syracuse, NY 13057-1026   315-437-1611
          Fax: 315-437-1903 sales@flexhose.com
                              www.flexhose.com
Manufacturer and exporter of hoses including Teflon, stainless steel and rubber flexible; also, couplings and expansion joints
President: Philip Argersinger
pbargersinger@flexhose.com
VP: Philip Argersinger
Quality Assurance: Chuck Phillips
Sales Management: Philip Argersinger
Operations Coordinator: Charles Phillips
Purchasing: Bill Wells
Estimated Sales: Below $5 Million
Number Employees: 10-19
Square Footage: 20000
Brands Exported: PumpSaver; TeFlex; FlexZorber; Tri-Flex Loop
Regions Exported to: Middle East, Canada, Caribbean
Percentage of Business in Exporting: 10

44229 Flexicell Inc
10463 Wilden Dr
Ashland, VA 23005-8134   804-550-7300
          Fax: 804-550-4898 www.flexicell.com
Manufacturer and exporter of robotic packaging machinery for case packing, collating, palletizing and conveying
President: Hans Dekoning
hdekoning@flexcon.com
R & D: Jack Morris
VP of Sales: Stuart Cooper
Operations Manager: Allen Bancroft
Manufacturing Specialist: Jack Mouris
Plant Manager: John Architzel
Purchasing Manager: Jim Golob
Estimated Sales: Below $5 Million
Number Employees: 20-49
Square Footage: 48000
Regions Exported to: Central America, South America, Europe, Canada
Percentage of Business in Exporting: 20

44230 (HQ)Flexicon
2400 Emrick Blvd
Bethlehem, PA 18020-8006   610-814-2400
          Fax: 610-814-0600 888-353-9426
              sales@flexicon.com www.flexicon.com
Manufacturer and exporter of flexible screw conveyor systems, bulk bag dischargers, weigh batching systems and bulk handling systems with automated controls
CEO: William S Gill
Number Employees: 50-99
Other Locations:
  Flexicon Corporation
  KentFlexicon Corporation
Regions Exported to: Central America, South America, Europe, Asia, Middle East, Africa

44231 Flexicon
165 Chicago St
Cary, IL 60013   847-639-3530
                              Fax: 847-639-6828
Flexible packaging materials for the food and pharmaceuticalical industries, supplied in rollstock for thermoforming, lidding, and form fill and seal applications. Preformed pouches are also supplied. Specializing in rollstock orpouches for boil and freeze applications.
President: Robert Biddle
CEO: Greg Baron
Estimated Sales: $20 Million
Number Employees: 50-99
Type of Packaging: Consumer, Food Service, Private Label

44232 Flexo Transparent Inc
28 Wasson St
Buffalo, NY 14210-1544   716-825-7710
          Fax: 716-825-0139 877-993-5396
Flexographic printer, manufacturer and exporter of custom designed and printed plastic films up to ten colors including process print. Flexible packaging materials including: bags, rollstock, bottle sleeves, sheeting, reclosablezipper, resealable tape, pallet covers, specialty prepared foods totes, custom shaped packaging, etc. EDI and VMI capable; Just in Time Deliveries; Fast turnaround shipments.
President: Ronald Mabry
HR Executive: Debbi Gauthier
dgauthier@flexotransparent.com
Sales: Mark Barrile
Estimated Sales: $20-50 Million
Number Employees: 50-99
Number of Brands: 4
Square Footage: 84000
Type of Packaging: Consumer, Food Service, Private Label, Bulk
Percentage of Business in Exporting: 5

44233 Flippin-Seaman Inc
5529 Crabtree Falls Hwy
Tyro, VA 22976-3103   434-277-5828
                              Fax: 434-277-9057
Growers, packer and shippers of fine fruit.
Owner: Bill Flippin
Owner: Richard Seaman
info@flippin-seaman.com
Estimated Sales: $10-20 Million
Number Employees: 20-49
Regions Exported to: Central America, South America, Europe

44234 Flo-Matic Corporation
1982t Belford North Drive
Belvidere, IL 61008-8565   815-547-5650
          Fax: 815-544-2287 800-959-1179
Manufacturer and exporter of washers and washing systems
Chief Engineer: Edward Herman
Estimated Sales: $ 1 - 5,000,000
Regions Exported to: Worldwide
Percentage of Business in Exporting: 5

44235 Floating Leaf Fine Foods
28 Christopher St
Winnipeg, MB R2C 2Z2
Canada   204-989-7696
          Fax: 204-943-4719 866-989-7696
              info@slwr.com eatwildrice.ca
Wild rice

Importers & Exporters / A-Z

President: Murray Ratuski
murray@slwr.com
Director of Sales: Matthew Ratuski
Coordinator: Sheldon Ratuski
Number Employees: 1-4
Type of Packaging: Food Service, Private Label, Bulk
Brands Exported: Canadian wild Rice

44236 Flojet
20 Icon
Foothill Ranch, CA 92610-3000 949-859-4945
Fax: 949-859-1153 800-235-6538
www.flojet.com
Manufacturer, importer and exporter of bag-in-box packaging pumps, motor pump units and power sprayers for soda, beer, cider, wine, condiments and water
President: Russ Davis
Marketing Director: Brud LeTourneav
Sales Director: Jon Byrd
Estimated Sales: $ 50 - 100 Million
Number Employees: 250
Regions Exported to: Worldwide
Regions Imported from: Asia

44237 Flomatic International
2100 Future Drive
Sellersburg, IN 47172 503-775-2550
Fax: 812-246-7020 800-367-4233
www.manitowocbeverage.com
Manufacturer and exporter of post-mix soft drink dispensing valves
VP: John Cochran
Estimated Sales: $ 10-20 Million
Number Employees: 20-49
Square Footage: 43200
Parent Co: Manitowoc Foodservice Group
Regions Exported to: Worldwide
Percentage of Business in Exporting: 70

44238 Flora Foods Inc
11927 West Sample Road
Coral Springs, FL 33065 954-785-3100
Fax: 954-785-2353
customerservice@florafoods.com
www.florafoods.com
Wholesaler/distributor, importer and exporter of pasta, olive oil, tomatoes, grilled vegetables, spices, sauces, pastries, meats and granulated garlic; serving the food service and retail markets
CEO/President: John Flora
jflora@florafoods.com
CFO: Richard DeCario
Operations Manager: Guy Rizzo
Estimated Sales: $10-20 Million
Number Employees: 20-49
Square Footage: 160000
Type of Packaging: Food Service
Brands Exported: Flora
Brands Imported: Flora

44239 Florart Flock Process
13870 W Dixie Hwy
North Miami, FL 33161-3343 305-643-3900
Fax: 305-981-9929 800-292-3524
www.flagusa.com
Manufacturer and exporter of flags, flagpoles, pennants, indoor flag sets and banners
Owner: Barbara Dabney
CEO: Stephanie Ledlow
Number Employees: 5-9
Square Footage: 20800
Brands Exported: Florart; Annin; Valley Forge; Dettra; Eder Mfg.
Regions Exported to: Central America, South America, Europe, Antilles
Percentage of Business in Exporting: 4

44240 Florida Choice Foods
1413 N. State Road 7
Hollywood, FL 33023 954-989-7964
Fax: 954-987-0367 info@fcfpopcorn.com
www.fcfpopcorn.com
Wholesaler/distributor and exporter of concession equipment and supplies including popcorn machines, popcorn, ice cream and dry yogurt mixes, etc.; serving the food service market
Owner: Craig S Garber
craig@fcfpopcorn.com
VP: Sharon Martin
Estimated Sales: $1-2.5 Million
Number Employees: 5-9
Square Footage: 12000

Regions Exported to: Central America, South America, Europe, Caribbean
Percentage of Business in Exporting: 40

44241 Florida European Export-Import
1500 NW 96th Ave
Doral, FL 33172-2852 305-477-0994
Fax: 305-477-0994 www.floridaeuropean.com
Importer and exporter of produce including mangos, avocados, limes, strawberries, cherries, apples, asparagus and green onions
Owner: Steve Blackburn
Secretary: Lisbeth Blackburn
VP: Christine Blackburn
International Sales: Christina Blackburn
Accounting Manager: Oscar Rangel
Estimated Sales: $10-20 Million
Number Employees: 20-49
Square Footage: 20000
Regions Exported to: Europe
Percentage of Business in Exporting: 95
Regions Imported from: Central America, South America
Percentage of Business in Importing: 5

44242 (HQ)Florida Food Products Inc
2231 W County Road 44 # 1
Eustis, FL 32726-2628 352-357-4141
Fax: 352-483-3192 800-874-2331
contact@floridafood.com www.floridafood.com
Vegetable juice concentrates, aloe vera gel, fruit juice powders, vegetable juice powders
President: Jerry Brown
jbrown@floridafood.com
Vice President: Tom Brown
Research & Development: Scott Ruppe
VP Marketing: Thomas Brown
Sales Manager: Mike McIntyre
National Accounts Manager: Randy Blackmar
VP Operations & Manufacturing: Charles Hamrick
Plant Manager: Keith Burt
Purchasing Manager: James Arnett
Estimated Sales: $15-20 Million
Number Employees: 50-99
Square Footage: 300000
Other Locations:
Florida Food Products
SabilaFlorida Food Products
Regions Imported from: Central America, South America, Europe, Asia

44243 Florida Knife Co
1735 Apex Rd
Sarasota, FL 34240-9386 941-371-2104
Fax: 941-378-9427 800-966-5643
sales@florida-knife.com www.florida-knife.com
Manufacturer and exporter of knives for ice, candy and packaging; also, food processing machine knife blades
President: Tom Johanning
tjohanning@florida-knife.com
Sales: Tom Johanning Jr
Personnel: Debbie Dean
Estimated Sales: $2.5-5 Million
Number Employees: 10-19
Square Footage: 48000
Regions Exported to: Worldwide

44244 Florida Natural Flavors
180 Lyman Rd # 120
Casselberry, FL 32707-2805 407-834-5979
Fax: 407-834-6333 800-872-5979
info@floridanaturalflavors.com
www.barcontrolsofflorida.com
Manufacturer, exporter and importer of juice and beverage concentrates including carbonated, noncarbonated and frozen products
Vice President: Garry Erdman
gerdman@floridanaturalflavors.com
COO: Gary Erdman
Manager: Leonard Combs
Estimated Sales: $4,000,000
Number Employees: 20-49
Parent Co: Florida Natural Flavors
Type of Packaging: Private Label
Regions Exported to: Europe, Latin America
Percentage of Business in Exporting: 15
Regions Imported from: Latin America
Percentage of Business in Importing: 10

44245 Florida Plastics Intl
10200 S Kedzie Ave
Evergreen Park, IL 60805-3735 708-499-0400
Fax: 708-499-4620 800-499-0400
salessupport@keyser-group.com
Manufacturer and exporter of point of purchase displays, signs and menu boards
Owner: Bill Kaiser
bkaiser@keyser-group.com
CEO: Donald Keyser
Quality Control: Tom Page
Estimated Sales: $ 10 - 20 Million
Number Employees: 1-4
Square Footage: 120000
Type of Packaging: Food Service
Regions Exported to: Worldwide
Percentage of Business in Exporting: 15

44246 Florida's Natural Growers
20205 US Hwy. 27 N.
Lake Wales, FL 33853 863-676-1411
Fax: 863-676-1640 888-657-6600
www.floridasnatural.com
Fresh and frozen fruit juices, concentrates and blends including grapefruit, orange, lemonade, lime, apple and grape.
Owner/President: Frank Hunt
CEO: Bob Behr
CFO: William Hendry
chip.hendry@citrusworld.com
Year Founded: 1933
Estimated Sales: $105 Million
Number Employees: 1,100
Type of Packaging: Consumer, Food Service, Private Label
Brands Exported: Florida's Natural
Regions Exported to: Worldwide
Percentage of Business in Exporting: 7

44247 Flow Aerospace
1635 Production Rd
Jeffersonville, IN 47130-9624 812-283-7888
Fax: 812-284-3281 www.flowwaterjet.com
Manufacturer and exporter of positioning systems for waterjet cutting pick and place robots
Manager: Anthony Neeley
Vice President of Global Sales: Dick LeBlanc
Manager: Kent Eubank
keubank@flowcorp.com
General Manager: Gerald Malmrose
Chief Engineer: Mark Saberton
Estimated Sales: $ 1 - 5 Million
Number Employees: 100-249
Square Footage: 108000
Parent Co: Flow International
Regions Exported to: Worldwide
Percentage of Business in Exporting: 10

44248 (HQ)Flow International Corp.
23500 64th Ave. S
Kent, WA 98032 253-850-3500
Fax: 253-813-9377 800-446-3569
info@flowcorp.com www.flowwaterjet.com
Food processing and high-pressure waterjet cutting and cleaning equipment.
President/CEO: Marc Michael
Year Founded: 1974
Estimated Sales: $200 Million
Number Employees: 680
Square Footage: 150000
Regions Exported to: Worldwide
Percentage of Business in Exporting: 30

44249 Flowers Baking Co
900 16th St N
Birmingham, AL 35203-1017 205-252-1161
Fax: 205-323-7610 www.flowersfoods.com
Manufacturer and exporter of hamburger buns
President: Carter Wood
carter_wood@flocorp.com
Vice President of Marketing: Janice Anderson
Chief Engineer: Richard Davis
Estimated Sales: $10-20 Million
Number Employees: 250-499
Square Footage: 195000
Parent Co: Flowers Baking Company
Type of Packaging: Consumer
Brands Exported: Wendy's
Regions Exported to: Caribbean, Mexico
Percentage of Business in Exporting: 5

Importers & Exporters / A-Z

44250 Fluid Air Inc
2580 Diehl Rd # E
Aurora, IL 60502-5309   630-665-5001
      Fax: 630-851-1244 fluidairinfo@spray.com
                www.fluidairinc.com
Manufacturer and exporter of milling equipment for fine grinding and dryers/agglomerators for drying, agglomerating, coating and encapsulating foods and flavors
President: Martin Bender
CEO: Thomas Tappen
Director Process Development: Donald Verbarg
Estimated Sales: $ 5 – 10 Million
Number Employees: 20-49
Square Footage: 64000
Parent Co: Spraying Systems Company
Regions Exported to: Central America, South America, Europe, Asia
Percentage of Business in Exporting: 35

44251 Fluid Energy Processing& Eqpt
2629 Penn St
Hatfield, PA 19440-2344   215-368-2510
      Fax: 215-368-6235 sales@fluidenergype.com
                www.fluidenergype.com
Manufacturer and exporter of jet/micronizing grinding mills, pulverizers and flash drying equipment
President: Jerry Leimkuhler
Estimated Sales: $ 5 – 10 Million
Number Employees: 50-99
Regions Exported to: Central America, South America, Europe, Asia, Middle East, Australia, Canada, Mexico

44252 Fluid Metering Inc
5 Aerial Way # 500
Syosset, NY 11791-5593   516-922-6050
      Fax: 516-624-8261   800-223-3388
      pumps@fmipump.com www.fmipump.com
Manufacturer and exporter of metering pumps, dispensers and accessories including valveless and variable positive displacement piston pumps
President: Hank Pinkerton
hank.pinkerton@fmipump.com
Marketing Manager: Herb Werner
VP Sales: David Peled
Purchasing Director: Anthony Mennella
Estimated Sales: $10-20 Million
Number Employees: 10-19
Square Footage: 24000
Brands Exported: Micro-Pipetter, Ratiomatic, Ceram Pump
Regions Exported to: Central America, South America, Europe, Asia, Middle East

44253 Fluid-O-Tech International Inc
161 Atwater St
Plantsville, CT 06479-1644   860-276-9270
      Fax: 860-620-0193 info@fluid-o-tech.com
                www.fluidotech.it
Importer, exporter and wholesaler/distributor of rotary vane, oscillating piston and magnetic drive gear pumps
President: Mark Petrucci
fotint@aol.com
VP: Mark Petrucci
Number Employees: 5-9
Square Footage: 40000
Parent Co: Fluid O Tech
Regions Exported to: Japan
Percentage of Business in Exporting: 20
Brands Imported: Fluid-O-Tech
Regions Imported from: Italy

44254 Flux Pumps Corporation
4330 Commerce Cir SW
Atlanta, GA 30336   404-691-6010
      Fax: 404-691-6314   800-367-3589
      contact-flux-usa@flux-pumpen.de
Manufacturer and exporter of pumps including centrifugal, pneumatic, positive displacement, progressive cavity and sanitary
President: L G Eastman
Vice President: Mike O'Toole
Contact: Fred Bryant
fbryant@flux-pumps.com
Estimated Sales: $1-2,500,000
Number Employees: 5-9
Parent Co: Flux Pumps Corporation
Type of Packaging: Bulk
Regions Exported to: Central America, South America
Percentage of Business in Exporting: 10

44255 Flying Dog Brewery
4607 Wedgewood Blvd
Frederick, MD 21703-7120   301-694-7899
                www.flyingdogales.com
Manufacturer and exporter of beer, ale, stout, lager and porter.
President/CFO: Kelly McElroy
CEO: Jim Caruso
jimcaruso@flyingdogales.com
COO: Matt Brophy
CMO: Ben Savage
VP Sales: John Stolins
VP Plant Operations: Mark Matovich
Director, Packaging & Logistics: Christopher Farley
Estimated Sales: $7 Million
Number Employees: 50-99
Square Footage: 114000
Type of Packaging: Consumer, Food Service, Private Label
Regions Exported to: Europe, Asia, Canada

44256 Flyover International Corporation
34851 Belvedere Ter
Fremont, CA 94555   510-713-7988
      Fax: 510-745-7988 flyovercorp@hotmail.com
Importer and exporter of tomato sauce, sausage casings, etc
President: Jianmin Yuan
CEO: Lili Lu
VP: Lucy Gao
Number Employees: 5-9
Parent Co: Keda Corporation
Regions Exported to: Asia
Percentage of Business in Exporting: 50
Regions Imported from: Asia
Percentage of Business in Importing: 50

44257 (HQ)Fmali Herb
831 Almar Avenue
Santa Cruz, CA 95060-5899   831-423-7913
      Fax: 831-429-5173 sales@fmali.com
Manufacturer and contract packager of ginseng, hibiscus flowers, orange and lemon peels, herbal, green and black teas and chamomile; importer of ginseng, royal jelly and panax extractum; exporter of herbal teas and orange and lemonpeels
President/Co-Founder: Ben Zaricor
Executive VP/Co-Founder: Louise Veninga
Contact: Roberto Avila
ravila@goodearthteas.com
Estimated Sales: $14.0 Million
Number Employees: 50-99
Square Footage: 84000
Type of Packaging: Consumer, Food Service, Private Label, Bulk

44258 Foam Concepts Inc
44 Rivulet St
PO Box 410
Uxbridge, MA 01569-3134   508-278-7255
      Fax: 508-278-3623 sales@foamconcepts.com
                www.foamconcepts.com
Manufacturer and exporter of custom molded insulated foam shipping containers and custom packaging for perishables
Owner: Mark Villamaino
mvillamaino@filmconcepts.com
VP Sales: Philip Michaelson
mvillamaino@filmconcepts.com
Estimated Sales: $ 5 – 10 Million
Number Employees: 20-49
Square Footage: 160000
Regions Exported to: Canada
Percentage of Business in Exporting: 5

44259 Foam Packaging Inc
35 Stennis Rd
Vicksburg, MS 39180-9175   601-638-4871
      Fax: 601-636-2655   800-962-2655
                info@foampackaging.com
                www.foam-packaging.com
Manufacturer and exporter of food service trays and insulated food containers for eggs, poultry and produce
President: Ray B English
renglish@vicksburg.com
Estimated Sales: $1-2.5 Million
Number Employees: 1-4
Regions Exported to: Central America

44260 Foell Packing Company
PO Box 4595
Naperville, IL 60567-4595   919-776-0592
      Fax: 919-774-1627 www.foellpacking.com
Manufacturer and exporter of canned meats including tripe, Vienna sausage and pork brains; also, contract packaging available
President: D Johnson
Vice President: T O'Shea
Estimated Sales: $5-10 Million
Number Employees: 20-49
Square Footage: 108000
Type of Packaging: Consumer, Private Label
Brands Exported: Beverly; Rose
Regions Exported to: Central America
Percentage of Business in Exporting: 2

44261 (HQ)Fogel Jordon CommercialRefrigeration Company
2501 Grant Avenue
Philadelphia, PA 19114-2307   215-535-8300
      Fax: 215-289-1597   800-523-0171
Manufacturer and exporter of refrigerators, walk-in cabinets, refrigerated display cases, beverage coolers, cooling rooms, etc
Secretary/Treasurer: Gene Sterner
Sales Manager: Howard Smith
Estimated Sales: $20-50 Million
Number Employees: 50-99
Square Footage: 200000
Type of Packaging: Consumer, Bulk

44262 Fogg Filler Co
3455 John F Donnelly Dr
Holland, MI 49424-9207   616-786-3644
      Fax: 616-786-0350 info@foggfiller.com
Manufacturer and exporter of packaging machinery including bottle fillers and cappers, and rinsers for flowable liquid, and noncarbonated products
President: Mike Fogg
Vice President: Al Nienhuis
Marketing Director: Susan Lamar
Sales Director: Ben Fogg
Plant Manager: Randy Dewaard
Estimated Sales: $10-20 Million
Number Employees: 100-249
Square Footage: 80000
Type of Packaging: Consumer, Food Service, Private Label, Bulk
Regions Exported to: Worldwide
Percentage of Business in Exporting: 50

44263 Fogo Island Cooperative Society
P.O. Box 70
Seldom Fogo Island, NL A0G 3Z0
Canada   709-627-3452
      Fax: 709-627-3495 fogoislandcoop@nf.aibn.com
                www.fogoislandcoop.com
Manufacturer and exporter of live and frozen crabs
President: Roy Freake
General Manager: Keith Watts
Estimated Sales: $1,400,000
Number Employees: 10
Type of Packaging: Consumer, Food Service, Bulk
Regions Exported to: US, Japan

44264 (HQ)Fold-Pak Corporation
Van Buren Street
Newark, NY 14513   315-331-3159
      Fax: 315-331-0093
Manufacturer and exporter of folding ice cream and carry out food cartons
President/CEO: Karl De May
Senior VP Sales/Marketing: Robert Mullally
VP Sales: Max Richter
Estimated Sales: $50-100 Million
Number Employees: 100-249
Type of Packaging: Consumer, Private Label
Other Locations:
  Fold-Pak Corp.
  Hazleton, PAFold-Pak Corp.
Regions Exported to: Central America, South America, Europe
Percentage of Business in Exporting: 1

44265 Fold-Pak LLC
33 Powell Dr
Hazleton, PA 18201-7360   570-454-0433
      Fax: 570-454-0456   800-486-0490
                www.fold-pak.com
Wire handled square paper food containers, round cup style closeable food and soup containers, square closeable paper food containers (microwaveable, carry out and storage capable)

Importers & Exporters / A-Z

Manager: Charlie Mattson
Director of Operations: Wes Gentles
Sales Director: Jim Keitges
Corporate Credit Manager: William Moon
Plant Manager: Lee King
Number Employees: 5000-9999
Number of Brands: 16
Number of Products: 66
Square Footage: 416000
Parent Co: Rock-Tenn Company
Type of Packaging: Consumer, Food Service, Private Label

44266 Fold-Pak South
3961 Cusseta Rd
Columbus, GA 31903-2045   706-689-2924
Fax: 706-689-2308
Manufacturer and exporter of food trays, soup containers and wire-handled food pails including Oriental and microwaveable; available with or without pagoda design
Quality Control: Coral Vessel
Contact: April Butler
aprilb@fold-pak.com
Plant Manager: Carl Vessell
Estimated Sales: $ 10 - 20 Million
Number Employees: 20-49
Type of Packaging: Food Service
Regions Exported to: South America, Europe, Asia
Percentage of Business in Exporting: 3

44267 Folding Guard Co
5858 W 73rd St
Chicago, IL 60638-6216   708-924-1359
Fax: 312-829-3278   800-622-2214
Manufacturer and exporter of partitions, gates and lockers
Manager: J Lipa
jlipa@foldingguard.com
Operations Manager: Keith Stadwick
Estimated Sales: $10-20 Million
Number Employees: 50-99
Type of Packaging: Bulk
Regions Exported to: Worldwide
Percentage of Business in Exporting: 20

44268 Foley Sign Co
572 Mercer St
Seattle, WA 98109-4618   206-324-3040
Fax: 206-328-4953   www.foleysign.com
Manufacturer and exporter of signs
Owner: Mark Metcalf
mark@foleysign.com
Estimated Sales: $ 1-2.5 Million
Number Employees: 10-19
Regions Exported to: Worldwide

44269 Foley-Belsaw Institute
1173 Benson St
River Falls, WI 54022-1594   715-426-2275
Fax: 715-426-2198   800-821-3452
www.foley-belsaw.com
Wholesaler/distributor and exporter of sharpening equipment, carbide saws, knives, scissors, shears, bandsaws, etc.; also, hog splitting, carcass and bandsaw machinery
Partner: Ron Bearl
rbearl@foley-belsaw.com
Number Employees: 20-49
Brands Exported: Foley-Belsaw; Tru-Hone
Regions Exported to: Central America, South America, Europe, Middle East, Canada, South Africa
Percentage of Business in Exporting: 3

44270 (HQ)Folgers Coffee Co
1 Strawberry Ln
Orrville, OH 44667-0208
800-937-9745
www.folgerscoffee.com
Roasted, ground, regular and decaffeinated coffee. Also, Folgers is the licensed manufacturer and distributor of Dunkin' Donuts retail coffee brand.
Chief Executive Officer: Richard Smucker
SVP/Chief Financial Officer: Mark Belgya
Chief Operating Officer: Vincent Byrd
VP/Controller: John Denman
VP/General Counsel: Jeannette Knudsen
SVP/Corporate Communications: Christopher Resweber
Logistics Leader/Operations Manager: Shane Boddie
Number Employees: 100-249
Parent Co: J.M Smucker Company

Type of Packaging: Consumer
Regions Exported to: Central America, Canada

44271 Folklore Foods
2011 Hwy 12 & 83
PO Box 104
Selby, SD 57472   605-649-1144
Fax: 509-865-7363   www.folklorefoods.com
Manufacturer and exporter of espresso syrups and granita concentrate
President/CEO: Daniel Hanson
VP: Chris Hanson
Estimated Sales: $690,000
Number Employees: 5
Square Footage: 22000
Type of Packaging: Consumer, Food Service, Private Label
Brands Exported: Folklore Gourmet Syrups
Regions Exported to: Central America, South America, Europe, Asia
Percentage of Business in Exporting: 10

44272 Follett Corp
801 Church Ln
Easton, PA 18040-6637   610-252-7301
Fax: 610-250-0696   800-523-9361
www.follettice.com
Manufacturer and exporter of high quality, innovative ice storage bins, ice storage and transport systems, ice and water dispensers, ice and beverage dispensers, and Chewblet® ice nugget ice machines
President/CEO: Steven Follett
fsteven@follettice.com
CFO: Thomas Rohrbach
Executive VP: Robert Bryson
Marketing Director: Lois Schneck
VP Sales: Ed Barr
Manager, Marketing Services: Robin Porter
VP Operations: David Tumbusch
Manager, Materials: Jeff Craig
Number Employees: 100-249
Type of Packaging: Food Service
Regions Exported to: Central America, South America, Europe, Asia, Middle East, Worldwide
Percentage of Business in Exporting: 5

44273 Fona International
1900 Averill Rd
Geneva, IL 60134   630-578-8600
Fax: 630-578-8601   www.fona.com
Flavoring extracts and syrups.
Founder, Chairman & CEO: Joe Slawek
jslawek@fona.com
VP, Accounting & Finance: Chad Hall
EVP: TJ Widuch
EVP: Manon Daoust
COO: Jeremy Thompson
Estimated Sales: $100-500 Million
Number Employees: 100-249

44274 Fonseca Coffee
301 E Durham Street
Philadelphia, PA 19119-1219   215-455-7825
Fax: 215-248-0913
Roasted coffee
Director: Karl Ludwig Papgendick
Estimated Sales: $300,000-500,000
Number Employees: 1-4

44275 Fonterra Co-operative Group Limited
8700 W Bryn Mawr Ave
Chicago, IL 60631
888-869-6455
FUSA@fonterra.com   www.fonterra.com
Dairy exporter based in New Zealand.
CEO: Miles Hurrell
CFO: Marc Rivers
CEO, Americas: Kelvin Wickham
COO: Fraser Whineray
Year Founded: 2001
Estimated Sales: $19.2 Billion
Number Employees: 21,400
Type of Packaging: Consumer, Food Service
Brands Exported: Dairy ingredients, specialty ingredients and consumer products.
Regions Exported to: 140 countries worldwide.
Percentage of Business in Exporting: 95

44276 Food & Agrosystems
1289 Mandarin Drive
Sunnyvale, CA 94087-2028   408-245-8450
Fax: 408-748-1826   www.foodagrosys.com

Consultant specializing in process engineering, product/process development, plant/process layout, equipment design, feasibility analysis, production problem-solving, management assistance, etc
President: Thomas Parks
VP Marketing: Robert Marquardt
Estimated Sales: $1-2.5 Million
Number Employees: 10
Regions Exported to: Asia
Percentage of Business in Exporting: 45

44277 Food Equipment BrokerageInc
PO Box 6541
Key West, FL 33041
800-968-8881
febinc@mo.net
We do turn key c-stores across the United States and Canada. We also export to Asia
CEO: Michael Hesse
Marketing: J R Kim
Sales: Dave Schuller
Number Employees: 110
Number of Brands: 400
Type of Packaging: Food Service, Private Label

44278 Food Equipment Manufacturing Company
22201 Aurora Rd
Bedford Heights, OH 44146   216-672-5859
Fax: 216-663-9337   info@femc.com
www.femc.com
Manufacturer and exporter of packaging machinery including fillers, de-stackers, sealers and slicers
President: Robert Sauer
rls@femc.com
CFO: Obert Sauer
VP: Joseph Lukes
Sales Manager: Daniel Auvil
Estimated Sales: $5-10 Million
Number Employees: 20-49
Square Footage: 120000
Regions Exported to: Europe, Canada, Mexico

44279 Food Instrument Corp
115 Academy Ave
Federalsburg, MD 21632-1202   410-754-8606
Fax: 410-754-8796   800-542-5688
kickout@verizon.net
www.foodinstrumentcorporation.com
Manufacturer, wholesaler/distributor and exporter of microprocessor based quality control instrumentation including closure seal testers, rejectors, data analyzers, can orienters and diverters
President: Richard V Kudlich
Sales Director: James Boehm
Estimated Sales: $1-5 Million
Number Employees: 1-4
Number of Brands: 1
Number of Products: 6
Square Footage: 40000
Brands Exported: FIC;
Regions Exported to: Central America, South America, Europe, Middle East
Percentage of Business in Exporting: 40

44280 Food Ireland, Inc.
230 East 3rd Street
New York, NY 10553   914-699-5000
Fax: 914-665-4083   wholesale@foodireland.com
www.foodirelandwholesale.com
Importer and wholesaler of baked goods, beverages, candy, canned vegetables, cereal, cookies, desserts, instant meals, jams, salads, sauces, seasonings and more.
Owner: Patrick Coleman
Estimated Sales: $1.1 Million
Number Employees: 6
Square Footage: 40000
Regions Imported from: Europe

44281 Food Machinery Sales
328 Commerce Blvd # 8
Bogart, GA 30622-2200   706-549-2207
Fax: 706-548-1724   fmssales@fmsathens.com
www.fmsathens.com
Manufacturer and exporter of product handling and packaging machinery for the biscuit and cracker industries
Manager: Eric Gunderson
Estimated Sales: $10-20 Million
Number Employees: 20-49
Regions Exported to: Worldwide
Percentage of Business in Exporting: 10

Importers & Exporters / A-Z

44282 Food Masters
1331 Monroe St
Jefferson City, MO 65101   573-635-4358
         Fax: 573-635-4604 800-635-4711
leonardm@bnpmedia.com www.foodmaster.com
Owner: James Foster
Estimated Sales: $ 3 - 5 Million
Number Employees: 1-4

44283 (HQ)Food Pak Corp
2300 Palm Ave
San Mateo, CA 94403-1817   650-341-6559
                      Fax: 650-341-2110
Chili seasonings, board and food coatings; manufacturer and exporter of custom packaging products including flexible X-ray film, insulated and sandwich bags, containers, folding cartons, shopping bags, flexible packaging bags, paper &foil bags
CEO: Steve Kanaga
Estimated Sales: Less Than $500,000
Number Employees: 1-4
Square Footage: 14000
Type of Packaging: Food Service, Private Label, Bulk
Regions Exported to: Europe, Pacific Rim, Eastern Europe

44284 Food Processing Equipment Co
13623 Pumice St
Santa Fe Springs, CA 90670-5105   562-802-3727
         Fax: 562-802-8621 salesark@fpec.com
                      www.fpec.com
Manufacturer and exporter of food processing and material handling equipment including vacuum tumblers, blenders and mixers, chilled massage blenders, conveyors, dumpers, screw conveyors, cart lifts, screw loaders, vacuum hoppers, openblenders and mixers, etc
Owner: Alan Davison
Sales Manager: Larry Butler
Estimated Sales: $ 5 - 10 Million
Number Employees: 1-4
Square Footage: 72000
Regions Exported to: Worldwide

44285 Food Resources International
250 Rayette Rd.
Units 13 & 14
Concord, ON L4K 2G6
Canada   905-482-8967
         Fax: 905-482-8968 ifr@rogers.com
Manufacturer and exporter of food processing equipment including dairy machinery, membrane systems and spray dryers; also, reconditioned equipment available; importer of casein and whey and milk protein concentrates
President: Jon Chesnut
VP: Karen Chesnut
Number Employees: 10-19
Brands Exported: Food Resources International
Regions Exported to: Worldwide
Percentage of Business in Exporting: 80
Regions Imported from: Europe, Asia
Percentage of Business in Importing: 10

44286 Food Source Company
1335 Fewster Drive
Mississauga, ON L4W 1A2
Canada   905-625-8404
                      Fax: 905-238-9160
Manufacturer, exporter and importer of salad dressings, sauces and fat-free mayonnaise
President: Ralph Murray
Estimated Sales: $2,000,000
Number Employees: 18
Square Footage: 40000
Type of Packaging: Consumer, Food Service, Private Label
Regions Exported to: Europe, Middle East
Percentage of Business in Exporting: 5
Regions Imported from: USA
Percentage of Business in Importing: 5

44287 Food Technology Corporation
45921 Maries Rd
Suite 120
Sterling, VA 20166-9278   703-444-1870
         Fax: 703-444-9860 info@foodtechcorp.com
                      www.foodtechcorp.com
Manufacturer and exporter of food texture testing systems and measurement equipment including texture profile analysis, pea tenderometers, peak force measurement systems, and kramer shear press
President: Shirl Lakeway
srkim@mcik.co.kr
Estimated Sales: $3 Million
Number Employees: 5
Square Footage: 6000
Regions Exported to: Central America, South America, Europe, Asia, Middle East

44288 Food Tools
315 Laguna St
Santa Barbara, CA 93101-1716   805-962-8383
         Fax: 805-966-3614 877-836-6386
                      www.foodtools.com
Manufacturer and exporter of de-panners, cake slabbers, crumb spreaders and ultrasonic slicers and mechanical slicers
Owner: Marty Grano
martyg@foodtools.com
Vice President: Mike Christenson
Vice President: Doug Petrovich
VP of Engineering: Matt Browne
VP of Production: Gary Grand
Estimated Sales: $ 5 - 10 Million
Number Employees: 20-49
Square Footage: 78000
Brands Exported: FoodTools
Regions Exported to: South America, Europe
Percentage of Business in Exporting: 25

44289 Food Warming Equipment Co
338 Memorial Dr # 300
Crystal Lake, IL 60014-6262   815-444-6394
         Fax: 815-459-7989 800-222-4393
                      www.fwe.com
Manufacturer and exporter of stainless steel heated and refrigerated utility carts and mobile cabinets
President: Chuck Deck
c-deck@fweco.net
CEO: Deron Lichte
CFO: Chris Huffman
VP Marketing/Sales: Curt Benson
Estimated Sales: $ 5 - 10 Million
Number Employees: 50-99
Square Footage: 280000
Regions Exported to: Worldwide
Percentage of Business in Exporting: 24

44290 Food-Trak
15900 N 78th St # 201
Scottsdale, AZ 85260-1215   480-951-8011
         Fax: 480-951-2807 ftsales@foodtrak.com
                      www.foodtrak.com
Contact: Jeanine Bennett
jeanineb@foodtrak.com

44291 FoodMatch, Inc.
575 Eighth Ave
23rd Fl
New York, NY 10018   212-244-5050
         Fax: 212-334-5042 800-350-3411
         info@foodmatch.com www.foodmatch.com
Mediterranean specialty foods
President: Phil Meldrum
Quality Control: Beth Greenburg
Marketing Director: Aaron Conrow
Sales Director: Kevin O'Conor
Contact: Emma Archbold
emma.archbold@foodmatch.com
Operations Manager: Patti Kennedy
Estimated Sales: $ 5 - 10 Million
Number Employees: 20-49
Type of Packaging: Consumer, Food Service, Private Label, Bulk
Brands Imported: Divina; LaMedina; Cannone; Barnier; Dalmatia
Regions Imported from: Europe, Greece, France, Italy, Spain

44292 FoodShowcase.Com
1925 N Lynn Street
Arlington, VA 22209-1745   703-524-9200
         Fax: 703-524-9203 bizdev@foodshowcase.com

44293 Foodcomm International
4260 El Camino Real
Palo Alto, CA 94306-4404   650-813-1300
                      Fax: 650-813-1500
President: Greg Bourke
gregb@foodcomm.com
Number Employees: 20-49

44294 (HQ)Foodpro International
P.O.Box 1119
Stockton, CA 95202   209-943-8400
         Fax: 408-227-4908 888-687-5797
         bwashburn@foodpro.net www.foodpro.net
Consultant provides engineering services including studies, plans and specifications development, construction and equipment installation management; exporter of fruit fly extermination systems
President: M W Washburn
CEO: M Wm Washburn
CFO: Lou Kong
Research & Development: Olga Osipova
Marketing Director: Richard Jennings
Branch Manager: Alex Tarasov
Estimated Sales: $ 1 - 3 Million
Number Employees: 12

44295 Foodscience Corp
20 New England Dr
PO Box 1
Essex Junction, VT 05452-2896   802-878-5508
         Fax: 802-878-0549 800-874-9444
         international@foodsciencecorp.com
                      www.foodsciencecorp.com
Manufacturer and exporter of vitamin supplements, joint and immune support supplements and specialty nutritional formulas
President: Dom Orlandi
CEO: Dale Metz
Financial Executive: Tricia Wunsch
Director of Strategic Planning: Mary Helrich
VP Marketing: Mark Ducharme
Operations: Sarah Oliveira
Estimated Sales: $300,000-500,000
Number Employees: 100-249
Parent Co: FoodScience Corporation
Brands Exported: FoodScience
Regions Exported to: Central America, South America, Europe, Asia, Middle East, New Zealand
Percentage of Business in Exporting: 25

44296 Foodservice Database Co
5724 W Diversey Ave # 9
Chicago, IL 60639-1203   773-745-9400
         Fax: 773-745-7432 www.fsdbco.com
Owner: Raymond Mitchell
Estimated Sales: $ 3 - 5 Million
Number Employees: 5-9

44297 Foodworks International
641 Cowpath Road
Suite 204
Lansdale, PA 19446   609-688-8500
         Fax: 732-783-0404 a.francois@foodworksintl.com
                      www.foodworksintl.com
Imported French food specialties, cheeses and dry groceries
President: Alain Francois
Estimated Sales: Under $500,000
Number Employees: 1-4
Type of Packaging: Food Service, Private Label
Brands Imported: Bourdin French Goat Cheeses and other different brands.
Regions Imported from: Europe

44298 Fool Proof Gourmet Products
1813 Parkwood Dr.
Grapevine, TX 76051   817-329-1839
                      Fax: 817-329-1819
Manufacturer and exporter of gourmet seasonings, spices, sauces, etc
President: Mark Pierce
VP: Jeff Covington
Estimated Sales: $1-3,000,000
Number Employees: 5-9
Square Footage: 20000
Parent Co: Coulton Associates
Type of Packaging: Consumer, Food Service

44299 Footner & Co Inc
6610 Tributary St # 300
PO Box 9973
Baltimore, MD 21224-6514   410-631-7711
         Fax: 410-631-7716 info@footner.com
                      www.footner.com
Transportation broker of international freight forwarding
Owner: Roberto Gutierrez
roberto@footner.com
Manager: John Ryan
Number Employees: 10-19

Importers & Exporters / A-Z

44300 Foppiano Vineyards
12707 Old Redwood Hwy
PO Box 606
Healdsburg, CA 95448-9241   707-433-7272
Fax: 707-433-0565 info@foppiano.com
www.foppiano.com
Manufacturer and exporter of wines
President: Louis Foppiano
louis@foppiano.com
Winemaker: Bill Regan
Estimated Sales: $ 10 - 20 Million
Number Employees: 20-49
Type of Packaging: Consumer
Brands Exported: Foppiano Vineyards
Regions Exported to: South America, Europe, Asia, Canada, UK, Denmark, Holland, Germany, Belgium, Bahamas, Bermuda

44301 Forbes Chocolate BP
800 Ken Mar Industrial Pkwy
Broadview Hts, OH 44147   440-838-4400
Fax: 440-838-4438 info@forbeschocolate.com
www.forbeschocolate.com
Manufacturer and exporter of cocoa and flavor powders for dairies. Chocolate, mocha, strawberry, vanilla, orange cream, root beer, banana, mango and others
Owner: Keith Geringer
kgeringer@forbeschocolate.com
VP: Douglas Geringer
Quality Control: Ellon Waters
Director of Marketing: Rick Stunek
Sales: Mike Richter
Estimated Sales: $1.4 Million
Number Employees: 10-19
Square Footage: 17000
Type of Packaging: Bulk

44302 Forbes Industries
1933 E Locust St
Ontario, CA 91761-7608   909-923-4549
Fax: 909-923-1969 sales@forbesindustries.com
www.forbesindustries.com
Manufacturer and exporter of banquet cabinets and carts, tables, sign stands, boards, easels, bins, carts, menus, etc.; also, bars including salad, soup and portable.
President: Tim Sweetland
tsweetland@forbesindustries.com
Estimated Sales: $50-100 Million
Number Employees: 100-249
Brands Exported: Forbes; Hargoff
Regions Exported to: Central America, South America, Europe, Asia, Middle East
Percentage of Business in Exporting: 20

44303 Ford Gum & Mach Co Inc
18 Newton Ave
Akron, NY 14001-1099   716-542-4561
Fax: 716-542-4610 fordgum@fordgum.com
www.fordgum.com
Manufacturer and distributor of gum balls and gum ball machines.
President: Lindsey Barnick
lbarnick@harrisbeach.com
Sr. Vice President: Steve Greene
Year Founded: 1913
Number Employees: 5-9
Type of Packaging: Consumer, Food Service, Private Label, Bulk
Brands Exported: Ford Extreme
Regions Exported to: Europe, Asia, Canada
Percentage of Business in Exporting: 9
Brands Imported: Carousel
Regions Imported from: Asia

44304 Foremost Machine Builders Inc
23 Spielman Rd
Fairfield, NJ 07004-3488   973-227-0700
Fax: 973-227-7307 sales@foremostmachine.com
Manufacturer and exporter of plastic scrap recovery and bulk material handling systems
President: Marlene Heydenreich
mheydenreich@foremostmachine.com
VP/General Manager: Clifford Weinpel
Assistant Sales Manager: Drew Schmid
Estimated Sales: $ 10 - 20 Million
Number Employees: 50-99
Square Footage: 110000
Regions Exported to: Central America, South America, Europe, Middle East
Percentage of Business in Exporting: 10

44305 Forest Glen Winery
PO Box 416
Sonoma, CA 95476-0416   707-224-2393
Fax: 707-224-6503

44306 Forest Manufacturing Co
1665 Enterprise Pkwy
Twinsburg, OH 44087-2284   330-425-3805
Fax: 330-425-9604
Manufacturer/exporter of flags, pennants, banners, pressure-sensitive product markings and decals
President: Forest Bookman
CFO: Bob Briggs
Sales Manager: Dick Dragonnette
General Manager: John Hammons
Estimated Sales: $ 20 - 30 Million
Number Employees: 50-99
Square Footage: 135000

44307 Forever Cheese
3636 33rd St
Suite 307
Long Island City, NY 11106-2329   718-777-0772
Fax: 718-361-6999 info@forevercheese.com
www.forevercheese.com
Cheeses
Owner: Pierluigi Sini
info@forevercheese.com
Number Employees: 10-19

44308 (HQ)Forever Foods
325 E Washington Street
137
Sequim, WA 98382-3488   360-582-3822
Fax: 360-681-0186 888-407-6672
Wholesaler/distributor and exporter of freeze-dried and dehydrated foods
President: Steve Sparkowich
VP: Crystal Sparkowich
Sales Manager: Debra Poe
Number Employees: 1-4
Regions Exported to: Europe, Asia, Australia
Percentage of Business in Exporting: 4

44309 Formflex
70 N Main St
Bloomingdale, IN 47832   765-498-8900
Fax: 765-498-5200 800-255-7659
de@formflexsales.com
www.formflexproducts.com
Manufacturer and exporter of polyolefin sheets, signs, and packaging
CEO: Martha Alexander
kwformflex@bloomingdaletel.com
CEO: Brent Thompson
Marketing Director: David Elliott
Sales Director: Brent Thompson
Public Relations: Janice Stewart
Estimated Sales: $10-20 Million
Number Employees: 250-499
Square Footage: 60000
Parent Co: Futurex Industries
Type of Packaging: Bulk
Brands Exported: Formflex
Regions Exported to: Central America, Canada
Percentage of Business in Exporting: 2

44310 Formost Packaging Machines
19211 144th Ave NE
Woodinville, WA 98072   425-483-9090
Fax: 425-486-5656 sales@formostfuji.com
Manufacturer and exporter of high-speed automated horizontal and vertical bagging and wrapping machines including formers/fillers/sealers
President: Norm Formo
normf@formostpkg.com
CFO: Dan Semanskee
Executive VP: Norm Formo
VP Sales: Dennis Gunnell
Plant Manager: Al Shelton
Purchasing Manager: Michelle Richards
Number Employees: 50-99
Type of Packaging: Consumer, Food Service, Private Label, Bulk

44311 Formula Espresso
65 Commerce Street
Brooklyn, NY 11231-1642   718-834-8724
Fax: 718-834-9022 www.espressosystems.com
Manufacturer and exporter of commercial stainless steel espresso equipment
Owner: George Ilardo
Estimated Sales: $ 1-2.5 Million
Number Employees: 5-9

Type of Packaging: Food Service
Regions Exported to: Worldwide
Percentage of Business in Exporting: 60

44312 Forrest Engraving Company
92 1st St
New Rochelle, NY 10801-6121   914-632-9892
Fax: 914-632-7416
Manufacturer and exporter of plastic and metal nameplates and signs
President: Thomas Giordano
tom@forrestpermasigns.com
Manager: Tom Giordano
Estimated Sales: $500,000-$1 Million
Number Employees: 5 to 9

44313 Forte Technology
58 Norfolk Ave.
Suite 4
South Easton, MA 02375-1055   508-297-2363
Fax: 508-297-2314 info@forte-tec.com
www.forte-tec.com
Manufacturer and exporter of electronic moisture measurement systems
President: Patricia White
Contact: Tom Gorman
t.gorman@forte-tec.com
Plant Manager: Mark Donohowski
Estimated Sales: $2.5-5 Million
Number Employees: 5-9
Square Footage: 28000
Regions Exported to: Central America, South America, Europe, Asia
Percentage of Business in Exporting: 70

44314 Fortune Plastics, Inc
P.O Box 637
Williams Ln.
Old Saybrook, CT 06475
Fax: 860-388-9930   800-243-0306
Manufacturer and exporter of plastic bags
Contact: Jay Adamski
jadamski@fortuneplastics.com
Estimated Sales: $ 5 - 10 Million
Number Employees: 20-49
Parent Co: Hilex Poly Co. LLC
Regions Exported to: Worldwide

44315 Fortune Products Inc
2010 Windy Ter # A
Cedar Park, TX 78613-4559   512-249-0334
Fax: 830-693-6394 contact@accusharp.com
www.accusharp.com
Manufacturer and exporter of manually operated knife and scissor sharpeners
President: Jay Cavanaugh
info@accusharp.com
VP: Dale Fortenberry Jr
Operations: Randy Fortenberry
Estimated Sales: Less Than $500,000
Number Employees: 5-9
Square Footage: 13000
Type of Packaging: Consumer, Food Service, Private Label, Bulk
Regions Exported to: South America, Europe, Asia, Middle East

44316 Fortune Seas
42 Rogers Street
Gloucester, MA 01930-5000   978-281-6666
Fax: 978-281-8519
Seafood
President/CEO: Donald Short
VP Sales: Charles Bencal

44317 Forum Lighting
900 Old Freeport Rd
Pittsburgh, PA 15238-3130   412-781-5970
Fax: 412-244-9032 www.forumlighting.com
Manufacturer and exporter of fluorescent and HID linear lighting; custom designs available
Special Projects: Paula Garret
Controller: Julie McElhattan
Senior VP: Jonathan Garret
Special Projects: Paula Garret
Vice President of Sales: Steve Seligman
Plant Manager: Bill Dapper
Estimated Sales: $20-50 Million
Number Employees: 20-49
Square Footage: 70000
Regions Exported to: Central America, South America, Middle East
Percentage of Business in Exporting: 10

Importers & Exporters / A-Z

44318 Foss Nirsystems
12101 Tech Rd
Silver Spring, MD 20904-1915   301-755-5200
                    Fax: 301-236-0134
Manufacturer and exporter of rapid quality control analysis equipment including moisture, fat, protein and sugar for laboratory and in-plant application using near infrared technology
IT Executive: Dan Cipriaso
dcipriaso@foss.dk
IT Executive: Dan Cipriaso
dcipriaso@foss.dk
Estimated Sales: $ 20 Million
Number Employees: 1-4
Brands Exported: NirSystems
Regions Exported to: Central America, South America, Europe, Asia, Middle East

44319 Foster Family Farm
90 Foster St
South Windsor, CT 06074-3873   860-648-9366
                    www.fosterfarms.com
Manufacturer and exporter of pickled asparagus and beans
Principal: Chris Foster
Co-Owner/Member: Teresa Robertson
Partner: Alexandra Palmer
alexandrapalmer@fosterfarm.com
Estimated Sales: $10-20 Million
Number Employees: 10-19
Regions Exported to: Canada
Percentage of Business in Exporting: 45

44320 Foster Farms Inc.
1000 Davis St.
PO Box 306
Livingston, CA 95334
                    800-255-7227
                    www.fosterfarms.com
Poultry producer.
CEO: Dan Huber
Estimated Sales: Over $1 Billion
Number Employees: 10000+
Number of Brands: 6
Type of Packaging: Consumer, Food Service, Private Label, Bulk
Brands Exported: Sunland
Regions Exported to: Central America, Asia, Canada, Mexico
Percentage of Business in Exporting: 5

44321 Foster Fine Foods, LLC
3410 Alexander Road Ne
Suite 653
Atlanta, GA 30326   404-405-6089
Fax: 404-963-5037 dfoster@fosterfinefoods.com
Olive oil, jams.
Marketing: Dawn Foster
Contact: Dawn Foster
dawnmfoster@gmail.com

44322 Foster Miller Inc
350 2nd Ave
Waltham, MA 02451-1196   781-684-4000
Fax: 781-290-0693 www.qinetiq-na.com
Custom food processing and vending equipment; design services available engineering and R&D services from 200+ engineers and scienctists
President: Michael G. Stolarik
CEO: Duane P. Andrews
Executive VP: David Shrum
david.shrum@qinetiq-na.com
Marketing: Peter Debakker
Number Employees: 20-49
Square Footage: 380000

44323 Foster Refrigerator Corporation
PO Box 718
Kinderhook, NY 12106   518-828-3311
   Fax: 518-828-3315 888-828-3311
fosterusa@yahoo.com www.foster-us.com
Manufacturer and exporter of commercial refrigerators, freezers, coolers and ovens
Owner: James Dinardi
Estimated Sales: $ 1 - 5 Million
Number Employees: 1-4
Square Footage: 200000
Type of Packaging: Food Service
Brands Exported: Foster's
Regions Exported to: Middle East
Percentage of Business in Exporting: 40

44324 (HQ)Fountain Valley Foods
2175 N Academy Circle # 201
PO Box 9882
Colorado Springs, CO 80932   719-573-6012
   Fax: 719-573-5192 www.fountainvalleyfoods.com
Salsa, ketchup, bean dip and specialty chili products; Importer/Distributor of cheese sauce, jalapeno peppers, banana peppers, chipotle peppers, green chile.
President: James Loyacono
Contact: Ginger Steineke
ginger@fountainvalleyfoods.com
Estimated Sales: $4.9 Million
Number Employees: 4
Square Footage: 20000
Type of Packaging: Consumer, Food Service, Private Label, Bulk
Other Locations:
   Den-Mar Products
   Trinidad, CODen-Mar Products
Brands Exported: Nacho Grande; Queso Del Sol; Lonetree; Farys
Brands Imported: Nacho Grande; La Comadre

44325 Fountainhead
1726 Woodhaven Drive
Bensalem, PA 19020-7108   215-245-7300
   Fax: 215-245-7390 800-326-8998
info@towelettes.com www.towelettes.com
Manufacturer and exporter of stainless steel beverage dispensers, fountains, hoods and fans
General Manager: Ralph Kearney
Number Employees: 50-99
Parent Co: Floaire
Regions Exported to: Worldwide
Percentage of Business in Exporting: 3

44326 Fourinox Inc
1015 Centennial St
Green Bay, WI 54304-5562   920-336-0621
   Fax: 920-336-0089 www.fourcorp.com
Manufacturer and exporter of ASME certified process vessels
President: Ben Meeuwsen
ben.meeuwsen@fourinox.com
Marketing/Sales: John Ruppel
Estimated Sales: $ 10-20 Million
Number Employees: 20-49
Square Footage: 110000

44327 Fowler Farms
10273 Lummisville Rd
Wolcott, NY 14590   315-594-8068
   Fax: 315-594-8060 800-836-9537
                    www.fowlerfarms.com
Apples.
Director, Business Development: Mark Sharp
VP, Sales & Marketing: Dave Williams
Sales Assitant: Jennifer Sutton
Year Founded: 1858
Estimated Sales: $100-500 Million
Number Employees: 250-499

44328 Fowler Products Co LLC
150 Collins Industrial Blvd
Athens, GA 30601-1516   706-549-3300
   Fax: 706-548-1278 877-549-3301
   sales@fowlerproducts.com
                    www.fowlerproducts.com
Manufacturer and exporter of bottling, capping and packaging machinery
President: Don Cotney
Vice President: Randy Uebler
ruebler@fowlerproducts.com
VP Sales: Andy Monroe
Estimated Sales: Less Than $500,000
Number Employees: 1-4
Square Footage: 150000
Brands Exported: Fowler & Fowler; Zalkin
Regions Exported to: Central America, South America, Latin America, Mexico
Percentage of Business in Exporting: 30

44329 Foxboro Company
10900 Equity Drive
Houston, TX 77041   713-329-1600
   Fax: 508-543-8764 888-369-2676
ips.csc@invensys.com www.foxboro.com
Manufacturer and exporter of microprocessor based enterprise network systems, instruments and controls
President: Mike Caliel
Industry Consultant: John Blanchard
VP: Ken Brown
Contact: Alexander Johnson
ajohnson@foxboro.com
Manager: Joe Fillion
Number Employees: 6000
Parent Co: Siebe
Brands Exported: I/A Series
Regions Exported to: Worldwide
Percentage of Business in Exporting: 65

44330 Foxon Co
235 W Park St
Providence, RI 02908-4881   401-421-2386
   Fax: 401-421-8996 800-556-6943
                    www.quicktest.com
Manufacturer and exporter of pressure sensitive, flexible and embossed/debossed foil and paper labels
President: William Ewing
wewing@foxonlabels.com
Estimated Sales: $10-20 Million
Number Employees: 20-49
Regions Exported to: Europe, Caribbean, Canada
Percentage of Business in Exporting: 10

44331 Framarx Corp
3224 Butler St
S Chicago Hts, IL 60411-5505   708-755-3530
   Fax: 708-755-3617 800-336-3936
   saus@framarx.com www.framarx.com
Manufacturer and exporter of waxed and coated papers
Vice President: Cindy Cofran
ccofran@framarx.com
Vice President: Cindy Cofran
Marketing Coordinator: Julia Saeid
Sales: Deborah M
Operations Manager: Christopher Czaszwicz
Production Manager: Jim Merrell
Estimated Sales: $ 20 - 50 Million
Number Employees: 20-49
Type of Packaging: Food Service, Private Label, Bulk
Brands Exported: Framarx Patty Paper
Regions Exported to: Central America, South America, Europe, Asia, Middle East
Percentage of Business in Exporting: 15

44332 France Delices
5065 Rue Ontario E
Montreal, QC H1V 3V2
Canada   514-259-2291
   Fax: 514-259-1788 800-663-1365
   information@francedelices.com
                    www.francedelices.com
Manufacturer and exporter of cakes including fresh, frozen and gourmet
President: Colette Durot
VP: Laurent Durot
Estimated Sales: $13million
Number Employees: 3
Square Footage: 100000
Type of Packaging: Consumer, Food Service
Regions Exported to: Asia, USA
Percentage of Business in Exporting: 5

44333 (HQ)Francis & Lusky Company
1437 Donelson Pike
Nashville, TN 37217-2957   615-242-0501
   Fax: 615-256-0862 800-251-3711
Manufacturer, importer and exporter of advertising calendars; distributor of promotional products
President: Richard Francis
VP Marketing: Eric Wittel
VP Sales: Jeff Brown
Estimated Sales: $ 20 - 50 Million
Number Employees: 20-49
Percentage of Business in Exporting: 5
Regions Imported from: Asia
Percentage of Business in Importing: 10

44334 Franciscan Estate
1178 Galleron Road at Highway 29
St. Helena, CA 94574   707-967-3830
                    www.franciscan.com
Winemaker
Director of Winemaking: Janet Myers
Type of Packaging: Consumer
Regions Exported to: Worldwide

Importers & Exporters / A-Z

44335 Franco's Cocktail Mixes
121 SW 5th Ct
Pompano Beach, FL 33060-7909   954-782-7491
Fax: 954-786-9253   800-782-4508
Francocktl@aol.com
www.francoscocktailmixes.com
Manufacturer and exporter of liquid and dry cocktail mixes; also, colored margarita salt and colored rimming sugars
Owner: Michael A Pitino
Quality Control: Guy Haret
Manager: Laura Schnell
michael@francoscocktailmixes.com
Estimated Sales: $10-24.9 Million
Number Employees: 5-9
Number of Brands: 12
Number of Products: 100+
Square Footage: 50000
Type of Packaging: Food Service, Private Label
Brands Exported: Franco's; Pat O'Brien's; Florida's Pride
Regions Exported to: Europe
Percentage of Business in Exporting: 20

44336 Frank M Hartley Inc
82 Village Dr
Mahwah, NJ 07430-2586   201-760-0020
Fax: 201-760-0252 hartleywine@aol.com
Import and domestic broker of alcoholic beverages including wine and liquor from Europe, South America and California. Selling under the brands/labels of our suppliers or customer's own brands and labels.
President: Bruce Hartley
hartleywine@aol.com
Estimated Sales: $ 5 Million
Number Employees: 1-4
Square Footage: 450
Brands Imported: Alianca (Portugese), Mertes (German), Schenck Italia (Italian), Tresh French Products

44337 Franklin Industries LLC
4013 10th Ave
Brooklyn, NY 11219-1006   718-853-0935
Fax: 718-435-9399
President: Frank Lico
Estimated Sales: $ 20 - 50 Million
Number Employees: 20-49

44338 Franklin Machine Products
PO Box 992
Marlton, NJ 08053-0992   856-983-2500
Fax: 800-255-9866   800-257-7737
sales@fmponline.com www.fmponline.com
Wholesaler/distributor of parts and accessories: serving the food service market
CEO: Carol Adams
Vice President: Michael Conte, Sr.
Estimated Sales: $ 20-50 Million
Number Employees: 100-249
Square Footage: 50000

44339 (HQ)Franklin Trading Company
666 Old Country Rd # 202
Garden City, NY 11530-2013   516-228-3131
Fax: 516-228-3136 kazemiinc@aol.com
Importer and exporter of cumin seeds, cumin seed oil, pistachio nuts, dried fruits and fruit and nut processing/packaging machinery
Partner: Glenn Franklin
Estimated Sales: $ 1 - 3 Million
Number Employees: 5-9
Square Footage: 20000
Regions Exported to: Central America, South America, Europe, Asia, Middle East
Regions Imported from: Central America, South America, Europe, Asia

44340 Franrica Systems
PO Box 30127
Stockton, CA 95213-0127   209-948-2811
Fax: 209-948-5198
Manufacturer, importer and exporter of aseptic fillers, heat exchangers, tanks, pumps, evaporators, flash coolers, tomato paste processing plants, etc
Director: Eric Curtz
Controller: Marty Menz
Contact: Jerry Hougland
jerry.hougland@fmc.com
Estimated Sales: $ 20 - 30 Million
Number Employees: 125
Square Footage: 70000
Parent Co: FMC Technologies
Brands Exported: Franrica
Regions Exported to: Worldwide
Percentage of Business in Exporting: 30
Brands Imported: FBM
Regions Imported from: Europe
Percentage of Business in Importing: 1

44341 Frazier & Son
101 Longview St
Conroe, TX 77301-4075   936-494-4040
Fax: 936-494-4045   800-365-5438
info@frazierandson.com
Manufacturer and exporter of power operated packaging machinery including fillers for frozen food; also, bucket elevators
Owner: Mark Frazier
Sales/Engineer: Robert Gennario
Manager: Nicole Baird
nicole.baird@lrsus.com
Estimated Sales: $ 2.5 - 5 Million
Number Employees: 10-19
Square Footage: 20000

44342 Frazier Nut Farms Inc
10830 Yosemite Blvd
Waterford, CA 95386-9637   209-522-1406
Fax: 209-874-9638 fraznut@aol.com
www.fraziernut.com
Manufacturer and exporter of nuts including shelled and in-shell English walnuts and shelled almonds
President: Jim Frazier
jfrazier@fraziernut.com
VP: Steve Slacks
Estimated Sales: $2.5-5 Million
Number Employees: 100-249
Type of Packaging: Bulk
Brands Exported: Frazier's Finest
Regions Exported to: South America, Europe
Percentage of Business in Exporting: 45

44343 Frazier Precision InstrCo
925 Sweeney Dr
Hagerstown, MD 21740-7128   301-790-2585
Fax: 301-790-2589 info@frazierinstrument.com
www.frazierinstrument.com
Manufacturer and exporter of test instruments and measuring equipment
President: Thomas F Scrivener
Estimated Sales: $ 1 - 2.5 Million
Number Employees: 5-9

44344 (HQ)Fred D Pfening Co
1075 W 5th Ave
Columbus, OH 43212-2691   614-294-5361
Fax: 614-294-1633 sales@pfening.com
www.pfening.com
Manufacturer and exporter of bakers' machinery including proof boxes, sifters and water metering devices; also, material handling equipment
President: Fred Pfening
ebrackman@pfening.com
VP of Sales/Marketing: Norm Meulenberg
Sales Exec: Edward Brackman
Purchasing Agent: Patrick Inskeep
Estimated Sales: $ 10 - 20 Million
Number Employees: 50-99
Square Footage: 150000
Regions Exported to: Central America, South America, Asia, Middle East
Percentage of Business in Exporting: 10

44345 Frederick Wildman & Sons LTD
307 E 53rd St # 3
New York, NY 10022-4985   212-355-0700
Fax: 212-355-4719   800-733-9463
info@frederickwildman.com
www.frederickwildman.com
Manufacturer, importer and distributor of fine wines.
President: John Sellar
CEO: Davide Mascalzoni
d.mascalzoni@frederickwildman.com
VP, Finance: James DiCicco
VP/Director, Marketing: Martin Sinkoff
VP/National Sales Manager: Bill Seawright
Assistant VP/Director, Public Relations: Odila Galer-Noel
Year Founded: 1934
Estimated Sales: $20-50 Million
Number Employees: 100-249
Number of Brands: 26
Type of Packaging: Consumer, Food Service
Regions Imported from: South America, Europe

44346 Fredrick Ramond Company
33000 Pin Oak Parkway
Avon Lake, OH 44012   440-653-5550
Fax: 440-653-5555   800-446-5539
service@hinkleylighting.com
www.fredrickramond.com
Manufacturer, importer and exporter of decorative light fixtures
President: Fredrick Glassman
National Sales Manager: Alan Dubrow
Inside Sales: David Brusius
Support Manager: Carol Romero
Estimated Sales: $10-20 Million
Number Employees: 100-249
Brands Exported: Fredrick Ramond
Regions Exported to: Central America, South America, Canada
Regions Imported from: Europe

44347 Freeda Vitamins Inc
4725 34th St # 301
Long Island City, NY 11101-2436   718-433-4337
Fax: 212-685-7297   800-777-3737
info@freedavitamins.com
www.freedavitamins.com
Manufacturer and exporter of kosher yeast-free vitamins and supplements including garlic. Our products are also gluten free, dairy free, and free of artificial colors & flavors.
President/CEO: Eliyahu Zimmerman
Estimated Sales: $2.5 Million
Number Employees: 20-49
Number of Brands: 1
Number of Products: 200
Square Footage: 9150
Type of Packaging: Consumer
Brands Exported: Freeda Vitamins
Percentage of Business in Exporting: 10
Regions Imported from: Europe, Asia, Middle East

44348 Freeland Bean & Grain Inc
1000 E Washington
PO Box 515
Freeland, MI 48623-8439   989-695-9131
Fax: 989-695-5241   800-447-9131
freeland.i@att.net www.freelandbeanandgrain.com
Manufacturer and exporter of dried beans and grains
Owner: John Hupfer
freeland.i@att.net
VP: Elenor Hupfer
Estimated Sales: $3.8 Million
Number Employees: 5-9
Type of Packaging: Bulk
Regions Exported to: Canada
Percentage of Business in Exporting: 15

44349 Freely Display
12401 Euclid Ave
Cleveland, OH 44106-4314   216-721-6056
Fax: 216-721-6081
Manufacturer and exporter of wood store fixtures and displays
Controller: Bernadette Gello
Operations Manager: Thomas Olechiw
Estimated Sales: $2.5-5 Million
Number Employees: 5-9

44350 Freeman Industries
100 Marbledale Rd
Tuckahoe, NY 10707   914-961-2100
Fax: 914-961-5793   800-666-6454
freeman@lanline.com www.freemanllc.com
Dairy vitamin concentrates and zein. Importer and exporter of dried fruits and vegetables, pectin, herbal extracts and natural colors. Processor of citrus bioflavonoids and rice bran and rice bran derivates
President/CEO: Joel G Freeman
VP: Paul Freeman
Contact: Joel Freeman
joelfreeman@freemanb2b.com
Estimated Sales: $1-3 Million
Number Employees: 10-19
Square Footage: 10000
Type of Packaging: Bulk
Regions Exported to: South America, Europe, Asia, Middle East
Regions Imported from: Central America, South America, Europe, Asia, Middle East

Importers & Exporters / A-Z

44351 Freemark Abbey Winery
3022 Saint Helena Hwy N # 5
St Helena, CA 94574-9652 707-963-9698
Fax: 707-963-7633 800-963-9698
info@freemarkabbey.com
www.freemarkabbey.com
Manufacturer and exporter of wines including cabernet sauvignon, chardonnay and johannisberg riesling
Director of Winemaking: Ted Edwards
wineinfo@freemarkabbey.com
Estimated Sales: $5-9.9 Million
Number Employees: 20-49
Type of Packaging: Food Service
Regions Exported to: Europe, Asia, Canada, Bermuda

44352 FreesTech
PO Box 2156
Sinking Spring, PA 19608 717-560-7560
Fax: 717-560-7587 info@freestech.com
www.freestech.com
Palletizers, freezing and cooling systems, conveyors and storage and retrieval machines for warehouse applications.
Contact: Richard Greener
dgreener@freestech.com
Year Founded: 1967
Estimated Sales: $500 Million-$1 Billion
Number Employees: 10
Brands Exported: Fusion Cell; Tri-Flow; Tri-Stacker; Tri-Tray
Regions Exported to: Central America, South America, Europe, Canada
Percentage of Business in Exporting: 15

44353 Freeze-Dry Foods Inc
111 West Ave # 4
Albion, NY 14411-1500 585-589-6399
Fax: 585-589-6402 info@freeze-dry.com
www.freeze-dry.com
Freeze dried ingredients specializing in meat, seafood and protein items
President: Karen Richardson
krichardson@freeze-dry.com
Business Development: Lisa Horvath
Estimated Sales: $4.5 Million
Number Employees: 20-49
Type of Packaging: Consumer

44354 Freiria & Company
Mercado Central Plaza
Po Box 364165
Puerto Nuevo, PR 920 787-792-4460
Fax: 787-783-3945 888-792-0160
Import and export broker of confectionery products, frozen foods, general merchandise, corn meal, granulated garlic, dehydrated onions, paprika, adobo powder, garlic powder, apple cider and white distilled vinegar, groceries, spicesetc
President: Enrique Freiria
CEO: F Freiria
CFO: Juan Garcia
VP: H Freiria Jr
Quality Control: Elvis Diaz
Marketing: F Freiria
Sales: Angel Rosario
Public Relations: Jose Lopez
Estimated Sales: $19.5 Millionn
Number Employees: 52
Square Footage: 120000
Parent Co: Henframar Corporation
Type of Packaging: Food Service, Private Label
Brands Exported: Bohio
Regions Exported to: Central America
Brands Imported: La Choy, Lea & Perrins, Glad

44355 (HQ)Freixenet USA Inc
967 Broadway
Sonoma, CA 95476-7403 707-996-4981
Fax: 707-996-0720 info@freixenetusa.com
www.gloriaferrer.com
Manufacturer and importer of Spanish champagnes and wines; also, processor of California wines
President: Robert Abel
robert.abel@freixenetusa.com
Number Employees: 50-99
Parent Co: Freixenet SA
Type of Packaging: Consumer
Regions Exported to: Europe
Regions Imported from: Europe, Australia

44356 Frelco
PO Box 316
Stephenville, NL A2N 2Z5
Canada 709-643-5668
Fax: 709-643-3046
Manufacturer, importer and exporter of conveyors, hoppers, tables and cabinets
Regions Exported to: Worldwide
Regions Imported from: Germany, England, Spain

44357 Frem Corporation
60 Webster Place
Worcester, MA 01603-1920 508-791-3152
Fax: 508-791-7969
Manufacturer and exporter of injection molded plastic housewares including food storage bins, crates and waste baskets
CEO: M.L. Sherman
CFO: D.A. Denovellis
Vice President: J.J. Althoff
Manager: Tim Eunice
Parent Co: Ekco Group

44358 Fremont Authentic Brands
802 N Front St
Fremont, OH 43420-1917 419-334-8995
Fax: 419-334-8120 info@fremontcompany.com
www.fremontfoodservice.com
Tomatoes, sauerkraut, salsa and barbecue sauces.
Logistics Manager: Pam Hufford
Year Founded: 1905
Estimated Sales: $28 Million
Number Employees: 250-499
Square Footage: 250000
Type of Packaging: Consumer, Food Service, Private Label

44359 French Cheese ClubC/O Solutions Export USA
9413 50th Place
College Park, MD 20740 646-216-9472
contact@frenchcheeseclub.com
www.frenchcheeseclub.com
Cheese
Marketing: Cecile Delannes
Contact: Rachel Perez
rachel@frenchcheeseclub.com

44360 French Creek Seafood
1097 Lee Road
Parksville, BC V9P 2E1
Canada 250-248-7100
Fax: 250-248-7197 mail@frenchcreek.ca
www.frenchcreek.ca
Manufacturer and exporter of fresh and frozen seafood
President: Brad McLean
President: Brad McLean
Estimated Sales: $6,000,000
Number Employees: 15
Type of Packaging: Bulk
Regions Exported to: Worldwide
Percentage of Business in Exporting: 90

44361 French Farm
916 W 23rd St
Suite B
Houston, TX 77008-1810 713-660-0577
Fax: 713-660-0477 ffinfo@frenchfarm.com
www.thefrenchfarm.com
Oils & vinegars, truffle oils, mustards & vinegars, chutneys & confits, sea salts, salts & sugars, exotic spices, provence products, honeys, jams, pestos & spreads, pastas, and sweets.
Owner: Gisele Oriot
ffinfo@frenchfarm.com
Marketing: Gisele Oriot
Number Employees: 1-4

44362 French Oil Mill Machinery Co
1035 W Greene St
P.O. Box 920
Piqua, OH 45356-1855 937-773-3420
Fax: 937-773-3424 sales@frenchoil.com
www.frenchoil.com
Manufacturer and exporter of vegetable oilseed processing equipment including cracking and flaking mills, conditioners, full, extruder and pre-presses, dewatering and drying presses, liquid-solid separation equipment and hydraulicpresses
President: Daniel French
CEO: Jason P Mcdaniel
jmcdaniel@frenchoil.com
CFO: Dennis Bratton
CEO: Jason P McDaniel
Quality Control: Jason McDaniel
Sales Director: James King
Public Relations: Eric Brockman
Estimated Sales: $ 10 - 20 Million
Number Employees: 50-99
Square Footage: 450000
Regions Exported to: Central America, South America, Europe, Asia, Middle East, Worldwide
Percentage of Business in Exporting: 50

44363 Fresh Island Fish
312 Alamaha St
Unit G
Kahului, HI 96732-2430 808-871-1111
Fax: 808-871-6818 www.freshislandfish.com
Seafood
President: Mike Lee
Owner/Founder/C.E.O: Bruce Johnson
fif@maui.net
Estimated Sales: $ 10 - 20 Million
Number Employees: 50-99

44364 Fresh Juice Delivery
269 S Beverly Dr
Suite 1072
Beverly Hills, CA 90212-3851 310-271-7373
Manufacturer and exporter of fresh and fresh-frozen juices including citrus and blended
Estimated Sales: Less Than $500,000
Number Employees: 5-9
Parent Co: Saratoga Beverage
Type of Packaging: Consumer, Food Service
Regions Exported to: Worldwide

44365 Fresh Pack Seafood
PO Box 1008
Waldoboro, ME 04572-1008 207-832-7720
Fax: 207-832-7795
Fresh seafood
President: Frank Minio
VP/General Manager: Roger Greene

44366 Fresherized Foods
300 Burlington Rd
Saginaw, TX 76179-1304 817-509-0626
Fax: 817-509-0636 jalley@fresherized.com
Salsa/dips
President: Steve Parnell
sparnell@fresherized.com
Founder/Owner: Don Bowden
VP of Operations: Jeff Morris
Vice President, Sales & Marketing: Jay Alley
Vice President, Food Service Sales: Cindy Wong
Number Employees: 20-49

44367 Freudenberg Nonwovens
2975 Pembroke Road
Hopkinsville, KY 42240 270-887-5115
Fax: 270-886-5069
HVAC@freudenberg-filter.com
www.freudenberg-filter.com
Manufacturer and importer of air and liquid filters; also, filtration media
Contact: Terezie Zapletalova
terezie.zapletalova@freudenberg-nw.com
Estimated Sales: $ 50-100 Million
Number Employees: 100-249
Regions Imported from: Europe

44368 (HQ)Friedman Bag Company
865 Manhattan Beach Boulevard
Suite 204
Manhattan Beach, CA 90266-4955 213-628-2341
Fax: 213-687-9772
Manufacturer and exporter of burlap, cotton, polyethylene, open mesh bags; wholesaler/distributor of paper bags, cartons and packaging supplies
President: Al Lanfeld
VP/Operations Manager: David Friedman
Sales/Service: Diane Dal Porto
Estimated Sales: $20-50 Million
Number Employees: 250-499
Square Footage: 400000
Regions Exported to: South America, Canada, Mexico
Percentage of Business in Exporting: 5

Importers & Exporters / A-Z

44369 Friedr Dick Corp
33 Allen Blvd
Farmingdale, NY 11735-5611   631-454-6955
Fax: 631-454-6184   800-554-3425
www.fdick.us
Manufacturer and distributor of cutlery
Sales: Morgan
Manager: Steve Kurek
s.kurek@feiedrdick.us
Operations: Scott Belovin
Number Employees: 5-9
Number of Brands: 7
Number of Products: 600
Square Footage: 10000
Type of Packaging: Consumer, Food Service, Bulk
Brands Exported: Friedr Dick
Brands Imported: Friedr Dick
Percentage of Business in Importing: 100

44370 Friedrich Metal Products
6204 Technology Dr
Browns Summit, NC 27214-9702   336-375-3067
Fax: 336-621-7901   800-772-0326
info@friedrichproducts.com
www.friedrichproducts.com
Manufacturer and exporter of smokehouses, bakery ovens, smokers, deli equipment, etc
President: Jennifer Prago
jprago@friedrichproducts.com
CFO: Bob Friedrich
Vice President: Laura Friedrich-Bargebuhr
Quality Control: Axel Dender
Estimated Sales: $ 1 - 3 Million
Number Employees: 20-49
Square Footage: 60000
Regions Exported to: Central America, Europe, Asia, Canada
Percentage of Business in Exporting: 20

44371 Friendship International
21 Merrill Drive
Rockland, ME 04841-2142   207-594-1111
Fax: 207-236-6103
Manufacturer and exporter of live sea urchins
President: Jim Wadsworth
Contact: Rino Safrizal
safrizal@friends-international.org

44372 (HQ)Friskem Infinetics
PO Box 2330
Wilmington, DE 19899   302-658-2471
Fax: 302-658-2475
Manufacturer and exporter of detectors including metal, pilferage, passive magnetometer and active field
CEO: M Schwartz
Brands Exported: Friskem; Friskem-af; Tellem
Regions Exported to: Central America, South America, Europe, Asia, Middle East, Worldwide
Percentage of Business in Exporting: 40

44373 Fristam Pumps USA LLP
2410 Parview Rd
Middleton, WI 53562-2521   608-831-5001
Fax: 608-831-8467   800-841-5001
fristam@fristampumps.com   www.fristam.com
Manufacturer and exporter of stainless steel, centrifugal and positive displacement pumps, blenders and mixers.
President: Pete Herb
CEO: Wolfgang Stamp
VP: Pete Skora
Quality Control/Operations: Duane Ehlke
Marketing Supervisor: Dan Funk
Sales Director: Larry Cook
Public Relations: Wendy Andrew
Number Employees: 100-249
Number of Products: 80

44374 Fristam Pumps USA LLP
2410 Parview Rd
Middleton, WI 53562-2521   608-831-5001
Fax: 608-831-8467   sales@fristampumps.com
www.fristam.com
Centrifugal pumps, shear pumps, powder mixers and positive displacement pumps
President: Scott Haman
shaman@fristam.com
Number Employees: 100-249
Regions Exported to: North America, Worldwide

44375 Frito-Lay Inc.
7701 Legacy Dr.
Plano, TX 75024-4099
800-352-4477
www.fritolay.com
Corn chips, potato chips, and other snack foods.
CEO, PepsiCo Foods North America: Steven Williams
Senior VP/CFO: Jamie Caulfield
Senior VP/General Counsel: Leanne Oliver
Senior VP/Foods & Global R&D: Denise Lefebvre
Senior VP/Chief Marketing Officer: Rachel Ferdinando
Senior VP, Sales: John Dean
Senior VP/Chief Customer Officer: Mike Del Pozzo
Estimated Sales: $15.79 Billion
Number Employees: 10000+
Number of Brands: 28
Parent Co: PepsiCo
Type of Packaging: Consumer, Food Service
Regions Exported to: Worldwide

44376 Frobisher Industries
6260 Rte 105
Waterborough, NB E4C 2Y4
Canada   506-362-2198
Fax: 506-362-9090
Manufacturer and exporter of hamper baskets, veneer and wooden boxes for fruits and vegetables
President: George Staples
CFO: George Lorriaine
Number Employees: 10
Square Footage: 48000
Regions Exported to: USA
Percentage of Business in Exporting: 15

44377 (HQ)Front Range Snacks Inc
6547 S Racine Cir # 1800
Centennial, CO 80111-6463   303-744-8850
Fax: 303-389-6859
Processor and exporter of ready-to-eat popcorn
Owner: Tim Bradley
tim@openroadsnacks.com
Estimated Sales: Less Than $500,000
Number Employees: 1-4
Number of Brands: 1
Number of Products: 10
Square Footage: 80000
Type of Packaging: Consumer, Food Service, Private Label, Bulk
Regions Exported to: Central America, South America, Europe, Asia, Mexico
Percentage of Business in Exporting: 90

44378 Frontier Bag
5720 E State Route 150
Kansas City, MO 64147-1003   816-765-4811
Fax: 816-765-6603   www.yellowbagpeople.com
Plastic, shrink and meat bags, polyethylene bag liners, pallet covers and sheeting; exporter of plastic bags; importer of polyethylene raw materials bager plain and printed
President: Mark Gurley
m.gurley@yellowbagpeople.com
Owner: Ron Gurley
VP Sales: Tom Hauser
VP Production: Ron Avery
Estimated Sales: $ 20-50 Million
Number Employees: 50-99
Square Footage: 90000
Brands Exported: Herco Brand Bags
Regions Exported to: Central America, Canada, Mexico
Percentage of Business in Exporting: 10
Regions Imported from: Canada, Latin America, Mexico
Percentage of Business in Importing: 5

44379 Frontline Inc
3200a Danville Blvd # 101
Suite 101
Alamo, CA 94507-1971   925-362-8000
Fax: 925-362-8078   800-562-7702
frontline.jan@sbcglobal.net
www.frontline-inc.com
Wholesaler/distributor of store and safety equipment including check stands, shopping carts, refrigeration cases and specialty lighting; also, gloves, mats and floor cones; exporter of floor cones, check stands and fluorescent lamps
President: Barry Nauroth
Comptroller: John Hudson
Estimated Sales: Less Than $500,000
Number Employees: 1-4
Square Footage: 4000
Brands Exported: Handy Cones; Killion; Promolux
Regions Exported to: Asia, Canada, Mexico
Percentage of Business in Exporting: 5

44380 Frost ET Inc
2020 Bristol Ave NW
Grand Rapids, MI 49504-1402   616-301-2660
Fax: 616-453-2161   800-253-9382
frost.sales@frostinc.com   www.frostinc.com
Overhead, inverted and converyor trolleys, guide rollers, conveyor roll bearings, and food processing components.
President: Chad Frost
cfrost@frostinc.com
Number Employees: 10-19
Regions Exported to: Worldwide

44381 Frost Food Handling Products
2020 Bristol Ave NW
Grand Rapids, MI 49504   616-453-7781
Fax: 616-453-2161   800-253-9382
frost@frostinc.com   www.frostinc.com
Conveying components for food handling applications
CEO: Chad Frost
CFO: Fred Sytsma
Sales Director: Joe Jakeway
Estimated Sales: $10-20 Million
Number Employees: 50-99
Square Footage: 120000
Parent Co: Frost Industries
Brands Exported: Sani-Trolley; Sani-Link Chain; Smooth-Link Chain
Regions Exported to: Worldwide
Percentage of Business in Exporting: 15

44382 Frosty Factory Of America Inc
2301 S Farmerville St
Ruston, LA 71270-9042   318-255-1162
Fax: 318-255-1170   800-544-4071
dolph@frostyfactory.com   www.frostyfactory.com
Manufacturer and exporter of frozen beverage, soft serve ice cream and shake machines
President: Heath Williams
ruston186@aol.com
Finance Executive: Penny Taylor
Sales/Marketing: Craig Moss
Sales Executive: Christopher Williams
Engineer: Ralph Pettijohn
Purchasing Manager: Ralph Pettijohn
Estimated Sales: $5 Million
Number Employees: 20-49
Square Footage: 80000
Brands Exported: Sorbeteer; Petite Sorbeteer
Regions Exported to: Worldwide
Percentage of Business in Exporting: 25

44383 Frozfruit Corporation
14805 S San Pedro Street
Gardena, CA 90248-2030   310-217-1034
Fax: 310-715-6943
Manufacturer and exporter of frozen ice cream novelties and fruit bars
President: Tom Guinan
Estimated Sales: $500,000-$1 Million
Number Employees: 5-9
Square Footage: 150000
Type of Packaging: Consumer, Food Service, Private Label, Bulk
Brands Exported: Frozfruit
Regions Exported to: Central America, Europe, Middle East

44384 Fruit Belt Canning Inc
54168 60th Ave
P.O. Box 81
Lawrence, MI 49064-9525   269-674-3939
Fax: 269-674-8354   office@fruitbeltfoods.com
www.fruitbeltfoods.com
Manufacturer, wholesaler/distributor of fruits and vegetables such as; asparagus, red tart cherries and strawberries
President: David Frank
davf@fruitbeltfoods.com
Vice President: Warren Frank
Sales Manager: Jim Armstrong
Estimated Sales: $5-9.9 Million
Number Employees: 100-249
Type of Packaging: Food Service, Private Label, Bulk
Regions Exported to: Europe

Importers & Exporters / A-Z

Percentage of Business in Exporting: 5
Regions Imported from: Central America, Europe
Percentage of Business in Importing: 5

44385 Fruit Growers Package Company
4693 Wilson Avenue SW
Suite H
Grandville, MI 49418-8762   616-724-1400
Manufacturer and exporter of wood veneer products, craft baskets and wooden shipping crates for berries
President: Diane Taylor
VP: Dennis Palasek
Contact: Dennis Palasek
dennis.palasek@fruitgrowers.com
Estimated Sales: $600,000
Number Employees: 10
Square Footage: 80000
Type of Packaging: Consumer, Bulk
Regions Exported to: South America
Percentage of Business in Exporting: 5

44386 Fruitcrown Products Corp
250 Adams Blvd
Farmingdale, NY 11735-6615   631-694-5800
Fax: 631-694-6467   800-441-3210
info@fruitcrown.com www.fruitcrown.com
Aseptic fruit flavors and bases for beverage, dairy and baking industries
President: Robert Jagenburg
orjagenburg@fruitcrown.com
Number Employees: 50-99
Type of Packaging: Bulk
Brands Exported: Fruitcrown
Regions Exported to: Worldwide
Percentage of Business in Exporting: 5
Regions Imported from: Central America, South America, Europe, Asia, Carribean, Worldwide
Percentage of Business in Importing: 10

44387 Frutarom Meer Corporation
Manofim St. Herzeliya
P.O. Box 3088
Hertzeliya Pituach, 46104
Israel
www.iff.com/en/taste/frutarom
Botanicals, extracts, gums, stabilizers, oleoresins, natural colors, enzymes and hydrocolloids
President: Amos Anatot
Year Founded: 1933
Estimated Sales: $20-50 Million
Number Employees: 5600
Number of Products: 70K
Square Footage: 100000
Parent Co: International Flavors-Fragrances
Type of Packaging: Bulk
Regions Exported to: Worldwide
Percentage of Business in Exporting: 30
Regions Imported from: Worldwide
Percentage of Business in Importing: 25

44388 Frutech International Corp
180 S Lake Ave # 335
Suite 335
Pasadena, CA 91101-4735   626-844-0200
Fax: 626-844-0202 info.mx@frutech.com
www.frutech.com
Citrus oil production
Owner: Scott Alexander
scott.a@frutech.com
Treasurer: Gene Adams
VP Finance: Pat Breyer
Estimated Sales: $500,000
Number Employees: 1-4
Parent Co: Frutech International Corporation

44389 Frutex Group
3575 Saint Laurent
Suite 502
Montreal, QC H2X 2T7
Canada   514-892-3511
Fax: 514-524-8849 mbussieres@frutex.ca
Exporter and importer of juice concentrates and frozen fruit including organic cranberries and wild blueberries
Director Marketing: Michel Bussieres
Estimated Sales: $1,000,000 - $4,999,999
Number Employees: 1-4
Type of Packaging: Bulk
Regions Exported to: Europe, Asia
Percentage of Business in Exporting: 55
Regions Imported from: Worldwide
Percentage of Business in Importing: 45

44390 Fry Foods Inc
P.O. Box 837
Tiffin, OH 44883
800-626-2294
orders@fryfoods.com www.fryfoods.com
Frozen, battered and breaded appetizers such as onion rings, cheese sticks, mushrooms, jalapeno poppers, zucchini sticks and breaded cauliflower
President: Norman Fry
Vice President: David Fry
Year Founded: 1961
Estimated Sales: $20-50 Million
Number Employees: 50-99
Number of Brands: 1
Square Footage: 45000
Type of Packaging: Consumer, Food Service
Brands Exported: Fry Foods, Fuddruckers, Dairy Queen
Regions Exported to: Central America, Europe, Asia, Caribbean, Canada
Percentage of Business in Exporting: 8
Regions Imported from: Central America

44391 Frye's Measure Mill
12 Frye Mill Rd
Wilton, NH 03086-5010   603-654-6581
Fax: 603-654-6103 www.fryesmeasuremill.com
Manufacturer and exporter of wooden dry measures, specialty packaging, veneer containers, colonial pantry and shaker boxes
President: Harley Savage
harleysavage@tds.net
Quality Control: Harley Savage
Estimated Sales: Below $ 5 Million
Number Employees: 5-9
Regions Exported to: Europe, Asia, Canada

44392 Frymaster/Dean
8700 Line Ave
Shreveport, LA 71106-6800   318-865-1711
Fax: 318-868-5987   800-221-4583
webmaster@frymaster.com
Supplier of commercial fryers, frying systems, water-bath rethermalizers, pasta cookers, and of the equipment related to these technologies.
President: Gene Baugh
Cio/Cto: Bruce Arnold
bconnor@frymaster.com
Vice President & General Manager: Todd Phillips
Estimated Sales: $ 60 Million
Number Employees: 500-999
Square Footage: 180000
Parent Co: ENODIS
Type of Packaging: Food Service

44393 Fuji Foods Corp
6206 Corporate Park Dr
Browns Summit, NC 27214   336-375-3111
Fax: 336-375-3663 information@fujifoodsusa.com
www.fujifoodsusa.com
Chicken, pork and beef broths including concentrated pastes and powders; also, savory flavors, soup bases; and spray dried flavor powders; spray drying services available.
VP Operations & Chief Operating Officer: Michael Russell
Plant Manager: Terry Lawson
Estimated Sales: $20-50 Million
Number Employees: 20-49
Square Footage: 20000
Parent Co: Fuji Foods Corporation
Type of Packaging: Food Service, Bulk
Regions Exported to: Asia

44394 Fuller Industries LLC
1 Fuller Way
Great Bend, KS 67530-2466   620-792-1711
Fax: 620-792-1906   800-522-0499
customer@fuller.com www.fullerindustriesllc.com
Manufacturer and exporter of detergents, mops, floor polish, brooms and plastic bottles
President: G Robert Gey
CEO: David Sabin
dsabin@fuller.com
VP: Lewis L Gray
VP Sales: Dolores McConnaughy
VP Sales: Bill McCoy
Number Employees: 250-499
Square Footage: 1000000
Brands Exported: Fuller Brush
Regions Exported to: Central America, South America, Europe, Asia, Middle East, Australia, Canada
Percentage of Business in Exporting: 10

44395 Fuller Packaging Inc
1152 High St
PO Box 198
Central Falls, RI 02863-1506   401-725-4300
Fax: 401-726-8050
customerservice@fullerbox.com
www.fullerbox.com
Manufacturer, importer and exporter of boxes including paper and counter display
President: Peter Fuller
Product Development Manager: Alvin Fuller
Estimated Sales: $10-20 Million
Number Employees: 50-99
Square Footage: 154000
Regions Exported to: South America, Europe, Asia, Mexico
Percentage of Business in Exporting: 5
Regions Imported from: Asia
Percentage of Business in Importing: 5

44396 Fuller Weighing Systems
1600 Georgesville Road
Columbus, OH 43228-3616   614-882-8121
Fax: 614-882-9594 www.fullerweighing.com
Manufacturer and exporter of bulk weighing systems, feeders and automatic net-weigh container filling systems for liquids and dry materials
VP Sales: Tim Schultz
General Manager: Karl Hedderich
Production: David Patterson
Number Employees: 50
Square Footage: 60000
Parent Co: Cardinal Scale Manufacturing Company
Regions Exported to: South America, Europe, Asia, Middle East
Percentage of Business in Exporting: 20

44397 Fullway International
1891 Peeler Road
Atlanta, GA 30338-5714   770-604-9299
Fax: 770-604-9296
Importer, exporter and wholesaler/distributor of soybean and fish oils; also, canned foods
President: Ralph Lai
Regions Exported to: Asia
Percentage of Business in Exporting: 80
Regions Imported from: Asia
Percentage of Business in Importing: 20

44398 Fumoir Grizzly
159 Amsterdam
St Augustin, QC G3A 2V5
Canada   418-878-8941
Fax: 418-878-8942 info@grizzly.qc.ca
www.grizzly.qc.ca
Manufacturer and exporter of smoked salmon, trout, halibut
President: Pierre Fontaine
CEO: Laura Boivin
Controller: Sebastian Legault
Director Quality Management: Michele Tessier
Marketing, R&D: Marie-Pier Grondin
Sales Representative - Quebec: Normand Richard
Director Human Resources: Connie Biladeau
Production Manager: Sergiu Parsikov
Estimated Sales: $6,3,000,000
Number Employees: 37
Type of Packaging: Consumer, Food Service, Private Label, Bulk
Regions Exported to: US, France
Percentage of Business in Exporting: 10

44399 Fun Express
4206 S 108th St
Omaha, NE 68137   800-875-8494
Fax: 800-228-1002 sharon@funexpress.com
www.funexpress.com
Contact: Lisa Aguirre
laguirre@funexpress.com

44400 Fun Foods
99 Murray Hill Pkwy
Suite D
East Rutherford, NJ 07073-2143   201-896-4949
Fax: 201-896-4911   800-507-2782
funfoodspasta@yahoo.com
Bi- and tri-colored holiday shaped gourmet pasta including Christmas trees, hearts, bunnies, stars and stripes, Jack O'Lanterns, star of David, angels, etc
Manager: Sharon Nicklas
Estimated Sales: $5-10 Million
Number Employees: 5-9
Square Footage: 8000

Importers & Exporters / A-Z

Type of Packaging: Consumer, Food Service, Private Label, Bulk
Regions Exported to: Central America, South America, Europe, Asia, Middle East
Percentage of Business in Exporting: 10

44401 Fun-Time International
433 W Girard Ave.
Philadelphia, PA 19123   215-925-1450
Fax: 215-925-1884   800-776-4386
orders@krazystraws.com   www.krazystraws.com
Manufacturer and exporter of novelty drinking straws, eating utensils and drinking containers; also, novelty candy items
Owner: Erik Lipson
Estimated Sales: $ 3 - 5 Million
Number Employees: 10-19
Square Footage: 2000
Brands Exported: Connector; Crazy Glasses; Funstraws; Krazy Utensils; Krazy Koolers; Spookyware; Candy Bracelets
Regions Exported to: Central America, South America, Europe, Asia, Middle East
Percentage of Business in Exporting: 5

44402 Furgale Industries Ltd.
324 Lizzie Street
Winnipeg, NB R3A 0Y7
Canada   204-949-4200
Fax: 204-943-3191   800-665-0506
Provider of cleaning tools to the north american market - tools include: brooms, mops & brushes
President: Jim Furgale
VP: Terry Gibb
Customer Service: Kate Furgale
Number Employees: 70
Number of Brands: 10
Number of Products: 250
Square Footage: 280000
Type of Packaging: Consumer, Private Label
Brands Exported: Furgale Brand, 8-Ender
Regions Exported to: Europe, USA
Percentage of Business in Exporting: 5
Brands Imported: Furbale Brand
Regions Imported from: Europe, Asia
Percentage of Business in Importing: 40

44403 Furnace Belt Company
2316 Delaware Avenue
Suite 217
Buffalo, NY 14216
Canada
Fax: 800-354-7215 800-354-7213
fbc@furnacebeltco.com   www.furnacebeltco.com
Manufacturer and exporter of wire processing belts for heat treating, brazing, annealing, sintering, quenching, freezing and baking
President: J Tatone
Number Employees: 40
Square Footage: 90000
Regions Exported to: Central America, South America, Europe, Middle East
Percentage of Business in Exporting: 75

44404 Furniturelab
106 S Greensboro St # E
Carrboro, NC 27510-2266   919-913-0270
Fax: 919-913-0271   800-449-8677
sales@furniturelab.com   www.furniturelab.com
Manufacturer and exporter of wood and laminated tables, tabletops, chairs and bases
President: Greg Rapp
sales@furniturelab.com
Marketing: Courtney Smith
Sales Director: Nathan Bearman
Estimated Sales: $ 1 - 3 Million
Number Employees: 10-19
Square Footage: 14000
Regions Exported to: Worldwide
Percentage of Business in Exporting: 15

44405 Future Commodities IntlInc
10676 Fulton Ct
Rancho Cucamonga, CA 91730-4848 909-987-4258
Fax: 909-987-5189   888-588-2378
sales@bestpack.com   www.bestpack.com
Manufacturer and exporter of carton sealers, erectors and end line packaging machinery
President: David Lim
VP: Chery Lim
Sales Manager: Patrick Brennan
Contact: Mike Byrne
mbyrne@bestpack.com

Estimated Sales: $ 5 - 10 Million
Number Employees: 1-4
Square Footage: 108000
Parent Co: Future Commodities International
Regions Exported to: Central America, South America, Europe, Asia, Middle East, Australia
Percentage of Business in Exporting: 10

44406 G & F Systems Inc
208 Babylon Tpke
Roosevelt, NY 11575-2146   516-868-4923
Fax: 516-868-4968   sales@gfsystems.com
www.gfsystems.com
Custom manufacturer of food processing equipment
Manager: Pat Allen
VP: Guy Irwin
VP: Anthonny Salsone
Director/Acct Manager: Aryola Kaufman
Contact: Merve Cagaloglu
merve.cagaloglu@citigroup.com
Estimated Sales: $4.4 Million
Number Employees: 10-19
Square Footage: 400000
Regions Exported to: Worldwide

44407 G & L Import Export Corp
4828 E 22nd St
Tucson, AZ 85711-4904   520-790-9016
Wholesaler/distributor, importer and exporter of Oriental and Hispanic food, frozen seafood, shrimp and produce; serving the food service market
Manager: Park Pang
Estimated Sales: Less Than $500,000
Number Employees: 1-4
Square Footage: 160000

44408 G A B Empacadora Inc
9330 San Mateo Dr
Laredo, TX 78045-8728   956-727-0100
Fax: 956-726-0079
Wholesaler/distributor, importer and exporter of fresh and frozen vegetables
President: Liz Martinez
liz@empgab.com
Sales Coordinator: Carmen Lopez
Traffic: Juan Ramirez
Manager: George Hughes
Estimated Sales: $ 10 - 20 Million
Number Employees: 10-19

44409 G K Skaggs Inc
100 Pacifica # 450
Suite 450
Irvine, CA 92618-7450   949-752-1500
Fax: 949-752-1525   800-578-7521
customerservice@gkskaggs.com
Importers of premium & specialty beers & wines.
CEO: Gregory Skaggs
gks@gkskaggs.com
CFO: Jo Ann Martin
VP: Ryan Heilip
R&D: Angela Caraglio
Sales: Tim Loiselle
Estimated Sales: $7.8 Million
Number Employees: 5-9
Square Footage: 16000
Type of Packaging: Consumer, Private Label
Regions Exported to: Canada
Brands Imported: Hinano, Bahia, Bavaria, Caguama, Hollande 1620 Nautica.
Regions Imported from: Central America, Europe, Asia

44410 G Nino Bragelli Inc
235 Brixton Rd
Garden City, NY 11530-1312   516-746-6400
Fax: 516-746-5828
Importer of cheese including pecorino romano, parmesan, provolone, ricotta and toscanello
President: Peter Cannizzaro
Number Employees: 1-4
Type of Packaging: Bulk
Brands Imported: Brunelli; Lopez; Mannoni
Regions Imported from: Europe
Percentage of Business in Importing: 100

44411 G Scaccianoce & Co
1165 Burnett Pl
Bronx, NY 10474-5716   718-991-4462
Fax: 718-991-0154
Processor and exporter of confectionery items including Jordan almonds, French mints and licorice
President: Donald Beck
gscaccianoceinc@hotmail.com

Estimated Sales: $2.5-5 Million
Number Employees: 5-9
Type of Packaging: Consumer, Food Service, Private Label, Bulk
Regions Exported to: Worldwide
Percentage of Business in Exporting: 1

44412 G&R Graphics
PO Box 7095
West Orange, NJ 7052   973-380-8317
Fax: 973-731-7438   813-503-8592
gnrstamp@aol.com
Manufacturer and exporter of rubber printing plates, corporate seals, rubber stamps, inks and pads
President: David Gonzalez
Contact: Anibal Gonzalez
agonzalez@grgraphicsinc.com
Estimated Sales: $ 1 - 5 Million
Number Employees: 5-9
Square Footage: 8000
Regions Exported to: Caribbean
Percentage of Business in Exporting: 10

44413 G-M Super Sales Company
PO Box Ff
Hidalgo, TX 78557   956-843-2283
Fax: 956-843-2520
Importer and exporter of mangos, limes, melons, citrus fruits and avocados
President: Wade Shiba
Sales Manager: Roy Duleba
Estimated Sales: $ 20-50 Million
Number Employees: 50-99
Regions Exported to: Worldwide
Regions Imported from: Central America

44414 (HQ)G.E. Barbour
165 Stewart Ave
Sussex, NB E4E 3H1
Canada   506-432-2300
Fax: 506-432-2323   www.barbours.ca
Family-owned business since 1867. Manufacturer of tea, nut butters, spices and extracts.
President: Sylvia MacVey
VP: Blair Hystom
Marketing Manager: Gordonna Hache
Director of Sales: Mike Trecartin
Number Employees: 100-249
Type of Packaging: Consumer, Food Service, Private Label
Other Locations:
G.E. Barbour
St. John, NB G.E. Barbour

44415 G.F. Frank & Sons
9075 LeSaint Dr Fairfield
Fairfield, OH 45014   513-870-9075
Fax: 513-870-0579   john@GFFrankAndSons.com
www.gffrankandsons.com
Manufacturer and exporter of meat hooks, skewers, trolleys and smokehouse shelving
President: George Frank
Vice President: John Frank
Estimated Sales: $10-20 Million
Number Employees: 10-19

44416 G.G. Greene Enterprises
2790 Pennsylvania Avenue
West Warren, PA 16365   814-723-5700
Fax: 814-723-3037
awillingham@greenegroup.com
www.greenegroup.com
Manufactures guns, howitzers, mortars & related equipment; manufactures small arms ammunition; manufactures stamped or pressed metal machine parts; plate metal fabricator
Manager: Brent Long
Estimated Sales: $4,500,000
Number Employees: 20-49
Square Footage: 850000
Type of Packaging: Consumer, Food Service
Regions Exported to: South America, Europe
Percentage of Business in Exporting: 5

44417 G.P. de Silva Spices Inc
8531 Loch Lomond Dr
Pico Rivera, CA 90660   562-506-3485
www.lankacinnamon.com
Importer of cinnamon & other spices.
President/CEO: Ravi de Silva
Chief Financial Officer: Nalin Kulasooriya
Managing Director: Garumuni Edward Lal de Silva
Parent Co: G.P. de Silva & Sons International Ltd.
Regions Imported from: Asia

Importers & Exporters / A-Z

44418 GAP Food Brokers
1412 E 11 Mile Rd
Madison Heights, MI 48071   248-544-1190
   Fax: 248-544-1195 gapfdbkr@bignet.net
Import broker of dairy/deli products, frozen foods, groceries, meat, meat products and seafood
President: Gerald Petty
gapfdbkr@bignet.net
VP: Donna Petty
Estimated Sales: $10-20 Million
Number Employees: 10-19
Square Footage: 8000

44419 GCI Nutrients
1163 Chess Dr # H
Foster City, CA 94404-1119   650-376-3534
   Fax: 650-697-3013   866-580-6549
   mikec@gcinutrients.com www.gcinutrients.com
Processor, importer and exporter of vitamins and supplements including beta carotene, essential fatty acids, herbal products, botanical extracts, food supplements, bulk ingredients, premium raw materials for nutritional and beverage industries with over 42 years of experience
Owner: Richard Merriam
rickm@gcinutrients.com
General Manager: Mike Cronin
Controller: Fransisca Cronin
R&D: William Forgach
Marketing: Michael Sevohon
Production: Derek Cronin
Plant Manager: Mike Cronin
Purchasing Manager: Catherine Sabbah
Estimated Sales: $10 Million
Number Employees: 10-19
Number of Brands: 10
Number of Products: 300
Square Footage: 20000
Regions Exported to: South America, Europe, Asia, Middle East, India
Regions Imported from: South America, Europe, Asia, Middle East, India
Percentage of Business in Importing: 50

44420 GE Interlogix Industrial
12345 SW Leveton Dr
Tualatin, OR 97062-6001   503-692-4052
   Fax: 503-691-7377   800-247-9447
   www.sentrol.com
Manufacturer and exporter of noncontract safety switches, position sensors and safety relays
President: Greg Burge
Contact: Rich Laitta
rlaitta@berwind.com
Estimated Sales: $ 50-100 Million
Number Employees: 500-999
Square Footage: 140000
Parent Co: Interlogix
Brands Exported: GuardSwitch; Failsafe GuardSwitch

44421 (HQ)GEA North America
1880 Country Farm Dr
Naperville, IL 60563-1089   630-369-8100
   Fax: 630-369-9875
Manufacturer and exporter of dairy farm equipment including cleaners
President: John Ansbro
john.ansbro@geagroup.com
CEO: Dirk Hejnal
CFO: Dr. Ulrich Hullman
Sales: Vern Foster
Business Unit, Milking & Cooling: Dr. Armin Tietjen
Estimated Sales: Below $ 5 Million
Number Employees: 100-249
Other Locations:
   Babson Brothers Co.
   Galesville, WIBabson Brothers Co.
Regions Exported to: South America, Europe, Asia
Percentage of Business in Exporting: 16

44422 GED, LLC
28107 Beaver Dam Branch Rd
Box 140
Laurel, DE 19956-9801   302-856-1756
   Fax: 302-856-9888 gedllc@yahoo.com
Importers and exporters of cans, plus dealers of food processing machines and parts
Estimated Sales: $ 1 - 5 Million
Number Employees: 3

44423 GEI Autowrappers
700 Pennsylvania Drive
Exton, PA 19341-1129   610-321-1115
   Fax: 610-321-1199
Manufacturer and exporter of electronic flow wrappers
Sales Manager: Richard Landers
Number Employees: 120
Square Footage: 160000
Parent Co: GEI International
Regions Exported to: Worldwide
Percentage of Business in Exporting: 30

44424 GEI PPM
569 W Uwchlan Ave
Exton, PA 19341-1563   610-524-7178
   Fax: 610-321-1199   800-345-1308
Manufacturer and exporter of pressure sensitive and multi-head/in-line rotary labelers
Owner: Jin Guo
Estimated Sales: $ 1 - 5 Million
Number Employees: 1-4
Square Footage: 320000
Parent Co: GEI International
Regions Exported to: Worldwide
Percentage of Business in Exporting: 30

44425 GEI Turbo
700 Pennsylvania Drive
Exton, PA 19341-1129   610-321-1100
   Fax: 610-321-1199   800-345-1308
Manufacturer and exporter of hand-held and automatic high and low temperature filling equipment
Estimated Sales: $ 1 - 5 Million
Parent Co: GEI International
Regions Exported to: Worldwide
Percentage of Business in Exporting: 30

44426 GEM Berry Products
PO Box 709
Orofino, ID 83544   208-263-7503
   Fax: 866-357-3505   888-231-1699
   gifrep52@gmail.com www.gemberry.com
Processor and exporter of spreads, jams and syrups including raspberry and huckleberry; berry filled chocolates, berry barbecue sauce and many other berry products.
President: Jack O' Brien
CFO: Betty Menser
Marketing: Harry Menser
Contact: Cathy Miller
cathy.miller@gemberryproducts.com
Production: Elizabeth O Brien
Estimated Sales: $50,000-100,000
Number Employees: 1-4
Square Footage: 5000
Type of Packaging: Food Service, Bulk
Brands Exported: Gem Berry; Litehouse
Regions Exported to: Asia
Brands Imported: None

44427 GEM Cultures
PO Box 39426
Lakewood, WA 98496   253-588-2922
   gemculture@juno.com
   www.gemcultures.com
Manufacturer and exporter of shelf stable starters for cultured vegetarian foods including tempeh, miso, shoyu, natto, sourdough, nonyogurt and dairy cultures; importer of koji and natto starters
Owner: Betty Stechmeyer
Public Relations: Gordon McBride
Estimated Sales: $70,000
Number Employees: 1
Square Footage: 2000
Type of Packaging: Private Label
Brands Exported: GEM Cultures; Mitoku
Regions Exported to: Central America, South America, Europe, Asia, Canada, Australia
Percentage of Business in Exporting: 36
Brands Imported: Mitoku
Regions Imported from: Asia
Percentage of Business in Importing: 3

44428 GEM Equipment Of OregonInc
2150 Progress Way
Woodburn, OR 97071-9765   503-982-9902
   Fax: 503-981-6316 gem@gemequipment.com
   www.gemequipment.com
Manufacturer and exporter of blanchers, conveyor systems and components, fryers, dumpers, mixers, preheaters and batter mix systems
President: Edward McKenney
CEO: Steve Ross
sross@gemequipment.com
COO: Steve Ross
Vice President of Sales: Jerry Bell
Plant Manager: Ray Rowe
Purchasing Manager: Ray Rowe
Estimated Sales: $20-50 Million
Number Employees: 50-99
Square Footage: 100000
Regions Exported to: South America, Europe, Canada
Percentage of Business in Exporting: 20

44429 GERM-O-RAY
1641 Lewis Way
Stone Mountain, GA 30083-1107   770-939-2835
   Fax: 770-621-0100   800-966-8480
   sales@insect-o-cutor.com www.insect-o-cutor.com
Manufacturer and exporter of air disinfection fixtures and germicidal fluorescent, UV and UVC lamps; available in in-room, in-duct and custom styles
CEO: Bill Harris
Marketing Director: J Harris
Advertising: D Johnson
Systems Engineer: J Baum
Estimated Sales: $ 1 - 3 Million
Number Employees: 10-19
Brands Exported: GERM-O-RAY
Regions Exported to: Central America, South America, Asia, Middle East, Canada, Caribbean, Latin America, Mexico
Percentage of Business in Exporting: 15

44430 GET Enterprises LLC
1515 W Sam Houston Pkwy N
Houston, TX 77043-3112   713-467-9394
   Fax: 713-467-9396   800-727-4500
   info@get-melamine.com www.get-melamine.com
Importer and wholesaler/distributor of dinnerware, high chairs, tray stands, tumblers, platters and soup and coffee mugs; serving the food service market
President: Glen Hou
HR Executive: Joyce Liu
joyceliu@get-melamine.com
VP Sales/Marketing: Eve Hou
Estimated Sales: $5-10 Million
Number Employees: 50-99
Square Footage: 40000
Regions Imported from: China, Taiwan, Indonesia
Percentage of Business in Importing: 90

44431 GH Ford Tea Company
PO Box 683
Shokan, NY 12481   845-464-6755
   info@ghfordtea.com
   www.ghfordtea.com
Processor, importer and exporter of whole leaf teas in tea ball packaging. Offers 30 to 50 blends and flavors utilizing original blending formulas and all natural flavoring.
President: Keith Capolino
ghfordtea@gmail.com
Estimated Sales: $2.5-5 Million
Number Employees: 5-9
Type of Packaging: Consumer, Food Service, Private Label, Bulk
Brands Exported: G.H. Ford Teas
Regions Exported to: Europe, Asia, Middle East
Percentage of Business in Exporting: 25
Regions Imported from: Asia

44432 (HQ)GHM Industries Inc
100 Sturbridge Rd # A
Charlton, MA 01507-5323   508-248-3941
   Fax: 508-248-0639   800-793-7013
   sales@millerproducts.net www.millerproducts.net
Manufacturer and exporter of textile machinery including automatic roll wrappers and polywraps
President: Paul Jankovic
pjankovic@millerproducts.net
Estimated Sales: $2.5-5 Million
Number Employees: 5-9
Regions Exported to: Central America, Europe, Asia, Canada

44433 GLAC Seat Inc
115 Bray Ave
Milford, CT 06460-5408   203-874-4513
   Fax: 203-874-4514   800-233-7381
   glacseat@aol.com www.glacseat.com

Importers & Exporters / A-Z

Wholesaler/distributor, importer and exporter of resin chairs, cantilevered umbrellas and rattan chairs and tables; serving the food service market
CEO: Annie Claude
glacseat@aol.com
CEO: Annie Claude
Operations Manager: Annie Claude
Estimated Sales: $1 Million
Number Employees: 1-4
Square Footage: 24000
Type of Packaging: Food Service
Brands Imported: Poitoux
Regions Imported from: Europe

44434 (HQ)GM Nameplate
2040 15th Ave W
Seattle, WA 98119-2783   206-284-2200
　　Fax: 206-284-3705   800-366-7668
　　webnet@gmnameplate.com
　　www.gmnameplate.com
Manufacturer and exporter of nameplates, labels, membrane switches, injection and compression molding.
President: Brad Root
bred@gmnameplate.com
Chairman & CEO: Donald Root
New Product Manager: Dennis Cook
Research & Development: Debbie Anderson
Marketing Manager: Shannon Kirk
VP Sales & Marketing: Gerry Gallagher
Operations Executive: Mark Samuel
Plant/Production Manager: Marc Doan
Purchasing Agent: Jim Davis
Number Employees: 1000-4999
Square Footage: 560000
Other Locations:
　Elite Plastics Division
　Beaverton, OR
　Canada Division
　Surrey, BC
　California Division
　San Jose, CA
　North Carolina Division
　Monroe, NC
　SuperGraphics Division
　Seattle, WAElite Plastics DivisionSurrey

44435 GNS Spices
766 Trotter Ct
Walnut, CA 91789-1277   909-594-9505
　　Fax: 909-594-5455
Processor and exporter of red savina and orange habanero peppers including pods, flakes and ground
President: Frank Garcia Jr
VP: Mary Garcia
Operations Manager: Frank Garcia Sr
Estimated Sales: $150,000
Number Employees: 2
Type of Packaging: Bulk

44436 GOJO Industries Inc
1 Gojo Plz # 500
Akron, OH 44311-1085   330-255-6000
　　Fax: 330-255-6119   800-321-9647
　　www.gojo.com
Manufacturer and exporter of hand cleaners and soap dispensers
President/Chief Operating Officer: Mark Lerner
Chief Executive Officer: Joe Kanfer
Managing Director: Adrian Coombes
Vice Chair: Marcella Rolnick
Research & Development: Thales De Nardo
Quality Control Assurance: Susan Jack
Vice President, Sales & Marketing: Jeff Buysse
Vice President, Sales: Greg Conner
Product Manager: Aaron Conrow
Lab Manager: Dan Willis
Purchasing: Debbie Topliff
Estimated Sales: $ 75 Million
Number Employees: 250-499
Square Footage: 500000
Regions Exported to: Worldwide

44437 GPI USA LLC.
10062 190th Place
Suite 107
Mokena, IL 60448   706-850-7826
　　Fax: 708-785-0608   800-929-4248
　　karen.haley@foodgums.com
Specialize in carageenan used for stabilization and as an additive for both dairy products and in the red meat and poultry industries.

44438 GS Dunn & Company
80 Park Street N
Hamilton, ON L8R 2M9
Canada   905-522-0833
　　Fax: 905-522-4423   info@gsdunn.com
　　www.gsdunn.com
Global supplier and manufacturer of dry mustard products
President: Ron Kramer
Director Technical Services: Nancy Post
Estimated Sales: $5 Million
Number Employees: 20-49
Square Footage: 70000
Type of Packaging: Food Service, Private Label, Bulk
Regions Exported to: Central America, South America, Europe, Asia, Middle East, USA
Percentage of Business in Exporting: 80

44439 GSB & Assoc
3115 Cobb International Blvd N
Kennesaw, GA 30152-4354   770-424-1886
　　Fax: 770-422-1732   877-472-2776
　　sales@gsbflavorcreators.com
　　www.gsbflavorcreators.com
Natural and artificial, artificial, water or oil soluble, liquid and spray dried flavors. Flavors are Kosher Certified. We also offer a line of Certified Organic Flavors.
President: Eugene Buday
sales@gsbflavorcreators.com
Estimated Sales: $5-10 Million
Number Employees: 10-19
Type of Packaging: Bulk
Regions Exported to: Worldwide

44440 GSW Jackes-Evans Manufacturing Company
4427 Geraldine Avenue
Saint Louis, MO 63115-1217   314-385-4132
　　Fax: 314-385-0802   800-325-6173
Manufacturer, importer and exporter of barbecue equipment and accessories
President: Rob Harris
BBQ Products: Joe Fernandez
Director Sales (Heating Products): Ron Bailey
Number Employees: 200
Square Footage: 500000
Parent Co: GSW
Type of Packaging: Consumer, Private Label, Bulk
Brands Exported: Jackes-Evans
Regions Exported to: South America, Europe, Canada
Percentage of Business in Exporting: 7
Brands Imported: Jackes-Evans E-Z Fit
Regions Imported from: Asia
Percentage of Business in Importing: 20

44441 GTCO CalComp
14557 N. 82nd Street
Scottsdale, AZ 85260   410-381-3450
　　Fax: 480-948-5508   800-856-0732
　　calcomp.sales@gtcocalcomp.com
Manufacturer and exporter of wide-format graphic printers and tablets
Sales Director: Kim Plasterer
VP Sales: Don Lightfoot
Contact: Debra Melcher
dmelcher@gtcocalcomp.com
Number Employees: 1,000-4,999
Parent Co: eInstruction
Type of Packaging: Food Service
Regions Exported to: Central America, South America, Europe, Asia

44442 GTI
12650 W 64th Ave # F
Arvada, CO 80004-3887   303-420-6699
　　Fax: 303-420-6699 www.greatclips.com
Manufacturer and exporter of seamers
President: Charlie Simpson
Chairman of the Board: Ray Barton
Vice President: Michelle Sack
Senior Vice President of Operations: Steve Hockett
Estimated Sales: $ 1 - 5 Million
Regions Exported to: Worldwide
Percentage of Business in Exporting: 40

44443 GWB Foods Corporation
PO Box 228
Brooklyn, NY 11204-0228   718-686-6611
　　Fax: 718-686-6161   877-977-7610
　　info@gwbfoods.com   www.gwbfoods.com
Processor, exporter, importer and wholesaler/distributor of specialty and frozen foods including cookies, candies, crackers, rice cakes, vegetables in jars, bottled water, pickles and pimiento peppers
President: Joshua Weinstein
Export Manager: S Williams
Sales Manager: Jack Yumens
Estimated Sales: $2.5-5 Million
Number Employees: 10-19
Square Footage: 80000
Parent Co: President Baking Company
Type of Packaging: Consumer, Food Service, Private Label, Bulk
Brands Exported: Presidor; Letova; Keren
Regions Exported to: Central America, South America, Europe, Asia, Middle East, Mexico
Percentage of Business in Exporting: 60
Brands Imported: Presidor; Keren; Produce Farm; Hadar
Regions Imported from: South America, Europe, Asia, Middle East
Percentage of Business in Importing: 25

44444 Gabila's Knishes
100 Wartburg Ave
Copiague, NY 11726   631-789-2220
　　gabilas.com
Processor and exporter of frozen knishes
President: Gloria Gabay
Partner: Sophie Levy
Controller: Linda Ghignone
Estimated Sales: $1-2.5 Million
Number Employees: 20-49
Type of Packaging: Consumer
Regions Exported to: Worldwide

44445 Gabriella Imports
5100 Prospect Ave
Cleveland, OH 44103   216-432-3651
　　Fax: 216-432-3654   800-544-8117
Manufacturer, importer and exporter of automatic espresso equipment and granita machines and products
Estimated Sales: $ 500,000-$ 1 Million
Number Employees: 35
Regions Exported to: Worldwide
Percentage of Business in Exporting: 10
Regions Imported from: Europe
Percentage of Business in Importing: 40

44446 Gadoua Bakery
150 Bd Industriel
Napierville, QC J0J 1L0
Canada   450-245-7542
　　Fax: 450-245-7609   800-661-7246
　　info@gadoua.qc.ca   www.gadoua.qc.ca
Bread, buns, bagels, english muffins, and tortillas
President: Pascal Gadoua
Year Founded: 1911
Estimated Sales: $40-60 Million
Number Employees: 550
Square Footage: 150000
Parent Co: George Weston Ltd.
Type of Packaging: Food Service
Regions Exported to: Canada

44447 Gaetano America
9460 Telstar Ave
El Monte, CA 91731-2904   626-442-2858
　　Fax: 626-401-1988 gaetanorf@aol.com
Manufacturer and exporter of ceramic bowls, platters, serving pieces and dinnerware
Owner: Irving Chait
VP Sales/Marketing: Rick Frovich
Regions Exported to: Worldwide

44448 Gage Industries
P.O.Box 1318
Lake Oswego, OR 97035   503-639-2177
　　Fax: 503-624-1070   800-443-4243
　　sales@gageindustries.com
Manufacturer and exporter of plastic thermoformed packaging products including freezable and dual-ovenable food trays, cutting trays, totes, plastic containers, etc
President: Jeff Gage
Executive VP: Lizbeth Gage
Sales: Scott Tullis
Estimated Sales: $ 50 - 100 Million
Number Employees: 250-499
Number of Brands: 3
Number of Products: 70
Square Footage: 200000

Importers & Exporters / A-Z

Type of Packaging: Consumer, Food Service, Private Label, Bulk

44449 Gaggia Espresso MachineCompany
1335 Davenport Road
Toronto, ON M6H 2H4
Canada 416-537-3439
Fax: 416-588-9012
Importer and wholesaler/distributor of Italian espresso machines; serving the food service market
President: Karen Zuccarini
Sales Manager: Jackie Zuccarini
Number Employees: 5-9

44450 Gail Pittman
290 South Perkins Street
Ridgeland, MS 39157-2701 615-807-1078
Fax: 601-856-5740 www.gailpittman.com
President: Gail Pittman
Contact: Lisa Reyes
lisa@gailpittman.com
Estimated Sales: $ 10 - 20 Million
Number Employees: 100-249

44451 Gainco Inc
1635 Oakbrook Dr
Gainesville, GA 30507-8492 770-534-0703
Fax: 770-534-1865 800-467-2828
Sales@gainco.com www.gainco.com
Portion sizing and distribution equipment, sorting, counting, weighing, and bagging systems, as well as bench and floor scales for the poultry, meat and food processing industries.
Manager: Joe Cowman
jcowman@gainco.com
Number Employees: 20-49
Regions Exported to: Worldwide

44452 Gaiser's European Style
2019 Morris Ave
Union, NJ 07083-6013 908-686-3421
Fax: 908-686-7131
Processor, exporter and wholesaler/distributor of sausage, liverwurst and smoked ham
Owner: Efem Rablov
gaisers@verizon.net
Estimated Sales: $500,000-$1 Million
Number Employees: 10-19
Regions Exported to: Worldwide
Percentage of Business in Exporting: 15

44453 Galaxy Chemical Corp
2041 Whitfield Park Ave
Sarasota, FL 34243-4085 941-755-8545
Fax: 941-751-9412 gccgps@aol.com
Manufacturer and exporter of hand cleaners
Owner: Allan M Sanger
gccgps@aol.com
Manager: Tim San
Estimated Sales: $ 5 - 10 Million
Number Employees: 10-19
Regions Exported to: Worldwide
Percentage of Business in Exporting: 3

44454 (HQ)Galbreath LLC
461 East Rosser Road
Winamac, IN 46996 574-946-6631
sales@wastequip.com
www.galbreath-inc.com
Manufacturer and exporter of detachable container systems, roll-off hoists and recycling containers, lugger boxes, self-dumping hoppers, dock carts, material-handling equipment, compactors, trailers and balers
Chief Technology Officer: Lbehny Podell
Contact: Shawn Harper
sharper@wastequip.com
Estimated Sales: $ 10 Million
Number Employees: 75
Square Footage: 250000
Parent Co: Wastequip, Inc.
Other Locations:
Galbreath
Ider, ALGalbreath
Brands Exported: Galbreath
Regions Exported to: Central America, South America, Europe, Asia, Middle East
Percentage of Business in Exporting: 5

44455 Galil Importing Corp
120 Eileen Way
Syosset, NY 11791 516-496-7400
Fax: 516-496-8811 sales@galilco.com
galilfoods.com
Confections; salt; nuts; olives; pickles and pickled vegetables.
President: Raymond Nourmand
Year Founded: 1985
Estimated Sales: $6,000,000
Number Employees: 9
Brands Imported: Galil; Zweet; Lior; Nature's Envy; Shams; Bright Morning
Regions Imported from: Central America

44456 Galilee Splendor
333 Sylvan Avenue
Englewd Clfs, NJ 07632-2724 201-871-4433
Fax: 201-871-8726 800-200-6736
galileespl@aol.com
Wholesaler/distributor and importer of crisp breads, bottled water and Israeli foods
President: Peter Shamir
Estimated Sales: $ 5 - 10 Million
Number Employees: 5-9
Parent Co: Sky is the Limited
Brands Imported: Bible Bread; River Jordan Spring Water

44457 Galley
50 South US Highway One
Jupiter, FL 33477-5107 561-748-5200
Fax: 561-748-5250 800-537-2772
galley@galleyline.com www.galleyline.com
Manufacturer and exporter of modular and mobile cafeteria and buffet equipment, salad bars, hot food tables and portable freezers
President: Alice Spritzer
CEO: Larry Spritzer
Estimated Sales: $500,000-$1 Million
Number Employees: 1-4
Square Footage: 11000
Brands Exported: Galley
Regions Exported to: Worldwide
Percentage of Business in Exporting: 2

44458 Gallimore Industries
PO Box 158
Lake Villa, IL 60046 847-356-3331
Fax: 847-356-6224 800-927-8020
mark@gallimoreinc.com
Manufacturer and exporter of in-pack coupons and coupon inserters
President: Claris Gallimore
CEO: C Clay Gallimore
Quality Control: Mark Gallimore
Equip. VP/Production Manager: Kent Gallimore
Print VP/Production Manager: Mark Gallimore
Estimated Sales: Below $5 Million
Number Employees: 10-19
Square Footage: 42000
Regions Exported to: Central America, Canada
Percentage of Business in Exporting: 2

44459 Gallo
3600 S Memorial Dr
Racine, WI 53403-3822 262-752-9950
Fax: 262-752-9951
Manufacturer and exporter of resealable plastic bag sealers
President: Mary Sollman
VP: Thomas Sollman
Estimated Sales: $ 1 - 2.5 Million
Number Employees: 10-19
Square Footage: 32000
Regions Exported to: Canada
Percentage of Business in Exporting: 10

44460 Gamajet Cleaning Systems
604 Jeffers Circle
Exton, PA 19341-2524 610-408-9940
Fax: 610-408-9945 800-289-5387
sales@gamajet.com www.gamajet.com
Manufacturer and exporter of tank cleaning equipment and CIP systems for fermenters, reactors, tank trucks, storage tanks and industrial process vessels
Chairman: Robert Delaney
Sales/Customer Service: Linda Chappell
Estimated Sales: $1-2.5 Million
Number Employees: 10-19
Square Footage: 19200
Parent Co: Alfa Laval Group
Brands Exported: Gamajet
Regions Exported to: Central America, South America, Asia, Australia
Percentage of Business in Exporting: 10

44461 Gamewell Corporation
251 Crawford Street
Northborough, MA 01532-1234 508-231-1400
Fax: 508-231-0900 888-347-3269
www.gamewell.com
Manufacturer and exporter of fire alarm systems
President: Bill Abraham
Estimated Sales: $20-50 Million
Number Employees: 50-99
Regions Exported to: Worldwide
Percentage of Business in Exporting: 4

44462 Ganeden, Inc
5800 Landerbrook Dr
Suite 300
Mayfield Hts, OH 44124 440-229-5200
Fax: 440-229-5240 info@ganedenprobiotics.com
www.ganedenprobiotics.com
Manufacturer and distributor probiotic ingredients.
Chairman of the Board: Andy Lefkowitz
CEO: Michael Bush
Director of Marketing: Erin Marshall
Regions Exported to: Worldwide

44463 (HQ)Ganong Bros Ltd
One Chocolate Dr
St. Stephen, NB E3L 2X5
Canada 506-465-5600
Fax: 506-465-5610 888-270-8222
feedback@ganong.com www.ganong.com
Confectionery products including bagged candy, boxed chocolate and fruit snacks. Many old fashion varieties such as rich milk caramel, sinful chaocolate truffles, peanut butter cups, delicious double dipped cherries and the one andonly chicken bones.
President & CEO: Bryana Ganong
VP, Innovation & Contract Manufacturing: Nicholas Ganong
CFO: Joe Lacey
Executive Vice Chair: David Ganong
Director, National Sales: John Burgess
Director, Operations: Tim Byrne
Year Founded: 1873
Estimated Sales: $32 Million
Number Employees: 325
Type of Packaging: Consumer, Private Label, Bulk
Brands Exported: Delecto; Fevitfull

44464 Ganong Bros Ltd
500 St. George St
Moncton, NB E1C 1Y3
Canada 506-389-7898
Fax: 506-854-5826 www.ganong.com
Confectionery products including bagged candy, boxed chocolate and fruit snacks. Many old fashion varieties such as rich milk caramel, sinful chocolate truffles, peanut butter cups, delicious double dipped cherries and the one and onlychicken bones.
Estimated Sales: $32 Million
Number Employees: 325
Type of Packaging: Consumer, Private Label, Bulk

44465 Ganz Brothers
12 Mulberry Ct
Paramus, NJ 7652 201-845-6010
Fax: 201-384-1329
Manufacturer and exporter of wrapping machinery including high speed, paperboard, multipack and shrink film for cans, bottles, cups and tubs
President: Christopher Ganz
cganz@ganz.com
VP: Jay Ganz
VP: Jay Ganz
Manager: Lisa Noch
Estimated Sales: $2.5-5 Million
Number Employees: 19
Square Footage: 24000
Regions Exported to: Worldwide
Percentage of Business in Exporting: 70

44466 Gar Products
170 Lehigh Ave
Lakewood, NJ 08701-4526 732-364-2100
Fax: 732-370-5021 800-424-2477
elliotb@garproducts.com www.garproducts.com
Manufacturer and exporter of indoor and outdoor barstools, chairs, tables and bases; importer of chair frames and table base castings

317

Importers & Exporters / A-Z

President: Jay Garfunkel
jaygar@garproducts.com
Vice President: Ellen Garfunkle
Quality Control: Sam Garfunkle
Sales Director: Elliot Bass
Operations Manager: Sam Garfunkle
Plant Manager: Jose Lopez
Purchasing Manager: Daniel Hyams
Number Employees: 20-49
Square Footage: 300000
Regions Exported to: Central America, Middle East
Percentage of Business in Exporting: 2
Regions Imported from: Europe, Asia
Percentage of Business in Importing: 80

44467 Garb-El Products Co
240 Michigan St # 1
Lockport, NY 14094-1797   716-434-6010
    Fax: 716-434-9148 jcarbonejr@garb-el.com
        www.garb-el.com
Manufacturer and exporter of food waste disposal equipment and prep stations
President/ CEO: James M. Carbone, Jr.
VP: Deborah Carbone
Contact: Deborah Carbone
jcarbonejr@garb-el.com
Estimated Sales: $ 1-2.5 Million
Number Employees: 10-19
Square Footage: 30000
Regions Exported to: Worldwide
Percentage of Business in Exporting: 2

44468 Garber Farms
3405 Descannes Hwy
Iota, LA 70543-3118   337-824-6328
    Fax: 337-824-2676 800-824-2284
        www.garberfarm.com
Processor and exporter of long grain white rice and yams
Owner: Wayne Garber
Partner: Wayne Garber
Sales/Marketing Partner: Wayne Garber
layamla@aol.com
Production Manager: Earl Garber
Estimated Sales: $1-2.5 Million
Number Employees: 10-19
Square Footage: 200000
Type of Packaging: Consumer, Food Service, Private Label, Bulk
Brands Exported: Creole Rose Rice; Creole Classic Yams
Regions Exported to: Europe, Canada
Percentage of Business in Exporting: 20

44469 (HQ)Garcoa Laboratories Inc
26135 Mureau Rd # 100
Calabasas, CA 91302-3184   818-225-0113
    Fax: 818-225-9251 800-831-4247
        info@garcoa.com www.garcoa.com
Processor and exporter of vitamins and supplements.
President: Richard Soriano
rsoriano@ci.banning.ca.us
CEO: Gregory Rubin
VP/Sales: Terry Williams
R&D: Moh Chizari
Quality Control: Juan Leal
Marketing: Donna Fedecki
Sales: Gregory Rubin
Operations/Purchasing: Jack Clark
Estimated Sales: & 125 Million
Number Employees: 10-19
Square Footage: 8000000
Type of Packaging: Consumer, Private Label
Brands Exported: Vitamin Classics; Nature's Glory; Nature's Beauty; Nature's Balance
Regions Exported to: Central America, South America, Europe, Asia, Middle East
Percentage of Business in Exporting: 10

44470 Garden & Valley Isle Seafood
225 N Nimitz Hwy # 3
Honolulu, HI 96817-5349   808-524-4847
    Fax: 808-528-5590 800-689-2733
        info@gvisfd.com www.gvisfd.com
Ahi, sashimi, swordfish and snapper; importer and exporter of fresh seafood; wholesaler/distributor of smoked fish and general merchandise
President: Robert Fram
info@gvisfd.com
CFO: Richard Jenks
Vice President: David Marabella
Operations: Cliff Yamauchi

Estimated Sales: $13,500,000
Number Employees: 20-49
Square Footage: 18000
Type of Packaging: Bulk
Regions Exported to: Worldwide
Percentage of Business in Exporting: 33
Regions Imported from: Worldwide
Percentage of Business in Importing: 33

44471 (HQ)Garden Complements Inc
920 Cable Rd
Kansas City, MO 64116-4244   816-421-1090
    Fax: 816-421-4220 800-966-1091
        info@gardencomplements.com
        www.gardencomplements.com
Sauces including barbecue, Mexican, Italian and Asian marinades, salsas, salad dressing, gourmet products
President: Don Blackman
Marketing Director: Jim Pirotte
Estimated Sales: $1-2.5 Million
Number Employees: 5-9
Square Footage: 45000
Type of Packaging: Consumer, Food Service, Private Label, Bulk
Brands Exported: Ausie Sauces & Marinades

44472 Garden Protein International
200-12751 Vulcan Way
Richmond, BC V6V 3C8
Canada   604-278-7300
    Fax: 604-278-8238 877-305-6777
        www.gardein.com
Frozen and fresh meals
President: Yves Potvin
Vice President: Ihab Leheta
VP Sales: Richard Bauman
Estimated Sales: $3 Million
Number Employees: 20-49
Type of Packaging: Food Service

44473 Garden Row Foods
9150 Grand Avenue
Franklin Park, IL 60131-3038   847-455-2200
    Fax: 847-455-9100 800-555-9798
Manufacturer and distribuor of hot sauces and other products, including Endorphin Rush, Pyromania, Brutal Bajan and 350 more products.
Owner: Gary Poppins
Principal: George Kosten
Estimated Sales: $2.5-5,000,000
Number Employees: 10-19
Type of Packaging: Consumer, Food Service, Bulk
Regions Exported to: Europe, Asia, Middle East, Canada, Caribbean, Mexico, Latin America, Africa
Percentage of Business in Exporting: 5

44474 Gardner Denver Inc.
222 E Erie St
Suite 500
Milwaukee, WI 53202
        www.gardnerdenver.com
Compressed air, blower and vacuum applications.
President & CEO, Industrials Group: Vicente Reynal
Parent Co: Ingersoll Rand Inc
Regions Exported to: USA
Percentage of Business in Exporting: 5

44475 Gardner Manufacturing Inc
1201 W Lake St
Horicon, WI 53032-1819   920-485-4303
    Fax: 920-485-4370 800-242-5513
        www.gardnermfg.com
Manufacturer and exporter of insect electrocuting systems, traps and lamps
Owner: John S Jones
johnjones@gardnermfg.com
Quality Control: Mark Sullivan
Sales Division: Robert Marschke
Estimated Sales: $ 10 - 20 Million
Number Employees: 100-249
Square Footage: 190000
Regions Exported to: Europe, Asia
Percentage of Business in Exporting: 1

44476 Gardner's Gourmet
45450 Industrial Pl # 3
Fremont, CA 94538-6474   510-490-6106
    Fax: 510-490-4563 800-676-8558
        info@greatdrink.com www.greatdrink.com

Processor and exporter of frosted caffe ghiaccio, granitas, iced cappuccino and smoothie mixes, our original fruit ices, concentrates, frozen cocktails, fruit purees and flavoring syrups.
Owner: Beverly Fritz
Estimated Sales: $ 3 - 5,000,000
Number Employees: 1-4
Regions Exported to: Canada
Percentage of Business in Exporting: 10

44477 Garland Commercial Industries
185 South St
Freeland, PA 18224-1916   570-636-1000
    Fax: 570-636-3903 www.garland-group.com
Senior VP: Dale Kostick

44478 Garland Commercial Ranges Ltd.
1177 Kamato Road
Mississauga, ON L4W 1X4
Canada   905-624-0260
        www.garland-group.com
Manufacturer and exporter of commercial cooking equipment including ranges, ovens, gas and electric broilers and griddles; custom cooking equipment available
CFO: Angelo Ascidne
CEO: Dale Kostick
Senior VP: Dale Kostick
Regional Manager: Jeff McGowan
Number Employees: 250-499
Number of Brands: 2
Number of Products: 1005
Square Footage: 904000
Parent Co: ENODIS
Regions Exported to: Central America

44479 Garland Writing Instruments
1 S Main St
Coventry, RI 2816   401-828-9582
    Fax: 401-823-7460
        customerservice@garlandpen.com
        www.garlandpen.com
Quality writing instruments and accessories. USA-made writing collections offer a full color logo top. All writing instruments and accessories can be customized
President: Louise Lanoie
VP: Kevin Bittle
Estimated Sales: $ 10 - 20 Million
Number Employees: 20-49
Number of Brands: 1
Square Footage: 130000
Brands Exported: Garland

44480 Garlic Valley Farms Inc
624 Ruberta Ave
Glendale, CA 91201   818-247-9600
    Fax: 818-247-9828 800-424-7990
        Info@GarlicValleyFarms.com
        www.garlicvalleyfarms.com
Processor, importer and exporter of liquid garlic products including juices and purees
President: William Anderson
CFO: Sonja Anderson
R&D: Bill Brock
Contact: Noli Leoncio
noli@garlicvalleyfarms.com
Estimated Sales: $1,200,000
Number Employees: 5-9
Number of Products: 2
Square Footage: 30000
Type of Packaging: Consumer
Brands Exported: Garlic Juice
Regions Exported to: Europe, Canada, UK

44481 Garlic and Spice, Inc.
9674 Telstar Ave
Unit H
El Monte, CA 91731   626-579-2888
    Fax: 626-579-2333 info@garlicandspice.com
        www.garlicandspice.com
Importer of spices including dehydrated garlic, onion and various chilies for spices re-packers, seasoning and ingredients companies, wholesalers for restaurants, and any other food and beverage applications.
President: Min Li
CEO: Xuehui Bai
Sales Manager: Jason Hao
Number Employees: 600+
Square Footage: 240000
Type of Packaging: Food Service, Private Label, Bulk
Regions Imported from: Asia, Africa, China

Importers & Exporters / A-Z

44482 Garroutte
830 NE Loop 410 # 203
San Antonio, TX 78209-1207   210-826-2321
Fax: 210-824-5253   888-457-4997
Manufacturer and exporter of custom designed food processing equipment
President: Bob Garrett
Sales Support Manager: Richard Knappen
International Rep.: John Wurster
Operations Manager: Dan Southwood
Estimated Sales: $ 5-10 Million
Number Employees: 5-9
Square Footage: 120000
Regions Exported to: Central America, South America, Europe
Percentage of Business in Exporting: 10

44483 Garuda International
PO Box 159
Exeter, CA 93221-0159   559-594-4380
Fax: 559-594-4689   www.garudaint.com
Development and marketing of ingredients derived from natural sources
President/CEO: J Roger Matkin
Marketing/Sales: Bassam Faress
Contact: Liang Chen
lchen@garudaint.com
Estimated Sales: $500,000-$1 Million
Number Employees: 5-9
Square Footage: 30000
Type of Packaging: Private Label, Bulk
Brands Exported: Rice*Trin; Tapi*3; Malta Gran; Essential Aloe; Insta-Starch; Insta-Thick; RicePro; Lem; Rem; Foamex; Vege-Coat; Cowcium; Moo-Calcium; Lesstanol
Regions Exported to: Worldwide
Percentage of Business in Exporting: 90
Regions Imported from: Central America, South America, Asia
Percentage of Business in Importing: 5

44484 Garver Manufacturing Inc
224 N Columbia St
PO Box 306
Union City, IN 47390-1432   765-964-5828
Fax: 765-964-5828   www.garvermfg.com
Manufacture a wide variety of industrial centrifuges, bottle shakers, and bottle washers as well as custom equipment.
President: Michael Read
garvermfg@woh.rr.com
Estimated Sales: Less Than $500,000
Number Employees: 1-4
Number of Brands: 2
Number of Products: 5
Square Footage: 16000
Brands Exported: Garver; Kimble
Regions Exported to: Central America, South America, Asia

44485 Garvey Corp
208 S Route 73
Hammonton, NJ 08037-9565   609-561-2450
Fax: 609-561-2328   800-257-8581
garvey@garvey.com   www.garvey.com
Conveyors and accumulators; exporter of conveyor systems and components; also, installation and start-up services available
President: Mark Garvey
Cmo: Ruth Caldwell
rcaldwell@garvey.com
VP: William Garvey
Sales: Michael Earling
Estimated Sales: $ 20 - 50 Million
Number Employees: 50-99
Type of Packaging: Bulk
Regions Exported to: Central America, Europe, Asia, Canada, Mexico
Percentage of Business in Exporting: 1

44486 Gary Manufacturing Company
2626 Southpoint Wat
Suite E
National City, CA 91950   619-429-4479
Fax: 619-429-4810   800-775-0804
www.garymanufacturing.com
Manufacturer and exporter of plastic and fabric table covers, aprons and napkins
Co-Owner: Helen Smith
Estimated Sales: $2.5-5 Million
Number Employees: 5-9
Square Footage: 20000
Regions Exported to: Central America, South America, Europe, Mexico
Percentage of Business in Exporting: 5

44487 Gary Plastic Packaging Corporation
3539 Tiemann Ave
Bronx, NY 10469-1636   718-231-4285
Fax: 203-629-1160   800-221-8151
sales@plasticboxes.com   www.plasticboxes.com
Manufacturer and exporter of plastic boxes, containers and packaging materials; also, package design service available
Owner: Valerie A Gray
Sales: Rich Satone
Estimated Sales: 25-50 Million
Number Employees: 1-4
Regions Exported to: Worldwide

44488 Gary Plastic Packaging Corporation
3539 Tiemann Ave
Bronx, NY 10469-1636   718-231-4285
Fax: 203-629-1160   800-227-4279
sales@plasticboxes.com   www.plasticboxes.com
Advertising specialties, plastic packaging and candy boxes; exporter of packaging products
Owner: Valerie A Gray
VP: Marilyn Hellinger
Sales: Rich Satone
Estimated Sales: $ 24 Million
Number Employees: 1-4
Square Footage: 4000
Regions Exported to: Europe
Percentage of Business in Exporting: 1

44489 Gasketman Inc
PO Box 78136
Corona, CA 92877-0137   951-870-7116
Fax: 951-341-5117
Wholesaler/distributor and exporter of nonasbestos belting, cups, gaskets, hose, matting, O-rings, packing rod, packing sheet, plastics, protective clothing and tape
Sales: Mike Lucas
Estimated Sales: $2.5-5 Million
Number Employees: 1-4
Regions Exported to: Worldwide
Percentage of Business in Exporting: 10

44490 Gaspar's Linguica Co Inc
384 Faunce Corner Rd
North Dartmouth, MA 02747-1257   508-998-2012
Fax: 508-998-2015   800-542-2038
gaspars@linguica.com   www.linguica.com
Portugese sausage, linguica, chourico, turkey linguica and chourico, andouille, kielbasa, salapicao, chourizos and morcela
President: Charles Gaspar
Sales Director: Randy Gaspar
IT: Annette Scrocca
gaspararap@linguica.com
Plant Manager: Charles Gaspar
Estimated Sales: $6 Million
Number Employees: 20-49
Square Footage: 102000
Type of Packaging: Consumer, Food Service, Private Label
Regions Exported to: Bermuda
Percentage of Business in Exporting: 5

44491 Gasser Chair Co Inc
4136 Logan Way
Youngstown, OH 44505-1797   330-759-2234
Fax: 330-759-9844   800-323-2234
sales@gasserchair.com   www.gasserchair.com
Wood and metal chairs, barstools and tables
President: Gary Gasser
gary.gasser@gasserchair.com
CEO: George L Gasser
President: Mark Gasser
VP Sales/Marketing: Cindy Gasser
Estimated Sales: $10-20 Million
Number Employees: 50-99
Square Footage: 300000
Regions Exported to: Central America, South America, Europe, Asia, Middle East
Percentage of Business in Exporting: 12

44492 Gast Jun-Air
2300 M 139
Benton Harbor, MI 49022-6114   269-926-6171
Fax: 269-925-8288   technical.junair@idexcorp.com
Estimated Sales: $ 3 - 5 Million
Number Employees: 500-999
Percentage of Business in Exporting: 5

44493 Gastro-Gnomes
22 Brightview Drive
West Hartford, CT 06117-2001   860-236-0225
Fax: 860-236-7967   800-747-4666
Manufacturer and exporter of plastic and thematic menu stands, menus and pop-out menu inserts
President: Allan Grody
Vice President: Marjorie Grody
Number Employees: 4
Regions Exported to: South America, Europe, Asia, Canada, Caribbean, Mexico

44494 Gates Mectrol Inc
9 Northwestern Dr
Salem, NH 03079-4809   603-890-1515
Fax: 603-890-1616   800-394-4844
contact@gatesmectrol.com   www.gatesmectrol.com
Timing pulleys and polymer based automation components and synchronous timing belts.
President: Mark Appleton
appleton@gatesmectrol.com
Number Employees: 100-249
Regions Exported to: North America, Worldwide

44495 Gateway Food Products Co
1728 N Main St
Dupo, IL 62239-1045   618-286-4844
Fax: 618-286-3444   877-220-1963
traines@gatewayfoodproducts.com
www.gatewayfoodproducts.com
Syrups, vegetable oils and shortenings; exporter of corn syrup; wholesaler/distributor of general line items; also shortening flakes, popcorn oils and butter toppings
President: John Crosley
jcrosley@gatewayfoodproducts.com
Vice President: Carroll Crosley
Quality Control: Jeremy Gray
Marketing Director: Teresa Raines
Sales Director: Teresa Raines
Operations Manager: Jeremy Gray
Production Manager: Jim Raines
Plant Manager: Jim Raines
Purchasing Manager: John Crosley
Estimated Sales: $10-20 Million
Number Employees: 10-19
Number of Products: 9
Square Footage: 75000
Type of Packaging: Food Service, Private Label, Bulk
Regions Exported to: Canada
Percentage of Business in Exporting: 1

44496 Gaudet & Ouellette
Chemin Bas-Cap-Pele
Cap-Pele, NB E4N 1L8
Canada   506-577-4016
Fax: 506-577-4006
Smoked herring
President: Normand Ouellette
Estimated Sales: $5,000,000
Number Employees: 30
Type of Packaging: Bulk
Regions Exported to: US, West Indies
Percentage of Business in Exporting: 100

44497 Gaylord Container Corporation
8700 Adamo Dr
Tampa, FL 33619-3524   813-621-3591
Fax: 813-621-3318   www.templeinland.com
Manufacturer and exporter of corrugated shipping containers, boxes and cartons
Manager: Wayne Parker
Controller: P Wilkins
General Manager: John Thrift
Production Supervisor: R Piepenbring
Estimated Sales: $20-50 Million
Number Employees: 100-249

44498 Gaylord Industries
10900 SW Avery St
Tualatin, OR 97062-8578   503-691-2010
Fax: 503-692-6048   800-547-9696
www.gaylordventilation.com
or more than 75 years, Gaylord's ventilation systems have been known for durability, dependability, and meticulous attention to detail. They continue to revolutionize the industry with groundbreaking new designs as well as an innovative approach to solving the two main priorities facing foodservice operators: enrg savings and labor optimization.

Importers & Exporters / A-Z

President: Dan Shoop
CFO: Jeana Randall
R&D: Biucazx Lukins
Sales Manager: Keven Hass
Estimated Sales: $ 10 - 20 Million
Number Employees: 100-249
Square Footage: 150000
Brands Exported: Gaylord
Regions Exported to: Worldwide
Percentage of Business in Exporting: 15

44499 Gbn Machine & Engineering
17073 Bull Church Rd
Woodford, VA 22580-2412   804-448-2033
    Fax: 804-448-2684 800-446-9871
    gbnmach@verizon.net www.nailerman.com
Manufacturer and exporter of pallet assembly systems, lumber stackers and conveyors
Vice President: Paul Bailey
paul@nailerman.com
Estimated Sales: Below $5 Million
Number Employees: 5-9
Regions Exported to: Worldwide
Percentage of Business in Exporting: 25

44500 Gbs
7233 Freedom Ave NW
North Canton, OH 44720-7123   330-494-5330
                               800-552-2427
    marketing@gbscorp.com www.gbscorp.com
Manufacturer and exporter of plastic film, pressure sensitive labels and tags
VP: Jim Lee
VP/General Manager: James Lee
Marketing Director: Jackie Davidson
Plant Manager: Bruce Budney
Estimated Sales: $4 Million
Number Employees: 1-4
Square Footage: 120000

44501 (HQ)Gch Internatonal
330 Boxley Ave
Louisville, KY 40209-1845   502-636-1374
    Fax: 502-636-0125 www.gchintl.com
Manufacturer and exporter of surge bins, vibrating sizing conveyors, enrobers and separators; also, freezers including spiral, tunnel and trolley
Chief Operating Officer: Haldun Turgay
CEO: John Thornton
jthornton@gchintl.com
VP Business Development: Edward Ward
Sales Manager Food: Thomas Fahed
Estimated Sales: $1-2.5 Million
Number Employees: 50-99
Square Footage: 360000
Parent Co: GCH International
Other Locations:
    Cardwell Machine Co.
    Farnborough, NHCardwell Machine Co.
Brands Exported: Vibe-O-Vey; Vibe-O-Bin; PAL
Regions Exported to: Central America, South America, Europe, Asia
Percentage of Business in Exporting: 25

44502 GePolymershapes Cadillac
25900 Telegraph Road
Southfield, MI 48033-5222   248-603-8600
    Fax: 248-603-8693 800-488-1200
Wholesaler/distributor and exporter of plastic sheets, rods, tubes and films; also, replacement parts for food processing equipment
President: Kent Darragh
VP Marketing: Tom Taylor
Parent Co: M.A. Hanna
Regions Exported to: Europe, Asia

44503 Gea Intec, Llc
4319 S Alston Ave
Suite 105
Durham, NC 27713   919-433-0131
                    Fax: 919-433-0140
Single and variable retention time freezers/chillers for the food and beverage industries.
Contact: Jennifer Shambley
jshambley@gearefrigeration.com
Parent Co: Intec USA
Regions Exported to: Central America, South America, Europe, Asia, Middle East, North America, India, USA

44504 Gea Us
20903 W Gale Ave
Galesville, WI 54630-7276   608-582-3081
                    Fax: 608-582-2581
Manufacturer, importer and exporter of dairy farm equipment and machinery including milk meters, processors and coolers
Manager: Ralph Rottier
Cio/Cto: Kathy Snyder
kathy.snyder@westfaliasurge.com
VP: Ralph Rottier
Estimated Sales: $ 20-50 Million
Number Employees: 100-249
Square Footage: 140000
Parent Co: Babson Brothers Company
Brands Exported: Surge
Regions Exported to: Central America, South America, Europe, Asia, Middle East
Percentage of Business in Exporting: 20
Regions Imported from: Europe
Percentage of Business in Importing: 5

44505 Gebo Conveyors, Consultants & Systems
1045 Autoroute Chomedey
Laval, QC H7W 4V3
Canada   450-973-3337
    Fax: 450-973-3336 www.sidel.com
Manufacturer and exporter of stainless steel tabletop conveying systems and equipment including package line controls, pressure-free combiners, packer infeed systems and line audits
President: Mark Aury
Sales Manager: Jean Dion
Project Director: Mike De Cotiis
Number Employees: 250
Square Footage: 260000
Parent Co: Gebo Industries
Brands Exported: Gebo
Regions Exported to: Central America, South America, USA
Percentage of Business in Exporting: 92

44506 Gebo Corporation
6015 31st Street E
Bradenton, FL 34203-5382   941-727-1400
                    Fax: 941-727-1200
Manufacturer, importer and exporter of conveyors including air trans and cap feeder
President: Mark Aury
Marketing Director: George Louli
General Manager: Christian Fitsch-Mouras
Estimated Sales: $20-50 Million
Number Employees: 100-249
Square Footage: 40000
Parent Co: Sidel Corporation
Regions Exported to: Worldwide
Percentage of Business in Exporting: 30
Regions Imported from: Worldwide
Percentage of Business in Importing: 20

44507 Gedney Foods Co
12243 Branford St
Sun Valley, CA 91352   952-448-2612
                               888-244-0653
    info@gedneypickle.com www.gedneyfoods.com
Condiments, barbecue sauces, vinegars, syrups, pickles, relishes, sauerkraut, salsas, salad dressings, mayonnaise, mustard; cucumbers
CEO: Gary Ethan Kamins
VP, Operations: Rod Prochaska
Estimated Sales: $6-8 Million
Number Employees: 100-249
Parent Co: PMC Global, Inc.
Type of Packaging: Consumer, Food Service, Private Label, Bulk
Regions Imported from: Mexico
Percentage of Business in Importing: 35

44508 Geerpres Inc
1780 Harvey St
Muskegon, MI 49442-5396   231-773-3211
    Fax: 231-773-8263 sales@geerpres.com
                    www.geerpres.com
Manufactures cleaning tools for the maintenance supply industry in a business-to-business environment: steel, stainless steel, plastic, microfiber and metal components.
President: Scott Ribbe
scott@geerpres.com
CFO: Bryan Depree
R&D: Joe Fodrocy
Quality Control: Jeff Kulbe
Marketing Director: Megan Schihl
Sales Director: Ted Moon
Purchasing Manager: Barb McAttnen
Estimated Sales: Below $ 5 Million
Number Employees: 20-49
Square Footage: 340000

44509 Gehnrich Oven Sales Company
2675 Main Street
East Troy, WI 53120   262-642-3938
    Fax: 262-363-4018 sales@wisoven.com
                    www.wisoven.com/gehnrich-oven
Manufacturer and exporter of convection baking and cooking ovens
President: Richard Gehnrich
Treasurer: Leon Pedigo, Jr.
VP: Wayne Pedigo
Estimated Sales: $1-2.5 Million
Number Employees: 20-49
Square Footage: 45000
Parent Co: Nevo Corporation
Regions Exported to: Central America, South America, Europe, Asia, Middle East
Percentage of Business in Exporting: 15

44510 Geiger Bros
70 Mount Hope Ave
Lewiston, ME 04240-1021   207-755-2000
    Fax: 207-755-2422 geigerorders@geiger.com
                    www.geiger.com
Manufacturer and exporter of advertising specialties
Regional VP East: Fred Snyder
Owner, CEO: Gene Geiger
CFO: Bob Blaisdell
Owner, Executive Vice President: Peter Geiger
V.P. Marketing: Gary Biron
V.P. Sales & Marketing: Jim Habzda
Vice President of Operations: Sheila Olson
Estimated Sales: $ 500,000 - $ 1 Million
Number Employees: 500-999
Square Footage: 40000
Brands Exported: Time By Design; Farmer's Almanac
Regions Exported to: Worldwide
Percentage of Business in Exporting: 10

44511 Gelnex Gelatins
30 North Michigan Ave
Suite 1111
Chicago, IL 60601   312-577-4275
    Fax: 888-505-1771 www.gelnex.com
Gelatins
President: Alessandro Luize
CEO: Ross Priebbenow
Executive VP: Felipe Chaluppe
fchaluppe@gelnex.com
Estimated Sales: $500,000-1 Million
Number Employees: 4

44512 Gemini Bakery Equipment
9991 Global Rd
Philadelphia, PA 19115-1005   215-676-9508
    Fax: 215-673-3944 800-468-9046
    sales@geminibe.com www.geminibe.com
Manufacturer and importer of bakery equipment
CEO/ Founder: Mark Rosenberg
Marketing Coordinator: Laura Albright
Sales Exec: Lou Giliberti
Estimated Sales: $10-20 Million
Number Employees: 20-49
Regions Exported to: Worldwide

44513 Gems Sensors & Controls
1 Cowles Rd
Plainville, CT 06062-1107   860-747-3000
    Fax: 860-793-4531 www.gemssensors.com
Manufacturer and exporter of conductance actuated liquid level controls including sanitary probes and fittings; also, underground leak detection services available
President: Blue Lane
twanbentlage@yahoo.com
Marketing Specialist: Tony Mancin
Estimated Sales: H
Number Employees: 100-249
Square Footage: 29000
Parent Co: Danaher Corporation
Regions Exported to: Central America, South America, Asia, Middle East, Australia
Percentage of Business in Exporting: 8

44514 Genarom International
6 Santa Fe Way
Cranbury, NJ 08512-3288   609-409-6200
                    Fax: 609-409-6500

Processor and exporter of marinades, sauces and flavors including beef, chicken, turkey, pork, ham, cheese, seafood and creams
CEO: Gary Rodkin
President/Comercial Foods: Paul Maass
Number Employees: 20-49
Square Footage: 60000
Type of Packaging: Food Service, Bulk
Brands Exported: Dohler, Genarom
Regions Exported to: Europe, Asia
Percentage of Business in Exporting: 20

44515 General Bag Corporation
3368 W 137th St
Cleveland, OH 44111 216-941-1190
    Fax: 216-476-3401 800-837-9396
                generalbag@aol.com
Manufacturer and distributor of all packaging materials paper bags, poly, mesh. Boxes all sizes, bulk and waxed produce cartons; also packaging machinery
President: Rob Sprosty
Sales Manager: Dan Juba
Sales Representative: Larry Sprosty
Contact: Robert Sprosty
generalbag@aol.com
Estimated Sales: $ 5 - 10 Million
Number Employees: 20-49
Square Footage: 160000
Brands Imported: Upmann; Drumar; Schema
Regions Imported from: Central America, South America, Europe, Asia
Percentage of Business in Importing: 20

44516 General Cage
238 N 29th St
Elwood, IN 46036-1702 765-552-5039
    Fax: 765-552-6962 800-428-6403
Manufacturer and exporter of wire products including forms, specialties, cages, display racks, partitions, grills, etc
Member: Bruce D Cook
Estimated Sales: $ 10-20 Million
Number Employees: 100-249
Square Footage: 216000

44517 General Commodities International
10865 NW 29th Street
Doral, FL 33172-5913
    305-592-8778
    Fax: 305-477-4660
Importer and exporter of specialty European confectionery products
CEO/President: Benigno Gonzalez
Vice President: Juan Gonzalez
Estimated Sales: $10-20 Million
Number Employees: 10-19
Square Footage: 17000
Percentage of Business in Exporting: 3
Brands Imported: Delaviuda; Albatros
Regions Imported from: Europe
Percentage of Business in Importing: 90

44518 General Corrugated Machinery Company
269 Commercial Avenue
Palisades Park, NJ 07650-1154 201-944-0644
  Fax: 201-944-7858 70451.2363@compuserve.com
Manufacturer and exporter of corrugated box formers; also, case formers, sealers, case packers and palletizers
Sales Manager: John Lavin
Estimated Sales: $ 1 - 5 Million

44519 General Espresso Equipment
7912 Industrial Village Rd
Greensboro, NC 27409-9691 336-393-0224
    Fax: 336-393-0295 info@geec.com
            www.astoriausaparts.com
Owner: Roberto Daltio
Manager: Randy Brewer
Estimated Sales: $1-3 Million
Number Employees: 10-19

44520 General Films Inc
645 S High St
Covington, OH 45318-1182 937-473-3033
    Fax: 937-473-2403 888-436-3456
            www.generalfilms.com
Manufacturer and exporter of plastic bags, packaging coextruded films and bag-in-box bulk liquid packaging
President: Tim Weikert
Quality Control: Norman Slade
Sales (Food Pkg.): Linda Lyons
Sales Manager (Industrial Pkg.): Howard Stutzman
Sales (Bag-in-Box): Cindy Grogean
Estimated Sales: $ 20 - 50 Million
Number Employees: 50-99
Square Footage: 60000
Regions Exported to: Central America, South America
Percentage of Business in Exporting: 10

44521 General Floor Craft
4 Heights Ter
Little Silver, NJ 07739-1323 973-742-7400
    Fax: 973-742-0004
Manufacturer and exporter of vacuums and carpet cleaning machinery
Owner: Barry Gore
VP: Jeff Gore
Estimated Sales: $2.5-5 Million
Number Employees: 20-49
Square Footage: 54000
Regions Exported to: Worldwide
Percentage of Business in Exporting: 15

44522 General Formulations
309 S Union St
Sparta, MI 49345-1529 616-887-7387
    Fax: 616-887-0537 800-253-3664
            mclay@generalformulations.com
            www.generalformulations.com
Manufacturer and exporter of self-adhesive and floor advertising films
CEO: James Clay
CEO: James Clay
Marketing Manager: Mike Clay
Regional Sales Manager: Jeff Balasko
Estimated Sales: $20-50 Million
Number Employees: 50-99
Square Footage: 100000
Brands Exported: Permalar
Regions Exported to: Worldwide
Percentage of Business in Exporting: 5

44523 General Machinery Corp
1831 N 18th St
PO Box 717
Sheboygan, WI 53081-2312 920-458-2189
    Fax: 920-458-8316 888-243-6622
        sales@genmac.com www.genmac.com
Manufacturer and exporter of meat and cheese processing equipment including meat flakers, slicers, dicers, mechanical tenderizers, grinders, pork rind chippers and cheese cutters; also, cake and bun slabbers, pan washers and beltconveyors.
President: Michael Horwitz
CFO: Marsha Binversie
VP Operations: Robert Jeske
Production Manager: Gary Mueller
Estimated Sales: $2.5-5 Million
Number Employees: 10-19
Regions Exported to: Worldwide
Percentage of Business in Exporting: 15

44524 General Methods Corporation
3012 SW Adams Street
Peoria, IL 61602 309-497-3344
    Fax: 309-497-3345
Manufacturer and exporter of coupon and premium dispensers; also, contract thermoform packaging and seal integrity verification equipment
President: Dale Kuykendall
Chief Tech.: Ken Brackett
Estimated Sales: Less than $ 500,000
Number Employees: 3
Square Footage: 26000

44525 General Packaging Equipment Co
6048 Westview Dr
Houston, TX 77055-5420 713-686-4331
    Fax: 713-683-3967 sales@generalpackaging.com
            www.generalpackaging.com
Manufacturer and exporter of packaging machinery including bag forming and net weighers
President: Robert C Kelly
rkelly@generalpackaging.com
Director of Sales: Tom Wilson
Estimated Sales: $5-10 Million
Number Employees: 20-49
Square Footage: 66000
Type of Packaging: Consumer, Food Service, Private Label
Regions Exported to: Central America, South America
Percentage of Business in Exporting: 20

44526 General Press Corp
110 Allegheny Dr
PO Box 316
Natrona Heights, PA 15065-1902 724-224-3500
    Fax: 724-224-3934 www.generalpress.com
Manufacturer and exporter of die cut paper labels for food and beverage containers; also, heat seal foil lids for single serve jelly cups, injection mold labels and lightweight plastic labels.
President: Scott Poorbaugh
spoorbaugh@generalpress.com
Sales Manager: David Wolff
VP Operations: T Conroy
Estimated Sales: $5-10 Million
Number Employees: 50-99
Square Footage: 120000
Regions Exported to: Canada, Mexico
Percentage of Business in Exporting: 1

44527 General Processing Systems
12838 Stainless Drive
Holland, MI 49424 616-399-2220
    Fax: 616-399-7365 800-547-9370
        jswiatlo@nbe-inc.com www.productsaver.com
Manufacturer and exporter of bag opening equipment and custom designed product recovery systems.
President: Ed Swiatlo
Sales Manager: Jeff Swiatlo
Contact: Joe Reed
todd@nbe-inc.com
Estimated Sales: $ 3 - 5 Million
Number Employees: 10-19
Square Footage: 40000
Parent Co: General Processing Systems
Regions Exported to: Central America, South America, Europe, Asia, Canada, Mexico

44528 General Tape & Supply
28505 Automation Blvd
Wixom, MI 48393-3154 248-357-2744
    Fax: 248-357-2749 800-490-3633
Manufacturer and exporter of pressure sensitive labels
President: Mary Raden
COO: Jack Hooker
Research & Development: Debbie Wojcik
Sales Director: Julie Stallings
Estimated Sales: $ 2.5 - 5 Million
Number Employees: 30

44529 General Trade Mark Labelcraft
55 Lasalle St
Staten Island, NY 10303 718-448-9800
    Fax: 718-448-9808
Embossed and printed labels, price tag seals and stickers; exporter of printed labels
Owner: Richard Capuozzo
CEO: V Kruse
Estimated Sales: $ 10 - 20 Million
Number Employees: 20-49
Square Footage: 40000
Regions Exported to: Worldwide
Percentage of Business in Exporting: 5

44530 General Wax & Candle Co
6863 Beck Ave
North Hollywood, CA 91605-6206 818-765-5800
    Fax: 818-764-3878 800-929-7867
            www.generalwax.com
Manufacturer and exporter of candles
Owner: Jerry Baker
jbaker@generalwax.com
VP: Mike Tapp
Estimated Sales: $ 10 - 15 Million
Number Employees: 50-99
Type of Packaging: Food Service
Regions Exported to: Worldwide
Percentage of Business in Exporting: 30

44531 General, Inc
3355 Enterprise Ave.
Suite 160
Weston, FL 33331 954-202-7419
    Fax: 954-202-7337 info@generalfoodservice.com
            www.generalfoodservice.com
Manufacturer, importer and exporter of slicers, grinders and mixers; manufacturer of food and organic waste disposers

Importers & Exporters / A-Z

President: John Westbrook
VP Sales/Marketing: Harry Ristan
Purchasing Manager: Dean Council
Estimated Sales: $5-10 Million
Number Employees: 100-249
Square Footage: 80000
Parent Co: Standex International Corporation
Type of Packaging: Food Service
Brands Exported: Red Goat Disposers
Regions Exported to: Central America, South America, Europe, Worldwide, Latin America
Percentage of Business in Exporting: 15
Brands Imported: General Slicing
Regions Imported from: Europe
Percentage of Business in Importing: 50

44532 Generation Tea
PO Box 907
Monsey, NY 10952-0907 845-352-1216
Fax: 845-352-2973 866-742-5668
info@generationtea.com www.generationtea.com
Chinese tea
Owner: Michael Sanft
msanft@generationtea.com
Co-Owner: Marci Sanft
Estimated Sales: $300,000-500,000
Number Employees: 1-4

44533 Genesee Brewing Company
445 Saint Paul Street
Rochester, NY 14605 585-263-9200
Fax: 585-546-8928 www.geneseebeer.com
Beers
President: Johnhen Henderson
CEO: Ramon Sanchez
Marketing Brand Manager: Jennifer McCauley
Vice President, Sales: Donald Cotter
Contact: Michael Baker
mbaker@highfalls.com
Estimated Sales: $2 Million
Number Employees: 460+
Number of Brands: 12
Parent Co: Cerveceria Costa Rica S.A.
Type of Packaging: Consumer, Food Service
Brands Exported: JW Dundee's Honey Brown Lager, Michael Shea's Irish Amber, Genny Light, The Genesee Family of Brands and Koch's Golden Anniversary.
Regions Exported to: Ontario, Canada

44534 Genesee Corrugated
2022 North St
Flint, MI 48505 810-228-3702
Fax: 810-235-0350 www.genpackaging.com
Manufacturer and exporter of corrugated shipping containers and interior packing materials
President: Luella Kautman
lkautman@co.genesee.mi.us
Material Control: Bobbi Jackson
Estimated Sales: $23.1 Million
Number Employees: 20-49
Type of Packaging: Bulk
Regions Exported to: Worldwide

44535 Genpak
25 Aylmer Street
P O Box 209
Peterborough, ON K9J 6Y8
Canada
705-743-4733
Fax: 705-743-4798 800-461-1995
info@genpak.com www.genpakca.com
Manufacturer and exporter of plastic containers, cups and lids; also, single-serve packaging machinery for butter, margarine, creamers, etc
Quality Control: Jennifer Seeley
R&D: Jennifer Seeley
National Sales Manager: Kevin Callahan
Production Manager: Bernie Logan
Plant Manager: Brian May
Number Employees: 60
Type of Packaging: Bulk
Regions Exported to: Europe, South Africa
Percentage of Business in Exporting: 3

44536 Genpak LLC
10601 Westlake Dr
Charlotte, NC 28273
800-626-6695
info@genpak.com www.genpak.com

Manufacturer and exporter of plastic and styrofoam take out containers including plates, bowls and take-out containers. Dual oven meal solutions and bakery trays in opet plastic for retail packs. Packaging for processor, food service and retail applications.
Vice Presdient, Marketing: Tawn Whittemore
Director of Product Innovation: Jeff Cole
Estimated Sales: $100-500 Million
Number Employees: 1000-4999
Regions Exported to: Central America, South America, Europe, Asia, Middle East
Percentage of Business in Exporting: 5

44537 Gensaco Marketing
1751 2nd Ave
New York, NY 10128-5388 212-876-1020
Fax: 212-876-1003 800-506-1935
espmachine@aol.com
Coffee bars, espresso and cappuccino machines; importer of grinders; exporter of espresso machines, ice cream machines - restaurant equipment
Partner: Edward V Giannasca
CEO: Al Elvino
VP Sales: Lawrence Coal
VP Purchasing: Carbone Lorenzo
Estimated Sales: $1 Million
Number Employees: 5-9
Square Footage: 34000
Parent Co: Gensaco
Brands Exported: Gensaco
Regions Exported to: Central America, South America, Asia
Brands Imported: Gensaco
Regions Imported from: Europe

44538 Geo. Olcott Company
PO Box 267
Scottsboro, AL 35768-0267 256-259-4937
Fax: 256-259-4942 800-634-2769
Manufacturer and exporter of glass bead blast-cleaning cabinets, degreasing tanks, magnetic detectors and jet spray washers
President: Richard Olcott
Vice President: Marilyn Olcott
Estimated Sales: $1-2.5 Million
Number Employees: 9
Square Footage: 16800
Regions Exported to: Canada
Percentage of Business in Exporting: 5

44539 George A Jeffreys & Company
504 Roanoke St
Salem, VA 24153-3552 540-389-8220
Fax: 540-387-7418 www.novozymes.com
Enzymes
Manager: Doug Acksel
dacksel@novozymes.com
Estimated Sales: $5-10 Million
Number Employees: 10-19
Square Footage: 100000
Regions Exported to: South America, Europe, Asia
Percentage of Business in Exporting: 25

44540 George Basch Company
PO Box 188
Freeport, NY 11520 516-378-8100
Fax: 516-378-8140 info@nevrdull.com
www.nevrdull.com
Metal cleaners and polishes
President: Laurie Basch-Levy
Vice President: Mark Ax
Estimated Sales: $ 5-10 Million
Number Employees: 10-19
Number of Brands: 1
Number of Products: 1

44541 George Chiala Farms Inc
15500 Hill Rd
Morgan Hill, CA 95037-9516 408-778-0562
Fax: 408-779-4034 www.gcfarmsinc.com
Tomatillos, garlic, peppers
President: Alice Chiala
Chief Operating Officer: Tim Chiala
Chief Financial Officer: Christi Becerra
Quality Assurance Manager: Bob See
Sales Director: Joe Trammell
Production Manager: Sam Garcia
Plant Engineer: Rusty McMillan
Estimated Sales: $20-50 Million
Number Employees: 100-249
Number of Products: 300
Square Footage: 40000
Type of Packaging: Food Service, Bulk

44542 George Degen & Co
144 Woodbury Rd # 34
Woodbury, NY 11797-1418 516-692-6862
Fax: 516-692-3140 sales@tungoil.com
www.tungoil.com
Wholesaler/distributor and importer of oils including dehydrated castor, rape seed, tung and oiticica
President: John Blake-Hanson
blakehanson@tungoil.com
Estimated Sales: $2.5-5 Million
Number Employees: 1-4
Type of Packaging: Bulk
Regions Imported from: South America, Europe, Asia, Canada
Percentage of Business in Importing: 90

44543 George E De Lallo Co Inc
6390 State Route 30
Jeannette, PA 15644-3193 724-523-6577
Fax: 724-523-0981 877-335-2556
info@DeLallo.com www.delallo.com
Pasta, sauces, olives, oils
President: Fran Delallo
fran@delallo.com
Purchasing Agent: J Panichella
Estimated Sales: $500,000-$1 Million
Number Employees: 50-99
Type of Packaging: Consumer

44544 George Glove Company, Inc
301 Greenwood Ave
Midland Park, NJ 07432 201-251-1200
Fax: 201-251-8431 800-631-4292
steve@georgeglove.com www.georgeglove.com
Importer of white gloves
President/CEO: Andrew Wilson
CFO: Andrew Wilson
Marketing Director: Roy Miller
Sales: Roy Miller
Contact: Sharon Jubelt
sjubelt@newconceptoffice.com
Operations Manager: Juan Mino
Estimated Sales: $2 Million
Number Employees: 7
Square Footage: 48000
Regions Exported to: Europe
Percentage of Business in Exporting: 2
Regions Imported from: Asia
Percentage of Business in Importing: 90

44545 George Gordon Assoc
12 Continental Blvd
Merrimack, NH 03054-4302 603-424-5204
Fax: 603-424-9031 sales@ggamfg.com
www.ggamfg.com
Packaging machinery, kits packaging, pouching systems, case/carton gaylord loaders
President: Don Blanger
VP Sales/Marketing: Ron Downing
Purchasing Manager: Maurice Demarais
Estimated Sales: $10-20 000,000
Number Employees: 5-9
Brands Exported: Packaging Machinery
Regions Exported to: Europe, Australia, Canada, Mexico
Percentage of Business in Exporting: 5

44546 George Robberecht Seafood
440 Mcguires Wharf Road
Montross, VA 22520-3603 804-472-3556
Fax: 804-472-4800
Blue crab, soft-shell crab, oysters, eel, seafood
President/CEO: Maurice Bosse
President: Wilhemina Bosse
Estimated Sales: $2.5-5 Million
Number Employees: 1-4

44547 George W Saulpaugh & Son
1790 Route 9
Germantown, NY 12526-5512 518-537-6500
Fax: 518-537-5555 info@saulpaughapples.com
www.saulpaughapples.com
Apples, pears, grapes and prunes
Vice President: David Jones

Estimated Sales: $10-20 Million
Number Employees: 20-49
Type of Packaging: Consumer, Food Service, Bulk

44548 George's Candy Shop Inc
558 S Broad St
Mobile, AL 36603-1124 251-433-1689
Fax: 251-433-3364 800-633-1306
www.3georges.com

Pecans and baked goods
President: Scott Gonzales
scott@3georges.com
VP: Sibhan Gonzales
Estimated Sales: $1500000
Number Employees: 50-99
Square Footage: 120000
Type of Packaging: Consumer

44549 Georgetown Farm
P.O.Box 106
Free Union, VA 22940   434-973-6761
Fax: 434-973-7715 888-328-5326
www.eatlean.com
Beef and bison meat; sausage and jerky products
Production: Craig Gibson
Plant Manager: Matt Albert
Estimated Sales: $3-5,000,000
Number Employees: 5-9

44550 (HQ)Georgia Duck & Cordage Mill
21 Laredo Drive
Scottdale, GA 30079   404-297-3170
Fax: 404-296-5165
Manufacturer and exporter of conveyor and elevator belting including vinyl, rubber and urethane
President: Raymond Willoch
VP Sales/Marketing: Ken Dangelo
Sales Manager/National Accounts: Jim Hinson
Sales Manager: Jim Panter
Number Employees: 490
Regions Exported to: Worldwide
Percentage of Business in Exporting: 10

44551 Georgia Spice Company
3600 Atlanta Industrial Parkway
Atlanta, GA 30331   404-696-6200
Fax: 404-696-4546 800-453-9997
SShapiro@gaspiceco.com gaspiceco.com
Spices and seasonings
Owner/CEO/Plant Manager: Selma Shapiro
R&D Director: Brian Lusty
Human Resources Director: S Lafosse
Manufacturing Director: Bob Kupinsky
Estimated Sales: $5 Million
Number Employees: 19
Square Footage: 78000
Type of Packaging: Food Service, Private Label, Bulk
Brands Exported: Georgia Spice
Regions Exported to: Central America, South America, Asia, Middle East, Canada, Caribbean, Latin America
Percentage of Business in Exporting: 15
Regions Imported from: Asia, Middle East, Latin America

44552 Georgia-Pacific LLC
133 Peachtree St. NE
Atlanta, GA 30303   404-652-4000
800-283-5547
www.gp.com
Manufacturer and exporter of corrugated shipping cases.
President/Chief Executive Officer: Christian Fischer
SVP, Operations: Jeff Koeppel
SVP/Chief Financial Officer: Tyler Woolson
SVP/Communications, Gov't & Pub. Affairs: Sheila Weidman
Year Founded: 1927
Estimated Sales: Over $5 Billion
Number Employees: 30,000+
Parent Co: Koch Industries
Type of Packaging: Consumer
Regions Exported to: Asia
Percentage of Business in Exporting: 5

44553 Gerber Agri
1000 Parkwood Circle
Suite 335
Atlanta, GA 30339   770-952-4187
Fax: 770-952-3290 www.gerberatl.com
Exporter of beef
Sr. VP: Earl Skahill
Contact: Andrey Aviles
andreya@gerberatl.com
Number Employees: 5-9
Parent Co: Gerber Agri
Regions Exported to: Japan
Percentage of Business in Exporting: 100

44554 Gerber Cheese Company
704 Executive Boulevard
Valley Cottage, NY 10989-2010   914-347-4000
Fax: 914-592-1324
Importer of specialty cheese products including Gruyere wedges, edam, gouda and fondue; also, chocolate fondue and whole wheat crackers
President: Martin Whalen
Treasurer: Jorg Dirren
General Sales Manager: James DeLaurentis
Estimated Sales: $500,000-$1 Million
Number Employees: 5-9
Square Footage: 24000
Parent Co: Gerber Cheese Company
Type of Packaging: Consumer, Food Service
Brands Imported: Swiss Knight; HUM; Cheese Roussettes; Fondue au Chocolat; Dar-Vida
Regions Imported from: Europe, Canada
Percentage of Business in Importing: 100

44555 Gerber Innovations
24 Industrial Park Rd W
Tolland, CT 6084
Fax: 978-694-0055 800-331-5797
www.gerberinnovations.com
Manufacturer and exporter of computer plotters and sample makers for packaging design
Director of Sales & Marketing: Don Skenderian
Vice President, Business Development: Mark Bibo
Technical Manager: Ken Hooks
VP Sales: Steven Gore
General Manager: W Staniewicz
Estimated Sales: $ 10 - 20 Million
Number Employees: 50-99
Parent Co: Data Technology
Regions Exported to: Worldwide
Percentage of Business in Exporting: 10

44556 Gerber Legendary Blades
14200 SW 72nd Ave.
Portland, OR 97224-8010   503-639-6161
Fax: 503-403-1102 800-950-6161
www.gerbergear.com
Culinary knives including steak, carving, slicing, etc.
Year Founded: 1939
Estimated Sales: $100 Million
Number Employees: 250-499
Parent Co: Fiskars

44557 Gerber Products Co
1812 N Moore St
Arlington, VA 22209
800-284-9488
www.gerber.com
Infant and toddler food.
President & CEO: Bill Partyka
Year Founded: 1927
Estimated Sales: $477 Million
Number Employees: 5,000-9,999
Parent Co: Nestle
Type of Packaging: Food Service, Bulk
Other Locations:
   Production Facility
   Fremont, MI
   Production Facility
   Florham Park, NJ
   Production Facility
   Fort Smith, NJ Production Facility Florham Park
Regions Imported from: Central America, South America, Europe, Asia, Middle East

44558 Gerlau Sales
5015 Cliff Drive
Delta, BC V4M 2C2
Canada   604-943-0961
Fax: 604-943-4799
Wholesaler/distributor, importer and exporter of ceiling/wall panels; food processing equipment & services, smokehouse installation, refurbishing, HACCP implemented, control & recording data acquisition, smokehouse & parts.
President: Sigrid Lauk
VP: Gerhard Lauk
Marketing: Irene Langlais
Regions Exported to: Central America
Regions Imported from: Europe

44559 Germack Pistachio Co
2140 Wilkins St
Detroit, MI 48207-2123   313-393-2000
Fax: 313-393-0636 800-872-4006
wholesale@germack.com www.germack.com
Dried fruit, chocolate and nuts
Estimated Sales: $1,000,000 - $5,000,000
Number Employees: 20-49
Type of Packaging: Consumer, Food Service
Regions Imported from: South America, Europe, Asia, Middle East
Percentage of Business in Importing: 50

44560 Gerrit J. Verburg Company
12238 Germany Rd
Fenton, MI 48430   810-750-9779
Fax: 810-750-9770 gerrit@fresch.com
Importer of confectionery items including chocolate covered cherries, milk chocolate coins, bubble and chewing gum, sour candies, sugar-free mints, etc
President: Gerrit Verburg
VP: Tatiana Verburg
Contact: Gerrit Co
gerrit@fresch.com
Estimated Sales: $2.5-5 Million
Number Employees: 5-9
Type of Packaging: Consumer, Bulk
Brands Imported: Fort Knox; Sour Blockheads; Cherra; Fresch; Extreme Ice; Extreme Fresh; Castle Casino Chips; Satellite Wafers, Broadway Licorice; Gustafin Licorice; Finnska Licorice
Percentage of Business in Importing: 100

44561 Gesco ENR
139 Rue De La Reine
Gaspe, QC G4X 2R8
Canada   418-368-1414
Fax: 418-368-1812 gesco@globetrotter.qc.ca
Fresh and frozen shrimp
President: Gaetan Denis
Number Employees: 20-49
Type of Packaging: Consumer, Food Service, Private Label, Bulk
Regions Exported to: US, Switzerland
Percentage of Business in Exporting: 20

44562 Gessner Products
241 N Main St
PO Box 389
Ambler, PA 19002-4224   215-646-7667
Fax: 215-646-6222 800-874-7808
sales@gessnerproducts.com
www.gessnerproducts.com
Manufacturer and exporter of plastic ashtrays, credit card trays, coasters, signs, condiment jars, sugar caddies and restaurant smallwares
President: Edward H Gessner
Controller: Neo Brown
Executive VP: Geoffrey Ries
Quality Control: Steve Fuhrmeister
National Sales Manager: Michael Salemi
Production Manager: Chuck Denoncour
Estimated Sales: $ 5 - 10 Million
Number Employees: 100-249
Regions Exported to: Central America, South America, Europe, Asia, Middle East

44563 Geyser Peak Winery
2306 Magnolia Dr
Healdsburg, CA 95448-9406   707-857-9463
Fax: 707-857-9401 800-255-9463
www.geyserpeakwinery.com
Wines
Winemaker: Ondine Chattan
Manager: Lisa Flohr
lisa.flohr@accoladewinesna.com
Number Employees: 50-99
Regions Exported to: Europe, Asia, Middle East
Percentage of Business in Exporting: 10

44564 Ghibli North American
14 Germay Drive
Wilmington, DE 19804   302-654-5908
Fax: 302-652-7159 ghibli@frontiernet.net
Manufacturer and exporter of high pressure and hot water cleaning equipment
General Manager: Gordon Thomas
Estimated Sales: $ 1 - 5 Million
Number Employees: 5 to 9

44565 Giacona Container Co
121 Industrial Ave
New Orleans, LA 70121-2908   504-835-5465
Fax: 504-835-5581 giacona@giacona.com
www.flexyard.com
Vice President: Gina Lynch
giacom@giaccna.com
VP: Gina Giacona

Importers & Exporters / A-Z

Estimated Sales: $ 20 - 50 Million
Number Employees: 10-19

44566 Giant Advertising
15221 Transistor Lane
Huntington Beach, CA 92649-1141 714-891-5928
Fax: 714-891-5958

44567 (HQ)Giant Gumball Machine Company
200 Macarthur Blvd
Grand Prairie, TX 75050-4739 972-262-2234
Fax: 972-262-3167
Manufacturer and exporter of vending machines
President: Dan Clemson
d.clemson@productsales.com
National Sales Manager: Bob Rogers
National Sales Manager: Dan Wright
Estimated Sales: $300,000-500,000
Number Employees: 1-4
Regions Exported to: South America

44568 Gielow Pickles Inc
5260 Main St
Lexington, MI 48450 810-359-7680
marketing@gielowpickles.com
www.gielowpickles.com
Pickles, sweet relish & peppers
Vice President: Craig Gielow
Year Founded: 1970
Estimated Sales: $40-50 Million
Number Employees: 20-49
Square Footage: 330000
Type of Packaging: Food Service, Private Label
Brands Exported: Cool Crisp
Regions Exported to: Canada
Percentage of Business in Exporting: 10
Regions Imported from: Mexico
Percentage of Business in Importing: 8

44569 Giesecke & Devrient America
45925 Horseshoe Dr # 100
Dulles, VA 20166-6588 703-480-2000
Fax: 703-480-2060 800-856-7712
www.gi-de.com
Manufacturer and exporter of high speed currency counters, dispensers and endorsers
President: Scott Marquardt
scott.marquardt@gdai.com
Director Distribution: Bill Chamberlain
Estimated Sales: $50-100 Million
Number Employees: 250-499
Parent Co: G&D America
Regions Exported to: Worldwide
Percentage of Business in Exporting: 25

44570 Giesser
6119 Adams St
West New York, NJ 07093-1505 201-453-1460
Fax: 201-453-9255 888-411-2666
Importer of meat processing equipment, cutlery and scissors
President/CEO: Michael Maffei
National Sales Rep: Ernest Regensburg
Contact: Michael Massie
m.massie@ezh.com
Estimated Sales: $2.5-5 Million
Number Employees: 10-19
Brands Imported: Giesser; Kretzer
Regions Imported from: Europe

44571 Gilbert Insect Light Traps
5511 Krueger Dr
Jonesboro, AR 72401-6818 870-932-6070
Fax: 870-932-5609 800-643-0400
mailbox@gilbertinc.com www.gilbertinc.com
Manufacturer and exporter of professional flytraps, emergency lighting and LED exit signs; also, consultant on flying insect control
President/ILT Research/Customer Service: David Gilbert
ILT Sales/Customer Service: Stephen Goad
Executive Administrator/Customer Service: Libby Mackey
Estimated Sales: $ 1 - 3 Million
Number Employees: 20-49
Number of Brands: 2
Number of Products: 15
Square Footage: 152000
Parent Co: Gilbert Industries
Brands Exported: Gilbert
Regions Exported to: Worldwide
Percentage of Business in Exporting: 3

44572 Gilchrist Bag Co Inc
907 Sharp Ave
Camden, AR 71701-2603 870-836-6416
Fax: 870-836-8379 800-643-1513
sales@gilchristbag.com www.gilchristbag.com
Manufacturer and exporters of a wide variety of quality paper bags, sacks and specialty supplies used by a variety of markets.
Owner: Tom Gilchrist
tgilchrist@gilchristbag.com
Director Operations Marketing: Randy Robertson
Plant/Production Manager: Larry Starnes
Plant Manager: Louis Hammond
Estimated Sales: $5-10,000,000
Number Employees: 20-49
Square Footage: 350000
Type of Packaging: Consumer, Food Service, Private Label
Regions Exported to: Worldwide
Percentage of Business in Exporting: 2

44573 (HQ)Giles Enterprises Inc
2750 Gunter Park Dr W
P.O.Box 210247
Montgomery, AL 36109-1098 334-272-1457
Fax: 334-239-4117 800-288-1555
intsales@gilesent.com www.gfse.com
Manufacturer and exporter of kitchen and deli equipment including ventless hood fryers
President: David Byrd
dbyrd@gfsequipment.com
Financial Director: Ken Robinson
Quality Control: Sheila Munday
VP Sales: David Byrd
Estimated Sales: $ 10 - 20 Million
Number Employees: 100-249
Square Footage: 160000
Regions Exported to: South America, Europe, Asia, Middle East, Australia
Percentage of Business in Exporting: 5

44574 Giles Food Service
2750 Gunter Park Drive W
Montgomery, AL 36109-1016 334-272-3528
Fax: 334-272-3561 800-288-1555
ramseyd@gilesent.com
Contact: Dave Bromley
dbromley@gfse.com
Estimated Sales: $ 10 - 20 Million
Number Employees: 100-249

44575 Gillies Coffee
150 19th St
P.O. Box 320206
Brooklyn, NY 11232-1005 718-499-7766
Fax: 718-499-7771 800-344-5526
info@gilliescoffee.com www.gilliescoffee.com
Coffee
Owner: David Chabbott
davidhchabbott@gmail.com
Estimated Sales: $3.4 Million
Number Employees: 20-49
Square Footage: 28000
Type of Packaging: Food Service, Private Label, Bulk
Brands Exported: Gillies; Jamaica Blue Mountain; La Minita Tarrazu; Hawaiian Kona
Regions Exported to: Worldwide
Percentage of Business in Exporting: 7
Regions Imported from: Central America, South America, Asia, Latin America, Mexico, Caribbean, East Africa, Pacific Rim

44576 Gilly Galoo
PO Box 64
South Egremont, MA 01258-0064
Importer and exporter of gourmet foods from Mediterranean region
President: Kathy Ankerer
Brands Exported: Purple Waves, 17th St., Jerry's
Regions Exported to: Europe, Asia, Middle East
Percentage of Business in Exporting: 20
Brands Imported: Nook's Cranny Sauce, Steve's Farfel, Medito
Regions Imported from: Europe, Middle East, Mediterranean
Percentage of Business in Importing: 80

44577 Gilson Co Inc
7975 N Central Dr
Lewis Center, OH 43035-9409 740-548-5314
Fax: 740-548-5314 800-444-1508
www.globalgilson.com
Liquid handling

President: Trent R Smith
tsmith@gilsonco.com
CEO: Robert H Smith
Marketing Director: Carl Kramer
Technical Development Manager: Jim Bibler
Estimated Sales: $12-20 Million
Number Employees: 50-99
Brands Exported: Fritsch; Gilson
Regions Exported to: Central America, South America, Europe

44578 (HQ)Gilster-Mary Lee Corp
1037 State St
PO Box 227
Chester, IL 62233 618-826-2361
Fax: 618-826-2973
webmaster@gilstermarylee.com
www.gilstermarylee.com
Cake & bread mixes, pancake mixes, drink mixes, cereal, potatoes, frostings, muffin mixes, popcorn, stuffing, chocolate items, brownie mixes, pie shell, baking soda, soups, sauces, and gravies, pastas, cookie mixes, marshmallow itemsmacaroni & cheese, coatings, biscuit mixes, puddings & gelatins, rice, dinners, and organic foods.
VP Sales/Marketing: Tom Welge
Number Employees: 1000-4999
Type of Packaging: Consumer, Food Service, Private Label, Bulk
Other Locations:
 Baking Mix/Shredded Wheat Plants
 Chester, IL
 Baking/Mac&Cheese & Pasta Plants
 Steeleville, IL
 Cocoa Plant
 Momence, IL
 Baking Mix Plant
 Centralia, IL
 Popcorn/Cereal Plant Dist, Ctr
 McBride, MO
 Corrugated Sheet Plant
 McBride, MO
 Baking Mix/Shredded Wheat PlantsSteeleville
Regions Exported to: Central America, South America, Europe, Asia, Middle East, Latin America, Mexico, Canada, Caribbean
Percentage of Business in Exporting: 7

44579 Ginco International
725 Cochran St
Unit C
Simi Valley, CA 93065-1974 805-520-7500
Fax: 805-520-7509 800-284-2598
sales@ginsengcompany.com
Ginseng
President: Gary Raskin
VP Marketing: Linda Raskin
Sales Exec: Rick Seibert
sales@gincointernational.com
Estimated Sales: Less Than $500,000
Number Employees: 1-4
Square Footage: 30000
Brands Exported: Imperial Elixir
Regions Exported to: Asia
Percentage of Business in Exporting: 3
Brands Imported: AcuLife; Sandals; Imperial Elixir
Regions Imported from: Asia
Percentage of Business in Importing: 10

44580 Ginger People, The
215 Reindollar Ave
Marina, CA 93933 831-582-2494
Fax: 831-582-2495 800-551-5284
info@gingerpeople.com www.gingerpeople.com
Ginger products
President: Bruce Leeson
VP: Diana Cumberland
Contact: Robert Ballard
rballard@gingerpeople.com
Estimated Sales: $9 000,000
Number Employees: 18
Parent Co: Royal Pacific Foods

44581 Ginkgo International LTD
8102 Lemont Rd # 1100
Woodridge, IL 60517-7785 630-910-5244
Fax: 630-910-5279 ginkgo@flash.net
www.ginkoint.com
President: David Helmick
ginkgo@flash.net
Estimated Sales: $ 1 - 3 Million
Number Employees: 5-9

Importers & Exporters / A-Z

44582 Ginseng Up Corp
16 Plum St
Worcester, MA 01604-3600   508-799-6178
Fax: 508-799-0686   800-446-7364
info@ginsengup.com www.ginsengup.com
Natural soft drinks; contract packaging available
President: Sang Han
Manufacturing Executive: Courtney Craite
courtney@ginsengup.com
Estimated Sales: $ 3 - 5 Million
Number Employees: 10-19
Parent Co: One Up
Type of Packaging: Consumer
Brands Exported: Ginseng Up
Regions Exported to: Central America, South America, Europe, Asia, Canada, Africa, Caribbean
Percentage of Business in Exporting: 30

44583 Giovanni Food Co Inc
6050 Court Street Rd
Syracuse, NY 13206-1711   315-457-2373
sales@giovannifoods.com
www.giovannifoods.com
Sauces
CEO: Louis DeMent
Chief Financial Officer: David Monahan
Vice President of Operations: Tim Budd
Director of Research & Development: Eric Lynch
National Sales Director: Joe Barbara
Production/Purchasing Manager: Katie Weber
Estimated Sales: $20-50 Million
Number Employees: 20-49
Number of Brands: 5
Square Footage: 67000
Type of Packaging: Consumer, Food Service, Private Label
Brands Exported: Tuscan Traditions Organic Pasta Sauce, Tuscan Traditions Bruschetta, Luigi Giovanni Pasta Sauce, Jose Pedro Organic Salsa
Regions Exported to: Middle East, Worldwide

44584 Giovanni's Appetizing Food Co
37775 Division Road
Richmond, MI 48062   586-727-9355
Fax: 586-727-3433 philipjr@gioapp.com
www.gioapp.com
Gourmet foods including antipasto, pickled mushrooms, chopped chicken liver and pates
President: Philip Ricossa
ricossa@gioapp.com
Vice President: Giovanni Ricossa
Estimated Sales: $2.5-5 Million
Number Employees: 10-19
Square Footage: 16000
Type of Packaging: Consumer, Food Service
Regions Exported to: South America
Percentage of Business in Exporting: 20
Regions Imported from: Europe, Canada
Percentage of Business in Importing: 25

44585 Girard's Food Service Dressings
145 Willow Avenue
City of Industry, CA 91746
   888-327-8442
sales@girardsdressings.com
www.girardsdressings.com
Mayonnaise, salad dressings, sauces and marinades.
Quality Control/R&D Manager: Jeff Stalley
Year Founded: 1935
Estimated Sales: $24 Million
Number Employees: 60
Number of Brands: 3
Number of Products: 175
Square Footage: 25000
Parent Co: HACO
Type of Packaging: Consumer, Food Service, Bulk
Brands Exported: Girard's; Chef's Ideal; State Fair
Regions Exported to: South America, Europe, Asia, Mexico, Canada
Percentage of Business in Exporting: 10

44586 Girton Manufacturing Co
160 W Main St
Millville, PA 17846-5004   570-458-5521
Fax: 570-458-5589 info@girton.com
www.girton.com
Manufactures stainless steel washing equipment for the Food & Dairy Processing Industries, including COP tanks, bin and tub washing systems for pallets, drums, cases, etc. Girton MFG co Inc also manufactures King Zeero Ice Builders.
President: Dean Girton
info@girton.com
Sales: Wm Bruce Michael
Plant Manager: Jim Eves
Purchasing Director: Donna Bender
Estimated Sales: $ 10 - 20 Million
Number Employees: 50-99
Square Footage: 45000
Brands Exported: Girton; Girton King Zeero
Regions Exported to: Central America, South America, Europe, Asia

44587 (HQ)Giumarra Companies
P.O. Box 861449
Los Angeles, CA 90086   213-627-2900
Fax: 213-628-4878 www.giumarra.com
Produce marketing
Senior VP, Strategic Development: Hillary Brick
Director of Quality Control: Jim Heil
Manager: Donald Corsaro

Number Employees: 50-99
Other Locations: Giumarra Agricom

44588 Givaudan Fragrances Corp
245 Merry Ln.
East Hanover, NJ 07936   973-386-9800
Fax: 973-428-6312 www.givaudan.com
Flavors and fragrances.
CEO: Gilles Andrier
CFO: Tom Hallam
President, Fragrance Division: Maurizio Volpi
President, Flavor Division: Louie D'Amico
Estimated Sales: $4.66 Billion
Other Locations:
  Flavour Production Plant
  Cincinnati, OH
  Flavour Creation Plant
  Cincinnati, OH
  Flavour Creation Plant
  East Hanover, NJ
  Flavour Application Plant
  Elgin, ILFlavour Production PlantCincinnati
Regions Exported to: Mexico
Percentage of Business in Exporting: 1
Regions Imported from: South America, Africa

44589 Glacier Fish Company
2320 West Commodore Way
Suite 200
Seattle, WA 98199   206-298-1200
Fax: 206-298-4750 info@glacierfish.com
www.glacierfish.com
Fish
President: Jim Johnson
CEO: Mike Breivik
CFO: Rob Wood
VP Sales/Marketing: Merle Knapp
Contact: Stephanie Gilbert
stephanie@glacierfish.com
Estimated Sales: $20 Million
Number Employees: 250
Type of Packaging: Food Service, Bulk
Brands Exported: Glacierfreeze
Regions Exported to: Europe, Asia
Percentage of Business in Exporting: 60

44590 Glacier Foods
11303 Antoine Drive
Houston, TX 77066   832-375-6300
Fax: 559-875-3179 www.glazierfoods.com
Frozen and fresh fruit and vegetables
Owner: Jack Mulvaney
Contact: Greg Bohnsack
gregbohnsack@glazierfoods.com
Manager: Alvin Avoy
Plant Manager: Alvin McAvoy
Assistant Plant Manager: Sheila Young
Estimated Sales: $ 10 - 20 Million
Number Employees: 50-99
Square Footage: 1496520
Parent Co: JR Wood
Type of Packaging: Consumer, Food Service, Private Label, Bulk
Brands Exported: Big Valley
Regions Exported to: Asia
Percentage of Business in Exporting: 16
Regions Imported from: Central America
Percentage of Business in Importing: 3

44591 Glaro Inc
735 Calebs Path # 1
Hauppauge, NY 11788-4201   631-234-1717
Fax: 631-234-9510 info@glaro.com
www.glaro.com
Manufacturer and exporter of waste containers, engraved signs, aluminum tray stand equipment, crowd control stanchions, planters, coat racks, etc
Vice President: Robert Betensky
robert@glaro.com
CEO: Michael Glass
VP: Robert Betensky
Estimated Sales: $20-50 Million
Number Employees: 10-19
Square Footage: 50000
Brands Exported: Glaro, Inc.
Regions Exported to: Worldwide
Percentage of Business in Exporting: 15

44592 Glass Industries America LLC
340 Quinnipiac St # 3
Wallingford, CT 06492-4050   203-269-6700
Fax: 203-269-8782 www.wallingfordglass.com
Manufacturer and exporter of lighting fixtures including bent and decorated glassware
Owner: George Sutherland
glass.industries@snet.net
Manager: Jack Jackson
Estimated Sales: $2.5-5 Million
Number Employees: 5-9
Parent Co: L.D. Kichler
Regions Exported to: Canada
Percentage of Business in Exporting: 10

44593 Glass Pro
2300 W Windsor Ct
Addison, IL 60101-1491   630-268-9494
Fax: 800-875-6243   888-641-8919
Manufacturer and exporter of glass washing machinery, sanitizers and accessories
President: Robert Joesel
CEO: Evelyn Joesel
R&D: Robert Joesel
Quality Control: Robert Joesel
Estimated Sales: Below $ 5 Million
Number Employees: 5-9
Number of Brands: 4
Number of Products: 3
Square Footage: 12000
Type of Packaging: Food Service, Private Label
Brands Exported: Glass Maid; Glass Pro; Powerline
Regions Exported to: Central America, South America, Asia, Canada, Mexico, Latin America
Percentage of Business in Exporting: 5

44594 Glastender
5400 N Michigan Rd
Saginaw, MI 48604-9700   989-752-4275
Fax: 989-752-4444   800-748-0423
info@glastender.com www.glastender.com
Manufacturer and exporter of bar and restaurant equipment including glass washers, cocktail stations, underbar and refrigerated backbar equipment, mug frosters, beer and soda line chillers, ice cream freezers and coolers
President: Todd Hall
thall@glastender.com
CFO: Jamie Rievert
VP Admin: Kim Norris
Quality Control: David Burk
VP Operations: Mark Norris
Plant Manager: Mark Norris
Purchasing Manager: Zoa May
Estimated Sales: $ 10 - 20 Million
Number Employees: 100-249
Square Footage: 200000
Brands Exported: Glastender
Regions Exported to: Central America, South America, Europe, Asia, Middle East, Canada
Percentage of Business in Exporting: 1

44595 Glazier Packing Co
3140 State Route 11
Malone, NY 12953-4708   518-483-4990
Fax: 518-483-8300
Sausage and frankfurters; importer of other meat products
President/Owner: John Glazier
jglazier@glazierfoodservice.com
Vice President: Shawn Glazier
General Manager: Lynn Raymond
Estimated Sales: $10-11 Million
Number Employees: 50-99
Square Footage: 90000
Type of Packaging: Consumer, Food Service
Regions Imported from: New Zealand, Australia, Brazil
Percentage of Business in Importing: 1

Importers & Exporters / A-Z

44596 Glen Raven Custom Fabrics LLC
1831 N Park Ave
Burlington, NC 27217-1137   336-227-6211
    Fax: 336-226-8133 oford@glenraven.com
                        www.glenraven.com
Solutions dyed acrylic fabrics for awnings and umbrellas
Chairman/ CEO: Allen E Gant Jr
President/ COO: Leib Oehmig
SVP, CFO & Treasurer: Gary Smith
SVP, Secretary & General Counsel: Derek Steed
R&D: John Coates
Sales/Marketing Administration: Harry Gobble
National Sales Manager: Ocie Ford
Contact: Emily Eby
eeby@glenraven.com
Number Employees: 20-49
Parent Co: Glen Raven Custom Fabrics LLC
Type of Packaging: Food Service
Regions Imported from: France
Percentage of Business in Importing: 10

44597 Glenmarc Manufacturing
2001 S.Blue Island Ave.
Chicago, IL 60608   312-243-0800
     Fax: 312-243-4670   800-323-5350
              glenmarc@aol.com
Manufacturer and exporter of adhesive dispensing equipment. Also 304/316 stainless steel pressure tanks
President: John Sims
Chairman, Chief Executive Officer: John Chen
CEO: Don Deloach
Senior Vice President of Operations: Billy Ho
Purchasing Manager: Steve Eichele
Estimated Sales: Below $ 500,000
Number Employees: 5-9
Square Footage: 26000
Regions Exported to: Europe, Asia
Percentage of Business in Exporting: 10

44598 Glenn Sales Company
6425 Powers Ferry Rd NW
Suite 120
Atlanta, GA 30339   770-952-9292
              Fax: 770-988-9325
Seafood
President: Bruce Pearlman
Estimated Sales: $1,600,000
Number Employees: 5-9

44599 Glit Microtron
305 Rock Industrial Park Dr
Bridgetown, MO 63044   877-947-7117
     Fax: 800-327-5492   800-325-1051
              CustomerService@contico.com
           www.continentalcommercialproducts.com
Abrasive coated synthetic sponge, scour pads and scrub sponges
President: Gordan Kirsch
Research Manager: Alan Christopher
Number Employees: 250-499
Parent Co: Katy Industries
Regions Exported to: South America, Europe, Asia, Middle East
Percentage of Business in Exporting: 5

44600 Glo-Quartz Electric Heater
7084 Maple St
Mentor, OH 44060-4932   440-255-9701
     Fax: 440-255-7852   800-321-3574
        tstrokes@gloquartz.com www.gloquartz.com
Electric immersion heaters and tubular metal and quartz heating elements for food processing and packaging; also, temperature controls; exporter of electric heaters
President: George Strokes
VP: Thomas Strokes
Sales: John Paglia
Contact: Jeffrey Payne
jpayne@gloquartz.com
Plant Manager: Jeff Payne
Estimated Sales: $ 3 - 5 Million
Number Employees: 20-49
Square Footage: 88000
Brands Exported: Glo-Quartz
Regions Exported to: Central America, South America, Europe, Asia, Worldwide
Regions Imported from: Europe, Asia

44601 Global Botanical
545 Welham Road
Barrie, ON L4N 8Z6
Canada   705-733-2117
     Fax: 705-733-2391 info@globalbotanical.com
Herbs, spices, oils
President: Sandra Thuna
Office Manager: Therese White
General Manager: Joel Thuna
Number Employees: 12
Square Footage: 40000
Type of Packaging: Private Label, Bulk
Brands Exported: Pure-Li Natural; Pure-Le Natural; Easy Vitamins & Minerals; Slim & Smart

44602 Global Egg Corporation
283 Horner Ave
Toronto, ON M8Z 4Y4
Canada   416-231-2309
     Fax: 416-231-8991 info@globalegg.com
              www.globalegg.com
Eggs
CEO: Aaron Kwinter
Estimated Sales: $13 Million
Number Employees: 70
Square Footage: 50000
Type of Packaging: Food Service, Bulk
Regions Exported to: Asia
Percentage of Business in Exporting: 10

44603 Global Equipment Co Inc
11 Harbor Park Dr
Port Washington, NY 11050-4646   516-608-7000
     Fax: 516-625-8415   888-628-3466
              www.globalindustrial.com
Manufacturer, exporter and importer of steel bins, benches, wire shelving and material handling equipment
President: Bob Dooley
bdooley@systemax.com
Chief Financial Officer: Lawrence Reinhold
Vice President: Bruce Leeds
Quality Control Assurance: Paul Betzold
Marketing Manager: Maureen Cronin
Director, Sales: Steve McNamara
Operations: Jack Kaserow
Product Manager: Elise Wong
Purchasing Manager: Eric Bertel
Estimated Sales: $ 28 Million
Number Employees: 100-249
Square Footage: 85000
Parent Co: Systemax
Regions Exported to: Central America, South America, Europe, Middle East
Regions Imported from: Asia

44604 Global Food Service Publications Group
150 Great Neck Road
Great Neck, NY 11021   516-829-9210
              Fax: 516-829-9306
Estimated Sales: $ 5 - 10 Million
Number Employees: 5-9

44605 Global Food Source
114 Carpenter Ave
Tuckahoe, NY 10707   303-893-0552
              Fax: 914-961-0637
Gourmet, specialty and organic delicacies
President/CEO: Albert Savarese
VP Sales/Marketing: Teresa Belvedere
Number Employees: 4

44606 Global Health Laboratories
9500 New Horizons Boulevard
Amityville, NY 11701   631-777-2134
     Fax: 631-777-3348 www.globalhealthlabs.com
Vitamins and nutritional supplements
Administrator: Susan Mc Guckian
Sales Director: James Gibbons
Contact: Cheryl Manzione
cmanzione@globalhealthlabs.com
Type of Packaging: Consumer, Private Label
Brands Exported: Herbal Actives

44607 Global Impex
2336 Winter Woods Boulevard
Suite 2008
Winter Park, FL 32792-1922   407-774-2390
     Fax: 407-673-6612 janglobl@sundial.net
Exporter of food processing and material handling/distribution equipment
General Manager: Ramzon Janmohamed

Estimated Sales: $2.5-5 Million
Number Employees: 1-4
Brands Exported: Flor-D'Orlando
Regions Exported to: Africa, India
Percentage of Business in Exporting: 100

44608 Global Manufacturing
1801 E 22nd St
Little Rock, AR 72206-2501   501-374-7416
     Fax: 501-376-7147   800-551-3569
              www.globalmanufacturing.com
Manufacturer and exporter of vibrators including hydraulic, pneumatic, electric, air blasters and turbine
President: Catherine Janosky
cjanosky@globalmanufacturing.com
Quality Control: Wilfred Coney
Marketing: April Crocker
Sales: Perry Schnebelen
Operations: Tom Janosky
Production: Stan Kligman
Plant Manager: Rod Treat
Purchasing Director: Howard Stewart
Estimated Sales: $ 3 - 5,000,000
Number Employees: 10-19
Brands Exported: All Global And Viber Brands - Vibrators
Regions Exported to: Central America, South America, Europe, Asia, Middle East
Brands Imported: Findeva Vibrators From Switzerland
Regions Imported from: Europe

44609 Global Marketing Assoc
3536 Arden Rd
Hayward, CA 94545-3908   510-887-2462
     Fax: 510-887-1882   800-869-0763
        global@gmaherbs.com www.gmaherbs.com
Wholesaler/distributor, importer and exporter of herbal extracts and nutritional supplements including garlic tablets and powders, ginkgo biloba, milk thistle and St. John's wort
President: Clement Yo
clement@gmaherbs.com
Chairman: Kenneth Yeung
Vice President: Lolita Lim
Estimated Sales: $500,000-$1 Million
Number Employees: 5-9
Square Footage: 280000
Type of Packaging: Bulk
Regions Exported to: Worldwide
Regions Imported from: Worldwide

44610 Global Organics
68 Moulton St
Cambridge, MA 02138-1119   781-648-8844
     Fax: 781-648-0774 info@global-organics.com
              www.global-organics.com
Organic ingredients
President: Dave Alexander
Vice President: Roland Hoch
Account Manager: Dino Scarsella
Sales and Marketing Coordinator: Ravi Arori
Estimated Sales: Under $500,000
Number Employees: 25

44611 Global Package
PO Box 634
Napa, CA 94559   707-224-5670
     Fax: 707-224-8170 info@globalpackage.net
              www.globalpackage.net
International packaging solutions for wine, spirits and food
CEO: Erica Harrop
Sales: Kathy Feder
Estimated Sales: $5 Million
Number Employees: 3
Type of Packaging: Food Service

44612 Global Sticks, Inc.
13555-23A Avenue
Surrey, BC V4A 9V1
Canada   604-535-7748
     Fax: 604-535-7749   866-433-5770
Wooden ice cream spoons & sticks, corn dog sticks & coffee stirrers.
President: Reggie Nukovic
General Manager: Earl Metcalf
Regions Exported to: Central America, Europe

Importers & Exporters / A-Z

44613 (HQ)Globe Fire Sprinkler Corp
4077 Airpark Dr
Standish, MI 48658-9533 989-846-4583
Fax: 989-846-9231 800-248-0278
Bob733@aol.com www.globesprinkler.com
Manufacturer, importer and exporter of commercial, industrial and residential fire sprinklers, deluge/preaction, alarm, dry pipe and check valves, water motor alarms and accessories for sprinkler systems
President: Steven R. Worthington, I.M.B..A
Chairman/ CEO: Robert C. Worthington, P.E.
bob733@aol.com
EVP: Buck Buchanan
Dir. Of Marketing & Information System: John D. Corcoran
VP, Sales: Randy Lane
VP, Operations: Terry Bovee
Estimated Sales: $10-20 Million
Number Employees: 100-249
Square Footage: 80000
Brands Exported: Globe; Millenium; Kennedy; System Sensor
Regions Exported to: Worldwide
Percentage of Business in Exporting: 35
Regions Imported from: Europe, Asia, Canada, South Africa

44614 Globe Food Equipment Co
2153 Dryden Rd
Moraine, OH 45439-1739 937-299-5493
Fax: 937-299-4147 800-347-5423
www.globefoodequip.com
Manufactures slicers, vegetable cutters, mixers, choppers and scales
President: Hilton Gardner
hgardner@globeslicers.com
Marketing: Alicia Sanders
Sales: Bob Adams
Number Employees: 20-49
Brands Exported: Chefmate, Globe, Protech
Regions Exported to: Central America, South America, Europe, Asia, Middle East, Australia

44615 Globe Machine
902 E E St
Tacoma, WA 98421-1839 253-572-9637
Fax: 253-572-9672 800-523-6575
sales@globemachine.com www.globemachine.com
Manufacturer and exporter of material handling equipment including hydraulic lift tables, conveyors, personnel carriers, tilters, dumpers and transfer cars
Special Projects Manager: Mark Allen
Operations Manager: Michael Natucci
Estimated Sales: $ 20 - 50 Million
Number Employees: 1-4
Square Footage: 225000
Parent Co: Globe Machine Manufacturing Company
Regions Exported to: Worldwide
Percentage of Business in Exporting: 10

44616 Glopak
4755 Boulevard De Grandes Prairies
St Leonard, QC H1R 1A6
Canada 514-323-4510
Fax: 514-323-5999 800-361-6994
www.glopak.com
Manufacturer and exporter of packaging equipment and supplies including bags, fillers, filling equipment, films, flexible packaging, pouches and wrapping material
President: Ritchie Baird
CEO: Harold Martin
CFO: John Mireault
Quality Control: Hens Pohl
R&D: Eves Quiten
Number Employees: 130
Type of Packaging: Bulk
Regions Exported to: USA

44617 Glove Cleaners & SafetyProducts
PO Box 2378
Plainville, MA 02762 508-668-0632
Fax: 508-668-8907
Estimated Sales: $ 1 - 3 Million
Number Employees: 10-19

44618 Glowmaster Corporation
312 Lexington Ave
Clifton, NJ 07011-2366 973-772-1112
Fax: 973-772-4040 800-272-7008
www.e-hospitality.com/storefronts/glowmaster.html
Manufacturer and importer of cooking and heating equipment including portable tabletop butane stoves and fuel, chafers, griddles, service carts and induction cooking systems; exporter of portable butane stoves
Owner: Juan Travezano
CFO: Linda Smith
Director Sales: Frank Palatiello
Number Employees: 10-19
Square Footage: 28000
Brands Exported: Glowmaster
Regions Exported to: Central America, South America, Europe, Canada
Percentage of Business in Exporting: 20
Brands Imported: Glowmaster; Chefmaster
Regions Imported from: Europe, Asia
Percentage of Business in Importing: 80

44619 Glucona America
114 E Conde Street
Janesville, WI 53546-3010 608-752-0449
Fax: 608-752-7643
Gluconates and other supplements
Development Manager: Charles King
Marketing Manager: Scott Wellington
General Manager: Sean Trac
Estimated Sales: $20-50 Million
Number Employees: 20-49
Parent Co: Avebe
Type of Packaging: Food Service
Brands Exported: Gluconal
Regions Exported to: Worldwide
Percentage of Business in Exporting: 10
Regions Imported from: Europe
Percentage of Business in Importing: 10

44620 Goetze's Candy Co
3900 E Monument St
Baltimore, MD 21205 410-342-2010
Fax: 410-522-7681 marketing@goetzecandy.com
www.goetzecandy.com
Confectionary, specifically chewy caramel
President: Mitchell Goetze
CEO: Spaulding Goetze
CFO: Dave Long
EVP: Todd Goetze
Year Founded: 1895
Estimated Sales: $20-50 Million
Number Employees: 50-99
Type of Packaging: Consumer, Food Service, Bulk
Brands Exported: Goetz's Caramel Creams; Caramel Cow Tales
Regions Exported to: Central America, South America, Europe, Asia, Japan, Australia
Percentage of Business in Exporting: 10

44621 Goex Corporation
2532 Foster Ave
Janesville, WI 53545 608-754-3303
Fax: 608-754-8976 goex@goex.com
www.goex.com
Manufacturer and exporter of packaging materials including rigid plastic sheet products
President: Joshua D Gray
Sales Manager: Richard Hamlin
Contact: Vicky Bladl
vbladl@goex.com
Estimated Sales: $50-100 Million
Number Employees: 50-99
Regions Exported to: Worldwide

44622 Gold Band Oysters
412 Palm Ave
Houma, LA 70364-3400 985-868-7191
Fax: 985-868-7472 requests@theperfectoyster.com
www.motivatit.com
Owner: Michael Boisin

44623 Gold Medal Products Co
10700 Medallion Dr
Cincinnati, OH 45241-4807 513-769-7676
Fax: 513-769-8500 800-543-0862
info@gmpopcorn.com www.gmpopcorn.com
Manufacturer and exporter of food products and concession equipment including popcorn machines, supplies and staging cabinets, butter dispensers, caramel, kettle and cheese corn, cotton candy machines and supplies, shave ice & sno-conemachines, drinks and frozen beverages, fried foods & bakers, nachos & cheese dispensers, hot dog grills & cookers, candy & caramel apples, whiz bang carnival games and more.
President: Dan Kroeger
dkroeger@gmpopcorn.com
Senior VP: John Evans
National Sales: Chris Petroff
International Sales: David Garretson
Estimated Sales: $ 20 - 50 Million
Number Employees: 250-499
Square Footage: 325000
Type of Packaging: Consumer, Food Service, Private Label, Bulk
Brands Exported: Sno-Kones; Hawaii's Finest; Popcorn Poppers; EZ Kleen Kettle

44624 Gold Pure Food ProductsCo. Inc.
1 Brooklyn Rd
Hempstead, NY 11550-6619 516-483-5600
Fax: 516-483-5798 800-422-4681
Kosher salad dressings, sauces, mustards, and vinegar; importer of horseradish roots, dried peaches and dried apricots
President: Steven Gold
Vice President: Herbert Gold
Vice President Sales: Marc Gold
marc@goldshorseradish.com
Estimated Sales: $5-10 Million
Number Employees: 50-99
Square Footage: 300000
Type of Packaging: Consumer, Food Service, Private Label, Bulk
Brands Exported: Gold's
Regions Exported to: Central America, South America, Europe, Middle East
Percentage of Business in Exporting: 10
Regions Imported from: Central America, South America, Europe, Asia
Percentage of Business in Importing: 10

44625 (HQ)Goldco Industries
5605 Goldco Dr
Loveland, CO 80538 970-663-4770
Fax: 970-663-7212 info@goldcointernational.com
www.goldcointernational.com
Manufacturer and exporter of container and material handling equipment including depalletizers, palletizers and container, case and pallet handling systems
President: Richard Vander Meer
Marketing: Jim Parker
Sales: Jim Parker
Contact: Sharon Hogan
sharon.hogan@fgwa.com
Estimated Sales: $ 1 - 3 Million
Number Employees: 5-9
Square Footage: 200000
Other Locations:
  Goldco Industries
  Appleton, WIGoldco Industries
Regions Exported to: Central America, South America, Europe, Asia, Middle East, Mexico
Percentage of Business in Exporting: 60

44626 Golden 100
1600 Essex Ave
Deland, FL 32724-2102 386-734-0113
Fax: 386-734-9718
Flavors
President & CEO: Ronald Edmundson
Manager: Jeffrey Ross
jeffreyr@jogue.com
Operations Executive: Mike Bowes
Estimated Sales: $1.7 Million
Number Employees: 10-19
Square Footage: 80000
Parent Co: Jogue Inc.
Type of Packaging: Bulk
Brands Exported: Golden 100
Regions Exported to: Central America, South America, Jamaica, Caribbean
Percentage of Business in Exporting: 80

44627 Golden Beach Inc
2510 W 237th St # 102
Torrance, CA 90505-5234 310-530-3210
Fax: 310-530-8601 info@goldenbeachinc.net
www.goldenbeachinc.net
Importer and exporter of canned and frozen seafood including crab meat, shrimp, clams, oysters and sardines
President: Henry Kee
hkee@goldenbeachinc.net
VP: Nancy Change
Estimated Sales: $5-8 Million
Number Employees: 5-9
Square Footage: 8000

327

Importers & Exporters / A-Z

Type of Packaging: Consumer, Food Service, Private Label
Brands Exported: Sunny Sea
Brands Imported: Sunny Sea; Sunny Farm, Sunny Harvest.
Regions Imported from: South America, Europe, Asia
Percentage of Business in Importing: 100

44628 Golden Bridge Enterprises Inc
8040 San Fernando Rd
Sun Valley, CA 91352-4001 818-504-0830
Fax: 818-504-0892 goldenbr321@cs.com
www.cs.com
Importers of Italian cookies, crackers, cakes, panettone, pasta, olive oil, olives, vinegars, pickles, canned fish, canned vegetables, condiments, rice, dry fruits, jams, halvah, fruit nectar juices
Owner: Onnik Guzelses
goldenbr321@cs.com
VP: Onnik Guzelses
Estimated Sales: $10-20 Million
Number Employees: 10-19
Type of Packaging: Consumer, Food Service, Private Label
Brands Imported: Golden Bridge, Selena, Ponte Doro, Angelo Parodi, Balocco, etc.
Regions Imported from: South America, Europe, Asia, Middle East

44629 Golden Fluff Popcorn Co
118 Monmouth Ave
Lakewood, NJ 08701-3347 732-367-5448
Fax: 732-367-5448 goldenfluff@gmail.com
www.goldenfluff.com
Popcorn and other snacks
President: Ephraim Schwinder
goldenfluff@gmail.com
Estimated Sales: Less than $500,000
Number Employees: 10-19
Type of Packaging: Consumer, Bulk
Regions Exported to: Europe, Canada

44630 Golden Fruits
510-1650 Panama Avenue
Brossard, QC J4W 2W4
Canada 450-923-5856
Importer of dates

44631 Golden Gate Co
390 Swift Ave # 19
S San Francisco, CA 94080-6221 650-588-3632
Fax: 650-588-5912
sales@goldengatecompany.com
www.goldengatebridge.org
Importer of European james, jellies, candy, gourmet foods, crackers, teas, chocolate gourmet foods
Owner: Dieter Steindeck
dieters@ix.netcom.com
Senior Project Manager: Kris Krause
Estimated Sales: $2.8 Million
Number Employees: 5-9
Square Footage: 28800

44632 Golden Gulf Coast Packing Co
260 Maple St
Biloxi, MS 39530-4501 228-374-6121
Fax: 228-374-0599 wildshrimp@hotmail.com
Shrimp
President/Owner: Richard Gollott
goldengulf123@hotmail.com
Estimated Sales: $ 10 - 20 Million
Number Employees: 5-9
Square Footage: 16000

44633 Golden Harvest Pecans
348 Vereen Bell Road
Cairo, GA 39828-4910 229-377-5617
Fax: 229-762-3335 800-597-0968
Pecans and preserves, cookies and jellies
President/CEO: J Van Ponder
Estimated Sales: $250,000
Number Employees: 500-999
Square Footage: 6218
Type of Packaging: Consumer, Food Service, Private Label, Bulk
Regions Exported to: Germany, Netherlands, Brussels, China

44634 Golden Kernel Pecan Co
5244 Cameron Rd
Cameron, SC 29030-8207 803-823-2311
Fax: 803-823-2080 info@goldenkernel.com
www.goldenkernel.com
Pecans and other snacks
Co-Owner: David K Summers
Co-Owner/Sales Executive: Bill Summers
bill@goldenkernel.com
Number Employees: 20-49
Type of Packaging: Consumer, Private Label, Bulk
Brands Exported: Golden Kernel
Regions Exported to: Europe, Middle East
Percentage of Business in Exporting: 1

44635 Golden Moon Tea
PO Box 146
Bristow, VA 20136 425-820-2000
Fax: 425-821-9700 877-327-5473
service@goldenmoontea.com
www.goldenmoontea.com
Tea and chocolates
President: Cynthia Knotts
Owner: Marcus Stout
Number of Products: 30
Type of Packaging: Consumer, Food Service, Private Label, Bulk
Brands Exported: Golden Moon Tea
Regions Exported to: Central America, South America, Europe, Asia, Middle East
Regions Imported from: Asia

44636 Golden Needles Knitting & Glove Company
1300 Walnut Street
Coshocton, OH 43812-2262 919-667-5102
Fax: 919-838-2753 www.ansell.com
Manufacturer and exporter of protective gloves
Managing Director, Chief Executive Offic: Magnus Nicolin
Senior Vice President, Director of Asia: Denis Gallant
Communications Director: Wouter Piepers
Senior Vice President of Operations: Steve Genzer
Estimated Sales: $ 1 - 5 Million
Number Employees: 1000
Type of Packaging: Consumer, Food Service, Private Label, Bulk
Regions Exported to: Worldwide

44637 Golden Oldies LTD
13229 33rd Ave
Flushing, NY 11354-2741 718-445-4400
Fax: 718-445-4986 www.goldenoldiesltd.com
President: James Tang
jamest@goldenoldiesltd.com
Estimated Sales: $ 10 - 20 Million
Number Employees: 100-249

44638 Golden Peanut and Tree Nuts
100 North Point Center East
Suite 400
Alpharetta, GA 30022 770-752-8160
www.goldenpeanut.com
Peanuts and tree nuts.
President: Clint Piper
Year Founded: 2000
Estimated Sales: $500 Million-$1 Billion
Number Employees: 1000+
Parent Co: Archer Daniels Midland
Type of Packaging: Consumer
Regions Exported to: Worldwide

44639 Golden Platter Foods
37 Tompkins Point Rd
Newark, NJ 07114-2814 973-344-8770
Fax: 973-465-7580 contact@goldenplatter.com
goldenplatter.com
Poultry products
President: Eli Barr
sbarich@goldenplatter.com
Estimated Sales: $6.5 Million
Number Employees: 100-249
Type of Packaging: Consumer, Food Service

44640 Golden River Fruit Company
7150 20th Street #A
Vero Beach, FL 32966-8805 772-562-8610
Fax: 772-567-6008
Grapefruit
CEO: George Lamberth
glambeth@goldenriverfruit.com
VP: David Milwood
General Manager/Purchasing Director: Fred Antwerp
Estimated Sales: $2 Million
Number Employees: 25
Square Footage: 13474
Type of Packaging: Bulk
Regions Exported to: Asia
Percentage of Business in Exporting: 100

44641 Golden Specialty Foods Inc
14605 Best Ave
Norwalk, CA 90650-5258 562-802-2537
Fax: 562-926-4491
wayne@goldenspecialtyfoods.com
Canned dips, salad dressings, sauces, seasonings, chicken and beef bases
CEO: Phil Pisciotto
CFO: Derky Howard
Quality Assurance Director: Javed Atcha
Sales: Andrea Bouras
COO: Jeff Chan
Estimated Sales: $3.5 Million
Number Employees: 50-99
Square Footage: 62000
Type of Packaging: Consumer, Food Service, Private Label, Bulk
Regions Exported to: Europe, Asia
Percentage of Business in Exporting: 12

44642 (HQ)Golden Star
PO Box 12539
N Kansas City, MO 64116 816-842-0233
Fax: 816-842-1129 800-821-2792
goldenstar@goldenstar.com www.goldenstar.com
Manufacturer and exporter of floor and furniture polish, mops, dry carpet cleaner solvent, mats and mattings
President: Gary Gradinger
Executive VP: Bill Gradinger
National Sales Manager: Steve Lewis
Contact: Heather Moll
moll@goldenstar.com
Estimated Sales: $ 20-50 Million
Number Employees: 20-49
Square Footage: 350000
Type of Packaging: Consumer, Food Service, Private Label
Regions Exported to: Central America, South America, Europe, Asia, Middle East, Worldwide

44643 Golden State Foods Corp
18301 Von Karman Ave
Suite 1100
Irvine, CA 92612 949-247-8000
www.goldenstatefoods.com
Sauces, dressings, syrups, jams/jellies, meat products, produce, rolls and buns.
CEO & Chairman: Mark Stephen Wetterau
mwetterau@goldenstatefoods.com
SVP & Chief Financial Officer: Joe Heffington
EVP & Chief Administrative Officer: Bill Sanderson
SVP & Chief Legal Officer: John Page
Chief Human Resources Officer: Ed Rodriguez
Year Founded: 1947
Estimated Sales: Over $1 Billion
Number Employees: 1000-4999
Other Locations:
 Phoenix, AZ
 Portland, OR
 St. Peter, MO
 Schertz, TX
 Spokane Valley, WA
 Suffolk, VAPortland
Regions Exported to: Asia, Middle East, Latin America, Australia
Percentage of Business in Exporting: 24

44644 Golden State Herbs
60125 Polk St
P.O. Box 756
Thermal, CA 92274-8944 760-399-1133
Fax: 760-399-1555 800-730-3575
www.goldenstateherbs.com
Herbs
Estimated Sales: $3.4 Million
Number Employees: 5-9
Square Footage: 100000
Regions Exported to: Europe, Canada

44645 Golden Town Apple Products
755 Principale St
Rougemont, QC J0L 1M0
Canada 519-599-6300
Fax: 519-599-2103 866-552-7643
pierre.lheureux@lassonde.com www.lassonde.com
Apple processing

Chairman/CEO: Pierre-Paul Lassonde
President/CEO: Jean Gattuso
VP/CFO: Guy Blanchette
Business Manager: Gerry Williams
Technical Director: Doug Johnson
Office Administrator: Darlene Gardner
Maintenance/Engineering Manager: Ron McQuarrie
Juice Production Coordinator: Jennifer Rear
Plant Manager: Bryan Lowe
GM/Purchasing/Sales: Keith Cummings
Number Employees: 20-49
Square Footage: 80000
Parent Co: A. Lassonde, Inc
Type of Packaging: Consumer, Bulk
Regions Exported to: USA
Percentage of Business in Exporting: 20

44646 Golden Valley Foods Ltd.
3841 Vanderpol Court
Abbotsford, BC V2T 5W5
Canada   604-857-0704
        Fax: 604-607-5504 888-299-8855
                            www.goldenvalley.com
Eggs and egg products.
Plant & Quality Assurance Manager: Frank Curtis
Regional Sales Manager: Craig Ansell
Year Founded: 1950
Estimated Sales: $24.9 Million
Number Employees: 100
Parent Co: Fresh Start Food Corp.
Type of Packaging: Consumer, Food Service, Private Label

44647 Golden Walnut Specialty Foods
18279 Minnetonka Blvd
Wayzata, MN 55391-3342   95 -76 -079
        Fax: 847-731-6433 800-843-3645
                         sales@goldenwalnut.com
Specialty food products including cookies, cakes, cheesecakes, shortbread and candy
President: Mark Sigel
Estimated Sales: $5-10 Million
Number Employees: 20-49
Parent Co: EMAC International
Type of Packaging: Consumer, Private Label, Bulk
Brands Exported: Golden Walnut
Regions Exported to: Central America, South America, Asia, Middle East, Canada
Percentage of Business in Exporting: 5

44648 Goldenberg's Peanut Chews
1300 Stefko Blvd
Bethlehem, PA 18017
                                        888-645-3453
                            www.peanutchews.com
Confectionary
President & COO: David Yale
Year Founded: 1917
Estimated Sales: $20-50 Million
Number Employees: 100-249
Square Footage: 100000
Parent Co: Just Born, Inc.
Type of Packaging: Consumer, Food Service, Bulk
Regions Exported to: Worldwide

44649 Goldenwest Sales
16730 Gridley Rd
Cerritos, CA 90703-1730   562-924-7909
        Fax: 562-924-7930 800-827-6175
        info@gwsales.com www.gwsales.com
Manufacturer and exporter of tote boxes, magnetic flatware retriever systems and cutlery bins, covers, and rapid cooling flash chill bottles
Owner: Jitu Patel
jitu@sftech.com
Treasurer: Estee Edwards
Estimated Sales: $.5 - 1 million
Number Employees: 10-19
Square Footage: 60000
Brands Exported: The Chute; Tough Guy Totes; Flash Chill Rapid Cooling Bottles
Regions Exported to: Central America, Europe, Canada, Mexico
Percentage of Business in Exporting: 5

44650 Goldmax Industries
17747 Railroad St
City Of Industry, CA 91748-1111   626-964-8820
        Fax: 626-964-6629 sales@goldmax.com
Manufacturer and importer of wooden and bamboo toothpicks, chopsticks, stirrers, plastic bags, glove dispensers, skewers, disposable gloves and aprons; also, cocktail and party straws and picks
President: Helen Chen
helenchen@goldmax-polyking.com
COO: Marcelo Mancilla
Sales Director: David Wang
Production: Manuel De La Roja
Purchasing Manager: William Hsing
Estimated Sales: $ 1 - 2.5 Million
Number Employees: 10-19
Type of Packaging: Food Service
Brands Imported: Poly King
Regions Imported from: Asia

44651 (HQ)Gonterman & Associates
5411 S Grand Blvd
Saint Louis, MO 63111   314-771-0600
                           Fax: 314-771-0610
Manufacturer and exporter of custom calendars and other advertising specialties
Estimated Sales: $ 1 - 5 Million
Number Employees: 5
Square Footage: 6000000
Regions Exported to: Canada, Caribbean
Percentage of Business in Exporting: 5

44652 (HQ)Good For You America
110 S Bismark St
Concordia, MO 64020-8110   660-463-2158
        Fax: 660-463-2459 866-329-5969
                            www.foodtabs.com
Emergency and survival food tablets and canned freeze-dried foods; importer of bulk ingredients and freeze-dried foods
Manager: Rachel Goring
Manager: Craig Sallin
craig.sallin@frac.org
Wholesale Director: Juanita Haley
Estimated Sales: Less Than $500,000
Number Employees: 1-4
Square Footage: 10000
Type of Packaging: Consumer, Private Label, Bulk
Other Locations:
   Food Reserves - Laboratory
   Kansas City, MO
   Food Reserves
   Syracuse, NYFood Reserves -
   LaboratorySyracuse
Brands Exported: Storehouse Foods; Food Reserves
Regions Exported to: Asia, Australia
Percentage of Business in Exporting: 2
Regions Imported from: Canada
Percentage of Business in Importing: 3

44653 Good Health Natural Foods
3400 West Wendover Avenue
Suite E
Greensboro, NC 27407   336-285-0735
                     www.goodhealthnaturalfoods.com
Health snacks
CEO: Mark Gillis
Vice President: Terry Meyer
Contact: Don Heon
don.heon@e-goodhealth.com
Estimated Sales: $2.5-5,000,000
Number Employees: 1-4

44654 Good Humor-Breyers Ice Cream
800 Sylvan Ave.
Englewood Cliffs, NJ 07632
                                        800-931-2854
                       customer.services@unilever.com
                                www.breyers.com
Ice cream, gelato and frozen dairy desserts.
Estimated Sales: $11 Billion
Number Employees: 1000-4999
Parent Co: Unilever
Type of Packaging: Consumer, Food Service, Private Label, Bulk
Other Locations:
   Breyer's Manufacturing
   Philadelphia, PA
   Breyer's Manufacturing
   Long Island, NY
   Breyer's Manufacturing
   Brooklyn, NYBreyer's ManufacturingLong Island
Regions Exported to: Worldwide
Percentage of Business in Exporting: 2

44655 Good Idea
351 Pleasant St
PMB 224
Northampton, MA 01060   413-586-4000
        Fax: 413-585-0101 800-462-9237
        info@larien.com www.larien.com
Manufacturer and exporter of bagel slicers and replacement blades.
President: Rick Ricard
Sales/Marketing Executive: Jim Dodge
Contact: Elizabeth Devito
bdevito@larien.com
Estimated Sales: $ 1 - 3 Million
Number Employees: 1-4
Brands Exported: Bagel Biter
Regions Exported to: Europe
Percentage of Business in Exporting: 1

44656 Good-O-Beverages Inc
1801 Boone Ave
Bronx, NY 10460-5101   718-328-6400
        Fax: 718-328-7002 info@good-o.com
                                www.good-o.com
Soft drinks, juices, teas and energy drinks
Owner: George Deyarca
slperry8978@yahoo.com
Plant Manager: Irving Mendelson
Estimated Sales: $10-20 Million
Number Employees: 50-99
Square Footage: 159000
Type of Packaging: Consumer
Regions Exported to: Virgin Islands

44657 Goodell Tools
9440 Science Center Dr
New Hope, MN 55428-3624   763-531-0053
        Fax: 763-531-0252 800-542-3906
Manufacturer and exporter of grill scrapers and ice picks
Owner: Rick Garon
Marketing/Sales: Linda Alexander
Estimated Sales: $ 5 - 10 Million
Number Employees: 20-49
Square Footage: 88000
Type of Packaging: Private Label, Bulk
Brands Exported: Goodell
Regions Exported to: South America, Middle East, Canada, Mexico, Pacific Rim, Egypt
Percentage of Business in Exporting: 7

44658 Goodheart Brand Specialty Food
11122 Nacogdoches Rd
San Antonio, TX 78217-2314   210-637-1963
        Fax: 210-637-1391 888-466-3992
        amvillarreal@goodheart.com www.goodheart.com
Specialty meats: quail, venison, bison, wild boar, pheasant and Argentinian all-natural beef
Owner: Amalia Palmaz
apalmaz@goodheart.com
Director Sales: Chef Tim Kennedy
Plant Manager: Demetrio Molales
Estimated Sales: $5-10,000,000
Number Employees: 50-99
Square Footage: 30000
Parent Co: Bluebonnet Company
Type of Packaging: Consumer, Food Service
Regions Exported to: Worldwide
Percentage of Business in Exporting: 15
Regions Imported from: South America

44659 Goodnature Products
3860 California Rd
Orchard Park, NY 14127   716-855-3325
        Fax: 716-855-3328 800-875-3381
        sales@goodnature.com www.goodnature.com
Manufacturer and exporter of food and juice processing equipment
President/Treasurer: Dale Wettlaufer
President: Diane Massett
Marketing: Angela Dedlin
Estimated Sales: $3.5 Million
Number Employees: 20-49
Number of Brands: 1
Number of Products: 21
Regions Exported to: Europe
Percentage of Business in Exporting: 3

44660 Goodway Industries Inc
175 Orville Dr
Bohemia, NY 11716-2503   631-567-2929
        Fax: 631-567-2423 800-943-4501
Manufacturer, importer and exporter of batch mixers, emulsifiers, dispersers, homogenizers, foamers, injectors, fillers, toppers and depositors
Director Sales/Marketing: Phillip Branning
Estimated Sales: $ 1 - 3,000,000
Number Employees: 5-9
Regions Exported to: Worldwide
Percentage of Business in Exporting: 3
Brands Imported: Mono Equipment

Importers & Exporters / A-Z

Regions Imported from: Europe
Percentage of Business in Importing: 10

44661 Goodway Technologies Corp
420 West Ave
Stamford, CT 06902-6329   203-359-4709
Fax: 203-359-9601   800-333-7467
goodway@goodway.com   www.goodway.com
Manufacturer and exporter of tube cleaning equipment, vacuums and pressure washers
President: Per Reichdlin
CEO: Amanda Williams
awilliams@l1id.com
CFO: David Lobelson
CEO: Per K Reichborn
Director Marketing: Chris Van Name
Estimated Sales: $ 10 - 20,000,000
Number Employees: 50-99
Square Footage: 70000
Regions Exported to: Worldwide
Percentage of Business in Exporting: 25

44662 (HQ)Goodwin Co
12102 Industry St
Garden Grove, CA 92841-2814   714-894-0531
Fax: 714-897-7673   www.goodwinc.com
Manufacturer and exporter of detergents
President: Tom Goodwin
tom.goodwin@goodwinlnc.com
General Manager: Rusty Peters
Estimated Sales: $ 20 - 50 Million
Number Employees: 50-99

44663 Goodwrappers Inc
1920 Halethorpe Farms Rd
Halethorpe, MD 21227-4501   410-536-0400
Fax: 410-536-0484   800-638-1127
www.goodwrappers.com
Manufacturer and exporter of pallet stretch wrapping systems, printed stretch and black, red, orange, green, blue and white opaque and color tinted films and stretch netting
President: Bea Parry
CEO: John Parry
VP Marketing: David Parry
Estimated Sales: $10-20 Million
Number Employees: 20-49
Regions Exported to: Central America, South America, Europe

44664 Gorbel Inc
600 Fishers Run
Victor, NY 14564-9732   585-924-6262
Fax: 585-924-6273   www.gorbel.com
Manufacturer and exporter of aluminum and steel track cranes
President: David Reh
VP: David Butwid
Manager: Deb Rader
debrad@gorbel.com
Estimated Sales: $20.9 Million
Number Employees: 100-249
Parent Co: Raytek Group
Regions Exported to: Worldwide

44665 Gorton's Inc.
128 Rogers St.
Gloucester, MA 01930
800-222-6846
www.gortons.com
Seafood.
CEO: Judson Reis
judson.reis@gortons.com
Director Marketing: Mark Lamothe
Year Founded: 1849
Estimated Sales: $280 Million
Number Employees: 1,000-4,999
Parent Co: Nippon Suisan Kaisha
Type of Packaging: Consumer, Food Service
Other Locations:
  Gorton's Seafood
  Cleveland, OH Gorton's Seafood
Regions Exported to: Worldwide
Regions Imported from: Worldwide

44666 (HQ)Gosselin Gourmet Beverages
11203 Paloma Court
Louisville, KY 40229-2844   800-804-7831
Wholesaler/distributor, importer and exporter of gourmet coffee, teas and specialty flavorings; also, cafe equipment
President of Sales/Marketing: Craig Gosselin
Number Employees: 1-4

Regions Exported to: Latin America, Canada, Mexico
Regions Imported from: Latin America, Canada, Mexico

44667 Gossner Foods Inc.
1051 N. 1000 West
Logan, UT 84321-6852   435-227-2500
Fax: 435-227-2550   800-944-0454
www.gossner.com
Cheeses.
President/CEO: Dolores Gossner Wheeler
dolores@gossner.com
Vice President: Greg Rowley
Year Founded: 1966
Estimated Sales: $335 Million
Number Employees: 250-499
Number of Brands: 1
Type of Packaging: Consumer, Food Service, Private Label, Bulk

44668 Gough-Econ Inc
9400 N Lakebrook Rd
Charlotte, NC 28214-9008   704-399-4501
Fax: 704-392-8706   800-204-6844
sales@goughecon.com   www.goughecon.com
Bucket elevator and conveyor systems; exporter of bucket elevator systems; also, multiple discharges available. Also manufacturer of complete line of vibratory conveyors, feeders, screens and belt conveyors
CEO: David Risley
drisley@goughecon.com
VP: Don Calvert
Marketing: Angela Gallagher
Sales: Andrew Leitch
Estimated Sales: $5-10 Million
Number Employees: 20-49
Square Footage: 160000

44669 Gourm-E-Company Imports
405 Glenn Dr # 6
Sterling, VA 20164-4432   703-450-0090
Fax: 703-430-5618
Importer of tea, chutney, preserves, chocolate, cocoa powder, trout, salmon and peppers
President: Bob Eacho
Estimated Sales: $20-50 Million
Number Employees: 20-49
Type of Packaging: Consumer
Brands Imported: Ferris & Roberts; Chantal Plasse; Pettigrew; Valrhona; Mandrange; Singleton; Salerno's; Grafton Village; The Farm at Mt. Walden
Regions Imported from: Europe
Percentage of Business in Importing: 100

44670 Gourmet Brokers
5067 Ontario E Street
Montreal, QC H1V 1M2
Canada   514-259-2291
Fax: 514-259-1788

44671 Gourmet Club Corporation
20 Potash Rd
Oakland, NJ 07436-3100   201-337-5882
Fax: 201-337-0479
Wholesaler/distributor and importer of freeze-dried seafood, mushrooms, seasonings and spices, seafood and vegetable powders, green and pink peppercorns, dehydrated tropical fruits and vegetables and dried vanilla beans
President: Warren Gaffery
Contact: James Magna
james@mpba.org
Estimated Sales: $ 3 - 5 Million
Number Employees: 1-4
Square Footage: 100000
Regions Imported from: Europe, Asia, Madagascar

44672 Gourmet Display
6040 S 194th St # 102
Suite 102
Kent, WA 98032-1191   206-767-4711
Fax: 206-764-6094   800-767-4711
info@gourmetdisplay.com
www.gourmetdisplay.com
Mirrored and marble serving equipment for buffets and banquets

Owner: Precious Chuop
Vice President: Mark Vollmar
Marketing Manager: T Ecker
Sales Manager: Julien Chomette
pchuop@gourmetdisplay.com
General Manager: T Schueler
Estimated Sales: $ 2.5-5 Million
Number Employees: 5-9
Parent Co: Plastic Dynamics

44673 Gourmet Foods Intl
255 Ted Turner Dr SW
Atlanta, GA 30303-3705   404-954-7600
Fax: 404-954-7672   800-966-6172
www.afiaww.com
Wholesaler/distributor and importer of salmon, cheeses, caviar, truffles and foie gras
Owner: Russell Mc Call
rmccall@gfifoods.com
Estimated Sales: $300,000-500,000
Number Employees: 250-499

44674 Gourmet Gear
1413 Westwood Blvd
Los Angeles, CA 90024-4911   310-268-2222
Fax: 310-301-4115   800-682-4635
Culinary apparel
Owner: Farhad Besharati
CEO: Newton Katz
Director Marketing: Marcee Katz
Estimated Sales: $500,000-$1 Million
Number Employees: 1-4

44675 Gourmet International Inc
6605 Broadmoor Ave SE
Caledonia, MI 49316-9511   616-698-0666
Fax: 616-698-8870   800-875-5557
www.gourmetint.com
Importer of European gourmet foods
President: Michael Nitzsche
info@gourmetint.com
Marketing: Michael Nitzsche
Estimated Sales: $10-20 Million
Number Employees: 10-19
Type of Packaging: Consumer, Food Service
Regions Imported from: Europe
Percentage of Business in Importing: 100

44676 Gourmet Table Skirts
9415 W Bellfort St
Houston, TX 77031-2308   713-666-0602
Fax: 713-666-0627   800-527-0440
gkammerman@gourmet-table-skirts.com
www.tableskirts.com
Manufacturer and exporter of table cloths, skirts and runners, napkins, place mats and aprons
Owner: Glenn Kammerman
glenn@tableskirts.com
Estimated Sales: $2.5-5 Million
Number Employees: 50-99
Square Footage: 64000
Type of Packaging: Consumer, Food Service
Percentage of Business in Exporting: 10

44677 Gouw Quality Onions
5801-54 Avenue
Taber, AB T1G 1X4
Canada   403-223-1440
Fax: 403-223-2036
onions@gouwqualityonions.com
www.gouwqualityonions.com
Onions, radishes and red beets
Chairman: Casey Gouw, Sr.
Sales Manager/Controller: Casey Gouw
Warehouse/Plant Operations: Ken Gouw
Farm Manager: Kyle Gouw
Estimated Sales: D
Number Employees: 20-49
Type of Packaging: Consumer
Regions Imported from: USA
Percentage of Business in Importing: 2

44678 Governair Corp
4841 N Sewell Ave
Oklahoma City, OK 73118-7820   405-525-6546
Fax: 405-528-4724   info@governair.com
Manufacturer and exporter of air handling units, evaporative condensing package water chillers, etc

General Manager: Jim Durr
Quality Control: Bill Taylor
R & D: Mark Sly
Marketing: Mark Fly
Sales: Buddy Cross
Plant Manager: Brad Campbell
Purchasing: Vickey Hopper
Estimated Sales: $20-30 Million
Number Employees: 100-249
Square Footage: 150000
Parent Co: Nortek
Brands Exported: Governair
Regions Exported to: South America, Asia, Caribbean, Mexico

44679 Goya Foods Inc.
350 County Rd.
Jersey City, NJ 07307   201-348-4900
          Fax: 201-348-6609 www.goya.com
Latin American food and condiments.
President/CEO: Bob Unanue
Year Founded: 1936
Estimated Sales: $1.5 Billion
Number Employees: 4,000
Number of Products: 2500
Type of Packaging: Consumer, Food Service
Other Locations:
   Goya Foods of South Jersey
   Pedricktown, NJ
   Goya Foods of Great Lakes
   Angola, NY
   Goya Foods of Long Island
   Bethpage, NY
   Goya Foods of Massachusetts
   Webster, MA
   Goya Foods of Miami
   Miami, FL
   Goya Foods of Orlando
   Orlando, FL
   Goya Foods of South JerseyAngola

44680 Grace Instrument Co
9434 Katy Fwy # 300
Houston, TX 77055-6309   713-783-1560
      Fax: 713-974-7144 800-304-5859
                  info@graceinstrument.com
                  www.graceinstrument.com
Manufacturer and importer of thermometers including bi-metal, digital, pocket test, vapor tension dial, refrigeration, oven, barbecue grill and deep fry
Owner: Hongfeng Bi
Marketing Manager: Michelle Dahm
Estimated Sales: $ 1 - 5 Million
Number Employees: 20-49
Regions Exported to: Worldwide
Regions Imported from: Asia

44681 Grace Tea Co
14 Craig Rd
Acton, MA 01720-5405
                         978-635-9500
          Fax: 978-635-9701
          customerservice@gracetea.com
                  www.gracetea.com
Teas
Owner: Hartley Johnson
hejohnson1@gracetea.com
VP: Richard Verdery
Operations Director: Richard Sanders
Estimated Sales: $48,000
Number Employees: 5-9
Number of Brands: 1
Number of Products: 20
Square Footage: 4000
Regions Imported from: Europe, Asia

44682 (HQ)Graco Inc
88 11th Ave NE
Minneapolis, MN 55413-1829   612-623-6000
      Fax: 612-378-3505 877-844-7226
              info@graco.com www.graco.com
Manufacturer and exporter of industrial and portable cleaners, sanitary pumps and dispensers.
Chairman/President/CEO: David Roberts
Chief Administrative Officer: Mark Sheahan
Chief Financial Officer/Treasurer: James Graner
CEO: Patrick J McHale
Sales & Marketing Director: Rick Berkbigler
Vice President Operations: Charles Rescoria
Estimated Sales: Over $1 Billion
Number Employees: 1000-4999
Regions Exported to: Worldwide

44683 Graco Inc
88 11th Ave NE
Minneapolis, MN 55413-1829   612-623-6000
          Fax: 612-378-3505 www.graco.com
Manufacturer and exporter of conveyor lubrication equipment and specialty lubricants
HR Manager: Kathy Buechel
CEO: Patrick J Mc Hale
pmchale@graco.com
Vice President, General Counsel, Secreta: Karen Gallivan
Service Manager: Gary Knutson
Plant Manager: Ryan Eidenschink
Estimated Sales: Over $1 Billion
Number Employees: 1000-4999
Parent Co: IDEX
Brands Exported: OPCD; Wearmaster
Regions Exported to: Worldwide
Percentage of Business in Exporting: 10

44684 (HQ)Graham Engineering Corp
1203 Eden Rd
York, PA 17402-1965   717-848-3755
          Fax: 717-846-1931 www.grahamengineering.com
Manufacturer and exporter of blow-molded plastic bottles and containers
President: Steven F Wood
CEO: Wendy Brown
wendy_brown@uscourts.gov
VP: Joe Spohr
CEO: Wolfgang Liebertz
CFO: Rich Rutkowski
VP Sales/Marketing: F White
Estimated Sales: $ 20 - 50 Million
Number Employees: 50-99
Regions Exported to: Worldwide

44685 Grain Machinery Mfg Corp
1130 NW 163rd Dr
Miami, FL 33169-5816   305-620-2525
          Fax: 305-620-2551 grainman@bellsouth.net
                  www.grainman.com
Manufacturer and exporter of grain elevators, dryers, graders, cleaners, pea and bean hullers, casting and rice machinery, bagging scales and conveyor belts; importer of casting and rice machinery
Owner: Manny Diaz
grainman@bellsouth.net
Treasurer: Librada Dieguez
Vice President: Cary Dieguez
Sales Director: Jose Martinez
Purchasing Manager: Brissa Pichardo
Estimated Sales: $ 3 - 5 Million
Number Employees: 10-19
Square Footage: 86000
Brands Exported: Grainman; Rimac; Ohaus; Detecto; Fischbein, Tapco
Regions Exported to: Central America, South America, Europe, Asia, Caribbean, Latin America, Mexico
Percentage of Business in Exporting: 90
Brands Imported: Rimac
Regions Imported from: Central America, South America, Europe, Asia
Percentage of Business in Importing: 3

44686 Grain Process Enterprises Ltd.
115 Commander Blvd
Scarborough, ON M1S 3M7
Canada   416-291-3226
      Fax: 416-291-2159 800-387-5292
                  gbjr@grainprocess.com
Flours, granola cereals, grain, bread and muffin mixes
President: George Birinyi
Number Employees: 10
Square Footage: 225000
Type of Packaging: Consumer, Private Label, Bulk
Brands Exported: GrainPro
Regions Exported to: USA
Percentage of Business in Exporting: 5

44687 Grainaissance
1580 62nd St
Emeryville, CA 94608   510-922-8856
      Fax: 510-547-0526 800-472-4697
Rice-based products
President: Tony Plotkin
amazake@grainaissance.com
Estimated Sales: $1.4 Million
Number Employees: 11
Type of Packaging: Consumer
Regions Exported to: Asia
Percentage of Business in Exporting: 3

44688 Granco Manufacturing Inc
2010 Crow Canyon Pl # 100
Suite 100
San Ramon, CA 94583-1344   510-652-8847
          Fax: 510-652-1565 info@grancopump.com
                  www.grancopump.com
Manufacturer and exporter of hydraulically driven and low shear pumping systems; also, rotary positive pumps for displacement of viscous liquids.
President: Ivan Dimcheff
CEO: Michael Alessandro
Operations: Ivan Dimcheff
Production Manager: David Kenzler
Estimated Sales: $ .5 - 1 million
Number Employees: 5-9
Square Footage: 64000
Parent Co: Challenge Manufacturing Company
Type of Packaging: Private Label
Brands Exported: Grando; Hy-Drive Systems
Regions Exported to: Worldwide
Percentage of Business in Exporting: 10

44689 Grand Prix Trading
75a Onderdonk Ave
Ridgewood, NY 11385-1177   718-821-8563
          Fax: 718-418-9300 info@grandprixtrading.com
                  www.grandprixtrading.com
Cocoa/baking chocolate, coffee, juice/cider, other chocolate, spices, dessert toppings (i.e. fudge sauce, caramel sauce, whipped cream, etc.).
Marketing: Simon Simunovic

44690 Grand Prix Trading Corp
6153-B Mulford Street
Niles, IL 60714   847-583-0720
          Fax: 847-583-0741 info@grandprixtrading.com
                  www.grandprixtrading.com
Cocoa/baking chocolate, coffee, juice/cider, other chocolate, spices, dessert toppings (i.e. fudge sauce, caramel sauce, whipped cream, etc.).
Marketing: Simon Simunovic
Contact: Zeljko Mazic
zeljko.mazic@grandprixtrading.com

44691 Grand Rapids Label
2351 Oak Industrial Dr NE
Grand Rapids, MI 49505-6017   616-776-2778
          Fax: 616-459-4543 grlabel@grlabel.com
                  www.grlabel.com
Manufacturer and exporter of pressure sensitive and heat seal labels including advertising and supermarket
President: William Muir
CFO: John Laninga
R&D: Tony Maravalo
Quality Control: Christine Howlett
VP Sales: Tom Topel
Estimated Sales: $ 10 - 20 Million
Number Employees: 50-99
Type of Packaging: Bulk

44692 Grande Chef Company
21 Stewart Court
Orangeville, ON L9W 3Z9
Canada   519-942-4470
          Fax: 519-942-4440
Manufacturer, importer and exporter of stainless steel cooking equipment including cookers, kettles, ovens and broilers
President: Frank Edmonstone
Sales/Marketing Executive: Lisa Ashton
Sales/Marketing Executive: Alex Mackay
Operations Manager: Lisa Ashton
Purchasing Manager: Frank Edmonstone
Number Employees: 5-9
Brands Exported: Grande Chef
Percentage of Business in Exporting: 15
Regions Imported from: Asia, USA
Percentage of Business in Importing: 15

44693 Grande Custom Ingredients Group
250 Camelot Dr
Fond du Lac, WI 54935   920-952-7200
      Fax: 920-922-2921 800-772-3210
              gcig@grande.com www.grandecig.com
Processor and exporter of specialty whey products and lactose.
Group Vice President: Paul Graham
Research & Development: Rory McCarthy
Sales & Marketing: Brad Nielsen
Operations: Lary Turner
Purchasing Director: Chris Richards

Importers & Exporters / A-Z

Square Footage: 10000
Parent Co: Grande Cheese Company
Type of Packaging: Bulk
Regions Exported to: Central America, South America, Europe, Asia, Middle East

44694 Grandview Farms
417353 10th Line RR 1
Thornbury, ON N0H 2P0
Canada   519-599-6368
   Fax: 519-599-6971 www.grandviewfarms.ca
Meat
President: Desmond Von Teichman
Plant Manager: Bob Hutchinson
Estimated Sales: $100-350,000k
Number Employees: 25
Square Footage: 30000
Type of Packaging: Food Service, Private Label
Regions Exported to: Europe, Asia, USA
Percentage of Business in Exporting: 20

44695 Grantstone Supermarket
8 W Grant Rd
Tucson, AZ 85705-5529   520-628-7445
   Fax: 520-628-1259
Chinese, Japanese, Korean, Thai and Vietnamese products; fresh Chinese fruit and produce
President: Janet Hom
grantstonemarket@aol.com
Estimated Sales: $ 3 - 5 Million
Number Employees: 20-49

44696 Granville Gates & Sons
60 Fish Plant Rd
Hubbards, NS B0J 1T0
Canada   902-228-2559
   Fax: 902-228-2368
Dried and salted seafood
Manager: Garry Harnish
Office Manager: Norma Young
Plant Manager: Ed Grant
Estimated Sales: 5,000,000 - 9,999,999
Number Employees: 32
Type of Packaging: Bulk
Regions Exported to: Worldwide
Percentage of Business in Exporting: 80

44697 Graphic Apparel
2365 Industrial Park Road
Innisfil, ON L9S 3W1
Canada   705-436-6137
   Fax: 705-436-6139 800-757-4867
Distributor of career apparel and promotions
President: Werner Syndikus
Sales Manager: Mitch Dawkins
Number Employees: 10
Square Footage: 32000
Type of Packaging: Food Service
Regions Exported to: USA

44698 Graphic Calculator Company
234 James Street
Barrington, IL 60010-3388   847-381-4480
   Fax: 847-381-5370
Manufacturer and exporter of advertising novelties including slide rules, printed calculators and feature demonstrators
President: Capron Gulbronsen
VP: Lorraine Gorski
Estimated Sales: $ 5 - 10 Million
Number Employees: 10
Regions Exported to: Canada

44699 Graphic Packaging Intl
1500 Nicholas Blvd
Elk Grove Vlg, IL 60007-5516   847-437-1700
   Fax: 847-956-9291 www.graphicpkg.com
Manufacturer and exporter of folding cartons
President: Larry Field
Cmo: Larry Janis
larry.janis@fieldcontainer.com
Number Employees: 250-499
Regions Exported to: Worldwide
Percentage of Business in Exporting: 25

44700 Graphic Technology
301 Gardner Dr
New Century, KS 66031   913-764-5550
   Fax: 913-764-0320 800-767-9920
Manufacturer, exporter and importer of bar coded and nonbar coded shelf labels for product unit pricing; bar code printers and software; also, picking labels

VP Sales/Marketing: Tom Pooton
Contact: Robert Mccurdy
rob@graphictech.com
Estimated Sales: $ 1 - 5 Million
Number Employees: 500-999
Square Footage: 500000
Parent Co: Nitto Denko Corporation
Regions Exported to: South America
Percentage of Business in Exporting: 1
Regions Imported from: Asia

44701 Graphite Metalizing Corp
1050 Nepperhan Ave
Yonkers, NY 10703-1421   914-968-8400
   Fax: 914-968-8468 sales@graphalloy.com
   www.graphalloy.com
Manufacturer and exporter of graphalloy high-temperature self-lubricating bearings for ovens
President: Eben Walker
Quality Control: Mohmed Youssef
Director Marketing: Eric Ford
Estimated Sales: $ 10 - 20 Million
Number Employees: 50-99
Square Footage: 50000
Brands Exported: Graphalloy
Regions Exported to: Central America, South America, Europe, Asia, Middle East
Percentage of Business in Exporting: 15

44702 Grassland Dairy Products Inc
N8790 Fairground Ave
Greenwood, WI 54437-7668   715-267-6182
   Fax: 715-267-6044 800-428-8837
email@grassland.com www.grassland.com
Butter products
President: Dallas Wuethrich
CFO: Leony Gregorich
Estimated Sales: $38.8 Million
Number Employees: 250-499
Square Footage: 60000
Type of Packaging: Consumer, Food Service, Private Label, Bulk
Brands Exported: Grassland; Fall Creek
Regions Exported to: Central America, South America, Europe, Middle East
Percentage of Business in Exporting: 2

44703 Gravymaster, Inc.
101 Erie Blvd
Canajoharie, NY 13317   800-526-6872
   Fax: 888-673-2451 800-839-8938
info@richardsonbrands.com www.gravy.com
Sauces
President: Stephen Besse
Sales Executive: Cathy Testa
Consultant: John Mills
Sales Coordinator: MaryLou Sweet
Promotional Products Representative: Laurie Bluitt
Supply Chain Manager: Rebecca Woodruff
Estimated Sales: $10-20 Million
Number Employees: 20-49
Parent Co: Richardson Brands
Type of Packaging: Consumer, Food Service
Brands Exported: Gravy Master; DGP Rock Candy
Regions Exported to: Worldwide

44704 Gray & Company
3325 W Polk Rd
Hart, MI 49420-8149   231-873-5628
   Fax: 231-873-0348 800-551-6009
sales@cherryman.com www.grayandcompany.us
Maraschino cherries, glace fruit and chocolate cherry cordials
Director of Finance: Kevin Schulz
Executive Vice President: Joshua Reynolds
Food Scientist: Jillian Clark
Sales: Rich Bertellotti
Director of Cherry Operations: Dirk Williams
Plant Engineer: Benjamin Kirwin
Purchasing Manager: Steve Schauer
Estimated Sales: $28.2 Million
Number Employees: 250-499
Square Footage: 5000
Type of Packaging: Consumer, Food Service, Private Label, Bulk
Other Locations:
Hart, MI
Dayton, ORDayton
Brands Exported: Pennant; Cherry Man; Queen Anne
Regions Exported to: Worldwide
Percentage of Business in Exporting: 10

44705 Grayco Products Sales
100 Tec Street
Hicksville, NY 11801-3650   516-997-9200
   Fax: 516-870-0510
Wholesaler/distributor and exporter of paper and disposable products including tabletop and industrial equipment, packaging and printing supplies
Owner: Helen Kushner
CEO: Adrienne Kushner
Vice President: Alan Kushner
Operations Manager: D Pascale
Estimated Sales: $ 1 - 5 Million
Number Employees: 2
Square Footage: 10000
Parent Co: ASK Sales
Regions Exported to: Central America, South America, Europe, Asia, Middle East, Caribbean
Percentage of Business in Exporting: 25

44706 Great American Appetizers
216 8th St N
Nampa, ID 83687-3029   208-465-5111
   Fax: 208-465-5059 800-282-4834
marco@appetizer.com www.appetizer.com
Appetizers
President: Tammy Mika
tammy.mika@westin.com
Marketing/Sales Coordinator: Debbie Lindley
VP Retail Sales: Frank Benso
COO: Marco Meyer
Purchasing Director: Tammy Mika
Year Founded: 1959
Estimated Sales: $26.6 Million
Number Employees: 250-499
Number of Products: 100
Square Footage: 60000
Parent Co: Westin Foods
Type of Packaging: Consumer, Food Service, Private Label, Bulk
Regions Exported to: Canada
Percentage of Business in Exporting: 5
Regions Imported from: Central America, Europe, Asia
Percentage of Business in Importing: 10

44707 Great Atlantic Trading Company
1204 Longstreet Circle
Brentwood, TN 37027-6506   615-661-6678
   Fax: 910-575-7978 888-268-8780
   www.caviarstar.com
Fresh and frozen seafood, American and imported caviar
President: Dana Leavitt
Estimated Sales: $3.2 Million
Number Employees: 1-4
Square Footage: 5000
Parent Co: Great Atlantic Trading Company
Brands Exported: Great Atlantic; Caviarstar, Avari

44708 Great Atlantic Trading Inc
563 Seaside Rd SW
Ocean Isle Beach, NC 28469-6102   910-575-7979
   Fax: 910-575-7972 888-268-8780
   customerservice@caviarstar.com
Caviar, truffles, oils, vinegars, saffron
President: Dana Leavit
dana@caviarstar.com
Number Employees: 1-4

44709 Great Eastern Sun Trading Co
92 Mcintosh Rd
Asheville, NC 28806-1406   828-665-7790
   Fax: 828-667-8051 800-334-5809
   weborders@great-eastern-sun.com
Asian organic and natural foods
Owner: Berry Evans
generalmgr@great-eastern-sun.com
Finance: Brett Martin
Sales Manager: Mary Griffin
VP Operations/Purchaser: Jan Paige
Assistant Production Manager: Wendy Young
Warehouse/Shipping: Joe Putnam
Estimated Sales: $ 5 - 10 Million
Number Employees: 20-49
Brands Exported: Hailu; One World; Sweet Cloud; Emerald Cove; Organic Planet; Miso Master, Sushi Sonic
Regions Exported to: International
Brands Imported: Sweet Cloud; Emerald Cove; Organic Planet; Tohum; Sushi Sonic
Regions Imported from: Europe, Asia, Middle East

Importers & Exporters / A-Z

44710 Great Glacier Salmon
PO Box 1137
Prince Rupert, BC V8J 4H6
Canada 250-627-4955
Fax: 250-627-7945 greatglacier@hotmail.com
Salmon
Accounting: Mary Allen
General Manager: Robert Gould
Estimated Sales: $250,000 To 1,000,000
Number Employees: 20-49
Number of Brands: 2
Square Footage: 6400
Type of Packaging: Private Label, Bulk
Brands Exported: Glacier Salmon; Glacier Caviar
Regions Exported to: Asia, USA
Percentage of Business in Exporting: 20

44711 Great Lakes Brush
6859 Audrain Road #9139
Centralia, MO 65240 573-682-2128
Fax: 573-682-2121
Manufacturer and importer of brushes and wire drawn products
President: Matthew Kallas
Estimated Sales: $500,000-$1 Million
Number Employees: 1-4
Square Footage: 8000
Regions Imported from: Asia
Percentage of Business in Importing: 10

44712 (HQ)Great Lakes Cheese Company, Inc.
17825 Great Lakes Pkwy
PO Box 1806
Hiram, OH 44234-1806 440-834-2500
Fax: 440-834-1002 glcinfo@greatlakescheese.com
www.greatlakescheese.com
Cheese
Chairman: Hans Epprecht
CEO/President: Gary Vanic
CFO: Russell Mullins
VP Sales: William Andrews
VP Human Resources: Beth Wendell
VP/General Mgr: John W Epprecht
Manufacturing/Operations Director: Steve Scott
Plant Manager: Thomas Eastham
Purchasing Clerk: Shelley Williamson
Estimated Sales: Over $1 Billion
Number Employees: 1000-4999
Square Footage: 400000
Type of Packaging: Private Label
Other Locations:
  Great Lakes Cheese of New York
  Adams, NY
  Great Lakes Cheese of Utah
  Fillmore, UT
  Great Lakes Cheese Company - HQ
  Hiram, OH
  Great Lakes Cheese of La Crosse
  La Crosse, WI
  Great Lakes Cheese of Wisconsin
  Plymouth, WIGreat Lakes Cheese of New YorkFillmore

44713 Great Lakes Designs
544 S Green Rd
Cleveland, OH 44121-2843 216-382-6961
Fax: 216-382-7756 gld@gldesigns.com
Importer and wholesaler/distributor of latex gloves, bread accessories, chrome wire ware and solid wood and high density poly cutting boards; serving the food service market
President: Barry Epstein
Marketing Manager: Jonathon Varble
Estimated Sales: $1-3 Million
Number Employees: 10-19
Square Footage: 40000
Parent Co: Eppco Enterprises
Type of Packaging: Food Service
Regions Exported to: Asia
Regions Imported from: Asia

44714 Great Lakes Gourmet Food Service
24404 Catherne Ind Dr # 308
Novi, MI 48375-2456 248-735-1700
Fax: 248-735-1800 800-625-4591
Importer of bakery and pastry equipment; wholesaler/distributor and importer of bakery and pastry ingredients; serving the food service market
President: Tom Chaput
Estimated Sales: $1-2 Million
Number Employees: 1
Square Footage: 28000

Type of Packaging: Food Service
Brands Imported: Matfer; Schokinag; Cocoa Barry; Callebaut
Regions Imported from: South America
Percentage of Business in Importing: 60

44715 Great Lakes International Trading
858 Business Park Drive
Traverse City, MI 49686 231-947-2141
Fax: 231-947-0628 glit@glit.com
www.glit.com
Importer and exporter of dried fruits, nuts and seeds
President: Verne Powell
Vice President: George Powell
Sales/Marketing Assistant: Emi King
Sales Manager: Denny Malone
Estimated Sales: $5-10 Million
Number Employees: 10-19
Type of Packaging: Private Label, Bulk
Regions Exported to: Europe, Asia
Percentage of Business in Exporting: 20
Brands Imported: Great Lakes; Golden Palm
Regions Imported from: Central America, South America, Europe, Asia, Turkey
Percentage of Business in Importing: 80

44716 Great Northern Corp.
395 Stroebe Rd.
Appleton, WI 54914
800-236-3671
www.greatnortherncorp.com
Expandable polystyrene plastic packaging products including boxes and containers.
President/CEO: John Davis
Chairman: William Raaths
Year Founded: 1962
Estimated Sales: $100-500 Million
Number Employees: 500-999
Type of Packaging: Bulk
Regions Exported to: Worldwide

44717 Great Northern Products Inc
2700 Plainfield Pike
Cranston, RI 02921-2070 401-490-4590
Fax: 401-633-6051 info@northernproducts.com
www.northernproducts.com
Seafood
President: George Nolan
george@northernproducts.com
Executive Vice President: Peter Bruno
Quality Control/ Compliance: Kyle Wilkens
Domestic Sales: Don Nolan
COO: Jose Pons
Estimated Sales: $10.1 Million
Number Employees: 20-49
Number of Brands: 4
Number of Products: 40
Square Footage: 24000
Regions Exported to: Europe, Asia, Middle East
Percentage of Business in Exporting: 100
Brands Imported: Langlois; Cusimer; Gaspesienne
Regions Imported from: North America, Canada

44718 Great Southern Corp
3595 Regal Blvd
Memphis, TN 38118-6117 901-365-1611
Fax: 901-365-4498 800-421-7802
sales@greatsoutherncorp.com
www.gsmemphis.com
Manufacturer, importer and exporter of licensed gloves consisting of leather, cotton, plastic and rubber gloves; also, rubber bands
President: Scott Vaught
Chairman: C Vaught
Manager: Jeff Harrell
j.harrell@greatsoutherncorp.com
Estimated Sales: $20-50 Million
Number Employees: 5-9
Square Footage: 48000
Parent Co: Great Southern Corporation
Percentage of Business in Exporting: 10
Brands Imported: John Deere, Farmall and Collegiate Licensed Gloves
Regions Imported from: Asia
Percentage of Business in Importing: 90

44719 Great Spice Company
12101 Moya Blvd
Reno, NV 89506-2600
Fax: 760-744-0401 800-730-3575
www.greatspice.com
Dehydrated and fresh herbs

President: Jay Fishman
Inventory Manager: Steve Addison
s.addison@hqorganics.com
Quality Manager: Ja Attaphongse
VP Sales: Jim Slatic
Founder/VP Operations: Jerry Tenenberg
Operations Manager: Dan Sullivan
Shipping Manager: Michael Tenenberg
Global Purchasing Coordinator: Rommina Chavarria
Estimated Sales: $3-5,000,000
Number Employees: 20-49
Type of Packaging: Food Service, Private Label, Bulk
Regions Exported to: Worldwide

44720 Great Valley Mills
1774 A County Line Rd
Barto, PA 19504-8720 610-754-7800
Fax: 610-754-6490 800-688-6455
Stone ground flour, pancake, muffin, bread and specialty dry food mixes
Owner: Steve Kantoor
Estimated Sales: $690,000
Number Employees: 6
Square Footage: 45000
Type of Packaging: Consumer, Food Service, Private Label
Brands Exported: Great Valley Mills
Regions Exported to: Europe, Asia, Middle East
Percentage of Business in Exporting: 3

44721 Great Western Co LLC
30290 US Highway 72
Hollywood, AL 35752-6134 256-259-3578
Fax: 256-259-7087 www.gwproducts.com
Processor and exporter of popcorn, popping corn oil, cotton candy, sno-cone syrup, candy apple coatings, funnel cakes, waffle cones, corn dog mix, and other concession items
Contact: Tim Ferguson
timf@gwproducts.com
Estimated Sales: Less Than $500,000
Number Employees: 1-4
Number of Brands: 6
Type of Packaging: Consumer, Food Service, Private Label, Bulk
Brands Exported: Great Western; Senor Carlos
Regions Exported to: Central America, South America, Europe, Asia, Middle East
Percentage of Business in Exporting: 10

44722 Great Western Juice Co
16153 Libby Rd
Maple Heights, OH 44137-1298 216-475-5770
Fax: 216-475-5772 800-321-9180
gwjuice@sbcglobal.net
Beverages
President: Doreen Coons
dcoons@fibreglast.com
VP: Bill Overton
Marketing/Sales: Phil Leroy
Public Relations: Connie Rice
Operations Manager: John Stevens
Plant Manager: John Taziros
Purchasing Manager: Bill Overton
dcoons@fibreglast.com
Estimated Sales: $1.6 Million
Number Employees: 20-49
Square Footage: 60000
Type of Packaging: Food Service, Private Label
Regions Exported to: Canada, Mexico

44723 Great Western Malting Co
1705 NW Harborside Dr
Vancouver, WA 98660 360-693-3661
www.graincorp.com.au
Processed malt
President & CEO: Greg Friberg
Group Chief Financial Officer: Alistair Bell
Chief Information Officer: Andrew Baker
Estimated Sales: $27 Million
Number Employees: 50-99
Square Footage: 13440
Type of Packaging: Bulk
Other Locations:
  Malt Plant
  Vancouver, WA
  Malt Plant
  Pocatello, ID
  Bagged Malt Country Warehouse
  Vancouver, WA
  Bagged Malt Country Warehouse
  Aurora, CO
  Bagged Malt Country Warehouse
  Hayward, CA

Importers & Exporters / A-Z

Bagged Malt Country Warehouse
Champlain, NY
Malt PlantPocatello
Regions Exported to: Worldwide

44724 Great Western Manufacturing Company
2017 So. 4th Floor
PO Box 149
Leavenworth, KS 66048 913-682-2291
Fax: 913-682-1431 800-682-3121
sifter@gwmfg.com www.gwmfg.com
Screening machines, shakers, sifters, screens and sieves.
CFO: Michael Bell
General Manager: Robert Ricklefs
Sales, Services & Applications Engineer: Bob Recklifs
Production Manager: Steve Wood
Purchasing Manager: Michael Glassford
Estimated Sales: $5-10 Million
Number Employees: 10
Type of Packaging: Food Service
Regions Exported to: Central America, South America, Asia, Middle East, Australia
Percentage of Business in Exporting: 10

44725 Greater Omaha Packing Co Inc.
3001 L Street
Omaha, NE 68107 402-731-1700
 800-747-5400
info@greateromaha.com www.greateromaha.com
Beef.
President/CEO: Henry Davis
Credit/Account Manager: Carol Mesenbrink
Vice President, Sales: Dan Jensen
Year Founded: 1920
Estimated Sales: $1+ Billion
Number Employees: 1,000
Number of Brands: 5
Square Footage: 60000
Type of Packaging: Consumer, Food Service, Private Label, Bulk
Brands Exported: Greater Omaha Packing Co.
Regions Exported to: Central America, Europe, Asia, Middle East
Percentage of Business in Exporting: 25

44726 Greaves Jams & Marmalades
PO Box 26
Niagara-on-the-Lake, ON L0S 1J0
Canada 905-468-3608
Fax: 905-468-0071 800-515-9939
greaves@greavesjams.com www.greavesjams.com
Jams, jellies, marmalades and condiments
President: Lloyd Redekopp
Vice President: Angela Redekopp
Production: Rudy Doerwald
Estimated Sales: $1.4 Million
Number Employees: 15
Number of Products: 1
Square Footage: 20000
Type of Packaging: Consumer, Private Label
Brands Exported: Greaves
Regions Exported to: USA
Percentage of Business in Exporting: 5

44727 Grecon
15875 SW 74th Ave # 100
Suite 100
Tigard, OR 97224-7934 503-641-7731
Fax: 503-641-7508 sales@grecon-us.com
www.grecon-us.com
Spark detection and extinguishing systems, as well as quality assurance measuring systems.
Contact: Walter Crosson
wcrosson@grecon.us
Number Employees: 10-19

44728 Greek Farms Intl
2177 31st St
Long Island City, NY 11105-2674 718-932-9293
Fax: 718-932-3595 info@terramedi.com
www.terramedi.com
Olive oil, olive bruschetta, olivades, marinated olives, sesame oil, and vinegars
President/Owner: Apostolos Paralikas
apostolos@terramedi.com
Number Employees: 1-4

44729 Greek Gourmet Limited
38 Miller Avenue PMB 510
Mill Valley, CA 94941-1927 415-480-8050
Fax: 617-833-6056

Greek specialty products
President: George Nassopoulos
Vice President: Diane Nassopoulos
diane@greekgourmet.com
Sales Director: James Contis
Production Manager: P Margaritidis
Estimated Sales: $2.5-5 Million
Number Employees: 5-9
Number of Brands: 4
Number of Products: 35
Square Footage: 20000
Type of Packaging: Consumer, Food Service, Private Label, Bulk
Brands Imported: Greek Gourmet; Bolero, Santorina, 7 Day Round, Magdalena
Regions Imported from: Europe, Asia
Percentage of Business in Importing: 90

44730 (HQ)Green Bay Packaging Inc.
1700 Webster Ct.
Green Bay, WI 54302 920-433-5111
Fax: 920-433-5471 www.gbp.com
Corrugated shipping containers and labels including coated and stock.
President/CEO: William Kress
bkress@gbp.com
Senior VP/General Counsel: Scott Wochos
Year Founded: 1933
Estimated Sales: $850 Million
Number Employees: 3,200
Type of Packaging: Consumer, Food Service, Private Label, Bulk
Regions Exported to: Canada, Mexico, Latin America
Percentage of Business in Exporting: 10

44731 Green Belt Industries Inc
45 Comet Ave
Buffalo, NY 14216-1710 716-873-6923
Fax: 716-873-1728 800-668-1114
www.greenbelting.com
Manufacturer and exporter of Teflon-coated conveyor belting for baking pans and trays
Manager: Gail Lipka
Marketing Director: Joe Smith
Manager: Sue King
sking@greenbelting.com
Operations Manager: Scott O Hearn
Purchasing Manager: Jennifer White
Estimated Sales: $5-10 Million
Number Employees: 20-49
Square Footage: 200000
Regions Exported to: Central America, South America, Asia

44732 Green County Foods
PO BOX 2813
Monroe, WI 53566-1364 608-328-8800
Fax: 608-328-8648 800-233-3564
custserv@greencountyfoods.com
www.greencountyfoods.com
Desserts and baked goods
President: Gene Curran
Sales: Wally Wagner
Public Relations: Jim Mason
Operations: Sharee Marzolf
Estimated Sales: $2.5-5,000,000
Number Employees: 10-19
Parent Co: Swiss Colony
Type of Packaging: Consumer, Food Service, Private Label, Bulk
Brands Exported: Richly Deserved; Sweet Treasures; Green County Foods
Regions Exported to: Mexico; Canada

44733 Green Foods Corp.
2220 Camino Del Sol
Oxnard, CA 93030-8905
 800-777-4430
info@greenfoods.com greenfoods.com
Powdered protein shakes and juices
President: Takahiko Amano
Chief Administrative Officer: Deborah Pollack
deborah@greenfoods.com
Technical Service Manager: Bob Terry
Estimated Sales: $10-20 Million
Number Employees: 5-9
Square Footage: 19600
Type of Packaging: Consumer
Brands Exported: Green Essence
Regions Exported to: Central America, Canada
Percentage of Business in Exporting: 20
Brands Imported: Cellulogan; Shijimi; Green Magma Original

Regions Imported from: Asia
Percentage of Business in Importing: 30

44734 Green Gold Group LLC
13905 Stettin Dr
Marathon, WI 54448-9476 715-842-8546
Fax: 715-842-4614 888-533-7288
www.greengoldgroup.com
Ginseng, herbs, whole roots and other health products
Owner: Sam Chen
mail@greengoldgroup.com
CEO: Phouangmala Chen
Estimated Sales: $1 - 3,000,000
Number Employees: 10-19
Square Footage: 7200
Type of Packaging: Consumer, Bulk
Regions Exported to: Worldwide

44735 Green Grown Products Inc
13600 Marina Pointe Dr
Suite 315
Marina Del Ray, CA 90292 310-828-1686
Fax: 310-822-6440
Herbs, royal jelly, propolis, bee pollen, chia and sesame seeds, apricot kernels and turbinado sugar
President: Teri Bernardi
CEO: Hal Neiman
Estimated Sales: $2,000,000
Number Employees: 1-4
Square Footage: 16000
Parent Co: Earth Commodities
Type of Packaging: Private Label, Bulk
Regions Exported to: South America, Asia
Regions Imported from: South America
Percentage of Business in Importing: 75

44736 Green Spot Packaging
100 S Cambridge Ave
Claremont, CA 91711-4842 909-625-8771
Fax: 909-621-4634 800-456-3210
info@greenspotusa.com www.lagunaliquid.com
Beverages, flavors and fragrances; aseptic packaging services available
CEO: John Tsu
Finance Executive: Don Koury
Sales Executive: Greg Faust
Chief Operating Officer: Dana Staal
Plant Manager: Roy Cooley
Estimated Sales: $6.5 Million
Number Employees: 20-49
Square Footage: 200000
Type of Packaging: Consumer, Food Service, Private Label, Bulk
Brands Exported: Green Spot
Regions Exported to: South America, Europe, Asia
Percentage of Business in Exporting: 10
Regions Imported from: Worldwide
Percentage of Business in Importing: 10

44737 Green Turtle Bay Vitamin Company
PO Box 642
Summit, NJ 07902 908-277-2240
Fax: 908-273-9116 800-887-8535
mail@energywave.com www.energywave.com
Processor and exporter of vitamin supplement formulas including herbal antioxidants, oils and herbs
President: Karen Horbatt
CEO: Gloria Mckenna
Quality Control: Monica Harris
Marketing: Michele Murphy
Estimated Sales: $600,000
Number Employees: 5

44738 Green Valley Food Corp
1501 Market Center Blvd
Dallas, TX 75207-3913 214-939-3900
Fax: 214-939-3999 800-853-8399
www.greenvalleyfood.com
Importer and wholesaler/distributor of cheese, meats, pates, cookies, crackers, breads, jams, jellies, preserves, soups, snack foods, pasta and confections; custom packer of domestic and imported cheeses
Owner: George Chang
Estimated Sales: $2,100,000
Number Employees: 20-49
Square Footage: 120000
Brands Imported: Black Diamond; Jackie; M.D.; Long Clawson; Couronne; Claudel Champignon; Barrs; Somerdale; Galbani; Scandic; Bourdin
Regions Imported from: Europe, Canada

334

Percentage of Business in Importing: 60

44739 Greenbush Tape & Label Inc
40 Broadway # 3
PO Box 1488
Albany, NY 12202-1020   518-465-2389
       Fax: 518-465-5781 www.greenbushlabel.com
Manufacturer and exporter of pressure sensitive tapes and labels
President: James Chenot
Estimated Sales: Below $5 Million
Number Employees: 20-49
Type of Packaging: Consumer, Food Service, Private Label, Bulk
Regions Exported to: South America
Percentage of Business in Exporting: 1

44740 Greene Brothers
134 Broadway
Brooklyn, NY 11211-6031   718-388-6800
                     Fax: 718-782-4123
Manufacturer and exporter of lighting fixtures
Fmn.: Matthew Santoro
Number Employees: 5-9
Parent Co: Greene's Lighting Fixtures
Regions Exported to: Europe, Asia

44741 Greenheck Fan Corp
P.O. Box 410
Schofield, WI 54476   715-359-6171
                     info@greenheck.com
                     www.greenheck.com
Manufacturer and exporter of kitchen ventilation equipment including exhaust and supply fans, air units and exhaust hoods; also, pre-piped fire suppression systems including wet chemical and water spray.
Chairman & CEO: James McIntyre
President, Operations: Dave Kallstrom
Chief Financial Officer & Treasurer: Rich Totzke
VP, Manufacturing Execllence & Logistics: Scott Graf
Plant Manager: Mark Haase
Year Founded: 1947
Estimated Sales: $203.7 Million
Number Employees: 250-499
Square Footage: 1000000

44742 (HQ)Greer's Ferry Glass Work
PO Box 797
Dubuque, IA 52004-0797   501-589-2947
       Fax: 800-310-0525 gfgw@hotmail.com
Manufacturer and exporter of thermometers, refractometers and hydrometers for testing salt, alcohol, sugar, etc
Sales: Brenda Marler
Operations: Bob Mallis
Estimated Sales: $1-2.5 Million
Number Employees: 5-9
Other Locations:
   Greer's Ferry Glass Works
   West Paterson, NJGreer's Ferry Glass Works

44743 Gregor Jonsson Inc
13822 W Laurel Dr
Lake Forest, IL 60045-4529   847-247-4200
       Fax: 847-247-4272 sales@jonsson.com
                     www.jonsson.com
Manufacturer and exporter of shrimp peeling systems
President: Frank Heurich
Vice President: Beth Dancy
Computer Support/Database Design: Ann Curry
Operations Manager: Scott Heurich
Operations Manager: Scott Heurich
Estimated Sales: $ 10 - 20 Million
Number Employees: 10-19
Square Footage: 80000
Regions Exported to: Worldwide
Percentage of Business in Exporting: 20

44744 Greig Filters Inc
412 High Meadows Blvd
P.O.Box 91675
Lafayette, LA 70507-3417   337-237-3355
       Fax: 337-233-9263 800-456-0177
       gfi@greigfilters.com www.greigfilters.com
Manufacturer and exporter of filtration systems for cooking oil and beverages
Owner: Alan Greig
gfi@greigfilters.com
Office Manager: Tammy Roy
Engineer: Shane Hulin
Estimated Sales: $ 1-2.5 Million
Number Employees: 5-9
Square Footage: 40000
Regions Exported to: Central America, South America, Europe, Asia
Percentage of Business in Exporting: 50

44745 Gress Enterprises
992 N South Rd
Scranton, PA 18504-1412   570-561-0150
       Fax: 570-341-1299 www.gresscold.com
Frozen chicken products
Owner: E Gress
VP/General Manager: Keith Gress
VP Marketing: Glenn Gress
Estimated Sales: $5-10 Million
Number Employees: 10-19
Type of Packaging: Food Service, Bulk

44746 Grey Owl Foods
510 11th St SE
Grand Rapids, MN 55744   218-327-2281
       Fax: 218-327-2283 800-527-0172
Rice and rice products
Director Sales/Marketing: Jim McCool
Estimated Sales: $10-20 Million
Number Employees: 10-19
Square Footage: 12000
Parent Co: SIAP Marketing Company
Type of Packaging: Consumer, Food Service, Bulk
Regions Exported to: Europe
Percentage of Business in Exporting: 15

44747 Grgich Hills Estates
1829 Saint Helena Hwy S
St Helena, CA 94574-2207   707-963-2784
       Fax: 707-963-8725 800-532-3057
       info@grgich.com www.grgich.com
Wine
President: Miljenko Mike Grgich
VP Sales/Marketing: Violet Grgich
Public Relations: Kristie Nackordo
VP of Production: Ivo Jeramez
Estimated Sales: $5-9.9 Million
Number Employees: 20-49
Number of Brands: 1
Number of Products: 5
Type of Packaging: Consumer
Brands Exported: Grgich Hills Cellar
Regions Exported to: Central America, South America, Europe, Asia
Percentage of Business in Exporting: 3
Brands Imported: Grgic' Vina
Regions Imported from: Europe
Percentage of Business in Importing: 1

44748 Gridpath, Inc.
328 Glover Road
Stony Creek, ON L8E 5M3
Canada   905-643-0955
       Fax: 905-643-6718 info@gridpathinc.com
High pressure processing equipment for non-thermal pasteurization and packaging for the food processing industry.
President: Rick Marshall
Regions Exported to: North America, Worldwide

44749 Griesedieck Imports
6501 Hall Street
Saint Louis, MO 63147-2910   314-770-1515
                     Fax: 314-770-0954
Importer and wholesaler/distributor of German beer and wine
President: Alvin Griesedieck
Estimated Sales: $2.5-5 Million
Number Employees: 1-4
Brands Imported: Griesdieck; Warsteiner
Regions Imported from: Europe
Percentage of Business in Importing: 100

44750 (HQ)Griffin Bros Inc
3033 Industrial Way NE
Salem, OR 97301-0042   503-540-7886
       Fax: 503-540-7929 800-456-4743
                     griffinbros1@yahoo.com
Manufacturer and exporter of disinfectants, polymer floor finish, etc
President: Rod Bennett
rod@griffinbrothers.com
Account Sales Manager: Rod Bennett
Production Manager: Mike Allison
Estimated Sales: $ 1 - 3 Million
Number Employees: 5-9
Type of Packaging: Consumer, Food Service
Regions Exported to: Worldwide

44751 Gril-Del
400 Southbrook Circle
Mankato, MN 56001-4782   507-776-8275
       Fax: 507-776-8276 800-782-7320
Manufacturer and exporter of outdoor cooking utensils for the barbecue grill including spatulas, tongs and knives; also, aprons, salt and pepper shakers, handmade baskets, mitts and meat platters
President: Steven Saggau
VP: Connie Saggau
Number Employees: 10
Square Footage: 12000
Type of Packaging: Consumer, Food Service, Private Label, Bulk
Brands Exported: Gril-Classics
Percentage of Business in Exporting: 2

44752 Grill Greats
PO Box 568
Saxonburg, PA 16056-0568   724-352-1511
       Fax: 724-352-1266 sales@du.co.com
                     www.du.co.com
Manufacturer and exporter of ceramic briquettes for barbecue grills
President: Tom Arbanas
Quality Control: Paul Sekeras
Sales: Mike Carson
Estimated Sales: $ 50 - 100 Million
Number Employees: 100-249
Square Footage: 150000
Type of Packaging: Private Label, Bulk
Brands Exported: Grill Greats; Heat Sheets

44753 Grills to Go
5659 W San Madele Avenue
Fresno, CA 93722-5066   559-645-8089
       Fax: 559-645-8088 877-869-2253
Manufacturer, Distributor and Exporter of commerical barbecue equipment, smoker ovens, Southern Pride brand ovens and Rotisseries and supplies
President: Michael Hall
CEO: Nora Hall
Estimated Sales: $1-2.5 Million
Number Employees: 1-4
Square Footage: 12000
Regions Exported to: Worldwide
Percentage of Business in Exporting: 20

44754 Grimaud Farms-California Inc
1320 S Aurora St # A
Stockton, CA 95206-1616   209-466-3200
       Fax: 209-466-8910 800-466-9955
Duck and guinea fowl
Owner: Howard Chan
howard@grimaudfarms.com
Vice President: Lauren Bartels
Vice President Sales: Jim Galle
Production/Plant Manager: Diego Davalos
Purchasing Agent: Istvan Deli
Estimated Sales: $6.4 Million
Number Employees: 100-249
Square Footage: 168000
Parent Co: Groupe Grimaud
Type of Packaging: Consumer, Food Service, Private Label, Bulk
Regions Exported to: Central America, Canada, Mexico
Percentage of Business in Exporting: 5

44755 Grimm's Fine Food
#100 - 10991 Shellbridge Way
Richmond, BC V6X 3C6
Canada   780-415-4331
       Fax: 780-477-5287 866-663-4746
                     www.grimmsfinefoods.com
Processed meats and sausages
President: Rick Grimm
Plant Manager: George McCorry
Number Employees: 50-99
Parent Co: Fletcher's Fine Foods
Type of Packaging: Consumer, Food Service, Private Label, Bulk
Regions Exported to: Worldwide

44756 (HQ)Grindmaster-Cecilware Corp
4003 Collins Ln
Louisville, KY 40245-1602   502-425-4776
       Fax: 502-425-4664 800-695-4500
       info@gmcw.com www.gmcw.com
Manufacturers of a complete line of hot, cold and frozen beverage dispensing equipment.

Importers & Exporters / A-Z

CEO: Michael G Tinsley
mtinsley@grindmaster.com
CEO: Tom McDonald
Plant Manager: Jim Howell
Estimated Sales: $ 5 - 10 Million
Number Employees: 100-249
Brands Exported: Crathco; Grindmaster; Anw; Wilch
Regions Exported to: Worldwide
Percentage of Business in Exporting: 24
Regions Imported from: Europe, Asia
Percentage of Business in Importing: 5

44757 Grocers Supply Co
3131 E Holcombe Blvd
Houston, TX 77021-2199   713-747-5000
www.grocerssupply.com
Wholesaler/distributor of groceries, meats, produce, frozen foods, equipment and fixtures, general merchandise, private label items and specialty foods; serving the retail market.
Vice President, Produce: Tom Henthorn
Year Founded: 1928
Estimated Sales: $3 Billion
Number Employees: 10,000
Square Footage: 747752
Type of Packaging: Consumer
Regions Exported to: Central America, South America, Europe, Asia, Middle East
Percentage of Business in Exporting: 100

44758 Groeb Farms
10464 Bryan Hwy
Onsted, MI 49265-0269   517-467-2565
Fax: 517-467-2840   800-530-9969
Honey; UPC labeling, tamper-evident packaging, re-closable cap, easy pour handle and shatterproof containers
President & CEO: Ernest Groeb
VP & CFO: Jack Irvin Jr
VP/COO: Troy Groeb
Director Retail Sales: Jim McCoy
Chief Procurement Officer: Alison Tringale
Type of Packaging: Consumer, Food Service, Private Label, Bulk
Other Locations:
  Belleview, FL
  Miller's American Honey
  Colton, CAColton
Brands Exported: Groeb Farms
Regions Exported to: Worldwide
Regions Imported from: Worldwide

44759 Grosfillex Inc
230 Old West Penn Ave
Robesonia, PA 19551-8904   610-693-6213
Fax: 610-693-5414   800-233-3186
info@grosfillexfurniture.com
www.grosfillexfurniture.com
Supplier, importer and exporter of commercial outdoor resin furniture
President: Kim Addington
kladdington@grosfillex.com
Estimated Sales: $ 50-100 Million
Number Employees: 100-249
Parent Co: Grosfillex SARL
Other Locations:
  Grosfillex Contract Furniture
  Chino, CAGrosfillex Contract Furniture
Brands Exported: Grosfillex

44760 Grote Co
1160 Gahanna Pkwy
Columbus, OH 43230-6615   614-868-8414
Fax: 614-863-1647   888-534-7683
www.grotecompany.com
Manufacturer and exporter of food processing equipment including high yield slicer applicators, multi-purpose slicers, cheese shredders, pizza topping lines and paper sheeter systems
President: Jelff Rawef
aschneider@grotecompany.com
CEO: Bruce Hohl
Chairman: James Grote
Quality Control: Jon Feifeit
Marketing Communication/Sales Coord.: Terri Hoover
Sales Exec: Andy Schneider
Estimated Sales: $ 10 - 20 Million
Number Employees: 100-249
Square Footage: 140000
Brands Exported: Grote
Regions Exported to: Worldwide
Percentage of Business in Exporting: 50

44761 Groupe Paul Masson
110-50, Rue De La Barre
Longueuil, QC J4K 5G2
Canada   514-878-3050
Fax: 450-651-5453 www.bloomberg.com
Alcoholic beverages
President: Jean Denis Cote
VP Marketing Development: Alain Lecours
Number Employees: 100-249
Type of Packaging: Consumer
Brands Exported: California Cooler
Regions Exported to: South America, Africa
Percentage of Business in Exporting: 2
Brands Imported: Caballero; Il Florentino; Laloux; Paul Masson
Regions Imported from: South America, Europe
Percentage of Business in Importing: 5

44762 Grow Co
55 Railroad Ave
Ridgefield, NJ 07657-2109   201-941-8777
Fax: 201-342-9127 info@growco.us
Vitamins, minerals and flavors
Vice President: Massoud Avanaghi
arvanaghi@growco.us
Estimated Sales: $1-2.5 Million
Number Employees: 10-19
Square Footage: 91200
Brands Exported: Re-Natured
Regions Exported to: Europe, Asia
Percentage of Business in Exporting: 10

44763 Grower Shipper Potato Company
One Fourth Mile Hwy 285
Monte Vista, CO 81144   719-852-3569
Fax: 719-852-5917
Potatoes
Manager: Mark Lounsbury
Vice President: Ron Heersink
Manager: Ken Shepherd
Estimated Sales: $10-20 Million
Number Employees: 20-49
Square Footage: 120000
Type of Packaging: Consumer, Food Service, Bulk
Brands Exported: Colorado Gold
Regions Exported to: Europe
Percentage of Business in Exporting: 1

44764 Growers Cooperative Juice Co
112 N Portage St
Westfield, NY 14787-1054   716-326-3161
Fax: 716-326-6566 www.concordgrapejuice.com
Grape juice and juice concentrate
President: Steve Baran
dmom@concordgrapejuice.com
Quality Assurance Manager: Jim Gillespie
Sales Exec: Dave Momberger
General Manager: David Momberger
Plant Manager: Todd Donato
Estimated Sales: $5-10 Million
Number Employees: 20-49
Type of Packaging: Bulk
Regions Exported to: Worldwide

44765 Gruenewald ManufacturingCompany
100 Ferncroft Rd Ste 204
Danvers, MA 1923   978-777-0200
Fax: 978-777-9432   800-229-9447
info@whipcream.com www.whipcream.com
Manufacturer, importer and exporter of dispensers for food products, including ice cream and whipped cream
Owner: Fredrick Gruenewald
fredrick@whipcream.com
Sales/Marketing: Kevin Muldoon
VP Sales: Thomas Muldoon
Sales: Joseph Ransom
Estimated Sales: $10-20 Million
Number Employees: 10-19
Square Footage: 30000
Type of Packaging: Food Service
Brands Exported: Rocket; Refillo Whip Recharger
Regions Exported to: Worldwide
Percentage of Business in Exporting: 41
Regions Imported from: Worldwide

44766 Guans Mushroom Co
37048 Niles Blvd
P.O.Box 2861
Fremont, CA 94536-1648   510-745-8800
Fax: 510-745-8855 www.guansmushroom.com
Importers, wholesaler/distributor of fresh shiitake and oyster mushrooms and other mushroom products
Manager: Juliet Chu
juliet@guansmushroom.com
Vice President: Juliet Zhu
Estimated Sales: $ 3 - 5 Million
Number Employees: 10-19
Square Footage: 60000
Regions Imported from: Europe, Asia

44767 Guayaki
6782 Sebastopol Ave # 100
Sebastopol, CA 95472-3880   707-824-6644
Fax: 707-824-6644   888-482-9254
info@guayaki.com www.guayaki.com
Organic rainforest herbs
Co-Founder: Alex Pryer
Chief Executive Officer: Chris Mann
info@guayaki.com
Co-Founder: David Karr
VP of Sales: Luke Gernandt
Sales Coordinator: Saskia Baur
Customer Care: Scott Turner
Vice President Operations: Richard Bruehl
Productions: Lucia Diaz
Estimated Sales: $3 Million
Number Employees: 20-49
Number of Brands: 1
Number of Products: 13
Square Footage: 15000
Type of Packaging: Consumer, Food Service, Bulk

44768 Guerra Nut Shelling Co Inc
190 Hillcrest Rd
Hollister, CA 95023-4944   831-637-4471
Fax: 831-637-1358 walnut@guerranut.com
www.guerranut.com
Walnuts
President: Frank V Guerra
frank@guerranut.com
CEO: Jeff Guerra
Estimated Sales: $5-10 Million
Number Employees: 50-99
Square Footage: 150000
Type of Packaging: Bulk
Brands Exported: Cal Best; Hillcrest
Regions Exported to: Europe, Asia, Canada, Australia, Latin America
Percentage of Business in Exporting: 30

44769 Guglielmo Winery
1480 E Main Ave
Morgan Hill, CA 95037-3299   408-779-2145
Fax: 408-779-3166 info@guglielmowinery.com
Wines
Winemaker/ President: George E. Guglielmo
george@guglielmowinery.com
CFO: Julie Bradford
Director of Sales: Gene Guglielmo
Dir. Of Retail Operations: Cindy Adams
Estimated Sales: $10-20 Million
Number Employees: 20-49
Type of Packaging: Consumer, Private Label, Bulk
Brands Exported: Emile's; Guglielmo; Guglielmo Reserve
Regions Exported to: Europe, Asia, Canada
Percentage of Business in Exporting: 10

44770 Guido's International Foods
1669 La Cresta Dr
Pasadena, CA 91103-1260   626-296-1427
Fax: 626-296-0306   877-994-8436
Seasonings and sauces
President: Guido Meindl
Estimated Sales: $20,000
Number Employees: 2
Number of Brands: 7
Type of Packaging: Consumer, Food Service, Private Label, Bulk
Regions Exported to: Europe
Percentage of Business in Exporting: 2

44771 Guiltless Gourmet
80 Avenue K
Newark, NJ 7105   201-553-1100
deborah.ross@manischewitz.com
www.guiltlessgourmet.com
Natural, low-fat baked snacks, dips and salsas
President: Michael Shaw
VP Finance: Bart Glaser
VP Sales/Marketing: Robert Greenberg
Number Employees: 20-49
Parent Co: The Manischewitz Company

Importers & Exporters / A-Z

Type of Packaging: Consumer, Food Service, Private Label, Bulk
Regions Exported to: Central America, Europe, Canada, Caribbean

44772 Guinness Import Co
6 Landmark Sq
Stamford, CT 06901-2704   203-323-3311
     Fax: 203-359-7209   800-521-1591
     guinness@consumer-care.net   www.guiness.com
Beers, stout
President: Tim Kelly
Chief Information Officer: Lynda Gutman
Contact: Charles Ireland
guinness-storehouse@guinness.com
Vice President Operations: Colin Funnell
Number Employees: 5-9
Parent Co: Guiness PLC
Type of Packaging: Consumer
Regions Imported from: Europe

44773 Guittard Chocolate Co
10 Guittard Rd
PO Box 4308
Burlingame, CA 94010-2203   650-697-4427
     Fax: 650-692-2761   800-468-2462
     sales@guittard.com   www.guittard.com
Chocolate and chocolate products
President & CEO: Gary Guittard
gary@guittard.com
Director Sales/Marketing: Mark Spini
Estimated Sales: $20-50 Million
Number Employees: 100-249

44774 Gulf Coast Plastics
9314 Princess Palm Ave
Tampa, FL 33619-1364   813-621-8098
     Fax: 813-623-1408   800-277-7491
     sales@gulfcoastplastics.com
     www.gulfcoastplastics.com
Manufacturer and exporter of anti-static plastic bags
Owner: Karen Santiago
karens@gulfcoastplastics.com
CFO: Tom Coryn
Quality Control: Tom Coryn
Manager: Thomas Coryn
Estimated Sales: Below $ 5 Million
Number Employees: 20-49
Square Footage: 24000
Parent Co: Dairy Mix
Type of Packaging: Consumer, Food Service, Bulk
Regions Exported to: Worldwide
Percentage of Business in Exporting: 10

44775 Gulf Crown Seafood Co
306 Jon Floyd Rd
Delcambre, LA 70528-4522   337-685-4722
     Fax: 337-685-4241   gulfcrown@gulfcrown.us
     www.gulfcrown.us
Shrimp
President: John Floyd
Manager: Bonnie Richard
Sales: Crystal Marcaux
Manager: Stephen Greene
gulfcrown@gulfcrown.us
Estimated Sales: $7 Million
Number Employees: 5-9

44776 (HQ)Gulf Food Products Co Inc
509 Commerce Pt
New Orleans, LA 70123-3203   504-733-1516
     Fax: 504-733-1517   roberthoy@worldnet.att.net
Seafood
Owner: Albert Lin
gulffoodproducts@aol.com
Estimated Sales: Less than $500,000
Number Employees: 1-4
Square Footage: 16000
Regions Exported to: Asia, Canada
Regions Imported from: Asia
Percentage of Business in Importing: 50

44777 Gulf Marine
501 Louisiana St
Westwego, LA 70094-4141   504-436-2682
     Fax: 504-436-1585   sales@gulfmarineproducts.com
     www.lapack.com
Shrimp, crawfish and other seafood
President: David Lai
Number Employees: 20-49

44778 Gulf Packing Company
618 Commerce St
San Benito, TX 78586-4216   956-399-2631
     Fax: 956-399-2675
Meat, including heifer calf and packaged meats
CEO: Charlie Booth
VP: Carlos Salinas
Quality Control Manager: Fred Frausto
Manager: Ace Delacerta
Mngr: Frank Esquivel
Estimated Sales: $10-20 Million
Number Employees: 50 to 99
Type of Packaging: Consumer
Regions Exported to: Mexico, Canada

44779 Gulf Pride Enterprises
391 Bayview Ave
Biloxi, MS 39530-2502   228-432-2488
     Fax: 228-374-7411   888-689-0560
     www.gulfprideenterprises.com
Shrimp
President: Kathy Cruthirds
kathy@gulfprideshrimp.com
Vice President: Wally Gollott
Estimated Sales: $ 10 Million - $50 Million
Number Employees: 50-99
Type of Packaging: Consumer, Private Label
Regions Exported to: Canada
Percentage of Business in Exporting: 5
Regions Imported from: Central America, South America
Percentage of Business in Importing: 10

44780 Gum Technology Corporation
10860 North Mavinee Drive
Tucson, AZ 85737   520-888-5500
     Fax: 520-888-5585   800-369-4867
     info@gumtech.com   www.gumtech.com
Food gums, hydrocolloids and stabilizing systems
President/CEO: Allen Freed
R&D/Laboratory Director: Aida Prenzno
Marketing Director: Janelle Litel
VP/Sales: Joshua Brooks
Contact: Beth Woodley
beth@milehighingredients.com
Estimated Sales: $ 5 - 10 Million
Number Employees: 5-9
Square Footage: 12000
Type of Packaging: Bulk
Regions Exported to: South America, Asia, Canada, Mexico
Percentage of Business in Exporting: 5
Regions Imported from: Worldwide
Percentage of Business in Importing: 15

44781 Gumix International Inc
2160 N Central Rd # 202
Fort Lee, NJ 07024-7547   201-947-6300
     Fax: 201-947-9265   800-248-6492
     info@gumix.com
Foods gums
President: Sean Katir
info@gumix.com
Estimated Sales: D
Number Employees: 5-9
Regions Exported to: Worldwide

44782 Gumpert's Canada
2500 Tedlo Street
Mississauga, ON L5A 4A9
Canada   905-279-2600
     Fax: 905-279-2797   800-387-9324
     info@gumpert.com   www.gumpert.com
Toppings, puddings, flavors & extracts, glazes, icings, cake bases, powder fillings, creme pie fillings, fruit pie fillings, and bavarians
President: George Johnson
R&D/QA Manager: Erica Tulloch
Estimated Sales: $5 Million
Number Employees: 40
Number of Products: 200
Square Footage: 106000
Type of Packaging: Bulk
Brands Exported: Gumpert's
Regions Exported to: USA
Percentage of Business in Exporting: 20
Brands Imported: Renshaw; Semper
Regions Imported from: Europe
Percentage of Business in Importing: 1

44783 Gunter Wilhelm Cutlery
20-10 Maple Ave # 35g
Fair Lawn, NJ 07410-1591   201-569-6866
     Fax: 201-369-4679   sales@gunterwilhelm.com
     www.gunterwilhelm.com
Cookware, cooking implements
Founder: Paul Hellman
CEO: David Malek
Contact: Cherry Dan
sales@gunterwilhelm.com
Number Employees: 1-4

44784 Gusmer Enterprises Inc
81 M St
Fresno, CA 93721-3215   559-485-2692
     Fax: 559-485-4254   866-213-1131
     www.gusmerenterprises.com
Manufacturer and exporter of filter and fiber media for food and beverages
CEO: Marla Jeffrey
mjeffrey@gusmerenterprises.com
CEO: Marla Jeffrey
VP/Technical Sales: Phil Crantz
Estimated Sales: $ 5 - 10 Million
Number Employees: 50-99
Square Footage: 240000
Parent Co: Gusmer Enterprises
Other Locations:
   Cellulo Co.
   Crawford, NJCellulo Co.
Regions Exported to: Worldwide
Percentage of Business in Exporting: 25

44785 Gustiamo
1715 W Farms Rd
Bronx, NY 10460-6000   718-860-2949
     Fax: 718-860-4311   877-907-2525
     www.gustiamo.com
Oil and vinegar, pasta and rice, landfood, seafood, sweets and coffee.
President: Beatrice Ughi
beatrice.u@gustiamo.com
Number Employees: 5-9

44786 Guth Lighting
PO Box 7079
Saint Louis, MO 63177   314-533-3200
     Fax: 314-533-9127
Manufacturer and exporter of sealed and gasketed fluorescent and high-intensity discharge lighting equipment for use in water wash down and corrosive environments
Manager: Robert Catone
VP and Controller: Sue Pries
VP/General Manager: Robert Catone
Research & Development: Mike Kurtz
Estimated Sales: $ 20 - 50 Million
Number Employees: 50-99
Square Footage: 100000
Parent Co: JJI
Regions Exported to: Central America, South America, Asia, Middle East
Percentage of Business in Exporting: 5

44787 Guyllan USA Inc
560 Sylvan Ave
Englewood Cliffs, NJ 07632-3119   201-871-4964
     Fax: 201-871-3632   800-803-4123
     seashells@guylian.us   www.guylian.be
Confectionery imports
President/CEO: Leslie Coopersmith
Marketing: Greg Rosendahl
Estimated Sales: Less Than $500,000
Number Employees: 1-4
Type of Packaging: Private Label

44788 H & H Products Co
6600 Magnolia Homes Rd
Orlando, FL 32810-4285   407-299-5410
     Fax: 407-298-6966   800-678-8448
     info@hartleysbrand.com
     www.hhproductscompany.com
Juices, drink bases, liquid teas and syrups
Owner: Morris Hartley
mhartley@hartleysbrand.com
Founder: Len Hartley
Secretary: Betty Hartly
QC Manager: Joy Corbin
Regional Sales Manager: Emily Cooper
Regional Sales Manager: David Lynch
mhartley@hartleysbrand.com
Production Manager: Derrick Abner
Plant Manager: Jason Browning
Purchasing Manager: Mike Bowes

Importers & Exporters / A-Z

Estimated Sales: $6 Million
Number Employees: 20-49
Square Footage: 120000
Type of Packaging: Food Service, Private Label

44789 H A Phillips & Co
770 Enterprise Ave
DeKalb, IL 60115-7904   630-377-0050
Fax: 630-377-2706 info@haphillips.com
www.haphillips.com
Manufacturer and exporter of float controls, valves and pressure vessels for ammonia refrigeration systems; wholesaler/distributor and importer of pressure regulating and solenoid valves
President/Chief Executive Officer: Michael R. Ryan
Executive Director: John Schroeder
Vice-President of Finance: Janet L. Jones
Vice-President of Engineering: Steve L. . Yagla, P.E
R&D/Quality Control: Mike Ryan
Sales/Marketing: Ed Murziuski
Corporate Sales Manager: Thomas W. Herman
Secretary/Vice President of Human Resour: Mary Wright
Operations Manager: Andrew McCullough
Vice President of Manufacturing: Brian J. Youssi
Plant Manager: David Williams
Purchasing Manager: Rou Coleman
Estimated Sales: $ 4.2 Million
Number Employees: 20-49
Square Footage: 60000
Regions Exported to: Central America, South America, Europe, Asia
Percentage of Business in Exporting: 20
Brands Imported: Danfoss
Regions Imported from: Europe
Percentage of Business in Importing: 15

44790 H A Sparke Co
1032 Texas Ave
PO Box 674
Shreveport, LA 71101-3341   318-222-0927
Fax: 318-222-2731 info@hasparke.com
www.hasparke.com
Manufacturer and exporter of restaurant fixtures including pot, pan and utensil racks; also, guest check handling equipment
President: Richard W Sparke
Estimated Sales: $ 1-2.5 Million
Number Employees: 5-9
Square Footage: 14000
Regions Exported to: Central America, Europe, Canada, Caribbean
Percentage of Business in Exporting: 9

44791 H A Stiles
386 Bridgton Rd # A1
Westbrook, ME 04092-3606   207-854-8458
Fax: 207-854-3863 800-447-8537
askhastiles@hastiles.com www.hastiles.com
Manufacturer and exporter of wooden kitchen utensils and bread and cake boards; also, toothpicks
President: Ambrose Berry
Estimated Sales: Less Than $500,000
Number Employees: 10-19

44792 H B Taylor Co
4830 S Christiana Ave
Chicago, IL 60632-3092   773-254-4805
Fax: 773-254-4563 www.hbtaylor.com
Flavors, colors and food essentials.
President: Leon Juskaitis
Owner/Human Resources Executive: Saul Juskaitis
sjuskaitis@hbtaylor.com
Research & Development Director: Joy Souders
Quality Control Manager: Larry King
Operations Manager: Edward Juskaitis
Purchasing Manager: Mary Power
Estimated Sales: $3 Million
Number Employees: 10-19
Square Footage: 50000
Type of Packaging: Private Label, Bulk
Brands Exported: Flavors
Regions Exported to: Europe, Canada
Percentage of Business in Exporting: 15

44793 H C Duke & Son Inc
2116 8th Ave
East Moline, IL 61244-1800   309-755-4553
Fax: 309-755-9858 sales@electrofreeze.com
www.electrofreeze.com
Manufacturer and exporter of soft serve ice cream machines
Marketing: Joe Clark
VP Sales: Jim Duke
Estimated Sales: $20-50 Million
Number Employees: 100-249
Square Footage: 115000
Type of Packaging: Food Service
Brands Exported: Electro Freeze
Regions Exported to: Central America, South America, Europe, Asia, Middle East, Worldwide

44794 H Cantin
1910 Av Du Sanctuaire
Beauport, QC G1E 3L2
Canada   418-663-3523
Fax: 418-663-0717 800-463-5268
cantinh@microtec.ca
Jams, pie fillings, pudding mixes, maple syrup, soup bases, bakery products and candies; importer of frozen fruit; exporter of marshmallow cones and caramels
President/General Manager: Leonce Tremblay
Number Employees: 50-99
Square Footage: 60000
Parent Co: Bon Bons Associates
Type of Packaging: Consumer, Food Service, Private Label, Bulk
Brands Exported: Denis; Original
Regions Exported to: Worldwide
Percentage of Business in Exporting: 15
Percentage of Business in Importing: 5

44795 H F Staples & Co Inc
9 Webb Dr # 5
PO Box 956
Merrimack, NH 03054-4876   603-889-8600
Fax: 603-883-9409 800-682-0034
info@hfstaples.com www.naturalfurniturecare.com
Manufacturer and exporter of wood filler, wax and ladder accessories. Contract private label tube filling of viscous products
President: John Murphy
john.murphy@staples.com
Vice President: Thomas Stratton
Estimated Sales: $ 5 - 10 Million
Number Employees: 5-9
Square Footage: 52000
Type of Packaging: Private Label
Regions Exported to: Worldwide

44796 H Fox & Co Inc
416 Thatford Ave
Brooklyn, NY 11212-5895   718-385-4600
Fax: 718-345-4283
Chocolate and fruit flavored syrups, dessert toppings and juice mixes
President: David Fox
dfox@foxsyrups.com
Executive VP: Kelly Fox
IT: David Frankum
Estimated Sales: $10-20 Million
Number Employees: 20-49
Square Footage: 36000
Type of Packaging: Food Service
Brands Exported: Fox's U-Bet; Fox Brand; No-Cal
Regions Exported to: Europe, Caribbean
Percentage of Business in Exporting: 5

44797 H G Weber & Co
725 Fremont St
Kiel, WI 53042-1352   920-894-2221
Fax: 920-894-3786 info@hgweber.com
www.holwegweber.com
Manufacturer and exporter of paper and film bag machinery, flexographic printers and vertical case conveyors
President: Mike Odom
modom@hgweber.com
CFO: John Smith
Senior VP: Donald Ludwig
Marketing Director: Jeff Vogel
Sales Director: Brian Niemuth
Estimated Sales: $ 20 - 50 Million
Number Employees: 50-99
Square Footage: 130
Regions Exported to: Central America, South America, Europe, Asia, Middle East

44798 H Nagel & Son Co
2428 Central Pkwy
Cincinnati, OH 45214-1804   513-665-4550
Fax: 513-665-4570 www.brightonmills.com
Flour and flour based mixes
President: Edward Nagel
Estimated Sales: $20-50 Million
Number Employees: 20-49
Number of Brands: 1
Type of Packaging: Food Service, Private Label, Bulk
Regions Exported to: Central America, Middle East
Percentage of Business in Exporting: 2

44799 H R Nicholson Co
6320 Oakleaf Ave
Baltimore, MD 21215-2213   410-580-0975
Fax: 410-764-9125 800-638-3514
Fruit juices and tea concentrates
President: H Robert Nicholson
Secretary/Treasurer: Su Shaffer
VP Sales/Marketing: Bob Homewood
Number Employees: 20-49
Square Footage: 114000
Type of Packaging: Consumer, Food Service
Brands Exported: Bombay; Nicholson's
Regions Exported to: Europe, Asia
Percentage of Business in Exporting: 3
Brands Imported: Nicholson's, Bombay, Fix A Mix
Regions Imported from: Europe
Percentage of Business in Importing: 5

44800 H T I Filtration
30241 Tomas
Rancho Sta Marg, CA 92688-2123   949-546-0745
Fax: 949-269-6438 877-404-9372
info@htifiltration.com
Manufacturer and exporter of filtration equipment including oil, and hydraulic, specializing in water removal from oils
CEO: Steven Parker
Technical Service: Ron Hart
r.hart@htifiltration.com
Estimated Sales: $ 1 - 5 Million
Number Employees: 10-19
Square Footage: 40000
Parent Co: Temcor
Type of Packaging: Private Label
Brands Exported: Hydra-Supreme; Hydro-Fil
Regions Exported to: Europe, Asia
Percentage of Business in Exporting: 10

44801 H&H Fisheries Limited
PO Box 172
Eastern Passage, NS B3G 1M5
Canada   902-465-6330
Fax: 902-465-2572 866-773-4400
Fresh and frozen seafood
Contact: Regionald Hartlen
Estimated Sales: $13,8,000,000
Number Employees: 30
Type of Packaging: Consumer, Food Service, Private Label, Bulk
Regions Exported to: Worldwide
Percentage of Business in Exporting: 80

44802 H&K Packers Company
420 Turenne Street
Winnipeg, NB R2J 3W8
Canada   204-233-2354
Fax: 204-235-1258
Pork and beef
President: Albert Kelly
Production: Jake Penner
Plant Manager: Andy Van Patter
Number Employees: 20-49
Square Footage: 20000
Type of Packaging: Bulk
Brands Exported: H&K Packers; Kings Choice; Private Reserve Meats
Regions Exported to: USA
Percentage of Business in Exporting: 10

44803 H. Arnold Wood Turning
220 White Plains Road
Suite 245
Tarrytown, NY 10591   914-381-0801
Fax: 914-381-0804 888-314-0088
staff@arnoldwood.com www.arnoldwood.com
Wooden items including mini crates and boxes, broom and mop handles, turned handles, rolling pins, flag poles, skewers and dowels; importer of broom and mop handles and dowels
VP: Johnathan Arnold
VP Sales: Jonathan Arnold
Contact: Ann Arnold
ann@arnoldwood.com
Estimated Sales: $500,000-$1 Million
Number Employees: 5-9
Regions Imported from: Central America, South America, Asia, Canada, Malaysia, Indonesia

Importers & Exporters / A-Z

44804 H. Interdonati
PO Box 262
Cold Spring Harbour, NY 11724   631-367-6611
Fax: 631-367-6626   800-367-6617
flavorplus@aol.com   www.hinterdonati.com
Ingredients and additives
President: Robert Interdonati
Sales Manager: Andrew Interdonati
andrewinterdonati@hinterdonati.com
Estimated Sales: $3 Million
Number Employees: 3
Square Footage: 2000
Regions Exported to: Asia
Percentage of Business in Exporting: 10
Regions Imported from: South America, Europe, Asia
Percentage of Business in Importing: 90

44805 H. Reisman Corporation
377 Crane Street
Orange, NJ 7051   973-882-1670
Fax: 973-882-0323
Vitamins and herbal extracts
Owner/President: Frank Molinaro
Estimated Sales: $5-10 Million
Number Employees: 20-49
Square Footage: 300000
Parent Co: LycoRed Company
Type of Packaging: Bulk
Brands Exported: PhytoFoods; Bionova
Regions Exported to: Worldwide
Percentage of Business in Exporting: 10
Regions Imported from: South America, Europe, Asia
Percentage of Business in Importing: 90

44806 H.B. Dawe
PO Box 100
Cupids, NL A0A 2B0
Canada   709-528-4347
Fax: 709-528-3463
Groundfish and shellfish
General Manager: Philip Hillyard
Number Employees: 100-249
Type of Packaging: Consumer, Food Service, Private Label, Bulk
Regions Exported to: Worldwide
Percentage of Business in Exporting: 80

44807 H.D. Sheldon & Company
143 W 29th St
12th Floor
New York, NY 10001-5103   212-924-6920
Fax: 212-627-1759   sheldonex@aol.com
www.hdsheldon.com
Exporter of ranges, coffee urns, grinders, brewers, ice cream and barbecue machines, juice makers, sinks, waste compactors, glass washers, meat choppers, milk dispensers, portable bars, waitress stations, china, toasters and other foodservice equipment
President: Robert Metros
Assistant Secretary: M Moulabi
Secretary: Meris Brown
Sales Manager: Rick Peralta
Contact: Edmund Ho
eho@hdsheldon.com
Chairman: Susan Metros
Estimated Sales: $10-20 Million
Number Employees: 20-49
Square Footage: 15000
Brands Exported: Blickman; Hatco; Sunkist; Kold-Draft; Fisher; Federal; Advance; Lincoln; Precision; Salvajor; Service Ideas; Silver King; Smokaroma; Stoelting; Toastwell; Wilber Curtis Duraware
Regions Exported to: Worldwide
Percentage of Business in Exporting: 100

44808 H.F. Coors China Company
PO Box 59
New Albany, MS 38652-0059   310-338-8921
Fax: 310-641-9429   800-782-6677
Manufacturer and exporter of cookware and tableware including high strength china, health care service dishes, cups and mugs; also, custom decorated, colored, decal and banding available
Controller: George Holzheimer
General VP: Robert Gasbarro
Ceramics Engineer: Leo Suzuki
Number Employees: 50-99
Square Footage: 400000
Parent Co: Standex International Corporation
Type of Packaging: Food Service, Private Label, Bulk
Brands Exported: Alox China; Chefsware
Regions Exported to: Worldwide
Percentage of Business in Exporting: 1

44809 H.J. Jones & Sons
1155 Dundas Street
London, ON N5W 3A9
Canada   519-451-5250
Fax: 519-451-0545   800-667-0476
jonesy@farmline.com
Packaging materials including stretch pak and blister cards and folding cartons
President: Michael Jones
Controller: Scott Switzer
Vice President: Doug Jones
Marketing Director: Les Meeneil
Purchasing Manager: Glen Davies
Number Employees: 50
Regions Exported to: USA
Percentage of Business in Exporting: 50

44810 H.K. Canning
130 N Garden St
P.O. BOX 729
Ventura, CA 93002-0729   805-652-1392
www.whereorg.com
Canned and dry beans, soup and mushrooms
President: Henry Knaust
CFO: Richard Hanson
Vice-President: Carol Knaust
Estimated Sales: $4 Million
Number Employees: 66
Type of Packaging: Consumer, Food Service, Private Label, Bulk
Regions Exported to: Europe, Middle East, Canada, Mexico

44811 (HQ)H.L. Diehl Company
9 Babcock Hill Rd
South Windham, CT 6266   860-423-7741
Fax: 860-423-2654   info@giant-vac.com
www.giant-vac.com
Manufacturer and exporter of power cleaning equipment including industrial vacuum cleaners
President: Anton Janiak
anton.janiak@giant-vac.com
VP: Gail Marie Diehl
Estimated Sales: $ 10 - 20 Million
Number Employees: 50-99
Regions Exported to: Europe, Canada
Percentage of Business in Exporting: 5

44812 H.P. Neun
75 N Main St
Fairport, NY 14450   585-388-1360
Fax: 585-388-0184
Manufacturer and exporter of foam products and paper boxes including corrugated, folding, candy, set-up and fancy.
President: Mike Hanna
Estimated Sales: $20-50 Million
Number Employees: 100-249
Regions Exported to: Canada

44813 H20 Technology
885 Arapahoe Avenue
Boulder, CO 80302-6011   303-415-1253
Fax: 303-447-1392   800-670-7426
Wholesaler/distributor and exporter of bottled water
CEO/President: Merlin Yockstick
VP Finances: Hazel Chandler
VP Marketing: Vickie Brown
Number Employees: 1-4
Type of Packaging: Private Label
Brands Exported: Merlin; Wild Water Plus; Nordstrom Water
Regions Exported to: Asia

44814 HABCO Beverage Systems
501 Gordon Baker Road
Toronto, ON M2H 2S6
Canada   416-491-6008
Fax: 416-491-6982   800-448-0244
info@habcotech.com
Manufacturer and exporter of reach-in refrigerators, freezers, and merchandisers.
Vice President/Marketing: Scott Brown
EVP/Sales: Jim Maynard
Number Employees: 100
Number of Brands: 2
Number of Products: 27
Brands Exported: Habco; Cold Space Merchandisers

44815 HALCO
788 Morris Turnpike
Suite 202
Short Hills, NJ 07078   973-232-1065
Fax: 973-232-1066   888-289-1005
www.halco.com
Estimated Sales: $ 5 - 10 Million
Number Employees: 50-99

44816 HD Electric Co
1475 S Lakeside Dr
Park City, IL 60085-8314   847-473-4882
Fax: 847-473-4981   www.hdeinnovations.com
Manufacturer and exporter of electrical test equipment and portable/emergency lighting products
CEO: M Hoffman
mhoffman@hdelectriccompany.com
CEO: M Hoffman
Marketing Manager: Kimberly Higgins
Sales: Berstrom
Estimated Sales: $2.5-5 Million
Number Employees: 20-49

44817 HDT Manufacturing
RR 9
Salem, OH 44460   330-337-8565
Fax: 330-337-8576   800-968-7438
Manufacturer and exporter of industrial trailers and trucks
President: Dave Lawless
VP: Shawn Lawless
Purchasing Manager: Don Souce

44818 HFI Foods
17515 Northeast 6th Court
Redmond, WA 98074   425-883-1320
Fax: 425-861-8341
Surimi products; frozen entrees, mousse desserts and pasta salads
President: Byron Kuroishi
CFO: Yoshinari Kuroishi
Vice President: Christina Gaimaytan
Quality Control: Jenel Lee
Marketing Director: Gwen McLellan
Sales Director: Nori Ishiwari
Public Relations: Cindy Fuller-Stephens
Production Manager: Kazue Yamada
Plant Manager: Kazuo Yamada
Purchasing Manager: Cindy Fuller-Stephens
Estimated Sales: $12 Million
Number Employees: 50-99
Square Footage: 80000
Type of Packaging: Consumer
Brands Exported: King Cove, Rice Now
Regions Exported to: Central America, Europe, Asia
Percentage of Business in Exporting: 15
Regions Imported from: Central America, Europe, Asia

44819 HH Dobbins Inc
99 West Ave
Lyndonville, NY 14098-9744   585-765-2271
Fax: 585-765-9710   877-362-2467
bbaker@wnyapples.com
www.unitedapplesales.com
Produce, including apples, cabbage, pears and prunes
President: Howard Dobbins
hdobbins@wnyapples.com
Estimated Sales: $ 3 - 5 Million
Number Employees: 20-49
Parent Co: United Apple Sales Inc.
Type of Packaging: Consumer, Food Service, Bulk
Regions Exported to: Europe, United Kingdom, Canada

44820 (HQ)HHP Inc
14 Buxton Industrial Dr
PO Box 489
Henniker, NH 3242   603-428-3298
Fax: 603-428-3448   hhp@conknet.com
www.hhp-inc.com
Manufacturer and exporter of wooden pallets; also, saw mill
President: Ross D Elia
hhp@conknet.com
Sales: Nancy Kocsis

Importers & Exporters / A-Z

Estimated Sales: $5-10 Million
Number Employees: 50-99
Regions Exported to: Canada
Percentage of Business in Exporting: 8

44821 HM Electronics Inc
14110 Stowe Dr
Poway, CA 92064-7147   858-535-6000
Fax: 858-452-7207   800-848-4468
pfoley@hme.com   www.hme.com
CEO: Norman Allum
normana@hme.com
Estimated Sales: $ 20 - 50 Million
Number Employees: 250-499

44822 HMC Corp
284 Maple St
Hopkinton, NH 03229-3339   603-746-4691
Fax: 603-746-4819   petertaylor@hmccorp.com
www.hmccorp.com
Manufacturer and exporter of saw mill conveyors
President: Peter Taylor
petertaylor@hmccorp.com
Estimated Sales: $20-50 Million
Number Employees: 50-99
Regions Exported to: Europe
Percentage of Business in Exporting: 5

44823 (HQ)HMG Worldwide In-Store Marketing
371 7th Ave
New York, NY 10001-3984   212-736-2300
Fax: 212-564-3395
Manufacturer and exporter of point-of-sale displays, integrated merchandising systems and interactive electronics; also, in-store related research, market planning, package design and space management services available
CEO Director: Andrew Wahl
CEO: Michael Lipman
Estimated Sales: $ 1 - 5 Million
Number Employees: 5-9
Square Footage: 1200000
Other Locations:
HMG Worldwide In-Store Market
Chicago, IL HMG Worldwide In-Store Market
Regions Exported to: South America, Europe, Asia
Percentage of Business in Exporting: 8

44824 Haban Saw Company
9301 Watson Industrial Park
St.Louis, MO 63126   314-968-3991
Fax: 314-968-1240   info@habansaw.com
www.habansaw.com
Manufacturer and exporter of butcher handsaws and blades
Estimated Sales: $ 1-2.5 Million
Number Employees: 4

44825 Habasit America
805 Satellite Blvd NW
Suwanee, GA 30024-2879   678-288-3600
Fax: 800-422-2748   800-458-6431
info.america@us.habasit.com   www.habasit.com
Manufacturer, importer and exporter of belting
Chairman: Thomas Habegger
CEO: Andrea Volpi
CFO: Beat Stebler
Vice Chairman: Alice Habegger
R&D: Bill Humsby
Marketing: Allison Cox
National Sales Manager: Bert Fliegi
Segment Manager: Mike Creo
Head of Product Division Fabrics: Maarten Aarts
Estimated Sales: $ 5 - 10 Million
Number Employees: 100-249
Parent Co: Habasit-AG
Type of Packaging: Bulk
Regions Exported to: Central America, South America, Latin America, Caribbean
Percentage of Business in Exporting: 10
Regions Imported from: Europe

44826 Habasit America PlasticDiv
825 Morgantown Rd
Reading, PA 19607-9533   610-373-1400
Fax: 610-373-7448   800-445-7898
Manufacturers of modular plastic conveyor belts, chains and flat top chains
President: Christopher Nigon
VP Marketing/Sales: Joe Gianfalla
Marketing: Galina Rodzirosky
Estimated Sales: F
Number Employees: 100-249

Type of Packaging: Bulk
Regions Exported to: Worldwide
Percentage of Business in Exporting: 20

44827 Hach Co.
PO Box 389
Loveland, CO 80539-0389   970-669-3050
Fax: 970-669-2932   800-227-4224
techhelp@hach.com
Manufacturer of oxygen sensors and water analysis products for the beverage and water bottling industries. Also manufactures, designs, and distributes test kits for testing the quality of water in food industry applications.
Contact: Leon Moore
lmoore@hach.com
Regions Exported to: Worldwide

44828 Hackney Brothers
911 West 5th Street
Box 880
Washington, NC 27889   252-946-6521
Fax: 252-975-8340   800-763-0700
kgodley@vthackney.com
www.hackneybeverage.com
Manufacturer and exporter of refrigerated truck bodies and trailers; also, refrigeration systems and ice cream vending carts
President/Chief Executive Officer: Michael Tucker
Managing Director: Leandro Rodriguez
President, International Division: R. Hodges Hackney
Contact: Neal Dixon
ndixon@vthackney.com
Estimated Sales: $ 50-100 Million
Number Employees: 100-249
Square Footage: 220000
Type of Packaging: Food Service
Regions Exported to: Central America, South America, Europe, Asia, Middle East
Percentage of Business in Exporting: 2

44829 Hadley Fruit Orchards
48980 Seminole Dr
Cabazon, CA 92230   951-849-5255
Fax: 951-849-1979   800-854-5655
www.hadleyfruitorchards.com
Importer, exporter and wholesaler/distributor of dried fruits including apricots, dates, figs and prunes; also, nuts including pecans, cashews and pistachios; gift packs available
Manager: Wayne Dixon
CFO: Fred Bond
Manager: Jay Baczkowski
jbaczkowski@morongo-nsn.gov
Estimated Sales: $2.5-5 Million
Number Employees: 20-49
Square Footage: 200000
Type of Packaging: Consumer
Regions Exported to: Asia
Percentage of Business in Exporting: 2
Regions Imported from: South America, Asia
Percentage of Business in Importing: 5

44830 Hadley's Date Gardens
83555 Airport Blvd # 11
Thermal, CA 92274-9127   760-399-5191
Fax: 760-399-1311   www.hadleys.com
Dates
Owner: Melinda Dougherty
mdougherty@hadleys.com
CEO: John Keck
Vice President: Sean Dougherty
Number Employees: 50-99
Type of Packaging: Consumer, Food Service, Private Label, Bulk
Brands Exported: Hadley Date Gardens
Regions Exported to: Central America, Europe, Asia
Percentage of Business in Exporting: 10

44831 Hagensborg Chocolates LTD.
3686 Bonneville Place
Unit #103
Burnaby, BC V3N 4T6
Canada
   604-215-0234
Fax: 604-215-0235   877-554-7763
sales@hagensborg.com   www.hagensborg.com
Canned pate, chocolate and confectionery items, olive oils, sherry vinegar; exporter of smoked salmon fillets
President: Shelley Miller
Marketing: Shelley Wallace

Estimated Sales: $10-20 Million
Number Employees: 10-19
Square Footage: 30000
Type of Packaging: Consumer, Food Service, Private Label
Brands Exported: Pacific Northwest; Hagensborg; Bouquet de Chocolate; Land of Andalusia
Regions Exported to: Central America, South America, Europe, Asia, Mexico
Percentage of Business in Exporting: 15
Regions Imported from: Europe, Canada
Percentage of Business in Importing: 85

44832 Hahn's Old Fashioned Cake Co
75 Allen Blvd
Farmingdale, NY 11735-5614   631-249-3456
Fax: 631-249-3492   www.crumbcake.net
Coffee cake
President: Regina Hahn
Chief Operating Officer: Andrew Hahn
Estimated Sales: $2.5-5 Million
Number Employees: 10-19
Type of Packaging: Consumer, Food Service

44833 (HQ)Hain Celestial Group Inc
1111 Marcus Ave
Suite 100
Lake Success, NY 11042
   800-434-4246
www.hain.com
Organic health products.
President/CEO: Mark Schiller
Executive VP/CFO: Javier Idrovo
Senior VP, R&D: Jeff George
Senior VP, Sales: Kevin Lasher
Chief Supply Chain Officer: Jerry Wolfe
Estimated Sales: $2.6 Billion
Number Employees: 6,300
Number of Brands: 29
Brands Exported: Grains Noirs, Lima, Natumi
Regions Exported to: Worldwide

44834 Hairnet Corporation of America
151 W 26th St # 2
New York, NY 10001-6810   212-675-5840
Fax: 212-685-6225
Manufacturer and exporter of hairnets
President: E Gard
Secretary: M Moron
VP: T Persad
Estimated Sales: $2.5-5 Million
Number Employees: 1-4
Square Footage: 3500
Regions Exported to: Central America, Canada, Mexico

44835 Haitai Inc
7227 Telegraph Rd
Montebello, CA 90640   323-724-7337
www.haitaiusa.com
Wholesaler/distributor of frozen foods, seafood, specialty food items, dairy products, etc.; importer of canned and bottled beverages, dry and frozen fish, grains and pasta; exporter of fresh fruits, orange and pineapple frozenconcentrates and frozen beef.
President & CEO: Warren Jung
Year Founded: 1981
Estimated Sales: $100-500 Million
Number Employees: 50-99
Square Footage: 100000
Regions Exported to: Asia
Percentage of Business in Exporting: 40
Brands Imported: Haitai
Regions Imported from: South America, Europe, Asia
Percentage of Business in Importing: 50

44836 Haldin International
3 Reuten Dr
Closter, NJ 7624   201-782-2178
Fax: 201-784-2180   www.haldin-natural.com
Vanilla beans, essential oils for the flavor and fragrance industries
Manager: Khelly Boon
Founder/Chief Executive Officer: Ali Haliman
Contact: Meizy Worotitjan
meizy.worotitjan@haldin-natural.com
Estimated Sales: $ 5 - 10 Million
Number Employees: 1-4
Square Footage: 24000
Parent Co: Pt. Haldin Pacific Semesta
Type of Packaging: Bulk

Other Locations:
Haldin International
Cikarang, BekasiHaldin International
Regions Exported to: Central America, South America, Europe, Asia, Middle East
Percentage of Business in Exporting: 45
Regions Imported from: Central America, Asia
Percentage of Business in Importing: 75

44837 Hale Tea Co
235 Oak Ridge Cir
Richmond Hill, GA 31324-5370 912-727-3993
Fax: 912-727-3995 888-425-3832
sales@haletea.com www.haletea.com
Importer and manufacturer of gourmet specialty teas and tea bags
Owner: Lisa Brown
Estimated Sales: Under $500,000
Number Employees: 1-4
Type of Packaging: Food Service, Private Label, Bulk
Brands Imported: Gourmet Teas
Regions Imported from: Europe, Asia

44838 Hall China Co
1 Anna St
East Liverpool, OH 43920-3675 330-385-2900
Fax: 330-385-6185 800-445-4255
custserv@hallchina.com www.hlcdinnerware.com
Chinaware
President: Chuck Henderson
chenderson@hallchina.com
National Sales Manager: Jim Clunk
National Distributor Account Manager: Joe Owen
National Chain Account Manager: Joe Brice
Estimated Sales: $ 20 - 50 Million
Number Employees: 100-249

44839 Hall Manufacturing Co
297 Margaret King Ave
Ringwood, NJ 07456-1423 973-962-6022
Fax: 973-962-7652 kerry@hallmanufacturing.com
Manufacturer and exporter of extruded plastic tracks for refrigeration industry; also, co-extrusions and tubing
President: Mike Goceljak
kerry@hallmanufacturing.com
Sales Manager: Kerry Goceljak
Estimated Sales: $ 2.5-5 Million
Number Employees: 10-19
Square Footage: 42000
Regions Exported to: Europe, Asia, Canada, Mexico
Percentage of Business in Exporting: 11

44840 Hall Safety Apparel
1020 W 1st St
Uhrichsville, OH 44683-2210 740-922-3671
Fax: 740-922-4880 800-232-3671
www.hallssafety.com
Protective Clothin Manufacturing; Supplier, Importer and Exporter
President: Delores Schneider
delores.schneider@pro-am.com
VP: Delores Schneider
Public Relations: Arnold Ziffel
Estimated Sales: $1-3 Million
Number Employees: 5-9
Square Footage: 42000
Parent Co: Schneider Enterprises USA
Type of Packaging: Food Service, Private Label, Bulk
Regions Exported to: Central America, Europe
Percentage of Business in Exporting: 30

44841 Hall-Woolford Wood TankCo Inc
5500 N Water St
Philadelphia, PA 19120-3093 215-329-9022
Fax: 215-329-1177 jackhillman@woodtank.com
www.woodtank.com
Manufacturer and exporter of noncorrosive wood tanks, vats and tubs; wholesaler/distributor of flexible tank liners; industrial wood products; all products FDA approved. Also industrial wood products
President: Scott Hochhauser
woodtanks@aol.com
Sales Manager: Jack Hillman
Operations Manager: Robert Riepen
Estimated Sales: $ 1 - 3 Million
Number Employees: 5-9
Square Footage: 38000
Regions Exported to: Central America, South America, Europe, Asia, Middle East

44842 Hallberg Manufacturing Corporation
PO Box 23985
Tampa, FL 33623-3985 800-633-7627
Fax: 800-253-7323
Manufacturer and exporter of industrial hand soap
President: Charles Hallberg
VP: Linda Werlein
Estimated Sales: $300,000-500,000
Square Footage: 20000
Brands Exported: Surety Hand Soap; Pumice Jell Hand Cleaner; Citra Jell Hand Cleaner; Aloe Jell Hand Cleaner
Regions Exported to: Central America, South America, Middle East
Percentage of Business in Exporting: 5

44843 Halton Company
101 Industrial Dr
Scottsville, KY 42164 270-237-5600
Fax: 270-237-5700 800-442-5866
Manufacturer and exporter of stainless steel hoods, filters and fans; also, fire suppression and ventilation systems
President: Rick Bagwell
R&D: Andre Livchak
Controller: Chris Gentry
National Sales Manager: Rich Catan
Contact: Ben Barshaw
b.barshaw@petersoncat.com
Plant Manager: Phil Meredith
Purchasing Manager: Eric Key
Estimated Sales: $ 10 - 20 Million
Number Employees: 1250
Square Footage: 100000
Parent Co: Halton O.Y.
Brands Exported: Halton
Regions Exported to: Central America, Europe, Canada, Carribean, Latin America, Mexico, Worldwide
Percentage of Business in Exporting: 5
Brands Imported: Halton
Regions Imported from: Europe
Percentage of Business in Importing: 5

44844 Halton Packaging Systems
1045 S Service Road W
Oakville, ON L6L 6K3
Canada 905-847-9141
Fax: 905-847-9145
Manufacturer and exporter of pallet packaging machinery including stretch wrapping, conveyors, and pallet handling machinery
President: Peter Hughes
Estimated Sales: $2 Million
Number Employees: 10-19
Square Footage: 120000
Brands Exported: Halton
Regions Exported to: Central America, South America, Europe, Asia, Middle East

44845 Hamberger Displays
20-10 Maple Avenue
Fair Lawn, NJ 07410 973-423-5000
Fax: 973-423-6000 800-955-1663
www.cspdisplay.com

44846 Hamersmith, Inc.
3200 NW 125 Street
Miami, FL 33167 305-685-7451
Fax: 305-681-6093 office@hamersmith.com
www.hamersmith.com
Shortenings, margarines, oils, puff paste, pan releases and spices; packagaing services
President: Calvin Theobald
Sales Director: Gerald Delmonico
Estimated Sales: $2.5-5 Million
Number Employees: 10
Number of Brands: 20
Number of Products: 9
Square Footage: 60000
Type of Packaging: Food Service, Private Label, Bulk
Regions Exported to: Central America, South America, Caribbean, Latin America
Percentage of Business in Exporting: 50
Regions Imported from: Central America, South America, Caribbean

44847 Hamilton Beach Brands
261 Yadkin Rd
Southern Pines, NC 28387-3415 910-692-7676
Fax: 910-692-7959 800-851-8900
www.hamiltonbeach.com
Foodservice equipment for restaurant, bars, nursing homes, healthcare facilities, hotels, and more
CEO: Michael J Morecroft
Sales Director: Steve Sarfaty
Public Relations: Kirby Kriz
Estimated Sales: $1 - 5 Million
Number Employees: 100-249
Parent Co: Nacco Industries
Type of Packaging: Food Service
Regions Exported to: Central America, South America, Europe, Asia, Middle East
Percentage of Business in Exporting: 20

44848 Hamilton Beach Brands
4421 Waterfront Dr.
Glen Allen, VA 23060
804-237-9777
www.hamiltonbeach.com
Home appliances and commercial restaurant equipment.
President/CEO: Gregory Trepp
Vice President/CFO: Michelle Mosier
Senior Vice President, Gloabl Operations: Gregory Salyers
Senior VP, N. American Sales/Marketing: R. Scott Tidey
Year Founded: 1910
Estimated Sales: $743.1 Million
Number Employees: 5,000-9,999
Number of Brands: 5

44849 Hamilton Caster
1637 Dixie Hwy
Hamilton, OH 45011-4087 513-896-3541
Fax: 513-863-5508 888-699-7164
info@hamiltoncaster.com
www.hamiltoncaster.com
Manufacturer and exporter of nonpowered material handling carts, hand trucks, trailers, industrial casters and wheels
Vice President: Steve Lippert
steve.lippert@hamiltoncaster.com
Executive VP: Steven Lippert
Quality Control: Mary Latimer
Marketing Director: Mark Lippert
Sales Director: James Lippert
Estimated Sales: $ 10 - 20 Million
Number Employees: 50-99
Brands Exported: Hamilton
Regions Exported to: Central America, South America, Asia, Middle East, Worldwide
Percentage of Business in Exporting: 1

44850 Hamilton Kettles
2898 Birch Drive
Weirton, WV 26062-5142 304-794-9400
Fax: 304-794-9430 800-535-1882
sales@hamiltonkettles.com
Manufacturer and exporter of sanitary stainless steel and steam jacketed kettles, mix-cookers, pressure cookers, agitators, vacuum kettles and custom designed processing kettles and mixers
President: Charles Friend
Quality Control: Ed Henderson
VP/General Manager: George Gruner
R&D: Ed Henderson
Sales Director: Peggy Miller
Production Manager: Kenneth Henderson
Estimated Sales: $ 5 - 10 Million
Number Employees: 25
Square Footage: 128000
Parent Co: Allegheny Hancock Corporation
Regions Exported to: Central America, Europe, Canada, Australia, Mexico
Percentage of Business in Exporting: 5

44851 Hammons Products Co
105 Hammons Dr
PO Box 140
Stockton, MO 65785-7608 417-276-5181
Fax: 417-276-5187 888-429-6887
www.hammonsproducts.com
Walnuts
President: Brian Hammons
bhammons@black-walnuts.com
VP Marketing: David Hammons
VP Sales: David Steinmuller

Importers & Exporters / A-Z

Estimated Sales: $10-20 Million
Number Employees: 100-249
Square Footage: 687000
Type of Packaging: Consumer, Food Service, Bulk
Regions Exported to: Europe
Percentage of Business in Exporting: 1

44852 Hampton Associates & Sons
12728 Dogwood Hills Lane
Fairfax, VA 22033-3244   703-968-5847
jamcola@hotmail.com

Soft drinks
CEO/Chairman: Hampton Brown
Estimated Sales: Under $500,000
Number Employees: 1-4
Type of Packaging: Consumer, Food Service
Regions Exported to: Central America, South America, Europe, Asia, Middle East
Regions Imported from: Europe

44853 Hampton Roads Box Company
619 E Pinner St
Suffolk, VA 23434   757-934-2355
Fax: 757-539-4918

Manufacturer and exporter of pallets, wooden boxes and shipping crates
President: Mark Sullivan
Estimated Sales: $ 1.2 Million
Number Employees: 5-9
Regions Exported to: South America, Europe

44854 Hamrick Manufacturing &Svc
1436 Martin Rd
PO Box 5
Mogadore, OH 44260-1591   330-628-4877
Fax: 330-628-2180   800-321-9590
marketing@hamrickmfg.com
www.hamrickmfg.com

Manufacturer and exporter of packaging machinery including case packers, case sealers, bottled water case packers, lock tab pullers/breakers, liter tray packers, four flap openers, uncasers, etc.; custom built machinery available
President: Phil Hamrick
phamrick@hamrickmfg.com
CEO: Luther Hamrick
VP Sales: Tom Hamrick
VP of Production: Phil Hamrick
Purchasing Director: Kurt Kothmayer
Estimated Sales: $5-10 Million
Number Employees: 20-49
Number of Products: 18
Square Footage: 56000
Brands Exported: Case Packers, Case Nloaders, Case Sealers
Regions Exported to: Central America, South America, Europe, Asia, Middle East
Percentage of Business in Exporting: 10

44855 Hanan Products Co
196 Miller Pl
Hicksville, NY 11801-1826   516-938-1000
Fax: 516-938-1925 info@hananproducts.com
www.hananproducts.com

Kosher non-dairy products
President: John Bauer
jbauer@hananproducts.com
Estimated Sales: $2.5-5,000,000
Number Employees: 20-49
Type of Packaging: Consumer, Food Service
Regions Exported to: Singapore
Percentage of Business in Exporting: 1

44856 Hancock Peanut Company
P.O. Box 100
Courtland, VA 23837   757-653-9351
Fax: 757-653-2147

Peanuts
President: J Matthew Pope
VP Sales: Robert Pope
Contact: Melissa Rose
Number Employees: 50-99
Type of Packaging: Consumer, Food Service

44857 Handgards Inc
901 Hawkins Blvd
El Paso, TX 79915-1202   915-779-6606
Fax: 915-779-1312   800-351-8161
sales@handgards.com www.handgards.com

Manufacturer and exporter of disposable plastic gloves, aprons and bags; importer of latex and PVC gloves

CEO: Bob Mclellan
bmclellan@handgards.com
CEO: Bob McLellan
Estimated Sales: $ 500,000-$ 1,000,000
Number Employees: 250-499
Square Footage: 280000
Type of Packaging: Food Service, Private Label
Regions Exported to: Worldwide
Percentage of Business in Exporting: 73
Regions Imported from: Asia
Percentage of Business in Importing: 20

44858 Handtmann Inc
28690 N Ballard Dr
Lake Forest, IL 60045-4500   847-808-1100
Fax: 847-808-1106   800-477-3585
www.handtmann.us

Filling, portioning and linking machines for the sausage and meat industries. Also manufacture deli product systems and grinding machines.
President: Tom Kittle
tom.kittle@handtmann.us
Number Employees: 20-49
Regions Exported to: North America, USA

44859 Handy International Inc
700 E Main St # 101
Salisbury, MD 21804-5035   410-912-2000
Fax: 410-968-1592   800-426-3977
www.handycrab.com

Frozen seafood
President: Terry Conway
Senior VP: Rosario D Nero
VP: Todd Conway
Sales Executive: Todd Mcallister
Estimated Sales: $8,000,000
Number Employees: 100-249
Type of Packaging: Consumer, Food Service
Brands Exported: Handy
Regions Exported to: Europe, Asia
Percentage of Business in Exporting: 20

44860 Handy Manufacturing Co Inc
337 Sherman Ave
Newark, NJ 07114-1507   973-242-1600
Fax: 973-733-2185   800-631-4280
www.handystorefixtures.com

Manufacturer and exporter of store and wall fixtures, show cases, gondolas and shelving units
President: Paul Kurland
richardkurland@handystorefixtures.com
CFO: Scott McClymont
Executive VP: Richard Kurland
VP Sales: Walter Pincus
Number Employees: 50-99
Square Footage: 1200000
Type of Packaging: Food Service
Regions Exported to: Central America, South America, Canada

44861 Handy Wacks Corp
100 E Averill St
P.O. Box 129
Sparta, MI 49345
       800-445-4434
customerserv@handywacks.com
www.handywacks.com

Waxed packaging products including sandwich and interfolded high density polyethylene wrap, baking cups, hot dog trays, and steak, freezer, locker, delicatessen and bakery tissue and paper.
CIS Director: Bruce Stevens
Sales Director: George Siwik
Purchasing Manager: Mike Moberly
Year Founded: 1929
Estimated Sales: $20-25 Million
Number Employees: 50+
Number of Brands: 12
Number of Products: 225
Square Footage: 90000
Type of Packaging: Food Service
Brands Exported: Handy Wacks
Regions Exported to: Central America, Europe, Caribbean, Caribbean
Percentage of Business in Exporting: 3
Regions Imported from: Europe, Canada
Percentage of Business in Importing: 10

44862 Hanel Storage Systems
121 Industry Dr
Pittsburgh, PA 15275-1015   412-787-3444
Fax: 412-787-3744 info@hanel.us
www.hanel.us

Manufacturer, importer and exporter of vertical storage systems
President: Joachim Hanel
CEO: Brian Cohen
bcohen@hanel.us
Vice President: Brian Cohen
VP: Brian Cohen
Sales Director: Michael Fanning
Estimated Sales: $5-10 Million
Number Employees: 20-49
Parent Co: Hanel GmbH
Brands Exported: Hamel Lean-Lift; Hanel Rotomat
Regions Exported to: Worldwide
Brands Imported: Hanel Rotomat; Hanel Lean-Lift
Regions Imported from: Worldwide

44863 Hanif's International Foods
563 Ebury Place
Delta, BC V3M 6M8
Canada   604-540-4001
Fax: 604-540-4002   888-540-4009
hanifs@direct.ca

Importer and wholesaler/distributor of spices, beans, lentils and Middle Eastern foods
Owner: Hanif Ratanshi
Co Owner: S Ratanshi
Sales Director: Sheila Ratanshi
Number Employees: 30
Square Footage: 116000
Type of Packaging: Consumer, Food Service, Private Label, Bulk
Brands Exported: Hariyis
Regions Exported to: South America, Asia
Regions Imported from: Central America, South America, Europe, Asia, Middle East
Percentage of Business in Importing: 70

44864 Hanimex Company
15600 NE 8th Street
Suite B1, PMB801
Bellevue, WA 98007   425-957-9585
Fax: 425-696-1496

Exporter/importer and marketing management
President: Herman Kwik
hanimexco@aol.com
Operations Manager: Michelle Zieroth
Type of Packaging: Consumer, Private Label, Bulk
Other Locations:
    Hanimex Indonesia
    Jakarta Pusat, IndonesiaHanimex Indonesia
Brands Exported: Tropicana
Regions Exported to: Asia
Percentage of Business in Exporting: 90
Brands Imported: Indies, Cassava, Quindo
Regions Imported from: Asia
Percentage of Business in Importing: 10

44865 Hank Rivera Associates
13600 W Warren Ave
Dearborn, MI 48126-1421   313-581-8300

Manufacturer and exporter of uniforms, aprons and pizza delivery equipment including heat retention/insulated food bags, nylon pan pullers, beverage carriers and pizza lid supports
President: Dante Rivera
Secretary/Treasurer: Hank Rivera
Number Employees: 10-19
Square Footage: 25000
Brands Exported: Hank's
Regions Exported to: Central America, South America, Europe, Asia
Percentage of Business in Exporting: 20

44866 Hankison International
1000 Philadelphia St
Canonsburg, PA 15317-1700   724-746-1100
Fax: 724-745-6040 www.spx-hankison.de

Manufacturer and exporter of compressed air dryers, filters, condensate drains and air purifiers
Manager: Neal Horrigan
Marketing: Bill Kennedy
Sales: Rod Smith
Manager: Ken Gorman
Estimated Sales: $5-10 Million
Number Employees: 20-49
Square Footage: 808000
Parent Co: Hansen

44867 Hanmi Inc
5447 N Wolcott Ave
Chicago, IL 60640-1017   773-271-0730
Fax: 773-271-1756 www.wangfood.com

Korean foods

Owner: Young Kim
chihanmi@yahoo.com
Contact: Sung Sohn
CFO: Michael Winiarski
Vice President: John Kim
Estimated Sales: $ 10 - 20 Million
Number Employees: 5-9

44868 Hanna Instruments
584 Park E Dr
Woonsocket, RI 02895   401-765-7500
          Fax: 401-765-7575 800-426-6287
          info@hannainst.com
Manufacturer and exporter of electro-analytical instruments including sodium chloride and chlorine analyzers, conductivity, pH and relative humidity meters, temperature recorders and thermo hygrometers.
President: Martino Nardo
Vice President: Pamela Nardo
General Manager: Harry Lau
Year Founded: 1978
Estimated Sales: $100 Million
Number Employees: 20-49
Number of Products: 3000
Square Footage: 26000
Type of Packaging: Consumer, Food Service, Bulk
Brands Exported: Food Care; Bravo; Champ; Elth; Checker; Phandy; Phep; Key; Conmet; Piccolo; Agricare; Temp Care; Micro Phep; Temp Check
Regions Exported to: South America, Europe, Asia, Canada

44869 Hannan Products
220 N Smith Ave
Corona, CA 92880-1740   951-735-1587
          Fax: 951-735-0827 800-954-4266
          sales@hannanpak.com
Manufacturer and exporter of machinery and materials for skin and blister packaging; also, for die cutting
President: Damon Lewis
damon@hannanpak.com
CFO and QC and R&D: Alfred Ramos
Sales Manager: Lawrence Jenkins
Estimated Sales: $ 5 - 10 Million
Number Employees: 20-49

44870 Hannay Reels
553 State Route 143
Westerlo, NY 12193-2691   518-797-3791
          Fax: 518-797-3259 877-467-3357
          reels@hannay.com www.hannay.com
Metal reels for hose & cable, water, washdown, fluid handling
President: Eric Hannay
COO: Elaine Gruener
Quality Control: Ken Fritz
Marketing Manager: Jennifer Wing
Sales Manager: Mark Saker
Public Relations: Maureen Bagshaw
President/CEO: Eric Hannay
Production: Mike Ferguson
Facilities Manager: Walt Scram
Materials Manager: Dick Storm
Estimated Sales: $25-50 Million
Number Employees: 100-249
Square Footage: 118612

44871 Hanover Foods Corp
1125 Wilson Ave
P.O. Box 334
Hanover, PA 17331   717-632-6000
          Fax: 717-637-2890 www.hanoverfoods.com
Processor and importer of canned, frozen, freeze-dried and fresh vegetables, beans, mushrooms, potato chips, pretzels, juices, sauces, salads, entrees, soups, desserts, etc.; also, spaghetti and meat balls in tomato sauce.
Chief Executive Officer: John Warehime
john.warehime@hanoverfoods.com
Executive Vice President: Gary Knisely
VP, Canning Operations: Dave Still
VP, Sales: Dan Schuchart
Year Founded: 1924
Estimated Sales: $20-50 Million
Number Employees: 250-499
Square Footage: 5161
Type of Packaging: Consumer, Private Label, Bulk
Regions Imported from: Central America

44872 Hanover Uniform Co
3501 Marmenco Ct
Baltimore, MD 21230-3411   410-235-8338
          Fax: 410-235-6071 800-541-9709
          info@hanoveruniform.com
          www.hanoveruniform.com
Wholesaler/distributor and exporter of uniforms; serving the food service market
President: John Mintz
jmintz@hanoveruniform.com
Office Manager: John Mintz
Estimated Sales: $2.5-5 Million
Number Employees: 20-49
Type of Packaging: Food Service
Regions Exported to: Worldwide

44873 Hans Holterbosch Inc
375 Park Ave # 2503
New York, NY 10152-2506   212-421-3800
          Fax: 212-755-5271
Importer and wholesaler/distributor of beer
Executive Director: Daphne Marcial
Estimated Sales: $1-2.5 Million
Number Employees: 1-4
Type of Packaging: Consumer, Food Service
Brands Imported: Hoffbrau
Regions Imported from: Europe
Percentage of Business in Importing: 100

44874 Hansaloy Corp
820 W 35th St
Davenport, IA 52806-5800   563-386-1131
          Fax: 563-386-7707 800-553-4992
          sales@hansaloy.com www.hansaloy.com
Manufacturer and exporter of blades including slicing/dicing, band and reciprocating with scalloped and straight edges for slicing bread and boneless meat
Owner: Diane Artioli
CEO: Howard H Cherry Iii
Quality Control: Stephen Wright
VP Sales/Marketing: K Brenner
VP Sales: Allen Wright
d.artioli@hansaloy.com
Estimated Sales: $ 5 - 10 Million
Number Employees: 50-99
Square Footage: 80000
Regions Exported to: Worldwide
Percentage of Business in Exporting: 10

44875 Hansen Beverage Co
1 Monster Way
Corona, CA 92879-7101   951-739-6200
          Fax: 951-739-6210 800-426-7367
          info@hansens.com www.hansensenergy.com
Wholesaler/distributor and exporter of natural beverages including fruit and apple juices, sodas, lemonade and iced teas; serving the food service market
President & COO: Hilton Schlosberg
CEO: Rodney Sacks
Number Employees: 1-4
Parent Co: HB
Type of Packaging: Consumer, Food Service
Brands Exported: Equator; Hansen's Natural
Regions Exported to: Worldwide

44876 Hansen Distribution Group
96-1282 Waihona St
Pearl City, HI 96782   808-456-3334
          Fax: 808-456-5043 hansenhawaii.com
Importer of seafood including shellfish; wholesaler/distributor of groceries, meats, frozen foods, general merchandise, etc.; serving the food service market.
Director of Special Projects: Diana Allen
Controller: Lorenzo Eagan
Quality Assurance Director: Mike Piccinino
Year Founded: 1957
Estimated Sales: $50-100 Million
Number Employees: 50-99
Number of Products: 8000
Square Footage: 100000
Type of Packaging: Consumer, Food Service
Brands Imported: Hukilau; Bumble Bee; Meridian; Aquastar
Regions Imported from: Asia
Percentage of Business in Importing: 10

44877 Hanson Brass Rewd Co
7530 San Fernando Rd
Sun Valley, CA 91352-4344   818-767-3501
          Fax: 818-767-7891 888-841-3773
          info@hansonbrass.com www.hansonhl.com
Sneeze guards, copper carts and brass, chrome and copper lamps; exporter of carving units, food displays; wholesaler/distributor of restaurant equipment and supplies; serving the food service market, alto shaam test kitchen
President: Tom Hanson
VP: Jim Hanson
CFO: Tom Hanson
info@hansonbrass.com
Vice President: Robert Hanson
Plant Manager: Mark Denny
Estimated Sales: $6-7 Million
Number Employees: 10-19
Number of Brands: 2
Square Footage: 32000
Brands Exported: Hanson Brass
Regions Exported to: Central America, South America, Europe, Asia, Middle East

44878 Hanson Brass Rewd Co
7530 San Fernando Rd
Sun Valley, CA 91352-4344   818-767-3501
          Fax: 818-767-7891 888-841-3773
          info@hansonbrass.com www.hansonhl.com
President: Tom Hanson Jr
CEO: Jim Hanson
CFO: Tom Hanson Sr
VP: Robert Hanson
Plant Manager: Mark Denny
Number Employees: 10-19
Brands Exported: Hanson Brass
Regions Exported to: Central America, South America, Europe, Asia, Middle East
Percentage of Business in Exporting: 20
Regions Imported from: Asia
Percentage of Business in Importing: 25

44879 Hanson Lab Furniture Inc
814 Mitchell Rd
Newbury Park, CA 91320-2215   805-498-3121
          Fax: 805-498-1855 info@hansonlab.com
          www.hansonlab.com
Manufacturer and exporter of laboratory furniture, fume hoods and accessories; also, installation and lab planning services available
Owner: Joe Matta
joe@hansonlab.com
VP: Mike Hanson
Estimated Sales: $ 5 - 10 Million
Number Employees: 5-9
Parent Co: Norlab
Regions Exported to: Canada
Percentage of Business in Exporting: 5

44880 (HQ)Hantover Inc
10301 Hickman Mills Dr # 200
Kansas City, MO 64137-1600   816-761-7800
          Fax: 816-761-0044 800-821-7849
          contactus@hantover.com
Manufacturer and exporter of vacuum packaging machinery and stainless steel cutlery and utensils
Chairman: Bernard Huff
General Manager: David Philgreen
Estimated Sales: $ 20 - 50 Million
Number Employees: 100-249
Type of Packaging: Food Service
Other Locations:
  Hantover
  Kansas City, MOHantover
Regions Exported to: Worldwide
Percentage of Business in Exporting: 15

44881 Hanwa American Corporation
18100 Von Karman Ave.
Suite 320
Irvine, CA 98101   949-955-2780
          Fax: 949-955-2785
Importer and exporter of frozen fish, shrimp and crabs
Manager: Kazuyoshi Kai
Sales Manager: Kazuya Kashihara
Contact: Akihiko Baba
baba@hanwaamerican.com
Estimated Sales: $5-10 Million
Number Employees: 5-9
Parent Co: Hanwa Company

44882 Hapman Conveyors
6002 E N Ave
Kalamazoo, MI 49048-9775   269-343-1675
          Fax: 269-349-2477 800-968-7722
          info@hapman.com www.hapman.com

Importers & Exporters / A-Z

Manufacturer and exporter of flexible screw, pneumatic and tubular drag conveyors, bulk bag unloaders, manual bag dump stations, batch weigh equipment and silo dischargers
President: Edward Thompson
info@hapman.com
Quality Control: Randy McBroom
Marketing: Greg Nowak
Estimated Sales: $ 20 - 50 Million
Number Employees: 50-99
Square Footage: 100000
Parent Co: Prab
Brands Exported: Helix; MiniVac
Regions Exported to: Worldwide
Percentage of Business in Exporting: 25

44883 Happy Egg Dealers
3204 E 7th Ave
Tampa, FL 33605-4302 813-248-2362
Fax: 813-247-1754
Eggs
Owner: Frank Selph
Estimated Sales: $ 10 - 20 Million
Number Employees: 10 to 19
Type of Packaging: Consumer, Bulk

44884 Happy's Potato Chip Co
3900 Chandler Dr NE
Minneapolis, MN 55421-4494 612-781-3121
Fax: 612-781-3125
Snack foods
President: Steve Aanenson
Finance Executive: Betty Kapsner
Human Resource Executive: Allen Dick
Manager: Finn Henrikssen
Plant Manager: Finn Henrikssen
Estimated Sales: $5 Million
Number Employees: 50-99
Square Footage: 92000
Parent Co: Old Dutch Foods
Type of Packaging: Consumer, Food Service
Regions Exported to: Canada

44885 Haram-Christensen Corp
125 Asia Pl
Carlstadt, NJ 07072-2412 201-842-1098
Fax: 201-507-0507 800-937-3474
haramchris@aol.com www.haramchris.com
Importer and wholesaler/distributor of Scandinavian, German and Austrian food specialties
President: Walter Seifert
haramchris@aol.com
Treasurer: Victor Nahum
Assistant to President: Anna Vikki
Estimated Sales: $10-20 Million
Number Employees: 10-19
Square Footage: 63000
Brands Imported: Abba; Landsberg; Tchibo; Boviks; Hafi; Husmor; Gundelsheim; Hengstenberg; Darbo; Sachers; Erasco; Kuchenmeister; Wolf; Nidar; Freia; Stabburet; Korsnas; Adler; Norden; Oebel; Hela
Regions Imported from: Europe

44886 Harbor Seafood
969 Lakeville Rd
New Hyde Park, NY 11040-3000 516-775-2400
Fax: 516-775-3641 800-645-2211
Seafood
President & CEO: Pete Cardone
peteharbor@aol.com
Director Sales, Marketing & Purchasing: Enrique Oyaga
Sales & Marketing: Trish Albano
VP International Purchasing: Bogdan Swita
Estimated Sales: $6.4 Million
Number Employees: 20-49
Square Footage: 20000
Regions Imported from: Worldwide

44887 Harborlite Corporation
PO Box 519
Lompoc, CA 93438-0519 800-342-8667
Fax: 805-735-5699 info@worldminerals.com
www.worldminerals.com
Manufacturer and exporter of perlite filter aids and functional fillers
Contact: Mike Mcdonald
mike.mcdonald@worldminerals.com
Type of Packaging: Food Service, Bulk
Brands Exported: Harborlite Perlite Filter Aids
Regions Exported to: Central America, South America, Europe, Asia, Middle East

44888 Harbour House Bar Crafting
737 Canal Street
Bldg 16
Stamford, CT 06902-5930 203-348-6906
Fax: 203-348-6190 800-755-1227
bigbars@snet.net www.harbourhouse.com
Manufacturer solid wooden bars, tables, booths and carts
President: Steven Kline
VP: Jeff Watkins
Estimated Sales: $1-2.5 Million
Number Employees: 10
Type of Packaging: Food Service
Regions Exported to: Worldwide
Percentage of Business in Exporting: 5

44889 Harbour Lobster Ltd
5583 Hwy 3
P.O. Box 69
Shag Harbour, NS B0W 3B0
Canada 902-723-2500
Fax: 902-723-2568
Lobster and salted groundfish
President: Wayne Banks
Year Founded: 1972
Number Employees: 5-9
Type of Packaging: Bulk
Regions Exported to: Worldwide
Percentage of Business in Exporting: 70

44890 Harco Enterprises
675 the Parkway
Peterborough, ON K9J 7K2
Canada 705-743-5361
Fax: 705-743-4312 800-361-5361
sales@harco.on.ca www.harco.on.ca
Manufacturer, wholesaler/distributor and exporter of promotional items including hot stamping, pad printing, multi-color imprints, glow-in-the-dark custom products, coasters, swizzle sticks, toys, flyers, key tags, spoons, etc; serving the food service market. Supplier of spare parts to the dairy and food industries
President: Ray Harris
VP Finance: Kathy Perry
VP: Terry Harris
VP Marketing: Kathy Perry
VP Administration: Joan Harris
Number Employees: 10
Square Footage: 64000
Type of Packaging: Food Service
Regions Exported to: Central America, Europe
Brands Imported: Sparta Brush; Tetra Pak; Stranman Valves; Alfa Laval
Regions Imported from: South America

44891 Hardt Equipment Manufacturing
1756 50th Avenue
Lachine, QC H8T 2V5
Canada 888-848-4408
www.hardt.ca
Designer and manufacturer of food service equipment including commercial rotisseries, heated merchandisers, counter-top healted display cases and a cleaning apparatus for cookin utensils and accessories.
Purchasing Manager: Tony Morrone
Number Employees: 75
Square Footage: 112000
Brands Exported: Mark V; Mark G; Inferno 24; Inferno 43; Inferno 35; Excalibur; Inferno 2000; Inferno 3000; Zone Hot Case; Snack Zone; Cleaning Solution Tanks
Regions Exported to: Worldwide
Percentage of Business in Exporting: 85

44892 Hardware Components Inc
1021 Park Ave
New Matamoras, OH 45767 740-865-2424
Fax: 740-865-2534 hci@hardwarecomponents.com
www.hardwarecomponents.com
Manufacturer and importer of ferrous and nonferrous castings, stampings, forgings, furniture and cabinets
Vice President: Dan Gautschi
hci@hardwarecomponents.com
VP/General Manager: Danny Gautschi
VP Sales: Chris Dickinson
Estimated Sales: $ 5 - 10,000,000
Number Employees: 1-4
Regions Imported from: China, Korea, Taiwan, Mexico
Percentage of Business in Importing: 100

44893 Hardwood Products Co LP
31 School St
Guilford, ME 04443-6388 207-876-3311
Fax: 207-876-3130 800-289-3340
info@hwppuritan.com www.hwppuritan.com
Manufacturer and exporter of wooden ice cream sticks and spoons, stir sticks and skewers; also, industrial cleaning swabs, cocktail forks, cocktail spears, corn dog sticks, flag sticks, fan paddles, dawels
Chief Finacial Officer: Scott Welman
Quality Control: William Young
Sales Manager: Ann Erickson
Sales Exec: Timothy Templet
CSR Rep: Jessica Brown
ttemplet@hwppuritan.com
VP of Operations: James Cartwright
Plant Manager: Bruce Jones
Purchasing Agent: Joseph Cartwright
Estimated Sales: $ 20-50 Million
Number Employees: 250-499
Square Footage: 600000
Type of Packaging: Consumer, Food Service, Private Label, Bulk
Brands Exported: Gold Bond; Trophy; Puritan; Purswab
Regions Exported to: Central America, South America, Europe, Asia, Middle East, Worldwide
Percentage of Business in Exporting: 2

44894 Hardy Systems Corporation
610 Anthony Trl
Northbrook, IL 60062 847-272-4400
Fax: 847-272-4471 800-927-3956
Manufacturer and exporter of bins, batching scales, conveying systems and flow control panels
President: Richard Walter
Sales Manager: J Soling
Head Engineer: D Acker
Estimated Sales: Below $ 5,000,000
Number Employees: 5-9
Regions Exported to: Europe, Asia, Canada, Mexico
Percentage of Business in Exporting: 5

44895 Harford Systems Inc
2225 Pulaski Hwy
Havre De Grace, MD 21078-2145 410-272-3400
Fax: 410-273-7892 800-638-7620
pwatson@harfordsystems.com
www.harfordsystems.com
Manufacturer and exporter of alarm systems and refrigeration equipment and machinery
President: Ralph Ahrens
VP: George Gabriel
HR Manager: Kate Pelonquin
Estimated Sales: $20-50 Million
Number Employees: 100-249
Parent Co: Bio Medic Corporation
Regions Exported to: Worldwide

44896 Harlan Bakeries
7597 E US Highway 36
Avon, IN 46123 317-272-3600
800-435-2738
www.harlanbakeries.com
Bagels and other bakery products
President & Founder: Hugh Harlan
CFO: John Menne
Executive VP, Sales & Marketing: Joseph Latouf
Year Founded: 1991
Estimated Sales: $92 Million
Number Employees: 1,000-4,999
Number of Brands: 5
Square Footage: 2224
Regions Exported to: Europe, Asia
Regions Imported from: Asia

44897 Harland Simon Control Systems USA
Windsor Office Plaza
210 West 22nd Street, Suite 138
Oakbrook, IL 60523 630-572-7650
Fax: 630-572-7653 sales@harlandsimon.com
Manufacturer and exporter of control systems including drive systems
Systems Sales Manager: Robert Picknell
National Sales Support Manager: Scott Mincher
Number Employees: 70
Square Footage: 164000
Parent Co: Monotype Systems
Regions Exported to: Worldwide
Percentage of Business in Exporting: 20

44898 Harmony Enterprises
704 Main Ave N
Harmony, MN 55939-8839 507-886-6666
Fax: 507-886-6706 800-658-2320
info@harmony1.com www.harmony1.com
Manufacturer and exporter of waste handling and recycling equipment including indoor and outdoor compactors, vertical balers, beverage extraction equipment and full product destruction equipment. Some of their brands include HarmonyPower Packer, Harmony Insite Wireless Monitoring, Harmony SunPak Solar Options, Harmony Equipment Rental, Harmony ExtractPack and more.
President: Steve Cremer
Office Manager & Finance: Lana Soppa
New Business Development Manager: Lane Powell
Vice President, Sales & Marketing: Brent Christiansen
National Sales Manager: Nick Roberts
Vice President, Operations: Ramon Hernandez
Purchasing: Sid Polley
Estimated Sales: $24 Million
Number Employees: 75
Other Locations:
    Harmony, MN
Brands Exported: GPI; Harmony Enterprises
Regions Exported to: Worldwide
Percentage of Business in Exporting: 30

44899 Harney & Sons Tea Co.
5723 Route 22
Millerton, NY 12546-6500 518-789-2100
Fax: 518-789-2100 800-832-8463
ht@harneyteas.com www.harney.com
Teas
President: John Harney
masterteablender@harneyteas.com
Marketing: Lisa Prindle
Sales: Michael Harney
Manager: Paul Harney
Purchasing: Elvira Cardenos
Year Founded: 1983
Estimated Sales: $2.5-5 Million
Number Employees: 200
Square Footage: 90000
Type of Packaging: Consumer, Food Service, Private Label, Bulk
Brands Exported: Harney
Regions Exported to: Europe
Percentage of Business in Exporting: 1
Regions Imported from: Asia
Percentage of Business in Importing: 99

44900 Harold L King & Co Inc
1420 Stafford St # 2
Redwood City, CA 94063-1077 650-368-2233
Fax: 650-368-3547 888-368-2233
kingcoffee@aol.com www.king-coffee.com
Coffee
President & CEO: Robert King
Secretary/Treasurer, CFO: John King
Vice President: Tim Kallok
Traffic Manager: Chris King
Year Founded: 1958
Estimated Sales: $25 Million
Number Employees: 5-9
Type of Packaging: Consumer
Regions Exported to: Internationally

44901 Harold Leonard Southwest Corporation
1812 Brittmoore Road
Suite 230
Houston, TX 77043-2216 713-467-8105
Fax: 713-467-0072 800-245-8105
Manufacturer and wholesaler/distrbutor of smallwares
President: Carl Marcus
CEO: Herb Kelleher
Marketing Director: Roger Randall
Sales Representative: Jerry Williams
Estimated Sales: $1-2.5 Million
Number Employees: 6
Square Footage: 100000
Parent Co: Harold Leonard & Company
Regions Imported from: Europe, Asia, Latin America, Canada, India
Percentage of Business in Importing: 55

44902 Harpak-ULMA Packaging LLC
3035 Torrington Dr
Ball Ground, GA 30107-4543 770-345-5300
Fax: 770-345-5322 www.harpak-ulma.com
Packaging machines and packaging solutions such as traysealers, vertical and side seal packaging, blister packaging and film.
Manager: Ron Hartwig
ronhartwig@harpak-ulma.com
Number Employees: 10-19
Regions Exported to: Central America, South America, Europe, Asia, Middle East, North America, USA

44903 Harper Brush Works Inc
400 N 2nd St
Fairfield, IA 52556-2416 641-472-5186
Fax: 641-472-3187, 800-223-7894
info@harperbrush.com www.harperbrush.com
Manufacturer and exporter of brooms, brushes, mops and squeegees
CEO: Barry Harper
barry.harper@harperbrush.com
Marketing: Pat Adam
Sales: Jerry Armstrong
Public Relations: Pat Adam
Operations: Don Sander
Purchasing Director: Randy Rhoads
Estimated Sales: $ 20 - 50 Million
Number Employees: 100-249
Type of Packaging: Consumer, Food Service, Bulk

44904 Harper Trucks Inc
1522 S Florence St
Wichita, KS 67209-2634 316-942-1381
Fax: 316-942-8508 800-835-4099
www.harpertrucks.com
Manufacturer and exporter of industrial trucks
President: Phil G Ruffin
pruffin@harpertrucks.com
CFO: Phillip Ruffin
Vice President: Gary Leiker
Marketing Director: David Rife
Sales Director: Judy Darnell
Plant Manager: Hugh Sales
Purchasing Manager: Sonya Kellogg
Estimated Sales: $20 Million
Number Employees: 100-249
Number of Brands: 1
Square Footage: 350000
Regions Exported to: Worldwide

44905 Harris Crab House
433 Kent Narrow Way N
Grasonville, MD 21638-1307 410-827-9500
Fax: 410-827-9057 www.harrisseafoodco.com
Crabs and oysters
Chairman: William Jerry Harris
Vice President: Art Oertel
Estimated Sales: $ 5-10 Million
Number Employees: 50-99
Type of Packaging: Consumer

44906 Harris Freeman
3110 E Miraloma Ave
Anaheim, CA 92806-1906 714-765-1190
Fax: 714-765-1199 800-275-2378
info@harrisfreeman.com www.harrisfreeman.com
Spices, teas and coffee
Owner/President: Anil Shah
Owner: Chirayu Borooah
Vice President: Al Paruthi
Year Founded: 1981
Estimated Sales: 20-50 Million
Number Employees: 20-49

44907 Harris Moran Seed Co
555 Codoni Ave
Modesto, CA 95357-0507 209-579-7333
Fax: 209-527-5312
Vegetable seeds
President: Matthew Johnston
m.johnston@hmclause.com
CEO: Bruno Carette
VP Research: Jeff McElroy
Marketing Director: Bernie Hamel
US/Canada Sales Director: Dan Bailey
VP Of Production & Operations: Dennis Choate
Purchasing Agent: Maxine Corbett
Estimated Sales: $ 10 - 20 Million
Number Employees: 100-249
Parent Co: Groupe Limagrain

44908 Harris Ranch Beef Co
16277 S McCall Ave
Selma, CA 93662-9458 559-896-3081
Fax: 559-896-3095 800-742-1955
www.harrisranchbeef.com
Beef products
Chairman: David Wood
Chairman of the Board: John Harris
Chief Financial Officer: Doug Sariss
Estimated Sales: $ 85 Thousand
Number Employees: 500-999
Number of Brands: 1
Square Footage: 17190
Parent Co: Harris Farms, Inc.
Type of Packaging: Consumer, Food Service, Private Label, Bulk
Brands Exported: Harris Ranch
Regions Exported to: Dominican Republic

44909 Harrison Electropolishing
13002 Brittmoore Park Dr
Houston, TX 77041-7231 832-467-3100
Fax: 832-467-3111 info@harrisonep.com
www.m.harrisonep.com
Specializes in mechanical, electropolishing and passivation for brew kettles, fermenters and lagering tanks.
President: Tom Harrison
Manager: Ginger Happacher
ginger@harrisonep.com
Number Employees: 50-99
Regions Exported to: North America

44910 Harrisons & Crosfield Teas Inc.
PO Box 461
Chatham, NJ 07928 973-463-0426
Fax: 973-463-0430 800-416-8327
Tea
Marketing: Al Sharif

44911 Harsco Industrial IKG
1801 Forrest Park Dr
Garrett, IN 46738 260-357-6900
Fax: 260-357-0027 800-467-2345
salesikg@harsco.com www.harscoikg.com
Manufacturer and exporter of fiberglass grating used for flooring in food processing plants
Marketing Manager: Tom Toler
VP Sales/Marketing: Ray Palombi
Contact: Heidi Malcolm
h.malcolm@ikgindustries.com
Estimated Sales: $ 1 - 5 Million
Regions Exported to: Worldwide

44912 (HQ)Hart Design & Mfg
1940 Radisson St
Green Bay, WI 54302-2092 920-468-5927
Fax: 920-468-5888 www.hartdesign.com
Designs and constructs specialty, standard and proprietary equipment for use in the Food and Dairy industry. Our packaging machinery includes process cheese wrappers, automatic puching, filling and sealing lines for process and creamcheese, a ribbon cheese casting, slitting, slice stacking equipment, automatic product feeders, and portion cutting equipment for block and barrel cheese.
President: Timm Schaetz
CEO: John Adams
Founder/CEO: Gerald Schaetz
Marketing Manager: Dennis Adelmeyer
Sales Manager: Dennis Adelmeyer
Estimated Sales: $4 Million
Number Employees: 20-49
Square Footage: 80000
Brands Exported: Hart; Auto Pour; Auto Pouch; Climate-Tel
Regions Exported to: Central America, South America, Europe, Asia
Brands Imported: Hensen, Packing Concepts, B&B Packaging Technology
Regions Imported from: Europe

44913 Harten Corporation
18 Commerce Rd
Unit H
Fairfield, NJ 07004 973-808-9488
Fax: 973-808-3966 866-642-7836
hartencorp@aol.com www.hartencorp.com
Herbal extracts, botanicals, powders, and nutritional supplements
President: Shao Hua Chen
Vice President: Jing Chen
Contact: Denise Delaney-Reed
ddelaney-reed@hartencorp.com
Estimated Sales: $1-3 Million
Number Employees: 5-9
Square Footage: 3200
Regions Imported from: China
Percentage of Business in Importing: 100

Importers & Exporters / A-Z

44914 Hartford Plastics
10861 Mill Valley Rd
Omaha, NE 68154
Fax: 860-683-8484
Manufacturer and exporter of plastic bottles and containers; also, custom blow molding, labeling, hot stamping and silk screening available
VP Marketing: Anthony Roncaioli
Estimated Sales: $ 10-20 Million
Number Employees: 50-99
Parent Co: Comtrol

44915 Hartness International
1200 Garlington Road
P.O. Box 26509
Greenville, SC 26509   864-297-1200
Fax: 864-297-4486 800-845-8791
www.hartness.com
Manufacturer and exporter of packaging equipment and machinery including case packers, decasers, single filers/laners and conveyor and mass product flow systems
Managing Director: Jim Gordon
Chief Executive Officer: Bernard McPheely
Chief Financial Officer: Lamar Jordan
Vice President: Sean Hartness
Marketing Manager: Anne Elmerick
Vice President, Sales & Marketing: Scott Smith
Product Manager: Bill Gemmell
Director, Procurement: Dianne Hall
Estimated Sales: $ 50-75 Million
Number Employees: 250-499
Regions Exported to: Central America, South America, Europe, Asia, Middle East, Australia
Percentage of Business in Exporting: 50

44916 Hartstone Pottery Inc
1719 Dearborn St
Zanesville, OH 43701-5299   740-452-9999
Fax: 800-506-9627
Manufacturer, importer and exporter of stoneware, dinnerware, cookware, bakeware, tabletop accessories, oven dishwashers and microwave safe cookie molds
Manager: Wess Foltz
wess@hartstonepottery.com
VP/General Manager: Patrick Hart
Sales Manager: Mike Flynn
Operations Manager: Shawn McGee
Estimated Sales: $ 7 Million
Number Employees: 20-49
Square Footage: 400000
Parent Co: Carlisle Companies
Type of Packaging: Consumer, Food Service
Regions Exported to: Worldwide
Percentage of Business in Exporting: 3
Regions Imported from: Europe

44917 Hartzell Fan Inc
910 S Downing St
Piqua, OH 45356   937-773-7411
Fax: 937-773-8994 800-336-3267
info@hartzellfan.com www.hartzell.com
Manufacturer and exporter of general and process ventilation fans and centrifugal fans and blowers
President: George D Atkinson
CEO: Sean Steimle
customerservice@hartzell.com
Sales: George Atkins
Operations Manager: R Wallace
Estimated Sales: $20-50 Million
Number Employees: 100-249

44918 Harvard Folding Box Company
71 Linden St
Lynn, MA 1905   781-598-1600
Fax: 781-598-2950 www.idealboxmakers.com
Manufacturer and exporter of folding paper boxes
President: Leon Simkins
VP: David Simkins
Logistics Manager: Tony Geraneo
Contact: Mike Hios
mhios@idealboxmakers.com
Operational Manager: Chris Robertson
Plant Manager: Jimmy Mc Gee
Estimated Sales: $ 10 - 20 Million
Number Employees: 100-249
Parent Co: Simkins Industries
Regions Exported to: South America, Canada, Latin America, Mexico
Percentage of Business in Exporting: 2

44919 Harvest Food Products Co Inc
710 Sandoval Way
Hayward, CA 94544-7111   510-675-0383
Fax: 510-675-0396
sales@harvestfoodproducts.com
Pot stickers, egg rolls, wontons, barbecue pork buns and tempura shrimp
President: Yvonne Cooks
yvonne@womenprisoners.org
Estimated Sales: $ 10 - 20 Million
Number Employees: 50-99
Square Footage: 34000
Type of Packaging: Consumer, Food Service, Private Label, Bulk
Regions Imported from: Asia
Percentage of Business in Importing: 10

44920 Harvest Song Ventures
6 Yennicock Avenue
Port Washington, NY 11050   516-773-7356
Fax: 516-773-7726
Preserves, jams and jellies
President/Owner: Sylvia Tirakian

44921 Harwil Corp
541 Kinetic Dr
Oxnard, CA 93030-7923   805-988-6800
Fax: 805-988-6804 800-562-2447
www.harwil.com
Manufacturer and exporter of bag closing machinery, heat sealers and flow and liquid level switches. Also manufature fluid liquid level switches, liquid level pumpup/plumpdown controles, pump emergency shutdown controllers andachemical feed pump interface module
VP: Bruce Bowman
Sales Exec: Ellis Anderson
Number Employees: 20-49
Regions Exported to: Worldwide

44922 Hassia
1210 Campus Dr
Morganville, NJ 07751-1262   732-536-8770
Fax: 732-536-8850 sales@hassiausa.com
www.oystarusa.com
Wholesaler/distributor and importer of high and low acid aseptic packaging and thermoform filling, sealing and pouching equipment for the portion pack market, case and tray packing, palletizing
CEO: Charles Ravalli
Vice President: Juan Rodriguez
Marketing Director: Robert Dono
Sales Director: Don Lander
Estimated Sales: $15 Million
Number Employees: 10-19
Square Footage: 12000
Parent Co: Hassia Verpackungsmaschinen GmbH
Brands Imported: A&F Automation; ERCA-FORMSEAL
Regions Imported from: South America, Europe
Percentage of Business in Importing: 80

44923 Hastings Meat Supply
202 W 12th St
PO Box 1167
Hastings, NE 68901-3967   402-463-9857
Fax: 402-463-7181
Meat
Owner: Gary Deal
gary@hastingsfoods.com
Director: Jeff Andreasen
Estimated Sales: $ 1 - 3 Million
Number Employees: 1-4
Type of Packaging: Consumer, Food Service, Bulk

44924 Hatco Corp
635 S 28th St
Milwaukee, WI 53215-1298   414-671-6350
Fax: 414-615-1226 800-558-0607
www.hatcocorp.com
Manufacturer and exporter of heating, warming, toasting, cooking and equipment including display warmers, holding cabinets, low temperature and slow cookers and booster and sink heaters for hot water, toasters, etc
President: Dave Rolston
drolston@hatcocorp.com
Co-Founder: Lareine Hatch
Vice President - Sales: Michael Whiteley
National Sales Manager: Mark Pumphret
Number Employees: 50-99
Type of Packaging: Food Service
Regions Exported to: Worldwide
Percentage of Business in Exporting: 30

44925 Hatco Corp
635 S 28th St
Milwaukee, WI 53215-1298   414-671-6350
Fax: 414-615-1226 800-543-7521
equipsales@hatcocorp.com www.hatcocorp.com
President: Dave Rolston
drolston@hatcocorp.com
Vice President: Mike Whitely
Estimated Sales: G
Number Employees: 50-99

44926 Hatfield Quality Meats
2700 Clemens Rd
P.O. Box 902
Hatfield, PA 19440   215-368-2500
Fax: 215-368-3018 800-743-1191
www.hatfieldqualitymeats.com
Fresh and frozen pork products.
President: Craig Edsill
CEO: Doug Clemens
SVP & CFO: Josh Rennells
Year Founded: 1895
Estimated Sales: $138.3 Million
Number Employees: 1,000-4,999
Square Footage: 850000
Parent Co: Clemens Food Group
Type of Packaging: Consumer, Food Service, Private Label
Other Locations:
   Hatfield Quality Meats
   Chester, PA Hatfield Quality Meats
Brands Exported: Butcher Wagon; Hatfield
Regions Exported to: Central America, Asia
Percentage of Business in Exporting: 5

44927 Haumiller Engineering Co
445 Renner Dr
Elgin, IL 60123-6991   847-695-9111
Fax: 847-695-2092 sales@haumiller.com
www.haumiller.com
Manufacturer and exporter of high-speed automatic custom assembly machines, flip top closure closing machines, cappers, spray tip and fitment applicators, reducer plug inserters and collar placers
President: Russ Holmer
rholmer@haumiller.com
VP Sales: John Giacopelli
Estimated Sales: $5-10 Million
Number Employees: 50-99
Square Footage: 90000
Regions Exported to: Central America, South America, Europe, Asia, Mexico
Percentage of Business in Exporting: 35

44928 Hausbeck Pickle Co
1626 Hess Ave
Saginaw, MI 48601-3970   989-754-4721
Fax: 989-754-3105 866-754-4721
tim@hausbeck.com www.hausbeck.com
Relish and pickles
CEO: Tim Hausbeck
Treasurer: Richard Hausbeck
Sales Manager: John Schnepf
Estimated Sales: $17,500,000
Number Employees: 20-49
Square Footage: 90000
Type of Packaging: Consumer, Food Service
Regions Exported to: Caribbean
Percentage of Business in Exporting: 2

44929 Hauser Chocolates
59 Tom Harvey Rd
Westerly, RI 02891-3685   401-596-8866
Fax: 401-596-0020 888-599-8231
hauser@hauserchocolates.com
www.hauserchocolates.com
Chocolates
Owner: Ruedi Hauser
hauser@hauserchocolates.com
Estimated Sales: $2.5-5 Million
Number Employees: 10-19
Type of Packaging: Consumer
Regions Exported to: Canada
Percentage of Business in Exporting: 1

44930 Hausman Foods LLC
4261 Beacon St
Corpus Christi, TX 78405-3326   361-883-5521
Fax: 361-883-1003 www.hausmanfoods.com
Fresh and frozen beef

Importers & Exporters / A-Z

President/CEO: Steve R McClure, Sr.
CFO: Amy Seward
aseward@samhausman.com
Vice President/General Manager: Jerry Simpson
Quality Control Manager: Beryl Henry
Vice President/Cold Storage Manager: Amy Seward
Dry Purchasing: Paul des los Santos
Estimated Sales: $ 46 Million
Number Employees: 100-249
Type of Packaging: Consumer, Food Service, Bulk
Regions Exported to: Mexico

44931 Havco Services
1000 Washington Avenue
Croydon, PA 19021-7569   215-785-4031
      Fax: 215-785-3644 800-635-1304
info@havcoservices.com www.havcoservices.com
Owner: Ivan Schultz
Contact: Betty Fazio
betty@havcoservices.com
Estimated Sales: $ 5 - 10 Million
Number Employees: 20-49

44932 Have Our Plastic Inc
6990 Creditview Road
Unit 4
Mississauga, ON L5N 8R9
Canada   905-821-7550
      Fax: 905-821-7553 800-263-5995
      sales@hop.ca
Manufacture and distrubute synthetic paper, plastic and wire binding products, laminating equipment and supplies, other equipment and supplies, restaurant menu covers, display and merchandising products and PVC.
Estimated Sales: $5,000,000
Number Employees: 16
Number of Brands: 1
Square Footage: 96000
Type of Packaging: Private Label, Bulk
Regions Exported to: South America, Latin America

44933 Hawaii Candy Inc
2928 Ualena St # 4
Honolulu, HI 96819-1937   808-836-8955
      Fax: 808-839-4040 800-303-2507
website@hawaiicandy.com www.hawaiicandy.com
Confectionery items and snacks
President: Keith Ohta
info@hawaiicandy.com
Secretary: Richard Ohta
Marketing: Ron Vogel
Estimated Sales: $5-10 Million
Number Employees: 20-49
Square Footage: 33000
Type of Packaging: Consumer, Food Service, Private Label, Bulk
Brands Exported: Hawaii Candy; Hawaiian Island Crisp
Regions Exported to: Asia
Percentage of Business in Exporting: 5

44934 Hawaii International Seafood
371 Aokea Place
PO Box 30486
Kailua, HI 96819-1828   808-839-5010
      Fax: 808-833-0712 info@cryofresh.com
      www.cryofresh.com
Fish and seafood
President: Bill Kowalski
Estimated Sales: $2,000,000
Number Employees: 5-9

44935 Hawaii Papaya Ind Assn
190 Kamehameha Ave # 1
Suite 1
Hilo, HI 96720-2858   808-969-1160
      Fax: 808-969-1781
Manager: Karen Umehara
Number Employees: 1-4

44936 (HQ)Hawkhaven Greenhouse International
W9554 Blackhawk Ct.
Wautoma, WI 54982   920-540-3536
      Fax: 920-787-4295 800-745-4295
verdegrass@gmail.com www.hawkhaven.com
Wheat grass
President/Owner: Timothy Paegelow
Estimated Sales: Under $300,000
Number Employees: 1-4
Square Footage: 10000
Type of Packaging: Consumer

Brands Exported: VerdeGrass - Wheat Grass Juice For Daily Use!
Regions Exported to: Worldwide
Percentage of Business in Exporting: 50

44937 Hayes & Stolz Indl Mfg LTD
3521 Hemphill St
PO Box 11217
Fort Worth, TX 76110-5212   817-926-3391
      Fax: 817-926-4133 800-725-7272
sales@hayes-stolz.com www.hayes-stolz.com
Manufacturer and exporter of batch mixers, continuous blenders, liquid coaters, bucket elevators, valves and rotary screeners
President: B J Masters
marhay@hayes-stolz.com
VP: Mark Hayes
Chairman of the Board: Vernon Hayes
Sales Exec: Mark Hayes
Sales Engineer: Kris Helsley
Estimated Sales: $ 10 - 20 Million
Number Employees: 100-249
Regions Exported to: Worldwide
Percentage of Business in Exporting: 25

44938 Haynes Manufacturing Co
24142 Detroit Rd
Westlake, OH 44145-1528   440-871-2188
      Fax: 440-871-0855 800-992-2166
info@haynesmfg.com www.haynesmfg.com
Manufacturer and exporter of food grade lubricants
Owner: Tammy Doctor
Sales and Marketing Coordinator: Tammy Doctor
tdoctor@haynesmfg.com
Estimated Sales: Less Than $500,000
Number Employees: 1-4
Type of Packaging: Food Service, Private Label, Bulk
Brands Exported: Haynes; Haynes Spray; Haynes Lubri-Film; Haynes CIP-Film; Haynes 500; Haynes Silicone Spray; Haynes Oil; Haynes 500 Plus
Regions Exported to: Central America, Europe, Asia

44939 (HQ)Hayon Manufacturing
9682 Borgata Bay Blvd
Las Vegas, NV 89147-8080   702-562-3377
      Fax: 702-562-3351 hayonmfg@aol.com
      www.eggwashsprayer.com
Manufacturer and exporter of bakery machinery including automatic pan greasers and coaters, egg washers and icing/glaze applicators
Owner: Z Hayon
hayonmfg@aol.com
VP: Ziona Hayon
Estimated Sales: Below $ 500,000
Number Employees: 1-4
Brands Exported: Hayon Select-A-Spray
Regions Exported to: Worldwide
Percentage of Business in Exporting: 25

44940 Hayssen Flexible Systems
225 Spartangreen Blvd
Duncan, SC 29334-9400   864-486-4000
      Fax: 864-486-4412 sales@hayssen.com
      www.hayssen.com
Manufacturer and exporter of horizontal flow wrapping and horizontal and vertical form/fill/seal machinery
President: Daniel L Jones
Vice President: Dan Minor
dan.minor@hayssensandiacre.com
Vice President of Sales and Marketing: Dan Minor
Estimated Sales: $ 50 Million
Number Employees: 250-499
Parent Co: Barry Wehmiller Companies
Regions Exported to: Worldwide

44941 Hayward Industries Inc
1 Hayward Industrial Dr
Clemmons, NC 27012-9737   336-712-9900
      Fax: 336-712-9523 www.haywardindustries.com
Manufacturer and exporter of cartridge filters, pipeline strainers, gas/liquid separators, plastic valves and flow meters
President: Robert Davis
HR Executive: Mathieu Bienvenue
mbienvenue@haywardnet.com
Marketing Communication Manager: D Treslan
Number Employees: 500-999
Regions Exported to: Worldwide

44942 Hazelnut Growers Of Oregon
401 N 26th Ave
Cornelius, OR 97113-8510   503-648-4176
      Fax: 503-648-9515 800-273-4676
nutsales@hazelnut.com www.hazelnut.com
Hazelnuts
President & CEO: Tim Ramsey
Quality Control: Don Marshall
VP Sales & Marketing: Patrick Gabrish
Customer Service & Logistics Coordinator: Claudia Arreola
VP Operations: Dick Vanderschuere
Production Manager: Emilio Briones
Plant Manager: Ken Guinn
Purchasing Manager: Mike Sook
Estimated Sales: $32 Million
Number Employees: 50-99
Type of Packaging: Consumer, Bulk
Brands Exported: Oregon Orchard
Regions Exported to: Worldwide
Percentage of Business in Exporting: 45

44943 Hcs Enterprises
Plot No. 333, Rai Industrial Estate
Sonipat
Haryana, 131029
India
      www.hcsbakerymachines.com
Manufacturer, supplier and exporter of a comprehensive range of bakery plants, machines and equipment including steel flour sifters, bread slicing machines, baking proofer ovens, planetary mixers, infrared ovens, rack ovens
Managing Director: Bhupinder Singh
Estimated Sales: $1 Million
Number Employees: 26-50
Regions Exported to: Central America, South America, Europe, Asia, Middle East, North America, Caribbean
Percentage of Business in Exporting: 95

44944 Healdsburg Machine Company
2584 Rim Rock Way
Santa Rosa, CA 95404-1819   707-433-3348
      Fax: 707-433-3340
Manufacturer and exporter of grape crushing and stemming machinery; also, special pumps for the canning industry
President: Arthur Rafanelli
yvette.moseman@mosemanlaw.com
VP: Ron Rafanelli
Marketing: Ron Rafanelli
Estimated Sales: $ 1-2.5 Million
Number Employees: 10
Square Footage: 180000
Parent Co: Healdsburg Machine Company

44945 Healing Garden
PO Box 576
Maple Valley, WA 98038-0576   888-291-4970
Wholesaler/distributor and exporter of herbs, spices and formulas
Number Employees: 1-4
Regions Exported to: Asia, Canada, Mexico, Africa

44946 Health & Wholeness Store
104 N Main St
Fairfield, IA 52556-2802   641-472-6274
      Fax: 719-260-7400 800-255-8332
      www.healthandwholenessllc.com
Herbs and herbal products
President: Prakash Srivastava
Senior VP: Steven Barthe
Marketing Director: Russ Guest
Public Relations: Marsha Bonne
Operations Manager: Kevin Olson
Plant Manager: Kishore Nareundkar
Estimated Sales: Less Than $500,000
Number Employees: 1-4
Number of Brands: 4
Number of Products: 600
Square Footage: 188000
Type of Packaging: Consumer
Regions Imported from: Asia

44947 Health Concerns
8001 Capwell Dr
Oakland, CA 94621-2107   510-957-5118
      Fax: 510-639-9140 800-233-9355
      info@healthconcerns.com
Chinese herbs, medicinal mushrooms and energy tonics

347

Importers & Exporters / A-Z

President: Laurie Dearborn
laurie@healthconcerns.com
Estimated Sales: $3-5 Million
Number Employees: 10-19
Square Footage: 12000
Type of Packaging: Consumer
Regions Exported to: Europe, Middle East, Canada
Regions Imported from: Worldwide
Percentage of Business in Importing: 85

44948 Health Flavors
50 Sodom Rd
Brewster, NY 10509-4403   845-940-0190
   Fax: 845-278-6277   877-380-3422
Importer and distributer to natural food and gourmet trade
Owner: Josef Rosenfeld
CFO: Christine Zirkelbach
Estimated Sales: $24 Million
Number Employees: 1-4
Number of Products: 700
Square Footage: 5000
Type of Packaging: Consumer, Food Service, Private Label, Bulk
Brands Imported: Candy Tree, Orgran, Corn Candies
Regions Imported from: South America, Europe, Asia
Percentage of Business in Importing: 40

44949 Health Guardians
PO Box 274
Silver Spring, PA 17575-0274   717-285-4642
   Fax: 717-285-4642   800-231-2086
   hello@healthguardians.org
Wholesaler/distributor and exporter of shark cartilage capsules, fat burners, stimulants, diet aids, etc
President: Bruce Youm
Founding Partner: Jay Andrew Barcelon
Founding Partner: Graeme Moore
Chief Operating Officer: Brian Kim
Number Employees: 5-9
Square Footage: 4800
Type of Packaging: Private Label, Bulk
Brands Exported: Health Guardians
Regions Exported to: Worldwide
Percentage of Business in Exporting: 20

44950 Health King Enterprise
238 W 31st St # 1
Chicago, IL 60616-3600   312-567-9978
   Fax: 312-567-9986   888-838-8938
   service@healthkingenterprise.com
   www.healthkingenterprise.com
Importer and exporter of green, medicinal teas and diet and weight loss aids and digestive aids, chinese herb remedies
President: Xingwu Liu
CEO/VP: Joanne Liu
Vice President: Sarah Appleby
sarah.appleby@healthkingenterprise.com
Marketing: Maggie Qiu
Sales: Joaquin Gamino
Operations: Diego Meza
Estimated Sales: $ 1 - 3 Million
Number Employees: 1-4
Square Footage: 24000
Type of Packaging: Consumer
Brands Exported: Health King; Balanceuticals
Regions Exported to: Central America
Percentage of Business in Exporting: 5
Brands Imported: Health King; Yunnan Pu'er; Balanceuticals
Regions Imported from: Asia
Percentage of Business in Importing: 60

44951 Health Plus
13837 Magnolia Ave
Chino, CA 91710-7028   909-627-9393
   Fax: 909-591-7659   800-822-6225
   order_desk@healthplusinc.com
   www.healthplusinc.com
Psyllium and nutritional herbs, tablets and capsules
President: Rita Mediratta
ritam@healthplusinc.com
President: Pat Mediratta
Estimated Sales: $1-2.5 Million
Number Employees: 20-49
Square Footage: 34000
Type of Packaging: Bulk
Brands Exported: Colon Cleans
Regions Exported to: Central America, South America, Europe, Asia, Middle East
Regions Imported from: Asia

Percentage of Business in Importing: 40

44952 Health Products Corp
1060 Nepperhan Ave
Yonkers, NY 10703-1432   914-423-2900
   Fax: 914-963-6001   www.hpc7.com
Psyllium and nutritional herbs, tablets and capsules; contract packager of blending and filling powders
President: Joseph Lewin
zurion2@aol.com
Number Employees: 50-99
Regions Exported to: South America, Middle East
Percentage of Business in Exporting: 25

44953 Health Valley Company
16100 Foothill Boulevard
Irwindale, CA 91706   626-334-3241
   Fax: 626-334-0220   800-334-3204
   www.healthvalley.com
Natural foods
President: Ben Brecher
CFO/Sr VP: Diane Beardsley
Number Employees: 250-499
Parent Co: Intrepid Food Holdings
Type of Packaging: Consumer, Food Service, Private Label, Bulk
Regions Exported to: Worldwide

44954 HealthBest
133 Mata Way
Suite 101
San Marcos, CA 92069   760-752-5230
   Fax: 760-752-1322   www.globalkaizen.com
Natural and organic beans, dried fruits, snack foods, grains, herbs, spices, seasonings, nuts, seeds, bee pollen, pasta, sugar-free candy
President: Jamie Hickerson
President: Laurence Hickerson
Director of Operations: Eric Pena
Production Manager: Armando Ramos
Estimated Sales: $3 Million
Number Employees: 20-49
Number of Brands: 2
Number of Products: 300
Square Footage: 80000
Parent Co: Nature's Best
Type of Packaging: Consumer, Private Label, Bulk
Regions Exported to: Central America, South America
Percentage of Business in Exporting: 3
Regions Imported from: Central America, South America, Europe, Middle East
Percentage of Business in Importing: 20

44955 Healthmate Products
1510 Old Deerfield Rd Ste 103
Highland Park, IL 60035   847-579-1051
   Fax: 847-579-1059   www.healthmateproducts.com
Papaya concentrates
President: Tim Burke
treedburke@gmail.com
CEO/ Manager of Public Relations: Celeste Burke
Estimated Sales: $1 Million
Number Employees: 1-4
Type of Packaging: Consumer, Food Service
Brands Imported: Thorncroft
Regions Imported from: Europe
Percentage of Business in Importing: 5

44956 Healthy Habits Delivered
PO Box 5742
Astoria, NY 11102
   www.lebbysnacks.com
Chickpea snacks

44957 Healthy N Fit International
435 Yorktown Rd
Croton On Hudson, NY 10520-3703   914-271-6040
   Fax: 914-271-6042   800-338-5200
   Info@behealthynfit.com
   www.behealthynfit.com/default.asp
Vitamins, minerals and food supplements; importer of herbs, nutraceuticals, ascorbic acid and nutritional raw materials; exporter of food and dietary supplements
CEO: Robert J Sepe
VP/CFO: Irene Sepe
Public Relations: Denise O'Neill
Estimated Sales: $7 Million appx.
Number Employees: 10-19
Number of Products: 1000
Square Footage: 160000
Type of Packaging: Consumer, Food Service, Private Label, Bulk

Regions Exported to: Central America, South America, Europe, Asia, Middle East, Worldwide

44958 Hearthside Food Solutions
3500 Lacey Rd
Suite 300
Downers Grove, IL 60515   630-967-3600
   info@hearthsidefoods.com
   www.hearthsidefoods.com
Nutrition and energy bars, cookies, crackers, snack foods, cereal and granola, and food packaging.
Chairman/CEO & Co-Founder: Rich Scalise
Senior VP/CFO: Fred Jasser
Senior VP Human Resources: Steve England
Year Founded: 2009
Number Employees: 5000-9999
Type of Packaging: Consumer, Private Label
Regions Exported to: Worldwide

44959 Hearthware Home Products
1795 North Butterfield Road
Libertyville, IL 60048-1212   847-775-8123
   Fax: 847-775-8131   hearthware@aol.com
   hearthware.com
Contact: Vance Bingham
vancebingham@nuwavenow.com

44960 Heartland Food Products
1900 W 47th Place
Suite 302
Westwood, KS 66205   913-831-4446
   Fax: 913-831-4004   866-571-0222
   www.heartlandfoodproducts.com
Mashed potatoes
President: Bill Steeb
Founder: Mary Steeb
Contact: Tom Gray
tom.gray@heartlandfpg.com
Estimated Sales: Less than $500,000
Number Employees: 10-19
Type of Packaging: Bulk

44961 Heartland Gourmet LLC
52205 19th Street
Lincoln, NE 68512   402-423-1234
   Fax: 402-423-4586   800-735-6828
   www.heartlandgourmet.com
Organic, all natural and gluten free baking mixes; gluten free and gourmet frozen doughs
Sales & Product Development Manager: Susan Zink
Business Development Manager: Mark Zink
Estimated Sales: $2.3 Million
Number Employees: 20-49
Square Footage: 54000
Type of Packaging: Consumer, Private Label
Brands Exported: Wanda's
Regions Exported to: Europe, United Kingdom, Japan, Canada
Percentage of Business in Exporting: 5

44962 Heartland Mills Shipping
124 N Hwy 167
Marienthal, KS 67863-6368   620-379-4467
   Fax: 620-379-4459   800-232-8533
   info@heartlandmill.com   www.heartlandmill.com
Organic grains, flour, oat products and sunflower seeds
President: Larry Decker
VP: Mark Nightengale
Sales Executive: Carl Rosenlund
Manager: Carl Rosenlund
seanc@ekisticsinc.net
Estimated Sales: Less Than $500,000
Number Employees: 1-4
Square Footage: 28000
Type of Packaging: Food Service, Private Label, Bulk
Regions Exported to: Europe
Percentage of Business in Exporting: 10
Regions Imported from: Asia
Percentage of Business in Importing: 10

44963 Heat-It Manufacturing
12050 Crownpoint Dr
San Antonio, TX 78233-5362   210-650-9112
   Fax: 210-967-8345   800-323-9336
Manufacturer and exporter of canned heating fuels for buffets, catering, camping and emergencies
Manager: Lisa Garza
General Manager: Georgina Yoast
Estimated Sales: $ .5 - 1 million
Number Employees: 1-4
Square Footage: 60000
Brands Exported: Heat-It

Importers & Exporters / A-Z

44964 Heatcraft Refrigeration Prods
2175 W Park Place Blvd
Stone Mountain, GA 30087-3535   770-465-5600
Fax: 770-465-5990
hrrdp.feedback@heatcrafttrpd.com
www.heatcrafttrpd.com
Manufacturer and exporter of commercial refrigeration equipment
Cmo: Grady Mcadams
VP: Ken Rothgeb
Director Marketing: Jeff Almond
Director Sales: Mark Westphal
General Manager: J Jones
Estimated Sales: $ 10-20,000,000
Number Employees: 100-249
Square Footage: 140000
Parent Co: Lennox International
Brands Exported: Bohn
Regions Exported to: Worldwide
Percentage of Business in Exporting: 7

44965 Heatcraft Worldwide Refrig
5201 Transport Blvd
Columbus, GA 31907-1961   706-568-1514
Fax: 706-568-8990   800-866-5596
marietta.oneill@heatcrafttrpd.com
www.kysorwarren.com
Manufacturer and exporter of refrigerated display fixtures, walk-in coolers/freezers and refrigeration systems
President: Ralph Schmitt
Director of Sales-Eastern U.S. & Canada: Larry Norton
Director of Sales-Western U.S.: Robert Greene
Executive VP: Cliff Hill
Sales Manager: Brian Eddins
Dealer Development Manager: Oscar Stuart
Estimated Sales: $ 1 - 5 Million
Number Employees: 500-999
Square Footage: 980000
Parent Co: Heatcraft Worldwide Refrigeration
Brands Exported: Kysor/Warren; Series 2500; Dual Jet
Regions Exported to: Central America, South America, Europe, Asia
Percentage of Business in Exporting: 10

44966 Heatrex
P.O.Box 515
231 Chestnut St., Suite 410
Meadville, PA 16335-0515   814-724-1800
Fax: 814-333-6580   800-394-6589
sales@heatrex.com   www.heatrex.com
Manufacturer and exporter of heaters including tubular/finned tubular, flanged/screw plug immersion, circulation, defrost, high temperature duct, infrared and radiant process; also, heater controls
Owner: Fred O'Polka
CFO: Fred O Polka
R&D: Larry Clever
Quality Control: Kim Lenhart
Marketing: Earl Pifer
Sales: Earl Pifer
Contact: Cindy Andrews
andrews@heatrex.com
Operations Manager: Earl Pifer
Plant Manager: Kim Lenhart
Estimated Sales: $ 10 - 20 Million
Number Employees: 50-99

44967 Heaven Hill Distilleries Inc.
1311 Gilkey Run Rd.
Bardstown, KY 40004   502-337-1000
Fax: 502-348-0162 www.heavenhill.com
Distilled spirits.
President: Max Shapira
Executive Vice President: Harry Shapira
Vice President, Human Resources: Debbie Morris
COO: Allan Lats
Year Founded: 1935
Estimated Sales: $193 Million
Number Employees: 250-499
Number of Brands: 34
Number of Products: 51
Type of Packaging: Consumer, Private Label, Bulk
Brands Exported: Evan Williams; Bourbon; Elijah Craig Bourbob' Copa De Oro Coffee Liqueur; Du Bouchett Liqueues' Two Fingers Tequila' Christian Brothers Brandy, Hpnotiq
Regions Exported to: Central America, South America, Europe, Asia, Canada, Caribbean
Brands Imported: Copa De Oro; Kilbeggan; Cluny; Lazzaroni; Isle of Jura Single Malt Scotch; Tyrconnel Single Malt Irish Whiskey; Two Fingers Tequila; Cynar Aperitif; Sambuca Sarti
Regions Imported from: Central America, Europe, Canada, Mexico, Caribbean

44968 Heck Cellars
15401 Bear Mountain Winery Rd
Arvin, CA 93203-9743   661-854-6120
Fax: 661-854-2876
Wines, brandy; also, juices and bottled water
Owner: Gary Heck
gheck@korbel.com
Plant Manager: Tim Holt
Estimated Sales: $10-20 Million
Number Employees: 20-49
Square Footage: 1200000
Parent Co: F. Korbel & Brothers
Type of Packaging: Private Label, Bulk
Regions Exported to: Canada

44969 Hectronic
4300 Highline Blvd # 300
Oklahoma City, OK 73108-1843   405-946-3574
Fax: 405-946-3564 info@hetronic.com
www.hetronic.com
Manufacturer and exporter of material handling equipment including remote control systems
President: Dave Krueger
Executive VP: Torsten Rempe
VP: Torsten Rempe
Marketing: Laurel Benjamin
Sales: Bob Peddycoart
Contact: Stefan De
deboor@hectronic.com
Estimated Sales: $ 5 - 10 Million
Number Employees: 20-49
Parent Co: Hectronic
Regions Exported to: Canada

44970 Hedwin Division
1600 Roland Heights Ave
Baltimore, MD 21211-1299   410-467-8209
Fax: 410-889-5189   800-638-1012
sales@hedwin.net   www.hedwin.com
Manufacturer and exporter of plastic products including containers, film bags, shipping trays and drum protector lids; also, dispensing systems, drum and film liners, pails and flexible packaging
President: David E Rubley
CEO: Randy Wolfinger
rwolfinger@hedwin.com
Sales Service Manager: Wayne Deal
Number Employees: 500-999
Parent Co: A. Solvay America Company
Regions Exported to: Worldwide

44971 Heidi's Gourmet Desserts
1651 Montreal Cir
Tucker, GA 30084   770-449-4900
Fax: 770-326-6157   800-241-4166
Frozen speciality desserts
President: Larry Obertfell
Operations Director: Brian Schendider
Estimated Sales: $10-20 Million
Number Employees: 100-249
Square Footage: 134000
Type of Packaging: Consumer, Food Service, Private Label
Other Locations:
  Heidi's Gourmet
  Atlanta, GA
  Heidi's Gourmet
  Sun Valley, CA
  Heidi's Gourmet
  Salt Lake City, UTHeidi's GourmetSun Valley
Brands Exported: Gourmet Concepts; Peachtree Desserts of Atlanta
Regions Exported to: Europe, Asia

44972 Heineken USA Inc
360 Hamilton Ave
Suite 1103
White Plains, NY 10601   914-681-4100
www.heinekenusa.com
Exclusive importer of Heineken beer.
Chairman/CEO, Heineken International: Jean-Francois Van Boxmeer
CEO, Heineken USA: Maggie Timoney
Chief Financial Officer: Laurence Debroux
Year Founded: 1864
Estimated Sales: $19 Billion
Number Employees: 76,136
Parent Co: Heineken International

44973 Heinz Portion Control
7500 Forshee Dr
Jacksonville, FL 32219   904-695-1300
www.heinzfoodservice.com
Manufacturer and exporter of portion controlled sugar, pepper, salt, ketchup, mustard, sauces, dressings, jams, jellies, syrup, preserves, mayonnaise and artificial sweeteners
Parent Co: The Kraft Heinz Company
Type of Packaging: Food Service, Private Label
Other Locations:
  Portion Pac
  Stone Mountain, GAPortion Pac
Regions Exported to: Worldwide

44974 Heinzen Sales
405 Mayock Rd
Gilroy, CA 95020-7040   408-842-6678
Fax: 408-842-6678 hmisales@heinzen.com
www.heinzen.com
Manufacturer and exporter of food processing equipment including fruit peelers, dryers, dumpers, trim lines and conveyors with complete engineering service for new plant layout and equipment
President: Allan Heinzen
Sales: Gary M Hertzog
Estimated Sales: $10-20 Million
Number Employees: 1-4
Square Footage: 44000

44975 Heise Wausau Farms
2805 Valley View Rd
Wausau, WI 54403-8799   715-675-3862
Fax: 715-675-3256   800-764-1010
heisewausaufarms@yahoo.com
Ginseng, bee pollen capsules
President/Owner: Lyn Heise
heisewausaufarms@yahoo.com
Sales: Dan Heise
Estimated Sales: Less Than $500,000
Number Employees: 1-4
Square Footage: 16000
Brands Exported: Heise's Wausau Farms
Regions Exported to: Asia

44976 Heitz Wine Cellars
436 Saint Helena Hwy S
St Helena, CA 94574-2206   707-963-3542
Fax: 707-963-7454 www.heitzcellar.com
Wines
President: Asuncion Tolley
tasuncion@heitzcellar.com
Winemaker: David Heitz
Estimated Sales: $5-10 Million
Number Employees: 5-9
Square Footage: 18726
Type of Packaging: Consumer
Brands Exported: Heitz Wine Cellars
Regions Exported to: South America, Europe, Asia

44977 Helken Equipment Co
171 Erick St # Q1
Crystal Lake, IL 60014-4539   847-697-3690
Fax: 847-697-3692 info@helkenequipment.com
Used and rebuilt food processing equipment
Owner: Kent Redmond
kent@helkenequipment.com
Estimated Sales: $1-2.5 Million
Number Employees: 1-4
Square Footage: 29600
Regions Exported to: Central America, Europe, Canada
Percentage of Business in Exporting: 18

44978 Hellenic Farms LLC
317 Cox St
Roselle, NJ 07203   908-241-0035
Fax: 908-241-2151 info@hellenicfarms.com
hellenicfarms.com
Greek cooking products including herbs and spices; olive oils; honey; baked goods;
Founder: Vivianna Karamanis
vivianna@hellenicfarms.com
Year Founded: 2012
Estimated Sales: $500,00 to 1 Million
Number Employees: 1-4
Type of Packaging: Private Label
Brands Imported: Daphnis & Chloe; Eleia Estate; Salt Odyssey; Meligyris Cretan Honey; Baking Stories & Co.; Oreanthi; 5 Olive Oil; Timion Organic; Emelko

Importers & Exporters / A-Z

Percentage of Business in Importing: 100

44979 Heller Brothers Packing Corp
306 9th St
Winter Garden, FL 34787-3683   407-656-4986
Fax: 407-656-1751   855-543-5537
ptanner@hellerbros.com   www.hellerbros.com
Citrus fruits
Owner/President: Harvey Heller
Owner/CEO: Harry Falk
hfalk@hellerbros.com
CFO: Jeff McKinney
General Manager: Don Barwick
VP Sales/Marketing: Rob Brath
Human Resources/Finance Executive: Jeff McKinney
General Manager: Billy Howard
Production: Al Jefferson
Estimated Sales: $3 Million
Number Employees: 250-499
Square Footage: 1000000
Type of Packaging: Consumer
Regions Exported to: Worldwide

44980 Heller Estates
69 West Carmel Valley Road
PO Box 999
Carmel Valley, CA 93924   831-659-6220
Fax: 831-659-6226   800-625-8466
info@hellerestate.com   www.hellerestate.com
Organic wines
President: Robert Freeman
Controller: Pat Verde
Contact: Mary Roos
info@hellerestate.com
General Manager: Rene Schober
Estimated Sales: $1-2.5 Million
Number Employees: 7
Type of Packaging: Consumer
Regions Exported to: Europe, Asia, Canada
Percentage of Business in Exporting: 15

44981 Helm New York Chemical Corp
1110 Centennial Ave # 2
Piscataway, NJ 08854-4146   732-981-0528
Fax: 732-981-0965   www.helmus.com
Ingredients, additives and flavors
President: Beverly Marsh
bmarsh@helmus.com
CFO: Bill Van Fossen
Senior Vice President: Arun Manalkar
Number Employees: 20-49
Parent Co: Helm AG

44982 Heluva Good Cheese
6 Kimball Ln
Suite 400
Lynnfield, MA 01940   617-660-7400
800-644-5473
www.heluvagood.com
Cheese, dips, cocktail sauce and mustard.
Director, Production & Quality Assurance: Bob Fratangelo
Production Manager: Steve De Mass
Year Founded: 1925
Estimated Sales: $20-50 Million
Number Employees: 100-249
Number of Products: 31
Square Footage: 42000
Type of Packaging: Consumer, Food Service, Private Label, Bulk
Brands Exported: Heluva Good
Regions Exported to: Canada
Percentage of Business in Exporting: 2

44983 Hemisphere Foods
17017 W Dixie Hwy
North Miami Beach, FL 33160   305-948-8508
Fax: 305-948-8508
Contact: Benjamin Kudary
bkudary@hefoods.com
Estimated Sales: $1 - 3 Million
Number Employees: 10-19

44984 Hemisphere Group
221 Mt. Pleasant Road
Smithtown, NY 11787   631-382-9850
Fax: 631-382-9857   800-339-8846
info@greenfarms.com   www.greenfarms.com
Wholesaler/distributor, importer and exporter of sesame, sunflower and pumpkin seeds and nuts: macadamias, brazils, hazelnuts, cashews, pecans, almonds, pinenuts, filberts, walnuts and pistachios; dried fruits: raisins, prunes, applesapricots, peaches, pears and cranberries
President: Adam Green
adam@hemispheredev.com
Estimated Sales: $10-$20 Million
Number Employees: 5-9
Square Footage: 100000
Type of Packaging: Food Service, Bulk
Regions Exported to: Central America, Asia
Percentage of Business in Exporting: 10
Regions Imported from: Central America, South America, Asia
Percentage of Business in Importing: 50

44985 Hemp Oil Canada
PO Box 300
100 Prairie Rd
Ste. Agathe, MB R0G 1Y0
Canada   204-882-2480
Fax: 204-882-2529   800-289-4367
info@hempoilcan.com   hempoilcanada.com
Hemp food ingredients
Controller: Jodi Schreyer Cloutier
Asst. Mgr., Marketing: Timothy Bonnar
Year Founded: 1998
Number Employees: 51-200
Type of Packaging: Bulk

44986 Henggeler Packing Company
6730 Elmore Road
Fruitland, ID 83619   208-452-4212
Fax: 208-452-5416
Apples, plums and prunes
President: Gerald Henggeler
Vice President: Anthony Henggeler
Estimated Sales: $4 Million
Number Employees: 12
Type of Packaging: Consumer, Bulk
Regions Exported to: Worldwide

44987 Henkel Consumer Adhesive
32150 Just Imagine Dr
Avon, OH 44011   440-937-7000
Fax: 440-937-7077   800-321-0253
ask.a.duck@us.henkel.com
Manufacturer and exporter of pressure sensitive tapes including masking, strapping, packaging, identification, cloth, foil, electrical and specialty
President: Jack Kahle
CEO: John Kahle
Contact: Melanie Amato
melanie.amato@manco.com
Number Employees: 250-499
Type of Packaging: Consumer, Food Service
Regions Exported to: Worldwide

44988 Henny Penny, Inc.
1219 US 35 W.
PO Box 60
Eaton, OH 45320   937-456-8400
Fax: 937-456-8402   800-417-8417
www.hennypenny.com
Pressure and open fryers, heated holding equipment, combination convection and steamer ovens, rotisseries, filters, etc.
CEO: Rob Connelly
Executive VP: Steve Maggard
Executive VP: Carolyn Wall
Year Founded: 1957
Estimated Sales: $200 Million
Number Employees: 600
Square Footage: 400000
Brands Exported: Henny Penny Pressure Fryers

44989 Henry Gonsalves Co
35 Thurber Blvd
Smithfield, RI 02917-1838   401-231-6700
Fax: 401-231-6707   800-333-2344
bompet@yahoo.com
Importer of dry beans, cheese, olives, cod, corn meal, grits, oils, etc.; wholesaler/distributor of general line products and seafood
President: Henry Co
geeco71@gmail.com
Sales Manager: Oliver Furtado
Import Director: Jack Costa
Estimated Sales: $10-20 Million
Number Employees: 20-49
Regions Imported from: Europe, Canada

44990 Henry Hanger & Fixture Corporation of America
450 Seventh Ave 23rd Floor
New York City, NY 10123   212-279-0852
Fax: 212-594-7302   877-279-0852
www.henryhanger.com
Manufacturer and exporter of store fixtures and garment hangers
President: Henry Spitz
VP: Nancy Spitz Bittan
VP: Astrid Spitz Metsos
Estimated Sales: $ 5-10 Million
Number Employees: 50-99
Regions Exported to: Worldwide
Percentage of Business in Exporting: 8

44991 Henry Lambertz Inc
254 Comly Road
Suite 1
Lincoln Park, NJ 07035   973-557-2946
Fax: 973-406-4681   www.lambertzus.com
Sugar-free, bread/biscuits, cakes/pastries, cookies.
Marketing: Richard Larue

44992 Henry Troemner LLC
201 Wolf Dr
West Deptford, NJ 08086-2245   856-686-1600
Fax: 856-686-1601   856-686-1600
www.troemner.com
Manufacturer and exporter of laboratory stirrers and mixers for research and development and quality assurance applications
COO: Steve Butler
sbutler@troemner.com
Sales/Marketing: Linda Sears
Estimated Sales: $1-2.5 Million
Number Employees: 100-249
Brands Exported: T-Line
Regions Exported to: Asia, Canada, Mexico
Percentage of Business in Exporting: 10

44993 Herb Patch of Vermont
30 Island Street
Bellows Falls, VT 05101-3122   802-463-1400
Fax: 802-463-1911   800-282-4372
Cocoas, dessert beverages, dips, teas and herb blends; exporter of cocoa
Owner: John Moisis
Estimated Sales: Less than $500,000
Number Employees: 1-4
Square Footage: 13000
Brands Exported: Country Cow

44994 Herbal Products & Development
1200 Trout Gulch Rd
Aptos, CA 95003-3038   831-688-8706
herbprodinfo@gmail.com
www.herbprod.com
Food concentrates, digestive enzymes, antioxidants, probiotics, tinctures, oils and liquid vitamins and minerals
President: Paul Gaylon
herbprodinfo@gmail.com
Number Employees: 1-4
Square Footage: 2400
Type of Packaging: Consumer, Private Label

44995 Herbal Teas International
33 Hammond
Suite 206
Irvine, CA 926   949-461-0213
Fax: 949-461-0214
Importer of wine, tea and coffee
Managing Partner: Hugh Lamond
Partner: Greg Hex

44996 Herbs Etc
1345 Cerrillos Rd
Santa Fe, NM 87505-3508   505-820-0410
Fax: 505-984-9197   888-694-3727
mailorder@herbsetc.com   www.herbsetc.com
Liquid herbal extracts and fast acting softgel herbal medicines
Owner: Daniel Gagnon
Manager: Lynn Childson
lynn.childson@herbsetc.com
Estimated Sales: Less Than $500,000
Number Employees: 5-9
Square Footage: 14000
Type of Packaging: Consumer
Brands Exported: Herbs, Etc.
Regions Exported to: Europe, Middle East, Canada, Caribbean

Importers & Exporters / A-Z

44997 Heritage Books & Gifts
308 Laskin Rd
Virginia Beach, VA 23451-3020 757-428-0400
Fax: 757-428-3632 800-862-2923
www.heritagestore.com
Essential oils, health foods, food supplements, vitamins, herbal teas, herbal tonics and supplements
Owner: Tom Johnson
tom.johnson@heritagestore.com
Chief Financial Officer: Jean Baviera
Marketing Director: David Riblet
Estimated Sales: $9 Million
Number Employees: 50-99
Square Footage: 12000
Type of Packaging: Consumer, Private Label, Bulk
Brands Exported: Heritage

44998 Heritage Food Svc
5130 Executive Blvd
Fort Wayne, IN 46808-1149 260-482-1444
Fax: 260-482-4542 www.heritageparts.com
President: John Mc Donough
johnm@hfse.com
Number Employees: 100-249

44999 Heritage Packaging
625 Fishers Run
Victor, NY 14564-8905 585-742-3310
Fax: 585-742-3311 sales@heritagepackaging.com
www.heritagepackaging.com
Manufacturer and exporter of shipping containers and packaging for equipment
President: William S Smith
sales@heritagepackaging.com
Estimated Sales: $ 1-2.5 Million
Number Employees: 50-99
Regions Exported to: Worldwide

45000 Heritage Salmon Company
100-12051 Horseshoe Way
Richmond, BC V7A 4V4
Canada
604-277-3093
Fax: 604-275-8614
Salmon
President: Ken Hirtle
CFO: Rob Reisen
Type of Packaging: Bulk
Regions Exported to: Worldwide
Percentage of Business in Exporting: 75

45001 Hermann Laue Spice Company
119 Franklin Street
Uxbridge, ON L9P 1J5
Canada
905-852-5100
Fax: 905-852-1113 www.helacanada.ca
Custom blended spices; technical assistance available
President: Walter Knecht
Director of Sales and Marketing: Eric Nummelin
Number Employees: 35
Square Footage: 228000
Parent Co: Laue, Herman, GmbH
Type of Packaging: Food Service
Brands Exported: Hela
Regions Exported to: Central America, Europe
Percentage of Business in Exporting: 7
Regions Imported from: South America, Europe, Asia
Percentage of Business in Importing: 10

45002 Hershey Co.
19 E Chocolate Dr.
Hershey, PA 17033
800-468-1714
www.thehersheycompany.com
Chocolate, confectionery, snack, refreshment and grocery products.
Chairman/President/CEO: Michele Buck
Senior VP/CFO: Steve Voskuil
Senior VP/General Counsel: Damien Atkins
Year Founded: 1894
Estimated Sales: $7.8 Billion
Number Employees: 15,360
Number of Brands: 31
Type of Packaging: Consumer, Food Service, Private Label

45003 Herz Meat Company
PO Box 353
Ramsey, NJ 07446-0353 201-236-0769
Fax: 201-236-1269
Importer and exporter of canned ham and pork products, fish, fruit and vegetables
President: Steen Elgaard
CEO: Karsten Bruun
Number Employees: 5-9
Parent Co: Coastline Commodities Corporation
Brands Exported: Herz; Prima; Danish Pride; Prima; Nanda
Regions Exported to: Europe, Canada
Percentage of Business in Exporting: 10
Brands Imported: Herz; Prima; Danish Pride; Prima; Nanda
Regions Imported from: South America, Europe, Asia, Middle East, Africa
Percentage of Business in Importing: 90

45004 Hess Machine Intl
1040 S State St
Ephrata, PA 17522-2355 717-733-0005
Fax: 717-733-2255 800-735-4377
ozone@hessmachine.com www.hessmachine.com
Manufacturer and exporter of water treatment equipment including ozone analyzers, ozone generators and filteration equipment.
President: Richard Hess
Marketing Director: Lynn Martin
Manager: Terry Good
terry@ozonesolutions.com
Plant Manager: Calburn McElhheauey
Estimated Sales: Less Than $500,000
Number Employees: 1-4
Regions Exported to: Central America, South America, Europe, Middle East
Percentage of Business in Exporting: 30

45005 Heterochemical Corp
111 E Hawthorne Ave
Valley Stream, NY 11580-6319 516-561-8225
Fax: 516-561-8413
Vitamin K
President: Lynne Galler
VP: Raymond Berruti
Estimated Sales: $990,000
Number Employees: 10-19
Square Footage: 80000
Regions Exported to: Central America, South America, Asia

45006 Hevi-Haul International LTD
N90w14555 Commerce Dr
Menomonee Falls, WI 53051-2338 262-502-0333
Fax: 262-502-0260 800-558-0577
www.langelift.com
Manufacturer and exporter of rollers and material handling equipment
President: Daniel Knaebe
sales@hevihaul.com
VP: S Knaebe
Sales/Marketing Executive: M Knaebe
Purchasing Agent: M Knaebe
Estimated Sales: $ 1-2.5 Million
Number Employees: 5-9
Regions Exported to: Worldwide

45007 Hewitt Soap Company
654 Residenz Pkwy # H
Dayton, OH 45429-6290 937-293-2697
Fax: 937-258-3123 800-543-2245
contact@hewittsoap.com www.hewittsoap.com
Manufacturer and exporter of bar soap
Vice President of Marketing: Deb McDonough
Estimated Sales: $33.9 Million
Number Employees: 1-4
Square Footage: 400000
Parent Co: ASR
Regions Exported to: Europe, Asia
Percentage of Business in Exporting: 5

45008 Hi Roller Enclosed Belt Conveyors
5100 W 12th St
Sioux Falls, SD 57107-0551 605-332-3200
Fax: 605-332-1107 800-328-1785
sales@hiroller.com www.hiroller.com
Manufacturer and exporter of enclosed belt conveyors and related accessories
Owner: Philip Clark
Controller: Sally Dieltz
Sales Manager: Mike Spillum
General Manager: John Nelson
General Manager: Steve Tweet
Estimated Sales: $ 10 - 20 Million
Number Employees: 20-49
Square Footage: 120000
Parent Co: Hansen Manufacturing Corporation
Brands Exported: Hi Roller
Regions Exported to: Worldwide
Percentage of Business in Exporting: 10

45009 Hi-Country Foods Corporation
P.O.Box 338
Selah, WA 98942 509-697-7292
Fax: 509-697-3498
Fruit juice concentrates, bottled water, teas and new age beverages
President/Owner: Otis Harlan
CFO: Richard Johnson
CEO: Pat Kelly
Quality Control: Judy Groves
VP/Operations/Marketing: Patrick Kelly
Estimated Sales: $10-20 Million
Number Employees: 50-99
Square Footage: 150000
Type of Packaging: Food Service, Private Label, Bulk
Regions Exported to: Central America, Pacific Rim
Percentage of Business in Exporting: 5

45010 Hialeah Products Co
2207 Hayes St
Hollywood, FL 33020-3437 954-923-3379
Fax: 954-923-4010 800-923-3379
richnuts@aol.com
Nuts, dried fruits, candy and snacks
Owner: Richard Lesser
richard@newurbanfarms.com
CEO: Kathy Lesser
Research & Development: Noah Lesser
Estimated Sales: $10-25 Million
Number Employees: 10-19
Number of Brands: 2
Number of Products: 200+
Square Footage: 120000
Type of Packaging: Consumer, Food Service, Private Label, Bulk
Brands Exported: Hollywood Nut Co.; Oh Nuts!
Regions Exported to: Central America, South America, Europe, Asia
Percentage of Business in Exporting: 20

45011 Hickory Harvest Foods
90 Logan Pkwy
Akron, OH 44319-1177 330-644-6266
Fax: 330-644-2501 800-448-6887
www.hickoryharvest.com
Snack foods
President: Joe Swiatkowski
joe@hickoryharvest.com
VP, Sales: Mike Swiatkowski
Plant Manager: Nicholas Hamilton
Number Employees: 20-49
Type of Packaging: Consumer, Food Service, Private Label, Bulk

45012 Hickory Industries
4900 W Side Ave
North Bergen, NJ 00047 201-223-4382
Fax: 201-223-0950 800-732-9153
www.hickorybbq.com
Manufacturer and exporter of cooking equipment including grills, warmers, ovens and rotisseries; also, barbecue machinery and accessories
President: Steven Maroti
VP Sales/Marketing: Joe Slusz
Contact: Beth Beyer
beth.beyer@hickorybbq.com
Estimated Sales: $ 20 - 50 Million
Number Employees: 100-249
Square Footage: 50000
Brands Exported: Hickory; Old Hickory
Regions Exported to: Worldwide
Percentage of Business in Exporting: 8

45013 Hidden Villa Ranch
310 N Harbor Blvd
Suite 205
Fullerton, CA 92832
800-326-3220
info@hiddenvilla.com www.hiddenvilla.com
Cheese and cheese products, liquid eggs.
President: Tim Luberski
tluberski@hiddenvilla.com
EVP: Greg Schneider
EVP: Michael Sencer
LA Division General Manager: Richard Schmidt
Year Founded: 1945
Estimated Sales: $500 Million

Importers & Exporters / A-Z

45014 Hiestand USA
PO Box 776
Colleyville, TX 76034-0776   817-354-6853
Fax: 817-354-6183 thecutters@msn.com
www.hiestand.ch

45015 High Liner Foods Inc.
100 Battery Point
PO Box 910
Lunenburg, NS B0J 2C0
Canada   902-634-8811
Fax: 902-634-6228 info@highlinerfoods.com
www.highlinerfoods.com
Prepared, value-added frozen seafood.
Chairman: Henry Demone
President/CEO: Rod Hepponstall
Executive VP/CFO: Paul Jewer
Executive VP/General Counsel: Tim Rorabeck
VP, Quality Assurance/Food Safety: Meggan Hodgson
Senior VP, Marketing/Innovation: Craig Murray
Senior VP, North American Sales: Chris Mulder
Year Founded: 1926
Estimated Sales: $943 Million
Number Employees: 1,652
Number of Brands: 10
Type of Packaging: Consumer, Food Service, Private Label, Bulk
Other Locations:
   High Liner Foods
   Secaucus, NJHigh Liner Foods
Regions Exported to: Europe, USA
Regions Imported from: South America, Europe, Asia

45016 High-Purity Standards
7221 Investment Drive
North Charleston, SC 29418   843-767-7900
Fax: 843-767-7906 866-767-4771
www.highpuritystandards.com
Manufactures single and multielement standards of extremely high purity for the calibration of analytical instruments such as the AAS, ICP, ICP-MS and IC
President: Theodore Rains
CEO: Connie Hayes
Contact: Stephanie Audette
stephanie@hps.net
Estimated Sales: $1,904,757
Number Employees: 20-49
Square Footage: 40000
Regions Exported to: Worldwide
Percentage of Business in Exporting: 5

45017 Highland Fisheries
1E Fareham Park Road
Glace Bay, NS B1A 6C9
Canada   902-849-6016
Fax: 902-849-7794 fish.n.chips@btinternet.com
Fresh and frozen finfish
President: Josh Wallenham
Plant Manager: Greg Mitchelitis
Number Employees: 100-249
Type of Packaging: Bulk
Regions Exported to: USA
Percentage of Business in Exporting: 80

45018 Highlight Industries
2694 Prairie St SW
Wyoming, MI 49519-2461   616-531-2464
Fax: 616-531-0506 800-531-2465
info@highlightindustries.com
www.highlightindustries.com
Manufacturer and exporter of stretch wrapping machinery, case sealing, case strapping, and shrink wrap machinery
Owner: Kurt Riemenschneide
Estimated Sales: $10-20 Million
Number Employees: 50-99
Square Footage: 120000
Regions Exported to: Central America, South America, Europe, Asia, Middle East
Percentage of Business in Exporting: 9

45019 Highwood Distillers
PO Box 5693
High River, AB T1V 1M7
Canada   403-652-3202
Fax: 403-652-4227 hrplant@telus.net
Whiskey, vodka, rum, tequila, liquers and pre-mixers
President/Sales: Barry Wilde
Chairman/CEO: W Miller
Number Employees: 20-49
Square Footage: 120000

45020 Hilden America
1044 Commerce Ln
South Boston, VA 24592   434-572-3965
Fax: 434-572-4781 800-431-2514
President: Russell Basch
Contact: Greg Bonemeyer
gregb@gtlinens.com
Estimated Sales: $ 5 - 10 Million
Number Employees: 20-49

45021 Hilden Halifax
1044 Commerce Lane
P.O.Box 1098
South Boston, VA 24592-1098   434-572-3965
Fax: 434-572-4781 800-431-2514
www.hildenamerica.com
Manufacturer, importer and exporter of table linens and kitchen textiles
President: Russell Basch
Vice President of Sales: Tom Hall
Sales: Sharlene Gulley
Estimated Sales: $2.5-5 Million
Number Employees: 20-49
Square Footage: 160000
Parent Co: Hilden Manufacturing Company
Brands Exported: Hilden
Regions Exported to: Worldwide
Percentage of Business in Exporting: 10
Regions Imported from: Europe
Percentage of Business in Importing: 80

45022 Hill 'N' Dale Meat
21229 Valley Forge Circle
King of Prussia, PA 19406-1131   610-269-3420
decovney@aol.com
Importer of meat
Owner/President: Sidney DeCovny
Estimated Sales: $1-2.5 Million
Number Employees: 1-4
Square Footage: 40000
Regions Imported from: Central America, New Zealand, Canada

45023 Hill Manufacturing Co Inc
1500 Jonesboro Rd SE
Atlanta, GA 30315-4085   404-522-8364
Fax: 404-522-9694 www.hillmfg.com
Manufacturer, importer and exporter of USDA cleaning products including hand cleaners, liquid washing and industrial cleaning compounds, germicide disinfectants and floor polish
President: Stewart Hillman
VP: Jack Hillman
Estimated Sales: $ 20-50 Million
Number Employees: 100-249
Square Footage: 110000
Type of Packaging: Bulk
Regions Exported to: Central America, South America
Percentage of Business in Importing: 5

45024 Hillside Candy Co
35 Hillside Ave
Hillside, NJ 07205-1833   973-926-2300
Fax: 973-926-4440 800-524-1304
info@hillsidecandy.com www.hillsidecandy.com
Sugarfree candy
President: Ted Cohen
ted@hillsidecandy.com
Marketing/Export Sales: Sandy Gencarelli
Estimated Sales: $ 5 - 10 Million
Number Employees: 10-19
Type of Packaging: Consumer, Food Service, Private Label, Bulk
Brands Exported: Go Lightly Sugar Free Candy
Regions Exported to: Central America, South America, Europe, Asia, Middle East
Percentage of Business in Exporting: 10
Regions Imported from: Europe

45025 Hillside Metal Ware Company
1060 Commerce Ave
Union, NJ 07083-5026   908-964-3080
Fax: 908-964-3082
Manufacturer and exporter of aluminum cookware and bakeware including molds, black steel pizza, springform and cake pans
Estimated Sales: $ 2 Million
Number Employees: 20-49
Square Footage: 120000
Brands Exported: Hillware
Regions Exported to: Central America, South America, Canada

45026 Hillyard Inc
302 N 4th St
P.O. Box 909
St Joseph, MO 64501-1720   816-233-1321
Fax: 816-383-8414 800-365-1555
www.hillyard.com
Manufacturer and exporter of floor seals, finishes, waxes, polishes and cleaners
President: Jim Corolus
jcorolus@hillyard.com
Chief Financial Officer: Neil Ambrose
Executive Vice President: Scott Hillyard
Vice President, R&D: Stuart Hughes
Vice President, Sales: David Schauer
Operations Manager: Jon Gottlieb
Product Manager: Blake Roth
Purchasing Manager: Tom Armstrong
Estimated Sales: $ 66 Million
Number Employees: 500-999
Square Footage: 325600
Regions Exported to: Worldwide
Percentage of Business in Exporting: 5

45027 Hilmar Cheese Company
8901 N Lander Ave
P.O. Box 910
Hilmar, CA 95324   209-667-6076
800-577-5772
info@hilmarcheese.com www.hilmarcheese.com
Cheese.
President & CEO: David Ahlem
Chief Financial Officer: Jason Price
VP, Sales & Marketing: Phil Robnett
Operations Manager: Ted Dykzeul
Year Founded: 1984
Estimated Sales: $100-500 Million
Number Employees: 500-999
Type of Packaging: Consumer, Food Service, Private Label
Regions Exported to: Worldwide

45028 (HQ)Hilmar Ingredients
8901 N Lander Ave
PO Box 910
Hilmar, CA 95324   209-667-6076
Fax: 209-656-2557 888-300-4465
info@hilmaringredients.com
www.hilmaringredients.com
Functional whey proteins, high purity lactose and nutritious milk powders
President: Art De Rooy
CEO: John Jeter
CFO: Jay Hicks
Director, New Business & Applications: Grace Harris
Milk Powders, Sales Manager: Emil Skaria
Contact: Mark Petersen
mpetersen@hilmaringredients.com
Number Employees: 600
Other Locations:
   Manufacturing Site & Visitor Center
   Hilmar, CA
   Turlock Manufacturing Site
   Turlock, CA
   Texas Manufacturing Site
   Dalhart, TXManufacturing Site & Visitor CenterTurlock

45029 Hilo Fish Company
55 Holomua St
Hilo, HI 96720-5142   808-961-0877
Fax: 808-935-1603 info@hilofish.com
www.hilofish.com
Fresh billfish, bottomfish, tuna, open ocean fish; Frozen tuna, grouper, hamachi, snapper, and other seafood
CEO: Charlie Umamoto
President & COO: Kerry Umamoto
General Manager: Jamiesen Batangan
Marketing: Helene Rousselle
National Sales Manager: Sabrina Vaughn
Operations Manager: Keith Hayashi
Estimated Sales: $ 20 - 50 Million
Number Employees: 20-49

45030 Himalayan Heritage
N5821 Fairway Dr
Fredonia, WI 53021-9742   608-274-9640
Fax: 262-692-6387 888-414-9500
web@aliveandhealthy.com

Herbal dietary supplements
Co-Owner: Blair Lewis
Co-Owner: Karen Lewis
Estimated Sales: $ 1 - 3 Million
Number Employees: 10-19
Type of Packaging: Consumer, Food Service, Private Label, Bulk
Brands Exported: Attention Span; Joyful Mind; Rejuv-Powder; Immuno Force; Strength & Courage; Smooth Changes for Women; Colo Scold; Cough Scoff
Regions Exported to: Worldwide
Regions Imported from: India

45031 (HQ)Hinchcliff Products Company
13477 Prospect Road
Strongsville, OH 44149 440-238-5200
Fax: 440-238-5202 sales@hinchcliffproducts.com
www.hinchcliffproducts.com
Manufacturer and exporter of wooden pallets, skids, boxes, crates and containers
President: Jay D Phillips
VP of Sales: Don Phillips
Contact: Donald Phillips
sales@hinchcliffproducts.com
Purchasing Manager: Scott Phillips
Estimated Sales: $500,000-$1 Million
Number Employees: 1-4
Number of Products: 3
Square Footage: 200000
Regions Exported to: Canada

45032 Hinckley Springs Bottled Water
800-201-6218
www.hinckleysprings.com
Bottled water
President: Dave Muscato
CEO: Tom Harrington
CFO: Jerry Hoyle
General Manager: Mike Garrity
Estimated Sales: $500,000-$1 Million
Number Employees: 50-99
Square Footage: 6000
Parent Co: DS Services of America
Type of Packaging: Consumer, Food Service, Bulk
Regions Exported to: Central America, Canada
Percentage of Business in Exporting: 2

45033 Hinds-Bock Corp
2122 222nd St SE
Bothell, WA 98021-4430 425-885-1183
Fax: 425-885-1492 garyh@hinds-bock.com
www.hinds-bock.com
Manufacturer and exporter of standard and custom piston filling machines, depositors and transfer pumps for liquids and viscous products with delicate particulates
President: Gary Hinds
CFO: John Davis
VP Sales/Marketing: Lance Aasness
Estimated Sales: $ 5 - 10 Million
Number Employees: 20-49
Square Footage: 96000
Regions Exported to: Worldwide
Percentage of Business in Exporting: 5

45034 Hines Nut Co
990 S Saint Paul St
Dallas, TX 75201-6120 214-939-0253
Fax: 214-761-0720 800-561-6374
customerservice@hinesnutcompany.com
Wholesaler/distributor of nuts and dried fruits
President: Chris Hines
Director, Food Safety: Deborah Hines
Marketing: Cullen Hines
National Sales: Peter Ferris
Operations Support: Rod Gutierrez
Estimated Sales: $10-20 Million
Number Employees: 100-249
Type of Packaging: Consumer, Food Service, Private Label, Bulk

45035 (HQ)Hiram Walker & Sons
2072 Riverside Drive E
Windsor, ON N8Y 1A7
Canada 519-254-5171
Fax: 519-971-5732 www.hiramwalker.com
Processor and exporter of blended whiskey, gin, scotch, vodka, rum, liqueurs, etc schnapps flavors include...peah,peppermint,blackberry,pumpkin spice,melon,triple sec blend, there are 43 alltogether.
Chairman/CEO: Paul Duffy
CFO: Thibault Cuny
SVP/Operations: Dan Denisoff
General Counsel: Thomas Lalla
SVP/Spirit Sales: Marty Crane
Marketing Director: Matt Aeppli
Estimated Sales: $199.43million
Number Employees: 500
Parent Co: Pernod Ricard
Type of Packaging: Consumer, Food Service
Other Locations:
   Manufacturing Facility
   Fort Smith, ARManufacturing Facility
Regions Exported to: Worldwide

45036 Hirzel Canning Co & Farms
20790 Bradner Rd
Luckey, OH 43443 419-419-7525
www.hirzelfarms.com
Manufacturer and exporter of canned tomatoes and tomato products, sauerkraut, sauces, salsa, tomato juice, tomato soup and more.
President & CEO: Stephen Hirzel
Office Manager: Lynn Hirzel
Manager: William Hirzel
Director, Manufacturing: Karl Hirzel
Crop Production: Lou Kozma, Jr.
Year Founded: 1923
Estimated Sales: $20-50 Million
Number Employees: 50-99
Number of Brands: 4
Number of Products: 30
Square Footage: 500000
Type of Packaging: Consumer, Food Service, Private Label, Bulk
Regions Exported to: Asia
Percentage of Business in Exporting: 1

45037 Hitec Food Equipment
818 Lively Blvd
Wood Dale, IL 60191-1202 630-521-9460
Fax: 630-521-9466 information@hitec-usa.com
www.hitec-usa.com
Food processing machines for the ham and sausage industry.
Owner: Charles Chacon
cchacon@hitec-usa.com
Number Employees: 5-9
Regions Exported to: Europe, Asia, North America

45038 Hobe Laboratories Inc
6479 S Ash Ave
Tempe, AZ 85283-3657 480-413-1950
Fax: 480-413-2005 800-528-4482
hobelabs@aol.com www.hobelabs.com
Processor and exporter of weight loss and herbal teas
President: Bill Robertson
brobertson@hobelabs.com
Marketing Director: Brenda Martin
Operations Manager: Peter Samuell
Estimated Sales: $1.4 Million
Number Employees: 10-19
Square Footage: 27940
Type of Packaging: Consumer, Private Label
Brands Exported: Slim Tea
Regions Exported to: South America, Europe, Asia, Middle East, Canada
Percentage of Business in Exporting: 10

45039 Hodell International
1750 N University Dr
Coral Springs, FL 33071-8903 954-752-0010
Fax: 954-752-0080 800-441-4014
nosko@aol.com
Wholesaler/distributor and importer of produce cases, freezers, chillers, coolers and dispensers for milk and juice; exporter of refrigeration equipment
Partner: Howard Hoskowicz
Partner: Dell Dahl
Number Employees: 1-4
Square Footage: 80000
Brands Exported: AHT; ISA; Hodell
Regions Exported to: Central America, South America, Canada, Caribbean, Mexico
Percentage of Business in Exporting: 20
Brands Imported: AHT, ISA
Regions Imported from: Europe, Asia, Canada, Latin America

45040 Hoffer Flow Controls Inc
107 Kitty Hawk Ln
P.O.Box 2145
Elizabeth City, NC 27909-6756 252-331-1997
Fax: 252-331-2886 800-628-4584
info@hofferflow.com www.hofferflow.com
Manufacturer and exporter of sanitary turbine flowmeters for batch controlling, flow rate indication and totalization.
President: Bob Carrell
bcarrell@hofferflow.com
CEO: Ken Hoffer
CEO: Sandra Kelly
Quality Control: Wendy Brabble
Marketing Manager: Janna Critcher
Sales: Linda Markham
Production Manager: Deborah Blakeney
Purchasing: Melissa Stallings
Estimated Sales: $5-10 Million
Number Employees: 50-99
Square Footage: 80000
Regions Exported to: Central America, South America, Europe, Asia, Middle East
Percentage of Business in Exporting: 45

45041 Hoffman & Levy Inc Tasseldepot
3251 SW 13th Dr # 3
Deerfield Beach, FL 33442-8166 954-698-0001
Fax: 954-698-0009 info@tasseldepot.com
www.tasseldepot.com
Manufacturer and exporter of napkin rings and decorative items including tassles and chair tie-backs
President: Roger Leavy
info@tasseldepot.com
Marketing/Design: April Leavy
Estimated Sales: $1-2.5 Million
Number Employees: 50-99
Square Footage: 46000
Regions Exported to: Worldwide
Percentage of Business in Exporting: 10

45042 Hoffmaster Group Inc
2920 N Main St
Oshkosh, WI 54901-1221
Fax: 920-235-1642 800-327-9774
marketing@hoffmaster.com www.hoffmaster.com
Manufacturer and exporter of strip lace, place mats, baking cups, tray covers and doilies including paper lace, linen, glassine, grease-proof and foil
CEO: Rory Leyden
rory.leyden@creativeconverting.com
Customer Service Manager: Lori Hart-Noyes
General Manager: Wayne Grant
Number Employees: 500-999
Square Footage: 50000
Type of Packaging: Consumer, Private Label, Bulk
Regions Exported to: Central America, South America, Asia
Percentage of Business in Exporting: 20

45043 Hohn Manufacturing Company
200 Sun Valley Cir
Fenton, MO 63026 636-349-1400
Fax: 636-349-1440 800-878-1440
hohnmfginc@toast.net
Manufacturer and exporter of furniture polishes, cleaning compounds, soaps, detergents, tablets, etc
President: Larry Harrington
Estimated Sales: $1-4 Million
Number Employees: 5-9
Square Footage: 72000
Type of Packaging: Private Label

45044 Holistic Horizons/Halcyon Pacific Corporation
8154 Belvedere Ave
Sacramento, CA 95826-4724 916-731-4299
Fax: 916-731-4295 800-852-4261
www.holistichorizons.com
Wholesaler/distributor and exporter of herbal supplements including intestinal cleansing formula, intestinal bulking agent and lactobacteria food
President: Caroline Gray
Vice President: Ernest Gray
Contact: Jeffery Lu
service@holistichorizons.com
Office Manager: Ejffrey Lu
Estimated Sales: $500,000-$1 Million
Number Employees: 1-4
Square Footage: 16000
Brands Exported: Holistic Horizons
Regions Exported to: Europe, Asia, Canada
Percentage of Business in Exporting: 30

Importers & Exporters / A-Z

45045 Holistic Products Corporation
10 W Forest Avenue
Englewood, NJ 07631-4020 201-569-1188
Fax: 201-569-3224 800-221-0308
Processor, wholesaler/distributor and importer of health food products including propolis lozenges
President: Arnold Gans
a.gans@mdnu.com
VP Sales: Myra Gans
Number Employees: 38
Square Footage: 16000
Parent Co: MNI Group
Regions Imported from: Europe
Percentage of Business in Importing: 10

45046 Holland American Food
2755 28th St SW
Suite 2
Wyoming, MI 49519-2100 616-531-2012
Fax: 616-531-3511 888-531-5782
www.hollandamericanfood.com
Dutch cheese, windmill cookies, syrup wafers, spices and condiments, breakfast cakes, licorice, soups, vegetables, peppermints, dutch rusk, jams, spreads and chocolate sprinkles
Owner: Elisha Breuker
elishabreuker@hollandamericanfood.com
Estimated Sales: $2.2 Million
Number Employees: 5-9

45047 Holland Beef International Corporation
1084 Queen Anne Rd
Teaneck, NJ 07666 201-833-8100
Fax: 201-833-1920 usfoodproducts.com
Broker, wholesaler and exporter of beef, lamb, veal, dairy products, frozenfruits and vegetables and specialities
President: Edward Holland
CFO: Chona Canillas
Vice President: Philip White
Estimated Sales: $20-50 Million
Number Employees: 20-49
Square Footage: 20000
Type of Packaging: Food Service
Brands Exported: World Wide
Regions Exported to: Central America, South America, Europe, Asia, Middle East
Percentage of Business in Exporting: 50
Regions Imported from: Central America, South America, Europe, Asia, Middle East
Percentage of Business in Importing: 35

45048 Holland Co Inc
153 Howland Ave
Adams, MA 01220-1199 413-743-1292
Fax: 413-743-1298 800-639-9602
info@hollandcompany.com
www.hollandcompany.com
Manufacturer and exporter of food grade additives including ammonium, potassium and iron-free aluminum sulfates
President: Daniel J Holland
Estimated Sales: $ 10-20,000,000
Number Employees: 20-49
Regions Exported to: South America, Latin America

45049 Holland-American International Specialties
10343 Artesia Blvd
Bellflower, CA 90706 562-925-6914
Fax: 562-925-4507 hais2000@aol.com
Wholesaler/distributor and importer of European gourmet foods
Manager: Maria Cervantes
Sales Director: Karen Spurgeon
Specialty Division Manager: Pauline Bridgeman
Estimated Sales: $10-20 Million
Number Employees: 1-4
Type of Packaging: Consumer
Regions Imported from: Europe
Percentage of Business in Importing: 60

45050 Hollingsworth Custom Wood Products
284 N Street
Sault Ste. Marie, ON P6A 7B8
Canada
705-759-1756
Fax: 705-759-0275
Manufacturer and exporter of butchers' blocks, cutting boards and wooden bakers' tops
Marketing Director: Paul Hollingsworth
Customer Service: Ruth Bradley
General Manager: Jim Webb
Estimated Sales: $ 1 - 5 Million
Number Employees: 15
Parent Co: Soo Mill Lumber
Regions Exported to: Worldwide
Percentage of Business in Exporting: 40

45051 Hollowick Inc
100 Fairgrounds Dr
Manlius, NY 13104-1699 315-682-2163
Fax: 315-682-6948 800-367-3015
info@hollowick.com
Manufacturer and exporter of liquid candle lamps, lamp fuel, wax candles, chafing fuel and silk flowers ceramic vases
President: Alan Menter
info@hollowick.com
CFO: Eugene Duffy
Marketing: Mike Cleveland
Sales: Mike Cleveland
Plant Manager: Tom Palmeter
Estimated Sales: $5-10 Million
Number Employees: 20-49
Brands Exported: Easy Heat (Lamps, Lamp Fuel)
Regions Exported to: Central America, South America, Europe, Asia, Middle East
Percentage of Business in Exporting: 5
Brands Imported: Easy Floral

45052 Hollymatic Corp
600 E Plainfield Rd
Countryside, IL 60525-6900 708-579-3700
Fax: 708-579-1057 hollyinfo@hollymatic.com
www.hollymatic.com
Manufacturer, exporter and importer of food processing equipment and supplies including tenderizers, grinders, mixers/grinders/ patty machines, meat saws, etc.
President: James Azzar
R&D: Hardev Somal
Marketing Manager: Rob Kovack
Manager: Jim Trejo
jtrejo@hollymatic.com
Estimated Sales: $ 5 - 10 Million
Number Employees: 20-49
Type of Packaging: Food Service
Brands Exported: Hollymatic
Regions Exported to: Central America, South America, Europe, Asia, Middle East, Latin America
Regions Imported from: Europe

45053 Hollywood Banners
539 Oak St
Copiague, NY 11726-3261 631-842-3000
Fax: 631-842-3148 800-691-5652
info@hollywoodbanners.com
www.hollywoodbanners.com
Manufacturer and exporter of indoor and outdoor banners including plastic and cloth
President: Daniel F Mahoney
dmaoney@hollywoodbanners.com
Sales Exec: Daniel F Mahoney
Production Manager: Hugo Canedo
Estimated Sales: $1-3 Million
Number Employees: 20-49
Square Footage: 100000
Regions Exported to: Europe, Canada, Latin America, Mexico
Percentage of Business in Exporting: 1

45054 Holman Boiler Works
1956 Singleton Blvd
Dallas, TX 75212 214-637-0020
Fax: 214-637-2539 800-331-1956
dal-sales@holmanboiler.com
Manufacturer and exporter of watertube and firetube boilers; also, burners
President: John Campollo
sales@holmanboiler.com
CEO: Richard Maxson
Quality Control: Greg Martinez
Manager Business Development: Gary Perskhini
Estimated Sales: $ 50 - 100 Million
Number Employees: 50-99
Parent Co: Copes-Vulcan
Regions Exported to: Central America, South America, Europe, Middle East
Percentage of Business in Exporting: 5

45055 Holmco Container Manufacturing, LTD
1501 TR 183
Baltic, OH 43804-9677 330-897-4503
Fax: 330-698-3200
Manufacturer and exporter of stainless steel milk containers.
Owner: Eli Troyer
Number Employees: 2
Square Footage: 38400
Type of Packaging: Food Service
Brands Exported: Stainless Steel Milk Cans, Type 304
Regions Exported to: Central America, South America, Canada
Percentage of Business in Exporting: 1

45056 Holstein Manufacturing
5368 110th St
Holstein, IA 51025-8131 712-368-4342
Fax: 712-368-2351 800-368-4342
hmi@pionet.net www.holsteinmfg.com
Barbecue equipment, portable grills and flatbed, livestock and concession trailers
Vice President: Darrin Schmidt
dlshmidt@ruralwaves.us
VP: Darrin Schmidt
Estimated Sales: $1-2.5 Million
Number Employees: 5-9

45057 Homarus Inc
12-20 36th Ave
Long Island City, NY 11106 917-832-0333
Fax: 347-808-9948 info@homarus.com
Seafood, primarily lobster
Co-Owner/President: Peter Heineman
CEO: Chris Harvey
VP Sales: Thomas Marshall
Type of Packaging: Consumer, Food Service
Brands Exported: Homarus; Riverbank
Regions Exported to: South America, Europe, Asia, Caribbean

45058 Home Decoration Accessories
N116w18500 Morse Dr
Germantown, WI 53022-2482 262-253-6550
Fax: 262-253-6544 homedecoration@email.com
www.hdaltd.com
Owner: Naren Shah
Number Employees: 1-4

45059 Home Plastics Inc
5250 NE 17th St
Des Moines, IA 50313-2192 515-265-2562
Fax: 515-265-8872 info@homeplastics.com
www.homeplastics.com
Manufacturer and exporter of polyethylene heat sealed bags, tubes and liners; also, plastic film and plain and printed slip-on sleeve labels, political signs
President and QC: Samuel Siegel
Manager: Bob Rees
brees@homeplastics.com
Estimated Sales: $ 20 - 50 Million
Number Employees: 100-249
Type of Packaging: Consumer, Food Service, Private Label, Bulk
Regions Exported to: Central America, South America, Europe

45060 Home Rubber Co
31 Wolverton St
Trenton, NJ 08611-2429 609-394-1176
Fax: 609-396-1985 800-257-9441
info@homerubber.com www.homerubber.com
Manufacturer and exporter of industrial rubber food and milk unloading hoses, belting, molded goods and sheet rubber
President: Rich Balka
VP: Stephen Kelley
Estimated Sales: $10-20 Million
Number Employees: 20-49
Regions Exported to: Central America, South America, Canada, Caribbean, Latin America, Mexico

45061 Home Run Inn Frozen Foods
1300 Internationale Pkwy
Woodridge, IL 60517-4928 630-783-9696
Fax: 630-783-0069 800-636-9696
gyarka@homerunn.com
www.homeruninnpizza.com
Frozen pizza

President: Joe Perrino
jperrino@homeruninn.com
Marketing Director: Gina Bolger
Operations: Dan Costello
Estimated Sales: $10-24.9 Million
Number Employees: 500-999
Type of Packaging: Consumer, Food Service, Private Label

45062 Home Style Foods Inc
5163 Edwin St
Hamtramck, MI 48212-3388   313-874-3250
            Fax: 313-874-1026
Fresh prepared salads
President: Mike Kadian
Estimated Sales: $10-20 Million
Number Employees: 20-49
Type of Packaging: Private Label, Bulk
Regions Exported to: Canada

45063 Homestead Mills
221 N River St
Cook, MN 55723-9503   218-666-5233
    Fax: 218-666-5236 800-652-5233
            www.homesteadmills.com
Grain, wild rice, cereals, flours and pancake mixes
Owner/President: Keith Aho
aho@homesteadmills.com
Owner/Vice President: Carol Aho
Plant Manager: Anita Reinke
Estimated Sales: $1 Million
Number Employees: 5-9
Number of Brands: 2
Number of Products: 27
Square Footage: 52000
Type of Packaging: Consumer, Food Service, Private Label, Bulk
Brands Exported: Homestead Mills; Northern Lites Pancakes
Regions Exported to: Europe

45064 Honee Bear Canning
72100 M 40
Lawton, MI 49065-8444   269-624-4611
    Fax: 269-624-6009 800-626-2327
hbsales@honeebear.com www.honeebear.com
Berries, cherries, plums, asparagus, blueberries; pie fillings
President: Robert Packer
CEO: Steve Packer
steve@honeebear.com
Sales Manager: Ronald Armstrong
Director: Toby Fields
Estimated Sales: $ 10 - 20 Million
Number Employees: 50-99
Square Footage: 450000
Type of Packaging: Consumer, Food Service
Regions Exported to: Europe, Asia, Canada
Percentage of Business in Exporting: 20
Regions Imported from: Mexico

45065 Honey Acres
N1557 Hwy 67
Neosho, WI 53059   920-474-4411
            info@honeyacres.com
            www.honeyacres.com
Honey and honey products, including honey chocolates, honey mustards, andhoney straws.
CEO: John Gabielian
Marketing Manager: Debra Champeau
Director of Inside Sales & Marketing: Tiarra Detert
Plant Manager: Eugene Brueggeman
eugene@honeyacres.com
Year Founded: 1852
Estimated Sales: $5-9.9 Million
Number Employees: 30
Number of Products: 50
Square Footage: 144000
Type of Packaging: Consumer, Food Service, Private Label, Bulk
Regions Exported to: Europe, Asia, Middle East
Percentage of Business in Exporting: 15

45066 (HQ)Honeyville Grain Inc
1080 N Main St
Suite 100
Brigham City, UT 84302   435-494-4200
    Fax: 435-734-9482 www.honeyville.com
Bakery mixes and ingredients

Founder: Lowell Sherratt
VP Finance: Robert Anderson
Executive VP: Trevor Christensen
Director Marketing/Sales: Don Mann
Sales Manager: Craig Dunford
Assistant Operations Manager: Garth Rollins
Estimated Sales: $10 - 20 Million
Number Employees: 10-19
Square Footage: 120000
Type of Packaging: Consumer, Food Service, Private Label, Bulk
Other Locations:
    California Distribution
    Rancho Cucamonga, CA
    Utah Tempsure & Wholesale
    Salt Lake City, UT
    Arizona Wholsale Distribution
    Tempe, AZ
    Honeyville Grain Mill
    Honeyville, UT
    Ohio Distribution Center
    West Chester, OHCalifornia DistributionSalt Lake City
Regions Exported to: Central America, South America, Latin America, Mexico

45067 (HQ)Honeywell International
World Headquarters
Charlotte, NC 07950
            877-841-2840
            www.honeywell.com
Fire alarm systems and controls, among other safety and productivity products.
Chairman/CEO: Darius Adamczyk
President, Safety & Productivity: John Waldron
Senior VP/Chief Financial Officer: Greg Lewis
Senior VP/General Counsel: Anne Madden
Senior VP, HR/Security & Communications: Mark James
Year Founded: 1906
Estimated Sales: $41.8 Billion
Number Employees: 114,000
Square Footage: 15803

45068 Honeywood Winery
1350 Hines St SE
Salem, OR 97302-2521   503-362-4111
    Fax: 503-362-4112 800-726-4101
            info@honeywoodwinery.com
            www.honeywoodwinery.com
Grape and fruit wines
President: Lesley Gallick
info@honeywoodwinery.com
VP: Marlene K Gallick
Estimated Sales: $1 Million+
Number Employees: 5-9
Number of Brands: 5
Number of Products: 45
Square Footage: 88000
Type of Packaging: Private Label
Regions Exported to: Asia

45069 Honiron Corp
400 Canal St
Jeanerette, LA 70544-4504   337-276-6314
    Fax: 337-276-3614 sales@honiron.com
            www.honiron.com
Manufacturer and exporter of sugar machinery
Owner: John Deere
COO: Dennis Banta
dbanta@honiron.com
Estimated Sales: $ 1 - 5 Million
Number Employees: 50-99
Type of Packaging: Bulk
Regions Exported to: Worldwide

45070 Honolulu Fish Company
824 Gulick Avenue
Honolulu, HI 96819-1998   808-833-1123
    Fax: 808-836-1045 sales@honolulufish.com
            www.honolulufish.com
Sashimi-grade fish
Founder, Chief Executive Officer: Wayne Samiere
Contact: William Grafton
william@honolulufish.com

45071 Hood River Distillers Inc
660 Riverside Dr
Hood River, OR 97031-1177   541-386-1588
    Fax: 541-386-2520 HRDsales@HRDspirits.com
            www.findmonarch.com
Spirits, including whisky, rum, gin, vodka, schnapps, Irish cream whiskey, scotch and liqueurs

President: Olivia Barker
oliviab@hrdspirits.com
CFO: Gary Goatcher
VP & General Manager: Lynda Webber
Director of Marketing: Tia Bledsoe
VP Sales: Erik Svenson
Materials/Special Projects Manager: Brad Whiting
Estimated Sales: $4.6 Million
Number Employees: 50-99
Square Footage: 212000
Regions Exported to: Asia, Middle East, Canada
Regions Imported from: Europe

45072 Hoover Company
7005 Cochran Rd.
Glenwillow, OH 44139   330-499-9499
    Fax: 330-497-5065 www.hoover.com
Extractors, vacuum cleaners and supplies including bags, belts, air freshener tablets and steamvac cleaning solutions.
Year Founded: 1908
Estimated Sales: $350-400 Million
Number Employees: 1000-4999
Square Footage: 527000
Parent Co: Techtronic Industries

45073 Hoover Materials Handling Group
2135 Highway 6 S
Houston, TX 77077-4319
            800-844-8683
Manufacturer and exporter of containers and tanks.
Year Founded: 1911
Estimated Sales: $103.2 Million
Parent Co: Hoover Group

45074 Hope Industrial Systems
1325 Northmeadow Pkwy # 100
Suite 100
Roswell, GA 30076-3896   678-762-9790
    Fax: 678-762-9789 877-762-9790
            sales@hopeindustrial.com
Flat panel touchscreens and monitors for the food processing and dairy industries.
Contact: Bo Bowling
bo.bowling@hopeindustrial.com
Number Employees: 5-9
Regions Exported to: Worldwide

45075 Hopes Country Fresh Cookies
221 King Manor Dr # A
King Of Prussia, PA 19406-2502   610-272-4673
    Fax: 610-277-4329 sand@hopescookies.com
            www.hopescookies.com
Owner: Bob Olsen
bolsen@hopescookies.com
Estimated Sales: $ 10 - 20 Million
Number Employees: 20-49

45076 Hoppmann Corporation
13129 Airpark Dr # 120
Elkwood, VA 22718-1761   540-825-2899
    Fax: 540-829-1724 800-368-3582
            sales@ShibuyaHoppmann.com
            www.shibuyahoppmann.com
Manufacturer and exporter of assembly packaging systems including feeders, pre-feeders, conveyors, turnkey systems, etc.; also, integration services available
President: Mark Flanagan
flanagan@hoppmann.com
CEO: Peter Hoppmann
Executive Vice President: Kazuhiro Miyamae
VP Finance: Maryanne Flusher
Product Manager: Chad Roberts
Sales Director: Dave Martin
Number Employees: 100-249
Regions Exported to: South America, Europe, Asia, Canada, Latin America, Mexico
Percentage of Business in Exporting: 15

45077 Horix Manufacturing Co
1384 Island Ave
Mc Kees Rocks, PA 15136-2593   412-771-1111
    Fax: 412-331-8599 info@horix.net
            www.horix.info
Manufacturer, importer and exporter of liquid filling, capping, labeling and rinsing machinery for cans and bottles

Importers & Exporters / A-Z

Importers & Exporters / A-Z

President: Linda Fzramowski
Plant Manager: Felgon Robert
Research & Development: Russell Myers
CEO: Linda M Szramowski
Sales Director: David Becki
Plant Manager: Robert Feltop
Purchasing Manager: Brad Barber
Estimated Sales: $ 5 - 10 Million
Number Employees: 20-49
Square Footage: 120000
Brands Exported: Horix; Ave
Regions Exported to: Central America, South America, Asia, Middle East, Latin America, Mexico, Caribbean
Percentage of Business in Exporting: 30
Brands Imported: Officine Ave s.p.a.
Regions Imported from: Europe
Percentage of Business in Importing: 40

45078 Horizon Poultry
92 Cartwright Avenue
Toronto, ON M6A 1V2
Canada   519-364-3200
    Fax: 519-364-4692 cphilipp@schneiderfoods.ca
    www.schneiderfoods.ca/
Chickens; eggs
Quality Assurance: Cynthia Philippe
Number Employees: 165
Parent Co: J.M. Schneider
Type of Packaging: Consumer, Food Service, Private Label, Bulk
Regions Imported from: USA

45079 Hormann Flexan Llc
20a Avenue C
Leetsdale, PA 15056-1305   412-749-0400
    Fax: 412-749-0410   800-365-3667
Manufacturer and exporter of industrial/commercial doors and loading dock equipment including delivery truck ramps.
President: Christoph Hormann
CEO: Charles A De La Porte
VP: Patrick Boyle
Marketing: Alic Permigiani
Contact: Peter Burnham
p.burnham@hormann-flexon.com
Plant Manager: Mark Permigiani
Purchasing: David Palmosina
Estimated Sales: $ 10 - 20 Million
Number Employees: 20-49
Square Footage: 180000
Parent Co: Hexon
Regions Exported to: Central America, South America, Europe, Asia, Middle East

45080 Hormel Foods Corp.
1 Hormel Pl.
Austin, MN 55912   507-437-5611
    www.hormelfoods.com
Meat and grocery products.
Chairman/President/CEO: Jim Snee
Executive VP/CFO: Jim Sheehan
Senior VP/General Counsel: Lori Marco
Senior VP, R&D: Kevin Myers
Vice President, Quality Management: Richard Carlson
Year Founded: 1891
Estimated Sales: $9 Billion
Number Employees: 20,000
Number of Brands: 52
Type of Packaging: Consumer, Food Service, Private Label
Other Locations:
   Manufacturing Facility
   Austin, MN
   Manufacturing Facility
   Algona, IA
   Manufacturing Facility
   Alma, KS
   Manufacturing Facility
   Atlanta, GA
   Manufacturing Facility
   Aurora, IL
   Manufacturing Facility
   Barron, WI
   Manufacturing FacilityAlgona

45081 Horner International
5304 Emerson Drive
Raleigh, NC 27609   919-787-3112
    Fax: 919-787-4272 sales@hornerintl.com
    www.hornerinternational.com
Natural extracts and flavors
Contact: Ladiner Blaylock
ladiner.blaylock@hornerintl.com

Parent Co: Horner International

45082 Hosch Properties
1002 International Dr
Oakdale, PA 15071-9226   724-695-3002
    Fax: 724-695-3603   800-695-3310
    hosch@hoschusa.com   www.hoschusa.com
Scrapers for conveyor belt cleaning.
Owner: Kevin Carpol
kevinc@hoschusa.com
Operations: Grace Barkhurst
Estimated Sales: $5-10 Million
Number Employees: 20-49

45083 Hose Master Inc
1233 E 222nd St
Euclid, OH 44117-1121   216-481-2020
    Fax: 216-481-7557 info@hosemaster.com
    www.hosemaster.com
Manufacturer and exporter of gas, steam and water connectors
CEO: Sam Foti
Quality Control: Mike Thompson
CEO: Sam J Foti
Estimated Sales: $ 20 - 50 Million
Number Employees: 250-499
Square Footage: 130000
Regions Exported to: Central America, South America

45084 Hosford & Wood Fresh Seafood Providers
2545 E 7th Street
Tucson, AZ 85716-4701   520-795-1920
    Fax: 520-795-1010
Seafood
President: Anita Wood
Secretary: Bruce Hosford

45085 Hoshizaki America Inc
618 Highway 74 S
Peachtree City, GA 30269-3016   770-487-2331
    Fax: 770-487-1325   800-438-6087
    marketing@hoshizaki.com
    www.hoshizakiamerica.com
Commercial ice machines and refrigeration equipment.
CEO: Youki Suzuki
Executive VP: Mark McClanahan
Quality Control: Carter Davis
Marketing Director: Carter Davis
Operations Manager: Jim Procuro
Production Manager: Jim Procuro
Plant Manager: Jim Procuro
Number Employees: 500-999
Parent Co: Hoshizaki Electric Company
Brands Exported: Hosizaki America
Regions Exported to: Central America, South America, Canada, Latin America, Mexico
Percentage of Business in Exporting: 5
Brands Imported: Hoshizaki Electric
Regions Imported from: Asia
Percentage of Business in Importing: 5

45086 Hosoda Brothers Inc
1444 Tennessee St
San Francisco, CA 94107-3421   415-648-7144
    Fax: 415-282-6336 www.hosodabros.com
Importer of Oriental food products including rice crackers, soy sauce, pickled vegetables, wholesaler/distributor of specialty foods
President: Lesley Hosoda
lesley@hosodabros.com
Vice President: Carolyn Hosada
Business Development: Jeff Tanabe
Office Manager: Jill & Lesley Hosoda
Estimated Sales: $10-20 Million
Number Employees: 20-49
Square Footage: 40000
Brands Imported: Oedo Bruno Products; Takari Brand Rice; Yamada Soy Sauce; Distributors Of Hawaiian Food Products.

45087 Hospitality Mints LLC
213 Candy Ln
P.O. Drawer 3140
Boone, NC 28607
    Fax: 828-264-6933   800-334-5181
    mints@hospitalitymints.com
    www.hospitalitymints.com
Mint candies
President/CEO: Patrick Viancourt
CFO/COO: Walter Kaudelka
VP of Marketing: Kathi Guy

Estimated Sales: $500,000-$1 Million
Number Employees: 10-19
Square Footage: 252000
Parent Co: Party Sweets
Type of Packaging: Consumer, Food Service, Private Label, Bulk
Regions Exported to: Central America, Asia, Canada, Caribbean, Mexico, Australia
Percentage of Business in Exporting: 2

45088 Hot Food Boxes
451 East County Line Road
Mooresville, IN 46158   317-831-7030
    Fax: 317-831-7036   800-733-8073
    schirico@theramp.net   www.secoselect.com
Manufacturer and exporter of insulated stainless steel and aluminum equipment for hot and cold foods; also, steam tables and heated bulk food carts for banquet service.
President: John Schirico
Vice President: Pat Darre
Estimated Sales: $2.5-5 Million
Number Employees: 20-49
Square Footage: 100000
Brands Exported: Hot Food Boxes

45089 Hot Springs Packing Co Inc
580 Mid America Blvd
Hot Springs, AR 71913-8412   501-767-2363
    Fax: 501-767-9715   800-535-0449
    hspc@hotspringspacking.com
    www.hotspringspacking.com
Specialty sausages, deli meats and hams
President/CEO: John Stubblefield
hspc@hotspringspacking.com
Estimated Sales: $4.3 Million
Number Employees: 20-49
Type of Packaging: Consumer, Food Service
Regions Exported to: South America
Percentage of Business in Exporting: 50

45090 Houdini Inc
4225 N Palm St
Fullerton, CA 92835-1045   714-525-0325
    Fax: 714-996-9605
    www.winecountrygiftbaskets.com
Gourmet food, wine and gift baskets
Owner: Tim Dean
tdean@houdiniinc.com
Estimated Sales: $ 500,000 - $ 1 Million
Number Employees: 10-19
Regions Exported to: Europe, Asia, Latin America
Percentage of Business in Exporting: 30
Regions Imported from: Europe, Asia, Australia, Latin America
Percentage of Business in Importing: 10

45091 House Foods America Corp
7351 Orangewood Ave
Garden Grove, CA 92841-1411   714-901-4350
    Fax: 714-901-4235   877-333-7077
    www.house-foods.com
Tofu and tofu products; importer of curry, spices, ramen noodles and tea.
President: Shigeru Natake
shigeru@house-foods.com
Marketing Manager: Masahiko Kudo
Sales & Foodservice: Hirofumi Fujimura
Production & Supply Chain Management: Hajime Inoue
Purchasing, Cost Reduction, Admin: Keiji Matsumoto
Estimated Sales: $11.2 Million
Number Employees: 100-249
Square Footage: 60000
Parent Co: House Foods Corporation
Other Locations:
   Somerset, NJ
   Garden Grove, CA
   NYGarden Grove
Brands Imported: House Brand
Regions Imported from: Asia
Percentage of Business in Importing: 25

45092 House of Flavors Inc
110 N William St
Ludington, MI 49431-2092   231-845-7369
    Fax: 616-845-7371   800-930-7740
    www.houseofflavors.com
Kosher ice cream and frozen novelties
Owner: Pat Calder
hfpat@houseofflavors.com
Number Employees: 1-4
Type of Packaging: Consumer, Food Service

Importers & Exporters / A-Z

45093 House of Raeford Farms Inc.
PO Box 699
Rose Hill, NC 28458 910-289-3191
www.houseofraeford.com
Chickens and turkeys.
Chairman: Marvin Johnson
Chief Executive Officer/President: Robert Johnson
President, Cooked Products Group: Donald Taber
Chief Financial Officer: Ken Qualls
Year Founded: 1925
Estimated Sales: $705 Million
Number Employees: 5,500
Number of Brands: 3
Square Footage: 400000
Type of Packaging: Food Service
Other Locations:
  Further Processing Plant/Distrib.
  Raeford, NC
  Chicken Processing Plant
  Arcadia, LA
  Columbia Farms Chicken Processing
  Columbia, SC
  Breaded Chicken & Turkey Products
  Hemingway, SC
  Columbia Farms Chicken Plant
  Greenville, SCFurther Processing
  Plant/Distrib.Arcadia
Brands Exported: Columbia Farms
Regions Exported to: Worldwide
Percentage of Business in Exporting: 1

45094 House of Spices
12740 Willets Point Blvd
Flushing, NY 11368-1506 718-507-4600
Fax: 718-507-4798
customerservice@hosindia.com
www.hosindia.com
Pickles, condiment pastes, chutney, snack foods, candy, ice cream and frozen foods; importer of Indian-Pakistani basmati rice, lentils, spices, oils and nuts; exporter of pickles, condiments and spices.
President: Candace Kuechler
ckuechler@rich.com
Estimated Sales: $5-10 Millio
Number Employees: 50-99
Number of Brands: 25
Number of Products: 2000
Square Footage: 1200000
Type of Packaging: Consumer, Food Service, Private Label, Bulk
Other Locations:
  Manufacturing Facility
  Stafford, TX
  Manufacturing Facility
  Elk Grove, IL
  Manufacturing Facility
  Forestville, MD
  Manufacturing Facility
  Hayward, CA
  Manufacturing Facility
  Orlando, FL
  Manufacturing Facility
  Norcross, GA
  Manufacturing FacilityElk Grove
Brands Exported: Laxmi; Janta; Shamiana
Regions Exported to: Central America, South America
Percentage of Business in Exporting: 5
Brands Imported: Nestle; 777 Brand; Savour't; Parle; Maaza; M.D.H.; Specialty Wheat Flour
Regions Imported from: Central America, South America, Europe, Asia, Middle East, Australia
Percentage of Business in Importing: 80

45095 Houston Label
909 Shaver St
Pasadena, TX 77506-4411 713-477-6995
Fax: 713-477-0023 800-477-6995
sales@houstonlabel.com www.houstonlabel.com
Manufacturer and exporter of labels including pressure sensitive, printed, unprinted, color processed, UPC and inventory automatic labeling equipment
Owner: Richard Ryholt
Executive VP: Hans Ryholt
Outside Sales Manager: Willie Hager
rryholt@houstonlabel.com
Estimated Sales: $5-10 Million
Number Employees: 50-99
Square Footage: 92000
Type of Packaging: Consumer, Food Service, Private Label, Bulk
Other Locations:
  Houston Tape & Label Co.
  Pasadena, TXHouston Tape & Label Co.
Regions Exported to: Central America, South America, Middle East
Percentage of Business in Exporting: 15

45096 Houston Tea & Beverage
7703 Cannon Street
Houston, TX 77055 832-348-7780
Fax: 832-348-7760 800-585-4549
Teas
President: Linda Williams
Contact: Al Hernandez
al@houstonteaandbeverage.com
Estimated Sales: Less than $500,000
Number Employees: 1-4
Square Footage: 8500
Type of Packaging: Private Label
Regions Imported from: Asia, Middle East, Latin America
Percentage of Business in Importing: 100

45097 Houston Wire Works, Inc.
1007 Kentucky
South Houston, TX 77587 713-946-2920
Fax: 713-946-3579 800-468-9477
info@houstonwire.com www.houstonwire.com
Manufacturer and exporter of water bottle display, refrigerator, wine and wire racks; also, steel platform ladders and hand carts; exporter of storage racks
President: Ken Legler
CEO: Barbara Leagler
VP Sales/Marketing: Steve Foster
Sales Director: Melanie Houser
Contact: Barbara Legler
barbaralegler@att.net
Sales Manager: Bill Watkins
Purchasing Manager: Raquel Garza
Estimated Sales: $ 3 - 5 Million
Number Employees: 45
Square Footage: 280000
Type of Packaging: Food Service
Regions Exported to: Worldwide
Percentage of Business in Exporting: 6

45098 Hovair Systems Inc
6912 S 220th St
Kent, WA 98032-1906 253-872-0405
Fax: 253-872-0406 800-237-4518
info@hovair.com www.hovair.com
Manufacturer and exporter of air film material handling equipment. Manufactures air bearing systems and air film products for a wide variety of applications, with particular emphasis on the movement of heavy loads and equipment withintoday's industry.
Manager: Betty Roberts
robertsb@hovair.com
Marketing: Betty Roberts
Operations: Betty Roberts
Plant Manager: Jeff Grow
Estimated Sales: $ 3 - 5 Million
Number Employees: 10-19
Regions Exported to: Europe, Asia

45099 Howard Imprinting Machine Company
4519 Terrace Manor Drive
PO Box 15027
Houston, TX 77041 713-869-4337
Fax: 813-881-1554 800-334-6943
howard.imprinting@gte.net
www.howardimprinting.com
Manufacturer and exporter of hot stamp imprinting machinery
President: James Wrobbel
Estimated Sales: $ 3 - 5 Million
Number Employees: 5-9

45100 Howard Turner & Son
1659 Route 1 Highway 7
Marie Joseph, NS B0J 2G0
Canada 902-347-2616
Fax: 902-347-2714
Fresh and frozen lobster and groundfish
President: Randy Turner
Type of Packaging: Bulk
Regions Exported to: Worldwide
Percentage of Business in Exporting: 75

45101 (HQ)Howard-Mccray
831 E Cayuga St
Philadelphia, PA 19124-3815 215-464-6800
Fax: 215-969-4890 800-344-8222
www.howardmccray.com
Manufacturer and exporter of commercial refrigerators and freezers, open merchandisers; deli, fish, poultry and red meat service cases; produce cases; bakery display, proofers, retarders; glass door; step in and reach in units. Alsodistribute beer frosters, bottle coolers, beer dispensers, under counter coolers, and prep tables.
President: Annette Ramsey
aramsey@howardmccray.com
CFO: Marie Ginon
Marketing Director: Diane Scott
Plant Manager: Brian Tyndall
Estimated Sales: $ 1 - 10 Million
Number Employees: 100-249
Number of Products: 60
Square Footage: 460000
Parent Co: HMC Enterprises,LLC
Brands Exported: Howard, McCray, Ovations
Regions Exported to: Central America, Middle East, Worldwide, Carribean
Percentage of Business in Exporting: 1

45102 Howe Corp
1650 N Elston Ave
Chicago, IL 60642-1585 773-235-0200
Fax: 773-235-1530 webinfo@howecorp.com
www.howecorp.com
Specialty refrigeration equipment including flake ice machines, bin transport systems, packaged refrigeration systems, compressors and pressure vessels
President: Mary C Howe
craig@cmvsharperfinish.com
CFO: M Aguilar
Senior VP: Kevin McCool
Research & Development: A Ahuja
Marketing Director: K McCool
VP Sales: A Ortman
Director Sales/Marketing: Chuck Janovsky
IT: Andrew Ortman
Production Manager: Steve Bokor
Plant Manager: John Myrda
Purchasing Manager: Bob Dondzik
Estimated Sales: $20-50 Million
Number Employees: 20-49
Square Footage: 65000
Brands Exported: Howe
Regions Exported to: Worldwide
Percentage of Business in Exporting: 20
Regions Imported from: Asia
Percentage of Business in Importing: 5

45103 Howell Associates
55 Acorn Ponds Dr
Roslyn, NY 11576-2817 516-829-2330
Fax: 516-829-2334 howell18@aol.com
Import and export broker of confectionary and dairy/deli products, frozen foods, groceries, industrial ingredients, meats, etc. Servicing food services & canadian products
President: Howard Duchin
howell18@aol.com
VP: William Jaffee
Public Relations: Irene Lumia
Estimated Sales: $12 Million
Number Employees: 1-4
Type of Packaging: Consumer, Food Service, Private Label
Brands Imported: Lexus Foods, Lavo, Plat Du Chef
Regions Imported from: Central America, Europe

45104 Howell Brothers Chemical Laboratories
5007 Overbrook Ave
Philadelphia, PA 19131-1402 215-477-0260
Manufacturer and exporter of glass cleaners and hair products
President: Douglas C Howell
Manager: David Hart
Production Manager: Charles Thomson
Estimated Sales: $ 2.5-5 Million
Number Employees: 7
Square Footage: 24000
Type of Packaging: Consumer, Private Label
Regions Exported to: Europe, Africa
Percentage of Business in Exporting: 11

357

Importers & Exporters / A-Z

45105 Howes S Co Inc
25 Howard St
Silver Creek, NY 14136-1097 716-934-2611
Fax: 716-934-2081 888-255-2611
sales@showes.com www.pressureleaffilter.com
Manufacturer and exporter of job engineered processing and materials handling equipment including classifiers, conveyors, crushers, rotary cutters, horizontal/vertical mixers, continuous liquid mixers and feeders, sifters, elevatorsauger packers and scales
President: Wayne Mertz
bryantd@showes.com
Vice President: Frederick Mertz
Sales: Diana Bryant
Estimated Sales: $10-20,000,000
Number Employees: 10-19
Regions Exported to: Worldwide
Percentage of Business in Exporting: 20

45106 Howson Mills
320 Blyth Rd
Blyth, ON N0M 1H0
Canada 519-523-4241
  866-422-7522
howson@howsons.ca www.howsons.ca
Durum flour.
Sales Manager: Dan Greyerbighl
Year Founded: 1875
Estimated Sales: $35 Million
Number Employees: 65
Type of Packaging: Bulk
Brands Exported: Howson Mills Durum Products
Regions Exported to: USA

45107 (HQ)Hoyt Corporation
251 Forge Rd
Westport, MA 2790 508-636-8811
Fax: 508-636-2088 hoytinc@hoytinc.com
  www.hoyt-corp.com
Manufacturer and exporter of vapor recovery systems and dry cleaning equipment including commercial washer extracts, laundry dryers and extractors
Chairman: Jean H Olinger
VP Marketing: Pat King
Contact: Gil Abernathy
gil.abernathy@hoyavc.com
Estimated Sales: $10-20 Million
Number Employees: 10-19
Regions Exported to: Worldwide
Percentage of Business in Exporting: 10

45108 Hoyt's Honey Farm
11711 Interstate 10 E
Baytown, TX 77523 281-576-5383
Fax: 281-576-2191 hoyts@imsday.com
Honey
President: Gordon Brown
Estimated Sales: $5-10 Million
Number Employees: 5-9
Square Footage: 30000
Type of Packaging: Consumer, Food Service, Private Label, Bulk
Regions Imported from: Central America, South America, Europe, Asia
Percentage of Business in Importing: 80

45109 Hsin Tung Yang Foods Inc
405 S Airport Blvd
S San Francisco, CA 94080-6909 650-589-6789
Fax: 650-589-3157 info@htyusa.com
  www.htyusa.com
Asian meat products
President: Kailen Mai
Contact: Peter Hamilton
p.hamilton@cymi.com
Director Manufacturing: Pin Chong
Estimated Sales: $10 - 20 Million
Number Employees: 20-49
Regions Exported to: Canada

45110 Hsu's Ginseng Enterprises Inc
T6819 County Rd W
Wausau, WI 54403-9461 715-675-2325
Fax: 715-675-7832 800-826-1577
info@hsuginseng.com www.hsuginseng.com
Ginseng products, royal jelly, bee pollen, astragalus, dong quai and goldenseal
President: Paul Hsu
info@hsuginseng.com
Vice President: Sharon Hsu
Estimated Sales: $5-10 Million
Number Employees: 50-99
Regions Exported to: Asia

45111 Hub Electric Company
6207 Commercial Rd
Crystal Lake, IL 60014 815-455-4400
Fax: 815-455-1499 richardvaralightinc@juno.com
Manufacturer and exporter of dimming systems and special lighting equipment
President and CFO: Richard Latronica
VP: Kenneth Hansen
Estimated Sales: Below $1 Million
Number Employees: 5-9

45112 Hub Pen Company
230 Quincy Avenue
Quincy, MA 02169-6741 617-471-9900
Fax: 617-471-2990 www.hubpen.com
Manufacturer and exporter of felt tip markers, pens, pencils, etc
President: Helen Fleming
Quality Control: Howard Ernest
Sales Manager: Robert McGaughey
Contact: Cheryl Brugliera
cbrugliera@hubpen.com
Estimated Sales: $10 - 20 Million
Number Employees: 65
Square Footage: 20000
Regions Exported to: Europe
Percentage of Business in Exporting: 3

45113 Hubbard Peanut Co Inc
30275 Sycamore Ave
PO Box 94
Sedley, VA 23878 757-562-4081
Fax: 757-562-2741 800-889-7688
hubs@hubspeanuts.com www.hubspeanuts.com
Cocktail peanuts
President: Lynne Rabil
lynne@hubspeanuts.com
Plant Manager: David Benton
Estimated Sales: $10-24.9 Million
Number Employees: 10-19
Square Footage: 90000
Type of Packaging: Consumer, Food Service, Private Label
Brands Exported: Hubs
Regions Exported to: Worldwide
Percentage of Business in Exporting: 1

45114 Hubbell Electric HeaterCo
45 Seymour St
PO Box 288
Stratford, CT 06615-6170 203-380-3306
Fax: 203-378-3593 800-647-3165
info@hubbellheaters.com
  www.hubbellheaters.com
Manufacturer and exporter of electric hot water booster heaters for sanitizing water
President: William E Newbauler
Head of Quality Control: Clifford Dineson
Sales Director: Sean Clarker
IT: Jessica Delvalle
jessicad@hubbellheaters.com
Estimated Sales: $5 - 10 Million
Number Employees: 50-99
Brands Exported: Hubbell
Regions Exported to: Worldwide
Percentage of Business in Exporting: 15

45115 Hubbell Lighting Inc
701 Millennium Blvd
Greenville, SC 29607-5251 864-678-1000
Fax: 864-678-1065 www.hubbelllighting.com
Manufacturer and exporter of industrial, commercial, emergency, exit, recessed and track lighting
Vice President: Scott H Muse
smuse@prescolite.com
VP: Scott Veil
VP Sales/Marketing: Richard Barrett
VP Sales: James O'Hargan
Number Employees: 500-999
Parent Co: Hubbell
Regions Exported to: Central America, South America, Europe, Asia, Middle East

45116 Hubco Inc
215 S Poplar St
PO Box 1286
Hutchinson, KS 67501-7456 620-663-8301
Fax: 620-663-5053 800-563-1867
  www.hubcoinc.com
Manufacturer, importer and exporter of bags including drawstring, cotton, flannel, polypropylene and burlap for flour, rice, popcorn, nuts, etc.; also, specialty food packaging available
President: Merlin Prehein
VP: Trey McPherson
VP: Jim Schmidt
Plant Manager: Fred Moore
Estimated Sales: $5 - 10 Million
Number Employees: 50-99
Square Footage: 284000
Regions Imported from: Asia

45117 Hudson Commercial Foods
39 Highwood Road
East Norwich, NY 11732-1110 516-922-9595
Fax: 516-922-7334
Importer and exporter of essences, natural colors and fruit juice concentrates and purees
President: Efren Estevez
Contact: Ed Gagliardi
ed.gagliardi@sunopta.com
Office Manager: Lonnie Jackson
Estimated Sales: $10-20 Million
Number Employees: 10-19
Type of Packaging: Bulk
Regions Exported to: Caribbean, Worldwide
Percentage of Business in Exporting: 10
Regions Imported from: Worldwide
Percentage of Business in Importing: 90

45118 Hudson Control Group Inc
10 Stern Ave
Springfield, NJ 07081-2905 973-376-8265
Fax: 973-376-8265 info@hudsoncontrol.com
  www.hudsoncontrol.com
Manufacturer and exporter of custom designed and integrated robotic automation systems including case packers/unpackers; also, software
President: Phil Farrelly
CSO: Cliff Olson, Ph.D.
VP Sales/Marketing: Tom Gilman
Contact: John Celecki
jcelecki@hudsoncontrol.com
Estimated Sales: $1 - 2.5 Million
Number Employees: 5-9
Square Footage: 12000
Regions Exported to: Europe
Percentage of Business in Exporting: 10

45119 Hudson Valley Coffee Company
632 Kids Lane
Castleton on Hudson, NY 12033-9687 518-766-9009
Fax: 518-766-9789 800-637-6550
bhnelisa@iname.com
Wholesaler/distributor, importer and exporter of specialty coffees and teas; also, infusers and grinders
Director Sales/Marketing: Lisa Goldstein
Service Manager: Diamond Psarianos
VP Purchasing: Jim Topaltzas
Estimated Sales: $2.5-5 Million
Number Employees: 5-9
Square Footage: 80000
Type of Packaging: Consumer, Food Service, Private Label, Bulk
Brands Exported: Barrie House Gourmet Coffee
Regions Exported to: Asia
Regions Imported from: Central America, South America

45120 Hudson Valley Hops
PO Box 292
Beacon, NY 12508 845-202-2398
admin@hvhops.com
  www.hvhops.com
Harvester, processor and distributor of hops to brewers in the Hudson Valley
Co-Founder: Justin Riccobono
Co-Founder: Shawn McLearen *Year Founded:* 2013
Type of Packaging: Bulk

45121 Hudson Valley Malt
320 Co. Rte. 6
Germantown, NY 12526 845-489-3450
info@hudsonvalleymalt.net
  www.hudsonvalleymalt.net
Artisan craft malt
Co-Owner: Dennis Nesel
Co-Owner: Jeanette Nesel
Number of Brands: 1
Type of Packaging: Consumer, Bulk
Brands Exported: Hudson Valley Malt
Regions Exported to: USA

45122 Hudson-Sharp Machine Co
975 Lombardi Ave
Green Bay, WI 54304-3735 920-494-4571
Fax: 920-496-1322 800-950-4362

Manufacturer and exporter of packaging machinery including bag makers and pouch makers and fillers
President: Don Pansier
VP: Gilas Blaser
Sales Director: Dennis Jimmel
Plant Manager: Jack Hendrickson
Estimated Sales: $ 20-50 Million
Number Employees: 50-99
Square Footage: 60000
Brands Exported: Amplas
Regions Exported to: Worldwide
Percentage of Business in Exporting: 50

45123 Hudson-Sharp Machine Company
P.O.Box 13397
Green Bay, WI 54307-3397   920-494-4571
Fax: 920-496-1322 sales@hudsonsharp.com
www.hudsonsharp.com
Manufacturer and exporter of converting and pouch and plastic bag making equipment
President: Peter Hatchell
CFO: Gary Reinert
CEO: Rod Drummond
Research & Development: Danford Anderson
Marketing Director: Mark Smith
Sales Director: Paul Staab
Contact: Michele Allamprese
michele.allamprese@hudsonsharp.com
Operations Manager: Scott Romenesko
Estimated Sales: $50-100 Million
Number Employees: 50-99
Regions Exported to: Central America, South America, Europe, Asia, Middle East
Regions Imported from: Europe

45124 Hughes Co
1200 W James St
Columbus, WI 53925-1028   920-623-2000
Fax: 920-623-4098 866-535-9303
hughes@hughesequipment.com
www.hughesequipment.com
Food processing equipment
President/CEO: Ross Lund
rosslund@hughescompany.biz
Sales Manager: Tracey Lange
Sales Manager: Ryan Metzdorf
Director of Engineering: Todd Belz
Plant Manager: Bill Wandersee
Estimated Sales: $ 10 - 20 Million
Number Employees: 20-49
Brands Exported: Hughes
Regions Exported to: Central America, South America, Europe, Asia, Middle East
Percentage of Business in Exporting: 25

45125 Hughes Manufacturing Company
2301 W Highway 290
Giddings, TX 78942   979-542-0333
Fax: 979-542-0335 800-414-0765
www.hughesmanufacturing.com
Manufacturer and exporter of nylon and plastic flags, pennants and banners
Manager: Lisa Marek
Operations Manager: Larry Conlee
Operations Manager: Larry Conlee
Estimated Sales: Below $5 Million
Number Employees: 10-19
Square Footage: 40000
Regions Exported to: Europe
Percentage of Business in Exporting: 10

45126 Humboldt Creamery
Modesto, CA 95351
   888-316-6064
info@humboldtcreamery.com
www.humboldtcreamery.com
Ice cream and milk products
CFO: Ralph Titus
National Sales & Marketing Manager: Rod Masters
Operations Manager: Mike Callihan
Purchasing Manager: Mark McCurtain
Number Employees: 100-249
Parent Co: Foster Dairy Farms
Type of Packaging: Consumer, Food Service, Bulk
Regions Exported to: Columbia
Percentage of Business in Exporting: 2

45127 Humco Holding Group Inc
7400 Alumax Rd
Texarkana, TX 75501-0282   903-831-7808
Fax: 903-334-6300 www.nomoreitch.com
Liquid and powder herbal supplements
President/CEO: Greg Pulido
gpulido@humco.com
CFO: Steve Woolf
Vice President: Susan Hickey
VP Quality/Regulatory Affairs: Steve Bryant
VP Sales: Alan Fyke
Estimated Sales: $10-20 Million
Number Employees: 100-249
Regions Exported to: Middle East, Caribbean

45128 Hungerford & Terry
226 Atlantic Ave
PO Box 650
Clayton, NJ 8312   856-881-3200
Fax: 856-881-6859 sales@hungerfordterry.com
www.hungerfordterry.com
Manufacturer and exporter of water treatment systems including filters, softeners, demineralizers and reverse osmosis
President: Allen Davis
Executive VP: Vernon Dawson
VP Sales: Kenneth Sayell
Contact: Douglas Bateman
dbateman@hungerfordterry.com
Estimated Sales: $ 10-20 Million
Number Employees: 50-99
Square Footage: 40000
Regions Exported to: Central America, South America, Europe, Asia, Middle East
Percentage of Business in Exporting: 20

45129 Hunt Country Vineyards
4021 Italy Hill Rd
Country Road 32
Branchport, NY 14418-9615   315-595-2835
Fax: 315-595-2835 800-946-3289
info@HuntWines.com www.huntwines.com
Wines, sherry and port
Owner: Joyce Hunt
joycehunt@huntwines.com
CEO, Owner: Arthur Hunt
Owner, Winemaker: Jonathan Hunt
Owner: Caroline Boutard Hunt
Marketing Operations Manager: Andy Marshall
General Manager: Jim Alsina
joycehunt@huntwines.com
Vineyard Manager: Dave Mortensen
Estimated Sales: $500,000-$1 Million
Number Employees: 20-49
Square Footage: 32000
Type of Packaging: Consumer, Private Label
Brands Exported: Hunt Country Vineyards; Foxy Lady
Regions Exported to: Europe, Canada
Percentage of Business in Exporting: 5

45130 Hunter Amenities International
1205 Corporate Drive
Burlington, ON L7L 5V5
Canada   800-668-1483
Fax: 905-331-2832 www.hunteramenities.com

45131 Hunter Lab
11491 Sunset Hills Rd # 1
Reston, VA 20190-5280   703-471-6870
Fax: 703-471-4237 sales@hunterlab.com
www.hunterlab.com
Manufacturer and exporter of color measurement systems
Owner: Phil S Hunter
CFO: Teresa Demangos
R & D: Jim Freal
Quality Control: Ambur Daley
Sales Manager: Paul Barnes
hunter@hunterlab.com
Estimated Sales: $10-20 Million
Number Employees: 50-99
Square Footage: 140000
Regions Exported to: Worldwide
Percentage of Business in Exporting: 50

45132 Hunter Walton & Co Inc
120 Circle Dr N
Piscataway, NJ 08854-3703   732-805-0808
Fax: 732-805-0282 hunterwalton@earthlink.com
www.hunterwalton.com
Distributor and manufacturer of dairy products and food oils. Continuous and batch churn butter, domestic natural and processed cheese, dry cheese, milk powders and custom blends, margarine and shortenings (vegetable and animal)
President: Glenn Grimshaw
hunterwalton@earthlink.net
CEO: Peter Love
Sales Director: Gary Behie
Estimated Sales: $18 Million
Number Employees: 10-19
Type of Packaging: Consumer, Food Service, Private Label, Bulk
Brands Exported: Land O'Lakes
Regions Exported to: Central America, Caribbean
Percentage of Business in Exporting: 1
Regions Imported from: Europe
Percentage of Business in Importing: 3

45133 Huntsman Packaging
PO Box 97
South Deerfield, MA 01373-0097   413-665-2145
Fax: 413-665-4854 www.pliantcorp.com
Manufacturer and exporter of co-extruded polyethylene packaging film
VP Finance: Peter Dube
Chairman: Charles Barker
Plant Manager: Clark Sylvester
Estimated Sales: $ 50-100 Million
Number Employees: 100-249
Square Footage: 100000
Regions Exported to: Middle East, Canada
Percentage of Business in Exporting: 5

45134 Hurst Labeling Systems
20747 Dearborn St
PO Box 5169
Chatsworth, CA 91311-5914   818-701-0710
Fax: 818-701-8747 800-969-1705
info@hurstinternational.net
www.hurstinternational.net
Manufacturer and exporter of pressure sensitive labels and label application equipment
Owner: Ari Lichtenberg
CFO: Rita Rebera
Quality Control: Rick Aranbul
Sales Representative: Melody Nichols
Sales Representative: Chaylon Holland
ari@hurstinternational.net
Estimated Sales: $ 3 - 5 Million
Number Employees: 10-19
Square Footage: 26000
Regions Exported to: Central America, South America
Percentage of Business in Exporting: 5

45135 (HQ)Huskey Specialty Lubricants
1580 Industrial Ave
Norco, CA 92860-2946   951-340-4000
Fax: 951-340-4011 888-448-7539
sales@huskey.com www.huskey.com
Manufacturer and exporter of food grade grease and lubricating oils for food processing machinery
President: Sheldy Huskey
R&D: Jim Landry
Vice President: Mike Montgomery
Research & Development: Hugh Woodworth
Foreign Sales Manager: Denis Alonso
Contact: Michael Montgomery
mmontgomery@huskey.com
Plant Manager: Chris Kimball
Purchasing Manager: Cathy Merlo
Estimated Sales: $ 10 - 20 Million
Number Employees: 5-9
Square Footage: 120000
Type of Packaging: Private Label, Bulk
Other Locations:
  Huskey Specialty Lubricants
  Twinsburg, OHHuskey Specialty Lubricants
Brands Exported: Huskey; Slipnote
Regions Exported to: Central America, South America, Asia

45136 Hussmann Corp
12999 Saint Charles Rock Rd.
Bridgeton, MO 63044-2483   314-291-2000
www.hussmann.com
Commercial and display refrigerators and coolers.
President/CEO: Tim Figge
CFO: Cathy Haigh
Senior VP, Retail Services: Jay Welu
Year Founded: 1906
Estimated Sales: Over $1 Billion
Number Employees: 5000-9999
Parent Co: Panasonic Corporation Of North America

Importers & Exporters / A-Z

45137 Hutchinson Group
12335 Baseline Road
Suite 101
Rancho Cucamonga, CA 91739   909-224-3002
                                Fax: 909-972-1642
Estimated Sales: $ 10 - 20 Million
Number Employees: 20-49

45138 Huther Brothers
1290 University Avenue
Rochester, NY 14607-1674   585-473-9462
                                Fax: 585-473-9476 800-334-1115
Manufacturer and exporter of industrial food processing cutting blades and circular, straight and specialty knives
President: George W Huther Iii
CFO: James Aldridge
Bookkeeper: Margie Campaigne
Foreman: Eric Nash
Estimated Sales: $ 3 - 5 Million
Number Employees: 10-19
Square Footage: 38000
Regions Exported to: Central America, South America, Asia, Australia, Canada, Caribbean, Mexico
Percentage of Business in Exporting: 10

45139 Hybrinetics Inc
225 Sutton Pl
Santa Rosa, CA 95407-8199   707-585-0333
                                Fax: 707-585-7313 800-247-6900
hybrinet@voltagevalet.com www.voltagevalet.com
Manufacturer and exporter of dimmer controls for incandescent and fluorescent lighting
President: Rick Rosa
hybrinet@voltagevalet.com
Estimated Sales: $ 20 - 50 Million
Number Employees: 20-49
Brands Exported: Hybringtics; Aladdin Products; Star Controls; Voltage Valet
Regions Exported to: South America, Europe, Asia, Middle East

45140 Hydrel Corporation
12881 Bradley Ave
Sylmar, CA 91342-3828   818-362-9465
                                Fax: 818-362-6548 www.hydrel.com
Manufacturer and exporter of outdoor lighting fixtures including flood, ingrade and underwater; also, custom environment fixtures
President: Craig Jennings
VP: Dwight Hochstein
VP: Mark Blackford
CFO: John Gay
VP Marketing: Hal Madsen
Sales Manager: Dan Roth
Contact: Trilby Jasinski
tjasinski@hrblock.com
Estimated Sales: $ 20 - 50 Million
Number Employees: 100-249
Parent Co: GTY Industries
Regions Exported to: Central America, South America, Europe, Asia, Middle East
Percentage of Business in Exporting: 35

45141 Hydro-Miser
906 Boardwalk # B
San Marcos, CA 92069-4071   442-744-5083
                                Fax: 442-744-5031 800-736-5083
Manufacturer and exporter of portable and thermal storage chillers and cooling towers and systems; also, food processing equipment and supplies
President/CEO: Kimberly Howard
Estimated Sales: $1-2.5 Million
Number Employees: 1-4
Parent Co: Applied Thermal Technologies
Brands Exported: Copeland; Gould
Regions Exported to: Worldwide
Percentage of Business in Exporting: 25

45142 Hydromax Inc
4 Creamery Way
Emmitsburg, MD 21727-8803   301-447-3800
                                Fax: 301-668-3700 800-326-0602
info@hydromax.net www.hydromax.net
Manufacturer and exporter of water filtration and purification equipment including reverse osmosis, ultraviolet, ozone and filtration technologies
President: Frederick N Reidenbach
Estimated Sales: $1-2.5 Million
Number Employees: 5-9
Brands Exported: HydroMax
Regions Exported to: Worldwide
Percentage of Business in Exporting: 25

45143 Hydropure Water Treatment Co
5727 NW 46th Dr
Coral Springs, FL 33067-4005   954-340-3331
                                Fax: 954-971-0801 800-753-1547
Exporter of rotary vane pumps and water filtration, purification and reverse osmosis systems.
President: Vittorio Sordi
VP: Susan Shasser
Estimated Sales: $1.6 Million
Number Employees: 5-9
Number of Brands: 4
Number of Products: 78
Type of Packaging: Consumer, Food Service
Brands Exported: Hydropure Pumps/Hydropurefilters.
Regions Exported to: Central America, South America, Europe, Asia, Middle East
Percentage of Business in Exporting: 15
Regions Imported from: Europe

45144 Hye Cuisine
4730 S Highland Ave
Del Rey, CA 93616-9716   559-834-3000
          Fax: 559-834-5882 hyecuisine@gmail.com
                              www.hyecuisineinc.com
Grape leaves and roasted eggplant
President: Raffi Santikian
hyecuisine@gmail.com
Secretary: Hilda Santikian
Estimated Sales: $1 Million
Number Employees: 10-19
Square Footage: 32000
Type of Packaging: Food Service, Private Label
Regions Exported to: Middle East
Percentage of Business in Exporting: 80

45145 Hyer Industries
91 Schoosett St
Pembroke, MA 02359-1839   781-826-8101
          Fax: 781-826-7944 mail@thayerscale.com
                              www.thayerscale.com
Manufacturer and exporter of continuous scale weighing systems, flow aid devices, volumetric feeders and pre-blending and continuous compound feeder networks for extrusion processes
Owner: Frank Hyer
sales@thayerscales.com
CFO: Bruce Edward
R & D: Rick Tolles
VP Sales/Marketing: Charles Wesley
Purchasing Agent: Lou Sawyer
Estimated Sales: $10-20 Million
Number Employees: 50-99
Square Footage: 164000
Parent Co: Hyer Industries
Regions Exported to: Worldwide
Percentage of Business in Exporting: 31

45146 Hygeia Dairy Company
5330 Ayers St
Corpus Christi, TX 78415-2104   361-854-4561
          Fax: 361-854-7267 www.deanfoods.com
Milk, chocolate milk and orange juice
Manager: Scott Mc Clarren
VP: Doug Purl
Human Resources Director: Robin Somsngyi
Year Founded: 1927
Estimated Sales: $20-50 Million
Number Employees: 45
Square Footage: 34002
Parent Co: Hygeia Dairy Company
Type of Packaging: Consumer, Food Service, Private Label, Bulk
Regions Exported to: Mexico

45147 Hygiene-Technik
4743 Christie Drive
Beamsville, ON L0R 1B4
Canada   905-563-4987
          Fax: 905-563-6266 info@gotoHTI.com
                              www.gotoHTI.com
Specializing in the design, development and manufacturing of proprietary dispensing systems.
President: Heiner Ophardt
VP/General Manager: Tony Kortleve-Snider
Business Development Manager: Marina Nava
Number Employees: 50
Square Footage: 180000
Regions Exported to: Worldwide
Percentage of Business in Exporting: 90

45148 Hygrade Gloves
30 Warsoff Pl
Brooklyn, NY 11205   718-488-9000
                                Fax: 718-694-9500 800-233-8100
Manufacturer, importer and exporter of protective and disposable clothing including gloves, aprons, goggles, hair nets, uniforms, boots and dust masks
President: Lazar Follman
Contact: Ryan Bowling
r.bowling@hygradesafety.com
Estimated Sales: $ 1 - 5 Million
Number Employees: 20-49
Square Footage: 440000
Parent Co: LDF Industries
Brands Exported: American Optical; Comfiwear
Regions Exported to: Asia
Percentage of Business in Exporting: 50
Regions Imported from: Asia
Percentage of Business in Importing: 50

45149 Hyster Company
7227 Carroll Rd
San Diego, CA 92121   855-804-2118
                                Fax: 858-578-6165 www.johnson-lift.com
Manufacturer and exporter of automatic storage and handling systems and industrial trucks; also, service and rental available
Manager: Scott Stearne
Service Manager: Steve Lacroix
Estimated Sales: $5-10 Million
Number Employees: 10-19
Parent Co: Johnson Machinery
Brands Exported: Hyster
Regions Exported to: Worldwide

45150 I Magid
965 Rue Bergar
Laval, QC H7L 4Z6
Canada   450-629-3737
                                Fax: 450-629-1809
Wholesaler/distributor and importer of canned mackerel, sardines, snails, clams, crab meat, oysters, mussels, shrimp, pineapples, mandarin oranges, olives, tropical fruit cocktail, artichoke hearts, etc
VP/Buyer: Allan Magid
Number Employees: 20-49
Square Footage: 200000
Type of Packaging: Consumer
Brands Imported: Beaver; Club Supreme; Lady Sarah
Regions Imported from: Worldwide
Percentage of Business in Importing: 50

45151 I P Callison & Sons
2400 Callison Rd NE
Lacey, WA 98516-3154   360-412-3340
                                Fax: 360-412-3344
Flavours, specifically mint
President: Jim Burgett
callisons@callisons.com
Chief Financial Officer: Rick Robinson
Vice President: Jeff Johnson
Vice President, Innovation & Technology: Greg Biza
VP, Director of Global Sales: Philippe Job
Vice President, Operations: Damon Smith
Vice President, Controller: Cena Latshaw
Vice President, Purchasing: Les Toews
Number Employees: 50-99

45152 I Rice & Co Inc
11500 Roosevelt Blvd
Building D
Philadelphia, PA 19116-3080   215-673-7423
          Fax: 215-673-2616 800-232-6022
          amarino@iriceco.com www.iriceco.com
Syrups, flavorings, sundae toppings, fudge, bakery fillings, bases, tea blends and stabilizers.
President/CEO: Steve Kuhl
skuhl@iriceco.com
Plant Engineer/Maintenance Manager: Ashly Marchese
Estimated Sales: $20-50 Million
Number Employees: 20-49
Number of Brands: 1
Number of Products: 1000
Square Footage: 85000
Type of Packaging: Food Service, Private Label, Bulk
Brands Exported: Rice's Products
Regions Exported to: Central America, Europe
Percentage of Business in Exporting: 5

Importers & Exporters / A-Z

45153 I Wanna Distributors
480 27th Street
Orlando, FL 32806-4451 407-999-9511
Fax: 407-999-9512 www.iwannaicecream.com
Wholesaler/distributor, exporter and importer of food service supplies, desserts, cakes, ice cream, cookies and pastries; serving the food service market
President: Susan Sullivan
Vice President: Bill Sullivan
Sales: Bill Sullivan
Estimated Sales: $6 Million
Number Employees: 5-9
Number of Brands: 20
Number of Products: 1000
Square Footage: 36000

45154 I Zakarin & Sons Inc
5296 State Route 42
South Fallsburg, NY 12779-5725 845-434-4430
Fax: 845-434-4610 800-543-3459
Wholesaler/distributor and exporter of general merchandise including paper, janitorial supplies, kitchen, baking and cooking equipment, etc.; serving the food service market
President: Shirley Zakarin
VP: Judy Averick
Estimated Sales: $5-10 Million
Number Employees: 10-19
Square Footage: 120000

45155 I-Health Inc
55 Sebethe Dr
Suite 102
Cromwell, CT 06416
800-990-3476
www.i-healthinc.com
Vitamins, supplements and health food. Formerly known as Amerifit Brands.
Estimated Sales: $463 Million
Number Employees: 50-99
Parent Co: DSM
Other Locations:
  Amerifit/Strength Systems USA
    Bloomfield, CT Amerifit/Strength Systems USA
Brands Exported: AmeriFit; Strength Systems; HealthCare U.S.A.; Newt
Regions Exported to: Central America, South America, Europe, Asia, Middle East
Percentage of Business in Exporting: 15

45156 I. Deveau Fisheries LTD
PO Box 577
Barrington Passage, NS B0W 2J0
Canada 902-745-2877
Fax: 902-645-2211 www.ideveau.com
Live lobster.
President: Berton German
Director, Sales: Joel German
Estimated Sales: $7 Million
Number Employees: 15
Type of Packaging: Bulk
Regions Exported to: USA, Japan
Percentage of Business in Exporting: 95

45157 I. Grob & Company
PO Box 260026
Bellerose, NY 11426-0026 718-328-4194
Fax: 718-991-6972
Importer and wholesaler of sugar, flour and baking products

45158 I.W. Tremont Company
79 4th Ave
Hawthorne, NJ 07506 973-427-3800
Fax: 973-427-3778 www.iwtremont.com
Manufacturer and exporter of filter media including inspection, analysis, sampling and testing systems
President: Sal Averso
CFO: Andrew Averso
Contact: Salvatore Averso
jimaverso@iwtremont.com
Production Manager: Andrew Averso
Production Manager: James Averso
Estimated Sales: $ 20 - 50 Million
Number Employees: 10-19
Square Footage: 10000
Regions Exported to: Europe, Canada
Percentage of Business in Exporting: 5

45159 IB Concepts
657 Dowd Avenue
Elizabeth, NJ 07201-2116 215-739-9960
Fax: 215-739-9963 888-671-0800
www.celwa.com
Manufacturer and exporter of printed, embossed and molded crepe wadding inserts and liners; also, absorbent cellulose doilies, pulpboard coasters, die cut polyester discs, and die cut foam
General Manager: Robert Pettus
Operations Manager: Michael Hersh
Number Employees: 25
Square Footage: 80000

45160 IB Roof Systems
2877 Chad Dr
Eugene, OR 97408-7396 541-687-6429
Fax: 888-741-1160 800-426-1626
ibroof.com
President: Larry Stanley
CFO: John Srague
Marketing Director: Shawn Stanley
Contact: Leslie Estes
leslie@ibroof.com
Estimated Sales: $ 5 - 10 Million
Number Employees: 20-49

45161 IBF
803 Pressley Road
Suite 101
Charlotte, NC 28217-0771 704-334-6870
Fax: 704-335-6861
Importer and wholesaler/distributor of European wine and beer
CEO/President: Ralf Geschke
Estimated Sales: $5-10 Million
Number Employees: 5-9
Regions Imported from: Europe

45162 IBS Trading
555 Fifth Ave
14th Floor
New York, NY 10017 212-377-2073
info@ibsna.us
www.ibsna.us
Cheese, cured meats, preserved vegetables

45163 ICB Greenline
5808 Long Creek Park Dr # Q
Suite Q
Charlotte, NC 28269-3748 704-333-3377
Fax: 704-334-6146 800-331-5312
info@icb-usa.com
Manufacturer and exporter of overhead conveyors for poultry and meat processing
President: Heinz Dremel
Manager: Iris Chasteen
Estimated Sales: $5.6 Million
Number Employees: 10-19
Square Footage: 200000
Brands Exported: Greenline; Dura-Plate
Regions Exported to: Central America, South America, Europe, Asia, Middle East
Percentage of Business in Exporting: 10

45164 ICEE
1205 S. DuPont Ave.
Ontario, CA 91761-7817
800-426-4233
marketing@icee.com www.icee.com
Frozen carbonated beverage in fruit and soda flavors.
President/CEO: Gerald Shreiber
President, ICEE Company: Daniel Fachner
Senior VP/Chief Financial Officer: Dennis Moore
Year Founded: 1958
Estimated Sales: $98 Million
Number Employees: 850
Square Footage: 30000
Parent Co: J & J Snack Foods Corp.

45165 ICL Performance Products
622 Emerson Road
Suite 500
St. Louis, MO 63141
800-244-6169
www.icl-perfproductslp.com
Food-grade phosphoric acid, phosphate salts and food additives
President/CEO: Charles Weidhas
VP Finance: Paul Schlessman
Contact: K Amy
amy.zuzack@icl-pplp.com
VP Operations: Terry Zerr
Number Employees: 500-999
Parent Co: ICL Holdings

45166 ICatcher Network
2400 Boston St
Baltimore, MD 21224-4723 410-327-9156
Fax: 410-327-4100

45167 ID Foods Corporation
1800 Autoroute Laval
Laval, QC H7S 2E7
Canada 450-687-2680
Fax: 450-682-4797 800-361-9157
info@idfoods.com www.IDFoods.com
Importer, exporter and wholesaler/distributor of canned fish, spices, confectionery and specialty food items; serving the food service market
President: Philip Issenman
CFO: Phillip Gattolar
VP Procurement/Compliance: Diana Henault
VP Sales/Marketing: Mario Latendresse

45168 IEW
49 W Federal Street
Niles, OH 44446 330-652-0113
Manufacturer and exporter of industrial electronic weighing devices and scales for mobile material handling equipment
Estimated Sales: $ 1 - 5 Million

45169 IFFE/Rainbow Embroidery
467 Pennsylvania Avenue
Fort Washington, PA 19034 215-643-5881
Fax: 215-643-1149 www.iffe.net
Embroiders promotional items for industries, including the food industry
Estimated Sales: $ 3 - 5 Million
Number Employees: 10-19

45170 IFM
20 West 20th Street
Suite 303
New York, NY 10011 212-229-1633
Fax: 212-898-9024 franck@ifm-usa.com
Gourmet products
Marketing: Frank Foulloy

45171 ILHWA American Corporation
91 Terry St
Belleville, NJ 07109 973-759-1996
Fax: 973-450-0562 800-446-7364
info@ilhwana.com www.ilhwa-usa.com
Korean ginseng
President: Sang Kil Han
Warehouse Manager: Edner Louis
Estimated Sales: $2.5-5 Million
Number Employees: 1-4
Brands Exported: Il Hwa
Regions Exported to: Central America, South America, Europe, Asia, Caribbean
Percentage of Business in Exporting: 30
Brands Imported: Il Hwa
Regions Imported from: Asia
Percentage of Business in Importing: 50

45172 IMECO Inc
3820 S IL Route 26
Polo, IL 61064-9006 815-946-2351
Fax: 815-946-3409 www.imeco.com
Manufacturer and exporter of refrigeration equipment including prime surface evaporative condensers and sub-zero blast freezers
President: Mark Stencel
Controller: Kevin Tribley
kevin.tribley@york.com
General Manager: Ian McGavisk
Quality Controller: Mark Smith
Director Operations: Colin McDonough
Estimated Sales: $ 50-100 Million
Number Employees: 100-249
Square Footage: 135000
Parent Co: York International
Regions Exported to: Europe, Asia, Middle East
Percentage of Business in Exporting: 5

45173 IMI Cornelius
2401 N Palmer Dr
Schaumburg, IL 60196-0001 847-397-4600
Fax: 847-539-6960 800-323-4789
www.cornelius.com
Manufacturer and exporter of ice making and dispensing equipment including beverage, ice, juice and beer
President: Tim Hubbard
t.hubbard@imi-cornelius.com
Executive VP Sales/Marketing: Joseph Asfoud
President (Wilshire Canada): David Noble

Importers & Exporters / A-Z

Estimated Sales: $ 1 - 5 Million
Number Employees: 250-499
Parent Co: IMI Cornelius
Regions Exported to: Central America, South America, Europe, Asia, Australia

45174 IMI Precision Engineering
72 Spring Ln
Farmington, CT 06032-3140 860-677-0272
Fax: 860-677-4999 800-722-5547
www.imi-precision.com
Solenoid valves, liquid level controls, pressure switches
Executive Director: Gary Fett
Cmo: Joshua Denison
jdenison@norgren.com
Quality Control: Ned Lanfranco
Marketing: Karen Markie
Operations: Gary Fett
Purchasing: Dave Simons
Estimated Sales: $10-20 Million
Number Employees: 100-249
Parent Co: IMI Norgren
Brands Exported: Kip
Regions Exported to: Central America, South America, Europe, Asia, Middle East

45175 IMO Foods
P.O.Box 236
Yarmouth, NS B5A 4B2
Canada 902-742-3519
Fax: 902-742-0908 imofoods@ns.sympatico.ca
www.imofoods.com
Canned fish
President: Sidney Hughes
Executive VP/General Manager: Phillip Le Blanc
Director Marketing: David Jollimore
Number Employees: 100-249
Parent Co: IMO Foods
Type of Packaging: Consumer, Food Service, Private Label
Other Locations: IMO Foods Ltd.
Regions Exported to: Worldwide
Percentage of Business in Exporting: 80

45176 INA Co
837 Industrial Rd # G
San Carlos, CA 94070-3333 650-631-7066
Fax: 650-873-4729 www.sovaleather.com
Importer of china and plastic bags and garbage bags
Owner: Philip Wong
Estimated Sales: Less than $500,000
Number Employees: 1-4
Brands Imported: Ina
Regions Imported from: Asia
Percentage of Business in Importing: 100

45177 (HQ)INDEECO
425 Hanley Industrial Ct
St Louis, MO 63144-1511 314-644-4300
Fax: 314-644-5332 800-243-8162
sales@indeeco.com www.indeeco.com
Electric heating elements and systems including heat transfer systems, circulation and pipeline impedance; exporter of electric heaters and controls
President: Fred Epstein
CEO: John Eulich
Research & Development: Steve Links
Quality Control: Jana Jensen
Marketing Director: Kevin Healy
Operations Manager: Ron Kohlman
Production Manager: Cathy Luster
Purchasing Manager: John ie Harrington
Estimated Sales: $ 50 - 100 Million
Number Employees: 100-249
Square Footage: 200000
Other Locations:
   INDEECO
   Saint Louis, MOINDEECO
Regions Exported to: Worldwide

45178 IPL Plastics
20 Boyd St
Edmundston, NB E3V 4H4
Canada 506-739-9559
Fax: 506-739-1028 800-739-9595
Manufacturer and exporter of thin wall plastic food containers; also, molding and printing services available
Sales Manager: Pierre Boilard
Administrative Services: Claude Nadeau
Operations Manager: Mario Gaudieauit

Number Employees: 100
Square Footage: 180000
Parent Co: IPL
Regions Exported to: USA
Percentage of Business in Exporting: 35

45179 IPS International
20124 Broadway Ave
Snohomish, WA 98296 360-668-5050
Fax: 360-415-9056 info@ipsintl.com
www.independentpetsupply.com
Manufacturer and exporter of thermal and insulated handling and shipping containers
Estimated Sales: less than $ 500,000
Number Employees: 1

45180 IQ Scientific Instruments
PO Box 389
Loveland, CO 80539-0289
Fax: 970-669-2972 800-227-4224
www.phmeters.com
Manufacturer and exporter of pH meters
President: Malcolm Mitchell
Marketing Director: Kate Roberts
Sales Director: Rod Stark
Estimated Sales: $ 10 - 20 Million
Number Employees: 10-19
Regions Exported to: Worldwide
Percentage of Business in Exporting: 30

45181 ISF Trading
Hobson's Wharf
P.O Box 772
Portland, ME 04104 207-879-1575
Fax: 207-761-5877 isfco@aol.com
www.searchinmaine.com
Urchin, lobster, crab, whelk, salmon and shrimp products
Founder: Atchan Tamaki
Office Manager: Lan Gao
Estimated Sales: $ 20 - 49.9 Million
Number Employees: 120
Regions Exported to: Asia

45182 (HQ)ITC Systems
49 Railside Road
Unit 63
Toronto, ON M1H 2X1
Canada 416-289-2344
Fax: 416-289-4790 877-482-8326
sales@itcsystems.com www.itcsystems.com
Manufacturer, importer and exporter of cash card systems hardware and software for prepaid services at vending machines and manual food operations; manufacturer of photo identification cards with on-line debit/credit balances
Chief Executive Officer, President: Cam Richardson
Vice President of Business Development: Dan Bodolai
Director Sales: David Hulbert
Purchasing Manager: Janet Exconde
Number Employees: 10
Square Footage: 44000
Other Locations:
   ITC Systems
   Longwood, FLITC Systems
Brands Exported: ITC Systems
Regions Exported to: Worldwide
Percentage of Business in Exporting: 20
Regions Imported from: USA

45183 ITC Systems
49 Railside Road
Toronto, ON M3A 1B3
Canada 416-289-2344
Fax: 416-289-4790 877-482-8326
service@itcsystems.com www.itcsystems.com
Manufacturer, importer and exporter of cash card systems hardware and software for prepaid services at vending machines and manual food operations; manufacturer of photo identification cards with on-line debit/credit balances
Chief Executive Officer, President: Cam Richardson
R&D: Igor Irlin
Director of Sales: Dave Hulbert
Director Sales: David Hulbert
Plant Manager: Bryan Bull
Purchasing Manager: Janet Exconde
Number Employees: 25
Square Footage: 22000
Parent Co: ITC Systems
Brands Exported: ITC Systems
Regions Exported to: Worldwide
Percentage of Business in Exporting: 20

Regions Imported from: USA

45184 ITW Angleboard
113 Censors Road
Villa Rica, GA 30180-2120 770-459-5747
Fax: 770-459-1305 www.itw.com
Manufacturer and exporter of protective packaging profiles for shipping, unitizing and palletization
CEO: David Speer
CFO: James Wooten Jr.
Investor Relations: John Brooklier
Estimated Sales: $ 1 - 5 Million
Brands Exported: Edgeboard
Regions Exported to: South America, Europe, Asia, Baltic, Mediterranean
Percentage of Business in Exporting: 50

45185 ITW Engineered Polymers
2425 N Lapeer Rd
Oxford, MI 48371-2425 248-628-2587
Fax: 248-628-7136 info@ironout.com
Manufacturer and exporter of polyurea elastomeric coatings, urethane foam systems, application equipment and set-up processing stations. ITW Foamseal is currently supplying a wide range of urethane products for many uses in the automotive, manufactured housing, fenestration, furniture, sports equipment, recreational vehicle, medical, tolling and infrastructure markets
Manager: Gary Maxson
General Manager: Ted Stolz
Business Manager: Tim Walsh
Estimated Sales: $ 20-50 Million
Number Employees: 5-9
Square Footage: 50000
Parent Co: Illinois Tool Works
Type of Packaging: Private Label

45186 ITW United Silicone
4471 Walden Ave
Lancaster, NY 14086-9778 716-681-8222
Fax: 716-681-8789 info@unitedsilicone.com
www.unitedsilicone.com
Designer and manufacturer of product decorating and packaging equipment, supplies, tooling and heat seal solutions.
President: Kim Jackson
kjackson@unitedsilicone.com
Marketing Manager: Laura Baumann
Sales Director: Eric Steinwachs
Estimated Sales: $20-50 Million
Number Employees: 100-249
Square Footage: 18000
Parent Co: Illinois Toolworks
Type of Packaging: Consumer, Food Service
Regions Exported to: Canada, Mexico

45187 IVEX Packaging Corporation
610 Beriault Rd.
Longueuil, QC J4G 1D8
Canada 450-651-8887
Fax: 450-651-0093 www.ivexpackaging.com
Manufacturer and exporter of packaging materials including corrugated paper and trays.
President: Paul Gaulin
Year Founded: 2008
Estimated Sales: $710 Million
Parent Co: Induspac Inc.
Regions Exported to: Worldwide
Percentage of Business in Exporting: 9

45188 IWS Scales
9885 Mesa Rim Road
Suite 128
San Diego, CA 92191
Fax: 858-784-0542 800-881-9755
iwsscales.com
Manufacturer, importer and exporter of mechanical and electronic scales including platform, receiving, portion, racking, computing, etc
Estimated Sales: $ 1 - 3 Million
Number Employees: 50
Square Footage: 40000
Parent Co: Western Scale
Regions Exported to: Mexico
Percentage of Business in Exporting: 10
Regions Imported from: Asia
Percentage of Business in Importing: 25

45189 Ibertrade Commercial Corporation
711 3rd Avenue
New York, NY 10017-4014 212-583-1300
Fax: 212-583-9075

Importer of clementines, tomatoes, pears, apples and lemons
President: Juan Calvo
Director Sales: Diego Delavina
Estimated Sales: $5-10 Million
Number Employees: 5-9
Brands Imported: Oleastrun
Regions Imported from: South America, Europe

45190 Icco Cheese Co
1 Olympic Dr
Orangeburg, NY 10962-2514   845-680-2436
Fax: 845-398-1669 johna@iccocheese.com
www.iccocheese.com
Processor, importer and exporter of grated parmesan cheese in shaker canisters and glass pet containers; processor and exporter of bread crumbs
President: Joseph V Angiolillo
icco@aol.com
Vice President: John Angiolillo
Estimated Sales: $10-15 Million
Number Employees: 50-99
Type of Packaging: Consumer, Food Service, Private Label, Bulk
Regions Exported to: Canada
Regions Imported from: Worldwide

45191 Ice-Cap
P.O.Box 292
Piermont, NY 10968-292   718-729-7000
Fax: 718-392-4193 888-423-2270
Manufacturer and exporter of air conditioners
CEO: Mo Siegel
CFO: Mo Siegel
Estimated Sales: $ 20 - 50 Million
Number Employees: 10
Regions Exported to: Canada, Mexico
Percentage of Business in Exporting: 5

45192 Icebox Water
50 Corporate Plaza
Islandia, NY 11749-1516   631-479-3411
Fax: 888-503-1681 www.iceboxwater.com

45193 Icee-USA Corporation
4701 E Airport Dr
Ontario, CA 91761-7817   909-390-4233
Fax: 909-390-4260 800-426-4233
www.icee.com
Manufacturer and exporter of frozen carbonated beverage dispensers; also, point of sale signs and displays available
President: Dan Fachner
CFO: Kent Galloway
VP: Rod Sexton
Contact: Michael Acosta
macosta@icee.com
Estimated Sales: $ 5 - 10 Million
Number Employees: 100-249
Square Footage: 88000
Parent Co: J&J Snack Foods Company
Regions Exported to: Mexico

45194 Iceomatic
11100 E 45th Ave
Denver, CO 80239-3006   303-371-3737
Fax: 303-371-6296 800-423-3367
customer.service@iceomatic.com
www.iceomatic.com
Ice making equipment since 1952 including cubers, flakers, dispensers, bins and accessories. Provides equipment for restaurants, bars, hotels/motels, hospitals, etc
President: Kevin Fink
kevin.fink@iceomatic.com
CFO: Dave Weller
Quality Control: David Spiciarich
Marketing Director: Keith Kelly
Public Relations: Linda Gleeson
Plant Manager: Randy Karas
Number Employees: 250-499
Brands Exported: Ice-O-Matic; Mile High
Regions Exported to: Central America, South America, Europe, Asia, Middle East
Percentage of Business in Exporting: 35

45195 Iconics Inc
100 Foxboro Blvd # 130
Foxboro, MA 02035-2883   508-543-8600
Fax: 508-543-1503 800-946-9679
us@iconics.com www.iconics.com
ICONICS is the lead supplier of HMI SCADA, Energy Management, and Productivity Analytics software solutions to the Food and Beverage Industry. ICONICS GENISIS64 HMI/SCADA and Analytix software improves operational performance andproductivity by providing 360 degrees of visibility and real time control for business and production systems.
CEO: Russell Agrusa
russ@iconics.com
VP Finance/Administration, CFO: Paula Agrusa
VP Worldwide Sales: Chris Volpe
Business Development Manager for Buildin: Oliver Gruner
VP Product Marketing: Gary F. Kohrt
VP, Worldwide Sales: Mark Hepburn
Number Employees: 20-49
Square Footage: 96000
Brands Exported: Genesis32 Enterprise Edition; Alamwork Multimedia; Trendwork3 WebHMI; Pocker GENE MobileHMI
Regions Exported to: Central America, South America, Europe, Asia, Middle East, All

45196 Idaho Pacific Holdings Inc
4723 E 100 N
Rigby, ID 83442-5811   208-538-6971
Fax: 208-538-5082 800-238-5503
ipc@idahopacific.com
Dehydrated potato
President/CEO: Wally Browning
wallybrowning@idahopacific.com
CFO: Baden Burt
Quality Control Manager: Paul Eatinger
VP/Sales & Marketing: Jon Schodde
VP/Operations: Todd Sutton
Plant Manager: Steve McLean
Purchasing: Brian Hart
Year Founded: 1987
Estimated Sales: $40-50 Million
Number Employees: 100-249
Type of Packaging: Food Service, Private Label, Bulk
Brands Exported: Idaho-Pacific
Regions Exported to: Central America, South America, Europe, Asia, Middle East, Worldwide

45197 Idaho Steel Products Inc
255 E Anderson St
Idaho Falls, ID 83401-2016   208-522-1275
Fax: 208-522-6041 sales@idahosteel.com
www.idahosteel.com
Manufacturer and exporter of food processing equipment including blanchers, cookers, coolers, drum dryers and complete processing lines
President: Delynn Bradshaw
delynn@idahosteel.com
CFO: Craig Parker
Engineering Manager: Alan Bradshaw
Marketing/Public Relations: Davis Christiansen
Sales Director: Bruce Ball
Operations Manager: D Bradshaw
Purchasing Manager: Adam French
Estimated Sales: $ 10 - 20 Million
Number Employees: 100-249
Square Footage: 100000
Brands Exported: Idaho Steel Products; Kiremko
Regions Exported to: Europe, Asia, Mexico, Canada
Percentage of Business in Exporting: 25
Brands Imported: Idaho Steel Products; Kiremko

45198 Idaho Supreme Potatoes Inc
614 E 800 N
PO Box 246
Firth, ID 83236-1112   208-346-4100
Fax: 208-346-4104 www.idahosupreme.com
Potato products
President/General Manager: Wade Chapman
CFO: Steve Prescott
sprescott@idahosupreme.com
Estimated Sales: $37.60 Million
Number Employees: 100-249
Square Footage: 100000
Type of Packaging: Consumer, Food Service, Private Label
Brands Exported: Idaho Supreme
Regions Exported to: Asia
Percentage of Business in Exporting: 30

45199 Idaho Trout Company
PO Box 72
Buhl, ID 83316-0072   208-543-6444
Fax: 208-543-8476 866-878-7688
rainbowtrout@idahotrout.com
Trout
Manager: Harold Johnson
Vice President: Gregory Kaslo
Sales/Shipping: Janie Higgins
General Manager: Harold Johnson
Estimated Sales: $10-25 Million
Number Employees: 50-99
Type of Packaging: Food Service, Private Label, Bulk
Regions Exported to: Canada

45200 Ideal Stencil Machine &Tape Company
5307 Meadowland Parkway
Marion, IL 62959-5893   618-233-0162
Fax: 618-233-5091 800-388-0162
Manufacturer and exporter of ink including meat branding, hog tattoo, coding and jet printer; also, fountain brushes, conveyor line coders, ink applicators, metal markers and electronic stencil and embossing machines
Sales Manager: Jim Boyd
Executive VP Operations: Marco Ziniti
Estimated Sales: $2.5-5 Million
Number Employees: 20-49
Square Footage: 240000
Brands Exported: Ideal
Regions Exported to: Central America, South America, Europe, Asia, Middle East, Australia
Percentage of Business in Exporting: 25

45201 Ideal Wire Works
820 S Date Ave
Alhambra, CA 91803-1414   626-282-0886
Fax: 626-282-2674
Manufacturer and exporter of custom wire display racks, rings and parts in steel or stainless steel
Vice President: Liz Maro
lizmaro@idealwireworks.com
VP: Jim Freitag
Estimated Sales: $ 2.5 - 5 Million
Number Employees: 20-49
Square Footage: 40000
Regions Exported to: Central America, Europe, Canada
Percentage of Business in Exporting: 3

45202 Ideal Wrapping Machine Company
81 Sprague Avenue
Middletown, NY 10940-5223   845-343-7700
Fax: 845-344-4248
Manufacturer and exporter of forming, cutting and wrapping machinery for caramel, nougat and toffee candies
President: Lee Quality Tire
General Manager: Jim Horton
Number Employees: 5-9
Regions Exported to: Worldwide

45203 Ideal of America/ValleyRio Enterprise
1662 Broughton Court
Atlanta, GA 30338-4633   770-352-0210
Fax: 770-352-0106 idealvr@yahoo.com
Manufacturer and exporter of stainless steel packaging equipment including fully automated shrink and stretch wrappers
Vice President: Alan Pullock
Estimated Sales: $ 10 Million
Number Employees: 100-250
Square Footage: 210000
Parent Co: Ideal of America
Brands Exported: Ideal
Regions Exported to: Central America, South America, Europe, Canada, Caribbean, Mexico
Percentage of Business in Exporting: 15

45204 Ideas Etc Inc
8305 Dawson Hill Rd
Louisville, KY 40299-5317   502-231-4303
Fax: 502-239-0555 800-733-0337
ideasetc@msn.com www.ideas-etc.com
Manufacturer and exporter of shot and martini glasses, beverage containers and 4-necker T-shirts; importer of martini glasses. Designers and printers of food service calendars and planners

Importers & Exporters / A-Z

President: Tiffany Gaskin
tiffanygaskin@hotmail.com
Estimated Sales: $500,000+
Number Employees: 1-4
Brands Exported: Split Shot; Palm Tree Cooler; Split Sipper; Custom Cups
Regions Exported to: Central America, Europe
Brands Imported: Custom Drinkware in Glass & Plastic
Regions Imported from: Asia
Percentage of Business in Importing: 10

45205 Idesco Corp
37 W 26th St # 10
New York, NY 10010-1097   212-784-1800
Fax: 212-889-7033   800-336-1383
info@idesco.com www.idesco.com
Manufacturer and exporter of integrated security systems
President: Andrew Schonzeit
andrew@idesco.com
CFO: Ray O'Connor
VP of Sales: Michael Perlow
VP Sales: Andy Goldstone
Operations Manager: Brian Simpson
Estimated Sales: $10-20 Million
Number Employees: 20-49
Square Footage: 20000
Regions Exported to: Central America, South America, Europe, Asia, Middle East
Percentage of Business in Exporting: 15

45206 Idexx Laboratories Inc
1 Idexx Dr
Westbrook, ME 04092-2041   207-556-0300
Fax: 207-556-4346   800-548-6733
www.idexx.com
Manufacturer and exporter of cleaning and validation systems including testing kits for salmonella, coliforms/E coli in water, residues in milk and microbiological; also, dehydrated culture media.
President/CEO: Jay Mazelsky
EVP/Chief Financial Officer/Treasurer: Brian McKeon
Corp VP/Software & Engineering Officer: Jeff Dixon
Corp VP/General Counsel/Secretary: Sharon Underberg
Corp VP/Worldwide Operations: John Hart
Corp VP/Chief Information Officer: Ken Grady
Corp VP/Chief Technology Officer: Jeffrey Thomas
Year Founded: 1983
Estimated Sales: $2.4 Billion
Number Employees: 7,000

45207 Ido
Edgewater, NJ 07020-1362
www.ido-tea.com
Tea

45208 Ilapak Inc
105 Pheasant Run
Newtown, PA 18940-1820   215-579-2900
Fax: 215-579-9959 marketing@ilapak.com
www.ilapak.com
Flexible horizontal and vertical packaging machinery including fin seal and shrink wrappers, vertical form/fill/seal, four-side seal pouch, horizontal modified atmosphere, etc
President: Andrew G Axberg
CEO: Edward Young
eyoung@ilapak.com
CFO: Frank Zellucci
VP Sales: Randy Rice
Estimated Sales: $ 10 - 20 Million
Number Employees: 20-49
Square Footage: 36000
Parent Co: Ilapak Holding
Regions Exported to: Central America, South America, Canada, Caribbean, Latin America, Mexico
Percentage of Business in Exporting: 25

45209 Illes Seasonings & Flavors
2200 Luna Rd
Suite 120
Carrollton, TX 75006-6559   214-689-1300
800-683-4553
info@illesfoods.com www.illesfoods.com
Dry and liquid flavor solutions
Owner: Cristin Kahale
cristin@illesseasonings.com
CEO: Rick Illes

Estimated Sales: $28 Million
Number Employees: 50-99
Type of Packaging: Consumer, Food Service, Private Label

45210 Illinois Department of Agriculture
P.O.Box 19281
Springfield, IL 62794-9281   217-782-2172
Fax: 217-785-4505 www.agr.state.il.us
Executive Director: Tom Jennings

45211 Illuma Display
P.O.Box 1531
Brookfield, WI 53008-1531   262-446-9220
Fax: 262-446-9260   800-501-0128
Manufacturer and exporter of curved light boxes, graphic stands and backlit displays
President: Joe Galati
VP: Tony Galati
Estimated Sales: Less than $500,000
Number Employees: 1-4
Regions Exported to: Central America, South America, Europe, Canada, Mexico
Percentage of Business in Exporting: 5

45212 Image Experts Uniforms
1623 Eastern Pkwy
Schenectady, NY 12309-6011   518-377-4523
Fax: 518-374-1236   800-789-2433
www.imageexpertsuniforms.com
Manufacturer and exporter of uniforms
Owner: Tom Salamone
tom@imageexperts.com
CEO: Thomas J Salamone
Estimated Sales: $ 1-2.5 Million
Number Employees: 10-19
Square Footage: 8000
Parent Co: Image Experts Uniforms
Regions Exported to: Canada
Percentage of Business in Exporting: 15

45213 Image National Inc
16265 Star Rd
Nampa, ID 83687-8415   208-345-4020
Fax: 208-336-9886 jcarico@imagenational.com
Manufacturer and exporter of electric signs, store fronts and interior graphics
President: Doug Bender
doug.bender@imagenational.com
CEO/CFO: Chuck White
Service Install Manager: Jeff Carico
Sales Manager: Tony Adams
General Manager: Doug Bender
Estimated Sales: $ 5 - 10 Million
Number Employees: 100-249
Parent Co: Futura Corporation
Regions Exported to: Worldwide

45214 Imaging Technologies
445 Universal Drive
Cookeville, TN 38506-4603   931-432-4191
Fax: 931-432-4199   800-488-2804
www.icglink.com
Manufacturer and exporter of high resolution ink jet printing systems for printing bar codes, alphanumerics and graphics on porous surfaces
President: Loyd Tarver
Controller: Ted Bonnay
Vice President of Marketing: Chris Jones
Marketing Manager: Steve Shoup
Contact: Mark Doyle
sales@itiworldwide.com
Number Employees: 30
Square Footage: 24000
Brands Exported: ITI; Marksman
Regions Exported to: Central America, Europe, Asia
Percentage of Business in Exporting: 30

45215 Imaje
1650 Airport Rd NW # 101
Kennesaw, GA 30144-7017   678-594-7153
Fax: 770-421-1702 www.markem-imaje.us
Coding, dating and marking equipment, barcoding systems and inks for food packaging; importer of ink jet coders; exporter of ink jet coders, inks and additives
Manager: Linda Kaimesher
CFO: Steve Wakeford
Marketing Director: Alisha Curd
Sales Director: Tim Sines
Contact: Luis Davila
ldavila@markem-imaje.com
Purchasing Manager: Norm Coon

Estimated Sales: G
Number Employees: 1-4
Parent Co: Dover Technologies
Regions Exported to: Worldwide
Percentage of Business in Exporting: 50
Regions Imported from: Worldwide

45216 Iman Pack
5762 E Executive Dr
Westland, MI 48185-9125   734-467-9016
Fax: 734-467-8642   800-810-4626
sales@imanpack.com www.imanpack.com
Manufacturer and importer of automatic packaging equipment including horizontal and vertical form/fill/seal machinery, shrink wrappers, counting and weighing scales, case packers, palletizers, etc
President: Antonio Bonotto
Sales/Marketing: Lori Scheinman
National Sales Director: Fred Barbarotto
Contact: Mauro Ferrari
m.ferrari@imanpack.it
Estimated Sales: $ 1 - 3 Million
Number Employees: 5-9
Parent Co: Iman Pack SRL
Regions Imported from: Worldwide

45217 Imar
2301 Collins Avenue
Miami Beach, FL 33139-1639   305-531-5757
Fax: 305-538-2957
Manufacturer, importer and exporter of packaging machinery for pouches
CEO: Thomas Tennant
Parent Co: Imar
Brands Exported: Imar
Regions Exported to: Worldwide
Percentage of Business in Exporting: 60
Brands Imported: Imar
Regions Imported from: Spain

45218 Immu Dyne Inc
7453 Empire Dr # 300
Florence, KY 41042-2944   859-746-8772
Fax: 859-746-8772   888-246-6839
info@immudyne.com www.immudyne.com
Natural dietary supplements
President & CEO: Mark McLaughlin
markmcl@immudyne.com
Chairman: Anthony Bruzzese
VP: Alfred Munoz
Estimated Sales: Less Than $500,000
Number Employees: 1-4
Type of Packaging: Consumer, Food Service, Bulk
Brands Exported: MacroForce; MacroForce Plus
Regions Exported to: Worldwide

45219 Impact Confections
4017 Whitney St.
Janesville, WI 53546   608-208-1100
800-535-4401
info@impactconfections.com
www.impactconfections.com
Confectionery products
Founder/President: Brad Baker
CEO: Gary Viljoen
CFO: Rick Weina
Quality Manager: Dave Batchelder
Director Marketing: Jenny Doan
Contact: Andy Telatnik
atelatnik@impactconfections.com
Chief Operating Officer: George Wilson
Year Founded: 1981
Estimated Sales: $25-49.9 Million
Number Employees: 20-49
Number of Products: 40
Type of Packaging: Consumer
Regions Exported to: South America, Europe, Asia

45220 Impact Enterprises
122 Old Route 202a
Pomona, NY 10970-2823   845-354-3133
Fax: 702-547-9533 info@impactenterprises.com
www.impactenterprises.com

45221 Imperial Industries Inc
505 W Industrial Park Ave
Rothschild, WI 54474-7917   715-359-0200
Fax: 715-355-5349   800-558-2945
indsales@imperialind.com www.imperialind.com
Bulk storage silos and tanks, liquid waste tanks both self-contained and truck mounted, portable toilets, wash sinks and barricades. Also Asme certified tanks and DOT 407/412 truck mounted tanks.

Importers & Exporters / A-Z

President: Russ Putnam
HR Executive: Doug Hagen
doug@iimperialind.com
Reasearch/Development: Rial Potter
Quality Control: Doug Hagen
Marketing/Sales Manager: T Aerts
Plant Manager: K Mannel
Purchasing Director: Lisa Schultz
Number Employees: 100-249
Square Footage: 75000
Parent Co: Wausau Tile
Type of Packaging: Bulk
Brands Exported: Imperial
Regions Exported to: Central America, South America, Europe, Middle East
Percentage of Business in Exporting: 3

45222 Imperial Manufacturing Co
1128 Sherborn St
Corona, CA 92879-2089   951-281-1830
   Fax: 951-281-1879   800-281-1830
imperialsales@imperialrange.com
www.imperialrange.com
CEO: Peter Spenuzza
Manager: Matt Wise
mwise@imperialrange.com
Number Employees: 100-249

45223 Imperial Plastics Inc
21320 Hamburg Ave
PO Box 907
Lakeville, MN 55044-9032   952-469-4951
   Fax: 952-469-4724   www.imperialplastics.com
Manufacturer and exporter of plastic stoppers and advertising novelties
President: Dennis Erler
erler.dennis@yahoo.com
Number Employees: 100-249
Type of Packaging: Private Label
Regions Exported to: Worldwide

45224 Imperial Salmon House
1632 Franklin Street
Vancouver, BC V5L 1P4
Canada   604-251-1114
   Fax: 604-251-3177
Smoked salmon
President: Robert Blair
Number Employees: 5-9
Type of Packaging: Consumer, Food Service, Bulk
Regions Exported to: Europe, Asia, USA
Percentage of Business in Exporting: 10

45225 Imperial Sensus
PO Box 9
Sugar Land, TX 77487-0009   281-490-9522
   Fax: 281-490-9615 www.imperialsugarland.com
Inulin natural extract
VP Sales/Marketing: Sally Brain
VP of Technical Affairs: Bryan Tungland
Parent Co: Johnson Development Group
Type of Packaging: Food Service, Bulk
Brands Exported: Frutafit
Regions Exported to: Canada, Mexico
Percentage of Business in Exporting: 5
Brands Imported: Frutafit
Regions Imported from: Europe

45226 Important Wines
P O Box 1924
Venice, FL 34285   941-493-3000
   Fax: 941-497-6686
Importer of European wine and beer
President: George Pitthan
Estimated Sales: $2.5-5 Million
Number Employees: 1-4
Brands Imported: Bitburger; Erdinger; Diebels
Regions Imported from: Europe

45227 Imported Restaurant Specialties
331 Curie Dr
Alpharetta, GA 30005-2264   404-325-0585
   Fax: 404-777-6652   800-875-5451
Importer and wholesaler/distributor of espresso, cappuccino and coffee makers, pasta cookers and machinery, pizza oven and rollers, pastry cases, espresso carts, juice extractors, gelato machines, deli cases, ionia coffee, ice tealoose tea and frozen beverage mixes
President/CEO: Howard Brown
CFO/VP: DiJana DJelicovic
Estimated Sales: $5-10 Million
Number Employees: 1-4
Square Footage: 60000

45228 (HQ)Importex International
PO Box 310
Carboner, NL A1Y 1B7
Canada   709-596-2900
   Fax: 709-596-1901
Wholesaler/distributor, importer and exporter of frozen foods, general line products and merchandise, produce, provisions/meats and seafood; serving the retail and food service markets
President: Calvin Powell
Number Employees: 100-249
Square Footage: 340000

45229 Impra USA
12440 Firestone Blvd
Suite 309
Norwalk, CA 90650   562-868-2425
Ceylon tea

45230 Imprint Plus
21320 Gordon Way
Unit 260
Richmond, BC V6W 1J8
Canada   604-278-7147
   Fax: 604-278-7149   800-563-2464
sales@imprintplus.com   www.imprintplus.com
Name badges, name badge systems, and accessories
Owner: Ellen Flanders
CEO: Marla Kott
Sales Director: Phil Coles
Director of Operations: Kristin MacMillan
Number Employees: 65

45231 Improved Blow Molding
27 Hillside Dr
Hollis, NH 03049-6158   603-465-6190
   Fax: 603-465-6190   800-256-1766
Manufacturer and exporter of plastic blow molding machinery for food packaging
Owner: Ron Beaulieu
VP Marketing: H Lance Goldberg
VP Engineering: Ronald Beaulieu
Estimated Sales: $500,000-$1 Million
Number Employees: 1-4
Square Footage: 140000
Parent Co: Goodman Equipment Company
Regions Exported to: Central America, South America, Europe, Asia, Middle East, Canada
Percentage of Business in Exporting: 40

45232 Impulse Signs
25 Advance Road
Toronto, ON M8Z 2S6
Canada   416-231-3391
   Fax: 416-236-2116   866-636-8273
   mgisborne@impulsesigns.com
Manufacturer and exporter of menu boards and table signs
President/General Manager: Alex Cachia
Director, Marketing: Ron Wynne
VP, Sales: Carole Lynch
Estimated Sales: $ 1 - 5 Million
Number Employees: 20-50
Square Footage: 96000
Regions Exported to: Worldwide

45233 In A Bind Inc
8749 Center Rd
Springfield, VA 22152-2234   703-569-0371
   Fax: 703-569-2037   800-726-3687
inabindinc@aol.com   www.inabindinc.com
Wholesaler/distributor of custom menu covers, wine books, guest checks, guest services, directories, etc.; serving the food service market
Owner: William Gaspelin
william@inabindinc.com
Estimated Sales: $ .5 - 1 million
Number Employees: 1-4
Regions Exported to: Central America, South America, Europe, Asia, Middle East
Percentage of Business in Exporting: 7

45234 In Sink Erator
4700 21st St
Racine, WI 53406-5093   262-554-5432
   Fax: 262-554-3639   800-558-5712
   www.insinkerator.com
President: Tim Ferry
tim.ferry@insinkerator.com
Number Employees: 1000-4999

45235 InHarvest
1012 Paul Bunyan Dr SE
Bemidji, MN 56601
   Fax: 218-751-8519   800-346-7032
   www.inharvest.com
Wild rice and specialty grain importer and distributor
CFO: Jeffrey Buelow
VP, Foodservice Sales: Pete Linder
Type of Packaging: Food Service, Bulk

45236 Inaexpo USA LTD. Co.
2800 Biscayne Boulevard
Suite 900-A
Miami, FL 33137   305-571-1390
   Fax: 305-571-1831   sales@inaexpousa.com
   www.inaexpo.com
Canned or preserved vegetables/fruit, other vegetables/fruit.
Marketing: Eduardo Becerra
Contact: Inaexpousa Co
ebecerra@inaexpousa.com

45237 Incasa Instant SolubleCoffee
2029 University Avenue
Suite 206
Berkeley, CA 94704   510-845-5545
   Fax: 510-845-5565   incasa@incasacoffee.com
   www.incasacoffee.com
Premier supplier of wholesale instant and soluble coffees.
President: John Hornung
john@incasacoffee.com
Number Employees: 3
Regions Imported from: Central America, South America, Asia, Southeast Asia

45238 Incinerator International Inc
2702 N Main St
Houston, TX 77009-6838   713-227-1466
   Fax: 713-227-0884   sales@incinerators.com
   www.incinerators.com
Manufacturer and importer of material handling equipment including incinerators, balers, compactors, containers, crushers, trucks, hoppers and environmental; exporter of incinerators
Owner: Tom Leervig
sales@incinerators.com
Estimated Sales: $2.5-5 Million
Number Employees: 5-9
Square Footage: 10000
Parent Co: International Environmental Equipment Company
Regions Exported to: Worldwide
Percentage of Business in Exporting: 25
Regions Imported from: Worldwide

45239 Incinerator Specialty Company
6018 Golden Forest Dr
Houston, TX 77092-2360   713-681-4207
Manufacturer and exporter of destructors, afterburners and incinerators including pathological, garbage, waste, burners and parts
President: Mick Kromer
Estimated Sales: $1-2.5 Million
Number Employees: 4
Percentage of Business in Exporting: 1

45240 Ind-Us Enterprises/Spice'n Flavor
PO Box 166
Merrick, NY 11566-0166   516-223-6542
   Fax: 516-908-3846   888-287-7964
   www.spicenflavor.com
Importer of spices and curry mixes
CEO/President/Chef: Thomas Vellaringattu
Vice President: George Parambil
Marketing Director: George Parambil
Estimated Sales: $500,000-$1 Million
Number Employees: 1-4
Regions Imported from: Asia

45241 Indalo USA Corporation
1650 A Dickinson Ave
Dickinson, TX 77539   281-678-8015
   Fax: 786-866-5682
Olive oils

45242 Indel Food Products Inc
9515 Plaza Cir
El Paso, TX 79927-2005   915-590-5914
   Fax: 915-590-5913   800-472-0159
   gustavo@indelfoods.net   www.indelfoods.net
Jalapenos and salsa
President: Gustavo Deandar

365

Importers & Exporters / A-Z

Estimated Sales: $2.5-5 Million
Number Employees: 5-9
Parent Co: Agroindustrias Deandar
Type of Packaging: Consumer, Food Service, Private Label, Bulk
Brands Exported: Del Sol
Regions Exported to: Europe, Asia, Canada, Mexico
Percentage of Business in Exporting: 25

45243 Indemax Inc
1 Industrial Dr
Vernon, NJ 07462-3466   973-209-2424
Fax: 973-209-2644   800-345-7185
sales@indemax.com www.indemax.com
Manufacturer and exporter of parts for hot melt equipment
President: A Infurna
Vice President: P Infurna
Quality Control: P Infurna
Sales Director: R Infurna
Plant Manager: C Peterson
Purchasing Manager: J Tapscnyi
Estimated Sales: $5-10 Million
Number Employees: 5-9
Brands Exported: Indemax
Regions Exported to: Central America, South America, Europe, Asia, Middle East

45244 (HQ)Independent Can Co
1300 Brass Mill Rd
Po Box 370
Belcamp, MD 21017-1236   410-272-0090
Fax: 410-272-7500
salesdept@independentcan.com
www.independentcan.com
Manufacturer, importer and exporter of decorative tin containers for coffee, peanuts, cookies, cakes, popcorn, candies, ice cream, etc
Manager: Cathy Mc Clelland
CEO: Richard D Huether
Marketing: Neil Defrancisco
Sales: Frank Shriver
Public Relations: George R McClelland
Operations: G William Goodwin
Plant Manager: Frank Currens
Purchasing: Page Edwards
Estimated Sales: $20-50 Million
Number Employees: 100-249
Square Footage: 360000
Type of Packaging: Consumer, Private Label
Other Locations:
Independent Can Co.
Ontario, CAIndependent Can Co.
Regions Exported to: Central America, South America, Europe
Percentage of Business in Exporting: 13

45245 Independent Ink
13700 Gramercy Pl
Gardena, CA 90249-2455   310-523-4657
Fax: 310-329-0943   800-446-5538
www.independentink.com
Marking machines and coding and ink jet inks; exporter of inks and solutions
Owner: Barry Brucker
bbrucker@independentink.com
Executive VP/COO: Randa Nathan
International Sales: Nora Valdez
Estimated Sales: $ 5-10 Million
Number Employees: 20-49
Square Footage: 50000
Type of Packaging: Consumer, Private Label
Regions Exported to: Worldwide
Percentage of Business in Exporting: 20

45246 India Tree, Inc.
5309 Shilshole Ave NW
Suite 150
Seattle, WA 98107   206-270-0293
Fax: 206-282-0587   800-369-4848
india@indiatree.com www.indiatree.com
Sugars, spices and specialty products
Founder, President & CEO: Gretchen Goehrend
Contact: Traci Rivers
traci@indiatree.com
Number Employees: 10
Regions Exported to: Asia, Middle East

45247 Indian Bay Frozen Foods
PO Box 160
Centreville, NL A0G 4P0
Canada   709-678-2844
Fax: 709-678-2447 ackermans@ibffinc.com
www.ibffinc.com
Blueberries, lingonberries, jams and pie fillings; fish
President: Calvin Ackerman
Estimated Sales: 2.5-5 Million
Number Employees: 20-49
Square Footage: 40000
Type of Packaging: Consumer, Private Label, Bulk
Regions Exported to: Europe, Asia
Percentage of Business in Exporting: 90

45248 Indian Ridge Shrimp Co
120 Doctor Hugh St Martin Dr
Chauvin, LA 70344-2723   985-594-5869
Fax: 985-594-2168   800-594-0920
chris@pearlbrandseafood.com
www.louisianashrimpers.com
Shrimp
Owner: Andrew Blanchard
andrew_blanchard@louisianashrimpers.com
COO: Richard Fakier
Sales Manager: Daniel Babin
Estimated Sales: Less Than $500,000
Number Employees: 1-4
Square Footage: 100000
Type of Packaging: Consumer, Food Service
Brands Exported: Pearl
Regions Exported to: Canada
Percentage of Business in Exporting: 10
Regions Imported from: Central America, South America, Latin America
Percentage of Business in Importing: 10

45249 Indian Valley Industries
PO Box 810
Johnson City, NY 13790-0810   607-729-5111
Fax: 607-729-5158   800-659-5111
www.iviindustries.com
Manufacturer and exporter of burlap and textile bags; also manufacturers and supplies products relating to environmental protection, erosion control, and the containment of both air and waterborn pollutants.
President: Wayne Rozen
CEO: Nilton Rozen
VP Marketing: Phil March
Contact: John Brauer
brauer@iviindustries.com
Estimated Sales: $ 10 - 20 Million
Number Employees: 10-19
Regions Exported to: Worldwide

45250 Indian Valley Meats
HC 52 Box 8809
Indian, AK 99540-9604   907-653-7511
Fax: 907-653-7694 ivm@alaska.net
www.indianvalleymeats.com
Poultry, venison and fish
President: Douglas Drum
Plant Manager: Renia Drum
Estimated Sales: $2.5-5 Million
Number Employees: 10-19
Square Footage: 68000
Brands Exported: Indian Valley
Regions Exported to: Europe, Asia
Percentage of Business in Exporting: 30

45251 Indiana Carton Co Inc
1721 W Bike St
PO Box 68
Bremen, IN 46506-2123   574-546-3848
Fax: 574-546-5953   800-348-2390
salesservice@indianacarton.com
www.indianacarton.com
Manufacturer and exporter of boxes and cartons
President: David Petty
davidpetty@indianacarton.com
Chairman of the Board: Kenneth Petty
Estimated Sales: $10-20 Million
Number Employees: 50-99
Regions Exported to: Worldwide

45252 Indiana Glass Company
37 West Broad Street
Columbus, OH 43215   614-224-7141
Fax: 513-563-9639   800-543-0357
www.lancastercolony.com
Manufacturer and exporter of housewares including candleholders, glasses and other beverage containers
Human Resources: Cathy Durham
VP/Marketing: Jerry Vanden Eynden
National Sales Manager: Mark Cunningham
International Sales Manager: Alex Morroni
Estimated Sales: $ 1 - 5 Million
Number Employees: 500-999
Parent Co: Lancaster Colony Corporation
Type of Packaging: Bulk
Regions Exported to: Central America, South America, Europe, Asia, Middle East
Percentage of Business in Exporting: 8

45253 Indiana Vac Form Inc
2030 N Boeing Rd
Warsaw, IN 46582-7860   574-269-1725
Fax: 574-259-2723 bret@invacform.com
www.invacform.com
Manufacturer and exporter of custom plastic vacuum and thermoformed products including containers and refrigerator liners
Owner: Donald Robinson
ins@invacform.com
Operations Manager: Roy Szymanski
Production Manager: Bob Stevents
Estimated Sales: $2.5-5 Million
Number Employees: 20-49
Square Footage: 90000
Type of Packaging: Food Service
Regions Exported to: Canada
Percentage of Business in Exporting: 7

45254 Indianapolis Fruit Company
4501 Massachusetts Ave
Indianapolis, IN 46218   317-546-2425
800-377-2425
www.indyfruit.com
Wholesaler/distributor and importer of produce including peppers, tomatoes, cherry tomatoes, apples, kiwi, etc.
Owner: Joe Corsaro
Vice President: Peter Piazza
Director, Sales & Marketing: Daniel Corsaro
Year Founded: 1947
Estimated Sales: $41 Million
Number Employees: 180
Square Footage: 250000
Regions Imported from: Central America, South America, Europe, Asia, Middle East
Percentage of Business in Importing: 5

45255 Indianapolis Meat Company
1725 Southeastern Avenue
Indianapolis, IN 46201-3956   317-679-5352
Fax: 317-632-9389
Importer of frozen boneless beef, lamb and mutton; wholesaler/distributor of meat
President: Gerald Fivel
Estimated Sales: $1-2 Million
Number Employees: 1-4
Brands Imported: Jerry's

45256 Indo-European Foods
1000 Air Way
Glendale, CA 91201-3030   818-247-1000
Fax: 818-247-9722 indoeuro1@aol.com
www.indo-euro.com
Wholesaler/distributor and importer of French and Bulgarian foods, feta cheese, lady fingers, Indian basmati, Thailand jasmine rice, couscous, frozen quail, vegetable soup bases and mineral water
President: Albert Bezjian
CEO: Terry Bezjian
CFO: George Callas
Estimated Sales: $ 20 - 50 Million
Number Employees: 20-49
Square Footage: 42000
Brands Imported: Indo-European; B&B Better Birds; Elephant Basmati; Vicenzi; Al-Wadi; Beit Hashita
Regions Imported from: Europe, Asia, Middle East
Percentage of Business in Importing: 85

45257 Industrial Automation Specs
17 Research Dr
Hampton, VA 23666-1324   757-766-7520
Fax: 757-766-7505   800-916-4272
sales@iascorp.net www.iascorp.net
Manufacturer and exporter of analog chart recorder
CEO: Kathy Burton
preston@iascorp.net
Owner: Kathy Burton
Marketing Supervisor: Don Crawford
Estimated Sales: $1-2.5 Million
Number Employees: 10-19

Importers & Exporters / A-Z

Percentage of Business in Exporting: 5

45258 Industrial Ceramic Products
14401 Suntra Way
Marysville, OH 43040 937-642-3897
Fax: 937-644-2646 800-427-2278
sales@industrialceramic.com
www.industrialceramic.com
Manufacturer and exporter of ceramic pizza stones
President: R C Oberst
Contact: Clay Foreman
cforeman@industrialceramic.com
Estimated Sales: $ 5 - 10 Million
Number Employees: 20-49
Square Footage: 100000
Regions Exported to: South America, Canada, Mexico
Percentage of Business in Exporting: 5

45259 Industrial Commodities
4134 Innslake Dr
Glen Allen, VA 23060
800-523-7902
inquiries@industrialcommodities.com
www.industrialcommodities.com
Wholesaler/distributor and exporter of sugar, salt, honey, molasses, eggs, dextrose, milk powder, monosodium glutamate, coconut and syrups; serving the food service market.
Vice President: Rick Crowder
Partner Manager: David Hill
dhill@industrialcommodities.com
Year Founded: 1979
Estimated Sales: $20-50 Million
Brands Exported: Domino; Hubinger

45260 Industrial Contracting & Rggng
41 Ramapo Valley Rd
Mahwah, NJ 07430-1118 201-444-7504
Fax: 201-529-3754 888-427-7444
info@icrnj.com www.industrialcontracting.com
Trucking, rigging, crating & storage machinery
Owner: Joseph Sensale
icrnj@aol.com
Engineer: James Certaro
VP Marketing: Joseph Sensale
Estimated Sales: $1-2.5 Million
Number Employees: 10-19
Regions Exported to: Central America, South America, Europe, Asia
Percentage of Business in Exporting: 30

45261 (HQ)Industrial Kinetics
2535 Curtiss St
Downers Grove, IL 60515 630-655-0300
Fax: 630-655-1720 800-655-0306
ikiinfo@iki.com www.iki.com
Manufacturer and exporter of material handling and conveyor systems
Owner: George Huber
Marketing/Sales: Dwight Pentzien
Operations Manager: Dennis Harsnbarger
Production Manager: John Zienda
Plant Manager: John Zienda
Estimated Sales: $10-20 Million
Number Employees: 50-99
Square Footage: 180000
Other Locations:
Industrial Kinetics
Atlanta, GAIndustrial Kinetics
Brands Exported: Industrial Kinetic, Inc.; Olson Conveyors
Regions Exported to: Central America, South America, Europe

45262 Industrial Laboratory Eqpt Co
3210 Piper Ln
PO Box 220245
Charlotte, NC 28208-6442 704-357-3930
Fax: 704-357-3940 ile@ile-textiles.com
www.ile-textiles.com
Manufacturer and exporter of industrial testing equipment including custom, food and portion scales for analytical, counting and inventory use
President: Harry Simmons
ile@ile-textiles.com
VP: Harry Simmons
Estimated Sales: $1-2.5 Million
Number Employees: 5-9
Square Footage: 20000
Brands Exported: Ohaus; Ile; Multi-Scale
Regions Exported to: Central America, South America, Europe, Middle East
Percentage of Business in Exporting: 15

45263 Industrial Magnetics
1385 S M 75
Boyne City, MI 49712-9689 231-582-3100
Fax: 231-582-0622 800-662-4638
imi@magnetics.com www.magnetics.com
Manufacturer and exporter of magnetic separation devices for the removal of ferrous and metals.
CEO: Walter Shear
doleary@magnetics.com
Chief Financial Officer: Robin Wottowa
Engineering Manager: Dan Allore
Business Development, Marketing Manager: Dennis O'Leary
Plant Manager, Purchasing: Casey House
Estimated Sales: $25-30 Million
Number Employees: 51 - 200
Number of Products: 2000
Square Footage: 76000
Regions Exported to: Central America, South America, Europe
Percentage of Business in Exporting: 11

45264 (HQ)Industrial Piping Inc
800 Culp Rd
PO Box 518
Pineville, NC 28134-9469 704-588-1100
Fax: 704-588-5614 800-951-0988
Manufacturers and exporter of custom fabricated process equipment including coils, columns, condensers, exchangers, mix tanks, piping systems, pressure vessels, reactors and towers
President: Robert Jones
CEO: Mike Jones
mjones@goipi.com
VP: Michael Roberts
Quality Control: Ron Miller
Business Development: Earl Dowdy
Estimated Sales: $10-20 Million
Number Employees: 20-49
Square Footage: 136000
Regions Exported to: Central America, South America, Europe
Percentage of Business in Exporting: 15

45265 Industrial Product Corp
1 Hollywood Ave # 30
Suite 30
Ho Ho Kus, NJ 07423-1438 201-652-5913
Fax: 201-652-2494 800-472-5913
Manufacturer and exporter of standard and custom industrial blades for food processing machinery for pasta, pretzel and baked goods
Owner: Ken Dohner
kendohner@ipdco.com
Estimated Sales: Less Than $500,000
Number Employees: 1-4
Square Footage: 16200
Regions Exported to: South America, Asia, Canada
Percentage of Business in Exporting: 15

45266 Industries For The Blind
445 S Curtis Rd
Milwaukee, WI 53214-1016 414-778-3040
Fax: 414-933-4316 800-642-8778
info@ibmilw.com www.ibmilwaukee.com
Manufacturer and exporter of household cleaning supplies including plastic window brushes and brooms
President: Charles Lange
VP, Manufacturing: Helen Ritter
National Federal Sales Director: Dan Bailey
IT: Cindy Pinkley
cindy.pinkley@ibmilw.com
Estimated Sales: $ 10-20 Million
Number Employees: 50-99
Parent Co: Industries For The Blind
Type of Packaging: Consumer, Food Service, Bulk
Regions Exported to: Worldwide

45267 Ines Rosales
1717 Pennsylvania Ave NW
Suite 1025
Washington, DC 20006
844-354-7872
inesrosalesusa.com
Olive oil tortas *Year Founded:* 1910

45268 Infanti International
3075 Richmond Terrace
Staten Island, NY 10303-1300 718-447-5632
Fax: 718-447-5667 800-874-8590
www.infanti.com
Manufacturer and exporter of serving carts and chairs

Estimated Sales: $ 3 - 5 Million
Number Employees: 20-49
Type of Packaging: Food Service
Regions Exported to: Worldwide
Percentage of Business in Exporting: 5

45269 Infinite Peripherals
2312 Touhy Ave
Elk Grove Vlg, IL 60007-5329 224-404-6227
Fax: 847-818-1287 800-278-7860
andy@ipcprint.com www.ipcmobile.com
Importer and wholesaler/distributor of receipt printers
Owner: Andy Graham
andy@ipcprint.com
CEO: Jeff Scott
Estimated Sales: $ 1 - 3 Million
Number Employees: 10-19
Brands Imported: Citizen
Regions Imported from: Japan
Percentage of Business in Importing: 100

45270 Infitec Inc
6500 Badgley Rd
East Syracuse, NY 13057-9667 315-433-1150
Fax: 315-433-1521 800-334-0837
sales@infitec.com www.infitec
Timing controls (industrial/time delay), speed controls, flashers, and custom controls.
CEO/CFO/President: George Ehegartner, Sr
HR Executive: Kim Bremerman
kb@infitec.com
Quality Control/Marketing: George Ehegartner, Jr
kb@infitec.com
VP Sales: David Lawrie
Estimated Sales: $10-20 Million
Number Employees: 50-99
Square Footage: 50000
Type of Packaging: Bulk
Regions Exported to: Europe, Middle East, Canada, Mexico
Percentage of Business in Exporting: 8
Regions Imported from: Worldwide
Percentage of Business in Importing: 2

45271 Ingersoll & Assoc
6n971 Riverside Dr
St Charles, IL 60174-6456 847-742-7960
Fax: 847-742-9170 888-259-4040
ingersoll1@prodigy.net
Wholesaler/distributor of stock and custom forms, ticket books, ledgers, journal and inventory control sheets, grain elevator equipment, etc.; importer of promotional items, advertising specialties and health foods including vitaminand lecithin supplements
President: Zoe Ingersoll
zoe@ingersollsales.com
Estimated Sales: $ 3 - 5 Million
Number Employees: 1-4
Type of Packaging: Consumer, Food Service, Private Label, Bulk
Brands Imported: Harmony
Regions Imported from: Europe

45272 Ingersoll Rand Inc
N58 W14686 Shawn Cir
Menomonee Falls, WI 53051 262-232-7275
www.ingersollrand.com
Rotary screw, reciprocating and sliding vane compressors, multistage and positive displacement, centrifugal and side-channel blowers, vacuum technology and mobile transport products.
CEO: Vicente Reynal
SVP, Industrial Technologies: Todd Wyman
SVP & Chief Financial Officer: Emily Weaver
SVP, General Counsel & CCO: Andrew Schisel
VP, Global Sourcing & Logistics: Chris Neubauer
Year Founded: 1859
Estimated Sales: $2.3 Billion
Parent Co: Kohlberg Kravis Roberts
Regions Exported to: Worldwide
Regions Imported from: Central America, Europe

45273 Ingredia Inc
625 Commerce Rd
Wapakoneta, OH 45895-8265 419-738-4060
Fax: 419-738-4426
Dairy ingredients
CEO: Alain Thibault
Contact: Harmony Villemin
s.cedat@idi-ingredients.com
General Manager: Benot Leclercq
Number Employees: 50-99
Parent Co: Coop Laitiere Artois Flandre

Importers & Exporters / A-Z

45274 Ingredient Exchange Co
401 N Lindbergh Blvd # 315
St Louis, MO 63141-7839   314-872-8850
Fax: 314-872-7550 info@ingexchange.com
www.ingexchange.com
Importer of cheese, dairy ingredients; buyer of salvage and surplus; jobber of frozen foods, spices, concentrates and sweetners
President: Jerry Behimer
Manager: Chris Heupel
cheupeo@ingexchange.com
Estimated Sales: $15-20 Million
Number Employees: 1-4
Regions Imported from: Europe
Percentage of Business in Importing: 5

45275 Ingredient Inc
1130 W Lake Cook Rd
Suite 320
Buffalo Grove, IL 60089-1986   847-419-9595
Fax: 847-419-9547 sales@ingredientsinc.com
www.ingredientsinc.com
Supplies specialty ingredients to the food/beverage, nutraceutical and pharmaceutical industries in North America.
President: James Stewart
Chief Executive Officer, Owner: Debbie Stew
Contact: Glenn Bluemer
gbluemer@ingredientsinc.com
Estimated Sales: $ 5-10 Million
Number Employees: 5-9
Parent Co: J. Stewart & Company
Type of Packaging: Bulk
Brands Imported: Hahn & Co., Cellulose
Regions Imported from: Central America, Europe, Asia

45276 Ingredient Specialties
180 West Chestnut St
Exeter, CA 93221   559-594-4380
Fax: 559-594-4689 www.ingredientspecialties.com
Distributor of food and industrial ingredients; specializes in artificial sweetners
Director of Marketing and Sales: Bassam Faress
Estimated Sales: $1-2.5 Million
Number Employees: 9

45277 (HQ)Ingredients Solutions Inc
631 Moosehead Trl
Waldo, ME 04915-3402   207-722-4172
Fax: 207-722-4271   800-628-3166
info@ingredientssolutions.com www.isi.us.com
Independent supplier of Carrageenan. Offers a full range of Natural and Organic allowed products including Xanthan Gums, Sodium Alginates and Carrageenans for use in dairy, meat & poultry, sauces & dressings, bakery, confections, petfood, pharmaceuticals and personal-care applications.
Owner: Donna Ravin
info@ingredientssolutions.com
CEO: Scott Rangus
CFO: Janine Mehuren
Lab Manager: Kevin Johndro
Purchasing: Kristin Grover
Number Employees: 10-19
Type of Packaging: Bulk

45278 Ingredion Inc.
5 Westbrook Corporate Ctr.
Westchester, IL 60154   708-551-2600
Fax: 708-551-2700   800-713-0208
www.ingredion.com
Sweeteners, starches, corn syrups, glucose, and oils used in food and beverage products.
CEO: James Zallie
Executive VP/CFO: James Gray
Senior VP/General Counsel/CCO: Janet Bawcom
Senior VP/Chief Innovation Officer: Anthony Delio
COO: Robert Stefansic
Year Founded: 1906
Estimated Sales: $5.8 Billion
Number Employees: 11,000
Type of Packaging: Bulk
Regions Exported to: Worldwide
Regions Imported from: Central America, Canada, Mexico, Latin America

45279 Inksolv 30, LLC.
2495 N Ave
PO Box 66
Emerson, NE 68733   515-537-5344
info@inksolv30.com
www.inksolv30.com
Manufacturer and exporter of powdered hand soap

President: Kevin Wilson
Contact: Allison Franklin
allison.franklin@inksolv30.com
Estimated Sales: $2.5-5 Million
Number Employees: 1-4
Regions Exported to: Worldwide

45280 Inline Filling Systems
216 Seaboard Ave
Venice, FL 34285-4618   941-486-8800
Fax: 941-486-0077 sales101@fillers.com
www.fillers.com
Manufacturer and exporter of liquid filling equipment, capping machinery, conveyors and unscramblers
President: Sam Lubus
slubus@inlinefillingsysteminc.com
R&D: Jay Carlson
VP Sales: Joe Schemenauer
Estimated Sales: $10,000,000
Number Employees: 20-49
Square Footage: 20000
Regions Exported to: Central America, South America, Europe

45281 Inn Print
295 5th Avenue
Suite 1018
New York, NY 10016-7103   973-772-8019
Fax: 973-772-6519

45282 Inniskillin Wines
1499 Line 3
Niagra Parway
Niagara-On-The-Lake, ON L0S 1J0
Canada   905-468-2187
Fax: 905-468-5355   888-466-4754
inniskil@inniskillin.com www.inniskillin.com
Wines
President: Donald Ziraldo
VP: Karl Kaiser
Estimated Sales: $650,000
Number Employees: 20
Square Footage: 64000
Type of Packaging: Consumer, Food Service
Regions Exported to: Europe, Asia
Percentage of Business in Exporting: 10
Regions Imported from: Europe, USA, Australia
Percentage of Business in Importing: 10

45283 Inno-Vite
97 Saramia Crescent
Concord, ON L4K 4P7
Canada   905-761-5121
Fax: 888-279-3373   800-387-9111
www.inno-vite.com
Importer and wholesaler/distributor of dietary products, food and nutrition supplements and organic herbs; serving the food service market, supermarkets, pharmacies and health food and specialty stores
President: Cornelius Pasare
VP: Donna Pasare
Number Employees: 10-19
Square Footage: 80000
Brands Imported: Baxter
Regions Imported from: Europe, USA
Percentage of Business in Importing: 80

45284 Innova Envelopes
7213 Rue Cordner
La Salle, QC H8N 2J7
Canada   514-595-0555
Fax: 514-595-1112 www.supremex.com
Manufacturer and exporter of envelopes
President: Gilles Cyrcs
CFO: Stephan Lavigne
VP/General Manager: Gilles Cyr
R&D: Alain Tremblay
Estimated Sales: $ 30 - 50 Million
Number Employees: 200
Parent Co: Supremex
Regions Exported to: USA, Bermuda

45285 Innovation Moving Systems
310 S 10th St
P.O. Box 700169
Oostburg, WI 53070-1301   920-564-6272
Fax: 920-564-2322   800-619-0625
president@lectrotruck.com www.lectrotruck.com

USA manufacturer of the ORIGINAL battery operated stail climbing hand truck for over 40 years. Safely move heavy loads from 600lbs/272kg to 1500lbs/680kg in less time. All models include free battery, battery charger, strap bar(s), 2year motor warranty and a 1year entire unit warranty.
President: Kevin Peters
president@lectrotruck.com
Sales/Marketing Executive: Jason Tagel
Estimated Sales: Below $5 Million
Number Employees: 1-4
Square Footage: 34000
Brands Exported: Lectro Trucks
Regions Exported to: Worldwide
Percentage of Business in Exporting: 20

45286 Innovative Components
P.O. Box 294
Southington, CT 06489-0294   860-621-7220
Fax: 860-620-0288   800-789-2851
info@liquidlevel.com www.liquidlevel.com
Manufacturer and exporter of sanitary liquid level instrumentation for level indication, alarms and controls
Owner: Pete Meade
Sales: Pete Meade
Production: Joe Kubisek
Estimated Sales: $ 1-2.5 Million
Number Employees: 5-9
Square Footage: 10000
Regions Exported to: Europe, Asia
Percentage of Business in Exporting: 20

45287 Innovative Fishery Products
3569 Hwy 1 Saint-Bernard St
PO Box 125
Belliveau Cove, NS B0W 1J0
Canada   902-837-5163
Fax: 902-837-5165 ifp@eastlink.ca
Fresh, frozen and salted clams, scallops, groundfish and lobster
President: Marc Blinn
CEO: Doug Bertram
VP: Victor (Allan) McGuire
Number Employees: 20-49
Square Footage: 64000
Type of Packaging: Bulk
Regions Exported to: Worldwide
Percentage of Business in Exporting: 90

45288 Innovative Food Processors Inc
2125 Airport Dr
Faribault, MN 55021-7798   507-334-2730
Fax: 507-334-7969   800-997-4437
sales@ifpinc.biz www.ifpinc.biz
Custom manufacturing services including agglomeration, encapsulation, and packaging for food and beverage powders
CEO: Ephi Eyal
eeyal@ifpinc.biz
Marketing Director: Anna Batsakes
Sales Director: Scott Sijan
Estimated Sales: $23.4 Million
Number Employees: 250-499
Regions Exported to: Europe
Percentage of Business in Exporting: 5

45289 Innovative Foods, Inc.
338 N Canal
Suite 20
South San Francisco, CA 94080   650-871-8912
Fax: 650-871-0837 ed@innovativefoods.org
Infused foods, including using product forming, flavoring, coloring and value added to underutilized raw materials.
Owner: Gilbert Lee
VP/Secretary & Treasurer: Fay Hirschberg
Research & Development: Edward Hirschberg
Contact: David Terry
dterry@innovfoods.com
Estimated Sales: $190 Thousand
Square Footage: 74000

45290 Innovative Marketing
11801 Pierce St.
2nd Floor
Riverside, CA 92505   951-710-3135
Fax: 952-949-8865   800-438-4627
innovativemarketingca.com
Manufacturer and exporter of lid openers for plastic containers
President: Brad Pappas
Operations Manager: Amy Vinar

Estimated Sales: 150000
Number Employees: 1-4
Square Footage: 40000
Brands Exported: TLC; TBO

45291 Innovative Molding
6775 McKinley Ave
Sebastopol, CA 95472   707-829-2666
                    Fax: 707-829-5212
whunt@innovativemolding.com
www.innovativemolding.com
Manufacturer and exporter of threaded plastic caps and lids for jars and bottles.
Administrator: Alan Williams
awilliams@innovativemold.com
Vice President: Ron Cook
Operations Manager: Warren Hunt
Estimated Sales: $ 5-10 Million
Number Employees: 50-99
Square Footage: 56000
Regions Exported to: Canada, Mexico

45292 Innovative Plastics Corp
400 Route 303
Orangeburg, NY 10962-1340   845-359-7500
                    Fax: 845-359-0237
service@innovative-plastics.com
www.innovative-plastics.com
Thermoformed plastics packaging and contract packaging services
President: Don D'Antonio
don@inoplas.com
VP: Bud Macfarlane
Estimated Sales: $ 35 - 40 Million
Number Employees: 100-249
Square Footage: 60000
Type of Packaging: Consumer
Other Locations:
  Innovative Plastics Corporation
  Nashville, TN Innovative Plastics Corporation

45293 Innovative Space Management
2645 Brooklyn Queens Expressway
Woodside, NY 11377-7826   718-278-4300
   Fax: 718-274-0973 contact@ny.diam-int.com
Manufacturer, exporter and designer of shelf management systems and point of purchase displays
VP/General Manager (ISM Division): Bryan Yablans
VP Sales: Winn Esterline
VP Operations: Valerie Vignola
Number Employees: 850
Square Footage: 300000
Parent Co: POP Displays
Regions Exported to: Worldwide

45294 (HQ)Inovatech USA
8400 St-Laurent Boulevard
Montreal, QC H2P 2M6
Canada   360-527-1919
       Fax: 360-527-1881 800-344-7540
www.inovatech.com
Produces whey protein isolates, concentrates and modified milk ingredients in our leading edge ulta-filtration facilities; produces high quality egg white proteins; and continually works to identified and refine new technology to meetthe needs of our customers
President: Philip Vanderpol
General Manager Bio-Products: Stephen Smith
Research & Development: Jerry Middleton
Quality Control: Dr. Peter Bertram
Operations Manager: Mike Vanderpol
Estimated Sales: $ 5 - 10 Million
Number Employees: 10-19
Type of Packaging: Bulk
Brands Exported: Centrova; Emulsa; Avidin; Inovapure; Ovalbumin; Ovotransferrin; Alphapro 34; Inpro 80; Inpro 90 Plus
Regions Exported to: South America, Europe, Asia, Middle East, South Africa
Percentage of Business in Exporting: 70
Regions Imported from: USA
Percentage of Business in Importing: 10

45295 Inox Tech
67056 Route 132
Sainte Catherine, QC J5C 1B6
Canada   450-638-5441
       Fax: 450-638-2865 800-361-0319
info@inox-tech.com   www.inox-tech.com
Manufacturer and exporter of stainless steel process equipment including silos, fermenters, pressure vessels, bakery, dairy, storage tanks, etc

President: Dostie Guy
VP: Camille Dionne
Sales/Marketing Coordinator: Shirley Seller
Purchasing Director: Jason Dostie
Number Employees: 125
Square Footage: 200000
Regions Exported to: Asia, Africa
Regions Imported from: Europe

45296 Insect-O-Cutor Inc
1641 Lewis Way
Stone Mountain, GA 30083-1107   770-939-2835
       Fax: 770-621-0100 800-966-8480
sales@insect-o-cutor.com   www.insect-o-cutor.com
Industrial commercial grade insect light traps; 110 volt, 220 volt, stainless steel, scatterproof, energy-efficient
President: W A Harris
Number Employees: 10-19
Type of Packaging: Private Label
Brands Exported: Insect-O-Cutor; Guardian; Germ-O-Ray
Regions Exported to: Central America, South America, Europe, Asia, Middle East
Percentage of Business in Exporting: 15

45297 Insects Limited Inc
16950 Westfield Park Rd
Westfield, IN 46074-9374   317-896-9300
       Fax: 317-867-5757 800-992-1991
insectsltd@aol.com   www.fumigationzone.com
Manufacturer, exporter and wholesaler/distributor of pest control systems including traps, lures, insect monitoring and detection devices, fumigation products, etc.; importer of cigarette beetle pheromone traps; also, pest controlaudits and seminars available
President: David Mueller
d.mueller@insectslimited.com
CFO: Barbara Bass
VP: John Mueller
General Manager: Patrick Kelley
Estimated Sales: $ 1 Million
Number Employees: 10-19
Square Footage: 6000
Brands Exported: Bullet Lures, No Survivor Traps
Regions Exported to: Worldwide
Percentage of Business in Exporting: 15
Brands Imported: Lasio; Serrico
Regions Imported from: Europe, Asia
Percentage of Business in Importing: 15

45298 Inshore Fisheries
PO Box 118
Middle West Pubnico, NS B0W 2M0
Canada   902-762-2522
              Fax 902-762-3464 www.inshore.ca
Fresh and frozen fish
President: Claude d'Entremont
Number Employees: 50-99
Type of Packaging: Consumer, Food Service
Brands Exported: Inshore
Regions Exported to: Europe, Asia, USA
Percentage of Business in Exporting: 90

45299 Insignia Systems Inc
8799 Brooklyn Blvd
Minneapolis, MN 55445-2398   763-392-6200
       Fax: 763-392-6222 800-874-4648
info@insigniasystems.com
www.insigniasystems.com
Manufacturer and exporter of promotional items including signage and software for bar coding and large format printing
President/CEO: Glen P. Dall
VP, Finance: John C. Gonsior
CFO: John C. Gonsior
Quality Control: Bob Norman
VP Marketing: Scott Simcox
Number Employees: 50-99
Regions Exported to: South America, Europe, Canada, Caribbean, Latin America, Mexico, Australia, New Zealand
Percentage of Business in Exporting: 10

45300 (HQ)Insinger Co
6245 State Rd
Philadelphia, PA 19135-2996   215-624-4800
       Fax: 215-624-6966 800-344-4802
sales@insingermachine.com
www.insingermachine.com
Manufacturer and exporter of commercial dishwashers potato peelers, garbage disposal units, french fry cutters, tray washers and driers and dish, glass, pot and pan washers

President: John Stern
CEO: Robert Cantor
acantor@insingermachine.com
VP Sales/Marketing: Ari Cantor
Chief Engineer: Jim Bittner
Quality Control: Kris Hogan
Marketing Director: Annemarie Fisher
Regional Sales Manager: Don Gazzillo
Vice President of Operations: Kristine Hogan
Purchasing Manager: Kristine Hogan
Estimated Sales: $ 10 - 20 Million
Number Employees: 50-99
Square Footage: 130000
Regions Exported to: Central America, South America, Europe, Asia, Middle East
Regions Imported from: Europe

45301 Inspired Automation Inc
5321 Derry Ave # D
Agoura Hills, CA 91301-5064   818-991-4598
       Fax: 818-597-4820 www.inspiredautomation.com
Automatic net weighing, counting, in-line batching and filling machinery; exporter of automatic net weighing, in-line batching and counting machinery
President: Robert Homes
bob@inspiredautomation.com
Sales: Buzz Holmes
Plant Manager: Joesph Gonzales
Estimated Sales: $ 3 - 5 Million
Number Employees: 5-9
Number of Brands: 1
Number of Products: 22
Square Footage: 4000
Type of Packaging: Consumer, Food Service, Private Label, Bulk

45302 Insta-Pro International
10104 Douglas Ave
Urbandale, IA 50322-2007   515-254-1260
       Fax: 515-276-5749 800-383-4524
www.insta-pro.com
Manufacturer and exporter of processing equipment for textured soy products
Vice President: Ray Goodwin
rgoodwin@insta-pro.com
President, Chief Executive Officer: Kevin Kacere
R&D: Wilmot Wijeratne
VP: Karl Arnold
Chairman: Wayne Fox
VP International Marketing: Tom Welby
Vice President of Operations: Hennie Pieterse
Estimated Sales: $ 5 - 10 Million
Number Employees: 10-19
Parent Co: Triple F
Brands Exported: Insta-Pro
Regions Exported to: Worldwide

45303 Instant Products of America
835 S Mapleton Street
Columbus, IN 47201-7359   812-372-9100
                    Fax: 812-372-9132
Instant beverages, dry mixes, syrups and toppings
President: Rolf Walendy
Vice President: George Moon
Contact: Tom Behrman
tbehrman@instantproductsinc.net
Plant Manager: Mike Brannan
Estimated Sales: $10-24.9 Million
Number Employees: 50
Square Footage: 70000
Parent Co: Kruger Gmbh & Company
Type of Packaging: Consumer, Food Service, Private Label, Bulk
Regions Exported to: Canada
Percentage of Business in Exporting: 5
Regions Imported from: Europe
Percentage of Business in Importing: 5

45304 Instrumart
35 Green Mountain Dr
South Burlington, VT 05403-7824   802-863-0085
       Fax: 802-863-1193 800-884-4967
sales@instrumart.com   www.instrumart.com
Wholesaler/distributor, importer and exporter of temperature control and recording equipment
President: Bob Berman
bberman@instrumart.com
Engineering Manager: Scott Sabourin
Estimated Sales: $10-20 Million
Number Employees: 20-49
Square Footage: 24000
Brands Exported: Fuji; Toho; Sixth Sense
Regions Exported to: Central America, South America, Canada, Latin America, Mexico

Importers & Exporters / A-Z

Brands Imported: Fuji
Regions Imported from: Asia

45305 Insulair
35275 S Welty Rd
Vernalis, CA 95385-9733 209-839-0911
Fax: 209-839-1353 800-343-3402
Manufacturer and exporter of insulated triple-wall paper cups and plastic lids
President: Claus Sadlier
CFO: Larry Nally
Quality Control: Dale Houglant
Sales Director: Frank Gavin
Estimated Sales: $ 5 - 10 Million
Number Employees: 5-9
Regions Exported to: Europe, Asia, Middle East, Australia, Canada, Carribean, Mexico, South Africa
Percentage of Business in Exporting: 60

45306 Intedge Manufacturing
1875 Chumley Rd
Woodruff, SC 29388-8561 864-969-9601
Fax: 864-969-9604 866-969-9605
customer.service@intedge.com www.intedge.com
Food service equipment including textiles, smallware, baking supplies, timers, thermometers, utensils, and much more.
Plant Manager: Debi Collier
Number Employees: 20-49
Type of Packaging: Food Service, Private Label
Regions Exported to: Canada
Percentage of Business in Exporting: 10
Regions Imported from: Europe, Asia
Percentage of Business in Importing: 20

45307 Integrated Restaurant Software/RMS Touch
9 West Ridgely Road
Timonium, MD 21093 201-461-9096
Fax: 410-902-5468
Manufacturer and exporter of P.O.S. touch screen software for restaurants, bars, cafeterias, etc
President: Richard Adler
VP Sales: Peter Polizanno
Estimated Sales: $ 2.5 - 5 Million
Number Employees: 10-19
Square Footage: 12000
Regions Exported to: Worldwide
Percentage of Business in Exporting: 15

45308 Intelligent Controls
PO Box 638
Saco, ME 4072 207-283-0156
Fax: 207-283-0158 800-872-3455
webadmin@incon.com www.incon.com
Manufacturer and exporter of microprocessor and programmable controls including liquid level measurement and process multiplexing systems, supervisory control and data acquisition systems
CEO: Scott Tremble
Director Marketing: John Eastman
VP: Dean Richards
Contact: Vitaliy Demin
vdemin@franklinfueling.com
Estimated Sales: F
Number Employees: 1,000-4,999
Square Footage: 28000
Parent Co: Franklin Fueling Systems
Regions Exported to: South America
Percentage of Business in Exporting: 10

45309 Inter Ocean Seafood Trader
1200 Industrial Rd # 12
Suite 12
San Carlos, CA 94070-4129 650-508-0691
Fax: 650-595-1261
Fresh seafood
President: John Chen
Treasurer: Jeanne Chen
Vice President: Grace Chai
Estimated Sales: $25,000,000
Number Employees: 5-9

45310 Inter-Continental Imports Company
149 Louis Street
Newington, CT 06111 860-665-1101
Fax: 860-665-1085 800-424-4522
www.icaffe.com
Coffee
President/CEO: Vincent Saccuzzo
Office Manager: Lucy Pluchino
Purchasing Manager: Vincent Saccuzzo
Estimated Sales: $5-10 Million
Number Employees: 5-9
Type of Packaging: Private Label
Brands Imported: Torronalba, Carimali And Nuova Simonelli espresso machines
Regions Imported from: Europe
Percentage of Business in Importing: 50

45311 (HQ)Inter-Pack Corporation
PO Box 691
Monroe, MI 48161-0691 734-242-7755
Fax: 734-242-7756
Manufacturer and exporter of corrugated paper and foam plastic; contract packaging services available
Manager: Frank Calandra
Estimated Sales: $ 20 - 50 Million
Number Employees: 20-49

45312 InterMetro Industries
Wilkes-Barre, PA 18705 570-825-2741
Manufacturer of space and productivity solutions
Year Founded: 1929
Number Employees: 400
Number of Products: 30K
Regions Exported to: Worldwide

45313 InterNatural Foods
1455 Broad St
4th Floor
Bloomfield, NJ 07003 973-338-1499
Fax: 973-338-1485 www.internaturalfoods.com
Importer and distributor of natural and organic food products such as instant coffees, fruit popsicles, stevia sweeteners, cereals, oils and vinegars, crème filled wafers, red palm oil, coconut oil, sea salts, vegetarian organic soupsno salt spice rubs, organic baby foods, all natural licorice, corn starch, cane sugars, broth bouillon cubes, sunflower oil, yeast, chocolate hazelnut butters, crackers and pastas
Chairwoman: Linda Palame
info@internaturalfoods.com
Type of Packaging: Consumer, Food Service, Bulk
Brands Imported: Vivani, Ryvita, Rapunzel, pero, Panda, Loriva, Le Saunier De Camargue, Jungle Products, Helwa Organic, Gourmet Artisan, Familia Swiss Cereals, Erba Dolce, Cafix
Regions Imported from: Central America, South America, Europe, Asia, Middle East, Worldwide
Percentage of Business in Importing: 98

45314 Interamerican Coffee
19500 State Hwy 249 # 255
Houston, TX 77070 713-462-2671
Fax: 713-912-7072 800-346-2810
traders@iaccoffee.com
Green coffee importer and distributer
President: Guy Burdett
Controller: Samantha Marino
Vice President of Operations: John Mason
Estimated Sales: $5-10 Million
Number Employees: 20-49

45315 Interamerican Quality Foods
306 W Rhapsody Dr
San Antonio, TX 78216-3132 210-341-4057
Fax: 210-341-0147 www.iqf-tx.com
Importer and exporter of frozen vegetables and fruits
President: Gary Payne
gary@iqf-tx.com
Marketing Director: Chris Payne
Sales Director: Paul Farnsworth
Operations Manager: Patty Briscoe
Estimated Sales: $5-10 Million
Number Employees: 5-9
Type of Packaging: Consumer, Food Service, Private Label, Bulk
Brands Exported: Prime Crest
Regions Exported to: Europe, Asia
Percentage of Business in Exporting: 30
Regions Imported from: Central America, Canada, Mexico

45316 Intercard Inc
1884 Lackland Hill Pkwy # 1
St Louis, MO 63146-3569 314-275-8066
Fax: 314-275-4998 info@intercardinc.com
Manufacturer and exporter of credit and debit card systems

CEO: Ray Sherrod
CFO: Gerry Schmidt
Quality Control: Lynn Soreden
Estimated Sales: $ 10 - 20 Million
Number Employees: 20-49
Regions Exported to: Europe

45317 Intercomp
3839 County Road 116
Hamel, MN 55340-9342 763-476-2531
Fax: 763-476-2613 800-328-3336
info@intercompany.com
www.intercompco.com
Manufacturer and exporter of electronic scales including crane, platform, pallet and portable truck, floor, bench and hanging
Owner: Robert Kroll
Quality Control: Mark Browne
Plant Manager: Jeff Weyandt
Estimated Sales: $20 Million
Number Employees: 50-99
Square Footage: 90000
Brands Exported: Intercomp Co.
Regions Exported to: Central America, South America, Europe, Asia, Middle East, Worldwide
Percentage of Business in Exporting: 30
Regions Imported from: Central America, Europe, Asia
Percentage of Business in Importing: 5

45318 Interex
3200 Northern Cross Blvd
Fort Worth, TX 76137 817-361-4200
contact@topochicousa.net
www.topochicousa.com
Mineral water

45319 Interfrost
349 W Commercial St
East Rochester, NY 14445-2407 585-381-0320
Fax: 585-381-1052
Frozen fruits and vegetables
VP/General Manager: Thomas Crandall
Estimated Sales: $5-10 Million
Number Employees: 5-9
Parent Co: Cobi Foods

45320 Interlab
4200 Research Forest Dr # 150
The Woodlands, TX 77381-3237 281-298-9410
Fax: 281-298-9411 888-876-2844
www.polyseed.org
Manufacturer and exporter of microbial products for drain maintenance, odor control, septic systems, etc.; also, in-house and field technical support available
President: Peter Perez
Estimated Sales: $ 3 - 5 Million
Number Employees: 5-9
Square Footage: 28400
Regions Exported to: Central America, South America, Europe, Asia
Percentage of Business in Exporting: 40

45321 Interlake Mecalux
1600 N. 25th Ave.
Melrose Park
Chicago, IL 60160 708-344-9999
Fax: 708-343-9788 www.interlakemecalux.com
Steel racking, warehouse automation, warehouse management software and other storage solutions.
Founder/President: Jose Luis Carrillo Rodriguez
Year Founded: 2000
Estimated Sales: $100-$500 Million
Number Employees: 500-999
Regions Exported to: Central America, South America, Europe, Asia

45322 Intermix Beverage
1026 Central Ave NE
Minneapolis, MN 55413-2499 612-746-8880
Fax: 612-746-8889 800-826-4177
info@espresso-services.com
www.espresso-services.com
Importer and wholesaler/distributor of Italian espresso and cappuccino equipment, drip brewers, espresso coffee, syrups, chocolates, etc
Owner: Katie Coughlin
Marketing: Rachel Strand
Sales Director: Curtis Carr
katiec@intermixbev.com
Operations Manager: Jeff Adelman
Estimated Sales: $10-20 Million
Number Employees: 20-49
Square Footage: 8000

Type of Packaging: Consumer, Food Service, Bulk
Brands Imported: Lavazza; Torani; Ghiradecci; La Cimbali; Ghiradelli; Mazzer
Regions Imported from: Europe
Percentage of Business in Importing: 75

45323 Intermold Corporation
30 Old Mill Rd
Greenville, SC 29607   864-627-0300
    Fax: 864-627-0005   sales@intermoldcorp.com
    www.intermoldcorp.com
Manufacturer and exporter of plastic injection molding products including bakery proofer cups; custom molding for the baking industry available
President: Alan Butcher
sales@intermoldcorp.com
VP: Jane Butcher
Estimated Sales: $ 1-2.5 Million
Number Employees: 10-19
Square Footage: 32000
Regions Exported to: Canada
Percentage of Business in Exporting: 5

45324 Intermountain Specialty Food Group
265 Plymouth Ave
Salt Lake City, UT 84115   801-977-9077
    Fax: 801-977-8202   www.intermountainfood.com
Pasta, sauces, dessert mixes, dip mixes, baking mixes and soup mixes
President: Debbie Chidester
Co-Owner: Jody Chidester
Contact: Jim Hubbard
jimhubbard@intermountainfood.com
Estimated Sales: $700 Thousand
Number Employees: 13
Number of Brands: 4
Type of Packaging: Consumer, Food Service, Bulk
Other Locations:
    Intermountain Foods
    Meridian, ID Intermountain Foods
Regions Exported to: Canada

45325 International Adhesive Coating
6 Industrial Dr
PO Box 240
Windham, NH 03087-2020   603-893-1894
    Fax: 603-898-9025   800-253-4450
    sales@itctapes.com
Manifactures a complete line of double coated, single-coated, transfer tapes, bag sealing, foam and high tack/low tack products along with a wide range of coating and converting capabilities.
Manager: Dennis Salois
dsalois@itctapes.com
Estimated Sales: $ 5 - 10 Million
Number Employees: 20-49
Regions Exported to: Worldwide
Percentage of Business in Exporting: 3

45326 International Beverages
79 N 11th St
#1 Brewers Row
Brooklyn, NY 11249   718-486-7422
    Fax: 718-486-7440   www.brooklynbrewery.com
Importer and wholesaler/distributor of beer
Co-Founder & President: Steve Hindy
Controller: Debra Bascome
Technical Director: Mary Wiles
Marketing Director: Ben Hudson
VP of Sales: Robin Ottaway
Office Manager: Sherwin Chang
Production Manager: Jimmy Valm
Estimated Sales: $5-10 Million
Number Employees: 10-19
Parent Co: Brooklyn Brewery
Type of Packaging: Consumer
Regions Imported from: Central America, Europe
Percentage of Business in Importing: 60

45327 International Business Trading
4833 Fruitland Ave
Vernon, CA 90058-2722   323-277-0000
    Fax: 323-869-8889
Importer and exporter of frozen, fresh and live seafood
President: Albert Leung
Estimated Sales: $10-20 Million
Number Employees: 10-19
Square Footage: 100000
Type of Packaging: Consumer, Food Service, Bulk
Regions Imported from: Central America, South America, Asia, Middle East

45328 International Casings Group
4420 S Wolcott Ave
Chicago, IL 60609-3159   773-294-8996
    Fax: 773-376-9292   800-825-5151
    sales@casings.com   www.casings.com
Sausage casings
President: Serge Azohoun
satohoun@casings.com
CFO: Bryan Schultz
VP: Eric Svendsen
Director of Sales: Jim Dunbar
Operations Manager: Jim Wilt
Estimated Sales: $10-20 Million
Number Employees: 100-249
Square Footage: 104000
Type of Packaging: Food Service
Other Locations:
    International Casings Group
    Santa Fe Springs, CA International Casings Group
Regions Exported to: Central America, South America, Europe

45329 International Cellulose
12315 Robin Blvd
Houston, TX 77045-4820   713-433-6701
    Fax: 713-433-2029   icc@spray-on.com
    www.spray-on.com
President: Steven A Kempe
skempe@spray-on.com
Estimated Sales: $ 10 - 20 Million
Number Employees: 50-99

45330 International Chemical Corp
7654 Progress Cir
Melbourne, FL 32904-1655   321-952-6466
    Fax: 321-952-9883   800-914-2436
    95263@msn.com
    www.internationalchemicalcorp.com
Processor, importer and exporter of acids including ascorbic, citric, sorbic and tartaric; also, sodium citrate, sodium ascorbate and vanillin
Owner: Bob Catroneo
rcatroneo@floridachem.com
Number Employees: 1-4
Square Footage: 200000
Type of Packaging: Private Label, Bulk
Brands Exported: ICI
Regions Exported to: Worldwide
Percentage of Business in Exporting: 20
Regions Imported from: Worldwide
Percentage of Business in Importing: 50

45331 International ChocolateCompany
2030 N Redwood Rd
Salt Lake City, UT 84116-1229   801-359-7375
    Fax: 801-359-7376
    www.internationalchocolate.com
Owner: Tim Bergquist
Estimated Sales: $ 1 - 3 Million
Number Employees: 1-4

45332 International Coconut Corp
225 W Grand St
PO Box 3326
Elizabeth, NJ 07202-1205   908-289-1555
    Fax: 908-289-1556
    sales@internationalcoconut.com
Coconut
Owner: A Kaye
Vice President: Richard Kesselhaut
richard@internationalcoconut.com
Estimated Sales: $2.5-5 Million
Number Employees: 5-9
Square Footage: 46000
Type of Packaging: Consumer, Food Service, Private Label, Bulk
Brands Exported: Sno-Top
Regions Exported to: Central America, Europe, Asia
Regions Imported from: Asia

45333 International Cold Storage
215 E 13th St
Andover, KS 67002-9329   316-218-4100
    Fax: 316-733-2434   800-835-0001
    www.icsco.com
Walk-in coolers and freezers; exporter of walk-in coolers
President: Matt Madeksza
CFO: Carlos Tlusty
carlos.tlusty@carrier.utc.com
VP, Sales, West: Jim Cook
VP, Sales, Midwest: Mark Norvold
Plant Manager: Jay Risley
Estimated Sales: $ 10 - 20 Million
Number Employees: 100-249
Square Footage: 160000
Parent Co: Tyler Refrigeration Company
Brands Exported: ICS
Regions Exported to: Canada, Mexico
Percentage of Business in Exporting: 5

45334 International Commercial Supply
200 International Way
Winsted, CT 06098   860-738-7112
    Fax: 860-738-7140   custserv@allpointsfps.com
    www.icscparts.com

45335 International Cooling Systems
300 Granton Drive
Richmond Hill, ON L4B 1H7
Canada   416-213-5566
    Fax: 416-213-9666   888-213-5566
Manufacturer, importer and exporter of turnkey process cooling systems, cooling towers, chillers, flake and pumpable flow ice machines and water/fluid recirculation stations
President: Victor Gardiman
VP: Otto Novak
Plant Manager: Steve Novak
Number Employees: 10-19
Square Footage: 96000
Regions Exported to: Europe, Asia, Middle East, Latin America, Caribbean
Percentage of Business in Exporting: 15
Percentage of Business in Importing: 10

45336 International Culinary
747 Vassar Ave
Lakewood, NJ 08701-6908   732-229-0008
    Fax: 732-886-5885   chefharvey@aol.com
    www.chefharvey.com
Importer and wholesaler/distributor of culinary, stainless steel carving and melon and apple garnishing tools
President: Harvey Rosen
chefharvey@aol.com
Number Employees: 10-19

45337 International Dehydrated Foods
3801 E Sunshine St
Springfield, MO 65809   417-881-7820
    800-641-6509
    realfood@idf.com   www.idf.com
Processed meat and poultry ingredients
Founder: William Darr
CEO: Andrew Herr
Senior Director, Sales: Lou Croce
Credit Manager, Corporate Office: Debbie Thomas
Year Founded: 1982
Estimated Sales: $50 Million
Number Employees: 5-9
Number of Brands: 1
Square Footage: 6973
Type of Packaging: Bulk
Regions Exported to: Central America, South America, Asia
Percentage of Business in Exporting: 60

45338 International Enterprises Unlimited
5628 Mineral Spring Rd
Suffolk, VA 23438-9457   757-986-3800
    Fax: 757-986-3801   877-423-5263
Wholesaler/distributor and importer of all-natural and low-sodium foods including smoked salmon, haddock, caviar, escargot, caviar pate, etc.; also, gourmet specialty items including Icelandic lamb; serving the food service and retailmarkets
President/CEO: L Hayes
COO: Steinunn Hilmarsdottir
Contact: Lloyd Hayes
shawng@aquik.net
Estimated Sales: $1-2.5 Million
Number Employees: 1-4
Square Footage: 100000
Type of Packaging: Consumer, Food Service, Private Label, Bulk
Brands Imported: Iceland Gourmet; Artic Seafood Delicacies; Triton; Gem of Iceland; Godi
Regions Imported from: Europe, Iceland
Percentage of Business in Importing: 70

45339 International Enterprises
PO Box 158
Herring Neck, NL A0G 2R0
Canada   709-628-7406
    Fax: 709-628-7875

Importers & Exporters / A-Z

Mussels
President: Wayne Fudge
Estimated Sales: $975,000
Number Employees: 7
Type of Packaging: Consumer, Food Service, Bulk
Regions Exported to: USA
Percentage of Business in Exporting: 25

45340 International Environmental Solutions
6860 Gulfport Blvd S.
Suite 131
South Pasadena, FL 33707-2108   727-573-1676
Fax: 727-573-0747   800-972-8348
davidleeti@aol.com   www.drycamping.com
Automatic faucet controls
President: Steve Gordon
Estimated Sales: Less than $500,000
Number Employees: 20-49
Square Footage: 16000
Brands Exported: EzFlo; Quik Flo; Med Flo
Regions Exported to: Europe, Worldwide, Australia, Canada, Caribbean

45341 International Food Associates
1201 Mt Kemble Ave
Morristown, NJ 07960   973-425-1200
Fax: 973-425-1202
dlucas@internationalfoodassociates.com
Specialty food, natural food, organic food, confectionery candy
President/Owner: Larry LaPare
VP Finance: Jeann McLennan
Marketing: Dale Lucas
Contact: Ian Altman
ian@ifabrands.com
VP Operations: Jackie Peckham
Number Employees: 8

45342 International Food Packers Corporation
4691 SW 71st Avenue
Miami, FL 33155-4657   305-740-5847
Fax: 305-669-1447
Canned corned beef, frozen cooked beef and beef cuts; importer of canned fish and rice
President: Richard Spradling
Estimated Sales: $2.5-5 Million
Number Employees: 5-9
Square Footage: 12000
Brands Exported: Delta; Deltina; Bonanza; Caribe; Landcaster; Golden Cow; Deli Pride; Pando
Regions Exported to: Central America, South America, Europe, Asia, Caribbean
Percentage of Business in Exporting: 20
Brands Imported: Delta; Deltina; Bonanza; Caribe; Landcaster; Golden Cow; Deli Pride; Pando
Regions Imported from: South America, Asia
Percentage of Business in Importing: 80

45343 International Food Products
150 Larkin Williams Industrial Ct
Fenton, MO 63026
800-227-8427
info@ifpc.com   www.ifpc.com
Food ingredients and additives
Chairman: Fred Brown, Sr.
CEO: Clayton Brown
VP, Finance: Kathy Langan
VP, Sales & Marketing: Jamie Moritz
VP, Quality & Regulatory: Mary Ellen Rowland
VP, Manufacturing: Mark Warren
VP, Supply Chain: Jennifer Hoerchler
Year Founded: 1974
Estimated Sales: $150 Million
Number Employees: 50-200
Square Footage: 68000
Type of Packaging: Consumer, Food Service
Other Locations:
   St. Louis, MO
   Joplin, MO
   Kansas City, MO
   Houston, TX
   Dallas, TX
   Laredo, TXJoplin
Brands Exported: Dairy House© Stabilizers, Dairy House© Chocolate Dairy Powder, Dairy House© Vitamins, Dairy House© Milk Flavors, Ingredion©
Regions Exported to: Central America, South America, The Caribbean

45344 International Foodcraft Corp
1601 E Linden Ave
Linden, NJ 07036-1508   908-862-8810
Fax: 908-862-8825   800-875-9393
info@intlfoodcraft.com   www.ifc-solutions.com
Anti-stick lubricants, release agents and food color concentrates
Owner: David Dukes
ddukes@intlfoodcraft.com
Technical Director: Ted Palumbo
Estimated Sales: $2 Million
Number Employees: 10-19
Type of Packaging: Bulk
Regions Exported to: Canada, Latin America, Mexico
Percentage of Business in Exporting: 5

45345 International Foods & Confections
2635 Walnut St.
Denver, CO 80205   303-893-0552
Fax: 303-893-0507   800-362-5287
Importer of frozen European desserts and pastry ingredients including cake decorations, pastry shells, chocolate cups, purees, etc
President: Terry Herron
VP: Richard Wangenheim
Marketing: Mary Jo Kennedy
Sales: Mike Clever
Estimated Sales: $10-20 Million
Number Employees: 10-19
Square Footage: 36000
Brands Imported: Dobla; Euro Patisserie, Chocouic, Les Treis Toques Materne
Regions Imported from: Europe

45346 International Glace
1616 East Lyons Avenue
Spokane, WA 99217   760-731-3220
Fax: 760-731-3221   800-884-5041
alan@internationalglace.com
Importer of ginger, brewers' yeast spread and glace fruits
Manager: Marilyn Guest
Vice President: Bill Davids
Sales Director: Alan Sipole
Estimated Sales: $1-2.5 Million
Number Employees: 1-4
Type of Packaging: Consumer, Bulk
Brands Imported: Vegemite; Robern Fruit
Regions Imported from: Asia, Fiji, Australia
Percentage of Business in Importing: 85

45347 International Home Foods
1633 Littleton Rd
Parsippany, NJ 07054   973-359-9920
Fax: 973-254-5473
Canned beans, peas, apples, pasta, chicken, tomato paste, chili, mustard, instant hot cereal, nonstick cooking spray and glazed popcorn
Chairman/CEO: C Dean Metropoulos
SVP/CFO: Craig Steeneck
President/COO: Lawrence Hathaway
Sales/Marketing Executive: Mike Larney
Number Employees: 100
Parent Co: ConAgra Foods
Type of Packaging: Consumer
Brands Exported: Chef Boyardee; Pam Cooking Spray; Gulden's; CNM; Jiffy Pop; Dennison's; Luck's; Ranch Style
Regions Exported to: Central America, South America, Asia

45348 International Industries Corporation
154 Saint Andrews Dr
Spartanburg, SC 29306-6638
Fax: 864-542-0001   sales@iicorp.net
www.iicorp.net
Exporter of snack foods, chocolate products, peanuts, fruit drinks, peanut butter, spaghetti and pizza sauces, frozen bakery products, cakes, honey, crackers and cookies
President: David Cloer
Contact: Owantha Barfield
obarfield@iicorp.net
Estimated Sales: $2.5-5 Million
Number Employees: 5-9
Brands Exported: Sunrise; Party; Uncle Sam's; Barnaby's
Regions Exported to: Central America, South America, Europe, Asia, Middle East
Percentage of Business in Exporting: 80

45349 International Knife & Saw
1435 N Cashua Dr
Florence, SC 29501-6950   843-662-6345
Fax: 843-664-1103   800-354-9872
iks@iksinc.com   www.iksinc.com
Manufacturer and exporter of fruit and vegetable slicing machinery; also, machine knives
President: Don Weeks
Vice President of Division: Terry Isaacs
Vice President, Metal & Printing Divisio: Jim Ranson
Sales: Warren Balderson
Manager: Robb Kirkpatrick
rkirkpatrick@iksinc.com
Vice President, Finance & Manufacturing: Mike Gray
Purchasing Manager of Materials: Sarah Strother
Estimated Sales: $60 Million
Number Employees: 50-99
Percentage of Business in Exporting: 4

45350 International Lowell
9234 Belmont Ave
Franklin Park, IL 60131-2808   847-260-5018
Fax: 847-349-1009   800-733-3772
info@lowellfoods.com   www.lowellfoods.com
European style yogurts
President: Conrad Lowell
lowellch@lowellfoods.com
Marketing: Katherine Mrugala
Estimated Sales: $10 Million
Number Employees: 1-4

45351 International MachineryXchnge
214 N Main St
Deerfield, WI 53531-9644   608-764-5481
Fax: 608-764-8240   800-279-0191
sales@imexchange.com   www.imexchange.com
Manufacturer and exporter of re-manufactured machinery including refrigeration, cheese making, centrifuges, compressors and heat exchangers; also, tanks and custom control systems
President: Greg Mergen
sales@imexchange.com
Sales Director: George Bamman
Estimated Sales: $5-10 Million
Number Employees: 10-19
Square Footage: 80000
Regions Exported to: Central America, South America, Europe
Percentage of Business in Exporting: 25

45352 International Market Brands
516 6th St S # 100
Kirkland, WA 98033-6727   425-827-3849
Fax: 425-827-3484   www.imbusa.com
Exporter of fresh fruits, cheese, turkey, cake mixes, powdered beverage bases, dried pasta, gelatin and tomato products, frozen French fries, dairy and nondairy products, beef, pork, fish, bakery products including nondairy toppingsand flour mixes
President: James Kern
jkern@imbusa.com
Export Manager: Ludy Medina
Estimated Sales: $2.5-5 Million
Number Employees: 1-4
Brands Exported: Garden Chef, Nulaid, Mary Alice, Grand Duchess, Baker Boy, Big Country
Regions Exported to: Central America, Europe, Middle East, Carribean, Latin America, Worldwide
Percentage of Business in Exporting: 100

45353 International Molasses Corp
88 Market St
Saddle Brook, NJ 07663-4830   201-368-8036
Fax: 201-845-0028   800-526-0180
info@maltproducts.com   www.maltproducts.com
Processor and exporter of molasses including cane, syrup and dry
Owner: Ronald Targan
intlmol@aol.com
CEO: Herb Schneider
Sales Exec: Joe Hickenbottom
Estimated Sales: $10 - 20 Million
Number Employees: 10-19
Type of Packaging: Consumer, Food Service, Bulk
Regions Exported to: Worldwide

Importers & Exporters / A-Z

45354 International Oils & Concentrates
45 US Highway 206 # 104
P.O.Box 185
Augusta, NJ 07822-2044   973-579-0014
Fax: 973-579-2509 info@iocsales.com
iocsales.com
Importer, wholesaler and distributor of fruit juice concentrates, tropical and fruit purees, single strength juices, essential oils and essences; exporter of fruit juice concentrates. Some of their products include Lemon ConcentrateRed Grape Concentrate, Peach Puree, Blueberry Concentrate, Coconut Cream, Apple Essence and more.
President: Don De Stefano
juiceconcentratesioc@yahoo.com
Vice President: Donny De Stefano
Sales: Diane De Stefano
Estimated Sales: $7-8 Million
Number Employees: 4
Square Footage: 6000
Type of Packaging: Bulk
Regions Exported to: Central America, South America, Europe
Percentage of Business in Exporting: 10
Regions Imported from: Central America, South America, Europe

45355 International Olive Oil
2271 Landmark Pl
Manasquan, NJ 08736   855-556-5483
Fax: 877-791-9127 info@internationaloliveoil.com
internationaloliveoil.com
Olive oils, vinegars, salts and spices

45356 International Omni-Pac Corporation
2079 Wright Ave
La Verne, CA 91750-5822   909-593-2833
Fax: 909-593-2829 bobdavis@omni-pac.com
www.omni-pac.com
Manufacturer and exporter of packaging systems and juice and soft drink bottle carriers
President: Richard Erickson
Sales Manager: Bob Davis
Contact: Bill Johnston
bjohnston@omni-pac.com
Estimated Sales: Below $5 Million
Number Employees: 5-9
Square Footage: 40000
Regions Exported to: Worldwide
Percentage of Business in Exporting: 2

45357 International Pack & Ship
377b Nassau Road
Roosevelt, NY 11575-1316   516-378-9110
Fax: 516-378-9372 tvlrainbow@aol.com
Wholesaler/distributor, importer and exporter of health food products including vitamins, nutritional supplements, herbal teas, coffees, spices and seasonings
President: Joseph Horton
Number Employees: 1-4
Type of Packaging: Consumer, Bulk
Regions Exported to: Central America, South America, Middle East, Mexico, Latin America, Caribbean
Percentage of Business in Exporting: 80
Regions Imported from: Central America, South America, Middle East, Caribbean
Percentage of Business in Importing: 20

45358 International PackagingMachinery
PO Box 8597
Naples, FL 34101-8597   941-643-2020
Fax: 941-643-2708 800-237-6496
Manufacturer and exporter of stretch wrapping machinery including film tensioners and stretch film delivery systems
Estimated Sales: $ 5-10 Million
Number Employees: 20-49
Square Footage: 42000
Brands Exported: IPM
Regions Exported to: Central America, South America, Asia, Middle East, Canada, Caribbean, Latin America, Mexico
Percentage of Business in Exporting: 30

45359 (HQ)International Paper BoxMachine Company
PO Box 787
Nashua, NH 03061-0787   603-889-6651
Fax: 603-882-2865
Manufacturer, exporter and importer of carton folding and gluing machinery; also, corrugated converters including liquid-tight packaging
President: Hugh McAdam
Marketing Manager: Larry Macko
Marketing Communications Manager: Michael Sutcliffe
Estimated Sales: $20-50 Million
Number Employees: 100-249
Square Footage: 165000
Regions Exported to: Central America, South America, Europe, Asia
Percentage of Business in Exporting: 45
Brands Imported: Sanwa; Temcorr
Regions Imported from: Asia

45360 International Paper Food Service Business
3 Paragon Dr
Montvale, NJ 07645-1782   201-391-1776
Fax: 201-307-6125
VP: Austin Lance
Number Employees: 100-249

45361 International Patterns,Inc.
50 Inez Dr
Bay Shore, NY 11706-2238   631-952-2000
Fax: 516-938-1215
Manufacturer and exporter of illuminated and nonilluminated menu, changeable letter and write-on boards, nonneon signs, banners, point of purchase displays, tray stands, ice-free wine coolers and youth chairs
President: Shelley Beckwith
shelleyb@u.washington.edu
CFO: Shelly Beckwi
Vice President: Shellay Beckwith
R & D: Paul Kaplan
VP Marketing: Murray Gottieb
VP Sales: Andrew Replan
Production Manager: Ran Alvaeri
Purchasing Manager: Nancy St. Nicholas
Estimated Sales: $5-10 Million
Number Employees: 50-99
Number of Brands: 1
Number of Products: 50
Square Footage: 140000
Type of Packaging: Food Service
Brands Exported: City Lites; Village Lites; Tray Chic; Custer; Grandstand; Life Writer; Magnetic MenuMaster; Comet; Designer 2000
Regions Exported to: Central America, South America, Europe, Asia, Middle East, Caribbean, Australia
Percentage of Business in Exporting: 15

45362 International Reserve Equipment Corporation
46 Chestnut Avenue
Clarendon Hills, IL 60514-1238   708-531-0680
Fax: 630-325-7045
Manufacturer, importer and exporter of food processing equipment including centrifuges, separators, dryers, screeners, mills, filters, mixers and blenders; also, pollution control, wastewater treatment and sludge de-wateringequipment
Owner: Robert Mertz
Marketing Manager: Thomas Mertz
Estimated Sales: $ 1 - 5 Million
Number Employees: 2
Regions Exported to: Central America, South America, Europe, Asia, Middle East
Percentage of Business in Exporting: 80
Regions Imported from: Central America, South America, Europe, Asia, Middle East
Percentage of Business in Importing: 20

45363 International ResourcesCorporation
270 Presidential Drive
Wilmington, DE 19807-3302   302-449-0465
Fax: 302-449-0466
Importer of films including BOPP, PVC, polyester and BAREX
President: Ray Lay
Estimated Sales: $1-2.5 Million
Number Employees: 5-9
Square Footage: 60000
Brands Imported: Ariene
Regions Imported from: Asia
Percentage of Business in Importing: 100

45364 International Service Group
4080 Mcginnis Ferry Rd # 1403
Alpharetta, GA 30005-1774   770-518-0988
Fax: 770-518-0299
Peanuts, popcorn
President: John Kopec
j.kopec@isgnuts.com
Estimated Sales: $ 3 - 5 Million
Number Employees: 1-4
Type of Packaging: Consumer, Private Label, Bulk
Percentage of Business in Exporting: 90

45365 International Silver Company
PO Box 21379
York, PA 17402   617-561-2200
Fax: 617-568-1528 800-264-0758
President: Alan Kanter

45366 International Sourcing
32 Haviland Street
P.O.Box 90
Norwalk, CT 06854-4906   203-299-3220
Fax: 203-299-1355 800-772-7672
sales@charkit.com
Wholesaler/distributor, importer and exporter of preservatives, mineral supplements, acidulants, vegetable oils, flavorings, firming agents, chelates, antioxidants, buffers, humectants, sweeteners, etc
President: Seymour Friedman
Vice President: Larry Smith
Sales Correspondent: Linda Harth
Technical Division: Laurence Smith
Estimated Sales: $10-20 Million
Number Employees: 20-49
Square Footage: 13200
Regions Exported to: Central America, South America, Europe, Asia, Middle East
Percentage of Business in Exporting: 25
Regions Imported from: Central America, South America, Europe, Asia, Middle East
Percentage of Business in Importing: 65

45367 International SpecialtySupply
1011 Volunteer Dr
Cookeville, TN 38506-5026   931-526-1106
Fax: 931-526-8338 www.sproutnet.com
Alfalfa and bean sprouts
Owner: Robert Rust
Contact: Raymond Jones
r_cjones@me.com
Estimated Sales: Less Than $500,000
Number Employees: 1-4
Parent Co: International Specialty Supply
Type of Packaging: Consumer, Food Service, Private Label, Bulk
Regions Exported to: Central America, South America
Percentage of Business in Exporting: 10

45368 International Tank & Pipe Co
PO Box 590
Clackamas, OR 97015-0590   503-288-0011
Fax: 503-493-0372 888-988-0011
Info@WoodTankandPipe.com
woodtankandpipe.com
Manufacture wood stove tanks and pipe. Install new wood stove tanks and pipe and repair existing tanks and pipe.
President/CEO: Michael Bye
CFO: Jacqueline Bye
R&D/Purchasing Director: Kent Huschka
Quality Control: Matthew Bye
Marketing/Sales/Production: Michael Bye
Estimated Sales: $2-4 Million
Number Employees: 12
Number of Brands: 2
Square Footage: 40000
Type of Packaging: Consumer
Other Locations:
 Portland, OR
Brands Exported: National Brands Wood Tanks and Pipe
Regions Exported to: Central America, South America, Europe, Asia, Canada
Regions Imported from: Canada
Percentage of Business in Importing: 5

45369 International Telcom Inc
185 Commerce Ctr
Greenville, SC 29615-5817   864-676-2170
Fax: 864-297-7186 800-433-4043
info@interplas.com www.interplas.com

Importers & Exporters / A-Z

Manufacturer, importer and wholesaler/distributor of plastic and polyethylene bags, film, boxes, plastic food wrap, ziplock bags, trash bags, etc
President: Steve McClure
CEO: Mark McClure
Quality Control: Lisa Hughes
Marketing Manager: Roger Throckmorton
Sales Director: Chris Davis
Contact: Phillip Malphrus
pmal@intermicro.com
Estimated Sales: $20 Million
Number Employees: 1-4
Square Footage: 56000
Type of Packaging: Consumer, Food Service, Private Label, Bulk
Regions Exported to: Central America, South America, Europe, Asia, Middle East
Percentage of Business in Exporting: 10
Brands Imported: Clear Tuff
Regions Imported from: Central America, Asia

45370 International Trading Company
300 Portwall Street
Houston, TX 77029   713-224-5901
Fax: 713-678-1718
Importer of gourmet foods
Sales Manager: Lenny Yassie
Brands Imported: Jaka; Hafnia; Continental
Regions Imported from: Europe

45371 International Tray Pads
3299 NC Highway 5
P.O. Box 307
Aberdeen, NC 28315-8619   910-944-1800
Fax: 910-944-7356 www.pactiv.com
Manufacturer and supplier of tray pads for meats and case liners for produce and dairy products.
Contact: Larry Norpoth
lrnorpoth@traypads.com
Number Employees: 20-49
Regions Exported to: Central America, South America, Europe, Asia, Middle East, Worldwide

45372 International Ventures
5628 Mineral Spring Rd
Suffolk, VA 23438-9457   757-986-3800
Fax: 757-986-3801
Importation of gourmet seafood appetizers and entres (smoked fish, caviar, seafood tearines, pates, stuffed fillets), most products are preservative free and all natural
President/Owner: Chuck Hayes
CFO: Steinunn Hilmars
Estimated Sales: $1-2.5 Million
Number Employees: 1-4
Number of Brands: 6
Number of Products: 32
Square Footage: 150000
Type of Packaging: Consumer, Food Service, Private Label, Bulk
Brands Exported: Chef's Favorite, Chef's Style, Gem of Ireland, Triton, NOVA
Regions Exported to: Europe
Percentage of Business in Exporting: 40
Brands Imported: Chef's Favorite, Chef's Style, Gem of Ireland, Triton, NOVA
Regions Imported from: Europe
Percentage of Business in Importing: 60

45373 International Vitamin Corporation
500 Halls Mill Road
Freehold, NJ 07728   732-308-3000
Fax: 855-482-3291 800-666-8482
www.ivcinc.com/
Vitamin supplements, herbal products and antioxidants
Manager: Barb McCleer
Vice President, General Counsel, Secreta: Ellen Chiniara
Contact: Phillip Abbatiello
phillip.abbatiello@ivcinc.com
Number Employees: 250-499
Type of Packaging: Consumer

45374 International Wood Industries
12027 Three Lakes Rd
Snohomish, WA 98290   360-568-3185
Fax: 509-965-6141 800-922-6141
www.nepapallet.com
Manufacturer and exporter of skids, wooden pallets and bins, couch boxes, baggage boxes, household goods

President: Denton Sherry
General Manager: Joe Carlos
Estimated Sales: $10-20 Million
Number Employees: 100-249
Parent Co: International Wood Industries
Regions Exported to: Worldwide

45375 Interocean
412 W End Ave Apt 5n
New York, NY 10024-5772
Fax: 212-532-6909
Importer of frozen seafood
President: F Stern
VP: D Levis
Contact: Elizabeth Cruz
elizabeth@interoceaninc.com
Estimated Sales: $5-10 Million
Number Employees: 5-9
Brands Imported: Arctic Delight; ICM
Regions Imported from: Worldwide

45376 (HQ)Interplast
1400 Lytle Road
Troy, OH 45373-9401   937-332-1110
Fax: 937-332-0672
Manufacturer and exporter of plastic custom-injection moldings
Sales Manager: Bob Garton
Contact: Jared Langman
jlangman@interplastinc.com
Estimated Sales: $5-10 Million
Number Employees: 50-99
Regions Exported to: Canada, Mexico

45377 Interroll Corp
3000 Corporate Dr
Wilmington, NC 28405-7422   910-799-1100
Fax: 910-392-3822   800-830-9680
usa-sales@interroll.com www.interroll.us
Manufacturer and exporter of conveyor components and flow storage systems
President: Tim Mcgill
t.mcgill@interroll.com
VP: Richard Keely
VP Sales/Marketing: Steve Vineis
Estimated Sales: $ 20-50 Million
Number Employees: 100-249
Square Footage: 250
Parent Co: Interroll Holding AG
Brands Exported: Joki; Driveroll; Logix; Taperhex Gold
Regions Exported to: Worldwide

45378 Intershell Seafood Corp
9 Blackburn Dr
Gloucester, MA 01930-2237   978-281-2523
Fax: 978-283-1303 info@intershell.biz
www.intershell.biz
Shellfish
President: Yibing Gao
yibing@intershell.biz
Chairman: Monte Rome
Accounting: Linda Amaral
Research & Development: Shannon Blakeley
Quality Control: Eric Strong
Sales: Chrispher J Blankenbaker
Plant Manager: Eric Strong
Purchasing Manager: Monte Rome
Estimated Sales: $5 Million
Number Employees: 50-99
Type of Packaging: Bulk

45379 Interstate Monroe Machinery
2230 1st Avenue S
Seattle, WA 98134-1408   206-682-4870
Fax: 313-891-5449
Manufacturer and exporter of controls and instrumentation equipment
General Manager: Larry Gruendike
Estimated Sales: $1-2.5 Million
Number Employees: 9
Square Footage: 30000
Parent Co: Statco Engineering & Fabrication
Regions Exported to: Worldwide
Percentage of Business in Exporting: 10

45380 Interstate Packaging
2285 Highway 47 N
White Bluff, TN 37187-4126   615-797-9000
Fax: 615-797-9411 800-251-1072
ldoochin@interstatepkg.com
www.interstatepkg.com

Manufacturer and exporter of pressure sensitive labels and poly bags; manufacturer of printed flexible films
President: Michael Doochin
mdoochin@interstatepkg.com
Sales Manager: Lawrence Doochin
Customer Service Representative: Robert Garlock
Purchasing Manager: Liz Gilliam
Estimated Sales: $20-50 Million
Number Employees: 250-499
Square Footage: 100000
Type of Packaging: Consumer
Regions Exported to: Central America, Europe, Caribbean, Mexico
Percentage of Business in Exporting: 2

45381 Intertape Polymer Group
741 4th St
Menasha, WI 54952-2801   920-725-4335
Fax: 920-729-4217 800-558-5006
www.itape.com
Manufacturer and exporter of printed and plain pressure sensitive and gummed tapes: kraft paper and reinforced carton sealing; pressure sensitive carton sealing machine systems
President: Dale McSween
Manager: Bob Mc Donald
rmcdonal@itape.com
Product Manager: Steve Pistro
Product Manager: Tom Zettler
Plant Manager: John Cullen
Estimated Sales: $2.5-5 Million
Number Employees: 100-249
Parent Co: Intertape Polymer Group
Regions Exported to: Worldwide
Percentage of Business in Exporting: 5

45382 Intervest Trading Company Inc.
106 Chain Lake Drive
Halifax, NS B3S 1A8
Canada   902-425-2018
Fax: 902-420-0763 info@intervest.ca
Fresh and frozen groundfish and shellfish
President: Jeff Whitman
Year Founded: 1988
Estimated Sales: $5 Million
Number Employees: 1,000-4,999
Type of Packaging: Bulk
Regions Exported to: Worldwide
Percentage of Business in Exporting: 90

45383 Intralox LLC
301 Plantation Rd
Harahan, LA 70123-5326   504-733-0463
Fax: 504-734-0063 800-535-8848
www.intralox.com
Manufacturer and exporter of USDA accepted and FDA compliant modular plastic screw conveyors and conveyor belting
President: James Lapeyre Jr
Marketing Manager: Michelle Waite
National Sales Manager: Da Waters
Number Employees: 500-999
Parent Co: Laitram Corporation
Brands Exported: Intralox, Inc.

45384 Invictus Systems Corporation
5505 Seminary Rd Apt 2210n
Suite 202
Falls Church, VA 22041-3544
Fax: 703-503-8064
www.govcon.com/storefronts/invictus
Manufacturer and exporter of custom computer software for the food industry including facts panel creation, nutrition calculators, formula costing, time to market analysis and operations planning. Our services include custom websoftware for both internal and external use
President: Anthony Latta
CFO: Kim Witney
Chief Scientist: Kenneth Latta
Quality Control: Benson Wetta
Business Developer: Scott Weaver
Estimated Sales: Below $ 5 Million
Number Employees: 20-49
Number of Products: 3
Square Footage: 30000
Type of Packaging: Bulk
Regions Exported to: Central America, South America, Europe
Percentage of Business in Exporting: 10

Importers & Exporters / A-Z

45385 Ipswich Shellfish Co Inc
8 Hayward St
Ipswich, MA 01938-2012   978-356-4371
Fax: 978-356-9235   800-477-9424
www.ipswichshellfish.com
Seafood
Owner, President: Chrissi Pappas
CEO: Alexis Pappas
Controller: Lou Cellineri
VP: Alexander Pappas
Sales Manager: Michael Gagne
Director of Human Resources: Kathy Waymous
Operations Manager: Bob Butcher
General Manager: Michael Trupiano
Purchasing Director: Vito Finazzo
Estimated Sales: $22.2 Million
Number Employees: 250-499
Square Footage: 35000

45386 Irish Hospitality/Foodprops
174B Semoran Commerce Blvd.
Suite 124
Apopka, FL 32703   321-277-4375
Fax: 407-880-6210

45387 Irish Tea Sales
9216 95th Street
Woodhaven, NY 11421-2707   718-845-4402
Fax: 718-835-5965
Importer and wholesaler/distributor of Irish teas, preserves, biscuits and oatmeal; serving the food service market and retail store
President: Ellen Smith
Sales Director: Eileen Clarke
Estimated Sales: $2.5-5 Million
Number Employees: 1-4
Type of Packaging: Consumer, Food Service
Brands Imported: Jacobs; Bolands; McCann's; Barry's; Lyons
Regions Imported from: Europe
Percentage of Business in Importing: 95

45388 Isadore A. Rapasadi & Son
PO Box 66
800 North Peterboro Road
Canastota, NY 13032   315-697-2216
Fax: 315-697-3300   800-828-7277
datudman@twcny.com
Potatoes and onions
President/CEO: Izzy Rapasadi
Sales Manager: Bob Rapasadi
Estimated Sales: F
Number Employees: 50-99
Square Footage: 180000
Type of Packaging: Bulk
Regions Exported to: Worldwide

45389 Isernio Sausage Company
5600 7th Ave S
Seattle, WA 98108-2644   206-762-5259
Fax: 206-762-6207   888-495-8674
info@isernio.com
Pork, beef and lamb sausages
President: Frank Isernio
Contact: Greg Arend
grega@isernio.com
Estimated Sales: $2.5-5 Million
Number Employees: 20-49
Type of Packaging: Consumer, Food Service
Regions Exported to: Canada
Percentage of Business in Exporting: 1

45390 Isigny Ste Mere
2200 Fletcher Avenue
3rd Floor
Fort Lee, NJ 07024   201-253-5604
Fax: 201-585-8575   www.isigny-ste-mere.com
Butter, cheese, other dairy and eggs.
Marketing: Nicolas Lecuq
Contact: Laurent Muriel
laurent.muriel@isigny-ste-mere.com

45391 Island Marine Products
2772 Main Road
P.O. Box 40
Clarks Harbour, NS B0W 1P0
Canada   902-745-2222
Fax: 902-745-3247   islandmarine@ss.eastlink.ca
Processor and exporter of haddock, lobster and lobster meat and tuna
President: Cyril Swim
Estimated Sales: $10-20 Million
Number Employees: 15
Type of Packaging: Food Service, Bulk
Regions Exported to: Asia
Percentage of Business in Exporting: 90

45392 Island Oasis Frozen Cocktail
3400 Millington Rd.
Beloit, WI 53511   508-660-1177
Fax: 508-660-1435   800-777-4752
www.kerryfoodservice.com
Non-alcoholic beverage mixes; ice shavers and blenders
President & CEO: Gerry Behan
Marketing Director: Abhishek Trivedi
VP of Global & Strategic Accounts: Michael Walsh
Estimated Sales: $20-50 Million
Number Employees: 100-249
Number of Products: 16
Square Footage: 25000
Parent Co: Kerry Food Services
Brands Exported: Island Oasis; Beverage Mixes & Equipment
Regions Exported to: Central America, Europe, Asia

45393 Island Supply
6601 Lyons Rd # B6
Suite B-6
Coconut Creek, FL 33073-3605   954-312-0300
Fax: 954-344-2917   info@IslandSupply.com
www.islandsupply.com
Wholesaler/distributor of food service equipment and supplies including ranges, plates, utensils, etc.; also, grocery items including produce, meat, seafood, canned goods, etc.; serving the food service market
Owner: Ken Cufo
ken@islandsupplyco.com
Manager: Ian Givens
Estimated Sales: $2.5-5 Million
Number Employees: 10-19
Type of Packaging: Food Service

45394 Island Sweetwater Beverage Company
825 Lafayette Road
Bryn Mawr, PA 19010-1816   610-525-7444
Fax: 610-525-7502   www.peacemountain.com
Soft drinks, bottled waters, energy drinks; exporter of beer
President: Michael Salaman
Square Footage: 40000
Parent Co: A/S Beverage Marketing
Type of Packaging: Private Label
Brands Exported: Jazz-Cola; Mont D'Aire; Bahama; Virgil's Root Beer; O'Sippie
Regions Exported to: Central America, South America, Europe, Asia, Middle East, Australia
Percentage of Business in Exporting: 25
Brands Imported: Red Bull; Flying Horse; Isotonic; Ritual Drink; That's; Horse Power; Top Secret; Excalibur; Mach 6; XTC; Full Speed; Taurus; Magic; Lady Dynamite; NRG; Boss; Stampede; Sankt Olav
Regions Imported from: Central America, South America, Europe, Asia, Middle East, Australia, Mexico
Percentage of Business in Importing: 50

45395 Islander Import
257 William Street
West Hempstead, NY 11552-1500   516-481-9677
Importer and wholesaler/distributor of German beer
President: Charles Leidner
Number Employees: 1-4
Regions Imported from: Europe

45396 Isola Imports Inc
4525 S Tripp Ave
Chicago, IL 60632-4416   773-342-2121
Fax: 773-523-9064   jaynitti@isolaimports.com
www.isolaimports.com
Antipasti, cheese, confections, cream of balsamic, crisp breads, grains, olive oil and vinegars, pasta, sauces and pesto, seafood and truffles.
President/Owner: John Nitti
johnnitti@isolaimports.com
Estimated Sales: $1.7 Million
Number Employees: 10-19

45397 Itac Label & Tag Corp
179 Lexington Ave
Brooklyn, NY 11216-1114   718-625-2148
Fax: 718-625-3806
Manufacturer and exporter of labels including pressure sensitive, magnetic, shipping, bar code and file folder; also, tags and decals
President: Sidney Alder
CEO: James H C Tao
Estimated Sales: $ 5-10 Million
Number Employees: 10-19
Square Footage: 28000
Regions Exported to: Asia
Percentage of Business in Exporting: 10

45398 Italfoods Inc
205 Shaw Rd
S San Francisco, CA 94080-6605   650-877-0724
Fax: 650-871-9437   info@italfoodsinc.com
www.italfoodsinc.com
Wholesaler/distributor and importer of a full line of Italian food products including antipasto, syrups, mineral water, bread, candy, cheese, coffee, tea, dairy products, dry beans, flour, frozen desserts, meat products,etc.; servingthe food service market
Owner: Georgette Guerra
Estimated Sales: $10-20 Million
Number Employees: 100-249
Type of Packaging: Food Service
Brands Imported: Diva/Velo; Vello; Columbo; Rocca; Unica; AgriFant

45399 Italgi
PO Box 89
Westwood, NJ 07675-0089   201-666-2378
Fax: 201-666-8525   800-706-9338
Importer of espresso, cappuccino and latte machinery, pasta cookers, ravioli, gnocchi and pasta makers, wood burning ovens, grills and granita/frozen cocktail machines
Parent Co: Italgi SPA
Brands Imported: Panini; Cap-O-Mat
Regions Imported from: Italy

45400 Italian Bottega
150 N Michigan Ave
28th Floor
Chicago, IL 60601   312-235-2665
info@italianbottega.com
www.italianbottega.com
Olive oils, vinegar, pasta, coffee, sauces, preserved vegetables and cheese

45401 Italian Harvest, Inc.
214 Shaw Rd Ste 1
South San Francisco, CA 94080-6619   866-408-4457
Fax: 650-871-2977   www.italianharvest.com
Pasta, chocolate, cookies, crackers, carbonated beverages, sauces, salt, spices
President: John Blount
Number Employees: 1-4

45402 Italian Products USA
758 Lidgerwood Ave
Elizabeth, NJ 07202   201-770-9130
Fax: 201-770-1551   info@italianproducts.com
www.italianproducts.com
Pastas, sauces, oils, truffles and creams

45403 Italian Quality Products
22600c Lambert Street
Suite 901
Lake Forest, CA 92630-1607   949-472-1270
Fax: 949-472-1080   info@pastamachine.com
www.pastamachine.com
Importer and exporter of pasta equipment for sheeted, extruded and filled pasta including ravioli and tortellini
Owner: Riccardo Carretti
riccardocarretti@yahoo.com
Estimated Sales: $500,000-$1 Million
Number Employees: 1-4
Square Footage: 2400
Brands Exported: Saima; Italpast; Italgi
Regions Exported to: Central America, Europe, Asia
Brands Imported: Saima; Capitanio; Italpast; Italgi
Regions Imported from: Europe

45404 Italica Imports
411 Theodore Fremd Avenue
Suite 120
Rye, NY 10580
Fax: 914-925-0458   800-431-1529
www.italicaoliveoil.com
Wholesaler/distributor and importer of olive oil, cornichons, capers, olives, pickled vegetables, pepperoncini, jalapeno peppers and wine vinegar

Importers & Exporters / A-Z

President: Lucy Landesman
Executive Secretary: Emil Cairo
VP of Marketing/Sales: Neil Albert
Estimated Sales: $5-10 Million
Number Employees: 1-4
Parent Co: Cory International Corporation
Type of Packaging: Consumer, Private Label
Brands Imported: Italica; Casa Italica; Villa Blanca
Regions Imported from: Europe
Percentage of Business in Importing: 100

45405 Item Products
16111 Park Entry Drive
Suite 100
Houston, TX 77041-4077   281-893-0100
    Fax: 281-893-4836   800-333-4932
Manufacturer and exporter of carts and storage racks; also, consultant specializing in the design of custom machinery
Marketing Coordinator: Claudia Sears
National Marketing Manager: Jim Boyd
Estimated Sales: $10-20,000,000
Number Employees: 20-49
Square Footage: 60000
Regions Exported to: Central America, South America, Mexico
Percentage of Business in Exporting: 5

45406 Iti Tropicals Inc
30 Gordon Ave
Lawrenceville, NJ 08648-1033   609-987-0550
    Fax: 609-987-4333   www.ititropicals.com
Importer of tropical fruit juices, purees and concentrates
President: Garrit Van Manen
Contact: Gene Jezek
gene@ititropicals.com
Estimated Sales: $2.5-5 Million
Number Employees: 5-9

45407 Ito Cariani Sausage Company
3190 Corporate Place
Hayward, CA 94545-3916   510-887-0882
    Fax: 510-887-8323   us.kompass.com/
Meat products
President: Tony Nakashima
VP Finance: Allen Shiroma
Executive VP/General Manager: Ken Kamata
VP Sales: Al Lera
Estimated Sales: $10-20 Million
Number Employees: 50-99
Square Footage: 170000
Type of Packaging: Consumer, Food Service, Private Label, Bulk
Other Locations:
Ito Cariani Sausage Co.
NishinomiyaIto Cariani Sausage Co.
Brands Exported: Cariani
Regions Exported to: Asia
Percentage of Business in Exporting: 60

45408 Ivanhoe Cheese Inc
11301 Hwy 62 RR 5
Madoc, ON K0K 2K0
Canada   613-473-4269
    Fax: 613-473-5016   www.ivanhoecheese.com
Cheeses
President: Bruce Kingston
Vice President: Larry Hook
Sales: Paul McKinlay
Plant Manager: Chris Spencer
Estimated Sales: $16.5 Million
Number Employees: 80
Type of Packaging: Consumer, Food Service, Private Label, Bulk
Brands Exported: Ivanhoe

45409 Ivar's Chowders
11777 Cyrus Way
Mukilteo, WA 98275   425-493-1402
cpl@keepclam.com
www.ivarschowder.com
Contact: Chris Lewark
clewark@ivarschowder.com
Estimated Sales: $300,000-500,000
Number Employees: 10-19

45410 Ivarson Inc
3100 W Green Tree Rd
Milwaukee, WI 53209-2535   414-351-0700
    Fax: 414-351-4551   sales@ivarsoninc.com
www.ivarsoninc.com
Manufacturer and exporter of process and packaging equipment and parts for butter, cheese and margarine industries; also, set-up boxes
President: Glenn Ivarson
givarson@ivarsoninc.com
Engineering Manager: Chuck Ellingson
Manager Technical Services: Jim Wycklendt
Sales Director: Mark Mullinix
Estimated Sales: $10-20 Million
Number Employees: 50-99
Square Footage: 100200

45411 Ives-Way Products
2030 N Nicole Ln
Round Lake Beach, IL 60073-2288   847-740-0658
Manufacturer and exporter of automatic can sealers for food, giftware or other sealed shipping containers
VP: Laura Ours
Estimated Sales: Less Than $500,000
Number Employees: 1-4
Square Footage: 4000
Regions Exported to: Europe, Asia, Canada
Percentage of Business in Exporting: 50

45412 Iveta Gourmet Inc
2125 Delaware Ave
Suite F
Santa Cruz, CA 95060-5758   831-423-5149
    Fax: 831-423-5169   iveta@iveta.com
www.iveta.com
Baked goods; jams, curds and clotted cream
Owner: John Bilanko
iveta@iveta.com
Co-Owner: Yvette Bilanko
Estimated Sales: $2.5-5 Million
Number Employees: 5-9

45413 Iwasaki Images Of America Inc
16927 S Main St # C
Suite C
Gardena, CA 90248-3139   310-225-2727
    Fax: 310-323-7524   www.iwasaki-images.com
Estimated Sales: $1-3 Million
Number Employees: 10-19

45414 Iwatani International Corporation of America
2050 Center Avenue
Suite 425
Fort Lee, NJ 07024   201-585-2442
    Fax: 201-585-2369   jjnol@msn.com
www.iwatani.com
Contact: Hiroshi Kimura
h.kimura@iwatani.com

45415 Iwatani International Corporation of America
2200 Post oak Blvd.
Suite 1150
Houston, TX 77056   713-965-9970
    Fax: 713-963-8497   800-775-5506
christopher@iwatani.com   www.iwatani.com
Manufacturer and importer of portable butane stoves and induction cookers.
Regional Sales Manager: Karen Buquicchio
National Sales Manager: Gary Rodgers
Estimated Sales: $5-10 Million
Number Employees: 5-9
Parent Co: Iwatani International
Regions Imported from: Asia

45416 Izabel Lam International
204 Van Dyke Street
Brooklyn, NY 11231-1038   718-797-3983
    Fax: 718-797-0030   info@izabellam.com
www.izabellam.com
Manufacturer and exporter of tabletop products including cutlery, dinnerware and drinkware
Estimated Sales: $500,000-$1 Million
Number Employees: 1-4
Square Footage: 112000
Type of Packaging: Consumer, Food Service
Brands Exported: Splash; Sphere; Wind Over Water; Glacier; Morning Tide; Rushing Tide; Pale Wind; Golden Wind; Mt. Rainbow Series
Regions Exported to: South America, Europe, Asia, Middle East

45417 J & B Sausage Co Inc
100 Main
PO Box 7
Waelder, TX 78959-5329   830-788-7511
    Fax: 830-788-7279   contact@jbfoods.com
Smoked sausage, bacon, ham, jerky and barbecued meat
President: Danny Janecka
CEO: Ty Ahrens
tahrens@jbfoods.com
Year Founded: 1959
Estimated Sales: $42040000
Number Employees: 250-499
Type of Packaging: Consumer, Food Service, Private Label, Bulk
Regions Exported to: Europe

45418 J & J Snack Foods Corp
6000 Central Hwy
Pennsauken, NJ 08109   856-665-9533
    800-486-9533
consumerrelations@jjsnack.com   www.jjsnack.com
Nutritional snack foods and beverages.
Chairman/CEO: Gerald Shreiber
gshreiber@jjsnack.com
President: Dan Fachner
CFO: Dennis Moore
COO: Robert Radano
Year Founded: 1971
Estimated Sales: $1.08 Billion
Number Employees: 4,200
Number of Brands: 35
Square Footage: 70000
Type of Packaging: Food Service, Private Label
Regions Exported to: Worldwide

45419 J & K Ingredients
160 E 5th St
Paterson, NJ 07524-1603   973-340-8700
    Fax: 973-340-4994   sales@jkingredients.net
www.jkingredients.net
Bakery ingredients
President: James Sausville
jkfoods1@aol.com
Vice President of Research & Development: Nigel Weston
Vice President of Sales & Marketing: Al Orr
Director of National Sales: Kurt Miller
Customer Service: Cheryl Tirri
General Manager: Fred Denman
Controller: Andrew Madacsi
Senior Bakery Technician: Jeremy Jones
Estimated Sales: $19.5 Million
Number Employees: 20-49
Number of Brands: 11

45420 J & M Wholesale Meat Inc
2300 Hoover Ave
Modesto, CA 95354-3908
Canada   209-522-1248
    Fax: 209-522-8834   855-522-1248
Fresh and frozen pork
President: J McCullough
Administrator Quality Control: Kevin McCullough
Sales Manager: Nannette McCullough
Number Employees: 20-49
Square Footage: 72000
Type of Packaging: Consumer, Food Service, Bulk
Regions Exported to: Worldwide
Percentage of Business in Exporting: 30

45421 J & R Mfg Inc
820 W Kearney St # B
Mesquite, TX 75149-8804   972-289-0801
    Fax: 972-288-9488   800-527-4831
sales@jrmanufacturing.com
www.jrmanufacturing.com
Manufacturer and exporter of barbecue pits, broilers, grills, rotisseries and combo broiler/rotisseries
Vice President: Trent Hamrick
trent.hamrick@jrmanufacturing.net
VP: Larry Bellows
Estimated Sales: $5-10 Million
Number Employees: 20-49
Square Footage: 60000
Regions Exported to: Worldwide
Percentage of Business in Exporting: 5

45422 J A Heilferty & Co
133 Cedar Ln # 104
Teaneck, NJ 07666-4416   201-836-5060
    Fax: 201-836-3275   info@primepak.com
www.primepakcompany.com

Manufacturer, importer and exporter of HDPE and LLDPE poly bags, sheeting, box and trash can liners, T-sacks and plain and printed bags
Owner: William Poppe
Chief Financial Officer: Mike Heilferty
VP Sales: William Heilferty
VP Operations: Chris Poppe
Estimated Sales: $ 20 - 50 Million
Number Employees: 20-49
Square Footage: 120000
Regions Exported to: Europe
Percentage of Business in Exporting: 2
Regions Imported from: South America, Europe, Asia, Latin America
Percentage of Business in Importing: 5

45423 **J C Ford Co**
901 S Leslie St
La Habra, CA 90631-6841   714-871-7361
Fax: 714-773-5827 www.jcford.com
Manufacturer and exporter of cooling conveyors, corn masa feeders, tamale steamers and extruders, tortilla and chip ovens, tortilla sheeter and corn cookers and grinders
Sales: Robert Meyer
Customer Service: Desi Sanchez
Engineer: Thomas Dosch
Estimated Sales: $5-10 Million
Number Employees: 5-9
Square Footage: 40000
Regions Exported to: Worldwide
Percentage of Business in Exporting: 35

45424 **J C Watson Co**
201 E Main St
Parma, ID 83660   208-722-5141
Fax: 208-722-6646 nancy@soobrand.com
www.soobrand.com
Produce, including onions, apples, potatoes and plums
Owner: Jon Watson
Sales Manager: Nancy Carter
jonw@soobrand.com
Transportation Manager: Melanie Steinhaus
Number Employees: 5-9
Type of Packaging: Consumer, Food Service
Regions Exported to: Europe, Asia, Middle East

45425 **(HQ)J C Whitlam Mfg Co**
200 W Walnut St
Wadsworth, OH 44281-1379   330-334-2524
Fax: 330-334-3005 800-321-8358
www.whitlampaint.com
Manufacturer and exporter of refrigeration chemicals, waterless hand cleaners and other cleaning chemicals
President: Jack Whitlam
sales@jcwhitlam.com
CFO: Doug Whitlam
Senior VP: Doug Whitlam
VP Operations: Steve Carey
Estimated Sales: $5-10 Million
Number Employees: 20-49
Square Footage: 280000
Regions Exported to: Central America, Europe, Middle East
Percentage of Business in Exporting: 5

45426 **J F O'Neill & Packing Co**
3120 G St
Omaha, NE 68107-1447   402-733-1200
Fax: 402-733-1724
Beef
President: Ron O'Neill
General Production Manager: Brian O'Neill
Estimated Sales: $12.2 Million
Number Employees: 50-99
Type of Packaging: Consumer, Food Service, Private Label, Bulk
Regions Exported to: Worldwide
Percentage of Business in Exporting: 98

45427 **J G Van Holten & Son Inc**
703 W Madison St
Waterloo, WI 53594-1365   920-478-2144
Fax: 920-478-2316 800-256-0619
info@vanholtenpickles.com
www.vanholtenpickles.com
Pre-packaged pickles and relish
President: Steve Byrnes
sbyrnes@vanholtenpickles.com
President: Steve Byrnes
VP of Sales: Stef Espiritu
Operations Manager: Bruce Dorn
Estimated Sales: $7000000
Number Employees: 50-99
Type of Packaging: Consumer, Private Label, Bulk
Regions Exported to: Asia

45428 **J L Becker Co**
41150 Joy Rd
Plymouth, MI 48170-4634   734-656-2000
Fax: 734-656-2009 800-837-4328
www.jlbecker.com
Manufacturer and exporter of heat treating furnaces and conveyor belts including wire mesh and flat wire
President: John Becker
CEO: Wayne Webbe
CFO: Ellen Beckor
Vice President: John Beckor
Sales Manager: David Peterson
Estimated Sales: $10-20 Million
Number Employees: 20-49
Type of Packaging: Bulk
Regions Exported to: Worldwide
Percentage of Business in Exporting: 5

45429 **J L Clark Corp**
923 23rd Ave
Rockford, IL 61104-7173   815-962-8861
Fax: 815-966-5862 www.jlclark.com
Manufacturer and exporter of decorative tin cans and injection molded plastic dispensing closures
President: Philip Baerenwald
pbaerenwald@jlclark.com
CFO: Bill Holiday
Vice President/General Manager: Walt Pietruch
R&D: Ron Axon
Sales: Mike Tolluer
Public Relations: Luanna Grimes
Purchasing: George Mastromatteo
Estimated Sales: H
Number Employees: 250-499
Parent Co: Clarcor Consumer Products
Type of Packaging: Consumer, Food Service, Private Label
Regions Exported to: Europe

45430 **(HQ)J M Canty Inc E1200 Engineers**
6100 Donner Rd
Lockport, NY 14094-9227   716-625-4227
Fax: 716-625-4228 sales@jmcanty.com
www.cantylight.com
Manufacturer and exporter of fiber optic lighting, image processing and inspection and color analysis
President: Thomas Canty
Quality Control: Dan Raby
VP: Tod Canty
Manager: Chris Miller
chrism@jmcanty.com
Estimated Sales: $ 5 - 10 Million
Number Employees: 20-49
Square Footage: 152000
Other Locations:
   Canty
   Dublin, IrelandCanty
Regions Exported to: Worldwide
Percentage of Business in Exporting: 40

45431 **J M Packaging Co**
26300 Bunert Rd
Warren, MI 48089-3639   586-771-7800
Fax: 586-771-5440 www.jmindustries.com
Manufacturer and exporter of printed tapes and labels; contract packaging available
Owner: Corey Bunch
cbunch@jmindustries.com
VP: Michael Jones
Estimated Sales: $5-10 Million
Number Employees: 50-99
Type of Packaging: Bulk
Regions Exported to: Canada
Percentage of Business in Exporting: 1

45432 **J R Carlson Laboratories Inc**
600 W University Dr
Arlington Heights, IL 60004   847-255-1600
888-234-5656
carlson@carlsonlabs.com www.carlsonlabs.com
Norwegian fish oils, vitamins, minerals, amino acids, special formulations and nutritional supplements.
President: Carilyn Carlson Anderson
VP, Marketing & Corporate Relations: Kirsten Carlson Cecchin
Year Founded: 1965
Estimated Sales: $24.3 Million
Number Employees: 100-249
Number of Products: 200
Square Footage: 40000
Type of Packaging: Consumer, Private Label
Brands Exported: Carlson
Regions Exported to: Europe, Asia, Middle East
Percentage of Business in Exporting: 5

45433 **J T Gibbons Inc**
600 Elmwood Park Blvd # 2
New Orleans, LA 70123-3310   504-831-9907
Fax: 504-837-5516
Wholesaler/distributor and export and import broker of frozen foods, groceries, industrial ingredients and private label items
President: Richard Keeney
rkeeney@gibbonsinc.com
CFO: Arthur Schott
Purchasing: Tammy Ducote
Estimated Sales: Less Than $500,000
Number Employees: 1-4
Square Footage: 60000
Type of Packaging: Consumer, Food Service, Private Label
Brands Exported: Lucky Leaf; Musselman's; Kingsway; Super Fresh
Regions Exported to: Central America, Europe, Middle East
Percentage of Business in Exporting: 100

45434 **J W Outfitters**
3102 Oakcliff Industrial St
Atlanta, GA 30340-2902   770-457-0447
Fax: 770-457-4157 800-554-7662
CustomerService@JWOutfitters.com
www.jwoutfitters.com
Wholesaler/distributor and exporter of uniforms; serving the food service market
President: Jack Willis
jwoutfitters@mindspring.com
National Sales Manager: Giles Davis
Estimated Sales: $5-10 Million
Number Employees: 50-99
Square Footage: 92000
Type of Packaging: Food Service
Regions Exported to: Central America, South America, Canada
Percentage of Business in Exporting: 3

45435 **J&S Export & Trading Company**
8621 Fancy Finch Drive
Suite 104
Tampa, FL 33614-2391   813-806-5327
Exporter of snack foods, canned and dry goods and processed foods
President: Sonia Lee
VP Marketing: John Lee
Number Employees: 1-4
Square Footage: 1200
Brands Exported: Jamaica Hell Fire; Saguaro Food Products
Regions Exported to: South America
Percentage of Business in Exporting: 100

45436 **J. Crocker Exports**
961 S Meridian Ave
Alhambra, CA 91803   626-539-3663
Fax: 626-570-6999 866-924-3373
info@gourmetimports.com
www.gourmetimports.com
Importer and exporter of hot sauce, nutmeg, syrup, tea, mustard, raw sugar, Maine lobster and chocolates
President: Jeffrey Crocker
Number Employees: 1-4
Regions Exported to: Asia, Latin America
Percentage of Business in Exporting: 85
Regions Imported from: Europe, Asia, Latin America, Australia
Percentage of Business in Importing: 15

45437 **J. Flex International**
5130 E La Palma Ave Ste 207
Anaheim, CA 92807   714-693-0141
Fax: 714-693-0138
Importer of preformed plastic laminated pouches printed in rotogravure with a tamper evident seal
President: Kurt Itoh
Estimated Sales: $1-2.5 Million
Number Employees: 1-4
Type of Packaging: Bulk

Importers & Exporters / A-Z

45438 J. Rutigliano & Sons
301 Hollywood Ave
South Plainfield, NJ 07080-4201   908-226-8866
Fax: 908-226-1534
Importer and wholesaler/distributor of olives, macaroni, tomato products, olive oil, cheese and vinegar
Owner: Joseph Rutigliano
VP: Vincent Rutigliano
Estimated Sales: $5-10 Million
Number Employees: 5-9
Square Footage: 120000
Type of Packaging: Consumer, Food Service
Brands Imported: Divella; Nina; Baresi; Pugliese
Regions Imported from: Europe
Percentage of Business in Importing: 90

45439 J.A. Thurston Company
Route 2
Rumford, ME 04276   207-364-7921
Fax: 207-369-9903
Manufacturer and exporter of chairs and stools
VP: John Thurston
Sales: Cindy Giroux
Estimated Sales: $ 5 - 10 Million
Number Employees: 5-9
Regions Exported to: Canada
Percentage of Business in Exporting: 1

45440 J.E. Roy
60 Boulevard Begin
St Claire, QC G0R 2V0
Canada   418-883-2711
Fax: 418-838-8008
Manufacturer, importer and exporter of plastic bottles and bottle nasal plugs
President: Ronald Leclair
Quality Control: Nicoles Mertileau
VP Sales: Sylvie Lefevbre
Number Employees: 55
Square Footage: 18000
Type of Packaging: Consumer, Food Service, Private Label
Regions Exported to: USA
Percentage of Business in Exporting: 20

45441 J.F. Braun & Sons
PO Box 6061
1 Atalanta Plaza
Elizabeth, NJ 07207   908-393-7400
Fax: 908-393-7439 800-997-7177
sales@jfbny.com www.jfbny.com
Importer and exporter of shelled nuts, pumpkin seeds, carob powders, coconut products, crystallized ginger, pignolias and dried fruits including apples, raisins, papayas, pineapples, sweetened banana chips and turkish apricots
President: Stephen O'Mara
Sales Manager/Purchasing Agent: Steve Schaarschimdt
Contact: Joe Harding
harding@jfbny.com
Estimated Sales: $1-2.5 Million
Number Employees: 20-49
Square Footage: 20000
Parent Co: Atalanta
Type of Packaging: Food Service, Bulk
Regions Exported to: Canada, Mexico
Percentage of Business in Exporting: 1
Regions Imported from: South America, India, Turkey, Phillipines
Percentage of Business in Importing: 99

45442 J.H. Thornton Company
879 N Jan Mar Ct
Olathe, KS 66061   913-764-6550
Fax: 913-764-1314
Manufacturer, exporter and wholesaler/distributor of conveyor systems; installation services available
President: Douglas Metcalf
Estimated Sales: $ 3 - 5 Million
Number Employees: 10
Regions Exported to: Mexico

45443 J.L. DeGraffenreid & Sons
2848 N Lecompte Road
Springfield, MO 65803   417-862-8615
Fax: 417-862-8615
www.arborpic.com/company/51-j-l-degraffenreid-sons-llc
Contact: Michael Hoverson
michael.hoverson@lindsayolives.com

45444 J.M. Rogers & Sons
PO Box 8725
Moss Point, MS 39562-0011   228-475-7584
Pallets, drag line mats, skids, lumber, etc.; exporter of pallets
Owner: Louis Rogers
Number Employees: 50

45445 J.M. Smucker Co.
1 Strawberry Ln.
Orrville, OH 44667-0280
888-550-9555
www.jmsmucker.com
Fruit spreads, juices, ice cream toppings, syrups, peanut butter and coffee.
Executive Chairman: Richard Smucker
President/CEO: Mark Smucker
mark.smucker@jmsmucker.com
Chief Legal & Compliance Officer: Jeannette Knudson
Chief Marketing & Commercial Officer: Geoff Tanner
Year Founded: 1897
Estimated Sales: $7.3 Billion
Number Employees: 7,140
Number of Brands: 40
Type of Packaging: Consumer, Food Service
Regions Exported to: Europe
Percentage of Business in Exporting: 1

45446 J.P. Sunrise Bakery
14728 119th Avenue NW
Edmonton, AB T5L 2P2
Canada   780-454-5797
Fax: 780-452-7696 office@sunrise-bakery.com
www.sunrisebakery.com
Baked goods
President: Gary Huising
Director: Tony Bron
Director: Hank Renzenbrink
Number Employees: 80
Square Footage: 120000
Type of Packaging: Consumer, Food Service
Regions Exported to: USA
Percentage of Business in Exporting: 40

45447 J.R. Short Canadian Mills
70 Wickstead Avenue
Toronto, ON M4G 2B5
Canada   416-421-3463
Fax: 416-421-2876
Confectioners corn flakes, corn meal, stablized wheat bran, wheat germ and corn germ
Vice President: Alexa Norris
Parent Co: J.R. Short Milling Company
Regions Imported from: USA

45448 J.V. Reed & Company
1939 Goldsmith Ln
Suite 121
Louisville, KY 40218-3175   502-454-4455
Fax: 502-587-6025 877-258-7333
Manufacturer and exporter of dust pans, metal waste baskets, signs, tabs, labels, burner covers, hot pads, stove and counter mats, canister sets, etc
Owner: Jean Reid
Chairman Board: Marc Ray
Estimated Sales: $10-20 Million
Number Employees: 1-4
Square Footage: 160000
Regions Exported to: Central America, Canada
Percentage of Business in Exporting: 5

45449 JAAMA World Trade
295 Forest Avenue
Suite 127
Portland, ME 04101-2018   207-253-1956
Fax: 207-878-8455 jaama@gwi.net
www.gwi.net/~jaama
Wholesaler/distributor, importer and exporter of frozen chicken and meat, dried beans, canned foods, beverages and groceries
President: Brian Cooke
Estimated Sales: $ .5 - 1 million
Number Employees: 10-19
Regions Exported to: Europe, Asia, Middle East, Australia , Latin America
Percentage of Business in Exporting: 10
Regions Imported from: Europe, Australia , Latin America
Percentage of Business in Importing: 80

45450 JANA Worldwide
17 Mercer Rd
Natick, MA 01760-2414   508-620-0001
Fax: 508-651-3001 www.janabrands.com
Importer and exporter of frozen Alaskan, Chinese and Canadian seafood including swordfish and tuna
CEO: Steve Forman
VP: Kevin McCartney
Sales Manager: Lewis Allinson
Estimated Sales: $10-20 Million
Number Employees: 10-19
Square Footage: 8000
Type of Packaging: Consumer, Food Service
Brands Exported: Tuna Sooner
Regions Exported to: Canada
Brands Imported: Tuna Sooner

45451 JBG International
PO Box 6339
Torrance, CA 90504-0339   562-590-9356
Fax: 562-432-8339
Wholesaler/distributor and importer of olives, olive oil, almonds, honey, rice, artichokes, pimientos, pinenuts, paprika, anchovies, tuna, mandarines, etc
CEO: Juan Garibo
Regions Imported from: Spain

45452 JBS USA LLC
1770 Promontory Cir.
Greeley, CO 80634   970-506-8000
www.jbssa.com
Beef, pork and chicken.
CEO: Andre Nogueira
CFO: Denilson Molina
Estimated Sales: $27.8 Billion
Number Employees: 78,000
Number of Brands: 17
Parent Co: JBS S.A.
Type of Packaging: Consumer
Brands Exported: Swift®, 1855®, Aspen Ridge®, Blue Ribbon Beef®, La Herenica®, Chef;S Exclusive®, Swift Premium Natural Pork®, Swift Black Angus®
Regions Exported to: Worldwide
Brands Imported: Acres Organic Grass-fed Beef, AMH®, Great Southern®, Swift Australia®, Spring Crossing Cattle Co®, Beef City®, Riverina®, Your Choice®
Regions Imported from: Central America, South America, Australia, New Zealand

45453 JCH International
978 E Hermitage Rd NE
Rome, GA 30161-9641   706-295-4111
Fax: 706-295-4114 800-328-9203
info@jchinternational.com
Manufacturer and exporter of industrial and commercial mats and matting for entrance, meat cutting and produce areas; also, specialty flooring available; importer of heavy duty carpets
President: John Hoglund
jchoglund@yahoo.com
Number Employees: 5-9
Type of Packaging: Food Service
Regions Exported to: Worldwide
Percentage of Business in Exporting: 5
Regions Imported from: Worldwide
Percentage of Business in Importing: 25

45454 JD Sweid Foods
9696-199A Street
Langley, BC V1M 2X7
Canada   604-888-8662
Fax: 604-888-0074 800-665-4355
info@jdsweid.com www.jdsweid.com
Poultry and meat products
President & CEO: Blair Shier
Estimated Sales: $49.1 Million
Number Employees: 600+
Type of Packaging: Consumer, Food Service, Private Label, Bulk
Regions Exported to: Europe, Asia

45455 JDT Corporation
P.O.Box 965
Wallace, NC 28466-0965   910-285-4502
Fax: 910-285-5491 jdtea@hotmail.com
Owner: Joseph Teachey

Importers & Exporters / A-Z

45456 JE Bergeron & Sons
7 Rue St John Baptiste
Bromptonville, QC J0B 1H0
Canada 819-846-2761
Fax: 819-846-6217 800-567-2798
www.nuvel.ca
Shortening and margarine
President: Philippe Bergeron
Secretary: Berengere Bergeron
VP: Danielle Bergeron
Number Employees: 20-49
Square Footage: 120000
Parent Co: Margarine Thibault
Type of Packaging: Consumer, Food Service, Private Label, Bulk
Regions Exported to: South America
Percentage of Business in Exporting: 10

45457 JET Tools
427 New Sanford Rd
La Vergne, TN 37086
800-274-6848
www.jettools.com
Wholesaler/distributor of general merchandise including service carts, scissor lift tables, hydraulic and pallet jacks, hand trucks, hardwood and drum dollies and hoists including electric, chain and manual.
President: Robert Romano
VP, Finance/Controller/CFO: Tony Stratton
VP, Global Supply Chain: Ivan Werhli
SVP, National Sales Account: Bob Varzino
VP, Human Resources: Virginia Schmidt
Year Founded: 1958
Estimated Sales: $50-100 Million
Number Employees: 50-99
Parent Co: Walter Meier Holding
Brands Exported: Jet
Regions Exported to: Central America, South America
Percentage of Business in Exporting: 5
Brands Imported: Jet
Regions Imported from: Europe, Asia
Percentage of Business in Importing: 98

45458 JFC International Inc
7101 E Slauson Ave
Commerce, CA 90040 323-721-6100
www.jfc.com
Importer of Japanese foods including mushrooms, chewing gum, mandarin oranges, noodles and fish; exporter of general Japanese groceries.
President: Yoshiyuki Ishigaki
VP, Sales & Marketing: Paul Iiyama
DC Manager: Ian Tennant
Year Founded: 1906
Estimated Sales: $49.4 Million
Number Employees: 100-249
Number of Products: 15
Square Footage: 13075
Type of Packaging: Consumer, Food Service
Other Locations:
 Norcross, GA
 Los Angeles, CA
 Savage, MD
 Pompano Beach, FL
 Hanover Park, IL
 Linden, NJ Los Angeles
Regions Exported to: Worldwide
Regions Imported from: Asia

45459 JH Display & Fixture
P.O. Box 432
Greenwood, IN 46142 317-888-0631
Fax: 317-888-0671
Manufacturer, importer and exporter of wood, acrylic, metal and glass fixtures. Also custom shelving and tables available. Antique and vintage decorative props for all types of settings
Owner: John Holbrook
VP/Owner: Trudy Holbrook
Estimated Sales: $ 1-2.5 Million
Number Employees: 5-9
Regions Exported to: Worldwide
Percentage of Business in Exporting: 10
Regions Imported from: Asia, Mexico
Percentage of Business in Importing: 5

45460 JJI Lighting Group, Inc.
11500 Melrose Ave.
Franklin Park, IL 60131-1334 847-451-0700
Manufacturer, importer and exporter of lighting fixtures and systems

CEO: Robert Haidinger
Contact: Claude Sarti
claude.sarti@philips.com
Estimated Sales: $ 55 Million
Number Employees: 650
Number of Products: 15
Type of Packaging: Private Label, Bulk
Regions Exported to: Worldwide
Regions Imported from: Germany

45461 JL Industries Inc
4450 W 78th Street Cir
Bloomington, MN 55435-5416 952-835-6850
Fax: 952-835-2218 800-554-6077
www.activarcpg.com
Manufacturer, exporter and importer of fire extinguishers and cabinets, other fire and emergency AED cabinets, metal access panels and roof hatches, dirt control floor mats and gratings, and detention specialties.
President: Carl Coleman
ccoleman@jlindustries.com
Marketing: Nona Peterson
Estimated Sales: $ 10 - 20 Million
Number Employees: 50-99
Square Footage: 116000
Parent Co: Activar
Brands Exported: Fire Extinguishers; Fire Extinguisher Cabinets; Access Panels; Roof Hatches; Floor Mats/Grates.
Regions Exported to: Worldwide
Percentage of Business in Exporting: 5
Regions Imported from: Worldwide

45462 JLS Foods International
1101 Perimeter Drive
Suite 400
Schaumburg, IL 60173-5133 847-517-7711
Fax: 847-517-7733 877-JLS-INTL
customerservice@jlsfoods.com www.jlsfoods.com
Importer of powdered milk proteins including casein, caseinates, whey proteins and concentrates
President: Arden Reisenbigler
Sales: Sean Baumgartner
seanb@jlsfoods.com
Purchasing: Eric Reisenbigler
Estimated Sales: $5-10 Million
Number Employees: 5-9
Brands Imported: Ameripro
Regions Imported from: Europe
Percentage of Business in Importing: 95

45463 JM Schneider
4060 78th Avenue SE
Calgary, AB T2C 2I8
Canada 403-720-3860
Fax: 403-236-4255 www.schneiders.ca
Wholesaler/distributor of frozen beef and pork products; importer of frozen entrees
Sales/Marketing Executive: Dan Bradrich
Manager: Doug McFarlane
Number Employees: 50-99
Square Footage: 260000
Parent Co: J.M. Schneider
Brands Imported: Michelina
Regions Imported from: U.S.A.
Percentage of Business in Importing: 2

45464 JMC Packaging Equipment
3470 Mainway Drive
Burlington, ON L7M 1A8
Canada 905-335-4196
Fax: 905-335-4201 800-263-5252
davidk@jmcpackaging.com
www.jmcpackaging.com
Manufacturer and exporter of bagging and bag sealing machinery
Sales Manager: David Kay
Office Manager: Linda Campbell
Number Employees: 10-19
Type of Packaging: Consumer, Food Service, Private Label, Bulk
Regions Exported to: Worldwide
Percentage of Business in Exporting: 30

45465 JMS
P.O. Box 336
Brookline, MA 02446 617-254-1116
Fax: 617-254-1414
Wholesaler/distributor, importer and exporter of produce and fresh herbs including thyme, basil, oregano, rosemary, mint, chives, sage, cilantro and parsley

President: Joel Shaw
VP: Karen Shaw
Contact: Josephs Leah
jleah@jms-herbs.net
Estimated Sales: $ .5 - 1 million
Number Employees: 1-4
Regions Exported to: Latin America
Percentage of Business in Exporting: 65

45466 JNS Foods
3785 Airport Pulling Road N
Suite C
Naples, FL 34105-4518 239-403-9080
Fax: 941-403-9085 jnsfoods@aol.com
Wholesaler/distributor and exporter of dairy/deli products, frozen foods, groceries, meats, seafood, general merchandise, etc.; serving the food service market
President: Jeffrey Siegal
CEO: Nancy Siegal
Estimated Sales: $7 Million
Number Employees: 1-4
Square Footage: 6000
Type of Packaging: Food Service

45467 JTECH Communications Inc
6413 Congress Ave # 150
Boca Raton, FL 33487-2823 561-997-0772
Fax: 561-995-2260 800-321-6221
sales@jtech.com www.jtech.com
President: Jack Troy
Number Employees: 100-249

45468 JUMO Process Control Inc
6733 Myers Rd
East Syracuse, NY 13057-9787 315-437-5866
Fax: 315-697-5860 800-554-5866
www.jumo.net
Meat thermometers, temperature control probes and refrigeration controllers.
President: Carsten Juchheim
CEO: Bernhard Juchheim
Manager: Katherine Blume
katherine.blume@jumo.net
Number Employees: 20-49

45469 JW Aluminum
435 Old Mt Holly Rd
Mt Holly, SC 29445 843-572-1100
Fax: 843-572-1049 800-568-1100
www.jwaluminum.com
Aluminum foil
Chief Executive Officer: Lee McCarter
Chief Financial Officer: Philip Cavatoni
Chief Commercial Officer: Ryan Roush
Chief Operating Officer: Stan Brant
Estimated Sales: $1 - 5 Million
Number Employees: 10-19
Type of Packaging: Food Service
Regions Exported to: Canada, Mexico

45470 JW Leser Company
4408 W Jefferson Blvd
Los Angeles, CA 90016-4090 323-731-4173
Fax: 323-731-4175
Sell and manufacture fillers, pumps, homogenizers, tanks, mixers, and filters
President: Ray Leser
Number Employees: 1-4
Regions Exported to: Worldwide
Percentage of Business in Exporting: 5
Regions Imported from: Europe, Asia
Percentage of Business in Importing: 10

45471 Jaccard Corporation
3421 N Benzing Rd
Orchard Park, NY 14127 716-825-3814
Fax: 716-825-5319
Wholesaler/distributor and exporter of food processing equipment including tenderizers, slicers/dicers, cutlet flattening devices, vacuum packagers and pickling injectors; serving the food service market
President: Eric Wangler
Marketing Director: Karen Beamish
Sales Director: Erin Janney
Contact: Paul Eichin
pauleichin@jaccard.com
Operations Manager: Doug Spaetch
Estimated Sales: $2.5-5 Million
Number Employees: 10-19
Type of Packaging: Food Service
Brands Exported: Jaccard
Regions Exported to: Worldwide
Percentage of Business in Exporting: 55

379

Importers & Exporters / A-Z

45472 Jack & Jill Ice Cream
101 Commerce Dr
Moorestown, NJ 08057-4212   856-813-2300
Fax: 856-813-2373 info@jjicc.com
www.jjicc.com
Ice cream and frozen yogurt; cakes and fancy desserts
President: Jay Schwartz
jschwartz@jjicc.com
Founder: Mickey Schwartz
Marketing Director: Shawn Brady
VP Sales: John Corral
General Manager: Ken Schwartz
Number Employees: 500-999
Type of Packaging: Consumer, Food Service
Regions Exported to: Worldwide
Percentage of Business in Exporting: 2

45473 Jack Brown Produce
8035 Fruit Ridge Ave NW
Sparta, MI 49345-9758   616-887-9568
Fax: 616-887-9765 800-348-0834
info@jackbrownproduce.com
www.jackbrownproduce.com
Produce
Owner: Steve Thome
Chairman/VP: Philip Succop
Sales Exec: Mitch Brinks
mitch@jackbrownproduce.com
Operations Manager: Pat Chase
Estimated Sales: $6.5 Million
Number Employees: 20-49
Square Footage: 2000000
Type of Packaging: Consumer, Food Service, Private Label, Bulk
Regions Exported to: Worldwide
Percentage of Business in Exporting: 15

45474 Jack Daniel Distillery
280 Lynchburg Hwy.
Lynchburg, TN 37352   931-759-6357
888-551-5225
www.jackdaniels.com
Whiskey.
CEO, Brown-Forman Corp.: Lawson Whiting
Year Founded: 1866
Estimated Sales: $121,700,000
Number Employees: 500+
Parent Co: Brown-Forman Corporation
Type of Packaging: Consumer
Brands Exported: Jack Daniels
Regions Exported to: Worldwide

45475 Jack Stack
221 Sheridan Blvd
Inwood, NY 11096-1226   516-371-5214
Fax: 516-371-6880 800-999-9840
info@jackstack.com www.interfreight.net
Manufacturer and importer of mobile plate racks
Manager: Tom Staub
tom@interfreight.net
Managing Director: Tom Staub
Sales Manager: John Falzarano
Sales Manager: Pascale Steingueldoir
Estimated Sales: Less than $ 500,000
Number Employees: 5-9
Parent Co: Jackstack International
Brands Imported: Jackstack
Regions Imported from: Europe

45476 Jack the Ripper Table Skirting
4003 Greenbriar Drive
Suite A
Stafford, TX 77477   281-240-1024
Fax: 281-240-0343 800-331-7831
www.tableskirting.com
Manufacturer and exporter of table skirting, table cloths, napkins, place mats and tray stand covers
Director Sales: Erik Dean
Customer Service: Jessie Carpenter
Estimated Sales: $ 1 Million
Number Employees: 20-50
Regions Exported to: Worldwide

45477 Jacks Manufacturing Company
PO Box 50695
Mendota, MN 55150-0695   651-452-1474
Fax: 651-452-1477 800-821-2089
Manufacturer and exporter of boiler compounds and carpet and upholstery cleaners
Chairman Board: C Nimis
Director: S Nimis
Office Manager: Sharon Bruesile

Estimated Sales: $2.5-5 Million
Number Employees: 1-4

45478 Jacob Holtz Co.
10 Industrial HWY MS-6 Airport Business
Lester, PA 19029   215-423-2800
Fax: 215-634-7454 800-445-4337
info@jacobholtz.com
Supplier and exporter of self-adjusting table glides
Estimated Sales: Below $ 5 Million
Number Employees: 3
Square Footage: 9600
Regions Exported to: Canada
Percentage of Business in Exporting: 1

45479 Jade Products Co
2650 Orbiter St
Brea, CA 92821-6265   714-528-4486
800-884-5233
dpack@maytag.com www.jaderange.com
OEM equipment including commercial cooking ranges and refrigerators
President: Ray Williams
VP Sales: Lex Poulos
Customer Service Manager: Susan Hopkins
Production Engineering Manager: Peng Wang
Estimated Sales: $ 2.5-5 Million
Number Employees: 100-249
Parent Co: Maytag Corporation

45480 Jain Americas Inc
1819 Walcutt Rd
Suite I
Columbus, OH 43228-9149   614-850-9400
Fax: 614-850-8600 888-473-7539
info@jainamericas.com www.jainamericas.com
Dehydrated vegetables, fruit purees, puree concentrates and clarified juices
CEO: Narinder Gupta
Executive Vice President: Murali Ramanathan
murali@jainamericas.com
Number Employees: 20-49

45481 Jakeman's Maple Products
454414 Trillium Line
RR #1
Beachville, ON N0J 1A0
Canada   519-539-1366
Fax: 519-421-2469 800-382-9795
info@themaplestore.com www.themaplestore.com
Maple syrup, sugar, candy and yogurt; coffee, tea and cookies
President: Robert Jakeman
CFO: Jane Henderson
Quality Control: Melissa Martin
Sales: Mary Jakeman
Production: Heather Crane
Estimated Sales: $1 Million
Number Employees: 11
Number of Brands: 1
Number of Products: 78
Square Footage: 26480
Parent Co: Auvergne Farms
Type of Packaging: Consumer, Food Service, Private Label, Bulk
Brands Exported: Jakeman's
Regions Exported to: Europe, Asia, USA
Percentage of Business in Exporting: 15

45482 (HQ)Jam Group of Company
4200 Chino Hills Parkway
Suite 375
Chino Hills, CA 91709-5825   213-627-9194
Fax: 213-627-9312
Export broker of sugar, wheat, rice, powdered milk, soybeans, butter, oils, etc. Importer of frozen fish
President: Javed Matin
VP: Bill Schnack
Number Employees: 10-19
Square Footage: 12800
Regions Imported from: Asia, Pakistan, Bangladesh, India

45483 Jamaican Teas LimitedC/O Eve Sales Corporation
945 Close Ave
Bronx, NY 10473   718-589-6800
Fax: 718-617-6717 ihopp@evesales.com
www.jamaicanteas.com
Wholesaler/distributor and importer of Caribbean and Mexican foods

Owner: Irving Nadler
Executive VP: Irving Nadler
VP Marketing: Stuart Gale
Sales Manager: Isadore Hoppenfeld
Estimated Sales: $5-10 Million
Number Employees: 10-19
Square Footage: 88000
Regions Imported from: South America, Europe
Percentage of Business in Importing: 75

45484 James L. Mood Fisheries
Woods Harbour
Nova Scotia, NS B0W 2E0
Canada   902-723-2360
Fax: 902-723-2880 info@moodfisheries.com
www.moodfisheries.com
Fresh seafood
President: Corey Mood
Vice President: Almond Mood
Estimated Sales: $674,000
Number Employees: 10
Type of Packaging: Consumer, Food Service, Private Label, Bulk
Regions Exported to: Europe, Asia
Percentage of Business in Exporting: 90

45485 (HQ)James P. Smith & Company
1253 Springfield Avenue
New Providence, NJ 07974-1935   201-935-0233
Importer of olives
Estimated Sales: $10-20 Million
Number Employees: 10-19
Other Locations:
   Smith, James P., & Co.
   Carlstadt, NJSmith, James P., & Co.

45486 James Skinner Company
4657 G St
Omaha, NE 68117-1410   402-734-1672
Fax: 402-734-0516 800-358-7428
www.skinnerbaking.com
Frozen baked goods
President: James Skinner
Chief Executive Officer: Jim Skinner
VP Marketing: Doug Dinnin
Contact: Scott Barrows
sbarrows@skinnerbaking.com
Director of Operations: Dennis Nolan
Plant Manager: Tom Urzendowski
Estimated Sales: $7.6 Million
Number Employees: 100-249
Square Footage: 300000
Type of Packaging: Consumer, Food Service, Private Label, Bulk
Regions Exported to: Europe
Percentage of Business in Exporting: 5

45487 (HQ)James Thompson
381 Park Ave S
Rm 718
New York, NY 10016-8806   212-686-5306
Fax: 212-686-9528 inquiry@jamesthompson.com
www.jamesthompson.com
Manufacturer and exporter of buckrams, netting, cotton goods, burlap, cheesecloth, etc
President: Robert B Judell
Treasurer: Barry Garr
Vice President, Sales/Marketing: Marc Bieler
Site Manager: Steve Luchansky
Vice President, Manufacturing: Steve Luchansky
Merchandise Manager: Gail Boyle
Estimated Sales: $300,000-500,000
Number Employees: 5-9
Regions Exported to: Worldwide
Percentage of Business in Exporting: 10

45488 Jamieson Laboratories
4025 Rhodes Drive
Windsor, ON N8W 5B5
Canada   519-974-8482
Fax: 519-974-4742 800-265-5088
www.jamiesonvitamins.com
Kefir, yogurt, cod liver oil, vitamins, mineral supplements; water purifying systems and filters.
President/CEO: Mark Hornick
Year Founded: 1922
Estimated Sales: $42 Million
Number Employees: 400
Number of Brands: 22
Square Footage: 40000
Parent Co: CCMP Capital Advisors LLC
Type of Packaging: Consumer
Other Locations:
   Toronto, ON

Importers & Exporters / A-Z

45489 Jamison Door Co
55 Jv Jamison Dr
Hagerstown, MD 21740   301-733-3100
Fax: 240-329-5155   800-532-3667
www.jamisondoor.com
Cold storage refrigerator and freezer doors.
CEO: John T Williams
jw@jamisondoor.com
Purchasing: Don Wilson
Number Employees: 100-249
Number of Brands: 3
Regions Exported to: Worldwide

45490 Jammit Jam
PO Box 720416
Dallas, TX 75372
jammitjam.com
Jam
Co-Founder: Andrea Chatterji
Co-Founder: Stephanie Magilow *Year Founded:* 2014

45491 Jana Foods LLC
700 Plaza Dr Ste 215
Secaucus, NJ 07094   201-866-5001
Fax: 201-866-3004   info@janafoods.com
www.janafoods.com
Importer and exporter of dairy products
Marketing: Jana Team
Contact: Dan Lynch
dan@janafoods.com
Estimated Sales: $1.2 Million
Number Employees: 7

45492 Jans Enterprises Corp.
4181 Temple City Blvd
Suite A
El Monte, CA 91731   626-575-2000
contact@jansfood.com
jansfood.com
Gluten-free, organic/natural, crackers, gluten-free, juice.cider, chips.
Founder & CEO: Anthony Kartawinata
anthony@jansfood.com *Year Founded:* 1998

45493 Janta International Company, Inc
PO Box 1111
Belmont, CA 94002-1111   650-591-9465
Fax: 650-595-1025
Importer and exporter of ginseng tea, white flower balm
President: Janet Wu
CEO: Dr Tom Wu
Vice President: Gabriel Wu
Quality Control: Michal Wu
Marketing Manager: John Li
Office Manager: Linda Ching
Purchasing Manager: Dr Janet Wu
Estimated Sales: Less than $500,000
Number Employees: 1-4
Square Footage: 2400
Regions Exported to: Asia
Percentage of Business in Exporting: 20
Brands Imported: White Flower Analgesic Balm

45494 Jantec
1777 Northern Star Dr
Traverse City, MI 49696-9244   231-941-4339
Fax: 231-941-1460   800-992-3303
accounting@jantec.com www.jantec.com
Manufacturer and exporter of belt, angle-edge and spiral conveyors; also, power turns and specialty stainless steel conveying equipment for food and washdown applications
Owner: Ronald Sommerfield
ronalds@jantec.com
Number Employees: 20-49
Regions Exported to: South America, Asia, Canada, Mexico, Latin America, Australia
Percentage of Business in Exporting: 15

45495 Jarchem Industries
414 Wilson Ave
Newark, NJ 07105   973-578-4560
Fax: 973-344-5743   info@jarchem.com
www.jarchem.com
Ingredients and additives
CEO: Arnold Stern
Contact: Hein Arthur
hein.arthur@jarchem.com
Mngr.: Howard Honing
Estimated Sales: $ .5 - 1 million
Number Employees: 1-4

45496 Jarden Home Brands
14611 W. Commerce Road
P.O Box 529
Daleville, IN 47334   800-392-2575
Fax: 765-557-3250   info@jardenhomebrands.com
www.diamondbrands.com
Cocktail forks, toothpicks, corn-on-the-cob holders, skewers, candy sticks, spoons, etc; exporter of woodware and cutlery; importer of toothpicks and candy apple sticks
Sales Manager: Phil Dvorak
Contact: Jared Anderson
janderson@jardencs.com
Brands Exported: Diamond; Forster; Permawave
Regions Exported to: Canada, Caribbean, Mexico
Percentage of Business in Exporting: 12
Brands Imported: Forster
Regions Imported from: Asia
Percentage of Business in Importing: 45

45497 Jardine Ranch
910 Nacimiento Lake Dr
Paso Robles, CA 93446-8713   805-238-2365
Fax: 805-239-4334   866-833-5050
order@jardineranch.com www.jardineranch.com
Gift baskets of nuts
Owner: Bill Jardine
Owner: Mary Jardine
jardine@jardineranch.com
Manager: Duane Jardine
Estimated Sales: Less Than $500,000
Number Employees: 5-9
Type of Packaging: Consumer, Food Service, Bulk
Regions Exported to: Worldwide
Percentage of Business in Exporting: 1

45498 Jaret Specialties
900 Us Highway 9 N
Suite 404
Woodbridge, NJ 07095-1003   732-726-2700
Fax: 732-634-5389   800-655-2738
Importer of gourmet grille french toast crisps, bouchees, gublies, lingonberries, spices and vinegars; also, coffee filters and baking pans
President: Greg Barratt
National Sales Director: Steve Bruner
Marketing Director: Douglas King
Number Employees: 20-49

45499 Jarrow Formulas Inc
1824 1/2 S Robertson Blvd
Los Angeles, CA 90035-4317   310-204-6936
Fax: 310-204-2520   800-726-0886
info@jarrow.com www.jarrow.com
Wholesaler/distributor and exporter of nutritional supplements including antioxidants, vitamins, minerals, herbal formulas, acidophilus capsules and powders
President: Jarrow Rogovin
jarrow@jarrow.com
VP Finance: Benjamin Khowong
R&D VP: Sid Shastro
Sales VP: Clay DuBose
Estimated Sales: $30 Million
Number Employees: 50-99
Square Footage: 8000
Brands Exported: Bone-Up; Muscle Optimeal; Jarro-Dophilus EPS; Glycemic Balance; Iso Rich Soy; Biosel; Joint Builder; Ala Sustain; Lyco-Sorb; Q-Absorb
Regions Exported to: Central America, South America, Europe, Australia
Percentage of Business in Exporting: 5

45500 Jarvis Caster Company
881 Lower Brownsville Rd
Jackson, TN 38301-9667   731-554-2138
800-995-9876
inof@jarviscaster.com www.jarviscaster.com
Manufacturer and exporter of industrial casters and wheels
President: Rodney Brooks
CFO: Ronnie Fondrun
Vice President: Scott Lackey
Research & Development: Harry Green
Marketing Director: Cary Gillespie
Sales Director: Scott Lackey
Contact: Zachary Minner
zminner@emdeon.com
Operations Manager: Harold Clark
Purchasing Manager: Tracy Hall
Number Employees: 100-249
Square Footage: 800000
Parent Co: Standex International Corporation
Type of Packaging: Bulk
Other Locations:
Jarvis East
Mississauga, ONJarvis East
Regions Exported to: Worldwide
Percentage of Business in Exporting: 5

45501 (HQ)Jarvis Products Corp
33 Anderson Rd
Middletown, CT 06457-4926   860-347-7271
Fax: 860-347-9905   sales@jarvisproducts.com
Meat and poultry processing equipment.
President: Peter Brown
peterdouglas@hotmail.com
Estimated Sales: $14.8 Million
Number Employees: 100-249
Square Footage: 24000
Brands Exported: Jarvis
Regions Exported to: Worldwide
Percentage of Business in Exporting: 40
Regions Imported from: Worldwide
Percentage of Business in Importing: 10

45502 Jasmine Vineyards, Inc.
33319 Pond Road
Delano, CA 93215   661-792-2141
Fax: 661-792-6365   jvine@jasminevineyards.com
www.jasminevineyards.com
Grapes
Number of Brands: 4
Type of Packaging: Consumer, Food Service, Bulk
Brands Exported: Jasvine, Havren, Vinmar, M and V
Regions Exported to: Worldwide
Percentage of Business in Exporting: 45

45503 Jason Marketing Corporation
10900 NW 97th St Unit 101
Medley, FL 33178   305-882-6716
Fax: 305-882-6724
Wholesaler/distributor, importer and exporter of dry groceries including canned items, rice, nonalcoholic beverages, paper products, trays, etc.; serving the retail market
President: Norman Welch
Estimated Sales: $5-10 Million
Number Employees: 5-9
Square Footage: 52000
Regions Exported to: Caribbean
Regions Imported from: South America, Asia

45504 Java Jacket
910 NE 57th Ave # 300
Portland, OR 97213-3615   503-281-6240
Fax: 503-281-6462   800-208-4128
info@javajacket.com www.javajacket.com
Manufacturer and exporter of hot and cold paper cup coffee sleeves, joe to go boxes and custom sized sleeves.
President: Jay Sorensen
jay@javajacket.com
CEO: Colleen Sorensen
Estimated Sales: $500,000-$1 Million
Number Employees: 5-9
Regions Exported to: Worldwide
Percentage of Business in Exporting: 10

45505 Javalution Coffee Company
2400 Boswell Road
Chula Vista, CA 91914   619-934-3980
Fax: 619-934-3205   800-982-3197
customerservice@javalution.com
www.javalution.com/index.php
Coffee
President: Scott Pumper
CEO/Chairman of the Board: Steve Wallach
Vice President of Business Development: Brent Jensen
Chief Science Officer: Jose Antonio
Vice President of Operations: Mike Kolinski
Type of Packaging: Food Service

Importers & Exporters / A-Z

45506 Jay Packaging Group Inc
100 Warwick Industrial Dr
Warwick, RI 02886-2486   401-244-1300
Fax: 401-738-0137 siteadmin@jaypack.com
www.jaypack.com
Manufacturer and exporter of displays, blister cards, skin sheets and thermoformed trays and blisters
President: Richard E Kelly
CFO: Fernando Lemos
flemos@jaypack.com
VP Sales: Jim Nattiucci
Estimated Sales: $ 20 - 50 Million
Number Employees: 100-249

45507 Jay-Bee Manufacturing Inc
522 N Beverly Ave
Tyler, TX 75702-5932   903-597-9343
Fax: 903-593-8725 800-445-0610
jaybeemfg@suddenlinkmail.com
www.jaybeehammermills.com
Manufacturer and exporter of stainless steel hammer mills for particle reduction of fruits, rice cakes and spices
President: Edwina Granberry
Estimated Sales: $1-2.5 Million
Number Employees: 10-19
Square Footage: 280000
Brands Exported: Jay Bee
Regions Exported to: Central America, South America, Asia, Middle East
Percentage of Business in Exporting: 10

45508 Jayhawk Manufacturing Co Inc
1426 N Grand Street
Hutchinson, KS 67501-2135   620-669-8269
Fax: 620-669-9815 866-886-8269
www.jayhawkmills.com
Manufacturer and exporter of wet process, stone grinding and colloid mills used primarily in the production of condiments
President: Merle Starr
Estimated Sales: $500,000-$1 Million
Number Employees: 1-4
Brands Exported: Jayhawk Mills
Regions Exported to: Central America, South America

45509 Jb Prince
36 E 31st St # 11
New York, NY 10016-6861   212-683-9273
Fax: 212-683-4488 800-473-0577
customerservice@jbprince.com www.jbprince.com
Exporter and wholesaler/distributor of food service equipment and supplies including serving and cooking equipment, tableware and chefs' tools; serving the food service market; importer of restaurant kitchen smallware
President: J Prince
VP: L Prince
Manager: John Thompson
jthompson@jbprince.com
Estimated Sales: $5-10 Million
Number Employees: 20-49
Regions Exported to: Worldwide
Percentage of Business in Exporting: 20
Regions Imported from: Worldwide
Percentage of Business in Importing: 70

45510 Jeco Plastic Products LLC
885 Andico Rd
Plainfield, IN 46168-9659   317-839-4943
Fax: 317-839-1209 800-593-5326
www.jecoplastics.com
FDA approved plastic pallet and containers
President/CEO: Craig Carson
craigc@jecoplastics.com
CFO: Sherry Arndt
R & D: Roger Streling
Sales: Paul Koehl
Sales/Customer support: Ann Carson
Plant Manager: Don Andrews
Estimated Sales: Below $5 Million
Number Employees: 20-49
Square Footage: 74000
Type of Packaging: Bulk
Regions Exported to: Central America, South America, Europe

45511 Jel Sert
501 Conde St
West Chicago, IL 60185   630-876-4838
800-323-2592
www.jelsert.com
Frozen juice pops, juice beverages and mixes

President: Kenneth Wegner
Research & Development Director: John Dobrozsi
Senior Quality Engineer: Erika Scherer
Director of Human Resources: Juan Chavez
Engineer & Plant Manager: Simon Richards
Square Footage: 1600000
Type of Packaging: Consumer, Food Service, Bulk

45512 (HQ)Jelly Belly Candy Co.
One Jelly Belly Lane
Fairfield, CA 94533-6741   707-428-2800
Fax: 707-428-2863 800-522-3267
www.jellybelly.com
Candy
President: Lisa Brasher
CEO: Herman Rowland
hrowland@jellybelly.com
Vice President, Specialty Sales: John Pola
Chief Sales and Marketing Officer: Ryan Schader
Vice President, Sales: Andrew Joffer
Plant Manager: Anthony Habib
hrowland@jellybelly.com
Purchasing Manager: Reg Nelson
Estimated Sales: $ 215 Million
Number Employees: 500-999
Number of Brands: 2
Number of Products: 150
Square Footage: 350000
Type of Packaging: Consumer, Private Label
Other Locations:
  Distribution Center
  Pleasant Prairie, WIDistribution Center
Brands Exported: Jelly Belly
Regions Exported to: South America, Europe, Asia, Middle East, Australia, Canada, Mexico

45513 Jemolo Enterprises
100 S Westwood Street
Spc 126
Porterville, CA 93257-7708   559-784-5566
Fax: 209-823-2506 jemoloente@aol.com
www.jemolo.en.ec21.com
Manufacturer and exporter of environmental technological building systems including water purification and waste water and sanitation treatment; also, reverse osmosis water treatment systems
President: Fred Niswonger
Brands Exported: Purtec
Regions Exported to: Worldwide
Percentage of Business in Exporting: 90

45514 Jen-Coat, Inc.
132 North Elm Street
PO Box 274
Westfield, MA 01086   877-536-2628
Fax: 413-562-8771 info@jencoat.com
Manufacturer and exporter of plastic coated paper
President: James Kauffman
Contact: Michelle Cotham
michellec@workplacestaff.com
Estimated Sales: $ 1 - 5 Million
Number Employees: 250-499
Parent Co: Ana Business Products

45515 Jennie-O Turkey Store
1126 Benson Ave SW
Willmar, MN 56201   320-235-6080
Fax: 320-231-0779 turkeyinfo@j-ots.com
www.jennieo.com
Turkey products
President: Michael Tolbert
CEO: Jerry Jerome
CFO: Dwight York
VP Marketing: Bob Tegt
Sales Director: Jime Splinter
Public Relations: Dave Suheke
Operations Manager: Bob Wood
Purchasing Agent: Larry Hammond
Number Employees: 250-499
Parent Co: Hormel Foods Corporation
Type of Packaging: Consumer, Food Service
Brands Exported: Jennie-O; Natural Choice
Regions Exported to: Worldwide

45516 Jennies Gluten-Free Bakery
590 Rocky Glen Rd
Moosic, PA 18507   570-457-2400
Fax: 570-457-3626 lainiehamlin@outlook.com
jenniesmacaroons.com
Macaroons and cakes
President: Arnold Badner
Estimated Sales: $4,000,000
Number Employees: 20-49
Square Footage: 120000

Type of Packaging: Food Service

45517 Jensen Meat Company
2550 Britannia Blvd
Suite 101
San Diego, CA 92154   619-754-6400
Fax: 619-754-6450 info@jensenmeat.com
www.jensenmeat.com
Ground beef hamburger patties
President: Robert Jensen
CEO: Abel Olivera
CFO: Sam Acuna
VP of Executive Accounts: Patricia Lavigne
VP of Production: Anthony Crivello
Year Founded: 1958
Estimated Sales: $26.9 Million
Number Employees: 1-4
Type of Packaging: Consumer, Food Service, Private Label, Bulk
Regions Exported to: Mexico

45518 Jervis B WEBB Co
30100 Cabot Dr
Novi, MI 48377   248-553-1000
www.daifuku.com/us
Manufacturer and exporter of conveyor and integrated material handling systems.
President & CEO: Aki Nishimura
Year Founded: 1919
Estimated Sales: $100-250 Million
Number Employees: 1,000
Parent Co: Daifuku Co.
Other Locations:
  Webb, Jervis B., Co.
  Chardon, OHWebb, Jervis B., Co.
Regions Exported to: Worldwide
Percentage of Business in Exporting: 30

45519 Jesco Industries
950 Anderson Rd
Litchfield, MI 49252   517-542-2353
Fax: 517-542-2501 800-455-0019
www.jescoonline.com
Manufacturer, importer and exporter of hoppers, dumpers, security trucks, carts, dollies, baskets, wire mesh partitions, security cages, window guards and enclosures, etc
Vice President: Tom Sebastian
toms@jescolion.com
VP: B Desjardin
Marketing Director: Bonny DesJardin
Sales Engineer: Phil Risedorph
Estimated Sales: $8 Million
Number Employees: 100-249
Square Footage: 360000
Regions Exported to: Worldwide
Percentage of Business in Exporting: 10
Regions Imported from: Worldwide
Percentage of Business in Importing: 40

45520 (HQ)Jescorp
300 E Touhy Avenue
Suite C
Des Plaines, IL 60018-2669   847-299-7800
Fax: 847-299-7822
Manufacturer and exporter of thermoformed and laminated containers and films, integrated gas flushing systems, gas flush tray sealers and vacuum seamers
VP Direct Sales: Jim Sanfilippo
Number Employees: 64
Square Footage: 280000
Regions Exported to: Europe, Canada, Mexico
Percentage of Business in Exporting: 15

45521 Jess Jones Vineyard
6496 Jones Ln
Dixon, CA 95620-9601   707-678-3839
Fax: 707-678-3898 www.jessjonesvineyard.com
Wines
President: Jess Jones
CEO: Mary Ellen Jones
Estimated Sales: $700,000
Number Employees: 1-4
Square Footage: 20000
Type of Packaging: Consumer, Bulk

45522 Jessie's Ilwaco Fish Company
45 Shed B
Unit 4
San Francisco, CA 94133   360-642-3773
Fax: 360-642-3362 don@alberseafoods.com
Fish and seafood

Owner: Pierre Marchand
VP: Doug Ross
Marketing: George Alexander
Production: Phil Marchand
Estimated Sales: $20-40 Million
Number Employees: 100-249
Square Footage: 25000
Type of Packaging: Consumer, Food Service, Private Label, Bulk
Brands Exported: Seaside
Regions Exported to: South America, Europe, Asia
Percentage of Business in Exporting: 50

45523 Jet Plastica Industries
1100 Schwab Rd
Hatfield, PA 19440
www.dwfinepack.com
Manufacturer and exporter of molded plastics including packaging kits, tumblers, cutlery and straws
Contact: Donna Alexander
dalexander2@kaplanco.com
Estimated Sales: $ 43 Million
Number Employees: 600
Square Footage: 300000
Parent Co: D&W Fine Pack

45524 Jet Set Sam
10918 Phillips Avenue
Burnaby, BC V5A 2V8
Canada
604-283-4362
Fax: 604-444-2661 sales@jetsetsam.com
www.jetsetsam.com/
Wholesaler/distributor, importer and exporter of canned smoked salmon and caviar
Owner: Firoz Jinnah
Number Employees: 1-4
Square Footage: 24000
Parent Co: Jet Set Sam Services
Brands Exported: Jet Set Sam
Regions Exported to: Central America, South America, Europe, Asia, USA
Percentage of Business in Exporting: 50
Regions Imported from: Russia
Percentage of Business in Importing: 10

45525 Jetstream Systems
400 South Emporia St.
Wichita, KN 67202
316-462-9784
Fax: 303-371-9012 855-861-6916
jetstreamsys.com
Manufacturer and exporter of mechanical and air conveyors, palletizers and depalletizers, bottle and can fillers and rinsers
Director Sales: Neal McConnellogue
Director Applications: Vince Jones
Number Employees: 153
Square Footage: 264000
Parent Co: Barry-Wehmiller Company
Regions Exported to: Worldwide
Percentage of Business in Exporting: 45

45526 Jewel Case Corp
110 Dupont Dr
Cranston, RI 02907-3181
401-943-1400
Fax: 401-943-1426 800-441-4447
contact@jewelcase.com www.jewelcase.com
Manufacturer and exporter of gift and promotional packaging for candy, confections, gourmet foods and cutlery/tableware
President: Terri Eisen
teisen@jewelcase.com
Controller: Terry Eisen
Marketing Manager: Lynn Johnson
Sales: Richard Dobuski
Estimated Sales: $ 10 - 20 Million
Number Employees: 100-249
Square Footage: 200000
Type of Packaging: Consumer, Private Label, Bulk
Regions Exported to: Central America, South America
Percentage of Business in Exporting: 2

45527 Jewel Date Co
84675 60th Ave
Thermal, CA 92274-8780
760-399-4474
Fax: 760-399-4476
Natural and organic pecans, dates, raisins, nuts and dried fruits
President: Gregory Raumin
CEO: Greg Raumin
greg@jeweldate.com
Sales Manager: John Ortiz

Estimated Sales: $1,300,000
Number Employees: 20-49
Parent Co: Covalda
Type of Packaging: Consumer
Brands Exported: Covalda
Regions Exported to: Europe, Asia

45528 (HQ)Jif-Pak Manufacturing
1451 Engineer St # A
Vista, CA 92081-8841
760-597-2665
Fax: 760-597-2667 800-777-6613
info@jifpak.com www.jifpak.com
Manufacturer and exporter of elastic and nonelastic nettings, stockinettes, stuffing horns, semi and automatic netting machines and elastic trussing loops
President: Gary Cleppe
garycleppe@kalleusa.com
Marketing Executive: John Connelly
Operations Ex: Lee Jared
Estimated Sales: $ 1 - 5 Million
Number Employees: 5-9
Brands Exported: Casing-Net; Jif-Pak
Regions Exported to: Worldwide

45529 Jilasco Food Exports
1415 2nd Avenue
Unit 2005
Seattle, WA 98101-2072
206-684-9433
Fax: 206-233-9440
Export broker of frozen foods, groceries, meat and meat products, seafood, spices, frying equipment, general merchandise, etc.
President: Eduardo Bicierro
Vice President: Luisa Bicierro
Operations Manager: Bernard Corsles
Number Employees: 1-4
Square Footage: 2200
Parent Co: Jilasco LLC
Type of Packaging: Food Service, Private Label, Bulk
Regions Exported to: Asia

45530 Jilson Group
20 Industrial Rd
Lodi, NJ 7644
973-471-2400
Fax: 973-471-3993 800-969-5400
heretohelp@jilson.com www.jilson.com
Manufacturer and importer of casters, wheels, noncorrosive bearings and bearing housings as well as plastic packaging ties.
Chief Financial Officer: Pete Rennard
VP: David Baughn
Products Manager: Steven Becher
Vice President Sales: David Baughn
Contact: Tony Alfano
talfano@jilson.com
Purchasing Manager: Tony Alfano
Estimated Sales: $ 2.5-5 Million
Number Employees: 10-19
Square Footage: 40000
Brands Imported: Steinco Casters
Regions Imported from: Europe, Asia, Canada
Percentage of Business in Importing: 50

45531 Jim Did It Sign Company
PO Box 17
Allston, MA 2134
617-782-2410
Fax: 781-782-5433
Manufacturer and exporter of commercial signs for supermarkets and other businesses
Owner: Robert Thompson
Estimated Sales: $ 500,000-$ 1 Million
Number Employees: 5-9
Regions Exported to: Europe, Asia
Percentage of Business in Exporting: 1

45532 Jim Scharf Holdings
PO Box 305 Ave K & 9th St
Perdue, SK S0K 3C0
Canada
306-237-4365
Fax: 306-237-4362 800-667-9727
sales@ezeewrap.com www.ezeewrap.com
Manufacturer and exporter of plastic wrap dispensers, process refrigerator/freezer odor absorbers, shopping bag handles, bagel cutters and lettuce knives; processor of instant lentils
President: Bruna Scharf
Marketing: Leanna Carr
Plant Manager: Mary Ann Cotterill
Estimated Sales: Below $5,000,000
Number Employees: 10
Square Footage: 24000
Brands Exported: Ezeewrap 1000; Nona's
Regions Exported to: USA, England

45533 Jo Mar Laboratories
583 Division St # B
Campbell, CA 95008-6915
408-374-5920
Fax: 408-374-5922 800-538-4545
info@jomarlabs.com www.jomarlabs.com
Health products; contract packaging
President: Joanne Brown
joanne@jomarlabs.com
Estimated Sales: $ 1 - 3 Million
Number Employees: 10-19
Square Footage: 14000
Parent Co: Jo Mar Labs
Type of Packaging: Consumer, Private Label
Brands Exported: 20 Blend; Pure Form
Regions Exported to: Worldwide
Percentage of Business in Exporting: 5

45534 JoDaSa Group International
146 Chelwood Drive
Thornhill, ON L4J 7C4
Canada
905-669-3760
Fax: 905-669-4352
Importer and wholesaler/distributor of canned kiwifruit and kiwi syrup, jams, spreads and nectars; also, organic extra virgin olive oil and dried pasta
Managing Director: Sergio Zavarella
Type of Packaging: Consumer, Food Service, Private Label, Bulk
Brands Imported: Green House
Regions Imported from: Italy
Percentage of Business in Importing: 100

45535 Joe Clark Fund Raising Candies
621 E 1st Ave
Tarentum, PA 15084-2005
724-226-0866
888-459-9520
www.clarkcandies.com
Chocolates
Owner: Bob Clark
bob@clarkcandies.com
Estimated Sales: $ 3 - 5 Million
Number Employees: 5-9
Type of Packaging: Consumer
Regions Imported from: Europe

45536 Joe Hutson Foods
8331 Sanlando Avenue
Jacksonville, FL 32211-5135
904-731-9065
Fax: 904-731-9066 keithhutson@juno.com
Sauces
President: Teresa Foster
CEO: Keith Hutson
Chairman Board: Joe Hutson
Number Employees: 1-4
Square Footage: 1200
Parent Co: Joe Hutson Foods
Regions Exported to: Worldwide

45537 Joe Tea and Joe Chips
PO Box 43255
Upper Montclair, NJ 07043-0255
973-744-7502
www.joetea.com
Iced teas, juices and chips
CEO and Co-Founder: Joe Prato
Co-Founder: Ann Prato
Regions Exported to: South America, Asia

45538 Joey's Fine Foods
135 Manchester Place
Newark, NJ 07104
973-482-1400
Fax: 973-482-1597 sales@joeysfinefoods.com
www.joeysfinefoods.com
Mixes and baked goods
President: Aaron Aihini
Vice President Sales: Anthony Romano
Contact: Joe Aihini
Estimated Sales: $5.5 Million
Number Employees: 40
Square Footage: 168000
Type of Packaging: Consumer, Food Service, Private Label, Bulk
Brands Exported: Joey's
Regions Exported to: Central America, Europe, Asia, Caribbean Basin
Percentage of Business in Exporting: 15

45539 Johanna Foods Inc.
1 Johanna Farms Rd.
PO Box 272
Flemington, NJ 08822
908-788-2200
800-727-6700
info@johannafoods.com www.johannafoods.com
Fruit juices, beverages and yogurt.

Importers & Exporters / A-Z

President/CEO: Robert Facchina
robertfacchina@johannafoods.com
Quality Systems Coordinator: Nicole Branstetter
Year Founded: 1995
Estimated Sales: $100 Million
Number Employees: 500-999
Number of Brands: 3
Square Footage: 500000
Type of Packaging: Consumer, Food Service, Private Label, Bulk

45540 (HQ)John Boos & Co
3601 S Banker St
PO Box 609
Effingham, IL 62401-2899   217-347-7701
Fax: 217-347-7705 888-431-2667
www.johnboos.com
Manufacturer and exporter of cutting boards, butchers' blocks, dining room tables and chairs and stainless steel work tables and sinks
President: Edward Surowiec
gerencia@cibersam.es
Executive Chef: Dustin Muroski
VP Sales: Eric Johnson
Estimated Sales: $10-20 Million
Number Employees: 20-49
Square Footage: 260000
Other Locations:
  John Boos & Co.
  Philipsburg, PAJohn Boos & Co.
Brands Exported: Pro Chef; Cucina Americana; Stallion; The Table Tailors
Regions Exported to: Central America, South America, Europe, Asia, Middle East
Percentage of Business in Exporting: 4

45541 John Burton Machine Corporation
3251 John Muir Pkwy
Rodeo, CA 94572   510-799-5000
Fax: 510-799-5003 800-664-4178
Packaging machines and case conveyor, case conveyors for cardboard boxes and tote boxes
President: Burton Rice
Sales Director: Burton Rice
Estimated Sales: Below $5 Million
Number Employees: 1-4

45542 John Crane Mechanical Sealing Devices
227 W Monroe St
Suite 1800
Chicago, IL 60606
www.johncrane.com
Manufacturer and exporter of mechanical seals, bearing isolators, couplings, lubrication systems, heat exchangers and pressure reservoirs.
President & CEO: Jean Vernet
Chief Financial Officer: Celine Boland
Vice President & General Counsel: Jay Angelo
VP & Chief Technology Officer: Joe Haas
Vice President, Global Quality: Rich Steffens
Executive Vice President, Marketing: Patrick Thompson
Year Founded: 1910
Estimated Sales: $900 Million
Number Employees: 6,550
Square Footage: 9000
Parent Co: TI Group

45543 John D Walsh Co
25 Executive Pkwy
Ringwood, NJ 07456-1429   973-962-1400
Fax: 973-962-1557 info@johndwalsh.com
www.johndwalsh.com
Importer, exporter and wholesaler/distributor of essential oils and aroma chemicals
President: G Lermond
Vice President: L Serafini
Estimated Sales: $5-10 Million
Number Employees: 10-19
Square Footage: 97200
Regions Exported to: Worldwide
Regions Imported from: Worldwide

45544 John E. Ruggles & Company
PO Box 8179
New Bedford, MA 02742-8179   508-992-9766
Fax: 508-992-9734
Manufacturer, importer and exporter of varietal fiber regular and dyed rope, twine and braid
President: John Ruggles

Estimated Sales: $5-10 Million
Number Employees: 50-99
Square Footage: 100000
Regions Exported to: Asia, Canada
Regions Imported from: Europe, Canada

45545 John Henry Packaging
10005 Main St
Penngrove, CA 94951   707-664-8018
Fax: 707-762-1253 800-327-5997
Producer of digital, flexo, embossed, screened labels and cartons
Owner: John Herpeck
Digital Print Manager/Marketing Director: Dan Welty
Number Employees: 5-9
Number of Brands: 30
Square Footage: 8000
Parent Co: John Henry Company
Type of Packaging: Consumer, Food Service, Private Label, Bulk
Regions Exported to: South America, Canada, Caribbean, Mexico
Percentage of Business in Exporting: 5

45546 John I. Haas
5185 Macarthur Blvd NW
Suite 300
Washington, DC 20016
info@johnihaas.com
www.barthhaasgroup.com
Hops and hop aroma extract and oils
CEO: Henry Von Eichel
Estimated Sales: $160 Million
Number Employees: 2,000
Number of Brands: 7
Type of Packaging: Food Service, Private Label, Bulk
Regions Exported to: Worldwide
Regions Imported from: South America, Europe, Australia

45547 John J. Adams Die Corporation
10 Nebraska St
Worcester, MA 01604-3628   508-757-3894
Fax: 508-753-8016 jadamsdie@aol.com
Knives; exporter of cutting dies
President and CFO: Richard Adams
General Manager: John J Adams II
Marketing: John Adams
Estimated Sales: $2.5 - 5 Million
Number Employees: 1-4
Square Footage: 40000
Brands Exported: John J. Adams
Regions Exported to: Central America, South America, Europe, Asia, Middle East

45548 John R Nalbach Engineering Co
621 E Plainfield Rd
Countryside, IL 60525-6913   708-579-9100
Fax: 708-579-0122 neco@nalbach.com
www.nalbach.com
Manufacturer and exporter of high speed powder fillers for instant coffee, ground coffee and drink mixes; also, plastic bottle unscramblers, container orientors and aerosol filling lines.
Owner: Matt Nalbach
CEO: John Nalbach
VP Engineering: David Nowaczyk
VP Marketing: Edward Atwell
VP Sales: Gary Lange
mnalbach@nalbach.com
VP Manufacturing: Phil Testa
Estimated Sales: $5 - 10 Million
Number Employees: 20-49
Square Footage: 280000
Regions Exported to: Central America, South America, Europe, Asia, Middle East, Worldwide
Percentage of Business in Exporting: 50

45549 John Rohrer ContractingCo
2820 Roe Ln # S
Kansas City, KS 66103-1560   913-236-5005
Fax: 913-236-7291
www.johnrohrercontracting.com
Manufacturer and exporter of concrete floors
Owner: Kirt Courkamp
kirtcourkamp@jrccolorado.net
EVP: Brandon McMullen
Estimated Sales: $1-2.5 Million
Number Employees: 10-19
Regions Exported to: Mexico

45550 John's Import Foods
5515 N Northwest Hwy
Chicago, IL 60630-1115   773-792-1010
Fax: 773-792-1110 800-222-0458
sales@johnsimportfoodsinc.com
www.johnsimportfoodsinc.com
President: John Ligis
info@johnsimportfoodsinc.com
Number Employees: 1-4

45551 Johns Cove Fisheries
RR 3
Yarmouth, NS B5A 4B1
Canada   902-742-8691
Fax: 902-742-3574
Lobster, herring roe and scallops
President: Don Cunningham
Number Employees: 60
Type of Packaging: Consumer, Food Service, Bulk
Regions Exported to: Central America, Europe, Asia
Percentage of Business in Exporting: 60

45552 Johnson & Sbrocco Associates
3155 State Route 10 # 212
Denville, NJ 07834-3430   973-361-9700
Fax: 973-361-2870 jascoinc@aol.com
Importer of Chilean fruit
President: Robert Johnson
Estimated Sales: $1-2.5 Million
Number Employees: 1-4
Regions Imported from: South America
Percentage of Business in Importing: 20

45553 (HQ)Johnson Foods, Inc.
336 E Blaine Ave
P.O. Box 916
Sunnyside, WA 98944   509-837-4214
Fax: 509-837-4855 johnsonfoodsinc.blogspot.ca
Processed cherries, asparagus and pickled vegetables
President: Gary Johnson
gary@johnsonfoods.com
Estimated Sales: $10 - 20 Million
Number Employees: 250-499
Square Footage: 40000
Type of Packaging: Consumer, Food Service, Private Label, Bulk
Brands Exported: Princess
Regions Exported to: Europe, Asia, Mexico, Canada
Percentage of Business in Exporting: 60

45554 Johnson Industries Intl
6391 Lake Rd
Windsor, WI 53598-9708   608-846-4499
Fax: 608-846-7195 info@johnsonindint.com
www.johnsonindint.com
Manufacturer and exporter of mozzarella cheese making machinery
President: Gary Nesheim
gnesheim@johnsonindint.com
Estimated Sales: $5 - 10 Million
Number Employees: 50-99
Square Footage: 77408
Brands Exported: Supreme

45555 Johnson International Materials
2908 Boca Chica Blvd
Brownsville, TX 78521-3506   956-541-6364
Fax: 956-541-1446
Manufacturer and exporter of wiping rags
President: Jim Johnson
VP Marketing: Bob Ewing
Estimated Sales: $20-50 Million
Number Employees: 100-249
Regions Exported to: Europe, Middle East

45556 (HQ)Johnson Refrigerated Truck
215 E Allen St
Rice Lake, WI 54868-2203   715-234-7071
Fax: 715-234-4628 800-922-8360
jtbsales@johnsontruckbodies.com
Manufacturer and exporter of fiberglass composite plastic refrigerated truck bodies and trailers, and all-electric truck refrigeration systems.
President: Ron Ricci
rricci@johnsontruckbodies.com
VP Sales/Marketing: Mayo Rude
Public Relations: Nicole King
VP Operations: Chris Olson
Number Employees: 250-499
Square Footage: 268000
Type of Packaging: Food Service

Brands Exported: Johnson Truck Bodies; All-Electric Truck Refrigeration
Regions Exported to: Central America, South America, Europe, Asia, Middle East
Percentage of Business in Exporting: 5

45557 Johnson-Rose Corporation
5303 Crown Dr
Lockport, NY 14094   716-434-2711
    Fax: 716-434-2762 800-456-2055
info@johnsonrose.com www.johnsonrose.com
Aluminum cookware and bakeware; importer and exporter of commercial kitchen utensils including ladles, spoons, tongs, mixing bowls, collanders, steam pans, etc
President: Ernie Berman
ernieberman@johnsonrose.net
CFO: Viola Wilson
Director of Marketing: Mark Kuligowski
Operations Manager: D Kuligowski
Inventory Control: Darrell Szyprygada
Estimated Sales: $2.5-5 Million
Number Employees: 20-49
Square Footage: 82000
Parent Co: Johnson-Rose
Brands Exported: Johnson-Rose
Regions Exported to: Central America, South America, Mexico, Caribbean
Percentage of Business in Exporting: 10
Brands Imported: Johnson-Rose
Regions Imported from: Europe, Asia, Canada
Percentage of Business in Importing: 90

45558 Johnston Equipment
#105-581 Chester Road
Annacis Island
Delta, BC V3M 6G7
Canada
        604-524-0361
    Fax: 604-524-8961 800-237-5159
couttsd@johnstonequipment.com
www.johnstonequipment.com
Manufacturer, wholesaler/distributor and exporter of material handling equipment including electric forklifts and pallet racking/shelving systems
President & CEO: Michael Marcotte
Regional Sales Manager: John Binns
Sales Manager: Curt Snigol
Estimated Sales: $ 1 - 5 Million
Number Employees: 50-99
Square Footage: 66000
Regions Exported to: Asia
Percentage of Business in Exporting: 1

45559 Johnston Farms
13031 Packing House Rd
Bakersfield, CA 93307   661-366-3201
    Fax: 661-366-6534 johnstongiftfruit@gmail.com
Navel oranges, peppers and potatoes
Owner: Dennis Johnston
Co-Prtnr.: Gerald Johnston
Commercial Sales Department: Derek Vaughn
dennisj@johnstonfarms.com
Packinghouse Operations: Steve Staker
Plant Manager: Steve Stacker
Number Employees: 100-249
Brands Exported: Bluejay; Top J; Victor
Regions Exported to: Europe, Asia, Canada, Mexico
Percentage of Business in Exporting: 35

45560 Jomac Products
7525 N Oak Park Avenue
Niles, IL 60714-3819   215-343-0800
    Fax: 215-343-0912 800-566-2289
Manufacturer and exporter of terrycloth, cut-resistant and nomex gloves, mitts, aprons, pads and sleeves
Marketing Manager: Charlie Lake
Sales Manager: Jim Podall
Number Employees: 499
Type of Packaging: Food Service, Bulk

45561 Jomar Corp
115 E Parkway Dr
Egg Harbor Twp, NJ 08234-5112   609-646-8000
    Fax: 609-645-9166 www.jomarcorp.com
Manufacturer and exporter of plastic injection blow molding machinery and plastic molds and dies
President: William Petrino
Founder: Joseph Johnson
Senior VP: Walter Priest
Contact: Ed Burns
eburns@jomarcorp.com
Estimated Sales: $10-20 Million
Number Employees: 20-49
Square Footage: 90000
Parent Co: Inductotherm Industries
Brands Exported: Jomar
Regions Exported to: Worldwide
Percentage of Business in Exporting: 50

45562 Joneca Corp
4332 E LA Palma Ave
Anaheim, CA 92807-1806   714-993-5997
    Fax: 714-993-2126 info@joneca.com
        www.joneca.com
Manufacturer and exporter of dehydrators and waste reduction and water purification systems
President: Edward E Chavez
contactus@joneca.com
Estimated Sales: Below $ 5 Million
Number Employees: 10-19
Parent Co: Anaheim Marketing International
Regions Exported to: Canada
Percentage of Business in Exporting: 2

45563 Jones Brewing Company
260 2nd St
Smithton, PA 15479   724-483-2400
    Fax: 724-565-5743 info@stoneysbeer.com
        www.stoneysbeer.com
Beers, including non-alchoholic beer
Owner: Jon King
Brewmaster: Greg King
Purchasing: Joyce Winkler
Type of Packaging: Consumer, Private Label

45564 Jones Dairy Farm
800 Jones Ave
Fort Atkinson, WI 53538
        800-563-6637
www.jonesdairyfarmfoodservice.com
Sausage, bacon, ham, and liverwurst products.
President & CEO: Philip Jones
pjones@jonesdairy.com
Marketing Director: Bridget Molthen
Executive Vice President: Richard Lowry
Manager of Human Resources: Katherine Bruns
SVP, Operations: Roger Borchardt
Manager of Purchasing: Joyce Lemke
Year Founded: 1832
Estimated Sales: $30.7 Million
Number Employees: 250-499
Square Footage: 215000
Type of Packaging: Consumer, Food Service, Bulk
Regions Exported to: Worldwide

45565 Jones-Hamilton Co
30354 Tracy Rd
Walbridge, OH 43465-9792   419-666-9838
    Fax: 419-666-1817 888-858-4425
    info@jones-hamilton.com
    www.jones-hamilton.com
Producer of natural acidulants and pHase.
CFO: Brian Brooks
EVP: Bernard Murphy
Director Research & Development: Carl Knueven
IT: Daniel Dias
dad@jones-hamilton.com
Plant Manager: Chuck Almroth
Estimated Sales: $64 Million
Number Employees: 50-99

45566 Jones-Zylon Co
305 N Center St
West Lafayette, OH 43845-1001   740-545-6341
    Fax: 740-545-6671 800-848-8160
miker@joneszylon.com www.joneszylon.com
Institutional tableware, compartments and serving trays, tumblers, cups, bowls, plates and reusable plastic flatware; exporter of dinnerware and flatware
President: Todd Kchl
toddk@joneszylon.net
CEO: Tracey Jackrich
Quality Control: Chuck Laney
Sales (Mid Atlantic): Mike Robertson
Sales (West): Myron Vile
Chairperson: Marion Mulligan-Sutton
Estimated Sales: $ 5 - 10 Million
Number Employees: 10-19
Square Footage: 81600
Parent Co: Jones Metal Products Company
Brands Exported: Jones Zylon
Regions Exported to: Europe, Canada

45567 Jordan Paper Box Co
5045 W Lake St
Chicago, IL 60644-2596   773-287-5362
            Fax: 773-287-5362
Manufacturer, importer and exporter of paper boxes
President: John M Jordan
jordanpaperbox@att.net
President: Jam Jordan
Estimated Sales: $ 1 - 2.5 Million
Number Employees: 5-9
Square Footage: 60000
Type of Packaging: Bulk
Regions Exported to: Worldwide
Percentage of Business in Exporting: 3
Percentage of Business in Importing: 1

45568 Jordon Commercial Refrigerator
2200 Kennedy Street
Philadelphia, PA 19137-1820   215-535-8300
    Fax: 215-289-1597 800-523-0171
Manufacturer, importer and exporter of refrigerators and freezers
President: Gene Sterner
VP, Sales: Jim Duff
Purchasing Manager: Jerry Joyce
Number Employees: 100-249
Square Footage: 296000
Parent Co: Jordon/Fleetwood/Fogel, LLC
Other Locations:
    Jordon Commercial Refrigerato
    Fleetwood, PA Jordon Commercial Refrigerato
Brands Exported: Fogel; Jordon
Regions Exported to: Central America, South America, Europe, Asia, Middle East
Percentage of Business in Exporting: 10
Brands Imported: Fogel; Jordon; Fleetwood
Regions Imported from: Central America

45569 Jose Andres
717 D St NW
6th Floor
Washington, DC 20004   202-638-1910
Olive oils, sherry vinegars, seafood and capers.

45570 Joseph Adams Corp
5740 Grafton Rd
Valley City, OH 44280-9327   330-225-9135
            Fax: 330-225-9105
Oleoresins, essential oils, natural flavors and colors
President: Patrick Adams
Sales: Kathy Adams
Estimated Sales: $3 Million
Number Employees: 10-19
Regions Exported to: Central America, South America, Europe, Asia
Percentage of Business in Exporting: 5

45571 Joseph Antognoli & Co
1800 N Pulaski Rd
Chicago, IL 60639-4916   773-772-1800
            Fax: 773-772-0031
Importer and wholesaler/distributor of groceries, meat, giardiniera, eggplant salad, pepper spread for sandwiches and Italian food including pasta; serving the food service market
Owner: Joseph H Antognoli
info@josephantognoli.com
CEO: Vincent Candice
Estimated Sales: $ 3 - 5 Million
Number Employees: 10-19
Square Footage: 120000
Type of Packaging: Consumer, Food Service, Private Label
Brands Imported: Duomo Olive Oil; Lavazza Espresso Coffee; Duomo Artichokes; San Benedetto Water and Beverages
Regions Imported from: Europe, Canada

45572 Joseph Gies Import
3345 N Southport Avenue
Chicago, IL 60657-1440   773-472-4577
            Fax: 773-472-3903
Importer of wine, liqueur and spirits
Owner: MariAnne Gies
Estimated Sales: $1-2.5 Million
Number Employees: 1-4
Brands Imported: Hasenburg; Guntrum
Regions Imported from: Europe
Percentage of Business in Importing: 100

Importers & Exporters / A-Z

45573 Joseph Phelps Vineyards
200 Taplin Rd
St Helena, CA 94574-9544 707-967-9153
Fax: 707-963-4831 800-707-5789
minglis@josephphelps.com
www.josephphelps.com
Wines
Owner: Bill Phelps
bphelps@jpbwines.com
Founder & Chairman Emeritus: Joe Phelps
VP, CFO: Robert Boyd
VP, Director of Winemaking: Damian Parker
Winemaker: Ashley Hepworth
VP, Director of Sales & Marketing: Mike McEvoy
Director of Vineyard Operations: Philippe Pessereau
Vice President, Director of Winemaking: Damian Parker
Estimated Sales: $5 Million
Number Employees: 50-99
Square Footage: 200000
Type of Packaging: Consumer

45574 Joseph Struhl Co Inc
195 Atlantic Ave
PO Box N
New Hyde Park, NY 11040-5027 516-741-3660
Fax: 516-742-3617 800-552-0023
info@magicmaster.com www.magicmaster.com
Manufacturer and exporter of signs including open/closed self-adhesive reusable and removable static vinyl and stock and custom using static cling vinyl
Managing Director: Cliff Stevens
cliff@magicmaster.com
Sales Manager: H Green
Manager: Cliff Stevens
Estimated Sales: $ 1 - 2.5 Million
Number Employees: 10-19
Brands Exported: Magic Master; Glo; Suler Moderna; Ready Made; Frame-It
Regions Exported to: Central America, South America, Europe
Percentage of Business in Exporting: 25

45575 Josheph Gies Import
625 Ridge Ave
Evanston, IL 60202-2632 773-472-4577
Fax: 773-472-3903
Wines, liqueurs and spirits
Owner: Marianne Gies
Estimated Sales: $500,000-$1 Million
Number Employees: 1-4
Regions Imported from: Europe

45576 Jost Chemical
8150 Lackland Rd
St Louis, MO 63114-4524 314-428-4300
Fax: 314-428-4366 www.jostchemical.com
Chemical ingredients
President/Owner: Jerry Jost
jerryj@jostchemical.com
CFO: Jeff Lenger
Vice President: Keith Wunderli
Estimated Sales: $15.5 Million
Number Employees: 100-249

45577 Jost Kauffman Import & Export Company
47 Capital Drive
Nepean, ON K2G 0E7
Canada 613-226-3887
Fax: 613-226-3907
Wholesaler/distributor and exporter of fresh fish
President: Jost Kauffman
Number Employees: 5-9

45578 Jp Tropical Foods
945 Close Ave
Bronx, NY 10473 718-589-6800
Fax: 718-617-6717 ihopp@evesales.com
www.jptropicalfoods.com
Wholesaler/distributor and importer of Caribbean and Mexican foods
Owner: Irving Nadler
Executive VP: Irving Nadler
VP Marketing: Stuart Gale
Sales Manager: Isadore Hoppenfeld
Estimated Sales: $5-10 Million
Number Employees: 10-19
Square Footage: 44000
Regions Imported from: South America, Europe
Percentage of Business in Importing: 75

45579 Jr Mats
1519 Mcdaniel Dr
West Chester, PA 19380-7037 610-344-7225
Fax: 610-696-6760 800-526-7763
justrightmats@aol.com
Manufacturer and distributor of quality entry matting, kitchen matting and antifatigue matting. Custom logo mats
Owner: Jay Mc Grath
Sales/Marketing: Jay McGrath
jrmats@comcast.net
General Manager: Jeri Delahanty
Estimated Sales: $1 Million
Number Employees: 1-4
Number of Brands: 10
Number of Products: 25
Square Footage: 116000
Type of Packaging: Consumer, Food Service, Private Label, Bulk
Regions Exported to: Worldwide

45580 Jso Associates Inc
17 Maple Dr # 1
Great Neck, NY 11021-2000 516-773-0000
Fax: 516-773-0193 800-421-0404
jaredort@jsoinc.com www.jsoassociates.com
Industrial sales agent specializing in the sale of fruit, fruit purees, juice concentrate, vegetables and various other food products to the manufactuing trade.
President: Barbara Dejose
barbara@jsoinc.com
CEO: Jerry Sunshine
Sales: Jared Ort
Purchasing Manager: Joel Ort
Estimated Sales: $1.7 Million
Number Employees: 10-19
Square Footage: 12000
Type of Packaging: Bulk
Regions Imported from: Mexico
Percentage of Business in Importing: 15

45581 Juanita's Foods
645 Eubank Ave
P.O. Box 847
Wilmington, CA 90748 310-834-5339
Fax: 310-834-5064 800-303-2965
consumercomments@juanitasfoods.com
www.juanitas.com
Mexican foods
President: George De La Torre
CEO: Aaron De La Torre
Director, Quality Assurance: Rasheedi Samira
VP, Sales: John Thompson
Director, Human Resources: Diana Rodriguez
Operations Manager: Mark De La Torre
General Manager: Gina Harpur
Plant Manager: Frank Andrade
Purchasing Manager: Leo Medina
Year Founded: 1946
Estimated Sales: $41500000
Number Employees: 100-249
Type of Packaging: Consumer, Food Service, Private Label, Bulk
Brands Exported: Juanita's
Regions Exported to: Central America, Asia, Latin America, Mexico
Percentage of Business in Exporting: 5

45582 Judel Products
45 Knollwood Road
Suite 24
Elmsford, NY 10523-2822 914-592-6200
Fax: 914-592-1216 800-583-3526
Manufacturer, importer and exporter of glassware
President: Mel Schulweis
VP: John Rufus
Sales Director: Stven Fox
Office Manager: Dorothy See
Estimated Sales: $ 500,000 - $ 1 Million
Number Employees: 1-4
Parent Co: Tiffany & Company
Type of Packaging: Food Service
Brands Exported: Judel
Regions Exported to: Europe, Asia, Canada, Caribbean, Mexico
Brands Imported: Durobor
Regions Imported from: Europe

45583 Judy's Cream Caramels
19995 SW Chapman Rd
Sherwood, OR 97140 503-625-7161
Fax: 503-625-1602
Cream caramels
Owner: Debbie Judy
Number Employees: 5-9
Type of Packaging: Consumer
Regions Exported to: Canada
Percentage of Business in Exporting: 1

45584 Juice Tree
10861 Mill Valley Road
Omaha, NE 68154-3975 714-891-4425
Fax: 714-892-3699
Manufacturer and exporter of citrus juice extractors, pineapple peelers, mobile ice display tables for fresh fruit products and capped plastic containers for juice
President: James Beck
Plant Administrator: B Copeland
Estimated Sales: $1-2.5 Million
Number Employees: 19
Brands Exported: Juice Tree
Regions Exported to: Central America, South America, Europe, Asia, Middle East, Canada

45585 Jumo Process Control
885 Fox Chase
Coatesville, PA 19320-5811 610-380-8002
Fax: 610-380-8009 www.jumousa.com
Estimated Sales: $ 3 - 5 Million
Number Employees: 5-9

45586 Juncker Associates
11 Parker St
Gloucester, MA 01930-3025 978-281-4555
Fax: 978-281-0867
President: Dennis Digregorio
dennis@junckerassociates.com
Estimated Sales: Less Than $500,000
Number Employees: 1-4

45587 Jupiter Mills Corporation
20 Walnut Dr
Roslyn, NY 11576 516-484-1166
Fax: 516-484-1242 800-853-5121
info@jupitermillscorp.com
Manufacturer and exporter of bags, barrels, drums, bottles, boxes, cans, cartons, cases, containers, foam, packaging materials, paper, partitions, tapes and tubes
President: Fred Fisher
Customer Service: Harvey Chestman
Office Manager: Pat Fisher
Estimated Sales: $5,000,000
Number Employees: 20-49
Square Footage: 2000

45588 Jus-Made
9761 Clifford Dr Ste 100
Dallas, TX 75220 972-241-5544
Fax: 972-241-3399 800-969-3746
info@jus-made.com
Beverages and beverage mixes; beverage equipment
President: Gene Barfield
VP Sales: Jim Tanner
Contact: Matt Cook
mcook@jus-made.com
Operations Manager: Mike Sayre
Estimated Sales: $ 1 - 3 Million
Number Employees: 50-99
Square Footage: 14000
Type of Packaging: Consumer, Food Service, Private Label, Bulk
Other Locations:
Jus-Made
Houston, TX Jus-Made
Regions Exported to: Worldwide

45589 JusTea
107 East 3rd Ave
Vancouver, BC V5T 1C7
Canada
844-832-7827
info@justea.com justea.com
Tea
Sales: Paul Bain
Operations: Russ Lafond

45590 Just Delicious Gourmet Foods
PO Box 2747
Seal Beach, CA 90740-1747 949-215-5341
Fax: 714-870-0332 800-871-6085
Dry soup, bread and dip mixes
President: Diana Ferguson
Estimated Sales: $500,000
Number Employees: 5-9
Square Footage: 40000
Type of Packaging: Consumer, Food Service, Bulk
Brands Exported: Just Delicious

Importers & Exporters / A-Z

45591 Just Plastics Inc
250 Dyckman St
New York, NY 10034-5354   212-569-8500
Fax: 212-569-6970 info@justplastics.com
www.justplastics.us
Manufacturer and exporter of custom acrylic point of purchase displays, signs, sneeze guards, menu holders, tent card holders and containers
President: Robert Vermann
info@justplastics.com
VP: Lois Vermann
Sales Associate: Tommy de Los Angeles
VP: Robert Vermann
Estimated Sales: $ 20 - 50 Million
Number Employees: 10-19
Square Footage: 15000
Regions Exported to: Bermuda, Canada, Mexico
Percentage of Business in Exporting: 5

45592 Justman Brush Co
828 Crown Point Ave
Omaha, NE 68110-2828   402-451-4420
Fax: 402-451-1473 800-800-6940
www.justmanbrush.com
Manufacturer and exporter of twisted-in-wire brushes including bottle, toilet bowl, hospital and laboratory
Owner: Justman Company
justmanbrush@aol.com
Estimated Sales: $ 1-2.5 Million
Number Employees: 20-49
Square Footage: 24000
Regions Exported to: Central America, South America, Europe, Middle East, Australia
Percentage of Business in Exporting: 20

45593 Jyoti Cuisine India
816 Newtown Rd
Berwyn, PA 19312-2200   610-296-4620
Fax: 610-889-0492 jyoti@jyotifoods.com
Indian foods
Founder: Jyoti Gupta
VP: Vijai Gupta
Number Employees: 5
Type of Packaging: Consumer, Food Service, Private Label
Brands Exported: India House
Regions Exported to: Canada
Percentage of Business in Exporting: 5

45594 K & F Select Fine Coffees
2801 SE 14th Ave
Portland, OR 97202-2203   503-234-7788
Fax: 503-231-9827 800-558-7788
Coffee products, torami syrups and sauces, taza rica cocoas, powdered drink mixes, and liquid fruit smoothie products.
Founder: Don Dominguez
ddominguez@kfcoffee.com
Director Sales/Marketing: Sandy Jumonville
Sales: Steve O Brien
Estimated Sales: $3228000
Number Employees: 10-19
Type of Packaging: Consumer, Food Service, Private Label, Bulk
Brands Exported: K&F; Torani; Guittard; Extreme Foods - Coffee D'Amore & Mighty Leaf; Taza Rica

45595 K & L Intl
1929 S Campus Ave
Ontario, CA 91761-5410   909-923-9258
Fax: 909-923-9228 888-598-5588
info@knl-international.com
www.knl-international.com
Manufacturer, Importer and Exporter of chopsticks, toothpicks, guest checks, napkins, plastic T-Shirt bags, bamboo skewers, matches, sushi containers, wood sushi plates, wood sushi boats (bridge), swirl bowls, dried seaweed, eel(unagi), wasabi powder and soybean (edamame).
President: David Kao
VP: Susan Lin
Marketing Director: Richard Yeang
Manager: May Lin
Estimated Sales: $ 5 - 10 Million
Number Employees: 10-19
Number of Products: 20
Square Footage: 100000
Type of Packaging: Food Service, Private Label
Brands Imported: K&L
Regions Imported from: Asia
Percentage of Business in Importing: 60

45596 K C Booth Co
1760 Burlington St
N Kansas City, MO 64116-3892   816-471-1921
Fax: 816-471-2461 800-866-5226
info@kcbooth.com www.kcbooth.com
Manufacturer and exporter of benches, front-end booths, tables and chairs
President: Scott Neuman
scott@kcbooth.com
VP: Scott Neuman
Operations Manager: Jack Buddemeyer
Estimated Sales: $5-10 Million
Number Employees: 20-49
Type of Packaging: Food Service
Regions Exported to: Worldwide
Percentage of Business in Exporting: 2

45597 K Doving Co Inc
1171 Folsom St
San Francisco, CA 94103-3930   415-861-6694
Fax: 415-861-7485
Exporter and wholesaler/distributor of restaurant and butcher equipment
Owner: Jim Christensen
Manager: Katie O'Brien
kdoving@att.net
Estimated Sales: $ .5 - 1 million
Number Employees: 5-9

45598 (HQ)K Katen & Company
65 E Cherry Street
Rahway, NJ 07065-4011   732-381-0220
Manufacturer and importer of linen goods including tablecloths, napkins, pillowcases and kitchen towels
VP: Pauline Katen
Manager: Benny Yabut
Manager: Steven Richards
Number Employees: 3
Square Footage: 4000
Type of Packaging: Consumer
Regions Imported from: Europe, Asia
Percentage of Business in Importing: 95

45599 K L Keller Imports
5332 College Ave
Suite 201
Oakland, CA 94618-2805   510-839-7890
Fax: 510-839-7895 orders@klkeller.com
www.klkeller.com
Olive, nut and, truffle oils; vinegar; condiments; herbs; spices; sea salts, and confections.
Owner: Kitty Keller
Sales: Lauren Zaira
Number Employees: 1-4

45600 K Trader Inc.
1452 W. 9th Street
Suite D
Upland, CA 91786   909-949-0327
Fax: 909-992-3471 sales@ktraderinc.com
www.ktraderinc.com
Exporter of fresh fruits, vegetables and meats to overseas markets.
President: Robert Amakasu
Manager: Kay Shimivu
Estimated Sales: $1 Million
Number Employees: 10
Regions Exported to: Central America, South America, Europe, Asia, Middle East, Worldwide
Percentage of Business in Exporting: 100

45601 K&N Fisheries
130 Seal Point Rd 1
Upper Port La Tour, NS B0W 3N0
Canada   902-768-2478
Fax: 902-768-2385
Fresh and salted fish.
Owner/Manager: Kirk Nickerson
Vice President: Gregory Nickerson
Estimated Sales: $2.3 Million
Number Employees: 17
Type of Packaging: Bulk
Regions Exported to: Worldwide
Percentage of Business in Exporting: 95

45602 K+S Windsor Salt Ltd.
755 boul St. Jean
Pointe Claire, QC H9R 5M9
Canada   514-630-0900
Fax: 514-694-2451 www.windsorsalt.com
Salt including table, food processing, water conditioning and ice melting.
President/CEO: Wes Clark
Marketing Manager: Michel Prevost
Year Founded: 1893
Estimated Sales: $4.89 Million
Number Employees: 861
Parent Co: K+S
Type of Packaging: Consumer, Food Service, Bulk
Other Locations:
  Canadian Salt Company
  Pugwash, Nova ScotiCanadian Salt
  CompanyMines Seleine, Quebec
Brands Exported: Windsor Salt
Regions Exported to: Worldwide

45603 K-Tron
PO Box
Salina, KS 67402-0017   785-825-1611
Fax: 785-825-8759 info@ktron.com
www.ktron.com
Manufacturer and exporter of pneumatic conveying and feeding systems
General Manager: Todd Smith
Estimated Sales: $20-50 Million
Number Employees: 100-249
Square Footage: 115000
Parent Co: K-Tron America

45604 K-Tron International
Routes 55 and 553
P.O. Box 888
Pitman, NJ 08071-0888   856-589-0500
Fax: 856-256-3281 800-203-4130
www.ktron.com
Maqnufacture feeders for low to high feed rate applications, precision feeding and material control with complete PLC-DCS system integration, vacuum loaders and receivers. Offer volumetric screw feeders, weighbelt feeders, vibratingfeeders, etc
President: Kevin Bowen
Estimated Sales: $77.50 Million
Number Employees: 727
Square Footage: 92000
Parent Co: K-Tron International

45605 K-Way Products
759 W Commercial St
Mount Carroll, IL 61053-9762   815-244-2800
Fax: 815-244-2799 800-622-9163
Manufacturer and exporter of soda, juice, beer and coffee dispensing equipment including pre and post-mix ice chests, carbonator/chiller dry refrigerated systems and soda and liquor guns
VP Marketing: Gene Deleeuw
VP Sales: John Hiney
Estimated Sales: $5-10 Million
Number Employees: 20-49
Square Footage: 76000
Type of Packaging: Food Service
Regions Exported to: Central America, Europe, Asia, Middle East, Canada
Percentage of Business in Exporting: 10

45606 K.F. Logistics
10045 International Boulevard
Cincinnati, OH 45246-4845   513-874-0788
Fax: 513-881-5383 800-347-9100
www.buschman.com
Manufacturer and exporter of case conveyors and sortation products
CFO and Sr VP Finance: Robert Duplain
Sr VP Sales/Marketing: Lawrence Frey
Number Employees: 10
Square Footage: 1200000
Regions Exported to: Europe, Asia
Percentage of Business in Exporting: 5

45607 K.R. International
PO Box 282043
Dubai, UA 07740-5950   150-100-2598
Fax: 150-100-8399
Importer and exporter of coffee, tea, sugar, canned fruits, spices, nuts, rice and other food commodities
Exp. Manager: Josephine Ferrerro
Manager: Barbara Cintron
Assistant Manager: Jane Parker
Number Employees: 5-9
Square Footage: 4000
Regions Exported to: Worldwide
Percentage of Business in Exporting: 90

Importers & Exporters / A-Z

45608 K.S.M. Seafood Corporation
PO Box 3057
Baton Rouge, LA 70821-3057   225-383-1517
Fax: 225-387-6641

Seafood
President: Bo Wallenhom
Estimated Sales: $ 10 - 20 Million
Number Employees: 50-99

45609 KAPCO
1000 Cherry Street
PO Box 626
Kent, OH 44240   330-678-1626
Fax: 330-678-3922   800-843-5368
converting@kapco.com   www.kapco.com
Manufacturer and exporter of coated and converted pressure sensitive flexible materials, labels, tapes and paper
President: Edward Small
Contact: Dan Barlett
dbarlett@kapco.com
Operations Manager: Phil Zavracky
Estimated Sales: $ 10 - 20 Million
Number Employees: 50-99
Square Footage: 180000
Regions Exported to: Central America, South America
Percentage of Business in Exporting: 5

45610 KAPS All Packaging
200 Mill Rd.
Riverhead, NY 11901-3125   631-727-0300
Fax: 631-369-5939   www.kapsall.com
Packaging machinery including fluid filling, bottle capping, bottle orienting and bottle cleaning; also, unscramblers, torque meters cap sealers and conveyor systems.
President: Kenneth Herzog
Packaging Solutions: Michael Herzog
mherzog@kapsall.com
Year Founded: 1941
Estimated Sales: Less Than $500,000
Number Employees: 1-4
Square Footage: 65000
Regions Exported to: Central America, South America, Europe, Asia, Middle East

45611 KARI-Out Co
399 Knollwood Rd
Suite 309
White Plains, NY 10603-1941   914-580-3200
Fax: 914-580-3248   800-433-8799
info@kariout.com   www.kariout.com
Sauces; cooking sherry; vinegar and food colors. Also food containers, specialty bags, cleaning supplies, placemats, napkins, cutlery, and chopsticks & skewers.
President: Epstein Paul
Estimated Sales: $361000
Number Employees: 100-249
Square Footage: 3197
Parent Co: Perk-Up Inc.
Regions Imported from: Asia
Percentage of Business in Importing: 5

45612 KAS Spirits
46 Miller Rd.
Mahopac, NY 10541   845-750-6000
info@kasspirits.com
www.kasspirits.com
Krupnikas spiced honey liqueur
Founder/Owner: Kestutis (Kas) Katinas
Year Founded: 2013
Number of Brands: 1
Number of Products: 1
Brands Exported: KAS

45613 KASE Equipment
7400 Hub Pkwy
Cleveland, OH 44125-5735   216-642-9040
Fax: 216-986-0678   info@plastechnic.com
www.kaseequip.com
Manufacturer and exporter of printers for cups, pails, lids and closures
President: Patrick Hawkins
patrick.hawkins@kaseequip.com
CEO: Edward Thomas
Estimated Sales: $ 50 - 100 Million
Number Employees: 50-99
Type of Packaging: Consumer, Food Service, Private Label
Regions Exported to: Central America, South America, Europe, Asia, Middle East, Worldwide
Percentage of Business in Exporting: 60

45614 KD Kanopy
3755 W 69th Pl
Westminster, CO 80030   303-650-1310
Fax: 303-650-5093   800-432-4435
askme@kdkanopy.com   www.kdkanopy.com
Manufacturer and exporter of instant set-up canopies, tents and banners; also, customized graphics available
President: John T Matthews
CFO: John T Matthews
Director Marketing: Helene Schmid
Sales: Scott Rudin
Contact: Shelly Bangs
shelly@kdkanopy.com
Sales: Matt Lehman
Estimated Sales: $ 1 - 2.5 Million
Number Employees: 20-49
Square Footage: 40000
Brands Exported: KD Bannerpole; KD Majestic; KD Party Shade; KD Starshade; KD Starstage
Regions Exported to: Worldwide
Percentage of Business in Exporting: 15

45615 KERN Ridge Growers LLC
25429 Barbara St
Arvin, CA 93203-9748   661-854-3141
Fax: 661-854-7229   kernridge.com
Grower, packer, and shipper of carrots, bell and chile peppers and Sunkist navel oranges.
General Manager: Bob Giragosian
bob@kernridge.com
Sales Manager: Rob Giragosian
Operations Manager: Pete Smith
Number Employees: 250-499
Type of Packaging: Consumer, Bulk
Brands Exported: Kern Ridge
Regions Exported to: Middle East

45616 (HQ)KH McClure & Company
456 Glenbrook Rd
Stamford, CT 06906-1800   203-969-1615
Fax: 203-327-3462
Exporter and broker of hard candies and chocolates
Owner: Harard Goerin
CEO: Linda Shippee
CFO: Debbie Kuter
Estimated Sales: $ 5 - 10 Million
Number Employees: 10-19
Square Footage: 8000
Type of Packaging: Consumer, Bulk
Brands Exported: E.J. Brach's; Philadelphia Chewing Gum
Regions Exported to: Europe, Asia, Caribbean
Percentage of Business in Exporting: 80

45617 KHL Flavors Inc
5925 63rd St
Flushing, NY 11378-3461   718-894-8200
Fax: 718-894-1618   plandes1@aol.com
www.khlflavors.com
Exporter and importer of spices, botanicals, spice oils, botanical extractsand herb supplements
President/Secretary: Peter Landes
plandes1@aol.com
Estimated Sales: $3.2 Million
Number Employees: 5-9
Square Footage: 152000
Regions Exported to: Caribbean
Regions Imported from: Central America, South America, Europe, Asia, Middle East
Percentage of Business in Importing: 100

45618 KHM Plastics Inc
4090 Ryan Rd # B
Gurnee, IL 60031-1201   847-249-4910
Fax: 847-249-4976   dankay@khmplastics.com
www.khmplastics.com
Custom bulk acrylic food bins; importer of acrylic sign holders. Custom displays for food service
President: Daniel Kay
dankay@khmplastics.com
Marketing Director: Dan Kay
Sales Director: Glenn Murphy
Operations Manager: Dan Bunting
Estimated Sales: $2.5-5 Million
Number Employees: 20-49
Square Footage: 200000

45619 KISS Packaging Systems
1399 Specialty Drive
Vista, CA 92081-8521   760-714-4177
Fax: 760-714-4188   888-522-3538
sales@kisspkg.com   www.kisspkg.com
Manufacturer and exporter of liquid fillers, cappers, conveyors, turntables, feeders/orienters, labelers and integrated packaging systems
Estimated Sales: $2.5-5 Million
Number Employees: 19
Square Footage: 34000
Regions Exported to: Central America, South America, Europe
Percentage of Business in Exporting: 10

45620 KL Products, Ltd.
234 Exeter Road
London, ON N6L 1A3
Canada   519-652-1070
Fax: 519-652-1071   800-388-5744
kadmin@klproducts.com   www.klproducts.com
Automated food processing equipment. Poultry and hatchery equipment and washing systems.
President: Patrick Poulin
Vice President, Sales & Marketing: Rick Bennett
Regions Exported to: North America

45621 KLT Global
Po Box 718
Warren, MI 48090-0718   586-777-5311
Fax: 586-777-5316   michelle@kltglobal.com

45622 KM International Corp
320 N Main St
Kenton, TN 38233-1130   731-749-8700
Fax: 256-539-9799   www.kminternational.com
Manufacturer, importer and exporter of plastic bags and film
President: Kourosh Vakili
CEO: Kevin Vakili
kevinb@kmigroup.com
Estimated Sales: $ 20 - 50 Million
Number Employees: 10-19
Regions Exported to: Worldwide
Regions Imported from: Asia

45623 KMJ International
5325 E Pacific Coast Highway
Long Beach, CA 90804-4441   562-597-5973
Fax: 562-498-7167

45624 KMS Inc
811 E Waterman St # 1
Wichita, KS 67202-4716   316-264-8833
Fax: 316-264-1452   www.kms.com
Supplier and exporter of excess inventory goods
President: Scott Jabara
scott@kms.com
Director Purchasing: Garrell Dombraugh
Estimated Sales: $ 20 - 50 Million
Number Employees: 20-49
Square Footage: 10000
Type of Packaging: Consumer, Food Service, Bulk
Regions Exported to: Worldwide

45625 KMT Aqua-Dyne Inc
635 W 12th St
Baxter Springs, KS 66713-1940   620-856-6222
Fax: 713-864-0313   800-826-9274
sales@aqua-dyne.com   www.aqua-dyne.com
Manufacturer and exporter of water blasting and tank cleaning equipment; also pumps
Manager: Deiter Tischler
VP: Jennifer Rankin
Regional Sales Manager: Jorge Elarba
Marketing: Dennis Williams
Sales/Marketing: Paul Bako
Public Relations: Dennis Williams
Purchasing: Jennifer Rankin
Estimated Sales: $5-10,000,000
Number Employees: 20-49
Square Footage: 170000
Brands Exported: Aqua-Dyne
Regions Exported to: Central America, South America, Europe, Asia, Middle East
Regions Imported from: Asia
Percentage of Business in Importing: 10

45626 KOZY Shack Enterprises Inc
P.O. Box 64050
St Paul, MN 55164-0050   855-716-1555
www.kozyshack.com
Ready-to-eat puddings.
Chairman/President/CEO: Robert Striano
Year Founded: 1967
Estimated Sales: $48.5 Million
Number Employees: 249-499
Square Footage: 70000
Type of Packaging: Consumer, Food Service, Bulk

Importers & Exporters / A-Z

45627 KP USA Trading
500 S Anderson Street
Los Angeles, CA 90033-4222   323-881-9871
                                    Fax: 323-268-3669
Soybean, corn, cottonseed, sesame and other vegetable oils; importer of oriental foods including jasmine, sweet rice, noodles, rice stick and candy
VP: Jerry Wong
Manager: Joe Beatly
Manager: Nancy Wong
Number Employees: 10-19
Square Footage: 100000
Type of Packaging: Consumer, Food Service, Private Label, Bulk
Brands Exported: King Products
Regions Exported to: Asia
Percentage of Business in Exporting: 5
Brands Imported: King; King Products; Marpolo; Elephant; Twin Rose; Kopico; Danisa
Regions Imported from: Asia
Percentage of Business in Importing: 45

45628 KSW Corp
1731 Guthrie Ave
PO Box 3224
Des Moines, IA 50316-2197   515-265-5269
        Fax: 515-265-9072 kswborp@aol.com
                www.kswcorporation.com
Manufacturer and exporter of mechanical blades and knives
President: Paul Naylor
kswcorpdsm@aol.com
National Sales Manager: Michelle Struble
Estimated Sales: $ 3 - 5 Million
Number Employees: 10-19
Type of Packaging: Consumer, Food Service
Regions Exported to: Europe
Percentage of Business in Exporting: 1

45629 KTG
11353 Reed Hartman Hwy
Cincinnati, OH 45241-2443   513-793-5366
        Fax: 866-533-6950 888-533-6900
Wireless temperature tracking computer software
CEO: Jim Flood
VP: Jack Kennamer
VP Sales: Jeff Carletti
VP Operations: Susan Payne
Estimated Sales: $ 10-20 Million
Number Employees: 5-9
Square Footage: 200000
Regions Exported to: Central America, South America, Europe, Asia, Middle East
Percentage of Business in Exporting: 3

45630 KUKA Robotics Corp
51870 Shelby Parkway
Shelby Township, MI 48315-1787
                                    800-459-6691
                www.kuka.com
Manufacturer and importer of automated robotic material handling and palletizing systems and system integrators
President, KUKA Robotics Corp US: Joseph Gemma
Estimated Sales: Over $1 Billion
Number Employees: 14,256
Parent Co: KUKA Robotics Corporation
Regions Imported from: Europe
Percentage of Business in Importing: 40

45631 KWIK Lok Corp
2712 S 16th Ave
Yakima, WA 98903-9530   509-248-4770
        Fax: 509-457-6531 800-688-5945
        sales@kwiklok.com www.kwiklok.com
Manufacturer and exporter of bag closures and bag closing machinery using plastic clips and labels
Vice President: Hal Miller
halm@kwiklok.com
VP: Hal Miller
Quality Control: Jim Paxton
Sales: Rich Zaremba
Public Relations: Bill Klancke
Purchasing Director: Kohen Kelly
Estimated Sales: $10-20 Million
Number Employees: 50-99
Brands Exported: Kwik Lok; Striplok
Regions Exported to: South America, Europe, Asia, Middle East, South Africa
Percentage of Business in Exporting: 50

45632 KWS Manufacturing Co LTD
3041 Conveyor Dr
Burleson, TX 76028-1857   817-295-2247
        Fax: 817-447-8528 800-543-6558
                sales@kwsmfg.com www.kwsmfg.com
Manufacturer and exporter of bulk elevators and conveyors including belt and screw; also, spare parts and repair services available. Installation and field service available
Owner: Claressa Moore
cmoore@drivetime.com
CEO: Tim Harris
CFO: Olin Miller
Marketing Director: Bill Porterfield
Plant Manager: Joe Radloff
Purchasing Manager: Eddie Maxwell
Estimated Sales: $ 10 - 20 Million
Number Employees: 100-249
Square Footage: 250000
Parent Co: J.B. Poindexter & Co., Inc.
Type of Packaging: Bulk
Regions Exported to: Central America, South America, Europe, Australia, Canada, Mexico, Caribbean, Latin America
Percentage of Business in Exporting: 10

45633 Kabobs
5423 N Lake Dr
Lake City, GA 30260   404-361-6283
                                    800-732-9484
        thunt@kabobs.com www.kabobs.com
Founder & Chairman: R. Terry Hunt
President & CEO: Steve Law
VP & Chief Financial Officer: D. Scott Barnett
VP & Chief Operating Officer: Bill Rosenhoover
R&D Manager: Claudia Cornwell
Quality Assurance Manager: Rhonda Houston
Marketing Manager: Jonathan Herrera
Director, Human Resources: Diane Davila
Estimated Sales: $50-100 Million
Number Employees: 100-249

45634 Kachemak Bay Seafood
4470 Homer Spit Rd
Homer, AK 99603-8003   907-235-2799
                                    Fax: 907-235-2799
Various fishes and other seafoods
Owner: William Sullivan
Estimated Sales: $380,000
Number Employees: 5

45635 Kadon Corporation
55 W Techne Center Drive
Milford, OH 45150-8901   937-299-0088
                                    Fax: 513-831-5474
Manufacturer and exporter of plastic pallets, tote boxes, storage containers and wash baskets; OEM services available
Sales Manager: Chuck Acton
Administrative Assistant: Linda Brandeburg
Type of Packaging: Bulk
Regions Exported to: Worldwide

45636 Kady International
30 Parkway Dr
Scarborough, ME 04074-7155   207-883-4141
        Fax: 207-883-8241 800-367-5239
        kady@kadyinternational.com
                www.kadyinternational.com
Manufacturer and exporter of high speed dispersion mills for mixing, blending, dispersing, emulsifying and cooking
President: Robert Kritzer
VP: Todd Kritzer
Sales: Todd Kritler
Estimated Sales: $5-10 Million
Number Employees: 10-19
Square Footage: 200000
Brands Exported: Kady
Regions Exported to: Worldwide
Percentage of Business in Exporting: 36

45637 KaiRak
1158 N. Gilbert St
Anaheim, CA 92801   714-870-8661
        Fax: 866-210-7542 literature@kairak.com
                www.kairak.com
Manufacturer and exporter of remote refrigeration systems, pan chillers and sandwich and pizza prep tables
President/General Manager: Mark Curran
VP Sales & Marketing: Steve Asay
National Sales Manager: Steve Asay
Contact: Brian Casserilla
bcasserilla@kairak.com
Administrative Assistant: Susie Parodi
Estimated Sales: $ 15 Million
Number Employees: 20-49
Square Footage: 160000
Parent Co: Hobart Corporation
Type of Packaging: Consumer, Food Service
Other Locations:
  KaiRak
  Gardena, CAKaiRak
Regions Exported to: Central America, Europe, Middle East
Percentage of Business in Exporting: 5

45638 Kairak
1158 North Gilbert Street   714-870-8661
        Fax: 866-210-7542 www.kairak.com
President: Mark Curran
Contact: Brian Casserilla
bcasserilla@kairak.com

45639 Kakosi Chocolate
52 Central St
Manchester-By-The-Sea, MA 01944   617-335-6475
        Fax: 877-869-2002 www.kakosichocolates.com
Cacao

45640 Kal Pac Corp
10 Factory St
Montgomery, NY 12549-1202   845-457-7013
        Fax: 845-457-7009 800-852-5722
                info@kalpac.com www.kalpac.com
Manufacturer, importer and exporter of plastic take out bags
CEO: Mike Nozawa
Sales Representative: Henry Meola
Estimated Sales: $10-20 Million
Number Employees: 10-19
Square Footage: 60000
Type of Packaging: Food Service
Regions Exported to: Europe, Asia, Caribbean
Brands Imported: Kal Pac
Regions Imported from: Asia, China, Thailand

45641 Kalle USA Inc
5750 Centerpoint Ct
Suite B
Gurnee, IL 60031-5279   847-775-0781
        Fax: 847-775-0782 www.kalle.de
Sausage casings and other meat processing supplies.
Sales Manager: John Lample
Number Employees: 10-19
Regions Exported to: Worldwide

45642 (HQ)Kalsec
3713 W Main St
Kalamazoo, MI 49006   269-349-9711
                                    800-323-9320
                www.kalsec.com
Natural flavors, colors, extracts; spice oleoresins and essential oils.
Executive Chairman: George Todd
Research & Development: Don Berdahl
Plant Manager: Harry Todd
Estimated Sales: $3-5 Million
Number Employees: 100-249
Parent Co: Kalamazoo Holdings
Type of Packaging: Food Service, Bulk
Regions Exported to: Central America, South America, Europe, Asia, Middle East

45643 Kalustyan
123 Lexington Ave # 1
New York, NY 10016-8120   212-685-3451
        Fax: 212-683-8458 800-352-3451
                www.kalustyans.com
Herbs; spices; rice; nuts; dried fruits; beans; seeds; oils, etc.
Owner: Saedul Alam
alam@kalustyans.com
Estimated Sales: $3 Million
Square Footage: 400000
Type of Packaging: Food Service, Bulk
Regions Exported to: Worldwide
Regions Imported from: Worldwide

Importers & Exporters / A-Z

45644 Kamflex Corp
1321 W 119th St
Chicago, IL 60643-5109   630-682-1555
Fax: 630-682-9312   800-323-2440
kamflex@kamflex.com
Manufacturer and exporter of FDA and USDA approved stainless steel conveyors and systems with fabric, plastic or steel belts, rotary turntables, air operations, etc
President: Kirit Kamdar
Vice President: Jose Ceja
jceja@kamflex.com
Marketing Director: John Tomaka
Operations Manager: Dave Matan
Estimated Sales: $ 5 - 10 Million
Number Employees: 5-9
Square Footage: 70000
Brands Exported: Elevair
Regions Exported to: Central America, South America, Canada, Caribbean, Latin America, Mexico
Percentage of Business in Exporting: 5

45645 Kamish Food Products
5846 N Kolmar Ave
Chicago, IL 60646-5806   773-725-6959
Fax: 773-267-0400
Baking mixes, chocolate products, jams, jellies and dehydrated fruit nuggets
President: Ted Kamish
VP: Ronald Kamish
Estimated Sales: $5 Million
Number Employees: 20-49
Type of Packaging: Food Service, Private Label, Bulk

45646 Kane International Corporation
411 Theodore Fremd Avenue
Rye, NY 10580   914-921-3100
Fax: 914-921-3180   800-323-8946
info@kaneintl.com kaneinternational.com/
Importer and exporter of fruit candy, banana chips, glace apricots; and ginger; dehydrated fruits: pineapple, apricots, papaya, mango, etc
Owner: Thom Kohlberg
VP: Daniel Fox
Estimated Sales: $2.5-5 Million
Number Employees: 5-9
Type of Packaging: Consumer, Food Service, Private Label, Bulk

45647 Kanematsu
75 Rockefeller Plaza 22nd FL
New York, NY 10019   212-704-9400
Fax: 213-620-1050
Importer, exporter and wholesaler/distributor of ingredients including potassium sorbate, sorbic acid, riboflavin and whey protein isolate
Manager: James Scott Levy
Number Employees: 20-49
Parent Co: Kanematsu USA
Type of Packaging: Bulk

45648 Karabetian Import & Export
2450 Crystal St
Los Angeles, CA 90039-2813   323-664-8956
Fax: 323-664-8958   karabetian@aol.com
www.karabetian.com
Lebanese foods
Owner: Nabil Karabetian
nabil@karabetian.com
Number Employees: 10-19

45649 Karl Ehmer
6335 Fresh Pond Rd
Flushing, NY 11385-2623   718-456-8100
Fax: 718-456-2270   800-487-5275
info@karlehmer.com www.karlehmer.com
Sausages; deli and smoked meats.
President: Mark Hanssler
Quality Control: Gary Durante
Production Manager/VP: Allen Hanssler
Marketing Director: Will Osanitsch
Contact: Paul Haglich
Purchasing Manager: Daniel Durante
Estimated Sales: $ 5-10 Million
Number Employees: 20-49

45650 Karl Strauss Brewing Co
5985 Santa Fe St
San Diego, CA 92109-1623   858-273-2739
jobs@karlstrauss.com
www.karlstrauss.com
Beer; amber lager; and pale ale.
Owner: Karl Strauss
CEO: Ashley Freeborn
afreeborn@yourglobalgroup.com
CFO: Matthew Rattner
Marketing Director: Brian Bolten
Sales: Paul Timm
PR Manager: Melody Daversa
Operations: Grant Gotteshon
Production: Paul Segura
Estimated Sales: $.5-1 million
Number Employees: 50-99
Number of Brands: 25
Number of Products: 2
Square Footage: 88000
Parent Co: Associated Micro Breweries

45651 Karma
500 Milford Street
Watertown, WI 53094   920-262-8688
Fax: 920-261-3302   800-558-9565
Manufacturer and exporter of hot and cold beverage and mashed potato dispensers; also, warmers including hot fudge
President: Chris Gorski
Vice President: Jerry Scheiber
Marketing VP: Elizabeth Brennecke
VP Sales: Jeremy Scheiber
Contact: Brittany Brantley
brantleyb@karma-inc.com
Estimated Sales: $10-20 Million
Number Employees: 20-49
Square Footage: 120000
Brands Exported: Cafe-Matic; Choco-Matic; Whip-Master; Insti-Mash; Tea-Master; Drink-Master; Juice-Master

45652 Karoun Dairies Inc
13023 Arroyo St
San Fernando, CA 91340   818-767-7000
Fax: 818-767-7024   888-767-0778
contact@karouncheese.com
www.karouncheese.com
Cheese and cultured dairy products.
President & Chairman: Ara Baghdassarian
CFO: Tsolak Khatcherian
COO: Rostom Baghdassarian
Year Founded: 1990
Estimated Sales: $62.5 Million
Number of Brands: 6
Parent Co: Parmalat Canada
Type of Packaging: Consumer, Food Service
Regions Imported from: Europe

45653 Kasel Industries Inc
3315 Walnut St
Denver, CO 80205-2429   303-296-4417
Fax: 303-293-9825   www.kasel.net
Manufacturer and exporter of meat slicers, conveyors and automatic loaders
Owner: Ray Kasel
ray@kasel.net
Sls./Mktg. Mgr.: Jon Toby
Quality Control: Galana Kasel
Estimated Sales: $ 32 Million
Number Employees: 10-19
Regions Exported to: Worldwide

45654 Kashi Company
PO Box 649
Solana Beach, CA 92075
877-747-2467
info@kashi.com www.kashi.com
Various multi-grain products
President/Owner: Tony Chow
CEO: David Denholm
Estimated Sales: $5-10 Million
Number Employees: 20-49
Parent Co: Kellogg Company
Type of Packaging: Food Service, Private Label
Brands Exported: Puffed Kashi Cereal; The Breakfast Pilaf
Regions Exported to: Europe, Asia, Canada
Percentage of Business in Exporting: 5

45655 Kasilof Fish Company
1930 Merrill Creek Pkwy
Everett, WA 98203-5897   360-658-7552
Fax: 360-653-3560   800-322-7552
smokedsales@tridentseafoods.com
Smoked salmon and smoked seafood
President: Drew Ellison
Finance Manager: Julie Lorig
VP Sales & Marketing: Patti Moore
Estimated Sales: $2.5 Million
Number Employees: 25
Parent Co: Trident Seafoods
Type of Packaging: Consumer, Food Service, Private Label, Bulk

45656 Kason Central
7099 Huntley Road
Columbus, OH 43229-1073   614-885-1992
Fax: 614-888-1771
Manufacturer, exporter and wholesaler/distributor of refrigerator latches and hinges, strip curtains, hood lights, grease filters, gaskets, stainless steel food service hardware, thermometers for ovens and refrigerators and plumbing fixtures
Manager: David Katz
Sales Representative: Rich Kaiser
Office Manager: Greg Murray
General Manager: David Katz
Estimated Sales: $1-2.5 Million
Number Employees: 5-9
Square Footage: 8000
Parent Co: Kason Industries
Type of Packaging: Consumer, Food Service, Private Label
Regions Exported to: Central America, Europe, Middle East

45657 Kasseler Food Products Inc.
1031 Brevik Place
Mississauga, ON L4W 3R7
Canada   905-629-2142
Fax: 905-629-1699 sales@kasselerfoods.com
www.kasselerfoods.com
Bread and biscuits.
President: Erich Lamshoeft

45658 Katagiri & Company
224 E 59th St Frnt A
New York, NY 10022   212-755-3566
Fax: 212-752-4197   www.katagiri.com
Importer and exporter of Japanese spices, seasonings, herbs, rice and sauces
Manager: David Tanaka
Contact: Takashi Tanaka
tk-tanaka@kddi.com
Manager: Tamaka Takashi
Estimated Sales: $1-2.5 Million
Number Employees: 10-19
Parent Co: Central Trading Company
Regions Exported to: Central America, South America, Europe
Regions Imported from: Asia

45659 Kauai Organic Farms
P O Box 86
Kilauea, HI 96754   808-651-8843
Fax: 808-828-0151   phil@kauaiorganicfarms.com
www.kauaiorganicfarms.com
Organic Hawaiian yellow ginger and other ginger based products.
Owner/President: Phil Green
Public Relations: Linda Green
Estimated Sales: $ .5 - 1 million
Number Employees: 5
Number of Products: 4
Square Footage: 8000
Type of Packaging: Bulk

45660 Kay Home Products Inc
90 Mcmillen Rd
Antioch, IL 60002-1845   847-395-4940
Fax: 847-395-3305   800-600-7009
www.kayhomeproducts.com
Manufacturer and exporter of patio and tray tables, lap trays, barbecue grills, etc
Chairman: Edward Crawford
CEO: Jack Murray
Estimated Sales: $ 1 - 5 Million
Number Employees: 50-99
Square Footage: 600000
Parent Co: Park-Ohio Industries
Brands Exported: Marshallan; Quaker
Regions Exported to: Central America, South America, Europe, Asia, Middle East
Percentage of Business in Exporting: 5

45661 Kayco
72 New Hook Rd
Bayonne, NJ 07002   718-369-4600
customercare@kayco.com
kayco.com
Kosher, all natural, gluten free, vegan, and fair trade products; also specializes in grape juice.

President: Ilan Ron
CEO: Mordy Herzog
Financial Manager: Dov Levi
Executive Vice President: Harold Weiss
Year Founded: 1948
Estimated Sales: $86 Million
Number Employees: 500-999
Number of Brands: 76
Type of Packaging: Consumer, Food Service, Bulk
Regions Exported to: Worldwide

45662 Kaye Instruments
101 Billerica Avenue
Suite 7
N Billerica, MA 01862-1256   978-262-0273
    Fax: 978-439-8181   800-343-4624
    kaye@ge.com   www.kayeinstruments.com
Manufacturer and exporter of data acquisition systems for process monitoring, controlling, archiving and reporting
President: Kenneth B Hurley
CEO: Ken Hurley
CFO: Al Parenteau
VP Sales/Marketing: Karen Huffman
Number Employees: 120
Square Footage: 240000
Regions Exported to: South America, Europe, Asia, Middle East
Percentage of Business in Exporting: 25

45663 (HQ)KeHE Distributors
1245 E Diehl Rd
Suite 200
Naperville, IL 60563   630-343-0000
                          800-995-5343
    contactus@kehe.com   www.kehe.com
Specialty, fresh, natural & organic foods
President/CEO: Brandon Barnholt
COO: Gene Carter
CFO: Timothy Wiggins
CIO: Brian Wilkinson
Executive Director of Marketing: Ari Goldsmith
EVP Independent Sales & Marketing: Brad Helmer
SVP People Operations: Jennifer Ricks
EVP Warehouse Operations: Larry Hartley
Year Founded: 1953
Estimated Sales: $10-20 Million
Number Employees: 5500
Type of Packaging: Private Label
Brands Imported: Reese; DaVinci; El Rio; Walker Shortbread; Evian Water; Perrier
Regions Imported from: South America, Europe, Asia, Middle East
Percentage of Business in Importing: 35

45664 KeHE Distributors
900 N Schmidt Rd
Romeoville, IL 60446-4056
Specialty, fresh, natural & organic foods
Type of Packaging: Private Label

45665 KeHE Distributors
19488 Telegraph Trail
Surrey, BC V4N 4H1
Canada
Specialty, fresh, natural & organic foods
Type of Packaging: Private Label

45666 KeHE Distributors
9555 NE Alderwood Rd
Portland, OR 97220
Specialty, fresh, natural & organic foods
Type of Packaging: Private Label

45667 KeHE Distributors
4650 Newcastle Rd
Stockton, CA 95215
Specialty, fresh, natural & organic foods
Type of Packaging: Private Label

45668 KeHE Distributors
16081 Fern Ave
Chino, CA 91708
Specialty, fresh, natural & organic foods
Type of Packaging: Private Label

45669 KeHE Distributors
2600 - 61 Ave SE
Calgary, AB T2C 4V2
Canada
Specialty, fresh, natural & organic foods
Type of Packaging: Private Label

45670 KeHE Distributors
2200 N Himalaya Rd
Aurora, CO 80011
Specialty, fresh, natural & organic foods
Type of Packaging: Private Label

45671 KeHE Distributors
101 Enterprise Dr
Flower Mound, TX 75028
Specialty, fresh, natural & organic foods
Type of Packaging: Private Label

45672 KeHE Distributors
4024 Rock Quarry Rd
Dallas, TX 75211
Specialty, fresh, natural & organic foods
Type of Packaging: Private Label

45673 KeHE Distributors
225 Daniels Way
Bloomington, IN 47404
Specialty, fresh, natural & organic foods
Type of Packaging: Private Label

45674 KeHE Distributors
1851 Riverside Pkwy
Douglasville, GA 30135
Specialty, fresh, natural & organic foods
Type of Packaging: Private Label

45675 KeHE Distributors
6185 McLaughlin Rd
Mississauga, ON L5R 3W7
Canada
Specialty, fresh, natural & organic foods
Type of Packaging: Private Label

45676 KeHE Distributors
4055 Deerpark Blvd
P.O. Box 410
Elkton, FL 32033
Specialty, fresh, natural & organic foods
Type of Packaging: Private Label

45677 KeHE Distributors
3225 Meridian Pkwy
Fort Lauderdale, FL 33331
Specialty, fresh, natural & organic foods
Type of Packaging: Private Label

45678 KeHE Distributors
860 Nestle Way
Suite 250
Breinigsville, PA 18013
Specialty, fresh, natural & organic foods
Type of Packaging: Private Label

45679 Keating Of Chicago Inc
8901 W 50th St
Mc Cook, IL 60525-6001   708-246-3000
    Fax: 708-246-3100   800-532-8464
    keating@keatingofchicago.com
        www.keatingofchicago.com
Manufacturer and exporter of fryers, frying baskets, serving equipment, griddles, griddle brushes, pasta cookers, food warmers, hot plates, salting/bagging stations and grease/oil filtration systems.
President: Eliza Keating
IT: Eliza Moravec
elizaann@keatingofchicago.com
Estimated Sales: $2.5-5 Million
Number Employees: 5-9
Regions Exported to: Worldwide

45680 Kedco Wine Storage Systems
564 Smith St
Farmingdale, NY 11735-1111   631-454-7800
    Fax: 631-454-4876   800-654-9988
        www.kedcowinestoragesystems.com
Manufacturer and importer of store fixtures, glass doors, temperature-controlled wine storage equipment, display cabinets and refrigeration and wine racks
VP: David Windt
VP: Ken Windt
Contact: Helene Windt
helene.windt@kedco.com
Estimated Sales: Less Than $500,000
Number Employees: 5-9
Square Footage: 50000
Regions Imported from: Europe
Percentage of Business in Importing: 10

45681 Kedem
72 New Hook Rd
Bayonne, NJ 07002   718-369-4600
    customercare@kayco.com
        www.kayco.com
Kosher, gluten free and all natural products. Kosher grape juice, non-alcoholic wines, jams and, cooking products and biscuits.
President: Ilan Ron
CEO: Mordy Herzog
Financial Manager: Dov Levi
Executive Vice President: Harold Weiss
Year Founded: 1948
Estimated Sales: $50-90 Million
Number of Brands: 23
Parent Co: Kayco
Type of Packaging: Consumer
Regions Exported to: Worldwide

45682 Keegan Ales
20 St. James St.
Kingston, NY 12401   845-331-2739
        www.keeganales.com
Craft IPA, American ales and stout
Founder/Owner: Tommy Keegan
Year Founded: 2003
Number of Brands: 1
Number of Products: 6
Type of Packaging: Consumer, Private Label
Brands Exported: Keegan Ales
Regions Exported to: USA

45683 Keen Kutter
20608 Earl St
Torrance, CA 90503   310-370-6941
    Fax: 310-370-3851   rshaver814@aol.com
        www.keenkutter.shaverspecialty.com
Manufacturer and exporter of vegetable cutters
President: George W Shaver
Manager: Scott Shaver
Estimated Sales: $2.5-5 Million
Number Employees: 20-49
Regions Exported to: Canada
Percentage of Business in Exporting: 1

45684 Keenline Conveyor Systems
1936 Chase Dr
Omro, WI 54963-1788   920-685-0365
    Fax: 920-235-0825   mail@keenline.com
        www.keenline.com
Manufacturer and exporter of conveying equipment including tabletop chain, belt and case conveyors, accumulators, indexers, pushers, counters, clamps, mergers, dividers, combiners and gripper elevators/de-elevators
President: David Kersztyn
davidk@keenline.com
Vice President: Ed Gamoke
Estimated Sales: $ 5 - 10 Million
Number Employees: 20-49
Square Footage: 30000
Brands Exported: Keenline
Regions Exported to: Worldwide
Percentage of Business in Exporting: 5

45685 Keeper Thermal Bag Co
1006 Poplar Ln
Bartlett, IL 60103-5649   630-213-0125
    Fax: 630-213-0134   800-765-9244
        keeperb@sbcglobal.net
        www.keeperthermalbags.com
Manufacturer and exporter of insulated bags including food, pizza and catering; also, beverage carriers
Owner: Mike Leel
Manager: Mike Leel
Estimated Sales: $ 1 - 3 Million
Number Employees: 5-9
Brands Exported: Kee-Per
Regions Exported to: Europe, Asia
Percentage of Business in Exporting: 20

45686 (HQ)Kehr-Buffalo Wire FrameCo Inc
127 Kehr St
Buffalo, NY 14211-1522   716-893-4276
    Fax: 716-897-2389   800-875-4212
    sales@kbwf.net   www.kbwf.net
Manufacturer and exporter of custom fabricated store fixtures and point of purchase displays for baked goods, produce and beverage products

Importers & Exporters / A-Z

Owner: James A Rogers Jr
jrogers@rogersindustrialspgs.com
CFO: James Rogers
Research & Development: James Rogers
Quality Control: James Rogers
Sales Director: George Rogers
Estimated Sales: $ 3 - 5 Million
Number Employees: 10-19
Square Footage: 50000
Type of Packaging: Bulk
Regions Exported to: Canada
Percentage of Business in Exporting: 1

45687 Keith Machinery Corp
34 Gear Ave
Lindenhurst, NY 11757-1078   631-957-1200
Fax: 631-957-9264 sales@keithmachinery.com
www.keithmachinery.com
Agitators, attritors, autoclaves, bag filling and sealing machines, bag labeling equipment, blenders, bundling machines, carton machines: closing, filling, sealing, checkweighers
VP: John Hatz
Estimated Sales: $10-20 Million
Number Employees: 50-99

45688 Kelley Company
1612 Hutton Dr
Suite 140
Carrollton, TX 75006   972-466-0707
800-558-6960
kelley@entrematic.com kelleyentrematic.com
Hydraulic, mechanical and air-powered dock levelers, restraints, controls and seals for loading dock shelters.
Year Founded: 1953
Estimated Sales: $100-500 Million
Regions Exported to: Asia, North America, USA

45689 (HQ)Kellogg Co.
1 Kellogg Sq.
PO Box 3599
Battle Creek, MI 49017-3599   269-961-2000
Fax: 269-961-2871 800-962-1413
www.kelloggcompany.com
Breakfast foods manufacturer
Chairman/CEO: Steven Cahillane
President, Kellogg North America: Chris Hood
Senior VP/CFO: Amit Banati
Estimated Sales: $13.5 Billion
Number Employees: 34,000
Number of Brands: 28
Type of Packaging: Consumer
Other Locations:
    R&D
    Battle Creek, MI R&D
Regions Exported to: Worldwide

45690 Kelly Dock Systems
6720 N Teutonia Avenue
Milwaukee, WI 53209-3119   414-352-1000
Fax: 414-352-2093
Manufacturer and exporter of dock equipment including levers and restraints
Sales/Marketing Manager: Steve Sprunger
Estimated Sales: $20-50 Million
Number Employees: 100-249
Regions Exported to: Worldwide

45691 Kelly Foods
513 Airways Blvd
Jackson, TN 38301   731-424-2255
info@kellyfoods.com
www.kellyfoods.com
Canned meat products; importer of corned beef.
President: Ann Koch
Contact: Tony Jordan
tony_jordan@kellysfoods.com
VP Operations: Mark Koch
Plant Manager: Bob James
Purchasing Manager: Mike Rushing
Estimated Sales: $5700000
Number Employees: 50
Square Footage: 260000
Type of Packaging: Consumer
Regions Imported from: South America
Percentage of Business in Importing: 6

45692 Kelly Gourmet Foods Inc
2095 Jerrold Ave
Suite 218
San Francisco, CA 94124-1628   415-648-9200
Fax: 415-648-6164
Cooked, smoked and raw meats.
President: Rina Kelly
VP: Chris Kelly
Sales Director: Ed Kelly
Estimated Sales: Less than $500,000
Number Employees: 1-4
Type of Packaging: Consumer, Food Service, Bulk
Brands Exported: Fulton Valley; Sierra Sausage Co.
Regions Exported to: Asia
Percentage of Business in Exporting: 4

45693 Kelman Bottles LLC
1101 William Flynn Hwy
Glenshaw, PA 15116-2637   412-486-9100
Fax: 412-486-6087
Formerly Glenshaw Galss Company, producers of glass containers for the food and beverage industry in the US, Canada and Mexico
President: William Kelman
tromig@kelmanbottles.com
Sales Exec: Tracy Romig
Operations Manager: John Lilley
Plant Manager: Dawn Dietz
Estimated Sales: $ 660 Thousand
Number Employees: 250-499
Square Footage: 3829
Regions Exported to: Canada

45694 Kelsen, Inc.
40 Marcus Drive
Suite 101
Melville, NY 11747   631-694-8080
Fax: 631-694-8085 888-253-5736
sales.usa@kelsen.com www.kelsen.com
Danish butter cookies
President: Lars Norgaard
Marketing: Gilbert Quiles
Contact: Nicolaj Andersen
na@kelsen.com
Estimated Sales: $5-10 Million
Number Employees: 5-9
Number of Brands: 4

45695 Kemach Food Products
9920 Farragut Rd
Brooklyn, NY 11236-2302   718-272-5655
Fax: 718-272-6226 info@kemach.com
www.kemach.net
Drink mixes; soup mixes; crackers; flour; cereals; pasta; baked goods; candy, chocolates, health food, chocolate syrup, juices, pasta sauces, ices, cones, etc.
President: Samuel Salzman
CFO: Aaron Daum
VP: Nik Salzman
Estimated Sales: $2.5-5 Million
Number Employees: 10-19
Square Footage: 15000
Type of Packaging: Consumer, Food Service, Private Label, Bulk
Brands Exported: Kemach; Mekach; A'Gvania
Regions Exported to: Central America, South America, Europe, Middle East
Percentage of Business in Exporting: 10
Brands Imported: Kemach; Mekach; Ta'aman
Regions Imported from: Europe, Middle East
Percentage of Business in Importing: 10

45696 Kemex Meat Brands
2400 T Street NE
Washington, DC 20002-1919   301-277-2444
Fax: 301-277-0235
Manufacturer and exporter of USDA inspection leg-end insert labels
Owner: Mary Ellen Campbell
Estimated Sales: Less than $500,000
Number Employees: 4
Regions Exported to: Canada

45697 Kemin Industries Inc
2100 Maury St
P.O. Box 70
Des Moines, IA 50317-1100   515-559-5100
Fax: 515-559-5232 800-777-8307
kftcs.am@kemin.com www.kemin.com
Liquid products which help to enhance the shelf life of food items.
Co- Founder: Mary Nelson
CEO: Jennifer Brown
jennifer-l-brown@uiowa.edu
Number Employees: 100-249
Regions Exported to: Worldwide

45698 Kemps LLC
1270 Energy Ln
St Paul, MN 55108
www.kemps.com
Frozen yogurt, ice cream, sherbert, milk, juices, cottage cheese, sour cream and dips, and yogurt.
President & CEO: Greg Kurr
CFO: Daniel Jones
SVP, Growth & Innovation: Rachel Kyllo
VP, Operations: Bob Williams
General Manager: Brad Cuthbert
Year Founded: 1914
Estimated Sales: $116.7 Million
Number Employees: 1,125
Square Footage: 40000
Parent Co: Dairy Farmers of America

45699 Kemutec Group Inc
130 Wharton Rd # A
Keystone Industrial Park
Bristol, PA 19007-1685   215-788-8013
Fax: 215-788-5113 sales@kemutecusa.com
www.kemutecusa.com
Manufacturer, importer and exporter of blenders, mixers, centrifugal sifters, grinding mills and valves
President: Karin Galloway
klg@kemutecusa.com
Director of Marketing: Kathy Moncur
Estimated Sales: $5-10 Million
Number Employees: 5-9
Square Footage: 40000
Brands Exported: Kek; Mucon
Regions Exported to: Central America, South America
Brands Imported: Kek; Mucon; Gardner
Regions Imported from: Europe

45700 Ken Coat
P.O.Box 575
Bardstown, KY 40004-575
Fax: 270-259-9858 888-536-2628
Manufacturer and exporter of plastisol-coated, metal outdoor furniture including tables, benches, chairs, etc.; also, trash receptacles
President: J R Davis
Sls.: Philip Clemens
Estimated Sales: $ 5-10 Million
Number Employees: 10-19
Square Footage: 75000
Regions Exported to: Worldwide

45701 Kenko International
6984 Bandini Blvd
Los Angeles, CA 90040   323-721-8300
Fax: 323-721-9600 ronu@kenko-intl.com
www.kenkoco.com
Sweeteners, food acidulants, antioxidants, preservatives and other food chemicals.
President: Satomi Tsuchibi
Contact: Juliet Cunningham
jcunningham@alere.com
Estimated Sales: $2.7 Million
Number Employees: 15

45702 Kennedy Group
38601 Kennedy Pkwy
Willoughby, OH 44094-7395   440-951-7660
Fax: 440-951-3253
kennedygroup1@kennedygrp.com
www.kennedygrp.com
Developer and manufacturer of labeling, packaging, promotional labels, and identification systems. Manufactures prime labels, clear labels, booklets, coupons, blister cards, instant digital labels, case pack labels, versa-cards, tab-onads, shrink labels, etc
Owner: Patrick Kennedy
kennedypatrick@kennedygrp.com
Marketing/Sales: Patrick Kennedy
Operations Manager: Todd Kennedy
Estimated Sales: $ 10 - 20 Million
Number Employees: 50-99
Square Footage: 160000
Type of Packaging: Consumer, Food Service, Private Label, Bulk
Regions Exported to: Europe, Canada

45703 Kenshin Trading Corp
22353 S Western Ave # 201
Torrance, CA 90501-4156   310-212-3199
Fax: 310-212-3299 800-766-1313
sales@kenshin.com www.kenshin.com
Wholesaler/distributor and importer of Asian health related products; serving food processors, health food stores, etc

Owner: Kunio Suziki
kunio@kenshin.com
Estimated Sales: $500,000-$1 Million
Number Employees: 5-9
Square Footage: 7200
Type of Packaging: Consumer
Brands Imported: Katsu; Ken-Reishi; Kenshin Premium Green Teas; Katsu Herbal Supplements

45704 Kensington Lighting Corp
593 Rugh St
Greensburg, PA 15601-5637 724-850-2433
Fax: 724-837-8087 800-434-5005
info@kensingtonUS.com www.kensingtonus.com
Manufacturer and exporter of energy efficient lighting fixtures and flourescent lighting
Owner: Gary Whiteknight
gary@kensingtonus.com
Estimated Sales: $500,000-$1 Million
Number Employees: 5-9
Parent Co: Adience Equities
Type of Packaging: Consumer, Food Service

45705 Kent Corp
4446 Pinson Valley Pkwy
Birmingham, AL 35215-2940 205-856-3621
Fax: 205-856-3622 800-252-5368
sales@kentcorp.com www.kentcorp.com
Manufacturer and exporter of store fixtures including modular steel display shelving
President: Mera Craws
crawsm@asme.org
CEO: V Albano
CFO: Sharron Harbison
Sales Director: Allan Solomon
Estimated Sales: $ 20 - 50 Million
Number Employees: 100-249
Square Footage: 250000
Regions Exported to: Central America, South America, Europe, Middle East
Percentage of Business in Exporting: 5

45706 Kent Precision Foods Group Inc
2905 US-61
Muscatine, IA 52761
800-442-5242
www.precisionfoods.com
Pickle and tomato mixes, pectins, jams, jellies, fruit preservatives, blended spices and seasonings, dessert mixes; exporter of dry soft serve and dessert mixes.
Manager of Business Development: Kirk Kuiper
Vice President of Sales & Marketing: Connie Huck
Year Founded: 1992
Estimated Sales: $69.4 Million
Number Employees: 20-49
Number of Brands: 8
Square Footage: 200000
Parent Co: Kent Corporation
Type of Packaging: Consumer, Food Service, Private Label, Bulk
Other Locations:
 Manufacturing Location
 Bolingbrook, IL Manufacturing Location
Brands Exported: Frostline®
Regions Exported to: Central America, South America, Europe, Asia, Middle East
Percentage of Business in Exporting: 5

45707 Kentea
459 Main St Ste 101
New Rochelle, NY 10801 914-576-3600
Fax: 914-576-2963
Tea importer
President: Victor Ferretti
Vice President: Nick Salza
Estimated Sales: $5-10 Million
Number Employees: 1-4
Regions Imported from: South America, Europe, Asia, Africa
Percentage of Business in Importing: 100

45708 Kentmaster Manufacturing Co
1801 S Mountain Ave
Monrovia, CA 91016-4270 626-359-8888
Fax: 626-303-5151 800-421-1477
sales@kentmaster.com
Manufacturer and exporter of portable power beef and hog slaughtering equipment
Owner: Ralph Karubian
rk@kentmaster.com
Sls./Svce. Mgr.: Joe Leamen
Estimated Sales: $5-10 Million
Number Employees: 20-49

45709 Kenwood Vineyards
9592 Sonoma Hwy
Kenwood, CA 95452 707-833-5891
Fax: 707-833-1146 info@kenwoodvineyards.com
www.kenwoodvineyards.com
Wines
Manager: Alan Jensen
ajensen@kenwoodvineyards.com
Sales/Marketing: Paul Young
Public Relations: Margie Healy
Winemaker: Mike Lee
Number Employees: 50-99
Square Footage: 200000
Parent Co: Korbel Champagne
Type of Packaging: Consumer
Brands Exported: Kenwood
Regions Exported to: Europe, Asia, Canada, Mexico
Percentage of Business in Exporting: 8

45710 Kerekes Bakery & RstrntEquip
6103 15th Ave
Brooklyn, NY 11219-5402 718-232-7044
Fax: 718-232-4416 800-525-5556
sales@bakedeco.com
Kerekes is a distributor of quality tools, supplies, and equipment for every food service establishment.
Owner: Tovia Fleischman
pearl@bakedeco.com
CEO: Carlos Rodriguez
CFO: Pearl Fleischman
Estimated Sales: $ 1 - 3 Million
Number Employees: 5-9
Square Footage: 80000
Brands Imported: Maftier; PCB
Regions Imported from: Europe, Asia

45711 Kerian Machines Inc
1709 Highway 81 S
Grafton, ND 58237 701-352-0480
Fax: 701-352-3776 sales@Kerian.com
www.kerianmachines.com
Manufacturer and exporter of fruit and vegetable graders and sizers
President: John Kerian
CEO: James Kerian
Estimated Sales: $1-2.5 Million
Number Employees: 10-19
Brands Exported: Kerian Speed Sizer
Percentage of Business in Exporting: 20

45712 Kerr Brothers
Toronto, ON M8Z 4P6
Canada 416-252-7341
Fax: 416-252-6054 hr@kerrs.com
www.kerrs.com
Confections, candy, and cough drops.
VP of Sales: Lyndon Brown *Year Founded:* 1895

45713 Kerry Foodservice
30 Paragon Pkwy
Mansfield, OH 44903-8074 419-522-2722
Fax: 419-522-1152 800-533-2722
slinfo@kerrygroup.com
Processor and exporter of Italian syrups, specialty sugars and powdered toppings for coffees; also, coffee and tea flavors and extracts; private labeling available
Business Director: Peter Dillane
Marketing Director: Corrie Byron
Manager: James Powers
jpowers@stearns-lehman.com
Estimated Sales: $7.9 Million
Number Employees: 20-49
Square Footage: 200000
Type of Packaging: Private Label
Brands Exported: Dolce; Flavormate
Regions Exported to: South America, Europe, Indonesia

45714 Ketchup World
P.O.Box 301
Merion Station, PA 19066 610-667-0769
Fax: 610-667-2751

45715 Keto Foods
56 Park Pl
Suite 2
Neptune, NJ 07753 732-922-0009
Fax: 732-643-6677 email@keto.com
Diet coffee, tea and creamer; low carbohydrate foods and snacks.
President: Arnie Bey
Quality Control: Allan Nargolies
VP Corporation Counsel: Dan Majollo
Sales/Marketing Executive: Arnie Bey
Purchasing Agent: Megan Holman
Estimated Sales: $ 2.5-5 Million
Number Employees: 30
Square Footage: 120000
Type of Packaging: Consumer, Food Service, Bulk
Brands Exported: Keto
Regions Exported to: Central America, South America, Europe, Asia, Middle East, Australia, Canada, Carribbean, Latin America, Mexico

45716 (HQ)Key Industries Inc
400 Marble Rd
Fort Scott, KS 66701-8639 620-223-2000
Fax: 620-223-5822 800-835-0365
customerservice@keyapparel.com
Manufacturer and exporter of clothing and uniforms
President/Chief Executive Officer: Chris Barnes
cbarnes@keyapparel.com
Chairman: William Pollock
Controller: Julian McPharson
Senior Vice President: Mike Johnson
Information Technology Manager: Jeff Sweetser
Director, Marketing: Mike Hughey
Estimated Sales: $ 9 Million
Number Employees: 50-99
Square Footage: 130000

45717 Key Largo Fisheries
1313 Ocean Bay Dr
Key Largo, FL 33037-4213 305-451-3782
800-432-4358
www.keylargofisheries.com
Seafood
President & Co-Owner: Tom Hill
tomhill13@aol.com
Co-Owner: Rick Hill
Estimated Sales: $10 Million
Number Employees: 20-49
Square Footage: 6000
Type of Packaging: Consumer, Food Service, Private Label
Regions Exported to: Worldwide

45718 Key Packaging Co
15th St E
Sarasota, FL 34243 941-355-2728
Fax: 941-351-8708 webinfo@keypackaging.com
www.keypackaging.com
Manufacturer and exporter of thermoformed plastic packaging, containers, food trays and blister packs
President: Earl Smith
earl@keypackaging.com
Quality Control: Gifford Quast
Sales Coordinator: Gene Donohue
Sales Director: Karlson Strouse
Manager: Karlson Strouse
Purchasing Manager: Chris Rathbun
Estimated Sales: $10-20 Million
Number Employees: 50-99
Square Footage: 104000
Type of Packaging: Consumer, Food Service, Bulk
Regions Exported to: Europe, Asia
Percentage of Business in Exporting: 5

45719 (HQ)Key Technology Inc.
150 Avery St.
Walla Walla, WA 99362 509-529-2161
Fax: 509-394-3538 www.key.net
Design, manufacture and market process automation systems for food and other industries. This technology integrates automated optical inspection systems, specialized conveyor systems, and processing/preparation systems, as well as research, development, and world-class engineering.
President: John Ehren
Vice President, Finance: Carson Brennan
Vice President, Global Operations: Shawn Prendiville
Year Founded: 1948
Estimated Sales: $116.33 Million
Number Employees: 500-999
Square Footage: 173000
Other Locations:
 Redmond, OR
Brands Exported: Iso-Flo; Tegra; Turbo-Flo; ADR; Prism; Marathon; Horizon; Impulse; ITS; Optyx
Regions Exported to: Central America, South America, Europe, Asia
Percentage of Business in Exporting: 35

Importers & Exporters / A-Z

45720 Key-Bak
4245 Pacific Privado
Ontario, CA 91761-1588
909-923-7800
Fax: 909-923-0024 sales@keybak.com
www.keybak.com
President: Boake Paugh
boake@keybak.com
Estimated Sales: $300,000-500,000
Number Employees: 50-99

45721 (HQ)Key-Pak Machines
1221 Us Highway 22
Suite 1
Lebanon, NJ 8833
908-236-2111
Fax: 908-236-7013 www.key-pak.com
An extension of the specialized packaging equipment manufactured by Research & Development Packaging Corp. Specializing in vertical form/fill/seal machines, Key-Pak has consistently expanded its machinery portfolio over the years by adding combinational net-weigh scales, cup indexing system, piston liquid fillers and even conveyors.
CEO: Donald Bogut
Vice President: Chris Wanthouse
Research & Development: Don Bogut
Marketing Director: Christopher Wanthouse
Sales Director: Christopher Wanthouse
Operations Manager: Stan Florey
Estimated Sales: $ 1 - 3 Million
Number Employees: 5-9
Number of Brands: 1
Square Footage: 17000
Brands Exported: Key-Pak Machines
Regions Exported to: Central America, South America, Asia
Percentage of Business in Exporting: 20

45722 Keystone Adjustable CapCo Inc
1591 Hylton Rd # B
Pennsauken, NJ 08110-1381
856-317-9879
Fax: 856-663-6075 800-663-5439
info@keystonecap.com www.keystonecap.com
Disposable sanitary headwear including paper and cloth chef hats, overseas caps and bouffants, beard covers, hair nets, etc.; also, aprons, shoe covers, nonwoven coveralls and sleeves; exporter of overseas caps, chef hats and hairnets
CEO: Andrew Feinstein
afeinstein@keystonecap.com
Estimated Sales: $ 50-100 Million
Number Employees: 100-249
Number of Brands: 1
Number of Products: 400
Square Footage: 95000
Type of Packaging: Consumer, Food Service, Private Label, Bulk
Brands Exported: Cordon Bleu; Chef Hat by Keystone; Classy Cap
Regions Exported to: Worldwide

45723 Keystone Coffee Co
2230 Will Wool Dr
Suite 100
San Jose, CA 95112-2605
408-998-2221
Fax: 408-998-5021 www.keystonecoffee.com
Processor and exporter of gourmet coffee
President: Tim Wright
CEO: Dan Mckenrick
mdan@keystonecoffee.com
Estimated Sales: $3000000
Number Employees: 10-19
Regions Exported to: Canada

45724 Keystone Fruit Marketing Inc
11 N Carlisle St # 102
P.O. Box 189
Greencastle, PA 17225-1493
717-597-2112
Fax: 717-597-4096 keystone@keystonefruit.com
Exporter of fruit including apples, peaches, nectarines, plums and pears; importer of sweet onions
President: Kurt Schweitzer
kurt@keystonefruit.com
CFO: Eric Linde
Sales & Marketing: Lisa Fetterhoff
Sales & Marketing: Charlie Rice
Director of Operations: Pat McTavish
Estimated Sales: $5-10 Million
Number Employees: 10-19
Regions Exported to: Worldwide

45725 Keystone Rubber Corporation
PO Box 9
Greenbackville, VA 23356
717-235-6863
Fax: 717-235-9681 800-394-5661
Manufacturer and exporter of conveyor belting, rubber sheeting hoses, rubber gaskets and fittings; FDA approved materials
President: Gloria Lawson
Sales: Mary Baley
Estimated Sales: $ 5 - 10 Million
Number Employees: 10-19
Parent Co: Maryland Rubber Corporation

45726 Khong Guan Corp
30068 Eigenbrodt Way
Union City, CA 94587-1226
510-487-7800
Fax: 510-487-0301 877-889-8968
Importer of cookies, crackers, Asian foods and confectionery products; exporter of ingredients
Exec. V.P.: Albert Lin
Mktg. Mgr.: Harry Gao
Manager: Deborah Heng
dheng@kgcusa.com
Estimated Sales: $5-10 Million
Number Employees: 10-19
Square Footage: 104000
Regions Exported to: Asia
Brands Imported: Cerebos; Luv Yu; Woh Hup; Louwhiss; Lousiana Seafood; Kim Heng; Dragon Brand; Khong Guan; Miss Kate; Datu Puti; Leslie's Clover Chips; Isabelle; Jufran; Laguna
Regions Imported from: Central America, South America, Asia

45727 Kidde Residential & Commercial
1016 Corporate Park Dr
Mebane, NC 27302-8368
919-563-5911
Fax: 919-563-3954 www.kidde.com
Manufacturer and exporter of portable and hand-held fire extinguishers
Vice President: Bob Amrine
amrine.robert@kiddeus.com
Vice President: Bob Amrine
amrine.robert@kiddeus.com
Number Employees: 250-499
Parent Co: William Holdings
Type of Packaging: Consumer, Food Service, Private Label, Bulk
Regions Exported to: Worldwide

45728 Kiefer Brushes, Inc
15 Park Dr
Franklin, NJ 07416
Fax: 888-239-1986 800-526-2905
Manufacturer, exporter and importer of brushes including oven, floor, window and counter; also, broom and wax applicators, squeegee mop handles, paint rollers and brushes
President and CFO: Edward F Boscia
CEO: Gregory Kiefer
Number Employees: 20-49
Square Footage: 100000
Regions Exported to: Central America, South America, Europe, Asia
Percentage of Business in Exporting: 5
Regions Imported from: Asia
Percentage of Business in Importing: 5

45729 Killion Industries Inc
1380 Poinsettia Ave
Vista, CA 92081-8504
760-727-5107
Fax: 760-599-1612 800-421-5352
sales@killionindustries.com
www.killionindustries.com
Manufacturer and exporter of checkstands, and refrigerated fixtures
President: Richard W Killion
richard@killionindustries.com
Estimated Sales: $ 20-50 Million
Number Employees: 100-249
Square Footage: 200000

45730 Kim Lighting
PO Box 60080
City of Industry, CA 91716-0080
626-968-5666
Fax: 626-369-2695 sales@kimlighting.com
www.kimlighting.com
Manufacturer and exporter of lighting fixtures
President: Bill Foley
Regional Sales Manager: Debbie Bell
Estimated Sales: $ 20-50 Million
Number Employees: 250-499
Parent Co: US Industries
Regions Exported to: Central America, South America, Europe, Asia, Middle East, Canada
Percentage of Business in Exporting: 10

45731 (HQ)Kimberly-Clark Corporation
351 Phelps Drive
Irving, TX 75038
972-281-1200
www.kimberly-clark.com
Manufacturer and exporter of toilet paper, paper towels, diapers, feminie products, tissues.
Pres., North America Consumer Business: Kim Underhill
Chairman & CEO: Michael Hsu
CFO: Maria Henry
President & Chief Operating Officer: Michael Hsu
Chief Growth Officer: Alison Lewis
Year Founded: 1872
Estimated Sales: $18.5 Billion
Number Employees: 42,000
Number of Brands: 31
Type of Packaging: Consumer, Food Service, Private Label, Bulk
Regions Exported to: Worldwide

45732 Kincaid Enterprises
PO Box 549
Nitro, WV 25143
304-755-3377
Fax: 304-755-4547 800-951-3377
Manufacturer and exporter of insecticides and other agricultural chemicals
President: R E Kincaid
VP Production: Brian Kincaid
Estimated Sales: $ 5 - 10 Million
Number Employees: 5-9
Brands Exported: K.E.; Terraneb S.P.; Demosan
Regions Exported to: Central America, South America, Europe, Asia, Middle East
Percentage of Business in Exporting: 5

45733 Kinematics & Controls Corporation
15151 Technology Dr.
Brooksville, FL 34604-0690
352-796-0300
Fax: 352-796-4477 800-833-8103
sales@kcontrols.com www.kcontrols.com
Manufacturer and exporter of liquid level sensors and liquid/powder filling machines
President: John Rakucewicz
Contact: Ricky Clotter
ricky@kcontrols.com
Number Employees: 10
Square Footage: 8000
Regions Exported to: Worldwide
Percentage of Business in Exporting: 10

45734 Kinergy Corp
7310 Grade Ln
Louisville, KY 40219-3437
502-366-5685
Fax: 502-366-3701 kinergy@kinergy.com
www.kinergy.com
Manufacturer, designer, importer and exporter of bulk solid material handling equipment including bin and container activators, storage pile and rail car dischargers, rail car shakers, feeders, conveyors, deliquefying and deslimingscreens and fluid bed coolers
President: George Dumbaugh
CEO: Scott Greenwell
CFO: Charles Hays
Manager: Lim Adeline
adeline@kinergy.com.sg

Estimated Sales: $10-20 Million
Number Employees: 20-49
Square Footage: 50000
Regions Exported to: Central America, South America, Europe, Asia, Middle East
Percentage of Business in Exporting: 25
Regions Imported from: Central America, South America, Europe, Asia, Middle East
Percentage of Business in Importing: 25

45735 Kinetic Co
6775 W Loomis Rd
Greendale, WI 53129-2700   414-425-8221
Fax: 414-425-7927
joseph.masters@knifemaker.com
www.knifemaker.com
Manufacturer and exporter of perforating blades, machine and packaging knives and slitters
President: Kyle Peerenboom
kylepeerenboom@nestlepurinacareers.com
VP: Cash Masters
VP of Sales: Tina Lawton
General Manager: Ian Finkill
Estimated Sales: $ 10 - 20 Million
Number Employees: 50-99
Type of Packaging: Food Service

45736 Kinetico
11015 Kinsman Rd
Newbury, OH 44065-9787   440-564-9111
Fax: 440-564-7641 custserv@kinetico.com
www.kinetico.com
Manufacturer and exporter of water conditioners, purifiers and filters. Systems are utilized in a wide variety of residential and commercial applications that include restaurants, hotels, carwashes, hospitals and others
President: Toby Thomas
tthomas@kinetico.com
Commercial Sls. Mgr.: George Hohman
CFO: Trevor Wilson
CEO: Shamus Hurley
R&D: Keith Brown
VP Industrial: Chris Hanson
Estimated Sales: $ 20 - 50 Million
Number Employees: 250-499
Type of Packaging: Bulk
Regions Exported to: Worldwide
Percentage of Business in Exporting: 10

45737 King Arthur
646 Shelton Ave
Statesville, NC 28677-6104   704-873-0300
Fax: 704-872-4194   800-257-7244
karthur@i-america.net
Manufacturer and exporter of room service carts, furniture, sternos, chafers and serving equipment
V.P. Sls./Mktg.: Greg Holroyd
Estimated Sales: $10-20,000,000
Number Employees: 1-4
Parent Co: Falcon Products
Regions Exported to: Worldwide

45738 King B Meat Snacks
P.O. Box 397
Minong, WI 54859-0397   715-466-2234
Fax: 715-466-5151   800-346-6896
info@linksnacks.com
Manufacturer and exporter of jerky and meat snacks
President: Troy Link
CEO: John Link
CFO: John Hermeier
Executive Vice President of Supply Chain: Karl Paepke
Director of Marketing: Jeff LeFever
Estimated Sales: $10-20 Million
Number Employees: 250-499
Type of Packaging: Consumer, Food Service, Private Label, Bulk
Regions Exported to: Asia
Percentage of Business in Exporting: 5

45739 King Bag & Mfg Co
1500 Spring Lawn Ave
Cincinnati, OH 45223-1699   513-541-5440
Fax: 513-541-6555   800-444-5464
mike@kingbag.com
www.kingbag.com
Manufacturer, importer and exporter of bulk handling bags, filters bags and curtains, crumb belts
President: Annie Bunn
annie@kingbag.com
VP: Ron Kirsch Jr
Sales Manager: Mike Jennings
Production Manager: Chris Miller

Estimated Sales: $2.5-5 Million
Number Employees: 20-49
Square Footage: 80000
Regions Exported to: Canada
Percentage of Business in Exporting: 3
Regions Imported from: Worldwide
Percentage of Business in Importing: 15

45740 King Cole Ducks Limited
15351 Warden Ave.
PO Box 185
Newmarket, ON L3Y 4W1
Canada   905-836-9461
Fax: 905-836-4440   800-363-3825
rgrant@kingcoleducks.com
www.kingcoleducks.com
Processor and exporter of fresh and frozen duck including parts, smoked, boneless breast, peppered, fully cooked, etc
President: James Murby
VP: Robert Murby
Square Footage: 4000
Type of Packaging: Consumer, Food Service, Private Label, Bulk
Brands Exported: King Cole
Regions Exported to: USA

45741 King Company
4830 Transport Drive
Dallas, TX 75247-6310   507-451-3770
Fax: 507-455-7400 king@kingcompany.com
Manufacturer and exporter of air curtains, process air conditioning, filtration systems and finned coils
Sls. Mgr.: Thomas Heisler
Marketing Manager: Mike Kaler
Sales Manager: Bruce Glover
Estimated Sales: $ 1 - 5 Million
Number Employees: 100-249
Square Footage: 240000
Parent Co: United Dominion Industries
Regions Exported to: Central America
Percentage of Business in Exporting: 4

45742 King Engineering - King-Gage
8019 Ohio River Boulevard
Newell, WV 26050
  800-242-8871
www.King-Gage.com
Level measurement systems and compressed air filters
President: Steve Lefevre
Estimated Sales: Below $ 5 Million
Number Employees: 20-49
Square Footage: 28000
Type of Packaging: Bulk
Regions Exported to: Central America, South America
Percentage of Business in Exporting: 8

45743 King Food Service
7810 42nd St W
Rock Island, IL 61201-7319   309-787-4488
Fax: 309-787-4501 www.kingfoodservice.com
Seafood, poultry & meat
President: Matthew Cutkomp
CEO/CFO: Mike Cutkomp
Director of Sales & Marketing: Kelly McDonald
VP Operations: Chad Gaul
Estimated Sales: $24 Million
Number Employees: 10-19
Number of Products: 1500

45744 King Nut Co
31900 Solon Rd
Solon, OH 44139-3536   440-248-8484
Fax: 440-248-0153   800-860-5464
info@kingnut.com www.kingnut.com
Snack mixes, chocolates, nuts, dried fruit, granola and pretzels; exporter of salted nuts.
Chairman: Michael Kanan
President/CEO: Martin Kanan
SVP/CFO: Joseph Valenza
EVP/CMO: Matthew Kanan
VP Quality Assurance/Product Development: Debra Smith
Manufacturing/Plant Operations: Michael Smith
Estimated Sales: $35 Million
Number Employees: 100-249
Number of Brands: 3
Square Footage: 250000
Parent Co: Kanan Enterprises
Type of Packaging: Consumer, Food Service, Private Label, Bulk
Brands Exported: Peterson's

Regions Exported to: Central America, Europe, Asia
Percentage of Business in Exporting: 10

45745 King Packaging Co
708 Kings Rd
Schenectady, NY 12304-3665   518-370-5464
Fax: 518-393-5464
Contract packaging of cat litter, ice melt products and decorative landscape stone.
Owner: Bill Venezio
bvenezio@kingpackagingcorp.com
Plant Manager: Anthony Farone
Estimated Sales: Less Than $500,000
Number Employees: 5-9
Number of Brands: 6
Number of Products: 24
Square Footage: 240000
Type of Packaging: Consumer, Private Label
Brands Exported: Sure-Trax
Regions Exported to: Canada
Percentage of Business in Exporting: 1

45746 King Plastic Corp
1100 N Toledo Blade Blvd
North Port, FL 34288-8694   941-493-5502
Fax: 941-497-3274   800-780-5502
llathrum@kingplastics.com www.kingplastic.com
Manufacturer and exporter of tamper-resistant plastic containers including cups
President: Debra Cunningham
cunningham@kingplastic.com
VP: Robert King
Marketing Manager: Marjorie Williamson
Sales Manager: Larry Lathrum
Estimated Sales: $ 10 - 20 Million
Number Employees: 100-249
Square Footage: 200000
Type of Packaging: Bulk
Regions Exported to: Worldwide

45747 King Products
1435 Bonhill Road
Unit 25
Mississauga, ON L5T 1V2
Canada   866-454-6757
Fax: 416-850-9828 sales@mzero.com
www.kingproducts.com
Manufacturer and exporter of outdoor plastic signs, point of purchase displays and furniture
President: Philippe Moulin
CFO: Roger Whitzel
Number Employees: 90
Parent Co: Meridian Kiosks
Regions Exported to: Worldwide
Percentage of Business in Exporting: 50

45748 Kings Canyon
1750 S Buttonwillow Ave
Reedley, CA 93654-4400   559-638-3571
Fax: 559-638-6326
Peaches, apricots and other fruits
President: Steve Kenfield
VP Sales: Fred Berry

45749 Kings Choice Food
2583 N Orange Blossom Trl
Orlando, FL 32804-4808   407-426-9979
Fax: 407-426-9688   888-426-9979
netkings@aol.com
Exporter and wholesaler/distributor of vacuum packed steaks, chicken and seafood
President: Ray Reyhani
General Manager: Shawn Kasper
Estimated Sales: $1-2.5 Million
Number Employees: 1-4
Type of Packaging: Consumer, Food Service, Private Label, Bulk
Regions Exported to: Latin America

45750 Kings River Casting
1350 North Ave
Sanger, CA 93657-3742   559-875-8250
Fax: 559-875-1491 888-545-5157
Sales@KingsRiverCasting.Com
Manufacturer and exporter of tables, chairs and barstools
President/CEO: Pat Henry
henry@kingsrivercasting.com
Vice President: Dale Monteleone
Estimated Sales: Below $5 Million
Number Employees: 10-19
Square Footage: 54000
Parent Co: Kings River Casting

Importers & Exporters / A-Z

Type of Packaging: Food Service
Regions Exported to: Europe, Asia, Worldwide
Percentage of Business in Exporting: 15

45751 Kingspan Insulated Panels, Ltd.
Langley Office
5202-272nd Street
Langley, BC
Canada
604-607-1101
877-638-3266
Cold storage and blast freezer doors, as well as controlled environment and low temperature doors for the food and beverage industry. Also a manufacturer of paneling and roof panels for industrial buildings.
Regions Exported to: North America

45752 Kingston Fresh
477 Shoup Ave
Suite 207
Idaho Falls, ID 83402-3658
208-522-2365
Fax: 208-552-7488 www.kingstonfresh.com
Potatoes; onions; broccoli; sweet pineapples; and lettuce.
President: Mike Kingston
CEO: Dave Kingston
Number Employees: 5-9
Type of Packaging: Consumer, Food Service

45753 Kingston McKnight
419 Avenue Del Ora
Redwood City, CA 94062
650-462-4900
Fax: 650-268-3733 800-900-0463
Manufacturer, importer and exporter of slip-resistant safety shoes serving the hospitality industry
Owner: Jeff Mc Knight
VP: Terry Kingston
Contact: Terry Kingston
tphilipk@yahoo.com
Estimated Sales: $1,000,000
Number Employees: 1-4
Square Footage: 10000
Other Locations:
 Kingston McKnight
 Las Vegas, NVKingston McKnight
Brands Exported: Kingston McKnight
Regions Exported to: Central America, Europe
Percentage of Business in Exporting: 10
Brands Imported: Kingston McKnight; Slip-Resistant Safety Shoes
Regions Imported from: Asia
Percentage of Business in Importing: 100

45754 Kingsville Fisherman's Company
PO Box 37
Kingsville Dock
Kingsville, ON N9Y 2E8
Canada
519-733-6534
Fax: 519-733-6959
Processor and exporter of fresh and frozen perch and pickerel
President: Carl Fraser
Sales Manager: John Murray
Number Employees: 50-99
Type of Packaging: Bulk
Regions Exported to: U.S

45755 Kinnikinnick Foods
10940-120 Street NW
Edmonton, AB T5H 3P7
Canada
780-424-2900
Fax: 780-421-0456 877-503-4466
info@kinnikinnick.com www.kinnikinnick.com
Gluten-free bakery products
President & CEO: Jerry Bigam
CFO: Lynne Bigam
VP, Operations: Jay Bigam
Number Employees: 60
Number of Products: 120
Square Footage: 120000
Type of Packaging: Consumer, Food Service
Brands Exported: Kinni-Kwik Mixes, Kinnibetik Baked Goods.
Brands Imported: Ingredients
Regions Imported from: South America, Europe, Asia

45756 Kinsley Inc
901 Crosskeys Dr
Doylestown, PA 18902-1025
215-348-7723
Fax: 215-348-7724 800-414-6664
info@kinsleyinc.com www.kinsleyinc.com
Manufacturer and exporter of bottle sorters and unscramblers, capping and filling machinery, bottle conveyors and timing screws.

President: T Mc Carthy
info@kinsleyinc.com
R&D: James Malloy
Quality Control: James Malloy
Sales: Brandon Concannon
Engineering Manager: David Hansen
Plant Manager: Dan Froehlich
Estimated Sales: Below $ 5 Million
Number Employees: 5-9
Regions Exported to: Central America, South America, Europe, Middle East, Canada, Mexico, Caribbean
Percentage of Business in Exporting: 10

45757 Kirin Brewery Of America LLC
5230 Pacific Concourse
Suite 310
Los Angeles, CA 90045-6256
310-381-3040
Fax: 310-320-5955 888-547-4623
Exporter of alcoholic beverages including beer
President: Takafumi Yamada
Pres.: Satoru Shimura
Number Employees: 5-9
Parent Co: Kirin Brewery Company
Regions Exported to: South America, Canada

45758 Kisco Manufacturing
5155 Argyle Street
Port Alberni, BC V9Y 1V3
Canada
604-823-7456
Fax: 250-724-5155 www.kiscomanufacturing.com
Manufacturer and exporter of flour silos and scales, conveyor systems and water meters
Pres.: Svend Kuhr
Svce. Mgr.: Peter Kuhr
Number Employees: 5
Square Footage: 14000
Parent Co: Kisco Foods
Brands Exported: Kisco; Kimac; Mix Master
Regions Exported to: USA, Pacific Rim
Percentage of Business in Exporting: 50

45759 Kiss International/Di-tech Systems
965 Park Center Drive
Vista, CA 92081-8312
800-527-5477
Fax: 760-599-0207 800-527-5477
Manufacturer and exporter of reverse osmosis water purification systems; also, components and filter cartridges
VP/General Manager: Theresa Hawks
Sales/Customer Service: Becky Rivera
Sales/Customer Service: Kerri Rivera
Number Employees: 22
Square Footage: 80000
Parent Co: Aqua Care Corporation
Brands Exported: Aristocrat 3000, 4000, 5000; DiplomaT; Ambassador; Duchess
Regions Exported to: Central America, South America, Europe, Asia, Middle East, Mexico, Canada
Percentage of Business in Exporting: 20

45760 Kisters Kayat
5501 N Washington Boulevard
Sarasota, FL 34243-2249
386-424-0101
Fax: 386-424-0266 parts@kkiusa.com
Manufacturer, importer and exporter of high speed tray and wraparound packers, shrink wrappers, tray stackers and turners and case sealers
VP Finance: Peter Welen
VP Engineering: Gary Hunt
Number Employees: 90
Square Footage: 144000
Parent Co: Kisters Maschinenbau GmbH
Regions Exported to: Central America, South America, Asia, Canada, Mexico, Caribbean, Latin America
Percentage of Business in Exporting: 10
Regions Imported from: Europe

45761 Kitchener Plastics
962 Guelph Street
Kitchener, ON N2H 5Z6
Canada
519-742-0752
Fax: 519-742-9247 800-429-5633
Manufacturer and exporter of plastic signs
President: Gabrielle Wolf
Estimated Sales: Below $ 5 Million
Number Employees: 4

45762 Kitchens Seafood
1001 E Baker St
Suite 202
Plant City, FL 33566
813-750-1888
Fax: 813-750-1889 800-327-0132
sales@kitchensseafood.com
www.kitchensseafood.com
Manufacturer, packer and importer of frozen seafood including lobster, crab, shrimp, shrimp meat and langostinos
President: Dan La Fleur
Type of Packaging: Consumer, Food Service, Private Label, Bulk
Other Locations:
 Kitchens Seafood - Production
 Jacksonville, FLKitchens Seafood - Production
Brands Imported: Poseidon
Regions Imported from: Ecuador, Thailand

45763 Kittling Ridge Estate Wines & Spirits
271 Chrislea Road
Vaughan, ON L4L 8N6
Canada
905-945-9225
Fax: 905-738-5551 800-461-9463
www.kittlingridge.com
Wine and spirits
President/CEO: Rosanna Magnotta
Year Founded: 1992
Estimated Sales: $20-50 Million
Number Employees: 100-249
Parent Co: Magnotta Winery Corporation
Regions Exported to: Asia
Percentage of Business in Exporting: 25

45764 Klaire Laboratories
10439 Double R Blvd
Reno, NV 89521-8905
775-850-8800
Fax: 775-850-8810 888-488-2488
www.klaire.com
Processor and exporter of allergen-free nutritional supplements
President: Cary Fereuson
Number Employees: 20-49
Parent Co: Kek Industries
Brands Exported: Vital Life
Regions Exported to: South America, Europe, Asia
Percentage of Business in Exporting: 20

45765 Kleen Products Inc
8136 SW 8th St
Oklahoma City, OK 73128-4210
405-495-1168
Fax: 405-495-1175 800-392-1792
ken@joeshandcleaner.com
www.joeskleenproducts.com
Manufacturer and exporter of hand, glass and floor cleaners
CEO: Kenneth Newman
CFO: Kenneth Newman
Vice President: Michael Newman
R&D: Kenneth Newman
Quality Control: Joe Brantley
Estimated Sales: $ 1.5 Million
Number Employees: 5-9
Type of Packaging: Private Label
Brands Exported: Joe's All Purpose; Joe's Hand Scrub; Joe's Citrus Blue
Regions Exported to: South America, Asia, Canada, Greece
Percentage of Business in Exporting: 6

45766 Kleenpak Systems
611 Calle Embocadura
San Clemente, CA 92673-3030
949-492-8604
Fax: 949-492-2075 sales@kleenpak.com
www.kleenpak.com
Dispensing systems; polystyrene and biocompostable products
President: Terence Tucker
sells@kleenpaksystems.com
Vice President: Marie Tucker

45767 Kliklok-Woodman
5224 Snapfinger Woods Dr
Decatur, GA 30035-4023
770-981-5200
Fax: 770-987-7160 sales@kliklok-woodman.com
www.kliklokwoodman.com
Manufacturer and exporter of flexible packaging machinery for the snack food, confectionery, nut and baking industries including fillers, sealers, weighers, loaders, closers, etc

President: Peter Black
pblack@klikwood.com
CEO: William Crist
Sales Director: T Long
Public Relations: C Kuhr
Estimated Sales: $45 Million
Number Employees: 100-249
Number of Brands: 5
Number of Products: 50
Square Footage: 220000
Parent Co: Kliklok Corporation
Brands Exported: Clipper; Commander; Gemini; Pacer; Polaris; Profitmaker; Quasar; Spectra
Regions Exported to: Worldwide
Percentage of Business in Exporting: 50

45768 Klockner Pentaplast of America
P.O.Box 500
Gordonsville, VA 22942 540-832-3600
Fax: 540-832-5656 kpainfo@kpfilms.com
www.kpfilms.com
Manufacturer and exporter of rigid vinyl, polyester and barex films for form/fill/seal, hot fill, trays, cups, portion packs, rounds, clamshells and modified atmospheric packaging of food and full body shrink sleeves for beverages
Chairman: Bruno Deschamps
CFO: Markus Holzl
Vice President: Michael Tubridy
Research & Development: Dean Inman
Marketing Director: Michael Ryan
Sales Director: Bobby Nolan
Communications Manager: Nancy Ryan
Chief Operating Officer: Stefan Brandt
Number Employees: 500-999
Number of Brands: 17
Type of Packaging: Consumer, Food Service
Brands Exported: Pentaprint
Regions Exported to: Central America, South America, Canada, Mexico

45769 Kloss Manufacturing Co Inc
7566 Morris Ct
Suite 310
Allentown, PA 18106-9247 610-391-3820
Fax: 610-391-3830 800-445-7100
Processor and exporter of flavoring extracts for Italian ices and slushes; also, concession equipment and supplies, fountain syrups, popcorn, cotton candy, nachos and waffles
Owner: Stephen Lloss
skloss@klossfunfood.com
Estimated Sales: $3-5 Million
Number Employees: 10-19
Square Footage: 120000
Type of Packaging: Food Service, Private Label, Bulk
Brands Exported: Kloss
Regions Exported to: Central America, Caribbean, Latin America, Mexico
Percentage of Business in Exporting: 3

45770 Knall Beverage
4550 Tiedeman Rd
Cleveland, OH 44144 216-252-2500
Fax: 216-252-2512
Importer of German beer
CEO: Robert Knall
Estimated Sales: $14.2 Million
Number Employees: 65
Brands Imported: Becks
Regions Imported from: Europe

45771 Knappen Milling Co
110 S Water St
P.O. Box 245
Augusta, MI 49012-9781 269-731-4141
Fax: 269-731-5441 800-562-7736
Knappen@knappen.com
Soft wheat, cereal bran, wheat and flour
President/CEO: Charles B. Knappen III
Treasurer: Darrell Roese
Vice President: John Shouse
jshouse@knappen.com
VP of Sales & Grain Purchasing: Todd C. Wright
Plant Manager: Bob Likens
Number Employees: 20-49
Type of Packaging: Private Label, Bulk

45772 Knight Equipment International
20531 Crescent Bay Dr
Lake Forest, CA 92630-8825 949-595-4800
Fax: 949-595-4801 800-854-3764
www.knightequip.com
Manufacturer and exporter of low energy dish washing machines; also, pumps, controls and dispensers
President: George Noa
Pres.: Paul Beldham
Sales/Mktg: George Noa
Contact: Joah Bridwell
jbridwell@kofc9487.com
Estimated Sales: $20-50 Million
Number Employees: 1,000-4,999
Regions Exported to: South America

45773 (HQ)Knight Seed Company
12550 W Frontage Road
Suite 203
Burnsville, MN 55337-2402 952-894-8080
Fax: 952-894-8095 800-328-2999
Processor, importer and exporter of soybeans, dried beans, peas and buckwheat; exporter of lentils
President/CEO: Dave Dornacker
Export Manager: Jeff Pricco
VP: Tom Kennelly
Marketing: Tim Kukowski
Sales: Dan Dahlquist
Estimated Sales: $ 3 - 5 Million
Number Employees: 16
Square Footage: 12000
Other Locations:
 Knight Seed Co.
 Vanscoy, SKKnight Seed Co.
Regions Exported to: Central America, South America, Europe, Asia, Middle East
Percentage of Business in Exporting: 20
Regions Imported from: Asia

45774 Knight's Appleden Fruit LTD
11687 County Road 2
Colborne, ON K0K 1S0
Canada 905-349-2521
Fax: 905-349-3129 www.knights-appleden.ca
Processor, importer and exporter of apples
President: Roger Knight
Estimated Sales: 1-2.5 Million
Number Employees: 20-49
Regions Exported to: Worldwide
Percentage of Business in Exporting: 50
Regions Imported from: South America
Percentage of Business in Importing: 2

45775 Knobs Unlimited
13350 Bishop Rd
Bowling Green, OH 43402 419-353-8215
Fax: 419-353-8325
Manufacturer and exporter of plastic replacement knobs for appliances
Owner/Plt. Mgr.: John Cardenas
R & D: William Anderson
R & D: John Cardinas
Estimated Sales: Below $5 Million
Number Employees: 5-9
Square Footage: 17000

45776 Knott Slicers
290 Pine Street
Canton, MA 02021-3353 781-821-0925
Fax: 781-821-0768
Manufacturer and exporter of slicing machinery for potato chips, yams, plantains, yuccas, bananas, taro roots, beets, potatoes, tomatoes and bagel sticks
President: Alan Burgess
VP: Steve Burgess
Quality Control: Doug Merrill
Marketing/Sales: Alan Burgess
Operations: Jim Stratis
Estimated Sales: $10-15 Million
Number Employees: 50-99
Number of Products: 5
Square Footage: 120000
Parent Co: Burgess Brothers
Type of Packaging: Food Service
Regions Exported to: Central America, South America, Europe, Asia, Middle East
Percentage of Business in Exporting: 80

45777 Knouse Foods Co-Op Inc.
800 Peach Glen Rd. - Idaville Rd.
Peach Glen, PA 17375 717-677-8181
www.knouse.com
Apples and apple products, vinegar, cherries, tomato juice, pie fillings, and more.
President/Chairman: Kenneth Guise
kguise@knouse.com
CEO: Charles Haberkorn
Vice President, Marketing: Robert Fisher
Vice President, Sales: Richard Esser
Year Founded: 1949
Estimated Sales: $290 Million
Number Employees: 1,500
Number of Brands: 5
Square Footage: 557450
Type of Packaging: Consumer, Food Service, Private Label, Bulk

45778 Knutsen Coffees
1448 Pine St Ste 209
San Francisco, CA 94109 415-922-9570
Fax: 415-922-1045 800-231-7764
kcltd@pacbell.net
Import and broker of raw coffee beans
President: Erna Knutsen
erna@knutsencoffees.com
CFO: John Rapinchuk
Estimated Sales: $2 Million
Number Employees: 1-4
Type of Packaging: Bulk
Regions Imported from: Central America, South America, Asia
Percentage of Business in Importing: 100

45779 Kobrand Corporation
1 Manhattanville Rd
4th Floor
Purchase, NY 10577-2126 914-252-7700
Importer of wine and champagne.
President & CEO: Robert Deroose
SVP Director, Marketing: Cathlene Burke
Year Founded: 1944
Estimated Sales: $20-50 Million
Number Employees: 50-99
Brands Imported: Tattinger; Jadot; Fortant de France; Mouieix
Regions Imported from: South America, Europe

45780 Koch Bag & Supply Co
999 Bedford Rd
Kansas City, MO 64116-4114 816-221-1883
Fax: 816-221-7070
Wholesaler/distributor and exporter of bags including cotton specialty polyethylene; also, burlap products
President: Diana Byron
d.bryon@kochbag.com
Estimated Sales: $10-20 Million
Number Employees: 10-19
Type of Packaging: Consumer, Bulk
Regions Exported to: Worldwide

45781 Kochman Consultants LTD
5545 Lincoln Ave
Morton Grove, IL 60053-3430 847-470-1195
Fax: 847-470-1189 info@kclcad.com
www.kclcad.com
Designer and exporter computer software for the food service industry
President: Ronald Kochman
ron@kclcad.com
R & D: Kevin Kochman
Vice President: Kevin Kochman
Estimated Sales: Below $5 Million
Number Employees: 5-9
Square Footage: 8000
Type of Packaging: Food Service
Brands Exported: KCL Cadalog
Regions Exported to: Worldwide
Percentage of Business in Exporting: 10

45782 Kodex Inc
160 Park Ave # 7
Nutley, NJ 07110-2808 973-235-0606
Fax: 973-235-0132 800-325-6339
sales@kodexray.com www.kodexray.com
Manufacturer, importer and exporter of x-ray inspection systems for detection of contaminants in packaged and fresh food products
President: Gary Korkala
kodex@kodexray.com
General Manager: Don Airey
VP: Gary Korkala
Quality Control: Garrett Sollitto
Sales: Richard Zieminski
Estimated Sales: $3-4 Million
Number Employees: 5-9
Square Footage: 17600
Brands Exported: ImageX; Inspex; Varian
Regions Exported to: Central America, South America, Europe, Middle East
Percentage of Business in Exporting: 15
Brands Imported: Inspex; X-Scan; Fast Scan
Regions Imported from: Europe

Importers & Exporters / A-Z

45783 Koehler Instrument Co Inc
1595 Sycamore Ave
Bohemia, NY 11716-1732   631-589-3800
        Fax: 631-589-3815 800-878-9070
            sales@koehlerinstrument.com
            www.koehlerinstrument.com
Manufacturer and exporter of lubricant, grease and viscosity testing equipment
President: Roy Westerhaus
rwesterhaus@koehlerinstrument.com
CFO: Peter Brey
R&D: Dr Raj Shah
Marketing: Dr Wayne Goldenberg
Sales: Atul Gautama
Production: Joseph Russo
Estimated Sales: $10-20,000,000
Number Employees: 50-99
Number of Brands: 2
Number of Products: 200
Square Footage: 35000
Brands Exported: Koehler Instruments
Regions Exported to: Central America, South America, Europe, Asia, Middle East
Percentage of Business in Exporting: 50

45784 Koehler-Gibson Marking
875 Englewood Ave
Buffalo, NY 14223-2334   716-838-5960
        Fax: 716-838-6859 800-875-1562
            sales@kgco.com www.kgco.com
Manufacturer and exporter of marking products, steel stamps, embossing dies, stencils, etc.; also, printing plates and cutting dies for plastic and corrugated packaging
Owner: David Koehler
ddk@kgco.com
Estimated Sales: $2.5-5 Million
Number Employees: 20-49
Square Footage: 28000
Regions Exported to: Canada
Percentage of Business in Exporting: 10

45785 Koha Food
500 Alakawa St
Suite 104
Honolulu, HI 96817-4576   808-845-4232
                Fax: 808-841-5398
Oriental foods
President: Paul Kim
Estimated Sales: $ 5 - 10 Million
Number Employees: 20-49

45786 Kohana Coffee
1221 S Mopac Expressway
Suite 100
Austin, TX 78746   512-904-1174
        Fax: 512-532-0581 info@kohanacoffee.com
                www.kohanacoffee.com
Coffee, decaff and cold brew coffee.
Owner: Victoria Lynden
Sales: Nate Creasey
Contact: Joe Browne
joe@kohanacoffee.com
Operations: Piper Jones
Estimated Sales: Under $500,000
Number Employees: 2

45787 Kohler Industries Inc
4925 N 56th St # C
PO Box 29496
Lincoln, NE 68504-1771   402-465-8845
        Fax: 402-465-8841 800-365-6708
            info@kohlerequip.com www.kohlerequip.com
Manufacturer and distributor of freezers, conveyors, bagging equipment and mixers.
President/Owner: Jim Kohler
jim@kohlerequip.com
IT: Scott Jaquez
Sales: Norm Pavlish
Office Mgr./ Inventory Control: Dave Bonczynski
Number Employees: 10-19
Regions Exported to: Central America, South America, Middle East, North America, USA

45788 Kola
215 W 64th St
New York, NY 10065-6662   212-688-1895
                rincakola@aol.com
Processor and exporter of soft drinks
Principal: Louis Jardines
Estimated Sales: $2.5-5 Million
Number Employees: 5-9
Type of Packaging: Consumer, Food Service, Private Label

Brands Exported: Inca Kola; Golden Kola
Regions Exported to: Central America, South America, Europe, Asia, Canada, Caribbean, Latin America
Percentage of Business in Exporting: 10

45789 Kold-Draft
1525 E Lake Rd
Erie, PA 16511-1088   814-453-6761
        Fax: 814-455-6336 tomm@kold-draft.com
                www.kolddraft.com
CEO: John Brigham
Contact: Shawn Heifner
sheifner@eriemg.com
Estimated Sales: $ 5 - 10 Million
Number Employees: 20-49
Parent Co: Uniflow Manufacturing

45790 Kold-Hold
P.O.Box 570
Edgefield, SC 29824-0570   803-637-3166
                Fax: 803-637-3046
Manufacturer and exporter of cold plates for refrigeration trucks; used in short delivery
President: Paul Cooper
G.M.: Dave Stasktlunas
Number Employees: 100-249
Square Footage: 440000
Parent Co: Tranter
Regions Exported to: Central America, South America, Europe, Asia, Middle East
Percentage of Business in Exporting: 5

45791 Kole Industries
PO Box 20152
Miami, FL 33102   305-633-2556
                Fax: 305-638-5821
Manufacturer and exporter of corrugated parts, bins and mailing and shipping room supplies
President: Arthur Kaplan
Contact: Donald Spraque
donald.spraque@koleindustries.com
Estimated Sales: $ 5 - 10 Million
Number Employees: 15
Parent Co: National Lithographers

45792 Kolpak
2915 Tennessee Ave N
Parsons, TN 38363   731-847-6361
        Fax: 731-847-5387 800-826-7036
                www.kolpak.com
Manufacturer and exporter of walk-in coolers and freezers
General Manager: Gerry Senion
VP: Jack Antell
Contact: Jack Antell
j.antell@kolpak.com
Estimated Sales: $50-100 Million
Number Employees: 100-249
Type of Packaging: Food Service
Regions Exported to: Worldwide
Percentage of Business in Exporting: 30

45793 Kolpak Walk-ins
P.O.Box 550
Parsons, TN 38363-0550   731-847-6361
        Fax: 731-847-5387 800-826-7036
                www.kolpak.com
Manufacturer and exporter of walk-in coolers, freezers and refrigeration systems
Quality Control: Barry Autry
CFO: Tonny Jordan
VP: Jack Antell
Research & Development: Richard Fahey
Marketing Director: Stephanie Ferrell
Plant Manager: Steve Clayton
Estimated Sales: $ 50 - 75 Million
Number Employees: 20-49
Parent Co: Manitowoc Foodservice Group
Brands Exported: Kolpak; McCall
Regions Exported to: Central America, South America, Asia, Middle East, Canada, Mexico, Latin America
Percentage of Business in Exporting: 10

45794 Kona Cold Lobsters
73-4460 Queen Kaahumanu
Suite 103
Kailua Kona, HI 96740-2637   808-329-4332
        Fax: 808-326-2882 info@konacoldlobsters.com
                www.konacoldlobsters.com
Lobsters

President: Joseph Wilson
Manager: Philip Wilson
phil@konacoldlobsters.com
Estimated Sales: Less than $300,000
Number Employees: 10-19

45795 Kona Joe Coffee LLC
79-7346 Mamalahoa Hwy
Kealakekua, HI 96750-7910   808-322-2100
        Fax: 808-322-9800 sales@konajoe.com
                www.konajoe.com
President/Owner/CEO: Joseph Alban
General Manager: Nikki Santiago
Manager: Bruno Oleverira
bruno@konajoe.com
Estimated Sales: $2 Million
Number Employees: 10
Type of Packaging: Consumer, Food Service, Private Label, Bulk
Brands Exported: Kona Joe Coffee, Kona Roasting Company, Jammers, Mac-Jammers
Regions Exported to: Europe, Asia, Middle East, Canada
Percentage of Business in Exporting: 50

45796 Konica Minolta Corp
101 Williams Dr
Ramsey, NJ 07446-1293   201-825-4000
        Fax: 201-825-7567 888-473-3637
                www.konicaminolta.com
Manufacturer and exporter of color measuring instrumentation including spectrophotometers, colorimeters, light meters, etc.; also, computer software for color formulation and quality control
CEO: Scott Cohen
scohen@mi.konicaminolta.us
CEO: Jun Haraguchi
Marketing Director: Maria Repici
Number Employees: 500-999
Regions Exported to: South America

45797 Kontane
1000 Charleston Regional Pkwy
Charleston, SC 29492   843-352-0011
        Fax: 828-397-3683 info@kontanelogistics.com
                www.kontane.com
Manufacturer and exporter of containers: heavy duty wooden, household storage and custom built; also, pallet and export boxes and cleated plywood
President: Ed Byrd
VP: Jason Essenberg
COO: Rusty Byrd
Estimated Sales: $2.5-5 Million
Number Employees: 100-249

45798 Kopke, William H
1000 Northern Blvd # 200
Great Neck, NY 11021-5312   516-328-6800
                Fax: 516-328-6874
Importer and wholesaler/distributor of produce
President: Peter Kopke
Contact: Joe Fox
joefox@kopkefruit.com
Estimated Sales: $20-50 Million
Number Employees: 5-9
Regions Imported from: South America

45799 (HQ)Koppers Chocolate
45 Jackson Drive
Cranford, NJ 07016   212-243-0220
                800-325-0026
            info@kopperschocolate.com
                www.kopperschocolate.com
Processor, importer and exporter of confectionery items including chocolate covered espresso beans, chocolate covered gummy bears and Danish mint lentils.
President: Jeff Alexander
jeff@kopperschocolate.com
Director of Sales: Ellen Silverman
Estimated Sales: $7800000
Number Employees: 51-200

45800 Kopykake
3699 W 240th St
Torrance, CA 90505-6002   310-373-8906
        Fax: 310-375-5275 800-999-5253
            sales@kopykake.com www.kopykake.com
Manufacturer and exporter of computerized cake photo printing, edible frosting sheets and edible ink. kartriges, cake decorating equipment and supplies, including drawing projectors, airbrushes and compressors, food colors, disposable decorating bags, etc

President: Gerry Mayer
gerry@kopykake.com
Vice President: Greg Mayer
Sales Director: Rudy Arce
Estimated Sales: $ 1-2.5 Million
Number Employees: 20-49
Square Footage: 80000
Type of Packaging: Food Service
Brands Exported: Kopykake; Airmaster
Regions Exported to: Worldwide
Percentage of Business in Exporting: 20

45801 Korab Engineering Company
7727 Beland Avenue
Los Angeles, CA 90045-1128   310-670-7710
Fax: 310-670-7710
Manufacturer, exporter and importer of packaging machinery including liquid fillers, monoblock machinery, automation systems, vertical form fillers, seal machinery, horizontal thermoforming equipment, tray makers, pick and placeequipment, etc
Pres./G.M.: Jacek Zdzienicki
Shop Mgr.: Eric Zuber
Cust. Rel.: Janine Luciano
Number Employees: 5-9
Square Footage: 16000
Regions Exported to: South America, Europe, Asia
Percentage of Business in Exporting: 10
Regions Imported from: Europe, Asia

45802 Kord Products Inc.
325B West Street #200
PO Box 265
Brantford, ON N3T 5M8
Canada
Fax: 519-753-2667 800-452-9070
www.kord.ca
Manufacturer and exporter of plastic injection molded products including blisters, clamshells and fiber protective packaging, custom molded products
President: Don Gayford
CEO: Gerry Docksteader
Research & Development: David Penkmann
Marketing Director: Jon Hensen
Plant Manager: Brock Howes
Purchasing Manager: Rachel St. Laurent
Number Employees: 200
Brands Exported: Planter's Pride, Valmark

45803 Kornylak Corp
400 Heaton St
Hamilton, OH 45011-1894   513-863-1277
Fax: 513-863-7644 800-837-5676
kornylak@kornylak.com www.kornylak.com
Manufacturer and exporter of material handling equipment including conveyors, multi-directional and plastic skate wheels and gravity controlled live storage systems
President: Thomas Kornylak
Staff, Engineering Department: Richard Kornylak
Marketing/Sales Manager: Anne McAdams
IT: Walter Stortz
walter@kornylak.com
Purchasing Director: Ginger Vizedom
Estimated Sales: $5 Million
Number Employees: 20-49
Square Footage: 400000
Brands Exported: Armorbelt; Palletflo; Transwheel; Zipflo
Regions Exported to: Central America, South America, Europe, Asia, Middle East
Percentage of Business in Exporting: 10
Regions Imported from: Asia
Percentage of Business in Importing: 5

45804 Kosto Food Products Co
1325 N Old Rand Rd
Wauconda, IL 60084-3302   847-487-2600
Fax: 847-487-2654 www.kostofoods.com
Processor and exporter of salad dressings, food colorings, pudding and ice cream mixes; importer of colorants, stabilizers, ice cream mixes, drink crystals, meat extenders and puddings
President: Donald F Colby
General Manager: Steve Colby
Sales Director: Richard Gray
Estimated Sales: $1300000
Number Employees: 10-19
Type of Packaging: Consumer, Food Service, Private Label, Bulk
Regions Exported to: Central America, South America, Europe, Asia, Middle East
Regions Imported from: Central America, South America, Asia

45805 Koza's Inc
2910 S Main St
Pearland, TX 77581-4710   281-485-1462
Fax: 281-485-8000 800-594-5555
sales@kozas.com www.kozas.com
Manufacturer and exporter of advertising novelties including caps and hats; also, custom cresting available
Owner: Joseph Koza
jek@kozas.com
Estimated Sales: $ 6 Million
Number Employees: 50-99
Square Footage: 40000
Regions Exported to: Worldwide

45806 Kozlowski Farms
5566 Hwy 116
Forestville, CA 95436-9697   707-887-1587
Fax: 707-887-9650 800-473-2767
koz@kozlowskifarms.com
www.kozlowskifarms.com
Fruit spreads; jams; mustards; preserves; chutneys; jellys; fruit butters; dessert sauces; steak and BBQ sauces; fruit vinegar; salad dressings and chipotle sauces; apples an Pinot Noir grapes.
Vice President: Carol Every
carol@kozlowskifarms.com
CEO: Perry Kozlowski
CFO: Cindy Kozlowski-Hayworth
Estimated Sales: $1,000,000
Number Employees: 20-49
Number of Brands: 1
Number of Products: 90
Square Footage: 80000
Type of Packaging: Consumer, Private Label
Brands Exported: Kozlowski Farms; Sonoma County Classics
Regions Exported to: South America, Europe, Middle East, Canada
Percentage of Business in Exporting: 2

45807 Kradjian Importing
5018 San Fernando Rd
Glendale, CA 91204
www.kraimpco.com
Feta cheese, olives, olive oil, pickles, jams, canned beans and cookies.

45808 Kraft Heinz Canada
95 Moatfield Dr.
North York, ON M3B 3L6
Canada
416-441-5000
www.kraftcanada.com
Condiments, peanut butter, salad dressings, cheeses, desserts, frozen meals, macaroni and cheese, coffee blends, drink mixes, sweeteners, BBQ sauces, and more.
President, Canada Zone: Bruno Keller
CMO: Dana Somerville
VP of Sales: Peter Hall
Estimated Sales: $3.5 Billion
Number Employees: 2,000
Number of Brands: 6
Parent Co: The Kraft Heinz Company
Type of Packaging: Consumer, Food Service
Regions Exported to: Worldwide

45809 Kraissl Co Inc
299 Williams Ave
Hackensack, NJ 07601-5289   201-342-0008
Fax: 201-342-0025 800-572-4775
kraissl@aol.com www.strainers.com
Strainers, filters, valves for pipelink service
President/CEO: Richard Michel
richard@moviesunlimited.com
Foreman: Winston Philips
Chairman of the Board: Richard Michel
Tech Sales: Bill Henderson
Office Supervisor: Barbara Punthsecca
Estimated Sales: Below $ 5,000,000
Number Employees: 50-99
Square Footage: 14000
Type of Packaging: Bulk
Regions Exported to: Worldwide
Percentage of Business in Exporting: 15

45810 Kraus & Sons
215 W 35th St
Suite 300
New York, NY 10001   212-620-0408
Fax: 212-924-4081
Manufacturer and exporter of badges, buttons, flags, banners and awnings
Owner: Paul Schneider
Estimated Sales: Below 1 Million
Number Employees: 5-9
Type of Packaging: Food Service
Regions Exported to: Europe
Percentage of Business in Exporting: 1

45811 Kreiner Imports
9934 S Wood Lane
Palos Hills, IL 60465-1469   708-598-9422
Importer of German gourmet foods
Ownr.: Martin Karpus
Number Employees: 10-19
Type of Packaging: Consumer
Brands Imported: Knorr; Maggi; Rittersport
Regions Imported from: Europe
Percentage of Business in Importing: 100

45812 Krewson Enterprises
855 Canterbury Rd
Cleveland, OH 44145-1420   440-871-8780
Fax: 440-871-5127 800-521-2282
airtools@superiorpneumatic.com
www.superiorpneumatic.com
Manufacturer and exporter of adjustable freezer and cooler alarms
President: Bradley Krewson
Contact: Walter Krewson
pshko1@aol.com
Estimated Sales: $5-10 Million
Number Employees: 5-9
Square Footage: 20000
Parent Co: Superior Pneumatic & Manufacturing
Brands Exported: Protecto-Freeze; Protecto-Temp
Regions Exported to: Worldwide
Percentage of Business in Exporting: 5

45813 Krinos Foods
1750 Bathgate Ave
Bronx, NY 10457   718-729-9000
Fax: 718-361-9725 info@krinos.com
www.krinos.com
Greek olives, sauces, salsas, and oils.
Owner: Eric Moscahlaidis
Year Founded: 1850
Estimated Sales: $304 Million
Number Employees: 100
Type of Packaging: Consumer, Food Service, Bulk
Other Locations:
Krinos Manufacturing Facility
Long Island City, NYKrinos Manufacturing FacilityToronto, Canada
Regions Exported to: Worldwide
Regions Imported from: Europe

45814 Krispy Kernels
2620 Watt Street
Quebec, QC G1P 3T5
Canada
418-658-1515
Fax: 418-657-5971 877-791-9986
www.krispykernels.com
Peanuts, popcorn, candy and dried fruits and nuts
Owner: Denis Jalbert
CEO: Pierce Rivard
Quality Control: Stephen Jackson
Marketing Director: Renee Maude Jalbert
Sales Director: Stephane Gravel
Plant Manager: Jacques Bieion
Purchasing Manager: Marc Parent
Square Footage: 200000

45815 Krispy Kist Company
120 S Halsted Street
Department R8
Chicago, IL 60661-3508   312-733-0900
Fax: 312-733-3508
Manufacturer and exporter of snack food processing machinery including extruders, fryers, kettles, coating tumblers, mixers, ovens and peanut roasters
Sales/Operations: J Geiersbach
Office Mgr.: Kevin Coster
Estimated Sales: $1-5 Million
Number Employees: 8
Square Footage: 20000
Type of Packaging: Food Service
Regions Exported to: Worldwide
Percentage of Business in Exporting: 50

45816 Kristian Regale
14 Birkmose Park Ln
Hudson, WI 54016-2286   715-386-8388
Fax: 715-386-9295 info@kristianregale.com
www.kristianregale.com

Manufacturer and Importer of Swedish nonalcoholic apple and pear sparkling ciders, there are six flavors including the following, apple,peach,pear,poegranate-apple,lingonberry-apple,black currant.
Owner: Nancy Bieraugel
CHR/CEO: Ed Doherty
CFO: Dave Baldwin
Evp: Bob Gillespie
Estimated Sales: $3.4 Million
Number Employees: 7
Type of Packaging: Consumer, Food Service
Brands Imported: Kristian Regale, Inc.
Regions Imported from: Sweden
Percentage of Business in Importing: 100

45817 Krogh Pump Co
251 W Channel Rd
Benicia, CA 94510-1129   707-747-7585
Fax: 707-747-7599   800-225-7644
Manufacturer and exporter of horizontal and vertical centrifugal pumps for abrasive, corrosive, food and sewage services
Owner: Charles O' Brian
Estimated Sales: $2.5-5 Million
Number Employees: 20-49
Square Footage: 30000
Type of Packaging: Food Service, Private Label
Regions Exported to: Europe, Asia
Percentage of Business in Exporting: 30

45818 Krones
PO Box 321801
9600 S. 58th St.
Franklin, WI 53132-6241   414-409-4000
Fax: 414-409-4100   800-752-3787
www.kronesusa.com
Food processing and packaging machinery including blenders, fillers, labelers, bottle washers and rinsers, palletizers, depalletizers, pasteurizers, etc.
CEO: Christoph Klenk
CFO: Norbert Broger
Chief Sales Officer: Thomas Ricker
Year Founded: 1951
Estimated Sales: $4.1 Billion
Number Employees: 15,299
Square Footage: 232000
Parent Co: Krones AG
Regions Exported to: Central America, Canada, Mexico

45819 Krowne Metal Corp
100 Haul Rd
Wayne, NJ 07470-6616   973-305-3300
Fax: 973-872-1129   800-631-0442
customerservice@krowne.com   www.krowne.com
Manufacturer and exporter of bar equipment, hand sinks and faucets
Vice President: James Angood
james.angood@krowne.com
Exec. V.P.: Roger Forman
Vice President: James Angood
james.angood@krowne.com
Estimated Sales: $ 5-10,000,000
Number Employees: 10-19
Square Footage: 160000
Regions Exported to: Worldwide
Percentage of Business in Exporting: 15

45820 Krueger International Holding
1330 Bellevue St.
Green Bay, WI 54302
800-424-2432
info@ki.com
Tables, stools and chairs.
Chairman/CEO: Richard Resch
President: Brian Krenke
Year Founded: 1941
Estimated Sales: $650 Million
Number Employees: 3,000+
Square Footage: 250000
Regions Exported to: Worldwide

45821 Kruger Foods
18362 E Highway 4
Stockton, CA 95215-9323   209-941-8510
www.krugerfoods.com
Processor and exporter of condiments including relish, pickles, peppers and sauerkraut.
Chief Executive Officer: Kara Kruger
Contact: Jessica Altamirano
j.altamirano@krugerfoods.com
Director, Operations: Erik Kruger
Director, Technical Services: Christine Ramsey
Year Founded: 1930
Estimated Sales: $22 Million
Number Employees: 100
Square Footage: 120000
Type of Packaging: Consumer, Food Service, Bulk
Regions Exported to: Central America, Asia, Middle East

45822 Kubla Khan Food Company
3369 SE Raymond Street
Portland, OR 97202-4360   503-234-7494
Fax: 503-234-7716
Frozen fruits and vegetables
President: Percy Loy
Estimated Sales: $470,000
Number Employees: 5
Type of Packaging: Food Service, Bulk
Brands Exported: Kubla Khan
Regions Exported to: Asia
Percentage of Business in Exporting: 5
Brands Imported: Kubla Khan And Packers
Regions Imported from: Asia
Percentage of Business in Importing: 75

45823 Kuepper Favor Company, Celebrate Line
P.O.Box 428
Peru, IN 46970-0428   765-473-5586
Fax: 765-472-7247   800-321-5823
www.partydirect.com
Manufacturer and importer of paper party favors, favor goodie bags, custom imprinted lite-up favors and novelties.
President: Mike Kuepper
VP: Douglas Kuepper
Head Of Marketing Department: Jane Grund
Contact: Michael Keeper
mike@partydirect.com
Number Employees: 50-99
Type of Packaging: Consumer, Private Label, Bulk
Regions Exported to: Canada, Caribbean, Mexico
Percentage of Business in Exporting: 10

45824 Kuest Enterprise
PO Box 110
Filer, ID 83328-0110   208-326-4084
Fax: 208-326-6604
goldengraingrinder@hotmail.com
Manufacturer and exporter of grain grinders
Founder: Johnnie Kuest
Estimated Sales: $ 500,000 - $ 1 Million
Number Employees: 1-4

45825 Kuhl Corporation
39 Kuhl Rd
PO Box 26
Flemington, NJ 8822   908-782-5696
Fax: 908-782-2751   khk@kuhlcorp.com
www.kuhlcorp.com
Industrial washing machines for the food industry
President: Henry Kuhl
CEO: Kevin Kuhl
CFO: Rick Kuhl
Marketing/Public Relations: Michael Vella
Contact: Paul Chou
pchou@kuhlcorp.com
Operations Manager: John Pichell
Plant Manager: Al Fisher
Estimated Sales: $12 Million
Number Employees: 70
Square Footage: 40000
Regions Exported to: Central America, South America, Europe, Asia
Percentage of Business in Exporting: 50

45826 Kuhlmann's Market Gardens & Greenhouses
1320-167 Avenue NW
Edmonton, AB T5Y 6L6
Canada   780-475-7500
Fax: 780-472-9923   info@kuhlmanns.com
www.kuhlmanns.com
Processor, exporter and packer of cabbage, carrots, broccoli, peas and potatoes
Pres.: Dietrich Kuhlmann
Estimated Sales: C
Number Employees: 20-49
Type of Packaging: Consumer, Food Service
Regions Exported to: Japan,USA
Percentage of Business in Exporting: 5

45827 Kullman Industries
1 Kullman Corporate Campus Dr
Lebanon, NJ 08833-2163   908-236-0220
Fax: 908-236-0848
CEO: Avi Telyas
Contact: Nalini Bora
nbora@uams.edu
Estimated Sales: $ 20 - 50 Million
Number Employees: 5-9

45828 Kurtz Orchards Farms
16006 Niagra River Parkway
PO Box 457
Niagra-on-the-Lake, ON L0S 1J0
Canada   905-468-2937
info@kurtzorchards.com
www.kurtzorchards.com
Jams, jellies, fruit butters, fruit sauces, honey butters, and wine jellies.
Pres.: Wilf Kurtz
CEO: Brad Kurtz
VP: Brad Kurtz
Plant Manager: Darren Hedges
Number Employees: 18
Number of Brands: 3
Brands Exported: Black Cat; Superior, Kurtz
Regions Exported to: USA
Percentage of Business in Exporting: 50
Regions Imported from: Central America, South America
Percentage of Business in Importing: 50

45829 Kusel Equipment Company
PO Box 87
Watertown, WI 53094-0087   920-261-4112
Fax: 920-261-3151   sales@kuselequipment.com
www.kuselequipment.com
Manufactures stainless steel drainage systems and cheese equipment.
President: Dave Smith
Contact: Clark Derleth
cderleth@kuselequipment.com
Estimated Sales: $10 Million
Number Employees: 1-4

45830 Kusha Inc.
11130 Warland Drive
Cypress, CA 90630   949-930-1400
Fax: 949-250-1520   800-550-7423
Rice, basmati, jasmine, tea, grape seed oil, cheese
Vice President: Jerry Taylor
Contact: Mukesh Agrawal
mukesh@ltfoodsamericas.com
Estimated Sales: Under $500,000
Number Employees: 30
Type of Packaging: Consumer, Food Service, Private Label, Bulk
Regions Imported from: Middle East

45831 Kwikprint ManufacturingInc
4868 Victor St
Jacksonville, FL 32207-1702   904-737-3755
Fax: 904-730-0349   800-940-5945
www.kwik-print.com
Manufacturer and exporter of foil, gold and hot stamping equipment; also, custom stamping dies and foils; wholesaler/distributor of advertising specialties and promotional items
Owner: Mike Bulger
mbulger@kwik-print.com
V.P.: Lynn Cann
Estimated Sales: Below $ 5 Million
Number Employees: 5-9
Square Footage: 48000
Type of Packaging: Food Service, Private Label, Bulk
Brands Exported: Kwikprint
Regions Exported to: Worldwide
Percentage of Business in Exporting: 5

45832 Kwok Shing Hong
1818 Harrison St
San Francisco, CA 94103-4228   415-861-1920
Fax: 415-861-1524   800-326-1668
Importer and exporter of Chinese herbs
Owner: David Cheung
Estimated Sales: $10-20 Million
Number Employees: 20-49
Regions Imported from: China

Importers & Exporters / A-Z

45833 Kyowa Hakko
600 Third Avenue
19th Floor
New York, NY 10017-9023   212-319-5353
Fax: 212-421-1283   800-596-9252
info@kyowa-usa.com www.kyowa-usa.com
Amino, nuclei and organic acids; exporter of food ingredients
President & CEO: Leo Cullen
VP Sales: D Christopher Nolte
Contact: Maurice Kirch
kirch@kyowa-usa.com
Estimated Sales: $ 20-50 Million
Number Employees: 10-19
Parent Co: Kyowa Hakko Kogyo Company
Regions Exported to: Asia
Percentage of Business in Exporting: 5
Brands Imported: Aromild
Regions Imported from: Asia
Percentage of Business in Importing: 30

45834 Kysor Panel Systems
4201 N Beach St
Fort Worth, TX 76137   817-230-8703
Fax: 817-281-5521   800-633-3426
jburke@kysorpanel.com
Manufacturer and exporter of refrigerated walk-in coolers
President: David Frase
Quotations: Gary Holloway
Contact: Shannon Barnes
sbarnes@fidelitylifeandhealth.com
Estimated Sales: $20-50 Million
Number Employees: 100-249
Square Footage: 300000
Parent Co: Scotsman Industries
Other Locations:
  Kysor Panel Systems
  Goodyear, AZKysor Panel Systems
Brands Exported: Kysor/Neeedham
Regions Exported to: Central America, South America, Asia, Middle East
Percentage of Business in Exporting: 10

45835 L & N Label Co
2051 Sunnydale Blvd
Clearwater, FL 33765-1202   727-442-5400
Fax: 727-442-8915   800-944-5401
customerservice@lnlabel.com www.lnlabel.com
Manufacturer and exporter of die cut pressure sensitive labels; blank and printed types and roll, sheet, long and short runs available. Four color process labels, up to 8 colors.
President: Steve Sabadosh
artdepartment@lnlabel.com
Vice President: Julee Sabadosh
Sales Director: Reyna Martin
IT Executive: John Brand
Production Manager: Curtis Booth
Plant Manager: Dave Gioia
Estimated Sales: $4-5 Million
Number Employees: 20-49
Square Footage: 80000
Type of Packaging: Private Label

45836 (HQ)L & S Packing Co
101 Central Ave
Farmingdale, NY 11735-6915   631-845-1717
Fax: 631-420-7309   800-286-6487
sales@paesana.com www.paesana.com
Importer of gourmet condiments such as olives, capers, pickles, cocktail onions, mushrooms, etc.; serving food service, industrial and private label markets. Also, high quality authentic pasta sauces and Chinese sauces, see our ad onthe back cover of Vol
President: Louis Scaramelli
lou@paesana.com
Estimated Sales: $ 3 - 5 Million
Number Employees: 20-49
Type of Packaging: Consumer, Food Service, Private Label, Bulk
Other Locations:
  L&S Packing Co.
  Flushing, NYL&S Packing Co.

45837 L F Lambert Spawn Co
1507 Valley Rd
Coatesville, PA 19320   610-384-9051
Fax: 610-384-0390 www.lambertbiologicals.com
Processor and exporter of mushroom spawns
President: Hugh Mcintyre
hugh@lambertspawn.com
Owner: Rick McIntyre
VP of Operations: Joseph Mascrangelo
Estimated Sales: $3300000
Number Employees: 50-99
Regions Exported to: Europe, Asia, Middle East, Canada, Australia

45838 L G I Intl Inc
6700 SW Bradbury Ct
Portland, OR 97224-7734   503-620-0528
Fax: 503-620-3296   800-345-0534
sales.usa@lgintl.com www.lgitechnology.com
Manufacturer and exporter of pressure sensitive, front panel, bar code and clean room labels
President: Tim Hartka
tim.hartka@lionbrothers.com
International Sales: Greg Jarmin
Sales Manager: Dale Gremaux
Estimated Sales: $ 1 - 5 Million
Number Employees: 20-49
Square Footage: 172000
Regions Exported to: Europe, Asia
Percentage of Business in Exporting: 15

45839 L T Hampel Corp
W194n11551 Mccormick Dr
Germantown, WI 53022-3000   262-255-4540
Fax: 262-255-9731   800-681-6979
sales@hampelcorp.com www.hampelcorp.com
Manufacturer and exporter of plastic pallets including rugged light weight, steel reinforced, thermoformed, nestable, standard and custom interlocking sleeve pack and double decker
President: Lance Hampel
CEO: Dave Brudvig
dbrudvig@thermoformpallets.com
Estimated Sales: $ 10 - 20 Million
Number Employees: 100-249
Regions Exported to: Worldwide
Percentage of Business in Exporting: 5

45840 L&A Process Systems
1704 Reliance St
Modesto, CA 95358   209-581-0205
Fax: 209-581-0194
Manufacturer and exporter of evaporators, distilleries, rotary coil vessels for jam and jelly production, ceramic cross flow micro-filtration and essence/aroma recovery systems
CEO: Don Carter
Estimated Sales: $1-2.5 Million
Number Employees: 5-9
Regions Exported to: Central America, South America, Asia, Canada, Mexico
Percentage of Business in Exporting: 10

45841 L&C Fisheries
French River
RR #2
Kensington, PE C0B 1MO
Canada
    902-886-2770
Fax: 902-886-3003
calvin@greengablesmussels.com
www.greengablesmussels.com
Fresh mussels, oysters, and fresh and frozen lobsters
Owner: Calvin Jollimore
Number Employees: 10-19
Type of Packaging: Consumer, Food Service
Regions Exported to: USA
Percentage of Business in Exporting: 50

45842 L. Cherrick Horseradish Company
2020 N 9th St
Saint Louis, MO 63102   314-421-5431
Fax: 314-421-3277
Wholesaler/distributor and exporter of horseradish
Co-Owner: Vernon Bruns
Co-Owner: Elaine Bruns
Estimated Sales: $2.5-5 Million
Number Employees: 1-4
Type of Packaging: Consumer, Bulk
Regions Exported to: Canada
Percentage of Business in Exporting: 2

45843 L. Della Cella Company
PO Box 8133
Garden City, NY 11530-8133   516-746-6400
Fax: 516-746-5828
Importer of Italian and Spanish foods including cheeses, olives, canned and fresh vegetables, olive oils and pastas
President: Peter Cannizzaro
Estimated Sales: $1-2.5 Million
Number Employees: 1-4
Square Footage: 4000
Type of Packaging: Consumer, Food Service, Private Label, Bulk
Brands Imported: Cantarelli; Prieto; Riscossa; Anjani
Regions Imported from: Italy, Spain

45844 L.C. Thompson Company
1303 43rd St.
Kenosha, WI 53140   262-652-3662
Fax: 262-652-3526   800-558-4018
www.lcthomsen.com
Manufacturer, importer and exporter of dairy processing machinery including control systems, filters, gaskets, hoses, pumps, strainers, thermometers, tubing and valves
President: Wayne Borne
Sls. Mgr.: Mike Dyutka
Service Manager: Mike Dyutka
Sales: Joyce Saftig
Contact: Hose Hooks
hhooks@lcthomsen.com
Number Employees: 20-49
Square Footage: 48000
Regions Exported to: Worldwide
Percentage of Business in Exporting: 20
Regions Imported from: Europe, Asia
Percentage of Business in Importing: 5

45845 L.J. Rench & Company
26 Pine St
Dover, DE 19901   302-736-6781
Fax: 302-736-6763
Importer of gourmet foods, frozen fish, game and sauces,bonsai
CEO: Leroy Rench
Number Employees: 10-19
Square Footage: 100000
Type of Packaging: Consumer, Food Service

45846 L.N. White & Company
225 W 34th St # 1313
New York, NY 10122-1313   212-239-7474
Fax: 212-563-5389
Importer of frozen seafood including shrimp, scallops, frog legs and lobster tails
President: David White
VP: Abe Moskowitz
Estimated Sales: $10-20 Million
Number Employees: 1-4
Square Footage: 9000
Regions Imported from: Central America, South America, Europe, Asia
Percentage of Business in Importing: 100

45847 L.T. Overseas
1059 King Georges Post # 101
Edison, NJ 08837-3582   732-661-1030
Fax: 732-661-1034   877-322-9281
Importer of basmati rice and mushrooms
Owner: Sandip Patel
VP Sales: Sandip Patel
Estimated Sales: $2.5-5 Million
Number Employees: 5-9
Type of Packaging: Consumer, Food Service, Bulk
Brands Imported: Daawat; Sona Chandi
Regions Imported from: India

45848 (HQ)LA Cena Fine Foods LTD
4 Rosol Ln
Saddle Brook, NJ 07663-5522   201-797-4600
Fax: 201-797-6988 v.piigjr@lacenafoods.com
Ethnic food distributor (Spanish), Food importer and distributors to supermarket chains.
Owner: Antonio Argueta
VP/Co-Owner: Vincent Puig Jr
Marketing Director: Marcela Carlin
Sales: Jose Badia
a.argueta@lacenafoods.com
Purchasing: Maria Jose Alvarez
Number Employees: 20-49
Brands Exported: Casa Real - Victorina
Percentage of Business in Exporting: 15
Brands Imported: La Cena; Palacio Real; Bajamar; Casa Real; Victorina; Gran Colombiana; Tiegerbrao
Regions Imported from: Central America, South America, Europe, Middle East
Percentage of Business in Importing: 50

Importers & Exporters / A-Z

45849 LA Marche Mfg Co
106 Bradrock Dr
Des Plaines, IL 60018-1967   847-299-1193
Fax: 847-299-3061 www.lamarchemfg.com
Manufacturer and exporter of battery chargers for forklift trucks and vehicles
President: Stan Burg
agalvan@conversantmedia.com
EVP: Raj Dhiman
CFO: Rick Rutkowski
Vice President: J. Vargas
Research & Development: Vance Pearson
Quality Control Manager: Bob Brewer
Marketing Director: S. Burg
Sales Director: John Pawula
Customer Service Manager: Lacy Zyrkowski
agalvan@conversantmedia.com
Director Purchasing: Bob Lewinski
Estimated Sales: $ 10-20 Million
Number Employees: 100-249
Square Footage: 170000
Regions Exported to: Worldwide
Percentage of Business in Exporting: 15

45850 LA Mexicana Tortilleria
2703 S Kedzie Ave
Chicago, IL 60623-4735   773-247-5443
Fax: 773-247-9004
Tortillas and corn chips
President: Rodolfo Guerrero
Estimated Sales: $4600000
Number Employees: 20-49
Type of Packaging: Consumer

45851 LA Monica Fine Foods
PO Box 309
Millville, NJ 08332
info@lamonicafinefoods.com
www.lamonicafinefoods.com
Surf clams and ocean clams from US certified waters, serving the fresh, canned and frozen markets.
Founder: Peter LaMonica
Number Employees: 20-49
Square Footage: 360000
Type of Packaging: Consumer, Food Service, Private Label, Bulk
Brands Exported: LaMonica, Cape May
Regions Exported to: Central America, South America, Europe, Asia
Percentage of Business in Exporting: 10

45852 LA Torilla Factory
3300 Westwind Blvd
Santa Rosa, CA 95403-8273   707-586-4000
Fax: 707-586-4017 800-446-1516
info@latortillafactory.com
www.latortillafactory.com
Corn and flour tortillas and tortilla chips and masa
President: Carlos Tamayo
Owner/President/VP Sales/Marketing: Sam Tamayo
CFO: Stan Mead
R&D Manager: Luz Ana Osbun
Executive Director Sales/Marketing: Jan Remak
Human Resources Manager: Jonna Green
COO/VP/Plant Manager: Sam Tamayo
Estimated Sales: $8000000
Number Employees: 250-499
Square Footage: 18100
Type of Packaging: Consumer, Food Service, Private Label, Bulk

45853 LA Wholesale Produce Market
1601 E Olympic Boulevard
Los Angeles, CA 90021
Fax: 213-622-7075 888-454-6887
admin@lanuthouse.com www.lanuthouse.com
Manufacturer, importer and exporter of tree nuts and peanuts; also, processor of peanut butter and manufactured and coated materials
Estimated Sales: $ 3 - 5 Million
Number Employees: 5-9
Square Footage: 88000
Parent Co: Morven Partners
Type of Packaging: Consumer, Food Service, Private Label, Bulk
Regions Imported from: South America

45854 LB Furniture Industries
99 S 3rd St
Hudson, NY 12534   518-828-1501
Fax: 518-828-3219 800-221-8752
sales@lbfurnitureind.com
Manufacturer and exporter of tables, chairs and booths
President: Les Lak
Contact: Penny Abell
penny@lbfurnitureind.com
Estimated Sales: $1-2.5 Million
Number Employees: 10-19
Square Footage: 650000

45855 LBB Imports
2015 S Acacia Court
Rancho Dominquez, CA 90220   310-761-9565
Fax: 310-761-9566 sales@lbbimports.com
www.lbbimports.com
Specialty foods
Contact: Andrew Dulley
andrewdulley@lbbimports.com
Estimated Sales: $1.6 Million
Number Employees: 13

45856 LBP Manufacturing LLC
1325 S Cicero Ave
Cicero, IL 60804-1404   708-652-5600
Fax: 708-652-5537 sales@lbpmfg.com
www.lbpmfg.com
Manufacturer and exporter of hot cup sleeves, take-out containers and acrylic displays and dispensers
President: Barry Silverstein
Pricing Manager: Mary Lou Medina
CFO: Mike Schaechter
VP: Matthew Cook
R&D and QC: Barry M
Estimated Sales: $ 10 - 20 Million
Number Employees: 500-999
Parent Co: Terrace Paper Company
Brands Exported: Coffee Clutch; Coffee on the Move; Safepak
Regions Exported to: Europe, Canada, Mexico

45857 LDI Manufacturing Co
417 North St # 104
Logansport, IN 46947-2775   574-722-3124
Fax: 574-722-7213 800-366-2001
www.ldi-industries.com/LDI.htm
Manufacturer and exporter of exhaust ventilation equipment including commercial exhaust hoods and fans. Distribution of complete, pre-engineered heating and air conditioning equipment system. Custom stainless steel and metal fabrication. Indoor environment air quality equipment systems
Manager: Susan Begley
susan@ldimfg.com
VP Finance: Camille Hall
Marketing Director: Susan Erny
VP Customer Services: Susan Erny
Estimated Sales: $5-10 Million
Number Employees: 5-9
Square Footage: 100000
Type of Packaging: Food Service
Brands Exported: Greese Gobler
Regions Exported to: Canada

45858 LE VILLAGE.COM
1301 6th Street
Building F
San Francisco, CA 94107-0000
Fax: 415-861-2197 888-873-7194
www.levillage.com
Distributors of specialty foods and wines/beverages from Europe
President/CEO: Hugues De Vernon
CFO: Kerry Baer
Vice President: Daniel Nollinger
Sales Director: Patrick Maury
Contact: Julia Machotka
j@ideablast.com
Parent Co: MIF San Francisco
Type of Packaging: Consumer, Food Service, Bulk
Brands Imported: Le Village; Fallot; Vilux; Valrhona; Agrimontana; Fini; Galvanina; Le Petit Marseillais

45859 LEESON Electric Corp
1051 Cheyenne Ave
Grafton, WI 53024-9541   262-377-8810
Fax: 262-377-9025 www.leeson.com
Manufacturer and exporter of electric motors, gears and drives for food processing machinery.
CEO: Henry Knueppel
CFO: Dave Barta
VP: Bud Pritchard
Marketing: Philippe De Gail
Sales: Steve Weber
COO: Mark Gliebe
Number Employees: 500-999
Brands Exported: Leeson; Speedmaster; Washguard
Regions Exported to: Worldwide
Percentage of Business in Exporting: 15

45860 LEF McLean Brothers International
PO Box 128
20 Erie St South
Wheatley, ON N0P 2P0
Canada   519-825-4656
Fax: 519-825-7374
Processor and exporter of fresh and frozen lake fish and seafood
President: Robert Ricci
VP Business Development: Danny Ricci
Type of Packaging: Consumer, Food Service, Private Label, Bulk
Regions Exported to: Europe, U.S.A.
Percentage of Business in Exporting: 70

45861 LFI Inc
271 US Highway 46 # C101
Fairfield, NJ 07004-2495   973-882-0550
Fax: 973-882-0554 lfiinc@aol.com
www.lfiincorporated.com
Imported foods
Owner: Anthony Lisanti
lfiantonio@aol.com
Marketing Director: Danielle Iannacconi
Public Relations: Carol Lisanti
Estimated Sales: Below $ 5 000,000
Number Employees: 5-9
Type of Packaging: Private Label

45862 LLJ's Sea Products
PO Box 296
Round Pond, ME 04564-0296   207-529-4224
Fax: 207-529-4223
Canned and cured fish and seafood.
Owner: Stephen J Brackett
Estimated Sales: $3,000,000
Number Employees: 5-9

45863 LMC International
893 N Industrial Dr
Elmhurst, IL 60126   630-834-7789
Fax: 630-834-4322 info@Latiniusa.com
www.lmcinternational.com
Equipment for the confectionery and bakery industries
Sales/Marketing: Pat Kiel
Sales Director: Roger Hohberger
Sales: Daniel Herman
Estimated Sales: $15 000,000
Number Employees: 50
Number of Brands: 2
Number of Products: 50
Square Footage: 30000

45864 LMG Group
792 NW 12th Street
Suite 121
Miami, FL 33136-2351   305-477-9057
Fax: 305-477-9146
Wholesaler/distributor and exporter of food service equipment including, washers, dryers, ice makers, etc.; serving the food service market
President: Christian Lugo
General Manager: Jenny Gomez
VP: Hector McDougall
Number Employees: 20-49
Parent Co: Grupo Institucional Del Caribe, S.A.
Type of Packaging: Food Service
Regions Exported to: Central America, Caribbean

45865 LMK Containers
PO Box 1001
Centerville, UT 84014-5001   626-821-9984
Manufacturer, importer and exporter of glass and plastic bottles, jars, caps and containers
Purchasing Director: Robert Frome
Type of Packaging: Consumer, Food Service, Private Label, Bulk
Regions Exported to: South America, Asia
Regions Imported from: Central America, South America, Asia

45866 LPI Information Systems
10020 Fontana Ln
Overland Park, KS 66207-3640   913-381-9118
Fax: 913-381-9118 888-729-2020
www.datasmithpayroll.com

Manufacturer and exporter of payroll software and tax forms
President: David Land
landlines@datasmithpayroll.com
Number Employees: 20-49
Regions Exported to: Canada
Percentage of Business in Exporting: 15

45867 LPS Technology
1009 McAlpin Court
Grafton, OH 44044-1322   440-355-6992
   Fax: 440-355-6998   800-586-1410
Manufacturer and exporter of washers, ovens, compressed air systems, conveyors and air vacuums
President: Dean Burke
General Manager: Dave Bobak
Estimated Sales: $1-2,500,000
Number Employees: 10-19
Parent Co: Eton Fab Company
Regions Exported to: Worldwide

45868 LT Foods Americas
11130 Warland Dr
Cypress, CA 90630
   800-550-7423
   www.ltfoodsglobal.com
Rice
Chairman & Managing Director: Vijay Arora

45869 LTI Printing Inc
518 N Centerville Rd
Sturgis, MI 49091-9601   269-651-7574
   Fax: 269-651-3262   www.ltiprinting.com
Manufacturer and exporter of labels and offset cartons
President: Don Frost
dfrost@ltiprinting.com
Estimated Sales: $20-50 Million
Number Employees: 50-99
Type of Packaging: Consumer, Food Service, Bulk
Regions Exported to: Canada

45870 (HQ)La Belle Suisse Corporation
PO Box 6013
San Antonio, TX 78209-0013   210-820-3544
   Fax: 210-829-8013
Importer of pate, cookies, candies, chocolates, air-dried beef, ham, filled wafer rolls, mustard, pasta, etc.; exporter of mustard, ketchup, pate, mayonnaise, juices, coffee, oils and kosher products
President: Edouard Musy
Type of Packaging: Consumer, Food Service, Bulk
Brands Exported: Le Parfait; Thomy
Regions Exported to: Central America, South America, Europe, Middle East, Canada, Mexico
Percentage of Business in Exporting: 80
Brands Imported: Le Parfait; Thomy; Swissflcr; Frutti; Hilcona; Suttero; Trias
Regions Imported from: South America, Europe, Mexico

45871 La Brasserie McAuslan Brewing
5080 St-Ambroise
Montreal, QC H4C 2G1
Canada   514-939-3060
   Fax: 514-939-2541   info@mcauslan.com
   www.mcauslan.com
Processor and exporter of beer and ale including stout
President: Peter McAuslan
Master Brewer and VP, Production: Ellen Bounsall
Number Employees: 100-249
Type of Packaging: Consumer, Food Service
Regions Exported to: Europe, USA
Percentage of Business in Exporting: 15

45872 La Crosse
W6636 L B White Rd
Onalaska, WI 54650   608-783-2800
   Fax: 608-783-6115   800-345-0018
   mail@lacrossecooler.com
   www.hospitalityinternational.com
Manufacturer and exporter of underbar items including sinks, drain boards, ice chests, cocktail stations and storage units; also, portable bars
CEO: Tony Wilson
CFO: Jack Lauer
Vice President of Development: Ron Provus
Marketing Director: Bridget Crave
Sales Director: Della Indahl
Estimated Sales: $ 50 - 100 Million
Number Employees: 100-249
Parent Co: Hospitality International

Regions Exported to: Central America, South America, Europe, Asia, Canada, Korea

45873 La Flor Spices
25 Hoffman Avenue
Hauppauge, NY 11788-4717   631-885-9601
   Fax: 631-851-9606
Manufacturer, importer, exporter and contract packager of spices, herbs, blends, seasonings and ground peppers
President: Ruben La Torre
VP: Dan La Torre
Sales/Distribution Manager: Ruben La Torre
Estimated Sales: $5 Million
Number Employees: 45
Square Footage: 124000
Type of Packaging: Private Label
Brands Exported: La Flor
Regions Exported to: Central America, South America, Europe, Asia, Middle East
Brands Imported: La Flor
Regions Imported from: Central America, South America, Europe, Asia, Middle East
Percentage of Business in Importing: 40

45874 La Have Seafoods
3371 Hwy 331
La Have, NS B0R 1C0
Canada   902-688-2773
   Fax: 902-688-2766   lahaveseafoods@eastlink.ca
Processor and exporter of fresh and salted fish including pollack, cod, haddock and scallops
President: Dave Himmelman
Estimated Sales: $6.2 Million
Number Employees: 45
Type of Packaging: Bulk
Regions Exported to: U.S. , Jamaica
Percentage of Business in Exporting: 100

45875 La Piccolina
1075 N Hills Drive
Decatur, GA 30033-4220   406-636-1909
   Fax: 404-296-2008   800-626-1624
Processor and exporter of breadsticks, dips, biscotti, gourmet coffee, cranberry pecan bread, pasta, pasta sauces, olive oil, etc.
President: Olympia Manning
VP: Denise Walsh-Bandini
National Sales Manager: Denise Walsh-Bandini
Estimated Sales: $270,000
Number Employees: 5
Square Footage: 14400

45876 La Pine Scientific Company
PO Box 780
Blue Island, IL 60406-0780   708-388-4030
   Fax: 708-388-4084   800-205-6303
Wholesaler/distributor, importer and exporter of laboratory supplies
President/Treasurer: Robert La Pine
Estimated Sales: $970,000
Number Employees: 5-9
Square Footage: 44000
Regions Exported to: Europe
Regions Imported from: Europe

45877 La Rustichella Truffles
3718 Northern Blvd
Long Island City, NY 11101-1631   347-320-4572
   www.larustichellatruffles.com
Truffles, pat,, honey, mushrooms, artichokes, cheese, olive oil and balsamic vinegar.
Owner: Francesca Brugnoli

45878 La Societe
1415 Rue De La Montagne
Montreal, QC H3G 1Z3
Canada   514-507-9223
   Fax: 514-325-6398   www.lasociete.ca
Processor and exporter of aroma coffee; importer of green coffee beans and cocoa; custom blending available
President: M Claude Parent
Sales/Marketing Executive: Andre Richer
Purchasing Agent: Linda McGail
Number Employees: 12
Square Footage: 24000
Type of Packaging: Consumer, Food Service, Private Label, Bulk
Brands Exported: Aroma; Altima; Bourbon Excelso
Regions Exported to: USA
Percentage of Business in Exporting: 15
Regions Imported from: Asia

45879 LaCrosse Milling Company
105 Highway 35
P.O.Box 86
Cochrane, WI 54622-0086   608-248-2222
   Fax: 608-248-2221   800-441-5411
   jbackus@lacrossemilling.com
   www.lacrossemilling.com
Oatmeal and rolled oat flakes; exporter of milled oat products
President: Dan Ward
Vice President, Sales: Glenn Hartzell
Plant Manager: Bill Brueger
Estimated Sales: $ 10 - 20 Million
Number Employees: 60
Number of Products: 50
Type of Packaging: Food Service, Private Label, Bulk
Regions Exported to: Mexico
Percentage of Business in Exporting: 2

45880 LaCrosse Safety and Industrial
18550 NE Riverside Parkway
Portland, OR 97230-4975   503-766-1010
   Fax: 800-558-0188   800-557-7246
Manufacturer and importer of waterproof protective clothing and footwear including vulcanized double coated rubber aprons
President: John McGinnis
Manager: Tammy Woolrage
Sales Director: Ken Furtech
Contact: John Mcginnis
jmcginnis@lacrossefootwear.com
Number Employees: 100-249
Number of Products: 600
Parent Co: Standalone
Regions Imported from: Asia

45881 Labatt Brewing Company
207 Queen's Quay W.
Suite 299
Toronto, ON M5J 1A7
Canada   416-361-5050
   Fax: 416-361-5200   800-268-2337
   www.labatt.com
Beer.
President, Labatt Canada: Kyle Norrington
VP, Legal & Corproate Affairs: Charlie Angelakos
Director, Marketing: Andrew Oosterhuis
Year Founded: 1847
Estimated Sales: $296.58 Million
Number Employees: 3,400
Number of Brands: 60
Number of Products: 60
Square Footage: 88587
Parent Co: AB InBev
Type of Packaging: Consumer, Food Service
Brands Exported: Ozujsko Pivo, Lowenbrau, Bass, Boddingtons, Staropramen, Leffe Blond, Leffe Brun, Hoegaarden, Brahma, Beck's, Bud Light, Stella Artois, Budweiser, Corona
Regions Exported to: South America, Europe, United Kingdom

45882 Labconco Corp
8811 Prospect Ave
Kansas City, MO 64132-2696   816-333-8811
   Fax: 816-363-0130   800-821-5525
   labconco@labconco.com   www.labconco.com
Manufacturer and exporter of scientific laboratory equipment and apparatus including chloride instruments, Kjeldahl nitrogen determination apparatus and fat and fiber apparatus
President: Stephen Gound
stephengound@labconco.com
Executive VP: Mark Weber
VP Marketing: Debbie Kenny
National Sales Manager: Tom Schwaller
Estimated Sales: $30 Million
Number Employees: 100-249
Regions Exported to: Worldwide
Percentage of Business in Exporting: 20

45883 Label Art
2278 Brockett Rd
Tucker, GA 30084   770-939-6960
   Fax: 770-939-6960   800-652-1072
Manufacturer and exporter of grocery shelf marking products, warehouse picking labels and continuous and sheet fed laser printer products
National Sales Manager: Deborah Goss
Sales Representative: Lisa Wood
Estimated Sales: $20-50 Million
Number Employees: 100-249
Square Footage: 30000

Importers & Exporters / A-Z

45884 Label Makers
8911 102nd St
Pleasant Prairie, WI 53158-2212 262-947-3300
Fax: 262-947-3301 800-208-3331
www.lmipackaging.com
Manufacturer and exporter of heat seal lidding, flexible packaging solutions, daisychain, rollstock & die cut lidding
Owner: Virginia Moran
CEO: Jean Moran
Vice President of Business Development: Randall Troutman
VP Research & Development: Mike Gorzynski
Director of Marketing: Lea Connelly
National Accounts Manager: Gary Morrison
VP Operations: Vince Incandela
Number Employees: 20-49

45885 Label Specialties Inc
704 Dunn Way
Placentia, CA 92870-6805 714-961-8074
Fax: 714-961-8276 800-635-2386
www.labelspec.com
Labels including scale printer, ingredient printer, bar code, plain, pressure sensitive, stock and custom; also, transfer ribbons
Owner: Micheal Gyure
VP: Thomas Wetterhus
Manager: Maria Arellano
marellano@labelspec.com
Estimated Sales: $1-2.5 Million
Number Employees: 10-19
Square Footage: 18000
Percentage of Business in Exporting: 2

45886 Label Systems
1150 Kerrisdale Blvd.
Unit 2
Newmarket, ON L3Y 8Z9
Canada 905-836-7844
Fax: 905-853-9357 m.kirby@label-systems.com
www.label-systems.com
Manufacturer and exporter of pressure sensitive label machinery and equipment.
Sales Director: Matthew Kirby
Number Employees: 5
Square Footage: 44000
Regions Exported to: Central America, South America, USA, Caribbean
Percentage of Business in Exporting: 50

45887 Label-Aire Inc
550 Burning Tree Rd
Fullerton, CA 92833-1449 714-441-0700
Fax: 714-526-0300 info@label-aire.com
www.label-aire.com
Manufacturer and exporter of pressure-sensitive label applicators and rotary and incline systems
President: George Allen
gallen@label-aire.com
Marketing Manager: William Claproth
Sales: Steve Winders
Operations: Gene Bukovi
Estimated Sales: $20-50 Million
Number Employees: 100-249
Square Footage: 60000
Parent Co: Impaxx
Type of Packaging: Consumer, Food Service, Private Label, Bulk

45888 Labelette Company
1237 Circle Avenue
Forest Park, IL 60130-2416 708-366-2010
Fax: 708-366-0226 sales@labelette.com
www.labelette.com
Manufacturer and exporter of semi-automatic and automatic labeling machinery
Estimated Sales: $5-10 Million
Number Employees: 20-49
Square Footage: 40000
Regions Exported to: Central America, Europe, Canada
Percentage of Business in Exporting: 20

45889 Labelquest Inc
493 W Fullerton Ave
Elmhurst, IL 60126-1404 630-833-9400
Fax: 630-833-9421 800-999-5301
gary@labelquest.net www.labelquest.com
Manufacturer and exporter of labels, decals and heat transfers
President: Pat Vandenberg
Sales Manager: Neil Vandenberg

Estimated Sales: $2.5-5 Million
Number Employees: 50-99
Square Footage: 10000
Regions Exported to: Europe, Canada, Latin America
Percentage of Business in Exporting: 20

45890 Laboratory Devices
PO Box 6402
Holliston, MA 01746-6402 508-429-1716
Fax: 508-429-6583
Manufacturer and exporter of laboratory instruments
Estimated Sales: $1-5 Million
Number Employees: 5
Regions Exported to: Worldwide

45891 Lacollina Toscana Inc
7 W 34th St
Suite 715
New York, NY 10001-8100 212-686-5050
Fax: 212-686-6427 lacollina1@aol.com
www.lacollinatoscanausa.com
Antipasto, oil & vinegar, pasta, preserves & honey, pasta sauces, salit & spices
CEO: Victor Setton
Number Employees: 1-4

45892 Lactalis American Group Inc
2376 S Park Ave
Buffalo, NY 14220
877-522-8254
www.lactalisamericangroup.com
Processor, exporter and importer of cheeses including Brie, Swiss, Roquefort, feta, edam, Gouda, mozzarella, ricotta, fontina, Asiago, shredded/grated, Parmesan and romano, as well as snack and spreadable cheese.
CEO: Thierry Clement
SVP & Chief Legal Officer: Pierre Lorieau
Marketing Director: Karine Blake
VP of Sales: Yann Connan
Year Founded: 1992
Estimated Sales: $415 Million
Number Employees: 1,600
Number of Brands: 10
Square Footage: 16231
Parent Co: Groupe Lactalis
Type of Packaging: Consumer, Food Service, Private Label
Regions Exported to: Central America, South America, Asia
Percentage of Business in Exporting: 25
Regions Imported from: Europe, Asia
Percentage of Business in Importing: 90

45893 Ladder Works
1125 E Saint Charles Rd
Lombard, IL 60148-2085 630-629-7154
Fax: 630-268-9655 800-419-5880
Manufacturer and exporter of flag poles and flags
Owner: Ed Reeder
Inside Sales Manager: Lisa Simpson
Estimated Sales: $10-20,000,000
Number Employees: 20-49
Parent Co: Uncommon USA
Regions Exported to: Worldwide
Percentage of Business in Exporting: 15

45894 Laetitia Vineyard & Winery
453 Laetitia Vineyard Dr
Arroyo Grande, CA 93420-9701 805-481-1772
Fax: 805-481-6920 888-809-8463
info@laetitiawine.com www.laetitiawine.com
Wine
President & Head Winemaker: Eric Hickey
HR Executive: Jan Wilkinson
jan@laetitiawine.com
Marketing Coordinator: Jackie Ross
Division Sales Manager: Tabitha Alger
Operations: Dave Hickey
President & Head Winemaker: Eric Hickey
Estimated Sales: Below $5 Million
Number Employees: 50-99
Brands Exported: Barnwood; Laetitia; Avila
Regions Exported to: Europe, Asia
Percentage of Business in Exporting: 3

45895 Lagorio Enterprises
2771 E French Camp Rd
Manteca, CA 95336-9689 209-982-5691
Fax: 209-982-0235 mail@lagorio.com
www.lagorio.com
Grower, packer and exporter of fresh tomatoes
President: Ed Beckman

Estimated Sales: $5-10 Million
Number Employees: 100-249
Square Footage: 635772
Regions Exported to: Canada, Mexico

45896 Lahaha Tea Co
135 E Santa Clara St # B
Suite B
Arcadia, CA 91006-3288 626-215-6960
lahahatea@yahoo.com
Natural teas imported from China
President: Angie Lin
angielin@lahahatea.com
Number Employees: 5-9

45897 Laidig Inc
14535 Dragoon Trl
Mishawaka, IN 46544-6896 574-256-0204
Fax: 574-256-5575 sales@laidig.com
www.laidig.com
Manufacturer and exporter of bulk material steel storage structures and handling systems including conveyors
President: Wyn Laidig
sales@laidig.com
SVP: Tom J Lindenman
Vice President Marketing/Information: Daniel Laidig
Vice President Sales: Mike Laidig
VP, Manufacturing: Dan Collins
Estimated Sales: $5-10 Million
Number Employees: 50-99
Parent Co: LIS Corporation
Regions Exported to: Worldwide
Percentage of Business in Exporting: 15

45898 Laird & Company
One Laird Road
Scobeyville, NJ 07724 732-542-0312
Fax: 732-542-2244 877-438-5247
sales@lairdandcompany.com
www.lairdandcompany.com
Established in 1780. Processor of apple brandy, bourbon, vodka, gin, blended whiskey and other spirits; importer of wine and bulk alcoholic beverages; imported olive oils and balsamic vinegars.
President: Larrie Laird
EVP: John Laird III
VP: Lisa Laird Dunn
SVP of Sales/Marketing: Tom Alberico
Operations Manager: Raymond Murdock
General Manager: Lester Clements
Estimated Sales: $20-50 Million
Number Employees: 35
Number of Brands: 7
Type of Packaging: Consumer, Private Label, Bulk
Brands Exported: Laird's, Bankers Club
Regions Exported to: Worldwide
Percentage of Business in Exporting: 5
Regions Imported from: Worldwide
Percentage of Business in Importing: 5

45899 Laita
Hoboken Business Center, Suite 508 E
720 Monroe St
Hoboken, NJ 07030
www.intervalexport.com
Butter, buttermilk, crepes and cheese.
USA Branch Manager: Diane Sauvage
diane@intervalexport.com

45900 Lake City Foods
5185 General Road
Mississauga, ON L4W 2K4
Canada 905-625-8244
Fax: 905-625-8244 hello@lakecityfoods.com
www.lakecityfoods.com
Processor and exporter of drink mixes, jelly powders, soup bases and mixes, army rations, nondairy coffee creamers and camping and trail foods
Proprietor: Eyal Adda
Number Employees: 10-19
Parent Co: Eden Manufacturing Company
Type of Packaging: Consumer, Food Service, Private Label, Bulk

45901 Lake Shore Industries Inc
1817 Poplar St
Erie, PA 16502-1624 814-456-4277
Fax: 814-453-4293 800-458-0463
info@lsisigns.com www.lsisigns.com
Interior and exterior signage; exporter of signs and markers

President: Leo Bruno
info@lsisigns.com
Estimated Sales: $ 2.5 - 5 Million
Number Employees: 10-19
Square Footage: 38480
Regions Exported to: Canada
Percentage of Business in Exporting: 4

45902 Lake States Yeast
428 W Davenport St
Rhinelander, WI 54501-3325   715-369-4949
　　　Fax: 715-369-4969 lgary@lallemand.com
　　　　　　　　　　　www.lallemand.com
Manufacturer and exporter of yeasts including inactive dried, torula, autolyzed, formulated and specialty grades that inlcudes smoked, roasted, and grill flavors.
President/Manager: Antoine Chagnon
Quality Control: Joelle Provix
Customer Service Manager: Linda Gary
Plant Manager: Stuart Bacon
Production Manager: Rick Bishop
Plant Manager: Stuart Bacon
Number Employees: 5-9
Parent Co: Rhinelander Paper Company
Type of Packaging: Private Label, Bulk
Brands Exported: Lake States

45903 Lakeport Brewing Corporation
180 Henri Dunant St
Moncton, NB E1E 1E6
Canada   905-523-4200
　　　Fax: 905-523-6564   800-268-2337
Processor and exporter of beer, ale, lager and stout
President: Teresa Cascioli
Sales/Marketing Executive: Ian McDonald
Estimated Sales: F
Number Employees: 200
Type of Packaging: Consumer, Food Service
Regions Exported to: USA

45904 Lakeside Foods Inc.
1055 W. Broadway
Plainview, MN 55964   507-534-3141
　　　　　www.lakesidefoods.com
Frozen and canned vegetables, frozen appetizers and seafood, canned meats and pet food, canned beans, whipped toppings and sauces.
CEO: Glenn Tellock
Estimated Sales: $103 Million
Number Employees: 500-999
Type of Packaging: Consumer
Other Locations:
　Lakeside Foods - Manufacturing
　Manitowoc, WI
　Lakeside Foods - Manufacturing
　Belgium, WI
　Lakeside Foods - Manufacturing
　Random Lake, WI
　Lakeside Foods - Manufacturing
　Reedsburg, WI
　Lakeside Foods - Manufacturing
　Seymour, WI
　Lakeside Foods - Manufacturing
　Plainview, MN
　Lakeside Foods - ManufacturingBelgium
Regions Exported to: Worldwide
Percentage of Business in Exporting: 3

45905 (HQ)Lakeside Foods Inc.
PO Box 1327
Manitowoc, WI 54221-1327   920-684-3356
　　　Fax: 920-686-4033   800-466-3834
　　　　　www.lakesidefoods.com
Food manufacturing company for private label consumers, including canned and frozen vegetables, frozen seafood, canned meats, pet food, canned beans, whipped topping and sauces.
CEO: Glenn Tellock
General Manager: Janet De Pirro
CFO: Denise Kitzerow
Quality Assurance Manager: Alex Kiel
Vice President, Sales: Matt Brown
Vice President, Operations: Bruce Jacobson
Year Founded: 1887
Estimated Sales: $103.5 Million
Number Employees: 1,000-4,999
Square Footage: 28500
Type of Packaging: Consumer, Food Service, Private Label
Other Locations:
　Lakeside Foods Processing Plant
　Manitowoc, WI
　Lakeside Foods Processing Plant
　Belgium, WI
　Lakeside Foods Processing Plant
　Random Lake, WI
　Lakeside Foods Processing Plant
　Reedsburg, WI
　Lakeside Foods Processing Plant
　Seymour, WI
　Lakeside Foods Processing Plant
　Plainview, MN
　Lakeside Foods Processing PlantBelgium
Regions Exported to: Europe, Asia, Middle East
Percentage of Business in Exporting: 10

45906 (HQ)Lakeside Manufacturing Inc
4900 W Electric Ave
Milwaukee, WI 53219-1629   414-645-0630
　　　Fax: 414-902-6545   888-558-8565
　　　info@elakeside.com www.elakeside.com
Manufacturer and exporter of mobile material handling and food service equipment including carts, racks, containers, dispensers, portable beverage bars, etc
President: Joe Carlson
jcarlson@elakeside.com
Chairman/CEO: Lawrence Moon
Chairman of the Board: Lawrence Moon
VP Sales: Alex Carayannopoulos
Estimated Sales: $ 10 - 20 Million
Number Employees: 100-249
Regions Exported to: South America, Asia, Mexico, Canada
Percentage of Business in Exporting: 5

45907 Lakeside Mills
PO Box 230
Rutherfordton, NC 28139-0230   828-286-4866
　　　Fax: 828-287-3361 www.lakesidemills.com
Corn meal, hush puppy mix and breadings; importer of peppers and spices
VP: Aaron King
Contact: Kim King
kimking@lakesidemills.com
Number Employees: 10-19
Parent Co: Lakeside Mills
Type of Packaging: Consumer, Food Service, Private Label, Bulk
Regions Imported from: South America
Percentage of Business in Importing: 2

45908 Lakeside Packing Company
667 County Road #50
Harrow, ON N0R 1G0
Canada   519-738-2314
　　　Fax: 519-738-3684 info@lakesidepacking.com
　　　　　www.lakesidepacking.com
Pickles, peppers, relish, salsa, tomatoes
President/Board Member: Donald Woodbridge
VP/Board Member: Alan Woodbridge
Estimated Sales: $813,000
Number Employees: 20
Type of Packaging: Consumer, Food Service

45909 Lakeside-Aris Manufacturing
1977 S Allis Street
Milwaukee, WI 53207-1248   414-481-3900
　　　Fax: 414-481-9313   800-558-8565
Manufacturer and exporter of serving carts and culinary display trays
VP: Jon Carlson
VP Sales: Alex Carayannopoulos
Estimated Sales: $10-20 Million
Number Employees: 100-249
Parent Co: Lakeside Manufacturing
Type of Packaging: Consumer, Food Service
Regions Exported to: Central America, South America, Asia, Middle East, Canada
Percentage of Business in Exporting: 3

45910 Lakewood Juice Company
1035 NW 21st Ter
Miami, FL 33127   305-324-5932
　　　Fax: 305-325-9573   866-324-5900
　　　　　info@floridabottling.com
Manufacturer and exporter of glass-packed fruit juices
President: Vivian Calzadilla
CEO: R Fuhrman
VP, Sales: Joseph Letiz
Contact: Pamela Ford
pford@floridabottling.com
Estimated Sales: $7,000,000
Number Employees: 50
Parent Co: Florida Family Trust
Type of Packaging: Consumer, Food Service, Bulk
Regions Exported to: Worldwide
Percentage of Business in Exporting: 2

45911 (HQ)Lallemand
1620 Rue Prefontaine
Montreal, QC H1W 2N8
Canada   514-522-2133
　　　Fax: 514-522-2884 www.bio-lallemand.com
Manufacturer and exporter of food and dairy microbial cultures, lactobacilli and bifidobacteria; also, custom formulations available
President: Roland Chagnon
Vice President: Francois Leblanc
Estimated Sales: $10-20 Million
Number Employees: 50-99
Square Footage: 100000
Type of Packaging: Consumer, Private Label, Bulk
Brands Exported: Rosell; Ferlac; Rosellac; Gastro-Ad; Polylacton; Probiotic-2000; Standard Formulations; Vitanal
Regions Exported to: Central America, South America, Europe, Asia, USA, Mexixo
Percentage of Business in Exporting: 62

45912 (HQ)Lamb Cooperative Inc
372 Danbury Rd
#207
Wilton, CT 06897-2523   203-529-9100
　　　Fax: 203-529-9101   800-438-5262
　　　　　www.lambcompany.com
Importer and wholesaler/distributor of frozen and refridgerated lamb, beef, venison, goat and mutton.
President: Tony Ruffo
Vice President of Sales and Marketing: John Dolan
Estimated Sales: $10-20 Million
Number Employees: 10-19
Number of Brands: 2
Type of Packaging: Consumer, Food Service
Other Locations:
　The NZ & Aus Lamb Company LTD
　Etobicoke, ON, CanadaNew Zealand Lamb Company
　Compton, CAThe NZ & Aus Lamb Company LTDRichmond, BC, Canada
Regions Exported to: Canada
Regions Imported from: Australia, New Zealand

45913 Lambent Technologies
7247 Central Park Ave
Skokie, IL 60076   847-675-3951
　　　Fax: 847-675-3013   800-432-7187
　　　　　www.lambenttech.com
Manufacturer and exporter of nonionic emulsifiers including polysorbates, sorbitan esters and glycerol esters; also, silicone and nonsilicone antifoams and defoamers
President: Michael Hayes
Marketing Manager: Randy Cobb
Sales Manager: Kevin Hrebenar
Estimated Sales: $9800000
Number Employees: 55
Square Footage: 40000
Parent Co: Petroferm
Regions Exported to: Central America, South America, Europe, Asia, Middle East
Percentage of Business in Exporting: 10

45914 Lambert Company
PO Box 740
Chillicothe, MO 64601-0740   660-646-2150
　　　Fax: 660-646-2152   800-821-7667
Manufacturer and exporter of work gloves and headwear
President: James Lambert
CFO: James Lambert
Estimated Sales: $ 5 - 10 Million
Number Employees: 6
Type of Packaging: Consumer, Food Service, Private Label
Regions Exported to: Worldwide

45915 Lambertson Industries Inc
1335 Alexandria Ct
Sparks, NV 89434-9597   775-857-1100
　　　Fax: 775-857-3289   800-548-3324
　　　　　sales@lamberston.com
Stainless steel manufacturing
Owner: Jason Weiss
Marketing Director: Justin Pecot
Sales Manager: Ken Hewson
jasonweiss@lambertson.com
Operations Manager: Joseph McCaslin
Production Manager: Oswaldo Garcia
Estimated Sales: $1.5-3,500,000
Number Employees: 20-49
Square Footage: 60000

Importers & Exporters / A-Z

45916 Lambeth Band Corporation
PO Box 50490
New Bedford, MA 02745-0017 508-984-4700
Fax: 508-984-4780
Manufacturer and exporter of belting including nylon and urethane elastic bands.
President: Braley Gray
CEO: Lisa Larsen
Estimated Sales: $ 3 - 5 Million
Number Employees: 5-9
Square Footage: 14000

45917 Lamports Filter Media
777 E 82nd St
Cleveland, OH 44103-1817 216-881-2050
Fax: 216-881-8957 info@lamports.com
www.lamports.com
Manufacturer and exporter of fabricated textiles for air and liquid filtration
President: Walter Senney
Contact: Jennifer Geraci
jennifer.geraci@lamports.com
Estimated Sales: $ 5 - 10 Million
Number Employees: 20-49
Square Footage: 120000
Regions Exported to: Central America, Europe, Canada

45918 Lamson & Goodnow
45 Conway St
Shelburne Falls, MA 01370-1420 413-625-6331
Fax: 413-625-9816 800-872-6564
info@lamsonsharp.com
www.lamsonandgoodnow.com
Manufacturer and exporter of culinary knives including butchers' cleavers, bread, cheese and steak
President: Jim Pelletier
jpelletier@lamsonsharp.com
CFO: David Dunn
Marketing: Kurt Saunders
Sales Manager: Kurt Zanner
Plant Manager: Fran Gipe
Estimated Sales: $ 10 - 20 Million
Number Employees: 20-49
Type of Packaging: Consumer, Food Service, Private Label, Bulk
Brands Exported: Lamson; Lamson Sharp
Regions Exported to: Central America, South America, Europe, Australia
Percentage of Business in Exporting: 8

45919 Lanaetex Products Incorporated
151 3rd St
Elizabeth, NJ 7206 908-351-9700
Fax: 908-351-8753
Processor and exporter of food grade waxes
President: Mike Gutowski
Estimated Sales: $ 10 - 20 Million
Number Employees: 10-19

45920 Lancaster Colony Corporation
380 Polaris Parkway
Suite 400
Westerville, OH 43082 614-224-7141
www.lancastercolony.com
Amenities including glassware, ice and food molds, iced tea dispensers, wood grain serving trays, ice buckets, aluminum cookware and commercial coffee urns, candles and matting. Foodservice products include frozen appetizers, dips, and salad dressings.
Executive Chairman: John Gerlach
President & CEO: David Ciesinki
Vice President/CFO: Thomas Pigott
General Counsel/Chief Ethics Officer: Matthew Shurte
Vice President, Investor Relations: Dale Ganobsik
Year Founded: 1969
Estimated Sales: $1.13 Billion
Number Employees: 500-1000
Type of Packaging: Consumer, Food Service, Bulk
Regions Exported to: Europe, Middle East
Percentage of Business in Exporting: 4

45921 Lancer
1150 Emma Oaks Trail
Ste 140
Lake Mary, FL 32746-7120 407-327-8488
Fax: 407-327-1229 800-332-1855
sales@lancer.com www.lancer.com
Wholesaler/distributor and exporter of industrial glassware and instrument washers
Manager: Michael Henley
Technical Sales: Patrick Grady
Contact: Tim Benton
tim.benton@lancer.com
Estimated Sales: $2.5-5 Million
Number Employees: 10-19
Parent Co: Lancer Industries S.A.
Brands Exported: Lancer
Regions Exported to: Central America, South America, Canada, Caribbean, Latin America, Mexico
Percentage of Business in Exporting: 12

45922 Lancer Corp
100 N Gary Ave
Cuite C
Roselle, IL 60172 847-524-1707
Fax: 847-524-1710 877-814-2271
www.lancercorp.com
Beverage dispensing equipment.
Type of Packaging: Food Service
Other Locations:
Lancer Corp.
BeverleyLancer Corp.
Regions Exported to: Worldwide
Percentage of Business in Exporting: 20

45923 (HQ)Lancer Corp
6655 Lancer Blvd
San Antonio, TX 78219
Fax: 210-310-7250 888-676-5196
generalinfo@lancercorp.com www.lancercorp.com
Beverage dispensing equipment.
President: Wayne Degon
Buyer/Planner: Gerry Law, Jr.
Estimated Sales: $113 Million
Number Employees: 1,500
Regions Exported to: Worldwide
Percentage of Business in Exporting: 20

45924 Land O'Frost Inc
911 Hastings Ave
Searcy, AR 72143-7401 501-268-2473
Fax: 501-268-0357 800-643-5654
www.landofrost.com
Processor and importer of ham, beef, chicken and turkey; also, pre-sliced luncheon meats, pre-portioned julienne meat strips and diced meats
President & CEO: David Van Eekeren
COO: William Marion
wmarion@landofrost.com
Number Employees: 500-999
Square Footage: 1052000
Type of Packaging: Consumer, Food Service, Private Label, Bulk
Regions Imported from: Latin America
Percentage of Business in Importing: 5

45925 (HQ)Land O'Frost Inc.
16850 Chicago Ave.
Lansing, IL 60438 708-474-7100
Fax: 708-474-9329 800-323-3308
www.landofrost.com
Lunch and deli meats such as; beef, chicken, turkey, ham and meat ingredients.
President: Charles Niementowski
Chairman/CEO: Donna Van Eekeren
Chief Financial Officer: George Smolar
Director of Quality Control: Dayna Nicholas
Estimated Sales: $103.6 Million
Number Employees: 500-999
Square Footage: 100000
Type of Packaging: Consumer, Food Service, Private Label

45926 Land O'Lakes Inc
4001 Lexington Ave. N.
Arden Hills, MN 55126-2998 651-375-2222
800-328-9680
www.landolakesinc.com
A global crop inputs, dairy foods and animal nutrition co-operative.
President/CEO: Beth Ford
Senior VP/CFO: Bill Pieper
Senior VP/General Counsel: Sheilah Stewart
Senior VP/Chief Marketing Officer: Tim Scott
Executive VP/COO: Jerry Kaminski
Chief Supply Chain Officer: Yone Dewberry
Year Founded: 1921
Estimated Sales: $14 Billion
Number Employees: 10,000
Number of Brands: 5
Type of Packaging: Consumer, Food Service, Private Label, Bulk
Brands Exported: Land O'Lakes
Regions Exported to: Central America, South America, Europe, Asia, Middle East

45927 Landau Uniforms Inc
8410 W Sandidge Rd
Olive Branch, MS 38654-3412 662-895-7200
Fax: 662-895-5099 800-238-7513
Manufacturer, importer and exporter of aprons, shirts and fast-food uniforms
President: Nat Landau
CEO: Bruce Landau
CFO: Nancy Russell
nrussell@landau.com
Vice President: Gregg Landau
Quality Control: Dale Scott
Estimated Sales: $ 20 - 50 Million
Number Employees: 250-499
Type of Packaging: Food Service
Brands Exported: Landau
Regions Exported to: Worldwide
Regions Imported from: Honduras

45928 Landis Plastics
5750 W 118th St
Alsip, IL 60803-6012 708-396-1470
Fax: 708-824-3722
Manufacturer and exporter of injected molded plastic packaging supplies including can lids, jar caps, containers, scoops and pails; exporter of containers and lids
Manager: H R Landis
Vice President: Jennifer Bjerga
Purchasing: Tim Brenner
Estimated Sales: $ 50-100 Million
Number Employees: 300
Square Footage: 102053
Parent Co: Berry Plastics Group, Inc.
Regions Exported to: Europe

45929 Landoo Corporation
331 Maple Avenue
Horsham, PA 19044-2139 785-562-5381
Fax: 785-562-4853 kfox@drexeltrucks.com
Manufacturer and exporter of lift trucks
President: Jon Landoo
CFO: Dan Caffrey
Quality Control: Hank Burker
R & D: Dave Kongs
Marketing Supporting Manager: Jennifer Reynolds
VP Sales Manager: Kim Wanamaker
Export Sales Manager: Dave Pederson
Estimated Sales: $20-50 Million
Number Employees: 10
Square Footage: 65000
Regions Exported to: Worldwide
Percentage of Business in Exporting: 2

45930 Landreth Wild Rice
2320 Industrial Blvd
Norman, OK 73069-8518 405-360-2333
Fax: 405-360-6644 800-333-3533
Processor and exporter of wild rice
Principal: George Landreth
Estimated Sales: $110,000
Number Employees: 2
Type of Packaging: Consumer, Food Service, Private Label
Regions Exported to: Worldwide
Percentage of Business in Exporting: 10

45931 Landry's Pepper Co
1606 Cypress Island Hwy
PO Box 127
St Martinville, LA 70582-6013 337-394-6097
Fax: 337-394-7629 landry6097@aol.com
Hot sauces.
President: Lamar Bertrand
VP: Toby Bertrand
Estimated Sales: $500,000
Number Employees: 5-9
Square Footage: 120000
Type of Packaging: Consumer, Food Service, Private Label, Bulk
Brands Exported: Landry's; Cajun Gourmet Magic; Premium
Regions Exported to: Middle East
Percentage of Business in Exporting: 50

45932 Lane Labs
110 Commerce Drive
Allendale, NJ 07401-1600 201-236-9090
Fax: 201-236-9091 800-526-3005
lanelabs@aol.com www.lanelabs.com

Importer and exporter of food supplements including shark cartilage
President: Andy Lane
Estimated Sales: $10-20 Million
Number Employees: 20-49
Type of Packaging: Consumer
Brands Exported: BeneFin
Regions Exported to: Worldwide
Brands Imported: BeneFin

45933 Lane's Dairy
310 N Concepcion St
El Paso, TX 79905-1605 915-772-6700
Fax: 915-772-3097
Manufacturer and exporter of milk and canned and bottled fruit juice
President: John Lane
Owner: Hilda Lane
Production Manager: Chris Lane
Estimated Sales: $2 Million
Number Employees: 20-49
Square Footage: 60000
Type of Packaging: Consumer
Regions Exported to: Mexico
Percentage of Business in Exporting: 25

45934 Lang Manufacturing Co
6500 Merrill Creek Pkwy
Everett, WA 98203-5860 425-349-2400
Fax: 425-349-2733 800-882-6368
info@langworld.com www.langworld.com
Offer a quality line of innovative gas and electric commercial cooking equipment to the commercial, retail, marine, correctional, and government foodservice inductries
President: Dave Ek
CEO: Tracy Olson
Executive VP: Steve Hegge
Manager of Marketing: Annette Steinbach
Vice President of Sales and Marketing: Jim Baxter
Purchasing Manager: Mark Johnston
Estimated Sales: $ 20-50 Million
Number Employees: 5-9
Square Footage: 90000
Type of Packaging: Food Service
Regions Exported to: Worldwide
Percentage of Business in Exporting: 10

45935 (HQ)Langen Packaging
6154 Kestrel Road
Mississauga, ON L5T 1Z2
Canada 905-670-7200
Fax: 905-670-5291 sales@langeninc.com
Manufacturer and exporter of packaging machinery and carton and case packers
President: Stuart Cooper
CFO: Alan Makhan
VP Marketing/Sales: Kevin Walsh
VP Engineering: Peter Guttinger
Purchasing Manager: Elinor Workman
Estimated Sales: $ 20 - 30 Million
Number Employees: 100
Square Footage: 80000
Regions Exported to: Central America, South America, Europe, Asia, Middle East, Australia, Mexico
Percentage of Business in Exporting: 70

45936 (HQ)Langer Manufacturing Company
1025 7th Street SW
Cedar Rapids, IA 52404-1918 319-362-1481
Fax: 319-364-7131 800-728-6445
langermfg@aol.com
Manufacturer and exporter of wire products including milk bottle crates, bakery racks, partitioned cases, custom baskets and display racks
President: John R Langer
CEO: James M Langer
Sales: John Langer
Operations: James Langer
Estimated Sales: $2.5 Million
Number Employees: 20-49
Number of Products: 150
Square Footage: 80000
Brands Exported: Wire Lite Crates
Regions Exported to: Central America
Percentage of Business in Exporting: 1

45937 Langsenkamp Manufacturing
1699 South 8th St
Indianapolis, IN 46060 317-773-2100
Fax: 317-585-1715 877-585-1950
rogerm@warnerbodies.com
www.warnerbodies.com
Manufacturer and exporter of canning and food processing machinery including pumps, finishers, tanks, can openers and crushers, etc
President: Rick Manasek
Sales: Roger McNew
Controller: Bryan Lindsay
Estimated Sales: $2.5-5 Million
Number Employees: 18-25
Number of Brands: 1
Number of Products: 10
Square Footage: 62000
Brands Exported: Langsenkamp
Regions Exported to: Central America, South America, Europe
Percentage of Business in Exporting: 20

45938 (HQ)Langston Co Inc
1760 S 3rd St
Memphis, TN 38109-7712 901-774-4440
Fax: 901-942-5402 lango@bellsouth.net
www.langstonbag.com
Manufacturer and exporter of bags including burlap, produce and multi-wall paper
CEO: Robert Langston
CEO: Robert Langston
Production Manager: Steve Winston
Estimated Sales: $20-50 Million
Number Employees: 50-99
Regions Exported to: Worldwide
Percentage of Business in Exporting: 10

45939 Lanly Co
26201 Tungsten Rd
Cleveland, OH 44132-2997 216-731-1115
Fax: 216-731-7900 sales@lanly.com
www.lanly.com
Designs and builds custom heat processing equipment for an extensive range of industries.
President: Dennis Hill
mmarincic@lanly.com
Sales Exec: Martin F Marincic
Plant Manager: Tim Brooks
Estimated Sales: $5-10 Million
Number Employees: 20-49
Square Footage: 136000
Regions Exported to: Central America, South America, Europe, Asia, Middle East, Worldwide

45940 Larco
210 10th Ave NE
Brainerd, MN 56401-2802 218-829-9797
Fax: 218-829-0139 800-523-6996
sales@larcomfg.com www.larco.com
Manufacturer and exporter of switch mats and controls for machine guarding safety
President: B Wilder
bwilder@mulberrymc.com
Sales Manager: Joe Schultz
Estimated Sales: $2.5-5 Million
Number Employees: 50-99
Parent Co: Acrometal Companies
Regions Exported to: Worldwide
Percentage of Business in Exporting: 15

45941 Larien Products
351 Pleasant St
PMB 224
Northampton, MA 01060 413-586-4000
Fax: 413-585-0101 800-462-9237
lsmith@larien.com www.larien.com
Larien is noted for a patented bagel slicing design that safely isolates the user from the slicing action. We manufacture a consumer model and a commercial model
President: Rick Ricard
CEO: Lois Smith
National Sales Manager: Jim Dodge
Operations: Elizabeth DiVito
Estimated Sales: $1 Million
Number Employees: 1-4
Number of Brands: 4
Number of Products: 4
Type of Packaging: Consumer, Food Service
Brands Exported: The Bagel Biter; The Commercial Bagel Biter
Regions Exported to: Canada
Percentage of Business in Exporting: 5

45942 Laros Equipment Co Inc
8278 Shaver Rd
Portage, MI 49024-5440 269-323-1441
Fax: 269-323-0456 laros@globalcrossing.net
www.laros.com
Manufacturer and exporter of conveyor systems
President: Tim Vanness
Estimated Sales: $10-20 Million
Number Employees: 20-49
Parent Co: George R. Laure Enterprises
Regions Exported to: Europe, Canada

45943 Larose & Fils Lte
2255 Industrial Boulevard
Laval, QC H7S 1P8
Canada 514-382-7000
Fax: 450-667-8515 877-382-7001
info@larose.ca www.larose.ca
Cleaning equipment and supplies including sweepers, pressure washers, germicides, disinfectants, drain openers, etc.; industrial floor polishers and waxstrippers; importer of vacuum cleaners
President: Jean Larose
CEO: Manon Larose
CFO: Richard Colerette
VP: Pierre Larose
Research & Development: Andr^ Foisy
Quality Control: Yves Lafrances
Marketing Director: France Morin
Sales Director: Andr^ Foisy
Public Relations: France Morin
Operations Manager: Manon Larose
Purchasing Manager: Anick Murray
Number Employees: 40
Square Footage: 120000
Parent Co: Labchem
Type of Packaging: Consumer, Food Service, Private Label
Regions Imported from: Europe
Percentage of Business in Importing: 10

45944 Lasermation Inc
2629 N 15th St
Philadelphia, PA 19132-3904 215-228-7900
Fax: 215-225-1593 800-523-2759
www.lasermation.com
Manufacturer and exporter of brass and mylar stencils, awards, wine holders, pepper grinding mills and wooden back bar displays. Signs, executive gifts and awards
President: Joseph Molines
jmolines@lasermation.com
Estimated Sales: $1-3 Million
Number Employees: 10-19
Square Footage: 50000
Type of Packaging: Private Label

45945 Lasertechnics Marking Corporation
80 Colonnade Road
Nepean, ON K2E 7L2
Canada 613-749-4895
Fax: 613-749-8179
webinquiry@lightmachinery.com
Manufacturer and exporter of laser code markers and date/code marking equipment
CEO: Martin Janiak
Sales/Marketing: Bob Michael
Director Sales Administration: Bob Baker
Estimated Sales: $2.5-5 Million
Number Employees: 20-49
Square Footage: 96000
Parent Co: Quantrad Sensor
Brands Exported: Blazer
Regions Exported to: Worldwide
Percentage of Business in Exporting: 50

45946 Lassonde Pappas & Company, Inc.
1 Collins Dr.
Suite 200
Carneys Point, NJ 08069
800-257-7019
info@lassondepappas.com lassondepappas.com
Juices including apple, blueberry, grape, papaya and cranberry sauce, flavored waters, and juice cocktails, lemonades, organic products, and ready to drink teas.
President, Lassonde Pappas: Seth French
Year Founded: 1942
Estimated Sales: $450 Million
Number Employees: 650
Number of Brands: 1

Importers & Exporters / A-Z

Square Footage: 600000
Parent Co: Lassonde Industries, Inc.
Type of Packaging: Consumer, Private Label, Bulk
Other Locations:
  Clement Pappas Food Plant
  Springdale, AR
  Clement Pappas Food Plant
  Seabrook, NJ
  Clement Pappas Food Plant
  Mountain Home, NC
  Clement Pappas Food Plant
  Ontario, CAClement Pappas Food PlantSeabrook
Regions Exported to: Canada
Percentage of Business in Exporting: 1

45947 Latendorf Corporation
PO Box 205
Brielle, NJ 08730-0205   732-528-0180
         Fax: 732-528-6804 800-526-4057
Manufacturer, importer and exporter of bakery machinery
Owner: Malcolm Latendorf
Estimated Sales: $ 1 - 5 Million
Number Employees: 50-99
Square Footage: 120000
Regions Exported to: Central America, South America, Europe, Asia
Regions Imported from: Europe

45948 Latitude, LTD
37 West Shore Road
Huntington, NY 11743   631-659-3374
         Fax: 631-659-3376 latitudeltd@aol.com
Food ingredients manufacturer; including: sweeteners, vitamins, antioxidants and preservatives
Director: Laurel Eastman
Office Manager: Elissa Farrugia

45949 Laub-Hunt Packaging Systems
13547 Excelsior Dr
Norwalk, CA 90650-5236   562-802-9591
         Fax: 562-802-8183 888-671-9338
         info@laubhunt.com www.laubhunt.com
Manufacturer and exporter of liquid fillers
Vice President: Jeff Hunt
info@laubhunt.com
Quality Control: E J Daniel
Vice President: Jeff Hunt
Marketing Director: Jean Pei
Estimated Sales: Below $5 Million
Number Employees: 5-9
Square Footage: 20000
Regions Exported to: Central America, Asia, Canada, Caribbean, Latin America, Mexico
Percentage of Business in Exporting: 30

45950 Laughlin Sales Corp
3618 N Grove St
Fort Worth, TX 76106-4466   817-625-7756
         Fax: 817-625-0687 www.laughlinconveyor.com
Manufacturer and exporter of conveyor systems including metal belt, chain, vibrating, magnetic, roller, etc.; also, custom designing available
President: Matt Laughlin Jr
VP Engineering/Manufacturing: David Laughlin
Sales Manager: Gene Fields
Estimated Sales: $ 1 - 2.5 Million
Number Employees: 1-4
Square Footage: 200000
Regions Exported to: Central America, South America, Mexico, Latin America
Percentage of Business in Exporting: 10

45951 Laval Paper Box
118 Hymus
Pointe Claire, QC H9R 1E3
Canada   450-669-3551
         Fax: 514-694-5636
Manufacturer and exporter of cardboard boxes
President: Frank Carbone
Number Employees: 200
Type of Packaging: Bulk
Regions Exported to: USA
Percentage of Business in Exporting: 50

45952 Lavazza Premium Coffees
3 Park Ave # 35
New York, NY 10016-5902   212-725-9196
         Fax: 212-725-9475 info@lavazza.it
                            www.lavazza.com
Manufacturer and importer of Italian coffee and espresso machines
VP: Ennio Ranaboldo
Contact: Bidya Alie
balie@sovrana.com
Estimated Sales: $10-20 Million
Number Employees: 20-49
Parent Co: LaVazza Premium Coffee
Type of Packaging: Consumer, Food Service
Regions Imported from: Italy
Percentage of Business in Importing: 100

45953 Lavi Industries
27810 Avenue Hopkins
Valencia, CA 91355-3409   661-257-7809
         Fax: 661-257-4938 800-624-6225
                            sales@lavi.com www.lavi.com
Manufacturers of Architectural Metals, Public Guidance Systems, Hospitality Fixtures, Traditional Portable Post for Hospitality, Rope Ends & Snaps, Beltrac Series in many lengths, colors and widths, Sign Frames, Graphics, Sneeze GuardsStemware Racks, Bellman Carts, Trucks, Specialty Hardware Products and much more
President: Gavriel Lavi
gavriel@lavi.com
Director Sales: Edward Bradford
Estimated Sales: $ 20 - 50 Million
Number Employees: 100-249
Square Footage: 75000
Type of Packaging: Food Service
Brands Exported: Beltrac; Lavi; Lido
Regions Exported to: Worldwide
Percentage of Business in Exporting: 11

45954 Lawnelson Corporation
131 Oneida Drive
Greenwich, CT 06830-7127   203-259-3366
         Fax: 203-259-3369
Importer of spices, nuts, dates and dried fruits
Sales Manager: Paul Nelson
Number Employees: 1-4
Brands Imported: Gulf; Sinbad
Regions Imported from: Middle East

45955 Lawrence Equipment Inc
2034 Peck Rd
South El Monte, CA 91733-3727   626-442-2894
         Fax: 626-350-5181 800-423-4500
                            www.lawrenceequipment.com
Manufacturer and exporter of food processing machinery including corn and flour tortilla systems, corn based snack lines and pizza forming lines; importer of dough processing equipment
President: John Lawrence
johnlawrence@lawrenceequipment.com
Vice President: Glenn Shelton
International Sales: Dan Woodward
Estimated Sales: $10-20 Million
Number Employees: 100-249
Square Footage: 172000
Brands Exported: Lawrence Equipment, Inc.
Regions Exported to: Worldwide
Percentage of Business in Exporting: 20
Brands Imported: Werner; Pfliter
Regions Imported from: Worldwide
Percentage of Business in Importing: 10

45956 Lawrence Metal ProductsInc
260 Spur Dr S
Bay Shore, NY 11706-3900   631-666-0300
         Fax: 631-666-0336 800-441-0019
         info@lawrencemetal.com www.tensatorgroup.com
Manufacturer and exporter of brass, chrome and stainless steel bar railings; also, glass racks, food shields and crowd control
President: David Lawrence
CEO: Jeremy Williman
Marketing: Suzanne De Angelo
Director Sales/Marketing: Betty Castro
Estimated Sales: $10-20 Million
Number Employees: 100-249
Square Footage: 160000
Brands Exported: Lawrence
Regions Exported to: Central America, South America, Asia, Middle East

45957 Lawrence Schiff Silk Mills
31 W. 34th Street
Suite 7002
New York, NY 10001   212-679-2185
         Fax: 212-696-4565 800-272-4433
Manufacturer and exporter of ribbons, tapes, bindings, webbings and trims
President/CEO: Richard J. Schiff
CFO: Bruce Ershler
VP Sales/Marketing: Nancy Sherman
Estimated Sales: $ 5 - 10 Million
Number Employees: 10-19
Regions Exported to: Europe

45958 Laydon Company
PO Box 69
Brown City, MI 48416-0069   810-346-2952
         Fax: 810-346-2900 laydonco@greatlakes.net
Manufacturer and exporter of precision custom plastic injection molding including long and short run
VP: Sandy Fuller
Sales Manager: Connie Dixon
Estimated Sales: $ 10 -20 Million
Number Employees: 50-99
Square Footage: 70000

45959 Layflat Products
901 Tatum St
Shreveport, LA 71107   318-222-6141
         Fax: 318-424-2949 800-551-8515
Manufacturer and exporter of screw-type wet mops, mop heads and handles
Owner: James Beadles
National Sales Manager: Bill Hill
Director Operations: Steve Williams
Estimated Sales: $ 3 - 5 Million
Number Employees: 20-49
Square Footage: 50000
Type of Packaging: Consumer, Food Service, Private Label
Brands Exported: Layflat
Regions Exported to: Central America
Percentage of Business in Exporting: 1

45960 Lazzari Fuel Co LLC
11 Industrial Way
Brisbane, CA 94005-1001   415-467-2970
         Fax: 415-468-2298 800-242-7265
         info@Lazzari.com www.lazzari.com
Mesquite lump charcoal and wood chips; importer and exporter of mesquite lump charcoal
Owner: Robert Colbert
CEO: Richard Morgan
Estimated Sales: $ 1 - 3 Million
Number Employees: 10-19
Square Footage: 74000
Type of Packaging: Consumer, Food Service, Private Label, Bulk
Brands Exported: Lazzari
Regions Exported to: Asia
Percentage of Business in Exporting: 1
Brands Imported: Lazzari
Regions Imported from: Mexico
Percentage of Business in Importing: 70

45961 Lazzaroni USA
299 Market St
Suite 160
Saddle Brook, NJ 07663-5312   201-368-1240
         Fax: 201-368-1262 www.lazzaroni-ita.com
Manufacturer and distributor of chocolates and cookies
President: Stefano Tombetti
Executive VP: Kathy Ecoffey
Contact: Theresa Strunck
tstrunck@lazzaroniusa.com

45962 Le Cordon Bleu
40 Enterprise Ave N
Secaucus, NJ 07094-2500   070-4 2-17
         Fax: 201-617-1914 800-457-2433
         gourmet@cordonbleu.net www.cordonbleu.net
Importer of gourmet foods, chef's accessories and cutlery
President: Andre Cointreau
Sales Director: Margaret Warren
Contact: Karen Dubois
kdubois@cordonbleu.edu
Estimated Sales: $500,000-$1 Million
Number Employees: 1-4
Type of Packaging: Consumer
Brands Imported: Le Cordon Bleu
Regions Imported from: Europe

45963 Le Creuset of America
PO Box 67
Early Branch, SC 29916   803-943-4308
         Fax: 803-943-4510 www.lecreuset.com
Exporter of enameled cast iron cookware, corkscrews and food storage canisters
Manager: Marshall Colleton
Contact: Todd Densley
tdensley@lecreuset.com
Estimated Sales: Less than $500,000
Number Employees: 1-4
Type of Packaging: Food Service

Regions Exported to: Europe
Percentage of Business in Exporting: 100

45964 Le Fiell Co
5601 Echo Ave
Reno, NV 89506-3207 402-592-9993
Fax: 402-592-7776 meatsys@lefiellco.com
www.lefiellco.com
Manufacturer and exporter of conveyors, meat packing and slaughter house machinery, trolley and trucks, meat house, engineering and overhead track switches, hide pullers and dehairers and restrainers for custom installation
Owner: Joe Gonzales
j.gonzales@lefiellco.com
CEO: Brandon Camp
COO: Joe Gonzales
Plant Manager: Dave Gomes
Estimated Sales: $2.5 Million
Number Employees: 20-49
Square Footage: 100000
Brands Exported: Le Fiell Overhead Conveyor And Monorial Systems
Regions Exported to: South America, Canada, Mexico
Percentage of Business in Exporting: 5
Brands Imported: Wheels
Regions Imported from: Asia, Mexico
Percentage of Business in Importing: 1

45965 Le Smoker
321 Park Avenue
Salisbury, MD 21801-4208 410-677-3233
Fax: 410-677-3234
Stainless steel smokers, fire place, grills, wood chips, chunks and charcoal; exporter of smokers
President: Richard Isaacs
VP: Dominique Isaacs
Number of Brands: 3
Square Footage: 12000
Type of Packaging: Food Service
Brands Exported: Le Smoker
Regions Exported to: Central America, Europe, Middle East

45966 Leader Candies
132 Harrison Place
Brooklyn, NY 11237-1522 718-366-6900
Fax: 718-417-1723
Processor and exporter of candies including hard, caramels, jelly beans, novelties, lollypops, filled, fundraising, hard toffee, starch jellies, bagged and nonchocolate, and nonfrozen freeze pops
President: Howard Kastin
Sales: Helen Garfield
VP Manufacturing: Malcom Kastin
Number Employees: 155
Square Footage: 320000
Type of Packaging: Consumer, Food Service, Private Label, Bulk
Brands Exported: Kastin's
Regions Exported to: Central America, South America, Asia, Canada
Percentage of Business in Exporting: 2

45967 Least Cost FormulationsLTD
824 Timberlake Dr
Virginia Beach, VA 23464-3239 757-467-0954
Fax: 757-467-2945 sales@lcfltd.com
www.lcfltd.com
Manufacturer and exporter of material requirement planning and technical software for the blending industry
Owner: Robert Labudde
ral@lcfltd.com
VP Marketing: Joy LaBudde
Estimated Sales: $1 Million
Number Employees: 1-4
Brands Exported: Least Cost Formulator; QC Assistant; Bindometer; Color Gaude
Regions Exported to: Central America, South America, Europe, Asia, Worldwide
Percentage of Business in Exporting: 10

45968 (HQ)Leavitt Corp., The
100 Santilli Hwy
Everett, MA 02149-1938 617-389-2600
Fax: 617-387-9085 contact@teddie.com
teddie.com
Peanut butter, salted and unsalted cashews and peanuts; raw cashews
President: James T Hintlian
jameshint@teddie.com
Executive VP: Mark Hintlian
Quality Control: Christopher Hayes
Operations Manager: Joseph Saraceno
Production Manager: Jack Skamarakas
Purchasing Manager: Frank Ciampa
Estimated Sales: $10-24.9 Million
Number Employees: 50-99
Type of Packaging: Consumer, Food Service, Private Label, Bulk
Brands Exported: Americana; River Queen
Regions Exported to: Central America, South America, Europe, Asia, Middle East, Caribbean
Regions Imported from: South America, Asia

45969 (HQ)Lebermuth Company
14000 McKinley Highway
Mishawaka, IN 46545 574-259-7000
Fax: 574-258-7450 800-648-1123
info@lebermuth.com www.lebermuth.com
Fragrance and flavor company
President: Rob Brown
CEO: Irvin Brown
Vice President: Alan Brown
Contact: Jodi Aker
jaker@lebermuth.com
Production Manager: Mike Ryan
Plant Manager: Robert Hall
Purchasing Manager: Jim Gates
Estimated Sales: $5-10 Million
Number Employees: 50
Square Footage: 180000
Type of Packaging: Bulk
Regions Exported to: Asia
Percentage of Business in Importing: 50

45970 Lee Financial Corporation
8350 N. Central Expressway
Suite 1800
Dallas, TX 75206 972-960-1001
Fax: 972-404-1123 Info@Leefin.com
www.leefin.com
Manufacturer and exporter of corn cutters, pea shellers and electric nutcrackers
President: Dana Pingenot
CEO & Founder: Richard Lee
CFO: Blake Decker
VP: Teresa Quinn
Contact: Rebecca Anderson
randerson@leefin.com
COO & Director of Human Resources: Jeff Ramsey
Estimated Sales: Below $ 5 Million
Number Employees: 20-49
Square Footage: 14000
Brands Exported: Kninetic Kracker; Lee's Kracker; Dynamic Nutcracker
Regions Exported to: South America, Europe, Australia, Canada
Percentage of Business in Exporting: 5

45971 Lee Kum Kee
#350, 30-56 Whitestone Expy
Whitestone, NY 11354 718-821-2199
Fax: 718-821-2989 800-346-7562
contact@lkkusa.com www.lkk.com
Processor, importer and exporter of condiments and sauces including chili.
Estimated Sales: $190,000
Number Employees: 3
Square Footage: 80000
Parent Co: Lee Kum Kee Company
Type of Packaging: Consumer, Food Service, Private Label, Bulk
Brands Exported: Lee Kum Kee
Regions Exported to: Central America, South America, Caribbean, Mexico
Regions Imported from: Asia

45972 Lee's Food Products
1233 Queen Street E
Toronto, ON M4L 1C2
Canada 416-465-2407
Canned soy sauce and Chinese vegetables including bamboo shoots, water chestnuts and mushrooms; importer of mushrooms, instant noodles and mini corn
President: Marilyn Wong
Secretary/Treasurer: L Wong
Estimated Sales: $ 5-10 Million
Number Employees: 45
Type of Packaging: Consumer, Food Service
Brands Imported: China Lily
Regions Imported from: Europe, Asia

45973 Leedal Inc
3453 Commercial Ave
Northbrook, IL 60062-1818 847-498-0111
Fax: 847-498-0198 sink@leedal.com
www.consolidateddoorintl.com
Manufacturer, importer and exporter of pot and pan washers, disposers, power scrubbers, wire shelfing, hot dog cookers, and steam tables
President: Aj Levin
ajlevin@hotmail.com
CFO: Sheldon Levin
Vice President: A Levin
Quality Control: Levin
Sales Director: Josie Negron
Estimated Sales: $ 5 - 10 Million
Number Employees: 20-49
Square Footage: 28000
Type of Packaging: Consumer, Food Service, Private Label, Bulk
Regions Exported to: Worldwide
Regions Imported from: Europe, Asia, Worldwide
Percentage of Business in Importing: 10

45974 Leelanau Fruit Co
2900 S West Bay Shore Dr
Peshawbestown, MI 49682-9614 231-271-3514
Fax: 231-271-4367 info@leelanaufruit.com
www.leelanaufruit.com
Processer and exporter of frozen and brined cherries and strawberries
President: Glen Lacross
General Manager: Allen Steimel
Estimated Sales: $ 1 - 3 Million
Number Employees: 20-49
Type of Packaging: Consumer, Food Service, Private Label, Bulk
Regions Exported to: Canada
Percentage of Business in Exporting: 5

45975 Leer Inc
206 Leer St
New Lisbon, WI 53950-1163 608-562-3161
Fax: 608-562-6022 800-237-8350
info@leerlp.com www.leerinc.com
Manufacturer and exporter of self-service ice merchandising equipment and block ice-makers
VP: Charlotte Maginnis
CEO and Owner and President: Steve Dolenzel
IT: Kevin Kracht
kkracht@leerlp.com
Estimated Sales: $ 500,000 - $ 1 Million
Number Employees: 100-249
Square Footage: 320000
Parent Co: Leer Manufacturing Partner
Type of Packaging: Bulk
Other Locations:
Star/Starrett
Dumas, AZStar/Starrett
Brands Exported: Starrett; Leer; Star
Regions Exported to: Central America, South America, Europe, Middle East
Percentage of Business in Exporting: 25

45976 Leeward Winery
2511 Victoria Ave
Oxnard, CA 93035-2931 805-656-5054
Fax: 805-656-5092 www.leewardwinery.com
Processor and exporter of table wines
President: Charles Brigham
Co-Owner: Chuck Gardner
Estimated Sales: $260,000
Number Employees: 4
Square Footage: 34000
Type of Packaging: Consumer, Food Service
Brands Exported: Leeward
Regions Exported to: Worldwide
Percentage of Business in Exporting: 1

45977 Lef Bleuges Marinor
1015 Rg Double
St-Felicien, QC G8K 2M1
Canada 418-679-4577
Fax: 418-679-9602
Frozen blueberries
President: Jeanne-Pierre Senneville
Regions Exported to: Worldwide

45978 Leggett & Platt Inc
1 Leggett Road
Carthage, MO 64836-9649 417-358-8131
Fax: 417-358-5840 www.leggett.com

Importers & Exporters / A-Z

Manufacturer and exporter of store fixtures including bakery showcases, cash register stands and checkouts, bulk shelving and storage units and custom wood display equipment
President/Director/CEO: David Haffner
Chairman: Richard Fisher
Senior VP/Chief Financial Officer: Matthew Flanigan
EVP/Chief Operating Officer: Karl Glassman
Director, Quality Assurance: Brad Richards
Marketing Manager: John Patrick
Director, Sales: Diane Holman
Operations Manager: Hal Gimmer
Plant Manager: Jim Winters
Director, Procurement: Jeff Mitchell
Estimated Sales: Over $1 Billion
Number Employees: 10000+
Square Footage: 15491
Parent Co: Reflector Hardware Corporation
Type of Packaging: Consumer, Food Service, Bulk
Other Locations:
   Goer Manufacturing Co.
   Union, MO Goer Manufacturing Co.

45979 Leggett & Platt Storage
11230 Harland Drive
Vernon Hills, IL 60061-1547   847-816-6246
       Fax: 847-968-3899 www.focuspg.com
Manufacturer and exporter of cabinets, racks, mobile storage equipment, shelving, carts, servingware, buffetware, utensils, utility trucks, dollies and tote/bus boxes
President: Keith Jaffee
Number Employees: 10-19
Square Footage: 2000000
Parent Co: SPG International, LLC
Other Locations:
   Leggett & Platt
   Charlotte, NC Leggett & Platt
Regions Exported to: Worldwide

45980 Legion Export & Import Company
479 Washington St
New York, NY 10013-1325   212-925-4627
       Fax: 212-925-4627
Importer and exporter of flavoring extracts, food preservatives and essential oils
President: Libery Raho
Treasurer: Peter Raho
Estimated Sales: $500,000-$1 Million
Number Employees: 20-49
Square Footage: 44000
Regions Exported to: Central America, South America
Regions Imported from: Europe, Asia
Percentage of Business in Importing: 40

45981 Legion Lighting Co Inc
221 Glenmore Ave
Brooklyn, NY 11207-3307   718-498-1770
       Fax: 718-498-0128 800-453-4466
       sales@legionlighting.com
       www.legionlighting.com
Manufacturer and exporter of architecturally engineered fluorescent lighting equipment
President: Michael Bellovin
VP Sales: Michael Bellovin
Engineering: Wayne Cowell
Sales: Evan Bellovin
Accountant: Gia Carla Rodriguez
Estimated Sales: $ 5-10 Million
Number Employees: 50-99
Square Footage: 12000
Regions Exported to: Central America, Europe, Middle East
Percentage of Business in Exporting: 2

45982 Lehigh Food Sales Inc
2374 Seipstown Rd # 208
Fogelsville, PA 18051-2200   610-285-2039
       Fax: 610-285-4562 www.profruit.com
Importer of strawberries, broker of frozen foods
President: Terry Muth
tmuth@lehighfoods.com
Estimated Sales: $ 3 - 5 Million
Number Employees: 20-49

45983 Lehman Sales Associates
3025 Saddle Brook Trl
Sun Prairie, WI 53590   608-575-7712
       Fax: 608-837-8421 bob@lehmanequip.com
Manufacturer and exporter of used and rebuilt food processing and packaging equipment
President: Richard Lehman
Estimated Sales: $ 1 - 2.5 Million
Number Employees: 1-4

45984 Lehr Brothers
12901 Packing House Road
Edison, CA 93220   661-366-3244
       Fax: 661-366-1449 spudron1@aol.com
Processor and exporter of potatoes
President: Ronald Lehr
VP: Ronald Lehr Jr
Estimated Sales: $17,155,306
Number Employees: 50
Square Footage: 45000
Type of Packaging: Bulk

45985 Leisure Craft Inc
940 Upward Rd
Flat Rock, NC 28731   828-693-8241
       Fax: 828-693-1803 www.leisurecraftinc.com
CEO: Dick Herman
dherman@leisurecraftinc.com
CEO: Dick Herman
Estimated Sales: $ 10 - 20 Million
Number Employees: 50-99

45986 Leland Limited Inc
2614 S Clinton Ave
South Plainfield, NJ 07080-1427   908-561-2000
       Fax: 908-668-7716 sales@lelandltd.com
       www.lelandgas.com
Manufacturer and exporter of food mixing equipment
Owner: Lee Stanford
lee@lelandgas.com
Engineer: P Bowlin
Customer Service: R Callaway
Estimated Sales: $5-10 Million
Number Employees: 10-19
Regions Exported to: Europe, Asia
Percentage of Business in Exporting: 5

45987 Leland Limited Inc
2614 S Clinton Ave
South Plainfield, NJ 07080-1427   908-561-2000
       Fax: 908-668-7716 800-984-9793
       sales@lelandltd.com www.lelandgas.com
Manufacturer, importer and exporter of whipped cream machinery and soda syphons
Owner: Lee Stanford
lee@lelandgas.com
Estimated Sales: $5,000,000
Number Employees: 10-19
Square Footage: 30000
Type of Packaging: Food Service
Regions Exported to: Worldwide
Percentage of Business in Exporting: 10
Regions Imported from: Europe

45988 Lello Appliances Corp
355 Murray Hill Pkwy # 204
East Rutherford, NJ 07073-2139   201-939-2555
       Fax: 201-939-5074 gbuzzi1063@aol.com
Importer and wholesaler/distributor of food service equipment; serving the food service market
President: G Bucci
lelloappliances@aol.com
Estimated Sales: $5-10 Million
Number Employees: 1-4
Type of Packaging: Food Service

45989 Lematic Inc
2410 W Main St
Jackson, MI 49203-1099   517-787-3301
       Fax: 517-782-1033 sales@lematic.com
       www.auto-op.com
Manufacturer and exporter of bulk packaging, bagging machinery and dry pan cleaners; also, bakery equipment including garlic and French bread makers and slicers for buns, bagels, croissants, etc
Owner: Dale Lecrone
dlecrone@lematic.com
CEO: Dale LeCrone
Director Marketing: George Arnold
dlecrone@lematic.com
Estimated Sales: $5-10 Million
Number Employees: 50-99
Square Footage: 60000
Regions Exported to: Worldwide
Percentage of Business in Exporting: 25

45990 Lemberger Candy Corporation
160 E Midland Ave
Paramus, NJ 07652   201-261-3718
       Fax: 201-261-8614 800-977-9921
       chocaidlemberger@aol.com
Importer of over 100 unique chocolate novelties
President: David Lemberger
Estimated Sales: $ 1 - 3 Million
Number Employees: 1-4
Number of Brands: 2
Number of Products: 100
Type of Packaging: Consumer
Brands Imported: Choc-Aid; Gumi-Aid; Chocolate Crayons; Chocolate Film
Regions Imported from: Central America, South America

45991 Lemon-X Corporation
168 Railroad Street
Huntington Station, NY 11746   631-424-2850
       Fax: 631-424-2852 800-220-1061
       sales@lemon-x.com www.lemon-x.com
Juices and cocktail mixes.
President: James Grassi
Co-Founder: Sonja Grassi
Contact: Greg Aluise
galuise@lemon-x.com
Estimated Sales: $20-50 Million
Number Employees: 100-249
Number of Brands: 5
Type of Packaging: Consumer, Food Service, Private Label, Bulk

45992 Lenchner Bakery
50 Drumlin Circle
Concord, ON L4K 3G1
Canada   905-738-8811
       Fax: 905-738-3822 www.lenchners.com
Processor and exporter of kosher frozen entrees and dessert pastries including chocolate, almond, cheese, apple, blueberry, cherry, prune, lemon, spinach feta cheese, potato onion, etc.; also, bagels; private labeling available
President: Zeev Lenchner
Estimated Sales: $1-2.5 Million
Number Employees: 20-49
Square Footage: 40000
Parent Co: Lechner's
Type of Packaging: Consumer, Food Service, Private Label, Bulk
Brands Exported: Prrogala
Regions Exported to: Europe, Middle East, USA
Percentage of Business in Exporting: 25

45993 Lengsfield Brothers
PO Box 50020
New Orleans, LA 70150-0020   504-529-2235
       Fax: 504-524-9281
Manufacturer and exporter of candy boxes

45994 Lenox Corp
1414 Radcliffe St # 1
Bristol, PA 19007-5496   267-525-7800
       Fax: 267-525-5618 800-223-4311
       lenox@lenox.com www.lenox.com
Manufacturer and exporter of chinaware, stemware, silverplated hollowware, crystal gifts and flatware including stainless and sterling
Owner: Walter S Lenox
walter.lenox@lenox.com
CFO: James Burwitt
Quality Control: Dave Summers
Number Employees: 1000-4999
Parent Co: Brown-Foreman
Type of Packaging: Food Service

45995 Lentia Enterprises Ltd.
17733-66th Ave
Surrey, BC V3S 7X1
Canada   604-576-8838
       Fax: 604-576-1064 888-768-7368
Naturally fermented, dehydrated sourdoughs from both wheat and rye flours, specialty malted products such as whole malted rye kernels, aroma malts, colouring malts and clean label bread mixes.
President/Board Member: Karl Eibensteiner
Director: Gertrude Eibensteiner
Estimated Sales: $4.08 Million
Number Employees: 23
Regions Exported to: Europe, USA

Importers & Exporters / A-Z

45996 Leo G. Atkinson Fisheries
89 Daniel Head Road
South Side
Clarks Harbor, NS B0W 1P0
Canada   902-745-3047
            Fax: 902-745-1245
Processor and exporter of fresh, frozen and salted seafood including haddock, cod, halibut and lobster. Founded in 1983.
President: Leo Atkinson
Estimated Sales: $9.9 Million
Number Employees: 20
Type of Packaging: Consumer, Food Service, Private Label, Bulk
Regions Exported to: Worldwide
Percentage of Business in Exporting: 75

45997 Leon's Bakery
1000 Universal Dr N
North Haven, CT 06473-3151   203-234-0115
            Fax: 203-234-7620   800-223-6844
Frozen dough; exporter of wheat and white rolls
President: Luis Alpizar
CEO: John Ruth
CFO: Eric Olson
Sales Manager: Terry Ginn
Plant Manager: Fred Macey
Estimated Sales: $ 5 - 10 Million
Number Employees: 5-9
Square Footage: 300000
Type of Packaging: Food Service, Private Label, Bulk
Regions Exported to: Canada

45998 Leonidas
485 Madison Ave # 4
New York, NY 10022-5803   212-980-2608
            Fax: 212-980-2609   800-900-2462
Importer and wholesaler/distributor of Belgian pralines, solid chocolate wafers and chocolates; serving the food service market
President: Noel Duchateau
General Manager/VP: Jacques Bergier
sales@leonidas-chocolate.com
VP: Jacques Bergier
Estimated Sales: $500,000-$1 Million
Number Employees: 10-19
Square Footage: 3600
Type of Packaging: Consumer, Food Service, Bulk
Brands Imported: Leonidas
Regions Imported from: Europe
Percentage of Business in Importing: 100

45999 Leprino Foods Co.
1830 W. 38th Ave.
Denver, CO 80211   303-480-2600
            Fax: 303-480-2605   800-537-7466
            www.leprinofoods.com
Mozzarella cheese, cheese blends, and pizza cheese made especially for pizzeria and foodservice operators, frozen food manufacturers and private label cheese packagers.
Chairman/CEO: James Leprino
CFO/SVP, Operations: Lance FitzSimmons
Year Founded: 1950
Estimated Sales: Over $1 Billion
Number Employees: 4,000+
Square Footage: 60000
Type of Packaging: Food Service, Bulk
Other Locations:
  Leprino Foods
  Allendale, MI
  Leprino Foods
  Fort Morgan, CO
  Leprino Foods
  Ravenna, NE
  Leprino Foods
  Remus, MI
  Leprino Foods
  Roswell, NM
  Leprino Foods
  Waverly, NY
  Leprino FoodsFort Morgan
Brands Exported: Le-Pro; Quality-Locked Cheese

46000 (HQ)Leroy Smith Inc
4776 Old Dixie Hwy
Vero Beach, FL 32967-1239   772-569-2059
            Fax: 772-567-8428 www.leroysmith.com
Manufacturer and exporter of citrus fruit including grapefruit and oranges.
CEO: Elson Smith
elson.smith@leroysmith.com
Year Founded: 1947
Number Employees: 100-249
Type of Packaging: Consumer
Regions Exported to: Worldwide

46001 Les Aliments Livabec Foods
95 Rang St Louis Rr 2
Sherrington, QC J0L 2N0
Canada   450-454-7971
      Fax: 450-454-9100 info@livabec.ca
            www.livabec.ca/accueil
Processor and exporter of marinated mixed and roasted vegetables and mushrooms in oil; processor of antipasto calabrese, basil and sun-dried tomato pesto; importer of sun-dried tomatoes
President: Lino Cimagila
VP: Lino Cimaglia, Jr.
Estimated Sales: $2 Million
Number Employees: 3
Square Footage: 50000
Brands Exported: Livia; Livabel
Regions Exported to: USA
Regions Imported from: Italy

46002 Les Aliments Ramico Foods
8245 Rue Le Creusot
St. Leonard, QC H1P 2A2
Canada   514-329-1844
            Fax: 514-329-5096
Beans, soups, sauces, chicken and meat with beans
Director: Rami Matta
VP: Galal Matta
Estimated Sales: G
Number Employees: 10-19
Square Footage: 12000
Type of Packaging: Private Label
Brands Exported: Feletto; Naima; Cosmos; Shahia; El Masri; Grand Valley
Regions Exported to: USA
Percentage of Business in Exporting: 10

46003 Les Industries Bernard et Fils
104 Rue Industrielle Du Boise
Saint Victor, QC G0M 2B0
Canada   418-588-3590
      Fax: 418-588-6836 martin@bernards.ca
            www.bernards.ca
Processor and exporter of pure maple and fruit syrups
President: Yves Bernard
Marketing Director: Martin Bernard
Estimated Sales: $4.4 Million
Number Employees: 35
Type of Packaging: Consumer, Food Service, Private Label, Bulk
Regions Exported to: Canada

46004 (HQ)Les Industries Touch Inc
4025 Lesage
Sherbrooke, QC J1L 2Z9
Canada   819-822-4140
            Fax: 819-822-2904   800-267-4140
            info@industriestouch.com
            www.industriestouch.com
Manufacturer and exporter of toothpicks, skewers, plastic cutlery, straws etc.
President: Gervais Morier
Sales Director: Gerald Bouchard
Operations Manager: Jean-Yves Blouin
Estimated Sales: $10-20 Million
Number Employees: 50-99
Number of Products: 300+
Square Footage: 90000
Type of Packaging: Consumer, Food Service, Private Label, Bulk
Regions Exported to: Central America, Europe, Mexico, USA
Percentage of Business in Exporting: 25
Regions Imported from: Asia
Percentage of Business in Importing: 75

46005 Les Viandes du Breton
150 Ch Des Raymond
Riviere-Du-Lup, QC G5R 5X8
Canada   418-863-6711
      Fax: 416-863-6767 service@dubreton.com
            www.dubreton.com
Fresh and frozen pork; exporter of hams, spare ribs, bellies, etc.
President: Vincent Breton
VP, Administration & Finance: Marie Jos,e Landry
Year Founded: 1944
Estimated Sales: $169 Million
Number Employees: 550
Parent Co: Bose Corporation
Type of Packaging: Consumer, Food Service, Private Label, Bulk
Brands Exported: DuBreton
Regions Exported to: Central America, South America, Asia, Middle East, Caribbean, Mexico, USA
Percentage of Business in Exporting: 40

46006 Les Viandes or Fil
2080 Rue Monterey
Laval, QC H7L 3S3
Canada   450-687-5664
            Fax: 450-687-2733
Processor and exporter of fresh and frozen pork
President: Antonio Filice
Vice President: Bernard Paquette
Estimated Sales: $15 Million
Number Employees: 50
Type of Packaging: Bulk
Regions Exported to: Worldwide

46007 Lesieur Cristal
10-34 44th Dr
2nd Floor
Long Island City, NY 11101   786-368-7988
            salesusa-tb@lesieur-cristal.co.ma
Olive oil

46008 Leslie Leger & Sons
34 Chemin De La Cote
P.O.Box 1061
Cap-Pele, NB E4N 3B3
Canada   506-577-4730
      Fax: 506-577-4960 sales@leslieandsons.com
            http://www.leslieandsons.com
Processor and exporter of smoked herring and brined alewife
President: Leslie Leger
Estimated Sales: $4.8 Million
Number Employees: 35
Type of Packaging: Bulk
Regions Exported to: Haiti , Greece
Percentage of Business in Exporting: 100

46009 Letica Corp
52585 Dequindre Rd
Rochester Hills, MI 48307-2321 248-652-0557
            Fax: 248-608-2153   800-538-4221
            www.letica.com
Manufacturer and exporter of plastic shipping containers, paper and plastic cups and containers for cultured dairy products and freight lines
CEO: Ilija Letica
iletica@letica.com
CEO: Ilija Letica
Sales Director: David Bradwell
Public Relations: David Schueler
Estimated Sales: $ 5 - 10 Million
Number Employees: 1000-4999
Regions Exported to: Worldwide

46010 Letrah International Corp
W7603 Koshkonong Mounds Rd
Fort Atkinson, WI 53538-8709   920-563-6597
      Fax: 920-563-7515 doughartel@gmail.com
            www.hartelinternational.com
Manufacturer, importer and exporter of process control systems including blending, processing, clean-in-place, refrigeration, level, load cell, metering, proportioning and packaging.
President: Douglas Hartel
doughartel@gmail.com
Estimated Sales: Less Than $500,000
Number Employees: 1-4
Square Footage: 5332
Regions Exported to: Central America, South America, Europe, Asia, Russia
Percentage of Business in Exporting: 40
Regions Imported from: Central America, South America, Europe, Asia, Russia
Percentage of Business in Importing: 40

46011 Lettieri & Co LTD
120 Park Ln
Brisbane, CA 94005-1312   415-657-3392
      Fax: 415-657-9957 lettieri@lettieri.com
            www.lettieriandco.com
Importer of pasta, olive oil, vinegar, condiments, and coffee
Owner: Catherine Plummer
catherine_plummer@rand.org
Estimated Sales: $ 1 - 3 Million
Number Employees: 10-19

Importers & Exporters / A-Z

46012 Levant
3390 Rand Road
S Plainfield, NJ 07080-1307
908-754-1166
Fax: 908-754-9666 www.levantpdx.com
Wholesaler/distributor and importer of spices, dried fruits and nuts
President: Reha Guzelay
Contact: Ray Guzelay
ray@levantinc.com
Estimated Sales: $2.5-5 Million
Number Employees: 1-4
Square Footage: 80000

46013 Lewin Group
4801 W Peterson Ave # 200
Chicago, IL 60646-5725
773-202-1300
Fax: 773-472-1435
President: Benjamin Lewin
Estimated Sales: $ 3 - 5 Million
Number Employees: 20-49

46014 Lewis M Carter Mfg Co Inc
Highway 84 W
Donalsonville, GA 39845
229-524-2197
Fax: 229-524-2531 800-332-8232
lmc@lmcarter.com www.lmcarter.com
Manufacturer and exporter of peanut shellers, cleaners, vibratory conveyors, elevators, sizing shakers, reclaimers, stoners, gravity separators, belt sizers, bean polishers, blanchers and bean ladders. Also air pollution control equipment
President: Lewis Carter Jr
CFO: Gordon Carpenter
gordon.caarpenter@lmcarter.com
Sales Representative: David Sandlin
Sales Manager: Jack Williams, Jr.
Estimated Sales: $ 10 - 20 Million
Number Employees: 100-249
Square Footage: 600000
Brands Exported: LMC
Regions Exported to: Central America, South America, Europe, Asia, Middle East
Percentage of Business in Exporting: 20

46015 Lewisburg Printing
170 Woodside Ave
Lewisburg, TN 37091-2866
931-359-1526
Fax: 931-270-3112 800-559-1526
info@lpcink.com www.lpcink.com
Manufacturer and exporter of litho sheet labels, point of purchase advertising brochures, posters and manuals
President: Seawell Brandau
CEO: Thomas Hale Hawkins, IV
CEO: Hale Hawkins
VP Sales: Kirk Kelso
Director Of Operations: Brian Tankersley
Estimated Sales: $ 5-10 Million
Number Employees: 50-99
Regions Exported to: Canada, Caribbean
Percentage of Business in Exporting: 1

46016 (HQ)Lewtan Industries Corporation
PO Box 2049
Hartford, CT 06145-2049
860-278-9800
Fax: 860-278-9019 lewtan@snet.net
Manufacturer and exporter of advertising specialties and promotional products including coasters, mighty grips, skimmers, clips, emblems, tape measures, mouse pads, calendars, etc
President: Douglas Lewtan
Estimated Sales: $10 Million
Number Employees: 20-49
Square Footage: 74000
Regions Exported to: Worldwide
Percentage of Business in Exporting: 5

46017 Lexidyne of Pennsylvania
PO Box 5372
Pittsburgh, PA 15206-0372
412-661-4526
Fax: 858-815-7346 800-543-2233
General Manager: Rick Simoni
Number Employees: 10-19

46018 Lexington Logistics LLC
N7660 Industrial Rd
Portage, WI 53901-9451
608-742-5303
Fax: 608-742-9153 800-356-8150
bklimko@wilbertinc.com www.trienda.com
President: Curtis Zamec
curtis.zamec@trienda.com
Marketing Manager: Paul Schoeder
Sales Director: Rick Sasse
Estimated Sales: $ 1 - 5 Million
Number Employees: 250-499
Square Footage: 1200000
Parent Co: Wilbert
Regions Exported to: Central America
Percentage of Business in Exporting: 1

46019 Leyman Manufacturing Corporation
10900 Kenwood Rd
Cincinnati, OH 45242
513-891-6210
Fax: 513-891-4901 866-539-6261
www.leymanlift.com
Manufacturer, importer and exporter of trailer and truck loading and unloading equipment, hydraulic lifts, elevators, tailgates, platforms, carts, dollies and van bodies
President: John McHenry
Marketing: Joann Russo
VP Sales: Chip Drews
Contact: Larry Disque
ldisque@leymanlift.com
Estimated Sales: $20-50 Million
Number Employees: 50-99
Type of Packaging: Food Service
Other Locations:
 Leyman Manufacturing Corp.
 Cincinnati, OHLeyman Manufacturing Corp.
Regions Exported to: South America, Europe
Percentage of Business in Exporting: 5
Regions Imported from: Europe
Percentage of Business in Importing: 10

46020 Libbey Inc.
300 Madison Ave.
Toledo, OH 43604
419-325-2100
Fax: 419-325-2749 info@libbey.com
www.libbey.com
Table glassware.
Chairman/CEO: William Foley
william.foley@libbey.com
Senior VP/CFO: Jim Burmeister
Vice President/Chief Information Officer: Dave Anderson
Year Founded: 1818
Estimated Sales: $797.9 Million
Number Employees: 6,230
Number of Brands: 8
Brands Exported: Libbey
Regions Exported to: Worldwide

46021 Liberty Engineering Co
10567 Main St
Roscoe, IL 61073-8830
815-623-7677
Fax: 815-623-7050 877-623-9065
info@libertyengineering.com
www.libertyengineering.com
Manufacturer and exporter of rotary dies, candy molds, starch molding processing equipment and depositing pumps
President: Brian Belardi
bbelardi@libertyengineering.com
Engineering Manager: John Micinski
Quality Control: Rob Klein
Plant Manager: John Akelaitis
Estimated Sales: Below $5 Million
Number Employees: 10-19
Square Footage: 40000
Parent Co: Libco Industries
Regions Exported to: Central America, South America, Europe, Middle East, Canada
Percentage of Business in Exporting: 25

46022 Liberty Gold Fruit Co Inc
500 Eccles Ave
S San Francisco, CA 94080-1905
650-583-4700
Fax: 650-583-4770 timr@libertygold.com
www.libertygold.com
Wholesaler/distributor and exporter of fruit
Owner: Harry Battatt
harry@libertygold.com
Estimated Sales: $5-10 Million
Number Employees: 10-19
Regions Exported to: Worldwide
Percentage of Business in Exporting: 70

46023 Liberty Machine Company
125 Derry Court
York, PA 17406-8405
717-848-1493
Fax: 800-745-8150 800-745-8152
Manufacturer and exporter of wire racks and grilles for refrigerators, ovens, etc.; also, wire material handling equipment
President: Brad Stump
Secretary/Treasurer: Patti Miller
Estimated Sales: $ 3 - 5 Million
Number Employees: 20
Square Footage: 36000
Type of Packaging: Food Service
Regions Exported to: Central America

46024 Liberty Natural Products Inc
20949 S Harris Rd
Oregon City, OR 97045-9428
503-631-4488
Fax: 503-631-2424 800-289-8427
jim@libertynatural.com www.libertynatural.com
Processor and exporter of gourmet breath fresheners, natural flavors and oils; processor of vitamins; importer of essential oils and botanical extracts; wholesaler/distributor of gourmet breath fresheners
Owner: Jim Derking
Sales Manager: Tabor Helton
jim@libertynatural.com
Operations Manager: Shane Reaney
Purchasing Manager: Michelle Falls
Estimated Sales: $1-2.5 Million
Number Employees: 20-49
Square Footage: 68000
Type of Packaging: Consumer, Bulk
Brands Exported: Max; Tib
Regions Exported to: Worldwide
Percentage of Business in Exporting: 3
Regions Imported from: Central America, South America, Europe, Asia, Middle East
Percentage of Business in Importing: 25

46025 Liberty Orchards Co Inc
117 Mission Ave
P.O. Box C
Cashmere, WA 98815-1007
509-782-2191
Fax: 509-782-1487 800-231-3242
sales@libertyorchards.com
www.libertyorchards.com
Processor and exporter of confectionery products including chocolate, holiday and boxed nonchocolate candy
President: Sue Meiner
sue@libertyorchards.com
VP Marketing & Sales: Michael Rainey Sr
Estimated Sales: $12,377,000
Number Employees: 50-99
Type of Packaging: Consumer, Food Service
Regions Exported to: Worldwide

46026 Liberty Richter
1455 Broad St
Bloomfield, NJ 07003-3047
973-338-0300
Fax: 973-338-0382 info@worldfiner.com
www.libertyrichter.com
Wholesaler, distributor and importer of gourmet foods including jam, balsamic vinegar, French sea salt, French olives, olive oil, soups, cookies, pickled vegetables and sugars. Customers they serve include supermarket chainsindependent grocers, specialty & ethnic stores, convenience stores, drug & mass market stores and foodservice.
Division President: David Billings
Marketing Manager: Killeen Hasan
Director of Sales: Mark Klarich
Contact: Dilenia Chireno
dchireno@worldfiner.com
Estimated Sales: $5-10,000,000
Number Employees: 10-19
Square Footage: 80000
Parent Co: World Finer Foods
Brands Imported: Duke of Modena; Balsamic Vinegar; Mornflake Oatmeal
Regions Imported from: Europe
Percentage of Business in Importing: 100

46027 Liberty Ware LLC
PO Box 160450
Clearfield, UT 84016-0450
801-825-5885
Fax: 801-825-5875 888-500-5885
bbbrisko@aol.com
Manufacturer, importer and exporter of frying and stock pans, flatware, thermometers, disposable gloves and aprons, tongs, ladles, salt and pepper shakers and portion control equipment
Owner: Robert Brisko
rbrisko@libertywareusa.com
Estimated Sales: $ 1 - 2,500,000
Number Employees: 10-19
Regions Exported to: Worldwide

Importers & Exporters / A-Z

Regions Imported from: Asia, India
Percentage of Business in Importing: 95

46028 Libido Funk Circus
P.O.Box 2610
Orlando, FL 60462 630-294-7132
Fax: 708-460-6076 www.lfcentertainment.com
Wholesaler/distributor, importer and exporter of game including antelope, bear, kangaroo, rattle-snake, elk, partridge, alligator, zebra, etc
CEO: Gregory A Landry
Secretary: Carmen Landry
VP Sales/Marketing: Greg Landry
Number Employees: 20-49
Parent Co: LFC
Regions Exported to: Europe, Asia, Latin America
Percentage of Business in Exporting: 30
Regions Imported from: Asia
Percentage of Business in Importing: 15

46029 Lifestar Millennium
PO Box 3837
Sedona, AZ 86340 925-202-4302
Fax: 970-422-4739 877-422-4739
lsmail@lifestar.com
Processor and exporter of natural nutritional supplements; importer of grapeseed oil
President: J Bentley
Estimated Sales: $300,000-500,000
Number Employees: 1-4
Type of Packaging: Consumer, Food Service
Brands Exported: Food Matrix
Regions Exported to: Asia
Regions Imported from: Europe

46030 Lifestyle Health Guide
1603 Capitol Ave
Suite 314
Cheyenne, WY 82001 307-529-1239
Fax: 805-650-0997 800-822-3712
Processor, exporter and importer of health products including nutritional supplements
Owner: Larry Permen
President: Jean Koven
VP: Larry Permen
Estimated Sales: $ 3 - 5,000,000
Number Employees: 1-4
Regions Exported to: Europe, Asia, Latin America , Africa
Percentage of Business in Importing: 20

46031 (HQ)Lifetime Brands Inc
1000 Stewart Ave
Garden City, NY 11530-4814 516-683-6000
Fax: 516-555-0101 questions@lifetimebrands.com
www.lifetimebrands.com
Exporter, importer and manufacturer of cutlery and gadgets
President: Steven Lizak
Chairman of the Board: Jeffrey Siegel
CFO: Rob Roknznally
VP: Bruce Cohen
VP: Larry Sklute
Number Employees: 1000-4999
Square Footage: 800

46032 Lifeway
6431 W Oakton St
Morton Grove, IL 60053 847-967-1010
Fax: 847-967-6558 877-281-3874
lifewaykefir.com
Kefir, frozen kefir, specialty cheeses and probiotic beverages for kids
President and CEO: Julie Smolyansky
julies@lifeway.net
CFO: Eric Hanson
Sr. EVP, Sales: Amy Feldman
COO: Edward Smolyansky
Estimated Sales: $ 4 Million
Number Employees: 250-499
Square Footage: 240000
Type of Packaging: Consumer
Regions Exported to: Central America, Europe, Canada
Percentage of Business in Exporting: 10

46033 Lift Rite
5975 Falbourne Street - Unit 3
Mississauga, ON L5R 3L8
Canada 905-456-2603
Fax: 905-456-1383 www.liftrite.com
Manufacturer and exporter of stackers, pallet trucks, easy lifts and hi-lifters
President: Mel Griffin

Number Employees: 90
Regions Exported to: USA
Percentage of Business in Exporting: 80

46034 Liftomatic Material Handling
700 Dartmouth Ln
Buffalo Grove, IL 60089-6902 847-325-2930
Fax: 847-325-2959 800-837-6540
sales@liftomatic.com www.liftomatic.com
Manufacturer and exporter of drum handlers, lift truck attachments and lifting equipment
President: Todd Berg
tpberg@liftomatic.com
Sales Manager: E Darren Berg
Inside Sales: Angela Foster
Estimated Sales: $3-5,000,000
Number Employees: 10-19
Square Footage: 34000
Brands Exported: Liftomatic; Ergo-Matic Transporters
Regions Exported to: Worldwide
Percentage of Business in Exporting: 35

46035 Light Technology Ind
811 Russell Ave # 302
Suite 302
Gaithersburg, MD 20879-3518 301-990-4050
Fax: 301-990-7525 sales@ltindustries.com
www.ltindustries.com
Manufacturer and exporter of control systems and instrumentation for quality control measurements in labs and on line, including, liquid, solid, powders, pellets, etc.
President: Aviva Landa
Marketing Director: Aviva Landa
Estimated Sales: $1-5 Million
Number Employees: 10-19
Regions Exported to: Central America, South America, Europe, Asia, Middle East
Percentage of Business in Exporting: 50

46036 Light Waves Concept
The Esquire Building 41st St
4100 1st Ave 3rd Floor North
Brooklyn, NY 11232 212-677-5230
Fax: 347-416-6201 800-670-8137
customerservice@lightwavesconcept.com
www.lightwavesconcept.com
Manufacturer, importer and exporter of lighting fixtures and low voltage track lighting
President: Joel Slavis
Estimated Sales: Below $ 5 Million
Number Employees: 10-19
Square Footage: 12000
Regions Exported to: Worldwide
Percentage of Business in Exporting: 5
Regions Imported from: Worldwide
Percentage of Business in Importing: 50

46037 Lightlife
153 Industrial Blvd
Turners Falls, MA 01376 413-774-9000
Fax: 413-774-9080 800-769-3279
info@lightlife.com lightlife.com
Processor and exporter of soy-based products like chili, sausages, deli meats, ground meat, tempeh, chicken, burgers and bacon
President: Daniel Abrahamson
dabrahamson@lightlife.com
General Manager: Darcy Zbinovec
R&D: Ron Desautels
Human Resources Director: Bobby Riley
Product Manager: Dean Kuhlka
Year Founded: 1979
Estimated Sales: $ 20 - 50 Million
Number Employees: 100-249
Square Footage: 80000
Parent Co: Maple Leaf Foods
Regions Exported to: Asia
Percentage of Business in Exporting: 5

46038 Lights On
1960 Central Park Ave
Yonkers, NY 10710 914-961-0588
Fax: 914-961-0589
Manufacturer, importer and exporter of lighting fixtures
Manager: Glenn Aroni
Estimated Sales: Less than $ 500,000
Number Employees: 10-19
Square Footage: 6000
Regions Exported to: Worldwide
Regions Imported from: China, Taiwan, Spain, Italy, France , India

46039 Liguria Foods Inc
1515 15th St N
Humboldt, IA 50548-1017 515-332-4121
Fax: 515-332-2629 www.liguriafoods.com
Sausage and salami; exporter of hard and Genoa salami and pepperoni.
Owner: Roger Lawson
Estimated Sales: $25 Million
Number Employees: 50-99
Square Footage: 45000
Parent Co: SMG
Type of Packaging: Consumer, Food Service, Private Label, Bulk
Brands Exported: Liguria
Regions Exported to: Europe, Asia, Canada, Latin America
Percentage of Business in Exporting: 5

46040 Lil' Orbits
2850 Vicksburg Ln N
Minneapolis, MN 55447 763-559-7505
Fax: 763-559-7545 800-228-8305
contact@lilorbits.com
Manufacturer and exporter of vending carts, displays and automatic doughnut and crepe/pancake machines and accessories
Founder: Ed Anderson
e.anderon@lilorbits.com
President: Charlie Anderson
Vice President: Brian OGara
Marketing: Mike Foster
Sales: Brian O'Gara
Office Manager: Sue Larson
Service Production Manager: Terry OGara
Purchasing: Terry O'Gara
Estimated Sales: $ 3 - 5 Million
Number Employees: 10-19
Number of Brands: 2
Number of Products: 10
Square Footage: 100000
Brands Exported: Lil' Orbits; Orbie

46041 Lillsun Manufacturing Co
1350 Harris St
PO Box 767
Huntington, IN 46750-4302 260-356-6514
Fax: 260-356-8337 mail@lillsun.com
www.lillsun.com
Manufacturer and exporter of bakers' woodenware including pizza and oven peels, paddles and proofing boards
President: Bill Sundermann
mail@lillsun.com
VP: W Sunderman
Estimated Sales: $ 1-2.5 Million
Number Employees: 5-9
Regions Exported to: Canada
Percentage of Business in Exporting: 5

46042 Lilly Co Inc
3613 Knight Arnold Rd
Memphis, TN 38118-2729 901-363-6000
Fax: 901-795-7000 800-238-3006
www.lillyforklifts.com
Exporter and wholesaler/distributor of ice processing machinery including breakers and sizers; also, storage systems, fork lift truck parts and material handling equipment
Owner: Frank Clark
fclark@embracesafety.com
CEO: Craig Avery
CFO: Bob Davidson
Estimated Sales: $20-50 Million
Number Employees: 100-249
Square Footage: 40000
Brands Exported: Lift Trucks
Regions Exported to: Central America, South America
Percentage of Business in Exporting: 1

46043 Lily of the Desert
1887 Geesling Rd
Denton, TX 76208 940-566-9914
Fax: 940-566-9925 800-229-5459
contact@lilyofthedesert.com
www.lilyofthedesert.com
Organic aloe vera beverages, cold brew coffee and tea, and dietary supplements
President: Don Lovelace
dlovelace@lilyofthedesert.com
Year Founded: 1971
Estimated Sales: $ 1 - 3 Million
Number Employees: 20-49

Importers & Exporters / A-Z

Type of Packaging: Consumer, Food Service, Private Label, Bulk
Brands Exported: Lily of the Desert
Regions Exported to: Worldwide

46044 Lilydale Foods
100 Commerce Valley Dr W
Markham, ON L3T 0A1
Canada
800-661-5341
www.lilydale.com
Fresh and frozen meats, poultry, sausages and sandwiches; also, further processed poultry products including fully cooked, par cooked, breaded and unbreaded.
Executive Chairman, Sofina Foods: Michael Latifi
President/CEO: Robert Wilt
Year Founded: 1940
Estimated Sales: Over $1 Billion
Number Employees: 2700
Square Footage: 81978
Parent Co: Sofina Foods Incorporated
Type of Packaging: Consumer, Food Service, Bulk
Brands Exported: Lilydale
Regions Exported to: Worldwide
Percentage of Business in Exporting: 5

46045 Lima Grain Cereal Seeds LLC
2040 SE Frontage Rd
Fort Collins, CO 80525-9717   970-498-2200
Fax: 970-223-4302 LCS-info@limagrain.com
www.limagrain.com
Processor and distributor of breakfast cereals in boxes and bags
President: Bernie Blach
Secretary: Cindy Blach
CFO: Kelly Mundorf
Executive VP: Cedric Audebert
cedric.audebert@limagrain.com
Marketing/Technical Manager: Zach Gaines
Number Employees: 5-9
Square Footage: 80000
Type of Packaging: Consumer, Food Service, Private Label, Bulk
Brands Exported: Colorado's Kernels; Las Palomas Grandes; Pop'n Snak
Regions Exported to: Worldwide
Percentage of Business in Exporting: 95

46046 Limberis Seafood Processing
5025 Limberis Drive
Ladysmith, BC V9G 1M6
Canada   250-245-3021
Fax: 250-245-3603 info@limberisseafood.com
www.limberisseafood.com
Exporter of fresh clams and oysters
President: Leo Limberis
Plant Manager: Mike Langlet
Assistant Plant Manager: Kathleen Nicholls
Number Employees: 10-19
Square Footage: 80000
Type of Packaging: Consumer, Food Service, Private Label, Bulk
Brands Exported: North Cove Manila Clams
Regions Exported to: USA
Percentage of Business in Exporting: 100

46047 Limpert Bros Inc
202 N West Blvd
Vineland, NJ 8360   856-691-1353
Fax: 856-794-8968 800-691-1353
www.limpertbrothers.com
Processor, importer and exporter of marshmallow fluff, hot fudge, cherries, butterscotch, carmel, and other toppings, flavors and ingredients.
President: Pearl Giordano
limpertbr@aol.com
R&D: Jim Behringer
Quality Control: Donna Phrampus
Estimated Sales: $1 Million
Number Employees: 10-19
Number of Brands: 1
Number of Products: 400
Square Footage: 280000
Type of Packaging: Food Service, Bulk
Regions Exported to: Europe, Middle East, Latin America, Canada, Caribbean
Percentage of Business in Exporting: 5
Regions Imported from: Mexico
Percentage of Business in Importing: 5

46048 (HQ)Lin Pac Plastics
200 Windrift Court
3
Roswell, GA 30076-3727   770-751-6006
Fax: 770-751-7154
Manufacturer and exporter of plastic egg cartons and food service packaging containers; also, processing and packaging trays
Sales/Marketing Manager: James Gullo
Other Locations:
  Lin Pac Plastics
  Sebring, FL Lin Pac Plastics
Regions Exported to: Central America, South America
Percentage of Business in Exporting: 2

46049 LinPac
6842 Templin Ct
San Angelo, TX 76904-4112   325-651-7378
Fax: 325-651-7482 800-453-7393
Manufacturer and exporter of corrugated boxes and other packaging materials
President: Robert Hanton
Quality Control: Alvin Kennedy
R&D: Sal Flores
President: Nigel Roe
Plant Manager: Danny Lopez
Estimated Sales: $ 10 - 20 Million
Number Employees: 20-49
Square Footage: 100000
Parent Co: LinPac
Regions Exported to: Central America
Percentage of Business in Exporting: 50

46050 Lincoln Food Service
1333 East 179th Street
PO Box 1229
Cleveland, OH 44110   260-459-8200
Fax: 800-285-9511 800-374-3004
www.lincolnfp.com
President: Charlie Kingdon
Contact: Bob Dellert
dellertrobert@lincolnfp.com

46051 Lincoln Foodservice
1333 East 179th Street
Cleveland, OH 44110   260-459-8200
Fax: 800-285-9511 800-374-3004
www.lincolnfp.com
Designs, manufactures, and markets commercial and institutional foodservice cooking equipment, serving systems, and utensils. The company also manufactures and markets a line of electric Fresh-O-Matic food steamers.
President: Charlie Kingdon
Plant Manager: Jim Muston
Purchasing Manager: Tom Hengy
Number Employees: 250-499
Regions Exported to: Worldwide

46052 Linda's Lollies Company
1 International Blvd
Ste 208
Mahwan, NJ 07495-002   20- 25- 876
Fax: 201-252-8768 800-347-1545
info@lindaslollies.com www.lindaslollies.com
Processor and exporter of gourmet lollypops and confectionery gifts
President: Linda Harkavy
Sales & Marketing: Tammy Demone
Customer Services: Connie Atticella
Estimated Sales: $1500000
Number Employees: 1-4
Type of Packaging: Consumer, Food Service, Bulk
Brands Exported: Linda's Lollies
Regions Exported to: Worldwide

46053 Line-Master Products
PO Box 407
Cocolalla, ID 83813-0407   208-265-4743
Fax: 208-265-9393
Manufacturer and exporter of work benches, push carts and fixed and mobile material handling racks
President: Jackie Warren
Estimated Sales: $ 1-2.5 Million
Number Employees: 5-9
Parent Co: Sandefur Engineering Company
Regions Exported to: Canada, Mexico
Percentage of Business in Exporting: 10

46054 (HQ)Linear Lighting Corp
3130 Hunters Point Ave
Long Island City, NY 11101-3132   718-361-7552
Fax: 718-937-2747 mike@linearltg.com

Manufacturer and exporter of lighting fixtures
President: Larry Deutsch
larry@linearltg.com
CFO: Lois Shorr
R&D: Kewin Ehrhardt
Estimated Sales: $ 20 - 50 Million
Number Employees: 100-249
Regions Exported to: Worldwide

46055 Linker Machines
20 Pine St
Rockaway, NJ 07866-5131   973-983-0001
Fax: 973-983-0011 sales@linkermachines.com
www.linkermachines.com
Manufacturer and exporter of automatic sausage linking and peeling machinery; also, general purpose grease
Owner: Jean Hebrank
sales@linkermachines.com
VP: R Hebrank
General Manager: Rob Hebrank, Jr.
Estimated Sales: $2.5-5 Million
Number Employees: 1-4
Square Footage: 8000
Brands Exported: Ty-Linker; Ty-Peeler
Regions Exported to: Worldwide
Percentage of Business in Exporting: 35

46056 Linvar
237 Hamilton St
Suite 202
Hartford, CT 6106   860-951-3818
Fax: 860-951-3547 800-282-5288
Manufacturer and exporter of metal shelving systems and plastic containers
Vice President: John Ramondetta
General Manager: John Ahern
Estimated Sales: $ 5 - 10 Million
Number Employees: 10-19
Square Footage: 50000
Regions Exported to: Central America, South America, Europe, Asia, Middle East
Percentage of Business in Exporting: 20

46057 (HQ)Linzer Products Corp
248 Wyandanch Ave
West Babylon, NY 11704-1506   631-253-3333
Fax: 631-253-9750 800-423-3254
info@linzerproducts.com www.linzerproducts.com
Manufacturer and exporter of confectioners' and bakers' brushes and rollers
President: Alan Benson
CEO: Mark Aaronson
elliottw@linzerproducts.com
VP Sales: Brent Swenson
VP Production: Sidney Zichvin
Number Employees: 100-249
Type of Packaging: Consumer

46058 Lion Labels Inc
15 Hampden Dr
South Easton, MA 02375-1159   508-230-8211
Fax: 508-230-8116 800-875-5300
epage@lionlabels.com www.lionlabels.com
Manufacturer and exporter of signage, pressure sensitive labels and decals
President: Jerome Berke
jberke@lionlabels.com
CEO: Michael Berke
CFO: Nina Berke
Sales Director: Moe Decelles
Operations Manager: Ed Page
Production Manager: Bruce Boteliao
Estimated Sales: $ 4.7 Million
Number Employees: 20-49
Square Footage: 58000
Type of Packaging: Consumer, Food Service, Private Label, Bulk
Regions Exported to: Europe, Canada
Percentage of Business in Exporting: 8

46059 Lion Raisins Inc
9500 S DE Wolf Ave
Selma, CA 93662-9534   559-834-6677
Fax: 559-834-6622 www.lionraisins.com
Grower and processor of California raisins and raisin products.
CEO: Al Lion
alion@lionsraisins.com
Number Employees: 250-499
Square Footage: 130000
Type of Packaging: Consumer, Food Service, Private Label, Bulk

Regions Exported to: Central America, South America, Europe, Asia, Middle East, Australia
Percentage of Business in Exporting: 50

46060 Lionel Hitchen Essitional Oils
1867 Porter Lake Drive
Sarasota, FL 34240   941-379-1400
Fax: 941-379-1433   www.lheo.co.uk
Natural flavors and oils
President: Alison Barnes
General Manager: Suzy Nolan
snolan@lhitchenusa.com
Estimated Sales: $700,000
Number Employees: 8

46061 (HQ)Liqui-Box
901 E. Byrd St.
Suite 1105
Richmond, VA 23219
   804-325-1400
   www.liquibox.com
Food and industrial plastic packaging and packaging systems.
President/CEO: Ken Swanson
Chief Financial Officer: Leanne Parker
Chief Operating Officer: Andrew McLeland
Senior VP, Research & Development: Greg Gard
Senior VP, Sales & Marketing: Paul Kase
Year Founded: 1961
Estimated Sales: $128.6 Million
Number Employees: 684

46062 Liqui-Box Corp
901 E Byrd St # 1105
Richmond, VA 23219-4068   804-325-1400
Fax: 614-888-0982   804-325-1400
liquibox@liquibox.com   www.liquibox.com
Manufacturer and exporter of form, fill and seal pouch packaging machinery; also, bag-in-box, retort and dispenser systems
CEO: Terry Barfield
tbarfield@hillcresttransportation.com
Plant Manager: Barry Pritchard
Estimated Sales: $ 5-10 Million
Number Employees: 500-999
Parent Co: Liqui-Box Corporation
Regions Exported to: South America, Europe

46063 Liquid Scale
2033 Old Highway 8 NW
New Brighton, MN 55112   651-633-2969
Fax: 651-633-2969   888-633-2969
Manufacturer and exporter of milk silo air agitators, liquid level gauges and controls and needlepoint dividers
Estimated Sales: Under $ 300,000
Number Employees: 1-4
Square Footage: 6000

46064 (HQ)Liquid Solids Control Inc
10 Farm St
Upton, MA 01568-1665   508-529-3377
Fax: 508-529-6591   paulb@liquidsolidscontrol.com
   www.liquidsolidscontrol.com
Manufacturer and exporter of in-line process control refractometers for continuous measurement and production; also, quality assurance of dissolved food solids available
President: Paul R Bonneau
usa@liquidsolidscontrol.com
CFO: Paul R Bonneau
VP: Gordon Vandenburg
Estimated Sales: $ 10 - 20 Million
Number Employees: 10-19
Square Footage: 50000
Other Locations:
   Liquid Solids Control
   Victoria, BC Liquid Solids Control
Brands Exported: LSC Model 725
Regions Exported to: Worldwide
Percentage of Business in Exporting: 25

46065 Lista International Corp
106 Lowland St
Holliston, MA 01746-2094   508-429-1350
Fax: 508-626-0353   800-722-3020
sales@listaintl.com   www.listaintl.com
Storage and workbench products.
President: Peter Lariviere
CFO: David Gavlik
Vice President: John Alfieri
Marketing: Anne Swagoriusky
Sales: John Alfieri
Estimated Sales: $50-100 Million
Number Employees: 100-249
Number of Brands: 2
Square Footage: 225000
Parent Co: Stanley Black & Decker
Regions Exported to: Central America, South America
Percentage of Business in Exporting: 10

46066 Listo Pencil Corp
1925 Union St
Alameda, CA 94501-1345   510-522-2910
Fax: 510-522-3798   800-547-8648
sales@listo.com   www.listo.com
Manufacturer and exporter of mechanical marking pencils, carton openers and industrial razor blades
President: Rick Stuart
rick@listo.com
VP: Rick Stuart
Estimated Sales: Less Than $500,000
Number Employees: 1-4
Square Footage: 34000
Brands Exported: Listo
Regions Exported to: Central America, Europe
Percentage of Business in Exporting: 5

46067 Lite-Weight Tool & Mfg Co
8621 San Fernando Rd
Sun Valley, CA 91352-3104   818-767-7901
Fax: 818-767-0010   800-859-3529
info@liteweighttool.com   www.liteweighttool.com
Manufacturer and exporter of squeegees including emulsion spreading, handheld and floor
President: C R Brunson
VP: Andy Brunson
Estimated Sales: $500,000
Number Employees: 1-4
Square Footage: 10000
Regions Exported to: Central America, Canada
Percentage of Business in Exporting: 7

46068 Litecontrol
65 Spring St
Plympton, MA 02367-1701   781-294-0164
Fax: 781-293-2849   www.litecontrol.com
Manufacturer and exporter of lighting fixtures
President/CEO: Brian Golden
brian.golden@litecontrol.com
Senior Accountant: Kristen Woods
VP/Sales: Vince Santini
R&D: Paul Duane
Quality Control: James Pierce
Marketing Manager: Cory Passerello
Sales: Vince Santini
Project Manager: Barbara Goodwin
Estimated Sales: $ 5 - 10 Million
Number Employees: 100-249

46069 (HQ)Litehouse Foods
100 Litehouse Dr
Sandpoint, ID 83864
   800-669-3169
   www.litehousefoods.com
Dressings and dips; portion control and bulk available, including vinaigrette, bleu cheese, ranch, caesar, coleslaw dressing, french, cumin citrus, tartar sauce, burger spread, BBQ sauce, cocktail sauce, deli salsa, mayonaise horseradish, raspberry, honey mustard, Italian, also low calorie, specialty, and gluten free sauces and dressings.
President & CEO: Kelly Prior
VP, Finance & Accounting: Matt Burrows
SVP, Sales & Marketing: Brent Carr
VP, Operations: Rob Tyrrell
VP, Information Technology: Derek Christensen
Year Founded: 1963
Estimated Sales: $100-500 Million
Number Employees: 250-499
Type of Packaging: Consumer, Food Service, Private Label, Bulk

46070 Lithonia Lighting
1400 Lester Rd NW
Conyers, GA 30012-3908   770-922-9000
Fax: 770-483-2635   comments@lithonia.com
   www.lithonia.com
Manufacturer and exporter of electric and fluorescent lighting fixtures
President: Vern Nagel
CFO: Wesley Wittich
wes.wittich@acuitybrands.com
Number Employees: 20-49

46071 Little Crow Foods
PO Box 1038
Warsaw, IN 46581-1038   574-267-7141
Fax: 574-267-2370   800-288-2769
customerservice@littlecrowfoods.com
   www.littlecrowfoods.com
Manufacturer and contract packager of dry blended products including flour, pancake mixes and breakfast cereals; exporter of flour, cereals and seasoned coating mixes
President: Dennis Fuller
EVP: Kimberly Fuller
VP Operations: Ron Shipley
Estimated Sales: $8 Million
Number Employees: 50-99
Square Footage: 360000
Type of Packaging: Consumer, Food Service, Private Label, Bulk
Brands Exported: Fastshake; Frying Magic; CoCo Wheats; Miracle Maize
Regions Exported to: Central America, South America, Europe, Asia, Canada

46072 Little Giant Pump Company
9255 Covedale Rd.
Fort Wayne, IN 46809   260-824-2900
Fax: 260-824-2909   www.littlegiant.com
Decorative and outdoor lighting fixtures, and water removal and transfer pumps.
Chairman/CEO: Franklin Electric: Gregg Sengstack
Estimated Sales: $100-500 Million
Number Employees: 500-999
Square Footage: 270000
Parent Co: Franklin Electric
Regions Exported to: Worldwide

46073 Littleford Day
PO Box 128
Florence, KY 41022-0128   859-525-7600
Fax: 859-525-1446   800-365-8555
sales@littleford.com   www.littleford.com
Food processing equipment including mixers, granulators, sterilizers, agglomerators, vacuum dryers, liquid dispensers and pressure cookers; importer and exporter of mixers, dryers and sterilizers
President & CEO: Charles Kroeger
Research & Development: Glen Vice
Marketing & Sales: William R Barker
Contact: Steve Grall
sgrall@littleford.com
Estimated Sales: $50-100 Million
Number Employees: 100-249
Number of Brands: 10
Number of Products: 10
Type of Packaging: Food Service, Private Label

46074 Livingston Farmers Assn
641 6th St
PO Box 456
Livingston, CA 95334-1397   209-394-7941
Fax: 209-394-7952   jim@lfa-ca.com
   www.lfa-ca.com
Processor and exporter of sweet potatoes, peaches and almonds
President: Steve Moler
General Manager/CEO: James Snyder
Manager: Jenny Allen
jenny@lfa-ca.com
Estimated Sales: $6 Million
Number Employees: 20-49
Square Footage: 95200
Regions Exported to: Canada

46075 Livingston-Wilbor Corporation
PO Box 496
Edison, NJ 08818-496   908-322-8403
Fax: 908-322-9230
Manufacturer and exporter of labeler change parts
Purchasing Agent: Chris Haigh
Estimated Sales: $1-2.5 Million
Number Employees: 10-19
Square Footage: 24000
Type of Packaging: Consumer, Food Service, Private Label
Regions Exported to: Central America, South America, Europe, Caribbean

46076 Lixi Inc
120 S Lincoln Ave
Carpentersville, IL 60110-1703   847-961-6666
Fax: 847-961-6667   lixi@lixi.com
   www.lixi.com

Importers & Exporters / A-Z

Manufacturer and exporter of inspection systems specializing in automatic detection of defects and rejection from conveyors
President: Brent Burns
bburns@lixi.com
Sales Manager: Joseph Plevak
Production: Ken Belzey
Estimated Sales: $2.5-5 Million
Number Employees: 10-19
Square Footage: 20000
Regions Exported to: Worldwide
Percentage of Business in Exporting: 70

46077 Lixi, Inc.
11980 Oak Creek Pkwy
Huntley, IL 60142   847-961-6666
Fax: 847-961-6667 lixi@lixi.com
www.lixi.com
Small x-ray imaging systems used for monitoring quality assurance, product malfunctions and fault analysis, security inspection and product tampering.
Contact: Brent Burns
bburns@lixi.com
Regions Exported to: Worldwide

46078 Lloyd Disher Company
5 Powers Lane Place
Decatur, IL 62522-3287   217-429-0593
Fax: 217-423-2611 www.manta.com
Manufacturer and exporter of aluminum alloy Teflon coated ice cream scoops
President: Gordan R Lloyd
Sales Manager: Lucy Murphy
Estimated Sales: $ 1 - 5 Million
Number Employees: 4
Square Footage: 10000
Regions Exported to: Worldwide
Percentage of Business in Exporting: 5

46079 Lo Temp Sales
20 W Park Avenue
Suite 303
Long Beach, NY 11561-2019   516-889-0300
Fax: 516-466-9590 800-645-8086
lindalotemp@aol.com
Importer, exporter and wholesaler/distributor of commercial equipment including refrigerators, shelving, counters, walk-in freezers and coolers, microwave ovens and popcorn, hot dog and soda machines
Marketing Director: L Conti
Estimated Sales: $2.5-5 Million
Number Employees: 5-9
Square Footage: 80000
Regions Exported to: Worldwide
Percentage of Business in Exporting: 1
Regions Imported from: Canada
Percentage of Business in Importing: 5

46080 LoTech Industries
12136 W Bayaud Ave Ste 120
Lakewood, CO 80228   303-202-3537
Fax: 303-202-9252 800-295-0199
Manufacturer and exporter of catering and food service custom imprinted utensils including plastic spoons, tongs, cake servers, pizza cutters, ladles, spatulas, and pasta forks
Vice President: Bev Whiteside
Estimated Sales: $ 2 Million
Number Employees: 3
Type of Packaging: Consumer, Food Service, Private Label, Bulk

46081 Load King Mfg
1357 W Beaver St
Jacksonville, FL 32209-7694   904-354-8882
Fax: 904-353-1984 800-531-4975
www.loadking.com
Manufacturer and exporter of garbage and waste compactors, cardboard recycling balers, stainless steel tables, sinks, wire racks, carts, salad bars, checkout counters, etc. Manufactures fixtures and equipment worldwide to the supermarket, restaurant and retail industries
CEO: Charlie Chupp Jr
VP Sales: Charles Chupp
Estimated Sales: $ 10 - 20 Million
Number Employees: 100-249
Square Footage: 600000
Type of Packaging: Consumer, Food Service
Regions Exported to: Central America, South America, Europe, Asia, Middle East
Percentage of Business in Exporting: 20

46082 LoadBank International
4654 35th St
Orlando, FL 32811-6521   407-957-4000
Fax: 407-957-4175 800-458-9010
Manufacturer and exporter of material handling and distribution equipment including dock staging and cross-docking systems
President: Doug Hughes
Vice President: Mike Willett
Sales Director: Mike Willett
Operations Manager: John Veitch
Estimated Sales: $ 1-2.5 Million
Number Employees: 20-49
Number of Brands: 12
Number of Products: 12
Regions Exported to: Europe, Canada
Percentage of Business in Exporting: 4

46083 Lochhead Mfg. Co.
527 Axminister Dr
Fenton, MO 63026
800-776-2088
sales@lochheadvanilla.com
www.lochheadvanilla.com
Processor and exporter of vanilla extracts including pure, natural and artificial blends.
Co-Owner: John Lochhead
sales@lochheadvanilla.com
Co-Owner: George Lochhead
Estimated Sales: $ 10 - 20 Million
Number Employees: 10-19
Type of Packaging: Consumer, Private Label, Bulk
Regions Exported to: Worldwide

46084 Lock Inspection Systems
207 Authority Drive
Fitchburg, MA 01420-6094   978-343-3716
Fax: 978-343-6278 800-227-5539
sales@lockinspection.com
www.lockinspection.com
Manufacturer, importer and exporter of advanced quality control detection systems including metal detectors, checkweighers and conveyors for the packaging and processing industries
President: Mark D'Onofrio
Marketing Director: Michelle Contois
VP of Sales & Marketing: David Arseneault
Contact: Walter Army
warmy@lockwoodint.com
Production Manager: Brian Clough
Purchasing Manager: John Parker
Estimated Sales: $ 5-10 Million
Number Employees: 20-49
Square Footage: 120000
Parent Co: Transfer Technology Group PLC

46085 Locknane
720 132nd St SW
Suite 207
Everett, WA 98204-9359   425-742-5187
Fax: 425-745-0277 800-848-9854
Manufacturer and exporter of nylon apparel and vinyl aprons; also, jackets
President: Duane Locknane
Marketing Director: Brent Locknane
duane.locknane@locknane.com
Purchasing Manager: Tami Matuizek
Estimated Sales: $ 3 - 5 Million
Number Employees: 25
Square Footage: 14000
Type of Packaging: Food Service
Regions Exported to: Canada
Percentage of Business in Exporting: 10

46086 Locknetics
11819 N Pennsylvania St
Carmel, IN 46032-4555
Fax: 860-584-2136
Manufacturer and exporter of electro-magnetic locking systems
Finance Executive: Robert Zdanowski
Sales Manager: George Nortonen
Estimated Sales: $ 20 - 50 Million
Number Employees: 100-249
Parent Co: Ingersoll-Rand.
Regions Exported to: Worldwide

46087 Lockwood Packaging
271 Salem Street
Unit G
Woburn, MA 01801-2004   781-938-1500
Fax: 781-938-7536 800-641-3100
Manufacturer and exporter of automatic weighing and bagging equipment and supplies; also, repair and operating services available
President: Richard Gold
VP: Thomas Gold
VP: Hans Van Der Sande
Estimated Sales: $ .5 - 1 million
Number Employees: 20-49
Regions Exported to: Central America
Percentage of Business in Exporting: 5

46088 Lodal Inc
620 N Hooper St
Kingsford, MI 49802-5400   906-779-1700
Fax: 906-779-1160 800-435-3500
sales@lodal.com www.lodal.com
Manufacturer and exporter of refuse removal systems
President: Bernie Leger
CFO: Bernard Leger
Director Marketing: Darren Tavonatti
Estimated Sales: $ 10 - 20 Million
Number Employees: 100-249

46089 Lodge Manufacturing Company
503 S Cedar Ave
South Pittsburg, TN 37380   423-837-5919
Fax: 423-837-8279 www.lodgemfg.com
Manufacturer, importer and exporter of cast iron cookware, bakeware and servingware
President: Henry Lodge
CEO: Bob Kellermann
CEO: Robert F Kellermann
R&D: Jeanne Scholze
Quality Control: Lou Zarzaur
VP Sales: Gray Bekurs
Contact: Richard Lodge
rlodge@lodgemfg.com
VP Production: Mike Whitfield
Estimated Sales: $ 20 - 50 Million
Number Employees: 100-249
Type of Packaging: Consumer, Food Service
Regions Exported to: Europe, Asia, Canada
Percentage of Business in Exporting: 4
Regions Imported from: Europe, Asia
Percentage of Business in Importing: 1

46090 Lodi Metal Tech
P.O.Box 967
Lodi, CA 95241-0967   209-334-2500
Fax: 209-334-1259 800-359-5999
Manufacturer and exporter of racks
Manager: Dean Bender
Estimated Sales: $10-20,000,000
Number Employees: 50-99
Square Footage: 310000
Brands Exported: Lodi Metal Tech
Regions Exported to: Asia, Australia, Canada, Mexico, Guam
Percentage of Business in Exporting: 5

46091 Logemann Brothers Co
3150 W Burleigh St
Milwaukee, WI 53210-1999   414-445-3005
Fax: 414-445-1460 logemannbalers@aol.com
Manufacturer and exporter of scrap-metal, liber and refuse bales, also, alligator shears, briquettes and guillotines
Owner: Carl Dieterle
carl@milwpc.com
General Sales Manager: Robert Pichta
Estimated Sales: $2.5 Million
Number Employees: 20-49

46092 Loma International
283 E Lies Rd
Carol Stream, IL 60188-9421   630-588-0900
Fax: 630-588-1394 800-872-5662
www.loma.com
Manufacturer, exporter and importer of metal detectors and weighing equipment
President: Gary Wilson
CFO: Hary Pommier
Technical Director: Mike Nevin
Manager of IT: Brooke Kruger
Marketing Manager: James Chrismas
Sales Manager: Andrey Ivanov
Contact: Carlos Aillon
carlos.aillon@loma.com
Estimated Sales: $ 20 - 50 Million
Number Employees: 50-99
Square Footage: 21000
Regions Exported to: Central America, South America

Importers & Exporters / A-Z

46093 Lombardi Brothers Meat Packers
1926 W Elk Pl
P.O. Box 11277
Denver, CO 80211   303-458-7441
lombardibrothers.com
Beef, pork, lamb and veal; importer of wild game.
President & Owner: Victoria Phillips
General Manager: Jeff Harvey
Year Founded: 1947
Estimated Sales: $30 Million
Number Employees: 60
Square Footage: 30000
Type of Packaging: Food Service
Other Locations:
  Lombardi Brothers Meat
    Fridley, MN
  Lombardi Brothers Meat
    Le Mars, IALombardi Brothers MeatLe Mars
Percentage of Business in Importing: 8

46094 Lombardi's Seafood
1152 Harmon Avenue
Winter Park, FL 32789   407-628-3474
Fax: 407-240-2562 800-879-8411
quality@lombardis.com www.lombardis.com
Processor, importer and wholesaler/distributor of fresh and frozen seafood; serving the food service market
Owner: Vince Lomabardi
VP: Vince Lombardi
Contact: James Carr
jamescarr@lombardis.com
Supervisor: Mike Lombardi
Estimated Sales: $10-20 Million
Number Employees: 100-249
Type of Packaging: Food Service

46095 London Fruit Inc
9010 S Cage Blvd
Pharr, TX 78577-9769   956-781-7799
800-531-7422
barry@londonfruit.com www.londonfruit.com
Importer, exporter and wholesaler/distributor of fresh mangos, limes, papaya, coconuts, dry chiles and Mexican peppers.
President: Barry London
barry@londonfruit.com
Purchasing Agent: Jerry Garcia
Year Founded: 1981
Estimated Sales: $20-50 Million
Number Employees: 20-49
Square Footage: 45000
Type of Packaging: Food Service, Bulk
Brands Imported: Bandera; London
Regions Imported from: Mexico
Percentage of Business in Importing: 90

46096 Lone Pine Enterprise Inc
121 Durkee St
Carlisle, AR 72024   870-552-3217
Processor and exporter rice and soybeans
President: Jason Smith
Estimated Sales: Less Than $500,000
Number Employees: 1-4
Type of Packaging: Consumer, Food Service, Bulk
Brands Exported: Lone Pine
Regions Exported to: Europe, Asia, Canada
Percentage of Business in Exporting: 60

46097 Lone Star Bakery
106 W Liberty St
Round Rock, TX 78664-5122   512-255-7268
Fax: 512-255-6405 www.roundrockdonuts.com
Processor and exporter of pre-baked and frozen buttermilk biscuits, muffins, cinnamon rolls, brownies, sheet cakes, fruit cobblers,pie shells, pecan and fruit pie, and portioned cookie and dough
Owner: Dale Cohrs
VP: Bill Scott
Sales: Rick Perrett
Operations: Damon Smith
Plant Manager: Fred Alexander
Purchasing: Clint Scott
Estimated Sales: $450000
Number Employees: 50-99
Square Footage: 600000
Type of Packaging: Food Service, Private Label, Bulk

46098 Lone Star Container Corp
700 N Wildwood Dr
Irving, TX 75061-8832   972-579-1551
Fax: 972-554-6081 800-552-6937
jphipps@lonestarbox.com
www.lonestarcontainer.com
Manufacturer and exporter of corrugated boxes
President: Jerry C Hardison
jhardison@lonestarbox.com
CEO: John McLeod
Manager: Joe Phipps
Estimated Sales: $500,000-$1 Million
Number Employees: 100-249
Regions Exported to: Mexico

46099 Lonestar Banners & Flags
212 S Main St
Fort Worth, TX 76104-1223   817-335-2548
Fax: 817-877-1610 800-288-9625
www.fortworthflag.com
Flags, banners, outdoor advertising displays and pennants; exporter of flags
President: James Eggleston
Vice President: Mark Buechelle
info@abcflag.com
VP Marketing: Pam Engelhardt
Estimated Sales: $5-10 Million
Number Employees: 20-49
Square Footage: 80000
Regions Exported to: Central America
Percentage of Business in Exporting: 2

46100 Long Reach ManufacturingCompany
136 Main Street
Suite 4
Westport, CT 06880-3304   713-434-3400
Fax: 713-433-9710 800-285-7000
www.longreach.com
Manufacturer and exporter of lift truck attachments and pallet trucks
Chief Executive Officer: William Masson
Chief Financial Officer: William Masson
Vice President: Pat Poyton
Estimated Sales: $33 Million
Number Employees: 142
Regions Exported to: Worldwide
Percentage of Business in Exporting: 25

46101 Longbottom Coffee & TeaInc
4893 NW 235th Ave # 101
Hillsboro, OR 97124-5835   503-648-1271
Fax: 503-681-0944 800-288-1271
info@longbottomcoffee.com
www.longbottomcoffee.com
Processor and importer of specialty coffees including certified organics, espresso, flavored, regionals and blends; wholesaler/distributor of espresso machines and fine teas
Owner: Jody Baccelleri
Marketing Director: Lisa Walker
Sales Director: Gabrielle Paeson
jbaccelleri@medicalteams.org
Manufacturing/Operations Director: Tom Brandon
Estimated Sales: $8 Million
Number Employees: 50-99
Square Footage: 112000
Type of Packaging: Consumer, Food Service, Private Label, Bulk
Regions Imported from: Worldwide
Percentage of Business in Importing: 80

46102 Longhorn Liquors
1017 Nederland Ave
Nederland, TX 77627   409-853-1632
nederland@long-hornliquor.com
long-hornliquor.com
Importer and wholesaler/distributor of European wine and beer; wholesaler/distributor of American wine and beer.
Year Founded: 2012
Estimated Sales: $50-100 Million
Number Employees: 50-99
Square Footage: 4000
Other Locations:
  Groves, TX
  Mauriceville, TX
  Lumberton, TX
  Silsbee, TX
  Woodville, TX
  Bookland, TXMauriceville
Regions Imported from: Europe

46103 Longhorn Packaging Inc
110 Pierce Ave
San Antonio, TX 78208-1928   210-222-9686
Fax: 210-226-7511 800-433-7974
www.longhornpackaging.com
Manufacturer and exporter of converted flexible packaging film and vertical form/fill/seal packaging machinery; also, contract packaging available
President: Holly Ferguson
hferguson@prosper-isd.net
VP: Bill Green
VP Production: Harold Smith
Estimated Sales: $20-50 Million
Number Employees: 50-99
Square Footage: 40000
Regions Exported to: Central America, South America

46104 Longview Farms Emu Oil
3410 Shaffer Rd
Bloomsburg, PA 17815-7928   570-380-1077
Fax: 570-380-1078 emuoil@aol.com
www.longviewfarms.com
Vice President: Joanne Long
joanne@longviewfarms.com
VP: Joanne Long
Estimated Sales: $300,000-500,000
Number Employees: 1-4
Type of Packaging: Bulk
Regions Exported to: Europe, Asia

46105 Longview Fibre Company
8705 SW Nimbus Ave
Beaverton, OR 97008-4000   503-350-1600
Fax: 323-725-6341 www.longviewfibre.com
Manufacturer and exporter of disposable liquid bulk bins
Sales Manager: Dennis Dorgan
Vice President of Sales and Marketing: Lou Loosbrock
Sales Bulk Liquid Packaging: Paul Hansen
Estimated Sales: $ 1 - 3 Million
Number Employees: 5-9
Type of Packaging: Bulk
Brands Exported: Liquiplex; Drumplex
Regions Exported to: Central America, South America, Europe, Asia, Latin America, Canada
Percentage of Business in Exporting: 25

46106 Loos Machine
205 W Washington St
Colby, WI 54421-9458   715-223-2844
Fax: 715-223-6140 www.loosmachine.com
Custom designed automated food processing equipment for the dairy, meat and poultry industries.
Owner: Dennis Baumgartner
info@loosmachine.com
Number Employees: 20-49
Regions Exported to: Worldwide

46107 Lorac Union Tool Co
97 Johnson St
Providence, RI 02905-4518   401-781-3330
Fax: 401-941-7717 888-680-3236
lorac@loracunion.com www.loracunion.com
Manufacturer and exporter of point of purchase displays and sign holders
President: Richard Carroll
Estimated Sales: $ 5 - 10 Million
Number Employees: 10-19
Square Footage: 204000
Parent Co: Lorac Company
Regions Exported to: Worldwide
Percentage of Business in Exporting: 2

46108 Lord Label Group
2980 Planters Place
Charlotte, NC 28216-4149   704-394-9171
Fax: 704-394-0641 800-341-5225
Manufacturer and exporter of labels and labeling equipment
Director Marketing: George McCrary
VP Sales Eastern Region: Jim Prendergast
Sales Manager Western Region: Tom Deegan
Number Employees: 250
Parent Co: Mail-Well
Other Locations:
  Lord Label Group
    Arlington, TXLord Label Group
Regions Exported to: Central America, South America
Percentage of Business in Exporting: 3

Importers & Exporters / A-Z

46109 Lord Label Machine Systems
10350A Nations Food Road
Charlotte, NC 28273   704-644-1650
Fax: 704-664-1662 www.satoamerica.com
Manufacturer and exporter of label applicators
General Manager: Les Roisum
Number Employees: 20-49
Square Footage: 72000
Parent Co: Mail Well
Regions Exported to: Worldwide
Percentage of Business in Exporting: 15

46110 (HQ)Loren Cook Co
2015 E Dale St
Springfield, MO 65803-4637   417-869-6474
Fax: 417-862-3820 800-289-3267
info@lorencook.com www.lorencook.com
Manufacturer and exporter of fans, blowers and ventilators
President: Gerald Cook
Cmo: Victor Colwell
vcolwell@lorencook.com
Estimated Sales: $ 77 Million
Number Employees: 1000-4999
Other Locations:
  Loren Cook Co.
  Ashville, NCLoren Cook Co.

46111 Lorenz Couplings
PO Box 1002
Cobourg, ON K9A 4K2
Canada   905-372-2240
Fax: 905-372-4456 800-263-7782
www.lorenz.ca
Manufacturer and exporter of stainless steel gasket couplings for connection of pipe and tube in bulk handling conveying and vacuum systems
President: Peter Lorenz
CEO: Stacy Warner
Estimated Sales: Below $ 5 Million
Number Employees: 30
Square Footage: 80000
Brands Exported: Lorenz Couplings
Regions Exported to: Worldwide
Percentage of Business in Exporting: 5

46112 Loriva Culinary Oils
1192 Illinois Street
San Francisco, CA 94107   415-401-0080
Fax: 415-401-0087 866-972-6879
www.worldpantry.com
Processor and exporter of specialty oils including roasted, infused and toasted sesame, peanut, safflower, walnut, garlic, olive, avocado, hazelnut, macadamia, etc.; also, kosher varieties available
President: Patrick Lee
CEO: David Miller
Consumer Relations: Liz Scatena
Number Employees: 10-19
Parent Co: NSpired Natural Foods
Type of Packaging: Consumer, Food Service, Private Label, Bulk
Brands Exported: Loriva
Regions Exported to: Europe, Asia, Canada
Percentage of Business in Exporting: 5

46113 Los Altos Food Products
450 N Baldwin Park Blvd.
City Of Industry, CA 91746   626-330-6555
Fax: 626-330-6755 www.losaltosfoods.com
Mexican and Swiss cheeses
President: Raul Andrade
Co-Founder, Vice President: Gloria Andrade
Quality Control Manager: Sergio Mares
Director Sales & Marketing: William Finicle
Contact: Alin Andrade
aandrade@losaltosfoods.com
VP Operations: Alin Andrade
Estimated Sales: $21.5 Million
Number Employees: 1-4
Square Footage: 38000
Type of Packaging: Consumer, Food Service

46114 Los Angeles Smoking & Curing Company
1100 West Ewing Street
Seattle, WA 98119   213-628-1246
Fax: 213-614-8857 info@oceanbeauty.com
www.oceanbeauty.com
Herring, kippers, lox, roe, cod, mackerel, salmon, shad, caviar and whitefish
President: Howard Klein
VP Sales/Marketing: Richard Schaeffer
Contact: Glen Stein
gstein@oceanbeauty.com
Number Employees: 100-249
Parent Co: Ocean Beauty
Type of Packaging: Consumer, Food Service

46115 Lost Trail Root Beer
PO Box 670
Louisburg, KS 66053-0670   913-837-5202
Fax: 913-837-5762 800-748-7765
lcmill@micoks.net www.louisburgcidermill.com
Processor, wholesaler/distributor and exporter of apple cider and root beer; also, apple butter
President/Owner: Tom Schierman
Estimated Sales: $500,000-$1 Million
Number Employees: 5-9
Square Footage: 40000
Type of Packaging: Consumer, Private Label
Brands Exported: Louisburg; Lost Trail

46116 Lotito Foods Inc
240 Carter Dr
Edison, NJ 08817-2097   732-248-0222
Fax: 732-248-0442 www.lotitofoods.com
Salsa/dips, other dairy and eggs, gors d'oeuvres/appetizers, other snacks, other vegetables/fruit.
President: Christopher Lotito
Coo: John Leszczak
Number Employees: 20-49

46117 Lotus Brands
PO Box 325
Twin Lakes, WI 53181   262-889-8561
Fax: 262-889-2461 800-824-6396
lotusbrands@lotuspress.com
www.lotusbrands.com
Teas and herbal supplements
President: Santosh Krinsky
Year Founded: 1992
Estimated Sales: $ 1-2.5 Million
Number Employees: 50-99
Number of Brands: 16
Number of Products: 1000
Square Footage: 152000
Type of Packaging: Consumer, Private Label, Bulk

46118 Lotus Herbs
620 Cabrillo Ave
Santa Cruz, CA 95065-1108   831-479-1667
Fax: 831-479-1951
Import and sale of ayurvedic products
President: Cynthia Copple
Estimated Sales: Under $500,000
Number Employees: 1-4

46119 (HQ)Louis Baldinger & Sons
875 3rd Ave Fl 9
New York, NY 10022-0123   718-204-5700
Fax: 718-721-4986
Manufacturer and exporter of decorative and custom lighting fixtures
President: Howard Baldinger
Chairman of the board: Daniel Baldinger
Quality Control: Shankar Balmick
VP Sales/Marketing: Linda Senter
Contact: Edison Alulema
ealulema@baldinger.com
Estimated Sales: $10-20 Million
Number Employees: 120
Type of Packaging: Consumer
Regions Exported to: Central America, South America, Europe, Asia, Middle East
Percentage of Business in Exporting: 10

46120 (HQ)Louis Caric & Sons
33398 Cecil Ave
Delano, CA 93215   661-725-9372
Fax: 661-725-5943
Exporter of table grapes
Owner: Louis Caric
velikel@dslextreme.com
Estimated Sales: $ .5 - 1 million
Number Employees: 100-249
Square Footage: 160000
Type of Packaging: Consumer, Private Label
Regions Exported to: Central America, Europe
Percentage of Business in Exporting: 20

46121 Louis Dreyfus Company Citrus Inc
355 9th St.
Winter Garden, FL 34787   407-656-1000
www.ldc.com
Frozen fruit juice concentrates, citrus oils, pulp and purees.
CEO: Ian McIntosh
Head, Juice Platform: Murilo Parada
Year Founded: 1851
Estimated Sales: G
Number Employees: 100-249
Type of Packaging: Consumer, Food Service, Private Label, Bulk
Regions Exported to: Worldwide
Percentage of Business in Exporting: 4

46122 (HQ)Louis Dreyfus Corporation
Westblaak 92
3012
Rotterdam,
Netherlands
www.ldc.com
International agribusiness spanning production, refining, transport and merchandizing.
Non-Executive Chairperson: Margarita Louis-Dreyfus
CEO: Ian McIntosh
CFO: Patrick Treuer
COO: Michael Gelchie
Year Founded: 1851
Estimated Sales: $36.5 Billion
Number Employees: 22,000+
Type of Packaging: Food Service, Private Label, Bulk
Regions Exported to: Worldwide
Percentage of Business in Exporting: 70

46123 Louisiana Packing Company
501 Louisiana St
Westwego, LA 70094   504-436-2682
Fax: 504-436-1585 800-666-1293
www.lapack.com
Processor, importer and exporter of breaded, cooked and IQF shrimp
President: David Lai
CEO: John Mao
Plant Manager: David Lai
Estimated Sales: $500,000-$1 Million
Number Employees: 1-4
Square Footage: 132000
Type of Packaging: Consumer, Food Service, Private Label, Bulk
Brands Exported: Fresh Sea Taste; Bayou Segnette
Regions Exported to: Canada, Australia
Percentage of Business in Exporting: 10
Regions Imported from: Central America, South America, Asia, Australia
Percentage of Business in Importing: 40

46124 Louisiana Rice Mill
4 S Avenue D
PO Box 490
Crowley, LA 70526-5657   337-783-9777
Fax: 337-783-3204 contact@laricemill.com
www.laricemill.com
Long grain milled rice
President: William A Dore
bill.dore@supremerice.com
Estimated Sales: $11.9 Million
Number Employees: 50-99
Square Footage: 39732
Regions Exported to: Worldwide
Percentage of Business in Exporting: 50

46125 (HQ)Louisiana Seafood Exchange
428 Jefferson Highway
Jefferson, LA 70121   504-283-9393
Fax: 504-834-5633 800-969-9394
bmiller@louisianaseafoodexchange.net
www.louisianaseafoodexchange.net
Seafood including bass, garfish, catfish, trout, amberjack, crab, shark and snapper
Owner/General Manager: Benny Miller
Sales: Steve Shonkoff
Estimated Sales: $ 20-50 Million
Number Employees: 50-99
Type of Packaging: Consumer, Food Service, Private Label, Bulk
Regions Exported to: Worldwide

Importers & Exporters / A-Z

46126 Louisiana Seafood Exchange
3790-D I-55 South
Jackson, MS 39212 601-853-4554
Fax: 601-853-4554
ray@louisianaseafoodexchange.net
www.louisianaseafoodexchange.net
Seafood including bass, garfish, catfish, trout, amberjack, crab, shark and snapper
Sales: Ray Hopkins
Type of Packaging: Consumer, Food Service, Private Label, Bulk
Regions Exported to: Worldwide

46127 Louisiana Seafood Exchange
11975 Lake Park Blvd.
Baton Rouge, LA 70809 225-756-5225
Fax: 225-756-5237 800-314-5225
robwalker@louisianaseafoodexchange.net
www.louisianaseafoodexchange.net
Seafood including bass, garfish, catfish, trout, amberjack, crab, shark and snapper
Sales: Robert Walker
Type of Packaging: Consumer, Food Service, Private Label, Bulk
Regions Exported to: Worldwide

46128 Louisville Dryer Company
1100 Industrial Boulevrd
Louisville, KY 40219 502-969-3535
Fax: 502-962-9028 800-735-3613
mail@louisvilledryer.com
www.louisvilledryer.com
Manufacturer and exporter of rotary drying and cooling equipment, distillation columns, heat exchangers, pressure vessels and conveyors
VP Sales: Robin Henry
Process Engineer: John Robertson
Plant Manager: Gary Billion
Estimated Sales: $5-10 Million
Number Employees: 20-49
Brands Exported: Louisville
Regions Exported to: Worldwide

46129 Loumidis Foods
1270 Valley Brook Ave
Unit 100B
Lyndhurst, NJ 07071 201-635-1700
Fax: 201-635-1710 info@loumidisfoods.com
loumidisfoods.com
Greek cheeses, honey and baked goods.

46130 Love Controls Division
P.O.Box 373
Michigan City, IN 46361-0373 219-879-8000
Fax: 219-872-9057 800-828-4588
love@love-controls.com www.dwyer-inst.com
Manufacturer, distributor and exporter of temperature and process control instrumentation and associated products
President: Stephen Clark
Contact: David Lange
dlange@love-controls.com
Estimated Sales: $ 75 Million - 1 Billion
Number Employees: 100-249
Square Footage: 50000
Parent Co: Dwyer Instruments
Regions Exported to: Central America, South America, Europe, Asia, Australia
Percentage of Business in Exporting: 10

46131 Love Quiches Desserts
178 Hanse Ave
Freeport, NY 11520-4698 516-623-8800
Fax: 516-623-8817 info@loveandquiches.com
www.loveandquiches.com
Frozen layer cakes, mousses, tarts, pies, cheesecakes and quiches; exporter of cakes, cheesecakes and brownies.
Chairwoman/Founder: Susan Axelrod
CEO: Andrew Axelrod
CFO: Jeffrey Appleman
VP: Bonnie Warstadt
VP, R&D: Michael Goldstein
Director of Quality Assurance: Ellen Lazzaro
EVP, Sales & Marketing: Karen Sullivan
Estimated Sales: $37 Million
Number Employees: 100-249
Number of Brands: 2
Square Footage: 40000
Brands Exported: Love and Quiches Desserts
Regions Exported to: Europe, Asia, Middle East

46132 Lovebiotics LLC
Los Osos, CA
wholesale@thecoconutcult.com
www.thecoconutcult.com
Dairy-free, probiotic-infused coconut yogurt in various flavors
Founder: Noah Simon-Wadell
Number Employees: 11-50
Number of Brands: 1
Number of Products: 3
Type of Packaging: Consumer, Private Label
Brands Exported: The Coconut Cult
Regions Exported to: USA

46133 Loveshaw Corp
2206 Easton Tpke
PO Box 83
South Canaan, PA 18459 570-937-4921
Fax: 570-937-3229 800-572-3434
info@loveshaw.com www.loveshaw.com
Manufacturer and exporter of packaging machinery including case sealers and formers; also, ink jet printers, labeling equipment
President: Doug Henry-Om
Cmo: Wes Carpenter
wcarpenter@loveshaw.com
VP: Mark Craddick
Marketing Manager: Valerie Burke
Sales: Chet Metcalf
Estimated Sales: $10-24 Million
Number Employees: 100-249
Parent Co: ITW
Regions Exported to: Central America, South America, Europe, Asia, Middle East, Worldwide

46134 Lovion International
14 Coachlamp Ln
Stamford, CT 06902 203-327-1405
Fax: 203-325-8636
Wholesaler/distributor and importer of Japanese balanced natural herb mixes; exporter of vitamins and health foods
President: John Tanaka
VP: Kayoko Tanaka
Marketing Director: Kyoko Hirota
Estimated Sales: $2.5-5 Million
Number Employees: 1-4
Regions Exported to: Asia
Percentage of Business in Exporting: 50
Brands Imported: Vulgaris Chlorella; Chlorella Algae; Organic Germanium; Super Hi'Ron
Regions Imported from: Asia
Percentage of Business in Importing: 50

46135 Low Humidity Systems
8425 Hazelbrand Road NE
Covington, GA 30014 770-788-6744
Fax: 770-788-6745 Info@dehumidifiers.com
www.dehumidifiers.com
Manufacturer and exporter of desiccant dehumidifiers
Sales Manager: Debra Adams
Estimated Sales: $ 2.5-5 Million
Number Employees: 10-19
Square Footage: 60000
Regions Exported to: Central America, South America, Europe, Asia, Middle East
Percentage of Business in Exporting: 10

46136 (HQ)Low Temp Industries Inc
9192 Tara Blvd
Jonesboro, GA 30236-4913 678-674-1317
Fax: 770-471-3715 lt@lowtempind.com
www.lowtempind.com
Manufacturer and exporter of stainless steel, fiberglass and wood-free standing and hot food counters. Custom stainless steel kitchen equipment, serving lines, buffets and salad bars, portable hot and cold carts and custom millwork
CEO: William Casey
Executive VP: David W Pearson
dpearson@lowtempind.com
VP Sales: Steve Ballard
Director Purchasing: Dan Casey
Estimated Sales: $10-20 Million
Number Employees: 100-249
Square Footage: 500000
Type of Packaging: Food Service
Regions Exported to: Central America, South America, Asia, Middle East
Percentage of Business in Exporting: 10

46137 Lowell International
9234 Belmont Ave
Franklin Park, IL 60131 847-349-1002
Fax: 847-349-1003 www.lowellfoods.com
Cured and deli meats, hams, mustards, hard cheeses and other European specialty products.
President & CEO: Conrad Lowell

46138 Lozier Corp
6336 John J Pershing Dr
Omaha, NE 68110-1122 402-457-8000
Fax: 402-457-8478 800-228-9882
www.lozier.com
Manufacturer and exporter of store fixtures
CEO: Sheri Andrews
sandrews@lozier.biz
CEO: Allan G Lozier
Estimated Sales: $500,000-$1 Million
Number Employees: 1000-4999
Parent Co: Lozier Corporation
Regions Exported to: Worldwide

46139 Ltg Inc
105 Corporate Dr
Spartanburg, SC 29303-5045 864-599-6340
Fax: 414-672-8800 sales@itsllcusa.com
www.ltg.de
Manufacturer and exporter of controlled heat processing systems for the metal container industry
President: Gerhard Seyffer
gerhard.seyffer@ltg-inc.net
General Manager: Bill Lawrence
VP: Brian Schofield
Estimated Sales: $ 20 - 50 Million
Number Employees: 1-4
Square Footage: 180000
Regions Exported to: South America, Europe, Asia, Middle East, South Africa
Percentage of Business in Exporting: 30

46140 Luban International
9900 NW 25th St
Doral, FL 33172 305-629-8730
Fax: 305-629-8740
Cereals
Owner: Luis Banegas
xbanegas@gmail.com
Brands Exported: Luban
Regions Exported to: Central America
Percentage of Business in Exporting: 100

46141 Lubriplate Lubricants
129 Lockwood St
Newark, NJ 07105-4720 419-691-2491
Fax: 973-589-4432 800-733-4755
richardm@lubriplate.com www.lubriplate.com
Manufacturer and exporter of food grade lubricating oils and grease
President: Richard Mc Cluskey
Vice President, General Manager, Chief M: Jim Girard
Contact: Michael Barto
mbarto@lubriplate.com
Number Employees: 100-249
Parent Co: Fisk Brothers
Regions Exported to: Worldwide

46142 Lucas Industrial
1445 American Way
PO Box 293
Cedar Hill, TX 75104-8409 972-291-6400
Fax: 972-291-6447 800-877-1720
sales@lucasindustrial.com
www.lucasindustrial.com
Manufacturer, importer and wholesaler/distributor of power transmission products including steel and stainless steel shaft and split collars, linear bearing and shaftings, roller chains and mounted bearing
Owner: Mike Lucas
Sales Manager: Bobby Swann
lucasindustrial@aol.com
Estimated Sales: Below $ 5 Million
Number Employees: 5-9

46143 Lucich Santos Farms
12631 Rogers Rd
Patterson, CA 95363-8511 209-892-6500
Fax: 209-892-2446 www.blossomhillapricots.com
Processor and exporter of table grapes
Owner: Pete Lucich
Owner/Partner: David Santos
Sales Manager: Jim Lucich
blossomhill@inreach.com

419

Importers & Exporters / A-Z

Estimated Sales: $10.6 Million
Number Employees: 100-249
Square Footage: 23064
Parent Co: Stevco Inc.
Type of Packaging: Consumer, Bulk

46144 Luckner Steel Shelving
5454 43rd St
Flushing, NY 11378-1028   718-363-0500
     Fax: 718-784-9169   800-888-4212
     info@karpinc.com   www.karpinc.com
Manufacturer and exporter of wire shelving
President: Burt Gold
bgold@karpinc.com
CFO: Ron Peterson
Marketing: Claudia Holtz
Sales: Chantale Laraque
Estimated Sales: $ 5 - 10,000,000
Number Employees: 50-99
Square Footage: 45000
Parent Co: Karp Associates
Brands Exported: Penco
Regions Exported to: Worldwide
Percentage of Business in Exporting: 5

46145 Ludell Manufacturing Co
5200 W State St
Milwaukee, WI 53208-2688   414-476-9934
     Fax: 414-476-9864   800-558-0800
     sales@ludellmfg.com
     www.ludellmanufacturing.com
Manufacturer and exporter of ASME certified heat exchangers, custom engineered wastewater heat recovery systems, direct contact water heaters, and boiler feedwater systems, replacement storage tanks and boiler stack economizers
Owner: Robert Fesmire
george.simpson@gcmk.org
Chief Executive Officer: Bob Fesmire
CFO: David Arthur
Quality Control: Richard Ogren
Vice President: Robert Fesmire
george.simpson@gcmk.org
Sales Director: Greg Thorn
george.simpson@gcmk.org
Plant Manager: Gary Nance
Purchasing Manager: Mark Grosskreutz
Estimated Sales: $8.5 Million
Number Employees: 20-49
Number of Brands: 6
Number of Products: 2
Square Footage: 200000
Regions Exported to: Central America, South America, Asia, Middle East
Percentage of Business in Exporting: 3

46146 Ludfords
3038 Pleasant St
Riverside, CA 92507-5554   951-823-0306
     Fax: 909-948-0597   support@ludfordsinc.com
     www.ludfordsinc.com
Processor, importer and exporter of fresh, frozen and canned fruit juices including orange, apple, grape, etc
President: Paul Ludford
Contact: Matt Real
matt@ludfordsinc.com
Estimated Sales: Below $ 5,000,000
Number Employees: 1-4
Square Footage: 40000
Type of Packaging: Consumer, Food Service, Private Label
Regions Exported to: Worldwide
Regions Imported from: Worldwide

46147 Ludwig Mueller Co Inc
366 N Broadway # 204
Jericho, NY 11753-2000   516-394-8181
     Fax: 516-394-8190
Importer and exporter of spices, seeds, herbs, tomato powder, oleoresins, dried fruits and nuts
President: Jalina Beck
jbeck@houlihanlawrence.com
President: Gilbert Oliver
Estimated Sales: $300,000-500,000
Number Employees: 10-19
Square Footage: 12000
Type of Packaging: Bulk
Regions Exported to: South America, Europe
Percentage of Business in Exporting: 5
Regions Imported from: Central America, South America, Europe, Asia, Middle East, Australia
Percentage of Business in Importing: 90

46148 Luetzow Industries
1105 Davis Ave
South Milwaukee, WI 53172-1195   414-762-0410
     Fax: 414-762-0943   800-558-6055
     www.luetzow.cc
Manufacturer and exporter of polyethylene bags and film, and sheating
President: Albert Luetzow
VP: Brent Luetzow
Estimated Sales: $ 10 - 20 Million
Number Employees: 20-49
Square Footage: 160000
Type of Packaging: Consumer, Private Label, Bulk
Regions Exported to: Central America, South America
Percentage of Business in Exporting: 10

46149 Luhr Jensen & Sons Inc
400 Portway Ave
Hood River, OR 97031-1192   541-386-3811
     Fax: 541-386-4917   info@luhrjensen.com
     www.luhrjensen.com
Sausage and brine mixes and seasonings and spices; also, sausage making kits, electric smokers and wood flavor fuels
President: Philip Jensen
philipjensen@luhrjensen.com
Customer Service: Linda Gordon
Estimated Sales: $10-20 Million
Number Employees: 250-499
Square Footage: 100000

46150 Luigi Bormioli Corporation
5 Walnut Grove Dr
Horsham, PA 19044   215-672-7111
     Fax: 215-757-7115
     customerservice@luigibormioli.com
     www.luigibormioli.com
Importer and wholesaler/distributor of porcelain dinnerware, barware and glassware; serving the food service market
President: Marcel Trepanier
National Sales Manager: Jay Allie
Contact: Deon Allen
dallen@luigibormioli.com
Project Coordinator: Lora Campbell
Estimated Sales: $2.5-5 Million
Number Employees: 10-19
Parent Co: Luigi Bormioli Spa
Type of Packaging: Food Service
Brands Imported: Luigi Bormioli; Tognana
Regions Imported from: Italy

46151 Lukas Confections
231 W College Ave
York, PA 17401-2103   717-843-0921
     Fax: 717-854-9743   sales@warrellcorp.com
     www.classiccaramel.com
Processor and exporter of sugarless and regular caramel toffee, taffy nougat and caramel including liquid; also salt water taffy and nutraceuticals
President/CEO: Robert Lukas
angie@classiccaramel.com
CFO: G Mark Zelinski
angie@classiccaramel.com
Contact: Angela Smith
angie@classiccaramel.com
Operations Manager: Joseph Stuck
Estimated Sales: $4 Million
Number Employees: 50
Number of Brands: 4
Number of Products: 110
Square Footage: 208000
Type of Packaging: Consumer, Private Label, Bulk
Brands Exported: Flipsticks; Classic; Dork Chews
Regions Exported to: Central America, South America, Europe, Asia, Middle East
Percentage of Business in Exporting: 5
Brands Imported: Toffee Wrap
Regions Imported from: Central America, Europe

46152 Luma Sense TechnologiesInc
3301 Leonard Ct
Santa Clara, CA 95054-2054   408-727-1600
     Fax: 408-727-1677   800-631-0176
     info@lumasenseinc.com   www.lumasenseinc.com
Temperature monitoring sensors used in microwave food processing development and gas monitoring systems.
CEO: Michael Chavez
mchavez@clp.com
CEO: Vivek Joshi
Marketing Director: Mark Reis
Public Relations: Judi Seavers

Estimated Sales: $ 10-20 Million
Number Employees: 50-99
Square Footage: 74000
Regions Exported to: Worldwide
Percentage of Business in Exporting: 50

46153 Lumacurve Airfield Signs
9115 Freeway Dr
Macedonia, OH 44056   330-467-2030
     Fax: 330-467-2076   800-258-1997
     www.lumacurve.com
Manufacturer and exporter of porcelain top tables
President: John A Messner
Quality Control: Craig Fussner
R&D: Dane Scholz
Sales: Neil Messner
Contact: Melanie Rostankowski
melanie@lumacurve.com
Estimated Sales: Below $ 5,000,000
Number Employees: 20-49
Parent Co: Standard Signs Inc.
Type of Packaging: Food Service
Regions Exported to: Worldwide
Percentage of Business in Exporting: 10

46154 Lumax Industries
301 Chestnut Ave
Altoona, PA 16601   814-944-2537
     Fax: 814-944-6413   sales@lumaxlighting.com
     www.lumaxlighting.com
Manufacturer and exporter of lighting fixtures and H.I.D. luminares including commercial, industrial and custom
CEO: Vineet Sahni
vineetsahni@lumaxmail.com
CEO: Donald E Snyder
National Sales Manager: Randy Solliday
VP Operations: Ken Merritts
Estimated Sales: $10-20 Million
Number Employees: 100-249
Square Footage: 320000
Type of Packaging: Consumer, Food Service, Private Label
Regions Exported to: Central America, South America, Middle East
Percentage of Business in Exporting: 3

46155 Lumber & Things
PO Box 386
Keyser, WV 26726   304-788-5600
     Fax: 304-788-7823   800-296-5656
     www.lumberandthings.com
We have been in business for over 30 years. Our customers depend on the standards that we build on: Honesty-Quality-Service. We produce: Reconditioned, Remanufacture and New pallets; Reconditioned, Remanufactured and Recycled tier/slipsheets; Reconditioned, Remanufactured and New top frames; Reconditioned and New can and glass bulk pallets. With an attendant standing by our 24 hour hotline we can provide your company with delivery within 24 hours of your phone call.
President: Jack Amoruso
National Accounts Manager: Victor Knight
Customer Service Specialist: Patricia Davis
Plant Manager: Jack Amoruso
Purchasing Director: Ken Winter
Number Employees: 100-249
Square Footage: 150000
Type of Packaging: Consumer, Food Service, Private Label, Bulk
Regions Exported to: Central America, South America, Europe, Asia
Brands Imported: New Lumber
Regions Imported from: Central America, South America, Europe, Asia, Canada

46156 Lumenite Control Tech Inc
2331 17th St
Franklin Park, IL 60131-3432   847-455-1450
     Fax: 847-455-0127   800-323-8510
     customerservice@lumenite.com
     www.lumenite.com
Manufacturer, importer and exporter of blending and batching equipment, flow meters, level detectors and temperature indicators and controllers
Owner: Ron Calabrese
roncalabrese@lumenite.com
Office Manager: Craig Meixner
V.P. Engineering: Ronald Calabrese
Sales manager: David Calabrese
Advertising Manager: Carol Calabrese
Service Representative: Rosa Furio

Importers & Exporters / A-Z

46157 Luminiere Corporation
4269 Park Ave
Bronx, NY 10457-4207
718-295-5450
Fax: 718-295-5451
Manufacturer, importer and exporter of crystal and bronze chandeliers, electric lamps, lighting fixtures and display lighting
Owner: Herbert Leggan
VP: A Langsam
VP: N Gussack
Estimated Sales: $ 3 - 5 Million
Number Employees: 5-9
Square Footage: 100000
Percentage of Business in Exporting: 20
Regions Imported from: Europe, Asia, Middle East
Percentage of Business in Importing: 30

Estimated Sales: $2.5-5 Million
Number Employees: 10-19
Square Footage: 40000
Regions Exported to: Central America, South America, Europe, Middle East
Percentage of Business in Exporting: 15
Regions Imported from: Germany
Percentage of Business in Importing: 2

46158 Lumsden Flexx Flow
PO Box 4647
Lancaster, PA 17604
717-394-6871
Fax: 717-394-1640 800-367-3664
sales@lumsdenbelting.com
www.lumsdencorp.com
Wire and mesh conveyor belting, chain driven belts, positive drive pin rolls, furnace curtains and wire straightening devices; exporter of conveyor belting
President: Glenn Farrell
Quality Control: Glenn Farrell
Sales Manager: Pete Moore
Contact: Clayton Farrell
cfarrell@lumsdencorp.com
Estimated Sales: Below $15 Million
Number Employees: 20-49
Regions Exported to: Worldwide

46159 Lund's Fisheries
997 Ocean Dr
Cape May, NJ 08204
609-884-7600
Fax: 609-884-0664 info@lundsfish.com
www.lundsfish.com
Frozen cod, flounder, mackerel, squid, sturgeon, tuna, herring and shad.
Owner & Chairman: Jeffery Reichle
Owner & President: Wayne Reichle
wreichle@lundsfish.com
Director, Compliance & Quality Assurance: Marty Martinez
Director, Sales & Marketing: Randy Spencer
Director, Government Affairs: Jeff Kaelin
Year Founded: 1954
Estimated Sales: $219 Million
Number Employees: 250-499
Type of Packaging: Consumer, Food Service

46160 Luseaux Labs Inc
16816 Gramercy Pl
Gardena, CA 90247-5282
323-321-0562
Fax: 310-538-3889 800-266-1555
detergents@luseaux.com www.luseaux.com
Manufacturer, importer and exporter of cleaners, sanitizers and detergents including liquid and powder
Vice President: Kathy Kalohi
kathy@luseaux.com
Chief Information Officer: Charles Edwards
Office Manager: Kathleen Kalohi
Estimated Sales: $810,000
Number Employees: 5-9
Square Footage: 180000
Type of Packaging: Food Service, Private Label, Bulk
Other Locations:
  Kingman, AZ
Brands Exported: Luseaux
Regions Exported to: Asia
Percentage of Business in Exporting: 1
Regions Imported from: Asia, Middle East
Percentage of Business in Importing: 1

46161 Lustrecal
715 S Guild Ave
Lodi, CA 95240-3153
209-370-1600
Fax: 209-370-1690 800-234-6264
rbeckler@lustrecal.com www.lustrecal.com
Manufacturer and exporter of color anodized and etched aluminum nameplates and labels
CEO: Clydene Hohenrieder
chohenrieder@lustrecal.com
Estimated Sales: $20-50 Million
Number Employees: 50-99

46162 Luthi Machinery Company, Inc.
1 Magnuson Avenue
Pueblo, CO 81001
719-948-1110
Fax: 719-948-9540 sales@atlaspacific.com
www.luthi.com
Manufacturer and exporter of can filling and dicing machinery for tuna, salmon, chicken, turkey, pork and beef
President: Erik Teranchi
CFO/VP: Don Freeman
V.P. & General Manager: Craig Furlo
Marketing/Sales: Robb Morris
Sales: Gini Fisher
Contact: Juan Monroy
jmonroy@luthi.com
Production: Vern Brown
Number Employees: 50
Square Footage: 136000
Brands Exported: Luthi Fillers & Dicing Machines
Regions Exported to: Central America, South America, Europe, Asia
Percentage of Business in Exporting: 90

46163 Lutz Pumps Inc
1160 Beaver Ruin Rd
Norcross, GA 30093-4898
770-925-1222
Fax: 770-923-0334 800-843-3901
info@lutzpumpsamerica.com www.lutzpumps.com
Importer of drum transfer pumps; exporter of air operated double diaphragm pumps
President: Calle Larsson
Manager: Dave O'Rourke
dave@lutzpumpsamerica.com
Estimated Sales: $ 1 - 3 Million
Number Employees: 5-9
Square Footage: 60000
Brands Exported: Lutz
Regions Exported to: Canada, Mexico
Brands Imported: Lutz
Regions Imported from: Europe

46164 (HQ)Luxco Inc
5050 Kemper Ave
St Louis, MO 63139-1106
314-772-2626
Fax: 314-772-6021 contactus@luxco.com
www.luxco.com
Manufacturer, bottler, importer and exporter of quality destilled spirits and wines.
Chairman/CEO: Donn Lux
President/COO: David Bratcher
VP Finance/CFO: Steve Soucy
Chief Marketing Officer: Steve Einig
Director, Corporate R&D: John Rempe
EVP Sales: Dan Streepy
Contact: Tina Aebi
t.aebi@luxco.com
Warehouse Manager: Douglas Finkeldey
Estimated Sales: $23.8 Million
Number Employees: 1-4
Square Footage: 200000
Type of Packaging: Private Label

46165 Luxo Corporation
Ste 105
5 Westchester Plz
Elmsford, NY 10523-1645
914-937-4433
Fax: 914-937-7016 800-222-5896
www.luxous.com
Manufacturer and importer of magnification, ambient and task lighting fixtures
Regional Sales Manager: Doug Benway
Estimated Sales: $10-20 Million
Number Employees: 50-99
Square Footage: 120000
Parent Co: Luxo ASA
Type of Packaging: Food Service

46166 Luxor California Exports Corp.
3659 India Street
2nd Floor
San Diego, CA 92103-4767
619-465-7777
Fax: 619-692-4292 rkafaji@aol.com
Supplier and exporter of agricultural commodities closeouts including dry beans, grains, oils, yeast, dry milk, butter, etc
President: Ray Kafaji
Marketing Director: Holland Clem
Estimated Sales: $1000000
Number Employees: 5
Type of Packaging: Bulk
Regions Exported to: Middle East, Africa
Percentage of Business in Exporting: 100

46167 Luxury Crab
64 Airport Rd
Unit 2
St John's, NL A1A 4Y3
Canada
709-739-6668
info@whitecapseafoods.com
www.luxurycrab.com
Frozen crab and crab claws.
Chief Executive Officer: Randolph Bishop
Technical Director: Brian Cuff
Project Manager: Brad Hookey
Estimated Sales: $40 Million
Number Employees: 25
Other Locations:
  Toronto, ON
  Winnipeg, MB
  Calgary, AB
  Vancouver, BC
  Danvers, MA
  Seattle, WAWinnipeg
Regions Exported to: Central America, Europe, Asia

46168 Luyties Pharmacal Company
4200 Laclede Street
Saint Louis, MO 63108
314-533-9600
Fax: 314-535-9600 800-325-8080
info@1800homeopathy.com
Processor and exporter of vitamins and homeopathic products
Director Marketing: Michael Smith
Number Employees: 50-99
Parent Co: Manola Company
Brands Exported: Succus Cineraria Maritima
Regions Exported to: Central America, South America, Europe, Asia, Middle East
Percentage of Business in Exporting: 15

46169 Lyco Manufacturing
PO Box 2022
Wausau, WI 54402-2022
715-845-7867
Fax: 715-842-8228 info@lycowausau.com
www.lycowausau.com
Stainless steel liquid ring vacuum pumps for food, pharmaceutical, chemical, medical, laboratory and general industrial applications where corrosion resistance is beneficial.
President: Thomas Frane
Number Employees: 50-99
Brands Exported: Lyco Wausau Stainless Steel Vacuum Pumps
Regions Exported to: Central America, Europe, Asia, Worldwide
Percentage of Business in Exporting: 5

46170 Lyco Wausau
P.O.Box 2022
Wausau, WI 54402-2022
715-845-7867
Fax: 715-842-8228 www.lycowausau.com
Manufacturer and exporter of stainless steel liquid ring vacuum pumps and systems for filling, deaerating, cooking, dewatering, conveying, evaporating and packaging
President: Thomas Frane
Estimated Sales: $ 3 - 5 Million

46171 (HQ)Lynch Corp
140 Greenwich Ave # 4
Suite 4
Greenwich, CT 06830-6560
203-340-2590
Fax: 401-453-2009
Manufacturer and exporter of glass forming and packaging machines
President: Richard E McGrail
CEO: Ralph R Papitto
ralphp@gemini-cap.com
CFO: Raymond Keller
Estimated Sales: $ 20 - 30 Million
Number Employees: 1-4
Regions Exported to: Worldwide

46172 (HQ)Lynn Sign Inc
8 Gleason St
Andover, MA 01810-3324
978-470-1194
Fax: 978-346-8197 800-225-5764
lynnsign@aol.com

Importers & Exporters / A-Z

Manufacturer and exporter of changeable plastic letters and signs, menu boards, building directories, bulletin boards, display cases, engraving stock and sign holders
Owner: R Rand Richmond
Public Relations: Darlene Reiss
Manager: Lynn Sullivan
Estimated Sales: Less Than $500,000
Number Employees: 1-4
Number of Brands: 1
Square Footage: 34000
Type of Packaging: Bulk
Percentage of Business in Exporting: 2

46173 Lyo-San
500 Boul De L Aeroparc
C P 598
Lachute, QC J8H 4G4
Canada
450-562-8525
Fax: 450-562-1433 800-363-3697
lyo-san@lyo-san.ca www.lyo-san.ca
Manufacturer and exporter of freeze-dried yogurt cultures and bifido-bacteria; custom freeze-drying available. Founded in 1983.
President/Owner: Celine St-Pierre
Number Employees: 10-19
Square Footage: 180000
Type of Packaging: Consumer, Food Service, Private Label, Bulk
Brands Exported: Yogourmet
Regions Exported to: Asia, USA
Percentage of Business in Exporting: 20

46174 Lyoferm & Vivolac Cultures
3852 E Washington St
Indianapolis, IN 46201-4470
317-356-8460
www.iquest.net
Cultures including dairy, meat and bakery starter, freeze dried/lyophilized and food fermentation
President/Vice President: Ethel Sing
Vice President: Edmond Sing
Estimated Sales: $2 Million
Number Employees: 23
Brands Exported: Vivolac; Lyoferm
Regions Exported to: Worldwide
Percentage of Business in Exporting: 2

46175 Lyon LLC
420 N Main St
Montgomery, IL 60538-1367
630-892-8941
Fax: 630-264-4542 www.lyonworkspace.com
Manufacturer and exporter of metal storage equipment including shelving, cabinets, etc
CEO: R Peter Washington
CEO: R Peter Washington
Marketing Director: Robert Bell
Estimated Sales: $50-100 Million
Number Employees: 1000-4999
Regions Exported to: Worldwide

46176 M & E Mfg Co Inc
19 Progress St
Kingston, NY 12401-3611
845-331-2110
Fax: 845-331-4143
customerservice@zframerack.com
Manufacturer and exporter of shelving, racks, tables, cutting boards, trucks, platters, dollies and carts
President: Conor Curley
conor.curley@digicelgroup.com
Executive VP: Don Hall
Estimated Sales: $ 20 - 50 Million
Number Employees: 50-99
Square Footage: 40000
Regions Exported to: Canada
Percentage of Business in Exporting: 5

46177 M & Q Plastic Products
1120 Welsh Road
Suite 170
North Wales, PA 19454-3710
267-498-4000
Fax: 215-641-4572
Contact: Ernie Bachert
ebachert@pansaver.com

46178 M & R Sales & Svc Inc
1n372 Main St
Glen Ellyn, IL 60137-3576
630-858-6101
Fax: 630-858-6134 800-736-6431
www.mrprint.com
Manufacturer and exporter of belting, switches, etc
CEO: Richard Hoffman
Estimated Sales: $ 1-2.5 Million
Number Employees: 20-49
Parent Co: M&R Printing Equipment

46179 M 5 Corp
1619 S Rancho Santa Fe Rd # C
Suite C
San Marcos, CA 92078-5114
760-744-6665
Fax: 760-744-6065 800-995-6530
info@m5corporation.com
Organic and natural gourmet foods, Italian gourmet foods and South American gourmet foods
Owner: Michael Mc Grath
Marketing: Michael McGrath
Estimated Sales: $310,000
Number Employees: 1-4
Type of Packaging: Food Service

46180 M F & B Restaurant Systems Inc
133 Icmi Rd
Dunbar, PA 15431-2309
724-628-3050
Fax: 724-626-0247
Remanufacture conveyor pizza ovens, sell new and used parts
Owner: Mike French
mfrench@edgeoven.com
Vice President: Michael French
Estimated Sales: $400,000
Number Employees: 5-9
Number of Brands: 5
Square Footage: 24000

46181 M O Industries Inc
9 Whippany Rd # B1-2
Unit B1-2
Whippany, NJ 07981-1530
973-386-9228
Fax: 973-428-0221 sales@moindustries.com
www.moindustries.com
Manufacturer importer and exporter of movable and stationary drum lifters/positioners; also, dust control blending, crushing and milling size reducers, pallets, stainless steel funnels, quick-release valves, viscous materialdischargers, and stainless steel drums
President: German Leiva
gleiva@moindustries.com
Estimated Sales: $4 Million
Number Employees: 5-9
Regions Exported to: Canada
Regions Imported from: Europe

46182 M Phil Yen Company
18 E 16th Street
Room 307
New York, NY 10003-3111
212-463-8234
Fax: 212-463-8298 dyen2@aol.com
Importer and exporter of lemon and orange peels and powders
G.M.: Genevieve Harley
Pres.: David Yen
Estimated Sales: $1-2.5 Million
Number Employees: 1-4
Square Footage: 8000
Type of Packaging: Food Service, Bulk
Regions Exported to: South America, Europe, Canada
Percentage of Business in Exporting: 5
Regions Imported from: Europe, Asia, Caribbean
Percentage of Business in Importing: 95

46183 M S Plastics & Packaging Inc
10 Park Pl # 11
Building 2-1A2
Butler, NJ 07405-1370
973-492-2400
Fax: 973-492-7801 800-593-1802
web@msplastics.com
Polyethylene bags, liners, sheets, stretch wrap, printed bags, tubing, stretch and shrink film and bands; importer of plastic shrink films and bands
Owner: Ellen Saraisky
info@msplastics.com
CFO: Al Saraisky
Estimated Sales: $ 3 - 5 Million
Number Employees: 20-49
Regions Imported from: Asia
Percentage of Business in Importing: 10

46184 M S Walker Inc
20 3rd Ave
Somerville, MA 02143-4404
617-776-6700
Fax: 617-776-5808
Processor and importer of brandy, liqueurs, wines and spirits
President: Harvey Allen
CEO: Richard Sandler
rsandler@mswalker.com
CEO: Richard Sandler
Estimated Sales: $ 1 - 3 Million
Number Employees: 100-249

46185 M S Willett Inc
220 Cockeysville Rd
Cockeysville, MD 21030-4367
410-771-0460
Fax: 410-771-6972 info@mswillett.com
www.mswillett.com
Manufacturer and exporter of precision equipment to produce stamped and formed metal food, shallow drawn and specialty containers and easy open can ends
President: Gabriel Gauzon
pgauzon@worldbank.org
R&D: Gary Ruby
Quality Control: Robert Burns
Sales Director: Gary Ruby
Public Relations: Linda Ambrose
Plant Manager: Larry Felty
Purchasing Director: Jack Kersch
Estimated Sales: $5 Million
Number Employees: 50-99
Square Footage: 240000
Brands Exported: M.S. Willett
Regions Exported to: Central America, Europe, Canada
Percentage of Business in Exporting: 25

46186 M&L Gourmet Ice Cream
2524 E Monument St
Baltimore, MD 21205-2539
410-276-4880
Fax: 410-525-8320
Processor and exporter of kosher ice cream
Owner: Chris Napfel
Estimated Sales: Less than $500,000
Number Employees: 1-4
Type of Packaging: Consumer, Food Service
Regions Exported to: Saudi Arabia, Korea
Percentage of Business in Exporting: 1

46187 M&L Plastics
150 Pleasant St
Easthampton, MA 01027-1887
413-527-1330
Fax: 413-527-8621
Manufacturer and exporter of plastic display containers
Number Employees: 10-19
Parent Co: Paragon Rubber Corporation
Regions Exported to: Central America
Percentage of Business in Exporting: 1

46188 M&R Flexible Packaging
PO Box 907
Springboro, OH 45066-0907
937-298-7272
Fax: 937-298-7388 800-543-3380
Manufacturer, importer and exporter of plastic bags, industrial packaging materials, plastics and shipping room supplies
President/Owner: Ronald Morris
Estimated Sales: $2.5-5,000,000
Number Employees: 10-19
Regions Exported to: Worldwide
Percentage of Business in Exporting: 15
Regions Imported from: Worldwide
Percentage of Business in Importing: 15

46189 M-C McLane International
1902 Cypress Station Dr.
Suite 200
Houston, TX 77090
281-210-3295
info@mclaneglobal.com
www.mclaneglobal.com
Perishable & nonperishable groceries and beverages.
Chairman/Owner: Denton McLane
CEO: Todd Avery
President/Chief Financial Officer: Todd Frease
Director, Marketing: Melissa Hunt
Director, Operations: Mauricio Gallego
Estimated Sales: $100 Million
Number Employees: 100
Number of Brands: 19
Square Footage: 24000
Parent Co: McLane Global
Regions Exported to: Central America, South America, Europe, Asia, Middle East
Percentage of Business in Exporting: 100

46190 M-CAP Technologies
3521 Silverside Rd
Wilmington, DE 19810-4900
302-695-5329
Fax: 302-695-5350 jdoncheck@lakefield.net
Processor and exporter of industrial ingredients including bromate replacers, additives and preservatives; also, temperature release vitamins and minerals
President: Ernie Porta
VP Technology: James Doncheck

Importers & Exporters / A-Z

Number Employees: 5
Parent Co: DuPont Chemical

46191 M-E-C Co
1400 Main St
Neodesha, KS 66757-1679   620-325-2673
                            Fax: 620-325-2678
Manufacturer and exporter of dryer systems for nonedible biological materials and foodwastes including convection, total, rotary, and flash tube
President: John Quick
jquick@m-e-c.com
CFO: Jerry Creekmore
R&D: Mike Hudson
Quality Control: Kent Shields
Sales Manager: Gary Follmer
Purchasing: John George
Estimated Sales: $ 20 - 50 Million
Number Employees: 100-249
Square Footage: 170000
Regions Exported to: Worldwide
Percentage of Business in Exporting: 40

46192 M-Vac Systems Inc
14621 S 800 W # 100
Suite 100
Bluffdale, UT 84065-4863   801-523-3962
                            www.m-vac.com
The m-vac is a dry or wet vacuuming collection/containment device used to detect and recover surface pathogens.
Owner: Dr. Bruce Bradley
Parent Co: MSI
Regions Exported to: Europe, Asia, North America

46193 M. Licht & Son
PO Box 507
Knoxville, TN 37901   865-523-5593
                            Fax: 865-523-0270
Processor and exporter of liquid artificial sweeteners
President: Richard M Licht
VP: Karen McGuire
Estimated Sales: $ 5 - 10 Million
Number Employees: 5-9
Square Footage: 12800
Type of Packaging: Food Service
Brands Exported: Smoky Mountain
Regions Exported to: Europe

46194 (HQ)M.E. Heuck Company
1111 Western Row Road
Mason, OH 45040-2649   513-681-1774
          Fax: 513-681-2329 877-800-359-3200
Manufacturer, importer, exporter of kitchen utensils including barbecue tools, nut crackers, shellfish crackers, etc
President: Ramesh Malhotra
CFO: Tim Omelia
VP: Bill Dickmann
R&D: Tim Omelia
Manager: Linda Brandt
Contact: Chris Carthy
c.carthy@heuck.com
Estimated Sales: $ 20 - 50 Million
Number Employees: 30
Square Footage: 90000
Regions Exported to: Europe, Canada, Mexico
Percentage of Business in Exporting: 5
Regions Imported from: Asia
Percentage of Business in Importing: 25

46195 M.H. Rhodes Cramer
105 Nutmeg Rd S
South Windsor, CT 6074   860-291-8402
          Fax: 860-610-0120 877-684-6464
          customer-service@mhrhodes.com
                  www.mhrhodes.com
Manufacturer, importer and exporter of timers including audible signal and electronic as well as mechanical timers/time switches for OEM's
President: Ken Mac Cormac
Founder: Mark Rhodes, Sr.
Manager Sales: Jim Kline
Customer Service: Bernie Rodrigues
Purchasing Manager: Jeff Carlson
Estimated Sales: $10-20 Million
Number Employees: 100-249
Square Footage: 170000
Type of Packaging: Consumer, Food Service, Private Label, Bulk
Brands Exported: Mark-Time
Regions Exported to: South America, Europe
Percentage of Business in Exporting: 5
Brands Imported: Mark-Time

Regions Imported from: Asia
Percentage of Business in Importing: 2

46196 MAC Tac LLC
4560 Darrow Rd
Stow, OH 44224-1898   330-688-1111
          Fax: 330-688-2540 866-262-2822
       mactac.americas@mactac.com www.mactac.com
Manufacturer and exporter of pressure sensitive paper, film and foil products
President: Jim Peruzzi
Cmo: Jennifer Bowman
jmbowman@bemis.com
Executive VP: Robert Hawthorne
Purchasing Agent: Hank Cardarelli
Number Employees: 500-999
Parent Co: Bemls Company

46197 MAF Industries Inc
36470 Highway 99
PO Box 218
Traver, CA 93673   559-897-2905
          Fax: 559-897-3422 mafusa@aol.com
                  www.mafindustries.com
Manufacturer, importer and exporter of packaging equipment including sizers, color sorters, box fillers, robotic bin dumpers, washers, waxers, etc
CEO: Jack Kraemer
CFO/Controller: Raul Mejia
Sales Manager: Leendert Van Der Tas
Manager: Raul Mejia
rmejia@mafindustries.com
Estimated Sales: $10-20 Million
Number Employees: 50-99
Square Footage: 100000
Parent Co: SMCM
Brands Exported: MAF Sizers Equipment
Regions Exported to: Central America, Canada, Mexico
Percentage of Business in Exporting: 10
Brands Imported: MAF
Regions Imported from: Europe
Percentage of Business in Importing: 10

46198 (HQ)MAFCO Worldwide
300 Jefferson St
Camden, NJ 08104   856-986-4050
          Fax: 856-964-6029
          magnasweet@mafcolicorice.com
                         mafco.com
Licorice products and other ingredients, including sweeteners
President & COO: Lucas Bailey
Global Research & Development Director: Mark Hines
SVP Strategy & Business Development: Jeff Robinson
Year Founded: 1902
Estimated Sales: $36 Million
Number Employees: 230
Type of Packaging: Bulk
Regions Exported to: Central America, South America, Europe, Asia
Percentage of Business in Exporting: 40

46199 MBC Food Machinery Corp
78 Mckinley St
Hackensack, NJ 07601-4009   201-489-7000
          Fax: 201-489-0614
          jbattaglia@mbcfoodmachinery.com
                  www.mbcfoodmachinery.com
Manufacturer and exporter of filling pumps and automatic frozen pasta processing machinery including ravioli, manicotti and cavatelli
President and CFO: John Battaglia
Estimated Sales: Less than $ 500,000
Number Employees: 5-9
Regions Exported to: Europe
Percentage of Business in Exporting: 5

46200 MBH International Corporation
494 8th Ave Ste 802
New York, NY 10001-2542   212-594-6700
          Fax: 212-594-7100 export@mbhny.com
President: Joseph Civovsky
Estimated Sales: $ 10 - 20 Million
Number Employees: 20-49

46201 MBI Heating & Air Conditioning
450 Business Park Ln
Allentown, PA 18109-9119   610-821-9555
          Fax: 610-821-9189 www.mbihvac.com
We offer a wide range of commerical services for industries of all types.

President: Mark Berean
markb@mbihvac.com
Estimated Sales: $5-10 Million
Number Employees: 20-49

46202 MCD Technologies
2515 South Tacoma Way
Tacoma, WA 98409-7527   253-476-0968
          Fax: 253-476-0974 www.mcdtechnologiesinc.com
Manufacturer and exporter of food dryers and evaporators; also, contract toll drying
President: Karin Bolland
info@mcdtechnologiesinc.com
VP: Richard Magoon
Marketing: Leo Schultz
Estimated Sales: $1-2.5 Million
Number Employees: 10-19
Square Footage: 36000
Brands Exported: Refractance Window
Regions Exported to: Central America, South America, Europe, Asia, Middle East

46203 MDS Nordion
447 March Road
Ottawa, ON K2K 1X8
Canada   613-592-2790
          Fax: 613-592-6937 800-465-3666
Supplies patented food irradiation solutions for the meat, poultry and produce industry. Our equipment and process eliminates food-borne pathogens such as E. coli, Salmonella and Listeria from food, prolongs shelf life and treatsproduct for quarantine and bio-security after harvest
President: Steve West
CFO: Micheal Thomas
Senior Vice President, General Counsel,: Andrew Foti
Product Manager Food and Radiation: Joseph Borsa Ph D
R&D and Director: Pierre Lahaie
Marketing Director: Carolin Vandenberg
Senior Vice President of Sales and Marke: Kevin Brooks
Number Employees: 800
Parent Co: MDS

46204 MDS-Vet Inc
3429 Stearns Rd
Valrico, FL 33596-6450   813-653-1180
          Fax: 813-684-5953 tbattle@mdsincorporated.com
                  www.mdsvet.com
Manufacturer and exporter of scopes used to check bacteria in pipes and tubes
Owner: Jayson Fitzgerald
jfitzgerald@seminolecountyfl.gov
Director Marketing: Trudi Battle
Estimated Sales: Less than $500,000
Number Employees: 5-9
Regions Exported to: Worldwide
Percentage of Business in Exporting: 15

46205 MERRICK Industries Inc
10 Arthur Dr
Lynn Haven, FL 32444-1685   850-522-4300
          Fax: 850-265-9768 800-271-7834
          info@merrick-inc.com www.merrick-inc.com
Manufacturer and exporter of process weighing and control equipment, belt feeders and loss-in-weight feeders
CEO: Larry Adams
ladams@acistudios.com
CEO: Joe K Tannehill Sr
Purchasing Manager: Steve Rhinehart
Estimated Sales: $10-20,000,000
Number Employees: 100-249
Square Footage: 55000
Brands Exported: Gravimerik; MC2; MC3; SuperBridge
Regions Exported to: Worldwide
Percentage of Business in Exporting: 18

46206 MFI Food Canada
70 Irene Street
Winnipeg, MB R3T 4E1
Canada   204-992-8200
          Fax: 204-475-7740 www.michaelfoods.com
Egg products including egg whites and yolks, scrambled egg mix, omelettes and egg patties.
Human Resources Manager: Darren Luke
Plant Manager: Mark Driedger
Estimated Sales: $37 Million
Number Employees: 200
Number of Brands: 1
Parent Co: Michael Foods, Inc.

423

Importers & Exporters / A-Z

46207 MFS/York/Stormor
2928 E US Highway 30
Grand Island, NE 68801-8318   308-384-9320
        Fax: 308-382-6954   800-247-6621
Manufacturer, exporter and wholesaler/distributor of grain storage, drying, handling and conditioning and conveying equipment; also, seed storage equipment
President: Dan Faltin
dfaltin@mfsyork.com
VP Finance: Charles Stracuzzi
Sales Manager: Randy Van Langen
Executive VP Operations: Wayne Sasges
Production Manager: Dave Forbes
Estimated Sales: $20-50 Million
Number Employees: 50-99
Parent Co: Blount

Before MFS/York, there are these lines:
Type of Packaging: Food Service
Regions Exported to: Asia
Regions Imported from: Europe

46208 MGP Ingredients Inc
100 Commercial St
Atchison, KS 66002-2514   913-367-1480
        Fax: 913-367-0192   800-255-0302
        www.mgpingredients.com
Process starches and specialty wheat proteins for food and non-food applications.
President/CEO: Tim Newkirk
CEO: Augustus C Griffin
augustus.griffin@mgpingredients.com
Vice President of Technical Services: Clodualdo Maningat
Vice President of Sales and Marketing: David Dykstra
Number Employees: 250-499

46209 MIC Foods
8701 SW 137th Avenue
#308
Miami, FL 33183   786-507-0540
        Fax: 786-507-0545   800-788-9335
info@micfood.com   www.micfood.com/
Processor and importer of frozen plaintains, yuca, cassava and frozen fruit products.
President: Alfredo Lardizabal
Sales VP: Maria Krogh
maria@micfood.com
Estimated Sales: $ 5 - 10 Million
Number Employees: 5-9

46210 MIFAB Inc
1321 W 119th St
Chicago, IL 60643-5109   773-341-3030
        Fax: 773-341-3047   800-465-2736
        sales@mifab.com   www.mifab.com
Manufacturer, importer and exporter of grease traps, oil, sediment and lint interceptors, floor drains, access doors, etc
President: Michael Whiteside
mwhiteside@mifab.com
Accounting Manager: Daniel ODekirk
Vice President of Division: Paul Lacourciere
Engineering Manager: Jason Gremchuk
Quality Control Manager: John Murphy
National Sales Manager: Andrew Haines
Purchasing Manager: Alice OConnor
Number Employees: 50-99
Square Footage: 180000
Brands Exported: MIFAB
Regions Exported to: Europe, Middle East, Canada
Percentage of Business in Exporting: 80
Regions Imported from: Asia

46211 MIRA International Foods
1200 Tices Ln Ste 203
Suite 203
East Brunswick, NJ 08816   732-846-5410
        Fax: 732-846-3052   www.miramango.com
Marketing Director: Mariam Gandour
Estimated Sales: $ 5 - 10 Million
Number Employees: 5-9
Brands Exported: Mira Premium Tropical Nectars
Regions Exported to: Central America, South America
Percentage of Business in Exporting: 5
Brands Imported: Mira Premium Tropical Nectars
Regions Imported from: South America, Middle East
Percentage of Business in Importing: 100

46212 MISCO Refractometer
3401 Virginia Road
Cleveland, OH 44122   216-831-1000
        Fax: 216-831-1195   866-831-1999
        www.misco.com
Manufacturer and exporter of digital hand-held abbe/labprator, inline/process refractometers. Established in 1949 in Cleveland, Ohio and is recognized as a world leader in the refractometer industry.
CEO: Michael Rainer
Contact: Tosha Hudson
thudson@misco.com
Number Employees: 10-19
Type of Packaging: Food Service, Bulk
Regions Exported to: Worldwide
Percentage of Business in Exporting: 1

46213 (HQ)ML Catania Company
575 Orwell Street
Mississauga, ON L5A 2W4
Canada   416-236-9394
        Fax: 416-236-3992   www.cataniaworldwide.com
Wholesaler/distributor and importer of fresh fruits and vegetables
President: Paul Catania, Sr.
Executive VP: Paul Catania, Jr.
Estimated Sales: $8 Million
Number Employees: 10-19
Square Footage: 120000
Parent Co: Catania Worldwide
Other Locations:
    ML Catania Co. Ltd.
    Fresno, CAML Catania Co. Ltd.
Regions Exported to: Central America, South America, Europe, Latin America, Mexico
Percentage of Business in Exporting: 100
Regions Imported from: Central America, South America, Europe
Percentage of Business in Importing: 100

46214 MLG Enterprises Ltd.
PO Box 52568
Mississauga, ON L5J 4S6
Canada   905-696-6947
        Fax: 905-696-6955
        office-mgr@mlgfoodingredients.com
        www.mlgfoodingredients.com
Processor and distributor of specialty food ingredients
President: Terry McCann
Sales Manager: Patrick McCann
Estimated Sales: $10 Million
Number Employees: 10
Square Footage: 44000
Type of Packaging: Food Service, Private Label, Bulk
Regions Exported to: Europe, Asia, USA, Caribbean
Percentage of Business in Exporting: 20
Regions Imported from: Worldwide
Percentage of Business in Importing: 50

46215 MLP Seating Corporation
2125 Lively Blvd
Elk Grove Vlg, IL 60007-5207   847-956-1700
        Fax: 847-956-1776   www.mlpseating.com
Owner: Ralph Samuel
Contact: Jennie Betti
jbetti@mlpseating.com
Estimated Sales: $ 5 - 10 Million
Number Employees: 20-49

46216 MMR Technologies
1400 N Shoreline Blvd Ste A5
Mountain View, CA 94043-1346   650-962-9620
        Fax: 650-962-9647   855-962-9620
        sales@mmr-tech.com   www.mmr-tech.com
Manufacturer and exporter of microminiature refrigeration equipment for materials research
CEO: William Little
Sales VP: Robert Paugh
Contact: Lee Asplund
leea@mmr.com
Estimated Sales: $2.5-5 Million
Number Employees: 10-19
Square Footage: 36000
Regions Exported to: South America, Europe, Asia, Canada, Latin America, Mexico
Percentage of Business in Exporting: 30

46217 MODAGRAPHICS
5300 Newport Dr
Rolling Meadows, IL 60008-3797   847-392-3980
        Fax: 847-392-3989   marketing@modagrafics.com
        www.modagrafics.com
Manufacturer and exporter of graphics for food stores and truck fleets
President/Chief Executive Officer: Carlson Lennard
CEO: Paul Pirkle
paul.pirkle@modagrafics.com
Vice President/Chief Financial Officer: Jack Masters
Executive Vice President: Robert Jurgens
Chief Information Officer/IT Director: Betsy Carlson
Marketing Department: Kate Kummer
Vice President, Operations: Howard Baden
Production Manager: Marty Dorner
Plant Engineering Manager: Salvatore Geraci
Director, Purchasing: Marty Anderson
Estimated Sales: $ 12 Million
Number Employees: 100-249
Square Footage: 80000
Regions Exported to: Central America, South America, Europe, Asia
Percentage of Business in Exporting: 10

46218 MSSH
901 N Carver St
Greensburg, IN 47240-1014   812-663-2180
        Fax: 812-663-5405   ashleymachine@yahoo.com
Manufacturer and exporter of eviscerating tables, poultry pickers and scalders
Manager: Jim Israel
CFO: Jim Israel
Estimated Sales: $30-50 Million
Number Employees: 5-9
Square Footage: 8000
Regions Exported to: Central America, Canada, Mexico
Percentage of Business in Exporting: 20

46219 MTL Etching Industries
861 Fiske St
Woodmere, NY 11598-2429   516-295-9733
        Fax: 516-295-9733
Manufacturer and exporter of advertising specialties, nameplates, dials, scales, rulers, etc
CEO: Alan Stern
Estimated Sales: $ 1 - 3 Million
Number Employees: 10-19

46220 Mac Farms Of Hawaii Inc
89-406 Mamalahoa Hwy
Captain Cook, HI 96704-8941   808-328-2435
        Fax: 808-328-8081   sales@macfarms.com
        www.macfarms.com
Macadamia nuts, flavored macadamia nuts, chocolate covered macadamia nuts and macadamia nut cookies
President: Nicole Knight
sales@macfarms.com
Executive Vice President: Scott Wallace
VP Sales: Brian Loader
Manager: Rick Vigden
Estimated Sales: $ 20 - 50 Million
Number Employees: 100-249
Parent Co: Blue Diamond Growers
Type of Packaging: Consumer, Private Label, Bulk
Brands Exported: MacFarms of Hawaii
Regions Exported to: Europe, Asia, Canada
Percentage of Business in Exporting: 33

46221 Mac Knight Smoke House Inc
550 NE 185th St
Miami, FL 33179-4513   305-651-3323
        Fax: 305-655-0039   sales@macknight.com
        www.macknight.com
Processor and importer of smoked and fresh fish
President: Jonathan Brown
General Manager: Alex McMorran
Estimated Sales: $ 10 - 20 Million
Number Employees: 20-49
Square Footage: 20000
Type of Packaging: Consumer, Food Service, Private Label, Bulk
Brands Imported: MacKnight; Ridley; James White
Regions Imported from: Europe

Importers & Exporters / A-Z

46222 MacGregors Meat & Seafood
265 Garyray Drive
Toronto, ON M9L 1P2
Canada
416-746-5951
888-383-3663
www.macgregors.com
Poultry, seafood and meat products; importer of beef and seafood
CFO: Ed de Vries
Vice President: John Hercus
VP of Sales, National Accounts: Rob Simpson
Number Employees: 180
Square Footage: 184000
Regions Imported from: Central America, South America, Pacific Rim

46223 MacMillan Bloedel Packaging
4001 Carmichael Rd
Montgomery, AL 36106-3613
334-244-0562
Fax: 334-213-6199 800-239-4464
Manufacturer and exporter of corrugated shipping containers
VP: J Tignor
Director Marketing: Stewart Williams

46224 Macco Organiques
100 rue Mc Arthur
Valleyfield, QC J6S 4M5
Canada
450-371-1066
Fax: 450-371-5519 macco@macco.ca
www.macco.ca
Processor and exporter of food preservatives including: calcium acetate; calcium chloride dihy; calcium propionate; potassium acetate; potassium benzoate; sodium acetate anh; sodium benzoate; sodium diacetate; and sodium propionate.
President: Robert Briscoe
VP: Jacques Rochon
General Manager: Simon Rinella
Estimated Sales: 9.27 Million
Number Employees: 60
Regions Exported to: Worldwide
Percentage of Business in Exporting: 85

46225 Macdonald Meat Co
2709 Airport Way S
Seattle, WA 98134-2112
206-623-7993
Fax: 206-623-3835
customerservice@macmeat.com
www.macmeat.com
Wholesaler/distributor and exporter of meats/provisions and general merchandise; serving the food service market
President: Allan Motter
VP: William Jones
Contact: Kris Black
kad@macmeat.com
Estimated Sales: $20-50 Million
Number Employees: 20-49

46226 (HQ)Machem Industries
1607 Derwent Way
Delta, BC V3M 6K8
Canada
604-526-5655
Fax: 604-526-1618
Manufacturer and exporter of alkaline, acid and specialty cleaners, sanitizers, chain lubes, defoamers, descalers and chlorine dioxide
General Manager: Paul Grehen
Other Locations:
 Machem Industries
 Regina, SKMachem Industries
Brands Exported: Topsan; Rinsol; Dairi-San; Optimum; Tuff Stuff; Orbit; Kloriclean; Progress
Regions Exported to: South America, USA
Percentage of Business in Exporting: 45

46227 Machine Builders & Design Inc
806 N Post Rd
Shelby, NC 28150-4247
704-482-3456
Fax: 704-482-3000 www.machinebuilders.com
Manufacturer and exporter of cookie packaging machinery
President/Owner: Darryl Mims
Finance Manager: Steve Hyde
Vice President: Brad Hogan
Service Manager: Phillip Cannon
Sales Manager: Rick MaDaniel
Engineering Manager: Eric Grayson
Estimated Sales: $5-10,000,000
Number Employees: 20-49
Regions Exported to: Worldwide

46228 Machine Ice Co
8915 Sweetwater Ln
Houston, TX 77037-2706
281-448-7823
Fax: 713-868-4424 800-423-8822
www.machineice.com
Wholesaler/distributor and exporter of mobile ice centers, ice plants, ice machines and refrigeration equipment; also, walk-in and reach-in coolers, cold storage facilities, ice cream makers, etc.; serving the food service market
President: Dan Celli
Sales Manager: Walter Felix
Estimated Sales: Less Than $500,000
Number Employees: 1-4
Square Footage: 88000
Brands Exported: Vogt; Kold-Draft; Coldelite
Regions Exported to: Central America, South America, Europe, Asia, Middle East, Mexico
Percentage of Business in Exporting: 20

46229 Machine Ice Co
8915 Sweetwater Ln
Houston, TX 77037-2706
281-448-7823
Fax: 713-868-4424 800-423-8822
www.machineice.com
Manufacturer and exporter of ice equipment including automatic ice cube makers, dispensers, crushers and storage bins; also, air conditioning units
President: Dan Celli
Sales Manager: Walter Felix
Estimated Sales: Less Than $500,000
Number Employees: 1-4
Square Footage: 200000
Brands Exported: Kold Draft
Regions Exported to: Worldwide
Percentage of Business in Exporting: 18

46230 Macrie Brothers
750 S 1st Rd
Hammonton, NJ 08037-8407
609-561-6822
Fax: 609-561-6296 bluebuck@bellatlantic.net
Blueberries
Owner/CEO: Paul Macrie III
Superviser: Al Macrie
Operations: Nicholas Macrie
Production: Michael Macrie
Estimated Sales: Below $ 5 Million
Number Employees: 5
Square Footage: 120000
Type of Packaging: Consumer, Food Service, Private Label, Bulk
Brands Exported: Macrie

46231 Maddalena Restaurant-Sn
737 Lamar St
Los Angeles, CA 90031-2514
323-223-1401
Fax: 323-221-7261 800-626-7722
info@sanantoniowinery.com
Wines
Owner/Manager: Anthony Riboli
anthony@sanantoniowinery.com
President/VP: Santo Riboli
Owner/President/Marketing Director: Steve Riboli
Sales Manager: Rick Rechetnick
HR & Finance Director/Purchasing Agent: Tony Tse
Estimated Sales: $12.7 Million
Number Employees: 100-249
Square Footage: 930000
Type of Packaging: Consumer, Food Service

46232 Madelaine Chocolate Company
9603 Beach Channel Dr
Rockaway Beach, NY 11693-1398
718-945-1500
800-322-1505
service@madelainechocolate.com
www.madelainechocolate.com
Chocolate in various colors, and shapes, such as butterflies, flowers, hearts, its a boy/girl, chocolate coins and cigars, seasonal and holiday chocolates and truffles.
President & CEO: Jorge Farber
jfarber@madelainechocolate.com
VP, Sales & Marketing: Joan Sweeting
VP, Production: Sam Farber
Year Founded: 1949
Estimated Sales: $49.8 Million
Number Employees: 100-249
Square Footage: 200000
Type of Packaging: Private Label, Bulk
Regions Exported to: South America, Europe

46233 Madera Enterprises Inc
32565 Avenue 9
Madera, CA 93636-8346
559-431-1444
Fax: 559-674-8214 800-507-9555
maderaent@aol.com
Processor and exporter of custom fruit juice concentrates and purees including grape, apple, strawberry, plum, prune, date, raisin, pomegranate, etc.; also, dried fruits and vinaigrettes
President: Susan Nury
maderaent@aol.com
Marketing: Rosanna Andrews-White
Estimated Sales: $ 3 - 5 Million
Number Employees: 5-9
Type of Packaging: Bulk
Brands Exported: Pomegranate Concentrate
Regions Exported to: Asia
Percentage of Business in Exporting: 10

46234 MadgeTech, Inc.
879 Maple Street
Contoocook, NH 03229
603-456-2011
Fax: 603-456-2012 info@madgetech.com
www.madgetech.com
Data logging instrumentation used for reading and monitoring temperatures both during and after the cooking process.
Contact: Ann Battles
ann@madgetech.com
Regions Exported to: Worldwide

46235 (HQ)Madhava Natural Sweeteners
4665 Nautilus Court S
Suite 301
Boulder, CO 80301
800-530-2900
madhavasweeteners.com
Organic sweeteners, including honey, agave nectar and coconut sugar
CEO: Colin Sankey
Estimated Sales: $710,000
Number Employees: 20-49
Square Footage: 8974
Type of Packaging: Consumer, Food Service, Private Label, Bulk
Other Locations:
 Madhava Honey
 Parachute, COMadhava Honey

46236 Madison Foods
238 Chester St
Saint Paul, MN 55107
651-265-8212
Fax: 651-297-6286 madisonfoodsmt.com
Butter substitutes; also, contract packager of retail and food service sauces
President: Steve Anderson
Estimated Sales: $ .5 - 1 million
Number Employees: 1-4
Type of Packaging: Consumer, Food Service, Private Label, Bulk

46237 Madix Inc
500 Airport Rd
Terrell, TX 75160-5200
214-515-5400
Fax: 972-563-0792 800-776-2349
www.madixinc.com
Manufacturer and exporter of retail display shelving, storage, wire and wood display systems
Owner: Thomas A Satterfield
tsatterfield@madixinc.com
Estimated Sales: $ 56 Million
Number Employees: 500-999
Square Footage: 1070000
Brands Exported: Omega; Maximum Merchandiser; Multiple Media Fixture
Regions Exported to: Worldwide
Percentage of Business in Exporting: 15

46238 Madsen Wire Products Inc
101 Madsen St
Orland, IN 46776-5417
260-829-6561
Fax: 260-829-6652 bsnyder@madsenwire.com
www.madsenwire.com
Manufacturer and designer of wire baskets, bases, containers, carts, displays, grids, stands, trays, fan and clamp guards, shelving, cages, etc. Constructed out of cold roll steel or stainless steel
President: Steve Cochran
scochran@generalcage.com
Estimator/Customer Service: Gwen Wheaton
Account Manager: Kim Straley

Importers & Exporters / A-Z

Estimated Sales: $10-20 Million
Number Employees: 20-49
Square Footage: 84000
Type of Packaging: Food Service, Private Label, Bulk

46239 Madys Company
1555 Yosemite Ave
San Francisco, CA 94124-3268   415-822-2227
                Fax: 415-822-3673
Herbal, medicinal and regular teas; also, vitamins, ginseng root
Owner: Sandy Su Wing
General Manager: Marian Hong
Number Employees: 10-19
Square Footage: 13600
Parent Co: Azeta Brands
Type of Packaging: Consumer, Food Service, Private Label, Bulk
Brands Exported: Madys Tea; Butterfly; Crocodile; Evergreen; Weiloss
Regions Exported to: Worldwide
Percentage of Business in Exporting: 20
Regions Imported from: Asia
Percentage of Business in Importing: 90

46240 Maestri d'Italia
480 Oberlin Ave S
Lakewood, NJ 08701   732-901-0949
                info@maestriditalia.com
                goodngreenfoods.com
Plant-based deli meats
CEO: Athos Maestri

46241 Magi Kitch'n
10 Ferry St
Concord, NH 03301-5022   603-225-6684
    Fax: 603-230-5548   800-441-1492
        sales@pitco.com www.magikitchn.com
Manufacturer and exporter of commercial cooking equipment including mobile outdoor units and gas, electric and charcoal broilers; also, broiler-griddles including mesquite and charcoal
President: Robert Bosa
bosa@magikitchn.com
CFO: Bob Granger
Vice President, General Manager: Greg Moyer
VP: George McMahon
Quality Control: Ray Amitrano
Senior Manager of Sales: Bonnie Bolster
Public Relations: Thomas Cassin
VP Operations: Robert Granger
Vice President of Operations: Steve Reale
Purchasing Manager: Terri Miller
Estimated Sales: $ 30 - 50 Million
Number Employees: 20-49
Parent Co: Middleby Corporation
Type of Packaging: Food Service
Regions Exported to: Worldwide
Percentage of Business in Exporting: 2

46242 MagiKitch'n
509 Route 3a
512
Bow, NH 03304-3102   800-258-3708
    Fax: 603-225-8472 dpack@maytag.com

46243 Magic American Corporation
23700 Mercantile Road
Cleveland, OH 44122-5900   216-464-2353
    Fax: 216-464-5895   800-321-6330
                www.magicamerican.com
Manufacturer and exporter of household cleaning products including stain removers and floor polish
President: Ross Chawson
VP: Scott Zeilinger
Sales Manager: Bob Beebe
Contact: James Zeilinger
jimmyze@aol.com
Estimated Sales: $ 10 - 20 Million
Number Employees: 50
Square Footage: 110000
Brands Exported: Magic; Goo Gone
Regions Exported to: Worldwide
Percentage of Business in Exporting: 12

46244 Magic Ice Products
1326 Ethan Ave
Cincinnati, OH 45225-1810   513-541-2645
                800-776-7923
                magiciceproducts@gmail.com
                www.magiciceproducts.com
Processor and exporter of gourmet coffee flavor, slush and ice syrups; importer of shave ice machines and equipment
President: Shirley Weist
Number Employees: 5-9
Type of Packaging: Consumer, Food Service, Private Label

46245 Magic Valley Growers
375 W Avenue D
Wendell, ID 83355-5512   208-536-6693
    Fax: 208-536-6695 www.magicvalleygrowers.com
Grower and packer of specialty onions including pearl, boiler, peeled pearl and sets; exporter of pearl and boiler onions
President: Robert Reitveld
onions@magicvalleygrowers.com
VP: James Kelly
Estimated Sales: $1.1 Million
Number Employees: 20-49
Square Footage: 212400
Type of Packaging: Consumer, Private Label, Bulk
Regions Exported to: Central America, Europe, Asia, Canada
Percentage of Business in Exporting: 8

46246 Magna Foods Corporation
16010 Phoenix Drive
City of Industry, CA 91745-1623   626-336-7500
    Fax: 626-336-3999   800-995-4394
                magnafoods@aol.com
Processor and exporter of confectionery, candy, cookies, crackers and cocoa products
President: Yogi Atmadja
VP: Peter Surjadinata
Estimated Sales: $1.5 Million
Number Employees: 25
Square Footage: 20000
Parent Co: IBIS
Brands Exported: Coffeego
Regions Exported to: Central America, South America, Canada
Percentage of Business in Exporting: 5

46247 Magna Power Controls
P.O.Box 13615
Milwaukee, WI 53213-0615   262-783-3500
    Fax: 262-783-3510   800-288-8178
        lbostrom@magnetek.com www.magnetek.com
Manufacturer and exporter of material handling equipment including control, electrification and automation
President: Andy Glass
CFO: Ryan Gyle
CEO: Peter M McCormick
Quality Control: Mark Logic
R & D: Ban Beilfuss
Marketing/Sales: Perry Pabich
Estimated Sales: $ 20 - 50 Million
Number Employees: 250-499
Type of Packaging: Bulk
Regions Exported to: Worldwide

46248 Magnatech Corp
6 Kripes Rd
East Granby, CT 06026-9645   860-653-2573
    Fax: 860-653-0486   888-393-3602
        info@magnatechllc.com www.magnatechllc.com
Sanitary processing tubes and fittings for food processing and dairy industries.
Executive VP: Garry Mccabe
gmccabe@magnatech-lp.com
Number Employees: 20-49
Regions Exported to: Worldwide

46249 Magnetic Products Inc
683 Town Center Dr
Highland, MI 48356-2965   248-887-5600
    Fax: 248-887-6100   800-544-5930
        info@mpimagnet.com www.mpimagnet.com
Magnetic separators, metal detectors and check weighers
President: Keith Rhodes
keith.rhodes@mpimagnet.com
R&D: Ron Kwaz
Marketing: Ellen Kominars
Sales: Del Butler
Estimated Sales: $6 Million
Number Employees: 20-49
Square Footage: 160000
Brands Exported: Magnetic Products Inc
Regions Exported to: Central America, South America, Europe, Asia
Percentage of Business in Exporting: 10

46250 Magnetool Inc
505 Elmwood Dr
Troy, MI 48083-2755   248-588-5400
    Fax: 248-588-5710 sales@magnetoolinc.com
                www.magnetoolinc.com
Manufacturer and exporter of magnetic separation equipment
President: A T Churchill
atchurchill@magnetoolinc.com
Engineer: Mike Wright
VP: C Sulisz
Estimated Sales: $ 20 - 50 Million
Number Employees: 20-49
Square Footage: 40000
Brands Exported: Magnetool
Regions Exported to: Central America, South America, Europe, Middle East, Mexico, Canada
Percentage of Business in Exporting: 5

46251 Magnolia Citrus Assn
1014 E Teapot Dome Ave
Porterville, CA 93257-9766   559-784-4455
    Fax: 559-781-9182 www.tcoe.org
Processor, packer and exporter of Valencia and navel oranges
Manager: Dominick Arcure
Manager: Larry Fultz
Manager: Dominick Arcure
Estimated Sales: $ 10 - 20 Million
Number Employees: 10-19
Type of Packaging: Private Label, Bulk
Regions Exported to: Asia, Australia

46252 (HQ)Magnotta Winery Corporation
271 Chrislea Road
Vaughan, ON L4L 8N6
Canada   905-738-9463
    Fax: 905-738-5551   800-461-9463
        mailbox@magnotta.com www.magnotta.com
Wines and wine baskets, ice wines, sparking wines, various beers, and liquors
President/Ceo: Rossana Magnotta
Chief Financial Officer: Fulvio De Angelis
Estimated Sales: $23 Million
Number Employees: 107
Square Footage: 60000
Type of Packaging: Consumer
Other Locations:
    Magnotta Winery Corp.
    Scarborough, ONMagnotta Winery Corp.
Brands Exported: Vidal
Regions Exported to: Asia
Regions Imported from: South America, Europe

46253 Magnum Custom Trailer &BBQ Pits
10806 Hwy 620 N
Austin, TX 78726   512-258-4101
    Fax: 512-258-2701   800-662-4686
        sales2@magnumtrailers.com
                www.magnumtrailers.com
Manufacturer and exporter of barbecue and catering trailers, custom kitchens and mobile concession stands
President: Charles Mc Lemore
Sales: Todd McLemore
Sales: Richard Westlund
Plat Manager: Jeff Israel
Estimated Sales: $15 Million
Number Employees: 50-99
Square Footage: 200000
Brands Exported: Magnum

46254 Magnuson
1 Magnuson Ave
Pueblo, CO 81001-4889   719-948-9500
    Fax: 719-948-9540 sales@magnusoncorp.com
                www.magnusoncorp.com
Manufacturer and exporter of processing and packaging machinery including vegetable cutters and peelers, washers and feeders; also, full can palletizers
Owner: Bob Smith
bsmith@magnusoncorp.com
VP/General Manager: Craig Furlo
Estimated Sales: $2.5-5 Million
Number Employees: 20-49
Parent Co: Atlas Pacific Engineering
Regions Exported to: Worldwide
Percentage of Business in Exporting: 30

Importers & Exporters / A-Z

46255 Magnuson Industries
3005 Kishwaukee St
Rockford, IL 61109-2061   815-229-2970
Fax: 815-229-2978   800-435-2816
www.posi-pour.com
Manufacturer, importer and exporter of portion control liquor pourers and bar supplies
Vice President: Stewart Magnuson
smagnuson@posi-pour.com
VP: Stewart Magnuson
Director Sales: Robert Gough
Estimated Sales: $ 5-10 Million
Number Employees: 10-19
Square Footage: 80000
Brands Exported: Posi-Pour
Regions Exported to: Worldwide
Percentage of Business in Exporting: 25
Brands Imported: Posi-Pour
Regions Imported from: Europe, Asia
Percentage of Business in Importing: 10

46256 Magrabar Chemical Corp
6100 Madison Ct
Morton Grove, IL 60053-3216   847-965-7550
Fax: 847-965-7553   www.magrabar.com
Manufactures additives, release agents and viscosity modifiers
President: Susan Jenkins
sjjenkins@magrabar.com
Chairman of the Board: Sandy Roy
Vice President: Dale Roy
Technical Director: Jeffrey Conrad
Estimated Sales: $3.4 Million
Number Employees: 10-19

46257 Magsys Inc
4144 S 112th St
Milwaukee, WI 53228-1914   414-543-2177
Fax: 414-541-9203
Manufacturer and exporter of stainless steel magnetic conveyor equipment for transport of ferrous crowns, caps and closures
President: Rudy Zwiebel
Estimated Sales: Below $ 5 Million
Number Employees: 1-4
Square Footage: 10000
Regions Exported to: Central America, South America
Percentage of Business in Exporting: 10

46258 Mahantongo Game Farm
559 Flying Eagle Rd
Dalmatia, PA 17017-7003   570-758-6284
Fax: 570-758-2095   800-982-9913
mgf@tds.net   www.pagamebirds.com
Processor and exporter of game birds including pheasants and partridges
Owner: Troy Laudenslager
mgf@tds.net
Estimated Sales: $360,000
Number Employees: 20-49

46259 Maid-Rite Steak Company
105 Keystone Industrial Park
Dunmore, PA 18512
800-233-4259
sales@mr-specialty.com   www.mr-specialty.com
Portioned controlled meat products, including quick frozen beef, ground beef, pork, veal, and lamb products.
Executive Vice President: Michael Bernstein
Estimated Sales: $41.5 Million
Number Employees: 255
Square Footage: 115000
Type of Packaging: Consumer, Food Service, Private Label, Bulk
Regions Exported to: Canada
Percentage of Business in Exporting: 5

46260 Maier Sign Systems
515 Victor Street
Saddle Brook, NJ 07663-6118   201-845-7555
Fax: 201-845-3336
Manufacturer and exporter of bulletin and menu boards, directories, awnings and signs including plastic, metal and neon
President/CEO: Stuart Brown
Estimated Sales: Less than $500,000
Number Employees: 4
Square Footage: 32000
Parent Co: Elms Industries
Regions Exported to: Europe, Canada

46261 Maine Potato Board
744 Main St # 1
Suite 1
Presque Isle, ME 04769-2270   207-769-5061
Fax: 207-764-4148   800-553-5516
mainepotatoes@mainepotatoes.com
www.mainepotatoes.com
Exporter of potatoes
President: Gregg Garrison
Vice President: Keith Labrie
Lab Technician: Ann I. Currier
Director Marketing/Promotions: Donale Flannery
Number Employees: 5-9

46262 Maine Wild Blueberry Company
320 Ridge Rd.
Cherryfield, ME 04622-0128   207-546-7573
Fax: 207-546-2713   800-243-4005
www.oxfordfrozenfoods.com
Canned, dehydrated and frozen wild blueberries
President/CEO: John Bragg
Co-CEO: Dave Hoffman
Chief Operating Officer: Ragnar Kamp
Treasurer: Geoff Baldwin
VP, Sales: Matthew Bragg
Director/Manufacturing: Milton Wood
Year Founded: 1997
Estimated Sales: $27 Million
Number Employees: 20-49
Square Footage: 100000
Parent Co: Oxford Frozen Foods
Regions Exported to: Europe, Asia
Percentage of Business in Exporting: 20

46263 Mainline Industries Inc
1 Allen St # 1
Suite 1
Springfield, MA 01108-1953   413-733-5771
Fax: 413-733-5929   800-527-7917
customerservice@mainlineind.com
www.mainlineind.com
Manufacturer and exporter of disposable wipers, cleaning towels and scuff pads
President: Paul Motter
paumotter@mainlineind.com
VP: Carlo Rovelli
Quality Control: Angie Smith
Marketing Support: Lee Albert
Estimated Sales: $2.5-5 Million
Number Employees: 5-9
Brands Exported: Aquawipes; Hydroscrubs; Hydrowype
Regions Exported to: Central America, South America, Middle East
Percentage of Business in Exporting: 5

46264 Mainstreet Menu Systems
1375 N Barker Rd
Brookfield, WI 53045-5215   262-782-6000
Fax: 262-782-6515   800-782-6222
info@mainstreetmenus.com
Manufacturer and exporter of point of purchase displays, menu boards and order racks. Design, engineer, produce & install menu boards, graphics & displays.
President: Doug Watson
CFO: Bill Hintz
Research & Development: Paul Steinbrenner
Marketing: Angie Herrmann
Estimated Sales: $ 10 - 20 Million
Number Employees: 20-49
Parent Co: Howard Company
Type of Packaging: Food Service
Brands Exported: Mainstreet Menu Systems
Regions Exported to: Worldwide
Percentage of Business in Exporting: 18

46265 Maison Riviere USA
1424 Collins Ave
Miami Beach, FL 33139   305-531-3488
aroma-one.com
Herb pastes
Contact: Mathieu Rouget

46266 Majestic
60 Cherry Street
Bridgeport, CT 06605-2395   203-367-7900
Fax: 203-335-6973
Manufacturer, importer and exporter of plastic serving and tabletop accessories including beverage glasses, pitchers, bowls, mugs, stemware, ice buckets, plates, trays and coasters; manufacturer of electric lamps and plastic kitchentools and gadgets
Contact: Elliott Zivin
ezivin@majesticgifts.com
Estimated Sales: $2.5-5 Million
Number Employees: 10-19
Parent Co: Zivco
Brands Exported: Diner Mugs; Basket Weave; Ice-Stir-Cools; Seaglass; Transitions; Facets; Koziol; Chroma Lamps
Regions Exported to: Worldwide
Percentage of Business in Exporting: 30
Regions Imported from: Europe, Asia
Percentage of Business in Importing: 20

46267 Majestic Industries Inc
15378 Hallmark Ct
Macomb, MI 48042-4017   586-786-9100
Fax: 586-786-9105   www.majesticind.net
Manufacturer and exporter of treated dusting cloths and wet and dust mops
President: Gavonna Agnew
gagnew@majesticind.com
CEO: Gary Potashnick
Estimated Sales: $ 1 - 3 Million
Number Employees: 50-99
Number of Brands: 10
Number of Products: 250
Square Footage: 128000
Type of Packaging: Consumer, Food Service, Private Label, Bulk
Regions Exported to: Europe, Canada, Mexico
Percentage of Business in Exporting: 5

46268 Majesty
11 Commerce Dr Ste 305
Cranford, NJ 7016   908-272-4433
Fax: 908-272-0632
Importer of cooked ham, pork shoulder and back and spare ribs
President: Soren Svenningsen
VP Sales: Bjarne Jenshoej
jobj@majestyinc.com
Estimated Sales: $ 10 - 20 Million
Number Employees: 10-19
Parent Co: Tulip International
Brands Imported: Majesty; Royal Dane; Midland
Regions Imported from: Europe
Percentage of Business in Importing: 100

46269 Makana Beverages Inc.
Oxnard, CA
www.thebukombucha.com
Organic, raw, non-GMO, gluten-free and vegan kombucha in various flavors
Founder: Gary Hawes
CEO: Ryan Mason
Number of Brands: 1
Number of Products: 5
Type of Packaging: Consumer, Private Label

46270 Maker's Mark Distillery Inc
3350 Burkes Spring Rd
Loretto, KY 40037-8027   270-865-2881
Fax: 270-865-2196   www.makersmark.com
Processor and exporter of whiskey
President/COO: Rob Samuels
Manager: Victoria Mc Rae-Samuels
Estimated Sales: $ 25-49 Million
Number Employees: 50-99
Parent Co: Beam Suntory Inc.
Type of Packaging: Consumer
Regions Exported to: Central America, South America, Europe, Asia, Middle East

46271 Malena Produce Inc
947 E Frontage Rd # A
Rio Rico, AZ 85649-6264   520-281-1185
Fax: 520-281-2156   dstoller@malenaproduce.com
Wholesaler/distributor and importer of fruits and vegetables including eggplant, bell and hot peppers, squash and pickles
President: Juanita Avila
javila@malenaproduce.com
Sales Manager: Ana Astrid Celaya
Sales: Oscar Rodriguez
Estimated Sales: $10-20 Million
Number Employees: 10-19
Square Footage: 30000
Type of Packaging: Consumer, Food Service
Regions Imported from: Mexico

Importers & Exporters / A-Z

46272 (HQ)Malgor & Company
PO Box 366
Catano, PR 00963-0366   787-788-0303
Fax: 787-788-2190
Importer of oils including corn, olive and soybean; also, sauces, fish, wines, olives and spices; exporter of wine and olives
President: Conrado Garcia Guerra
VP: Antonio Garcia Mendez
Quality Control: Conrado Garcia Guerra
Number Employees: 95
Square Footage: 400000
Brands Exported: Canario; Castellar
Regions Exported to: Central America
Brands Imported: Canario; Maizete; Michelangelo
Regions Imported from: Central America, South America, Europe

46273 Mali's All Natural Barbecue Supply Company
161 Bramblewood Ln
East Amherst, NY 14051-1417   716-688-2210
Fax: 716-688-2795   800-289-6254
buymali@localnet.com
Manufacturer, importer and exporter of lump charcoal, briquettes and wood for smoking and cooking; also, grilling woods
President: James Maliszewski
CEO: Frances Maliszewski
Estimated Sales: $ 1 - 3 Million
Number Employees: 1-4
Number of Brands: 1
Regions Exported to: Canada, Caribbean
Percentage of Business in Exporting: 5
Regions Imported from: Mexico
Percentage of Business in Importing: 10

46274 (HQ)Malnove Of Nebraska
13434 F St
Omaha, NE 68137-1181   402-330-1100
Fax: 402-330-2941   800-228-9877
packaging.systems@malnove.com
www.malnove.com
Manufacturer and exporter of folding paperboard cartons
President, CEO: Paul Malnove
CFO: Jim Belcher
VP: Dick Lawson
VP Sales: Michael Querry
Operations: Steve Maynar
Plant Manager: Craig Beaber
Estimated Sales: B
Number Employees: 500-999
Square Footage: 800000
Type of Packaging: Consumer, Food Service, Private Label
Regions Exported to: Central America
Percentage of Business in Exporting: 5

46275 Malo Inc
12111 E 51st St # 106
Tulsa, OK 74146-6005   918-583-2743
Fax: 918-583-6208   sales@maloinc.com
www.maloinc.com
Manufacturer and exporter of crateless and overpressure retort systems for low-acid foods in metal and flexible containers
President: Chuck Clugston
cclugston@maloinc.com
VP: Allen Stucky
Marketing/Sales: Rick Holsted
Estimated Sales: $2.5-5 Million
Number Employees: 10-19
Square Footage: 80000
Brands Exported: Malo
Regions Exported to: Central America, Europe, Asia, Worldwide
Percentage of Business in Exporting: 80

46276 Maloney Seafood Corporation
PO Box 690109
Quincy, MA 02269-0109   617-472-1004
Fax: 617-472-7722   800-566-2837
info@maloneyseafood.com
www.maloneyseafood.com
Importers of frozen seafood.
President: Thomas Maloney
Contact: Frank Maloney
frank@maloneyseafood.com
Estimated Sales: $10-20 Million
Number Employees: 5-9
Type of Packaging: Consumer, Food Service
Regions Imported from: Asia

46277 Malt Diastase Co
141 Lanza Ave # 31
Bldg 31
Garfield, NJ 07026-3539   973-772-2103
Fax: 973-772-0623   800-772-0416
Processor and exporter of flavoring extracts and syrups
President: Art Levy
Contact: Barry Kirsch
b_kirsch@maltproducts.com
Estimated Sales: $ 10 - 20 Million
Number Employees: 1-4
Type of Packaging: Food Service, Bulk

46278 Malt Diastase Co
88 Market St
Saddle Brook, NJ 07663
Fax: 201-845-0028   800-526-0180
www.maltproducts.com
Malt, molasses, natural sweeteners
Owner/President: Amy Targan
VP of Sales: John Johansen
Number Employees: 20-49
Type of Packaging: Bulk

46279 Malteurop North America
3830 W Grant St
Milwaukee, WI 53215   414-671-1166
www.malteurop.com
Processor and exporter of malt, also offers several modes of commercial collaboration, as well as consulting, engineering, and training services.
CEO: Olivier Parent
President, North America: Kevin Eikerman
Chief Commercial & Innovation Officer: Alain Caekaert
Year Founded: 1984
Estimated Sales: $31.5 Million
Number Employees: 100-249
Parent Co: Malteurop
Type of Packaging: Food Service, Bulk
Regions Exported to: Worldwide

46280 Malthus Diagnostics
35888 Centre Ridge Road
North Ridgeville, OH 44039   440-327-2585
Fax: 440-327-7286   800-346-7202
Automated microbiological analyzers; manufacturer, importer and exporter of incubators and growth media
Director Marketing/Sales: Joseph Carney
Director US Operations: Joseph Carney
Estimated Sales: $1-2.5 Million
Number Employees: 25
Square Footage: 2000
Parent Co: IDG
Brands Exported: Malthus; Lab M
Regions Exported to: Canada, Mexico
Percentage of Business in Exporting: 15
Brands Imported: Malthus; Lab M
Regions Imported from: Europe
Percentage of Business in Importing: 85

46281 Mama Amy's Quality Foods
5715 Coopers Avenue
Mississauga, ON L4Z 2C7
Canada   905-456-0056
Fax: 905-456-1536
Pizza and broccoli and cheese sticks, calzones, jambalaya
Sales/Marketing Director: Aldon Reed
Number Employees: 30
Square Footage: 28000
Type of Packaging: Consumer, Food Service, Private Label, Bulk
Brands Exported: Mama Amy's
Regions Exported to: USA

46282 Man-O Products
811 Ridgeway Ave
Cincinnati, OH 45229   513-281-5959
Fax: 513-936-6555   888-210-6266
Manufacturer and exporter of protective hand creams and soap products
President: Steve Seltzer
Quality Control: Andy Joseph
Sales Manager: Tom Joseph
Estimated Sales: $ 5 - 10 Million
Number Employees: 5-9

46283 Management Tech of America
4742 N 24th Street
Suite 410
Phoenix, AZ 85016-4862   602-381-5800
Fax: 602-251-0903
Manufacturer and exporter of software for the control of material handling systems
Estimated Sales: $10-20 Million
Number Employees: 50-99
Regions Exported to: Worldwide

46284 Manager's Redbook by Dataworks
4550 S Windermere St
Englewood, CO 80110-5541   303-761-6975
Fax: 303-761-6985   www.managersredbook.com
President: Greg Thiesen
Estimated Sales: $ 20 - 50 Million
Number Employees: 50-99

46285 Manchester Farms
8126 Garners Ferry Rd
Columbia, SC 29209-9402   803-783-9024
Fax: 803-227-3103   800-845-0421
customerservice@manchesterfarms.com
www.manchesterfarms.com
Quail and bacon wrapped chicken; Franks-in-a-blanket; mini stuffed potato skins.
President: Brittney Miller
VP: Steve Odom
Total Quality Manager: Liz Benson
Marketing Manager: Matt Miller
Sales: Heather Ivey
Sales: Angela Covington
Director of Operations: Michael Davis
Plant Manager: Jennifer Alexander
Estimated Sales: Less Than $500,000
Number Employees: 1-4
Square Footage: 88000
Type of Packaging: Consumer, Food Service, Private Label

46286 Manchester Tool & Die Inc
601 S Wabash Rd
North Manchester, IN 46962-8148   260-982-8524
Fax: 260-982-4575
www.manchestertoolanddie.com
Manufacturer and exporter of packaging equipment and machinery; also, prototype development available
President: Barry Blocher
bablocher@manchestertoolanddie.com
Sales/Supervisor: Robin Brubaker
Production Manager: Steve Music
Plant Manager: Josh Berry
Estimated Sales: $ 2.5-5 Million
Number Employees: 50-99
Square Footage: 34000
Regions Exported to: Canada
Percentage of Business in Exporting: 1

46287 Mancini Packing Co
3500 Mancini Pl
Zolfo Springs, FL 33890-4710   863-735-2000
Fax: 863-735-1172   800-741-1778
rmancini@mancinifoods.com
www.mancinifoods.com
Peppers and olive oil
Chairman/President: Frank Mancini
fmancini@mancinifoods.com
VP: Alan Mancini
Estimated Sales: $11 Million
Number Employees: 50-99
Type of Packaging: Consumer, Food Service, Private Label, Bulk

46288 Mancuso Cheese Co
612 Mills Rd # 1
Joliet, IL 60433-2897   815-722-2475
Fax: 815-722-1302   pfalbo@mancusocheese.com
www.mancusocheese.com
Cheese including ricotta, mozzarella, etc.; exporter of pizza supplies; importer of pasta, olive oil, olives and anchovies; wholesaler/distributor of frozen foods, produce, meats, baked goods, general merchandise, etc.
President: Dominic Mancuso
mberta@mancusocheese.com
VP: Philip Falbo
Sales Exec: Mike Berta
Estimated Sales: $6 Million
Number Employees: 20-49
Square Footage: 80000

Type of Packaging: Consumer, Food Service, Bulk
Brands Exported: Mancuso
Regions Exported to: Asia
Percentage of Business in Exporting: 1
Regions Imported from: Europe
Percentage of Business in Importing: 5

46289 Mandalay Food Products Corporation
1633 Bayshore Hwy Ste 338
Burlingame, CA 94010
650-652-9990
Fax: 650-652-9998
Importer of canned pineapples and pineapple juice concentrate
President: Anthony Tay
Estimated Sales: $5-10 Million
Number Employees: 4
Square Footage: 3300
Brands Imported: Mandalay
Regions Imported from: Asia
Percentage of Business in Importing: 100

46290 Mandarin Soy Sauce Inc
4 Sands Station Rd
Middletown, NY 10940-4415
845-343-1505
Fax: 845-343-0731 info@wanjashan.com
www.wanjashan.com
Soy sauce, asian sauce, rice and vinegar
President: Alvin Lam
alvin.c.lam@chase.com
VP: Mike Shapiro
Estimated Sales: $165 Million
Number Employees: 20-49
Square Footage: 170000
Brands Exported: Wan Ja Shan
Brands Imported: Wan Ja Shan

46291 Mane Inc.
2501 Henkle Dr.
Lebanon, OH 45036
513-248-9876
Fax: 513-248-8808 requests@mane.com
www.mane.com
Flavors and seasoning blends
President/CEO: Jean Mane
President: Michell Mane
Executive Vice President: Kent Hunter
Contact: James Abel
james.abel@mane.com
Year Founded: 1871
Estimated Sales: 20-50 Million
Number Employees: 50-99
Square Footage: 65000
Regions Exported to: Central America, South America, Europe, Asia, Middle East
Percentage of Business in Exporting: 10

46292 Manger Packing Corp
124 S Franklintown Rd
Baltimore, MD 21223-2036
410-233-0126
Fax: 410-362-8065 800-227-9262
Manufacturer and packer of meat including pork, beef, chicken, lamb, veal and smoked ham; exporter of beef sausage
Owner: A Manger
Estimated Sales: $9 Million
Number Employees: 10-19
Type of Packaging: Consumer, Bulk
Regions Exported to: Middle East

46293 Mangia Inc.
23166 Los Alisos Blvd
Suite #228
Mission Viejo, CA 92691
949-581-1274
Fax: 949-581-2906 866-462-6442
info@mangiainc.com www.MANGIAINC.com
Canned San Marzano tomato products, originally produced in Italy, with no preservatives or added salt
President: Matt Maslowski
Manager: Morgan Patterson
VP: Bob Maruca
Contact: Rosa Borrelli
rosacinzia@mangiainc.com
Estimated Sales: $1.3 Million
Number Employees: 12
Number of Brands: 1
Number of Products: 7
Type of Packaging: Consumer, Food Service
Other Locations:
Conditalia
Nocera Superiore, ItalyConditalia

46294 Manhattan Truck Lines
91 Michigan Ave
Paterson, NJ 07503-1807
973-278-0190
Fax: 973-278-0582 800-370-7627
info@pariserchem.com www.pariserchem.com
Manufacturer and exporter of warewashing detergents, water-treatment chemicals and institutional maintenance products. Products include laundry chemicals, soaps and detergents
Owner: Bill Moakley
bmoakley@pariserchem.com
VP: Andrew Pariser
VP: Scott Pariser
Estimated Sales: $ 10-20 Million
Number Employees: 10-19
Type of Packaging: Consumer, Food Service, Private Label, Bulk
Regions Exported to: Caribbean
Percentage of Business in Exporting: 4

46295 Mani Imports
3601 Parkway Pl
West Sacramento, CA 95691-3420
916-373-1100
Fax: 916-373-1018 info@maniimports.com
www.maniimports.com
Wholesaler/distributor and importer of olive oil, fire-roasted peppers, olives, spices, feta cheese, olive oil soap, tropical fruit pulps and natural sponges
Owner: Peter Cononelos
Corporate Chief: Glenn Weddell
Estimated Sales: $ 5 - 10 Million
Number Employees: 10-19
Regions Imported from: Greece, Columbia

46296 Manicaretti Italian Food Importers
5332 College Ave
Suite 200
Oakland, CA 94618
510-655-0911
Fax: 510-655-2034 800-799-9830
mail@manicaretti.com www.manicaretti.com
Importer of artisan produced Italian foods including pasta, extra virgin olive oils, citrus fruit pressed with extra virgin olive oil and rice for risotto
President: Sava Wilson
CFO: Rolando Rutz Berameadi
CFO: Gustavo Houghton
Sales/Marketing Director: Carolyn Buck
Contact: Rolando Beramendi
rolando@manicaretti.com
Estimated Sales: $ 5 - 10 Million
Number Employees: 5-9
Type of Packaging: Consumer, Food Service, Bulk
Brands Imported: Rustichella d'Abruzzo; Principato di Lucedio; Capezzana; Frescobaldi Laudemio; Tenuta di Capezanna; Agrumato; Olio Verde
Regions Imported from: Europe
Percentage of Business in Importing: 100

46297 Manildra Milling Corporation
4210 Shawnee Msn Pkwy Ste 312a
Fairway, KS 66205
913-362-0777
Fax: 913-362-0052 800-323-8435
info@manildrausa.com www.manildrausa.com
Processor, exporter and importer of wheat gluten; processor of wheat starch
President: Gerry Degnan
Vice President of Business Development: Tom McCurry
Engineering Manager: Deryl Hancock
Number Employees: 10-19
Parent Co: Manildra Group
Type of Packaging: Bulk
Percentage of Business in Exporting: 1
Brands Imported: Gem of The West
Regions Imported from: Australia
Percentage of Business in Importing: 40

46298 Manischewitz Co
80 Avenue K
Newark, NJ 07105-3803
201-553-1100
Fax: 201-333-1809
deborah.ross@manischewitz.com
www.manischewitz.com
Manufacturer and exporter of kosher foods including matzoth, crackers, cereals, wine, bagel mixes, candy, pickles, gefilte fish, borscht, doughnut mixes, bagel mixes and egg noodles.
President & CEO: David Sugarman
Contact: Bankier Alain
bankier.alain@manischewitz.com
Number Employees: 400
Number of Brands: 12
Type of Packaging: Consumer, Food Service, Private Label
Brands Exported: Manischewitz
Regions Exported to: Central America, South America, Europe, Asia, Middle East
Percentage of Business in Exporting: 10

46299 Manitowoc Foodservice
2100 Future Drive
Sellersburg, IN 47172
818-637-7200
Fax: 818-637-7222 800-367-4233
www.manitowocbeverage.com
Manufacturer, importer and exporter of automatic ice transportation systems, beverage and ice dispensers, faucets, fluid control devices, pumps, timers, bar guns and carbonators
Manager: Andrew Nelson
CEO: G McCann
Contact: Paul Hanniffy
hanniffypaul@gmail.com
Estimated Sales: $ 3 - 5 Million
Number Employees: 5-9
Square Footage: 480000
Brands Exported: McCann's
Regions Exported to: Central America, South America, Europe, Asia, Middle East
Percentage of Business in Exporting: 10
Regions Imported from: Asia

46300 Manitowoc Ice Machine
2110 S 26th St
Manitowoc, WI 54220-6321
920-682-0161
Fax: 920-683-7589 800-545-5720
www.manitowocice.com
Manufacturer and exporter of ice machines, ice storage bins and reach-in refrigerators and freezers
Vice President: Lee Wichlacz
lee.wichlacz@manitowoc.com
Executive Vice President: Larry Bryce
Vice President of Sales: Kevin Clark
VP International Operations: Mark Kreple
Estimated Sales: $ 1 - 5 Million
Number Employees: 250-499
Square Footage: 365000
Parent Co: Manitowoc Foodservice Group
Brands Exported: Manitowoc; Kolpak; McCall
Regions Exported to: Worldwide
Percentage of Business in Exporting: 20

46301 (HQ)Manning Lighting Inc
1810 North Ave
Sheboygan, WI 53083-4619
920-458-2184
Fax: 920-458-2491 info@manningltg.com
www.digitalspeck.com
Manufacturer and exporter of lighting equipment including institutional decorative chandeliers
Owner: Andy Manning
Controller: Mary Kuhfuss
Sales: Liz Manning
amanning@manningltg.com
Estimated Sales: $ 10 - 20 Million
Number Employees: 20-49
Type of Packaging: Food Service
Regions Exported to: Central America, South America, Canada
Percentage of Business in Exporting: 2

46302 Mansi, Inc.
8416 193rd St
New York, NY 11423
info@drinkmansi.com
www.drinkmansi.com
Calamansi juice beverage
CEO: Charles Medenilla

46303 Manufacturers Credit Corp
903 18th St # 230
Plano, TX 75074-5848
972-422-7852
Fax: 972-422-7858 www.mcccredit.com
Owner: James Dempster
james.dempster@mcccredit.com
Number Employees: 5-9

46304 (HQ)Manufacturers Wood Supply Company
1936 Scranton Road
Cleveland, OH 44113-2429
216-771-7848
Fax: 216-771-7848
Manufacturer, importer and exporter of specialty and industrial wood products including plywood and masonite boxes, packaging inserts and basket bases; custom sizing available

Importers & Exporters / A-Z

Plant Manager: Joseph Rielinger
Estimated Sales: $ 1-2.5 Million
Number Employees: 6
Square Footage: 40000
Regions Exported to: Canada
Percentage of Business in Exporting: 10

46305 Manufacturing Warehouse
110 NW 24th Avenue
Miami, FL 33125-5260
305-635-8886
Fax: 305-633-2266
Manufacturer and exporter of freezers including walk-in, ice cream and quick freezing; also, walk-in coolers and doors: strip, supermarket and cold storage
Estimated Sales: $ 1 - 5 Million
Number Employees: 4
Square Footage: 20000
Regions Exported to: Central America, South America, Middle East, Caribbean
Percentage of Business in Exporting: 15

46306 Maple Leaf Cheesemakers
554 Frst Street
New Glarus, WI 53574
608-527-2000
Fax: 608-527-3050   888-624-1234
mapleleaf1@tds.net
www.mapleleafcheeseandchocolatehaus.com
Cheese including monterey jack and gouda, fudge and chocolates
Owner: Barbara Kummerfeldt
Estimated Sales: $500,000-$1 Million
Number Employees: 20-49
Type of Packaging: Consumer, Food Service, Private Label, Bulk
Regions Exported to: Canada, Israel

46307 (HQ)Maple Leaf Foods International
5160 Yonge St
Suite 300
North York, ON M2N 6L9
Canada
416-480-8900
Fax: 416-480-8950   800-268-3708
www.mapleleaf.ca
Processor, importer and exporter of fresh and frozen meat, seafood, dairy products, produce, potato products and specialty grains
President: Michael Detlefsen
Senior Vice President, Transactions and: Rocco Cappuccitti
Executive VP/Chief Strategy Officer: Douglas Dodds
Chief Information Officer: Patrick Ressa
Chief Financial Officer: Michael Vels
Estimated Sales: $6.4 Million
Number Employees: 23,000
Square Footage: 42000
Type of Packaging: Consumer, Food Service, Private Label, Bulk
Other Locations:
  Maple Leaf Foods Internationa
  Chatham, NJMaple Leaf Foods Internationa
Brands Exported: Cana; Five Oceans; York; Maple Leaf; Shur Gain
Regions Exported to: Central America, South America, Europe, Asia, Middle East
Regions Imported from: Central America, South America, Europe, Asia

46308 Maple Leaf Pork
P.O.Box 55021
Montreal, QC H3G 2W5
Canada
403-328-1756
Fax: 403-327-9821   800-268-3708
www.mapleleaf.ca
Processor and exporter of fresh and frozen pork including carcass, boxed and by-products
President: Michael McCain
Sales: Wilf Fiebich
General Manager: Ralph Miller
Plant Manager: Dave Wood
Number Employees: 100-249
Parent Co: Maple Leaf Foods
Type of Packaging: Consumer, Bulk
Regions Exported to: Worldwide
Percentage of Business in Exporting: 65

46309 Maple Products
1500 Rue De Pacifique
Sherbrooke, QC J1H 2G7
Canada
819-569-5161
Fax: 819-569-5168
Processor and exporter of maple syrup and sugar; also, kosher grades available
Production Manager: Ghislain Pare
Number Employees: 10-19
Parent Co: Citadelle
Type of Packaging: Food Service, Bulk
Regions Exported to: Worldwide

46310 Maplehurst Bakeries LLC
50 Maplehurst Dr
Brownsburg, IN 46112
800-428-3200
info@maplehurstbakeries.com
www.maplehurstbakeries.com
Bread and other bakery products including; rolls, cakes, donuts, pies, and danishes.
President: Luc Mongeau
Supply Chain Director: Craig Myers
Year Founded: 1967
Estimated Sales: $107.2 Million
Number Employees: 1,000-4,999
Parent Co: George Weston Ltd.
Type of Packaging: Food Service, Private Label, Bulk

46311 Mar-Con Wire Belt
2431 Vauxhall Place
Richmond, BC V6V 1Z5
Canada
604-278-8922
Fax: 604-278-8938   877-962-7266
www.metalbelt.com
Manufacturer and exporter of wire mesh conveyor belting, food processing equipment, conveyors and sheet metal fabrications including stamping
President: Michael Chiu
CFO: Michael Chiu
R&D: Michael Chiu
Sales Director: Krey Miller
Production/Purchasing: Nathan Chiu
Estimated Sales: $ 5 Million
Number Employees: 25
Square Footage: 10000
Regions Exported to: South America, Asia, USA
Percentage of Business in Exporting: 80

46312 Mar-Jac Poultry Inc.
1020 Aviation Blvd.
Gainesville, GA 30501
770-531-5000
Fax: 770-531-5015   info@marjacpoultry.com
www.marjacpoultry.com
Fresh and frozen chicken; whole birds (with or without giblets), fast food (8, 9, or 6 pieces), splits, or quarters, boneless butterflies, tenders, filets, or thigh meat, and parts; split breasts, drums, thighs, whole legs, legquarters, whole wings, cut wings, gizzards, livers, paws.
CFO: Tanveer Papa
Vice President, Operations: Joel Williams
Year Founded: 1954
Estimated Sales: $284 Million
Number Employees: 1000-4999
Number of Brands: 2
Square Footage: 300000
Type of Packaging: Food Service, Private Label
Regions Exported to: Worldwide

46313 Mar-Khem Industries
PO Box 2266
Cinnaminson, NJ 8077
Fax: 856-829-9203
Supplier, exporter of closeouts; also, investment recovery and used equipment available
President: Anthony Corradetti
a_corradetti@mar-khem.com
Number Employees: 5-9
Number of Brands: 200
Number of Products: 800
Square Footage: 500000
Type of Packaging: Consumer, Food Service, Private Label, Bulk

46314 Mar-Len Supply Inc
23159 Kidder St
Hayward, CA 94545-1630
510-782-3555
Fax: 510-782-2032   mark@marlensupply.com
www.marlensupply.com
Manufacturer and exporter of biodegradable oil and grease dispersing and removing compounds
Owner/President/office Manager: Shirley Winter
marlnsupply@aol.com
Technical Director: Frank Winter
Production/Sales Manager: Mark Wieland
Production Engineer: Curt Winter
Estimated Sales: $500,000-$1 Million
Number Employees: 1-4

46315 (HQ)Maramor Chocolates
1855 E 17th Ave
Columbus, OH 43219
614-291-2244
Fax: 614-291-0966   800-843-7722
Processor and exporter of kosher boxed chocolates, chocolate covered bagel chips and mints; packaged for racks and fund raising purposes; contract manufacturing available
President: Michael Ryan
Sales: Scott Sher
Contact: Crystal Burchett
cburchett@maramor.com
Estimated Sales: $1.6 Million
Number Employees: 20-49
Square Footage: 120000
Type of Packaging: Consumer, Private Label, Bulk
Brands Exported: Maramor
Regions Exported to: Europe, Middle East
Percentage of Business in Exporting: 5

46316 (HQ)Marantha Natural Foods
1192 Illinois Street
San Francisco, CA 94107
415-401-0080
Fax: 415-401-0087   866-972-6879
customerservice@worldpantry.com
www.worldpantry.com
Organic and regular nut and seed butters, trail mixes and dry roasted nuts and seeds; importer of cashews and sesame seeds; exporter of organic and regular nut and seed butters and trail mixes
President: Patrick Lee
CEO: David Miller
Estimated Sales: $ 10 - 20 Million
Number Employees: 20-49
Square Footage: 28000
Type of Packaging: Consumer, Food Service, Private Label, Bulk
Other Locations:
  Marantha Natural Foods
  San Leandro, CAMarantha Natural Foods
Brands Exported: Marantha
Regions Exported to: Asia
Regions Imported from: Central America

46317 Marathon Enterprises Inc
9 Smith St
Englewood, NJ 07631-4607
201-569-2915
Fax: 201-935-5693   800-722-7388
info@sabrett.com   www.sabretthotstuff.com
Hot dogs including; all beef natural casing, pork and beef natural casing, or all beef skinless, available in cocktail size up to foot long franks, and condiments such as sauerkraut, mustard, relish and onions in sauce
President: Boyd G Adelman
VP Sales: Mark Rosen
Plant Manager: Herb Tetens
Number Employees: 250-499
Type of Packaging: Consumer, Food Service, Private Label, Bulk

46318 Marathon Equipment Co
P.O. Box 1798
Highway 9 S
Vernon, AL 35592-1798
205-695-9105
Fax: 205-695-8813   800-269-7237
www.marathonequipment.com
Commercial waste and recycling equipment including balers and self-contained and stationary compactors.
President/General Manager: Vic Ujihara
Estimated Sales: $47 Million
Number Employees: 250-499
Parent Co: Dover Corporation
Brands Exported: RamJet; Nexgen Baling Systems
Regions Exported to: Central America, South America, Europe, Asia, Middle East

46319 Marburg Industries Inc
1207 Activity Dr
Vista, CA 92081-8510
760-727-3762
Fax: 760-727-5502   marburgind@aol.com
www.marburgind.com
Manufacturer and exporter of tamper evident packaging machinery
VP Marketing: Barbara Paschal
Manager: Barbara Paschal
Estimated Sales: $1-2.5 Million
Number Employees: 10-19
Square Footage: 20000

Type of Packaging: Food Service, Private Label, Bulk
Regions Exported to: Worldwide
Percentage of Business in Exporting: 25

46320 Marc Refrigeration Mfg Inc
7453 NW 32nd Ave
Miami, FL 33147-5877   305-691-0500
Fax: 305-691-1212 info@marcrefrigeration.com
www.marcrefrigeration.com
Manufacturer and exporter of commercial refrigerators and ice cream freezers
President: Hy Widel
Vice President: Loretta Widelitz
lwidelitz@marcrefrigerationmfginc.com
Treasurer: Hal Videlitz
Secretary: Robert Gordon
Estimated Sales: $5-10 Million
Number Employees: 20-49
Square Footage: 228000
Type of Packaging: Food Service

46321 Marchant Schmidt Inc
24 W Larsen Dr
Fond Du Lac, WI 54937-8518   920-921-4760
Fax: 920-921-9640 sales@marchantschmidt.com
www.marchantschmidt.com
Manufacturers stainless steel products and equipment for the food and dairy industry
Vice President: Richard F Schmidt
rschmidt@marchantschmidt.com
CEO: Myleen Schmidt
Vice President: Lyle Schmidt
Sales Director: Jeno Thuecks
Estimated Sales: $11 Million
Number Employees: 100-249
Square Footage: 48000

46322 Marconi Italian Specialty Foods
710 W Grand Ave
Chicago, IL 60654-5574   312-421-0485
Fax: 312-421-1286 sales@marconi-foods.com
www.marconi-foods.com
Manufacturers a variety of specialty Italian foods including cheeses; coffees; salad dressings; meats; olive oils; pasta; salads; sauces; seafoods; spices, and vinegars.
President/CEO/Co-Owner: Robert Johnson
Co-Owner: Sue Formusa
Estimated Sales: $ 5 - 10 Million
Number Employees: 5-9
Parent Co: V Formusa Company

46323 Marcus Food Co
P.O. Box 781659
Wichita, KS 67278-1659   316-686-7649
Fax: 316-684-1266
information@marcusfoodco.com
www.marcusfoodco.com
Importer, exporter and wholesaler/distributor of frozen food, seafood and meat products including pork and chicken.
President: Jerry Marcus
Founder & Chairman: Howard Marcus
hmarcus@marcusfoodco.com
Operations Manager: Rick Finney
Year Founded: 1980
Estimated Sales: $140 Million
Number Employees: 10-19
Type of Packaging: Food Service, Private Label, Bulk
Regions Exported to: Asia, Canada
Regions Imported from: South America

46324 Marel Food Systems, Inc.
8145 Flint Street
Lenexa, KS 66214   913-888-9110
Fax: 913-888-9124 info@marel.com
www.marel.com
Manufacturer of meat hoppers, checkweighers, scales and end line scales. Also manufacture batter mixers, flour and bread applicators, spiral and linear ovens and steam cookers.
CEO: Theo Hoen
CFO: Eric Kaman
Regional Sales Manager: David Bertelsen
Contact: Debra Bernas
dbernas@marel.com
Regions Exported to: Worldwide

46325 Marel Stork Poultry Processing
1024 Airport Pkwy
Gainesville, GA 30501-6814   770-532-7041
Fax: 770-532-5672
Manufacturer and exporter of poultry processing equipment
President: Frank Nicoletti
frank.nicoletti@stork.com
Executive VP: Frank Nicoletti
Manager Domestic Sales: Bryon Lovingood
Estimated Sales: $ 20-50 Million
Number Employees: 100-249
Square Footage: 145000
Regions Exported to: Central America, South America, Caribbean, Canada, Latin America, Mexico

46326 Marel Stork Poultry Processing
1024 Airport Pkwy
Gainesville, GA 30501-6814   770-532-7041
Fax: 770-532-5672 800-247-8609
info.us@marel.com www.marel.com/poultry
Poultry processing equipment
President: Frank Nicoletti
frank.nicoletti@stork.com
Director: Bob Conklin
Number Employees: 100-249
Parent Co: Marel

46327 Maren Engineering Corp
111 W Taft Dr
South Holland, IL 60473-2049   708-333-6250
Fax: 708-333-7507 800-875-1038
sales@marenengineering.com
www.marenengineering.com
Manufacturer and exporter of vertical and horizontal balers for corrugated paper and other applications; also, shredders, drum crushers and packers
CFO: Lee Norbeck
Vice President: Charles Brown
R & D: David Rudofski
Manager: Greg Hermdon
Estimated Sales: $5-10 Million
Number Employees: 20-49
Parent Co: Kine Corporation
Regions Exported to: Central America, South America, Europe
Percentage of Business in Exporting: 5

46328 Margate Wine & Spirit Co
2800 Shore Road
Northfield, NJ 08225   609-404-3000
Fax: 609-404-4610
Their focus is to work with a select group of producers/owners who will offer their finest wines.
President: Jonathan Shiekman
VP: Richard Shiekman
Director: Morton Shiekman
Estimated Sales: $5-10 Million
Number Employees: 1-4
Brands Imported: Chantefleur; Leonard de St. Aubin; Robert Michele; Chateau de Maligny; Vignamaggio; Saccardi; Cecilia Beretta; Delarche; Piduco Creek, Pepper Tree, Bondi Blue, Fanitinel Faruse
Regions Imported from: Europe, Mexico
Percentage of Business in Importing: 95

46329 (HQ)Marglo Products Corporation
381 Park Ave S
New York, NY 10016-8806   212-684-7079
Fax: 212-684-3879 margloprod@aol.com
Importer of grapes, apples, pears, plums, nectarines, peaches, cherries, artichokes and avocados
President: Eric Margules
Contact: Richard Norland
rnorland@margulesproperties.com
Estimated Sales: $200,000
Number Employees: 10-19
Square Footage: 4800
Other Locations:
 Marglo Products Corporation
 Philadelphia, PAMarglo Products Corporation
Brands Imported: Agral; Opagsa; Primavera; Quilapilunl; Fenix; Aexco; Rigol, Chil-Choke; D.G.O.; Cabo de Hornos; Paidahuen; Mare; Farfana; Quilvo; Capra; IGSA; RSVP; Comey; Capra
Regions Imported from: South America, Europe

46330 Mariani Nut Co
28306 County Road 90a
Winters, CA 95694   530-795-1546
Fax: 530-795-2681 www.marianinut.com
Processor and exporter of walnuts and almonds
President & CEO: Jack Mariani
Co-Owner: Gus Mariani
Partner: Martin Mariani
Vice President: Dennis Mariani
VP Marketing & Ecommerce: Matt Mariani
Marketin Mgr, VP Operations/Sales: John Martin
Estimated Sales: $5.5 Million
Number Employees: 10-19
Square Footage: 120000
Type of Packaging: Consumer, Bulk
Regions Exported to: Europe, Asia, Australia

46331 Marie Brizard Wines & Spirits
849 Zinfandel Lane
St. Helena, CA 94574   800-878-1123
Fax: 415-979-0305 info@boisset.com
www.boissetamerica.com
Processor, importer and exporter of alcoholic beverages including vodka, bourbon, tequila, scotch, brandy, cognac, schnapps, gin, rum, cordials, wines and champagne
President: Jean-Charles Boisset
VP/Director Marketing: Michael Avitable
VP/Director Sales: Robert Bermudez
Director Operations: Hubert Surville
Number Employees: 20-49
Square Footage: 26000
Parent Co: Marie Brizard Wines & Spirits USA

46332 Marie F
123 Denison Street
Markham, ON L3R 1B5
Canada   905-475-0093
Fax: 905-475-0038 800-365-4464
fmarie@ca.inter.net
Beef, butcher supplies and sausage and sheep casings; importer of sausage casings, butcher suppliers and cures; exporter of sausage casings
President: Sandra Marie Rundle
Plant Manager: Alaister Sears
Estimated Sales: $4 Million
Number Employees: 25
Square Footage: 60000
Type of Packaging: Food Service
Regions Exported to: South America, South Africa, USA
Percentage of Business in Exporting: 5
Regions Imported from: Germany, USA
Percentage of Business in Importing: 15

46333 Marin Food Specialties
14800 Highway 4
Byron, CA 94505-2236   925-634-6126
Fax: 925-634-4647
Processor, importer and exporter of specialty foods including cookies, fig and fruit bars, pasta, trail mixes, marinated vegetables, almond butter, spices and candy; gift baskets available
President: Joseph Brucia
VP: Fred Vuylsteke
Estimated Sales: $ 1 - 3 Million
Number Employees: 50 to 99
Square Footage: 60000
Type of Packaging: Consumer, Private Label, Bulk
Brands Exported: Marin
Regions Exported to: Asia
Percentage of Business in Exporting: 10
Regions Imported from: Central America, Europe, Asia
Percentage of Business in Importing: 10

46334 Marina Foods
11125 NW 124th Street
Medley, FL 33178-3173   786-888-0129
Fax: 786-888-0134 info@marinafoods.com
www.marinafoods.com
Packers of edible oils, shortenings and related products.
President: John Ioannou
Contact: George Ioannou
george@marinafoods.com
Estimated Sales: $20 Million
Number Employees: 20-49
Number of Brands: 3
Type of Packaging: Consumer, Food Service, Private Label, Bulk
Regions Exported to: Central America, South America, Caribbean

Importers & Exporters / A-Z

46335 Marineland Commercial Aquariums
3001 Commerce St.
Blacksburg, VA 24060-6671   805-529-0083
          Fax: 805-529-0852 800-322-1266
          consumersupport@unitedpetgroup.com
          www.marineland.com
Manufacturer and exporter of display tanks for lobsters and fish
President: Gary Smith
CFO: John McGreevy
Vice President: Bill Sheweloff
Quality Control: Fred Bohmour
Sales Manager (West Coast): Jay Dersahagian
Contact: Keri Barton
barton@marineland.com
Estimated Sales: $ 5 - 10 Million
Number Employees: 250-499
Brands Exported: Marineland
Regions Exported to: Worldwide

46336 Mario Camancho Foods
2502 Walden Woods Dr
Plant City, FL 33566-7167   813-305-4534
          Fax: 813-305-4546 800-293-9783
          info@mariocamachofoods.com
          www.mariocamachofoods.com
A leading manufacturer and distributor of olives, olive oil and other specialty food products
President: Shawn Kaddoura
CEO: Michelle Andersen
andersenm@mariocamachofoods.com
CEO: Bret Milligan
Marketing: Jeff Hanneken
Sales: Jon Horoquist
Production: Bob Fidoelke
Estimated Sales: $ 10 - 20 Million
Number Employees: 20-49
Square Footage: 375000
Parent Co: Angel Camacho S.A.
Type of Packaging: Consumer, Food Service, Private Label, Bulk
Brands Imported: Fragata

46337 Mario Camancho Foods
2502 Walden Woods Dr
Plant City, FL 33566
                           800-293-9783
          info@mariocamachofoods.com
          www.mariocamachofoods.com
Bacon bits, black and green olives, bruschettas/tapenades, capers/onions, olive oil, fruit jams, maraschino cherries, peppers and pimientos.
President & CEO: Shawn Kaddoura
Year Founded: 2008
Estimated Sales: $92 Million
Number Employees: 20-49

46338 Mario's Gelati
88 E 1st Avenue
Vancouver, BC V5T 1A1
Canada   604-879-9411
          Fax: 604-879-0435 info@mariosgelati.com
                           www.mariosgelati.com
Processor, importer and exporter of ice cream
President: Mario Loscerbo
Vice President: Chris Loscerbo
Estimated Sales: $5.4 Million
Number Employees: 30
Square Footage: 120000
Regions Exported to: Asia
Regions Imported from: Europe

46339 Marion Paper Box Co
600 E 18th St
Marion, IN 46953-3304   765-664-6435
          Fax: 765-664-6440 sales@marionbox.com
                           www.marionpaperboxco.com
Manufacturer and exporter of folding and set-up paper boxes; also, die cutting and partitions available. Also manufactures pads
Owner: Joe Mc Coy
Sales: Jason Priest
marionpaperbox2004@yahoo.com
Manager Operations: David Wilson
Estimated Sales: $ 2.5 - 5 Million
Number Employees: 5-9
Square Footage: 30000
Regions Exported to: Worldwide

46340 Mark Container Corporation
1899 Marina Blvd
San Leandro, CA 94577-4225 510-483-4440
          Fax: 510-352-1524 www.wellsfargo.com
Manufacturer and exporter of corrugated boxes
Manager: Shuzair Malik
Estimated Sales: $10-20 Million
Number Employees: 10-19
Regions Exported to: Canada
Percentage of Business in Exporting: 1

46341 Mark NYS
19485 E Walnut Drive N
Walnut, CA 91789-2813   909-598-3353
          Fax: 909-598-3084 800-446-3444
Exporter of water, soft drinks and seltzer water; importer of wine and beer
President/CEO: Frank Jerant
Executive VP: Paul Musselman
Production/Operations Manager: Bonnie Hack
Number Employees: 1-4
Square Footage: 8000
Type of Packaging: Consumer, Food Service, Private Label
Brands Exported: Original New York Seltzer
Regions Exported to: Europe, Middle East
Percentage of Business in Exporting: 50
Brands Imported: Valeverde
Regions Imported from: Europe, Asia
Percentage of Business in Importing: 50

46342 Mark Products Company
46 Rainbow Trl
Denville, NJ 7834   973-983-8818
          Fax: 973-627-6273
Manufacturer and exporter of packaging equipment and materials including shrink and pallet wrappers and wrapping films; importer of shrink PVC films
President: Doug Mark
VP: Charles Scweizer
Number Employees: 1-4
Number of Brands: 1
Number of Products: 10
Square Footage: 4000
Type of Packaging: Food Service, Bulk
Regions Exported to: Worldwide
Percentage of Business in Exporting: 30
Regions Imported from: Asia
Percentage of Business in Importing: 10

46343 Mark's International Seafood Brokers
PO Box 602
Fairhaven, MA 02719-0602   508-992-2115
          Fax: 508-991-2072
President: Mark Wright
Estimated Sales: $ 10 - 20 Million
Number Employees: 20-49

46344 Market Forge IndustriesInc
35 Garvey St
Everett, MA 02149-4403   406-209-1300
          Fax: 617-387-4456 866-698-3188
          custserv@mfii.com www.mfii.com
Comerical food service equipment
President: Jeffrey Leckel
Chief Financial Officer: Dave Zappala
Vice President: Robert Stefka
Chief Information Officer: Nancy Murphy
Vice President, Sales & Marketing: Peter Kelley
Sales Manager: Kelly Powers
Vice President, Operations: William McGourty
Production Manager: Hal Hamilton
Facilities Manager: Fred Bartlett
Estimated Sales: $ 13 Million
Number Employees: 10-19
Square Footage: 14859
Type of Packaging: Food Service
Regions Exported to: Worldwide
Percentage of Business in Exporting: 7
Regions Imported from: Europe
Percentage of Business in Importing: 2

46345 Markham Vineyards
2812 Saint Helena Hwy N
P.O.Box 636
St Helena, CA 94574-9655   707-963-5292
          Fax: 707-963-4616 info@markhamvineyards.com
                           www.markhamvineyards.com
Processor and exporter of wines
President: Bryan Del Bondio
bdelbondio@markhamvineyards.com
Winemaker: Kimberlee Nicholls
Associate Winemaker: James Coughlin
General Manager: Kathryn Fowler
Estimated Sales: $ 5 - 10 Million
Number Employees: 20-49
Regions Exported to: Asia, Canada
Percentage of Business in Exporting: 5

46346 Marking Devices Inc
3110 Payne Ave
Cleveland, OH 44114-4504   216-861-4498
          Fax: 216-241-1479 mdinc@en.com
                           www.realtyappreciation.com
Manufacturer and exporter of rubber and polymer printing plates and rubber and steel stamps
Owner: John Enci
VP: John Wacker
Sales Manager: Dave Tully
johne@royalacme.com
Estimated Sales: $ 2.5-5 Million
Number Employees: 20-49
Square Footage: 22000
Regions Exported to: South America, Europe
Percentage of Business in Exporting: 2

46347 Marking Methods Inc
301 S Raymond Ave
Alhambra, CA 91803-1531   626-308-5800
          Fax: 626-576-7564 experts@markingmethods.com
                           www.markingmethods.com
Permanent stress-free marking equipment including electro-chemical hot stamping for plastics, laser, dot peen for metal parts and equipment; exporter of electro-chemical marking equipment, etc
President: Nataly Baltazar
natalyb@markingmethods.com
CEO: A Bennett
CFO: Susan Chu
Sales Director: Victor Amorim
Estimated Sales: Below $5 Million
Number Employees: 20-49
Square Footage: 40000
Regions Exported to: Central America, South America, Europe, Asia, Middle East, Australia
Percentage of Business in Exporting: 1

46348 Marko By Carlisle
PO Box 53006
Oklahoma City, OK 73152   405-475-8210
          Fax: 405-475-5607 800-872-4701
          customerservice@carlislefsp.com
                           www.carlislefsp.com
Number Employees: 250-499

46349 Marko Inc
1310 Southport Rd
Spartanburg, SC 29306-6199 864-585-2259
          Fax: 864-585-0750 866-466-2756
          help@markoinc.com www.markoinc.com
Manufacturer and exporter of table cloths and skirting; also, napkins, aprons and place mats
Owner: Anne Meehan
ameehan@markoinc.com
VP Sales/Marketing: Tony La Porte
VP Manufacturing: Rob James
Estimated Sales: $10-20 Million
Number Employees: 5-9
Type of Packaging: Food Service
Brands Exported: Marko Intl.; Markoated; Midwest Marko
Percentage of Business in Exporting: 10

46350 Markson Lab Sales
5285 NE Elam Young Parkway
Hillsboro, OR 97124-6427   800-528-5114
                           www.markson.com
Wholesaler/distributor, importer and exporter of laboratory and microbiology equipment
Sales Supervisor: Bob Dickie
General Manager: Steve Ciucci
Production Manager: Jeff Geiger
Number Employees: 20-49
Brands Exported: Markson; Labcraft
Regions Exported to: Central America, South America, Middle East
Percentage of Business in Exporting: 10
Regions Imported from: Europe, Asia
Percentage of Business in Importing: 10

46351 Markwell Manufacturing Company
692 Pleasant St
Norwood, MA 2062 781-769-6610
Fax: 781-769-7060 800-666-1123
info@mrkwll.com www.mrkwll.com
Manufacturer, importer and exporter of plier, box and hand, foot and air operated staplers, tackers and carton sealers; also, staples, collated nails, marking crayons, tapes, strech-wrap, and spray ashesives
President: Sam Opland
Contact: Jeff Cobb
markwellusa@gmail.com
Estimated Sales: $1-2.5 Million
Number Employees: 5-9
Square Footage: 27000
Brands Exported: Markwell
Regions Exported to: Europe, Asia, Africa, Australia
Percentage of Business in Exporting: 20
Regions Imported from: South America, Asia
Percentage of Business in Importing: 5

46352 Marky's Caviar
1000 Northwest 159th Drive
Miami, FL 33169-4709 305-758-9288
Fax: 305-758-0008 800-722-8427
info@markys.com www.markys.com
Wholesaler/distributor, importer and exporter of caviar, smoked salmon, foie gras, truffles, mushrooms, saffron, anguila, etc.; wholesaler/distributor of frozen foods and meats
Owner: Mark Gelman
Vice President: Sarah Echevarria
Estimated Sales: $7 Million
Number Employees: 50
Square Footage: 60000
Parent Co: Optimus
Type of Packaging: Consumer, Food Service, Private Label, Bulk
Brands Exported: Caspian; Marky's; Bon Appetit; Malossol; Beluga
Regions Exported to: Worldwide
Brands Imported: Caspian; Marky's; Bon Appetit; Malossol; Beluga
Regions Imported from: Europe, Asia

46353 Marlen
4780 NW 41st Street
Ste 100
Riverside, MO 64150 913-888-3333
Fax: 913-888-5471 www.marlen.com
Portioning and forming equipment, in-line grinders, pumping equipment and material handling products.
President: Richard Schneider
CEO: Jim Anderson
Regional Sales Manager: Fernando Casado
Contact: Jeff Blansit
jeff.blansit@marlen.com
Regions Exported to: Central America, South America, Europe, Asia, Middle East, North America, Australia, New Zealand

46354 Marlen International
441 30th St
Astoria, OR 97103-2807 503-861-2273
Fax: 913-888-6440 800-862-7536
www.marlen.com
Continuous flow slicers, dicers, strip cutters, shredders, volumetric rotary/piston fillers, pak-shapers, specialty conveyors, etc
Manager: Pete Johnson
CFO: Irene Codonau
Vice President: Jarrod McCarroll
Research & Development: Robert Zschoche
Quality Control: David Bogih
Marketing/Sales: Pete Johnson
Regional Sales Manager: Mike Leiker
Public Relations: Jack Walls
Inside Sales: Jack Walls
Production Manager: David Bogh
Plant Manager: Rusty Price
Purchasing Manager: Mark Ross
Estimated Sales: $10-20 Million
Number Employees: 20-49
Square Footage: 120000
Brands Exported: Auto Slicer/Dicer; Home Style; Mega-Slicers; Pak-Shaper; Pathfinder; Nu-Pak; Rotary Piston Fillers; Auto Shreder; Table Top Shreder
Regions Exported to: Central America, South America, Europe, Asia, Middle East
Percentage of Business in Exporting: 10

46355 Marlite
1 Marlite Dr
Dover, OH 44622 330-343-6621
Fax: 330-343-7296 800-377-1221
info@marlite.com www.marlite.com
Manufacturer and exporter of sanitary wall and ceiling panel systems, decorative wall panel systems, doors/frames, restroom partitions, korelock panels, retail merchandising display systems, etc
CFO: Kimberly McBride
VP, Sales & Marketing: Greg Triplett
Contact: Nini Abreu
nabreu@marlite.com
Estimated Sales: $21 Million
Number Employees: 251-500
Square Footage: 450000
Brands Exported: Marlite; Displawall; Surface Systems; FRP Sanitary Systems

46356 Marlo Manufacturing
301 Division St
Boonton, NJ 07005-1826 973-423-0226
Fax: 973-423-1638 800-222-0450
Manufacturer, importer and exporter of stainless steel food service equipment
Founder: Sal Pirruccio
Partner: Larry Dubov
larry@marlomfg.com
VP, Manufacturing: Paul Pirruccio
VP, Sales & Marketing: Larry Dubov
VP, Operations: Paul Tommasi
Plant Manager: Paul Pirruccio
Estimated Sales: $ 4-6 Million
Number Employees: 1-4
Square Footage: 60000
Type of Packaging: Food Service

46357 Marlyn Nutraceuticals
4404 E Elwood St
Phoenix, AZ 85040-1909 480-991-0200
Fax: 480-991-0551 800-899-4499
Processor and exporter of health foods and natural vitamins, minerals and food supplements including B-complex and C-combination formulas, fish oils, fiber blends, multi-vitamins and enzymes
Owner: Joe Lehmann
Export Sales Manager: Mark Wojick
VP Sales: Don Haygood
lehmannj@naturallyvitamins.com
Estimated Sales: $ 5 - 10 Million
Number Employees: 50-99
Square Footage: 80000
Type of Packaging: Food Service, Private Label, Bulk
Brands Exported: Naturally Vitamins
Regions Exported to: Central America, South America, Europe, Asia
Percentage of Business in Exporting: 20

46358 Marnap Industries
225 French Street
Buffalo, NY 14211 716-897-1220
Fax: 716-897-1306 www.flavorchem.com
Processor and exporter of essential oils, spice blends, seasonings, flavor compounds and oleoresins; importer of essential oils and oleoresins
President: Dennis J Napora
VP: Kevin Martin
Sales: Joanne Evans
Production: J Cogley
Estimated Sales: $ 3 - 5 Million
Number Employees: 5-9
Number of Products: 100+
Square Footage: 48000
Parent Co: Flavorchem Corp.
Type of Packaging: Bulk
Regions Exported to: Canada
Percentage of Business in Exporting: 10

46359 Marquip Ward United
1300 N Airport Rd
Phillips, WI 54555 715-339-2191
www.marquipwardunited.com
Manufacturer and exporter of packaging and stacking machinery.
Year Founded: 1898
Estimated Sales: $100-500 Million
Number Employees: 500-999
Parent Co: Barry Wehmiller Companies

46360 Marriott Walker Corporation
925 E Maple Rd
Bingham Farms, MI 48009 248-644-6868
Fax: 248-642-1213 mwc@marriottwalker.com
www.marriottwalker.com
Manufacturer and exporter of evaporators, spray dryers, etc
President: Winthrop Walker
VP Engineering: Mark Price
Contact: Mary Ayotte
mayotte@marriottwalker.com
Estimated Sales: $1-2.5 Million
Number Employees: 5-9
Square Footage: 13200
Brands Exported: Marriot Walker
Regions Exported to: Worldwide
Percentage of Business in Exporting: 25

46361 Marroquin Organic Intl.
303 Potero St
Suite 18
Santa Cruz, CA 95060 831-423-3442
Fax: 831-423-3432 info@marroquin-organics.com
www.marroquin-organics.com
Organic and non-GMO ingredients
President: Grace Marroquin
Vice President: Mark Nelson
Organic Ingredient Specialist: Helen Hudson
Contact: Ciaran Cooney
ccooney@paypal.com
Estimated Sales: $4-5 Million
Number Employees: 5-9

46362 (HQ)Mars Air Products
14716 S Broadway
Gardena, CA 90248-1814 310-532-1555
Fax: 310-324-3030 800-421-1266
info@marsair.com www.marsair.com
Manufacturer and exporter of air purifiers and heated and unheated air curtains in electric, gas, steam and hot water for insect control and environmental separation; also, packaged make-up air, cooling, heating and ventilatingsystems
Owner: Jimmy Johnson
johnson@skycatch.com
Vice President: Steve Rosol
Quality Control: Michael Goldman
Marketing Director: Dana Agens
Plant Manager/Purchasing Director: Frank Cuaderno
Estimated Sales: Below $ 5 Million
Number Employees: 50-99
Square Footage: 392000
Brands Exported: Mars Air Doors; Combi; Whispurr Air; Windguard
Regions Exported to: Worldwide
Percentage of Business in Exporting: 10
Regions Imported from: Middle East
Percentage of Business in Importing: 2

46363 Mars Inc.
6885 Elm St.
McLean, VA 22101 703-821-4900
www.mars.com
Pet products, chocolate, chewing gum, beverages, food and health products.
CEO: Grant Reid
CFO: Claus Aagaard
Vice President/General Counsel: Stefanie Straub
President, Innovation: Jean-Christophe Flatin
Global President, Mars Food: Fiona Dawson
Mars Wrigley: Andrew Clarke
Year Founded: 1911
Estimated Sales: $35 Billion
Number Employees: 100,000
Number of Brands: 74
Type of Packaging: Consumer, Bulk
Regions Exported to: Worldwide

46364 (HQ)Marsan Foods
106 Thermos Road
Toronto, ON M1L 4W2
Canada 416-755-9262
Fax: 416-755-6790 sean@marsanfoods.com
www.marsanfoods.com
Processor and exporter of single-series frozen entries and bowls, family size entries, control and private label. Processor and exporter of specialty meal components for healthcare settings
President: James Jewett
Director Sales/Marketing: Sean Lippay
Number Employees: 100
Number of Products: 160
Square Footage: 300000

Importers & Exporters / A-Z

Type of Packaging: Consumer, Food Service, Private Label
Brands Exported: Coming Home; Private Label American Grocery
Regions Exported to: Asia
Percentage of Business in Exporting: 5

46365 (HQ)Marsh Company
PO Box 388
Belleville, IL 62222-0388 618-234-1122
Fax: 618-234-1529 800-527-6275
marshco@marshco.com www.marshco.com
Manufacturer, exporter and importer of large and small character ink jet coding systems, marking and sealing machines and supplies
President: Robret Willett
CEO/Chairman: John Marsh
CFO: Mark Kuhn
Quality Control: Mark Wilmsen
R&D: Jerry Robortson
VP Sales/Marketing: P Wagner
Estimated Sales: $ 20 - 50 Million
Number Employees: 500
Other Locations:
  Marsh Co.
  S.A, GenevaMarsh Co.
Brands Exported: Marsh
Regions Exported to: Central America, South America, Europe, Asia, Middle East
Percentage of Business in Exporting: 33
Regions Imported from: Europe, Asia
Percentage of Business in Importing: 5

46366 Marshall Air Systems Inc
419 Peachtree Dr S
Charlotte, NC 28217-2098 704-525-6230
Fax: 704-525-6229 800-722-3474
customerservice@marshallair.com
www.marshallair.com
Manufacturer and exporter of food warming and conveyorized cooking systems including broilers; also, ventilation systems including hoods and fans
Chairman: Robert Stuck
Chairman: Marina Flick
mflick@marshallair.com
Estimated Sales: $20-50 Million
Number Employees: 50-99
Type of Packaging: Food Service
Brands Exported: Autobake™; Autobroil Omni™; Autotoast™; ThermoGlo™; Automelt™; Autobroil™
Regions Exported to: Central America, South America, Europe, Asia, Middle East

46367 Marshall Plastic Film Inc
904 E Allegan St
Martin, MI 49070-9797 269-672-5511
Fax: 269-672-5035 www.marshallplastic.com
Manufacturer and exporter of form, fill, seal and shrink plastic films and bags
President: Rich Bowman
rbowman@marshallplastic.com
VP: Casey McCarthy
Customer Service: William Rackley
Customer Service: Sylvia Davis
Estimated Sales: $20-50 Million
Number Employees: 20-49
Square Footage: 45500
Regions Exported to: Canada, Latin America, Mexico
Percentage of Business in Exporting: 5

46368 Marshall Sales Co
PO Box 495
Castle Rock, CO 80104-0495 303-660-1781
Fax: 410-749-9960
sam@marshallsalescompany.com
Broker, importer and exporter of industrial foods focusing on fruits, vegetables and ingredients, fresh and processed
Manager: Kathy Williams
VP: Paul Capucille
Marketing Director: Paul Capucille
Sales Director: Dave Krester
Office Manager: Kathy Williams
Estimated Sales: Less Than $500,000
Number Employees: 1-4
Type of Packaging: Consumer, Food Service, Private Label, Bulk

46369 Marson Food Inc
1135 Westminster Avenue
Unit D
Alhambra, CA 91803 626-282-5868
Fax: 626-282-5533
Full-line spices, spices.
Marketing: Ryan Gao
Estimated Sales: $190,000
Number Employees: 3

46370 Mart CART-Smt
112 E Linden St
Rogers, AR 72756-6035 479-636-5776
Fax: 479-246-6473 800-548-3373
apc@assembledproducts.com
www.assembledproducts.com
Manufacturer and exporter of pressure washers
President: George Panter
Vice President: Bob Sage
Marketing Director: Steve Scroggins
Sales Director: Kent Langum
Plant Manager: R Smith
Purchasing Manager: Don McKenzie
Estimated Sales: $ 20 - 30 Million
Number Employees: 100-249
Square Footage: 123000
Parent Co: Assembled Pro Corporation
Regions Exported to: Worldwide

46371 Mart CART-Smt
112 E Linden St
Rogers, AR 72756-6035 479-636-5776
Fax: 479-246-6473 800-548-3373
www.assembledproducts.com
President: George Panter
Estimated Sales: $ 1 - 5 Million
Number Employees: 100-249

46372 Martin Cab Div
7108 Madison Ave
Cleveland, OH 44102-4093 216-377-8200
Fax: 216-651-2079 www.martincab.com
Manufacturer and exporter of cab enclosures, including freezer cabs
President: James Martin
CFO: Jim Markin
Chairman: Pauline Martin
VP Sales/Marketing: James Girard
Estimated Sales: $ 20 - 50 Million
Number Employees: 5-9
Parent Co: Martin Sheet Metal

46373 (HQ)Martin Engineering
1 Martin Pl
Neponset, IL 61345-9766 309-852-2384
Fax: 309-594-2432 800-766-2786
info@martin-eng.com www.martin-eng.com
Manufacturer and exporter of belt conveyors and cleaners, transfer point skirting systems and electric, hydraulic and pneumatic vibrators; importer of electric vibrators
Owner: E H Peterson
CEO: Scott Hutter
CFO: Ron Vick
CTO: R Todd Swinderman
VP: Jim Turner
Public Relations: AD Marti
Estimated Sales: $ 20 - 50 Million
Number Employees: 100-249
Square Footage: 130000
Other Locations:
  Martin Engineering
  WallufMartin Engineering
Regions Exported to: Central America, South America, Europe, Asia, Middle East, Worldwide
Percentage of Business in Exporting: 25
Regions Imported from: Italy

46374 Martin Laboratories
PO Box 1873
Owensboro, KY 42302-1873 270-685-4441
Fax: 270-684-7859 800-345-9352
Manufacturer and exporter of hand cleaners and soaps including liquid and waterless
President: Harold C Martin
National Sales Manager: Art Wilbert
Contact: Clifford Martin
rwatson@tqsinc.com
Customer Service: Stacia Jarvis
Estimated Sales: $ 10-20 Million
Number Employees: 5-9
Square Footage: 60000
Regions Exported to: Asia, New Zealand

46375 Martin/Baron
5454 2nd St
Irwindale, CA 91706-2000 626-960-5153
Fax: 626-962-1280 www.mbicryo.com
Manufacturer and exporter of food processing equipment, stainless steel conveying systems, cryogenic and mechanical coolers and freezers, steam and radiant heat cookers, spirals, tunnels, cabinets for heat transfer and vertical pizzaovens
President: Jonathan Martin
VP: David Baron
Sales: Allan Weiner
Operations: Carl Gumber
Estimated Sales: $ 3 - 5 Million
Number Employees: 10-19
Square Footage: 48000
Brands Exported: Martin/Baron; MBI
Regions Exported to: Central America, South America, Asia
Percentage of Business in Exporting: 10

46376 Marubeni America Corp.
375 Lexington Ave.
New York, NY 10017 212-450-0100
Fax: 212-450-0700 www.marubeniamerica.com
Marubeni exports grains, meat, sugar and other foodstuffs to Asia.
President/CEO: Fumiya Kokubu
Year Founded: 1951
Estimated Sales: $273,000
Parent Co: Marubeni Corporation
Regions Exported to: Asia
Brands Imported: Sugar
Regions Imported from: Central America, South America

46377 Maruchan Inc
15800 Laguna Canyon Rd
Irvine, CA 92618 949-789-2300
www.maruchan.com
Asian foods including wonton soup and instant ramen noodles.
President & Chairman: Mutsuhiko Oda
muoda@maruchaninc.com
Year Founded: 1953
Estimated Sales: $33.2 Million
Number Employees: 500-999
Parent Co: Toyo Suisan Kaisha
Type of Packaging: Consumer
Regions Exported to: Worldwide

46378 Marukai Market
1740 W Artesia Blvd # 114
Gardena, CA 90248-3238 310-660-6300
Fax: 310-660-6301 info@marukai.com
Established in 1965. Manufacturer, importer, and exporter of Japanese food products.
President: Masataka Hattori
Estimated Sales: $41 Million
Number Employees: 100-249
Parent Co: Marukai Corporation
Other Locations:
  Marukai Corporation
  Honolulu, HIMarukai Corporation

46379 Marukome USA Inc.
17132 Pullman Street
Irvine, CA 92614 949-863-0110
Fax: 949-863-9813 www.marukomeusa.com
Miso manufacturer
President: Shigeru Sharasaka
Secretary: Tetsuhiko Iijima
Marketing: (Fred) Teruo Yamanaka
Contact: Toshio Abe
tabe@marukomeusa.com
Number Employees: 17

46380 Marva Maid Dairy
5500 Chestnut Ave
Newport News, VA 23605-2118 757-245-3857
800-768-6243
dlovell@marvamaid.com
Milk and specialty food products, including; milk, buttermilk, egg nog and orange juice

Importers & Exporters / A-Z

President: David Grogan
Owner: Dennis Bailey
Finance Manager: Jan Pass
Chief Engineer/Vice President: W Gross
Procurement & Plan Supervisor: Peter Natale
Marketing Manager: Scott Garrett
Sales Mgr/Dir of Product Management: Ed Boyd
Human Resources Director: Ruby Jones
Operations Manager: Bruce Matson
Plant Manager: Walter Auman
Purchasing Agent: Andrea Lopez
Number Employees: 100-249
Square Footage: 406728
Parent Co: Maryland & Virginia Milk Producers Coop Assoc, Inc.
Type of Packaging: Consumer

46381 Marx Imports
PO Box 540
Atlantic Highlands, NJ 07716   732-936-1211
    Fax: 732-936-1227   800-459-7349
    www.marximports.com
Wild and game meats, game birds, pates and foie gras.
Founder: Frank Marx

46382 MarySue.com
2600 Georgetown Rd
Baltimore, MD 21230
    800-662-2639
    info@marysue.com   www.marysue.com
Manufacturer and importer of gourmet chocolate candy. Founded in 1948
President: William Buppert
VP Production: Mark Berman
Estimated Sales: $10 Million
Number Employees: 5-9
Square Footage: 204000
Type of Packaging: Consumer, Private Label, Bulk
Brands Imported: Lindt; Perugina; Droste
Regions Imported from: South America, Europe
Percentage of Business in Importing: 25

46383 Maryland China
54 Main St
Reisterstown, MD 21136-1210   410-833-5559
    Fax: 410-833-1851   info@marylandchina.com
    www.marylandchina.com
Porcelain and ceramics
President/Owner: Edward Weiner
VP: Jonathan Weiner
Manager: Jonathan Weiner
jtw@marylandchina.com
Estimated Sales: $5-10 Million
Number Employees: 10-19
Square Footage: 88000
Type of Packaging: Consumer, Private Label, Bulk
Regions Exported to: Central America, South America, Europe, Asia, Middle East
Regions Imported from: Europe, Asia

46384 Maryland Packaging Corporation
7030 Troy Hill Dr
Elkridge, MD 21075   410-540-9700
    Fax: 410-540-9789   www.marylandpackaging.com
Manufacturer and exporter of shrink wrapping, sleeve bundling, horizontal form/fill/seal, overwrapping and horizontal bagging machinery, also have a contract packaging division
President: John Voneiff II
CEO: Marwan Moheyeldien Sr.
Quality Control Manager: Drexel Nelson
Sales Director: Jay Gibson
HR: Mari Cruz Abarca
Estimated Sales: $ 5 - 10,000,000
Number Employees: 60
Square Footage: 50000
Type of Packaging: Consumer, Food Service, Private Label, Bulk
Regions Exported to: Worldwide
Percentage of Business in Exporting: 5

46385 Maryland Seafood Marketing
50 Harry S Truman Pkwy
Annapolis, MD 21401   410-841-5700
    Fax: 410-841-5914   www.mda.state.md.us

46386 Maryland Wire Belts
8000 Hub Parkway
Cleveland, OH 44125   216-642-9100
    Fax: 216-642-9573   800-677-2358
    salessupport@bdi-usa.com   www.bdi-usa.com
Manufacturer and Exporter of conveyor belting, conveyors and conveyor services

President: William Weber
CEO: Duane Marshall
CEO: Bill Colson
Number Employees: 100-249
Square Footage: 400000

46387 Masa Linen
7863 Kipling Avenue
Woodbridge, ON L4L 1Z6
Canada   416-410-0493
    Fax: 416-410-8257

46388 Masala Chai Company
PO Box 8375
Santa Cruz, CA 95061-8375   831-475-8881
    Fax: 831-475-5967   masala@masalachaico.com
    www.masalachaico.com
Processor and importer of chai teas including bottled and ready-to-drink, Indian spiced, regular, decaf and energy tonics
Co-Owner: Raphael Reuben
Co-Owner: Susan Beardsley
Estimated Sales: $240,000
Number Employees: 1-4
Square Footage: 6000
Type of Packaging: Consumer, Food Service, Private Label, Bulk
Regions Imported from: Asia
Percentage of Business in Importing: 20

46389 (HQ)Maselli Measurements Inc
7746 Lorraine Ave # 201
Stockton, CA 95210-4234   209-474-9178
    Fax: 209-474-9241   800-964-9600
    daveodum@maselli.com   www.maselli.com/en
Process & laboratory refractometers
President: Mario Maselli
mariomaselli@maselli.com
Quality Control: Mario Maselli
Sales: Dave Odum
Estimated Sales: $2.5-5 Million
Number Employees: 5-9
Number of Brands: 1
Number of Products: 10
Other Locations:
    Maselli Measurements
    Leon, GTOMaselli Measurements
Brands Exported: Maselli Measurements Inc
Regions Exported to: Central America, South America, Europe, Asia, Middle East
Percentage of Business in Exporting: 25

46390 Maselli Measurements Inc
7746 Lorraine Ave # 201
Stockton, CA 95210-4234   209-474-9178
    Fax: 209-474-9241   800-964-9600
    daveodum@maselli.com   www.maselli.com/en
Liquid analysis machines such as carbonated beverage analysis systems, automatic and in-line refractometers.
President: Mario Maselli
mariomaselli@maselli.com
Sales Manager: Dave Odum
Number Employees: 5-9
Regions Exported to: Central America, North America, USA

46391 Mason Candlelight Company
PO Box 59
New Albany, MS 38652-0059   310-338-6987
    Fax: 310-348-0135   800-556-2766
Manufacturer and exporter of tabletop lighting including lamps and candles
VP/General Manager: Robert Gasbarro
Plant Supervisor: Robert Bacher
Estimated Sales: $2.5-5 Million
Number Employees: 9
Square Footage: 180000
Parent Co: Standex International Corporation
Brands Exported: Mason; Lumatane
Regions Exported to: Worldwide

46392 (HQ)Mason Transparent Package Company
PO Box 852
Armonk, NY 10504-0852   718-792-6000
    Fax: 718-823-7279
Printed and converted films and bags including polyethylene, clysar, polypropylene, linear low density, co-extruded, etc.; importer of film
President: Richard Cole
VP: Kevin O'Connell

Estimated Sales: $ 2.5 - 5 Million
Number Employees: 10-19
Square Footage: 100000
Regions Imported from: South America, Asia, Canada
Percentage of Business in Importing: 5

46393 Massimo Zanetti Beverage USA
1370 Progress Rd
Suffolk, VA 23434
    888-246-2598
    www.mzb-usa.com
Coffee manufacturer
Founder: Massimo Zanetti
Estimated Sales: Less Than $500,000
Number Employees: 1-4
Type of Packaging: Food Service, Private Label
Regions Exported to: Worldwide

46394 Master Air
415 S Grant St
Lebanon, IN 46052-3605   317-375-7600
    Fax: 317-375-7607   800-248-8368
Manufacturer and exporter of commercial kitchen ventilation equipment including hood systems and fan controls
President: Loren Gard
Sales Engineer: Jim Rader
Office Manager: Sharon Amack
Engineer: Kevin Blandford
Estimated Sales: $2.5-5 Million
Number Employees: 20-49
Square Footage: 118000
Regions Exported to: Worldwide
Percentage of Business in Exporting: 2

46395 Master Mix
181 W Orangethorpe Avenue
Placentia, CA 92870-6931   714-524-1698
    Fax: 714-524-8540
Processor and exporter of powdered mixes including soft serve, shake and yogurt; also, syrups, toppings, water soluable ginseng extract and drink bases
President: Pat Lagraffe
VP: Jim LaGraffe
Estimated Sales: $ 1 - 3 Million
Number Employees: 1-4
Square Footage: 20000
Type of Packaging: Consumer, Food Service, Private Label, Bulk
Brands Exported: Chalet Gourmet
Regions Exported to: Central America, South America, Europe, Asia, Middle East
Percentage of Business in Exporting: 50

46396 Master-Bilt
908 State Highway 15 N
New Albany, MS 38652-9507   662-534-9061
    Fax: 662-534-6049   800-647-1284
    sales@master-bilt.com   www.master-bilt.com
Manufacturer and exporter of commercial refrigeration products including refrigeration and freezer cabinets, walk-in and reach-in units, etc; also, merchandising units for dairy items and deli cabinets
President: David Parks
Chief Financial Officer: Edward Jacobs
Vice President, Sales & Marketing: Bill Huffman
Vice President, Operations: Eddie Carr
Purchasing: Larry Fry
Estimated Sales: $ 50-100 Million
Number Employees: 500-999
Square Footage: 64006
Parent Co: Standex International Corporation

46397 Mastercraft Industries Inc
777 South St
Newburgh, NY 12550-4159   845-565-8850
    Fax: 845-565-9392   800-835-7812
    www.mastercraftusa.com
Manufacturer, importer and exporter of industrial vacuum cleaners, parts, floor machines, carpet extractors, automatic scrubbers, steamers, marble/stone maintenance equipment and chemicals
President: Howard Goldberg
Community Director: Jay Goldberg
Executive VP: Carol Andreasian
Quality Control: Jay Goldberg
Estimated Sales: $ 10 - 20 Million
Number Employees: 50-99
Square Footage: 200000
Brands Exported: Mastercraft
Regions Exported to: Central America, South America, Europe, Asia, Middle East, Canada
Percentage of Business in Exporting: 25

435

Importers & Exporters / A-Z

Brands Imported: Mastercraft
Regions Imported from: Europe, Canada, Mexico
Percentage of Business in Importing: 5

46398 Mastercraft International
PO Box 668407
Charlotte, NC 28266-8407
704-392-7436
Fax: 704-395-1600
Manufacturer and exporter of packaging machinery including vertical and horizontal cartoners
President: Dan Rothwell
Engineer: A Christopher
Estimated Sales: $ 1 - 2.5 Million
Number Employees: 9
Square Footage: 40000
Brands Exported: Mastercraft
Regions Exported to: South America, Europe, Canada
Percentage of Business in Exporting: 5

46399 Mastercraft Manufacturing Co
3715 11th St # B1
Long Island City, NY 11101-6006
718-729-5620
Fax: 718-729-5620
Awards, badges, medals, incentives, premiums and plaques; exporter of badges; importer of pins and patches
Owner: Murray Wiener
mwiener@mastercraft-boats.net
General Manager: Peter Borsits
General Manager: Peter Borsits
Estimated Sales: $ 500,000 - $ 1,000,000
Number Employees: 5-9
Square Footage: 2000
Regions Exported to: Worldwide
Percentage of Business in Exporting: 15
Regions Imported from: Europe, Asia
Percentage of Business in Importing: 15

46400 Mastex Industries
2035 Factory Ln
Petersburg, VA 23803
804-732-8300
Fax: 804-732-8395
Manufacturer and exporter of electric and thermostatically controlled dish warmers and cooking utensils
President: Frank Mast
National Sales Manager: Paul Christian
Estimated Sales: $ 1 - 5 Million
Number Employees: 10-19
Square Footage: 100000
Type of Packaging: Consumer
Regions Exported to: Asia, Middle East

46401 Mat Logo Company
PO Box 230
Forest City, IA 50436-0230
641-581-5650
Fax: 641-581-5647   888-628-5646
randy@logofloormats.com
www.logofloormats.com
Wholesaler/distributor and exporter of rubber floor mats with logos
Owner: Randy Bush
randy@logofloormats.com
Regions Exported to: Worldwide

46402 Matador Processors
1820 N Council Rd
Blanchard, OK 73010
405-485-2597
Fax: 405-485-2597   800-847-0797
matador@matadorprocessors.com
www.matadorprocessors.com
Frozen foods including chile rellenos (stuffed peppers), stuffed jalapenos and breaded hors d'oeuvres including cheese bites, mushrooms, desserts, etc.; exporter of chile rellenos, stuffed jalapenos and mozzarella sticks
Owner: Betty Wood
CFO: Richard Clark
VP: Ron W Diggs
R&D: Debbie Funderburk
Plant Manager: Debbie Funderburk
Estimated Sales: $3 Million
Number Employees: 50-99
Square Footage: 108000
Type of Packaging: Food Service, Private Label
Regions Exported to: Europe, Canada, Central America, Mexico
Percentage of Business in Exporting: 2

46403 Mateer Burt
700 Pennsylvania Drive
Exton, PA 19341-1129
610-321-1100
Fax: 610-321-1199   800-345-1308
www.mateerburt.com
Manufacturer and exporter of filling and labeling machinery and parts; installation available
Marketing Manager: April Koss
Estimated Sales: $ 1 - 5 Million
Number Employees: 50-99
Number of Brands: 7
Number of Products: 4
Square Footage: 320000
Brands Exported: Mateer; Datalink; Burt; Primemark; Flexline
Regions Exported to: Worldwide
Percentage of Business in Exporting: 30

46404 Material Storage Systems
8827 Will Clayton Pkwy
Humble, TX 77338-5821
281-446-7144
Fax: 281-446-7391   800-881-6750
info@msshouston.com www.msshouston.com
Manufacturer and exporter of storage and material handling equipment
Owner: Mike Gonzales
Plant Manager: Paul Eye
Estimated Sales: $ 1 - 2.5 Million
Number Employees: 20-49
Brands Exported: Komatsu; Webblock Racking; Kingway Packing
Regions Exported to: Latin America
Percentage of Business in Exporting: 5
Brands Imported: Hytsu

46405 Material Storage Systems
PO Box 1010
Gadsden, AL 35902
256-543-2467
Fax: 256-547-6725   877-543-2467
Exclusive rights to the Lemanco product line. Major products are modular bolted storage bins, welded silos and refuse containers. Many accessory items are also available
President: Barney Leach
CFO: Cindi Graves
Vice President: Craig Graves
R&D: Randall Wright
Quality Control: Robert Bellow
Marketing Director: Dawn Howell
VP Sales: Craig Graves
Operations Manager: Paul Allen
Production Manager: Paul Allen
Plant Manager: Randal Wright
Purchasing Manager: Robert Bellew
Estimated Sales: $ 1 Million
Number Employees: 30
Number of Brands: 1
Number of Products: 3
Square Footage: 90000
Brands Exported: Lemanco
Regions Exported to: Worldwide
Percentage of Business in Exporting: 10

46406 Materials Transportation Co
1408 Commerce Dr
PO Box 1358
Temple, TX 76504-5134
254-298-2900
Fax: 254-771-0287   800-433-3110
info@mtcworldwide.com
Manufacturer and exporter of food processing equipment, cookers, dumpers, blenders and screw and belt conveyors
President & CEO: Jim Granfor
CEO: Reg Ackerman
r.ackerman@mtcworldwide.com
VP Sales: Stephen Hicks
Estimated Sales: $23.4 Million
Number Employees: 100-249
Number of Brands: 6
Number of Products: 6
Regions Exported to: Central America, South America, Europe, Asia, Canada, Caribbean, Latin America, Mexico, Australia
Percentage of Business in Exporting: 5

46407 Matfer Inc
16300 Stagg St
Van Nuys, CA 91406-1717
818-782-0792
Fax: 818-782-0799   800-766-0333
Dbesson@matferinc.com
www.matferbourgeatusa.com
Importer and exporter of cookware

President: M Scheinmann
Manager: Dan Burgoni
dburgoni@matferinc.com
Operations Officer: Robert Garcia
Number Employees: 1-4
Square Footage: 16000
Parent Co: Bourgeat SA
Brands Exported: Bourgeat
Regions Exported to: Central America, South America, Asia, Middle East, Australia
Regions Imported from: Europe

46408 Matfer Inc
16150 Lindbergh St
Van Nuys, CA 91406-1707
818-782-0792
Fax: 818-782-0799   800-766-0333
contact@matferinc.com
www.matferbourgeatusa.com
Manufacturer, importer and exporter of kitchen and bakery utensils including molds, nonstick baking sheets, pastry bags, thermometers, food mills, juicers, casserole dishes, commercial mixers, mandolines, saute pans, etc
Manager: Jean Paul Riou
CEO: Jean Paul Rio
VP: Pierre Perisot
National Sales Manager: Dominique Besson
Manager: Sergey Perevalov
sperevalov@matferinc.com
Estimated Sales: $ 8 Million
Number Employees: 10-19
Square Footage: 30000
Parent Co: Matfer France
Brands Exported: Matfer
Regions Exported to: Central America, South America, Europe, Asia, Middle East, Australia, Canada, Carribean, Latin America, Mexico
Percentage of Business in Exporting: 20
Brands Imported: Matfer
Regions Imported from: Europe

46409 Mathews Packing
950 Ramirez Rd
Marysville, CA 95901-9444
530-743-9000
Fax: 530-742-6625
Dried prunes, pitted prunes, rice
Owner: Ed Mathews
VP/Marketing: Mark Mathews
Estimated Sales: $1-$2.5 000,000
Number Employees: 1-4
Type of Packaging: Private Label
Brands Exported: Mathews Prunes
Regions Exported to: Europe, Asia
Percentage of Business in Exporting: 100

46410 Matiss
8800 25th Avenue
St Georges, QC G6A 1K5
Canada
418-227-9144   888-562-8477
Fax: 418-227-9144
doris.boily@matiss.com www.matiss.com
Manufacturer and exporter of bakery processing equipment including greasers, depositors, fillers, cutting and batching systems; also, snack food and pizza processing and packaging equipment; laboratory testing available
President: Jacques Martel
CFO: Pierre Martel
Sales Manager: Francois Henault
Sales Engineer: Patrice Painchaud
General Manager: Jacques Martel
Estimated Sales: Below $ 5 Million
Number Employees: 90
Square Footage: 80000
Regions Exported to: USA
Percentage of Business in Exporting: 20

46411 Matot - Commercial GradeLift Solutions
2501 Van Buren
Bellwood, IL 60104-2459
708-547-1888
Fax: 708-547-1608   800-369-1070
sales@matot.com www.matot.com
Manufacturer and exporter of electric dumbwaiters
Co-President/ Owner: Anne B. Matot
Co-President: Cathryn Matot
Executive Vice President: Jim Piper
Senior Vice President, Sales: Jim Peskuski
Estimated Sales: $1-2.5 Million
Number Employees: 5-9
Square Footage: 32000
Regions Exported to: Asia, Middle East
Percentage of Business in Exporting: 1

Importers & Exporters / A-Z

46412 Matrix Engineering
P.O.Box 650728
Vero Beach, FL 32965-0728 772-461-2156
Fax: 772-461-7185 800-926-0528
www.griprock.com
Manufacturer and exporter of safety and slip resistant floor mats and flooring
President: Thomas Hayes
CEO: Edward Saylor
Vice President: Thomas Hayes
Operations Manager: Randi McManus
Number Employees: 19
Number of Brands: 4
Number of Products: 4
Square Footage: 40000
Brands Exported: Grip Rock; Super G; Brite-Trac Safety Floor Mats
Regions Exported to: Central America, South America, Europe, Middle East
Percentage of Business in Exporting: 1

46413 Matrix Health Products
9316 Wheatlands Road
Santee, CA 92071-5644 619-448-7550
Fax: 619-448-2995 888-736-5609
info@earthsbounty.com www.matrixhealth.com
Manufacturer, importer and exporter of nutritional and herbal supplements including tablets, liquids, powders and capsules - also kosher & organic products. Teas, coffee & vanilla and nonjuice
President: Steven Kravitz
Number Employees: 10-19
Type of Packaging: Consumer, Private Label, Bulk
Brands Exported: Earth's Bounty, Bio Health, Mandy Dave's
Regions Exported to: Central America, South America, Europe, Asia, Middle East

46414 Matrix Packaging Machinery
650 N Dekora Woods Blvd
Saukville, WI 53080-1674 262-268-8300
Fax: 262-268-8301 888-628-7491
sales@matrixpm.com www.matrixpm.com
Manufacturer and exporter of vertical form/fill/seal machinery
Gen Mgr/R&D/Quality Control: Marc Willden
Marketing: Lori Stein
Sales Exec: Matt Lanfrankie
Public Relations: John LaBouve
sales@matrixpm.com
Operations: Jane Barnett
Production/Plant Manager: Tim Marchant
Purchasing: Lori Klandrud
Estimated Sales: $15-20 Million
Number Employees: 50-99
Square Footage: 80000
Parent Co: Pro Mach Inc
Regions Exported to: Central America, South America, Europe, Asia, Middle East
Percentage of Business in Exporting: 20
Regions Imported from: Asia
Percentage of Business in Importing: 10

46415 Matson Fruit Co
201 N Railroad Ave
Selah, WA 98942 509-697-7100
matsonfruit.com
Processor and exporter of apples and pears.
President & General Manager: Rod Matson
on@matsonfruit.com
Estimated Sales: $25 Million
Number Employees: 100-249
Square Footage: 18000
Type of Packaging: Consumer, Food Service
Regions Exported to: Worldwide

46416 Matson LLC
45620 SE North Bend Way
North Bend, WA 98045 425-888-6212
Fax: 425-888-6216 800-308-3723
www.corrys.com
Manufacturer and exporter of insecticides
President: Ken Matson
matson@corrys.com
Sales Representative: Dave Grasmann
Estimated Sales: $ 5 - 10 Million
Number Employees: 5-9

46417 Matthews Marking Systems Div
6515 Penn Ave
Pittsburgh, PA 15206-4407 412-665-2500
Fax: 412-665-2550 info@matw.com
www.matthewsmarking.com
Manufacturer and exporter of marking equipment for identification of products and packaging; also, turnkey systems available
President: Annette Aranda
aaranda@matthewsinternational.com
Vice President: Peter Hart
Marketing Director: Michelle Staulding
Estimated Sales: $ 10-20 Million
Number Employees: 100-249
Parent Co: Matthew International Corporation
Other Locations:
Matthews International Corp.
10156 TorinoMatthews International Corp.
Regions Exported to: Worldwide
Percentage of Business in Exporting: 30

46418 Matthiesen Equipment
566 N Ww White Rd
San Antonio, TX 78219-2816 210-333-1510
Fax: 210-333-1563 800-624-8635
ctorres@matthiesenequipment.com
www.matthiesenequipment.com
Manufacturer and exporter of material handling processing machinery for ice including bins, baggers, belt and screw conveyors, crushers, bag closers, drying belts, etc.; exporter and wholesaler/distributor of ice machinery
Office Manager: Claudia Torres
Research & Development: Stephen Niestroy
National Sales Manager: Diane Hardekopf
Sales Engineer: Jerry Bosma
Production Manager: Pete Ruiz
Purchasing: John Barratachea
Estimated Sales: $ 2.5-5 Million
Number Employees: 5-9
Square Footage: 80000
Parent Co: Tour Ice National
Brands Exported: Vogt; Matthiesen; Mannhardt; Clinebell; Hamer; Kasten/Kamco; Turbo; Arrow
Regions Exported to: Central America, South America, Europe, Asia, Middle East, Mexico
Percentage of Business in Exporting: 40

46419 Matworks Co LLC
11900 Old Baltimore Pike
Beltsville, MD 20705-1265 410-792-2733
Fax: 301-595-1817 800-523-5179
www.thematworks.com
Owner: Jared Agan
jagan@thematworks.com
Number Employees: 50-99

46420 Maui Gold Pineapple Company
PO Box 880190
Pukalani, HI 96788 808-877-3805
info@pineapplemaui.com
www.pineapplemaui.com
Whole fresh, canned and fresh-cut pineapple; also, pineapple juice and concentrates
President: Darren Strand
CFO: Michael Hotta
Estimated Sales: $78 Million
Number Employees: 1,000
Square Footage: 10000
Type of Packaging: Consumer, Food Service, Private Label, Bulk
Regions Exported to: Europe, Asia, Canada, Mexico
Percentage of Business in Exporting: 2

46421 Maull-Baker Box Company
16685 Lower Valley Ridge Drive
Brookfield, WI 53005-5557 414-463-1290
Fax: 414-463-5975
Manufacturer and exporter of wooden boxes, crates, pallets and skids
President: Jerry Maull
Estimated Sales: $2.5-5 Million
Number Employees: 9

46422 Maurer North America
6324 N Chatham Avenue
Kansas City, MO 64151-2473 816-914-3518
Fax: 816-746-5011
Manufacturer and importer of food processing equipment
President: Rolf Hammann
Parent Co: A.G. Maurer
Regions Imported from: Germany

46423 Max Landau & Company
6977 180th Street
Flushing, NY 11365-3529 718-969-1114
Importer of dairy products including butter and cheese
President: Ronald Landau
Secretary: Julian Landau
Number Employees: 1-4
Regions Imported from: Europe
Percentage of Business in Importing: 100

46424 Maxfield Candy
1050 S 200 W
Salt Lake City, UT 84101 801-355-5321
Fax: 801-355-5546 800-288-8002
Boxed chocolates, nut logs, cream sticks, holiday novelties, salt water taffy, cordial cherries, mint sandwiches, etc.; exporter of boxed chocolates
President: Taz Murray
Contact: Judy Adams
jadams@maxfieldcandy.com
Estimated Sales: $ 5 - 10 Million
Number Employees: 5-9
Square Footage: 424000
Parent Co: Alpine Confections
Type of Packaging: Consumer
Brands Exported: Maxfield's; All American
Regions Exported to: Asia, Canada, Mexico
Percentage of Business in Exporting: 10

46425 Maxi-Vac Inc.
PO Box 688
Dundee, IL 60118 855-629-4538
sales@maxi-vac.com
www.maxi-vac.com
Manufacturer and exporter of pressure washers and steam cleaning equipment
President: Jim Nolan
Secretary and Treasurer: Janice Nolan
Estimated Sales: $1-2.5 Million
Number Employees: 1-4
Regions Exported to: Central America, South America, Asia, Middle East, Canada, Caribbean, Mexico, Latin America
Percentage of Business in Exporting: 12

46426 (HQ)Maxim's Import Corporation
2719 NW 24th Street
Miami, FL 33142-7005 915-577-9228
Fax: 91- 57- 921 800-331-6652
info@maximsimports.com maximsimports.com
Processor, importer and exporter of shrimp; processor of packaged fish; exporter of frozen chicken, duck, turkey, pork and beef; wholesaler/distributor of shrimp, pork, beef, poultry, fish, produce and frozen, specialty and healthfoods
President: Luis Chi
CEO: Jeo Chi
Contact: Joe Chi
luis.chi@hotmail.com
Estimated Sales: $4.1 Million
Number Employees: 22
Square Footage: 140000
Type of Packaging: Bulk
Other Locations:
Maxim's Import Corp.
SalvadorMaxim's Import Corp.
Regions Exported to: Central America, South America, Europe, Asia, Caribbean
Percentage of Business in Exporting: 30
Regions Imported from: Central America, South America, Europe, Africa

46427 Maximicer
4175 Country Road 268
Georgetown, TX 78628 512-259-0500
Fax: 512-258-8804 800-289-9098
info@Maximicer.com
Manufacturer and exporter of optimizers for ice making machinery
President: J L Love
VP Manufacturing & Product Dev: Daniel L Welch
Contact: J Love
j.love@maximicer.com
Estimated Sales: $ 1 - 3,000,000
Number Employees: 1-4
Type of Packaging: Food Service, Private Label
Regions Exported to: Worldwide
Percentage of Business in Exporting: 25

46428 May Flower
56-72 49th Pl
Maspeth, NY 11378 347-480-4076
www.shopmayflower.com
Asian sauces and seasonings, snacks, beverages, frozen food, pickled vegetables and cake.

Importers & Exporters / A-Z

Type of Packaging: Private Label

46429 Mayacamas Fine Foods
20590 Palmer Avenue
Suite A
Sonoma, CA 95476 707-291-3024
Fax: 707-938-8350 800-826-9621
info@mayacamasfinefoods.com
www.mayacamasfinefoods.com
Processor and exporter of dehydrated soups, salad dressings, pasta sauces, gravies and seasonings
President: Vicki Webber
VP: Walter Rahrau
Contact: Craig Parrott
craig@mayacamasfinefoods.com
Estimated Sales: $2.4 Million
Number Employees: 1-4
Square Footage: 72000
Type of Packaging: Consumer, Food Service, Private Label
Brands Exported: Mayacamas
Regions Exported to: Central America, Europe, Canada, Australia

46430 Mayacamas Vineyards & Winery
1155 Lokoya Rd
Napa, CA 94558-9566 707-224-4030
Fax: 707-224-3979 www.mayacamas.com
Processor and exporter of wines including cabernet sauvignon, chardonnay, sauvignon blanc and pinot noir
Owner: John Fisher
johnf@mayacamas.com
Marketing Director: Trina Vaught
Estimated Sales: $88000
Number Employees: 10-19
Regions Exported to: Europe, Asia
Percentage of Business in Exporting: 10

46431 Mayekawa USA, Inc.
8750 West Bryn Mawr Avenue
Suite 190
Chicago, IL 60631 773-516-5070
sales@mayekawausa.com
www.mayekawausa.com
Freezing, thawing and heating units.
Contact: Bryan Arevalo
barevalo@mayekawausa.com
Regions Exported to: North America, USA

46432 Mayrsohn International Inc
2007 NW 70th Ave
Miami, FL 33122-1811 305-470-1444
Fax: 305-470-1440 mayrsohn@hotmail.com
Importer and exporter of produce
Owner: Arold Ariste
CEO: Bernard Mayrsohn
Director of Asian Export Sales: mark Holobetz
aristea@palmbeachstate.edu
Number Employees: 20-49
Percentage of Business in Exporting: 80
Percentage of Business in Importing: 20

46433 Maytag Corporation
553 Benson Rd.
Benton Harbor, MI 49022
800-344-1274
www.maytag.com
Ranges and stoves.
Chairman/CEO: Marc Bitzer
Executive VP/CFO: Jim Peters
Senior VP/General Counsel: Kirsten Hewitt
Year Founded: 1893
Estimated Sales: $4.7 Billion
Number Employees: 2,500
Square Footage: 116393
Parent Co: Whirlpool Corporation
Regions Exported to: Worldwide

46434 Maywood International Sales
PO Box 9292
Sante Fe, NM 87504 505-982-2700
Fax: 505-982-9780 805-500-5500
Oilseed manufacturer
Sales: Jacques Brazy
Sales: Peter Connick

46435 Mazzetta Company
P.O. Box 1126
Highland Park, IL 60035 847-433-1150
Fax: 847-433-8973 seamazz@mazzetta.com
www.mazzetta.com
Seafood and fish such as orange roughy fillets, whiting fillets, greenshell mussels, raw and cooked shrimp, lobster tails, Chilean sea bass fillets, squid and crab meat.
President: Thomas Mazzetta
Contact: Dominic Benedetto
dominic@mazzetta.com
Estimated Sales: $ 1 - 3 Million
Number Employees: 10-19

46436 Mba Suppliers Inc.
1000 Fort Crook Rd N
Suite 100
Bellevue, NE 68005-4573 402-597-5777
Fax: 402-597-2444 800-467-1201
www.mbasuppliers.com
New, reconditioned, used and pre-owned food processing and meat equipment and supplies.
Contact: Kevin Hammerle
khammerle@mbasuppliers.com
Regions Exported to: Central America, South America, Australia, New Zealand, North America, USA

46437 Mc Steven's Coca Factory Store
5600 NE 88th St
Vancouver, WA 98665-0971 360-944-5788
Fax: 360-944-1302 800-547-2803
sales@mcstevens.com
Beverage mixes including white chocolate, regular and sugar-free cocoa, lemonade, cappuccino, chai, and apple cider; exporter of cocoa mixes
Owner: Brent Houston
brent@mcstevens.com
VP Marketing: Dave Demsky
VP Operations: Brent Huston
Estimated Sales: $500,000-$1 Million
Number Employees: 20-49
Type of Packaging: Consumer, Food Service, Private Label, Bulk
Brands Exported: McStevens
Regions Exported to: Europe, Asia, Canada
Percentage of Business in Exporting: 10

46438 (HQ)McAnally Enterprises
32710 Reservoir Rd
Lakeview, CA 92567 951-928-1935
Fax: 951-928-1947 800-726-2002
Processor and exporter of cartoned, frozen and liquid eggs and egg products
President: Carlton Lofgren
Rep. (S.W.): Glenn Lemley
Vice President: Don Brown
Marketing Director: John Klien
Operations Manager: Tom McAnally
Number Employees: 100-249
Square Footage: 80000
Type of Packaging: Food Service
Other Locations:
McAnally Enterprises
Phoenix, AZ McAnally Enterprises
Brands Exported: Yucaipa Valley; Mesilla Valley; Henny Penny
Regions Exported to: Central America, Europe, Asia, Middle East
Percentage of Business in Exporting: 10

46439 McCabe's Quality Foods
17600 NE San Rafael St
Portland, OR 97230-5924 503-256-4770
Fax: 503-256-1263 www.ssafood.com
Wholesaler/distributor and exporter of meat, fruit, frozen food, general merchandise, general line items, produce and seafood; serving fast food chains
President: Gerald Cobb
Sales Manager: Sandy Thames
Operations Manager: Steve Peil
Estimated Sales: $20-50 Million
Number Employees: 250-499
Square Footage: 100000
Regions Exported to: Asia, Australia
Percentage of Business in Exporting: 10

46440 McCarter Corporation
PO Box 351
Norristown, PA 19404-0351 610-272-3203
Fax: 610-275-5120
Manufacturer and exporter of paste and confectionery mixing equipment
President: H Craig McCarter
Number Employees: 17
Square Footage: 150000
Regions Exported to: Canada

46441 (HQ)McCleskey Mills
197 Rhodes Street
PO Box 98
Smithville, GA 31787-0098 229-846-2003
Fax: 229-846-4805 mmi@mccleskeymills.com
www.mccleskeymills.com
Manufacturer and exporter of shelled peanuts, seed peanuts, and peanut hulls
President: Keith Chandler
Chairman & CEO: Jerry Chandler
Vice President & CFO: Billy Marshall
VP, MIS: Cleve McRee
Accounting Manager & Quality Assurance: Robert Hamlin
Executive Vice President Sales: Joe West
Contact: Tyler Carlisle
tcarlisle@mccleskeymills.com
Plant Manager: James Champion
Estimated Sales: $2 Million
Number Employees: 9
Square Footage: 72000
Type of Packaging: Consumer, Bulk
Regions Exported to: Worldwide

46442 McConnell's Fine Ice Cream
835 E Canon Perdido St
Santa Barbara, CA 93103 805-963-8813
Fax: 805-965-3764 info@mcconnells.com
mcconnells.com
Manufacturer and exporter of ice cream
Owner: Jimmy Young
Contact: Mike Vierra
mvierra@mcconnells.com
Year Founded: 1949
Estimated Sales: Below $ 5 Million
Number Employees: 5-9
Type of Packaging: Consumer, Food Service
Percentage of Business in Exporting: 5

46443 McCormack Manufacturing Company
PO Box 1727
Lake Oswego, OR 97035 503-639-2137
Fax: 503-639-1800 800-395-1593
Manufacturer and exporter of industrial refrigeration equipment including quick freezing and sub-zero freezers
CEO: Gary Montgomery
VP Engineering: Tom Resseler
Estimated Sales: $10-20 Million
Number Employees: 1-4
Square Footage: 50000
Regions Exported to: Central America, South America, Asia
Percentage of Business in Exporting: 1

46444 McCormick & Company
24 Schilling Rd
Hunt Valley, MD 21031 410-527-6189
www.mccormickcorporation.com
Dessert products, honey, flavors and sauces.
Chairman/President/CEO: Lawrence Kurzius
lawrence_kurzius@mccormick.com
CAO: Malcolm Swift
Executive VP/CFO: Mike Smith
VP/General Counsel: Jeffrey Schwartz
Year Founded: 1889
Estimated Sales: $5.3 Billion
Number Employees: 12,400
Number of Brands: 32
Type of Packaging: Consumer, Food Service, Private Label, Bulk
Regions Exported to: Worldwide

46445 McCoy's Products
1075 Central Park Ave # 407
Scarsdale, NY 10583-3232 914-472-2737
Fax: 914-472-2738
Wholesaler/distributor and exporter of cod liver oil tablets
President: Richard Sosin
Estimated Sales: $2.5-5 Million
Number Employees: 1-4

46446 McDaniel Fruit
965 E Mission Rd
Fallbrook, CA 92028 760-728-8438
Fax: 760-728-4898 www.mcdanielavocado.com
Processor, importer and exporter of avocados

Owner: Kay Ahrend
kay@mcdanielavocado.com
VP Sales/Marketing: Rankin McDaniel
General Sales Manager: Laurie Johnson
Secretary: Larry McDaniel
Estimated Sales: $9.3 Million
Number Employees: 20-49
Square Footage: 40000
Type of Packaging: Consumer, Food Service, Private Label, Bulk
Brands Exported: Linda-Vista
Regions Exported to: Europe, Asia
Percentage of Business in Exporting: 3
Brands Imported: Propal; Santa Cruz
Regions Imported from: South America, Mexico
Percentage of Business in Importing: 18

46447 McDowell Industries
PO Box 2087
Memphis, TN 38101-2087   901-527-6596
     Fax: 901-525-6596 800-622-3695
Manufacturer and importer of textile bags for vegetables and grain
Manager Customer Service: Scott Feuer
Plant Superintendent: Rod Johnston
Number Employees: 100-249
Square Footage: 500000
Type of Packaging: Consumer, Food Service, Private Label, Bulk
Regions Imported from: South America, Asia
Percentage of Business in Importing: 5

46448 McGunn Safe Company
29 S La Salle St # 425
Chicago, IL 60603-1599   312-782-3668
     Fax: 312-782-4502 800-621-2816
Manufacturer and exporter of safes and other security devices
Partner: Maureen J Mc Gann
Sales/Marketing: Pat McGunn
Estimated Sales: $ .5 - 1 million
Number Employees: 1-4
Square Footage: 100000
Regions Exported to: Europe, Canada
Percentage of Business in Exporting: 5

46449 McKee Foods Corp.
10260 McKee Rd.
PO Box 750
Collegedale, TN 37315   423-238-7111
     Fax: 423-238-7127 800-522-4499
     www.mckeefoods.com
Cookies, crackers, snack and granola bars, snack cakes and cereal.
President/CEO: Michael McKee
mike_mckee@mckee.com
CFO: Andrew Lang
Chairman/Chief Administrative Officer: R. Ellsworth McKee
Corp. Communications/Public Relations: Mike Gloekler
Year Founded: 1934
Estimated Sales: $1 Billion
Number Employees: 5,800
Number of Brands: 4
Type of Packaging: Consumer, Food Service, Private Label
Other Locations:
   McKee Foods
   Gentry, AR
   Stuarts Draft, VA
   Kingman, AZ
   Chattanooga, TNMcKee FoodsStuarts Draft

46450 McKenna Bros.
PO Box 70
Cardigan, PE C0A 1G0
Canada   902-583-2951
     Fax: 902-583-2891 info@mckennabros.ca
Importer and exporter of fresh apples, onions, turnips, potatoes and garlic
Number Employees: 5-9
Brands Exported: Island Brand

46451 McNeil Nutritionals
7050 Camp Hill Rd
Fort Washington, PA 19034   215-273-7000
     Fax: 908-874-1120 www.splenda.com
Artificial sweeteners
President: Peter Luther
Vice President: Sheila Bergey
Contact: Joan Anton
janton@mcnus.jnj.com
Estimated Sales: $10-20 Million
Parent Co: Johnson & Johnson

46452 McNeil Specialty Products Company
PO Box 2400
501 George St.
New Brunswick, NJ 08903-2400   732-524-3799
     Fax: 732-524-3303
artifical sweetners.such as sucralose.
President: Stephen Fanning
Director Sales (North America): Jim Thornton
Director International Sales: Joseph Zannoni
Contact: Donna Fernandez
donna@sucralose.com
Estimated Sales: $10-25million
Number Employees: 20-49
Parent Co: Johnson & Johnson

46453 McNichols Conveyor Company
21411 Civic Center Drive
Suite 204
Southfield, MI 48076   248-357-6077
     Fax: 248-357-6078 800-331-1926
     sales@mcnicholsconveyor.com
     www.mcnicholsconveyor.com
Manufacturer, exporter and designer of conveyors including power roller, gravity roller and belt
President: Robert Iwrey
General Manager: Vince Giannone
Estimated Sales: $2.5-5 Million
Number Employees: 5-9
Regions Exported to: Worldwide

46454 (HQ)Mcbrady Engineering Co
1251 S Larkin Ave
Rockdale, IL 60436-9326   815-744-8900
Fax: 815-744-8901 www.mcbradyengineering.com
Manufacturer and exporter of container cleaning equipment
Owner: Garrett Mc Brady
Vice President: Garrett McBrady
Sales: David Anderson
Estimated Sales: $2 Million
Number Employees: 10-19
Number of Brands: 7
Number of Products: 3
Square Footage: 60000
Brands Exported: Orbit
Regions Exported to: Central America, South America, Europe, Asia, Middle East
Percentage of Business in Exporting: 35

46455 Mccourt Manufacturing Co
1001 N 3rd St
Fort Smith, AR 72901-1009   479-783-2593
     Fax: 479-783-7608 800-333-2687
     info@mccourtmfg.com www.mccourtmfg.com
Manufacture tables and chairs
Owner: Terry Clark
Marketing: Tammy Helliker
Sales: Terry Clark
charles@mccourtmfg.com
Plant Manager: Ronnie Fergason
Estimated Sales: $7 Million
Number Employees: 20-49
Square Footage: 800000
Type of Packaging: Private Label
Brands Exported: McCourt Folding Chairs & Tables
Regions Exported to: Europe

46456 (HQ)Mccullagh Coffee Roasters
245 Swan St
Buffalo, NY 14204
     800-753-3473
     sales@mccullaghcoffee.com
     www.mccullaghcoffee.com
Processor, importer and exporter of coffee, tea, non-dairy creamer and hot chocolate
President: Warren Emblidge
VP of Sales and Marketing: Paul Zanghi
Estimated Sales: $9 Million
Number Employees: 50-99
Brands Exported: McCullagh Coffee
Regions Exported to: Canada
Percentage of Business in Exporting: 25

46457 Mccullough Industries Inc
13047 County Road 175
P.O.Box 222
Kenton, OH 43326-9022   419-673-0767
     Fax: 419-673-8176 800-245-9490
     sales@mcculloughind.com
     www.mcculloughind.com
Manufacturer and exporter of self dumping hoppers
Owner: Steve Mc Cullough
smm@mcculloughind.com
Owner: W McCullough
Number Employees: 20-49
Regions Exported to: Worldwide
Percentage of Business in Exporting: 10

46458 Mcfadden Farm
16000 Powerhouse Rd
Potter Valley, CA 95469-8771   707-743-1122
     Fax: 707-743-1126 800-544-8230
     mcfaddenfarm@pacific.net
     www.mcfaddenfarm.com
Processor and exporter of organic herbs including garlic braids and wild rice
Owner: Eugene Mc Fadden
mcfaddenfarm@pacific.net
Estimated Sales: $1.5 Million
Number Employees: 20-49
Square Footage: 4000
Type of Packaging: Consumer, Food Service, Bulk
Regions Exported to: Europe, Asia, Canada
Percentage of Business in Exporting: 15

46459 Mcintyre Metals Inc
310 Kendall Mill Rd
Thomasville, NC 27360-5524   336-476-3646
     Fax: 336-476-3622 800-334-0807
     www.mcmetals.com
Manufacturer and exporter of point-of-purchase displays including stock and special designs, powder coated and wire formed
President: Jeff Mc Intyre
jeff@mcmetals.com
VP: Gilbert Luck
Sales Manager: Jim Plumb
VP, Operations: Mike Smith
Estimated Sales: $2.5-5 Million
Number Employees: 20-49
Regions Exported to: Worldwide
Percentage of Business in Exporting: 2

46460 Mckey Perforating Co Inc
3033 S 166th St
New Berlin, WI 53151-3555   262-786-2700
     Fax: 262-786-7673 800-345-7373
     jmckey@mckey.com
     www.mckeyperforatingco-inc.com
Manufacturer and exporter of component parts for food handling equipment and perforated metals and plastics
President/CEO: Jean Mc Key
General Manager: Don Pirlot
dpirlot@mckey.com
Product Development Manager: Tony Elsinger
VP Marketing: Jim Thurman
VP, Sales: Jim Thurman
Director of Operations: James Kuehn
Purchasing Manager: Wayne Schowalter
Estimated Sales: $4700000
Number Employees: 50-99
Square Footage: 280000
Regions Exported to: Canada
Percentage of Business in Exporting: 10

46461 (HQ)Mclaughlin Gormley KingCo
8810 10th Ave N
Minneapolis, MN 55427-4372   763-544-0341
     Fax: 763-544-6437 800-645-6466
     www.mgk.com
Manufacturer and exporter of insecticide concentrates and repellents
President: William D Gullickson Jr
CEO: Steve Gullickson
steve.gullickson@mgk.com
CFO: Tom Majpor
Quality Control: Michael Lunch
Director Marketing: Dan Untiedt
Production Manager: Don Sundquist
Estimated Sales: $20-50 Million
Number Employees: 50-99
Square Footage: 100000
Other Locations:
   McLaughlin Gormley KingCo.
   Baltimore, MDMcLaughlin Gormley KingCo.

Importers & Exporters / A-Z

Regions Exported to: Central America, South America, Europe, Asia, Middle East
Percentage of Business in Exporting: 20

46462 Mcroyal Industries Inc
1421 Lilac St
Youngstown, OH 44502-1339   330-747-8655
          Fax: 330-747-3331   800-785-2556
          www.mcroyal.com
Manufacturer and exporter of laminated restaurant fixtures including counters, booths, tables, kiosks, etc ; also, point of purchase displays
CEO: John N Lallo
jkllallo@mcroyal.com
Purchasing Agent: Don Ceo
Estimated Sales: $2.5-5 Million
Number Employees: 5-9
Square Footage: 56000

46463 MeGa Industries
5109 Harvester Road, Unit 3A
Burlington, ON L7L 5Y9
Canada   905-631-6342
      Fax: 905-631-6341   800-665-6342
             sales@megaindustries.com
             www.megaindustries.com
Manufacturer, importer, exporter and wholesaler/distributor of material and bulk handling equipment including vibrating tables, conveyors, bins, feeders, vibrators and bin level controls and indicators
President: Mel Gallagher
Sales: Steve Atkinson
Number Employees: 5-9
Square Footage: 12000
Brands Exported: Mega
Regions Exported to: Worldwide
Brands Imported: Dynapac; Svedala; Metso
Regions Imported from: Europe

46464 (HQ)Meadowbrook Meat Company
2641 Meadowbrook Rd.
Rocky Mount, NC 27801   252-985-7200
   Fax: 252-985-7247   www.mbmfoodservice.com
Manufacturer & distributor of frozen foods
Chairman, President & CEO: Jerry Wordsworth
CFO: Jeffrey Kowalk
Exective Vice President & COO: Jim Sabiston
Business Development Manager: Kristine Newton
Director of Quality Assurance: Samuel Richardson
Contact: Mike Amodeo
mamodeo@mbmfoodservice.com
Executive Director of Operations: Andy Blanton
Distribution Manager: Earl Smith
Director of Purchasing: Mitch Brantley
Number Employees: 3,000
Square Footage: 800000
Type of Packaging: Consumer, Food Service
Other Locations:
   MBM Corp.
   Fort Worth, TXMBM Corp.
Brands Exported: Gwaltney
Regions Exported to: South America

46465 (HQ)Meadows Mills Inc
1352 W D St
PO Box 1288
North Wilkesboro, NC 28659-3506   336-838-2525
      Fax: 336-667-6501   800-626-2282
             sales@meadowsmills.com
             www.meadowsmills.com
Manufacturer and exporter of stone burr and hammer mills, grits separators, bolters, eccentric sifters, elevating fans, collectors, elbows, piping, self rising corn meal mixer, and hand boggers, christmas tree palletizers
Vice President: Corey Sheets
csheets@meadowsmillscoinc.com
CFO: June Hege
Senior VP: Corey Sheets
VP Sales/Marketing: Brian Hege
VP Product Engineering: Robert Miller
Purchasing: Corey Sheets
Estimated Sales: $5 Million
Number Employees: 20-49
Number of Brands: 4
Square Footage: 210000
Type of Packaging: Consumer, Food Service, Private Label, Bulk
Other Locations:
   Meadows Mills
   Tynda, AmurMeadows Mills
Brands Exported: Meadows; Miner; Andrus

Regions Exported to: Central America, South America, Asia
Percentage of Business in Exporting: 35

46466 Meadwestvaco Corp
501 S 5th St
Richmond, VA 23219-0501   804-444-7939
      Fax: 843-745-3028   804-444-1000
Manufacturer and exporter of kraft paper
Chairman and Chief Executive Officer: John A. Luke, Jr.
SVP and Chief Financial Officer: E. Mark Rajkowski
Chief Marketing & Innovation Officer: Diane Teer
Contact: Suzanne Abbot
suzanne.abbot@mwv.com
EVP, Global Operations: Robert A. Feeser
Estimated Sales: $5-10 Million
Number Employees: 1-4
Type of Packaging: Consumer, Food Service, Private Label, Bulk
Regions Exported to: Worldwide

46467 Measurex/S&L Plastics
2860 Bath Pike
Nazareth, PA 18064-8898   610-759-0280
      Fax: 610-759-0650   800-752-0650
Plastic measuring scoops, plastic apothecary jars and clear plastic cubes
President: John Bungert
Marketing/Sales: Denise Yonney
Purchasing Manager: Ron Timura
Estimated Sales: $10-20 Million
Number Employees: 100-249
Square Footage: 380000

46468 Meat & Livestock Australia
1401 K Street NW, Ste 602
Washington DC, DC 20005   202-521-2555
      Fax: 202-521-2699   www.australian-meat.com
Beef, lamb and goatmeat
Regional Manager: Stephen Edwards
Marketing: Elise Garling
Retail Development: Linden Cowper
Contact: Peter Barnard
pbarnard@mla.com.au
Estimated Sales: $4 Million
Number Employees: 5

46469 Mecco Marking & Traceability
290 Executive Drive
PO Box 307
Cranberry Township, PA 16066   724-779-9555
      Fax: 724-779-9556   888-369-9190
             info@mecco.com   www.mecco.com
For over 100 years MECCO Marking Systems has partnered with a variety of industries for permanent marking solutions. Products range from high quality hand - held marking devices, portable marking tools, and computer - controlledmarking systems. The lates technology of bumpy barcode marking systems enhance MECCO's position as an industry leader and innovator for marking solutions
CEO: Dean Frenz
CFO: Christine Grabowski
R&D: Eric McElnoy
Marketing: Todd Hockenberry
VP Sales: Todd Hockenberry
Purchasing: Frank Zowojski
Estimated Sales: $ 3 - 5 Million
Number Employees: 20-49
Brands Exported: Code-A-Can; Code-A-Plas; Code-A-Top, Dot-A-Mark
Regions Exported to: Central America, South America, Europe
Percentage of Business in Exporting: 5
Regions Imported from: Europe

46470 Medallion InternationalInc
233 W Parkway
Pompton Plains, NJ 07444-1028   973-616-3401
      Fax: 973-616-3405   www.medallionint.com
Flavors: natural and artificial; edible and essential oils
President: Michael Boudjouk
VP Business Development: William Lulum
Director Sales/Marketing: Paula Boudjouk
Plant Manager: Gwen Kenyon
Estimated Sales: $2 Million
Number Employees: 10-19
Type of Packaging: Consumer, Food Service, Private Label, Bulk
Regions Exported to: Central America, Europe, Middle East

Percentage of Business in Exporting: 30
Regions Imported from: South America, Europe, Asia, Middle East, Canada
Percentage of Business in Importing: 20

46471 (HQ)Medina & Medina
PO Box 362200
San Juan, PR 00936-2200   787-782-7575
      Fax: 787-782-7552   www.medinapr.com
Importer and wholesaler/distributor of frozen foods, cheese, fish, meat and poultry
President: Jose Medina
Marketing Manager: Eduardo Medina
Number Employees: 50-99
Brands Imported: Hormel; Nestle; Pescanova; Navidol; Palacios; Fripan
Regions Imported from: Europe, Canada
Percentage of Business in Importing: 25

46472 Mediterranean Delight
CHO Tunisia, 204 B W Ymc Dr
Baytown, TX 77521-4122   281-712-1549
      Fax: 281-966-6970   oliveoil@igotoil.com
Other baking mixes and ingredients, olive oil.

46473 Mediterranean Gourmet
Po Box 1016
Ashton, MD 20861   571-212-6755
             Fax: 703-953-1903
Organic/natural, full-line condiments, other condiments, olive oil, other oils, full-line seafood, tuna, canned or preserved vegetables/fruit.
Marketing: Mounsif Tolab

46474 Mediterranean Snack Food Co
708 Main St
Boonton, NJ 07005-1450   973-402-2644
Healthy, non-GMO and gluten-free snacks such as chips and crackers
President: Vincent James
vincent@mediterraneansnackfoods.com
Vice President: Franck Le Berre
Estimated Sales: Less Than $500,000
Number Employees: 1-4

46475 Meduri Farms
P.O. Box 866
Dallas, OR 97338   877-388-8800
             Fax: 800-310-4270
customerservice@meduriworlddelights.com
             www.meduriworlddelights.com
Dried cherries, blueberries and strawberries; also, infused cherries with raspberry juice
President: Joe Meduri
Sales: Mike Meduri
Year Founded: 1984
Estimated Sales: Less Than $500,000
Number Employees: 5-9
Parent Co: Meduri Farms
Type of Packaging: Food Service, Private Label, Bulk
Brands Exported: Meduri Farms Inc
Regions Exported to: Europe, Asia
Regions Imported from: Europe, Asia, Middle East

46476 Mega Pro Intl
251 W Hilton Dr # 100
St George, UT 84770-2201   435-673-1001
      Fax: 435-673-1007   800-541-9469
             info@mega-pro.com   www.mega-pro.com
Processor, importer and exporter of nutritional supplements including vitamins for weight gain and loss
President: Dave Smith
megapro@mega-pro.com
Estimated Sales: $1.8 Million
Number Employees: 20-49
Regions Exported to: Central America, South America, Europe, Asia, Middle East
Percentage of Business in Exporting: 40
Percentage of Business in Importing: 50

46477 MegaFood
Manchester, NH 03108
                  800-848-2542
   questions@megafood.com   www.megafood.com
Dietary supplements
Chief Executive Officer: Robert Craven
Quality Assurance Manager: Dale Bates
Marketing Communications Manager: Jamila Lasante
Customer Exeprience Manager: Amy Keronen

Importers & Exporters / A-Z

Year Founded: 1973
Estimated Sales: $20-50 Million
Number Employees: 50-99
Type of Packaging: Consumer
Percentage of Business in Exporting: 50

46478 Meguiar's Inc
17991 Mitchell S
Irvine, CA 92614-6015 949-752-8000
Fax: 949-752-5784 jlakkis@meguiars.com
www.meguiars.com
Manufacturer and exporter of furniture and floor cleaning products including polish
CEO: Barry Meguiar
barry.meguiar@meguiars.com
CEO: Barry Meguiar
Estimated Sales: $ 20 - 50 Million
Number Employees: 100-249
Regions Exported to: Worldwide

46479 Mehu-Liisa Products
9147 State Route 96
Trumansburg, NY 14886 607-387-6716
Fax: 607-387-9277 www.podunk.com
Importer of stainless nonelectric steam juicers/cookers
Owner: Barry Ford
Number Employees: 1-4
Square Footage: 5600
Brands Imported: Mehu-Liisa
Regions Imported from: Europe
Percentage of Business in Importing: 100

46480 Mei Shun Tofu Products Company
523 W 26th St
Chicago, IL 60616-1803 312-842-7000
Fax: 312-791-9429
Canner and exporter of tofu
Owner: Yim Sung
Estimated Sales: Less than $500,000
Number Employees: 5 to 9
Type of Packaging: Consumer, Food Service, Private Label, Bulk

46481 Melcher Manufacturing Co
6017 E Mission Ave
Spokane Valley, WA 99212-1264 509-535-7626
Fax: 509-536-3931 800-541-4227
sales@melcher-ramps.com
www.melcher-ramps.com
Manufacturer and exporter of fiberglass truck-loading ramps
President: Wayne Hardan
Sales Manager: Wendell Anglesey
Plant Manager: Dick Colby
Estimated Sales: Below $5 Million
Number Employees: 10-19

46482 Melco Steel Inc
1100 W Foothill Blvd
Azusa, CA 91702-2818 626-334-7875
Fax: 626-334-6799 info@melcosteel.com
www.melcosteel.com
Canned food sterilizing and cooking equipment including pressure vessels, retorts, quick opening doors, reaction chambers; manufacturer and exporter of autoclaves
President: Michel Kashou
michelkashou@melcosteel.com
VP: Joe Varela
Chief Engineer: Jeff Cowan
Estimated Sales: $2.5-5 Million
Number Employees: 20-49
Square Footage: 50000
Regions Exported to: Worldwide
Percentage of Business in Exporting: 25

46483 Mele-Koi Farms
787 Alderwood Drive
Newport Beach, CA 92660-7157 949-660-9000
Fax: 949-660-9000
Manufacturer and exporter of powdered tropical drink mixes
Owner: Lloyd L Aubert Jr
Estimated Sales: $400,000
Number Employees: 1 to 4
Number of Brands: 1
Number of Products: 1
Type of Packaging: Consumer
Brands Exported: Mele-Koi; Hawaiian Coconut Snow
Regions Exported to: Canada, Mexico
Percentage of Business in Exporting: 5

46484 Melitta USA Inc
13925 58th St N
Clearwater, FL 33760-3721 727-535-2111
Fax: 727-535-7376 888-635-4880
consumerrelations@melitta.com www.melitta.com
Processor, importer and exporter of coffee; also, coffee machines and filters
President & CEO: Martin Miller
CEO: Marty Miller
mmiller@melitta.com
Senior Product Manager: Kerrie Tobin
Quality Assurance Manager: Mark Kiczalis
Marketing Director: Chris Hillman
VP Sales: Edward Mitchell
National Sales Manager: Thomas Best
Plant Manager: Matthias Bloedorn
Estimated Sales: $27 Million
Number Employees: 100-249
Square Footage: 104000
Type of Packaging: Consumer, Food Service
Brands Exported: Melitta
Regions Exported to: Central America, South America, Europe
Percentage of Business in Exporting: 5
Regions Imported from: Central America, Europe
Percentage of Business in Importing: 10

46485 Mello Smello LLC
6010 Earle Brown Dr # 100
Minneapolis, MN 55430-4516 763-504-5400
Fax: 763-504-5493 888-574-2964
Mealbags, trayliners and kids premiums, stickers, tattoo's, static cling
President: Joe Morris
jmorris@mellosmello.com
Estimated Sales: $24.4 Million
Number Employees: 50-99
Square Footage: 70000
Parent Co: Miner Group International
Type of Packaging: Food Service, Private Label
Regions Exported to: Central America
Regions Imported from: Asia
Percentage of Business in Importing: 25

46486 Mellos North End Mfr
63 N Court St
Fall River, MA 02720-2701 508-673-2320
Fax: 508-675-0893 800-673-2320
info@melloschourico.com
www.melloschourico.com
Processor and exporter of sausage patties, links and pork
Owner: Eduardo Rego
Sales Manager: Diane Rego
Contact: Dan Rego
dan@melloschourico.com
Estimated Sales: $500,000-$1 Million
Number Employees: 1-4
Type of Packaging: Consumer, Food Service, Bulk

46487 Meluka Honey
Santa Clarita, CA 91350
salesusa@melukahoney.com
www.melukahoney.com
Australian honey

46488 Melvina Can Machinery Company
30 Casey Rd
Hudson Falls, NY 12839 518-743-0606
Fax: 631-391-9039
Manufacturer, importer and exporter of compound liners, can machinery and oil filter equipment, including can seamers and closers
President: Thomas Cahill
Estimated Sales: $5-10 Million
Number Employees: 10-19
Parent Co: Can Industries
Regions Exported to: Worldwide
Regions Imported from: Worldwide

46489 Membrane System Specialist Inc
1430 2nd St N
PO Box 998
Wisconsin Rapids, WI 54494-2914 715-421-2333
Fax: 715-423-6181
membrane@mssincorporated.com
www.mssincorporated.com
Manufacturer and exporter of brine and control systems, evaporators, condensers, filtration and membrane processing equipment, separators, clarifiers, waste water treatment systems and whey processing equipment for dairy industry
Owner: Greg Pesko
membrane@mssincorporated.com
Regional Sales Manager: Marian Oehme
Production Manager: Derek Hibbard
Estimated Sales: Below $ 5 Million
Number Employees: 5-9
Square Footage: 20840
Regions Exported to: Worldwide
Percentage of Business in Exporting: 10

46490 Menke Marking Devices
13253 Alondra Blvd
Santa Fe Springs, CA 90670-5574 562-921-1380
Fax: 562-921-1184 800-231-6023
sales@menkemarking.com
www.menkemarking.com
Manufacturer and exporter of large and small character ink jet printers, roller coders and rubber and steel codes
President: Stephen Menke
VP: Rocco Falatico
Sales Manager: Paul Carrocino
Estimated Sales: $1-2.5 Million
Number Employees: 10-19
Square Footage: 21000

46491 Menu Solution Inc
4510 White Plains Rd
Bronx, NY 10470-1609 718-994-9049
Fax: 718-994-6913 800-567-6368
sales@menucovers.biz www.menucovers.biz
Owner: Joel Varrocas
Contact: Jaclyn Barrocas
jaclyn@menucovers.biz
Estimated Sales: $ 5 - 10 Million
Number Employees: 20-49

46492 MenuMark Systems
5700 W Bender Court
Milwaukee, WI 53218-1608 414-228-4350
Fax: 414-228-4373

46493 Mepsco
1888 E Fabyan Pkwy
Batavia, IL 60510-1498 630-231-4130
Fax: 630-231-9372 800-323-8535
www.mepsco.com
Manufacturer and exporter of mechanical tenderizers and pickle injector machinery for the curing of pork and beef, marinating of chicken and the basting of turkey
President: Robert Benton
Estimated Sales: $9,000,000
Number Employees: 20-49
Square Footage: 32000
Brands Exported: Mepsco
Regions Exported to: Central America, South America, Asia
Percentage of Business in Exporting: 10

46494 Mercado Latino
245 Baldwin Park Blvd
City Of Industry, CA 91746-1404 626-333-6862
800-432-7266
www.mercadolatinoinc.com
Manufacturer, importer and distributor of authentic Latin products with nine distribution centers in the western United States.
Estimated Sales: Less Than $500,000
Number Employees: 1-4
Brands Exported: Faraon; Sol-Mex; Milpas; Bebyto; Payaso; Brillasol
Regions Exported to: Canada
Percentage of Business in Exporting: 1
Regions Imported from: Central America, South America, Europe, Asia, Mexico

46495 Merchandising FrontiersInc
1300 E Buchanan St
Winterset, IA 50273-9589 515-462-4965
Fax: 515-462-4962 800-421-2278
sales@mfi4u.com www.mfi4u.com
Manufacturer and exporter of indoor/outdoor carts, displays and kiosks
Owner: Jerry Mayer
jmayer@merchandisingfrontiers.com
Co-Owner And CEO: Janet Mayer
Estimated Sales: $2.5-5,000,000
Number Employees: 20-49
Square Footage: 62000
Regions Exported to: Worldwide
Percentage of Business in Exporting: 5

441

Importers & Exporters / A-Z

46496 Merchandising Inventives
1665 S Waukegan Rd
Waukegan, IL 60085   847-688-0591
Fax: 847-688-0748   800-367-5653
www.merchinv.com
Manufacturer and exporter of point of purchase advertising display hardware components including mobile kits, ceiling fixtures, pole displays, banner hangers, shelf fixtures, display fasteners, etc
CEO: Ethan Berger
CFO: Diane Johnson
Vice President: Dan Jezierny
Quality Control: Aier Torres
Public Relations: Kay Berger
Operations Manager: Dan Jezierny
Production Manager: Jose Gayton
Plant Manager: Sue Kradwitz
Purchasing Manager: Sue Kradwitz
Estimated Sales: $12 Million
Number Employees: 20-49
Number of Products: 2000
Square Footage: 90000
Parent Co: DisplaWerks
Regions Exported to: Central America, South America, Asia, Canada, Latin America
Percentage of Business in Exporting: 8

46497 Merchandising Resources
2311 Thomas Street
Hollywood, FL 33020-2038   800-882-6693
Fax: 800-314-4814

46498 Merchandising Systems Manufacturing
2951 Whipple Rd
Union City, CA 94587-1207   650-324-8324
Fax: 650-324-4584   800-523-1468
Manufacturer and exporter of store displays and fixtures
President/Owner: Kyle Robinson
National Account Manager: Carol Sauceda
Contact: Kumar Gaurav
kumar@wireline.net
Estimated Sales: $ 5 - 10 Million
Number Employees: 20-49
Square Footage: 176000

46499 Merchants Export Inc
200 Dr Mlk Jr Blvd
Riviera Beach, FL 33404   561-844-7000
www.merchantsmarket.com
Exporter of juices, poultry, meats, seafood, cleaning supplies and fresh, canned and frozen fruits and vegetables; warehouse offering dry, cooler, humidity-controlled and freezer storage for produce, dairy items, meat products.
President & CEO: Terry Collier
terry.collier@merchantexport.com
Director, Accounting & Finance: Tom Homberger
Director, Sales: Steve Shoupp
Year Founded: 1967
Estimated Sales: $73.7 Million
Number Employees: 50-99
Number of Brands: 1000
Number of Products: 4000
Square Footage: 100000
Parent Co: Clare Holdings
Type of Packaging: Food Service
Brands Exported: Nugget
Regions Exported to: Caribbean

46500 Merchants Publishing Company
20 Mills St
Kalamazoo, MI 49048   269-345-1175
Fax: 269-345-6999
Labels, tags and folding cartons
President: M Jack Fleming
CFO: Dick Nagle
VP Sales / Marketing: Ben Behrman
National Sales Manager (Label Division): Frank Brady
Estimated Sales: $10-20 Million
Number Employees: 50-99
Regions Exported to: Worldwide

46501 Merci Spring Water
11570 Rock Island Ct
Maryland Heights, MO 63043-3522   314-872-9323
Fax: 314-872-9544
Processor and exporter of water including spring, purified and distilled; also, concentrated juices
President: Don Schneeberger

Estimated Sales: Under $500,000
Number Employees: 1-4
Square Footage: 90000
Brands Exported: Merci; Citrus Springs
Regions Exported to: Central America, Europe, Middle East
Percentage of Business in Exporting: 1

46502 Merco/Savory
980 South Isabella R
Mt. Pleasant, MI 48858   989-773-7981
Fax: 800-669-0619   800-733-8821
Manufacturer and exporter of rotisseries, broilers, toasters, hot dog grilling systems, convection, pizza and cookie ovens, heated display cases and food warmers
President: Stephen Whiteley
COO: Marion Antonini
Director Marketing: Barbara Wolf
Director Sales: Alan Oates
Number Employees: 250-499
Square Footage: 30000
Parent Co: ENODIS
Type of Packaging: Food Service
Regions Exported to: Central America, South America, Europe, Asia, Middle East
Percentage of Business in Exporting: 13

46503 Merco/Savory Equipment
1111 N Hadley Rd
Fort Wayne, IN 46804-5540   260-459-8200
Fax: 260-459-8240   www.lincolnfp.com
President: Stephen Whiteley
Contact: Dave Furge
dfurge@lincolnfp.com

46504 Mercury Equipment Company
15023 Sierra Bonita Lane
Chino, CA 91710-8902   909-606-8884
Fax: 909-606-8885   800-273-6688
Manufacturer and exporter of doughnut making equipment and bakery display cases and fixtures
President: Mike Campbell
Vice President: Joe Campbell
Estimated Sales: $ 1 - 3 Million
Number Employees: 6
Square Footage: 20000
Brands Exported: Hobart; Belshaw; DCA; Mercury
Regions Exported to: Central America, South America, Europe, Asia, Middle East
Percentage of Business in Exporting: 10

46505 Mercury Plastic Bag Company
168 7th St
Passaic, NJ 7055   973-778-7200
Fax: 973-778-0549
Polyethylene and polypropylene packaging bags
President: Marvin Rosen
VP Sales: Stuart Rosen
Estimated Sales: $5-10 Million
Number Employees: 20-49

46506 Meridian Nut Growers
1625 Shaw Ave
Clovis, CA 93611-4089   559-458-7272
Fax: 559-458-7270   jzion@meridiannut.com
www.meridiangrowers.com
Grower owned sales and marketing company supporting growers, processors, and buyers of California almonds, pistachios, walnuts, prunes, and raisins as well as South African macadamia nuts. In addition, they handle a full line of various dried fruit and nut products from origins around the world.
Managing Director: Jim Zion
jzion@meridiangrowers.com
Sales & Marketing: Michelle Carter
Sales Representative: Stacy Dovali
Customer Service Representative: Trisha Aranda
Chief Operations Officer: Mark Dutra
Accounting Manager: Julie Sawyer
Estimated Sales: $500,000-$1 Million
Number Employees: 10-19
Type of Packaging: Food Service, Private Label, Bulk
Brands Exported: A&P Growers
Regions Exported to: Worldwide
Percentage of Business in Exporting: 60

46507 Meridian Trading Co
1136 Pearl Street
Boulder, CO 80302   303-442-8683
Fax: 303-379-5199   info@meridiantrading.com
www.meridiantrading.com

Distribution of herbal products which includes extracts, teas, spices and medicinal herbs
President: David Black
Contact: Jesse Canizio
jesse@meridiantrading.com
Estimated Sales: $5 Million
Number Employees: 1-4

46508 Meritech
600 Corporate Circle
Suite H
Golden, CO 80401-5643   303-790-4670
Fax: 303-790-4859   800-932-7707
www.meritech.com
No-touch automated hygiene equipment to the food processing, food service, medical, cleanroom, daycare, school and prison industries.
President/CEO: Jim Glenn
Sales: Michele Colbert
Contact: Samantha Dill
samanthadill@wiradcom.com
Estimated Sales: $5-10 Million
Number Employees: 10-19
Square Footage: 40000
Type of Packaging: Food Service
Brands Exported: Chg 2%, Chg4%, Self Clean, Clean Tech, Pro Tech
Regions Exported to: Worldwide
Percentage of Business in Exporting: 3

46509 Merix Chemical Company
230 W Superior St
Chicago, IL 60654-3595   312-573-1400
Fax: 773-221-3047   www.marxsaunders.com
Manufacturer and exporter of anti-static coatings for polyethylene films; also, anti-fog coatings to prevent moisture and condensation on food display cases
Owner: Bonnie Marx
Manager: Z Blowret
Estimated Sales: $ 1 - 5 Million
Number Employees: 5-9
Square Footage: 6000
Brands Exported: Merix
Regions Exported to: Europe, Asia, Middle East, Australia, Canada, Mexico
Percentage of Business in Exporting: 28

46510 Merlin Candies
5635 Powell St
Harahan, LA 70123   504-733-5553
Fax: 504-733-5536   800-899-1549
Processor, importer and exporter of confectionery products including custom molded and sugar-free chocolates, seasonal candies and chocolate trolls
President: Jean La Hoste
VP: Mary Crowley
Contact: Raymond Brinson
rbrinson@merlincandies.com
Estimated Sales: $1 Million
Number Employees: 5-9
Type of Packaging: Consumer, Food Service, Private Label
Brands Exported: Merlin's
Regions Exported to: Central America, South America, Canada, Mexico
Percentage of Business in Exporting: 1
Brands Imported: Merlin's
Regions Imported from: Canada
Percentage of Business in Importing: 10

46511 Merlin Process Equipment
700 Louisiana St
Houston, TX 77002-2700   713-221-1651
Fax: 713-690-3353
Manufacturer and exporter of mixers
Estimated Sales: $300,000-500,000
Number Employees: 1-4
Regions Exported to: Worldwide

46512 Merlin-Montgomery Imports
3104 Central Avenue
Union City, NJ 07087-2403   201-865-3505
Fax: 201-865-1086
Wine
President: Maria Della Gala
Vice President: Alessandra Goodkin
Public Relations: Alessandra Goodkin
Type of Packaging: Private Label

46513 Mermaid Seafoods
Builder Street
Llandudno, GY LL30 1DDR   149-287-8014
Fax: 203-622-9415   800-367-6675
www.mermaidseafoods.co.uk

Importer and wholesaler/distributor of frozen fish including hoki, roughy, pollack, yellowfin sole and cod; wholesaler/distributor of equipment and fixtures and general merchandise
CEO/President: Erna Reingold
CFO: Maria Coro Gorriti
Operations Director: Joel Reingold
Estimated Sales: $ 3 - 5 Million
Number Employees: 5-9
Square Footage: 10000
Regions Exported to: Canada
Percentage of Business in Exporting: 10
Brands Imported: Mermaid
Regions Imported from: South America, Europe, Asia, Latin America
Percentage of Business in Importing: 80

46514 Mermaid Spice Corporation
5702 Corporation Cir
Fort Myers, FL 33905   239-693-1986
Fax: 239-693-2099
Processor and importer of herbs, spices, seasonings, salt substitutes, rices, soup bases and salad dressings; exporter of spices and soup bases; also, custom blending available
General Manager: Mike Asaad
Estimated Sales: $1-3 Million
Number Employees: 1-4
Square Footage: 72000
Type of Packaging: Food Service
Brands Exported: Mermaid Spice
Regions Exported to: Middle East, Worldwide
Percentage of Business in Exporting: 30
Regions Imported from: Europe, Asia, Worldwide
Percentage of Business in Importing: 40

46515 Merrill's Blueberry Farms
176 High Street
PO Box 149
Ellsworth, ME 04640-3141   207-667-9750
Fax: 207-667-4052 800-711-6551
merrblue@merrillwildblueberries.com
www.merrillwildblueberries.com
Wild blueberries
Estimated Sales: $ 1 - 3 Million
Number Employees: 10-19
Number of Brands: 1
Number of Products: 1
Square Footage: 200000
Type of Packaging: Private Label, Bulk
Brands Exported: Merrill's Wild IQF Blueberries
Regions Exported to: Europe, Asia, Middle East
Percentage of Business in Exporting: 5
Regions Imported from: Canada
Percentage of Business in Importing: 25

46516 Merritt Estate Winery Inc
2264 King Rd
Forestville, NY 14062-9703   716-965-4800
Fax: 716-965-4800 888-965-4800
nywines@merrittestatewinery.com
www.merrittestatewinery.com
Processor and exporter of table wines including red, white, rose, dry, sweet and sparkling
President: William T Merritt
Director of Marketing, Branding & Events: Michael J. Ferguson
Wholesale Sales: Mike Burkland
Manager: Jason Merritt
nywine@merritwestatewinery.com
Estimated Sales: $$1-2.5 Million
Number Employees: 1-4
Square Footage: 28000
Type of Packaging: Consumer, Food Service, Private Label
Brands Exported: Merritt
Regions Exported to: Caribbean

46517 Merritt Pecan Co
Highway 520
Weston, GA 31832   229-828-6610
Fax: 229-828-2061 800-762-9152
merritt@merritt-pecan.com
Processor and exporter of shelled and in-shell pecans
Owner: Tammy Merritt
merritt@merritt-pecan.com
President: Richard Merritt
Estimated Sales: $2 Million
Number Employees: 20-49
Square Footage: 54000
Type of Packaging: Consumer, Bulk

46518 Messermeister
418 Bryant Circle Suite A
Ojai, CA 93023   805-640-0051
Fax: 805-640-0053 800-426-5134
info@messermeister.com
Wholesaler/distributor and exporter of knives, scissors and cutting boards; importer of cutlery, knife luggage, tools, food torches.
President: Debra Dressler
Contact: Brian Amodio
bamodio@actionac.net
Estimated Sales: $3-5 Million
Number Employees: 10-19
Square Footage: 32000
Brands Exported: Messermeister
Regions Exported to: Central America, Europe, Australia, Canada
Brands Imported: Messermeister
Regions Imported from: Central America, Europe, Asia

46519 Messina Brothers Manufacturing Company
1065 Shepherd Avenue
Brooklyn, NY 11208-5713   718-345-9800
Fax: 718-345-2441 800-924-6454
Manufacturer, importer and wholesaler/distributor of mops, brooms and brushes
Sales Representative: Robert Messina
General Manager: Lawrence Mirro
Number Employees: 15
Square Footage: 90000
Parent Co: Howard Berger Company
Brands Imported: My Helper
Regions Imported from: Central America, South America, Europe, Pakistan

46520 Metabolic Nutrition
10450 W McNab Rd
Tamarac, FL 33321
800-626-1022
info@metabolicnutrition.com
www.metabolicnutrition.com
Processor and exporter of general and sports nutritional supplements
President/CEO: Murray Cohen
VP Marketing/CFO: Brian Cohen
VP/Sales: Jay Cohen
jay@metabolicnutrition.com
Estimated Sales: $1-2.5 Million
Number Employees: 5-9
Number of Products: 15
Square Footage: 56000
Type of Packaging: Private Label
Brands Exported: Advantage; Protizyme; Burners; Synedrex; Gainer; Recovery; Creative Phosphate
Regions Exported to: Europe

46521 Metafoods LLC
2970 Clairmont Rd NE # 510
Brookhaven, GA 30329-4418   404-843-2400
Fax: 404-843-1119 www.metafoodsllc.net
Frozen foods, beef, pork, poultry, frozen seafood, canned goods
President: Joe Wright
sales@metafoodsllc.com
CFO: Patricia Smith
Estimated Sales: $ 5 - 10 Million
Number Employees: 20-49

46522 Metal Equipment Company
600 Dover Center Rd
Cleveland, OH 44140-3310   440-835-3100
Fax: 440-835-1780 800-700-6326
Manufacturer, importer and exporter of custom metal industrial carts, storage racks, industrial bottle washers, waste management tanks, guards, platform trucks and pallet carriers
Manager: Bill Reilly
General Manager: Paul Drda
VP: Robert Walzer
Estimated Sales: Below $5 Million
Number Employees: 5-9
Square Footage: 110000
Brands Exported: Roll-a-bench
Regions Exported to: Canada
Percentage of Business in Exporting: 1
Regions Imported from: Canada
Percentage of Business in Importing: 1

46523 Metal Master Sales Corp
1159 N Main St
Glendale Heights, IL 60139-3509   630-858-4750
Fax: 630-858-4735 800-488-8729
sales@metalmaster.com www.metalmaster.com
Manufacturer and exporter of food processing equipment and parts, cabinets, hoods, trays, tables, sinks, carts, tableware, canopies, fixtures, art metal, serving lines, bartops and countertops, etc
Owner: Jim Jensen
jjensen@metalmaster.com
VP: Bob Lonrod
Estimated Sales: $ 2.5 - 5 Million
Number Employees: 10-19
Square Footage: 104000
Parent Co: Richards Manufacturing & Services Corporation
Regions Exported to: Central America, South America, Middle East
Percentage of Business in Exporting: 15

46524 Metaline Products Co Inc
101 N Feltus St
South Amboy, NJ 08879-1529   732-721-1373
Fax: 732-727-0272 sales@metalineproducts.com
www.metalineproducts.com
Manufacturer and exporter of wood, wire, plastic and corrugated display racks, shelving and point of purchase displays
President: Natalie Papailiou
natalie@mstudio.com
VP: August Zilincar
Estimated Sales: $2.5-5 Million
Number Employees: 20-49
Square Footage: 50000
Regions Exported to: Europe, Asia, Canada
Percentage of Business in Exporting: 2

46525 Metalloid Corp
504 Jackson St
Huntington, IN 46750   260-358-4610
Fax: 260-356-3201 800-686-3201
sales@metalloidcorp.com www.metalloidcorp.com
Manufacturer and exporter of cutting fluids, tapping compounds and hand cleaners
President: Gary Russ
gruss@metalloidcorp.com
VP Marketing: William Fair
Estimated Sales: $2.5-5 Million
Number Employees: 10-19

46526 Metlar Us
2248 Roanoke Ave
Riverhead, NY 11901-1822   631-252-5574
Fax: 828-253-7773 www.metlar-us.com
Manufacturer, importer and exporter of fine pore filters
Office Manager: Anne Ogg
Contact: Doreen Kula
dkula@metlar-us.com
Estimated Sales: $ 1 - 5 Million
Number Employees: 1-4
Parent Co: US Filter/Schumacher
Regions Exported to: Worldwide
Regions Imported from: Germany

46527 Metro Corporation
P.O. Box A
Wilkes Barre, PA 18705   570-825-2741
800-992-1776
www.intermetro.com
Supplier of food service storage, warehandling and transport solutions. The complete range of Metro products puts space to work in virtually avery area - cooler, freezer, dry storage, food preparation, catering and front of thehouse.
President & CEO: John Nackley
Vice President, Sales: Bill O'Donoghue
Year Founded: 1929
Estimated Sales: $100-500 Million
Number Employees: 1000-5000
Type of Packaging: Food Service

46528 Metropolitan Lighting Fixture Company
138 Bowery 2nd Floor
New York, NY 10013   212-545-0032
Fax: 212-545-0031 866-344-3875
customerservice@lightingnewyork.com
www.lightingnewyork.com
Importer of lighting fixtures
Manager: Joann Turits

Importers & Exporters / A-Z

Estimated Sales: $1-2.5 Million
Number Employees: 1-4
Square Footage: 24000
Parent Co: Minka Lavery
Brands Imported: Metropolitan Lighting Fixture Co.; Camer Glass Lighting; Minka-Lavery; Minka-Aire; Minka Great Outdoors
Regions Imported from: Europe, Asia
Percentage of Business in Importing: 100

46529 Mettler-Toledo Process Analytics, Inc
900 Middlesex Turnpike
Building 8
Billerica, MA 01821
800-352-8763
mtprous@mt.com www.mt.com/pro
Manufacturer, importer and exporter of process measurement equipment including pH and dissolved oxygen probes, transmitters and head space analyzers.
Head of Process Analytics Division: Gerry Keller
Estimated Sales: $10-20 Million
Number Employees: 50-99
Square Footage: 20000
Regions Exported to: Worldwide
Regions Imported from: Europe

46530 Mettler-Toledo SafelineInc
1571 Northpointe Pkwy
Lutz, FL 33558
800-638-8537
www.mt.com
Metal detectors and x-ray equipment for food products (including bulk, packed, liquid, slurry and powder) and for pharmaceutical products.
National Sales Manager: Oscar Jeter
Market Communications Specialist: Sarrina Crowley
Estimated Sales: $5 Million
Number Employees: 100-249
Square Footage: 276000
Brands Exported: Safeline
Regions Exported to: Central America, South America

46531 (HQ)Mettler-Toledo, LLC
1900 Polaris Pkwy
Columbus, OH 43240
800-638-8537
www.mt.com
Manufacturer and exporter of stainless steel scales and printing devices for processing applications including portion control, sorting, box weighing, shipping/receiving and in-motion weighing.
Chief Executive Officer: Olivier Filliol
olivier.filliol@mt.com
Chief Financial Officer: Shawn Vadala
Head of Supply Chain & IT: Oliver Wittorf
Head of Divisions & Operations: Peter Aggersbjerg
Head of Process Analytics Division: Gerry Keller
Head of Industrial Division: Elena Markwalder
Head of Product Inspection Division: Jonas Greutert
Head of Human Resources: Christian Magloth
Year Founded: 1946
Estimated Sales: Over $2 Billion
Number Employees: 10,000
Brands Exported: Mettler Toledo
Regions Exported to: Central America, South America, Europe, Asia
Percentage of Business in Exporting: 20

46532 Metz Premiums
250 W 57th St # 25
New York, NY 10107-0001
212-315-4660
Fax: 212-541-4559 metzpremiums@yahoo.com
Manufacturer and importer of uniforms; also advertising specialties including metal pins and key rings, tote bags, picture frames and ceramic products
VP Sales: Laurie Zelen
Purchasing Manager: Gerry Kroll
Estimated Sales: less than $ 500,000
Number Employees: 1-4
Regions Imported from: Asia, China
Percentage of Business in Importing: 90

46533 Metzgar Conveyors
901 Metzgar Dr NW
Comstock Park, MI 49321-9758
616-784-0930
Fax: 616-784-4100 888-266-8390
sales@metzgarconveyors.com
Manufacturer and exporter of conveyors and package and pallet handling systems
President: D R Metzgar
dr.metzgar@metzgarconveyor.com
VP: Roger Scholten
R & D: Tom Dewey
Marketing: Roger Schotten
Production: Jon Goeman
Purchasing Manager: David Stevens
Estimated Sales: $10 Million
Number Employees: 50-99
Square Footage: 100000
Regions Exported to: Central America, South America, Europe
Percentage of Business in Exporting: 15

46534 Metzger Popcorn Co
24197 Road U20
Delphos, OH 45833-9343
419-692-2494
Fax: 419-692-0890 800-819-6072
mail@metzgerpopcorn.com
www.metzgerpopcorn.com
Processor and exporter of popcorn
Owner: Bob Metzger
b.metzger@metzgerpopcorn.com
Estimated Sales: Less Than $500,000
Number Employees: 1-4
Square Footage: 40000
Type of Packaging: Consumer, Food Service, Private Label, Bulk
Brands Exported: Mello-Krisp
Regions Exported to: Central America, South America, Europe, Asia, Middle East, Canada
Percentage of Business in Exporting: 20

46535 Mexi-Frost Specialties Company
37 Grand Avenue
Brooklyn, NY 11205-1309
718-625-3324
Fax: 718-852-8699
Frozen West Indian, Mexican, Caribbean, Chinese and Italian foods including chicken, meat pies, tamales, burritos, egg rolls
President: Gonzalo Armendariz Jr
VP: Gonzalo Armendariz, Jr.
VP Sales: Mark Armendariz
Plant Manager: Gonzaol Armendariz, Jr.
Estimated Sales: $ 5 - 10 Million
Number Employees: 20-49
Type of Packaging: Consumer, Food Service, Private Label, Bulk
Brands Exported: MEXI-FROST
Regions Exported to: South America, Europe, Asia, Middle East
Percentage of Business in Exporting: 35

46536 Mexican Accent
16675 W Glendale Dr
New Berlin, WI 53151
262-784-4422
Fax: 262-784-5810
Processor and exporter of flour and corn tortillas; processor of tortilla chips; private labeling available
President: Mike Maglio
Contact: Steve Carew
scarew@mexicanaccent.com
Estimated Sales: $13 Million
Number Employees: 150
Square Footage: 240000
Type of Packaging: Consumer, Food Service, Private Label, Bulk
Brands Exported: Manny's
Regions Exported to: Europe, Asia, Middle East
Percentage of Business in Exporting: 5

46537 Meximex Texas Corporation
48 La Costa Drive
Montgomery, TX 77356-5325
210-582-4642
Fax: 210-582-4639
Importer and exporter of canned sardines, squid and abalone; also, tequila and potato sticks
President: Julio Fernandez
Director: Julio Fernandez
VP: Gabriela Valdez
Number Employees: 1-4
Parent Co: Merimex San Diego
Brands Exported: Deon Chenio; Marimar; Classic; Tequila Atalaje; Tequila Coronel
Regions Exported to: Latin America
Percentage of Business in Exporting: 80
Brands Imported: Don Chenio; Marimar; Classic; Tequila Atalaje; Tequila Coronel
Regions Imported from: Latin America
Percentage of Business in Importing: 20

46538 Mexspice
PO Box 3336
S El Monte, CA 91733-0336
626-579-1276
Fax: 626-579-1276
Wholesaler/distributor of fava, garbanzo and pinto beans, dry chili pods, paprika, garlic, black pepper, seasoning salt, rice, etc.; importer of Mexican, Indian and Japanese foods including spices and rice
President: Octano Kelly
VP: Marco Kelly
Number Employees: 10-19
Square Footage: 329528
Type of Packaging: Bulk
Regions Imported from: Mexico, China, Japan, Sri-Lanka, Sudan

46539 Meyenberg Goat Milk
PO Box 934
Turlock, CA 95381
800-891-4628
info@meyenberg.com meyenberg.com
Goat milk
President: Robert Jackson
CFO: Doug Buehrle
Vice President: Carol Jackson
COO/Marketing: Tracy Plante-Darrimon
Plant Manager: Frank Fillman
Estimated Sales: $18-20 Million
Number Employees: 50
Number of Products: 25
Type of Packaging: Consumer, Bulk
Regions Exported to: Central America, South America, Asia, Canada, Caribbean
Percentage of Business in Exporting: 10

46540 Meyer Label Company
15143 Winkler Rd
Fort Myers, FL 33919
239-489-0342
Fax: 201-894-8867
Manufacturer and exporter of pressure sensitive and roll labels
Owner: Kurt Meyer
VP Sales: Bob Reineke
Estimated Sales: $2.5-5 Million
Number Employees: 1-4
Square Footage: 50000
Regions Exported to: Worldwide
Percentage of Business in Exporting: 10

46541 Meyer Machine & Garroutte Products
3528 Fredericksburg Rd.
P.O.Box 5460
San Antonio, TX 78201-0460
210-736-1811
Fax: 210-736-4662 Sales@meyer-industries.com
www.meyer-industries.com
Manufacturer and exporter of belt and vibratory conveyors and feeders, pivoting bucket elevators, spiral lowerators, fryers, broilers, ovens, live bottom and bin storage and food seasoning equipment.
President: Eugene Teeter
Quality Control and CFO: Larry Marek
North & South Central Regional Sales Mgr: Roland Metivier
Northeast/Southeast Regional Sales Mgr: Scott Carter
Western Regional Sales Mgr: Jim Lassiter
VP Manufacturing: Carroll Fries
Estimated Sales: $ 10 - 20 Million
Number Employees: 50-99
Square Footage: 200000
Parent Co: Meyer Industries
Other Locations:
  Meyer Machine Co.
  West MidlandsMeyer Machine Co.
Regions Exported to: Central America, South America, Europe, Middle East, Canada, Mexico, Latin America
Percentage of Business in Exporting: 5

46542 Mia Rose Products
177 Riverside Ave Ste F
Newport Beach, CA 92663
714-662-5465
Fax: 714-662-5891 800-615-2767
Manufacturer and exporter of natural, biodegradable air fresheners, deodorizing mists and home cleaners made with real citrus
President/CEO: Mia Rose
Marketing/Sales: Carolena Hidalgo
Contact: Carmen Arzate
c.arzate@morrisrose.com

Estimated Sales: $2 Million
Number Employees: 10-19
Square Footage: 8000
Type of Packaging: Consumer, Private Label
Brands Exported: Air Therapy; Citri-Glow; Pet Air; Doggy Sudz
Regions Exported to: Europe

46543 Miami Beef Co
4870 NW 157th St
Miami Lakes, FL 33014-6486   305-621-3252
Fax: 305-620-4562 info@miamibeef.com
Steaks, hamburgers, meat, beef, chicken, lamb, pork, sausage, roast beef, veal, prime rib, patties, stew, sirlion, tenderloim, soy, ground beef, breaded, cooked, hoagie, palomolla, pepper, salisbury, t-bone, sliced sandwich sirloinskirt steak, cubed steak, filet mignon
President: Michael Young
miamibeef@bellsouth.net
Head Sales: Barry Dean
Plant Manager: Russ Milina
Estimated Sales: $10.8 Million
Number Employees: 50-99
Type of Packaging: Consumer, Food Service, Private Label, Bulk
Brands Exported: Miami Beef
Regions Exported to: Central America, Caribbean
Percentage of Business in Exporting: 50

46544 Miami Coffee Imports
618 Coral Way
Suite 505
Coral Gables, FL 33134-7501   305-448-2735
Fax: 305-448-0123
Coffee Imports
President: Carlos Knoepffler, Jr.
Estimated Sales: $5-10 Million
Number Employees: 1-4

46545 Miami Depot Inc
2915 W Okeechobee Rd
Hialeah, FL 33012-4596   305-884-1303
Fax: 305-887-5038
Exporter of dry foods, cleaning products, paper, etc.; wholesaler/distributor of closeout and salvage groceries
President: Robert Halsey
CFO: John Antiieau
VP Retail: Margaret Halsey
Estimated Sales: Less Than $500,000
Number Employees: 1-4
Square Footage: 81000
Regions Exported to: Central America, South America
Percentage of Business in Exporting: 35

46546 Miami Foods & Products
999 Ponce De Leon Boulevard
Coral Gables, FL 33134-3000   305-460-2995
Fax: 305-460-2996
Instant tea, soluble in cold water, instant coffee, green coffee beans
President: Horacio Feraud
VP Marketing: Pablo Ontaneda
Estimated Sales: $7 Million
Number Employees: 5-9

46547 Miami Metal
255 NW 25th Street
Miami, FL 33127-4329   305-576-3600
Fax: 305-576-2339
Manufacturer and exporter of chairs, cushions, pads, table legs and bases and booths
Sales Manager: Carol Sieger
Estimated Sales: $20-50 Million
Number Employees: 100-249
Type of Packaging: Food Service
Regions Exported to: Worldwide
Percentage of Business in Exporting: 15

46548 (HQ)Miami Purveyors Inc
7350 NW 8th St
Miami, FL 33126-2922   305-262-6170
Fax: 305-262-6174 800-966-6328
www.miamipurveyors.com
Manuafacturer and exporter of frozen foods including beef, pork, ham, poultry, seafood, fruits and vegetables
Owner: Rick Rothenberg
rick@miamipurveyors.com
Chief Financial Officer: Kaly Rosenberg
Estimated Sales: $14.1 Million
Number Employees: 50-99

Type of Packaging: Food Service
Regions Exported to: Central America, South America

46549 Micelli Chocolate Mold Company
135 Dale St
West Babylon, NY 11704   631-752-2888
Fax: 631-752-2885 micelliusa@aol.com
www.micelli.com
Manufacturer and exporter of plastic and metal molds for chocolate products
President: Joseph Micelli
Vice President: John Micelli
Sales Director: John Micelli
Contact: Mike Daly
mike_daly@micelli.com
Plant Manager: John Micelli
Estimated Sales: $3-5 Million
Number Employees: 10-19
Square Footage: 20000
Regions Exported to: South America, Europe, Canada
Percentage of Business in Exporting: 20
Regions Imported from: Europe
Percentage of Business in Importing: 5

46550 Michael Foods, Inc.
301 Carlson Pkwy.
Suite 400
Minnetonka, MN 55305   952-258-4000
info@michaelfoods.com
www.michaelfoods.com
Processed egg and potato products.
President: Mark Westphal
Year Founded: 1987
Estimated Sales: $1.5 Billion
Number Employees: 3,500
Number of Brands: 6
Type of Packaging: Consumer, Food Service, Private Label, Bulk
Other Locations:
   Michael Foods
   Minneapolis, MNMichael Foods
Regions Exported to: Central America, South America, Europe, Asia
Percentage of Business in Exporting: 20

46551 Michael Leson Dinnerware
P.O.Box 5368
Youngstown, OH 44514   330-726-4788
Fax: 330-726-2274 800-821-3541
www.americanrails.com
Manufacturer, exporter and importer of dinnerware, flatware, glassware, mugs, plate covers, platters, premiums, incentives, salt and pepper shakers, etc
CEO: Michael Leson
Estimated Sales: $500,000-$1,000,000
Number Employees: 1-4
Parent Co: MLD Group
Regions Exported to: Worldwide
Regions Imported from: Worlwide

46552 Michael's Cookies
2205 6th Ave. S
Clear Lake, IA 50428   641-454-5577
Fax: 641-954-5451 800-822-5384
info@michaelscookies.com
www.michaelscookies.com
Frozen pre-portioned cookie doughs
COO/CFO: Scott Summeril
Quality Assurance: Myrkantra Dorlean
SVP Sales: Don Smith
Estimated Sales: $ 20 - 50 Million
Number Employees: 20-49
Number of Brands: 1
Number of Products: 1
Square Footage: 30000
Type of Packaging: Food Service, Private Label, Bulk
Brands Exported: Bonzers
Regions Exported to: South America, Europe, Asia, Mexico
Percentage of Business in Exporting: 10

46553 Michaelo Espresso
309 S Cloverdale St # D22
Ste D22
Seattle, WA 98108-4572   206-695-4950
Fax: 206-695-4951 800-545-2883
info@michaelo.com
Kiosks, carts and vending equipment; importer and wholesaler/distributor of espresso and granita machinery and panini grills; serving the food service market

President: Michael Myers
info@michaelo.com
General Manager: Russ Myers
National Sales Manager: Douglas Pratt
Estimated Sales: $5-10 Million
Number Employees: 10-19
Square Footage: 40000
Type of Packaging: Food Service
Brands Imported: Elmeco; Aristarco
Regions Imported from: Italy,Switzerland
Percentage of Business in Importing: 60

46554 Michelle Chocolatiers
122 N Tejon Street
Colorado Springs, CO 80903-1406   719-633-5089
Fax: 719-633-8970 888-447-3654
Processor, importer and exporter of ice creams and candy including chocolates and gold coins
VP: Jim Michopoulos
Estimated Sales: $ 5-10 Million
Number Employees: 20-49
Type of Packaging: Consumer, Private Label
Regions Exported to: Worldwide
Regions Imported from: Worldwide
Percentage of Business in Importing: 35

46555 (HQ)Michiana Box & Crate
2193 Industrial Dr
Niles, MI 49120-1254   269-683-6372
Fax: 269-684-7860 800-677-6372
www.kampsinc.com
GMA and can pallets, bulk bins, export boxes, crates and skids; exporter of bulk bins
President: Gary Cehovic
CEO: Thomas Kiehl
CFO: Dan Searfoss
Production Manager: Bog Modlin
Estimated Sales: $27 Million
Number Employees: 100-249
Number of Products: 205
Square Footage: 76000
Type of Packaging: Bulk
Regions Exported to: Canada
Percentage of Business in Exporting: 15

46556 (HQ)Michigan Agricultural Commdty
445 N Canal Rd
Lansing, MI 48917   517-627-0200
Fax: 517-627-3510 800-878-8900
info@michag.com www.michag.com
Exporter and wholesaler/distributor of sunflower seeds, grains and soybeans.
President: Dave Geers
davegerrs@agcommodites.com
Merchandising Manager: Robert Geers
Estimated Sales: $20-50 Million
Number Employees: 10-19
Brands Exported: Mac King
Regions Exported to: Canada
Percentage of Business in Exporting: 5

46557 Michigan Agricultural Commodities Inc
10894 E US 223
Blissfield, MI 49228   517-486-2171
Fax: 517-486-2173 800-344-7246
www.michag.com
Exporter and wholesaler/distributor of sunflower seeds, grains and soybeans.
Facility Manager: Noel Eisenmann
Number Employees: 10-19
Regions Exported to: Canada
Percentage of Business in Exporting: 5

46558 Michigan Agriculture Commodities
1601 N Mitchell Rd
Cadillac, MI 49601   989-236-7263
800-344-7263
www.michag.com
Exporter and wholesaler/distributor of sunflower seeds, grains and soybeans.
Northern Michigan Representative: Wes Edington
Number Employees: 10-19
Regions Exported to: Canada
Percentage of Business in Exporting: 5

Importers & Exporters / A-Z

46559 Michigan Agriculture Commodities
216 Eastman St
Breckridge, MI 48615   989-842-3104
Fax: 989-842-3108 800-472-4629
www.michag.com
Exporter and wholesaler/distributor of sunflower seeds, grains and soybeans.
Branch Manager: Adam Geers
Office Manager: Pam Thebo
Number Employees: 10-19
Regions Exported to: Canada
Percentage of Business in Exporting: 5

46560 Michigan Agriculture Commodities
7115 Maple Valley Rd
Brown City, MI 48416   810-346-2711
Fax: 810-346-4719 800-851-1448
www.michag.com
Exporter and wholesaler/distributor of sunflower seeds, grains and soybeans.
Branch Manager: Chuck Kunisch
Location Manager: Joe Berry
Number Employees: 10-19
Regions Exported to: Canada
Percentage of Business in Exporting: 5

46561 Michigan Agriculture Commodities
1050 Ogden St
Jasper, MI 49248   517-436-3126
Fax: 517-436-3782 www.michag.com
Exporter and wholesaler/distributor of sunflower seeds, grains and soybeans.
Branch Manager: Noel Eisenmann
Facility Manager: Jess Strahan
Number Employees: 10-19
Regions Exported to: Canada
Percentage of Business in Exporting: 5

46562 Michigan Agriculture Commodities
3346 Main St
Marlette, MI 48453   989-635-3578
Fax: 989-635-2951 800-647-4628
www.michag.com
Exporter and wholesaler/distributor of sunflower seeds, grains and soybeans.
Branch Manager: Chuck Kunisch
Office Manager: Jenny St. George
Number Employees: 10-19
Regions Exported to: Canada
Percentage of Business in Exporting: 5

46563 Michigan Agriculture Commodities
306 N Caroline
Middleton, MI 48856   989-236-7263
Fax: 989-236-7716 800-344-7263
www.michag.com
Exporter and wholesaler/distributor of sunflower seeds, grains and soybeans.
Branch Manager: John Ezinga
Number Employees: 10-19
Regions Exported to: Canada
Percentage of Business in Exporting: 5

46564 Michigan Agriculture Commodities
103 Water St
Newaygo, MI 49337   231-652-6017
Fax: 231-652-3811 800-878-5800
www.michag.com
Exporter and wholesaler/distributor of sunflower seeds, grains and soybeans.
Branch Manager: Mitchell Murray
Number Employees: 10-19
Regions Exported to: Canada
Percentage of Business in Exporting: 5

46565 (HQ)Michigan Box Co
1910 Trombly St
Detroit, MI 48211-2130   313-873-8084
Fax: 313-873-8084 888-642-4269
info@michiganbox.com www.michiganbox.com
Manufacturer and exporter of corrugated and pizza boxes, point of purchase displays, crates and pallets; also, custom printed and corrugated carry-out food containers available
President: Elaine Fontana
efontana@michiganbox.com
Sales Manager: Scott Keech
Operations: Ralph Betzler
Estimated Sales: $ 10-20 Million
Number Employees: 50-99
Square Footage: 400000
Other Locations:
  Michigan Box Co.
  Detroit, MI Michigan Box Co.
Regions Exported to: Canada, Mexico
Percentage of Business in Exporting: 2

46566 Michigan Brush Mfg Co
7446 Central St
Detroit, MI 48210-1037   313-834-1070
Fax: 313-834-1178 800-642-7874
sales@mi-brush.com www.michiganbrush.com
Manufacturer and exporter of brushes, brooms, mops, and paint rollers, also squeegees for food processing and food services.
President: Bruce Gale
mmfgcoinc@aol.com
CFO: Bruse Gale
Estimated Sales: $ 1 - 3 Million
Number Employees: 10-19
Number of Brands: 4
Number of Products: 1001
Square Footage: 220000
Type of Packaging: Private Label, Bulk
Brands Exported: All Products

46567 Michigan Desserts
10750 Capital St
Oak Park, MI 48237-3134   248-544-4574
Fax: 248-544-4384 800-328-8632
sales@midasfoods.com www.midasfoods.com
Sweet dry mix items
President: Richard Elias
relias@midasfoods.com
Sr VP Sales/Marketing: Gary Freeman
Estimated Sales: $7 Million
Number Employees: 20-49
Square Footage: 180000
Parent Co: Midas Foods India
Type of Packaging: Consumer, Food Service, Private Label, Bulk
Brands Exported: Private
Regions Exported to: Central America, South America, Asia, Middle East
Percentage of Business in Exporting: 5

46568 Michigan Freeze Pack
835 S. Griswold
P.O.Box 30
Hart, MI 49420   231-873-2175
Fax: 231-873-3025
msutton@michiganfreezepack.com
www.michiganfreezepack.com
Processor and exporter of asparagus, zucchini squash, celery, broccoli, peppers, carrots and eggplant
President: Gary Dennert
VP Sales/Finance: John Ritche
Contact: Ray Drum
rdrum@michiganfreezepack.com
Production Manager: Ronald Clark
Estimated Sales: $1 Million
Number Employees: 10
Square Footage: 400000
Type of Packaging: Food Service, Bulk
Regions Exported to: Canada
Percentage of Business in Exporting: 5

46569 Michigan Maple Block Co
1420 Standish Ave
Petoskey, MI 49770-3049   231-347-4170
Fax: 231-347-7975 800-447-7975
mmb@mapleblock.com www.butcherblock.com
Manufacturer, importer and exporter of cutting boards, tabletops, carving boards and preparation and bakery tables
President: James Reichart
VP Sales & Marketing: Pat Stanley
VP Sales/Marketing: Russell Foth
Estimated Sales: $5-10 Million
Number Employees: 50-99
Parent Co: Bally Block Company
Type of Packaging: Food Service
Brands Exported: Wood Welded
Regions Exported to: Central America, Europe, Asia, Middle East

46570 Micosa Inc
3415 N Kennicott Ave # C
Arlington Hts, IL 60004-7819   847-632-1200
Fax: 847-632-1217 www.micosafoods.com
Import broker of seafood and meats including pork and poultry
President: J Goldman
Commodity Sales Manager: B Anderson
VP/Sales Manager: J Cchudik
Estimated Sales: $2.5-5 Million
Number Employees: 5-9

46571 Micro Matic
19761 Bahama St
Northridge, CA 91324   818-701-9765
Fax: 818-341-9501 sac@micro-matic.com
www.micro-matics.com
Manufactures liquid transfer valves and related equipment
President: Peter Muzzcnigro
CFO: Jim Motush
Sales Manager: Barry Broughton
Contact: Allen Cossairt
allen@micro-matics.com
Estimated Sales: $ 20 - 50 Million
Number Employees: 50-99
Parent Co: Micro Matic AIS
Type of Packaging: Bulk

46572 Micro Wire Products Inc
120 N Main St
Brockton, MA 02301-3911   508-584-0200
Fax: 508-584-1188 jwmwp@aol.com
www.microwire-products.com
Manufacturer and importer of welded wire baskets, store displays and fixtures and dishwasher and tray racks
Owner: Jeff Weafer
jwmwp@aol.com
Controller: Linda Weaver
Treasurer: Arnold Wilson
Estimated Sales: $ 5 - 10 Million
Number Employees: 20-49
Square Footage: 280000
Regions Imported from: Asia, Canada
Percentage of Business in Importing: 50

46573 Micro-Brush Pro Soap
1830 E Interstate 30
Rockwall, TX 75087-6241   972-722-1161
Fax: 972-722-1584 800-776-7627
www.prosoap.com
Manufacturer and exporter of hand cleaning scrubs and pastes for removing inks, food coloring and food odors; also, soap dispensers
President: Scott L Self
VP Operations: James Wilkins, III
Estimated Sales: $10-20 Million
Number Employees: 5-9
Square Footage: 36000
Parent Co: Texas Nova-Chem Corporation
Type of Packaging: Food Service
Regions Exported to: Central America, Europe, Asia, Canada
Percentage of Business in Exporting: 20

46574 Micro-Strain
291 Stony Run Rd
Spring City, PA 19475   610-948-4550
Manufacturer and exporter of digital and analog electronic measuring systems and devices including scales and weighing systems
President: Rolf Jespersen
Estimated Sales: Less than $500,000
Number Employees: 1-4
Square Footage: 10000

46575 MicroSoy Corporation
300 Microsoy Dr
Jefferson, IA 50129   515-386-2100
Fax: 515-386-3287
Processor and exporter of microsoy flakes used in soy milk, tofu and other soy based foods
President/CEO: Terry Tanaka
CFO: Mike Mumma
Estimated Sales: $3.5 Million
Number Employees: 15
Square Footage: 115200
Parent Co: Mycal Corporation
Type of Packaging: Bulk
Brands Exported: Microsoy Flakes
Regions Exported to: Europe, Asia, Canada
Percentage of Business in Exporting: 90

Importers & Exporters / A-Z

46576 MicroThermics, Inc.
3216-B Wellington Ct
Raleigh, NC 27615   919-878-8045
   Fax: 919-878-8032 info@microthermics.com
                www.microthermics.com
Manufacturer and exporter of laboratory and food processing equipment for pasteurization and aseptic purposes.
President: John Miles
Executive Vice President: David Miles
VP Sales, Marketing, Business Operations: David Miles
Estimated Sales: $5-10 Million
Other Locations: MicroThermics Minature Plant
Regions Exported to: Worldwide
Percentage of Business in Exporting: 50

46577 Microbest Inc
670 Captain Neville Dr # 1
Waterbury, CT 06705-3855   203-597-0355
   Fax: 203-597-0655 800-426-4246
               www.microbest.com
Manufacturer and exporter of cleaning supplies and equipment including microbial floor cleaners, degreasers, treatment products, etc
President: Ed Mc Nerney
emcnerney@microbest.com
CEO: Michael Troup
VP Sales/Marketing: Gary Garavaglin
Estimated Sales: $ 1 - 5 Million
Number Employees: 50-99
Brands Exported: Microbest Bio Cleansing Systems
Regions Exported to: Central America, South America, Europe, Asia
Percentage of Business in Exporting: 50

46578 Microcide Inc
2209 Niagara Dr
Troy, MI 48083-5933   248-526-9663
   Fax: 248-526-9663 www.microcide.com
President: John Lopes
microcide@gmail.com
Estimated Sales: $ 3 - 5 Million
Number Employees: 10-19

46579 Microdry
5901 W Highway 22
Crestwood, KY 40014-7217   502-241-8933
   Fax: 502-241-5907 engineering@microdry.com
              www.nemeth-engineering.com
Manufacturer and exporter of industrial microwaves
Owner: Peter Nemeth
info@nemethengineering.com
Systems Specialist: Mark Isgryg
Plant Manager: Herb Bullis
Estimated Sales: $2.5-5 Million
Number Employees: 20-49
Square Footage: 100000
Regions Exported to: Worldwide
Percentage of Business in Exporting: 15

46580 Microfluidics International
90 Glacier Dr # 1000
Suite 1000
Westwood, MA 02090-1818   617-969-5452
   Fax: 617-965-1213 800-370-5452
              www.microfluidicscorp.com
Manufacturer and exporter of high pressure mixing equipment for processing emulsions, dispersions, liposomes, particle size reduction, deagglomeration, high end food, flavorings and colorants
President: Robert Bruno
CEO: Irwin Gruverman
Controller: Dennis Riordan
Marketing Communications Manager: Wendy Rogalinski
Number Employees: 20-49
Square Footage: 60000
Brands Exported: Microfluidizer Processing Equipment
Regions Exported to: South America, Europe, Asia, Middle East
Percentage of Business in Exporting: 40

46581 Micromeritics
4356 Communications Dr
Norcross, GA 30093-2901   770-638-7569
   Fax: 770-662-3696 www.micromeritics.com
Manufacturer and exporter of analytical instruments for production and process control application
President: Preston Hendrix
Estimated Sales: $ 20-50 Million
Number Employees: 100-249

Type of Packaging: Bulk
Regions Exported to: Worldwide

46582 Microplas Industries
2364 Brookhurst Dr
Dunwoody, GA 30338   770-234-0600
   Fax: 770-234-0601 800-952-4528
Manufacturer and importer of polyethylene shrink film and black conductive and antistat LDPE and HDPE bags
President: John J Cawley
Estimated Sales: Below $ 500,000
Number Employees: 1-4
Square Footage: 10000
Regions Imported from: Asia
Percentage of Business in Importing: 30

46583 Micropoint
1077 Independence Ave # B
Mountain View, CA 94043-1601   650-969-3097
   Fax: 650-969-2067 www.microfit.com
Manufacturer, importer and exporter of writing and marking pens
President: Paul Vodak
Estimated Sales: less than $ 500,000
Number Employees: 1-4
Regions Exported to: Canada
Percentage of Business in Exporting: 3
Regions Imported from: Asia

46584 Micropub Systems International
10 Milford Rd
Rochester, NY 14625   585-385-3990
   Fax: 585-385-4387 www.micropub.com
Manufacturer and exporter of beer brewing systems; processor of brewing ingredients
Manager: Barb Smith
Estimated Sales: Below $ 500,000
Number Employees: 10-19
Square Footage: 80000
Brands Exported: Micropub
Regions Exported to: Worldwide
Percentage of Business in Exporting: 30

46585 Micropure Filtration Inc
1100 Game Farm Cir
Mound, MN 55364-7900   952-472-2323
   Fax: 952-472-0105 800-654-7873
tsenney@micropure.com www.micropure.com
Manufacturer, importer and exporter of food and beverage filtration and regulating devices including segmented stainless steel, cartridge, air, processing, sampler, trap filter removers and air filters, culinary steam.
President: Trey Senney
Estimated Sales: Less Than $500,000
Number Employees: 1-4
Square Footage: 4000
Brands Exported: Glas-Flo; Mem-Pure; Micro-Pure; Pro-Flo; Sulfur Guard; Segma-Flo; Segma-Pure
Regions Exported to: Central America, South America, Europe, Asia, Mexico, Canada
Percentage of Business in Exporting: 20
Brands Imported: Segma-Flo; Segma-Pure
Regions Imported from: Europe
Percentage of Business in Importing: 80

46586 Microtechnologies
123 Whiting St. Ste 1A
Plainville, CT 6062   860-829-2710
   Fax: 860-516-1549 888-248-7103
             support@temperatureguard.com
                www.temperatureguard.com
Manufacturer and exporter of HVAC controls
President: Frank Geissler
Estimated Sales: Below $ 5,000,000
Number Employees: 5-9
Square Footage: 8000
Regions Exported to: China , Mexico
Percentage of Business in Exporting: 15

46587 Mid Valley Nut Co
2065 Geer Rd
PO Box 987
Hughson, CA 95326-9614   209-883-4491
   Fax: 209-883-2435 info@midvalleynut.com
                www.midvalleynut.com
Processor and importer of walnuts
President: Regina Arnold
mheskin@belkorpag.com
Sales: Mary Valdez
Production Manager: Billy Casazza

Estimated Sales: $4.6 Million
Number Employees: 100-249
Type of Packaging: Consumer, Private Label, Bulk
Regions Imported from: Worldwide
Percentage of Business in Importing: 50

46588 Mid West Quality GlovesInc
835 Industrial Rd
Chillicothe, MO 64601-3218   660-646-2165
   Fax: 660-646-6933 800-821-3028
                www.midwestglove.com
Manufacturer and exporter of work, garden and sports protective gloves
Chairman of the Board: Stephen Franke
sfranke@midwestglove.com
Marketing Manager: Shirley Fisher
Sales Manager: Clark Carlton
Estimated Sales: $20-50 Million
Number Employees: 100-249
Regions Exported to: Worldwide
Percentage of Business in Exporting: 5

46589 Mid-Atlantic Foods Inc
8978 Glebe Park Dr
Easton, MD 21601-7004   410-822-7500
   Fax: 410-822-1266 800-922-4688
             sales@seaclam.com www.seaclam.com
Canned and frozen clams and seafood chowders, sauces and soups, clam juice
President: Bob Brennan
CEO: Steve Gordon
Marketing Director: Brian Shea
Contact: Betty Bain
bbain@seaclam.com
Estimated Sales: Less Than $500,000
Number Employees: 10-19
Square Footage: 33000
Type of Packaging: Consumer, Food Service, Private Label
Brands Exported: Mid-Atlantic
Regions Exported to: Central America, Asia, Canada
Percentage of Business in Exporting: 5

46590 Mid-Lands Chemical Company
1202 S 11th St
Omaha, NE 68108-3611   402-346-8352
   Fax: 402-346-7694 800-642-5263
   orders@midlandsci.com www.midlandsci.com
Manufacturer and exporter of ice packs
Account Manager: Brian Plautz
Operations Manager: Matt Sutej
Estimated Sales: $1-2,500,000
Number Employees: 10-19
Type of Packaging: Food Service, Private Label
Regions Exported to: Worldwide
Percentage of Business in Exporting: 5

46591 Mid-Pacific Hawaii Fishery
Old Airport Road
Hilo, HI 96720   808-935-6110
                Fax: 808-961-6859
Processor and exporter of fresh tuna, marlin and shark
Owner: John Romero
Estimated Sales: $ 2.5-5 Million
Number Employees: 7
Type of Packaging: Consumer, Food Service
Regions Exported to: Japan

46592 Mid-States Mfg & Engr Co Inc
509 E Maple St
PO Box 100
Milton, IA 52570-9636   641-656-4271
   Fax: 641-656-4225 800-346-1792
                www.mid-states1.com
Manufacturer and exporter of steel shipping containers, hand and platform trucks and nonpowered material handling equipment
Cio/Cto: Kevin Early
kevinearly@mid-states1.com
COO: Kevin Early
Purchasing Director: Suzie Lister
Estimated Sales: $ 5 Million
Number Employees: 20-49
Square Footage: 280000
Type of Packaging: Bulk
Regions Exported to: Worldwide
Percentage of Business in Exporting: 5

447

Importers & Exporters / A-Z

46593 Mid-West Wire Products
800 Woodward Hts
Ferndale, MI 48220-1488   248-548-3200
Fax: 248-542-7104 800-989-9881
schargo@midwestwire.com
Manufacturer and exporter of wire baskets and specialties including display, transporter and merchandising trays
President: Richard Geralds
VP: Steven Chargo
Vice President: Christopher Wozniacki
cwozniacki@midwestwires.com
VP Sales: Steven Chargo
VP Manufacturing: William Klein
Estimated Sales: $ 5 - 10 Million
Number Employees: 20-49
Regions Exported to: Canada

46594 Mid-Western Enterprises
P.O.Box 621
Oak Lawn, IL 60454   708-430-5990
Fax: 708-430-8120
Importer olive oil, domestic dairy

46595 Midamar
1105 60th Ave SW
Cedar Rapids, IA 52404-7212   319-362-3711
Fax: 319-362-4111 800-362-3711
info@midamar.com www.midamar.com
Halal food products including crescent chicken, ethnic sauces, beef, lamb, shawarma, turkey and pizzas.
President: Bill Aossey
baossey@midamar.com
Estimated Sales: $ 20 - 50 Million
Number Employees: 50-99

46596 Midas Foods Intl
10750 Capital St
Oak Park, MI 48237-3134   248-544-4574
Fax: 248-544-4384 877-728-2379
sales@midasfoods.com www.midasfoods.com
Dry mix foods and bases including gravies, sauces, cheese sauce, soup bases, batter products .They manufacturer dry powdered mixes for food processing and national restauraunt chains.
Owner: Richard Elias
relias@midasfoods.com
Number Employees: 10-19
Square Footage: 180000
Parent Co: MiDAS Foods International
Type of Packaging: Food Service, Bulk
Brands Exported: American Saucery
Regions Exported to: Asia, Middle East, Australia
Percentage of Business in Exporting: 5

46597 Midbrook Inc
1300 Falahee Rd # 51
Jackson, MI 49203-4700   517-787-3481
Fax: 517-787-2349 800-966-9274
sales@midbrook.com www.midbrookmetalfab.com
Manufacturer and exporter of washing, drying and wastewater treatment equipment
CEO: Mick Lutz
mlutz@midbrook.com
CEO: Mick Lutz
Manufacturing Manager: E Houghton
Estimated Sales: $ 20-50 Million
Number Employees: 100-249
Regions Exported to: Worldwide

46598 Middleby Corp
1400 Toastmaster Dr
Elgin, IL 60120-9272   847-741-3300
sales@middleby.com
www.middleby.com
Manufacturer, importer and exporter of conveyor and convection ovens, ranges, fryers, toasters and steamers.
Chief Executive Officer: Timothy Fitzgerald
Chief Operating Officer: Devid Brewer
Corporate Treasurer: Martin Lindsay
Estimated Sales: #2.72 Billion
Number Employees: 5000-9999
Other Locations:
  Middleby Corp.
  Miramar, FLMiddleby Corp.
Regions Imported from: Worldwide

46599 Middleby Marshall Inc
1400 Toastmaster Dr
Elgin, IL 60120-9272   847-741-3300
www.middmarshall.com
Manufacturer and exporter of high speed conveyor ovens for pizza, bagels, pretzels and full service restaurants; also, ranges, broilers, combi ovens, toasters, hot food warmers and steam equipment
President: John Kania
Year Founded: 1888
Estimated Sales: $50 - 75 Million
Number Employees: 100-249
Square Footage: 285000
Parent Co: Middleby Corporation
Type of Packaging: Food Service
Other Locations:
  Middleby Marshall, CTX
  Elgin, ILMiddleby Marshall, CTX
Brands Exported: Middleby Marshall; CTX;
  Toastmaster; Southbend
Regions Exported to: Central America, South America, Europe, Asia, Middle East, Worldwide
Percentage of Business in Exporting: 14

46600 Midland
PO Box 8298
Fort Wayne, IN 46898-8298   219-484-8895
Fax: 219-484-8892
Importer of tapioca flour
CEO: Gordon Bell
Sales Administration: Steve Swihart
Estimated Sales: $5-10 Million
Number Employees: 5-9
Regions Imported from: Europe, Asia, Mexico
Percentage of Business in Importing: 5

46601 Midori Trading Inc
89-16 126th Street
Richmond Hill, NY 11418   718-461-3835
Fax: 718-461-3729
Wholesaler/distributor, importer and exporter of produce, specialty and health foods including ginger and green teas
President: Mo Ma
Estimated Sales: $1-2.5 Million
Number Employees: 1-4

46602 Midway Games
2727 W Roscoe St
Chicago, IL 60618-5909   773-961-2000
Fax: 773-961-2376 www.midway.com
Manager: Matt Booty
Contact: Rigo Cortes
rcortes@midway.com
Estimated Sales: $ 1 - 3 Million
Number Employees: 100-249

46603 Midwest Aircraft Products Co
125 S Mill St
Lexington, OH 44904-9571   419-884-2164
Fax: 419-884-2331 www.midwestaircraft.com
Manufacturer and exporter of food handling equipment including liquid containers, ice drawers, oven racks and beverage drawers and carts for airline food services
Owner: Jerry Miller
j.miller@midwestaircraft.com
CFO: Gayle Gorman Freeman
Engineering Manager: Matt Marles
CEO: Gayle Gorman Freeman
Sales: Richard Baker
Manufacturing: Lee Craii
Production: Gene Wheitner
Purchasing Manager: Chuck Kumisarek
Estimated Sales: $ 10 - 20 Million
Number Employees: 10-19
Square Footage: 26000
Regions Exported to: Worldwide
Percentage of Business in Exporting: 5

46604 Midwest Badge & NoveltyCo
3337 Republic Ave
Minneapolis, MN 55426-4108   952-927-9901
Fax: 952-927-9903
Manufacturer, importer and wholesaler/distributor of name badges, buttons and advertising specialties
President: Kevin Saba
kevin.saba@mgincentives.com
Estimated Sales: Less than $500,000
Number Employees: 1-4
Square Footage: 16000
Type of Packaging: Consumer, Private Label, Bulk
Regions Exported to: Central America, South America
Percentage of Business in Exporting: 5
Regions Imported from: Asia
Percentage of Business in Importing: 10

46605 Midwest Folding Products
1414 S Western Ave
Chicago, IL 60608   312-666-3366
Fax: 312-666-2606 800-344-2864
sales@midwestfolding.com
www.midwestfolding.com
Banquet and meeting room tables in lighweight plastic, steel edge plywood and high-pressure plastic laminate with plywood core tops. Comfort Leg meeting room tables afford your guests unobstructed knee space and increase seatingcapacity, dual-height cocktail tables, table storage and handling systems are also available
CEO: Darryl Rossen
CFO: Len Farrell
Vice President: Chuck Pineau
Marketing Director: Ken Hufstater
Sales Director: Bob Bishop
Plant Manager: Sam Thomas
Purchasing Manager: Oscar Ortiz
Estimated Sales: $35 Million
Number Employees: 100-249
Number of Brands: 1
Square Footage: 200000
Type of Packaging: Bulk
Regions Exported to: Worldwide
Percentage of Business in Exporting: 5

46606 Midwest Frozen Foods, Inc.
2185 Leeward Ln
Hanover Park, IL 60133-6026   630-784-0123
Fax: 630-784-0424 866-784-0123
Midwest Frozen Foods provides in house and private label frozen fruits and vegetables to the retail, food services and industrial manufacturing sectors.
President: Zafar Iqbal
VP: Athar Siddiq
Operations: Rob Linchesky
Production: Jose Manjarrez
Estimated Sales: $5 Million
Number Employees: 18
Number of Brands: 2
Number of Products: 100+
Square Footage: 20000
Type of Packaging: Food Service, Private Label, Bulk

46607 Midwest Imports LTD
205 Fencl Ln
Hillside, IL 60162-2001   708-236-1500
Fax: 708-236-3100 800-621-3372
www.midwestimports.com
Wholesaler/distributor and importer of baking ingredients, chocolate coatings, preserves, Swiss dried sauces and soups
Owner: Todd Ostrowski
info@midwestimports.com
Office Manager/Customer Service: Todd Ostrowski
VP: Frank Jurkowski
Estimated Sales: $10-20 Million
Number Employees: 20-49
Square Footage: 77600
Brands Imported: Felchlin Swiss Couvertures;
  Haco Swis Drie; Hero Swiss
Regions Imported from: Europe
Percentage of Business in Importing: 100

46608 Midwest Ingredients Inc
103 W Main St
PO Box 186
Princeville, IL 61559-7511   309-385-1035
Fax: 309-385-1036 www.midwestingredients.com
Midwest Ingredients has purchased excess and close coded food products and ingredients across the continental United States since 1994. The inventory is sold with any restrictions the manufacturer requires. We work with retail orinstitutional packaging and also bulk pack products.
CFO: Ruthi Coats
ruthi@midwestingredients.com
Estimated Sales: Above $ 5 Million
Number Employees: 5-9
Regions Exported to: Canada and Mexico
Percentage of Business in Exporting: 20
Regions Imported from: Canada and Mexico
Percentage of Business in Importing: 10

46609 Midwest Stainless
408 3M Drive NE Suite B
Menomonie, WI 54751   715-235-5472
Fax: 715-235-5484

Importers & Exporters / A-Z

Manufacturer and exporter of dairy tanks, CIP systems, heat exchangers, cheese presses, pumps, valves, fittings and complete turn-key process systems for the food, dairy and biotechnical industries
President : Joe Maxfield
VP & General Manager: Josh Hoover
Sales Engineer: Tim Jenneman
Operations Manager : Rob Hesse
Estimated Sales: $10-20 Million
Number Employees: 20-49
Square Footage: 38000
Regions Exported to: Central America, Europe, Canada, Mexico
Percentage of Business in Exporting: 15

46610 Mies Products
505 Commerce St
West Bend, WI 53090-1698 262-338-0676
Fax: 262-338-1244 800-480-6437
info@miesproducts.com www.miesproducts.com
Processor and exporter of breading for chicken, fish, meats and vegetables; also, holding and display warmers and electric pressure fryers and filter machines for fats and oils
President: Mike Mies
VP: Mike Mies
Sales: Mark Mey
Purchasing Director: Ed Casey
Estimated Sales: $ 3 - 5 Million
Number Employees: 10-19
Number of Brands: 1
Number of Products: 10
Square Footage: 135040
Type of Packaging: Food Service, Private Label
Brands Exported: Mies
Regions Exported to: Central America, Europe, Asia
Percentage of Business in Exporting: 15

46611 Migali Industries
516 Lansdowne Ave
Camden, NJ 08104-1198 856-963-3600
Fax: 856-963-3604 800-852-5292
contact@migali.com www.migali.com
Manufactures a complete line of G3 reach-in refrigerators and freezers, glass door merchandisers, sandwich tables, pizza preparation tables, and beer equipment. Also distributes Brema Ice Cream Makers, high quality machines inclusingundercounter and modular cubes and flakers.
President: Ernest Migali
Estimated Sales: $5-10 Million
Number Employees: 20-49
Brands Exported: Migali
Regions Exported to: Central America
Percentage of Business in Exporting: 5

46612 Migatron Corp
935 Dieckman St # A
Suite A
Woodstock, IL 60098-9203 815-338-5800
Fax: 815-338-5803 888-644-2876
info@migatron.com www.migatron.com
Manufacturer, exporter and importer of ultrasonic sensors
President: Frank Wroga
info@migatron.com
Estimated Sales: $ 2.5 - 5 Million
Number Employees: 10-19
Regions Exported to: Worldwide
Regions Imported from: Worldwide

46613 Mighty Leaf Tea
136 Mitchell Boulevard
San Rafael, CA 94903 415-339-8856
Fax: 415-472-1780 877-698-5323
www.mightyleaf.com
Contact: Rafael Chacon
rafael@mightyleaf.com

46614 Miguel & Valentino - Scout Marketing
PO Box 1552
Lorton, VA 22199 301-986-1470
Fax: 301-986-9277 maryl@miguelvalentino.com
www.miguelvalentino.com
Importing unique authentic specialty foods from spain. Olive Oil & vinegar, olives and tapenades, cheese and crackers, rice and vegetables, salts and spices, fruit cakes and spreads, sweets and nuts and seafood.
Marketing: Christine Steshko
General Sales Manager: Maryl Holley
Contact: Christine Dibenigno
christine@miguelvalentino.com

46615 Miguel's Stowe Away
17 Town Farm Ln
Stowe, VT 05672 802-253-8900
Fax: 802-253-3946 800-448-6517
mexicanfoods@miguels.com
Processor and exporter of Mexican food products including salsa cruda, blue and white corn tortilla chips, red chili sauce, flavored salsa and smoked jalapeno
President: Christopher Pierson
Regional Sales Manager: Tim Couture
Estimated Sales: $ 3 - 5 Million
Number Employees: 1-4
Square Footage: 20000
Type of Packaging: Consumer, Food Service, Bulk
Brands Exported: Miguel's Stowe Away
Regions Exported to: Europe, Asia, Bermuda
Percentage of Business in Exporting: 1

46616 Mikasa Hotelware
1 Mikasa Drive
Secaucus, NJ 07094-2581 201-867-9210
Fax: 201-867-2385 866-645-2721
gwen_opfell@mikasa.com www.mikasa.com
Manufacturer, exporter and importer of china, dinnerware and crystal
VP: Neil Orzeck
Contact: John Beaupre
jbeaupre@mikasa.com
Number Employees: 100-249
Regions Exported to: Worldwide

46617 Mil-Du-Gas Company/StarBrite
4041 SW 47th Ave
Fort Lauderdale, FL 33314-4031 954-587-6280
Fax: 954-587-2813 800-327-8583
peter@starbrite.com www.starbrite.com
Manufacturer and exporter of mildew preventers with air fresheners and maintenance and cleaning chemicals
CEO: Peter Dornau
CFO: Jeff Barocas
Executive Vice President: Gregor Dornau
Vice President, Technology: Justin Gould
VP of Marketing / Art Dept & Literature: Bill Lindsey
Senior Vice President, Sales: Marc Emmi
Vice President, Sales: Dennis Torok
Vice President, Operations/Manufacturing: Will Dudman
Number Employees: 20-49
Square Footage: 560000
Parent Co: Ocean Bio-Chem
Other Locations:
 Mil-Du-Gas Co./Star Brite
 Montgomery, ALMil-Du-Gas Co./Star Brite
Brands Exported: Star Brite
Regions Exported to: Central America, South America, Europe, Asia, Middle East
Percentage of Business in Exporting: 15

46618 Milan Box Corporation
2090 West Van Hook Street
P.O. Box 30
Milan, TN 38358 731-686-3338
Fax: 731-686-3330 800-225-8057
andrew@milanbox.com www.milanbox.com
Plywood pallet boxes, crates and wirebound and wooden boxes; exporter of wirebound boxes
President: Franklin Dedmon
franklin@milanbox.com
Finance Manager: Donna Hardy
VP: Andrew Dedmon
President/Head Sales/Marketing: Franklin Dedmon
Head of Operations: Freddy McCartney
Head of Production: Rudy Graves
Estimated Sales: $ 10 - 20 Million
Number Employees: 50-99
Regions Exported to: South America, Europe, Israel

46619 Milas Foods, LLC
280 N Midland Avenue Bldg
Saddle Brook, NJ 07663-5708 201-773-4872
Fax: 201-773-6876 camato@milasfood.com
Contact: Chad Amato
camato@milasfood.com

46620 Milburn Company
520 Bellevue Street
Detroit, MI 48207-3733 313-259-3410
Fax: 313-259-3415
Manufacturer and exporter of soap and soap dispensers, manufacturing, skincreams and lotions
VP/Marketing: Frank Newman
Estimated Sales: Less than $500,000
Number Employees: 1-4
Square Footage: 20000
Regions Exported to: Worldwide
Percentage of Business in Exporting: 10

46621 Mild Bill's Spices
PO Box 1303
Ennis, TX 75120 972-875-2975
http://www.mildbills.com/
Processor and exporter of chili powder, seasoning blends and barbecue spices, salsa, relish
Owner: Bill Dees
Co-Owner: Tamara Dees
Type of Packaging: Consumer, Food Service
Regions Exported to: Canada, Switzerland
Percentage of Business in Exporting: 5

46622 Milea Estate Vineyard
40 Hollow Circle Rdl
Staatsburg, NY 12580 845-264-0403
Fax: 845-389-0313 info@mileaestatevineyard.com
www.mileaestatevineyard.com
Pinot Noir, Riesling, Chardonnay, Vignoles, Traminette, Ros, and sparkling wine
Co-Founder: Barry Milea
Co-Founder: Ed Evans
Co-Founder: Bruce Tripp
Year Founded: 2015
Number of Brands: 1
Number of Products: 10
Type of Packaging: Consumer, Private Label
Brands Exported: Milea Estate Vineyard
Regions Exported to: USA (New York and Connecticut)

46623 Miljoco Corp
200 Elizabeth St
Mt Clemens, MI 48043-1643 586-777-4280
Fax: 586-777-7891 888-888-1498
info@mijoco.com www.miljoco.com
Manufacturers standard and custom thermometers.
President: Howard M Trerice
htrerice@miljoco.com
Reaersch Development: Heath Trerice
Quality Control: Bruce Trerice
Marketing: Mike Mroz
Sales: Tom Adams
Public Relations: Mike Mroz
Plant Manager: Alex Jakob
Purchasing: Kimberly Trerice
Estimated Sales: $10-20 Million
Number Employees: 20-49
Square Footage: 94000
Regions Exported to: Central America, South America, Europe, Asia

46624 Milk Specialties Global
7500 Flying Cloud Dr
Suite 500
Eden Prairie, MN 55344 952-942-7310
Fax: 952-942-7611 www.milkspecialties.com
Dairy protein ingredients
President/Owner: Eddie Wells
CEO: Dave Lenzmeier
davelenzmeier@milkspecialties.com
Estimated Sales: $35 Million
Number Employees: 500-999
Regions Exported to: Asia

46625 Milky Whey Inc
910 Brooks St # 203
Suite 203
Missoula, MT 59801-5784 406-542-7373
Fax: 406-542-7377 800-379-6455
dairy@themilkywhey.com
www.themilkywhey.com
Whey proteins and dry dairy ingredients including nonfat dry milk, whole milk, whey powder, butter, buttermilk powder, caseinates, lactose, nondairy creamers, whey protein concentrates and isolates, and cheese powders

Importers & Exporters / A-Z

President: Curt Pijanowski
curt@themilkywhey.com
CFO: Steve Schmidt
Vice President: Dan Finch
Operations Manager: Carla Messerly
Reception: Tony Cavanaugh
Estimated Sales: $1.2 Million
Number Employees: 10-19
Type of Packaging: Consumer, Private Label, Bulk

46626 Mill Wiping Rags Inc
1656 E 233rd St
Bronx, NY 10466-3306   718-994-7100
Fax: 718-994-1973 ragmaster67@optonline.net
www.millwipingrags.com
Manufacturer and exporter of wiping rags, cheesecloth and paper wipes, bar towels
President: F Scifo
millrags@optimaline.net
Quality Control: A Pimento
Marketing Director: Eric Saltzman
Sales Director: Eric Saltzman
Plant Manager: F Scifo
Purchasing Manager: Eric Saltzman
Estimated Sales: $2 Million
Number Employees: 50-99
Number of Brands: 3
Number of Products: 100
Parent Co: D. Benedetto
Type of Packaging: Private Label, Bulk

46627 Mill-Rose Co
7995 Tyler Blvd
Mentor, OH 44060-4896   440-946-5727
Fax: 440-255-5039 800-321-3598
www.millrose.com
Manufacturer and exporter of grill and basting brushes
President: Paul Miller
millrose@en.com
CFO: Vincent Pona
Sales Manager: Gregory Miller
Purchasing Manager: Susan Stallknict
Estimated Sales: $20 Million
Number Employees: 100-249
Regions Exported to: Europe
Percentage of Business in Exporting: 10

46628 Mille Lacs Wild Rice Corp
25300 Paddy Ave
PO Box 200
Aitkin, MN 56431   218-927-2740
800-626-3809
info@canoewildrice.com www.canoewildrice.com
Processor and exporter of kosher wild rice
President: Chris Ratuski
Estimated Sales: $2.5 Million
Number Employees: 10-19
Type of Packaging: Consumer, Food Service, Private Label, Bulk
Brands Exported: Canoe; Oh Canada
Regions Exported to: Europe, Asia, Canada
Percentage of Business in Exporting: 2
Percentage of Business in Importing: 2

46629 Miller Group Multiplex
1610 Design Way
Dupo, IL 62239-1826   636-343-5700
Fax: 618-286-6202 800-325-3350
info@miller-group.com www.otpracks.com
Manufacturer and exporter of store fixtures and display systems including point of purchase
President: Randy Castle
CFO: Roger Lovejoy
Director Marketing: Tony Evans
Marketing: Catherine Lafarth
Marketing Services: Cathy Berding
Estimated Sales: $ 10 - 20 Million
Number Employees: 20-49
Square Footage: 80000
Parent Co: Miller Multiplex
Brands Exported: Multiplex
Regions Exported to: Central America, Europe, Middle East, Australia
Percentage of Business in Exporting: 5

46630 (HQ)Miller Studio
734 Fair Ave NW
PO Box 997
New Philadelphia, OH 44663-1589   330-339-1100
Fax: 330-339-4379 800-332-0050
www.miller-studio.com

Manufacturer and exporter of pressure sensitive double-coated tape for decorative trim, mounting, fastening, etc.; also, adhesive systems
President: John Basiletti
Purchasing Manager: Tina Schlemmer
Sales: Mark Gazdik
Estimated Sales: $ 5 - 10 Million
Number Employees: 50-99
Type of Packaging: Consumer
Brands Exported: Magic-Mounts

46631 Miller Technical Svc
47801 W Anchor Ct
Plymouth, MI 48170-6018   734-414-1769
Fax: 734-738-1975 millerstec@cs.com
www.nextmobilitynow.com
Manufacturer and exporter of rebuilt and used packaging and food processing equipment; also, machinery parts; repair and rebuilding services available
President: James Miller
CEO: Patrick Miller
pmiller@mtsmedicalmfg.com
Estimated Sales: $ .5 - 1 million
Number Employees: 20-49
Square Footage: 6000
Type of Packaging: Food Service

46632 Millerbernd Systems
330 6th St S
P.O. Box 37
Winsted, MN 55395-1102   320-485-2685
Fax: 320-485-3900
Design, manufacture and install processing equipment for the dairy and cheese industries such as pasteurization and heat transfer units, controls and automation systems, agitating tanks, batching/blending and barrel handlingsystems.
President: Brad Millerbernd
bmillerbernd@millerbernd.com
VP: Terry Voight
National Sales Manager: Lisa Stanger
Product Manager: Frank Bruggman
Purchasing: Sam Zimmerman
Number Employees: 100-249
Regions Exported to: Central America, South America, Europe, Asia, USA

46633 Millflow Spice Corp.
60 Davids Dr
Hauppauge, NY 11788
Fax: 631-231-5500 866-227-8355
info@castellaimports.com
www.millflowspicecorp.com
Food colors, flavoring extracts, spices, seasonings and sauces including pesto, Worcestershire, soy, barbecue, hot and smoke
President: Zane Moses
Estimated Sales: $2.6 Million
Number Employees: 21
Parent Co: Regal Extract Company
Type of Packaging: Consumer, Food Service, Private Label, Bulk

46634 Milligan & Higgins
PO Box 506
Johnstown, NY 12095   518-762-4638
Fax: 518-762-7039 info@milligan1868.com
www.milligan1868.com
Manufacturer, importer and exporter of kosher edible and technical gelatins.
Year Founded: 1868
Parent Co: Hudson Industries Corporation
Type of Packaging: Bulk
Regions Exported to: Worldwide
Percentage of Business in Exporting: 10
Regions Imported from: Central America, South America, Europe
Percentage of Business in Importing: 5

46635 Milliken & Co
P.O. Box 1926
Spartanburg, SC 29304   864-503-2020
brand@milliken.com
www.milliken.com
Aprons, table cloths and skirting and place mats.
Chief Executive Officer: J. Harold Chandler
Year Founded: 1865
Number Employees: 7,000

46636 Mills Brothers Intl
16000 Christensen Rd
Suite 300
Seattle, WA 98188-2967   206-575-3000
Fax: 206-957-1362 mbi@millsbros.com
www.millsbros.com
Specialty and organic grains, dried peas, dried beans, lentils, millet rice and corn products including popcorn kernels, flour, grits, meal and starch
President: Eric Mills
Year Founded: 1982
Estimated Sales: $36306000
Number Employees: 50-99
Square Footage: 26000
Type of Packaging: Consumer, Food Service, Private Label, Bulk
Regions Exported to: Central America, Asia

46637 Mills Seafood Ltd.
5 Mills Street
Bouctouche, NB E4S 3S3
Canada   506-743-2444
Fax: 506-743-8497 millsseafood.ca
Seafood processor
Owner: Steven Mills
Vice President: Marie Allain
Quality Control: George Robichaud
Plant Manager: Laurie Allain
Number Employees: 50-99
Type of Packaging: Food Service

46638 Milmar Food Group
One 6 1/2 Station Road
Goshen, NY 10924   845-294-5400
Fax: 845-294-6687 www.milmarfoodgroup.com
Frozen foods including breakfast selections, vegetarian, chicken, burrito, and pre-plated meal products
President: Martin Hoffman
EVP: Dov Peikes
Marketing Director: Rita O'Connor
Sales Director: Cindy Cohen
Purchasing: Barry Werk
Year Founded: 2000
Estimated Sales: $30 Million
Number Employees: 250
Number of Brands: 3
Number of Products: 100
Square Footage: 60000
Type of Packaging: Consumer, Food Service, Private Label, Bulk
Regions Exported to: Canada

46639 Milne Fruit Products Inc
804 Bennett Ave
P.O. Box 111
Prosser, WA 99350-1267   509-786-2611
Fax: 509-786-1724 selkins@milnefruit.com
www.milnefruit.com
Processes fruit juice, fruit juice concentrates, purees, custom blends and nutritional ingredients. Flavors include concord grape, strawberry, cranberry, raspberry, blueberry and cherry and others
President: Randy Hageman
rhageman@milnefruit.com
General Manager: Randall Hageman
Research & Development: Eric Johnson
Quality Control: Eric Johnson
Sales Director: Shannon Elkins
Number Employees: 20-49
Parent Co: Ocean Spray Cranberries
Type of Packaging: Bulk
Regions Exported to: Europe, Asia, Canada
Percentage of Business in Exporting: 10

46640 Milsek Furniture PolishInc.
5525 E Pine Lake Rd
North Lima, OH 44452   330-542-2700
Fax: 330-542-1059 www.milsek.com
Manufacturer, exporter and wholesaler/distributor of furniture polish and cleaner
President: Jean Hamilton
VP: Susan Bender
Estimated Sales: Under $1 Million
Number Employees: 5-9
Number of Brands: 1
Number of Products: 2
Square Footage: 108000
Brands Exported: Milsek

46641 Milton A. Klein Company
PO Box 363
New York, NY 10021-0006   516-829-3400
Fax: 516-829-3427 800-221-0248

Importers & Exporters / A-Z

President: Irene Klein
VP: Allen Klein
Number Employees: 15
Square Footage: 6800
Regions Exported to: Worldwide
Percentage of Business in Exporting: 10

46642 Milwaukee Dustless Brush Co
1632 Hobbs Dr
Delavan, WI 53115-2029   323-724-7777
Fax: 323-724-1111 sales@milwaukeedustless.com
www.milwaukeedustless.com
Manufacturer, importer and exporter of floor brushes, squeegees, sponge mops, utility brushes and related janitorial maintenance tools
National Sales Manager: Jeff Feder
Estimated Sales: $5-10 Million
Number Employees: 50-99
Brands Exported: Speed Sweep
Regions Exported to: Worldwide
Regions Imported from: Europe

46643 Milwaukee Sign Company
2076 1st Ave
Grafton, WI 53024   262-375-5740
Fax: 262-376-1686
Manufacturer and exporter of internally illuminated signs and menu systems
President: Kevin Sutherby
R&D: Rick Richards
Contact: Nancy Stansy
rcarlson@kdhe.state.ks.us
Estimated Sales: $ 20 - 30 Million
Number Employees: 100-249
Type of Packaging: Food Service, Bulk
Regions Exported to: Worldwide

46644 Milwaukee Tool & MachineCompany
PO Box 94
Okauchee, WI 53069-0094   262-821-0160
Fax: 262-821-0162 mtmco@execpc.com
Manufacturer and exporter of packaging machinery
President: Richard Mumper
VP: Ralph Mumper
Estimated Sales: $5-10 Million
Number Employees: 10

46645 Milwhite Inc
5487 Padre Island Hwy
Brownsville, TX 78521-8300   956-547-1970
Fax: 956-547-1999 800-442-0082
www.milwhite.com
Manufacturer and importer of clay, talcs, calcium carbonate, barium sulfate, attapulgite, bentonite and other nonmetallic minerals; exporter of aflatoxin binders.
President: Mike Hughes
mhughes@milwhite.com
Accounting & Financial Manager: Hector Guerrero
Director, Health Science Division: Dr Orlando Osuna
Quality Assurance: Steve Lopez
Customer Service: Paola Tella
Estimated Sales: $20-50 Million
Number Employees: 20-49
Number of Brands: 5
Type of Packaging: Private Label, Bulk
Regions Exported to: Central America, South America, Europe, Asia, Middle East
Percentage of Business in Exporting: 5
Regions Imported from: Mexico
Percentage of Business in Importing: 10

46646 Mimi et Cie
P.O.Box 80157
Seattle, WA 98108-0157   206-545-1850
Fax: 800-284-3834 www.mimietcie.com
Manufacturer, importer and exporter of decorative packaging including shrink and printed basket wrap and food bags for cookies, candy, etc. Also waxed tissue paper, food containers and custom products including bags, totes andribbons
President: Mark Revere
Estimated Sales: $1-2.5 Million
Number Employees: 50-99
Square Footage: 80000
Type of Packaging: Consumer, Food Service, Private Label, Bulk
Brands Exported: Mimi et Cie
Regions Exported to: Europe, Asia, Australia
Percentage of Business in Exporting: 5
Brands Imported: Raffia
Regions Imported from: Madagascar, Venezuela

Percentage of Business in Importing: 5

46647 Min Tong Herbs
318 7th St
Oakland, CA 94607-4112   510-873-8677
Fax: 510-873-8671 800-562-5777
mintongherbs@hotmail.com www.mintong.com.tw
Processor and importer of Chinese herbal extracts
President: Charles Chang
mintongherbs@aol.com
Vice President: Susan Chang
Sales: Tiffany Zhon
Estimated Sales: $500,000-$1 Million
Number Employees: 10-19
Number of Brands: 1
Type of Packaging: Consumer, Private Label, Bulk
Regions Exported to: Central America, Europe
Brands Imported: Min Tong
Regions Imported from: Taiwan

46648 Mincing Overseas Spice Company
K N Building
10 Tower Road
Dayton, NJ 08810   732-355-9944
Fax: 732-555-9964 mail@mincing.com
www.mincing.com
Importers, processor of spices, seeds and aromatic herbs
President: Manoj Rupaerlia
CFO: K Jobanputra
Quality Control: Nagy Beskal
Sales: Dorothy Holloway
Plant Manager: Charles Armgnti
Purchasing: H Ruparelia
Estimated Sales: $ .5 - 1 million
Number Employees: 1-4
Square Footage: 200000
Parent Co: Mincing Trading Corporation
Regions Imported from: Central America, South America, Europe, Asia, Middle East

46649 Mingo Bay Beverages
721 Seaboard Street
Myrtle Beach, SC 29577-6520   843-448-5320
Fax: 843-448-4162 mingomoe@aol.com
Processor and exporter of coffee, tea and fruit bases, mixes and concentrates
President: Larry Moses
Estimated Sales: $ 1-5 Million
Number Employees: 8
Square Footage: 320000
Type of Packaging: Consumer, Food Service, Private Label, Bulk
Brands Exported: Mingo Bay Beverages
Regions Exported to: Worldwide
Percentage of Business in Exporting: 50

46650 Minn-Dak Growers LTD
4034 40th Ave N
PO Box 13276
Grand Forks, ND 58203-3818   701-746-7453
Fax: 701-780-9050 info@minndak.com
www.minndak.com
Buckwheat, mustard, safflower and sunflower
Owner/President/General Manager: Harris Peterson
harris.peterson@minndak.com
Principal/CFO: Mona Kozojed
R&D Director: Mohammad Badaruddin
Quality Control Manager: Liz Carruth
Marketing Director: Kristin Sharp
Sales: Harris Peterson
Public Relations Director: Jaci Peau
Manufacturing Supervisor: Bruce Sondreal
Estimated Sales: $11 Million
Number Employees: 20-49
Number of Brands: 3
Number of Products: 9
Square Footage: 180000
Type of Packaging: Consumer, Food Service, Bulk
Regions Exported to: Central America, South America, Europe, Asia, Middle East, New Zealand, Mexico
Percentage of Business in Exporting: 35
Regions Imported from: Asia, Canada
Percentage of Business in Importing: 10

46651 Minnesota Department-Agrcltr
625 Robert St N
St Paul, MN 55155-2538   651-201-6000
Fax: 651-201-6118 www.mnfarmlink.com
Manager: Gene Hugoson
Manager: Stephen Morse
steve.morse@state.mn.us
Number Employees: 20-49

46652 Minnesota Turkey Research and Promotion
108 Marty Drive
Buffalo, MN 55313-9338   763-682-2171
Fax: 763-682-5546 ldurben@minnesotaturkey.com
www.minnesotaturkey.com

46653 Minterbrook Oyster Co
12002 114th Street Court Kp N
PO Box 432
Gig Harbor, WA 98329-5058   253-857-5251
Fax: 253-857-5521 www.minterbrookoyster.com
Processor and exporter of fresh and frozen oysters, Manila clams and mussels
President: Harold E Wiksten
COO: Erica Wiksten
mntrerka@aol.com
Sales Manager: Mike Paul
Estimated Sales: $8.6 Million
Number Employees: 5-9
Square Footage: 280
Type of Packaging: Consumer, Food Service, Private Label
Regions Exported to: Worldwide
Percentage of Business in Exporting: 60

46654 Minuet Cookies
113 McHenry Road #151
Buffalo Grove, IL 60089   847-541-7244
Fax: 847-541-9364 fmex@aol.com
www.minuetcookies.com
Creams, cookies and crackers

46655 Minuteman Power Boss
175 Anderson St
Aberdeen, NC 28315   314-283-7304
Fax: 910-944-7409 800-323-9420
info@minutemanintl.com www.powerboss.com
Manufacturer and exporter of power sweepers and scrubbers
President: Greg Rau
VP: Gregory Rau
Advertising Manager: Krista Harris
Estimated Sales: $ 5 - 10 Million
Number Employees: 100-249
Square Footage: 200000
Parent Co: Minuteman International
Other Locations:
  Minuteman PowerBoss
  Villa Park, ILMinuteman PowerBoss
Brands Exported: Armadillo; Badger; PowerBoss; Prowler
Regions Exported to: South America, Europe, Asia, Middle East, Canada
Percentage of Business in Exporting: 40

46656 Minuteman Trading
12 Greenway Ave S
Boyce, VA 22620-9735   540-837-1138
Fax: 540-837-2526
Wholesaler/distributor and importer of kitchen utensils; serving the food service market and retail stores
President: Chuck Lockard
Estimated Sales: $3.2 Million
Number Employees: 1-4
Square Footage: 39600
Type of Packaging: Consumer, Food Service
Regions Imported from: Europe, Asia
Percentage of Business in Importing: 100

46657 MirOil
602 North Tacoma St
Allentown, PA 18109-8103   610-437-4618
Fax: 610-437-4618 800-523-9844
info@miroil.com www.miroil.com
President: Bernard Friedman
Contact: Bernard Firedman
bfiredman@miroil.com

46658 Miracapo Pizza
2323 Pratt Blvd
Elk Grove Village, IL 60007   847-631-3500
miracapopizza.com
Premium pizzas, gourmet sandwiches, wraps, paninis, grab-n-go items, breakfast items and desserts. Gluten-free options.
VP, Finance: Dan Hoffman
VP, R&D and Quality Assurance: Lynn Waldman
Year Founded: 1984
Estimated Sales: $200 Million
Number Employees: 200-500
Square Footage: 150000
Regions Exported to: Asia
Percentage of Business in Importing: 10

451

Importers & Exporters / A-Z

46659 Miracle Exclusives
PO Box 2508
Danbury, CT 06813-2508   203-796-5493
Fax: 203-648-4871   800-645-6360
www.miracleexclusives.com
Wholesaler/distributor and importer of juice extractors, cookware, grain mills, grinders, graters, pasta and yogurt makers, dehydrators, sprouters and wheat grass growers
President: George Drake
VP: John Downey
Estimated Sales: $5-10 Million
Square Footage: 40000
Type of Packaging: Consumer
Brands Imported: Miracle; Jupiter; Santos; Aeternum
Regions Imported from: Europe, Asia, Canada
Percentage of Business in Importing: 99

46660 Mirasco
900 Circle 75 Pkwy SE # 1660
Atlanta, GA 30339-3095   770-956-1945
Fax: 770-956-0308   atlanta@mirasco.com
www.mirasco.com
Supplier of meats, poultry and seafood
President: Sami Rizk
sami.rizk@mirasco.com
Estimated Sales: $4.5 Million
Number Employees: 20-49
Type of Packaging: Food Service, Private Label, Bulk

46661 Miroil
602 Tacoma St
Allentown, PA 18109-8103   610-437-4618
Fax: 610-437-3377   800-523-9844
hgos1946@gmail.com   www.miroil.com
Manufacturer and exporter of frying oil stabilizer, filter aids and clean and reusable filters for fryers; also, testing for polar and alkaline contaminants
President: Bernard Friedman
Manager: J Wessner
Contact: Bernard Firedman
bfiredman@miroil.com
Estimated Sales: $ 5 - 10 Million
Number Employees: 1-4
Square Footage: 140000
Brands Exported: Frypowder; MirOil; EZ Flow
Regions Exported to: Worldwide

46662 Mirro Company
1115 W 5th Ave
Lancaster, OH 43130   800-848-7200
Fax: 920-684-1929
Cookware, bakeware, tools and gadgets
Owner: Dave Moore
Estimated Sales: $ 1 - 5 Million
Number Employees: 1-4
Parent Co: Newell Companies
Type of Packaging: Food Service
Regions Exported to: Worldwide
Percentage of Business in Exporting: 30

46663 Mirrotek International
90 Dayton Ave # 1f
Building 1-F
Passaic, NJ 07055-7014   973-472-1400
Fax: 973-472-5170   www.tolifeproducts.com
Sauces, gourmet soup mixes, exotic rice crisps and flavored Japanese bread crumbs
President: Joe Bezzy
jcebezzy@mirrotek.com
Number Employees: 20-49

46664 Mishima Foods USA
2340 Plaza Del Amo
Suite 105
Torrance, CA 90501   310-787-1533
Fax: 310-787-1651   mishima.com
Japanese products
Business Development Manager: Ken Hsu
Contact: Yuho Quintero
yuho@mishima.com
Estimated Sales: $2.5-5 Million
Number Employees: 1-4
Parent Co: Mishima
Type of Packaging: Consumer, Food Service
Brands Imported: Mishima
Regions Imported from: Asia
Percentage of Business in Importing: 100

46665 Miss Mary
115 Pacific Ave
Long Beach, WA 98631   360-642-5541
Fax: 360-642-3391
Wholesaler/distributor of frozen pacific ocean spot prawns, albacore tuna
President: Wendy J Murry
CEO: Debra Oakes
CFO: Jared Oakes
Vice President: Tiffany Turner
Estimated Sales: $400,000
Number Employees: 1-4
Number of Brands: 1
Number of Products: 1
Type of Packaging: Private Label
Brands Exported: Watanabe Enterprises, Spot Prawns
Regions Exported to: Asia
Percentage of Business in Exporting: 95

46666 Mission Foodservice
PO Box 2008
Oldsmar, FL 34677-7008   800-443-7994
Fax: 800-272-5207   mission@answers-sys.com
Manufacturer and exporter of Mexican foods including flour and corn tortillas, tortilla chips, pastries, taco and tostada shells
SVP/GM: Robert Smith
Marketing Director: Robin Tobor
VP Sales: Tom Daley
Number Employees: 1,000-4,999
Square Footage: 1680000
Type of Packaging: Consumer, Food Service, Private Label, Bulk

46667 Mission Produce Inc
2500 E Vineyard Ave # 300
Suite 300
Oxnard, CA 93036-1377   805-981-3650
Fax: 805-981-3660
www.worldsfinestavocados.com
Exporter of avocados
Manager: Victor Rosa
CEO: Steven Albeck
salbeck@missionpro.com
Estimated Sales: $5-10 Million
Number Employees: 1-4
Regions Exported to: Worldwide

46668 Mister Label, Inc
PO Box 326
Bluffton, SC 29910   843-815-2222
Fax: 843-815-5488   800-732-0439
misterlabel@msn.com   www.misterlabel.com
Manufacturer and exporter of labels including pressure sensitive, heat seal, gummed, tyvek and tag-stock
President: Todd Elliot
Chief Operating Officer: Kelly Elliot
Estimated Sales: $5-10 Million
Number Employees: 11
Square Footage: 30000
Type of Packaging: Food Service, Private Label, Bulk
Regions Exported to: Europe
Percentage of Business in Exporting: 10

46669 Mitsubishi Polyester Film, Inc.
2001 Hood Rd.
PO Box 1400
Greer, SC 29652   864-879-5000
Fax: 864-879-5006   contact@m-petfilm.com
www.m-petfilm.com
Biaxially oriented polyester films, and copolyester shrink sleeve film.
President/CEO: Dennis Trice
Year Founded: 1991
Estimated Sales: $61 Million
Number Employees: 600
Number of Brands: 1
Number of Products: 100
Square Footage: 24239
Parent Co: Mitsubishi Chemical Corporation
Regions Exported to: Central America, South America, Europe, Canada, Mexico, Latin America
Percentage of Business in Exporting: 2

46670 Mitsui & Co Commodity Risk Management Limited
200 Park Ave
New York, NY 10166   212-878-4192
www.mbcl.com
Importer of modified and tapioca starch, dextrin, sorbic acid, potassium sorbate, glycerine, gelatin, etc.
Chairman, Energy: Richard Breton
Vice President, Energy Trading Desk: Peter Jones
Year Founded: 1991
Estimated Sales: Over $1 Billion
Parent Co: Mitsui Bussan Commodities Ltd
Type of Packaging: Bulk
Regions Imported from: Asia
Percentage of Business in Importing: 100

46671 Mitsui Foods Inc
35 Maple St
Norwood, NJ 07648   201-750-0500
Fax: 201-750-0150   foods@mitsuifoods.com
www.mitsuifoods.com
Importer of sardines, tuna, shellfish, mandarin oranges, rice cakes, dehydrated ingredients and juice concentrates.
President & CEO: Hiroki Sato
SVP/Food Company President: Jeff Lacy
VP, Coffee Division: Shuto Oikawa
SVP, Chief Financial Officer: Joseph Bellitto
General Counsel & Compliance Officer: Odalys Perez Dines
VP, Human Resources & General Affairs: Anne Murphy
Year Founded: 1953
Estimated Sales: $20-50 Million
Number Employees: 20-49
Parent Co: Mitsui & Co Ltd
Type of Packaging: Consumer, Food Service, Private Label, Bulk
Brands Imported: Empress; Gift of Nature; Nice; Nobility
Regions Imported from: Central America, South America, Europe, Asia, Middle East
Percentage of Business in Importing: 100

46672 Mity Lite Inc
1301 W 400 N
Orem, UT 84057-4442   801-224-0589
Fax: 801-224-6191   shnna@mitylite.com
www.mitylite.com
CEO: John Dudash
johnd@mitylite.com
CEO: Brad Nielson
Number Employees: 10-19

46673 Mixon Fruit Farms Inc
2525 27th St E
Bradenton, FL 34208-7467   941-748-5829
Fax: 941-748-1085   800-608-2525
info@mixon.com   www.mixon.com
Manufacturer, packer and exporter of citrus fruits, vegetables, fudge, honey, jellies, marmalades and spreads, salsa, dips, pickles and nuts
President: Dean Mixon
Estimated Sales: $3.43 Million
Number Employees: 50-99
Square Footage: 360000
Brands Exported: Indian Ruby
Regions Exported to: Europe, Asia, Canada

46674 Miyako Oriental Foods Inc
4287 Puente Ave
Baldwin Park, CA 91706-3420   626-962-9633
Fax: 626-814-4569   877-788-6476
joearai@coldmountainmiso.com
www.coldmountainmiso.com
Miso in different flavors and colors. Used in making sauces, soups, marinades, dressings, dips and main dishes.
Vice President: Teruo Shimizu
shimizu@coldmountainmiso.com
VP: Teruo Shimizu
Marketing/Sales/Quality Assurance Mgr: Joe Arai
Estimated Sales: $3 Million
Number Employees: 10-19
Square Footage: 72000
Type of Packaging: Consumer, Food Service, Private Label, Bulk
Regions Exported to: South America, Canada, Mexico
Percentage of Business in Exporting: 10

46675 Mlp Seating
950 Pratt Blvd
Elk Grove Vlg, IL 60007-5119   847-956-1700
Fax: 847-956-1776   800-723-3030
www.mlpseating.com
Manufacturer and exporter of chairs, tables and bar stools

President: Ralph D Samuel
rdsamuel@mlpseating.com
R&D: Ralph D Samuel
Quality Control: Goerge Stembridge
Sales: Steven Seres
Estimated Sales: $ 5 - 10 Million
Number Employees: 20-49
Regions Exported to: Canada
Percentage of Business in Exporting: 3

46676 Mmi Engineered Soultions Inc
1715 Woodland Dr
Saline, MI 48176-1614   734-429-4664
         Fax: 734-429-4664   800-825-2566
info@moldedmaterials.com www.mmi-es.com
Manufacturer and exporter of custom molded totes and trays for processing and shipping
Manager: Mike Wolf
COO: R Campbell
VP Engineering: T Elkington
Estimated Sales: Below $ 5 Million
Number Employees: 50-99
Square Footage: 160000
Regions Exported to: Central America, Europe, Canada, Mexico
Percentage of Business in Exporting: 1

46677 Mo Hotta Mo Betta
2822 Limerick St
Savannah, GA 31404-4172   912-748-2766
         Fax: 912-748-1364 www.mohotta.com
Processor and exporter of hot sauces
President: Jim Kelley
jimkelley@mohotta.com
Estimated Sales: $110,000
Number Employees: 20-49
Type of Packaging: Consumer, Food Service
Regions Exported to: Europe, Asia
Percentage of Business in Exporting: 10

46678 Mocon Inc
7500 Boone Ave N # 110
Minneapolis, MN 55428-1026   763-493-7229
         Fax: 763-493-6358 info@mocon.com
                        www.mocon.com
Manufacturer and exporter of instrumentation, consulting, and laboratory services to medical, pharmaceutical, food and other industries worldwide. Develops and manufactures high technology instrumentation and provides consulting andanalytical service to research laboratories, manufacturers and quality control departments in the life sciences, food/beverage, polymer/adhesives, electronic and other industries
CEO: Robert Demorest
CFO: Darrell Lee
VP: Doug Lindemann
Research And Development: Dan Mayer
Marketing: Guy Wray
Sales: Betty Kauffman
Public Relations: Sophia Dilberakis
Production: Tim Ascheman
Estimated Sales: $25 Million
Number Employees: 120
Square Footage: 50000
Brands Exported: Permatran®; Pac Check®; Ox-Tran®; Pac Guard®; Vericap®
Regions Exported to: Central America, South America, Europe, Asia, Middle East
Percentage of Business in Exporting: 55
Brands Imported: RDM
Regions Imported from: Europe

46679 Modar
1394 E. Empire Ave.
Benton Harbor, MI 49022   269-925-0671
         Fax: 269-925-0020   800-253-6186
                        modar@qtm.net
Manufacturer and exporter of ready-to-assemble store fixtures, shelving, point-of-purchase displays, furniture and storage cabinets; also, particle board laminating services available
President: Dennis Rousseau
Sales Manager: Gary Cichon
Inside Sales Manager: Jim Hendrix
Estimated Sales: $12.7 Million
Number Employees: 90
Square Footage: 300000
Other Locations:
    Warehousing
    Bridgman, MI
    Sales, Marketing, Design
    Middletown, CTWarehousingMiddletown
Regions Exported to: Asia
Percentage of Business in Exporting: 10

46680 Modern Brewing & Design
3171 Guerneville Road
Santa Rosa, CA 95401-4028   707-542-6620
                   Fax: 707-542-3147
Manufacturer and exporter of barrel microbrewing and brewpub equipment; also, support tanks and stainless steel wine storage vessels
President: Daniel Shulte
Secretary: Russell Kargell
VP: Robert Kral
Number Employees: 32
Regions Exported to: Worldwide
Percentage of Business in Exporting: 15

46681 Modern Macaroni Co LTD
1708 Mary St
Honolulu, HI 96819-3103   808-845-6841
         Fax: 808-845-6841 www.modernmacaroni.net
Dry Asian noodles, shrimp flakes and soybean flour
Owner: Darrell Siu
Estimated Sales: $900,000-$1 Million
Number Employees: 10-19
Square Footage: 4800
Type of Packaging: Consumer, Food Service
Brands Exported: Hula
Brands Imported: Avebe
Regions Imported from: Europe, Asia
Percentage of Business in Importing: 100

46682 Modern Products Inc
6425 W Executive Dr
Mequon, WI 53092-4478   262-242-2400
         Fax: 262-242-2751   800-877-8935
         modernfearn@aol.com www.modernfearn.com
Seasonings, spices, bake mixes, natural products and soy products
President: Gaylord G Palermo
modernfearn@aol.com
CEO & Chairman: Anthony Palermo
Secretary: Petronella Palermo
Quality Control Manager: Jim Kohnke
Estimated Sales: $2.5 Million
Number Employees: 20-49
Type of Packaging: Consumer, Food Service
Regions Exported to: Central America, South America, Europe, Canada
Percentage of Business in Exporting: 10

46683 Modular Packaging
6 Aspen Dr
Randolph, NJ 07869-1103   973-970-9393
                   Fax: 973-970-9388
customer.services@modularpackaging.com
                www.modularpackaging.com
Packaging machinery including unscrambler desiccant feeders, shrink bundlers, cottoners, blister and case packers, cappers, etc.; importer of cartoners, case and blister packers, counters, etc.; exporter of liquid fillers, tube fillersand cottoners
President: Clifford Smith
cliffs@modularpackaging.com
Vice President: Bradford Smith
Estimated Sales: $ 3 - 5,000,000
Number Employees: 10-19
Square Footage: 36000
Brands Exported: Modular
Regions Exported to: South America, Canada
Percentage of Business in Exporting: 5
Brands Imported: Cariba; King; MAC; Mimi P&D
Regions Imported from: South America, Europe
Percentage of Business in Importing: 40

46684 Modular Panel Company
63 David Street
New Bedford, MA 02744-2320   508-993-9955
                   Fax: 508-993-9957
Manufacturer and exporter of insulated panels for freezers and coolers
President: James Chadwick
Drafting Engineer: Pasquale Sbardella
Estimated Sales: Below $5 Million
Number Employees: 10
Regions Exported to: Central America
Percentage of Business in Exporting: 10

46685 Modulightor Inc
246 E 58th St
New York, NY 10022-2011   212-371-0336
         Fax: 212-371-0335 www.modulightor.com
Manufacturer, importer and wholesaler/distributor of lighting fixtures
Owner: Ernst Wagner
ernst@modulightor.com
Estimated Sales: $1-2.5 Million
Number Employees: 10-19
Square Footage: 26000

46686 Moen Industries
10330 Pioneer Blvd
Suite 230
Santa Fe Springs, CA 90670   562-946-6381
         Fax: 562-946-3200   800-732-7766
                  rstorms@moenindustries.com
Manufacturer and exporter of corrugated box forming and sealing equipment
Owner: Carl Moen
Sales Co-coordinator: Iris Walker
Contact: Noreen Boos
boos@moenindustries.com
Purchasing Manager: Lori Maxey
Estimated Sales: $5-10 Million
Number Employees: 50-99
Square Footage: 76000
Brands Exported: Moen
Regions Exported to: Central America, South America, Asia, Canada, Caribbean, Latin America, Mexico
Percentage of Business in Exporting: 20

46687 Moet Hennessy USA
85 10th Ave
New York, NY 10011   212-251-8200
                        www.mhusa.com
Wines and spirits.
President & CEO: Jim Clerkin
Managing Director: Jo Thornton
Year Founded: 1980
Estimated Sales: $884.58 Million
Number Employees: 3,452
Other Locations:
    New JerseyMassachusettsIllinoisFloridaGeorgiaTexas Massachusetts

46688 Mogen David Wine Corp
85 Bourne St
Westfield, NY 14787   716-326-3151
                       www.mogendavid.com
Kosher and nonkosher wines including white, rose and red.
President: E. Schwartz
Year Founded: 1933
Estimated Sales: $200-500 Million
Number Employees: 100-249
Parent Co: The Wine Group
Type of Packaging: Consumer
Regions Exported to: Worldwide

46689 Moisture Register Products
9567 Arrow Route
Suite E
Rancho Cucamonga, CA 91730   909-941-7776
         Fax: 909-941-1830   800-966-4788
                  sales@aquameasure.com
              www.moistureregisterproducts.com
Manufacturer and exporter of computers for measuring moisture content in solids for the food processing industry
Owner: John Lundstrom
Sales: Gabriel Cote
craig.mitchell@bankofamerica.com
Contact: Craig Mitchell
craig.mitchell@bankofamerica.com
Estimated Sales: $ 3 - 5 Million
Number Employees: 10-19
Parent Co: Aqua Measure Instrument Company
Regions Exported to: Worldwide
Percentage of Business in Exporting: 20
Regions Imported from: Worldwide
Percentage of Business in Importing: 20

46690 Mold-Rite Plastics LLC
2222 Highland Rd
Twinsburg, OH 44087-2231   330-425-4206
         Fax: 330-425-4586 marketing@weatherchem.com
                        www.weatherchem.net
A packaging company that designs, develops, and delivers innovative dispensing closures.
CEO: Jennifer Altstadt
CFO: Bill Wolf
Research & Development: Barry Daggett
VP Marketing: Anna Fedova-Levi
Director of Sales: Jack Hotz
VP Operations: Carol Rinder

Importers & Exporters / A-Z

Estimated Sales: $10-20 Million
Number Employees: 100-249
Square Footage: 80000
Parent Co: Weatherhead Industries
Type of Packaging: Consumer, Food Service, Private Label
Regions Exported to: Central America, South America, Europe, Asia, Middle East

46691 Molding Automation Concepts
1760 Kilkenny Ct
Woodstock, IL 60098   815-337-3000
     Fax: 815-337-3020 800-435-6979
               sales@macautomation.com
                   www.macautomation.com
Manufacturer and exporter of horizontal, incline and elevator belt conveyors for automatic box, tote bag and tray filling systems
President: Frank Altvedt
R&D: Frank Altvedt
Sales Manager: Randy Artheid
Contact: April Booze
april@centerforenrichedliving.org
Estimated Sales: $ 10 - 20,000,000
Number Employees: 50-99
Type of Packaging: Bulk
Regions Exported to: Canada, England
Percentage of Business in Exporting: 5

46692 Moledina Commodities
5501 Muirfield Court
Flower Mound, TX 75028   817-490-1101
     Fax: 817-490-1105 mohamed@moledina.com
Manufacturer of quality green coffees from throughout the work, with a strong emphasis on East African Coffees.
President: Mohamed Moledina
VP: Fidahusein R Moledina
fidahusein@moledina.com

46693 Moli-International
1150 W Virginia Ave
Denver, CO 80223-2026   303-777-0364
     Fax: 303-777-0658 800-525-8468
               sales@moliinternational.com
                   www.moliinternational.com
Manufacturer and exporter of displays, sampling and merchandising covers, pans, trays, clear plexiglass, service carts, ice bins, water stations, sinks and sneeze guards
Owner: Larry Larson
llarson@moliinternational.com
Secretary/Treasurer: Larry Larson
Estimated Sales: $500,000-$1 Million
Number Employees: 5-9
Square Footage: 25000
Type of Packaging: Food Service
Regions Exported to: Europe, Asia, Canada

46694 Molinaro's Fine Italian Foods Ltd.
2345 Stanfield Rd
Unit 50
Mississauga, ON L4Y 3Y3
Canada   905-281-0352
                   www.molinaros.com
Processor, importer and exporter of pizza, fresh and frozen pizza shells, fresh pasta, flatbread, focaccia, pasta sauce, fresh and frozen pasta entrees, meat, vegetable and cheese lasagna, panzerottis and calzones
President: Vince Molinaro
CEO: Gino Molinaro
Sales/Marketing: Catherine Pyman
Purchasing Manager: Frank Molinaro
Number Employees: 140
Square Footage: 304000
Type of Packaging: Consumer, Food Service, Private Label, Bulk
Brands Exported: Molinaro's; Famosa; Supremo
Regions Exported to: Central America, South America, Mexico, Japan, Caribbean
Percentage of Business in Exporting: 40
Regions Imported from: Central America, Caribbean, Latin America, Mexico

46695 Moline Machinery LLC
114 S Central Ave
PO Box 16308
Duluth, MN 55807-2302   218-624-5734
     Fax: 218-628-3853 800-767-5734
               sales@moline.com www.moline.com
Manufacturer and exporter of proofing, frying and dough processing systems for doughnuts, specialty breads, snack foods and yeast raised products

President: Gary Moline
gmoline@moline.com
Sales Manager: Terry King
Engineering Director: Larry Meyer
Estimated Sales: $10-20 Million
Number Employees: 50-99
Square Footage: 190000
Brands Exported: Moline
Regions Exported to: Worldwide
Percentage of Business in Exporting: 20

46696 Molinera International
PO Box 557732
Miami, FL 33255-7732   305-883-6060
                Fax: 305-887-4997
Wholesaler/distributor of canned fruits, sweet red pimientos, artichokes, asparagus, virgin and pure oil, rice, beans, etc.; importer of olive oil, sweet red pimientos, etc.; exporter of rice, beans and corn and vegetable oils; serving the food service market
CEO: Fernando Siman
VP: Juan-Carlos Ley
Estimated Sales: $20-50 Million
Number Employees: 20-49
Square Footage: 27000
Brands Exported: Surfine; Hormel; Molinera
Regions Exported to: Central America, South America, Caribbean
Percentage of Business in Exporting: 40
Brands Imported: Molinera
Regions Imported from: South America, Europe

46697 Molins/Sandiacre Richmond
8191 Brook Rd # G
Richmond, VA 23227-1334   804-421-8795
     Fax: 804-421-8798 864-486-4000
               sandiacre.usa@molins.com
Manufacturer, importer and exporter of packaging machinery
Founder: Herman Hayssen
Vice President of Sales and Marketing: Dan Minor
Estimated Sales: $ 10 - 20 Million
Number Employees: 1-4
Brands Exported: Sandiacre
Regions Exported to: Central America, South America, Canada, Mexico
Percentage of Business in Exporting: 10
Brands Imported: Sandiacre
Regions Imported from: Europe
Percentage of Business in Importing: 20

46698 (HQ)Molson Coors Beverage Company
250 South Wacker Dr.
Chicago, IL 60606
                              800-645-5376
                   www.molsoncoors.com
Brews and beer.
President/CEO, Molson Coors: Gavin Hattersley
President, Molson Coors Canada: Frederic Landtmeters
CFO: Tracey Joubert
President, Emerging Growth: Pete Marino
Chief Strategy Officer: Rahul Goyal
Chief People & Diversity Officer: Dave Osswald
Chief Marketing Officer: Michelle St. Jacques
President, U.S. Sales: Kevin Doyle
Chief Communications Officer: Adam Collins
Chief Legal & Government Affairs Officer: E. Lee Reichert
Chief Supply Chain Officer: Brian Erhardt
Estimated Sales: $6.7 Billion
Number Employees: 17,000
Number of Brands: 100
Type of Packaging: Consumer
Other Locations:
    Molson Coors Canada
    Montreal, QCMillerCoors
    Chicago, ILMolson Coors CanadaPrague, Czech Rep.
Brands Exported: Coors Light; Coors Banquet; Zima
Regions Exported to: Worldwide
Percentage of Business in Exporting: 5

46699 Momar
1830 Ellsworth Industrial Drive NW
Atlanta, GA 30318-3746
                              800-556-3967
               info@momar.com www.momar.com
Manufacturer and exporter of industrial maintenance chemicals, water treatment products, lubricants and cleaning chemicals for the food processing industry

Estimated Sales: $ 34 Million
Number Employees: 300
Square Footage: 50000
Regions Exported to: Central America, Europe, Asia, Caribbean, South Africa, Australia
Percentage of Business in Exporting: 10

46700 Monadnock Paper Mills Inc
117 Antrim Rd
Bennington, NH 03442-4205   603-588-3311
                Fax: 603-588-3158
Manufacturer and exporter of paper including uncoated cover, text, technical specialty and converting, nonwovens
President/Chairman/CEO: Richard Verney
rverney@mpm.com
Managing Director: Keith Hayward
Vice President/CFO/Treasurer: Andrew Manns
Vice President: Julie Hughes
Director, Information Technology: Joseph Gleason
Quality Control Manager: Richard Beahm
Vice President, Sales: James Clemente
Plant Manager: Dave Burnham
Purchasing Manager: Denise Long
Estimated Sales: $ 68 Million
Number Employees: 100-249
Square Footage: 300000
Regions Exported to: Europe

46701 Monarch Beverage Company
3630 Peachtree Road NE
Suite 775
Atlanta, GA 30326   404-262-4040
     Fax: 404-262-4001 800-241-3732
               info@monarchbeverages.com
                   www.monarchbeverages.com
Manufacturer and exporter of concentrates including sports and energy drinks, healthy fruit beverages, enhanced waters, ready-to-drink beverages, ready-to-drink coffees and soft drinks. Beverage brand franchisor.
CEO: Jacques Bombal
COO: Didier Arnaud
Estimated Sales: $3.2 Million
Number Employees: 30
Type of Packaging: Bulk

46702 Monarch Import Company
1 S Dearborn St # 1700
Chicago, IL 60603-2308   312-346-9200
                Fax: 312-855-1220
Importer of beer
CEO: James Ryan
Director: Jennifer Hou
CEO: Alexander Berk
Number Employees: 100-249
Number of Brands: 1
Number of Products: 1
Brands Imported: Tsingtao
Regions Imported from: Asia

46703 Monarch-McLaren
329 Deerhide Crescent
Weston, ON M9M 2Z2
Canada   416-741-9675
                Fax: 416-741-2873
Manufacturer, importer and wholesaler/distributor of conveyor and transmission belting, V-belts, timing belts, variable speed belts, hoses, pulleys, chains, sprockets, bearings, speed reducers, casters, motors, couplings, belt lacingleather packings, etc
President: Terence Whitfield
Sales Manager: Brian Flint
Estimated Sales: Below $5 Million
Number Employees: 10
Square Footage: 72400
Brands Imported: Flexible Steel; Lambeth
Regions Imported from: Europe

46704 Mondial Foods Company
P.O.Box 75036
Los Angeles, CA 90075-0036   213-383-3531
Processor and exporter of pineapple and other tropical juices
President: Ben Gattegno
Estimated Sales: $210000
Number Employees: 20-49
Type of Packaging: Food Service, Bulk
Regions Exported to: Asia

Importers & Exporters / A-Z

46705 Money's Mushrooms
#800-1500 W Georgia Street
Vancouver, BC V6G 2Z6
Canada   604-669-3741
         Fax: 604-669-9732 800-669-7992
                          www.calbur.com
Processor, grower and exporter of canned and pickled mushrooms
President: Keith Potter
CFO: Cliff Lillicrop
VP Sales/Marketing: Dean Fleming
Number Employees: 900
Type of Packaging: Consumer, Food Service, Private Label, Bulk
Brands Exported: Money's
Regions Exported to: Asia, USA

46706 Monin Inc.
Clearwater, FL   855-352-8671
                          www.monin.com
Manufacturer and exporter of flavored syrups, smoothie mixes and purees, sauces, cocktail mixes, and sweeteners.
CEO: Bill Lombardo
Owner: Olivier Monin
VP of Marketing: Suzanna Geel
Regions Exported to: Europe, Asia

46707 Monitor Company
P.O.Box 4411
Modesto, CA 95352-4411   209-523-0500
         Fax: 209-523-4267 800-537-3201
Manufacturer and exporter of temperature recorders
Estimated Sales: $ 1 - 5 Million
Number Employees: 15
Regions Exported to: Worldwide
Percentage of Business in Exporting: 40

46708 Monitor Technologies LLC
44W320 Keslinger Rd
Elburn, IL 60119   630-365-9403
         Fax: 630-365-5646 800-601-6204
monitor@monitortech.com www.monitortech.com
Level and flow monitoring products for powder and bulk solids
President/Owner: Craig Russell
Estimated Sales: $5+ Million
Number Employees: 20-49
Type of Packaging: Private Label
Regions Exported to: Central America, South America, Europe, Asia
Percentage of Business in Exporting: 25

46709 Monroe Environmental Corp
810 W Front St
Monroe, MI 48161-1627   734-242-7654
         Fax: 734-242-5275 800-992-7707
         sales@mon-env.com www.mon-env.com
Manufacturer oil mist, smoke and vapor collectors, venturi scrubbers, dust collectors, water & wastewater clarifiers.
Owner: Gary Pashaian
gpashaian@monroeenvironmental.com
Sales Manager: Adam Pashaian
Operations Manager: Rob Cardella
Estimated Sales: $15 Million
Number Employees: 50-99
Square Footage: 70000
Regions Exported to: Central America, Asia, Mexico
Percentage of Business in Exporting: 10

46710 Monster Beverage Corp.
1 Monster Way
Corona, CA 92879
                          800-426-7367
         info@monsterbevcorp.com
         www.monsterbevcorp.com
Energy drinks.
President/Vice Chair/COO: Hilton Schlosberg
Chairman/CEO: Rodney Sacks
Year Founded: 2002
Estimated Sales: $3.3 Billion
Number Employees: 1,991
Number of Brands: 7
Parent Co: The Coca-Cola Company
Type of Packaging: Consumer, Food Service
Regions Exported to: Worldwide
Percentage of Business in Exporting: 1

46711 Monster Cone
8500 Delmeade
Montreal, QC H4T 1L6
Canada   541-636-2022
         Fax: 514-342-0346 800-542-9801
                          info@monstercone.com
Processor and exporter of waffle bowls and cones including plain and chocolate dipped
President: Daniel Mardinger
Number Employees: 50-99
Square Footage: 80000
Type of Packaging: Consumer, Food Service, Private Label, Bulk
Brands Exported: Monster Cone
Regions Exported to: USA
Percentage of Business in Exporting: 65

46712 Montague Co
1830 Stearman Ave
Hayward, CA 94545-1018   510-785-8822
         Fax: 510-785-3342 800-345-1830
                          www.montaguecompany.com
Manufacturer and exporter of commercial gas and electric cooking equipment. Products include convection ovens, deluxe griddles, heavy duty & medium duty ranges, counter equipment, fryers, over-fired and under-fired broilers, deckovens, chinese ranges, induction cooking equipment, under-counter refrigeration, and custom island suites.
President: Thomas Whalen
twhalen@montague-inc.com
VP Finance: R Erickson
VP Sales/Marketing: Gary Rupp
Purchasing: Lisa Catanzano
Estimated Sales: $30-30 Million
Number Employees: 100-249
Type of Packaging: Food Service
Brands Exported: Grizzly; Legend; Vectaire; Hearthbake; Extreme Cuisine; Excalibur; Crusader
Regions Exported to: Worldwide
Percentage of Business in Exporting: 15

46713 Montalbano Development Inc
3275 Veterans Meml Hwy # B15
Ronkonkoma, NY 11779-7665 631-737-2236
         Fax: 631-467-1035 800-739-9152
                          www.montalbanoinc.com
Provider of computer services for the food industry including
Owner: Chris Montalbano
chrism@montalbanoinc.com
VP: Chris Montalbano
Manager: Steghen Naroney
Estimated Sales: $2.5-5,000,000
Number Employees: 20-49
Regions Exported to: Worldwide

46714 Montana Naturals
1400 Kearns Blvd
Park City, UT 84060-6725
                          800-650-9597
                          www.mtnaturals.com
Processor and exporter of dietary supplements
General Manager: Sterling Gabbitas
Number Employees: 50-99
Square Footage: 104000
Parent Co: HealthRite
Type of Packaging: Consumer, Private Label
Other Locations:
    Montana Naturals by HealthRit
    Arlee, MTMontana Naturals by HealthRit
Brands Exported: Montana Naturals; Montana Big Sky; Herbal Specialties; Nautilus Nutritionals
Regions Exported to: Asia, Middle East, Canada
Percentage of Business in Exporting: 15

46715 Montana Specialty Mills LLC
701 2nd St S # 5
P.O.Box 2208
Great Falls, MT 59405-1852 406-761-2338
         Fax: 406-761-7926 800-332-2024
                          www.mtspecialtymills.com
Primary agricultural processor providing contracting, origination, storage and processing of grain and oilseed-based products to secondary food manufacturers
President: Steve Chambers
steve@mtspecialtymills.com
Controller: Cecil Swensen
General Manager: Gordon Svenby
Operations: Robert Bender
Conrad Plant Manager: Gordon Mattern
Estimated Sales: Below $ 5 Million
Number Employees: 20-49
Square Footage: 80000
Regions Exported to: Worldwide
Percentage of Business in Exporting: 5
Regions Imported from: Canada
Percentage of Business in Importing: 10

46716 Montana Tea & Spice Trading
2600 W Broadway St
Missoula, MT 59808-1624   406-721-4882
         Fax: 406-543-1126 montanatea@msn.com
                          www.montanatea
Tea and herbal tea blending, spice blending. Wholesale, retail and mail order
Owner: Sherri Lee
Estimated Sales: $750,000
Number Employees: 5-9
Number of Brands: 2
Number of Products: 300+
Square Footage: 16000

46717 Monte Vista Farming Co
5043 N Montpelier Rd
Denair, CA 95316-9608   209-874-1866
         Fax: 209-874-2024 www.montevistafarming.com
Processor and exporter of almonds
President: Jonathan Hoff
jhoff@montevistafarming.com
CFO: Bob McClain
VP Sales: Dan Whisenhunt
Operations Manager: Renee Crozier
Estimated Sales: $1.3 Million
Number Employees: 50-99
Square Footage: 8000
Regions Exported to: Worldwide
Percentage of Business in Exporting: 90

46718 Montello Inc
6106 E 32nd Pl # 100
Tulsa, OK 74135-5495   918-665-1170
         Fax: 918-665-1480 800-331-4628
                          www.montelloinc.com
Importer and distributor of emulsifiers and gums
President: Allen Johnson
allenj@montelloinc.com
VP: Leo Wooldridge
Estimated Sales: $6 Million
Number Employees: 5-9
Brands Imported: Cellogen CMC; DK Ester
Regions Imported from: Asia

46719 Monterey Mushrooms Inc
260 Westgate Dr
Watsonville, CA 95076
         Fax: 831-763-2300 800-333-6874
                          www.montereymushrooms.com
Manufacturer and exporter of canned, frozen and refrigerated mushroom stems/pieces, slices and buttons
President & CEO: Shah Kazemi
shah.kazemi@montmush.com
VP of Sales & Marketing: Mike O'Brien
Number Employees: 1000-4999
Type of Packaging: Consumer, Food Service, Private Label, Bulk
Other Locations:
    Multi Site Fresh Operation Farms
    Orlando, FL
    Multi Site Fresh Operation Farms
    Princeton, IL
    Multi Site Fresh Operation Farms
    Royal Oaks, CA
    Multi Site Fresh Operation Farms
    Las Lomas, CA
    Multi Site Fresh Operation Farms
    Morgan Hill, CAMulti Site Fresh Operation FarmsPrinceton

46720 Monument Industries Inc
159 Phyllis Ln
Bennington, VT 05201-1663 802-442-8187
                          Fax: 802-442-8188
Manufacturer and exporter of polyethylene bags
Vice President: Jay L Whitten
VP: Jay L Whitten
Estimated Sales: $5-10 Million
Number Employees: 20-49
Regions Exported to: Bermuda
Percentage of Business in Exporting: 5

46721 Moore Paper Boxes Inc
2916 Boulder Ave
Dayton, OH 45414-4834   937-278-7327
                          Fax: 937-278-5932

455

Importers & Exporters / A-Z

Manufacturer and exporter of paper boxes
President: Charles Moore
Estimated Sales: $10-20 Million
Number Employees: 5-9
Regions Exported to: Worldwide

46722 Moore Production Tool Spec Inc
37531 Grand River Ave
Farmington Hills, MI 48335-2879   248-476-1200
Fax: 248-476-6887
Manufacturer and exporter of sealing jaws, knives, anvils and packaging tooling
President: Durk Moore
CEO: Richard Moore
President: Richard Moore
Sales: Brian Carfango
Estimated Sales: $2.5-5 Million
Number Employees: 20-49
Square Footage: 56000
Regions Exported to: Central America, South America, Asia
Percentage of Business in Exporting: 1

46723 Moorhead & Company
PO Box 1799
Rocklin, CA 95677   818-787-2510
Fax: 916-624-1604   800-322-6325
order@moorAgar.com   www.mooragar.com
Manufacturer and importer of stabilizers including agar
President: Deborah Nichols
Sales/Marketing: Brenda Franklin
Estimated Sales: $180000
Number Employees: 3
Type of Packaging: Bulk
Regions Imported from: South America, Europe

46724 Moosehead Breweries Ltd.
89 Main St W
St. John, NB E2M 3H2
Canada
www.moosehead.ca
Processor and exporter of beer.
President & CEO: Andrew Oland
Executive Chairman: Derek Oland
CFO: Patrick Oland
VP, Supply Chain: Matthew Oland
Quality Control Technician: Jeanann Fairweather
Director of Marketing & Communications: Karen Cousins
Retail Operations Manager: Stephen Buckley
Special Projects Manager: Mary Gardner
Year Founded: 1867
Estimated Sales: $263.8 Million
Number Employees: 400
Type of Packaging: Consumer, Food Service
Brands Exported: Moosehead
Regions Exported to: USA

46725 Morehouse Foods Inc
760 Epperson Dr
City Of Industry, CA 91748-1336   626-854-1655
Fax: 626-854-1656   888-297-9800
info@morehousefoods.com
www.morehousefoods.com
Yellow mustard, dijon mustard, stoneground mustard, honey spice mustard, spicy brown mustard, horseradish mustard, distilled vinegar and horseradish.
President: David Latter
davesr@morehousefoods.com
Year Founded: 1898
Estimated Sales: $20 - 50 Million
Number Employees: 20-49
Square Footage: 80000
Type of Packaging: Consumer, Food Service, Private Label, Bulk
Brands Exported: El Rey; Morehouse; Rhingeld
Regions Exported to: Worldwide
Percentage of Business in Exporting: 20
Regions Imported from: Worldwide
Percentage of Business in Importing: 5

46726 Morey's Seafood Intl LLC
1218 Highway 10 S
Motley, MN 56466-8209   218-352-6345
Fax: 218-352-6523   800-808-3474
www.moreysmarkets.com
Processor, importer and exporter of fresh and frozen fish including marinated salmon, marinated tilapia and marinated smoked fish and other speciality products.
President: Jim Walstrom
CFO: Gary Ziolkowski
Plant Manager: Patti Zahler
VP of Purchasing: Greg Frank
Year Founded: 1937
Estimated Sales: $20 - 50 Million
Number Employees: 10-19
Square Footage: 52000
Parent Co: Morey's Seafood International
Brands Exported: Morey's
Regions Exported to: Europe, Canada
Percentage of Business in Exporting: 5
Regions Imported from: Europe, Canada
Percentage of Business in Importing: 5

46727 Morgan & Company
943 Avenida Pico # E
San Clemente, CA 92673-3914   949-940-9006
Manager: Morgan Calucci
Estimated Sales: $.5 - 1 million
Number Employees: 1-4

46728 Morgan Foods Inc
90 W Morgan St
Austin, IN 47102   812-794-1170
888-430-1780
mfi-web@morganfoods.com
www.morganfoods.com
Canned foods including condensed soups, baked and refried beans, gravies, condiments and sauces.
SVP & Chief Financial Officer: Dan Slattery
dan.slattery@morganfoods.com
CEO & Chairman: John Morgan
Vice Chairman: Kelly Morgan Maciejak
Regional Sales Manager: Monty Craig
VP, Sales & Marketing: Bryan Flowers
VP, Human Resources: Phillip Bundy
Production Manager: Richard Miller
Year Founded: 1899
Estimated Sales: $48.5 Million
Number Employees: 250-499
Square Footage: 1000000
Type of Packaging: Consumer, Food Service, Private Label

46729 Morgan Winery
590 Brunken Ave
Suite C
Salinas, CA 93901   831-751-7777
Fax: 831-751-7780   www.morganwinery.com
Wine
Propietors: Donna Lee
Propietors: Dan Lee
Wine Maker: Giane Abate
Marketing Coordinator: Jason Auxier
Director of Sales: Jim McAllister
Contact: Jason Auxier
jason.auxier@morganwinery.com
Production Team: Carmen Maldonado
Estimated Sales: $850000
Number Employees: 5-9
Regions Exported to: Worldwide

46730 Morley Sales Co
119 N 2nd St
Geneva, IL 60134-2226   630-845-8750
Fax: 630-845-8749
Import and export broker of seafood, frozen foods, dairy/deli products, groceries and private label items
Secretary/Treasurer: Gary Slavik
Manager: Jessica Weaver
Contact: Al Mazulis
al@morleysales.com
Estimated Sales: $1.9 Million
Number Employees: 1-4
Square Footage: 1000

46731 Morre-Tec Ind Inc
1 Gary Rd
Union, NJ 07083-5527   908-686-0307
Fax: 908-688-9005   sales@morretec.com
www.morretec.com
Manufacturer, importer and exporter of magnesium chloride, food grade and potassium bromate; importer and wholesaler/distributor of low sodium substitutes and licorice, spray, dried and powder
Owner: Rachel Abenilla
rachela@morretec.com
Marketing Director: Michael Fuchs
Operations Manager: Norm Cantoe
Estimated Sales: $ 10 - 20 Million
Number Employees: 20-49
Number of Products: 150
Square Footage: 50000
Type of Packaging: Consumer, Bulk
Regions Exported to: Central America, South America, Europe, Asia, Middle East, Australia
Percentage of Business in Exporting: 10
Regions Imported from: Worldwide
Percentage of Business in Importing: 80

46732 Morris & Associates
803 Morris Dr
Garner, NC 27529   919-582-9200
Fax: 919-582-9100   info@morris-associates.com
www.morris-associates.com
Custom refrigeration equipment for the foodprocessing industry. Specializing in industrial ice makers and storage and delivery systems.
CEO: Bill Morris III
Research & Development: John Shell
Marketing Director: Virginia Arello
Sales Director: Bobby Cathey
Operations Manager: David Maw
Production Manager: Ron Correia
Purchasing Manager: Tome Patterson
Estimated Sales: $ 5 - 10 Million
Number Employees: 10-19
Number of Products: 20+
Square Footage: 100000
Brands Exported: Ice-Master
Regions Exported to: Central America, South America, Europe, Asia, Middle East, Canada
Percentage of Business in Exporting: 20

46733 Morris J Golombeck Inc
960 Franklin Ave
Brooklyn, NY 11225-2403   718-284-3505
Fax: 718-693-1941   golspice@aol.com
www.golombeckspice.com
Processor, importer and exporter of herbs and spices including basil, cassia, cayenne, garlic, ginger, paprika, etc
Owner: Hy Golombeck
mail@golombeckspice.com
Vice President: Sheldon Golombeck
Estimated Sales: $ 5 - 10 Million
Number Employees: 10-19
Square Footage: 480000
Type of Packaging: Bulk
Regions Imported from: Central America, South America, Europe, Asia, Middle East
Percentage of Business in Importing: 90

46734 Morris Okun
209 Hunts Point Term Mkt
Bronx, NY 10474-7402   718-589-7700
Fax: 718-328-6148
Importer, exporter and wholesaler/distributor of produce and nuts
President: Tom Cignarella
Chief Executive Officer & Owner: Ronnie Okun
Estimated Sales: $35.3 Million
Number Employees: 150
Square Footage: 30000
Regions Exported to: Worldwide
Percentage of Business in Exporting: 20
Regions Imported from: Worldwide
Percentage of Business in Importing: 20

46735 Morrison Timing Screw Co
335 W 194th St
Glenwood, IL 60425-1501   708-331-6600
Fax: 708-756-6620   info@morrison-chs.com
www.morrison-chs.com
Manufacturer and exporter of timing screws and automatic can opening systems
President: Nick Wilson
CEO: Nancy Wilson
Vice President: Lois Hayworth
Vice President of Operations: Chris Wilson
IT: Tim Dupin
tim.dupin@morrison-chs.com
Estimated Sales: $10-20 Million
Number Employees: 20-49
Regions Exported to: Worldwide

46736 Morrissey Displays & Models
20 Beverly Rd
Port Washington, NY 11050   516-883-6944
Fax: 516-767-2379
Manufacturer and exporter of display booths
Owner: Stuart Morrissey
Estimated Sales: $500,000-$1 Million
Number Employees: 1-4

Importers & Exporters / A-Z

46737 Morrow Technologies Corporation
12000 28th Streett North
St Petersburg, FL 33716   727-531-4000
         Fax: 727-531-3531 877-526-8711
sales@janusdisplays.com www.janusdisplays.com
Manufacturer and exporter of interior electronic signs including Leo, LCD and Plasma
Owner: Sharon Morrow
CEO: John Morrow
Controller: Kathy Naranjo
Marketing: Rhonda Candreva
Sales Manager: Steve Asbrand
Number Employees: 20-49

46738 Morse Manufacturing Co Inc
727 W Manlius St
East Syracuse, NY 13057-2145   315-437-8475
Fax: 315-437-1029 inquiry@morsedrum.com
www.morsemfgco.com
Drum handling equipment, fork attachments for drum moving and drum mixers; exporter of drum handling equipment including rotators, handlers and tumblers
President: Nate Andrews
Chairman Of the Board: Robert Andrews
randrews@morsedrum.com
Marketing: Ralph Phillips
Sales Manager: Phil Mulpagano
Number Employees: 20-49
Number of Brands: 1
Number of Products: 100
Brands Exported: Morse
Regions Exported to: Central America, South America, Europe, Asia, Middle East
Percentage of Business in Exporting: 5

46739 Mortec Industries Inc
29240 County Road R
P.O. Box 977
Brush, CO 80723-9444   970-842-5063
       Fax: 970-842-5061 800-541-9983
joe@mortecscales.com www.mortecscales.com
Manufacturer and exporter of electronic weighing scales; wholesaler/distributor of computer hardware and software; serving the food service market
Owner: Joe Kral
mortecscales@gmail.com
Estimated Sales: $ 1-2.5 Million
Number Employees: 1-4
Type of Packaging: Consumer, Food Service

46740 Mortimer's Fine Foods
5341 John Lucas Drive
Burlington, ON L7L 6A8
Canada
                    905-336-0000
           Fax: 905-336-0909
customerservice@mortimers.com
           www.mortimers.com
Processor and exporter of frozen beef, prepared and vegetarian entrees and meat pies
VP Sales: Karim Talakshi
Type of Packaging: Consumer, Food Service, Private Label, Bulk
Brands Exported: Mortimer Fine Foods
Regions Exported to: USA

46741 Morton Salt Inc.
123 North Wacker Dr.
Chicago, IL 60606-1743   312-807-2000
           Fax: 312-807-2899 800-725-8847
                      www.mortonsalt.com
Salt including food grade and rock salt.
Chief Executive Officer: Christian Herrmann
Vice President/CFO: Tim McKean
Vice President/General Counsel: Chad Walker
Vice President, Human Resources: Nicole Turner
Vice President, Operations: Jennifer McCormick
Year Founded: 1848
Estimated Sales: $429.7 Million
Number Employees: 2,900
Square Footage: 95838
Parent Co: K+S AG
Type of Packaging: Consumer, Food Service, Private Label, Bulk
Other Locations:
   Morton Salt Distribution
   Newark, CA
   Grantsville, UT
   Perth Amboy, NJ
   Port Canaveral, FLMorton Salt
   DistributionGrantsville
Brands Exported: Morton & Private Label

Regions Exported to: Central America, South America, Asia, Middle East

46742 Mosaic Co
1 E Kennedy Blvd
Suite 2500
Tampa, FL 33602   813-775-4200
                         800-918-8270
                         www.mosaicco.com
Producer and marketer of concentrated phosphate and potash for the crop fertilizer industry.
President & CEO: Joc O'Rourke
SVP, Posphates: Bruce Bodine
SVP, Human Resources: Chris Lewis
SVP/General Cousel/Corporate Secretary: Mark Isaacson
SVP/CFO: Clint Freeland
SVP, Potash: Karen Swager
SVP, Mosaic Fertilizantes: Corrine Ricard
Year Founded: 1909
Estimated Sales: $7.4 Billion
Number Employees: 12,000
Square Footage: 15333
Regions Exported to: Brazil

46743 Mosher Products Inc
4318 Hayes Ave
Cheyenne, WY 82001-2349   307-632-1492
   Fax: 307-632-1492 info@wheatandgrain.com
                    www.wheatandgrain.com
Organic grain
President: Leonard O Mosher
leonard@wheatandgrain.com
Estimated Sales: Below $ 5 Million
Number Employees: 20-49
Square Footage: 240000
Other Locations:
   Bushnell, NE
Regions Exported to: Central America, South America, Europe, Asia, Middle East
Percentage of Business in Exporting: 10

46744 Mosshaim Innovations
13901 Sutton Park Drive S
Suite 120
Jacksonville, FL 32224-0229   614-985-3000
          Fax: 614-985-0703 888-995-7775
Portable, 120 volt, vitro ceramic glass stovetops. Also produces 120 volt drop-in stovetops. Patented technology will replace gas and induction portables
President: James Sarvadi
Quality Control: Tom Dorothy
R & D: James Sarvadi
VP Marketing: Donald Lewis
VP Operations: James Sarvadi
Estimated Sales: Below $5 Million
Number Employees: 10
Number of Brands: 2
Square Footage: 40000
Parent Co: Mosshaim Innovations

46745 Mosuki
PO Box 671
N Bellmore, NY 11710-0671   631-785-1262
      Fax: 718-345-2958 members.aol.com/mosukiltd
Importer, exporter and wholesaler/distributor of dispensing and food processing equipment for ice cream, yogurt, slushies, frozen cocktails, espresso/cappuccino and granita; also, fresh pasta machinery and wood burning brick pizzaovens
President: Salvatore Favarolo
VP: Anthony Favarolo
Number Employees: 20-49
Square Footage: 160000
Brands Exported: Victoria Arduino; Stoelting; CRM; Dominioni
Regions Exported to: Worldwide
Percentage of Business in Exporting: 5
Brands Imported: LaVictoria Ardvino; Ambrogi; Dominioni
Regions Imported from: Europe
Percentage of Business in Importing: 50

46746 Mother Parker's Tea & Coffee
2530 Stanfield Road
Mississauga, ON L4Y 1S4
Canada
                    905-279-9100
           Fax: 905-279-9821 800-387-9398
                    www.mother-parkers.com
Processor and exporter of ground and whole bean coffees and teas including orange pekoe, regular, decaffeinated, black and herbal; importer of green coffee and teas

Co-CEO: Michael Higgins
Co-CEO: Paul Higgins, Jr.
Sr. VP/Finance/Administration: Brian Goard
Vice President: Chris Bklecki
Number Employees: 280
Type of Packaging: Consumer, Food Service, Private Label, Bulk
Brands Exported: Higgins & Burke
Regions Exported to: Europe, Africa, USA
Regions Imported from: Worldwide
Percentage of Business in Importing: 90

46747 Motherland International Inc
8822 Flower Road
Suite 202
Rancho Cucamonga, CA 91730   909-596-8882
          Fax: 909-596-8870 800-590-5407
                          www.motherlandinc.org
Processor and exporter of herbs and vitamins in powder and extract forms used in nutritional supplements; contract manufacturing available
President: Jackson Wen
Marketing: Michael Pinson
Estimated Sales: $ 1 - 3 Million
Number Employees: 20-49
Square Footage: 100000
Parent Co: Motherland International
Type of Packaging: Consumer, Food Service, Private Label, Bulk
Regions Exported to: Worldwide

46748 Motivatit Seafoods Inc
412 Palm Ave
Houma, LA 70364-3400   985-868-7191
          Fax: 985-868-7472 www.motivatit.com
Established in 1971. Supplier of fresh oysters and clams.
Owner: Steve Voisin
CEO/VP: Mike Voisin
CFO: Dotty Voisin
Marketing/Purchasing: Kevin Voisin
Sales: Greg Voisin
steven.voisin@motivatit.com
Operations: Wayne DeHart
Estimated Sales: $20-50 Million
Number Employees: 100-249
Square Footage: 100000
Type of Packaging: Consumer, Food Service, Private Label, Bulk
Brands Exported: Wine Island Oysters
Regions Exported to: Europe, Japan
Percentage of Business in Exporting: 10
Regions Imported from: Central America
Percentage of Business in Importing: 10

46749 Motom Corporation
631 Il Route 83
Suite 180
Bensenville, IL 60106-1342   630-787-1995
                   Fax: 630-787-1795
Manufacturer and exporter of drying and baking ovens, cleaning and automated material handling equipment
President: T Teshigawara
VP: W Kojima
Number Employees: 16
Parent Co: Tsukamoto Industrial Trading Company
Regions Exported to: Worldwide

46750 Motry International
139-141 Dolomite Drive
Toronto, ON M3J 2N1
Canada
                    416-667-8800
           Fax: 416-667-0547
Importer and exporter of peanuts
President: Peter Zhang
Regions Imported from: Asia

46751 Mouli Manufacturing Corporation
1 Montgomery Street
Belleville, NJ 07109-1305   201-751-6900
          Fax: 201-751-0345 800-789-8285
                          moulimfg@aol.com
Manufacturer, importer and exporter of stainless steel food service equipment including cheese shredders, choppers, cutter, peelers, pots, pans and vegetable processors, etc
VP: P Varkala
Sales: Chris Varkala
Estimated Sales: $ 1 - 5 Million
Number Employees: 5-9
Square Footage: 60000

Importers & Exporters / A-Z

Regions Exported to: South America, Mexico, Canada
Percentage of Business in Exporting: 1
Regions Imported from: Europe

46752 Mountain Rose Herbs
35859 Highway 58
Pleasant Hill, OR 97455-9651 541-741-7307
 Fax: 510-217-4012 800-879-3337
customerservice@mountainroseherbs.com
www.mountainroseherbsmercantile.com
Organic herbal products.
Owner: Julie Baily
Vice President: Shawn Donnille
Laboratory/Quality Control Manager: Steven Yeager
Marketing Director: Irene Wolansky
Terms Department Manager: Ray Sammartano
julie@mountainroseherbs.com
Public And Media Relations: Kori Rodley
Operations Manager: Jennifer Gerrity
Production Manager: Julie DeBord
Warehouse Manager: Kim Christenson
Purchasing Manager: Peggy Hall
Estimated Sales: Less Than $500,000
Number Employees: 5-9
Type of Packaging: Consumer, Bulk

46753 Mountain Safety Research
4000 1st Avenue South
Seattle, WA 98134 206-505-9500
 Fax: 206-682-4184 800-877-9677
info@msrgear.com www.cascadedesigns.com
Manufacturer, importer, and exporter of camp stoves, fuel bottles, water filtration products and cook sets
President: Joe Mc Sweeney
Research & Development: Kevin Gallagher
Manager Marketing/Sales: Michael Glavin
Director, Government Sales: Tim Davis
Contact: Dave Bartholomew
dbartholomew@msrgear.com
VP Operations/Engineering: R Michael Ligrano
Manager Product: Gail Snyder
Estimated Sales: $10-20 Million
Number Employees: 1-4
Number of Brands: 1
Number of Products: 250
Square Footage: 160000
Parent Co: Recreational Equipment
Type of Packaging: Consumer
Regions Exported to: Central America, South America, Europe, Asia, Middle East, Canada
Percentage of Business in Exporting: 30
Brands Imported: Trangia
Regions Imported from: Europe, Asia, Canada
Percentage of Business in Importing: 25

46754 Mountain Valley Products Inc
108 East Blaine Avenue
PO Box 246
Sunnyside, WA 98944-0246 509-837-8084
 Fax: 509-837-3481 www.valleyprocessing.com
Processor and exporter of fruit juice concentrates including apple and grape; also, apple juice
President: Mary Ann Bliesner
VP Operation: Kelly Blienser
Maintenance Manager: Jay Fanciullo
Sales Manager: Terry Bliesner
Maintenance Supervisor: Mark Mulford
Production/Personnel: David Perez
Estimated Sales: $1.2 Million
Number Employees: 20-49
Square Footage: 180000
Type of Packaging: Bulk
Regions Exported to: Asia
Percentage of Business in Exporting: 1

46755 Mountain Valley Water Company
PO Box 660070
Miami Springs, FL 33266 305-883-2200
 Fax: 305-885-7800
www.mountainvalleyspring.com
Exporter and wholesaler/distributor of bottled spring water
Owner: Lee Holtzman
Number Employees: 5-9
Type of Packaging: Bulk
Regions Exported to: Central America

46756 Moyer Diebel
3765 Champion Blvd
Winston Salem, NC 27105-2667 336-661-1992
 Fax: 336-661-1979 info@moyerdiebel.com
www.moyerdiebel.com
Manufacturer and exporter of commercial dishwashers
President: Lin Senseing
lsenseing@championindustries.com
Sales Associate: Robert Croker
Estimated Sales: $20-50 Million
Number Employees: 100-249
Regions Exported to: Central America, South America, Latin America, Caribbean, Mexico

46757 Moyer Packing Co.
741 Souder Rd.
Elroy, PA 18964
 Fax: 970-346-4611 800-967-8325
www.mopac.com
Boxed and ground beef, and fresh and frozen boxed beef.
Year Founded: 1877
Estimated Sales: Less Than $500,000
Parent Co: JBS USA
Type of Packaging: Consumer, Private Label, Bulk
Brands Exported: MOPAC
Regions Exported to: Worldwide
Percentage of Business in Exporting: 20

46758 Moyno
PO Box 960
Springfield, OH 45501 937-327-3111
 Fax: 937-327-3177 www.moyno.com
Manufacturer and exporter of progressing cavity pumps and pinch valves
VP Operations: Norman Shearer
Product Manager: Andy Kosiak
VP Sales: Bob Lepera
Contact: Paul Reiss
paul.reiss@nov.com
Engineering Manager: Dale Parrett
Plant Manager: Todd Brown
Estimated Sales: $20-30 Million
Number Employees: 250-499
Square Footage: 240000
Parent Co: National Oilwell Varco
Brands Exported: Moyno; R&M; RKL
Regions Exported to: Worldwide
Percentage of Business in Exporting: 20

46759 Mr Chips For Pickles
2606 N Huron Rd
Pinconning, MI 48650-9512 989-879-3555
 Fax: 989-879-2659 www.mrchipsforpickles.com
Contact: Randy Hugo
rhugo@mrchipsforpickles.com

46760 Mr Dell Foods
300 W Major St
Kearney, MO 64060-8550 816-628-4644
 Fax: 816-628-4633 mrdells@mrdells.com
www.mrdells.com
Various styles of hash browns, shredded potatoes, O'Brien potatoes, and souther style potatoes.
President: Tommy Baker
tbaker@mrdells.com
VP: Kurt Johnsen
Marketing/Sales Director: Tom Sherrer
Operations Manager: Rick Wilkins
Plant Manager: John Duncan
Estimated Sales: $8445651
Number Employees: 20-49
Square Footage: 160000
Type of Packaging: Consumer, Food Service, Bulk
Brands Exported: Mr. Dell's
Regions Exported to: Canada

46761 (HQ)Mr Ice Bucket
345 Sandford St
New Brunswick, NJ 08901-2320 732-545-0420
 Fax: 732-846-3383 www.mricebucket.com
Manufacturer and exporter of vinyl ice buckets and plastic trays and tumblers
President/CEO: Fred Haleluk
fhaleluk@mistericebucket.com
Information Systems Manager: Elaine Herman
Sales Manager: Sudesh Rajpal
Estimated Sales: $1-2.5 Million
Number Employees: 5-9
Square Footage: 40000
Brands Exported: Mr. Ice Bucket; Shelton-Ware
Regions Exported to: Central America, South America, Asia, Canada, Caribbean
Percentage of Business in Exporting: 15

46762 Mr. Bar-B-Q
5650 University Parkway
Suite 400
Winston-Salem, NC 27105 516-752-0670
 Fax: 516-752-0683 800-333-2124
mzemel@mrbarbq.com www.mrbarbq.com
Manufacturer and importer of portable butane stoves, lighters, cookers and buffet and omelet stations
President/CEO: Marc Zemel
Senior VP: Adam Schillen
Director - Sales & Marketing: Wendy Sender
Senior VP -Sales: Jeff Lynch
VP operations: Michael Guadagno
Estimated Sales: $10 - 20 Million
Number Employees: 20-49
Square Footage: 68000
Regions Imported from: Asia

46763 Mr. Broadway Kosher Restaurant
1372 Broadway (At 38th Street)
New York, NY 10018-6113 212-921-2152
 Fax: 212-768-2852 www.mrbroadwaykosher.com
Owner: Jack Dock
Estimated Sales: $300,000-500,000
Number Employees: 1-4

46764 Mrs Auld's Gourmet Foods Inc
572 Reactor Way # B4
Reno, NV 89502-4133 775-856-3350
 Fax: 775-856-3351 800-322-8537
john@mrs-aulds.com
Gourmet foods including brandied cherries, sweet and spicy pickles, marmalades, preserves, pancake, scone and soda bread mix, salsa, pasta sauce and bean, red corn and barbeque chips, chili sauce, pesto sauce, chestnuts
Owner: John Auld
Sales Manager: Teresa West
Estimated Sales: $1 - 3 Million
Number Employees: 5-9
Square Footage: 12000
Percentage of Business in Exporting: 5
Regions Imported from: Asia

46765 (HQ)Mrs Baird's
PO Box 976
Horsham, PA 19044
 800-984-0989
www.mrsbairds.com
Bread, buns, donuts, cinnamon rolls, honey buns, applie pie and chocolate cup cakes
President, Grupo Bimbo: Fred Penny
Parent Co: Bimbo Bakeries USA
Type of Packaging: Consumer, Food Service, Private Label, Bulk
Other Locations:
 Mrs Baird's Bakeries
 Abilene, TX
 Mrs Baird's Bakeries
 Fort Worth, TX
 Mrs Baird's Bakeries
 Lubbock, TX
 Mrs Baird's Bakeries
 Waco, TX
 Mrs Baird's Bakeries
 Houston, TX
 Mrs Baird's Bakeries
 San Antonio, TX
 Mrs Baird's BakeriesFort Worth

46766 (HQ)Mrs Clark's Foods
740 SE Dalbey Dr
Ankeny, IA 50021-3908 515-964-8036
 Fax: 515-964-8397 800-736-5674
info@mrsclarks.com www.mrsclarks.com
Shelf-stable beverages, sauces and dressings
President: Ron Kahrer
QC: Ned Williams
Sales: Julie Southwick
Plant Manager: John Weber
Purchasing: Ron Mathis
Estimated Sales: $450,000
Number Employees: 100-249
Number of Brands: 12
Number of Products: 50
Square Footage: 240000
Parent Co: AGRI Industries
Type of Packaging: Consumer, Food Service, Private Label

46767 Mrs. Denson's Cookie Company
120 Brush St
Ukiah, CA 95482 707-462-2272
 Fax: 707-462-2283 800-219-3199

Processor and exporter of fruit juice and honey sweetened cookies including energy, reduced fat, fat-free, vegan and organic
President/Owner: Mike Bielenberg
Vice President: Desi Ringor
Number Employees: 50-99
Square Footage: 100000
Type of Packaging: Consumer, Food Service, Private Label, Bulk
Brands Exported: Mrs. Denson's
Regions Exported to: Canada
Percentage of Business in Exporting: 8

46768 **Mrs. Dog's Products**
PO Box 6872
Grand Rapids, MI 49516-6872   616-970-2677
                   800-267-7364
mrsdogsorders@comcast.net www.mrsdogs.com
Processor and exporter of gourmet mustard, Jamaican jerk marinade and habanero pepper sauces; also, shelled green chile pistachio nuts
Owner: Julie Curtis Applegate
Estimated Sales: Less than $500,000
Number Employees: 1-4
Type of Packaging: Consumer
Regions Exported to: Worldwide
Percentage of Business in Exporting: 1

46769 **Mrs. Leeper's Pasta**
1000 Italian Way
Excelsior Springs, MO 64024   816-502-6000
       Fax: 816-502-6722   800-848-5266
Flavored dry pasta including shapes, fettucine, angel hair, wheat-free, gluten-free, bulk, organic, kosher and private label
President: Michelle Muscat
VP/Director, Sales and Marketing: Ed Muscat
Number Employees: 700
Number of Brands: 6
Type of Packaging: Consumer, Food Service, Private Label, Bulk
Brands Exported: Mrs. Leeper's Wheat Free/Gluten-Free, Eddie's Spaghetti, Michelle's Natural
Regions Exported to: Europe, Asia
Percentage of Business in Exporting: 7

46770 **(HQ)Mt Capra Products**
279 SW 9th St
Chehalis, WA 98532-3313   360-748-4224
       Fax: 360-748-3099   800-574-1961
                       www.mtcapra.com
Processor and exporter of dehydrated powder whey product and cheese including cheddar, feta and raw goat milk with no salt
Owner: Frank Stout
frank@mtcapra.com
Key Account Manager: Arny Davis
Estimated Sales: $$1-2.5 Million
Number Employees: 20-49
Square Footage: 20000
Other Locations:
    Mount Capra Cheese
    Chehalis, WAMount Capra Cheese
Regions Exported to: Worldwide
Percentage of Business in Exporting: 10

46771 **Mt Valley Farms & Lumber Prods**
1240 Nawakwa Rd
Biglerville, PA 17307-9728   717-677-6166
       Fax: 717-677-9283 admin@mtvalleyfarms.com
                   www.mtvalleyfarms.com
Hardwood bins, skids and pallets; also, sawdust
President: Henry L Taylor
CFO: Patrick McCreary
VP/Operations: H Michael Taylor
R & D: Jemay Lua
Estimated Sales: Below $5 Million
Number Employees: 50-99
Square Footage: 208000
Other Locations:
    Mountain Valley Farms &Lumbe
    Biglerville, PAMountain Valley Farms &Lumbe
Brands Exported: Enviro-Logs
Regions Exported to: Worldwide

46772 **Mt. Konocti Growers**
2550 Big Valley Road
Kelseyville, CA 95451   707-279-4213
       Fax: 707-279-2251 www.mtkonoctiwines.com
Grower, packer and exporter of bartlett pears
Manager: Robert Gayaldo
Number Employees: 5-9
Square Footage: 170000
Type of Packaging: Bulk
Brands Exported: Mt. Konocti
Regions Exported to: Worldwide
Percentage of Business in Exporting: 5

46773 **Mt. Olympus Specialty Foods**
1601 Military Road
Buffalo, NY 14217-1205   716-874-0771
                 Fax: 716-839-4006
Processor and exporter of meat, poultry and fish marinades, Greek salad dressings, pasta sauces and appetizers, gourmet foods, salsa, hot sauce and seasonings
CEO/President: George Bechakas
Executive VP: Nick Bechakas
Estimated Sales: $ 1 - 3 Million
Number Employees: 20-49
Regions Exported to: Europe

46774 **Mts Seating**
7100 Industrial Dr
Temperance, MI 48182-9105   734-847-3875
       Fax: 734-847-0993 info@mtsseating.com
                   www.mtsseating.com
Manufacturer and exporter of metal stack chairs, bar stools, pedestal tables and bases and a complete line of hospitality and food service seating
President: Bart Kulish
Marketing Manager: Eric Foster
Sales VP: Greg Piper
Estimated Sales: $ 20 - 50 Million
Number Employees: 250-499
Square Footage: 200000
Parent Co: Michigan Tube Swagers Fabricators
Type of Packaging: Food Service
Regions Exported to: Worldwide
Percentage of Business in Exporting: 2

46775 **Muckler Industries, Inc**
355 Leesmeadow Rd.
Suite 207
Saint Louis, MO 63125   314-631-7616
       Fax: 314-631-7409   800-444-0283
ktechinfo@mucklerktech.com
Manufacturer and exporter of commercial kitchen hoods, baffle filters, waterwash and grease extractors, engineered commercial ventilation and utility distribution systems
National Sales Manager: Douglas Muckler
Sales: Sean Wood
Estimated Sales: $ 2.5-5 Million
Number Employees: 10
Square Footage: 60000
Type of Packaging: Food Service
Regions Exported to: Asia, Middle East
Percentage of Business in Exporting: 5

46776 **(HQ)Muellermist Irrigation Company**
2612 S. 9th Ave.
P.O. Box 6307
Broadview, IL 60155   708-450-9595
       Fax: 708-450-1403 info@muellermist.com
                   www.muellermist.com
Manufacturer and exporter of underground lawn sprinkling and solar roof cooling systems
President: Tammy Boralli
Contact: Tammy Buralli
tburalli@muellermist.com
Estimated Sales: $ 10 - 20 Million
Number Employees: 50-99
Square Footage: 36000
Type of Packaging: Bulk
Brands Exported: Fanjet
Regions Exported to: Central America, South America, Europe, Asia, Middle East
Percentage of Business in Exporting: 5

46777 **Mugnaini Imports**
11 Hangar Way
Watsonville, CA 95076   831-761-1767
       Fax: 831-728-5570   888-887-7206
mugnaini@mugnaini.com www.mugnaini.com
Supplier and importer of wood burning ovens and gas fire
Owner: Andrea Smith
Contact: Curt Corcoran
curt@mugnaini.com
Manager: Ken Belardi
Estimated Sales: Less than $500,000
Number Employees: 1-4
Brands Imported: Valoriani
Percentage of Business in Importing: 100

46778 **Muir Copper Canyon Farms**
951 S 3600 W
Salt Lake City, UT 84104-4587   801-908-6091
       Fax: 801-908-6176   800-564-0949
ldehaan@coppercanyonfarms.com
www.coppercanyonfarms.com
Packer and exporter of potatoes, onions and frozen ready-to-process cherries; wholesaler/distributor of fresh fruits and vegetables; serving the food service market in the Salt Lake City metropolitan area
President/CEO: Phil Muir
VP/Chief Financial Officer: Chuck Madsen
Controller: Adam Jensen
Sales: John Marsh
Manager: Andy Salmon
asalmon@coppercanyonfarms.com
Operations Manager: Andy Salmon
Estimated Sales: $16.6 Million
Number Employees: 50-99
Square Footage: 400000
Type of Packaging: Food Service, Private Label, Bulk
Brands Exported: Big M; RTP Cherries
Regions Exported to: Asia, Canada, Mexico

46779 **Mulholland-Harper Company**
PO Box C
Denton, MD 21629-0298   410-479-1300
       Fax: 410-479-0207   800-882-3052
Manufacturer and exporter of electric fixtures and signs including electric, plastic, metal and outdoor and exterior identification
President: Patrick Hanrahan
Manufacturing Manager: Michael Conner
Estimated Sales: $5-10 Million
Number Employees: 50-99
Square Footage: 200000
Regions Exported to: Europe, Canada, Mexico
Percentage of Business in Exporting: 10

46780 **Mulligan Associates**
286 Barbados Dr
Mequon, WI 53092   414-305-0840
       Fax: 262-242-3944   800-627-2886
gene@mulliganassociates.com
Manufacturer, importer and exporter of high and low volume citric and noncitric juicers, fruit and vegetable peelers, water vending machines and sugar cane and wheat grass extractors
President: Gene Mulligan
CFO: Gene Mulligan
Quality Control: Gene Mulligan
Marketing: Gene Mulligan
Sales Director: Gene Mulligan
General Manager: Bonnie Mulligan
Estimated Sales: $ 2 Million
Number Employees: 50-99
Square Footage: 30000
Parent Co: AOJ Manufacturing
Type of Packaging: Food Service
Brands Exported: SJD; S-16; W-47; T6A; T6JR; V-10; V-20; P-100
Regions Exported to: Central America, South America, Europe, Asia, Middle East
Percentage of Business in Exporting: 25
Brands Imported: Rotor
Regions Imported from: Europe
Percentage of Business in Importing: 10

46781 **Multi-Fill Inc**
4343 W 7800 S Ste B
West Jordan, UT 84088   801-280-1570
       Fax: 801-280-4341 info@multi-fill.com
                   www.multi-fill.com
Volumetric filling equipment for the food processor. Line configurations for cooked rice, short/long pasta, vegetables, fruits, ready-to-eat salads (cut, sliced, IQF, blanched, or raw). New technology for the MPF fillers allows forfaster changeover, tighter accuracy's, increased cleanliness of fill, and results in less down time.
President: Richard Price
rt72@netzero.net
Sales Director: Bill Allred
Estimated Sales: Below $5 Million
Number Employees: 10-19
Square Footage: 22000
Regions Exported to: Central America, Europe

46782 **Multi-Pak**
180 Atlantic St
Hackensack, NJ 07601-3301   201-342-7474
       Fax: 201-342-6525 www.multipakcorp.com

Importers & Exporters / A-Z

Manufacturer and exporter of refuse compactors for multi-dwelling units, hotels, hospitals and restaurants; also, attaching containers, odor control equipment and other collection systems. Hopper door repairs, chute cleaning, recyclingsystem
President: Niel Cavanaugh
ncavanaugh@multipak.com
Chairman of the Board/CFO/R&D: Niel Cavanaugh
Estimated Sales: $ 2.5 - 5 Million
Number Employees: 20-49
Square Footage: 24000
Regions Exported to: Europe, Asia, Middle East
Percentage of Business in Exporting: 10

46783 Multi-Panel Display Corporation
107 Georgia Ave
Brooklyn, NY 11207-2401   718-495-3800
     Fax: 718-346-0871   800-439-0879
Display racks and swing type display boards and panels; exporter of display units
President: Tommy Weber
VP: Zipora Weber
Contact: Daniel Weber
multipanel@aol.com
Estimated Sales: Less than $ 500,000
Number Employees: 5-9
Square Footage: 40000
Regions Exported to: Central America, South America, Europe, Canada
Percentage of Business in Exporting: 15

46784 Multi-Plastics Extrusions Inc
600 Dietrich Ave
Hazleton, PA 18201-7754   570-455-2021
     Fax: 570-455-0178   www.multi-plastics.com
Manufacturer and exporter of transparent biaxially oriented polystyrene sheets used for pressure and vacuum forming
Cmo: Paul Hinspeter
paul.hinspeter@alcoa.com
VP/General Manager: Eugene Whitacre
Plant Manager: Juan Escobar
Estimated Sales: $ 20-50 Million
Number Employees: 100-249

46785 MultiMedia Electronic Displays
11370 Sunrise Park Dr
Rancho Cordova, CA 95742-6542   916-852-4220
     Fax: 916-852-8325   800-888-3007
info@multimedialed.com   www.multimedialed.com
Manufacturer and exporter of programmable electronic signs
President: William Y Hall
CEO: Rex Williams
Marketing Director: Karen Klueh
Contact: Steven Craig
scraig@multimedialed.com
Operations Manager: Paul Selems
Plant Manager: George Pappas
Estimated Sales: $ 5 - 10 Million
Number Employees: 20-49
Number of Brands: 5
Number of Products: 200
Parent Co: SignUp
Type of Packaging: Food Service
Regions Exported to: Worldwide

46786 Multibulk Systems International
6 W 3rd Street
Wendell, NC 27591-8086   919-366-2100
     Fax: 919-676-7716
Manufacturer and exporter of bulk bag flexible containers
Sales Manager: John Watson
Estimated Sales: $ 500,000-$ 1,000,000
Number Employees: 5-9
Type of Packaging: Private Label
Regions Exported to: Worldwide
Percentage of Business in Exporting: 80

46787 (HQ)Multiflex Company
18 Utter Ave
Hawthorne, NJ 07506-2127   973-636-9700
     marzipanco@aol.com
Processor and exporter of confectionery items including marzipan, icing decorations, edible Easter eggs, chocolate dessert cups, chocolate liqueur cups, lollypops, sugar decorations and decorated chocolate covered sandwich cookies
President: Rita Keller
Vice President: Rozie Keller
VP Sales: Royce Keller
Estimated Sales: $120,000
Number Employees: 2
Square Footage: 30000
Type of Packaging: Food Service, Private Label, Bulk
Brands Exported: Keller's, Swissart, Crescent Confections & Biermann Marzipan
Regions Exported to: South America, Europe, Asia, Canada
Percentage of Business in Exporting: 3

46788 (HQ)Multikem Corp
700 Grand Ave
Ridgefield, NJ 07657-1524   201-941-4520
     Fax: 201-941-5239   800-441-7405
     www.multikem.com
Importer of thickeners, stabilizers and emulsifiers including guar gum, locust bean gum, sucrose esters, tapioca starches, carboxymethylcellulose and sodium alginate; exporter of gum blends and tapioca starches
President: Larry Muhlberg
multikem@mindspring.com
Sales/Marketing: Bob Wilson
Estimated Sales: $ 5 - 10 Million
Number Employees: 5-9
Other Locations:
   Multi-Kem Corp.
   Ridgefield, NJMulti-Kem Corp.
Regions Exported to: Europe
Percentage of Business in Exporting: 25
Regions Imported from: Europe, Asia
Percentage of Business in Importing: 75

46789 Multiplex Co Inc
2100 Future Dr
Sellersburg, IN 47172-1874   812-256-7777
     Fax: 636-527-4313   800-787-8880
     www.google.com
High capacity dispensing systems for beverages including beer; also, water filtration systems
President & Chief Operating Officer: J. Kisling
Chief Executive Officer: Terry Growcock
Contact: John Bell
jbell@manitowocfsg.com
Estimated Sales: $34.6 Million
Number Employees: 1-4
Square Footage: 10000000
Parent Co: Manitowoc Foodservice Group

46790 (HQ)Multisorb Technologies Inc
325 Harlem Rd
Buffalo, NY 14224-1893   716-824-8900
     Fax: 716-824-4128   800-445-9890
     info@multisorb.com   www.multisorb.com
Manufacturer and exporter of active packaging technologies for food packaging, including odor absorbers, desiccants, and moisture regulators, and odor and other volatile absorbers.
President: James Renda
jrenda@multisorb.com
Marketing: Tom Powers
Marketing Communications Coordinator: Kay Krause
Number Employees: 500-999
Square Footage: 340000
Other Locations:
   Multisorb Technologies
   Orchard Park, NYMultisorb Technologies
Brands Exported: FreshPax; FreshMax; StripPax; MiniPax
Regions Exported to: Central America, South America, Europe, Asia, Middle East
Percentage of Business in Exporting: 15
Regions Imported from: Europe, Asia

46791 Multivac Inc
11021 N Pomona Ave
Kansas City, MO 64153-1146   816-891-0555
     Fax: 816-891-0622   800-800-8552
     muinc@multivac.com
Wholesaler/distributor, importer and exporter of thermoform, fill and seal packaging equipment; also, tray sealers, chamber vacuum packaging and labeling equipment; sales support services available
President: Michel Defenbau
CEO: Werner Britz
werner.britz@multivacsa.com
CEO: Jan Erik Kuhlmann
CFO: Danny Liker
Sales Director: Norm Winkel
Estimated Sales: $ 50 - 60Million
Number Employees: 100-249
Square Footage: 60000
Parent Co: Multivac Export AG
Brands Exported: Multivac
Regions Exported to: Central America, Canada, Mexico
Percentage of Business in Exporting: 15
Brands Imported: MR; Multivac
Regions Imported from: Europe
Percentage of Business in Importing: 100

46792 Mumper Machine Corporation
5081 N 124th St
Butler, WI 53007   262-781-8908
     Fax: 262-781-1253
Manufacturer and exporter of vegetable topping and conveying equipment
President: Jordy Mumper
Estimated Sales: $500,000-$1 Million
Number Employees: 5-9

46793 Mundial
63 Broadway # 1
Norwood, MA 02062-3558   781-762-0053
     Fax: 781-762-0364   800-487-2224
     info@mundial-usa.com   www.mundialusa.com
Manufacturer, importer and exporter of knives, scissors and shears
President: Adilson Delatorre
CFO: John Keese
Sales VP: Rich Zirpolo
Estimated Sales: $1-2.5 Million
Number Employees: 1-4
Square Footage: 200000
Parent Co: Zivi-Hercules
Type of Packaging: Consumer, Food Service, Bulk
Brands Imported: Mundial; Futur, Elegonce, Le Corden Bleu, Sishment
Regions Imported from: South America, Asia

46794 Munson Machinery Co
210 Seward Ave
PO Box 855
Utica, NY 13502-5750   315-797-0090
     Fax: 315-797-5582   800-944-6644
     info@munsonmachinery.com
     www.munsonmachinery.com
Mixers, blenders and size reduction equipment for bulk solid materials.
Partner/VP/COO: Thomas Dalton III
Marketing Manager: Charles Divine
Regional Sales Manager: Darren Woods
Estimated Sales: $ 5 - 10 Million
Number Employees: 20-49
Square Footage: 90000
Regions Exported to: Central America, South America, Europe, Asia
Percentage of Business in Exporting: 20

46795 Munters Corp
79 Monroe St
Amesbury, MA 01913-3204   978-388-0600
     Fax: 978-241-1219   800-843-5360
     www.munters.com
Manufacturer and exporter of continuous desiccant dehumidification systems
President: Mike Mc Donald
Cmo: Scott Haynes
shaynes@munters.com
Estimated Sales: $20-50 Million
Number Employees: 250-499
Square Footage: 175000
Parent Co: Munters Corporation

46796 Muntons Ingredients
2018 156th Ave NE, Ste 230
Bellevue, WA 98007   425-372-3082
     terry.mcneill@muntons.com
     www.muntons.com
Manufacture of grain malts and related ingredients
Executive Chairman: Tom Wells
MMI Inc, Vice President Sales: Terry McNeill
Parent Co: Muntons Malt

46797 Murakami Farms
1431 SE 1st St
PO Box 9
Ontario, OR 97914   541-889-3131
     Fax: 541-889-2933   800-421-8814
     murakamionions.com
Packer and exporter of dry fresh yellow, red and white onions
President: Grant Kitamura
VP: David Murakami
Plant Manager: Paul Hopper

Importers & Exporters / A-Z

Estimated Sales: $2.5 Million
Number Employees: 25
Square Footage: 12000
Type of Packaging: Consumer, Food Service, Private Label
Regions Exported to: Asia, Canada, Caribbean, Mexico
Percentage of Business in Exporting: 10

46798 Murotech
550 Mckinley Rd
St Marys, OH 45885-1803   419-394-6529
  Fax: 419-394-6820   800-565-6876
muropeeler@aol.com www.murotech.com
Manufacturer, exporter and importer of semi-automatic peeling machines for fruits and vegetables including oranges, apples, mangos, cantaloupes and rutabegas
President: Naonobu Kenmoku
Quality Manager: Rick Wiley
Sales Manager: S. Sugimoto
Production Manager: Koichi Uchida
Estimated Sales: $500,000-$1 Million
Number Employees: 100-249
Square Footage: 4000
Parent Co: Muro Corporation
Regions Exported to: Central America, South America, Middle East, Mexico, Canada, Caribbean, Latin America
Percentage of Business in Exporting: 30
Regions Imported from: Asia

46799 (HQ)Murray Envelope Corporation
1500 N Main St
Suite C
Hattiesburg, MS 39401-1911   601-583-8292
  Fax: 800-423-7589 murray@netdoor.com
Manufacturer and exporter of filing folders and envelopes
Owner: Marvin Murry
CFO: Joae Comprtallo
R & D: Lenda Wisa
Estimated Sales: Below $5 Million
Number Employees: 1-4
Regions Exported to: Central America

46800 (HQ)Murzan Inc
2909 Langford Rd # A700
Rd. 1-700
Peachtree Cor, GA 30071-1512   770-448-0583
  Fax: 770-448-0967 murzan@murzan.com
  www.murzan.com
Manufacturer and exporter of food processing pumps and drum unloading, turnkey and bag-in-box blending/batching systems
Owner: Alberto Bazan
murzan@aol.com
CEO: Alberto Bazan
Estimated Sales: $2,600,000
Number Employees: 50-99
Regions Exported to: Worldwide

46801 Murzan Inc. Sanitary Sys
2909 Langford Rd # 1-700
Norcross, GA 30071-1590   770-448-0583
  Fax: 770-448-0967 murzan@murzan.com
  www.murzan.com
Importer and exporter of oregano, dry chiles and salsa
President: Alberto Bazan
albertobazan@murzan.com
CEO: David Wood
VP: Luis Uriba
Operations Food Division: Leopoldo Cruz
Estimated Sales: $1-2.5 Million
Number Employees: 20-49
Parent Co: Murzan
Type of Packaging: Food Service, Private Label
Brands Exported: Murzan
Regions Exported to: Central America, South America, Europe, Asia, Middle East
Percentage of Business in Exporting: 20

46802 Musco Family Olive Co
17950 Via Nicolo
Tracy, CA 95377   866-965-4837
  Fax: 209-836-0518   800-523-9828
  sales@muscoolive.com www.olives.com
Processor and exporter of canned olives including California stuffed green, Sicilian-style, black ripe and deli, and specialty olives and frozen ripe olives
President: Nicholas Musco
nicholasm@olives.com
CEO: Felix Musco
Director of Brand and Product Management: Tracy Wood
Director of Operations: Janet Mitchell Edwards
Director of Technical Services: Ben Hall
Year Founded: 1922
Number Employees: 250-499
Number of Brands: 7
Type of Packaging: Consumer, Food Service, Private Label
Brands Exported: Musco; Bravo
Regions Exported to: Asia, Canada
Percentage of Business in Exporting: 5

46803 Musco Food Corp
5701 49th St
Flushing, NY 11378-2020   718-628-9710
  Fax: 718-326-1109 www.muscofood.com
Importer and wholesaler/distributor of general line products and specialty foods including cheese, olive oil and canned foods
Owner: Philip Musco
Estimated Sales: $20-50 Million
Number Employees: 20-49
Regions Imported from: Europe

46804 Mushroom Co
902 Woods Rd
Cambridge, MD 21613   410-221-8971
  Fax: 410-221-8952
custserv@themushroomcompany.com
www.themushroomcompany.com
Canned, refrigerated, froze, organic, Kosher, seasoned, sauteed and sauced quality mushrooms.
President: Dennis Newhard
dnewhard@mushroomcanning.com
National Sales Manager: Ruth Newhard
Sales Representative: Fred Lister
Year Founded: 1931
Estimated Sales: $20 Million
Number Employees: 50-99
Square Footage: 150000
Type of Packaging: Consumer, Food Service, Private Label, Bulk
Regions Exported to: Canada

46805 Mushroom Wisdom, Inc
1 Madison St
Bldg F6
East Rutherford, NJ 07073   973-470-0010
  Fax: 973-470-0017   800-747-7418
  www.mushroomwisdom.com
Processor and exporter of nutritional mushroom supplements and teas
President & CEO: Mike Shirota
VP: Joe Carroll
R&D: Dr. Cun Shuang
VP Marketing: Donna Noonan
Contact: Martin Agurto
martin.a@mushroomwisdom.com
Production: Masashi Ohara
Estimated Sales: $ 3 - 5 Million
Number Employees: 10-19
Number of Brands: 2
Number of Products: 24
Square Footage: 18000
Type of Packaging: Consumer, Food Service, Private Label, Bulk
Other Locations:
  Maitake Products
  Ridgefield Park, NJ Maitake Products
Brands Exported: Grifron; Grifron-Pro D-fraction; Grifron D-fraction; Mai Tonic Tea; Mai Green Tea; Grifron Prost Mate; Grifron Mushroom Emperors
Regions Exported to: Europe, Asia, Canada

46806 Music City Metals Inc
2633 Grandview Ave
Nashville, TN 37211-2202   615-255-4481
  Fax: 615-255-4482   800-251-2674
  musiccitymetals@musiccitymetals.net
  www.musiccitymetals.net
Cast iron hot plates, gas burners, cooking grids, cast iron and stainless steel burners, grids and grates for gas grills.
President: Bo Richardson
musiccitymetals@musiccitymetals.net
Estimated Sales: $ 1 - 2.5 Million
Number Employees: 10-19
Regions Imported from: Asia
Percentage of Business in Importing: 60

46807 Muth Associates
53 Progress Ave
Springfield, MA 01104-3266   413-734-2107
  Fax: 413-734-2107   800-388-0157
  info@muthassociates.com muthassociates.com
Wholesaler/distributor of adsorbent materials
President: Cis Lafond
cislafond@muthassociates.com
CEO: Doug Muth
CFO: Sandra Peterson
Estimated Sales: $5-10 Million
Number Employees: 10-19
Number of Products: 300
Square Footage: 52000
Type of Packaging: Private Label, Bulk
Regions Exported to: Central America, South America, Europe, Asia, Middle East

46808 Mutual Biscuit
100 Central Avenue
Kearny, NJ 07032-4640   973-466-1020
  Fax: 973-466-1115
Wholesaler/distributor and importer of cookies
General Manager: Eddie Nassour

46809 Mutual Trading Co Inc
431 Crocker St
Los Angeles, CA 90013   213-626-9458
  Fax: 213-626-5130 www.lamtc.com
Wholesaler/distributor, importer and exporter of miso, soybean sauce, rice and vinegar.
President: Kosei Yamamoto
Year Founded: 1926
Estimated Sales: $20-50 Million
Number Employees: 100-249
Number of Brands: 2
Regions Exported to: Asia
Brands Imported: Miyoko Foods; Tycoon Foods
Regions Imported from: Asia

46810 Mutual Wholesale Liquor
P.O.Box 58829
Los Angeles, CA 90058-0829   323-587-7641
  Fax: 323-587-0820
Importer and wholesaler/distributor of beer and wine
President: Harvey Monterski
Estimated Sales: $20-50 Million
Number Employees: 50-99
Type of Packaging: Consumer, Food Service
Brands Imported: Henninger; Peters
Regions Imported from: Europe
Percentage of Business in Importing: 100

46811 My Daddy's Cheesecake
265 S Broadview St
265 S. Broadview
Cape Girardeau, MO 63703-5756   573-335-6660
  800-735-6765
  sales@mydaddyscheesecake.com
  www.mydaddyscheesecake.com
Processor and exporter of confectionery items, cheesecakes, desserts, wedding and birthday cakes and gourmet cookies
Owner: Susan Stanfield
Estimated Sales: Less Than $500,000
Number Employees: 10-19
Square Footage: 10000
Type of Packaging: Consumer, Food Service, Private Label
Regions Exported to: Central America
Percentage of Business in Exporting: 40

46812 My Grandma's Coffee Cake
1636 Hyde Park Ave
Hyde Park, MA 02136-2458   617-364-9900
  Fax: 617-364-0505   800-847-2636
  www.mygrandma.com
Coffeecakes in a variety of flavors including Granny Smith Apple, Golden Raspberry, Cappuccino, New England Blueberry, Chocolate, Banana Walnut and Cape Cod Cranberry
President: Robert Katz
bmills@mygrandma.com
Controller: Seth Anapolle
EVP: Bruce Willis
VP of Marketing and Operations: Bruce Mills
Distribution Sales Manager: Gail Molino
VP Operations: Will Weeks
Estimated Sales: $ 5-6 Million
Number Employees: 20-49
Square Footage: 35600

461

Importers & Exporters / A-Z

46813 My Quality Trading Corp
133 48th St
Brooklyn, NY 11232-4227   718-854-8714
                            Fax: 718-854-6816
Wholesaler/distributor, importer and exporter of general line merchandise including nuts, dried fruits, bakery supplies, spices and chocolate candy; serving the food service market
President: Moses Geller
Estimated Sales: $20-50 Million
Number Employees: 20-49
Square Footage: 10000
Regions Exported to: Central America, South America, Europe, Middle East
Regions Imported from: Central America, South America, Middle East

46814 My Style
614 NW Street
Raleigh, NC 27603   919-832-2526
          Fax: 919-832-1546 800-524-8269
Wholesaler/distributor, importer and exporter of teak, cast aluminum, stainless steel and hardwood outdoor furniture; also, wooden and market umbrellas
Director: Ward Usmar
Owner: Klaus Weihe
Owner: Eik Niemann
Marketing Administrator: Ceri Usmar
Number Employees: 1-4
Square Footage: 13500
Brands Imported: Caribbean Shade; Teak; Ligot; Siesta Shade
Regions Imported from: South Africa, Indonesia

46815 Myers Container
21301 Cloud Way
Hayward, CA 94545-1216   510-785-8235
     Fax: 510-271-6215 jcutt@myerscontainer.com
                    www.myerscontainer.com
Manufacturer, exporter and reconditioner of steel drums including aseptic, hot pack food, conical and vegetable oil
President: John Cutt
Chief Executive Officer: Kyle Stavig
CFO: Thomas Holmes
Quality Control: Dana Zanone
Manager Food Sales: Roger Thornton
Manager: Benjamin Rivera
br.vera@myerscontainer.com
Estimated Sales: $50-100 Million
Number Employees: 10-19
Square Footage: 500000
Parent Co: IMACC Corporation
Brands Exported: Pureliner; Purevac; Purestack
Regions Exported to: Central America, Asia

46816 N S I Sweeteners
1554 Barclay Blvd
Buffalo Grove, IL 60089-4530   847-215-9955
          Fax: 847-215-9959 800-952-5130
                    info@flavourcreations.com
Coffee flavoring such as french vanilla, hazelnut and dutch chocolate and other calorie free products
Owner: Paul Przybyla
CEO: Alfred Sprague
CFO: Paul Przybyla
Marketing: Nancy Parker
Sales: Linda Havranik
Public Relations: Nancy Williams
Estimated Sales: $ 3 - 5 Million
Number Employees: 1-4
Number of Brands: 4
Number of Products: 18
Type of Packaging: Consumer, Food Service, Private Label
Brands Exported: Flavour Creations
Regions Exported to: Central America, South America, Europe, Asia
Percentage of Business in Exporting: 10

46817 N Star Seafood LLC
2213 NW 30th Pl # 7a
Pompano Beach, FL 33069-1026   954-984-0006
          Fax: 954-984-5912 800-631-8524
Manager: Doug Boadway
dougboadway@northstarseafood.com
Number Employees: 20-49

46818 N.G. Slater Corporation
42 W 38th St Rm 200
Suite 1002
New York, NY 10018   212-768-9434
          Fax: 212-869-7368 800-848-4621
                    info@ngslater.com
                    www.ngslater.com
Manufacturer and distributors of custom imprinted and specialties, badges, buttons and emblems
Owner: Robert Slater
VP: Alan Slater
Estimated Sales: $ 1 - 3,000,000
Number Employees: 5-9
Regions Exported to: Worldwide
Percentage of Business in Exporting: 5

46819 NACCO Materials Handling Group
4000 NE Blue Lake Road
Fairview, OR 97024-8710   503-721-6205
          Fax: 503-721-1364 www.hysterusa.com
Manufacturer and exporter of forklift trucks
Engineering Manager: Darrel Libby
Contact: Bob Downey
bob.downey@nmhg.com
Estimated Sales: $ 50-100 Million
Number Employees: 141
Square Footage: 68384
Parent Co: NACCO Industries
Regions Exported to: Worldwide

46820 NAP Industries
667 Kent Ave
Brooklyn, NY 11249-7500   718-625-4948
          Fax: 718-596-4342 877-635-4948
                    info@napind.com www.napind.com
Manufacturer and exporter of bags including heat sealed, meat, plastic, polyethylene and shopping; also, pressure sensitive tapes
President: Leo Lowy
morris@napind.com
Sales Exec: Morris Lowy
Estimated Sales: $5-10 Million
Number Employees: 20-49

46821 NAR Gourmet
379 West Broadway
Suite 524
New York, NY 10012   917-336-0818
          Fax: 917-591-4766 us.nargourmet.com
Olive oils, preserves, vinegars and spices.

46822 NCC
21005 Obrien Rd
Groveland, FL 34736-9590   352-429-9036
          Fax: 352-429-9039 800-429-9037
novelty@aol.com www.partyplasticsplus.com
Hotel and restaurant supplies including catering and buffet trays, plastic drinkware, pitchers, bowls and serving utensils
President: Sara Michaeli
sara@global-nation.com
CEO: Asher Michaeli
CFO: Joe Michaeli
VP: Sara Coslett
R&D: Joe Michaeli
Marketing: Ed Coslett
Sales Manager: Ed Coslett
Public Relations: Sara Coslett
Manager: Sara Michaeli
Plant Manager: Paul Patin
Estimated Sales: $1-2.5 Million
Number Employees: 20-49
Square Footage: 125000
Parent Co: Novelty Crystal Corporation
Type of Packaging: Food Service
Brands Exported: Novelty Crystal Corp
Regions Exported to: Central America, South America, Europe

46823 NDC Infrared Engineering Inc
5314 Irwindale Ave
Irwindale, CA 91706   626-960-3300
          Fax: 626-939-3870 info@ndcinfrared.com
                    www.ndcinfrared.com
Manufacturer and exporter of on-line instrumentation for measurement of moisture, fat/oil, protein and caffeine including testers and analyzers
President: Bromley Beadle
Marketing Manager: Raymond Shead
Sales/Marketing Executive: Bill Diltz
Contact: Drew Cheshire
jhazlett@verrents.com
Estimated Sales: $ 20 - 50 Million
Number Employees: 50-99
Square Footage: 50000
Parent Co: Fairey Group
Regions Exported to: Central America, South America, Worldwide

46824 NECO/Nebraska Engineering
9364 N 45th St
Omaha, NE 68152-1328   402-453-6912
          Fax: 402-453-0471 800-367-6208
                    www.necousa.com
Manufacturer and exporter of grain processing and handling equipment including cleaners, augers, spreaders, conveyors, dryers and aeration fans
President: Steve Campbell
VP: Bryan Hayes
Marketing Director: Steve Campbell
Sales Manager: Pat McCarthy
Manager: William Hiltgen
Plant Manager: Rick Wulf
Purchase Head: Rick Wuls
Estimated Sales: Below $ 5 Million
Number Employees: 50-99
Square Footage: 300000
Parent Co: GLOBAL Industries
Brands Exported: Neco
Regions Exported to: Europe, Middle East
Percentage of Business in Exporting: 5

46825 NEPA Pallet & Container Co
12027 3 Lakes Rd
Snohomish, WA 98290-5502   360-568-3185
          Fax: 360-568-9135 www.nepapallet.com
Manufacturer and exporter of pallets and bins
President: Denton Sherry
dsherry@nepapallet.com
Estimated Sales: $ 5 - 10 Million
Number Employees: 100-249
Regions Exported to: Asia
Percentage of Business in Exporting: 2

46826 NJM/CLI
8 Plateau Street
Pointe Claire, QC H9R 5W2
Canada   514-630-6990
                            Fax: 514-695-0801
Manufacturer, exporter and importer of packaging machinery including fillers, cappers, labelers, tablet and capsule counters, etc
President: Michel LaPierre
Director: Charles Lapierre
VP: Dan Lapierre
Marketing: Louise Lafleur
VP Sales: Mark Laroche
Number Employees: 150
Square Footage: 80000
Parent Co: NJM/CLI Packaging Systems International
Brands Exported: Njm / Cli-Made Machines
Regions Exported to: North America, Mexico
Brands Imported: Monobloc; Blister; Blipack; PCE; CMA
Regions Imported from: South America

46827 NORPAC Foods Inc
3225 25th St SE
Salem, OR 97302
                    consumeraffairs@norpac.com
                    www.norpac.com
Frozen vegetables, fruits and juices.
President & CEO: Shawn Campbell
Research & Development Manager: Kim Claggett
Director of Marketing: Brad Burden
VP of Operations: Mark Croeni
Year Founded: 1924
Estimated Sales: $476.3 Million
Number Employees: 1,500
Type of Packaging: Consumer, Food Service, Private Label, Bulk
Other Locations:
   Lake Oswego, OR
   Salem, OR
   Hermiston, OR
   Quincy, WA Salem
Regions Exported to: Worldwide

46828 NOW Foods
244 Knollwood Dr.
Bloomingdale, IL 60108
                            888-669-3663
                    www.nowfoods.com
Vitamins, healthy foods, natural personal care and sports nutrition products.

Importers & Exporters / A-Z

CEO: Jim Emme
CFO: Andy Kotlarz
General Counsel: Beverly Reid
VP, Quality/Regulatory Affairs: Aaron Secrist
VP, Global Sales/Marketing: Dan Richard
Vice President, Human Resources: Michelle Canada
COO: Ernest Shepard
Year Founded: 1968
Estimated Sales: $100 Million
Number Employees: 100-249
Number of Brands: 9
Number of Products: 1500
Square Footage: 203000
Type of Packaging: Consumer, Private Label, Bulk
Brands Exported: Now; Private Label
Regions Exported to: Central America, South America, Europe, Asia, Middle East, Africa
Percentage of Business in Exporting: 6

46829 NSG Transport Inc
115 W 16th St
Gothenburg, NE 69138-1302   308-537-7191
    Fax: 308-537-7193 www.nsgco.com
Processor and exporter of corn
President: Norman Geiken
wade@nsgco.com
Sales Exec: Wade Geiken
Estimated Sales: $ 3 - 5 Million
Number Employees: 20-49
Type of Packaging: Bulk

46830 NST Metals
721-723 East Main Street
Louisville, KY 40202   502-584-5846
    Fax: 502-584-3481
Manufacturer and exporter of food processing equipment, pressure vessels, hoppers, bins and silos
President: Joe Harvey
VP: Kenneth Harvey
VP: Brian Harvey
Estimated Sales: $1-2.5 Million
Number Employees: 5-9
Square Footage: 28000
Type of Packaging: Consumer, Bulk
Regions Exported to: Central America, South America
Percentage of Business in Exporting: 1

46831 NTN Wireless
6080 Northbelt Dr.
Norcross, GA 30071   770-277-2760
    Fax: 770-277-2765 800-637-8639
    james.frakes@ntn.com
Manufacturer and exporter of wireless server call systems and in-house server, guest and table ready paging systems
President: Mark Degortor
Number Employees: 20-49
Square Footage: 16000
Parent Co: Hysen Technologies
Regions Exported to: Central America, South America, Europe, Middle East
Percentage of Business in Exporting: 5

46832 NYP
10 Site Rd
Leola, PA 17540-1849   717-656-0299
    Fax: 717-656-0350 800-541-0961
    padiv@nyp-corp.com www.nyp-corp.com
Plain and printed bags including multi-wall, paper, polyethylene, woven polypropylene, burlap, cotton and mesh; importer of woven polypropylene bags
VP: Christopher LaBelle
VP Sales: Gerald LaBelle
Sales/Customer Service: Don Ament
dament@nyp-corp.com
Manager: Beverley Campbell
Division Manager: Robert Ellis
Purchasing Manager: Katie Gorsuch
Estimated Sales: less than $ 500,000
Number Employees: 1-4
Square Footage: 30000
Parent Co: NYP Corporation
Type of Packaging: Private Label, Bulk
Regions Imported from: Asia, Middle East

46833 NaceCare Solutions
1205 Britannia Road East
Mississauga, ON L4W 1C7
Canada
    Fax: 800-709-2896 800-387-3210
    www.nacecare.com
Importer and exporter of cleaning equipment including polishers, pressure washers, janitor and maid carts, vacuums, automatic floor scrubbers and vapor cleaners
President: Gareth Mason
National Sales Manager: Neil Lyall
Sales Manager (West): Dale Rawlyke
Regions Exported to: Mexico, Caribbean
Regions Imported from: Italy

46834 Nahmias et Fils
201 Saw Mill River Rd. #C
Yonkers, NY 10701   914-294-0055
    www.nahmiasetfils.com
Whiskey, fig-flavored distilled spirits
Founder: Dorit Nahmias
Year Founded: 2010
Number of Brands: 1
Number of Products: 3s
Type of Packaging: Consumer, Private Label
Brands Exported: Nahmias et Fils
Regions Exported to: USA

46835 Naleway Foods
233 Hutchings Street
Winnipeg, MB R2X 2R4
Canada
    204-633-6535
    Fax: 204-694-4310 800-665-7448
    sales@naleway.com www.naleway.com
Processor and exporter of frozen foods including pierogies and panzarotti
Sales: W Halley
Number Employees: 100-249
Type of Packaging: Consumer, Food Service
Regions Exported to: USA

46836 Nalge Process Technologies Group
75 Panorama Creek Dr
Rochester, NY 14625-2385   585-586-8800
    Fax: 585-586-8431 nnitech@nalgenunc.com
    www.nalgenunc.com
Manufacturer and exporter of blowers, fans, fittings, hoses, liquid mixers, pipe tube and hose clamps, safety equipment and tanks
Marketing: Karen Dally
Sales Manager: John Cooling
Contact: Charlie Amico
camico@nalgenunc.com
Product Manager: Greg Felosky
Number Employees: 500-999
Parent Co: Sybron Corporation
Regions Exported to: Worldwide

46837 Naltex
220 E Saint Elmo Rd
Austin, TX 78745   512-447-7000
    Fax: 512-447-7444 800-531-5112
    sales@naltex.com www.delstarinc.com
Manufacturer and exporter of plastic mesh, heat sealing and header bags; also, case liners
Marketing: Marjorie Wilcox
Product Manager: Susan Emory
semory@delstarinc.com
Plant Manager: Scott Mc Henry
Estimated Sales: $20-50 Million
Number Employees: 100-249
Square Footage: 110000
Brands Exported: Naltex
Regions Exported to: Central America, South America, Europe, Asia, Middle East, Canada
Percentage of Business in Exporting: 5

46838 Namco Controls Corporation
760 Beta Dr # F
Cleveland, OH 44143-2334   440-460-1360
    Fax: 440-460-3800 800-626-8324
    www.namcocontrols.com
Manufacturer and exporter of packaging and material handling presence and position sensors including photoelectric, laser scanner, rotary cam switch and proximity
President: Alex Joseph
Marketing Manager: Chuck Juda
VP Sales/Marketing: Bob Joyce
Plant Manager: Jamy Robins
Number Employees: 1-4
Parent Co: Danaher Corporation
Other Locations:
  Namco Controls Corp.
  HerzhornNamco Controls Corp.
Regions Exported to: Europe, Asia, Mexico, Canada

46839 Namco Machinery
5421 73rd Pl
Maspeth, NY 11378
    Fax: 718-803-0165
Manufacturer and exporter of bottle washing machinery for laboratory glassware
President: Manning E Cole
jackjackson54@aol.com
Sales Manager: R Jackson
Estimated Sales: $ 3 - 5 Million
Number Employees: 5-9
Regions Exported to: Worldwide

46840 Nancy's Specialty Foods
6500 Overlake Pl
Newark, CA 94560   510-494-1100
    Fax: 510-494-1140 www.nancys.com
Processor and exporter of frozen appetizers, entrees and desserts.
President: Bob Kroll
markus.bahr@wellsfargo.com
CFO: Adam Ferris
Marketing/Communications Director: Diane DiMartini
VP Sales: R L Booth
VP Operations: David Joiner
Plant Manager: Rick Shepherd
Estimated Sales: $19.8 Million
Number Employees: 325
Square Footage: 172000
Type of Packaging: Consumer, Food Service, Private Label, Bulk
Regions Exported to: Asia, Canada
Percentage of Business in Exporting: 12

46841 Nanonation Inc
301 S 13th St
Lincoln, NE 68508-2537   402-323-6266
    Fax: 402-323-6268 866-843-6266
    info@nanonation.net
Software developer focusing on customer touch points such as kiosks and dynamic signage
CEO: Bradley Walker
VP Business Development: Brian Ardinger
Estimated Sales: $ 3 - 5 Million
Number Employees: 20-49

46842 Napa Valley Kitchens
564 Gateway Dr
Napa, CA 94558-7517   707-254-3700
    Fax: 707-259-0219
Manufacturer and exporter of flavored oils, marinades, and dressings
Chairman: John Foraker
Cfo: Dale Eagle
Vice President of R&D: Bob Kaake
Senior Vice President of Marketing: Sarah Bird
Sales Director: Terry Dudley
Production Manager: Mark Osborne
Estimated Sales: $10 Million
Number Employees: 75
Type of Packaging: Consumer
Brands Exported: Consorzio
Regions Exported to: Canada
Percentage of Business in Exporting: 3

46843 Napco Marketing Corp
7800 Bayberry Rd
Jacksonville, FL 32256-6817   904-737-8500
    Fax: 904-737-9178 800-356-2726
    www.napcoimports.com
Importer of wicker gift baskets and decorative containers
Owner: William F Rein
wrein@napcomarketing.com
VP Supermarket Sales: Ron Ross
Estimated Sales: $20-50 Million
Number Employees: 100-249
Square Footage: 180000
Parent Co: Napco Marketing
Regions Imported from: Europe, Asia
Percentage of Business in Importing: 100

46844 Napco Security Systems Inc
333 Bayview Ave
Amityville, NY 11701-2800   631-842-0253
    Fax: 631-789-9292 salesinfo@napcosecurity.com
    www.napcosecurity.com
Manufacturer and exporter of electronic security systems and accessories including control panels

Importers & Exporters / A-Z

President/Chairman/Secretary: Richard Soloway
SVP, Operations & Finance/Director: Kevin Buchel
SVP, Engineering Development: Michael Carrieri
SVP Corporate Sales & Marketing: Jorge Hevia
Vice President, Sales: Scott Schramme
Contact: John Banks
jbanks@napcosecurity.com
Purchasing: Edward Daber
Estimated Sales: $ 71 Million
Number Employees: 5-9
Square Footage: 90000

46845 Napoleon Appliance Corporation
214 Bayview Drive
Barrie, ON L4N 4Y8
Canada 705-726-4278
Fax: 705-725-2564 866-820-8686
wecare@napoleonproducts.com
www.napoleongrills.com
Manufacturer and exporter of gas grills
President: Wolfgang Schroeter
VP: Ingrid Schroeter
Research & Development: Steve Schwartz
Quality Control: Steve Taylor
Marketing/Sales: David Blain
Plant Manager: Michael Pulfer
Purchasing Manager: Lynda Allen
Number Employees: 100
Number of Brands: 11
Square Footage: 600000
Parent Co: Wolf Steel
Regions Exported to: Worldwide
Percentage of Business in Exporting: 20

46846 Napoleon Co.
310 120th Ave NE
#A203
Bellevue, WA 98005-3013 425-455-3776
Fax: 425-454-3142 info@napoleon-co.com
www.napoleon-co.com
Specialty foods importer/broker
President: Joe Magnano
joe@napoleon-co.com
VP: Roger Thorson
Estimated Sales: $17-20 Million
Number Employees: 10-19
Number of Brands: 5
Number of Products: 100
Type of Packaging: Consumer, Food Service, Private Label, Bulk
Brands Exported: Napoleon
Regions Exported to: Asia
Percentage of Business in Exporting: 1
Brands Imported: Napoleon; Felix; Siljans
Regions Imported from: Central America, South America, Europe, Asia, Middle East
Percentage of Business in Importing: 99

46847 NaraKom
PO Box 368
Peapack, NJ 07977-0368 908-234-1776
Fax: 908-234-0964
Distributor of Nara milling, sizing, coating, and powder surface modification technology in the Americas
President: C Komline
Number Employees: 20-49
Parent Co: Komline-Sanderson Engineering Corporation
Regions Exported to: Europe, Asia

46848 Naraghi Group
20001 Mchenry Ave
Escalon, CA 95320-9614 209-579-5253
Fax: 209-551-4544
Processor and exporter of grapes, peaches, apples, walnuts, pistachios and almonds
Owner: Miguel Lizarraga
miguel@naraghifarms.com
Owner: Wendell Naraghi
Plant Manager: Isidro Vaca
Number Employees: 1-4
Regions Exported to: Europe

46849 Nareg International Inc
3661 San Fernando Rd
Glendale, CA 91204-2939 818-500-8291
Fax: 818-240-8292 888-677-8292
sales@naregint.com
Wholesaler/distributor and importer of table accessories, gift wrapping and disposable tablecloths and napkins
Owner: Adour Aghjayan
sales@naregint.com
Assistant President: Helen Aghjayan
Marketing Director: David Ghoukassian
Estimated Sales: $1.5 Million
Number Employees: 1-4
Square Footage: 20000
Type of Packaging: Consumer, Food Service, Private Label, Bulk

46850 Nasco Inc
901 Janesville Ave
P.O. Box 901
Fort Atkinson, WI 53538-0901
800-431-4310
custserv@eNasco.com
Manufacturer and exporter of WHIRL-PAK sample bags; wholesaler/distributor of laboratory supplies.
Regional Sales Director: James Felt
jfelt@enasco.com
Director, Whirl-Pak Sales: Tom Valitchka
Year Founded: 1941
Estimated Sales: $50-100 Million
Number Employees: 50-99
Parent Co: Nasco International
Other Locations:
Nasco
Modesto, CA Nasco

46851 Nash-DeCamp Company
1612 W Mineral King Ave
Visalia, CA 93291-4438 559-622-1850
Fax: 559-622-1883
Wholesaler/distributor and exporter of produce including plums, grapes, kiwi, lemons and oranges; importer of grapes and kiwi
CEO: Stephen Biswell
Sales/Marketing Executive VP: Tom Whitehouse
Number Employees: 20-49
Square Footage: 56000
Regions Exported to: Worldwide
Regions Imported from: South America, Mexico

46852 Nashua Corporation
250 S. Northwest Highway
Suite 203
Park Ridge, IL 60068 402-397-3600
Fax: 402-392-6080 800-323-4265
www.nashua.com
Manufacturer and exporter of computer and pressure sensitive labels
President: Andrew Albert
CFO: John Patenaude
VP: Michael Jarrett
VP: Mike Jarrutt
Contact: Charles Bonnier
cbonnier@nashua.com
Number Employees: 100-249

46853 Nashua Corporation
44 Franklin Street
Nashua, NH 03064-2665 603-661-2004
Fax: 603-880-5671 info@amstock.com
www.nashua.com
Manufacturer and exporter of industrial tape and labels
President: Andrew Albert
CFO: John Petenaude
Regions Exported to: Worldwide

46854 Nashville Display Manufacturing Company
306 Hartmann Drive
Lebanon, TN 37087 615-743-2900
Fax: 615-743-2901 888-743-2572
dissales@nashvillewire.com
www.nashvilledisplay.com
Manufacturer and exporter of displays and merchandisers for retail products
President: David L Rollins
CFO: Jeff McCeann
VP: E White
Quality Control: Charles Brittain
R & D: Juris Leikartt
Sales Manager: Richard Hornsby
Office Manager: Jere Lane
Estimated Sales: $10-20 Million
Number Employees: 20-49
Square Footage: 1600000

46855 (HQ)Nassau Candy Distributors
530 W John St
Hicksville, NY 11801-1039 516-433-7100
Fax: 516-433-9010 sales@nassaucandy.com
www.nassaucandy.com
Manufacturer, importer and distributor of confectionery items and gourmet foods.
President: Barry Rosenbaum
Chairman & CEO: Lesley Stier
Vice President: Carol Baca
carol.baca@nassaucandy.com
Number Employees: 100-249
Other Locations:
Nassau Candy Co.
Deer Park, NY Nassau Candy Co.

46856 Nat-Trop
4610 Mission St
San Francisco, CA 94112-2640 415-334-7199
Fax: 415-334-7395 800-260-7862
Importer of botanical extracts and supplements
President: Paulo Altaffer
VP Operations: Michael Altaffer
Estimated Sales: $500,000-$1 Million
Number Employees: 1-4
Parent Co: New World Enterprises
Brands Imported: Sumax5; Potent Potion; Vitavin
Regions Imported from: Brazil
Percentage of Business in Importing: 100

46857 Natale Machine & Tool Co Inc
339 13th St
Carlstadt, NJ 07072-1917 201-933-5500
Fax: 201-933-8146 800-883-8382
www.circle-d.com
Manufacturer and exporter of emergency lighting including flash, flood and spot lights; also, HID, quartz and commercial lighting available
CEO: Dominick Natale
VP: Lynn Natale
Sales: John Cocozzo
Production/Plant Manager/Purchasing: John Cocozzo
Estimated Sales: $ 3 - 5 Million
Number Employees: 10-19
Square Footage: 30000
Regions Exported to: Canada
Percentage of Business in Exporting: 10

46858 Natalie's Orchid Island Juice Co.
330 North U.S. Highway One
Ft. Pierce, FL 34950 772-465-1122
Fax: 772-465-4303 800-373-7444
www.oijc.com
Fresh-squeezed fruit juices
Owner/CEO: Marygrace Sexton
COO: Frank Tranchilla
EVP: John Martinelli
Quality Assurance/Food Safety Manager: Brian Christensen
Director of Marketing: Natalie Sexton
Director of Customer Service/Logistics: David Cortez
Contact: Keith Camara
kcamara@oijc.com
Director of Operations: Jim Zurbey
Senior Production Manager: Peter Binns
Estimated Sales: $20-50 Million
Number Employees: 50-99
Number of Brands: 1
Type of Packaging: Consumer, Food Service
Regions Exported to: Worldwide

46859 Natco Worldwide Representative
23004 Frisca Dr
Santa Clarita, CA 91354-2225 661-296-8778
Fax: 661-296-8778 npatow@aol.com
www.natcoglobal.com
Importer, Exporter of canned seafood, Broker for frozen seafood
Owner: Natalia Patow
npatow@aol.com
Estimated Sales: $2.5-$5 Million
Number Employees: 5-9
Square Footage: 12000
Type of Packaging: Consumer, Private Label
Brands Exported: Grand Dutchess; Delicias; Private Brands
Regions Exported to: Europe, Asia, Worldwide
Percentage of Business in Exporting: 20
Brands Imported: Delicias; Grand Duchess
Regions Imported from: South America, Latin America, Mexico
Percentage of Business in Importing: 80

Importers & Exporters / A-Z

46860 National Association-Pediatric
2055 L St NW
Washington, DC 20036-4983 202-223-2250
800-424-5156
www.napnap.org
Offers educational resources, materials, and programs for the restaurant and foodservice industry.
President/CEO: Dawn Sweeney
Executive Vice President: Rob Gifford
Contact: Phyllis Aaronson
paaronson@restaurant.org
Estimated Sales: Less Than $500,000
Number Employees: 5-9

46861 National Band Saw Co
25322 Avenue Stanford
Santa Clarita, CA 91355-1214 661-294-9552
Fax: 661-294-9554 800-851-5050
harley@nbsparts.com www.nbsparts.com
Manufacturer, exporter and wholesaler/distributor of replacement parts for meat slicing and cutting machinery; importer of slicing knives, tenderizers and bread slicing and patty-making machines; wholesaler/distributor of office and shipping supplies
Owner: Enrique Barbosa
enriqueb@nbarizona.com
VP: Chris Tuttle
R & D: Ron Voytek
Director of IT Computer Services: Jason Jasperson
Production: Ron Voytek
Estimated Sales: Below $5 Million
Number Employees: 10-19
Square Footage: 12200
Type of Packaging: Consumer, Food Service, Private Label, Bulk
Regions Exported to: Europe, Canada, Mexico
Percentage of Business in Exporting: 5
Regions Imported from: Europe, India, China
Percentage of Business in Importing: 6

46862 National Bar Systems
16571 Burke Lane
Huntington Beach, CA 92647-4537 714-848-1688
Fax: 714-848-2788 www.nbsmfg.com
Manufacturer and exporter of stainless steel under-bar equipment including sinks, work tables and ice storage equipment
President: Johnny Lee
VP: John Ashkarian
CFO: Joe Kim
Contact: Joe Kim
joek@nbsmfg.com
Estimated Sales: $ 5 - 10 Million
Number Employees: 5-9
Regions Exported to: Worldwide
Percentage of Business in Exporting: 5

46863 National Cart Co
3125 Boschertown Rd
St Charles, MO 63301-3263 636-947-3800
Fax: 636-723-4477 sales@nationalcart.com
www.nationalcart.com
Manufacturer and exporter of oven racks, bun pans and pan tray carts
CEO: Brian Gillis
zroach@kumc.edu
CEO: Robert Unnerstall
Estimated Sales: $ 20-50 Million
Number Employees: 100-249
Square Footage: 100000
Regions Exported to: Worldwide
Percentage of Business in Exporting: 5

46864 National Computer Corporation
211 Century Drive
Suite 100-B
Greenville, SC 29607 866-944-5164
Fax: 864-235-7688 www.nccusa.com
Manufacturer, importer and exporter of point of sale systems
President: Douglas Harris Jr
Contact: Mary Harris
mharris@nccusa.com
Estimated Sales: $ 5 - 10,000,000
Number Employees: 10-19
Regions Exported to: Worldwide
Brands Imported: Eurotouch
Regions Imported from: Europe

46865 (HQ)National Conveyor Corp
2250 Yates Ave
Commerce, CA 90040-1914 323-725-0355
Fax: 323-725-1440 info@natconcorp.com
Manufacturer and exporter of utensil washers, conveyor equipment, dish handling systems and waste reduction systems
Owner: Frank Bargas
Customer Service Manager: Luis Vargas
fra_cie@netzero.com
Engineer Manager: Joseph Marin
Estimated Sales: $ 2.5 - 5 Million
Number Employees: 10-19
Square Footage: 60000
Type of Packaging: Food Service
Regions Exported to: Worldwide
Percentage of Business in Exporting: 10

46866 National Distributor Services
3033 S Parker Road
Suite 400
Aurora, CO 80014-2921 303-755-4411
Fax: 303-755-4545
Manufacturer and exporter of forklifts
President: B Anthony Reed
CEO: Tony Reed
Number Employees: 50
Brands Exported: W.D.S.
Regions Exported to: Europe, Africa, Canada
Percentage of Business in Exporting: 20

46867 National Drying Machry Co Inc
2190 Hornig Rd
Philadelphia, PA 19116-4202 215-464-6070
Fax: 215-464-4096 info@nationaldrying.com
www.nationaldrying.com
Manufacturer and exporter of thermal processing equipment including dehydrators, dryers, ovens, roasters, blanchers, coolers and multi-tier and multi-pass conveyor systems and feeders
President: Richard Parkes
Director Marketing/Sales: Paul Branson
Director: Richard Eckard
Estimated Sales: $20-50 Million
Number Employees: 5-9
Square Footage: 80000
Parent Co: Apollo Sheet Metal
Regions Exported to: Worldwide
Percentage of Business in Exporting: 50

46868 (HQ)National Equipment Corporation
801 E 141st St
Bronx, NY 10454 718-585-0200
Fax: 718-993-2650 800-237-8873
sales@unionmachinery.com
www.unionmachinery.com
Manufacturer, importer and exporter of used and reconditioned food processing and packaging equipment
VP: Arthur Greenberg
VP: Richard Greenberg
VP: Charles Greenberg
Contact: David Feinne
dfeinne@unionmachinery.com
Number Employees: 20-49
Square Footage: 1800000
Other Locations:
National Equipment Corp.
NaucalpanNational Equipment Corp.
Regions Exported to: Worldwide
Percentage of Business in Exporting: 50
Regions Imported from: Worldwide

46869 National Fish & Oyster
5028 Meridian Rd NE
Olympia, WA 98516-2339 360-491-5550
Fax: 360-438-3681 www.nationaloyster.com
Processor and exporter of fresh and frozen oysters
President: James Bulldis
VP: George Bulldis
Plant Manager: Catherine Gylys
Estimated Sales: $5-10 Million
Number Employees: 20-49
Square Footage: 12000
Type of Packaging: Consumer

46870 National Foam
180 Sheree Blvd # 3900
Exton, PA 19341-1272 610-363-1400
Fax: 610-524-9073 webmaster@kidde-fire.com
www.kidde-fire.com
Manufacturer and exporter of foam fire extinguishing chemicals and equipment
Manager: Bobby Nelson
CFO: Larry Mansfield
Contact: Herbert Cooper
herbert.cooper@nationalfoam.com
Estimated Sales: $ 20 - 50 Million
Number Employees: 100-249
Parent Co: Racal-Chubb

46871 National Food Corporation
728 - 134th St. SW
Suite 103
Everett, WA 98204 425-349-4257
Fax: 425-349-4336 www.natlfood.com
Eggs and egg products including; yolks only, whole eggs, whites, and whole egg blends
President: Brian Bookey
VP Marketing: Roger Deffner
Sales Director: Gerry Wigren
Estimated Sales: $23.2 Million
Number Employees: 500
Type of Packaging: Consumer, Food Service
Regions Exported to: South America, Europe, Asia

46872 National Food Trading Co
12 Industrial Ave
Upper Saddle Rvr, NJ 07458-2302 201-825-6214
Fax: 201-825-6226 sales@nationalfoodscorp.com
www.nationalcortina.com
Importer of tomato products
Controller: Frank Saroff
VP: William Rahal
Sales Representative: John Lideski Jr
john@nationalfoods.com
Estimated Sales: $10-20 Million
Number Employees: 1-4
Brands Imported: Tomato House

46873 National Foods
1414 S West Street
Indianapolis, IN 46225-1548 317-634-5645
800-683-6565
Processor and exporter of portion cut meat and frankfurters
President: Steve Silk
Senior VP/General Manager: Martin Silver
Sales/Marketing Executive: Mark Kleinman
Number Employees: 600
Square Footage: 720000
Parent Co: ConAgra Refrigerated Prepared Foods
Type of Packaging: Consumer, Food Service
Other Locations:
National Foods
Indianapolis, INNational Foods
Brands Exported: Hebrew National
Regions Exported to: Central America, South America, Canada, Caribbean
Percentage of Business in Exporting: 2

46874 National Frozen Foods Corp
1600 Fairview Ave E
Suite 200
Seattle, WA 98102 206-322-8900
Fax: 206-322-4458 sales@nffc.com
Frozen foods including fruit and vegetable purees, vegetable blends, peas, corn, carrots, cooked squash, creamed corn, beans, pearl onions.
President & CEO: Dick Grader
Director of Chain Accounts: Sunshine Sang
Year Founded: 1912
Estimated Sales: $178.08 Million
Number Employees: 1,000-4,999
Square Footage: 12000
Type of Packaging: Consumer, Food Service, Private Label, Bulk
Other Locations:
Albany, OR
Chehalis, WA
Moses Lake, WA
Quincy, WAChehalis
Regions Exported to: Worldwide

46875 National Fruit Flavor Co Inc
935 Edwards Ave
New Orleans, LA 70123-3124 504-733-6757
Fax: 504-736-0168 800-966-1123
admin@nationalfruitflavor.com
www.nationalfruitflavor.com
Beverage concentrates, syrups and mixes. Manufacturer since 1917.

Importers & Exporters / A-Z

President: Gene Gamble
admin@nationalfruitflavor.com
Controller: Anthony Fulco
Vice President: Peter Gambel
Research and Development/Quality Control: Sharon Prados
Sales Manager: Avery Stirratt
Customer Service: Chris Rooks
Operations: Peter Gambel
Plant Manager: Giovanni Galvan
Purchasing: Michelle Adams
Estimated Sales: $ 10-20 Million
Number Employees: 20-49
Number of Brands: 6
Number of Products: 700
Square Footage: 41000
Type of Packaging: Consumer, Food Service, Private Label, Bulk
Brands Exported: National; Zodiac; Old Comiskey
Regions Exported to: Central America, South America, Europe, Asia
Percentage of Business in Exporting: 3

46876 National Hotpack
3538 Main Street
Stone Ridge, NY 12484   845-255-5000
          Fax: 845-687-7481 800-431-8232
          hotpack@spindustries.com www.hotpack.com
Hotpack manufactures and sells enviromental rooms and chambers, stability rooms and chambers, humidity rooms and chambers, glassware washers and dryers, vacuum ovens, sterilizers and autoclaves, C-O2 incubators, general purpose incubators, ovens, refrigerators, freezers
President/CEO: Bill Downs
CFO: Michael Bonner
Marketing: Shireen Scott
Sales: James Shiever
Estimated Sales: $65 Million
Number Employees: 100-249
Square Footage: 70000
Parent Co: SP Industries
Brands Exported: Hotpack; Heinicke
Regions Exported to: Central America, South America, Europe, Asia, Middle East

46877 National Importers
120-13100 Mitchell Road
Richmond, BC V6V 1M8
Canada   604-324-1551
          Fax: 604-324-1553 888-894-6464
          ussales@nationalimporters.com
          www.nationalimporters.com
Importer of gourmet, Mexican, Chinese, Indian, Thai foods, candy and groceries
Owner: David Dueck
Marketing: Barbara Allen
Office Manager: Peggy Hunter
Regions Imported from: Worldwide
Percentage of Business in Importing: 80

46878 National Instruments
4119 Fordleigh Rd
Baltimore, MD 21215-2292   410-764-0900
          Fax: 410-951-2093 866-258-1914
          jrosen@filamatic.com www.filamatic.com
Manufacturer and exporter of liquid filling, capping and turnkey packaging equipment
CEO: Robert Rosen
VP Marketing/Sales: Jim Striese
Manager: Mark Evans
mark.evans@filamatic.com
Estimated Sales: $ 10-20 Million
Number Employees: 50-99
Brands Exported: Filamatic; Capamatic
Regions Exported to: Central America, South America, Europe, Asia, Middle East, Australia
Percentage of Business in Exporting: 10

46879 National Interchem Corporation
13750 Chatham Street
Blue Island, IL 60406-3218   773-638-5100
          Fax: 773-638-8769 800-638-6688
          www.nichemical.com
Manufacturer and exporter of industrial cleaning and maintenance chemicals
Director Sales: Greg Fishman
Estimated Sales: $ 2.5-5 Million
Number Employees: 10-19

46880 National Label Co
2025 Joshua Rd
Lafayette Hill, PA 19444-2426   610-825-3250
          Fax: 610-834-8854 www.nationallabel.com

Manufacturer and exporter of pressure sensitive labeling equipment and labels
Exec VP: James Shacklett IV
Estimated Sales: $ 50-100 Million
Number Employees: 250-499
Type of Packaging: Bulk
Regions Exported to: Worldwide

46881 National Menuboard
4302 B St NW # D
Auburn, WA 98001   253-859-6068
          Fax: 253-859-8412 800-800-5237
Menu boards including illuminated, nonilluminated, indoor and outdoor
President: Dave Medzegian
dave@nationalmenuboard.com
Sales Representative: Wendi Adsley
Estimated Sales: Below $5 Million
Number Employees: 5-9
Square Footage: 40000

46882 National Metal Industries
203 Circuit Avenue
West Springfield, MA 01089-4016   413-785-5861
          Fax: 413-737-2309 800-628-8850
          www.national-metal.com
Manufacturer and exporter of metal stamps and parts for food processing equipment
Sales Manager: Bryan Costello
Estimated Sales: $ 10-20 Million
Number Employees: 50-99
Parent Co: Standex International Corporation
Regions Exported to: Worldwide

46883 (HQ)National Novelty Brush Co
505 E Fulton St
Lancaster, PA 17602-3022   717-299-5681
          Fax: 717-397-0991 www.nnbc-pa.com
Manufacturer and exporter of brushes, applicators and metal screw caps
President: Richard Seavey
rseavey@nnbc-pa.com
CFO: Bryan Howett
Quality Control: Sandy Donley
Sales Manager: Ronald Vellucci
Customer Service: Marianne Walsh
Estimated Sales: $ 20 - 50 Million
Number Employees: 100-249

46884 National Package Sealing Company
10791 SE Skyline Drive
Santa Ana, CA 92705-7413   714-630-1505
          Fax: 714-632-3217
Manufacturer and exporter of electric and manual dispensers for gummed carton sealing tapes and labels
President: William Amneus
Marketing Director: Fay Amneus
Estimated Sales: $2.5-5 Million
Number Employees: 19
Square Footage: 80000
Regions Exported to: Worldwide
Percentage of Business in Exporting: 5

46885 National Packaging
PO Box 4798
Rumford, RI 02916-0798   401-434-1070
          Fax: 401-438-5203 www.multiwall.com
Manufacturer and exporter of cloth winding reels and single faced corrugated paper
President: Charles M Dunn
Estimated Sales: $20-50 Million
Number Employees: 10-19
Parent Co: Real Reel Corporation
Regions Exported to: Worldwide

46886 National Plastics Co
15505 Cornet St
Santa Fe Springs, CA 90670-5511   562-926-4511
          Fax: 562-926-0222 800-221-9149
          mra@natcos.com www.menucovers.com
Menu covers, loose leaf binders, wine lists, check presenters, transparent price card holders and pad holders; exporter of menu covers
President: Gregory Mitchell
gregm@natcos.com
Marketing Director: Mark Anderson
Sales Director: Brian Bromm
Office Manager: Bryan Carr
Plant Manager: Benjamin Jimenez
Estimated Sales: $5-10 Million
Number Employees: 50-99

Square Footage: 36000
Parent Co: National Plastic Company of California
Regions Exported to: Central America, South America, Europe, Caribbean, Canada, Latin America, Mexico
Percentage of Business in Exporting: 4

46887 National Printing Converters
4310 Bonavita Dr
Encino, CA 91436   818-906-7936
Manufacturer and exporter of data processing printed, pressure sensitive, laser, on-line pattern adhesive and vinyl shelf marking labels and shelf talkers
President: Brain Buckley
Chairman: Robert Buckley
Operations Manager: Richard Atkins
Estimated Sales: $ .5 - 1 million
Number Employees: 1-4
Square Footage: 110000
Brands Exported: National Printing ""Pin Stick''; Label Data-Set
Regions Exported to: Central America, South America, Europe, Asia
Percentage of Business in Exporting: 15

46888 National Raisin Co.
PO Box 219
Fowler, CA 93625   559-834-5981
          Fax: 559-834-1055 info@nationalraisin.com
          www.nationalraisin.com
Raisins, nuts and other dried fruits.
President/CEO: Lindakay Abdulian
Founder/Senior Advisor: Kenneth Bedrosian
kenneth.bedrosian@national-raisin.com
Accounts Payable Manager: Carlotta Bedrosian
Vice President: Bryan Bedrosian
Senior VP, Sales/Marketing: Jane Asmar
Vice President, Grower Relations: Michael Bedrosian
Year Founded: 1969
Estimated Sales: $140 Million
Number Employees: 500-999
Number of Brands: 1
Square Footage: 400000
Type of Packaging: Consumer, Food Service, Private Label, Bulk
Regions Exported to: Worldwide
Percentage of Business in Exporting: 25

46889 National Sales Corporation
7250 Oxford Way
Commerce, CA 90040   323-586-0200
          Fax: 800-560-4040 800-690-4444
          www.e-nsc.com
Exporter and wholesaler/distributor of groceries, general merchandise, health/beauty aids, private label items, sugar, condiments, soups, kitchenware, etc.
Estimated Sales: $50-100 Million
Number Employees: 50-99
Square Footage: 80000
Type of Packaging: Private Label

46890 National Scoop & Equipment Company
PO Box 325
Spring House, PA 19477-0325   215-646-2040
Manufacturer, wholesaler/distributor and importer of pails, buckets, scales, scoops, skimmers, dippers, disposable paper clothing, sinks and trucks
Manager: Ken Johnson
Regions Imported from: Asia

46891 National Shippng SupplyCo
19950 W 161st St
Olathe, KS 66062-2741   913-764-1551
          Fax: 913-764-0779 800-444-8361
Wholesaler/distributor and exporter of labels, tags and cloth bags; also, plastic sampling and reclosable bags
Owner: Rosey Hohendorf
rosey@natshipsupply com
Customer Service: Rosie Hohendorf
Estimated Sales: $500,000-$1 Million
Number Employees: 1-4
Square Footage: 20000
Parent Co: Victor Enterprises
Brands Exported: Hubco; Whirlpak; Nasco; Ennis
Regions Exported to: Europe, Asia, Canada
Percentage of Business in Exporting: 10

Importers & Exporters / A-Z

46892 National Stabilizers
1846 Business Center Dr
Duarte, CA 91010-2997
626-359-4584
Fax: 626-359-4586
Stabilizers
President: Robert Burger
Quality Control: Raivo Partma
VP Sales: Robert Burger
Sales/Purchasing: Tomas Martinez
Estimated Sales: $2.5-5 Million
Number Employees: 5 to 9

46893 National Tape Corporation
5128 Storey Street
New Orleans, LA 70123-5320
504-733-8020
Fax: 504-734-8751 800-535-8846
Manufacturer and exporter of pressure sensitive labels and tapes including masking, duct, electrical, pressure sensitive and marking
VP Sales: Joel Teachworth
VP: Robert Wiswall
Number Employees: 100
Square Footage: 520000
Brands Exported: Action Brand
Regions Exported to: Central America, South America, Europe, Asia, Middle East
Percentage of Business in Exporting: 10

46894 National Time RecordingEqpt
64 Reade St # 2
New York, NY 10007-1870
212-227-3310
Fax: 212-227-5353 info@nationaltime.net
www.nationaltime.net
Manufacturer and exporter of time clocks, time stamps and thermometers
VP: K Kelly
Estimated Sales: $ 5-10 Million
Number Employees: 10-19

46895 National Velour Corp
36 Bellair Ave
Warwick, RI 02886-2206
401-737-8300
Fax: 401-738-7418 800-556-6523
service@nationalvelour.com
www.nationalvelour.com
Manufacturer and exporter of flock for packaging and displays; also, custom flocking and stock lines available
President: Oscar Der Manouelian
Estimated Sales: $5-10 Million
Number Employees: 10-19
Percentage of Business in Exporting: 2

46896 Nationwide Pennant & Flag Mfg
7325 Reindeer Trl
San Antonio, TX 78238-1214
210-684-3524
Fax: 210-680-2329 800-383-3524
sales@napmfg.com www.napmfg.com
Manufacturer and exporter of pennants, flags, flagpoles, banners and decals
President: Donald W Engelhardt
CEO: Rick Sutton
Sales: Joe Pyland
Estimated Sales: $10-20 Million
Number Employees: 50-99
Square Footage: 120000
Regions Exported to: Central America, South America, Europe, Asia, Middle East
Percentage of Business in Exporting: 15

46897 Native Scents
1040 Dea Ln
Taos, NM 87571-6277
575-758-9656
Fax: 575-758-5802 800-645-3471
Processor, importer and exporter of herbal teas and aromatic products, honey and essential oils, incense, bath products
President: Marlene Payfoya
CEO: Alfred Savinelli
nativescents@gmail.com
CEO: Alfred Savinelli
Estimated Sales: Less Than $500,000
Number Employees: 1-4
Number of Products: 127
Square Footage: 24000
Brands Exported: Native Scents
Regions Exported to: Central America, South America, Europe, Canada, Caribbean, Mexico
Percentage of Business in Exporting: 32
Regions Imported from: South America, Europe, Canada, Mexico
Percentage of Business in Importing: 10

46898 Natra US
2535 Camino Dek Rio South
Suite 355
Chula Vista, CA 91910
619-397-4120
Fax: 619-397-4121 800-262-6216
www.natrus.com
Importer and exporter of cocoa powder, butter and extract; also, chocolate, caffeine, theobromine and nutraceuticals
Manager: Maria Dominguez
Vice President: Martin Brabenec
Key Account Manager: Juan Carlos Vinolo
Estimated Sales: $650000
Number Employees: 1-4
Number of Brands: 2
Number of Products: 30
Parent Co: Natra S.A.
Type of Packaging: Consumer, Food Service, Bulk
Brands Exported: Natra
Regions Exported to: Central America, South America, Europe, Asia, Middle East, Canada
Brands Imported: Natra
Regions Imported from: Europe

46899 (HQ)Natrium Products Inc
58 Pendleton Street
Cortland, NY 13045-2702
607-753-9829
Fax: 607-753-0552 800-962-4203
info@natrium.com www.natrium.com
Baking Soda/Sodium Biocarbonate
President: Tim Herman
herman@natrium.com
Estimated Sales: $ 10 - 20 Million
Number Employees: 20-49
Square Footage: 70000
Type of Packaging: Bulk

46900 (HQ)Natrol Inc
21411 Prairie St
Chatsworth, CA 91311-5829
818-739-6000
Fax: 818-739-6001 800-326-1520
support@natrol.com www.natrol.com
Wholesaler/distributor, exporter and importer of specialty vitamins and dietary supplements
President: Elliott Balbert
CEO: Harun Simbirdi
hsimbirdi@natrol.com
CEO: Craig Cameron
VP Sales: Jon Denis
Number Employees: 250-499
Square Footage: 320000
Type of Packaging: Consumer
Brands Exported: Natrol Melatonin; Natrol Kavatrol; Ester-c/My Favorite Multiple
Regions Exported to: Canada
Percentage of Business in Exporting: 2
Regions Imported from: South America, Europe, Asia

46901 Natur Sweeteners, Inc.
11155 Massachusetts Avenue
Los Angeles, CA 90025
310-445-0020
Fax: 310-473-1086 stephenf@naturresearch.com
www.cweet.com
Natural intense sweetener; characteristics and other performance qualities similar to cane sugar

Regions Exported to: South America, Asia, North America

46902 Natural Alpha Omega
9900 Bell Ranch Drive
Suite 108
Santa Fe Springs, CA 90670
562-906-9988
Fax: 562-906-1199
Sprouted flaxseed power, dressings and sauces, soyage yogurt, curry tree, sprakling fruit flavored drink and ashitaba products

46903 Natural Casing Co
410 E Railroad St
Peshtigo, WI 54157-1644
715-582-3931
Fax: 715-582-3931 www.naturalcasingco.com
Wholesaler/distributor and importer of sausage casings
President: Stephen Dirtzu
Estimated Sales: $1-2.5 Million
Number Employees: 5-9
Square Footage: 100000
Parent Co: SD Enterprises
Regions Imported from: South America, Europe
Percentage of Business in Importing: 95

46904 Natural Flavors
268 Doremus Ave
Newark, NJ 07105-4879
973-589-1230
Fax: 973-589-0016 Flavorinfo@flavor.com
www.flavor.com
Natural and certified organic flavors
President: Herb Stein
Secretary: Joanne Hoffman
EVP: Julie Eisman
Director Quality Assurance: Robert Maxwell
E Commerce Manager: Josh Richards
National Sales Manager: Jeff Rakity
Manager: Isabel Couto
Estimated Sales: $2 Million
Number Employees: 10-19
Regions Exported to: South America, Europe, Asia, Africa, Australia, Canada, Mexico

46905 Natural Food Holdings
4241 US 75 Ave.
Sioux Center, IA 51250
800-735-7765
www.siouxpreme.com
Manufacturer and exporter of pork products.
CEO, Perdue Farms: Randy Day
Year Founded: 1969
Estimated Sales: $113 Million
Number Employees: 250-499
Square Footage: 50000
Parent Co: Perdue Farms
Type of Packaging: Consumer, Private Label, Bulk
Regions Exported to: Central America, South America

46906 Natural Food Source
52 E Union Blvd
Bethlehem, PA 18017
610-997-0500
Fax: 610-954-9959 www.nimeks.com
Dried fruits, frozen vegetables, concentrates and purees.
VP: Kadir Veziroglu

46907 Natural Foods Inc
3040 Hill Ave
Toledo, OH 43607-2983
419-537-1711
Fax: 419-531-6887 vip@bulkfoods.com
www.3qf.com
Wholesaler/distributor, importer and packer of food, candy, nuts, spices, fruit, and chocolates
Owner: Frank Dietrich
Estimated Sales: $5 Million
Number Employees: 20-49
Square Footage: 1800000
Type of Packaging: Food Service, Bulk
Regions Imported from: Asia
Percentage of Business in Importing: 25

46908 Natural Fruit Corp
770 W 20th St
Hialeah, FL 33010-2430
305-887-7525
Fax: 305-888-8208 info@nfc-fruti.com
www.nfc-fruti.com
Processor and exporter of frozen fruit bars, cocktail mixes and ice cream novelties
Founder/President: Simon Bravo
Quality Assurance Director: Angelica Delia
EVP Operations/Founder: Jorge Bravo Sr
Plant Supervisor: Peter Infante
Estimated Sales: $14 Million
Number Employees: 20-49
Square Footage: 40000
Regions Exported to: Europe, Canada, Caribbean

46909 Natural Group
909 15th Street
Suite 2
Modesto, CA 95354-1130
209-522-6860
Fax: 209-522-7928 naturalgroup@att.net
Wholesaler/distributor, importer and exporter of sparkling, mineral and natural beverages including water; wholesaler/distributor of groceries
President: Richard Keer
Marketing Manager: Denise Haight
Estimated Sales: $2.5-5 Million
Number Employees: 1-4
Type of Packaging: Consumer, Private Label
Brands Exported: AME; Alog Ginseng; Aqua Libra
Regions Exported to: Asia, Middle East
Brands Imported: Ame; Purdey's; Aqua Libra; Hildon Waters; Apres
Regions Imported from: Europe
Percentage of Business in Importing: 90

Importers & Exporters / A-Z

46910 Natural Oils International
2279 Ward Ave
Simi Valley, CA 93065-1863   805-433-0160
     Fax: 805-433-0182 www.naturaloils.com
Processor, importer and exporter of vegetable oils
President: Brendon Bonnar
Sales: Barbara Hardy
Sales: Jack Phillips
Estimated Sales: $ 1 - 3 Million
Number Employees: 1-4
Square Footage: 120000
Regions Exported to: Central America, South America, Europe, Asia, Middle East, Australia
Percentage of Business in Exporting: 70
Regions Imported from: Central America, South America, Europe, Asia, Middle East, Australia
Percentage of Business in Importing: 30

46911 Natural Rush
PO Box 421753
San Francisco, CA 94142-1753   415-863-2503
     Fax: 415-431-5763
Importer and exporter of honey
Owner: Gilles Desaulniers
Number Employees: 1-4
Square Footage: 15200
Parent Co: Alveole Foods
Brands Imported: Cinnamon Rush

46912 Natural Value
1511 Corporate Way
Suite 100
Sacramento, CA 95831   916-836-3561
     Fax: 916-914-2446 gary@naturalvalue.com
     naturalvalue.com
Organic beans, lentils, tomatoes and condiments
President/Owner: Gary Cohen
CEO: Jody Cohen
Estimated Sales: $ 1 - 3 Million
Number Employees: 1-4
Number of Brands: 1
Number of Products: 200
Type of Packaging: Consumer, Food Service, Bulk

46913 Natural Way Mills Inc
24509 390th St NE
Middle River, MN 56737-9367   218-222-3677
     Fax: 218-222-3408 naturalwaymills@wiktel.com
     www.naturalwaymills.com
Organic wheat, seven-grain cereal, rye, flax seed, barley, millet, brown rice, flour and grits; custom milling available
Owner: Ray Juhl
rayjuhl@naturalwaymills.com
CEO: Helen Juhl
Quality Control: Aaron Pervis
Sales: Leigh Mott
rayjuhl@naturalwaymills.com
Plant Manager: Charles Knapp
Estimated Sales: $620,000
Number Employees: 5-9
Regions Exported to: Europe
Percentage of Business in Exporting: 2

46914 Nature Most Laboratories
Trigo Business Park
60 Trigo Drive
Middletown, CT 06457-6157   860-346-8991
     Fax: 860-347-3312 800-234-2112
     sales@naturemost.com
Manufacturer, importer and exporter of products, vitamins, oils, minerals, herbal supplements
President: Robert Trigo
Marketing: Sam Schwartz
Sales: Donna Platnum
Operations: Fred Wuschner
Estimated Sales: $ 5 - 10 Million
Number Employees: 20-49
Number of Brands: 3
Number of Products: 300
Square Footage: 80000
Type of Packaging: Consumer, Private Label
Brands Exported: Naturemost Labs; Trigo Labs
Regions Exported to: Europe, Asia, Worldwide
Percentage of Business in Exporting: 35
Percentage of Business in Importing: 25

46915 Nature Quality
13805 Llagas Ave
San Martin, CA 95046   408-683-2182
     Fax: 408-683-4249 natqual@aol.com
     naturequality.com
Processor and exporter of IQF cut celery, olives, onions, garlic and peppers
President: Karen Ash
kash@naturesquality.com
Food Safety & Quality Assurance Manager: Nicole Kamath
Sales Manager: Melissa Guevara
Estimated Sales: $7 Million
Number Employees: 100-249
Square Footage: 40000
Type of Packaging: Food Service, Bulk
Regions Exported to: Europe, Asia, Australia
Percentage of Business in Exporting: 2

46916 Nature's Apothecary
244 Knollwood Drive
Suite 300
Bloomingdale, IL 60108   970-664-1600
     Fax: 970-664-5106 888-669-3663
     www.nowfoods.com
Processor and exporter of fresh organic, medicinal, botanical and herbal liquid extracts
President: Jim Emme
Engineering Manager: Dan Mirjanic
Sales Manager: Dan Richard
Type of Packaging: Consumer, Private Label, Bulk
Regions Exported to: Worldwide
Percentage of Business in Exporting: 20

46917 Nature's Best Inc
195 Engineers Rd
Hauppauge, NY 11788-4020   631-232-3355
     Fax: 631-232-3320 800-345-2378
     info@naturesbest.com
     www.theisopurecompany.com
Processor and exporter of athletic supplements and sport drinks
President: Hal Katz
Estimated Sales: $1.5 Million
Number Employees: 5-9
Brands Exported: Nature's Best; Perfect Decades; No Holds Bar; Perfect Rx
Regions Exported to: South America, Europe

46918 Nature's Bounty Co.
2100 Smithtown Ave.
Ronkonkoma, NY 11779   631-200-2000
     877-774-3361
consumeraffairsmgmt@nbty.com
     www.naturesbountyco.com
Nutritional supplements and vitamins.
President/CEO: Paul Sturman
CFO: Ted McCormick
General Counsel/Chief Compliance Officer: Stratis Philipps
Estimated Sales: $3 Billion
Number Employees: 10,000+
Number of Brands: 19
Number of Products: 22K
Parent Co: KKR
Type of Packaging: Consumer, Private Label, Bulk
Regions Exported to: Worldwide
Percentage of Business in Exporting: 30

46919 Nature's Guru
19416 Amhurst Ct
Cerritos, CA 90703-6787   949-478-4878
     info@naturesguru.com
     www.naturesguru.com
Chai

46920 Nature's Herbs
PO Box 970
Merritt, BC V1K 1B8
Canada   250-378-8822
     Fax: 250-378-8753 800-437-2257
     www.naturesherbs.net/p/contact_us
Processor and exporter of dietary supplements and encapsulated herbs
President/CEO: Ross Blechman
Executive VP Sales: Dean Blechman
Estimated Sales: $ 5 - 10 Million
Number Employees: 250
Square Footage: 200000
Parent Co: Twin Laboratories
Type of Packaging: Consumer
Regions Exported to: Worldwide

46921 Nature's Legacy Inc.
417 S. Meridian Road
Hudson, MI 49247   517-448-2050
     Fax: 517-448-2070 info@purityfoods.com
     www.natureslegacyforlife.com
Organic pasta, flours, spelt granola, pretzels, sesame sticks, beans, grains, and seeds.
Owner/President: Donald Stinchcomb
Estimated Sales: $5.8 Million
Number Employees: 11
Square Footage: 24000
Type of Packaging: Consumer, Bulk
Brands Exported: Erntedank; Vita Spelt
Regions Exported to: South America, Europe, Middle East, Canada
Percentage of Business in Exporting: 10
Regions Imported from: Europe, Asia, Canada, Phillipines
Percentage of Business in Importing: 10

46922 Nature's Own
11 Fred Roddy Avenue
Attleboro, MA 2703   508-399-8690
     Fax: 508-399-8693 www.naturesown.com.au
Natural hardwood charcoal and grilling/smoking woods; importer of herbwoods; exporter of hardwood charcoal
President/Owner: Don Hysko
VP: Holly Hysko
Sales Manager: Dana Bracket
Estimated Sales: $2.5-5 Million
Number Employees: 5-9
Square Footage: 50000
Brands Imported: Treestock; Nature's Own

46923 (HQ)Nature's Path Foods
205 H Street
Suite 275
Blaine, WA 98230
     888-808-9505
naturespath@worldpantry.com
     www.naturespath.com
Organic cereal products
President & Founder: Arran Stephens
Co-CEO & COO: Ratana Stephens
Executive VP Sales & Marketing: Arjan Stephens
Director of Human Resources: Jyoti Stephens
Year Founded: 1985
Estimated Sales: $145.87 Million
Number Employees: 60
Square Footage: 29999
Type of Packaging: Consumer, Private Label, Bulk
Other Locations:
   Nature's Path Foods
   Blaine, WA Nature's Path Foods
Regions Exported to: Europe, Japan
Percentage of Business in Exporting: 65

46924 Nature's Plus
548 Broadhollow Rd
Melville, NY 11747-3722   631-293-0013
     Fax: 800-688-7239 800-645-9500
     salesinfo@naturesplus.com www.naturesplus.com
Processor and exporter of health products including protein weight loss supplements, vitamins and herbs
Director Marketing: Gerard McIntee
Estimated Sales: $15.1 Million
Number Employees: 5-9
Parent Co: Natural Organics
Regions Exported to: South America, Europe, Asia

46925 (HQ)Nature's Products Inc
1301 Sawgrass Corporate Pkwy
Sunrise, FL 33323-2813   954-233-3300
     Fax: 954-233-3301 800-752-7873
     info@natures-products.com
Manufacturer and supplier of raw materials specializing in gelatin, flavors, active pharmaceuticals, botanicals and pharmaceutical additives. Providing import/export services, warehousing and freight forwarding to and from the UnitedStates and worldwide
President: Jose Minski
josem@npi-gmi.com
Number Employees: 100-249
Type of Packaging: Private Label, Bulk
Brands Exported: Generic Brand Names; GMI Gelatin; Curt Georgi
Regions Exported to: Central America, South America, Europe, Asia, Middle East
Percentage of Business in Exporting: 40
Brands Imported: Curt Georgi; GMI/Originates; Food Ingredients and Gelatin
Regions Imported from: South America, Europe, Asia
Percentage of Business in Importing: 60

46926 Nature's Sunshine Products Company
2901 W. Blue Grass Blvd.
Lehi, UT 84043
     800-223-8225
     www.naturessunshine.com

Health products including vitamins, minerals and herbs.
CEO: Terrence Moorehead
Executive VP/CFO: Joseph Baty
Executive VP/General Counsel: Nathan Brower
Vice President, Human Resources: Tracee Comstock
Executive VP/COO: Sue Armstrong
Year Founded: 1972
Estimated Sales: $367.81 Million
Number Employees: 1,003
Square Footage: 63000
Type of Packaging: Consumer
Brands Exported: Nature's Sunshine Products

46927 Natures Sungrown Foods Inc
700 Irwin St # 103
Suite 103
San Rafael, CA 94901-3300   415-491-4944
     Fax: 415-532-2233 hal@naturessungrown.com
          www.naturessungrown.com
Manufacturer and exporter of natural beef and pork, organic foods (dried fruit, coffee, juice, sauce, tortilla chips, guacamole, jalapeno peppers and Mexican foods
President: Hal Shenson
hal@naturessungrown.com
Estimated Sales: $5-10 Million
Number Employees: 1-4
Number of Brands: 2
Type of Packaging: Consumer, Food Service, Private Label, Bulk
Brands Exported: La Victoria; Veracruz; Santa Cruz; RW Knousen, Francesco Rinaldi; Bar-S; Organic Valley; Borden; Niman Ranch
Regions Exported to: Central America, South America, Europe, Asia
Percentage of Business in Exporting: 90
Regions Imported from: Europe
Percentage of Business in Importing: 5

46928 Naturex Inc
375 Huyler St
South Hackensack, NJ 07606   201-440-5000
               www.naturex.com
Natural antioxidants, colors, herbs and spices oleoresins and essential oils, and botanical extracts for the food, flavor and nutraceutical industries.
Chief Procurement Officer: Serge Sabrier
Year Founded: 1992
Estimated Sales: $404.9 Million
Number Employees: 1,700
Square Footage: 14991
Parent Co: Naturex, France Avignon Headquarters
Type of Packaging: Bulk
Other Locations:
     Naturex, Inc. USA Chicago
     Chicago, IL
     Naturex USA Atlanta Sales Office
     Marietta, GA
     Naturex USA Californaia Sales Offic
     Costa Mesa, CANaturex, Inc. USA
     ChicagoMarietta
Regions Exported to: Worldwide
Percentage of Business in Exporting: 20
Regions Imported from: Worldwide

46929 Navarro Pecan Co
2131 E State Highway 31
Corsicana, TX 75109   903-872-5641
     Fax: 903-874-7143   800-333-9507
     sales@navarropecan.com www.navarropecan.com
Processor and exporter of kosher certified shelled raw and roasted pecans used as ingredients.
Chief Information Officer: Linda Garza
lgarza@navarropecan.com
Year Founded: 1977
Estimated Sales: $20-50 Million
Number Employees: 250-499
Square Footage: 200000
Type of Packaging: Consumer, Bulk
Brands Exported: Navarro
Regions Exported to: Europe, Asia, Middle East, Canada, Caribbean
Percentage of Business in Exporting: 20

46930 Navco
11929 Brittmoore Park Dr
Houston, TX 77041-7226   832-467-3636
     Fax: 832-467-3800   800-231-0164
               sales@navco.us www.navco.us
Manufacturer and exporter of material handling equipment including pneumatic and electric vibrators

President: Mark Neundorfer
Marketing Manager: Ben Snider
Number Employees: 10-19
Regions Exported to: Worldwide
Percentage of Business in Exporting: 10

46931 Naya
2030-340 Pie IX
Montreal, QC H1V 2C8
Canada   450-562-7911
     Fax: 450-562-3654 info@naya.com
               www.naya.com
Processor and exporter of bottled spring water
President: Anita Jarjour
Executive VP/COO: Stu Levitan
Director Sales Marketing: Raynald Brisson
VP Operations: Sylvain Mayrand
Number Employees: 100-249
Square Footage: 240000
Type of Packaging: Consumer, Food Service, Private Label
Brands Exported: Naya
Regions Exported to: Central America, South America, Europe, Asia, Middle East
Percentage of Business in Exporting: 80

46932 Naylor Candies Inc
289 Chestnut St
Mt Wolf, PA 17347-9702   717-266-2706
     Fax: 717-266-2706 www.naylorcandies.com
Processor and exporter of confectionery products including butter toffee peanuts, butter mints, cashew crunch, peanut crunch and honey roasted peanuts; importer of cashews and peanuts
Owner: Dennis Naylor
dennis@cannonfamily.4t.com
Estimated Sales: $750,000
Number Employees: 10-19
Square Footage: 32000
Type of Packaging: Consumer, Private Label, Bulk
Regions Exported to: Canada
Percentage of Business in Exporting: 5
Regions Imported from: South America
Percentage of Business in Importing: 5

46933 Nbi Fresh Juices Distribution
12798 Perimeter Rd # C100
Dallas, TX 75228-8116   214-319-0784
     Fax: 214-319-0622 orders@naturalbrands.com
               www.naturalbrands.com
Owner: Don Duchesneau
Estimated Sales: $ 10 - 20 Million
Number Employees: 5-9

46934 Ne-Mo's Bakery Inc
416 N Hale Ave
Escondido, CA 92029-1496   760-741-5725
     Fax: 760-741-0659   800-325-2692
     customerservice@horizonfoodgroup.com
               www.nemosbakery.com
Processor and exporter of baked goods including hand-wrapped cake squares, cake slices, cinnamon rolls, cookies, muffins, mini loaf cakes, danish, cake breads, coffee cakes, and specialty cakes
Cio/Cto: Darren Watson
dwatson@nemosbakery.com
Senior VP: Sam Delucca Jr
Estimated Sales: $ 10 - 20 Million
Number Employees: 100-249
Square Footage: 120000
Type of Packaging: Consumer, Food Service, Private Label, Bulk
Brands Exported: Ne-Mo's
Regions Exported to: Canada, Mexico

46935 Neal Walters Poster Corporation
PO Box 480
Bentonville, AR 72712-0480   501-273-2489
          Fax: 501-271-2132
Manufacturer and exporter of billboard and point of purchase posters, product markings, decals, bar code and pressure sensitive labels, business and computer forms, etc
President: James Walters
Secy./Treas.: Thomas Walters
V.P.: John Walters
Estimated Sales: $500,000-$1 Million
Number Employees: 9
Square Footage: 60000
Regions Exported to: Canada
Percentage of Business in Exporting: 5

46936 Near East Importing Corporation
8000 Cooper Avenue
Suite 6
Glendale, NY 11385-7734   718-894-3600
          Fax: 718-326-2832
Importer and wholesaler/distributor of pistachios, pickled olives and vegetables, sesame butter, meat products, beans, raisins, apricots, cherries, mudberries and spices; also, kitchenware items; serving the food service market
Executive Adminstration: A Anasa
Estimated Sales: $2.5-5 Million
Number Employees: 10-19
Brands Imported: Pyramid; Tamek
Regions Imported from: South America, Europe, Asia, Middle East
Percentage of Business in Importing: 15

46937 Nebraska Bean
85824 519th Ave
Clearwater, NE 68726-5239   402-887-5335
     Fax: 402-887-4709   800-253-6502
     brett@nebraskabean.com www.nebraskabean.com
Experienced grower, processor and packager of quality popcorn. The fully integrated operation offers microwave, bulk, private label and poly bags of popcorn
President: Brett Morrison
brett@nebraskabean.com
VP: Brett Morrison
Sales: Michelle Steskal
Estimated Sales: $ 10 - 20 Million
Number Employees: 20-49
Number of Brands: 1
Square Footage: 10000
Type of Packaging: Consumer, Food Service, Private Label, Bulk
Brands Exported: Morrison Farms
Regions Exported to: Central America, South America, Europe, Asia, Middle East
Percentage of Business in Exporting: 50

46938 Nebraska Corn-Fed Beef
1010 Lincoln Mall
Suite 101
Lincoln, NE 68508   402-475-2333
     Fax: 402-475-0822 nc@necattlemen.org
               www.nebraskacattlemen.org
Executive VP: Michael Kelsey
Number Employees: 10-19

46939 Nebraska Department of Agriculture
301 Centennial Mall South
PO Box 94947
Lincoln, NE 68508-6967   402-471-2341
     Fax: 402-471-2759   800-422-6692
     agr.webmaster@nebraska.gov www.agr.ne.gov
Promote Nebraska Agricultural products, including food and beverage produced in the state.
Number Employees: 5-9

46940 Nederman
102 Transit Ave
Thomasville, NC 27360-8927   336-821-0800
     Fax: 336-821-0890   800-533-5286
               www.nederman.com
Manufacturer and importer of dust collection filters, cyclones, grinders, pipe clamps and ducts
President: Tom Ballus
tom.ballus@nederman.com
Marketing Director: Tarey Cullen
VP Sales: Steve McDaniel
Estimated Sales: $20-50 Million
Number Employees: 100-249
Brands Imported: Quick-Fit Components
Regions Imported from: Europe
Percentage of Business in Importing: 20

46941 Neesvig Meats
4350 Duraform Ln
PO Box 288
Windsor, WI 53598-9671   608-846-1150
     Fax: 608-846-1155   800-633-4494
               www.neesvigs.com
Wholesaler/distributor and exporter of portion control meats

469

Importers & Exporters / A-Z

President: Lindabob Flanagan
lflanagan@neesvigs.com
President: Marvin Leppert
COO: Paul Greisen
Sales/Marketing Executive: Lee Fritz
Operations Manager: Matt Meyer
Director Operations/Mail Order: Paul Werwinski
Purchasing Manager: Bob Flanagan
Estimated Sales: $ 1 - 3 Million
Number Employees: 100-249

46942 Nefab Packaging, Inc.
204 Airline Drive
Suite 100
Coppell, TX 75019   469-444-5308
    Fax: 603-367-4329 800-322-4425
            www.nefab.us
Manufacturer and exporter of wooden industrial packaging and distribution equipment including pallets, skids, crates and boxes; also, milling services available
Director of Global Business Development: Ken Wilson
Chief Executive Officer: Brian Bulatao
VP: Andi Wilson
Executive Vice President: Eric Howe
Contact: Stephanie Carreon
scarreon@nefab.us
Number Employees: 400

46943 Neil Jones Food Company
1701 W 16th Street
Vancouver, WA 98660-1067   360-696-4356
    Fax: 360-696-0050 800-291-3862
            sales@nwpacking.com
            www.neiljonesfoodcompany.com
Manufacturer of canned fruits and vegetables
President/Owner: Matt Jones
CEO: L. Neil Jones
Estimated Sales: $500,000-$1 Million
Number Employees: 250-499
Type of Packaging: Consumer, Food Service, Private Label

46944 Nelles Automation
7000 Hollister St
Houston, TX 77040-5617   713-939-9399
        Fax: 713-939-0393
tom.christopher@telvent.abengoa.com
            www.telvent.com
Manufacturer and exporter of automated control systems and circuit boards for electric utility
President: Dave Jardine
CFO: Manuel Fanchez
VP: Tom Christopher
Estimated Sales: $ 1 - 3 Million
Number Employees: 5-9
Parent Co: Valmet

46945 Nellson Candies Inc
5800 Ayala Ave
Irwindale, CA 91706-6215   626-334-4508
            www.nellsonllc.com
Manufacturer and exporter of custom formulated snack, diet/weight loss, sport nutrition and medical food nutrition bars
Processor: Hoa Nguyen
Estimated Sales: Less Than $500,000
Number Employees: 1-4
Square Footage: 89864
Type of Packaging: Consumer, Food Service, Private Label, Bulk
Regions Exported to: Europe, Middle East

46946 Nelson Cheese Factory
S237 State Road 35 S
Nelson, WI 54756   715-673-4725
        Fax: 715-673-4218
nelsoncheesefactory@gmail.com
            www.nelsoncheese.com
Broker and importer of Wisconsin and imported cheeses, as well as wines and a selection of breads, scones and cookies.
Owner: Edward Greenheck
nelsoncheesefactory@gmail.com
Estimated Sales: Less Than $500,000
Number Employees: 5-9
Type of Packaging: Consumer, Food Service
Other Locations:
    Nelson Cheese Factory - Eau Claire
    Eau Claire, WI
    Nelson Cheese Factory - Rochester
    Rochester, MNNelson Cheese Factory - Eau ClaireRochester

46947 Nelson Crab Inc
3088 Kindred Ave
Tokeland, WA 98590   360-267-2911
    Fax: 360-267-2921 800-262-0069
Processor, importer and exporter of canned, fresh, smoked and frozen seafood including salmon steaks, shad, crabs, crab meat and shrimp
President: Kristi Nelson
kristi@nelsoncrab.com
Plant Manager: Les Candler
Estimated Sales: $ 10 - 20 Million
Number Employees: 50-99
Type of Packaging: Food Service, Private Label
Regions Exported to: Asia, Canada
Regions Imported from: Canada

46948 Nemco Food Equipment
301 Meuse Argonne St
PO Box 305
Hicksville, OH 43526-1143   419-542-7751
    Fax: 419-542-6690 800-782-6761
        mwibel@nemcofoodequip.com
Manufacturer and exporter of vegetable slicers and cutters
President: Jarod Martenies
vanney75@yahoo.com
Estimated Sales: $10-20 Million
Number Employees: 50-99
Type of Packaging: Food Service
Regions Exported to: Worldwide
Percentage of Business in Exporting: 1

46949 Nemco Food Equipment
301 Meuse Argonne St
Hicksville, OH 43526-1143   419-542-7751
    Fax: 419-542-6690 mwibel@nemcofoodequip.com
President: Jarod Martenies
vanney75@yahoo.com
Estimated Sales: $ 10 - 20 Million
Number Employees: 50-99

46950 Neo-Ray Products
537 Johnson Avenue
Brooklyn, NY 11237-1304   718-456-7400
    Fax: 718-456-5492 800-221-0946
Manufacturer and exporter of architectural grade fluorescent lighting systems
National Sales Manager: Andrew Gross
Estimated Sales: $20-50 Million
Number Employees: 100-249
Regions Exported to: Worldwide

46951 Neogen Corp
620 Lesher Pl
Lansing, MI 48912-1509   517-372-9200
    Fax: 517-372-2006 800-234-5333
        foodsafety@neogen.com www.neogen.com
Manufacturer, importer and exporter of food pathogen testing kits
CEO: John Adent
Marketing Manager: Margaret Cyr
General Manager: Mark Mozola
Estimated Sales: $2.5-5 Million
Number Employees: 1000-4999
Parent Co: Vysis
Regions Exported to: South America, Europe, Asia, Canada
Regions Imported from: Worldwide

46952 (HQ)Neon Design-a-Sign
26022 Cape Dr Bldg H
Laguna Niguel, CA 92677   949-348-9223
    Fax: 949-348-1736 888-636-6327
Manufacturer and exporter of signs including changeable, fiber-optic neon and programmable LED message displays. Also have a full line of LED lighting.
President: Timothy Piper
CEO: Christine Busnardo
Contact: Tim Piper
piper@neon-das.com
Estimated Sales: $600,000
Number Employees: 1-4
Square Footage: 8000
Brands Exported: Neon Design-A-Sign - Led's Signs, Neon Signs, Fiber Optic Signs
Regions Exported to: Central America, South America, Europe, Asia, Middle East
Percentage of Business in Exporting: 30

46953 Neonetics Inc
900 S Main St
Hampstead, MD 21074-2202   410-374-8057
    Fax: 410-374-8056 AlanObligin@yahoo.com
Manufacturer, importer and exporter of neon signs
Owner: Allen Obligen
neonman@neonetics.com
CFO: Brad Sogollss
VP: Brad Sotoloff
Estimated Sales: Less Than $500,000
Number Employees: 1-4
Regions Exported to: Worldwide
Regions Imported from: Asia
Percentage of Business in Importing: 10

46954 Neos
12797 Meadowvale Road NW
Suite B
Elk River, MN 55330-1171   763-441-0705
    Fax: 763-441-0706 888-441-6367
    neosinc@att.net www.neos-server.org
Manufacturer and exporter of packaging machinery for rigid plastic containers; also, burrito and sliced bread dispensers, conveyors with filler depositers, folding tables for assembly and fillers
President: Jack T Mowry
CFO: Greg Erlandson
National Sales Manager: Joe Gibbs
Estimated Sales: $1-2.5 Million
Number Employees: 5-9
Square Footage: 48000
Brands Exported: NEOS

46955 Nepco Egg Of Ga
469 Ronthor Dr SE
Social Circle, GA 30025   770-464-2652
    Fax: 770-464-2998 www.goodegg.com
Processor and exporter of egg products including standard yolk, whole, whites and albumen
Manager: Brad Ginnane
Plant Manager: Terry Anglin
Estimated Sales: $1-3 Million
Number Employees: 1-4
Square Footage: 240000
Parent Co: Rose Acre Farms
Type of Packaging: Bulk
Brands Exported: Nepco
Regions Exported to: Central America, South America, Europe, Asia
Percentage of Business in Exporting: 5

46956 Neptune Fisheries
802 Jefferson Ave
Newport News, VA 23607   757-245-3231
    Fax: 757-893-9227 800-545-7474
Processor and importer of frozen, cooked, peeled and deveined shrimp and scallops; also, lobster tails
President: Robin West
CFO: Richard Costa
National Sales Manager: Aaron Cabral
Sales Director: Sam Weinstein
Plant Manager: Reuben Benkovitz
Number Employees: 5-9
Square Footage: 240000
Type of Packaging: Consumer, Food Service, Private Label, Bulk
Regions Imported from: Central America, South America, Asia, Caribbean

46957 Neptune Foods
4510 S Alameda St
Vernon, CA 90058-2011   323-232-8300
    Fax: 323-232-8833 info@neptunefoods.com
            www.neptunefoods.com
Frozen cod, perch, pollack, fish sticks, clams, lobster, oysters, scallops and shrimp
President: Howard Choi
info@neptunefoods.com
Marketing Manager: Kelly Osterhout
Controller/VP Human Resources: Martin Tsai
COO/Plant Manager: Barbara Letourneau
Estimated Sales: $29.3 Million
Number Employees: 250-499
Square Footage: 150000
Type of Packaging: Consumer, Food Service, Private Label, Bulk
Regions Exported to: Asia, Canada, Mexico
Percentage of Business in Exporting: 8
Regions Imported from: Worldwide
Percentage of Business in Importing: 90

46958 (HQ)Nercon Engineering & Manufacturing
PO Box 2288
Oshkosh, WI 54903-2288   920-233-3268
        Fax: 920-233-3159

Manufacturer and exporter of table top, belt and case conveyors, bi-directional tables, vertical accumulators, label removers, twist rinsers, bottle emptiers, can coolers, etc
President: Jim Nerenhausen
CEO: Jay Nerenhausen
Marketing: Jim Streblow
Estimated Sales: $ 10 - 20 Million
Number Employees: 100-249
Square Footage: 166500
Other Locations:
 Nercon Engineering & Manufact
 Oconto, WINercon Engineering & Manufact
Regions Exported to: Central America, South America, Canada, Mexico
Percentage of Business in Exporting: 10

46959 Nestle USA
150 Oak Grove Dr
Mt Sterling, KY 40353-9087 859-499-1100
 Fax: 859-498-4363 www.nestleusa.com
Prepared frozen foods including stuffed sandwiches and croissants, pizza snacks and waffles
CEO: Paul Merage
CFO: Glenn Lee
VP: Larry Johnson
Research & Development: Phil Mason
V P Finance: Glenn Lee
Manufacturing Development Manager: John Spinner
Purchasing Director: George Turner
Purchasing Manager: Russ Shroyer
Plant Manager: Mike Crawford
Purchasing Manager: George Turner
Number Employees: 500-999
Type of Packaging: Consumer, Food Service

46960 Nestor Imports Inc
8403 7th Ave
Brooklyn, NY 11228-3236 718-836-1133
 Fax: 718-836-3233 info@nestorimports.com
 www.nestorimports.com
Importer of Greek wines
Manager: Chuck Andreae
Executive VP: Kathy Spiliotopoulos
Estimated Sales: $ 3 - 5 Million
Number Employees: 5-9
Type of Packaging: Consumer, Food Service, Private Label
Brands Imported: Kourtakis; Samos Muscat; Chateau Julia; Amethystos; Geromilos Farms Dimitra; Domaine Constantin Lazaridi; Kouros; Apelia; Calliga Mavrodaphne; Asprolithi Patras
Regions Imported from: Europe, Greece
Percentage of Business in Importing: 100

46961 Netzsch Pumps North America
119 Pickering Way
Exton, PA 19341-1311 610-363-8010
 Fax: 610-363-0971 netzsch@netzschusa.com
 www.pumps.netzsch.com
Manufacturer and exporter of pumps, filter presses and grinding mills
CEO: Dr Tilo Stahl
CFO: Mark Vitcov
VP: John Maguire
R&D: Harry Way
Quality Control: Bill Pye
Marketing: Kelly Rismiller
Public Relations: Kelly Rismiller
Production: Bob Hopple
Plant Manager: Bob Maxwell
Purchasing: Bob Hoffman
Estimated Sales: $30 Million
Number Employees: 50-99
Square Footage: 85000
Parent Co: Netzsch

46962 Neuhaus
3914 Sweeten Creek Rd.
Chapel Hill, NC 27514 516-883-7400
 516-767-1550 888-999-8141
 www.neuhauschocolate.com
Importer of Belgian chocolates
Owner: Michael Dubin
VP: Claude Emery
Number Employees: 10-19
Type of Packaging: Consumer
Brands Imported: Opera Collection; Tin Collection
Regions Imported from: Belgium
Percentage of Business in Importing: 100

46963 Nevlen Co. 2, Inc.
96 Audubon Road
Wakefield, MA 01880-1200 978-462-7777
 Fax: 978-462-7774 800-562-7225
 nevlen@nevlen.com
Manufacturer and exporter of van equipment including roof racks, shelving, drawer units and partitions
VP: James Capomaccio
VP: M Nickerson
Executive VP/Treasurer: J Capomaccio
Estimated Sales: $2.5-5 Million
Number Employees: 20-49
Square Footage: 208000
Brands Exported: Nevlen
Regions Exported to: Central America, South America, Middle East
Percentage of Business in Exporting: 5

46964 (HQ)Nevo Corporation
50 Hayney Ct
PO Box 601
Ronkonkoma, NY 11779-7220 631-585-8787
 Fax: 631-585-9285
Manufacturer and exporter of roll-in and rotating rack convection ovens
President: Richard Gehnrich
Treasurer: Leon Pedigo
VP: Wayne Pedigo
Estimated Sales: $ 1 - 3 Million
Number Employees: 20-49
Square Footage: 46000
Regions Exported to: Central America, South America, Europe, Asia, Middle East
Percentage of Business in Exporting: 15

46965 New Age Industrial
16788 US Highway 36
PO Box 520
Norton, KS 67654-5488 785-877-5121
 Fax: 785-877-2616 800-255-0104
 janet@newageindustrial.com
 www.newageindustrial.com
Manufacturer and exporter of aluminum backroom equipment including mobile platters, lug carts, racks, shelving, dollies and tables
President: Dakota Criqui
dcriqui@newagefoodserviceequipment.com
VP: Tom Sharp
Sales Director: Allen Hasken
Estimated Sales: $ 10 - 20 Million
Number Employees: 100-249
Type of Packaging: Food Service
Regions Exported to: Mexico, Canada

46966 New Attitude Beverage Corporation
PO Box 117385
Burlingame, CA 94011-7385 310-414-6501
 Fax: 310-414-6547 newattbev@aol.com
Unique package designs and products beverages for the industry
Estimated Sales: $2 Million
Number Employees: 22
Type of Packaging: Consumer, Food Service
Brands Exported: Ju Age, Music Premium Glacier Water, All Natural Juice Drinks
Regions Exported to: Europe, Asia, Canada
Percentage of Business in Exporting: 60

46967 New Chief Fashion
3223 E 46th St
Vernon, CA 90058-2407 323-582-5322
 Fax: 323-581-0077 800-639-2433
 www.newchef.com
Manufacturer and exporter of aprons, uniforms and chef hats
Owner: Lucien Salama
lucien@newchef.com
Estimated Sales: Less Than $500,000
Number Employees: 1-4
Type of Packaging: Food Service
Regions Exported to: Worldwide

46968 New Chief Fashion
3223 E 46th St
Vernon, CA 90058-2407 323-582-5322
 Fax: 213-489-1745 800-639-2433
 www.newchef.com
Owner: Lucien Salama
lucien@newchef.com
Estimated Sales: Less Than $500,000
Number Employees: 1-4

46969 (HQ)New City Packing Company
2600 Church Rd
Aurora, IL 60502-8732 630-851-8800
 Fax: 630-898-3030
Purveyor of fine meats
President: Marvin Fagel
Vice President: Dave Aardema
National Sales: David McClendon
Estimated Sales: $6.6 Million
Number Employees: 30
Square Footage: 240000
Type of Packaging: Consumer
Regions Exported to: Worldwide

46970 New Earth
565 Century Ct
Klamath Falls, OR 97601-7100 541-882-5406
 Fax: 541-885-5458 www.newearth.com
Processor and exporter of blue green algae products
President: Jerry Anderson
COO: Justin Straus
VP Sales: Roger Martin
VP Marketing/Strategy: Victor Bond
Number Employees: 50-99
Square Footage: 1000000
Regions Exported to: South America, Europe, Asia
Percentage of Business in Exporting: 4

46971 New England Cranberry
82 Sanderson Ave
Lynn, MA 01902-1974 781-596-0888
 Fax: 781-596-0808 800-410-2892
 info@newenglandcranberry.com
 www.newenglandcranberry.com
Processor and exporter of naturally sweetened dried cranberries, premium suger sweetened dried berries, dried wild blueberries, dried cherries, frozen whole cranberries, cranberry jams and jellies, cranberry chutney and pepperjelly, and fine chocolates with sweet cranberries
President: Ted Stux
Sales: Arthur Stock
Estimated Sales: $530000
Number Employees: 10-19
Square Footage: 7400
Type of Packaging: Consumer, Food Service, Bulk
Brands Exported: New England Cranberry
Regions Exported to: Europe

46972 New England Herbal Foods
8 Whittier Place
Boston, MA 02114 617-306-7706
 Fax: 617-245-8999 ed@neherbalfoods.com
 www.neherbalfoods.com
Thai curry and rice, asian fried rice, stir-fry noodles, noodle soup bowls, fat free crackers, and fruit and veggie chips
Contact: Harry Tan
harry.tan@nehfllc.com

46973 New England Machinery Inc
2820 62nd Ave E
Bradenton, FL 34203-5305 941-755-5550
 Fax: 941-751-6281 info@neminc.com
 www.neminc.com
Manufacturer and exporter of hopper/elevators and bottling machinery including unscramblers, orienters, cappers, lidders, puckers, de-puckers, gap transfers and more
Owner: Pat Charles
pat.charles@jacksonhealth.org
Director Sales/Marketing: Marge Bonura
VP Manufacturing: Geza Bankuty
Number Employees: 100-249
Square Footage: 160000
Regions Exported to: Central America, South America, Europe, Asia, Australia
Percentage of Business in Exporting: 35

46974 New England Natural Bakers
74 Fairview St E
Greenfield, MA 01301 413-772-2239
 Fax: 413-772-2936 800-910-2884
 nenb@nenb.com www.nenb.com
Organic granola and trail mix
President & CEO: Pam Clark
pclark@nenb.com
CFO: Didi Foley
Quality Control: Dale Parda
Quality Assurance & IT Coordinator: Dale Prada
Brand Sales & Marketing Manager: Larry Cornick
Vice President Of Sales & Marketing: Pam Clark
Director Of Operations: Scott Johnson

Number Employees: 10-19
Number of Brands: 1
Number of Products: 50
Square Footage: 60000
Type of Packaging: Consumer, Food Service, Private Label, Bulk
Regions Exported to: Asia
Percentage of Business in Exporting: 25
Regions Imported from: South America, Asia, Australia, Mexico, Canada
Percentage of Business in Importing: 25

46975 New England Pallets & Skids
250 West St
Ludlow, MA 01056-1248   413-583-6628
Fax: 413-583-5187   info@nepallets.com
www.nepallets.com
Wooden pallets
President: Cynthia Kawie
Estimated Sales: $ 1-2.5 Million
Number Employees: 10-19
Square Footage: 200000
Type of Packaging: Consumer, Food Service
Regions Imported from: Canada
Percentage of Business in Importing: 35

46976 (HQ)New England Wooden Ware
205 School St # 201
Suite 201
Gardner, MA 01440-2781   978-630-3600
Fax: 978-630-1513   800-252-9214
www.newoodenware.com
Manufacturer, importer and exporter of corrugated paper boxes
President: David Urquhart
VP Sales: R Goguen
Quality Control Manager: Don Broderick
Sales Manager: Mark Salisbury
Contact: Judith Berman
judithb@mediatemanagement.com
VP Production: D Urquhart
Estimated Sales: Less Than $500,000
Number Employees: 1-4
Square Footage: 386000
Other Locations:
  New England Wooden WareCorp.
  Fitchburg, MA New England Wooden WareCorp.
Regions Exported to: Canada
Regions Imported from: Canada
Percentage of Business in Importing: 5

46977 New Era Canning Company
4856 1st St
New Era, MI 49446   231-861-2151
Fax: 231-861-4068
Canned fruits and vegetables including beans, asparagus, apples, and apple sauce
President/CEO: Rick Ray
CFO: Rick McClouth
Sales: Patrick Alger
Contact: Mike Aebig
maebig@gloryfoods.com
Production: Jim Merrill
Purchasing: Ron Fekken
Estimated Sales: $33 Million
Number Employees: 250
Number of Brands: 3
Number of Products: 65
Square Footage: 200000
Type of Packaging: Consumer, Food Service, Private Label
Regions Exported to: Canada
Regions Imported from: South America

46978 New Hope Imports
PO Box 99
Lahaska, PA 18931-0099   215-249-8484
Fax: 215-249-9910   newhope5@juno.com
Importer and wholesaler/distributor of health supplements including proteins, herbs, dried sea kelp, etc
President: Cheryl Alber
Secretary/Treasurer: Otto Alber
Number Employees: 1-4
Square Footage: 8000
Brands Imported: Kiwa
Regions Imported from: Worldwide
Percentage of Business in Importing: 80

46979 New Horizon Foods
33440 Western Ave
Union City, CA 94587-3202   510-489-8600
Fax: 510-489-9797
Dough conditioners, bread bases, natural mixes, beverage, cake, muffin, pudding, meat spices, spice blends, snack and chip seasonings, custard, ice cream, waffle cone and sauce mixes and bases; exporter of dough conditioners and cakeand muffin mixes
Owner: Ken Crawford
kenc@newhorizonfoodsinc.com
Senior Vice President: Yael Melzer
Number Employees: 10-19
Parent Co: Tova Industries
Type of Packaging: Consumer, Food Service, Private Label, Bulk
Brands Exported: New Horizon Foods, Industries Hodovan
Regions Exported to: Central America, South America, Europe, Asia
Percentage of Business in Exporting: 15

46980 New Klix Corporation
551 Railroad Avenue
South San Francisco, CA 94080-3450   650-761-0622
Fax: 650-589-6735   800-522-5544
Manufacturer and exporter of warewash, laundry detergents and cleaning compounds
President: Rodrigo Ortiz
VP: Lautaro Ortiz
Estimated Sales: $2.5-5 Million
Number Employees: 19
Square Footage: 110000
Type of Packaging: Food Service, Private Label
Brands Exported: Klix
Regions Exported to: Asia
Percentage of Business in Exporting: 5

46981 New Organics
600 Lawnwood Road
Kenwood, CA 95452   734-677-5570
Fax: 707-833-0105
Organic ingredient supplier-grains, sweetners, oils, soy powders
President: Jethren Phillips
Manager: Mathew Keegan
Estimated Sales: $17.5 Million
Number Employees: 74
Number of Brands: 3
Number of Products: 100
Square Footage: 25000
Type of Packaging: Bulk
Other Locations:
  American Health & Nutrition
  Eaton Rapids, MI American Health & Nutrition
Brands Exported: Organic Harvest
Regions Exported to: South America, Europe, Asia, Middle East
Percentage of Business in Exporting: 30
Regions Imported from: Central America, South America, Europe, Asia, Middle East
Percentage of Business in Importing: 10

46982 New Orleans Food Co-op
2372 St. Claude Avenue
Suite 110
New Orleans, LA 70117   504-264-5579
Fax: 504-734-7684   800-628-4900
cook@bumblebee.com   www.nolafood.coop
Canned shrimp, crab meat, oysters, clams, sardines, tuna and mackerel; also, bottled clam juice; exporter of canned shrimp; importer of canned seafood
VP Sales/Marketing: David Cook
Estimated Sales: $ 5 - 10 Million
Number Employees: 5-9
Type of Packaging: Consumer, Food Service, Private Label
Brands Imported: Orleans; Harris; Cutcher
Regions Imported from: South America, Asia

46983 New Season Foods Inc
2329 Yew St # A1
P.O. Box 157
Forest Grove, OR 97116-4401   503-357-7124
Fax: 503-357-0419   www.newseasonfoods.com
Drum-dried vegetable powders and other custom ingredients
CEO: Bruce McVean
Estimated Sales: $5-10 Million
Number Employees: 20-49
Square Footage: 600000
Type of Packaging: Bulk
Regions Exported to: Europe, Asia, Canada, Latin America

46984 New Way Packaging Machinery
PO Box 467
Hanover, PA 17331   717-637-2133
Fax: 717-637-2966   800-522-3537
sales@labeler.com
Manufacturer and exporter of labeling machinery
President: Edward Abendschein
Contact: Merle Mcmaster
merle@labeler.com
Estimated Sales: $10-20 Million
Number Employees: 5-9

46985 New York Apple Assn Inc
7645 Main Street Fishers
Victor, NY 14564-8909   585-924-2171
Fax: 585-924-1629   www.nyapplecountry.com
President: Jim Allen
jimallen@nyapplecountry.com
Number Employees: 5-9

46986 New York Apple Sales Inc
17 Languish Pl
Glenmont, NY 12077-4819   518-477-7200
Fax: 518-477-6770   888-477-6770
kaari@newyorkapplesales.com
www.newyorkapplesales.com
Apples and pears.
President: Kaari Stannard
kaari@newyorkapplesales.com
VP, Sales: John Cushing
Sales: Michael Harwood
Food Safety Coordinator: Colleen O'Brien
Production & Logistics Manager: Michael Shannon
Estimated Sales: $29 Million
Number Employees: 20-49
Type of Packaging: Consumer, Food Service, Bulk
Regions Exported to: Europe, Asia, Middle East

46987 New York Bakeries Inc
261 W 22nd St
Hialeah, FL 33010-1521   305-883-0790
Fax: 305-883-0790
Manufacturer and exporter of bread, rolls, and cakes.
President: Sarah Zimmerman
Estimated Sales: $35 Million
Number Employees: 50-99
Parent Co: New York Bakeries
Type of Packaging: Consumer, Food Service, Private Label

46988 New York Department of Agriculture & Markets
10b Airline Dr
Albany, NY 12235-0001   518-457-8876
Fax: 518-457-3087   800-554-5401
Government agacny promoting and regulating New York State food and agriculture industry.
Commissioner: Darrel Ambertine
Number Employees: 100-249

46989 (HQ)New York Export Co
1158 North Ave # 2nd
Beacon, NY 12508-2535   845-831-7770
Fax: 914-592-1113   nyexport@aol.com
Exporter of fresh garlic, apples, grapes, pears, lettuce and potatoes; importer of fresh apricots, nectarines, grapes, pears, apples, plums, kiwi, etc
Owner: Zach Shuman
zach@newyorkexport.com
VP: Tom Dub
Estimated Sales: $20-50 Million
Number Employees: 5-9
Square Footage: 2000
Brands Exported: SMG; Sunnyview; Ranier; Nexco
Regions Exported to: Central America, South America, Europe
Percentage of Business in Exporting: 70
Brands Imported: Nexco
Regions Imported from: South America, Asia
Percentage of Business in Importing: 30

46990 New York Izabel Lam
204 Van Dyke St
Brooklyn, NY 11231-1038   718-797-3983
Fax: 718-797-0030   www.izabellam.com
Estimated Sales: $ 1 - 3 Million
Number Employees: 1-4

Importers & Exporters / A-Z

46991 New York Pretzel
200 Moore St
Brooklyn, NY 11206   718-366-9800
    Fax: 718-821-4544 info@nypretzel.com
    www.nypretzel.com
Soft pretzels
President: Themis Makkos
VP: Richard Berger
Contact: Ronald Orfinger
jack@nypretzel.com
Estimated Sales: $9.7 Million
Number Employees: 75

46992 New Zealand Lamb Co
19840 S Rancho Way # 101
#101
Compton, CA 90220-6321   310-885-4855
    Fax: 310-885-4966
Importer and wholesaler/distributor of frozen and refrigerated lamb, beef, venison, goat and mutton.
President: Shane O'Hara
Vice President of Operations: Bill Mcmichael
Estimated Sales: $5 Million
Number Employees: 20-49
Number of Brands: 2
Parent Co: The Lamb Co-Operative Inc
Type of Packaging: Consumer, Food Service
Regions Exported to: Canada
Regions Imported from: New Zealand, Australia

46993 NewStar Fresh Foods LLC
850 Work St.
Suite 101
Salinas, CA 93901   831-758-7800
    Fax: 831-758-7869 info@newstarfresh.com
    www.newstarfresh.com
Fresh asparagus, iceless green onions, cilantro, spinach, etc.
President/CEO: Anthony Vasquez
Year Founded: 1996
Estimated Sales: $26.1 Million
Number Employees: 250-499
Square Footage: 20000
Type of Packaging: Consumer, Food Service, Private Label, Bulk
Brands Exported: Lee; Tall & Tender; Green N' Fresh; Newstar
Regions Exported to: Europe, Asia, Canada
Brands Imported: Lee; Tall & Tender; Green N' Fresh; Newstar
Regions Imported from: South America, Mexico
Percentage of Business in Importing: 70

46994 Newark Wire Cloth Co
160 Fornelius Ave
Clifton, NJ 07013-1844   973-778-4478
    Fax: 973-778-4481   800-221-0392
    info@newarkwire.com www.newarkwire.com
Manufacturer, exporter and importer of wire cloth, filters, strainers, testing sieves, etc. Manufacturers of the Sani Cloan Strainer product line. Consisting of: inline, side inlet, and hi-capacity basket strainers. Custom fabricationsare a specialty.
President/Owner: Richard Campbell
rcampbell@newarkwire.com
Estimated Sales: $5 - 10 Million
Number Employees: 20-49
Square Footage: 120000
Type of Packaging: Food Service
Regions Exported to: Worldwide
Regions Imported from: Worldwide

46995 Newcastle Co Inc
3812 Wilmington Rd
New Castle, PA 16105-6134   724-658-4516
    Fax: 724-658-5100 ncco@newcastleco.com
    www.newcastleco.com
Manufacturer and integrator of load transfer systems, palletizers, pallet dispensers, sheet dispensers, and conveyors.
Owner: Dennis Alduk
ncco@losch.net
Number Employees: 5-9
Regions Exported to: Central America, South America, Europe
Percentage of Business in Exporting: 5

46996 Newco Enterprises Inc
3650 New Town Blvd
St Charles, MO 63301-4357   636-946-1330
    Fax: 314-925-0029   800-325-7867
    www.newcocoffee.com
Coffee and tea brewing equipment and water treatment systems; exporter of commercial coffee brewers
Owner: Karen Enke
CFO: Mcenke Karen
VP Marketing: Anthony Westcott
VP, Sales: Jason College
s.murthy@trafinfo.com
Estimated Sales: $ 10 - 20 Million
Number Employees: 100-249
Square Footage: 160000
Brands Exported: Vaculator; Newco
Regions Exported to: Worldwide
Percentage of Business in Exporting: 10

46997 Newell Brands
6655 Peachtree Dunwoody Rd
Atlanta, GA 30328
    consumer.inquiries@newellco.com
    www.newellbrands.com
Manufacturer and exporter of food service, sanitary maintenance and material handling products.
President & CEO: Ravi Saligram
Unit CEO, Appliances & Cookware: David Hammer
Unit CEO, Food: Kris Malkoski
CFO & President, Business Operations: Christopher Peterson
Chief Legal & Administrative Officer: Bradford Turner
Chief Human Resources Officer: Steve Parsons
Chief Customer Officer: Mike Hayes
Chief Procurement Officer: Steve Nikolopoulos
Year Founded: 1903
Estimated Sales: $14.7 Billion
Number Employees: 49,000
Type of Packaging: Consumer, Food Service
Regions Exported to: Central America, South America, Europe, Asia, Middle East, Worldwide

46998 Newell Lobsters
72 Water St
PO Box 99
Yarmouth, NS B5A 4B1
Canada   902-742-6272
    Fax: 902-742-1542
Processor and exporter of fresh herring roe and lobster
President: Robert Newell
Estimated Sales: $7.4 Million
Number Employees: 15
Type of Packaging: Consumer, Food Service, Private Label
Regions Exported to: USA

46999 Newfound Resources
90 O'Leary Ave
Suite 203
St Josephs, NL A1B 2C7
Canada   709-579-7676
    Fax: 709-579-7668 shrimp@nfld.com
    www.newfoundresources.com
Processor and exporter of frozen shrimp
President: Brian McNamara
Controller: Bill Coady
Operations Manager: Jeff Simms
Estimated Sales: $6.6 Million
Number Employees: 60
Type of Packaging: Bulk
Regions Exported to: Worldwide

47000 Newlands Systems
602-30731 Simpson Road
Abbotsford, BC V2T 6Y7
Canada   604-855-4890
    Fax: 604-855-8826 mail@nsibrew.com
Manufacturer and exporter of brewing equipment and machinery
President: Brad McQuhae
Director Marketing: Loch McJannett
Number Employees: 10
Square Footage: 80000
Type of Packaging: Food Service
Regions Exported to: Worldwide
Percentage of Business in Exporting: 50

47001 (HQ)Newly Weds Foods Inc
2501 N Keeler Ave
Chicago, IL 60639-2131   773-489-6224
    Fax: 773-489-2799   800-621-7521
    nwfnorthamerica@newlywedsfoods.com
    www.newlywedsfoods.com
Processor and exporter of breadings, batters, seasoning blends, marinades, glazes and capsicum products
President: Charles T. Angell
CFO: Brian Johnson
SVP Sales & Marketing: Bruce Leshinski
R&D: Jim Klein
Sales Director: Jim Chin
Contact: Mary Adderhold
madderhold@newlywedsfoods.com
VP Manufacturing: Mike Hopp
Plant Manager: Leo Vogler
Director of Purchasing: Tom Lisack
Estimated Sales: $959 Million
Number Employees: 1-4
Square Footage: 1500000
Other Locations:
    Newly Weds Foods
    Bethlehem, PA
    Newly Weds Foods
    Chicago, IL
    Newly Weds Foods
    Cleveland, TN
    Newly Weds Foods
    Watertown, MA
    Newly Weds Foods
    Yorkville, IL
    Newly Weds Foods
    Horn Lake, MS
    Newly Weds FoodsChicago
Regions Exported to: Central America, South America, Asia, Middle East, Canada, Latin America

47002 Newman Sanitary Gasket Co
964 W Main St
P.O.Box 222
Lebanon, OH 45036-9173   513-932-7379
    Fax: 513-932-4493 customer@newmangasket.com
    www.newmangasket.com
Manufacturer and exporter of foodgrade sanitary process piping gaskets, seals and F.D.A. O-rings. Also custom molded rubber parts
President: David W Newman
davidn@newmangasket.com
CEO: Tom Moore
VP: Betsy Newman
Marketing Director: Larry Hensel
Customer Service Manager: Cindy Swagler
Plant Manager: Matt Agricola
Estimated Sales: $ 1-5,000,000
Number Employees: 50-99
Square Footage: 65000
Type of Packaging: Private Label, Bulk
Regions Exported to: Central America, Europe, Asia, Middle East, Worldwide
Percentage of Business in Exporting: 25

47003 (HQ)Newman's Own
246 Post Rd E # 308
Suite 308
Westport, CT 06880-3615   203-222-0136
    Fax: 203-227-5630 www.newmansown.com
Exporter of pizzas, complete skillet meals, salad dressings, sauces, salsas, marinades, beverages, cereals, popcorn, and wine
President & COO: Tom Indoe
CEO: Clea Newman
Business Development Manager: Steve Ripson
VP Marketing: Michael Havard
Director of Sales: Mark Tilley
Contact: M Anita
anita@newmansown.com
VP Operations: Bill Lee
Estimated Sales: $4.9 Million
Number Employees: 28
Square Footage: 16800
Type of Packaging: Consumer, Food Service
Other Locations:
    Newman's Own
    Aptos, CANewman's Own
Brands Exported: Newman's Own
Regions Exported to: Central America, South America, Europe, Asia, Middle East, Canada, Mexico
Percentage of Business in Exporting: 3

47004 Newport Electronics Inc
2229 S Yale St
Santa Ana, CA 92704-4401   714-540-4914
    Fax: 714-968-7311   800-639-7678
    info@newportus.com www.microinfinity.com
NEWPORT® is known for designing and manufacturing the world's most accurate industrial instrumentation. Prestotek brand of products includes: pH, ORP, conductivity, Resistivity, salt, and much more. Offered as panel mount ofhandheld instruments.

Importers & Exporters / A-Z

President: Milton Hollander
Manager: Dick Hollander
Estimated Sales: $ 1 - 3 Million
Number Employees: 50-99
Parent Co: Newport Electronics
Type of Packaging: Private Label

47005 Newstamp Lighting Factory
227 Bay Rd
PO Box 189
North Easton, MA 02356-2673   508-238-7073
   Fax: 508-230-8312 info@newstamplighting.com
            www.newstamplighting.com
Electric lighting fixtures, metal stamping equipment, plumbing products and security windows; exporter of electric lighting fixtures
President: Robert Zeitsiff
bob@newstamplighting.com
VP: Sandra Zeitstiff
Clerk: Charlotte Zeitsiff
Estimated Sales: $2.5-5 Million
Number Employees: 20-49
Square Footage: 68000
Regions Exported to: Worldwide
Percentage of Business in Exporting: 1

47006 Newton OA & Son Co
16356 Sussex Hwy
Bridgeville, DE 19933-3056   302-337-3782
   Fax: 302-337-3780   800-726-5745
      solutions@oanewton.com www.oanewton.com
Manufacturer and exporter of weighing equipment and pneumatic and mechanical material handling systems including dust collection
President: Rob Rider
Number Employees: 20-49
Regions Exported to: Central America, Canada

47007 Newtown Foods
601 Corporate Dr W
Langhorne, PA 19047-8013   215-579-2120
   Fax: 215-579-2129 info@newtownfoods.com
            www.newtownfoods.com
Importer of Dutch cocoa powders, Brazilian banana puree, fruit extracts and distillates to the dairy and baking industries
Owner: John Mc Donald
Sales Manager: Kathleen Lentini
Estimated Sales: $2.5-5 Million
Number Employees: 1-4
Type of Packaging: Bulk
Brands Imported: Bananex
Regions Imported from: South America, Europe
Percentage of Business in Importing: 100

47008 Newtree America
508 San Anselmo Avenue
Suite 12
San Anselmo, CA 94960   415-785-1185
   Fax: 415-785-1186 info@newtree.com
            www.newtree.com
Belgian chocolate
Contact: Benoit Cebruyn
benoit@newtree.com

47009 Nexel Industries Inc
11 Harbor Park Dr
Port Washington, NY 11050-4656   516-484-5225
   Fax: 516-625-0084   800-245-6682
      nexelinfo@nexelwire.com www.nexelwire.com
Manufacturer, importer and exporter of material handling and storage systems including solid steel and wire shelving, trucks and carts
Vice President: Dibuseng Moloi
dmoloi@businessmonitor.com
VP: John Svitek
Inside Sales Manager: Howard Ziporkin
National Sales Manager: Jerry Mark
Number Employees: 100-249
Square Footage: 2400000
Type of Packaging: Food Service, Private Label
Brands Exported: Nexelon; Poly-Z-Brite; Loadmaster; Space-Trac, Nexelite
Regions Exported to: South America, Asia, Middle East, Australia, Canada
Percentage of Business in Exporting: 10
Regions Imported from: Asia
Percentage of Business in Importing: 90

47010 Nexira
15 Somerset St
Somerville, NJ 08876-2828   908-707-9400
   Fax: 908-707-9405   800-872-1850
      info-usa@nexira.com www.nexira.com

Nexira is a global leader in natural ingredients and botanical extracts for food nutrition and dietary supplements. Nexira built its reputation as the world leader in acacia gum and now manufactures a wide range of functional andnutritional ingredients, antioxidants, and active botanicals for weight management, sports nutrition, digestive and cardiovascular health. It manufactures the following ingredients for the food and health industry: acacia gun, botanical extracts andpowders.
President: Stephane Dondain
heese@cnius.com
VP: Teresa Yazbek
Marketing/Logistics Specialist: Nina Segura
Sales: Bob Bremer
Estimated Sales: $14 Million
Number Employees: 10-19
Number of Brands: 25
Number of Products: 100
Type of Packaging: Bulk
Regions Imported from: South America, Europe, Asia, Africa, Australia, Canada & Mexico

47011 Niagara Blower Company
673 Ontario St
Buffalo, NY 14207   716-875-2000
   Fax: 716-875-1077   800-426-5169
      sales@niagarablower.com
      www.niagarablower.com
Manufacturer and exporter of custom refrigeration systems including bacteria-free, frost-free moisture management, evaporators, condensers and dehumidification
President: Peter Demakos
Marketing Assistant: Jen Dorman
Sales Manager: Phil Rowland
Contact: David Anderson
danderson@niagarablower.com
COO: Peter Demakos
Estimated Sales: $ 10 - 20 Million
Number Employees: 50-99
Square Footage: 200000
Brands Exported: Aero; No Frost; Hygrol
Regions Exported to: Central America, Europe, Asia, Middle East, Canada
Percentage of Business in Exporting: 15

47012 Niagara Foods
10 Kelly Ave
Middleport, NY 14105-1210   716-735-7722
   Fax: 716-735-9076 www.agvest.com
Processor, importer and exporter of frozen vegetable products and fruit and vegetable powders and flakes; also, frozen and dehydrated fruits including apples, cherries, strawberries, cranberries and wild and cultivated blueberries
President: Barry Schneider
Contact: Bradley Devey
bradley@valley.net
General Manager: Bob Neuman
Estimated Sales: $14.9 Million
Number Employees: 50
Square Footage: 140000
Parent Co: Agvest
Type of Packaging: Consumer, Food Service, Private Label, Bulk
Brands Exported: Agvest; Quality Brand
Regions Exported to: Central America, South America, Europe, Asia
Percentage of Business in Exporting: 15
Regions Imported from: South America, Europe
Percentage of Business in Importing: 20

47013 (HQ)Nice-Pak Products Inc
2 Nice-Pak Park
Orangeburg, NY 10962-1376   845-365-1700
            800-444-6725
               www.nicepak.com
Manufacturer and exporter of cleaning and sanitizing supplies including moist towelettes, disposable wash cloths, surface disinfectants and hand sanitizers.
Chief Executive Officer: Robert Julius
Chief Operating Officer: Ron Gordon
Analytic Chemist: Elmira Abdelnasser
eabdelnasser@nicepak.com
Year Founded: 1955
Estimated Sales: $165.5 Million
Number Employees: 2,500
Square Footage: 28000
Type of Packaging: Consumer, Food Service, Private Label
Brands Exported: Nice-N-Clean, Wet-Nap; Flat-Pak Baby 100's; Flat Pax Baby 126; Baby Wipe Tub 40's & 80's; Rub A Dubs; Sani-Cloth; Sani-Dex
Regions Exported to: Central America, South America, Europe, Asia, Middle East
Percentage of Business in Exporting: 10

47014 Niche Gourmet
5253 Patterson Ave SE
Grand Rapids, MI 49512   616-698-0666
   Fax: 616-698-8870   800-875-5557
      sales@nichegourmet.com www.nichegourmet.com
Importer of European gourmet brands
Owner: Peter Nelson
Estimated Sales: $ 10 - 20 Million
Number Employees: 10-19

47015 Nichem Co
750 Frelinghuysen Ave
Newark, NJ 07114-2221   973-399-9810
   Fax: 973-399-8818 sales@nichem.com
            www.nichem.com
Processor and importer of ingredients including citric acid, vanillin and sodium citrate; exporter of citric acid
President: Peg Blue
sales@nichem.com
Estimated Sales: $700,000
Number Employees: 5-9
Square Footage: 80000
Type of Packaging: Consumer, Food Service
Regions Exported to: South America, Asia
Percentage of Business in Exporting: 10
Regions Imported from: Asia

47016 Nichimen America
1345 Avenue of the Americas
New York, NY 10105-0302   212-262-5200
   Fax: 212-698-5200
Importer of flour
Number Employees: 100-249
Parent Co: Nichimen
Type of Packaging: Bulk
Brands Imported: Konjac; Glycymin
Regions Imported from: Asia
Percentage of Business in Importing: 100

47017 Nichols Specialty Products
10 Parker Street
Southborough, MA 01772-1949   508-481-4367
   Fax: 508-481-7806
Manufacturer and exporter of bottle and can capping machinery
President: Larry Quinlan
CEO: Janet Wellman
CFO: Shannon Quinlan
Number Employees: 10
Brands Exported: Kinex
Regions Exported to: Worldwide
Percentage of Business in Exporting: 10

47018 Nick Sciabica & Sons
2150 Yosemite Blvd
Modesto, CA 95354-3931   209-577-5067
   Fax: 209-524-5367   800-551-9612
            www.baginfusti.com
Extra-virgin olive oil; importer of olive oil, pasta and tomato products; wholesaler/distributor of wine vinegar, olive oil, canned tomatoes, olives and pasta
Partner: Jonathan Sciabica
Controller: Susan Ochoa
VP: Gemma Sciabica
Marketing Manager: Dean Cohan
Production Manager: Daniel Sciabica
Estimated Sales: $2.5 Million
Number Employees: 20-49
Number of Brands: 6
Number of Products: 150
Square Footage: 274912
Type of Packaging: Consumer, Food Service, Private Label, Bulk
Brands Imported: Mission Trail
Regions Imported from: Europe
Percentage of Business in Importing: 40

47019 Nicky USA Inc
223 SE 3rd Ave
Portland, OR 97214-1006   503-234-4263
   Fax: 503-234-8268   800-469-4162
      info@nickyusa.com www.nickyusa.com
Distributor of natural game birds and meats including pheasant, poussin, quail, venison, buffalo, rabbit, ostrich, alligator, ducks and wild boar; also, sausage, veal, free-range lamb

Owner, President: Geoff Latham
glatham@nickyusa.com
VP: Melody Latham
Sales Office Manager: Ursula McVittie
Production Manager: Jace Hentges
Estimated Sales: $4 Million
Number Employees: 20-49
Square Footage: 20000
Type of Packaging: Consumer, Food Service, Private Label, Bulk
Brands Imported: Bain of Taruas
Regions Imported from: Europe

47020 Nicol Scales & Measurement LP
7239 Envoy Ct
Dallas, TX 75247-5103   214-428-8181
       Fax: 214-428-8127   800-225-8181
       sales@nicolscales.com www.nicolscales.com
Manufacturer and exporter of industrial scales and force measuring equipment; also, leasing available
President, CEO: Ted Tabolka
ted@nicolscales.com
Director of Finance: Oliver Jackson
Vice President, Service: Steve Ford
Director of Sales and Marketing: Jim Budke
Estimated Sales: $ 5 - 10 Million
Number Employees: 20-49

47021 Nicola International
4561 Colorado Blvd.
Los Angeles, CA 90039-0758   818-545-1515
       Fax: 818-247-8585
Finest olives, olive oils and grape leaves for deli departments, bakeries and the pizza industry, salad manufacturers, custom marination and creative gourmet dishes
President: Nicola Khachatoorian
VP: Alice Toomanian
Contact: Adik Khachatoorian
adikk@nicolainternational.com
Purchasing Manager: Claudine Reyes
Estimated Sales: $1-10 Million
Number Employees: 25
Type of Packaging: Food Service, Private Label

47022 Nicole's Divine Crackers
1505 N Kingsbury Street
Chicago, IL 60642-2533   312-640-8883
       Fax: 312-640-0988 nicolescrackers@msn.com
Crackers
President: Nicole Bergere
Estimated Sales: Below $ 5 Million
Number Employees: 5-9

47023 Nieco Corporation
7950 Cameron Drive
Windsor, CA 95492   707-284-7100
       Fax: 707-284-7430   800-643-2656
       sales@nieco.com
Manufacturer and exporter of automatic bun grilling and meat broiling machines for hamburgers, steaks, chicken and fish
President: Ed Baker
Executive VP: John Brown
Contact: Steve Alcocer
salcocer@nieco.com
Estimated Sales: $ 10-20 Million
Number Employees: 50-99
Square Footage: 150000
Type of Packaging: Food Service
Brands Exported: Nieco Broilers
Regions Exported to: Central America, South America, Europe, Asia, Middle East, Africa
Percentage of Business in Exporting: 23

47024 Nielsen Citrus ProductsInc
15621 Computer Ln
Huntington Beach, CA 92649-1607   714-892-5586
       Fax: 714-893-2161 info@nielsencitrus.com
                  www.nielsencitrus.com
Processor and exporter of frozen, concentrated lemon and lime juice, lemon puree, lime puree, orange puree
President: Chris Nielsen
greg.hogue@verizon.net
Vice President: Earl Nielsen
Number Employees: 10-19
Square Footage: 40000
Type of Packaging: Consumer, Food Service, Private Label, Bulk
Brands Exported: Nielsen's
Regions Exported to: Europe, Asia
Percentage of Business in Exporting: 5

47025 Nielsen-Massey Vanillas Inc
1550 Shields Dr
Waukegan, IL 60085-8307   847-578-1550
       Fax: 847-578-1570   800-525-7873
       info@nielsenmassey.com nielsenmassey.com
Manufacturer of vanilla extracts and pure flavors
CEO: Kirk Trofholz
VP, Global Sales: Brent Allen
Director of Sales: Dan Fox
Year Founded: 1907
Estimated Sales: $20-50 Million
Number Employees: 20-49
Number of Brands: 1
Square Footage: 100500
Type of Packaging: Consumer, Food Service, Bulk
Other Locations:
   Nielsen-Massey Vanillas Inter. B.V.
   Leeuwarden, NetherlandsNielsen-Massey Vanillas Inter. B.V.
Brands Exported: Nielsen-Massey Vanillas
Regions Exported to: Central America, South America, Europe, Asia, Middle East, North America, Africa, Australia, New Zealand

47026 Nigrelli Systems Purchasing
16024 County Road X
Kiel, WI 53042-9741   920-693-3165
       Fax: 920-693-3634   800-693-3144
                  www.aquamasterfountains.com
Manufacturer and exporter of continuous motion case and tray packing systems, tray formers, plastic tray denesting systems, bulk container and bottled water packers, wrap around packers and shrinkwrapping equipment
President: Nicholas Nigrelli
VP Sales: David O'Keefe
Estimated Sales: Less Than $500,000
Number Employees: 1-4
Regions Exported to: Central America, South America, Europe, Canada, Mexico, South Africa
Percentage of Business in Exporting: 2

47027 Nikken Foods
4984 Manchester Ave
St Louis, MO 63110-2010   314-881-5818
       Fax: 502-292-3283 nikken@lilar.com
                  www.nikkenfoods.com
Processor, importer and exporter of soy sauce, fermented soy sauce powders, extracted seafood powders and concentrates and dehydrated mushrooms and oriental vegetables
Manager: Beth James
bethj@nikkenfoods.com
General Manager: Herb Bench
Number Employees: 10-19
Parent Co: Nikkens Foods Company
Type of Packaging: Bulk
Regions Exported to: Central America, South America, Latin America, Mexico, Canada, Caribbean
Regions Imported from: Asia

47028 Nikki's Cookies
2018 South 1st St
Milwaukee, WI 53207   414-481-4899
       Fax: 414-481-5222   800-776-7107
       customerservice@nikkiscookies.com
                  www.nikkiscookies.com
Processor and exporter of shortbreads and cookies
President: Nikki Taylor
Contact: Bill Danner
billdanner@nikkiscookies.com
Estimated Sales: Less than $500,000
Number Employees: 5-9
Square Footage: 120000
Type of Packaging: Consumer, Food Service
Regions Exported to: South America, Europe, Asia, Canada
Percentage of Business in Exporting: 2

47029 Nikko Ceramics
815 Fairview Ave # 9
Building 9
Fairview, NJ 07022-1571   201-840-5200
       Fax: 201-840-5201 custserv@nikkoceramics.com
                  www.nikkoceramics.com
Vice President: Kenji Anzai
kenji@nikkoceramics.com
Vice President: Kenji Anzai
kenji@nikkoceramics.com
Number Employees: 10-19

47030 Nimbus Water Systems
41840 McAlby Ct # A
Murrieta, CA 92562-7080   951-894-2800
       Fax: 760-591-0106   800-451-9343
                  www.nimbuswater.com
Manufacturer and exporter of water treatment equipment; also, consultant providing water and water recycle systems design services
Founder: Donald Bray
CEO: Mike Faulkner
VP Marketing/Sales: Tony Pagliano
Contact: Sid Brandhuber
sid@nimbuswater.com
Purchasing Manager: Bree Ann Plange
Estimated Sales: $ 2.5-5 Million
Number Employees: 1-4
Number of Products: 50
Square Footage: 140000
Brands Exported: Nimbus
Regions Exported to: Worldwide
Percentage of Business in Exporting: 45

47031 Niro
1600 Okeefe Rd
Hudson, WI 54016   715-386-9371
       Fax: 715-386-9376 www.niroinc.com
Custom fabrication, filtration equipment, aseptic processing equipment, heat recovery systems, deaerators, dryers, fluid bed, spray, pilot plants, process control, high pressure pumps and homogenizers
President: Steve Kaplan
VP: Eric Bryars
VP: Christian Svensgaard
Marketing Coordinator: Heather Szymanski
Contact: Tim Huntley
thuntley@nilpeter.net
Manager Food/Dairy Evaporators: Bo Bjarekull
Estimated Sales: $ 20 - 50 Million
Number Employees: 100-249
Parent Co: GEA Group
Other Locations:
   Niro
   Columbia, MDNiro
Regions Exported to: Central America, South America, Europe, Asia, Canada, Mexico, Australia
Percentage of Business in Exporting: 5

47032 Niroflex, USA
PO Box 90
Deerfield, IL 60015   847-400-2638
       Fax: 847-919-3809 metalmesh@niroflex.com
                  www.niroflex.com
Maker of stainless steel mesh gloves and apparel that is designed to protect workers in the meat and poultry food processing industry.
Vice President: Loren Rivkin
Regions Exported to: Central America, South America, Europe, Asia, Worldwide

47033 Nirwana Foods
778 Newark Ave
Jersey City, NJ 07306   201-659-2200
       Fax: 201-659-1260 www.nirwanafoods.com
Spices, almonds, cashews and tea.
President: Jimmy Singh

47034 Nisbet Oyster Company
7081 Niawaukum St Hwy 101
P.O. Box 338
Bay Center, WA 98527-0338   360-875-6629
       Fax: 360-875-6684   888-875-6629
       sales@goosepoint.com www.goosepoint.com
Processor and exporter of Pacific and farm oysters; Pacific oyster farm operations; retail and food service products fresh and frozen
President, Owner: David Nisbet
Owner: Maureene Nisbet
Sales Manager: Josh Valdiz
Plant Manager: Kathleen Nisbet
Purchasing: Geoff Clarine
Estimated Sales: $10 Million
Number Employees: 75
Number of Brands: 1
Number of Products: 3
Square Footage: 12800
Brands Exported: Goose Point

47035 Nissho Iwai American Corporation
1211 SW 5th Ave
Portland, OR 97204   503-241-7203
       Fax: 503-241-0302

Importers & Exporters / A-Z

Importer of frozen and canned peapods, water chestnuts, bamboo shoots, baby corn, ginger, green coffee beans, etc.; exporter of dehydrated potato flakes and granules, frozen corn, peas, mixed vegetables, soup, pasta, frozen bakedpotatoes and French fries
Estimated Sales: $20-50 Million
Number Employees: 1-4
Parent Co: Nissho Iwai Corporation
Regions Exported to: Worldwide
Regions Imported from: Worldwide

47036 Nitech
911 E 23rd St
Columbus, NE 68601-3736 402-563-3188
Fax: 402-563-2792 800-237-6496
info@nitechIPM.com www.nitechipm.com
Turntables and stretch wrapping equipment
Owner: Roger Bettenhousen
rogerb@nitechindustries.com
Sales Director: Chris Bettenhausen
Estimated Sales: $2.5-5,000,000
Number Employees: 20-49
Type of Packaging: Bulk
Regions Exported to: Central America, South America, Europe, Asia

47037 Nitsch Tool Co Inc
1715 Grant Blvd
Syracuse, NY 13208-3017 315-472-4044
Fax: 315-472-4051
Manufacturer and exporter of machine knives for baking
Owner: Leonard Nitsch
Estimated Sales: Less than $500,000
Number Employees: 1-4
Regions Exported to: Canada
Percentage of Business in Exporting: 5

47038 Niutang Chemical, Inc.
5181 Edison Ave
Chino, CA 91710 909-631-2895
Fax: 909-631-2309 sales@niutang.us
www.niutang.com
High-quality food additives and pharmaceutical intermediates including sucralose, aspartame and folic acid
President: Licheng Wang
Owner: Feng Lu
Director Technical & Quality Support: Kerry Kenny
Quality Manager: Sharon Bosch
Contact: Mandy Chen
mandy@niutang.us
Manager/Director: Jie Lin
Regions Exported to: South America, Europe, Asia, Africa

47039 (HQ)Noble Harvest
P.O.Box 612
Edgemont, PA 19028-0612 610-353-5400
Fax: 610-284-5202 lorimer@voicenet.com
Wholesaler/distributor, importer and exporter of specialty foods, wine, olive oil and beer
Owner: David N Goane
Public Relations: Nicola Gentili
Manager European Operations: Luciano Lambrughi
Estimated Sales: $ 1 - 3 Million
Number Employees: 1-4
Square Footage: 20000
Other Locations:
Noble Harvest Ltd.
MilanoNoble Harvest Ltd.
Brands Exported: Blue Ridge; Hempen Ale; Domain Saren
Regions Exported to: Europe
Percentage of Business in Exporting: 10
Brands Imported: Villa Foscari; La Cascina; Roagna; La Filera; Trevi; Sommaia; Marina Colonna; Dosio; Guicciardini; Crea; Miotto
Regions Imported from: Europe
Percentage of Business in Importing: 90

47040 Noel Corp
1001 S 3rd St
Yakima, WA 98901-3403 509-248-1313
Fax: 509-248-2843 www.noelcorp.com
Bottled and canned carbonated and noncarbonated beverages; also, bag-in-box juices including orange and apple
President: Rodger Noel
Controller: Martha Barman
VP: Justin Noel
Marketing Executive: Mike Sutton
Manager Sales: William Dalton
IT: Martha Berman
martha@noelcorp.com
Estimated Sales: $42.8 Million
Number Employees: 10-19
Square Footage: 200000
Type of Packaging: Consumer, Food Service, Private Label
Percentage of Business in Importing: 10

47041 Noh Foods of Hawaii
1402 W 178th St
Gardena, CA 90248-3202 808-944-0655
customerservice@nohfoods.com
www.nohfoods.com
International seasonings, sauces and drink mixes
President: Raymond Noh
Number Employees: 4
Square Footage: 35200
Parent Co: E&M Corporation
Type of Packaging: Consumer, Food Service, Bulk
Other Locations:
NOH Foods of Hawaii
Honolulu, HINOH Foods of Hawaii
Brands Exported: Noh Foods
Regions Exported to: Central America, Europe, Asia
Percentage of Business in Exporting: 20

47042 Nolon Industries
PO Box T
Mantua, OH 44255 330-274-2283
Fax: 330-274-2283
Manufacturer and exporter of fiberglass reinforced plastic boxes
President: Nick Nicolanti
Type of Packaging: Bulk
Regions Exported to: Worldwide
Percentage of Business in Exporting: 1

47043 Nonni's Foods LLC
3920 E Pine St
Tulsa, OK 74115 918-621-1200
Fax: 918-560-4159 877-295-9604
info@nonnis.com nonnis.com
Biscotti, crackers and cookies
Chief Executive Officer: Brian Hansberry
brianhansberry@nonnis.com
Estimated Sales: $150 Million
Number Employees: 100-249
Number of Brands: 2
Number of Products: 16
Type of Packaging: Private Label

47044 Nonpareil Farms
40 N 400 W
Blackfoot, ID 83221-5632 208-785-5880
Fax: 208-785-3656 800-522-2223
www.greenerfieldstogether.org
Grower of potatoes including potato flakes, hash browns, potato slices, diced potatoes, scalloped & au gratin, mashed potatoes, and flavored potatoes in casseroles and mashed.
CEO: Christopher Abend
Treasurer & Secretary: Ilene Abend
IT: Kent Nelson
knelson@gotspuds.com
Estimated Sales: $46.2 Million
Number Employees: 500-999
Type of Packaging: Consumer
Regions Exported to: Canada
Percentage of Business in Exporting: 5

47045 (HQ)Noon Hour Food ProductsInc
215 N Desplaines St # 1
Floor One
Chicago, IL 60661-1072 312-382-1177
Fax: 312-382-9420 800-621-6636
Processor and importer of salted, canned and pickled fish, cheese and groceries
President: Paul Buhl
Executive VP: P Scott Buhl
Marketing Manager: Tyler Swanberg
Operations Manager: William Buhl
Estimated Sales: $6.7 Million
Number Employees: 20-49
Square Footage: 620000
Type of Packaging: Food Service
Other Locations:
Noon Hour Food Products
Minneapolis, MNNoon Hour Food Products
Regions Imported from: Europe, Canada
Percentage of Business in Importing: 25

47046 Noon International
3840 Blackhawk Rd # 100
Danville, CA 94506-4649 925-736-6696
Fax: 925-736-6177 info@noon-intl.com
Importer and exporter of fruits and vegetables
President: Lillian Noon
lnoon@noon-intl.com
Manager: Betty Johnson
Estimated Sales: $10-20 Million
Number Employees: 10-19
Type of Packaging: Bulk

47047 Nor-Cliff Farms
888 Barrick Rd.
Port Colborne, ON L3K 6H2
Canada 905-835-0808
Fax: 905-892-4011 sales@norcliff.com
Processor and exporter of fresh, frozen and marinated fiddlehead greens; also, soup mix
President: Nick Secord
Vice President: Nina Dilorenzo Secord
Regions Exported to: Europe, Asia, USA
Percentage of Business in Exporting: 40

47048 (HQ)Nor-Lake
11 Keewaydin Drive
Salem, NH 03079 603-893-9701
Fax: 603-893-7324 www.norlake.com
Refrigeration systems including walk-in coolers, walk0in freezers, milk coolers, ice cream freezers, environmental rooms, plasma refrigerators and chromatography refrigerators.
Chairman of the Board: Roger Fix
President/Chief Executive Officer: David Dunbar
VP/Chief Legal Officer/Secretary: Deborah Rosen
Chief Financial Officer: Thomas DeByle
Chief Accounting Officer: Sean Valashinas
Group VP, Food Service Group: John Abbott
Warehouse Supervisor: Cory Schlosser
Procurement Manager: Terry Clay
Estimated Sales: $ 26 Million
Number Employees: 300
Square Footage: 20000
Parent Co: Standex International Corporation
Type of Packaging: Food Service

47049 Norac Technologies
9110-23 Avenue
Edmonton Research Park
Edmonton, AB T6N 1H9
Canada 780-414-9595
Fax: 780-450-1016
Processor and exporter of spice extracts, egg yolk powder and essential, wheat germ and oat bran oils
President: Tom Evans
VP: Uy Nguyen
Plant Manager: Dan Moser
Number Employees: 10-19
Type of Packaging: Private Label, Bulk
Brands Exported: Labex; SC
Regions Exported to: USA, Japan
Percentage of Business in Exporting: 90

47050 (HQ)Noral
88 Pleasant Street S.,
Natick, MA 01760-563 508-653-5574
Fax: 508-653-1828 800-348-2345
Manufacturer and exporter of portable digital thermometers and probes including temperature measurement griddle probes, insertion, handheld and compact
President: Albert Ladanyi
CEO: Dr Deszo Ladanyi
VP Sales: Vincent Passiatore
Contact: Harry Erickson
harrye@noral.com
Operations: Dave Gilgenback
Purchasing Director: Mark O'Malley
Estimated Sales: $1-2.5 Million
Number Employees: 20
Square Footage: 80000
Regions Exported to: Central America, Europe
Percentage of Business in Exporting: 1

47051 Norandal
801 Crescent Centre Drive
Suite 600
Franklin, TX 37067   615-771-5700
Fax: 615-771-5701 investrel@noralinc.com
www.norandaaluminum.com
Manufacturer and exporter of laminated foil and aluminum foil pie plates
VP, Communication & Investor Relations: John Parker
Contact: David Hamling
david.hamling@noralinc.com
Estimated Sales: $ 97 Million
Number Employees: 820
Parent Co: Noranda
Type of Packaging: Private Label, Bulk
Regions Exported to: Worldwide

47052 Norback Ley & Assoc
3022 Woodland Trl
Middleton, WI 53562-1900   608-233-3814
Fax: 608-233-3895 www.norbackley.com
Manufacturer and exporter of food safety, HACCP and thermal processing software in English, Spanish, French, and Japanese
Owner: Kathleen A Ley
Chief Executive Officer: Sebastian Norback
CFO: Kathryn Olszewski
Estimated Sales: Less Than $500,000
Number Employees: 1-4
Number of Brands: 9
Number of Products: 14
Brands Exported: Do HACCP; Do SOP, Step HACCP, Record HACCP, Know Hazards, Say Data, Tpro, Tform
Regions Exported to: Central America, South America, Europe, Asia, Middle East
Percentage of Business in Exporting: 40

47053 Norbest, LLC
PO Box 890
Moroni, UT 84646
Fax: 888-597-5416 800-453-5327
norbest@norbest.com www.norbest.com
Raw and cooked processed turkey products including roasts and deli breasts, and luncheon meats including ham, pastrami, salami, etc.
President/CEO: Matthew Cook
Year Founded: 1923
Estimated Sales: $100+ Million
Number Employees: 20-49
Type of Packaging: Consumer, Food Service, Private Label, Bulk
Brands Exported: Norbest; Family Pride
Regions Exported to: South America, Middle East, Caribbean, Mexico
Percentage of Business in Exporting: 8

47054 Nordic Group Inc
253 Summer St # 203
Boston, MA 02210-1114   617-423-3358
Fax: 617-423-2057 800-486-4002
Processor and importer of fresh and frozen Norwegian seafood including smoked salmon, cod, haddock and fillets
Owner: Salmon Bake
Finance/Administration VP: Joe Mara
Regional Sales Manager: Joe Scharon
sbake@nordicgroupusa.com
Estimated Sales: $500,000-$1 Million
Number Employees: 5-9
Parent Co: Nordic Group ASA
Type of Packaging: Food Service, Bulk
Brands Imported: Fjord Fresh; Troll
Regions Imported from: Europe

47055 Nordic Ware Food Service
5005 County Road 25
Minneapolis, MN 55416-2276   952-920-2888
Fax: 952-924-8561 800-328-4310
www.nordicware.com
President: H David Dalquist Iii
Estimated Sales: $ 20 - 50 Million
Number Employees: 100-249

47056 Nordson Corp
11475 Lakefield Dr
Duluth, GA 30097-1557   770-497-8971
Fax: 866-667-3329 800-683-2314
pkgwebcontacts@nordson.com www.nordson.com
Manufacturer and exporter of adhesive dispensers and applicators, adhesives, coatings, heat sealers and coating, gluing, labeling and packaging machinery
President: John Raven
VP: John Keane
Manager Marketing Communication: Dave Grgetic
Business Developmental Specialist: Salieta Stone
Estimated Sales: $20-50 Million
Number Employees: 250-499
Regions Exported to: Worldwide
Percentage of Business in Exporting: 60

47057 Nordson Sealant Equipment
45677 Helm St
PO Box 701460
Plymouth, MI 48170-6025   734-459-8600
Fax: 734-459-8686 sales@sealantequipment.com
www.sealantequipment.com
Manufacturer and exporter of adhesive and food dispensing machinery
President/Chairman: Carl Schultz
Sales/Marketing/Public Relations: James Schultz
Contact: Randy Cochran
r.cochran@sealantequipment.com
Estimated Sales: $10-20 Million
Number Employees: 50-99
Regions Exported to: Central America, South America, Europe, Asia
Percentage of Business in Exporting: 15

47058 Noren Products Inc
1010 Obrien Dr
Menlo Park, CA 94025-1409   650-322-9500
Fax: 650-324-1348 866-936-6736
sales@norenproducts.com
www.norenproducts.com
Manufacturer and exporter of heat pipes, compact cabinet coolers, thermal pins, AcoustiLock, and HyTec Coolers.
Owner: Kimberely Dawn
Estimated Sales: $10-20,000,000
Number Employees: 50-99
Brands Exported: Compact Cabinet Coolers; Thermal Pins; Acoustilock Hytea Coolers; Heat Pipes
Regions Exported to: Central America, South America, Europe, Asia, Middle East
Percentage of Business in Exporting: 20

47059 Norfolk Hatchery
1000 East Omaha Avenue
PO Box 132
Norfolk, NE 68702-0132   402-371-5710
Fax: 402-371-5711 800-345-2449
www.norfolkhatchery.com
Poultry. Founded in 1926.
Owner/President: Paula Rasmussen
Estimated Sales: Less than $125,000
Number Employees: 2
Type of Packaging: Bulk

47060 Norimoor Company
Rockefeller Center
New York, NY 10185   212-695-6667
Fax: 718-721-6668 888-649-6667
norimoor@aol.com www.norimoor.com
Importer and exporter of herbal drinks, minerals, vitamins and bottled water
President: E Kruphan
Executive VP: Karl J Krupka
Estimated Sales: $250,000
Number Employees: 6
Square Footage: 20000
Brands Exported: Herbal Melange; Ida Mineral Water
Regions Exported to: Central America, Europe
Percentage of Business in Exporting: 15
Brands Imported: Herbal Melange; Moor Products
Regions Imported from: Europe

47061 Norpak Corp
70 Blanchard St
Newark, NJ 07105-4702   973-589-4200
Fax: 973-578-8845 800-631-6970
sales@norpak.net www.norpak.net
Manufacturer, importer and exporter of plain and printed food wrap including foil laminated, waxed and freezer paper; also, baking pan liners and interfolded deli sheets
President: Anthony Coraci
CFO: Lidia Gelasmagas
VP/General Manager: Robert Godown
Sales Manager: Michael Pacyna
Manager: Pedro Oliveira
poliveira@norpak.com
Estimated Sales: $ 20 - 30 Million
Number Employees: 20-49
Square Footage: 100000
Regions Exported to: Canada, Caribbean, Mexico
Percentage of Business in Exporting: 2
Regions Imported from: South America, Europe, Canada
Percentage of Business in Importing: 5

47062 Norseland Foods Inc
3 Parklands Dr
Suite 102
Darien, CT 06820   203-324-5620
Fax: 203-325-3189 www.norseland.com
Importer of gourmet Norwegian cheeses, French boursin and tholstrup danish cheese.
Director, Finance: Michael Albano
albano@norseland.com
Director, Information Technology: Marjorie Gordon
Marketing Coordinator: Taryn Prostano
Director, Sales: Paul Sullivan
Year Founded: 1965
Parent Co: Norwegian Dairies
Brands Imported: Ski Queen; Jarlsberg; Jarlsberg Lite; Snofrisk; Amablu; Gabriella; Garcia Baquero; Lotito Foods; Merci Chef; Old Amsterdam; Parmissimo; Capra; Couturier; St. Pete's Select; Verdant
Regions Imported from: Europe, Norway, France

47063 North American Enterprises
4330 N Campbell Ave Ste 256
Tucson, AZ 85718   520-885-0110
Fax: 520-298-9733 800-817-8666
www.capitanelli.com
Importer/distributor of olive oil, oil, balsamic vinegar, pasta sauces, salad dressings and biscotti; importer of Italian dry pasta and gourmet products
Owner: Joe Lovallo
VP Marketing: Grant Lovallo
National Sales Manager: Tim Champa
Contact: Joe Goodrich
jgoodrich@hazloc.net
Estimated Sales: $ 10 - 20 Million
Number Employees: 10-19
Square Footage: 4600
Type of Packaging: Consumer, Food Service
Brands Imported: Rummo
Regions Imported from: Europe
Percentage of Business in Importing: 85

47064 North American Packaging Corp
140 E 30th St
New York, NY 10016-7319   212-213-4141
Fax: 212-213-4145 800-499-3521
info@packagingonline.com
www.packagingonline.com
Manufacturer and importer of shopping, paper and plastic bags, gift boxes and stationery including letterhead, business cards, gift certificates, roll and sheet labels, press kits, catalogs, fliers, etc
Manager: John Destefano
Manager: John DeStefano
Estimated Sales: Below $5,000,000
Number Employees: 1-4
Regions Imported from: Europe

47065 North American Provisioners
5800 Franklin Street
Suite 101
Denver, CO 80216-1249   303-831-1299
Fax: 303-831-1292 888-289-2833
Wholesaler and exporter of buffalo and game meat products
CFO: Rusty Seedig
Sales: Mary Gonsior
Operations: Mike Sobieski
VP Production/Distribution: Jerry Getka
Purchasing: Bruce Klein
Estimated Sales: $2.5-5 Million
Number Employees: 10-19
Number of Products: 300
Square Footage: 120000
Parent Co: New West Foods
Type of Packaging: Consumer, Food Service, Bulk
Brands Exported: Denver Buffalo Co.
Regions Exported to: Europe, Asia
Percentage of Business in Exporting: 5

Importers & Exporters / A-Z

47066 North American Reishi/Nammex
PO Box 1780
Gibsons, BC V0N 1V0
Canada
604-886-7799
Fax: 604-648-8954 info@nammex.com
www.nammex.com
Processor and exporter of standardized and certified organic mushroom extracts; also, whole dried mushrooms and mushroom mycelia
President: Jeffrey Chilton
Estimated Sales: $1.2 Million
Number Employees: 6
Type of Packaging: Bulk
Regions Exported to: Worldwide
Percentage of Business in Exporting: 90

47067 North Atlantic Products
232 Buttermilk Ln
South Thomaston, ME 04858-3003   207-596-0331
Fax: 207-596-0532
Seafood

47068 North Bay Fisherman's Cooperative
Wharf Road
RR 4
Ballantyne's Cove, NS B2G 2L2
Canada
902-863-4988
Fax: 902-863-1112
Fresh and frozen lobster, scallops and groundfish; exporter of tuna
Manager: Kim MacDonald
Number Employees: 5-9
Type of Packaging: Consumer, Food Service, Private Label, Bulk
Regions Exported to: USA, Japan
Percentage of Business in Exporting: 20

47069 North Bay Produce Inc
1771 N US Highway 31 S
Traverse City, MI 49685-8748   231-946-1941
Fax: 231-946-1902
marketing@northbayproduce.com
www.northbayproduce.com
Cooperative, importer and exporter of fresh produce including apples, asparagus, blueberries, cherries, peaches, plums, snow peas, sugar snaps, mangos, raspberries, blackberries, red currants, etc.; also, apple cider.
President: Mark Girardin
National Marketing Manager: Sharon Robb
Facilities & Compliance Manager: Jonathan Wall
Estimated Sales: $73 Million
Number Employees: 20-49
Number of Brands: 1
Square Footage: 15000
Type of Packaging: Consumer, Food Service, Private Label, Bulk
Other Locations:
  North Bay Produce Warehouse
  Miami, FL
  North Bay Produce Warehouse
  Mascoutah, IL North Bay Produce
  Warehouse Mascoutah
Brands Exported: North Bay
Regions Exported to: Europe, Asia
Percentage of Business in Exporting: 20
Regions Imported from: Central America, South America
Percentage of Business in Importing: 40

47070 North Bay Trading Co
13904 E US Highway 2
Brule, WI 54820-9038   715-372-5031
800-348-0164
borg@cheqnet.net www.northbaytrading.com
Organic and Canadian wild rice, heirloom beans, dehydrated vegetables, dry soup mixes
Owner: Greggar Isaksen
greggar@northbaytrading.com
Estimated Sales: $160,000
Number Employees: 5-9
Number of Brands: 2
Number of Products: 6
Type of Packaging: Consumer, Food Service, Bulk
Brands Exported: Canadian Wild Rice
Regions Exported to: Europe
Brands Imported: Canadian Wild Rice
Regions Imported from: Canada

47071 North Coast Processing
5451 Avenida Encinas
Suite D
Carlsbad, CA 92008   814-725-9617
Fax: 814-725-4374 760-931-6809
info@northcoastphoto.com
www.northcoastphoto.com
Processor and contract packager of salad dressings, sauces, marinades and dry seasonings
President: Richard H Shute
Operations Manager: Tom Barnes
Plant Manager: Wilson Haller
Estimated Sales: $13 Million
Number Employees: 10-19
Square Footage: 50000
Type of Packaging: Consumer, Food Service, Private Label, Bulk
Brands Exported: Den; Garden Goodness
Regions Exported to: South America
Percentage of Business in Exporting: 10

47072 North Country Natural Spring Water
P.O. Box 123
Port Kent, NY 12911   518-834-9400
Fax: 518-834-9429
Processor and importer of natural spring water
President: Roger Jakubowski
Estimated Sales: $ 1 - 3 Million
Number Employees: 10-19
Square Footage: 44000
Type of Packaging: Consumer, Food Service, Private Label, Bulk
Brands Imported: North Country
Regions Imported from: Canada
Percentage of Business in Importing: 8

47073 North Lake Fish Cooperative
RR 1
Elmira, PE C0A 1K0
Canada   902-357-2572
Fax: 902-357-2386 www.gov.pe.ca/fard
Processor and exporter of fresh and frozen scallops, skate, silversides and lobster
President: Walter Bruce
CEO/General Manager: Mickey Rose
Number Employees: 100-249
Type of Packaging: Bulk
Percentage of Business in Exporting: 75

47074 North Pacific Seafoods Inc
4 Nickerson St
Suite 400
Seattle, WA 98109   206-726-9900
Fax: 206-352-7421
www.northpacificseafoods.com
Wild Alaska seafood products.
President: Hisashi Sugiyama

47075 North Peace Apiaries
RR1 Station Main
Fort St. John, BC V1J 4H5
Canada   250-785-4808
Fax: 250-785-2664
Processor and exporter of honey and bee pollen
President: Ernie Fuhr
Secretary/Treasurer: Rose Fuhr
Estimated Sales: $496,000
Number Employees: 3
Square Footage: 15120
Type of Packaging: Consumer
Regions Exported to: Europe

47076 North River Roasters
8 North Cherry St.
Poughkeepsie, NY 12601   845-418-2739
hello@northriverroasters.com
www.northriverroasters.com
Micro-roasted, small batch fair trade organic whole bean coffee; sourced from Mexico & Peru
Founder/Owner: Feza Oktay
Year Founded: 2015
Number of Brands: 1
Number of Products: 4
Type of Packaging: Consumer, Private Label
Regions Exported to: Central America, South America, Europe, Asia, Middle East, USA and Canada

47077 North Star Engineered Products
28905 Glenwood Rd
Perrysburg, OH 43551-3020   419-726-2645
Fax: 419-666-1549
Manufactures equipment to process fresh cut vegetables and fruit, including fruit processing centrifuges
Owner: Tom Ziems
tsz@glassline.com
CFO: John K Clement
Sales Manager: Joe Moroni
Technical Services: Buddy Santus
Estimated Sales: $ 2.5 - 5 Million
Number Employees: 10-19
Type of Packaging: Bulk

47078 North Star Ice Equipment Corporation
8151 Occidental Ave S
P.O. Box 80227
Seattle, WA 98108-4210   206-763-7300
Fax: 206-763-7323 800-321-1381
info@northstarice.com www.northstarice.com
Manufacturer and exporter of industrial ice makers and related handling equipment. Products include Flake Ice Makers, Liquid Ice Generators, Ice Storage Systems, Ice Delivery Systems and more.
President: Logan Shepardson
Vice President Sales & Marketing: Tom Crawford
Sales & Marketing Administrator: Jennifer Ward
Director of Operations & Finance: Rachel Camarillo
Estimated Sales: $10 - 20 Million
Number Employees: 11 - 50
Square Footage: 60000
Brands Exported: Cold Spell Ice System
Regions Exported to: Central America, South America, Europe, Asia, Middle East, Worldwide
Percentage of Business in Exporting: 70

47079 North Taste Flavourings
71 Rte 320
Anse-Bleue, NB E8N 2B7
Canada   506-732-0010
Fax: 506-732-5370 joel.albert@northtaste.ca
www.northtaste.ca
All-natural seafood flavors for soups, bisques, chowders, spreads, dips, sauces, stuffings, and other seafood dishes
President: Julien Albert
Research & Production Manager: Dr. Eric Albert
Quality Control Supervisor: Johanne Doucet
VP Sales & Marketing: Joel Albert
VP US Sales & Product Development: Jerry Levine
Director of Asian Sales: K. Nunokawa
Square Footage: 56000
Regions Exported to: Europe, Asia, Australia, USA, Mexico

47080 Northeast Calamari Inc
13 Forest St
Gloucester, MA 01930-2807   978-281-6553
Fax: 978-281-2656
President: Maria Maniaci
Estimated Sales: Less Than $500,000
Number Employees: 1-4

47081 Northeast Group Exporters Inc
20 Robert Pitt Dr # 203
Suite 203
Monsey, NY 10952-3340   845-352-0222
Fax: 845-425-6369 info@foodexport.net
www.northeastgroupexporters.com
Exporter of fine foods, snack foods, candies, canned fruits & vegetables, desserts, mixes, baked goods, kosher, beverages, sauces, condiments, frozen and refrigerated foods
President: Henry Weiss
VP: Eli Ebstein
Marketing: Shimmy Adler
Sales: Julie Neiman
Marketing Coordinator: Shimmy Adler
Estimated Sales: $4-5 Million
Number Employees: 5-9
Type of Packaging: Consumer, Food Service, Private Label, Bulk
Brands Exported: Betty Crocker; Crisco; General Mills; Green Giant; Hellman's; Kellogg's; Kraft; Beech-Nut; Oreo; Hershey's; Terra Chips
Regions Exported to: Central America, Europe, Asia, Middle East
Percentage of Business in Exporting: 95

47082 Northeast Packaging Co
875 Skyway St
Presque Isle, ME 04769-2063   207-764-6271
Fax: 207-496-3171 www.nepcobags.com
Paper and poly bags

President: Robert Umphrey
rumphrey@mfx.net
Sales Representative: Ken Joy
General Manager: Chris Burtchell
Production Manager: Jesse Harris
Number Employees: 50-99
Type of Packaging: Consumer, Private Label
Regions Exported to: Canada
Percentage of Business in Exporting: 5
Regions Imported from: Asia
Percentage of Business in Importing: 5

47083 Northeast Packaging Materials
20 Robert Pitt Dr # 202
Monsey, NY 10952-3340   845-426-2900
Fax: 845-426-3700   sbraun@nepack.com
www.nepack.com
Manufacturer and exporter of barrier films; available in roll stock and pouches
President and QC: Stewart Braun
Estimated Sales: Below $ 5,000,000
Number Employees: 1-4
Regions Exported to: Worldwide

47084 Northeastern Products Corp
115 Sweet Rd
PO Box 98
Warrensburg, NY 12885-4754   518-623-3161
Fax: 518-623-3803   800-873-8233
info@nep-co.com   www.nep-co.com
Manufacturer and exporter of meat smoking sawdust including hickory, maple, cherry and alder
President: Gary Shiavi
CEO: Paul Schiavi
Marketing Director: Richard Morgan
Estimated Sales: Below $ 5 Million
Number Employees: 50-99
Square Footage: 80000
Regions Exported to: Central America, South America, Europe, Asia, Middle East, Canada, Mexico
Percentage of Business in Exporting: 10

47085 Northern Feed & Bean Company
33278 Us Highway 85
Lucerne, CO 80646   970-352-7875
Fax: 970-352-7833   800-316-2326
mail@nfbean.com www.northernfeedandbean.com
Manufacturer and exporter of dried pinto beans
Manager: Larry Lande
Estimated Sales: $4.6 Million
Number Employees: 14
Square Footage: 27048
Type of Packaging: Consumer, Food Service, Private Label

47086 Northern Orcharad Co Inc
537 Union Rd
Peru, NY 12972-4664   518-643-2367
Fax: 518-643-2751 northernorchard@verizon.net
www.northernorchard.com
Wholesaler/distributor, exporter and packer of macintosh apples and honey
President: Albert Mulbury
Contact: Samson Church
schurch@northernorchard.com
Estimated Sales: $1,950,266
Number Employees: 20-49
Type of Packaging: Consumer
Brands Exported: Champlain Valley
Regions Exported to: Europe

47087 Northern Products Corporation
1932 1st Ave
Suite 705
Seattle, WA 98101-1040   206-448-6677
Fax: 206-448-9664   888-599-6290
Processor and exporter of frozen salmon, cod, halibut, flounder, pollock, squid, and rockfish
President: William Dignon
Plant Manager: Terry Barry
Estimated Sales: $ 1 - 3 Million
Number Employees: 1-4
Type of Packaging: Private Label, Bulk
Regions Exported to: Worldwide

47088 Northern Stainless Fabricating
P.O.Box 6715
Traverse City, MI 49696-6715   231-947-4580
Fax: 231-947-9074
Manufacturer and exporter of custom made stainless steel kitchen equipment for food service and institutional use including salad bars, dish tables and prep tables
President: Mike Fisher
Chief Estimator: Harry Muse
CFO: Michael J Fisher
VP Production: Bruce Muzzarelli
Estimated Sales: $10-20 Million
Number Employees: 50-99
Square Footage: 60000
Regions Exported to: Worldwide
Percentage of Business in Exporting: 10

47089 Northern Wind Inc
16 Hassey St
New Bedford, MA 02740-7209   508-997-0727
Fax: 508-990-8792   888-525-2525
www.northernwind.com
Processor and exporter of fresh and frozen seafoods including; bay and sea scallops, farm-raised chilean mussels, farm-raised chilean atlantic salmon, hard shell north atlantic lobsters, monkfish, skate
Owner: Colleen Avila
CEO: Ken Melanson
VP: Betsy Borba
Sales Manager: Rick Moreno
sma1217@aol.com
Plant Manager: Michael Fernandes
Estimated Sales: $15.3 Million
Number Employees: 50-99
Number of Brands: 3
Number of Products: 3
Type of Packaging: Food Service, Private Label, Bulk
Regions Exported to: Worldwide

47090 Northfield Freezing Systems
PO Box 98
Northfield, MN 55057-0098   507-645-9546
Fax: 507-645-6148   800-426-1283
Manufacturer and exporter of freezers, coolers, chillers, hardeners and spiral conveying freezing systems
President: Tim Colies
Sales/Marketing Executive: Larry Deboer
Purchasing Agent: Bill Westby
Estimated Sales: $ 20 - 50 Million
Number Employees: 120
Parent Co: Frigo Schndia
Brands Exported: Northfield Spiral
Regions Exported to: Central America, South America, Asia, Middle East
Percentage of Business in Exporting: 10

47091 Northland Corp
1260 E Van Deinse St
Greenville, MI 48838-1400   616-754-5601
Fax: 616-754-0970   800-223-3900
sales@northlandnka.net
www.documentofconformity.com
Custom refrigeration, commercial and residential
President: Mike Bufton
CFO: Karen Braund
Vice President: Brad Stauffer
Research & Development: Jim Holland
Quality Control: Rick Waldorf
Marketing Director: Gerry Reda
Public Relations: Sindy Angi
Operations/Plant Manager: Kent Coon
Plant Manager: Kent Coon
Purchasing Manager: Richard Burns
Estimated Sales: $ 10 - 20 Million
Number Employees: 100-249
Square Footage: 440000
Parent Co: AGA Food Service Group

47092 Northland Organic Foods Corporation
495 Portland Ave
Saint Paul, MN 55102   651-221-0070
Fax: 651-221-0856
Leading organic food brokerage company. Specializes in the production and exportation of premium-quality, non-genetically modified, organic soybean, wheat, corn, rice and other cereal grains as well as certified organic commoditiessuch as oils, meals and flour
Owner: Peter Shortridge
Estimated Sales: $ 1 - 3 Million
Number Employees: 5-9

47093 Northridge Laboratories
20832 Dearborn St
Chatsworth, CA 91311   818-882-5622
Fax: 818-998-2815
Processor and exporter of vitamins, herbal supplements and protein powders
President: Brett Richman
CEO: Jane Richman
CFO: Charles Wands
Contact: Angie Armendariz
nrlabs@aol.com
Estimated Sales: $6400000
Number Employees: 50
Square Footage: 120000
Type of Packaging: Private Label
Regions Exported to: Worldwide
Percentage of Business in Exporting: 30

47094 Northtech Workholding
301 Commerce Dr
Schaumburg, IL 60173-5305   847-310-8787
Fax: 847-310-9484   www.kitagawa.com
Exporter of food processing machinery and meat products
Vice President: Sam Ooka
sooka@kitnt.com
Food Division Manager: Shoi Kabayashi
VP: Sam Ooka
Estimated Sales: $10-20 Million
Number Employees: 50-99
Square Footage: 24000
Parent Co: Sumikin Bussan Kaisha

47095 Northwest Analytical Inc
111 SW 5th Ave # 800
Portland, OR 97204-3606   503-224-7727
Fax: 503-224-5236   888-692-7638
nwa@nwasoft.com   www.nwasoft.com
Manufacturer and exporter of SPC charting workstation and statistical quality control (SQC) software for control charting, process capability analysis and plant floor data collection
Chairman: Clifford S L Yee
CEO: Bob Ward
bward@nwasoft.com
CFO: T Olin Nichols
VP: Jeff Cawley
R&D: Louis Halvorsen
VP Marketing: Peter Guilfoyle
VP Sales: Jim Petrusich
Estimated Sales: $10-20,000,000
Number Employees: 20-49
Brands Exported: NWA
Regions Exported to: Central America, South America, Europe, Asia, Middle East
Percentage of Business in Exporting: 15

47096 Northwest Art Glass
9003 151st Ave NE
Redmond, WA 98052-3513   425-861-9600
Fax: 425-861-9300   800-888-9444
www.nwartglass.com
Manufacturer and importer of etched glass separators and screens, brass posts, traffic control systems, liscourts and sneeze guards
Owner: Richard Mesmer
richard@cascadegac.com
Metal Sales/Operations: Steve Bolens
richard@cascadegac.com
Estimated Sales: $1-2.5 Million
Number Employees: 10-19
Square Footage: 17000
Type of Packaging: Bulk
Regions Imported from: Europe, Asia
Percentage of Business in Importing: 15

47097 Northwest Chocolate Factory
2162 Davcor Street SE
Salem, OR 97302-1510   503-362-1340
Fax: 503-362-0186   www.nwchocolate.com
Processor and exporter of chocolate covered hazelnuts
President: Sam Kaufman
General Manager: Dan Kaufman
Number Employees: 5-9
Square Footage: 40000
Type of Packaging: Consumer
Regions Exported to: Asia
Percentage of Business in Exporting: 1

47098 Northwest Fisheries
RR 1
Hubbards, NS B0J 1T0
Canada   902-228-2232
Fax: 902-228-2116
Processor and exporter of fresh lobster, cod and halibut
President: Olimpio Martins
Number Employees: 5-9

Importers & Exporters / A-Z

Type of Packaging: Consumer, Food Service, Private Label, Bulk
Regions Exported to: Worldwide
Percentage of Business in Exporting: 35

47099 Northwest Naturals Company
40 E 78th St # 6f
New York, NY 10075-1830
212-439-8361
Fax: 212-439-8364
Wholesaler/distributor of seafood; exporter of fresh fish and honey; importer of fish, cheese, peanut butter, honey and shellfish
President: Soloman Moussatche
VP: Salomon Moussatche
Estimated Sales: $ 3 - 5 Million
Number Employees: 5-9
Square Footage: 5200
Regions Exported to: Europe
Percentage of Business in Exporting: 10
Regions Imported from: Central America, South America, Europe
Percentage of Business in Importing: 65

47100 Northwest Naturals LLC
11805 N Creek Pkwy S # 104
Bothell, WA 98011-8803
425-881-2200
Fax: 425-881-3063 nwn@nwnaturals.com
www.nwnaturals.com
Processor, importer and exporter of concentrates including juice and iced coffee and fruit beverages and flavors
Vice President: Mike Marquand
mikem@nwnaturals.com
CEO: James
VP Sales and Administration: Mike Marquand
VP Operations: Danny Shaffer
Estimated Sales: $ 5 - 10 Million
Number Employees: 20-49
Number of Brands: 4
Number of Products: 50
Square Footage: 120000
Parent Co: Tree Top
Type of Packaging: Consumer, Food Service, Private Label, Bulk
Regions Exported to: Worldwide
Percentage of Business in Exporting: 25
Regions Imported from: Worldwide
Percentage of Business in Importing: 10

47101 Northwestern Coffee Mills
30950 Nevers Rd
Washburn, WI 54891
715-373-2122
Fax: 715-747-5405 800-243-5283
Processor, importer and exporter of coffee and tea
Owner: Harry Demorest
Estimated Sales: Under $300,000
Number Employees: 1-4
Square Footage: 8000
Type of Packaging: Consumer, Food Service
Regions Exported to: Europe, Asia, Canada
Percentage of Business in Exporting: 3
Regions Imported from: Central America, South America, Asia, Middle East, Canada, Caribbean, Latin America, Mexico

47102 Northwestern Corp
922 Armstrong St
PO Box 490
Morris, IL 60450-1921
815-942-1300
Fax: 815-942-4417 800-942-1316
sales@nwcorp.com
Manufacturer and exporter of vending machinery
President: Richard Bolen
nwsales@nwcorp.com
CFO: Angie Stropel
R&D: Angie Stropel
Quality Control: Angie Stropel
Sales Director: Diane Olson
Estimated Sales: $ 10 - 20 Million
Number Employees: 20-49
Square Footage: 100000
Regions Exported to: Central America, South America, Europe, Middle East
Percentage of Business in Exporting: 25

47103 Northwestern Extract
W194n11250 Mccormick Dr # 1
Germantown, WI 53022-3049
262-345-6900
Fax: 262-781-0660 800-466-3034
flavors@nwextract.com
www.northwesternextract.com
Flavorings and extracts

President: William Peter
CEO: Megan Bruzan
megan@nwextract.com
Marketing Director: Patricia Hein
Purchasing Manager: Michael Peter
Estimated Sales: $ 5 - 10 Million
Number Employees: 10-19
Square Footage: 40000
Type of Packaging: Consumer, Food Service, Private Label, Bulk
Brands Exported: Norwesco
Regions Exported to: Worldwide
Percentage of Business in Exporting: 5

47104 Norvell Co Inc
4002 Liberty Bell Rd
Fort Scott, KS 66701-8638
620-223-3110
Fax: 620-223-3115 800-653-3147
www.norvellco.com
Manufacturer and exporter of flour mill sifters for the processing of flour, spices, cereals, etc.; also, agitators for blending
Office Manager: Barbara Fitts
General Manager: Mark Shank
Manager: Mark Shank
Estimated Sales: $5-10 Million
Number Employees: 20-49
Square Footage: 80000
Type of Packaging: Food Service
Regions Exported to: Central America, South America, Europe, Asia
Percentage of Business in Exporting: 20

47105 Norwood Marking Systems
2538 Wisconsin Ave
Downers Grove, IL 60515
630-968-0646
Fax: 630-968-7672 800-626-3464
Manufacturer and exporter of coding systems and accessories including hot stamp imprinters, thermal transfer printers, embossers, hot stamp and thermal transfer ribbon supplies and steel type
General Manager: Larry Kulik
Sales Director: Cliff Vanwey
Estimated Sales: $20-50 Million
Number Employees: 50-99
Parent Co: Illinois Tool Works
Regions Exported to: Central America, South America

47106 Nossack Fine Meats
7240 Johnstone Dr
Suite 100
Red Deer, AB T4P 3Y6
Canada
403-346-5006
Fax: 403-343-8066 www.nossack.com
Roast and corned beef, pastrami, sausage and ham; also, garlic rings and pizza products
President: Karsten Nossack
Manager of Finance: Ingrid Nossack
Estimated Sales: $27 Million
Number Employees: 70
Square Footage: 22000
Type of Packaging: Consumer, Food Service
Regions Imported from: South America

47107 Nothum Food Processing Systems
631 S Kansas Ave
Springfield, MO 65802
417-831-2816
Fax: 417-866-4781 800-435-1297
nothum@nothum.com www.nothum.com
Manufacturer and exporter of batter applicators, breaders, pre-dusters, fryers, shuttle conveyors, char markers, coaters, blanchers, filters, ovens, polar therm and stack freezers, etc.
President/Chief Executive Officer: Robert Nothum
nothum@nothum.com
Sales & Marketing: Robert Nothum
Number Employees: 30
Regions Exported to: Worldwide

47108 Notre Dame Seafoods Inc.
PO Box 201
Comfort Cove, NL A0G 3K0
Canada
709-244-5511
Fax: 709-244-3451
jeveleigh@notredamesseafoods.com
www.notredamesseafoods.com
Processor and exporter of canned and frozen crab, cod, turbit, capelin, squid, mackerel, lumpfish, roe and lobster
President & COO: Jason Eveleigh
VP/General Manager: Rex Eveleigh
Number Employees: 250-499
Parent Co: Provincial Investments

Type of Packaging: Consumer, Food Service
Regions Exported to: Worldwide
Percentage of Business in Exporting: 95

47109 Nova Hand Dryers
12801 Worldgate Drive
Suite 500
Herndon, VA 20170
Canada
703-615-3636
Fax: 877-385-1291
Manufacturer and exporter of warm air hand dryers
Sales Manager: Maurine Cohen
Number Employees: 45
Parent Co: Avmor
Regions Exported to: Worldwide

47110 Nova Industries
999 Montague St
San Leandro, CA 94577
510-357-0171
Fax: 510-357-3832 www.bordenlighting.com
Manufacturer and exporter of glare control devices and lighting fixtures including custom made and incandescent
President: James Borden
VP: Floyd Shreeve
Contact: Bobby Aquino
baquino@bordenlighting.com
Estimated Sales: $2.5-5 Million
Number Employees: 20-49
Square Footage: 28000
Regions Exported to: Europe, Middle East
Percentage of Business in Exporting: 10

47111 Nova Seafood
P.O.Box 350
Portland, ME 04112-0350
207-774-6324
Fax: 207-774-6385 www.novaseafood.com
Canadian seafood: Fresh Whole and Fresh Fillet Products - Cod, Haddock, Hake, Cusk, Catfish, Pollock, Flounder, Dabs, Grey Sole, Yellowtail, Salmon, Monk, Monk Tail, Halibut; Specialty Items: Clams, Maine Shrimp, Swordfish, Scallops(Dry Sea), Tuna Loin, C/K Lobster Meat, Crab Meat
President: Angelo Ciocca
Sales: Ernie Salamone
Estimated Sales: $ 20 - 50 Million
Number Employees: 20-49

47112 Novamex
500 W Overland Ave
Suite 300
El Paso, TX 79901
www.novamex.com
Markets and exports a variety of foods and beverages from Mexico.
Logistics Coordinator: Susana Barreda
susana.barreda@novamex.com
Executive Vice President: Sanford Gross
International Market Development: Raymundo Gomez
Year Founded: 1986
Estimated Sales: $150 Million
Number Employees: 250-499
Type of Packaging: Food Service

47113 Novel Ingredient Services, LLC
10 Henderson Drive
West Caldwell, NJ 07006
973-808-5900
Fax: 973-808-5959 866-668-3550
wedeliver@novelingredient.com
www.novelingredient.com
Beverage ingredients and sweeteners
President: David Green
Sales: Jim O'Donnell
Contact: Richard Antonoff
rantonoff@novelingredient.com
Other Locations:
  Novel Ingredient Services, LLC
  Pompton Plains, NJ Novel Ingredient Services, LLC

47114 (HQ)Novelty Advertising
1148 Walnut St
Coshocton, OH 43812-1769
740-622-3113
Fax: 740-622-5286 800-848-9163
Manufacturer and exporter of calendars and advertising specialties
President: Gregory Coffman
gcoffman@noveltyadv.com
Owner: Greg Coffman
Owner: Thad Coffman
VP: Jim McConnell
Estimated Sales: $5-10 Million
Number Employees: 20-49

Type of Packaging: Consumer, Food Service, Bulk
Regions Exported to: Canada
Percentage of Business in Exporting: 25

47115 Novelty Crystal
3015 48th Ave
Long Island City, NY 11101-3419   718-458-6700
            Fax: 718-458-9408 800-622-0250
joe@noveltycrystal.com www.noveltycrystal.com
Plastic caterware which includes; plastic serving trays, plastic bowls, plastic bowls, plastic tumblers, plastic pitchers, plastic stemware and plastic serving accessories.
Owner: Ed Coslett
e.coslett@noveltycrystal.com
VP: Asher Michaeli
VP: Joseph Michaeli
CFO: Ashur Michaeli
Estimated Sales: $ 2.5 - 5 Million
Number Employees: 20-49
Square Footage: 240000
Type of Packaging: Consumer, Food Service
Regions Exported to: Central America, South America, Europe, Asia, Middle East, Canada, Australia
Percentage of Business in Exporting: 15

47116 Novozymes North America Inc
77 Perrys Chapel Church Rd
Franklinton, NC 27525-9677   919-494-3000
            Fax: 919-494-3450 800-879-6686
enzymesna@novozymes.com
www.novozymes.com
Enzymes
President: Adam Monroe
ad@novozymes.com
EVP & CFO: Benny Loft
EVP & CSO: Per Falholt
Director Purchasing: Percy Taylor
Estimated Sales: $40 Million
Number Employees: 1000-4999
Parent Co: Novozymes
Type of Packaging: Bulk
Regions Exported to: Worldwide

47117 Novus
650 Pelham Blvd
Suite 100
St. Paul, MN 55114   952-944-8000
            Fax: 952-944-2542 800-328-1117
www.novusglass.com
Manufacturer and exporter of plastic polish and scratch remover and auto glass replacement products
President: Keith Beverige
Contact: Allan Dmore
dmore.allan@novuspolish.com
Number Employees: 1,000-4,999
Square Footage: 40000
Parent Co: TCG International
Type of Packaging: Consumer
Brands Exported: Novus Plastic Polish

47118 Now Designs
3233 S La Cienega Boulevard
Los Angeles, CA 90016-3112   310-253-9001
            Fax: 310-837-0490

47119 Now Plastics Inc
136 Denslow Rd
East Longmeadow, MA 01028-3188   413-525-1010
            Fax: 413-525-8951 info@nowplastics.com
www.nowplastics.com
NOW Plastics offers an extensive line of high performance film sustracts including but not limited to; PET, BOPP, CPP, PVC, MOPP, FOPP, OPS, Nylon, Non Woven, Synthetic Paper, Skin Film, Retort films and Co-extrusions. AdditionallyNOW Plastics supplies various types of micro-perforated, laser perforated or high clarity bags and films for bakery and produce packaging.
President: Oded Edan
CEO: Larry Silverstein
ls@nowplastics.com
CEO: Larry Silverstein
Estimated Sales: $ 10 - 20,000,000
Number Employees: 10-19
Square Footage: 40000
Type of Packaging: Bulk
Regions Exported to: Central America, Europe, Canada
Percentage of Business in Exporting: 15
Regions Imported from: Israel
Percentage of Business in Importing: 25

47120 Noyes, P J
89 Bridge St
Lancaster, NH 03584-3103   603-788-2848
            Fax: 603-788-3873 800-522-2469
Liquids, tablets and capsules
President: David Hill
Quality Control Manager: Janet Christenson
Marketing Executive: Jim Hoverman
Sales/Marketing Manager: Jennifer Cusick
Contact: Alan Balog
alanb@pjnoyes.com
VP/COO: Dennis Wogaman
Production Manager: Steve Skinner
Estimated Sales: $10 Million
Number Employees: 5-9
Square Footage: 70000
Type of Packaging: Private Label, Bulk
Brands Exported: Noyes Pellets
Regions Exported to: South America, Europe, Middle East, Canada, Caribbean, Latin America, Mexico

47121 Nrd LLC
2937 Alt Blvd
P.O.Box 310
Grand Island, NY 14072-1292   716-773-7634
            Fax: 716-773-7744 800-500-8076
sales@nrdinc.com www.nrdinc.com
Manufacturer and exporter of static control products to increase safety, productivity and product quality including ionizers.
President: Doug Fiegel
dfiegel@nrdinc.com
Chairman: Sal Alfiero
Director Sales & Marketing: Greg Gumkowski
Production Manager: Kathleen Kowalik
Purchasing Manager: Jim Zoldowski
Number Employees: 20-49
Type of Packaging: Bulk
Regions Exported to: Canada
Percentage of Business in Exporting: 2

47122 Ntc Marketing
5680 Main St
Williamsville, NY 14221-5518   716-884-3345
            Fax: 716-884-4680 800-333-1637
info@ntcmarketing.com
Processor and importer of canned products including pineapples, pineapple juice, tropical fruits, tropical fruit mix, mandarin orange
Owner/Principal: Michael Derose
mjderose@ntcmarketing.com
Human Resource Executive: Sue Godzala
Estimated Sales: $3.3 Million
Number Employees: 10-19
Square Footage: 40000
Type of Packaging: Consumer, Food Service, Private Label, Bulk

47123 Nu-Star Inc
1425 Stagecoach Rd
Shakopee, MN 55379-2798   952-445-8295
            Fax: 952-445-0231 800-800-9274
jadams@nustarinc.com
Manufacturer and exporter of carts for lifting, pushing and pulling
President: Scott Lorch
slorch@nustarinc.com
CFO: James Coan
VP Power Pusher Division: Scott Lorch
VP Sales & Marketing: John D Adams
Estimated Sales: $ 5 - 10,000,000
Number Employees: 20-49
Type of Packaging: Bulk
Regions Exported to: Worldwide

47124 Nu-Tex Styles, Inc.
285 Davidson Ave # 104
Somerset, NJ 08873   732-485-5456
            Fax: 732-873-0854 info@nu-tex.com
www.nu-tex.com
Manufacturer, importer and exporter of industrial fabrics and wiping rags including cheesecloth and dusting cloth
President: Howard Bromwich
howard@nu-tex.com
Estimated Sales: $1-2.5 Million
Number Employees: 1-4
Number of Brands: 3
Number of Products: 57
Square Footage: 360000
Brands Exported: Zorbit
Regions Exported to: Worldwide
Percentage of Business in Exporting: 85

Regions Imported from: Canada
Percentage of Business in Importing: 10

47125 (HQ)Nu-Trend Plastics Thermoformer
119 Sewald St
Jacksonville, FL 32204-1731   904-353-5936
            Fax: 904-353-2035
Manufacturer and exporter of thermoformed plastic containers, trays and inserts
CEO: Michael Corrigan
CFO: Mike Corrigan
Estimated Sales: $2-2.5 Million
Number Employees: 5-9
Square Footage: 30000
Type of Packaging: Consumer, Food Service, Private Label
Regions Exported to: South America, Middle East

47126 Nu-World Amaranth Inc
552 S Washington St # 120
Suite #107
Naperville, IL 60540-6669   630-369-6851
            Fax: 630-369-6851
customerservice@nuworldfoods.com
Manufacturer and exporter of amaranth-based products including popped, flour, pre-baked flat bread, sancks and cereal. Offers foods that are allergy free and gluten free foods
Founder/Co-Owner: Larry Walters
President: Susan Walters-Flood
CFO: Jim Behling
Vice President: Terry Walters
t.walters@nuworldamaranthinc.com
Manager/Co-Owner: Diane Walters
VP Production: Terry Walters
Estimated Sales: Under $500,000
Number Employees: 10-19
Number of Brands: 2
Number of Products: 15
Square Footage: 10800
Type of Packaging: Consumer, Private Label, Bulk
Brands Exported: Nu-World Amaranth
Regions Exported to: Europe, Asia, Australia
Percentage of Business in Exporting: 5

47127 NuTone
9825 Kenwood Rd
Suite 301
Cincinnati, OH 45242   513-527-5100
            Fax: 513-527-5177 888-336-3948
www.nutone.com
Manufacturer and exporter of range hoods, exhaust fans, heaters, central cleaning systems, etc.
CEO: David Pringle
CFO: Bill Kissell
Quality Control: Gloria Wrenn
Contact: Jimmie Cheek
jcheek@nutone.com
Manager: Fabio Fronda
Number Employees: 500-999
Parent Co: Nortek
Regions Exported to: Worldwide

47128 Nuance Solutions Inc
1140 E 103rd St
Chicago, IL 60628-3010   773-785-2300
            Fax: 800-621-1276 800-621-8553
cjh@nuancesol.com www.nuancesolutions.com
Manufacturer and exporter of liquid and jelly hand soap, degreasers, disinfectants, pine oil germicide, sanitizers and hard surface cleaners
Owner: James Flanagan
jflana1@nuancesol.com
VP Marketing: Neil Houtsma
Estimated Sales: $ 20 - 50 Million
Number Employees: 50-99
Square Footage: 150000
Parent Co: Bullen Metawest
Type of Packaging: Bulk
Regions Exported to: Central America, Asia, Australia
Percentage of Business in Exporting: 1

47129 Nuchief Sales Inc
2710 Euclid Ave
Wenatchee, WA 98801-5914   509-663-2625
            Fax: 509-662-0299 888-269-4638
nuchief@nwi.net
Grower, packer and exporter of apples and pears

Importers & Exporters / A-Z

President: Randy Steensma
randy@honeybear-nuchief.com
VP: Dave Battis
Quality Control: Ray Vespier
Sales: Joe Defina
Estimated Sales: $279.000
Number Employees: 5-9
Number of Brands: 5
Number of Products: 10
Type of Packaging: Consumer, Food Service
Brands Exported: Crane; Big Check
Regions Exported to: Central America, Asia, Middle East
Percentage of Business in Exporting: 40
Brands Imported: Taylor
Regions Imported from: South America, Asia
Percentage of Business in Importing: 15

47130 Nucon Corporation
111 S Pfingsten Ste 100
Deerfield, IL 60015   847-564-3505
       Fax: 847-509-0011 877-545-0070
       customersupport@brightsparktravel.com
                www.brightsparktravel.com
Manufacturer and exporter of plastic pallets
Owner: Mitchell Slotnick
VP Sales/Marketing: Allan Wasserman
Estimated Sales: $2.5-5,000,000
Number Employees: 20-49
Regions Exported to: Central America, South America, Europe

47131 Nuherbs Company
3820 Penniman Ave
Oakland, CA 94619   510-534-4372
       Fax: 510-534-4384 800-233-4307
       herbals@nuherbs.com www.nuherbs.com
Wholesaler/distributor and importer of Chinese herbs, extract powders, ginseng and spices
President: Pat Kwan
Quality Control: Lorenzo Puertas
Sales Director: Maria Yung
Contact: Nuherbs Co
kevinamiles@hotmail.com
Estimated Sales: $1-3 Million
Number Employees: 5-9
Type of Packaging: Consumer, Bulk
Brands Imported: Herbal Times
Regions Imported from: Asia

47132 Nulaid Foods Inc
200 W 5th St
Ripon, CA 95366-2793   209-599-2121
       Fax: 209-599-5220 www.nulaid.com
Egg products
President: David Crockett
CEO: Christopher Barry
cbarry@bainbridge.com
CFO: Scott Hennecke
Number Employees: 50-99
Type of Packaging: Consumer, Food Service, Private Label, Bulk
Regions Exported to: Central America, Asia, Middle East

47133 Nunes Co Inc
930 Johnson Ave
Salinas, CA 93901   831-751-7500
       Fax: 831-424-4955 employment@foxy.com
                www.foxy.com
Grower and exporter of vegetables
Owner: Susan Canales
CFO: Mike Scarr
VP: David Nunes
VP Marketing: Matt Seeley
VP Sales: Mark Crossgrove
scanales@foxyproduce.com
Production Manager: Jim Nunes
Estimated Sales: $11,100,000
Number Employees: 100-249
Type of Packaging: Consumer, Food Service, Bulk
Regions Exported to: Worldwide

47134 Nunes Farms Marketing
4012 Pete Miller Rd
Gustine, CA 95322-9507   209-862-3033
       Fax: 209-862-1038 www.nunesfarms.com
Processor and exporter of roasted almonds, mixed nuts and pistachios, candies toffee caramel chews, chocolate almonds and toffee almonds
Owner: Maureen Nunes
maureen@nunesfarms.com
Estimated Sales: Under $500,000
Number Employees: 10-19

Regions Exported to: Worldwide

47135 Nuova Distribution Centre
6940 Salashan Pkwy
Bldg - A
Ferndale, WA 98248-8314   360-366-2226
       Fax: 360-366-4015 info@nuovadistribution.com
                www.nuovadistribution.com
Manufacturer and importer of coffee and espresso grinders, sandwich grills and espresso, cappuccino and Italian slush/granita machines
President: Roberto Bresciani
roberto@nuovadistribution.com
Coordinator: Vic Bialas
Estimated Sales: $1 - 3 Million
Number Employees: 10-19
Brands Imported: Nuova Simonelli
Regions Imported from: Europe

47136 Nuova Simonelli
6940 Salashan Pkwy
Ferndale, WA 98248-8314   360-366-2226
       Fax: 360-366-4015 nuovasimonelli@msn.com
                www.nuovadistribution.com
President: Roberto Bresciani
bresciani@nuovadistribution.com
Estimated Sales: $1 - 3 Million
Number Employees: 10-19

47137 Nustef Foods
2440 Cawthra Road #101
Mississauga, ON L5A 2X1
Canada   905-896-3060
       Fax: 905-896-4349 877-306-7562
                info@pizzellecookies.com
Processor and exporter of pizzelle cookies and polenta
President: Cesidio Nucci
Estimated Sales: $4 Million
Number Employees: 60
Square Footage: 48000
Type of Packaging: Consumer, Food Service, Private Label, Bulk
Brands Exported: Reko; Gold'n Polenta
Regions Exported to: Asia, USA
Percentage of Business in Exporting: 75

47138 Nut Factory
PO Box 815
Spokane Valley, WA 99016-0815 509-926-6666
       Fax: 509-926-3300 888-239-5288
       nuts@TheNutFactory.com www.thenutfactory.com
Processor, packager and importer of nuts and dried fruits
President: Gene Cohen
gene_cohen@yahoo.com
Estimated Sales: $1700000
Number Employees: 5-9
Type of Packaging: Consumer

47139 Nutec Manufacturing Inc
908 Garnet Ct
New Lenox, IL 60451-3569   815-722-2800
       Fax: 815-722-2831 815-722-5348
       sales@nutecmfg.com www.nutecmfg.com
Manufacturer, importer and exporter of food forming equipment including patties formers, cubers and conveyors
President: Ken Sandberg
CEO: Zibe Gibson
bids@nutecmfg.com
Vice President: Mike Barnett
Research & Development: Bob Nard
Marketing Director: Mike Barnett
Sales Director: Mike Barnett
IT: Jeff Regan
Production Manager: John Goetzinger
Plant Manager: Ken Galloy
Purchasing: John Goetzinger
Estimated Sales: $2.5-5 Million
Number Employees: 10-19
Square Footage: 20000

47140 Nutra Food Ingredients, LLC
4683 50th Street SE
Kentwood, MI 49512   616-656-9928
       Fax: 419-730-3685
       sales@nutrafoodingredients.com
       www.nutrafoodingredients.com
Functional and nutritional ingredients supplier to the food, beverage, nutraceutical and cosmetics industries

President: Bryon Yang
Director of Business Development: Tim Wolffis
Quality Control: Monica Mylet
monica.mylet@nutrafoodingredients.com
Director of Sales and Marketing: Clarence Harvey
Year Founded: 2004
Estimated Sales: Under $500,000
Number Employees: 1-4
Other Locations:
   Distribution Center
   Edison, NJ
   Distribution Center
   Carson, CA Distribution Center Carson
Regions Exported to: South America, Europe, Asia, North America

47141 NutraSpa Soap
830 Fairway Dr # 200
Bensenville, IL 60106-1345   630-616-9450
       Fax: 630-616-1751 888-616-9450
       Rick@Midwestsalon.com www.midwestsalon.com
President: Richard A Orenstein
Estimated Sales: $3 - 5 Million
Number Employees: 5-9

47142 Nutraceutical International
1400 Kearns Blvd # 2
2nd Floor
Park City, UT 84060-7228   435-655-6000
       Fax: 435-647-3802 800-669-8877
       info@nutraceutical.com www.nutraceutical.com
Manufacturer and exporter of vitamins, minerals and nutritional supplements
President: Bruce R Hough
bruce.hough@nutraceutical.com
CEO/Director/Chairman: Frank W. Gay II
CFO/ VP: Cory J. McQueen
bruce.hough@nutraceutical.com
Executive Vice President: Gary M. Hume
VP Marketing/Sales: Christopher B. Neuberger
Vice President, Operations: Darren Peterson
Estimated Sales: $500,000-$1 Million
Number Employees: 500-999
Type of Packaging: Consumer, Private Label, Bulk
Brands Exported: Sentinel
Regions Exported to: Central America, South America, Europe, Asia, Middle East, Canada, Caribbean, Mexico, Latin America
Percentage of Business in Exporting: 50

47143 Nutraceutics Corp
2900 Brannon Ave
St Louis, MO 63139-1440   314-664-6684
       Fax: 314-664-4639 877-664-6684
       info@nutraceutics.com www.nutraceutics.com
Nutraceutical tablets, capsules, effervescents, tropicals and powers
President: Jennifer Cherry
jcherry@nutraceutics.com
Estimated Sales: $500,000-$1 Million
Number Employees: 20-49
Number of Brands: 50
Number of Products: 1000
Type of Packaging: Consumer, Private Label, Bulk
Regions Exported to: Worldwide
Percentage of Business in Exporting: 10
Regions Imported from: Worldwide

47144 Nutranique Labs
398 Tesconi Court
Santa Rosa, CA 95401-4653   707-545-9017
                Fax: 707-575-4611
Processor and exporter of broccoli sprouts and certified nutraceutical powders including spinach, wheat grass juice, tomato, broccoli, garlic, carrot, green tea, kale and cruciferous blends
General Manager: Mark Martindill
Director Sales/Marketing: Nancy Costa
Operations Manager: Tom Ikesaki
Number Employees: 1-4
Parent Co: FDP USA
Type of Packaging: Bulk
Regions Exported to: Worldwide

47145 Nutrex Hawaii Inc
73-4460 Queen Kaahumanu Hwy
Suite 102
Kailua Kona, HI 96740-2632   808-326-1353
       Fax: 808-329-4533 800-453-1187
       info@nutrex-hawaii.com www.nutrex-hawaii.com
Nutrient-rich dietary supplement

President: Gerald R Cysewski
CEO: Andrew Jacobson
ajacobson@cyanotech.com
Vice President: Glen Johnson
Vice President of Sales and Marketing: Bob Capelli
Sales: Agnes Prehn
Estimated Sales: $500-$1 Million
Number Employees: 50-99
Number of Brands: 2
Parent Co: Cyanotech Corporation
Type of Packaging: Consumer, Private Label, Bulk
Brands Exported: Spirulina Pacifica; BioAstin
Regions Exported to: Worldwide
Percentage of Business in Exporting: 50

47146 Nutri-Cell
1915 Trade Center Way
Naples, FL 34109
866-953-2355
www.nutricell.com
Manufacturer and exporter of animal-free nutritional supplements
Medical Consultant: Dr Derrick De Silva
Medical Consultant: Dr William Judy
Medical Consultant: Dr Bruce Dooley
Number Employees: 1-4
Number of Brands: 2
Number of Products: 7
Square Footage: 12000
Type of Packaging: Consumer, Private Label
Brands Exported: Nutri-Cell
Regions Exported to: Asia, Middle East, Caribbean
Percentage of Business in Exporting: 20

47147 Nutribiotic
PO Box 238
Lakeport, CA 95453
707-263-0411
Fax: 707-263-7844 800-225-4345
info@nutribiotic.com www.nutribiotic.com
Manufacturer and exporter of vitamins and supplements
President: Patrick Fourteau
CFO: Wendy Sexton
Sales Director: Teri Whitestone
Contact: Pam Lausten
sales@nutribiotic.com
Operations Manager: Wendy Brossard
Purchasing/Manufacturing Director: Kenny Ridgeway
Estimated Sales: Less Than $500,000
Number Employees: 1-4
Square Footage: 80000
Brands Exported: Nutribiotic; Citricidal; Traveler's Friend; Prozone
Regions Exported to: Central America, South America, Europe, Asia, Mexico, Canada
Percentage of Business in Exporting: 15
Regions Imported from: Canada
Percentage of Business in Importing: 10

47148 Nutricepts
2208 E 117th St
Burnsville, MN 55337-1265
952-707-0207
Fax: 952-707-0210 800-949-9060
info@nutricepts.com www.nutricepts.com
Processor and exporter of calcium salts, oxygen consuming agents, oxygen scavengers, mold inhibitors, sodium lactate, humectants, flavor enhancers, etc
President: Mark Cater
mw.cater@nutricepts.com
Estimated Sales: $ 3 - 5 Million
Number Employees: 1-4
Type of Packaging: Bulk
Brands Exported: Oxyvac
Regions Exported to: Europe, Asia, Canada
Percentage of Business in Exporting: 20

47149 Nutrifaster Inc
209 S Bennett St
Seattle, WA 98108-2226
206-767-5054
Fax: 206-762-2209 800-800-2641
Sales@Nutrifaster.com www.nutrifaster.com
Manufacturer and exporter of centrifugal juice extractors
President: Bert Robins
Sales/Service: Fred Davies
Manager: Rocco Robins
sales@nutrifaster.com
Estimated Sales: Less than $500,000
Number Employees: 5-9
Type of Packaging: Food Service
Regions Exported to: Worldwide

47150 Nutrilabs
1230 Market St
Suite 401
San Francisco, CA 94102-4801
415-235-6205
Fax: 415-707-2122 877-468-8745
www.nutrilabs.com
Private label manufacturer vitamins and supplements
Owner: Etty Motazedi
VP: Elsie Orell
Contact: Shahin Kashani
skashani@nutrilabs.com
Purchasing Director: Argee Davidovici
Estimated Sales: Less than $500,000
Square Footage: 11200
Type of Packaging: Consumer, Private Label, Bulk

47151 Nutrisoya Foods
4050 Av Pinard
Saint-Hyacinthe, QC J2S 8K4
Canada
450-796-4261
Fax: 450-796-1837 877-769-2645
www.nutrisoya.com
Processor and exporter of soy milk, rice milk and almond mil
President: Nicholas Feldman
Estimated Sales: $4.1 Million
Number Employees: 17
Square Footage: 40000
Type of Packaging: Consumer, Food Service, Private Label, Bulk
Brands Exported: Natura; Nutrisoy
Regions Exported to: Worldwide
Percentage of Business in Exporting: 20

47152 Nutritech Corporation
719 E Haley St
Santa Barbara, CA 93103
805-963-9581
Fax: 805-963-0308 800-235-5727
www.all-one.com
All-in-one multi-vitamin and mineral amino acid powder including rice original and base, green phyto base, active seniors and fruit antioxidant formulas
President/CEO: Douglas Ingoldsby
VP Sales: Lori Herman
Contact: Ron Adams
ron.adams@nutritech.com
VP Operations: Carol Huerta
Estimated Sales: $ 1 - 3 Million
Number Employees: 5-9
Type of Packaging: Consumer
Brands Exported: All One
Regions Exported to: Europe, West Indies

47153 Nutrition & Food Associates
PO Box 47007
Plymouth, MN 55447
763-550-9475
Fax: 763-559-3675 info@nutriform.com
www.nutriform.com
Manufacturer and exporter of computer software for product development, nutrition labeling, recipe and menu analysis
President: Patricia Godfrey
Estimated Sales: Below $ 5 Million
Number Employees: 1-4
Type of Packaging: Food Service
Brands Exported: NutriForm
Regions Exported to: Worldwide
Percentage of Business in Exporting: 10

47154 Nutrition Supply Corp
317 Industrial Cir
Liberty, TX 77575-3447
936-334-0514
Fax: 800-671-3144 888-541-3997
nsc24@nsc24.com www.nsc24.com
Processor and exporter of nutritional supplements, vitamins and encapsulated herbs
CEO: Frank Jordan
fjordan@healthinspirationministry.com
National Sales VP: Mark Campbell
Estimated Sales: Less than $500,000
Number Employees: 10-19
Square Footage: 60000
Type of Packaging: Consumer, Food Service
Brands Exported: NSC-24; NSC-100
Regions Exported to: Worldwide
Percentage of Business in Exporting: 5

47155 Nutritional Counselors of America
1267 Archie Rhinehart Pkwy
Spencer, TN 38585-4612
931-946-3600
Fax: 931-946-3602
Vitamins, minerals, herbs, herbal teas, nutritional supplements, and colon cleaners, neutraceuticals and probiotics
President/CEO: June Wiles
Estimated Sales: $3-$5 Million
Number Employees: 5 to 9
Square Footage: 10000
Type of Packaging: Consumer, Private Label
Brands Exported: 6-N-1
Regions Exported to: Europe, Asia, Africa
Percentage of Business in Exporting: 15

47156 (HQ)Nutritional Labs Intl
1001 S 3rd St W
Missoula, MT 59801-2337
406-273-5493
Fax: 406-273-5498 info@nutritionallabs.com
Nutritional and herbal supplements and nutraceuticals including tablets, and capsules
President & CEO: Terry Benishek
CEO: Peter Malecha
pmalecha@nutritionallabs.com
VP of Research & Development: Titut Yokelson
Director of Quality Assurance: Jera'le Smith
Director of Sales & Marketing: Doug Lefler
Sales Manager: Tito Flores
Director of Operations: Steve Dybdal
Estimated Sales: $ 21.4 Million
Number Employees: 50-99
Square Footage: 18000
Type of Packaging: Consumer, Private Label, Bulk
Regions Exported to: Worldwide

47157 (HQ)Nutritional Research Associates
407 E Broad St
South Whitley, IN 46787
260-723-4931
Fax: 260-723-6297 800-456-4931
pookjg@usa.net
Processor and exporter of vitamins including carotene, A, D and E
Manager: Jonathan Pook
Acting Manager: Jonathan Pook
Estimated Sales: $979000
Number Employees: 5-9
Square Footage: 40000
Type of Packaging: Consumer, Bulk
Brands Exported: Carex; Quitrex
Regions Exported to: Europe, Asia, Australia, Canada, Caribbean, Latin America, Mexico
Percentage of Business in Exporting: 5

47158 Nutritional Specialties
1967 N Glassell St
Orange, CA 92865-4320
714-634-9340
Fax: 714-634-9347 800-333-6168
www.lifetimevitamins.com
Herbal formulas and nutritional supplements; importer of chlorella powder and tablets; exporter of dietary supplements
President: Tom Pinkowski
VP: Tom Krech
VP: Sale Stauch
Estimated Sales: $ 10 - 20 Million
Number Employees: 20-49
Type of Packaging: Private Label, Bulk
Brands Exported: LifeTime
Regions Exported to: Asia, Canada, Mexico
Percentage of Business in Exporting: 20
Brands Imported: Tung Hai
Regions Imported from: Asia

47159 Nutriwest
P.O. Box 950
2132 E Richards St
Douglas, WY 82633
307-358-5066
Fax: 307-358-9208 800-443-3333
www.nutriwest.com
Vitamin products and food and sports drink supplements.
Year Founded: 1982
Estimated Sales: $20-50 Million
Number Employees: 20-49
Square Footage: 60000
Type of Packaging: Consumer, Private Label
Other Locations:
Nutriwest
Alliance, NENutriwest
Brands Exported: Nutri-West; Nutriquest
Regions Exported to: Europe, Africa, Australia, Canada
Percentage of Business in Exporting: 20

Importers & Exporters / A-Z

47160 Nydree Flooring
1115 Vista Park Dr # C
Ste D
Forest, VA 24551-4686   434-525-5252
Fax: 434-525-7437 800-682-5698
www.nydreeflooring.com
Commercial flooring
Owner: Barry Brubaker
VP Radiation: James Myron
Estimated Sales: $500,000-$1 Million
Number Employees: 50-99
Square Footage: 72000
Parent Co: Appliant Radian Energy Corporation
Regions Exported to: Europe
Regions Imported from: Europe

47161 Nyman Manufacturing Company
275 Ferris Ave
Rumford, RI 02916-1033   401-438-3410
Fax: 401-438-5975
Manufacturer and exporter of plastic cups, dinnerware, lids, caps and covers; also, paper cups
Marketing Director: Laura Coupal
General Manager (Paper): Walter Bennett
General Manager (Plastic): Al Domenici
Type of Packaging: Food Service

47162 O'Brien Installations
4435 Corporate Drive
Burlington
Ontario, CA L7L 5T9
Canada   905-336-8245
Fax: 905-331-6494 info@obrieninstall.com
www.obrieninstall.com
Manufacturer and exporter of cranes
President: George O'Brien
Marketing Coordinator: John Marchetti
Sales Director: Wayne Davis
Production Manager: Randy Mullin
Purchasing Manager: Krys Klain
Estimated Sales: $1-10 Million
Number Employees: 50-99
Square Footage: 80000
Parent Co: O'Brien Material Handling
Other Locations:
 O'Brien Material Handling
 Memramock, NBO'Brien Material Handling
Regions Exported to: USA
Percentage of Business in Exporting: 15

47163 O'Dell Corp
13833 Indian Mound Rd
Ware Shoals, SC 29692-3533   864-861-2222
Fax: 864-861-3171 800-342-2843
www.odellcorp.com
Manufacturer, importer and exporter of household and janitorial mops, brooms, brushes and handles
CEO: Wh O'Dell
who@odellcorp.com
VP: Paul O'Dell
Customer Service: Gayle O'Dell
Estimated Sales: $ 10-20 Million
Number Employees: 100-249
Square Footage: 170000
Regions Exported to: Europe, Asia
Percentage of Business in Exporting: 5
Regions Imported from: Central America, South America, Europe
Percentage of Business in Importing: 5

47164 O'Hara Corp
120 Tillson Ave # 1
Rockland, ME 04841-3450   207-594-4444
Fax: 207-594-0407 www.oharabait.com
Processor and exporter of seafood including frozen scallops
Owner: Frank O'Hara
foharajr@oharacooperative.com
Estimated Sales: $4100000
Number Employees: 50-99
Type of Packaging: Consumer, Food Service
Regions Exported to: Japan
Percentage of Business in Exporting: 75

47165 O-At-Ka Milk Prods Co-Op Inc.
700 Ellicott St.
Batavia, NY 14020   585-343-0536
Fax: 585-343-4473 800-828-8152
www.oatkamilk.com
Meal replacement beverages, pet milk replacers, dairy base liqueurs, RTD beverages, high protein products, infant formula, evaporated milk, milk powders, butter, bulk cream and skim milk concentrate.
General Manager: Larry Webster
CEO: Bill Schreiber
CFO: Michael Fuchs
Vice President, Human Resources: Donna Maxwell
Year Founded: 1959
Estimated Sales: $274.56 Million
Number Employees: 400+
Square Footage: 600000
Type of Packaging: Consumer, Food Service, Private Label, Bulk
Brands Exported: Gold Cow
Regions Exported to: Central America, South America, Europe, Middle East, Caribbean
Percentage of Business in Exporting: 5
Regions Imported from: Europe, New Zealand
Percentage of Business in Importing: 2

47166 O-Cedar
2188 Diehl Road
Aurora, IL 60502   219-726-8128
800-543-8105
www.ocedar.com
Manufacturer and exporter of industrial brooms and brushes
Plant Manager: Mike White
Parent Co: O'Cedar Vining

47167 OCS Process Systems
24142 Detroit Rd
Cleveland, OH 44145-1515   440-871-6009
Fax: 440-871-0855 800-482-6226
sales@ocsprocess.com www.ocsprocess.com
Wholesaler/distributor and exporter of sanitary process systems for the dairy, beverage and chemical industries; custom design and installation services available
President: Tim Kloos
CEO: Beth Kloos
Vice President: Alan Pleska
Estimated Sales: $5-10 Million
Number Employees: 20-49
Square Footage: 100000
Parent Co: R&J Corporation of Ohio
Regions Exported to: South America, Europe, Canada, Caribbean, Australia

47168 OFI Markesa Intl
5970 Alcoa Ave
Vernon, CA 90058-3925   323-231-1600
Fax: 323-231-0088
Importer of fresh seafood including shrimp, crab and lobster
President: Brent Church
bc@ofimarkesa.com
VP: Raul Gutierrez
Number Employees: 20-49
Regions Imported from: Mexico

47169 (HQ)OSF
650 Barmac Drive
Toronto, ON M9L 2X8
Canada   416-749-7700
Fax: 416-740-6365 800-465-4000
Manufacturer and exporter of store fixtures, showcases and displays; also, steel shelving
CEO: Harry Shier
Co-Chairman: Milton Shier
Number Employees: 2100
Square Footage: 8800000
Other Locations:
 OSF
 Blackstone, VAOSF
Brands Exported: Vista Classic; Century
Regions Exported to: Worldwide
Percentage of Business in Exporting: 90

47170 OTD Corporation
P.O.Box 510
Hinsdale, IL 60522-0510   630-321-9232
Fax: 574-254-5092
Manufacturer and exporter of aluminum containers, racks and pallets
President: James Ogle
Controller: Jean Chatman
Estimated Sales: $20-30 Million
Number Employees: 1-4
Regions Exported to: Worldwide
Percentage of Business in Exporting: 10

47171 OTP Industrial Solutions
3601 N Fruitridge Ave
Terre Haute, IN 47804-1756   812-466-2734
Fax: 812-466-2831 860-953-7632
www.otpnet.com
Manufacturer and exporter of overhead bridge cranes, wire rope winches, conveyors and reciprocating feeders
Manager: Walt Tompkins
CEO/Engineer: Steve White
CFO: Jim Bennett
Vice President: Joe Goda
Marketing Director: Dave Parks
Sales Director: Tom Bland
Public Relations: Tom Bland
Plant Manager: Steve Rowe
Purchasing Manager: Jerry Taylor
Estimated Sales: $16.5 Million
Number Employees: 10-19
Square Footage: 40000
Brands Exported: Pumps; Cranks; Conveyor
Regions Exported to: Central America, South America, Europe
Percentage of Business in Exporting: 5

47172 (HQ)OWD
PO Box 1260
Tupper Lake, NY 12986-0260   518-359-2944
Fax: 518-359-2994 800-836-1693
www.jarden.com/phoenix.zhtml?c=72395&p=irol...ID.
Manufacturer and exporter of plastic spoons, forks, knives, straws, cups and plates
CEO: James E. Lillie
CFO: John Breshahan
Vice President: Rachel Wilson
R & D: Allison Malkin
VP Sales: Al Huggins
Estimated Sales: Less than $500,000
Number Employees: 100-249
Square Footage: 260000
Parent Co: Jarden Corporation
Other Locations:
 O.W.D.
 La Fayette, GAO.W.D.
Brands Exported: Lady Dianne
Regions Exported to: South America, Middle East

47173 OXO International
601 West 26th St
Suite 1050
New York, NY 10001   212-242-3333
Fax: 717-709-5350 www.oxo.com
Manufacturer of kitchen utensils and appliances
President: Edward Ahn
eahn@oxo.com
VP, Sales: Michael Cleary
Estimated Sales: $2.5-5 Million
Number Employees: 50-99
Number of Products: 1000
Type of Packaging: Consumer
Regions Exported to: Central America, South America, Europe, Asia
Percentage of Business in Exporting: 20
Regions Imported from: Asia

47174 Oak Barrel Winecraft
1443 San Pablo Ave
Berkeley, CA 94702-1045   510-849-0400
Fax: 510-528-6543 info@oakbarrel.com
www.oakbarrel.com
Oak barrels for wine and beer making, bottles and stoppers for wine, vinegar starter culture and bottling and brewery machinery; importer of wine presses, crushers and barrels; also, wholesaler/distributor of vinegar starter cultureand barrels
President and CFO: Bernard Rooney
info@oakbarrel.com
Vice President: Homer Smith
Estimated Sales: $ 5 - 10 Million
Number Employees: 1-4
Square Footage: 12000
Regions Imported from: Europe
Percentage of Business in Importing: 20

47175 Oak International
1160 White St
Sturgis, MI 49091   269-651-9790
Fax: 269-651-7849 www.cimcool.com
Manufacturer and exporter of FDA approved cutting, stamping and drawing oils; also, grinding coolants and cleaners
Sr. VP Sales/Operations: F Edwards
Contact: Michelle Dressler
michelle_dressler@milacron.com
Plant Manager: Jim Phillips
Estimated Sales: $ 5 - 10 Million
Number Employees: 10-19
Square Footage: 52000

Regions Exported to: Worldwide
Percentage of Business in Exporting: 20

47176 Oak Leaf Confections
416-751-0740
Fax: 416-751-3656 877-261-7887
info@sweetworks.net sweetworks.net/oakleaf
Processor and exporter of confectionery products including malt balls, gum balls, bubble gum, hard candies and freeze pops
Owner/President: Philip Terranova
Number Employees: 300
Square Footage: 560000
Parent Co: SweetWorks Confections LLC
Type of Packaging: Consumer, Private Label, Bulk
Regions Exported to: Europe

47177 Oakrun Farm Bakery
58 Carluke Road West
PO Box 81070
Ancaster, ON L9G 3L1
Canada   905-648-1818
Fax: 905-648-8252 800-263-6422
customerservice@oakrun.com www.oakrun.com
Processor and exporter of English muffins, pastries, bagels, muffins, danish, tarts, crumpets, and cakes.
President: Roger Dickhout
COO: Tony Tristani
Research & Development: Maria Pais
Quality Control: Rita Fajardo
Marketing Director: Andra Zondervan
VP Sales: Dave MacPhail
Plant Manager: Chet Czerny
Purchasing: Christine Richer
Number Employees: 100-249
Square Footage: 1068000
Type of Packaging: Consumer, Food Service, Private Label
Regions Exported to: Worldwide

47178 Occidental Foods International, LLC
4 Middlebury Blvd
Suite 3, Aspen Business Park
Randolph, NJ 07869   973-970-9220
Fax: 973-970-9222 info@occidentalfoods.com
www.occidentalfoods.com
Representatives and importers of bulk spices and seeds, including paprika; pure mancha saffron; chilies dried, crushed and ground; turmeric; granulated garlic and garlic powder; cardamom; annatto, allspice and sesame seeds
President: Scott Hall
Chief Financial Officer: Denise Hall
Estimated Sales: $4.9 Million
Type of Packaging: Food Service, Bulk
Regions Exported to: Central America, South America, Europe
Percentage of Business in Exporting: 10
Regions Imported from: Central America, South America, Europe, Asia, Africa
Percentage of Business in Importing: 50

47179 Ocean Beauty Seafoods Inc
1100 W Ewing St
Seattle, WA 98119   206-285-6800
800-365-8950
info@oceanbeauty.com www.oceanbeauty.com
Manufacturer and distributor of seafood.
President & CEO: Mark Palmer
CFO: Tony Ross
VP, Retail Sales: Ron Christianson
Year Founded: 1910
Estimated Sales: $409 Million
Number Employees: 1,000-4,000
Type of Packaging: Food Service
Other Locations:
  Ocean Beauty Seafood Facility Boston, MA
  Ocean Beauty Seafood Facility Cordova, AK
  Ocean Beauty Seafood Facility Alitak, AK
  Ocean Beauty Seafood Facility Kodiak, AK
  Ocean Beauty Seafood Facility Los Angeles, CA
  Ocean Beauty Seafood Facility Monroe, WA
  Ocean Beauty Seafood FacilityCordova
Brands Exported: Salmon; Halibut Steaks; Fillets
Brands Imported: Swordfish; Tuna; Mahi Mahi; Shark; Seabass

47180 Ocean Cliff Corp
362 S Front St
New Bedford, MA 02740-5745   508-990-7900
Fax: 508-990-7950
gregwhite@oceancliffcorporation.com
www.oceancliffcorporation.com
Fish and seafood liquid and powder extracts and spices including shrimp, clam, crab, fish, lobster and mussel
Owner: G White
Sales: Peter Shephard
gwhite@oceancliffcorporation.com
Estimated Sales: $ 2.5-5,000,000
Number Employees: 5-9
Square Footage: 40000
Type of Packaging: Bulk
Regions Exported to: Europe, Canada
Percentage of Business in Exporting: 10
Regions Imported from: Europe

47181 Ocean Frost
471 Mulberry St
Newark, NJ 07114-2736   973-622-3200
Fax: 973-622-4949 ocfrost@optonline.net
Importer and wholesaler/distributor of frozen seafood in the New York metro area; serving restaurants, fish markets, hotels and institutions
Owner: A Joo
jooalavoura@claro.net.co
Estimated Sales: $10-20 Million
Number Employees: 20-49
Square Footage: 11000
Type of Packaging: Food Service

47182 Ocean Garden Products Inc
10085 Scripps Ranch Ct # A
San Diego, CA 92131-1274   858-790-3200
Fax: 858-790-3337 800-474-7467
marketing@oceangarden.net
www.oceangarden.com
Importer and exporter of canned and frozen seafood including shrimp, lobster, octopus, squid, scallops, salmon, cod, abalone, sardines and caracol
President: Javier Gorella
jgorella@oceangarden.net
CFO: Frank Bamancotto
CEO: Javier Corella
Quality Control: Arturo Carlos
Marketing Director: Janet Vogel
VP Sales: John Filose
VP Operations: Emilio Mitre
Purchasing: Ron Boren
Year Founded: 1957
Estimated Sales: $12.4 Million
Number Employees: 20-49
Number of Products: 50
Regions Exported to: Worldwide

47183 Ocean King International
1680 S Garfield Avenue
Suite 202
Alhambra, CA 91801-5413   626-289-9399
Fax: 626-300-8177
Seafood
President/CEO: Jimmie Dang
CFO: Miling Shua
Vice President: Richard Mendelson
Secretary: Jorge Pardinas

47184 Ocean Pride Fisheries
136 Jacquard Rd
PO BOX 402
Lower Wedgeport, NS B0W 2B0
Canada   902-663-4579
Fax: 902-663-2698 jules@oceanpridefisheries.com
www.oceanpridefisheries.com
Processor and exporter of smoked salmon, cod and haddock
President: Milton Leblanc
Chief Operating Officer: Jules Leblanc
Estimated Sales: $1.3 Million
Number Employees: 10
Type of Packaging: Consumer, Food Service, Bulk
Percentage of Business in Exporting: 10

47185 Ocean Spray International
One Ocean Spray Dr.
Lakeville-Middleboro, MA 02349
800-662-3263
www.oceanspray.com
Manufacturer of bottled juices and fruit ingredient supplier.
Interim CEO: James White
Senior VP/CFO: Daniel Cunha
Global Chief Innovation Officer: Rizal Hamdallah
VP, Marketing Services: Yash Sikand
COO: Brian Schiegg
Year Founded: 1930
Estimated Sales: $2.2 Billion
Number Employees: 2,000
Number of Brands: 26
Square Footage: 99000
Type of Packaging: Consumer, Food Service
Other Locations:
  Middleboro, MA
  Lehigh Valley, PA
  Wisconsin Rapids, WI
  Markham, WA
  Kenosha, WI
  Henderson, NVLehigh Valley
Regions Exported to: Worldwide

47186 Ocean Union Company
2100 Riverside Pkwy
Suite 129
Lawrenceville, GA 30043-5927   770-995-1957
Fax: 770-513-8662
Seafood, snapper, grouper, lobster, crab, tuna, eel, mackerel
President: Jackie Tsai

47187 Oceanfood Sales
1909 East Hastings Street
Vancouver, BC V5L 1T5
Canada   604-255-1414
Fax: 604-255-1787 877-255-1414
sales@oceanfoodsales.com www.oceanfoodsales.com
Processor and exporter of smoked salmon
VP: Robert Graham
VP, Controller: Louise Graham
Sales And Marketing Manager: Dave Slade
Customer Service: Dorothy Chaves
Production Manager: John Makowhichuk
Estimated Sales: $7.9 Million
Number Employees: 16
Type of Packaging: Consumer, Food Service, Private Label, Bulk
Regions Exported to: Asia

47188 Odenberg Engineering
4038 Seaport Blvd
West Sacramento, CA 95691   916-371-0700
Fax: 916-371-5471 800-688-8396
sales@odenberg.com
Manufacturer and exporter of batch steam peelers, chillers/freezers and sorters
President: Maurice Moynihan
VP: Ashley Hunter
Contact: Noel Basquel
noel.basquel@odenberg.com
Production Sales Manager: Diamond Meagher
Estimated Sales: $ 10 - 20,000,000
Number Employees: 20-49
Parent Co: Odenberg Engineering
Regions Exported to: Canada, Italy, Ireland

47189 Oerlikon Leybold Vacuum
5700 Mellon Rd
Export, PA 15632-8900   724-327-5700
Fax: 724-325-3577 www.oerlikon.com
Manufacturer, importer and exporter of vacuum pumps and systems
Chief Executive Officer: Andreas Widl
Vice President: P Albert
Manager of Technical Services: Joachim GstA hl
Marketing Director: M Vitale
Head of Sales: Werner SchA dler
Manager: Jim Hupp
Chief Operating Officer, Chief Operating: Wolfgang Ehrk
Plant Manager: Dennis Pellegrino
Number Employees: 1-4
Square Footage: 596000
Parent Co: Leybold AG
Regions Exported to: Central America, South America, Europe, Asia
Regions Imported from: Europe

47190 Oess Foods Inc
169 Olive St
New Haven, CT 06511-4980   203-907-4005
Fax: 203-907-4008 oreste@oessefoods.com
Owner: Oreste Speciale
info@oessefoods.com
Estimated Sales: Less Than $500,000
Number Employees: 1-4

Importers & Exporters / A-Z

47191 Office General des EauxMinerales
5260 Avenue Notre-Dame-De-Grace
Montreal, QC H4A 1K9
Canada   514-482-7221
          Fax: 514-482-7093 www.saintjustin.ca
Bottler and exporter of carbonated natural mineral water
President: Nicole Lelievre
Number Employees: 23
Type of Packaging: Food Service
Brands Exported: Saint Justin

47192 Ogden Manufacturing Company
103 Gamma Drive
Pittsburgh, PA 15238   412-967-3906
         Fax: 412-967-3930 cs@ogdenmfg.com
                           www.ogdenmfg.com
Manufacturer and exporter of electric heating elements and microprocessor-based temperature controls
VP: Randy Lee
Marketing Manager: Gordon Hollander
Contact: Barbara Lee
cs@ogdenmfg.com
Estimated Sales: $ 5-10 Million
Number Employees: 150-250
Square Footage: 260000
Regions Exported to: Central America, South America, Europe, Asia, Australia

47193 Ohaus Corp
7 Campus Dr # 300
Parsippany, NJ 07054-4413   973-377-9000
         Fax: 973-593-0359   800-672-7722
                 marla.bormann@ohaus.com
Manufacturer and exporter of electronic, analytical, precision top loading and moisture balances; also, portable and bench scales
President: Ted Xia
ted.xia@ohaus.com
CFO: Peter Minder
Estimated Sales: $ 25 - 50 Million
Number Employees: 250-499
Brands Exported: Ohaus
Regions Exported to: Central America, South America, Europe, Asia, Middle East

47194 Ohio Magnetics Inc
5400 Dunham Rd
Maple Heights, OH 44137-3653   216-662-8484
         Fax: 216-662-2911   800-486-6446
                 sales@ohiomagnetics.com
                 www.ohiomagnetics.com
Manufacturer and exporter of magnetic separators, metal detectors and conveyors
Manager: John Wohlgemuph
Sales Manager: Ken Richendollar
General Manager: John Wohlgemuth
Plant Manager: Tim Essick
Purchasing: Bob Zajc
Estimated Sales: $ 10-20 Million
Number Employees: 20-49
Square Footage: 288000
Parent Co: Ohio Magnetics
Brands Exported: Stearns
Regions Exported to: South America, Asia, Mexico
Percentage of Business in Exporting: 10

47195 Ohlson Packaging
490 Constitution Dr
Taunton, MA 02780-7389   508-977-0004
         Fax: 508-977-0007 sales@ohlsonpack.com
                           www.ohlsonpack.com
Manufacturer and exporter of automatic stainless steel weighing machinery for bagging or boxing pasta, frozen foods, candy, produce, etc
Owner: John Ohlson Jr
Vice President: John Ohlson
Estimated Sales: $ 7 Million
Number Employees: 10-19
Regions Exported to: Worldwide
Percentage of Business in Exporting: 3

47196 Ok Industries
PO Box 1787
Fort Smith, AR 72902   479-783-4186
         Fax: 479-784-1358   800-635-9441
                             www.tenderbird.com
Fresh and frozen chicken.
President/CEO: Trent Goins
CFO: Scott Hunter
SVP, Supply Chain: Russ Bragg
Contact: Randall Goins
fgoins@okfoods.com
Estimated Sales: $20-50 Million
Number Employees: 100-249
Number of Brands: 2
Parent Co: OK Industries
Type of Packaging: Consumer, Food Service, Private Label
Regions Exported to: Asia, Mexico, Philipines, Russia

47197 Ok Uniform Co Inc
253 Church St # B
New York, NY 10013-3438   212-791-9789
         Fax: 212-791-9795   866-700-5765
                             www.okuniform.com
Manufacturer and exporter of uniforms including restaurant wear, formal wear and work/industrial wear; a complete line of anywhere shoes/clogs; full line of tuxedos and formal wear for men and women. We also carry disposable uniformscoveralls, etc
CEO: Ellie Cohen
CFO: Ezra Cohen
Sales Manager: Ivan Cohen
Public Relations: Taimara K
Manager: George Gross
Estimated Sales: $1-2.5 Million
Number Employees: 5-9
Number of Brands: 4

47198 Okura USA Inc
9970 Lakeview Ave
Lenexa, KS 66219-2502   913-599-1111
         Fax: 913-599-0096   800-772-1187
                 www.vanguardshrinkfilms.com
Manufacturer and importer of polyolefin heat shrinkable packaging films
President: John Campbell
john.campbell@okura-usa.com
Sales Manager: Mike Coyle
Sales Manager: Bill Filer
Estimated Sales: $ 1 - 2.5 Million
Number Employees: 5-9
Square Footage: 50000
Parent Co: Okura Industrial Company
Brands Imported: Vanguard 100; Vanguard 210; Vanguard-XV; Vanguard 501
Regions Imported from: Asia
Percentage of Business in Importing: 100

47199 Olcott Plastics
95 N 17th St
St Charles, IL 60174-1636   630-584-0555
         Fax: 630-584-5655   888-313-5277
         sales@olcottplastics.com www.olcottplastics.com
Manufacturer, importer and exporter of plastic containers, jars and jar closures.
President: Joe Brodner
joe.brodner@olcottplastics.com
CFO: Mark Herzog
Quality Manager: Perry Norsworthy
Sales Manager: Troy Rusch
Human Resources Director: Sandy Allen
Purchasing: Teresa Casey
Estimated Sales: $12.6 Million
Number Employees: 50-99
Square Footage: 120000
Type of Packaging: Consumer, Private Label, Bulk
Regions Exported to: Central America
Percentage of Business in Exporting: 2
Regions Imported from: South America, Latin America, Mexico
Percentage of Business in Importing: 3

47200 Old Dominion Box Company
PO Box 77
Burlington, NC 27216-0077   336-226-4491
                      Fax: 336-570-1217
Manufacturer and exporter of small paper and set-up boxes
Estimated Sales: $500,000-$1 Million
Number Employees: 4
Parent Co: Mark IV Industries

47201 Old Dominion Wood Products
800 Craddock St
PO Box 11226
Lynchburg, VA 24501-1700   434-846-3019
         Fax: 434-846-1213   800-245-6382
         csodwp@att.net www.olddominionwood.net
Manufacturer, importer and exporter of chairs, tray stands, laminated trash receptacles, booths, tabletops and table bases
Owner: George R Harris
Customer Service: Sherri Stilwell
Sales Director: Dennis Hunt
IT: Cindi Rice
crice@olddominionwoodproducts.com
Estimated Sales: $ 3 - 5 Million
Number Employees: 10-19
Number of Products: 1000
Square Footage: 120000
Brands Exported: Old Dominion
Regions Exported to: Worldwide
Percentage of Business in Exporting: 5
Regions Imported from: Europe, Asia
Percentage of Business in Importing: 30

47202 Old Mansion Inc
3811 Corporate Rd
PO Box 1839
Petersburg, VA 23805   804-862-9889
                               800-476-1877
                          www.oldmansion.com
Quality spices, seasonings, coffee and teas
Sales: Tom Mullen
Number Employees: 20-49
Type of Packaging: Consumer, Food Service, Private Label, Bulk
Brands Imported: Old Mansion
Regions Imported from: Central America, South America, Europe, Asia, Middle East, Latin America
Percentage of Business in Importing: 20

47203 Old Sacramento Popcorn Company
1011 St
Sacramento, CA 95814   916-446-1980
                      Fax: 916-442-2676 www.oslhp.net
Processor and exporter of popcorn
Owner: Jim Scott
Estimated Sales: Less than $150,000
Number Employees: 1-4
Regions Exported to: Europe, Asia, Middle East
Percentage of Business in Exporting: 5

47204 Olde Country Reproductions Inc
145 N Hartley St
York, PA 17401-3334   717-848-1859
         Fax: 717-845-7129   800-358-3997
                             pewtarex@epix.net
Manufacturer and exporter of pewter plates, mugs, goblets, trays, skillets, platters, bowls, servers, candle sticks, ice coolers, ladles, pans and kettles
President: W Swartz
VP Sales: Chris Kiehl
Manager: Chris Kiehl
ckiehl@pewtarex.com
Estimated Sales: $ 20 - 50 Million
Number Employees: 20-49
Number of Brands: 2
Number of Products: 2000
Square Footage: 50000
Type of Packaging: Bulk
Brands Exported: Pewtarex, York Pewter
Regions Exported to: Europe, Asia, Middle East
Percentage of Business in Exporting: 5

47205 Olde Tyme Food Corporation
775 Benton Drive
East Longmeadow, MA 01028-3215   413-525-4101
         Fax: 413-525-3621   800-356-6533
Snack foods including candy apples, cotton candy, waffles, waffle cones, peanuts
President: David Baker
Sales Director: David Wedderspoon
Estimated Sales: $1.7 Million
Number Employees: 21
Square Footage: 100000
Parent Co: Hampton Farms
Type of Packaging: Consumer, Food Service, Private Label, Bulk

47206 Ole Hickory Pits
333 N Main St
Cape Girardeau, MO 63701-7205   573-334-3377
         Fax: 573-334-3377   800-223-9667
                     main@olehickorypits.com
                     www.olehickorypits.com
Manufacturer and exporter of commercial barbecue pits

President: David Knight
main@olehickorypits.com
CFO: David Scherer
Sales Coordinator: Margaret Wiggins
Estimated Sales: Below $ 5 Million
Number Employees: 20-49
Square Footage: 40000
Type of Packaging: Consumer, Food Service, Private Label, Bulk
Brands Exported: Ole Hickory Pits
Regions Exported to: Central America, Europe, Canada, Caribbean, Mexico, Australia
Percentage of Business in Exporting: 5

47207 Olive Can Company
1111 Bowes Rd
Elgin, IL 60123   847-468-7474
          Fax: 847-468-7695
Manufacturer and exporter of decorative custom tins and trays
Executive VP/General Manager: Virginia Price
National Sales Manager: Tom Doyle
Trade Show Manager: Carolyn Wisniewski
Number Employees: 125
Square Footage: 288000
Regions Exported to: Canada, Caribbean
Percentage of Business in Exporting: 3

47208 Oliver Products Company
511 6th St NW
Grand Rapids, MI 49504   616-456-5290
    Fax: 616-456-5820 www.oliverproducts.com
President: John R Green
CFO: Jim Johnson
R&D: Jack Knodlauch
Quality Control: Loura Keena
Contact: Lisa Miller
lmiller@oliverquality.com
Estimated Sales: $ 50 - 100 Million
Number Employees: 100-249

47209 Olivier's Candies
2828 54th Ave SE
Calgary, AB T2C 0A7
Canada   403-266-6028
    Fax: 403-266-6029 info@oliviers.ca
          www.oliviers.ca
Chocolate, hard candy, brittles, barks
President: Wally Marcolin
Secretary: Rick Jeffrey
Number Employees: 10-19
Type of Packaging: Consumer, Bulk
Regions Exported to: Asia, United States

47210 Olney Machinery
9057 Dopp Hill Road
PO Box 280
Westernville, NY 13486   315-827-4208
    Fax: 315-827-4249 info@olneymachinery.com
          www.olneymachinery.com
Manufacturer, importer and exporter of canning and food packing machinery
President: W Floyd Olney
Secretary and Treasurer: J Olney
Estimated Sales: $2.5-5 Million
Number Employees: 20-49
Regions Exported to: Central America, South America, Europe, Asia, Middle East, Canada
Percentage of Business in Exporting: 15
Percentage of Business in Importing: 1

47211 Olymel
2200 Pratte Ave.
Suite 400
Saint-Hyacinthe, QC J2S 4B6
Canada   450-771-0400
    Fax: 450-773-6436 www.olymel.com
Pork and poultry.
President/CEO: Rejean Nadeau
First VP: Paul Beauchamp
Senior VP, Sales/Marketing: Richard Davies
Year Founded: 1991
Estimated Sales: $3.6 Billion
Number Employees: 13,000
Number of Brands: 3
Type of Packaging: Private Label, Bulk
Regions Exported to: Central America, South America
Percentage of Business in Exporting: 5
Regions Imported from: USA
Percentage of Business in Importing: 5

47212 Olympia International
2166 Spring Creek Road
Belvidere, IL 61008-9507   815-547-5972
          Fax: 815-547-5973
pickles, mushrooms, horseradish, marinated peppers, beets and salads
President: Greg Bodak
Contact: Arturo Gonzalez
arturo@olympiaintl.com
Estimated Sales: $260,000
Number Employees: 1
Percentage of Business in Exporting: 90
Regions Imported from: Europe, Asia

47213 Olympic Foods
5625 W Thorpe Rd
Spokane, WA 99224   509-455-8059
          Fax: 509-455-8329
fruit juice
President: Doug Koffinke
CEO: Howard Chow
CFO: Richard Cook
Contact: Valerie Biladeau
jkskwilcox@msn.com
Estimated Sales: $1-2.5 Million
Number Employees: 12
Square Footage: 348000
Type of Packaging: Consumer, Food Service, Private Label
Brands Exported: Heritage Foods
Regions Exported to: Canada

47214 Olympus Dairy
33 Ludwig Street
Littleferry, NJ 07643   718-777-2150
          Fax: 718-606-2220
Dairy importer.
President: Anastasius Baradakis
Vice President/Sales: Nickolaos Nikolaou
Marketing: Dimitrios Stamoulakis

47215 Omaha Meat Processors
6016 Grover St
Omaha, NE 68106-4358   402-554-1965
    Fax: 402-554-0224 omahameats@aol.com
Beef, pork steaks, sausage
President: David Kousgaard
omahameats@aol.com
Estimated Sales: $30 Million
Number Employees: 20-49
Square Footage: 9000
Type of Packaging: Food Service

47216 Omaha Steaks Inc
          800-960-8400
          www.omahasteaks.com
sausage, steak, veal and poultry; also desserts and wine
President: Bruce Simon
basimon@aol.com
Senior VP: Todd Simon
Number Employees: 1000-4999
Type of Packaging: Consumer, Food Service
Brands Exported: Omaha Steaks International
Regions Exported to: Caribbean
Percentage of Business in Exporting: 1

47217 Omcan Inc.
3115 Pepper Mill Court
Mississauga, ON L5L 4X5
Canada   800-465-0234
    Fax: 905-607-0234 sales@omcan.com
          www.omcan.com
Manufacturer and importer of food processing machinery
Estimated Sales: $ 500,000 - $ 1 Million
Number Employees: 1-4
Square Footage: 600000
Regions Imported from: Europe
Percentage of Business in Importing: 70

47218 Omcan Manufacturing & Distributing Company
3115 Pepper Mill Court
Mississauga, ON L5L 4X5
Canada   905-607-0234
    Fax: 905-828-0897 800-465-0234
          sales@omcan.com www.omcan.com

Manufacturer and exporter of butcher knives; personalized knives available; wholesaler/distributor of food service equipment and supplies including cutters, slicers, choppers, bowls, vegetable processors, mixers, etc.; serving the foodservice market
Owner: Tar Nella
General Manager: Tarcisio Nella
Number Employees: 30
Square Footage: 600000
Regions Exported to: United Kingdom
Percentage of Business in Exporting: 5

47219 Omega Design Corp
211 Philips Rd
Exton, PA 19341-1336   610-363-6555
    Fax: 610-524-7398 800-346-0191
    sales1@omegadesign.com www.omegadesign.com
Manufacturer and exporter of secondary orienters, desiccant feeders, plastic bottle unscramblers, wrap around case packers and shrink bundling, tray loading and wrapping equipment; importer of wrap around case packers and tray loadingand wrapping equipment
President: Glenn Siegele
gsiegele@omegadesign.com
VP Sales/Marketing Manager: Randy Caspersen
International Sales Manager: Niall McDermott
Food/Beverage Manager: Paul Sherman
Estimated Sales: $ 10 - 20 Million
Number Employees: 50-99
Square Footage: 90000
Regions Exported to: Worldwide
Percentage of Business in Exporting: 20
Regions Imported from: Europe
Percentage of Business in Importing: 10

47220 Omega Industrial Products Inc
795 N Progress Dr
Saukville, WI 53080-1613   262-284-4184
    Fax: 262-284-4199 800-279-6634
    omega@omegaindl.com www.omegaindl.com
Manufacturer and exporter of conveyor and wall guards, handrails and steel safety barriers stairs
President: John Weber
omega@omegaindl.com
CFO: John Weber
Operations Manager: James Pautmann
Number Employees: 10-19
Square Footage: 27000
Brands Exported: Omega; Trak-Shield; Quick Step
Regions Exported to: Canada, Caribbean, Mexico
Percentage of Business in Exporting: 5

47221 (HQ)Omega Nutrition
6515 Aldrich Rd
Bellingham, WA 98226
    Fax: 604-253-4228 800-661-3529
          info@omeganutrition.com
          www.omeganutrition.com
Organic oils: borage, flax, hazelnut, sesame, safflower, sunflower, pistachio, almond and canola; hazelnut flours
Owner: Bob Walbert
Marketing Director: Robert Gaffney
Contact: Simon Hatton
graphics@omeganutrition.com
Estimated Sales: $6.5 Million
Number Employees: 20-49
Square Footage: 64000
Type of Packaging: Food Service, Private Label
Other Locations:
  OMEGA Nutrition U.S.A.
  Vancouver, BCOMEGA Nutrition U.S.A.
Brands Exported: Omegaflo; Nutriflax
Regions Exported to: Middle East, Canada, Australia
Percentage of Business in Exporting: 50

47222 Omega Produce Company
PO Box 277
Nogales, AZ 85628   520-281-0410
          Fax: 520-281-1010
cucumbers and bell peppers
President: George Gotsis
ggomega1@aol.com
Secretary/Treasurer, VP: Toru Fujiwara
Office Manager: Norah Romero
VP Sales: J Nick Gotsis
Estimated Sales: $10-20 Million
Number Employees: 10-19
Regions Exported to: Europe, Asia, Canada

487

Importers & Exporters / A-Z

47223 Omega Products Inc
6291 Lyters Ln
Harrisburg, PA 17111-4622   717-561-1105
Fax: 717-561-1298   800-633-3401
omega@omegajuicers.com
www.omegajuicers.com
Manufacturer and exporter of fruit and vegetable juice extractors
President: Rob Boyd
rboyd@omegajuicers.com
VP Sales: James Pascotti
Estimated Sales: $1600000
Number Employees: 10-19
Square Footage: 80000
Brands Exported: Omega
Regions Exported to: Central America, South America, Europe, Asia, Middle East, Canada, Mexico
Percentage of Business in Exporting: 20

47224 Omega Protein
610 Menhaden Rd.
Reedville, VA 22539
hq@omegaprotein.com   804-453-6262
www.omegaprotein.com
Menhaden oil, red meat and fish.
President/CEO: Bret Scholtes
Executive VP/CFO: Andrew Johannesen
President, Animal Nutrition Division: Dr. Mark Griffin
Vice President, Operations: Montgomery Deihl
Year Founded: 1913
Estimated Sales: $168 Million
Number Employees: 546
Parent Co: Cooke Inc.
Regions Exported to: Central America, South America, Europe, Asia, Canada

47225 Omicron Steel Products Company
11701 Park Lane S
Jamaica, NY 11418-1014   718-805-3400
Fax: 718-805-3401
Manufacturer, importer and exporter of shelving, worktables, benches, counters, racks, storage cabinets, carts, hand trucks, conveyors, store fixtures, chairs and stools
Sales Manager: Jerry Czajowski
Estimated Sales: $ 1 - 5 Million
Number Employees: 6
Parent Co: Omicron Group
Regions Exported to: Central America, South America, Europe, Asia, Middle East
Percentage of Business in Exporting: 40
Percentage of Business in Importing: 2

47226 Omni Controls Inc
5309 Technology Dr
Tampa, FL 33647-3523   813-971-5001
Fax: 813-960-4779   800-783-6664
sales@omnicontrols.com   www.omnicontrols.com
Manufacturer and exporter of pressure, flow, temperature and sanitary transmitters
President: Bryan Nye
zacharyillare@aforesearch.com
Accountant: Dianne Delarenzo
Sales Director: Frank Most
Estimated Sales: $2.5-5 Million
Number Employees: 1-4
Square Footage: 2000
Brands Exported: Krohne America; Ametek; Delta; Aquavivol; GIC
Regions Exported to: Central America, South America
Percentage of Business in Exporting: 30

47227 Omni Craft Inc
5640 Feltl Rd
Hopkins, MN 55343-7911   952-988-9944
Fax: 952-938-2035
Manufacturer, exporter and designer of exhibits and displays
Owner: Mike Rendahl
mrendahl@omnicraft.com
Estimated Sales: Less Than $500,000
Number Employees: 1-4
Square Footage: 120000
Type of Packaging: Consumer, Food Service
Regions Exported to: Worldwide
Percentage of Business in Exporting: 2

47228 Omni International
935 Cobb Place Blvd NW # 110
Kennesaw, GA 30144-6802   770-421-0058
Fax: 770-421-0206   800-776-4431
omni@omni-inc.com   www.omni-inc.com
Manufacturer and exporter of mechanical shear homogenizers and dispersers suited for R/D, QA/QC, content analysis, fat replacement, beverages, dairy, etc
President: Karl Jahn
omni@omni-inc.com
Vice President: James Partridge
Quality Control: Eric Ruwe
Manufacturing Manager: Pete Tortorelli
Estimated Sales: Below $ 5 Million
Number Employees: 20-49
Square Footage: 40000
Type of Packaging: Food Service, Private Label
Regions Exported to: Worldwide
Percentage of Business in Exporting: 40

47229 Omni Metalcraft Corporation
4040 Us Highway 23 N
Alpena, MI 49707   989-358-7000
Fax: 989-358-7020   info@omni.com
www.omni.com
Manufacturer and exporter of skatewheel, belt, roller, vertical and chain conveyors
Chairman of the Board: Ronald W Winter
VP Sales/Marketing: Paul Diamond
Contact: Leeck Austin
austinl@omni.com
Estimated Sales: $20-50 Million
Number Employees: 50-99
Square Footage: 130000
Regions Exported to: Canada

47230 Omni Pacific Company
2499 N Main St Ste 250
Walnut Creek, CA 94597   925-933-0695
Fax: 925-933-0691
Wholesaler/distributor and exporter of canned fruits, vegetables and fish products; serving government institutions and schools
President: Brett Roberts
Estimated Sales: $5-10 Million
Number Employees: 10-19
Square Footage: 8800
Type of Packaging: Food Service
Brands Exported: California Cola; Island Sun
Regions Exported to: Central America, South America, Europe, Asia, Caribbean, Latin America
Percentage of Business in Exporting: 90

47231 Omnicor
11034 N 23rd Dr # 103
Phoenix, AZ 85029-4752   602-870-0534
Fax: 602-870-9877   info@wikkistix.com
www.wikkistix.com
Owner: Kem Clark
kclark@wickysticks.com
Estimated Sales: $ 5 - 10 Million
Number Employees: 10-19

47232 Omnion
185 Plain St Rockland
Rockland, MA 02370-0614   781-878-7200
Fax: 781-878-7465   omnion@world.std.com
Manufacturer and exporter of oxidative stability analytical instrumentation for the food industry
President: Frank Mcgovern McGovern
Technical Specialist: Cheryl Porter
Estimated Sales: $ 1 - 3,000,000
Number Employees: 5-9
Type of Packaging: Bulk
Brands Exported: Omnion, Inc.
Regions Exported to: Worldwide
Percentage of Business in Exporting: 70

47233 Omnitech International
2715 Ashman Street
Midland, MI 48640   989-631-3977
Fax: 989-631-0812   info@omnitechintl.com
www.omnitechintl.com
Manufacturer and exporter of turnkey can and can end systems for domestic and international installation
CEO: Lee Rouse
Vice President/Business Manager, Plastic: Phil Sarnacke
Operations Manager/Controller: Carolyn Owen
Estimated Sales: $ 5 - 10 Million
Number Employees: 10-19
Square Footage: 24000
Regions Exported to: Central America, South America, Europe, Asia, Middle East
Percentage of Business in Exporting: 100

47234 Omnitemp Refrigeration
9300 Hall Road
Downey, CA 90241-5309   562-923-9660
Fax: 562-862-7466   800-423-9660
www.omniteaminc.com
Manufacturer and exporter of display cases and heat recovery and refrigeration equipment
Owner: Don Hyatt
CEO, President: Mr. Haasis
Plant Manager: Jess McKeoun
Estimated Sales: $ 1 - 5 Million
Number Employees: 50-99
Type of Packaging: Food Service
Regions Exported to: Worldwide
Percentage of Business in Exporting: 2

47235 Omnova Solutions Inc.
25435 Harvard Rd.
Beachwood, OH 44122-6201   216-682-7000
www.omnova.com
Emulsion polymers, specialty chemicals and functional/decorative surfaces.
President/CEO: Anne Noonan
Senior VP/CFO: Paul DeSantis
Year Founded: 1999
Estimated Sales: $769.8 Million
Number Employees: 2,390
Square Footage: 10124

47236 OnTrack Automation Inc
592 Colby Drive
Waterloo, ON N2V 1A2
Canada   519-886-9090
Fax: 519-886-9306   ontrack@psangelus.com
www.ontrack-inc.com
Manufacturer and exporter of bottling machinery including orienters line conveyors, labeling change parts, feedscrews
President: Ward Flannery
Plant Manager: Ed Gardiner
Purchasing Manager: Daren Ste. Marie
Number Employees: 20-49
Parent Co: Joseph E. Seagram & Sons
Regions Exported to: Central America, South America, Europe, Asia
Regions Imported from: Europe, Asia

47237 Once Again Nut Butter
12 S State St
PO Box 429
Nunda, NY 14517   585-468-2535
Fax: 585-468-5995   888-800-8075
onceagainnutbutter.com
Organic peanut butter, nut and seed butters, roasted and raw nuts, honey
General Manager: Bob Gelser
rgelser@onceagainnutbutter.com
Chief Financial Officer: Bryan Fritz
VP: Bill Owen
Quality Assurance Manager: Jake Rawleigh
Director Of Sales: Lisa Blatz
Production Manager: Esther Hinrich
Director of Purchasing: Lloyd Kirwan
Estimated Sales: $1.5 Million
Number Employees: 50-99
Square Footage: 40000
Type of Packaging: Consumer, Food Service, Private Label, Bulk
Brands Exported: Once Again Nut Butter
Regions Exported to: Europe, Asia, Middle East, Canada
Percentage of Business in Exporting: 15
Regions Imported from: Central America, South America, Asia, Africa
Percentage of Business in Importing: 20

47238 One-Shot
901 Norwalk Street
Suite E
Greensboro, NC 27407-2039   336-854-1020
Fax: 336-854-1577
Importer and wholesaler/distributor of soft serve frozen dessert dispensing equipment; serving the food service market
President: Bill Rhodes
VP Sales: J Cooper
Number Employees: 10-19

Type of Packaging: Food Service
Brands Imported: One-Shot
Regions Imported from: U.K.
Percentage of Business in Importing: 100

47239 Oneida Food Service
200 S Civic Center Dr
Columbus, OH 43215
Fax: 315-361-3745 800-828-7033
FSCustomerService@oneida.com
www.oneida.com
Manufacturer, importer and exporter of stainless steel and silver plated holloware and flatware; also, dinnerware, glassware, crystal and china.
Chief Executive Officer: James Joseph
Year Founded: 1848
Estimated Sales: I
Number Employees: 1,000-4,999
Number of Brands: 9
Parent Co: Oneida
Brands Exported: Oneida; Buffalo China
Regions Exported to: Worldwide
Percentage of Business in Exporting: 15
Regions Imported from: Europe, Asia, Canada
Percentage of Business in Importing: 20

47240 (HQ)Onevision Corp
5805 Chandler Ct # A
Westerville, OH 43082-9076
614-794-1144
Fax: 614-794-3366 neil@onevisioncorp.com
www.craftbrewquality.com
Can inspection systems
President: Neil Morris
neil@onevisioncorp.com
Quality Control: Matt Allaire
Director Sales: Mike Raczynski
Estimated Sales: Below $ 5 Million
Number Employees: 5-9
Square Footage: 9000
Other Locations:
  OneVision Corp.
  Riverside, CAOneVision Corp.
Brands Exported: Seammate; One Vision Systems
Regions Exported to: Asia, Canada
Percentage of Business in Exporting: 10

47241 Onguard Industries LLC
1850 Clark Rd
Havre De Grace, MD 21078-4000 410-272-2000
Fax: 410-272-3346 800-304-2282
sales@onguardindustries.com
www.onguardindustries.com
Protective clothing and non-slip boots.
CEO: Chris Maistros
cmaistros@onguardindustries.com
Number Employees: 100-249
Regions Exported to: North America, Worldwide

47242 Ono International
2702 NW 112th Ave
Doral, FL 33172-1805 305-591-1516
Fax: 305-500-9566 877-387-6273
onointer@aol.com
Wholesaler/distributor and importer of pre-baked and frozen baguettes, rolls, loaves, croissants, pastries, par-cooked frozen paella 100% natural, brandy (France) and wines (Spain)
Managing Member: Joseph Ayash
Chief of Operation: Rafael Ayash
Estimated Sales: $10 Million
Number Employees: 5-9
Square Footage: 20000
Type of Packaging: Consumer, Food Service, Private Label
Regions Exported to: Caribbean
Percentage of Business in Exporting: 80
Brands Imported: Fripan; Only Paella; Indyr; Palacio Del Duque; Charles 8; Marnay
Regions Imported from: Europe
Percentage of Business in Importing: 20

47243 Ontario Glove and Safety Products
5 Washburn Drive
Kitchener, ON N2R 1S1
Canada 519-886-3590
Fax: 519-886-3597 800-265-4554
sales@ontarioglove.com www.ontarioglove.com
Manufacturer and importer of gloves including PVC, cotton, latex and neoprene; wholesaler/distributor and exporter of leather and synthetic aprons
President: John McCarthy
CFO: Randell Moore
Quality Control: Truedy Henric
Number Employees: 10
Regions Exported to: USA
Percentage of Business in Exporting: 2
Regions Imported from: South America, Europe, Asia, Middle East, Mexico
Percentage of Business in Importing: 50

47244 Ontario International
528 Plum St # 200a
Syracuse, NY 13204-1430 315-433-0040
Fax: 315-433-0033
Importer and exporter of fresh fruits and vegetables including celery, cherries and lettuce
President: Paul Genecco
Estimated Sales: $5-10 Million
Number Employees: 5-9
Brands Exported: Ontario Select
Regions Exported to: Europe, Middle East
Percentage of Business in Exporting: 90
Regions Imported from: Central America, Asia
Percentage of Business in Importing: 10

47245 Ontario Produce Company
PO Box 880
Ontario, OR 97914 541-889-6485
Fax: 541-889-7823
Red, yellow and white onions; dry storage for onions
President and CEO: Robert A Komoto
Office Manager & Transportation: Janet Komoto
Shed Foreman: Arturo Rodriguez
Inspector: Alan Lovitt
Estimated Sales: $5-10 Million
Number Employees: 20 to 49
Square Footage: 160000
Type of Packaging: Consumer, Food Service, Private Label, Bulk
Brands Exported: A; Golden Bird
Regions Exported to: Asia
Percentage of Business in Exporting: 3

47246 Oogolow Enterprises
2560 Dominic Drive
Suite A
Chico, CA 95928-7185 530-893-2646
Fax: 530-893-9344 800-816-6873
Chicken, turkey, beef, ham and vegetable flavored meat analogs, vegetarian tamales, vegan cokies and energy bars.
President: Michael Epperson
oogolow@gmail.com
Estimated Sales: Below $ 5 Million
Number Employees: 15
Square Footage: 16000
Type of Packaging: Consumer, Food Service, Private Label
Regions Imported from: Canada
Percentage of Business in Importing: 5

47247 (HQ)Opal Manufacturing Ltd
10 Compass Court
Toronto, ON M1S 5R3
Canada 416-646-5232
Fax: 416-646-5242 rosa@nrttech.com
www.customvendingmachines.com
Manufacturer and exporter of custom vending machines and refrigerated liquid portion control cream dispensers
Sales: Brian Simon
Number Employees: 10
Brands Exported: Opal; Little Squirt
Regions Exported to: Worldwide

47248 Open Date Systems
Georges Mill Rd
Sunapee, NH 3782 603-763-3444
Fax: 603-763-4222 877-673-6328
sales@opendate.com www.opendate.com
Coding systems including hot stamp, thermal transfer and fully and semi-automatic carton; feeding systems
President/CEO: Thierry Brousse
CFO: Nikki MacLennan
Vice President: Rick Berquist
Marketing/Sales: Don Morong
Contact: James Poitras
james@opendate.com
Production Manager: Terry Bartlett
Purchasing: Marcia Crawford
Estimated Sales: $3,000,000
Number Employees: 5-9
Square Footage: 6000
Parent Co: Open Date Equipment
Regions Exported to: Canada, Caribbean, Latin America, Mexico
Percentage of Business in Exporting: 20

47249 Opie Brush Company
16400 E Truman Rd
Independence, MO 64050-4161 816-246-6767
Fax: 816-833-8955 800-877-6743
Manufacturer and exporter of custom made and industrial brushes including flour milling
Marketing: Connie Dulin
General Manager: Connie Dulin
Plant Manager: James Dulin
Estimated Sales: $500,000-$1 Million
Number Employees: 5-9
Number of Brands: 1
Square Footage: 24000
Brands Exported: Opie
Regions Exported to: Central America, South America, Europe, Asia, Middle East
Percentage of Business in Exporting: 20

47250 Optek Inc
5229 Cheshire Rd
Galena, OH 43021-9407 740-548-4700
Fax: 740-548-4999 800-533-8400
wtkavage@optek-inc.com www.optek-inc.com
Manufacturer and exporter of volume flow measurement systems for belt conveyors, tablet counting systems and control systems including moisture, temperature and fill level
President/CFO: Dr. Marvin E. Monroe
VP: William Kavage
Estimated Sales: Below $ 5 Million
Number Employees: 1-4
Square Footage: 30000

47251 Optex
13661 Benson Ave
Chino, CA 91710 909-993-5770
Fax: 310-533-5910 800-966-7839
www.optexamerica.com
Manufacturer and exporter of alarm systems and sensors
President: Robert Blair
VP Marketing/Sales: Jay Kessel
Contact: Norma Armstrong
narmstrong@optexamerica.com
Estimated Sales: $ 20 - 50 Million
Number Employees: 25-30
Parent Co: Optex
Regions Exported to: Central America, South America, Canada, Caribbean, Latin America, Mexico
Percentage of Business in Exporting: 20

47252 Optima Foods
15 W Jefryn Blvd
Deer Park, NY 11729 631-243-4670
Fax: 631-243-4681 info@optimafoods.com
www.optimafoods.com
Greek cheeses, olives, olive oil and vinegars.
Business Development Manager: Eleftheria Perrikos

47253 Optimal Nutrients
1163 Chess Dr Ste F
Foster City, CA 94404 707-528-1800
Fax: 707-349-1686
Vitamins and supplements: royal jelly, beta carotene, essential fatty acids
President: Tim Lally
Vice President: Darlene Angeli
darlenea@optinutri.com
Estimated Sales: $500,000-$1 Million
Number Employees: 5-9
Square Footage: 20000
Parent Co: Pegasus Corp
Percentage of Business in Exporting: 15
Regions Imported from: South America, Asia
Percentage of Business in Importing: 50

47254 Oracle Hospitality
500 Oracle Pkw
Redwood, CA 94065 650-506-7000
800-392-2999
www.oracle.com/industries/hospitality
Manufacturer and exporter of management system software for hospitality, food and beverage, table seating for hotels, motels, casinos and other leisure and entertainment businesses.

Importers & Exporters / A-Z

Chairman & Chief Technology Officer: Lawrence Ellison
Vice Chairman: Jeffrey Henley
Chief Executive Officer: Safra Catz
Chief Corporate Architect: Edward Screven
Year Founded: 1977
Estimated Sales: $39.50 Billion
Number Employees: 136,000
Parent Co: Oracle Corporation
Type of Packaging: Food Service
Other Locations:
   Micros Systems/Fidelio Softwa
   Elk Grove Village, ILMicros Systems/Fidelio Softwa
Regions Exported to: Worldwide
Percentage of Business in Exporting: 25

47255 (HQ)Orafti Active Food Ingredients
101 Lindenwood Drive
Malvern, PA 19355-1755   610-889-9828
   Fax: 610-889-9821
Wholesaler/distributor and importer of inulin and oligofructose
President: Kathy Niness
CEO: Mark T Izzo
Marketing: Barry Schwartz
Estimated Sales: $5-10 Million
Number Employees: 5-9
Parent Co: Orafti S.A.
Type of Packaging: Bulk
Brands Imported: Raftiline; Raftilose

47256 Orange Bakery
17751 Cowan
Irvine, CA 92614-6064   949-863-1377
   Fax: 949-863-1932 orangebakery.com
Frozen pastries
Year Founded: 1978
Number Employees: 50-99
Type of Packaging: Consumer, Food Service, Private Label, Bulk
Regions Exported to: Canada

47257 Orange Cove-Sanger Citrus
180 South Ave
Orange Cove, CA 93646-9447   559-626-4453
   Fax: 559-626-7357 www.ocsca.com
Oranges
President: Lee Bailey
General Manager: Kevin Severns
kevin@orangecovesanger.com
Vice President: Shawn Stevenson
Sales Manager: Dave Christofferson
Plant Manager: Bob Johnson
Estimated Sales: $10 Million
Number Employees: 50-99
Type of Packaging: Consumer, Food Service
Brands Exported: Sunkist
Regions Exported to: Asia, New Zealand

47258 Orange Peel Enterprises
2183 Ponce DE Leon Cir
Vero Beach, FL 32960-5337   772-562-2766
   Fax: 772-562-9848 800-643-1210
info@greensplus.com www.greensplus.com
Protein powders, energy bars
President: Ryan Deauville
ryan@greensplus.com
Director National Sales/Marketing: Todd Westover
Estimated Sales: $3.5 Million
Number Employees: 10-19
Square Footage: 60000
Type of Packaging: Consumer, Private Label
Brands Exported: Fiber Greens+; Greens+; Pro-Relief; Protein Greens+
Regions Exported to: Worldwide
Percentage of Business in Exporting: 10

47259 Orangeburg Pecan Co
761 Russell St
Orangeburg, SC 29115   803-534-4277
   www.uspecans.com
Shelled pecans
Founder: Marion H Felder
Number Employees: 10-19
Type of Packaging: Consumer, Food Service, Bulk

47260 Orca Bay Foods
2729 6th Ave S
Suite 200
Seattle, WA 98134   425-204-9100
   Fax: 425-204-9200 800-932-6722
info@orcabayfoods.com orcabayseafoods.com
Frozen fish and seafood
President/CEO: Ryan Mackey
rmackey@orcabayfoods.com
VP/Finance: Jay Olsen
Senior Marketing Manager: Richard Mullins
National Sales Manager: Mark Tupper
Warehouse Manager: Troy Roy
Estimated Sales: $160 million
Number Employees: 200
Number of Brands: 1
Number of Products: 20
Square Footage: 70000
Type of Packaging: Consumer, Food Service, Private Label, Bulk

47261 Orca Inc
199 Whiting St
New Britain, CT 06051-3146   860-223-4180
   Fax: 860-826-1729 www.orca-mfg.com
Manufacturer and exporter of custom caps including can, glass and screw neck ends
Owner: Brian Melanson
bmelanson@orca-mfg.com
Estimated Sales: $5-10 Million
Number Employees: 50-99
Square Footage: 60000

47262 (HQ)Ore-Cal Corp
634 Crocker St
Los Angeles, CA 90021-1002   213-623-8493
   Fax: 213-228-6557 800-827-7474
CustomerService@ore-cal.com www.ore-cal.com
Shrimp, pangasius, mahi mahi, swordfish, calamari, breaded shrimp, and ready mixed entree dishes such as; shrimp scampi, seafood gumbo, cioppino, shrimp pad thai, and shrimp torn kha soup.
President: William Shinbane
Human Resources: Josephine Davif
Controller/Vice President Finance: Mark Feldstein
Vice President: Mark Shinbane
Lab Director: Avito Moniz
Human Resources Compliance & Regulatory: Wendy Gomez
Manager of National Sales: Shelley Gee
Manufacturing Supervisor: Rick Kanase
Estimated Sales: $10.9 Million
Number Employees: 50-99
Number of Brands: 1
Number of Products: 11+
Square Footage: 240000
Type of Packaging: Consumer, Food Service, Private Label, Bulk
Regions Exported to: Worldwide

47263 Ore-Ida Foods
PO Box 57
Pittsburgh, PA 15230   412-237-5700
   800-255-5750
   www.oreida.com
Frozen potato products
VP of Marketing: Fed Arreola
Estimated Sales: $20-50 Million
Number Employees: 400
Number of Brands: 12
Parent Co: H.J. Heinz Company
Type of Packaging: Consumer, Food Service
Regions Exported to: Worldwide

47264 Oregon Chai
1745 NW Marshall Street
Portland, OR 97209-2420   503-221-2424
   Fax: 503-796-0980 888-874-2424
nirvana@oregonchai.com www.oregonchai.com
Chai lattes, blends of tea, honey, vanilla and spices.
President: Cory Comstock
VP Finance: Kurt Peterson
Senior VP Marketing: Sean Ryan
VP Marketing: Lori Woolfrey
Sales Director: Tom Carl
Contact: Jeff Card
jeff.card@oregonchai.com
Production Manager: Emile Gaiera
Estimated Sales: $2.5-5 Million
Number Employees: 30
Square Footage: 36000
Type of Packaging: Consumer, Food Service
Brands Exported: Oregon Chai
Regions Exported to: Canada
Percentage of Business in Exporting: 5
Regions Imported from: Worldwide

47265 Oregon Cherry Growers Inc
1520 Woodrow St NE
Salem, OR 97301
   Fax: 503-585-7710 sales@pcoastp.com
   www.oregoncherry.com
Fresh, maraschino, froze, brined, glance, ingredient and canned cherries.
Chief Executive Officer: Tim Ramsey
tramsey@orcherry.com
VP, Human Resources & Communications: Michele Halverson
VP, Operations: Steve Travis
Year Founded: 1932
Estimated Sales: $46.1 Million
Number Employees: 100-249
Square Footage: 20000
Type of Packaging: Consumer, Food Service, Private Label, Bulk
Other Locations:
   The Dalles, OR
   Salem, ORSalem
Regions Exported to: Worldwide

47266 Oregon Cherry Growers Inc
1st and Madison
P.O. Box 1577
The Dalles, OR 97058
Fresh, maraschino, froze, brined, glance, ingredient and canned cherries.
Chief Executive Officer: Tim Ramsey
Year Founded: 1932
Estimated Sales: $46.1 Million
Number Employees: 100-249
Type of Packaging: Consumer, Food Service, Private Label, Bulk
Regions Exported to: Worldwide

47267 Oregon Coffee Roaster
P.O.Box 223
North Plains, OR 97133   503-647-5102
   Fax: 503-647-5857 800-526-9940
mugs3@aol.com www.oregoncoffee.com
Specialty coffee roaster and tea importer
Owner: John Turner
Co-Owner: Bobi Turner
Contact: Cindy Ertell
cindyertell@oregoncoffee.com
Estimated Sales: $5-9.9 Million
Number Employees: 5-9
Type of Packaging: Food Service, Private Label, Bulk
Regions Imported from: Central America, South America, Asia, Far East, Mexico
Percentage of Business in Importing: 90

47268 Oregon Freeze Dry, Inc.
525 W. 25th Ave. SW
Albany, OR 97322   541-926-6001
   Fax: 541-967-6527 customerservice@ofd.com
   www.ofd.com
Kosher meats, poultry, seafood, sweetened fruits, vegetables, military rations, pet treats
President and COO: Jim Merryman
VP of Finance: Dale Bookwalter
VP: Fred Vetter
Manager, R&D: Norm Jager
VP Business & Technical Development: Walter Pebley
Contact: Kelvin Adams
kelvin.adams@ofd.com
Estimated Sales: $27.6 Million
Number Employees: 201-500
Square Footage: 29000
Type of Packaging: Consumer, Private Label
Other Locations: Danish Freeze Dry
Brands Exported: Mountain House, EasyMeal
Regions Exported to: Central America, South America, Europe, Asia

47269 Oregon Fruit Products Co
150 Patterson St NW
PO Box 5283
Salem, OR 97304-4042   503-378-0255
   Fax: 503-588-9519 800-394-9333
cooking@oregonfruit.com www.oregonfruit.com
Canned fruits and berries
President: Joe Peterson
joep@ofpc.com
Sales Director: Bryan Brown
Operations Manager: Patti Law
Estimated Sales: A
Number Employees: 100-249
Type of Packaging: Consumer, Food Service, Private Label, Bulk

Importers & Exporters / A-Z

Regions Exported to: Worldwide

47270 Oregon Hill Farms
32861 Pittsburg Rd
St Helens, OR 97051-9110   503-397-2791
Fax: 503-397-0091   800-243-4541
Specialty fruit jams, syrups, fruit butters and dessert toppings
President: Thomas Mcmahon
tom@oregonhill.com
Operations Manager: Carmen McMahon
Estimated Sales: $ 3 - 5 Million
Number Employees: 5-9
Square Footage: 68000
Type of Packaging: Consumer, Food Service, Private Label
Brands Exported: Oregon Hill
Regions Exported to: Europe, Asia
Percentage of Business in Exporting: 5

47271 (HQ)Oregon Potato Co
650 E Columbia Ave
PO Box 169
Boardman, OR 97818   541-481-2715
Fax: 541-481-3443   800-336-6311
Potato products: flakes, flour, frozen, diced and fresh potatoes
Manager: Steve White
Director QA/Technical Services: Nick Ross
Director Global Sales: Barry Stice
Manager: Frank Tiegs
frank@ftiegs.com
Number Employees: 100-249
Square Footage: 400000
Type of Packaging: Private Label
Other Locations:
   Oregon Potato Co.
   Warden, WAOregon Potato Co.
Brands Exported: Oregon Trail; Regal Crest; Private Label
Regions Exported to: Central America, South America, Europe, Asia, Middle East
Percentage of Business in Exporting: 35

47272 Orelube Corp
20 Sawgrass Dr
Bellport, NY 11713-1549   631-205-9700
Fax: 631-205-9797   800-645-9124
info@orelube.com   www.orelube.com
Manufacturer and exporter of lubricants including aluminum complex EP grease, chain oil and synthetic grease
Owner: Robert Silverstin
robert@orelube.com
Purchasing Agent: Donna Klempka
Estimated Sales: $5-10 Million
Number Employees: 10-19
Square Footage: 132000
Regions Exported to: Worldwide
Percentage of Business in Exporting: 45

47273 Organic Gourmet
14431 Ventura Blvd #192
Sherman Oaks, CA 91423   800-400-7772
Fax: 818-906-7417   scenar@earthlink.net
www.organic-gourmet.com
Organic vegetarian soups and stocks, yeast extract spreads, bouillon cubes and miso pastes
Founder & CEO: Elke Heitmeyer
Estimated Sales: $ 1 - 3 Million
Number Employees: 1-4
Number of Brands: 1
Number of Products: 16
Type of Packaging: Consumer, Food Service
Brands Imported: The Organic Gourmet
Regions Imported from: Europe
Percentage of Business in Importing: 40

47274 Organic Juice USA
44 Mound St
Lindenhurst, NY 11757-6918   631-567-3487
Importer of 100% certified pure organic & natural fruit juice and seed extract.
President: Mark Rollino
mrollino@elitenaturel.com
Vice President: Ali Syman

47275 Organic Milling
505 W Allen Ave
San Dimas, CA 91773   909-599-0961
Fax: 909-599-5180   info@organicmilling.com
www.organicmilling.com
Breakfast cereals and granola
President: Wolfgang Buehler
Vice President, Operations: Lupe Martinez
Year Founded: 1960
Number Employees: 100-249
Number of Products: 29
Type of Packaging: Private Label, Bulk
Other Locations:
   Warehouse & Distribution
   San Dimas, CAWarehouse & Distribution
Regions Exported to: Europe, Asia
Percentage of Business in Exporting: 10

47276 Organic Products Trading Co
2908 NW 93rd St
Suite D-8
Vancouver, WA 98665-6184   312-753-6330
Fax: 360-573-4388   888-881-4433
www.optco.com
Green, organic, shade grown, and Fairtrade grown coffees
President: Garth Smith
Coffee Buyer & General Manager: Dustin Johnson
CFO: Gaylene Smith
Logistics Coordinator & Quality Analyst: Sophie Olivares
Marketing: Gaylene Smith
Sales: Tim Koolstra
Producer Relations Manager: Katherine Oglietti
Estimated Sales: Less Than $500,000
Number Employees: 1-4
Square Footage: 8000
Regions Exported to: Europe
Percentage of Business in Exporting: 10
Brands Imported: Raw Green Organic; Fair Trade; Shade Grown Coffee
Regions Imported from: Central America, South America, Asia, Africa
Percentage of Business in Importing: 90

47277 Organic Vintages
PO Box 832
Ukiah, CA 95482-0832   707-462-2300
Fax: 707-462-4258   800-877-6655
info@organicvintages.com
www.organicvintages.com
Wholesaler/distributor of organic wine, sake, cider, champagne and beer; serving the food service market; importer of organic wine
President: Steven Frenkel
Estimated Sales: $700,000-800,000
Number Employees: 1-4
Square Footage: 800
Regions Imported from: Europe
Percentage of Business in Importing: 15

47278 Organically Grown Co
1800 Prairie Rd # B
Eugene, OR 97402-9722   541-689-5320
Fax: 541-461-3014   800-937-9677
davidl@organicgrown.com
www.organicgrown.com
Fruits and vegetables, tropical produce and dried fruit
CEO: Christopher Anderson
christopher.anderson@marriott.com
CEO: Josh Hinerfeld
Marketing Manager: Stacy Kraker
VP of Sales & Marketing: David Lively
Operations Manager: Anthony Seran
Purchasing/Inventory Director: David Amorose
Number Employees: 50-99
Other Locations:
   Clackamas, OR
   Kent, WAKent
Regions Imported from: South America
Percentage of Business in Importing: 5

47279 Organics Unlimited
8587 Avenida Costa Norte
Suite 2
San Diego, CA 92154   619-710-0658
info@organicsunlimited.com
www.organicsunlimited.com
Organic bananas, plantains, and coconuts
President/CEO: Mayra Velazquez de Leon
Director Operations: Marco Garcia Ojeda
Year Founded: 2000
Number Employees: 10-19
Regions Imported from: Central America

47280 Orics Industries
240 Smith St
Farmingdale, NY 11735   718-461-8613
Fax: 718-461-4719   info@orics.com
www.orics.com
Manufacturer and exporter of tray sealers for vacuum gas flush map packaging
Owner: Ori Cohen
Contact: Staci Banta
staci_banta@orics.com
Number Employees: 20-49

47281 Oriental Foods
2550 W Main Street
Suite 210
Alhambra, CA 91801-7003   626-293-1994
Fax: 626-293-1983
Seafood
President: Dr Venku Reddy
Estimated Sales: $1,300,000
Number Employees: 5

47282 Original Swiss Aromatics
P.O.Box 6842
San Rafael, CA 94903   415-479-9120
Fax: 415-479-0614
www.originalswissaromatics.com
Importer of essential oils
Owner: Kurt Schnabelt
Estimated Sales: $ 1 - 3 Million
Number Employees: 1-4
Square Footage: 8000
Parent Co: Pacific Institute of Aromatherapy
Regions Imported from: Europe
Percentage of Business in Importing: 85

47283 Orinoco Coffee & Tea
8265 Patuxent Range Rd
Suite L
Jessup, MD 20794   410-312-5292
Fax: 240-636-5196   info@orinococoffeeandtea.com
www.orinococoffeeandtea.com
Coffe and tea
CEO: Pedro Ramirez
Master Roaster, R&D: Juan Carlos Ramirez

47284 Orion Research
100 Cummings Ctr
Beverly, MA 01915   978-232-6000
www.scientificcomputing.com
Manufacturer and exporter of analytical instruments for the measurement of sodium, pH chemical species in solutions and moisture in foods.
Estimated Sales: $100-500 Million
Parent Co: Scientific Computing
Brands Exported: Orion; Ross; Sage; Cahn
Regions Exported to: Central America, South America, Europe, Asia, Middle East

47285 Orion Trading Corp
1927 E 19th St
Tucson, AZ 85719-6918   520-622-6588
Fax: 520-884-0891   www.oriontrading.com
Owner: James DE Girolamo
jim@oriontading.com
Estimated Sales: $ 5 - 10 Million
Number Employees: 5-9

47286 Orioxi International Corporation
1422 Edinger Avenue,
Suite 250
Tustin, CA 92780   71- 99- 899
Fax: 714-824-3386
Importer of walnuts, pine nuts and seeds; exporter of fresh and dried fruits; wholesaler/distributor of nuts, seeds and dried fruits; serving the food service market
President: Ziegfred Young
Number Employees: 5-9
Square Footage: 48000
Regions Exported to: Asia
Percentage of Business in Exporting: 15
Regions Imported from: Central America, Asia
Percentage of Business in Importing: 80

47287 Orlando Food Corp
51 E Spring Valley Ave
Maywood, NJ 07607-2120   201-368-2345
Fax: 201-368-2059   www.caputoflour.com
Importer of beans, cheese, oils, pasta, artichokes and tomatoes
President: Carlo Orlando
carlo@orlandofoods.com

Importers & Exporters / A-Z

Estimated Sales: $5-10 Million
Number Employees: 5-9
Regions Imported from: Europe, Morocco
Percentage of Business in Importing: 100

47288 Orleans International
30600 Northwestern Hwy
Suite 300
Farmington Hills, MI 48334-3172   248-855-5556
Fax: 248-855-5668 info@orleansintl.com
www.orleansintl.com
Beef, lamb, pork, poultry, seafood, and wild game.
President: Earl Tushman
Secretary: Larry Tushman
Director of Operations: Reed Tushman
Director of Logistics: Marc Tushman
Senior Vice President: Steve Sanger
Controller: Beth Ehrlich
Estimated Sales: $100-500 Million
Number of Products: 2000
Type of Packaging: Consumer, Food Service
Regions Imported from: New Zealand
Percentage of Business in Importing: 90

47289 Orleans Packing Co
1715 Hyde Park Ave
Hyde Park, MA 02136-2457   617-361-6611
Fax: 617-361-2638 George@orleanspacking.com
www.orleanspacking.com
Olives
President: George Gebelein
george@orleanspacking.com
Vice President: Suzanne Gebelein
Estimated Sales: $ 1 Million
Number Employees: 10-19
Type of Packaging: Consumer, Food Service, Private Label, Bulk

47290 Orwak
10820 Normandale Boulevard
Minneapolis, MN 55437-3112   612-881-9200
Fax: 612-881-8578 800-747-0449
www.orwak.us
Manufacturer and exporter of trash compactors and recycling balers
Estimated Sales: $500,000-$1 Million
Number Employees: 4
Brands Exported: Orwak
Regions Exported to: Central America, South America, Middle East, Caribbean, Latin America, Mexico

47291 Osborne USA Inc
189 West 89 Street #10-G
New York, NY 10024   212-706-2160
Fax: 212-706-2160 www.osborne.es
Importer of wine.

47292 Oscartek
361 - 367 Beach Rd
Burlingame, CA 94010   650-342-2400
Fax: 650-342-7400 855-885-2400
www.oscartek.com
Display cases
CEO: Rabih Ballout

47293 Oskaloosa Food Products
543 9th Ave E
Oskaloosa, IA 52577-3901   641-673-3486
Fax: 641-673-8684 800-477-7239
info@oskyfoods.com www.oskyfoods.com
Dried, frozen and liquid egg products.
President: Blair Van Zetten
Controller: Brad Hodges
bhodges@oskyfoods.com
Sales/Purchasing Director: Jason Van Zetten
Human Resource Manager: Joyce Wilson
Estimated Sales: $10 Million
Number Employees: 50-99
Type of Packaging: Consumer, Food Service, Private Label, Bulk
Regions Exported to: Germany, Mexico

47294 Oskri Corporation
528 E Tyranena Park Rd
Lake Mills, WI 53551   920-648-8300
info@oskri.com
www.oskri.com
Organic coffee, dried fruit and soup bases, teas and herbal products
Owner: Fekri Zainoba
Sales Director: Jen Fredrich
Contact: Tricia Blasing
tricia.kastrosky@gmail.com

Estimated Sales: $500,000-$1 Million
Number Employees: 5-9
Type of Packaging: Consumer, Private Label, Bulk
Regions Exported to: Mexico
Regions Imported from: Worldwide

47295 Osso Good, LLC
San Rafael, CA
hello@ossogoodbones.com
www.ossogoodbones.com
GMO-free, hormone-free and organic bone broth soups in various flavors; bone broth cleanse packages; Paleo diet-friendly soups
Co-Founder/CEO: Jazz Hilmer
Co-Founder/CEO: Meredith Cochran
Co-Founder/CFO: Toran Hilmer
Number of Brands: 1
Number of Products: 19
Type of Packaging: Consumer, Private Label
Brands Exported: The Osso Good Co.
Regions Exported to: USA

47296 (HQ)Osterneck Company
Highway 72 E
Lumberton, NC 28358   910-738-2416
Fax: 910-739-2881 800-682-2416
Manufacturer and exporter of plastic bags and woven polypropylene products
Vice President: Leroy Freeman
Estimated Sales: $ 1 - 5 Million
Number Employees: 50-99
Square Footage: 400000

47297 Otis McAllister Inc.
300 Frank H Ogawa Plaza
Suite 400
Oakland, CA 94612   415-421-6010
Fax: 415-421-6016 www.otismcallister.com
Importer of specialty rice
President/Owner: Don Spilman
VP, Retail Sales: Harold Russell
Contact: Jeff Brehm
jbrehm@otismcallister.com
Number Employees: 51-200
Type of Packaging: Bulk
Brands Exported: Butterpop
Regions Exported to: Central America, South America, New Zealand
Percentage of Business in Exporting: 100
Regions Imported from: Central America, South America

47298 Ottens Flavors
7800 Holstein Avenue
Philadelphia, PA 19153   215-365-7800
Fax: 215-365-7801 800-523-0767
www.ottensflavors.com
Spray dry flavorings, imitation and natural confectionery oils and spices
President: George Robinson
CEO: Richard Robinson
Eastern Manager: Sharon D'Alo
Contact: Philip Bafundo
philip@ottensflavors.com
COO: Rudy Dieperink
Estimated Sales: $11.5 Million
Number Employees: 50-99
Square Footage: 109500
Type of Packaging: Food Service, Private Label, Bulk
Regions Exported to: South America, Europe, Australia
Percentage of Business in Exporting: 10
Regions Imported from: Central America, Europe, Asia, Middle East
Percentage of Business in Importing: 15

47299 Ouachita Machine Works
120 N Hilton St
West Monroe, LA 71291-7499   318-396-1468
Fax: 318-396-1668
Manufacturer and exporter of packaging machinery including automatic and stretch balers
President: Jimmy Dulaney
jdulaney@omwinc.com
CFO: Jimmy Dulaney
R&D: Don Hudson
Quality Control: Jimmy Dulaney
Estimated Sales: Below $ 5 Million
Number Employees: 20-49
Parent Co: Ouachita Machine Works

47300 Outerbridge Peppers Limited
20 Harry Shupe Blvd
Wharton, NJ 07885   626-296-2400
peppers@logic.bm
www.outerbridge.com
Packaging facility for Outerbridge Peppers LTD, specializing in sherry peppers and a variety of other sauces.
Managing Director: Norma Cross
Number of Brands: 1
Parent Co: Outerbridge Peppers Limited
Type of Packaging: Consumer, Food Service, Bulk
Brands Imported: Outerbridge's
Regions Imported from: Bermuda

47301 Outlook Packaging
PO Box 775
Neenah, WI 54957-0775   920-722-1666
Fax: 920-722-0008
Manufacturer, importer and exporter of flexible packaging materials for meat, cheese, candy, frozen food, fish, poultry and other various industrial applications
President: Joe Baksha
Contact: Dennis Grabski
Estimated Sales: G
Number Employees: 250-499
Square Footage: 83000
Parent Co: Flexible Technology
Type of Packaging: Bulk
Regions Imported from: Central America, Asia, Middle East, Canada

47302 Outotec USA Inc
8280 Stayton Dr # M
Suite M
Jessup, MD 20794-9609   301-543-1200
Fax: 301-543-0002 www.outotec.com
Manufacturer and exporter of energy recovery systems including waste incinerators and waste disposal equipment; also, fluidized bed systems and fabrication services available
CEO: Paul Abbott
paul.abbott@outotec.com
Plant Manager: Mark Castle
Purchasing Manager: Joe Malloy
Estimated Sales: $ 50 Million
Number Employees: 10-19
Number of Brands: 1
Square Footage: 30000
Parent Co: Idaho Energy Partnership
Regions Exported to: South America, Europe, Canada
Percentage of Business in Exporting: 50

47303 Oven Head Salmon Smokers
101 Oven Head Road
Bethel, NB E5C 1S3
Canada   506-755-2507
Fax: 506-755-8883 877-955-2507
ovenhead@xplornet.ca
www.ovenheadsmokers.com
Smoked Atlantic salmon, salmon pate and jerky
President: R Joseph Thorne
Vice President: Debra Thorne
Estimated Sales: $691,000
Number Employees: 5
Number of Brands: 1
Number of Products: 3

47304 Overlake Foods
PO Box 2631
Olympia, WA 98507-2631   360-352-7989
Fax: 360-352-8076 800-683-1078
Frozen blueberries, raspberries, strawberries, blackberries and peaches
COO: Rodney Cook
Sales: Paul Askier
Estimated Sales: $1 Million
Number Employees: 4
Square Footage: 5400
Parent Co: Producer Marketing Group
Type of Packaging: Bulk
Brands Exported: Overlake Beesweet Blueberries
Regions Exported to: Europe, Asia
Brands Imported: Golden Eagle Blueberries, Senco Wild Blue Berries
Regions Imported from: Central America, South America, Europe, Asia
Percentage of Business in Importing: 2

Importers & Exporters / A-Z

47305 Oversea Fishery & Investment
2752 Woodlawn Dr
Suite 5-110
Honolulu, HI 96822-1855   808-847-2500
  Fax: 808-836-3308
Seafood
President: Francis Tsang
Estimated Sales: $ 3 - 5 Million
Number Employees: 1-4

47306 Overseas Food Trading
2200 Fletcher Ave.
Fort Lee, NJ 07024   201-585-8730
European foods
President: Robert Leduc
Marketing & Production Manager: Geoffrey Ferez
VP Sales: Gilles Dion
Customer Service Manager: Josee Nardella
Product Development Manager: Sophie Tran
Purchasing Manager: Sophie Dehau
Estimated Sales: $31.5 Million
Number Employees: 375
Type of Packaging: Consumer, Food Service
Regions Exported to: USA

47307 Owens-Illinois Inc
1 Michael Owens Way
Perrysburg, OH 43551-2999   567-336-5000
glass@o-i.com
www.o-i.com
Manufacturer and exporter of plastic bottles, containers, closures and carriers including HDPE, PVC, PET, LDPE, multilayer and barex
Chairman and Chief Executive Officer: Al Stroucken
CEO: Andres A Lopez
andres.lopez@o-i.com
SVP and CFO: Steve Bramlage
SVP and General Counsel: Jim Baehren
SVP and Chief Administrative Officer: Paul Jarrell
Estimated Sales: Over $1 Billion
Number Employees: 10000+

47308 Oxbo International Corp
100 Bean St
Clear Lake, WI 54005-8400   715-263-2112
Fax: 715-263-3324   800-628-6196
atalbott@oxbocorp.com www.oxbocorp.com
Manufacturer and exporter of pea, bean and sweet and seed corn harvesting machinery and vibratory sorting tables
President: Andy Tallobt
Cmo: Doug Aherns
daherns@oxbocorp.com
VP Sales: Andrew Talbott
Inside Sales: Doug Ahrens
Human Resources: Deborah Arcand
Estimated Sales: $ 10 - 20 Million
Number Employees: 100-249
Square Footage: 220000
Brands Exported: Pixall
Regions Exported to: Central America, South America, Europe

47309 Oxford Frozen Foods
4881 Main Street
Po Box 220
Oxford, NS B0M 1P0
Canada   902-447-2100
Fax: 902-447-3245 sales@oxfordfrozenfoods.com
www.oxfordfrozenfoods.com
Frozen blueberries, carrots and onion rings
President and CEO: John Bragg
Co-CEO: David Hoffman
Vice President, Sales & Logistics: Matthew Bragg
Customer Service Coordinator: Kerri Baker
COO: Ragnar Kamp
Director of Manufacturing: Milton Wood
Number Employees: 250-499
Type of Packaging: Consumer
Regions Exported to: Europe, Asia
Percentage of Business in Exporting: 75

47310 Oxygen Import LLC
955 E Hazelwood Ave
Rahway, NJ 07065-5653   732-882-1000
Fax: 732-882-1001 oxygen@oxygenimports.com
www.oxygenimports.com
Importer of natural and gourmet food: sauces, preserves and spreads, beverages, coffee, cookies, honey, seeds and more
Vice President: Hadara Biala
oxygen@oxygenimports.com
CEO: Ron Biala
Vice President: Hadara Biala
oxygen@oxygenimports.com
Number Employees: 10-19
Brands Imported: Oxygen, Lin's Farm, Aunt Berta's, Rejwan, Super Drink, Nofet Dagan, Papouchado, Prince, Schwartz, Arazon
Regions Imported from: Central America, South America

47311 Oyang America
1043 S Harvard Boulevard
Los Angeles, CA 90006-2403   323-737-8501
Fax: 213-365-8670
Wholesaler/distributor, importer and exporter of frozen fish, surimi products, frozen seafood, freeze-dried seafood and prepared frozen seafood
President: Kenneth Yoon
Estimated Sales: $2.5-5 Million
Number Employees: 1-4
Parent Co: Oyang Corporation
Regions Exported to: Asia
Percentage of Business in Exporting: 5
Regions Imported from: Worldwide
Percentage of Business in Importing: 70

47312 Oyster Bay Pump Works Inc
78 Midland Ave # 1
PO Box 725
Hicksville, NY 11801-1537   516-933-4500
Fax: 516-933-4501 info@obpw.com
www.obpw.com
Manufacturer and exporter of dispensers including single channel, multi-channel and conveyor systems for metering fluids
President: Eyal Angel
eangel@obpw.com
Sales/Marketing: Michael Dedora
Estimated Sales: $ 5 - 10 Million
Number Employees: 20-49
Square Footage: 40000
Type of Packaging: Consumer, Food Service, Private Label, Bulk
Regions Exported to: Worldwide
Percentage of Business in Exporting: 55

47313 Ozone Confectioners & Bakers Supplies
55 Bank St
Elmwood Park, NJ 07407-1146   201-791-4444
Fax: 201-791-2893
Licorice, almonds, nonpareil seeds
President: Patrick Lapone
VP: Louis Lapone
Estimated Sales: $ 3 - 5 Million
Number Employees: 10 to 19
Number of Brands: 1
Type of Packaging: Private Label

47314 P & F Machine
301 S Broadway
Turlock, CA 95380-5414   209-667-2515
Fax: 209-667-4945 eparker@pfmetals.com
www.pfmetals.com
Manufacturer and exporter of custom engineered and fabricated food, poultry and wine processing equipment
Contact: Brian Alves
balves@pfmetals.com
Purchasing Agent: Jim Wells
Estimated Sales: less than $ 500,000
Number Employees: 50-99

47315 P & H Crystalite, LLC
101 Palm Harbor Parkway
Suite 117
Palm Coast, FL 32137   561-330-8660
Fax: 561-330-8665   800-468-8673
Specializes in LED decorative, linear and flood lighting.
Estimated Sales: $3.5 Million
Number Employees: 18
Square Footage: 12000

47316 P J Rhodes Corporation
P.O. Box 2627
Mill Valley, CA 94942-2627
Fax: 480-393-4414 www.pjrhodes.com
Exporter of groceries.
Year Founded: 1946
Estimated Sales: $20-50 Million
Regions Exported to: South America, Europe, Asia, Australia

47317 P R Farms Inc
2917 E Shepherd Ave
Clovis, CA 93619-9152   559-299-0201
Fax: 559-299-7292 info@prfarms.com
www.prfarms.com
Almonds, olive oil, citrus, tree fruit, wine and raisin grapes
President: Pat Ricchiuti
Number Employees: 100-249
Type of Packaging: Consumer, Food Service, Private Label, Bulk
Other Locations:
  Headquarters
  Clovis, CA
  Enzo Olive Oil Company
  Madera, CA
  Almond Facility
  Madera, CAHeadquartersMadera
Brands Exported: P-R Farms
Regions Exported to: Europe, Asia, Middle East

47318 P&L Seafood of Venice
401 Whitney Ave # 103
Gretna, LA 70056-2500   504-363-2744
Fax: 504-392-3334 www.chartwellsmenus.com
Seafood
Manager: John Duke

47319 P. Janes & Sons
PO Box 10
Hant's Harbor, NL A0B 1Y0
Canada   709-586-2252
Fax: 709-586-2870
Seafood
Sales Director: Jeff Galliford
Purchasing Agent: Blair Janes
Type of Packaging: Consumer, Food Service, Private Label, Bulk
Brands Exported: Janes Brand
Regions Exported to: Worldwide

47320 P.F. Harris Manufacturing Company
PO Box 1122
Alpharetta, GA 30009   904-389-5686
Fax: 904-384-0979   800-637-0317
info@pfharris.com www.pfharris.com
Manufacturer, importer and exporter of insecticides and pest control devices including roach tablets
General Manager: Franklin Goodman
Contact: Beth Cline
beth@pfharris.com
Estimated Sales: $300,000-500,000
Number Employees: 4
Square Footage: 24000
Brands Exported: Harris Famous
Regions Exported to: Central America, South America, Caribbean, Mexico
Percentage of Business in Exporting: 3
Regions Imported from: South America, Mexico
Percentage of Business in Importing: 10

47321 P.L. Thomas & Company
119 Headquarters Plaza
Morristown, NJ 07960   973-984-0900
Fax: 973-984-5666 www.plthomas.com
Supplier of extracts, natural color and flavorings, herbs and probiotics
President: Paul Flowerman

47322 PAFCO Importing Co
15373 Innovation Dr # 105
San Diego, CA 92128-3424   858-487-4844
Fax: 650-692-8950 tsfpafco@aol.com
Focusing on hanlding every aspect of importing your private label.
President: Terence S Fitzgerald
terry@pafcoimporting.com
VP: Barbara Burns
Operations: Myrna Goble
Estimated Sales: $10-20 Million
Number Employees: 1-4
Square Footage: 2800
Type of Packaging: Consumer, Food Service, Private Label, Bulk
Brands Exported: Seawave-Bono
Regions Exported to: Asia
Percentage of Business in Exporting: 5
Brands Imported: Terry's; Dingle's Delight
Regions Imported from: South America, Europe, Asia

Importers & Exporters / A-Z

47323 PAR Tech Inc
8383 Seneca Tpke
New Hartford, NY 13413
800-448-6505
www.partech.com
Manufacturer and exporter of computerized cash registers.
President & CEO: Dr. Donald Foley
Chief of Staff & Strategy: Karen Sammon
Chief Financial Officer: Bryan Menar
VP/General Counsel/Corporate Secretary: Cathy King
VP, Business & Financial Relations: Chris Byrnes
Year Founded: 1978
Estimated Sales: $118 Million
Number Employees: 500-999
Type of Packaging: Food Service
Brands Exported: System 3000

47324 PAR-Kan
2915 W 900 S
Silver Lake, IN 46982-9300
260-352-2141
Fax: 260-352-0701 800-291-5487
info@par-kan.com www.par-kan.com
Manufacturer and exporter of recycled grease containers, lids, screens and caster frames
President: David Caldwell
CFO: Richard Burton
rburton@par-kan.com
Marketing: Todd Sheets
Sales: Carolyn Montel
Estimated Sales: $10 - 20 Million
Number Employees: 50-99

47325 (HQ)PAR-Way Tryson Co
107 Bolte Ln
St Clair, MO 63077-3219
636-629-4545
Fax: 636-629-8341 moreinfo@parway.com
www.parwaytryson.com
Food release coatings, bakery and seasoning sprays
President: Keyna Lowrey Klabzuba
Owner & CEO: Mandy Hanson
Contact: Mike Abts
mike@parwaytryson.com
Year Founded: 1948
Number Employees: 20-49
Type of Packaging: Food Service, Private Label, Bulk
Brands Exported: Vegalene® Sunflower Aerosol & Liquid, Japan Bak-klene®, Japan Vegalene®
Regions Exported to: Central America, South America, Europe, Asia, Canada
Percentage of Business in Exporting: 20

47326 PASCO
2600 S Hanley Rd # 450
St Louis, MO 63144-2593
314-781-2212
Fax: 314-781-9986 800-489-3300
pasco@pascosystems.com www.pascosystems.com
Manufacturer and exporter of packaging machinery including slipsheet and pallet dispensers and bag, drum, pail and case palletizers
President: Dominic Spitalieri
spitalierid@pasco-group.com
CFO: Teresa Ovelgoenner
Executive VP: Sandy Elfrink
Sales Manager: Darin Everett
Estimated Sales: $10-20,000,000
Number Employees: 20-49
Square Footage: 50000
Regions Exported to: Worldwide

47327 PAX Spices & Labs Inc
550 N Rimsdale Ave
Covina, CA 91722-3507
626-967-7800
Fax: 626-967-7811 sales@paxspices.com
www.paxspices.com
Importer and distributor of exotic herbs, spices and oils.
President & CEO: Tom Tharayil
providence@paxspices.com
Estimated Sales: Less Than $500,000
Number Employees: 1-4
Other Locations:
Headquarters
Covina, CA
Sales & Distribution
Schaumburg, IL Headquarters Schaumburg
Percentage of Business in Importing: 95

47328 PB Leiner USA
PO Box 645
Plainview, NY 11803
516-822-4040
Fax: 516-465-0331 www.pbgelatins.com
Porcine gelatin
VP, Sales & Marketing: Cheryl Michaels
Contact: Kim Hildebrandt
kim.hildebrandt@pbleiner.com
Parent Co: Tessenderlo Group
Regions Exported to: Worldwide
Regions Imported from: South America, Latin America

47329 PBC
185 Route 17 North
Mahwah, NJ 07430
201-512-0387
Fax: 201-512-1459 800-514-2739
brewing@pubbrewing.com www.pubbrewing.com
Stainless steel tanks; importer of beer and wine filters; exporter of microbrew systems
President: Erwin Eibert
CFO: David Generso
VP: Ralph Eibert
Design Engineer: Dino Benvenuto
Estimated Sales: $3.5 Million
Number Employees: 10-19
Regions Exported to: Worldwide
Regions Imported from: Italy

47330 PC/Poll Systems
3162 Cedar Crest Rdg
Suite B
Dubuque, IA 52003
563-556-3556
Fax: 563-556-0405 800-670-1736
www.pcpoll.com
Manufacturer and exporter of software providing the ability to connect a PC to a cash register; compatible with all Casio ECR's NCR 2170, 2113, CRS 2000 and 3000 and Samsung 6500; also, provides collection, display, printing, export of reports, etc
Support: Gary Bishop
Estimated Sales: $2.5-5 Million
Number Employees: 5-9
Square Footage: 2400
Regions Exported to: Central America, South America, Europe, Asia

47331 (HQ)PDC International
1106 Clayton Ln # 521w
Austin, TX 78723-2489
512-302-0194
Fax: 512-302-0476 sales@pdc-corp.com
www.pdceurope.com/
Manufacturer and exporter of heat shrinkable tamper-evident seal and sleeve label machinery.
President: Neal Konstantin
Chief Executive Officer: Anatole Konstantin
VP: Alcyr Coelho
Marketing & Sales Director North America: Alcyr Coelho
Sales Representative: Reid Vail
Purchasing: Paul Strauss
Estimated Sales: $20 - 50 Million
Number Employees: 50-99
Square Footage: 17000
Other Locations:
PDC International Corporation
Austin, TX PDC International Corporation
Brands Exported: Tamper-Evident Seal & Sleeve Label Machinery
Regions Exported to: South America, Europe

47332 PDE Technology Corp
11522 Markon Dr
Garden Grove, CA 92841-1809
714-799-1704
Fax: 714-799-1705 866-547-8090
sales@castertech.com www.pdetechnology.com
Wholesaler/distributor and exporter of zinc and stainless steel finished casters and wheels for all applications; wholesaler/distributor of high temperature and washdown replacement parts for OEM equipment; serving the food service market
President: Chris Merchant
chris@pdetechnology.com
VP Marketing: David Elles
Account Services Manager: Bob Pettingill
Estimated Sales: $5-10 Million
Number Employees: 10-19
Square Footage: 80000
Type of Packaging: Consumer, Food Service, Bulk
Brands Exported: Javis & Javis; RWM; Darcor
Regions Exported to: Central America, South America, Europe, Asia, Middle East, Australia
Percentage of Business in Exporting: 5
Regions Imported from: Europe, Asia, Canada
Percentage of Business in Importing: 10

47333 PFI Displays Inc
40 Industrial St
PO Box 508
Rittman, OH 44270-1525
330-925-9015
Fax: 330-925-8520 800-925-9075
jtricomi@pfidisplays.com www.pfidisplays.com
Manufacturer and exporter of point of purchase displays, exhibits and store fixtures
President: Anthony R Tricomi
Chairman of the Board: Vincent Tricomi
Vice President of Sales: Jim Tricomi
Estimated Sales: $5 - 10 Million
Number Employees: 20-49
Square Footage: 140000
Regions Exported to: South America
Percentage of Business in Exporting: 2

47334 PLT Health Solutions Inc
119 Headquarters Plz
Morristown, NJ 07960-6834
973-984-0900
Fax: 973-984-5666 www.plthomas.com
Extracts for food, supplements and cosmeceuticals.
President & CEO: Paul Flowerman
Executive Vice President: Seth Flowerman
Contact: Jenson Chang
jensonchang@hotmail.com
Number Employees: 50-99

47335 PM Chemical Company
5319 Grant Street
San Diego, CA 92110-4010
619-296-0191
Manufacturer and exporter of detergents, soaps and food processing cleaners
President: John Mehren
soapies@pacbell.net
CEO: Bernard Mehren
Estimated Sales: $1-2.5 Million
Number Employees: 5-9
Square Footage: 40000
Brands Exported: Bronco; Red X; Purechem; Sofwite
Regions Exported to: Worldwide
Percentage of Business in Exporting: 5

47336 PMC Specialties Group Inc
501 Murray Rd
Cincinnati, OH 45217-1014
513-242-3300
Fax: 513-482-7373 800-543-2466
davidsc@pmsg.com www.pmcsg.com
Saccharin, BHT, methyl anthranilate and benzonitrile
President: Michael Buchanan
Contact: Antaeus Kelly
antaeusk@pmcsg.com
Estimated Sales: $70 Milion
Number Employees: 250-499
Square Footage: 7500
Parent Co: PMC Global, Inc.
Regions Exported to: Central America, South America, Europe, Asia, Middle East

47337 PMP Fermentation Products
900 NE Adams St
Peoria, IL 61603-4200
309-637-0400
Fax: 309-637-9302 800-558-1031
info@pmpinc.com www.pmpinc.com
Sodium gluconate, erythorbate, calcium gluconate, gluconic acid, glucono-delta-lactone, sodium erythorbate, calcium potassium gluconate.
President/CEO: Randall Niedermeier
Director, Corporate Planning & Sales: Jim Zinkhon
Director, Administration: Dan Rudy
Year Founded: 1985
Estimated Sales: $25000000
Number Employees: 50-99
Parent Co: Fuso Chemical Company
Type of Packaging: Bulk
Brands Exported: Eribate
Regions Exported to: Worldwide
Percentage of Business in Exporting: 30
Brands Imported: Eribate
Regions Imported from: Asia
Percentage of Business in Importing: 5

47338 (HQ)PMS
275 E 131st St
Cleveland, OH 44108-1605
216-451-7878
Fax: 216-451-4952 packnow@packnow.com
www.packnow.com
Exporter of new and rebuilt packaging machinery including bag closers and fillers, box closers and bottle, jar, box, carton and case sealers

President: Ken Franklin
Plant Manager: Fritz Aufdenkampe
Estimated Sales: $10-20 Million
Number Employees: 20-49
Square Footage: 300000

47339 POM Wonderful LLC
11444 W. Olympic Blvd.
Los Angeles, CA 90064
866-976-6999
pr.pom@wonderful.com www.pomwonderful.com
Pomegranates, fruit juices, extracts and more.
Owner: Lynda Resnick
Chief Executive Officer: Stewart Resnick
Chief Financial Officer: Marc Washington
Marketing Director: Molly Flynn
Year Founded: 2002
Estimated Sales: $762 Million
Number Employees: 100-249
Parent Co: The Wonderful Company
Type of Packaging: Bulk
Regions Exported to: South America, Europe, Asia, Canada, Mexico, Australia

47340 POSWarehouse.com
1125 Northmeadow Pkwy # 114
Roswell, GA 30076-3870
678-424-4000
Fax: 678-424-4004 sales@poswarehouse.com
www.postec.com
President: David Shaw
Contact: Carlos Mudafort
carlos@postec.com
Number Employees: 250-499

47341 PPC Perfect Packaging Co
26974 Eckel Rd
PO Box 286
Perrysburg, OH 43551-1214
419-874-3167
Fax: 419-874-8044
Manufacturer and exporter of custom wooden boxes for machinery and related equipment and domestic, export and military packaging; also, heated warehousing available
Owner: Anil Sharma
Estimated Sales: Less Than $500,000
Number Employees: 1-4
Square Footage: 28000

47342 PPI Technologies Group
1610 Northgate Blvd
Sarasota, FL 34234
941-359-6678
Fax: 941-359-6804 rcmpp@aol.com
www.ppitechnologies.com
Manufacturer and supplier of stand up pouch machinery
President: Stuart Murray
CEO: R Charles Murray
CFO: Karena Thomas
Vice President: Sandra Christensen
Research & Development: Rudi Kleer
Quality Control: Gary Bush
Marketing: Richard Murray
Marketing/Sales: Robert Libera
Contact: Andre Beukes
abeukes@redi2drinqgroup.com
Operations Manager: Peter Aeberhard
Production Manager: Pete Ceconci
Plant Manager: Sean Reed
Purchasing Manager: Tom Richard
Estimated Sales: $20 Million
Number Employees: 40
Number of Brands: 7
Number of Products: 10
Square Footage: 60000
Parent Co: Profile Packaging Inc - Paksource Group LLC
Type of Packaging: Food Service
Brands Exported: Laudenberg; Nishibe; Psglee; Psg Sung; Psgmini Pmo; Shot Pak
Regions Exported to: Central America, South America, Europe, Asia, Middle East
Brands Imported: Laudenberg; Nishibe; Leepack; Abtech; Yokomama; EL Sung; Shot Pak
Regions Imported from: Central America, South America, Europe, Asia, South Africa

47343 PROCON Products
869 Seven Oaks Blvd # 120
Suite 120
Smyrna, TN 37167-6482
615-355-8000
Fax: 615-355-8001 mail@proconpump.com
www.proconpumps.com
Manufacturer and exporter of positive displacement rotary vane pumps
President: Paul Roberts
proberts@proconpump.com
VP, Sales & Business Development: Jim Kelly
Product Manager: Jeff Kulikowski
Purchasing Agent: Tracy Harris
Estimated Sales: $10-25 Million
Number Employees: 20-49
Parent Co: Standex International
Type of Packaging: Food Service
Brands Exported: Procon
Regions Exported to: Worldwide
Percentage of Business in Exporting: 40

47344 PTC International
401 East Pratt Street
Baltimore, MD 21202-3117
410-962-8409
Fax: 410-962-8281 www.ptcintl.com
Wholesaler/distributor and exporter of fruit juices, juice concentrates, canned vegetables, snack foods, frozen cheesecakes, processed poultry products, ingredients, seasonings, flavors, etc
Assistant Manager: Charles Ji
Assistant Manager: Tomo Naito
Contact: Steve Hsin
shsin@ptcintl.com
Estimated Sales: $5-10 Million
Number Employees: 5-9
Brands Exported: Chuck Full of Nuts; Ambrosia of ADM; Mother's Kitchen; Baltimore Spice; Pilgrim's Pride; Kellogg's
Regions Exported to: Asia, Middle East
Percentage of Business in Exporting: 80

47345 PTI Packaging
1055 Saddle Rdg
Portage, WI 53901
920-623-3566
Fax: 920-623-5659 800-501-4077
protech@powerweb.net
Manufacturer and exporter of palletizers, conveyors, sheet dispensers, pallet dispensers/conveyors and package accumulators
President: John Wildner
jwildner@ptipackaging.com
Estimated Sales: $2.5-5,000,000
Number Employees: 1-4

47346 PTR Baler & Compactor Co
2207 E Ontario St
Philadelphia, PA 19134-2615
267-345-0490
Fax: 215-533-8907 800-523-3654
sales@ptrco.com www.ptrco.com
Manufacturer and exporter of vertical recycling balers and waste compaction systems
President/CEO: Michael Savage
IT: Joseph Bennett
jbennett@tramrail.com
Estimated Sales: $30 Million
Number Employees: 100-249
Number of Brands: 3
Square Footage: 135000
Parent Co: RJR Enterprises
Regions Exported to: Central America, Europe, Asia, Middle East, Caribbean, Canada, Mexico
Percentage of Business in Exporting: 5

47347 PURA
9848 Glenoaks Boulevard
Sun Valley, CA 91352-1045
818-768-0451
Fax: 661-257-6385 800-292-7872
Manufacturer and exporter of ultraviolet and filtration water treatment products
Vice President: Edwin Roberts
Regional Sales Manager: Brad Hess
Estimated Sales: $ 1-2.5 Million
Number Employees: 10-19
Square Footage: 320000
Parent Co: Hydrotech
Brands Exported: Pura
Regions Exported to: Worldwide
Percentage of Business in Exporting: 70

47348 Pa R Systems Inc
707 County Road E W
St Paul, MN 55126-7007
651-528-5200
Fax: 651-483-2689 800-464-1320
info@par.com www.par.com
Manufacturer and exporter of cranes, hoists and crane controls
General Manager: Joe Hoff
CEO: Mark Wrightsman
mwrightsman@par.com
VP: Neil Skogland
Director Sales/Marketing: Jaems Nelson
Estimated Sales: $10-20 Million
Number Employees: 100-249
Type of Packaging: Bulk
Regions Exported to: Worldwide

47349 Paar Physica USA
1 Industrial Way W
Eatontown, NJ 07724-2255
804-266-5553
Fax: 804-550-1057 800-688-3569
Wholesaler/distributor, importer and exporter of laboratory instrumentation for measuring viscosity and elasticity of food products; also, rheometers for research and quality assurance
CEO: Sean Race
COO: Abel Gaspar
Number Employees: 10-19
Square Footage: 6000
Regions Exported to: Central America, South America, Canada
Percentage of Business in Exporting: 5
Regions Imported from: Europe
Percentage of Business in Importing: 95

47350 (HQ)Pabst Brewing Company
Consumer Affairs Department
PO Box 792627
San Antonio, TX 78279
210-226-0231
Fax: 210-226-2512 800-947-2278
products@pabst.com www.pabst.com
Beers
Chairman: Dean Metropoulos
Co-CEO: Evan Metropoulos
Co-cEO: Daren Metropoulos
President: John Coleman
Chief Financial Officer: Brent Zachary
SVP/General Counsel: Jim Vieceli
Chief Marketing Officer: Daniel McHugh
VP Sales/National Accounts: Mark Beatty
Number Employees: 100-249
Type of Packaging: Consumer
Other Locations:
Pabst Brewery Location
San Antonio, TX
Pabst Brewery Location
Milwaukee, WIPabst Brewery
LocationMilwaukee

47351 Pace Packaging Corp
3 Sperry Rd
Fairfield, NJ 07004-2004
973-227-1040
Fax: 973-227-7393 800-867-2726
sales@pacepackaging.com
www.pacepackaging.com
Manufacturer and exporter of high speed plastic bottle unscramblers
President/CFO: Kenneth F Regula
Vice President-Sales: Glenn G. Kelley
Quality Control: Mike Regula
Sales Manager: Glenn Kelley
Manager: Sam Jarkas
jarkas@pacepkg.com
VP Manufacturing: Ken Regula
Estimated Sales: $ 5 - 10 Million
Number Employees: 20-49
Square Footage: 60
Brands Exported: Omni-Line
Regions Exported to: Worldwide
Percentage of Business in Exporting: 40

47352 Pacer Pumps
41 Industrial Cir
Lancaster, PA 17601-5927
717-656-2161
Fax: 717-656-0477 800-233-3861
sales@pacerpumps.com www.pacerpumps.com
Manufacturer and exporter of pumps including self-priming centrifugal nonmetallic, hand operated and powered drum
Manager: Glenn Geist
sales@pacerpumps.com
General Manager: Denzel Stoops
Marketing: Art Foster
Sales: Ron Hock
Manager: Glenn Geist
sales@pacerpumps.com
Purchasing Manager: Ernie Stoltzfus
Estimated Sales: $ 5 - 10 Million
Number Employees: 20-49
Square Footage: 144000
Parent Co: Serfilco
Brands Exported: Pacer; Camelot
Regions Exported to: Central America, South America, Europe, Asia, Middle East, Canada, Caribbean, Latin America, Mexico
Percentage of Business in Exporting: 15

Importers & Exporters / A-Z

47353 Pacific American Fish Co Inc
5525 S Santa Fe Ave
Vernon, CA 90058-3523   323-587-3298
Fax: 323-319-1517   800-625-2525
pehuh@pafco.net www.pafco.net
Shrimp, fish fillets and calamari steaks, rings and strips
Chairman/CEO: Peter Huh
Vice Chairman/VP, Operations & Sales: Paul Huh
VP, New Venture Development: Jihee Huh
Estimated Sales: $37.8 Million
Number Employees: 50-99
Number of Brands: 4
Square Footage: 10600
Type of Packaging: Consumer, Food Service
Other Locations:
   San Francisco, CA
   Boston, MABoston
Regions Exported to: Worldwide
Regions Imported from: Asia, Mexico

47354 Pacific Choice Brands
4652 E. Date Ave.
Fresno, CA 93725   559-476-3581
Fax: 559-237-2096 sales@pacificchoice.com
www.pacificchoice.com
Maraschino cherries, garlic, grape leaves, peppers, olives, salsa, sauces, capers and sun dried tomotoes
President: Allan Andrews
CFO: Faith Buller
VP: Villalobos Boni
Plant Manager: Chris Rabago
Purchasing Manager: Mireille Akel
Estimated Sales: $39.5 Million
Number Employees: 275
Square Footage: 225000
Type of Packaging: Consumer, Food Service, Private Label
Regions Exported to: Europe, Asia, Australia, Mexico

47355 Pacific Coast Fruit Co
201 NE 2nd Ave # 100
Portland, OR 97232-2993   503-234-6411
Fax: 503-234-0072 www.pcfruit.com
Frozen fruits, juice concentrates
President: Dave Nemarnik
Secretary/Treasurer: Ellen McIntyre
Accounting Manager: Jeff Rine
Vice President, Director: Don Daeges
Sales Manager: Bob Meikle
Vice President of Operations: Joe Santucci
Number Employees: 250-499
Type of Packaging: Bulk
Regions Exported to: Europe, Asia
Regions Imported from: South America, Europe

47356 Pacific Commerce Company
16320 Bake Parkway
Irvine, CA 92618   949-679-4700
Fax: 949-589-9002
Exporter of maraschino cherries, pie fillings, bakery items, mayonnaise, salad dressings, etc.; wholesaler/distributor of general line products; serving the food service market; warehouse offering dry storage for groceries
President: Bryan McCullough
VP: Mark Roberts
Contact: Mackay Ramsay
mramsay@pacificommerce.com
Estimated Sales: $2.5-5 Million
Number Employees: 1-4
Square Footage: 73728
Brands Exported: Pennant; Oregon Fruit; Pastry Pride; Gold N' Soft
Regions Exported to: South America, Asia, Middle East, Australia

47357 Pacific Foods
21612 88th Ave S
Kent, WA 98031-1918   253-395-9400
Fax: 253-395-3330   800-347-9444
Flavoring extracts, seasoning mixes, soup bases, baking powder, nuts and spices
President: James Hughs
Plant Manager: Brandan Caile
Vice President: Richard Weaver
Plant Manager: Mark Hendrickson
Estimated Sales: $ 5 - 10 Million
Number Employees: 50-99
Type of Packaging: Food Service, Private Label, Bulk
Brands Exported: Crescent
Regions Exported to: Worldwide

Regions Imported from: Worldwide

47358 Pacific Fruit Processors
7301 Ohms Lane
Suite 600, CA 55439   952-820-2518
Fax: 952-939-8106 pfpsalesorders@sunopta.com
Fruit ingredients
Prsident/CEO: Steve Bromley
COO: Frank Gonzalez
Estimated Sales: $93,000
Number Employees: 1
Square Footage: 7384
Type of Packaging: Food Service
Other Locations:
   Pacific Fruit Processors
   Lapham, CoPacific Fruit Processors

47359 Pacific Nutritional
6317 NE 131st Ave # 103
Vancouver, WA 98682-5879   360-896-2297
Fax: 360-253-6543
Tablet, capsule, powder and liquid nutritional formulations
President: Michael Schaesser
CEO: Tiffany Swett
CFO: Ron Golden
VP, Sales/Marketing: Tina Mori
COO: Scott Haugen
Estimated Sales: $27 Million
Number Employees: 50-99
Square Footage: 35000
Type of Packaging: Private Label
Regions Exported to: Worldwide
Regions Imported from: Europe, Asia

47360 Pacific Oasis Enterprise Inc
8413 Secura Way # B
Santa Fe Springs, CA 90670-2297   562-698-9146
Fax: 562-698-9147   800-424-1475
POEUS@PacificOasis.com
Manufacturer, importer and exporter of stainless steel scouring pads for the cleaning of pans, grills, ovens, etc.; also, disposables including aprons and gloves
President: S C Chen
scchen@pacificoasis.com
Quality Control: Nick Sumgsun
General Manager: Daisy Reyes
Manager: Nely Go
Estimated Sales: $ 2.5 - 5 Million
Number Employees: 1-4
Regions Exported to: Europe, Latin America
Percentage of Business in Exporting: 20
Regions Imported from: Asia
Percentage of Business in Importing: 80

47361 Pacific Plaza Imports
675 Cumberland Street
PO Box 390
Pittsburgh, CA 94565   925-252-9700
Fax: 925-252-9797   888-888-4470
Caviar, spices, confections, mushrooms, pasta, smoked fish and oils
President/Owner: Mark Bolourchi
VP: Ali Bolourchi
Estimated Sales: $3 Million
Number Employees: 8

47362 Pacific Refrigerator Company
328 S Mountain View Avenue
San Bernardino, CA 92408-1415   909-381-5669
Fax: 909-888-1203
Manufacturer and exporter of walk-in cooler and freezers
President: John Gomez
Estimated Sales: Below $5 Million
Number Employees: 10
Regions Exported to: Worldwide
Percentage of Business in Exporting: 1

47363 Pacific Resources
1021 Mark Ave
Carpinteria, CA 93013-2912   805-684-0624
Fax: 805-684-8624   800-871-8879
www.shoppri.com
Bottled water, honey, sea salt and propolis products
President: David Noll
pri98@earthlink.net
Estimated Sales: $ 3 - 5 Million
Number Employees: 1-4
Type of Packaging: Consumer
Brands Imported: Comvita; Clarus; Cool Blue, Honeyland.
Regions Imported from: New Zealand

Percentage of Business in Importing: 100

47364 Pacific Salmon Company
21630 98th Ave W
Edmonds, WA 98020-3923   425-774-1315
Fax: 425-774-6856
Black cod, halibut, salmon, shark, smelt, squid, kosher foods and fish patties
Owner: John Mc Callum
Contact: James Chapa
johnmccallum@msn.com
Estimated Sales: $ 5 - 10 Million
Number Employees: 10 to 19
Brands Exported: Pacific
Regions Exported to: Europe, Asia, Canada, Worldwide
Percentage of Business in Exporting: 30

47365 Pacific Scientific Instrument
481 California St
Grants Pass, OR 97526   541-479-1248
Fax: 541-479-3057   800-866-7889
infogp@hachultra.com
Manufacturer and exporter of instruments for detecting and measuring minute particles
President: Simon Appleby
Contact: Carroll Davis
carroll.davis@particle.com
Production Manager: Brian Bosch
Production Manager: Joe Gecsey
Estimated Sales: $ 50-100 Million
Number Employees: 100-249
Square Footage: 10000
Brands Exported: HIAC Royco
Regions Exported to: Central America, South America, Europe, Asia, Middle East, Australia

47366 Pacific Seafoods International
PO Box 401
Port Hardy, BC V0N 2P0
Canada   250-949-8781
Fax: 250-949-8781
Salmon fillets
President: Hardy Fish
CEO: Todd Harmon
Number Employees: 20-49
Square Footage: 48000
Type of Packaging: Consumer, Food Service, Private Label, Bulk
Brands Exported: Treasure Island
Regions Exported to: South America, Europe, Asia
Percentage of Business in Exporting: 40

47367 Pacific Spice Co
6430 E Slauson Ave
Commerce, CA 90040-3108   323-890-0895
Fax: 323-726-9442 www.pacspice.com
Spices and herbs
President: Akiba Schlussel
akiba@pacspice.com
Estimated Sales: G
Number Employees: 100-249
Square Footage: 150000
Type of Packaging: Consumer, Food Service, Private Label, Bulk
Brands Exported: Pacific Natural Spices
Regions Exported to: Worldwide
Percentage of Business in Exporting: 2
Brands Imported: Raw Material
Regions Imported from: Worldwide
Percentage of Business in Importing: 70

47368 Pacific Standard Distributors
38954 Proctor Blvd
Suite 388
Sandy, OR 97055   760-479-1460
Fax: 800-741-2164 sales@modifilan.com
www.modifilan.com
Seaweed supplement capsules
Owner: Vladimir Bajanov
Contact: Michelle Arakaki
marakaki@modifilan.com
Estimated Sales: $ 1 - 3 Million
Number Employees: 1-4
Number of Products: 1
Type of Packaging: Consumer, Food Service, Bulk
Regions Imported from: Russia

47369 Pacific Steam Equipment, Inc.
10648 Painter Ave
Santa Fe Springs, CA 90670   562-906-9292
Fax: 562-906-9223   800-321-4114
sales@pacificsteam.com

Manufacturer and exporter of boilers; distributor of food processing machinery
Owner: David Ken
President: William Shanahan
Vice President: Shin King
Marketing Manager: Simon Lee
Sales Manager: Santiago Kuan
Contact: Dave Kang
res@pacificsteam.com
Estimated Sales: $2.9 Million
Number Employees: 25
Square Footage: 90000
Regions Exported to: Worldwide

47370 Pacific Store Designs Inc
11781 Cardinal Cir
Garden Grove, CA 92843-3815   714-636-4440
    Fax: 714-636-4442   800-772-5661
    psd4cmiller@sbcglobal.net
    www.pacificstoredesigns.com
Manufacturer and exporter of retail store fixtures including shelving, general contractor, architecturer and desgin services trade show exhibits and custom woodworking items specializing in small to medium sized convenience, gourmetand health food stores; also, installation services available
President: Chris Miller
Sr. Vice President: James Raynor
Research & Development: Sonia Quintana
Quality Control: Erv Miller
Plant Manager: Ken Kasper
Estimated Sales: Less Than $500,000
Number Employees: 1-4
Square Footage: 13200
Type of Packaging: Private Label

47371 Pacific Trellis
1500 W Manning Ave
Reedley, CA 93654-9211   559-638-5100
    Fax: 559-638-5400 www.pacifictrellisfruit.com
Stone fruits and grapes
Manager: Earl Mc Menamin
Contact: Tim Dayka
t.dayka@pacifictrellisfruit.com
Estimated Sales: $ 10 - 20 Million
Number Employees: 10-19

47372 Pacific Valley Foods Inc
2700 Richards Rd # 101
Bellevue, WA 98005-4200   425-643-1805
    Fax: 425-747-4221 sales@pacificvalleyfoods.com
    www.pacificvalleyfoods.com
French fries, frozen vegetables, frozen berries, tortillas, dried peas, lentils, chickpeas
Co-Owner/Co-Director: Scott Hannah
scott@pacificvalleyfoods.com
Co-Owner/Co-Director: Lynn Hannah
Executive VP: John Hannah
Estimated Sales: $2.7 Million
Number Employees: 5-9
Square Footage: 40000
Parent Co: Pacific Valley Foods
Type of Packaging: Consumer, Food Service, Private Label, Bulk
Brands Exported: Pacific Valley; Lynden Farms; Country Goodness; Cedar Farms; Hi West
Regions Exported to: Worldwide
Percentage of Business in Exporting: 70
Regions Imported from: Europe, Asia
Percentage of Business in Importing: 5

47373 Pacific World Enterprises
225 Market Street
203
Oakland, CA 94607-2554   510-843-0240
Wholesaler/distributor and exporter of frozen foods, produce, meats and seafood; serving the food service market
President: Edward Chiang
VP/General Manager: Keith Toy
Manager (West Coast): Bill Chiang
Number Employees: 20-49
Square Footage: 72000
Parent Co: Good World Investment Company
Type of Packaging: Food Service
Other Locations:
    Pacific World Enterprises
    Saipan MPPacific World Enterprises
Brands Exported: Certified Angus Beef; Tyson; McCain's
Regions Exported to: Asia

47374 Pack Line Corporation
3026 Phillips Ave
Racine, WI 53403   262-635-6966
    Fax: 262-634-0512 800-248-6868
    packrite@packrite.com www.packrite.com
Manufacturer, importer and exporter of semi-automatic and automatic fillers and capping, and sealing machinery
Manager: Dave Bornhuepter
CFO: Michael Beilinson
Vice President: Nick Maslovets
Marketing Director: Erica Kosinski
Estimated Sales: $1 Million
Number Employees: 5-9
Square Footage: 8000
Parent Co: Pack Line
Regions Exported to: Europe
Percentage of Business in Exporting: 50
Brands Imported: Pack Line
Regions Imported from: Israel

47375 Pack Rite Machine Mettler
3026 Phillips Ave
Mt Pleasant, WI 53403-3585   262-635-6966
    Fax: 262-634-0521 800-248-6868
    packrite@packrite.com www.packrite.com
Manufacturer and exporter of bag closing, and packaging machinery
Manager: Dave Bornhuepter
dave.bornhuepter@mt.com
General Manager: Dave Bornhuetter
Estimated Sales: $ 3 - 5 Million
Number Employees: 5-9
Square Footage: 24000
Parent Co: Mettler-Toledo
Brands Exported: Pack Rite
Regions Exported to: Worldwide
Percentage of Business in Exporting: 25

47376 Pack West Machinery
5316 Irwindale Ave # B
Baldwin Park, CA 91706-2034   626-814-4766
    Fax: 626-814-1615 www.ratioflo.com
Manufacturer and exporter of packaging machinery including top driven and in-line cappers
Owner: Bill Ellison
Marketing/General Manager: Loren Lauxen
Estimated Sales: $2.5-5,000,000
Number Employees: 20-49
Regions Exported to: Worldwide
Percentage of Business in Exporting: 10

47377 Pack-A-Drum
862 Hawksbill Island Dr
Satellite Beach, FL 32937-3850   321-773-1551
    Fax: 321-779-3816 800-694-6163
    profits@packadrum.com www.pack-a-drum.com
Manufacturer and exporter of manually operated trash compactors/deflators, waste containers and platform carts with free waste management consulting for customers.
President: William E Wagner
pack-a-drum@cfl.rr.com
CFO: Kelli Wagner
VP Marketing: Erik Wagner
VP Sales: Mark Wagner
Director Customer Service: Kirk Wagner
Estimated Sales: $2 Million
Number Employees: 5-9
Number of Brands: 1
Number of Products: 10
Square Footage: 200000
Regions Exported to: Latin America
Percentage of Business in Exporting: 2

47378 Package Concepts & Materials Inc
1023 Thousand Oaks Blvd
Greenville, SC 29607-5642   864-458-7291
    Fax: 864-458-7295 800-424-7264
    sales@packageconcepts.com
    www.packageconcepts.com
Cook-in casings for meat and poultry processing
President: Peter Bylenga
Estimated Sales: $10 - 20 Million
Number Employees: 50-99
Square Footage: 100000
Type of Packaging: Food Service
Regions Exported to: Central America, Canada, Mexico, Latin America
Percentage of Business in Exporting: 12

47379 Package Conveyor Co
123 S Main St
Fort Worth, TX 76104-1222   817-332-7195
    Fax: 817-334-0855 800-792-1243
    wapowers@flash.net
Manufacturer and exporter of conveying equipment including flat, inclined and floor-to-floor belts
Owner: Jack Powers
pcco@flash.net
President: Doyle Powers
Estimated Sales: $2.5-5 Million
Number Employees: 10-19
Parent Co: W.A. Powers Industries
Regions Exported to: Mexico
Percentage of Business in Exporting: 20

47380 (HQ)Package Machinery Co Inc
80 Commercial St
Holyoke, MA 01040-4704   413-315-3801
    Fax: 413-732-1163
    customerservice@packagemachinery.com
    www.packagemachinery.com
Manufacturer and exporter of rebuilt packaging and injection molding equipment; also, parts
President: Katherine E Putnam
kputnam@packagemachinery.com
Marketing Manager: Meg Cook
General Manager: Paul Stiebel
Estimated Sales: $2.5-5 Million
Number Employees: 20-49
Square Footage: 44000
Brands Exported: Package
Regions Exported to: Central America, South America, Canada, Latin America, Mexico
Percentage of Business in Exporting: 30

47381 Package Systems Corporation
109 Connecticut Mills Avenue
Danielson, CT 06239-1653   860-774-0363
    Fax: 860-774-5326 800-522-3548
Pressure sensitive rolls and sheets, labels, label machinery and grease proof polystyrene inserts for meats, poultry, etc.; importer of cellophane; exporter of labels
Sales/Marketing Executive: Charles Pingeton
VP Sales: Randall Duhaime
Estimated Sales: $2.5-5 Million
Number Employees: 20-49
Square Footage: 132000
Regions Exported to: Central America, Europe, Asia
Percentage of Business in Exporting: 30
Brands Imported: Courtald Films
Regions Imported from: Europe

47382 (HQ)Packaging & Processing Equipment
121 Earl Thompson Road
Ayr, ON N0B 1E0
Canada   519-622-6666
    Fax: 519-622-6669
Manufacturer and exporter of new, used, rebuilt and custom built blister packagers, bottle sorters, cappers, cartoners, case packers and sealers, cleaners, conveyors, fillers, heat sealers, kettles, labelers, mixers, palletizerstanks, etc
President: P Wiese
CEO: Peter Weise
Other Locations:
    Packaging & Processing Equipm
    WindhagenPackaging & Processing Equipm
Brands Exported: PPET
Regions Exported to: Central America, South America, Europe, Asia, Middle East, Africa, Mexico
Percentage of Business in Exporting: 60

47383 Packaging Aids Corporation
P.O.Box 9144
San Rafael, CA 94912-9144   415-454-4868
    Fax: 415-454-6853 sales@paçaids.com
    www.paçaids.com
Manufacturer, importer and exporter of sealing machinery for meat, produce, poultry and seafood; also, vacuum chambers and form/fill machinery
President: Serge Berguig
Quality Control: Dana McDaniel
National Sales/Marketing Manager: R Perrone
Sales Manager (Eastern Region): Jerry Henry
Estimated Sales: $5-10 Million
Number Employees: 20-49
Regions Exported to: Worldwide
Percentage of Business in Exporting: 18
Brands Imported: Audion; Schlosspack

Importers & Exporters / A-Z

Regions Imported from: Europe, Canada
Percentage of Business in Importing: 15

47384 (HQ)Packaging Dynamics
PO Box 5332
Walnut Creek, CA 94596-1332   925-938-2711
Fax: 925-938-2713   dlehm19148@aol.com
Manufacturer, importer and exporter of packaging machinery including horizontal and vertical form/fill/seal machinery, liquid fillers and bottling lines, cartoners, wrappers, bundlers and tea baggers
President: Richard Novak
Engineering Manager: Mike Sanchez
Marketing: Banchez
Sales Manager: Fred Wermuth
Estimated Sales: $2.5-5 Million
Number Employees: 5-9
Square Footage: 20000
Brands Exported: Packaging Dynamics
Regions Exported to: Central America, South America, Asia
Brands Imported: Marden Edward
Regions Imported from: South America, Europe, Asia

47385 (HQ)Packaging Dynamics Corp
3900 W 43rd St
Chicago, IL 60632-3421   773-843-8000
Fax: 773-254-8136
Manufacturer and exporter of packaging machinery including liquid filling
CEO: Patrick T Chambliss
pchambliss@pkdy.com
Vice President of Human Resources: Paul Christensen
Estimated Sales: $2.5-5 Million
Number Employees: 1000-4999
Square Footage: 40000
Other Locations:
   Packaging Dynamics Ltd.
   Hartwell, GAPackaging Dynamics Ltd.
Regions Exported to: Worldwide
Percentage of Business in Exporting: 35

47386 Packaging Dynamics International
17153 Industrial Hwy
Caldwell, OH 43724-9779   740-732-5665
Fax: 740-732-7515
laminations@ici-laminating.com
Manufacturer and exporter of aluminum beverage and can liners, containers for biscuits and sandwich wrap; also, laminated paper
President: Darin Barton
VP: Gerry Medlin
Estimated Sales: $ 15 - 20 Million
Number Employees: 50-99
Parent Co: Alupac
Regions Exported to: Canada

47387 Packaging Enterprises
12 N. Penn Ave
Rockledge, PA 19046   215-379-1234
Fax: 215-379-1166   800-453-6213
fillers@packagingenterprises.com
www.packagingenterprises.com
Manufacturer and exporter of plastic bags and pouches
President: Lee Sanford
Contact: Terry Geyer
terry@packagingenterprises.com
Estimated Sales: $1-2.5 Million
Number Employees: 1-4
Square Footage: 72000
Type of Packaging: Private Label, Bulk
Percentage of Business in Exporting: 2

47388 Packaging Enterprises
12 N. Penn ave.
Rockledge, PA 19046   215-379-1234
Fax: 215-379-1166   800-453-6213
fillers@packagingenterprises.com
www.packagingenterprises.com
Manufacturer and exporter of filling machinery for liquids and viscous food products
President: Terrence Geyer
VP: Timothy Geyer
Contact: Terry Geyer
terry@packagingenterprises.com
Estimated Sales: $2.5-5 Million
Number Employees: 10-19
Number of Products: 15
Square Footage: 13600
Type of Packaging: Private Label
Regions Exported to: Worldwide
Percentage of Business in Exporting: 15

47389 Packaging Equipment & Conveyors, Inc
52853 County Road 7
Elkhart, IN 46514-9522   574-266-6995
Fax: 574-264-6210
Manufacturer and exporter of liquid and aerosol filling line equipment; also, modular conveying systems, bi-directional accumulation tables, flight-bar sorters, tube taping machines, orienting systems, de-palletizers, can de-elevatorsand product hoppers
Manager: Dennis Kline
Vice President: Brenda Arbogast
Research & Development: Brad Wegner
Sales Director: Chuck Reed
Operations Manager: Dennis Kline
Estimated Sales: $3 Million
Number Employees: 5-9
Number of Products: 16
Square Footage: 40000
Type of Packaging: Private Label
Regions Exported to: Asia, Canada, Caribbean
Percentage of Business in Exporting: 10

47390 Packaging Machinery
2303 W Fairview Ave
Montgomery, AL 36108-4158   334-265-9211
Fax: 334-265-9218
Manufacturer and exporter of material handling equipment, designer packaging machinery, conveyors, etc
Finance/Treasurer: Bruce Murchison
Estimated Sales: $1-2.5 Million
Number Employees: 5-9
Type of Packaging: Bulk
Regions Exported to: Worldwide

47391 Packaging Machinery & Equipment
179-181 Watson Ave
West Orange, NJ 7052   973-325-2418
Fax: 973-325-6937   packmach@aol.com
www.packagingmachineryandequipment.com
Manufacturer and exporter of cartoners and machinery including marking, printing, dating and coding; also, rebuilding of packaging equipment available
President: James Lyle Clark
Secretary: Mary Cameron
Quality Control: Dennis McDermott
Estimated Sales: Below $5 Million
Number Employees: 1-4
Regions Exported to: Worldwide

47392 Packaging Machinery International
1260 Lunt Avenue
Elk Grove Village, IL 60007-5618   847-640-1512
Fax: 847-640-8732   800-871-4764
www.pmi-intl.com
Manufacturer and exporter of packaging machinery and equipment including shrink wrappers and bundlers
President: Branko Vukotic
CFO: Branko Vukotic
VP: Randy Spahr
Estimated Sales: $ 5 - 10 Million
Number Employees: 20-49
Square Footage: 56000
Regions Exported to: South America, Asia
Percentage of Business in Exporting: 20

47393 (HQ)Packaging Products Corp
6820 Squibb Rd
Mission, KS 66202-3224   913-262-3033
Fax: 913-789-8698
Manufacturer and exporter of printed and converted flexible packaging materials including sheet and roll
President: Jack Joslin
CEO: Laird Dowgray
dlaird@packagingcorp.com
Sales/Marketing: Laird Dowgray
Sales Manager: Tom Zammit
COO: Jack Joslyn
Billing & Accounts Receivable: Cindy Hansen
Number Employees: 50-99
Square Footage: 74000
Other Locations:
   Packaging Products Corp.
   Rome, GAPackaging Products Corp.
Regions Exported to: Canada
Percentage of Business in Exporting: 5

47394 Packaging Service Co Inc
1904 Mykawa Rd
Pearland, TX 77581-3210   281-485-4320
Fax: 281-485-3242   800-826-2949
sales@packserv.com   www.packserv.com
Contract packager and exporter of charcoal starter, all-purpose cleaners, lamp oil and household chemicals; private labeling available
President: Gean-Pierre Baizan
websales@packserv.com
Quality Control: Carl Caldwell
VP/General Manager: Jean-Pierre Baizan
Manager Grocery/Sales: Larry Lubs
Export Manager: George Foster
Plant Manager: Luis Dela Cruz
Estimated Sales: $20-25 Million
Number Employees: 100-249
Square Footage: 150000
Regions Exported to: Central America, Middle East, Caribbean, Latin America, Mexico
Percentage of Business in Exporting: 5

47395 (HQ)Packaging Systems Intl
4990 Acoma St
Denver, CO 80216-2030   303-244-9000
Fax: 303-298-1016   www.pkgsys.com
Manufacturer and exporter of bag filling and weighing machinery, portable flexible conveyors, bag openers, stackers, palletizers and material handling machinery
President: Michael Lott
mlott@pkgsys.com
Chairman of the Board: H Lott
Quality Control: Jenee Jenee
Sr. VP Sales/Marketing: A Guyton
Estimated Sales: $5-10 Million
Number Employees: 20-49
Square Footage: 150000
Parent Co: St. Regis Paper Company
Regions Exported to: Central America, South America, Europe, Asia, Middle East
Percentage of Business in Exporting: 20

47396 Pacmac Inc
1501 S Armstrong Ave
Fayetteville, AR 72701-7230   479-521-0525
Fax: 479-521-2448   800-834-1544
fterminella@pacmac.com   www.pacmac.com
Manufacturer and exporter of vertical form/fill/seal machinery
Administrator: Joe Terminella
Manager: Frank Terminella
terminella@pacmac.com
Estimated Sales: $2.5-5,000,000
Number Employees: 20-49
Square Footage: 200000
Regions Exported to: Worldwide

47397 (HQ)Pacmatic/Ritmica
4140 Tuller Road
Suite 130
Dublin, OH 43017-5013   614-793-0440
Fax: 614-793-0443   800-468-0440
Importer and wholesaler/distributor of packaging machinery including horizontal baggers, overwrappers, shrink bundlers, cartoners, case packers, tray formers and stretch wrapping equipment
President: Andre Pitaluga
Number Employees: 5-9
Square Footage: 24000
Brands Imported: Amotek; Dimac; Robopac
Regions Imported from: Europe

47398 Pactiv LLC
1900 W Field Ct
Lake Forest, IL 60045
800-476-4300
www.pactiv.com
Manufacturer and exporter of bags, cartons, containers, film, trays, etc.
Chief Executive Officer: John McGrath
Year Founded: 1965
Estimated Sales: $7.3 Billion
Number Employees: 11,000
Parent Co: Reynolds Group Holdings, LLC
Brands Exported: MicroFoam; Astro-Cell; Astro-Foam; Polyplank
Regions Exported to: Worldwide
Percentage of Business in Exporting: 2

47399 Pacur
3555 Moser St
Oshkosh, WI 54901-1270   920-236-2888
Fax: 920-236-2882

Manufacturer and exporter of packaging materials; extruder of PET, PP, PETG, CPET, APET, RPET and recycled materials
President: Ron Johnson
rjohnson@pacur.com
R&D: Tim Wiycha
Director Sales/Marketing: Richard Knapp
Estimated Sales: $ 20 - 50 Million
Number Employees: 100-249
Square Footage: 80000
Parent Co: Rexham
Regions Exported to: Central America, Asia, Middle East, Canada, Caribbean, Latin America, Mexico
Percentage of Business in Exporting: 10

47400 Paderno
Winsloe, PE C1E 1Z3
Canada   902-629-1500
    Fax: 902-629-1502 800-263-9768
    customer.service@padinox.ca paderno.com
Parent Co: Padinox Inc.

47401 Padinox
489 Brackley Point Road
P.O. Box 20106
Winsloe, PE C1A 9E3
Canada   902-629-1500
    Fax: 902-629-1502 800-263-9768
    paderno@padinox.ca www.paderno.com
Manufacturer and exporter of stainless steel cookware including pots, pans, gadgets, utensils and bakeware
President: Jim Casey
VP: Tim Casey
Marketing: Scott Chandler
Production: Ernie Bremman
Number Employees: Oover 200
Brands Exported: Chandier
Regions Exported to: Central America, Europe
Percentage of Business in Exporting: 1
Regions Imported from: Central America, South America, Europe, Asia, Middle East

47402 Pagatech
4463 Worth Dr E
Jacksonville, FL 32207   904-733-2424
    Fax: 904-733-1308
Exporter of dried fruits and nuts, popcorn, sunflower seeds, almonds, cashews, corn nuts, hazelnuts, macademiad, pistachios, walnuts, peanuts, pecans, drier beans and peas, breakfast cereals, lentils, raisins, dates, garbanzos (chickpeas), cake mikes, canned mushrooms and canned corn
President: Gary A Granfield
Estimated Sales: $2.5-5 Million
Number Employees: 1-4
Brands Exported: Pagatech
Percentage of Business in Exporting: 90
Brands Imported: Pagatech, Comfy-Briefs
Regions Imported from: Asia

47403 Paget Equipment Co
417 E 29th St
Marshfield, WI 54449-5312   715-384-3158
    Fax: 715-387-0720 paget@northsidecomp.com
    www.pagetequipment.com
Manufacturer and exporter of process control systems, spray dryers, evaporators, tanks, heat exchangers, wet separators, blenders and conveyors
President: James Reigel
jimr@pagetequipment.com
CFO: James Reigel
Quality Control: Steve Desmet
Sales: Richard Wermersen
Project Engineer: Brian Johnson
Estimated Sales: $ 5 - 10 Million
Number Employees: 50-99
Square Footage: 88000
Parent Co: JBL International
Regions Exported to: Central America, South America, Middle East
Percentage of Business in Exporting: 10

47404 Paklab Products
1315 Gay-Lussac
Boucherville, QC J4B 7K1
Canada   450-449-1224
    Fax: 450-449-3380 888-946-3233
Grape juice
President: Claudio Garuti
Finance Director: Assunta Marcone

47405 Pakmark
PO Box 228
Chesterfield, MO 63006-0228   636-532-7877
    Fax: 636-532-9634 800-423-1379
    pakmark@pakmark.com
Manufacturer and exporter of decorative pressure sensitive labels and tapes; also, hot-stamped and embossed foil
Estimated Sales: $ 1-2.5 Million
Number Employees: 10-19
Regions Exported to: Canada, Mexico

47406 Paktronics Controls
23555 Telegraph Road
Southfield, MI 48033-4129   248-356-1400
    Fax: 248-356-0829 info@maxitrol.com
    www.maxitrol.com
Manufacturer, importer and exporter of temperature controls
President: David Sundberg
Inside Sales: Toni Thompson
Purchasing Manager: Linda McCleskey
Estimated Sales: $2.5-5 Million
Number Employees: 10
Square Footage: 21600
Parent Co: Maxitrol Company
Brands Exported: Pakstat; Trakstat; Paktronics
Regions Exported to: Canada, Mexico
Percentage of Business in Exporting: 7
Regions Imported from: Asia
Percentage of Business in Importing: 10

47407 Palamatic Handling USA
901 S Bolmar St Bldg 1c
P.O.Box 2020
West Chester, PA 19380-2020 610-701-6350
    Fax: 610-701-6354 info@tnthandling.com
    www.tnthandling.com
Wholesaler/distributor and importer of material handling and food processing equipment
President: Tim Carney
Sales Manager: Tom Carney
Estimated Sales: $ 1 - 3 Million
Number Employees: 5-9
Square Footage: 11400
Brands Exported: Palamatic
Regions Exported to: Europe
Percentage of Business in Exporting: 95

47408 Paleewong Trading Corporation
62-04 34th Ave
Woodside, NY 11377   718-507-6520
    Fax: 718-507-6528 www.paleewongtrading.com
Importer and wholesaler/distributor of beer
President: Chi Chi Paleewong
Estimated Sales: $ .5 - 1 million
Number Employees: 5-9
Brands Imported: Thailand Sing Ha Beer
Regions Imported from: Asia

47409 Pall Filtron
50 Bearfoot Rd # 1
Northborough, MA 01532-1551   508-393-1800
    Fax: 508-393-1874 800-345-8766
    piannucci@pall.com www.pall.com
Filtration and separation systems for food and beverage applications
Sr. VP: Jamie Monat
VP Sales: Piers O'Donnell
Contact: Engin Ayturk
engin_ayturk@pall.com
Estimated Sales: $ 20 - 50 Million
Number Employees: 50-99
Parent Co: Pall Group
Other Locations:
    Pall Filtron
    Shinagawa-KuPall Filtron
Regions Exported to: Worldwide

47410 Pallet One Inc
1470 US Highway 17 S
Bartow, FL 33830-6627   863-533-1147
    Fax: 863-533-3065 800-771-1148
    www.palletone.com
Manufacturer and exporter of wooden pallets and harvesting bins
CEO/President/Chairman: Howe Q. Wallace
CFO: Casey A Fletcher
cfletcher@palletone.com
Vice President: Donnie Isaacson
Vice President of Sales: Keith M. Reinstetle
COO: Matt B. Sheffield
Estimated Sales: $ 10 - 20 Million
Number Employees: 1000-4999
Parent Co: IFCO

47411 Pallox Incorporated
7221 Hickory Ln
Onsted, MI 49265   517-456-4101
    Fax: 517-456-7821
Manufacturer and exporter of wooden pallets, skids and boxes; also, pallet repair and design available; also heat treat pallets for ISPM-15 standard
President: R J Moore
Estimated Sales: $2.5 Million
Number Employees: 20-49
Number of Products: 100
Square Footage: 36000
Brands Exported: Elro

47412 Palme d'Or
228 Principale
Saint Louis de Gonzague, QC J0S 1T0
Canada   450-377-8766
    www.palmedor.ca/en/
Duck foie gras
Regions Exported to: Europe, USA

47413 (HQ)Palmer Candy Co
2600 N US Highway 75
Suite 1
Sioux City, IA 51105-2444   712-258-5543
    Fax: 712-258-3224 800-831-0828
    vicki@palmercandy.com
    www.palmerspecialtyfoods.com
Bagged, multi-pack vending snacks
President: Martin Palmer
Director of Quality Control: Dawn Gorham
VP, Marketing: Bob O'Neill
VP, Operations: Bill Kennedy
Purchasing Manager: Jeff Wilkerson
Estimated Sales: $15.50 Million
Number Employees: 50-99
Square Footage: 420000
Type of Packaging: Consumer, Food Service, Private Label, Bulk
Other Locations:
    Palmer Candy Company
    Kansas City, MOPalmer Candy Company
Regions Imported from: South America

47414 (HQ)Palmer Distributors
23001 W Industrial Dr
St Clair Shores, MI 48080-1187 586-498-2900
    Fax: 586-772-4627 800-444-1912
    sales@palmerpromos.com
    www.palmerpromos.com
Manufacturer and exporter of display cases, card holders, bowls, tray covers, light boxes and syrup bottles
President: Jim Palmer
jpalmer@palmerpromos.com
VP: Mark Armstrong
Food Service Sales Manager: Michael Lacoursiere
Estimated Sales: $ 10 - 20 Million
Number Employees: 50-99
Square Footage: 100000
Type of Packaging: Food Service
Regions Exported to: Worldwide
Percentage of Business in Exporting: 5

47415 Palmer Fixture Company
1255 Winford Ave
Green Bay, WI 54303-3707   950-884-8698
    Fax: 920-884-8699 800-558-8678
    info@palmerfixture.com www.palmerfixture.com
Manufacturer, importer and exporter of paper towel, tissue, and napkin dispensers including a universal hands-free towel dispenser
Owner: Bill Palmer
Vice President: Greg Kampschroer
Contact: Siggi Witt
siggi@palmerfixture.com
Purchasing Manager: Chris Worth
Estimated Sales: $820,000
Number Employees: 7
Square Footage: 44000
Brands Exported: No-Waste; Holdit
Regions Exported to: Worldwide
Percentage of Business in Exporting: 10
Regions Imported from: Worldwide
Percentage of Business in Importing: 15

Importers & Exporters / A-Z

47416 Palmer Snyder
400 N Executive Drive
Brookfield, WI 53005-6068   262-780-8780
Fax: 262-780-8790   800-762-0415
lpage@palmersnyder.com www.palmersnyder.com
Manufacturer and exporter of plywood and plastic folding tables, wooden folding chairs maintenence free, galerie series chairs and transport cars for tables and chairs
CEO: Richard Bibler
VP Sales: Craig Clarke
Sales Representative: Chelsea Stecker
Estimated Sales: $ 1-2.5 Million
Number Employees: 100-250
Square Footage: 600000
Parent Co: Palmer Snyder
Other Locations:
  Palmer Snyder
  Elkhorn, WI Palmer Snyder
Brands Exported: Bryan ABS Plastic Tables
Regions Exported to: Worldwide
Percentage of Business in Exporting: 3

47417 Palmetto Canning
3601 US Highway 41 N
Palmetto, FL 34221   941-722-1100
pcrbaggs@tampabay.rr.com
palmettocanning.com
Canning and packaging sauces and beverage
Estimated Sales: $5-10 Million
Number Employees: 1-4
Square Footage: 128000
Type of Packaging: Consumer, Private Label

47418 Palms & Co
515 Lake St S # 203
6421 Lake Washington Blvd NE, 408
Kirkland, WA 98033-6441   425-828-6774
Fax: 425-827-5528 food@peterpalms.com
www.twocupsofjoy.com
Export management company of grains, meats, rabbit meat, canned foods, wines. EMC services in Eastern Europe, China, Russia for US manufacturers - canned boneless wholechicken; purchasing agent-nitric fertilizer-russian export
President: Peter Palms
CEO: Pyotr Joannevicn
CFO: Alexander Wislobokov
VP: Alexander Goldenberg
Research & Development: Alex Repin
Marketing: Yakon Soblev
Public Relations: Anke Van Waal
Estimated Sales: $20-50 Million
Number Employees: 1-4
Number of Brands: 200
Number of Products: 1500
Type of Packaging: Consumer, Food Service, Private Label, Bulk
Brands Exported: Palms; All brands specified by buyers
Regions Exported to: Europe, Asia, Russia, Eastern Europe
Percentage of Business in Exporting: 90
Brands Imported: Azot, Kraz, Baryutin, Rusal
Regions Imported from: Europe, Asia
Percentage of Business in Importing: 25

47419 Paltier
1701 Kentucky St
Michigan City, IN 46360   219-872-7238
Fax: 219-872-9480   800-348-3201
Manufacturer and exporter of engineered storage rack systems including cantilever and drive-in/drive-thru
VP/General Manager: James Washington
Plant Manager: Glenn Clark
Estimated Sales: $20-50 Million
Number Employees: 100-249
Square Footage: 110000
Parent Co: Lyon Metal Products
Type of Packaging: Food Service
Brands Exported: Paltier
Regions Exported to: Central America, South America, Asia
Percentage of Business in Exporting: 7

47420 Pamela's Products
1 Carousel Ln
Ukiah, CA 95482-9509   707-462-6605
Fax: 707-462-6642 info@pamelaproducts.com
www.pamelasproducts.com
Cookies, bars, flours and baking mixes
President/Owner: Pamela Giusto-Sorrells
Estimated Sales: $450,000
Number Employees: 100-249
Type of Packaging: Consumer, Bulk
Brands Exported: Pamela's
Regions Exported to: Europe, Canada
Percentage of Business in Exporting: 10

47421 Pan American Papers Inc
5101 NW 37th Ave
Miami, FL 33142-3232   305-635-2534
Fax: 305-635-2538 jvl@panampap.com
www.panampap.com
Distributors of paper
Sr. VP: Jesus Roca
panampap@bellsouth.net
Executive VP: Francisco Valdes
Estimated Sales: $ 20-50 Million
Number Employees: 10-19
Square Footage: 80000

47422 Pan Pacific Plastics Inc
26551 Danti Ct
Hayward, CA 94545-3917   510-785-6888
Fax: 510-785-6886   888-475-6888
panpacplastics@aol.com
Manufacturer, exporter and importer of plastic bags
President: Ying Wang
mtan@pppmi.com
Marketing/Sales: Mike Tan
Sales Exec: Mike Tan
Estimated Sales: $20-50 Million
Number Employees: 20-49
Square Footage: 40000
Parent Co: Pan Pacific Group Companies
Type of Packaging: Consumer, Food Service, Private Label, Bulk
Regions Exported to: Africa
Percentage of Business in Exporting: 20
Regions Imported from: Asia
Percentage of Business in Importing: 20

47423 Panapesca USA LLC
42 Winter St # 7
Pembroke, MA 02359-4958   781-829-9019
Fax: 781-829-0427 jfee@panapesca.com
www.panapesca.com
Clams, mussels, scallops, crab, calamari and octopus
Owner: G Aprea
gaprea@panapesca.com
Vice President: Danielle Berti
Marketing: John Fee
Estimated Sales: $4.5 Million
Number Employees: 5-9

47424 Panasonic Commercial Food Service
2 Riverfront Plaza
Newark, NJ 07102
na.panasonic.com/us/industries/food-service-technology
Commercial microwave ovens, vacuum cleaners, compact fluorescent light bulbs and ventilating fans; importer of rice cookers.
CEO, US Company: Mototsugu Sato
Year Founded: 1918
Estimated Sales: $79 Billion
Number Employees: 257,533
Regions Imported from: Asia
Percentage of Business in Importing: 2

47425 (HQ)Pandol Brothers Inc
33150 Pond Rd.
Delano, CA 93215-9598   661-725-3755
Fax: 661-725-4741 sales.domestic@pandol.com
www.pandol.com
Green, black, red and seeded grapes; persimmons, blueberries, cherries, apples, peaches, plums, nectarines
President & CEO: Cheri Diebel
Safety Manager: Andrew Pandol
Account Manager: Andrew Brown
Manager: Carlos Mendoza
Director, Global Operations: David Sudduth
Year Founded: 1923
Estimated Sales: $ 20 - 50 Million
Number Employees: 20-49
Regions Imported from: South America

47426 Pandol Brothers Inc
1737 North Wenatche Ave.
Suite A
Wenatchee, WA 98801   509-662-3763
Fax: 509-663-8449 pandolWA@pandol.com
www.pandol.com
Green, black, red and seeded grapes; persimmons, blueberries, cherries, apples, peaches, plums, nectarines
Regions Imported from: South America

47427 Pandol Brothers Inc
San Francisco de Asis
150 of 621
Santiago,
Chile
pandolCL@pandol.com
www.pandol.com
Green, black, red and seeded grapes; persimmons, blueberries, cherries, apples, peaches, plums, nectarines
Regions Imported from: South America

47428 Pangaea Sciences
18 Pine Ridge Road
Erin, ON N0B 1T0
Canada   51- 83- 730
Fax: 51- 83- 901 sales@pangaeasciences.com
www.pangaeasciences.com
Pangaea Sciences strives to replace the use of chemicals with natural alternatives in their cosmetics, food stuff and pharmaceuticals.
Operations Manager: Roy Val
Number Employees: 5-9
Regions Exported to: Central America, South America, Europe, Asia
Percentage of Business in Exporting: 50
Regions Imported from: Central America, South America, Europe, Asia
Percentage of Business in Importing: 50

47429 Panhandler, Inc.
PO Box 1329
Cordova, TN 38088-1329   800-654-7237
Fax: 901-336-6377 panhandlerpads@yahoo.com
www.panhandlerinc.com
Manufacturer and exporter of pot holders, bakers' gloves and bakery oven pads
Owner: Don White
CEO: Sherrie Nischwitz
Vice President: Christy Graves
Number Employees: 8
Square Footage: 24000
Type of Packaging: Food Service
Regions Exported to: Europe
Percentage of Business in Exporting: 20

47430 Panoche Creek Packing
3611 W Beechwood Ave
Suite 101
Fresno, CA 93711-0648   559-449-1721
Fax: 559-431-9970 inquiry@panochecreek.com
www.panochecreek.com
Almonds
Owner: Estelle Holland
estelle@panochecreek.com
Vice President: John Blackburn
Marketing Manager: Ross Blackburn
Plant Manager: Jason Baldwin
Estimated Sales: Less than $500,000
Number Employees: 5-9
Type of Packaging: Private Label, Bulk
Regions Exported to: Central America, South America, Europe, Asia, Middle East
Percentage of Business in Exporting: 80

47431 Pantry Shelf Food Corporation
3983 Nashua Drive
Mississauga, ON L4V 1P3
Canada   905-677-7200
info@pantryshelf.com
www.pantryshelf.com
Importer and wholesaler/distributor of canned seafood, fruits, vegetables, pickles, condiments, rice, beans, snack foods, corned beef, concentrates, private label items and confections; serving the food service and retail markets;exporter of beans
President: Kanu Patel
VP: Kantu Patel
Estimated Sales: $8 Million
Number Employees: 25
Square Footage: 45000
Type of Packaging: Consumer, Food Service, Private Label, Bulk
Regions Exported to: South America, Europe
Percentage of Business in Exporting: 5
Brands Imported: Pantry Shelf
Regions Imported from: Central America, South America, Europe, Asia, South Africa, Australia
Percentage of Business in Importing: 80

Importers & Exporters / A-Z

47432 Paoli Properties
2531 11th St
Rockford, IL 61104-7219 815-965-0621
Fax: 815-965-5393
Manufacturer and exporter of one-step deboners and desinewers for meat, poultry and seafood
President: Louis Paoli
info@stephenpaoli.com
CFO: Louis Paoli
Sales: Neal Ryan
General Manager: Shawn Lee
Estimated Sales: $ 5 - 10 Million
Number Employees: 10-19
Square Footage: 760000
Brands Exported: Paoli One Step
Regions Exported to: Central America, South America, Europe, Asia, Middle East, Worldwide
Percentage of Business in Exporting: 70

47433 Paper Box & Specialty Co
1505 Sibley Ct
Sheboygan, WI 53081-2456 920-459-2440
Fax: 920-459-2463 888-240-3756
Linda.quast@paperboxandspecialty.com
www.paperboxandspecialty.com
Manufacturer and exporter of set-up and folding cartons, poly-coated cheese liners and gift boxes
President: David Van Der Puy
Contact: Nicole Spielvogel
tgesch@pathconit.com
Estimated Sales: $ 2.5 - 5 Million
Number Employees: 20-49
Square Footage: 150000
Regions Exported to: Central America, Asia
Percentage of Business in Exporting: 2

47434 (HQ)Paper Converting MachineCompany
2300 S Ashland Ave
Green Bay, WI 54304 920-494-5601
Fax: 920-494-8865 www.pcmc.com
Printing presses print narrow to wide flexographic printing on film, paper, labels, non-woven board stock.
President: Tim Sullivan
Vice President of Sales: Mark Zastrow
Sales Engineer: Mike Callahan
mikecallahan@pcmc.com
Year Founded: 1919
Estimated Sales: $237 Million
Number Employees: 1,000
Parent Co: Barry-Wehmiller Companies, Inc.
Regions Exported to: Worldwide
Percentage of Business in Exporting: 10

47435 Paper Converting Machine Company
1163 Glory Rd
Green Bay, WI 54304 920-494-5601
Fax: 920-494-8865 www.pcmc.com
Printing presses print narrow to wide flexographic printing on film, paper, labels, non-woven board stock.
Square Footage: 880000
Parent Co: Barry-Wehmiller Companies Inc
Other Locations:
  Aquaflex
  Boucherville, PQ CanadaAquaflex
Brands Exported: Webtron
Regions Exported to: Worldwide
Percentage of Business in Exporting: 60

47436 Paper Service
PO Box 45
Hinsdale, NH 03451-0045 603-239-6344
Fax: 603-239-8861 www.paperservice.com
Manufacturer and exporter of paper napkins, wrapping and tissue paper
CEO: G O'Neal
Operations Manager: R O'Neal
Estimated Sales: $ 10-20 Million
Number Employees: 20-49
Square Footage: 400000
Type of Packaging: Food Service, Private Label
Regions Exported to: Central America
Percentage of Business in Exporting: 75

47437 Paper Systems Inc
6127 Willowmere Dr
Des Moines, IA 50321-1230 515-280-1111
Fax: 515-280-9219 800-342-2855
nate@paper-systems.com
Manufacturer and exporter of pallets and disposable and returnable bulk containers for food grade liquids and powders
Owner: William Chase
psi@paper-systems.com
Estimated Sales: Below $5 Million
Number Employees: 10-19
Type of Packaging: Bulk
Brands Exported: EZ-Bulk; EZ-Pak; EZ-Flow; EZ-Pallet
Regions Exported to: Central America, South America, Europe, Asia, Canada, Latin America, Mexico
Regions Imported from: Europe

47438 Papertech
108-245 Iell Avenue
North Vancouver, BC V7P 2K1
Canada 604-990-1600
Fax: 604-990-1606 877-787-2737
info@papertech.ca www.papertech.ca
Manufacturer and exporter of dairy processing equipment including clean-in-place systems, milk processors and process control instruments
President: Kari Hilden
Marketing Coordinator: Tanja Kannisto
Number Employees: 30
Regions Exported to: Europe, Asia, USA
Percentage of Business in Exporting: 75

47439 Paperweights Plus
3661 Horseblock Road
Suite Q
Medford, NY 11763-2232 631-924-3222
Fax: 631-345-0752
Manufacturer, importer and exporter of advertising specialties including emblems, ID badges, name plates, lapel pins, key rings and paperweights
President: Darlene Reynolds
Estimated Sales: Less than $500,000
Number Employees: 1-4
Square Footage: 1700
Regions Exported to: Worldwide
Regions Imported from: Italy , Japan

47440 Pappy's Sassafras Tea
10246 Road P
Columbus Grove, OH 45830-9733 419-659-5110
Fax: 419-659-5110 877-659-5110
pappy@q1.net www.sassafrastea.com
Sassafras tea, green tea, raspberry tea and tea concentrate
President: Sandy Nordhaus
pappy@q1.net
VP: Don Nordhaus
Marketing & Sales: Jeff Nordhaus
Estimated Sales: $360,000
Number Employees: 5-9
Number of Brands: 1
Number of Products: 2
Square Footage: 45000
Type of Packaging: Consumer, Food Service, Private Label, Bulk
Brands Exported: Pappy's
Regions Exported to: Central America, Caribbean, Mexico, Canada
Percentage of Business in Exporting: 1

47441 (HQ)Par-Pak
14345 Northwest Freeway
Houston, TX 77040 713-686-6700
Fax: 713-686-6553 888-727-7252
www.parpak.com
Manufacturer and exporter of clear plastic containers for food packaging; also, catering trays
President: Sajjad Ebrahim
VP Technical: Dominic DiDomizio
VP Sales: David Goralski
Estimated Sales: $ 5 - 10 Million
Number Employees: 20-49
Square Footage: 210000
Brands Exported: Cake-Mix, Ebony, Invisi-Bowl, Invisible Packaging, Quartz Collection
Regions Exported to: Central America, Europe, USA

47442 Parachem Corporation
2733 6th Ave
Des Moines, IA 50313 515-280-9445
Fax: 515-280-7600
Manufacturer and exporter of hand soap, hand soap dispensers, anti-bacterial soap systems in leaf form, etc
President: Beryl Halterman
Marketing Manager: Carla Stephens
Office Manager: Dean Blum
Purchasing Manager: Dean Blum
Estimated Sales: Below $ 5 Million
Number Employees: 1-4
Square Footage: 48000
Parent Co: Flightags
Brands Exported: Cleaf
Regions Exported to: Europe, Asia, Canada
Percentage of Business in Exporting: 20

47443 Paraclipse
2271 E 29th Ave
Columbus, NE 68601-3166 402-563-3625
Fax: 402-564-2109 800-854-6379
ljochen@paraclipse.com www.paraclipse.com
Manufacturer and exporter of decorative indoor lighted fly traps and industrial fly traps for public dining areas, kitchen and food preparation areas. Outdoor lighted mosquito trap for restaurant outside serving areas and patios.
CFO: Cheryl Ditter
Sales Manager: Len Jochens
Manager: Abby Cremers
acremer@paraclipse.com
Estimated Sales: $3-6 Million
Number Employees: 10-19
Square Footage: 216000
Brands Exported: Insect Inn Ultra; Terminator; Fly Patrol
Regions Exported to: Central America, South America, Europe, Asia, Middle East, Australia
Percentage of Business in Exporting: 50

47444 Paradise Inc
1200 W Dr. Martin Luther King Jr. blvd.
Plant City, FL 33563-5155 813-752-1155
Fax: 941-754-3168 paradisefruitco@hotmail.com
www.paradisefruitco.com
Candied fruits
Chairman/CEO: Melvin Gordon
President/Director: Randy Gordon
rgordon@paradisefruitco.com
Senior Vice President, Sales: Tracy Schulis
Executive Vice President: Mark Gordon
VP/Corporate Sales: Ron Peterson
Estimated Sales: $21 Million
Number Employees: 100-249
Number of Brands: 6
Square Footage: 275000
Type of Packaging: Consumer, Food Service, Private Label, Bulk
Regions Imported from: Europe, Asia

47445 (HQ)Paradise Island Foods
6451 Portsmouth Road
Nanaimo, BC V9V 1A3
Canada 250-390-2644
Fax: 250-390-2117 800-889-3370
lthomson@paradise-foods.com
www.paradise-foods.com
Muffin mixes, cheeses, pasta, yogurt, juice, candy, salad dressings and ethnic foods
President: Len Thomson
Vice President: Kevin Thomson
Estimated Sales: $15 Million
Number Employees: 60
Square Footage: 72000
Type of Packaging: Consumer, Private Label, Bulk
Brands Imported: La Costena
Regions Imported from: Central America, Europe, Mexico
Percentage of Business in Importing: 30

47446 Paradise Products
PO Box 568
El Cerrito, CA 94530-0568 510-524-8300
Fax: 510-524-8165 800-227-1092
100 page catalog of theme decorations and party supplies for special events and sales promotions cateterias and clubs
Controller: Alice Rickey
Sales: Shirley Imai
Number Employees: 14
Number of Products: 3000
Square Footage: 80000
Regions Imported from: Central America, Europe, Asia
Percentage of Business in Importing: 25

Importers & Exporters / A-Z

47447 (HQ)Paradise Products Corporation
17851 Deauville Ln
Boca Raton, FL 33496-2458
Fax: 718-378-3521 800-826-1235
Marinated foods, condiments, olives, artichokes, pimientos, capers, cauliflower, cherries, corn, kumquats, mushrooms, olive oil, pickled onions, salsa, sauces
President: David Lax
Estimated Sales: $10-20 Million
Number Employees: 60
Square Footage: 450000
Type of Packaging: Consumer, Food Service, Private Label, Bulk
Brands Exported: Paradise; Julianna; Three Star
Regions Exported to: Central America, South America, Europe, Asia, Middle East, Caribbean, Mexico, Latin America, Canada
Percentage of Business in Exporting: 3
Brands Imported: Paradise
Regions Imported from: South America, Europe, Asia, Middle East, Canada, Caribbean, Central America, Latin America, Mexico

47448 Paragon Coffee Trading Co
445 Hamilton Ave # 401
White Plains, NY 10601-2902   914-949-2235
Fax: 914-949-1211 kerry@paragoncoffee.com
www.paragoncoffee.com
Importer of coffee including green and decaffeinated
President: Roland Veit
roland@paragoncoffee.com
CFO: Sheldon Berger
VP Trading: Michael Silberstein
Estimated Sales: $5-10 Million
Number Employees: 10-19

47449 Paragon Films Inc
3500 W Tacoma St
Broken Arrow, OK 74012-1164   918-250-3456
Fax: 918-355-3456 800-274-9727
jpt@paragon-films.com www.paragonfilms.com
Manufacturer and exporter of packaging materials including stretch and specialty films and hand applied and pallet stretch wrap
President: Mike Baab
mbaab@paragon-films.com
Estimated Sales: $ 20 - 50 Million
Number Employees: 100-249
Regions Exported to: South America

47450 Paragon Group USA
3433 Tyrone Boulevard N
St Petersburg, FL 33710-1136   727-341-0547
Fax: 727-302-9816 800-835-6962
Manufacturer and exporter of ozone generators designed to electronically eliminate odors without the use of chemicals; also, food preservation equipment
President: David Kocksten
R & D: Phillip Rod
VP Sales: Susan Duffy
Purchasing Manager: Chuch Pacino
Estimated Sales: $1-2.5 Million
Number Employees: 10
Square Footage: 20800
Brands Exported: Zontec
Regions Exported to: Europe, Asia, Middle East, Australia
Percentage of Business in Exporting: 10

47451 Paragon International
731 W 18th St
Nevada, IA 50201-7847   515-382-8000
Fax: 515-382-8001 800-433-0333
www.manufacturedfun.com
Manufacturer and exporter of popcorn machines and carts
Owner: Dave Swegle
Quality Control: Bill Tierce
VP Sales/Marketing: Tom Berger
Manager Customer Service: Sandra Holubar
Estimated Sales: $ 3 - 5,000,000
Number Employees: 20-49
Square Footage: 25000
Regions Exported to: Worldwide
Percentage of Business in Exporting: 28

47452 Paragon Labeling
1607 9th St
St Paul, MN 55110-6717   651-429-7722
Fax: 651-429-6006 800-429-7722
info@paragonlabeling.com
www.paragonlabeling.com
Manufacturer and exporter of printing machines and supplies and custom labeling systems
Director of Label Manufacturing Operatio: Karla Bridgeman
CFO: Ed Clarke
Vice President: Craig Blonigen
VP: Craig Blonigen
Sales/Marketing: Craig Blonigen
Contact: Randy Black
randyb@lowrycomputer.com
Operations Manager: Ken Koehler
Production Manager: Matt Thoreson
Plant Manager: Ken Koehler
Estimated Sales: $5 Million
Number Employees: 5-9
Square Footage: 160000
Parent Co: Lowry Computer Products Company
Regions Exported to: Europe
Percentage of Business in Exporting: 10

47453 Paramount Export Co.
175 Filbert St.
Suite 201
Oakland, CA 94607   510-839-0150
www.paramountexport.net
Produce including oranges, apples, grapes, lemons, grapefruit, pears, strawberries, cherries, kiwi, lettuce, tomatoes, asparagus and celery, as well as wine, snack foods, dairy products, meat, seafood, etc.
President/Chief Executive Officer: Nick Kuklan
nick@paramountexport.net
Chief Financial Officer: Norman Lancaster
nick@paramountexport.net
Year Founded: 1939
Estimated Sales: $23.8 Million
Number Employees: 100-249
Type of Packaging: Consumer
Regions Exported to: Worldwide
Percentage of Business in Exporting: 90

47454 Paramount Industries
304 N Howard Ave
PO Box 259
Croswell, MI 48422   810-679-2551
Fax: 810-679-4045 800-521-5405
piisales@paramountlighting.com
www.paramountlighting.com
High performance lighting for specialized environments
President: Craig Bailey
piiadv@paramountlighting.com
VP Sales: Derryl Fewins
Sales: Angie Smiley
Plant Manager: Jim Jarchow
Estimated Sales: Below $5 Million
Number Employees: 50-99
Square Footage: 90000
Regions Exported to: Central America, Asia, North America, Latin America, Caribbean
Percentage of Business in Exporting: 3

47455 Paratherm Corporation
31 Portland Rd
Conshohocken, PA 19428   610-941-4900
Fax: 610-941-9191 800-222-3611
info@paratherm.com www.paratherm.com
Manufacturer and exporter of food-grade heat transfer fluids for precise and uniform temperature control in food processing applications
President: John Fuhr
Research & Development: Jim Oetinger
Marketing Director: Andy Andrews
Sales Director: Jim Oetinger
Contact: Andy Andrews
aandrews@paratherm.com
Purchasing Manager: Anne Grabowski
Estimated Sales: $2.5-5 Million
Number Employees: 1-4
Number of Brands: 1
Number of Products: 9
Square Footage: 20000
Brands Exported: Paratherm Heat Transfer Fluids; Paratherm Hot-Oil-System Cleaners
Regions Exported to: Central America, South America, Europe, Asia
Percentage of Business in Exporting: 15

47456 Parducci Wine Cellars
501 Parducci Rd
Ukiah, CA 95482-3015   707-463-5357
Fax: 707-462-7260 888-362-9463
info@mendocinowineco.com www.parducci.com
Wines
Manager: Tim Thornhill
timthornhill@mendocinowineco.com
Marketing: David Hance
Winemaker: Robert Swain
Estimated Sales: $ 2 Million
Number Employees: 20-49
Regions Exported to: Europe, Asia

47457 Paris Gourmet
145 Grand St
Carlstadt, NJ 07072-2106   201-939-5656
Fax: 201-939-0084 800-727-8791
jmacoban@yahoo.com www.parisgourmet.com
Importer of frozen desserts
President: Xavier Noel
xav@parisgourmet.com
VP: Dominique Noel
Marketing & PR: Shirley Hall
Purchasing: Sheryl Polizzi
Number Employees: 20-49
Regions Imported from: Europe
Percentage of Business in Importing: 85

47458 (HQ)Parish Chemical Company
P.O.Box 277
Orem, UT 84059-0277   801-226-2018
Fax: 801-226-8496
Nutritional food additives, acidulants and preservatives, ferulic acid, carboxyethylgermanium sesquioxide and indole-3-carbinol
President: W Wesley Parish
Marketing Director: Bill Ellenberger
Estimated Sales: $ 1 Million
Number Employees: 20-49
Square Footage: 100000
Type of Packaging: Bulk
Other Locations:
Parish Chemical Co.
Orem, UT Parish Chemical Co.
Regions Exported to: Worldwide
Percentage of Business in Exporting: 5

47459 Parish Manufacturing Inc
7430 New Augusta Rd
Indianapolis, IN 46268-2291   317-872-0172
Fax: 317-872-1242 800-592-2268
www.parishmfg.com
Manufacturer and exporter of bag-in-box liquid packaging systems
President: Richard Smith
rsmith@parishmfg.com
Estimated Sales: $10-20 Million
Number Employees: 20-49
Square Footage: 56000
Type of Packaging: Consumer, Food Service, Bulk
Regions Exported to: Central America, South America, Asia, Middle East
Percentage of Business in Exporting: 15

47460 Parisi Inc
305 Pheasant Run
Newtown, PA 18940-3423   215-968-6677
Fax: 215-968-3580
Manufacturer and exporter of bars, booths, counters, tabletops and buffet equipment; also, bakery, confectionery and deli display cases
President: Ron Germain
rgermain@parisi-royal.com
CFO: Gary Graf
Marketing Director: Eleanor Parisi
Sales Director: Dave Moore
Sales: Bill Matnias
Operations Manager: Steve Dickier
Estimated Sales: $ 10 - 20 Million
Number Employees: 50-99
Square Footage: 130000
Regions Exported to: Worldwide
Percentage of Business in Exporting: 1

47461 Parity Corp
11812 N Creek Pkwy N # 204
Bothell, WA 98011-8202   425-487-0997
Fax: 425-487-2317 www.paritylink.com
Manufacturer and exporter of accounting, systems integration and inventory control software

Owner: Arvid Tellevik
atellevik@paritycorp.com
R & D: John Ratliff
VP: George Fletcher
Office Administrator: Cindy Kouremetis
Estimated Sales: $5-10,000,000
Number Employees: 20-49
Square Footage: 4000
Regions Exported to: Worldwide

47462 Park Cheese Company Inc
168 Larsen Drive
Fond Du Lac, WI 54937-8519
Fax: 920-923-8485 800-752-7275
Italian cheeses: asiago, aged provolone, romano, parmesan, pepato, fontina, Italian sharp, kasseri, and milk provolone.
President & COO: Eric Liebetrau
CEO: Alfred Liebetrau
Secretary/Treasurer: Lylia Liebetrau
Manager: Jason Blank
Director Sales & Marketing: Linda Cizek
Contact: Sue Behling
sueb@belgioioso.com
Plant Manager/General Manager: Steve Heard
Number Employees: 70
Square Footage: 80000
Type of Packaging: Consumer, Food Service, Private Label, Bulk
Regions Exported to: Canada, Mexico

47463 Parker's Wine Brokerage
16101 Maple Park Drive
Suite 4
Maple Heights, OH 44137 216-475-4173
Fax: 216-472-8990 winebrokaergae@yahoo.com
Import and export food and beverage
President: Michael Parker
Marketing Director: Carolyn Williams
Sales Director: Maud Wilson
Estimated Sales: $500,000
Number Employees: 4
Square Footage: 10000
Type of Packaging: Food Service, Private Label, Bulk

47464 Parkland
PO Box 266342
Houston, TX 77207-6342 713-926-5055
Fax: 713-926-7358
Manufacturer and exporter of air conditioners, refrigerators and heating and ventilation equipment
President: J P Landers
Office Manager: John Rosales
Number Employees: 10
Type of Packaging: Food Service

47465 (HQ)Parkson Corp
1401 W Cypress Creek Rd # 100
Fort Lauderdale, FL 33309-1969 908-464-0700
Fax: 954-974-6182 www.parkson.com
Manufacturer and exporter of bulk material conveyors, bucket elevators and slide and diverter gates; importer of shaftless spirals
Owner: Steven Lombardi
CEO: Zain Mahmood
Director Marketing: Charlene Low
Estimated Sales: $ 1-2.5 Million
Number Employees: 250-499
Square Footage: 120000
Parent Co: Conelco
Brands Exported: Corra-Trough
Regions Exported to: Central America, South America, Asia
Percentage of Business in Exporting: 10
Regions Imported from: Europe

47466 Parkson Corp
562 Bunker Ct
Vernon Hills, IL 60061-1831 847-816-3700
Fax: 847-816-3707 technology@parkson.com
www.parkson.com
Provider of equipment and systems for water/process water and wastewater treatment including screens, sand filters, dewatering presses, inclined plate clarifiers, conveyors, filter presses, sludge thickeners and thermodryers andaeration
President: Axel Johnson, Inc
CEO: William Acton
Marketing Director: Charlene Low
Sales Director: Michael Miller
Number Employees: 10-19
Parent Co: Parkson Corporation
Brands Exported: Hycor Screens; Dynasand Filter; Lamella Settlers, Aqua Guard Screens
Regions Exported to: Central America, South America, Europe, Asia, Middle East

47467 Parkway Plastic Inc
561 Stelton Rd
Piscataway, NJ 08854-3868 732-752-3636
Fax: 732-752-2192 800-881-4996
sales@parkwayjars.com
www.store.parkwayjars.com
Manufacturer and exporter of polystyrene, linear polyethylene and polypropylene jars, bottles, boxes and caps
President: Debbie Coyle
dcoyle@parkwayproducts.com
Estimated Sales: $ 10 - 20 Million
Number Employees: 50-99
Regions Exported to: Canada

47468 Parlor City Paper Box Co Inc
2 Eldredge St
Binghamton, NY 13901-2600 607-772-0600
Fax: 607-772-0806 parcitybox@aol.com
Manufacturer and exporter of trays and printed folding boxes
President: David Culver
Sales/Marketing: Jeffrey Culver
Office Manager: Juanita Mendez
Estimated Sales: $5-10 Million
Number Employees: 20-49
Square Footage: 204000
Regions Exported to: Canada, Mexico
Percentage of Business in Exporting: 2

47469 Parmalat Canada
405 The West Mall
10th Floor
Toronto, ON M9C 5J1
Canada
800-563-1515
parmalat.ca
Milk, cheeses, spreads and yogurt.
CEO: Mark Taylor
Year Founded: 1997
Estimated Sales: $1.9 Billion
Number Employees: 3,500
Number of Brands: 10
Parent Co: Lactalis
Type of Packaging: Consumer, Food Service, Private Label, Bulk

47470 Parrish's Cake Decorating
225 W 146th St
Gardena, CA 90248-1803 310-324-2253
Fax: 310-324-8277 800-736-8443
Aluminum cake pans, cookie cutters, artificial icing, candy molds, plates and pillars, pastry bags, food colors and flavorings
President: Bob Parrish
customerservice@parrishsmagicline.com
VP: Norma Parrish
Estimated Sales: $ 1 - 3 Million
Number Employees: 10-19
Number of Products: 4000
Square Footage: 180000
Type of Packaging: Consumer, Food Service, Private Label, Bulk
Regions Exported to: Central America, Europe, Asia, Mexico, Canada
Percentage of Business in Exporting: 15
Regions Imported from: Asia
Percentage of Business in Importing: 35

47471 Parsons Manufacturing Corp.
1055 Obrien Dr
Menlo Park, CA 94025 650-324-4726
Fax: 650-324-3051
Manufacturer and exporter of sample cases, tote boxes, travel cases and shipping cases
Owner: Alan Parsons
VP Sales/Marketing: Steve Wurzer
Contact: Alan Hall
alan.hall@parsons.com
Estimated Sales: $20-50 Million
Number Employees: 20-49

47472 Particle Dynamics
2601 S Hanley Rd
Saint Louis, MO 63144 314-968-2376
Fax: 314-646-3761 800-452-4682
info@particledynamics.com
www.particledynamics.com
Vitamins, minerals, flavors, acidulants, colors, spices
President: Paul T Brady
Marketing: Andrea Keith
Sales VP: Richard Miller
Contact: Sonia Belotti
sonia.belotti@savannah.co.za
Purchasing: Jim Cronk
Estimated Sales: $3500000
Number Employees: 20-49
Square Footage: 180000
Parent Co: KV Pharmaceutical
Type of Packaging: Bulk
Brands Exported: Descote; Destab
Regions Exported to: Central America, South America, Europe, Asia, Middle East
Percentage of Business in Exporting: 20

47473 Partners in Hospitality
1120 N La Salle Drive
Apt 12m
Chicago, IL 60610-2687 312-397-0731

47474 Partnership Resources
1069 10th Ave SE
Minneapolis, MN 55414-1388 612-331-2075
Fax: 612-331-2887 www.partnershipresources.org
Manufacturer and exporter of electric infrared heating systems and based power controllers
Manager: Dan Mc Calister
danmccalister@partnershipresources.org
Chief Executive Officer: Norm Munk
Marketing Manager: James Lee
Manager: Dan Mc Calister
danmccalister@partnershipresources.org
Chief Operating Officer: Julie Zbaracki
Number Employees: 50-99
Square Footage: 360000
Regions Exported to: Europe, Asia

47475 Party Linens
7780 S Dante Ave
Chicago, IL 60619 773-731-9281
Fax: 773-731-7669 800-281-0003
www.partylinens.com
Manufacturer and importer of specialty linens and table skirting for various table shapes
Owner: Ed Denormandie
Estimated Sales: $2.5-5 Million
Number Employees: 10-19
Square Footage: 20000
Parent Co: DeNormandie Towel & Linen
Brands Imported: Milliken

47476 Party Yards
950 S Winter Park Drive
Suite 101
Casselberry, FL 32707-5451 407-696-9440
Fax: 407-696-6963 877-501-4400
partyyards@aol.com www.partyyards.com
Manufacturer, importer and exporter of plastic cups
VP: Andrew Baron
Sales Contact: Peter Dorney
Estimated Sales: $2.5-5 Million
Number Employees: 5-9
Square Footage: 48000
Parent Co: Party Yards
Regions Exported to: Worldwide
Percentage of Business in Exporting: 20
Regions Imported from: Asia, Canada
Percentage of Business in Importing: 4

47477 Parvin Manufacturing Company
6033 W Century Blvd # 1180
Los Angeles, CA 90045-6424 310-645-4411
Fax: 323-585-0427 800-648-0770
Manufacturer, importer and exporter of protective clothing and supplies including oven/barbecue mitts, aprons, skillet handle covers and insulated pizza delivery bags
Owner: Michael Provan
VP: Rick Resnick
Estimated Sales: $10-20 Million
Number Employees: 5-9
Square Footage: 68000
Regions Exported to: Europe, Asia, Canada, Australia
Regions Imported from: Asia

47478 Paskesz Candy Co
4473 1st Ave
Brooklyn, NY 11232-4201 718-215-1752
Fax: 718-832-3492 customerservice@paskesz.com
www.paskesz.com

Importer of kosher candy; wholesaler/distributor of kosher candy, cookies and grocery items; serving the food service market
Owner: Henry Schmidt
VP Marketing: Henri Schmidt
VP Sales: David Snyder
Contact: Gavriel Fein
gavriel@paskesz.com
Estimated Sales: Less Than $500,000
Number Employees: 1-4
Square Footage: 130000
Brands Imported: Man Israeli; Osem Israeli; Taste of Israel; Telma
Regions Imported from: Middle East
Percentage of Business in Importing: 100

47479 Pasquini Espresso Co
1501 W Olympic Blvd
Los Angeles, CA 90015-3803   213-739-8226
            Fax: 213-385-8774   800-724-6225
pasquini@pasquini.com
www.pasquini.biz
Manufacturer and exporter of commercial espresso equipment
President: Ambrose Pasquini
pasquini@pasquini.com
VP: Guy Pasquini
National Sales Manager: Sergio Laganiere
Estimated Sales: Below $5 Million
Number Employees: 20-49
Square Footage: 24000
Type of Packaging: Food Service
Regions Exported to: Central America, South America, Asia
Percentage of Business in Exporting: 2

47480 Passport Food Group
2539 E Philadelphia St
Ontario, CA 91761   310-463-0954
customerservice@passportfood.com
www.passportfood.com
Noodles, appetizers, fortune cookies and tofu, egg roll, wonton and potsticker wrappers
Senior Vice President: Brian Dean
bdean@passportfood.com
VP, Sales & Marketing, Retail: Terry Girch
Broker Sales Manager: Rich Frankey
Territory Sales Manager: Jeffrey Tavares
Year Founded: 1978
Estimated Sales: $50 Million
Number Employees: 200-500
Number of Brands: 4
Type of Packaging: Consumer, Food Service, Private Label, Bulk
Regions Exported to: Asia
Regions Imported from: Asia

47481 Pasta Del Mondo
27 Seminary Hill Rd
Suite 27
Carmel, NY 10512-1928   845-225-8889
         Fax: 845-225-0900 800-392-8887
Pasta
President: Frank Marrone
Production Manager: Brendan Conboy
Estimated Sales: $300,000-500,000
Number Employees: 9
Square Footage: 12000
Type of Packaging: Consumer, Food Service, Private Label, Bulk
Brands Imported: Barilla, Ghigi

47482 Pasta Factory
1225 W Grand Ave
Melrose Park, IL 60164   847-451-0005
         Fax: 847-451-6563 800-615-6951
Pasta
President: Michael Sica
VP: Irene Sica
Sales Manager/Marketing: Thomas Lichner
Contact: Brenda Sica
bsica@nova.edu
Operations/Purchasing Director: Joseph Sica
Estimated Sales: $2700000
Number Employees: 20-49
Square Footage: 64000
Parent Co: MAS Sales
Type of Packaging: Consumer, Food Service, Private Label, Bulk
Brands Imported: Pasta Factory

47483 Pasta Quistini
1700 Ormont Dr
Toronto, ON M9L 2V4
Canada
                 416-742-3222
Pasta
President: Elena Quistini
Vice President: Orlando Quistini
Estimated Sales: $3 Million
Number Employees: 18
Type of Packaging: Consumer, Food Service
Regions Exported to: USA

47484 Pasta Shoppe
3418 North Harlem Avenue
Chicago, IL 60634   773-745-5888
              Fax: 773-736-0566

47485 Pastene Co LTD
330 Turnpike St
Suite 100
Canton, MA 02021-2703   781-298-3397
       Fax: 781-830-8225 www.pastene.com
Cheese, sauces, oil and vinegar, vegetables, fish, olives, peppers, beans, bread sticks, pasta, rice and polenta
Owner: Mark Tosi
mtosi@pastene.com
Year Founded: 1848
Number Employees: 20-49
Type of Packaging: Consumer, Food Service
Regions Imported from: Europe

47486 Pastorelli Food Products
162 N Sangamon St
Chicago, IL 60607-2210   312-666-2041
         Fax: 312-666-2415   800-767-2829
www.pastorelli.com
Pizza sauces, crusts, pasta sauces, oils and vinegars
Owner: Richard Pastorelli
rpastorelli@pastorelli.com
Estimated Sales: $ 5 - 10 Million
Number Employees: 10-19
Square Footage: 244000
Type of Packaging: Consumer, Food Service, Private Label, Bulk
Brands Exported: Italian Chef; Continental Chef
Regions Exported to: Central America, South America, Europe, Asia, Mexico
Percentage of Business in Exporting: 15
Brands Imported: Regina
Regions Imported from: Central America, South America, Europe, Asia
Percentage of Business in Importing: 10

47487 Pastry Chef
112 Warren Avenue
Pawtucket, RI 02860-5604   401-722-1330
                            800-639-8606
Cakes and pies
President: Per Jensen
CEO: Paul Meunier
Number Employees: 20-49
Number of Brands: 3
Number of Products: 110
Square Footage: 80000
Parent Co: Pastry Chef
Type of Packaging: Food Service, Private Label

47488 (HQ)Paterno Imports LTD
2401 Waukegan Rd
Bannockburn, IL 60015-1505   847-444-5500
www.terlatowines.com
Importer of wines, spirits, beer and water
President & Chief Executive Officer: William Terlato
Chairman: Anthony Terlato
Vice Chairman: John Terlato
Estimated Sales: $39.7 Million
Number Employees: 5-9

47489 Patrick Cudahy LLC
1 Sweet Applewood Ln
Cudahy, WI 53110
                            800-486-6900
www.patrickcudahy.com
Bacon, hams, lard, shortening, pepperoni, salami, bologna and sausage
President: Ken Sullivan
Year Founded: 1888
Estimated Sales: $200-300 Million
Number Employees: 1,000-4,999
Square Footage: 1000000
Parent Co: Smithfield Foods
Type of Packaging: Food Service, Private Label
Brands Exported: La Abuelita
Regions Exported to: Central America, South America, Europe, Middle East

47490 Patterson Frozen Foods
100 W. Las Palmas Avenue
Patterson, CA 95363-0114   209-892-2611
                  Fax: 209-892-2582
Vegetables, pasta, pesto sauces, blends, stir frys and fruits
CFO: Russell Kenerly
Information Technology Software: Gregg Skarmas
Sales Manager: Tom Ielmini
Contact: Vance Blade
vance.blade@pattersonfoods.com
Vice President of Operations: B Ingebretsen
Manager of Purchasing: Joe Ghisletta
Estimated Sales: $ 310,000
Square Footage: 10496
Type of Packaging: Consumer, Food Service, Bulk
Other Locations:
    Patterson Frozen Foods Plant
    Monte Alto, TXPatterson Frozen Foods PlantGuatemala
Regions Exported to: Worldwide

47491 Patterson Industries
250 Danforth Road
Scarborough, ON M1L 3X4
Canada   416-694-3381
         Fax: 416-691-2768 800-336-1110
process@pattersonindustries.com
www.pattersonindustries.com
Designers, engineers and manufacturers of quality time proven equipment for the food industries; Ribbon and Paddle mixers, ThoroBlender Double Cone Blenders, Conaform Double Cone Vacuum Dryers, Ribbon and Paddle type round bodydryers, pressure vessels and heat exchangers and general mixing and agitation equipment
President: H Haischt
CFO: Seth Mendonza
Research & Development: Mike Lindsey
Sales Director: M Lindsey
Estimated Sales: $2,500,000
Number Employees: 10-20
Square Footage: 120000
Regions Exported to: South America, Asia
Percentage of Business in Exporting: 60

47492 Patty Palace Foods
595 Middlefield Road
Unit 16
Toronto, ON M1V 3S2
Canada   416-297-0510
         Fax: 416-297-4024 info@pattypalace.net
www.pattypalace.net
Sandwiches
President: Michael Davidson
Estimated Sales: $3.6 Million
Number Employees: 30
Type of Packaging: Consumer, Food Service
Regions Exported to: USA

47493 Patty Paper Inc
1955 N Oak Dr
Plymouth, IN 46563-3412   574-935-8439
         Fax: 574-936-6053   800-782-1703
www.pattypaper.com
Manufacturer and supplier of specialty papers for wrapping meat, cheese and deli items, bakery style picking paper and waxed paper.
Manager: Sherry Simmons
Number Employees: 1-4
Regions Exported to: Worldwide

47494 Paul G. Gallin Company
222 Saint Johns Avenue
Yonkers, NY 10704-2717   914-964-5800
                  Fax: 914-964-5293
Manufacturer and exporter of uniforms and accessories
Estimated Sales: $ 25-50 Million
Number Employees: 18
Square Footage: 12000
Type of Packaging: Bulk
Regions Exported to: Central America, South America, Europe, Middle East
Percentage of Business in Exporting: 40

47495 Paul N. Gardner Company
316 NE 1st St
Pompano Beach, FL 33060-6608 954-946-9454
         Fax: 954-946-9309   800-762-2478
gardner@gardco.com   www.gardco.com
Producer of physical testing instruments. Their brands include Gardco and EZ Zahn Viscosity Cup.

President: Paul Gardner
tjohns@gardco.com
Vice President, International Sales: Sandra Bride
Marketing: Sherri Thompson
Sales Manager: Bill Bride
Manager, Customer Service: Cheryl Wilson
Manager & Director: Lisa Richards
Estimated Sales: $7 Million
Number Employees: 33
Regions Exported to: Central America, South America, Europe, Asia, Middle East, Worldwide

47496 Paul O. Abbe
P.O.Box 80
Bensenville, IL 60106-0080   630-350-2200
    Fax: 630-350-9047   sales@pauloabbe.com
           www.aaronequipment.com
Manufacturer and exporter of tumble and agitated mixers and blenders for powders and solids; also, batch vacuum and fluidized dryers and ball and pebble mills
VP: Alan Cohen
Vice President of Business Development: Bruce Baird
Estimated Sales: $ 5-10 Million
Number Employees: 20-49
Square Footage: 140000
Regions Exported to: Central America, South America, Europe, Asia, Middle East, Worldwide
Percentage of Business in Exporting: 20

47497 Pavailler Distribution Company
232 Pegasus Avenue
Northvale, NJ 07647-1904   201-767-0766
          Fax: 201-767-1723
Bakery equipment
Estimated Sales: $2.5-5 Million
Number Employees: 9
Square Footage: 22400
Brands Imported: Pavailler
Regions Imported from: Europe
Percentage of Business in Importing: 80

47498 Pavan USA Inc
Connelly Rd
Emigsville, PA 17318   717-767-4889
    Fax: 717-767-4656   www.pavan.com
Design and engineering of technologies and intergrated product lines for cereal base food.
President: Dave C Parent
VP/General Manager: David Parent
Estimated Sales: $1-3 Million
Number Employees: 1-4
Square Footage: 20000
Parent Co: Pavan SrL
Brands Imported: Pavan; Toresani; Mapimpianti; Stiavelli

47499 Paxton Corp
86 Tupelo St # 5
Unit 5
Bristol, RI 02809-2837   401-396-9062
    Fax: 203-925-8722   paxton@paxtoncorp.com
Food processing machines such as cutters, slicers, shredders, dicers, graters, and strip cutters, for vegetables, fruits, cheeses, and nuts
President: Leif Jensen
paxton@paxtoncorp.com
CFO: Monica Wingard
Sales Director: Steven King
Estimated Sales: $ 3 - 5 Million
Number Employees: 1-4
Square Footage: 30000
Regions Exported to: Central America, South America, Canada, Caribbean, Latin America, Mexico
Percentage of Business in Exporting: 20
Brands Imported: Hallde, Alexanderwerk
Regions Imported from: Europe
Percentage of Business in Importing: 75

47500 Paxton Products Inc
10125 Carver Rd
Blue Ash, OH 45242-4798   513-891-7474
    Fax: 513-891-4092   800-441-7475
           sales@paxtonproducts.com
           www.paxtonproducts.com
A leader in energy saving, application-specific air systems. Designs and manufactures compact, energy-efficient compressors, blowers, air knives and drying systems.

General Manager: Barbara Stefl
Engineering Manager: Steve Puccinani
Quality Control: Charlie Hertel
International Sales Manager: Rick Immell
Customer Service: Anne Tomsic
Operations Manager: Stan Coley
Buyer: Sherry Driskell
Number Employees: 20-49

47501 Payne Controls Co
Rocky Step Rd
Scott Depot, WV 25560   304-757-7353
    Fax: 304-757-7305   800-331-1345
    info@PaynEng.com   www.payneng.com
Manufacturer and exporter of motor controls for material handling equipment and SCR controls for ovens and process temperature controls
President: Roger Westfall
roger@payneng.com
Manager Marketing Services: Jean Miller
Estimated Sales: $5-10 Million
Number Employees: 10-19
Square Footage: 72000
Brands Exported: Payne Engineering
Regions Exported to: Worldwide
Percentage of Business in Exporting: 5

47502 Peace Industries
1100 Hicks Rd
Rolling Meadows, IL 60008-1016   847-259-1620
    Fax: 847-259-9236   800-873-2239
    pchartier@spotnails.com   www.spotnails.com
Manufactures a wide range of industrial fastening products including nails, staples, pins, brads and tools for use in packaging, furniture/woodworking, construction, factory-built housing and many other industries.
President: Mark R Wilson
CFO: Rex Janderman
Vice President: Win Waterman
Marketing Director: Candi Mortenson
Sales Director: Win Waterman
Contact: Leon Larosa
llarosa@spotnails.com
Plant Manager: Sy Akbari
Purchasing Manager: Alice Mortenson
Estimated Sales: $ 10 - 20 Million
Number Employees: 50-99
Type of Packaging: Bulk
Regions Exported to: Worldwide
Percentage of Business in Exporting: 30

47503 Peace Mountain Natural Beverages
PO Box 1445
Springfield, MA 01101-1445   413-567-4942
          Fax: 413-567-8161
Bottled water, juices, nutraceuticals
Owner: J David
VP R&D: John Alden
Number Employees: 5-9
Type of Packaging: Private Label
Regions Exported to: NE Asia, China, Western Europe

47504 Peace River Citrus Products
582 Beachland Boulevard
Suite 300
Vero Beach, FL 32963   772-492-4050
    Fax: 772-492-4056   www.peacerivercitrus.com
Citrus
President: Bill Becker
Contact: Dale Shaffer
dshaffer@google.com
Plant Manager: Romilio Herrera
Estimated Sales: $ 1 million
Number Employees: 100-249
Type of Packaging: Bulk
Other Locations:
    Peach River Citrus Products Plant
    Arcadia, FL
    Peach River Citrus Products Plant
    Bartow, FLPeach River Citrus Products PlantBartow
Regions Exported to: Europe, Asia, Middle East
Percentage of Business in Exporting: 15

47505 Peace Village Organic Foods
76 Florida Avenue
Berkeley, CA 94707-1708   510-524-4420
          info@peacevillage.net
          www.peacevillage.net
Asian pasta and food ingredients
President: Joel Wollner

Importers & Exporters / A-Z

Type of Packaging: Consumer, Private Label
Brands Exported: Peace Village
Regions Exported to: Asia, Middle East
Brands Imported: Peace Village
Regions Imported from: Europe, Asia

47506 (HQ)Peacock Crate Factory
225 Cash St
PO Box 1110
Jacksonville, TX 75766   903-586-0988
    Fax: 903-586-7476   800-657-2200
Manufacturer and exporter of wood veneer gift, fruit and vegetable baskets; also, store fixtures and displays
President: Richard S Peacock
CFO: Claudia Vastal
Vice President: Speedy Peacock
Estimated Sales: Below $ 5 Million
Number Employees: 20-49
Other Locations:
    Peacock Crate Factory
    Jacksonville, TXPeacock Crate Factory
Regions Exported to: Europe, Asia
Percentage of Business in Exporting: 2

47507 Peanut Patch Gift Shop
27478 Southampton Pkwy
Courtland, VA 23837   757-653-2028
    Fax: 757-653-9530   800-544-0896
           customerservice@feridies.com
           www.thepeanutpatchgiftshop.com
Peanuts and peanut candies
President: Jane Riddick-Fries
janerf@peanutpatch.com
CFO: Paul Sheffer
R&D: Ted Fries
Number Employees: 50-99
Type of Packaging: Consumer, Food Service, Private Label
Regions Exported to: Worldwide
Percentage of Business in Exporting: 5

47508 Pearl Coffee Co
675 S Broadway St
Akron, OH 44311-1099   330-253-7184
    Fax: 330-253-7185   800-822-5282
           dianacoffee@aol.com
Coffee
President: John Economou
Vice President, Marketing: Johnna Economou
Estimated Sales: $9 Million
Number Employees: 10-19
Square Footage: 80000
Type of Packaging: Consumer, Food Service, Private Label
Regions Imported from: Central America, South America
Percentage of Business in Importing: 95

47509 Pearson Packaging Systems
8120 W Sunset Hwy
Spokane, WA 99224-9048   509-838-6226
    Fax: 509-747-8532   800-732-7766
    info@pearsonpkg.com   www.pearsonpkg.com
Manufacturer and exporter of case forming, case packing, tray forming, bottom, top or end sealing, carrier erecting, multipacking, partition and bag inserting machinery, and magazine feeding machinery
CEO: Michael Senske
psenske@pearsonpkg.com
CFO: Randy Bell
Vice President of Engineering: Leo Robertson
Marketing/Sales: Mark Ewing
Vice President of Sales and Marketing: Randy Denny
Estimated Sales: $ 10 - 20 Million
Number Employees: 100-249
Square Footage: 220000
Type of Packaging: Food Service, Private Label, Bulk
Brands Exported: Pearson Machinery
Regions Exported to: South America, Europe, Asia

47510 Pearson's Berry Farm
34463 Range Rd 40
Site 24
Bowden, AB T0M 0K0
Canada   403-224-3011
    Fax: 403-224-2096   www.pearsonsberryfarm.ca
Jams, pie fillings and dessert toppings
President: E Leonard Pearson
Sales Manager: Joyce Park
Number Employees: 20-49
Type of Packaging: Consumer, Food Service

505

Importers & Exporters / A-Z

47511 Pecan Deluxe Candy Co
2570 Lone Star Dr
Dallas, TX 75212-6308
214-631-3669
Fax: 214-631-5833 800-733-3589
pdcc_info@pecandeluxe.com
www.pecandeluxe.com
Dessert and baked goods ingredients: toffees, nuts, chocolate coated items, flavor bases, sauces
President: Jay Brigham
Chairman of the Board: Bennie Brigham
bennie_brigham@pecandeluxe.com
Chief Financial Officer: Keith Hurd
Chief Operating Officer: Tim Markowicz
VP Quality Assurance: Rick Hintermeier
VP Operations: Mike Cavin
Inventory/Production Coordinator: Wayne Miller
Purchasing Manager: James Mitchell
Estimated Sales: $20 - 50 Million
Number Employees: 250-499
Number of Products: 2000
Square Footage: 63000
Type of Packaging: Bulk
Regions Exported to: South America, Europe, Asia
Percentage of Business in Exporting: 9

47512 (HQ)Peco Controls Corporation
1439 Emerald Ave
Mcdesto, CA 95351
510-226-6686
Fax: 510-226-6687 800-732-6285
info@pecocontrols.com www.pecocontrols.com
Manufacturer and exporter of monitors for inspecting fill and vacuum/pressure levels, contents and labels of packages; also, automatic container sampling systems and two-piece can metrology systems
President: F Allan Anderson
Vice President: Aslam Khan
Quality Control: Cheong Chan
Contact: Allan Anderson
a.anderson@pecocontrols.com
Estimated Sales: $ 3 - 5 Million
Number Employees: 35
Square Footage: 64000
Type of Packaging: Consumer, Private Label
Other Locations:
  Peco Controls Corp.
  Pershore, WozosPeco Controls Corp.
Regions Exported to: Central America, South America, Europe, Asia, Middle East, Africa
Percentage of Business in Exporting: 30

47513 Peco Foods Inc.
1101 Greensoro Ave.
Tuscaloosa, AL 35401
205-345-4711
Fax: 205-366-4533 www.pecofoods.com
Deli and tray-pack chicken.
President/CEO: Mark Hickman
mhickman@pecofoods.com
Chairman: Denny Hickman
Chief Financial Officer: Patrick Noland
Director, Technical Services: Curtis Stell
Director, Human Resources: Bart Carter
Director, Sales & Marketing: Bobby Wilburn
Director, Live Operations: Roddy Sanders
Chief Operations Officer: Benny Bishop
Year Founded: 1937
Estimated Sales: $582.2 Million
Number Employees: 1000-4999
Square Footage: 6185
Type of Packaging: Consumer, Food Service
Other Locations:
  Peco Foods, Inc. Processing Plant
  Tuscaloosa, AL
  Peco Foods, Inc. Processing Plant
  Bay Springs, MS
  Peco Foods, Inc. Processing Plant
  Brooksville, MS
  Peco Foods, Inc. Processing Plant
  Sebastopol, MS
  Peco Foods, Inc. Processing Plant
  Canton, MS
  Peco Foods, Inc. Processing Plant
  Batesville, AR
  Peco Foods, Inc. Processing PlantBay Springs
Regions Exported to: South America, Europe, Asia, Canada, Mexico

47514 Pecoraro Dairy Products
287 Leonard St
Brooklyn, NY 11211-3618
718-388-2379
Fax: 315-339-3008 pcr2c1@aol.com
Cheeses
Owner: Ceasre Pecoraro
Operations: Ralph Parlato
Estimated Sales: Less Than $500,000
Number Employees: 1-4
Number of Brands: 4
Number of Products: 12
Square Footage: 14400
Type of Packaging: Consumer, Food Service, Private Label
Regions Exported to: Middle East, Caribbean
Percentage of Business in Exporting: 8

47515 Peerless Dust Killer Company
111 Hill St
Orange, NJ 07050-3901
973-676-1868
Fax: 973-676-4564
Wholesaler/distributor and exporter of maintenance chemicals and janitorialsupplies
Owner: Stan Reichel
Estimated Sales: $ .5 - 1 million
Number Employees: 1-4

47516 Peerless Food Equipment
500 S Vandemark Rd
Sidney, OH 45365-8991
937-492-4158
Fax: 937-492-3688 www.peerlessfood.com
Manufacturer and exporter of snack food and bakery processing equipment including conveyors, coolers, depositors, icers, mixers, pumps, topping applicators and bagel machinery
General Manager: George Hoff
Director of Marketing: Sherri Swabb
Director of Sales: Richard Taylor
Estimated Sales: 5-10 Million
Number Employees: 100-249
Square Footage: 208000
Regions Exported to: Worldwide
Percentage of Business in Exporting: 20

47517 Peerless Food Equipment
500 S Vandemark Rd
Sidney, OH 45365-8991
937-492-4158
Fax: 937-492-3688 info@petersmachinery.com
www.peerlessfood.com
Manufacturer and exporter of food processing machinery including stackers and cookie sandwiching and wrapping equipment
General Manager: George Hoff
Controller: David Alexander
Director, Marketing And Customer Support: Sherri Swabb
Sales Director: Richard Taylor
Human Resource Manager: Kathy Weldy
Plant And Materials Manager: Mike Gniazdowski
Estimated Sales: $7 Million
Number Employees: 100-249
Parent Co: Peerless Group
Regions Exported to: Worldwide
Percentage of Business in Exporting: 75

47518 Peerless Lighting Corporation
PO Box 2556
Berkeley, CA 94702-0556
510-845-2760
Fax: 510-845-2776 www.peerless-lighting.com
Manufacturer and exporter of institutional and commercial fluorescent lighting fixtures
President: Douglas Herst
VP: Jim Young
Manager Marketing Services: Margaret Einhorn
Contact: Michael Brunasso
michael.brunasso@peerless-lighting.com
Estimated Sales: $10-20 Million
Number Employees: 50-99

47519 (HQ)Peerless Machinery Corporation
PO Box 769
Sidney, OH 45365
937-492-4158
Fax: 937-492-3688 800-999-3327
www.thepeerlessgroup.us
Manufacturer and exporter of bakery mixers, dividers, blenders and rounders
President: Dane Belden
Director Marketing: Terry Bartsch
VP Sales: Michael Booth
Contact: David Alexander
dalexander@thepeerlessgroup.us
Estimated Sales: $20-50 Million
Number Employees: 100-249
Square Footage: 75000
Other Locations:
  Peerless Machinery Corp.
  Odessa, FLPeerless Machinery Corp.
Brands Exported: Peerless
Regions Exported to: Worldwide
Percentage of Business in Exporting: 45

47520 Peerless Ovens
334 Harrison St
Sandusky, OH 44870
419-625-4514
Fax: 419-625-4597 800-548-4514
www.peerlessovens.com
Manufacturer and exporter of bakery and pizza ovens, griddles and ranges
President: Bryan Huntley
peerless@lrbcg.com
Estimated Sales: $1-2.5 Million
Number Employees: 10-19
Square Footage: 200000
Type of Packaging: Food Service
Regions Exported to: Central America, Middle East
Percentage of Business in Exporting: 5

47521 Peerless of America
109 Schelter Rd
Lincolnshire, IL 60069-3603
847-634-7500
Fax: 847-634-7506
Manufacturer and exporter of refrigeration and air conditioning equipment including evaporators, finned coils, heat transfer products and unit and flash coolers
Owner: Igor Gordon
VP Sales/Marketing: Michael Schopf
Estimated Sales: $20-50 Million
Number Employees: 100-249
Square Footage: 395000
Brands Exported: Peerless of America
Regions Exported to: Central America, South America, Europe, Asia, Middle East, Australia
Percentage of Business in Exporting: 2

47522 Peerless-Premier Appliance Co
119 S 14th St
Belleville, IL 62220-1715
618-233-0475
Fax: 618-235-1771 info@premierrange.com
www.premierrange.com
Manufacturer and exporter of gas and electric ranges
President: Joseph Geary
CEO: Robert Burggraf
burggraf@premierrange.com
CEO: Alex Volansky
Chairman of the Board: William T Sprague
VP Marketing: Allan Gramlich
National Sales Manager: Robert Volkmann
Estimated Sales: $ 20 - 50 Million
Number Employees: 100-249
Square Footage: 300000
Brands Exported: Premier

47523 Peerless-Winsmith Inc
172 Eaton St
Springville, NY 14141
716-592-9310
Fax: 716-592-9546 www.winsmith.com
Manufacturer and exporter of worm gear speed reducers for material handling conveyors and machinery; also, food processing and bottling machinery.
IT Manager: Gary Fraser
fraser@winsmith.com
Quality Assurance Manager: Bruce DeMont
Year Founded: 1901
Estimated Sales: $100-500 Million
Number Employees: 100-249
Regions Exported to: Worldwide

47524 Peking Noodle Co Inc
1518 N San Fernando Rd
Los Angeles, CA 90065-1225
323-223-0897
Fax: 323-223-3211 info@pekingnoodle.com
www.pekingnoodle.com
Noodles, egg rolls, wontons, potsticker wraps, suey gow skins, fortune cookies and snack foods
Owner: Tony Li
chieffrank@yahoo.com
Vice President: Frank Tong
Plant Manager: Maria Gonzalez
Estimated Sales: $2200000
Number Employees: 50-99
Square Footage: 120000
Type of Packaging: Consumer, Food Service, Private Label, Bulk
Regions Exported to: Europe, Asia
Percentage of Business in Exporting: 5

47525 Pelican Bay Ltd.
150 Douglas Ave
Dunedin, FL 34698-7908
727-733-3069
Fax: 727-734-5860 800-826-8982
sales@pelicanbayltd.com www.pelicanbayltd.com
Baking and drink mixes, spice blends and gifts

Importers & Exporters / A-Z

Owner: Char Pfaelzer
char@pelicanbayltd.com
CEO: Jim Hubbard
Executive VP: David Pfaelzer
Plant Manager: Justin Pfaelzer
Purchasing: Greg Kathan
Estimated Sales: $4.7 Million
Number Employees: 20-49
Number of Brands: 1
Number of Products: 200
Square Footage: 120000
Type of Packaging: Consumer, Private Label, Bulk
Brands Exported: Pelican Bay
Regions Exported to: Europe
Regions Imported from: South America, Asia

47526 Pelican Products Inc
1049 Lowell St
Bronx, NY 10459-2608   718-860-3220
     Fax: 718-860-4415 800-552-8820
info@pelicanproducts.com
www.pelicanproducts.com
Manufacturer and exporter of molded plastic advertising specialties, imprinted premiums and promotional give-aways including coasters, stirrers, cocktail forks, corkscrews and ball point pens
Vice President: David Silver
david@pelicanproducts.com
CEO: Harold Silver
Vice President: Dave Silver
Estimated Sales: $ 2.5 - 5 Million
Number Employees: 10-19
Square Footage: 40000
Regions Exported to: Europe, Asia

47527 Pellerin Milnor Corporation
700 Jackson St
P.O. Box 400
Kenner, LA 70063-0400   504-467-9591
                 800-469-8780
milnorinfo@milnor.com www.milnor.com
A leading commercial and industrial laundry equipment manufacturer. Washer-extractors range in size from 25 lb to 700 lb capacity; dryers from 30-550 lb. These models are available with a variety of controls from very simple to quitesophisticated, depending upon your food and beverage linen needs.
Chairman & CEO: James Pellerin
Vice President: Mike Dineen
mdineen@milnor.com
VP, Sales & Marketing: Richard Kelly
Year Founded: 1947
Estimated Sales: $100+ Million
Number Employees: 530
Square Footage: 400000
Brands Exported: CBW

47528 Pelouze Scale Company
7400 W 100th Place
Bridgeview, IL 60455-2438   708-430-8330
     Fax: 800-654-7330 800-323-8363
www.pelouze.com
Manufacturer and exporter of mechanical and electronic timers, food thermometers and food portion, dietetic, electronic digital and shipping and receiving scales
VP: Dan Maeir
VP: Dan Maeir
National Sales Manager: Jack Kramer
Customer Service Manager: Laura Anton
Estimated Sales: $ 50 - 100 Million
Number Employees: 140
Parent Co: Sunbeam
Type of Packaging: Consumer, Food Service
Brands Exported: Pelouze
Regions Exported to: Central America, South America, Europe, Asia, Middle East
Percentage of Business in Exporting: 25

47529 Pemberton & Associates
152 Remsen Street
Brooklyn, NY 11201
Canada   718-923-1111
     Fax: 718-923-6065 800-736-2664
career@pencom.com www.pencom.com
Manufacturers full service representative of meat and poultry processing, and packaging equipment
Founder, President: Wade Saadi
Vice President of Operations: Jim Kenner
Number Employees: 15
Regions Exported to: Worldwide
Percentage of Business in Exporting: 95

47530 Penauta Products
PO Box 155 RR2
4276 Betaesda Road
Stouffville, ON L4A 7Z5
Canada   905-640-1564
     Fax: 905-640-7479
Jarred honey and bee pollen
President: Paul Nauta
General Manager: Henry Nauta
Production Manager: Martin Nauta
Estimated Sales: $130,000
Number Employees: 3
Square Footage: 24000
Type of Packaging: Consumer, Food Service, Private Label, Bulk
Brands Exported: Meadowview Honey
Regions Exported to: Asia, Middle East

47531 Penco Products
P.O.Box 158
Skippack, PA 19474   610-666-0500
     Fax: 610-666-7561 800-562-1000
customerservice@pencoproducts.com
www.pencoproducts.com
Manufacturer and exporter of shelving, work benches, storage cabinets, pallet racks and lockers
President: Greg Grogan
VP Sales/Marketing: Bill Vain
Estimated Sales: $20-50 Million
Number Employees: 250-499
Regions Exported to: Worldwide
Percentage of Business in Exporting: 1

47532 Penda Form Corp
200 S Friendship Dr
New Concord, OH 43762-9641   740-826-5000
     Fax: 740-826-5001 800-837-2574
Material handling equipment including trays, pallets and covers; exporter of electrical components
President: John Knight
jknight@fabri-form.com
VP Sales: Larry Howard
Manager Customer Service: Dennis Hardin
jknight@fabri-form.com
Plant Manager: Jerry Andrech
Number Employees: 50-99
Regions Exported to: Central America, Europe
Percentage of Business in Exporting: 5

47533 Pendery's
1221 Manufacturing St
Dallas, TX 75207
                 800-533-1870
email@penderys.com www.penderys.com
Bay leaves, cinnamon, garlic, ginger, paprika, chile pepper and herb blends
Estimated Sales: $1-3 Million
Number Employees: 5-9
Square Footage: 92000
Type of Packaging: Consumer, Food Service, Private Label, Bulk
Regions Exported to: Worldwide
Percentage of Business in Exporting: 2
Regions Imported from: Central America, South America, Europe, Asia, Middle East, Africa

47534 Penguin Frozen Foods Inc
555 Skokie Blvd
Suite 440
Northbrook, IL 60062-2835   847-291-9400
     Fax: 847-291-1588 800-323-1485
www.penguinfrozenfoods.com
Seafood and fish: shrimp, sole, turbot, fillets, lobster, crab meat
President: Ellen Paton
ellen@penguinfrozenfoods.com
Estimated Sales: $2,700,000
Number Employees: 10-19
Type of Packaging: Consumer, Food Service
Regions Exported to: Canada, Mexico

47535 Penley Corporation
PO Box 277
West Paris, ME 04289-0277   207-674-2501
     Fax: 207-674-2510 800-368-6449
Manufacturer, importer and exporter of wooden toothpicks, matches, chopsticks, etc.; also, plastic cutlery and drinking straws
Owner: Richard Penley
Director Sales/Marketing: Stephen Gilman
Director Manufacturing: Robert Warrington
Estimated Sales: $5-10 Million
Number Employees: 10-19
Brands Exported: Penley
Regions Exported to: Central America, Canada
Percentage of Business in Exporting: 7
Brands Imported: Penley
Regions Imported from: Asia
Percentage of Business in Importing: 10

47536 Penn Herb Co
10601 Decatur Rd
Suite 2
Philadelphia, PA 19154-3212   215-632-4430
     Fax: 215-632-7945 800-523-9971
www.pennherb.com
Encapsulated herbs ginseng and golden seal root; vitamins and supplements
President: William Betz
wbetz@penton.com
President: Ronald Betz
Estimated Sales: $3500000
Number Employees: 20-49
Square Footage: 92000
Brands Imported: Olbas
Regions Imported from: Europe
Percentage of Business in Importing: 30

47537 Penn Refrigeration Service Corporation
P.O.Box 1261
Wilkes Barre, PA 18703-1261   570-825-5666
     Fax: 570-825-5705 800-233-8354
sales@pennrefrig.com
Manufacturer and exporter of refrigeration equipment and systems including walk-in coolers and freezers
President: Albert Finarelli Jr
afinarelli@pennrefrig.com
Plant Manager: John Gosciewski
Estimated Sales: $ 5 - 10 Million
Number Employees: 50-99
Regions Exported to: Worldwide
Percentage of Business in Exporting: 5

47538 Pennsylvania Apple Mktng Prgm
2301 N Cameron St
Harrisburg, PA 17110-9405   717-783-5418
www.paveggies.org
Manager: Dennis Wolff
Contact: Clifford Ackman
cackman@pa.gov
Estimated Sales: $ 10 - 20 Million
Number Employees: 5-9

47539 Pennsylvania Macaroni Company Inc.
2010 Penn Avenue
Pittsburgh, PA 15222   412-227-1982
dsunseri@pennmac.com
www.pennmac.com
Wholesaler/distributor and importer of olive oil, cheese and pasta products; serving the food service market.
President: David Sunseri
Office Manager: Kathy Feinstein
VP, Purchasing: Bill Sunseri
Year Founded: 1902
Estimated Sales: $24 Million
Number Employees: 80
Number of Brands: 300
Number of Products: 5000
Square Footage: 80000
Type of Packaging: Consumer
Regions Imported from: Europe

47540 Penobscot Mccrum LLC
28 Pierce St
PO Box 229
Belfast, ME 04915-6648   207-338-4360
     Fax: 207-338-5742 800-435-4456
www.penobscotmccrum.com
Potato pancakes, mashers, skins, and wedges.
Managing Partner: Jay McCrum
Managing Partner: David McCrum
Manager, JDR Transport, Inc.: Wade McCrum
Financial Analysis & Marketing: Nick McCrum
Manager, North Maine Farm Operations: Darrell McCrum
Estimated Sales: $33 Million
Number Employees: 100-249
Type of Packaging: Consumer, Food Service

Importers & Exporters / A-Z

47541 Penta Manufacturing Company
50 Okner Pkwy
Livingston, NJ 07039-1604   973-740-2300
         Fax: 973-740-1839   sales@pentamfg.com
                              www.pentamfg.com
Fructose, rice starch, nutraceuticals, food and flavor compounds, chemicals, cooking and essential oils, extracts, spices
Owner: Mark Esposito
SVP: George Volpe
Sales Manager: Christine Tavares
Contact: Fatima Jasmins
fatimaj@pentamfg.com
Estimated Sales: $10 - 20 Million
Number Employees: 20-49
Number of Products: 7000
Square Footage: 700000
Parent Co: Penta International Corporation
Type of Packaging: Food Service, Private Label, Bulk
Regions Exported to: Central America, South America, Europe, Asia
Regions Imported from: Central America, South America, Europe, Asia

47542 Pepe's Inc
1325 W 15th St
Chicago, IL 60608-2190   312-733-2500
         Fax: 312-733-2564   www.pepes.com
Mexican food
President: Betty Wright
b.wright@adm.com
General Manager: Mario Dovalina Jr
Number Employees: 1000-4999
Square Footage: 260000
Type of Packaging: Private Label, Bulk
Brands Exported: Aventura Gourmet - Pepes Mexican Foods.
Regions Exported to: Europe
Percentage of Business in Exporting: 5

47543 Pepe's Mexican Restaurant
2429 W Ball Rd
Anaheim, CA 92804-5210
Canada   714-952-9410
         Fax: 416-674-2805   www.pepesmexicanfood.com
Tortilla chips, flour tortillas, multi-grain snacks, burritos, jalapeno peppers, salsa and beans
Owner: Nathan Russi
Vice President: Ronaldo Sardelitti
VP Sales: Tom Reynolds
National Sales Manager: Tony Kent
Estimated Sales: Less Than $500,000
Number Employees: 5-9
Square Footage: 132000
Parent Co: Signature Brands
Type of Packaging: Consumer, Food Service
Brands Exported: Casa Del Norte
Regions Exported to: South America, USA
Percentage of Business in Exporting: 10
Brands Imported: La Preferida
Regions Imported from: USA
Percentage of Business in Importing: 10

47544 Pepper Creek Farms
1002 SW Ard St
Lawton, OK 73505-9660   580-536-1300
         Fax: 580-536-4886   800-526-8132
                info@peppercreekfarms.com
                www.peppercreekfarms.com
Jellies, mustards, peppers, salsa, relish, syrup, mixes, and seasonings
Owner: Craig Weissman
craig@peppercreekfarms.com
Vice President: Marshall Weissman
Estimated Sales: $600,000
Number Employees: 10-19
Square Footage: 30000
Type of Packaging: Consumer, Food Service, Private Label
Brands Exported: Wildfire; Jalapeno TNT; Jalapeno Hot Sauce
Regions Exported to: South America, Middle East

47545 Pepperama
PO Box 293764
Lewisville, TX 75029-3764   214-212-0574
         Fax: 214-343-0383
Importer of hot pepper sauces

47546 Pepperell Paper Company
9 S Canal Street
Lawrence, MA 01843-1412   978-433-6951
         Fax: 978-433-6427
Manufacturer and exporter of specialty papers including acid free, beater dyed colors, packaging, supercalendered, grease, mold and flame resistant, crepe, flour bag, kraft, etc
Sales Manager: Steve Ulicny
Number Employees: 4
Square Footage: 400000
Parent Co: James River Corporation
Regions Exported to: Central America, South America, Europe, Asia, Middle East
Percentage of Business in Exporting: 10

47547 Per-Fil Industries Inc
407 Adams St
Riverside, NJ 08075-3098   856-461-5700
         Fax: 856-461-0741   www.per-fil.com
Manufacturer and exporter of filling machinery for liquids, powder, paste, granules and food products
President: Shari Becker
Director/Chairman: Horst Boellmann
per-fil@sales.com
Service Manager: Tobin Wrice
National and International Sales: Shari Becker
Estimated Sales: Below $5 Million
Number Employees: 20-49
Square Footage: 29000
Regions Exported to: Worldwide
Percentage of Business in Exporting: 60

47548 Perdue Farms Inc.
31149 Old Ocean City Rd.
Salisbury, MD 21804
                             800-473-7383
                             www.perdue.com
Chicken, turkey and pork.
Chairman: Jim Perdue
CEO: Randy Day
Senior VP/CFO: Brenda Galgano
General Counsel: Herb Frerichs
Senior VP, Corporate Communications: Andrea Staub
Year Founded: 1920
Estimated Sales: $6.7 Billion
Number Employees: 21,000
Number of Brands: 8
Type of Packaging: Consumer, Food Service, Private Label, Bulk
Other Locations:
    Perdue Farms
    Monterey, TN Perdue Farms
Brands Exported: Perdue
Regions Exported to: Worldwide

47549 Peregrine Inc
5301 N 57th St # 102
Lincoln, NE 68507-3164   402-466-4011
         Fax: 402-466-1639   800-777-3433
                info@peregrine-inc.com   www.peregrine-inc.com
Manufacturer and exporter of material handling equipment including four-wheel steering trailers
President: Troy Rivers
troy@peregrine-inc.com
Office/Sales Manager: Joyce Schiermann
Estimated Sales: $1 - 2,500,000
Number Employees: 5-9
Type of Packaging: Bulk
Regions Exported to: Canada, Mexico
Percentage of Business in Exporting: 1

47550 Perfect Equipment Inc
4259 Lee Ave
Gurnee, IL 60031-2175   847-244-7200
         Fax: 847-244-7205   800-356-6301
                info@perfectequip.com   www.perfectequip.com
Manufacturer and exporter of beverage and condiment dispenser systems, custom fabricated stainless steel bar and restaurant equipment including underbar and portable and back bar units, glycol units and water chillers
President: Sanford Hahn
sandy@perfectequip.com
CEO: Kay Hahn
Sales/ Administration: Kathy Pino
Operations Manager/ R&D: Alan Hale
Plant Manager: Alan Hale
Purchasing: Gene Wood
Estimated Sales: $5-10,000,000
Number Employees: 20-49
Square Footage: 28000
Type of Packaging: Food Service
Regions Exported to: Worldwide
Percentage of Business in Exporting: 20

47551 Perfect Fry Company
615 71st Avenue SE
Calgary, AB T2H 0S7
Canada   403-255-7712
         Fax: 403-255-1725   800-265-7711
                profits@perfectfry.com   www.perfectfry.com
Manufacturers ventless countertop deep fryers designated for commercial deep-frying without the installation of hoods and vents
Vice President of Business Development: Gary Calderwood
CFO: Sharon Hyasdick
Vice President, General Manager: Greg Moyer
Research & Development: Shaun Calderwood
Senior Manager of Sales: Bonnie Bolster
Vice President of Operations: Steve Reale
Plant Manager: Jeff Scott
Estimated Sales: Below $5 Million
Number Employees: 20
Square Footage: 60000
Parent Co: Perfect Fry Corporation
Type of Packaging: Food Service
Brands Exported: Perfect Fry
Regions Exported to: Worldwide
Percentage of Business in Exporting: 70

47552 Perfex Corporation
32 Case St
Poland, NY 13431   315-826-3600
         Fax: 315-826-7471   800-848-8483
                perfex@perfexonline.com   www.perfexonline.com
Manufacturer and exporter of PVC floor and neoprene rubber squeegees, polypropylene, chemical resistant and hygienic brooms and brushes, shovels and stainless steel clean room flat mopping systems
President: Michael Kubick
Marketing Manager: Mike Dougherty
Sales: Irene Gouthier
Customer Service Supervisor: Trudy Pickerd
Estimated Sales: $1-2.5 Million
Number Employees: 10-25

47553 Performance Labs
5115 Douglas Fir Rd
Suite M
Calabasas, CA 91302-2597   818-591-9669
         Fax: 818-591-2116   800-848-2537
Nutritional and herbal supplements, vitamins and garlic
Owner: Richard Burke
CEO: David Mercer, Jr.
Contact: Jon Ackland
cousteau@performancelab.co.nz
Purchasing Manager: Allan Suda
Estimated Sales: $3 Million
Number Employees: 20-49
Type of Packaging: Consumer
Brands Exported: GarliMax
Regions Exported to: Canada
Percentage of Business in Exporting: 1
Regions Imported from: Worldwide

47554 Perky's Pizza
4029 Tampa Rd
Oldsmar, FL 34677-3206   813-855-7700
         Fax: 813-855-0014   800-473-7597
                perky@perkys.com   www.perkys.com
Pizza producer of Perky's pizza products, program and product sales
President: Jim Howell
CEO: Frank Rozel
R&D: Bill Sweet
Marketing Manager: Anne Reilley
Sales: Rick White
Contact: G Gable
g.gable@perkys.com
Estimated Sales: $2.5-5 Million
Number Employees: 10-19
Square Footage: 8000
Type of Packaging: Food Service, Private Label
Brands Exported: Perky's
Regions Exported to: Central America, South America, Middle East

47555 Perl Packaging Systems
80 Turnpike Dr # 2
Middlebury, CT 06762-1830   203-598-0066
         Fax: 203-598-0068   800-864-2853
Manufacturer and exporter of straight line liquid filling machines, piston fillers, portable cappers, rotary unscramblers, cap and bottle orienter feeders and labelers
President: David Baker

Estimated Sales: $ 3 - 5 Million
Number Employees: 5-9
Square Footage: 40000
Regions Exported to: Worldwide
Percentage of Business in Exporting: 30

47556 Perley-Halladay Assoc
1037 Andrew Dr
West Chester, PA 19380-4293 610-840-6300
Fax: 610-647-1711 800-248-5800
sales@perleyhalladay.com
www.perleyhalladay.com
Manufacturer and exporter of refrigerated buildings, walk-in coolers and process freezers
Owner: Boone Flint
bf@perleyhalladay.com
Office Mngr.: Jim Sonvogni
Estimated Sales: $2.5-5 Million
Number Employees: 1-4
Regions Exported to: Middle East, Mexico
Percentage of Business in Exporting: 10

47557 Perlick Corp
8300 W Good Hope Rd
Milwaukee, WI 53223-4524 414-353-7060
Fax: 414-353-7069 800-558-5592
perlick@perlick.com www.perlick.com
Manufactuer of bar and beverage dispensing equipment for the foodservice industry.
President, CEO: Paul Peot
pap@perlick.com
CFO: Mike Pitialip
VP of Manufacturing: Tim Carpenter
VP of Marketing & Business Development: Tim Ebner
VP of Commercial Sales: Jim Koelbl
Number Employees: 250-499
Square Footage: 1112000
Type of Packaging: Food Service
Regions Exported to: Worldwide
Percentage of Business in Exporting: 10

47558 Perma-Vault Safe Co Inc
72 Ash Cir
Warminster, PA 18974-4800 215-293-9951
Fax: 215-293-9952 800-662-3360
sales@perma-vault.com www.perma-vault.com
Largest manufacturer of case management drop boxes. Product line includes drop box, depository, in ground, in wall and B rate configuration to fill all requirements. Custom requirements our specialty since 1978
President: Robert Johnson
sales@perma-vault.com
Marketing: Norman Bartwink
Sales: Norman Bartwink
Operations: Tina Williams
Production: Tina Williams
Purchasing: Tina Williams
Estimated Sales: $ 3 - 5 Million
Number Employees: 10-19
Regions Exported to: Central America, Europe
Percentage of Business in Exporting: 5

47559 Perry Videx LLC
25 Mount Laurel Rd
Hainesport, NJ 08036-2711 609-267-1600
Fax: 609-267-4499 info@perryvidex.com
www.perryvidex.com
Wholesaler/distributor, importer and exporter of used food processing equipment; serving the food service market
President/ CEO: Gregg Epstein
gepstein@perryvidex.com
VP-Finance: Bob Bowdoin
VP- Production: Ron Mueller
Sales: Pete D'Angelo
Estimated Sales: $5-10 Million
Number Employees: 20-49
Regions Exported to: Central America, South America, Europe, Asia, Middle East, Worldwide
Percentage of Business in Exporting: 40
Regions Imported from: Worldwide
Percentage of Business in Importing: 20

47560 Persistination
4205 Frost Way
Modesto, CA 95356-8921 209-765-9640
Fax: 209-521-8545 nancetalkies1@aol.com

47561 Perten Instruments
6444 S 6th Street Rd # A
Springfield, IL 62712-6882 217-585-9440
Fax: 217-585-9441 888-773-7836
lblack@perten.com www.perten.com
Manufacturer, importer and exporter of spectrometers, gluten and alpha analysis testing equipment, laboratory sample mill grinders and NIR analyzers
President: Gavin O'Reilly
goreilly@perten.com
Manager Western: Carl Meuser
Manager Eastern: Walter Munday
Sales/Marketing Manager: Wes Shadow
Estimated Sales: $2.5-5 Million
Number Employees: 20-49
Square Footage: 16000
Parent Co: Perten Instruments AB
Brands Exported: DA 7000; SKCS
Regions Exported to: Europe
Percentage of Business in Exporting: 35
Brands Imported: Inframatic; Falling Number; La Mills; Glutomatics
Regions Imported from: Europe
Percentage of Business in Importing: 65

47562 Pestano Foods

New Rochelle, NY 10801
info@drinktoma.com
www.drinktoma.com
Artisanal Bloody Mary cocktail mix
Founder/Owner: Alejandro Lopez
Number of Brands: 1
Number of Products: 1
Type of Packaging: Consumer, Private Label, Bulk
Brands Exported: Toma
Regions Exported to: USA

47563 (HQ)Pete's Brewing Company
14800 San Pedro Ave
San Antonio, TX 78232-3733 210-490-9128
Fax: 210-490-9984 800-877-7383
Beer
President: Scott Barnum
CEO: Jeffrey Atkins
CEO: Carlos Alvarez
VP Sales: Don Quigley
Contact: James Bolz
j.bolz@petes.com
Number Employees: 50-99
Parent Co: Miller Brewing Company
Brands Exported: Pete's Wicked Ale
Regions Exported to: United Kingdom

47564 Peter Pan Seafoods Inc.
3015 112th Ave. NE
Suite 100
Bellevue, WA 98004 206-728-6000
Fax: 206-441-9090 sales@ppsf.com
www.ppsf.com
Seafood including crab, herring and surimi blends, canned salmon, swordfish, mahi mahi and tuna.
President/CEO: Barry Collier
barryc@ppsf.com
Controller/Treasurer: Adrian Yonke
Year Founded: 1912
Estimated Sales: $225 Million
Number Employees: 1,000-4,999
Number of Brands: 8
Parent Co: Maruha Capital Investment, Inc.
Type of Packaging: Consumer, Food Service, Private Label, Bulk
Regions Exported to: Europe, Asia
Percentage of Business in Exporting: 50
Regions Imported from: Central America, South America, Europe
Percentage of Business in Importing: 5

47565 Peter Rabbit Farms
85810 Peter Rabbit Ln
Coachella, CA 92236 760-398-0136
Fax: 760-398-0972 sales@peterrabbitfarms.com
www.peterrabbitfarms.com
Peppers, grapes, eggplant, leafy greens and Medjool dates
President/CEO: John Powell Jr
Controller: Stephanie Sibotka
stephanies@peterrabbitfarms.com
VP & COO: Steve Powell
Manager, Sales: John Burton
Number Employees: 100-249
Square Footage: 400000
Type of Packaging: Consumer, Food Service, Private Label, Bulk

Regions Exported to: Worldwide
Percentage of Business in Exporting: 5

47566 Peters Imports Inc.
900 N Schmidt Road
Romeoville, IL 60446 616-261-5405
Fax: 800-541-8034 800-541-8267
cs@petersimports.com
Imports and distributes fine gourmet foods and confections
President: Edwin Peters
Vice President: Ernest Peters
Marketing: B.J. Joyner
Contact: Julie Jeltema
julie.jeltema@petersimports.com
Estimated Sales: $9.9 Million
Number Employees: 55

47567 Peterson
1102 D St NE
Auburn, WA 98002
800-735-0313
sales@petersoncheese.com
www.petersoncheese.com
Flavorings, cheese, chocolate, meats and bacon.
Chief Executive Officer: Jack Fabulich III
Year Founded: 1947
Estimated Sales: $20-50 Million
Number Employees: 200
Square Footage: 180000
Type of Packaging: Food Service
Brands Imported: MD Foods; Couronne; Couturier; Norsland; Westland; Grassi; Illchester; Finlandia; Kaserei; Sini Fulvi; Suisse; Scundil; Nederland; Scholewag; Haco; Hero; Callebuut; Mona Lisa
Regions Imported from: Europe, Australia
Percentage of Business in Importing: 55

47568 Peterson Manufacturing Company
24133 W 143rd St
Plainfield, IL 60544 815-436-9201
Fax: 815-436-2863 800-547-8995
callpmc@peterson-mfg.com
www.peterson-mfg.com
Manufacturer and exporter of metal storage racks
President: Gerry Kusiolek
CFO: Dicks Jenkins
Chairman of the Board: David Peterson
Estimated Sales: $ 5 - 10 Million
Number Employees: 50-99

47569 Petra International
1260 Fewster Drive
Unit 1
Mississauga, ON L4W 1A5
Canada 905-629-9269
Fax: 905-542-2546 800-261-7226
petra@petradecor.com www.petradecor.com
Gum paste flowers
President: Ham Go
Parent Co: Indomex Foods
Type of Packaging: Consumer, Private Label, Bulk
Regions Exported to: Central America, South America, Europe, Middle East
Regions Imported from: Asia, Western Europe

47570 Petrini Foods International, DBA Foodworld Sales
543 Valley Road
Montclair, NJ 07043-1881 973-746-9488
Fax: 973-746-6667 Petriniusa@aol.com
Master distributor of Italian pasta
President: Carlo Petrini
CFO: Gasper Tirone
Sales/Marketing: Kerry Dutter
General Manager: Mario Tisba
Number Employees: 5-9
Brands Imported: Spigadoro
Regions Imported from: Europe
Percentage of Business in Importing: 100

47571 (HQ)Petro Moore Manufacturing Corporation
3641 Vernon Blvd
Long Island City, NY 11106-5123 718-784-2516
Fax: 718-784-7099
Manufacturer and exporter of steel folding legs and folding and stackable tables
President: Robert Murphy
Secretary: Jan DeRosa

Importers & Exporters / A-Z

Estimated Sales: Below $5 Million
Number Employees: 5-9
Square Footage: 40000
Type of Packaging: Food Service

47572 Petrofsky's Bakery Products
16647 Annas Way
Chesterfield, MO 63005-4509
636-519-1613
Dough and bagels
President: Jerry Shapiro
Vice President: Robert Petrofsky
Estimated Sales: $ 10 - 20 Million
Number Employees: 20-49
Parent Co: Maplehurst Bakeries
Type of Packaging: Consumer, Food Service
Regions Exported to: Worldwide

47573 (HQ)Petroleum Analyzer Co LP
8824 Fallbrook Dr
Houston, TX 77064-4855
281-940-1803
Fax: 281-580-0719 800-444-8378
sales@paclp.com www.paclp.com
Manufacturer and exporter of analyzers including total nitrogen, sulfur and fluoride; also, sulfur-selective and nitrogen-specific GC and HPLC detectors
President: Jereon Schmits
jereon@paclp.com
CEO: Randy Wreyford
Marketing Director: Cindy Goodman
Sales Manager: Emmanuel Filaudeau
Number Employees: 500-999
Square Footage: 120000
Other Locations:
 Antek Instruments
 DusseldorfAntek Instruments
Regions Exported to: Worldwide
Percentage of Business in Exporting: 40

47574 Petschl's Quality Meats
1150 Andover Park E
Tukwila, WA 98188-3903
206-575-4400
Fax: 206-575-4463 info@petschls.com
Beef, lamb, pork, veal and chicken
Owner: Shelley Greene
shelley@petschls.com
Vice President: Nancy Kvinge
Estimated Sales: $9 Million
Number Employees: 20-49
Type of Packaging: Consumer, Food Service, Private Label, Bulk
Regions Exported to: Asia, Canada

47575 Pez Candy Inc
35 Prindle Hill Rd
Orange, CT 06477-3616
203-795-0531
Fax: 203-799-1679
Candy and dispensers
President: Joseph Vittoria
CEO: Christian Jegen
jegen@pezcandyinc.com
CFO: Brian Fry
VP Marketing: Peter Vandall
VP Sales: Dan Silliman
VP Operations: Mark Morrissey
Estimated Sales: $3,100,000
Number Employees: 100-249
Type of Packaging: Consumer
Other Locations:
 PEZ Candy
 Orange, CTPEZ Candy
Brands Exported: Pez
Regions Exported to: Central America, South America, Canada, Mexico
Brands Imported: Manner; Napoli

47576 Pfankuch Machinery Corporation
5885 149th St W Ste 101
Apple Valley, MN 55124
952-891-3311
Fax: 952-891-5168 pfankuchmachine@msn.com
Manufacturer, importer and exporter of packaging machinery including feeders, collators, counters and wrappers
CEO: Claus Pfankuch
Estimated Sales: $ 3 - 5,000,000
Number Employees: 5-9
Square Footage: 22000
Parent Co: Pfankuch Maschinen
Regions Exported to: Canada
Percentage of Business in Exporting: 10
Regions Imported from: Europe, Germany

47577 Pfanstiehl Inc
1219 Glen Rock Ave
Waukegan, IL 60085-6249
847-623-0370
Fax: 847-623-9173
Lactic acid
Chairman: Jim Breckenridge
President: Cynthia Kerker
VP, Sales & Marketing: Chris Wilcox
VP, Research & Development: Trevor Calkins
Quality Control Chemist: Jimmy Moshopoulos
Contact: Jessica Bakutis
jessica.bakutis@pfanstiehl.com
Year Founded: 1919
Estimated Sales: $23.9 Million
Number Employees: 10-19
Parent Co: Med Opportunity Partners
Type of Packaging: Bulk
Regions Exported to: Worldwide

47578 Pfeil & Holding Inc
5815 Northern Blvd
Woodside, NY 11377-2297
718-545-4600
Fax: 718-932-7513 800-247-7955
info@cakedeco.com www.cakedeco.com
Bakers' equipment and utensils, cake decorations, pastry bags, pans, tubes, tier separators, flavors and ingredients
President: David Gordils
davidg@cakedeco.com
CEO: Sy Stricker
Sales Director: Jenn Covalluzzi
Estimated Sales: $ 5 -10 Million
Number Employees: 20-49
Number of Products: 7000
Square Footage: 200000
Regions Exported to: Worldwide

47579 Pharaoh Trading Company
5043 Red Maple Court
Medina, OH 44256-7084
216-749-6070
Fax: 216-749-7327 800-929-4913
Wholesaler/distributor, importer and exporter of groceries, plasticware, industrial equipment and supplies, disposables and cleaning supplies; serving the health care and food service industries
President: Bill Bebawi
Secretary: Mary Bebawi
Executive VP: Hany Anis
Estimated Sales: $1-2.5 Million
Number Employees: 5-9
Square Footage: 4800
Brands Exported: Golden Seal
Regions Exported to: South America, Middle East
Percentage of Business in Exporting: 30
Regions Imported from: South America, Asia, Middle East

47580 Pharmaceutical & Food Special
P.O.Box 7697
San Jose, CA 95150-7697
408-275-0161
Fax: 408-280-0979 phfspec@pacbell.net
www.phfspec.com
Importer and exporter of temperature sensing equipment; also, consulting services available including plant and process design, training, seminars and FDA/USDA regulation compliance packaging design
President: Pamela Hardt-English
Quality Control: Peter Cocotas
Vice President: Peter Cocotas
Food Tecnologist: Kim Cortes
Estimated Sales: Below $ 5 Million
Number Employees: 1-4
Square Footage: 10000
Regions Exported to: Central America, Asia
Brands Imported: Ellab
Regions Imported from: Europe
Percentage of Business in Importing: 10

47581 Pharmachem Laboratories
265 Harrison Ave
Kearny, NJ 07032-4315
201-246-1000
Fax: 201-991-5674 800-526-0609
www.pharmachemlabs.com
Ingredients: proteins, extracts, acids
President: David Holmes
CEO: Andrea Bauer
andrea.bauer@pharmachem.com
Number Employees: 50-99

47582 Pharmachem Labs
2929 E White Star Ave
Anaheim, CA 92806-2628
714-630-6000
Fax: 714-630-6655 800-717-5770
www.pharmachemlabs.com
Importer, exporter and wholesaler/distributor of bulk vitamins and minerals; also, vegetable powders, fruit powders, botanic powders and nutritional raw materials
President: Howard Simon
Vice President: George Joseph
gjoseph@amer-ing.com
Purchasing: George Joseph
Estimated Sales: $2.5-5 Million
Number Employees: 20-49
Square Footage: 160000
Parent Co: Pharmachem Laboratories
Type of Packaging: Bulk
Brands Exported: Puregar Garlic
Regions Exported to: Europe, Asia
Regions Imported from: Europe, Asia

47583 Pharmavite LLC
8510 Balboa Blvd
Suite 100
Northridge, CA 91325-3581
818-221-6200
Fax: 818-221-6618 800-276-2878
www.pharmavite.com
Vitamin tablets and ingredients
President: Brent Belly
CEO: Connie Barry
Executive VP Marketing: Catherine Mardesich
Estimated Sales: $300,000-500,000
Number Employees: 5-9
Parent Co: Pharmavite Corporation
Type of Packaging: Bulk

47584 Phase II Pasta Machine Inc
55 Verdi St
Farmingdale, NY 11735-6316
631-293-4259
Fax: 631-293-4572 800-457-5070
pastamachine@aol.com
Manufacturer, exporter and importer of commercial pasta equipment
President: Michael Wilson
pastamachines@aol.com
Estimated Sales: Less Than $500,000
Number Employees: 1-4
Square Footage: 11000
Regions Exported to: Central America, South America, Mexico, Canada
Percentage of Business in Exporting: 10
Regions Imported from: Europe
Percentage of Business in Importing: 25

47585 Phelps Industries
P.O.Box 190718
Little Rock, AR 72219-0718
501-568-5550
Fax: 501-568-3363 www.phelpsfan.com
Manufacturer and exporter of platform dump trucks and live floor hoppers for bulk handling
Owner: Donald Phelps
Vice President: John Phelps
Estimated Sales: $ 10 - 20 Million
Number Employees: 50-99
Regions Exported to: Europe, Asia, Middle East, North America, Africa, Caribbean
Percentage of Business in Exporting: 15

47586 Phenix Label Co
11610 S Alden St
Olathe, KS 66062-6923
913-327-7000
Fax: 913-327-7010 800-274-3649
info@phenixlabel.com www.phenixlabel.com
Manufacturer and exporter of custom printed labels
President: Hans Peter
hpeter@phenixlabel.com
CFO: Mark Volz
VP: Mike Darpel
Quality Control: Gina Waltmire
Estimated Sales: $10-20 Million
Number Employees: 100-249
Square Footage: 70000
Parent Co: Phenix Box & Label Company
Type of Packaging: Consumer, Food Service, Private Label
Regions Exported to: Europe

47587 Philadelphia Cheese Steak
520 E Hunting Park Ave
Philadelphia, PA 19124-6009
215-423-3333
Fax: 215-423-3131 www.phillycheesesteak.com

President: Nicholas Karamatsoukas
Contact: Caitlin Anderson
canderson@phillycheesesteak.com
Estimated Sales: Less Than $500,000
Number Employees: 1-4

47588 Philadelphia Macaroni Co
760 S 11th St
Philadelphia, PA 19147-2614   215-923-3141
   Fax: 215-925-4298 www.philamacaroni.com
Pasta and noodles.
Director of Sales/Marketing: Joe Viviano
EVP Sales: Bill Stabert
Customer Service: Fran Pickel
Estimated Sales: $20-50 Million
Number Employees: 10-19
Type of Packaging: Food Service, Private Label, Bulk
Regions Exported to: Europe, Asia, Middle East, Australia
Percentage of Business in Exporting: 3

47589 Phildesco
500 State Route 17
Suite 306
Hasbrouck Heights, NJ 07604-3121   908-955-4100
   coconut@phildesco.com
   www.phildesco.com
Importer of coconut products
President: John Quimson
Estimated Sales: $2.5-5 Million
Number Employees: 1-4
Type of Packaging: Food Service, Private Label
Brands Imported: Sweet Cote

47590 Philipp Lithographing Co
1960 Wisconsin Ave
PO Box 4
Grafton, WI 53024-2623   262-377-1100
   Fax: 262-377-6660   800-657-0871
   help@philipplitho.com www.philipplitho.com
Manufacturer and exporter of labels and point of purchase displays
President/CEO: Peter Buening
pbuening@philipplithographing.com
CFO/Treasurer: Dave Kaehny
Vice President/General Counsel: Stacy Buening
Estimated Sales: $5-10 Million
Number Employees: 50-99
Square Footage: 70000
Type of Packaging: Private Label

47591 Philips Lighting Company
PO Box 6800
Somerset, NJ 08875-6800   732-563-3000
   Fax: 732-563-3641 www.lighting.philips.com
Manufacturer and exporter of lamps including incandescent, fluorescent, HID, specialty, miniature, etc
CEO: Ed Crawford
Director Channel Marketing: Paul Lienesch
Contact: Koen Joosse
koen.joosse@philips.com
Estimated Sales: $ 30 - 50 Million
Number Employees: 10,000

47592 Phoenician Herbals
P.O.Box 28381
Scottsdale, AZ 85255   480-368-8144
   Fax: 480-368-2912   800-966-8144
Vitamins, supplements and teas
Owner: Redgie Hansen
Estimated Sales: $440,000
Number Employees: 5-9
Brands Exported: Phoenician Herbals
Regions Exported to: Worldwide

47593 Phoenix Agro-IndustrialCorporation
521 Lowell St
Westbury, NY 11590   516-334-1194
   Fax: 516-338-8647
Frozen foods and groceries
President: Tomipor Pasto
Marketing: Julianna Edlyn
Purchasing Director: Neone Din
Estimated Sales: $ 3 - 5 Million
Number Employees: 5-9
Square Footage: 40000
Type of Packaging: Consumer, Private Label, Bulk
Brands Exported: Citizen
Regions Exported to: Worldwide
Percentage of Business in Exporting: 98

47594 Phoenix Closures Inc
1899 High Grove Ln
Naperville, IL 60540-3996   630-544-3475
   Fax: 630-420-4774
   greatcaps@phoenixclosures.com
   www.phoenixclosures.com
Manufacturer and exporter of caps and seals
President: Bert Miller
CFO: Rich Classen
Quality Control: Jim Twohij
VP Sales/Marketing: Jeff Davis
Sales Director: Tim Ferrel
Estimated Sales: $ 20 - 50 Million
Number Employees: 250-499
Number of Products: 1000
Square Footage: 100000
Brands Exported: SureSeal-liner, Vent Seal, AccuPor & AccuGard
Regions Exported to: Central America, South America, Europe, Asia, Middle East
Percentage of Business in Exporting: 5

47595 Phoenix Industries Corp
114 N Bedford St
Madison, WI 53703-2610   608-251-2533
   Fax: 608-256-2604   888-241-7482
   www.negusboxnbag.com
Manufacturer and exporter of corrugated ice cream containers; wholesaler/distributor and exporter of packaging supplies including bags
President: Rod Shaughnessy
contact.nequs@negusboxnbag.com
Sales: Greg Koch
Operations: Al Baler
Estimated Sales: $1-5 Million
Number Employees: 5-9
Square Footage: 40000
Parent Co: Phoenix Industries Corporation
Brands Exported: Negus Octapak; Negus Square Pak
Regions Exported to: Central America, Europe, Asia
Percentage of Business in Exporting: 5

47596 Phytotherapy Research Laboratory
W Fourth S
PO Box 627
Lobelville, TN 37097-0627   931-593-3780
   Fax: 931-593-3782   800-274-3727
Herb extracts
President: Brent Davis
Estimated Sales: $500,000-$1 Million
Number Employees: 1-4
Square Footage: 50000
Type of Packaging: Private Label
Regions Exported to: Europe, Canada

47597 Piazza's Seafood World LLC
205 James Dr W
St Rose, LA 70087-4036   504-602-5050
   Fax: 504-602-1555 info@cajunboy.net
   www.cajunboy.net
crawfish, alligator, catfish, shrimp, squid, crabmeat and softshell crabs
Manager: Jennifer Champagne
CFO: Mike Sabolyk
Manager: Jarrod Champagne
jarrod@cajunboy.net
Estimated Sales: $ 5-10 Million
Number Employees: 10-19
Number of Products: 20
Type of Packaging: Food Service, Private Label
Regions Exported to: Europe, Asia
Percentage of Business in Exporting: 5
Brands Imported: Cajun Boy; Cajun Delight
Regions Imported from: Central America, South America, Europe, Asia
Percentage of Business in Importing: 95

47598 Pica Trade Company
P.O.Box 882344
San Francisco, CA 94188-2344   650-777-9977

47599 Pick Heaters
P.O.Box 516
West Bend, WI 53095   262-338-1191
   Fax: 262-338-8489   800-233-9030
info1@pickheaters.com www.pickheaters.com

Manufacturer and exporter of direct steam injection liquid heating systems including heat exchangers, water heaters, hose stations and clean-in-place; also, cookers including food/starch, fruit and vegetable purees, etc
CEO: Prudence Hway
Executive VP: Michael Campbell
Estimated Sales: $ 2.5 - 5 Million
Number Employees: 25
Regions Exported to: Central America, South America, Europe, Asia, Middle East, Worldwide
Percentage of Business in Exporting: 15

47600 Pickard China
782 Pickard Ave
Antioch, IL 60002-1574   847-395-3800
   Fax: 847-395-3827 finest@pickardchina.com
   www.pickardchina.com
Manufacturer and exporter of stock and custom fine china
President: Andrew P Morgan
amorgan@pickardchina.com
International Sales VP: Larry Smith
Estimated Sales: $5-10 Million
Number Employees: 20-49
Square Footage: 120000
Regions Exported to: Asia, Middle East
Percentage of Business in Exporting: 5

47601 Pickles Olives Etc
267 Ridge Rd
Lyndhurst, NJ 07071-1928   201-729-1414
   Fax: 201-729-1515 www.picklesandolives.com
Pickles, olives, mushrooms, pepperoncini, sundried tomatoes, sauerkraut, capers, dried figs, dried turkish apricots, turkish pistachios, peppadew, roasted red pepper
President: Al Sozer
info@valescotrading.com
Number Employees: 5-9

47602 Pickwick Manufacturing Svc
4200 Thomas Dr SW
Cedar Rapids, IA 52404-5055   319-393-7443
   Fax: 319-393-7456   800-397-9797
   wcorey@pickwick.com www.pickwick.com
Manufacturer and exporter of poultry processing equipment including batch scalders, pickers and conveyorized eviscerating lines
President: Walter F Corey
wcorey@pickwick.com
CEO: Walter F Corey
Estimated Sales: $20-50 Million
Number Employees: 100-249
Square Footage: 100000
Brands Exported: Pickwick
Regions Exported to: Worldwide
Percentage of Business in Exporting: 5

47603 Pictsweet Co
10 Pictsweet Dr
Bells, TN 38006-4274   731-663-7600
   Fax: 731-663-7639 mailbox@pictsweet.com
   www.pictsweet.com
Asparagus, beans, broccoli, brussels sprouts, carrots, cauliflower, turnip, mustard and collard greens, okra, peas, spinach, squash, succotash
President: Billy Ennis
Chairman/Ceo: James Tankersley
jtankersley@pictsweet.com
Marketing Director: Julia Wells
Director Manufacturing: Frank Tankersley
Estimated Sales: $10-20 Million
Number Employees: 500-999
Number of Products: 100
Parent Co: Pictsweet
Type of Packaging: Consumer, Food Service, Private Label
Regions Exported to: Asia
Percentage of Business in Exporting: 1
Regions Imported from: Asia

47604 Pie Piper Products
654 South Wheeling Road
Wheeling, IL 60090   847-459-3600
   Fax: 630-595-1551   800-621-8183
   www.distinctivefoods.com
Cheesecakes, brownies, quiche and beef frankfurters

President: Josh Harris
joshh@distinctivefoods.com
Chief Financial Officer: Ron Buck
Vice President: Daniel Mager
Quality Control: Jay Trujillo
Marketing/Sales/Public Relations: Stephanie Jacobs
Engineer: Jim Howard
Production Manager: Mike Lopardo
Purchasing: Araeeli Ocampo
Estimated Sales: $ 10 - 20 Million
Number Employees: 40
Square Footage: 32000
Parent Co: Vienna Manufacturing Company
Type of Packaging: Consumer, Food Service, Private Label
Brands Exported: Pie Piper; Central Park
Regions Exported to: Europe, Asia, Mexico
Percentage of Business in Exporting: 25

47605 Pied-Mont/Dora
176 Saint-Joseph
Anne Des Plaines, QC J0N 1H0
Canada   450-478-0801
            Fax: 450-478-6381   800-363-8003
info@piedmontdora.com www.piedmontdora.com
Vegetable and fruit dips, jams, jellies and marmalades; chocolate spreads, pie fillings, syrups and drink crystals
President/Board Member: Louis Limoges
Marketing: Justin Bart
Estimated Sales: $6.9 Million
Number Employees: 40
Percentage of Business in Importing: 10

47606 Pier 1 Imports
453 Chestnut Ridge Rd
Woodcliff Lake, NJ 07677-7679   201-666-4500
            Fax: 201-666-8525   800-448-9993
                                www.pier1.com
Espresso machines, wood burning ovens and pasta equipment; importer of pasta and espresso equipment
Manager: Lauren Sanders
Estimated Sales: $ 1 - 3 Million
Number Employees: 10-19
Type of Packaging: Food Service
Brands Imported: Cap-O-Mat; Italgi; Rancilio
Regions Imported from: Italy
Percentage of Business in Importing: 100

47607 Piknik Products Company
3806 Day Street
P.O. Box 9388
Montgomery, AL 36108-1720   334-240-2218
            Fax: 334-265-9490
Mayonnaise, mustard and salad dressing
President: Herman Loeb
Estimated Sales: $29 Million
Number Employees: 205
Type of Packaging: Consumer, Food Service, Private Label
Regions Exported to: Worldwide

47608 (HQ)Pilant Corp
4100 W Profile Pkwy
Bloomington, IN 47404-2546   812-334-7090
            Fax: 317-392-4772   800-366-3525
Manufacturer and exporter of custom and stock recloseable and polyethylene bags
Manager: Peter Lenzen
Executive VP: Ronald Thieman
VP Sales: Dick Zurich
Manager: Curt Howard
howard@pliantcorporation.com
Estimated Sales: $ 3 - 5 Million
Number Employees: 5-9
Square Footage: 1400000
Other Locations:
    KCL Corp.
    Dallas, TX KCL Corp.
Regions Exported to: Europe, Canada
Percentage of Business in Exporting: 5

47609 Pilgrim Plastics
1200 W Chestnut St
Brockton, MA 02301-5574   508-436-6300
            Fax: 508-580-0829   800-343-7810
                                www.pilgrimplastics.com
Manufacturer and exporter of plastic point of purchase displays, including window displays, door displays, counter change mats, shelf displays, membership cards, change cashing cards, promotional items, rulers, luggage tags, etc

President: Mark Abrams
mabrams@starprintingcorp.com
CFO: Mark Abrams
Quality Control: Jason Abrams
Estimated Sales: Below $ 5 Million
Number Employees: 50-99
Square Footage: 320000
Percentage of Business in Exporting: 3

47610 Pilgrim's Pride Corp.
1770 Promontory Cir.
Greeley, CO 80634   970-506-8000
                                www.pilgrims.com
Chicken.
Global CEO: Jayson Penn
Year Founded: 1946
Estimated Sales: $10 Billion
Number Employees: 35,700
Number of Brands: 11
Parent Co: JBS S.A.
Type of Packaging: Consumer, Food Service, Private Label, Bulk
Other Locations:
    WLR Foods
    Broadway, VA WLR Foods
Brands Exported: Pilgrim's
Regions Exported to: Worldwide
Percentage of Business in Exporting: 10

47611 Piller Sausages & Delicatessens
443 Wismer Street
Waterloo, ON N2K 2K6
Canada   519-743-1412
            Fax: 519-743-7111   800-265-2628
                                www.pillers.com
Sausage and processed meats
President: William Huber, Jr.
Number Employees: 100-249
Type of Packaging: Consumer, Food Service, Private Label, Bulk
Regions Exported to: Worldwide

47612 Piller's Fine Foods
443 Wismer Street
Waterloo, ON N2K 2K6
Canada   519-743-1412
                                800-265-2627
                                www.pillers.com
Pork, beef, poultry, chubs and sticks, hot dogs and franks, luncheon meat, sausages, pate and coils
CEO: Willy Huber
VP of Innovation & Business Development: Gerhart Huber
VP of Sales & Marketing: Sean Moriarty
Number Employees: 200
Type of Packaging: Private Label
Brands Exported: Royale
Regions Exported to: USA

47613 Pines International
1992 E 1400 Rd
Lawrence, KS 66044-9303   785-841-6016
            Fax: 785-841-1252   800-697-4637
pines@wheatgrass.com www.wheatgrass.com
Grass: wheat, barley, rye and oat; powders and tablets; alfalfa
President: Ron Seibold
rseibold@wheatgrass.com
CEO: Steve Malone
Sales/Marketing: Allen Levine
Purchasing Director: Jeff Richards
Year Founded: 1976
Estimated Sales: $3,635,158
Number Employees: 20-49
Square Footage: 160000
Type of Packaging: Consumer, Private Label, Bulk
Brands Exported: Pines; Pines Mighty Greens
Regions Exported to: Central America, South America, Europe, Asia, Middle East

47614 Pinnacle Furnishing
10564 Nc Highway 211 E
Aberdeen, NC 28315   910-944-0908
            Fax: 910-944-0920   866-229-5704
                                www.pinnaclefurnishings.com
Manufacturer and exporter of chairs and tables for restaurants, casinos, hotels and banquets
President: Jack Berggren
R&D: Jack Berggren
Vice President: Steve Laufer
Quality Control: Sarah Swanson
Regional Sales Representative: Bunnie Strauh

Estimated Sales: $ 2.5 - 5,000,000
Number Employees: 20-49
Square Footage: 80000
Regions Exported to: Worldwide
Percentage of Business in Exporting: 2

47615 Pintys Delicious Foods
5063 North Service Road
Suite 101
Burlington, ON L7L 5H6
Canada   905-835-8575
            Fax: 905-834-5093   800-263-9710
humanresources@pintys.com www.pintys.com
Poultry
President/Owner: Phil Kudelka
CEO: Aba Vanderlaan
CFO: Patricia Bowman
VP Operations: Jack Vanderlaan
Sales: Greg Fox
General Manager: Doug Bowman
Number Employees: 100-249
Square Footage: 360000
Type of Packaging: Food Service, Bulk
Regions Exported to: Worldwide

47616 Pioneer Growers
227 NW Avenue L
Belle Glade, FL 33430-1935   229-243-9306
            Fax: 561-996-5703   www.pioneergrowers.com
Chinese cabbage, carrots, celery, corn and radishes
Vice President, General Manager: Gene Duff
Vice President of Quality Assurance: James Jacks
Sales/ Marketing: Jon Browder
Sales Exec: J D Poole
Number Employees: 20-49
Type of Packaging: Consumer, Bulk
Brands Exported: Frontier; Well's Ace; Team
Regions Exported to: Worldwide

47617 Pioneer Mat Company
610 Ohio Ave
Signal Mountain, TN 37377   423-622-4272
            Fax: 423-622-7787   800-333-8516
Owner: Mertland M Hedges
Estimated Sales: $ 1 - 3 Million
Number Employees: 10-19

47618 Pioneer Packing Co
510 Napoleon Rd
PO Box 171
Bowling Green, OH 43402-4821   419-352-5283
            Fax: 419-352-7330   wcontris@aol.com
                                www.pioneerpacking.com
Bacon, smoked meats and pork sausage
President: Jason Blewer
jasonb@pioneersantaana.net
Estimated Sales: $5 Million
Number Employees: 20-49
Square Footage: 150000
Type of Packaging: Consumer, Bulk
Regions Exported to: Central America
Percentage of Business in Exporting: 5

47619 Pioneer Plastics Inc
1584 US Highway 41a N
Dixon, KY 42409-9328   270-639-9133
            Fax: 270-639-5882   800-951-1551
                                sales@pioneerplastics.com
                                www.pioneerplastics.com
Manufacturer and exporter of rigid molded clear plastic containers including round, square, oval and rectangular
President: Edward Knapp
CFO: Edward Knapp Jr
Marketing Manager: Wayne Fiester
Customer Service: David Fiester
Estimated Sales: $ 5 - 10 Million
Number Employees: 50-99
Type of Packaging: Consumer, Food Service
Regions Exported to: Central America, South America, Europe, Middle East, Canada
Percentage of Business in Exporting: 3

47620 (HQ)Piper Products Inc
300 S 84th Ave
Wausau, WI 54401-8460   715-842-5382
            Fax: 715-848-1870   800-544-3057
info@piperonline.net www.piperonline.net
Aluminum racks, transport cabinets, dollies, proofer cabinets, hot boxes, pans and accessories; exporter of aluminum racks and transport cabinets

President: Roger D Sweeney
CEO: Tony Sweeney
National Sales Manager: R Joseph Graf
Customer Service: Evelyn Yakich
Estimated Sales: $ 10 - 20 Million
Number Employees: 50-99
Type of Packaging: Food Service
Other Locations:
   Piper Products
      Wausau, WIPiper Products
Brands Exported: Piper
Regions Exported to: Europe, Asia, Middle East
Percentage of Business in Exporting: 5

47621 **Piper Products Inc**
300 S 84th Ave
Wausau, WI 54401-8460   715-842-5382
      Fax: 715-848-1870   800-544-3057
            www.piperonline.net
Manufacturer and exporter of ovens, proofers, combination oven/proofers, transport and heated cabinets and bakery racks, cafeteria, buffet lines, tray delivery carts and support equipment
CEO: Tony Sweeney
CEO: Tony Sweeney
Estimated Sales: $ 10 - 20 Million
Number Employees: 50-99
Type of Packaging: Food Service
Brands Exported: Super Systems, Piper Products
Regions Exported to: Central America, South America, Europe, Asia
Percentage of Business in Exporting: 15

47622 **Pippin Snack Pecans**
1332 Old Pretoria Rd
PO Box 3330
Albany, GA 31721-8696   229-432-9316
      Fax: 229-435-0056   800-554-6887
            treypippen@gmail.com
Pecans
Manager: Trey Pippin
Estimated Sales: $7 Million
Number Employees: 50
Square Footage: 80000
Type of Packaging: Consumer, Food Service, Private Label, Bulk

47623 **Pitco Frialator Inc**
509 Route 3a
Bow, NH 03304-3102   603-225-6684
      Fax: 603-230-5548   800-258-3708
            dpacka@maytag.com www.pitco.com
Manufacturer and exporter of commercial cooking equipment including standard, high capacity, doughnut/bakery and high efficiency fryers, pasta cookers, frying filters and baskets
President: Scott Blasingame
sblasingame@pitco.com
Director Materials: Steve Karas
VP/General Manager: Robert Granger
VP Engineer: George McMahon
Estimated Sales: $20-50 Million
Number Employees: 20-49
Parent Co: G.S. Blodgett Corporation
Type of Packaging: Food Service
Regions Exported to: Central America, South America, Europe, Asia, Middle East
Percentage of Business in Exporting: 20

47624 **Pittsburgh Brewing Co**
3340 Liberty Ave
Pittsburgh, PA 15201-1394   412-682-7400
      Fax: 412-682-2379 www.pittsburghbrewing.com
Beer
President/CEO: Eddie Lozano
CEO: Brian G Walsh
bwalsh@pittsburghbrewingco.com
Director of Sales & Marketing: David Sykes
Operations Manager: Melissa O'Dell
Brew master: Michael Carota
Plant Manager: Bill St Leger
Estimated Sales: $13 Million
Number Employees: 100-249
Square Footage: 27000
Parent Co: ICB Holdings, LLC
Type of Packaging: Consumer
Brands Exported: American
Regions Exported to: Central America, Middle East
Percentage of Business in Exporting: 3

47625 **Pittsburgh Casing Company**
102 33rd St
Pittsburgh, PA 15201   412-281-4327
      Fax: 412-281-0445   800-886-4329
            www.pittsburghspice.com
Importer of natural sewn sausage casing; wholesaler/distributor of spices and seasonings
Owner: Gregory Mancini
Vice President: Gregory Mancini
Estimated Sales: $500,000-$1 Million
Number Employees: 5-9
Square Footage: 100000
Parent Co: Pittsburgh Spice & Seasoning Company
Type of Packaging: Bulk
Regions Imported from: Europe
Percentage of Business in Importing: 5

47626 **Pittsburgh Corning Corp**
800 Presque Isle Dr
Pittsburgh, PA 15239-2799   724-327-6100
                  Fax: 724-387-3805
Manufacturer and exporter of moisture resistant glass insulation for floors, walls and roofs of food and beverage buildings, coolers and freezers
CEO: Jim Kane
jim_kane@pghcorning.com
Manager: Erik Elthiele
Chief Financial Officer/VP, Finance: Joseph Kirby
Vice President: Jean Collet
Vice President, Information Technology: Peter Atherton
Sales Manager: Steve Oslica
Director, Global Supply Chain: John Holzwarth
Estimated Sales: $ 45 Million
Number Employees: 20-49
Brands Exported: Foamglas

47627 **Pizzey's Milling & Baking Company**
121 4th Ave. S.
Twin Falls, ID 83301
Canada   208-733-7555
      Fax: 204-773-2317 www.glanbiafoods.com
Flaxseed
President: Linda Pizzey
Vice President: Glenn Pizzey
Vice President of Business Development: Dave Snyder
Business Development Manager: Shawn Harrison
Estimated Sales: $10-20 Million
Number Employees: 20-49
Square Footage: 80000
Parent Co: Glanbia Nutritionals
Type of Packaging: Consumer, Food Service, Private Label, Bulk
Regions Exported to: Worldwide
Percentage of Business in Exporting: 90

47628 **Planet Products Corp**
4200 Malsbary Rd
Blue Ash, OH 45242-5598   513-984-5544
      Fax: 513-984-5580 info@planet-products.com
            www.planet-products.com
Manufacturer and exporter of sausage and frankfurter loading, cheese stick equipment. Manufacturer of turnkey systems in automating sandwich assembly and other ready to eat products
Owner: Kathy Randolph
krandolph@planet-products.com
CEO: Mike F
VP: John Abraham
Marketing: Jennifer Coromel
Estimated Sales: $10-20 Million
Number Employees: 20-49
Brands Exported: Planet; Atlas Vac Machine
Regions Exported to: Central America, South America, Europe
Percentage of Business in Exporting: 25

47629 **Plantation Candies**
4224 Old Bethlehem Pike
Telford, PA 18969   215-723-6810
      Fax: 215-723-6834   888-678-6468
            chuck@plantationcandies.com
            www.plantationcandies.com
Bulk hard candy
Owner/President: Charles Crawford
chuck@plantationcandies.com
Estimated Sales: $1500000
Number Employees: 5-9
Type of Packaging: Consumer, Food Service, Private Label, Bulk
Regions Exported to: Worldwide

47630 **Plascal Corp**
361 Eastern Pkwy
PO Box 590
Farmingdale, NY 11735-2713   516-249-2200
      Fax: 516-249-2256   800-899-7527
            plascal@aol.com www.plascal.com
Manufacturer and exporter of plain, printed, laminated and PVC plastic film and sheeting
CEO: Mark Hurd
President: Fred Hurd
Estimated Sales: $10-20 Million
Number Employees: 100-249

47631 **Plastech**
205 W Duarte Rd
Monrovia, CA 91016-4529   626-358-9306
                  Fax: 626-303-6288
Manufacturer and exporter of plastic point of purchase displays
Owner: Pat Delaney
CFO: Pat Delaney
Contact: Laurie Castro
jauthier@solarcity.com
Estimated Sales: Below $5 Million
Number Employees: 10-19
Type of Packaging: Consumer, Bulk
Regions Exported to: Canada

47632 **Plasti-Clip Corp**
38 Perry Rd
Milford, NH 03055-4308   603-672-1166
      Fax: 603-672-6637   800-882-2547
            sales@plasticlip.com www.plasticlip.com
Manufacturer and exporter of point of purchase clips and fasteners including displays, price tags, tickets, etc; also, coupon holders, employee (and visitor) ID badging software and supplies
President: Daniel Faneuf
sales@plasticlip.com
Estimated Sales: $1-2.5 Million
Number Employees: 5-9
Number of Brands: 50
Number of Products: 1000
Square Footage: 14000
Regions Exported to: Central America, South America, Europe, Asia, Middle East
Percentage of Business in Exporting: 5

47633 **Plasti-Line**
445 S Gay Street
Suite 100
Knoxville, TN 37902-1133   865-938-1511
      Fax: 865-947-8531   800-444-7446
Manufacturer and exporter of plastic, metal, interior and exterior illuminated signs including menu boards and point of purchase displays
VP Marketing: Mickey Davis
Marketing Manager: Mary Ann Herrick
Estimated Sales: $ 20 - 50 Million
Number Employees: 500-999

47634 **Plasti-Mach Corporation**
704 Executive Blvd # G
Valley Cottage, NY 10989-2023 845-267-2985
      Fax: 845-267-2825   800-394-1128
            plastimach@plastimach.com www.plastimach.com
Manufacturer and exporter of used equipment including thermoforming, extrusion and heat sealing
President: Robert Rosen
VP: Jerry Hammerman
Contact: Tammy Sabat
tammysabat@plastimach.com
Estimated Sales: $ 1 - 5 Million
Number Employees: 5-9
Square Footage: 40000
Regions Exported to: Worldwide
Percentage of Business in Exporting: 15

47635 **Plastic Suppliers Inc**
2400 Marilyn Ln
Columbus, OH 43219   614-471-9100
                               800-722-5577
            www.plasticsuppliers.com
Complete line of unsupported film substrates for the label market including Labelflex, a biaxially oreinted polysterne label stock film, polyester film, polypropylene films for labeling, packaging and lamination applications, PVC andsynthetic papers; also new shrink label films. Whether your products call for durability, printability or over all appearance, Plastic suppliers is your total films solution

Importers & Exporters / A-Z

President & CEO: George Thomas
thomas@plasticsuppliers.com
Managing Director: Bart DeKeyser
Chief Financial Officer: Michael DuFrayne
Chief Technical Officer: Francisco Cavalcanti
Director of R&D/New Product Development: Ed Tweed
VP, Sales & Markting for the Americas: Brad Bastion
VP of Manufacturing: Erich Emhuff
Operations Manager: Denis Vynckier
Year Founded: 1949
Estimated Sales: $100-500 Million
Number Employees: 250-499
Brands Exported: Polyflex; Labelflex
Regions Exported to: Central America, South America, Europe, Asia, Canada, Latin America, Mexico
Percentage of Business in Exporting: 10
Brands Imported: Clarifol Acetate
Regions Imported from: Europe, Middle East
Percentage of Business in Importing: 5

47636 Plastic Supply Inc
8 Liberty Dr
Londonderry, NH 03053-2251   603-260-6101
Fax: 603-668-1691   800-752-7759
sales@plasticsupply.com www.plasticsupply.com
Lobster tanks
President: John Murphey
sales@plasticsupply.com
General Manager: Bill Johnson
Estimated Sales: $2.5-5 Million
Number Employees: 10-19
Square Footage: 23000
Parent Co: Plastic Supply Inc
Brands Exported: Atlantic Bio V
Regions Exported to: Canada
Percentage of Business in Importing: 10

47637 Plastipak Packaging
41605 Ann Arbor Road
Plymouth, MI 48170   734-354-3510
Fax: 734-455-0556 info@plastipak.com
Manufacturer and exporter of PET and HDPE bottles and containers
President/CEO: William C Young
Estimated Sales: $5-10 Million
Number Employees: 100-249
Regions Exported to: Worldwide

47638 Plate-Mate Inc USA
5211 Tuscarawas St W
Canton, OH 44708-5054   330-477-7575
Fax: 330-477-8599
customerservice@plate-mate.com
www.plate-mate.com
CEO: Michael Kazes
CFO: Mark Erlitz
Estimated Sales: $500,000-$1 Million

47639 Plaza Sweets Bakery
521 Waverly Ave
Mamaroneck, NY 10543-2235   914-698-0233
Fax: 914-698-3712   800-816-8416
Cakes
Owner: James Ward
Pres/CEO: Rodney Holden
Manager: Kathy Dumas
Estimated Sales: $5.8 Million
Number Employees: 20-49
Square Footage: 60000
Type of Packaging: Consumer, Food Service
Regions Exported to: Worldwide
Percentage of Business in Exporting: 1

47640 Plaza de Espana Gourmet
100 Kings Point Drive
Apt 1004
Sunny Isles Beach, FL 33160-4729   305-971-3468
Fax: 305-971-5004
Spanish foods, olive oil, artichokes, asparagus, piquillo peppers, wine and ham
President: Jesus Metias, Sr.
Vice President: Serafina Atalaya
Estimated Sales: $ 2.5-5 Million
Number Employees: 5-9
Parent Co: Plaza De Espana Gourmet Foods
Type of Packaging: Consumer, Food Service, Private Label, Bulk
Brands Imported: Plaza De Espana
Regions Imported from: Europe
Percentage of Business in Importing: 70

47641 Pleasant Grove Farms
PO Box 636
Pleasant Grove, CA 95668   916-655-3391
Fax: 916-655-3699 info@pleasantgrovefarms.com
www.pleasantgrovefarms.com
Almonds, wheat, beans, popcorn and rice
President: Thomas Sills
VP Sales: Edward Sills
Estimated Sales: $1,100,000
Number Employees: 5-9
Number of Products: 9
Square Footage: 20000
Parent Co: Sills Farms
Type of Packaging: Bulk
Brands Exported: Pleasant Grove Farms
Regions Exported to: Europe, Asia
Percentage of Business in Exporting: 10

47642 PlexPack Corp
1160 Birchmount Road
Unit 2
Toronto, ON M1P Z08
Canada   416-291-8085
Fax: 416-298-4328   855-635-9238
info@emplex.com www.plexpack.com
Bag sealing and automated bagging equipment and the bamark line of shrink and sleeve wrapping equipment
President/CEO: Paul Irvine
Vice President: John Lewitt
Number Employees: 20-49
Type of Packaging: Consumer, Food Service, Private Label
Brands Exported: Emplex Bag Sealing Solutions; Damark Shrink Packaging Systems
Regions Exported to: Central America, South America, Europe, Asia
Percentage of Business in Exporting: 60

47643 Plt Health Solutions Inc
119 Headquarters Plz
Morristown, NJ 07960-6834   973-984-0900
Fax: 973-984-5666 plt@plthomas.com
www.plthomas.com
Company products includes water soluble gums, hydrocolloids, botanical extracts, mineral gluconates, stabilizers and thickeners. Additional products include agar-agar, carob, fenugreek and fiber, nutraceuticals and spirulina.
President: Paul M Flowerman
Marketing/Public Relations: Paula Nurnberger
Sales Director: Rodger Jonas
Contact: Jenson Chang
jensonchang@hotmail.com
Estimated Sales: $ 5 - 10 Million
Number Employees: 50-99
Number of Brands: 15
Number of Products: 200
Other Locations:
P L Thomas
Morristown, NJP L Thomas

47644 Pluto Corporation
PO Box 391
French Lick, IN 47432   812-936-9988
Fax: 812-936-2828 alan.friedman@plutocorp.com
www.plutocorp.com
Contract packager and exporter of household cleaners; also blowmold HDPE plastic bottles
President: Alan J Friedman
Plant Manager: Dennis Kaiser
Estimated Sales: $ 5 -10 Million
Number Employees: 100-249
Square Footage: 240000
Parent Co: AHF Industries
Regions Exported to: Europe, Asia, Middle East, Canada, Caribbean
Percentage of Business in Exporting: 10

47645 Plymold
615 Centennial Dr
Kenyon, MN 55946-1297   507-789-5111
Fax: 507-789-8315   800-759-6653
seating@plymold.com www.foldcraft.com
Manufacturer and exporter of tabletops, booths, indoor/outdoor clusters, millwork, tables, chairs, waste receptacles, salad bars and cabinets
Founder: Harold Nielsen
CEO: Chuck Mayhew
Marketing Coordinator: John Price
Contact: Jodie Anderson
andersonjodie@plymold.com
Estimated Sales: $ 20 - 50 Million
Number Employees: 100-249
Square Footage: 275000
Parent Co: Foldcraft

47646 Plymouth Beef Co.
3585 Food Center Drive
Bronx, NY 10474   718-589-8600
Fax: 718-860-8930 info@plymouthbeef.com
www.plymouthbeef.com
Beef
Chairman: Gerald Sussman
Ceo/President: Andrew Sussman
Estimated Sales: $5 Million
Number Employees: 25
Type of Packaging: Consumer, Food Service

47647 Pneumatic Conveying Inc
960 E Grevillea Ct
Ontario, CA 91761-5612   909-923-2901
Fax: 909-923-4491   800-655-4481
sales@pneu-con.com
www.pneumaticconveyingsolutions.com
Manufacturer and exporter of customized pneumatic conveying equipment
President: Wayland Gillrspie
Sales Engineer: David Gordon
Sales Administrator: Jennifer Edmondson
Estimated Sales: $ 2.5-5 Million
Number Employees: 20-49
Square Footage: 120000
Parent Co: Pneumatic Conveying
Regions Exported to: South America, Middle East, Canada, Australia
Percentage of Business in Exporting: 10

47648 Pneumatic Scale Angelus
10 Ascot Pkwy
Cuyahoga Falls, OH 44223-3325   330-923-0491
Fax: 330-923-5570 sales@pneumaticscale.com
www.pneumaticscale.com
Manufacturer and exporter of liquid and dry fillers, cappers, and can seamers
President: William Morgan
Marketing Director: Bethany Hilt
Sales Director: Paul Kearney
Contact: Karl Barkhurst
kbarkhurst2@master-lighting.com
Operations Manager: Paul Kelly
Purchasing Manager: Dave Bellet
Estimated Sales: Less Than $500,000
Number Employees: 1-4
Square Footage: 130000
Parent Co: Barry-Wehmiller Company
Type of Packaging: Consumer, Food Service, Private Label, Bulk
Regions Exported to: Central America, South America, Europe, Asia, Australia
Percentage of Business in Exporting: 45

47649 Pocino Foods
14250 Lomitas Ave
City Of Industry, CA 91746-3096   626-968-8000
Fax: 626-330-8779   800-345-0150
onlythebest@pocinofoods.com
www.pocinofoods.com
Deli meats (Italian and Mexican style), pizza toppings
CEO: Jason Katsuki
Vice President: Jim Pierson
National Sales Director: Karen Barro
Regional Sales Manager: Ramona Shope
Estimated Sales: $32 Million
Number Employees: 100-249
Number of Brands: 1
Type of Packaging: Private Label
Regions Exported to: Central America, Asia

47650 Podnar Plastics Inc
1510 Mogadore Rd
Kent, OH 44240-7599   330-673-2255
Fax: 330-673-2273   800-673-5277
www.rez-tech.com
Manufacturer and exporter of injection blow-molded plastic products including bottles and point-of-purchase containers
President: Jack Podnar
Marketing Director: Jack Podnar
Sales Director: C Allen Clarke
Plant Manager: Scott Podnar
Estimated Sales: $5-10 Million
Number Employees: 20-49
Square Footage: 94000
Type of Packaging: Bulk
Regions Exported to: Central America, Canada, Mexico

Importers & Exporters / A-Z

47651 (HQ)Point Group
1790 Highway A1a
Suite 103
Satellite Beach, FL 32937-5446 321-777-7408
  Fax: 321-777-9777 888-272-1249
Coffee, tea, fruit extracts and juices
President: Gary Trump
VP: Roger Koltermann
Type of Packaging: Consumer, Food Service, Private Label, Bulk
Brands Exported: Mingo Bay Beverages, Inc.
Regions Exported to: Worldwide
Percentage of Business in Exporting: 50

47652 Poiret International
7866 Exeter Boulevard E
Tamarac, FL 33321-8797 203-926-3700
  Fax: 954-721-0110 800-237-9151
Preserves and organic jams
CEO/Purchasing: Ed Kerzner
CFO: Sheila Kerzner
Marketing Director: Stan Margulese
Plant Manager: Frank Bilisi
Number Employees: 20-49
Square Footage: 100000
Parent Co: Siroper/E. Meurens SA
Type of Packaging: Consumer, Food Service, Private Label, Bulk
Brands Exported: Sugar Free Candy
Brands Imported: Frozen Health Dinners
Regions Imported from: Europe

47653 Pokanoket Ostrich Farm
177 Gulf Rd
South Dartmouth, MA 02748 508-992-6188
  Fax: 508-993-5356 pokanokets@aol.com
Ostrich meat
President: Alan Weinshel
National Sales Manager: Mike Yokemick
Contact: Gail Weinshel
pokanokets@aol.com
Estimated Sales: Below $ 5 Million
Number Employees: 1-4
Type of Packaging: Consumer, Food Service, Private Label
Regions Exported to: Asia, Mexico

47654 Pokonobe Industries
2701 Ocean Park Blvd
Suite 208
Santa Monica, CA 90405-5247 310-392-1259
  Fax: 310-392-3659 www.pokonobe.com
Oils: almond, grapeseed, soy, sunflower, sesame, walnut, corn, olive, linseed, wheat germ, safflower, rice bran, avocado, pumpkinseed, flaxseed, hazelnut, macadamia nut, coconut, palm
President: David Nagley
General Manager: Larry Kronenberg
Contact: Robert Grebler
info@pokonobe.com
Estimated Sales: $ 5 - 10 Million
Number Employees: 5-9
Square Footage: 7948
Type of Packaging: Bulk
Other Locations:
  Pokonobe Industries
  Santa Monica, CAPokonobe Industries

47655 Polar Beer Systems
26035 Palomar Rd
Sun City, CA 92585-9710 951-928-8174
  Fax: 619-449-0464
Manufacturer and exporter of food service equipment including beverage dispensers, servers and preparation equipment; also, carts
Owner: Sandy Blais
admin@polarbeersystems.com
Estimated Sales: $2.5-5 Million
Number Employees: 10-19
Type of Packaging: Food Service
Regions Exported to: Canada

47656 Polar Hospitality Products
2046 Castor Ave
Philadelphia, PA 19134 215-535-6940
  Fax: 215-535-6971 800-831-7823
  bradk@the-polar.com www.the-polar.com
Manufacturer and exporter of menu covers and wine list covers, check presenters and coasters
President: Brad Karasik
National Sales Manager: Lisa Dale
Customer Service Manager: Arlinda Candelaria
Estimated Sales: $ 1 Million
Number Employees: 20-49
Square Footage: 72000
Parent Co: Polar Manufacturing
Regions Exported to: Worldwide

47657 Polar King Transportation
4410 New Haven Ave
Fort Wayne, IN 46803-1650 260-428-2575
  Fax: 260-428-2533 888-541-8330
  www.polarking.com
Constructed and ready to operate walk-in coolers and freezers for outdoor use
Marketing Director: Kris Markham
Manager: Mike Lovett
mikel@polarking.com
Manager: Mike Lovett
Number Employees: 5-9
Square Footage: 150000

47658 Polar Plastics
4210 Thimens Blouevard
St Laurent, QC H4R 2B9
Canada 514-331-0207
  Fax: 514-331-7604 info@polarplastic.ca
  www.polarplastic.ca
Manufacturer and exporter of disposable plastic tableware including plates, cups, utensils and dish covers
President: David Stevenson
Plant Manager: Claude Jacques
Estimated Sales: $ 30 - 50 Million
Number Employees: 250
Type of Packaging: Consumer, Food Service
Regions Exported to: Worldwide
Percentage of Business in Exporting: 5

47659 Polar Ware Company
2806 N 15th St
Sheboygan, WI 53083-3943 920-458-3561
  Fax: 920-458-2205 800-237-3655
  customerservice@polarware.com
  www.polarware.com
Manufacturer and exporter of deep drawn and stainless steel items including steam table pans and covers, trays, pans, pots, bowls, containers, smallwares, bar supplies, etc.; importer of smallwares, barware, chafers, beverage serversaccessories and sinks
CEO: Jerry Baltus
Executive VP: Rick Carr
Marketing Director: Steph Wittmus
National Sales Manager: Dick Ballwahn
Contact: Tom Dinolfo
tom_sharp@sharp-residential.com
Production Manager: Peter Hansen
Purchasing Manager: Tom Kennedy
Estimated Sales: $ 20-50 Million
Number Employees: 100-249
Square Footage: 250000
Brands Exported: Polar Ware
Regions Exported to: Worldwide
Percentage of Business in Exporting: 17
Regions Imported from: Asia
Percentage of Business in Importing: 15

47660 Polean Foods
PO Box 148
Hamspted, NC 28443 910-319-0850
  Fax: 910-319-0854 866-765-3263
  sales@poleanfoods.com
Wholesaler/distributor, importer and exporter of pork products and ingredients
President: Peter Jazwinski
Sales Director: Steve Eldridge
Estimated Sales: $ 5 - 10 Million
Number Employees: 5-9
Square Footage: 4000
Type of Packaging: Consumer, Food Service, Private Label, Bulk
Brands Exported: Polean
Regions Exported to: Europe, Canada
Brands Imported: Polean; Deliham, LeNormando
Regions Imported from: South America, Europe, Canada

47661 Poly Processing Co
8055 Ash St
French Camp, CA 95231-9667 209-982-4904
  Fax: 209-982-0455 877-325-3142
  sales@polyprocessing.com
  www.polyprocessing.com
Manufacturer and exporter of molded plastic tanks
Quality Control: John Brinlanco
Sales Manager: Del Mann
Manager: John Blanco
Estimated Sales: $ 2.5 - 5 Million
Number Employees: 50-99
Regions Exported to: Worldwide
Percentage of Business in Exporting: 5

47662 PolyConversions, Inc.
505 E Condit Dr
Rantoul, IL 61866-3604 217-893-3330
  Fax: 217-893-3003 888-893-3330
  info@polycoUSA.com www.polycousa.com
Supplier of personal protective apparel for industrial safety, food processing, controlled environments, etc.
President: Ronald Smith
Sales Manager: Scott Carlson
Estimated Sales: $10-20 Million
Number of Brands: 2
Number of Products: 15
Square Footage: 47000
Regions Exported to: Central America, South America, Europe, Canada

47663 PolyMaid Company
PO Box 1466
Largo, FL 33779-1466 727-507-9321
  Fax: 727-524-8271 800-206-9188
  www.polymaid.com
Manufacturer and exporter of food mixers and coffee flavoring tumble mixers with removable plastic liners
President: Ken Orthner
VP Operations: Susan Orthner
Number Employees: 4
Square Footage: 20000
Brands Exported: Polymaid
Regions Exported to: Worldwide
Percentage of Business in Exporting: 10

47664 Polycon Industries
1001 E 99th Street
Chicago, IL 60628-1693 773-374-5500
  Fax: 773-374-9805
Manufacturer and exporter of plastic bottles and containers; also, various types of labeling and silk screening available
VP: Dan Faro
Plant Manager: Fred Palmer
Estimated Sales: $ 1 - 5 Million
Number Employees: 100-250
Square Footage: 210000
Regions Exported to: Europe, Asia
Percentage of Business in Exporting: 3

47665 (HQ)Polypack Inc
3301 Gateway Centre Blvd
Pinellas Park, FL 33782-6108 727-578-5000
  Fax: 727-578-1300 info@polypack.com.com
  www.polypack.com
Engineer and manufacturer of shrink packaging equipment including shrink-wrap robotic infeeds and collation, continuous motion form fill seal machines
President/Founder: Alain Cerf
Estimated Sales: $10-20 Million
Number Employees: 50-99
Type of Packaging: Consumer, Food Service, Private Label, Bulk
Other Locations:
  Polypack
  ShanghaiPolypack
Brands Exported: Polypack
Regions Exported to: Central America, South America, Europe, Asia, Middle East
Percentage of Business in Exporting: 2
Brands Imported: CEFMA-BAUMER

47666 Polyplastics
10201 Metropolitan Dr
Austin, TX 78758-4944 512-339-9293
  Fax: 512-339-9317 800-753-7659
  sales@1polyplastics.com www.polyplastics.com
Manufacturer, exporter and wholesaler/distributor of rigid and flexible foamed plastics
President: Dave McArthur
VP: Tim Buckley
Sales Director: Tim Buckley
Manager: Tito Robledo
trobledo@1polyplastics.com
Manufacturing Manager: Harry Stevens
Estimated Sales: $2.5-5 Million
Number Employees: 5-9

Importers & Exporters / A-Z

Square Footage: 56000
Parent Co: Buckley Industries
Regions Exported to: Central America
Percentage of Business in Exporting: 2

47667 Polypro International Inc
7300 Metro Blvd
Suite 570
Edina, MN 55439-2346 952-835-7717
Fax: 952-835-3811 800-765-9776
polypro@polyprointl.com www.polyprointl.com
Guar and cellulose gums
President: Mark Kieper
polypro@polyprointl.com
Controller: Jennifer Jansson
Senior Account Manager, Sales/Technical: Louise Polizzotto
Customer Service/Logistics: Janet Burger
Estimated Sales: $ 2.5-5 Million
Number Employees: 1-4
Type of Packaging: Bulk
Regions Exported to: Worldwide
Percentage of Business in Exporting: 4
Regions Imported from: Europe, India, Pakistan

47668 Polyscience
6600 W Touhy Ave
Niles, IL 60714-4516 847-647-0611
Fax: 847-647-1155 800-229-7569
culinary@polyscience.com www.polyscience.com
Producer of constant temperature control equipment
President: Philip Preston
HR Executive: Pat Shamburg
pshamburg@polyscience.com
Marketing: Bob Bausone
Sales: Jason Sayers
Operations: Wayne Walter
Estimated Sales: $10-20 Million
Number Employees: 100-249
Square Footage: 128000
Parent Co: Preston Industries
Regions Exported to: Central America, South America, Europe, Asia, Middle East
Percentage of Business in Exporting: 10
Percentage of Business in Importing: 2

47669 (HQ)Polytainers
197 Norseman Street
Toronto, ON M8Z 2R5
Canada 416-239-7311
Fax: 416-239-0596 800-268-2424
www.polytainersinc.com
Designer and manufacturer of thinwall rigid plastic containers for the food and dairy industry
President: Robert Barrett
Number Employees: 600
Square Footage: 1000000
Regions Exported to: USA

47670 Pomi USA
253 Main St
Suite 380
Matawan, NJ 07747 732-541-4115
Fax: 732-862-1173 www.pomi.us.com
Tomatoes and tomato sauces.

47671 (HQ)Pomona Service & Pkgng Co LA
2733 Central Sta
Yakima, WA 98902 509-452-7121
Fax: 509-576-3942
Manufacturer and exporter of produce handling and packaging equipment
President: John Muller
pomonasvc@aol.com
Estimated Sales: $1-2.5 Million
Number Employees: 5-9
Regions Exported to: Worldwide
Percentage of Business in Exporting: 8

47672 Pompeian Inc
4201 Pulaski Hwy
Baltimore, MD 21224-1699 410-276-6900
Fax: 410-276-3764 800-766-7342
www.pompeian.com
Spanish olive oil, vinegar and cooking wines.
President: Frank Patton
sales@pompeian.com
Chief Executive Officer: David Bensadoun
Year Founded: 1906
Estimated Sales: $20-50 Million
Number Employees: 50-99
Number of Brands: 4
Type of Packaging: Consumer, Food Service, Bulk
Brands Imported: Laco, Romanza, Avallo
Regions Imported from: Europe

47673 Popcorn Connection
7615 Fulton Avenue
North Hollywood, CA 91605-1805 818-764-3279
Fax: 818-765-0578 800-852-2676
Popcorn and nuts
Owner: Kevin Needle
VP: Ross Wallach
Estimated Sales: $300,000
Number Employees: 3
Number of Products: 20
Square Footage: 14000
Type of Packaging: Consumer, Food Service, Private Label, Bulk
Brands Exported: Video Munchies; Corn Appetit
Regions Exported to: Asia
Percentage of Business in Exporting: 2

47674 Popcorn Popper
6323 N 150 E
Monon, IN 47959 219-253-6607
Fax: 219-253-8172 800-270-2705
www.popcornpopper.com
Popcorn and gift baskets
President: Dani Paluchniak
Vice President: Joe Dold
Sales Manager: Steve Dold
Estimated Sales: $4041306
Number Employees: 5-9
Parent Co: Felknor International
Type of Packaging: Consumer
Brands Exported: Wabash Valley Farm
Regions Exported to: Europe
Percentage of Business in Exporting: 1

47675 Poppers Supply Company
PO Box 90187
Allentown, PA 18109 503-239-3792
Fax: 503-235-6221 800-457-9810
info@poppers.com www.poppers.com
Popcorn and fountain syrup
President: Vernon Ryles Jr
Sales Manager: Jody Riggs
Estimated Sales: $1.4 Million
Number Employees: 10
Type of Packaging: Consumer, Food Service

47676 Poppie's Dough
2411 S Wallace St
Chicago, IL 60616-1855 312-949-0404
Fax: 312-949-0505 www.poppiesdough.com
Owner: Mark Cwiakala
mcwiakala@poppiesdough.com
Estimated Sales: $ 5 - 10 Million
Number Employees: 20-49

47677 Porcelain Metals Corporation
400 South 13th Street
PO Box 7069
Louisville, KY 40210 502-635-7421
Fax: 502-635-1200
Manufacturer and exporter of cooking equipment including barbecue and charcoal grills, domestic cooktops and accessories
Manager: Randy Smitley
OEM Sales Management: Bob Miller
Estimated Sales: $ 10-20 Million
Number Employees: 20-49
Square Footage: 350000
Type of Packaging: Consumer, Private Label
Brands Exported: Kingsford
Regions Exported to: South America, Europe, Asia
Percentage of Business in Exporting: 5

47678 Porinos Gourmet Food
280 Rand St
Central Falls, RI 02863-2512 401-273-3000
Fax: 401-273-3232 800-826-3938
porinos@aol.com
Pasta and sauces, salad dressings, marinades and pickled pepper
Owner: Michael Dressler
VP Operations: Marshall Righter
Estimated Sales: $1.9 Million
Number Employees: 10-19
Square Footage: 120000
Type of Packaging: Consumer, Food Service, Private Label
Regions Exported to: Canada, Caribbean
Percentage of Business in Exporting: 10
Regions Imported from: South America, Europe
Percentage of Business in Importing: 10

47679 Port Royal Sales LTD
95 Froehlich Farm Blvd # 200
Woodbury, NY 11797-2930 516-921-8483
Fax: 516-921-8488 www.portroyalsales.com
Importer and wholesaler/distributor of canned peaches, pineapples, pears, tomatoes, mushrooms, olives, tuna and sardines; serving the food service market
President: Steven Zwecker
CEO: Wayne Wellner
wwellner@portroyalsales.com
CEO: Wayne Wellner
VP Marketing: Wayne Wellner
Estimated Sales: $5-10 Million
Number Employees: 10-19
Square Footage: 20000
Type of Packaging: Consumer, Food Service, Private Label
Brands Imported: Premium
Regions Imported from: South America, Europe, Asia, Middle East
Percentage of Business in Importing: 75

47680 (HQ)Porter Bowers Signs
3300 101st Street
Des Moines, IA 50322-3866 515-253-9622
Fax: 515-253-9915
Manufacturer and exporter of signs including neon, painted, indoor and outdoor
Estimated Sales: $1-2.5 Million
Number Employees: 5-9
Regions Exported to: Worldwide

47681 Portier Fine Foods
436 Waverly Ave
Mamaroneck, NY 10543 914-899-9006
Fax: 914-381-4045 800-272-9463
portier.finefoods@verizon.net
Salmon, trout, scallops, shrimp, caviar, game, birds and Belgian chocolates
President: Sean Portier
Sales Director: Patrick Portier
Estimated Sales: Below $ 5 Million
Number Employees: 10-19
Parent Co: Chenoceaux, Inc
Type of Packaging: Consumer, Food Service

47682 Portion-Pac Chemical Corp.
400 N Ashland Ave
Suite 1
Chicago, IL 60622 312-226-0400
Fax: 312-226-5400 info@portionpaccorp.com
www.portionpaccorp.com
Manufacturer/exporter of cleaning products including pre-measured floor cleaners and detergents, bathroom and glass cleaner, air freshener odor counteractant, carpet shampoo, final rinse sanitizers, extraction detergent and strippers/degreasers
President: Marvin Klein
Vice President: John Miller
SFS Pac Division Manager: Chuck Ainsworth
Estimated Sales: $10-20 Million
Number Employees: 20-49
Type of Packaging: Consumer, Food Service
Regions Exported to: Central America, South America, Europe, Asia, Middle East
Percentage of Business in Exporting: 5

47683 Portland Shellfish Company
92 Waldron Way
Portland, ME 04103 207-799-9290
Fax: 207-799-7179 www.portlandshellfish.com
Crab and lobster
President: Jeff Holden
Human Resources: John Maloney
john@pshellfish.com
Estimated Sales: $9 Million
Number Employees: 100-249
Square Footage: 48000
Type of Packaging: Consumer, Food Service, Private Label, Bulk
Brands Exported: Portland Lighthouse
Regions Exported to: Worldwide
Percentage of Business in Exporting: 20
Brands Imported: Portland Lighthouse
Regions Imported from: Canada
Percentage of Business in Importing: 20

47684 Portugalia Imports
23 Tremont St
Fall River, MA 02720-4821 508-679-9307
Fax: 508-673-1502 portugaliaimports.com
Seafood, breads, vegetables, and other specialty foods

Importers & Exporters / A-Z

President/Owner: Fernando Benevides
benevidesf@portugaliaimports.com
Vice President: Michael Benevides *Year Founded:* 1988
Regions Imported from: Portuguese

47685 (HQ)Portuguese United Grocer Co-Op
45 Wheeler Point Rd
Newark, NJ 07105-3034 973-344-1561
Fax: 973-344-8046
Wholesaler/distributor of frozen foods, general line products, meats, fish,specialty foods and candy; serving the food service market; importer of olive oil
President: Joaquim Vieira
CFO: J Jesus Vieira
VP: Alzira Vieira
Estimated Sales: $5 Million
Number Employees: 5-9
Square Footage: 260000
Type of Packaging: Consumer, Food Service
Brands Imported: Andorinha; Rico
Regions Imported from: Europe, Caribbean
Percentage of Business in Importing: 2

47686 Posterloid Corporation
4862 36th St
Long Island City, NY 11101-1918 718-729-1050
Fax: 718-786-9310 800-651-5000
Manufacturer and exporter of menu boards and displays
President: Robert Sudack
Sales Manager: Allied Collins
Contact: Basil Mcpherson
bmcpherson@posterloid.com
Estimated Sales: $ 10 - 20 Million
Number Employees: 100-249

47687 Potlatch Corp
601 W 1st Ave # 1600
Suite 1600
Spokane, WA 99201-3807 509-835-1500
Fax: 509-835-1555 www.potlatchcorp.com
Manufacturer and exporter of paper products including napkins, toilet paper, paper towels and facial tissues
Executive Director: Mark Ohleyer
CEO: Michael J Covey
michael.covey@potlatchcorp.com
Manager: Mike Lappa
Director Marketing: Cynthia Dickerson
National Sales Manager: Mike Redden
Estimated Sales: $ 50-100 Million
Number Employees: 500-999
Parent Co: Potlatch Corporation
Regions Exported to: Canada
Percentage of Business in Exporting: 5

47688 Power Brushes
756 S Byrne Rd # 1
Toledo, OH 43609-1062 419-385-5725
Fax: 419-382-0756 800-968-9600
president@powerbrushes.com
www.powerbrushes.com
Manufacturer and exporter of custom designed brushes for harvesting, cleaning, peeling and packing of fruits and vegetables
President: Tom Parseghian
Sales Director: Scott Dunckel
Manager: Paul Sneider
tafttool@aol.com
Estimated Sales: $ 3 Million
Number Employees: 20-49
Regions Exported to: Europe, Asia
Percentage of Business in Exporting: 15

47689 Power Electronics Intl Inc
561 Plate Dr # 8
East Dundee, IL 60118-2467 847-836-2071
Fax: 847-428-7744 800-362-7959
www.peinfo.com
Manufacturer and exporter of variable speed and AC powered drives
President: Victor Habisohn
Sales Manager: Michael Habisohn
Service Manager: Adam Jezek
Estimated Sales: $ 20 - 50 Million
Number Employees: 50-99
Regions Exported to: Worldwide
Percentage of Business in Exporting: 15

47690 Poweramp
W194n11481 Mccormick Dr
Germantown, WI 53022-3035 262-255-1510
Fax: 262-255-4199 800-643-5424
sales@poweramp.com www.docksystemsinc.com
Manufacturer and exporter of dock levelers including pit-style, edge of dock, truck, truck restraining systems, dock seals and shelters, etc
Owner: Ed Mguire
Vice President: Mike Pilgrim
Estimated Sales: $ 25 Million
Number Employees: 50-99
Square Footage: 100000
Parent Co: Systems

47691 Powertex Inc
1 Lincoln Blvd # 101
Suite 101
Rouses Point, NY 12979-1087 518-297-2634
Fax: 518-297-2634 800-769-3783
seabulk@powertex.com www.powertex.com
Manufacturer and exporter of dry powder and bulk plastic liners for use in ocean containers and truck trailers
President: Stephen Podd
stephen@powertex.com
Chairman/CEO: Victor Podd
Sales Manager: Patricia Olsen
Estimated Sales: $ 10 - 20 Million
Number Employees: 50-99
Square Footage: 130000
Brands Exported: Seabulk Powerliner
Regions Exported to: Central America, South America, Europe, Asia, Middle East
Percentage of Business in Exporting: 36

47692 Practical Promotions
1586 Groveland Ridge Rd
Columbia, TN 38401-8154 931-388-4491
Fax: 931-381-2605
customerservice@practicalpromotions.com
practicalpromotions.com

47693 Praga Food Products
32 Riveredge Rd
Tenafly, NJ 07670-2032 201-894-1177
Fax: 201-894-1110
Importer of cheese
Manager: Mukadder Gungur
Regions Imported from: South America, Europe
Percentage of Business in Importing: 100

47694 Praim Co
92 Jackson St
Salem, MA 01970-3068 978-745-9100
Fax: 978-745-9150 800-970-9646
sales@praimgroup.com www.praimgroup.com
Chocolate, toffee and truffles
CEO: Paul Pruett
Estimated Sales: Less Than $500,000
Number Employees: 1-4
Square Footage: 60000
Brands Exported: Dreamworks, Trolls, Boss Baby, Waldo
Regions Exported to: Europe

47695 Prairie Cajun Wholesale
5966 Highway 190
Eunice, LA 70535 337-546-6195
Seafood and exotic meats; alligator and nutria
President: Jeffery Derouen
Estimated Sales: $1 - 2 Million
Number Employees: 10-19
Type of Packaging: Consumer, Food Service
Regions Exported to: Europe, Asia

47696 Prairie Malt
PO Box 1150
Biggar, SK S0K 0M0
Canada 306-948-3500
Fax: 306-948-5038 david_klinger@cargill.com
www.prairiemaltltd.com
Barley malt
President: Doug Eden
Number Employees: 50-99
Parent Co: Cargill, Incorporated
Type of Packaging: Bulk
Regions Exported to: Worldwide

47697 Prairie Mushrooms
52557 Range Road 215
Ardrossan, AB T8E 2H6
Canada 780-467-3555
Fax: 780-467-3893 info@prairiemushrooms.com
www.prairiemushrooms.com
Mushrooms
President: George DeRuiter
Marketing Manager: John Kostelyk
Sales: Kevin Christman
General Manager: Terry Uppal
Production: Don Kostelyk
Estimated Sales: $5 - 10 Million
Number Employees: 100-249
Type of Packaging: Consumer, Food Service

47698 Prawn Seafoods Inc
6894 NW 32nd Ave
Miami, FL 33147-6606 305-691-2435
Fax: 305-693-6348 www.sunset-foods.com
Food service distributor of canned goods, dry goods, frozen foods, frozen vegetables; serving the food service market
President: Jeff Wine
Estimated Sales: $4.5-4.8 Million
Number Employees: 5-9
Square Footage: 80000
Type of Packaging: Food Service
Regions Exported to: Caribbean

47699 Prawnto Systems
4770 Interstate 30 W
Caddo Mills, TX 75135-7634 903-527-4149
Fax: 903-527-4951 800-426-7254
sales@prawntomachine.com www.prawnto.net
Manufacturer and exporter of shrimp processing equipment including cutters, processing stations and deveiners
CEO: Don Morris
sales@prawntomachine.com
VP: Derrell Sawyer
Sales: Derrell Sawyer
Estimated Sales: $1,000,000
Number Employees: 1-4
Number of Brands: 2
Number of Products: 7
Square Footage: 7000
Brands Exported: Prawnto; Shrimperfect
Regions Exported to: Central America, South America, Asia, Middle East, Worldwide
Percentage of Business in Exporting: 40

47700 Prawnto Systems
4770 Interstate 30 W
Caddo Mills, TX 75135-7634 903-527-4149
Fax: 903-527-4951 800-426-7254
sales@prawntomachine.com
President: Don Morris
sales@prawntomachine.com
Estimated Sales: Below $ 5 Million
Number Employees: 1-4

47701 Praxair Inc
10 Riverview Dr
Danbury, CT 06810 716-879-4077
Fax: 800-772-9985 800-772-9247
info@praxair.com www.praxair.com
Manufacturer and exporter of nitrogen freezing systems for food packaging.
Chairman & CEO: Steve Angel
SVP & Chief Financial Officer: Matthew White
Executive Vice President: Eduardo Menezes
Executive Vice President: Anne Roby
VP/General Counsel/Corporate Secretary: Guillermo Bichara
Year Founded: 1907
Estimated Sales: $11.44 Billion
Number Employees: 26,000
Parent Co: Linde plc
Regions Exported to: Worldwide

47702 Prayon Inc.
1610 Marvin Griffin Rd.
Augusta, GA 30906 206-213-5572
www.prayon.com
Phosphates and phosphoric acid.
Chairman: Olivier Vanderijst
CEO: Y. Caprara
Director of Finance: P. Schils
Director, Research: A. Germeau
Director, Sales & Marketing: V. Renard
Year Founded: 1882
Estimated Sales: $786 Million

Importers & Exporters / A-Z

Number Employees: 1,115
Parent Co: Prayon
Type of Packaging: Bulk

47703 Precision Brush
6700 Parkland Blvd
Cleveland, OH 44139-4341 440-498-0140
Fax: 800-252-0834 800-252-4747
info@precisionbrush.com www.brushes.info
Manufacturer and exporter of custom metal channel strip brushes in various shapes and sizes
President: Jim Benjamin
jim@precisionbrush.com
General Manager: Mike Porter
Estimated Sales: $2.5-5 Million
Number Employees: 10-19
Square Footage: 36000
Regions Exported to: Worldwide
Percentage of Business in Exporting: 15

47704 Precision Component Industries
5325 Southway St SW
Canton, OH 44706-1943 330-477-6287
Fax: 330-477-1052
tricia@precision-component.com
www.precision-component.com
Manufacturer and exporter of special production machinery, tools, dies, fixtures, short and long run production machining, stamping services and cans
President: Tricia Gerak
tfino@saralee.com
CEO: Patricia Gerak
President: Tony Gerak
Sales Manager: Lewis Page
Purchase Manager: George Melson
Estimated Sales: Below $ 5 Million
Number Employees: 20-49
Parent Co: Brennan Industrial Group
Type of Packaging: Bulk
Regions Exported to: Worldwide
Percentage of Business in Exporting: 15

47705 Precision Pours
12837 Industrial Park Blvd
Minneapolis, MN 55441-3910 763-694-9291
Fax: 763-694-9343 800-549-4491
ricksandvik@precisionpours.com
Manufacturer and exporter of pour spouts for liquor, syrups and cooking oils; wholesaler/distributor of pour cleaning systems
President: Rick Sandvik
ricksandvik@precisionpours.com
Accounting: Patrick Sandvik
VP Sales: Duane Nording
Estimated Sales: Below $ 5,000,000
Number Employees: 10-19
Square Footage: 9600
Regions Exported to: Worldwide
Percentage of Business in Exporting: 15

47706 Precision Temp Inc
11 Sunnybrook Dr
Cincinnati, OH 45237-2103 513-641-4446
Fax: 513-641-0733 800-934-9690
service@precisiontemp.com
www.precisiontemp.com
Manufacturer and exporter of gas booster heaters for high temperature water
Vice President: Steve Aldrich
aldrich@precisiontemp.com
CEO: Rick Muhlhauser
Vice President: Fred Rohtzeid
Estimated Sales: $2-4,000,000
Number Employees: 10-19
Square Footage: 40000
Type of Packaging: Food Service
Regions Exported to: Canada, Carribean
Percentage of Business in Exporting: 5

47707 (HQ)Precision Wood Products
PO Box 529
Vancouver, WA 98666-0529 360-694-8322
Fax: 360-696-1530 palletmfg@aol.com
Manufacturer and exporter of wooden pallets and containers
President: Marley Petersen Jr
Contact: Tim Darrow
info@palletpricing.com
Estimated Sales: $5-10 Million
Number Employees: 50-99

47708 Precit
710 Tech Park Drive
La Vergne, TN 37086-3622 615-287-8255
Fax: 615-287-8355 800-338-4585
jeff.watson@franke.com
Parent Co: Franke

47709 Preferred Machining Corporation
3730 S Kalamath Street
Englewood, CO 80110-3493 303-761-1535
Fax: 303-789-9300 sales@pmc1.net
Manufacturer and exporter of fillers, pumps/stuffers, formers and vacuumizers for poultry, beef, etc. As well as end liners and accessories for the can making industry
Vice President: Jim Abbott
Marketing Director: Tom Hoffmann
Estimated Sales: $ 10 - 20 Million
Number Employees: 50
Regions Exported to: Central America, Europe, Asia, Africa
Percentage of Business in Exporting: 50

47710 Preferred Meal Systems Inc
4135 Birney Ave
Moosic, PA 18507-1397 570-457-8311
Fax: 570-457-9241 www.preferredmeals.com
Portion control lunches
Executive Director: Bob Keen
Director Technology Services: Richard Ludt
Estimated Sales: $4,800,000
Number Employees: 250-499
Square Footage: 200000
Type of Packaging: Food Service, Private Label
Regions Exported to: Asia, Canada

47711 Preferred Packaging Systems
440 S Lone Hill Avenue
San Dimas, CA 91773
Fax: 909-592-5640 800-378-4777
www.ghlpackaging.com
Manufactures, engineers and designs packaging equipment.
Estimated Sales: $10-15 Million
Number Employees: 15
Square Footage: 30000
Brands Exported: Preferred Packaging
Regions Exported to: Central America, South America, Europe, Asia, Middle East
Percentage of Business in Exporting: 30
Regions Imported from: Europe, Asia

47712 (HQ)Preferred Popcorn
1132 9th Rd
Chapman, NE 68827-2753 308-986-2526
Fax: 308-986-2626 info@preferredpopcorn.com
www.preferredpopcorn.com
Popcorn, salts and oils
CEO: Norm Krug
Estimated Sales: $30 Million
Number Employees: 20-49
Type of Packaging: Consumer, Food Service, Private Label, Bulk
Regions Exported to: Central America, South America, Europe, Asia, Middle East
Percentage of Business in Exporting: 20

47713 Preferred Produce & Food Service
501 S Washington Ave Ste 1
Scranton, PA 18505 570-344-1626
Fax: 570-344-3065
President: Phillip Abdalla
Estimated Sales: $1-2.5 Million
Number Employees: 1-4

47714 Preiser Scientific Inc
94 Oliver St
St Albans, WV 25177-1796 304-727-2902
Fax: 304-727-2932 800-624-8285
preiser@preiser.com www.preiser.com
Wholesaler/distributor, importer and exporter of laboratory and water testing equipment and supplies. Manufacturer of coal testing equipment
President: A Preiser
CEO: G Preiser
CFO: P Fourney
VP: J Gatens
R&D: K Westfall
Sales: C Cline
Operations: D Meddings
Purchasing: D Martin
Estimated Sales: $5-10 Million
Number Employees: 20-49
Square Footage: 240000
Regions Exported to: Central America, South America, Europe, Asia, Middle East
Brands Imported: Carbolite; Cecil; Strohlein
Regions Imported from: South America, Europe
Percentage of Business in Importing: 10

47715 Premier
5721 Dragon Way
Suite 113
Cincinnati, OH 45227-4518 513-271-0600
Fax: 859-581-5525 800-354-9817
www.excellead.com
Manufacturer and exporter of paper plates, hot dog holders, food trays and foil laminated ashtrays
Owner: Thomas P Santen
VP/General Manager: J Paul Taylor
Sales: Lori Roberts
VP Operations: Viea Gerwin
Plant Manager: Mike McCann
Estimated Sales: $5-10 Million
Square Footage: 80000
Type of Packaging: Private Label
Regions Exported to: Canada
Percentage of Business in Exporting: 5

47716 Premier Brand Imports
2899 Portland Drive
Oakville, ON L6H 5S4
Canada 905-855-0086
Fax: 905-855-6904
Importer of German beer
Manager: Clayton Blakely
Number Employees: 10-19
Brands Imported: Halsten
Regions Imported from: Europe

47717 Premier Brass
255 Ottley Dr NE Ste A
Atlanta, GA 30324-3926 404-873-6000
Fax: 404-873-9993 800-251-5800
info@premierbrass.com www.premierbrass.com
Manufacturer, importer and exporter of brass and chrome components for custom foodguards, display cases and railing systems
President: Alex Mazingue
Vice President: Pep Matus
General Manager: Fred Boyajian
Estimated Sales: $1-2.5 Million
Number Employees: 10-19
Square Footage: 50000
Parent Co: Great Eastern Distributors
Type of Packaging: Food Service
Regions Exported to: Central America, South America, Europe
Regions Imported from: Europe, Asia
Percentage of Business in Importing: 10

47718 Premier Meat Co
5030 Gifford Ave
PO Box 58183
Vernon, CA 90058-2726 323-277-5888
Fax: 323-277-9100 800-555-5539
www.premiermeats.com
Beef, veal and pork
Owner: Manuel Hernandez
manuel.hernandez@premiermeats.com
Controller: Richard Orosco
Vice President: Eldad Hadar
Operations Manager: Orner Greenberg
Production Supervisor: Maricela Romero
Number Employees: 50-99
Type of Packaging: Consumer, Food Service, Bulk
Regions Exported to: Worldwide
Percentage of Business in Exporting: 3

47719 Premier Pacific Seafoods Inc
333 1st Ave W
Seattle, WA 98119-4103 206-286-8584
Fax: 206-286-8810 www.prempac.com
Fish
President: Tom Coryell
tom@prempac.com
Estimated Sales: Under $500,000
Number Employees: 10-19
Type of Packaging: Bulk

47720 Premier Skirting Products
241 Mill St
Lawrence, NY 11559-1209 516-239-6581
Fax: 516-239-6810 800-544-2516
info@premierskirting.com
www.premierskirting.com
Manufacturer and exporter of table and skirting cloths, napkins, chair covers and place mats

Importers & Exporters / A-Z

Owner: Ross Yudin
ross@premeirskirting.com
CEO: C VanDewater
CFO: Linda Ehrlich
Manager: Ross Yudin
ross@premeirskirting.com
Plant Manager: Wayne Rizzo
Estimated Sales: $ 1 - 2.5 Million
Number Employees: 10-19
Square Footage: 20000
Regions Exported to: Europe, Asia, Australia
Percentage of Business in Exporting: 10

47721 Premium Foil Products Company
PO Box 32309
Louisville, KY 40232 502-459-2820
Fax: 502-454-5488
Manufacturer and exporter of aluminum foil containers
President: A J Kleier
VP/General Manager: Robert Moses
Contact: Robert Moses
musherone@aol.com
Estimated Sales: $5-10 Million
Number Employees: 20-49
Type of Packaging: Food Service, Bulk
Regions Exported to: Worldwide

47722 Premium Water
7810 N W 100th Street
Kansas City, MO 64153 816-801-6900
800-332-3332
www.premiumwaters.com
Bottled water
President: Peter Johnson
Contact: Dawn Andresen
dawn.andresen@premiumwaters.com
GM: Bob McBride
Estimated Sales: $ 5 - 10 Million
Number Employees: 50-99
Square Footage: 80000
Type of Packaging: Consumer, Food Service, Private Label
Brands Exported: Acappella
Regions Exported to: Central America, South America, Cayman Islands
Percentage of Business in Exporting: 4

47723 Prentiss
3600 Mansell Rd Ste 350
Alpharetta, GA 30022 770-552-8072
Fax: 770-552-8076 info@prentiss.com
www.prentiss.com
Manufacturer, importer and exporter of pesticides, insecticides and rodenticides
President: Richard A Miller
VP/Purchasing: Jeffery Miller
Sales Director: Larry Eichler
Estimated Sales: $ 10 - 20 Million
Number Employees: 5-9
Square Footage: 150000
Type of Packaging: Private Label, Bulk
Regions Exported to: Worldwide
Percentage of Business in Exporting: 2
Regions Imported from: South America, Europe, Africa
Percentage of Business in Importing: 35

47724 Pres-Air-Trol Corporation
704 Bartlett Ave.
Altoona, WI 54720 715-831-6353
Fax: 419-818-0897 800-431-2625
info@senasys.com www.presair.com
Manufacturer and exporter of foot pedals and switches including pneumatic/electric and shock, explosion and water-proof; pressure and vacuum switches, thermometers, thermostats
President: Arthur Blumenthal
Vice President: Doreen Bassin
Sales: Juana Magana
Contact: Ivon Graner
ivong@presair.com
Production/Plant Manager: Chris Felon
Purchasing: Marie Schuartz
Estimated Sales: $ 10 - 20 Million
Number Employees: 20-49
Square Footage: 24000
Brands Exported: Pres-Air-Trol
Regions Exported to: Worldwide
Percentage of Business in Exporting: 20

47725 Pres-On Products
21 W Factory Rd
Addison, IL 60101 630-543-9370
Fax: 630-628-8025 800-323-7467
Manufacturer and exporter of liners including induction seal, PE, styrene and self-sealing
Division VP: Tom Cummins
Contact: John Lesavage
johnl@preson.com
VP Manufacturing: Frank Edes
Estimated Sales: $ 20-50 Million
Number Employees: 15

47726 Prescolite
695 Walnut Ave
Vallejo, CA 94592-1134 707-562-3500
Fax: 510-577-5022 www.prescolite.com
Manufacturer and exporter of lighting fixtures including electric, incandescent, mercury and outdoor
Marketing Manager: John Taylor
Estimated Sales: $20-50 Million
Number Employees: 250-499
Parent Co: US Industries

47727 Presence From Innovation LLC
2290 Ball Dr
St Louis, MO 63146-8602 314-423-9777
Fax: 314-423-0420 info@pfinnovation.com
www.pfinnovation.com
Manufacturer and exporter of universal gravity feed systems, ice barrel coolers and display and merchandising equipment
President: Jim Watt
Number Employees: 250-499
Regions Exported to: Central America, Europe, Asia, Middle East, Australia
Percentage of Business in Exporting: 30

47728 Presentations South
4748 Jetty St
Orlando, FL 32817-3183 407-657-2108
Fax: 407-849-0930
Manufacturer, designer and exporter of industrial displays, attraction exhibits, etc
Estimated Sales: $2.5-5 Million
Number Employees: 1-4
Square Footage: 120000
Regions Exported to: Central America, Europe, Caribbean
Percentage of Business in Exporting: 10

47729 Pressure King Inc
231 Herbert Ave # 1
Closter, NJ 07624-1332 201-768-1911
Fax: 201-768-4811 800-468-1007
pressurekg@aol.com
Wholesaler/distributor and importer of pressure washers, steam cleaning equipment, carpet extraction systems and detergents for the restaurant industry; exporter of pressure washers, water heaters, steamers, etc
Owner: Harry Mccormick
pressurekg@aol.com
Estimated Sales: $500,000
Number Employees: 1-4
Square Footage: 10000
Brands Exported: Karcher; Sioux; MITM; DeVilbiss
Regions Exported to: Central America, South America, Europe
Percentage of Business in Exporting: 20
Brands Imported: Karcher; Alto/Nil Fisk (Kew)
Regions Imported from: Europe
Percentage of Business in Importing: 80

47730 Prestige Plastics Corporation
8207 Swenson Way
Delta, BC V4G 1J5
Canada 604-930-2931
Fax: 604-930-2936
Manufacturer, importer and exporter of bins, tote and plastic boxes, cartons, point of purchase displays and signs; also, die cutting and design services available
President: Bill Schoenbaum
Sales Manager: James Berry
Estimated Sales: $10-20 Million
Number Employees: 10-19
Regions Exported to: Worldwide
Regions Imported from: Canada

47731 Prestige Proteins
1101 South Rogers Circle
Suite 1
Boca Raton, FL 33487-2748 561-997-8770
Fax: 561-997-8786 casein@casein.com
www.casein.com
Caseinate: calcium, sodium and potassium
Owner: Hue Henly
Sales Manager: Tina Thimlar
Estimated Sales: $1-2.5 Million
Number Employees: 1-4
Square Footage: 200000
Type of Packaging: Consumer, Food Service, Private Label, Bulk
Regions Exported to: Central America, South America, Europe, Asia, Middle East
Percentage of Business in Exporting: 75

47732 Prestige Skirting & Tablecloths
60 Dutch Hill Rd # 4a
Orangeburg, NY 10962-1722 845-358-6900
Fax: 845-359-2287 800-635-3313
prestigeskirting@aol.com
Manufacturer and exporter of tablecloths, napkins, banquet skirting, clips with Velcro, skirt hangers, chair covers, working racks and custom made linens
President: Marilyn Enison
Office Manager: Emily Valerie Ross
Sales Manager: Paul Tessler
Customer Service: Jane Smithers
Estimated Sales: $5-10 Million
Number Employees: 10-19
Square Footage: 20000
Regions Exported to: Central America, Europe

47733 (HQ)Prestige Technology
1101 S Rogers Cir
Suite 1
Boca Raton, FL 33487-2748 561-997-8770
Fax: 561-997-8786 888-697-4141
casein@casein.com
Sodium and calcium caseinates
President: Hugh Henley
casein@gate.net
Director of Sales: Tina Thimlar
Estimated Sales: $18 Million
Number Employees: 10-19
Square Footage: 20000
Other Locations:
 Prestige Technology Corp.
 MinskPrestige Technology Corp.
Brands Imported: Belampol
Regions Imported from: Europe
Percentage of Business in Importing: 10

47734 Preston Farms Popcorn
1000 Zane Street
Louisville, KY 40210 502-813-3207
Fax: 502-813-3219 866-767-7464
Hybrid popcorn
CEO: Raymond Preston
President: Leigh Anne Preston
Private Label Sales: Charles Shacklette
Contact: Kermit Highfield
kermit@prestonfarms.com
Estimated Sales: $300,000-500,000
Number Employees: 10-19
Number of Products: 60
Type of Packaging: Private Label

47735 Preston Scientific
1450 N Hundley St
Anaheim, CA 92806-1322 714-632-3700
Fax: 714-632-7355
Manufacturer and exporter of computer systems including data acquisition sub-systems
President and CEO: Bernard Spear
Executive VP: Phillip Halverson
President: Bill Boston
Sales Manager: Charles McGuire
Plant Manager: Amber Brideisca
Purchasing Manager: Robert Exley
Estimated Sales: $ 1 - 2.5 Million
Number Employees: 1-4
Square Footage: 48000
Parent Co: Halear
Brands Exported: PreSys1000
Regions Exported to: Europe, Asia, Middle East, Canada, Australia
Percentage of Business in Exporting: 35

Importers & Exporters / A-Z

47736 Pretium Packaging
200 W 20th St
Hermann, MO 65041-1602   573-486-2811
    Fax: 573-486-2443 www.pretiumpkg.com
Manufacturer and exporter of custom packaging and mustard bottles
President: Keith Harbison
Plant Manager: Bob Gillig
Estimated Sales: $ 20 - 50 Million
Number Employees: 50-99

47737 Pretium Packaging, LLC.
15450 S Outer Forty
Suite 120
Chesterfield, MO 63017   314-727-8200
               pretiumpkg.com
Manufacturer and exporter of plastic bottles and containers used for syrup.
SVP, Sales of Marketing: Mark Howell
Year Founded: 1992
Estimated Sales: $232.23 Million
Number Employees: 1200
Square Footage: 300
Parent Co: Harrison
Type of Packaging: Bulk
Regions Exported to: Canada

47738 Pretzels Inc
123 W Harvest Rd
Bluffton, IN 46714-9007   260-824-4838
    Fax: 260-824-0895 800-456-4838
               www.pretzels-inc.com
Pretzels, cheese curls, corn puffs and cheese balls
President: William Huggins
CEO: William Mann
Marketing Director: Chip Manneson
Sales Director: Marvin Sparks
Operations Manager: John Sommer
Purchasing Manager: Steve Huggins
Number Employees: 250-499
Square Footage: 800000
Type of Packaging: Consumer, Food Service, Private Label, Bulk
Regions Exported to: Canada

47739 Prevor Marketing International
975 Union Ave
Bronx, NY 10459-2926   718-589-5200
    Fax: 516-624-3486
Importer, exporter and wholesaler/distributor of produce and poultry
Owner: Barry Prevor
Number Employees: 10-19
Regions Exported to: Worldwide
Percentage of Business in Exporting: 20
Regions Imported from: Worldwide
Percentage of Business in Importing: 30

47740 Prima Foods
PO Box 353
Ramsey, NJ 07446-0353   201-236-0900
    Fax: 201-236-1269 cccprima@aol.com
Importer of canned hams, fruits, mushrooms, vegetables and tuna; exporter of canned meat, poultry and frozen pork
President: Steen Elgaard
CEO: Karsten Brunn
Estimated Sales: $ 3 - 5 Million
Number Employees: 5-9
Regions Exported to: Europe, Canada
Percentage of Business in Exporting: 5
Brands Imported: Prima; Danish Pride; Holco; Nanda
Regions Imported from: Central America, South America, Europe, Asia
Percentage of Business in Importing: 75

47741 Prima Foods International
PO Box 2208
Silver Springs, FL 34489   352-732-9148
    Fax: 352-720-0625 800-774-8751
Syrup, cocktail mixes, fruit purees and concentrates, drink bases and milk replacers
President: Hector Viale
Vice President: Celeste Viale
VP Sales: Mary Lou Sharp
Estimated Sales: $1 Million
Number Employees: 8
Square Footage: 40000
Type of Packaging: Food Service, Private Label, Bulk
Brands Exported: Prima Naturals
Regions Exported to: Central America, South America, Middle East, Africa, Caribbean, Latin America
Percentage of Business in Exporting: 40
Regions Imported from: Central America, South America, Dominican Republic, South Africa, India, Caribbean, Latin America
Percentage of Business in Importing: 40

47742 Primarily Seating Inc
475 Park Ave # 3a
Suite 3A
New York, NY 10022-1669   212-838-2588
    Fax: 212-838-2588 primarilyseating@verizon.net
American manufacturer that produces chairs, sofas, loveseats, benches, and ottomans combining the highest degree of style and quality with the correct construction for Seniors.
President: Edith Claman
Estimated Sales: $680,000
Number Employees: 1-4

47743 Primarque Products Inc
100 Grand St # 2
Worcester, MA 01610-1696   508-754-4750
    Fax: 508-624-4717 800-752-0105
               www.primarque.com
Importer of chocolate and cocoa products, soup and gravy bases and specialty foods from Spain, Portugal, Formosa and France
President: Jack Barron
Estimated Sales: Less Than $500,000
Number Employees: 1-4
Type of Packaging: Private Label
Regions Imported from: Europe, Asia

47744 Prime Ingredients Inc
280 N Midland Ave
Saddle Brook, NJ 07663-5721   201-791-6655
    Fax: 201-791-4244 888-791-6655
               www.primeingredients.com
Dessert, dips and sauces, cheese, creamers, mixes, glazes, oils, margarines and olive oil
Director: Christopher Walsh
chris@primeingredients.com
Estimated Sales: Below $5 Million
Number Employees: 5-9
Square Footage: 80000
Type of Packaging: Bulk
Regions Exported to: Worldwide
Percentage of Business in Exporting: 25
Regions Imported from: Europe, Asia
Percentage of Business in Importing: 2

47745 Prime Machinery Corporation
1031 Snyder Road
Lansdale, PA 19446-4609   215-393-8770
    Fax: 732-960-2380 info@primemachinery.com
Wholesaler/distributor and exporter of used machinery including ribbon, paddle, dispersion, double cone, high intensity, planetary, twinshell and pony mixers; also, mills, kettles, pulverizers, screens, dryers, homogenizers, filtersetc
President: Rick Kronstain
Contact: Richard Kronstain
misc@primemachinery.com
Number Employees: 5-9

47746 Prime Ostrich International
8702a 98th Street
Morinville, AB T8R 1K6
Canada   780-939-3804
    Fax: 780-939-4888 800-340-2311
Ostrich meat and meat pies
President: James Danyluik
Marketing Director: Michelle Danyluik
Number Employees: 5-9
Type of Packaging: Consumer, Food Service, Private Label, Bulk
Brands Exported: Prime Ostrich Jerky
Regions Exported to: South America
Percentage of Business in Exporting: 25

47747 Prime Play
6700 McMillan Way
Richmond, BC V6W 1J7
Canada   604-273-1068
    Fax: 604-273-4518 alexia@whitewaterwest.com
               www.primeplay.com

47748 Prime Smoked Meats Inc
220 Alice St
Oakland, CA 94607-4394   510-832-7167
    Fax: 510-832-4830
Pork
Owner: Dave Andes
Sales Manager: Tina DeMello
dave.andes@primesmoked.com
Office Manager: Elsie Jorstad
Production Manager: Jose Garcia
Estimated Sales: $5897842
Number Employees: 20-49
Square Footage: 48000
Type of Packaging: Consumer, Food Service, Private Label, Bulk
Brands Exported: Prime Smoked Meat Brand
Regions Exported to: Asia, Russia
Percentage of Business in Exporting: 5

47749 Primex International Trading
5777 W Century Blvd
Suite 1485
Los Angeles, CA 90045   310-410-7100
    Fax: 310-568-3336 info@primex.us
               www.primex-usa.com
Pistachios, dried fruits and nuts.
Owner & CEO: Ali Amin
Quality System Director: Tiffany Weldin
Grower Relations Representative: Bob Engleman
Plant Manager: Mike Vasilescu
Year Founded: 1989
Estimated Sales: $184.5 Million
Number Employees: 10-19

47750 Primlite Manufacturing Corporation
407 S Main St
Freeport, NY 11520   516-868-4411
    Fax: 516-868-4609 800-327-7583
sales@primelite-mfg.com www.primelite-mfg.com
Manufacturer and exporter of outdoor lighting fixtures, plastic globes and store fixtures including custom designed prismatic glass ceiling and wall fixtures
President: Benjamin Heit
Quality Control Manager: Joanne Heit
Estimated Sales: $ 3 - 5 Million
Number Employees: 10-19
Square Footage: 60000

47751 Primo Water Corporation
101 N Cherry St
Suite 501
Winston-Salem, NC 27101
               844-237-7466
               primowater.com
Water dispensers, purified bottled water, self-service refill drinking water.
Chief Executive Officer: Jerry Fowden
Chief Financial Officer: Jay Wells
Chief Accounting Officer: Jason Ausher
VP/General Counsel/Secretary: Marni Morgan-Poe
SVP/Global Human Resources: Steve Edman
Estimated Sales: K
Number Employees: 10,000+
Type of Packaging: Consumer, Food Service, Private Label, Bulk
Other Locations:
    Cliffstar Manufacturing Plant
    East Freetown, MA
    Cliffstar Manufacturing Plant
    Fontana, CA
    Cliffstar Manufacturing Plant
    Fredonia, NY
    Cliffstar Manufacturing Plant
    Greer, SC
    Cliffstar Manufacturing Plant
    Joplin, MO
    Cliffstar Manufacturing Plant
    N East, PA
    Cliffstar Manufacturing PlantFontana
Regions Exported to: Europe, Asia, Canada
Regions Imported from: South America, Europe, Asia

47752 Primrose Candy Co
4111 W Parker Ave
Chicago, IL 60639-2176   773-276-9522
    Fax: 773-276-7411 800-268-9522
               support@primrosecandy.com
               www.primrosecandy.com
Salt water taffy, lollipops, popcorn, sugar-free candies, and hard and chewy confections.
President/CEO: Mark Puch
mvp@primrosecandy.com
VP Sales/Marketing: Richard Griseto
Estimated Sales: $27,800,000
Number Employees: 100-249

Number of Brands: 2
Square Footage: 95000
Type of Packaging: Consumer, Food Service, Private Label, Bulk
Regions Imported from: Asia

47753 Prince Castle Inc
355 Kehoe Blvd
Carol Stream, IL 60188-1833 630-462-8801
Fax: 630-462-1460 800-722-7853
info@princecastle.com www.princecastle.com
Manufacturer and exporter of preparation and holding equipment including warming and toasting equipment, electronic cooking timers and computers, grill tools, high chairs, fry baskets and shortening filters, dispensers, drink mixerscutters and slicers
President: Ted Bethke
ted@aviation-schools.com
Product Marketing Manager: Richard Blauvelt
VP Sales/Marketing: William Kinney
Number Employees: 100-249
Square Footage: 240000
Parent Co: Marmon Group
Type of Packaging: Food Service
Brands Exported: Fasline; Comfortline; Excalibur; Merlin; Redi-Grill; Frequent Fryer
Regions Exported to: Central America, South America, Europe, Asia, Middle East
Percentage of Business in Exporting: 35

47754 Prince Industries Inc
5635 Thompson Bridge Rd
Murrayville, GA 30564-1209 770-536-3679
Fax: 770-535-2548 800-441-3303
www.princeindustriesinc.com
Manufacturer and exporter of poultry processing equipment including deboners, grinders and meat pumps
President: Jesse Prince
prinind@bellsouth.net
CFO: Jesse Prince
Vice President: Dottie Prince
National Sales Manager: Jesse Prince
General Manager: Kam Singh
Estimated Sales: $ 2.5 - 5 Million
Number Employees: 5-9
Square Footage: 24000
Regions Exported to: Worldwide
Percentage of Business in Exporting: 60

47755 Prince Waffles
16520 Bake Pkwy Ste 320
Irvine, CA 92618-4689 949-268-3350
Fax: 949-455-9472
Belgium Waffles

47756 Prince of Peace
3536 Arden Rd
Hayward, CA 94545-3908 510-887-1899
Fax: 510-887-1799 800-732-2328
popsf@popus.com www.princeofpeacecharity.org
Ginseng tea
Vice President: Lolita Lim
lolita@popus.com
VP Finance: Agnes Tsang
National Sales Manager: Mike Jarrett
Purchasing: Maria Wong
Estimated Sales: $11,200,000
Number Employees: 20-49
Square Footage: 145548
Brands Exported: Jamaica Gold; American Ginseng Tea; Prince of Peace
Regions Exported to: Europe, Asia, Middle East
Brands Imported: Paton's Macadamia Nuts; Tiger Balm; Loacker; Delacre; Bee Health
Regions Imported from: Europe, Asia, Middle East

47757 (HQ)Printpack Inc.
2800 Overlook Pkwy. NE
Atlanta, GA 30339 404-460-7000
info@printpack.com
www.printpack.com
Printed, coated, laminated and flexible film, rolls, sheets and heat sealing paper; also, candy bar and meat wrappers.
Chairman & CEO: Jimmy Love
Senior VP & CFO: Tripp Seitter
Year Founded: 1956
Estimated Sales: Over $1 Billion
Number Employees: 1000-4999
Regions Exported to: South America, Europe, Asia, Middle East

47758 Priority One America
3255 Medalist Drive
PO Box 2408
Oshkosh, WI 54903
Canada 920-235-5562
Fax: 866-580-2312
www.priorityonepackaging.com
Manufacturer, exporter and importer of palletizers, conveyors, depalletizers and packaging machinery
President: Colin Cunningham
Controller: Carolyn Schnefer
Estimated Sales: $ 10 - 20 Million
Number Employees: 100
Square Footage: 30000
Parent Co: Priority One Packaging
Regions Exported to: Worldwide
Regions Imported from: South America, Canada, Latin America , Mexico
Percentage of Business in Importing: 30

47759 Priority One Packaging
815 Bridge Street
Waterloo, ON N2V 2M7
Canada 519-746-6950
Fax: 519-746-3578 800-387-9102
products@priorityonepackaging.com
www.priorityonepackaging.com
Priority One is a manufacturer of palletizing and depalletizing equipment. Included in the product range are both high and low level palletizers, small footprint palletizers, multi-line (shuttle and rotary) palletizers, pailpalletizers, bulk palletizers, high and low depalletizers, table-top and mat-top conveyor systems, pressured and pressureless single filers, bottle and case elevators/lowerators, rinsers, magnetic elevators, cable track, full load stackers, labellersand line integration
Owner/CEO: Colin Cunningham
President: Brian Webster
VP: Drew Cameron
Estimated Sales: $30 Million
Number Employees: 120
Square Footage: 100000
Regions Exported to: Central America, South America, Europe, Asia, USA
Percentage of Business in Exporting: 60

47760 Priority Plastics Inc
704 Pinder Ave
Grinnell, IA 50112-9700 641-236-4798
Fax: 641-236-3478 800-798-3512
www.showme.com
Custom silk screened printed plastic canisters and plastic bottles; exporter of plastic bottles
President: Lawrence Den Hartog
Plant Manager: Gary Vowels
Estimated Sales: $ 20 - 50 Million
Number Employees: 20-49
Square Footage: 28000
Brands Exported: Sho-Me Container
Regions Exported to: Canada, Mexico, United Kingdom
Percentage of Business in Exporting: 5

47761 Pro Form Labs
PO Box 626
Orinda, CA 94563 707-752-9010
Fax: 707-752-9014 info@proformlabs.com
www.proformlabs.com
Nutritional powders and vitamins; weight control and sports nutrition tablets, capsules and powders
President: Doug Gillespie
Customer Service: Kellie Henry
Purchasing Agent: Alex Gillespie
Estimated Sales: $ 3 - 5 Million
Number Employees: 1-4
Square Footage: 100000
Parent Co: Gillespie & Associates
Type of Packaging: Consumer, Food Service, Private Label, Bulk
Brands Exported: Juice-Mate; Naturslim
Regions Exported to: Central America, South America, Europe, Asia, Middle East
Percentage of Business in Exporting: 30

47762 Pro Line Co
10 Avco Rd # 1
Haverhill, MA 01835-6997 978-521-2600
Fax: 978-374-4885 bench@1proline.com
www.1proline.com
Manufacturer and exporter of ergonomic workstations for production and lab areas
Owner: Derek Coughlin
President, Chief Executive Officer: Robert W Hatfield
bench@1proline.com
Sr. VP: Bob Simmons
Estimated Sales: $ 3 - 5 Million
Number Employees: 20-49
Type of Packaging: Bulk
Regions Exported to: Worldwide

47763 Pro Scientific Inc
99 Willenbrock Rd
Oxford, CT 06478-1032 203-267-4600
Fax: 203-267-4606 800-584-3776
sales@proscientific.com www.proscientific.com
Manufactures laboratory homogenizers from handheld to larger benchtop programmable models. North American distributor of Andreas Hettich Centifuges which range in size from micro to floor-model. Also distribute a full line ofincubators, water and oil baths and ovens
Owner: Donald Peronace
don@madisonavecreative.com
Sales/Marketing: Holly Yacko
Estimated Sales: $ 5 - 10 Million
Number Employees: 10-19
Number of Brands: 3
Number of Products: 40
Brands Exported: Pro
Regions Exported to: Central America, South America, Europe, Asia, Middle East, Worldwide
Percentage of Business in Exporting: 30
Brands Imported: Hettich; Memmed
Regions Imported from: Europe
Percentage of Business in Importing: 50

47764 Pro-Flo Products
30 Commerce Rd
PO Box 390
Cedar Grove, NJ 7009 973-239-2400
Fax: 973-239-5817 800-325-1057
Manufacturer, importer and exporter of water treatment and filtration equipment, drinking water coolers, chillers and dispensers
President: Louis Reyes
Quality Control: Nicaolas Iannaccio
Estimated Sales: $657,000
Number Employees: 5-9
Square Footage: 8400
Brands Exported: Pro-Flo
Regions Exported to: Central America, South America, Europe, Asia, Middle East
Percentage of Business in Exporting: 30
Regions Imported from: Europe, Asia
Percentage of Business in Importing: 30

47765 ProAmpac
12025 Tricon Rd.
Cincinnati, OH 45246 513-671-1777
800-543-7030
www.proampac.com
Polyethylene and paper bags, and specialty films. Custom plastic and paper shopping bags, polymailers and specialty films. (Blown film with six monolayer lines, two 3-layer lines and on 7-layer line).
Chairman/CEO: Tony Pritzker
Year Founded: 1966
Estimated Sales: $121.7 Million
Number Employees: 1,100
Square Footage: 815000
Parent Co: PPC Partners
Type of Packaging: Consumer, Food Service, Private Label
Regions Exported to: Worldwide

47766 (HQ)ProBar Systems Inc.
92 Caplan Ave.
Suite 607
Barrie, ON L4N 0Z7
Canada
800-521-7294
info@probarsystems.com www.probarsystems.com
Manufacturer and exporter of beverage dispensing machines including computer controlled bar pouring and inventory systems, juice dispensers and soft drink machines

President: Charles M Stimac Jr
CFO: John Hornbeck
Research & Development: Mike Smith
Quality Control: Greg Gemmell
Marketing: Chris Burden
Sales Director: Kris Croft
Operations Manager: Carlos DeMelo
Production/Plant Manager/Purchasing: Jimmy Neuman
Estimated Sales: $300,000-500,000
Number Employees: 1-4
Number of Brands: 3
Number of Products: 3
Type of Packaging: Private Label
Regions Exported to: Central America, South America, Europe, Worldwide
Percentage of Business in Exporting: 2

47767 ProRestore Products
1016 Greentree Road
Suite 115
Pittsburgh, PA 15220   412-264-8340
Fax: 412-920-2905   800-332-6037
sales@prorestoreproducts.com
www.prorestoreproducts.com
Manufacturer and exporter of deodorants, cleaners and disinfectants
President: Cliff Zlotnik
Contact: Mike Kerner
mikek@prorestoreproducts.com
Estimated Sales: $ 5 - 10 Million
Number Employees: 20-49
Parent Co: RPM International Inc.
Type of Packaging: Food Service, Private Label, Bulk
Regions Exported to: Worldwide

47768 ProTeam
12438 W Bridger Street
Boise, ID 83713   208-377-9555
Fax: 208-377-8444   800-541-1456
customerservice.proteam@emerson.com
www.pro-team.com
ProTeam became a global phenomenon in the commercial cleaning world after introducing a game-challenging design innovation, the lightweight backpack vacuum. Today ProTeam offers a full range of innovative vacuums, including the newProGuard wet/dry line.
CEO: Matt Wood
Contact: Richard Coombs
r.coombs@pro-team.com
Estimated Sales: $50-100 Million
Number Employees: 50
Square Footage: 5000
Regions Exported to: Central America, Europe
Percentage of Business in Exporting: 5

47769 Proacec USA
1158 26th Street
Suite 509
Santa Monica, CA 90403-4621   310-996-7770
Fax: 310-996-7772   www.proacec.com
Olives and olive oil
President: Paul Short
Estimated Sales: Below $ 5 Million
Number Employees: 10
Number of Brands: 4
Number of Products: 30
Square Footage: 2000
Type of Packaging: Consumer, Food Service, Bulk
Brands Imported: Caroliva; Plantio Del Condado; Don Quixate; El Carmen
Regions Imported from: Europe
Percentage of Business in Importing: 100

47770 Procedyne Corp
11 Industrial Dr
New Brunswick, NJ 08901-3657   732-249-8347
Fax: 732-249-7220   mail@procedyne.com
www.procedyne.com
Manufacturer and exporter of fluidized bed systems including dryers, granulators and thermal processors. Engineering and research and development facility with laboratory and pilot plant. Offer process design, process development andscale-up testing
President: H Kenneth Staffin
CEO: Kenneth Staffin
kstaffin@procedynecorp.com
VP Process Technology: Thomas Parr
VP Products: Bob Archibald
Chairman of the Board: Dr H Kenneth Staffin

Estimated Sales: $ 10 - 20 Million
Number Employees: 50-99
Square Footage: 120000
Type of Packaging: Bulk
Regions Exported to: Worldwide
Percentage of Business in Exporting: 60

47771 Process Displays
5800 S Moorland Rd
New Berlin, WI 53151   262-782-3600
Fax: 262-782-3857   800-533-1764
Manufacturer and exporter of point of purchase displays, vacuum form trays, case dividers, rail strips, counter mats, menu board and deli signs and decals
President: Bob Zanotti
Vice President: Brendon Rowan
Contact: Lori Gebhard
gebhard@pdisplays.com
Estimated Sales: $ 2.5 - 5 Million
Number Employees: 50-99
Square Footage: 200000
Parent Co: Process Retail Group
Regions Exported to: Central America, South America, Europe, Asia
Percentage of Business in Exporting: 10

47772 Process Engineering & Fabrication
20 Hedge Ln
Afton, VA 22920   540-456-8163
Fax: 540-456-8171   800-852-7975
www.processengineeringinc.com
Manufacturer and exporter of custom industrial refrigeration systems, spiral conveyor systems and stainless steel food processing equipment; also, installation services available
President: Bart Shellabarger
CEO: Bob Amacker
CFO: Bruce Neidlinger
Chief Freezing Officer: Charley Marckel
Sales: Jimmy Sokora
Contact: Bruce Neidlinger
bruce@processengineeringinc.com
Estimated Sales: Below $ 5 Million
Number Employees: 10
Square Footage: 40000
Brands Exported: Mini-Spiral; Super Mini-Spiral
Regions Exported to: Central America, South America
Percentage of Business in Exporting: 50

47773 Process Heating Co
2732 3rd Ave S
PO Box 84585
Seattle, WA 98134-1983   206-682-3414
Fax: 206-682-1582   866-682-1582
inquire@processheating.com
www.processheating.com
Manufacturer and exporter of industrial immersion heaters, circulation heating systems and fuel oil preheaters
President: Rick Jay
rick@processheating.com
CEO: Ron Jay
Marketing: Mike Peringer
Sales/Industrial: Eric Olden
Estimated Sales: $ 3 - 5 Million
Number Employees: 10-19
Number of Products: 15
Square Footage: 15000

47774 Process Heating Corp
547 Hartford Tpke
Shrewsbury, MA 01545-4002   508-842-5200
Fax: 508-842-9418   proheat@gis.net
www.proheatcorp.com
Manufacturer and exporter of ovens, furnaces, air pollution control incinerators and process heating equipment; also, rebuilding and remodeling available
President: Brad Green
proheat@gis.net
Estimated Sales: Below $ 5,000,000
Number Employees: 5-9
Regions Exported to: Worldwide
Percentage of Business in Exporting: 10

47775 Process Sensors Corp
113 Cedar St # S1
Milford, MA 01757-1192   508-473-9901
Fax: 508-473-0715   www.processsensors.com
Manufacturer, importer and exporter of moisture measuring instruments

President: Robert Winson
robertwinson@outback.com
Estimated Sales: $ 5 - 10,000,000
Number Employees: 20-49
Regions Exported to: Worldwide
Percentage of Business in Exporting: 25
Regions Imported from: U.K.
Percentage of Business in Importing: 5

47776 Process Solutions
6701 Garden Rd # 1
Riviera Beach, FL 33404-5900   561-840-0050
Fax: 561-840-0070   sales@processsolutions.net
www.processsolutions.net
Manufacturer and exporter of drum lifters and inverters, stainless steel drums, bins, tanks, control panels and systems, etc.; importer of stainless steel bins and butterfly valves
President: Howard Rosenkranz
Vice President: H Rosenkranz
Estimated Sales: $5-10 Million
Number Employees: 20-49
Regions Exported to: Central America, South America, Middle East, Canada, Mexico
Percentage of Business in Exporting: 20
Brands Imported: BorZ; Sterivalve
Regions Imported from: Europe
Percentage of Business in Importing: 20

47777 Prodo-Pak Corp
77 Commerce St
Garfield, NJ 07026-1811   973-777-7770
Fax: 973-772-0471   sales@prodo-pak.com
Manufacturer, importer and exporter of form/fill/seal packaging machines for pouches and tube fillers; also, conveyor systems and labeling equipment
President: John Mueller
sales@prodo-pak.com
Research & Development: Rudy Degenars
Operations/Plant/Purchasing Manager: Ralph Isler
Estimated Sales: $ 5 - 10 Million
Number Employees: 20-49
Number of Brands: 1
Number of Products: 10
Square Footage: 20000

47778 Produce Trading Corp
290 N Grove St
Merritt Island, FL 32953-3444   321-452-7037
Fax: 321-454-3006   www.gorlin.com
Wholesaler/distributor and exporter of cured pork and beef and dried fruit
President: Richard Champon
Estimated Sales: $ .5 - 1 million
Number Employees: 1-4
Regions Exported to: South America, Caribbean

47779 Producers Cooperative
1800 N Texas Ave
Bryan, TX 77803-1831   979-778-6000
Fax: 979-778-0243
producers@producerscooperative.com
www.producerscooperative.com
Pinto beans
Manager: Bob Beyer
Manager: Martin Jackson
martin.jackson@nestle.com
General Manager: Bob Beyer
Number Employees: 5-9
Square Footage: 40000
Type of Packaging: Private Label
Regions Exported to: Mexico
Percentage of Business in Exporting: 2

47780 Producers Cooperative Oil Mill
6 SE 4th St
Oklahoma City, OK 73129-1000   405-232-7555
Fax: 405-236-4887   www.producerscoop.net
Cottonseed
President/Chief Executive Officer: Gary Conkling
gary.conkling@producerscoop.net
Director, Health, Safety & Environment: Becky Mosshammer
Estimated Sales: $ 15 Million
Number Employees: 50-99
Number of Products: 1
Regions Exported to: Worldwide

47781 Producers Peanut Company
PO Box 250
Suffolk, VA 23434   757-539-7496
Fax: 757-934-7730   800-847-5491
pntkid@producerspeanut.com
www.producerspeanut.com

Peanuts and peanut butter
CEO: James Pond
Estimated Sales: $800,000
Number Employees: 20-49
Square Footage: 144000
Type of Packaging: Food Service, Private Label, Bulk
Regions Exported to: Worldwide
Percentage of Business in Exporting: 50
Regions Imported from: South America, Europe, Asia, Australia, Caribbean, Mexico, Latin America
Percentage of Business in Importing: 6

47782 Producers Rice Mill Inc.
PO Box 1248
Stuttgart, AR 72160   870-673-4444
    Fax: 870-673-7394 info@producersrice.com
        www.producersrice.com
Rice and soybeans.
President/CEO: Keith Glover
kglover@producersrice.com
Chairman: Jerry Hoskyn
Year Founded: 1943
Estimated Sales: $550 Million
Number Employees: 500-999
Square Footage: 30000
Type of Packaging: Consumer, Food Service
Regions Exported to: Worldwide

47783 Production Equipment Co
401 Liberty St
Meriden, CT 06450-4500   203-235-5795
    Fax: 203-237-5391 800-758-5697
        www.productionequipmentcompany.com
Manufacturer and exporter of overhead cranes and hoists; also, steel fabricators
Owner: Bud Davis
VP Sales/Marketing: Rosewell Davis
bdavis@productionequipment.com
Estimated Sales: $ 5-10 Million
Number Employees: 20-49
Regions Exported to: Worldwide

47784 Production Packaging & Processing Equipment Company
1713 East Victory Drive
Savannah, GA 31404   912-856-4281
    Fax: 912-354-4615 www.kettles.com
Manufacturer, exporter and wholesaler/distributor of new and rebuilt packaging and processing equipment including mixers, fillers, cap tighteners, labeling, cappers, kettles and tanks
President: Louis R Klein
CEO: Jeff Klein
Estimated Sales: $2.5-5 Million
Number Employees: 5-9
Square Footage: 100000
Brands Exported: P3

47785 Production Systems
850 Mountain Industrial Dr NW
Marietta, GA 30060   770-424-9784
    Fax: 770-424-8392 800-235-9734
Manufacturer and exporter of package and case conveyors and packaging and palletizing systems; also, integrated control systems for production and processing plants
President: Michael Anderson
Manager Marketing Series: Sharon Phillips
Engineer Manager: Wayne Marlow
Estimated Sales: $5-10 Million
Number Employees: 20-49
Square Footage: 100000
Regions Exported to: Asia, Middle East
Percentage of Business in Exporting: 10

47786 Productos Familia
1511 Calle Loiza
Santurce, PR 00911-1846   787-268-5929
    Fax: 787-268-7717 www.nosotrasonline.com
Supplier of soft paper tissues; wholesaler/distributor, importer and exporter of toilet paper, paper towels and napkins; serving the food service market
President: Fabio Posada
VP: Carlos Upegui
Number Employees: 7
Square Footage: 12000
Parent Co: Productos Familia SA
Type of Packaging: Food Service
Regions Exported to: Central America, Caribbean
Percentage of Business in Exporting: 20
Regions Imported from: South America, Latin America

47787 Products A Curtron Div
5350 Campbells Run Rd
Pittsburgh, PA 15205-9738   412-787-9750
    Fax: 412-787-3665 800-888-9750
        info@tmi-pvc.com www.curtronproducts.com
Manufacturer and exporter of leading food safety products such as strip doors, air doors, rack covers, swinging doors, hood enclosures, display cooler curtains, milk cooler curtains and eutectic packs
Manager: Joseph Klaynjans
Contact: Steve Battaglia
stevebattaglia@curtronproducts.com
Estimated Sales: Less Than $500,000
Number Employees: 1-4
Square Footage: 100000
Parent Co: TMI
Brands Exported: Save-T
Regions Exported to: Worldwide

47788 Produits Alimentaire
1186 Rue Du Pont
St Lambert De Lauzon, QC G0S 2W0
Canada   418-889-8080
    Fax: 418-889-9730 800-463-1787
Flour, food colors, confectionery and syrup
Director: Michel Blouin
Number Employees: 20-49
Square Footage: 32000
Type of Packaging: Consumer, Food Service, Private Label, Bulk
Regions Imported from: Europe
Percentage of Business in Importing: 20

47789 (HQ)Produits Alimentaire
1805 Berlier St
Laval, QC H7L 3S4
Canada   514-334-5503
    Fax: 514-334-3584 800-361-9326
        www.berthelet.com
Flavorings, seasonings, puddings, soup bases, sauces, jams, food colorings, jelly powder, pie fillings, beverage syrups, bouillon bases, concentrates, sundae toppings and beverage crystals
Special Advisor: Guy Berthelet
Sales Manager: Pierre Berthelet
Operations & Human Resources Director: Dany Miville
Planning & Purchasing Manager: Roger Tremblay
Type of Packaging: Consumer, Food Service, Private Label, Bulk
Other Locations:
    Produits Alimentaires Berthel
    Blainville, PQProduits Alimentaires Berthel
Brands Exported: Berthelet
Regions Exported to: USA
Percentage of Business in Exporting: 5

47790 Produits Belle Baie
10 rue du Quai
Caraquet, NB E1W 1B6
Canada   506-727-4414
    Fax: 506-727-7166 info@bellebaie.com
Herring, shrimp and crab
President: Alie Lebouthiller
Vice President: Valmond Chaison
Quality Control: Georges Boudreau
Marketing & Sales Director: Fernand Brideaux
Production Manager: Georges Foulem
Estimated Sales: $10 Million
Number Employees: 150
Type of Packaging: Consumer, Food Service
Regions Exported to: Europe, Asia, USA

47791 Produits Ronald
200 St Joseph Street
St. Damase, QC J0H 1J0
Canada   450-797-3303
    Fax: 450-797-2389 800-465-0118
Canned corn-on-the-cob, marinades, sauces, baked beans, bouillons and fondue
President: Jean Messier
Vice President/General Manager: Bernard Belanger
Quality Assurance Manager: Lucie Labbe
Plant Manager: Louis Richard
Purchasing Manager: David Lussier
Number Employees: 100-249
Square Footage: 160000
Parent Co: A. Lassonde
Type of Packaging: Consumer, Food Service
Brands Exported: Mont-Rouge; Madeleine; Rougemont
Regions Exported to: Central America, Europe

Percentage of Business in Exporting: 50

47792 Professional Bakeware Company
11739 N Highway 75
Willis, TX 77378-5740   866-710-1936
    Fax: 936-890-8760 800-440-9547
Bakeware, cookware, servingware, displayware and indestructable alumaware
President: David Beauregard
Vice President: Jennifer Beauregard
Marketing/Design: Judy Beck
Public Relations: Stephanie Samudio
Plant Manager: Sterling Samudio
Estimated Sales: $ 10 - 20,000,000
Number Employees: 20-49
Number of Brands: 5
Number of Products: 500
Square Footage: 15000
Type of Packaging: Food Service, Bulk

47793 Professional Home Kitchens
1504 145th Pl SE
Bellevue, WA 98007-5500   425-451-1593
    Fax: 425-641-7225 800-570-2433
        stan@lacanche.com www.lacanche.com
Importer of French ranges
Manager: Yasuhisa Oki
Number Employees: 5-9
Brands Exported: Lacanche; Morice; Charvet; Caumartin
Brands Imported: Lecanche; Morice
Regions Imported from: France

47794 Professional Marketing Group
912 Rainier Avenue S
Seattle, WA 98144-2840   206-322-7303
    Fax: 206-322-4351 800-227-3769
        www.vacuumpackers.com
Importer, exporter and wholesaler/distributor of commercial grade flush and nonflush vacuum packing machinery
Owner: Thom Dolder
Estimated Sales: $2.5-5 Million
Number Employees: 5-9
Regions Exported to: Worldwide
Regions Imported from: Italy

47795 Professional Materials Hndlng
4203 North Landmark Dr
Orlando, FL 32817-1210   407-677-0040
    Fax: 407-678-0273 info@pmh-co.com
        www.pmh-co.com
Wholesaler/distributor and importer of turretts and fully automatic lift trucks/alvs. Warehouse management & inventory control software, factoty automation, and material handling planning and integration
President: Charles Nordhorn
cnordhorn@pmh-co.com
VP: Wolfgang Nordhorn
Estimated Sales: $2.5-5 Million
Number Employees: 10-19
Square Footage: 80000

47796 Proffitt Manufacturing Company
404 Mitchell Street
Dalton, GA 30721-2705   706-278-7105
    Fax: 706-225-4419 800-241-4682
Manufacturer and exporter of dust control mats
CEO: John R Proffitt Jr
VP: W Masters
Manager: Fred Lester
Estimated Sales: $ 3 - 5 Million
Number Employees: 50
Square Footage: 132000
Brands Exported: Endurance; Master Turf
Regions Exported to: Europe, Asia, Canada, Mexico, Australia
Percentage of Business in Exporting: 8

47797 Profire Stainless Steel Barbecue
9621 S Dixie Hwy
Miami, FL 33156   305-665-5313
    Fax: 305-666-3315 info@profirebbq.com
Outdoor barbecues, built-in-grills, portable grills and other accessories
President and CFO: David Zisman
Contact: Alex Alonzo
lester.perdomo@profirebbq.com
Estimated Sales: $ 10 - 20 Million
Number Employees: 10
Regions Exported to: South America, Canada
Percentage of Business in Exporting: 1

Importers & Exporters / A-Z

47798 Profood International
670 W Fifth Ave
Suite 116
Naperville, IL 60563 630-428-2386
Fax: 630-527-9905 888-288-0081
support@profoodinternational.com
www.profoodinternational.com
Preservatives, emulsifiers, enzymes, texturizers and acids
Contact: Dave Shi
daves@profoodinternational.com

47799 Progenix Corporation
7566 N 72nd Ave
Wausau, WI 54401 715-675-7566
Fax: 715-675-4931 800-233-3356
Ginseng, whole root, fiber, prong, powder and extract; capsules, teas and gift packaging
President: Robert Duwe
Number Employees: 20-49
Square Footage: 26000
Type of Packaging: Consumer, Food Service, Bulk
Brands Exported: Ameriseng; Wiscon
Regions Exported to: Europe, Asia, Canada
Percentage of Business in Exporting: 20

47800 Progress Lighting
101 Corporate Dr # L
Spartanburg, SC 29303-5043 864-599-6000
Manufacturer and exporter of commercial, interior and exterior lighting
Contact: Robert Childs
rchilds@progresslighting.com
Warehouse Manager: Grant Barrett
Director, Purchasing: Jeff Pickens
Estimated Sales: $ 77 Million
Number Employees: 5-9
Square Footage: 35000
Parent Co: Hubbell Incorporated
Type of Packaging: Bulk

47801 Progressive International/Mr. Dudley
P.O.Box 97046
Kent, WA 98064-9746 253-850-6111
Fax: 253-852-2611 800-426-7101
info@progressiveintl.com
www.progressiveintl.com
Importer and exporter of wood and acrylic peppermills, salt shakers, spice grinders and racks and cheese graters
Owner/President: Duke Kebow
VP (New Products): Mark Kibbe
CEO: Bill Reibl
VP Sales: Dianne Schick
Estimated Sales: $ 20 - 50 Million
Number Employees: 50-99
Square Footage: 40000
Brands Exported: Mr. Dudley
Regions Exported to: Central America, South America, Europe, Asia, Middle East
Percentage of Business in Exporting: 25
Brands Imported: Mr. Dudley; Spice Tree
Regions Imported from: Asia
Percentage of Business in Importing: 75

47802 Progressive Specialty Glass
123 Whitling Street
Unit R
Fax: 860-747-4924 860-410-9980
www.progressiveglass.com

47803 Proheatco Manufacturing
3427 Pomona Boulevard
Suite D
Pomona, CA 91768-3260 909-598-7445
Fax: 909-598-3514 800-423-4195
Manufacturer and exporter of ovens, heaters and steam heated systems; exporter of heaters
President: Ralph J Schaefer
Estimated Sales: $1-2.5 Million
Number Employees: 10-19
Square Footage: 24000
Regions Exported to: Worldwide
Percentage of Business in Exporting: 5

47804 Proluxe
PO Box 869
Paramount, CA 90723-0869 562-531-0305
Fax: 562-869-7715 800-594-5528
www.proluxe.com
Manufacturer and exporter of pizza and tortilla presses, dough and vending carts, pizza slicing guides, clam shell and tortilla warming grills, pan racks, conveyor and tray ovens and sauce rings; also, custom stainless steel fabrication available
President: Eugene Raio
VP/General Manager: Daniel Raio
Director of Marketing: Michael Cole
Vice President of Sales: Mike Cervantes
Number Employees: 50
Square Footage: 180000
Brands Exported: Doughpro; Pizzacart; Doughcart; Hotslot; Personal Pizza Machine; Ovens Wood Fried; Dough Divider/Rounders

47805 Promarks
1915 E Acacia St
Ontario, CA 91761-7921 909-923-3888
Fax: 909-923-3588 www.promarksvac.com
Vacuum sealing and vacuum packaging machines. Also manufacture dicer, stuffer, tumbling and brine injector machines.
Owner: Karen Chiu
karen@promarksvac.com
Number Employees: 10-19
Regions Exported to: Worldwide

47806 Promens
100 Industrial Drive
PO Box 2087
St. John, NB E2L 3T5
Canada 506-633-0101
Fax: 506-658-0227 800-295-3725
Trays, cups, jars and plastic packaging for the food and beverage industry. Also manufacture bins, bin liners, ingredient bins and dump tubs.
Regions Exported to: Worldwide

47807 (HQ)Promo Bar/Howw
P.O.Box 276
Barrington, IL 60011-0276 847-382-4380
Fax: 847-382-4383 mike@howw.com
www.howw.com
Plastic glassware and barware; lighted glassware and shots
President: Michael Kalamaras
Estimated Sales: $ 3 - 5 Million
Type of Packaging: Bulk

47808 Promofood International
4306 E 26th St
Vernon, CA 90058-4301 323-981-6900
Fax: 323-231-1477 www.promofood.com
Importer of gourmet canned goods
Owner: Baudoin Stgaldepons
Estimated Sales: $ 3 - 5 Million
Number Employees: 5-9
Square Footage: 12000
Type of Packaging: Consumer, Food Service
Regions Imported from: Europe
Percentage of Business in Importing: 80

47809 Promotion in Motion Companies
PO Box 558
Closter, NJ 07624-0558 201-784-5800
800-369-7391
mail@promotioninmotion.com
www.promotioninmotion.com
Brand name confections, fruit snacks and other fine foods
President/CEO: Michael Rosenberg
mrosenberg@promotioninmotion.com
Executive Director: Frank McSorley
COO: Basant Dwivedi
Number Employees: 250-499
Type of Packaging: Private Label

47810 Promotional Resources
7215 SW Topeka Blvd
Topeka, KS 66624-8700 785-862-3707
Fax: 785-862-0070 sales@kidstuffnet.com
www.kidstuff.com
Owner: Joe Tindall
joe@kidstuff.com
Number Employees: 20-49

47811 Pronatura Inc
1435 E Algonquin Rd
Arlington Hts, IL 60005-4715 847-410-1361
Fax: 847-545-1008 800-555-7580
Importer, exporter and wholesaler/distributor of herbal remedies including kombucha teas, extracts and capsules, ginseng multi-minerals/vitamins and nutritional, herbal and homeopathic supplements
Manager: Andre Mehrabian
amehrabian@pronaturainc.com
VP: Andre Mehrabian
Estimated Sales: $500,000
Number Employees: 5-9
Square Footage: 22000
Parent Co: Naturwaren
Brands Exported: Swedish Bitters; Kombueha; Dantox
Regions Exported to: South America, Asia, Africa
Percentage of Business in Exporting: 20
Brands Imported: Kombusha Tea & Extract, Swedish Bitters
Regions Imported from: Europe
Percentage of Business in Importing: 80

47812 Pronova Biopolymer
135 Commerce Way
Suite 201
Portsmouth, NH 03801-3200 603-433-1231
Fax: 603-433-1348 800-223-9030
bess.mosley@pronova.com www.pronova.com
Processor, importer and exporter of industrial ingredients including alginates, propylene glycol alginates, chitin and chitosan
General Manager: Sandra Platt
Manager Customer Service: Bess Mosley
Number Employees: 5-9
Parent Co: Pronova Biopolymer
Brands Exported: Sea Cure; Pro Floc
Regions Exported to: Central America, South America, Europe, Asia, Middle East
Brands Imported: Protanal; Scogin; Protacell; Protacid; Pronova
Regions Imported from: Europe, Asia

47813 Pronto Products Company
11765 Goldring Rd
Arcadia, CA 91006 626-358-5718
Fax: 626-358-9194 800-377-6680
www.prontoproducts.com
Wire products including chrome and stainless steel dispensers and frying baskets
President: William Parrott
VP: Martha Wagner
Estimated Sales: $20-50 Million
Number Employees: 20-49

47814 Proper-Chem
46 Arbor Ln
Dix Hills, NY 11746 631-420-8000
Fax: 631-420-8003
Vitamins and supplements
President: Emil Backstrom
Estimated Sales: $ 3 - 5 Million
Number Employees: 10-19
Square Footage: 40000
Type of Packaging: Consumer, Private Label

47815 Protectowire Co Inc
60 Washington St
Pembroke, MA 02359-1833 781-924-5384
Fax: 781-826-2045 pwire@protectowire.com
www.protectowire.com
Manufacturer and exporter of fire detection systems for refrigerated storage
President: Andrew Sullivan
asullivan@protectowire.com
CFO: Steve Loughlin
VP North American Sales: John Whaling
Chairman of the Board: Carol M Sullivan
Quality Assurance Manager: Richard Twigg
Sales Engineer: John Whaling
Sales Engineer: James Roussel
Estimated Sales: $5-10 Million
Number Employees: 20-49
Brands Exported: Protectowire
Regions Exported to: Worldwide
Percentage of Business in Exporting: 40

47816 Protein Research
1852 Rutan Dr
Livermore, CA 94551-7635 925-243-6300
Fax: 925-243-6308 800-948-1991
info@proteinresearch.com
www.proteinresearch.com
Amino acid, vitamin and mineral supplements
Owner: Robert Matheson
robert@proteinresearch.com
Director: Theodore Aarons
VP Operations: Daniel Aarons
Estimated Sales: $5-10 Million
Number Employees: 50-99

Importers & Exporters / A-Z

Number of Products: 12
Square Footage: 132000
Type of Packaging: Private Label, Bulk
Regions Exported to: Europe, Asia, Mexico
Percentage of Business in Exporting: 10

47817 Protexall
1025 S. Fourth St
Greenville, IL 62246 618-664-6990
Fax: 877-776-8397 800-334-8939
Manufacturer and exporter of uniforms
President: Wayne Williams
CEO: Lois Williams
Vice President: Wade Williams
Sales Rep Coordinator: Dona Tredge
Operations Head: Randy Woods
Estimated Sales: $5-10 Million
Number Employees: 50-99
Square Footage: 200000
Parent Co: DeMoulin Bros. and Co.
Regions Exported to: Worldwide

47818 Protica Inc
1002 MacArthur Rd
Whitehall, PA 18052-7052 610-832-2000
Fax: 978-975-4325 800-776-8422
www.protica.com
Hydrolyzed proteins and fish gelatin
President: Peter Noble
Sales: Chris Gorski
Contact: Bill Dillon
wdillon@protica.com
Type of Packaging: Bulk
Brands Exported: Peptan Collagen Hydrolysate
Regions Exported to: Europe, Asia, Middle East
Brands Imported: Peptan Collagen Hydrolysate
Regions Imported from: South America, Europe

47819 (HQ)Prototype Equipment Corporation
1601 Northwind Blvd
Libertyville, IL 60048-9613 847-680-4433
Fax: 847-816-6374
Manufacturer, exporter and importer of robotic packaging equipment including flexible bag packers, case formers, pick and place packers, bulk case packers, top sealers and vertical snack food packers
Owner: Matthew Clatch
Director Sales/Marketing: Bruce Larson
VP Production: William Goodman
Estimated Sales: $300,000-500,000
Number Employees: 5-9
Square Footage: 168000
Brands Exported: Universal, Pouch Pack
Regions Exported to: South America, Europe, Middle East, Canada, Mexico
Percentage of Business in Exporting: 5
Regions Imported from: South America, Europe, Middle East, Mexico,Canada
Percentage of Business in Importing: 5

47820 Provender International
6050 Kennedy Boulevard E
West New York, NJ 07093-3901 631-907-8840
Fax: 631-907-8711 800-678-5603
provend@optonline.net
Consultants both international and domestic, specialty food and confectionary, manufacturers and representatives
President: Nicola Lombardi
Executive VP: Joseph Lombardi
Number Employees: 1-4
Type of Packaging: Consumer
Brands Imported: Whittard; Provender; English; Hudson's International; Fudgies Bakery; Bontle's Confectionery; Dartington Foods; Chalice
Regions Imported from: Europe

47821 Provigo Distribution
320 Bd Leclerc O
Granby, QC J2G 1V3
Canada 450-372-8014
Fax: 514-383-5110 800-361-1168
www.provigo.ca
Wholesaler/distributor and exporter of meats
Maintenance Supervisor: Francis De Roy
Transportation Manager: Mickael Rheaume
Director Operations: Denis Lepine
Number Employees: 100-249
Parent Co: Provigo

47822 Provimi Foods
W2103 County Road VV
Seymour, WI 54165 920-833-6861
Fax: 920-833-9850 800-833-8325
info@provimifoods.com www.provimifoods.com
Veal and sauces
President: Dan Schober
CFO: Rod Mackenzie
Contact: Bruce Achten
achten@provimifoods.com *Year Founded:* 1982
Type of Packaging: Consumer, Food Service, Private Label, Bulk
Regions Exported to: Worldwide
Percentage of Business in Exporting: 10

47823 Provisur Technologies
9150 W 191st St
Mokena, IL 60448-8727 708-479-3500
Fax: 708-479-3598 marketing@formaxinc.com
Advanced forming and slicing systems for the food processing industry. Also provide tooling, filling systems and packaging supplies.
VP N. American Sales/Marketing/Service: Kevin Howard
Contact: Chris Blodgett
chris@formax.us
Number Employees: 5-9
Regions Exported to: Worldwide

47824 Pruden Packing Company
1201 North Main Street
Suffolk, VA 23434-5814 757-539-8773
Fax: 757-925-4971
Ham and pork shoulder
President: Peter Pruden
General Manager: K Jones
Plant Superintendent: Terry McNitt
Estimated Sales: $3.0 Million
Number Employees: 5-9
Parent Co: Smithfield Companies
Brands Exported: Champon; Pruden
Regions Exported to: Central America, Caribbean
Percentage of Business in Exporting: 5

47825 Psc Floturn Inc
1050 Commerce Ave # 1
Union, NJ 07083-5080 908-687-3225
Fax: 908-687-1715 sales@flow-turn.com
www.stainlessbeltcurves.com
Manufacturer, importer and exporter of USDA listed powered belt curve and custom straight conveyors
President: Herman Migdel
Product Manager: J Grabowski
Vice President: Larry Cerpetier
danotsc@aol.com
Operations Manager: Dan Otero
Estimated Sales: $2.5-5 Million
Number Employees: 10-19
Square Footage: 144000
Regions Exported to: South America, Asia, Canada, Mexico
Percentage of Business in Exporting: 5
Percentage of Business in Importing: 25

47826 Psyllium Labs
1701 E Woodfield Road
Suite 636
Schaumburg, IL 60173
888-851-6667
info@psyllium.com www.psylliumlabs.com
Psyllium, chia and quinoa
Operations Executive: Drew West
Other Locations:
  Manufacturing Facility
  North Gujarat, IndiaManufacturing FacilitySanta Cruz, Bolivia
Regions Exported to: Europe, Asia, South Africa, Australia, New Zealand

47827 Pucel Enterprises Inc
1440 E 36th St
Cleveland, OH 44114-4117 216-881-4604
Fax: 216-881-6731 800-336-4986
www.pucelenterprises.com
Manufacturer and exporter of material handling equipment, stock carts, drum lifters and hand, shop and platform trucks, benches and cabinets
President: M Ann
amleissa@pucelenterprises.com
Vice President: Robert Mlakar
Plant Manager: Ronald Cook
Estimated Sales: $5-10,000,000
Number Employees: 50-99
Square Footage: 105000
Regions Exported to: Europe, Asia, Middle East, Latin America, Africa, Caribbean

47828 Pudgies Famous Chicken
1735 Deer Park Avenue
Deer Park, NY 11729-5206 631-586-0055
Fax: 631-586-0068
Estimated Sales: $ .5 - 1 million
Number Employees: 20-49

47829 Puebla Foods Inc
75 Jefferson St
Passaic, NJ 07055-6551 973-473-0201
Fax: 973-473-3854 pueblafoods@aol.com
Mexican products: tortillas, chips and taco shells, jalapenos, hot sauces, dried peppers, tomatillos and sodas
President: Felix Sanchez
VP: Carmen Sanchez
Contact: Martha Acevedo
macevedo@pueblafoods.com
General Manager: Gabriela Molina
Estimated Sales: Less Than $500,000
Number Employees: 1-4
Square Footage: 30000

47830 Pueblo Trading Co Inc
PO Box 11508
Newport Beach, CA 92658-5032 949-640-6499
Fax: 949-642-6545 pueblotrading@yahoo.com
www.pueblotradingco.com
Wholesaler/distributor and exporter of meat, poultry, cheese, etc
President: Carie Ross
Operations: Gerry Ross
Number Employees: 1-4
Type of Packaging: Consumer, Food Service, Private Label, Bulk

47831 Pulse Systems
422 Connie Avenue
Los Alamos, NM 87544 505-662-7599
Fax: 505-662-7748 www.psilasers.com
Manufacturer and exporter of laser marking and coding systems
President: Edward J McLellan
VP: Linda McLellan
Contact: Holly Page
hpage@pulsesystem.com
Chief Operating Officer: Linda Mclellan
Estimated Sales: $ 1 - 3 Million
Number Employees: 1-4
Type of Packaging: Consumer, Private Label, Bulk
Regions Exported to: Central America, South America, Europe, Asia, Middle East
Percentage of Business in Exporting: 15

47832 Pulva Corp
105 Industrial Dr W
Valencia, PA 16059-3321 724-898-2555
Fax: 724-898-3192 800-878-5828
sales@pulva.com www.pulva.com
Grinding mills, parts and feeders
Owner: Ed Ferree
R&D: Bruce Dene
Quality Control: Bruce Dene
Sales Director: L Ward
ed@pulva.com
Estimated Sales: $ 20 - 50 Million
Number Employees: 20-49
Regions Exported to: Worldwide
Percentage of Business in Exporting: 20

47833 PurJava
PO Box 67233
Lincoln, NE 68506-7233 402-730-3857
Fax: 402-730-6532 info@purjava.com
www.purjava.com

47834 Purac America
111 Barclay Blvd
Lincolnshire, IL 60069 608-752-0449
Fax: 847-634-1992 pam@purac.com
www.purac.com
Producer of lactic acid, lactates and lactitol
President: Gerrit Vreeman
Vice President: Peter Kooijman
Marketing Manager: Casper Ravesteijn
VP Sales: Peter Hooijman
Contact: Lisette Nanning
l.nanning@puracaps.com
Estimated Sales: $ 20 - 50 Million
Number Employees: 20-49
Type of Packaging: Bulk

Importers & Exporters / A-Z

Regions Exported to: Canada, Mexico
Brands Imported: Purac; Purasal; Puracal; Puramex; Purasolv; Lacty
Regions Imported from: Europe

47835 Puratos Canada
520 Slate Dr
Mississauga, ON L5T 0A1
Canada
905-362-3668
Fax: 905-362-0296 info@puratos.ca
www.puratos.com
Dough conditioners, bases and mixes, custards, fruit compounds and fillings, glazes, chocolate products and ganache
President: Eddy Van Belle
Number Employees: 20-49
Square Footage: 160000
Parent Co: Puratos NV
Type of Packaging: Food Service, Private Label, Bulk
Brands Imported: Ladyfruit; Clamr
Regions Imported from: Central America
Percentage of Business in Importing: 1

47836 Purcell International
2499 N Main St
Walnut Creek, CA 94597
Fax: 925-933-3353 800-886-7725
prcl@purcell-intl.com www.purcell-intl.com
Importer of canned and frozen beef, pork, lamb, corned beef, tuna, sardines, shrimp, crab, clams, scallops, mussels, mushrooms, pineapple, grapefruit and mandarin orange sections.
President: Duncan MacLeod
Vice President: John Purcell
Vice President: Warren White
Logistics Manager: Marianne Haines
Estimated Sales: $3 Million
Number Employees: 10-19
Square Footage: 8000
Type of Packaging: Consumer, Food Service, Private Label, Bulk
Brands Imported: Island Sun; Del Sol
Regions Imported from: Central America, South America, Europe, Asia, Australia
Percentage of Business in Importing: 100

47837 Purchase Order Co Of Miami Inc
3724 NW 72nd St
Miami, FL 33147-5820
305-696-2190
Fax: 305-696-2192 poco3724chef@aol.com
Wholesaler/distributor, importer and exporter of caviar, frozen par-baked bagels, truffles, freeze and air-dried vegetables, fruits, spices, herbs, milk, juice, flavors, meats, etc.; serving the food service market
Owner: Jerome Lundy
jeromelundy@puradyn.com
Secretary: S Tragash
CFO: R Tragash
Estimated Sales: $5-10 Million
Number Employees: 5-9
Square Footage: 20000
Type of Packaging: Food Service
Brands Exported: Gossner Milk; Sunny Morning; E.D. Foods Ltd.; Van Vooren Game Ranch; Van Drunen Farms; Grey Owl Foods; Select Brands
Regions Exported to: Central America, South America, Europe, Caribbean, Mexico, Canada
Percentage of Business in Exporting: 70
Brands Imported: E.D. Foods; Van Vooren Game Ranch; B&K
Regions Imported from: Central America, South America, Europe, Asia, Middle East
Percentage of Business in Importing: 30

47838 Pure & Secure LLC-Cust Svc
4120 NW 44th St
Lincoln, NE 68524-1623
402-467-9300
Fax: 402-467-9393 800-875-5915
info@mypurewater.com www.mypurewater.com
Manufacturer and exporter of water treatment equipment; also, bottling and molding equipment
President: A E Meder
ae@pureandsecure.com
Sales Manager: Jason Harrington
Sales Manager: Alan Billups
Estimated Sales: $ 5-10 Million
Number Employees: 20-49
Square Footage: 90000
Brands Exported: Total; Pure Water; Ultima
Regions Exported to: Worldwide
Percentage of Business in Exporting: 75

47839 Pure Fit Nutrition Bars
216 Technology Dr # E
Irvine, CA 92618-2416
949-679-7997
Fax: 949-679-7998 866-787-3348
info@purefit.com www.purefit.com
Manufacturer and exporter of fittings, hoses and assemblies
Founder/ CEO: Robb Dorf
robbdorf@purefit.com
Vice President: Robert Elbich
Sales Manager: John Cooling
Number Employees: 1-4
Parent Co: Nalge Process Technologies
Regions Exported to: Worldwide
Percentage of Business in Exporting: 20

47840 Pure Food Ingredients
514 Commerce Pkwy
Verona, WI 53593
608-845-9601
Fax: 608-845-9628 800-355-9601
stan@itis.com
Canned tomatoes, chiles, jalapenos and olives; beeswax and honey
President: Stanley Kanter
Estimated Sales: $1,000,000
Number Employees: 5-9
Square Footage: 40000
Type of Packaging: Consumer, Food Service, Private Label, Bulk
Regions Imported from: Europe, Asia
Percentage of Business in Importing: 50

47841 (HQ)Pure Foods
32533 Cascade View Drive
Sultan, WA 98294-7733
360-793-2241
Fax: 360-793-2485
Molasses and honey
President: Michael Ingalls
CEO: Denice Ingalls
Contact: Brian Albans
balbans@purefoodsco.com
Plant Manager: Dan Johnson
Estimated Sales: $5,000,000
Number Employees: 20 to 49
Square Footage: 36000
Type of Packaging: Consumer, Food Service, Private Label, Bulk
Brands Exported: Millers; Heins; Pure Gold
Regions Exported to: Europe, Asia
Percentage of Business in Exporting: 10
Regions Imported from: Central America, South America, Asia
Percentage of Business in Importing: 60

47842 Pure Life Organic Foods
6625 W Sahara Ave
Suite 1
Las Vegas, NV 89146
708-990-5817
info@purelifeorganicfoods.com
www.purelifeorganicfoods.com
Organic sugars, coconut milk and coconut oil
Managing Director: Pradeep Mathur
Sales and Marketing Head: Sayida Bano
Parent Co: Pure Diets Intl. Ltd.
Type of Packaging: Bulk
Regions Exported to: Europe, USA, Israel, Australia

47843 Pure Sales
660 Baker St
Suite 367
Costa Mesa, CA 92626-4470
714-540-5455
Fax: 714-540-5974 puresales@aol.com
Export broker of organically grown ingredients
President: James Silver
puresales@aol.com
Estimated Sales: $2.5 Million
Number Employees: 1-4
Type of Packaging: Private Label, Bulk
Brands Exported: Organically Grown Ingredients
Regions Exported to: Europe, Asia

47844 Pure Source LLC
9750 NW 17th St
Doral, FL 33172-2753
305-477-8111
Fax: 305-477-4002 800-324-6273
info@thepuresource.com www.thepuresource.com
Vitamins, antioxidants, raw materials and packaging services
Owner: Joel Meyer
sylvia@thepuresource.com
Estimated Sales: Below $ 5 Million
Number Employees: 100-249
Square Footage: 280000
Type of Packaging: Consumer, Food Service, Private Label, Bulk
Regions Exported to: Central America, South America, Europe, Canada, Caribbean, Mexico
Percentage of Business in Exporting: 10
Regions Imported from: Worldwide

47845 Pure Sweet Honey Farms Inc
514 Commerce Pkwy
Verona, WI 53593-1841
608-845-9601
Fax: 608-845-9628 800-355-9601
map007@earthlink.net www.puresweethoney.com
Honey, maple syrup and molasses
President: Stanley Kanter
stan@chorus.net
Sales Director: Mark Pelka
Estimated Sales: $470000
Number Employees: 5-9
Square Footage: 80000
Type of Packaging: Consumer, Food Service, Private Label, Bulk
Regions Imported from: South America, Asia, Mexico
Percentage of Business in Importing: 50

47846 PureCircle USA
200 W Jackson Blvd
8th Floor
Chicago, IL 60606
630-361-0374
info.usa@purecircle.com
purecircle.com
Stevia
CEO: Lai Hock Meng
CFO: Lim Kian Thong
Year Founded: 2001
Estimated Sales: $127 Million
Parent Co: PureCircle Limited
Type of Packaging: Bulk
Regions Exported to: South America, Europe, Asia, Australia, Africa, Canada, Mexico

47847 Puritan Manufacturing Inc
1302 Grace St
Omaha, NE 68110-2591
402-341-3793
Fax: 402-341-4508 800-331-0487
purmfg@ixnetcom.com www.purmfg.com
Custom fabricated conveyors, mixers, hoppers, tanks, cereal puffing machinery and catwalks; exporter of cereal puffing machinery
President/Owner: Bill Waters
VP & General Manager: Dave Waters
Estimated Sales: $5-10 Million
Number Employees: 20-49
Square Footage: 350000
Brands Exported: Puritan
Regions Exported to: Central America, South America, Europe, Asia, Middle East
Percentage of Business in Exporting: 1

47848 Puritan/Churchill Chemical Company
1341 Capital Circle SE
Suite E
Marietta, GA 30067-8718
404-875-7331
800-275-8914
Manufacturer and exporter of deodorants, warewash systems and chemicals, disinfectants and cleaners including kitchen, industrial laundry and window
President: Richard Bruce
VP Finance: Regina Crothers
Director Marketing: Adam Gould
Number Employees: 240
Parent Co: Gibson Chemical Industries
Regions Exported to: Asia
Percentage of Business in Exporting: 5

47849 Purity Factories
96 Blackmarsh Rd
St. John's, NL A1C 5M9
Canada
709-579-2035
Fax: 709-738-2426 800-563-3411
orderdesk@purity.nf.ca www.purity.nf.ca
Jams, fruit syrups and biscuits
General Manager: Doug Spurrell
Sales Manager: Gerry Power
Type of Packaging: Consumer, Food Service, Private Label, Bulk
Brands Exported: Heritage Mills; Classic Milk Lunch
Regions Exported to: USA

Importers & Exporters / A-Z

47850 Purity Products
200 Terminal Dr
Plainview, NY 11803-2312   516-767-1967
Fax: 516-767-1722   800-256-6102
customercare@purityproducts.com
www.puritypgoducts.com
Sauces, mayonnaise, vinegar, mustard, salad dressings, vegetable oils, jellies, pickles
President: William Schroeder
President, Chief Executive Officer: Jahn Levin
jahn@purityproducts.com
CFO: Bruce Morecroft
Vice President of Quality Assurance: Richard Conant
Marketing: Al Rodriquez
Operations: Ricky Montejo
Purchasing Director: Charles Menezes
Estimated Sales: Less Than $500,000
Number Employees: 20 - 49
Square Footage: 400000
Parent Co: Sea Specialties Company
Type of Packaging: Food Service, Private Label, Bulk
Brands Exported: Chef Choice; Purity; Ideal; Cheryl Lynn
Regions Exported to: Central America, South America, Middle East, Caribbean Island
Percentage of Business in Exporting: 60
Regions Imported from: South America, Europe
Percentage of Business in Importing: 18

47851 Purolator Facet Inc
8439 Triad Dr
Greensboro, NC 27409-9018   336-668-4444
Fax: 336-668-4452   800-852-4449
info@purolator-facet.com
www.purolator-facet.com
Manufacturer and exporter of self-cleaning and sterilizable stainless steel filters for viscous fluids, food and steam
President: Russ Stellfox
rstellfox@purolator-facet.com
Program Manager: Mark Willingham
Director Sales/Marketing: Kevin Nelson
Number Employees: 100-249
Square Footage: 360000
Parent Co: Dayco Products
Regions Exported to: South America, Europe, Asia
Percentage of Business in Exporting: 20

47852 Purse Valet
PO Box 9113
Chandler Heights, AZ 85127   602-826-0254
Fax: 602-539-2564   info@pursevalet.com
Contact: Jean Wise
jeanwiselutcf@msn.com

47853 Putnam Group
35 Corporate Dr
Trumbull, CT 06611-6319   203-452-7270
Fax: 203-268-8071
Importer and wholesaler/distributor of promotional items; also, marketing consultant services available
VP: Ann Rerat
Estimated Sales: Less than $ 500,000
Number Employees: 1-4
Regions Imported from: Asia, Mexico
Percentage of Business in Importing: 50

47854 Pyro-Chem
1 Stanton St
Marinette, WI 54143   715-732-3465
Fax: 715-732-3569   800-526-1079
charding@tycoint.com www.pyrochem.com
Manufacturer and exporter of pre-engineered fire fighting systems
CEO: John Fort
Technical Services Engineer: Curt Harding
Technical Services Engineer: Brian Chernetski
General Manager Sales/Marketing: William Vegso
Contact: Edgar Alvarez
ealvarez@tycoint.com
Product Manager: Katherine Adrian
Estimated Sales: $ 1 - 5 Million
Number Employees: 12
Square Footage: 60000
Parent Co: Borg-Warner/Wells Fargo Alarm
Regions Exported to: Europe, Asia, Middle East, Australia
Percentage of Business in Exporting: 60

47855 Pyromation Inc
5211 Industrial Rd
Fort Wayne, IN 46825-5152   260-484-2580
Fax: 260-482-6805   sales@pyromation.com
www.pyromation.com
Manufacturer and exporter of 3A compliant CIP thermocouples. RTDs, temperature sensors, thermowells, transmitters, connection heads, wire and cable
President: Peter Wilson
kim@pyromation.com
Marketing Manager: Greg Craghead
Sales Manager: Scott Farnham
Estimated Sales: $25-30 Million
Number Employees: 100-249
Square Footage: 40000
Regions Exported to: Central America, South America, Europe
Percentage of Business in Exporting: 6

47856 Pyrometer Instrument CoInc
92 N Main St # 18
PO Box 479
Windsor, NJ 08561-3209   609-443-5522
Fax: 201-768-2570   800-468-7976
information@pyrometer.com www.pyrometer.com
Manufacturer, importer and exporter of controllers, sensors, chart recorders, indicators, alarms and portable pyrometers; also, pressure transmitters and temperature measurement systems
Owner: Dave Crozier
sales@pryometer.com
CEO: D Crozier
Marketing: Mickey Otto
Estimated Sales: $2.4 Million
Number Employees: 10-19
Number of Brands: 2
Number of Products: 12
Square Footage: 30000
Brands Exported: Philips; Pyro
Brands Imported: PMA
Regions Imported from: Europe

47857 Q & B Foods
Irwindale, CA   626-334-8090
Fax: 626-969-1587   customerservice@qbfoods.com
www.qbfoods.com
Dressings, marinades, sauces and mayonnaise
President/Owner: Jerry Shepherd
Estimated Sales: $ 20-50 Million
Number Employees: 50-99
Square Footage: 50000
Type of Packaging: Private Label

47858 Q A Supplies LLC
1185 Pineridge Rd
Norfolk, VA 23502-2043   757-855-3094
Fax: 757-855-4155   800-472-7205
info@QAsupplies.com www.qasupplies.com
Supplier of insulated refrigiwear insulated clothing, boots and gloves, hot/cold transport bags & covers, temperature measurements, thermometers and alarms.
President: David Cowles
dcowles@qasupplies.com
Sales: Russ Holt
Number Employees: 10-19
Regions Exported to: Worldwide

47859 Q-Matic Technologies
355 East Kehoe Boulevard
Carol Stream, IL 60188-1817   847-263-7324
Fax: 847-263-7367   800-880-6836
Manufacturer and exporter of conveyor ovens
Sales Manager: David Cook
Production Manager: Frank Agnello
Estimated Sales: $ 1-2.5 Million
Number Employees: 7
Square Footage: 20000
Type of Packaging: Food Service
Brands Exported: Q-Matic Ovens
Regions Exported to: South America, Europe, Asia, Middle East
Percentage of Business in Exporting: 35

47860 Q-Sales & Leasing
16720 Mozart Avenue
Suite A
Hazel Crest, IL 60429-1092   708-331-0094
Fax: 708-339-8294   www.qsales.com
President: John Lanigan Sr
Contact: Tom Larocca
tlarocca@qsales.com

47861 Q.E. Tea
533 Washington Ave
Suite 100
Bridgeville, PA 15017   412-221-4444
800-622-8327
qetea@aol.com
Coffees and teas
President: Paul Rankin
Marketing Manager: Peter Shaffalo
Estimated Sales: $500,000-$1 Million
Number Employees: 5-9
Square Footage: 24000
Regions Exported to: Canada
Percentage of Business in Exporting: 2
Regions Imported from: Asia

47862 (HQ)QBD Modular Systems
5255 Steven Creeks Blvd
#187
Santa Clara, CA 95051   408-890-8924
Fax: 905-459-1478   800-663-3005
daryl@qpd.com   www.qpd.com
Manufacturer and exporter of merchandising coolers and modular display cases
President: Jeff Jaffer
CFO: Mohammed Chowdhary
Number Employees: 40
Regions Exported to: Worldwide
Percentage of Business in Exporting: 50

47863 QBI
500 Metuchen Road
South Plainfield, NJ 07080-4810   908-668-0088
Fax: 908-561-9682
Bioflavonoids, botanical powders, herbs, nutraceuticals, antioxidants, diet and sports supplements, fruit and vegetable powders, extracts and bee pollen
President: Joseph Schortz
VP Finance: Carlos Mendez
Marketing: Joan Naso
Sales Director: Allen Lovitch
International Account Executive: Rena Strauss-Cohen
Plant Manager: Donald Andrejewski
Number Employees: 50-99
Number of Products: 500
Square Footage: 224000
Type of Packaging: Bulk
Brands Exported: PhytoFlow
Regions Exported to: Europe, Canada
Percentage of Business in Exporting: 20
Regions Imported from: South America, Europe, Asia
Percentage of Business in Importing: 45

47864 QMI
426 Hayward Ave N
St Paul, MN 55128-5379   651-501-2337
Fax: 651-501-5797   qmi2@aol.com
Manufacturer and exporter of aseptic sampling and transfer systems for liquids; also, sampling system for bioreactors
President: Darrell Bigalke
Manager: Gwen Raddatz
Estimated Sales: Below $5 Million
Number Employees: 1-4
Square Footage: 8000
Parent Co: Quality Management
Brands Exported: QMI
Regions Exported to: Worldwide
Percentage of Business in Exporting: 25

47865 QMS International, Inc.
1833 Folkway Drive
Mississauga, Ontario, ON
Canada   905-820-7225
Fax: 905-820-7021   info@qmsintl.com
www.qmsintl.com
Manufacturer and supplier of new and refurbished tying machines and supplies for the meat, poultry and seafood industries.
Regions Exported to: USA

47866 QUIKSERV Corp
11441 Brittmoore Park Dr
PO Box 40466
Houston, TX 77041-6919   713-849-5882
Fax: 713-849-5708   800-388-8307
sales@quikserv.com   www.quikservtest.com
Manufacturer and exporter of food service drive-thru windows, security transaction drawers, BR glass, and air curtains; custom fabrications available

527

Importers & Exporters / A-Z

CEO: Jason T. Epps
sales@quikserv.com
Marketing/Sales: Ray Epps
Sales Director: Sophia Navarro
Plant Manager: Jack Weaver
Purchasing Manager: Jason Epps
Number Employees: 20-49
Square Footage: 152000
Brands Exported: Quikserv
Regions Exported to: Worldwide
Percentage of Business in Exporting: 5

47867 Qosina Corporation
2002-Q Orville Dr. N.
Ronkonkoma, NY 11779   631-242-3000
   Fax: 631-242-3230 info@qosina.com
   www.qosina.com
OEM components supplier to the medical, cosmetic, cleanroom, veterinary and pharmaceutical industries.
President/CEO: Scott Herskovitz
Year Founded: 1980
Estimated Sales: $100+ Million
Number Employees: 50-99
Regions Exported to: Europe
Regions Imported from: Europe

47868 (HQ)Qsx Labels
220 Broadway
Everett, MA 2149   617-389-7570
   Fax: 617-381-9280 800-225-3496
   rkaress@qsxlabels.com www.qsxlabels.com
Manufacturer and exporter of labels including thermal, laser, pin feed, graphic, bar code, etc.; also, label applicators and dispensers
President and CEO: Mike Karess
CFO: Robert Karess
Vice President: Robert Karess
Marketing: Robert Karess
Plant Manager: Peter Kozowylt
Estimated Sales: $5-10 Million
Number Employees: 20-49
Square Footage: 120000
Type of Packaging: Private Label
Regions Exported to: Canada
Percentage of Business in Exporting: 1

47869 Quadrel Labeling Systems
7670 Jenther Dr
Mentor, OH 44060-4872   440-602-4700
   Fax: 440-602-4701 800-321-8509
   labeling@quadrel.com www.quadrel.com
Manufacturer and exporter of labeling equipment
President: Lon Deckard
VP/General Manager: Charles Wepler
Marketing: Joe Uhlir
Sales: Christine Burrier
Operations: Shirley Chambers
Estimated Sales: $15-20 Million
Number Employees: 50-99
Square Footage: 80000
Type of Packaging: Consumer, Food Service
Regions Exported to: Central America, South America, Asia

47870 Quaker Chemical Company
PO Box 554
Columbia, SC 29202-0554   803-765-9520
   Fax: 803-765-9522 800-849-9520
   www.quakerchem.com
Janitorial supplies and equipment including mops and floor finish-acrylics for high speed buffers and general use; exporter of cleaning chemicals
President: Josie Hendrix
Contact: Joseph Anderson
anderson@quakerchem.com
Estimated Sales: $5-10 Million
Number Employees: 5-9
Square Footage: 40000
Brands Exported: Quaker
Regions Exported to: Central America, Europe, Asia, Middle East
Percentage of Business in Exporting: 1

47871 (HQ)Quaker Oats Company
555 W. Monroe St.
Suite 1
Chicago, IL 60661   312-821-1000
   www.quakeroats.com
Cookies, oats, oatmeal, farina, granola bars, puffed wheat, puffed rice, barley, groats, shredded wheat, pancake syrups and mixes, flour, corn syrups, baking mixes, pasta and corn meal.
Senior VP/General Manager: Robbert Rietbroek
IT: Mike Lyons
mike.lyons@pepsi.com
Estimated Sales: Over $1 Billion
Number Employees: 10000+
Number of Products: 195
Parent Co: PepsiCo
Type of Packaging: Consumer, Food Service
Regions Exported to: Worldwide

47872 QualiGourmet
3780 rue La Verendrye
Boisbriand, QC J7H 1R5
Canada   514-287-3530
   Fax: 514-287-3510 info@qualigourmet.ca
   www.qualigourmet.ca
Salmon, mackerel, foie gras, duck, trout, caviar, charcuterie, jellies, fruit and wild berries
General Manager: Cathy Sahut
Buyer: Steve Labonte
Number Employees: 5-9
Type of Packaging: Food Service
Regions Exported to: USA
Regions Imported from: Russia

47873 Qualicaps Inc
6505 Franz Warner Pkwy
Whitsett, NC 27377-9215   336-449-7300
   Fax: 336-449-3333 800-227-7853
   info@qualicaps.com www.qualicaps.com
Gelatin capsules
President: Greg Bowers
Sales: Matt Schappert
CFO: Dennis Stella
CEO: Herb Hugill
Quality Control: Schuck Waldroup
Estimated Sales: $ 5-10 Million
Number Employees: 100-249
Parent Co: Shionogi
Type of Packaging: Bulk
Regions Exported to: Europe
Percentage of Business in Exporting: 5
Regions Imported from: Europe, Asia
Percentage of Business in Importing: 5

47874 Qualiform, Inc
689 Weber Drive
Wadsworth, OH 44281   330-336-6777
   Fax: 330-336-3668
   www.qualiformrubbermolding.com
Manufacturer and exporter of custom molded rubber stoppers
President: Nick Antonino
CFO: Andy Antonino
Quality Control: Duane Lawrence
Contact: Andy Antonino
aantonino@qualiforminc.com
Estimated Sales: Below $5 Million
Number Employees: 10

47875 Qualifresh Michel St. Arneault
4605 Thibault Avenue
St. Hubert, QC J3Y 3S8
Canada   450-445-0550
   Fax: 450-445-5687 800-565-0550
French fries
President: Michelle St. Arneaul
National Manager, Sales And Marketing: Marc Dumas
Number Employees: 50-99
Type of Packaging: Consumer, Food Service, Private Label
Brands Exported: Golden Crop; Qualifreeze
Regions Exported to: Central America, South America, Middle East, Canada, Caribbean, Mexico
Percentage of Business in Exporting: 40

47876 (HQ)Quality Cabinet & Fixture Co
885 Gateway Center Way # 201
San Diego, CA 92102-4538   619-266-1011
   Fax: 619-266-0878 quality1@qcfc.com
   www.qcfc.com
Manufacturer, exporter and importer of store fixtures and wood cabinets
President: Tim Paradise
tpa@qcfc.com
Sales/Marketing: Laura Cohen
Estimated Sales: $ 10-20 Million
Number Employees: 100-249
Regions Exported to: Worldwide
Regions Imported from: Worldwide

47877 Quality Container Company
1236 Watson St
Ypsilanti, MI 48198   734-481-1373
   Fax: 734-481-8790 www.qualitycontainer.com
Manufacturer and exporter of high density polyethylene containers
Manager: Rob Salemi
CFO: Jamie Barche
Quality Control: Robert Johnson
VP Sales/Marketing: Robert Bell
Contact: Jamie Barche
jbarche@alphap.com
Estimated Sales: $ 20 - 50 Million
Number Employees: 50-99
Square Footage: 160000
Other Locations:
   Quality Container Company
   Thomasville, GAQuality Container Company
Regions Exported to: Worldwide

47878 Quality Containers
128 Milvan Drive
Weston, ON M9L 1Z9
Canada   416-749-6247
   Fax: 416-749-3293
Manufacturer and exporter of tin cans and slip cover, friction top and open top containers
President: Patrick Henry
Number Employees: 20
Square Footage: 32000
Regions Exported to: USA
Percentage of Business in Exporting: 20

47879 Quality Control Equipment Co
4280 E 14th St
Des Moines, IA 50313-2604   515-266-2268
   Fax: 515-266-0243 www.qcec.com
Manufacturer and exporter of automatic wastewater and dry material samplers, open channel flow meters and flumes
President: Richard Miller
rmiller@qualitycontrolequipmentco.com
Quality Control: Tim Johnston
Sales Director: Joyce Hanson
Manager: Mike Wright
Purchasing Manager: Tim Johnston
Estimated Sales: $1-3 Million
Number Employees: 20-49
Type of Packaging: Bulk
Regions Exported to: Worldwide
Percentage of Business in Exporting: 40

47880 Quality Corporation
2401 S Delaware St
Denver, CO 80223   303-777-6608
   Fax: 303-777-6488 800-383-3018
Manufacturer and exporter of truck-carried forklifts
President: Kc Ensor
CFO: Kenton C Ensor Jr
Contact: Daniel Collins
dcollins@qscorp.net
Estimated Sales: $ 10 - 20 Million
Number Employees: 50-99
Type of Packaging: Bulk
Regions Exported to: Worldwide

47881 Quality Fabrication & Design
955 Freeport Pkwy # 400
Coppell, TX 75019-4455   972-304-3266
   Fax: 972-745-4244
   AlexPier@quality-fabrication.com
   www.quality-fabrication.com
Manufacturer and exporter of stainless steel food processing equipment including corn handling, fryers, seasoning systems, corn cooking systems, conveyors, etc
President: Alex Pier
alexpier@quality-fabrication.com
VP: Vondel Kremeier
Technical Sales: Harvey Norman
Operations Manager: Roger Pier
Estimated Sales: $12-15 Million
Number Employees: 50-99
Square Footage: 170600
Regions Exported to: Central America, South America, Europe
Percentage of Business in Exporting: 70

47882 (HQ)Quality Industries Inc
130 Jones Blvd
La Vergne, TN 37086-3227   615-793-3000
   Fax: 615-793-2347 www.qualityindustries.com

Manufacturer and exporter of food service equipment, stainless steal sifter cabinets; also, custom metal fabrication available
President: Fred Apple
CEO: Stanley Bryan
stanley.bryan@qualityindustries.com
CFO: Jeff Mayfield
CEO: Jeff Mayfield
Quality Control: Terry Tidwell
R&D: Micheal Taylor
Estimated Sales: $ 20 - 50 Million
Number Employees: 250-499
Square Footage: 190000
Regions Exported to: Central America, Europe, Asia

47883 Quality Kitchen Corporation
204 Southern Blvd
Wyoming, DE 19934-1028   302-697-3118
officemail@salame.com
Juices and concentrates: grapefruit and orange
Sales: Jerry McGuire
Estimated Sales: $5,000,000
Number Employees: 20 to 49
Type of Packaging: Consumer, Food Service

47884 Quality Naturally Foods
18830 San Jose Ave
City Of Industry, CA 91748-1325   626-854-6363
Fax: 626-965-0978   888-498-6986
www.qnfoods.com
Bakery mixes, icings, fillings, cappuccino and cocoa drinks
President: Frank Watase
fwatase@qnfoods.com
VP: Lincoln Watase
Sales Manager: Jerry Tuma
Number Employees: 1-4
Square Footage: 224000
Type of Packaging: Food Service, Private Label, Bulk
Regions Exported to: Asia, Mexico
Percentage of Business in Exporting: 30

47885 Quality Sausage Company
1925 Lone Star Dr
Dallas, TX 75212-6302   214-634-3400
Fax: 214-634-2296   www.qualitysausage.com
Meat products including meat balls, taco meat, patties, pizza toppings and pepperoni.
Chairman: Paul Birinyi
CEO: Skippers Adams
CFO: Steve O'Brien
Director of Food Safety: Mark Mar
VP Sales: Tim Burns
Year Founded: 1976
Estimated Sales: $41100000
Number Employees: 100-249
Square Footage: 100000
Parent Co: H.M. International
Type of Packaging: Food Service
Regions Exported to: Europe, Asia, Middle East
Percentage of Business in Exporting: 1
Regions Imported from: Canada
Percentage of Business in Importing: 5

47886 Quality Seating Co
4136 Logan Way
Youngstown, OH 44505-5703   330-747-0181
Fax: 330-747-0183   800-323-2234
www.gasserchair.com
Manufacturer and exporter of furniture including booths, chairs and tables
President: Jay Buttermore
jbuttermore@taylorseating.com
CEO: Roger Gasser
CFO: Frank Joy
Vice President: Marylou Joy
Research & Development: Mel Textoris
Marketing Director: Anthony Johntony
Sales Director: Paula Rapone
Operations Manager: Jim Humparies
Purchasing Manager: Paula Rapone
Estimated Sales: $2.5-5 Million
Number Employees: 20-49
Number of Brands: 1
Number of Products: 100
Square Footage: 200000
Parent Co: Quality Upholstering Company
Regions Exported to: Worldwide
Percentage of Business in Exporting: 5

47887 Quantum Performance Films
601 E Lake St
Streamwood, IL 60107-4101   630-289-5237
Fax: 630-213-6209   800-323-6963
Manufacturer and exporter of flexible polypropylene films
CEO: Robert Dea
Director Marketing: Mark Montsinger
Director Sales: Bill Rowe
Number Employees: 100-249
Square Footage: 1800000
Parent Co: Hood Industries
Regions Exported to: Canada, Mexico
Percentage of Business in Exporting: 1

47888 Quantum Storage SystemsInc
15800 NW 15th Ave
Miami, FL 33169-5606   305-687-0405
Fax: 305-688-2790   800-685-4665
sales@quantumstorage.com
www.quantumstorage.com
Plastic storage containers, metal shelving and mobile storage cabinets and carts
President: Hose Babani
ed@quantumstorage.com
VP: Dean Cohen
Marketing: Jose Babani
Sales: Elizabeth Faller
Estimated Sales: $ 3 - 5,000,000
Number Employees: 10-19
Square Footage: 300000
Parent Co: M&M Plastics
Type of Packaging: Consumer
Regions Exported to: Central America, South America, Europe
Percentage of Business in Exporting: 5

47889 Queen Bee Gardens
262 E Main St
Lovell, WY 82431-2102   307-548-7994
Fax: 307-548-6721   800-225-7553
queenbee@queenbeegardens.com
Confectionery: truffles, pralines, toffee, mints and turtles
President: Clarence Zeller
Partner: Von Zeller
Vice President: Gene Zeller
Executive Secretary: Bessie Zeller
Estimated Sales: $ 3 - 5 Million
Number Employees: 10-19
Square Footage: 80000
Type of Packaging: Consumer, Private Label, Bulk
Brands Exported: Q-Bee; Honey Essence
Regions Exported to: Canada
Percentage of Business in Exporting: 1

47890 Queensway Foods Company
1611 Adrian Rd
Burlingame, CA 94010   650-871-7770
Fax: 650-697-9966   info@qfco.com
www.qfco.com
Chicken powder, rice sticks, peanuts, sugar, vegetable oils, preserved fruits, candy
Owner: May Huang
Contact: Ashly Grzyb
ashly.grzyb@redtri.com
Manager: Tim Yuen
Estimated Sales: $ 5-10 Million
Number Employees: 5-9
Brands Imported: Many
Regions Imported from: Asia

47891 Queensway Foods Inc.
1611 Adrian Rd
Burlingame, CA 94010   650-697-2233
Fax: 650-697-9966   888-737-3663
www.qfco.com
Importer and exporter of canned fruit juice concentrates, tomatoes, mushrooms, corn, water chestnuts, orange sections, pineapples, tuna and oriental food products
Owner: May Huang
General Manager: Frances Huang
Sales Manager: Joey Lo
Contact: Ashly Grzyb
ashly.grzyb@redtri.com
Estimated Sales: $5-10 Million
Number Employees: 5-9
Square Footage: 200000
Regions Imported from: Asia
Percentage of Business in Importing: 100

47892 Quelle Quiche
814 Hanley Industrial Court
Brentwood, MO 63144-1403   314-961-6554
Quiches: lorraine, spinach, broccoli and crab meat
President: Eric Victor Cowle
VP: G Daniella Cowle
Number Employees: 10-19
Square Footage: 34000
Parent Co: Renaissance Foods
Type of Packaging: Consumer, Food Service, Private Label
Brands Exported: Quelle
Regions Exported to: Central America, South America, Europe, Asia
Percentage of Business in Exporting: 5

47893 Quest Corp
12900 York Rd
North Royalton, OH 44133-3623   440-230-9400
Fax: 440-582-7765   info@2quest.com
www.2quest.com
Electronic scales, weighing and batching systems and data acquisition/transmission systems; exporter of weighing and batching systems
Owner: David Fischer
dfischer@2quest.com
Sales/Marketing Manager: Daniel Donovan
Operations Manager: Jerome Kelly
Estimated Sales: $2.5-5 Million
Number Employees: 19
Regions Exported to: Central America, South America, Asia
Percentage of Business in Exporting: 8

47894 Quick Point Inc
1717 Fenpark Dr
Fenton, MO 63026-2939   636-343-9400
Fax: 636-343-3587   800-638-1369
www.quickpoint.com
Manufacturer, supplier and exporter of advertising specialties
CEO: John Goessling
CFO: Doug Bozler
Vice President: Duane Mayer
Marketing Director: Duane Mayer
Sales Director: Joe Keely
Operations Manager: Rick Smith
Production Manager: Bryan Frenzel
Purchasing Manager: Dave Miller
Number Employees: 100-249

47895 Quickdraft
1525 Perry Dr SW
Canton, OH 44710-1098   330-477-4574
Fax: 330-477-3314   www.quickdraft.com
Hot dog/sausage casing removal systems, draft inducer's to vent out the heat produced from ovens & boilers and food conveying systems.
Manager: Joseph Ovnic
joe.ovnic@quickdraft.com
Number Employees: 20-49
Regions Exported to: Worldwide

47896 Quigley Industries Inc
38880 Grand River Ave
Farmington, MI 48335-1526   248-426-8600
Fax: 248-426-8607   800-367-2441
sales@quigleyind.com   www.quigleyind.com
Confections and lozenges
Owner: Carol Quigley
VP: David Hess
Marketing: Libby Moyer
Plant Manager: Tom Nissley
Purchasing Director: William Latsha
Estimated Sales: $9500000
Number Employees: 20-49
Square Footage: 72000
Parent Co: Joel
Type of Packaging: Consumer, Private Label, Bulk
Brands Exported: Lannaman's; Simon's; College Farm Organic
Regions Exported to: Asia

47897 Quinault Pride
100 W Quinault St
Taholah, WA 98587   360-276-4431
Fax: 360-276-4880
Salmon: precooked, canned and foil pouched
Manager: Alan Heather
sunderwood@quinault.org
CFO: William Parkshurst
Sales Exec: David Underwood
Estimated Sales: $ 5 - 10 Million
Number Employees: 20-49

Importers & Exporters / A-Z

Type of Packaging: Consumer, Food Service, Private Label, Bulk
Regions Exported to: Worldwide
Percentage of Business in Exporting: 3

47898 Quinoa Corporation
PO Box 279
Gardena, CA 90248   310-217-8125
        Fax: 310-217-8140 quinoacorp@aol.com
Pasta and grains
President: Dave Schnorr
Contact: Tom Spielberger
toms@quinoa.net
Estimated Sales: Below $ 5 Million
Number Employees: 1-4
Type of Packaging: Bulk

47899 Quip Industries
1 Lakeway Dr
Carlyle, IL 62231   618-594-2437
        Fax: 618-594-4707
Wholesaler/distributor of tablecloths, napkins, aprons and skirts; serving the food service market
President: James Bolk
CEO: Tim Bolk
Sales Manager: Mike Bolk
Account Specialty: Millie Lampe
Estimated Sales: $20-50 Million
Number Employees: 100-249

47900 Quipco Products Inc
1401 Mississippi Ave
Suite 5
Sauget, IL 62201-1084   314-993-1442
        Fax: 618-271-2311
Manufacturer and exporter of custom and standard service food equipment including counters, racks, sinks and tables; also, custom stainless steel fabrication available
President: James Nations
nations@nationsfoodservice.com
VP/Owner: Jerry Chervitz
Office Manager: Tena Holmes
Estimated Sales: $ 1 - 3 Million
Number Employees: 5-9
Square Footage: 40000
Regions Exported to: Central America, South America, Mexico, Caribbean
Percentage of Business in Exporting: 4

47901 Qzina Specialty Foods
1726 W Atlantic Blvd
Pompano Beach, FL 33069-2857   954-590-4000
        rex.ciavola@qzina.com
        www.qzina.com
Wholesaler distributor of baking ingredients such as; semi sweet chocolate, milk chocolate, white chocolate, pure fountain chocolate, cups and decorations, pastry ingredients, molds and other equipment
President: Rex Ciavola
Founder/CEO: Richard Foley
CFO: Bryan Grobler
VP Sales USA & Canada: Tony Canino
Estimated Sales: $18.3 Million
Number Employees: 100
Square Footage: 25000
Type of Packaging: Food Service
Regions Imported from: Europe

47902 R A Jones & Co Inc
2701 Crescent Springs Pike
Ft Mitchell, KY 41017-1591   859-341-1807
        Fax: 859-341-0519 www.rajones.com
Manufacturer and exporter of automatic carton loading machines, case and tray packers, continuous web form, fill and seal machinery, bottle uncasers, pouch makers, fillers and robotic solutions; also provide complete partial lineintegration services
CEO: Barry Shoulders
shoulders.b@rajones.com
Estimated Sales: $300,000-500,000
Number Employees: 250-499
Parent Co: The Coesia Group
Regions Exported to: Central America, South America, Europe, Asia, Middle East

47903 R F Hunter Co Inc
113 Crosby Rd # 9
Dover, NH 03820-4389   603-742-9565
        Fax: 603-742-9608 800-332-9565
        info@rfhunter.com www.rfhunter.com
Manufacturer and exporter of filtration equipment for edible oils

President: Paul Santoro
sales@rfhunter.com
Estimated Sales: $ 500,000 - $ 1 Million
Number Employees: 5-9
Brands Exported: Hunter Filtrator; Ecco One; HF Series; Mini Max III
Regions Exported to: Worldwide
Percentage of Business in Exporting: 20

47904 R H Saw Corp
28386 W Main St
Barrington, IL 60010-1830   847-381-8777
        Fax: 847-381-9492 rhsaw@aol.com
Manufacturer, importer and exporter of cutlery, blades, grinder plates and knives including metal, wood and plastic
President: Ralph Hirsch
rhsaw@aol.com
CEO: Larry Adler
Estimated Sales: $ 500,000-$ 1 Million
Number Employees: 1-4
Regions Exported to: Central America
Regions Imported from: Central America

47905 R K Electric Co Inc
7405 Industrial Row Dr
Mason, OH 45040-1301   513-204-6060
        Fax: 513-204-6061 800-543-4936
        www.rke.com
Manufacturer and exporter of relays and voltage suppressors for HVAC applications
President: John L Keller
jkeller@rke.com
Estimated Sales: $ 5 - 10 Million
Number Employees: 10-19
Regions Exported to: Canada

47906 R M Felts' Packing Co
35497 General Mahone Blvd
Ivor, VA 23866-2859   757-859-6131
        Fax: 757-859-6381
        customerservice@feltspacking.com
        www.shopvafinest.com
Smoked ham and picnic hams
President: Robert M Felts Jr
CEO: Charles Stallard
Vice President: Robbie Feuts
Estimated Sales: $ 3 - 5 Million
Number Employees: 20-49
Square Footage: 68000
Type of Packaging: Consumer, Food Service, Private Label
Brands Exported: Southampton
Regions Exported to: Caribbean
Percentage of Business in Exporting: 2

47907 R R Street & Co
215 Shuman Blvd # 403
Naperville, IL 60563-5100   630-416-4244
        Fax: 630-416-4150 www.4streets.com
Manufacturer and exporter of dry cleaning detergents, fabric finishes, spotters and filtration products
President: L R Beard
lbeard@4streets.com
CFO: James Beecher
Estimated Sales: $ 5 - 10 Million
Number Employees: 5-9

47908 R T C
2800 Golf Rd
Rolling Meadows, IL 60008-4023   847-640-2400
        Fax: 847-640-5175 gcohen@rtc.com
Manufacturer and exporter of merchandising displays, signs, nonmechanical coolers and interactive, electronic, in store point of purchase displays
President: Bruce Vierck
CEO: Richard Nathan
rnathan@rtc.com
Sr VP: Howard Topping
Estimated Sales: $500,000-$1 Million
Number Employees: 250-499
Square Footage: 700000
Regions Exported to: Worldwide
Percentage of Business in Exporting: 10

47909 R T Foods Inc
11333 N Scottsdale Rd
Suite 105
Scottsdale, AZ 85254-5186   480-596-1089
        Fax: 480-596-3315 888-258-4437
        www.rtfoods.com
Tempura and breaded shrimp
Owner: Jeff Krause
jeff@rtfoods.com

Number Employees: 1-4

47910 R Torre & Co
233 E Harris Ave
S San Francisco, CA 94080-6807   650-875-1200
        Fax: 650-875-1600 800-775-1925
        www.torani.com
Italian flavoring syrups and fruit bases
Principal & Owner: Paul Lucheta
CEO: Melanie Dulbecco
CFO: Scott Triou
VP Research, Development & Innovation: Don Birnbaum
VP Marketing: Julie Garlikov
Director of Human Resources: Ro Carbone
Estimated Sales: $19.7 Million
Number Employees: 100-249
Square Footage: 330000
Type of Packaging: Consumer, Food Service
Brands Exported: Torani
Regions Exported to: Europe, Asia, Canada, Mexico
Percentage of Business in Exporting: 5

47911 R X Honing Machine Corp
1301 E 5th St
Mishawaka, IN 46544-2899   574-259-1606
        Fax: 574-259-9163 800-346-6464
        www.rxhoning.com
Manufacturer and exporter of honing and sharpening machines for restaurant knives
President: R J Watson
Estimated Sales: $5-10 Million
Number Employees: 5-9
Square Footage: 11000
Brands Exported: Mini Rx Hone
Regions Exported to: Central America, South America, Europe, Asia, Middle East, Worldwide

47912 R&A Imports
1439 El Bosque Ct
Pacific Palisades, CA 90272   310-454-2247
        Fax: 310-459-3218 zonevdka@gte.net
Vodka
President: Veronica Pekarovic
Estimated Sales: $1-$2.5 Million
Number Employees: 1 to 4
Regions Imported from: Italy, Mexico

47913 R&J Farms
9800 West Pleasant Home Road
West Salem, OH 44287   419-846-3179
        Fax: 419-846-9603 rjfarms@rjfarms.com
        www.rjfarms.com
Soy beans, sesame and sunflower seeds, grains, flour, microwaveable popcorn, chips and pretzels, garbanzo beans
Owner: Todd Driscoll
Number Employees: 5-9
Square Footage: 80000
Type of Packaging: Consumer, Private Label, Bulk
Brands Exported: Country Grown
Regions Exported to: Europe, Asia
Brands Imported: Whole Earth
Regions Imported from: Europe
Percentage of Business in Importing: 5

47914 R&R Mill Company
48 W 1st S
Smithfield, UT 84335-1956   435-563-3333
        Fax: 435-563-4093
Exporter of hand wheat mills; importer of corn and grain mills; wholesaler/distributor of hand and electric corn/wheat mills, dehydrators, wheatgrass juicers, kitchen appliances, etc.; serving the food service market
President: Ralph Roylance
Head Shipper: Bart Roylance
Office Manager/Head Shipper: Char Izat
Estimated Sales: Less than $500,000
Number Employees: 1-4
Parent Co: Smithfield Implement Company
Brands Exported: Corona
Regions Exported to: Central America, Europe, Canada
Percentage of Business in Exporting: 3
Brands Imported: Corona
Regions Imported from: South America

47915 R&R Sales Company
2800 NE Loop 410 # 207
San Antonio, TX 78218-1525   210-226-5101
        Fax: 210-225-4415 800-821-1765

Wholesaler/distributor/importer/exporter of jalapeno peppers and private label and general line items; serving supermarket chains and the food service market
President: David Rodriguez
CEO: L Rodriguez
Estimated Sales: $1 Million
Number Employees: 1-4
Number of Brands: 10
Number of Products: 500
Square Footage: 50000
Type of Packaging: Food Service
Regions Exported to: Mexico
Brands Imported: Rosita; San Marcos
Regions Imported from: Europe, Asia, Mexico, China, Belgium
Percentage of Business in Importing: 2

47916 R.A.V. Colombia
3750 W 5400 S
Kearns, UT 84118-3574   801-965-9000
Fax: 801-965-9022
Importer of tropical fruit purees used in juices, sorbets, sherbets and yogurt; including feijoa, tamarillo, guanabana, borojo, pitella, uchuba, etc
Manager: Michael Cheneey
Estimated Sales: $ 3 - 5 Million
Number Employees: 5-9
Regions Imported from: Central America, Colombia

47917 R.B. Morriss Company
1531 Deer Crossing Dr
Diamond Bar, CA 91765-2627   909-861-8671
Fax: 909-860-5272
Importer and exporter of juice concentrates, tropical purees and juices, tomato paste and sauces, dried vegetables and fruits, freeze dried shrimp, nuts, spices, corn products, drink mixes, gelatin, crackers, soup bases, etc; alsowaste treatment remediation
CEO/President: Bob Morriss
VP: Paul Chung
VP: Sam Kim
Number Employees: 5-9
Square Footage: 9600
Type of Packaging: Consumer, Private Label, Bulk
Regions Exported to: Central America, Asia, Mexico
Percentage of Business in Exporting: 85
Regions Imported from: Central America, South America, Asia
Percentage of Business in Importing: 15

47918 R.E. Meyer Company
4611 W Adams Street
Lincoln, NE 68524-1444   402-474-8500
Fax: 402-470-4380 888-990-2333
onlineorders@meyerfoods.com
Beef and pork
Owner: Robert Meyer
Number Employees: 100-249
Parent Co: Meyer Holdings
Type of Packaging: Food Service, Private Label, Bulk
Regions Exported to: Worldwide

47919 R.H. Chandler Company
1040 Claridge Pl
Saint Louis, MO 63122-2431   314-962-9353
Fax: 314-962-1661
Manufacturer and importer precision machined parts
President: Robert H Chandler
Number Employees: 7
Square Footage: 23200
Regions Imported from: Central America

47920 R.L. Zeigler Company
1 Plant St.
Selma, AL 36703   205-758-3621
Fax: 205-758-0185 800-392-6328
zeigler@zmeats.com www.zmeats.com
Lunch meats, bacon and frankfurters
Chairman/Director: James Hinton
CEO/Director: W Lackey
CFO: Ken Fitzgerald
Contact: Spencer Harris
spencerharris@zmeats.com
Year Founded: 1927
Estimated Sales: $ 35 Million
Number Employees: 20-49
Square Footage: 100000
Type of Packaging: Consumer, Food Service, Private Label
Brands Exported: Zeigler; Talmadge Farms
Regions Exported to: Central America, South America, Asia, Russia
Percentage of Business in Exporting: 15

47921 R.M. Palmer Co.
77 S. 2nd Ave.
West Reading, PA 19611   610-372-8971
sales@rmpalmer.com
www.rmpalmer.com
Confectionery items, such as chocolates.
President: Richard Palmer
Treasurer/CFO: Charles Shearer
Year Founded: 1948
Estimated Sales: $150-200 Million
Number Employees: 850
Number of Products: 500
Square Footage: 330230
Type of Packaging: Consumer, Bulk

47922 R.W. Garcia
100 Enterprise Way
Suite C230
Scotts Valley, CA 95066   408-287-4616
Fax: 408-287-7724 rwgarcia.com
Tortilla chips and crackers
Owner: Robert Garcia
Sales Manager: Jake Stenton
robert_garcia@bd.com
Estimated Sales: $ 10 - 20 Million
Number Employees: 100-249
Square Footage: 60000
Parent Co: R.W. Garcia Company
Type of Packaging: Private Label
Brands Exported: Santa Cruz; R.W. Garcia
Regions Exported to: South America, Europe
Percentage of Business in Exporting: 15

47923 RAM Center
5140 Moundview Dr
Red Wing, MN 55066   651-385-2271
Fax: 651-385-2180 800-309-5431
info@autoequipllc.com www.autoequipllc.com
Manufacturer and exporter of systems for robotic packaging and material handling; including palletizers for cold room and washdown applications
General Manager: Steve Halverson
R&D: Cory Doln
Executive VP: Dave Muelken
Quality Control: Dave Mulken
Director Sales/Marketing: Steve Valade
Estimated Sales: $ 10 - 20 Million
Number Employees: 20-49
Parent Co: RAM Center
Regions Exported to: Canada, Caribbean, Korea
Percentage of Business in Exporting: 5

47924 RAM Center: Automated Equipment Group (AEG)
5128 Moundview Drive
Red Wing, MN 55066-1100   651-385-2187
Fax: 651-385-2166

47925 RAO Contract Sales Inc
94 Fulton St # 4
Paterson, NJ 07501-1200   201-652-1500
Fax: 973-279-6448 888-324-0020
info@rao.com www.rao.com
Manufacturer and exporter of menu and bulletin boards, pedestal displays, etc
Owner: Brian Bergman
brian@rao.com
Account Executive: George Cross
Account Executive: Marsha Holland
Estimated Sales: $ 1 - 5 Million
Number Employees: 5-9
Square Footage: 40000
Regions Exported to: Europe, Asia
Percentage of Business in Exporting: 15

47926 RAS Process Equipment Inc
324 Meadowbrook Rd
Trenton, NJ 08691-2503   609-371-1220
Fax: 609-371-1200 www.ras-inc.com
Manufacturer and exporter of process equipment including pressure vessels, heat exchangers, reactors, columns and storage tanks
Owner: John Bonacorda
jbonacorda@ras-inc.com
Director: John Bonacorda
VP: John Bonacorda
Estimated Sales: $ 5 - 10 Million
Number Employees: 20-49
Square Footage: 80000
Regions Exported to: Asia

47927 RCW International
3603 Greenhill Drive
High Point, NC 27265-1821   336-869-1251
Exporter of powdered milk, butter and shortening
Contact: Al Bundy
alanb@self-help.org

47928 RDM International
11643 Otsego Street
North Hollywood, CA 91601-3628   818-985-7654
Fax: 818-760-2376 bobmoore@rdmintl.com
www.rdmintl.com
Processor, importer and exporter of fruits including frozen, dried, powderes, flakes and canned; also, fruit concentrates and purees, oils, nuts, pumpkin, sweet potatoes/yams and coconut
President/Sales: Bob Moore
Operations: Peri Abel
Number of Brands: 135
Number of Products: 280
Square Footage: 276000
Type of Packaging: Food Service, Private Label, Bulk
Brands Exported: Berry Fine Raspberries; Big Banana Puree; Big Red Rhubarb; Perfect Peach; Rippin Cherries; Mountain Mats' Apples; Fruit To The World; Rain Sweet; Petes Pumpkin; Bubba's Yarns
Regions Exported to: Central America, South America, Europe, Asia, Middle East, Australia, New Zealand
Percentage of Business in Exporting: 20
Brands Imported: Moore's Advantage; Big Banana; Pacific Coconut; OSO Grande Raisins
Regions Imported from: Central America, South America, Europe, Asia, Middle East, South Africa, Phillipines, Australia, New Zealand
Percentage of Business in Importing: 40

47929 RENFRO Foods Inc
815 Stella St
Fort Worth, TX 76104-1495   817-336-3849
Fax: 817-336-7910 jc@interstargroup.com
www.renfrofoods.com
Relishes, sauces, peppers and salsas
President: Doug Renfro
CEO: Bill Renfro
bill.renfro@renfrofoods.com
Vice President: Becky Renfro
Marketing: Dan Fore
InterStar PR: Jane Cohen
VP Production: James Renfro
Estimated Sales: $3.3 Million
Number Employees: 50-99
Number of Products: 27
Type of Packaging: Consumer, Food Service, Private Label
Brands Exported: Mrs. Renfro's
Regions Exported to: South America, Europe
Percentage of Business in Exporting: 5

47930 RFi Ingredients
300 Corporate Dr
Suite 14
Blauvelt, NY 10913-1162   845-358-8600
Fax: 845-358-9003 800-962-7663
trishad@rfiingredients.com
www.rfiingredients.com
Antioxidants, antimicrobials, preservatives, natural colors; fruit, vegetable and botanical extracts
President & CEO: Jeff Wuagneux
jeffw@rfiingredients.com
Vice President, R&D: Ginny Bank
Executive Vice President: Trisha Devine
Chief Operating Officer: Drew Luce
Estimated Sales: $ 4 - 5 Million
Number Employees: 50-99
Number of Brands: 5
Type of Packaging: Bulk
Regions Imported from: Worldwide
Percentage of Business in Importing: 50

47931 (HQ)RMF Companies
4417 Martha Truman Rd
Grandview, MO 64030-1119   816-839-9258
info@rmfworks.com
www.rmfworks.com
Manufacturer and exporter of food processing equipment focusing on flow-thru massaging, marinating, deboning and portioning; vacuum packaging equipment; freezers and chilling equipment; and engineering services, including turnkeysystems and plant design. Parent company of RMF Steel, Challenge RMF & RMF Freezers.

Importers & Exporters / A-Z

President/CEO: Jeff Brauner
Estimated Sales: $ 50-100 Million
Number Employees: 50-99
Regions Exported to: Worldwide

47932 RMI-C/Rotonics Manaufacturing
736 Birginal Dr
Bensenville, IL 60106-1213   630-773-9510
Fax: 630-773-4274 chicago@rotonics.com
www.rotonics.com
Manufacturer and exporter of polyethylene containers molded from FDA/USDA approved resin including material handling, shipping and storage; also, barrels, drums, tilt trucks, mobile bins, totes and custom molded parts available
Manager: Jay Rule
Sales Director: Michael Morrison
Estimated Sales: $ 20 - 50 Million
Number Employees: 50-99
Square Footage: 38000
Parent Co: Rotonics Manufacturing
Type of Packaging: Bulk
Regions Exported to: Canada
Percentage of Business in Exporting: 1

47933 RMS-Touch/Web4Pos
9 West Ridgely Road
Timonium, MD 21093   201-461-9096
Fax: 410-902-5468
President: Richard Adler
Estimated Sales: $ 3 - 5 Million
Number Employees: 10-19

47934 RPA Process Technologies
PO Box 1087
Marblehead, MA 01945-5087   781-631-9707
Fax: 781-631-9507 800-631-9707
www.rosedisplays.com
Manufacturer and exporter of displays including 3-D hanging, hanging sign, window and hall; also, price card holders
President: Michael Hoffman
Assistant to President: Carol Jones
Sales Manager: Tracy Hatfield
Number Employees: 15
Square Footage: 12800
Regions Exported to: Central America, South America, Europe, Asia, Middle East
Percentage of Business in Exporting: 5

47935 RPE Inc
8550 Central Sands Rd
Bancroft, WI 54921-8909   715-335-8480
800-678-2789
rpe@rpespud.com www.rpespud.com
Exporter of potatoes.
Category Manager: Rachel Leach
Estimated Sales: $50 Million+
Number Employees: 50-99
Parent Co: Wysocki Sales

47936 RPM Total Vitality
18032 Lemon Drive
Suite C
Yorba Linda, CA 92886-3386   714-524-8564
Fax: 714-524-3247 800-234-3092
Antioxidants: pollen and dimethylaminoethanol
Owner: Pat McBride
pat@rpmtv.com
Co-Owner: Roger McBride
Number Employees: 1-4
Square Footage: 4000
Brands Exported: Le Tan
Regions Exported to: Europe, Asia
Percentage of Business in Exporting: 10

47937 RTI Shelving Systems
40-19 80th Street
Elmhurst, NY 11373   212-279-0435
Fax: 212-465-1795 800-223-6210
info@rtishelving.com www.rtishelving.com
Manufacturer and exporter of steel filing systems, steel and wire shelving, racks, bins and storage systems
Owner: Bhim Motilal
Office Manager: Darryl Buyckes
Estimated Sales: $ 5 - 10 Million
Number Employees: 10-19
Regions Exported to: Worldwide

47938 RXI Silgan Specialty Plastics
541 Technology Dr
Triadelphia, WV 26059-2711   304-547-9100
Fax: 304-547-9200
silgan_sales@silganplastics.com
www.silganplastics.com
Manufacturer and exporter of plastic caps, jar covers, sifter and plug fitments and bottles; custom injection molding available
VP Engineering: Vice Exner
VP Sales: Tony Marceau
Operations Manager: Phil Sanderson
Estimated Sales: $ 36 Million
Number Employees: 100-249
Square Footage: 168400
Parent Co: Silgan Plastics
Type of Packaging: Consumer, Food Service, Private Label, Bulk
Other Locations:
   RXI Plastics
   Richmond, VARXI Plastics
Regions Exported to: Worldwide
Percentage of Business in Exporting: 1

47939 Rachael's Smoked Fish
150 Switzer Ave
Springfield, MA 01109
800-327-3412
rachaelsfoodcorp.com
Kosher foods: cream cheese, pickled herring, smoked fish and whitefish, salmon and herring salads
Plant Manager: Alan Axler
Number Employees: 38275
Square Footage: 24000
Type of Packaging: Consumer, Food Service, Private Label, Bulk
Brands Exported: Springfield; Axler's

47940 Racine Paper Box Manufacturing
3522 W Potomac Ave
Chicago, IL 60651   773-227-3900
Fax: 773-227-3983
Manufacturer and exporter of boxes including set-up, fancy and folding
President: Navnit Patel
Contact: Atul Patel
atul.patel@ipaksolutions.com
Estimated Sales: $1-2.5 Million
Number Employees: 10-19
Regions Exported to: Worldwide
Percentage of Business in Exporting: 10

47941 Rader Company
8901 La Cienega Boulevard
Suite 101
Inglewood, CA 90301   310-337-7075
Fax: 310-337-7079
dnrader@theradercompany.com
www.theradercompany.com
Importer of beer
Owner: Henry Stetler
Estimated Sales: $2.5-5 Million
Number Employees: 10-19
Brands Imported: Dinklelacher
Regions Imported from: Worldwide
Percentage of Business in Importing: 100

47942 Radiation Processing Division
P.O.Box 5064
Parsippany, NJ 07054-6064   973-267-5660
Fax: 973-267-5667 800-442-1969
Manufacturer and exporter of radiation sanitation and pathogen elimination equipment for the removal of bacteria from raw materials and food ingredients
President: Robert Solotist
President: Bruce Welt PhD
Estimated Sales: $ 1 - 5 Million
Number Employees: 20-49
Square Footage: 120000
Parent Co: Alpha Omega Technology
Regions Exported to: Brazil

47943 Radio Frequency Co Inc
150 Dover Rd
Millis, MA 02054-1335   508-376-9555
Fax: 508-376-9944 rfc@radiofrequency.com
www.radiofrequency.com
Manufacturer and exporter of radio frequency post-baking dryers and pasteurization equipment.
President: Tim Clark
tclark@radiofrequency.com
Estimated Sales: $ 5 - 10 Million
Number Employees: 20-49

Square Footage: 26
Parent Co: Radio Frequency Company
Brands Exported: Macrowave
Regions Exported to: Worldwide

47944 Radius Display Products
800 Fabric Xpress Way
Dallas, TX 75234-7260   972-406-1221
Fax: 972-406-1321 888-322-7429
info@radiusdp.com www.radiusdp.com
Manufacturer and exporter of table skirting and clips.
President: Darla Andrews
dandrews@radiusdisplay.com
CEO: Michelle Stacy
VP Sales: Sherry Day
Estimated Sales: $ 2.5 - 5 Million
Number Employees: 50-99
Brands Exported: Omniclip Ii
Regions Exported to: Worldwide

47945 Radlo Foods
313 Pleasant St
Watertown, MA 02472   617-926-7070
Fax: 617-923-6440 800-370-1439
Eggs and egg products
President & CEO: David Radlo
Contact: Jim Leroy
jiml@radlo.com
Estimated Sales: $2-5 Million
Number Employees: 1-4
Type of Packaging: Consumer, Food Service, Private Label, Bulk
Regions Exported to: Central America, Asia, Middle East

47946 Raffield Fisheries Inc
1624 Grouper Ave
Port St Joe, FL 32456-5144   850-229-8494
Fax: 850-229-8782 eugene@raffieldfisheries.com
www.raffieldfisheries.com
Atlantic herring, black drum, roe, bluefish, blue runner, Jack Crevalle, ladyfish, Spanish sardines, butterfish, goatfish, croakers and crawfish
President: Harold Raffield
harold@raffieldfisheries.com
Secretary/Treasurer: Danny Raffield
Estimated Sales: $ 10 - 20 Million
Number Employees: 50-99
Type of Packaging: Consumer, Food Service, Private Label, Bulk
Percentage of Business in Exporting: 25

47947 Ragold
20 N Wacker Dr
Chicago, IL 60606-2806   312-977-9984
Fax: 312-427-0413 www.ragold.com
Importer of candy including mints, juice-filled, gummies and sugar-free
CEO/President: Jorg Schindler
Director Finance: Arthur Pauly
Executive VP/COO: Rainer Schindler
Number Employees: 10-19
Square Footage: 12000
Type of Packaging: Consumer
Brands Imported: Juicefuls; Velamints
Regions Imported from: Europe, Canada
Percentage of Business in Importing: 70

47948 Ragozzino Foods Inc
10 Ames Ave
Meriden, CT 06451-2912   203-238-2553
Fax: 203-235-5158 800-348-1240
nancy@ragozzino.com www.ragozzino.com
Soups, pastas, sauces, entrees, side dishes and dips.
President: Nancy Ragozzino
CEO: Gloria Ragozzino
gloria@ragozzino.com
VP: John Ragozzino
VP Product Development: Susan Ragozzino
VP Purchasing/Distribution: Ellen Ragozzino
Estimated Sales: $23 Million
Number Employees: 100-249
Number of Brands: 1
Square Footage: 65000
Type of Packaging: Consumer, Food Service, Private Label

47949 Ragtime
4218 Jessup Rd
Ceres, CA 95307-9604   209-667-5525
Fax: 209-634-2667 ragtimewest@earthlink.net
www.ragtimewest.com

Manufacturer and exporter of coin and floppy disk operated pianos, monkey organs, animated food dispensers and dioramas and calliopes; importer of decorative plastic pipe
Owner: Ken Caulkins
ken@ragtime.com
Manager: Glenn Kern
Estimated Sales: $1-2.5 Million
Number Employees: 5-9
Square Footage: 40000
Regions Exported to: South America, Europe, Asia
Percentage of Business in Exporting: 10
Regions Imported from: Asia
Percentage of Business in Importing: 1

47950 **(HQ)Rahco International**
850 A1a Beach Blvd
Suite 121
St Augustine, FL 32080-6954   904-461-9931
Fax: 904-461-9932   800-851-7681
rahcoint@aol.com
Signs, menus and wine lists; importer of wines and gourmet Italian sauces, marmalades and panetone; exporter of Italian style cheeses, signs and wines
President: Alvin Moser
Vice President: Olga Lara-Moser
Contact: Robert Heflin
rheflin@rahco.com
Operations Manager: David Firch
Production Manager: Dale Mull
Estimated Sales: $500,000-$1 Million
Number Employees: 5-9
Number of Brands: 12
Number of Products: 60
Square Footage: 6000
Type of Packaging: Consumer, Food Service, Private Label, Bulk
Other Locations:
  Rahco International
  Agoura Hills, CARahco International
Brands Exported: Park Cheese; Trebon Wines;Doral Italian Foods
Regions Exported to: Central America, South America, Europe, Middle East
Percentage of Business in Exporting: 8
Regions Imported from: Europe, Asia
Percentage of Business in Importing: 10

47951 **Rahmann Belting & Industrial Rubber Products**
3100 Northwest Blvd
Gastonia, NC 28052-1167   704-864-0308
Fax: 704-868-4651   888-248-8148
Manufacturer and exporter of industrial conveyors and transmission belting including oriented nylon, monofilament and food, etc
Owner: Ron Dayton
CEO: Ronald Dayton
Estimated Sales: $ 2.5 - 5 Million
Number Employees: 5-9
Square Footage: 60000
Regions Exported to: Central America, South America, Canada
Percentage of Business in Exporting: 2

47952 **Railex Corp**
8902 Atlantic Ave
Ozone Park, NY 11416-1497   718-845-5454
Fax: 718-738-1020   800-352-3244
tech@railexcorp.com www.railexcorp.com
Supplier and exporter of electric and stationary coat and hat check equipment; also, garment racks
President: Abe Rutkovsky
railex@railexcorp.com
VP: Sam Rutkovsky
Sales: Bill Quirke
Estimated Sales: $ 10 - 20 Million
Number Employees: 20-49
Square Footage: 70000
Brands Exported: Railex
Regions Exported to: Central America, South America, Europe, Asia, Middle East

47953 **RainSoft Water Treatment System**
2080 E. Lunt Ave
Elk Grove Vlg, IL 60007   847-437-9400
Fax: 847-437-1594 comments@rainsoft.com
www.rainsoft.com
Manufacturer and exporter of water treatment equipment including filters, purifiers, reverse osmosis systems and ultraviolet
President: Robert Ruhstorfer
Commercial Department: Bob Krinner
Estimated Sales: $ 1 - 5 Million
Number Employees: 100-249
Square Footage: 280000
Regions Exported to: Central America, South America, Europe, Asia, Middle East, Canada
Percentage of Business in Exporting: 10

47954 **Rainbow Pops**
45 Benbro Dr
Cheektowaga, NY 14225-4805   716-685-4340
Fax: 716-685-0810   800-879-7677
Lollipops
President: Roe Baran
Number Employees: 20-49

47955 **Rainbow Seafoods**
422a Boston St
Topsfield, MA 01983   978-887-9121
Fax: 978-887-9125 www.rainbowseafood.com
Seafood
President: Frank Powell
Sales: Neil Murphy
Estimated Sales: $2,500,000
Number Employees: 9

47956 **Rainbow Valley Frozen Yogurt**
9444 W Shady Grove Ct
White Lake, MI 48386   248-355-1095
Fax: 248-353-3466   800-979-8669
Frozen yogurt mix
President: William Boyda
VP/Treasurer: Laurel Boyda
Estimated Sales: $500,000-$1,000,000
Number Employees: 5-9
Square Footage: 48000
Type of Packaging: Consumer, Food Service, Private Label, Bulk
Brands Exported: Stucchi's
Regions Exported to: Asia, Middle East, Worldwide
Percentage of Business in Exporting: 12

47957 **Rainforest Company**
141 Millwell Dr
Maryland Heights, MO 63043   314-344-1000
Fax: 314-344-3044
michaelm@the-rainforest-co.com
Snacks: cashew and Brazil nut bars, popcorn, salad dressings, salsas, marinades and hot sauces
President: Rick Drevet
Controller: Sherry Dawes
Number Employees: 35
Square Footage: 80000
Regions Exported to: Europe, Asia
Percentage of Business in Exporting: 10
Percentage of Business in Importing: 3

47958 **Rainsweet Inc**
1460 Sunnyview Rd. NE
P.O. Box 7079
Salem, OR 97301   503-363-4293
Fax: 503-585-4657   800-363-4293
linda@rainsweet.com www.rainsweet.com
Frozen blackberries, blueberries, black and red raspberries, boysenberries, IQF and puree cane berries, mushrooms, peppers, onions and bean sprouts
CEO: Rich Brim
richb@rainsweet.com
Quality Assurance Manager: Ian Bennet
Fruit Sales & Customer Service: Linda Ervin
Vegetable Sales: Chantal Wright
Field Manager: Bill Dinger
Estimated Sales: $30.4 Million
Number Employees: 100-249
Square Footage: 130000
Type of Packaging: Consumer, Food Service, Private Label, Bulk
Brands Exported: Rain Sweet Brand
Regions Exported to: Central America, South America, Europe

47959 **Rairdon Dodge Chrysler Jeep**
12828 NE 124th St
Kirkland, WA 98034-8309   425-821-1777
Fax: 425-814-3180
www.dodgechryslerjeepofkirkland.com
Manufacturer and exporter of checkstands and display fixtures
Owner: Jack Carroll
Director Sales: Ginny Hansen
Estimated Sales: $5-10 Million
Number Employees: 50-99
Square Footage: 680000
Regions Exported to: Central America, South America, Caribbean
Percentage of Business in Exporting: 10

47960 **Ralphs Pugh Conveyor Rollers**
3931 Oregon St
Benicia, CA 94510-1101   707-745-6363
Fax: 707-745-3942   800-486-0021
sales@ralphs-pugh.com www.ralphs-pugh.com
Manufacturer and exporter of rollers, idlers and bearings for conveyors
President: William Pugh
williamg@ralphs-pugh.com
Vice President: Tom Anderson
Estimated Sales: $ 5 - 10 Million
Number Employees: 20-49
Regions Exported to: Canada
Percentage of Business in Exporting: 1

47961 **Ram Equipment Co**
W227N913 Westmound Dr
Waukesha, WI 53186-1700   262-513-1114
Fax: 262-513-1115 tiefmach@execpc.com
www.tiefmach.com
Manufacturer and exporter of baking, blending and batching equipment, bins, control systems, enrobers, extruders and feeders; manufacturer of custom, pump feeding systems for pumping high viscosity products for food and industrialapplications
President: James E Tiefenthaler
jtief@tiefmach.com
VP: Norman Searle
Estimated Sales: Less Than $500,000
Number Employees: 1-4
Number of Brands: 2
Number of Products: 20
Square Footage: 4800
Regions Exported to: Central America, South America, Europe, Asia, Middle East
Percentage of Business in Exporting: 20

47962 **Ramarc Foods Inc**
14556 John Humphrey Dr
Orland Park, IL 60462-2640   708-403-1700
Fax: 708-403-2056   800-354-7272
www.ramarcfoods.com
Wholesaler/distributor and exporter of fresh and frozen meats
President: Mark Gehrman
Treasurer: Ray O'Brien
VP: Ray Gehrman
Estimated Sales: $ 20 - 50 Million
Number Employees: 10-19
Square Footage: 3000

47963 **Ramona's Mexican Foods**
13633 S Western Ave
Gardena, CA 90249   310-323-1950
Fax: 310-323-4210 sales@ramonas.com
ramonas.com
Frozen tortillas, burritos, tamales and Mexican dinners
Co-Founder: Ramona Acosta Banuelos
Co-Founder: Alejandro Banuelos
President & CEO: Martin Accosta Torres
Type of Packaging: Consumer, Food Service, Bulk
Regions Exported to: Worldwide

47964 **Ramoneda Bros Stave Mill**
13452 Rixeyville Rd
Culpeper, VA 22701   540-825-9166
Fax: 540-547-3271
Manufacturer and exporter of oak staves
Owner: Vincent Ramoneda
ramonedabros@aol.com
Partner: Vincent Ramoneda
Manager: Vincent Ramoneda
Estimated Sales: $ 5 - 10 Million
Number Employees: 5-9
Regions Exported to: Europe, Asia
Percentage of Business in Exporting: 90

47965 **Ramos Orchards**
9192 Boyce Rd
Winters, CA 95694-9625   530-795-4748
Fax: 530-795-4148
Walnuts, prunes and almonds
Owner: Fred Ramos
Estimated Sales: $4 Million
Number Employees: 20-49
Type of Packaging: Bulk
Regions Exported to: Europe
Percentage of Business in Exporting: 95

Importers & Exporters / A-Z

47966 Ramsey Popcorn Co Inc
5645 Clover Valley Rd NW
Ramsey, IN 47166-8252   812-347-2441
        Fax: 812-347-3336   800-624-2060
info@ramseypopcorn.com www.cousinwillies.com
Microwaveable popcorn
President: Wilfred Sieg
will@ramseypopcorn.com
Controller: Pat Smith
VP Operations: Daniel Sieg
Estimated Sales: $5 Million
Number Employees: 20-49
Type of Packaging: Consumer, Food Service, Private Label, Bulk
Brands Exported: Cousin Willie's
Regions Exported to: Central America, Europe, Asia, Middle East
Percentage of Business in Exporting: 12

47967 Randall Manufacturing Inc
722 N Church Rd
Elmhurst, IL 60126-1402   630-782-0001
        Fax: 630-782-0003   800-323-7424
info@randallmfg.com www.randallmfg.com
Manufacturer and exporter of bulkheads for refrigerator trailer partitions, plastic strip curtains for coolers and freezers and insulated pallet covers and curtain walls
President: Fred Jevaney
fjevaney@randallmfg.com
CFO: Philip Pick
VP: Fred Jevaney
Number Employees: 50-99
Square Footage: 80000
Type of Packaging: Food Service, Bulk
Regions Exported to: Worldwide

47968 Randell Manufacturing Unified Brands
252 South Coldwater Road
Weidman, MI 48893
        Fax: 888-864-7636   888-994-7636
                    www.unifiedbrands.com
Stainless steel preparation tables, custom equipment, refrigerators, freezers, precise temperature solutions, equipment stands, and hot food tables.
Estimated Sales: $ 50 - 100 Million
Number Employees: 250-499
Parent Co: Dover Corporation

47969 Ranger Tool Co Inc
5786 Ferguson Rd
Memphis, TN 38134-4533   901-213-0458
        Fax: 901-386-8088   800-737-9999
Manufacturer and exporter of peelers which remove cellulose casing from frankfurters and sausages
President: Eleanor Kiss
Estimated Sales: $2.5-5 Million
Number Employees: 5-9
Regions Exported to: Worldwide

47970 Rapat Corp
919 Odonnel St
Hawley, MN 56549-4313   218-483-3344
        Fax: 218-483-3535   800-325-6377
                    www.rapat.com
Manufacturer and exporter of material handling equipment including conveyors and conveyor belting
Owner: Thomas Sparrow
Sales Manager: Greg Deal
tsparrow@rapat.com
Estimated Sales: $10-20 Million
Number Employees: 50-99

47971 Rapid Industries Inc
4003 Oaklawn Dr
Louisville, KY 40219-2701   502-968-3645
        Fax: 502-968-6331   800-787-4381
info@rapidindustries.com www.rapidi.com
Manufacturer, importer and exporter of conveyors including trolley, enclosed track, power, free and floor
President: Mary Sheets
Controller: Jansen Nally
Marketing Manager: Paul McDonald
Sales Manager: Walt Hiner
Estimated Sales: $ 20 - 50 Million
Number Employees: 50-99
Type of Packaging: Bulk
Regions Exported to: South America, Europe, Asia, Middle East, Canada, Mexico
Percentage of Business in Exporting: 10

Regions Imported from: Asia
Percentage of Business in Importing: 1

47972 Rapid Pallet
100 Chestnut St
Jermyn, PA 18433-1433   570-876-4000
                    Fax: 570-876-4002
Manufacturer and exporter of lumber pallets
President: John Conrad
conrad@aacr.org
Estimated Sales: $10-20 Million
Number Employees: 50-99
Regions Exported to: Worldwide

47973 Rapid Rack Industries
14421 Bonelli St
City of Industry, CA 91746   626-333-7225
        Fax: 626-333-5265   800-736-7225
                    www.rapidrack.com
Racks and mobile aisle and mezzanine systems; importer of wire storage racks; exporter of wire and storage rack
CEO: William Marvin
CEO: Vaughn Sucevich
Marketing Director: Clara Banegas
VP Sales: Steve Painter
Contact: Margaret Andrade
m_andrade@haylorfinancial.com
Operations Manager: Rosemarie Kodarte
Production Manager: Alfredo Calderon Kodarte
Plant Manager: Ed Sledge
Purchasing Manager: Dennis Fachler
Estimated Sales: $ 30 - 50 Million
Number Employees: 250-499
Square Footage: 192000
Parent Co: Hampshire Equity Partners
Type of Packaging: Consumer
Regions Exported to: Central America, Europe, Canada
Percentage of Business in Exporting: 30
Brands Imported: Silver Fox
Regions Imported from: Asia

47974 (HQ)Rapids Wholesale Equipment
6201 S Gateway Dr
Marion, IA 52302-9430   319-447-3500
        Fax: 319-447-1680   800-472-7431
Wholesaler/distributor and exporter of restaurant equipment and supplies including refrigeration and draft beer coolers and dispensers; serving the food service market
President: Joe Schmitt
Sales/Marketing Executive: Ross Anderson
Estimated Sales: $10-20 Million
Number Employees: 50-99
Square Footage: 40000
Other Locations:
   Rapids
   Cincinnati, OH Rapids
Regions Exported to: Worldwide
Percentage of Business in Exporting: 2

47975 Rath Manufacturing Company
P.O.Box 389
Janesville, WI 53547   608-754-2222
        Fax: 608-754-0889   800-367-7284
Manufacturer and exporter of stainless steel pipes and tubing
President: Harley Aplan
CEO: Michael G Schwartz
VP Sales: James Coenen
Estimated Sales: $ 50 - 100 Million
Number Employees: 100-249
Regions Exported to: Worldwide

47976 Rational Cooking Systems
895 American Lane
Schaumburg, IL 60173-4575   847-755-9583
        Fax: 847-755-9584   888-320-7274
                    info@rationalusa.com
Manufacturer and importer of combination ovens
President: Peter Schon
Marketing Director: Werner Jochem
Sales Director: Robert Bratton
Contact: Gunter Blaschke
g.blaschke@rational-online.com
Estimated Sales: $2.5-5 Million
Number Employees: 20-49
Parent Co: Rational AG
Regions Exported to: Canada, Caribbean
Brands Imported: Rational
Regions Imported from: Europe

47977 Rawlings Sporting GoodsCo Inc
510 Maryville University # 110
St Louis, MO 63141-5821   636-349-3500
        Fax: 314-819-2980   800-323-5590
                    info@hiltoncc.com
CEO: Michael Zlaket
mzlaket@rawlings.com
Estimated Sales: $ 1 - 3 Million
Number Employees: 500-999

47978 Ray Cosgrove Brokerage Company
PO Box 281
Saddle River, NJ 07458-0281 201-825-0979
                    Fax: 201-327-8588
Import and export broker and wholesaler/distributor of seafood, private label items, frozen foods, groceries and health food
President: Ray Cosgrove
Number Employees: 20-49
Type of Packaging: Food Service, Private Label
Brands Exported: Del Pacifico; Ocean Queen
Regions Exported to: Central America, Asia
Brands Imported: Del Pacifico
Regions Imported from: Central America, South America

47979 Ray-Craft
2067 W 41st St
Cleveland, OH 44113   216-651-3330
                    Fax: 216-651-8714
Manufacturer and exporter of advertising novelties and promotional materials
President: Thomas Topp
Office Manager: Agnes Milter
Estimated Sales: $500,000-$1 Million
Number Employees: 9

47980 (HQ)Raymond Corp
22 S Canal St
Greene, NY 13778   607-656-2311
        Fax: 607-656-9005   800-235-7200
                    www.raymondcorp.com
Manufacturer and exporter of electric forklift trucks
President/ Operations: Michael G Field
Chief Financial Officer: Edward J Rompala
VP, General Counsel: Lou Callea
EVP Sales & Marketing: Timothy Combs
VP Sales: Gary Kirchner
EVP, Human Resources: Stephen E VanNostrand
Vice President, Distribution Development: Patrick McManus
Estimated Sales: $130,000
Number Employees: 1000-4999
Square Footage: 1000000
Brands Exported: Swing-Reach; Ordericker; Pacer; Reach-Fork; Fiddler; Pallet Trucks
Regions Exported to: Central America, South America, Asia, Middle East
Percentage of Business in Exporting: 10

47981 Raymond-Hadley Corporation
89 Tompkins St
Spencer, NY 14883   607-589-4415
        Fax: 607-589-6442   800-252-5220
                    www.raymondhadley.com
South and Central American and African foods: barley, beans, bran, flour, cereal, dried fruit, grains, rice, spices, starches, vegetables and corn meal
President: Lori Maratea
Founder: Arthur B. Raymond
Founder: Francis E. Hadley
Vice President of Sales: Tracy McCutcheon
President: Elliot Dutra
Number Employees: 20-49
Square Footage: 204000
Type of Packaging: Bulk
Brands Exported: Phoebe
Regions Exported to: Caribbean
Percentage of Business in Exporting: 10
Regions Imported from: Central America, South America, Asia, Caribbean
Percentage of Business in Importing: 20

47982 Raypak Inc
2151 Eastman Ave
Oxnard, CA 93030-5194   805-278-5300
        Fax: 805-278-5489   www.raypak.com
Manufacturer and exporter of water heating equipment including boosters
Vice President: Michael Sentovich
msentovich@raypak.com
VP: Louis Falzer

Number Employees: 250-499
Square Footage: 235000
Parent Co: Rheem
Other Locations:
   Raypak
   VictoriaRaypak
Regions Exported to: Worldwide
Percentage of Business in Exporting: 1

47983 Raytheon Co
870 Winter St
Waltham, MA 02451-1449   781-522-3000
   Fax: 781-860-2172   www.raytheon.com
Manufacturer and exporter of dehydration equipment for sugar, minerals, chemicals, corn and grain; also, evaporators, vacuum pans, dryers, crystallizers, granulators and coolers; engineering design services available
Chief Executive Officer: Thomas A. Kennedy
tkennedy@raytheon.com
SVP and Chief Financial Officer: David C. Wajsgras
Senior Vice President: Keith J. Peden
Estimated Sales: Over $1 Billion
Number Employees: 10000+
Square Footage: 1200000
Brands Exported: Stearns-Roger
Regions Exported to: Worldwide
Percentage of Business in Exporting: 30

47984 Read Products Inc
3615 15th Ave W
Seattle, WA 98119-1392   206-283-2510
   Fax: 206-282-8339   800-445-3416
   info@cuttingboards.com
   www.sagecuttingsurfaces.com
Manufacturer and exporter of food preparation cutting boards and tools
President: Charles R Read
cread@cuttingboard.com
Marketing Manager: Chuck Read
Inside Sales/Production Manager: Robert Read
Estimated Sales: $5-10 Million
Number Employees: 10-19
Square Footage: 80000
Type of Packaging: Food Service
Regions Exported to: Worldwide
Percentage of Business in Exporting: 3

47985 Readco Kurimoto LLC
460 Grim Ln
York, PA 17406-7949   717-848-2801
   Fax: 717-848-2811   800-395-4959
   readco@readco.com   www.readco.com
Manufacturer and exporter of containerized batch and continuous processing mixers
President: David Sieglitz
Manager: Ce Tyson
gtyson@readco.com
Estimated Sales: $5-10 Million
Number Employees: 20-49
Regions Exported to: Worldwide
Percentage of Business in Exporting: 20

47986 Reading Bakery Systems Inc
380 Old West Penn Ave
Robesonia, PA 19551-8903   610-693-5816
   Fax: 610-693-5512   info@readingbakery.com
   www.readingbakery.com
Manufacturer and exporter of extruders, cookers, topical seasoning applicators, multifuel ovens, guillotine dough cutters, dough handling systems and biscuit, cookie and cracker sheeters and laminators
President: Joseph Zaleski
EVP/ CFO: Chip Czulada
Director of Engineering: Tremaine Hartranft
Director, Science & Innovation Center: Ken Zvoncheck
VP, Sales & Marketing: David Kuipers
VP of Sales: Shawn Moye
Human Resources Manager: Roseann Reinhold
Vice President of Operations: Travis Getz
Estimated Sales: $ 10-20 Million
Number Employees: 50-99
Square Footage: 62000
Regions Exported to: Worldwide
Percentage of Business in Exporting: 30

47987 Reading Coffee Roasters
316 W Main St
Birdsboro, PA 19508-1900   610-582-2243
   Fax: 610-582-3615   800-331-6713
   www.thecoffeegourmet.com
Coffee
Owner: Albert Van Maanen
Co-Owner: Rosemary Hartigan
rdgcofrstr@aol.com
Estimated Sales: $300,000-500,000
Number Employees: 5-9
Type of Packaging: Private Label

47988 Ready Access
1815 Arthur DriveWest
Chicago, IL 60185   630-876-7766
   Fax: 630-876-7767   800-621-5045
   ready@ready-access.com   www.ready-access.com
Manufacturer and exporter of pass-thru windows and air curtain systems for fast food establishments
President: John Radek
CFO: Robert McKeever
R & D: Scott Hammac
Marketing/Sales/Public Relations: Kristy Rivera
Sales Director: Vince Asta
Operations/Production: Bob McKeever
Estimated Sales: $ 5 - 10 Million
Number Employees: 20-49
Square Footage: 70000
Brands Exported: Ready Access
Regions Exported to: Worldwide
Percentage of Business in Exporting: 20

47989 Real Aloe Company
7470 Dean Martin Drive
Suite 102
Las Vegas, NV 89139   877-301-8296
   Fax: 702-462-5880   800-541-7809
   www.realaloeinc.com
Aloe vera gel, juice and beverages
Owner: Frank Mundell
VP: M Mundell
Operations Manager: Dan Mundell
Estimated Sales: $1,100,000
Number Employees: 5-9
Square Footage: 21000
Type of Packaging: Consumer, Food Service, Private Label, Bulk
Brands Exported: Real Aloe Co.; Cal-Aloe Co.
Regions Exported to: Central America, South America, Europe, Asia, Canada
Percentage of Business in Exporting: 50

47990 Real Coconut Co. Inc., The
   www.therealcoconut.com
Gluten-free and dairy-free coconut flour tortillas and snack chips
Founder/President: Daniella Hunter
Number of Brands: 1
Number of Products: 6
Type of Packaging: Consumer, Private Label
Brands Exported: The Real Coconut
Regions Exported to: USA

47991 Real Cookies
3212 Hewlett Avenue
Merrick, NY 11566-5505   516-221-9300
   Fax: 516-221-9561   800-822-5113
Cookie dough and mixes: oatmeal raisin, mocha almond, ginger, macadamia, white chocolate, pecan and chocolate chip
President: Ellyn Knigin
CFO: Leonard Knigin
Vice President: Marian Knigin
Estimated Sales: $500,000-$1 Million
Number Employees: 5-9
Type of Packaging: Consumer, Food Service, Private Label, Bulk
Brands Exported: Real Cookies, Inc.
Percentage of Business in Exporting: 2

47992 Real Kosher Sausage Company
9 Euclid Ave
Newark, NJ 07105-4527   973-690-5394
   Fax: 212-598-9011
Kosher meats, sausage and deli
President/CEO: Jacob Hill
Estimated Sales: $750,000
Number Employees: 10
Square Footage: 60000
Type of Packaging: Consumer, Food Service, Private Label, Bulk
Brands Exported: Real Kosher; 999
Regions Exported to: Central America, South America, Europe, Asia
Percentage of Business in Exporting: 25

47993 Real Soda
124 N 35th St
Seattle, WA 98103   206-632-1050
   soda@ginseng.com
   www.ginseng.com
Wholesaler/distributor, exporter and importer of soft drinks, beer and wine
Number Employees: 5-9
Parent Co: Real Soda in Real Bottles
Regions Exported to: Europe, Asia, Australia
Percentage of Business in Exporting: 20
Regions Imported from: Europe, Australia , Latin America
Percentage of Business in Importing: 10

47994 Recco International
3940 Platt Springs Rd
West Columbia, SC 29170-1606   803-356-4003
   Fax: 803-356-4439   800-334-3008
   sales@reccointernational.com
   www.reccointernational.com
Manufacturer and exporter of printed labels and tapes
Owner: John W Etters
john@reccointernational.com
General Manager: Craig Hall
Estimated Sales: $ 20 - 50 Million
Number Employees: 20-49
Regions Exported to: Europe, Latin America, Mexico
Percentage of Business in Exporting: 40

47995 Rector Foods
2280 N Park Drive
Brampton, ON L6S 6C6
Canada   905-789-9691
   Fax: 905-789-0989   888-314-7834
Seasoning blends
President: Eoin Connell
VP Sales: Michael Parry
Number Employees: 50
Square Footage: 212000
Regions Exported to: Caribbean
Percentage of Business in Exporting: 10

47996 Red Chamber Co
1912 E Vernon Ave
Vernon, CA 90058   323-234-9000
   Fax: 323-231-8888   info@redchamber.com
   www.redchamber.com
Seafood
CEO: Ming Bin Kou
CFO: Ming Shin Kou
VP: Andro Chen
VP, Food Innovation and R&D: Wales Yu
Year Founded: 1973
Estimated Sales: $100-500 Million
Number Employees: 100-249
Regions Exported to: Central America

47997 Red Diamond Coffee & Tea
400 Park Ave
Moody, AL 35004
   800-292-4651
   qcdept@reddiamond.com   www.reddiamond.com
Coffee, tea pods and coffee brewers.
VP, Sales Development: John Padgett
VP, Manufacturing: Joe George
Year Founded: 1906
Estimated Sales: $45.9 Million
Number Employees: 100-249
Square Footage: 195000
Type of Packaging: Consumer, Food Service, Private Label, Bulk
Regions Imported from: Central America, South America, Europe, Asia

47998 Red Hat Cooperative
809 Broadway Avenue E
Redcliff, AB T0J 2P0
Canada   403-548-6208
   Fax: 403-548-7255   sales@redhatco-op.com
   www.redhatco-op.com
Vegetables
President: Albert Cramer
CEO: Lyle Aleman
Quality Control: Cassandra Cadrmin
Sales Manager: Blaine Andres
Operations: Tim Donnelly
Purchasing: Crystal McHargue
Number Employees: 180
Type of Packaging: Consumer, Food Service
Regions Exported to: USA
Percentage of Business in Exporting: 1

Importers & Exporters / A-Z

47999 Red Hot Chicago
4649 W Armitage Ave
Chicago, IL 60639   312-829-3434
    Fax: 312-829-2704   800-249-5226
info@redhotchicago.com www.redhotchicago.com
Wholesaler/distributor of gourmet hot dogs, specialty sausages and processed meats
President: Scott Ladany
Manager: Glenn Olsen
Contact: Billy Ladany
billy@redhotchicago.com
Estimated Sales: $2.5-5 Million
Number Employees: 1-4

48000 Red Kap Image Apparel
PO Box 140995
Nashville, TN 37214-0995   615-565-5000
    Fax: 615-565-5364 www.vfc.com
VP: Scott Shoener
Number Employees: 250-499

48001 Red Pelican Food Products
5650 Saint Jean Street
Detroit, MI 48213-3415   313-881-4095
Mustard, horseradish, relish, sauerkraut, vinegar, cheese, Belgian chocolate and sauce
President: Bernard Cornillie
Sales Manager: D Cornillie
Number Employees: 5-9
Square Footage: 56000
Type of Packaging: Consumer, Food Service, Private Label, Bulk
Brands Imported: Cote 'Dor; Frico
Regions Imported from: Europe
Percentage of Business in Importing: 15

48002 Red River Commodities Inc
501 42nd St N
Fargo, ND 58102-3952
     800-437-5539
contact@redriv.com www.redriv.com
Sunflower seeds, beans, millet, flax, soybeans and organics.
President & CEO: Eric Christianson
VP, Finance: Randy Wigen
Estimated Sales: $105.6 Million
Number Employees: 100-249
Square Footage: 140000
Type of Packaging: Food Service, Private Label, Bulk
Regions Exported to: Europe, Canada, Mexico

48003 Red River Foods Inc
9020 Stony Point Pkwy
Suite 380
Richmond, VA 23235-1944   804-320-1800
    Fax: 804-320-1896 www.redriverfoods.net
Nuts, seeds, dried foods and snack foods
President: James Phipps
Controller: Keith Dickerson
Vice President: Jack Bousfield
Estimated Sales: $10-49.9 Million
Number Employees: 10-19
Number of Products: 30
Regions Exported to: Asia

48004 Red River Lumber Company
2959 Saint Helena Highway N
Saint Helena, CA 94574-9703   707-963-1251
    Fax: 707-963-3142
Manufacturer and exporter of redwood boxes
Estimated Sales: $ 5-10 Million
Number Employees: 20-49
Regions Exported to: Asia
Percentage of Business in Exporting: 1

48005 Red Rose Trading Company
520 N Charlotte St
Lancaster, PA 17603   717-293-7833
Granola, pancake, baking and gluten-free mixes and blends
Owner: J Leichter
Estimated Sales: $ 3 - 5 Million
Number Employees: 10-19
Square Footage: 56000
Type of Packaging: Consumer, Food Service, Private Label, Bulk

48006 Red Smith Foods Inc
4145 SW 47th Ave
Davie, FL 33314-4006   954-581-1996
    Fax: 954-581-6775 www.redsmithfoods.com
Pickled eggs, sausage and pigs' feet
President: Stephen Foster
bburton@redsmithfoods.com
COO: Jon Foster
CFO: Tim Foster
Executive VP: David Foster
Marketing & Sales Director: Brian Burton
Plant Manager: Michael Sandy
Estimated Sales: $8 Million
Number Employees: 20-49
Number of Brands: 2
Number of Products: 6
Square Footage: 48000
Parent Co: Red Smith of Florida, Inc.
Type of Packaging: Consumer
Brands Exported: Big John; Red Smith
Regions Exported to: Caribbean
Percentage of Business in Exporting: 1

48007 Redding Pallet Inc
5323 Eastside Rd
Redding, CA 96001-4534   530-241-6321
    Fax: 530-241-3475 www.redding.com
Manufacturer and exporter of hardwood and softwood pallets
President: Don Lincoln
Estimated Sales: $ 1 - 5 Million
Number Employees: 10-19

48008 Redi-Call Inc
5655 Riggins Ct # 22
Reno, NV 89502-6554   775-331-0183
    Fax: 775-331-2730   800-648-1849
sales@redi-callusa.com www.redi-callusa.com
Manufacturer, importer and exporter of stainless steel cup and lid dispensers, condiment holders for bars, circular wheel check holders for restaurant kitchens, stainless steel pump units, squeeze bottles, waitress/waiter paging/callstations, etc
President: Melinda James
VP: Eric Seltzer
Purchasing Agent: Dave Schankin
Estimated Sales: Less Than $500,000
Number Employees: 1-4
Square Footage: 80000
Brands Exported: Redi-Call; Top O' Cup
Regions Exported to: Europe, Asia, Canada, Mexico
Percentage of Business in Exporting: 5
Regions Imported from: Europe, Asia

48009 Redi-Print
49 Mahan St
Unit B
West Babylon, NY 11704   631-491-6373
    Fax: 631-491-6372 rediprint1@aol.com
Manufacturer and exporter of pre-printed menu paper and menu designing software
President: Tom Vlahakis
Estimated Sales: $300,000-500,000
Number Employees: 10
Square Footage: 5000
Regions Exported to: Worldwide
Percentage of Business in Exporting: 5

48010 Redmond Minerals Inc
475 W 910 S
Heber City, UT 84032-2494   435-657-3600
    Fax: 435-529-7486   866-312-7258
mail@redmondminerals.com
www.redmondinc.com
Sea salt
CEO: Rhett Roberts
Estimated Sales: $ 20-50 Million
Number Employees: 30
Type of Packaging: Consumer, Food Service, Private Label, Bulk
Brands Exported: RealSalt
Regions Exported to: Europe, Canada, New Zealand, Japan
Percentage of Business in Exporting: 5

48011 Reed & Barton Food Service
144 West Brittania Street
Taunton, MA 02780   508-824-6611
    Fax: 508-822-7269   800-797-9675
Flatware and holloware
President/Chief Executive Officer: Timothy Riddle
Manager: Jill Pedro
VP, Finance/CFO/Treasurer/Controller: Stephen Normandine
Vice President, Information Technology: Paul Bartlet
SVP, Sales & Marketing: Joe D'Allessandro
Director, Sales: Angie Miller
Contact: John Alakel
jalakel@reedandbarton.com
Director, Purchasing & Planning: Rocco Davanzo
Estimated Sales: $ 25 Million
Number Employees: 98
Number of Brands: 5
Square Footage: 500000
Parent Co: Reed & Barton Silversmiths
Type of Packaging: Food Service

48012 Reed Oven Co
1720 Nicholson Ave
Kansas City, MO 64120-1453   816-842-7446
    Fax: 816-421-0422 www.reedovenco.com
Manufacturer and exporter of revolving shelf and rack ovens, proofers, retarders, fermentation rooms and steam cabinets
President: Kay Davies
reedoven@mindspring.com
Marketing Director/ IT Supervisor: Chris Davies
Operations: Brad Mitchell
Administrative Assistant: Linda Zeller
Plant Manager/ Engineer: Tim Davies
Purchasing Manager: Linda Zeller
Estimated Sales: $2.5-5 Million
Number Employees: 10-19
Square Footage: 72000
Regions Exported to: Central America, South America, Europe, Asia, Middle East
Regions Imported from: Asia

48013 (HQ)Reede International Seafood Corporation
PO Box 199
Roslyn Heights, NY 11577-0199   516-365-0265
    Fax: 516-365-2956
Import and export broker of seafood, private label items and frozen foods
President: Stephen Reede
VP: Rose Reede
Sales/Marketing: Glenn Rosenblatt
Public Relations: Mariann Kuznetz
Estimated Sales: $15-20 Million
Number Employees: 5
Number of Brands: 5
Number of Products: 30
Square Footage: 4000
Type of Packaging: Consumer, Food Service, Private Label, Bulk
Brands Exported: Various
Regions Exported to: Europe, Asia
Percentage of Business in Exporting: 10
Brands Imported: Sea-Reed/Pacific Andes/Nouvelle/Andes
Regions Imported from: South America, Europe, Asia
Percentage of Business in Importing: 90

48014 Reelcraft Industries Inc
2842 E Business 30
Columbia City, IN 46725-8451   260-248-8188
    Fax: 260-248-2605   800-444-3134
reelcraft@reelcraft.com www.reelcraft.com
Manufacturer and exporter of industrial-grade hose, cord and cable reels, including stainless steel.
President: Walter Sterneman
wsterneman@reelcraft.com
Estimated Sales: Over $50 Million
Number Employees: 100-249
Square Footage: 130000
Type of Packaging: Consumer, Food Service

48015 Reeno Detergent & Soap Company
9421 Midland Boulevard
Saint Louis, MO 63114-3327   314-429-6078
    Fax: 314-429-6078
Manufacturer, importer and exporter of powder and liquid laundry detergents and industrial cleaners
President: Colleen Trotter
VP Sales: Tim Trotter
VP Purchasing: Brad Trotter
Estimated Sales: $1-2.5 Million
Number Employees: 5-9
Brands Exported: Borax-Sudz

Importers & Exporters / A-Z

48016 Rees Inc
405 S Reed Rd
Fremont, IN 46737-2129   260-495-9811
Fax: 260-495-2186 sales@reesinc.com
www.reesinc.com
Manufacturer and exporter of industrial control switches including cable, palmbutton and stop-start
President: Daniel Breeden
db@reesinc.com
Estimated Sales: $ 1 - 5 Million
Number Employees: 10-19
Square Footage: 70000
Regions Exported to: Canada
Percentage of Business in Exporting: 5

48017 Reese Enterprises Inc
16350 Asher Ave E
Rosemount, MN 55068-6000   651-423-1126
Fax: 651-423-2662 800-328-0953
info@reeseusa.com www.reeseusa.com
Manufacturer, importer and exporter of plastic doors and door strips, aluminum roll-up mats, aluminum stair treads, floor mats and grates, weatherstrips and thresholds
President: Jim Beitzell
beitzell@reeseusa.com
National Sales/Marketing Manager: Edward Green
Estimated Sales: $10-20 Million
Number Employees: 1-4
Number of Products: 4
Square Footage: 160000
Parent Co: Astro Plastics
Brands Exported: Perfec
Regions Exported to: Asia, Middle East, Canada
Percentage of Business in Exporting: 5
Regions Imported from: Middle East, Canada, Mexico
Percentage of Business in Importing: 6

48018 Reeve Store Equipment Co
9131 Bermudez St
Pico Rivera, CA 90660-4507   562-949-2535
Fax: 562-949-3862 800-927-3383
info@reeveco.com www.reeveco.com
Manufacturer and exporter of point of purchase displays, tags, card holders and fixtures
President: John Frackelton
COO: Jim Thompson
jthompson@reeve.com
Manager Sales/Marketing: Robert Frackelton
Estimated Sales: $ 20 - 50 Million
Number Employees: 50-99
Square Footage: 160000
Regions Exported to: Central America, South America, Asia
Percentage of Business in Exporting: 5

48019 Refcon
220 Route 70
Medford, NJ 8055   609-714-2330
Fax: 609-714-2331
Manufacturer and exporter of curved display cases for candy, baked goods, deli meat, fish and poultry
President: Herman Jakubowski
Manager/Manufacturing: Len Pushkantser
Engineer: Rapael Colon
Estimated Sales: $ 3-5 Million
Number Employees: 20-49
Square Footage: 88000
Regions Exported to: Worldwide
Percentage of Business in Exporting: 5

48020 Refractron TechnologiesCorp
5750 Stuart Ave
Newark, NY 14513-9798   315-331-6222
Fax: 315-331-7254 sales@refractron.com
www.refractron.com
Manufacturer, importer and exporter of advanced porous ceramic filters including water, process, gas, micro, cross-flow, ceramic membrane, air, etc.; also, diffusers including liquid and gas
Owner: Bob Stanton
CFO: Darrell Johanneman
Director R & D: Gregg Crume
VP, Sales & Marketing: Adam Osekoski
bstanton@refractron.com
Estimated Sales: $10-20 Million
Number Employees: 50-99
Square Footage: 130000
Type of Packaging: Private Label
Brands Exported: Refractron; Pall Corp.
Regions Exported to: Central America, South America, Europe, Asia, Canada, Mexico, Latin America, South Africa
Percentage of Business in Exporting: 45
Regions Imported from: Europe
Percentage of Business in Importing: 2

48021 Refresco Beverages US Inc.
Tampa, FL 33614   813-313-1800
      888-260-3776
ConsumerAffairs.NA@refresco.com
www.refresco-na.com
Soft drinks, sports and energy drinks, tea, and sparkling and flavoured water.
CFO, North America: Bill McFarland
COO, North America: Brad Goist
Estimated Sales: Over $1 Billion
Number Employees: 3,600
Type of Packaging: Consumer, Food Service, Private Label, Bulk
Brands Exported: RC Cola
Regions Exported to: Central America, South America, Europe, Asia, Middle East, Worldwide

48022 (HQ)Refrigeration Research
525 N 5th St
PO Box 869
Brighton, MI 48116-1293   810-227-1151
Fax: 810-227-3700 info@refresearch.com
www.refresearch.com
Manufacturer and exporter of component parts for commercial refrigeration systems
Vice President: Michael Ramalia
mramalia@refresearch.com
Vice President: M Ramalia
Estimated Sales: $5-10 Million
Number Employees: 100-249
Type of Packaging: Bulk
Regions Exported to: Worldwide

48023 Refrigerator Manufacturers LLC
17018 Edwards Rd
Cerritos, CA 90703-2422   562-926-2006
Fax: 562-926-2007 sales@rmi-econocold.com
Manufacturer, importer and exporter of walk-in cold storage rooms and environmental chambers
President: Lawrence Jaffe
VP: Leo Lewis
Contact: Tony Bedy
tbedy@airdyne.com
Estimated Sales: $10-20 Million
Number Employees: 5-9
Square Footage: 80000
Regions Exported to: Central America, Caribbean, Mexico
Percentage of Business in Exporting: 3
Regions Imported from: Caribbean, Mexico
Percentage of Business in Importing: 3

48024 Refrigiwear Inc
54 Breakstone Dr
Dahlonega, GA 30533-7603   706-973-5000
Fax: 706-864-5898 800-645-3744
keepmewarm@refrigiwear.com
www.refrigiwear.com
Manufacturer and exporter of insulated and protective work clothing, head, hand, and footwear, thermal insulated blankets and carts and pallet covers
President: Ronald Breakstone
rbreakstone@refrigiwear.com
Vice President: Mark Silberman
Quality Control: Kate Bishop
Marketing: Kristy Chrisciaske
VP Sales: Don Byerly
Vice President/Operations: Scotty Depriest
Estimated Sales: $25 Million
Number Employees: 100-249
Square Footage: 80000
Brands Exported: RefrigiWear; Iron Tuff; Storm Trac; Weather Guard
Regions Exported to: Worldwide

48025 Refrigiwear Inc
54 Breakstone Dr
Dahlonega, GA 30533-7603   706-973-5000
Fax: 706-864-5898 800-645-3744
customerservice@refrigiwear.com
www.refrigiwear.com
President/CFO: Ronald Breakstone
rbreakstone@refrigiwear.com
Vice President: Scotty Depriest
Marketing Manager: Kate Bishop
Chief Operating Officer: Mark Silberman
Estimated Sales: $ 10 - 20 Million
Number Employees: 100-249

48026 Regal Crown Foods Inc
41 Mason St
Worcester, MA 01610-3203   508-752-2679
Fax: 508-831-0775
Vinegar pickles
Owner: William McEntee
regalcrownfoods@aol.com
Public Relations: Monica Freund Kaufman
Plant Manager: David Giorgio
Estimated Sales: $ 1 - 3 Million
Number Employees: 1-4
Number of Brands: 12
Number of Products: 6
Type of Packaging: Food Service, Private Label
Regions Imported from: Central America

48027 Regal Custom Fixture Company
22 Burrs Rd., Bldg. C
PO Box 446
Westampton, NJ 08060-0446   609-261-3323
Fax: 609-261-4929 800-525-3092
Manufacturer and exporter of display cases including bakery, deli and candy
VP: Mike Rainbolt
National Sales Manager: Shawn Adair
Number Employees: 20-49
Type of Packaging: Food Service
Regions Exported to: Worldwide
Percentage of Business in Exporting: 2

48028 Regal Health Food
3705 W Grand Ave
Chicago, IL 60651-2236   773-252-1044
Fax: 773-252-0817 info@regalsnacks.com
www.regalsnacks.com
Dried fruits and nuts
President: Gregory Piatigorsky
regalgourmetfoods@gmail.com
VP Marketing/Sales: Igor Piatigorsky
Estimated Sales: $ 10 - 20 Million
Number Employees: 10-19
Square Footage: 54000
Type of Packaging: Consumer, Food Service, Private Label, Bulk
Regions Imported from: Worldwide
Percentage of Business in Importing: 25

48029 Regal Springs Trading Company
PO Box 20608
Bradenton, FL 34204-0608   941-747-9161
Fax: 941-747-9476 tilapfilet@aol.com
www.regalsprings.com
Fish and Seafood
President: Michael Picchietti
Contact: Ty Barber
ty.barber@regalsprings.com
Estimated Sales: $1 Million
Number Employees: 5-9

48030 (HQ)Regal Ware Inc
1675 Reigle Dr
Kewaskum, WI 53040-8923   262-626-2121
Fax: 262-626-8565 www.regalware.com
Manufacturer, importer and exporter of frying and sauce pans, coffee makers and urns
President/CEO: Jeffery Reigle
Chairman: James Reigle
SVP/Chief Financial Officer: Gerald Koch
SVP/Chief HR Officer: David Lenz
Sales Director: Jim Dorn
SVP Operations: Joe Swanson
Purchasing: John McCormack
Estimated Sales: $36.8 Million
Number Employees: 500-999
Square Footage: 500000
Other Locations:
  Regal Ware
  Jacksonville, ARRegal Ware
Brands Exported: Regal Ware, West Bend
Regions Exported to: Central America, South America, Europe, Asia, Middle East
Percentage of Business in Exporting: 5

48031 Regency Hearts of Palm
2764 Bingle
Houston, TX 77055   713-789-7123
Fax: 713-621-5504 regencyfood@yahoo.com
Coffee, nuts, canned or preserved vegetables/fruit.
Marketing: C Kennedy

Importers & Exporters / A-Z

48032 Regency Service Carts
337 Carroll St
Brooklyn, NY 11231   718-855-8304
        Fax: 718-834-8507 regeastny@aol.com
VP: Connie Pezulich
Contact: John Pezulich
quote@regencynylv.com
Estimated Sales: $ 20 - 50 Million
Number Employees: 20-49

48033 Regina USA
305 E Mahn Ct
Oak Creek, WI 53154-2101   414-571-0032
        Fax: 414-571-0225 sales.us@reginachain.net
Manufacturer, of metal and plastic power transmission chains, conveying chains and plastic belts
President: Carlo Garbagnati
VP Sales/Marketing: Michael Hager
Sales: Brian Kelley
IT: Sandy Martino
smartino@reginausa.com
Estimated Sales: $ 20 Million
Number Employees: 10-19
Square Footage: 65000
Parent Co: Regina Industria SPA
Brands Exported: FliteTop; UlTop; Matveyor
Regions Exported to: Central America, Caribbean, Latin America, Canada, Mexico
Percentage of Business in Exporting: 10

48034 Rego China Corporation
200 Broadhollow Road
Suite 400
Melville, NY 11747-4806   516-753-3700
        Fax: 516-753-3728 800-221-1707
        www.oneida.com
Manufacturer, importer and exporter of chinaware
President, CEO: Foster Sullivan
Sales Manager: Frank Fan
Estimated Sales: $300,000-500,000
Number Employees: 40
Parent Co: Oneida
Type of Packaging: Food Service
Regions Exported to: Asia
Percentage of Business in Exporting: 2
Regions Imported from: Asia

48035 Rego Smoked Fish Company
6980 75th St
Flushing, NY 11379   718-894-1400
        Fax: 718-894-9100
Smoked salmon, sturgeon, trout, sablefish and whitefish
President: Jason Spitz
Manager: Sheldon Spitz
Owner: Conrad Spitz
Estimated Sales: $500,000-$1 Million
Number Employees: 1-4
Square Footage: 28000
Type of Packaging: Consumer, Bulk
Regions Imported from: Canada
Percentage of Business in Importing: 9

48036 Reheis Co
235 Snyder Ave
Berkeley Heights, NJ 07922-1150   908-464-1500
        Fax: 908-464-7726 rduffy@reheis.com
        www.reheis.com
Potassium chloride
VP R&D: J C Parekh
VP Sales: D Fondots
VP Operations: J Bogan
Plant Manager: Gerry Kirwan
Estimated Sales: Less Than $500,000
Number Employees: 1-4
Brands Exported: KCI
Regions Exported to: Central America, South America, Europe, Asia, Middle East
Percentage of Business in Exporting: 33

48037 Reichert Analytical Instruments
3362 Walden Avenue
Depew, NY 14043   716-686-4500
        Fax: 716-686-4545 www.reichertai.com
Hand held digital refractometers.
Contact: Ashley Agnew
aagnew@reichert.com
Regions Exported to: Worldwide

48038 Reidler Decal Corporation
264 Industrial Pk. Road
PO Box 8
Saint Clair, PA 17970   570-429-1528
        Fax: 570-429-1528 800-628-7770
        marketing@reidlerdecal.com
        www.reidlerdecal.com
Manufacturer and exporter of decals, plastic safety signs, fleet graphics, reflective markings, reflective striping and roll labels
President: Edward Reidler
Marketing Coordinator: Maralynn Hudock
Estimated Sales: $ 5 - 10 Million
Number Employees: 20-49
Square Footage: 100000

48039 (HQ)Reilly Dairy & Food Company
6603 S Trask Avenue
Tampa, FL 33616   813-839-8458
        Fax: 813-839-0394
Cheese, dairy, butter
President: Gerald Reilly
rdfjerry@gmail.com
Human Resources Director: Brenda Reilly
Estimated Sales: $16,000,000
Number Employees: 70
Square Footage: 36000
Type of Packaging: Consumer, Food Service, Private Label, Bulk
Regions Exported to: South America, Caribbean
Percentage of Business in Exporting: 15

48040 Reilly's Sea Products
PO Box 149
South Bristol, ME 04568-0149   207-644-1400
        Fax: 207-644-8192
Seafood
President: Terry Reilly
Estimated Sales: $ 5 - 10 Million
Number Employees: 20-49

48041 Reiner Products
196 Mill St
Waterbury, CT 06706-1208   203-574-2666
        Fax: 203-755-8178 800-345-6775
        info@reinerproducts.com
        www.reinerproducts.com
Manufacturer, importer and exporter of salt and pepper shakers
Owner: Patrick Bergin
Estimated Sales: $2.5-5 Million
Number Employees: 10-19
Regions Exported to: Worldwide
Regions Imported from: Europe, Asia

48042 Reinhart Foods
235 Yorkland Blvd
Suite 1101
Toronto, ON M2J 4Y8
Canada   416-645-4910
        Fax: 888-519-0079 cs@reinhartfoods.com
        www.reinhartfoods.com
Vinegar, maraschino cherries, glace fruit, dates, raisins, coconut, mince meat, pie fillings, apples and pineapples
President/CEO: Jeff King
Director of Sales/Bus. Dev./Marketing: Michael J.
Parent Co: Reinhart Vinegars
Type of Packaging: Consumer, Food Service, Private Label, Bulk
Brands Exported: Orchard Fresh; Perfec Py; Reinhart
Regions Exported to: Asia, USA
Regions Imported from: Europe, Asia

48043 Reinke & Schomann
3745 N Richards St
Milwaukee, WI 53212   414-964-1100
        Fax: 414-964-1995
        sales@reinkeandschomann.com
        www.reinkeandschomann.com
Manufacturer and exporter of steel and stainless steel screw conveyors and components
President: Frederick Schomann
VP Engineering/Sales: Ken Buchholz
Estimated Sales: Below $5,000,000
Number Employees: 5-9
Square Footage: 30000
Regions Exported to: Worldwide
Percentage of Business in Exporting: 1

48044 Reis Robotics
856 Commerce Pkwy
Carpentersville, IL 60110   847-741-9500
        Fax: 847-844-0745 www.kuka.com
Manufacturer and importer of automated robotic material handling and palletizing systems and system integrators
President, KUKA Robotics Corp US: Joseph Gemma
Year Founded: 1957
Estimated Sales: K
Number Employees: 10-19
Square Footage: 45000
Parent Co: KUKA Robotics Corporation
Regions Imported from: Europe
Percentage of Business in Importing: 40

48045 Reist Popcorn Co
113 Manheim St
Mt Joy, PA 17552-1317   717-653-8078
        Fax: 717-653-4121 reistpopcorn.com
Popcorn
President: David Reist
dreist@reistpopcorn.com
Estimated Sales: Less Than $500,000
Number Employees: 5-9
Type of Packaging: Private Label, Bulk

48046 Relco Unisystems Corp
2281 3rd Ave SW
Willmar, MN 56201-2799   320-231-2210
        Fax: 320-231-2282
        lorencorle@relcounisystems.com
        www.relco.net
Provides dairy and food plants with customized cheese, whey, soy, and processing equipment and systems through design, engineering, fabrication, installation, and commissioning. Relco process and control systems are recognized as industry leaders because of their application knowledge, understanding of sanitary and regulatory requirements, and focus on consumer needs
President: Loren Corle
lcorle@relco.com
VP: M Douglas Rolland
Estimated Sales: $20-50 Million
Number Employees: 50-99
Regions Exported to: Worldwide
Percentage of Business in Exporting: 1

48047 (HQ)Reliable Container Corporation
12029 Regentview Ave
Downey, CA 90241-5517   562-745-0200
        Fax: 562-861-3969 www.reliablecontainer.com
Manufacturer and exporter of corrugated boxes and foil-lined, coated, printed and plain cake circles and pads
President: Dan Brough
VP: Andrew Rosen
VP: Robert Schwartz
Estimated Sales: $ 20 - 50 Million
Number Employees: 100-249
Square Footage: 112500
Other Locations:
    Reliable Container Corp.
    Tijuana, Baja CA Reliable Container Corp.
Regions Exported to: Mexico
Percentage of Business in Exporting: 10

48048 Reliable Mercantile Company
21 Kensett Road
Manhasset, NY 11030-2105   516-365-7808
        Fax: 516-365-7808
Importer and wholesaler/distributor of spices
President: M Abrahamian
Regions Imported from: Worldwide

48049 Rema Foods Inc
140 Sylvan Ave
Englewood Cliffs, NJ 07632   201-947-1000
        www.remafoods.com
Importer of specialty food products.
President & CEO: Robert Feuerstein
Year Founded: 1964
Estimated Sales: $50-100 Million
Number Employees: 50-99

Importers & Exporters / A-Z

48050 (HQ)Remco Industries International
PO Box 480008
Fort Lauderdale, FL 33348-0008   954-462-0000
Fax: 954-564-0000 800-987-3626
remco2mill@aol.com www.remcousa.com
Manufacturer and exporter of cooking equipment including wood burning and infrared rotisseries and pizza ovens; also, spit racks, bagel ovens and warming carts; manufacturer and importer of wood burning, infrared and carousel brickpizza ovens; manufacturer of grease free chicken wing roaster the Wing King and BBQ Boy
President/CEO: Romano Moreth
CFO: Susan Test
Vice President: Rob Moreth
R&D/Plant Manager: Remy Moreth
Quality Control: Wayne Wilkenson
Marketing/Public Relations: Pascal Ledesma
Sales Director: Joe Obrien
Operations: David Finch
Production Manager: Vean George
Plant Manager: Sean Harker
Purchasing Manager: Ed Moreth
Estimated Sales: $7-8 Million
Number Employees: 20-49
Number of Brands: 3
Number of Products: 6
Square Footage: 160000
Type of Packaging: Food Service
Brands Exported: Remco; Royal Millennium
Regions Exported to: Central America, South America

48051 Remco Products Corp
4735 W 106th St
Zionsville, IN 46077-8761   317-876-9856
Fax: 317-876-9858 800-585-8619
sales@remcoproducts.com
www.remcoproducts.com
Remco Products sells a high quality line of products to the food processing, sanittation, pharmaceutical, safety, and material handling industries. Our tubs and polypropylene shovels have been used in these areas for over 30 years. The Vikan line of cleaning brooms, brushes, and squeegees is specifically designed to meet the stringent hygienic requirements of these different industries. We can also provide you with other hand tools such as scoops, scrapers, mixing paddles, forkkand rakes.
President: David Garrison
Marketing/Sales Support: Richard L. Williams
Director/Sales and Marketing: Chuck Bush
President of Operations: Richard L. Garrison
Estimated Sales: $2.5-5 Million
Number Employees: 10-19
Number of Brands: 2
Number of Products: 737
Square Footage: 96000
Brands Exported: Vikan, Remco
Regions Exported to: Central America, South America, Europe
Brands Imported: Vikan Hygiene System
Regions Imported from: Europe
Percentage of Business in Importing: 30

48052 Remco Specialty Products
3290 NE 33rd Street
Fort Lauderdale, FL 33308-7123   954-462-0000
Fax: 954-564-0000 remco2mill@aol.com
remcusa.com
Contact: David Bradley
dbradley@remcousa.com
Estimated Sales: $ 5 - 10 Million
Number Employees: 20-49

48053 Remcraft Lighting Products
12870 NW 45th Ave
PO Box 54-1487
Miami, FL 33054
    305-687-9031
Fax: 305-687-5069 800-327-6585
customerservice@remcraft.com
www.bacimirrors.com
Manufacturer and exporter of electric and fluorescent lighting fixtures
President: Jeffrey Robboy
CEO: Michell Roboy
Estimated Sales: $ 1 - 2.5 Million
Number Employees: 20-49
Square Footage: 80000
Type of Packaging: Consumer, Private Label
Regions Exported to: Central America, Asia
Percentage of Business in Exporting: 15

48054 Remel
12076 Santa Fe Dr
P.O. Box 14428
Lenexa, KS 66215
Fax: 800-621-8251 800-255-6730
www.remel.com
Manufacturer and exporter of microbiology products including culture media, dehydrated culture media identification kits, reagents and stains.
President & CEO, Thermo Scientific: Marc Casper
Year Founded: 1973
Estimated Sales: Over $1 Billion
Parent Co: Thermo Fisher Scientific
Regions Exported to: Worldwide

48055 Remstar International
41 Eisenhower Dr
Westbrook, ME 04092   207-854-1861
Fax: 207-854-1610 800-639-5805
info@remstar.com www.remstar.com
Manufacturer, importer and exporter of automated storage and retrieval systems
President: Gary Gould
Marketing Director: Ed Romaine
Contact: Brian Baker
brian.baker@kardexremstar.com
Estimated Sales: $20-50 Million
Number Employees: 20-49
Parent Co: Kardex A.G.

48056 Renard Machine Company
PO Box 19005
Green Bay, WI 54307-9005   920-432-8412
Fax: 920-432-8430
Manufacturer and exporter of packaging machinery including fillers, sealers, labelers, weighers and wrappers; also, paper converting equipment including folding, cutting, etc
Division Controller: Gary Rossman
Production Manager: Carl Strebel
Plant Manager: Ken Harvey
Estimated Sales: $ 5-10 Million
Number Employees: 50-99
Square Footage: 300000
Parent Co: Paper Converting Machine Company
Regions Exported to: Central America, South America, Europe, Middle East
Percentage of Business in Exporting: 10

48057 Renato Specialty Product
3612 Dividend Drive
Garland, TX 75042   972-272-4800
Fax: 972-272-4848 866-575-6316
renatos@renatos.com www.renatos.com
Manufacturer and exporter of food service equipment including broilers, ovens, griddles, grills and rotisseries
President, Founder: Renato Riccio
Estimated Sales: $1-2.5 Million
Number Employees: 5-9
Type of Packaging: Consumer, Food Service
Regions Exported to: Worldwide
Percentage of Business in Exporting: 10

48058 Rene Produce Dist
895 E Frontage Rd
Rio Rico, AZ 85648-9675   520-281-0806
Fax: 520-281-2933 reneprod@dakotacom.net
www.reneproduce.com
Cucumbers, eggplant, squash, tomatoes and peppers
President: Rene Carrillo
carrillo@reneproduce.com
Sales Manager: David Kennedy
Sales: George Quintero
Estimated Sales: $ 3 - 5 Million
Number Employees: 10-19
Type of Packaging: Consumer, Food Service
Regions Exported to: Canada

48059 Rennco LLC
300 S Elm St
Homer, MI 49245-1337   517-568-4121
Fax: 517-568-4798 800-409-5225
sales@rennco.com www.rennco.com
Manufacturer and exporter of vertical L-Bar sealers
VP/General Manager: Eric Vorm
Marketing Director: Jeanne George
Contact: Teresa Farmer
teresafarmer@rennco.com
Director of Operations: Terry Draper
Number Employees: 70
Parent Co: Pro Mach
Type of Packaging: Consumer, Food Service, Bulk

48060 Rennoc Corporation
645 Pine Street
Greenville, OH 45331   800-372-7100
Fax: 800-675-1727 www.rennoc.com
President: Michael Bruzzese
Contact: Thomas Genovese
genoveset@rennoc.com
Estimated Sales: $ 10 - 20 Million
Number Employees: 100-249

48061 Renold Products
P.O.Box A
Westfield, NY 14787-0546   716-326-3121
Fax: 716-326-6121 800-879-2529
ainfo@renoldajax.com www.renold.com
Manufacturer and exporter of material handling equipment including mechanical power transmission products and packer weigh scales and conveyors.
President: Thomas Murrer
Business Development Director: Alan Dean
Estimated Sales: $20-50 Million
Number Employees: 100-249
Square Footage: 120000
Parent Co: Renold PLC
Regions Exported to: Central America, South America, Europe, Asia, Middle East
Percentage of Business in Exporting: 5

48062 Renovator's Supply
PO Box 2515
Conway, NH 3818   800-659-0203
Fax: 603-447-1717
Manufacturer and exporter of hardware, lighting, plumbing and gift accessories; also, solid brass, iron, porcelain and stainless steel sinks and work centers
President: Cindy Harris
Estimated Sales: $10-20 Million
Number Employees: 100-249
Regions Exported to: Europe, Asia

48063 Reotemp Instrument Corp
10656 Roselle St
San Diego, CA 92121-1524   858-784-0710
Fax: 858-784-0720 800-648-7737
sales@reotemp.com www.reotemp.com
Manufactures temperature and pressure instrumentation. Provide bimetal thermometers, pressure gauges, diaphragm seals, transmitters, RTD's and thermocouples and related accessories.
President: Joanne Lin
joanne.lin@intel.com
VP/General Manager: John Sisti
Quality/Engineering Manager: Cora Marsh
Marketing Manager: Nathan O'Connor
Sales Manager, Global Sales: Mark Leonelli
Purchasing Associate: Stacy Munoz
Estimated Sales: $6 Million
Number Employees: 20-49
Square Footage: 15000
Regions Exported to: Central America, South America, Europe, Asia, Middle East, South Pacific

48064 Replacements LTD
1089 Knox Rd
Mc Leansville, NC 27301-9228   336-697-3000
Fax: 336-697-3100 800-737-5223
inquire@replacements.com
www.replacements.com
Manufacturer and exporter of household and institutional cutlery
CEO: Robert L Page
robert.page@replacements.com
Director Marketing: Maron Atkins
General Manager: James Robellard
Estimated Sales: $ 5-10 Million
Number Employees: 500-999
Square Footage: 140000
Parent Co: Syratech
Regions Exported to: Worldwide

48065 Republic Del Cacao
3780 Kilroy Airport Way
Suite 200
Long Beach, CA 90806   562-537-3656
Fax: 562-256-7001
Chocolate bars
President/Owner: Bernard Duclos

48066 Republic Foil
55 Triangle St
Danbury, CT 06810   203-743-2731
Fax: 203-743-8838 800-722-3645
Manufacturer and exporter of aluminum foil on coils

539

Importers & Exporters / A-Z

President: John Jehle
CFO: Fred Wallace
Contact: Joan Garofalo
joan.garofalo@garmcousa.com
Estimated Sales: $ 20 - 50 Million
Number Employees: 50-99
Square Footage: 100000
Type of Packaging: Bulk
Brands Exported: Republic High Yield
Regions Exported to: Europe, Asia

48067 Rer Services
19431 Business Center Dr # 17
Northridge, CA 91324-6408   818-993-1826
   Fax: 818-993-0016 rerserv@flash.net
Manufacturer and exporter of packaging machinery
Owner: Rick Ray
Estimated Sales: $ 2.5-5,000,000
Number Employees: 5-9
Regions Exported to: Worldwide
Percentage of Business in Exporting: 10

48068 Research Products Co
1835 E North St
Salina, KS 67401-8567   785-825-2181
   Fax: 785-825-8908   800-234-7174
   www.researchprod.com
Flour bleaching and maturing premixers; vitamins and minerals
President: Monte White
montewhite@researchprod.com
Estimated Sales: $ 10 - 20 Million
Number Employees: 50-99
Parent Co: McShares
Brands Exported: Oxylite; Kurolite; Repco Bro N-50; Repco Zyme 5000

48069 Resina
27455 Bostik Court
Temecula, CA 92590   951-296-6585
   Fax: 951-296-5018   800-207-4804
   sales@resina.com www.resina.com
Manufacturer and exporter of container capping machines
CEO: Micheal Tom
Director Sales: Andrew May
Sales Director: Tina Tricome
Estimated Sales: $10-20 Million
Number Employees: 1-4
Square Footage: 70000
Regions Exported to: Central America, South America, Europe, Asia, Middle East, Worldwide
Percentage of Business in Exporting: 20

48070 Resource Trading Company
72 Commercial Street
Portland, ME 04104-1698   207-772-2299
   Fax: 207-772-4709
Lobster, scallops and shrimp
President: Spencer Fuller
Domestic Sales: Tom Keegan
International Sales: Irene Ketalaar-Moon
Type of Packaging: Bulk
Brands Exported: Arctic Pride; Claw Island
Regions Exported to: Worldwide
Percentage of Business in Exporting: 50
Regions Imported from: Asia
Percentage of Business in Importing: 10

48071 Respirometry Plus, LLC
PO Box 1236
Fond Du Lac, WI 54937-7527
   Fax: 920-922-1085   800-328-7518
   operations@respirometryplus.com
   www.respirometryplus.com
Manufacturer and exporter of bench and on-line respirometer
Owner: Louis Sparagarto
CEO: Robert Arthur
Contact: Tim Keuler
tim@respirometryplus.com
Estimated Sales: $ 1 - 2,500,000
Number Employees: 10
Regions Exported to: Worldwide
Percentage of Business in Exporting: 40

48072 Resturantorows.com
233 E Shore Rd
Great Neck, NY 11023-2433   516-482-3399
   Fax: 516-482-8271
CEO: Norman Fredrick
Estimated Sales: $ 1 - 3 Million
Number Employees: 1-4

48073 Retalix
2490 Technical Dr
Miamisburg, OH 45342   937-445-1936
   Fax: 937-384-2280   877-794-7237
   www.ncr.com
Manufacturer and exporter of computer software including point of sale backoffice and headquarters systems for supermarkets, grocery stores and convenience stores
President: Ronen Levkovich
CEO: Shuky Sheffer
CFO: Sarit Sagiv
Head Innovation & Portfolio Strategy: Dr,Gill Roth
Marketing: Oren Betzaleli
Sales Director: Rick Cumberland
Contact: Jefferson Alcott
j.alcott@retalix.com
Operations Manager: Eli Spirer
Estimated Sales: $ 10 - 20 Million
Number Employees: 50-99
Square Footage: 60000
Parent Co: Retalix, Ltd
Type of Packaging: Consumer
Regions Exported to: Worldwide

48074 Reter Fruit
3100 S Pacific Hwy
Medford, OR 97501-8758   541-772-9560
   Fax: 541-772-5258
Pears
President: F Baker
Estimated Sales: $380000
Number Employees: 50-99
Type of Packaging: Consumer
Regions Exported to: Canada

48075 Revent Inc
100 Ethel Rd W
Piscataway, NJ 08854-5967   732-777-9433
   Fax: 732-777-1187   info@revent.com
   www.revent.com
Manufacturer and exporter of ovens including deck, mini and bake and roast rack; also, proof boxes
President: Torvjorn Alm
t.alm@revent.com
Quality Control: Tom Parker
Estimated Sales: $ 1 - 3 Million
Number Employees: 5-9
Square Footage: 200000
Parent Co: Revent International
Brands Exported: Revent Do-Sys
Regions Exported to: Central America, South America, Canada, Mexico, Caribbean
Brands Imported: Do-Sys
Regions Imported from: Europe

48076 Revent Inc
100 Ethel Rd W
Piscataway, NJ 08854-5967   732-777-9433
   Fax: 732-777-1187   info@revent.com
   www.revent.com
President: Torvjorn Alm
t.alm@revent.com
Estimated Sales: $ 1 - 3 Million
Number Employees: 5-9

48077 Rexcraft Fine Chafers
4139 38th Street
Long Island City, NY 11101-3617   718-361-3052
   Fax: 718-361-3054   888-739-2723
   rexchafer@aol.com
Manufacturer and exporter of banquetware including chafers, coffee/tea brewers and urns, holloware, steam table inserts, serving trays and food warmers
President: Ahsan Ullaha
VP: John Berman
Engineer & Designer: David Berman
Number Employees: 40
Square Footage: 36000
Brands Exported: Rexcraft
Regions Exported to: South America, Asia, Middle East, Canada, Latin America

48078 Rexford Paper Company
5802 Washington Ave
Suite 102
Racine, WI 53406-4088   262-886-9100
   Fax: 262-886-9130
Manufacturer, wholesaler/distributor and exporter of gummed, and reinforced paper and tapes including plain and printed, heat seal coated, lightweight meat packaging, gummed stay and pressure sensitive carton closure
CFO: Muriel Fincle
Sales Service Manager: James Carse
Sales Manager: Rory Wolf
Estimated Sales: $ 5 - 10 Million
Number Employees: 10-19
Parent Co: Inland Paperboard & Packaging
Type of Packaging: Consumer, Food Service
Brands Exported: REDCORE
Regions Exported to: Central America, South America, Europe, Asia, Middle East, Canada

48079 (HQ)Rexnord Corporation
Corporate Headquarters
511 Freshwater Way
Milwaukee, WI 53204   414-643-3000
       866-739-6673
       www.rexnord.com
Manufacturer, importer and exporter of belt, bottle and chain conveyors.
President & CEO: Todd Adams
SVP/Chief Financial Officer: Mark Peterson
SVP, Business & Corporate Development: Rodney Jackson
Chief Human Resources Officer: George Powers
Chief Information Officer: Mike Troutman
VP/General Counsel/Secretary: Patty Whaley
Year Founded: 1891
Estimated Sales: $1 Billion
Number Employees: 8,000
Regions Exported to: Worldwide
Percentage of Business in Exporting: 20
Regions Imported from: Worldwide
Percentage of Business in Importing: 10

48080 Rexroth Corporation
5150 Prairie Stone Pkwy
Hoffman Estates, IL 60192-3707   847-645-3600
   Fax: 847-645-0804 www.boschrexroth-us.com
Manufacturer and importer of servodrives and controls for motion control of processing and packaging machinery
President, Chief Executive Officer: Berend Bracht
VP Sales/Marketing: Richard Huss
Contact: Quentin Gilbert
quentin.gilbert@boschrexroth-us.com
Estimated Sales: $ 20-50 Million
Number Employees: 1,000-4,999
Square Footage: 50000
Parent Co: Rexroth Corporation
Brands Imported: Indramat
Regions Imported from: Europe
Percentage of Business in Importing: 75

48081 Reyco Systems Inc
1704 Industrial Way
Caldwell, ID 83605-6906   208-795-5700
   Fax: 208-795-5749 info@reycosys.com
   www.reyco.com
Manufacturer and exporter of pneumatic waste conveying, dewatering and fryer oil recovery equipment
General Manager: Rex McArthur
Account Manager: Marilyn McGrew
Design Manager: Jeff Denkers
Sales Director: Kathryn Brown
Manager: Wyland Atkins
awyland@reycosys.com
Plant Manager: Rex McArthur
Purchasing Manager: David Lethcoe
Estimated Sales: $ 5 - 10,000,000
Number Employees: 5-9
Regions Exported to: Worldwide

48082 Reyco Systems Inc
1704 Industrial Way
Caldwell, ID 83605-6906   208-795-5700
   Fax: 208-795-5749 info@reycosys.com
Manufacturers of oil and moisture removal systems, food and waste conveying systems, and UVC decontamination systems for food processing companies.
Owner: Tom Staley
Sales/Marketing/Advertising Manager: Brian Scott
Manager: Wyland Atkins
awyland@reycosys.com
Number Employees: 5-9
Regions Exported to: South America, Europe, Asia, Australia, Canada, Mexico

48083 Rhee Brothers
7461 Coca Cola Dr
Hanover, MD 21076   410-799-6656
   Fax: 410-381-9080 www.rheebros.com
Asian food products

President: Syng Rhee
CFO: Ha Chang
Contact: Phillip Ahn
phillipahn@rheebros.com
Estimated Sales: $20-50 Million
Number Employees: 100-249
Type of Packaging: Private Label

48084 Rheon USA
2 Doppler
Irvine, CA 92618-4306   949-768-1900
    Fax: 949-855-1991 us.info@rheon.com
       www.rheon.com
Manufacturer, importer and exporter of food processing equipment including automated mass production lines and flexible compact tables
General Manager: Kiyo Kamiyama
Sales Coordinator: Terry Smith
Manager Engineering Sales: Kazu Onuki
Manager: Kazu Onuki
us.info@rheon.com
Estimated Sales: $500,000-$1 Million
Number Employees: 20-49
Regions Exported to: Central America, South America
Percentage of Business in Exporting: 20
Regions Imported from: Asia
Percentage of Business in Importing: 75

48085 Rheon, U.S.A.
9490 Toledo Way
Irvine, CA 92618   949-768-1900
    Fax: 949-855-1991 www.rheon.com
Dough sheet & pastry equipment, bread equipment and encrusting machines.
Contact: Hiroshi Kimura
hiroshi.kimura@rheon.com
Regions Exported to: Central America, South America, North America

48086 Rhodes Bakery Equipment
14330 SW McFarland Boulevard
Portland, OR 97224-2906   503-232-9101
    Fax: 503-232-9206 800-426-3813
sales@kook-e-king.com www.kook-e-king.com
Manufacturer and exporter of cookie depositors and cutters
Marketing/Sales: Jan Duncan
Number Employees: 10-19
Square Footage: 120000
Brands Exported: Kook-E-King
Regions Exported to: Worldwide
Percentage of Business in Exporting: 20

48087 Rhodes Machinery International
1350 S 15th St
Louisville, KY 40210   502-213-3865
    Fax: 502-213-0096 www.rsisystemsinc.net
Manufacturer and exporter of tow line conveyors
President: William Rhodes
Plant Manager: Mark Wolford
Estimated Sales: $ 1 - 3 Million
Number Employees: 5-9
Parent Co: Rhodes Systems Worldwide
Type of Packaging: Bulk
Regions Exported to: Worldwide
Percentage of Business in Exporting: 40

48088 Ribus Inc.
10900 Manchester Rd
Suite 206
St. Louis, MO 63122   314-727-4287
    Fax: 314-727-1199 info@ribus.com
       www.ribus.com
Rice-based food ingredients, emulsifiers and extrusion aids
President: Steve Pierce
steve@ribus.com
Finance Supervisor: Michelle Kyle
Technical Manager: Neal Hammond
Manager, Global Marketing: Laurie Wittenbrink
Sales: Jim Goodall
Director of Operations: Peggy Vorwald
Estimated Sales: $720000
Number Employees: 1-4
Square Footage: 40000
Type of Packaging: Food Service, Private Label, Bulk
Other Locations:
    RIBUS
    Sabetha, KSRIBUS
Brands Exported: Nu-Rice; Nu-Bake
Regions Exported to: Central America, South America, Europe, Asia, Middle East

Percentage of Business in Exporting: 40

48089 Rice Company
11140 Fair Oaks Blvd
Suite 101
Fair Oaks, CA 95628   916-784-7745
    Fax: 916-784-7681 jobs@riceco.com
       www.riceco.com
Rice, popcorn, rice flour, sugar, beans, peas, lentils and ginger
Owner: Duane Kistner
President: J Kapila
Operations Manager: Vicki Manzoli
Estimated Sales: $4500000
Number Employees: 50-99
Type of Packaging: Consumer, Food Service, Private Label, Bulk
Regions Exported to: Central America, South America, Europe, Asia, Middle East, Canada, Caribbean, Latin America, Mexico
Percentage of Business in Exporting: 50
Regions Imported from: Central America, South America, Europe, Asia, Middle East, Caribbean, Latin America, Mexico
Percentage of Business in Importing: 10

48090 Rice Fruit Co
2760 Carlisle Rd
Gardners, PA 17324-9684   717-677-9842
    Fax: 717-677-9842 800-627-3359
info@ricefruit.com www.ricefruit.com
Apples, peaches and pears.
President: David Rice
david.rice@ricefruitcompany.com
Sales: John Rice
Number Employees: 50-99
Type of Packaging: Consumer, Food Service, Bulk
Regions Exported to: Worldwide
Percentage of Business in Exporting: 15

48091 Rice Innovations
13112 Santa Ana Ave
Unit A2-A3
Fontana, CA 92337
Canada   909-823-8230
    Fax: 909-823-2708
Rice, potato pastas, beverages
General Manager: Raj Sukul
R&D: Ly Hung
Customer Service: Sally Chee
Estimated Sales: $100,000
Number Employees: 1-4
Type of Packaging: Private Label
Brands Exported: Pastario, Pastato, Cafe Bonjour, Macariz, Rice Reality, CelifibR, Medicea, Body Fuel, Herb Science and Yin Yang
Regions Exported to: Worldwide

48092 (HQ)Rice Lake Weighing Systems
230 W Coleman St
Rice Lake, WI 54868-2422   715-234-9171
    Fax: 715-234-6967 800-472-6703
prodinfo@ricelake.com www.ricelake.com
Manufacturer and exporter of heavy capacity scales and computer interface equipment; also, full metal services available
Cmo: Pat Ranfranz
pranfranz@ricelake.com
VP: Rick Tyree
Regional Sales Director: Matt Crawford
Estimated Sales: $2.5-5 Million
Number Employees: 250-499
Square Footage: 100000
Regions Exported to: Central America, South America, Middle East, Latin America, Mexico
Percentage of Business in Exporting: 5

48093 Riceland Foods Inc.
PO Box 927
Stuttgart, AR 72160   870-673-5500
       855-742-3929
riceland@riceland.com www.riceland.com
Rice and rice bran oils.
CEO: Danny Kennedy
Estimated Sales: $1.3 Billion
Number Employees: 1,500
Type of Packaging: Consumer, Food Service, Private Label, Bulk
Other Locations:
    Newport, AR
    Weiner, AR
    Knobel, AR
    Holly Grove, AR

    Tuckerman, AR
    Corning, ARWeiner
Brands Exported: Riceland
Percentage of Business in Exporting: 27

48094 Ricetec
1925 Fm 2917 Rd
PO Box 1305
Alvin, TX 77512   281-756-3300
    Fax: 281-393-3532 800-580-7423
CustomerService@ricetec.com www.ricetec.com
Rice: Indian-style, basmati and American jasmine; rice mixes
President: John Nelson
jnelson@ricetec.com
CEO: Mike Gumina
EVP Business Development: Ken Fearday
VP Research & Development: Jose Re
Director Quality: Tim Williamson
Director Sales & Technical Services: Van McNeely
Estimated Sales: $33.4 Million
Number Employees: 50-99
Type of Packaging: Consumer, Food Service, Private Label, Bulk
Brands Exported: Texmati; Jasmati; Kasmati; Chefs Originals
Regions Exported to: Worldwide
Percentage of Business in Exporting: 5

48095 Rich Products Corp
1910 Gallagher Dr
Vineland, NJ 08360-1545   856-696-5600
    Fax: 856-696-3341 800-818-9261
       info@richs.com www.richs.com
Italian meat balls, pasta and sausage
Estimated Sales: $20 - 50 Million
Number Employees: 100-249
Square Footage: 100000
Parent Co: Rich Products Corporation
Type of Packaging: Consumer, Food Service
Regions Exported to: Worldwide
Percentage of Business in Exporting: 2

48096 Richards Packaging
4721 Burbank Rd
Memphis, TN 38118-6302   901-360-1121
    Fax: 901-360-0050 800-583-0327
memphissales@richardspackaging.com
       www.richardsmemphis.com
Manufacturer, exporter and importer of glass and plastic bottles and jars; also, droppers, sprayers and closures
CEO: Robert Boord
Estimated Sales: $10 Million
Number Employees: 10-19
Number of Brands: 100
Number of Products: 1000
Square Footage: 60000
Regions Exported to: Central America, South America, Europe, Canada, Caribbean, Latin America, Mexico
Percentage of Business in Exporting: 3
Regions Imported from: Europe, Asia, Canada, Mexico
Percentage of Business in Importing: 15

48097 Richardson Brands Co
101 Erie Blvd
Canajoharie, NY 13317-1148   518-673-3553
    Fax: 518-673-2451 www.richardsonbrands.com
Confectionery
Owner: Richard P Anderson
Supply Chain Manager: Rebecca Woodruff
Sr Traffic Controller: Marion Darrach
Senior VP Sales & Marketing: Michael Smith
Estimated Sales: $20 Million
Number Employees: 100-249
Type of Packaging: Consumer, Food Service, Private Label, Bulk
Regions Exported to: Europe
Percentage of Business in Exporting: 5
Regions Imported from: South America, Europe
Percentage of Business in Importing: 5

48098 Richardson International
2800 One Lombard Pl.
Winnipeg, MB R3B 0X8
Canada   204-934-5961
       866-217-6211
communications@richardson.ca
       www.richardson.ca
Grains and oilseed.
President/CEO: Curt Vossen

Importers & Exporters / A-Z

Year Founded: 1857
Estimated Sales: $28.6 Billion
Number Employees: 2,500
Type of Packaging: Consumer, Food Service, Private Label, Bulk
Regions Exported to: Central America, South America, Europe, Asia, Middle East, Worldwide

48099 Richland Beverage Association
2415 Midway Rd
Suite 115
Carrollton, TX 75006-2500   214-357-0248
    Fax: 214-357-9581 sales@texasselectna.com
Nonalcoholic malt beverages and beer
President: Martha Zelzer
sales@hphardware.com
Sales: John Rule
Sales: Dana Verrill
Estimated Sales: Less than $500,000
Number Employees: 1-4
Square Footage: 22800
Parent Co: Richland Corporation
Type of Packaging: Consumer, Food Service, Private Label
Brands Exported: Texas Select; Texas Brand
Regions Exported to: Central America, Asia, Middle East
Percentage of Business in Exporting: 75

48100 Richport International Inc
600 Route 73 N # 7b
Marlton, NJ 08053-1603   856-983-8006
    Fax: 856-983-0391
Importer of canned sardines, mackerel, chunk light tuna, albacore, pineapples, mandarin oranges and mushrooms including sliced, whole, stems, etc
President: Richard Ross
CEO: Robert Ross
Estimated Sales: $ 5 - 10 Million
Number Employees: 5-9
Square Footage: 8800
Type of Packaging: Private Label
Brands Imported: Richport
Regions Imported from: Europe, Asia
Percentage of Business in Importing: 100

48101 Richwood Imports Inc
1445 E Spruce St
Ontario, CA 91761-8303   909-930-6677
    Fax: 909-930-9927 www.richwood-imports.com
Owner: Hongfei He
hehongfei@richwood-imports.com
Estimated Sales: $ 5 - 10 Million
Number Employees: 5-9

48102 Rico Packaging Company
3617 S Ashland Avenue
Chicago, IL 60609-1320   773-523-9190
    Fax: 773-523-7965
Manufacturer and exporter of printed flexible packaging
President: William Wrigeyjr
CFO: Carol Riley
Manager: Don Bicking
R & D: William Wrigeyjr
Estimated Sales: $10-20 Million
Number Employees: 10
Parent Co: Wrigley
Regions Exported to: Worldwide

48103 Ridout Plastics
5535 Ruffin Rd
San Diego, CA 92123-1397   858-560-1551
    Fax: 858-560-1941 info@ridoutplastics.com
        www.eplastics.com
Architectural & Engineering Plastic Sheet ABS, Acrylic, Acrylite, Acetal, Bullet Resistant Plastic Sheet, Delrin, FRP, Fiberglass Grate, Sheet, Structural FRP Shapes, Lexan, Lexguard, Mirror, Micarta, Nylon, Plexiglas, Plexiglasspolycarbonate, Polypropylene, Polyethylene, Styrene, UHMW, abrasion-resistant sheet, anti-static.
President: Elliott Rabin
hr@ridoutplastics.com
Estimated Sales: $ 10 - 20 Million
Number Employees: 20-49

48104 Rieke Packaging Systems
500 W 7th St
Auburn, IN 46706-2006   260-925-3700
    Fax: 260-925-2493 sales@riekecorp.com
        www.riekepackaging.com
Manufacturer and exporter of dispensing equipment including pumps, pourspouts and faucets
CEO: David M Pritchett
dpritchett@riekecorp.com
CEO: Lynn Brooks
CFO: Chris Baron
VP: Don Laipple
Marketing Director: Wayne Schmidt
Director Of Sales: William Heimach
Purchasing Manager: Jim Szink
Estimated Sales: $ 1 - 5,000,000
Number Employees: 250-499
Type of Packaging: Consumer, Food Service
Regions Exported to: Central America, South America, Europe, Asia, Middle East, Worldwide

48105 Rigel Trading Corporation
P O Box 1994
Grand Cayman, KY 11104   345-949-5037
    Fax: 349-949-5038 www.regaltrading.com
Wholesaler/distributor and exporter of poultry equipment
President: Mike Williams
Manager: Craig Blyth
Estimated Sales: $500,000-$1 Million
Number Employees: 1-4

48106 Rigidized Metal Corp
658 Ohio St
Buffalo, NY 14203-3185   716-849-4760
    Fax: 716-849-0401 800-836-2580
    hr@rigidized.com www.rigidized.com
Manufacturer, importer and exporter of embossed metal parts for conveyors, packaging machinery and food processing equipment
Manager: Os Putman
osputman@rigidized.com
VP Sales: Louis Martin
Estimated Sales: $ 2.5-5,000,000
Number Employees: 50-99
Regions Imported from: Canada
Percentage of Business in Importing: 5

48107 Rio Syrup Co
2311 Chestnut St
St Louis, MO 63103-2298   314-436-7700
    Fax: 314-436-7707 800-325-7666
    flavors@riosyrup.com www.riosyrup.com
Syrups, extracts and concentrates, slush flavors and bases, fountain syrups and liquid food colors
President: Phillip Tomber
phil@riosyrup.com
Estimated Sales: $500,000-$1 Million
Number Employees: 5-9
Number of Products: 1200
Square Footage: 92000
Type of Packaging: Consumer, Food Service, Bulk
Brands Exported: Rio
Regions Exported to: Central America, Asia, Middle East, Africa, Australia
Percentage of Business in Exporting: 3

48108 Rip-N-Ready Foods
Ste 203
550 Fairway Dr
Deerfield Beach, FL 33441-1875   860-658-3060
    Fax: 860-658-3001

48109 Ripon Manufacturing Co Inc
652 S Stockton Ave
Ripon, CA 95366-2798   209-599-2148
    Fax: 209-599-3114 800-800-1232
    sales@riponmfgco.com www.riponmfgco.com
Manufacturer and exporter of edible nut processing equipment and conveyance systems
President: Glenn Navarro
sales@riponmfgco.com
VP: Ernst Boesch
Sales: Bruce Boyd
Purchasing: Denise Judd
Estimated Sales: $6 Million
Number Employees: 20-49
Square Footage: 126000

48110 Ripon Pickle Co Inc
1039 Beier Rd
Ripon, WI 54971-9063   920-748-7110
    Fax: 920-748-8092 rpi@riponpickle.com
        www.riponpickle.com
Celery, chili peppers, egg plant, onions, sauerkraut, green and red peppers
President: Darwin Wiese
Site Manager: Troy Gustke
tgusky@riponpickleco.com
Estimated Sales: $6.6 Million
Number Employees: 50-99
Square Footage: 280000
Type of Packaging: Consumer, Food Service, Private Label, Bulk
Brands Exported: Pickle-O-Pete
Regions Exported to: Central America, South America, Canada, Mexico
Regions Imported from: Central America, Canada, Mexico

48111 Rising Sun Farms
5126 S Pacific Hwy
Phoenix, OR 97535-6606   541-535-8331
    Fax: 541-535-8350 800-888-0795
    elizabeth@risingsunfarms.com
        www.risingsunfarms.com
Oils, mustard, pesto sauces, dried tomatoes, vinegars, salad vinaigrettes, cheese tortas and marinades
Owner: Kim Allen
Coo: Jeff Williams
VP: Richard Fujas
Sales: Jenn Woodward
kim@risingsunfarms.com
Public Relations: Jim Woodward
Operations: Chris Hanry
Plant Manager: Richard Fujas
Purchasing Director: Lynn Perkins
Estimated Sales: $3.2 Million
Number Employees: 20-49
Type of Packaging: Consumer, Food Service, Private Label, Bulk
Brands Exported: Rising Sun Farms

48112 Rito Mints
1055, rue Laverendrye
PO Box 312
Trois Rivieres, QC G9A 5GA
Canada   819-379-1449
    Fax: 819-379-0344 info@ritomints.com
        www.ritomints.com
Candy: mints, hearts and lozenges
President: Morris Masif
General Manager: Peter Nassif
Number Employees: 15
Square Footage: 64000
Type of Packaging: Consumer, Food Service, Private Label, Bulk
Brands Exported: Rito
Regions Exported to: USA
Percentage of Business in Exporting: 15

48113 Ritrovo
4231 W Marginal Way SW
SW
Seattle, WA 98106-1211   206-985-1635
    Fax: 206-768-1191 866-748-7686
    ritrovo@aol.com www.ritrovo.com
Principal: Ilyse Rathet
Owner: Ron Coast
Estimated Sales: $130,000
Number Employees: 1-4

48114 (HQ)Rival Manufacturing Company
800 E 101st Terrace
Suite 100
Kansas City, MO 64131-5308   816-943-4100
    Fax: 816-943-4123 www.rivco.com
Manufacturer and exporter of can openers, vegetable and fruit shredders/slicers, mini choppers, slow cookers and ice cream freezers
Number Employees: 100-249
Other Locations:
    Rival Manufacturing Co.
    Kansas City, MORival Manufacturing Co.

48115 (HQ)Riverside ManufacturingCompany
301 Riverside Drive
P.O. Box 460
Moultrie, GA 31776-0460
          800-841-8677
Manufacturer and exporter of industrial uniforms and clothing for bottlers, bakers, dairy workers, security officers and distillers
President/Chief Executive Officer: Lisa Vereen Zeanah
Contact: Norman Bergman
nbergman@riversideuniforms.com
Estimated Sales: $ 104 Million
Number Employees: 2,000
Square Footage: 1000000

Importers & Exporters / A-Z

Brands Exported: Riverside
Regions Exported to: Worldwide

48116 Riverside ManufacturingCompany
3405 N Arlington Heights Rd
Arlington Hts, IL 60004-1581 847-577-9300
Fax: 847-577-9318 800-877-3349
info@flagmaster.org www.riversidemedicalsc.com
Manufacturer and exporter of custom made plastic and fluorescent display pennants, flags and banners
VP Marketing: Andy Krupp
Estimated Sales: $ 1 - 5 Million
Number Employees: 20-49
Square Footage: 80000
Type of Packaging: Food Service
Regions Exported to: Central America, Middle East
Percentage of Business in Exporting: 3

48117 Riverside Wire & Metal Co.
PO Box 122
Ionia, MI 48846-0122 616-527-3500
Fax: 616-527-8550
Wire racks and baskets
Owner: Don Shephard
Estimated Sales: $ 500,000-$ 1 Million
Number Employees: 5-9
Parent Co: Col-Mell
Type of Packaging: Consumer, Food Service
Regions Exported to: Worldwide
Percentage of Business in Exporting: 10

48118 Riviana Foods Inc.
PO Box 2636
Houston, TX 77252 713-529-3251
sales@riviana.com
www.riviana.com
Rice and pasta.
President/CEO: Bastiaan de Zeeuw
bdezeeuw@riviana.com
Senior VP/CFO: Michael Slavin
Senior VP, Operations: Brett Beckfield
Senior VP, Marketing: Sandra Kim
Senior VP, Human Resources: Gerard Ferguson
Year Founded: 1965
Estimated Sales: $500 Million
Number Employees: 1,000-4,999
Number of Brands: 28
Parent Co: Ebro Foods, S.A.
Type of Packaging: Consumer, Food Service, Private Label, Bulk
Other Locations:
  Corporate Office
  Houston, TX
  Plant
  Brinkley, AR
  Plant
  Carlisle, AR
  Plant
  Clearbrook, MN
  Plant
  Hazen, AR
  Plant
  Memphis, TN
  Corporate OfficeBrinkley
Brands Exported: Mahatma®, Minute®
Regions Exported to: Worldwide

48119 Rixie Paper Products Inc
10 Quinter St
Pottstown, PA 19464-6514 610-323-9220
Fax: 610-323-6146 800-377-2692
www.sonoco.com
Manufacturer and exporter of disposable paper products including coasters: cellulose, pulpboard, budgetboard, nonwoven, etc.; also, placemats and sanitary caps for drinking glasses
President: Tom Johnson
Chairman: Roger Schrum
roger.schrum@sonoco.com
VP Sales/Marketing: Smitty Thomas
VP Operations: Kent Adicks
Plant Manager: Lee Burg
Estimated Sales: $ 5 - 10 Million
Number Employees: 10-19
Parent Co: Engraph
Type of Packaging: Food Service
Brands Exported: Cupkin Coasters; Sof-ette Coasters; RixCaps
Regions Exported to: Central America, South America, Europe, Middle East, Caribbean
Percentage of Business in Exporting: 10

48120 Rjr Technologies
7875 Edgewater Dr
Oakland, CA 94621-2001 510-638-5901
Fax: 510-638-5958 Service@rjrpolymers.com
www.rjrtechnologies.com
Manufacturer and exporter of flexible packaging products including folding foil cartons, barrier films and aluminum foil; also, printing and lamination available
President & CEO: Wil Salhuana
CFO: Tony Bregante
Estimated Sales: $ 1 - 5 Million
Number Employees: 100-249
Regions Exported to: Worldwide

48121 Rjs Carter Co Inc
251 5th St NW # D
New Brighton, MN 55112-6864 651-636-8818
Manufacturer and exporter of synthetic rubber balls for sifter and screener cleaning
President: John Galt
Estimated Sales: Less Than $500,000
Number Employees: 1-4
Brands Exported: Screwballs
Regions Exported to: Worldwide

48122 (HQ)Rl Alber T & Son Inc
60 Long Ridge Rd
Suite 300
Stamford, CT 06902-1838 203-622-7465
Fax: 203-622-7465 800-678-8655
mainmail@albertscandy.com
www.albertscandy.com
Importer and wholesaler/distributor of confectionery products including molded chocolates, seasonal candy, lollypops, mints, toffee, etc.
President: Larry Albert
Contact: Ernest Albert
ealbert@albertscandy.com
Number Employees: 5-9
Regions Imported from: South America, Europe, Asia

48123 Rob Salamida Co Inc
71 Pratt Ave
Suite 1
Johnson City, NY 13790-2255 607-729-4868
Fax: 607-797-4721 800-545-5072
info@spiedie.com www.huntersprideusa.com
Marinades, barbecue sauces and spice blends.
President: Robert Alan Salamida
sweethavens@msn.com
Estimated Sales: $4.2 Million
Number Employees: 1-4
Type of Packaging: Consumer, Food Service, Private Label
Regions Imported from: Worldwide
Percentage of Business in Importing: 40

48124 Robar International Inc
3013 N 114th St
Milwaukee, WI 53222-4289 414-259-1104
Fax: 414-259-0842 800-279-7750
rhoelzl@robarinternational.com
Dispoza-Pak trash compactors.
President: Robert Hoelzl
rhoelzl@robarinternational.com
VP: Daniel Hoelzl
Estimated Sales: Below $ 5 Million
Number Employees: 5-9
Brands Exported: Dispoza-Pak Containers
Regions Exported to: Central America, South America, Europe, Asia, Middle East
Percentage of Business in Exporting: 10

48125 Robby Vapor Systems
10224 NW 47th Street
Sunrise, FL 33351-7970 954-746-3080
Fax: 954-746-0036 800-888-8711
robbyvapor@aol.com
Manufacturer, importer and exporter of stainless steel vapor cleaning systems and carts
President: Fran Vogt-Strauss
Office Manager: Lisa Skewes
Estimated Sales: $500,000-$1 Million
Number Employees: 9
Square Footage: 22240
Regions Exported to: Central America, Canada, Mexico, Caribbean, Latin America
Regions Imported from: Europe

48126 Robelan Displays Inc
395 Westbury Blvd
Hempstead, NY 11550-1900 516-564-8600
Fax: 516-564-8077 865-564-8600
main@robelan.net www.robelan.net
Merchandising fixture and food display units; importer of theme props
President: Andrew Abatemarco
CFO: John Didiovanni
HR Executive: Rob Abatemarco
main@robelan.net
VP Sales: Rob Abutemarco
Customer Service: Carol Kirk
Estimated Sales: $ 5 - 10 Million
Number Employees: 50-99
Type of Packaging: Food Service

48127 Robert Mondavi Winery
7801 Saint Helena Highway
Oakville, CA 94562 707-226-1395
Fax: 707-251-4110 888-766-6328
www.robertmondaviwinery.com
Wines
CEO: Greg Evans
Winemaker: Genevieve Janssens
genevieve@robertsinskey.com
VP Marketing: Kevin Conner
Vice President, Operations: Karen Egan
Estimated Sales: $ 42 Million
Number Employees: 600
Number of Brands: 1
Square Footage: 5000
Other Locations:
  Woodbridge Winery
  Acampo, CAWoodbridge Winery
Regions Exported to: Worldwide

48128 Robert Wholey & Co Inc
1711 Penn Ave
Pittsburgh, PA 15222 412-391-3737
Fax: 412-391-7247 888-946-5397
customerservice@wholey.com www.wholey.com
Wholesaler/distributor of seafood, poultry and meat including fillets; importer of frozen seafood; serving the food service market.
CEO: James Wholey
Year Founded: 1912
Estimated Sales: $50-100 Million
Number Employees: 100-249
Square Footage: 400000
Type of Packaging: Consumer, Food Service, Private Label, Bulk
Brands Imported: Wholey
Regions Imported from: South America, Asia
Percentage of Business in Importing: 85

48129 Robert-James Sales
699 Hertel Ave
Buffalo, NY 14207-2341 716-871-0091
Fax: 716-871-0923 877-877-1325
RJSales@RJSales.com www.RJSales.com
Manufacturer and exporter of fittings, pipes, tubing, hose clamps and sanitary stainless steel valves
Sales Manager: Thomas Callahan
Estimated Sales: $50-100 Million
Number Employees: 100-249
Regions Exported to: Worldwide

48130 Robertet Flavors
10 Colonial Dr.
Piscataway, NJ 08854 732-981-8300
Fax: 732-981-1717
robertetFlavors@robertetUSA.com
www.robertet.com
Flavorings.
Chairman/CEO: Philippe Maubert
Head of the Flavourings Division: Olivier Maubert
CFO: Gilles Audoli
Managing Director, Flavourings Division: Antoine Kastler
Director, Industrial Operations: Herve Bellon
Year Founded: 1850
Estimated Sales: $524.9 Million
Number Employees: 1,800
Number of Brands: 5+
Square Footage: 16805
Parent Co: Robertet SA
Type of Packaging: Food Service
Other Locations:
  Robertet Culinary
  Schoten, BelgiumRobertet Culinary
Brands Exported: Citra-Next®, Natur-Cell®, Flavour sensations, SMArt® flavours, & Accord® flavours

543

Importers & Exporters / A-Z

Regions Exported to: Worldwide

48131 Roberts Ferry Nut Co
20493 Yosemite Blvd
Waterford, CA 95386-9506   209-874-3247
                    Fax: 209-874-3707
            www.robertsferrynutcompany.com
Almonds and popcorn
Owner: Brigitte Hayat
brigitteh@pjcc.org
Partner: Dorothy Mallory
Estimated Sales: $3135592
Number Employees: 20-49
Type of Packaging: Consumer, Bulk
Regions Exported to: Worldwide

48132 Roberts Poly Pro Inc
5416 Wyoming Ave
Charlotte, NC 28273-8861   704-588-1794
        Fax: 704-588-1821   800-269-7409
            info@robertspolypro.com
            www.robertspolypro.com
Manufacturer and exporter of converting equipment and systems including folder/gluers, case packers, prefeeders, turntables, stack turners, etc.; also, plastic packaging components and machinery including label and pour spoutapplicators, etc
President: Vipul Deshani
vipul.deshani@vvfltd.com
VP Engineering: Claude Monsees
Estimated Sales: $5-10 Million
Number Employees: 50-99
Square Footage: 140000
Parent Co: Pro Mach
Regions Exported to: South America, Europe
Percentage of Business in Exporting: 20

48133 Roberts Seed
982 22 Rd
Axtell, NE 68924-3618   308-743-2565
    Fax: 308-743-2048   robertsseed@gtmc.net
            www.robertsseed.com
Grain, soybeans, popcorn kernels, wheat, corn and beans
President: Joe Roberts
robertsseed@gtmc.net
Estimated Sales: $950,000
Number Employees: 1-4
Square Footage: 30000
Type of Packaging: Private Label, Bulk
Regions Exported to: Europe, Asia
Percentage of Business in Exporting: 65

48134 Robertson Furniture Co Inc
890 Elberton St
Toccoa, GA 30577-3479   706-886-1494
        Fax: 706-886-8998   800-241-0713
            tzirkle@robertson-furniture.com
            www.robertson-furniture.com
Manufacturer and importer of chairs, tables, booths, steel frame seating and casegoods
President: Scott Hodges
tzirkle@robertson-furniture.com
Director Sales/Marketing: Tim Zirkle
Sales Exec: Tim Zirkle
Estimated Sales: $ 10 - 20 Million
Number Employees: 50-99
Square Footage: 400000
Type of Packaging: Food Service, Private Label
Regions Imported from: Europe

48135 Robin Shepherd Group
1301 Riverplace Blvd.
Suite 1100
Jacksonville, FL 32207   904-359-0981
        Fax: 904-359-0808   877-896-8774
    trsginfo@shepherdagency.com www.trsg.net
Consultant providing food product development, point of purchase display design, public relations and marketing services; importer, exporter and packager of specialty foods including condiments and sauces
President: Robin Shepherd
VP Marketing: Tom Nuijens
Contact: Marina Martin
mmartin@shepherdagency.com
Estimated Sales: $5-10 Million
Number Employees: 20-49
Square Footage: 20000
Type of Packaging: Consumer, Food Service, Private Label
Brands Exported: Iguana; Tamarindo Bay; Caribbean Condiments
Regions Exported to: South America, Europe, Caribbean
Percentage of Business in Exporting: 15
Brands Imported: Iguana; Tamarindo; Pirate's Blend
Regions Imported from: Central America
Percentage of Business in Importing: 90

48136 Robinson Canning Company
129 E Oakridge Park
Metairie, LA 70005   504-835-1177
                    Fax: 504-436-1585
Wholesaler/distributor, importer and exporter of canned shrimp, oysters and crab meat
President: Alan Robinson
CEO: K Robinson
CFO: Leila Robinson
Estimated Sales: $ .5 - 1 million
Number Employees: 1-4
Square Footage: 8800
Brands Exported: High Sea; Louisiana; Nola; Blue Gulf
Regions Exported to: Europe, South Africa
Percentage of Business in Exporting: 5
Brands Imported: High Sea
Regions Imported from: Asia
Percentage of Business in Importing: 85

48137 Robinson Industries Inc
3051 W Curtis Rd
Coleman, MI 48618-8549   989-465-6111
    Fax: 989-465-1217   info@robinsonind.com
            www.robinsonind.com
Manufacturer and exporter of thermoformed and injection molded plastic pallets, trays and totes. Also, consumer items. Custom designed.
President: Bin Robinson
CEO: Inez Kaleto
CFO: Kurt Schefka
Research & Development: Jeff Sankler
Quality Control: Rod Crites
Marketing: Ronda Robinson
VP Sales/Manager: Mark Weidner
Production: Tom Roberts
Plant Manager: Melissa Jellum
Purchasing: Jason Pahl
Estimated Sales: $40 Million
Number Employees: 100-249
Square Footage: 152005
Regions Exported to: Worldwide

48138 Robinson's No 1 Ribs
940 Madison St
Oak Park, IL 60302-4430   708-383-8452
        Fax: 708-383-9486   800-836-6750
        charlie@rib1.com   www.rib1.com
Barbecue sauces
Owner: Charlie Robinson
sales@rib1.com
Vice President: Helen Robinson
Marketing Director: Cordell Robinson
Operations Manager: Bruce Swerdlow
Estimated Sales: $500,000-$1 Million
Number Employees: 20-49
Square Footage: 40000
Parent Co: Robinson's #1 Ribs Restaurants
Type of Packaging: Consumer, Food Service, Bulk
Brands Exported: Charlie Robinson's Barbecue Sauce; Mississippi Hot Sauce; Charlie Robinson's #1 Meat Seasoning
Regions Exported to: Europe, Asia, Canada

48139 Robot Coupe
280 S Perkins St
Ridgeland, MS 39157-2719   601-898-8411
        Fax: 601-898-9134   800-824-1646
            info@robotcoupeusa.com
Manufactures commercial food processors, vegetable preparation units, and combination processing units.
President: Jay Williams
VP: David Mouck
VP/Controller: C Redding
VP Marketing: David Mouck
National Accounts Manager: David Mouck
Estimated Sales: $10-20 Million
Number Employees: 50-99
Square Footage: 60000
Type of Packaging: Food Service
Brands Exported: Robot Coupe; Food Processor; Blixers; Vertical Cutter Mixers; Power Mixers
Regions Exported to: Canada, Mexico, Caribbean
Percentage of Business in Exporting: 10

48140 Robot Factory
3740 Interpark Dr
Colorado Springs, CO 80907   719-447-0331
        Fax: 719-447-0332   800-717-6268
            info@robotfactory.com
Robot devices for entertainment, promotional and educational purposes. We design high quality, reliable robots ranging from remotely controlled mobile robots to animated musicians. These life-sized, furry characters interactivelyengage with their audience through wireless microphone systems
Number Employees: 7

48141 Rochester Midland Corp
155 Paragon Dr
Rochester, NY 14624-1167   585-336-2200
        Fax: 585-266-8919   800-836-1627
            www.rochestermidland.com
Manufacturer and exporter of production cleaning and sanitizing chemicals for food and beverage processing facilities; also, water and wastewater treatment chemicals
President/Chief Operating Officer: Michael Coyner
CEO: Kathy Lindahl
klindahl@rochestermidland.com
Chief Financial Officer: Lisa Steel
Senior Vice President: Al Swierzewski
Senior Vice President, Marketing: Owen Foster
Vice President, Sales: Mike Burroughs
Senior Vice President, Operations: Howard Shames
Purchasing Manager: Richard Roy
Estimated Sales: $ 83 Million
Number Employees: 500-999
Square Footage: 190000
Brands Exported: Rochester Midland
Regions Exported to: Worldwide
Percentage of Business in Exporting: 5

48142 Rock Valley Oil & Chemical Co
1911 Windsor Rd
Loves Park, IL 61111-4293   815-654-2401
    Fax: 815-654-2428   www.rockvalleyoil.com
'Today, Rock Valley has grown to be recognized as an international manufacturer and supplier of superior quality industrial lubricants, metalworking and hydraulic fluids, as well as reference oils and calibrating fluids tailored to theautomotive and heavy truck industry'. www.rockvalleyoil.com
President: Roger Schramm
sales@rockvalleyoil.com
Estimated Sales: $12.5 Million
Number Employees: 50-99

48143 Rock-Ola Manufacturing Corp
2335 W 208th St
Torrance, CA 90501-1443   310-328-1306
    Fax: 310-328-3736   www.rock-ola.com
CEO: Glenn Streeter
gstreeter@rockola.com
CEO: Glenn Streeter
Estimated Sales: $ .5 - 1 million
Number Employees: 20-49

48144 Rock-Tenn Company
504 Tasman St
Norcross, GA 30071   608-223-6272
    Fax: 608-246-1145   www.rocktenn.com
Manufacturer and exporter of folding paper cartons, boxes and displays
Owner: Bill Rock
General Manager: Gary Adrian
Estimated Sales: $5-10 Million
Number Employees: 1-4
Regions Exported to: Worldwide

48145 Rocket Man
2501 Maple St
Louisville, KY 40211-1163   502-775-7502
        Fax: 502-775-7519   800-365-6661
    sales@rocketman.com   www.rocketman.com
Manufacturer, importer and exporter of backpack drink dispensers and portable beverage dispensing equipment
Owner: Mike Hinson
Contact: Mazen Masri
mazenm@rocketman.com
Estimated Sales: $1-3 Million
Number Employees: 10-19
Square Footage: 20000
Regions Exported to: Worldwide
Percentage of Business in Exporting: 50
Regions Imported from: Worldwide

Importers & Exporters / A-Z

48146 Rockford-Midland Corporation
1715 Northrock Ct
Rockford, IL 61103 815-877-0212
Fax: 815-877-0419 800-327-7908
Manufacturer and exporter of fully and semi-automatic case packers and sealers including hot melt, cold glue and tape
President: Adrienne Murphy
Sales Director: Donna Bonetti
Production Manager: Tim Vronch
Purchasing Manager: Karen Steiner
Estimated Sales: $ 5-10 Million
Number Employees: 20-49
Square Footage: 80000
Regions Exported to: Worldwide
Percentage of Business in Exporting: 10

48147 Rockline Industries
4343 S Taylor Dr
Sheboygan, WI 53081 920-453-2769
800-558-7790
customercareteam@rocklineind.com
www.rocklineind.com
Private label consumer products; including coffee filters and baby wipes.
President: Randy Rudolph
Year Founded: 1976
Estimated Sales: $100-500 Million
Regions Exported to: Worldwide
Percentage of Business in Exporting: 8

48148 Rocky Point Shrimp Association
429 West Madison Street
Phoenix, AZ 85003 602-254-8041
Fax: 602-523-9637
Shrimp
Estimated Sales: $ 3 - 5 Million
Number Employees: 5-9

48149 Rocky Top Farms
11486 Essex Rd
Ellsworth, MI 49729-9650 231-599-2251
Fax: 231-599-2352 800-862-9303
sales@rockytopfarms.com www.rockytopfarm.com
Processor and exporter of preserves including raspberry, cherry, strawberry, blackberry and black raspberry; also, butter toppings
President: Tom Cooper
tomcooper@rockytopfarm.com
Estimated Sales: $ 3 - 5 Million
Number Employees: 5-9
Type of Packaging: Consumer, Bulk

48150 Rod Golden Hatchery Inc
85 13th St. NE
Cullman, AL 35055 256-734-0941
Broiler, fryer, and roaster chickens.
President: Forrest Ingram
Estimated Sales: $34 Million
Number Employees: 1010
Square Footage: 2000
Parent Co: Ingram Farms
Type of Packaging: Consumer, Food Service, Private Label, Bulk
Regions Exported to: Worldwide

48151 Roddy Products Pkgng CoInc
1 Merion Ter
Aldan, PA 19018-3000 610-623-7040
Fax: 610-623-0521 joearoddy@aol.com
Manufacturer and exporter of wooden shipping crates
President: Joseph Masticola Sr
CFO: Joseph Masticola Sr
IT: Tina Moore
marieroddy@aol.com
Estimated Sales: $ 1 - 2.5 Million
Number Employees: 10-19
Regions Exported to: Worldwide
Percentage of Business in Exporting: 60

48152 Rodsan
PO Box 8576
San Juan, PR 00910-0576 787-792-4289
Fax: 787-273-4765
Importer of groceries, meats and bags including paper and plastic
President (Ventura): Ricardo Rodriguez
President (Rodsan): Roberto Rodriguez
Number Employees: 20-49
Square Footage: 120000
Brands Imported: Hillshire Farm; Kahn's; Seneca Foods; Nissin Foods; Estee Food Co.

48153 Roechling Engineered Plastics
PO Box 2729
Gastonia, NC 28053-2729 704-922-7814
Fax: 704-922-7651 800-541-4419
Manufacturer and exporter of conveyor components, industrial plastics, HDPE, PP, UHMW and PVDF; also, sheets, tubes and profiles
President: Lewis Carter
Quality Control: Brychan Griffiths
Marketing: Tim Brown
Sales: Paul Krawczyk
Contact: Kathy Millen
millen@roechling.com
Number Employees: 50-99
Square Footage: 560000
Brands Exported: Polystone
Regions Exported to: Central America, South America

48154 Rogers Collection
10 Dana Street
Suite 301
Portland, ME 04101 207-828-2000
Fax: 207-828-4000 contact@rogerscollection.us
www.rogerscollection.us
Olive oil, cheese, sauces, condiments, pasta, vinegar, salt, meat, olives, fish, marmalades, jam and honey.
Chairman: Ken Crerar
Managing Director: Carrie Blakeman
Sales: Jen Bonaccorsi
Warehouse Manager: Jason Arela
Other Locations:
  Warehouse
  Lydhurst, NJWarehouse
Brands Imported: Acetaia Cattani, Almas Ara, Arrigoni Battista SPA, Bauma, Bee Raw, Bertagni, Biolea, Can Pujol, CastelaS, Castello di Ama, Cinco Jotas, Fermin, Finca Pascualete
Regions Imported from: Worldwide

48155 (HQ)Rogers International Inc
10 Dana St # 301
Portland, ME 04101-4087 207-828-2000
Fax: 207-828-4000
contact@therogerscollection.com
www.therogerscollection.com
Full-line condiments, olive oil, balsamic vinegar, sherry vinegar, cheese, prociutto, cured meats i.e. prociutto/bacon, caviar, olives.
Chairman: Ken Crerar
General Manager: Carrie Davenport
Director, Sales: Jen Bonaccorsi
Customer Service: Jackie Schumacher
Warehouse Associate: Jason Arela
Estimated Sales: $330,000
Number Employees: 1-4
Other Locations:
  Rogers International Ltd.
  Lyndhurst, NJRogers International Ltd.
Brands Imported: Castello Di Ama; Moulins Mahjoub; Nunez De Prado; Pio Tosini; Appennino PlosdeEspana
Regions Imported from: Europe
Percentage of Business in Importing: 100

48156 Rogers International Inc
10 Dana St # 301
Portland, ME 04101-4087 207-828-2000
Fax: 207-828-4000 www.therogerscollection.com
Importers of artisan cheeses and olive oils from Spain and Italy as well as oil and condiments from Tonisa
Chairman: Ken Crerar
Logistics and Marketing: Paola D'Amato
Director of Sales: Jen Bonaccorsi
Customer Service: Jackie Schumacher
Operations: Kara Rubin
Estimated Sales: $ 3 - 5 Million
Number Employees: 1-4
Brands Imported: Casello di Ama; Nunez de Prado; Pio Tosini; Moulins Mahjoub; Pittaffo; Sommariva; Trevi
Regions Imported from: Europe, North Africa
Percentage of Business in Importing: 100

48157 Rogers' Chocolates Ltd
4253 Commerce Circle
Victoria, BC V8Z 4M2
Canada 250-727-6851
Fax: 250-384-5750 800-663-2220
info@rogerschocolates.com
www.rogerschocolates.com
Processor and exporter of confectionery products including boxed cream-filled and dark chocolates, chocolate mint wafers, almond brittles, caramel nutcorn, fudge, etc
President: Steve Parkhill
Estimated Sales: $10 Million
Number Employees: 130
Square Footage: 87000
Type of Packaging: Consumer, Private Label
Regions Exported to: USA
Percentage of Business in Exporting: 5

48158 Rogue Ales Brewery
748 SW Bay Blvd
Newport, OR 97365-4836 541-265-3188
Fax: 541-265-7528 www.rogue.com
Processor and exporter of ale, lager and barley wine
President: Jack Joyce
CEO: Jack Choice
jack@rogue.com
CEO: Jack Choice
Estimated Sales: $5-10 Million
Number Employees: 50-99
Type of Packaging: Consumer, Food Service
Brands Exported: Rogue Ales
Regions Exported to: Europe, Japan, Canada
Percentage of Business in Exporting: 2

48159 Rohrer Corp.
717 Seville Rd
PO Box 1009
Wadsworth, OH 44282
800-243-6640
info@rohrer.com www.rohrer.com
Manufacturer and exporter of skin packaging, blister cards and stretch pack cards
National Sales Director: Jim Price
Year Founded: 1973
Estimated Sales: $50-100 Million
Number Employees: 100-249
Type of Packaging: Bulk
Regions Exported to: Worldwide

48160 Roland Foods
71 West 23rd Street
New York, NY 10010 800-221-4030
info@rolandfood.com
www.rolandfood.com
Asian food, pasta and sauces, baked goods, cooking wines, dessert, Indian food, oils, seafood, juice and canned vegetables
CEO: Jim Wagner
Chief Financial Officer: Ted McCormick
VP, Global Procurement: Joseph Gozzi
Chief Operating Officer: Tyler Hawes
Year Founded: 1934
Estimated Sales: Under $500,000
Number Employees: 51-200
Brands Imported: Don Bruno© Pasta, Roland© Truffle Mac & Cheese, Don Bruno© Crostini, Jacob's©
Regions Imported from: Worldwide

48161 Roland Foods, LLC
71 W. 23rd St.
New York, NY 10010 212-741-8290
800-221-4030
www.rolandfood.com
Specialty foods including ingredients, groceries, meat products and canned fish.
CEO: Jim Wagner
Vice President, People & Culture: Aimee Miralles
Chief Operating Officer: Tyler Hawes
Year Founded: 1934
Estimated Sales: $187 Million
Number Employees: 58
Brands Exported: Roland; Consul; Costamar
Brands Imported: Roland; Consul; Costamar
Regions Imported from: Central America, South America, Europe, Asia
Percentage of Business in Importing: 99

48162 Roland Machinery
816 N Dirksen Pkwy
Springfield, IL 62702-6115 217-789-7711
Fax: 217-744-7314 800-325-1183
Breadings, batters, baking powder, fermentation additives, dough conditioners, sausage/meat binders, chocolate milk, baking and cake mixes, etc.; exporter of baking mixes

Importers & Exporters / A-Z

CEO: Ray Roland
rroland@rolandmachinery.com
COO: Ian MacEwan
Vice President: Terry McGuire
Plant Manager: Keith Gill
Purchasing Manager: Mary Gajewski
Number Employees: 20-49
Square Footage: 280000
Parent Co: Abitec Corporation
Type of Packaging: Private Label, Bulk

48163 Rolfs @ Boone
1773 219th Ln
P.O. Box 369
Boone, IA 50036 515-432-2010
 Fax: 515-432-5262 800-265-2010
info@boonegroup.com www.boonegroup.com
Manufacturer and exporter of dust systems, high and low bag filters, cyclones, ducting, fittings, bearing and belt alignment instrumentation and hazard and motion monitoring controls
President: Kevin Miles
Sales: Greg Knoxx
Dust Control: Delmar Mains
Production Manager: Brian Huffman
Estimated Sales: $ 5 - 10 Million
Number Employees: 10-19
Square Footage: 112000
Regions Exported to: Worldwide
Percentage of Business in Exporting: 10

48164 Roll-O-Sheets Canada
130 Big Bay Point Road
Barrie, ON L4N 9B4
Canada 705-722-5223
 Fax: 705-722-7120 888-767-3456
info@roll-o-sheets.com
Manufacturer, importer and exporter of converted PVC film; wholesaler/distributor of vacuum pouches, table covers, Cellophane and plastic sandwich and ovenable containers
General Manager: Bryce Atkinson
Number Employees: 20
Square Footage: 88000
Brands Exported: Wrap It
Regions Exported to: Europe, Cuba
Percentage of Business in Exporting: 2
Brands Imported: Qualitad
Regions Imported from: Europe, Asia, Mexico, USA
Percentage of Business in Importing: 20

48165 Rollprint Packaging Prods Inc
320 S Stewart Ave
Addison, IL 60101-3310 630-628-1700
 Fax: 630-628-8510 800-276-7629
mail@rollprint.com www.rollprint.com
Manufacturer and exporter of flexible food packaging materials including lidding, pouches, peelable and non-peelable composites. FlexForm and ClearForm line of forming webs provide tough, puncture resistant substrates that provide uniform film draw without snapback for frozen food applications including: poultry, meat, seafood, bakery, pizza, vegetables, fruits, and bakery goods.
President: Dhuanne Dodril
ddodrill@rollprint.com
CFO: David Reed
Marketing Manager: Edward Verkuilen
Estimated Sales: $20-50 Million
Number Employees: 100-249
Square Footage: 198000
Type of Packaging: Consumer, Food Service, Private Label, Bulk
Brands Exported: Flexible Packaging Materials
Regions Exported to: South America, Europe, Asia
Percentage of Business in Exporting: 25
Brands Imported: Flexible Packaging Materials For Future Converting
Regions Imported from: Europe, Asia
Percentage of Business in Importing: 5

48166 Roman Sausage Company
1810 Richard Avenue
Santa Clara, CA 95050-2818 408-988-1222
 Fax: 408-988-0546 800-497-7462
Processor and importer of patties including sausage, salmon and tuna; also, salmon fillets
President: Amir Kanji
akanji@biomeddiagnostics.com
Estimated Sales: $1,100,000
Number Employees: 10
Square Footage: 32000
Regions Imported from: Europe, Middle East
Percentage of Business in Importing: 10

48167 Romanow Container
346 University Ave
Westwood, MA 02090-2309 781-320-9200
 Fax: 781-461-5900 www.romanowcontainer.com
Manufacturer and exporter of corrugated and wooden boxes, foam converters and fabricators; also, contract packaging available
Owner: Theodore Romanow
info@romanowcontainer.com
Estimated Sales: $5-10 Million
Number Employees: 100-249
Regions Exported to: Europe

48168 Rome Machine & Foundry Co
906 Walnut Ave SW
PO Box 5383
Rome, GA 30161-6166 706-234-6763
 Fax: 706-232-0337 800-538-7663
Manufacturer and exporter of custom fabricated conveyors and food processing machinery
President: Albert Berry
aberry@romemachine.com
Sales/Marketing Manager: Willis Rogers
Chief Engineer: Jay Burnett
Purchasing Manager: Ted Porterfield
Estimated Sales: $1-2.5 Million
Number Employees: 10-19
Square Footage: 129600
Regions Exported to: Worldwide
Percentage of Business in Exporting: 30

48169 (HQ)Ron Son Foods Inc
81 Locke Ave
PO Box 38
Swedesboro, NJ 08085-1059 856-241-7333
 Fax: 856-241-7338 jim@ronsonfoods.com
 www.ronsonfoods.com
Manufacturer, importer and importer of canned mushrooms, olives, olive oil, Italian pasta, anchovies, roasted peppers and artichokes
Owner: Ron Son
ron@ronsonfoods.com
CEO: James Bianco
CEO: James Bianco
Chief Marketing Officer: Peter Goldsberry
VP Sales: James Bianco
ron@ronsonfoods.com
Estimated Sales: $2-4 Million
Number Employees: 5-9
Square Footage: 200000
Type of Packaging: Consumer, Food Service, Private Label, Bulk
Brands Exported: J-L; Joylin; Ron Son; Ghigi; Borelli
Regions Exported to: Central America, South America, Canada
Brands Imported: Joylin; Ron Son; J-L
Regions Imported from: Europe, Asia
Percentage of Business in Importing: 50

48170 Ron-Son Mushroom Products
Ellis & Deptford Rd
Glassboro, NJ 08028 856-881-2924
 Fax: 352-588-0369 800-237-8598
www.ronsonfoods.com
Canned mushrooms, olives, pasta, olive oil, artichokes
President: Jim Bianci
Estimated Sales: $10-20 Million
Number Employees: 10-19
Type of Packaging: Bulk
Brands Imported: Ron-Son
Regions Imported from: Europe
Percentage of Business in Importing: 100

48171 Rondo Inc
51 Joseph St
Moonachie, NJ 07074-1027 201-229-9700
 Fax: 201-229-0018 800-882-0633
info@us.rondo-online.com
Manufacturer, importer and wholesaler/distributor of high volume bakery equipment including mixers and sheeters
President: Jerry Murphy
jerry.murphy@rondo-online.com
VP Sales: Andrea Henderson
Estimated Sales: $ 2.5-5 Million
Number Employees: 20-49
Regions Imported from: Europe
Percentage of Business in Importing: 50

48172 Rondo of America
209 Great Hill Rd
Naugatuck, CT 6770 203-723-7474
 Fax: 203-723-5831 custserv@rondopackaging.com
 www.rondopackaging.com
Manufacturer and exporter of protective packaging, automatic packaging machinery and paper boxes
Owner: James Sinkins
Contact: Donna Pendleton
donna@rondopackaging.com
Estimated Sales: $5-10 Million
Number Employees: 20-49
Parent Co: Interrondo

48173 Ronnie's Ceramic Company
5999 3rd St
San Francisco, CA 94124 415-822-8068
 Fax: 415-822-8966 800-888-8218
Manufacturer and exporter of tableware, platters, coffee mugs and water pitchers
President: Risly Cheung
Vice President: Risly Chin
Estimated Sales: $ 3 - 5,000,000
Number Employees: 15
Square Footage: 8500
Regions Exported to: Canada
Regions Imported from: Asia

48174 Ronzoni
PO Box 5400
Largo, FL 33779
 800-730-5957
www.ronzoni.com
Pastas, including gluten free, vegetable based, and whole grain varieties
President/CEO: Bastiaan de Zeeuw
Senior VP/CFO: Michael Slavin
Senior VP/COO: Enrique Zaragoza
Number Employees: 75
Parent Co: Riviana Foods Inc.
Type of Packaging: Consumer, Food Service
Regions Exported to: Worldwide

48175 Roosevelt Dairy Trade, Inc
2 W Market Street
Suite 400
Westchester, PA 19382 610-692-1866
 Fax: 610-692-5733 www.rooseveltdairy.com
Whey powders, whole milk powder, casein/caseinates, whey protein concentrate, butter, lactose, buttermilk powder, nonfat dry milk, brewer's yeast, permeate, fluid products
President: Thomas Roosevelt
Estimated Sales: $40 Million
Number Employees: 6
Type of Packaging: Bulk
Regions Exported to: Central America, South America, Asia, Mexico; Canada

48176 (HQ)Rooto Corp
3505 W Grand River Ave
Howell, MI 48855-9610 517-546-8330
 Fax: 517-548-5162
Manufacturer and exporter of ammonia, liquid soap and chemical cleaners for drains, toilets and septic tanks
Manager: Penny Rulason
National Sales Manager: Roger Sheets
Manager: Roger Sheets
roger.sheets@rootocorp.com
Plant Manager: Ken Wood
Purchasing Manager: Dennis West
Estimated Sales: $2.5-5 Million
Number Employees: 20-49
Square Footage: 1000000
Type of Packaging: Consumer, Food Service, Private Label
Brands Exported: Rooto; Blue Ribbon
Regions Exported to: Central America, South America, Asia, Middle East

48177 Ropak
1515 W.22nd Street
Suite 550
Oak Brook, IL 60523
Canada
 800-527-2267
sales@bwaycorp.com www.ropakcorp.com
Manufacturer and exporter of polyethylene containers
President: Greg Toft
Sales Representative: Ricahrd Harrison
Operations Manager: Nevin McKay

Importers & Exporters / A-Z

Number Employees: 110
Parent Co: Bway Corporation
Type of Packaging: Food Service, Bulk
Regions Exported to: USA
Percentage of Business in Exporting: 50

48178 Ropak Manufacturing Co Inc
1019 Cedar Lake Rd SE
Decatur, AL 35603-1730   256-350-4241
Fax: 256-350-1611   sales@ropak.com
www.ropak.com
Manufacturer and exporter of form/fill/seal, liquid/dry and vertical/horizontal packagers, stik-pak packager
President/CEO: Ernest Matthews
VP, Electrical Engineer: Richard Matthews
Business Development: Chuck Garrett
VP Operations: Ernest Matthrews
Purchasing Manager: Ken Ray
Estimated Sales: $5-10,000,000
Number Employees: 20-49
Brands Exported: Expresspak
Regions Exported to: Worldwide
Percentage of Business in Exporting: 2

48179 Roquette America Inc.
2211 Innovation Dr.
Geneva, IL 60134   630-463-9430
Fax: 319-526-2542   www.roquette.com
Corn, wheat and potato food ingredients including modified starches, proteins and high fructose and maltose syrups.
President/Chief Executive Officer: Dominique Baumann
CFO: Eric Loges
Year Founded: 1933
Estimated Sales: $100 Million
Number Employees: 8,400
Square Footage: 19107
Parent Co: Roquette Freres
Regions Exported to: Central America, South America, Canada, Mexico

48180 (HQ)Rosco Inc
14431 91st Ave
Jamaica, NY 11435-4302   718-526-2652
Fax: 718-297-0323   800-227-2095
www.roscomirrors.com
Manufacturer and exporter of acrylic and glass convex safety mirrors
President: Sol Englander
Quality Control: George Lewandowski
VP and Finance: Danny Englander
VP Engineering and Ops: Ben Englander
National Sales Manager: Dave Mostel
Sales Manager: Joe Liberman
Contact: Amy Ahn
aahn@roscomirrors.com
Estimated Sales: $ 5 - 10 Million
Number Employees: 5-9
Square Footage: 140000

48181 Rose Forgrove
1 Illinois St Ste 300
Suite 400
Saint Charles, IL 60174   630-443-1317
Fax: 630-377-3069   www.hayssen.com
Manufacturer and exporter of flow wrappers for food and candy
VP Sales: Liam Buckley
Number Employees: 3
Square Footage: 5000
Parent Co: Howven
Regions Exported to: Worldwide
Percentage of Business in Exporting: 50

48182 Rose Hill Enterprises
6760 SW Hergert Rd
Cornelius, OR 97113-6024   503-357-7556
Fax: 503-357-5522   888-410-7556
info@rosehillenter.com   www.rosehillenter.com
Importer and distributor of Chinese ginger products
Owner: Elizabeth Rose
elizabeth@rosehillenter.com
CEO: Leonard Rose
Estimated Sales: $ 5 - 10 Million
Number Employees: 10-19
Brands Imported: CHINROSE

48183 (HQ)Rose Packing Co Inc
65 S Barrington Rd
South Barrington, IL 60010-9589   847-381-5700
Fax: 847-381-9424   800-323-7363
postmaster@rosepacking.com
www.rosepacking.com
Meat products including; canadian bacon, hams, boneless turkey, pork loin, sausages, meatballs, pork shoulder, toppings, fresh/frozen meats, pizza toppers, and zip-packs.
President & CEO: Dwight Stiehl
williamrose@rosepacking.com
CFO: James O'Hara
Executive Vice President: Jim Vandenbergh
Director of Information Systems: Marty Strickler
Quality Assurance Manager: Sean R. Tuftedal
Dir of Marketing & Advertising: Erik W. Vandenbergh
Retail Sales Manager: Larry Null
Lab Director: Maria Maris
Director of Operations: Michael Reiter
Director of Product Development: Peter D. Rose
Plant Superintendent: Joseph Mihalov
Purchasing Manager: Bob Jones
Number Employees: 500-999
Type of Packaging: Consumer, Food Service
Other Locations:
  Rose Packing Company Plant
  Chicago, ILRose Packing Company Plant
Regions Exported to: Worldwide

48184 Rosenthal & Kline
123 NYC Terminal Market
125
Bronx, NY 10474-7303   718-542-1800
Fax: 718-542-5523
Importer and wholesaler/distributor of produce
President: Burton Kline
Estimated Sales: $10-20 Million
Number Employees: 20-49
Regions Imported from: South America, Europe, Caribbean

48185 Roseville Charcoal & Mfg Co
500 Monroe St
Zanesville, OH 43701-3875   740-452-5473
Fax: 740-452-5474
Manufacturer and exporter of industrial and commercial charcoal briquettes including hardwood, granular and lump
President: Tim R Longstreth
Estimated Sales: $1-2.5 Million
Number Employees: 1-4
Regions Exported to: Worldwide

48186 Rosina Food Holdings Inc
170 French Rd
Buffalo, NY 14227-2777   716-668-0123
Fax: 716-668-1132   888-767-4621
gsetter@rosina.com   www.rosina.com
Italian foods including; appetizers, pastas, pizza toppings, meatballs, eggplant, specialty sausages, and entrees for consumers, industrial, foodservice and international markets.
President & CEO: Russell Corigliano
rcorigliano@rosina.com
Chairman: James Corigliano
CFO/COO: Roger Palczewski
VP: Joseph Corigliano
Manager Product Development: Nicholas Arbore
Quality Assurance Manager: Dan Etzinger
VP Marketing: Frank Corigliano
Communications Director: Nick Lukasiewicz
VP Engineering: Viren Sitwala
Estimated Sales: $32.4 Million
Number Employees: 250-499
Square Footage: 60000
Type of Packaging: Food Service

48187 Rosito & Bisani ImportsInc
940 S LA Brea Ave
Los Angeles, CA 90036-4808   323-937-1888
Fax: 323-938-0728   800-848-4444
admin@rosito-bisani.com   www.rositobisani.com
Wholesaler/distributor and importer of espresso/cappuccino machines, granita/pasta machines, electric coffee grinders, wood burning pizza ovens, etc.; serving the food service market
President: Rosanna Rosito
rosannar@rosito-bisani.com
CEO: Bosito
Marketing Manager: Michael Teahan
National Sales Manager: Michael Girgis
Estimated Sales: $1-2.5 Million
Number Employees: 20-49
Square Footage: 60000
Brands Imported: Brasilia; Desco; Danesi
Regions Imported from: Europe
Percentage of Business in Importing: 95

48188 Ross & Wallace Inc
204 Old Covington Hwy
Hammond, LA 70403-5121   985-345-1321
Fax: 985-345-1370   800-854-2300
customerservice@rossandwallace.com
www.rossandwallace.com
Manufacturer and exporter of paper and plastic bags and wrappings
President: Ken Ross
Chairman: Albert Ross
Estimated Sales: $10-20 Million
Number Employees: 50-99
Square Footage: 350000
Type of Packaging: Consumer, Bulk
Regions Exported to: Worldwide
Percentage of Business in Exporting: 2

48189 Ross Computer Systems
214 S Peters Rd Ste 208
Knoxville, TN 37923   865-690-3008
Fax: 865-690-1089   www.afsi.com
Manufacturer and exporter of computer hardware and software; also, consulting services available
President: Louis Schumacher
CEO: Jesse Hermann
CFO: Mark Schonau
Executive VP: Louis Schumacher
Chief Technology Officer: Suhas Gudihal
VP Sales: Greg Roberts
Chief Customer Officer: Lisa Whinney
Estimated Sales: Below $ 5 Million
Number Employees: 10-19
Regions Exported to: Worldwide

48190 Ross Engineering Inc
32 Westgate Blvd
Savannah, GA 31405-1400   912-238-3300
Fax: 912-238-5983   800-524-7677
www.mixers.com
Manufacturer and exporter of food processing equipment including mixing, blending and dispersion machinery
President: Richard Ross
COO: D Hathaway
d_hathaway@rossengineering.net
Vice President: David Hathaway
Estimated Sales: $10-20,000,000
Number Employees: 20-49
Square Footage: 60000
Parent Co: Charles Ross & Son Company
Regions Exported to: Worldwide

48191 Ross Industries Inc
5321 Midland Rd
Midland, VA 22728   540-439-3271
Fax: 540-439-2740   sales@rossindinc.com
www.rossindinc.com
Food processing and packaging equipment including pre-formed tray seal machines, tunnel freezers, mechanical tenderizers and meat presses.
Estimated Sales: $20-50 Million
Number Employees: 100-249
Brands Exported: Ross
Regions Exported to: Central America, South America, Europe
Percentage of Business in Exporting: 25

48192 Ross Technology Corp
104 N Maple Ave
Leola, PA 17540-9799   717-656-5600
Fax: 717-656-5281   800-345-8170
www.rosstechnology.com
Manufacturer and exporter of storage rack systems including pallet rack, drive-in, thru-flow and push back
Owner: Don Spicher
Vice President: Jay Otto
jotto@rosstechnology.com
Sales Manager: Tom Crippen
Estimated Sales: $ 20-50 Million
Number Employees: 100-249
Square Footage: 54000
Type of Packaging: Bulk
Regions Exported to: Central America
Percentage of Business in Exporting: 1

Importers & Exporters / A-Z

48193 Ross-Smith Pecan Company
107 Plantation Oak Dr
Thomasville, GA 31792-3540   229-859-2225
Fax: 229-859-2382 800-841-5503
Manufacturer and exporter of nuts including shelled pecans
President: Betty McDuffie
Estimated Sales: Less than $500,000
Number Employees: 23

48194 Roth KASE USA
1325 6th Ave
Monroe, WI 53566-2396   608-328-2122
Fax: 608-328-2120 info@emmi-rothkase.com
www.rothcheese.com
RTD - ready to drink (coffee, tea, concentrates, powders), cheese, yogurt.
Marketing: Daniel Schnyder
Sales Exec: Louie Cabral
Number Employees: 20-49

48195 Roth Sign Systems
606 Lakeville Street
Petaluma, CA 94952-3324   707-778-0200
Fax: 707-765-6079 800-585-7446
Manufacturer and exporter of menu, black and chalk boards; also, signs including changeable letter, advertising, luminous tube, plastic, etc
Owner: Lary Mathews
Estimated Sales: $500,000-$1 Million
Number Employees: 10
Square Footage: 80000
Parent Co: Rothcoast Company
Regions Exported to: Worldwide

48196 Rothfos Corp
1 Penn Plz # 2222
New York, NY 10119-2222   646-556-8400
Fax: 914-761-6575 coffee@rothfos.com
www.rothfos.com
Coffee beans
Director: Klaas Vanderkaaij
CEO: Dan Dwyer
Estimated Sales: $20-50 Million
Number Employees: 5-9
Type of Packaging: Bulk
Brands Imported: Rothfos
Regions Imported from: All Over The World
Percentage of Business in Importing: 100

48197 Rotisol France Inc
341 N Oak St
Inglewood, CA 90302-3312   310-671-7254
Fax: 310-671-8171 800-651-5969
info@rotisolusa.com www.rotisolusa.com
Manufacturer, importer and exporter pizza and rotisserie ovens; also, grills
Owner: Jim Doar
Head Accounts: Milene Berry
Business Development Manager: Orlane Parsons
Director Sales: Alain Lebret
Sales Coordinator: Cedric Dauphin
Office/Customer Service Manager: Kate Gramcko
jim@rotisolusa.com
Estimated Sales: $ 2.5 - 5 Million
Number Employees: 5-9
Parent Co: Rotisol S.A.
Regions Exported to: Worldwide
Brands Imported: Rotisol
Regions Imported from: France
Percentage of Business in Importing: 100

48198 Roto-Flex Oven Co
135 E Cevallos
San Antonio, TX 78204-1795   210-222-2278
Fax: 210-222-9007 877-859-1463
doug@rotoflexoven.com www.rotoflexoven.com
Manufacturer and exporter of food service equipment and pizza ovens
CEO: Richard Dunfield
service@rotoflexoven.com
CFO: Ed Dunfield
Vice President: Doug Dunfield
Marketing Director: Marijke Carey
Plant Manager: Jose Briano
Estimated Sales: $2 Million
Number Employees: 5-9
Number of Brands: 2
Number of Products: 10
Square Footage: 50000
Type of Packaging: Consumer, Food Service
Regions Exported to: Central America, South America, Europe, Asia, Middle East, Canada, Mexico

Percentage of Business in Exporting: 1

48199 Rotteveel Orchards
6183 Reddick Ln
Dixon, CA 95620-9731   707-678-1495
Fax: 707-678-1446
Processor and exporter of almonds
President: Neil Rotteveel
info@rotteveel.com
Estimated Sales: $500,000-$1 Million
Number Employees: 5-9
Type of Packaging: Bulk
Regions Exported to: Worldwide
Percentage of Business in Exporting: 80

48200 Roundup Food Equip
180 Kehoe Blvd
Carol Stream, IL 60188-1814   630-784-1000
Fax: 630-784-1650 800-253-2991
www.ajantunes.com
Manufacturer and exporter of toasters, steamers and hot dog grills
President: Glenn Bullock
customerservice@roundupfoodequip.com
Chairman of the Board: Virginia M Antunes
CFO: Bill Nelson
R & D: Tom Goodman
VP Marketing: Thomas Krisch
Estimated Sales: $ 5 - 10 Million
Number Employees: 100-249
Parent Co: A.J. Antunes & Company
Percentage of Business in Exporting: 35

48201 Routin America
955 NW 17th Avenue
Suite F
Delray Beach, FL 334452516
export@routin.com
www.1883.com
Flavored syrups and sauces.
President: Jean Clochet
Estimated Sales: $1.5 Million
Number Employees: 2
Number of Brands: 1
Parent Co: Routin SA
Type of Packaging: Private Label
Regions Imported from: Europe

48202 (HQ)Rovira Biscuit Corporation
619 La Ceiba Ave
Ponce, PR 00717-1901   787-844-8585
Fax: 787-848-7176
customerservice@rovirabiscuits.com
www.rovirabiscuits.com
Crackers and biscuits; exporter of crackers
President and Director: Rafael Rovira
President, Rovira Foods: Frances Rovira
Executive VP and General Manager: Carlos Rovira
Quality Control: Carla Traverso
Export Sales Manager: Roberto Ponce
Estimated Sales: $50 Million
Number Employees: 300
Square Footage: 180000
Other Locations:
  Rovira Biscuit Corp.
  Pueblo Viejo, PRRovira Biscuit Corp.
Brands Exported: Rovira
Percentage of Business in Exporting: 10

48203 Rowe International
2517 Shadowbrook Drive SE
Grand Rapids, MI 49546-7457   616-246-0483
www.roweinternational.com
Manufacturer and exporter of currency changers, bill acceptors, under-the-counter safes, jukeboxes and vending machines including refrigerated food, snack and popcorn
Controller: Scott Van Dam
Senior Vice President, Sales & Marketing: John Margold
Human Resources Executive: Linda Roer
Purchasing: Chris Steffes
Estimated Sales: $ 160 Thousand
Number Employees: 3
Square Footage: 3096
Brands Exported: Rowe AMI; Rowe
Regions Exported to: Worldwide
Percentage of Business in Exporting: 25

48204 (HQ)Rowena
758 W 22nd St
Norfolk, VA 23517-1925   757-627-8699
Fax: 757-627-1505 800-627-8699
rowena@rowens.com www.rowenas.com

Processor and exporter of gourmet pound cakes, jams, curds, dry mixes and sauces
Founder, President: Rowena Fullinwider
General Manager: Joan Place
Sales: Ann Cole
Contact: Tamikka Doman
tamikka@rowenas.com
Production: Renee Satterfield
Warehouse Manager: Dom Tamikk
Estimated Sales: $620000
Number Employees: 20-49
Square Footage: 52000
Type of Packaging: Consumer, Food Service, Private Label, Bulk
Regions Exported to: Canada

48205 Rowland Coffee RoastersInc.
P.O.Box 520845
Miami, FL 33152-0845   305-592-7302
Fax: 305-592-9471 866-318-0422
www.javacabana.com
Processor, importer and exporter of coffee; importer and wholesaler/distributor of coffee equipment and supplies including filters
President: Jose Souto
General Manager of Sales: Angeo Soupo
Estimated Sales: $2.5-5 Million
Number Employees: 50-99
Square Footage: 50000
Parent Co: Tetley USA
Type of Packaging: Consumer, Food Service, Private Label
Regions Exported to: Canada, Caribbean
Regions Imported from: Central America, South America, Europe, Caribbean, Mexico

48206 Rowland Technologies
320 Barnes Rd
Wallingford, CT 06492-1804   203-269-9500
Fax: 203-265-2768 www.rowlandtechnologies.com
Manufacturer and exporter of decorative plastic and polycarbonate packaging film
President: Peter Connerton
pconnerton@rowtec.com
Sales Manager: Carl Heflin
Estimated Sales: $ 5 - 10 Million
Number Employees: 20-49
Square Footage: 120000

48207 (HQ)Roxide International
24 Weaver St
Larchmont, NY 10538   914-630-7700
Fax: 914-235-5328 800-431-5500
roxide@aol.com
Manufacturer and importer of insecticides, repellents, swatters, traps, fly paper, baits and muldicides; also, graffiti removers, organic cleaners and lubricants; exporter of fly paper and insecticides
President: James Cowen
Estimated Sales: $2.5-5 Million
Number Employees: 10
Type of Packaging: Food Service
Brands Exported: Aeroxon; Revenge
Regions Exported to: South America, Europe, Asia, Middle East
Percentage of Business in Exporting: 15
Regions Imported from: Europe
Percentage of Business in Importing: 30

48208 Roxy Trading Inc
389 N Humane Way
Pomona, CA 91768-3345   626-610-1388
Fax: 626-610-1339 info@roxytrading.com
www.roxytrading.com
Importer and distributor of Asian specialty food products.
President: Elvis Sae-Tang
General Manager: Paulette Ho
Business Development Manager: Benjamin Sae-Tang
Estimated Sales: $8 Million
Number Employees: 20-49
Number of Brands: 28
Square Footage: 45000
Type of Packaging: Consumer
Other Locations:
  Roxy Trading - Northern California
  Union City, CARoxy Trading - Northern CaliforniaScarborough, ON, Canada
Regions Imported from: Europe, Asia
Percentage of Business in Importing: 80

Importers & Exporters / A-Z

48209 Royal Accoutrements
172 W Sherwood Road
Okemos, MI 48864-1235   517-347-7983
Fax: 517-349-0917 888-269-0185
info@royalcoffeemaker.com
www.royalcoffeemaker.com
Importer and wholesaler/distributor of tabletop coffee brewers; serving the food service market and retail stores
President/CEO: Maria Tindemans
Marketing Director: Katrien Maci
Estimated Sales: $1.2 Million
Number Employees: 5
Square Footage: 7200
Regions Exported to: Central America, South America, Europe, Asia, Middle East
Percentage of Business in Exporting: 15
Brands Imported: Royal
Regions Imported from: Europe
Percentage of Business in Importing: 100

48210 Royal Baltic LTD
9829 Ditmas Ave
Brooklyn, NY 11236-1925   718-385-8300
Fax: 718-385-4757
Manufactures smoked fish products; distributes gourmet foods, such as seafood delicacies, cheese, juice, feta, coffee, chocolate candy and sauces.
President: Alex Kaganovsky
alexkaganovsky@royalbaltic.com
Finance Manager: Alex Kaganovsky
Estimated Sales: $10-20 Million
Number Employees: 50-99
Type of Packaging: Consumer
Regions Imported from: Europe, Asia

48211 Royal Banquet
PO Box 8835
Red Bank, NJ 07701-8835   732-219-0198
Fax: 732-219-1018 877-428-2467
www.royalbanquet.com
Importer of Argentine beef, wine and seafood
President: Henry Piana Velland
VP: Pablo Liberatori
Sales Manager: Cristina Edelstein
Number Employees: 5-9
Type of Packaging: Consumer, Food Service, Bulk
Brands Imported: Gaucho Ranch
Regions Imported from: South America
Percentage of Business in Importing: 100

48212 (HQ)Royal Caribbean Bakery
620 S Fulton Ave
Mt Vernon, NY 10550-5012   914-668-6868
Fax: 914-668-5700 888-818-0971
info@royalcaribbeanbakery.com
www.royalcaribbeanbakery.com
Jamaican baked goods and specialty foods
President/CEO: Jeanette Hosang
CEO: Vincent Hosang
Estimated Sales: $5-10 Million
Number Employees: 50-99
Square Footage: 240000
Type of Packaging: Consumer, Food Service, Private Label, Bulk
Other Locations:
  Royal Caribbean Bakery
  Orlando, FLRoyal Caribbean Bakery

48213 Royal Coffee Inc
3306 Powell St
Emeryville, CA 94608-1548   510-652-4256
Fax: 510-652-3415 800-843-0482
info@royalcoffee.com www.royalcoffee.com
Green coffee
General Manager: Richard Sandlin
Sales: Jennifer Huber
Sales: John Cossette
Sales: Robert Fulmer
Contact: Carlos Aguirre
caguirre@royalcoffee.com
Year Founded: 1978
Estimated Sales: $ 30-50 Million
Number Employees: 20-49
Type of Packaging: Private Label

48214 Royal Crown Enterprises
780 Epperson Dr
City of Industry, CA 91748-1336   626-854-8080
Fax: 626-854-8090
Importer and wholesaler/distributor of canned seafood, general merchandise, Hispanic and Central American grocery products and bulk-packed spices
President/CEO: Juergen Lotter
CFO: Christine Lotter
Vice President: Jerry Lotter
Estimated Sales: $ 20 - 50 Million
Number Employees: 50-99
Square Footage: 90000
Type of Packaging: Consumer, Food Service, Bulk
Regions Imported from: Central America, South America, Europe, Asia
Percentage of Business in Importing: 80

48215 Royal Doulton
200 Cottontail Ln # 102b
Somerset, NJ 08873-1273   732-356-7880
Fax: 732-764-4974 800-682-4462
Importer and exporter of china and glassware
CEO: Art Vylin
Number Employees: 100-249
Parent Co: Royal Doulton
Regions Exported to: Canada, Mexico, Latin America, Caribbean
Brands Imported: Stratford; Capital; Horizons; Allegro; Hallmark; Oceana
Regions Imported from: Europe, Asia
Percentage of Business in Importing: 100

48216 Royal Ecoproducts
119 Snow Boulevard
Vaughan, ON L4K 4N9
Canada   905-761-6406
Fax: 905-761-6419 800-465-7670
Manufacturer and exporter of plastic pallets
President: Burno Casciato
President: Maircein Tarascandalo
Director Sales/Marketing: Anthony DiNunzio
Sales Coordinator: Vince Franze
Number Employees: 30
Regions Exported to: Worldwide

48217 Royal Foods Inc
215 Reindollar Ave
Suite G
Marina, CA 93933-3804   831-582-2495
Fax: 831-582-2495 800-551-5284
info@gingerpeople.com www.gingerpeople.com
Wholesaler/distributor and importer of Australian candied ginger and other specialty ginger ingredients
President: B Leeson
General Manager: A Leeson
Sales Director: Frances Krebs
Contact: Abbie Leeson
abbiel@gingerpeople.com
Estimated Sales: $10-20 Million
Number Employees: 10-19
Square Footage: 10000
Type of Packaging: Consumer, Food Service, Private Label, Bulk
Regions Exported to: Europe, Asutralia
Percentage of Business in Exporting: 5
Brands Imported: Havenglaze Party Limited; Ginger People
Regions Imported from: Asia, Australia
Percentage of Business in Importing: 80

48218 Royal Gourmet Caviar
27 Blake Ave
Lynbrook, NY 11563-2505   516-612-7407
Fax: 516-612-7408
Caviar, nuts and dried fruits
Distribution Manager: Donna Powers Bowe
Year Founded: 2000
Estimated Sales: Under $500,000
Number Employees: 1-4
Brands Imported: Caviar

48219 Royal Industries Inc
4100 W Victoria St
Chicago, IL 60646-6727   773-478-6300
Fax: 773-478-4948 800-782-1200
www.royalindustriesinc.com
Wholesaler/distributor of restaurant supplies; serving the food service market
President: Ervin Naiditch
CFO: Joe Lewis
VP: Jay Johnson
Estimated Sales: $10-20 Million
Number Employees: 20-49
Square Footage: 400000
Regions Imported from: Europe, Asia, Middle East

48220 Royal Label Co
50 Park St
Dorchester, MA 02122-2611   617-825-6050
Fax: 617-825-2678 sales@royallabel.com
www.royallabel.com
Manufacturer and exporter of pressure sensitive labels, price tags, decals, name plates and panels
Owner/President: Paul Clifford Jr.
pdc@royallabel.com
VP: Paul Ryan
Director of QA: Craig DiGiovanni
Business Development: Marychristine Clifford
Operations Manager: Paul Pelletier
Operations & Scheduling: Steve Gefteas
Plant Manager: Paul Pelletier
Controller: Eileen Clifford
Estimated Sales: Below $5 Million
Number Employees: 20-49
Square Footage: 50000
Regions Exported to: Asia, Mexico, Canada
Percentage of Business in Exporting: 15

48221 Royal Medjool Date Gardens
1203 Perez Rd
Bard, CA 92222   760-572-0524
Fax: 760-572-2292
Grower and exporter of dates and date trees.
General Manager: David Nelson
Estimated Sales: $3 Million
Number Employees: 75
Regions Exported to: Europe
Percentage of Business in Exporting: 35

48222 Royal Oak Enterprises
1 Royal Oak Ave
Roswell, GA 30076-7583   678-461-3200
Fax: 678-461-3220 www.royal-oak.com
Manufacturer and exporter of instant light charcoal briquettes and natural lump charcoal
Owner: James Keeter
jkeeter@royaloakenterprises.com
VP Sales/Marketing: Harold Ovington
Sales Manager: Brian Kerrigan
jkeeter@royaloakenterprises.com
Estimated Sales: $ 1 - 5 Million
Number Employees: 50-99
Regions Exported to: Europe
Percentage of Business in Exporting: 2

48223 Royal Palate Foods
960 E Hyde Park Blvd
Inglewood, CA 90302-1708   310-330-7701
Fax: 310-330-7710
Processor, exporter and wholesaler/distributor of kosher foods including chicken, beef, soups, sauces, frozen entrees, hors d'oeuvres, etc.; serving the food service market; importer of canned vegetables and fruits
President: William Pinkerson
Estimated Sales: $500,000-$1 Million
Number Employees: 10-19
Square Footage: 32000
Type of Packaging: Food Service, Bulk
Percentage of Business in Exporting: 2
Regions Imported from: South America, Middle East, Canada
Percentage of Business in Importing: 5

48224 Royal Paper Products
PO Box 151
Coatesville, PA 19320   610-384-3400
Fax: 610-384-5106 800-666-6655
www.royalpaper.com
Manufacturer and importer of place mats, coasters, bibs, napkin bands, chef hats, aprons, gloves, toothpicks, sword picks, arrow picks, skewers, coffee stirrers, griddle blocks/screens, scouring pads and metal sponges
President: David Milberg
CEO/CFO: Vince Mazzei
Executive VP: Fred Leibowitz
Quality Control: Debbie Sumka
Marketing Director: Todd Straves
Sales Director: Mark LaRusso
Contact: Candy Warfel
candyw@royalpaper.com
Plant Manager: Ross Glazer
Estimated Sales: $ 5 - 10 Million
Number Employees: 20-49
Number of Brands: 1
Number of Products: 300
Square Footage: 480
Type of Packaging: Food Service, Private Label, Bulk

Importers & Exporters / A-Z

Brands Exported: Royal Line
Brands Imported: Royal Line
Regions Imported from: Europe, Asia, Indonesia, Malaysia
Percentage of Business in Importing: 33

48225 Royal Vista Marketing Inc
126 W Center Ave
Visalia, CA 93291-6228 559-636-9198
Fax: 559-636-9637 info@royalvista.com
Grower and exporter of table grapes, kiwifruit, stone fruit and figs; importer of stone fruit, kiwifruit and table grapes
Owner: Todd Steele
Sales Manager: Patrick Allen
todd@royalvista.com
Estimated Sales: $84000
Number Employees: 10-19
Square Footage: 96000
Parent Co: Atalanta
Type of Packaging: Consumer, Food Service, Bulk
Other Locations:
  Alkop Farms
  Chico, CAAlkop Farms
Brands Exported: Alkop Farms; Cal Sweet
Regions Exported to: Pacific Rim
Percentage of Business in Exporting: 25
Regions Imported from: Chile, Italy
Percentage of Business in Importing: 25

48226 Royal Welding & Fabricating
1000 E Elm Ave
Fullerton, CA 92831-5022 714-680-6669
Fax: 714-680-6646 info@royalwelding.com
www.royalwelding.com
Custom stainless steel process tanks; also, vacuum chambers, mixers and cookers
President: Wallace Cook
CFO: Sekyung Kim
Vice President/Chief Engineer: Brad Card
Quality Control: Merritt Read
Chief Engineer: Collie Janda
General Manager: Wallace Cook
Estimated Sales: $4.0 Million
Number Employees: 20-49
Square Footage: 116000
Parent Co: Cook & Cook
Brands Exported: Custon Process Equipment by Royal Welding
Regions Exported to: Central America, South America, Europe, Asia, Middle East

48227 Royal Wine Corp
63 Lefante Dr
Bayonne, NJ 07002-5024 718-384-2400
Fax: 718-388-8444 info@royalwines.com
www.royalwine.com
Manufacturer, importer and distributor of premium kosher wines, spirits and liquors. Affiliate of Kedem Food Products International.
President: David Herzog
CEO: Mordy Herzog
Chief Financial Officer: Sheldon Ginsberg
Executive Vice President: Sheldon Ginsberg
SVP: Phillip Herzog
Executive Vice President of Sales: Nathan Herzog
Estimated Sales: $49.5 Million
Number Employees: 200
Number of Brands: 61
Square Footage: 184000
Parent Co: KayCo
Type of Packaging: Consumer, Food Service
Regions Exported to: Central America, South America, Europe, Asia, Middle East, South Africa, Canada
Percentage of Business in Exporting: 30
Regions Imported from: South America, Europe, Middle East, New Zealand
Percentage of Business in Importing: 40

48228 Royale Brands
5315 Tremont Ave
Davenport, IA 52807 563-386-5222
Fax: 563-386-1352 royale@netexpress.net
royalebrands.com
Produce and market frozen beverage products and equipment
President: Joe Colombari
Estimated Sales: Less than $500,000
Number Employees: 10-19
Number of Brands: 13
Number of Products: 250
Type of Packaging: Food Service
Regions Exported to: Worldwide

48229 Royce Corp
PO Box 729
Glendale, AZ 85311-0729
Canada 602-256-0006
Fax: 623-435-2030 info@roycemasonry.com
Manufacturer and exporter of wire and metal shelving, production line trucks, warehouse bins, point of purchase displays and racks; also, custom designed for chip, beverage, soups and biscuits
President: George Knowles
General Manager: Glenn Millar
Customer Service: Dave Haywood
Manager Operations: John Fox
Number Employees: 50
Square Footage: 212000
Parent Co: Royce Corporation
Type of Packaging: Consumer, Food Service, Private Label, Bulk
Brands Exported: Royce
Regions Exported to: USA
Percentage of Business in Exporting: 5

48230 Royce Rolls Ringer Co
16 Riverview Ter NE
Grand Rapids, MI 49505-6245 616-361-9266
Fax: 616-361-5976 800-253-9638
info@roycerolls.net www.roycerolls.net
Manufacturer and exporter of stainless steel mopping equipment, multi and single roll toilet paper dispensers, restroom fixtures and janitorial cleaning carts
President: Charles Royce Jr
VP: Charles Royce
Marketing Director: William Swartz
IT: Angelica Tant
angel@roycerolls.net
Estimated Sales: $1-3 Million
Number Employees: 20-49
Square Footage: 117200
Regions Exported to: Middle East
Percentage of Business in Exporting: 1

48231 Royer Corporation
9981 York Theta Dr
Cleveland, OH 44133-3512 440-237-0806
Fax: 440-237-1694 royerinfo@royercorp.com
Owner: Leonhard May
Estimated Sales: $ 20 - 50 Million
Number Employees: 50-99

48232 Rpac LLC
21490 Ortigalita Rd
Los Banos, CA 93635-9793 209-826-0272
Fax: 209-826-3882 info@rpacalmonds.com
www.rpacalmonds.com
Processor and exporter of almonds
Owner: Dave Parreira
dave@arpacalmonds.com
Partner: David Parreira
Shipping Manager: Janet Martin
Plant Manager: James Smith
Estimated Sales: $4500000
Number Employees: 20-49
Type of Packaging: Bulk
Regions Exported to: Worldwide

48233 RubaTex Polymer
PO Box 1050
Middlefield, OH 44062-1050 440-632-1691
Fax: 440-632-5761 www.universalpolymer.com
Manufacturer and exporter of plastic straws, can coolers and stoppers
President: Joe Colebank
VP: Andy Cavanagh
Sales/Marketing Manager: Philip Moses
Estimated Sales: $ 3 - 5 Million
Number Employees: 5-9

48234 Rubbermaid
4110 Premier Dr.
High Point, NC 27265 888-895-2110
www.rubbermaid.com
Ice coolers and chests, thermal jugs and containers, re-freezable ice substitutes and lunch kits, and hummingbird feeders and accessories.
President/CEO, Newell Brands: Michael Polk
Year Founded: 1920
Estimated Sales: $114.70 Million
Number Employees: 1,426
Number of Products: 15
Parent Co: Newell Brands Inc.
Type of Packaging: Food Service

Other Locations:
  Rubbermaid Specialty Products
  Winchester, VARubbermaid Specialty Products
Regions Exported to: Central America, South America, Europe, Asia, Middle East

48235 (HQ)Rubbermaid Commercial Products
2000 Overhead Bridge Rd NE
Cleveland, TN 37311-4692 423-476-4544
Fax: 423-559-9393
www.rubbermaidcommercial.com
Manufacturer and exporter of mops and cleaning aids
President: Neil Eibeler
Finance Manager: Kevin Rogers
Operations Manager: Frank McNeely
Production Manager: Phillip Carlton
Plant Manager: Steve Jones
Purchasing Senior Specialist: Jack Burke
Estimated Sales: $ 50-100 Million
Number Employees: 250-499
Parent Co: Newell Rubbermaid Inc.
Regions Exported to: Worldwide
Percentage of Business in Exporting: 10

48236 Rubbermaid Commercial Products
1400 Laurel Blvd
Pottsville, PA 17901-1427 570-622-7715
Fax: 570-622-3817 800-233-0314
united@unitedrecept.com
www.rubbermaidcommercial.com
Manufacturer and exporter of fiberglass, steel aluminum, marble and cement waste receptacles; also, smokers' urns, planters and restroom accessories
President/CEO: Richard Weiss
CFO: Rick Piger
rpiger@unitedrecept.com
Vice President: Layton Dodson
Marketing Director: Tom Palangio
Plant Manager: George Derosa
Purchasing Manager: Margaret Zimmerman
Estimated Sales: $50-100 Million
Number Employees: 100-249
Square Footage: 145000
Brands Exported: The Barclay Series; Designer Line; Americana Series; The Defenders; Medi-Can; Step Master; Waste Master; Collect-A-Cubes, Aladdin, Architek, Howard Products.

48237 Rubschlager Baking Corp
800-661-7246
CCC@westonfoods.com
www.rubschlagerbaking.com
Processor and exporter of rye breads.
President: Luc Mongeau
CFO: Tina Murrin
Number Employees: 1-4
Number of Brands: 2
Number of Products: 45
Parent Co: Weston Foods
Type of Packaging: Consumer, Food Service
Brands Exported: Rubschlager
Regions Exported to: Canada, Mexico

48238 Ruby Manufacturing & Sales
9853 Alpaca St
South El Monte, CA 91733-3101 626-443-1171
Fax: 626-443-0028 info@rubymfg.com
www.rubymfg.com
Manufacturer and exporter of vegetable juice extractors
Owner: Dan Turner
info@rubymfg.com
Estimated Sales: $500,000-$1 Million
Number Employees: 5-9
Type of Packaging: Food Service
Regions Exported to: Worldwide
Percentage of Business in Exporting: 10

48239 (HQ)Rudolph Foods Co
6575 Bellefontaine Rd
Lima, OH 45804 419-648-3611
www.rudophfoods.com
Manufacturer and exporter of pork rinds and related snacks
President: Richard Rudolph
VP, Sales & Marketing: Mark Singleton
Year Founded: 1955
Estimated Sales: $50 Million

Number Employees: 400
Number of Brands: 4
Square Footage: 110000
Type of Packaging: Consumer, Private Label, Bulk
Regions Exported to: Central America, South America, Europe, Asia

48240 Rudolph Industries
1176 Cardiff Boulevard
Mississauga, ON L5S 1P6
Canada
905-564-6160
Fax: 905-564-6155 info@rudolphind.com
www.rudolphind.com
Machine knives and injector needles for food processors
President: Bill Rudolph
Number Employees: 10
Square Footage: 80000
Parent Co: W. Rudolph Investments
Regions Exported to: Central America, Europe, Worldwide
Percentage of Business in Exporting: 70
Regions Imported from: Europe, Worldwide
Percentage of Business in Importing: 10

48241 Rudolph's Specialty Bakery
390 Alliance Avenue
Toronto, ON M6N 2H8
Canada
416-763-4315
Fax: 416-763-4317 800-268-1589
www.rudolphsbakeries.com
Processor and exporter of rye and flat breads, tortillas and flan cakes
President: George Paech
Type of Packaging: Consumer, Food Service, Private Label
Regions Exported to: USA
Percentage of Business in Exporting: 2

48242 Ruggiero Seafood
474 Wilson Ave
Po Box 5369
Newark, NJ 07105-4833
973-344-2282
Fax: 973-589-5690 866-225-2627
info@ruggieroseafood.com
www.ruggieroseafood.com
Processor, importer and exporter of fresh, frozen and breaded calamari and calamari entrees
President: Rocco Ruggiero
rocco@ruggieroseafood.com
Controller: Connie Dasaliva
Vice President: Frank Ruggiero
Sales Manager: Steve Clemente
Manager Operations: Anthon Trimarche
Plant Manager: Marcos Fontana
Estimated Sales: $387,000
Number Employees: 20-49
Square Footage: 100000
Type of Packaging: Consumer, Food Service, Bulk
Brands Exported: Fisherman's Pride
Regions Exported to: Central America, South America, Europe
Percentage of Business in Exporting: 10
Regions Imported from: Central America, South America, Asia
Percentage of Business in Importing: 40

48243 (HQ)Ruiz Food Products Inc.
501 S. Alta Ave.
PO Box 37
Dinuba, CA 93618
800-477-6474
contactus@ruizfoods.com www.ruizfoods.com
Frozen Mexican foods including burritos, enchiladas, tamales, soft tacos, chili rellenos, flautas and taquitos.
President/CEO: Rachel Cullen
Senior VP/CFO: John Landis
Year Founded: 1964
Estimated Sales: $276.2 Million
Number Employees: 3,500+
Number of Brands: 4
Square Footage: 200000
Type of Packaging: Consumer, Food Service, Private Label, Bulk
Brands Exported: El Monterey; Ruiz Family
Regions Exported to: Central America, Europe, Asia, Canada
Percentage of Business in Exporting: 5

48244 Rumi Spice
1400 W 46th St
Chicago, IL 60609-3212
213-447-6112
info@rumispice.com
www.rumispice.com
Saffron and spice blends
Co-Founder: Emily Miller
Director of New Product Development: Laura Willis
Year Founded: 2014
Estimated Sales: $500,000 - $1,000,000
Number Employees: 2-10
Brands Imported: Saffron
Regions Imported from: Afghanistan

48245 Rumiano Cheese Co.
511 9th St
Crescent City, CA 95531-3408
707-465-1535
Fax: 707-465-4141 866-328-2433
www.rumianocheese.com
Cheese manufacturer
President: Baird Rumiano
joby@rumianocheese.com
Logistics: Gary Smits
Production & Markering: Joby Rumiano
Office Manager: Tana Bachmann
Chief Operating Officer: Kirk Olsen
Production Manager: Enrique Leal
Lab Technician: Juan Pablo Gonzalez
Estimated Sales: $12 Million
Number Employees: 20-49
Number of Brands: 1
Square Footage: 16000
Type of Packaging: Consumer, Food Service
Other Locations:
    Distribution & Packaging
    East Williows, CADistribution & Packaging
Brands Exported: Rumiano
Regions Exported to: Asia

48246 Russell E. Womack, Inc.
P.O. Box 3967
Lubbock, TX 79452
806-747-2581
Fax: 806-747-2583 877-787-3559
rewi@casserolebean.com www.casserolebean.com
Dry pinto beans packed in poly and burlap sacks
Owner: Mike Byrne
Product Management/Quality Control: Mike Bryne
Director of Sales: Richard Byrne
Consumer Affairs: Walter James
warehouse Manager: Albert Rodriguez
Estimated Sales: $3800000
Number Employees: 20-49
Number of Brands: 1
Number of Products: 1
Square Footage: 144000
Type of Packaging: Consumer, Food Service

48247 Russian Chef
40 E 69th St
New York, NY 10021-5016
212-249-1550
Fax: 212-249-5451
Processor and packer of fresh and pasteurized kosher caviar including domestic salmon, whitefish, sturgeon, paddlefish, hackleback and lumpfish; also, Scottish smoked salmon, tuna and smoked trout; importer of caviar
President: Simon Kublanov
Vice President: Lenny Kuvykin
Estimated Sales: $ 1 - 3 Million
Number Employees: 5-9
Square Footage: 27000
Type of Packaging: Consumer, Food Service
Regions Imported from: Europe, Asia, Middle East, Canada

48248 Rutherford Engineering
1731 Apaloosa
Rockford, IL 61107
815-623-2141
Fax: 815-623-7170
Manufacturer and exporter of fillers, valves and packaging equipment
President: Ashwin Patel
Estimated Sales: $950,000
Number Employees: 15
Square Footage: 27000
Brands Exported: Rutherford; Akra-Pak
Regions Exported to: Central America, South America, Europe, Asia

48249 Rv Industries
1665 Heraeus Booulevard
Buford, GA 30518
770-729-8983
Fax: 770-729-9428 sales@rvindustries.com
www.rvindustries.com
Processor, importer and exporter of desiccated, sweetened and toasted coconut, coconut milk powder, aseptic coconut milk and water
President: Andres E Siochi
General Manager: Bob Weschrek
CFO: Bharat Shah
Sales: Robert Santiago
Production Manager: Guillermo Pineiro
Estimated Sales: $14,000,000
Number Employees: 20-49
Square Footage: 120000
Parent Co: RV Industries
Type of Packaging: Consumer, Food Service, Private Label, Bulk
Regions Exported to: Central America, South America
Brands Imported: Red V; Fiesta, Cocorich
Regions Imported from: Asia

48250 Ryan Potato Company
PO Box 388
East Grand Forks, MN 56721
218-773-1155
Fax: 218-773-6591
Wholesaler/distributor and exporter of potatoes; serving the food service market
President: Joan Ryan Mangino
Estimated Sales: $20-50 Million
Number Employees: 50-99
Type of Packaging: Consumer, Food Service, Private Label, Bulk
Percentage of Business in Exporting: 5

48251 Rymer Seafood
125 S Wacker Drive
Chicago, IL 60606-4424
312-236-3266
Fax: 312-236-4169
Seafood
President: Mark Bailin
Estimated Sales: $ .5 - 1 million
Number Employees: 1-4

48252 Rytec Corporation
780 N Water St
Milwaukee, WI 53202-3512
414-273-3500
Fax: 414-273-5198 888-467-9832
info@rytecdoors.com
Manufacturer and exporter of high-speed, rolling and folding doors including cold storage
Chairman: Donald Grasso
Regional Manager: Jamie Lilly
Marketing Manager: Scott Blue
Estimated Sales: $20-50 Million
Number Employees: 250-499
Regions Exported to: Worldwide
Percentage of Business in Exporting: 5

48253 S & D Coffee Inc
300 Concord Pkwy S
Concord, NC 28027-6702
704-782-3121
Fax: 800-950-4378 800-933-2210
www.sndcoffee.com
S&D is a coffee, tea and extracts supplier to the foodservice industry.
Chairman, President & CEO: Ron Hinson
hinsonr@sndcoffee.com
Number Employees: 1000-4999
Type of Packaging: Food Service, Private Label
Regions Imported from: Central America, South America, Europe, Asia

48254 S & H Uniform Corporation
200 William Street
Rye Brook, NY 10573-4620
800-210-5295
Fax: 914-937-0741

48255 S & L Store Fixture
3755 NW 115th Ave
Doral, FL 33178-1857
305-599-8906
Fax: 305-599-8906 800-205-4536
info@slstoredisplays.com www.usahanger.com
Manufacturer and exporter of store fixtures including metal shelving
President: Ronald Maier
VP: Ron Maier
Estimated Sales: $ 2.5 - 5 Million
Number Employees: 10-19
Square Footage: 128000
Brands Exported: Kent Shelving
Regions Exported to: Central America, South America, Latin America, Caribbean, Mexico
Percentage of Business in Exporting: 60

Importers & Exporters / A-Z

48256 S & S Indl Maintenance
Main St
Marlton, NJ 8053   856-768-6300
Fax: 856-768-8979 800-525-4448
Wholesaler/distributor, importer and exporter of general merchandise including fluorescent, halogen and ballast lighting and fixtures, electric hand dryers, rubber maid products, and tuff coated lights for food processing
CEO: Steve Sandro
lights@penn.com
Estimated Sales: $ .5 - 1 million
Number Employees: 1-4
Type of Packaging: Bulk
Brands Exported: Osram; Westinghouse
Regions Exported to: Central America, South America, Europe, Asia
Brands Imported: Wetinghouse; GE; Sylvania; Oshram
Regions Imported from: Central America, South America, Europe, Asia
Percentage of Business in Importing: 20

48257 S J Controls Inc
2248 Obispo Ave # 203
Suite 203
Signal Hill, CA 90755-4026   562-494-1400
Fax: 562-494-1066 info@sjcontrols.com
www.sjcontrols.com
Manufacturer and exporter of blending and batching equipment, process control systems, flow meters and level detectors; also, engineering services available
President: Dave Olszewski
CAO: Noel Brown
nbrown@sjcontrols.com
CFO: Cindy Pawn
Engineer: Steve Czaus
Estimated Sales: Below $ 5 Million
Number Employees: 5-9
Regions Exported to: Worldwide
Percentage of Business in Exporting: 2

48258 S L D Commodities Inc
2 Manhattanville Rd # 202
Purchase, NY 10577-2118   914-696-0071
Fax: 914-696-0076 sldcomm@aol.com
www.sldcommodities.com
Importer and exporter of cashews
Owner: Russell Lynch
russell.lynch@sldcommodities.com
Estimated Sales: $2.5-5 Million
Number Employees: 5-9
Regions Imported from: Worldwide
Percentage of Business in Importing: 70

48259 S L Sanderson & Co
173 Sandy Springs Ln
Berry Creek, CA 95916-9759   530-589-3062
Fax: 530-589-3062 800-763-7845
Manufacturer and exporter of handheld capsule fillers and tampers; wholesaler/distributor of gelatin capsules
President: Cydney Sanderson
capsulefillers@gmail.com
Estimated Sales: Less Than $500,000
Number Employees: 1-4
Number of Products: 6
Brands Exported: Cap. M. Quik (Capsule Fillers & Tampers)
Regions Exported to: Europe, Asia

48260 (HQ)S S Steiner Inc
655 Madison Ave # 1700
New York, NY 10065-8078   212-838-8901
Fax: 212-593-4238 sales@hopsteiner.com
www.hopsteiner.com
Processor, importer and exporter of hops extracts, pellets and oils.
President/COO: Louis Gimbel
VP of Sales: Mike Sutton
Estimated Sales: $20-50 Million
Number Employees: 10-19
Number of Brands: 1
Type of Packaging: Food Service
Other Locations:
  Salem, OR
  Yakima, WA Yakima
Regions Exported to: Worldwide
Percentage of Business in Exporting: 50
Regions Imported from: Europe

48261 S&P Marketing, Inc.
11100 86th Ave
Maple Grove, MN 55369   763-559-0436
Fax: 763-557-1318
Fruit ingredients including tropical and temperate fruit juices, purees, dried fruits, powders and more. Niche products include tamarind, coconut cream, alphonso mango puree, prickly pear juice, puree, powder, fiber and oil.
President: Chareonsri Srisangnam
Marketing/R&D: Vinod Padhye
om@snpmarketing.com
Contact: Om Padhye
om@snpmarketing.com
Type of Packaging: Food Service, Bulk
Regions Exported to: Europe, Asia, Canada, Mexico

48262 S&P USA Ventilation Systems, LLC
6393 Powers Ave
Jacksonville, FL 32217   904-731-4711
Fax: 904-737-8322 800-961-7370
www.solerpalau-usa.com
Manufacturer and exporter of commercial restaurant exhaust fans and ventilation equipment
Owner: Patrick M Williams Sr
VP Sales: Mike Wanek
Contact: Karen Antonell
karen.antonell@healogics.com
Manufacturing/Product Manager: Jim Webster
Estimated Sales: $10-20 Million
Number Employees: 100-249
Square Footage: 150000
Parent Co: Breidert Air Products
Type of Packaging: Consumer, Food Service, Private Label, Bulk
Brands Exported: JennFan; Breidert Air Products; Stanley Fans
Regions Exported to: Central America, Asia, Middle East, Canada, Caribbean, Latin America, Mexico
Percentage of Business in Exporting: 5

48263 S&R Imports
45 W 34th St # 9
New York, NY 10001-3008   212-983-0710
Fax: 212-557-4425
Importer and exporter of beer, mineral water, wheat and computer software
Owner: Iqbal Waryah
Estimated Sales: $300,000-500,000
Number Employees: 1-4
Square Footage: 3200
Regions Exported to: South America, Europe, Asia
Percentage of Business in Exporting: 70
Brands Imported: Maharafe; Ganga JAL
Regions Imported from: South America, Europe, Asia
Percentage of Business in Importing: 30

48264 S-W Mills Inc
3646 County Road 22
Archbold, OH 43502-9791   419-445-5206
Fax: 419-445-4275
Processor and exporter of dehydrated alfalfa pellets and meal
President: Mike Aeschliman
Operator: Martha Wyse
Sales: Ken Vaupel
Estimated Sales: $ 10 - 20 Million
Number Employees: 10-19

48265 S. B. C. Coffee
19529 Vashon Highway SW
Vashon, WA 98070-6029   206-463-5050
Fax: 206-463-5051
Import and retail coffee equipment and supplies
President: J Stewart
Estimated Sales: $500,000-$1 000,000
Number Employees: 5-9
Type of Packaging: Private Label, Bulk

48266 S. Ferens & Company
1108 Roxbury Dr
Westbury, NY 11590   516-338-0765
Fax: 516-338-0656
Importer and exporter of lemon, orange and tangerine oils, glace cherries and dried fruits including apricots, peaches, pears, raisins and currants
President: Glenn Ferens
Estimated Sales: $2.5-5 Million
Number Employees: 1-4

Regions Imported from: Central America, South America, Europe, Asia

48267 S.A.S. Foods
3005 Center Pl
Suite 200
Norcross, GA 30093   770-263-9312
Fax: 770-446-9234
Oriental grocery items, seafood, fin fish, shellfish
President: Goro Iwami
Estimated Sales: $ 5 - 10 Million
Number Employees: 5-9

48268 S.D. Mushrooms
P.O.Box 687
Avondale, PA 19311-0687   610-268-8082
Fax: 610-268-8644
Processor and importer of mushrooms and mushroom sauce
President/Owner: John D'Amico
Estimated Sales: $450,000
Number Employees: 1-4
Type of Packaging: Consumer, Food Service, Private Label, Bulk
Brands Imported: Pizzini Brand
Regions Imported from: India

48269 S.L. Kaye Company
230 5th Ave
New York, NY 10001-7704   212-683-5600
Fax: 212-481-7415 800-255-3529
kaye230@aol.com www.slkaye.com
Importer of confectionery products including butter toffee, fruit and chocolate eclairs and chocolate truffles
President: Abe Katzman
VP: Mitchell Katzman
VP Sales: Joseph Walsh
Estimated Sales: $1-2.5 Million
Number Employees: 1-4
Type of Packaging: Consumer, Food Service
Brands Imported: Needlers; Jersey Sensations; Witor's; Simas; It's A Mixed Bag
Regions Imported from: South America, Europe
Percentage of Business in Importing: 100

48270 S.V. Dice Designers
1836 Valencia Street
Rowland Heights, CA 91748-3050   909-869-7833
Fax: 909-869-0515 888-478-3423
Manufacturer and exporter of packaging machinery including case packers, erectors and sealers
President: Todd Dice
VP: Don Jameson
Engineer: Kent Martins
Estimated Sales: $2.5-5 Million
Number Employees: 1-4
Square Footage: 60000
Brands Exported: SAA
Regions Exported to: Central America, Asia
Percentage of Business in Exporting: 10

48271 SANGARIA USA
3142 Pacific Coast Hwy
Suite 208
Torrance, CA 90505-6796   310-530-2202
Fax: 310-530-5335 sangaria@msn.com
www.sangariausa.com
Manufacturer, importer and exporter of soft drinks: Ramune drink, green tea, oolong tea, iced coffee, energy drink, fruit juices, etc
Owner: Leona Singer
Estimated Sales: $300,000-500,000
Number Employees: 1-4
Square Footage: 500000
Parent Co: Japan Sangaria Beverage Company
Type of Packaging: Consumer, Food Service
Brands Exported: Sangaria
Regions Exported to: Asia
Percentage of Business in Exporting: 80
Brands Imported: Sangaria
Regions Imported from: Asia
Percentage of Business in Importing: 20

48272 SBK Preserves
1161 East 156th Street
Bronx, NY 10474-6226   718-589-2900
Fax: 718-589-8412 800-773-7378
info@sarabeth.com www.sarabeth.com
Processor and exporter of jams, preserves, fruit spreads, syrups and granola cereal
President: Charlie Apt
Finance Executive: Carlos Blanco
VP: Suzanne Levine

Importers & Exporters / A-Z

Estimated Sales: D
Number Employees: 10-19
Square Footage: 30000
Parent Co: Sarabeth's Kitchen
Other Locations:
  SBK Preserves
  New York, NYSBK Preserves
Brands Exported: Sarabeth's
Regions Exported to: Europe, Canada
Percentage of Business in Exporting: 7

48273 SCK Direct Inc
905 Honeyspot Rd
Stratford, CT 06615-7140   203-377-4414
       Fax: 203-377-8187 800-327-8766
       sales@fastinc.com www.kitchenbrains.com
Manufacturer and exporter of appliance timers and controls for frying, cooking, roasting, proofing, retarder-proofing, baking, etc.; also, portable shortening filter machines and software systems for appliance diagnostics
Chairman: Bernard G Koether
bkoether@mysck.com
President: George F Koether
CEO: Seth Lukash
Sales Operations Manager: Sherry Kraynak
Estimated Sales: $ 10 - 20 Million
Number Employees: 50-99
Regions Exported to: Worldwide
Percentage of Business in Exporting: 30

48274 (HQ)SDIX
111 Pencader Dr
Newark, DE 19702-3322   302-456-6789
       Fax: 302-456-6770 800-456-8881
              sales@sdix.com www.sdix.com
SDIX is a leader in developing accurate, simple, and rapid tests for pathogens. Our Rapidchek Tests for E.coli 0157, Listeria and Salmonella Enteritidis give you confidence in test reslutls, shortened product hold times and loweroverall testing costs. Rapidchek is Simply Accurate.
President/CEO: Fran DiNuzzo
R&D: Klaus Linopaintner
Marketing: Tim Lawink
Contact: Anthony Simonetta
anthony@haydenir.com
Estimated Sales: $30 Million
Number Employees: 5-9
Brands Exported: Trait Chek, Rapid Chek
Regions Exported to: Central America, South America, Europe, Asia

48275 SEMCO
1211 W. Harmony
PO Box 505
Ocala, FL 34478-0505   800-451-3383
       Fax: 352-351-3088 800-749-6894
              salesatsemco@aol.com
Spinner racks, grid systems, peg hooks, dump bins, pegboard and slatwall fixtures; also, custom display items
VP: Adrian Simonet
Marketing: Tammy Robinson
Sales: Tammy Robinson
Public Relations: Fran Smith
Estimated Sales: $ 1 - 5 Million
Number Employees: 100-250
Square Footage: 540000
Parent Co: Leggett & Platt
Regions Exported to: South America, Middle East
Percentage of Business in Exporting: 5

48276 SEW Friel
100 Friels Pl
PO Box 10
Queenstown, MD 21658-1674   410-827-8841
       Fax: 410-827-9472 www.sewfriel.com
Processor, importer and exporter of canned corn.
President: Michael Foster
Number Employees: 20-49
Type of Packaging: Consumer, Food Service, Private Label, Bulk
Regions Exported to: Central America, South America, Europe, Asia, Middle East
Regions Imported from: Central America, South America, Europe, Asia, Middle East

48277 SFP Food Products
348 Highway 64 E
Conway, AR 72032-9414   501-327-0744
       Fax: 501-327-2808 800-654-5329
              jballard@sfpfoods.com www.sfpfoods.com
Processor and exporter of waffle, pancake and cone mixes; manufacturer and exporter of waffle and cone irons
President: Jon Ballard
VP Marketing/Sales: Jon Ballard
VP Operations: Ray Ballard
Estimated Sales: $ 3 - 5 Million
Number Employees: 5-9
Square Footage: 60000
Type of Packaging: Food Service, Private Label
Regions Exported to: Asia, Canada
Percentage of Business in Exporting: 5

48278 SGS International Rice Inc
6 Stone Tavern Dr
Millstone Twp, NJ 08510-1733   732-603-5077
       Fax: 732-603-5037 weldonrice@optonline.com
              www.sgsgroup.us.com
Jasmine rice, basmati rice, coconut milk, coconut juice, canned and dried fruits, beans, spices, fruit juices, nuts and raisins, tuna, cashew, seaseme seeds-packer in put labels
President: Maria Gorfain
mariagorfain@weldonfoods.com
CEO: Surinder Sahni
CFO: Soena Sahni
VP: Gagan Sahni
Research & Development: Avneet Sodhi
Marketing: Harbinder Sahni
Manager: Dee Mirchandani
Production: Manoj Hedge
Purchasing: Harbinder Sahnl
Estimated Sales: $10 Million
Number Employees: 5-9
Square Footage: 1200
Type of Packaging: Consumer, Food Service, Private Label, Bulk
Brands Exported: Weldon, Mener
Regions Exported to: Asia, Middle East
Brands Imported: Weldon, Mehar
Regions Imported from: Asia

48279 SHURflo
3545 Harbor Gateway S
Suite 103
Costa Mesa, CA 92626   714-371-1550
       Fax: 714-242-1362 800-854-3218
       customer_service@shurflo.com www.shurflo.com
Manufacturer and exporter of pumps including gas operated demand, liquid, electric and dual inlet gas systems for beverage syrups and condiments.
Chairman & CEO, Pentair: Randall Hogan
EVP & Chief Financial Officer: John Stauch
SVP/Chief Accounting Officer/Treasurer: Mark Borin
SVP & Chief Marketing Officer: John Jacko
SVP/General Counsel/Secretary: Angela Jilek
Year Founded: 1968
Estimated Sales: $100-500 Million
Number Employees: 250-499
Parent Co: Pantair Inc.
Type of Packaging: Food Service
Regions Exported to: Central America, South America, Europe, Asia, Middle East

48280 SIG Combibloc USA, Inc.
2501 Seaport Drive
River Front Suite 100
Chester, PA 19013-9791   610-546-4200
       Fax: 610-546-4201 www.sigcombibloc.com
Manufacturer and exporter of aseptic carton filling and packaging systems for liquid foods and beverages
President: Yerry Derrico
Director Marketing: Bob Abamson
VP Sales/Marketing: Geoff Campbell
Contact: Kevin Abrams
kevin.abrams@sig.biz
Estimated Sales: $50-100 Million
Number Employees: 100-249
Parent Co: PKL Verpackungssysteme GmbH
Regions Exported to: Central America, South America, Asia

48281 SIGHTech Vision Systems
2953 Bunker Hill Lane
Suite 400
Santa Clara, CA 95054   408-282-3770
       Fax: 408-413-2600 sales@sightech.com
              www.sightech.com
Manufacturer and exporter of quality control and assurance machinery for visual inspection

Chairman, Chief Executive Officer: Art Gaffin
Director Marketing Communications: Jeanette Hazelwood
VP Sales/Marketing: Francis Tapon
Contact: Martha Cogan
mcogan@sightech.com
Estimated Sales: $1-2.5 Million
Number Employees: 4
Regions Exported to: Worldwide
Percentage of Business in Exporting: 50

48282 SIT Indeva Inc
3630 Green Park Cir
Charlotte, NC 28217-2866   704-357-8811
       Fax: 704-357-8866 info@sit-indeva.com
              www.sit-indeva.com
Manufacturer and importer of material handling equipment including balancers
Vice President: Stefania Zanardi
szanardi@sit-indeva.com
VP: Stefania Zanardi
Estimated Sales: $2.5-5 Million
Number Employees: 10-19
Parent Co: Scaglia America
Type of Packaging: Bulk
Regions Imported from: Europe

48283 SK Food International
4666 Amber Valley Parkway
Fargo, ND 58104   701-356-4106
       Fax: 701-356-4102 skfood@skfood.com
              www.skfood.com
Family-owned import/export company and bulk grain supplier.
Type of Packaging: Bulk
Other Locations:
  SK Food Specialty Processing
  Moorhead, MNSK Food Specialty Processing

48284 SKE Midwestern
4096 Piedmont Ave
No. 916
Oakland, CA 94611   510-289-9608
       Fax: 415-399-9605 skesf@aol.com
Importer and exporter of pumpkin and sunflower seeds and dried beans, chickpeas, chillies and hibiscus flowers
President: Wesley Fong
VP: Samuel Peck
Sales/Marketing: Juan Alvarado
Estimated Sales: $2.5-5 Million
Number Employees: 1-4

48285 SKW Gelatin & Specialties
PO Box 234
Waukesha, WI 53187-0234
Canada   262-650-8393
       Fax: 262-650-8456 800-654-2396
       gelatin.usa@rousselot.com www.rousselot.com
Food processing equipment manufacturer specializing in vacuum packaging machines (table top, single/double chamber, automatic and belted chambers) shring tunnels, tray sealers, thermoforming machines, injectors, tumblers, massagers andsmokehouses. Exports internationally to more than 50 countries.
President: Geoge Masson
CFO: Steve Smith
Estimated Sales: C
Number Employees: 10

48286 SKW Nature Products
2021 Cabot Boulevard W
Langhorne, PA 19047-1810   215-702-1000
              Fax: 215-702-1015
Cultures, enzymes, edible and industrial gelatins, hydrocolloids, flavors, fragrance raw materials and fruit systems
VP/General Manager: Kenneth Hughes
VP/General Manager: George Masson
Number Employees: 500-999
Parent Co: SKW
Regions Exported to: Central America, South America, Asia

48287 SLT Group
303 Ridge Rd
Dayton, NJ 08810   732-837-3096
              www.sltgroup.com
Basmati rice, lentils, beans, flour & spice
CEO: Sandip Patel
Estimated Sales: $38.9 Million
Number Employees: 9

Importers & Exporters / A-Z

Brands Imported: Basmati Rice, Dabur Chyawanprash, Dabur Herbal Toothpaste, Khazana Rice, Ramdev, Rellure Fruits
Regions Imported from: India

48288 (HQ)SP Industries
2982 Jefferson Rd.
Hopkins, MI 49328 269-793-3232
Fax: 269-793-7451 800-592-5959
info@sp-industries.com www.sp-industries.com
Manufacturer and exporter of hydraulic cart/dumpers, vertical balers, recycling equipment and refuse, precrusher and self-contained compactors
Owner/President: Denny Pool
Vice President: Roger Arndt
Marketing Mgr: David Jackiewicz
Sales Manager: Gene Koelsch
Office Manager: Elise Pool
Production Mgr: Julie Tahaney
Estimated Sales: $10-20 Million
Number Employees: 20-49
Square Footage: 100000
Regions Exported to: Worldwide
Percentage of Business in Exporting: 5

48289 SP Industries Inc
935 Mearns Rd
Warminster, PA 18974-2811 215-672-7800
Fax: 215-672-7807 800-523-2327
cs@spindustries.com
Manufactures Wilmad-LabGlass NMR & EPR tubes, hotpack incubators, chambers and glassware washers, VirTis Laboratory to production scale freeze dryers, FTS Smart Freeze Dryers Technology anf Precision Thermal Control Equipment, Genevacevaporator systems, and Hull Luophilization Systems.
CEO: Patrick Addvensky
patrick.addvensky@spindustries.com
CEO: Chuck Grant
CEO: Charles Grant
Marketing Director: Jennifer Colaiacomo
Sales: Robert Hoesly
Number Employees: 50-99
Square Footage: 280000

48290 (HQ)SPG International
11230 Harland Dr NE
Covington, GA 30014-6411 770-787-9830
Fax: 770-787-7432 877-503-4774
info@spgusa.com www.spgusa.com
Manufacturer and exporter of aluminum and stainless steel carts, racks and bakery shelving
Owner: Steve Durnell
steve.durnell@leggett.com
President, Chief Executive Officer: Steven DarnelL
VP Mfg.: Jose Lopez
Vice President of Business Development: Dave Mack
Vice President of Operations: Bob Buehler
Number Employees: 100-249
Square Footage: 320000
Parent Co: Keggerr & Platt Storage Products Group
Type of Packaging: Food Service
Other Locations:
 Kelmax Equipment Co.
 San Luis PotosiKelmax Equipment Co.
Regions Exported to: Caribbean, Central America, Mexico
Percentage of Business in Exporting: 5

48291 (HQ)SPX Flow Inc
13320 Ballantyne Corporate Pl
Charlotte, NC 28277 704-449-9187
 800-252-5200
communications@spxflow.com www.spxflow.com
Manufacturer, importer and exporter of fat crystallization machinery for the processing of mayonnaise, salad dressings, margarine and shortening
President & CEO: Marc Michael
President, Food & Beverage: Dwight Gibson
VP & CFO: Jaime Easley
Chief Strategy Officer: Brian Taylor
Estimated Sales: $1.5 Billion
Number Employees: 5000-9999
Regions Exported to: Worldwide
Regions Imported from: Europe

48292 SPX Flow Inc
135 Mount Read Blvd
Rochester, NY 14611-1921 585-436-5550
Fax: 585-527-1742 www.spxflow.com
Mixers and impeller systems for industrial water and wastewater treatment.

Number Employees: 250-499
Parent Co: SPX Flow Inc
Regions Exported to: Worldwide

48293 SQP
602 Potential Pkwy
Schenectady, NY 12302-1041 518-831-6800
Fax: 518-831-6890 800-724-1129
www.specialtyqualitypackaging.com
Tissue, paper food trays, plastic straws and stirrers, napkins, chicken boxes and paper hinged takeouts
Owner: Amar Martin
Plant Manager: Barbara Flaming
National Sales Manager: William Gnatek
Sales Manager: Richard Bonaker
rjssbonaker@msn.com
Plant Manager: Larry Meyers
Estimated Sales: $20-50 Million
Number Employees: 100-249
Type of Packaging: Bulk

48294 SSW Holding Co Inc
1100 W Park Rd
Elizabethtown, KY 42701-3168 270-769-5526
Fax: 270-769-0105 info@sswholding.net
www.sswholding.net
Manufacturer and exporter of wire racks and refrigerator and freezer shelving and baskets
President: Paul Kara
Marketing: Brad Nall
VP Sales/Marketing: Mark Gritton
Marketing Manager: Brad Nall
Contact: Richard Baker
r.baker@sswholding.net
Product Development Manager: Jeff Ambrose
Number Employees: 1-4
Square Footage: 1120000
Parent Co: SSW Holding Company
Other Locations:
 SSW Holding Co.
 Fort Smith, ARSSW Holding Co.
Regions Exported to: Central America, Canada
Percentage of Business in Exporting: 5

48295 ST Restaurant Supplies
#1 - 1678 Fosters Way
Delta, BC V3M 6S6
Canada 604-524-0933
Fax: 604-524-0633 888-448-4244
Manufacturer, importer and wholesaler/distributor of chef hats, hairnets, gloves and aprons; also, woodenware and nylon/metal scrubbers
President: Terry Kuehne
CEO: Sandy Lee
Sales: Sabastien Lachat
Purchasing: Sandy Lee
Number Employees: 21
Number of Products: 220
Square Footage: 160000
Type of Packaging: Food Service, Private Label, Bulk
Other Locations:
 ST Restaurant Supplies
 Dallas, TXST Restaurant Supplies
Regions Exported to: USA, Latin America, Mexico
Percentage of Business in Exporting: 20

48296 STD Precision Gear
318 Manley St # 4
West Bridgewater, MA 02379-1087 508-580-0035
Fax: 508-580-0071 888-783-4327
sales@stdgear.com www.stdgear.com
Manufacturer and exporter of corrosion-proof precision gears, sprockets, ratchets, splines, pulleys, etc
President: James Manning
CFO: Doug Grant
Sales Director: Susan Dauwer
Estimated Sales: $1-2 Million
Number Employees: 20-49
Square Footage: 26000
Brands Exported: STD Precision Gears & Instrument
Regions Exported to: Europe, Canada
Percentage of Business in Exporting: 2

48297 STE Michelle Wine Estates
14111 NE 145th St
PO Box 1976
Woodinville, WA 98072-6981 425-488-1133
Fax: 425-415-3657 800-267-6793
info@ste-michelle.com www.smwe.com
Processor, exporter and importer of wines

President/CEO: Ted Baseler
CEO: Melissa Cable
melissa.cable@ccisolarevineyards.com
EVP/CFO: Sheila Newlands
SVP/General Counsel: Tom Rowland
SVP Marketing: Martin Johnson
EVP Sales: Glenn Yaffa
SVP Human Resources: Susan Reams
EVP Winemaking/Vineyards/Operations: Doug Gore
Estimated Sales: $ 10 - 20 Million
Number Employees: 250-499
Type of Packaging: Consumer, Food Service, Private Label, Bulk
Other Locations:
 Stimson Lane Vineyards
 Woodinville, WAStimson Lane Vineyards
Regions Imported from: Worldwide

48298 STI Certified Products Inc
42982 Osgood Rd
Fremont, CA 94539-5627 510-226-9074
Fax: 510-226-9918 800-274-3475
edith@sticertified.com www.stielectronics.com
Exporter of canned and frozen fruits and vegetables including mandarin oranges and mushrooms; also, dried seasonings including chili and garlic
President: Alex Woo
CEO: George Lu
george@goldenmars.com
Marketing Manager: Edith Lai
Operations Manager: Melanie Lai
Estimated Sales: $10-20 Million
Number Employees: 10-19
Regions Exported to: Asia
Percentage of Business in Exporting: 100

48299 STI International
PO Box 7257
San Carlos, CA 94070-7257 650-592-8320
Fax: 650-592-8320
Wholesaler/distributor and exporter of canned meat, fruit, juices and vegetables including tomatoes. Wholesaler/distributor of private label items and health food
President: Todd Stewart
Number Employees: 1-4
Type of Packaging: Consumer, Food Service, Private Label, Bulk
Brands Exported: Chef's Choice; Nu Crest
Regions Exported to: Asia, Middle East, Russia, Mexico, Canada
Percentage of Business in Exporting: 75

48300 SUEZ Water Technologies & Solutions
4636 Somerton Rd
Trevose, PA 19053
 866-439-2837
www.suezwatertechnologies.com
Food and beverage water and wastewater treatment
CEO: Heiner Markhoff
CFO: Mamta Patel
Chief Marketing Officer: Ralph Exton
Other Locations:
 BetzDearborn
 Horsham, PABetzDearborn

48301 SVB Food & Beverage Company
717 Corning Way
Martinsburg, WV 25405 304-267-8500
Fax: 540-636-4470 cs@svbfoods.com
 www.svbfoods.com
Processor and exporter of sparkling cider
President: Ben R Lacy III
Manager: Richard Wadkins
Sales Manager: Debra Hunter
Contact: Ken Bookmyer
kbookmyer@svbfoods.com
Estimated Sales: $944,000
Number Employees: 20-49
Square Footage: 100000
Type of Packaging: Consumer

48302 SWELL Philadelphia Chewing Gum Corporation
North Eagle & Lawrence
Havertown, PA 19083 610-449-1700
 Fax: 610-449-2557
Manufacturer and exporter of chewing bubble gum and candy
President: Edward Fenimore

Importers & Exporters / A-Z

Estimated Sales: $14.5 Million
Number Employees: 100-249
Square Footage: 600000
Type of Packaging: Private Label, Bulk
Regions Exported to: Worldwide

48303 SWF Co
1949 E Manning Ave
Reedley, CA 93654-9462 559-638-8484
Fax: 559-638-7478 800-344-8951
www.swfcompanies.com
Manufacturer and exporter of automatic case and tray loading machinery
Vice President: Braden Beam
braden.beam@thieletech.com
VP/ General Manager: Ed Suarez
Director Engineering: Dan Nourian
Sales/Marketing Executive: Gregory Cox
Product Manager: Craig Friesen
Special Project Manager: Dennis Decker
Estimated Sales: $ 10-20 Million
Number Employees: 100-249
Square Footage: 400000
Parent Co: Thiele Technologies
Brands Exported: Salwasser
Regions Exported to: Central America, South America, Europe, Asia, Australia, Canada, Caribbean, Mexico, Latin America
Percentage of Business in Exporting: 5

48304 SWF McDowell
5505 Carder Road
Orlando, FL 32810-4738 407-291-2817
Fax: 407-293-7054 800-877-7971
Manufacturer and exporter of carton forming and packaging systems including case, inverted bottle and drop packers, top sealers and case erectors
Service Manager: David Robertson
Operations Manager: Dennis Ramey
Estimated Sales: $ 1 - 5 Million
Number Employees: 50-99
Square Footage: 72000
Parent Co: SWF Machinery
Regions Exported to: South America, Europe, Asia

48305 SWMCO Multi Products
20 Taurus Drive
Novato, CA 94947-1922 207-934-9287
Fax: 207-934-6288
Broker - Food Products
President: Elinor Strandburg
Type of Packaging: Consumer, Food Service

48306 Sabatino North America
330 Coster St
Bronx, NY 10474 718-392-3065
Fax: 718-328-4123 888-444-9971
customer@sabatinostore.com
www.sabatinotartufi.com
Truffles (fresh and frozen), condiments (infused oils, sauces and creams, USDA organic truffles, mustards and tapenades), and specialty foods (balsamic vinegar, italian saffron and infused honey).

48307 Sabel Engineering Corporation
1010 East Lake Street
Villard, MN 56385 320-554-3611
Fax: 320-554-2650 www.massmanllc.com
Manufacturer and exporter of automatic case packers and tiering mechanisms for collating multiple layers
President: Herbert Sabel
Engineering Manager: Stan Lundguist
Sales Director: Gary Ensey
Manager: Dave Rosenberg
General Manager: Noel Barbulesco
Estimated Sales: $ 5 - 10 Million
Number Employees: 20-49
Square Footage: 28800
Parent Co: Massman Automation Designs, LLC
Brands Exported: Carousel Caser; Descender
Regions Exported to: Central America, South America, Europe, Asia, Middle East, Canada
Percentage of Business in Exporting: 10

48308 (HQ)Sabert Corp
2288 Main St
Sayreville, NJ 08872-1476 732-721-5546
Fax: 732-721-0622 800-722-3781
sabert@sabert.com www.sabert.com
Plastic disposable plates, platters, containers and bowls; exporter of disposable platters and bowls
President: Katya Connor
kconnor2216@msn.com
Marketing Director: Mark Seckinger
Sales Director: Bob Shemming
Estimated Sales: $5-10 Million
Number Employees: 100-249
Square Footage: 200000
Other Locations:
  Sabert Corp.
  BrusselsSabert Corp.
Regions Exported to: Worldwide
Percentage of Business in Exporting: 10

48309 Sable Technology Solution
1628 Norwood Dr
St Paul, MN 55122-2754 651-994-8441
Fax: 510-293-8553 800-722-5390
info@sabletechnology.com
Manufacturer and exporter of compact point of sale systems for table and quick service restaurants
Executive VP: Adrian Bryan
VP Sales: James Files
Estimated Sales: $ 1 - 5 Million
Number Employees: 20-50
Square Footage: 16000
Type of Packaging: Food Service
Regions Exported to: Europe, Far East,Canada
Percentage of Business in Exporting: 20

48310 Sabra Dipping Company,LL
649 Benet Rd
Oceanside, CA 92058-1208 760-757-2622
Fax: 760-721-2600 800-748-5523
info@sbsalsa.com
Refrigerated salsa, shelf stable foods and sauces. Co-packer of specialty foods.
President/Manager: Doug Pearson
Vice President/Upper Management: Jackie Watson
Quality Assurance Manager: Tatiana Miranda
Contact: Carlos Heras
cheras@sbsalsa.com
VP Purchasing: Patrick Hickey
Estimated Sales: $10-15 Million
Number Employees: 100
Square Footage: 38000
Type of Packaging: Consumer, Food Service
Brands Exported: Chachies

48311 (HQ)Sadler Conveyor Systems
1845 William Street
Montreal, QC H3J 1R6
Canada 519-941-4858
Fax: 519-941-7339 888-887-5129
Custom conveying systems for case and pallet handling from horizontal to vertical applications
President: Stephen Sadler
Vice President: Neil Sadler
R & D: Neil Sadler
Marketing Director: Luc Martineau
Sales Director: Chris Morin
Production Manager: Marcel Richard
Engineering: Eric Allard
Estimated Sales: Below $5 Million
Number Employees: 10
Square Footage: 144000
Other Locations:
  Sadler Conveyor Systems
  Hartford, CTSadler Conveyor Systems
Regions Exported to: Central America, Mexico
Percentage of Business in Exporting: 20

48312 Saeco
7905 Cochran Rd # 100
Cleveland, OH 44139-5470 440-528-2000
Fax: 440-542-9173 estronic@aol.com
Manufacturer and importer of espresso and cappuccino machines including self-grinding, fully automatic and manual
President: John Mc Cann
Marketing Manager (Commercial Products): Julianna Benedick
Sales Manager (Housewares): Elizabeth Will
Contact: Kevin Lemaster
k.lemaster@saeco-usa.com
Estimated Sales: $2.5-5 Million
Number Employees: 20-49
Square Footage: 80000
Parent Co: Estro/Saeco
Type of Packaging: Consumer, Food Service
Brands Imported: Estro; Saeco
Regions Imported from: Italy

48313 Saeplast Canada
PO Box 2087
St John, NB E2L 3T5
Canada 506-633-0101
Fax: 506-658-0227 800-567-3966
saeplast@saeplastcanada.com
Manufacturer and exporter of plastic pallets and insulated containers for transporting fruits, vegetables, frozen foods and fresh fish
President: Torfi Gudmundsson
CFO: Dave Burnan
Number Employees: 50-60
Brands Exported: Dynoplast
Regions Exported to: Central America, South America, Middle East, Australia
Percentage of Business in Exporting: 40

48314 (HQ)Safe-Stride Southern
PO Box 3843
Seminole, FL 33775-3843 727-399-8393
Fax: 727-391-1184 800-566-7547
Wholesaler/distributor and exporter of industrial cleaning chemicals and slip resistant floor treatments
President: Jack O'Connell
Other Locations:
  Safe-Stride Southern
  Springfield, MOSafe-Stride Southern
Brands Exported: Safe-Stride; Florgrip
Regions Exported to: Worldwide
Percentage of Business in Exporting: 20

48315 Safe-T-Cut Inc
97 Main St
Monson, MA 01057-1320 413-267-9984
Fax: 413-267-9585 info@safetcut.com
www.safetcut.com
Manufacturer and exporter of safety knives for cutting films, foams and cartons
President: Richard Baer
CEO: Mary Clark
CFO: Debra Baer
Manager: Debbie Baer
info@safetcut.com
Number Employees: 10-19
Number of Products: 10
Regions Exported to: South America, Europe, Canada, Mexico

48316 Safesteril/Belt-O-Matic
7930 N 700 E
Tippecanoe, IN 46570 574-353-7855
Fax: 574-353-8152 usa@safesteril.com
www.safesteril.com
Sterilization processes for spices, herbs, ingredients and seeds.
Founder: Olivier Lepez
Founder: Philippe Sajet
Estimated Sales: $5-10 Million

48317 Sagawa's Savory Sauces
8292 SW Nyberg St
Tualatin, OR 97062-9457 503-692-4334
Fax: 503-691-0661
Hawaiian-style sauces including teriyaki, sweet and sour and Polynesian barbecue; salad dressings, seasonings and mixes.
President: Linda Rider
Estimated Sales: $540,000
Number Employees: 7
Square Footage: 21732
Type of Packaging: Consumer, Food Service
Regions Exported to: Canada

48318 Sagaya Corp
3700 Old Seward Hwy # 4
Anchorage, AK 99503-6037 907-563-0220
Fax: 907-561-2042 www.newsagaya.com
Offers retail grocery products and services to local customers, as well as wholesale distribution to restaurants and businesses.
Manager: Tom Griffin
Contact: Lorri Peterson
lpeterson@newsagaya.com
Estimated Sales: $30.7 Million
Number Employees: 1-4
Type of Packaging: Consumer, Food Service, Bulk
Regions Imported from: Worldwide

Importers & Exporters / A-Z

48319 Sage V Foods
1470 Walnut St
Suite 202
Boulder, CO 80302
303-449-5626
sales@sagevfoods.com
sagevfoods.com
Rice products
Owner: Pete Vegas
Controller: Whilma Aleman
Estimated Sales: $ 5-10 Million
Number Employees: 50-99
Type of Packaging: Food Service, Private Label, Bulk
Regions Exported to: Worldwide
Percentage of Business in Exporting: 10

48320 Sahadi Fine Foods Inc
4215 1st Ave
Brooklyn, NY 11232-3300
718-369-0100
Fax: 718-369-0800 800-724-2341
pwhelan@sahadifinefoods.com
www.sahadifinefoods.com
Maufacturer of nuts and seeds. Importer of dried fruit, beans, nuts, olives, Mediterranean foods
Owner: Robert Sahadi
VP: Pat Whelan
Sales: Ashraf Bakhoum
rsahadi@sahadifinefoods.com
Operations: Kristin Fernandez
Production: Brian Whelan
Estimated Sales: $11 Million
Number Employees: 20-49
Square Footage: 174000

48321 Sahadi Importing Company
187 Atlantic Ave
Brooklyn, NY 11201
718-624-4550
Fax: 718-643-4415 www.sahadis.com
Importer and exporter of Middle Eastern foods including grains, cheeses, nuts, olives and spices
President: Charles Sahadi
Contact: Audrey Sahadi
asahadi@sahadis.com
Estimated Sales: $10-20 Million
Number Employees: 20-49
Type of Packaging: Consumer, Bulk
Brands Exported: Sahadi
Percentage of Business in Exporting: 50
Brands Imported: Sahadi
Regions Imported from: Middle East
Percentage of Business in Importing: 50

48322 Sahagian & Associates
124 Madison St
Oak Park, IL 60302
708-848-5552
Fax: 708-386-5959 800-327-9273
sales@sahagianinc.com www.sahagianinc.com
Bubble gum, licorice, taffy, candy-coated chocolate malted balls, chocolate bites, almonds, chocolate and caramel popcorn; also, multi-colored and tri-colored popcorn, candy coated licorice, and chocolate dips
President: Linda G. Sahagian
greg@sahagianinc.com
Estimated Sales: $630,000
Number Employees: 11
Type of Packaging: Consumer, Private Label, Bulk
Brands Exported: The Whole 9 Yards; A Yard of; A Foot of
Regions Exported to: Worldwide
Percentage of Business in Exporting: 8

48323 Sahalee of Alaska
PO Box 104174
Anchorage, AK 99510-4174
907-349-4151
Fax: 907-349-4161 800-349-4151
sahalee@aol.com
Seafood
President/CEO: Hank Lind
VP/Secretary/Treasurer: Christa Lind
Sales Director: Bill Haller

48324 Sainsbury & Company
33 Holborn
London, BC EC 1N 2HT
Canada
416-485-3000
Fax: 416-485-3633 800-636-262
Importer of English beer
President: Peter Sainsbury
Number Employees: 20-49
Brands Imported: Marstons
Regions Imported from: Europe

48325 Saint-Gobain Corporation
20 Moores Rd
Malvern, PA 19355
610-893-6000
Fax: 855-639-6629
SGNorthAmericaInfo@saint-gobain.com
www.saint-gobain-northamerica.com
Building materials for a variety of industries including commercial construction.
Chairman, Saint-Gobain North America: Tom Kinisky
Senior Manager, Commercial Sales: Heather Whitaker
Commercial Business Development Manager: Brittany Wright
National Accounts Manager: Bernie Shalvey
Year Founded: 1967
Estimated Sales: $6.2 Billion
Number Employees: 15,000
Parent Co: Compagnie de Saint-Gobain S.A.
Regions Exported to: Canada

48326 Salad Oils Intl Corp
5070 W Harrison St
Chicago, IL 60644-5141
773-261-0500
Fax: 773-261-7555 saladoiljohn@earthlink.net
www.saladoils.net
Vegetable and olive oil packager and distributor
President: John Pacente
saladoiljohn@earthlink.net
VP Sales: Aimee Pacente
Estimated Sales: $5-10 Million
Number Employees: 5-9
Square Footage: 45000
Type of Packaging: Food Service, Private Label, Bulk
Regions Imported from: Europe
Percentage of Business in Importing: 15

48327 Salamatof Seafoods
Bridge Access Road Mp 1.5
PO Box 1450
Kenai, AK 99611-1450
907-283-7000
Fax: 907-283-8499
Fresh and frozen seafood including salmon, halibut, herring and cod
Chairman: Shane Morgan
Director Manufacturing: Roy Bertoglio
Estimated Sales: $ 20-50 Million
Number Employees: 100-249
Type of Packaging: Consumer, Food Service, Bulk

48328 Salba Smart Natural Prod LLC
6418 S Quebec St
Bldg 4
Centennial, CO 80111-4628
303-999-3996
info@salbasmart.com
www.salbasmart.com
Whole and ground chia seeds.
President: Rally Ralston
Partner: Judith Brooks
judith@organicfoodbrokers.com
National Sales Director: Staci Owens
Operations Manager: Kayleen Nichols
Number Employees: 5-9

48329 (HQ)Salem China Company
1000 S Broadway Avenue
Salem, OH 44460-3773
330-337-8771
Fax: 330-337-8775 salem-urfic@worldnet.att.net
Custom manufacturer and exporter of chinaware, dinner sets, teapots, beer steins, stainless flatware and mugs; importer of dinnerware sets
Secretary: Carolyn Brubaker
Estimated Sales: $ 500,000-$ 1 Million
Number Employees: 10-19

48330 (HQ)Salem Oil & Grease Company
60 Grove St
Salem, MA 01970-2245
978-745-0585
Fax: 978-741-4426
Processor and exporter of sulphonated castor oil
President: V Smith
VP Sales: J Donovan
VP Production: G Hanson
Estimated Sales: $10-20 Million
Number Employees: 20-49

48331 Salem-Republic Rubber Co
475 W California Ave
Sebring, OH 44672-1922
330-938-9801
Fax: 330-938-9809 800-425-5079
srr@salem-republic.com www.salem-republic.com
Manufacturer, importer and exporter of FDA approved hoses and hose assemblies, rubber tubing and pipes
President: Drew Ney
dney@salem-republic.com
VP Corporate Development: Anthony Kindler
Sales Manager: Raymond Willis
Estimated Sales: $10-20 Million
Number Employees: 50-99
Brands Exported: Champion; Flexrite; Vol-U-Flex
Regions Exported to: Worldwide
Percentage of Business in Exporting: 10
Regions Imported from: Worldwide
Percentage of Business in Importing: 10

48332 Sales & Marketing Dev
33 Timberline
Irvine, CA 92604-3033
949-552-0405
Fax: 949-552-0406 800-319-8906
smdtrading@aol.com www.smdtrading.com
Importer and exporter of disposable food service products including: chef hats, dollies, glasscovers, coasters, baking cups, cups, plates, dual-ovenable trays, microwavable bowls, containers and trays, aluminum containers & rolls, foodservices film and wraps, airlaid and paper napkins, placemats and traycovers
CEO: Kathryn Gillespie
CFO: John Gillespie
VP: John Gillespie
Estimated Sales: $ 3 - 5 Million
Number Employees: 1-4
Type of Packaging: Consumer, Food Service, Private Label, Bulk
Brands Exported: Premier Disposable Products; Kook Bird, SMD, Fabri Kal
Regions Exported to: Central America, South America, Europe, Asia, Middle East
Percentage of Business in Exporting: 50
Regions Imported from: Asia
Percentage of Business in Importing: 40

48333 Sales King International
782 N Industrial Park Ave
Nogales, AZ 85621-1732
520-761-3000
Fax: 520-281-4060
Wholesaler/distributor, importer and exporter of garlic, ginger and produce including tomatoes, bell peppers, beans, squash, cantaloupe, honeydew and tropical fruits; serving the food service market
Manager: Hector Muckui
VP Tropical Division: Joe Sandino
Parent Co: Sales King International
Regions Exported to: Canada, Hong Kong
Percentage of Business in Exporting: 5
Regions Imported from: Mexico, Brazil
Percentage of Business in Importing: 99

48334 Sales USA
220 Salado Creek Road
Salado, TX 76571-5783
254-947-3838
Fax: 254-947-3338 800-766-7344
pompeii1@aol.com
Fruit and vegetable juices.
President: Rusty Justus
CEO: Ronald Cox
Plant Manager: Lee Simpkins
Estimated Sales: $ 1 Million
Number Employees: 4
Square Footage: 60000
Type of Packaging: Consumer, Food Service, Private Label, Bulk
Brands Exported: Pompeii
Regions Imported from: South America, Mexico
Percentage of Business in Importing: 20

48335 Salinas Valley Wax Paper Co
1111 Abbott St
Salinas, CA 93901-4501
831-424-2747
Fax: 831-424-5883
Manufacturer and importer of printed and plain packaging paper including kraft, laminated, waxed, tissue, pads, box liners, etc
President: Chas Nelson
CEO: Charles Nelson
charles@svwpco.com
VP: Bill Zimmerman
Plant Manager: Richard Johnson
Estimated Sales: $ 10 - 20 Million
Number Employees: 20-49
Number of Brands: 1
Square Footage: 80000
Type of Packaging: Private Label, Bulk
Percentage of Business in Exporting: 1

Importers & Exporters / A-Z

48336 Salmolux Inc
34100 9th Ave S # A
Federal Way, WA 98003-7393   253-874-6570
Fax: 253-874-4042 seafood@salmolux.com
Smoked seafood products, pates, spreads, salmon burgers, herring, flavored butters and canned seafood salads
President: George Kuetgens
Cmo: John Randisi
seafood@salmolux.com
National Sales Director: Kira Kuetgens
Plant Manager: Ray Crockett
Year Founded: 1988
Estimated Sales: $ 20 Million
Number Employees: 50-99
Square Footage: 60000
Type of Packaging: Consumer, Food Service, Private Label, Bulk
Brands Exported: Salmolux
Regions Exported to: Central America
Percentage of Business in Exporting: 5
Regions Imported from: Europe

48337 Salmon Creek Cellars
PO Box 429
Ceres, CA 95307-0429   800-692-5780
Fax: 209-538-2178

48338 Saltworks, Inc.
16240 Wood-Red Road NE
Woodinville, WA 98072-4504   425-885-7258
Fax: 425-650-9876 www.seasalt.com
Salts
CEO: Mark Zoske
Number Employees: 50-99

48339 Salvajor Co
4530 E 75th Ter
Kansas City, MO 64132-2081   816-363-1030
Fax: 816-363-4914 800-SAL-AJOR
sales@salvajor.com www.salvajor.com
Manufacturer, importer and exporter of commercial food waste disposal and waste handling systems
President: Timothy Dike
cadman@modelwarships.com
Vice President: Don Misenhelter
Research & Development: Chris Hohl
National Sales Manager: Dennis Easteria
Purchasing Manager: P Cooper
Estimated Sales: $ 10 - 20 Million
Number Employees: 50-99
Square Footage: 80000
Brands Exported: Salvajor; Disposers; Scrapmaster; Toughveyor; Scrap Collector; Pot/Pan Collector; Trough Collector
Regions Exported to: Worldwide

48340 Sam KANE Beef Processors Inc
9001 Leopard St
Corpus Christi, TX 78409
800-242-4142
www.kanebeef.com
Processor and exporter of fresh, frozen and boxed beef.
Owner: Sam Kane
CEO: Alfred Bausch
CAO & CMO: Chuck Jackson
Director of Regulatory Compliance: Brian Honigbaum
Operations Manager: Dwayne Hubenak
Year Founded: 1949
Estimated Sales: $100-500 Million
Number Employees: 500-999
Type of Packaging: Consumer, Food Service, Bulk
Regions Exported to: Mexico
Percentage of Business in Exporting: 3

48341 SamMills USA
Str. Mioritei nr. 151
Suite 244
Boynton Beach, FL 447065   026-180-6031
Fax: 026-180-6032 office@sammills.eu
www.sammills.eu
Gluten free grains, pasta and oil
CEO: Henry Leighton
Sales Director: Carol D'Alessandra

48342 Sambonet USA
1180 Mclester St # 8
Elizabeth, NJ 07201-2931   908-351-4800
Fax: 908-351-3351 www.sambonet.it
Wholesaler/distributor and importer of general merchandise including cutlery, trays, coffee and tea service equipment, chafing dishes, etc.; serving the food service market
President: Pierre Luigi Coppo
CFO: Harish Patel
VP: Andrea Viannello
Quality Control: Harish Patel
Estimated Sales: $ 2.5 - 5 Million
Number Employees: 5-9
Parent Co: Paderno SpA
Brands Imported: Sambonet
Regions Imported from: Italy
Percentage of Business in Importing: 100

48343 Samir's Imported Food LLC
811 E Genesee St # 1
Syracuse, NY 13210-1574   315-422-1850
Fax: 315-422-1108
Importer of pita bread
Owner: Samir Ashkar
Estimated Sales: Less Than $500,000
Number Employees: 1-4

48344 Sampac Enterprises
551 Railroad Ave
S San Francisco, CA 94080-3450   650-876-0808
Fax: 650-876-0338 sales@sampacent.com
www.sampacent.com
Teas; wholesaler/distributor of herbs, teas, honey, bee pollen, etc
Owner: Sammy MA
sales@sampacent.com
Estimated Sales: $2.3 Million
Number Employees: 10-19
Square Footage: 80000
Type of Packaging: Private Label, Bulk
Regions Exported to: Worldwide
Percentage of Business in Exporting: 10
Regions Imported from: Asia
Percentage of Business in Importing: 80

48345 Sampco
651 W Washington Blvd # 300
Chicago, IL 60661-2138   312-346-1506
Fax: 312-346-8302 800-767-0689
www.sampcoinc.com
Importer of canned and frozen cooked meat extracts including beef; exporter of Vienna sausage, luncheon meats and corned beef
President: David Morrison
gmorrison@sampcoinc.com
VP Industrial Sales: Rod Nally
Estimated Sales: $5-10 Million
Number Employees: 20-49
Type of Packaging: Consumer, Food Service, Private Label, Bulk
Brands Exported: Clusico
Regions Exported to: Europe, Asia, Canada, Mexico
Percentage of Business in Exporting: 10
Brands Imported: Sampco; Cepa; Meatex; Pampeano; Clasico
Regions Imported from: South America, Canada, Caribbean
Percentage of Business in Importing: 90

48346 Samson Controls
4111 Cedar Boulevard
Baytown, TX 77523-8588   281-383-3677
Fax: 281-383-3690 www.samson-usa.com
Manufacturer and exporter of controls and control systems, flow regulators, valves and valve operators
President: Siegfried Hanicke
Contact: Javier Delamora
jdelamora@aerodynamix.com
Estimated Sales: $2.5-5 Million
Number Employees: 20-49
Parent Co: Samson Controls
Regions Exported to: Worldwide
Percentage of Business in Exporting: 2

48347 Samuel Pressure Vessel Group
2121 Cleveland Ave
PO Box 100
Marinette, WI 54143-3711   715-453-5326
Fax: 888-506-4271 spvg@samuel.com
Fabricator of custom designed screw conveyors, heat exchangers, sanitary tanks, pressure vessels from stainless steel and other high alloy metals with sanitary finish
President: Barry Berquist
Quality Control: Gary Anderson
Sales Director: Robert Eaton
Manager: Paul Anderson
paulanderson@samuelpressurevesselgroup.com
Plant Manager: Lenny Bartz
Purchasing Manager: Ann Kelash
Estimated Sales: $10 Million
Number Employees: 500-999
Square Footage: 130000
Parent Co: The Samuel Pressure Vessel Group

48348 Samuel Strapping Systems Inc
1401 Davey Rd # 300
Woodridge, IL 60517-4991   630-783-8900
Fax: 630-783-8901 800-323-4424
www.samuelstrapping.com
Manufacturer and exporter of steel and plastic straps; also, carton closing machines
President: Robert Hickey
rhickey@samuelstrapping.com
CFO: Richard Louis
Controller: Dick Louis
Sales/Marketing: Tom Gould
Marketing Manager: Cy Slifka
Purchasing Manager: Joe Capoccio
Estimated Sales: $ 30 - 50 Million
Number Employees: 20-49
Parent Co: Samuel Manu-Tech
Regions Exported to: Worldwide
Percentage of Business in Exporting: 10

48349 San Aire Industries
101 W Felix St
Fort Worth, TX 76115   817-924-8105
Fax: 817-921-3963 800-757-1912
sales@san-aire.com www.san-aire.com
Manufacturer and exporter of commercial dish, trayware, pot and pan dryers
President: Hatcher James
hjames@sanaire.com
VP Sales/Marketing: Bruce Barker
Estimated Sales: $ 1 - 2.5 Million
Number Employees: 1-4
Regions Exported to: Worldwide

48350 San Diego Products
P.O.Box 2821
Escondido, CA 92033   760-744-9558
Fax: 760-744-9419
Wholesaler/distributor, importer and exporter of snack foods including nuts and dried fruits; also, candy, whole and dried shrimp and spices; serving the American food service market
President: Michael Perez
Vice President: Elias Perez
Sales Director: Josie McKinnon
Contact: James Mckinnon
sdpsnacks@gmail.com
Plant Manager: Lucy Gaices
Purchasing Manager: Michael Perez
Estimated Sales: $1-3 Million
Number Employees: 12
Square Footage: 40000
Type of Packaging: Food Service
Regions Exported to: South America
Percentage of Business in Exporting: 40
Regions Imported from: Asia
Percentage of Business in Importing: 50

48351 San Fab Conveyor
2000 Superior St
Sandusky, OH 44870-1824   419-626-4465
Fax: 419-626-6376
Manufacturer, importer and exporter of package and bulk conveying components and systems including stainless, pallet handling and table top conveyors, carton sealers and stainless case tapers
Owner: Timothy Shenigo
Manager (Packaging Equipment): Don Williams
Engineering Manager: Charles Wheeler
Estimated Sales: $5-10 Million
Number Employees: 10-19
Square Footage: 320000
Brands Exported: San Fab
Regions Exported to: Central America, Middle East, Canada
Percentage of Business in Exporting: 10
Regions Imported from: Asia
Percentage of Business in Importing: 1

48352 San Francisco French Bread
580 Julie Ann Way
Oakland, CA 94621   510-729-6232

Processor and exporter of sourdough bread, rolls and croutons
President: Tom Hofmeister
National Sales Manager: Terry McDonough
Contact: Norm Andrews
norm@asapwinetags.com
Number Employees: 5-9
Parent Co: IBC
Type of Packaging: Consumer, Food Service
Brands Exported: Colombo; Parisian
Regions Exported to: Guam

48353 San Francisco Herb Co
250 14th St
San Francisco, CA 94103-2495   415-861-7174
    Fax: 415-861-4440 800-227-4530
        www.sfherb.com
Wholesaler/distributor, importer and exporter of spices, teas, herbs and essential oils; serving the food service market
Owner: Neil Hanscomb
neil@sfherb.com
Quality Control: Greg High
Operations Manager: John Rabiolo
Estimated Sales: $1-2.5 Million
Number Employees: 10-19
Square Footage: 104000
Type of Packaging: Consumer, Food Service
Regions Exported to: South America, Europe, Canada
Percentage of Business in Exporting: 2
Regions Imported from: Europe, Asia, Middle East
Percentage of Business in Importing: 5

48354 San Francisco Salt
30984 Santana St
Hayward, CA 94544   510-477-9600
    Fax: 510-477-9621 800-480-4540
    customerservice@sfsalt.com sfsalt.com
Salts: Himalayan, bath, dead sea, Epsom, scented, flavored and gourmet
President: Lee Williamson
Director of Sales: Marilou Collins
Operations Manager: Siro Rivera
Year Founded: 2002
Estimated Sales: $46 Million
Number Employees: 11-50
Brands Imported: Salts

48355 San Jamar
555 Koopman Ln
Elkhorn, WI 53121-2012   262-723-6133
    Fax: 262-723-4204 800-248-9826
    info@sanjamar.com www.sanjamar.com
Manufacturer and exporter of built-in dispensing units for condiments and disposable paper products including cups, towels and napkins; also, bar supplies and check management systems
President: Charles Colman
CFO: Andy Skerkowitz
Marketing Manager: Topper Woelfer
Senior Sales Coordinator: Michael Johnson
Estimated Sales: $ 10 - 20 Million
Number Employees: 100-249
Number of Brands: 3
Number of Products: 600
Type of Packaging: Consumer, Food Service
Brands Exported: Classic; Gourmet
Regions Exported to: Central America, South America, Europe, Asia, Middle East, Australia
Percentage of Business in Exporting: 20

48356 San Joaquin Vly Concentrates
5631 E Olive Ave
Fresno, CA 93727-2708   559-458-2500
    Fax: 559-458-2564 800-557-0220
    inquiries@sjvconc.com www.sjvconc.com
SJVC produces red and white juice concentrates, the grape seed extract ActiVin™ and is the world's largest supplier of anthocyanin colors.
Number Employees: 20-49
Regions Exported to: Europe, Asia, Australia, Africa, Canada, Mexico

48357 San Jose Imports
2600 W 35th St
Suite 126
Chicago, IL 60632-1602   773-523-8105
    Fax: 773-523-8125 877-385-2486
    info@dulcelandia.com www.dulcelandia.com
Importer and wholesaler/distributor of candies, pinatas, party favors and confectionery products
Owner: Eduardo Rodrigjuez
sanjoseimports@yahoo.com
CFO: Evelia Rodriguez
VP: Julio Rodriguez
Public Relations: Eve Rodriguez
Estimated Sales: $2.5-5 Million
Number Employees: 10-19
Number of Brands: 125
Number of Products: 400
Square Footage: 152000
Type of Packaging: Private Label
Brands Imported: Dulces Del Sol, Dulcelandia
Regions Imported from: Mexico
Percentage of Business in Importing: 80

48358 San Marzano Imports
116 West Fourth Street
Howell, NJ 07731   732-364-1724
    Fax: 732-364-1724
Dried tomatoes and Turkish and Greek olives
Sales Manager: Nick Soccodato
Number Employees: 5-9
Square Footage: 40000
Regions Imported from: Greece, Spain, Turkey, Morocco

48359 San-Ei Gen FFI
630 5th Ave
Suite 3201
New York, NY 10111   212-315-7850
    Fax: 212-974-2540 contact@saneigen.com
        www.saneigen.com
Food ingredients including coloring extracts and antioxidants.
President: Takashige Shimizu
Contact: Osamu Enomoto
oenomoto@saneigen.com
Estimated Sales: $5 Million
Number Employees: 1-4
Square Footage: 17600
Parent Co: San-El Gen FFI
Type of Packaging: Bulk
Brands Exported: San Rep; Arttaste
Regions Exported to: Central America, South America, Europe, Asia, Middle East
Percentage of Business in Exporting: 50
Regions Imported from: Asia, Canada, Latin America
Percentage of Business in Importing: 50

48360 San-J International Inc
2880 Sprouse Dr
Henrico, VA 23231-6072   804-226-8333
    Fax: 804-226-8383 800-446-5500
    info@san-j.com www.san-j.com
Gluten free tamari, Asian cooking sauces and salad dressings, brown rice crackers, organic shoyu, and soups.
President: Ola Badaru
obaru@san-j.com
Quality Manager: Mark Mansfield
Maintenance Manager: Gary Dudley
Purchasing Manager: Ola Badaru
Estimated Sales: $5.3 Million
Number Employees: 20-49
Number of Brands: 1
Number of Products: 22
Square Footage: 88000
Parent Co: San Jirushi Corporation
Type of Packaging: Consumer, Food Service, Bulk
Brands Exported: San-J; Tamari; Reduced Sodium Tamari; Shoyu
Regions Exported to: Europe, Canada, Australia
Regions Imported from: Asia

48361 San-Rec-Pak
9995 SW Avery St
PO Box 3210
Tualatin, OR 97062-3210   503-692-5552
    Fax: 503-692-4477
Manufacturer and exporter of maltsters' machinery
Manager: Karla Mc Combs
Estimated Sales: $ 3 - 5 Million
Number Employees: 10-19
Parent Co: Kloster Corporation

48362 Sanchelima International
1783 NW 93rd Ave
Miami, FL 33172   305-591-4343
    Fax: 305-591-3203 sales@sanchelimaint.com
        www.sanchelimaint.com
Manufacturer and exporter of dairy and cheese making equipment, fillers and sealers, homogenizers, molds, centrifugal separators, bottle unscramblers, pasteurizers, tanks and valves; processor and exporter of cultures
President: Juan A Sanchelima
Technical Director: Jesus Gonzalez
CFO: Maximo Questa
Estimated Sales: $5-10 Million
Number Employees: 10-19
Regions Exported to: Central America, South America

48363 Sancoa International
92 Ark Rd
Lumberton, NJ 08048   609-953-5050
    Fax: 856-273-2710
Manufacturer, exporter and importer of pressure sensitive labels and shrink sleeves
President: Joseph Sanski
Controller: Roger Spreen
CFO: Kevin Austin
Quality Assurance Manager: Bob Zimmerman
Contact: Mark Brennan
mbrennan@sancca.com
Estimated Sales: $ 20 - 50 Million
Number Employees: 250-499
Regions Exported to: South America, Europe
Regions Imported from: Europe

48364 Sandco International
151 Union Chapel Rd
Northport, AL 35473   205-339-0145
    Fax: 205-339-8222 800-382-2075
Processor and exporter of vitamins and sports supplements, anti-aging
President: Linda Sandlin
sandco@uronramp.com
Research & Development: Richard Sandlin
Marketing: Linda Madison
Purchasing Manager: Linda Wells
Estimated Sales: $1,100,000
Number Employees: 5-9
Square Footage: 80000
Type of Packaging: Consumer, Private Label, Bulk
Brands Exported: Dash
Regions Exported to: Central America, South America, Europe, Asia, Middle East
Percentage of Business in Exporting: 10

48365 Sanden Vendo America Inc
10710 Sanden Dr
Dallas, TX 75238   214-765-9066
    Fax: 800-541-5684 800-344-7216
        www.vendoco.com
Automatic and manual vending machines for bottles and cans
President: Bernt Voelkel
CEO: Frank Kabei
Contact: Bryce Batchelor
bbatchelor@vendoco.com
Number Employees: 500-999
Parent Co: Sanden Corporation
Regions Exported to: Central America, Europe, Asia

48366 Sanderson Farms
P.O. Box 988
Laurel, MS 39441
    800-844-4030
        www.sandersonfarms.com
Poultry.
President/COO: Lampkin Butts
Chairman/CEO: Joe Sanderson
Treasurer/CFO: Mike Cockrell
Secretary/Chief Accounting Officer: Tim Rigney
Year Founded: 1955
Estimated Sales: $3.4 Billion
Number Employees: 17,000+
Square Footage: 11418
Type of Packaging: Consumer, Food Service, Private Label, Bulk
Brands Exported: Sanderson Farms
Regions Exported to: Central America, Europe, Middle East
Percentage of Business in Exporting: 5

48367 Sandler Seating
1175 Peachtree Street NE
Suite 1850
Atlanta, GA 30361   404-982-9000
    Fax: 404-321-7882 www.sandlerseating.com
Manufacturer and exporter/importer of tables and chairs for hotels, restaurants, and food courts

U.S. Director of Sales: Rusty Wolf
Chief Executive Officer: Roy Sandler
Sales Manager: Anita Haslett
Estimated Sales: $ 5 - 10 Million
Number Employees: 5-9
Regions Exported to: Worldwide
Percentage of Business in Exporting: 10

48368 Sands African Imports
9 Dey St
Newark, NJ 07103-3609   973-824-5500
            Fax: 973-824-5502
Wholesaler/distributor and importer of Caribbean sauces and grains; exporter of canned fruits and fruit drinks; serving the food service market
President: Simon Belfer
Customer Service: Bob Montgomery
Warehouse Manager: Michael Sandala
Estimated Sales: $ .5 - 1 million
Number Employees: 1-4
Square Footage: 80000
Parent Co: Sands Brands International Foods
Type of Packaging: Consumer, Food Service, Private Label, Bulk
Regions Exported to: Middle East
Percentage of Business in Exporting: 10
Brands Imported: Doral; Sands African; Sands Caribbean
Regions Imported from: Worldwide
Percentage of Business in Importing: 90

48369 (HQ)Sands Brands International Food
PO Box 184
Millburn, NJ 07041-0184   973-824-5500
        Fax: 973-824-5502 888-407-2637
Wholesaler/distributor, importer and exporter of tropical baking flour, stockfish, coconut products, potato starch, etc; also, gourmet African products available
CEO: Robert Sandala
SE Representative: Josef Sandala
Customer Service: Laauren Sandala
Number Employees: 20-49
Square Footage: 100000
Other Locations:
    Sands Brands International Fo
    Newark, NJSands Brands International Fo
Brands Exported: Sands Brand
Regions Exported to: Europe
Percentage of Business in Exporting: 10
Brands Imported: Avebe; United Producers; Blohorn; Cadbury; Nkulenu; Nestle's Africa
Regions Imported from: Central America, South America, Europe, Iceland, Africa
Percentage of Business in Importing: 90

48370 Sandvik Process Systems
30 Stockholm
Box 510, SE-101
Sweden, NJ 7512   973-790-1600
        Fax: 973-790-9247 www.sandvik.com
Manufacturer and exporter of food processing equipment including dryers, coolers, freezers, drop-formers and steam cookers
President: Olof Faxander
Chairman: Anders Nyr,n
Marketing Manager: Craig Bartsch
Estimated Sales: $ 1 - 5 Million
Number Employees: 55
Parent Co: Sandvik
Brands Exported: Roto-Former
Regions Exported to: Worldwide

48371 Sanford Redmond Company
65 Harvard Ave
Stamford, CT 06902   203-351-9800
            Fax: 718-292-0010
Manufacturer and exporter of wrapping, food processing and packaging machinery
President: S Redmond
Contact: Sanford Redmond
ezpaks@sanred.com
Estimated Sales: $1-2,500,000
Number Employees: 5-9
Regions Exported to: Worldwide

48372 Sani-Fit
620 S Raymond Avenue
Suite 9
Pasadena, CA 91105-3261   626-395-7895
            Fax: 626-395-7899
Manufacturer, importer and exporter of stainless steel sanitary fittings, diaphragm valves and food processing fitting components
Estimated Sales: $ 1 - 5,000,000
Regions Exported to: Worldwide
Percentage of Business in Exporting: 20
Percentage of Business in Importing: 30

48373 Sani-Matic
P.O.Box 8662
Madison, WI 53708-8662   608-222-1935
        Fax: 608-222-5348 800-356-3300
info@sanimatic.com www.sanimatic.com
Cleaning systems for the food and pharmaceutical industries. Product lines include clean-out-of-place parts washers, clean-in-place systems, rinse/foam/sanitize pressure systems, conveyorized wash tunnels, and a variety of cabinetwashers to clean vats, racks, pallets, ibc, bin, totes and other product handling items.
President: Ted Lingard
Marketing: Kelsy Boyd
Sales: Chad Dykstra
Contact: John Leach
johnl@sanimatic.com
Plant Manager: Wayne Huebner
Estimated Sales: $20 Million
Number Employees: 100-249
Number of Products: 10
Square Footage: 40000
Brands Exported: Sani-Matic
Regions Exported to: Central America, South America, Europe, Asia, Canada, Mexico
Percentage of Business in Exporting: 15

48374 SaniServ
451 E County Line Rd
Mooresville, IN 46158   317-831-7030
        Fax: 317-831-7036 800-733-8073
sdowling@saniserv.com www.saniserv.com
Manufacturer and exporter of batch machines, freezers and dispensers for ice cream, shakes, frozen beverages/cocktails, yogurt and custard; processor of cappuccino; importer of visual slush machines
President: Robert Mc Afee
CFO: Allen McCormick
Contact: Robert Mcafee
rmcafee@saniserv.com
Number Employees: 50-99
Square Footage: 300000
Parent Co: MD Holdings
Type of Packaging: Consumer, Food Service, Private Label
Brands Exported: SaniServ
Regions Exported to: Worldwide
Percentage of Business in Exporting: 35
Brands Imported: Ugolini
Regions Imported from: Europe
Percentage of Business in Importing: 10

48375 Sanitary Couplers
275 S Pioneer Boulevard
Springboro, OH 45066-1180   513-743-0144
        Fax: 513-743-0146 reseal@compuserve.com
Manufacturer and exporter of high purity sanitary hoses, fittings and hose assemblies
General Manager: Jeffrey Zornow
Manager: Mark Hess
Sales Manager (Western Region): Jason Parks
Customer Service: Tracy Brandenburg
Estimated Sales: $2.5-5 Million
Number Employees: 9
Square Footage: 80000
Parent Co: Norton Performance Plastics
Brands Exported: ReSeal; PermaSeal; SaniGard; ClearGard
Regions Exported to: Central America, South America, Europe, Canada, Latin America, Mexico
Percentage of Business in Exporting: 15

48376 (HQ)Sanitech Inc
7207 Lockport Pl # H
Lorton, VA 22079-1534   703-339-7001
        Fax: 703-339-6848 800-486-4321
            www.sanitechcorp.com
Manufacturing sanitation systems for food processing and food service operations
President/CEO: alan weinstein
sumeersharma@sanitech.com
CFO: Pash Bhalla
VP: Bill Hannigan
Director Marketing: Sumeer Sharma
Sales Exec: Sumeer Sharma
Production: Tom Wines
Plant Manager: J R Bhalla
Purchasing Manager: Mike Sherman
Estimated Sales: $5 Million
Number Employees: 5-9
Square Footage: 20000
Brands Exported: Sanitech
Regions Exported to: Central America, South America, Europe, Asia, Middle East
Percentage of Business in Exporting: 20

48377 (HQ)Sanitek Products Inc
3959 Goodwin Ave
Los Angeles, CA 90039-1187   818-242-1071
        Fax: 818-242-1071 818-242-1071
info@sanitek.com www.sanitek.com
Manufacturer and exporter of floor finishes, hand cleaners and industrial chemicals; also, liquid soap and specialty chemicals available
President: Robert L Moseley
info@sanitek.com
VP: David Moseley
R&D and QC: Ronald Ostroff
Estimated Sales: $ 5 - 10 Million
Number Employees: 10-19
Square Footage: 160000
Type of Packaging: Consumer, Private Label
Regions Exported to: Europe
Percentage of Business in Exporting: 20

48378 Santa Barbara Olive Company
12477 Calle Real
Santa Barbara, CA 93117   805-562-1456
        Fax: 805-562-1464 800-624-4896
info@sbolive.com www.sbolive.com
Gourmet olives, extra virgin olive oils, sauces, vegetables, condiments, salsas
President: Craig Makela
Vice President: Cindy Makela
Contact: Jason Pace
jason@sbolive.com
Estimated Sales: $10 Million
Number Employees: 17
Square Footage: 14000
Type of Packaging: Consumer, Food Service, Private Label, Bulk
Brands Exported: Santa Barbara Olive
Regions Exported to: Central America, Europe, Asia, Canada, Australia
Percentage of Business in Exporting: 15
Regions Imported from: Europe
Percentage of Business in Importing: 10

48379 Santa Clara Nut Co
1590 Little Orchard St
San Jose, CA 95110-3599   408-298-2425
        Fax: 408-298-0101 santaclaranut@aol.com
Manufacturer and exporter of shelled and in-shell walnuts
Owner/President: Jim Pusateri
santaclaranut@aol.com
VP: Salvatore Pusateri
Estimated Sales: $15 Million
Number Employees: 5-9
Number of Brands: 1
Number of Products: 1
Square Footage: 150000
Type of Packaging: Consumer, Food Service, Bulk
Brands Exported: Santa Clara
Regions Exported to: South America, Europe, Asia, Australia
Percentage of Business in Exporting: 50

48380 Santa Monica Seafood Co.
18531 S. Broadwick St.
Rancho Dominguez, CA 90220   310-886-7900
        Fax: 310-886-3333 800-969-8862
            info@smseafood.com
            www.santamonicaseafood.com
Fresh and frozen fish including halibut, salmon, sea bass and swordfish.
President: Anthony Cigliano
anthony@smseafood.com
Controlling Partner: Marisa Cigliano
Controlling Partner: John Cigliano
Executive VP/Co-Owner: Michael Cigliano

Importers & Exporters / A-Z

Year Founded: 1939
Estimated Sales: $400 Million
Number Employees: 20-49
Type of Packaging: Consumer, Food Service, Private Label, Bulk
Other Locations:
 Long Beach Seafoods
 Del Mar, CALong Beach Seafoods
Regions Exported to: Central America, South America, Middle East
Percentage of Business in Exporting: 10

48381 Santini Foods
16505 Worthley Dr
San Lorenzo, CA 94580   510-317-8888
 Fax: 510-317-8343 800-835-6888
 www.santinifoods.com
Milk products, syrups, sauces, and ethnic and specialty foods
President/Owner: Vikram Chand
CFO: Tyler Abbott
Vice President: Christopher Quie
Quality Control: Hal Burgan
Operations: Roger Tan
Year Founded: 1987
Estimated Sales: $11 Million
Number Employees: 50-99
Square Footage: 400000
Type of Packaging: Consumer, Food Service, Private Label, Bulk
Brands Imported: Corticella; Santini; Oliveto; Savini
Regions Imported from: Italy, Chile

48382 Sanyo Corporation of America
500 Fifth Ave.
Suite 3620
New York, NY 10110   212-221-7890
 Fax: 212-221-7828 hohata@sanyocorp.com
Importer of packaging films including PVA barrier, plain and metallized nylon, FDA grade polyester, polyproplene and PE
Contact: Jun Aoki
jaoki@sanyocorp.com
Manager Plastics: Naruhiro Kiyota
Estimated Sales: $ 10 - 20 Million
Number Employees: 13
Parent Co: Sanyo Trading Company
Regions Imported from: Asia
Percentage of Business in Importing: 95

48383 Sapac International
PO Box 2035
Fond Du Lac, WI 54936-2035   920-921-5060
 Fax: 920-921-0822 800-257-2722
Palletizers; importer of bag filling and sealing equipment
Project Manager: Henry Brown
President/National Sales Manager: Bruce McMurry
Controls Manager: Jerome Haser
Number Employees: 1-4
Parent Co: Sapac
Regions Imported from: New Zealand
Percentage of Business in Importing: 70

48384 Sapore della Vita
West Country Club Drive N
Sarasota, FL 34243-3513   941-914-2656
 kristine@saporedellavita.com
 www.saporedellavita.com
Italian products: caramels, jams, marmalades, nut butter, biscotti, oils, sauces and confectionery.
Co-Owner: Kristine Insalaco-Gaioni
Year Founded: 2009
Estimated Sales: Under $500,000
Number Employees: 11-50
Type of Packaging: Food Service, Private Label
Brands Imported: Lick My Spoon, Marchesi, Villa Lan Franca, Crema di Miele, Sapore Del Tartufo
Regions Imported from: Italy

48385 Sapporo USA, Inc.
11 E 44th St
Suite 705
New York, NY 10017   212-922-9165
 Fax: 212-922-9576 info@sapporousa.com
Processor and importer of beer. They also prepare dishes using beer as an ingredient.
President: Tsukasa Orui
Contact: Saori Potts
saori@sapporousa.com
Estimated Sales: G
Number Employees: 30
Square Footage: 2000
Type of Packaging: Consumer, Food Service
Regions Imported from: Asia

48386 Saputo Cheese USA Inc.
One Overlook Point
Suite 300
Lincolnshire, IL 60069   847-267-1100
 Fax: 847-267-1110 www.saputocheeseusa.com
Natural cheese products and exporter of whey.
President/COO: Terry Brockman
Year Founded: 1954
Estimated Sales: $430 Million
Number Employees: 250-499
Number of Brands: 15
Number of Products: 12
Square Footage: 270000
Parent Co: Saputo, Inc.
Type of Packaging: Consumer, Food Service, Bulk
Regions Exported to: Worldwide

48387 Saquella U.S.A.
Via Toretta, 24
Italy, PC 65128   908-543-2171
 Fax: 390-855-2086 www.saquella-coffee.com
Importer of coffee
President: Dana Rafferty
Estimated Sales: $500,000-$1 Million
Number Employees: 5-9
Brands Imported: Saquella, U.S.A.
Regions Imported from: Italy
Percentage of Business in Importing: 100

48388 Saranac Brewery
830 Varick St
Utica, NY 13502
 800-765-6288
 www.saranac.com
Manufacturer, brewer and exporter of beer, ale, stout, lager and malt; also, soft drinks and juices
President: Fred Matt
Chairman & CEO: Nicholas Matt
Director of Operations: Jim Kuhr
Estimated Sales: $ 21 Million
Number Employees: 150
Number of Brands: 12
Square Footage: 360000
Type of Packaging: Consumer, Food Service, Private Label, Bulk
Regions Exported to: Worldwide
Percentage of Business in Exporting: 1

48389 Sarant International Cmmdts
213 Hallock Rd # 3b
PO Box 659
Stony Brook, NY 11790-3000   631-675-2875
 Fax: 631-246-5257 psarant@aol.com
Processor and importer of dehydrated vegetables including tomatoes, celery, carrots and red and green bell peppers
President: Peter Sarant
Co-Secretary: Pamela Sarant
Number Employees: 1-4
Type of Packaging: Bulk
Regions Imported from: Chile, Mexico, Turkey, Hungary

48390 Saratoga Food Specialties
771 W Crossroads Pkwy
Bolingbrook, IL 60490
 800-451-0407
 info@saratogafs.com www.saratogafs.com
Whole and ground spices, custom seasoning blends, seasoned rice, stuffing and gravy mixes.
President: Michael Marks
CFO: Ed Herbert
Vice President: Wade McGeorge
Research & Development: Paul Maki
Quality Control: Mark Beattie
Marketing Director: Kristi Freitager
Sales Director: George Rackos
Contact: Alan Ainsley
aainsley@saratogafs.com
Operations Manager: Jim Benja
Purchasing Manager: Ron Batzer
Estimated Sales: $30-40 Million
Number Employees: 100-249
Square Footage: 110000
Type of Packaging: Consumer, Food Service, Private Label, Bulk
Other Locations:
 Saratoga Specialties Co.
 Northlake, ILSaratoga Specialties Co.
Brands Exported: Saratoga Specialties
Regions Exported to: Central America, Africa, Mexico
Percentage of Business in Exporting: 10
Regions Imported from: Europe, Asia, Middle East, Caribbean
Percentage of Business in Importing: 15

48391 Sardee Industries Inc
5100 Academy Dr # 400
Suite 400
Lisle, IL 60532-4208   630-824-4200
 Fax: 630-824-4225 sales@sardee.com
 www.sardee.com
Manufacturer and exporter of palletizers, depalletizers and pallet, container and end handling equipment
President: Steve Sarovich
ssarovich@sardee.com
Sales Director: Gary Bishop
Estimated Sales: $ 5 - 10 Million
Number Employees: 10-19
Square Footage: 100000
Parent Co: Sardee Industries
Regions Exported to: Central America, South America, Europe, Asia, Middle East
Percentage of Business in Exporting: 30

48392 (HQ)Sargento Foods Inc
1 Persnickety Pl
Plymouth, WI 53073-3544   920-893-8484
 Fax: 920-893-8399 800-243-3737
 www.sargento.com
Natural and processed cheese manufacturer.
CEO: Louis Gentine
Executive VP: Karri Neils
karri.neils@sargentocheese.com
Estimated Sales: Over $1 Billion
Number Employees: 1000-4999
Type of Packaging: Consumer, Food Service, Private Label, Bulk
Regions Exported to: Europe, Canada, Mexico
Regions Imported from: Europe

48393 Sasib Beverage & Food North America
808 Stewart Drive
Plano, TX 75074-8101   800-558-3814
Manufacturer and exporter of high speed beverage fillers and processing systems, labelers, bottle washers, rinsers, casers, palletizers and turnkey beverage production facilities
President: Claudia Salvi
VP Manufacturing: Robert Prescott
Estimated Sales: $20-50 Million
Number Employees: 186
Square Footage: 300000
Parent Co: Sasib Beverage
Regions Exported to: Central America, South America, Asia, Middle East
Percentage of Business in Exporting: 60

48394 Sassone Wholesale Groceries Co
1706 Bronxdale Ave
Bronx, NY 10462-3393   718-792-2828
 Fax: 718-829-4378
Wholesaler/distributor and importer of general line items, dairy products, frozen foods, general merchandise and private label items; serving Italian-American restaurants and pizzerias
President: Ralph Sassone
Vice President: Joe Carnevalla
Plant Manager: Mike Merc
Purchasing: Joe Carnevalla
Estimated Sales: $10-20 Million
Number Employees: 10-19
Square Footage: 26000
Type of Packaging: Food Service, Private Label, Bulk
Brands Imported: Barilla; Valdigno
Regions Imported from: Central America
Percentage of Business in Importing: 10

48395 Satake USA
10905 Cash Rd
Stafford, TX 77477   281-276-3600
 Fax: 281-494-1427 cvincent@satake-usa.com
 www.satake-usa.com
Manufacturer and exporter of sorters including color, nut meat and tomato; also, rice processing and cereal milling equipment available

Importers & Exporters / A-Z

President: J J Naoki
VP Marketing: Peter Cawthorne
Marketing Specialist: Sandra Langlois
Contact: Mathew Abraham
mabraham@satake-usa.com
Estimated Sales: $ 20-50 Million
Number Employees: 100-249
Parent Co: Satake Corporation
Other Locations:
  Satake (USA)
  Cheshire, UKSatake (USA)
Regions Exported to: Central America, South America, Europe, Asia, Middle East
Percentage of Business in Exporting: 50

48396 Satin Fine Foods
32 Leone Lane
Chester, NY 10918
contact@satinfinefoods.com
www.satinice.com
Gluten-free, dairy-free, nut-free, vegan, Kosher fondant and gum paste in various colors
Founder/CEO: Kevin O'Reilly
Year Founded: 2001
Number of Brands: 1
Number of Products: 4
Type of Packaging: Consumer, Private Label, Bulk
Brands Exported: Satin Ice
Regions Exported to: USA, Canada

48397 Sato America
10350 Nations Ford Rd # A
Charlotte, NC 28273-5824   704-644-1662
Fax: 704-644-1662 888-871-8741
www.satoamerica.com
Manufacturer and exporter of bar code printers
President: Robert Linse
robertlinse@satoamerica.com
Marketing Manager: Nikki Aunn
Number Employees: 50-99
Type of Packaging: Consumer, Food Service, Private Label, Bulk
Regions Exported to: Central America, South America, Latin America, Canada, Caribbean, Mexico

48398 Saunder Brothers
Bacon Street
Bridgton, ME 4009   207-647-3331
Fax: 207-647-2064
Manufacturer and exporter of wooden candy sticks, skewers and plain dowels
Co-Owner/President/General Manag: Read Grover
Co-Owner/VP: Robert Berry
Sales Manager/Treasurer: Terri Grover
Number Employees: 24
Regions Exported to: Central America, Europe, Asia
Percentage of Business in Exporting: 1

48399 Saunders Manufacturing Co.
PO Box 12539
N Kansas City, MO 64116-0539   816-842-0233
Fax: 816-842-1129 800-821-2792
goldenstar@goldenstar.com www.goldenstar.com
Manufacturer and exporter of regular and dust mops including antimicrobial, cotton wet, disposable and rayon; also, mop handles and frames and carpet mats and mattings
President: Gary Gradinger
National Sales Manager: Ssteve Lewis
VP Manufacturing: Mike Julo
Estimated Sales: $ 20 - 50 Million
Number Employees: 20-49
Square Footage: 100000
Parent Co: Golden Star
Type of Packaging: Consumer, Food Service, Private Label, Bulk
Brands Exported: Infinity Twist; Barricade; Starborne; Comet; Healthcare; Sta-Flat; Victory; Wearever; Performer; Clencher; Quik-Change; Set-O-Swiv
Regions Exported to: Central America, South America, Europe, Asia, Middle East

48400 Savannah Food Co
575 Industrial Rd
PO Box 1000
Savannah, TN 38372-5977   731-925-1155
Fax: 731-925-1855 800-795-2550
info@savannahclassics.com
www.savannahclassics.com
Manufacturer and marketer of homestyle hushpuppies and authentic southern side dishes.
President: John Bryan
VP, Sales & Marketing: Jim Sisco
VP, Operations: Paul Stodard
Direction of Production: Lynn Austin
Year Founded: 1970
Number Employees: 50-99
Type of Packaging: Consumer, Food Service, Private Label
Other Locations:
  Savannah Foods & Industries
  Breman, GASavannah Foods & Industries

48401 Save-O-Seal Corporation
PO Box 553
Elmsford, NY 10523-0553   914-592-3031
Fax: 914-592-4511 800-831-9720
Manufacturer and exporter of bagging machines and heat sealing equipment; also, coated slitting blades
President: Tullio Muscariello
Sales: Anna DeLuca
Estimated Sales: $ 2.5 - 5 Million
Number Employees: 5-9

48402 Savello USA
1265 Sans Souci Parkway
Wilkes-Barre, PA 18706   570-822-9743
Fax: 570-822-6622 info@savellousa.com
www.savellousa.com
Cheese, meat, fish, pasta and rice, baked goods, honey, olives, spices, vegetables, sauces, oils and vinegars.
President: Cesare Gallo
Vice President: Palma Gallo
Vice President, Operations: Nicholas Gallo
Purchasing Director: John Corbino
Estimated Sales: $2.6 Million
Number Employees: 14
Brands Imported: Blue Marlin, Cao Formaggi, Callipo, Dalla Bona, E'Piu, Madeo, Turri, Silano, Carozzi, Spinoza and more.
Regions Imported from: Italy

48403 Savoia Foods
402 W Lincon Hwy
Chicago Heights, IL 60411   708-756-7600
Fax: 708-754-2133 800-867-2782
www.savoiafoods.com
Pasta, brands spaghetti, spinach spaghetti, inguine, fettucine and lasagne
President/Owner: Rudolph Bamonti
Sales Executive: Julia Bamonti
Estimated Sales: $2.5-5million
Number Employees: 10-19
Type of Packaging: Consumer, Food Service
Brands Exported: Savoia
Regions Exported to: Canada
Percentage of Business in Exporting: 1

48404 Savor California
817 Benjamin Way
Healdsburg, CA 95448   707-431-1814
www.savorcalifornia.com
Beverages, breads and other baked goods, cheese, yogurt, milk and butter, coffee and teas, condiments and sauces, desserts and confections, dried fruit, nuts and snacks, gourmet convenience food, herbs and seasonings, jams, jelliessyrups and honey, meats and poultry, oils and vinegars, pasta, cereal and grains, produce and seafood
President/Owner: Jane St.Clare

48405 Savory Foods
900 Hynes Ave SW
Grand Rapids, MI 49507-1091   616-241-2583
Fax: 616-241-6332 800-878-2583
www.pennstreetbakery.com
Processor and exporter of pork rinds
Owner: Dan Abraham
Safety Manager: Adam Dengel
VP Sales/Production: K Sanderlin
dan.abraham@savoryfoods.com
Production Manager: Ed Thompson
Plant Manager: Rigel Olmos
Number Employees: 20-49
Square Footage: 120000
Type of Packaging: Food Service, Private Label
Brands Exported: Porkies; Savory; Southern Style
Regions Exported to: Canada
Percentage of Business in Exporting: 1

48406 Savoury Systems Inc
230 Industrial Pkwy # C
Branchburg, NJ 08876-3580   908-526-2524
888-534-6621
savourysystems.com
Savory flavors manufacturer.
President: David Adams
customerservice@savourysystems.com
Vice President, Marketing: Jackie Sun
Vice President & Director of Sales: Kevin McDermott
Director of Operations: Alex Carillo
Estimated Sales: $12.6 Million
Number Employees: 10-19
Regions Exported to: South America, Europe, Asia, Australia, Canada, Mexico

48407 Saxby Foods
4120 98th Street NW
Edmonton, AB T6E 5A2
Canada   780-440-4179
Fax: 780-440-4480
Frozen desserts including cakes and cheesecakes
President: Jonathan Avis
Quality Control: Ana Avalos
Public Relations: Thea Avis
Plant Manager: Sean Gillis
Purchasing: Rhys Amatori
Estimated Sales: F
Number Employees: 120
Square Footage: 100000
Type of Packaging: Private Label
Brands Exported: Desserts
Regions Exported to: Europe, USA
Percentage of Business in Exporting: 15

48408 Sayco Yo-Yo Molding Company
2 Sunset Ave
Cumberland, RI 2864   401-724-5296
Manufacturer and exporter of advertising promotions and novelties including yo-yos, yo-yo promotions
President: Lawrence Sayegh
Plant Manager: Leroy Sayegh
Purchasing Manager: Larry Sayco
Estimated Sales: Under $300,000
Number Employees: 5
Square Footage: 3000
Parent Co: L.J. Sayegh & Company
Type of Packaging: Consumer, Private Label
Brands Exported: Sayco
Regions Exported to: Middle East, Australia
Percentage of Business in Exporting: 10

48409 Sazerac Company, Inc.
3850 N Causeway Blvd
Suite 1695
Metairie, LA 70002-3825   866-729-3722
info@sazerac.com
www.sazerac.com
Manufacturer and exporter of bourbon, scotch, whiskey, gin and vodka; importer of scotch
President & CEO: Mark Brown
mbrown@bourbonwhiskey.com
Owner: Chaolai Wu
Partner: Scott Newitt
Vice President of Human Resources: Kathy Thelen
Marketing Services Director: Meredith Moody
VP Sales & Marketing: Steve Wyant
PR Manager: Amy Preske
Plant Manager: Byron Du Bois
Number Employees: 350
Square Footage: 360000
Regions Exported to: Europe, Asia, Africa
Regions Imported from: Europe

48410 Scaltrol Inc
460 Brogdon Rd # 500
P.O. Box 3288
Suwanee, GA 30024-2314   678-541-5138
Fax: 877-769-2751 800-868-0629
rzimmerman@scaltrolinc.com
www.scaltrolinc.com
Manufacturer and exporter of water treatment units for removal of scale and staining
Owner: Austin Hansen
Business Manager: Hilda Epsten
Manager: Rob Zimmerman
rzimmerman@scaltrolinc.com
Operations Manager: Sunday Christopher
Number Employees: 1-4
Square Footage: 10000
Brands Exported: Scaltrol

Importers & Exporters / A-Z

Regions Exported to: Central America, South America, Europe, Canada, Caribbean, Latin America, Mexico, Australia
Percentage of Business in Exporting: 10

48411 Scan American Food Company
P.O. Box 5070
Lynnwood, WA 98046   425-514-0500
            Fax: 425-514-0400
scanamerican@scanamerican.com
www.scanamerican.com
Processor, importer and exporter of natural food flavors and extracts, aroma materials, proteins, fish oils and freeze dried seafood
President: Svein Bjorge
Estimated Sales: $ 5 - 10 Million
Number Employees: 5-9

48412 Scan Coin
20145 Ashbrook Pl # 110
Ashburn, VA 20147-3375   703-729-8600
      Fax: 703-729-8606   800-336-3311
info@scancoin-usa.com www.scancoin-usa.com
Manufacturer and importer of coin and currency handling equipment including counting, sorting and packing
President/Chief Executive Officer: Per Lundin
Contact: Gaaron Gilham
gilham@scancoin-cds.com
Estimated Sales: Below $ 5 Million
Number Employees: 5-9
Parent Co: Scan Coin AB
Type of Packaging: Consumer
Brands Imported: Scan Coin
Regions Imported from: Europe, Asia
Percentage of Business in Importing: 95

48413 Scan Corporation
110 Lithia Pinecrest Rd Ste G
Brandon, FL 33511   813-653-2877
      Fax: 813-654-3949   800-881-7226
sales@scancorporation.com
www.scancorporation.com
Manufacturer and exporter of point of sale systems including touch screen p.c.'s and terminals, membrane keyboards and scanning equipment
President: Frank Harrison
Estimated Sales: $10-20 Million
Number Employees: 10-19
Regions Exported to: Worldwide

48414 Scandia Packaging Machinery Co
15 Industrial Rd
Fairfield, NJ 07004-3017   973-473-6100
      Fax: 973-473-7226 jbrown@scandiapack.com
www.scandiapack.com
Manufacturer and exporter of automatic packaging equipment for overwrapping, bundling, banding, multipacking, cartoning and collating
President: Bill Bronander
wbb@scandiapack.com
Finance: Cecelia G. Bronander
Engineering: Arthur Goldberg
Sales Representative: Carolyn Placentino
Customer Service: Maria Van Ness
Sales Manager: James J. Brown
Parts Department: Lewis D'Allegro
Estimated Sales: $10-20 Million
Number Employees: 20-49
Square Footage: 61200
Regions Exported to: Central America, South America, Europe, Asia
Percentage of Business in Exporting: 25

48415 Scandic Food Inc
700 Rockmead Dr # 200
Humble, TX 77339-5018   281-348-2161
      Fax: 281-348-2347 usa@scandic-food.com
www.scandic-food.com
Jams and preserves, dessert toppings, honey, non-dairy cream and fresh and frozen vegetables
Vice President: Ben Svensson
usa@scandic-food.com
Vice President: Ben Svensson
usa@scandic-food.com
VP Marketing/Sales: Lars Obro
Sales Manager: Blaine Thompson
Number Employees: 1-4

48416 Scandicrafts Inc
740 Pancho Rd
Camarillo, CA 93012-8576   805-482-0791
      Fax: 805-484-7971   800-966-5489
sales@scandicrafts.com www.scandicrafts.com

Wholesaler/distributor, importer and exporter of kitchen tools, bakeware and metal polish
President: Frank Stiernelof
VP: Christa Stiernelof
Marketing: Joi Elliot
Sales: Marilyn Frates
Purchasing: Kathy Bockal
Estimated Sales: $ 20 - 50 Million
Number Employees: 20-49
Brands Exported: Wenol; Red Bear
Brands Imported: Wenol; Red Bear

48417 (HQ)Scandinavian Formulas Inc
140 E Church St
Sellersville, PA 18960-2402   215-453-2500
      Fax: 215-453-2508   800-288-2844
www.scandinavianformulas.com
Manufacturer, importer and exporter of vitamins and supplements, chemicals and ingredients. Botanicals, extracts, oils, bulk tablets and soft gels.
President: Catherine Peklak
Marketing: Sylvie Millet
Sales/Purchasing: Mike Peklak
IT: Bob Blackledge
bob@scandinavianformulas.com
Estimated Sales: $1005000
Number Employees: 1-4
Number of Brands: 7
Number of Products: 7
Square Footage: 36000
Type of Packaging: Consumer, Private Label, Bulk
Other Locations:
   Scandinavian Natural Health
   Perkasie, PAScandinavian Natural Health
Brands Exported: Nozovent®; Ecomer®; Salivasure™; Good Breath™; La Beaute; Bilberry Extract
Regions Exported to: Central America, South America, Europe, Middle East
Percentage of Business in Exporting: 10
Regions Imported from: South America

48418 Scandinavian Laboratories
316 Front Street
Belvidere, PA 07823-1510   908-475-4754
      Fax: 908-469-4912   866-623-2650
scanlabs@epix.net www.oceanaproducts.com
Nutritional products including shark liver and fish oils, essential fatty acids, effervescent tablets and liquid emulsions; importer and exporter of nutritional supplements including shark liver oils
President: Olav Sandnes
Contact: Susan Battillo
susan@oceanaproducts.com
Estimated Sales: $500,000
Number Employees: 5-9
Type of Packaging: Private Label, Bulk
Brands Exported: Pedia-Vit
Regions Exported to: Europe, Asia, Australia
Regions Imported from: Europe, Pacific Rim

48419 Schaefer Machine Co Inc
200 Commercial Dr
Deep River, CT 06417-1682   860-526-4000
      Fax: 860-526-4654   800-243-5143
schaefer@schaeferco.com www.schaeferco.com
Manufacturer and exporter of label gluing and cementing machinery
Owner: Robert Gammons
schaefer01@snet.net
Estimated Sales: $ 1-3 Million
Number Employees: 5-9
Square Footage: 40000
Regions Exported to: Central America, South America, Canada, Latin America
Percentage of Business in Exporting: 10

48420 (HQ)Schaefers
9820 D St
Oakland, CA 94603-2439   510-632-5064
      Fax: 510-632-2754 www.schaefersmeats.com
Warehouse providing freezer storage
President: Otto Schaefer
Manager: Adam Chan
schaefmeats@gmail.com
Estimated Sales: Less Than $500,000
Number Employees: 1-4
Square Footage: 80000

48421 Scheb International
27 Clarington Way
North Barrington, IL 60010-6932   847-381-2573
      Fax: 847-381-2573 schebltd@aol.com
www.schebltd

Manufacturer and exporter of tote, storage and material handling boxes; also, bulk carbon dioxide storage and delivery systems for beverage use; importer of carbon dioxide bulk delivery systems
Estimated Sales: $ 1 - 5 Million
Number Employees: 3
Parent Co: Carbo Carbonation Company
Type of Packaging: Food Service
Brands Exported: Carbo Mizer

48422 Scheidegger
345 Kear St Ste 200
Yorktown Heights, NY 10598   914-245-7850
            Fax: 914-243-0976
Manufacturer, importer and exporter of tamper evident sealing and full body sleeving machinery
VP Sales/Marketing: Dipak Modi
Number Employees: 2
Parent Co: Sch. S.A.
Regions Exported to: Worldwide
Regions Imported from: Europe
Percentage of Business in Importing: 100

48423 Schenck Process
746 E Milwaukee St
P.O.Box 208
Whitewater, WI 53190-2125   262-473-2441
      Fax: 262-473-2489   888-742-1249
mktg@accuratefeeders.com
www.schenckaccurate.com
Vibratory feeders with loss-in-weight batch control systems and loss-in-weight continuous flow systems; also, portable universal bin and feeder combination, bulk bag discharger, box dumps, weightbelts, and screw feeders
President: Dirk Maroske
CEO: Jay Brown
Research & Development: Bob Stephenson
Marketing Director: Mike Koras
Sales Director: Chris Isom
Regional Sales Manager: Rick Pruden
Plant Manager: Bill Samborski
Purchasing Manager: Angie Adams
Estimated Sales: $3-4 Million
Number Employees: 100-249
Square Footage: 128000
Parent Co: Schenck Process
Brands Exported: Any Country
Regions Exported to: Europe, Asia, Australia, Canada, Latin America, Mexico
Percentage of Business in Exporting: 8

48424 Schenk Packing Co Inc
1321 S 6th St
Mt Vernon, WA 98273-4919   360-336-2128
      Fax: 360-336-3092 info@schenkpacking.com
www.schenkpacking.com
Processor and exporter of meat products; custom slaughtering available.
Owner/President: Steve Lenz
stevel@schenkpacking.com
Operations Managerr: Marcie Lenz
Number Employees: 20-49
Square Footage: 84672
Type of Packaging: Consumer, Food Service

48425 Schiff Food Products CoInc
994 Riverview Dr
Totowa, NJ 07512-1129   973-237-1990
      Fax: 973-237-1999 sales@schifffood.com
www.schifffoods.com
Manufacturer, importer and exporter of spices, seeds, herbs and dehydrated vegetables
President: David Deutscher
david.deutscher@schiffs.com
Estimated Sales: $ 15 Million
Number Employees: 20-49
Square Footage: 600000
Type of Packaging: Consumer, Private Label
Brands Exported: Schiff Food Products
Regions Exported to: Central America, Asia
Percentage of Business in Exporting: 5
Brands Imported: Schiff Food Products
Regions Imported from: Central America, Europe, Asia, Middle East, Far East
Percentage of Business in Importing: 80

48426 Schillinger Genetics Inc
4401 Westown Pkwy # 225
Suite 225
West Des Moines, IA 50266-6721   515-225-1166
      Fax: 515-225-1177   866-769-7200
heartland@heartlandfields.com
www.schillgen.com

Manufacturer and exporter of soybeans
President: John Schillinger
Marketing/Sales Director: Karen Labenz
Estimated Sales: $10-20 Million
Number Employees: 10-19
Parent Co: Monsanto
Type of Packaging: Consumer, Bulk
Brands Exported: Hartz Seed
Regions Exported to: South America, Asia, Mexico
Percentage of Business in Exporting: 50

48427 Schiltz Foods Inc
7 W Oak St
Sisseton, SD 57262-1440   605-698-7651
Fax: 605-698-7112   877-872-4458
jschiltz@schiltzfoods.com   www.schiltzfoods.com
Processor and exporter of dressed geese and goose products
President: Richard Schiltz
richard.schiltz@schiltzfoods.com
VP/Director of Sales: James Schiltz
Estimated Sales: $2.1 Million
Number Employees: 100-249
Number of Brands: 4
Number of Products: 20
Square Footage: 136000
Type of Packaging: Consumer, Food Service, Private Label, Bulk
Regions Exported to: Europe

48428 Schlagel Inc
491 Emerson St N
Cambridge, MN 55008-1316   763-689-5991
Fax: 763-689-5310   800-328-8002
sales@schlagel.com   www.schlagel.com
Manufacturer and exporter of feed and grain equipment
CEO: Chris Schlagel
chris@schlagel.com
Sales Manager: Jeff Schwab
Purchasing Manager: Drew Stoffell
Estimated Sales: $ 10-20 Million
Number Employees: 50-99
Regions Exported to: Central America, South America, Asia, Middle East
Percentage of Business in Exporting: 15

48429 (HQ)Schlueter Company
310 N. Main Street
Janesville, WI 53545   608-755-5444
Fax: 608-755-5440   800-359-1700
www.schlueterco.com
Manufacturer and exporter of dairy and food plant equipment including process tanks, conveyors, hoppers, sanitizing systems (CIP-COP-HY pressure-foam), liquid/solid separators, strainers, filters, rotary drums, etc.; also, carts and work tables
President: Brad Losching
VP: H Losching
Marketing Manager: C Benskin
Estimated Sales: $10-20 Million
Number Employees: 50
Square Footage: 200000
Other Locations:
   Schlueter Co.
   Fresno, CA Schlueter Co.
Brands Exported: Safgard
Regions Exported to: Central America, South America, Europe, Asia, Middle East, Canada, Mexico, Latin America
Percentage of Business in Exporting: 10

48430 Schmidt Progressive
360 Harmon Ave
P.O. Box 380
Lebanon, OH 45036-8801   513-934-2600
Fax: 513-932-8768   800-272-3706
steve@schmidtprogressive.com
Design, engineering and manufacturing display fixtures for the supermarket, bakery, concession, food service and floral industries.
Owner/CEO: Julia Rodenbeck
julia@schmidtprogressive.com
VP Sales/Marketing: Stephen Moore
VP Sales/Marketing: Stephen Moore
VP Administration: Joseph Perdy
VP Manufacturing: Don Blades
Plant Manager: Robert Newton
Purchasing Manager: Don Blades
Estimated Sales: $2-5 Million
Number Employees: 20-49
Square Footage: 240000
Brands Exported: Food Furniture® Displays
Regions Exported to: South America, Jamacia, Virgin Islands

48431 Schneider Electric
70 Mechanic St
Foxboro, MA 02035   781-534-7535
www.schneider-electric.us
Manufacturer and exporter of programmable logic controllers and software.
Chairman & CEO: Jean-Pascal Tricoire
Deputy CEO/Finance & Legal Affairs: Emmanuel Babeau
CFO: Steven Laham
EVP, Supply Chain, North America: Annette Clayton
Business Analyst: Aric Luck
Global Marketing: Chris Leong
EVP, International Operations: Luc R,mont
Year Founded: 1836
Estimated Sales: $100-500 Million
Number Employees: 500-999
Parent Co: Groupe Schneider
Regions Exported to: Worldwide
Percentage of Business in Exporting: 50

48432 (HQ)Schneider Foods
321 Courtland Ave East
Kitchener, ON N2G 3X8
Canada   519-741-5000
Fax: 519-749-7400   www.schneiders.ca
Processor and exporter of frozen and refrigerated frankfurters, meat pies, sausage, ham, bacon, deli meats and poultry; fat and calorie reduced products available
President: Douglas Dodds
President (Cust. Foods): Paul Lang
VP Business: John Howard
Quality Control: Judy Tetker
R & D: Tim Gorgon
Number Employees: 5,500
Square Footage: 2920000
Type of Packaging: Consumer, Food Service, Private Label, Bulk
Other Locations:
   Schneider Corp.
   Ayr, ON Schneider Corp.
Regions Exported to: Asia
Percentage of Business in Exporting: 10

48433 Schneider Packaging Eqpt Co
5370 Guy Young Rd
Brewerton, NY 13029-8706   315-676-3035
Fax: 315-676-2875   sales@schneiderequip.com
www.schneiderequipment.com
Manufacturers case packing and robotic palletizing equipment and integrates conveyors, case elevators/lowerators, pallet dispensers, slip sheet dispensers and shuttle transfer cars for full unit loads.
CEO: Alex Naugle
alexnaugle@gmail.com
Estimated Sales: $500,000-$1 Million
Number Employees: 100-249
Square Footage: 400000

48434 Scholle IPN
2500 Cooper Ave
Merced, CA 95348   209-384-3100
Fax: 209-384-3166
NorthAmerica@scholleipn.com
www.scholleipn.com
Supplier of bag-in-box packaging, metallized plastics and paper, flexible shipping containers, industry leading bag-in-box tap and filling technology, marine salvage devices and battery electrolyte.
President & CEO: William Scholle
Global Program Director: Robert Kilmer
Year Founded: 1947
Estimated Sales: $227.30 Million
Number Employees: 1900
Square Footage: 35000
Brands Exported: Rhino

48435 Schreiber Foods Inc.
400 N. Washington St.
Green Bay, WI 54301   920-437-7601
Fax: 920-437-1617   contact@schreiberfoods.com
www.schreiberfoods.com
Dairy products such as cheese, yogurt, milk, milk powders and more.
President/CEO: Ron Dunford
SVP/CFO: Matt Mueller
SVP, U.S. Operations: Tony Nowak
SVP, Information Services: Tom Andreoli
SVP, Quality & Innovation: Vinith Poduval
SVP & Chief Commercial Officer: Trevor Farrell
Year Founded: 1945
Estimated Sales: Over $1 Billion
Number Employees: 8,000
Type of Packaging: Consumer, Food Service, Private Label, Bulk
Other Locations:
   Tempe, AZ
   Gainesville, GA
   Carthage, MO
   Clinton, MO
   Monett, MO
   Mt Vernon, MO Gainesville

48436 Schroeder Machine
165 Balboa St # C2
Ste C-2
San Marcos, CA 92069-1347   760-591-9733
Fax: 760-591-4019   sales@ssmci.com
www.schroedermachinetechnologies.com
Manufacturer and exporter of automatic case packing and erecting machines
Owner: John Schroeder
CFO: Richard Jones
Chief Mechanical Engineer: Patrick Burton
Marketing: Sandy Delepovitz
Sales Manager: Matt Brown
jschroeder@ssmci.com
Public Relations: Sandy Delepovit
Operations: David Barriello
Estimated Sales: $1 Million
Number Employees: 5-9
Square Footage: 160000
Type of Packaging: Private Label
Regions Exported to: Central America, South America, Canada
Percentage of Business in Exporting: 10

48437 Schuman Cheese
40 New Dutch Ln
Fairfield, NJ 07004
800-888-2433
info@schumancheese.com
www.arthurschuman.com
Cheese
CEO: Neal Schuman
nschuman@arthurschuman.com
Strategy Analyst: Keith Schuman
National Account Manager: Allison Schuman
Business Manager: Ian Schuman
Year Founded: 1945
Estimated Sales: $20.9 Million
Number Employees: 100-249
Square Footage: 50400
Brands Imported: Busti, Dodoni, Garofalo Bufala Mozzarella, Mario Costa Gorgonzola, Zanetti, Milcobel, Pastures of Eden and more.
Regions Imported from: Europe, South America

48438 Schwab Paper Products Co
636 Schwab Cir
Romeoville, IL 60446-1144   815-372-2233
Fax: 815-372-1701   800-837-7225
info@schwabpaper.com   www.schwabpaper.com
Manufacturer and exporter of layerboards, wax paper and steak paper for bakery, confectionery, frozen meat, seafood and poultry packaging
President: Kathy Schwab
CEO: Michael Schwab
mike@schwabpaper.com
Estimated Sales: Below $ 5 Million
Number Employees: 1-4
Square Footage: 120000
Brands Exported: Econo-Board; Frees-It Board; Wendy's V-Board
Regions Exported to: South America, Canada, Mexico
Percentage of Business in Exporting: 4

48439 Scienco Systems
3240 N Broadway
Saint Louis, MO 63147-3515   314-621-2536
Fax: 314-621-1952   www.sciencofast.com
Manufacturer and exporter of food and preservative tablets, oil/water separators, grease traps and waste water treatment equipment
General Manager: Jim Predeau
Sales Manager: Gary Wotli

Importers & Exporters / A-Z

Estimated Sales: $ 2.5 - 5 Million
Number Employees: 10-19
Parent Co: Smith Loveless
Regions Exported to: Worldwide

48440 Scientech, Inc
5649 Arapahoe Ave
Boulder, CO 80303-1399   303-444-1361
          Fax: 303-444-9229 800-525-0522
inst@scientech-inc.com www.scientech-inc.com
Electronic balances and scales
President: Tom O'Rourke
VP/COO: Tom Campbell
Contact: Mike Brunner
mbrunner@scientech-inc.com
Estimated Sales: $2 Million
Number Employees: 10-19
Number of Brands: 6
Number of Products: 75
Square Footage: 52000
Regions Exported to: Central America, South America, Europe, Asia, Middle East
Percentage of Business in Exporting: 30

48441 Scientific Process & Research
P.O.Box 5008
Kendall Park, NJ 08824-5008   732-846-3477
          Fax: 732-846-3029 800-868-4777
          info@spar.com www.spar.com
Manufacturer and exporter of extruder, timing and conveyor screws and extruder barrels; exporter of extruder screws and software
Production Manager: Felicia Cappo
Estimated Sales: $ 2.5-5 Million
Number Employees: 10-19
Square Footage: 80000
Regions Exported to: Central America, South America, Europe, Asia
Percentage of Business in Exporting: 10

48442 Sconza Candy Co
1 Sconza Candy Ln
Oakdale, CA 95361-7899   209-845-3700
          Fax: 510-638-5792 877-568-8137
customerservice@sconzacandy.com
          www.sconza.com
Candy including brittles, panned, butterscotch, hard, filled, mints, butter toffee nuts and seasonal
President: James Sconza
jrsconza@sconzacandy.com
Executive Vice President: Ron Sconza
Estimated Sales: $6 Million
Number Employees: 100-249
Square Footage: 200000
Type of Packaging: Consumer, Food Service, Private Label, Bulk
Brands Exported: Sconza
Regions Exported to: Asia, Middle East, Pacific Rim, Canada, Caribbean
Percentage of Business in Exporting: 5

48443 Scope Packaging
PO Box 3768
Orange, CA 92857   714-998-4411
          Fax: 714-998-5323
Manufacturer and exporter of corrugated boxes
President: Michael Flinn
VP Marketing: Cindy Baker
Contact: Christine Maple
christinem@scopepackaging.com
Estimated Sales: $20-50 Million
Number Employees: 50-99
Type of Packaging: Bulk
Regions Exported to: Worldwide
Percentage of Business in Exporting: 3

48444 (HQ)Scorpio Apparel
3318 Commercial Avenue
Northbrook, IL 60062-1909   847-559-3100
          Fax: 847-559-3103 800-559-3338
Manufacturer and exporter of uniforms
President: Allan L Klein
CEO: Lew Klein
Vice President: Carolyn Philips
Sales Director: Juli Shapiro
Estimated Sales: $2 Million
Number Employees: 34
Square Footage: 14000
Type of Packaging: Private Label
Other Locations:
    Scorpio Products
    Chicago, IL Scorpio Products
Brands Exported: Scorpio; 9th Wave
Regions Exported to: Worldwide

48445 Scot Young Research LTD
503 Renick St
St Joseph, MO 64501-3660   816-233-4898
          Fax: 816-232-3701 www.syrclean.com
Manufacturer and exporter of ergonomic and color coded mopping systems
General Manager: Myong Stracener
Contact: Jamie Carpentier
jamie.carpentier@syrclean.com
Estimated Sales: Less Than $500,000
Number Employees: 1-4
Regions Exported to: Worldwide
Percentage of Business in Exporting: 5

48446 Scotsman Beverage System
2007 Royal Lane
Suite 100
Dallas, TX 75229-3279   972-488-1030
          Fax: 972-243-8075 800-527-7422
Parent Co: ENODIS

48447 Scotsman Ice Systems
101 Corporate Woods Pkwy.
Vernon Hills, IL 60061   847-215-4500
          Fax: 847-913-9844 800-726-8762
customer.relations@scotsman-ice.com
          www.scotsman-ice.com
Ice machines including flakers and nugget makers and hotel dispensing bins, drink dispensers, water filtration systems, etc.
President: Kevin Clark
CFO: Jo Rendino
Estimated Sales: $92 Million
Number Employees: 800
Square Footage: 36000
Parent Co: Scotsman Industries
Type of Packaging: Consumer, Food Service
Other Locations:
    Scotsman Ice Systems
    La Verne, CA Scotsman Ice Systems
Brands Exported: Scotsman
Regions Exported to: Worldwide
Percentage of Business in Exporting: 80
Regions Imported from: Italy

48448 Scott Hams
1301 Scott Rd
Greenville, KY 42345-4683   270-338-3402
          Fax: 270-338-6643 800-318-1353
          scotthams@att.net
Country cured and fully cooked hams, bacon, smoked sausage, turkey, jams and fruit butters, sorghum molasses, honey, dried apples, relish, bean soup mix, biscuits, pork cracklins and dog biscuits
Owner: June Scott
scotthams@att.net
Estimated Sales: Less Than $500,000
Number Employees: 1-4
Regions Exported to: Canada
Percentage of Business in Exporting: 1

48449 Scott Sign Systems
7525 Pennsylvania Ave # C
PO Box 1047
Sarasota, FL 34243-5065   941-355-5171
          Fax: 941-351-1787 800-237-9447
mail@scottsigns.com www.scottsigns.com
Manufactures signs and sign systems including letters, logos, graphics and architectural signs.
President: Steve Evans
Cio/Cto: Maurice Aguinaldo
mauricea@scottsigns.com
Estimated Sales: $1-5 Million
Number Employees: 20-49
Square Footage: 150000
Parent Co: Identity Group
Regions Exported to: Worldwide
Percentage of Business in Exporting: 2

48450 Scott Turbon Mixer
9351 Industrial Way
Adelanto, CA 92301-3932   760-246-3430
          Fax: 760-246-3505 800-285-8512
sales@scottmixer.com www.haywardgordon.com
Manufacturer and exporter of sanitary mixing equipment for dairy, beverage and meat; also, complete systems including tanks, platforms and piping, lab and pilot plant mixers
Owner: William Scott
bill@scottmixer.com
Sales Director: Tim Moore
Estimated Sales: $ 1 - 5 Million
Number Employees: 20-49
Square Footage: 50000
Brands Exported: Scott Turbon
Regions Exported to: Worldwide
Percentage of Business in Exporting: 30

48451 Scott's Candy
819 South Veterans Blvd
Glennville, GA 30427   608-837-8020
          Fax: 608-837-0763 800-356-2100
Processor and exporter of boxed and tinned chocolates
CEO: Gary Ricco
National Sales Manager: James Regan
Contact: Gary Ricco
gricco@wisconsincheeseman.com
Estimated Sales: $ 3 - 5 Million
Number Employees: 20-49
Parent Co: Wisconsin Cheeseman
Type of Packaging: Consumer, Private Label
Regions Exported to: Worldwide

48452 Scott-Bathgate
149 Pioneer Avenue
Winnipeg, MB R3C 2M8
Canada   204-943-8525
          Fax: 204-957-5902 800-216-2990
          www.scottbathgate.com
Snack foods, food colorings, mustard, peanut butter, candy and shelled and in-shell sunflower seeds
National Director: Vic Homyshyn
Office/Credit Manager: D Sheridan
Production Manager: Jens Fieting
Type of Packaging: Food Service

48453 Screamin' Onionz
399 Manchester Rd.
Poughkeepsie, NY 12603
          www.loveonionz.com
Sliced, slow-cooked onions in flavoured sauces
Founder: Richard Romano
Year Founded: 2015
Number of Brands: 1
Number of Products: 3
Type of Packaging: Consumer, Private Label
Brands Exported: Screamin' Onionz

48454 Screen Print Etc
1081 N Shepard St # E
Anaheim, CA 92806-2819   714-630-1100
          Fax: 714-630-3719
Display and exhibit boards, decals, flags, pennants, banners and signs; also, commercial printing, graphic design and plastic printing services available
Owner: Ray Lynch
rlynch@screenprintetc.com
Estimated Sales: $530 Million
Number Employees: 5-9
Square Footage: 4000
Type of Packaging: Private Label, Bulk
Regions Exported to: Worldwide

48455 Screenflex Portable Partition
585 Capital Dr
Lake Zurich, IL 60047-6712   847-726-2900
          Fax: 847-726-2990 800-553-0110
          screenflex@aol.com
Accoustical, portable. accordian holding walls to help you make better use of your facility.
Vice President: Rich Mads
Human Resources: Donald Austin
Estimated Sales: $ 20 - 50 Million
Number Employees: 50-99

48456 Scroll Compressors LLC
1675 Campbell Rd
Sidney, OH 45365-2479   937-498-3011
          Fax: 937-498-3203 www.emersonclimate.com
Manufacturer and exporter of compressors for air conditioning and refrigeration
President: Tom Bettcher
Number Employees: 10-19
Type of Packaging: Food Service
Regions Exported to: Worldwide

48457 Se Kure Controls Inc
3714 Runge St
Franklin Park, IL 60131-1112   847-288-1111
          Fax: 847-288-9999 800-250-9260
          info@se-kure.com www.se-kure.com
Manufacturer, importer and exporter of safes, vaults, security mirrors and cameras and anti-shoplifting devices

Importers & Exporters / A-Z

Founder/President/CEO: Roger Leyden
rogerleyden@se-kure.com
Executive VP Administration & Finance: Laura Greenwell
National Sales Manager: John Mangiameli
Estimated Sales: $20-50 Million
Number Employees: 100-249
Number of Products: 500
Square Footage: 200000
Regions Exported to: Central America, South America, Europe, Asia, Middle East
Percentage of Business in Exporting: 20

48458 Sea Bear Smokehouse
605 30th St
Anacortes, WA 98221-2884   360-293-4661
Fax: 360-293-4097   800-645-3474
Processor and exporter of smoked fish and seafoods
President: Mike Mondello
CEO: Michael Mondello
mikem@seabear.com
VP Direct to Consumer: Patti Fisher
Marketing Manager: Barb Hoenselaar
Director Operations: Cathy Hayward-Hughes
Estimated Sales: $10.8 Million
Number Employees: 20-49
Type of Packaging: Consumer, Bulk
Regions Exported to: Worldwide

48459 Sea Breeze Fruit Flavors
441 Main Road
Towaco, NJ 07082-1201   973-334-7777
Fax: 973-334-2617   800-732-2733
info@seabreezesyrups.com
www.seabreezesyrups.com
Syrups including chocolate, pancake and milkshake; sundae toppings, bar mixes, juice concentrates, soda, iced tea, lemonade, fruit juice, flavored water and beverage dispensing equipment.
President: Steve Sanders
Vice President: Josh Sanders
Technical Director: Frank Maranino
Contact: George Apostolopoulos
george@seabreezesyrups.com
Production Manager: Paul Maranino
Estimated Sales: $25-49.9 Million
Number Employees: 50-99
Number of Brands: 6
Type of Packaging: Consumer, Food Service, Private Label
Regions Exported to: Europe, Asia
Percentage of Business in Exporting: 2

48460 Sea Farm & Farm Fresh Importing Company
855 Monterey Passage Road
Monterey Park, CA 91754   323-265-7075
Fax: 323-265-9578
Seafood products.
CEO: Hooi Eng Ooi
VP Operations: S Tan
Estimated Sales: $ 5 - 10 Million
Number Employees: 10-19

48461 Sea Safari
785 E Pantego St
Belhaven, NC 27810   252-943-3091
Fax: 252-943-3083   800-688-6174
seasafari@beaufortco.com
Processor and exporter of frozen crawfish and crab meat; also, canned blue crab meat
President/Finance & Sales Executive: Topper Bateman
General Manager: Guinn Leverett
Director Marketing: Christine Costley
Sales Manager: Frances Williams
Contact: Bateman Topper
tbateman@seasafari.com
Estimated Sales: $400,000
Number Employees: 4
Square Footage: 160000
Parent Co: Sea Safari
Type of Packaging: Consumer, Food Service
Regions Exported to: Europe

48462 Sea Snack Foods Inc
914 E 11th St
Los Angeles, CA 90021-2091   213-622-2204
Fax: 213-622-7845
Processor and exporter of cooked IQF shrimp and seafood cocktails

President/CEO: Fred Ockrim
fred@seasnack.com
VP: Jeffrey Kahn
Sales Director: Peter Peterson
Plant Manager: Alfred Dolor
Estimated Sales: $7 Million
Number Employees: 50-99
Square Footage: 8000
Type of Packaging: Consumer, Food Service
Brands Exported: Sea Snack; Twin Harbors; Restaurant Row; O.K. Brand
Regions Exported to: Central America, Canada
Percentage of Business in Exporting: 10

48463 Sea Watch Intl
8978 Glebe Park Dr
Easton, MD 21601-7004   410-822-7500
Fax: 410-822-1266   sales@seaclam.com
www.seawatch.com
Canned and frozen clams, crab cakes, extruded calamari rings, blue crab meat, squid, shrimp, soups and seafood chowders.
Vice President: Bernie Carr
bernie@seaclam.com
Controller: Betty Bain
Director, Quality Assurance: Larry Hughes
Senior Vice President of Sales: Michael Wyatt
Year Founded: 1978
Estimated Sales: $36.1 Million
Number Employees: 250-499
Number of Brands: 4
Square Footage: 15000
Type of Packaging: Food Service, Private Label

48464 SeaPerfect Atlantic Farms
PO Box 12139
Charleston, SC 29422-2139   843-762-0022
Fax: 843-795-6672   800-728-0099
Scallops and clams
President: Carlos Celle
Sales Director: Michelle Black
General Manager: Knox Grant
Estimated Sales: $2.3 Million
Number Employees: 45
Square Footage: 136000
Brands Exported: SeaPerfect
Brands Imported: SeaPerfect
Regions Imported from: South America
Percentage of Business in Importing: 1

48465 Seaboard Folding Box Corp
35 Daniels St
Fitchburg, MA 01420-7606   978-342-8921
Fax: 978-342-1105   800-255-6313
info@seaboardbox.com   www.seaboardbox.com
Manufacturer and exporter of paper boxes
President: Alan Rabinow
CEO: Allen Rabinow
allen.rabinow@jordanind.com
Number Employees: 100-249
Percentage of Business in Exporting: 1

48466 Seaboard Foods
9000 W. 67th St.
Suite 200
Shawnee Mission, KS 66202
   800-262-7907
info@seaboardfoods.com   seaboardfoods.com
Fresh, frozen and processed pork products.
President/CEO: Darwin Sand
Vice President, Marketing: Tom Blumhardt
Vice President, Plant Operations: Marty Hast
Year Founded: 1995
Estimated Sales: $38.8 Million
Number Employees: 4,986
Number of Brands: 5
Parent Co: Seaboard Corporation
Type of Packaging: Consumer, Food Service, Private Label, Bulk
Other Locations:
   Processing Plant
    Guymon, OK Mount Dora Farms Management
    Houston, TX Daily's Premium Meats Bacon Plant
    Salt Lake City, UT
   Daily's Premium Meats Bacon Plant
    Missoula, MT
   Processing Plant Reynosa, MEXICO
Regions Exported to: Central America, Asia, Global Markets

48467 Seachase Foods
1726 Ridge Road
Suite 106
Homewood, IL 60430-1846   708-481-7321
Fax: 708-481-7320
President: Mel Jones
Estimated Sales: $ 3 - 5 Million
Number Employees: 1-4

48468 Seacore Seafood
81 Aviva Park Drive
Vaughan, ON L4L 9C1
Canada   905-856-6222
Fax: 905-856-9445   800-563-6222
info@seacoreseafood.com
www.seacoreseafood.com
Wholesaler/distributor/importer/custom processor of fresh and frozen seafood, fish, and live lobsters.
Number Employees: 85
Square Footage: 308000

48469 Seacrest Foods
86 Bennett St
Lynn, MA 01905-3011   781-581-2066
Fax: 781-581-1767   www.seacrestfoods.com
International importer and wholesale distributor of specialty cheeses and fine foods including cheese, specialty meats, pasta, specialty grocery items, chocolates, desserts
Owner: Robert Di Tomaso
bditomaso@seacrestfoods.com
Number Employees: 50-99

48470 Seafood Connection
841 Pohukaina St # I
Suite I
Honolulu, HI 96813-5332   808-591-8550
Fax: 808-591-8445   sales@seafood-connection.com
www.seafood-connection.com
Seafood and gourmet products
President: Stuart Simmons
Estimated Sales: $ 10 - 20 Million
Number Employees: 10-19

48471 Seafood Hawaii Inc
875 Waimanu St # 634
Suite 634
Honolulu, HI 96813-5265   808-597-1971
Fax: 808-538-1973
Seafood
President: Jed J Inouye
Estimated Sales: $ 5 - 10 Million
Number Employees: 20-49

48472 Seafood International
1051 Old Henderson Hwy
Henderson, LA 70517-7805   337-228-7568
Fax: 337-228-7573   www.seafoodfromnorway.com
Seafood
Owner: Roy Robert
seafoodintl@cox-internet.com
Estimated Sales: $3,300,000
Number Employees: 5-9

48473 Seafood Merchants LTD
900 Forest Edge Dr
Vernon Hills, IL 60061-3105   847-634-0900
Fax: 847-634-1351
sales@theseafoodmerchants.com
Seafood
President: Roy Axelson
bonnie@theseafoodmerchants.com
CEO: Bonnie Axelson
bonnie@theseafoodmerchants.com
Sales Exec: Bonnie Axelson
Estimated Sales: $ 10-20 Million
Number Employees: 20-49
Square Footage: 23000
Type of Packaging: Consumer, Food Service, Bulk
Brands Imported: Shetland Smokehouse, Seafood Merchant
Regions Imported from: Europe
Percentage of Business in Importing: 5

48474 Seafood Producers Co-Op
2875 Roeder Ave
Suite 2
Bellingham, WA 98225   360-733-0120
Fax: 360-733-0513   jreynolds@spcsales.com
www.spcsales.com
Processor and exporter of salmon, halibut, sablefish and rockfish.

Importers & Exporters / A-Z

Chief Executive Officer: Joe Morelli
VP, Sales & Marketing: Jeff Reynolds
Sales Manager: Kurt Sigfusson
Traffic & Logistics: Jessie Koehler
Plant Manager: Craig Shoemaker
Year Founded: 1944
Estimated Sales: $45 Million
Number Employees: 5-9
Type of Packaging: Food Service, Bulk
Brands Exported: Alaska Gold; SPC
Regions Exported to: Europe, Asia, Canada
Percentage of Business in Exporting: 50

48475 Seal-O-Matic Corp
2542 Humbug Creek Rd
Jacksonville, OR 97530-9618   541-846-1000
            Fax: 541-846-1004 800-631-2072
            info@sealomatic.com
            www.sealomatic.net
Manufacturer, importer and exporter of shrink wrap and packaging equipment including gummed tape dispensers, safety knives, shipping room equipment, price labeling guns, staplers, staples, etc
President: Mel Ortner
Vice President: Janine Ortner
Marketing Director: Greg Sparre
Contact: Janine Ortner
janine@sealomatic.com
Purchasing Manager: Kim Westmoreland
Estimated Sales: $ 1 - 3 Million
Number Employees: 10-19
Square Footage: 10000
Brands Exported: Lewis; Flash; Labelmaster; Pricemaster
Regions Exported to: Worldwide
Percentage of Business in Exporting: 5
Regions Imported from: Asia

48476 Seald Sweet
1991 74th Ave
Vero Beach, FL 32966-5199   559-636-4400
            Fax: 772-569-5110 www.sealdsweet.com
Grower, importer and exporter of citrus products including oranges, grapefruit, lemons, clementines, minneolas, tangerines and tangeros.
President: Jeff Baskovich
jbaskovich@sealdsweet.com
CFO: Christine Wallace
VP: David E Mixon
Marketing Manager: Kim Flores
Estimated Sales: $5-10 Million
Number Employees: 50-99
Square Footage: 60000
Type of Packaging: Food Service, Bulk
Regions Exported to: South America, Europe, Asia

48477 Sealstrip Corporation
200 N Washington St
Boyertown, PA 19512-1115   610-367-6282
            Fax: 610-367-7727 www.sealstrip.com
Manufacturer and exporter of resealable packaging equipment and materials
President: Joanne Forman
Owner: Harold Forman
R&D: Ajrlod Forman
Sales: Heather Hartman
Manufacturing Manager: Jacob Greth
Estimated Sales: Below $ 5 Million
Number Employees: 20-49
Square Footage: 28000
Brands Exported: Sealstrip; Everfresh; Fresh Pak; Serv & Seal
Regions Exported to: Central America, South America, Europe, Asia
Percentage of Business in Exporting: 3

48478 Seamark Corporation
63 Main Street
Gloucester, MA 01930-5722   978-283-4476
            Fax: 978-281-6490
Estimated Sales: $300,000-500,000
Number Employees: 1-4

48479 Seapoint Farms
20042 Beach Blvd
Suite 102
Huntington Beach, CA 92648-3702   714-374-9531
            info@seapointfarms.com
            www.seapointfarms.com
Edamame and seaweed products
CEO: Kevin Cross
kcross@seapointfarms.com
National Sales Manager: Tim Boyer
COO: Phil Siegel

Estimated Sales: 1.6 Millin
Number Employees: 5-9

48480 Seasnax
5976 E Slauson Ave
Commerce, CA 90040-3020   310-882-5503
            Fax: 310-882-6485 www.seasnax.com
Seaweed snacks
Founder: Jin Jun
jin@seasnax.com
Estimated Sales: 323,000
Number Employees: 10-19

48481 Seasons 4 Inc
4500 Industrial Access Rd
Douglasville, GA 30134-3949   770-489-5405
            Fax: 770-489-2938 jkodobocz@seasons4.net
            www.seasons4.net
Manufacturer and exporter of custom engineered HVAC systems for supermarkets
President: Lewis Watford
lwatford@seasons4.net
VP Sales: Todd Smith
Purchasing Manager: Rick Rothschild
Estimated Sales: $ 50 - 100 Million
Number Employees: 250-499
Square Footage: 145000
Regions Exported to: Canada
Percentage of Business in Exporting: 4

48482 Seatech Corporation
16825 48th Ave W Ste 222
Lynnwood, WA 98037   425-487-3231
            Fax: 425-835-0367 johnw@seatechcorp.com
            www.seatechcorp.com
Frozen shrimp, crab and scallops
President: John Wendt
j.wendt@seatech.com
CFO: Jim Schantz
ice President: Todd Wendt
Estimated Sales: $6 Million
Number Employees: 3
Number of Brands: 2
Square Footage: 4000
Type of Packaging: Consumer, Food Service, Private Label, Bulk
Brands Exported: Seatech, Ocean Kitchen
Regions Exported to: Central America
Percentage of Business in Exporting: 20
Brands Imported: Seatech, Ocean Kitchen
Regions Imported from: South America
Percentage of Business in Importing: 20

48483 Seatex Ltd
445 TX-36
Rosenberg, TX 77471   713-357-5300
            Fax: 713-357-5301 800-829-3020
            kaimes@seatexcorp.com www.seatexcorp.com
Providers of turn key chemical compounding, toll manufacturing and private label packaging services. Areas of expertise included the food service, food processing, automotive, institutional and industrial laundry, janitorialindustrial and oilfield service markets.
President/CEO: Jim Nattier
CFO: John Nowak
VP: Kelly Aimes
R&D: Don Trepel
Director QA/QC: Don Trepel
Sales/Marketing: Tom Austin
Sales/Marketing: Kelly Aimes
Contact: Deneen Case
dcase@seatexcorp.com
Operations/Production: Dan Boone
Warehouse/Logistics: Jim Dockery
VP Purchasing : Larry Brown
Estimated Sales: $26 Million
Number Employees: 85
Number of Products: 400
Square Footage: 220000
Type of Packaging: Consumer, Food Service, Private Label, Bulk
Regions Exported to: Central America, Middle East, Mexico
Percentage of Business in Exporting: 15
Regions Imported from: Europe, Canada, Mexico
Percentage of Business in Importing: 15

48484 Seating Concepts Inc
125 Connell Ave
Rockdale, IL 60436-2466   815-730-7980
            Fax: 815-730-7969 800-421-2036
            sales@seating-concepts.com
            www.seating-concepts.com

Manufacturer and exporter of chairs, booths, cafeteria counters, tables and waste receptacles; importer of chairs
Owner: Marianne Dieter
Sales Director: Chris Mazzoni
mdieter@travstor.com
Estimated Sales: $3,000,000
Number Employees: 50-99
Type of Packaging: Food Service
Regions Exported to: Worldwide
Regions Imported from: Canada

48485 Seattle Boiler Works Inc
500 S Myrtle St
Seattle, WA 98108-3495   206-762-0737
            Fax: 206-762-3516 www.seattleboiler.com
Manufacturer and exporter of boilers, heat exchangers and pressure vessels; also, stainless steel fabrication, pipe and tube bending services available
Owner: Craig Hopkins
chopkins@seattleboiler.com
VP: Craig Hopkins
Quality Control: Craig Hopkins
Estimated Sales: $5-10 Million
Number Employees: 20-49
Square Footage: 140000
Type of Packaging: Bulk

48486 Seattle Menu Specialists
5844 South 194th Street
Kent, WA 98032   206-784-2340
            Fax: 206-782-7778 800-622-2826
            customerservice@seattlemenu.com
            www.seattlemenu.com
Manufacturer and designer of menu, wine and guest check covers and placemats; exporter of menu covers
President: Dale Phelps
Operations Manager: Lonnie Axtell
Purchasing Manager: George Rought
Estimated Sales: Below $5 Million
Number Employees: 10
Brands Exported: Duragrafic; Hard Back Menu Covers
Regions Exported to: Central America, Asia
Percentage of Business in Exporting: 10

48487 Seattle Refrigeration &Manufacturing
1057 S Director St
Seattle, WA 98108   206-762-7740
            Fax: 206-762-1730 800-228-8881
Manufacturer and importer of compressors, pressure vessels, belt and spiral freezers, condensers, heat exchangers, ice makers, chillers, freezers, hoses, pumps, etc.; importer of compressors, plate freezers and valves; exporter ofcompressors, and ice makers
President: Tracy Abbott
R&D: Frank Kanpp
Quality Control: Bob Petersen
Service Manager: Don Irons
Estimated Sales: $ 5 - 10 Million
Number Employees: 10-19
Square Footage: 30600
Parent Co: Seattle Refrigeration
Brands Exported: Gram; Mycom
Regions Exported to: Worldwide
Percentage of Business in Exporting: 5
Brands Imported: Gram; Mycom; Danfoss
Regions Imported from: Europe, Asia

48488 Seattle-Tacoma Box Co
23400 71st Pl S
Kent, WA 98032-2994   253-854-9700
            Fax: 253-852-0891 info@seattlebox.com
            www.seattlebox.com
Manufacturer and exporter of wooden produce and corrugated boxes
Vice President: Michael Nist
mike@seattlebox.com
Marketing Director: Rob Nist
Estimated Sales: $ 30 - 50 Million
Number Employees: 20-49
Regions Exported to: Asia
Percentage of Business in Exporting: 5
Regions Imported from: Australia
Percentage of Business in Importing: 10

48489 Seaview Lobster Co
43 Government St
Kittery, ME 03904-1652   207-439-1599
            Fax: 207-439-1476 800-245-4997
            orders@seaviewlobster.com
            www.seaviewlobster.com

Importers & Exporters / A-Z

Seafood
Owner: Tom Flanagan
seaviewlob@comcast.net
Estimated Sales: $ .5 - 1 million
Number Employees: 10-19

48490 Seawind Foods
120 1/2 South El Camino Real
Suite 202
San Clemente, CA 92672   949-542-8382
　　　Fax: 949-542-8392 www.seawindfoods.com
Importer of dehydrated vegetables, dried fruit, herb and spices.
President & CEO: Garry Green
Vice President, Sales: Julie Swink
Contact: Sandra Maring
smaring@seawindfoods.com
Parent Co: Seawind International
Type of Packaging: Food Service, Bulk
Percentage of Business in Exporting: 10
Regions Imported from: Central America, South America, Europe, Asia
Percentage of Business in Importing: 90

48491 Seco Systems
320 Sovereign Court
Ballwin, MO 63011-4417   800-544-5727

48492 See's Candies
20600 South Alameda Street
Carson, CA 90810
　　　Fax: 800-275-4733 800-347-7337
　　　qdordering@sees.com www.sees.com
Confectionary and chocolates
President & CEO: Charles Huggins
CFO: Ken Scott
General Manager: Jane Wellsplant
Estimated Sales: $ .5 - 1 million
Number Employees: 5-9
Square Footage: 880000
Parent Co: See's Candies
Type of Packaging: Consumer
Regions Exported to: Asia
Percentage of Business in Exporting: 2

48493 Seed Enterprises Inc
679 19th Rd
West Point, NE 68788-4510   402-372-3238
　　　Fax: 402-372-2627 888-440-7333
Soybeans
President: Conrad Reeson
Estimated Sales: $ 1 - 3 Million
Number Employees: 5-9
Square Footage: 70000
Regions Exported to: Europe, Asia
Percentage of Business in Exporting: 25

48494 Seenergy Foods
121 Jevlan Drive
Woodbridge, ON L4L 8A8
Canada   905-850-2544
　　　Fax: 905-850-2563 800-609-7674
info@seenergyfoods.com www.seenergyfoods.com
Processor and exporter of frozen vegetables including vegetable patties and IQF (individually quick frozen) beans
President/CEO: Shreyas Ajmera
Marketing/Sales: Carl McLaughlin
Estimated Sales: $3.2 Million
Number Employees: 80
Type of Packaging: Consumer, Food Service, Private Label, Bulk
Regions Exported to: U.S.

48495 Seepex Inc
511 Speedway Dr
Enon, OH 45323-1057   937-864-7150
　　　Fax: 937-864-7157 800-695-3659
　　　sales@seepex.net www.seepex.com
Designs, manufactures, and sells Progressive Cavity Pumps and Pump accessories.
President: Michael Dillon
CEO: Florencio Alvarez
falvarez@seepex.com
VP: Francis Harris
R&D: Mathew Brown
Quality Control: Robert Mentz
Marketing/Public Relations: Daniel Lakovic
Director, Sales: Mark Murphy
Product Manager: Joe Zinck
Purchasing: Robert Mentz
Estimated Sales: $30 Million
Number Employees: 250-499
Number of Brands: 1

Number of Products: 1000
Square Footage: 40000
Parent Co: Seepex
Brands Exported: Seepex
Regions Exported to: Central America, South America

48496 Sekisui TA Industries
100 S Puente St
Brea, CA 92821-3813   714-255-7888
　　　Fax: 800-235-8273 800-258-8273
　　　www.sta-tape.com
Manufacturer and exporter of FDA approved B.O.P.P. pressure sensitive tapes and semi and fully automatic carton sealing machinery
President: Ikusuke Shimizu
CEO: Ernest J Wong
CFO: Matt Minami
VP: Stephen J Wilson
R&D: Dinesh Shan
Marketing Administrator: Melissa Morris
Contact: Alison Barth
barth@cmu.edu
Plant Manager: C P Fang
Estimated Sales: $ 20 - 50 Million
Number Employees: 100-249
Square Footage: 185000
Parent Co: Sekisui Chemical
Brands Exported: Supreme

48497 (HQ)Select Food Products
120 Sunrise Avenue
Toronto, ON M4A 1B4
Canada   416-759-9316
　　　Fax: 416-759-9310 800-699-8016
　　　www.selectfoodproducts.com
Manufacturers and exporter of salad dressings, sauces, salsas, relishes, mustard, gravies, canned dinners, etc; importer of tomatoes and tomato paste
President: Paul Fredricks
Number Employees: 150
Square Footage: 464000
Type of Packaging: Consumer, Food Service, Private Label, Bulk
Brands Exported: Select; Horne's
Regions Exported to: Asia, Mexico, USA, Caribbean
Percentage of Business in Exporting: 5
Regions Imported from: Europe, USA
Percentage of Business in Importing: 15

48498 Select Meat Company
PO Box 21308
Los Angeles, CA 90021-0308   213-621-0900
　　　Fax: 213-621-0909
Wholesaler/distributor, importer and exporter of raw and processed meat, poultry, seafood, coffee, cheese, butter and margarine; serving the food service market
President: Ed Murphy
VP: Gerry Rose
VP (Asian Markets): Nhon Hien
Number Employees: 10-19
Type of Packaging: Food Service
Regions Exported to: Asia, Eastern Europe , Latin America
Percentage of Business in Exporting: 15
Percentage of Business in Importing: 30

48499 Selectdrinkware.com
P.O.Box 1235
Gig Harbor, WA 98335-3235   253-858-8141
　　　Fax: 253-858-8050
Owner: Mike Van Schaack
Estimated Sales: $ 3 - 5 Million
Number Employees: 5-9

48500 Selecto Scientific
3980 Lakefield Ct
Suwanee, GA 30024   678-475-0799
　　　Fax: 678-475-1595 www.selectoinc.com
Owner: Terry Libin
Contact: Alisha Kuzma
alisha_kuzma@mckinsey.com
Estimated Sales: $ 1 - 3 Million
Number Employees: 10-19

48501 (HQ)Selecto Scientific
3980 Lakefield Ct
Suwanee, GA 30024   678-475-0799
　　　Fax: 678-475-1595 800-635-4017
Customer-service@selectoinc.com
　　　www.selectoinc.com

Manufacturer and exporter of water filters for scale reduction, taste and odor and sediment for fountain dispensing equipment, coffee makers, ice equipment and steamers
Owner: Terry Libin
Co-founder and CEO: Ehud Levy
Director R&D/QC: Cang Li
VP Sales/Marketing: Terry Libin
Contact: Alisha Kuzma
alisha_kuzma@mckinsey.com
Purchasing Manager: Kenny Powell
Estimated Sales: $ 1 - 3 Million
Number Employees: 10-19
Square Footage: 136000
Regions Exported to: Central America, South America, Europe
Percentage of Business in Exporting: 30

48502 Sellers Engineering Division
PO Box 48
Danville, KY 40423-0048   859-236-3181
　　　Fax: 859-236-3184
Manufacturer and exporter of boiler feed systems, steam and hot water boilers, water heaters and deaerators
President & Public Relations: G. Miller
CEO/CFO: S Miller
Controller: J. Sizemore
VP Research & Development: Bill Doughty
Quality Control: L Gambrel
Marketing Director: R Larson
Sales Director: R Larson
Production/Plant Manager: R Woolum
Plant Manager: R Woolum
Purchasing Manager: P Coffman
Estimated Sales: $20-50 Million
Number Employees: 78
Square Footage: 64000
Type of Packaging: Food Service
Other Locations:
　Sellers
　Dallas, TX
　Weestern Engineering
　Danville, KYSellersDanville
Brands Exported: Sellers div of Green Boiler Technologies, Inc
Regions Exported to: Central America, South America, Asia, Middle East
Percentage of Business in Exporting: 10

48503 Semco Manufacturing Company
705 E Us Highway 83
PO Box 1686
Pharr, TX 78577   956-787-4203
　　　Fax: 956-781-0620 semcoice.com
Manufacturer and exporter of mobile/portable ice plants, slush ice makers, hydro coolers, freezers and vegetable harvesting and packing equipment
President: James Hatton
Sales Director: Jason Hatton
Contact: Raul Mora
raul@semcomfgco.com
Purchasing Manager: Rod Bradley
Estimated Sales: Below $5 Million
Number Employees: 20-49
Square Footage: 60000
Brands Exported: Semco
Regions Exported to: Central America, South America, Europe, Asia, Middle East, Caribbean, Latin America, Mexico
Percentage of Business in Exporting: 50

48504 Semco Plastic Co
5301 Old Baumgartner Rd
St Louis, MO 63129-2944   314-487-4557
　　　www.semcoplastics.com
Manufacturer and exporter of plastic products including drinking straws, boxes and advertising novelties.
President: Chuck Voelkel
cvoelkel@semcoplastic.com
Year Founded: 1944
Estimated Sales: $100-500 Million
Number Employees: 100-249
Square Footage: 450000

48505 Semi-Bulk Systems Inc
159 Cassens Ct
Fenton, MO 63026-2543   636-343-4500
　　　Fax: 636-343-2822 800-732-8769
info@semi-bulk.com www.semi-bulk.com
Manufacturer and exporter of mixers including batch and continuous; also, dry ingredient handling interface systems

567

Importers & Exporters / A-Z

President: Jeff Doherty
CEO: Charles Attack
Chief Financial Officer: Al Moresi
Vice President: Ron Bentley
Research/Development: Iris Freidel
Controller: Al Moresi
Sales/Marketing: Ronald Bentley
Public Relations: Diana McMahon
Operations/Production/Purchasing: Bernie Klipsch
Estimated Sales: $10 Million
Number Employees: 20-49
Square Footage: 220000
Regions Exported to: Worldwide
Percentage of Business in Exporting: 10

48506 Senba USA
23447 Cabot Blvd
Hayward, CA 94545   510-264-5850
      Fax: 510-264-0938 888-922-5852
      aoki@senbausa.com www.senbausa.com
Liquid sauces including teriyaki, beef and tempura; also, miso soup bases; importer of spray dried alcohol powder and tea extract; also, contract packaging and dry blending available
Sales: Hiro Aoki
Contact: Fernando Garcia
fgarcia@senbausa.com
Estimated Sales: $4.2 Million
Number Employees: 20-49
Square Footage: 52000
Parent Co: Senba Foods Company
Type of Packaging: Consumer, Food Service, Private Label, Bulk
Brands Imported: Senba
Regions Imported from: Japan
Percentage of Business in Importing: 5

48507 Seneca Environmental Products
Airport Industrial Park 1685 S. County
PO Box 429
Tiffin, OH 44883   419-447-1282
                      Fax: 419-448-4048
Manufacturer and exporter of sanitary type dust collectors including stainless steel, carbon steel, reverse jet, cartridge, cyclone, shaker and cylindrical; also, noise pollution control equipment, miscellaneous sanitary and steel fabrication
President: C Harple
Sales Manager: Don Harple
Estimated Sales: $1 - 3 Million
Number Employees: 20-49
Square Footage: 100000

48508 Seneca Foods Corp
606 S Tremont St
Princeville, IL 61559-9468 309-385-4301
      Fax: 309-385-2696 www.senecafoods.com
Canned vegetables including asparagus, pumpkins, green beans, corn and peas; also, salads including German potato, bean and garden salads
Manager: Wally Hochsprung
Vice President: Van Riper
Manager: L Dallinger
ldallinger@chiquita.com
Plant Manager: David Stoner
Estimated Sales: $10-20 Million
Number Employees: 100-249
Square Footage: 480000
Parent Co: Owatonna Canning Company
Type of Packaging: Consumer, Food Service, Private Label
Regions Exported to: Asia, Canada
Percentage of Business in Exporting: 5

48509 (HQ)Seneca Foods Corp
3736 S Main Steet
Marion, NY 14505   315-926-8100
      webmaster@senecafoods.com
                      www.senecafoods.com
Largest processor of fruits and vegetables in North America
President & CEO: Kraig H. Kayser
kkayser@senecafoods.com
Chairman: Arthur Wolcott
SVP Technology and Planning: Carl Cichetti
Sr VP of Sales & Marketing: Dean Erstad
Sr. VP & Chief Administrative Officer: Cynthia Fohrd
Exec. VP & COO: Paul Palmby
Year Founded: 1949
Estimated Sales: Over $1 Billion
Number Employees: 1000-4999
Number of Brands: 6
Square Footage: 7000

Type of Packaging: Consumer, Food Service, Private Label
Other Locations:
  Modesto, CA
  Geneva, NY
  Leicester, NY
  Marion, NY
  Buhl, ID
  Payette, ID Geneva
Regions Exported to: Worldwide

48510 Senomyx Inc
4767 Nexus Center Dr
San Diego, CA 92121-3051   858-646-8300
                      Fax: 858-404-0752
Flavor ingredients.
President/CEO: John Poyhonen
john.poyhonen@senomyx.com
CFO/SVP: Tony Rogers
VP/General Counsel/Corporate Secretary: Catherine Lee
SVP/Chief Commercial Development Officer: Sharon Wicker
VP, Information Technology: Lorenzo Pena
Estimated Sales: $28 Million
Number Employees: 50-99
Number of Brands: 3

48511 Sensidyne
1000 112th Circle North
Suite 100
St. Petersburg, FL 33716   727-530-3602
      Fax: 727-539-0550 800-451-9444
      info@sensidyne.com www.sensidyne.com
Manufacturer and exporter of gas detection and air sampling systems
President: Howie Mills
VP: Glenn Warr
Quality Control: George Mason
Marketing: Mary Slattery
National Sales Manager: Gary Queensberry
Contact: Mabie Eggleston
meggleston@sensidyne.com
Estimated Sales: $10-20 Million
Number Employees: 50-99
Regions Exported to: Central America, South America, Europe, Asia, Middle East
Percentage of Business in Exporting: 5

48512 Sensient Colors Inc
2515 N Jefferson Ave
St Louis, MO 63106-1939   314-889-7600
      Fax: 314-658-7318 800-325-8110
             foodcolors.stl@sensient.com
                 www.sensientfoodcolors.com
Global food and beverage color manufacturer.
President, Color Group: Michael Geraghty
Parent Co: Sensient Technologies Corporation
Type of Packaging: Consumer, Food Service, Private Label, Bulk
Regions Exported to: Europe, Asia, Middle East
Percentage of Business in Exporting: 7
Regions Imported from: Europe, Middle East
Percentage of Business in Importing: 5

48513 Sensient Flavors and Fragrances
2800 W Higgins Road
Suite 900
Hoffman Estates, IL 60169   847-755-5300
                      Fax: 847-755-5350
      corporate.communications@sensient.com
             www.sensientflavorsandfragrances.com
Flavoring extracts and syrups.
President, Flavors & Fragrances Group: E. Craig Mitchell
Estimated Sales: $100-200 Million
Number Employees: 1,000-4,999
Parent Co: Sensient Technologies Corporation
Regions Exported to: Europe, Asia

48514 Sensitech Inc
8801 148th Ave NE
P.O.Box 599
Redmond, WA 98052-3492   425-883-7926
      Fax: 425-883-3766 800-999-7926
                      www.sensitech.com
Manufacturer and exporter of time/temperature and humidity monitors for perishable commodities in transit, storage or processing
Manager: Mike Hanson
CFO: Mike Hurton
Senior Director of Quality Assurance: Dave Ray
Director Marketing: Susan Milant
VP Sales: Dan Vache

Estimated Sales: $10-20 Million
Number Employees: 50-99
Regions Exported to: Worldwide

48515 Sensus America Inc
100 Lenox Dr # 104
Suite 104
Lawrence Twp, NJ 08648-2332 646-452-6140
      Fax: 646-452-6150 www.inspiredbyinulin.com
Supplier of ingredients to the food and beverage industries.
Sales Manager: Carol Malczan
Number Employees: 1-4
Parent Co: Sensus

48516 Sentinel Lubricants Inc
15755 NW 15th Ave
PO Box 694240
Miami, FL 33169-5651   305-625-6400
      Fax: 305-625-6565 800-842-6400
             info@sentinelsynthetic.com
                 www.sentinelsynthetic.com
Manufacturer and exporter of food grade synthetic lubricants including nontoxic oil and grease
CEO: R Chaban
VP: J C Barroso
Research & Development: Charles Clay
Quality Control: Phil Sauder
Marketing Director: Emile Freidman
Sales: Raul Oquendo
Public Relations: Marta Garcia
Operations Manager: Randye Chaban
Production Manager: Juanillo Barroso
Plant Manager: Philip Sauder
Purchasing Manager: Martha Garcia
Estimated Sales: $18 Million
Number Employees: 10-19
Number of Brands: 200
Number of Products: 400
Square Footage: 50000
Type of Packaging: Consumer, Private Label
Brands Exported: Sentinel
Regions Exported to: Central America, South America, Europe, Asia, Middle East
Percentage of Business in Exporting: 60
Regions Imported from: Central America, South America, Europe, Asia, Middle East
Percentage of Business in Importing: 5

48517 Sentry Equipment Corp
966 Blue Ribbon Cir N
Oconomowoc, WI 53066-8666 262-567-7256
      Fax: 262-567-4523 sales@sentry-equip.com
                      www.sentry-equip.com
Manufacturer and exporter of sanitary samplers for milk, cream, whey, orange juice, viscous food products, wastewater liquids and slurries
President: Michael Farrell
CEO: John Hazlehurst
john_h@sentryequipment.com
Marketing Director: Lynn Castrodale
Sales Director: Doris Hoeft
Number Employees: 100-249
Brands Exported: ISOLOK
Regions Exported to: Central America, South America, Europe, Asia, Middle East
Percentage of Business in Exporting: 30

48518 Sentry Seasonings
928 N Church Rd
Elmhurst, IL 60126-1014   630-530-5370
      Fax: 630-530-5385 wayne@sentryseasonings.com
                      www.sentryseasonings.com
Flavors and seasonings for food processing companies
President: Carla Staniec
carla@sentryseasonings.com
VP: Michael Staniec
Estimated Sales: $730000
Number Employees: 10-19
Square Footage: 120000
Type of Packaging: Consumer, Food Service, Private Label, Bulk
Regions Exported to: Worldwide
Percentage of Business in Exporting: 10
Regions Imported from: Worldwide

48519 Sentry/Bevcon North America
16630 Koala Road
PO Box 578
Adelanto, CA 92301-0578   800-854-1177
      Fax: 760-246-4044 800-661-3003
             sales@ici.us www.ici.us

Importers & Exporters / A-Z

Manufacturer and exporter of portable bars and dispensers including soda, juice, coffee, liquor and beer
President: Joe Suarez
Quality Control: Jerry Wheeler
R & D: Jerry Wheeler
Marketing: Ken Wogberg
Sales: Amber Micham
Public Relations: Ken Wogberg
Technical Support: Jerry Wheeler
President: Joe Suarez
Number Employees: 35
Square Footage: 224000
Parent Co: International Carbonic
Type of Packaging: Consumer, Food Service, Private Label
Regions Exported to: Worldwide
Percentage of Business in Exporting: 10

48520 Separators Inc
5707 W Minnesota St
Indianapolis, IN 46241-3825 317-484-3745
 Fax: 317-484-3755 800-233-9022
 separate@sepinc.com www.separatorsinc.com
Leader in the sale and repair of reconditioned centrifuges.
President/CEO: Joe Campbell
COO/CFO: Joe Mansfield
Director of Manufacturing: Dan Goss
Estimated Sales: $10-20 Million
Number Employees: 20-49
Square Footage: 60000
Brands Exported: Alfa Laval; Westfalia; Voith Fluid Clutches; Roto Filters; Controls
Regions Exported to: Central America, South America, Canada
Percentage of Business in Exporting: 5
Brands Imported: Alfa Laval; Westfalia
Regions Imported from: Europe
Percentage of Business in Importing: 10

48521 Sepragen Corp
1205 San Luis Obispo St
Hayward, CA 94544-7915 510-475-0650
 Fax: 510-475-0625 info@sepragen.com
 www.sepragen.com
Manufacturer and exporter of process control systems and instruments and separation machinery for the dairy industry
CEO/ CTO: Vinit Saxena
CFO: Henry Edmunds
Director Quality & Tech Support: Salah Ahmed
Number Employees: 20-49
Regions Exported to: Worldwide
Percentage of Business in Exporting: 30

48522 SerVend International
2100 Future Drive
Sellersburg, IN 47172-1868 812-246-7000
 Fax: 812-246-9922 800-367-4233
 www.servend.com
Manufacturer and exporter of ice makers, beverage, cup and ice dispensers, ice storage bins and beverage dispensing valves
CEO: Terry Growcock
VP Sales/Marketing: Lonnie Shafer
Director Marketing: Elaine Momson
Contact: Greg Gummere
greg.gummere@manitowoc.com
Estimated Sales: $ 20 - 30 Million
Number Employees: 250
Square Footage: 155000
Parent Co: Manitowoc Foodservice Group
Other Locations:
 SerVend International
 Clackamas, ORSerVend International
Brands Exported: SerVend; Flomatic
Regions Exported to: Worldwide
Percentage of Business in Exporting: 6

48523 Serenade Foods
9179 N 200 E
Milford, IN 46542 574-658-4121
 Fax: 219-658-2246
Poultry
Communications Manager: Janelle Deatsman
Contact: Eric Essig
eessig@mapleleaffarms.com
Number Employees: 100-249
Parent Co: Maple Leaf Foods
Type of Packaging: Consumer, Food Service, Private Label, Bulk
Regions Exported to: Worldwide

48524 Serendib Tea Company
4806 W 129th Street
Alsip, IL 60803-3016 708-489-9980
 Fax: 708-489-9973 serendibtea@hotmail.com
Ceylon tea
President: Munira Nomanbhoy

48525 Serendipitea
73 Plandome Rd
Manhasset, NY 11030-2330 516-365-7711
 Fax: 516-365-7733 888-832-5433
 tea@serendipitea.com www.serendipitea.com
Tea; premium grade loose leaf
Principal: Linda Villano
tea@serendipitea.com
Estimated Sales: Less than $500,000
Number Employees: 5-9
Number of Brands: 1
Number of Products: 100+
Square Footage: 12000
Type of Packaging: Consumer, Food Service, Private Label, Bulk
Brands Exported: Serendipitea
Regions Exported to: Asia, Canada
Brands Imported: Tea; Tisane
Regions Imported from: Europe, Asia

48526 (HQ)Serfilco
2900 Macarthur Blvd
Northbrook, IL 60062-2007 847-509-2900
 Fax: 847-559-1995 800-323-5431
 sales@serfilco.com www.serfilco.com
Designs, manufactures and markets a broad line of corrosion resistant high performance pumps, agitators, filtration systems and instruments.
President: James Berg
jamesb@serfilco.com
Marketing: Chuck Schultz
Operations: Mike Berg
Production Manager: Jerry Swooda
Estimated Sales: $ 10 - 20 Million
Number Employees: 20-49
Other Locations:
 Serfilco Ltd.
 Lancaster, PASerfilco Ltd.
Regions Exported to: Central America, South America, Europe, Asia, Worldwide

48527 Sermia International
100-742 Boulevard Industrial
Blainville, QC J7C 3V4
Canada 450-433-7483
 Fax: 450-433-7484 800-567-7483
 info@sermia.com www.sermia.com
Manufacturer and exporter of filters for liquids
Number Employees: 10
Brands Exported: Sermia
Regions Exported to: Worldwide
Percentage of Business in Exporting: 80

48528 Serpa Packaging Solutions
7020 W Sunnyview Ave
Visalia, CA 93291-9639 559-651-2339
 Fax: 559-651-2345 800-348-5453
 sales@serpapackaging.com www.serpapkg.com
Manufacturer and exporter of cartoners and case packers and erectors; also, custom designs and turnkey applications available
President/CEO: Fernando M Serpa
fsepra@serpapackaging.com
Director Of Marketing: Rich James
Estimated Sales: $10,000,000
Number Employees: 50-99
Square Footage: 92000
Regions Exported to: Central America, South America, Europe, Asia, Worldwide
Percentage of Business in Exporting: 6

48529 Serr-Edge Machine Company
4471 W 160th St
Cleveland, Cl 44135-2625 216-267-6333
 Fax: 216-267-2929 800-443-8097
Manufacturer and exporter of industrial and commercial sharpening machines for scissors, knives and shears
President: Linda Ribar Oakley
Owner: Matthew Oakley
Estimated Sales: Below $5 Million
Number Employees: 5-9
Brands Exported: Easisharp; Keenedge
Regions Exported to: Central America, South America, Europe, Asia, Middle East, Africa

48530 Sertapak Packaging Corporation
PO Box 1500
Woodstock, ON N4S 8R2
Canada 519-539-3330
 Fax: 519-539-4499 800-265-1162
Manufacturer and exporter of returnable and expandable packaging systems, containers, pallets and sealed edge plastic corrugated slip sheets
President: C J David Nettleton
CEO: Alison Clarke
CFO: Bruce Orr
Number Employees: 10
Brands Exported: Sertote
Regions Exported to: Central America, South America, Europe, Mexico

48531 Sertodo Copper
3615 Oak Spring Road
Austin, TX 78746 512-923-4885
 Fax: 309-276-6343 info@sertodo.com
 www.sertodo.com

48532 Serval Foods
11580 NW 105th St
Medley, FL 33178-1191 305-884-1799
 Fax: 305-884-1739

48533 (HQ)Servco Equipment Co
3189 Jamieson Ave
St Louis, MO 63139-2519 314-781-3189
 Fax: 314-645-7003 www.servco-stl.com
Manufacturer and exporter of conveyors and under and back bar refrigerators
President: Earl Gates Jr
Sales Exec: Helen Gage
Estimated Sales: $ 5-10 Million
Number Employees: 20-49
Square Footage: 112000
Brands Exported: Servco; Gates
Regions Exported to: Worldwide
Percentage of Business in Exporting: 8

48534 Servend International
2100 Future Drive
Sellersburg, IN 47172-1868 812-246-7000
 Fax: 812-246-9922 www.servend.com
Contact: Greg Gummere
greg.gummere@manitowoc.com

48535 Server Products Inc
3601 Pleasant Hill Rd
PO Box 98
Richfield, WI 53076-9417 262-628-5100
 Fax: 262-628-5110 800-558-8722
 spsales@server-products.com
 www.server-products.com
Manufacturer and exporter of small pumps, food dispensers and warmers, bars and accessories, rails and pizza ovens
President: Chris Falkner
spsales@server-products.com
VP Sales: Ron Ripple
VP Production: Carol Miller
Estimated Sales: $ 10 - 20 Million
Number Employees: 50-99
Square Footage: 250000
Brands Exported: Server Products
Regions Exported to: Central America, South America, Europe, Asia, Middle East, Pacific Rim, Mexico
Percentage of Business in Exporting: 10

48536 Service Ideas
2354 Ventura Dr
Woodbury, MN 55125-4403 651-730-8800
 Fax: 651-730-8880 800-328-4493
 sales@serviceideas.com www.serviceideas.com
Manufacturer, importer and exporter of insulated serving plates, beverage servers, dispensers, pitchers and buffet bowls
President: Christina Brandt
laura@serviceideas.com
VP & HR Manager: Megan Blohowiak
Foodservice Sales Director: Andy Krawczyk
Site Manager: Laura Bjorkman
laura@serviceideas.com
Operations Director: Mark Bolowiak
Estimated Sales: $ 10 - 20 Million
Number Employees: 20-49
Square Footage: 80000
Brands Exported: Metallic Luster; Eco-Serv; Brew'N'Pour Lid; New Generation; Thermo-Serv; Thermo-Plate; Sculptured Ice Buffet

Importers & Exporters / A-Z

Regions Exported to: Worldwide
Percentage of Business in Exporting: 15
Brands Imported: Allgo; Animo; SteelVac; ZePe; Alfi; Coffee at a Touch; Diamond; SteelVac
Regions Imported from: Europe, Asia
Percentage of Business in Importing: 20

48537 Service Manufacturing
1601 Mountain St
Aurora, IL 60505-2402 630-898-1394
Fax: 630-898-7800 888-325-2788
tvickers@theramp.net www.rocktenn.com
Manufacturer, importer and exporter of custom packaging products including insulated coolers, cases and bags
President: Camerina Torres
Vice President: David Goodman
Marketing/Sales: Matthew Sheridan
Plant Manager: Octavio Serrano
Purchasing Manager: Clarence Eisernman
Estimated Sales: $10-20 Million
Number Employees: 10-19
Square Footage: 376000
Type of Packaging: Bulk
Regions Exported to: Central America
Percentage of Business in Exporting: 2
Regions Imported from: Asia, Middle East
Percentage of Business in Importing: 15

48538 Service Packing Company
250 Southern Street
Vancouver, BC V6A 2P1
Canada 604-681-0264
Fax: 604-681-9309
Dates, currants, raisins, shredded coconut, chocolate chips, prunes and nuts including walnuts and almonds
President: Ron Huntington
Estimated Sales: $500,000-1,000,000
Number Employees: 1-4
Square Footage: 340000
Type of Packaging: Private Label
Brands Exported: Martins
Regions Exported to: Europe, USA
Percentage of Business in Exporting: 5
Regions Imported from: South America, Europe, Asia, Middle East, South Africa
Percentage of Business in Importing: 95

48539 Servitrade
1000 Brickell Avenue
Suite 1220
Miami, FL 33131-3013 305-670-7961
Fax: 305-670-7967
Exporter of frozen meats, poultry, pasta, sauces and edible oils; importer of fresh seasonal produce, frozen and canned asparagus, frozen mango puree and passion fruit concentrate
Operations Manager: Jorge Prugue
Purchasing Manager: Jose Valdizan
Estimated Sales: $2.5-5 Million
Number Employees: 5-9
Parent Co: Romero Group
Type of Packaging: Food Service, Private Label, Bulk
Regions Exported to: South America, Latin America
Percentage of Business in Exporting: 50
Regions Imported from: South America

48540 Servpak Corp
5844 Dawson St
Hollywood, FL 33023-1910 954-962-4262
Fax: 954-962-5776 800-782-0840
www.serv-pak.com
Manufacturer and exporter table-topheat seal packaging machinery forrigid and semi rigid trays covered by pre-cut lids or lid film on a roll
Owner: Joel Mahler
Estimated Sales: Less than $500,000
Number Employees: 10-19
Square Footage: 4000

48541 Sesaco Corp
6201 E Oltorf St # 100
Suite 100
Austin, TX 78741-7511 512-389-0790
Fax: 512-389-0790 800-737-2260
www.sesaco.com
Sesame seeds including white hulled
Executive Director: Ray Langham
Administration: Tina Smith
Director of Production: Jerry Riney
jriney@sesaco.com

Estimated Sales: $ 3 - 5 Million
Number Employees: 1-4
Type of Packaging: Consumer, Bulk
Regions Exported to: Europe, Asia
Regions Imported from: Central America, South America, Asia, Africa

48542 Sesinco Foods
54 W 21st Street
New York, NY 10010-6908 212-243-1306
Fax: 212-243-2036
Frozen and canned foods, beverages, dairy products
President: Serbajit Singh
VP: Ann Gaudet
Estimated Sales: $1600000
Number Employees: 7
Type of Packaging: Consumer, Food Service
Regions Exported to: South America, Europe, Asia, Caribbean
Percentage of Business in Exporting: 30

48543 Sessions Co Inc
801 N Main St
Enterprise, AL 36330-9108 334-393-0200
Fax: 334-393-0240
Peanut sheller and processor producing quality shelled peanuts and peanut seed. Also producers of crude peanut oil and peanut meal.
Principal: Mo Sessions
CFO: Jeff Outlaw
sesscom@frost.snowhill.com
Estimated Sales: $9.3 Million
Number Employees: 50-99
Square Footage: 40000
Type of Packaging: Consumer, Food Service, Private Label, Bulk
Regions Exported to: Worldwide

48544 Setco
34 Engelhard Dr
Monroe Twp, NJ 08831 609-655-4600
Fax: 609-655-0225 www.setco.com
Manufacturer and exporter of plastic bottles
Contact: Bob Loftus
bobl@setcousa.com
Plant Manager: Ray Agondo
Estimated Sales: $ 50-100 Million
Number Employees: 250-500
Parent Co: APL Company
Regions Exported to: Worldwide

48545 Sethness Caramel Color
3422 W Touhy Avenue
Skokie, IL 60076 847-329-2080
Fax: 847-329-2090 mail@sethness.com
www.sethness.com
Producer of caramel color for beverage, bakery, nutritional, and other applications.
COO: Tom Schufreider
Type of Packaging: Food Service, Bulk
Other Locations:
Corporate Office
Skokie, IL
Eastern Office
Avenel, NJ
U.S. Plant & Research Center
Clinton, IACorporate OfficeAvenel
Regions Exported to: Worldwide
Regions Imported from: Worldwide

48546 Setterstix Corp
261 S Main St
Cattaraugus, NY 14719-1312 716-257-3451
Fax: 716-257-9818 nan@setterstix.com
www.setterstix.com
Manufacturer and exporter of rolled paper sticks for the confectionery industry
President: Paul Elly
pelly@setterstix.com
CFO: Ron Wasmund
Sales: Nan Mikowicz
Plant Manager: Eric Pritchard
Estimated Sales: $ 10 - 15 Million
Number Employees: 50-99
Square Footage: 60000
Parent Co: Knox Industries
Brands Exported: Setterstix
Regions Exported to: Central America, Asia, Middle East, Africa
Percentage of Business in Exporting: 15

48547 Setton International Foods
85 Austin Blvd
Commack, NY 11725 631-543-8090
Fax: 631-543-8070 800-227-4397
info@settonfarms.com
www.settoninternational.com
Pistachios, cashews, almonds, apricots, candy and snack foods
President: Joshua Setton
VP, Domestic Sales & Marketing: Joseph Setton
Human Resources Coordinator: Kellie Shepard
Logistics Manager: Patrick Braddock
Production Manager: Henry Scott
Plant Manager: Jeffrey Gibbons
Estimated Sales: $64 Million
Number Employees: 250-499
Square Footage: 55000
Type of Packaging: Consumer, Food Service, Private Label, Bulk
Other Locations:
Processing Facility
Terra Bella, CAProcessing FacilityZutphen, The Netherlands
Brands Exported: Pistachios
Regions Exported to: South America, Asia, Africa
Brands Imported: Cashews, Pineapple, Papaya, Apricots, and Other Dried Fruits & Nuts

48548 Setton Pistachio
9370 Road 234
Terra Bella, CA 93270 559-535-6050
Fax: 559-535-6089 info@settonfarms.com
www.settonfarms.com
Pistachios
President: Joshua Setton
settoninfo@settonfarms.com
VP, Domestic Sales & Marketing: Joseph Setton
Human Resources Coordinator: Kellie Shepard
Logistics Manager: Patrick Braddock
Project Manager: Henry Scott
Plant Manager: Jeffrey Gibbons
Estimated Sales: $64 Million
Number Employees: 100-249
Number of Brands: 2
Square Footage: 300000
Parent Co: Setton International Foods, Inc.
Type of Packaging: Consumer, Food Service, Bulk
Other Locations:
New York Sales Office
Commack, NYNew York Sales OfficeZutphen, The Netherlands
Brands Exported: Setton
Regions Exported to: Worldwide

48549 Seven Keys Co Of Florida
450 SW 12th Ave
Pompano Beach, FL 33069-3504 954-946-5010
Fax: 954-946-5012
Processor and exporter of tropical jams, jellies, marmalades and coconut toast spreads
President: Henry Stevens
Estimated Sales: $ 3 - 5 Million
Number Employees: 5-9
Square Footage: 45000
Type of Packaging: Consumer, Food Service, Private Label
Brands Exported: Seven Keys; Lapham
Regions Exported to: Canada
Percentage of Business in Exporting: 5

48550 Seven Seas Seafoods
901 S Fremont Ave Ste 168
Alhambra, CA 91803 626-570-9129
Fax: 626-570-0079
Seafood
President: Christopher Lin
VP: Sean Lin
Estimated Sales: $ 5 - 10 Million
Number Employees: 5-9

48551 Severn Trent Svc
3000 Advance Ln
Colmar, PA 18915-9432 215-822-2901
Fax: 215-997-4062
marketing@capitalcontrols.com
www.severntrentservices.com
Manufacturer and exporter of water treatment systems including chlorinators, ultraviolet sterilization systems, pH/orp monitors and chlorine, ammonia and fluoride residue analyzers
President, Chief Executive Officer: Martin Kane
Marketing Manager: Anne Penkal
Plant Manager: Jeff Dohnam

Importers & Exporters / A-Z

48552 (HQ)Seville Flexpack Corp
9905 S Ridgeview Dr
Oak Creek, WI 53154-5556 414-761-2751
Fax: 414-761-3140 kskempk@sevilleflexpack.com
www.sevilleflexpack.com
Manufacturer and exporter of flexible packaging materials, stand-up pouches and cold seal coatings
President: Jan Drzewiecki
Director Sales: Jay Yakich
VP Manufacturing: James Yakich
Estimated Sales: $20-50 million
Number Employees: 50-99
Square Footage: 12000000
Other Locations:
 Seville Flexpack Corp.
 Waco, TXSeville Flexpack Corp.

48553 Sevilo Inc
2745 Wild Vly
Little Elm, TX 75068 214-766-2199
Fax: 214-292-9428 info@sevilo.net
www.sevilo.net
French kosher, specialty olives, extra virgin olive oil, tapenade
Contact: Claude Vincent
claude@sevilo.net

48554 Seviroli Foods
385 Oak St
Garden City, NY 11530 516-222-6220
Fax: 516-222-0534 www.seviroli.com
All natural frozen pasta products.
President: Anthony D'Orazio
adorazio@doraziofoods.com
CFO: Michael Romano
VP Sales/Marketing: Terry D'Ozario
VP Operations/COO: Frank D'Orazio
VP Production: Anthony D'Orazio
Estimated Sales: $8.4 Million
Number Employees: 50-99
Square Footage: 100000
Regions Exported to: Canada

48555 Sew-Eurodrive Inc
1295 Old Spartanburg Hwy
P.O. Box 518
Lyman, SC 29365 864-439-8792
Fax: 864-949-3039 www.seweurodrive.com
Manufacturer and exporter of drives, motors and accessories.
Chief Executive Officer: Juegon Blickle
Marketing Communications/Tradeshow Mgr.: JoAnn Greenup
Year Founded: 1931
Estimated Sales: $100-500 Million
Number Employees: 250-499
Square Footage: 250000
Regions Exported to: Worldwide

48556 Seydel Co
244 John B Brooks Rd
Pendergrass, GA 30567 706-693-2266
Fax: 706-693-2074 customerservice@seydel.com
www.seydel.com
Starch, dextrin and protein.
Chairman & CEO: Scott Seydel, Sr.
President & COO: Scott Seydel, Jr.
Chief Financial Officer: Graham Marsh
Estimated Sales: $43.5 Million
Number Employees: 50-99
Parent Co: Seydel Company
Type of Packaging: Food Service, Bulk
Regions Exported to: Worldwide
Regions Imported from: South America, Asia

48557 Sfb Plastics Inc
1819 W Harry St
P.O.Box 533
Wichita, KS 67213-3243 316-262-0400
Fax: 316-712-0112 800-343-8133
sales@sfbplastics.com www.sfbplastics.com
Manufacturer and exporter of polyethylene air flow separators, pallets, pallet equipment and industrial blow molded plastic containers
President: David Long
dlong@sfbplastics.com
Quality Control: Debbie Speven
Marketing: John Fosse
Sales: John Fosse
Estimated Sales: $ 10 - 20 Million
Number Employees: 50-99
Square Footage: 168000
Regions Exported to: Europe
Percentage of Business in Exporting: 10

48558 Shadetree Canopies
6317 Busch Blvd
Columbus, OH 43229-1864 614-844-5990
Fax: 614-844-5991 800-894-3801
www.shadetreecanopies.com
Manufacturer and exporter of retractable awnings
Owner: Colin Leveque
CFO: Richard O Keith
Quality Control: Ken Wagner
VP Marketing: Dwayne Williams
Sales: Don Preston
Estimated Sales: $2.5-5 Million
Number Employees: 10-19
Parent Co: Certain Teed

48559 Shady Maple Farm
2585 Skymark Ave
Mississauga, ON L4W 4L5
Canada 905-206-1455
Fax: 905-206-1477 www.shadymaple.ca
Processor and exporter of pure maple syrup products
President/CEO: Robert Swain
CFO: Darren Brash
Marketing Director: Marlene Jolicoeur
Sales Director: Daniel Neale
Number Employees: 10-19
Square Footage: 220000
Type of Packaging: Consumer, Food Service, Private Label, Bulk
Brands Exported: Shady Maple Farm; Maple House; Canahorn
Regions Exported to: Central America, South America, Europe, Asia, Middle East
Percentage of Business in Exporting: 98
Brands Imported: Sahdy Maple Farm
Regions Imported from: Europe
Percentage of Business in Importing: 1

48560 Shafer Commercial Seating
4101 East 48th Ave
Denver, CO 80216 303-322-7792
Fax: 303-393-1836
Manufacturer and exporter of booths, chairs, cushions, pads, stools and tables including legs and bases
President: Randall Shafer
CFO: Dick Gish
CEO: Richard Gish
R & D: Dennis Trutcman
Marketing Director: Richard Howard
Contact: Darren Lingle
dalin@shafer.com
Purchasing Manager: Carla Rembolt
Estimated Sales: $18 Million
Number Employees: 100-249
Type of Packaging: Food Service
Brands Exported: Furniture
Regions Exported to: Worldwide
Percentage of Business in Exporting: 10
Brands Imported: Furniture Component Parts
Percentage of Business in Importing: 25

48561 Shafer-Haggart
1055 West Hastings Street
Suite 1038
Vancouver, BC V6E 4E2
Canada 604-669-5512
Fax: 604-669-9554 info@shafer-haggart.com
www.shafer-haggart.com
Processor and importer of canned mushrooms, tomatoes, peaches, tuna and salmon; exporter of frozen poultry and canned corn and fish products
President: Clive Lonsdale
Sr. VP: Brian Dougall
Estimated Sales: $2.5-5 Million
Number Employees: 20-49
Type of Packaging: Consumer, Food Service, Private Label
Brands Exported: Success; Schooner; Ensign
Regions Exported to: Europe, Asia
Percentage of Business in Exporting: 40
Brands Imported: Admiral; Four Star; Success; Schooner
Regions Imported from: Europe, Asia, USA
Percentage of Business in Importing: 60

48562 Shah Trading Company
3451 McNicoll Avenue
Scarborough, ON M1V 2V3
Canada 416-292-6927
Fax: 416-292-7932 info@shahtrading.com
www.shahtrading.com
Rice, spices, beans, peas, and lentils, specialty flours and nuts and dried fruits.
Other Locations:
 Pulse and Canning Plant
 Scarborough, ON
 Rice Plant
 Scarborough, ONPulse and Canning PlantScarborough

48563 (HQ)Shaklee Corp
4747 Willow Rd
Pleasanton, CA 94588-2763 925-924-2000
Fax: 925-924-2862 800-742-5533
www.shaklee.com
Nutritional supplements
Chairman/CEO: Roger Barnett
CEO: Etta Adams
adams@shaklee.net
CFO: Mike Batesole
Sr EVP & COO: Luiz Cerqueira
Research & Development, Chief Scientist: Dr. Carsten Smidt
adams@shaklee.net
Chief Marketing Officer: Brad Harrington
SVP, Sales & Field Development: Laura Hughes
Number Employees: 1000-4999
Parent Co: Ripplewood Holdings
Type of Packaging: Consumer
Other Locations:
 Shaklee Corporation
 Norman, OKShaklee Corporation
Regions Exported to: Worldwide

48564 Shammi Industries
390 Meyer Cir # A
Corona, CA 92879-6617 951-340-3419
Fax: 951-340-2716 800-417-9260
info@sammonsequipment.com
www.sammonsequipment.com
Manufacturer, importer and exporter of banquet and transport equipment including carts, heated cabinets, racks, tables, dollies and shelving
President: Dani Pollard
traci@curryelectric.com
Estimated Sales: $1-2.5 Million
Number Employees: 10-19
Square Footage: 42000
Brands Exported: Sammons
Regions Exported to: Worldwide
Percentage of Business in Exporting: 10
Brands Imported: Queen Mary's; Sammons

48565 Shamrock Technologies Newark
255 Pacific St
Newark, NJ 07114-2824 973-242-3859
Fax: 732-242-8074
marketing@shamrocktechnologies.com
www.shamrocktechnologies.com
Manufacturer and exporter of powdered waxes and PTFE (polytetrafluoroethylene); also, dispersions and emulsions including carnauba, PE, PP, paraffin, microcrystalline and blends
Owner: William B Neuberg
President: Bill Neueerg
Marketing Manager: Melanie McCarroll
Estimated Sales: $ 20 - 50 Million
Number Employees: 5-9

48566 Shank's Extracts Inc
350 Richardson Dr
Lancaster, PA 17603-4034 717-393-4441
Fax: 717-393-3148 800-346-3135
www.shanks.com
Supplier of extracts, flavors, colors, syrups, emulsions and sauces to industrial, private label and grocery customers.
President: Jeff Lehman
Vice President, Sales: Mark Freeman
Estimated Sales: G
Number Employees: 50-99
Square Footage: 110000
Type of Packaging: Consumer, Food Service, Private Label, Bulk
Regions Exported to: Canada
Percentage of Business in Exporting: 2
Regions Imported from: Europe, Asia
Percentage of Business in Importing: 10

Importers & Exporters / A-Z

48567 Shanker Industries
301 Suburban Avenue
Deer Park, NY 11729 631-940-9889
Fax: 631-940-9895 877-742-6561
sales@shanko.com www.shanko.com
Manufacturer and exporter of decorative wall and ceiling tiles for hotels and restaurants
President: John Shanker
VP Advertising and Finance: Francine Shanker
VP Sales: David Shanker
Contact: Grace Chai
grace@shanko.com
Estimated Sales: $ 500,000 - $ 1 Million
Number Employees: 5-9
Square Footage: 120000
Type of Packaging: Food Service
Regions Exported to: Europe, Asia, Canada, Mexico
Percentage of Business in Exporting: 15

48568 Shanzer Grain Dryer
PO Box 2371
Sioux Falls, SD 57101-2371 605-336-0439
Fax: 605-336-9569 800-843-9887
sales@dwindustries.us
Manufacturer and exporter of grain dryers
Owner: Marian Leuning
Secretary/Treasurer: Dave Leuning
VP: Marian Leuning
Estimated Sales: $ 3 - 5 Million
Number Employees: 20-49
Parent Co: D&W Industries
Regions Exported to: Worldwide
Percentage of Business in Exporting: 25

48569 Sharon Manufacturing Inc
540 Brook Ave
Deer Park, NY 11729-6802 631-242-8870
Fax: 631-586-6822 800-424-6455
info@sharonmfg.com www.sharonmfg.com
Manufacturer and exporter of replacement parts for gable top and reconditioned fillers for dairy and juice products
President: Robert Stamm
rob@sharonmfg.com
Number Employees: 5-9
Regions Exported to: Central America, South America, Worldwide
Percentage of Business in Exporting: 2

48570 Sharp Brothers
201 Orient St
Bayonne, NJ 7002 201-339-0404
Manufacturer and exporter of yeast extruders and cutters
Owner: Basem Abdelnour
Estimated Sales: $500,000-$1 Million
Number Employees: 1-4
Square Footage: 8750
Regions Exported to: Central America, South America
Percentage of Business in Exporting: 50

48571 (HQ)Sharp Electronics Corporation
Sharp Plaza
Mahwah, NJ 7495 201-529-8200
Fax: 201-529-8425 800-237-4277
www.sharpusa.com
Manufacturer and importer of commercial microwave ovens
President: Joel Biterman
CEO: Raymond Philippon
Chairman: Toshiaki Urushisako
Senior VP: Robert Scaglione
Number Employees: 1,000-4,999
Square Footage: 600000
Type of Packaging: Consumer, Food Service, Private Label
Other Locations:
Sharp Electronics Corp.
Romeoville, ILSharp Electronics Corp.
Regions Imported from: Asia
Percentage of Business in Importing: 30

48572 Shat R Shield Inc
116 Ryan Patrick Dr
Salisbury, NC 28147-5624 704-633-2100
Fax: 704-633-3420 800-223-0853
ayost@shatrshield.com www.shatrshield.com
Manufacturer and exporter of plastic-coated and shatter-proof fluorescent lamps and Teflon-coated 125 and 250 watt infrared heat lamps
Owner: Bob Nolan
bnolan@shatrshield.com
Marketing Coordinator: Anita Yost
VP Sales/Marketing: Marty Pint
Marketing/Communications Manager: Bill Hahn
Estimated Sales: Below $5 Million
Number Employees: 50-99
Square Footage: 84000
Type of Packaging: Food Service
Regions Exported to: Central America, Canada, Caribbean, Mexico
Percentage of Business in Exporting: 5

48573 Shaw-Clayton Corporation
90 Montecito Road
San Rafael, CA 94901-2378 415-472-1522
Fax: 415-472-1599 800-537-6712
www.shaw-clayton.com
Manufacturer and exporter of small hinged lid containers
President: H Shaw
Sales: L Smith
Public Relations: S Hanson
Estimated Sales: Less than $500,000
Square Footage: 8000
Type of Packaging: Consumer
Brands Exported: Flex-A-Top Hinged Lid Containers
Regions Exported to: Europe, Asia, Canada
Percentage of Business in Exporting: 5

48574 Shawano Specialty Papers
W7575 Poplar Rd
Shawano, WI 54166-6082 715-526-2181
800-543-5554
paper@littlerapids.com www.littlerapids.com
Manufacturer and exporter of paper including glazed, wet crepe, dry crepe tissue and serim reinforced tissue
Vice President: Ron Thiry
rthiry@littlerapids.com
Estimated Sales: $ 50-100 Million
Number Employees: 100-249
Parent Co: Little Rapids Corporation
Type of Packaging: Consumer, Bulk
Regions Exported to: Central America, South America, Europe, Asia
Percentage of Business in Exporting: 3
Regions Imported from: South America
Percentage of Business in Importing: 3

48575 (HQ)Shawnee Milling Co
201 S Broadway Ave
PO Box 1567
Shawnee, OK 74801-8427 405-273-7000
Fax: 405-273-7333 lspears@shawneemilling.com
www.shawneemilling.com
Flour, cornmeal, complete mixes, custom mixes
President: William Ford
bford@shawneemilling.com
CEo: Debra Howe
Vice President: Joe Lloyd Ford
Regional Sales Manager: James Smith
Plant Manager: Doug Myer
Purchasing Manager: Caleb Winsett
Number Employees: 250-499
Type of Packaging: Consumer, Food Service, Private Label, Bulk
Brands Exported: Shawnee
Regions Exported to: Central America, Asia

48576 Shekou Chemicals
24 Crescent Street
Waltham, MA 02453-4358 781-893-6878
Fax: 781-893-6881
Processor, importer and exporter of ingredients including citric acid, ascorbic acid, sodium benzoate, sodium propionate, calcium propionate, ammonium bicarbonate, sodium erythrobate, sodium citrate, potassium citrate and potassiumsorbate
System Staff: Herb Kimiatek
Sales/Marketing Executive: Judith Roiva
Purchasing Manager: Simon Altstein
Estimated Sales: $1.1 Million
Number Employees: 7
Square Footage: 40000
Type of Packaging: Bulk
Brands Exported: Monomers; Latex DeWebbers
Regions Exported to: Worldwide
Percentage of Business in Exporting: 50
Regions Imported from: Central America, South America, Europe, Asia, Latin America, Mexico
Percentage of Business in Importing: 100

48577 (HQ)Shelby Williams Industries Inc
810 W Highway 25 70
Newport, TN 37821-8044 423-623-0031
Fax: 866-319-9371 800-873-3252
www.shelbywilliams.com
Manufacturer and exporter of seating; importer of wicker chairs
President: David Morley
Chairman and CEO: Franklin Jacobs
VP Operations: Marty Blaylock
Plant Manager: Bob Drey
Number Employees: 1000-4999
Parent Co: Falcon Industries
Other Locations:
Williams, Shelby, Industries
Statesville, NCWilliams, Shelby, Industries

48578 Shelby Williams Industries Inc
810 W Highway 25 70
Newport, TN 37821-8044 423-623-0031
Fax: 866-319-9371 800-873-3252
www.shelbywilliams.com
President: David Morley
CFO: Jean Fleetwood
R & D: Terry Roche
Quality Control: Marriane Carter
Plant Manager: Bob Drey
Number Employees: 1000-4999
Parent Co: Falcon Products

48579 (HQ)Shelden, Dickson, & Steven Company
6114 Country Club Road
Omaha, NE 68152-2020 402-571-4848
Manufacturer and exporter of vending machines, fluorescent light fixtures, wall safes, etc
President: Richard Lebron
Estimated Sales: $ .5 - 1 million
Number Employees: 16
Square Footage: 200000

48580 (HQ)Shen Manufacturing Co Inc
40 Portland Rd
Conshohocken, PA 19428-2717 610-825-2790
Fax: 610-834-8617
Manufacturer, importer and exporter of placemats, chair pads, pot holders, oven mitts, aprons, bar mops, dish towels and cloths inclduing table, dish, scrub, dusting and polishing
President: Elissa Vogt
e.vogt@johnritz.net
CFO: Robert Steidle
VP Sales/Marketing: Howard Steidle Jr
Estimated Sales: $5-10 Million
Number Employees: 20-49
Regions Exported to: Worldwide
Regions Imported from: Worldwide

48581 Shenandoah Vineyards
12300 Steiner Rd
Plymouth, CA 95669-9503 209-245-4455
Fax: 209-245-5156 www.sobonwine.com
Wines
President: Leon Sobon
CEO: Shirley Sobon
Estimated Sales: Below $ 5 Million
Number Employees: 10-19
Regions Exported to: Europe, Asia, Canada

48582 Shepard Brothers Co
503 S Cypress St
La Habra, CA 90631-6126 562-697-1366
Fax: 562-697-5786 800-645-3594
info@shepardbros.com www.shepardbros.com
Manufacturer and exporter of cleaners, sanitizers and water treatment and waste treatment systems; also, consultant specializing in sanitation
President: Georgia Anglin
georgia@njcost.com
CEO: Ron Shepard
VP Sales: Tony Terranova
Estimated Sales: $ 15 - 20 Million
Number Employees: 50-99
Regions Exported to: Canada
Percentage of Business in Exporting: 3

48583 Shepard Niles Parts
220 N Genesee St
Montour Falls, NY 14865-9646 607-535-7111
Fax: 607-535-7323 800-727-8774
mike.baker@konecranes.com
www.shepard-niles.com

Hoists and genuine Shepard Niles replacement parts
Manager: Michael Baker
Number Employees: 10-19
Type of Packaging: Bulk
Brands Exported: Cleveland Tramrail
Regions Exported to: Worldwide
Percentage of Business in Exporting: 10

48584 (HQ)Shepherd Farms Inc
9330 E 8th Rd
Hillsboro, IL 62049-3448   217-532-5268
Fax: 815-389-1997   800-383-2676
www.shepherdfarms.com
Processor and packer of popcorn including yellow, white and specialty hybrids packaged for microwave, air poppers and commercial poppers; also, soybeans and tofu; exporter of soybeans for tofu, miso, natto and shoyu, seed corn and seedsoybeans
Owner: Jim Shepherd
Estimated Sales: Less Than $500,000
Number Employees: 1-4
Square Footage: 80000
Type of Packaging: Consumer, Food Service, Private Label, Bulk
Other Locations:
  Shepherd Farms
  Beloit, ILShepherd Farms
Regions Exported to: Asia, Middle East
Percentage of Business in Exporting: 10

48585 Sherman Specialty Toy Company
300 Jericho Quadrangle # 240
Jericho, NY 11753-2719   516-861-6420
Fax: 516-546-7496   hduran@makesparties.com
www.partybysherman.com
Owner: Adam Krosser

48586 Sherwood Brands
120 Jersey Ave
New Brunswick, NJ 08901   973-249-8200
info@sherwoodbrands.net
sherwoodbrands.net
Manufacturer of chocolates, truffles, cookies, snacks, tea and cappuccino.
Type of Packaging: Consumer, Private Label

48587 Sherwood Tool
10100 Reisterstown Road
Owings Mills, MD 21117-3815   860-828-4161
Fax: 860-828-5387
Manufacturer and exporter of packaging machinery
President: Paul R Corazzo Sr
Parent Co: Sherwood Industries
Type of Packaging: Food Service, Private Label
Regions Exported to: Worldwide

48588 Shibuya International
1070 Reno Avenue
Modesto, CA 95351-1176   209-529-6466
Fax: 209-529-1834
www.shibuya-international.com
Importer of food processing and packaging machinery including aseptic filling systems, cappers, cartoners, unscramblers, casers, uncasers, washers, cleaners, pasteurizers, warmers, coolers, conveyors and labelers
President: Ken Saisho
CEO: Ian Greenland
Estimated Sales: $ 1 - 3 Million
Number Employees: 4
Square Footage: 66800
Parent Co: Shibuya Kogyo Company
Brands Imported: Shibuya
Regions Imported from: Asia
Percentage of Business in Importing: 100

48589 Shick Esteve
4346 Clary Blvd
Kansas City, MO 64130-2329   816-861-7224
Fax: 816-921-1901   877-744-2587
info@shickesteve.com   www.shickesteve.com
Ingredient automation systems provider
President & CEO: Tim Cook
Executive VP & CFO: Blake Day
Director, Sales & Marketing: Jason Stricker
Estimated Sales: $40 Million
Number Employees: 100-249
Regions Exported to: Central America, South America, Asia
Percentage of Business in Exporting: 15

48590 Shields Bag & Printing Co
1009 Rock Ave
Yakima, WA 98902-4629   509-248-7500
Fax: 509-248-6304   800-541-8630
www.shieldsbag.com
Manufacturer and exporter of plain and printed mono and co-extrusion polyethylene, nylon and polypropylene film and bags; also, commercial printing services available.
President: Bill Shields
bshields@shieldsbag.com
Estimated Sales: $ 50-100 Million
Number Employees: 500-999
Square Footage: 300000
Regions Exported to: Central America, Asia
Percentage of Business in Exporting: 2

48591 Shiffer Industries
41 Moana Ave
Kihei, HI 96753-7170   216-524-6546
800-642-1774
Manufacturer and exporter of assemblers, handlers, formers, feeders, index transferers, sorters, orienters, fillers, meters, markers, cutters, counters, loaders, unloaders, dispatchers, dedimplers, deburrers, labelers, etc.; customdesigning available
Office Manager: L Mangal
President: Stuart Shiffer
Estimated Sales: $2.5-5 Million
Number Employees: 20-49

48592 Shilad Overseas Enterprises
1422 Chestnut St
Philadelphia, PA 19102-2509   215-751-2740
Fax: 215-751-0948
Importer and exporter of canned fruits, vegetable oils, poultry and beverages
Sales Executive: Aiman Shilad

48593 Shine Companies
4014 Evening Trail Drive
Spring, TX 77388-4936   281-353-8392
Fax: 281-353-8937
Processor and exporter of specialty seasonings, artichoke dips and toppings and marinades, salsas and condiments; importer of chile purees
President: Michael Shine
Executive VP: Janet Williams
Number Employees: 6
Square Footage: 5000
Brands Exported: Star Concepts
Regions Exported to: Europe, Mexico, Canada, Caribbean
Percentage of Business in Exporting: 2
Brands Imported: Chuqui's Gourmet
Regions Imported from: Canada, Mexico
Percentage of Business in Importing: 5

48594 Shingle Belting
420 Drew Ct # A
King Of Prussia, PA 19406-2681   610-239-6667
Fax: 610-239-6668   800-345-6294
belting@shinglebelting.com
www.shinglebelting.com
Manufacturer and exporter of flat sheet and profile thermoplastic conveyor belting including PU, PVC and polyester and bakery belts
President/ Owner: Rennie Keating
CFO: Frank Manley
fmanley@shinglebelting.com
Marketing Coordinator: Monica Berry
Sales VP: Bob Frasetto
Operations: Frank Manley
Plant Manager: Bob Bolan
Estimated Sales: $5-10 Million
Number Employees: 20-49
Square Footage: 60000
Brands Exported: Rounthane; Veethane; Polyflex
Regions Exported to: South America, Asia

48595 Shipley Basket Mfg Co
191 Shipley Ln
Dayton, TN 37321-5589   423-775-2051
Fax: 423-775-2145   800-251-0806
shipleybasket@aol.com   www.shipleybasket.com
Manufacturer and exporter of fruit and vegetable baskets
President: Diane Shipley
arthell3@aol.com
Estimated Sales: $5-10 Million
Number Employees: 20-49
Regions Exported to: Canada

48596 Shipley Sales
130 Old Tucson Rd
Nogales, AZ 85621   520-281-2621
Fax: 520-281-4456
Importer and exporter of cantalopes, honeydews, asparagus and grapes
Owner: Robert Shipley
Sales Manager: Reed Shipley
shipley@sogoodviva.com
Estimated Sales: $ 1 - 3 Million
Number Employees: 10-19
Brands Exported: Viva
Regions Exported to: Asia, Canada
Regions Imported from: Central America

48597 Shippers Paper ProductsCo
808 Blake Rd
Sheridan, AR 72150-8476   870-942-4043
Fax: 870-942-5933   800-468-1230
inquiry@itwshippers.com
www.shippersproducts.com
Manufacturer and exporter of paper and plastic dunnage bags
Contact: Jacqueline Garcia
jackie.garcia@shippersproducts.com
Plant Manager: Jeff Maness
Number Employees: 10-19
Regions Exported to: Worldwide

48598 Shippers Supply
2815A Cleveland Avenue
Saskatoon, SK S7K 8G1
Canada   306-242-6266
Fax: 306-933-4333   800-661-5639
saskatoon@shipperssupply.com
www.shipperssupply.com
Manufacturer, wholesaler/distributor and importer of printed labels, pressure sensitive tapes, corrugated boxes, material handling equipment, stretch film and shipping supplies; exporter of labels and printed tape
President: Ron Brown
Branch Manager: Ken Nordyke
Number Employees: Oover 200
Square Footage: 400000
Regions Exported to: USA
Percentage of Business in Exporting: 10
Regions Imported from: USA
Percentage of Business in Importing: 25

48599 Shipyard Brewing Co
86 Newbury St
Portland, ME 04101-4274   207-761-0807
Fax: 207-775-5567   800-789-0684
www.shipyard.com
Processor and exporter of beer, ale, stout and root beer
Owner: Fred Forsley
fforsley@shipyard.com
Master Brewer: Alan Pugsley
Director of Sales And Marketing: Bruce Forsley
fforsley@shipyard.com
Director Manufacturing: Paul Henry
Estimated Sales: Under $500,000
Number Employees: 50-99
Number of Brands: 17
Type of Packaging: Consumer, Food Service
Regions Exported to: United Kingdom

48600 Shivji Enterprises
2659 #5 Road
Richmond, BC V5M 1N1
Canada   604-270-3834
Fax: 604-270-3880   shivjis@hotmail.com
Importer and wholesaler/distributor of rice, spices, beans, frozen yucca and plantano, etc.; serving the food service and retail markets; exporter of flour, beans
Director: Shiraz Shivji
Estimated Sales: $3-5 Million
Number Employees: 5-9
Square Footage: 60000
Type of Packaging: Consumer, Food Service, Private Label, Bulk
Regions Exported to: Australia, Africa
Percentage of Business in Exporting: 5
Brands Imported: Golden Pacific; Golden Elephant; Peacock; Garden Temple; Fiesta
Regions Imported from: Central America, Europe, Asia, Australia
Percentage of Business in Importing: 50

Importers & Exporters / A-Z

48601 Shivvers
613 W English St
Corydon, IA 50060-1015   641-872-1007
Fax: 641-872-1593 www.shivvers.com
Manufacturer and exporter of continuous flow drying equipment and computer controls for dryers
President: Carl Shivvers
CFO: Ron Raasch
shivvers@shivvers.com
VP: Carl Shivvers
Assistant Sales Manager: Jim Ratliff
Estimated Sales: $20-50 Million
Number Employees: 100-249
Square Footage: 120000
Parent Co: Shivvers Manufacturing

48602 Shoei Foods USA Inc
1900 Feather River Blvd
Olivehurst, CA 95961   530-237-1295
www.shoeifoodsusa.com
Pine nuts, pumpkin seeds, sunflower seeds, walnut kernels.
President & CEO: Brian Dunning
briand@shoeiusa.com
Manager, Quality Control & Assurance: Tom Roach
Director, Global Sales & Marketing: John Gaffney
Director, Operations: Dwight Davis
Estimated Sales: $50-100 Million
Number Employees: 100-249
Number of Brands: 2
Number of Products: 5
Square Footage: 30000
Type of Packaging: Consumer, Food Service, Private Label, Bulk
Regions Exported to: Asia

48603 Shoes for Crews/Mighty Mat
1400 Centrepark Blvd # 31
West Palm Beach, FL 33401-7402   561-683-5090
Fax: 561-683-3080   800-667-5477
scotts@shoesforcrews.com
www.shoesforcrews.com
Shoes for Crews Slip-Resistant Footwear will provent your slips and falls with over 38 styles to choose from at prices starting at $24.98. We offer the exclusive $5000 Slip & Fall Warranty: If any employee slips and falls wearing SHOESFOR CREWS, we will reimburse your company up to $5000 on the paid workers comp claim. Call us at 1-877-667-5477 for details
Chairman of the Board: Stanley Smith
Contact: Stan Smith
s.smith@shoesforcrews.com
Estimated Sales: $ 5 - 10 Million
Number Employees: 1-4
Type of Packaging: Private Label
Brands Exported: Shoes for Crews, Mighty Mat, Crewguard
Regions Exported to: Central America, South America, Europe, Canada, Caribbean

48604 Shonna's Gourmet Goodies
320 W Center Street
West Bridgewater, MA 02379-1626   508-580-2033
Fax: 508-580-2044   888-312-7868
Frozen hors d'oeuvres
Owner/President: Howard Sherman
Estimated Sales: Less than $500,000
Square Footage: 12000
Type of Packaging: Private Label

48605 Shore Trading Co
665 Union Hill Rd
Alpharetta, GA 30004-5652   770-998-0566
Fax: 770-998-0571
Seafood
Owner: Ron Williams
ron@shoretrading.net
Owner: Marty Klausner
Estimated Sales: $1 Million
Number Employees: 1-4

48606 Shoreline Fruit
10850 E Traverse Hwy
Suite 4460
Traverse City, MI 49684-1365   231-941-4336
Fax: 231-941-4525   800-836-3972
cs@shorelinefruit.com www.shorelinefruit.com
Dried fruits, fruit juice and fruit concentrate
CEO: John Sommavilla
cs@shorelinefruit.com
Marketing Manager: Kristen Moravcik
Director, Sales & Marketing: Brian Gerberding
Number Employees: 10-19

Other Locations:
Headquarters
Traverse City, MI
Production & Storage
Williamsburg, MIHeadquartersWilliamsburg

48607 Showa-Best Glove
579 Edison St
P.O. Box 8
Menlo, GA 30731-6335   706-862-2302
Fax: 706-862-6000   800-241-0323
usa@showabestglove.com
Manufacturer and exporter of protective gloves
CEO: Bill Alico
Cmo: Tom Eggleston
teggleston@showabestglove.com
CFO: Andrew Akins
R&D: Bill Williams
Customer Service Rep: Deborah Ellenburg
Estimated Sales: $ 50 - 100 Million
Number Employees: 500-999
Regions Exported to: Worldwide

48608 Showeray Corporation
2028 E 7th St
Brooklyn, NY 11223   718-965-3633
Fax: 718-965-3647
Manufacturer, importer and exporter of tablecloths
Estimated Sales: $ 1 - 5 Million
Number Employees: 50-99
Square Footage: 120000
Regions Exported to: South America, Europe, Middle East, Carribean
Percentage of Business in Exporting: 15
Regions Imported from: Asia
Percentage of Business in Importing: 20

48609 Shrinkfast Marketing
460 Sunapee St
Newport, NH 03773-1488   603-863-7719
Fax: 603-863-6225   800-867-4746
info@shrinkfast-998.com
www.shrinkfast-998.com
Manufacturer and exporter of portable propane operated heat guns for shrinkwrap and palletizing applications
CFO: Chuck Milliken
cmilliken@ameriforge.com
Manager Sales/Marketing: Douglas Barton Jr
Estimated Sales: $ 5 - 10 Million
Number Employees: 5-9

48610 (HQ)Shuttleworth North America
10 Commercial Rd
Huntington, IN 46750-8805   260-356-8500
Fax: 260-359-7810   800-444-7412
inc@shuttleworth.com
www.collaborativeconveyor.com
Custom engineered solutions, conveyors, devices and material handling systems
President: Carol Shuttleworth
CEO: Steve Bucher
smbucher@gmail.com
Estimated Sales: $10-20 Million
Number Employees: 50-99
Number of Brands: 4
Square Footage: 9200
Parent Co: Shuttleworth
Other Locations:
Shuttleworth
Petaling JayaShuttleworth
Brands Exported: Slip-Torque; Easy Clean; Zone Control; Slip Track
Regions Exported to: Central America, South America, Europe, Asia, Middle East
Regions Imported from: Europe

48611 Si-Lodec
4611 S 134th Place
Tukwila, WA 98168-3202   206-244-6188
Fax: 714-731-2019   800-255-8274
Manufacturer and exporter of scales including mobile, portable axle and force measurement
President: Rick Beets
Director International Sales: Arthur Tyson
Number Employees: 80
Square Footage: 60000
Brands Exported: SI; Lodec; SI-Lodec
Regions Exported to: Central America, South America, Europe, Asia, Middle East
Percentage of Business in Exporting: 30

48612 (HQ)Sico Inc
7525 Cahill Rd
Minneapolis, MN 55439-2745   952-941-1700
Fax: 952-941-6688   800-328-6138
sales@sicoinc.com www.sico-wallbeds.com
Manufacturer and exporter of room service carts and mobile folding banquet and buffet tables; also, fuel-powered and electric food warmers. Also manufacture portable dance floors, and portable stages, and bellmans carts and trucks
President: Jerry Danielson
jdanielson@sicoinc.com
President: Ken Steinbauer
CFO: Keith Dahlen
Vice President, Global Sales: Jerry Danielson
Marketing: Joel Mondshane
National Sales Manager: Heidi Niesen
Vice President, Operations: James Kline
Plant Manager: Pam Heller
Estimated Sales: $20-50 Million
Number Employees: 100-249
Type of Packaging: Food Service
Other Locations:
SICO America
SingaporeSICO America
Regions Exported to: Central America, South America, Europe, Asia, Middle East, Worldwide
Percentage of Business in Exporting: 10

48613 Sico Inc
7525 Cahill Rd
Minneapolis, MN 55439-2745   952-941-1700
Fax: 952-941-6688   800-533-7426
www.sico-wallbeds.com
President: Jerry Danielson
jdanielson@sicoinc.com
Estimated Sales: $ 20 - 50 Million
Number Employees: 100-249

48614 Sid Wainer & Son Specialty
2301 Purchase St
New Bedford, MA 02746-1686   508-999-6408
Fax: 508-999-6795   888-743-9246
sidwainer@sidwainer.com www.sidwainer.com
Ostrich, Scottish smoked salmon, cheese, vinegars, preserves, olives peppers, oils and produce
Owner: Phil Spadaro
phil.spadaro@staples.com
Estimated Sales: $ 3 - 5 Million
Number Employees: 250-499
Regions Exported to: South America, Europe, Latin America, Caribbean
Brands Imported: Fondo di Trebbiano; Fondo di Toscana; Fondo di Alba; Domaine de Provence
Regions Imported from: Central America, South America, Europe, Canada, Caribbean, Mexico , Latin America

48615 Sid Wainer & Son Specialty
2301 Purchase St
New Bedford, MA 02746-1686   508-999-6408
Fax: 508-999-6795   800-423-8333
swgraph@ma.ultranet.com www.sidwainer.com
Importer and distributor of vegetables, rice, pasta, fruit, chocolate, cheese, and smoked fish
Owner: Phil Spadaro
phil.spadaro@staples.com
Estimated Sales: $ 3 - 5 Million
Number Employees: 250-499

48616 Sidney Manufacturing Co
405 N Main Ave
PO Box 380
Sidney, OH 45365-2345   937-492-4154
Fax: 937-492-0919   800-482-3535
www.sidneymanufacturing.com
Equipment used in handling wet and dry bulk materials with a customer base in industries such as grain, wood byproducts, cellulose fibers, animal feeds, pet foods, flour, pellets, powders, food products and the line. ALso manufacture aline of industrial personnel elevators from 300lbs to 1000lbs capacity four passengers.
President: Steve Baker
sbaker@sidneymfg.com
Executive Vice President: Paul Borders
Engineering Manager: Tom Gross
Design Engineer: Josh Hicks
Sales Engineer/Customer Service: Joe Swartz
Purchasing Agent: Ward Cartwright
Estimated Sales: Below $ 5 Million
Number Employees: 20-49
Square Footage: 100000
Regions Exported to: South America, Asia

Importers & Exporters / A-Z

48617 Sieb Distributor
412 Seneca Ave
Flushing, NY 11385-1453   718-417-0340
                                  Fax: 718-821-8120
Importer and wholesaler/distributor of German beer
Manager: Joseph Markovican
Estimated Sales: $2.5-5 Million
Number Employees: 1-4
Type of Packaging: Consumer, Food Service
Brands Imported: Binkelacker; Spaten; Franzis Kner
Regions Imported from: Europe

48618 Sieco USA Corporation
9014 Ruland Rd
PO Box 55485
Houston, TX 77055-4612   713-464-1726
Olive oil, stuffed olives, vinegar and gift sets
President: Sherif Cheman
Marketing: Diann Fischer
Estimated Sales: B
Number Employees: 4
Number of Brands: 2
Number of Products: 11
Square Footage: 34400
Type of Packaging: Consumer, Food Service, Private Label, Bulk
Brands Exported: Amber; Sammy's
Regions Exported to: South America
Brands Imported: Amber; Sammy's
Regions Imported from: Europe

48619 Siena Foods
16 Newbridge Road
Toronto, ON M8Z 2L7
Canada   416-239-3967
          Fax: 416-239-2084 800-465-0422
Processor, importer and exporter of Italian style meat including Genoa salami, mortadella, cappicola, prosciutto and hot and mild sausage
General Manager: Enzo DeLuca
Number Employees: 50-99
Type of Packaging: Consumer, Food Service
Regions Exported to: Central America, Asia
Percentage of Business in Exporting: 30
Regions Imported from: Europe
Percentage of Business in Importing: 10

48620 Sierra Dawn Products
1814 Empire Industrial Ct # D
Santa Rosa, CA 95403-1946   707-535-0172
          Fax: 707-588-0757 www.sierradawn.com
Manufacturer and exporter of liquid soaps, recycled packaging and household cleaning products with vegetable-based ingredients
President: Chris Maurer
chris@sierradawn.com
VP: Janet Jenkins
Estimated Sales: $1-2.5 Million
Number Employees: 1-4
Regions Exported to: Asia
Percentage of Business in Exporting: 2

48621 Sig Pack
2107 Livingston St
Oakland, CA 94606-5218   510-533-3000
          Fax: 510-534-3000 800-824-3245
                    butlerp@parsons-eagle.com
                    www.sigpacksystems.com
Manufacturer and exporter of vertical form/fill/seal machinery, linear scales and combination weighers
Regional Sales Manager: Pete Butler
Production Manager: Gary Barlettano
Estimated Sales: $ 1 - 5 Million
Number Employees: 50-100
Square Footage: 160000
Parent Co: SIG Pack International
Regions Exported to: Asia, Latin America
Percentage of Business in Exporting: 10

48622 Sigma Engineering Corporation
39 Westmoreland Ave
White Plains, NY 10606   914-682-1820
          Fax: 914-682-0599 info@sigmaus.com
                    www.sigmaus.com
Manufacturer and exporter of drum pumps and forming extruders
President: Edward Derrico
Estimated Sales: $ 5 - 10 Million
Number Employees: 5-9
Square Footage: 40000
Regions Exported to: Europe, Asia, Mexico
Percentage of Business in Exporting: 15

48623 Sigma Industries
4905 Hoffman Street
Suite B
Elkhart, IN 46516   574-295-9660
          Fax: 574-293-8552 cs@sigma-wire.com
Manufacturer and exporter of material handling equipment including pallets, pallet racks, decking and steel wire mesh containers
President: Stanley Jurasek
CFO: Stanley Jurasek
Sales Director: Jan Richardson
Estimated Sales: $ 2.5 - 5 Million
Number Employees: 10-19
Regions Exported to: Canada, Mexico
Percentage of Business in Exporting: 10

48624 Sign Classics
1014 Timothy Dr
San Jose, CA 95133-1042   408-298-1600
                                  Fax: 408-298-3177
Manufacturer and exporter of custom signs and designs including restaurant
President: Kenneth Fisher
Sales Manager: Clare Wild
Estimated Sales: $1-2.5 Million
Number Employees: 10-19
Regions Exported to: Worldwide

48625 Sign Expert
2044 Rose Ln
Pacific, MO 63069-1161   314-968-3565
          Fax: 636-257-3566 800-874-9942
                    www.signexperts.com
Manufacturer and exporter of advertising signs
President: Paul Stojeba
paul@signexperts.com
CFO: Deb Stojeba
Estimated Sales: Less than $ 500,000
Number Employees: 5-9

48626 Sign Systems, Inc.
23253 Hoover Road
Warren, MI 48089   586-758-1600
          www.signsystemsofmichigan.com
Manufacturer and exporter of metal and plastic advertising signs
Manager: Barbara Warren
Contact: Dave Sedlarz
d.sedlarz@signsystemsofmichigan.com
Type of Packaging: Consumer, Food Service, Bulk
Regions Exported to: Canada, Mexico

48627 Signature Brands LLC
808 SW 12th St
Ocala, FL 34471-0540   352-622-3134
          Fax: 352-402-9451 800-456-9573
                    info@signaturebrands.com
                    www.signaturebrands.com
Manufacturer, importer, and exporter of dessert decorating and specialty baking products. Importer of preserves.
Co-Founder: Louise Crawford
Co-Founder: Bobby Jones
Year Founded: 1951
Estimated Sales: $20 - 50 Million
Number Employees: 100-249
Square Footage: 80000
Parent Co: McCormick & Company
Type of Packaging: Consumer, Food Service, Private Label, Bulk
Brands Exported: Betty Crocker; Cake Mate; Fun! Tops
Regions Exported to: Central America, Europe, Asia, Middle East
Percentage of Business in Exporting: 5
Regions Imported from: Europe, Asia
Percentage of Business in Importing: 5

48628 Signet Marking Devices
3121 Red Hill Ave
Costa Mesa, CA 92626-4567   714-549-0341
          Fax: 714-549-0972 800-421-5150
                    sales@signetmarking.com
                    www.signetmarking.com
Manufacturer and exporter of steel type marking equipment
Owner: Melba Andrews
m.andrews@signetmarking.com
Operations Manager: Brian McGiffin
Estimated Sales: Below $5,000,000
Number Employees: 10-19
Regions Exported to: Asia
Percentage of Business in Exporting: 10

48629 Signode Industrial Group LLC
3650 W Lake Ave
Glenview, IL 60026-1215   847-724-6100
          Fax: 847-657-5323 800-323-2464
                    www.signodegroup.com
Manufacturer and exporter of protective packaging systems, equipment and consumables for steel and plastic strapping, stretch film and tape
CEO: Mark Burgess
mburgess@signodecorp.com
Director National Sales: Jeff Osisek
Manager: George Heller
Estimated Sales: $ 3 - 5 Million
Number Employees: 5000-9999
Parent Co: Illinois Tool Works
Regions Exported to: Central America, South America, Europe, Asia, Middle East

48630 Signs & Shapes Intl
2320 Paul St
Omaha, NE 68102-4030   402-331-3181
          Fax: 402-331-2729 800-806-6069
                    www.walkaroundmascots.com
Manufacturer and exporter of standard and custom cold air-inflated walk-around costumes; also, signs and character shapes; grand opening packages available
President: Lee Bowen
lee@walkaround.com
Estimated Sales: Below $5 Million
Number Employees: 20-49
Square Footage: 26000
Type of Packaging: Food Service
Brands Exported: WalkArounds
Regions Exported to: Central America, South America, Europe, Asia
Percentage of Business in Exporting: 10

48631 Silani Sweet Cheese
10 Roybridge Gate
Suite 100
Woodbridge, ON L4H 3M8
Canada   905-792-3811
          Fax: 905-792-7693 feedback@silani.ca
                    www.silanicheese.com
Processor and importer of cheese
President: Michael Talarico
CEO/VP: Joe Lanzino
Number Employees: 185
Square Footage: 100000

48632 Silent Watchman Security Services LLC
P.O. BOX 3017
Danbury, CT 06813   203-743-1876
          Fax: 203-743-9814 800-932-3822
                    info@silentwatchman.net
Manufacturer and exporter of smoke and infrared intrusion detectors, recording door locks, CCTV and multiplex security systems
President: Vincent Dascano
General Manager: Gary Sherman

48633 Silesia Grill Machines Inc
4770 County Road 16
St Petersburg, FL 33709-3130   727-544-1340
          Fax: 727-544-2821 800-237-4766
                    sales@veloxgrills.us www.veloxgrills.com
Manufacturer and exporter of high speed contact grills, crepe makers, panini grills and bucket openers
Owner: Silesia Grill
veloxgrills@aol.com
Estimated Sales: Less Than $500,000
Number Employees: 1-4
Type of Packaging: Food Service
Brands Exported: Silesia
Regions Exported to: Central America, South America, Middle East, Caribbean, Latin America, Mexico

48634 Silesia Grill Machines Inc
4770 County Road 16
St Petersburg, FL 33709-3130   727-544-1340
          Fax: 727-544-2821 800-267-4766
                    silesia@tampabay.rr.com www.veloxgrills.com
Manufacturer and exporter of high speed contact grills, crepe machines and bucket openers
Owner: Silesia Grill
veloxgrills@aol.com
Estimated Sales: Less Than $500,000
Number Employees: 1-4
Type of Packaging: Food Service
Brands Exported: Silesia

Importers & Exporters / A-Z

Regions Exported to: Central America, South America, Europe, Asia, Middle East

48635 Silgan Containers LLC
21800 Oxnard St # 600
Suite 600
Woodland Hills, CA 91367-3609 818-710-3700
Fax: 818-593-2255 www.silgancontainers.com
Plastic and aluminum closures for bottles and aluminum containers, capping machinery and feed systems
President: Thomas J Synder
tsynder@silgancontainers.com
Estimated Sales: Over $1 Billion
Number Employees: 1000-4999
Type of Packaging: Bulk
Regions Exported to: Worldwide

48636 Silgan Plastic Closure Sltns
1140 31st St
Downers Grove, IL 60515-1212 630-515-8383
Fax: 724-657-8597 800-727-8652
www.silganpcs.com
Manufacturer and exporter of tamper evident plastic bottle closures and related capping machinery
President: Tom Blaskow
CEO: Jack Watts
R&D: Borilla
Quality Control: Jee Book
Director: Bill Lauderbaugh
Sales/Marketing Manager: Don Kirk
General Manager: Alex Williams
Estimated Sales: $ 10 - 20 Million
Number Employees: 1000-4999
Parent Co: Partola Packaging
Other Locations:
 Partola Packaging
 Chino, CAPartola Packaging
Regions Exported to: Worldwide

48637 (HQ)Silgan Plastic Closure Sltns
1140 31st St
Downers Grove, IL 60515-1212 630-515-8383
Fax: 630-369-4583 800-767-8652
Manufacturer and exporter of capping equipment and closures
President: James Taylor
CEO: Kevin Kwilinski
kevin@portpack.com
CFO: Deniss Berk
CEO: Brian Bauerbach
Quality Control: Jo Beni Kisto
VP Sales/Services: Ross Markely
Number Employees: 1000-4999
Other Locations:
 Portola Packaging
 GuadalajaraPortola Packaging
Brands Exported: Cap Snap; NEPCO
Regions Exported to: Worldwide

48638 Silgan Plastics Canada
14515 North Outer Forty
Suite 210
Chesterfield, MO 63017
Canada 416-293-8233
Fax: 314-469-5387 800-274-5426
www.silganplastics.com
Manufacturer and exporter of plastic jars, bottles and closures including standard screw cap, child resistant and dispensing
National Sales Manager: David Meharg
Contact: Britt Babiarz
britt.babiarz@silganplastics.com
Estimated Sales: $ 1 - 5 Million
Number Employees: 100
Square Footage: 460000
Parent Co: Silgan Plastics Corporation
Regions Exported to: Asia
Percentage of Business in Exporting: 1

48639 Silgan White Cap LLC
1140 31st St
Downers Grove, IL 60515-1212 630-515-8383
Fax: 630-515-5326 800-515-1565
www.americas.silganwhitecap.com
Manufacturer and exporter of metal and plastic vacuum closures and related sealing equipment including cappers
CEO: Anthony J Allott
VP Sales: George Sullivan
Estimated Sales: $ 10-20 Million
Number Employees: 50-99
Square Footage: 20000
Parent Co: Schmalbach Lubecca

Type of Packaging: Bulk
Regions Exported to: Worldwide
Percentage of Business in Exporting: 15

48640 Siljans Crispy Cup Company
23 Skyline Crest NE
Calgary, AB T2K 5X2
Canada 403-275-0135
Fax: 403-275-0061 4sale@siljanscrispycup.com
www.siljanscrispycup.com
Processor and exporter of edible cups for hors d'oeuvres and desserts
President: B Ersson
CEO: Christina Ersson
Estimated Sales: $500,000
Number Employees: 5
Number of Brands: 1
Number of Products: 1
Square Footage: 32000
Type of Packaging: Consumer, Food Service, Private Label, Bulk
Brands Exported: Siljans; Eadible Hors D'oeuvres; Hafner; Salmolux

48641 Silk Road Teas
2980 Kerner Blvd # A
San Rafael, CA 94901-5588 415-458-8624
Fax: 415-458-8625 www.silkroadteas.com
Teas, herbs
Owner: Ned Heagerty
customerservice@silkroadteas.com
Number Employees: 1-4

48642 (HQ)Sillcocks Plastics International
PO Box 421
Hudson, MA 01749-0421 978-568-9000
Fax: 978-562-7128 800-526-4919
www.428main.com
Manufacturer and exporter of advertising novelties including plastic credit, debit and photo/ID cards; also, mag stripe signature panels, holography and security printing available
CEO and President: John Herslow
VP Sales/Marketing: Michele Logan
Estimated Sales: $ 3 - 5 Million
Number Employees: 10-19
Square Footage: 244000
Regions Exported to: Central America, South America, Europe, Asia, Middle East

48643 Silva Regal Spanish
512-35th St
Union City, NJ 07087 917-831-0721
Fax: 201-863-4661
Vinegar, oils, olive oils, nuts, salts, seasonings
President & CEO: Lorenzo Silva Martos

48644 Silver Fern Chemical Inc
2226 Queen Anne Ave N # C
Seattle, WA 98109-2372 206-282-3376
Fax: 206-282-0105 866-282-3384
info@silverfernchemical.com
www.silverfernchemical.com
Food chemicals and ingredients
President: Sam King
sam@silverfernchemical.com
Number Employees: 1-4

48645 Silver King Refrigeration Inc
1600 Xenium Ln N
Minneapolis, MN 55441-3706 763-923-2441
Fax: 763-553-1209 800-328-3329
info@silverking.com www.silverkingrefrig.com
Manufacturer and exporter of refrigerators, freezers, prep tables, ice cream cabinets, bulk milk and salad dispensers, display cases and fountainettes
President: Corey Kohl
Executive VP: Benjamin Rubin
Estimated Sales: $ 15 - 20 Million
Number Employees: 100-249
Parent Co: Prince Castle
Type of Packaging: Food Service
Brands Exported: Silver King
Regions Exported to: Central America, South America, Europe, Asia, Middle East

48646 (HQ)Silver Lining Seafood
5303 Shilshole Ave. N.W.
PO Box 6092
Seattle, WA 98107-4000 206-783-3818
Fax: 206-782-7195 800-426-5490
www.tridentseafoods.com

Processor and exporter of fresh, smoked and canned seafood.
Plant Manager: Leigh Gerber
Estimated Sales: $500,000-$1 Million
Number Employees: 5-9
Type of Packaging: Consumer, Food Service, Bulk
Regions Exported to: Worldwide

48647 Silver Palate Kitchens
221 Knickerbocker Rd
Cresskill, NJ 201-568-0110
www.silverpalate.com
Vinegars, oils, chutneys, mustards, savories, sweet sauces, preserves, brandied fruits, salad dressings, pasta sauces, oatmeals and berry cereals.
President & CEO: Peter Harris
Estimated Sales: $20-50 Million
Number Employees: 20-49
Type of Packaging: Consumer, Food Service, Private Label, Bulk
Regions Exported to: Europe

48648 Silver Spring Foods
2424 Alpine Road
Eau Clair, MI 54703
Fax: 715-830-9702 800-826-7322
info@bredefoods.com silverspringfoods.com
Processor and exporter of horseradish and horseradish sauce, as well as other specialty sauces including mustards, siracha, tartar, and wasabi sauces.
Chairman/CEO: Nancy Bartusch
Distribution & Warehouse Manager: Allyssa Fradette
Estimated Sales: $630,000
Number Employees: 5-9
Square Footage: 36000
Parent Co: Hunsinger Farms, Inc.
Type of Packaging: Consumer, Food Service, Private Label, Bulk
Regions Exported to: Canada
Percentage of Business in Exporting: 4

48649 Silver Springs Citrus Inc
25411 Mare Ave
Howey-in-the-Hills, FL 34737 610-793-0266
800-940-2277
bhughes@aol.com www.healthysqueezejuices.com
Manufacturer, importer and exporter of juices.
Treasurer: Michael Hall
Human Resources: Debra Fontaine
Operations Manager: Patrick Falcone
Purchasing Director: Pat Patrick
Estimated Sales: $35.1 Million
Number Employees: 100-249
Square Footage: 1260
Type of Packaging: Consumer, Food Service, Private Label, Bulk
Regions Exported to: Europe
Percentage of Business in Exporting: 2
Regions Imported from: Asia
Percentage of Business in Importing: 2

48650 Silver Weibull
14800 E Moncrieff Place
Aurora, CO 80011-1211 303-373-2311
Fax: 303-373-2319
Manufacturer and exporter of sugar centrifugals, reheaters and crystallizers
Manager Technical Process: Tommy Persson
Business Unit Manager (Worldwide): Derrald Houston
Manager: Randy Copsey
Estimated Sales: Below $ 5 Million
Number Employees: 3
Square Footage: 200000
Parent Co: Consolidated Process Machinery
Brands Exported: Silver-Weibull
Regions Exported to: Central America, South America, Europe, Asia
Percentage of Business in Exporting: 65

48651 Silverfern Specialties
Fair Lawn, NJ 07410 201-916-2803
Pavlova and meringues

48652 Silverland Bakery
439 Des Plaines Ave
Forest Park, IL 60130 708-488-0800
Fax: 708-488-0894 info@silverlandbakery.com
silverlandbakery.com
Brownies, bars, cookies and cakes.
Owner & President: Athena Uslander

Importers & Exporters / A-Z

Type of Packaging: Consumer, Food Service, Private Label

48653 Silverson Machines Inc
355 Chestnut St
PO Box 589
East Longmeadow, MA 01028-2702   413-525-4825
Fax: 413-525-5804   800-204-6400
fran@silverson.com   www.silverson.com
Manufacturer, supplier and exporter of food processing equipment including blending and batching equipment, high shear mixers, colloid mills and homogenizers; also, laboratory equipment and supplies
President: Harold Rothman
Clerk/VP: David Rothman
VP: Anne Rothman
Sales Manager: Brian Martin
IT: Frances Carhart
fran@silverson.com
General Manager: Michael Boyd
Estimated Sales: $2.6 Million
Number Employees: 10-19
Parent Co: Silverson Machines
Regions Exported to: Worldwide
Percentage of Business in Exporting: 40

48654 Simco Foods
1180 S Beverly Dr Ste 509
Los Angeles, CA 90035   310-284-8446
Fax: 310-284-8221   info@simco.us
www.simco.us
Tuna, pineapple, mandarins, olives, olive oil, artichokes, mushrooms, peppers, sardines, mackerel, peaches, pears, fruit cocktail, corn and green beans.
President: David Sims
Contact: John Ashworth
john@simco.us
Estimated Sales: $ 10 - 20 Million
Number Employees: 12
Number of Brands: 3
Number of Products: 200
Square Footage: 16000
Type of Packaging: Consumer, Food Service, Private Label, Bulk
Brands Imported: Stella, First Harvest, Sims
Regions Imported from: South America, Europe, Asia, Middle East
Percentage of Business in Importing: 20

48655 (HQ)Simkar Corp
700 Ramona Ave
Philadelphia, PA 19120   215-831-7700
Fax: 215-831-7703   www.simkar.com
Manufacturer and exporter of lighting fixtures including fluorescent, vaporproof, H.I.D., parabolic deep cell, waterproof, strip, undershelf display and overhead.
Chief Executive Officer: Glenn Grunewald
Year Founded: 1952
Estimated Sales: $100-$500 Million
Number Employees: 500-999
Square Footage: 275000
Type of Packaging: Consumer, Food Service, Private Label, Bulk
Other Locations:
  Simkar Corp.
  Philadelpia, PASimkar Corp.
Brands Exported: Simkar
Regions Exported to: Central America, South America, Middle East
Percentage of Business in Exporting: 5

48656 (HQ)Simmons Engineering Corporation
1200 Willis Ave
Wheeling, IL 60090   847-419-9800
Fax: 847-419-1500   800-252-3381
sales@simcut.com   www.simcut.com
Manufacturer and exporter of cutting knives and blades for bread, cake, fish, fruit, vegetables and meat products
President/Owner: Bruce Gillian
VP/General Manager: Colin Murphy
Customer Service & Marketing Manager: Erin O'Brien
Contact: Lorenzo Barrios
l.barrios@simcut.com
Estimated Sales: $ 5 - 10 Million
Number Employees: 50-99
Square Footage: 60000
Brands Exported: Tru-Trak
Regions Exported to: Central America, South America, Europe, Asia, Middle East, Canada
Percentage of Business in Exporting: 20

48657 (HQ)Simmons Foods Inc
601 N Hico St
Siloam Springs, AR 72761-2410   479-524-8151
Fax: 479-524-6562   888-831-7007
Chicken including; boneless skinless tenderloins and breasts, breaded tenderloins, chicken wings, fully cooked, ready to cook, frozen, fresh, marinated, glazed, grill marked, portioning and pack sizes
President: Tammy Bomar
tbomar@marykay.com
CFO: Mike Jones
Director Research & Development: Brian Davis
Marketing Manager: Joseph Meszaros
VP Sales: Chip Miller
Director of Public Relations: Mary Doyle
Plant Manager: Brian Burke
Number Employees: 100-249
Square Footage: 120000
Type of Packaging: Consumer, Food Service, Private Label, Bulk
Regions Exported to: Worldwide

48658 Simolex Rubber Corp
14505 Keel St
Plymouth, MI 48170-6002   734-453-4500
Fax: 734-453-6120   info@simolex.com
www.simolex.com
Manufacturer and exporter of rubber products including beverage hoses, juice tubing, milk hoses, gaskets, seals and bottle stoppers
President: Bob Dungarani
info@simolexrubber.com
Estimated Sales: $10-20 Million
Number Employees: 20-49
Square Footage: 50000
Type of Packaging: Food Service
Regions Exported to: Canada, Mexico
Percentage of Business in Exporting: 20

48659 Simonds International
135 Intervale Rd
PO Box 500
Fitchburg, MA 01420-6519
Canada   978-345-7521
Fax: 978-424-2212   nlaflamme@simondsint.com
www.simondsinternational.com
Manufacturer, exporter and importer of knives for packaging and food processing equipment, cryovac, etc
President: Roy Erdwins
roy.erdwins@simondsinternational.com
Sales Manager: Fred Adams
Number Employees: 100-249
Square Footage: 60000
Parent Co: IKS International
Regions Exported to: Worldwide
Regions Imported from: Worldwide
Percentage of Business in Importing: 45

48660 Simonds International
135 Intervale Rd
P.O. Box 500
Fitchburg, MA 01420-6519   978-345-7521
Fax: 978-424-2212   800-343-1616
www.simondsinternational.com
Manufacturer and exporter of band and hack saws and saw blades, circular machine knives, files and investment castings
President: Roy Erdwins
roy.erdwins@simondsinternational.com
Chairman: John Consentino
Chief Financial Officer: Henry Botticello
Vice President: Chip Holm
Engineering & R&D Manager: Rick Brautt
Vice President, Sales & Marketing: David Miles
Sales Manager: Tim House
Operations Supervisor: Dick Vain
Plant Manager: Roy Erdwins
Purchasing Agent: Valerie Johnson
Estimated Sales: $ 83 Million
Number Employees: 100-249
Square Footage: 400000
Regions Exported to: Central America, South America, Europe, Asia

48661 Simonian Fruit Company
350 N 7th St
Fowler, CA 93625   559-834-5921
Fax: 559-834-2363
Exporter and wholesaler/distributor of fresh fruit including grapes, plums, peaches, pomegranates and apricots; serving the food service market
President: David Simonian

Estimated Sales: $10-20 Million
Number Employees: 100-249
Type of Packaging: Consumer, Food Service, Bulk
Regions Exported to: Worldwide

48662 Simoniz USA Inc
201 Boston Tpke
Bolton, CT 06043-7203   860-646-0172
Fax: 860-645-6070   800-227-5536
wgorra@simonizusa.com   www.simonizusa.com
Manufacturer and exporter of waterless hand cleaners, soap and specialty chemicals
President: William Gorra
CEO: Mark Kershaw
mkershaw@simonizusa.com
VP Marketing: Michele O'Neal
Estimated Sales: F
Number Employees: 50-99
Percentage of Business in Exporting: 8

48663 Simplex Filler Co
640 Airpark Rd # A
Napa, CA 94558-7569   707-265-6801
Fax: 707-265-6868   800-796-7539
www.simplexfiller.com
Manufacturer and exporter of piston and pressure fillers for bottle, can, jar and bag filling; also, conveyors, unscramblers, lid droppers, accumulators and heated hoppers
CEO: G Donald Murray
Estimated Sales: $1-5 Million
Number Employees: 10-19
Square Footage: 30000
Parent Co: Wild Horse Industrial Corporation
Brands Exported: Simplex
Regions Exported to: South America, Asia, Middle East
Percentage of Business in Exporting: 30

48664 Simplex Time Recorder Company
1936 E Deere Avenue
Suite 120
Santa Ana, CA 92705-5732   949-724-5000
Fax: 978-630-7856
Manufacturer and exporter of fire alarms and time recorders
General Manager: Russell Stafford
Area/Branch Manager: Gary Holmes
Estimated Sales: $ 1 - 5 Million
Number Employees: 100
Brands Exported: Simplex
Regions Exported to: Worldwide

48665 Simplex Time Recorder Company
1936 E Deere Avenue
Suite 120
Santa Ana, CA 92705-5732   949-724-5000
Fax: 978-630-7856   800-746-7539
Manufacturer and exporter of fire alarm and security systems
General Manager: Russell Stafford
Estimated Sales: $ 1 - 5 Million
Number Employees: 20
Regions Exported to: Worldwide

48666 Simplimatic Automation
1046 W London Park Dr
Forest, VA 24551   434-385-9181
Fax: 434-385-7813   800-294-2003
sales@simplimatic.com   www.simplimatic.com
Manufacturer and exporter of product handling equipment including tray film packaging systems, palletizers and de-palletizers, rinsers and conveyor systems.
Chief Executive Officer: Tom DiNardo
Year Founded: 1965
Estimated Sales: $100+ Million
Number Employees: 51-200
Square Footage: 60000
Regions Exported to: Central America, South America, Europe, Asia, Middle East
Percentage of Business in Exporting: 50

48667 Simpson & Vail
3 Quarry Rd
Brookfield, CT 06804-1053   203-775-0240
Fax: 203-775-0462   800-282-8327
info@svtea.com   www.svtea.com
Processor, exporter and importer of coffee and gourmet tea
President: Jim Harron Jr
CEO: Joan Harron

577

Importers & Exporters / A-Z

Estimated Sales: $ .5 - 1 million
Number Employees: 5-9
Square Footage: 32000
Type of Packaging: Food Service
Regions Exported to: Worldwide
Percentage of Business in Exporting: 15
Regions Imported from: Europe, Asia, Canada
Percentage of Business in Importing: 80

48668 Simpson Imports
93 Old York Rd
Suite 1-560
Jenkintown, PA 19046-3925 201-353-3100
 Fax: 201-353-3100 www.simpsonbrands.com
Sauces, seasonings, canned fruits and vegetables
CEO: William Toll
Estimated Sales: $1 Million
Number Employees: 5
Brands Imported: SMT

48669 Sims Machinery Co Inc
3621 45th St SW
PO Box 446
Lanett, AL 36863-6305 334-576-2101
 Fax: 334-576-3116 sales@simsmachinery.com
 www.simsmachinery.com
Manufacturer and exporter of stainless steel food grade tanks; also, custom stainless steel fabrications available
CEO: Lynn Duncan
Sales Manager: Bryant Hollon
Estimated Sales: $5-10 Million
Number Employees: 10-19
Square Footage: 80000
Regions Exported to: Worldwide
Percentage of Business in Exporting: 10

48670 Sinbad Sweets
2401 West Almond Avenue
Madera, CA 93637 559-298-3700
 Fax: 559-298-9194 866-746-2232
 www.sinbadsweets.com
Pastries including baklava, strudel, tarts and fillo; exporter of baklava
President: Michael Muhawir
CEO: Edwina Aquino Seidel
COO: Anita Reina
Vice President: John Seidel
Public Relations: Sascha Muhawi
Operations Manager: Larry Burrow
Production Manager: Klaus Gernet
Number Employees: 50-99
Square Footage: 120000
Type of Packaging: Consumer, Food Service, Private Label, Bulk
Brands Exported: Sinbad Sweets
Regions Exported to: Central America, South America, Asia, Middle East, Canada
Percentage of Business in Exporting: 10

48671 Sinclair Trading
1204 E 8th St
Los Angeles, CA 90021-1514 213-627-6063
 Fax: 213-627-5340
Wholesaler/distributor and importer of Caribbean and African foods including Jamaican coffee
President: Lloyd Sinclair
CEO: Esperanza Sinclair
CFO: Alton McQueen
Sales Director: Michael Newman
Public Relations: Dave Sinclair
Purchasing Manager: Lloyd Sinclair
Estimated Sales: $5 Million
Number Employees: 10-19
Square Footage: 20000
Type of Packaging: Consumer, Private Label
Regions Exported to: Central America, South America, West Indies
Regions Imported from: Central America, Europe, Asia, Africa

48672 Sinco
3965 Pepin Avenue
Red Wing, MN 55066-1837 860-632-0500
 Fax: 860-632-1509 800-243-6753
Manufacturer and exporter of safety netting systems for guarding material handling equipment including conveyors, pallet racks, etc
President: David Denny
Estimated Sales: $ 10 - 20 Million
Number Employees: 40
Regions Exported to: Worldwide
Percentage of Business in Exporting: 1

48673 Sine Pump
14845 W 64th Ave
Arvada, CO 80007-7523 303-425-0800
 Fax: 303-425-0896 888-504-8301
 pumps@sundyne.com www.sinepump.com
Manufacturer and exporter of sanitary positive displacement pumps for the food and dairy industries including low-shear, low-pulsation and high-suction. designs, manufactures and supports industrial pump and compressor products for the process fluid and gas industries
President: William Taylor
Human Resources: Christine Lopez
Area Sales Manager: Brad Juntunen
After Market Specialist: Chuck Zachrich
Number Employees: 500-999
Parent Co: Sundyne Corporation
Brands Exported: Sine Pump
Regions Exported to: Central America, South America, Canada, Mexico, Latin America
Percentage of Business in Exporting: 10

48674 Singleton Seafood
P.O.Box 2819
Tampa, FL 33601-2819 813-719-6626
 Fax: 813-247-1782 800-732-3663
 info@tbfish.com
Frozen shrimp, breaded fish and shrimp, peeled and deveined shrimp, cooked shrimp, shrimp specialties
President: Dennis Reeves
CFO: Andrew Hawaux
Vice President: Rob Sharpe
Research & Development: Nina Burt
Quality Control: Don Toloday
Marketing Director: Dan Davis
Sales Director: Doug Knudsen
Production Manager: Bill Jacks
Plant Manager: Mike Pent
Purchasing Manager: Bill Stone
Estimated Sales: $300,000-500,000
Number Employees: 1-4
Number of Brands: 8
Number of Products: 200
Square Footage: 800000
Parent Co: ConAgra Foods
Type of Packaging: Consumer, Food Service, Private Label, Bulk

48675 Sini Fulvi U.S.A.
136 Mohawk St
Newark, NJ 07114-3314 973-274-0822
 Fax: 718-361-6999 sinifulvi@aol.com
Importer of Italian, Spanish and Portuguese cheeses and Italian cured meats
President: Agostino Sini
Vice President: Pierluigi Sini
Marketing Director: Michele Buster
Estimated Sales: $ .5 - 1 million
Number Employees: 4
Parent Co: Sini Fulvi
Type of Packaging: Consumer, Food Service, Bulk
Regions Exported to: Canada
Percentage of Business in Exporting: 5
Brands Imported: Fulvi; Sini; Buonatavola
Regions Imported from: Europe
Percentage of Business in Importing: 100

48676 Sioux Corp
1 Sioux Plz
Beresford, SD 57004-1500 605-763-3333
 Fax: 605-763-3334 888-763-8833
 email@sioux.com www.sioux.com
Manufacturer and exporter of hot, cold and combination pressure washers and steam cleaners; also, all-electric and explosion-proof units available
President/Owner: Jack Finger
CEO: Amanda Cooper
acooper@sioux.eu
Marketing Manager: Jessica Johnson
Sales Manager: Meg Andersen
Regional Manager - International Sales (: David Nelson
Estimated Sales: $ 2.5-5 Million
Number Employees: 20-49
Number of Products: 500+
Brands Exported: Sioux
Regions Exported to: Central America, South America, Europe, Asia, Middle East
Percentage of Business in Exporting: 25

48677 Sioux Honey Assn.
301 Lewis Blvd
Sioux City, IA 51101-2237 712-258-0638
 Fax: 712-258-1332 www.suebee.com
Honey collective with more than 300 members.
President & CEO: David Allibone
CEO: Lisa Hansel
lhansel@suebeehoney.com
Year Founded: 1921
Number Employees: 100-249
Type of Packaging: Consumer, Food Service, Private Label, Bulk
Other Locations:
 Processing Plant
 Sioux City, IA
 Processing Plant
 Anaheim, CA
 Processing Plant
 Elizabethtown, NC Processing Plant Anaheim
Regions Exported to: Worldwide

48678 Sipco Products
4301 Prospect Road
Peoria Heights, IL 61616-6537 309-682-5400
 Fax: 309-637-5120 terry@sipcoproducts.com
 www.pnduniforms.com
Ashtray receptacles, smoking urns, safety related items, wire racks and plastic bag holders; exporter of ashtray receptacles
President: Eileen Grawey
Office Manager: Audrey Wylie
Contact: Sharon Brick
sharon@sipcoproducts.com
Estimated Sales: $ 3 - 5 Million
Number Employees: 1-4
Square Footage: 40000
Type of Packaging: Food Service
Brands Exported: Sipco Dunking Station
Regions Exported to: Europe, Canada
Percentage of Business in Exporting: 5

48679 Sirco Systems
2828 Messer Airport Highway
Birmingham, AL 35203 205-731-7800
 Fax: 205-731-7885
Manufacturer and exporter of food storage equipment including steel drums
VP Sales: Jack Matheson
Estimated Sales: $5-10 Million
Number Employees: 50-99
Parent Co: Jemison Investment Company

48680 Sirocco Enterprises Inc
228 Industrial Ave
New Orleans, LA 70121-2904 504-834-1549
 Fax: 504-837-7762 www.siroccoenterprises.com
Manufacturer and exporter of ready-to-use liquid cocktail mixers
Vice President: Anthony Muto
VP: Anthony Muto
Production: Benny Peel
Estimated Sales: $1 Million
Number Employees: 10-19
Number of Brands: 1
Number of Products: 10
Square Footage: 52000
Type of Packaging: Food Service
Brands Exported: Pat O'Brien's Cocktail Mixers
Regions Exported to: Central America
Percentage of Business in Exporting: 2

48681 Sisson Imports
1520 15th St NW Ste 120
Auburn, WA 98001 253-939-1520
 Fax: 253-939-1099 800-423-2756
Importer of porcelain trays and flatware
President: Mary Sisson
Estimated Sales: $500,000-$1 Million
Number Employees: 5-9
Type of Packaging: Food Service
Brands Imported: Revol
Regions Imported from: France
Percentage of Business in Importing: 100

48682 Sisu Group Inc
8252 South Harvard Avenue
Suite 157
Tulsa, OK 74137 918-495-1364
 Fax: 918-746-7010 info@sisugrp.com
 www.sisugrp.com
Wholesaler/distributor and exporter of condiments and condiment dispensing equipment; serving the food service market
President: Kim Berghall
kberghall@sisugrp.com
CEO: Mike Boudreaux
Advertising Director: Lisa Roth
Type of Packaging: Food Service

Importers & Exporters / A-Z

48683 Sitma USA
Via Vignolese
Spilamberto, MO 41057　　　　390-597-8031
　　　　　　　Fax: 390-597-8030　800-728-1254
　　　　　　　sitmausa@sitma.com　www.sitma.com
Manufacturer and importer of packaging equipment including horizontal form, fill and seal systems and bundle wrappers
President: Aris Ballestrazzi
CEO/Managing Director: Pete Butikis
National Sales Manager: Al Lindsay
Estimated Sales: $ 2.5 - 5 Million
Number Employees: 10-19
Square Footage: 66000
Parent Co: Sitma Machinery SPA
Other Locations:
　Sitma USA
　BP 28-77013 Melun CedexSitma USA
Regions Imported from: Italy
Percentage of Business in Importing: 100

48684 (HQ)Skd Distribution Corp
13010 180th St
Jamaica, NY 11434-4108　　　　718-525-6000
　　　　　　　Fax: 718-276-4595　800-458-8753
　　　　　　　rachel@skdparty.com　www.biggiftbow.com
Manufacturer and exporter of plastic molders and fabricators, rigid foam fillers, wedges and foam packing inserts for boxes
Manager: Richard Mark
VP: Jack Schnitt
Marketing: Bill Stephan
Contact: Stanley Ast
sast@skdparty.com
Estimated Sales: $ 5-10 Million
Number Employees: 20-49
Square Footage: 1080000
Regions Exported to: Central America, South America, Asia
Percentage of Business in Exporting: 12

48685 Skim Delux Mendenhall Laboratories
715 Morton St
Paris, TN 38242-4296　　　　731-642-9321
　　　　　　　Fax: 731-644-3398　800-642-9321
Processor and exporter of dairy analogs, formulas and flavors for calcium-fortified milk, juice and fruit drink beverages; also, chocolate milkshake mixes
Owner: David Travis
Sales Assistant: Melissa Taylor
Estimated Sales: $500,000-$1 Million
Number Employees: 5-9
Type of Packaging: Bulk
Regions Exported to: South America

48686 (HQ)Skrmetta Machinery Corporation
3536 Lowerline Street
New Orleans, LA 70125-1004　　　　504-488-4413
　　　　　　　Fax: 504-488-4432
Manufacturer and exporter of shrimp peeling and deveining machinery
President: Eric Skrmetta
VP: Dennis Skrmetta
Estimated Sales: $5,800,000
Number Employees: 55
Square Footage: 40000
Other Locations:
　Skrmetta Machinery Corp.
　New Orleans, LASkrmetta Machinery Corp.
Regions Exported to: Worldwide

48687 Skylark Meats
4430 S 110th St
Omaha, NE 68137-1235　　　　402-592-0300
　　　　　　　Fax: 402-592-1414　800-759-5275
　　　　　　　skysales@americanfoodsgroup.com
　　　　　　　www.skylarkmeats.com
Corned beef and liver.
President: Paul Weiss
Chief Executive Officer: James Leonard
jamesleonard@skylarkmeats.com
Quality Assurance Manager: Jack Warner
Marketing Manager: Steve Giroux
VP Sales: John O'Brien
Human Resources Managers: Shane Keith
Operations Executive: Brayton Howard
Production Manager: Ray Marquez
Purchasing Manager: Barb Bevington
Year Founded: 1970
Estimated Sales: $41.1 Million
Number Employees: 250-499
Square Footage: 175000
Parent Co: Rosen's Diversified
Type of Packaging: Consumer, Food Service
Regions Exported to: Europe, Asia, Canada, Mexico
Percentage of Business in Exporting: 10

48688 Skymart Enterprises
8725 Naomi Ave
San Gabriel, CA 91775　　　　626-286-3742
　　　　　　　Fax: 626-285-6842
Exporter, importer and wholesaler/distributor of food ingredients
Owner: Gene Chen

48689 Slade Gorton & Co Inc
225 Southampton St
Boston, MA 02118　　　　617-442-5800
　　　　　　　Fax: 617-442-9090　800-225-1573
　　　　　　　sales@sladegorton.com　www.sladegorton.com
Wholesaler/distributor, importer and exporter of fresh and frozen shellfish and salt and smoked fish; serving the food service market and supermarket chains.
Chairman: Mike Gorton, Sr.
President & CEO: Kimberly Gorton
Vice President & National Accounts: Mike Gorton, Jr.
VP, Retail Sales & Product Development: Rachel Fitzgerald
VP, Fresh Business Development: Patrice Flanagan
Chief Operating Officer: Maureen Taylor
Year Founded: 1928
Estimated Sales: $54 Million
Number Employees: 100-249
Square Footage: 35000
Parent Co: Sg Seafood Holdings, Inc.
Type of Packaging: Consumer, Food Service, Bulk
Other Locations:
　Slade Gorton & Co.
　Maitland, FLSlade Gorton & Co.
Brands Exported: Icybay; Tem Tasty; Sea-Tasty
Regions Exported to: Europe, Asia
Regions Imported from: Central America, South America, Europe, Asia, Middle East

48690 Slautterback Corporation
11475 Lakefield Drive
Duluth, GA 30097-1511　　　　831-373-3900
　　　　　　　Fax: 831-373-0385　800-827-3308
　　　　　　　www.slautterback.com
Manufacturer and exporter of hot melt adhesive packaging equipment
President: Fred Erler
President, Chief Executive Officer: Michael Hilton
Marketing Manager: Jim Pagnella
Vice President of Systems: Douglas Bloomfield
Number Employees: 135
Square Footage: 252000
Parent Co: Nordson Corporation
Regions Exported to: Worldwide

48691 Sleeman Breweries, Ltd.
551 Clair Rd W
Guelph, ON N1L 1E9
Canada　　　　519-822-1834
　　　　　　　800-268-8537
　　　　　　　www.sleemanbreweries.ca
Beer, ale, & lager
President: Kenny Sadai
VP, Sales & Marketing: Greg Newbrough
Year Founded: 1834
Estimated Sales: $92.5 Million
Number Employees: 1,000
Square Footage: 98328
Parent Co: Sapporo Holdings Limited
Type of Packaging: Consumer, Food Service
Regions Exported to: United States

48692 Slicechief Co
3333 Maple St
P.O. Box 80206
Toledo, OH 43608-1147　　　　419-241-7647
　　　　　　　Fax: 419-241-3513
Manufacturer and exporter of nonelectric vegetable/fruit slicers and cheese shredders
President: Sue Brown
Estimated Sales: $2.5-5 Million
Number Employees: 1-4
Type of Packaging: Food Service
Regions Exported to: South America, Europe, Asia, Middle East, Canada, Caribbean, Latin America, Mexico

48693 Slip Not
2545 Beaufait St
Detroit, MI 48207-3467　　　　313-923-0400
　　　　　　　Fax: 313-923-4555　800-754-7668
　　　　　　　info@slipnot.com　www.slipnot.com
SlipNOT manufactures NSF registered stainless steel slip resistant flooring products from floor plates, drain covers, bar grating, ladder rungs/covers, to stair treads/covers, perforated and expanded metal retrofit plates. SlipNOTproducts can withstand the extreme cold of cyrogenics and heat of cookers, as well as caustic cleaning agents.
President: William S Molnar
National Sales Manager: Brian Pelto
Estimated Sales: $ .5 - 1 million
Number Employees: 20-49
Parent Co: WS Monar Comapany
Regions Exported to: Worldwide

48694 Slip-Not Belting Corporation
PO Box 386
Kingsport, TN 37662　　　　423-246-8141
　　　　　　　Fax: 423-246-7728
Manufacturer and exporter of leather, plastic and perlon transmission and conveyor belting
President/CEO: David Shivell
CEO: Phill Shivell
Marketing: David Shivell
Estimated Sales: $ 3 - 5 Million
Number Employees: 5-9
Regions Exported to: Canada

48695 Smarties
1091 Lousons Rd
Union, NJ 07083-5029　　　　908-964-0660
　　　　　　　Fax: 908-964-0911　800-631-7968
　　　　　　　www.smarties.com
Manufacturer of Smarties, the iconic Halloween candy.
Vice President, Management: Jessica Dee
Vice President, Communications: Liz Dee
Vice President, Operations: Sarah Dee
Estimated Sales: $10-20 Million
Number Employees: 100
Type of Packaging: Consumer
Brands Imported: Smarties
Regions Imported from: Europe

48696 Smeltzer Orchard Co
6032 Joyfield Rd
Frankfort, MI 49635-9163　　　　231-882-4421
　　　　　　　Fax: 231-882-4430　info@smeltzerorchards.com
　　　　　　　www.smeltzerorchards.com
Processor and exporter of frozen apples, apple juice, asparagus and cherries; also, dried blueberries, cherries, apples, strawberries and cranberries
President: Tim Brian
info@smeltzerorchards.com
Plant Manager: Mike Henschell
Estimated Sales: $9.3 Million
Number Employees: 50-99
Type of Packaging: Food Service

48697 Smetco
PO Box 560
14633 Ottaway Rd NE
Aurora, OR 97002　　　　503-678-3081
　　　　　　　Fax: 503-678-3095　800-253-5400
　　　　　　　www.smetco.com
Manufacturer and exporter of pallet handling systems for sorting and repair; also, conveyors, scissor lifts, dispensers, stackers and turn tables
President: John Smet
CFO: Kelly Wick
Vice President: John Smets
Marketing Director: Ken Butler
Contact: Carolyn Herman
carolynh@smetco.com
Estimated Sales: $1-3 Million
Number Employees: 20-49
Square Footage: 116000
Brands Exported: Smetco
Regions Exported to: Worldwide
Percentage of Business in Exporting: 20

48698 Smico Manufacturing Co Inc
6101 Camille Ave
Oklahoma City, OK 73149-5036　　　　405-946-1461
　　　　　　　Fax: 405-946-1472　800-351-9088
　　　　　　　www.smico.com
Manufacturer and exporter of vibrating screens and gyratory sifters

Importers & Exporters / A-Z

President: Randall Stoner
smico@smico.com
CEO: Erick Held
VP: Tim Douglass
Sales: Holly Lindsey
Operations: Randall Stoner
Purchasing Director: Jane Wenk
Estimated Sales: $ 5 - 10 Million
Number Employees: 20-49
Square Footage: 92000
Regions Exported to: Central America, South America, Europe, Asia
Percentage of Business in Exporting: 15

48699 Smirk's
17601 US Hwy 34
Fort Morgan, CO 80701   970-762-0202
   Fax: 877-682-1065   www.smirksbrand.com
Dried fruits, nuts, grains, seeds, flour and bird food
President: Nicholas Erker
nerker@smirksbrand.com
Chief Financial Officer: Cindy Schmid
Director, Quality Assurance: Jesse Bellefeuille
Sales: Jason Strauch
Chief Operations Officer: Eric Nickell
Number Employees: 2-10
Type of Packaging: Bulk
Brands Exported: Smirk's
Regions Exported to: Worldwide
Brands Imported: Dried fruits
Regions Imported from: Worldwide

48700 Smith Frozen Foods Inc
101 Depot St
Weston, OR 97886   541-566-3515
   Fax: 541-566-3707   www.smithfrozenfoods.com
Frozen vegetables including baby lima beans, diced and sliced carrots, kernel corn, corn-on-the-cob and peas
President & CFO: Gary Crowder
Co-Owner: Sharon Smith
Co-Owner: Gordon Smith
Corporate Controller: Rebecca Hatley
Director, Business Development: Ken Porter
Director, Quality Control & Assurance: John Humble
VP, Sales & Marketing: Kent Perkes
Sales Office Manager: Shelly Hall
VP, Logistics & Packaging: Aaron Ware
Warehouse Operations: Kelly Hahn
Director, Purchasing: Sandra Stewart
Year Founded: 1919
Estimated Sales: $85 Million
Number Employees: 250-499
Number of Brands: 1
Type of Packaging: Consumer, Food Service, Private Label, Bulk
Brands Exported: Smith; Mountain Meadows; Buyer's Label
Regions Exported to: Central America, South America, Europe, Asia, Middle East
Percentage of Business in Exporting: 15

48701 Smith Packaging
6045 Kestrel Road
Mississauga, ON L5T 1Y8
Canada   905-564-6640
   Fax: 905-564-5681
Manufacturer and exporter of boxes, cartons and containers
President: Mervin Hillier
Operations Manager: Gerard Gregoire
Number Employees: 100
Type of Packaging: Consumer, Bulk
Regions Exported to: USA

48702 (HQ)Smith Packing Regional Meat
105-125 Washington Street
P.O. Box 520
Utica, NY 13503-0520   315-732-5125
   Fax: 315-732-1166   sales@smithpacking.com
   www.smithpacking.com
Meat: beef, pork, veal, lamb, chicken and turkey; eggs, ham, bacon, frankfurters, sausage, kielbasa and turkey breast
President: Wesley Smith
VP: Mark Smith
Estimated Sales: $12.6 Million
Number Employees: 1-4
Square Footage: 150000
Type of Packaging: Private Label
Regions Exported to: Worldwide

48703 (HQ)Smith Restaurant SupplyCo
500 Erie Blvd E
Syracuse, NY 13202-1109   315-474-8731
   Fax: 315-478-7004   800-346-2556
   www.smithrestaurantsupply.com
Wholesaler/distributor of food service equipment and supplies including coffee, gourmet housewares and cutlery; importer of cutlery and home beer brewery equipment and supplies; serving the food service market
President: John Kuppermann
accounting@smithrestaurantsupply.com
President: Ellison Kuppermann
Sales Manager: Robin Russell
Estimated Sales: $10-20 Million
Number Employees: 5-9
Square Footage: 130000
Type of Packaging: Food Service
Brands Imported: M.J. Kupper
Regions Imported from: Europe
Percentage of Business in Importing: 1

48704 Smith-Lee Company
2920 N Main St.
PO Box 2038
Oshkosh, WI 54901   315-363-2500
   Fax: 315-363-9573   800-327-9774
   marketing@hoffmaster.com
Manufacturer and exporter of paper plates, place mats, napkins, bottle caps and packaged lace and linen doilies
President: Jonathan M Groat
VP Sales: Thomas Hennessey
VP Manufacturing: Alan Mattei
Estimated Sales: $10-20 Million
Number Employees: 50-99
Parent Co: Hoffmaster Group, Inc
Regions Exported to: Europe, Middle East

48705 Smith-Lustig Paper Box Manufacturing
2165 E 31st St
Cleveland, OH 44115   216-621-0454
   Fax: 216-621-0483
Manufacturer and exporter of paper boxes
President: Richard Ames
Contact: Jim Di Francesco
jdifrancesco@smithlustigbox.com
Estimated Sales: $5-10 Million
Number Employees: 20-49
Regions Exported to: Worldwide

48706 Smithfield Foods Inc.
200 Commerce St.
Smithfield, VA 23430   757-365-3000
   www.smithfieldfoods.com
Pork processor and hog producer.
President/CEO: Kenneth Sullivan
kennethsullivan@smithfieldfoods.com
Executive VP/CFO: Glenn Nunziata
COO, U.S. Operations: Dennis Organ
Year Founded: 1936
Estimated Sales: Over $1 Billion
Number Employees: 54,000
Number of Brands: 14
Number of Products: 200
Parent Co: WH Group Limited
Type of Packaging: Consumer, Food Service, Private Label
Regions Exported to: Worldwide

48707 Smitty's Snowballs
29124 Catholic Hall Road
Hammond, LA 70403-8380   225-567-7983
   smithwarren@yahoo.com
Wholesaler/distributor and exporter of snow cone syrup, shaved and flavored ice
Regions Exported to: Africa

48708 Smokaroma
62 Bar-B-Que Avenue
P.O.Box 25
Boley, OK 74829-0025   918-667-3341
   Fax: 918-667-3935   800-331-5565
   www.smokaroma.com
Manufacturer and exporter of barbecuing, smoking and cooking equipment for hamburgers, hot dogs, sausage patties, chicken fillets, etc.; also, spices for meat and barbecue sauce mix
Owner: Maurice W Lee Iii
CEO: Maurice Lee Jr
Marketing Director: Tonia Guess
Estimated Sales: $5-10 Million
Number Employees: 10-19
Square Footage: 160000
Brands Exported: Bar BQ Boss; Instant Burger; One Step Prep Mix; Red Rub & Bar-B-Q Sauce Mixs

48709 Smurfit Stone Container
8182 Maryland Ave
Suite 1100
St Louis, MO 63105-3915   314-679-2300
   Fax: 314-679-2300
Folding cartons, corrugated containers and labels including printed paper, foil and heat transfer; exporter of linerboard
VP Corporate Sales/Marketing: Jack Straw
Marketing: James P Duncan
Contact: Mary Duda
mduda@smurfit.com
Estimated Sales: $ 1 - 5 Million
Number Employees: 20-49
Parent Co: Jefferson Smurfit Group
Regions Exported to: Asia, Mexico

48710 (HQ)Smyth Co LLC
1085 Snelling Ave N
St Paul, MN 55108-2705   651-646-4544
   Fax: 651-646-2385   800-473-3464
   info@smythco.com   www.smythco.com
Manufacturer of sheet-fed and pressure sensitive labels, coupons, and high speed labelers for consumer goods packaging.
President: Jim Lundquist
Chief Executive Officer: John Hickey
Chief Financial Officer: David Baumgardner
Executive Vice President: Daniel Hickey
Quality Control Manager: Donna Niedenfuer
Purchasing Manager: Tom Schoolmeesters
Estimated Sales: $ 41 Million
Number Employees: 10-19
Square Footage: 110000
Parent Co: G.G. McGuiggan Corporation
Other Locations:
   Smyth Companies
   Bedford, PASmyth Companies
Regions Exported to: Worldwide
Percentage of Business in Exporting: 5

48711 Snack Factory
PO Box 3562
Princeton, NJ 08543-3562   609-683-5400
   Fax: 609-683-9595   888-683-5400
   info@pretzelcrisps.com   www.pretzelcrisps.com
Pretzel crisps-all natural and fat free; available in garlic, original and everything flavors.
President: Warren Wilson
VP: Sara Wilson
Contact: Todd Grandt
todd@pretzelcrisps.com
Estimated Sales: $5 Million
Number Employees: 9
Square Footage: 800000
Type of Packaging: Consumer, Food Service, Private Label, Bulk
Regions Exported to: Canada, Mexico
Percentage of Business in Exporting: 5

48712 (HQ)Snak King Corp
16150 Stephens St
City Of Industry, CA 91745-1718   626-336-7711
   Fax: 626-336-3777   info@snakking.com
   www.snakking.com
Snack foods, caramel corn, tortilla and corn chips, popcorn, beef jerky, pork rinds, cheese and rice puffs, nut meats and candy.
Chairman/CEO: Barry Levin
jpapiri@snakking.com
VP Sales & Marketing: Joe Papiri
Sales Exec: Joe Papiri
Number Employees: 250-499
Type of Packaging: Consumer, Food Service, Private Label, Bulk
Other Locations:
   Snak King Corp.
   City Industry, CASnak King Corp.
Brands Exported: Snak King; El Sabroso; Healthy Bites; Jensen Orchard
Regions Exported to: Europe, Asia
Percentage of Business in Exporting: 10

Importers & Exporters / A-Z

48713 Snap Drape Inc
2045 Westgate Dr # 100
Carrollton, TX 75006-9478 972-466-1030
Fax: 972-466-1049 800-527-5147
info@snapdrape.com www.snapdrape.com
Manufacturer and exporter of table skirting and drapes
President: Timothy Nealon
tmengel@msmandf.com
Contact: Daielon Sasser
Sales Manager: Kevin Burns
Estimated Sales: $10-20 Million
Number Employees: 50-99
Type of Packaging: Food Service
Regions Exported to: Worldwide
Percentage of Business in Exporting: 10

48714 Snap Drape International
2045 Westgate Dr
Suite 100
Carrollton, TX 75006 972-466-1030
Fax: 972-466-1049 800-527-5147
info@snapdrape.com www.snapdrape.com
President: Darrin Garlish
CEO: Felton Norris
CFO: John Phillips
Vice President: Ray Belknap
Marketing Manager: Tammy Brazeal
Sales Manager: Kevin Burns
Contact: Tim Nealon
t.nealon@msmandf.com
Operations Manager: Jose Aguado
Estimated Sales: $ 10 - 20 Million
Number Employees: 50-99

48715 Snapdragon Foods
PO Box 14103
Oakland, CA 94614
877-881-7627
info@snapdragonfood.com
www.snapdragonfood.com
Importer and manufacturer of Asian prepared meals
President: David Sakamoto
CEO: Seth Jacobson
Vice President of Sales: Ron Dallara
Estimated Sales: $1-2.5 Million
Number Employees: 5-9
Brands Imported: Asian foods
Regions Imported from: Asia

48716 Snappy Popcorn
610 Main St
Breda, IA 51436-8719 712-673-2347
Fax: 712-673-2347 800-640-0228
jon@snappypopcorn.com
www.snappypopcorn.com
Manufacturer, wholesaler/distributor and exporter of popcorn and supplies
President: Alan Tiefenthaler
alan@itien.com
Office Manager: Lori Steinkamp
VP Sales: Jon Tiefenthaler
Estimated Sales: $1-2.5 Million
Number Employees: 20-49
Square Footage: 100000
Type of Packaging: Food Service, Bulk

48717 Sneaky Chef Foods, The
c/o Action Brand Management
851 Broken Sound Pkwy. # 155
Boca Raton, FL 33487 561-757-6541
Fax: 866-920-6487 info@thesneakychef.com
www.thesnackbrigade.com
No-nut butters, prepared spreads with vegetable purees to appeal to children
Founder/President: Missy Chase Lapine
Number of Brands: 1
Number of Products: 8
Type of Packaging: Consumer, Private Label
Brands Exported: The Sneaky Chef
Regions Exported to: USA, Canada

48718 Sneezeguard Solutions
2508 Paris Rd
Columbia, MO 65202-2514 573-443-5756
Fax: 573-449-7126 800-569-2056
www.sneezeguardsolutions.com
Manufacturer and exporter of sneeze guards
President: Sydney Baumgartner
sneezeguard@centurytel.net
CFO: Susan Baumgaltner
Marketing: Bill Pfeiffer
Plant Manager: John Bazzell
Estimated Sales: $ 1 - 3 Million
Number Employees: 5-9
Number of Brands: 14
Number of Products: 14
Square Footage: 40000

48719 Snelgrove Ice Cream Company
850 E 2100 S
Salt Lake City, UT 84106-1832 801-486-4456
Fax: 801-486-3926 800-569-0005
www.dreyers.com
Processor, exporter and wholesaler/distributor of ice cream and ice cream novelties
President: David Mutzel
Contact: Troy Luckart
troy.luckart@dreyers.com
Estimated Sales: Less than $500,000
Number Employees: 50-99
Parent Co: MKD Distributing
Type of Packaging: Consumer, Food Service, Private Label, Bulk
Regions Exported to: Worldwide

48720 Snhook.com/P.K. Torten Ent
55 W 14th Street
Apt 7n
New York, NY 10011-7411 212-229-1314

48721 Sno Shack Inc
2774 N 4000 W
P.O. Box 1010
Rexburg, ID 83440-3106 208-359-0866
Fax: 208-359-1773 888-766-7425
sales@snoshack.com www.snoshack.com
Flavors, thickeners and sweeteners; also, shaved ice equipment including shavers, bottles, racks and yogurt flavoring, carts, concession trailers
Owner: Burt Hensley
Owner: Cheryl Lewis
Sales Director: Peter Orr
burt@snoshack.com
Manager: Bud Orr
Purchasing Manager: Brooke Anstine
Estimated Sales: Less Than $500,000
Number Employees: 1-4
Square Footage: 36000
Type of Packaging: Consumer, Food Service, Private Label
Regions Exported to: Worldwide
Percentage of Business in Exporting: 10

48722 Sno Wizard Inc
101 River Rd
New Orleans, LA 70121-4222 504-832-3901
Fax: 504-832-1646 800-366-9766
information@snowizard.com www.snowizard.com
Snowball, snowcone and shaved ice machines and flavorings
President: Ronnie Sciortino
Estimated Sales: $ 5 - 10 Million
Number Employees: 10-19
Square Footage: 20000
Type of Packaging: Consumer, Food Service, Bulk
Regions Exported to: Worldwide

48723 Sno-Pac Foods Inc
521 Enterprise Dr
Caledonia, MN 55921-1844 507-725-5281
Fax: 507-725-5285 800-533-2215
snopac@snopac.com www.snopac.com
Frozen organic vegetables including soy and edamame beans, green peas, whole kernel corn, cut green and mixed
President: Peter Gengler
VP: Darlene Gengler
Estimated Sales: $3.5 Million
Number Employees: 50-99
Type of Packaging: Consumer, Food Service, Bulk

48724 Snowcrest Packer
1925 Riverside Road
Abbotsford, BC V2S 4J8
Canada 604-859-4881
Fax: 604-859-1426 800-265-3686
info@snowcrest.ca www.snowcrest.ca
Processor and importer of frozen apples, blueberries, cherries, cranberries, raspberries, strawberries, asparagus, beans, broccoli, brussels sprouts, cauliflowers, corn, peas, peppers, rhubarb, spinach, squash and turnips
President: Tom Smith
Quality Control: Lim Lee
Sales: Pascal Countant
Operations Manager: Rob Christl
Number Employees: 120
Square Footage: 440000
Parent Co: Omstead Foods
Type of Packaging: Consumer, Food Service, Private Label, Bulk
Other Locations:
Snowcrest Packer Ltd.
Burnaby, BCSnowcrest Packer Ltd.
Regions Imported from: Canada, Mexico
Percentage of Business in Importing: 2

48725 Snyder Crown
602 Industrial St
Marked Tree, AR 72365-1909 870-358-3400
Fax: 870-358-3140
Manufacturer and exporter of custom, rotational-molded plastic transport tanks, storage bins and containers
Director Marketing: David Kelley
Director Operations: Dale Givens
Plant Manager: Ronnie Stone
Estimated Sales: $ 10-20 Million
Number Employees: 20 to 49
Brands Exported: Crown Rotational
Regions Exported to: South America, Canada, Mexico

48726 Snyder Foods
15350 Old Simcoe Road
P.O Box 750
Port Perry, ON L9L 1A6
Canada 905-985-7373
Fax: 905-985-7289
Processor and exporter of meat and fruit pies, sausage rolls, quiche, stuffed sandwiches and pie and tart shells
General Manager: Dave Jackson
Number Employees: 125
Square Footage: 220000
Type of Packaging: Consumer, Food Service, Private Label
Regions Exported to: USA
Percentage of Business in Exporting: 10

48727 Snyder's Bakery
31 N 4th Ave
Yakima, WA 98902 509-457-6150
Fax: 509-249-4102 www.usbakery.com
Importer of snack foods and pastries; wholesaler/distributor of baked goods including bread and sweet goods
Manager: Gene Parke
CEO: Bob Albers
CFO: Jerry Boness
Vice President: Kim Nisbet
Marketing: Todd Cornwell
Contact: Duane Howerton
howertond@usbakery.com
Estimated Sales: $2.5-5 Million
Number Employees: 20-49
Parent Co: United States Bakery
Brands Imported: Bimbo; Marinela
Percentage of Business in Importing: 5

48728 Snyder's of Hanover
PO Box 32368
Charlotte, NC 28232
800-233-7125
www.snydersofhanover.com
Snack foods including pretzels, flavored pretzel pieces and potato, tortilla and corn chips.
Chairman: Michael Wareheim
Year Founded: 1909
Estimated Sales: $652 Million
Number Employees: 2,400
Number of Products: 45
Square Footage: 37800
Type of Packaging: Consumer

48729 Snyder's-Lance Inc.
13515 Ballantyne Corporate Pl.
Charlotte, NC 28277
800-438-1880
www.snyderslance.com
Sandwich crackers, nuts and seeds, captain's wafers, cookies, popcorn, pretzels, snack cakes, and 100 calorie packs.
President/CEO: Brian Driscoll
Year Founded: 2010
Estimated Sales: $1.62 Billion
Number Employees: 5,900
Number of Brands: 15
Parent Co: Campbell Soup Company
Type of Packaging: Consumer

Importers & Exporters / A-Z

Other Locations:
  Lance
    Hyannis, MA Lance
Regions Exported to: Bahamas

48730 So Delicious Dairy Free
1130 Shelley St
Springfield, OR 97477   541-338-9400
        Fax: 541-338-9401 866-388-7853
        info@turtlemountain.com
        www.sodeliciousdairyfree.com
Processor and exporter of frozen nondairy desserts; also, fat-free
Founder, President, Chief Executive Offi: Mark Brawerman
Marketing: John Tucker
Contact: Michael Murray
mmurray@sodeliciousdairyfree.com
Director of Operations: Michael Dunteman
Estimated Sales: Under $500,000
Number Employees: 1-4
Type of Packaging: Consumer, Food Service, Private Label

48731 Sobaya
201 Rue Miner
Cowansville, QC J2K 3Y5
Canada   450-266-8808
        Fax: 450-266-4750 800-319-8808
        info@sobaya.ca www.sobaya.ca
Natural pasta, organic pasta, Kamut organic pasta and Spelt organic pasta
President: Jacques Petit
Vice President: William Swaney
Marketing/Sales: Sandra Prevost
Number Employees: 7
Number of Brands: 1
Number of Products: 14
Square Footage: 20000
Parent Co: Eden Foods
Type of Packaging: Consumer, Private Label, Bulk
Brands Exported: Soba; Udon; Somen; Genmai
Regions Exported to: USA
Brands Imported: La Soya
Regions Imported from: Asia
Percentage of Business in Importing: 2

48732 Socafe
41 Malvern St
Newark, NJ 07105-1510   973-589-4104
        Fax: 973-589-4429 www.socafe.net
Importer and wholesaler/distributor of espresso equipment; coffee roasting available; serving the food service market
President: Joseph Fernandes
socafe@socafe.com
VP: Isabel Fernandes
Estimated Sales: $10 - 20 Million
Number Employees: 10-19
Type of Packaging: Consumer, Food Service
Brands Imported: Fiamma
Regions Imported from: Portugal

48733 (HQ)Sogelco International
Suite 400
Montreal, QC H2Y 2H7
Canada   514-849-2414
        Fax: 514-849-0645 sogelco@sogelco.com
Producer and wholesaler/distributor, importer and exporter of seafood, poultry, meats and frozen foods; serving the food service market
President: Gabriel Elbaz
Sales Director: Andre Arseneault
Production/Plant Manager: Carl Desroches
Purchasing: Edmond Elbaz
Estimated Sales: $40 Million
Number Employees: 15
Type of Packaging: Consumer, Food Service, Bulk
Other Locations:
  Sogelco International
    Baie Ste. Anne, NB Sogelco International
Brands Exported: Sogel; Crown Pac; Deli Magic; Chefs Supreme; Lobsterine; Crabterine
Regions Exported to: Central America, Europe, Asia, Middle East
Percentage of Business in Exporting: 85
Brands Imported: Various Frozen Sea Food Products.
Regions Imported from: Central America, Asia
Percentage of Business in Importing: 5

48734 Solbern Corp
8 Kulick Rd
Fairfield, NJ 07004-3385   973-227-3030
        Fax: 973-227-3069 sales@solbern.com
        www.solbern.com
Manufacturer and exporter of container filling and dough folding equipment
President: Gil Foulon
VP: Jorge Espino
VP: Tom Berger
Marketing Director: Jorge Espino
Sales: Jorge Espino
Operations: Tom Berger
Estimated Sales: $5-10,000,000
Number Employees: 20-49
Square Footage: 24000
Regions Exported to: Central America, South America

48735 Sole Grano LLC
16-00 Pollitt Dr
Suite 3
Fair Lawn, NJ 07410-2765   201-797-7100
        info@solegrano.com
        www.solegrano.com
Dried fruits, nuts, trail mixes, granolas, grains, beans, seeds, peas, lentils, and confections.
President: Harun Ekici
Number Employees: 1-4
Type of Packaging: Private Label

48736 Solo Foods
5315 Dansher Road
Countryside, IL 60525
        800-328-7656
        info@solofoods.com www.solofoods.com
Cake and pastry fillings, almond paste and marzipan, pie and dessery fillings, marshmallow and toasted marshmallow creme, fruit butters, Asian dipping sauces and marinades, seasoning mixes.
President: John Sokol Novak
COO: Ralph Pirritano
Contact: Sami Abdel-Malek
sabdel-malek@solofoods.com
Estimated Sales: $20-50 Million
Parent Co: Sokol and Company
Type of Packaging: Consumer, Food Service, Private Label
Regions Imported from: Europe

48737 Solon Manufacturing Company
7 Grasso Ave
North Haven, CT 6473   203-230-5300
        Fax: 207-474-7320 800-341-6640
Wooden spoons and sticks for ice cream novelties
President: Steve Clark
CEO/CFO: Larry Feinn
Marketing Director: Jayne Norman
Sales Director: Grover Kilpatrick
Contact: Steve Laack
steve.laack@solon.com
Estimated Sales: $10-20 Million
Number Employees: 100-249
Type of Packaging: Private Label, Bulk

48738 Solutions
PO Box 407
Searsport, ME 04974-0407   207-548-2636
        Fax: 207-548-2921 800-628-3166
Wholesaler/distributor, exporter and importer of carrageenan, xanthan gum, sodium alginate
President: Donna Ravin
VP: Scott Rangus
R&D: Kevin Johndro
Marketing: Scott Rangus
VP Sales/Marketing: Scott Rangus
Estimated Sales: $15-20 Million
Number Employees: 5-9
Type of Packaging: Bulk
Brands Imported: BenGel; BenLacta; BenVisco
Regions Imported from: Europe, Asia

48739 Solvaira Specialties
50 Bridge St
North Tonawanda, NY 14120-6842 716-693-4040
        Fax: 716-693-3528 888-698-1936
        info@ifcfiber.com www.ifcfiber.com
A leading manufacturer of dietry fiber.
President/CEO: Dan Muth
Executive VP: Peter Vogt
pvogt@ifcfiber.com
R&D: Jit Ang
Exec VP of Operations: Brian Finn
Purchasing Manager: Steve Couladis
Year Founded: 2000
Number Employees: 50-99
Number of Brands: 10+
Type of Packaging: Bulk
Brands Exported: Justfiber; Solka-Floc; Nutrafiber; Fibrex
Regions Exported to: Central America, South America, Europe, Asia, Middle East
Brands Imported: Fibrex
Regions Imported from: Europe

48740 Solvay
504 Carnegie Ctr
Princeton, NJ 08540-6241   609-860-4000
        Fax: 609-409-8652 800-765-8292
        www.solvay.us
Manufacturer of food grade hydrogen peroxids, IXPER® Calcium Peroxide, and BICAR® Sodium Bicarbonate for use in bleaching/decolorization, dough conditioning, leavening, sulfite reduction, microbial sterilization and productpurification.
President: Richard Hogan
Business Development Manager: Patrick Fura
Business Development Manager: Ray Routhier
Senior Marketing Manager: Aparna Parikh
Contact: Ian Bartlett
ian.bartlett@solvay.com
Estimated Sales: Over $1 Billion
Number Employees: 250-499
Parent Co: Solvay S.A.
Regions Exported to: Canada, Mexico

48741 Solve Needs International
10204 Highland Rd
White Lake, MI 48386   248-698-3200
        Fax: 248-698-3070 800-783-2462
        sales@solveneeds.com
Manufacturer, importer and exporter of corrugated bins, boxes, dividers, drawers, shelving, cantilever and pallet racks, hydraulic and scissor lifts, pallet jacks, stairways, rolling ladders, casters, wheels, carts, platform andutility trucks, new equipment and repair parts, etc
President: Don Burski
Estimated Sales: $3 - 5 Million
Number Employees: 5-9
Square Footage: 200000
Brands Exported: Solve Needs International; Equipment Company of America
Regions Exported to: Global
Brands Imported: Pallet Jack; ECDA

48742 Somerset Industries
901 North Bethlehem Pike
Spring House, PA 19477-0927   215-619-0480
        Fax: 215-619-0489 800-883-8728
        www.somersetindustries.com
Wholesaler/distributor, importer and exporter of closeout items bought and sold. The correctional food specialist. Warehouse and transportation services provided
President: Jay Shrager
CFO: Carole Shrager
VP: Alan Breslow
Marketing Director: Candace Shrager
Sales Manager: Kevin Murray Jr
General Manager: Ben Caldwell
Number Employees: 20-49
Type of Packaging: Food Service, Private Label, Bulk
Brands Exported: Anna Maria Bobbie Brand Foods
Regions Exported to: Central America, Middle East
Regions Imported from: Central America, South America, Europe, Asia

48743 Somerset Industries
1 Esquire Rd
Billerica, MA 1862   978-667-3355
        Fax: 978-671-9466 800-772-4404
        somerset@smrset.com www.smrset.com
Manufacturer and exporter of bakery equipment including dough sheeters, rollers, fillers, depositors, bread molders and croissant machines
CEO: Andrew Voyatzakis
Estimated Sales: $2.5-5 Million
Number Employees: 10
Regions Exported to: Central America, South America, Europe, Asia, Middle East, Australia
Percentage of Business in Exporting: 40

Importers & Exporters / A-Z

48744 Something Different Linen
474 Getty Ave
Clifton, NJ 07011   973-772-8019
    Fax: 973-772-6519   800-422-2180
Manufacturer and exporter of tablecloths, skirting and napkins; custom sizes available
President: Mitchell Smith
Quality Control: Micheal Gates
Sales Manager: Wally Rachmaciej
Contact: Aricelis Baiz
abaez@somethingdifferentlinen.com
Estimated Sales: $ 20 - 50 Million
Number Employees: 50-99
Parent Co: Something Different Linen
Regions Exported to: Worldwide
Percentage of Business in Exporting: 5

48745 Sommers Organic
339 Messner Drive
Wheeling, IL 60090   847-229-8192
    Fax: 847-229-8264   877-377-9797
    info@sommersorganic.com
Organic beef products, chicken products, turkey products, and pork products.
Chairman: Walter Sommers
Type of Packaging: Consumer

48746 Sommers Plastic ProductCo Inc
31 Styertowne Rd
Clifton, NJ 07012-1713   973-777-7888
    Fax: 973-777-7890   800-225-7677
    sales@sommers.com www.sommers.com
Manufacturer and exporter of plastic packaging products including sheeting, fabrics, cloths and film
President: Ed Schecter
eschecter@aol.com
VP: Fred Schecter
R&D: Fred Schecter
Estimated Sales: $ 5 - 10 Million
Number Employees: 20-49
Regions Exported to: Worldwide

48747 Sonic Corp
1 Research Dr
Stratford, CT 06615-7184   203-375-0063
    Fax: 203-378-4079   866-493-1378
    kurt.limbacher@sonicmixing.com
    www.sonicmixing.com
Manufacturer and exporter of food processing machinery including propeller mixers, agitators, continuous inline multiple-feed liquid blending systems, colloid mills and homogenizing systems.
President: Robert Brakeman
rob.brakeman@sonicmixing.com
Sales Manager: Kurt Limbacher
Estimated Sales: $2.5-5 Million
Number Employees: 10-19
Square Footage: 26000
Percentage of Business in Exporting: 40

48748 Sonics & Materials Inc
53 Church Hill Rd # 2
Newtown, CT 06470-1699   203-270-4600
    Fax: 203-270-4610   800-745-1105
    info@sonics.com www.sonicsandmaterials.com
Manufacturer and exporter of liquid processing systems, food processing equipment, and food cutting equipment.
President/CEO: Robert Soloff
CEO: Thomas Bennetti
tbennetti@sonics.com
Quality Control: Dan Grise
Sales Manager: Lois Baiad
Biotechnology Manager: Mike Donaty
North Am. Sales Mngr., Welding Products: Brian Gourley
Estimated Sales: $ 10-20 Million
Number Employees: 50-99
Square Footage: 90000
Regions Exported to: Worldwide
Percentage of Business in Exporting: 30

48749 Sonoco Paperboard Specialties
3150 Clinton Ct
Norcross, GA 30071   770-476-9088
    Fax: 770-476-0765   800-264-7494
    www.sonocospecialties.com
Manufacturer and exporter of biodegradable and recyclable paperboard glassware caps used in the lodging, food and hospital industries for sanitary purposes
General Manager: Jeff Burgner
Division Controller: Gus Copeletti
gus.copeletti@sonoco.com
Plant Manager: Kelly Mowen
Plant Manager: Bill Janda
Estimated Sales: $5 - 10 Million
Number Employees: 20-49
Square Footage: 132000
Parent Co: Sonoco Products Co
Type of Packaging: Consumer, Food Service, Private Label, Bulk
Brands Exported: StanCap
Regions Exported to: Central America, South America, Europe, Asia, Middle East

48750 Sonoco ThermoSafe
3930 N Ventura Dr
Suite 450
Arlington Heights, IL 60004
    800-323-7442
    www.thermosafe.com
Insulated containers
Estimated Sales: $5-10 Million
Number Employees: 50-99
Square Footage: 92000
Parent Co: Sonoco Products Co
Brands Exported: Insul-Stor; Flexicold
Regions Exported to: South America, Europe, Asia, Canada, Latin America

48751 Sonora Seafood Company
420 16th St
Santa Monica, CA 90402-2234   310-458-9095
    Fax: 310-395-4697 bshpilots@aol.com
Importer of seafood
President: James Caulfield
VP: Paul Moriates
Marketing: Nick Edgar
Estimated Sales: $ 3 - 5 Million
Number Employees: 5-9
Type of Packaging: Private Label
Brands Imported: Sonora Blue
Regions Imported from: Canada, Mexico
Percentage of Business in Importing: 100

48752 Soodhalter Plastics
PO Box 21276
Los Angeles, CA 90021   213-747-0231
    Fax: 213-746-8125 soodhalterplastics@yahoo.com
Manufacturer, importer and exporter of party and bar accessories including plastic cocktail forks, stirrers and picks
President: Jackie Wolfson
CFO: Jackie Wolfson
Estimated Sales: $5-10 Million
Number Employees: 10-19
Regions Exported to: South America, Asia, Canada, Australia
Regions Imported from: Asia

48753 Soofer Co
2828 S Alameda St
Vernon, CA 90058-1347   323-234-6666
    Fax: 323-234-2447   800-852-4050
    info@sadaf.com www.sadaf.com
Wholesaler/distributor and importer of specialty Mid-Eastern and Spanish items including spices, juices, beans, nuts, pickles, jams and syrups; exporter of spices and juices
Owner: Darioush Soofer
Marketing VP: Dariush Soofer
Estimated Sales: $10-20 Million
Number Employees: 20-49
Square Footage: 68000
Type of Packaging: Consumer, Food Service, Bulk
Brands Exported: Sadaf
Regions Exported to: South America, Europe, Asia, Canada
Percentage of Business in Exporting: 15
Brands Imported: Tilda; Ahmad; Sadaf
Regions Imported from: Europe, Asia, Middle East, Canada
Percentage of Business in Importing: 50

48754 Sopralco
6991 W Broward Blvd
Plantation, FL 33317-2907   954-584-2225
    Fax: 954-584-3271 sopralco@aol.com
Ready-to-drink espresso
Owner: Peter Marciante
VP: Arcelia De Battisti
Marketing: Ana Ordaz
Estimated Sales: $1,500,000
Number Employees: 1-4
Square Footage: 1250
Parent Co: Sopralco
Type of Packaging: Consumer, Food Service
Brands Imported: Espre; Espre-Matic
Regions Imported from: Italy
Percentage of Business in Importing: 90

48755 (HQ)Sorbee Intl.
9990 Global Rd.
Philadelphia, PA 19115   215-677-5200
    Fax: 215-677-7736   800-654-3997
Confectionery items including sugar hard candy, low-fat candy bars and sugar-free items
CEO: Daniel Werther
CFO: Tom Keogh
VP Sales: Barry Sokol
Estimated Sales: $31 Million
Number Employees: 20-49
Other Locations:
    Sorbee International Ltd.
    Philadelphia, PASorbee International Ltd.

48756 Sortex
39161 Farwell Dr
Fremont, CA 94538-1050   510-797-5000
    Fax: 510-797-0555 sales@sortex.com
    www.sortex.com
Manufacturer and exporter of color sorters and vision systems
VP Sales: Mike Evans
Sales Director of Product: Christoph Naef
Head of Corporate Communications: Corina Atzli
Number Employees: 20-49
Square Footage: 80000
Parent Co: Buhler
Brands Exported: Sortex
Regions Exported to: Worldwide

48757 Sossner Steel Stamps
180 Judge Don Lewis Blvd
Elizabethton, TN 37643-6006   423-543-4001
    Fax: 423-543-8546   800-828-9515
    info@sossnerstamps.com www.sossnerstamps.com
Manufacturer and exporter of marking stamps
President: Neil Friedman
International Sales: Vianney Cabrera
General Manager: Russel Lacy
Estimated Sales: $ 5 - 10 Million
Number Employees: 20-49
Square Footage: 94000
Parent Co: Sossner Steel Stamps
Regions Exported to: Worldwide
Percentage of Business in Exporting: 1

48758 Source Atlantique Inc
140 Sylvan Ave
Englewood Cliffs, NJ 07632   201-947-1000
            888-470-0626
    www.sourceatlantique.com
Italian pastries, Swiss jams, Belgian cookies and chocolates, candies, cakes, pasta, olive oil and balsamic vinegar.
President & CEO, Import Food Group: Robert Feuerstein
President: Joel Schuman
Year Founded: 1991
Estimated Sales: $50-100 Million
Number Employees: 50-99
Parent Co: Food Import Group
Type of Packaging: Consumer, Bulk
Brands Imported: Bauli; Vicenzi; San Bernardo; Gazzola; Freddi; Cedrinca
Regions Imported from: Europe
Percentage of Business in Importing: 100

48759 Source Food Technology
2530 Meridian Parkway
#200
Durham, NC 27713   919-806-4545
    Fax: 919-806-4842   866-277-3849
Cholesterol-free shortenings, fats and oils; also, cholesterol reduced egg and dairy products
CEO: Henry Cardello
VP Sales: Patrick Halliday
Estimated Sales: B
Number Employees: 5-9

48760 Source for Packaging
227 E 45th Street
New York, NY 10017-3306   212-687-4700
    Fax: 212-687-4725   800-223-2527
Manufacturer and exporter of shopping bags, promotional items, labels, foil, pressure sensitive tapes; also, packaging design services available

Importers & Exporters / A-Z

President: Jay Raskin
VP Sales/Operations: Louis Cruz
Estimated Sales: $50-100 Million
Number Employees: 250-499
Regions Exported to: Worldwide

48761 South Carolina Beef Board
1200 Senate St # 514
Columbia, SC 29201-3734   803-734-9806
  Fax: 803-734-0325 www.energy.sc.gov
Manager: Brad Boozer
Number Employees: 1-4

48762 South Georgia Pecan Co
309 S Lee St
PO Box 5366
Valdosta, GA 31601-5723   229-244-1321
  Fax: 229-247-6361 229-627-6630
  info@georgiapecan.com www.georgiapecan.com
Esatblished in 1913. Manufacturer and exporter of shelled pecans and almonds.
Co-Owner: Jim Worn
Co-Owner: Ed Crane
Estimated Sales: $20 - 50 Million
Number Employees: 100-249
Type of Packaging: Consumer
Regions Exported to: Worldwide

48763 (HQ)South Mill
649 West South Street
Kennett Square, PA 19348   610-444-4800
  Fax: 610-444-1338 info@southmill.com
  www.southmill.com
National mushroom supplier.
Contact: Iris Ayala
iayala@southmill.com
Year Founded: 1978
Number Employees: 1,000
Type of Packaging: Consumer, Food Service, Private Label, Bulk
Other Locations:
  Distribution
    Atlanta, GA
  Distribution
    New Orleans, LA
  Distribution
    Houston, TX
  Distribution
    Dallas, TXDistributionNew Orleans
Regions Exported to: Canada
Percentage of Business in Exporting: 15
Regions Imported from: Europe
Percentage of Business in Importing: 5

48764 South Shore Controls Inc
4485 N Ridge Rd
Perry, OH 44081-9760   440-259-2500
  Fax: 440-259-5015 mail@southshorecontrols.com
  www.southshorecontrols.com
Manufacturer and exporter of controls and control panels for food processing equipment, material handling equipment, freezers, etc
President: Rick Stark
rjs@southshorecontrols.com
Sales Director: John Sauto, Jr.
Estimated Sales: $6 Million
Number Employees: 20-49
Square Footage: 58000

48765 South Valley Farms
15443 Beech Ave
Wasco, CA 93280-7604   661-391-9000
  Fax: 661-391-9012 www.southvalleyfarms.com
Grower and exporter of almonds and pistachios; processor of hulled and shelled almonds
Vice President: Benjamin Barnes
ben.y.barnes@gmail.com
VP: Daryl Wilkendors
Processing Manager: Jonathan Meyer
Estimated Sales: $ 2.5-5 Million
Number Employees: 100-249
Square Footage: 320000
Parent Co: Farm Management Company
Type of Packaging: Bulk
Brands Exported: South Valley Farms
Regions Exported to: Central America, Europe, Asia, Middle East
Percentage of Business in Exporting: 70

48766 Southbend
1100 Old Honeycutt Rd
Fuquay Varina, NC 27526-8971   919-762-1000
  Fax: 919-552-9798 800-348-2558
  sbgeneral@southbendnc.com
  www.buildmybattery.com
Manufacturer and exporter of commercial cooking equipment including broilers, fryer systems, restaurant ranges, convection, steamers, kettles, braising pans and cabinets
President: Nestor Ibrahim
COO: Selim Bassaul
CFO: Dave Baker
VP: Rob August
Research & Development: Ray Wi
VP Sales: Jonette Wylie
National Sales Manager: Mitch Cohen
Estimated Sales: $ 50 Million
Number Employees: 100-249
Square Footage: 135000
Parent Co: Middleby Corporation
Brands Exported: Southbend; Steamaster
Regions Exported to: Central America, South America, Europe, Asia, Middle East, Worldwide
Percentage of Business in Exporting: 20

48767 Southeast Foods
9475 NW 13th St
Doral, FL 33172-2809   305-593-0242
  Fax: 305-593-1527
Importer of candy, cheese, shrimp, lobster tails and meats
Manager: Mario Varela
Estimated Sales: $ 3 - 5 Million
Number Employees: 1-4
Parent Co: Atalanta Corporation
Brands Imported: Celebrity; Tuoli; Krakus

48768 Southern Ag Co Inc
942 N Main St
PO Drawer 546
Blakely, GA 39823-2029   229-723-4262
  Fax: 229-723-3223 souagcom@windstream.net
Manufacturer and exporter of conveyors, elevators, sizers and separators for peanuts; also, grain bins
Owner: Harold Still
Estimated Sales: $ 2.5-5 Million
Number Employees: 10-19
Regions Exported to: Worldwide

48769 Southern Aluminum
5 Highway 82 Byp W
Magnolia, AR 71753-8719   870-234-8660
  Fax: 870-234-2823
President: Mark Taylor
Estimated Sales: $ 10 - 20 Million
Number Employees: 50-99

48770 Southern Automatics
2845 Brooks Street
Lakeland, FL 33803-7379   863-665-1633
  Fax: 863-665-2500 800-441-4604
Manufacturer, importer and exporter of high-volume fruit and vegetable packing machinery; also, compact optic sorters and sizers
President: Hugh Oglesby
VP: Scott Oglesby
Estimated Sales: $ 1 - 3 Million
Number Employees: 20
Square Footage: 40000
Parent Co: Future Alloys
Brands Exported: Sai; Compac
Regions Exported to: Central America, South America, Middle East
Percentage of Business in Exporting: 10
Brands Imported: Compac
Percentage of Business in Importing: 5

48771 (HQ)Southern Champion Tray LP
220 Compress St
PO Box 4066
Chattanooga, TN 37405-3724   423-756-5121
  Fax: 423-756-0223 800-468-2222
  cchapellin@sctray.com
Manufacturer and exporter of paperboard folding cartons
President & CEO: John Zeiser
CEO: Mark Lonqnecker
Vice President: Bruce Zeiser
National Sales Manager: Paul Powell
Operations Manager: Jim Skidmore
Number Employees: 250-499
Square Footage: 650000
Type of Packaging: Consumer, Food Service, Private Label, Bulk
Other Locations:
  Southern Champion Tray L.P.
    Chattanooga, TNSouthern Champion Tray L.P.
Regions Exported to: Central America, South America
Percentage of Business in Exporting: 5

48772 Southern Film Extruders
2327 English Road
High Point, NC 27262   336-885-8091
  Fax: 336-885-1221 800-334-6101
  sales@southernfilm.com www.southernfilm.com
FDA polythylene packaging films
Owner: Joseph Martinez
Chief Financial Officer: John Barnes
Quality Control Manager: Tom Vanpelt
Vice President, Sales: Lanny Rampley
Warehouse Manager: Austin Fisher
Estimated Sales: $ 24 Million
Number Employees: 145
Square Footage: 115000
Type of Packaging: Private Label

48773 Southern Gardens Citrus
1820 County Road 833
Clewiston, FL 33440-9222   863-983-3030
  Fax: 863-983-3060 www.ussugar.com
Citrus juices, concentrates, blends and ingredients
President: Robert Baker Jr
Finance Executive: Ginny Pena
VP Marketing: Charles Lucas
Contact: Dan Casper
dcasper@southerngardens.com
Number Employees: 100-249
Parent Co: US Sugar Corporation
Type of Packaging: Bulk
Regions Imported from: South America

48774 Southern Gold Honey Co
3015 Brown Rd
Vidor, TX 77662-7902   409-768-1645
  Fax: 409-768-1009 808-899-2494
Honey and specialty items including pecan cream honey and fruit flavored honeys
Owner: Gretchen Horn
Estimated Sales: Less than $500,000
Number Employees: 1-4
Type of Packaging: Consumer, Private Label
Regions Exported to: Middle East
Percentage of Business in Exporting: 2

48775 Southern Heritage Coffee Company
6555 E 30th St Ste F
Indianapolis, IN 46219
     317-543-0757 800-486-1198
  Fax:
  kevin@heritage-coffee.com
  www.coppermooncoffee.com
Processor, importer, exporter and contract roaster of coffee including house blends and gourmet, liquid concentrate, espresso, instant cappuccino, pads, hotel in-room filter packed coffees
Manager: Doug Bachman
CEO: Kevin Daw
Sales Director: Kevin Daw
Contact: Christophe Burt
cgutwein@coppermooncoffee.com
Operations Manager: Dick Middleton
Purchasing Manager: Tom Oldridge
Number Employees: 20-49
Square Footage: 208000
Type of Packaging: Consumer, Food Service, Private Label, Bulk
Regions Exported to: Europe, Asia, Middle East
Percentage of Business in Exporting: 5
Regions Imported from: Central America, South America, Asia
Percentage of Business in Importing: 80

48776 Southern Imperial Inc
1400 Eddy Ave
Rockford, IL 61103-3198   815-310-9120
  Fax: 815-877-7454 800-747-4665
  grothmeyer@southernimperial.com
  www.southernimperial.com
Manufacturer and exporter of scanning hooks, display hooks, wire racks and baskets, clip strips, J-hooks, paper and adhesive labels and merchandising accessories
President: Stan C Valiulis
ekuehl@southernimperial.com
CFO: Dean Zanseil
Quality Control: Denise Bermingham
R&D: Tom Zeliulis
Marketing Manager: Tom Valiulis
Estimated Sales: $ 20 - 30 Million
Number Employees: 100-249
Square Footage: 320000
Regions Exported to: Worldwide

Importers & Exporters / A-Z

48777 Southern Metal Fabricators Inc
1215 Frazier Rd
Albertville, AL 35950-0719   256-891-4343
        Fax: 256-891-0922   800-989-1330
        sales@southernmetalfab.com
        www.southernmetalfab.com
Manufacturer and exporter of ventilating systems, ducts, hoods, blowpipes, fittings, tanks, hoppers, railings, funnels, racks, boxes, vats and conveyors
President/CEO: Charles Bailey
charles.bailey@southernmetalfab.com
CFO: Teresa Hammett
Vice President: Regenia Bailey
Quality Control: Donnie Buchanan
Sales Manager: Bud Weed
Operations Manager: Danny Murray
Estimated Sales: $5 Million
Number Employees: 20-49
Square Footage: 189000

48778 Southern Pride Catfish Company
2025 1st Ave Ste 900
Seattle, WA 98121
        Fax: 334-624-8224   800-343-8046
Processor and exporter of farm-raised catfish
President: Joe Glover
Quality Control: Alice Moore
VP Sales: Randy Rhodes
Public Relations: Mary Hand
Operations Manager: Bobby Collins
Number Employees: 500-999
Type of Packaging: Consumer, Food Service, Private Label
Brands Exported: Catfish Products
Regions Exported to: Europe
Percentage of Business in Exporting: 2

48779 Southern Pride Distributing
401 S Mill St
Alamo, TN 38001-1913   731-696-3175
        Fax: 731-696-3180   800-851-8180
        parts@sopride.com   www.southernpride.com
Manufacturer and exporter of ovens including mobile, revolving and warming; also, commercial barbecue equipment, smokers and rotisseries
President/CEO: Mike Robertson
VP: Jared Robertson
Quality Control: Bret Robertson
Marketing Director: Jack Griggs
Operations Manager: Jerry Cadle
Plant Manager: Marty Degrini
Purchasing: Rich Rowell
Estimated Sales: $10 Millions
Number Employees: 5-9
Square Footage: 130000
Type of Packaging: Food Service
Brands Exported: Southern Pride; Yield King
Regions Exported to: Central America, South America, Europe, Asia, Middle East

48780 Southern Rubber Stamp
2637 E Marshall St
Tulsa, OK 74110-4757   918-587-3818
        Fax: 918-587-3819   888-826-4304
        sales@southernmark.com   www.southernmark.com
Manufacturer and exporter of rubber stamps, seals, numbering machines, embossers, special inks, etc
President: Mike Forehand
mike@perfectseal.net
VP: David Parnell
Estimated Sales: Less Than $500,000
Number Employees: 5-9
Type of Packaging: Consumer, Food Service, Bulk
Regions Exported to: Worldwide
Percentage of Business in Exporting: 15

48781 Southern Shell Fish Company
501 Destrehan Avenue
Harvey, LA 70058-2737   504-341-5631
        Fax: 504-341-5635
Processor, canner and exporter of crabmeat, oysters and shrimp
Manager: Dennis Skrmetta
Sales Manager: H Burke Jr
Plant Manager: Golden Boutte
Estimated Sales: $1,400,000
Number Employees: 1-4
Parent Co: Deepsouth Packing Company
Type of Packaging: Consumer, Food Service, Private Label

Percentage of Business in Exporting: 10

48782 Southern Snow
103 W W St
Belle Chasse, LA 70037-1111   504-393-8967
        Fax: 504-393-0112
Manufacturer and exporter of artificial concentrates including colors and flavors; also, ice block shavers
Owner: Milton Wendling
info@flavorsnow.com
Marketing: Danielle Havnen
Estimated Sales: $1500000
Number Employees: 20-49
Square Footage: 40000
Brands Exported: Southern Snow
Regions Exported to: Central America, Middle East, South Africa
Percentage of Business in Exporting: 2

48783 (HQ)Southern Store FixturesInc
275 Drexel Rd SE
Bessemer, AL 35022-6416   205-428-4800
        Fax: 205-428-2552   800-552-6283
        chughes@southerncasearts.com
Manufacturer, exporter and designer of mobile and modular refrigerated cases for deli, bakery, salads, produce and floral; store and fixture design and installation services available
President: Gene Cary
Cmo: Dan Mcmurray
dmcmurray@southernstorefixtures.com
National Sales Manager: Joe Moore
Estimated Sales: $ 10 - 20 Million
Number Employees: 250-499
Square Footage: 216000
Regions Exported to: Worldwide

48784 Southern Tool
738 Well Road
West Monroe, LA 71292-0138   786-866-9865
        Fax: 318-387-5372   800-458-3687
        www.southern-tool.com
Manufacturer and exporter of packaging equipment
President: Dale Doty
Plant Manager: Buck Carlisle
Number Employees: 65
Square Footage: 200000
Parent Co: Southern Tool
Regions Exported to: Worldwide

48785 (HQ)Southwestern Porcelain Steel
201 E Morrow Road
Sand Springs, OK 74063-6531   918-245-1375
        Fax: 918-241-7339
Porcelain enamel tops for steel tables, counters and signs; importer of cast iron stove top grates; also, silk screen porcelain graphics available
Vice President: Jim Bigelow
Plant Superintendent: Don Bushnell
Estimated Sales: $ 5-10 Million
Number Employees: 20-50
Square Footage: 512000
Regions Imported from: Asia

48786 Sovena USA Inc
1 Olive Grove St
Rome, NY 13441-4815   315-797-7070
        Fax: 315-797-6981
        customerservice@sovenausa.com
        www.sovenagroup.com
Domestic edible oils including olive, corn, soybean, peanut and salad; importer of olive oil
CEO: Steve Mandia
CFO: Dave Lofgren
VP: Bert Mandia
VP Sales/Marketing: Mark Mottit
Manager: Luis Gato
l.gato@sovenagroup.com
Estimated Sales: $12.7 Million
Number Employees: 1-4
Square Footage: 45000
Regions Imported from: Europe, North Africa
Percentage of Business in Importing: 20

48787 Sovrana Trading Corp
14928 S Figueroa St
Gardena, CA 90248-1711   310-323-3357
        Fax: 310-217-1832   info@sovrana.com
Wholesaler/distributor and importer of olive oil, whole and ground coffee beans, coffee equipment and coffee mochas and syrups; serving the food service market
Owner: Aldo Bonfante
VP/General Manager/Treasurer: Aldo Bonfante
Estimated Sales: $1-2.5 Million
Number Employees: 10-19

Square Footage: 32000
Parent Co: Espresso World
Type of Packaging: Consumer, Food Service, Private Label
Brands Imported: Lavazza; Olivoro
Regions Imported from: Europe

48788 Sowden Brothers Farm
8888 Township Road
Live Oak, CA 95953   530-695-3750
        Fax: 530-695-1395   www.organicprunes.com
Prune concentrate and dried prunes including Ashlock pitted and whole
President: Richard Taylor
VP: John Taylor
Estimated Sales: $ 20 - 50 Million
Number Employees: 50
Square Footage: 25000
Type of Packaging: Food Service, Private Label, Bulk
Brands Exported: California Gold; Taylor Brothers Farms
Regions Exported to: Worldwide
Percentage of Business in Exporting: 50

48789 Spa Natural Spring Water
45 E Putnam Avenue
Greenwich, CT 06830-5438   203-629-2781
        Fax: 203-743-5475   800-779-2781
Importer of natural spring water and soft drinks
CEO: Richard Marusa
Assistant to CEO: Frances Whalen
National Sales Manager: Robert Mazza
Estimated Sales: $ 3 - 5 Million
Number Employees: 1-4
Parent Co: Spadel NV
Type of Packaging: Consumer
Brands Imported: Spa

48790 Spacesaver Corp
1450 Janesville Ave
Fort Atkinson, WI 53538-2798   920-563-6362
        Fax: 920-563-2702   800-492-3434
        ssc@spacesaver.com   www.spacesaver.com
Manufacturer and exporter of mobile high-density storage systems
President: Paul Olsen
R&D: David Klumb
Vice President: Bill Wettstein
CFO: Ryan Bittner
Marketing Director: Christopher Batterman
Sales Director: Kevin Carmody
Public Relations: Karen King
Operations Manager: Jim Muth
Purchasing Manager: Patricia Cropp
Estimated Sales: $ 75 - 100 Million
Number Employees: 250-499
Parent Co: KI
Type of Packaging: Bulk

48791 Spanco Crane & Monorail Systems
604 Hemlock Rd
Morgantown, PA 19543-9710   610-286-7781
        Fax: 610-286-0085   800-869-2080
        www.spanco.com
Manufacturer and exporter of stainless steel material handling equipment including cranes and conveyor systems and components
Vice President: George Nolan
gnolan@spanco.com
VP: George Nolan
Sales Manager: George Nolan
Estimated Sales: $ 20 - 50 Million
Number Employees: 50-99
Regions Exported to: Mexico, Canada

48792 (HQ)Spangler Candy Co
400 N Portland St
PO Box 71
Bryan, OH 43506-1257   419-636-4221
        Fax: 419-636-3695   888-636-4221
        www.spanglercandy.com
Lollipops, candy canes and circus peanuts
President & CEO: Kirk Vashaw
Chairman: Dean Spangler
CFO: Bill Martin
VP Marketing: Jim Knight
VP Sales: Denny Gunter
VP Production: Steve Kerr
Number Employees: 500-999
Square Footage: 2000000

Importers & Exporters / A-Z

Other Locations:
  Spangler Candy Co.
  Bryan, OH Spangler Candy Co.
Brands Exported: Dum Dum Pops; Saf-T-Pops; Spangler Candy Canes
Regions Exported to: Central America, South America, Europe, Asia, Middle East

48793 Sparboe Foods Corp
900 N Linn Ave
New Hampton, IA 50659-1204   641-394-3040
info@sparboe.com
www.sparboe.com
Fresh and frozen eggs
President: Bob Sparboe
Vice President: Beth Fechnell
Manager: Warren Miller
Estimated Sales: $20-50 Million
Number Employees: 100-249
Square Footage: 50000
Type of Packaging: Food Service, Private Label, Bulk
Regions Exported to: Asia, Middle East
Percentage of Business in Exporting: 10

48794 Sparkler Filters Inc
101 N Loop 336 E
Conroe, TX 77301-1446   936-756-4471
Fax: 936-756-4519 sales@sparklerfilters.com
www.sparklerfilters.com
Manufacturer and exporter of filter systems including fryer oil and liquid; also, manual and automatic
President: J T Reneau
jim@sparklerfilters.com
CFO: Robert Thompson
VP: Jose Sentmanat
Quality Control: James Dunklin
Marketing: Jose Sentmanat
Sales: Tom Buttera
Public Relations: Norm Hofer
Operations/General Manager: Link Reneau
Plant Manager: Alan Powell
Purchasing: Phil Lawson
Estimated Sales: $5-5.5 Million
Number Employees: 20-49
Number of Brands: 2
Square Footage: 140000
Type of Packaging: Food Service
Brands Exported: Sparkler
Regions Exported to: Central America, South America, Europe, Asia, Middle East
Regions Imported from: South America, Europe, Asia
Percentage of Business in Importing: 35

48795 Sparks Belting Co
3800 Stahl Dr SE
Grand Rapids, MI 49546-6148   616-949-2750
Fax: 616-949-8518   800-451-4537
sbcinfo@sparksbelting.com
www.sparksbelting.com
Wholesaler/distributor of food-approved and package handling conveyor belting; manufacturer of motorized pulleys; importer of thermoplastic belting, motorized pulleys and rollers
President: Steven Swanson
CFO: Martha Vrias
VP: Steven Bayus
Quality Control: Dave Vanderwood
Marketing: Frank Kennedy
Contact: Andy Balog
ajbalog@sparksbelting.com
Operations: Bruce Dielema
Production: Joe Graver
Plant Manager: John Grasmeyer
Purchasing Director: Mark White
Estimated Sales: $20-50 Million
Number Employees: 100-249
Square Footage: 52000
Regions Imported from: Europe
Percentage of Business in Importing: 30

48796 Sparrow Enterprises LTD
98 Condor St
PO Box 13
Boston, MA 02128-1306   617-569-3900
Fax: 617-569-5888   855-532-5552
info@chocolatebysparrow.com
www.chocolatebysparrow.com
Importer and wholesaler/distributor of chocolates and bakery and ice cream ingredients including seeds, milk products, cocoa, sweet and desiccated coconut, chocolate drops and coatings, etc
President: John Baybutt
VP: Henry Baybutt
contact@sparrowenterprises.com
Assistant VP: Sally Baybutt
Estimated Sales: $10-20 Million
Number Employees: 20-49
Square Footage: 45000
Type of Packaging: Food Service, Private Label, Bulk
Brands Imported: Valdrohna; Serin Dip; Red V
Regions Imported from: Central America, Europe, Asia, Middle East
Percentage of Business in Importing: 60

48797 Spartan Showcase
702 Spartan Showcase Drive
P.O. Box 470
Union, MO 63084   636-583-4050
Fax: 636-583-4067   800-325-0775
Manufacturer and exporter of bakery and deli wallcases, merchandising and self-serve display cases and dry and refrigerated showcases; also, custom glass and wood fixtures
CEO: Mike Lause
VP Marketing: Steve Lause
Sales Director: Royce Buehrlen
Manager: Greg Hall
Estimated Sales: $14 Million
Number Employees: 120
Square Footage: 400000
Parent Co: Leggett & Platt Inc

48798 Spartec Plastics
PO Box 620
Conneaut, OH 44030-0620   440-599-8175
Fax: 440-593-2003   800-325-5176
Manufacturer and exporter of extruded low and high density polyethylene and polypropylene products including thermoplastic and rolled sheets, rods, textured cutting boards and sanitary paneling systems with antibacterial additives
Operations Manager: Ernie Szydlowski
Estimated Sales: $2.5-5 Million
Number Employees: 19
Square Footage: 190000
Brands Exported: Resinol; ARP Cutting Board; PermaClean Paneling System; Bacticlean
Regions Exported to: Worldwide
Percentage of Business in Exporting: 5

48799 Spartech Plastics
1444 S Tyler Rd
Wichita, KS 67209   316-722-8621
Fax: 316-722-4875   www.spartech.com
Sheet and roll plastics and plastic film
Contact: Patricia Asher
patricia.asher@spartech.com
Plant Manager: Steve Zubke
Estimated Sales: $20-50 Million
Number Employees: 100-249
Square Footage: 60000
Parent Co: Atlas Alchem
Type of Packaging: Bulk
Regions Exported to: South America

48800 Spartech Plastics
1325 Adams St
Portage, WI 53901   608-742-7123
Fax: 608-745-1703   800-998-7123
www.spartech.com
Extruder of plastic sheet and rollstock
VP: Steven J Ploeger
Quality Control: Tim Hofp
Marketing: Kurt Kassner
Sales: Scott Eaton
Contact: Jay Eggleston
eggleston@spartech.com
Operations: Don Asch
Plant Manager: Don Asch
Purchasing: Jay Eggleston
Estimated Sales: $20-50 Million
Number Employees: 100-249
Square Footage: 170000
Parent Co: Spartech Plastics
Brands Exported: Coexcel

48801 Spartech Poly Com
120 South Central Avenue
Suite 1700
Clayton, MI 63105-1705   314-721-4242
Fax: 314-721-1447   888-721-4242
mark.garretson@spartech.com   www.spartech.com
Compounder of PVC for tubing & other applications
Manager: Nate Sofer
CEO: Natehen Sofer
Marketing/Sales: Mark Garretson
Contact: Matt Sweeney
matt.sweeney@spartech.com
Estimated Sales: $10-20 Million
Number Employees: 20-49
Number of Products: 250
Parent Co: Spartech Corporation

48802 Spaten West, Inc
284 Harbor Way
South San Francisco, CA 94080   650-794-0800
Fax: 650-794-9567 spaten@spatenusa.com
www.spatenusa.com
Importer and distributor of Bavarian beer.
President: Chris Hildebrandt
Estimated Sales: $2.5 Million
Number Employees: 15
Number of Brands: 1
Parent Co: Spaten-Franziskaner-Brau
Type of Packaging: Consumer, Food Service, Bulk
Brands Imported: Spaten
Regions Imported from: Europe

48803 Specialities Importers & Distributers
85 Division Avenue
PO Box 409
Millington, NJ 07946   908-647-6485
Fax: 908-647-8305   800-899-6689
www.specialitiesinc.com
Deli: cheeses, cured meats and hams.
President: Ron Schinbeckler
r.schinbeckler@specialitiesinc.com
Vice President, Sales & Marketing: Richard Kessler
Year Founded: 1991
Type of Packaging: Food Service
Brands Imported: Bellentani, Carpuela, Bayonne Ham, Ermitage, leBistro and Solera©
Regions Imported from: Europe

48804 (HQ)Specialty Bakers
450 S State Rd
Marysville, PA 17053-1009   717-957-2131
Fax: 717-957-0156   800-233-0778
CustomerService@SpecialtyBakers.com
www.specialtybakers.com
Manufacturer and exporter of sponge, snack and angel food cakes, lady fingers, dessert shells, French twirls and jelly rolls
President: John Piotrowski
CEO: Hamani Abdou
habdou@specialtybakers.com
Plant Manager: Richard Sychterz
Estimated Sales: $14 Million
Number Employees: 50-99
Square Footage: 150000
Type of Packaging: Consumer, Private Label
Other Locations:
  Specialty Bakers
  Marysville, PA
  Specialty Bakers
  Lititz, PA
  Specialty Bakers
  Dunkirk, NY Specialty Bakers Lititz
Brands Exported: Specialty
Regions Exported to: Canada

48805 Specialty Blades
9 Technology Drive
PO Box 3166
Staunton, VA 24402-3166   540-248-2200
Fax: 540-248-4400
Manufacturer and exporter of custom made industrial-duty food blades including stainless, high-speed and tool steel or carbide; also, prototyping available
President & CEO: Peter Harris
Contact: Dan Andrew
dan@specialtyblades.com
Estimated Sales: $8.5 Million
Number Employees: 50-99
Square Footage: 160000
Type of Packaging: Consumer, Food Service, Private Label, Bulk
Regions Exported to: Central America, South America, Europe, Asia
Percentage of Business in Exporting: 10
Regions Imported from: Europe, Asia
Percentage of Business in Importing: 5

48806 Specialty Coffee Roasters
1300 SW 10th St
Suite 2
Delray Beach, FL 33444
Fax: 800-805-4422   800-253-9363
Processor, packer and importer of gourmet coffees; exporter of gourmet coffees
President: Gabriela Harvey
Estimated Sales: $300,000
Number Employees: 3
Square Footage: 20000
Parent Co: MGH Holdings Corporation
Type of Packaging: Consumer, Food Service, Private Label, Bulk
Brands Exported: Shalina
Regions Exported to: Worldwide
Percentage of Business in Exporting: 30
Regions Imported from: Central America, South America, Europe, Caribbean, Latin America
Percentage of Business in Importing: 50

48807 Specialty Commodities Inc
1530 47th St N
Fargo, ND 58102-2858   701-282-8222
Fax: 701-264-5744
www.specialtycommodities.com
Manufacturer and importer of specialty ingredients for snack food, dairy, bakery, cereal, energy bar and confectionery. Products include dehydrated, dried fruit, legumes, nuts, seeds, spices and grains.
President: Ken Campbell
Vice President: Kevin Andreson
Number Employees: 10-19
Parent Co: Archer Daniels Midland Company
Type of Packaging: Private Label, Bulk
Other Locations:
  Corporate Office
  Fargo, ND
  Processing Plant
  Lodi, CA
  Processing Plant
  Stockton, CA
  Processing Plant
  Modesto, CACorporate OfficeLodi
Regions Exported to: Central America, South America, Europe, Asia, Middle East, Worldwide
Regions Imported from: South America, Asia, Middle East

48808 Specialty Equipment Company
1415 Mendota Heights Rd
Mendota Heights, MN 55120   651-452-7909
Fax: 651-452-0681 sales@specialtyequip.com
Manufacturer, importer and exporter of high pressure washing equipment
CEO: Sheldon Russell
President: Bryan Russell
Estimated Sales: $20-50 Million
Number Employees: 20-49
Square Footage: 70000
Type of Packaging: Consumer, Bulk
Regions Exported to: Worldwide
Percentage of Business in Exporting: 3
Regions Imported from: Europe
Percentage of Business in Importing: 5

48809 Specialty Equipment Company
1221 Adkins Rd
Houston, TX 77055   713-467-1818
Fax: 713-467-9130 www.specialtyequipment.com
Manufacturer of packaging machinery and material handling systems, including liquid fillers, custom dry solids fillers, drum and pallet conveyors, and palletizers.
Year Founded: 1969
Estimated Sales: $257 Million
Type of Packaging: Food Service
Other Locations:
  Specialty Equipment Cos.
  Etten-leurSpecialty Equipment Cos.
Regions Exported to: Worldwide
Percentage of Business in Exporting: 30

48810 (HQ)Specialty Foods Group Inc
6 Dublin Ln
Owensboro, KY 42301   270-926-2324
                             800-238-0020
www.specialtyfoodsgroup.com
Spices, lunch meats, turkey, and pork products including bacon, ham, and sausage.
Year Founded: 1914
Estimated Sales: $234 Million
Number Employees: 250-499
Number of Brands: 7
Type of Packaging: Consumer, Food Service, Private Label, Bulk
Other Locations:
  SFG Production Plant
  Owensboro, KY
  SFG Production Plant
  Humboldt, IA
  SFG Production Plant
  Chicago, IL
  SFG Production Plant
  Williamston, NCSFG Production PlantHumboldt

48811 Specialty Meats & Gourmet
1810 Webster St # 8
Hudson, WI 54016-9318   715-377-0734
Fax: 715-386-6613 800-310-2360
Marketer and processor of fresh and frozen farm raised game meat from alligator to yak; gourmet items, corporate gift boxes, etc.
Principal: Kent Phillips
Contact: Linda Janse
ljanse@smgfoods.com
Estimated Sales: Under $500,000
Number Employees: 1-4
Square Footage: 8000
Parent Co: Venison America
Type of Packaging: Consumer, Food Service
Regions Imported from: Canada
Percentage of Business in Importing: 2

48812 Specialty Minerals Inc
35 Highland Ave
Bethlehem, PA 18017-9482   610-861-3496
Fax: 610-882-8726 800-801-1031
www.mineralstech.com
Manufacturer, sellers and exporters of food and pharmaceutical grades of precipitated calcium carbonate, ground limestone and talc
Chairman/CEO: Jospeh Muscari
CFO: Douglas Dietrich
Director: Gary Castagna
Sales: Jay Esty
Commercial Manager: Jay Esty
Number Employees: 50-99
Parent Co: Minerals Technologies Inc
Type of Packaging: Private Label
Other Locations:
  SMI Mineral Plant
  Adams, MA
  SMI Mineral Plant
  Canann, CT
  SMI Mineral Plant
  Barretts, MT
  SMI Mineral Plant
  Lucerne Valley, CASMI Mineral PlantCanann
Brands Exported: Vicality Calcium Carbonate; CalEssence; Calofort; Vicron; Microtalc; Sturcal
Regions Exported to: Central America, South America, Europe, Asia, Middle East, Middle East

48813 Specialty Packaging Inc
3250 W Seminary Dr # A
Fort Worth, TX 76133-1145   817-922-9727
Fax: 817-922-8262 800-284-7722
Food service paper bags and wrap
President: H Dorris
spac@earthlink.net
R&D: Herman Chenezert
Estimated Sales: $ 10 - 20 Million
Number Employees: 50-99

48814 Specialty Products
128 Rogers Street
Gloucester, MA 01930   216-362-1050
Fax: 216-362-6506 800-222-6846
luis.granja@gortons.com www.gortons.com
Processor and exporter of breading batter
Manager: Luis Granja
Controller: Sue Spisak
Plant Manager: Luis Granja
Estimated Sales: $10-20 Million
Number Employees: 20-49
Parent Co: Gorton's
Type of Packaging: Food Service, Private Label, Bulk
Regions Exported to: Worldwide
Percentage of Business in Exporting: 5

48815 Specialty Rice Inc
1000 W 1st St
Brinkley, AR 72021-9000   870-734-1235
Fax: 870-734-1237 800-467-1233
info@dellarice.com www.delroserice.com
Processor, miller and exporter of five types of rice
Manager: Ojus Ajmara
Manager: Glenda Hilsdon
glendah@dellarice.com
General Manager: Glenda Hilsdon
Estimated Sales: $800,000
Number Employees: 10-19
Square Footage: 32000
Brands Exported: Della; Gourmet Basmati Rice; Jasmine
Regions Exported to: Central America, South America, Middle East
Percentage of Business in Exporting: 5

48816 (HQ)Specialty Wood Products
900 Lumac Rd
Clanton, AL 35045-9610   205-755-6016
Fax: 205-755-3678 800-322-5343
info@specwood.com www.specwood.com
Store fixtures and gift baskets
President: Bonny Smith
info@specwood.com
Sales Exec: K Smith
Estimated Sales: Below $ 5 Million
Number Employees: 20-49
Type of Packaging: Food Service
Regions Exported to: Asia

48817 Specific Mechanical Systems
6848 Kirkpatrick Crescent
Victoria, BC V8M 1Z9
Canada   250-652-2111
Fax: 250-652-6010 info@specific.net
www.specificmechanical.com
Manufacturer and exporter of stainless steel process and storage tanks, pressure vessels and mixers
President and CEO: Phil Zacharias
CFO: Bill Cumming
Engineering Manager: Tom Goldbach
Quality Control: Darren Combs
Sales Director: Blaine Clouston
Plant Manager: Bill Cummings
Estimated Sales: Below $ 5 Million
Number Employees: 40
Square Footage: 72000
Regions Exported to: South America, Asia, Worldwide
Percentage of Business in Exporting: 90

48818 Speco Inc
3946 Willow St
Schiller Park, IL 60176-2311 847-678-4240
Fax: 847-678-8037 800-541-5415
sales@speco.com www.speco.com
Manufacturer and exporter of meat cutting equipment including meat and mincer knives and bone collector systems
Vice President: Clarence Hoffman
clarence@speco.com
Office Manager: Sue Ryan
Sales Manager: Steve Jacob
Production Manager: Clarence Hoffman
Maintenance Supervisor: Ron Schulmeister
Estimated Sales: $7 Million
Number Employees: 50-99
Square Footage: 100000
Regions Exported to: Worldwide
Percentage of Business in Exporting: 20

48819 Spectro
1515 Us Highway 281
Marble Falls, TX 78654-4507 830-798-8786
Fax: 830-798-8467 800-580-6608
www.spectro.com
Manufacturer and exporter of X-ray fluorescent elemental analyzers
Manager: Robert Bartek
Marketing Communications Manager: Gisela Becker
VP Sales/Marketing: Phil Almquist
Contact: Andreas Eerden
aeerden@spectro.com
Estimated Sales: $ 3 - 5 Million
Number Employees: 5-9
Square Footage: 120000
Regions Exported to: Central America, South America, Europe, Asia, Middle East
Percentage of Business in Exporting: 30

48820 Spectrum Foods Inc
2520 South Grand Ave E
P.O. Box 3483
Springfield, IL 62703-5613   217-528-5301
Fax: 217-391-0096 lmyers@spectrum-foods.com
www.spectrum-foods.com

Offers natural and organic vegetable oil, organic soy products, and low sodium sea salt.
President: Rob Kirby
Chairman: Al Maiocco
VP Sales & Business Development: Lynn Myers
Manager: Karen Adamo
kglitter-adamo@spectrum-foods.com
Number Employees: 20-49
Type of Packaging: Bulk

48821 Spee-Dee Packaging Machinery
P.O.Box 656
1360 Grandview Parkway
Sturtevant, WI 53177   262-886-4402
    Fax: 262-886-5502 877-375-2121
    info@spee-dee.com www.spee-dee.com
Manufacturer and exporter of volumetric cup-type and auger filling equipment for powders, granulars and pastes
President: James P Navin
Vice President: Timm Johnson
Operations Manager: Paul Navin
Estimated Sales: Below $5 Million
Number Employees: 20-49
Square Footage: 20000
Brands Exported: Spee-Dee Packaging
Regions Exported to: Central America, South America, Europe, Asia, Canada, Mexico, Latin America
Percentage of Business in Exporting: 5

48822 Speed Queen
PO Box 990
Ripon, WI 54971-0990   800-345-5649
    Fax: 920-748-4411 sales@alliancels.com
    www.speedqueen.com

48823 Speedways Conveyors
PO Box 9
Lancaster, NY 14086-0009   716-893-2222
    Fax: 716-893-3067 800-800-1022
Aluminum conveyors including gravity, powered, pallet flow and line shaft; exporter of pallet flow systems
Executive VP: John Jacobowitz
VP Sales: Daniel Buckley
Estimated Sales: $ 5-10 Million
Number Employees: 50-99
Square Footage: 440000
Type of Packaging: Consumer, Food Service
Regions Exported to: Central America, South America, Europe
Percentage of Business in Exporting: 5

48824 Spence & Company
78 Campanelli Industrial drive
Brockton, MA 02301   508-427-5577
    Fax: 508-427-5557 salmon@spenceltd.com
    www.spenceltd.com
Smoked fish; importer of fish ingredients
President: Alan Spence
Estimated Sales: $4500000
Number Employees: 25
Type of Packaging: Consumer, Food Service
Regions Imported from: Europe
Percentage of Business in Importing: 5

48825 Spencer Turbine Co
600 Day Hill Rd
Windsor, CT 06095-4706   860-688-8361
    Fax: 860-688-0098 800-232-4321
    marketing@spencer-air.com
    www.spencerturbine.com
Manufacturer and exporter of central vacuum systems, tubing, fittings and centrifugal blowers; also, air and gas handling equipment, air knives and pressure fans
President/CEO: Mike Walther
mwalther@spencer-air.com
VP: Paul Burdick
Marketing Manager: Janis Cayne
Sales: Jim Yablonski
Estimated Sales: $ 20 - 50 Million
Number Employees: 100-249
Square Footage: 200000
Brands Exported: Spencer Turbine, Industravac, Power Mizer
Regions Exported to: Central America, South America, Europe, Asia, Middle East

48826 (HQ)Sperling Industries
2420 Z St
Omaha, NE 68107-4430   402-556-4070
    Fax: 402-556-2927 sperlingboss@aol.com
Manufacturer and exporter of meat processing equipment including sausage makers, cookers, renderers, cutters, presses and grinders, as well as food processing machinery. Also material handlers and conveyors
President: Craig Ellett
Executive VP: C Schmidt
Manager: Allen Tegtmneier
Estimated Sales: $ 3 - 5 Million
Number Employees: 10-19
Square Footage: 400000
Other Locations:
    Cincinnati Boss Co.
    Bellevue, NECincinnati Boss Co.
Brands Exported: Boss
Regions Exported to: Worldwide
Percentage of Business in Exporting: 30

48827 Sperling Industries
2420 Z St
Omaha, NE 68107-4430   402-556-4070
    Fax: 402-556-2927 800-647-5062
    sperling@sperlingind.com
Meat and food processing equipment; exporter of meat packing house equipment
President: Craig Ellett
Manager: Jim Adrian
adrian@sperlingind.com
Manager: Jeff Nicolajsen
Estimated Sales: $ 3 - 5 Million
Number Employees: 10-19
Square Footage: 7000
Parent Co: Cincinnati-Boss Company
Brands Exported: Boss
Regions Exported to: Central America, South America, Europe, Asia, Canada, Mexico, Australia
Percentage of Business in Exporting: 15

48828 Spice & Spice
655 Deep Valley Drive
Ste 125
Rolling Hills Estates, CA 90274   310-265-2914
    Fax: 310-265-2934 866-729-7742
    info@spicenspice.com www.spicenspice.com
Bulk line of whole and ground spice products: black pepper, white pepper, cumin, cinnamon, crush chili, cinnamon stick, chili powder, granulated garlic, dry chili pods
Owner: Anthony Dirocco
CEO: Mukesh Thakker
R & D: Nitul Unekekett
Quality Control: Nina Lukamanje
Contact: Cindy Philips
cindy@calwind.com
Estimated Sales: $ 5-10 Million
Number Employees: 1-4
Number of Brands: 1
Number of Products: 25
Square Footage: 200000
Type of Packaging: Food Service, Bulk
Brands Exported: Boat Brand
Regions Exported to: South America, Canada
Percentage of Business in Exporting: 10
Brands Imported: Boat Brand
Regions Imported from: Central America, Asia, Middle East, China, India
Percentage of Business in Importing: 90

48829 Spice House International Specialties
47 Bloomingdale Road
Hicksville, NY 11801-1512   516-942-7248
    Fax: 516-942-7249 www.spicehouseint.com
Spices and blends, specialty foods, hot sauces, dried fruits and nuts; serving the food service market from around the world
President: Anthony Provetto
Estimated Sales: $ 5 - 10 Million
Number Employees: 5-9
Square Footage: 18400
Type of Packaging: Consumer, Food Service, Private Label, Bulk
Brands Exported: ISH
Regions Exported to: Europe, Caribbean
Regions Imported from: Europe, Asia
Percentage of Business in Importing: 30

48830 Spice King Corporation
438 El Camino Dr
Beverly Hills, CA 90212   310-836-7770
    Fax: 310-836-6454
Processor, importer and exporter of custom formulated natural spices and seasonings; also, dehydrated vegetables and fruits
General Manager: James Stephens
VP: A Stern
Marketing Director: Anne Stern
Number Employees: 20-49
Square Footage: 100000
Regions Exported to: Worldwide
Percentage of Business in Exporting: 25
Regions Imported from: Worldwide

48831 Spice World Inc
8101 Presidents Dr
Orlando, FL 32809
    sworld@spiceworldinc.com
    www.spiceworldinc.com
Processor and exporter of garlic, custom seasoning blends and garlic including minced, chopped and packed in olive oil or water
Year Founded: 1949
Estimated Sales: $ 5 - 10 Million
Number Employees: 100-249
Number of Brands: 1
Square Footage: 480000
Type of Packaging: Consumer, Food Service, Private Label, Bulk

48832 Spin-Tech Corporation
1024 Adams St
Suite A
Hoboken, NJ 7030   201-659-6110
    Fax: 201-963-7674 800-977-4692
Beverage fountains, candelabra, serving trays and liquid fuel candles; exporter of beverage fountains, table candles and floral holders
Owner: Frank Pasquale
Estimated Sales: $1-2.5 Million
Number Employees: 5-9
Square Footage: 50000
Regions Exported to: Worldwide
Percentage of Business in Exporting: 20

48833 Spinco Metal Products Inc
1 Country Club Dr
Newark, NY 14513-1250   315-331-6285
    Fax: 315-331-9535 cthayer@spincometal.com
    www.spincometal.com
Manufacturer and exporter of copper refrigeration components, brass flow metering devices and stainless steel beverage lines, welded and brazed assemblies, cut to length tubing
President: Robert C Straubing
crstraubing@spincometal.com
Engineering/Quality Manager: David Gardner
Quality Assurance Coordinator: Craig Thayer
Inside Sales: Connie Rios
Estimated Sales: $ 10-20 Million
Number Employees: 50-99
Square Footage: 120000
Regions Exported to: Central America, South America, Europe, Asia, Middle East, Canada, Latin America
Percentage of Business in Exporting: 5

48834 Spir-It/Zoo Piks
200 Brickstone Sq # G05
Andover, MA 01810-1439   978-964-1551
    Fax: 978-964-1552 800-343-0996
Manufacturer and exporter of plastic cutlery, picks, sticks, stirrers, straws and other food service accessories; importer of wooden stirrers and toothpicks
President: Donald McCann
CFO: Peter Maki
VP Sales/Marketing: Joe Pierro
Sales/Marketing Manager: Marva White
Number Employees: 100-249
Square Footage: 320000
Type of Packaging: Food Service
Other Locations:
    Spir-It/Zoo Piks
    Dallas, TXSpir-It/Zoo Piks
Brands Exported: Glassips; Hob Nob; Spir-It
Regions Exported to: Central America, South America, Europe
Percentage of Business in Exporting: 5
Regions Imported from: Asia

48835 Spiral Biotech Inc
2 Technology Way
Norwood, MA 02062-2680   781-320-9000
    Fax: 781-320-8181 800-554-1620
    mail@aicompanies.com

Manufacturer and exporter of laboratory equipment including fast sample dilutors, spiral platers, automated plate counters and colony counting systems; importer of microbial air samplers and filter bags; wholesaler/distributor of microbial air samplers
President: John Coughlin
VP Operations: P Emond
Estimated Sales: $ 10 - 20 Million
Number Employees: 50-99
Square Footage: 6000
Parent Co: Advanced Instruments
Brands Exported: Casba II; Casba 4; Autoplate 4000; LabPro
Regions Exported to: Worldwide
Percentage of Business in Exporting: 30
Brands Imported: Microbio; Burkard
Regions Imported from: Europe
Percentage of Business in Importing: 15

48836 Spiral Manufacturing Co Inc
11419 Yellow Pine St NW
Minneapolis, MN 55448-3158 763-392-2336
Fax: 763-755-6184 800-426-3643
info@spiralmfg.com www.spiralmfg.com
Manufacturer and exporter of commercial and industrial HVAC, ventilation, air conditioning and pneumatic conveying, dust and fume collection distribution systems
President: Tom Menth
Contact: Jesiah Durene
jdurene@spiralmfg.com
Estimated Sales: $ 5 - 10 Million
Number Employees: 1-4
Regions Exported to: Worldwide
Percentage of Business in Exporting: 6

48837 Spirit Foodservice, Inc.
200 Brickstone Square
Suite G-05
Andover, MA 01810 978-964-1551
Fax: 978-964-1552 800-343-0996
www.spiritfoodservice.com
Manufacturer and exporter of plastic swizzle sticks, picks, napkin holders, tip trays, napkins, drinking straws and disposable drinkware; also, custom imprinting available
Contact: Peter Maki
maki@spir-it.com
Estimated Sales: $5-10 Million
Number Employees: 100-249
Brands Exported: Zoo Piks
Regions Exported to: Central America, South America, Europe, Australia
Percentage of Business in Exporting: 10

48838 Spokane Seed Co
6015 E Alki Ave
Spokane Valley, WA 99212-1019 509-535-3671
Fax: 509-535-0874 800-359-8478
spokseed@spokaneseed.com
www.spokaneseed.com
Processor and exporter of peas and lentils
President: Peter Johnstone
CFO: Jeff White
Sales: Nelson Fancher
Estimated Sales: $3900000
Number Employees: 20-49
Type of Packaging: Consumer, Food Service, Bulk

48839 Spoonable
345 Clinton Avenue
#4G
Brooklyn, NY 11238 718-974-0653
info@spoonablellc.com
www.spoonablellc.com
Salty caramel sauce, butterscotch sauce, chewy sesame caramel sauce, spicy chili caramel sauce, flowery lavender caramel sauce, peppered orange caramel sauce
President/Owner: Michelle Lewis
mnlewis@spoonablellc.com
Number Employees: 4
Number of Brands: 1
Number of Products: 7
Type of Packaging: Consumer, Food Service, Private Label, Bulk

48840 Sportabs International
PO Box 492118
Los Angeles, CA 90049-8118 310-451-2625
Fax: 310-207-8526 888-814-7767
Processor and exporter of multi-vitamin tablets
President: Richard Griswold
Estimated Sales: $500,000
Number Employees: 1-4
Type of Packaging: Consumer
Regions Exported to: Worldwide
Percentage of Business in Exporting: 25

48841 Spray Drying
5320 Enterprise St # J
Sykesville, MD 21784-9354 410-549-8090
Fax: 410-549-8091 sales@spraydrysys.com
www.spraydrysys.com
Manufacturer and exporter of spray dryers
President: Jeff Bayliss
bayliss@spraydrysys.com
Quality Control: Jess Bayliss
Vice President: Jeff Bayliss
Estimated Sales: Below $5 Million
Number Employees: 5-9
Square Footage: 7000
Regions Exported to: Worldwide
Percentage of Business in Exporting: 20

48842 Spray Dynamics LTD
108 Bolte Ln
St Clair, MO 63077-3218 636-629-7366
Fax: 636-629-7455 800-260-7366
spraydynamics@heatandcontrol.com
www.spraydynamics.com
Manufacturer and exporter of liquid and dry ingredient applicators and dispensers for food processing machinery.
Owner: Dave Holmeyer
Accounts Payable: Melanie Booher
Marketing Coordinator: Stephanie Butenhoff
Sales Representative: George Wipperfurth
Service Manager: Craig Booher
Estimated Sales: $2.5-5 Million
Number Employees: 20-49
Brands Exported: Unispense; Meter Master; Master Series I & II
Regions Exported to: Central America, South America, Europe, Asia, Middle East

48843 Spraying Systems Company
North Avenue and Schmale Road
PO Box 7900
Wheaton, IL 60187 630-655-5000
Fax: 630-260-0842 info@spray.com
www.spray.com
Manufacturer and exporter of nozzles, spray guns, portable spray systems and spray nozzle accessories including connectors, ball fittings, valves, regulators, etc
President/CEO: James Bramsen
VP Manufacturing: Don Fox
VP/COO: Dave Smith
Sr Applications Engineer: Wes Bartell
Regions Exported to: Central America, South America, Europe, Asia, Middle East

48844 Sprayway Inc
1005 S Westgate St
Addison, IL 60101-5021 630-628-3000
Fax: 630-543-7797 800-332-9000
info@spraywayinc.com
Manufacturer and exporter of aerosol products including all purpose and glass cleaners, dust control sprays and insecticides
President: Michael Rohl
CFO: Roger Hayes
rhayes@spraywayinc.com
VP Sales/Marketing: Bob Potvin
Estimated Sales: $ 10 - 20 Million
Number Employees: 100-249
Number of Brands: 1
Square Footage: 160000
Type of Packaging: Private Label
Regions Exported to: Worldwide
Percentage of Business in Exporting: 20

48845 (HQ)Spreda Group
7410 New Lagrange Rd
PO Box 378
Louisville, KY 40222 502-426-9411
Fax: 502-423-7531
Fruit and vegetable powder, tomato paste, colors, spray and vacuum dried and dehydrated fruits and vegetables, apple pectin and apple juice concentrate
President: George Falk
VP: James Falk
Number Employees: 100-249
Type of Packaging: Food Service, Bulk
Regions Exported to: Europe
Regions Imported from: Worldwide
Percentage of Business in Importing: 80

48846 Spring USA Corp
127 Ambassador Dr # 147
Naperville, IL 60540-4079 630-527-8600
Fax: 630-527-8677 800-535-8974
springusa@springusa.com
Products range from chafing dishes to professional cookware, from induction ranges to coffee urns.
President: Tom Brija
springusa@springusa.com
Sales/Marketing Supervisor: Kelly Boyle
Estimated Sales: $2.5-5,000,000
Number Employees: 5-9
Parent Co: Spring Switzerland

48847 (HQ)Springer-Penguin
PO Box 199
Mount Vernon, NY 10552-0199 914-699-3200
Fax: 914-699-3231 800-835-8500
Manufacturer and exporter of refrigerators, file cabinets and wood office furniture including conference tables, bookcases, etc.; importer of wooden bookcases
Number Employees: 10
Square Footage: 80000
Regions Imported from: South America
Percentage of Business in Importing: 15

48848 Springfield Creamery Inc
29440 Airport Rd
Eugene, OR 97402-9537 541-689-2911
Fax: 541-689-2915 sue@nancysyogurt.com
www.nancysyogurt.com
Manufacturer of yogurt, cultured soy yogurt, cream cheese, cottage cheese, sour cream, and kefir.
Owner: Joe Kesey
esther@nancysyogurt.com
Owner: Sue Kesey
Marketing: Sheryl Kesey Thompson
Operations: Kit Kesey
Estimated Sales: $22 Million
Number Employees: 50-99
Number of Brands: 1
Number of Products: 13
Square Footage: 40000
Type of Packaging: Consumer, Food Service, Private Label, Bulk
Brands Exported: Nancy's
Regions Exported to: Canada
Percentage of Business in Exporting: 3

48849 Springport Steel Wire Products
4906 Hoffman Street
Suite B
Elkhart, IN 46516 574-295-9660
Fax: 574-293-8552 cs@sigma-wire.com
www.sigmawire.com
Manufacturer and exporter of handling equipment including containers, pallets, wire and mesh shelving and conveyor guards
Estimated Sales: $ 2.5-5 Million
Number Employees: 20-50
Regions Exported to: Canada, Mexico
Percentage of Business in Exporting: 10

48850 Sprout Creek Farm
34 Lauer Rd.
Poughkeepsie, NY 12603 845-485-8432
info@sproutcreekfarm.org
www.sproutcreekfarm.org
Farm-made cow and goat milk cheese
President: Margot Morris
Year Founded: 1974
Number of Brands: 1
Number of Products: 7
Type of Packaging: Consumer, Private Label
Brands Exported: Sprout Creek Farm

48851 Spruce Foods
800 S El Camino Real
Suite 210
San Clemente, CA 92672-4274 949-366-9457
Fax: 800-708-9775 800-326-3612
bobbreen@sprucefoods.com
www.sprucefoods.com
Importer of organic grocery products
President: Bob Breen
Estimated Sales: $ 5 - 10 Million
Number Employees: 4
Number of Brands: 3
Number of Products: 160

Importers & Exporters / A-Z

Brands Imported: Montebello, Villa Flor, Acquerello, Massetti, Lapas, Paso Viejo, Nunez De Fado, Venecia, Lorenzi, Lischeto
Regions Imported from: South America, Europe
Percentage of Business in Importing: 90

48852 Spudnik Equipment Co
584 W 100 N
PO Box 1045
Blackfoot, ID 83221-5518 208-684-4120
Fax: 208-785-1497 www.spudnik.com
Manufacturer and exporter of potato handling equipment and parts including pliers, scoopers, conveyors, sorters, bins, bulk beds, van unloaders, semi-trailers, etc
CEO: Rolf Geier
Sales Manager: Dennis Schumacker
Engineering Manager: Andrew Blight
Estimated Sales: $ 10-20 Million
Number Employees: 100-249
Square Footage: 200000
Regions Exported to: South America, Europe, Pacific Rim
Percentage of Business in Exporting: 6

48853 Spurgeon Co
1330 Hilton Rd
Ferndale, MI 48220-2837 248-547-3805
Fax: 248-547-8344 800-396-2554
Manufacturer and exporter of conveyors, unscramblers, aluminum casting and stacking equipment; importer of aluminum casting and stacking equipment
CEO: Andy Willermet
awillermet@yoplait.fr
VP: Thomas Woodbeck
VP: Bernie Makie
Estimated Sales: $10-20 Million
Number Employees: 50-99
Square Footage: 200000
Parent Co: Overhead Conveyor Company
Regions Imported from: Europe

48854 Squab Producers of California
409 Primo Way
Modesto, CA 95358-5721 209-537-4744
Fax: 209-537-2037 squabbob@aol.com
www.squab.com
Processor and exporter of fresh and frozen squab, pheasant, quail, poussin and partridge
President: Robert Shipley
squabbob@aol.com
Sales Exec: Robert Shipley
Estimated Sales: $ 5 - 10 Million
Number Employees: 50-99
Square Footage: 40000
Type of Packaging: Consumer, Food Service, Private Label, Bulk
Brands Exported: King-Cal; Mendes Farms
Regions Exported to: Worldwide

48855 Squar-Buff
1000 45th Street
Oakland, CA 94608-3314 510-655-2470
Fax: 510-652-0969 800-525-6955
Manufacturer and exporter of floor and rug cleaning machinery
Number Employees: 5
Regions Exported to: Worldwide
Percentage of Business in Exporting: 4

48856 Square Enterprises Corp
19 Paterson Ave
Wallington, NJ 07057-1115 973-365-1639
Fax: 973-365-0156 square@squareenterprises.com
www.squareenterprises.biz
Polish products
Owner: Adam Szala
adamszala@squareenterprises.com
Number Employees: 20-49

48857 Squirrel Systems
3157 Grandview Highway
Vancouver, BC V5M 2E9
Canada 604-412-3300
Fax: 604-434-9888 800-388-6824
squirrel@squirrelsystems.com
www.squirrelsystems.com
Manufacturer and exporter of electronic point of sale terminals
Vice President of Research and Developme: Joe Cortese
Vice President of Corporate Sales: David Atkinson

Estimated Sales: $ 20 - 30 Million
Number Employees: 100-250
Regions Exported to: Worldwide

48858 St Charles Trading Inc
650 N Raddant Rd
Batavia, IL 60510-4207 630-377-0608
Fax: 630-406-1936
customerservice@stcharlestrading.com
Distributor, importer/exporter of food ingredients, specializing in beans and seeds; oar products; batters, coatins & breadcrumbs; dairy, potato, wheat, corn and protein products; cocoa and chocolate; dehydrated onion and garlic; spices; food chemicals and sweeteners; dehydrated vegetables and fruits; and rice.
CEO: William Manns
williammanns@stcharlestrading.com
Executive Vice President: Dave Nolan
Director, Manufacturing & Quality Contro: Andrew Rumshas
Vice President of Operations: Janet Matthews
Purchasing Manager: Novita Rahim
Estimated Sales: $64.4 Million
Number Employees: 20-49
Number of Brands: 49
Type of Packaging: Bulk
Regions Exported to: Worldwide
Regions Imported from: Worldwide

48859 (HQ)St John's Botanicals
7711 Hillmeade Rd
Bowie, MD 20720-4571 301-262-5302
Fax: 301-262-2489 www.stjohnsbotanicals.com
Spice blends, herb teas, essential oils, ginseng products, nutritional supplements
Owner: William Mussenden
Ceo: Sydney Vallentync
CFO: Patti Mussenden
Research/Dev: Diane Tolsen
Quality Control: Diane Tolsen
Marketing: Rayla Cuffey
Sales Manager: Rayla Cuffey
Pub Relations: Maria McCulvey
Operations Manager: Brandy Schwartz
Plant Manager: Diane Tolson
Purchasing: Sydney Vallentyne
Estimated Sales: Less Than $500,000
Number Employees: 5-9
Type of Packaging: Private Label, Bulk
Regions Exported to: Central America, South America, Europe, Asia, Middle East, Australia
Percentage of Business in Exporting: 5

48860 St Joseph Packaging Inc
PO Box 579
St Joseph, MO 64502-0579 816-233-3181
Fax: 816-233-2475 800-383-3000
Custom industrial packaging offset/flexo printing, diecut/cello windowing, laminating and direct print on mini-flute corrigated
President: C Hamilton Jr
CFO: Patty Waitkoss
CEO: Brad Keller
Quality Control: Don Kragel
Marketing: Pam Hurley
Plant Manager: Josh Hamilton
Purchasing: Kenny Hayter
Estimated Sales: $15 Million
Square Footage: 220000
Type of Packaging: Consumer, Food Service, Private Label

48861 (HQ)St Julian Winery
716 S Kalamazoo St
Paw Paw, MI 49079-1558 269-657-5568
Fax: 269-657-5743 800-732-6002
wines@stjulian.com www.stjulian.com
Processor and exporter of grape beverages including champagne, wine and juice
President: Kim Babcock
babcockk@stjulian.com
Executive VP: Charles Catherman
Marketing Director: Kim Babcock
VP Sales: Joe Zuiderueen
Wine Maker: David Miller, Ph.D.
Estimated Sales: $9 Million
Number Employees: 50-99
Type of Packaging: Consumer, Food Service
Brands Exported: Simply Red

48862 St. Clair Industries
3067 E Commercial Blvd
Ft Lauderdale, FL 33308 954-491-0400
Fax: 954-351-9082
Processor and exporter of catalyst altered water
President: Saul Rubinoff
CEO: Anne Rubinoff
Vice President: Anne Rubinoff
Estimated Sales: Less than $100,000
Number Employees: 2
Square Footage: 10000
Type of Packaging: Consumer, Bulk
Brands Exported: Willard; Briz
Regions Exported to: Central America, Europe
Percentage of Business in Exporting: 10

48863 St. Clair Pakwell
120 25th Ave
Bellwood, IL 60104-1201 708-547-7500
Fax: 708-547-9052 800-323-1922
Manufacturer and exporter of decorative packaging including wrapping paper
Estimated Sales: $20-50 Million
Number Employees: 100-249
Parent Co: Field Container Corporation
Type of Packaging: Food Service, Bulk
Regions Exported to: Canada

48864 St. Killian Importing
170 Market St.
Everett, MA 02149 617-410-3902
info@stkillian.com
stkillian.com
Beer and malt
President & General Manager: Phil Clarke
Marketing Coordinator: Piro Capo
National Sales Director: Matt Arthur
Year Founded: 1983
Estimated Sales: $4 Million
Number Employees: 10-20
Parent Co: L. Knife & Son Companies
Brands Imported: 961, Andechs, Belhaven, Bitburger Braugruppe, Carlsberg, Charles Wells, Corsendonk, Crabbie's, Grimbergen, James Boag's, Jenlain, Kronenbourg 1664, Okocim O.K. Beer and more.
Regions Imported from: Worldwide

48865 Sta-Rite Ginnie Lou Inc
245 E South 1st St
PO Box 435
Shelbyville, IL 62565-2332 217-774-3921
Fax: 217-774-5234 800-782-7483
www.sta-riteginnielou.com
Manufacturer, importer and exporter of nylon hair nets, hairpins, bobbypins and haircare accessories.
Chairman: Robert Bolinger
CEO: Noel Bolinger
noelbolinger@consulated.net
Sales Director: Linda Stewardson
Estimated Sales: $1 Million
Number Employees: 5-9
Number of Brands: 10
Number of Products: 1300
Square Footage: 32000
Type of Packaging: Consumer, Food Service, Private Label, Bulk

48866 Stadelman Fruit LLC
111 Meade St
Zillah, WA 98953-9419 509-829-5145
Fax: 509-829-5164 www.stadelmanfruit.com
Processor and exporter of produce including apples, cherries, nectarines, pears, plums and prunes
President: Peter Stadelman
CEO: Rob Stewart
Manager: Rob Stewart
Number Employees: 500-999
Type of Packaging: Consumer, Food Service, Private Label, Bulk
Regions Exported to: Worldwide

48867 Stahlbush Island Farms Inc
3122 SE Stahlbush Island Rd
Corvallis, OR 97333-2709 541-757-1497
Fax: 541-754-1847 sif@stahlbush.com
www.stahlbush.com
Frozen fruits, vegetables, grains and legumes.
Owners: Bill & Karla Chambers
Number Employees: 100-249
Brands Exported: Stahlbush Island Farms
Regions Exported to: Europe, Asia, Middle East
Percentage of Business in Exporting: 25

Importers & Exporters / A-Z

48868 Stainless
305 Tech Park Drive
Suite 115
La Vergne, TN 37086-3633   954-421-4290
Fax: 954-421-4464   800-877-5177
www.stainless.com
Manufacturer and exporter of stainless steel kitchen and dining room equipment including tables and sinks
VP/General Manager: Edward Umphlette
VP Sales: Tom Kassab
Estimated Sales: Less than $500,000
Number Employees: 4
Square Footage: 920000
Parent Co: Franke USA Holding
Other Locations:
    Stainless
    Holland, MIStainless
Regions Exported to: Worldwide
Percentage of Business in Exporting: 30

48869 Stainless One DispensingSystem
790 Eubanks Drive
Vacaville, CA 95688-9470   800-722-6738
Fax: 707-448-1521   888-723-3827
autobar@aol.com
Manufacturer and exporter of beer dispensing equipment
VP: Clark Smith
Number Employees: 3
Regions Exported to: Central America, South America, Europe, Middle East, Canada, Caribbean, Latin America, Mexico

48870 Stainless Products
1649 72nd Ave
P O Box 169
Somers, WC 53171   262-859-2826
Fax: 262-859-2871   800-558-9446
sales@stainless-products.com
www.stainless-products.com
Manufacturer and exporter of stainless steel fabrications including O-rings, pumps, gauges, welding and valves; also, clean-in-place systems
President: Cindy Gross
jerickson@stainless-products.com
President: Cindy Gross
Sales/Purchasing: Mike Shoop
Estimated Sales: $ 1 - 5 Million
Number Employees: 20-49
Type of Packaging: Bulk
Regions Exported to: Worldwide

48871 Stainless Specialists Inc
T7441 Steel Ln
Wausau, WI 54403-8732   715-675-4155
Fax: 715-675-9096   800-236-4155
www.ssi-wis.com
Manufacturer installation and exporter of stainless steel food processing and equipment, conveyors, tanks and work platforms
President: Roger Prochnow
CFO: Paul Kinate
Sr VP Sales: Mike Slattery
R&D: Steve Radant
Quality Control: Brian Stoffel
Marketing/Sales/Public Relations: Roger Prochnow
Operations: Keith Christian
Production: Shannon Herdt
Plant Manager: Keith Christian
Purchasing: Corey Eimmer
Estimated Sales: $20 Million
Number Employees: 100-249
Square Footage: 15000
Regions Exported to: Europe, Asia, Mexico
Percentage of Business in Exporting: 1

48872 Stainless Steel Coatings
835 Sterling Road
P.O.Box 1145
South Lancaster, MA 01561-1145   978-365-9828
Fax: 978-365-9874   info@steel-it.com
www.steel-it.com
Manufacturer and exporter of anti-corrosion and stainless steel pigmented paint coatings
President: Michael Faigen
Estimated Sales: $1-2,500,000
Number Employees: 10-19
Number of Brands: 2
Number of Products: 14
Square Footage: 20000
Brands Exported: STEEL IT
Regions Exported to: Worldwide
Percentage of Business in Exporting: 25

48873 Stampendous
1122 N Kraemer Pl
Anaheim, CA 92806-1922   714-688-0288
Fax: 714-688-0297   800-869-0474
stamp@markenterprises.com
www.stampendous.com
Manufacturer and exporter of stain and spot removers
Owner: Fran Sieford
stamp@stampendous.com
General Manager: Mark Bruhns
Product Manager: Regina Ashbaugh
Estimated Sales: $ 5 - 10 Million
Number Employees: 50-99
Square Footage: 40000
Regions Exported to: Worldwide
Percentage of Business in Exporting: 15

48874 Stan-Mark Food Products Inc
1100 W 47th Pl
PO Box 09251
Chicago, IL 60609-4302   773-690-5086
Fax: 773-847-6253   800-651-0994
admin@Ingredients-USA.com
www.stanmarkfoods.com
Pickles, spices, grains and seeds, herring
General Manager: Mark Kongrecki
kongrecki@stanmark.biz
Estimated Sales: $ 20 - 50 Million
Number Employees: 20-49
Square Footage: 60000
Type of Packaging: Consumer, Private Label, Bulk
Regions Imported from: Europe, Middle East

48875 (HQ)Standard Casing Company
165 Chubb Ave
Lyndhurst, NJ 07071-3503   201-434-6300
Fax: 201-434-1508   800-847-4141
Manufacturer, importer and exporter of sausage processing equipment including stuffers as well as sausage casings
President: Michael Koss
Executive VP: Joel Koss
Manager Sales: Richard Theise
Contact: Patricia Wisniewski
patriciaw@standardcasing.com
Estimated Sales: $10-20 Million
Number Employees: 50-99
Square Footage: 70000
Type of Packaging: Bulk
Regions Exported to: Central America, South America, Europe, Asia
Percentage of Business in Exporting: 30
Brands Imported: Pokomat; Talsa
Regions Imported from: South America, Europe, Asia
Percentage of Business in Importing: 25

48876 Standard Folding Cartons Inc
7520 Astoria Blvd # 100
Flushing, NY 11370-1645   718-396-4522
Fax: 718-507-6430   stanfold@aol.com
www.thestandardgroup.com
Manufacturer and exporter of folding cartons
President: Louis Cortes
Manager: Tanya Borges
tanyab@thestandardgroup.com
Estimated Sales: $ 20-50 Million
Number Employees: 20-49
Regions Exported to: Canada

48877 Standard Fruit & Vegetable Company
PO Box 225027
Dallas, TX 75222-5027   305-520-8400
Fax: 305-567-0320   800-428-3600
Importer and wholesaler/distributor of produce including potatoes and tomatoes
Chairman: Marty Rutchik
President: Jay Pack
CFO/VP: Steve Gray
Parent Co: Del Monte

48878 Standard Functional Foods Grp
715 Massman Dr
Nashville, TN 37210   615-889-6360
Fax: 615-889-7775   800-226-4340
www.sffgi.com
Manufacturer, exporter and contract packager of candy including bars, boxed, log rolls and caramel corn.
President & COO: Tom Drummond
Chief Executive Officer: Jimmy Spradley
VP Administration & Corporate Secretary: Dennis Adcock
Vice President: Neil Spradley
Director of Business Development: Bryan Lewis
Director of Quality Assurance: Scott Sherry
Marketing Manager: Joanne Barthel
Director of Corporate Procurement: Brian Hillman
Director of Human Resources: Carol Cooper
Director of Operations: Bill Hardin
Year Founded: 1901
Estimated Sales: $41.2 Million
Number Employees: 500
Square Footage: 96500
Type of Packaging: Private Label, Bulk
Brands Exported: Pop 'N Crunch; Goo Goo

48879 Standard Meat Co LP
5105 Investment Dr
Dallas, TX 75236-1420   972-283-8501
Fax: 214-561-0560   866-859-6313
www.standardmeat.com
Sausages and other prepared meats
Partner: Joseph Penshorn
Partner: William Rosenthal
Controller: Garry Custer
Food Safety & Research & Development: Scott Boleman
Quality Assurance: Jonathan Savell
Purchasing Manager: Sam Beede
Estimated Sales: $13.7 Million
Number Employees: 100-249
Square Footage: 195912
Percentage of Business in Importing: 5

48880 Standard Paper Box MachCo Inc
347 Coster St # 2
Bronx, NY 10474-6813   718-328-3300
Fax: 718-842-7772   800-367-8755
SPBM@prodigy.net   www.spbmco.com
Manufacturer and exporter of box making machinery
President: Bruce Adams
Sales: Ronnie Nadel
Estimated Sales: $ 5 - 10 Million
Number Employees: 10-19
Square Footage: 200000
Brands Exported: Standard; Econocut
Regions Exported to: Central America, South America, Europe, Middle East
Percentage of Business in Exporting: 10
Regions Imported from: Europe, Asia

48881 Standard Refrigeration Co
321 Foster Ave
Wood Dale, IL 60191-1432   708-345-5400
Fax: 708-345-3513
stanref.customerservice@alfalaval.com
www.alfalaval.us
Manufacturer and exporter of heat exchangers for refrigeration applications
Materials & Logistics Manager: Frank Nimesheim
Senior Vice President, Equipment: Mark Larsen
Research and Development Manager: Gary Kaiser
Quality Control Manager: Kevin Lenihan
Market Unit Manager, Refrigeration: Dan Aiken
Business Development Manager: Yao Jeppsson
Manager: Joseph Shukys
joe@btureps.com
General Manager: Phil Lucas
Product Portfolio Manager: Mark Hetherington
Factory Manager: Therese Huff
Estimated Sales: $ 50-100 Million
Number Employees: 100-249

48882 Standard Terry Mills
38 Green St
Souderton, PA 18964-1702   215-723-8121
Fax: 215-723-3651
Manufacturer and exporter of knitted and woven dish cloths, kitchen towels, oven mitts, aprons, food covers and pot holders; importer of kitchen towels
President: Kerry Gingrich
VP Production: G Nam
Estimated Sales: $10-20 Million
Number Employees: 1-4
Square Footage: 200000
Regions Exported to: South America, Europe, Asia
Percentage of Business in Exporting: 5
Regions Imported from: Asia
Percentage of Business in Importing: 20

Importers & Exporters / A-Z

48883 Stanfos
3908 69th Avenue NW
Edmonton, AB T6B 2V2
Canada
780-468-2165
Fax: 780-465-4890 800-661-5648
info@stanfos.com www.stanfos.com
Manufacturer, exporter and wholesaler/distributor of dairy, food and meat processing equipment including pasteurizers
President: Lang Jameson
Sales Manager: Shawna Bungax
Number Employees: 10-19
Brands Exported: Stanfos
Regions Exported to: Worldwide
Percentage of Business in Exporting: 10

48884 Stanley Access Technologies
65 Scott Swamp Rd
Farmington, CT 06032-2803
717-597-6958
Fax: 877-339-7923 800-722-2377
S-SAT-SatInfo@sbdinc.com
www.stanleyaccess.com
Manufacturer and exporter of automatic doors including fireproof, sliding, swinging and electrical; also, access control systems and door operating devices
President: Justin Boswell
International Sales/Marketing: Jennifer Loranger
Customer Service: Susan Martin
Administrative Assistant: Jennifer Almeida House
Estimated Sales: Below $ 500,000
Number Employees: 5-9
Parent Co: Stanley Works
Brands Exported: Dura-Glide; Magic Swing; Sentrex; Stan-Ray; Magic-Access
Regions Exported to: Central America, South America, Europe, Asia, Middle East

48885 Stanley Orchards Sales, Inc.
2044 State Route 32
#6
Modena, NY 12548
845-883-7511
Fax: 845-883-5077 sales@stanleyorchards.com
www.stanleyorchards.com
Apple growing and storage/packing facility; importer of apples and pears; cold storage facility.
President/CEO: Ronald Cohn
Sales & Marketing: Jordan Cohn
Sales Manager: Anthony Maresca
Domestic Sales: Janine Skurnick
Controller: Susan Surprise
Import/Export Liason: Lorrie Hazzard
Estimated Sales: $293 Thousand
Number Employees: 8
Type of Packaging: Consumer, Food Service, Private Label, Bulk
Regions Exported to: Europe, Asia, Middle East, Canada, Caribbean
Brands Imported: AMS, CyD, Frusan, Greenvic, Lonfrut, Rucaray, Surfruit, Trinidad, Brevi, Montever, Trevisur, Tres Ases
Regions Imported from: South America, Asia, New Zealand

48886 Stanpac, Inc.
Spring Creek Road
R.R. # 3
Smithville, ON L0R 2A0
Canada
905-957-3326
Fax: 905-957-3616 www.stanpacnet.com
Ice cream packaging, refillable glass milk bottles and closures, and glass bottles for the beverage and wine industries.
President: Steve Witt
Vice President, Marketing: Murray Bain
Vice President, Sales: Andrew Witt
Vice President, Operations: Ian Killins
Purchasing: Barry Kirk
Regions Exported to: Central America, South America, North America, USA

48887 Stapleton Spence Packing Co
1900 State Highway 99
Gridley, CA 95948-9401
408-297-8715
Fax: 408-297-0611 800-297-8815
www.stapleton-spence.com
Packer of prune concentrates, purees, juices, nuts and other dried fruits.
President/CEO: Brad Stapleton
vhong@stapleton-spence.com
CFO: Ellsworth Rowinski
IT: Victor Hong
Production Director: Mike Smith
Estimated Sales: $15,000,000
Number Employees: 10-19
Square Footage: 15000
Type of Packaging: Consumer, Food Service, Private Label
Regions Exported to: Central America, South America, Europe, Asia, Middle East
Percentage of Business in Exporting: 25

48888 (HQ)Staplex Co Inc
777 5th Ave
Brooklyn, NY 11232-1695
718-768-3333
Fax: 718-965-0750 800-221-0822
info@staplex.com www.staplex.com
Electric staplers for packaging applications. Made in the U.S.A.
President: Doug Butler
info@staplex.com
CEO: Phil Reed
Estimated Sales: $ 5 - 10 Million
Number Employees: 20-49
Regions Exported to: Central America, South America, Europe, Asia, Middle East

48889 Stapling Machines Co
41 Pine St # 30
Rockaway, NJ 07866-3139
973-627-4400
Fax: 973-627-5355 800-432-5909
sales@smcllc.com www.package-testing.com
Manufacturer and exporter of packaging machinery for wirebound containers
President: Norbert Weissburg
n.weissberg@package-testing.com
Estimated Sales: $ 10 - 20 Million
Number Employees: 10-19
Parent Co: Stapling Machines Company
Regions Exported to: Worldwide
Percentage of Business in Exporting: 25

48890 Star Filters
PO Box 518
Timmonsville, SC 29161-0518
843-346-3101
Fax: 843-346-3736 800-845-5381
invest@hilliard.com www.hilliard.com
Manufacturer and exporter of disposable filters and stainless steel plate and frame filter presses for process filtration applications; also, polypropylene dewatering presses for wastewater applications
Regional Sales Manager: Scott Thomas
Regional Sales Manager: Frank Reid
Sales/Marketing Executive: Howard Reed
Estimated Sales: $2.5-5 Million
Number Employees: 20-49
Square Footage: 140000
Parent Co: Hillard Corporation
Brands Exported: Star Filters; Star Poly Presses
Regions Exported to: Central America, South America, Europe, Asia, Middle East, Worldwide
Percentage of Business in Exporting: 10

48891 Star Industries, Inc.
P.O. Box 178
La Grange, IL 60525
708-240-4862
Fax: 708-240-4915 bob@starhydrodyne.com
www.starhydrodyne.com
Manufacturer and exporter of automatic floor scrubbing systems
Executive Director: Susan Frassato
Regional Sales Manager: Scott O'Brien
Estimated Sales: $ 2.5-5 Million
Number Employees: 50-100
Square Footage: 160000
Brands Exported: Star Hydrodyne
Regions Exported to: Europe, Asia
Percentage of Business in Exporting: 50

48892 Star Kay White Inc
85 Brenner Dr
Congers, NY 10920-1307
845-268-6304
Fax: 845-268-3572 800-874-8518
inquiry@starkaywhite.com www.starkaywhite.com
Syrups, candies, panned-items and extracts and flavors
Owner/President/CEO/Plant Manager: Walter Katzenstein
walter@starkaywhite.com
General Manager: Don Heffner
R&D: Richard Sroka
Marketing: Stephen Platt
VP/Sales Executive: James Taft
Manufacturing Supervisor: George Granada
Purchasing Manager: Judy Beaman
Estimated Sales: $8 Million
Number Employees: 50-99
Number of Brands: 1
Number of Products: 750
Square Footage: 180000
Type of Packaging: Bulk

48893 Star Manufacturing Intl Inc
10 Sunnen Dr
PO Box 430129
St Louis, MO 63143-3800
314-678-6303
Fax: 314-781-4344 800-264-7827
technical@star-mfg.com www.star-mfg.com
Manufacturer and exporter of food service equipment including gas and electric cooking equipment, sandwich grills, toasters/waffle bakers, hot dog equipment, condiment dispensers, popcorn equipment, specialty warmers, dispensing and display/merchandising equipment
President/CEO: Frank Ricchio
VP Sales/Marketing: Tim Gaskill
VP Engineering: Doug Vogt
VP: Mike Barber
Marketing Director: Cindi Benz
Sales Director: Phil Kister
Contact: Ibrahim Nestor
nibrahim@star-mfg.com
Estimated Sales: $ 1 - 3 Million
Number Employees: 50-99
Square Footage: 380000
Type of Packaging: Food Service
Brands Exported: Starmax; Galaxy; Jetstar; Grill-Max; Grill-Max Pro
Regions Exported to: Central America, South America, Europe, Asia, Middle East
Percentage of Business in Exporting: 17

48894 Star Pacific Inc
1205 Atlantic St
Union City, CA 94587-2002
510-471-6555
Fax: 510-471-4339 800-227-0760
starpac7@aol.com
Manufacturer and exporter of cleaning compounds including household/consumer detergents
Chairman of the Board: Joon Moon
Manager: Ed Kubiak
starpacnew@aol.com
Estimated Sales: $ 5 - 10 Million
Number Employees: 10-19
Square Footage: 114000
Type of Packaging: Consumer
Brands Exported: Blue Ribbon; Alta
Regions Exported to: Worldwide
Percentage of Business in Exporting: 5

48895 Star Poly Bag Inc
200 Liberty Ave
Brooklyn, NY 11207-2904
718-384-7034
Fax: 718-384-2342 rachel@starpoly.com
www.starpoly.com
Manufacturer and exporter of plastic bags including shopping, food, confectioners', heat sealed, etc.; also, packaging materials including cellulose acetate film and garbage and ice cream can liners
President: Rachel Posen
Contact: Rivkah Ffe
rivkah@starpoly.com
Production: Hershy Rosenfeld
Estimated Sales: Below $ 5 Million
Number Employees: 1-4
Square Footage: 100000

48896 Starbruck Foods Corporation
110 Bi County Boulevard
Suite 126
Farmingdale, NY 11735-3987
631-293-9696
Fax: 631-293-9825 starbruck@hotmail.com
Importer and wholesaler/distributor of dried fruits including raisins, papaya, pineapple, banana chips and apricots; also, nuts, seeds and fruit and nut mixes
President: Michael Stern
Number Employees: 1-4
Square Footage: 40000
Regions Imported from: Central America, South America, Asia
Percentage of Business in Importing: 50

48897 Starbucks
2401 Utah Ave. S.
Seattle, WA 98134
206-749-5925
Fax: 206-447-0828 800-782-7282
www.starbucks.com

Whole bean coffees and espresso beverages, a variety of pastries and confections, coffee-related accessories and equipment. Also ice cream and coffee drinks including blended and flavored and dairy-free blended juiced teas.
President/CEO: Kevin Johnson
Executive Chairman: Myron Ullman
Systems Analyst: Kris Aamot
kaamot@starbucks.com
Year Founded: 1971
Estimated Sales: $24.71 Billion
Number Employees: 291,000
Number of Brands: 8
Type of Packaging: Consumer, Private Label, Bulk
Regions Imported from: Latin America, Africa, Indonesia, Arabia

48898 (HQ)Stark Candy Company
135 American Legion Highway
Revere, MA 02151-2405   985-446-1354
Fax: 985-448-1627   800-225-5508
www.necco.com
Manufacturer and exporter of candy. Founded in 1847.
President: Dominic Antonellis
General Manager: Bobby Folfe
VP Sales: Tom Drummond
Number Employees: 30
Type of Packaging: Consumer

48899 Starkel Poultry
10524 128th Street East
Puyallup, WA 98373   253-845-2876
Fax: 253-841-1004
Processor and exporter of bagged poultry including fresh and frozen
President: Elsie Starkel
Vice President: Leona Starkel
Estimated Sales: $4400000
Number Employees: 45
Type of Packaging: Consumer, Bulk
Regions Exported to: Worldwide
Percentage of Business in Exporting: 15

48900 Starkey Chemical Process Company
PO Box 10
La Grange, IL 60525   708-352-2565
Fax: 708-352-2573   800-323-3040
Rubber cement, duplicating fluids, printing chemicals, hand cleaners, toners and gelled alcohol cooking and heating fuels; exporter of ink marking and duplicating fluids
President: Linda Yates
Estimated Sales: $1-2.5 Million
Number Employees: 20-49
Square Footage: 54000
Brands Exported: Starkey; Bantam; Canode; Super-Key
Regions Exported to: Central America, South America, Europe, Middle East
Percentage of Business in Exporting: 2

48901 Starlite Manufacturing/Sugar Daddy's
10 Aviator Way
Ormond Beach, FL 32174-2983   386-677-9316
Fax: 386-673-5356   starmfgss@aol.com
VP: Bill Starcevic
Estimated Sales: $ 10 - 20 Million
Number Employees: 20-49

48902 Starview Packaging Machinery
1840 St Regis Blvd
Dorval, QC H9P 1H6
Canada   514-920-0100
Fax: 514-920-0092   888-278-5555
info@starview.net   www.starview.net
Plastic packaging machinery.
Technical Director: Iwan Heynen
Number Employees: 15
Square Footage: 36216
Type of Packaging: Private Label
Regions Exported to: Central America, South America, USA, Mexico, Latin America
Percentage of Business in Exporting: 70

48903 Starwest Botanicals Inc
161 Main Ave # A
Sacramento, CA 95838-2080   916-638-8100
Fax: 916-853-9673   800-800-4372
www.starwest-botanicals.com
Processor, importer and exporter of herbs and herbal extracts, spices and essential and vegetable oils; also, custom milling, blending and formulating available
Founder, President: Van Joerger
CEO: Shirley Abrahamson
shirleyabrahamson@starwestherb.com
VP Finance: Mark Wendley
SVP R&D/Production Manager: Dawn Bennett
Marketing/Product Development: Daniela Nelson
VP Sales: Richard Patterson
Purchasing: Bonnie Sadkowski
Estimated Sales: $9.8 Million
Number Employees: 50-99
Square Footage: 200000
Type of Packaging: Bulk
Brands Exported: Starwest; Nature Actives
Regions Exported to: Central America, South America, Europe, Asia, Middle East
Regions Imported from: Central America, South America, Europe, Asia, Middle East
Percentage of Business in Importing: 30

48904 State Products
4485 California Avenue
Long Beach, CA 90807-2417   562-495-3688
Fax: 562-495-5788   800-730-5150
Manufacturer and exporter of standard baking pans, cookie sheets, French bread frames and fiberglass fabric liners coated with silicon rubber
Chairman: Arthur Haskell
Estimated Sales: $1-2.5 Million appx.
Number Employees: 20
Square Footage: 106000
Brands Exported: State
Regions Exported to: Central America, South America, Europe, Asia, Middle East

48905 Stauber Performance Ingrdients
4120 N Palm St
Fullerton, CA 92835-1026   714-441-3900
Fax: 714-441-3909   888-441-4233
customerservice@stauberusa.com
www.stauberusa.com
Leading supplier of bulk ingredients to the nutritional products, food, cosmetic and pet care industries.
President: Olivier Guiot
CEO: Sam Butler
sam.butler@viasat.com
COO & CFO: Steve Graham
Number Employees: 20-49
Type of Packaging: Bulk
Regions Exported to: Central America, South America, Europe, Asia
Percentage of Business in Exporting: 10
Regions Imported from: Central America, South America, Europe, Asia
Percentage of Business in Importing: 20

48906 Stauffer Biscuit Co
P.O. Box 12002
York, PA 17402-0672
   888-480-1988
www.stauffers.com
Cookies, crackers and snack products
President: Yujiro Kataoka
y.kataoka@stauffers.net
Vice President: Jim Biondolillo
Year Founded: 1871
Estimated Sales: $150 Million
Number Employees: 500-999
Parent Co: Meiji Co., Ltd.

48907 Stavis Seafoods
212 Northern Ave
Suite 305
Boston, MA 02210-2090   617-897-1200
Fax: 617-897-1291   800-390-5103
fish@stavis.com   www.stavis.com
Fresh and frozen seafood including cod, haddock, pollock, tuna, swordfish, mahi, snapper, grouper and seabass fillets, rockshrimp and baby scallops
President & CEO: Charles Marble
Chief Sustainability Officer: Richard Stavis
CFO: Mary Fleming
Executive Vice President: Stewart Altman
Director of Quality Assurance: Allison Roderick
VP Marketing: Michael Lynch
VP Sales: Stephen Young
VP Operations: Mohamad Fakira
Estimated Sales: $28.9 Million
Number Employees: 100-249
Square Footage: 10000
Type of Packaging: Food Service, Private Label, Bulk
Brands Exported: Bos'n; Foods From The Sea
Regions Exported to: Central America, South America, Europe, Asia
Brands Imported: Bos'n; Boston Pride; Foods From The Sea; Prince Edward
Regions Imported from: Central America, South America, Europe, Asia
Percentage of Business in Importing: 70

48908 Stay Tuned Industries
8 W Main St
Clinton, NJ 08809-1290   908-730-8455
Fax: 908-735-8180
Wholesaler/distributor and exporter of steel and aluminum cans and easy-open ends; also, consultant for can manufacturers
Owner: Ray Slocum
Estimated Sales: $ 500,000-$ 1 Million
Number Employees: 1-4
Square Footage: 1800
Regions Exported to: Central America, Europe, Mexico
Percentage of Business in Exporting: 85

48909 Steak-Umm Company
P.O. Box 350
Shillington, PA 19607-0350   860-928-5900
Fax: 860-928-0351   http://www.steakumm.com
Quick and easy to prepare and delicious in an endless variety of recipes.
President: Dennis Newnham
Estimated Sales: $14 Million
Number Employees: 120
Square Footage: 352000
Brands Exported: Steak-Umm

48910 Stearns Technical Textiles Company
100 Williams Street
Cincinnati, OH 45215-4602   513-948-5292
Fax: 513-948-5281   800-543-7173
Manufacturer and exporter of hot oil filters for deep fryers and medium and heavy duty nonabrasive scrub pads; manufacturer of milk filters
Director Sales: Kevin Finn
Customer Service Manager: Joanne Heidotting
Estimated Sales: $20-50 Million
Number Employees: 100-249
Square Footage: 50000
Regions Exported to: Worldwide
Percentage of Business in Exporting: 20

48911 Stearnswood Inc
320 3rd Ave NW
PO Box 50
Hutchinson, MN 55350-1625   320-587-2137
Fax: 320-587-7646   800-657-0144
info@stearnswood.com   www.stearnswood.com
Manufacturer and exporter of corrugated cartons, wooden boxes, crates, plastic pallets and bulk shipping cartons and bins
Owner: Paul Stearns
Sales Director: Paul Stearns
paul@stearnswood.com
Operational Manager: Mark Stearns
Plant Manager: Corey Stearns
Purchase Agent: Steve Fitzloff
Estimated Sales: 100000
Number Employees: 20-49
Square Footage: 60000
Type of Packaging: Bulk
Regions Exported to: Europe, Antartica, Canada
Percentage of Business in Exporting: 1

48912 Steel Art Co
189 Dean St
Norwood, MA 02062-4542   617-566-4079
Fax: 617-566-0618   800-322-2828
info@steelartco.com   www.steelartco.com
Manufacturer and exporter of metal signs, letters and plaques
President: John Borell
Director of Sales/Marketing: Charles Blanchard
CFO: Stew Dobson
Vice President: Stewart Dobson
Manager of Design & Engineering: Ciaran Dalton
Vice President of Sales: Charles Blanchard
Customer Service Manager: Kindra Jones
Vice President of Operations: Ashley Borell
Lead Production Manager: Jorge Aguirre
A/R-Credit Manager: Robert Smith

Importers & Exporters / A-Z

Estimated Sales: $ 5 - 10 Million
Number Employees: 100-249

48913 (HQ)Steel City Corporation
PO Box 1227
Youngstown, OH 44501-1227   330-792-7663
           Fax: 330-792-7951   800-321-0350
           jsmith@scity.com   www.scity.com
Manufacturer, wholesaler/distributor, importer and exporter of plastic bags, plastic and wire racks and coin operated vending machines; manufacturer and importer of rubber bands
President: C Kenneth Fibus
CFO: Mike Janak
Quality Control: Steve Speece
National Sales Manager: Jim Smith
VP Sales: Lee Rouse
Sales Department: Erika Flaherty
Estimated Sales: $ 30 - 50 Million
Number Employees: 100-249
Square Footage: 150000
Regions Exported to: Central America, Asia
Percentage of Business in Exporting: 4
Regions Imported from: Asia

48914 Steel Craft FluorescentCompany
191 Murray St
Newark, NJ 07114-2751   973-349-1614
           Fax: 973-824-0825
Manufacturer and exporter of fluorescent lighting fixtures

Estimated Sales: $ 1 - 3 Million
Number Employees: 10-19

48915 Steel King Industries
2700 Chamber St
Stevens Point, WI 54481   715-341-3120
           Fax: 715-341-8792   800-553-3096
           info@steelking.com   www.steelking.com
Manufacturer and exporter of racks including pallet, pushback, flow, cantilever and portable. Products also inlcude steel containers and guard railing
President: Jay Anderson
Marketing Director: Don Heemstra
National Sales Manager: Skip Eastman
Contact: Chrissy Christenson
c.christenson@renters-choice-inc.com
Plant Manager: Ralph Gagas
Estimated Sales: $20-50 Million
Number Employees: 100-249
Parent Co: VCI
Regions Exported to: Canada, Mexico
Percentage of Business in Exporting: 1

48916 Steel Products
750 44th Street
Marion, IA 52302-3841   319-377-1527
           Fax: 319-377-4580   800-333-9451
           www.marioniron.com
Hot chocolate and cappuccino dispensers; exporter of hot chocolate dispensers and parts
Customer Service: Lori Pickart
Operations Manager: Bryce Sandell
Estimated Sales: $1-2.5 Million
Number Employees: 5-9
Square Footage: 66000
Parent Co: ConAgra Foods
Regions Exported to: Europe
Percentage of Business in Exporting: 65

48917 Steel Storage Systems Inc
6301 Dexter St
Commerce City, CO 80022-3128   303-287-0291
           Fax: 303-287-0159   800-442-0291
           info@steelstorage.com
Manufacturer and exporter of material handling equipment including roller conveyors, sheet racks and drawers
President: Brian Mc Callin
Estimated Sales: $5-10 Million
Number Employees: 20-49
Type of Packaging: Bulk
Regions Exported to: Canada

48918 Steel's Gourmet Foods,Ltd.
55 E Front St # D175
Bridgeport, PA 19405-1489   610-277-1230
           Fax: 610-277-1228   800-678-3357
Processor and exporter of gourmet, sugar free dessert toppings, jams, sweetners, syrups and condiments; also organic salad dressings, condiments, fruit spreads and low sugar fudge sauces.
President, Owner: Elizabeth Steel
Contact: Anna Steel
annasteel@steelsgourmet.com
Plant Manager: Carlos Short
Estimated Sales: $2.5 Million
Number Employees: 8
Number of Products: 60
Square Footage: 40000
Parent Co: Clack-Steel
Type of Packaging: Consumer, Private Label
Brands Exported: Steels; Nature Sweet
Regions Exported to: Canada, Caribbean
Percentage of Business in Exporting: 4

48919 Steelite International USA
4041 Hadley Rd
South Plainfield, NJ 07080-1111   908-755-0357
           Fax: 908-755-7185   800-367-3493
           usa@steelite.com   www.steelite.com
Importer of ceramic commercial china
CEO: R J Chadwick
Marketing Director: Karen Gowarty
Contact: Kimberly Faloon
kfaloon@steeliteusa.com
Estimated Sales: $ 5 -10 Million
Number Employees: 10-19
Parent Co: Steelite International
Type of Packaging: Food Service
Brands Imported: Steelite; Albalite
Regions Imported from: Central America, Europe

48920 Steelmaster Material Handling
503 Commerce Park Drive SE
Suite B
Marietta, GA 30060-2745   770-425-7244
           Fax: 770-423-7545
Manufacturer and exporter of new and used warehouse equipment including pallet racks and shelving
President: Mike Miller
CEO: Deborah Molley
Plant Manager: James Young
Estimated Sales: $1-2.5 Million
Number Employees: 5-9
Square Footage: 40000

48921 (HQ)Stegall Mechanical INC
2800 5th Ave S
Birmingham, AL 35233-2820   205-251-0330
           Fax: 205-328-1988   800-633-4373
           www.stegallmechanical.com
Manufacturer and exporter of food service ventilation equipment including ventilation/exhaust hoods and fans; also, custom fabrications in stainless steel and wood available
President: Vince Chiarella
vchiarella@stegallmechanical.com
Estimated Sales: $ 10 - 15 Million
Number Employees: 20-49
Type of Packaging: Food Service
Regions Exported to: Worldwide
Percentage of Business in Exporting: 5

48922 Steiner Company
401 W Taft Drive
Holland, IL 60473-2015   708-333-2003
           Fax: 800-578-2507   800-222-4638
Manufacturer and exporter of waterless hand and skin soaps; also, soap dispensers
President: Guy Marchesi
Director OEM Sales: Craig Brown
Marketing Director: Karen Siravo
VP Sales: Greg Fachet
Contact: Brent Stack
bstack@stnr.com
Estimated Sales: $10-20 Million
Number Employees: 50-99
Parent Co: Steiner Company
Type of Packaging: Private Label
Regions Exported to: Asia, Australia, Worldwide
Percentage of Business in Exporting: 6

48923 Steiner Industries Inc
5801 N Tripp Ave
Chicago, IL 60646-6013   773-588-3444
           Fax: 773-588-3450   800-621-4515
           info@steinerindustries.com
           www.steinerindustries.com
Manufacturer and exporter of air freshener and soap dispensers; also, garment lockers, soaps, lotions and hand cleaners
President: Raefel Krammer
rk@steinerindustries.com
Marketing: Karen Siravo
Sales Director: Greg Fachet
Estimated Sales: $ 10 - 20 Million
Number Employees: 50-99
Parent Co: Steiner Corporation
Type of Packaging: Consumer, Food Service, Bulk
Regions Exported to: Europe, Asia
Percentage of Business in Exporting: 6

48924 Stella D'oro
8600 South Boulevard
Charlotte, NC 28273
           800-995-2623
           www.stelladoro.com
Manufacturer of Italian baked goods.
Type of Packaging: Consumer
Regions Exported to: Worldwide

48925 Stengel Seed & Grain Co
14698 SD Highway 15
Milbank, SD 57252-5452   605-432-6030
           Fax: 605-432-6064   gstengel@tnics.com
           www.tnics.com
Organic grains. Services include cleaning, dehulling, packaging, warehousing and shipping.
President: Doug Stengel
stengelseed@tnics.com
Estimated Sales: Less than $500,000
Number Employees: 5-9
Square Footage: 60000
Regions Exported to: Europe
Percentage of Business in Exporting: 30

48926 Stepan Co.
22 W. Frontage Rd.
Northfield, IL 60093   847-446-7500
           Fax: 847-501-2100   www.stepan.com
Surfactants, polymers and specialty products for industries including nutrition, food and beverage, and personal care.
Chairman/President/CEO: F. Quinn Stepan
Vice President/CFO: Luis Rojo
Vice President/General Counsel: David Kabbes
Year Founded: 1932
Estimated Sales: $1.925 Billion
Number Employees: 2,096
Type of Packaging: Bulk
Regions Exported to: Central America, South America, Europe, Asia, Middle East

48927 Stephan Machinery GmbH
1385 Armour Blvd.
Mandelein, IL 60060   847-247-0182
           Fax: 847-247-0184
Processing lines and machines for the food, dairy, meat, confectionary and convenience food industries.
Contact: Rolf Heinze
heinze@stephan-machinery.com
Regions Exported to: Worldwide

48928 Stephan Machinery, Inc.
1385 Armour Blvd
Mundelein, IL 60060   224-360-6206
           Fax: 847-247-0184   800-783-7426
           weirich@stephan-machinery.com
           www.stephan-machinery.com
Designs, engineers and builds the finest food processing equipment available.
CEO: Olaf Pehmoller
CFO: Gunter Dahling
Sales Manager: Eric Weirich
Contact: Rolf Heinze
heinze@stephan-machinery.com
Operations Director: Dirk Kuhnel
Estimated Sales: $ 7 -10 Million
Number Employees: 5-9
Square Footage: 28000
Brands Imported: Stephan, Microcuts, Ruhle, Vcm
Regions Imported from: Europe

48929 Steri Technologies Inc
857 Lincoln Ave
Bohemia, NY 11716-4100   631-563-8300
           Fax: 631-563-8378   800-253-7140
           steri@steri.com
Manufacturer, importer and exporter of dryers including vacuum shelf, lab and band; also, pressure leaf and vacuum filters
President: Clemens Nigg
steri@steri.com
Estimated Sales: $ 10 - 20 Million
Number Employees: 10-19
Square Footage: 30000
Type of Packaging: Private Label

Regions Exported to: Central America, South America, Europe
Percentage of Business in Exporting: 35
Regions Imported from: Europe
Percentage of Business in Importing: 5

48930 Steril-Sil Company
PO Box 495
Bowmansville, PA 17507   717-405-2258
Fax: 617-739-5063   800-784-5537
orders@sterilsil.com   www.sterilsil.com
Manufacturer and exporter of condiment and silverware dispensers, containers and covers
President: David Stiller
CFO: Laura McEachern
VP: Bernard Chiccariello
Sales: Brian Schilling
brian@sterilsil.com
Estimated Sales: $500,000-$1 Million
Number Employees: 1-4
Parent Co: Stiller Equipment Corporation
Regions Exported to: Europe
Percentage of Business in Exporting: 5

48931 Sterling Ball & Jewel
2900 S 160th St
New Berlin, WI 53151-3606   262-641-8610
Fax: 262-641-8653   800-423-3183
dazarello@corpemail.com   www.sterlco.com
Manufacturer and exporter of temperature control units & other heating & cooling equipment
President: Jeff Ackerberg
jeff.ackerberg@kohler.com
VP: Mike Zvolanek
Marketing: Bill Desrosiers
Sales: Wayne Lange
Public Relations: Nichole Saccomonto
Operations Manager: Rich Cramer
Number Employees: 100-249
Parent Co: Sterling
Type of Packaging: Private Label
Regions Exported to: Central America, South America, Europe, Asia, Middle East

48932 Sterling Corp
2001 E Gladstone St # B
Glendora, CA 91740-5381   909-305-0968
Fax: 909-981-1441   800-932-9561
www.stercorp.com
Manufacturer and importer of security equipment including fire and burglar alarms and systems; also, installation services available
Manager: Bill Jones
bill@stercorp.com
Estimated Sales: $ 2.5-5,000,000
Number Employees: 1-4
Regions Imported from: Japan, Taiwan

48933 Sterling Net & Twine Company
P.O.Box 411
Cedar Knolls, NJ 07927   973-783-9800
Fax: 973-783-9808   800-342-0316
Manufacturer and exporter of nets and netting, conveyors, pallets and custom bags for produce and customer packaging
President: James Van Loon
Sales Manager: Jerry Eick
Estimated Sales: $ 5 - 10,000,000
Number Employees: 20-49
Square Footage: 32000
Regions Exported to: Canada
Percentage of Business in Exporting: 10

48934 Sterling Novelty Products
1940 Raymond Dr
Northbrook, IL 60062-6715   847-291-0070
Fax: 847-291-0420
Manufacturer and exporter of U.S. flag sets, nylon mesh scouring cloths and plastic food bags
President: Marvin Glasser
Secretary/Treasurer: Michael Glasser
Estimated Sales: $ 1 - 3 Million
Number Employees: 10-19
Square Footage: 10000
Parent Co: Sterling Novelty
Regions Exported to: Canada
Percentage of Business in Exporting: 5

48935 Sterling Paper Company
1845 Progress Avenue Columbus
Ohio, PA 19134-2799   215-744-5350
Fax: 215-533-9577   800-282-1124
www.sterling-paper.com
Manufacturer, exporter and importer of paper plates, Chinese food pails and food trays; also, boxes including cake, pizza, doughnuts, sausage, steak, pastry, etc
President: Martin Stein
Secretary: John Paul
VP: Suzy Faigen
Estimated Sales: $10-20 Million
Number Employees: 50-99
Square Footage: 650000
Percentage of Business in Exporting: 3
Regions Imported from: Central America

48936 Sterling Rubber
675 Woodside Street
Fergus, ON N1M 2M4
Canada   519-843-4032
Fax: 519-843-6587
Manufacturer and exporter of rubber gloves
President: Robert Joyce
Manager Quality Assurance: Norma Ford
Number Employees: 30
Square Footage: 54000
Regions Exported to: Central America, South America, Europe
Percentage of Business in Exporting: 50

48937 (HQ)Sterling Scale Co
20950 Boening Dr
Southfield, MI 48075-5737   248-358-0590
Fax: 248-358-2275   800-331-9931
sales@sterlingscale.com   www.sterlingscale.com
Manufacturer, importer, exporter and wholesaler/distributor of industrial scales; manufacturer of engineering software for weighing equipment
President: E Donald Dixon
CFO: J Dixon
Vice President: Tom Ulicny
Research & Development: T Klauinger
Quality Control: Jeff Shultz
Marketing Director: Tom Ulicny
Plant Manager: J Holcomb
Purchasing Manager: S Latucca
Estimated Sales: $2-3 Million
Number Employees: 20-49
Number of Brands: 5
Number of Products: 100
Square Footage: 112000
Brands Exported: Sterling
Regions Exported to: Central America
Percentage of Business in Exporting: 1
Brands Imported: Sartorius

48938 Sterling Systems & Controls
24711 Emerson Rd
Sterling, IL 61081-9171   815-625-0852
Fax: 815-625-3103   800-257-7214
sci@sterlingcontrols.com   www.prater-sterling.com
Manufacturer, importer and exporter of batching and weighing process controls for dry and liquid products; also, weighing systems for poultry and meat
President: Don Goshert
VP/General Manager: Don Goshert
Western Sales: Bob Rogan
South/Southeastern Sales: Dean Considine
Northeastern Sales: Marty Gustafson
Estimated Sales: $2.5-5 Million
Number Employees: 10-19
Square Footage: 21000
Parent Co: Prater Industries
Regions Exported to: Worldwide
Percentage of Business in Exporting: 10
Regions Imported from: Worldwide
Percentage of Business in Importing: 10

48939 Stern International Consultants
E9-212 Gladwin Crescent
Ottawa, ON K1B 5N1
Canada   613-733-8237
Fax: 613-733-6161
Import and broker of dairy/deli products, frozen food, general merchandise, groceries, etc. Consultant providing market studies. Warehouse providing dry and cooler storage. Transportation firm providing local trucking fulfillment
President: Richard Stern
CEO: Doris Stern
CFO: Rene Melancon
Number Employees: 3
Square Footage: 20000

48940 Sterner Lighting Systems
701 Millennium Blvd
Greenville, SC 29607-5251   864-678-1000
Fax: 320-485-2881   866-898-0131
www.sternerlighting.com
Manufacturer and exporter of indoor and outdoor lighting equipment
General Manager: Mike Naylor
Marketing Manager: Sherry Thomson
Plt Mgr: Ken Lehner
Estimated Sales: $ 10 - 20 Million
Number Employees: 20-49
Parent Co: Hubbel Lighting
Type of Packaging: Food Service
Regions Exported to: Worldwide

48941 Sterno
1064 Garfield Street
Lombard, IL 60148   630-792-0080
Fax: 630-792-9914
Manufacturer and exporter of candles, including table, birthday, tapers, and table lamps
President: Richard T Browning
Number Employees: 50-99
Parent Co: Sterno
Type of Packaging: Food Service
Regions Exported to: Worldwide

48942 Stero Co
3200 Lakeville Hwy
Petaluma, CA 94954-5903   707-762-0071
Fax: 707-762-5036   800-762-7600
www.stero.com
Manager: Terry Goodfellow
Contact: Dan Ancheta
danancheta@stero.com
Estimated Sales: Less Than $500,000
Number Employees: 1-4

48943 Stertil Alm Corp
200 Benchmark Industrial Dr
Streator, IL 61364-9400   815-673-5546
Fax: 815-673-2292   800-544-5438
info@stertil-ALM.com   www.stertil-alm.com
US manufacturer of bulkbag discharge and fill lifts, welding and assembly positioner. ALM specializes in custom heavy duty lifting equipment.
President: Doug Grunnet
grunnet@almcorp.com
Sales Director: Patricia Galick
Estimated Sales: $ 10 - 20 Million
Number Employees: 20-49
Square Footage: 110000

48944 Steve's Authentic Key Lime Pies
204 Van Dyke Street
Brooklyn, NY 11231   770-333-0840
Fax: 770-436-4280   888-450-5463
inquiry@keylime.com   www.keylime.com
Processor and exporter of key lime pies, pie filling, sorbet and novelty desserts
President: Kenneth Burts
Plt. Mgr.: K Michael Miller
Quality Control: Slorence Clay
Estimated Sales: $ 5-10 Million
Number Employees: 20-49
Square Footage: 48000
Type of Packaging: Food Service, Private Label
Brands Exported: Kenny's
Regions Exported to: Phillipines
Percentage of Business in Exporting: 1

48945 Stevens Linen Association
137 Schofield Ave
Suite 5
Dudley, MA 1571   508-943-0813
Fax: 508-949-1847   800-772-9269
www.co-store.com/stevenslinen
Manufacturer and exporter of linen goods, pot holders and place mats
President: Gregory Kline
VP Sales/Marketing: Nancy Dalrymple
Contact: Timothy Barnardo
timothyb@stevenslinen.com
Estimated Sales: $10-20 Million
Number Employees: 100-249
Square Footage: 150000
Regions Exported to: South America, Europe, Asia
Percentage of Business in Exporting: 5

Importers & Exporters / A-Z

48946 Stevens Point Brewery
2617 Water St
Stevens Point, WI 54481-5248   715-344-9310
        Fax: 715-344-8897 800-369-4911
    info@pointbeer.com www.pointbeer.com
Processor and exporter of beer and gourmet soda.
Founder: Frank Wahle
Founder: George Ruder
Co-Owner: Jim Wiechmann
Operating Partner: Joe Martino
Brewing: Gabe Hopkins
Director, Marketing: Julie Birrenkott
Year Founded: 1857
Estimated Sales: $20-50 Million
Number Employees: 20-49
Number of Brands: 2
Type of Packaging: Consumer, Private Label
Regions Exported to: Europe

48947 Stevens Tropical Plantation
6550 Okeechobee Blvd
West Palm Beach, FL 33411-2798   561-683-4701
            Fax: 561-683-4993
Processor and importer of syrups, fruit juices, nectar and beverage bases
President: Henry Stevens Jr
Estimated Sales: $ 1 - 3 Million
Number Employees: 5-9
Square Footage: 40000
Type of Packaging: Consumer, Food Service
Regions Imported from: South America

48948 Stevenson-Cooper Inc
1039 W Venango St
PO Box 46345
Philadelphia, PA 19140-4391   215-223-2600
       Fax: 215-223-3597 waxcooper@aol.com
Manufacturer and exporter of oils including cottonseed and palm oils; also, manufacturer of paraffin and sealing wax
President: Dennis Cooper
dcooper@stevensonseeley.com
R&D: Tammy Pullins
Estimated Sales: Below $ 5 Million
Number Employees: 5-9
Regions Exported to: Worldwide

48949 (HQ)Stewart Assembly & Machining
7234 Blue Ash Rd
Cincinnati, OH 45236-3660   513-891-9000
      Fax: 513-891-0449 sales@stewartam.com
                www.stewartam.com
Manufacturer and exporter of packaging machinery
President: Jim Weckenbrock
VP Sales: Ray Meyer
Estimated Sales: $5-10 Million
Number Employees: 10-19
Type of Packaging: Bulk
Regions Exported to: Worldwide

48950 Stewart Systems Baking LLC
808 Stewart Dr
Plano, TX 75074-8197   972-422-5808
    Fax: 972-509-8734 www.stewart-systems.com
Conveyors, ovens and proofers
Vice President: Jim Makins
Sales: Bill Camp
Estimated Sales: $ 20-50 Million
Number Employees: 100-249
Parent Co: Sasi B. Baking
Regions Exported to: Worldwide

48951 Stewart's Private Blend Foods
4110 W Wrightwood Ave
Chicago, IL 60639-2172   773-489-2500
        Fax: 773-489-2148 800-654-2862
        info@stewarts.com www.stewarts.com
Processor, importer and exporter of coffees including flavored, decaffeinated and roasted; also, flavored and blended teas
President: Donald Stewart
CEO: Robert Stewart
Vice President: William Stewart Jr
Contact: Steve Blair
steve.blair@stewarts.com
Production Manager: Elita Pagan
Plant Manager: Ed Fabro
Estimated Sales: $2,000,000
Number Employees: 20-49
Square Footage: 192000
Type of Packaging: Consumer, Food Service, Private Label, Bulk
Brands Exported: Stewarts Private Blend
Regions Exported to: Asia
Regions Imported from: Central America, South America
Percentage of Business in Importing: 65

48952 Stichler Products Inc
1800 N 12th St
Suite 1
Reading, PA 19604-1545   610-921-0211
      Fax: 610-921-0294 info@megacandyco.com
                 www.megabuttons.com
Confectionery products: candy, decorative and ornamental
President: Martin Deutschman
spicandy@aol.com
Vice President: Brad Deutschman
Public Relations: Rachel Buckholtz
Estimated Sales: $4700000
Number Employees: 20-49
Square Footage: 248000
Type of Packaging: Consumer, Food Service, Private Label, Bulk
Regions Imported from: Asia
Percentage of Business in Importing: 50

48953 Stick Pack USA
1813 Eutaw Place
Baltimore, MD 21217
                    888-766-6361
                stickpack@aol.com
Contact: Elsa Abraham
elsa@stickpackusa.com

48954 Stickney & Poor Company
12 Reynolds Dr
Peterborough, NH 03458-1611   603-924-2259
Processor and exporter of portion-controlled products including ketchup, relish, nondairy coffee creamers, honey, artificial sweeteners, jams, jellies, marmalades, preserves, mayonnaise, mustard, salt, pepper, vinegar, salad dressings and dipping sauces
President: H Sandy Brown
VP: Chuck Lavery
Number Employees: 50-99
Type of Packaging: Food Service, Private Label, Bulk
Brands Exported: Stickney & Poor; Harvest Selects
Regions Exported to: Canada
Percentage of Business in Exporting: 5

48955 Stimo-O-Stam, Ltd.
70593 Bravo St
Covington, LA 70433
      Fax: 985-845-1489 800-562-7514
      laurie_sre@yahoo.com www.stimostam.com
Processor and exporter Supplements, Nutritional: Energy Mixes
Manager: Alan Lafferty
Estimated Sales: $300,000-500,000
Number Employees: 1-4
Square Footage: 40000
Type of Packaging: Consumer
Regions Exported to: South America, Europe, Canada, Caribbean
Percentage of Business in Exporting: 5

48956 Stirling Foods
P.O.Box 569
Renton, WA 98057   425-251-9293
        Fax: 425-251-0251 800-332-1714
Processor and exporter of gourmet beverage flavors and syrups
President: Mark Greiner
CEO: Earl Greiner
Contact: Jeff Greiner
stirling@stirling.net
Estimated Sales: $1,300,000
Number Employees: 5-9
Type of Packaging: Consumer, Food Service, Private Label
Regions Exported to: Europe, Asia, Canada, Mexico

48957 Stock Popcorn Ind Inc
304 Vine St
Lake View, IA 51450   712-657-2811
        Fax: 712-657-2550 stockpop@netins.net
Processor and exporter of yellow and white popcorn including processed unpopped and microwaveable; also, feed sack fashion packaging for popcorn
Owner: Jim Stock
stockpop@netins.net
Number Employees: 5-9
Type of Packaging: Consumer, Private Label, Bulk
Brands Exported: Lil' Chief Popcorn
Regions Exported to: Asia, Middle East
Percentage of Business in Exporting: 25

48958 Stock Yards Packing Company
2457 W North Ave.
Melrose Park, IL 60160   312-733-6050
        Fax: 708-223-1257 877-785-9273
    customerservice@stockyardscustomerservice.com
                www.stockyards.com
Processor and exporter of beef, pork, veal and lamb
President: Dan Pollack
Plant Manager: Oscar Moore
Estimated Sales: $ 10 - 20 Million
Number Employees: 100-249
Square Footage: 180000
Regions Exported to: Worldwide

48959 Stoffel Seals Corp
36 Stoffel Dr
Tallapoosa, GA 30176   770-574-2696
        Fax: 770-574-7937 800-422-8247
                www.stoffel.com
Stoffel Seals is a key supplier for product identification and branding systems, packaging enhancements, advertising premiums/promotional products, employee identification badges, tamper evident security seals and many other custommanufactured products. Our specialty items for the food and beverage industry include ham bone guards, trussing loops, rotisserie tags, tray pack inserts, pricing/shellfish tags, metal seals, string
Quality Control: Henry Bosshard
Marketing: Valerie Cates
Sales: Mark Swan
Production: Mike Brown
Plant Manager: Norbert Falk
Purchasing: James Westmoreland
Estimated Sales: $40 Million
Number Employees: 250-499
Square Footage: 180000
Parent Co: Stoffel Seals
Type of Packaging: Consumer, Food Service, Private Label, Bulk
Regions Exported to: Worldwide

48960 Stoffel Seals Corp
36 Stoffel Dr
Tallapoosa, GA 30176   770-574-2696
        Fax: 770-574-7937 800-422-8247
                www.stoffel.com
We are the supplier of choice for product identification and branding systems, packaging enhancements, advertising premiums/promotional products, employee identification badges, tamper evident security seals and many other custommanufactured products. Our specialty include ham bone guards, trussing loops, rotisserie tags, turkey lifters, tray pack inserts, pricing/shellfish tags, metal seals for kosher foods, elastic string tags, bottle neckers and cohes
President and CEO: Charles Fuehrer
Executive VP: Norbert Falk
Vice President: Joe Williams
Marketing Director: Pat Renz
Sales Director: Joe Cusack
Plant Manager: Norbert Falk
Estimated Sales: $ 50 - 100 Million
Number Employees: 250-499
Square Footage: 40000
Type of Packaging: Consumer, Private Label, Bulk

48961 Stogsdill Tile Co
14604 Harmony Rd
Huntley, IL 60142-9201   847-669-1255
        Fax: 847-669-1278 800-323-7504
    info@stogsdilltile.com www.stogsdilltile.com
Manufacturer and exporter of stainless steel floor drains; also, acid brick and monolithic flooring installation services available
President: Gloria Stogsdill
gstogsdill@stogsdilltile.com
Operations Manager: Ivan Gonzalez
Estimated Sales: $ 1 - 5 Million
Number Employees: 1-4
Square Footage: 32000
Regions Exported to: Central America, South America, Europe, Asia, Worldwide
Percentage of Business in Exporting: 2

Importers & Exporters / A-Z

48962 Stoller Fisheries
1301 18th St
PO Box B
Spirit Lake, IA 51360 712-336-1750
Fax: 712-336-4681 800-831-5174
stollerfisheries@mchsi.com
www.kreativekosherfoods.com
Processor and exporter of fresh fish including carp, buffalo, sheepheads and suckers- Asian Corp.
President: Larry Stoller
lstoller@stollerfisheries.com
Controller: Mark Salzwedel
VP: Thomas Opheim
Quality Control: LaRonna Opheum
Estimated Sales: $4 Million
Number Employees: 20-49
Square Footage: 140000
Parent Co: Progressive Companies
Type of Packaging: Bulk
Regions Exported to: Worldwide
Percentage of Business in Exporting: 5

48963 Stone Container
150 N Michigan Ave # 1700
Chicago, IL 60601-7597 312-346-6600
Fax: 312-580-2299 www.smurfit-stone.com
Manufacturer and exporter of envelopes, plastic film and bags: multi-wall, paper and plastic
President: Pat Moore
Estimated Sales: $ 10 - 20 Million
Number Employees: 10,000
Parent Co: Stone Container
Regions Exported to: Worldwide
Percentage of Business in Exporting: 5

48964 Stone Enterprises Inc.
10011 J St
Suite 3
Omaha, NE 68127 402-753-0500
Fax: 402-502-8102 877-653-0500
sales@stoneent.net www.stoneent.net
Designer and manufacturer of custom built machinery, refurbished machines and replacement parts.
Contact: Kim Banat
kbanat@24hourfitness.com
Regions Exported to: Worldwide

48965 Stone Soap Co Inc
2000 Pontiac Dr
Sylvan Lake, MI 48320-1758 248-706-1000
Fax: 248-706-1001 800-952-7627
sales@stonesoap.com www.stonesoap.com
Manufacturer, importer and exporter of cleaning products including hand cleaners, detergents and soaps
President: Ken Stone
stonesoap@stonesoap.com
National Sales Manager: Patty Muskat
Purchasing Agent: Jacqueline ElChemmas
Estimated Sales: $5-10 Million
Number Employees: 10-19
Square Footage: 200000
Regions Exported to: Central America, South America, Europe, Asia, Middle East, Australia
Percentage of Business in Exporting: 10
Regions Imported from: Central America, South America, Europe, Asia
Percentage of Business in Importing: 3

48966 StoneHammer Brewing
355 Elmira Rd N
Unit 135
Guelph, ON N1K 1S5
Canada 519-824-1194
Fax: 519-822-8201
Manufacturer and exporter of beer, lager and cask condition ale
CEO: Karen Cerniuk
General Manager: Brian Relly
Office Admin: Myriam Mullin
Sales & Service: Lee Ecclestone
Brewmaster: Charles MacLean
Brewery Manager: Brian Reilly
Estimated Sales: $382,000
Number Employees: 5
Type of Packaging: Consumer, Food Service
Regions Exported to: Canada

48967 Stonegrill America
12810 NE 178th Street
Suite 105
Woodinville, WA 98072-8788 425-482-0270
Fax: 425-482-9152 www.stonegrillamerica.com

48968 (HQ)Stonewall Kitchen
2 Stonewall Ln
York, ME 03909-1665 207-351-2713
Fax: 207-351-2715 800-826-1752
info@stonewallkitchen.com
www.stonewallkitchen.com
Specialty foods
CFO: Laurie King
Executive VP: Natalie King
nking@stonewallkitchen.com
Estimated Sales: $10-50 Million
Number Employees: 100-249
Square Footage: 60000
Type of Packaging: Consumer
Regions Exported to: Worldwide
Percentage of Business in Exporting: 2

48969 Stoneway Carton Company
3047 78th Ave SE # 203
Mercer Island, WA 98040-2847 206-232-2645
Fax: 206-232-2725 800-498-2185
Manufacturer and exporter of cartons, pads, and parts. Also graphic and structural design
President: Charles E Farrell
General Manager: Russ Salger
Sr. Account Executive Sales: Art Wical
Purchasing Manager: Troy Giesinger
Estimated Sales: $2.5-5 Million
Number Employees: 1-4
Square Footage: 240000
Regions Exported to: Worldwide

48970 Storage Unlimited
1001 N Kenneth Street
Nixa, MO 65714-8401 417-725-3014
Fax: 417-725-5750 800-478-6642
Manufacturer and exporter of racks including can, storage, dunnage, pan, tray; also, dish mobiles
President: Glenn Scott
Secretary: Mary Van Noy
Office Manager: Lisa Lewellen
Estimated Sales: 700000
Number Employees: 5-9
Square Footage: 24000
Regions Exported to: Canada, Caribbean, Mexico
Percentage of Business in Exporting: 15

48971 Stork Townsend Inc.
PO Box 1433
Des Moines, IA 50306-1433 515-265-8181
Fax: 515-263-3333 800-247-8609
info.townsendusa@stork.com
www.townsendeng.com
Manufacturer and exporter of meat processing machinery including pork, fish and poultry skinners, sausage stuffers, linkers, bacon injectors, sausage coextrusion, sausage loaders and meat harvesting systems.
President: Theo Bruinsma
Regional Sales Manager: David Bertelsen
Contact: Janet Bergeron
janet.bergeron@marel.com
Estimated Sales: $20-50 Million
Number Employees: 100-249
Type of Packaging: Food Service
Brands Exported: Townsend
Regions Exported to: Worldwide
Percentage of Business in Exporting: 60

48972 Storm Industrial
PO Box 14666
Shawnee Mission, KS 66285-4666 913-599-3650
Fax: 559-277-9580 800-745-7483
Manufacturer and exporter of plastic and brass valves including pilot mini, automatic drain, speed control exhaust, solenoid, hydraulic nonelectric, slip, pressure regulating, electric and barbed drain; also, wire connectors
Number Employees: 50
Square Footage: 80000
Parent Co: Imperial Valve Company
Brands Exported: Imperial
Regions Exported to: Central America, South America, Europe, Asia, Middle East
Percentage of Business in Exporting: 30

48973 Stormax International
90 Manchester St
Concord, NH 03301-5129 603-223-2333
Fax: 603-223-2330 800-874-7629
Manufacturer, importer and exporter of filling, sealing and lidding machinery for cups, trays, tubs and paper containers
President: Earl Gestewitz
Estimated Sales: Below $ 5 Million
Number Employees: 1-4
Parent Co: Stormax International A/S
Brands Exported: Stormax International
Regions Exported to: Worldwide
Percentage of Business in Exporting: 15
Regions Imported from: Europe
Percentage of Business in Importing: 35

48974 Stout Sign Company
6425 W Florissant Ave
Saint Louis, MO 63136-3622 314-385-4600
Fax: 314-385-9412 800-325-8530
www.stoutsign.com
Manufacturer and exporter of point of purchase signs and displays; silk screening available
President: Patrick Conners
Sales Manager: Randall Simonian
Contact: Redmond Egart
regart@stoutsign.com
VP Operations: Lee Witt
Estimated Sales: $ 15 - 20 Million
Number Employees: 100-249
Square Footage: 140000
Parent Co: Stout Industries of Delaware
Regions Exported to: Worldwide
Percentage of Business in Exporting: 10

48975 Strahman Valves Inc
2801 Baglyos Cir
Lehigh Valley Industrial Park VI
Bethlehem, PA 18020-8033 484-893-5080
Fax: 484-893-5099 877-787-2462
strahman@strahman.com
Manufacturer and exporter of cleaning products, hoses and valves
President/CEO: August Percoco
apercoco@strahman.com
CFO: Dan Eckel
VP: Kevin Carroll
Director of IT: Eric Hays
Director Quality Control: Arthur Pultz
Marketing Manager: Vanessa Reagle
VP Sales: Jan Willem Savelkoel
Customer Service Manager: Rosalind Bowens
VP Operations: William Doll
Purchasing & Inventory Control M: Chris Lipinski
Estimated Sales: $10-20 Million
Number Employees: 100-249
Type of Packaging: Bulk
Regions Exported to: Worldwide

48976 Strand Lighting
10911 Petal St
Dallas, TX 75238-2424 214-647-7880
Fax: 714-899-0042 www.strandlighting.com
Manufacturer and exporter of electric and incandescent lighting fixtures
President: Tim Burnham
peter.rogers@philips.com
VP Marketing: Peter Rogers
Sales Exec: Pete Borchetta
Estimated Sales: $ 20 - 30 Million
Number Employees: 20-49
Parent Co: Rank Industries America
Type of Packaging: Food Service
Regions Exported to: Worldwide

48977 Strathroy Foods
PO Box 188
225 Lothian Avenue
Strathroy, ON N7G 3J2
Canada 519-245-4600
Fax: 519-245-3661
Processor and exporter of frozen vegetables including peas and carrots and other vegetable varieties
President: Craig Richardson
Estimated Sales: $20-50 Million
Number Employees: 200
Type of Packaging: Consumer, Food Service, Private Label
Regions Exported to: USA

48978 Straub Designs Co
2238 Florida Ave S # A
Suite A
St Louis Park, MN 55426-2880 952-546-6686
Fax: 763-546-3056 800-959-3708
parts@straubdesign.com www.straubdesign.com
Manufacturer and exporter of packaging and taping machinery

Importers & Exporters / A-Z

President: Dennis Schuette
dschuette@straubdesign.com
Sales: Mark Baillie
Sales: Glenn Baillie
Estimated Sales: $2.5-5 Million
Number Employees: 20-49
Square Footage: 40000
Regions Exported to: Central America, South America, Europe, Asia, Canada, Mexico
Percentage of Business in Exporting: 5

48979 Straub Designs Co
2238 Florida Ave S # A
St Louis Park, MN 55426-2880 952-546-6686
Fax: 763-546-3056 parts@straubdesign.com
www.straubdesign.com
Manufacturer and exporter of hand and electric grinding mills for dry and oily materials including beans, nuts and herbs and for preparing laboratory samples for analysis
President: Dennis Schuette
dschuette@straubdesign.com
Office Manager: Judy Haag
Number Employees: 20-49
Parent Co: Clinton Separators, Inc.
Regions Exported to: Central America, South America, Europe, Middle East

48980 Strawberry Commission
180 Westridge Dr # 101
Suite 101
Watsonville, CA 95076-6683 831-724-1301
Fax: 831-724-5973 csmrkt@aol.com
www.heartoffarmers.com
Represents an industry of growers, shippers and processors of California strawberries.
President: Mark Murai
IT Executive: Stan Massat
smassat@calstrawberry.org
IT Executive: Stan Massat
smassat@calstrawberry.org
Estimated Sales: $ 5 - 10 Million
Number Employees: 20-49

48981 Streator Dependable Mfg
1705 N Shabbona St
Streator, IL 61364-2100 815-672-0551
Fax: 815-672-7631 800-798-0551
sales@streatordependable.com
www.streatordependable.com
Manufacturer and importer of material handling equipment including containers, pallets, stacking racks, skids and spools
President: Paul A Walker
pwalker@streatordependable.com
Marketing: Bill Bontemps
Sales Manager: Nathan Hovious
Number Employees: 100-249
Square Footage: 200000
Percentage of Business in Importing: 5

48982 Stremick's Heritage Foods
4002 Westminster Ave
Santa Ana, CA 92703-1310 714-775-5000
Fax: 714-775-7677 800-371-9010
info@heritage-foods.com
www.stremicksheritagefoods.com
Milk, cheese and cream, organic milk and soy milk
President/CEO: Louis Stremick
CFO: Mike Malone
VP Foodservice Sales: Tom Gustafson
VP Quality Assurance: Jin Jo
VP Sales & Marketing: Dan Nolan
Sales Manager: Tom Gustafson
Estimated Sales: $45.5 Million
Number Employees: 100-249
Type of Packaging: Consumer, Food Service
Other Locations:
 Heritage Foods
 Riverside, CAHeritage Foods
Regions Exported to: Worldwide

48983 Stretch Island Fruit
P.O. Box 649
Solana Beach, CA 92075
 800-700-9687
www.stretchislandfruit.com
Fruit snacks
Year Founded: 1976
Estimated Sales: $20-50 Million
Number Employees: 50-99
Square Footage: 12000
Type of Packaging: Consumer, Food Service
Brands Exported: Stretch Island

Regions Exported to: Europe, Canada
Percentage of Business in Exporting: 5

48984 Stretch-Vent Packaging System
PO Box 51462
Ontario, CA 91761-1062 909-947-3993
Fax: 909-947-0579 800-822-8368
Manufacturer, importer and exporter of vented produce wrap
VP Sales/Marketing: T Lasker
Director Sales/Operations: Phil Beach
Estimated Sales: $10-20 Million
Number Employees: 50-99
Type of Packaging: Consumer, Bulk
Regions Exported to: Worldwide
Regions Imported from: Worldwide

48985 Stricklin Co
1901 W Commerce St
Dallas, TX 75208-8104 214-637-1030
Fax: 214-747-7872 tjohnson@baldwinmetals.com
www.stricklincompany.com
Manufacturer and exporter of blenders, cookers and mixers; also, repair services available
President: Tom Johnson
tom.johnson@baldwinmetals.com
Controller: Don Smith
Engineer: Mitch Withem
Estimated Sales: Below $ 5 Million
Number Employees: 20-49
Square Footage: 120000
Parent Co: Baldwin Metals
Brands Exported: Stricklin
Regions Exported to: Central America, South America, Europe, Asia
Percentage of Business in Exporting: 5

48986 Stripper Bags
121 Quail Run Road
Henderson, NV 89014-2129 800-354-2247
Fax: 702-898-9938
Manufacturer and exporter of preprinted poly bags for food portioning and rotation; also, labels including peel/stick and disposable for food rotation
President: Mark Tenner
Regions Exported to: Europe, Canada, Caribbean
Percentage of Business in Exporting: 5

48987 (HQ)Strohmeyer & Arpe Co Inc
106 Allen Rd # 203
Basking Ridge, NJ 07920-3851 908-580-9100
Fax: 908-580-9300 sales@strohmeyer.com
www.strohmeyer.com
Importer of canned food including fruits, vegetables and paraffin wax for home canning
President: Charlie Kocot
ckocot@strohmeyer.com
VP: Pierre Crawley
Estimated Sales: $5-10 Million
Number Employees: 5-9
Brands Imported: S&A; King's Pantry
Regions Imported from: South America, Europe, Asia
Percentage of Business in Importing: 95

48988 Stronghaven Containers Co
11135 Monroe Rd
Matthews, NC 28105-6564 704-847-7743
Fax: 704-847-5871 800-222-7919
info@stronghaven.com www.stronghaven.com
Manufacturer and exporter of corrugated boxes
Estimated Sales: $ 1 - 5 Million
Number Employees: 20-49
Square Footage: 500000
Regions Exported to: Canada, Mexico
Percentage of Business in Exporting: 10

48989 Strub Pickles
100 Roy Boulevard
Brantford, ON N3R 7K2
Canada 519-751-1717
Fax: 519-752-5540 info@strubpickles.com
www.strubpickles.com
Sauerkraut, hot peppers, sweet pimientos, horseradish, herring, jalapeno peppers, kosher dill pickles and relish; exporter of pickles, refrigerated and shelf stable foods, zucchini relish and chili sauce
President: Leo Strub
CEO: Martin Strub
CFO: Arnold Strub
Vice President: Anoy Strub
Number Employees: 100-249
Number of Brands: 2

Number of Products: 250
Square Footage: 424000
Type of Packaging: Consumer, Food Service, Private Label, Bulk
Regions Exported to: Middle East, USA, Australia

48990 Sturm Foods Inc
215 Center St
Manawa, WI 54949-9277 920-596-2511
Fax: 920-596-3040 800-347-8876
www.sturmfoods.com
Healthy drink mixes and supplements
President & CEO: Michael Upchurch
Manager: Rob Rugger
rrugger@sturminc.com
Number Employees: 250-499
Parent Co: TreeHouse Foods
Type of Packaging: Consumer, Food Service, Private Label, Bulk
Regions Exported to: Worldwide

48991 Stylmark Inc
6536 Main St NE
PO Box 32008
Minneapolis, MN 55432-4314 763-574-7474
Fax: 763-574-1415 800-328-2495
info@stylmark.com www.stylmark.com
Manufacturer and exporter of back-lit, edge-lit and nonlit graphic display products; also, static graphic display products, sequential image, programmable multi-image and scrolling units available.
President: Andy Steinfeldt
CEO: Javier Barral Amil
jbarralamil@stylmark.com
Number Employees: 100-249

48992 Sucesores de Pedro Cortes
Manuel Camunas #205, Tres Monjitas
PO BOX 363626
Hato Rey, PR 00918-1485 787-754-7040
Fax: 787-754-2650 cortesco@tld.net
www.chocolatecortes.com
Chocolate and cocoa products; private labeling available; importer of chocolate, milk drinks and crackers; wholesaler/distributor of confectionery items, beverages and biscuits
President: Ignacio Cortes Del Valle
VP: Ignacio Cortes Gelpi
Number Employees: 50-99
Number of Brands: 11
Square Footage: 150000
Type of Packaging: Consumer, Private Label, Bulk
Brands Imported: Choki
Regions Imported from: South America, Europe
Percentage of Business in Importing: 5

48993 Suffolk Iron Works Inc
418 E Washington St
PO Box 1943
Suffolk, VA 23434-4518 757-539-2353
Fax: 757-539-1520 info@suffolkironworks.com
www.suffolkironworks.com
Manufacturer and exporter of peanut machinery and bulk material handling systems
Owner: John C Harrell
charrell@suffolkironworks.com
VP: Jenny Winslow
Senior Project Engineer: John Harrell
Estimated Sales: $5-10 Million
Number Employees: 20-49
Regions Exported to: Worldwide
Percentage of Business in Exporting: 1

48994 Sugar Creek
2101 Kenskill Ave
Washington Ct Hs, OH 43160-9404 740-335-7440
Fax: 740-335-7443 800-848-8205
www.sugarcreek.com
Manufacturer of bacon and turkey bacon.
Chairman/CEO: John Richardson
COO: Michael Richardson
CFO: Tom Bollinger
tbollinger@sugar-creek.com
VP of Quality Assurance: Rob Howe
VP of Sales: Jim Coughlin
Plant Manager: Dan Sileo
Estimated Sales: $20 Million
Number Employees: 1000-4999
Number of Brands: 1
Type of Packaging: Consumer, Food Service, Bulk
Other Locations:
 Cincinnati, OH
 Hamilton, OH

Frontenac, KS
Cambridge City, INHamilton
Regions Exported to: Japan, Mexico, Russia, Latin America

48995 Sugar Foods Corp
9500 El Dorado Ave
Sun Valley, CA 91352-1339   818-768-7900
Fax: 818-768-7619 info@sugarfoods.com
www.sugarfoods.com
Contract packager and exporter of dry entrees, side dishes, mixes including snack, nondairy creamer, sugar and sugar substitutes and croutons in bags, pouches, cups, cartons and canisters
President: Stephen O'Dell
sodell@sugarfoods.com
Operations Manager: Brian Thomson
Estimated Sales: $8500000
Number Employees: 250-499
Square Footage: 1400000
Parent Co: Sugar Foods Corporation
Regions Exported to: Canada, Mexico

48996 Sugar Stix
9550 Satellite Blvd # 160
Orlando, FL 32837-8471   407-816-8336
Fax: 407-816-8336 stewcfc@gte.net
www.dominosugar.com/sugar/sugar-stix
Plant Manager: Greg Wolf
Estimated Sales: $ 10 - 20 Million
Number Employees: 10-19

48997 Sugarman of Vermont
P.O.Box 1060
Hardwick, VT 05843   802-472-9891
Fax: 802-472-8526 800-932-7700
sales@sugarmanofvermont.com
www.sugarmanofvermont.com
Processor and exporter of jams, jellies, marmalades and preserves; processor and exporter of maple syrup
President: Anthony Sedutto
Contact: Marilyn Rogerson
m.rogerson@sugarmanofvermont.com
Number Employees: 20-49
Square Footage: 160000
Type of Packaging: Consumer, Food Service, Private Label, Bulk
Brands Exported: Sugarman
Regions Exported to: Worldwide

48998 Suity Confections Co
8105 NW 77th St.
P.O. Box 558943
Miami, FL 33166   305-639-3300
Fax: 305-593-7070 info@suity.com
www.suity.com
Candy, gum, chocolates, and cookies
VP: Jose Garrido Jr
garridojr@waltonpost.com
Quality Control: Luis Perez
Estimated Sales: $ 20-50 Million
Number Employees: 20-49
Regions Exported to: Europe
Percentage of Business in Exporting: 50
Regions Imported from: Latin America
Percentage of Business in Importing: 50

48999 Sullivan & Fitzgerald Food Brokers
513 W Mount Pleasant Ave Ste 200
Livingston, NJ 07039   973-994-3800
Fax: 973-994-4311 sullfitz@verizon.net
Importer broker of fresh and frozen seafood including shrimp, scallops, trout, salmon, sole, turbot and flounder
President: Eugene Sullivan
CEO: Gene Sullivan Jr
Estimated Sales: $ 3 - 5 Million
Number Employees: 5-9
Square Footage: 8000
Type of Packaging: Consumer, Food Service, Private Label, Bulk

49000 Sultan Linen Inc
313 5th Ave
New York, NY 10016-6518   212-689-8900
Fax: 212-689-8965
Manufacturer and exporter of decorative linens, towels, table cloths, place mats and aprons
President: Daniel Sultan
daniel@sultanslinens.com
Sales Manager: Daniel Sultan
Estimated Sales: $ 500,000 - $ 1 Million
Number Employees: 1-4
Parent Co: SLI Home Fashions

49001 Summerfield Foods
335 Shiloh Valley Ct
Santa Rosa, CA 95403-8085   707-579-3938
Fax: 707-579-8442 sales@summerfieldfoods.com
Contract packager and exporter of canned vegetarian foods including refried beans, soups and chili; also, cookies and cakes; private labeling available
President: Roland Au
roland@summerfieldfoods.com
Executive VP: John Stanghellini
Estimated Sales: $2000000
Number Employees: 5-9
Type of Packaging: Consumer, Private Label
Brands Exported: Car Cookies; Computer Cookies; Golf Cookies
Regions Exported to: Worldwide
Percentage of Business in Exporting: 6

49002 Summit Commercial
770 Garrison Ave
Bronx, NY 10474-5603   718-893-3900
Fax: 718-842-3093
President: Felix Storch
Estimated Sales: $ 10 - 20 Million
Number Employees: 50-99

49003 Summit Commercial
770 Garrison Ave
Bronx, NY 10474-5603   718-893-3900
Fax: 718-842-3093 800-932-4267
info@summitappliance.com
www.summitappliance.com
Equipment
President: Felix Storch
Vice President: Paul Storch
Estimated Sales: $40-50 Million
Number Employees: 100
Number of Brands: 1
Number of Products: 170
Square Footage: 150000
Brands Imported: Summit
Regions Imported from: Worldwide

49004 Summit Hill Flavors
21 Worlds Fair Drive
Somerset, NJ 08873   732-805-0335
Fax: 732-805-1994 www.summithillflavors.com
Natural flavorings for dry and liquid applications used for marinating meats and poultry. Flavorings for soups, gravies, sauces, food bases and pasta dishes.
Contact: Selvin Medina
medinaselvin@summithillflavors.com
Regions Exported to: Worldwide

49005 Summit Import Corp
100 Summit Pl
Jersey City, NJ 07305-9997   201-985-9800
Fax: 201-985-8055 800-888-8228
info@summitimport.com www.summitimport.com
President: Whiting Wu
Sales Manager: Tony Tsao
Warehouse Manager: Kent Jia
Year Founded: 1955
Estimated Sales: $20-50 Million
Number Employees: 50-99
Square Footage: 180000
Type of Packaging: Consumer, Food Service, Private Label, Bulk
Brands Exported: Soy Sauce, Noodles, Rice and Canned Foods
Regions Exported to: Central America, South America, Europe
Brands Imported: Oriental Mascot; Mount Tai; Gold Key, Yu Yee, Ming River Brand
Regions Imported from: Asia

49006 Summit Machine Builders Corporation
550 W 53rd Place
Denver, CO 80216-1612   303-294-9949
Fax: 303-294-9622 800-274-6741
Manufacturer and exporter of automation and automated assembly equipment including dry and fibrous product feeding, filling and dispensing systems; also, ingredients dispensing and automatic micro weighing equipment
President: Scott Harris
Director Sales: Mike Schmehl
Estimated Sales: $5-10 Million
Number Employees: 85
Square Footage: 200000
Brands Exported: Sro Feeder; Vibra-Meter Feeder
Regions Exported to: Worldwide
Percentage of Business in Exporting: 3

49007 Sun Chlorella USA
3305 Kashiwa Street
Torrance, CA 90505-4022   310-891-0600
Fax: 310-891-0621 800-829-2828
www.sunchlorellausa.com
Ginseng and chlorella including tablets, liquid extract and green single cell algae with broken cell walls
President/CEO: Futoshi Nakayama
VP/Chief Financial Officer: Ellen Kubijanto
VP/Chief Operating Officer: Rose Straub
Marketing Manager: Susan Arboua
Public Relations: Janise Zantine
Estimated Sales: $24 Million
Number Employees: 61
Square Footage: 5000
Parent Co: YSK International Corporation
Brands Exported: Sun Chlorella; Wakasa; Sun Siberian Ginseng
Regions Exported to: Canada
Percentage of Business in Exporting: 5
Regions Imported from: Asia
Percentage of Business in Importing: 100

49008 Sun Glo Of Idaho
378 S 7th W
PO Box 300
Sugar City, ID 83448-5009   208-356-7346
Fax: 208-356-7351 bruce@sunglo-idaho.com
www.sungloidaho.com
Idaho potatoes
CEO: George M Crapo
george@sunglo-idaho.com
CEO: Ceorge Crapo
CFO: Bruce Crapo
VP Fresh Sales: Betty Miles
Human Resource Manager: Melissa Coles
Number Employees: 100-249
Type of Packaging: Consumer, Food Service, Private Label, Bulk
Brands Exported: Sun-Glo; Sun Supreme
Regions Exported to: Asia, Pacific Rim

49009 Sun Grove Foods Inc
45 Tulip St
Passaic, NJ 07055-3133   973-574-1110
Fax: 973-574-1113 info@sungrovefoods.com
www.sungrovefoods.com
Olive oils.
Executive Vice President: Joanna Lacina
Contact: Ed Cekici
ecekici@sungrovefoods.com
Number Employees: 5-9
Brands Imported: Agraria Riva del Garda, Basirico, CUFROL, Viola, Tithini Foods
Regions Imported from: South America

49010 Sun Harvest Foods Inc
6201 Progressive Dr # 400
Suite 400
San Diego, CA 92154-6651   619-661-0909
Fax: 619-690-1173 www.productosfrugo.com.mx
Processor, importer and exporter of IQF entrees, canned vegetables, jalapenos, tomatillo, sauces, salsa, broccoli, cauliflower, vegetable blends and fruit; kosher items available
President: Jorge Gonzalez
Sales & Marketing: Art Sanchez
Estimated Sales: $1.4 Million
Number Employees: 1-4
Square Footage: 640000
Parent Co: Productos Frugo S.A. de C.V.
Type of Packaging: Consumer, Food Service, Private Label, Bulk
Brands Exported: Frugo and Private Labels
Regions Exported to: Central America, South America, Europe, Asia, Canada, Latin America, Mexico
Percentage of Business in Exporting: 50
Brands Imported: Frugo and Private Labels
Regions Imported from: Central America, South America, Europe, Asia, Canada, Latin America, Mexico
Percentage of Business in Importing: 50

Importers & Exporters / A-Z

49011 Sun Harvest Salt, LLC
100 Wilshire Boulevard
Suite 1200
Santa Monica, CA 90401 323-487-2587
www.secretsunsalt.com
Importer and distributor of pure and low sodium sea salts.
Founder & CEO: Ramona Cappello
Contact: Frederick Gaston
frederick.gaston@sunharvestcitrus.com
Regions Imported from: Mexico

49012 Sun Noodle New Jersey
40 Kero Road
Carlstadt, NJ 07072 201-530-1100
www.sunnoodle.com
Ramen noodles, yakisoba, udon, and soba noodles, ramen soup.
CEO: Hidehito Uki
Number Employees: 80
Square Footage: 10000
Brands Exported: Sun Noodle
Regions Exported to: South America

49013 (HQ)Sun Pac Foods
10 Sun Pac Boulevard
Brampton, ON L6S 4R5
Canada 905-792-2700
Fax: 905-792-8490
Processor and contract packager of canned fruit juices, drinks and concentrates, bread crumbs, croutons and tortilla chips; importer of canned seafood and mandarin orange sections; exporter of juices and drinks
President: J Riddell
VP Finance: Vince McEwan
VP Imports/Exports: Cathy Knowles
Number Employees: 135
Square Footage: 1420000
Type of Packaging: Consumer, Food Service, Private Label, Bulk
Brands Exported: Sun Pac; Sun Crop
Regions Exported to: Central America, South America, Europe, Asia, Caribbean
Brands Imported: Saico
Regions Imported from: Central America, South America, Europe, Asia, Mexico

49014 Sun Paints & Coatings
4701 East 7th Avenue
PO Box 75070
Tampa, FL 33605 813-367-4444
Fax: 813-367-0263 800-247-9691
www.suncoatings.com
Manufacturer and exporter of window, tile and mildew cleaners.
President: Barton Malina
Contact: Tom Crosier
tcrosier@sunpaintsandcoatings.com
Estimated Sales: $5-10 Million
Number Employees: 20-49
Square Footage: 200000

49015 Sun West Foods
1550 Drew Avenue
Suite 150
Davis, CA 95618-7852 530-758-8550
Fax: 530-758-8110 nor-calrice@saber.net
www.sunwestfoods.com
Grower/packer of processed wild rice; developer of proprietary wild rice varieties and specialty rices; processor of quick-cook wild and brown rice. Specializes in ingredient sales to packers and ingredient users
President: James Errecarte
Contact: Rebecca Baxter
rbaxter@sunwestfoods.com
Estimated Sales: $ 5 - 10 Million
Number Employees: 10-19
Square Footage: 92000
Type of Packaging: Food Service, Private Label, Bulk

49016 Sun West Trading
2281 W 205th Street
Suite 107
Torrance, CA 90501-1450 310-320-4000
Fax: 310-320-8444
Importer and wholesaler/distributor of rice gluten, syrups and spray-dried syrup solids
President: Qasim Habib
Administrative Manager: Gafar Habib
Estimated Sales: $2.5-5 Million
Number Employees: 1-4
Parent Co: Habib Arkady
Type of Packaging: Bulk
Regions Imported from: Asia

49017 Sun-Brite Canning
1532 County Rd 34
Kingsville, ON N0P 2G0
Canada 519-326-9033
Fax: 519-326-8700 www.sun-brite.com
Tomato canners
President: Henry Iacobelli
Director of Sales: John Iacobelli
Plant Manager: Sam Lopez
Number Employees: 50-99
Type of Packaging: Consumer, Food Service, Private Label
Regions Exported to: USA

49018 Sun-Maid Growers of California
13525 S Bethel Ave
Kingsburg, CA 93631-9232 559-896-8000
Fax: 559-897-2362 info@sunmaid.com
www.sunmaid.com
Sun-dried fruits including raisins, peaches, apricots and pears; raisin paste and juice concentrate
President & CEO: Harry Overly
Number Employees: 500-999
Type of Packaging: Consumer, Food Service, Private Label, Bulk
Brands Exported: Sun-Maid
Regions Exported to: Worldwide
Percentage of Business in Exporting: 30

49019 (HQ)SunWest Foods, Inc.
1550 Drew Avenue
Suite 150
Davis, CA 95618 530-758-8550
Fax: 530-758-8110 www.sunwestfoods.com
Processor and exporter of regular, organic and wild rice; also, walnuts, almonds, pistachios and pecans.
Contact: Jess Errecarte
jess@sunwestfoods.com *Year Founded:* 1991
Brands Exported: SunWest, SunNuts
Regions Exported to: Europe, Asia, Middle East, Australia
Percentage of Business in Exporting: 80

49020 Sunco & Frenchie
489 Getty Avenue
Clifton, NJ 07011
Fax: 973-478-1063 973-478-1011
www.sunconatural.com
Dried fruits, nuts, granola, raw sugar, quick oats, corn meal, and juice.
Co-Owner: Joel Ammar
Year Founded: 2009
Estimated Sales: $1-5 Million
Number Employees: 15
Brands Imported: Ingredients
Regions Imported from: Worldwide

49021 Sundial Herb Garden
59 Hidden Lake Rd
Higganum, CT 06441-4441 860-345-4290
Fax: 860-345-3462 sundial9@localnet.com
www.sundialgardens.com
Spices, herb blends, tea cake and scone mixes including hazelnut, pumpkin-ginger, cranberry and traditional; importer of rare and herbal teas
Owner: Ragna Goddard
VP: Thomas Goddard
Estimated Sales: Less Than $500,000
Number Employees: 1-4
Square Footage: 10000
Type of Packaging: Consumer
Regions Imported from: Canada
Percentage of Business in Importing: 60

49022 Sunflower Restaurant Supply
1647 Sunflower Rd
Salina, KS 67401-1758 785-823-6394
Fax: 785-823-5512
Locally owned and operated offering quality restaurant supplies and equipment.
President/Finance Executive: Leroy Baumberger
leroy@sunflowersrs.com
Estimated Sales: $7.3 Million
Number Employees: 20-49
Square Footage: 144000
Brands Imported: Lyon
Regions Imported from: Japan, China
Percentage of Business in Importing: 10

49023 Sunfood
1830 Gillespie Way
Suite 101
El Cajon, CA 92020-0922 619-596-7979
Fax: 619-596-7997 888-729-3663
support@sunfood.com www.sunfood.com
Goji berries, raw cacao, goldenberries, and maqui.
President: Doug Harbison
CEO: Matt Alonso
matt.alonso@sunfood.com
CFO: Deion Stromenger
Chief Marketing Officer: Eric Cutler
Sales Executive: Sara Thompson
Operations Director: Jack Wortman
Facilities Manager: Jerome Fodor
Number Employees: 20-49
Type of Packaging: Consumer, Bulk

49024 Sunkist Growers
27770 Entertainment Dr.
Valencia, CA 91355 661-290-8900
www.sunkist.com
Fruit juices, fruit drinks, healthy snacks, baking mixes, carbonated beverages, confections, vitamins, frozen novelties, salad toppings, freshly peeled citrus, chilled jellies and nonfood products.
Chief Executive Officer: Jim Phillips
Chief Operating Officer: Christian Harris
Year Founded: 1893
Estimated Sales: $1 Billion
Number Employees: 6,000
Type of Packaging: Food Service, Private Label
Other Locations:
  Sunkist Growers
  Toronto Canada, ON
  Sunkist Growers
  Cary, NC
  Sunkist Growers
  Pittsburgh, PA
  Sunkist Growers
  Buffalo, NY
  Sunkist Growers
  Stafford, TX
  Sunkist Growers
  Visalia, CA
  Sunkist GrowersCary
Regions Exported to: Europe, Asia

49025 Sunlike Juice
170 5th Avenue
Rougemont, QC J0L 1M0
Canada 416-297-1140
Fax: 416-297-5703 866-552-7643
www.alassonde.com
Processor and exporter of fruit juices and drinks including apple, apple/strawberry, cranberry cocktail, grapefruit, mango, orange juice, orange/pineapple, peach, pineapple, fruit punch, grape, papaya, pink lemonade, black cherry andiced tea
President/CEO: Jean Gattuso
EVP/General Manager of Sales: Pierre L Heureux
EVP/General Manager of Operations: Sylvain Mayrand
VP Marketing: Luc Prevost
VP Communications: Stefano Bertolli
Brands Exported: Sunlike
Regions Exported to: Europe, USA, Caribbean

49026 Sunny Avocado
20872 Deerhorn Valley Road
Jamul, CA 91935-7937 619-479-3573
Fax: 619-479-2960 800-999-2862
Provides extra chunky avocado pulp, original mild qualcomole and spicy blends; guac, salsa and guacamaya drink
President: Enrique Bautista
VP: Ana Rosa Bautista
VP Sales/Marketing: Michael Spinner
Estimated Sales: $120000
Number Employees: 2
Type of Packaging: Food Service, Private Label, Bulk
Brands Exported: Sunny Avocado
Regions Exported to: Europe, Asia
Percentage of Business in Exporting: 20
Brands Imported: Sunny Avocado
Regions Imported from: Mexico
Percentage of Business in Importing: 100

49027 Sunnyland Farms
P.O.Box 8200
Albany, GA 31706-8200 229-317-4979
Fax: 229-888-8332 800-999-2488
www.sunnylandfarms.com

Nuts, mixed nuts, pecans, dried fruits and specialty products.
Sales Manager: Beverly Willson
Purchasing: Larry Willson
Estimated Sales: $ 10 - 20 Million
Type of Packaging: Consumer, Bulk
Regions Imported from: Central America, South America, Europe, Asia

49028 (HQ)Sunrich LLC
3824 SW 93rd St
Hope, MN 56046-2010
507-451-4724
Fax: 507-451-2910 800-297-5997
sueklem@sunrich.com www.sunrich.com
Processor and exporter of soy products including milk, tofu powder and frozen green soybeans; also, corn products including grits and flour
President: Allan Routh
CFO: John Dietrich
Manager: Jon Meyer
john.meyer@sunopta.com
Estimated Sales: $9 Million
Number Employees: 20-49
Type of Packaging: Food Service, Private Label, Bulk
Other Locations:
SunRich
Cresco, IA SunRich
Regions Exported to: Europe, Asia

49029 Sunridge Farms
423 Salinas Rd
Royal Oaks, CA 95076-5232
831-786-7000
Fax: 831-786-8618 info@sunridgefarms.com
www.sunridgefarms.com
Organic and all natural nuts & seeds, dried fruit, candies, and snacks & tril mixes.
CFO: Phillip Adrian
Vice President: Larry Cox
Quality Assurance: Robert Yebra
Assistant Marketing Director: Vivian Guajardo
Sales: Eric Birckner
Director of Operations: Don Blodget
Production and Food Safety Supervisor: Pat Ryan
Estimated Sales: $900 Million
Number Employees: 20-49
Type of Packaging: Consumer, Bulk
Brands Exported: Sunridge Farms
Regions Exported to: Worldwide
Regions Imported from: Worldwide

49030 Sunrise Commodities
140 Sylvan Ave
Englewood Cliffs, NJ 07632
201-947-1000
800-524-0997
www.sunrisecommodities.com
Importer of dehydrated fruits and fruit juices, walnuts, filberts, cashews and pumpkin and squash seeds.
President: David Cottam
Year Founded: 1995
Estimated Sales: $50-100 Million
Number Employees: 50-99

49031 Sunrise Fruit Company
1727 Rhoadmiller Street
Richmond, VA 23220-1108
804-358-6468
Fax: 804-358-6947
Wholesaler/distributor, importer and exporter of tomatoes
Regions Imported from: Bahamas

49032 (HQ)Sunrise Growers
701 W Kimberly
Suite 210
Placentia, CA 92870
714-630-6292
Fax: 714-630-0920 website@sunrisegrowers.com
www.sunrisegrowers.com
Manufacturer, exporter and importer of frozen strawberries and purees
President: Ed Haft
CEO: Edward Haft
CFO: Tim Graven
VP: Carl Lindgren
Sales Executive: Steve Cjrcle
Contact: Doyal Andrews
dandrews@sunrisegrowers.com
Estimated Sales: $10-20 Million
Number Employees: 250-499
Square Footage: 1000000
Type of Packaging: Consumer, Food Service, Private Label, Bulk

Other Locations:
Frozsun Foods
Oxnard, CA Frozsun Foods
Brands Exported: Frozsun
Regions Exported to: Europe, Asia, Middle East, Canada
Percentage of Business in Exporting: 15
Regions Imported from: Worldwide
Percentage of Business in Importing: 1

49033 (HQ)Sunroc Corporation
PO Box 13150
Columbus, OH 43213-0150
302-678-7800
Fax: 302-678-7809 800-478-6762
literature@sunroc.com
Manufacturer and exporter of electric and bottled water coolers, drinking fountains and point-of-use coolers
President: Anthony Salamone
CFO: Mark Whitaker
Director Engineering: Ronald Greenwald
Quality Control: Tom Huber
VP Sales/Marketing: John Ott
Contact: Mel Sloan
msloan@sunroc.com
Estimated Sales: $20-50 Million
Number Employees: 100-249
Square Footage: 250000
Brands Exported: Sunroc
Regions Exported to: Central America, South America, Europe, Asia, Middle East
Percentage of Business in Exporting: 20

49034 Sunset Farm Foods Inc
1201 Madison Hwy
Valdosta, GA 31601
Fax: 229-242-3389 800-882-1121
webinfo@sunsetfarmfoods.com
www.sunsetfarmfoods.com
Processor of smoked sausage, fresh sausage, smoked meats, cooked products (souse, chitterling loaf, liver pudding, chili)
Owner & President: Tom Carroll
t.carroll@sunsetfarmfoods.com
Plant Manager: Ricky Lightsey
Year Founded: 1918
Estimated Sales: $20-50 Million
Number Employees: 50-99
Number of Brands: 6
Number of Products: 250
Square Footage: 40000
Type of Packaging: Consumer, Food Service, Private Label, Bulk

49035 Sunset Specialty Foods
PO Box 50, PMB 145
Lake Arrowhead, CA 92352
909-337-7643
Fax: 909-337-0963
Processor and exporter of specialty frozen items including pizza, chocolate chip cookies, etc
President/CEO: James Tolliver
Estimated Sales: $5-10 Million
Number Employees: 11-50
Square Footage: 108000
Type of Packaging: Consumer, Food Service, Private Label, Bulk
Brands Exported: Deli Pizza; Nutty Nanner
Regions Exported to: Central America, Europe, Asia
Percentage of Business in Exporting: 25

49036 Sunshine Farm & Garden
696 Glicks Rd
Renick, WV 24966-6601
304-497-2208
Fax: 304-497-2698 barry@sunfarm.com
www.sunfarm.com
Processor, importer and exporter of organic fruits including apples and pawpaws; also, organic herbs and seeds
President: Barry Glick
barry@sunfarm.com
VP: Zak Glick
Estimated Sales: $400000
Number Employees: 20-49
Square Footage: 260000
Brands Exported: Sunshine
Regions Exported to: Worldwide
Percentage of Business in Exporting: 35
Regions Imported from: Worldwide
Percentage of Business in Importing: 10

49037 Sunshine Food Sales
2900 NW 75th St Ste 305
Miami, FL 33147
305-696-2885

Processor and importer of fresh and frozen fish including mackerel, kingfish, lobster and crabs
President: Carlos Sanchez
Co-Owner: David Dossi
Plant Manager: Jesus Alonsa
Number Employees: 1-4
Type of Packaging: Bulk
Regions Imported from: Mexico
Percentage of Business in Importing: 85

49038 Sunshine Nut Company
16192 Coastal Highway
Lewes, DE 19958
210-732-9460
info@sunshinenuts.com
www.sunshinenuts.com
Walnuts, almonds and pecans
Contact: Don Larson
don@sunshinenuts.com
Parent Co: John B. Sanfilippo & Son

49039 Sunsweet Growers Inc.
901 N. Walton Ave.
Yuba City, CA 95993
800-417-2253
sunsweet@casupport.com www.sunsweet
Dried fruits including prunes, apricots and mangos, as well as prune juice. nuts and more.
President/CEO: Dane Lance
Vice President/CFO: Ana Klein
VP, Global Sales/Marketing: Brad Schuler
Year Founded: 1917
Estimated Sales: $281 Million
Number Employees: 500-999
Type of Packaging: Consumer, Food Service, Private Label, Bulk
Regions Exported to: Worldwide
Percentage of Business in Exporting: 30

49040 Suntec Power
1910 Bath Ave
Brooklyn, NY 11214-4713
718-333-3636
Fax: 718-333-3639 www.suntecusa.com
Exporter, importer and wholesaler/distributor of health food ingredients, vitamins, herbs, herbal extracts, food additives, spices, amino acids, etc
President: Tommy Liu
suntecpower@gmail.com
Owner: Wei Lin
Estimated Sales: Less Than $500,000
Number Employees: 1-4
Square Footage: 24000
Type of Packaging: Bulk
Regions Exported to: Central America, South America, Europe, Asia
Regions Imported from: South America, Asia

49041 Sunterra Meats
233 North Rd
P.O. Box 309
Trochu, AB T0M 2C0
Canada
403-442-4202
Fax: 403-442-2771 www.sunterrameats.ca
Fresh and frozen pork
President: Ray Price
VP Sales & Marketing: Tony Martinez
Plant Manager: Richard Johnson
Estimated Sales: $46 Million
Number Employees: 115
Type of Packaging: Food Service
Regions Exported to: Worldwide
Percentage of Business in Exporting: 50

49042 SupHerb Farms
300 Dianne Dr
Turlock, CA 95380-9523
209-633-3600
Fax: 209-633-3644 800-787-4372
custserv@supherbfarms.com
www.supherbfarms.com
Frozen culinary herb and specialty vegetable ingredients
President & CEO: Matt Reid
VP Finance & Administration: Debbie Salcedo
Executive Corporate Chef: Scott Adair
VP Sales & Marketing: Don Douglas
National Account Manager: Stephanie Schutz
Human Resources Director: Patricia Silva
Plant Manager: Eduardo Luna
Estimated Sales: $3.4 Million
Number Employees: 100-249
Square Footage: 65190
Type of Packaging: Food Service, Bulk
Brands Exported: SupHerb Farms
Regions Exported to: Europe, Asia

Importers & Exporters / A-Z

49043 Supelco Inc
595 N Harrison Rd
Bellefonte, PA 16823-6217   814-359-3441
Fax: 814-359-5459   800-247-6628
techservice@sial.com
Chromatography products for analysis and purification
President: Ryan Adams
ryan.adams@sial.com
Vice President: Russel Gant
Research & Development: Mark Robillard
Marketing Director: Don Hobbs
Sales Director: Marty McCoy
Public Relations: Diane Lidgett
Operations/Production: Rod Datt
Production Manager: Tom Henderson
Plant Manager: Rod Datt
Purchasing Manager: Jim Heiserl
Estimated Sales: $ 50 - 75 Million
Number Employees: 250-499
Parent Co: Sigma-Aldrich Corporation
Regions Exported to: Central America, South America, Europe, Asia, Middle East
Percentage of Business in Exporting: 25

49044 Super Cooker
6049 Peterson Rd
Lake Park, GA 31636-4003   229-559-1662
Fax: 229-559-1611   800-841-7452
Manufacturer and exporter of portable barbecue grills and smokers including charcoal, wood and gas
Owner: Ben Futch
ben@supercooker.com
Estimated Sales: $ 3 - 5,000,000
Number Employees: 10-19
Regions Exported to: Worldwide
Percentage of Business in Exporting: 1

49045 Super Radiator Coils
451 Southlake Blvd
N Chesterfield, VA 23236-3091   804-794-2887
Fax: 804-379-2118   800-229-2645
vainfo@superradiatorcoils.com www.srcoils.com
Coils and heat exchangers; exporter of coils, evaporators and condensors
Cmo: John Perez
john.perez@superradiatorcoils.com
Estimated Sales: $30+ Million
Number Employees: 100-249
Square Footage: 112000
Parent Co: Super Radiator Coils
Other Locations:
  Super Radiator Coils
  Phoenix, AZ Super Radiator Coils
Brands Exported: Super Radiator Coils
Regions Exported to: Worldwide
Percentage of Business in Exporting: 5

49046 Super Seal Manufacturing Limited
670 Rowntree Dairy Road
Woodbridge, ON L4L 5T8
Canada   905-850-2929
Fax: 905-850-4440   800-337-3239
info@supersealmfg.com www.supersealmfg.com
Manufacturer and exporter of energy saving devices, retail and industrial impact traffic, P.V.C. and bi-folding doors, dock seals, truck shelters and inflatable seals and shelters
President: Renato Torchetti
Director Sales (USA): Paul Ricci
Number Employees: 10
Square Footage: 160000
Regions Exported to: Europe
Percentage of Business in Exporting: 35

49047 Super Vision International
9400 Southridge Park Ct # 200
Orlando, FL 32819-8643   407-857-9900
Fax: 407-857-0050
Manufacturer and exporter of signs, lighting and lighting fixtures
President: Mike Bauer
Chairman of the Board: Brett M Kingstone
Sales (USA): Rick Hunter
International Sales: Paula Vega
Number Employees: 50-99
Square Footage: 320000
Regions Exported to: Worldwide
Percentage of Business in Exporting: 35

49048 Super-Chef Manufacturing Company
9235 Bissonnet Street
Houston, TX 77074   713-729-9660
Fax: 713-729-8404   800-231-3478
Manufacturer and exporter of broilers, fryers, griddles, warming units, ovens, hoods, ranges, hot plates, food concession trailers and compact kitchens with recirculating filter hoods
President: Chris Pappas
CEO: Regina Seale
CFO: Isabel Repka
VP: Ed Seale
R&D: Chris Pappas
Quality Control: Ed Seale
Marketing: Regina Seale
Sales: Isabel Repka
Public Relations: Regina Seale
Operations: Chris Pappas
Production: Barry Berg
Plant Manager: Barry Berg
Purchasing: Ed Seale
Number Employees: 20-49
Number of Brands: 2
Square Footage: 160000
Brands Exported: Super Chef; Fat Mizer; Kompact Kitchens

49049 Superflex Limited
152 44th St
Brooklyn, NY 11232-3310   718-768-1400
Fax: 718-768-5065   800-394-3665
sales@superflex.com www.seal-proof.com
Manufacturer and exporter of P.V.C. flexible suction and discharge reinforced hoses, liquid tight conduit and electrical tubing used for pumps, refrigerators, dairy equipment, beverage dispensers, etc
President: Yigal Elbaz
yelbaz@superflex.com
VP: Y Elbaz
Estimated Sales: Less Than $500,000
Number Employees: 1-4
Brands Exported: RollerFlex; SealProof; SuperFlex
Regions Exported to: Worldwide
Percentage of Business in Exporting: 7

49050 (HQ)Superior Brush Company
3455 W 140th St
Cleveland, OH 44111   216-941-6987
Fax: 216-252-8838
Manufacturer and exporter of metal strip brushes; also, custom design services available
VP Sales/Marketing: Richard Mertes
Estimated Sales: $10-20 Million
Number Employees: 20-49
Square Footage: 22000

49051 Superior Distributing Co
103 N 32nd St
Louisville, KY 40212   502-778-6661
Fax: 502-775-7519   800-365-6661
www.superiordisplayboards.com
Manufacturer and exporter of FDA approved wiping cloths, polyethylene bags, hairnets, beard masks, gloves and butchers' paper
Owner: Michael Hinson
Sales Manager: Susan Thrapp
Manager: Robert Mc Roberts
Estimated Sales: $5-10 Million
Number Employees: 1-4

49052 Superior Food Machinery Inc
7635 Serapis Ave
Pico Rivera, CA 90660-4516   562-949-0396
Fax: 562-949-0180   800-944-0396
info@Superiorinc.com www.superiorinc.com
Manufacturer, importer, exporter and designer of tortilla and tortilla chip processing equipment; also, corn feeders, ovens and washers
Owner: Maria Castro
General Sales Manager: Rick Rangel
Customer Service Manager: Mark Reyes
maria@superiorinc.com
Estimated Sales: $ 5-10 Million
Number Employees: 20-49
Square Footage: 7000
Brands Exported: Superior Food Machinery, Inc.
Regions Exported to: Central America, South America, Europe, Middle East, Australia
Percentage of Business in Exporting: 50
Brands Imported: L & M; Welbuilt
Regions Imported from: Canada
Percentage of Business in Importing: 1

49053 Superior Foods
275 Westgate Dr
Watsonville, CA 95076-2470   831-728-3691
Fax: 831-722-0926 info@superiorfoods.com
www.superiorfoods.com
Global supplier and manufacturer of frozen fruits, vegetables and grains for the consumer, foodservice, club and industrial markets.
President & CEO: R. Neil Happee
Number Employees: 50-99
Type of Packaging: Consumer, Food Service
Brands Exported: Superior
Regions Exported to: Central America, South America, Europe, Asia, Canada, Mexico
Percentage of Business in Exporting: 15
Regions Imported from: Central America, South America, Europe, Asia, Canada, Mexico
Percentage of Business in Importing: 25

49054 Superior Industries
315 State Highway 28
Morris, MN 56267-4699   320-589-2406
Fax: 320-589-3892   800-321-1558
info@superior-ind.com www.superior-ind.com
Manufacturer and exporter idlers and portable conveying equipment
President: Riley Arndt
rarndt@supind.com
Estimated Sales: $ 15 - 20 Million
Number Employees: 500-999
Regions Exported to: Worldwide

49055 Superior Manufacturing Division
P.O. Box 13343
Fort Wayne, IN 46868-3343   260-456-3596
Fax: 260-456-3598 smdmag@aol.com
www.superiorwaterconditioners.com
President: Charles Sanderson
Contact: Terri Parker
terri@superiorwaterconditioners.com
Estimated Sales: $ .5 - 1 million
Number Employees: 5-9

49056 Superior Packaging Equipment Corporation
3 Edison Pl
Suite 4
Fairfield, NJ 7004   973-575-8818
Fax: 973-890-7295 www.superiorpack.com
Manufacturer and exporter of cartoning machinery including forming, gluing, inserting, closing, sealing and opening
President: Glenn Rice
Executive VP: Russell Rice
Estimated Sales: $ 5 - 10 Million
Number Employees: 10
Square Footage: 76000
Regions Exported to: Central America, South America, Europe, Australia, Mexico, Canada
Percentage of Business in Exporting: 25

49057 Superior Paper & Plastic Co
1930 E 65th St
Los Angeles, CA 90001-2111   323-235-1228
Fax: 323-581-7777 www.superiorpaper.com
Wholesaler/distributor of disposable paper and plastic products including napkins, cups, plates, cutlery, etc.; serving the food service market
Owner: Mark Penhasian
mark@superiorpaper.com
CEO: John Fong
Vice President: Mourice Penhasian
Sales Director: Joe Diaz
mark@superiorpaper.com
Estimated Sales: $ 5 - 10 Million
Number Employees: 20-49
Number of Products: 3500
Square Footage: 128000
Type of Packaging: Food Service
Regions Exported to: Central America, South America, Asia
Percentage of Business in Exporting: 5

49058 Superior Quality Foods
2355 E Francis St
Ontario, CA 91761   909-923-4733
Fax: 909-947-7065   800-300-4210
Soup bases, beef extracts, dried seasonings and sauce mixes

Importers & Exporters / A-Z

President: Linda Owen
Vice President: Bob Grizzard
National Sales Manager: Paul Smalley
Contact: Cindy Deets
cdeets@superiortouch.com
Estimated Sales: $22.3 Million
Number Employees: 63
Parent Co: Southeastern Mills, Inc.
Type of Packaging: Food Service, Bulk

49059 Superior Uniform Group
10055 Seminole Blvd
Seminole, FL 33772
800-727-8643
info@superioruniformgroup.com
www.superioruniformgroup.com
Manufacturer and exporter of aprons, restaurant smocks, sheeting, knit shirts, hats and cloth bags.
Chief Executive Officer: Michael Benstock
Executive Vice President: Peter Benstock
COO/CFO/Treasurer: Andrew Demott, Jr.
VP/General Counsel/Secretary: Jordan Alpert
Year Founded: 1920
Estimated Sales: $100-$500 Million
Square Footage: 60000
Regions Exported to: Europe, Caribbean

49060 Supramatic
3313 Lakeshore Boulevard West
Toronto, ON M8W 1M8
Canada
416-251-3266
Fax: 416-251-1433 877-465-2883
info@supramatic.com www.supramatic.com
Manufacturer and importer of espresso, coffee and cappuccino machines; importer of coffee beans
President: Rene Peterson
Estimated Sales: Below $ 5 Million
Number Employees: 3
Brands Imported: Schaerer; Thermoplan; Jura; Rosca
Regions Imported from: Europe

49061 Supreme Chocolatier
1150 South Ave
Suite 1
Staten Island, NY 10314-3404   718-761-9600
Fax: 718-761-5279 www.supremechocolatier.com
Chocolate novelties and gift baskets
Owner: George Biddle
george.biddle@supremechocolatier.com
VP Marketing: Wayne Stottmeister
Estimated Sales: $6,100,000
Number Employees: 50-99
Type of Packaging: Consumer
Regions Exported to: Asia, Australia

49062 Supreme Corporation
2572 East Kercher Road
Goshen, IN 46528   574-533-3100
Fax: 574-642-4729   800-642-4889
info@supremecorp.com
Manufacturer and exporter of refrigerators, freezers and refrigerated truck cars
CEO: Herbert M Gardner
VP Marketing/Sales: Rick Horn
Contact: David Allen
dallen@supre.com
Estimated Sales: $ 10 - 20 Million
Number Employees: 2
Type of Packaging: Bulk
Regions Exported to: Canada

49063 Supreme Dairy Farms Co
111 Kilvert St
Warwick, RI 02886-1006   401-739-8180
Fax: 401-739-8230 www.supremedairyfarms.com
Processor and importer of tomato products; also, mozzarella and ricotta cheese
President: Paul Areson
Director: Bill Toll
Contact: Vincent Bruzzese
vincent@supremedairyfarms.com
Estimated Sales: $1.8 Million
Number Employees: 1-4
Square Footage: 56000
Type of Packaging: Food Service, Private Label
Brands Imported: Avanti Supreme

49064 Supreme Manufacturing Co Inc
5 Connerty Ct
East Brunswick, NJ 08816-1633   732-254-0087
Fax: 732-254-5736 supmfgco@aol.com
www.supreme-mfg.com
Owner: Cliff Krause
supmfgco@aol.com
Estimated Sales: $ 10 - 20 Million
Number Employees: 20-49

49065 Supreme Metal
3125 Trotters Parkway
Alpharetta, GA 30004-7746
Fax: 770-740-6010   800-645-2526
Manufacturer and exporter of stainless steel hot food tables, sinks, ice storage equipment and wait stations; also, bars, bins and glass racks
President: Rick Schwartz
VP Sales: Lisa Finegan
National Sales Manager: Sandy Hill
Contact: Talisha Hardy
talishahardy@gmail.com
Type of Packaging: Food Service
Regions Exported to: Worldwide
Percentage of Business in Exporting: 2

49066 Suram Trading Corporation
2655 Le Jeune Road
Suite 1006
Coral Gables, FL 33134   305-448-7165
Fax: 305-445-7185
Frozen seafood shrimp
President and CEO: Guido Adler
Controller: Carmen Artime
Marketing: Kristina Adler
Sales: Michael del Aguila
Contact: Michael Aguila
mdelaguila@suram.com
Operations Manager: Kenji Kurenuma
Estimated Sales: $ 20-49.9 Million
Number Employees: 10
Number of Brands: 1
Regions Imported from: South America, Asia

49067 (HQ)Surco Products
290 Alpha Dr
RIDC Industrial Park
Pittsburgh, PA 15238   412-252-7000
Fax: 412-252-1005   800-556-0111
www.surcopt.com
Manufacturer and exporter of air fresheners, deodorants and insecticides
President: Arnold Zlotnik
CEO: Bernard Surloff
Estimated Sales: $ 10 - 20 Million
Number Employees: 50-99
Square Footage: 114000
Type of Packaging: Consumer, Private Label, Bulk
Regions Exported to: Europe, Asia
Percentage of Business in Exporting: 8

49068 Sure Shot Dispensing Systems
100 Dispensing Way
Lower Sackville, NS B4C 4H2
Canada
902-865-9602
Fax: 902-865-9604   888-777-4990
sales@sureshotdispensing.com
www.sureshotdispensing.com
President: Michael Duck
VP: David Macaulay
R&D: Ian Maclean
Quality Control: Peter Black
Marketing: Chad Wiesner
Sales: William Morris
Operations: Garth I
Production: Dennis Dickinson
Plant Manager: Ken Lawrence
Purchasing Director: Tracey S
Number Employees: 90
Square Footage: 260000
Brands Exported: Sureshot Dispensing Systems®; Flavorshot by Surehot

49069 Sure Torque
12100 West 6th Avenue
Lakewood, CO 80228   303-987-8000
Fax: 303-987-8989   800-387-6572
spearson@suretorque.com www.suretorque.com
Manufacturer and exporter of container closure torque measurement instruments including near and on-line, automatic and electronic
Owner: Michelle Bergeron
R&D: Steve Pearson
Technical Engineer: Tibor Szenti
Sales/Technical: Gloria LaCroix
Director Operations: Jeff Dubrow
Estimated Sales: Below $ 5 Million
Number Employees: 1-4
Square Footage: 5000
Regions Exported to: Central America, South America, Europe, Mexico, Canada, Caribbean, Latin America
Percentage of Business in Exporting: 9

49070 Sure-Fresh Produce Inc
1302 W Stowell Rd
Santa Maria, CA 93458-9730   805-349-2677
Fax: 805-349-2674   888-423-5379
www.surefreshproduce.com
Industrial frozen vegetable ingredient manufacturer of both conventional and organic bulk products
President: Robert Witt
robert@surefreshproduce.com
CFO: Renee Kolding
Quality Control: Corrie Landymore
Marketing Director: Matthew Johnson
Sales Representative: Armando Gonzalez
Estimated Sales: $10-20 Million
Number Employees: 50-99
Number of Products: 750
Square Footage: 100000
Type of Packaging: Food Service, Bulk
Regions Exported to: Asia
Percentage of Business in Exporting: 5
Regions Imported from: Asia
Percentage of Business in Importing: 5

49071 Surekap Inc
579 Barrow Park Dr
Winder, GA 30680-3417   770-867-5793
Fax: 770-867-5799 support@surekap.com
www.surekap.com
Manufacturer and exporter of liquid filling and bottle and capping equipment including plastic, metal, tamper evident, CRC, etc
President: John Antoine
john@surekap.com
Estimated Sales: $ 10-20 Million
Number Employees: 5-9
Regions Exported to: Central America, South America, Asia, Middle East, Canada, Caribbean, Latin America, Mexico
Percentage of Business in Exporting: 15

49072 Surface Banana Company
1272 Gihon Road
Parkersburg, WV 26101   304-485-2400
Fax: 304-589-7252
Bananas and tomatoes; importer of bananas
Owner: David Surface
Estimated Sales: $300,000-500,000
Number Employees: 1-4
Regions Imported from: Central America, South America

49073 Surtec Inc
1880 N Macarthur Dr
Tracy, CA 95376-2841   209-820-3700
Fax: 209-820-3793   800-877-6330
orderdesk@surtecsystem.com
www.surtecsystem.com
Manufacturer, importer and exporter of floor cleaning systems, chemicals and high-speed buffing machines
Owner: William Fields
CFO: Bill Haag
VP/Director Reaserch/Development: Don Fromm
Manager Sales: Kurt Grannis
william.fields@surtecsystem.com
Estimated Sales: $ 5 - 10 Million
Number Employees: 50-99
Square Footage: 140000
Brands Exported: Surtec
Regions Exported to: South America, Europe, Australia
Percentage of Business in Exporting: 10
Regions Imported from: Asia
Percentage of Business in Importing: 5

49074 Sussman Electric Boilers
4320 34th St
Long Island City, NY 11101   718-937-4500
Fax: 718-937-4676   800-238-3535
seb@sussmancorp.com www.sussmanboilers.com
Manufacturer and exporter of electric boilers including steam, hot water, stainless steel and humidification, also, steam superheaters and steam-to-steam generators

Importers & Exporters / A-Z

President: Charles Monteverdi
Marketing: Louise Mound
Sales: Louise Mound
Production: Ben Cavanna
bcavanna@sussmancorp.com
Plant Manager: Ben Cavanna
Purchasing Manager: Arthur Perlman
Estimated Sales: $ 10 - 20 Million
Number Employees: 50-99
Parent Co: Sussman-Automatic Corporation
Brands Exported: Sussman Electric Boilers
Regions Exported to: South America, Asia, Middle East
Percentage of Business in Exporting: 15

49075 Sutter Home Winery
277 Saint Helena Hwy S
St Helena, CA 94574-2202   707-963-3104
                            800-967-4663
info@sutterhome.com www.sutterhome.com
Processor and exporter of wines
President: Larry Dizmang
CEO: Sandra Barros
sbarros@tfewines.com
CFO: George Schofield
Public Relations Director: David Foster
Production Manager: Scott Harvey
Purchasing Agent: Marc Norwood
Number Employees: 100-249
Square Footage: 58624
Regions Exported to: Worldwide
Percentage of Business in Exporting: 5

49076 Suzanne's Specialties
411 Jersey Ave
New Brunswick, NJ 08901   732-828-8500
     Fax: 732-828-8563   800-762-2135
info@suzannes-specialties.com
suzannes-specialties.com
Organic sweeteners and sugar alternatives including brown rice syrup, agave syrup and evaporated cane juice
President/Owner: Susan Morano
VP, Operations: Jim Morano
Number Employees: 20-49
Type of Packaging: Consumer, Food Service, Bulk
Brands Exported: Rice Nectar
Regions Exported to: Central America, Europe, Asia, Canada, Mexico
Percentage of Business in Exporting: 10

49077 Suzhou-Chem Inc
396 Washington St
Suite 318
Wellesley, MA 02481   781-433-8618
     Fax: 781-433-8619 info@suzhouchem.com
                        www.suzhouchem.com
Food and beverage ingredients including ascorbic acid, sodium ascorbate, calcium ascorbate, sodium saccharin granular, sodium saccharin dehydrate, sodium saccharin powder, calcium saccharin, insoluble saccharin, acesulfame-k aspartame, caffeine, potassium, sorbic acid, etc.
President: Joan Ni
Estimated Sales: $302 Million
Number Employees: 5-9
Type of Packaging: Bulk
Regions Imported from: Asia

49078 Svedala Industries
621 S Sierra Madre St
Colorado Springs, CO 80903-4016   719-471-3443
     Fax: 719-471-4469 denversala@aol.com
                        www.metso.com
Manufacturer and exporter of thermal heat exchangers
Manager: Kirk Smith
Production Manager (Thermal Equipment): Siegfried Nierenz
Estimated Sales: $ 20 - 50 Million
Number Employees: 20-49
Brands Exported: Holo-Flite
Regions Exported to: Central America, South America, Europe, Asia, Middle East
Percentage of Business in Exporting: 60

49079 Svedala Industries
621 S Sierra Madre St
Colorado Springs, CO 80903-4016   719-471-3443
     Fax: 719-471-4469 denversala@aol.com
                        www.metso.com
Manufacturer and exporter of belt conveyor components for bulk material handling systems

Manager: Kirk Smith
Manager: Rick Pummell
Manager Sales Administration: Jim Danielson
Estimated Sales: $ 20 - 50 Million
Number Employees: 20-49
Parent Co: Svedala Industries

49080 Swagger Foods Corp
900 Corporate Woods Pkwy
Vernon Hills, IL 60061-3155   847-913-1200
     Fax: 847-913-1263 info@swaggerfoods.com
Supplying the industrial, food service and retail markets as a manufacturer of seasonings, functional foods with vitamins, minerals, omega-3, other micronutrients/nutraceuticals, salt substitutes, soup mixes/bases, rubs, marinades gravy/sauce mixes, dip/dressing mixes, drink mixes, side dish mixes and other dry blends including Ethnic.
President: Terry R Shin
terry.shin@swaggerfoods.com
Number Employees: 10-19
Type of Packaging: Consumer, Food Service, Private Label, Bulk

49081 Swan Label & Tag Co
929 2nd Ave # A
PO Box 308
Coraopolis, PA 15108-1434   412-264-9000
     Fax: 412-264-7259 info@swanlabel.com
Manufacturer and exporter of pressure sensitive labels and tags
President: Jill Clendenning
jill@swanlabel.com
Art/Graphic Department: Justin Kevish
Sales: Jill Clendening
Customer Service: Gilda Clendenning
General Manager: Mike Chieski
Estimated Sales: $ 10-20 Million
Number Employees: 5-9

49082 Sweco Inc
8029 Dixie Hwy
PO Box 1509
Florence, KY 41042-2941   859-371-4360
     Fax: 859-283-8469 800-807-9326
info@sweco.com www.sweco.com
Manufacturer and exporter of FDA approved separation/screening equipment
President: David M Sorter
davidsorter@sweco.com
VP Engineering: Brad Jones
Marketing Manager: Jeff Dierig
Number Employees: 250-499
Parent Co: M-I LLC
Brands Exported: Vibro-Energy Separators; Supertaut Plus II

49083 Sweet Corn Products Co
124 N Broadway St
Bloomfield, NE 68718-4406   402-373-2211
     Fax: 402-373-2219 877-628-6115
                        www.no-nobirdfeeder.com
Processor and exporter of sweet corn products including dry mature for tortilla chips and toasted nuts
General Manager: Raymon Lush
ray@sweetcornproducts.com
Estimated Sales: $2000000
Number Employees: 1-4
Square Footage: 92000
Type of Packaging: Consumer, Food Service, Private Label, Bulk
Brands Exported: Ugly Nuts
Regions Exported to: Central America, Europe, Asia, Canada
Percentage of Business in Exporting: 6

49084 Sweet Dried Fruit
8105 Breeze Way
Jonestown, TX 78645-9642   512-267-8811
     Fax: 570-745-3362 sweet1888@aol.com
                        www.sweetdriedfruit.com
Importer and wholesaler/distributor of raisins, etc.; exporter of raisins
President: Sidney Sweet
Partner: Scott Fichter
scott@sweetdriedfruit.com
VP: Candace Sweet
Estimated Sales: Less Than $500,000
Number Employees: 1-4
Brands Exported: Sweet Brand
Regions Exported to: Central America, South America, Europe, Asia, Middle East
Percentage of Business in Exporting: 40
Brands Imported: Sweet Brand

Regions Imported from: Central America, South America, Asia, S Africa

49085 Sweet Endings Inc
1220 Okeechobee Rd
West Palm Beach, FL 33401-6947   561-655-0334
     Fax: 561-209-1901   888-635-1177
swtend@aol.com www.sweetendingsdesserts.com
Processor and exporter of cakes, pies, tortes and crumbles including sugar and fat-free
Owner: Dalanna Browning
dalannabrowning@sweetendingsdesserts.com
Estimated Sales: $ 3 - 5 Million
Number Employees: 20-49
Square Footage: 12000
Type of Packaging: Food Service, Private Label
Regions Exported to: Caribbean
Percentage of Business in Exporting: 2

49086 Sweet Harvest Foods
15100 Business Parkway
Rosemount, MN 55068   507-263-8599
     Fax: 651-322-1229 info@sweetharvestfoods.com
                        www.sweetharvestfoods.com
Natural and organic honey and peanut butter.
President: Curt Riess
Quality Manager: Gary Stromley
COO: Brian McGregor
Plant Manager: Brian Pleschourt
Estimated Sales: $4.8 Million
Number Employees: 20-49
Type of Packaging: Consumer, Food Service, Private Label

49087 Sweet Life Enterprises
2350 S Pullman St
Santa Ana, CA 92705   714-256-8900
Cinnamon rolls and cookies inluding chocolate chip, double fudge chocolate, oatmeal raisin, sugar, peanut butter, white chocolate, snickerdoodle, etc
President & CEO: Mike Gray
Quality Assurance Manager: Derek Osato
Marketing Manager: Stephanie Easterday
Vice President Sales: Lori Gray
Contact: Ryan Anita
ryan.anita@freshstartbakeries.com
VP Operations: Scott Fitzgerald
Estimated Sales: 20.9 Million
Number Employees: 115
Other Locations:
     North America Support Offices
     Santa Ana, CANorth America Support Offices
Regions Exported to: Canada

49088 Sweet Street Desserts
722 Hiesters Ln
Reading, PA 19605-3095   610-921-8113
     Fax: 610-921-8195 800-793-3897
ussales@sweetstreet.com www.sweetstreet.com
Variety of coffee bar and desserts: hazelnut cappucino torte, apple crumb cake, chocolate chip crumb cake, sour cream coffee cake
President: Sandy Solmon
sandys@sweetsreet.com
Estimated Sales: $39400000
Number Employees: 500-999
Type of Packaging: Consumer, Food Service

49089 Sweet Sue Kitchens
106 Sweet Sue Drive
Athens, AL 35611-2181   256-216-0500
     Fax: 256-216-0531
Processor and exporter of canned poultry products including chicken broth, chunks, stew and dumplings
Sales/Marketing Executive: Shirley Brown
Plant Manager: Bob Mahan
Purchasing Agent: Carol Moore
Parent Co: Sara Lee Corporation
Type of Packaging: Consumer, Food Service, Private Label
Regions Exported to: Europe, Canada

49090 Sweetware
2821 Chapman St # A
Oakland, CA 94601-2133   510-436-8600
     Fax: 510-436-8601 800-526-7900
inquiries@sweetware.com www.sweetware.com
Manufacturer and exporter of inventory control, order entry, invoicing, accounts receivable, recipe formula costing and nutrition analysis software
Owner: David Dunetz
info@sweetware.com

Estimated Sales: $500,000-$1 Million
Number Employees: 1-4

49091 (HQ)Swing-A-Way Manufacturing Company
4100 Beck Ave
St Louis, MO 63116-2694
314-773-1488
Fax: 314-773-5187
Manufacturer, importer and exporter of corkscrews, ice crushers and can and jar openers
President: Dorothy Rhodes
Estimated Sales: $10-20 Million
Number Employees: 50-99
Square Footage: 250000
Type of Packaging: Consumer
Other Locations:
  Swing-A-Way Manufacturing Co.
  Saint Louis, MOSwing-A-Way Manufacturing Co.
Brands Exported: Swing-A-Way
Regions Exported to: Worldwide
Percentage of Business in Exporting: 15
Regions Imported from: Europe
Percentage of Business in Importing: 5

49092 Swirl Freeze Corp
1261 S Redwood Rd # H
Salt Lake City, UT 84104-3705
801-886-1196
Fax: 801-973-7620 800-262-4275
sales@swirlfreeze.com www.swirlfreeze.com
Manufacturer and exporter of ice cream and frozen yogurt blending machinery
President: D Heinhold
Vice President: K Heinhold
Marketing Director: D Savage
Estimated Sales: $1 Million
Number Employees: 1-4
Number of Brands: 1
Number of Products: 6
Square Footage: 30000
Type of Packaging: Consumer
Brands Exported: Swirl Freeze
Regions Exported to: Central America, South America, Europe, Asia, Middle East, Australia
Percentage of Business in Exporting: 15

49093 Swisher Hygiene
4725 Piedmont Row Drive
Suite 400
Charlotte, NC 28210
908-353-8500
Fax: 908-353-6752 800-444-4138
contact@swsh.com www.swsh.com
Manufacturer and exporter of dishwashing and laundry products
President: Norman Lubin
Vice President: Mark Sherman
Contact: Bill Ainsley
bainsley@swsh.com
Estimated Sales: $10-20 Million
Number Employees: 50-99
Type of Packaging: Food Service
Regions Exported to: Bahamas
Percentage of Business in Exporting: 1

49094 (HQ)Swiss American Inc
4200 Papin St
St Louis, MO 63110-1736
314-533-2224
Fax: 314-533-0765 800-325-8150
Packer, importer and distributor of cheese and fine foods
President: Joseph Hoff
CEO: R Weil
VP: D Boyd
Contact: Chris Biscan
chris.biscan@swissamerican.com
Operations VP: David Boyd
Estimated Sales: Less Than $500,000
Number Employees: 1-4
Square Footage: 180000
Type of Packaging: Consumer, Bulk
Other Locations:
  Swiss-American
  North Charleston, SCSwiss-American

49095 Swiss Food Products
4333 W Division St
Chicago, IL 60651
312-829-0100
Fax: 773-394-6475 www.swissfoodproducts.com
Manufacturer and exporter of bases including soup, gravy, browning, seasoning and sauce; also, flavors
Estimated Sales: $ 5 - 10 Million
Number Employees: 10-19
Square Footage: 100000
Type of Packaging: Consumer, Food Service, Private Label, Bulk
Regions Exported to: Canada, Mexico, Caribbean, Latin America

49096 Swiss-American Sausage Company
251 Darcy Pkwy
Lathrop, CA 95330
209-858-5555
Fax: 209-858-1102
Processor and exporter of meat pizza toppings including pepperoni, salami, ham, linguica and raw and cooked sausage
President/CEO: Theodore Arena
Human Resources: Heidi Moore
Sales Manager: Paul Sheehan
Estimated Sales: $300,000-500,000
Number Employees: 50-99
Square Footage: 360000
Type of Packaging: Food Service, Private Label
Brands Exported: Capo Di Monte
Regions Exported to: Asia
Percentage of Business in Exporting: 2

49097 Swisscorp
7845 Camino Real
Suite 0-405
Miami, FL 33143
305-279-6859
Fax: 305-675-0812 cmunoz@swisscapitalcorp.com
www.swisscapitalcorp.com
Importer and exporter of fresh and frozen shrimp, molasses, raw sugar and powdered protein
President: Enrique Rais
Accountant: Jorge Melendez
Sales/Marketing: Miguel Panizo
Number Employees: 1-4
Parent Co: Biochemical S.A. de C.V.
Regions Exported to: Europe
Percentage of Business in Exporting: 90
Regions Imported from: Latin America
Percentage of Business in Importing: 10

49098 Swissh Commercial Equipment
5520 Chabot 203
Montreal, QC H2H 2S7
Canada
514-524-6005
Fax: 514-524-3305 888-794-7749
info@swissh.ca www.swissh.com
Technologically advanced dishwashers.
President: Bruno O Frank
Marketing: Elyse Pastor
Production: Miguel Viche
Number Employees: 7
Number of Brands: 4
Number of Products: 50
Square Footage: 16000
Brands Exported: Swissh Dish & Glasswashers
Regions Exported to: Central America, South America, Asia
Brands Imported: Foamer; Whipper; Franke, Spulboy;
Regions Imported from: Europe

49099 Swisslog Logistics Inc
161 Enterprise Dr
Newport News, VA 23603-1369
757-887-8080
Fax: 757-887-5588 800-777-6862
www.swisslog.com
Manufacturer and exporter of integrated and automated material handling software and equipment
President: Karl Puehringer
Chief Executive Officer: Remo Brunschwiler
Sr. VP Marketing: Brad Moore
Estimated Sales: $20-50 Million
Number Employees: 50-99
Square Footage: 50000
Parent Co: Swisslog
Regions Exported to: South America, Europe, Middle East, Mexico
Percentage of Business in Exporting: 10

49100 Swivelier Co Inc
600 Bradley Hill Rd # 3
Blauvelt, NY 10913-1171
845-353-1455
Fax: 845-353-1512 info@swivelier.com
www.swivelier.com
Lighting, including track, low-voltage display, clamp-on, display and accent, lighting fixtures, light converters and extenders
President: I Schucker
is@swive.com
VP Manufacturing: Gerard Phelan
Estimated Sales: $ 5 - 10 Million
Number Employees: 1-4
Square Footage: 480000
Brands Exported: Swivelier

49101 Symmetry Products Group
55 Industrial Cir
Lincoln, RI 02865-2643
401-365-6272
Fax: 401-365-6273 www.symmetryproducts.com
Manufacturer and exporter of signs; also, theme and architectural designing available
President: Steven Lancia
Marketing Director: Justine Ruizzo
Sales Director: Rich Dowd
Plant Manager: Tony Chernasky
Estimated Sales: $ 20 - 50 Million
Number Employees: 100-249
Square Footage: 150000
Parent Co: Lance Industries
Percentage of Business in Exporting: 10

49102 Symms Fruit Ranch Inc
14068 Sunny Slopes Rd
Caldwell, ID 83607
208-459-4821
Fax: 208-459-6932 www.symmsfruit.com
Produce including apples, cherries, peaches and plums, nectarines, pluots, pears, wine grapes, asparagus, onions and potatoes.
Partner: Jim Mertz
jim@symmsfruit.com
Year Founded: 1914
Estimated Sales: $20 Million
Number Employees: 100-249
Square Footage: 150000
Type of Packaging: Consumer, Food Service, Bulk
Regions Exported to: Central America, Europe, Asia

49103 Symons Frozen Foods
619 Goodrich Rd
Centralia, WA 98531-9336
360-736-1321
Fax: 360-736-6328
Processor and exporter of frozen fruits and vegetables including blackberries, blueberries, red and black raspberries, corn, peas, peas/carrots and succotash
Owner: Bill James
bjames@symonsfrozenfoods.com
Production Manager: Howard McLoughlin
Estimated Sales: $18,200,000
Number Employees: 50-99
Type of Packaging: Consumer, Food Service, Private Label, Bulk
Regions Exported to: Europe, Asia
Percentage of Business in Exporting: 20

49104 Sympak, Inc.
1385 Armour Blvd
Mundelein, IL 60060
847-247-0182
Fax: 847-247-0184 sympak-usa@sympak.com
www.sympak-usa.com
Processing and packaging equipment for the dairy, confectionery/baking industries and convenience stores.
Contact: Erich Weirich
eric.weirich-usa@sympak.com
Number Employees: 600
Regions Exported to: Worldwide

49105 Symrise Inc.
300 North St.
Teterboro, NJ 07608
201-288-3200
Fax: 201-462-2200 www.symrise.com
Global fragrance and flavorings company.
CEO: Dr. Heinz-Jürgen Bertram
CFO: Olaf Klinger
President, Scent & Care: Achim Daub
President, Nutrition: Dr. Jean-Yves Parisot
President, Flavor: Heinrich Schaper
Year Founded: 2003
Estimated Sales: $3.1 Billion
Number Employees: 9,649
Number of Products: 30K
Parent Co: Symrise AG
Other Locations:
  Customer Service
  Saddle Brook, NJ
  Engineering, Purchasing, Production
  Branchburg, NJ
  Production
  Elyria, OH
  Chemical Production
  Goose Creek, SCCustomer ServiceBranchburg
Regions Imported from: Europe
Percentage of Business in Importing: 20

Importers & Exporters / A-Z

49106 Synergee Foods Corporation
PO Box 3055
Bellevue, WA 98009-3055   425-462-7000
    Fax: 425-823-2300
Wholesaler/distributor and exporter of specialty foods including Indian-style popcorn
CEO: Paul Brueggemann
VP: Tracie Brueggeman
VP: Lee White
Marketing: Gretchen Green
Sales: Dawn Swain
Operations: David Longmire
Number Employees: 5-9
Square Footage: 6000
Type of Packaging: Consumer
Brands Exported: A*maiz*ing; Peristroika Bar
Regions Exported to: Europe
Regions Imported from: South America

49107 Synergy Flavors Inc
1500 Synergy Dr
Wauconda, IL 60084-1073   847-487-1011
    Fax: 847-487-1066
Global flavorings manufacturer.
Number Employees: 20-49
Type of Packaging: Consumer, Food Service, Bulk
Other Locations:
    U.S. Headquarters
    Wauconda, ILHamilton, OH
    Rochester, NY
    Ballineen, IrelandSao Paulo, BrazilU.S.
    HeadquartersHigh Wycombe, UK
Regions Exported to: Central America, Europe, Asia, Canada, Caribbean, Mexico
Percentage of Business in Exporting: 10

49108 Synthite USA Inc.
840 South Oak Park Avenue
Suite 212
Oak Park, IL 60304   708-446-1716
    synthiteusa@synthite.com
    www.synthite.com
Global premium ingredients company headquartered in India with operations in Sri Lanka, China, Brazil and the USA.
Contact: Joseph Jesus
josephj@synthite.com
Regions Exported to: South America, Europe, Asia, Africa, Australia, Canada, Mexico

49109 Synthron Inc.
420 W Fleming Drive
Suite C
Morganton, NC 28655-3966   828-437-8611
    Fax: 828-437-4126
Processor and exporter of detergents and oil and wax emulsifying agents
President: Raymond Pinard
Estimated Sales: $5-10 Million
Number Employees: 10-19
Type of Packaging: Bulk

49110 Systems Comtrex
101 Foster Rd # B
Moorestown, NJ 08057-1118   856-778-9322
    Fax: 856-778-9322   800-220-2669
    Sales@Comtrex.com www.comtrex.co.uk
Manufacturer and exporter of point of sale terminals, peripherals and software
CEO: Duane Reed
duane.reed@comtrex.co.uk
CEO: Jefferey C Rice
Estimated Sales: $ 1 - 3,000,000
Number Employees: 10-19
Type of Packaging: Food Service
Regions Exported to: Worldwide

49111 Systems IV
6641 W Frye Rd
Chandler, AZ 85226
    Fax: 480-961-1247   800-852-4221
    sales@systemsiv.com www.systemsiv.com
Manufacturer and exporter of food service water treatment systems for ice makers, steamers, coffee machines, proofers, misters and post mix systems
President: Leroy Terry
Quality Control: Dave Terry
Manager Sales/Marketing: Sean Terry
Contact: David Terry
davecterry@gmail.com
Number Employees: 20-49
Brands Exported: System IV
Regions Exported to: Canada, Mexico

49112 Systems Technology Inc
1351 Riverview Dr
San Bernardino, CA 92408-2945   909-799-9950
    Fax: 909-796-8297
    info@systems-technology-inc.com
    www.systems-technology-inc.com
Manufacturer and exporter of packaging machinery
President: John G St John
johnstjohn@systems-technology-inc.com
CFO: Steve Fox
Estimated Sales: $ 10 - 20 Million
Number Employees: 20-49
Square Footage: 80000
Parent Co: Baldwin Technology Corporation
Regions Exported to: Europe

49113 (HQ)T & S Brass & Bronze Work
2 Saddleback Cv
Travelers Rest, SC 29690-2232   864-834-4102
    Fax: 864-834-3518   800-476-4103
    tsbrass@tsbrass.com www.tsbrass.com
T&S produces a full line of faucets, fittings, and specialty products for the food service, industrial, commercial plumbing, and laboratory markets all across the world.
President: I Claude Theisen
CEO: Claude Theisen
claudetheisen@tsbrass.com
Vice President: Craig Ashton
Research & Development: Jeff Baldwin
Quality Control: Gary Cole
Marketing Director: Eva Fox
Sales Director: Ken Gallagher
Public Relations: Mary Alice Bowers
Operations Manager: Bob Clemment
Assembly Supervisor: David Whitlock
Purchasing Manager: Steve Abercrombie
Estimated Sales: $ 20-50 Million
Number Employees: 250-499
Type of Packaging: Consumer, Food Service, Private Label, Bulk
Regions Exported to: Worldwide
Percentage of Business in Exporting: 3

49114 T & S Brass & Bronze Work
2 Saddleback Cv
PO Box 1088
Travelers Rest, SC 29690-2232   864-834-4102
    Fax: 864-834-3518   800-476-4103
    www.tsbrass.com
T&S produces a full line of faucets, fittings and specialty products for the foodservice, industrial, commercial plumbing, and laboratory markets.
President: Claude Theisen
claudetheisen@tsbrass.com
Number Employees: 250-499
Type of Packaging: Consumer, Food Service, Private Label, Bulk

49115 T & S Perfection Chain Prods
301 Goodwin Rd
Cullman, AL 35058-0307   256-734-6538
    Fax: 256-734-1610   888-856-4864
    info@tsperfection.com www.tsperfection.com
Manufacturers welded and weldless chains and chain accessories. Also, upholstery nails, furniture glides, escutcheon pins and commercial can openers
President: Tom Pretak
VP Human Resources: Carol Soliani
CFO: Ken Rizzi
Chairman of the Board: Allen M Sperry Sr
VP Sales: Frank Silano
Estimated Sales: $ 10 - 20 Million
Number Employees: 50-99
Square Footage: 200000
Type of Packaging: Food Service

49116 T D Sawvel Co
5775 Highway 12
Maple Plain, MN 55359-9777   763-479-4322
    Fax: 763-479-3517   877-488-1816
    www.sawvelautomation.com
Manufacturer and exporter of denesters, fillers, sealers and lidders for plastic and paper containers for dairy and nondairy products; also, blenders, variegators, inline and rotary machines; custom design services available
President: Troy Sawvel
troy@tdsawvel.com
Estimated Sales: $1-3 Million
Number Employees: 10-19
Square Footage: 32000

49117 T Hasegawa USA Inc
14017 183rd St
Cerritos, CA 90703-7000   714-522-1900
    Fax: 714-522-6800 www.thasegawa.com
Processor, importer and exporter of custom blended flavors and seasonings for beverages, cuisine, dairy, salad dressings, sauces and prepared foods
President: Mark Scott
mscott@thasegawa.com
President: Michiru Waku
Sales Manager (Western): Jeff Carlson
Sales Manager (Eastern): Robert Taylor
Estimated Sales: $8300000
Number Employees: 50-99
Square Footage: 216000
Parent Co: T. Hasegawa Company
Other Locations:
    T. Hasegawa U.S.A.
    Northbrook, ILT. Hasegawa U.S.A.
Regions Exported to: Europe, Asia
Regions Imported from: Asia

49118 T M Duche Nut Co
1502 Railroad Ave
Orland, CA 95963-2035   530-865-5511
    Fax: 530-865-7864 www.duchenut.com
Processor and exporter of almonds
President: Mosha Schwartz
CFO: Tim Gray
Manager: John Wilson
barbara.pruitt@pmi.org
Estimated Sales: $1-2.5 Million
Number Employees: 20-49
Type of Packaging: Consumer, Food Service, Private Label, Bulk
Regions Exported to: Worldwide

49119 T&S Blow Molding
117 Simott Road
Scarborough, ON M1P 4S6
Canada   416-752-8330
    Fax: 416-752-1909
Manufacturer and exporter of plastic bottles and jars
President: Donald Seaton
CEO: Peter Barker
CFO: Eric Lakien
Sales: Donna Strong
Plant Manager: Grant Ross
Estimated Sales: $14 Million
Number Employees: 10
Number of Brands: 5
Number of Products: 300
Square Footage: 136000
Type of Packaging: Consumer, Food Service, Private Label, Bulk
Regions Exported to: USA
Percentage of Business in Exporting: 30

49120 T.B. Venture
7212 W 58th Place
Apt 2n
Summit Argo, IL 60501-1427   773-927-2745
    Fax: 773-581-9343
Importer and wholesaler/distributor of European specialty foods
Owner: Tom Biernat

49121 T.C. Food Export/ImportCompany
3169 College Point Boulevard
Flushing, NY 11354-2511   718-461-0375
Importer of canned foods and frozen seafood; exporter of deep sea fish oil and health products; wholesaler/distributor of general merchandise, frozen seafood and health, canned and dried foods; serving the food service market
President: Johnson Tseng
Number Employees: 5-9
Square Footage: 48000
Brands Exported: Emerald Johnson; Emerald
Regions Exported to: Asia
Percentage of Business in Exporting: 50
Regions Imported from: Asia
Percentage of Business in Importing: 50

49122 T.J. Kraft
1535 Colburn St
Honolulu, HI 96817-4905   808-842-3474
    Fax: 808-842-3475 tkraft@norpacexport.com
Various types of fresh Hawaiian seafood
President: Thomas Kraft
Estimated Sales: $ 10 - 20 Million
Number Employees: 10-19

Importers & Exporters / A-Z

49123 T.K. Products
1565 N Harmony Cir
Anaheim, CA 92807-6003 714-621-0267
Fax: 714-693-3762
Manufacturer, importer and exporter of high speed and high shear mixers, dispersers and kneaders
President: Hisashi Furuichi
Marketing Director: Masaki Mori
Estimated Sales: $1-2,500,000
Number Employees: 4
Parent Co: T.K. Japan
Regions Exported to: Worldwide
Percentage of Business in Exporting: 5
Regions Imported from: Japan

49124 T.O. Plastics
1325 American Boulevard E
Suite 6
Minneapolis, MN 55425-1152 952-854-2131
Fax: 952-854-2154 www.toplastics.com
Manufacturer and exporter of plastic sheeting and thermoformed and foam packaging materials
CFO: Doug Cundell
National Sales Manager: Jeff Smesmo
Contact: Karen Bohn
karen@toplastics.com
Estimated Sales: $20-50 Million
Number Employees: 10
Type of Packaging: Bulk
Regions Exported to: Canada, Mexico

49125 T.S. Smith & Sons
8887 Redden Rd
Bridgeville, DE 19933 302-337-8271
Fax: 302-337-8417 www.tssmithandsonsfarm.com
Apples, peaches, nectarines, sweet corn, asparagus, strawberries, soybeans, wheat, barley and broiles; exporter of apples
President: Matthew Smith
Sales (Wholesale/Retail): Thomas Smith
Production Manager: Charles Smith
Estimated Sales: $3-5 Million
Number Employees: 20-49
Type of Packaging: Consumer, Bulk
Brands Exported: T.S. Smith & Sons
Regions Exported to: Worldwide
Percentage of Business in Exporting: 2

49126 TC/American Monorail
12070 43rd St NE
Saint Michael, MN 55376 763-497-7000
Fax: 763-497-7001 www.tcamerican.com
Manufacturer and exporter of cranes and monorail systems
President: Paul Lague
Sales/Marketing: Beth Keene
Sales Administration Manager: Bill Swanson
Contact: Jami Brown
jbrown@andersencorp.com
Number Employees: 100-249
Square Footage: 180000
Regions Exported to: Worldwide
Percentage of Business in Exporting: 1

49127 (HQ)TDF Automation
PO Box 816
Cedar Falls, IA 50613-0040 319-277-3110
Fax: 319-277-7023 800-553-1777
sales@doerfer.com www.doerfercompanies.com
Manufacturer and exporter of display cartoning and casepacking systems; also, collaters/loaders and product handling machinery; consultant specializing in designing automated systems; custom fabricating services available
President: David Takes
Chairman: Sunder Subbaroyan
Plant Manager: Curt Barfels
Estimated Sales: $1-2.5 Million
Number Employees: 10
Square Footage: 320000
Type of Packaging: Consumer, Food Service
Other Locations:
  Doerfer Engineering
  Eagan, MNDoerfer Engineering
Regions Exported to: Central America, South America, Europe, Asia, Middle East
Percentage of Business in Exporting: 10

49128 TDH
20520 W Wekiwa Rd
Sand Springs, OK 74063-8192 918-241-8800
Fax: 918-241-8884 888-251-7961
www.tdhmfginc.com
Manufacturer and exporter of mixers, presses, pumps and automation equipment
Owner: John Owens
tdhmfginc@earthlink.net
VP: J Owens
VP: R Owens
Estimated Sales: Less Than $500,000
Number Employees: 1-4
Square Footage: 16000
Regions Exported to: Asia, Middle East
Percentage of Business in Exporting: 5

49129 TEMP-TECH Company
PO Box 2941
Springfield, MA 01101-2941 413-783-2355
Fax: 413-782-7220 800-343-5579
sales@temp-tech.com
Heatstones, thermal bags, tray totes and plastic smallwares including trays, plates and covers; exporter of trays
President: Jack Anderson
VP: Chuck Attridge
Contact: Greg Schurch
greg@temp-tech.com
Purchasing Agent: Layla O'Shea
Estimated Sales: $2 Million
Number Employees: 5-9
Square Footage: 24000
Type of Packaging: Food Service
Regions Exported to: Europe, Asia

49130 TESTO
P.O.Box 1030
Sparta, NJ 07871-5030 973-579-3400
Fax: 973-579-3222 800-227-0729
info@testo.com www.ita.cc
Manufacturer and importer of thermometers, probes and data loggers
Manager: Melissa Curro
VP: Andrew Kuezkuda
Marketing/Sales: John Bickers
Estimated Sales: $ 3 - 5 Million
Number Employees: 10-19
Square Footage: 20000
Parent Co: TESTO GMBH
Type of Packaging: Consumer, Food Service

49131 (HQ)THARCO
2222 Grant Ave
San Lorenzo, CA 94580-1804 510-276-8600
Fax: 510-317-2728 800-772-2332
sales-slz@tharco.com www.tharco.com
Corrugated boxes, packaging materials and displays; exporter of corrugated boxes and foam cushion packaging
President: Oscar Fears
Marketing Manager: Steve Malmquist
Sales Manager: Don Godshall
Estimated Sales: $ 20-50 Million
Number Employees: 1000-4999
Square Footage: 550000
Other Locations:
  THARCO
  Algona, WATHARCO
Regions Exported to: Central America, Europe, Canada
Percentage of Business in Exporting: 3

49132 THE Corporation
PO Box 445
Terre Haute, IN 47808-0445 812-232-2151
Fax: 800-783-2534 800-783-2151
corpies@thecorp.org
Graphic design, prepress, printing plates for packaging primary foods
CEO: Kenneth Williams
Sales Director: Dave Bryan
Estimated Sales: $3 Million
Number Employees: 31
Square Footage: 128000
Regions Exported to: Central America, South America, Europe, Middle East

49133 TKF Inc
726 Mehring Way
Cincinnati, OH 45203-1809 513-241-5910
Fax: 513-651-2792 www.tkf.com
Manufacturer, designer and exporter of custom vertical conveyor systems, including continuous vertical lift conveyors, reciprocating vertical lift conveyors, pallet handling conveyors, zero-pressure accumulator conveyors, and overhead monorail conveyors
Owner: Ronald Eubanks
VP Sales: Jim Walsh
reubanks@tkf.com
Estimated Sales: $ 20 - 50 Million
Number Employees: 50-99
Regions Exported to: Worldwide
Percentage of Business in Exporting: 10

49134 (HQ)TLB Corporation
150 Willard Avenue
PO Box 6954
Ellicott, MD 21042 410-773-9443
Fax: 203-233-1268 inquiries@respectrisk.com
Manufacturer, importer and exporter of pre-fabricated waste water treatment plants and pumping stations; also, effluent can be sanitized for reuse
President/Chief Engineer: Thomas Bond
Finance: Russell Correll
Production Manager: Thomas Farrell
Number Employees: 20-49
Square Footage: 60000
Brands Exported: Hartlift; Hart Treat; Hart Boost; Oxy Tower
Regions Exported to: Central America, South America, Europe, Asia, Middle East
Percentage of Business in Exporting: 30
Regions Imported from: Worldwide
Percentage of Business in Importing: 10

49135 TMCo Inc.
10801 Hammerly Blvd.
Suite 232
Houston, TX 77043 713-465-3255
Fax: 713-465-3237 gwyn.childress@tmcusa.com
www.tmco-usa.com
Manufacturer and exporter of displays
President: Roland Temme
VP Manufacturing: Joe Smith
Estimated Sales: $10-20 Million
Number Employees: 50-99

49136 TNA Packaging Solutions
702 S Royal Lane
Suite 100
Coppell, TX 75019-3800 972-462-6500
Fax: 972-462-6599
mark.lozano@tnasolutions.com
www.tnasolutions.com
Manufacturer and exporter of packaging systems including vertical form/fill/seal machinery; importer of multi-head scales and metal detectors
Founder & Director: Nadia Taylor
Founder & CEO: Alf Taylor
Group Finance Manager: Peter Calopedis
VP - Americas: Alfredo Blanco
Group Marketing Manager: Shayne De la Force
Group Sales Manager: Patrick Avelange
Group Operations Manager: Natasha Avelange
Group Manufacturing Manager: Andrew Smith
Estimated Sales: $3.5 Million
Number Employees: 240
Square Footage: 192000
Brands Exported: Robag
Regions Exported to: Central America, South America, Canada, Latin America, Mexico
Percentage of Business in Exporting: 65
Brands Imported: Yaviato, Yamato, Safeline Marker, Smartdate
Regions Imported from: Worldwide

49137 TNT Crust
P.O.Box 8929
Green Bay, WI 54308 920-431-7240
Fax: 920-431-7249 tntcrust@tyson.com
www.tntcrust.com
Processor and exporter of pre-made, partially baked pizza crusts including thin, thick and raised edge; also, fresh and frozen pizza dough.
President: Roger Lebreck
Vice President: Shreenivas Manthana
VP Sales/Marketing: Larry Kropp
Sales Director: Larry Kropp
VP Operations: Kent Reschke
VP Engineering: Phil Vangsnes
Number Employees: 100-249
Parent Co: FoodBrands America
Type of Packaging: Food Service
Regions Exported to: Europe

49138 TODDS Enterprises Inc
2450 White Rd
Irvine, CA 92614-6250 949-250-4080
Fax: 949-724-1338 800-568-6337
ed.stokes@us.hjheinz.com www.toddsfoods.com

Importers & Exporters / A-Z

Processor and exporter of soups, sauces, chili and salad dressings
Marketing Director: Ed Stokes
Contact: Carole Hoffman
Number Employees: 100-249
Type of Packaging: Food Service, Private Label
Regions Exported to: Worldwide

49139 TOR-REY USA
13003 Murphy Road
Suite E1
Stafford, TX 77477-3933   281-564-3150
Fax: 281-564-3246   www.tor-rey.com

49140 (HQ)TRC
15005 Enterprise Way
Middlefield, OH 44062   440-834-0078
Fax: 440-834-0083
Manufacturer and exporter of staple set brushes; also, custom injection molding of thermoplastic materials
Owner: Terry Ross
terry.martinez@apparelnews.net
VP Sales/Marketing: Dan Armstrong
Plant Manager: William O'Donnell
Estimated Sales: $ 10-20 Million
Number Employees: 100-249
Square Footage: 80000
Regions Exported to: South America, Europe, Asia, Japan, Canada
Percentage of Business in Exporting: 10

49141 TREX Corp Inc.
851 Burlway Rd.
Suite 400
Burlingame, CA 94010   650-342-7333
Fax: 650-342-8333   info@teamtrex.com
teamtrex.com
Beef, including Japanese wagyu.
President: Mark Melnick
VP: Matt Ebikawa
Sales Manager: Jay Moon
Year Founded: 1996
Parent Co: Greater Omaha Packing Co Inc.
Brands Exported: Greater Omaha
Regions Exported to: Asia, Canada, Mexico
Brands Imported: Satsuma Wagyu, Tokachi Poroshiri Wagyu, Hida gyu, Kobe gyu, Awa Gyu, Takamori Drunken Wagyu, Bushu Gyu
Regions Imported from: Asia

49142 TRITEN Corporation
3657 Briarpark
Houston, TX 77042   713-690-9050
Fax: 713-690-9080   832-214-5000
info@triten.com   www.triten.com
Manufacturer and exporter of plunger pumps, water blasting equipment and accessories
Chairman/President/CEO: John Scott Arnoldy
President/Chief Executive Officer: Thomas Amonet
Executive Vice President/Chief Financial: Donald O. Bainter
Executive Vice President and Chief Opera: Gary J. Baumgartner
Contact: Jack Adams
j.adams@triten.com
Product Manager: John Matlock
Estimated Sales: $1-2.5 Million
Number Employees: 100-249
Square Footage: 50000
Brands Exported: Hydr-Laser
Regions Exported to: Central America, South America, Europe, Asia, Middle East, Australia
Percentage of Business in Exporting: 30
Regions Imported from: Worldwide
Percentage of Business in Importing: 75

49143 TSA Griddle Systems
395 Penno Road
Suite 100
Kelowna, BC V1X 7W5
Canada   250-491-9025
Fax: 250-491-9045   info@griddlesystems.com
www.griddlesystems.com
Manufacturer and exporter of food processing equipment including pancake, waffle, french toast, egg patty and baked goods; also, mixers, blenders, depositors and cooling systems
President: Kevin Forrest
Estimated Sales: Below $ 5 Million
Number Employees: 10
Square Footage: 40000
Regions Exported to: South America, Europe

49144 TURBOCHEF Technologies
2801 Trade Center Drive
Carrollton, TX 75007   214-379-6000
Fax: 214-340-6073   800-908-8726
www.turbochef.com
Designs, develops, manufactures and markets speed cooking solutions
President: James K. Pool III
CEO: James Price
CFO: Al Cochran
COO: Paul Lehr
VP Marketing: David Shave
Sr VP Global Sales/Business Development: Peter Ashcraft
Contact: Max Abbott
max.abbott@turbochef.com
Plant Manager: Jeanean Weaver
Vice President Procurement: Rusty Rose
Estimated Sales: $10 - 20 Million
Number Employees: 10
Square Footage: 22000
Brands Exported: TurboChef
Regions Exported to: Europe, Asia
Percentage of Business in Exporting: 60

49145 TVT Trade Brands
18503 Pines Blvd.
Suite 308
Pembroke Pines, FL 33029   954-353-9003
Fax: 954-507-5933   info@tvttrade.com
www.tvttrade.com
Ethnic foods: Mediterranean, European, Asian, Latin-American, Middle Eastern, African and Australian; spices, superfoods and delicatessen.
Global Business Development Manager: Rubert Velasquez
Estimated Sales: $1-5 Million
Number Employees: 10-20
Type of Packaging: Food Service
Other Locations:
   Warehouse
   Miami, FL Warehouse
Brands Imported: Porto-Muinos, Vias, Sagekitchen, Maroc Gourmet, Maison In'onA, Dulse, Gazpacho Andaluz, Kampot, Sacchi Tartufi and more.
Regions Imported from: Around the world

49146 TWM Manufacturing
1960 Concession 3
Leamington, ON N9Y 2E5
Canada   519-326-0014
Fax: 519-326-7746   888-495-4831
sales@tugweld.com
Premium quality custom made food processing machinery and automated mechanical systems/specialists in stainless steel
President: John Friesen
VP: Jake Friesen
Estimated Sales: $2-3 Million
Number Employees: 13
Square Footage: 88000
Brands Exported: TWM; Tugweld; Cluster Buster

49147 Tabco Enterprises
1906 W Holt Ave
Pomona, CA 91768-3351   909-623-4565
Fax: 909-623-2605
Processor and exporter of nutritional food supplements including deep sea fish oil, shark cartilage, multivitamins and minerals, grape seed extract, herbal products, spirulina, garlic, etc
President: Bruce Lin
Financial Officer: Rebecca Lin
Estimated Sales: $ 5 - 10 Million
Number Employees: 20-49
Square Footage: 80000
Parent Co: Essential Pharmaceutical
Brands Exported: Tabco; Eden; Mt. Olive Enterprises; Essential Elite; Wonderful Life
Regions Exported to: South America, Asia, Canada
Percentage of Business in Exporting: 30

49148 Table Decor International
2748 S Cobb Industrial Blvd SE
Smyrna, GA 30082   770-432-1156
Fax: 770-436-9463   tabledecor@mindspring.com
www.tabledecor.com
Estimated Sales: $ 3 - 5 Million
Number Employees: 5-9

49149 Table Shox
#215-1515 Broadway
Port Coquitlam, BC V3C 6M2
Canada   604-941-9961
Fax: 604-941-1721   800-457-6454
www.tableshox.com
Elimite the #1 complaint in restaurants-wobbly tables. Fully automatic table levellers. Simple to install. Your wobbly table solution

49150 TableToyz
936 Peace Portal Drive
104
Blaine, WA 98230-4009   888-292-9444
Fax: 604-886-6594   www.tabletoyz.com

49151 Tablecheck Technologies, Inc
13276 Research Blvd # 103
Austin, TX 78750   512-219-9711
Fax: 512-219-6964   800-522-1347
info@tablecheck.com   www.tablecheck.com
Manufacturer and exporter of electronic seating systems
President: Barbara Horan
Estimated Sales: $1 - 5 Million
Number Employees: 5-9
Number of Brands: 1
Number of Products: 1
Square Footage: 3200
Regions Exported to: Canada
Percentage of Business in Exporting: 5

49152 Tablecloth Co Inc
514 Totowa Ave
Paterson, NJ 07522-1541   973-942-1555
Fax: 973-942-3092   800-227-5251
info@tablecloth.com   www.tablecloth.com
Manufacturer and exporter of tablecloths, napkins, table skirting and place mats
Owner: Matthew Sherburne
rlee@taylor-residences.org
Estimated Sales: $ 10 - 20 Million
Number Employees: 50-99

49153 Tablecraft Products Co Inc
801 Lakeside Dr
Gurnee, IL 60031-2489   847-855-9000
Fax: 847-855-9012   800-323-8321
info@tablecraft.com
Manufacturer, importer and exporter of smallwares, salt and pepper shakers, condiment and beverage dispensers, bar supplies, kitchen utensils, coffee equipment, baskets, salad bowls, rangettes, etc
President: Dave Burnside
dburnside@tablecraft.com
CFO: Ron Kostrewa
Vice President: Larry Davis
General Manager: Ted Rutkowski
Marketing Director: Amy Garrard
Sales Director: Dave Burnside
Plant Manager: Ted Rotkowski
Purchasing Manager: Larry Davis
Number Employees: 5-9
Square Footage: 400000
Parent Co: Hunter Manufacturing Company
Regions Exported to: Central America, South America, Europe, Asia, Middle East
Percentage of Business in Exporting: 8
Regions Imported from: Europe, Asia
Percentage of Business in Importing: 40

49154 Tablet & Ticket Co
1120 Atlantic Dr
West Chicago, IL 60185-5103   630-231-6611
Fax: 630-231-0211   800-438-4959
sales@tabletandticket.com
www.tabletandticket.com
Custom menu display boards including stainless steel, brass, aluminum, illuminated and nonilluminated; also, matching bulletin boards available
President: Brian Blair
brianb@tabletandticket.com
CFO: Tom Evans
Estimated Sales: $ 5 - 10 Million
Number Employees: 10-19
Square Footage: 30000
Regions Exported to: Canada
Percentage of Business in Exporting: 1

Importers & Exporters / A-Z

49155 Taconic
P.O.Box 69
Petersburg, NY 12138   518-658-3202
Fax: 518-658-3988 800-833-1805
info@4taconic.com www.4taconic.com
Manufacturer, importer and exporter of PTFE and silicone coated fiberglass fabrics and tapes; also, reusable and nonstick coated cake rings and liners for trays, bagel boards, ovens, roasting and proofing
Executive: Philippe Heffley
Sales: Al Hepp
Contact: Jeffrey Browne
jeffrey.browne@taconic.com
Estimated Sales: $ 20 - 50 Million
Number Employees: 100-249
Regions Exported to: Europe, Asia
Percentage of Business in Exporting: 10
Regions Imported from: Europe
Percentage of Business in Importing: 3

49156 Tai Foong USA Inc
2450 6th Ave S # 300
PO Box 84868
Seattle, WA 98134-2029   206-515-9688
Fax: 206-515-9788 800-388-3666
www.northernchef.com
Importer of seafood including shrimp, scallops, crab, fish fillets, steaks, etc
President: Davy Lam
dlam@northernchef.com
Controller: John Motta
Credit Manager: Gil Martin
Estimated Sales: $ 10 - 20 Million
Number Employees: 20-49
Square Footage: 24000
Brands Imported: Northern King
Regions Imported from: Central America, South America, Asia

49157 Taiko Enterprise Corp
1467 W 178th St # 200
Gardena, CA 90248-3248   310-715-1888
Fax: 310-324-1115 sales@taiko-enterprises.com
www.taikous.com
Importer of signs, skimmers, thermometers, grinding sticks, pressure cookers, strainers, dispensers, spatulas, knives, filters, boilers, aprons, bench mats, plates, grills, ladles, plates, bowls, glasses, serving trays, pots, gratersice shavers, etc
President: Steve Sodeyama
Estimated Sales: $2.5-5 Million
Number Employees: 10-19
Regions Imported from: Japan

49158 Taj Gourmet Foods
4600 Sleepytime Dr.
Boulder, CO 80301   610-692-2209
800-434-4246
www.ethnicgourmet.com
Processor and exporter of ethnic entrees including Thai, Indian and Italian
President: Paul Jaggi
VP: Sangeeta Jaggi
VP Operations: Harmeet Shanhu
Estimated Sales: $5-10 Million
Number Employees: 25
Square Footage: 120000
Regions Exported to: Canada

49159 Takari International Inc
2040 E Locust Ct
Ontario, CA 91761-7617   909-923-9399
Fax: 909-923-9995 www.takari.com
Snack foods, candy, energy drinks and coffee
Owner: Andy Li
andy@takari.com
Estimated Sales: $ 1 - 3 Million
Number Employees: 10-19

49160 Taku Smokehouse
550 S Franklin St
Juneau, AK 99801-1330   907-463-4617
Fax: 907-463-4644 800-582-5122
mailorder@takusmokeries.com
www.takustore.com
Processor and exporter of Alaskan salmon, halibut, crab and cod including frozen, portion cut, fillet, smoked, salted and packed
President: Sandro Lane
Smokehouse Manager: Jeremy LaPierre
General Manager: Eric Norman
CEO: Giovanni Gallizio
Contact: Laura Powers
lpowers@takusmokeries.com
Estimated Sales: Less than $500,000
Number Employees: 100-249
Square Footage: 200000
Type of Packaging: Consumer, Food Service, Private Label, Bulk
Brands Exported: Taku
Regions Exported to: South America, Europe, Asia, Canada
Percentage of Business in Exporting: 60

49161 Talbott Farms
3800 F-1/4 Road
Palisade, CO 81526   970-464-5656
talbottfarms.com
Peach and wine grape grower.
Regions Exported to: Canada, Caribbean, Latin America
Percentage of Business in Exporting: 5

49162 Talley Farms
2900 Lopez Dr
Arroyo Grande, CA 93420-4999   805-489-5400
Fax: 805-489-5201 www.talleyvineyards.com
Grower and exporter of produce including sugar peas, bell peppers, nappa, cabbage, romaine lettuce, zucchini, Blue Lake beans, spinach and cilantro
President: Brian Talley
btalley@talleyfarms.com
Sales: Todd Talley
Sales Director: Jeff Halfpenny
Operations Manager: Ryan Talley
Plant Manager: Arturo Ibarra
Estimated Sales: $ 10 - 20 Million
Number Employees: 250-499
Number of Brands: 2
Number of Products: 12
Type of Packaging: Consumer, Food Service, Bulk

49163 Tallygenicom
15345 Barranca Pkwy
Irvine, CA 92618-2216   714-368-2300
800-665-6210
printers@tally.com www.tally.com
Manufacturer and provider of industrial and back-office enterprise printing solutions for office/industrial marketplace and distribution supply chain.
Chief Executive Officer: Randy Eisenbach
Chief Financial Officer: Rhonda Longmore-Grund
VP, Worldwide Engineering/CTO: Bill Matthews
SVP, Global Sales Marketing: Mark Edwards
VP, Sales & Marketing, Asia-Pacific: Albert Ching
Vice President, Global Operations: Sean Irby
Estimated Sales: $ 50-100 Million
Number Employees: 500-999
Square Footage: 140000
Parent Co: Printronix
Regions Exported to: Central America, South America, Europe
Percentage of Business in Exporting: 30

49164 Tamarack Products Inc
1071 N Old Rand Rd
Wauconda, IL 60084-1239   847-526-9333
Fax: 847-526-9353 info@tamarackproducts.com
www.tamarackproducts.com
Manufacturer and exporter of printing, labeling and die cutting equipment
President: David Steidinger
dsteidinger@tamarackproducts.com
Estimated Sales: $2.5-5 Million
Number Employees: 20-49

49165 Tamarind Tree
518 Justin Way
Neshanic Station, NJ 8853   908-369-6300
800-432-8733
All-natural and preservative, wheat and gluten-free Indian vegetarian entrees, snack foods, condiments and spicy lentil crisps
President: Harshad Parekh
Number Employees: 1-4
Square Footage: 4000
Brands Exported: Tamarind Tree; The Taste of India
Regions Exported to: Europe, Canada
Percentage of Business in Exporting: 5

49166 Tampa Bay Fisheries Inc
3060 Gallagher Rd
Dover, FL 33527-4728   813-752-8883
Fax: 813-752-3168 800-732-3663
info@tbfish.com www.tbfish.com
Variety of fresh and frozen shrimp, crab, clams, scallops, lobster tails, squid, mussels, frog legs, oysters.
President: Robert Patterson
CFO: Tom Tao
VP Sales/Marketing: Robert Hatcher
Human Resources Director: Sandi Fail
Operations Manager: Fred Godbold
Plant Manager: Mary Brown
Purchasing Director: Brenda Newman
Estimated Sales: $25 Million
Number Employees: 500-999
Square Footage: 18562
Type of Packaging: Consumer, Food Service
Regions Exported to: Canada, Caribbean
Regions Imported from: Worldwide

49167 Tampa Corrugated CartonCompany
3517 N 40th Street
Tampa, FL 33605-1641   813-623-5115
Fax: 813-626-2153
Manufacturer and exporter of custom and stock boxes including corrugated, paper and paper folding; also, cartons
General Manager: Ron Pollard
Estimated Sales: $10-20 Million
Number Employees: 50-99
Regions Exported to: Worldwide

49168 Tampa Maid Foods Inc
1600 Kathleen Rd
Lakeland, FL 33805-3435   863-687-4411
Fax: 863-683-8713 800-237-7637
info@tampamaid.com www.tampamaid.com
Processor, importer and exporter of frozen prepared seafood including breaded, peeled and deveined shrimp, stuffed flounder, oysters, scallops and appetizers
President/CEO: George Watkins
CFO: Dave Cordy
dcordy@tampamaid.com
Data Processing: Gene Gerstmeier
Production Manager: Kevin Stallworth
Purchasing Manager: Tim Moore
Number Employees: 250-499
Square Footage: 560000
Type of Packaging: Consumer, Food Service, Private Label, Bulk
Regions Exported to: Europe, Canada, Mexico
Regions Imported from: Central America, South America, Asia, Latin America

49169 Tampa Pallet Co
2402 S 54th St
Tampa, FL 33619-5364   813-626-5700
Fax: 813-623-5180 TAMPAPALLET@AOL.COM
www.tampapallet.com
Manufacturer and exporter of wooden pallets, crates and boxes
Owner, President: Fred Haman
tampapallet@aol.com
Estimated Sales: $ 5-10 Million
Number Employees: 5-9
Regions Exported to: Caribbean
Percentage of Business in Exporting: 5

49170 Tampico Beverages Inc
3106 N Campbell Ave
Chicago, IL 60618-7921   773-296-0190
Fax: 773-296-0191 877-826-7426
comments@tampico.com www.tampico.com
Processor, exporter and importer of beverage bases and citrus blends
CEO: John Carson
CEO: Scott Miller
VP Marketing: Tracey Schroeder
Number Employees: 50-99
Type of Packaging: Bulk
Brands Exported: Tampico
Regions Exported to: Worldwide
Percentage of Business in Exporting: 37
Regions Imported from: Latin America

49171 Tangent Systems
8030 England Street
B
Charlotte, NC 28273-5978   704-554-0830
Fax: 704-554-0820 800-992-7577
sales@versid.com www.versid.com
Manufacturer and exporter of temperature measurement and data logging instruments
Sales Manager: Mary Lynn Rogers
Estimated Sales: $ 1-2.5 Million
Number Employees: 10

Importers & Exporters / A-Z

Brands Exported: Versid; Tempest
Regions Exported to: Worldwide

49172 Tango Shatterproof Drinkware
P.O.Box 737
Walpole, MA 02081 888-898-2646
Fax: 508-668-0543 Kpicchi@IslandOasis.com
www.tango-shatterproof.com
Shatterproof glasses, tumblers and pitchers
General Manager: Paul Shilo
Sales: Marie Sandre
Parent Co: Island Oasis

49173 Tangra Trading
3902 West Valley Hwy North
Suite 410
Auburn, WA 98001 253-444-0155
sales@tangratrading.com
tangratrading.com
Olive oil, sea salt, coffee and cocao.
Founder & CEO: Yuliyan Popov
Number Employees: 2-10
Type of Packaging: Private Label
Brands Imported: Dona Oliva, Nazca Foods
Regions Imported from: South America

49174 (HQ)Tanimura Antle Inc
1 Harris Rd
Salinas, CA 93908-8608 831-455-2950
Fax: 831-455-3913 800-772-4542
www.taproduce.com
Processor and exporter of cauliflower, broccoli, broccoflower, celery, lettuce, scallions, green onions and value-added products.
Executive Vice President: Gary Tanimura
CEO: Rick Antle
rick@taproduce.com
Executive Vice President: Mike Antle
Number Employees: 100-249
Type of Packaging: Consumer
Other Locations:
Tanimura & Antle
Salinas, CATanimura & Antle
Regions Exported to: Worldwide
Percentage of Business in Exporting: 5

49175 Tanita Corp Of America
2625 S Clearbrook Dr
Arlington Hts, IL 60005-4625 847-640-9241
Fax: 847-640-9261 www.tanita.com
President: Tim Hasselbeck
prosales@tanita.com
Estimated Sales: $ 5 - 10 Million
Number Employees: 20-49

49176 Tantos Foods International
15 Josiah Court
Markham, ON L3R 9A1
Canada 905-943-9999
Fax: 905-943-9943
Processor, exporter and importer of hot sauce, frozen fruit pulp, plantain, cassava and taro chips, annatto seeds, powder norbixin and ackees
President: Sultanali Ajani
Manager: Konrad Lutz
Estimated Sales: $390,000
Number Employees: 3
Square Footage: 28000
Parent Co: Mejores Alimentos de Costa Rica/Alina Foods C.A.
Type of Packaging: Consumer, Food Service, Private Label, Bulk
Brands Exported: Tantos; Diges
Regions Exported to: Central America, Europe, USA
Percentage of Business in Exporting: 80
Brands Imported: Tantos, Banana Gold
Regions Imported from: Central America, South America, Kenya, Latin America, Mexico, Ivory Coast
Percentage of Business in Importing: 80

49177 Tanzamaji USA
5602 Hummingbird Lane
Fairview, TX 75069
info@tanzamaji.com
tanzamaji.com
Bottled water
Managing Director: Beda Ruefer
Brands Imported: Tanzamaji©
Regions Imported from: Tanzania

49178 Taormina Sales Company
1 Dewolf Rd Ste 208
Old Tappan, NJ 07675 201-297-0600
Fax: 201-297-0007
Import broker of groceries, industrial ingredients, private label items, specialty products, canned vegetables, etc.
CEO: Anna Gannon
CFO: Jim Cosentino
Sales: Joe Fragola
Sales: Peter Ferrari
Sales Director: Helena Dane
Number Employees: 10-19
Square Footage: 9200
Type of Packaging: Consumer, Food Service, Private Label, Bulk
Brands Imported: De Nigris; Del Papa; Del Sol
Regions Imported from: South America, Europe, Middle East, Australia
Percentage of Business in Importing: 51

49179 Tapatio Hot Sauce
4685 District Blvd
Vernon, CA 90058-2731 323-587-8933
Fax: 323-587-5266 info@tapatiohotsauce.com
www.tapatiohotsauce.com
Processor and exporter of hot sauce
Owner/President: Luis Saavedra
Manager: Jose Saavedra
Estimated Sales: $2 Million
Number Employees: 20-49
Type of Packaging: Consumer, Food Service
Brands Exported: Tapatio
Regions Exported to: Central America, Europe
Percentage of Business in Exporting: 10

49180 Tape & Label Converters
8231 Allport Ave
Santa Fe Springs, CA 90670-2105 562-945-3486
Fax: 562-696-8198 888-285-2462
www.stickybiz.com
Printer of high quality short run digital and large run flexographic pressure sensitive labels. 35+ years of experience with food and beverage labels. Customers are small family owned companies to Fortune 500.
CEO: Robert Varela Sr.
Research & Development: Robert Varela Jr.
Quality Control: Roger Varela
Marketing: Mas Crawford
Sales: Mas Crawford
Public Relations: Mas Crawford
Operations: Robert Varela Sr.
Production: Roger Varela
Plant Manager: Randy Varela
Purchasing: Robert Varela Jr.
Estimated Sales: $1-2.5 Million
Number Employees: 10-19
Square Footage: 24000
Type of Packaging: Consumer, Food Service, Private Label
Regions Exported to: Europe, Mexico
Percentage of Business in Exporting: 5

49181 Tape Tools
3 Horizon Rd
Fort Lee, NJ 07024-6744 201-886-1316
Fax: 212-489-8548 800-327-2354
Importer and wholesaler/distributor of packaging equipment including bag sealers and tape dispensers
President: Irene Seiden
CEO: Jason Seiden
CFO: Hal Berman
Regions Imported from: Europe, Asia
Percentage of Business in Importing: 100

49182 (HQ)Tapp Technologies
6270 205th Street
Langley, BC V2Y 1N7
Canada 604-533-3294
Fax: 604-533-3295 800-533-8277
Premium offset, flexo and digital pressure sensitive labels; wine & food industry specialists
Estimated Sales: $30 Million
Number Employees: 100-249
Square Footage: 65000
Other Locations:
Tapp Technologies
Windsor, CATapp Technologies
Regions Exported to: North America
Brands Imported: Impresstik Label Applicators
Regions Imported from: Australia

49183 Tara Linens
PO Box 1350
Sanford, NC 27331-1350 919-774-1300
Fax: 919-774-3525 800-476-8272
Manufacturer and exporter of table linens including cloths, napkins, place mats, skirting, runners, aprons and tray and chair covers; importer of table aprons
President: Brooks Pomeranz
Number Employees: 100-249
Square Footage: 480000
Parent Co: Cascade Fibers Company
Brands Exported: Queens Linen; Windsor; Classic; Checkmate; Nouveau
Regions Exported to: Worldwide
Percentage of Business in Exporting: 6
Regions Imported from: Middle East
Percentage of Business in Importing: 1

49184 Tarazi Specialty Foods
13727 Seminole Dr
Chino, CA 91710-5515 909-628-3601
Fax: 909-590-4869 www.tarazifoods.com
Tahini and falafel dry mix
Owner: Ernest Busby
ernestbusby@tarazifoods.com
CFO: J Huleis
VP: J Huleis
Estimated Sales: $2-5 Million
Number Employees: 5-9
Square Footage: 47200
Type of Packaging: Consumer, Food Service, Private Label, Bulk
Regions Imported from: Central America, Canada

49185 Target Flavors Inc
7 Del Mar Dr
Brookfield, CT 06804-2401 203-775-4727
Fax: 203-775-2147 800-538-3350
info@targetflavors.com www.targetflavors.com
Processor and exporter of flavorings and extracts
Owner: John Mac Lean
info@targetflavors.com
General Manager: Bill McLean
Estimated Sales: $2100000
Number Employees: 10-19
Square Footage: 100000
Regions Exported to: Worldwide

49186 Target Industries
95 S River Bend Way
North Salt Lake, UT 84054 866-617-2253
Fax: 801-383-3251 info@targetlabel.com
www.targetlabel.com
Extruded plastic bags, sheetings, discs, liners and tubings; also, converter of polyamide/plastic casings for processed meat, cheese and poultry; importer of plastic casings
President: Tom Fox
CFO: Warren Greenberg
Sales Manager: Guy Eric
Estimated Sales: $10-20 Million
Number Employees: 50-99
Square Footage: 106000
Brands Imported: Nalobar
Regions Imported from: Europe
Percentage of Business in Importing: 15

49187 Taroco Food Corporation
1125 Hudson Street
Hoboken, NJ 07030-5305 201-792-5409
Fax: 201-792-0961
Wholesaler/distributor, importer and exporter of frozen fish
General Manager: Jack Sun
Number Employees: 10-19
Type of Packaging: Consumer, Food Service
Regions Imported from: Asia
Percentage of Business in Importing: 95

49188 Tarrison Products
1123 S Service Road W
Oakville, ON L6L 6K4
Canada 905-825-9665
Fax: 905-828-0965 www.tarrison.com

49189 Tartaric Chemicals
1801 Reliance St
Modesto, CA 95358-5710 209-537-7190
Fax: 209-537-7199 www.tartarics.com
Importer and exporter of tartaric acid, cream of tartar and rochelle salt
Executive VP: Dino Cavanna
VP: Alessandro Bonecchi
info@tartarics.com

Estimated Sales: $2.5-5 Million
Number Employees: 5-9
Type of Packaging: Bulk
Regions Exported to: Worldwide
Percentage of Business in Exporting: 5
Regions Imported from: Worldwide
Percentage of Business in Importing: 95

49190 Taste It Presents Inc
200 Sumner Ave
Suite A
Kenilworth, NJ 07033-1319 908-241-0672
Fax: 908-241-9410 sales@tasteitpresents.com
www.tasteitpresents.com
Ethnic pastries
Vice President: Paula Perlis
andrew@tasteitpresents.com
Vice President: Larry Dimurro
Estimated Sales: $7.5 Million
Number Employees: 20-49
Type of Packaging: Consumer, Food Service, Private Label

49191 Taste Teasers
6910 Northwood Rd
Dallas, TX 75225 214-750-6334
Fax: 214-696-3316 800-526-1840
Processor and exporter of jalapeno based condiments and confections
President: Susanne Hilou
VP: Eddie Michel
Estimated Sales: $100,000
Number Employees: 1-4
Type of Packaging: Consumer, Food Service, Bulk
Brands Exported: Taste Teasers; Hot Chocolate-Fine Chocolate That Bites Back; Pepper Chicks
Regions Exported to: Europe, Asia
Percentage of Business in Exporting: 10

49192 Taste Traditions Inc
9097 F St
Omaha, NE 68127-1305 402-339-7000
Fax: 402-339-1579 800-228-2170
www.tastetraditions.com
Packer and exporter of precooked roast beef, pastrami, corned beef, smoked meats, frozen prepared soups, entrees, Mexican foods and home meal replacements
President: Harold Mann
CEO: Jeff Souba
jeffsouba@tastetraditions.com
VP: Linda Mann
VP Marketing: John Shipp
Sales Executive: Lewis Marshall
Plant Manager: Bruce Hamilton
Estimated Sales: $11.2 Million
Number Employees: 50-99
Brands Exported: Mann's Intl.; Gourmet Intl.; El Hombre Hambre
Regions Exported to: Central America, South America, Europe, Asia, Middle East
Percentage of Business in Exporting: 25

49193 Taste of Gourmet
36 Sunflower Rd
Indianola, MS 38751 662-887-6760
Fax: 662-887-5547 800-833-7731
jennifer@tasteofgourmet.com
www.tasteofgourmet.com
Processor and exporter of catfish pate and capers; also, fudge and lemon pie mixes including fat-free
President: Evelyn Roughton
Estimated Sales: $885603
Number Employees: 20-49
Type of Packaging: Consumer
Regions Exported to: Worldwide

49194 Tastepoint
10801 Decatur Rd
Philadelphia, PA 19154 215-632-3100
Fax: 215-637-3920 800-363-5286
customerrequest@tastepoint.com
www.tastepoint.com
Flavors including beef extract replacement, savory, nut, fruit, vanilla extract and raisin juice concentrate; also, stabilizers. Formerly known David Michael & Co.
Chairman & CEO: Andreas Fibig
EVP/General Counsel/Corp Secretary: Anne Chwat
EVP, Operations: Francisco Fortanet
Group President, Flavors: Matthias Haeni
Group President, Fragrances: Nicolas Mirzayantz
EVP/Global Scientific & Sustainability: Dr. Gregory Yep
EVP & Chief Financial Officer: Richard O'Leary
EVP & Chief Human Resources Officer: Dr. Susana Suarez Gonzalez
Year Founded: 1896
Estimated Sales: $22.2 Million
Number Employees: 100-249
Square Footage: 66000
Parent Co: International Flavors & Frangrances Inc.
Type of Packaging: Consumer, Private Label, Bulk
Regions Exported to: Central America, South America, Europe, Asia, Middle East

49195 Tata Tea
1001 Dr Martin L King Jr Blvd
Plant City, FL 33563-5150 813-754-2602
Fax: 813-754-2272 www.tataglobalbeverages.com
Importer of tea
President: Ashok Bhardwha
Executive VP: Savi Lamba
Estimated Sales: $2.5-5 Million
Number Employees: 20-49
Parent Co: Tata Tea
Regions Imported from: Asia
Percentage of Business in Importing: 100

49196 Tate Western
36 Aero Camino
Goleta, CA 93117-3105 805-685-5544
Fax: 805-685-3695 800-903-0200
Manufacturer, importer and exporter of automatic chemical dispensers including warewash, laundry and metering pumps
President: Russ Kovacevich
Sales Manager: Glen Kent
Estimated Sales: $5-10 Million
Number Employees: 25
Square Footage: 34000
Parent Co: Shurflo Pump Manufacturing
Brands Exported: Tate Western; Versa Pro
Regions Exported to: South America, Europe, Asia, Middle East, Canada, Caribbean, Latin America, Mexico
Percentage of Business in Exporting: 20
Regions Imported from: Asia, Canada, Mexico
Percentage of Business in Importing: 5

49197 Tatra Sheep Cheese Company
PO Box 190389
Brooklyn, NY 11219-0389 718-782-7975
Fax: 718-782-7995
Importer and wholesaler/distributor of regular and grated cheese including romano, sheep, parmesan, frozen fish, kaskaval, feta and kefalotyi; also, giardiniera and pepperoncini
President: Benny Feldman
Vice President: George Frankl
Estimated Sales: $5-10 Million
Number Employees: 5-9
Square Footage: 60000
Brands Imported: Empire; Cara Lucia
Regions Imported from: Europe
Percentage of Business in Importing: 90

49198 Taurus Spice
1731 W San Bernardino Rd
West Covina, CA 91790 626-579-2888
Fax: 626-579-2333 info@taurusspice.com
taurusspice.com
Importer of spices such as dehydrated garlic, onion and chilies.
President: Min Li
Estimated Sales: Under $500,000
Number Employees: 5
Brands Imported: Spices and chilies
Regions Imported from: Asia, China, South-Eastern Asia and Africa

49199 Taylor Box Co
293 Child St
PO Box 343
Warren, RI 02885-1907 401-245-5900
Fax: 401-245-0450 800-304-6361
info@taylorbox.com www.taylorbox.com
Manufacturer and exporter of specialty paper and metal boxes for consumer goods and confectionery items
President: Dan Shedd
Design/Engineering: Julie Passey
Sales/Marketing: Daniel Shedd
Administration: Martha Lemoi
Production: Donna Costa
Estimated Sales: $ 10 - 20 Million
Number Employees: 20-49

49200 Taylor Manufacturing Co
128 Talmadge Dr
PO Box 625
Moultrie, GA 31768-5049 229-985-5445
Fax: 229-890-9090 www.peasheller.com
Manufacturer and exporter of motor driven shelling machinery for peas and beans
President/CFO: Terry Taylor Sr
VP: Terry Taylor
Estimated Sales: Below $ 5 Million
Number Employees: 5-9

49201 Taylor Orchards
1665 E Fall Line Fwy
Highway 96 West
Reynolds, GA 31076-2707 478-847-5963
Fax: 478-847-4464 www.taylororchards.com
Processor, packer and exporter of peaches
Owner: Jeff Wainwright
gafruit@pstel.net
Owner/Sales Manager: Walter Wainwright
Estimated Sales: $7215000
Number Employees: 100-249
Square Footage: 16000
Type of Packaging: Consumer, Bulk
Brands Exported: Satin Slipper; Big Top
Regions Exported to: Central America, Canada
Percentage of Business in Exporting: 20

49202 Taylor Precision Products
2311 W 22nd St # 200
Oak Brook, IL 60523-5625 630-954-1250
Fax: 630-954-1275 866-843-3905
info@taylorusa.com www.taylorusa.com
Manufactures thermometers, scales and related measurement devices.
CFO: Donald Robinson
VP: Donald Robinson
Director Sales/Marketing: Kent Beaverson
Contact: Elvira Abate
eabate@taylorusa.com
Estimated Sales: $1-2,500,000
Number Employees: 10-19
Type of Packaging: Consumer, Food Service, Private Label, Bulk

49203 (HQ)Taylor Products Co
2205 Jothi Ave
Parsons, KS 67357-8477 620-421-5550
Fax: 620-421-5586 888-882-9567
sales@magnumsystems.com
www.magnumsystems.com
Manufacturer and exporter of bag filling and unloading bagging scales, applicable for open mouth, valve, drum/box and bulk bags
CEO: Gary Saunders
CFO: Debra Weidert
Sales Manager: Brad Schultz
Estimated Sales: $ 20-50 Million
Number Employees: 20-49
Square Footage: 208000
Other Locations:
 Taylor Products Co.
 Decatur, ALTaylor Products Co.
Regions Exported to: Central America, Asia, Middle East, Canada, Caribbean, Latin America, Mexico

49204 Taylor-Wharton-Cryogenics
4075 Hamilton Blvd
Theodore, AL 36582-8575 251-443-8680
Fax: 251-443-2250
VP: Hoyt Fitzimmons
Contact: Nancy Bellamy
nbellamy@taylorwharton.com
Estimated Sales: $ 20 - 50 Million
Number Employees: 250-499

49205 Tea Importers Inc
47 Riverside Ave
Westport, CT 06880-4215 203-226-3301
Fax: 203-227-1629 Sales@teaimporters.com
www.teaimporters.com
Importer of coffee and tea

Importers & Exporters / A-Z

President: J Wertheim
IT: Andrew White
sales@teaimporters.com
Estimated Sales: $ .5 - 1 million
Number Employees: 5-9
Type of Packaging: Bulk
Regions Imported from: Central America, South America, Asia, Africa
Percentage of Business in Importing: 100

49206 Tea To Go
3475 NW 60th Street
Miami, FL 33142   786-999-8499
Fax: 888-893-6595
On the go teas

49207 TecArt Signs
46925 West Rd
Wixom, MI 48393-3654   248-624-8880
Fax: 248-624-8066   800-466-7609
sales@tecartinc.com www.tecartinc.com
CEO: Kimberly Perrigan
Estimated Sales: $ 3 - 5 Million
Number Employees: 20-49

49208 (HQ)Tech Lighting LLC
7400 Linder Ave
Skokie, IL 60077-3219   847-410-4400
Fax: 847-410-4500   800-323-3226
lblcseast@lbllighting.com
Manufacturer, importer and exporter of lighting fixtures
President/Owner: Steve Harriott
Vice President: Dennis Beard
dbeard@lbllighting.com
Sales: Krista Fischer
Plant Manager: Don Clark
Purchasing Director: Cathy Santiago
Number Employees: 100-249
Square Footage: 140000
Parent Co: Encompass Lighting
Brands Exported: LBL Lighting
Regions Exported to: Central America, South America, Europe, Asia, Middle East
Percentage of Business in Exporting: 10
Regions Imported from: Europe, Asia
Percentage of Business in Importing: 20

49209 Tech Sales Inc
4505 Zenith St
Metairie, LA 70001-1235   504-885-8085
Fax: 504-885-8106 www.tech-sales.net
Exporter of material handling and food processing equipment including conveyor systems, industrial hoses, chain drives, mixers, pumps, valves, fittings and sanitary gaskets; wholesaler/distributor of industrial equipment
President: Carlos Hidalgo
chidalgo@tech-sales.net
Shipping Manager: Alex Pineda
Quality Control: Aurelio Gonzalez
Sales Manager: Ron Barone
General Manager: Jose Mendez
Estimated Sales: $5-10 Million
Number Employees: 10-19
Square Footage: 10800
Regions Exported to: Central America, South America, Europe, Asia
Percentage of Business in Exporting: 100

49210 Tech-Roll Inc
PO Box 959
Blaine, WA 98231-0959   360-371-4321
Fax: 360-371-0752   888-946-3929
www.hydraulicdrummotors.com
Hyrdaulic motorized pulleys for the meat, poultry and food processing equipment industries.
Number Employees: 1-4
Regions Exported to: North America, USA

49211 Technibilt/Cari-All
700 E P St
Newton, NC 28658   828-464-7388
Fax: 828-464-7603   800-233-3972
custserv@technibilt.com www.technibilt.com
Manufacturer and exporter of wire shelves, carts, stacking baskets, dunnage and display racks, security units, stock trucks, containers, utility/shopping carts and high density storage sytems
President: Pierre Lafleur
General Manager: Marcel Bourgeoys
Sales Manager: Charles Nicely
Estimated Sales: $20-50 Million
Number Employees: 250-499
Square Footage: 260000
Parent Co: Cari-All Products
Type of Packaging: Food Service
Brands Exported: Adapta-Plus
Regions Exported to: Central America, South America, Europe, Asia, Middle East, Mexico
Percentage of Business in Exporting: 15

49212 TechnipFMC
11740 Katy Freeway
Energy Tower 3
Houston, TX 77079   218-591-4000
www.technipfmc.com
Manufacturer and exporter of flow and level control equipment, environmental analyzers and process control instrumentations including flow meters, level controls, valves, oil detectors, etc.
Chairman & CEO: Douglas Pferdehirt
EVP & Chief Financial Officer: Maryann Mannen
EVP & Chief Legal Officer: Dianne Ralston
EVP/Chief Technology Officer: Justin Rounce
EVP, People & Culture: Agnieszka Kmieciak
Estimated Sales: $13 Billion
Number Employees: 37,000
Square Footage: 268000
Regions Exported to: Central America, South America, Europe, Asia, Middle East
Percentage of Business in Exporting: 5

49213 Technistar Corporation
1725 Gaylord Street
100
Denver, CO 80206-1208   303-651-0188
Fax: 303-651-5600 support@ew3.com
www.technistar.com
Manufacturer and exporter of flexible robotic packaging equipment including carton loaders, case packers, palletizers, kit assembly, vision inspection and system integration
Chief Engineer: Rick Tallian
Sales Manager: Mike Weinstein
Number Employees: 85
Square Footage: 172000
Regions Exported to: Europe, Asia, Australia
Percentage of Business in Exporting: 30

49214 Technium
68 Stacy Haines Road
Medford, NJ 08055   609-702-5910
Fax: 609-702-5915
Manufacturer, exporter and importer of juice machines
Chief Executive Officer: Ian Bell
Vice President of Product Development: Jeronimo Barrera
Chief Technical Officer: Dan Gaul
Vice President of Sales: Sean Cullinane
Estimated Sales: $ 1-3 Million
Number Employees: 10
Square Footage: 32000
Regions Exported to: Central America, South America, Europe, Middle East, Caribbean, Lating America, Mexico
Percentage of Business in Exporting: 30
Brands Imported: Model 100-200-28-32-38-450
Regions Imported from: Europe
Percentage of Business in Importing: 10

49215 Techno USA
236 W Clary Avenue
San Gabriel, CA 91776   626-288-8478
Fax: 626-288-8479 sales@techno-fi.com
www.techno-fi.com
Sucralose
Owner: Helena Xue
Marketing Manager: Peter Zou
Estimated Sales: $370,000
Number Employees: 3
Parent Co: Techno Food Ingredients Co., Ltd.
Other Locations:
  Headquarters
  Guangzhou, ChinaSan Gabriel, CA
  Vancouver, CanadaHong KongHeadquartersYongan, Fujian, China
Regions Exported to: Asia

49216 Technology Flavors & Fragrances
10 E Edison St
Amityville, NY 11701   631-789-8228
Fax: 631-842-8332
Natural and artificial flavors for the beverage and food industries

CFO: Joseph A Gemmo
Chairman/CEO: Phil Rosner
CEO: Philip Rosner
Marketing Director: Virginia Bonofligio
Sales Director: Gary Frumberg
Contact: Richard Cerniglia
cerniglia@tffi.com
Operations/Production: Ronald Dinteman
Plant Manager: Joseph Piazza
Purchasing Manager: Rose Marotta
Estimated Sales: $15,587,285
Number Employees: 50-99
Number of Products: 1200
Square Footage: 104000
Regions Exported to: Central America, South America, Europe, Australia

49217 Tecnicam Inc
119 Naylon Ave
Livingston, NJ 07039-1005   973-994-4888
Fax: 973-992-4497 www.campak.com
Importer of packaging machinery for powder, paper and food products
Manager: Bill Zoom
CEO: Tom Miller
Part Manager: Franz Rugel
CEO: Thomas Miller
Estimated Sales: $5-10 Million
Number Employees: 10-19
Square Footage: 28000
Parent Co: Cam Organization
Regions Imported from: Europe
Percentage of Business in Importing: 100

49218 Tecumseh Products Co.
5683 Hines Dr.
Ann Arbor, MI 48108   734-585-9500
Fax: 734-352-3700 www.tecumseh.com
Refrigeration compressors, condensing units and gasoline engines, power train components and centrifugal pumps; exporter of ice making, refrigerating and cooling machinery.
CEO: Douglas Murdock
douglas.murdock@tecumseh.com
Executive VP/CFO: Michael Baursfeld
General Counsel: Carrie Williamson
Year Founded: 1934
Estimated Sales: $854 Million
Number Employees: 5,800
Square Footage: 7176000
Other Locations:
  Tecumseh Products Co.
  ParisTecumseh Products Co.
Brands Exported: Tecumseh; Sicom
Regions Exported to: Worldwide
Percentage of Business in Exporting: 20
Regions Imported from: South America, Europe, Asia, Latin America

49219 Tecweigh
1201 N Birch Lake Blvd
St Paul, MN 55110-6709   651-777-4780
Fax: 651-777-5582   800-536-4880
info@tecweigh.com www.tecweigh.com
Manufacturer and exporter of volumetric and gravimetric feeders, weigh belts, belt scales, batching systems and bulk bag dischargers
CFO: John Madgett Jr
Quality Control: Steve Frank
President: John P Madgett Sr
Regional Manager: Jeff Desjardin
Estimated Sales: $ 10 - 20 Million
Number Employees: 20-49
Square Footage: 60000
Brands Exported: Tecweigh; Flex-Feed; Multi-Weigh; Tec Line
Regions Exported to: Central America, South America, Europe, Canada, Caribbean, Latin America, Mexico, Australia
Percentage of Business in Exporting: 20

49220 Ted Shear Assoc Inc
1 West Ave # 210
Larchmont, NY 10538-2471   914-833-0017
Fax: 914-833-0233 ted.shear@verizon.net
Honey and vanilla extracts
President: Ted Shear
katestanley@avis.com
Estimated Sales: $ 1 - 3 000,000
Number Employees: 1-4
Type of Packaging: Private Label

Importers & Exporters / A-Z

49221 Tee Pee Olives, Inc.
411 Theodore Fremd Avenue
Suite 120
Rye, NY 10580 914-925-0450
Fax: 914-925-0458 800-431-1529
lucy.teepeeolives@verizon.net
www.teepeeolives.com
Importer and packer of bulk Spanish green olives in the US.
Pres/CEO/Mktg/Purchasing: Lucy Landesman
CFO: William Barrett
VP/Quality Control: Robert Cory PhD
VP Sales: Deborah Eklund
COO: Joseph Fairchild
Plant Manager: Robert Roaden
Purchasing Manager: Emil Cairo
Estimated Sales: $ 10 - 20 Million
Number Employees: 50
Type of Packaging: Consumer, Food Service, Private Label, Bulk
Brands Imported: Lily; Marta; Italica
Regions Imported from: Europe, Middle East
Percentage of Business in Importing: 90

49222 Tee's Plus
90 Knothe Road
Westbrook, CT 06498 800-785-3323
Fax: 860-581-8289 sales@teesplus.com
www.teesplus.com
Wholesaler/distributor and exporter of uniforms and aprons; also, silkscreening and embroidering available
VP National Accounts: Ronna Davis
Sales: Christy Kendrick
Contact: Kerri Santana
ksantana@teesplus.com
Number Employees: 50-99

49223 Tee-Jay Corporation
415 Howe Ave
Suite 202
Shelton, CT 6484 203-924-4767
Fax: 203-924-2967
Manufacturer and exporter of industrial sponge rubber products
Owner: Thomas J Mc Queeney Jr
Estimated Sales: Less than $500,000
Number Employees: 1-4
Regions Exported to: Canada
Percentage of Business in Exporting: 20

49224 Teelee Popcorn
101 W Badger St
Shannon, IL 61078-9020 815-864-2363
Fax: 815-864-2388 800-578-2363
Processor and exporter of microwaveable popcorn
Owner: Gary Armstrong
VP/Sales: Ken Weaver
garyarmstrong@teeleepopcorn.com
Estimated Sales: $2 Million
Number Employees: 20-49
Square Footage: 100000
Type of Packaging: Consumer, Private Label, Bulk
Brands Exported: Tee Lee
Regions Exported to: South America, Europe, Asia, Middle East, Canada

49225 Teilhaber ManufacturingCorp
2360 Industrial Ln
Broomfield, CO 80020-1612 303-466-2323
Fax: 303-466-2366 800-358-7225
www.teilhaber.com
Manufacturer and exporter of pallet racks, shelving and storage accessories
President: Norm Ooms
nooms@teilhaber.com
VP Sales: Don Rutkowski
Estimated Sales: $ .5 - 1 million
Number Employees: 50-99
Square Footage: 140000
Brands Exported: C.U.E. Rack; C.U.E. Shelf
Regions Exported to: Central America

49226 Tejon Ranch Co
4436 Lebec Rd
Lebec, CA 93243-9705 661-248-3000
Fax: 661-248-6209 bzoeller@tejonranch.com
www.tejonranch.com
Processor and exporter of pistachios, walnuts, almonds and wine grapes
President/CEO: Robert Stine
CEO: Gregory S Bielli
bielli@tejonranch.com
CFO/VP/Corporate Secretary: Allen Lyda
Vice President, Controller: Abel Guzman
Vice President of Corporate Communicatio: Barry Zoeller
Vice President of Operations: Brian Grant
Estimated Sales: Less than $500,000
Number Employees: 100-249
Type of Packaging: Consumer, Private Label, Bulk
Regions Exported to: Worldwide
Percentage of Business in Exporting: 60

49227 Tek Visions
40970 Anza Rd
Temecula, CA 92592-9368 951-506-9709
Fax: 951-506-4035 800-466-8005
tekv@primenet.com www.tekvisions.com
Manufacturer, importer and exporter of touch monitors, PCs and POS systems. TechVisions specializes in fast-loading, quickly-developed and memorable Web sites that are within any budget!
Owner: Tom Cramer
VP, Sales: Nick Christie
Tech Support Engineer: Fred Meyerhofer
VP, Sales: Tom Cramer
tom@tekvisions.com
Estimated Sales: $5-10 Million
Number Employees: 5-9
Regions Exported to: Worldwide
Regions Imported from: Asia

49228 Teksem LLC
19 Wayne Street
Jersey City, NJ 07302-3614 646-552-5807
Fax: 503-213-9627
President: Burak Arikan
burak@burakarikan.com
VP Marketing: Burak Arikan
Estimated Sales: $5 Million
Type of Packaging: Private Label, Bulk
Other Locations:
Fruit Acres Farm Market
Coloma, MI Fruit Acres Farm Market
Brands Imported: Celal, Birsen, Teksem
Regions Imported from: Turkey
Percentage of Business in Importing: 100

49229 Tel-Tru Manufacturing Co
408 Saint Paul St
Rochester, NY 14605-1734 585-232-1440
Fax: 585-232-3857 800-232-5335
info@teltru.com
Manufactures and distributes instrumentation products such as Bimetal Thermometers, Digital Thermometers, Temperature and Pressure Transmitters, pressure gauges, and accessory products that are designed and manufactured for worldwidedistribution to sanitary, industrial OEM, HVAC, and food service markets.
President: Andy Germanow
Cmo: Kati Chenot
kchenot@teltru.com
Marketing Manager: Kati Chenot
Sales Manager: Yvonne O Brien
Estimated Sales: $20-50 Million
Number Employees: 100-249
Square Footage: 100000
Brands Exported: Tel-Tru
Regions Exported to: Worldwide
Percentage of Business in Exporting: 25

49230 TeleTech Label Company
113 Commerce Dr
Fort Collins, CO 80524-2764 970-221-2275
Fax: 970-221-2530 888-403-8253
www.teletech.com
Manufacturer and exporter of pressure sensitive and extended format promotional labels and weather and ultra-violet resistant tags; also, digital printing on films and hot stamping available
President: Carol Hargadine
Director Sales/Marketing: Lindsay Woods
Estimated Sales: $ 3 - 5 Million
Number Employees: 5-9

49231 Teledyne Benthos Inc
49 Edgerton Dr
North Falmouth, MA 02556-2826 508-563-1000
Fax: 508-563-6444 taptone@teledyne.com
www.taptone.com
Manufacturer and exporter of package inspection equipment and leak detectors
General Manager: Francois Leroy
CFO: Franke Dunne
Director of Research: Bob Melvin
Director of QC/QA: Andrew Bonacker
Marketing Manager: Melissa Rossi
Sales/Marketing Director: Doug McGowen
Director of Production: Rick Martin
Estimated Sales: $5-10 Million
Number Employees: 100-249
Parent Co: Teledyne Technologies
Type of Packaging: Bulk
Brands Exported: TapTone 100, TapTone 500, TapTone 4000
Regions Exported to: Central America, South America, Europe, Asia, Middle East
Percentage of Business in Exporting: 40

49232 Teledyne TEKMAR
4736 Socialville Foster Rd
Mason, OH 45040-8265 513-229-7042
Fax: 513-229-7050 800-874-2004
tekmarinfo@teledyne.com
www.teledynetekmar.com
Manufacturer and exporter of equipment used for flavors and fragrance analysis, bacterial count analysis and food packaging material studies
Manager: Charlie Fulmer
Cio/Cto: Kym Silber
kym_silber@teledyne.com
CFO: Cindy Reed
Chairman of the Board: Robert Mehrabian
Director Operations: Ron Uchtman
Estimated Sales: $20-50 Million
Number Employees: 50-99
Parent Co: Rosemount
Regions Exported to: Worldwide
Percentage of Business in Exporting: 35

49233 Telesonic Packaging
805 E 13th St
Wilmington, DE 19802-5000 302-658-6945
Fax: 302-658-6946 telesonics@aol.com
www.telesoniconline.com
Manufacturer and exporter of flexible and shrink packaging equipment, form/fill/seal and bagging machinery and horizontal flow wrappers
Owner: Bernard Katz
telesonics@aol.com
Estimated Sales: $ 1 - 5,000,000
Number Employees: 5-9
Square Footage: 20000
Regions Exported to: Worldwide
Percentage of Business in Exporting: 25

49234 (HQ)Televend
111 Croydon Rd
Baltimore, MD 21212 410-532-7818
Fax: 410-532-7818
Manufacturer and exporter of computer terminal systems and custom application software including supermarket incentive gaming; importer of computer software
President: Stephen R Krause
CEO: Nat Miller
CFO: Sam Katz
VP: George Panda
R&D: SR Krause
Quality Control: Earl Davis
Marketing/Sales: Nat Miller
Contact: Sam Katz
sktv@comcast.net
Operations: RM Martin
Production: Charles Caplan
Plant Manager: Earl Davis
Purchasing: Geroge Panda
Estimated Sales: $1-3 Million
Number Employees: 50-99
Number of Brands: 12
Number of Products: 11
Square Footage: 5000
Type of Packaging: Bulk
Regions Exported to: South America, Europe, Middle East
Percentage of Business in Exporting: 10
Regions Imported from: Europe, Asia
Percentage of Business in Importing: 47

49235 Telman Incorporated
57 Fairhaven Drive
Allendale, NJ 07401-1108 617-734-4534
Fax: 617-734-4962
President: Spiros A Haliotis
Type of Packaging: Consumer, Food Service, Private Label, Bulk

Importers & Exporters / A-Z

Regions Exported to: South America
Brands Imported: Private Label, Importer & Distributor Label & Our Own.
Regions Imported from: South America, Europe, Asia, Middle East
Percentage of Business in Importing: 100

49236 Telwar International Inc
7104 Crossroads Blvd # 123
Brentwood, TN 37027-2913   615-661-6177
     Fax: 615-661-7818 www.telwar.com
Exporter and importer of groceries and specialty food products; also, commodities, clothing, furniture and household goods
President: Fatima Telwar
Secretary: Lisa Telwar
Contact: Fatima K Telwar
fatima@telwar.com
Number Employees: 5-9
Type of Packaging: Private Label, Bulk
Regions Exported to: Central America, Europe, Asia, Middle East

49237 Tema Systems Inc
7806 Redsky Dr
Cincinnati, OH 45249-1632   513-792-2840
     Fax: 513-489-4817 www.tema.net
Centrifuge parts, filtration and recycling equipment, separators, clarifiers and whey processing equipment; exporter of centrifuges and separators
President: Mike Mullins
changar.glori@lexisnexis.com
Technical Manager: Mike Vastola
Estimated Sales: $10-20 Million
Number Employees: 20-49
Square Footage: 30000
Parent Co: Siebtechnik
Regions Exported to: Central America, South America, Europe, Asia, Middle East, Canada, Mexico
Percentage of Business in Exporting: 10

49238 Temco
2100 Dennison St
Oakland, CA 94606   707-746-5966
     Fax: 707-746-5965 sales@temcoscales.com
     www.temcoscales.com
Manufacturer and exporter of packaging machinery including weighers, bag openers, fillers, sealers and case and can fillers
President: David Travis
Engineer: Rob Vincent
Equipment Sales: Jeff Reed
Plant Manager: Bob Breitenstein
Estimated Sales: Below $ 5 Million
Number Employees: 10
Square Footage: 36000
Brands Exported: Temco
Regions Exported to: Central America, South America, Canada, Mexico
Percentage of Business in Exporting: 15

49239 Tempco Electric Heater Corporation
607 N Central Ave
Wood Dale, IL 60191-1452   630-350-2252
     Fax: 630-350-0232   888-268-6396
     info@tempco.com www.tempco.com
Manufacturer and exporter of industrial and commercial electric heating elements including air, band, bolt and cartridge heaters; temperature sensors and controls, including thermocouples and RTDs.
President: Fermin Adames
faadames@tempco.com
Quality Control: Tony Ocosta
Estimated Sales: $30 Million
Number Employees: 400
Square Footage: 260000
Regions Exported to: Central America, South America, Europe, Asia, Canada, Mexico
Percentage of Business in Exporting: 15

49240 Templar Food Products
571 Central Avenue
New Providence, NJ 7974   908-665-9511
     Fax: 908-665-9122   800-883-6752
     info@icedtea.com www.icedtea.com
Templar Food Products manufactures private-label tea using black, green, and oolong sourced from around the world. Tea mixture and flavor is customized according to customer preference.
President/Founder: Edward D Reeves
Manager of Laboratory: Trudy Genna
Sales Manager: Spencer Griffith
Contact: Michael Eagan
michael@icedtea.com
VP, Operations: Michael Murray
Estimated Sales: $870,000
Number Employees: 10-19
Type of Packaging: Private Label
Regions Exported to: Central America, South America, Europe, Asia, Middle East, Canada, Mexico
Percentage of Business in Exporting: 10
Regions Imported from: South America, Asia, Worldwide

49241 Templock Corporation
The Vercal Building 170
Santa Barbara, CA 93130   805-962-3100
     Fax: 805-962-3110   800-777-1715
     sales@templock.com www.templock.com
Manufacturer and exporter of PVC heat shrinkable tubing for tamper-evident seal, label and sleeve applications
President: William Spargur
Executive VP: Paul Montgomery
Sales Manager: Kristine Hille
Estimated Sales: $5-10 Million
Number Employees: 20-49
Square Footage: 60000
Regions Exported to: Central America, South America, Europe, Asia, Middle East, Canada
Percentage of Business in Exporting: 9

49242 Tennant Co.
701 N. Lilac Dr.
P.O. Box 1452
Minneapolis, MN 55422
     Fax: 763-513-2142   800-553-8033
     info@tennantco.com www.tennantco.com
Clean room and sanitation equipment and supplies, power sweeper/scrubbers, floor coatings and flooring.
President/CEO/Director: Chris Killingstad
Managing Director: Junzo Tsuda
Vice President/Chief Financial Officer: Thomas Paulson
Vice President, Global Operations: Don Westman
Vice President, Technology: Thomas Bruce
Director, Public Relations: Michael Buckley
Vice President, Operations: Steven Weeks
Year Founded: 1870
Estimated Sales: $739 Million
Number Employees: 1000-4999
Number of Brands: 4
Type of Packaging: Bulk
Regions Exported to: Worldwide
Percentage of Business in Exporting: 50

49243 Tenneco Inc
500 N Field Dr
Lake Forest, IL 60045-2595   847-482-5000
     Fax: 847-482-5940   800-403-3393
     www.tenneco.com
Manufacturer and exporter of dual oven pressed paperboard trays
Chairman: Gregg Sherrill
gsherrill@tenneco.com
CEO: Hari N Nair
CFO/EVP: Kenneth R Trammell
SVP, General Counsel & Corp. Secretary: James Harrington
Marketing Administration: Carly Rhoads
VP Sales North America: William Read
SVP, Global HR & Administration: Gregg A Bolt
Estimated Sales: Over $1 Billion
Number Employees: 10000+
Square Footage: 1172000
Parent Co: Tenneco Packaging
Type of Packaging: Food Service
Brands Exported: Pressware
Regions Exported to: Europe, Asia, Latin America
Percentage of Business in Exporting: 10

49244 Tenneco Specialty Packaging
2907 Log Cabin Drive SE
Smyrna, GA 30080-7013   404-350-1300
     Fax: 404-350-1489   800-241-4402
Manufacturer and exporter of foam and barrier modified atmosphere packaging trays, disposable tableware, plastic utensils and foam cups
Manager: Ross Eckerman
Number Employees: 1500
Parent Co: Tenneco
Type of Packaging: Consumer, Food Service
Regions Exported to: Central America, South America, Europe, Middle East

49245 Tennsco Corp
201 Tennsco Dr
Dickson, TN 37055-3014   615-446-8000
     Fax: 615-446-7224   800-251-8184
     info@tennsco.com www.tennsco.com
Manufacturer and exporter of wire shelving systems, lockers and cabinets
CEO: Lester Speyer
VP Sales: Hal McCalla
Plant Manager: Johnnie Morris
Purchasing Manager: Mickey Self
Estimated Sales: $ 80 Million
Number Employees: 500-999
Square Footage: 1400000
Type of Packaging: Food Service
Brands Exported: Logic
Regions Exported to: Worldwide
Percentage of Business in Exporting: 1

49246 Tente Casters Inc
2266 S Park Dr
Hebron, KY 41048-9537   859-586-5558
     Fax: 859-586-5859   800-783-2470
     info@tente-us.com www.tente.us
NSF listed casters; importer of casters
President: Brad Hood
Vice President: Renne Beltramo
Marketing Director: Sabine Batsche
Sales Director: Aaron Romer
Production Manager: Sue Dinkel
Estimated Sales: $ 10 - 20 Million
Number Employees: 100-249
Square Footage: 130000
Parent Co: TENTE-ROLLEN Gmbh

49247 Tenth & M Seafoods
1020 M St
Anchorage, AK 99501-3317   907-272-6013
     Fax: 907-272-1685   800-770-2722
     tenmsea@alaska.net www.10thandmseafoods.com
Processor, exporter and wholesaler/distributor of salmon, halibut, shrimp and king crab and scallops. Also operates under the name Alaska Sea Pack, Inc
President: Skip Winfree
tenmsea@alaska.net
Vice President: Rob Winfree
Sales Manager: Dannon Southall
Estimated Sales: $8 Million
Number Employees: 20-49
Type of Packaging: Consumer, Food Service
Regions Exported to: Japan, Germany, Canada
Regions Imported from: Worldwide

49248 Terkelsen Machine Company
Airport Road
Hyannis, MA 2601   508-775-6229
     Fax: 508-778-4441
Manufacturer and exporter of baling wire for bulk packaging
President: Russell Terkelsen
Number Employees: 4

49249 Terminix
3050 Whitestone Expy # 303
Flushing, NY 11354-1995   516-671-2411
     Fax: 718-939-4161   866-319-6528
     www.terminix.com
Manufacturer and exporter of waste disposal and pest control systems
Owner: Anthony Tabacco
Chief Operating Officer: Larry Pruitt
VP, Customer Experience: Phil Barber
Chief Marketing Officer: Kevin Kovalski
Vice President of Sales: Steve Good
VP, Communications: Valerie Middleton
Vice President of Operations: Larry Pruitt
Estimated Sales: $2.5-5 Million
Number Employees: 20-49
Parent Co: Terminix Commercial Services
Regions Exported to: Worldwide

49250 Terphane Inc
2754 W Park Dr
Bloomfield, NY 14469-9385   585-657-5800
     Fax: 585-657-5838   800-724-3456
     mail@terphane.com www.terphane.com
Manufacturer, importer and exporter of polyester film

Importers & Exporters / A-Z

General Manager: Dan Roy
Sales/Marketing Manager: Brian Ochsner
Human Resources Manager: Karen VanDerEems
Plant Manager: Chuck Mac Cary
Estimated Sales: $10-20 Million
Number Employees: 50-99
Square Footage: 320000
Regions Exported to: South America, Canada
Percentage of Business in Exporting: 20
Regions Imported from: South America
Percentage of Business in Importing: 50

49251 Terra Ingredients LLC

Minneapolis, MN
Fax: 612-486-3954   855-497-3308
hello@terraingredients.com
www.terraingredients.com
Whole organic ingredients for feed and consumer products, including flax, beans and lentils, corn, quinoa, millet, buckwheat, oats, rye, barley, wheat, soybeans, chia seeds and complete feed ingredient blends
Year Founded: 2000
Number of Brands: 1
Type of Packaging: Private Label, Bulk
Regions Exported to: USA

49252 Terra Origin, Inc.

Hauppauge, NY 11788   631-300-2306
info@terraorigin.com
www.terraorigin.com
Health supplements and powders, including superfood powder blends, whey protein powder, bone broth protein, plant-based protein and antioxidant formula capsules
Year Founded: 2017
Number of Brands: 1
Number of Products: 21
Type of Packaging: Consumer, Private Label
Brands Exported: Terra Origin
Regions Exported to: USA, Canada

49253 Terriss Consolidate

807 Summerfield Ave
Asbury Park, NJ 07712-6970   732-988-2044
Fax: 732-502-0526   800-342-1611
terriss@terriss.com   www.terriss.com
Laboratory equipment: testing equipment, stainless steel fabricators, mixing tanks, tables, and sinks
Owner: Judy Bodnobich
Research and Development: Marc Epstein
Sales: Edward DellaZanna
terriss@terriss.com
Estimated Sales: $1.8 Million
Number Employees: 10-19
Square Footage: 25000

49254 Terry Manufacturing Company

PO Box 130041
Birmingham, AL 35213-0041   205-250-0062
Fax: 334-863-8835
Manufacturer and exporter of uniforms
President: Roy Terry
Estimated Sales: $1-2.5 Million
Number Employees: 1-4
Type of Packaging: Food Service

49255 Tesa Tape Inc

5825 Carnegie Blvd
Charlotte, NC 28209-4633   704-554-0707
Fax: 704-553-5677   800-429-8273
customercare@tesatape.com   www.tesatape.com
Manufacturer and exporter of pressure sensitive adhesive tape
President: Carston Myer
cmyer@tesatape.com
CEO: Torsten Schermer
Estimated Sales: H
Number Employees: 50-99
Parent Co: tesa AG
Type of Packaging: Consumer, Food Service, Private Label, Bulk
Brands Exported: Tesa
Regions Exported to: Worldwide

49256 Tesoro USA, LLC

286 Spring Street
Room 505
New York, NY 10013-1428   646-486-6457
Fax: 212-243-3569   866-483-7000
Import, market, and sell Cerveza Tesoro from Puerto Rico
President: Patrick Legin
Marketing Director: Minoy Figueroa
Sales Director: Louis Navarro
Public Relations: Jessie Maldonado
Estimated Sales: $250,000
Number Employees: 3
Number of Brands: 1
Number of Products: 1
Square Footage: 6000
Parent Co: Cerveceria Tesoro
Type of Packaging: Consumer
Brands Exported: Cerveza Tesoro
Percentage of Business in Exporting: 100

49257 Tessenderlo Kerley Inc

2255 N 44th St # 300
Phoenix, AZ 85008-3279   602-889-8300
Fax: 602-889-8430   800-669-0559
info-tki@tkinet.com   www.tkinet.com
Producer of high quality gelatins for the food, pharmaceutical and photoghaphic industry, operating worldwide
Vice President: Larry Tryon
ltryon@tkinet.com
CEO: Jordan Burns
Estimated Sales: $ 3 - 5 Million
Number Employees: 50-99
Type of Packaging: Private Label
Regions Exported to: Worldwide

49258 Test Laboratories Inc

7121 Canby Ave
Reseda, CA 91335-4304   818-881-4251
Fax: 818-881-6370   rob@testlabinc.com
www.testlabinc.com
Processor and exporter of enzymes, flavors and ingredients.
President: Rob Brewster
Estimated Sales: $1,100,000
Number Employees: 20-49
Square Footage: 4000
Percentage of Business in Exporting: 15

49259 Testing Machines Inc

40 Mccullough Dr
New Castle, DE 19720-2066   302-613-5619
Fax: 302-613-5019   800-678-3221
info@testingmachines.com
www.testingmachines.com
Manufacturer and exporter of crush, permeation, humidity, thickness and printability testing machinery
CEO: John Sullivan
Vice President: Richard Young
Marketing Director: Dave Muchorski
Sales Director: Richard Young
Estimated Sales: $10-20,000,000
Number Employees: 100-249
Regions Exported to: Worldwide
Percentage of Business in Exporting: 30

49260 Teti Bakery

27 Signal Hill Avenue
Etobicoke, ON M9W 6V8
Canada   416-798-8777
Fax: 416-798-8749   800-465-0123
www.tetibakery.com
Pizza, pizza crusts and Italian flat bread; exporter of pizza crusts
President: Franco Teti
VP: Dino Teti
Sales Manager: Tony Saldutto
Estimated Sales: $2 Million
Number Employees: 50
Square Footage: 56000
Type of Packaging: Consumer, Food Service, Private Label, Bulk
Brands Exported: Teti; San Mario
Regions Exported to: USA
Percentage of Business in Exporting: 20

49261 Tetley USA

P.O.Box 856
Shelton, CT 06484-0856   203-929-9200
Fax: 203-925-0512   michael.nestor@tetleyusa.com
www.tetleyusa.com
President: John Petrizzo
Contact: Glynne Jones
glynne.jones@tetleyusa.com
Number Employees: 500-999

49262 Teton Waters Ranch LLC

3301 Lawrence St. # 3
Denver, CO 80205   720-340-4590
www.tetonwatersranch.com
100% grass-fed and grass-finished beef frankfurters and sausages in various flavors
Founder: Jeff Russell
CEO: Walt Freese
Year Founded: 2008
Number of Brands: 1
Number of Products: 11
Type of Packaging: Consumer, Private Label
Brands Exported: Teton Waters Ranch
Regions Exported to: USA

49263 Tew Manufacturing Corp

470 Whitney Rd
PO Box 87
Penfield, NY 14526-2326   585-586-6120
Fax: 585-586-6083   800-259-5839
info@tewmfg.com   www.tewmfg.com
Manufacturer and exporter of fruit and vegetable cleaning equipment
Owner: William H Tew
tewmfg@aol.com
Estimated Sales: Less Than $500,000
Number Employees: 1-4
Square Footage: 16000
Regions Exported to: Central America, South America, Canada

49264 Texas Coffee Co

3297 S M L King Jr Pkwy
Beaumont, TX 77705-2513   409-835-3434
Fax: 409-835-4248   800-380-3400
texjoy@texjoy.com   www.texjoy.com
Tea, coffee, extracts, spices and seasonings; importer of coffee and tea
President/Operations: Carlo Busceme
cbusceme@texjoy.com
VP: Donald Fertitta
Estimated Sales: $ 10 - 20 Million
Number Employees: 20-49
Square Footage: 135000
Type of Packaging: Consumer, Food Service, Private Label, Bulk
Regions Imported from: Central America, South America
Percentage of Business in Importing: 20

49265 Texas Food Research

3202 W Anderson Lane
Suite 203
Austin, TX 78757   512-467-6731
www.satayusa.com

49266 Texas Halal Corporation

P.O. Box 630829
Houston, TX 77263   713-266-4300
Fax: 713-489-0808   ayesha@texashalal.com
www.texashalal.com
Halal beef, lamb, goat and poultry
Operations Manager: Ayesha Abou Taleb   *Year Founded:* 2003
Regions Exported to: Central America, South America, Europe, Asia, Middle East

49267 (HQ)Texas Refinery Corp

840 N Main St
Fort Worth, TX 76164-9486   817-332-1161
Fax: 817-332-6110   trc711@texasrefinery.com
www.texasrefinery.com
Food machinery lubricants
President: Jerry Hopkins
CEO: A M Pate III
CFO: Chuck Adamson
VP: Jim Peel
R&D: Seth Davis
Sales: Dennis Parks
Purchasing: Barbara Main
Estimated Sales: $20-50 Million
Number Employees: 50-99

49268 Texas Toffee

5 Santa Fe Pl
Odessa, TX 79765   972-596-1031
Fax: 915-563-4105   800-599-2133
www.texastoffee.com
Processor and exporter of toffee including milk and white chocolate, bittersweet, peanut, butterscotch and sugar-free
President: Susan Leshnower
Number Employees: 1-4
Square Footage: 64
Type of Packaging: Consumer, Food Service, Private Label, Bulk
Regions Exported to: Europe
Percentage of Business in Exporting: 10

Importers & Exporters / A-Z

49269 Texas Traditions Gourmet
PO Box 2705
Georgetown, TX 78627-2705 512-863-7291
Fax: 512-869-6212 800-547-7062
www.texastraditions.com
Processor and exporter of foods with Texas heritage, including mesquite smoke, jalapeno pepper, country-style German and black peppercorn mustard, jalapeno and red chile pepper, prickly pear cactus jelly, hot salt, seasoning blends and dry dip mixes
Founder, CEO: Dianna Howard
Estimated Sales: $300,000-500,000
Number Employees: 10-19
Regions Exported to: Europe, Asia, Middle East, Africa, Australia, Latin America
Percentage of Business in Exporting: 7

49270 Textile Buff & Wheel
511 Medford St # 1
Charlestown, MA 02129-1495 617-241-8100
Fax: 617-241-7280 www.textilebuff.com
Manufacturer and exporter of wiping cloths, mill remnants, cheesecloths and cotton gloves
Owner: Jerold Wise
Partner: Andrew Wise
Estimated Sales: $ 5-10 Million
Number Employees: 20-49
Square Footage: 200000
Regions Exported to: Central America, South America, Europe, Africa

49271 Textile Products Company
2512-2520 W Woodland Drive
Anaheim, CA 92801-2636 714-761-0401
Fax: 714-761-2928
Manufacturer and exporter of cheesecloth wiping rags and disposable rags
Marketing Director: Pearl Seratelli
Estimated Sales: $ 1 - 5 Million
Parent Co: Textile Products

49272 Texture Technologies Corporation
18 Fairview Rd
Scarsdale, NY 10583 914-472-0531
Fax: 914-472-0532
marcj@texturetechnologies.com
www.texturetechnologies.com
Manufacturer, importer and exporter of measurement instrumentation and software for testing food texture; also, bloom gel testers
President: Boine Johnson
CEO: Marc Johnson
CFO: Sue Perko
Quality Control: Joseph Piperis
Contact: James Fabry
jimf@texturetechnologies.com
Estimated Sales: $5 Million
Brands Exported: TA-XT2
Brands Imported: TA-XT2
Regions Imported from: Europe
Percentage of Business in Importing: 25

49273 Thaigrocer.com
PO Box 2054
Issaquah, WA 98027 425-687-1708
Fax: 425-687-8413 info@importfood.com
www.thaigrocer.com

49274 Tharo Systems Inc
2866 Nationwide Pkwy
PO Box 798
Brunswick, OH 44212-2362 330-273-4408
Fax: 330-225-0099 800-878-6833
info@easylabel.fr www.tharo.com
Manufacturer and exporter of computer software for custom designing and printing bar code, RFID and food ingredient labels, printers and printer/applicators, ribbons, labels, label rewinds, unwinds, and dispensers
President: Michelle Lyngoe
m_lyngoe@aimforsafety.com
VP Marketing: Lauren Shaarda
Sales Director: James Danko
Operations: Randy Thatcher
Estimated Sales: $ 5 - 10 Million
Number Employees: 10-19
Number of Brands: 1000
Number of Products: 4
Brands Exported: Easylabel Software; Tharo Printer; Datamax Printers, PA 1200 Label Printers/Applicators, Sony Chemicals Ribbons
Regions Exported to: Central America, South America, Europe, Asia, Middle East, Worldwide
Regions Imported from: Europe

49275 That's How We Roll, LLC
100 Passaic Ave. # 155
Fairfield, NJ 07004 973-602-3011
info@thwroll.com
www.thwroll.com
Snack crisps and cookies made with wholesome ingredients
Chief Operating Officer: Samuel Kestenbaum
Number of Brands: 3
Number of Products: 2
Type of Packaging: Consumer, Private Label
Brands Exported: Mrs. Thinster's, Kitchen Table Bakers, Party 'Tizers
Regions Exported to: USA

49276 The Amazing Chickpea
1600 Hwy. 100 South # 500A
St. Louis Park, MN 55416 612-548-1099
contact@theamazingchickpea.com
www.theamazingchickpea.com
Gluten-free chickpea butter spread in various flavors
Contact: Sunil Kumar
Year Founded: 2016
Number of Brands: 1
Number of Products: 4
Type of Packaging: Consumer, Private Label
Brands Exported: The Amazing Chickpea
Regions Exported to: USA, Canada

49277 The Ardent Homesteader
PO Box 44
Arden, NY 10910
www.ardenthomesteader.com
Handmade, all-natural caramel sauce
Founder/Owner: Kristin Nelson
Year Founded: 2010
Number of Brands: 1
Number of Products: 1
Type of Packaging: Consumer, Private Label
Brands Exported: Cara-Sel
Regions Exported to: USA

49278 The Art of Broth, LLC
818-715-9320
info@theartofbroth.com
www.theartofbroth.com
Sippable chicken, beef and vegan vegetable-flavored broth; broths are vegan, Kosher, non-GMO and gluten-free
Number of Brands: 1
Number of Products: 3
Type of Packaging: Consumer, Private Label
Brands Exported: The Art of Broth
Regions Exported to: USA

49279 The Brand Passport
18 E. 41st Street
Suite 802
New York, NY 10017 212-315-2343
thebrandpassport.com
Cookies and biscuits
CEO: Thomas Daly
Part-time Chief Financial Officer: Christopher Meron
Supply Chain Leader: Jason Stuart
Estimated Sales: $7.6 Million
Number Employees: 11-50
Brands Imported: Daelmans Stroopwafels
Regions Imported from: Holland

49280 The Bruss Company
3548 N. Kostner Ave.
Chicago, IL 60641 773-282-2900
customer.bruss@tyson.com
www.bruss.com
Portion controlled steaks, pork, and veal.
Year Founded: 1937
Estimated Sales: $175 Million
Number Employees: 250-499
Number of Brands: 1
Square Footage: 52000
Parent Co: Tyson Foods
Type of Packaging: Consumer, Food Service
Brands Exported: Bruss
Regions Exported to: Worldwide
Percentage of Business in Exporting: 5

49281 The Carriage Works
1877 Mallard Ln
Klamath Falls, OR 97601-5522 541-882-0700
Fax: 541-882-9661 sales@carriageworks.com
www.carriageworks.com
Manufacturer, importer and exporter of food service and retail merchandising carts, in-line concepts, kiosks and machines including espresso, hot dog, ice cream and beverage
President & CEO: Brian Dunham
VP, Sales & Marketing: Lori Butler
Estimated Sales: $ 5 - 10 Million
Number Employees: 20-49
Regions Exported to: Worldwide
Percentage of Business in Exporting: 40
Regions Imported from: Worldwide
Percentage of Business in Importing: 15

49282 The Chefs' Warehouse
100 E Ridge Rd
Ridgefield, CT 06877 203-897-1345
chefswarehouse.com
Wholesaler/distributor and importer of olives, cheese, olive oil, condiments, pasta, confections, processed meats, specialty foods, etc.
Founder/Chairman/CEO: Christopher Pappas
Founder & Vice Chairman: John Pappas
Chief Financial Officer: James Leddy
Chief Accounting Officer: Timothy McCauley
General Counsel & Corporate Secretary: Alexandros Aldous
Chief Human Resources Officer: Patricia Lecouras
Year Founded: 1956
Estimated Sales: $100-500 Million
Number Employees: 1000-4999
Type of Packaging: Consumer, Food Service, Private Label
Regions Imported from: South America, Europe
Percentage of Business in Importing: 95

49283 The Cherry Company Ltd.
4461 Malaai St
Honolulu, HI 96818 808-422-6555
Fax: 808-422-6721 www.cherryco.com
Wholesale distributor and importer of Japanese foods and restaurant supplies
Chairman: Noritoshi Kanai
President: Kosei Yamamoto
Vice President: Takateru Kishii
Sales Manager: Wesley Sakamoto
Contact: Rorie Mitsui
mitsui@cherryco.com
Accounting Manager: Rorie Mitsui
Warehouse Manager: Shane Riveral
Estimated Sales: $15 Million
Number Employees: 25
Square Footage: 25514
Parent Co: Mutual Trading Company Inc
Type of Packaging: Consumer, Food Service, Private Label

49284 The Coconut Cooperative, LLC
234 Fifth Ave. # 406
New York, NY 10001
hello@thecoconutcoop.com
www.thecoconutcoop.com
Organic coconut ingredients (chips, flakes, oil, sugar, flour)
Founder/CEO: Benjamin Weingarten
Number Employees: 2-10
Number of Products: 6
Type of Packaging: Bulk
Regions Exported to: USA

49285 The Coromega Company
PO Box 131135
Carlsbad, CA 92013-1135 760-599-6088
Fax: 760-599-6089 877-275-3725
www.coromega.com
Flavored Omega-3 fish oil gel supplements and gummy supplements
Chief Operating Officer: Andrew Aussie
Year Founded: 1999
Number of Brands: 1
Number of Products: 6
Type of Packaging: Consumer, Private Label
Brands Exported: Coromega
Regions Exported to: USA

49286 The Frank Pesce International Group, L.L.C.
902 Clint Moore Road
Boca Raton, FL 33487 561-997-0400
Fax: 561-997-7555 800-848-6352
Supplier and importer of Russian vodka and domestic vodka
Owner: Frank Pesce

Importers & Exporters / A-Z

Estimated Sales: $910,000
Number Employees: 5-9
Type of Packaging: Consumer, Food Service
Regions Imported from: Russia
Percentage of Business in Importing: 100

49287 The Good Crisp Company

www.thegoodcrispcompany.com
Gluten-free potato crisps in various flavors
Director, Sales/Marketing: Matt Parry
Number of Brands: 1
Number of Products: 3
Type of Packaging: Consumer, Private Label
Brands Exported: The Good Crisp Company
Regions Exported to: USA, Canada, Australia

49288 The Honest Stand

PO Box 100742
Denver, CO 80250
chat@thehoneststand.com
www.thehoneststand.com
Plant-based, certified organic, dairy- and gluten-free cheese style dips in various flavors
Co-Founder: Alexandra Carone
Co-Founder: Jeremy Day
Year Founded: 2014
Number of Brands: 1
Number of Products: 5
Type of Packaging: Consumer, Private Label
Brands Exported: The Honest Stand
Regions Exported to: USA, Canada

49289 The Irish Dairy Board Holdings

1007 Church Street
Suite 314
Evanston, IL 60201　　　　531-661-9599
Fax: 531-662-2778　kerrygold@idbusa.com
www.kerrygold.com
Other lifestyle, butter, cheese.

49290 The Lamb Company

372 Danbury Rd.
Suite 207
Wilton, CT 06897　　　　203-529-9100
Fax: 203-529-9101　800-438-5262
www.thelambcompany.com
Lamb, beef, venison, goat, and mutton from New Zealand and Australia
HR Manager: Brenda Norman
General Manager, Processing & Operation: Philip Fisher
Director of Product Development: Sari Goldenberg
Year Founded: 1964
Number Employees: 50-99
Regions Imported from: Oceania

49291 The Lancaster Food Company

Lancaster, PA
Certified organic and allergen-free breads and cookies
Co-Founder/CEO: Charlie Crystle
Co-Founder/Chief Product Officer: Craig Lauer
Vice-President, Operations: Polly Lauer
Year Founded: 2014
Number of Brands: 1
Number of Products: 7
Type of Packaging: Consumer, Private Label
Brands Exported: The Lancaster Food Company
Regions Exported to: USA

49292 The Little Kernel

400 Madison Ave.
Manalapan, NJ 07726　　　　732-607-3880
info@thelittlekernel.com
Olive-oil popped popcorn with no artificial ingredients, in various flavors
Co-Founder: Christopher Laurita
Co-Founder: Andy Epstein
Year Founded: 2016
Number of Brands: 1
Number of Products: 6
Type of Packaging: Consumer, Private Label
Brands Exported: The Little Kernel
Regions Exported to: USA, Canada

49293 The Long Life Beverage Company

P.O.Box 7802
Mission Hills, CA 91346-7802　　661-259-5575
　　　　　　　　　　　　　　　　800-848-7331
Processor, importer and exporter of organic herbal black and green teas, over 40 boxed varieties and 11 ready to drink bottled iced teas, and a variety of enhanced waters
Owner: Troy Long
Estimated Sales: $7.5 Million
Number Employees: 1-4
Number of Brands: 3
Number of Products: 52
Square Footage: 44000
Parent Co: Consac Industries
Type of Packaging: Consumer, Private Label
Brands Exported: Long Life
Regions Exported to: Central America, South America, Europe
Percentage of Business in Exporting: 10
Regions Imported from: Central America, South America, Europe, Asia, Middle East
Percentage of Business in Importing: 30

49294 The N Beverage Group

1301 West Elizabeth Avenue
Unit D
Linden, NJ 07036　　　　908-583-6438
Fax: 732-909-2323　www.thenbeveragegroup.com
Mineral water
Office Manager: AnnaMaria Lacchiana
Estimated Sales: $10-20 Million
Number Employees: 5-9
Type of Packaging: Food Service
Brands Imported: Rocchetta, Uliveto and Elisir
Regions Imported from: Italy

49295 The Naked Edge, LLC

3020 Carbon Place #103
Boulder, CO 80301
　　　　　　　　　　　　　　　　888-297-9426
www.wildmadesnacks.com
Organic, non-GMO Veggie-Go's dried fruit & vegetable snack; available in strips or bites
Co-Founder: John McHugh
Co-Founder: Lisa McHugh
Number of Brands: 1
Type of Packaging: Consumer, Private Label
Brands Exported: Veggie-Go's
Regions Exported to: USA

49296 The National Provisioner

155 N. Pfingsten Rd.
Suite 205
Deerfield, IL 60015　　　　847-763-9534
Fax: 847-763-9538　www.provisioneronline.com
Manufacturer and exporter of material handling products including conveyors and laser guided automated vehicle systems
Owner: Elmer Hartford
COO: Kevin Donahue
Engineer Manager: Todd Frandsen
Vice President of Services: Tom Egan
Sales Manager: Diana Rotman
Contact: Andy Hanacek
hanaceka@bnpmedia.com
Number Employees: 100-249
Square Footage: 300000
Regions Exported to: Central America, Europe
Percentage of Business in Exporting: 10

49297 The Premium Beer Company

275 Belfield Road
Etobicoke, ON M9W 7H9
Canada　　　　　　　　　　905-855-7743
Fax: 416-679-1929　800-561-6808
pbctelesales@moosehead.ca　www.premiumbeer.ca
Wholesaler/distributor and importer of alcoholic and nonalcoholic beer, ale, lager and cider; serving the food service market
General Manager: Bill Wade
CFO: Gorton Walker
Number Employees: 50-99
Square Footage: 54000
Parent Co: Moosehead Breweries
Type of Packaging: Consumer, Food Service
Brands Imported: Double Diamond; Becks; Calcedonian, Moosehead; Strongbow Cider; Caffrey's
Regions Imported from: Europe, United Kingdom,Canada
Percentage of Business in Importing: 85

49298 The Procter & Gamble Company

1 P&G Plaza
Cincinnati, OH 45202　　　　513-983-1100
Fax: 513-983-9369　800-692-0132
us.pg.com
Baby diapers, fabric care, feminine products, shampoos, paper towels, toilet paper, tissues, conditioners, dishwashing detergent, home cleaning products, razors, shaving gels, supplements, pregnancy tests, cough syrup, and more.
Chairman, President & CEO: David Taylor
CFO: Jon Moeller
Estimated Sales: $67.6 Billion
Number Employees: 97,000
Number of Brands: 57
Type of Packaging: Consumer

49299 The Real Co

3613F Kirkwood Hwy.
Wilmington, DE 19808　　　　347-433-8945
info@thereal.co
www.thereal.co
Single-origin, non-GMO food products: quinoa, raw coconut sugar, raw cane sugar, pink Himalayan salt and white basmati rice
Founder: Colin Carter
Chief Executive Officer: Belal El-Banna
Chief Commercial Officer: Mo Elkateb
Number of Brands: 1
Number of Products: 6
Type of Packaging: Consumer, Food Service, Private Label
Brands Exported: The Real Co
Regions Exported to: USA

49300 The Scoular Company/TSCContainer Freight

2027 Dodge Street
Omaha, NE 68102
food@scoular.com
www.scoular.com
Merchandise a full range of agricultural products: traditional and specialty crops, food and feed ingredients, and freight.
Chairman: David Faith
Chief Executive Officer: Paul Maass
Chief Financial Officer: Andrew Kenny
Chief Human Resources Officer: Kurt Peterson
Chief Information Officer: Jeff Schreiner
SVP & General Counsel: Megan Belcher
SVP & Division General Manager: Bob Ludington
SVP & Division General Manager: John Messerich
SVP & Division General Manager: Bryan Wurscher
Year Founded: 1892
Estimated Sales: $4.3 Billion
Number Employees: 1,000+
Number of Products: 100+
Other Locations:
　Overland Park, KS
　Minneapolis, MNMinneapolis
Regions Exported to: Central America, South America, Europe, Asia
Percentage of Business in Exporting: 50
Regions Imported from: Worldwide

49301 The Sola Company

4203 Montrose Blvd. # 490
Houston, TX 77006　　　　800-277-1486
hello@solasweet.com
www.solasweet.com
Low-carb and low-glycemic index yogurt, ice cream, granola, bread, nut bars and sweetener
Co-Founder: Ed Bosarge
Co-Founder: Ryan Turner
Year Founded: 2012
Number of Brands: 1
Number of Products: 6
Type of Packaging: Consumer, Private Label
Brands Exported: Sola
Regions Exported to: USA

49302 The Tea Spot, Inc.

4699 Nautilus Ct. South # 504
Boulder, CO 80301　　　　303-444-8324
www.theteaspot.com
A variety of white, green, oolong, black, pu'erh, mate, herbal and organic teas in various flavors and sampler packs
CEO: Maria Upenski
Number of Brands: 1
Type of Packaging: Consumer, Private Label
Brands Exported: The Tea Spot
Regions Exported to: USA

49303 The Toasted Oat Bakehouse

Columbus, OH
www.thetoastedoat.com

617

Importers & Exporters / A-Z

Gluten- and preservative-free all natural granola blends in various flavors
Founder: Erika Boll
Chief Financial Officer: Tom Kelley
Year Founded: 2013
Number of Brands: 1
Number of Products: 4
Type of Packaging: Consumer, Private Label
Brands Exported: The Toasted Oat

49304 (HQ)Theochem Laboratories Inc
7373 Rowlett Park Dr
Tampa, FL 33610-1101   813-237-6463
        Fax: 813-237-2059   800-237-2591
        www.theochem.com
Manufacturer and exporter of chemical cleaners and inorganic cleaning compounds
COO and President: John Theofilos
Director Operations: Lenny Wydotis
Estimated Sales: $20-50 Million
Number Employees: 5-9
Square Footage: 250000
Brands Exported: Solutions For A Cleaner World
Regions Exported to: Central America, South America, Europe, Middle East
Percentage of Business in Exporting: 5

49305 Therm L Tec Building Systems
15115 Chestnut St
Basehor, KS 66007-9207   913-728-2662
        Fax: 913-724-1446 www.thermltec.com
Insulated commercial cold storage panels, partitions, doors and liners
Sales: Dennis Bixby
Contact: Joshua Cole
jcole@thermltec.com
Estimated Sales: $5-10 Million
Number Employees: 1-4
Square Footage: 300000

49306 Therm-Tec Inc
20525 SW Cipole Rd
Sherwood, OR 97140-8339   503-625-7575
        Fax: 503-625-6161   800-292-9163
        www.thermtec.com
Manufacturer and exporter of solid, animal and human crematories, and hospital waste incinerators; also air pollution control equipment
Owner: Dean Robbins
thermtec@earthlink.net
Estimated Sales: Below $5 Million
Number Employees: 10-19
Square Footage: 160000
Brands Exported: Therm-Tec
Regions Exported to: Central America, South America, Asia, Middle East
Percentage of Business in Exporting: 20

49307 Therma Kleen
10212 S Mandel St # A
Plainfield, IL 60585-5374   630-820-6700
        Fax: 630-305-8696   800-999-3120
        steamtk@aol.com www.therma-kleen.com
Manufacturer and exporter of steam cleaners and pressure washers
President: Andy Heller
VP: Linda Heller
IT: Linda Hubbell
steamtk@aol.com
Estimated Sales: $500,000-$1 Million
Number Employees: 5-9
Square Footage: 5600
Brands Exported: Therma-Kleen
Regions Exported to: Central America, South America, Asia, Middle East
Percentage of Business in Exporting: 10

49308 Thermaco Inc
646 Greensboro St
PO Box 2548
Asheboro, NC 27203-4739   336-629-4651
        Fax: 336-626-5739   800-633-4204
        info@thermaco.com www.thermaco.com
Manufacturer and exporter of pre-treatments and automatic solid and grease/oil removal units for restaurants and food processing plants
President: William Batten
info@thermaco.com
Estimated Sales: $1-2.5 Million
Number Employees: 10-19
Square Footage: 12000
Brands Exported: Big Dipper
Regions Exported to: Worldwide
Percentage of Business in Exporting: 25

49309 Thermal Bags By Ingrid Inc
131 Sola Dr
Gilberts, IL 60136-9748   847-836-4400
        Fax: 847-836-4408   800-622-5560
        Mary@ThermalBags.com www.thermalbags.com
Manufacturer and exporter of thermal food bags, racks, thermal hoods, insulated carrying bags, pizza delivery pouches and catering bags. Also lightweight insulated bags for the carry-out market and advertising specialties
Inventor & CEO: Ingrid Kosar
ingrid@thermalbags.com
Marketing Director: Fred Kosar
Estimated Sales: $2.5-5 Million
Number Employees: 5-9
Type of Packaging: Food Service
Brands Exported: Thermal Bags By Ingrid
Regions Exported to: Worldwide
Percentage of Business in Exporting: 20

49310 Thermo Detection
27 Forge Pkwy
Franklin, MA 02038-3135   508-520-0430
        Fax: 508-520-1732   866-269-0070
        www.thermo.
Manufacturer and exporter of moisture and other consistent process analyzers and monitors
Administrator: Michael Nemergut
VP Sales/Marketing: Terry Rose
National Sales Manager: Don Piatt
Inside Sales: Jill Holman
Number Employees: 50-99
Square Footage: 80000
Parent Co: Thermedics Detection
Brands Exported: Micro Quad 8000; Quadra Beam 6600; Micro Lab; Micro Quad 9000; Quadra Beam 6600T; Micro Quad 8200; Spectra Beam 1000
Regions Exported to: Central America, South America, Europe, Asia, Middle East
Percentage of Business in Exporting: 35

49311 Thermo-KOOL/Mid-South Ind Inc
723 E 21st St
Laurel, MS 39440-2457   601-649-4600
        Fax: 601-649-0558 sales@thermokool.com
        www.thermokool.com
Manufacturer and exporter of self-contained, remote, quick connect and walk-in refrigeration equipment
President: Randolph McLaughlin
CEO: Patricia McLaughlin
VP: Randplph McLaughlin
Sales: Gary Crocker
Plant Manager: Duane Eldridge
Purchasing: Lee Thames
Estimated Sales: $20-50 Million
Number Employees: 100-249
Square Footage: 123000
Regions Exported to: Europe, Asia, Middle East
Percentage of Business in Exporting: 3

49312 ThermoWorks
1762 W 20 S
Suite 100
Lindon, UT 84042   801-756-7705
        Fax: 801-756-8948   800-393-6434
        www.thermoworks.com
President: Randy Owen
Contact: Tricia Buss
tricia.buss@thermoworks.com
Estimated Sales: Below $5 Million
Number Employees: 5-9

49313 Thermodynamics
6780 Brighton Blvd
Commerce City, CO 80022
        Fax: 918-251-2826   800-627-9037
        www.okpallets.com
Reusable plastic pallets, bins, boxes, containers and trays including standard and custom; exporter of plastic pallets
CEO: Sheri Orlowitz
General Manager: Robert Lux
Production Manager: Shawn Harley
Plant Manager: Robert Luxtwood
Purchasing Manager: Ray Carr
Estimated Sales: $5 - 10 Million
Number Employees: 20-49
Square Footage: 70000
Parent Co: Shan Industries

49314 Thermodyne Foodservice Prods
4418 New Haven Ave
Fort Wayne, IN 46803-1650   260-428-2535
        Fax: 260-428-2533   800-526-9182
        www.tdyne.com
Manufacturer and exporter of conduction ovens
President: Vincent Tippmann Sr
General Manager: Sue Brown
IT: Dave Schenkel
dave.schenkel@polarking.com
Number Employees: 1-4
Square Footage: 500000
Parent Co: Polar King International
Regions Exported to: Canada
Percentage of Business in Exporting: 1

49315 Thermodyne International LTD
1841 S Business Pkwy
Ontario, CA 91761-8537   909-923-9945
        Fax: 909-923-7505 sales@thermodyne.com
        www.thermodyne.com
Manufacturer and exporter of reusable plastic containers and instrument shipping and carrying cases; also, custom vacuum forming services available
President: Gary Ackerman
gackerman@thermodyne-online.com
Sr. VP: Gary Ackerman
Chairman of the Board: Gary S Ackerman
Estimated Sales: $ 10 - 20 Million
Number Employees: 50-99
Brands Exported: Rack-Pack; Shok-Stop
Regions Exported to: Central America, South America, Europe, Asia

49316 Thermoil Corporation
7 Franklin Avenue
Brooklyn, NY 11211-7801   718-855-0544
        Fax: 718-643-6691
Manufacturer and exporter of industrial oils and greases
Estimated Sales: $ 10-20 Million
Number Employees: 10-19
Regions Exported to: Worldwide
Percentage of Business in Exporting: 15

49317 Thermoquest
3661 Interstate Park Road N
Suite 100
Riviera Beach, FL 33404-5906   561-383-2000
        Fax: 561-383-2043   888-383-2025
        www.palmbeachschools.org
Manufacturer and exporter of stainless steel pots and pans
General Manager: Ralph Kearney
Number Employees: 50
Parent Co: Floarie
Type of Packaging: Food Service
Regions Exported to: Worldwide
Percentage of Business in Exporting: 3

49318 Theta Sciences
11835 Carmel Mountain Road
Suite 1304
San Diego, CA 92128-4609   760-745-3311
        Fax: 760-745-5519
Manufacturer, importer and exporter of electronic instruments specializing in food process control and personnel hazard monitoring
President: Hal Buscher
VP: Bob LeClair
VP: Dave Furuno
Estimated Sales: $1-2.5 Million
Number Employees: 9
Square Footage: 19200
Brands Exported: Theta Sciences
Regions Exported to: South America, Europe, Asia, Australia
Percentage of Business in Exporting: 10
Brands Imported: Nint
Regions Imported from: Europe, Asia
Percentage of Business in Importing: 20

49319 Thiel Cheese & Ingredients
N7630 County Hwy BB
Attn: Kathy Pitzen
Hilbert, WI 54129   920-989-1440
        Fax: 920-989-1288 kathyp@thielcheese.com
Manufacturer and custom formulator of processed cheeses that are used primarily as ingredients in other food products
President: Steven Thiel
Sales: Kathy Pitzen
Number Employees: 50-99

Importers & Exporters / A-Z

Type of Packaging: Consumer, Food Service, Private Label, Bulk
Brands Exported: Thiel
Regions Exported to: South America
Percentage of Business in Exporting: 5

49320 Thiele Engineering Company
810 Industrial Park Boulevard
Fergus Falls, MN 56537   218-739-3321
    Fax: 218-739-9370 info@swfcompanies.com
    www.thieletech.com
Manufacturer and exporter of cartoners and case packers
VP Sales: Wayne Slaton
Number Employees: 260
Square Footage: 173900
Parent Co: Barry-Wehmiller Company
Regions Exported to: Central America, South America, Europe, Asia, Middle East
Percentage of Business in Exporting: 45

49321 Thiele Technologies-Reedley
1949 E Manning Ave
Reedley, CA 93654-9462   559-638-8484
    Fax: 559-638-7478   800-344-8951
    Sales@ThieleTech.com www.thieletech.com
Manufacturer and exporter of corrugated box forming and sealing machinery, case erectors, automatic case packers, case openers/positioners, cartoners and robotics automation.
President: Larry Smith
VP: Ed Suarez
Sales Director: Craig Friesen
Contact: Stephen Akins
stephen.akins@thieletech.com
Number Employees: 250-499
Square Footage: 400000
Parent Co: Barry-Wehmiller
Other Locations:
   SWF Machinery
   Orlando, FLSWF Machinery
Brands Exported: SWF; Dyna-Pak; McDowell; Salwasser; GSMA; Tisma
Regions Exported to: Worldwide
Percentage of Business in Exporting: 33

49322 Thirs-Tea Corp
4611 N Dixie Hwy
Boca Raton, FL 33431-5030   561-948-5600
    info@thirs-tea.com
    www.thirs-tea.com
Processor of tea beverages amd concentrates.
President: Ray Welch
Year Founded: 1977
Estimated Sales: $500,000-$1 Million
Number Employees: 11-50
Type of Packaging: Consumer, Food Service, Private Label, Bulk
Brands Exported: Thirs-Tea
Regions Exported to: Central America, South America, Europe, Asia, Middle East, Caribbean
Percentage of Business in Exporting: 2

49323 This Bar Saves Lives, LLC
Culver City, CA   310-730-5060
    hello@thisbarsaveslives.com
    www.thisbarsaveslives.com
Non-GMO, gluten-free healthy snack bar; with every purchase, the company gives food aid to a child in need from Haiti, the Democratic Republic of the Congo, Guatemala, South Sudan, the Philippines and/or Mexico
Co-Founder: Ryan Devlin
Co-Founder: Todd Grinnell
Co-Founder: Ravi Patel
Year Founded: 2013
Number of Brands: 1
Number of Products: 6
Type of Packaging: Consumer, Private Label
Brands Exported: This Bar Saves Lives
Regions Exported to: USA, Canada

49324 Thomas L. Green & Company
380 Old West Penn Ave
Robenosia, PA 19551   610-693-5816
    Fax: 610-693-5512 info@readingbakery.com
    www.readingbakery.com
Manufacturer and exporter of bakery machinery including automatic band ovens, dough mixers, conveyors for crackers and cookies, biscuit cutters, dough formers and dough sheeters
Chairman: Thomas Lugar
EVP & CFO: Chip Czulada
CEO: Terry Groff
CFO: Charles Czulada
Quality Control: Mike Johnson
VP, Sales and Marketing: David Kuipers
VP of Sales, Americas: Shawn Moye
VP, Operations: Travis Getz
Estimated Sales: $ 5 - 10 Million
Number Employees: 10-19
Regions Exported to: Central America, South America, Europe, Asia, Canada, Caribbean, Latin America, Mexico

49325 Thomas Lighting Residential
10275 W Higgins Rd, 8th Floor
Rosemont, IL 60018
    Fax: 800-288-4329   800-825-5844
    info@thomaslighting.com
    www.thomaslighting.com
Manufacturer and exporter of outdoor lighting fixtures
Sales Manager: Sheryl Fraga
Number Employees: 350
Regions Exported to: Worldwide
Percentage of Business in Exporting: 10

49326 Thomas Precision, Inc.
3278 S Main St
Rice Lake, WI 54868-8793   715-234-8827
    Fax: 715-234-6737   800-657-4808
    sales@tpm-inc.com www.tpm-inc.com
Manufacturer and exporter of stainless steel and alloy replacement parts for food processing equipment including grinder plates, blades and screens; also, build and rebuild separating machines and augers
CEO: Roger Norberg
Sales: Jerry Klasen
Plant Manager: Kevin Nyra
Purchasing Agent: Rod Stoyke
Estimated Sales: $10 Million
Number Employees: 60
Square Footage: 48000
Regions Exported to: Central America, South America, Europe, Australia, Canada
Percentage of Business in Exporting: 10

49327 Thomas Tape & Supply CoInc
1713 Sheridan Ave
Springfield, OH 45505-2263   937-325-6414
    Fax: 937-325-2850 www.thomastape.com
Manufacturer and exporter of sealing tape including paper, cloth, reinforced glass fiber, gummed, and pressure sensitive tape
President: David Simonton
dave11@thomastape.com
Sales/Marketing Executive: Kevin Amidon
Estimated Sales: $300,000-500,000
Number Employees: 5-9
Square Footage: 120000
Brands Exported: Pasrite, Raycord
Regions Exported to: Central America, Canada, Caribbean, Latin America, Mexico
Percentage of Business in Exporting: 5

49328 (HQ)Thompson Bagel Machine Mfg
8945 Ellis Ave
Los Angeles, CA 90034-3380   310-836-0900
    Fax: 310-836-0156 sales@bagelproducts.com
    www.bagelproducts.com
Manufacturer and exporter of one and two bank bagel machines including horizontal and vertical; also, two and four row rotary dividers.
President: Steve Thompson
sales@bagelproducts.com
Research & Development: Dan Thompson
Marketing/Sales: Charles Ducat
Operations Manager: Craig Thompson
Estimated Sales: $1-5 Million
Number Employees: 5-9
Number of Products: 10
Type of Packaging: Private Label
Regions Exported to: Europe

49329 Thompson Packers
550 Carnation St
Slidell, LA 70460-1899   985-641-6640
    Fax: 985-645-2112   800-989-6328
Began in 1953. Manufacturer and exporter of frozen beef, pork, veal and lamb; processor of frozen ground beef and hamburger patties.
Owner: Mary Thompson
thompson@thompack.com
Estimated Sales: $21 Million
Number Employees: 10-19
Square Footage: 50000
Type of Packaging: Consumer, Food Service, Private Label
Brands Exported: Cloverleaf
Regions Exported to: Mexico
Percentage of Business in Exporting: 1

49330 (HQ)Thomson-Leeds Company
450 Park Avenue S
2nd Floor
New York, NY 10016-7320   914-428-7255
    Fax: 914-428-7047   800-535-9361
Manufacturer, importer and exporter of displays, fixtures, package designs and point of purchase merchandising materials. Broker of specialty displays
President: Vince Esposito
CEO: Douglas Leeds
Director Marketing: Peter Weiller
Estimated Sales: $2.5-5 Million
Number Employees: 50-99
Square Footage: 80000
Brands Exported: Stockpop
Regions Exported to: Worldwide
Percentage of Business in Exporting: 10
Regions Imported from: Europe, Asia, Middle East, Canada, Mexico
Percentage of Business in Importing: 5

49331 Thorco Industries LLC
1300 E 12th St
Lamar, MO 64759   417-682-3375
    Fax: 417-682-1326   800-445-3375
Manufacturer and exporter of point of purchase displays, wire grids, store fixtures, bag holders and baskets
President: John Kuhahl
CFO: Jeff Gardener
Quality Control: Rodney Walters
Contact: Sarah Dorris
sdorris@lauracookseymusic.com
Number Employees: 500-999
Parent Co: Marmon Corporation
Regions Exported to: Canada

49332 Thoreson Mc Cosh Inc
1885 Thunderbird
Troy, MI 48084-5472   248-362-0960
    Fax: 248-362-5270   800-959-0805
    sales@thoresonmccosh.com
    www.thoresonmccosh.com
Manufacturer and exporter of dryers, hoppers, loaders and loading systems, tilters and bulk handling systems
President: David Klatt
sales@thoresonmccosh.com
Sales Exec: Steven Taugher
Estimated Sales: $10-20 Million
Number Employees: 20-49
Type of Packaging: Bulk
Regions Exported to: Worldwide
Percentage of Business in Exporting: 10

49333 Thorn Smith Laboratories
7755 Narrow Gauge Rd
Beulah, MI 49617-9792   231-882-4672
    Fax: 231-882-4804 auric@thornsmithlabs.com
    www.thornsmithlabs.com
Manufacturer and exporter of temperature specific sterilizer controls for use in quality assurance programs
President: Robert Brown
Plant Manager: Melanie Cederholm
Estimated Sales: Below $ 5 Million
Number Employees: 1-4
Square Footage: 17200
Brands Exported: Diack & Vac; Drytrol
Regions Exported to: Central America, South America, Europe, Asia, Australia
Percentage of Business in Exporting: 10

49334 Thorpe & Associates
227 N Chatnam Ave
Siler City, NC 27344-3443   919-742-5516
    Fax: 919-742-4657
Manufacturer and importer of chairs and tables
President: Bill Thorpe
VP Design: William Thorpe
VP Sales: Van Thorpe
Estimated Sales: Less than $500,000
Number Employees: 500
Square Footage: 400000
Regions Imported from: China

Importers & Exporters / A-Z

49335 Thoughtful Food
Lafayette, CA 510-910-2581
www.thoughtfulfood.net
Organic, gluten-free, dairy-free and vegan snack mix and granola
Founder/CEO: Jennifer Bielawski
Year Founded: 2009
Number of Brands: 2
Number of Products: 7
Type of Packaging: Consumer, Private Label
Brands Exported: Nosh Oranic, Giddy Up & Go
Regions Exported to: USA

49336 Three P
333 Andrew Ave
Salt Lake City, UT 84115-5113 801-486-7407
Fax: 801-571-4896
Manufacturer and exporter of custom printed and pressure sensitive decals, labels, tags, signs, etc
Owner: Edd Lancaster
Quality Control: Ernie Ashcroft
Marketing: Denise Lancaster
Sales: Edd Lancaster
Estimated Sales: $500,000-$1 Million
Number Employees: 5-9
Type of Packaging: Private Label, Bulk

49337 Three Trees Almondmilk
San Mateo, CA
855-863-8733
contact@threetrees.com www.threetrees.com
Organic, additive-free almond milk in unsweetened and vanilla varieties
Co-Founder: Jenny Eu
Number of Brands: 1
Number of Products: 2
Type of Packaging: Consumer, Private Label
Brands Exported: Three Trees
Regions Exported to: USA

49338 ThreeWorks Snacks
259 Niagara St., ON M6J 2L7
Canada
hello@threeworks.ca
www.threeworks.ca
Gluten-free, non-GMO, nut-free, no sugar added dehydrated apple chips in various flavors
Founder/CEO: Michael Petcherski
Year Founded: 2016
Number of Brands: 1
Number of Products: 6
Type of Packaging: Consumer, Private Label
Brands Exported: ThreeWorks
Regions Exported to: Canada, USA

49339 Thunder Group
717 Ferguson Drive
Los Angeles, CA 90022 323-290-0493
Fax: 323-869-9881 jwen@tarhong.com
www.tarhong.com
Estimated Sales: $300,000-500,000
Number Employees: 1-4

49340 Thunderbird Food Machinery
P.O. BOX 4768
4602 Brass Way
Blaine, WA 98231 214-331-3000
Fax: 214-331-3581 866-875-6868
tbfm@tbfm.com www.thunderbirdfm.com
Importer and wholesaler/distributor of food processing equipment including mixers, dough sheeters, vegetable and bread slicers, meat grinders, etc
Owner: Ky Lin
Marketing Director: Kara M
Estimated Sales: $1-2.5 Million
Number Employees: 5-9

49341 Thunderbird Real Food Bar
1101 - West 34th St. # 329
Austin, TX 78705 512-383-8334
support@thunderbirdbar.com
www.thunderbirdbar.com
Gluten-free, non-GMO, vegan, no-sugar-added fruit and nut snack bars in various flavors
Chief Executive Officer: Mike Elhaj
Number of Brands: 1
Number of Products: 14
Type of Packaging: Consumer, Private Label
Brands Exported: Thunderbird
Percentage of Business in Importing: 50

49342 Thyme and Truffles
51 Kesmark
Dollard-Des-Ormeaux
Montreal, QC H9B 3J1
Canada 514-685-9955
Fax: 514-685-2602 877-785-9759
lyndon.schreyer@platsduchef.com
www.thymeandtruffles.com

49343 Tieco-Unadilla Corporation
22 Depot Street
Unadilla, NY 13838 607-369-3236
Fax: 607-369-2011 877-889-6540
tieco@tyups.com www.tyups.com
Manufacturer and exporter of tying devices for securing bundles and pallets
President: Scott McLean
Estimated Sales: Below $500,000
Number Employees: 5-9
Brands Exported: Ty-Ups; Duo Cord Hangers
Regions Exported to: Central America, South America, Europe, Canada, Caribbean, Mexico
Percentage of Business in Exporting: 8

49344 Tier-Rack Corp
425 Sovereign Ct
Ballwin, MO 63011-4432 636-527-0700
Fax: 636-256-4901 800-325-7869
info@tier-rack.com www.tier-rack.com
Manufacturer and exporter of portable storage racks
Owner: Scott Ten Eyck
steneyck@tier-rack.com
General Manager: George Willis
Controller: Ward Wilson
Estimated Sales: $1 - 2.5 Million
Number Employees: 10-19
Square Footage: 150000
Regions Exported to: Central America, Asia, Canada, Caribbean, Mexico
Percentage of Business in Exporting: 2

49345 (HQ)Tierra Farm
2424 NY-203
Valatie, NY 12184 519-392-8300
Fax: 518-392-8304 info@tierrafarm.com
www.tierrafarm.com
Organic and gluten-free nut butters and nuts, raw and roasted seeds, dried fruit mixes, granolas, chocolate snacks and fair-trade coffee beans
Founder/President: Gunther Fishgold
Chief Executive Officer: Todd Kletter
Year Founded: 1999
Number of Brands: 1
Type of Packaging: Consumer, Private Label, Bulk
Brands Exported: Tierra Farm
Regions Exported to: USA

49346 Tiesta Tea
213 West Institute Place # 310
Chicago, IL 60610 312-202-6800
customerservice@tiestatea.com
www.tiestatea.com
Loose leaf tea blends in various flavors; cold brew bottled tea
Co-Founder: Patrick Tannous
Co-Founder/Chief Executive Officer: Dan Klein
Year Founded: 2010
Number of Brands: 1
Number of Products: 50
Type of Packaging: Consumer, Private Label
Brands Exported: Tiesta Tea
Regions Exported to: USA

49347 Tiger Botanicalsl
33 Hammond
Suite 206
Irvine, CA 92618 949-768-4437
Fax: 949-461-0214 855-858-4437
Importer and distributor of Baobab and other unique ingredients including oils and extracts.
President & CEO: Hugh Lamond
Manager: Jazmin Jaleh
Estimated Sales: $500 Thousand
Type of Packaging: Bulk
Regions Imported from: West Africa

49348 Tiger Corporation/I-Ward
15531 Carmenita Rd
Santa Fe Springs, CA 90670-5609 562-926-7171
Fax: 562-926-3383 iwardusa@msn.com
Manager: Henry Choi
Estimated Sales: $ 5 - 10 Million
Number Employees: 5-9

49349 Tigo+
786-207-4772
info@tigosportsdrink.com
www.tigosportsdrink.com
Sports drink made with coconut water and amino acids, sweetened with Stevia; various flavors
Number of Brands: 1
Number of Products: 5
Type of Packaging: Consumer, Private Label
Brands Exported: Tigo+

49350 Tillamook Country Smoker
8335 North Hwy. 101
Bay City, OR 97107
www.tcsjerky.com
Beef jerky, steak cuts, nuggets, jerky sticks and other snacks
Co-Founder: Dick Crossley
Year Founded: 1975
Number of Brands: 1
Type of Packaging: Consumer, Private Label
Brands Exported: Tillamook Country Smoker
Regions Exported to: USA

49351 Tillamook County Creamery Association
Tillamook, OR 503-842-4481
Fax: 503-842-6039 www.tillamook.com
Dairy butter, cheese, nonhygroscopic cheddar cheese whey powder and ice cream; exporter of dried whey, sour cream, yogurt, fluid milk.
Chief Executive Officer: Patrick Criteser
Chief Financial Officer: Linda Pearce
Director of R&D: Jill Allen
Vice President Sales & Marketing: Jay Allison
Plant & Facilities Manager: Rich Snyder
Year Founded: 1909
Estimated Sales: $49.4 Million
Number Employees: 250-499
Square Footage: 30000
Type of Packaging: Consumer, Food Service, Private Label, Bulk
Regions Exported to: Asia
Percentage of Business in Exporting: 1

49352 Tilly Industries
4210 Blvd Poirier
St Laurent, QC H4R 2C5
Canada 514-331-4922
Fax: 514-331-4924 www.tillyindustries.com
Manufacturer and exporter of aluminum foil dies for pie plates and containers
VP: Dagmar Tilly
Estimated Sales: $ 1 - 5 Million
Number Employees: 8
Square Footage: 36000
Parent Co: Maven Engineering Corporation
Regions Exported to: USA
Percentage of Business in Exporting: 75

49353 Tim's Cascade Snacks
PO Box 2302
Auburn, WA 98071-2302 253-833-2986
Fax: 253-939-9411 800-533-8467
consumer_affairs@timschips.com
www.timschips.com
Snacks including original potato chips, jalapeno, sour cream and onion, cheddar. sea salt, dill picklie, onion ring chips, and popcorn.
President: Dennis M Mullen
COO: Jeff Leichleiter
Sales/Marketing Executive: George Masiello
Year Founded: 1986
Estimated Sales: $ 20 - 50 Million
Number Employees: 50-99
Square Footage: 130000
Parent Co: Agrilink Foods
Type of Packaging: Consumer, Food Service, Private Label
Regions Exported to: Worldwide

49354 Timely Signs Inc
2135 Linden Blvd
Elmont, NY 11003-3901 516-285-5339
Fax: 516-285-9637 800-457-4467
sales@timelysigns.net
Manufacturer and exporter of labels, marketing signs and banners; wholesaler/distributor of computerized sign making equipment

President: Gene Goldsmith
signs11003@aol.com
Estimated Sales: $1-2.5 Million
Number Employees: 5-9
Square Footage: 4000
Regions Exported to: Central America, South America, Europe
Percentage of Business in Exporting: 5

49355 Timemed Labeling Systems
27770 N Entertainment Drive
Suite 200
Valencia, CA 91355   818-897-1111
Fax: 818-686-9317 intl@pdcorp.com
www.pdchealthcare.com
Manufacturer and exporter of pressure-sensitive labels, embossed seals and printed gummed tapes
President: Jerry Nerad
General Manager: Lee Smith
Contact: Tima Fanning
tima.fanning@phoenix.edu
Plant Manager: Dave Luther
Estimated Sales: $ 10 - 20 Million
Number Employees: 20-49
Parent Co: Timemed Labeling Systems
Regions Exported to: Worldwide
Percentage of Business in Exporting: 5

49356 Tin Star Foods
Austin, TX
info@tinstarfoods.com
www.tinstarfoods.com
Grassfed cultured ghee; lactose- and casein-free
Founder/Chief Executive Officer: Hima Pal
Year Founded: 2014
Number Employees: 2-10
Number of Brands: 1
Number of Products: 1
Type of Packaging: Consumer, Private Label
Brands Exported: Tin Star Foods

49357 Tindall Packaging
1150 E U Ave
Vicksburg, MI 49097   269-649-1163
Fax: 616-649-1163
Manufacturer and exporter of filling equipment for dairy, deli and cultured products; also, single and two-flavor variegators
President: Marianne Tindall
marianne@tindallpackaging.com
VP: Marianne Tindall
Quality Control: Frank Tindall
Number Employees: 5
Regions Exported to: Central America, South America, Europe, Asia
Percentage of Business in Exporting: 3

49358 Tiny Hero Foods
200 Kansas St. # 205
San Francisco, CA 94103
855-778-4662
www.tinyherofoods.com
Golden quinoa, quinoa and rice blends, quinoa side dishes, quinoa macaroni and cheese dish, quinoa breakfast packs
Chief Executive Officer: Aaron Jackson
Director, Marketing: Christine Lee
Year Founded: 2016
Number Employees: 2-10
Number of Brands: 1
Type of Packaging: Consumer, Private Label
Brands Exported: The Tiny Hero

49359 Tip Top Poultry Inc
327 Wallace Rd
Marietta, GA 30062-3573   770-973-8070
Fax: 770-973-6897 800-241-5230
www.tiptoppoultry.com
Processor and exporter of poultry
President: Evelyn Delong
evelyn.delong@regalpoultry.com
COO: Mike Brooks
CFO: Charlie Singleton
VP: Lee Bates
VP/Sales: Brian Tucker
Technical VP: Mitch Forstie
Production Manager: Steve Moore
Estimated Sales: $15 Million
Number Employees: 1000-4999
Type of Packaging: Consumer, Bulk

49360 Tipiak Inc
45 Church St
Suite 303
Stamford, CT 06906-1733   203-961-9117
Fax: 203-975-9081 sales@tipiak-e.com
www.tipiak.com
Specialty rices and beans, tapioca flour and pearls, frozen appetizers and desserts.
President: Laurent Chery
laurent.chery@tipiak-e.com
VP: Laurent Chery
Estimated Sales: Below $ 5 Million
Number Employees: 5-9

49361 Tipper Tie Inc
2000 Lufkin Rd
Apex, NC 27539-7068   919-362-8811
Fax: 919-362-4839 www.tippertie.com
Clippers, aluminum clips, aluminum wire products, electric fence supplies and netting
President: Gernot Foerster
Chief Financial Officer: Roman Steiger
Vice President: Robert Cleveland
Directory, Quality: Tim Downes
Marketing Executive: Emy Mooffitt
Sales Manager: Bryan Wilkins
Officer Manager: Ashley Gideon
Purchasing: Sue Chandler
Estimated Sales: $ 35 Million
Number Employees: 100-249
Square Footage: 130000
Parent Co: Dover Corporation
Brands Exported: Tipper Clippers
Regions Exported to: Central America, South America, Europe, Asia, Middle East
Percentage of Business in Exporting: 40

49362 Tirawisu
13705 Ventura Blvd
Sherman Oaks, CA 91423-3023   818-906-2640
Fax: 516-599-6540
Exporter and processor of Italian desserts including chocolate mousse, tiramisu, gelato, tartufo, tortoni and spumoni; importer of Italian cakes and pasta
Owner/President: Aldo Antonoacci
Contact: Peter Kastelan
peter@il-tiramisu.com
Estimated Sales: Less Than $500,000
Number Employees: 5-9
Regions Imported from: Europe
Percentage of Business in Importing: 25

49363 Tisma Machinery Corporation
1099 Estes Avenue
Elk Grove Village, IL 60007-4907   847-427-9525
Fax: 847-427-9550 bwilliams@swfcompanies.com
Manufacturer and exporter of automatic cartoning machinery and systems
Estimated Sales: $ 10-20 Million
Number Employees: 50-99
Square Footage: 176000
Regions Exported to: Worldwide
Percentage of Business in Exporting: 50

49364 Titan Industries Inc
735 Industrial Loop Rd
New London, WI 54961-2600   920-982-6600
Fax: 920-982-7750 800-558-3616
www.titanconveyors.com
Manufacturer and exporter of conveyors
President: Dan Baumbach
dbaumbach@titansystems.com
Estimated Sales: $ 5-10 Million
Number Employees: 20-49
Square Footage: 84000
Regions Exported to: Canada, Mexico
Percentage of Business in Exporting: 2

49365 Tni Packaging Inc
333 Charles Ct # 101
West Chicago, IL 60185-2604   630-293-3030
Fax: 630-293-5303 800-383-0990
www.tnipackaging.com
Manufacturer and exporter of open mesh netting bags, pre-tied elastic poultry trusses and mechanical meat tenderizers
President: Jerry J Marchese
jmarchese@tnipackaging.com
Marketing Director: Ana Tirado
Sales Director: Jane Larsen
Plant Manager: Victor Castijelo
Estimated Sales: $3-5 Million
Number Employees: 5-9
Number of Brands: 7
Number of Products: 4
Square Footage: 48000
Type of Packaging: Consumer, Food Service, Private Label, Bulk
Brands Exported: Mister Tenderizer; Chicken-Tuckers
Regions Exported to: Central America, South America, Europe, Canada

49366 ToastmasterA Middleby Company
10 Sunnen Drive
St. Louis, MO 61343   314-781-2777
Fax: 314-781-3636 800-264-7827
Manufacturer of conveyor and pop-up toasters, fryers, convection ovens, smokers, fryers, griddles, charbroilers, and hot food drawers
President: Mark Sieron
Estimated Sales: $ 1 - 3 Million
Number Employees: 5-9

49367 Toastmaster
1400 Toastmaster Drive
Elgin, IL 60120-9274   847-741-3300
Fax: 847-741-0015 mww@middleby.com
www.toastmastercorp.com
Manufacturer and exporter of broilers, fryers, griddles, grills, hot plates, ovens, ranges, rotisseries and toasters
President: Mark Sieron
Estimated Sales: $ 1 - 5 Million
Number Employees: 5-9
Parent Co: Middleby Corporation
Regions Exported to: Worldwide

49368 Toastmasters International
23182 Arroyo Vis
Rancho Sta Marg, CA 92688-2699   949-858-8255
Fax: 949-858-1207 www.toastmasters.org
Wholesaler/distributor and importer of ovens, ranges and freezers; serving the food service market
President: Jo Stante
govarea05d@tmdistrict38.org
First Vice President: Jim KoKocki
Number Employees: 50-99
Type of Packaging: Food Service
Regions Imported from: Europe, USA
Percentage of Business in Importing: 85

49369 Todd's
PO Box 4821
Des Moines, IA 50305   515-266-2276
Fax: 515-266-1669 800-247-5363
Variety of food products, wet and dry, kosher and organic certified.
President/CEO: Alan Niedermeier
Quality Control: Diana Burzloff
Public Relations: Alissa Douglas
Operations: Duane Hettkamp
Production: Jeff Sullivan
Plant Manager: John Routh
Purchasing: Danielle Robinson
Estimated Sales: $ 1 - 3 Million
Number Employees: 30
Number of Brands: 40
Number of Products: 200
Square Footage: 320000
Type of Packaging: Consumer, Food Service, Private Label, Bulk
Brands Exported: Private Label, Todd's Ltd, Papa Joe's Specialty Foods
Regions Exported to: Central America, South America, Asia
Percentage of Business in Exporting: 10

49370 Todd's
6055 Malburg Way
Vernon, CA 90058   323-585-5900
Fax: 323-585-5900 800-938-6337
Processor, importer and exporter of nuts and nut meats, dried fruit, trail mixes, candy, etc
President: Todd Levin
Estimated Sales: $ 5 - 10 Million
Number Employees: 5-9
Type of Packaging: Consumer, Food Service, Private Label, Bulk
Brands Exported: Todd's Treats; Buenositos
Regions Exported to: Asia
Percentage of Business in Exporting: 1
Regions Imported from: South America, Middle East
Percentage of Business in Importing: 2

Importers & Exporters / A-Z

49371 (HQ)Toddy Products Inc
803 W Kansas Ave
Midland, TX 79701-6121 713-225-2066
Fax: 713-225-2110 www.toddycafe.com
Processor and exporter of liquid concentrates including coffee, tea, mocha, chai, etc.; also, espresso pecan brittle; manufacturer of cold brew coffee makers
Owner: Strother Simpson
Vice President: Scott Schroer
Contact: Kathy Kat
kkat@toddycafe.com
Estimated Sales: $1500000
Number Employees: 5-9
Square Footage: 80000
Type of Packaging: Consumer, Food Service, Private Label, Bulk
Regions Exported to: Asia
Percentage of Business in Exporting: 5
Regions Imported from: Africa

49372 Todhunter Foods
222 Lakeview Avenue
Suite 1500
West Palm Beach, FL 33401-6174 561-655-8977
Fax: 561-655-9718 800-336-9463
www.todhunter.com
Cooking wines, powdered wine flavors, denatures spirits, vinegar and wine reductions.
President: Jay Maltby
CFO: Ezra Shashoua
Vice President: D Chris Mitchell
Sales Director: Jim Polansky
Plant Manager: Ousik Yu
Purchasing Manager: Frank Dibling
Number Employees: 410
Parent Co: Todhunter International
Type of Packaging: Consumer, Food Service, Private Label, Bulk

49373 Todhunter Foods
PO Box 1447
Lake Alfred, FL 33850-1447 863-956-1116
Fax: 863-956-3979 www.todhunter.com
Vinegar and cooking wine; contract packager of fruit juices and carbonated/flavored beverages; importer of alcoholic beverages and juice concentrates; exporter of alcoholic beverages and vinegar
President: Jay Maltby
Number Employees: 100-249
Square Footage: 1800000
Parent Co: Todhunter International
Type of Packaging: Consumer, Food Service, Private Label, Bulk
Regions Exported to: Central America, South America, Europe, Middle East
Percentage of Business in Exporting: 5
Regions Imported from: Central America, South America, Europe

49374 Tofutti Brands Inc
50 Jackson Dr
Cranford, NJ 07016-3504 908-272-2400
Fax: 908-272-9492 info@tofutti.com
www.tofutti.com
Processor and exporter of nondairy food products including imitation cream cheese, no-cholesterol egg products made of egg whites and tofu with added vitamins and minerals and frozen tofu desserts
CEO: Shana Joseph
sjoseph@tofutti.com
CEO: David Mintz
CFO: Steven Kass
Director: Neal Axelrod
Estimated Sales: $10-20 Million
Number Employees: 5-9
Type of Packaging: Consumer, Food Service, Bulk
Regions Exported to: Central America, Middle East

49375 Token Factory
2131 South Ave
La Crosse, WI 54601 608-785-2439
888-486-5367
custserv@tokenfactory.com
www.tokenfactory.com
Manufacturer and exporter of plastic tokens and swizzle sticks
President: Dale Stevens
Sales Manager: Rosie Hundt
Estimated Sales: $1-2.5 Million
Number Employees: 11
Regions Exported to: Worldwide
Percentage of Business in Exporting: 10

49376 Tokheim Co
560 31st St
Marion, IA 52302-3724 319-362-4847
Fax: 319-377-7953 800-747-3442
info@tokheimco.com www.tokheimco.com
Manufacturer and exporter of liquid level gauges for large storage tanks
President: Vicky Barnes
Quality Control: Chris Peyton
VP: Thomas Barnes
Sales: Barb Riffey
Manager: Tom Barnes
tom.barnes@tokheimco.com
Estimated Sales: Less Than $500,000
Number Employees: 1-4
Square Footage: 40000
Regions Exported to: Worldwide
Percentage of Business in Exporting: 10

49377 (HQ)Tolan Machinery Company
PO Box 695
164 Franklin Ave.
Rockaway, NJ 7866 973-983-7212
Fax: 973-983-7217 www.tolanmachinery.com
Manufacturer and exporter of tanks, reactors, hoppers, bins, heat exchangers, storage vessels and fermentors
President: John Tolpa
VP, General Manager: Stephen Tolpa
Chief Engineer: Bill Ebbinghouser
VP Sales/Marketing: Thomas Spencer
Operations Manager: Brian T. Gill
Estimated Sales: $ 10 - 20 Million
Number Employees: 20-49
Square Footage: 80000
Regions Exported to: Asia, Puerto Rico

49378 Tolas Health Care Packaging
905 Pennsylvania Blvd
Feasterville Trevose, PA 19053 215-322-7900
Fax: 215-322-9034 marketing@tolas.com
www.tolas.com
Printed and converted paper, foil and plastics for packaging; exporter of paper, barrier films and foils
President: Carl D Marotta
CFO: Chuck Klink
Quality Control: Skip Peacock
R & D: Chris Perry
Marketing Team Leader: Denise Dilissio
Sales Director: Leslie Love
l.love@ciprianopi.com
Operations Manager: Dave Preikszas
Purchasing Manager: Jim McNally
Estimated Sales: $20 Million
Number Employees: 100-249
Square Footage: 50000
Regions Exported to: Europe, Asia, Canada

49379 Toledo Ticket Co
3963 Catawba St
PO Box 6876
Toledo, OH 43612-1492 419-476-5424
Fax: 419-476-6801 800-533-6620
www.toledoticket.com
Manufacturer and exporter of labels and coupons
President: Roy Carter
VP Sales and Marketing: Tom Carter
Estimated Sales: $5-10 Million
Number Employees: 20-49
Regions Exported to: Worldwide

49380 Tom's Snacks Company
8600 S Boulevard
Charlotte, NC 28273 706-323-2721
Fax: 706-323-8231 800-995-2623
www.tomsfoods.com
Potato chips, thick and bold chips, thunder chips, cheezers, pork skins, rings, fries, corn and tortilla, bugles and mega twisters
Supply Chain VP, Lance Inc.: Blake Thompson
Contact: Marc Albers
malbers@tomsfoods.com
Estimated Sales: $ .5 - 1 million
Number Employees: 50-99
Parent Co: Lance, Inc.
Type of Packaging: Consumer
Regions Exported to: Worldwide

49381 Tomich Brothers Seafoods
2208 Signal Pl
San Pedro, CA 90731 310-832-5365
Fax: 310-832-9578
Wholesaler/distributor and exporter of seafood
Owner: Frank Tomich
ftomich@tomichbros.com
Sales/Product Inquiries Contact: Julie Heberer
Shipping/Logistics Inquiries Contact: Angela Felix
Estimated Sales: $5-10 Million
Number Employees: 10-19

49382 Tomlinson Industries
13700 Broadway Ave
Cleveland, OH 44125-1945 216-587-3400
Fax: 216-587-0733 800-945-4589
jengle@tomlinsonind.com www.tomlinsonind.com
Manufacturer and exporter of faucets and fittings, kettles, warmers and dispensers for cups, cones, lids, straws, napkins and condiments; also, table top organizers, thermal platters and cook and serve skillets;foodservice glovescutting boards and anti-fatigue mats.
President: Michael Figas
CEO: H Meyer
CFO: Donald Calkins
VP: Louis Castro
Quality Control: John Silcox
Marketing: Jeanne Engle
Operations: Kenneth Sidoti
Purchasing: Michael Ritley
Estimated Sales: $ 20 - 50 Million
Number Employees: 100-249
Square Footage: 120000
Parent Co: Meyer Company
Regions Exported to: Worldwide
Percentage of Business in Exporting: 25

49383 Tommy's Jerky Outlet
8640 Mentor Ave
Mentor, OH 44060-6140 440-255-3994
Fax: 305-723-7686 866-448-6942
info@tommyjerky.com www.tommysjerky.com
Beef jerky and jerky spices
President: Thomas Stabosz
Production: Joe Muscarella
Number Employees: 5-9
Number of Brands: 1
Number of Products: 9
Parent Co: TFS
Type of Packaging: Consumer, Food Service, Private Label, Bulk

49384 Tomsed Corporation
420 McKinney Pkwy
Lillington, NC 27546 910-814-3800
Fax: 910-814-3899 800-334-5552
Manufacturer and exporter of access control equipment including high security and waist-high turnstiles, handicapped gates, portable posts and sign holders; wholesaler/distributor of portable and fixed crowd railing
President: Robert Sedivy
CEO: Thomas Sedivy
CFO: Karin Sedivy
Sales: Russell Socles
Estimated Sales: $15 Million
Number Employees: 100-249
Number of Brands: 9
Number of Products: 100
Square Footage: 220000
Regions Exported to: Central America, South America, Europe, Asia, Middle East,
Percentage of Business in Exporting: 25

49385 Tone Products Inc
2129 N 15th Ave
Melrose Park, IL 60160-1406 708-681-3660
Fax: 708-681-2368 800-536-8663
Processor and exporter of fountain beverages, energy drinks, fruit smoothies, pancake syrups, beverage concentrates, sauces and marinades.
President/CEO: Tim Evon
CEO: Timothy E Evon
timevon@toneproducts.com
Chief Financial Officer: William Hamen
Director, National Accounts: Tim Collins
VP, Sales: William Evon
Director, Operations: Greg Sperry
Director of Purchasing: Matt Claus
Estimated Sales: $12 Million
Number Employees: 50-99
Number of Brands: 9
Square Footage: 46000
Type of Packaging: Consumer, Private Label, Bulk

Importers & Exporters / A-Z

49386 Tonex
27 Park Row
Wallington, NJ 07057-1629   973-773-5135
Fax: 973-916-1091 tonexinc@aol.com
Cappuccino, nondairy creamers, instant coffee and tea and chocolate covered nuts; importer and exporter of beer, vodka, candy, fresh and dried fruits, tea, instant cappuccino, juice and juice concentrates, etc
Owner: Bogdan Torbus
President: Grace Torbus
Marketing Director: Angela Torbus
Type of Packaging: Consumer, Food Service, Private Label, Bulk
Regions Exported to: Worldwide
Percentage of Business in Exporting: 50
Regions Imported from: South America, Europe
Percentage of Business in Importing: 50

49387 Tonnino
7805 North West 15 Street
Suite 506
Miami, FL 33126   888-325-8621
info@tonnino.com
www.tonnino.com
Yellowfin tuna

49388 Tony Downs Foods
54934 210th Ln
Mankato, MN 56001   507-387-3663
Fax: 507-388-6420 866-731-4561
mdowns@downsfoodgroup.com
www.tonydownsfoods.com
Poultry fully cooked, diced-frozen and commercial and retail canned chicken.
President: Mike Downs
mdowns@downsfoodgroup.com
Vice President: Greg Cook
Director, Human Resources: David Ross
Year Founded: 1947
Estimated Sales: $22 Million
Number Employees: 20-49
Square Footage: 100000
Type of Packaging: Consumer, Food Service, Private Label, Bulk
Regions Exported to: Canada

49389 Toom Dips
Saint Paul, MN   651-447-8666
www.toomdips.com
Garlic dip made with all natural ingredients and based on Lebanese toum sauce, in various flavors
Founder/Chief Executive Officer: Matty Joyce
Number of Brands: 1
Number of Products: 4
Type of Packaging: Consumer, Private Label
Brands Exported: Toom
Regions Exported to: USA

49390 Tooterville Trolley Company
5422 Bice Lane
Newburgh, IN 47630-8815   812-858-8585
Fax: 812-858-8580
Manufacturer and exporter of mobile carts including shaved ice, fruit and salad bar; also, soda vending machines
Owner: Thomas Rennels
Number Employees: 1
Square Footage: 2400
Regions Exported to: Central America, South America, Europe, Asia, Middle East, Australia
Percentage of Business in Exporting: 25

49391 Tootsi Impex
8800 Blvd Henri Bourassa West
Saint Laurent, QC H4S 1P4
Canada   514-381-9790
Fax: 514-387-9314 888-505-7028
sales@tootsiimpex.com www.tootsiimpex.com
Nuts and dried fruits; conventional bulk foods.
President: Ali Shayesteh
VP: Farhad Shayesteh
Marketing: Matt Mousavi
Sales: Jean-Luc Lachance
Number Employees: 5-9
Type of Packaging: Bulk
Regions Exported to: Europe, Asia, Middle East, Africa, Australia
Percentage of Business in Exporting: 50
Regions Imported from: Europe, Asia, Middle East, Africa, Australia, Latin America, U.S.A.
Percentage of Business in Importing: 50

49392 Tootsie Roll Industries Inc.
7401 S. Cicero Ave.
Chicago, IL 60629   773-838-3400
Fax: 773-838-3435 866-972-6879
tootiseroll@worldpantry.com www.tootsie.com
Candy.
President/CEO/Director: Ellen Gordon
VP Finance/CFO: G. Howard Ember
VP: George Rost
Year Founded: 1896
Estimated Sales: $550 Million
Number Employees: 2,201
Number of Brands: 23
Square Footage: 2375000
Type of Packaging: Consumer, Food Service, Bulk
Brands Exported: All Brands Manufactured
Regions Exported to: Worldwide

49393 (HQ)Top Line Process Equipment Company
PO Box 264
Bradford, PA 16701   814-362-4626
Fax: 814-362-4453 800-458-6095
topline@toplineonline.com
www.toplineonline.com
Supplier of hygienic stainless steel process equipment
CEO: Dan McCone
VP: Kevin O'Donnell
Marketing: Debra Fowler
Sales: John Quteri
Contact: Thomas Nicola
tnicola@toplineonline.com
Operations: Tom Wilson
Plant Manager: Tim Fox
Purchasing: Marlene Raszmann
Number Employees: 5-9
Regions Exported to: Worldwide
Percentage of Business in Exporting: 15

49394 Top Tier Foods Inc.
3737 Oak St.
Vancouver, BC V6H SM4
Canada   778-628-0015
hello@toptierfoods.com
www.toptierfoods.com
Ready-to-serve quinoa pilafs in various flavors; sushi quinoa
President: Blair Bullus
Year Founded: 2013
Number of Brands: 1
Type of Packaging: Consumer, Private Label
Brands Exported: Quinoa Quickies
Regions Exported to: USA

49395 Topo Chico Mineral Water
5800 Granite Pkwy. # 900
Plano, TX 75024   888-456-4357
www.topochicousa.net
Sparkling mineral water in various flavors; bottled at source in Monterrey, Mexico
General Manager: Gerardo Galvan
Year Founded: 1895
Number of Brands: 1
Type of Packaging: Consumer, Private Label
Brands Exported: Topo Chico

49396 Toppo by Carlisle
PO Box 53006
Oklahoma City, OK 73152   405-475-5600
Fax: 405-475-5607 800-654-8210
www.carlislefsp.com
Number Employees: 250-499

49397 Tops Manufacturing Co
83 Salisbury Rd
Darien, CT 06820-2225   203-655-9367
Coffee and tea equipment including percolators, knobs, handles, carafes, coffee makers and filters, tea infusers, liquid coffee flavors, glass cups, instant and ground coffee dispensers, measuring spoons, etc
President: Michael Davies
michael@endeavourpartners.net
VP: Pat Himmel
Sales Manager: Ernie Hurlbut
Estimated Sales: Less than $500,000
Number Employees: 1-4
Square Footage: 31400
Type of Packaging: Consumer, Food Service
Regions Exported to: Worldwide
Percentage of Business in Exporting: 15

49398 Torbeck Industries
355 Industrial Dr
Harrison, OH 45030-1483   513-367-0080
Fax: 513-367-0081 800-333-0080
Producer of material handling and safety equipment used in manufacturing, distribution and warehousing facilities throughout North America.
President: R L Torbeck Jr
Estimated Sales: $10,000,000 - $49,900,000
Number Employees: 50-99
Square Footage: 80000

49399 Toroid Corp
225 Wynn Dr NW
Huntsville, AL 35805-1958   256-837-7510
Fax: 256-837-7512 toroidcorp@hotmail.com
www.toroidcorp.com
Custom weighing equipment, load cells and repairing load cells.
President: Anne Paelian
toroidcorp@hotmail.com
Vice President/Sales Manager: Paul Paelian
Estimated Sales: $1 Million
Number Employees: 10-19
Square Footage: 80000
Brands Exported: Toroid; Low Boy; Omniflex
Regions Exported to: Asia, Middle East
Percentage of Business in Exporting: 20

49400 Toromont Process Systems
395 W 1100 N
North Salt Lake, UT 84054-2621   801-292-1747
Fax: 801-292-9908
www.toromontpowersystems.com
Manufacturer and exporter of custom designed industrial and chemical refrigeration systems
President: Hugo Sorenson
CFO: Jerry Frailec
Manager: Jim Shepherd
Contact: Vladimir Kratser
vkratser@toromontsystems.com
Estimated Sales: $30-50 Million
Number Employees: 10
Square Footage: 70000
Parent Co: Toromont Industries
Other Locations:
    Toromont Process Systems
    Malden, MA Toromont Process Systems
Regions Exported to: South America, Europe, Asia, Middle East, Australia
Percentage of Business in Exporting: 50
Regions Imported from: Worldwide
Percentage of Business in Importing: 10

49401 Toronto Fabricating & Manufacturing
1021 Rangeview Road
Mississauga, ON L5E 1H2
Canada   905-891-2516
Fax: 905-891-7446 sales@tfmc.com
www.tfmc.com
Manufacturer and exporter of tables, chairs, table tops and bases, benches, barstools and decorative lighting sconces and fixtures
Manager: Allan Farnum

49402 Torpac Capsules
333 Route 46
Fairfield, NJ 07004   973-244-1125
Fax: 973-244-1365 www.torpac.com
Processor, importer and exporter of gelatin capsules; manufacturer and exporter of capsule filling machinery
President: Raj Tahil
Quality Control: Ajay Varma
Estimated Sales: Below $5 Million
Number Employees: 10
Square Footage: 40000
Type of Packaging: Consumer
Regions Exported to: Worldwide
Percentage of Business in Exporting: 50
Regions Imported from: Europe, Asia
Percentage of Business in Importing: 20

49403 Torre Products Co Inc
479 Washington St
New York, NY 10013-1381   212-925-8989
Fax: 212-925-4627
Manufacturer, importer and exporter of flavoring extracts and essential oils
Owner: Liberty F Raho
Estimated Sales: $10-20 Million
Number Employees: 5-9
Square Footage: 33000

Importers & Exporters / A-Z

Regions Exported to: Central America, South America
Regions Imported from: Europe
Percentage of Business in Importing: 5

49404 Torrefazione Barzula & Import
3117 Wharton Way
Mississauga, ON L4X 2B6
Canada   905-625-6082
       Fax: 905-625-5741   866-358-5488
       sales@barzula.com www.barzula.com
Processor, importer and exporter of coffee beans including green, espresso, Turkish and decaffeinated
President: Luigi Russignan
Treasurer: Gigliola Russignan
VP: Phil Cennova
Estimated Sales: $2.2 Million
Number Employees: 14
Number of Brands: 1
Number of Products: 12
Square Footage: 48000
Regions Exported to: Europe
Regions Imported from: Central America, South America, Africa
Percentage of Business in Importing: 90

49405 Torter Corporation
P.O.Box 367
Montville, NJ 07045   973-299-2811
       Fax: 973-299-0252   800-867-8371
Importer of frozen fruits and juice concentrates; broker of ingredients
President: Joseph Torter
VP Sales: Thomas Torter
Estimated Sales: $5-10 Million
Number Employees: 5-9
Type of Packaging: Bulk
Regions Imported from: South America, Europe
Percentage of Business in Importing: 60

49406 Toscarora
2901 W Monroe Street
Sandusky, OH 44870-1810   419-625-7343
       Fax: 419-625-1171
Manufacturer and exporter of custom designed plastic thermoformed food trays; also, custom designed cookie trays
Operations Manager: Joe Knight
Plant Manager: Mike LaFond
Estimated Sales: $10-20 Million
Number Employees: 50-99
Square Footage: 200000
Regions Exported to: South America, Europe
Percentage of Business in Exporting: 5

49407 Toshoku America
4 Park Plz
Suite 570
Irvine, CA 92614-8505
       www.cargill.co.jp/en/toshoku-global-offices
Exporter of frozen and fresh fruits and vegetables.
Secretary: Takeshi Higashio
takeshi_higashio@toshoku.com
Estimated Sales: $77 Million
Parent Co: Cargill Inc.
Regions Exported to: Asia
Percentage of Business in Exporting: 90
Regions Imported from: Asia
Percentage of Business in Importing: 10

49408 Tosi & Company
624 Main Street
Vancouver, BC V6A 2V3
Canada   604-681-5740
       Fax: 604-685-5704 tosifoods.com
Wholesaler/distributor and importer of Italian products including vinegar, olive oil, pasta, cheese, salami, almonds, pine nuts, canned tomatoes, rice, beans and stock fish; also, Greek olives; serving the food service market-Rosottoand Balsamic Vinegar
President: Bill Tosi
Sales Manager: J Martin
Plant Manager: R Calabrigo
Purchasing: Angelo Tosi
Estimated Sales: $1.5 Million
Number Employees: 1-4
Square Footage: 36000
Brands Imported: Angelo; Sagra; Tiger; Pagami; Bertarini; Galetti
Regions Imported from: Europe

49409 Tosi Trading Company
47 Bay State Road
Boston, MA 02215-2114   617-247-3300
       Fax: 617-247-7533
Importer of Italian foods including olive and blended oils, pasta, breadsticks, balsamic and white wine vinegar, mini-snack sticks, rice and torcetti cookies
President: Linda Tosi
VP/Treasurer: Tod Minotti
Estimated Sales: $2.5-5 Million
Number Employees: 1-4
Square Footage: 840000
Type of Packaging: Consumer, Food Service, Private Label, Bulk
Brands Imported: Gondola; G'Pagani
Regions Imported from: Europe
Percentage of Business in Importing: 100

49410 Tote Vision
1319 Dexter Ave N Ste 20
Seattle, WA 98109   206-623-6000
       Fax: 206-623-6609 www.totevision.com
President: Bill Taraday
Contact: Rachel Anderson
r.anderson@totevision.com
Estimated Sales: $ 5 - 10 Million
Number Employees: 5-9

49411 Toter Inc
841 Meacham Rd
Statesville, NC 28677-2983 704-872-8171
       Fax: 704-878-0734   800-772-0071
       toter@toter.com www.toter.com
Manufacturer and exporter of carts and lifter systems
President: Jeff Gilliam
jgilliam@wastequip.com
VP Sales: Rick Hoffman
Estimated Sales: $50-100 Million
Number Employees: 50-99
Regions Exported to: Worldwide

49412 Touch Menus
1601 116th Ave NE # 111
Bellevue, WA 98004-3010   425-881-3100
       Fax: 425-881-2980   800-688-6368
Manufacturer and exporter of touch screen point of sale systems and software; also, credit card services available
VP: Darrin Howell
Marketing Manager: Gill Gilman
Estimated Sales: $ 5-10 Million
Number Employees: 5-9
Square Footage: 8000
Type of Packaging: Private Label
Regions Exported to: Canada

49413 Touchtunes Music Corporation
1110 W Lake Cook Road
Suite 100
Buffalo Grove, IL 60089-1965 847-419-3300
       Fax: 847-419-3304 www.touchtunes.com

49414 Toufayan Bakeries
175 Railroad Ave
Ridgefield, NJ 07657-2312 201-861-4131
       Fax: 201-861-0392 msteve@toufayan.com
       www.toufayan.com
Pita bread, flatbread, bagels, wraps, lavash, and bread sticks
Owner: Greg Toufayan
CFO, Controller: Kristine Toufayan
Vice President: Bob Thomas
VP & Treasurer: Suzanne Toufayan
VP Marketing: Karen Toufayan
VP Sales: Roy Peterson
Operations Manager: Chris Clark
Production Manager: Paul Steinbach
Purchasing Manager: James Bogosian
Estimated Sales: $26 Million
Number Employees: 20-49
Type of Packaging: Consumer, Food Service
Other Locations:
       Orlando, FL
       Plant City, FLPlant City

49415 Town Dock
74 Railroad Ave
Johnston, RI 02919-2323   401-232-0764
       Fax: 401-782-4421 www.towndock.com
Contact: Joao Bokel
jbokel@towndock.com
Estimated Sales: $ 10 - 20 Million
Number Employees: 5-9

49416 Townfood Equipment Corp
72 Beadel St
Brooklyn, NY 11222-5232   718-388-5650
       Fax: 718-388-5860   800-221-5032
       customerservice@townfood.com
       www.townfood.com
Asian barbecue equipment, cooking utensils, china, soup stoves, ovens, ranges, smokers and electric rice cookers; importer of hand hammered woks and gas rice cookers; exporter of rice cookers, ranges and smokers
President: Charles Suss
Founder: Morris Suss
VP: Sada Nair
R&D/Quality Control: Ken Trosterman
Marketing Executive: Marianne Suss
Sales: Mary Ann Balk
Equipment Specialists: Sincere Chan
Production: Ken Tosterman
Purchasing Director: Sada Nair
Estimated Sales: $5-10 Million
Number Employees: 10-19
Square Footage: 100000
Type of Packaging: Consumer, Private Label
Brands Exported: Rice Master
Regions Exported to: Central America, South America, Europe, Middle East
Percentage of Business in Exporting: 5
Regions Imported from: Asia
Percentage of Business in Importing: 30

49417 Townsend Farms Inc
23400 NE Townsend Way
Fairview, OR 97024-4626   503-666-1780
       Fax: 503-618-8257 www.townsendfarms.com
Fresh and frozen blueberries, blackberries and strawberries; fresh black raspberries, mixed fruit, manoes, boysenberries, cherries, marionberries, red raspberries and pineapple; fresh raspberries
President: Tracy Casillas
tracyc@thecanbycenter.org
CEO: Jeff Townsend
CFO: Chris Valenti
Plant Manager: Reyes Pena
Purchasing: Mark Davis
Estimated Sales: $ 10 - 20 Million
Number Employees: 1000-4999
Square Footage: 4000
Type of Packaging: Consumer, Food Service, Private Label, Bulk
Brands Exported: Buyers Brand
Regions Exported to: Canada
Percentage of Business in Exporting: 5
Brands Imported: Buyers Brand
Regions Imported from: Worldwide
Percentage of Business in Importing: 5

49418 Trade Diversified
1650 Fremont Court
Ontario, CA 91761-8319   909-923-1208
       Fax: 909-923-1212   800-835-8338
       brasspeople@msn.com www.tdi4brass.com
Wholesaler/distributor of sneeeze guards, bar and stair rails, glass racks and turnstiles; importer and exporter of brass fittings; also, custom fabrication, bending and finishing services available; serving the food service market
President: King Lu
Marketing Director/Operations Manager: Erica Huang
Sales: Michelle Wong
Contact: Erica Chu
brasspeople@msn.com
Estimated Sales: $1-3 Million
Number Employees: 5
Square Footage: 48000
Regions Exported to: Canada, Mexico
Percentage of Business in Exporting: 3
Regions Imported from: Asia, Taiwan
Percentage of Business in Importing: 65

49419 Trade Farm
PO Box 43369
Oakland, CA 94624-0369   855-737-3276
       Fax: 510-836-1481
Frozen, air dehydrated and freeze dried supplier of Chinese vegetables

Importers & Exporters / A-Z

49420 Trade Fixtures
1501 Westpark Dr # 5
Little Rock, AR 72204-2457 501-664-1318
Fax: 501-664-9253 800-872-3490
cservice@tradefixtures.com www.h2optimized.net
Manufacturer and exporter of molded displays for bulk food items including gravity and scoop bins
Manager: Scott Johnson
sjohnson@tradefixtures.com
Quality Control: Walter Baumgarten
President: Scott Johnson
VP Sales: Clay Odom
VP Sales: Doug Holland
General Manager: Joe Herrmann
Purchasing Manager: Roy Jackson
Estimated Sales: $ 5 - 10 Million
Number Employees: 50-99
Square Footage: 112000
Parent Co: Display Technologies
Regions Exported to: Worldwide
Percentage of Business in Exporting: 5

49421 Tradeco International Corp
1107 S Westwood Ave
PO Box 1155
Addison, IL 60101-4920 630-628-1112
Fax: 630-628-6616 800-628-3738
ventura@tradecointl.com www.tradecointl.com
Manufacturer and importer of chinaware including plates, cups, saucers and holloware
President: Leslie D Plass
lplass@tradecointl.com
Estimated Sales: $ 1 - 3,000,000
Number Employees: 10-19
Type of Packaging: Consumer
Brands Imported: Ventura China
Regions Imported from: China

49422 Tradelink
7880 NW 76th Avenue
Medley, FL 33166-7511 305-443-1869
Fax: 305-463-7792
Exporter and wholesaler/distributor of dry groceries, frozen foods, seafood, powdered milk, French cheeses, store equipment, and fresh fruits
President: Jorge Garrido
Vice President: Maria Leon
Estimated Sales: $2.5-5 Million
Number Employees: 1-4
Parent Co: SE Tradelink USA
Regions Exported to: Central America, South America, Europe, Caribbean

49423 Trader Vic's Food Products
9 Anchor Dr
Emeryville, CA 94608 510-653-3400
Fax: 510-653-9384 877-762-4824
info@tradervics.com tradervics.com
Processor and exporter of nonalcoholic cocktail mixes, syrups, dry spices, sauces and salad dressings
CEO: Hans Richter
VP: Peter Seely
Estimated Sales: $540000
Number Employees: 6
Type of Packaging: Consumer
Brands Exported: Trader Vic's
Regions Exported to: Europe, Asia, Middle East
Percentage of Business in Exporting: 20

49424 Traeger Industries
10450 SW Nimbus Ave
Building R, Suite A
Portland, OR 97223 503-845-9234
Fax: 503-94 -155 800-872-3437
traeger@traegerindustries.com
www.traegergrills.com
Manufacturer and exporter of wood pellet smokers and cooking appliances
President: Joseph Traeger
VP Sales/Marketing: Randy Traeger
VP Production: Mark Traeger
Estimated Sales: $ 5 - 10 Million
Number Employees: 50-99
Square Footage: 108000
Regions Exported to: Canada
Percentage of Business in Exporting: 15

49425 Traex
101 Traex Dr
Dane, WI 53529 608-849-2500
Fax: 608-849-2580 800-356-8006
www.libbey.com
Manufacturer, importer and exporter of food trays, straw dispensers, portion control and napkin dispensers, bus boxes, dishracks and tabletop accessories
Marketing: Lori Barger
Contact: Allen Byers
allen.byers@libbey.com
Plant Manager: Steve Boeder
Purchasing Agent: Rose Ohlert
Estimated Sales: $10-20 Million
Number Employees: 100-249
Square Footage: 30000
Parent Co: Menasha Corporation
Brands Exported: Straw Boss; Rackmaster; Sauce Boss; Batter Boss; Self Serve System; Konds-Keeper
Regions Exported to: Central America, South America, Europe, Asia, Middle East, Africa, Australia
Percentage of Business in Exporting: 15
Regions Imported from: Asia
Percentage of Business in Importing: 5

49426 Traitech Industries
100 Four Valley Drive
Unit C
Vaughan, ON L4K 4T9
Canada 905-695-2800
Fax: 905-695-0737 877-872-4835
info@traitech.com www.traitech.com
Manufacturer and exporter of ventilated merchandising trays, baskets and displays custom manufacturer
President: Tom Penton
VP: Ryan Slight
Type of Packaging: Consumer, Food Service, Private Label, Bulk
Regions Exported to: Central America, South America, Canada, Mexico, Latin America
Percentage of Business in Exporting: 50

49427 Trak-Air/Rair
555 Quivas St
Denver, CO 80204-4915 303-779-9888
Fax: 303-694-3575 800-688-8725
sales@trak-air.com www.trak-air.com
Manufacturer and exporter of hot air and greaseless countertop fryers; also, pizza ovens
President: Dale Terry
dterry@coloradosalesinc.com
Estimated Sales: $ 1 - 2 Million
Number Employees: 20-49
Square Footage: 64000
Type of Packaging: Food Service
Brands Exported: Trak-Air; Rair

49428 Trane Inc
800-E Beaty St
Davidson, NC 28036 704-655-4000
www.trane.com
Manufacturer and exporter of roof top and self-contained air conditioner; also, heat pumps including water-source.
President, Commercial HVAC Americas: Donald Simmons
President, Residential HVAC & Supply: Jason Bingham
Year Founded: 1913
Estimated Sales: $10 Billion
Number Employees: 29,000
Parent Co: Ingersoll Rand
Regions Exported to: Worldwide

49429 Trans Act Technologies Inc
One Hamden Center
2319 Whitney Ave, Suite 3B
Hamden, CT 06518 203-859-6800
Fax: 203-949-9048 www.transact-tech.com
Industrial printers and tech products for hospital and food services.
Chairman & CEO: Bart Shuldman
President/CFO/Treasurer/Secretary: Steven DeMartino
SVP, Operations: Andrew Hoffman
SVP, Engineering: Donald Brooks
Estimated Sales: $50-100 Million
Number Employees: 100-249

49430 Trans Pecos Foods
112 E Pecan St # 800
San Antonio, TX 78205-1578 210-228-0896
Fax: 210-228-0781 pjk@texas.net
www.transpecosfoods.com
Manufacturer, importer and exporter of frozen breaded vegetables
President: Patrick J Kennedy
Contact: Steven Skinner
steven.skinner@transpecosbanks.com
Plant Manager: Bruce Salcido
Estimated Sales: $3900000
Number Employees: 20-49
Parent Co: Anchor Food Products
Type of Packaging: Consumer, Food Service, Private Label, Bulk
Regions Exported to: Central America
Percentage of Business in Exporting: 2
Regions Imported from: Central America
Percentage of Business in Importing: 2

49431 Trans World Services
72 Stone Pl
Melrose, MA 02176-6016 781-665-9200
Fax: 781-665-6649 800-882-2105
twsinc@gis.net
Manufacturer and exporter of thermometers and sandwich packaging materials including crystal wrap and cellophane; also, packaging machinery. Consumer, institution and processor packaging of T-shirts, USDA/FSIS partner
President: Thomas E Ford
CFO: Thomas Foid
Vice President: Dan Tuono
R&D: Thomas Foid
Quality Control: Thomas Foid
Sales/Marketing: Ira Siegal
Estimated Sales: $ 10 - 20 Million
Number Employees: 10-19
Square Footage: 208000
Type of Packaging: Food Service
Regions Exported to: Europe
Percentage of Business in Exporting: 30

49432 (HQ)Trans-Chemco Inc
19235 84th St
PO Box 9
Bristol, WI 53104-9184 262-857-2363
Fax: 262-857-9127 800-880-2498
info@trans-chemco.com www.trans-chemco.com
Manufacturer, importer and exporter of chemicals including defoamers and antifoamers; also, laboratory research and development for products and special needs
President: Susanne Gardiner
CFO: Irene Swan
VP/Director: Merle Gardiner
VP R&D: Merle Gardiner
Operations Manager: Sheila Cleveland
Estimated Sales: $ 1 - 3 Million
Number Employees: 10-19
Square Footage: 60000
Brands Exported: Trans-10; Trans-30; Trans-100; Trans-FG2
Regions Exported to: Europe, Australia
Percentage of Business in Exporting: 3
Regions Imported from: Europe
Percentage of Business in Importing: 3

49433 Transatlantic Foods
PO Box 286677
New York, NY 10128 212-330-8286
Fax: 646-607-9555 info@transatlanticfoods.com
Fresh, frozen, dried and processed wild and exotic mushrooms, as well as select specialty food products.
Contact: Francois Baumont
francoisbaumont@transatlanticfoods.com

49434 Transbotics Corp
3400 Latrobe Dr
Charlotte, NC 28211-4847 704-362-1115
Fax: 704-364-4039 www.transbotics.com
Design, development, support and installation of Automatic Guided Vehicles, or transportation robots, with an emphasis on complete customer satisfaction. Supplier of Automatic Guide Vehicle Systems, AGV controls technology, engineeringservices, AGV batteries, charges and other related products
CEO: Claude Imbleau
EVP: Neville Croft
Service/ Quality System Manager: Robert Stiteler
Marketing & Aftermarket Sales: Jayesh Mehta
Sales: Chuck Rossell
Public Relations: Ryan Willis
Operations: Mark Ramsey
Purchasing Manager: David Melton
Estimated Sales: $ 1 - 5,000,000
Number Employees: 20-49
Parent Co: NDC Automation
Type of Packaging: Bulk

625

Importers & Exporters / A-Z

Regions Exported to: Worldwide

49435 Transit Trading Corporation
196-198 West Broadway
New York, NY 10013   212-925-1020
   Fax: 212-925-1629 ttcspices@aol.com
Importer of seeds including anise, caraway, celery, dill, cumin, fenugreek, fennel, poppy, sesame and coriander; also, beans, couscous, allspice, basil, oregano, paprika, parsley flakes, rosemary, thyme, cardamon, dillweed, peppermarjoram, etc.
Estimated Sales: $5 Million
Number Employees: 20-49
Type of Packaging: Bulk
Regions Imported from: Central America, South America, Europe, Middle East
Percentage of Business in Importing: 90

49436 Transmundo Company
999 Brickell Avenue
Suite 1001
Miami, FL 33131-3044   305-539-1205
   Fax: 305-539-0022 transmundo@aol.com
Importer and exporter of meat; importer of confectionery items and guava products including shells and paste
President: Alberto Senosiain
Manager (Financial Administrator): Esther Gomez
Manager (Import/Export): Bettina Siwek
Estimated Sales: $2.5-5 Million
Number Employees: 5-9
Regions Exported to: South America, Asia
Percentage of Business in Exporting: 20
Brands Imported: Triple Star; Lacta; Mirabel; Cepa
Regions Imported from: South America
Percentage of Business in Importing: 80

49437 Transnorm System Inc
1906 S Great Southwest Pkwy
Grand Prairie, TX 75051-3580   972-606-0303
   Fax: 972-606-0768 800-259-2303
   sales@transnorm.com www.transnorm.com
Manufacturer and exporter of belt curve conveyors including mini edge, power, spiral, straight, etc
President: Kay L Wolfe
VP: Rick Lee
Estimated Sales: $20-50 Million
Number Employees: 10
Square Footage: 80000
Parent Co: Transnorm System GmBH
Regions Exported to: Worldwide

49438 Transpacific Foods Inc
2603 Main St # 730
Suite 730
Irvine, CA 92614-4264   949-975-9900
   Fax: 949-975-9907 www.transpacificfoods.com
U.S. pineapple supplier
President: Septi Suwandi
Number Employees: 10-19
Type of Packaging: Consumer, Food Service

49439 Tranter INC
1900 Old Burk Hwy
Wichita Falls, TX 76306-5904   940-723-7125
   Fax: 940-723-5131 sales@tranter.com
   www.tranter.com
Surface and plate heat exchangers, cabinet liners for walk-in refrigerator/freezing rooms, freezing storage units, cold and hot food displays; exporter of heat exchangers
President: Charles Monachello
CEO: Roy Mason
CFO: Arnold Downes
VP: Roy Mason
Research & Development: Jeff Mathur
Marketing Director: Ronald Stonecipher
Sales Director: Frank Kierzkowski
Purchasing Manager: Czeech Richardson
Number Employees: 100-249
Square Footage: 480000
Parent Co: Tranter
Brands Exported: Platecoil; Superchanger
Regions Exported to: South America, Canada, Africa

49440 Traulsen & Co
4401 Blue Mound Rd
Fort Worth, TX 76106-1928   817-625-1168
   Fax: 817-624-4302 800-825-8220
Manufacturer and exporter of commercial refrigerators and freezers including display, stainless steel, anodized aluminum, vinyl, reach-in, roll-in and pass-through
Manager: Gary Hoying
Vice President: Pepe Griffo
Marketing Director: Mark Kauffman
Operations: Gary Hoying
Purchasing: John Hebert
Estimated Sales: $20-50 Million
Number Employees: 10-19
Square Footage: 300000
Parent Co: ITW
Other Locations:
   Traulsen & Co.
   New Troy, MI Traulsen & Co.
Regions Exported to: Worldwide
Percentage of Business in Exporting: 10

49441 Travelon
700 Touhy Ave
Elk Grove Vlg, IL 60007-4916   847-621-7000
   Fax: 847-621-7001 800-537-5544
   www.travelonbags.com
Manufacturer, importer and exporter of metal displays and carts
Owner: Don Godshaw
   dong@travelonbags.com
VP Marketing: Kathy Novak
Estimated Sales: $ 1 - 5 Million
Number Employees: 100-249
Square Footage: 100000
Type of Packaging: Consumer
Brands Exported: Travelow; Travel Caddy
Regions Exported to: Central America, South America, Europe, Asia, Middle East
Percentage of Business in Exporting: 5
Brands Imported: Travelow; Travel Caddy
Regions Imported from: Asia
Percentage of Business in Importing: 30

49442 Traycon Manufacturing Co
555 Barell Ave
Carlstadt, NJ 07072-2891   201-939-5555
   Fax: 201-939-4180 info@traycon.com
   www.traycon.com
Manufacturer and exporter of conveyors and carts for dish and tray handling systems
CEO: Nicholas Pisto
VP: Candice Pisto
Estimated Sales: $5-10 Million
Number Employees: 20-49
Square Footage: 40000
Brands Exported: RA; RDL; SDL; SSW; DW; RDB
Regions Exported to: Worldwide
Percentage of Business in Exporting: 5

49443 Treasure Foods
2500 S 2300 W # 11
West Valley, UT 84119-7676   801-974-0911
   Fax: 801-975-0553 treasurefoods@hotmail.com
Processor and exporter of whipped honey butter, flavored fruit honey, scones; wholesaler/distributor of frozen foods and general line items; serving the food service market
Owner: Amin Motilla
CFO: Zarina Motiwala
Vice President: Mohamed Motiwala
Marketing Director: Amin Motiwala
Public Relations: Amin Motiwala
Production Manager: Fawad Motiwala
Plant Manager: Fawad Motiwala
Purchasing Manager: Amin Motiwala
Estimated Sales: $450,000
Number Employees: 5
Number of Brands: 3
Number of Products: 3
Square Footage: 14400
Parent Co: Algilani Food Import & Export
Type of Packaging: Food Service, Private Label, Bulk
Other Locations:
   Treasure Foods
   Salt Lake City, UT Treasure Foods
Percentage of Business in Exporting: 8

49444 Tree Ripe Products
53 S Jefferson Rd
Whippany, NJ 07981-1082   973-463-0777
   800-873-3747
   www.1800treeripe.com
Processor and exporter of nonalcoholic cocktail mixes
President: Joel Fishman
Estimated Sales: $3,000,000
Number Employees: 20-49
Square Footage: 20000
Type of Packaging: Consumer, Food Service
Brands Exported: Tree Ripe
Regions Exported to: Central America, South America, Europe
Percentage of Business in Exporting: 15

49445 Treehouse Farms
116 Camino Agave
Elgin, AZ 85611   559-757-5020
   Fax: 559-757-0510
Processor and exporter of almonds including natural, blanched, sliced, roasted, diced and slivered
President: David Fitzgerald
Executive Director: Jacob Carter
Sales Manager: Carol Coffey
Number Employees: 250-499
Square Footage: 400000
Parent Co: Yorkshire Foods
Type of Packaging: Private Label, Bulk
Regions Exported to: Central America, South America, Europe, Asia, Middle East

49446 Trefethen Family Vineyards
1160 Oak Knoll Ave # 3
Napa, CA 94558-1398   707-255-7700
   Fax: 707-255-0793 winery@trefethen.com
   www.trefethen.com
Producer and exporter of wine
Owner: John Trefethen
VP Finance: Gerald Bush
VP: David C Whitehouse Jr
Marketing: Terry Hall
Sales Director: Betty Calvin
   jtrefethen@trefethen.com
Public Relations: Terry Hall
Operations Manager: Richard De Garmo
Estimated Sales: $5 Million
Number Employees: 20-49
Square Footage: 16000
Brands Exported: Trefethen Vineyards
Regions Exported to: Central America, South America, Europe, Asia
Percentage of Business in Exporting: 10

49447 Treif USA
230 Long Hill Cross Rd
Shelton, CT 06484-6160   203-929-9930
   Fax: 203-849-8517 treifusa@treif.com
   www.treif.com
High speed, high-output slicing and dicing equipment
President: Robert Linke
Contact: Alicia Clayton
   aclayton@treif.com
Estimated Sales: $1-2.5 Million
Number Employees: 5-9

49448 Trevor Industries
8698 S Main St
Eden, NY 14057   716-992-4775
   Fax: 716-992-4788
Manufacturer, importer and exporter of plastic drinking straws and cocktail stirrers
Owner: Gary Ballowe
VP Administration: Karen Amico
Plant Manager: Robert Martin
Estimated Sales: $ 5 - 10 Million
Number Employees: 20-49
Square Footage: 150000
Brands Exported: Niagara
Regions Exported to: Europe, Asia
Percentage of Business in Exporting: 5
Regions Imported from: Europe
Percentage of Business in Importing: 10

49449 Trevor Owen Limited
80 Barbados Boulevard
Unit 5
Scarborough, ON M1J 1K9
Canada   416-267-8231
   Fax: 416-267-1035 866-487-2224
   sales@trevorowenltd.com www.trevorowenltd.com
Manufacturer and exporter of banners and insulated food delivery bags
President: Pierre Barcik
Sales Executive: Trevor Owen
Number Employees: 10
Square Footage: 40000
Regions Exported to: USA
Percentage of Business in Exporting: 5

Importers & Exporters / A-Z

49450 Tri Car Sales
16 Kipper St
Rio Rico, AZ 85648-6236   520-377-7602
     Fax: 520-281-5888 www.tricarsales.com
Importer and wholesaler/distributor of produce including hydroponic tomatoes, European cucumbers, red, yellow and green bell and jalapeno peppers, green beans and squash, etc.; serving the food service market
President: Juan Cardenas
jcardenas@tricarsales.com
Sales Manager: Frank Calixtro
Sales Director: Richard Morales
Public Relations: Joey Bernal
Operations Manager: Juan Carlos Cardenas
Estimated Sales: $ 3 - 5 Million
Number Employees: 10-19
Type of Packaging: Bulk
Regions Imported from: Central America, Mexico

49451 (HQ)Tri-Marine International
10500 NE 8th St
Suite 1888
Bellevue, WA 98004   425-688-1288
     Fax: 425-688-1388 sfarno@trimarinegroup.com
     trimarinegroup.com
Importer and wholesaler/distributor of seafood.
Chief Executive Officer: Renato Curto
Chief Operating Officer: Joe Hamby
Chief Financial Officer: Steve Farno
Director, Enviornmental Policy: Matt Owens
Director, Information Systems: Johnny Yip
Year Founded: 1972
Estimated Sales: $100-500 Million
Number Employees: 20-49
Type of Packaging: Consumer, Food Service
Other Locations:
  Tri-Marine International
  JurongTri-Marine International

49452 Tri-Pak Machinery Inc
1102 N Commerce St
Harlingen, TX 78550-4814   956-423-5140
     Fax: 956-423-9362
     dfitzgerald@tri-pakmachinery.com
     www.tri-pak.com
Manufacturer and exporter of fruit and vegetable processing machinery including belt and chain conveyors, graders, sizers, cleaners, packers and wax coaters; also, graders for shrimp
President: David A Fitzgerald
VP: Charles M. Kilbourn
Director of Sales and Marketing: James W. Fitzgerald
Sales: Robert E. Fitzgerald
Director of Operations: Daniel J. Groves
Purchasing: Chuck Kilbourn
Estimated Sales: $ 5 - 10 Million
Number Employees: 20-49
Square Footage: 516000
Regions Exported to: Central America, South America, Europe, Asia, Middle East
Percentage of Business in Exporting: 10

49453 Tri-Seal
900 Bradley Hill Rd
Blauvelt, NY 10913-1196   845-353-3300
     Fax: 845-353-3376
     LinersNorthAmer@tekni-plex.com
     tri-seal.tekni-plex.com
Manufacturer and exporter of coextruded thermoplastic bottle cap liners and extruded rigid and flexible PVC tubing and profiles
CEO: F Smith
President: Bruce Burus
VP Sales/Marketing: Walter Burgess
Estimated Sales: $ 5 - 10 Million
Number Employees: 50-99
Square Footage: 440000
Regions Exported to: Central America, South America, Europe, Asia, Middle East
Percentage of Business in Exporting: 5

49454 Tri-State Logistics Inc
3156 Spring Valley Road
Dubuque, IA 52001-1531   563-690-0926
     Fax: 775-417-6709 866-331-7660
     www.tri-statelogistics.com
Energy drink and power cool drink
President: Evan Fleisher
VP: Randy Sirk
Estimated Sales: C
Number Employees: 5-9
Square Footage: 3500
Type of Packaging: Private Label
Brands Imported: Rox
Regions Imported from: Europe

49455 (HQ)Tri-State Plastics
PO Box 337
Henderson, KY 42419-0337   270-826-8361
     Fax: 270-826-8362
Manufacturer and exporter of injection molded food containers
Owner: Mike Walden
VP/Secretary/Treasurer: Mike Walden
Estimated Sales: less than $ 500,000
Number Employees: 1-4
Square Footage: 70000
Type of Packaging: Private Label, Bulk

49456 Tri-State Plastics
PO Box 496
Glenwillard, PA 15046-0496   724-457-6900
     Fax: 724-457-6901 www.crightonplastics.com
Manufacturer and exporter of vacuum formed plastic products including trays, covers, guards, material handling components, etc.
President/ Sales: Chris Crighton
General Manager: Michael Lopez
Production Manager: Charles Goetz

49457 Tri-Sterling
1050 Miller Dr
Altamonte Spgs, FL 32701-7505   407-260-0330
     Fax: 407-260-7096
Manufacturer and exporter of packaging equipment and shrink wrappers
VP: Ken Schilling
Marketing: Thomas Jimenez
Estimated Sales: $20-50 Million
Number Employees: 100-249
Regions Exported to: Worldwide

49458 Tri-Tronics
7705 Cheri Ct
PO Box 25135
Tampa, FL 33634-2419   813-886-4000
     Fax: 813-884-8818 800-237-0946
     info@ttco.com www.ttco.com
Manufacturer and exporter of material handling and automation application controls including photoelectric sensors, registration scanners, photoelectric eyes and flexible plastic/glass fiber optic light guides
President: Scott Seehawer
scotts@ttco.com
VP/Sales Manager: Dennis Henderson
Estimated Sales: $10-20 Million
Number Employees: 50-99
Square Footage: 56000
Brands Exported: SmartEye; OptiEye; SmartEye Colormark; SmartEye Mark III; SmartEye Pro
Regions Exported to: Central America, South America, Europe, Canada, Mexico, Caribbean
Percentage of Business in Exporting: 5

49459 Triad Scientific
6 Stockton Lake Blvd
Manasquan, NJ 08736-3024   732-292-1994
     Fax: 732-292-1961 800-867-6690
     triadscientific@gmail.com www.triadsci.com
Manufacturer and exporter of laboratory equipment including balances, analysis instrumentation, filtration, incubators, lamps, microscopes, monitoring systems, ovens, sterilizers, spectrophotometers, etc.; also, analysis, designservice and repair available
VP: Tom Leskow
Estimated Sales: $ 3 - 5 Million
Number Employees: 1-4
Square Footage: 20000
Type of Packaging: Food Service, Bulk
Regions Exported to: Worldwide
Percentage of Business in Exporting: 15

49460 Triangle Package Machinery Co
6655 W Diversey Ave
Chicago, IL 60707-2293   773-889-0201
     Fax: 773-889-4221 800-621-4170
     wcray@trianglepackage.com
     www.trianglepackage.com
Manufacturer and exporter of bag and carton making, closing, filling, packing, weighing and sealing machinery
President: Bryan Muskat
bmuskat@trianglepackage.com
R&D: Jerone Lasky
Quality Control: Roger Gaw
Director Sales: John Michalson
Purchasing Agent: John Musso
Estimated Sales: $ 20 - 50 Million
Number Employees: 100-249
Square Footage: 10000000
Regions Exported to: Worldwide
Percentage of Business in Exporting: 10

49461 Tribali Foods
2275 Huntington Dr. # 342
San Marino, CA 91108   310-592-5420
     hello@tribalifoods.com
     www.tribalifoods.com
Organic, grass-fed Mediterranean style beef patties and Umami beef patties; organic, free-range chicken patties
Founder/Owner: Angela Bicos Mavridis
Year Founded: 2016
Number of Brands: 1
Number of Products: 3
Type of Packaging: Consumer, Private Label
Brands Exported: Tribali Foods
Regions Exported to: USA

49462 Tribe Mediterranean
110 Prince Henry Dr
Taunton, MA 02780-7385   774-961-0000
     800-848-6687
     info@tribehummus.com www.tribehummus.com
Processor and exporter of hummus dips/spreads
President/Ceo: Carlos Canals
Cfo: Charles Webster
Number Employees: 100-249
Square Footage: 240000
Type of Packaging: Consumer, Food Service, Private Label, Bulk

49463 Tribest Corp
1143 N Patt St
Anaheim, CA 92801-2568   714-879-7150
     Fax: 562-623-7160 888-254-7336
     service@tribest.com www.tribestlife.com
Importer, exporter and wholesaler/distributor of Korean noodle soups, ginseng sodas, tropical juices, cookies and candy; also, juice extractors.
Owner: Brandon Chi
General Manager: John Kim
Sales Manager: Kevin Kim
bran@tribest.com
Estimated Sales: $ 10 - 20 Million
Number Employees: 5-9
Square Footage: 20000
Type of Packaging: Food Service
Brands Exported: Comet; Arirang; Autumn Harvest; Chemarrow; Nong Shim; Ginseng Up; Tribest; Green Power
Regions Exported to: Central America, South America, Europe, Asia
Percentage of Business in Exporting: 5
Brands Imported: Choice; Nong Shim; Maaza; Ginseng Up; Tribest; Green Power
Regions Imported from: Europe, Asia
Percentage of Business in Importing: 35

49464 Tribology Tech Lube
35 Old Dock Rd
Yaphank, NY 11980-9702   631-345-3000
     Fax: 631-345-3001 609-859-1757
     info@tribology.com www.tribology.com
Manufacturer and exporter of synthetic and specialty lubricants
President: William Krause
Sales: Paul Anderson
Manager: T Tierney
Operations/General Manager: Terence Tierney
Purchasing: Gail Moore
Estimated Sales: $50-100 Million
Number Employees: 10-19
Number of Products: 300
Square Footage: 35000
Type of Packaging: Private Label, Bulk
Regions Exported to: Central America, South America, Europe, Asia

49465 Trico Converting Inc
1801 Via Burton
Suite A
Fullerton, CA 92831-5319   714-563-0701
     Fax: 714-772-7528 www.printaccess.com

Importers & Exporters / A-Z

Manufacturer and exporter of flexible packaging; also, printing and laminating available
President: Larry Schow
lschow@goarmy.com
VP: Tim Love
Estimated Sales: $ 10 - 20 Million
Number Employees: 5-9
Square Footage: 40000
Type of Packaging: Consumer, Food Service, Private Label, Bulk
Regions Exported to: Central America, Asia

49466 Trident Plastics
1009 Pulinski Rd
Ivyland, PA 18974 215-672-5225
Fax: 215-672-5582 800-222-2318
sales@tridentplastics.com
www.tridentplastics.com
Manufacturer and exporter of plastic tubes, sheets, rods, ducts, films, slabs and signs
President: Ronald Cadic
Sales Manager: Michael Peroni
Contact: William Thomas
vasales@tridentplastics.com
Estimated Sales: $1-2.5 Million
Number Employees: 10-19

49467 (HQ)Trident Seafoods Corp
5303 Shilshole Ave NW
Seattle, WA 98107 206-783-3818
Fax: 206-782-7195 800-426-5490
humanresources@tridentseafoods.com
www.tridentseafoods.com
Seafood from Alaska and the Pacific Northwest.
Founder/Chairman: Chuck Bundrant
Chief Executive Officer: Joe Bundrant
Year Founded: 1973
Estimated Sales: $2.4 Billion
Number Employees: 1000-4999
Number of Brands: 3
Type of Packaging: Consumer, Food Service, Bulk
Brands Exported: Trident
Regions Exported to: Central America, South America, Europe, Asia, Middle East, Canada, Mexico, Australia
Percentage of Business in Exporting: 30

49468 Trident Seafoods Corp
P.O. Box 908
641 Shakes Street
Wrangell, AK 99929 907-874-3346
Fax: 907-874-3035
Processor and exporter of canned, fresh and frozen shrimp, crab, halibut, herring and salmon
Type of Packaging: Food Service, Bulk
Regions Exported to: Worldwide
Percentage of Business in Exporting: 60

49469 Tridyne Process Systems
80 Allen Rd
South Burlington, VT 05403-7801 802-863-8573
Fax: 802-860-1591 sales@tridyne.com
www.tridyne.com
Manufacturer and exporter of automatic weighing and counting systems including net weighers and weigh counters; also, baggers, cartoners, conveyors, etc
President: Susith Wijetunga
Estimated Sales: $ 1 - 5 Million
Number Employees: 5-9
Square Footage: 44000
Parent Co: Tridyne Process Systems, Inc
Type of Packaging: Consumer, Food Service, Private Label, Bulk
Brands Exported: Tridyne
Regions Exported to: Central America, South America, Europe, Asia, Middle East, Canada, Mexico
Percentage of Business in Exporting: 5

49470 Trilogy Essential Ingredients
1304 Continental Dr
Abingdon, MD 21009-2334 410-612-0691
Fax: 410-612-9401 info@trilogyei.com
www.trilogyei.com
Flavors, seasonings, liquid spice extracts, proprietary delivery systems and functional ingredients.
Contact: Amy Ashcraft
aashcraft@trilogyei.com
Number Employees: 10-19
Number of Brands: 3
Type of Packaging: Bulk
Regions Exported to: South America, Europe, Asia, Canada

49471 Trimen Foodservice Equipment
1240 Ormont Drive
North York, ON M9L 2V4
Canada 416-744-3313
Fax: 416-744-3347 877-437-1422
paul_cesario@trimen.net www.trimen.net
Manufacturer and exporter of ovens, broilers, tables, booths and refrigeration equipment
President: Paul Cesario
Finance Manager: Grace Giulano
Head Operations: Mario Dipiede
Purchasing Manager: Mario Dipiede
Estimated Sales: $50-75 Million
Number Employees: 10
Type of Packaging: Food Service
Regions Exported to: USA
Percentage of Business in Exporting: 1

49472 Trine Rolled Moulding Corp
1421 Ferris Pl
Bronx, NY 10461-3610 718-828-5200
Fax: 718-828-4052 800-223-8075
info@trinecorp.com www.trinecorp.com
OEM manufacturer of factory direct original F-series baffle grease filters, aluminum, galvanized, stainless steel, all sizes-large inventory, UL/MEA/USA
President: Frank Rella
info@trinecorp.com
Plant Manager: James Lange
Estimated Sales: $5-10 Million
Number Employees: 50-99
Square Footage: 264000
Type of Packaging: Private Label

49473 Triner Scale & Mfg Co
8411 Hacks Cross Rd
Olive Branch, MS 38654-4010 662-890-2385
Fax: 901-363-3114 800-238-0152
info@trinerscale.com www.trinerscale.com
Manufacturer and exporter of scales including electronic, postage and platform; stainless steel, washdown and USDA approved
Owner: Arthur Wendt
awendt@trinerscale.com
Estimated Sales: $ 1 - 2.5 Million
Number Employees: 10-19
Square Footage: 120000
Brands Exported: Triner
Regions Exported to: Worldwide
Percentage of Business in Exporting: 10

49474 Trinidad Benham Corporation
3650 S Yosemite, Suite 300
P.O. Box 378007
Denver, CO 80237 303-220-1400
Fax: 303-220-1490 info@trinidadbenham.com
www.trinidadbenham.com
Dry beans, rice, popcorn, and peas
Vice President: Steve Dipasquale
Estimated Sales: $36.3 Million
Number Employees: 500
Square Footage: 35000
Type of Packaging: Consumer, Food Service, Private Label, Bulk
Regions Exported to: Worldwide

49475 Trinity Fruit Sale Co
7571 N Remington Ave # 104
Suite 104
Fresno, CA 93711-5799 559-433-3777
Fax: 559-433-3790 sales@trinityfruit.com
www.trinityfruit.com
Fresh cherries, apricots, peaches, plums, nectarines, kiwi, grapes, apples and pears
President: David White
Marketing Director: John Hein
Sales: Vance Uchiyama
Number Employees: 20-49

49476 Trinity Packaging
55 Innsbruck Dr
Cheektowaga, NY 14227-2703 716-668-3111
Fax: 716-668-3816 800-778-3111
Flexible packaging, process printing and film laminations; exporter of printed laminated rollstock; also, slitting and bag making available
President: Richard Gioia
Chairman: Tony Gioia
tgioia@cello-pack.com
VP: Sam Brown
Operations: Compton Plummer
Purchasing Director: Tim Shiley
Estimated Sales: $ 20 - 50 Million
Number Employees: 100-249
Square Footage: 100000
Type of Packaging: Consumer, Food Service, Private Label, Bulk
Regions Exported to: Central America, Europe
Percentage of Business in Exporting: 2

49477 Trinkle Sign & Display
24 5th Ave
Youngstown, OH 44503-1191 330-747-9712
Fax: 330-747-9712
Manufacturer and exporter of signs and displays
Owner: Robert Page
Estimated Sales: Less Than $500,000
Number Employees: 1-4
Regions Exported to: Worldwide
Percentage of Business in Exporting: 1

49478 (HQ)Trio Packaging Corp
90 13th Ave # 11
Ronkonkoma, NY 11779-6819 631-588-0800
Fax: 631-467-4690 800-331-0492
sales@triopackaging.com www.triopackaging.com
Manufacturer, importer and exporter of form/fill/seal packaging equipment and films
President: John Bolla
john@triopackaging.com
Vice President: Frederick Kramer
Sales Director: Anthony Carris
Estimated Sales: $ 20 - 50 Million
Number Employees: 20-49
Square Footage: 20000
Other Locations:
  Trio Packaging Corp.
  Ronkonkoma, NY Trio Packaging Corp.
Regions Exported to: Europe, Middle East, Canada, Mexico
Percentage of Business in Exporting: 2
Regions Imported from: Europe
Percentage of Business in Importing: 5

49479 Trio Products
250 Warden Ave
Elyria, OH 44035 440-323-5457
Fax: 440-323-3247
Manufacturer and exporter of plastic food packaging materials including regular and thermoforming sheets and bacon boards
National Sales Representative: C Derringer
Contact: Christine Hood
christineh@trioproducts.com
Engineering/Technical: Mike Linner
Estimated Sales: $ 10-20 Million
Number Employees: 10-19
Type of Packaging: Consumer, Private Label, Bulk
Regions Exported to: Canada

49480 Triple D Orchards Inc
8310 W Stormer Rd
Empire, MI 49630-9480 231-326-5174
Fax: 231-326-5480
Processor and exporter of canned and frozen sweet cherries
President: TJ Keyes
Year Founded: 1973
Estimated Sales: $20 - 50 Million
Number Employees: 100-249
Type of Packaging: Consumer, Food Service, Private Label, Bulk
Regions Exported to: Europe
Percentage of Business in Exporting: 40

49481 Triple Dot Corp
3302 S Susan St
Santa Ana, CA 92704-6841 714-241-0888
Fax: 714-241-9888 info@triple-dot.com
www.triple-dot.com
Plastic containers, dessicant packages and neck bands; importer of glass containers
Owner: Tony Tsai
tytsai@aol.com
VP: Jason Tsai
Estimated Sales: $5-10 Million
Number Employees: 20-49
Square Footage: 140000
Brands Imported: TDC
Regions Imported from: Asia
Percentage of Business in Importing: 25

49482 Triple Leaf Tea Inc
434 N Canal St # 5
S San Francisco, CA 94080-4667 650-588-8255
Fax: 650-588-8406 800-552-7448
triple@tripleleaf-tea.com
Processor and exporter of authentic, traditional Chinese medicinal teas including green, ginger, ginseng, diet and medicinal; also, American ginseng capsules
President: Johnson Lam
Estimated Sales: $450.00k
Number Employees: 5-9
Number of Brands: 1
Number of Products: 18
Square Footage: 20000
Type of Packaging: Consumer, Food Service, Private Label
Brands Exported: Triple Leaf Tea
Regions Exported to: Central America, South America, Europe, Asia, Middle East, Caribbean
Percentage of Business in Exporting: 15

49483 Triple S Dynamics Inc
2467 E US Highway 180
Breckenridge, TX 76424-4956 254-559-8266
Fax: 254-559-8057 800-527-2116
sales@sssdynamics.com www.sssdynamics.com
Manufacturer and exporter of conveyors, separators and vibrating screens
Marketing: Jim Tatum
Estimated Sales: $10-20,000,000
Number Employees: 10-19
Square Footage: 125000
Brands Exported: Slipstick; Texas Shaker
Regions Exported to: Europe, Asia, Worldwide
Percentage of Business in Exporting: 15

49484 Triple-A Manufacturing Company
44 Milner Avenue
Toronto, ON M1S 3P8
Canada 416-291-4451
Fax: 416-291-1292 800-786-2238
Manufacturer and exporter of storage systems, shelving, steel work benches, modular storage drawers, plastic and corrugated bins, welded wire partitions and mezzanines; also, racks including bottle, can, cold storage room, palletwine, wire, barrel, drum, etc
President: Joe Harnest
VP Finance: A Lerman
VP Sales: R Gasner
Buyer: T Kelly
Estimated Sales: $ 10 - 20 Million
Number Employees: 35
Square Footage: 240000
Other Locations:
Triple-A Manufacturing Co. Lt
Exeter, NHTriple-A Manufacturing Co. Lt
Regions Exported to: Central America, Europe, Asia
Percentage of Business in Exporting: 15

49485 Tripper Inc
PO Box 51440
Oxnard, CA 93031-1440 805-988-8851
Fax: 805-988-2992 www.tripper.com
Processor and importer of kosher & spices including pepper, nutmeg, cinnamon, and ginger; also, ingredients including vainilla beans and extracts; organic available
Owner: Francois Bervard
frab@tripper.com
Estimated Sales: $ 1-2.5 Million
Number Employees: 1-4
Square Footage: 60000
Type of Packaging: Food Service, Private Label, Bulk
Regions Imported from: Europe, Asia, Middle East, Mexico
Percentage of Business in Importing: 85

49486 Triton International
1060 W Florence Ave
Inglewood, CA 90301 310-337-0044
Fax: 310-337-0044 www.tritoninternational.com
Wholesaler/distributor, importer and exporter of fresh and frozen fruits and vegetables including asparagus, baby potatoes, mangos, pineapples, lemons, blackberries, blueberries, papayas, etc.; serving the food service and retailmarkets
President: Alex Hall
Manager Frozens: Jason Chang
Procurement: Jose Paredes
Estimated Sales: $10-20 Million
Number Employees: 20-49
Square Footage: 20000
Type of Packaging: Consumer, Food Service, Private Label, Bulk
Regions Exported to: Europe, Asia, Canada
Brands Imported: Tri Mango
Regions Imported from: South America, Latin America, Mexico

49487 Triton System Of Delaware LLC
21405 B St
Long Beach, MS 39560-3141 228-863-4710
Fax: 228-575-3101 800-367-7191
CEO: Bill Johnson
Number Employees: 100-249

49488 (HQ)Trojan Commercial Furniture Inc.
163 Van Horne
Montereal, QC H2T 2J2
Canada 514-271-3878
Fax: 514-271-8960 877-271-3878
Manufacturer and exporter of wooden restaurant furniture including tables, chairs, booths and counters
President: Dennis Petsinis
Co-President: Chris Petsinis
Number Employees: 10
Square Footage: 24000
Type of Packaging: Food Service, Bulk
Regions Exported to: USA
Percentage of Business in Exporting: 50

49489 (HQ)Trojan Inc
198 Trojan St
Mt Sterling, KY 40353-8000 859-498-0526
Fax: 859-498-0528 800-264-0526
sales@trojaninc.com www.trojaninc.com
Manufacturer and exporter of lighting including long life, energy-efficient incandescent, fluorescent, HID, NSF approved, shatter-resistant, lamps, etc.; also, adapters and plate and exit sign retrofit kits
President: Edward Duzyk
CEO: Dennis Duzyk
sales@trojaninc.com
Estimated Sales: $ 3 - 5 Million
Number Employees: 10-19
Square Footage: 340000
Type of Packaging: Food Service
Other Locations:
Trojan
Meadville, PATrojan
Brands Exported: Saf-T-Cote; Power-Saver; Hytron
Regions Exported to: Central America, South America, Europe, Asia, Middle East, Canada, Mexico
Percentage of Business in Exporting: 2

49490 Tropical Açaí LLC
587 East Sample Rd. # 263
Pompano Beach, FL 33064 917-699-1923
855-550-2224
www.tropicalaçaí.com
Organic açai berry packs, açai sorbets
General Manager: Renata Nogueria
Number of Brands: 1
Number of Products: 10
Type of Packaging: Consumer, Private Label
Brands Exported: Tropical Açai
Regions Exported to: USA

49491 Tropical Cheese
452 Fayette St
Perth Amboy, NJ 08861 732-442-4898
Fax: 732-442-8227 888-874-4928
admin@tropicalcheese.com
www.tropicalcheese.com
Hispanic specialty food products, including cheese products, tortillas, beverages, meat products, other dairy products and desserts.
President & Founder: Rafael Mendez
Vice President of Opertions: Alejandro Lopez
Production Manager: Alex Quiles
Year Founded: 1983
Number of Brands: 5
Type of Packaging: Consumer
Regions Exported to: Central America, South America, Europe

49492 Tropical Commodities
9230 Nw 12th Street
Miami, FL 33172 305-471-8120
Fax: 305-471-9825 tropicom@direcway.com
Fresh habanero chili peppers and mash as well as other varieties of chili peppers.
President: D Douglas Bernard
Vice President: Robert Kholer
Marketing: Alberto Beers
Estimated Sales: $1.3-1.5 Million
Number Employees: 5-9
Number of Products: 10
Square Footage: 60000
Type of Packaging: Private Label, Bulk
Brands Imported: Fresh Chili Peppers
Regions Imported from: Caribbean
Percentage of Business in Importing: 95

49493 Tropical Foods
350 Riverside Pkwy
Lithia Springs, GA 30122-3865 770-438-9950
Fax: 770-435-1371 800-544-3762
info@tropicalfoods.com www.tropicalfoods.com
Processor and importer of candy, dried fruits, nuts, seeds, Asian rice snacks and dessert toppings
President: David Williamson
President: John Bauer
Sales Director: Debbie Ponton
Manager: Peter Njuguna
njuguna@tropical.com
Operations Manager: William Stapleton
Estimated Sales: $ 10 - 20 Million
Number Employees: 10-19
Parent Co: Tropical
Type of Packaging: Food Service, Private Label, Bulk

49494 Tropical Illusions
1436 Lulu Street
PO Box 338
Trenton, MO 64683-1819 660-359-5422
Fax: 660-359-5347 tropical@tropicalillusions.com
Processor and exporter of frozen drinks mixes including: cocktail, slush and granita, cream base, and smoothies.
President: Vance Cox
Vice President: Carrol Baugher
Estimated Sales: $590,000
Number Employees: 6
Square Footage: 200000
Type of Packaging: Food Service, Private Label
Regions Exported to: Central America, South America, Europe, Asia, Middle East
Percentage of Business in Exporting: 10

49495 Tropical Link Canada Ltd.
7668 Winston St.
Burnaby, BC
Canada 778-379-3510
Fax: 778-379-3511 www.tropicallinkcanada.ca
Organic cinnamon powder, cinnamon sticks, turmeric powder, coconut sugar, coconut oil, coconut vinegar, prepared fruit dips, rice blends, bulk dried fruit
Director: Sudhani Perera
Number of Brands: 2
Number of Products: 20
Type of Packaging: Consumer, Private Label, Bulk
Brands Exported: Snow Farms, Wild Tusker
Regions Exported to: Central America, Asia, Canada, USA

49496 Tropical Preserving Co Inc
1711 E 15th St
Los Angeles, CA 90021-2715 213-748-5108
Fax: 213-748-4998 sales@tropicalpreserving.com
www.tropicalpreserving.com
Processor and exporter of jams, jellies and apple butter
President: Ronald Randall
Estimated Sales: $12,000,000
Number Employees: 20-49
Type of Packaging: Consumer, Private Label
Regions Exported to: Asia

49497 (HQ)Tropicana Products Inc.
555 W. Monroe St.
Chicago, IL 60661
800-237-7799
www.tropicana.com
Orange and grapefruit juices, as well as frozen concentrates.
Chairman/CEO, PepsiCo: Ramon Laguarta
Year Founded: 1947
Estimated Sales: $431.9 Million
Number Employees: 1000-4999
Square Footage: 100000
Parent Co: PepsiCo

Importers & Exporters / A-Z

49498 Trotters Importers
PO Box 497
Orange, MA 01364-0497 413-624-0121
Fax: 413-624-0262 800-863-2437
Importer of chocolates, chocolate-covered cherries in brandy, wafers and teas
Sr. Partner: Maia Magee
Sr. Partner: Neb Chupin
Type of Packaging: Consumer

49499 Trout Lake Farm
PO Box 181
Trout Lake, WA 98650 509-395-2025
Fax: 509-395-2749 800-655-6988
www.troutlakefarm.com
Processor, exporter and importer of certified organically grown medicinal and beverage tea herbs and spices including garlic, oregano, peppermint and spearmint
CEO: Lloyd Scott
Sales Manager: Martha-Jane Hylton
Contact: Sharon Frazey
sharon.frazey@troutlakefarm.com
Operations Manager: Gary Vollema
Estimated Sales: $3500000
Number Employees: 50
Square Footage: 160000
Type of Packaging: Bulk
Regions Exported to: Europe, Asia, Canada
Regions Imported from: Central America, South America, Europe, Asia, Middle East, Canada
Percentage of Business in Importing: 4

49500 (HQ)Troy Lighting
14508 Nelson Ave
City Of Industry, CA 91744-3514 626-336-4511
Fax: 626-330-4266 800-533-8769
Manufacturer, exporter and importer of electric lighting fixtures including decorative interior, track and recessed; also, exterior including wall, hanging, flush and post lanterns
Owner: Carol Coffey
VP Sales/Marketing: Steve Nadell
carolc@troycsl.com
Estimated Sales: $20-50 Million
Number Employees: 5-9
Square Footage: 100000
Regions Exported to: Central America, South America
Percentage of Business in Exporting: 5
Regions Imported from: Europe
Percentage of Business in Importing: 10

49501 Tru Fru, LLC
1546 S 4650 W # 200
Salt Lake City, UT 84104
888-437-2497
info@trufru.com www.trufru.com
Freeze-dried, dark chocolate-covered fruits
Co-Founder: Taz Murray
National Sales Director: Dion Rasmussen
Year Founded: 2015
Number of Brands: 1
Number of Products: 6
Type of Packaging: Consumer, Private Label
Brands Exported: TruFru
Regions Exported to: USA

49502 Tru Hone Corp
1721 NE 19th Ave
Ocala, FL 34470-4701 352-622-1213
Fax: 352-622-9180 800-237-4663
www.truhone.com
Manufacturer and exporter of knife sharpeners
President: James Gangelhoff
truhone@truhone.com
CEO: Fred R Gangelhoff
Estimated Sales: $ 1-2.5 Million
Number Employees: 10-19
Square Footage: 13200
Brands Exported: Tru Hone
Regions Exported to: Worldwide
Percentage of Business in Exporting: 5

49503 Tru Hone Corp
1721 NE 19th Ave
Ocala, FL 34470-4701 352-622-1213
Fax: 352-622-9180 800-237-4663
www.truhone.com
Knife sharpeners and accessories for industrial operations, meat, fish, poultry and produce plants.

President: James Gangelhoff
truhone@truhone.com
Number Employees: 10-19
Regions Exported to: Worldwide

49504 TruHeat Corporation
P.O.Box 190
Allegan, MI 49010-0190 269-673-2145
Fax: 269-673-7219 800-879-6199
www.truheat.com
Manufacturer and exporter of electric heating elements and assemblies for warming, broiling, frying, steaming and defrosting
President: Larry Nameche
Marketing/Sales: Jim Jennings
Estimated Sales: $10-20 Million
Number Employees: 100-249
Square Footage: 104000
Regions Exported to: Central America, South America, Europe, Asia, Middle East, Canada, Australia, Latin America, Mexico
Percentage of Business in Exporting: 10

49505 TruVibe Organics
Santa Monica, CA
www.truvibeorganics.com
Organic superfood blends (raw cacao nibs, goji berries, chia seeds) and superfood meal replacement drinks
Co-Founder: Anand Dani
Co-Founder: Jason Dekker
Year Founded: 2013
Number of Brands: 1
Number of Products: 10
Type of Packaging: Consumer, Private Label
Brands Exported: Eat Clean Organic, TruVibe

49506 True Blue Farms
9548 County Road 215
Grand Junction, MI 49056-9214 269-434-6112
Fax: 269-434-8192 877-654-2400
www.truebluefarms.com
Blueberries including fresh, frozen and puree
Owner: Shelly Hartmann
CEO: Myron Brady
Secretary: Evelyn Farmer
Marketing Manager: Juana Chavez
Sales: Ronald Benson
truebluefarms@btc-bci.com
Office Manager: Lee Erickson
Estimated Sales: Less Than $500,000
Number Employees: 5-9
Type of Packaging: Consumer, Food Service, Private Label, Bulk

49507 True Food Service Equipment, Inc.
2001 E Terra Ln
O Fallon, MO 63366-4434 636-240-2400
Fax: 636-272-2408 800-325-6152
truefood@truemfg.com www.truemfg.com
Manufacturer and exporter of commercial refrigeration equipment including deli cases, refrigerators, freezers and coolers; also, beer dispensers and pizza prep tables
President: Robert J Trulaske
Contact: Randy Bates
rbates@truemfg.com
Estimated Sales: $ .5 - 1 million
Number Employees: 1-4
Brands Exported: True
Regions Exported to: Central America, South America, Europe, Asia, Middle East, Australia

49508 True Jerky
226 Union St
Suite A
San Francisco, CA 94123 858-336-2005
www.madebytrue.com
Flavored beef jerky, jerky snack mix and biltong
Chief Executive Officer: Jess Thomas
Year Founded: 2015
Number of Brands: 2
Number of Products: 12
Type of Packaging: Consumer, Private Label

49509 True Nopal Cactus Water
8255 East Raintree Dr. # 300
Scottsdale, AZ 85260 480-636-8044
info@truenopal.com
www.truenopal.com
All-natural cactus water

Number of Brands: 1
Number of Products: 1
Type of Packaging: Consumer, Private Label

49510 True Organic Product Inc
20225 W Kamm Ave
Helm, CA 93627 559-866-3001
Fax: 559-866-3003 800-487-0379
info@trueorganicproducts.net
Processor and exporter of organic juices including orange, apple, pineapple, grape, tangerine, lime, watermelon, blackberry, soursop, lulo and pineapple blends
President/CEO: Jake Evan
CEO: Jake Evans
jevans@trueorganicproducts.net
Estimated Sales: $ 3 - 5 Million
Number Employees: 20-49
Square Footage: 48000
Brands Exported: True Organic
Regions Exported to: Middle East
Percentage of Business in Exporting: 30

49511 True Pac
420 Churchmans Rd
New Castle, DE 19720-3157 302-326-2222
Fax: 302-326-9330 800-825-7890
info@truepack.com www.truepack.com
Manufacturer and exporter of insulated shipping containers
Owner: Steve Nam
steve@truepack.co.kr
Manager: Joan Carter
Estimated Sales: $ 1 - 5 Million
Number Employees: 20-49

49512 True Story Foods
San Francisco, CA
888-277-1171
hi@truestoryfoods.com www.truestoryfoods.com
Organic, GMO-free deli meats, sausages, hot dogs and fresh pork
Founder/Chief Executive Officer: Phil Gatto
Number of Brands: 1
Number of Products: 34
Type of Packaging: Consumer, Private Label
Brands Exported: True Story Foods

49513 True World Foods LLC
24 Link Dr
Rockleigh, NJ 07647-2504 201-750-0024
Fax: 201-750-0025 info@trueworldfoods.com
www.trueworldfoods.com
Fresh seafood
President: Jackie Madsuka
CEO: Takeshi Yashiro
yashiro@trueworldfoods.com
Estimated Sales: $ 20 - 50 Million
Number Employees: 100-249

49514 Trumark
830 E Elizabeth Ave
Linden, NJ 7036 908-486-5900
Fax: 908-486-5900 800-752-7877
Processor and exporter of sodium and potassium lactate and lactate and acetate blends
President: Mark Satz
CEO: Jeff Wales
Contact: Kathy Moraglia
kathy@tru-mark.com
Estimated Sales: $780,000
Number Employees: 10-19
Regions Exported to: Worldwide
Percentage of Business in Exporting: 50

49515 Truth Bar LLC
260 Charles St. # 210
Waltham, MA 02453
888-886-8959
www.truthbar.com
Various flavors of energy bars with prebiotics and probiotics
Co-Founder: Sean Fay
Co-Founder: Diana Stobo
Year Founded: 2014
Number of Brands: 1
Number of Products: 5
Type of Packaging: Consumer, Private Label
Brands Exported: Truth Bar
Regions Exported to: USA

Importers & Exporters / A-Z

49516 Try The World
123 5th Ave
4th Fl
New York, NY 10003-1019   855-841-0303
sayhello@trytheworld.com
www.trytheworld.com
Ethnic snacks: chia seed pudding, dried berries, cacao nibs and blueberries, olive oil, caramels, honey and coffee beans.
Co-Founder: David Foult
Co-CEO & Co-Founder: Kat Vorotova
Integrated Marketing Manager: Diya Varadaraj
Chief Operating Officer: Hugo Facchin
Estimated Sales: $14 Million
Number Employees: 11-50
Brands Imported: Casa da Prisca, Giuliano Caffe, Dos Cafeteras, Delicious Crete, Banana JOE, Briosa, Orientines and more.
Regions Imported from: Worldwide

49517 Tsar Nicoulai Caviar LLC
60 Dorman Ave
San Francisco, CA 94124-1807   415-543-3007
Fax: 415-543-5172   800-952-2842
beluga@tsarnicoulai.com   www.tsarnicoulai.com
Caviar, aquaculture operation
President: Mats Engstrom
VP: Dafne Engstrom
Sales/Marketing Manager: A Engstrom
Manager: Marian Mahone
concierge@tsarnicoulai.com
Plant Manager: Dr David Stedhen
Estimated Sales: $5 Million
Number Employees: 20-49
Square Footage: 120000
Type of Packaging: Consumer, Food Service, Private Label, Bulk
Brands Exported: Tsar Nicoulai
Regions Exported to: Europe, Asia
Percentage of Business in Exporting: 20
Brands Imported: Tsar Nicoulai
Regions Imported from: Europe, Asia
Percentage of Business in Importing: 60

49518 Tsar Nicoulai Caviar LLC
60 Dorman Ave
San Francisco, CA 94124-1807   415-543-3007
Fax: 415-543-5172   800-952-2842
info@tsarnicoulai.com   www.tsarnicoulai.com
Caviar and smoked fish
President/CEO: Mats Engstrom
Co-Owner: Dafne Engstrom
Manager: Marian Mahone
concierge@tsarnicoulai.com
Estimated Sales: $500,000-$1 Million
Number Employees: 20-49
Type of Packaging: Private Label

49519 Tu Me Beverage Company
818-237-5105
info@tumewater.com
www.drinktume.com
Turmeric-infused, naturally-sweetened flavored water
Co-Founder: Shaina Zaidi
Number of Brands: 1
Number of Products: 5
Type of Packaging: Consumer, Private Label
Brands Exported: Tu Me
Regions Exported to: USA

49520 Tualatin Estate Vineyards
10850 NW Seavey Rd
Forest Grove, OR 97116-7703   503-357-5005
Fax: 503-357-1702   tualatinestate@yahoo.com
www.tualatinestate.com
Processor and exporter of table wines including chardonnay, pinot noir, pinot blanc, gewurztraminer, riesling and semi-sparkling muscat
Founder: Jim Bernau
Vice President: William L Fuller
Operations Manager/Winegrower: Stirling Fox
Winemaker: Joe Dobbes
Estimated Sales: $600000
Number Employees: 10-19
Square Footage: 80000
Parent Co: Willamette Valley Vineyards
Type of Packaging: Consumer
Brands Exported: Tualatin Estate Vineyards
Regions Exported to: Worldwide

49521 Tucel Industries, Inc.
2014 Forestdale Rd.
Forestdale, VT 05745-0146   802-247-6824
Fax: 802-247-6826   800-558-8235
Manufacturer and exporter of produce sponges and food preparation brushes including pastry; also, janitorial supplies including brushes, brooms, scours and squeegees
President: John Lewis Jr
CEO: Joanne Raleigh
Estimated Sales: $ 3 - 5 Million
Number Employees: 20-49
Square Footage: 180000
Type of Packaging: Consumer, Food Service, Private Label, Bulk
Brands Exported: Tucel; Cycle Line; Tu-Scrub; Fused
Regions Exported to: Europe, Canada, Mexico
Percentage of Business in Exporting: 10

49522 Tuchenhagen
6716 Alexander Bell Drive
Suite 125
Columbia, MD 21046-2186   410-910-6000
Fax: 410-910-7000
Manufacturer and exporter of compact modular skid-mounted processing units and systems including blending, mixing, yeast pitching, etc.; also, valves, in-line flow measuring instruments and sanitary fittings, etc.; also, consultationservices available
Marketing Coordinator: Mads Michael Skaarenborg
Sales Director: Dave Medlar
Estimated Sales: $2.5-5 Million
Number Employees: 20-49
Parent Co: Tuchenhagen North America
Regions Exported to: Worldwide

49523 Tucker Industries
2835 Janitell Road
Colorado Springs, CO 80906-4104   719-527-4848
Fax: 719-527-1499   800-786-7287
action@burnguard.com   www.burnguard.com
Manufacturer and exporter of burn protective garments including oven mitts, aprons and hot pads
President: Vincent A. Tucker
Safety Director: Les Burns
CFO: Hathy Tucker
Quality Control: Hathy Tucker
VP Marketing: Paul Weklinski
Contact: Andrea Mabe
andrea@burnguard.com
Estimated Sales: Below $ 5 Million
Number Employees: 20-49
Square Footage: 172000
Brands Exported: BurnGuard; IntraLine; LiteLine; VaporGuard
Regions Exported to: Worldwide
Percentage of Business in Exporting: 10

49524 (HQ)Tucson Container Corp
6601 S Palo Verde Rd
Tucson, AZ 85756-5044   520-746-3171
Fax: 520-741-0962   www.tucsoncontainer.com
Manufacturer and exporter of fiber and corrugated boxes; also, packaging materials and foam products
President: John Widera
Manager: Daniel Robinson
Controller: Christel Widera
Sales Service Manager: Karina Walters
Manager: Joaquin Rivadeneyra
joaquin.rivadeneyra@tucsoncontainer.com
Production Supervisor: Eladios Cortez
Plant Manager: Joaquin Rivadeneyra
Purchasing Agent: Chris Woolridge
Estimated Sales: $ 16 Million
Number Employees: 50-99
Square Footage: 160000
Other Locations:
Tucson Container Corp.
El Paso, TXTucson Container Corp.
Regions Exported to: Mexico

49525 Tucson Tamale Company
Tucson, AZ   520-398-6282
www.tucsontamale.com
Handmade tamales with various meat, cheese and bean fillings; organic hot sauce; oregano and seasoning mixes
Founder/Owner: Todd Martin
Year Founded: 2008
Number of Brands: 1
Type of Packaging: Consumer, Private Label
Brands Exported: Tucson Tamale

Regions Exported to: USA

49526 Tudor Pulp & Paper Corporation
17 White Oak Dr
Prospect, CT 6712   203-758-4494
Fax: 203-758-4498
Manufacturer and importer of specialty paper for packaging including grease resistant, oil resistant, industrial and electric
VP Sales: Stephen Hansen
Manager: Brad Russell
Estimated Sales: $ 1 - 5 Million
Number Employees: 10-19
Regions Imported from: Europe
Percentage of Business in Importing: 10

49527 Tufco Technologies Inc
1205 Burris Rd
Newton, NC 28658-1953   828-464-6730
Fax: 828-464-6732   800-336-6712
www.tufco.com
Wholesaler/distributor of point of sale displays, place mats and guest checks; serving the food service market
President: John Bonander
CFO: Gene Brittain
gene.brittain@tufco.com
VP Sales/Operations: Judy Joplin
Plant Manager: Charles Sigmon
Estimated Sales: $20-50 Million
Number Employees: 50-99
Square Footage: 125000
Parent Co: Tufco Industries

49528 Tufty Ceramics Inc
47 S Main St
PO Box 785
Andover, NY 14806   607-478-5150
ktufty@infoblvd.net
www.tuftyceramics.com
Manufacturer and exporter of terracotta bakeware including nonstick, microwaveable and dishwasher safe
President: Karen Tufty
Estimated Sales: Below $ 500,000
Number Employees: 1-4
Regions Exported to: Japan

49529 Tundra Wild Rice
PO Box 263
Pine Falls, NB R0E 1M0
Canada
204-367-8651
Fax: 204-367-8309
Processor and exporter of Canadian lake wild rice
President: Denis Pereux
Sales/Marketing: Ed Thibedeau
Number Employees: 4
Square Footage: 11360
Type of Packaging: Private Label, Bulk
Brands Exported: Tundra Wild Rice
Regions Exported to: South America, Middle East

49530 Turbana Corp.
999 Ponce de Leon Blvd.
Suite 900
Coral Gables, FL 33134   305-445-1542
Fax: 305-443-8908   800-226-2627
www.fyffes.com
Bananas and plantains.
CEO: Juan Alarcon
Year Founded: 1970
Estimated Sales: $174.56 Million
Number Employees: 20-49
Square Footage: 8500
Parent Co: C.I. Uniban SA
Brands Imported: Turbana
Regions Imported from: Central America, South America
Percentage of Business in Importing: 100

49531 Turbo Refrigerating Company
P.O.Box 396
Denton, TX 76202-0396   940-387-4301
Fax: 940-382-0364   info@turboice.com
Manufacturer and exporter of ice making, storage and distribution systems; processor of ice
President: El Beard
CFO: Chris Worghington
VP: Dan Aiken
VP Sales/Marketing: T Baker
Estimated Sales: $ 20 - 50 Million
Number Employees: 20-49
Parent Co: Henry Vogt Machine Company

Importers & Exporters / A-Z

Other Locations:
  Turbo Refrigerating Co.
  Louisville, KY Turbo Refrigerating Co.
Regions Exported to: Central America, South America, Europe, Asia, Middle East, Africa, Australia
Percentage of Business in Exporting: 25

49532 Turkana Food
555 N Michigan Avenue
Kenilworth, NJ 07033   908-810-8800
   Fax: 908-810-8820 info@turkanafood.com
   www.turkanafood.com
Ethnic foods: European, Mediterranean and Middle Eastern.
Business Development: Furkan Bugra Er
Admisinstrative Service Manager: Tuncay Yalim
Estimated Sales: $9-11 Million
Number Employees: 11-50
Type of Packaging: Food Service
Brands Imported: Aleppo, Bahcivan, Erzurum, Gazi, Golden Plate, Mersin, Nestle, Santa Sophia, Solen, Superfresh, Teksut, Toros and more.
Regions Imported from: Europe, Middle East, Mediterranean

49533 Turkey Hill Sugarbush
10 Waterloo Street
PO Box 160
Waterloo, QC J0E 2N0
Canada   450-539-4822
   Fax: 450-539-1561 www.turkeyhill.ca
Processor and exporter of maple products including syrups, cookies, chocolates, coffee, tea, fudge, caramels, butter, soft and hard candies
President/Board Member: Michael Herman
Chairman: Brian Herman
Estimated Sales: $10-20 Million
Number Employees: 35
Number of Brands: 1
Number of Products: 85
Square Footage: 70000
Type of Packaging: Consumer, Private Label, Bulk
Regions Exported to: Europe, Asia, Australia
Percentage of Business in Exporting: 70

49534 Turlock Fruit Co
500 S Tully Rd
Turlock, CA 95380-5121   209-634-7207
   Fax: 209-632-4273 www.turlockfruit.com
Processor and exporter of honeydew melons
President: Donald Smith
Treasurer: Stephen Smith
Secretary: Stuart Smith
Estimated Sales: $500,000-$1 Million
Number Employees: 20-49
Type of Packaging: Consumer, Bulk
Brands Exported: King O' The West; Peacock; Sycamore; Oak Flat
Regions Exported to: Asia
Percentage of Business in Exporting: 30

49535 Turtle Island Foods
601 Industrial St
PO Box 176
Hood River, OR 97031-2006   541-386-7766
   Fax: 541-386-7754 800-508-8100
   info@tofurky.com
Processor, importer and exporter of soy meat analos including tempeh, tofurkey, deli slices, sausages, franks
President: Seth Tibbott
sue@tofurky.com
CFO: Sue Tibbott
VP: Bob Tibbott
Quality Assurance Manager: James Athos
Production Manager: Graciela Pulido
Plant Manager: Graciela Pulido
Estimated Sales: $2,398,946
Number Employees: 20-49
Number of Brands: 2
Number of Products: 25
Square Footage: 40000
Type of Packaging: Consumer, Food Service, Private Label, Bulk
Brands Exported: Tofurky
Regions Exported to: Europe
Percentage of Business in Exporting: 1

49536 Turtle Wax
PO Box 247
Westmont, IL 60559-0247   905-470-6665
   Fax: 708-563-4302 distributorinfo@turtlewax.com
   www.turtlewax.com
Manufacturer and exporter household cleaners, dressings and polishes
CEO: Denis J Healy
Chairman: Sondra A Healy
Contact: Huntington Beach
hbeach@turtlewax.com
Estimated Sales: $ 5 - 10 Million
Number Employees: 1,000-4,999

49537 Turveda
www.turveda.com
Turmeric protein powder, turmeric capsules, turmeric tea K-cups, turmeric sparkling tonics in various flavors
Founder: Dev Chakraborty
Number of Brands: 1
Number of Products: 12
Type of Packaging: Consumer, Private Label
Brands Exported: Turveda
Regions Exported to: USA

49538 Tuscan Eat/Perdinci
3003 S Tamiami Trl
Sarasota, FL 34239-5108   941-565-7382
   www.perdinci.com
Italian foods
Owner & President: Lorenzo Masolini
Estimated Sales: Under $500,000
Number Employees: 6
Regions Imported from: Italy

49539 Tuthill Vacuum & BlowerSystems
P.O.Box 2877
Springfield, MO 65801-2877   417-865-8715
   Fax: 417-865-2950 800-825-6937
   vacuum@tuthill.com www.tuthillvacuum.com
Manufacturer and exporter of positive displacement rotary lobe blowers mechanical vacuum boosters, rotary piston vacuum pumps, liquid ring vacuum pumps and complete systems
President: John Ermold
Controller: James Ashcraft
Sales/Marketing Director: Mike Branstetter
Contact: Henry Mateja
hmateja@tuthill.com
Estimated Sales: $10-20 Million
Number Employees: 250-499
Number of Brands: 10
Number of Products: 6
Square Footage: 130000
Parent Co: Tuthill Corporation
Regions Exported to: Central America, South America, Europe, Asia, Middle East
Percentage of Business in Exporting: 25
Regions Imported from: South America, Europe, Asia
Percentage of Business in Importing: 15

49540 Tutt Global Industries
3710 E Ovid Ave
Des Moines, IA 50317-5851   515-265-9500
   Fax: 515-265-9502
Manufacturers' representative for imported and exported confectionery and dairy/deli products, frozen foods, general merchandise, groceries, industrial ingredients, etc.; serving all markets
President/CEO: Richard Gannon
CFO: Mohamed Diabate
Vice President: Madjan Diabate
Contact: Dana Chernet
d.chernet@intanprima.com
Estimated Sales: $ .5 - 1 million
Number Employees: 20-49

49541 Tuway American Group
191 E Pearl St
Rockford, OH 45882   419-363-3191
   Fax: 419-363-2129 800-537-3750
   www.tuwaymops.com
Manufacturer, importer and exporter of dust cloths and mops, carpet cleaning pads and bonnets, scouring pads, wall washing supplies and handles
President: Trudy Koster
Director Sales: M Healy
National Sales Manager: Steve Grimes
Manager: John Feeney
Plant Manager: John Feeney
Estimated Sales: $ 20 - 50 Million
Number Employees: 50-99
Parent Co: Tu-Way Products Company
Regions Exported to: Worldwide
Percentage of Business in Exporting: 15
Regions Imported from: Europe

49542 Tuxton China
21011 Commerce Point Drive
Walnut, CA 91789-3052   909-595-2510
   Fax: 909-595-5353 info@tuxton.com
   www.tuxton.com

49543 Twang Partners LTD
6255 Wt Montgomery
San Antonio, TX 78252-2227   210-226-7008
   Fax: 210-226-4040 800-950-8095
   info@twang.com www.twang.com
Processor and importer of flavored salts including lemon-lime, traditional and colored margarita, beer, pickle and chili; also, Bloody Mary toppings
Owner: Roger Trevino Sr
VP Finance: Patrick Trevino
Sales/Marketing: Roger Trevino Jr
Estimated Sales: $ 10 - 20 Million
Number Employees: 20-49
Number of Brands: 10
Number of Products: 15
Square Footage: 24000
Type of Packaging: Consumer, Food Service, Private Label, Bulk

49544 Twenty-First Century Foods
30 Germania St # 2
Jamaica Plain, MA 02130-2312   617-522-7595
   Fax: 617-522-8772 www.21stcenturyfood.com
Soy products including tofu and tempeh; exporter of tempeh starter
Owner: Rudy Canale
rudy@cantinabostonia.com
Estimated Sales: $ .5 - 1 million
Number Employees: 1-4
Square Footage: 3800
Regions Exported to: Europe
Percentage of Business in Exporting: 2

49545 Twi Laq
1345 Seneca Ave
Bronx, NY 10474-4611   718-638-5860
   Fax: 718-789-0993 800-950-7627
   customerservice@twi-laq.com
Manufacturer and exporter of cleaning chemicals including soaps, degreasers, detergents, marble care chemicals and floor finishes
Vice President: Shanelle Acabeo
sacabeo@twi-laq.com
VP: Robert Wels
VP Operations: Michael Wels
Estimated Sales: $5-10 Million
Number Employees: 10-19
Brands Exported: Stone-Glo; Sun-Glo; Top Guard
Regions Exported to: Worldwide
Percentage of Business in Exporting: 15

49546 Twin Marquis
7 Bushwick Place
Brooklyn, NY 11206-2802   718-386-6868
   Fax: 718-821-6841 800-367-6868
   info@twinmarquis.com www.twinmarquis.com
Processor and importer of Asian foods including buns, dumplings, sauces, soups, and noodles; also organic pasta and instant coffee and cappuccino
President: Joseph Tang
Executive Director: Terry Tang
Vice President: Alan But
Contact: Alan But
alan@twinmarquis.com
Estimated Sales: $ 3-4 Million
Number Employees: 50-99
Square Footage: 88000
Regions Imported from: Asia
Percentage of Business in Importing: 10

49547 Twinings North America Inc
777 Passaic Ave
Suite 230
Clifton, NJ 07012-1884   973-591-0600
   Fax: 973-591-1700 800-803-6695
   consumer.service@twiningusa.com
   www.twiningsusa.com
Black, green and herbal teas.

President: Dan Martin
Vice President, Finance: Lars Kirkegard
Vice President, Marketing: Karen Maroli
Vice President, US/Mexico Sales: James Donnelly
twiningsusa@yahoo.com
Vice President, Operations: Alan Duncan
Estimated Sales: $5-10 Million
Number Employees: 20-49
Number of Brands: 1
Parent Co: R. Twining & Company
Brands Imported: Twinings Teas
Regions Imported from: United Kingdom
Percentage of Business in Importing: 100

49548 Twinlab Corporation
4800 T-Rex Ave
Boca Raton, FL 33431
800-645-5626
product@twinlab.com www.twinlab.com
Processor and importer of vitamins and nutritional supplements.
Quality Assurance Manager: Mary Baum
mbaum@twinlab.com
Year Founded: 1968
Estimated Sales: $30 Million
Number Employees: 400
Type of Packaging: Consumer
Other Locations:
  American Fork, UT
  Grand Rapids, MI
  Farmingdale, NYGrand Rapids
Regions Imported from: Worldwide

49549 TyRy Inc
4041 Alvis Court
Rocklin, CA 95677-7799
916-624-6050
Fax: 916-624-1604   800-322-6325
info@tyry.com
Manufacturer and exporter of health, backpacking, self-heating and emergency prepared foods, freeze-dried and no cooking required foods including; pre-packed beans, cereals, desserts, dried fruits and vegetables, grains and meatsubstitutes
President: Don Gearing
donald@tyry.com
Square Footage: 200000
Parent Co: TyRy, Inc
Type of Packaging: Consumer, Private Label, Bulk
Brands Exported: Alpineaire
Regions Exported to: Europe, Asia, Canada, Australia
Percentage of Business in Exporting: 10

49550 Tyco Fire Protection Products
1400 Pennbrook Pkwy
Lansdale, PA 19446-3840
215-362-0700
Fax: 215-362-5385   800-558-5236
sales@starsprinkler.com
Manufacturer and exporter of automatic self-adjusting fire sprinkler systems including concealed and recessed
President: Colleen Repplier
colleen.repplier@tycofp.com
Marketing Manager: John Corcoran
International Sales Manager: Patti Kowalski
Number Employees: 500-999
Parent Co: Tyco Corporation
Brands Exported: Star
Regions Exported to: Central America, South America, Europe, Asia, Middle East, Australia
Percentage of Business in Exporting: 20

49551 Tyco Fire Protection Products
1 Stanton St
Marinette, WI 54143-2542
715-732-3465
Fax: 715-732-3471   800-862-6785
www.ansul.com
Manufacturer and exporter of fire protection products includes fire extinguishers and hand line units; pre-engineered restaurant, vehicle, and industrial systems; sophisticated fire detection/suppression systems and a complete line ofdry chemical, foam, and gaseoue extinguishing agents.
President: Colleen Repplier
Cmo: David A Pelton
dpelton@tycoint.com
CFO: Dennis Moraros
Operations: Sally Falkenberg
Director, R&D: Jay Thomas
Director, Global Marketing: David Pelton
VP Sales: William Smith
Number Employees: 10-19
Parent Co: Tyco International

Brands Exported: Ansulex; Automan; Foray; Plus-Fifty; R-102; Sentry; Piranha; K-Guard
Regions Exported to: Worldwide
Percentage of Business in Exporting: 30

49552 Tyco Plastics
8235 220th St W
Lakeville, MN 55044-8059   952-469-8771
Fax: 952-469-5337   800-328-4080
Manufacturer and exporter of packaging supplies including barrier bags, films and pouches for meats, cheeses, etc
Sales/Marketing: Mike Baarts
Business Unit Manager (Food): Dennis Leisten
Business Unit Manager (Industrial): Tom Lundborg
Purchasing Manager: Gordon Raway
Estimated Sales: $20-50 Million
Number Employees: 100-249
Regions Exported to: Worldwide
Percentage of Business in Exporting: 3

49553 Tyco Retail Solutions
6600 Congress Ave
Boca Raton, FL 33487   561-912-6000
www.tycoretailsolutions.com
Manufacturer and exporter of safety systems including closed circuit television, electronic article surveillance and access control.
Year Founded: 1968
Estimated Sales: $300 Million
Number Employees: 1000-4999
Regions Exported to: Worldwide

49554 (HQ)Tyson Foods Inc.
2200 W. Don Tyson Pkwy.
Springdale, AR 72762   479-290-4000
www.tysonfoods.com
Chicken, beef and pork products.
CEO: Noel White
President/Director: Dean Banks
Executive VP/CFO: Stewart Glendinning
Executive VP/General Counsel: Amy Tu
Executive VP/Chief Customer Officer: Scott Rouse
Estimated Sales: $40 Billion
Number Employees: 122,000
Number of Brands: 41
Type of Packaging: Consumer, Food Service, Bulk
Regions Exported to: Central America, South America, Europe, Asia, Middle East, Worldwide
Percentage of Business in Exporting: 10

49555 U L Wholesale Lighting Fixture
3443 10th St
Long Island City, NY 11106-5107   718-726-7500
Fax: 718-626-8812 www.ullighting.net
Manufacturer and importer of lighting fixtures
Owner: Charlie Papastylianou
Estimated Sales: $ 2.5 - 5,000,000
Number Employees: 10-19
Square Footage: 10000
Regions Imported from: Asia
Percentage of Business in Importing: 10

49556 U-Line Corporation
8900 N 55th St
Milwaukee, WI 53223   414-354-0300
Fax: 414-354-0349   800-779-2547
sales@u-line.com www.u-line.com
Ice making machinery, compact freezers and compact, built-in and under-counter refrigerators
VP: Jennifer Seraszewski
CEO: Jennifer U Straszewski
Quality Control: Dean Bycnski
Sales/Marketing Manager: Henry Uline
Contact: Roland Marciniak
roland.marciniak@u-line.com
Vice President of Operations: Andrew Doberstein
Estimated Sales: $ 20 - 50 Million
Number Employees: 250-499

49557 U.C. Import & Company
PO Box 6161
Beverly Hills, CA 90212-1161   323-262-5050
Fax: 213-749-6446
Importer of latex disposable and rubber gloves; also, plastic cutlery
President: Max Naami
Estimated Sales: $ 5 - 10 Million
Number Employees: 5-9
Square Footage: 33680
Type of Packaging: Consumer, Food Service
Brands Imported: Smartway; Maxi Care; Pamitex
Regions Imported from: Asia
Percentage of Business in Importing: 90

49558 U.S. Range
1177 Kamato Rd
Mississauga, ON L4W IX4
Canada   905-624-0260
   800-424-2411
www.garland-group.com
Manufacturer of cooking systems.

49559 UBC Food Distributors
12812 Prospect St
Dearborn, MI 48126-3652   877-846-8117
Fax: 313-846-8118 info@wellmadefood.com
www.wellmadefood.com
Honey, chocolates, cookies, juices, and snacks
Sales Manager: Hassan Houssami
Estimated Sales: $10-12 Million
Number Employees: 10
Other Locations:
  East Coast, NJ
  West Coast, CAWest Coast
Brands Imported: Baraka
Regions Imported from: Europe, Middle East

49560 UDEC Corp
271 Salem St # A
Woburn, MA 01801-2004   781-933-7770
Fax: 781-933-5366   800-990-8332
Manufacturer and exporter of solid-state fluorescent emergency, exit and night lights; also, electronic ballasts for back lighting
President: Eugene P. Brandeis
e.brandeis@udeccorp.com
CFO: Janice Ferro
Purchasing Manager: J Ferro
Estimated Sales: Below $ 5 Million
Number Employees: 5-9
Square Footage: 9200
Type of Packaging: Food Service, Private Label
Brands Exported: Udee
Regions Exported to: Europe, Canada, Latin America
Percentage of Business in Exporting: 20
Regions Imported from: Europe, Asia

49561 UFL Foods
450 Superior Boulevard
Mississauga, ON L5T 2R9
Canada   905-670-7776
Fax: 905-670-7751
Processor and exporter of custom formulated and blended ingredients including milk replacers, mustard, seasonings, meat binders, curing preparations, etc.; also, pasta and rice sauce mixes, soup and sauce bases, batters andbreadings
VP: Jack Conway
Number Employees: 100-249
Square Footage: 440000
Parent Co: Newly Weds Foods
Type of Packaging: Food Service, Private Label, Bulk

49562 (HQ)US Can Company
1101 Todds Lane
Rosedale, MD 21237-2905   410-686-6363
Fax: 410-391-9323   800-436-8021
Manufacturer and exporter of aluminum and tin cans
VP Sales/Marketing: David West
Sales Director: Jack Finnell
Estimated Sales: $ 20-50 Million
Number Employees: 20-49
Type of Packaging: Consumer, Food Service, Private Label, Bulk

49563 US Chemical
316 Hart St
Watertown, WI 53094-6631   920-261-3453
Fax: 920-206-3979   800-558-9566
www.uschemical.com
Specialty chemicals including warewashing, laundry, maintenance, carpet and floor care chemicals; exporter of cleaning products and dispensing systems
General Manager: Bill Moody
Technical Manager: Cheryl Maas
QC Lab: Brian Truman
Sales Leader: David Kohnke
Contact: Eric Losey
eric.losey@uschemical.com
Plant Manager: Dennis Bollhurst
Estimated Sales: $30-50 Million
Number Employees: 100-130
Square Footage: 150000
Parent Co: Diversey, Inc

Importers & Exporters / A-Z

Regions Exported to: Central America, Europe, Asia, Canada, Caribbean
Percentage of Business in Exporting: 8

49564 US Chocolate Corp
4801 1st Ave
Brooklyn, NY 11232-4208   718-788-8555
Fax: 718-788-3311   uschoc@aol.com
Processor and exporter of kosher liquid marble chocolate and white parve coatings, fudge bases and flavors.
President: David Rosenberg
abe@uschoc.com
Estimated Sales: $10 - 20 Million
Number Employees: 10-19
Square Footage: 81000
Brands Exported: US
Regions Exported to: Europe, Middle East, Canada
Percentage of Business in Exporting: 4

49565 US Distilled Products Co
1607 12th St S
Princeton, MN 55371-2311   763-389-4903
Fax: 763-389-2549   info@usdp.com
www.usdp.com
Alcoholic beverages
President: Bradley P Johnson
CFO: Pat Pelzer
Production Manager: Kevin Issendorf
Purchasing Manager: Todd Rhode
Year Founded: 1981
Estimated Sales: $20-30 Million
Number Employees: 250-499
Square Footage: 250000
Brands Exported: Durange; Mothers; Karkov
Regions Exported to: Central America, South America, Europe, Asia, Middle East, Africa
Brands Imported: Jean Darec

49566 US Filter Dewatering Systems
2155 112th Ave
Holland, MI 49424-9609   616-772-9011
Fax: 616-772-4516   800-245-3006
Manufacturer and exporter of filter presses and other dewatering equipment for processing and waste treatment
President: Ken Hollidge
President, Chief Executive Officer: Eric Spiegel
CEO: Chuck Gordon
Executive Vice President of Global Sales: Paul Vogel
Estimated Sales: $20 - 50 Million
Number Employees: 100-249
Square Footage: 140800
Brands Exported: J-Press; J-Mate; J-Vap; Centramax; Centrapac
Regions Exported to: Central America, South America, Europe, Asia, Middle East
Percentage of Business in Exporting: 15

49567 (HQ)US Food Products
1084 Queen Anne Rd
Teaneck, NJ 07666-3508   201-833-8100
Fax: 201-833-1920   edsbeef@aol.com
www.usfoodproducts.com
Broker, wholesaler and exporter of all categories of frozen-chilled and dry food
President/CEO: Edward W Holland
edsbeef@aol.com
CFO: Chona Canillas
Estimated Sales: $20-50 Million
Number Employees: 20-49
Number of Brands: 50
Number of Products: 5000
Square Footage: 25000
Type of Packaging: Food Service
Brands Exported: National Brands and Private Level
Regions Exported to: Central America, South America, Europe, Asia, Middle East
Percentage of Business in Exporting: 50
Brands Imported: Beef, Lamb, Veal, Dairy Products, Frozen Fruits and Vegetables, Specialties.
Regions Imported from: Central America, South America, Europe, Asia, Middle East
Percentage of Business in Importing: 50

49568 US Industrial Lubricants
3330 Beekman St
Cincinnati, OH 45223-2424   513-541-2225
Fax: 513-541-2293   800-562-5454
www.usindustriallubricants.com
Manufacturer and exporter of vegetable oil and liquid soap, synthetic liquid detergent and lubricants including petroleum and synthetic
Co-Owner: Don Mattcheck
dmattcheck@usindustriallubricants.com
R & D: Ted Korzep
Facilities Engineer: Adam Freeman
Inside Sales: Jenny Anderson
USIL National Sales Manager: Dave Darling
Controller: Shannon Schlichte
Estimated Sales: $5-10 Million
Number Employees: 10-19
Number of Brands: 3
Number of Products: 250
Square Footage: 70000
Regions Exported to: Middle East, Mexico, Canada, Australia
Percentage of Business in Exporting: 5

49569 (HQ)US Label Corporation
2118 Enterprise Rd
Greensboro, NC 27408-7004   336-332-7000
Fax: 336-275-7674
Manufacturer and exporter of printed cloth, woven and paper labels; also, label tape
CFO: Charlie Davis
VP Marketing: Phil Koch
Sales Manager: James Grant
Contact: Edward Tidaback
edward@uslabelcorp.com
Number Employees: 250-499

49570 US Line Company
16 Union Avenue
Westfield, MA 01085-2497   413-562-3629
Fax: 413-562-7328
Manufacturer and exporter of specialized industrial braided synthetics
President: Brad Gage
CFO: Brad Gage
Quality Control: Brad Gage
R&D: Brad Gage
Marketing Director: Bradley Gage
Estimated Sales: Below $5 Million
Number Employees: 15

49571 US Marketing Company
2571 Route 212
Woodstock, NY 12498-2115   845-679-7274
Fax: 845-679-4650   800-948-0739
usmcompany@hotmail.com
Wholesaler/distributor and exporter of herbal-based vitamins, protein supplements, antioxidants, fitness and exercise equipment as on TV MDSE
President: Alan Altschul
aa@usmarketingcorp.com
CEO: Karen Kingsley
Public Relations: Glenn Taggart
Estimated Sales: $900,000
Number Employees: 5-9
Square Footage: 32000
Type of Packaging: Consumer
Regions Exported to: Central America, South America, Europe

49572 US Mills
401 E City Ave Ste 220
Bala Cynwyd, PA 19004-1117
Fax: 781-444-3411   800-422-1125
Processor and exporter of natural/organic foods including ready-to-eat and hot cereals and graham crackers.
Executive VP: Cynthia Davis
Director of Marketing: Daniel Wiser
Sales: William Bunn
Number Employees: 6
Number of Brands: 5
Number of Products: 45
Type of Packaging: Consumer
Brands Exported: Erewhon; New Morning; Uncle Sam, Farina Mills
Regions Exported to: Central America, Europe, Asia

49573 US Seating Products
707 S W 20th Street
Ocala, FL 34471
Fax: 352-629-2860   800-999-2589
info@admiralfurniture.com
www.admiralfurnitureonline.com
Manufacturer and exporter of aluminum and vinyl benches, chairs, cushions and pads, tray stands, tables and booths including legs and bases
President: Peter Villella
Estimated Sales: $10-20 Million
Number Employees: 10
Type of Packaging: Food Service
Regions Exported to: Worldwide
Percentage of Business in Exporting: 15

49574 USA Laboratories Inc
1438 Highway 96
Burns, TN 37029-5030   615-441-1521
Fax: 615-446-3788   800-489-4872
usalabs@usalabs.com   www.usalabs.com
Processor and exporter of vitamins, minerals, nutritional supplements and weight loss aids
President/Owner: Charles Stokes
CEO: Charles Stokes
R&D: David Bethshears
yumyum1969@live.com
Quality Control: Brad Stokes
Marketing Director: Erica White
Sales Director: Shelby Bethsheard
Contact: Suzzane Guire
yumyum1969@live.com
Operations: Ted Sanders
Estimated Sales: $4.7 Million
Number Employees: 1-4
Number of Brands: 5
Number of Products: 1000
Square Footage: 400000
Parent Co: USA Laboratories
Regions Exported to: Europe
Percentage of Business in Exporting: 20

49575 (HQ)USDA-NASS
1400 Independence Ave SW
Washington, DC 20250-0002   202-690-8122
Fax: 202-720-9013   800-727-9540
nass@nass.usda.gov   www.nass.usda.gov
The mission is to research and develop knowledge and technology needed to solve technical agricultural problems of broad scope in order to ensure adequate production of high quality food and agricultural products
Administrator: Cynthia Clark
Director of Research and Development: Mark Harris
Contact: Art Fairson
art.fairson@ars.usda.gov
Director of Operations: Kevin Barnes
Number Employees: 250-499

49576 USECO
P.O.Box 20428
Murfreesboro, TN 37129-0428   615-893-4820
Fax: 615-893-8705   info@useco.com
www.useco.com
Manufacturer and exporter of stainless steel and aluminum food service equipment including hot and cold food service carts, tray line refrigerators, blast chillers, tray lifters, pellet heaters, etc
President: John Westbrook
VP (Food Service Systems Tech.): Sara Hurt
VP Sales/Marketing (USECO): Paul Murphy
Estimated Sales: $20-50 Million
Number Employees: 50-99
Square Footage: 100000
Parent Co: Standex International Corporation
Type of Packaging: Food Service
Regions Exported to: Worldwide

49577 UVA Packaging
8111 Virginia Pine Ct
Richmond, VA 23237-2202   804-275-8067
Fax: 804-271-3096   www.pmb-uvainc.com
Importer and wholesaler/distributor of packaging machinery including vertical form/fill/seal
President: George Van Bergen
Sales/Marketing Manager: Siegfried Gaessner
Estimated Sales: $3 - 5 Million
Number Employees: 10-19
Square Footage: 44032
Parent Co: PMB-UVA
Brands Imported: Butler 1; Butler 2; Butler 3; UVA 350A; UVA 600A; Newton 250i; 250c; 400c.
Regions Imported from: Europe
Percentage of Business in Importing: 100

49578 (HQ)Uas Laboratories
9953 Valley View Rd
Eden Prairie, MN 55344   952-935-1707
Fax: 952-935-1650   800-422-3371
info@uaslabs.com
Manufacturer and exporter of nutritional supplements

President: S K Dash
Quality Control: Scot Elert
Marketing Director: Raj Dash
Operations Manager: Steven Shack
Estimated Sales: $3 Million
Number Employees: 10-19
Number of Products: 12
Square Footage: 21600
Type of Packaging: Consumer, Private Label, Bulk
Brands Exported: DDS
Regions Exported to: Worldwide
Percentage of Business in Exporting: 10

49579 Ucc Ueshima Coffee Co Inc
723a Liggett Ave
San Francisco, CA 94129-1480   415-440-8221
Fax: 212-397-1862 info@ucc-america.com
www.ucc-america.com
Importer of coffee
Director: Hirotsugu Tsuzimoyo
Executive VP: S Sasaki
Estimated Sales: Less Than $500,000
Number Employees: 1-4
Type of Packaging: Private Label, Bulk

49580 Ulcra Dynamics
3000 Advance Lane
Colmar, PA 18915-9432   201-489-0044
Fax: 201-489-9229 800-727-6931
Manufacturer and exporter of water treatment systems
Estimated Sales: $ 500,000-$ 1 Million
Number Employees: 10-19
Parent Co: Severn Trent Services
Regions Exported to: Worldwide
Percentage of Business in Exporting: 15

49581 Ullman, Shapiro & UllmanLLP
425 Park Ave 27th Floor
New York, NY 10022   212-755-0299
www.usulaw.com
Manufacturer and exporter of platters, plates, bowls, tumblers and pitchers
Partner: Marc Ullman
Chief Executive Officer: Zev Weiss
Executive VP: Marvin Lipkind
Estimated Sales: $10-20 Million
Number Employees: 1-4
Square Footage: 300000
Regions Exported to: Worldwide
Percentage of Business in Exporting: 5

49582 Ultima Health Products Inc.
3284 Niles-Cortland Rd.
Cortland, OH 44410
Fax: 330-638-5500 888-663-8584
www.ultimareplenisher.com
Electrolyte-balanced energy drink without sugar, carbs or calories
Vice-President, Sales: Skeet Freeman
Year Founded: 1996
Number of Brands: 1
Type of Packaging: Consumer, Private Label
Brands Exported: Ultima
Regions Exported to: USA, Canada

49583 Ultimate International
4631 N Dixie Hwy
Boca Raton, FL 33431-5030   561-347-1531
Fax: 561-347-1533 www.ultimatelabs.com
Exporter of food flavors, commodities and chemicals
Manager: Kathleen Boulos
kbw@ultimatelabs.com
VP: Kathleen Weckering
Estimated Sales: $2.5-5 Million
Number Employees: 1-4
Square Footage: 6000
Type of Packaging: Private Label, Bulk
Brands Exported: V&E
Regions Exported to: Europe, Haiti,Caribbean
Percentage of Business in Exporting: 100

49584 Ultimate Nutrition
161 Woodford Avenue
Farmington, CT 06034-0643   860-409-7100
Fax: 860-793-5006 www.ultimatenutrition.com
Food processor and exporter of food supplements including capsules, tablets, powders and protein bars
President: Victor Rubino
Advertising: Seth Darvick
VP Sales: Dean Caputo
Type of Packaging: Consumer
Regions Exported to: Worldwide
Percentage of Business in Exporting: 60

49585 Ultra Enterprises
14108 Lambert Rd
Whittier, CA 90605-2427   562-945-4833
Fax: 562-698-7362 800-543-0627
b.kaliultra@verizon.net www.ultraent.com
Processor and sports nutrition of granulars
President/CEO: Bud Thompson
Vice President: Mary Thompson
Number of Products: 50
Type of Packaging: Consumer
Regions Exported to: Worldwide

49586 Ultra Seal
521 Main St
New Paltz, NY 12561-1609   845-255-2490
Fax: 845-255-3553 info@ultra-seal.com
www.ultra-seal.com
Contract packager of portion controlled products including ketchup, mustard, powder lemonade, fruit juice, iced tea mix, etc
President: Dennis Borrello
dennisb@ultra-seal.com
Manager: Christine Downs
Executive: Terry Murphy
Estimated Sales: $5-10 Million
Number Employees: 100-249
Square Footage: 104000
Type of Packaging: Consumer, Food Service, Private Label, Bulk
Regions Exported to: Worldwide

49587 Ultrafilter
3560 Engineering Drive
Norcross, GA 30092-2819   770-942-5322
Fax: 770-448-3854 800-543-3634
Worldwide supplier of compressed gas, steam and liquid purification equipment. Process filtration: culinary steam filters, sterile gas filters, process liquid filters, tank vent filters, 3-A approved sanitary filter housings, microfiltration cartridges. Compressed air filters and dryers, on-site compressed air quality testing: ultra-survey programs
President: Keith Hayward
Sales/Marketing: Jeff Touo
Number Employees: 20-49
Square Footage: 132000
Parent Co: Ultrafilter GmBH
Other Locations:
    Ultrafilter
    Scarborough, ONUltrafilter
Regions Exported to: Central America, South America, Latin America, Mexico
Percentage of Business in Exporting: 5
Brands Imported: Ultrafilter; Ultrasep; Ultrex; Ultrair; Ultrapac
Regions Imported from: Europe
Percentage of Business in Importing: 50

49588 Ultrafryer Systems Inc
302 Spencer Ln
San Antonio, TX 78201-2018   210-731-5000
Fax: 210-731-5099 800-545-9189
ultrafryersales@ultrafryer.com
www.ultrafryer.com
Manufacturer and exporter of gas and electric fryers, filters, breading tables, warmers, cookers and hoods
President: Ed Odmark
CEO: Edward T Odmark
eodmark@ultrafryer.com
National Manager Sales: Steve Ricketson
General Manager: William Collins
Estimated Sales: $10-20 Million
Number Employees: 50-99
Square Footage: 150000
Type of Packaging: Consumer, Food Service
Regions Exported to: Worldwide
Percentage of Business in Exporting: 15

49589 Umpqua Dairy
333 SE Sykes Ave
P.O. Box 1306
Roseburg, OR 97470   541-672-2638
Fax: 541-673-0256 888-672-6455
info@umpquadairy.com www.umpquadairy.com
Processor and exporter of ice cream, milk, cottage cheese, sour cream and butter
President: Douglas Feldkamp
Director, Sales & Marketing: Marty Weaver
COO: Steve Feldkemp
Year Founded: 1931
Estimated Sales: $50.2 Million
Number Employees: 100-249
Type of Packaging: Consumer, Food Service, Private Label
Regions Exported to: Worldwide
Percentage of Business in Exporting: 2

49590 UnReal Brands
Boston, MA
hi@getunreal.com
www.getunreal.com
Non-GMO, fair trade, gluten-free, artificial ingredient-free dark and milk chocolate peanut butter cups, chocolate-coated quinoa and chocolate-covered nuts
Co-Founder: Nicky Bronner
Co-Founder: Kristopher Bronner
Year Founded: 2010
Number of Brands: 1
Number of Products: 6
Type of Packaging: Consumer, Private Label
Brands Exported: UnReal
Regions Exported to: USA

49591 Unarco Industries LLC
400 SE 15th St
Wagoner, OK 74467-7900   918-485-9531
Fax: 918-485-2131 800-654-4100
www.unarco.com
Manufacturer and exporter of shopping carts, retail display fixtures, stainless steel tables and accessories, food service containers and carts and warehousing and stocking carts
President: Randy Garvin
CFO: Misty Allen
misty.allen@unarco.com
Sales: Richard Wilkinson
VP International Sales: David Warneke
VP Sales: Richard Wilkinson
Estimated Sales: $50-100 Million
Number Employees: 250-499
Square Footage: 650000
Type of Packaging: Food Service
Regions Exported to: Central America, South America, Europe, Asia, Middle East
Percentage of Business in Exporting: 10

49592 Unarco Material Handling Inc
407 E Washington St
Pandora, OH 45877   419-384-3211
Fax: 419-384-7239 800-448-0784
www.unarcorack.com
Manufacturer and exporter of roll-formed pallet rack systems
National Sales Manager: David Johnstone
Manager: Mike Burris
mikeb@clymer-rack.com
Estimated Sales: $10-20 Million
Number Employees: 50-99
Parent Co: Unarco Material Handling, Inc.
Type of Packaging: Bulk
Regions Exported to: Canada

49593 Uncle Dougie's
Chicago, IL
www.originaluncledougies.com
Preservative- and GMO-free barbecue sauces, marinades, seasonings, rubs, hot sauces and drink mixes in various flavors
Founder: Doug Tomek
Year Founded: 1989
Number of Brands: 1
Number of Products: 19
Type of Packaging: Consumer, Private Label
Brands Exported: Uncle Dougie's
Regions Exported to: USA, Canada

49594 Uncle Fred's Fine Foods
209 N Doughty Street
Rockport, TX 78382-5322   361-729-8320
www.unclfred.com
Processor and importer of habanero ketchup, jelly, hot sweet mustard and chips, salsa, spices, meat rubs and sauces including cocktail, pepper and barbecue
President: Fred Franklin
VP/Co-Owner: Pat Marsh
Manager: Judith Jecmen-Fuhrman
Number Employees: 1-4
Square Footage: 6400
Parent Co: Island Enterprises
Type of Packaging: Consumer
Regions Imported from: Central America
Percentage of Business in Importing: 2

Importers & Exporters / A-Z

49595 Uncle Lee's Tea Inc
11020 Rush St
South El Monte, CA 91733-3547 626-350-3309
Fax: 626-350-4364 800-732-8830
www.unclelee.com
Processor, exporter and importer of teas including herb, spiced, traditional and dieter's; co-packing and private label available
Vice President: Tim Carter
tim.carter@health.net
Chairman: Lee Rieho
Vice President: Jonason Lee
Sales Director: James O'Young
Public Relations: Patty Gillno
Plant Manager: Joe Villegas
Estimated Sales: $1400000
Number Employees: 20-49
Parent Co: Ten Ren Tea Company
Brands Exported: Uncle Lee's Teas
Regions Exported to: Worldwide
Percentage of Business in Exporting: 50

49596 Uncle Matt's Organic
PO Box 120187
Clermont, FL 34712 833-729-8625
Fax: 352-394-1003 media@unclematts.com
www.unclematts.com
Organic orange, grapefruit, apple juices; organic lemonade; organic probiotic waters in various flavors
Founder/Owner: Matt McLean
Year Founded: 1999
Number of Brands: 1
Number of Products: 11
Type of Packaging: Consumer, Private Label
Brands Exported: Uncle Matt's Organic
Regions Exported to: USA, Canada

49597 Une-Viandi
505 Industriel Boulevard
St. Jean Sur Richelieu, NB J3B 5Y8
Canada 450-347-8406
Fax: 450-347-8142 800-363-1955
Processor, importer and exporter of meat products including bone-in and boneless beef, lamb and veal
President: Claude Berni
Export Manager: Lloyd Arshinoff
Number Employees: 50-99
Square Footage: 88000
Type of Packaging: Consumer, Food Service, Private Label, Bulk
Regions Exported to: Worldwide
Regions Imported from: USA

49598 Unger Co
12401 Berea Rd
Cleveland, OH 44111-1607 216-252-1400
Fax: 216-252-1427 800-321-1418
info@ungerco.com www.ungerco.com
Supplier of packaging for bakery and deli products. Importer of polyethylene, polyprop and plastic shopping bags, and boxes. Consulting services available
President/CEO: Gerald Unger
info@ungerco.com
Controller: Scott Smith
VP: Diane Tracy
Estimated Sales: $5-10 Million
Number Employees: 10-19
Type of Packaging: Food Service
Brands Exported: Ungermatic; Decorated Cake Box; Deleez Bag
Brands Imported: Siluett; Package Nakazawa
Regions Imported from: Europe, Asia

49599 (HQ)Ungerer & Co
4 Bridgewater Ln
Lincoln Park, NJ 07035-1491 973-706-7381
Fax: 973-628-0251 www.ungererandcompany.com
Manufacturer, importer and exporter of natural and artificial fruit flavors and essential oils including lemon, orange, peppermint, spearmint, ginger, lime and dill
President: Casey Annicchiarico
cannicchiarico@ungererandcompany.com
Estimated Sales: $10 Million
Number Employees: 100-249
Type of Packaging: Consumer, Private Label, Bulk
Other Locations:
Ungerer & Company Plant
Bethlehem, PAUngerer & Company PlantOaxaca, Mexico
Brands Exported: Ungerer & Co.
Regions Exported to: Central America, South America, Europe, Asia, Middle East
Percentage of Business in Exporting: 15
Regions Imported from: Central America, South America, Asia, Middle East

49600 (HQ)UniTrak Corporation
299 Ward Street
PO Box 330
Port Hope, ON L1A 3W4
Canada 905-885-8168
Fax: 905-885-2614 866-883-5749
info@unitrak.com www.unitrak.com
Manufacturer and exporter of bucket elevators, packaging machinery and conveyors
President: W Gorsline
Engineering Team Leader: Keith Douglas
Scheduling and Special Project: D Snoddon
Marketing Team Leader: Marie Lytle
Operations Manager: D Snoddon
Plant Manager: Ivan Patton
Number Employees: 10
Square Footage: 40000
Other Locations:
UniTrak Corp. Ltd.
Furness Vale, High PeakUniTrak Corp. Ltd.
Brands Exported: Efficia; TipTrak
Regions Exported to: Central America, South America, Europe, Asia, Canada, Mexico

49601 Unibroue/Unibrew
80 Rue Des CarriŠres
Chambly, QC J3L 2H6
Canada 450-658-7658
Fax: 450-658-9195 info@unibroue.com
www.unibroue.com
Gourmet beer including black currant, apple, and chambly blonde
Brewing Supervisor: Martin Gagn
Year Founded: 1990
Estimated Sales: $21million
Number Employees: 250
Parent Co: Sapporo
Type of Packaging: Consumer, Food Service
Regions Exported to: Worldwide

49602 Unified Food Ingredients
145 Vallecitos DE Oro # 208
San Marcos, CA 92069-1459 760-744-7225
Fax: 760-744-7215
Processor, exporter and importer of dehydrated vegetables including bell peppers, carrots, celery, peas, corn, mushrooms, garlic, etc
Owner: Dan Stouder
VP: Dan Stouder
Sales Manager: Simone Grunewald
Customer Service: Kris Cannan
Operations Manager: Melissa Coetzee
Estimated Sales: $ 1 - 3,000,000
Number Employees: 1-4
Square Footage: 20000
Type of Packaging: Bulk
Regions Exported to: Europe, Mexico
Percentage of Business in Exporting: 10
Regions Imported from: Worldwide
Percentage of Business in Importing: 80

49603 Unifoil Corp
12 Daniel Rd
Fairfield, NJ 07004-2536 973-244-9990
Fax: 973-244-5555 www.unifoil.com
Manufacturer and exporter of laminated and coated aluminum foil; also, metallized and holographic paper and boards
President: Joseph Funicelli
CEO: Milica Bubalo
mbubalo@unifoil.com
CFO: William Mulooney
Quality Control: Robert Galloino
Sales Director: Robert Rumer
Plant Manager: Dwight Penrell
Estimated Sales: $20-50 Million
Number Employees: 50-99

49604 Uniforms To You
9525 S. Cicero Avenue
Oak Lawn, IL 60453 708-424-4747
800-889-6072
www.uniformstoyou.com
Uniforms, work gear and career apparel.
Estimated Sales: $20 - 50 Million
Number Employees: 500-999
Parent Co: Cintas Corp

49605 Unilever Canada
160 Bloor St. East
Suite 1400
Toronto, ON M4W 3R2
Canada 416-415-3000
www.unilever.ca
Food products, personal care, and home products.
Director, Customer Development: Bruce Findlay
VP, Brand Strategy & Innovation: Margaret McKellar
Year Founded: 1949
Estimated Sales: $466 Million
Number Employees: 3,400
Square Footage: 80912
Parent Co: Unilever US
Type of Packaging: Consumer, Food Service

49606 Unilever US
800 Sylvan Ave
Englewood Cliffs, NJ 07632
800-298-5018
www.unileverusa.com
Food products, personal care, and home products.
President, North America: Amanda Sourry
CEO: Alan Jope
CFO: Graeme Pitkethly
Chief R&D Officer: Richard Slater
VP, Human Resources, North America: Mike Clementi
Estimated Sales: $18 Billion
Number Employees: 5000-9999
Parent Co: Unilever N.V. & Unilever plc
Type of Packaging: Consumer, Food Service
Regions Exported to: Worldwide

49607 Unimove LLC
1145 Little Gap Rd # C
Palmerton, PA 18071-5027 610-826-7855
Fax: 610-826-8422 unimove@ptd.net
www.unimove.com
Manufacturer and exporter of vacuum tube lifting systems
Director: Robert Shannon
unitech@ptd.net
VP: Vincent Julian Jr
Director Marketing: Ken Kasick
Operations: Alan Zimmermann
Purchasing: Charles Kistler
Estimated Sales: 1,000,000
Number Employees: 5-9
Number of Brands: 1
Square Footage: 140000
Regions Exported to: South America, Europe
Percentage of Business in Exporting: 1

49608 Union
14522 Myford Rd
Irvine, CA 92606-1000 714-734-2200
Fax: 714-734-2223 800-854-7292
Processor and exporter of Oriental ramen noodles
President: Sang Mook Lee
CEO: Victor Sim
Sales Manager: Bob Hicks
Estimated Sales: $10,900,000
Number Employees: 100-249
Square Footage: 200000
Type of Packaging: Consumer, Private Label
Brands Exported: Smack
Regions Exported to: Central America, South America, Europe
Percentage of Business in Exporting: 30

49609 Union Confectionery Machinery
801-825 E 141st St
Bronx, NY 10454-1917 718-585-0200
Fax: 718-993-2650 sales@unionmachinery.com
www.unionmachinery.com
Exporter of food packaging and processing machinery
VP: John Greenberg
Estimated Sales: $1-3 Million
Number Employees: 20-49
Parent Co: National Equipment Corporation
Regions Exported to: Central America, South America, Europe, Asia, Middle East, Australia, Canada, Carribean, Latin America, Mexico
Percentage of Business in Exporting: 40

49610 Union Cord Products Company
425 N Martingdale Road
Schaumburg, IL 60173 847-240-1500
Fax: 847-240-1576 info@unionleasing.com
www.unionleasing.com

Manufacturer and exporter of gaskets including braided, knitted, rubber insert and poly-jacketed cellulose
CEO: Warren Benis
Estimated Sales: $ 1 - 5,000,000
Parent Co: Sasser Family Holdings Inc.

49611 Union Fish Co
100 Larkspur Landing Cir # 115
Suite 115
Larkspur, CA 94939-1731   415-925-5280
Fax: 415-925-5283 unionfish@aol.com
www.unionfishco.com
Importer of frozen seafood including squid, octopus, scad, orange roughy, mahi mahi, black cod, tuna, yellowfin, mussels, scallops, snapper, lobster and shrimp; exporter of seafood, frozen vegetables and fruits
President: Ken Hild
National Sales Manager: Scott Smith
Estimated Sales: Less Than $500,000
Number Employees: 1-4
Type of Packaging: Food Service
Regions Exported to: Asia, Australia
Percentage of Business in Exporting: 10
Regions Imported from: South America, Asia, Australia
Percentage of Business in Importing: 90

49612 Union Industries
10 Admiral St
Providence, RI 02908   401-274-7000
Fax: 401-331-1910   800-556-6454
Manufacturer and exporter of flexible packaging
President: Harley Frank
Chairman: H Alan Frank
CFO: John Wilbur
Sales Director: Michael Kauffman
Contact: Anne Delany
adelany@unionpaperco.com
Estimated Sales: $ 23.5 Million
Number Employees: 125
Square Footage: 125000
Type of Packaging: Food Service, Private Label
Regions Exported to: South America, Europe

49613 Union Process
1925 Akron Peninsula Rd
Akron, OH 44313   330-929-3333
Fax: 330-929-3034 eli@unionprocess.com
www.unionprocess.com
Manufacturers a broad line of wet and dry milling attritors and small media mills. Also offer a wide assortment of grinding media and provide toll milling and refurbishing services. Also the meading manufacturer of rubber inks for balloons, swim caps and other rubber products.
President: Arno Szegvari
R & D Lab: Margaret Yang
National Sales Manager: Robert Schilling
Production: Craig McCaulley
Plant Manager: Ron Sloan
Estimated Sales: $ 5 - 10 Million
Number Employees: 20-49
Square Footage: 56000
Brands Exported: Szegvari Attritors
Regions Exported to: Worldwide
Percentage of Business in Exporting: 33

49614 Uniplast Films
1017 Wilson Street
Palmer, MA 01069-1137   413-283-8365
Fax: 413-283-8278   800-343-1295
Film laminates and plastic and coextended film; exporter of plastic film
VP: Fredy Steng
Customer Service: Diane Fihal
Estimated Sales: $ 1 - 5 Million
Number Employees: 100
Square Footage: 160000
Parent Co: Uniplast Industries
Regions Exported to: Central America, South America, Europe, Canada, Caribbean, Latin America
Percentage of Business in Exporting: 5

49615 Unique Beverage Company
PO Box 2246
Everett, WA 98213-0246   425-267-0959
Fax: 425-353-5600
customerservice@cascadeicewater.com
www.cascadeicewater.com
Sodium-free, caffeine-free, sugar-free flavored sparkling water; organic varieties available
Chief Executive Officer: Mark Christensen
Number of Brands: 1
Type of Packaging: Consumer, Private Label
Brands Exported: Cascade Ice
Regions Exported to: USA

49616 Unique Ingredients LLC
6460 S Mountainside Dr
Gold Canyon, AZ 85118-2900   480-983-2498
Fax: 509-653-1992 oly@werunique.com
www.werunique.com
Dried apples in a variety of cuts, styles and varieties; offering air dried, drum dried and upon request, freeze dried fruits and vegetables, specializing in apples, apricots, cherries, peaches, plums, raisins, bananas and all tropical fruits
Founder: Dave Olsen
Finance and Accounting: Karen Bentz
Sales: Matt Gibbs
Contact: Delrae Blanchard
delrae@werunique.com
Operations: Becky Cornwall
Estimated Sales: $3 Million
Number Employees: 5-9
Number of Brands: 1
Number of Products: 100
Square Footage: 500
Type of Packaging: Private Label, Bulk
Brands Imported: Surfrut; Confoco
Regions Imported from: South America, Chile, Honduras, Ecuador
Percentage of Business in Importing: 80

49617 Unique Manufacturing
1920 W Princeton Ave Ste 17
Visalia, CA 93277   559-739-1007
Fax: 559-739-7725   888-737-1007
Manufacturer and importer of silverware sleeves, paper napkin bands, beverage coasters, menu covers, chopsticks, flag food picks and paper parasols
President: Irwin Smith
Marketing: Paul Smith
Sales: Erwin Smith
Number Employees: 5-9
Square Footage: 4000
Regions Imported from: Asia, Mexico

49618 Unique Manufacturing Company
1050 Corporate Ave
Suite 108
North Port, FL 34289   941-429-6600
Fax: 253-669-7645 sales@uniquemanuf.com
www.uniquemanuf.com
Importers and manufacturing of hospitality items. Custom printed stock flag food picks, beverage stirs, paper/foil parasols, napkins bands, silverware sleeves, chenille and foil decorator picks, plastic food picks, chop sticks coasters, paper glass covers, placemats, tray covers, and menu covers and binders
Owner: Michael Jakubowski
Estimated Sales: Below $5 Million
Number Employees: 1-4
Number of Products: 500
Square Footage: 2000
Type of Packaging: Consumer, Private Label

49619 Unique Pretzel Bakery, Inc.
215 East Bellevue Ave.
Reading, PA 19605   610-929-3172
Fax: 610-929-3444
Hard-baked pretzel "splits"; pretzel shells, chocolate-covered pretzels
Number of Brands: 1
Type of Packaging: Consumer, Private Label
Brands Exported: Unique

49620 Unique Solutions
2836 Corporate Pkwy
Algonquin, IL 60102-2564   847-960-1110
Fax: 847-540-1431 info@unique-solutions.com
www.unique-solutions.com
Product line includes inserting and labeling equipment produced in a continuous, perforated bandolier format in addition to that of two or three-dimensional premiums and labels that are inserted (In-Pakrs) or attached to the outside of primary packaging (On-Pakrs).
President: Mark Ulan
Chairman/CEO: Joyce Witt
info@unique-solutions.com
Business Development Manager: Brian Dawson
VP Sales: Walter Peterson
COO: Jason Raasch
Production Manager: Norman Hendle
info@unique-solutions.com
Customer Service Representative: Christie Haack
Estimated Sales: $2.5-5 Million
Number Employees: 5-9
Square Footage: 52000
Parent Co: Unique Coupons

49621 Unique Vitality Products
29215 Hillrise Dr
Agoura Hills, CA 91301-1533   818-889-7739
Fax: 818-889-4895
Processor and exporter of vitamins
Owner: Pierre Van Wessel
uvppierre@extreme.com
CEO: Robert Van Wessel
CFO: Wendy Van Wessel
Quality Control: Ashwin Patel
Production: Hasmuck Patec
Estimated Sales: $ .5 - 1 million
Number Employees: 1-4
Square Footage: 800000
Type of Packaging: Private Label, Bulk
Regions Exported to: Europe, Middle East
Regions Imported from: Europe

49622 Unirak Storage Systems
7620 Telegraph Rd
Taylor, MI 48180-2237   313-291-7600
Fax: 313-291-7605   800-348-7225
sales@unirak.com www.unirak.com
Manufacturer and exporter of racks including adjustable storage, pallet, galvanized, refrigerated, selective, drive-in/thru, deck, pallet flow, push-back and carton flow
Vice President: Eric Gonda
sales@unarak.com
Sales Director: Eric Gonda
Estimated Sales: $ 3 - 5 Million
Number Employees: 10-19
Number of Brands: 4
Number of Products: 110
Square Footage: 400000
Type of Packaging: Bulk
Brands Exported: Unirak
Regions Exported to: Worldwide
Percentage of Business in Exporting: 10

49623 United Ad Label
3075 Highland Parkway
Suite 400
Downers Grove, IL 60515-5560   714-990-2700
Fax: 800-962-0658   800-423-4643
Manufacturer and exporter of pressure sensitive labels
President: Cal Laird
VP Marketing: Brad Baylies
New Markets Manager: Cheryl Hall
cheryl.hall@rrd.com
Estimated Sales: $ 1 - 5 Million
Number Employees: 100-250
Type of Packaging: Consumer, Bulk
Regions Exported to: Central America, Europe, Canada

49624 (HQ)United Air Specialists Inc
4440 Creek Rd
Blue Ash, OH 45242-2832   513-891-0400
Fax: 513-891-4171   800-992-4422
www.uasinc.com
Manufacturer and exporter of air filtration media including electrostatic precipitators, liquid coating and dust collection systems
President: Rich Larson
riclar@uasinc.com
VP Marketing: Lynne Laake
Estimated Sales: G
Number Employees: 250-499
Square Footage: 152500
Other Locations:
    United Air Specialists
    Cincinnati, OH United Air Specialists

49625 United Apple Sales
124 Main St Ste 5
New Paltz, NY 12561   585-765-2460
Fax: 585-765-9710 uasales@aol.com
www.unitedapplesales.com

Importers & Exporters / A-Z

Grower, importer and exporter of apples
COO: Chuck Andola
Domestic/Export Sales: Dean Decker
Estimated Sales: $360,000
Number Employees: 1-4
Type of Packaging: Consumer, Food Service
Brands Exported: Storm King; Americas Fruit
Regions Exported to: Europe, Middle East

49626 United Bags Inc
1355 N Warson Rd
St Louis, MO 63132-1598   314-421-3700
          Fax: 314-421-0969 800-550-2247
     custserv@unitedbags.com www.unitedbags.com
Manufacturer and importer of bags including bulk, burlap, multi-wall, polypropylene, paper and cotton
President: Todd Greenberg
unitedbags@aol.com
CEO: Herbert Greenberg
CFO: Ruth Allen
VP: Todd Greenberg
Estimated Sales: $2.5-5 Million
Number Employees: 20-49
Square Footage: 600000

49627 United Bakery EquipmentCompany
15815 W 110th St
Shawnee Mission, KS 66219   913-541-8700
          Fax: 913-541-0781 www.ubeusa.com
Manufacturer and exporter of slicers and baggers for breads, buns, tortillas, muffins, bagels, etc
President: Frank Bastasch
Vice President: Paul Bastasch
Sales Director: Bob Plourde
Contact: Levent Gokkaya
lgokkaya@untek.com.tr
Estimated Sales: $ 20 - 50 Million
Number Employees: 50-99
Square Footage: 32000
Parent Co: United Bakery Equipment Company
Type of Packaging: Food Service, Private Label
Regions Exported to: Worldwide
Percentage of Business in Exporting: 35

49628 United Banana Company
27 Griswold St
Binghamton, NY 13904-1543   607-724-0994
Importer and wholesaler/distributor of produce
President: Thomas Burns
VP: Heather Burns
Estimated Sales: $2.5-5 Million
Number Employees: 5-9
Square Footage: 12800
Brands Imported: Dole
Regions Imported from: Central America
Percentage of Business in Importing: 100

49629 United Canadian Malt
843 Park Street South
Peterborough, ON K9J 3V1
Canada   705-876-9110
          Fax: 705-876-9118 800-461-6400
Processor, exporter and importer of dried and custom liquid brewing extracts, malt syrups and liquid malt
President/General Manager: Monte Smith
Estimated Sales: $500,000-999,999
Number Employees: 15
Square Footage: 499600
Type of Packaging: Bulk
Regions Exported to: Central America, South America, Europe, Asia
Percentage of Business in Exporting: 40
Regions Imported from: Europe
Percentage of Business in Importing: 4

49630 United Chairs
4600 Steeles Avenue W
Woodbridge, ON L4L 9L5
Canada   905-851-8838
          Fax: 905-850-3729
Wholesaler/distributor and importer of chairs; serving the food service market

49631 United Citrus
244 Vanderbilt Ave # 1
Norwood, MA 02062-5052   781-769-7300
          Fax: 781-769-9492 800-229-7300
          www.unitedcitrus
Bulk dry blends and liquid food products including: cocktail mixes, cocktail rimmers, beverage juices, energy drinks, hydration beverages, frozen carbonated beverages, superfruit beverages and dry blended specialty desserts
President: Richard Kates
rkates@unitedcitrus.net
VP/General Manager: Christopher Fernandes
R&D: Linda Halik
Quality Control: Cheryl Senato
Purchasing: Kristen Burbank
Estimated Sales: $5 Million
Number Employees: 10-19
Type of Packaging: Consumer, Food Service, Private Label, Bulk
Regions Exported to: Europe, Asia

49632 United Desiccants
985 Damonte Ranch Parkway
Suite #320
Reno, NE 89521   505-864-6691
          Fax: 505-864-9296 888-659-1377
     insidesale@desiccare.com www.desiccare.com
Manufacturer and exporter of desiccant absorption packs; also, humidity indicators for packaging
President: William Monin
General Manager: George Klett
Business Unit Manager: Richard Greenlaw
Number Employees: 300
Parent Co: United Catalysts
Regions Exported to: Central America, Europe, Asia

49633 United Electric Controls Co
180 Dexter Ave
Watertown, MA 02472-4200   617-926-1000
          Fax: 617-926-4354 support@ueonline.com
          www.ueonline.com
Manufacturer and exporter of temperature control and detection devices including thermostats, pressure and temperature switches, transducers and sensors for general purpose and sanitary service.
Chief Executive Officer: Dave Reis
Director of Materials: Cheryl O'Connell
Year Founded: 1931
Estimated Sales: $100+ Million
Number Employees: 100-249
Other Locations:
     United Electric Controls Co.
     Milford, CT United Electric Controls Co.
Regions Exported to: Central America, South America, Europe, Asia, Middle East

49634 United Filters Intl
901 S Grant St
Amarillo, TX 79101-3625   806-373-8386
          Fax: 806-371-7783 info@unitedfilters.com
          www.unitedfilters.com
Manufacturer and exporter of string wound filter cartridges and vessels
Manager: David Otwell
Sales Manager (South): David Otwell
Sales Manager (North): Lynn Love
Estimated Sales: $500,000-$1 Million
Number Employees: 10-19
Square Footage: 100000
Parent Co: Perry Equipment Corporation
Brands Exported: Peco
Regions Exported to: Worldwide
Percentage of Business in Exporting: 5

49635 United Flexible
900 Merchants Concourse
Westbury, NY 11590-5142   516-222-2150
          Fax: 516-222-2168 captivepackaging@aol.com
Manufacturer and exporter of plastic bags, printed roll stock and shrink packaging and lamination
President/CEO: Aldel Englander
Marketing Head: Elen Blonett
Estimated Sales: $5-10,000,000
Number Employees:
Regions Exported to: Worldwide

49636 United Floor Machine Co
7715 S South Chicago Ave # 1
Chicago, IL 60619-2797   773-734-0974
          Fax: 773-734-0874 800-288-0848
          unico1946@aol.com
Manufacturer and exporter of burnishers, heavy duty floor polishers and scrubbers, carpet shampooers
President/Owner: Richard Leitelt
unico1946@aol.com
VP: David Leitelt

Estimated Sales: Below $ 5 Million
Number Employees: 1-4
Square Footage: 6000
Regions Exported to: South America, Europe
Percentage of Business in Exporting: 5

49637 United Foods & Fitness
532 N State Road
Briarcliff Manor, NY 10510-1526   914-941-2145
          Fax: 914-941-8443 800-638-3800
Importer and wholesaler/distributor of nutritional supplements, energy bars, vitamins, amino acids, protein powders, sports drinks and weight gain supplements
President: Cherie Deglon
Estimated Sales: $2.5-5 Million
Number Employees: 1-4
Type of Packaging: Consumer, Food Service
Brands Imported. Multi Power
Regions Imported from: Europe
Percentage of Business in Importing: 100

49638 United Industries GroupInc
11 Rancho Cir # 1100
Lake Forest, CA 92630-8324   949-759-3200
          Fax: 949-759-3425 info@unitedind.com
          www.unitedind.com
Manufacturer and exporter of storage tanks and wastewater treatment and water purification systems; also, designer of water bottling and water purification package plants
Manager: Jim Mansour
Quality Control: John Mansell
VP: M Mulvaney
IT: James P Mansour
info@unitedind.com
Estimated Sales: $20-30 Million
Number Employees: 20-49
Regions Exported to: Central America, Europe, Asia, Middle East, Africa, Caribbean, Australia
Percentage of Business in Exporting: 50

49639 United International Indstrs
104 Mullach Ct # 1008
Suite 1008
Wentzville, MO 63385-4858   636-327-5910
          Fax: 636-327-5904 800-292-3509
          tcarlisle@uinternational.com
          www.uinternational.com
Wholesaler/distributor of whey, dry milk, casein, processed and imitation cheese and cheese powders, butter, etc
Chief Executive Officer: M Jane Carlisle
CFO: James Dolson
VP: Thomas Carlisle Jr
Sales: Kris Jenkins
Estimated Sales: $6-$10 Million
Number Employees: 10-19
Regions Exported to: Central America, South America, Europe, Middle East
Percentage of Business in Exporting: 20
Regions Imported from: Central America, South America, Europe, Asia, Middle East, Australia, New Zealand
Percentage of Business in Importing: 40

49640 United Marketing Exchange
215 Silver St
Delta, CO 81416-1517   970-874-3332
          Fax: 970-874-9525
Processor and exporter of fresh fruits and onions
President: Harold Broughton
Sales Manager: Mike Gibson
mike@umefruit.com
Estimated Sales: $1089000
Number Employees: 1-4
Parent Co: Hi Quality Packing
Type of Packaging: Consumer
Brands Exported: Tom-Tom
Regions Exported to: Caribbean
Percentage of Business in Exporting: 15

49641 United Meat Company
1040 Bryant St.
San Francisco, CA 94103   415-864-2118
          Fax: 415-703-9061
Manufacturer, exporter, and importer of frozen portion controlled lamb, venison, veal and beef.
President: Phil Gee
Finance Executive: Bill Gee
Sales Executive: Leonard Gee
Contact: Philip Gee
philjr77@yahoo.com

Importers & Exporters / A-Z

Estimated Sales: $20-50 Million
Number Employees: 20-49
Square Footage: 19430
Type of Packaging: Food Service
Regions Exported to: Asia
Percentage of Business in Exporting: 15
Brands Imported: American Beef
Regions Imported from: Asia
Percentage of Business in Importing: 5

49642 United Mineral & Chemical Corporation
1100 Valley Brook Ave Ste 203
Lyndhurst, NJ 07071 201-507-3300
Fax: 201-507-1506 800-777-0505
inquiry@umccorp.com www.umccorp.com
Importer and wholesaler/distributor of magnesium chlorides FCC, sorbic and citric acid, potassium sorbate, and sodium erythorbate
President: A Becidyan
Chemical Department Manager: Sal Morreale
Contact: Michael Sansonetti
msansonetti@umccorp.com
Estimated Sales: $20 Million
Number Employees: 20-49
Type of Packaging: Bulk
Regions Imported from: Europe, Asia, Latin America, China
Percentage of Business in Importing: 95

49643 United Olive Oil Import
139 Fulton St
Suite 314
New York, NY 10038-2537 212-346-0942
Fax: 212-504-3297 scott@unitedoliveoil.com
www.unitedoliveoil.com
Italian food: olive oils, pasta and tomatoes, beans and grains, vegetables, condiments, coffee, cookies, fish, cheese and spices.
President & CEO: Tommaso Asaro
Business Development Manager: Cristina Ile
Director of Operations: Zach Casso
Estimated Sales: $5.3 Million
Number Employees: 30
Other Locations:
  National Distribution Centers
  Edison, NJ
  Southern Warehousing & Distribution
  San Antonio, TX National Distribution Centers San Antonio
Brands Imported: A'Siciliana, Asaro, Chef Gennaro, Frankies, Grifo, Organic Farm, Oro di Sicilia, Paesanol, Rustico, Tartuflanghe, Verolio and Partanna.
Regions Imported from: Italy

49644 United Performance Metals
3045 Commercial Ave
Northbrook, IL 60062-1912 847-498-3111
Fax: 847-498-2810
www.upmet.com
Manufacturer and exporter of titanium caustic food processing equipment and machine parts including scrapper, tubing and pipe coils
President: Richard Leopold
Senior VP: Jerry St Clair
Marketing Director: Joanie Leopold
Sales: Steve Gerzel
Operations: Adelberto Cordova
Estimated Sales: $9000000
Number Employees: 20-49
Parent Co: United Performance Metals
Regions Exported to: Central America, South America, Europe, Asia, Middle East
Percentage of Business in Exporting: 25
Regions Imported from: Europe, Asia
Percentage of Business in Importing: 30

49645 (HQ)United Pickles
4366 Park Ave
Bronx, NY 10457-2494 718-933-6060
Fax: 718-367-8522 picklebiz@aol.com
www.unitedpickle.com
Pickle, sauerkraut and relish maker.
Owner: Steve Leibowitz
sleibowitz@unitedpickle.com
Number Employees: 1-4
Type of Packaging: Consumer, Food Service, Bulk
Other Locations:
  United Pickle Products Corp.
  Rosenhayn, NJ United Pickle Products Corp.

49646 United Ribtype Co
1319 Production Rd
Fort Wayne, IN 46808-1164 260-424-8973
Fax: 260-426-5502 800-473-4039
sales@ribtype.com www.ribtype.com
Manufacturer and exporter of rubber stamps
Owner: Tom Beaver
sales@ribtype.com
VP Sales: John Peirce
Estimated Sales: $3,000,000
Number Employees: 20-49
Square Footage: 40000
Parent Co: Indiana Stamp Company
Brands Exported: Ribtype
Regions Exported to: Central America, South America, Europe, Asia, Middle East
Percentage of Business in Exporting: 10

49647 United Salt Corp
4800 San Felipe St
Houston, TX 77056-3908 713-877-2600
Fax: 713-877-2609 800-554-8658
uscinfo@tum.com www.unitedsalt.com
Processor and exporter of salt including plain, iodized, agricultural and water conditioning
President: Jim O'Donnell
VP: Theresa Feldman
Contact: Ashley Baker
abaker@aquasalt.com
Estimated Sales: $16,100,000
Number Employees: 10-19
Parent Co: Texas United Corporation
Type of Packaging: Consumer, Food Service, Private Label, Bulk
Brands Exported: Gulf
Regions Exported to: Central America, South America, Middle East, Canada
Percentage of Business in Exporting: 5

49648 United Seafood Imports
5500 1st Ave N
St Petersburg, FL 33710-8006 727-894-2661
Fax: 727-894-5097
Importer and wholesaler/distributor of frozen shrimp, mahi-mahi, orange roughy and mussels
President: Richard Stowell
CFO: Vincent Arfuso
Vice President: Shane Stowell
Estimated Sales: $ 20 - 50 Million
Number Employees: 5-9
Square Footage: 3500
Brands Imported: Diamonds of the Sea
Regions Imported from: South America, Asia
Percentage of Business in Importing: 99

49649 United Seal & Tag Corporation
1544 Market Cir
Building 8
Port Charlotte, FL 33953 941-625-6799
Fax: 941-625-3644 800-211-9552
www.unitedsealandtag.com
Manufacturer and exporter of pressure sensitive, embossed, hot stamp, acetate and vinyl foil labels; also, foil tags
Owner: Robert Freda
Estimated Sales: $500,000-$1 Million
Number Employees: 10-19
Square Footage: 20000
Regions Exported to: Mexico

49650 United Showcase Company
PO Box 145
Wood Ridge, NJ 07075-0145 201-438-4100
Fax: 201-438-2630 800-526-6382
Manufacturer and exporter of stainless steel and brass showcases, nonrefrigerated salad cooler cases, collapsible cutting board brackets, pot and pan racks, sneeze guards, guide rails, tray slides, tray slide brackets and salad barshields
President/CEO: Robert Cline
CFO: Doris Cline
VP: Robert Cline
R&D: Robert Cline
Quality Control: William Stevick
Marketing: Robert Cline
Sales/Public Relations: Robert Cline
Operations/Production/Plant Manager: William Stevick
Plant Manager: Bill Stevick
Estimated Sales: $1-2.5 Million
Number Employees: 20-49
Square Footage: 60000
Regions Exported to: Europe, Bermuda, Caribbean, Canada

Percentage of Business in Exporting: 2

49651 United States Beverage LLC
700 Canal St # 4
Stamford, CT 06902-5950 203-961-8215
Fax: 203-961-8217 qq@unitedstatesbeverage.com
www.unitedstatesbeverage.com
President/CEO: Joseph Fisch Jr
CEO: Sergio Acevedo
sergioacevedo@unitedstatesbeverage.com
Estimated Sales: $300,000-500,000
Number Employees: 10-19

49652 United States Systems Inc
1028 Scott Ave
Kansas City, KS 66105-1222 913-281-1010
Fax: 913-281-2901 888-281-2454
gregahawkins@aol.com
www.unitedstatessystems.com
Manufacturer and exporter of portable and stationary pneumatic conveyor systems for dry bulk goods including railcar unloading systems and in-plant transfers; also, storage silos, dust filters and bulk bag/box filling machines
President: Greg Hawkins
gregahawkins@aol.com
General Manager: Mark Aron
Sales Manager: Greg Hawkins
Estimated Sales: $2.5-5 Million
Number Employees: 5-9
Square Footage: 10000
Brands Exported: Venturi 30; Vactank; P/D Pot
Regions Exported to: Canada, Mexico
Percentage of Business in Exporting: 30

49653 United Steel Products Company
P.O.Box 407
East Stroudsburg, PA 18301-0407 570-476-1010
Fax: 570-476-4358 www.usprack.com
Manufacturer and exporter of roll-formed and structural steel storage rack systems
President: Martin A Skulnik
Sales: Mary Petronio
Plant Manager: Bob Micco
Purchasing Manager: Maria Sosa
Estimated Sales: $50-100 Million
Number Employees: 100-249
Square Footage: 390000
Parent Co: United Steel Enterprises
Regions Exported to: Central America, South America, Middle East, Latin America
Percentage of Business in Exporting: 5

49654 United Supply
170 Associated Road
South San Francisco, CA 94080 650-588-2203
Fax: 650-588-8568
customerservice@unitedbrands.us
Manager: Baran Dilaver

49655 United Textile Distribution
350 Shipwash Dr
Garner, NC 27529-6890 919-779-4151
Fax: 919-779-6065 800-262-7624
www.unitedtextiledistribution.com
Manufacturer and exporter of disposable food service wipers including cloth and paper; also, towels and absorbent traffic mats; importer of towels
Owner: Rick EtheridgeGradin
ricketheridge@aol.com
Sales Representatives: Dave Shelton
Estimated Sales: $ 1 - 5 Million
Number Employees: 5-9
Number of Brands: 20
Number of Products: 4000
Brands Exported: Envirotex
Regions Exported to: Central America, South America, Europe, Asia, Middle East, Mexico, Africa
Percentage of Business in Exporting: 25
Regions Imported from: Middle East
Percentage of Business in Importing: 10

49656 United Universal Enterprises Corporation
7747 N 43rd Ave
Phoenix, AZ 85051 623-842-9691
Fax: 623-842-4605 univenterp@cs.com
Wholesaler/distributor, importer and exporter of general merchandise, frozen seafood, canned fruits, grains, meat, cooking oils and powdered milk; serving the food service market
Manager: Louis Galvac
Vice President: Linda Kirschner

639

Importers & Exporters / A-Z

Estimated Sales: $ 3 - 5 Million
Number Employees: 10
Square Footage: 28000
Type of Packaging: Food Service, Private Label
Regions Exported to: Worldwide
Percentage of Business in Exporting: 60
Regions Imported from: Worldwide
Percentage of Business in Importing: 40

49657 United Valley Bell Dairy
508 Roane St
Charleston, WV 25302-2091 304-344-2511
Fax: 304-344-2518
Fluid milk
Manager: John Duty
Marketing Director: Halan Varley
Estimated Sales: Less than $500,000
Number Employees: 100-249
Type of Packaging: Private Label

49658 United With Earth
2833 - 7th St.
Berkeley, CA 94710 510-210-4359
Fax: 510-984-0538 www.unitedwithearth.com
Medjool dates, coconut and almond date rolls, pitted dates, California golden figs, Mission figs, Persian cucumbers
Number of Brands: 1
Type of Packaging: Consumer, Private Label, Bulk
Brands Exported: United With Earth
Regions Exported to: USA

49659 Unitherm Food System
502 Industrial Rd
Bristow, OK 74010-9763 918-367-0197
Fax: 918-367-5440
www.unithermfoodsystems.com
Steamers & spiral ovens, roasters, smokehouses and grilling systems, pasteurizing equipment and chillers.
President: David Howard
unitherm@unithermfoodsystems.com
Number Employees: 20-49
Regions Exported to: South America, Europe, North America

49660 Unity Brands Group
319 W Town Pl
Suite 28
Saint Augustine, FL 32092-3103 904-940-8975
Fax: 866-878-9306 info@unitybrandsgroup.com
unitybrandsgroup.com
Marketing services
President: Praful Mehta
Marketing Executive: William Edwards
Estimated Sales: $1-2.5 Million
Number Employees: 1-10
Type of Packaging: Food Service
Brands Imported: Terra Creta, Akbar Teas, Basilur Tea, Kalliston Olive Soaps, Organic Drops, Pellas Nature, The Grindstone and Ellora Farms.
Regions Imported from: Around the World

49661 Univar USA
17411 NE Union Hill Rd
Redmond, WA 98052-3375 425-889-3400
855-888-8648
www.univarusa.com
Distributor of specialty and basic food ingredients and chemicals used in the food manufacturing industry.
Director, Food Ingredients: Austin Nichols
Product Management: Denise McLaughlin
Number Employees: 10-19
Regions Exported to: North America, Western Europe, the Asia-Pacific region, Latin America

49662 Universal Beverages Inc
10033 Sawgrass Dr W # 202
Ponte Vedra Bch, FL 32082-3550 904-280-7795
Fax: 904-280-7794 ubisyfocorp@aol.com
www.syfobeverages.com
Processor and exporter of bottled water including purified and sodium free; also, regular and flavored seltzer and naturally sparkling water
CEO: Jonathan Moore
Plant Manager: Justin Jones
Estimated Sales: $$2.5-5 Million
Number Employees: 20-49
Square Footage: 400000
Parent Co: Universal Beverages Holding Corporation
Type of Packaging: Consumer, Food Service, Private Label
Brands Exported: Syfo
Regions Exported to: Worldwide
Percentage of Business in Exporting: 30

49663 Universal Commodities Tea
141 Parkway Rd # 20
Bronxville, NY 10708-3618 914-779-5700
Fax: 914-779-5742 universaltea@uctt.com
www.uctt.com
Tea importers
President: Domenick Ciaccia
universaltea@uctt.com
Director: Paul Strader
Estimated Sales: $ 5-10 Million
Number Employees: 5-9

49664 (HQ)Universal Die & Stampings
735 15th St
Prairie Du Sac, WI 53578-9618 608-643-2477
Fax: 608-643-2024 breunigb@unidie.com
www.unidie.com
Manufacturer and exporter of stainless steel conveyor belts for tab conversion systems: for food, beer and beverage
Owner: Carol Baier
cbaier@unidie.com
Research & Development: Bryan Jaedike
Quality Control: Steve Heyn
Sales Director: Gene Everson
Plant Manager: Karl Anderson
Estimated Sales: $5-10 Million
Number Employees: 20-49
Square Footage: 80000
Regions Exported to: Central America, South America, Europe, Asia, Middle East
Percentage of Business in Exporting: 75

49665 Universal Dynamics Technologies
100-13700 International Place
Richmond, BC V6V 2X8
Canada 604-214-3456
Fax: 604-214-3457 888-912-7246
Manufacturer and exporter of software for automation process control equipment
Sales/Marketing Executive: Steve Crotty
Product Manager: Bill Gough
Brands Exported: Brainwave, Advanced Process Control Systems
Regions Exported to: Worldwide

49666 Universal Handling Equipment
PO Box 3488, Station C
Hamilton, ON L8H 7L5
Canada 905-547-0161
Fax: 905-549-6922 877-843-1122
www.universalhandling.com
Waste disposal units and refuse compactors
President: David Gerard
CFO: James Hreljac
Director Sales/Marketing: Richard Kool
Estimated Sales: $20-50 Million
Number Employees: 10
Square Footage: 80000
Type of Packaging: Food Service
Regions Exported to: Caribbean
Percentage of Business in Exporting: 10

49667 Universal Industries Inc
5800 Nordic Dr
Cedar Falls, IA 50613-6942 319-277-7501
Fax: 319-277-2318 800-553-4446
sales@universalindustries.com
www.universalindustries.com
Manufacturer and exporter of bucket elevators and belt conveyors
President: Dean Bierschenk
Marketing: Drew McConnell
Sales: Mike Giaaratmnd
Operations: Carolyn Peterson
Purchasing: Gail Snyder
Estimated Sales: $9 Million
Number Employees: 50-99
Square Footage: 240000

49668 Universal Jet Industries
PO Box 70
Hialeah, FL 33011 305-887-4378
Fax: 305-887-4370
Manufacturer and exporter of air curtains
Chairman: L Bass
General Manager: B Warshaw
Number Employees: 12
Square Footage: 36000
Brands Exported: UJI
Regions Exported to: Central America, South America, Europe, Asia, Middle East
Percentage of Business in Exporting: 30

49669 Universal Marketing
1647 Pilgrim Ave
Bronx, NY 10461-4807 914-576-5383
Fax: 914-576-1711 800-225-3114
Wholesaler/distributor, importer and exporter of commercial kitchen equipment including freezers, refrigerators, coolers and fast food cooking equipment; serving the food service market
President: James Deluca
VP: Henry Muench
Estimated Sales: Below $ 5 Million
Number Employees: 7
Square Footage: 12000
Brands Exported: Server; Baker's Pride; Unimar
Regions Exported to: Central America, South America, Europe, Middle East, Latin America, Mexico
Brands Imported: Unimar
Regions Imported from: South America, Europe, Canada

49670 Universal Packaging Inc
1308 Upland Dr
Houston, TX 77043-4719 713-461-2610
Fax: 713-461-1459 800-324-2610
Manufacturer and exporter of vertical form/fill/seal machinery, conveyors, flexible packaging equipment, augers, coders and indexers
Owner: Patricia Wylie
R & D: Bill Huhn
Sales: Jim Hooper
Estimated Sales: Below $5 Million
Number Employees: 10-19
Regions Exported to: Worldwide
Percentage of Business in Exporting: 10

49671 Universal Paper Box
644 NW 44th St
Seattle, WA 98107-4431 206-782-7105
Fax: 206-782-3817 800-228-1045
www.paperboxco.com
Manufacturer and exporter of boxes including rigid, set-up and die-cut; also, PVC lids and bases
Owner: Greg Donald
paperbox@paperboxco.com
Estimated Sales: Below $ 5 Million
Number Employees: 10-19
Square Footage: 72000
Type of Packaging: Consumer, Food Service, Private Label
Regions Exported to: Europe, Asia, Canada

49672 Universal Security Instrs Inc
11407 Cronhill Dr # A
Owings Mills, MD 21117-6218 410-363-3000
Fax: 410-363-2218 www.universalsecurity.com
Exporter and importer of video and audio tapes, corded promotional telephones, motion detector lights and smoke detectors
CEO: Harvey B Grossblatt
harvey@universalsecurity.com
VP (International Sales): Mike McConnell
Estimated Sales: G
Number Employees: 10-19
Square Footage: 65000
Type of Packaging: Consumer, Private Label, Bulk
Brands Exported: Universal; Smoke Signal; Lite-Aide
Regions Exported to: Asia
Percentage of Business in Exporting: 12
Regions Imported from: Asia
Percentage of Business in Importing: 100

49673 Univex Corp
3 Old Rockingham Rd
Salem, NH 03079-2140 603-893-6191
Fax: 603-893-1249 800-258-6358
info@univexcorp.com www.univexcorp.com
Manufacturer and exporter of food preparation machines including ground beef fat analyzers, vertical, electric bench and floor model mixers, electric bench model vegetable peelers, slicers and shredders and gravity feed electric meatslicers
President: John Tsiakos
john@univexcorp.com
VP Marketing: Richard McIntosh
National Sales Manager: John Tsiakos
Estimated Sales: $10-20 Million
Number Employees: 50-99
Type of Packaging: Food Service

Importers & Exporters / A-Z

Regions Exported to: Worldwide

49674 Unlimited Exports & Imports
5064 SW 131st Avenue
Miramar, FL 33027-5530
305-829-5816
Exporter of packaging machinery
Regions Exported to: Latin America

49675 Update International
5801 S Boyle Ave
Vernon, CA 90058-3926
323-585-0616
Fax: 323-585-4021 800-747-7124
stephen@update-international.com
www.update-international.com
Manufacturer, importer and exporter of stainless steel kitchenware and utensils; also, air pots and steam table pans
President: Alec Chung
alec@update-international.com
Controller: Herman Yu
VP: Andrew Lazar
Marketing: Charles Arjavac
Vice President of Sales and Marketing: Steven Linzy
Operations: Jose Aleman
Estimated Sales: $ 5 - 10 Million
Number Employees: 50-99
Square Footage: 320000
Brands Exported: Update International
Regions Exported to: Central America, Europe
Brands Imported: Update International
Regions Imported from: South America, Europe, Asia, Middle East, .
Percentage of Business in Importing: 100

49676 Upham & Walsh Lumber
2155 Stonington Ave # 209
Hoffman Estates, IL 60169-2058
847-519-1010
Fax: 847-519-3434
Manufacturer and importer of wooden, steel and plastic pallets; also, skids and watermelon and onion bins
Partner: Chris Hayden
c_hayden@uphamwalshlumber.com
Office Manager: Lauren Kowalski
Sales Manager: Sean Hayden
Estimated Sales: $7 Million
Number Employees: 1-4
Regions Imported from: Asia
Percentage of Business in Importing: 5

49677 Upright
10715 Kahlmeyer Dr
St Louis, MO 63132-1621
314-426-4347
Fax: 314-426-0145 800-248-7007
www.wyksorbents.com
Manufacturer and exporter of sorbents, anti-slip compounds and spill response products
President: James Dunn
Sales Manager: James Meador
Production: James Callaham
Estimated Sales: $1-3 Million
Number Employees: 10-19
Square Footage: 80000
Regions Exported to: Canada, Carribean
Percentage of Business in Exporting: 5

49678 Uptime Energy, Inc.
7930 Alabama Ave.
Canoga Park, CA 91304
www.uptimeenergy.com
Energy drink with caffeine, coenzyme Q10, Ginkgo Biloba and ginseng; capsules also available
Chief Executive Officer: Benjamin Kim
Year Founded: 1985
Number Employees: 10-50
Number of Brands: 1
Type of Packaging: Consumer, Private Label
Brands Exported: Uptime
Regions Exported to: USA

49679 Upton's Naturals
2054 West Grand Ave.
Chicago, IL 60612
info@uptonsnaturals.com
www.uptonsnaturals.com
Pre-packaged, marinated jackfruit and seitan; pre-pared vegan side dishes
Co-Founder: Nicole Sopko
Year Founded: 2006
Number of Brands: 1
Number of Products: 19
Type of Packaging: Consumer, Private Label
Brands Exported: Upton's Naturals

49680 Urbani Truffles
10 West End Ave
New York, NY 10023
212-247-8800
Fax: 212-247-8900 info@urbani.com
www.urbani.com
Italian truffles and truffle products
President: Paul Urbani
CEO: John Natale
Number Employees: 20-49
Parent Co: Urbani Tartufi
Type of Packaging: Consumer, Food Service
Other Locations:
 Urbani Truffles
 New York, NYUrbani Truffles
Regions Exported to: South America, Europe, Asia
Percentage of Business in Exporting: 90
Brands Imported: Urbani
Regions Imported from: Europe
Percentage of Business in Importing: 100

49681 Urnex Brands Inc
700 Executive Blvd
Elmsford, NY 10523-1208
914-345-6080
Fax: 914-963-2145 800-222-2826
info@urnex.com www.urnex.com
Manufacturer and exporter of coffee and tea equipment cleaning compounds, urn brushes, lemon covers, lemon wedge bags and shellfish steamer bags
President: Kofi Amoako
kofi.amoako@urnex.com
R & D: Jason Dick
Quality Control: Bill Colter
Sales Manager: Joshua Dick
General Manager: Jay Lazarin
Assist. Mngr: Frankie Dominiquez
Estimated Sales: Less Than $500,000
Number Employees: 1-4
Square Footage: 30000
Brands Exported: Urnex
Regions Exported to: Worldwide
Percentage of Business in Exporting: 5

49682 Urschel Laboratories
2503 Calumet Avenue
Valparaiso, IN 46384-2200
219-464-4811
Fax: 219-462-3879 info@urschel.com
www.urschel.com
Manufacturer and supplier of high capacity food cutting equipment
President: Robert Urschel
CFO: Dan Marchetti
VP Sales: Tim O'Brien
Contact: Jen Abatie
jabatie@urschel.com
Regional Manager: Alan Major
Plant Manager: Dave Whitenack
Number Employees: 250-499
Square Footage: 500000
Type of Packaging: Food Service
Brands Exported: Comitrol; Urschalloy; Urschel; Translicer; Quanticut; Veldcicut; Diversacut
Regions Exported to: Central America, South America, Europe, Asia, Middle East
Percentage of Business in Exporting: 50

49683 Us Bottlers Machinery Co Inc
11911 Steele Creek Rd
Charlotte, NC 28273-3773
704-588-4750
Fax: 704-588-3808 sales@usbottlers.com
www.usbottlers.com
Manufacturer and exporter of bottling machinery including liquid filling, bottle rinsing, container cleaning and capping equipment
President: Thomas Risser
julie.kimbrell@usbottlers.com
Sales: Julie Kimbrell
Estimated Sales: $10-20 Million
Number Employees: 50-99

49684 Us Rubber
238 N 9th St # 1
Brooklyn, NY 11211-2160
718-782-7888
Fax: 718-782-8788
Manufacturer and exporter of food hoses, tubing and conveyor belts
Owner: Ken Auster
kauster@usrubbersupply.com
Estimated Sales: $10-20 Million
Number Employees: 20-49
Regions Exported to: Worldwide

49685 Us Spice Mill Inc
4537 W Fulton St
Chicago, IL 60624-1609
773-378-6800
Fax: 773-378-0077 www.usspice.com
Manufacturer and importer of spices
President: Nick Patel
usspice@gmail.com
Estimated Sales: $600000
Number Employees: 5-9

49686 (HQ)Utica Cutlery Co
820 Noyes St
PO Box 10527
Utica, NY 13502-5053
315-733-4663
Fax: 315-733-6602 800-879-2526
info@uticacutlery.com www.walcostainless.com
Manufacturers of pocket knives and importers of stainless steel cutlery
President: David Allen
davidallen@uticacutlery.com
CFO: Jess Gouger
VP (Walco): Kathleen Allen
International Sales Manager: Dave Meislin
Estimated Sales: $ 10 - 20 Million
Number Employees: 100-249
Brands Exported: Utua; Walco; Kutmaster
Regions Exported to: Central America, South America
Regions Imported from: Asia

49687 Utility Refrigerator Company
7355 E Slauson Avenue
Los Angeles, CA 90040-3626
323-267-0700
Fax: 323-728-2318 800-884-5233
www.utilityrefrigerator.com
Manufacturer and exporter of commercial cooking equipment, refrigerators and freezers
Customer Service: Larry Gomez
Customer Service: Mark Parra
Customer Service: Martha Gonzalez
General Manager: Mark Champaigne
Estimated Sales: $ .5 - 1 million
Number Employees: 160
Square Footage: 800000
Parent Co: Stery Manufacturing Company
Regions Exported to: Worldwide
Percentage of Business in Exporting: 5

49688 V & E Kohnstamm Inc
882 3rd Ave # 7
Brooklyn, NY 11232-1902
718-788-1776
Fax: 718-768-3978 800-847-4500
flavorinfo@virginiadare.com
www.virginiadare.com
Flavors, masking agents, bases, extracts, vanilla, orange oils and colors
President: Howard Smith Jr
VP Finance: Bobby Corcoran
VP Research Dev/Quality Assurance: Michael Springsteen
VP Operations: Frederic Thor
Year Founded: 1835
Estimated Sales: $21100000
Number Employees: 100-249
Type of Packaging: Private Label, Bulk
Brands Exported: Veko
Regions Exported to: Worldwide

49689 V C 999 Packaging Systems
419 E 11th Ave
Kansas City, MO 64116-4162
816-472-8999
Fax: 816-472-1999 800-728-2999
www.shrinkbagpackaging.com
Manufacturer and supplier of packaging equipment, materials and supplies such as trays, bags/pouches, containers and film.
President: Silvio Weder
silvio.weder@vc999.com
Number Employees: 20-49
Regions Exported to: Central America, South America, Europe, Asia, USA

49690 V-Ram Solids
620 S Broadway Ave
PO Box 289
Albert Lea, MN 56007-4526
507-373-3996
Fax: 507-373-5937 888-373-3996
sales@vram.com
Manufacturer, importer and exporter of solids handling pumps for waste/rendering
President: David A Olson
Sales Director: Jeff Hall
Purchasing Manager: Rose Modderman

Estimated Sales: $ 3 - 5 Million
Number Employees: 10-19
Brands Exported: V-Ram Pumps
Regions Exported to: Central America, South America, Europe, Asia, Middle East
Regions Imported from: Central America, South America, Europe

49691 V-Suarez Provisions
PO Box 364588
San Juan, PR 00936-4588 787-792-1212
Fax: 787-792-0735
Wholesaler/distributor and importer of canned pastas, teas, soups, juices, sports drinks, paper products, insecticides, cleaning products, evaporated milk, foil, plastic wrap, Mexican foods, prunes, raisins, salad dressings, olive oilseasonings, etc
VP: Javier Arango
Number Employees: 50-99
Square Footage: 600000
Parent Co: V-Suarez & Company
Type of Packaging: Consumer
Brands Imported: Chef-Boy-Ar-Dee; Lipton; Ocean Spray; Gatorade; Northern; Real Kill; Pet; Reynolds; Old El Paso; Musselman's; Denia; Kresto; Sunsweet; Sunmaid; Accent; Borges; Crystal Geyser
Regions Imported from: Central America, South America, Europe
Percentage of Business in Importing: 100

49692 (HQ)V.M. Calderon
4040 Red Rock Ln
Sarasota, FL 34231 941-366-3708
Fax: 941-951-6529 888-654-8365
vmcalderon@aol.com
Wholesaler/distrubutor, import broker and contract packager of brined vegetables, black and green olives, pepperoncini, cherries, capers, onions and pickles
President: Victor Calderon
Estimated Sales: $ 1 - 3 Million
Number Employees: 1-4
Square Footage: 7200
Type of Packaging: Consumer, Food Service, Private Label, Bulk
Regions Imported from: Europe
Percentage of Business in Importing: 100

49693 V.W. Joyner & Company
PO Box 387
Smithfield, VA 23431-0387 757-357-2161
Fax: 757-357-0184
Processor and exporter of smoked cured country hams, picnics and bacon for distribution to wholesale, retail and restaurant markets
VP/General Manager: Larry Santure
Plant Manager: R Howell
Number Employees: 10-19
Square Footage: 160000
Parent Co: Smithfield Companies
Type of Packaging: Consumer, Food Service, Private Label, Bulk
Regions Exported to: Asia, Canada

49694 VC Menus
P.O.Box 71
Eastland, TX 76448-0071 254-629-2626
Fax: 254-629-1134 800-826-3687
menusales@vcmenus.com www.vcmenus.com
Manufacturer and exporter of menus and covers
President: Cary Meeks
Secretary and Treasurer: Donald Eaves
Corporate Sales/Marketing: Trent Smith
Estimated Sales: $5-10 Million
Number Employees: 20-49
Regions Exported to: Worldwide
Percentage of Business in Exporting: 10

49695 VCI Beverage Center
6050 E Hanna Avenue
Indianapolis, IN 46203-6125 317-791-1900
Fax: 317-791-0522

49696 VCPB Transportation
600 Meadowlands Pkwy # 138
Secaucus, NJ 07094-1637 201-770-0070
Fax: 201-770-0102 info@vcpbtrans.com
www.vcpbtrans.com
Importers and distributors of a wide range of food ingredients, supplying food manufacturers, bakeries and food service companies throughout the USA
Owner: Fredric Israel
fisrael@vcpbtrans.com

Number Employees: 5-9
Type of Packaging: Food Service, Bulk
Regions Imported from: Poland, Holland, United Kingdom
Percentage of Business in Importing: 20

49697 VIFAN Canada
1 Rue Vifan
Lanoraie, QC J0K 1E0
Canada 514-640-1599
Fax: 514-640-1577 800-557-0192
www.vifan.com
Packaging products for the food industry
VP, Sales: Ezra Bowen
Estimated Sales: $185 Million
Number Employees: 245
Number of Brands: 78
Number of Products: 78
Square Footage: 130000
Parent Co: Vibac S.p.A.
Type of Packaging: Food Service
Brands Exported: Vifan
Regions Exported to: Central America, South America, USA
Percentage of Business in Exporting: 80

49698 (HQ)VIP Foods
1080 Wyckoff Ave
Flushing, NY 11385 718-821-5330
Fax: 718-497-7110 vipfoods@aol.com
Processor and exporter of soups, instant lunches, low-calorie sweeteners and mixes including dessert, pasta, tea, hot chocolate, pasta, pudding, cake and cake mixes, sauce and chicken coating
Owner: Mendel Freund
Sales Manager: Esther Freund
esther@vipfoodsinc.com
Estimated Sales: $ 10 - 20 Million
Number Employees: 20-49
Square Footage: 90000
Type of Packaging: Consumer, Food Service, Private Label, Bulk
Brands Exported: Kojel; The Soup Bowl; Minute Lunch
Regions Exported to: South America, Europe, Asia, Canada
Percentage of Business in Exporting: 3

49699 VIP Real Estate LTD
3945 S Archer Ave
Chicago, IL 60632-1157 773-376-5000
Fax: 773-376-5091 www.viprealestateltd.com
Manufacturer and exporter of folding boxes, printed folding cartons, point of purchase displays and polylined, freezer-coated boxes for frozen foods. Items manufactured to order
Owner: Sammy Cruz
sammy@viprealestateltd.com
VP: Ray Maza
Marketing: James Coen
Estimated Sales: $5-10 Million
Number Employees: 10-19
Square Footage: 212000
Type of Packaging: Consumer, Food Service, Private Label
Regions Exported to: Canada
Percentage of Business in Exporting: 1

49700 VIP Sales Company
2395 American Ave
Hayward, CA 94545 918-252-5791
Fax: 918-254-1667 866-536-8008
sbeck@vipfoods.com www.vipfoods.com
Packer and exporter of frozen fruits, vegetables and Chinese entrees and prepared foods; importer of raspberries, blueberries and broccoli
President: Guy Lewis
Sr. VP/COO: Lee Turman
VP Sales/Marketing: Steve Beck
Public Relations: Mick Lewis
Plant Manager: Don Avera
VP Purchasing: Fred Meyer
Estimated Sales: $5900000
Number Employees: 30
Number of Brands: 5
Number of Products: 180
Type of Packaging: Consumer, Food Service, Private Label, Bulk
Brands Exported: VIP
Regions Exported to: Worldwide
Percentage of Business in Exporting: 50
Regions Imported from: South America, Mexico
Percentage of Business in Importing: 20

49701 VMC Corp
92 Maple St
Weehawken, NJ 07086-5722 201-863-3137
Fax: 201-863-3137 800-863-5606
sales@vmc-health.com
http://www.vmc-health.com/
Wholesaler/distributor and importer of yogurt, cheese, kefir products and processing equipment; exporter of bee pollen, royal jelly and yogurt acidophilus powders
Manager: Alan Cheung
acheung@vmchealth.com
Estimated Sales: $ 5 - 10 Million
Number Employees: 10-19
Square Footage: 12000
Type of Packaging: Consumer, Private Label, Bulk
Brands Exported: YoGourmet; Malaka Brand
Regions Exported to: Central America, Europe, Asia
Brands Imported: Yogurmet; Malaka Brand; Nature's Own
Regions Imported from: Central America, Asia, Canada

49702 VPI Manufacturing
11814 S. Election Rd
Ste 200
Draper, UT 84020 801-495-2310
Fax: 866-307-0033 www.vpimanufacturing.com
Manufacturer and exporter of heat shrinkable polyethylene cook-in bags for meat, poultry, etc
President: Aron Perlman
VP: Hessa Tary
Estimated Sales: $4114713
Number Employees: 20-49

49703 (HQ)VT Industries Inc
1000 Industrial Park
P.O. Box 490
Holstein, IA 51025-7730 712-368-4381
Fax: 712-368-4111 800-827-1615
www.vtindustries.com
Manufacturer and exporter of post-formed laminated and solid surface countertops; also, laminated multi-use components
President/Chief Executive Officer: Douglas Clausen
douglas.clausen@vtindustries.com
Chief Financial Officer: Randy Gerritsen
Vice President: Elizabeth Hansch
Director, Information Technology: Teri Luebeck
Vice President, Marketing: Trisha Schmidt
Vice President, Sales & Marketing: John Bowling
Vice President, Operations: Bruce Campbell
Plant Manager: Gary Henry
Estimated Sales: $ 32 Million
Number Employees: 250-499
Square Footage: 300000
Brands Exported: CurvFlo; Casemate; DurAllure
Regions Exported to: Central America, South America, Europe, Asia, Middle East, Canada, Caribbean
Percentage of Business in Exporting: 1

49704 VT Kidron
911 W 5th St
P.O.Box 880
Washington, NC 27889-4205 252-946-6521
Fax: 330-857-8451 800-763-0700
ksales@kidron.com www.kidron.com
Manufacturer and exporter of refrigerated truck bodies and trailers
President: Mike Tucker
Executive VP: John Sommer
Estimated Sales: $5-10 Million
Number Employees: 5-9
Parent Co: TTI
Type of Packaging: Food Service
Regions Exported to: Central America, South America
Percentage of Business in Exporting: 10

49705 Vac-U-Max
69 William St
Belleville, NJ 07109-3040 973-759-4600
Fax: 973-759-6449 800-822-8629
info@vac-u-max.com www.vac-u-max.com
Manufacturer, importer and exporter of pneumatic conveying systems and ingredient storage systems; also, handling and batching systems
President: Stevens Pendelton
CEO: H Kadel
VP: Doan Pendleton
IT: Stevens Pendleton
info@vac-u-max.com

Importers & Exporters / A-Z

49706 Vacaville Fruit Co
2055 Cessna Dr # 200
Vacaville, CA 95688-8838   707-447-1085
Fax: 707-447-1085   info@vacavillefruit.com
www.vacavillefruit.com
Processor importer and exporter of kosher dried fruit and fruit pastes; serving the food service market
President: Richard Nola
HR Executive: Nichole Nolz
info@vacavillefruit.com
Director Sales/Marketing: Nicole Nola
Plant Superintendent: Gary De La Rosa
Estimated Sales: $4200000
Number Employees: 50-99
Type of Packaging: Consumer, Food Service, Bulk
Regions Imported from: South America, South Africa
Percentage of Business in Importing: 4

49707 Vacuform Inc.
500 Courtney Road
PO Box 117
Sebring, OH 44672   330-938-9674
Fax: 330-938-9676   info@vacuforminc.com
www.vacuforminc.com
Manufacturer and importer of interior and exterior signs, menus and image products including point of purchase displays
President: Kenneth Galloway
CEO: Dennis Kaufman
Contact: Catherine Hubbs
c_hubbs@vacuforminc.com
Estimated Sales: $10-20 Million
Number Employees: 100-249
Square Footage: 400000
Type of Packaging: Food Service
Regions Imported from: Asia
Percentage of Business in Importing: 5

49708 Vacumet Corp
20 Edison Dr
Wayne, NJ 07470-4713   973-628-1067
Fax: 973-628-0491   bfoley@vacumet.com
Manufacturer and exporter of metallized and holographic films and papers; also microwave susceptor and barrier films for flexible packaging, label stock available.
President: Robert Korowicki
Estimated Sales: G
Number Employees: 10-19
Parent Co: Scholle Corporation
Regions Exported to: Worldwide
Percentage of Business in Exporting: 5

49709 Vacuum Barrier Corp
4 Barten Ln
Woburn, MA 01801-5601   781-933-3570
Fax: 781-932-9428   sales@vacuumbarrier.com
www.vacuumbarrier.com
Manufacturer, importer and exporter of cryogenic pipe systems including liquid nitrogen injection equipment for pressurizing hot filled beverages, food, etc
President: Bart Limpens
bart@vbseurope.com
CFO: Leonard Gardner
Vice President: David Gorham
Quality Control and R&d: David Tucker
VP Sales: Edward Hanlon Jr
Purchasing Manager: Douglas Vanaruem
Estimated Sales: $ 5 - 10 Million
Number Employees: 20-49
Square Footage: 84000
Brands Exported: Linerter; Linjector; Semiflex; Nitrodoser
Regions Exported to: Central America, South America, Europe, Asia, Middle East, Australia, Canada, Latin America, Mexico, Worldwide
Percentage of Business in Exporting: 35
Regions Imported from: Europe, Worldwide
Percentage of Business in Importing: 10

49710 Val-Pak Direct Market Systems
8605 Largo Lakes Dr
Largo, FL 33773-4912   727-393-1270
Fax: 727-399-3061   pat_fridley@coxtarget.com
www.valpak.com
Supplier and exporter of coupons
President: Joe Bourdow
Contact: Juliane Abudi
juliane_abudi@valpak.com
Number Employees: 1,000-4,999
Parent Co: Cox Industries
Type of Packaging: Consumer, Bulk
Regions Exported to: Worldwide

49711 Valad Electric Heating Corporation
PO Box 577
160 Wildey Street
Tarrytown, NY 10591   914-631-4927
Fax: 914-631-4395   info@valadelectric.com
www.valadelectric.com
Manufacturer and exporter of food warming ovens, hot plates and food warming cabinets
President: Dante Cecchini
VP: Arthur Cecchini
Sales: Mike Sona
Estimated Sales: Below $ 5 Million
Number Employees: 10-19
Square Footage: 70000
Type of Packaging: Consumer, Food Service
Regions Exported to: Europe
Percentage of Business in Exporting: 10

49712 Valco Melton
411 Circle Freeway Dr
West Chester, OH 45246-1213   513-874-6550
Fax: 513-874-3612   sales@valcocincinnatiinc.com
www.valcomelton.com
Manufacturer and exporter of hot melt and cold glue dispensers
President: Karla Bridges
karla.bridges@valcomelton.com
CFO: Scott Soutar
CEO: Gregory Amend
Purchase: Jim Epp
Sales Manager: Paul Chambers
Estimated Sales: $ 5 - 10 Million
Number Employees: 100-249
Square Footage: 200000
Regions Exported to: Worldwide

49713 Valentine Enterprises Inc
1291 Progress Center Ave
Lawrenceville, GA 30043-4801   770-995-0661
Fax: 770-995-0725   info-sales@veiusa.com
www.veiusa.com
Powdered products including diet meal replacements, protein, fiber, sport fitness products, lecithin granules, etc
President & CEO: Alan Smith
Estimated Sales: $30 Million
Number Employees: 100-249
Square Footage: 50000
Regions Exported to: Central America, South America, Europe, Asia
Percentage of Business in Exporting: 20

49714 Valentino USA
3 Dora Ln
Holmdel, NJ 07733-1624   732-203-1717
Fax: 732-810-0272
Italian cakes and biscuits
President: Giancarlo Valentino
Brands Imported: Valentino
Regions Imported from: Italy

49715 Valeo
555 taxter Road
Suite 210
Elmsford, Ny 10523   800-634-2704
Fax: 800-831-9642   800-634-2704
www.valeoinc.com
Manufacturer and exporter of safety accessories including back support belts, wrist supports, knee supports, elbow support, and material handling gloves
President: Lisa Yewer
Estimated Sales: $ 5 - 10 Million
Number Employees: 20-49
Square Footage: 240000
Regions Exported to: Worldwide
Percentage of Business in Exporting: 50

49716 Valesco Trading
1 Terminal Road
Lyndhurst, NJ 07071   201-729-1414
Fax: 201-729-1515   aos@valescofoods.com
www.valescofoods.com
Mediterranean olives, sun dried tomatoes, dried figs and apricots.
President: Ali Sozer
Estimated Sales: $3.6 Million
Number Employees: 12
Type of Packaging: Food Service
Brands Imported: Pera, Pickles Olives Etc., Valesco Foods, and Valesco Trading LLC.
Regions Imported from: Italy, Spain, Greece, Turkey and Morocco.

49717 (HQ)Valley Container Inc
850 Union Ave
Bridgeport, CT 06607-1137   203-368-6546
Fax: 203-367-5266   flutedpartition@aol.com
www.valleycontainer.com
Manufacturer and exporter of corrugated shipping containers
President: Arthur Vietze Jr
CEO: Rudy Niederneier
rudy.niederneier@valleycontainer.com
VP Sales: Richard Jackson
Estimated Sales: $ 20 - 50 Million
Number Employees: 50-99
Regions Exported to: Worldwide

49718 Valley Craft Inc
2001 S Highway 61
Lake City, MN 55041-9557   651-345-3386
Fax: 651-345-3606   800-328-1480
customer@valleycraft.com   www.valleycraft.com
Manufacturer and exporter of hand and delivery trucks, trailers and forklift attachments, and storage equipment, custom-designed manufacturing and production equipment.
Owner: Dennis Campbell
Manager: Roger Goff
R&D: Josh Rodewald
Marketing: Daria Dalager
Sales: Dave Minck
Production: Tom Balow
tombalow@valleycraft.com
Plant Manager: Roger Goff
Estimated Sales: $10-20,000,000
Number Employees: 1-4
Number of Brands: 6
Number of Products: 300+
Square Footage: 332000
Parent Co: Liberty Diversified International
Type of Packaging: Consumer, Private Label, Bulk
Brands Exported: Valley Craft; Vari-Tuff
Regions Exported to: Central America, South America, Europe, Asia, Mexico
Brands Imported: Viking II; Dura-Lite II
Regions Imported from: Asia

49719 Valley Fig Growers
2028 S 3rd St
Fresno, CA 93702-4156   559-237-3893
Fax: 559-237-3898   info@valleyfig.com
www.valleyfig.com
Fig growers cooperative exports dried figs worldwide.
President: Gary Jue
gjue@valleyfig.com
CFO: Jim Gargiulo
Operations Manager: Darin Ciotti
Number Employees: 50-99
Type of Packaging: Consumer, Food Service, Private Label, Bulk
Brands Exported: Blue Ribbon Orchard Choice
Regions Exported to: South America, Europe, Asia, Middle East
Percentage of Business in Exporting: 10

49720 Valley Fixtures
171 Coney Island Drive
Sparks, NV 89431-6317   775-331-1050
Manufacturer and exporter of cabinet fixtures for bars, restaurants, casinos, hotels and stores
Sales Manager: Dillon Moore
Estimated Sales: $10-20 Million
Number Employees: 100-249
Square Footage: 100000
Regions Exported to: Europe
Percentage of Business in Exporting: 10

49721 Valley Packaging SupplyCo
3181 Commodity Ln
Green Bay, WI 54304-5671   920-336-9012
Fax: 920-336-3935
general@valleypackagingsupply.com
www.valleypackagingsupply.com
Manufacturer and exporter of pouches and bags for food and industry

Importers & Exporters / A-Z

President: Lance Czachor
lance@valleypackagingsupply.com
Treasurer: Richard Czachor
Sales Director: Lance Czachor
Operations Manager: Ty Parsons
Purchasing Manager: Jean Rottier
Estimated Sales: $5 Million
Number Employees: 100-249
Square Footage: 272000
Type of Packaging: Bulk
Regions Exported to: Europe
Percentage of Business in Exporting: 1

49722 Valley Seafoods
Hc 70
Box 24
Brownsville, TX 78521-9802   956-831-9416
Fax: 956-831-7580 800-624-7056
Importer of fresh and frozen shrimp
General Manager: Louis Dartez
Estimated Sales: $2.5-5 Million
Number Employees: 1-4
Brands Imported: Mexico's Finest
Regions Imported from: Mexico
Percentage of Business in Importing: 100

49723 Valley View Packing Co
7547 Sawtelle Ave
PO Box 3540
Yuba City, CA 95991-9514   530-673-7356
Fax: 530-673-9432 info@sacramentopacking.com
www.valleyviewfoods.com
Manufacturer and exporter of dried fruits and fruit juices and concentrates
Owner: Dennis Serger
serger@valleyviewpacking.com
Estimated Sales: $17 Million
Number Employees: 10-19
Type of Packaging: Consumer, Food Service, Private Label, Bulk
Brands Exported: Valley View
Regions Exported to: Worldwide

49724 Valrhona
45 Main Street
Suite 1054
Brooklyn, NY 11201   718-522-7001
Fax: 718-522-7331 www.valrhona.com
Chocolates
CEO: Christophe Henry
Contact: Andrea Aguilar
aaguilar@valrhona.com
Estimated Sales: $1.4 Million
Number Employees: 9

49725 Valvinox
650 1st Rue
Iberville, QC J2X 3B8
Canada
 450-346-1981
Fax: 450-346-1067 www.valvinox.it
Manufacturer and exporter of fittings, pumps, stainless steel valves, tubing and pipe
Administrator: Chantal Allard
Number Employees: 10,000
Parent Co: SQRM
Type of Packaging: Bulk
Regions Exported to: USA
Percentage of Business in Exporting: 5

49726 Van Air Systems
2950 Mechanic St
Lake City, PA 16423-2095   814-774-2631
Fax: 814-774-0778 800-840-9906
www.vanairsystems.com
Manufacturer and exporter of compressed air dryers, condensation drain valves, after coolers, filters, oil/water separators, etc.; importer of filters
President: Mark Sunseri
msunseri@vanairinc.com
CEO: J Currie
CFO: Mark Sunseri
VP: Jeff Mace
Sales: W J Ulrich
Estimated Sales: $20 Million
Number Employees: 20-49
Number of Brands: 8
Square Footage: 65000
Regions Exported to: Central America, South America, Europe, Asia, Middle East
Percentage of Business in Exporting: 15
Regions Imported from: Europe
Percentage of Business in Importing: 10

49727 Van Blarcom Closures Inc
156 Sandford St
Brooklyn, NY 11205-3985   718-855-3810
Fax: 718-935-9855 www.vbcpkg.com
Manufacturer and exporter of metal and plastic caps
Chairman of the Board: Vincent Scuderi Jr
VP Sales/Marketing: John Scuderi
Estimated Sales: $20-50 Million
Number Employees: 500-999
Regions Exported to: Worldwide

49728 Van Damme Confectionery
172 Beekman Lane
Hillsborough, NJ 08844   908-281-5140
Fax: 908-281-5141
vandammeusa@vandammegroup.com
Marshmallow products
Contact: Van Candy
vandammeusa@vandammegroup.com

49729 Van Der Graaf Corporation
1481 Trae Lane
Lithia Springs, GA 30122   770-819-6650
Fax: 770-819-6675 www.vandergraaf.com
Drum motors for conveyor belts.
Contact: Jason Kanaris
jkanaris@vandergraaf.com

49730 Van Drunen Farms
300 W 6th St
Momence, IL 60954-1136   815-472-3100
Fax: 815-472-3850 sales@vandrunen.com
www.vandrunenfarms.com
Manufacturer of fruit, vegetable and herb ingredients.
President: Edward Van Drunen
evandrunen@vandrunen.com
Sales Manager: Irv Dorn
Estimated Sales: $25-100 Million
Number Employees: 50-99
Type of Packaging: Consumer, Food Service, Private Label, Bulk
Regions Exported to: Europe, Asia
Percentage of Business in Exporting: 20

49731 Van Oriental Food Inc
4828 Reading St
Dallas, TX 75247-6705   214-630-0111
Fax: 214-630-0473 feedback@vaneggrolls.com
www.vaneggrolls.com
Frozen foods including regular and low-fat egg rolls, fried wontons, crab rangoon, enchiladas, burritos and spring rolls
President: Kimberly Nguyen
Co-Owner: Gretchen Perrenot
Corporate Treasurer: Theresa Motter
Sales Manager: Carl Motter
Contact: David Duval
david@vanfoods.com
Plant Engineer: Apollo Nguyen
Estimated Sales: $8.9 Million
Number Employees: 10-19
Square Footage: 224000
Type of Packaging: Consumer, Food Service, Private Label, Bulk

49732 Van Vooren Game Ranch
Clemmons, NC 27012   336-306-9332
Fax: 336-306-9332 stanvvgr@xplornet.com

49733 Van de Kamps
Po Box 3900
Peoria, IL 61612
 800-798-3318
www.vandekamps.com
Processor and exporter of pies, fish and vegetables
Plant Manager: James Frey
Number Employees: 100-249
Parent Co: Van de Kamps
Type of Packaging: Consumer, Food Service, Private Label
Regions Exported to: Canada
Percentage of Business in Exporting: 1

49734 Vana Life Foods
Seattle, WA 98104-2205   347-446-6504
info@vanalifefoods.com
www.vanalifefoods.com
Green chickpea-based, pre-packaged superfood bowls in various flavors
Founder/Chief Executive Officer: Krishan Walia
Year Founded: 2015
Number of Brands: 1
Number of Products: 4
Type of Packaging: Consumer, Private Label
Brands Exported: Vana Life Foods
Regions Exported to: USA

49735 (HQ)Vance's Foods
2129 Harrison St.
PO Box 627
San Francisco, CA 94110   800-497-4834
Fax: 800-497-4329 415-621-1171
info@vancesfoods.com
Processor and exporter of nondairy and fat-free potato-based milk substitutes including dry and liquid, and dry soy-based milk substitutes
President: Vance Abersold
VP: Glenn Abersold
Director Marketing: Frederick Mattos
Type of Packaging: Consumer, Food Service, Bulk
Brands Exported: Darifree; Sno-E Tofu; NotMilk
Regions Exported to: Europe, Canada, Caribbean
Percentage of Business in Exporting: 10

49736 Vanderburgh & Company
350 5th Ave Ste 1820
New York, NY 10118   212-947-5270
Fax: 212-564-7264
Exporter of ingredients, machinery and spare parts
President: Pedro Concha
Contact: Carlos Martinez
cmartinez@vanderburghco.com
Estimated Sales: $300,000-500,000
Number Employees: 1-4
Brands Exported: International Flavors
Regions Exported to: South America
Percentage of Business in Exporting: 100

49737 Vanguard Technology Inc
29495 Airport Rd
Eugene, OR 97402-9524   541-461-6020
Fax: 541-461-6023 800-624-4809
info@vanguardtechnologyinc.com
www.vanguardtechnologyinc.com
High-efficiency gas fired domestic hot water heaters, gas fired booster water heaters
President: S Kujawa
vti1999@aol.com
Estimated Sales: $1 Million
Number Employees: 1-4
Square Footage: 20000
Type of Packaging: Food Service
Brands Exported: FirePower; PowerPac; PowerMax; Firemax
Regions Exported to: Central America, South America, Canada, Caribbean 10

49738 Vanilla Corp Of America LLC
2273 N Penn Rd
Hatfield, PA 19440-1952   215-996-1978
Fax: 215-996-9867
Grain and field bean merchant wholesalers
President: Doug Daugherty
vanillacorp@aol.com
Estimated Sales: $500,000-1 Million
Number Employees: 5-9
Type of Packaging: Food Service, Bulk

49739 Vanilla Saffron Imports
949 Valencia Street
San Francisco, CA 94110   415-648-8990
Fax: 415-648-2240 saffron@saffron.com
www.saffron.com
Importer and exporter of saffron, pure vanilla extracts, beans, truffles and wild mushrooms including frozen, dried and powdered
President: Juan San Mames
Contact: Juan Mames
juansanmames@vanillasaffronimports.com
Estimated Sales: Less than $500,000
Number Employees: 1-4
Square Footage: 8000
Type of Packaging: Consumer, Food Service, Private Label, Bulk
Regions Exported to: Worldwide
Percentage of Business in Exporting: 51

49740 Vanmark Equipment
300 Industrial Pkwy
Creston, IA 50801-8102   641-782-6575
Fax: 641-782-9209 800-523-6261
www.vanmarkequipment.com
Manufacturer of industrial food processing for a wide range of produce products.

Manager: Tom Mathues
Sales: Tom Jones
Manager: Jason Davis
Operations: Rich Shafar
Estimated Sales: $5-10 Million
Number Employees: 20-49
Square Footage: 120000
Regions Exported to: Central America, South America, Europe, Asia, Middle East
Percentage of Business in Exporting: 20

49741 Vanmark Equipment LLC
4252 S Eagleson Rd
Boise, ID 83705　　　　208-362-5588
　　　Fax: 208-362-3171　800-523-6261
　　　　　　sales@vanmarkequipment.com
　　　　　　www.vanmarkequipment.com
Manufacturer and exporter of food processing equipment for produce including tension blades and wedge, square and rectangular tension cutters
Owner: George Mendenhall
Estimated Sales: $2.5-5 Million
Number Employees: 10-19
Regions Exported to: Worldwide
Percentage of Business in Exporting: 75

49742 (HQ)Vantage Performance Materials
3938 Porett Dr
Gurnee, IL 60031-1244　　　847-244-3410
　　　Fax: 847-249-6790　aronson@ppg.com
　　　　　　www.petroferm.com
Manufacturer and exporter of precipitated silica for anticaking and carrier applications
President: Michael Horton
Vice President: Anup Jain
Vice President of Research and Developme: Charles Kahle
Marketing Manager: Paul Brown
Manager: Steve Korzeniewski
steve.korzeniewski@polyonics.com
Vice President of Operations: John Richter
Vice President of Purchasing: Stephen Lampe
Estimated Sales: $20-50 Million
Number Employees: 100-249
Type of Packaging: Food Service, Bulk
Brands Exported: Flo-Gard
Regions Exported to: Worldwide
Percentage of Business in Exporting: 23

49743 Vapor Power Intl LLC
551 S County Line Rd
Franklin Park, IL 60131-1013　　630-694-5500
　　　Fax: 630-694-2230　888-874-9020
　　info@vaporpower.com　www.vaporpower.com
Manufacturer and exporter of steam generators and liquid phase heaters
President: Curt Diedrick
CEO: Bob Forslund
Sales Manager: B Corrigan
Number Employees: 20-49
Parent Co: Westinghouse Air Brake Company
Regions Exported to: Europe
Percentage of Business in Exporting: 10

49744 (HQ)Variant
7169 Shady Oak Road
Eden Prairie, MN 55344-3516　612-927-8611
　　　Fax: 612-927-4624　info@variantinc.com
Manufacturer, importer and exporter of advertising products
President: Jerry Gruggen
Operations: Jan Davis
Controller: Tom Fournelle
Plant Manager: Ted Fors
Square Footage: 30000
Other Locations:
　Variant
　　Minneapolis, MN
Brands Exported: Warco
Regions Exported to: Central America, South America
Regions Imported from: Asia, Middle East

49745 Varied Industries Corp
905 S Carolina Ave
Mason City, IA 50401-5813　　641-423-1460
　　　Fax: 641-423-0832　800-654-5617
　　　　　　www.vi-cor.com
Manufacturer and exporter of lactic acid fermentation and yucca extracts for food, feed and litter products
President: Mark Holt
VP/ Controller: Michael Lunning
Vice President: Gerry Keller
PD & Research Coordinator: Sangita Jalukar Ph. D.
Quality Manager: Julie Sanchez
VP/ Director of Marketing: Jodi Ames-Peterson
Exec. VP International BD: Roger Beers
Contact: Charlie Elrod
celrod@vicor.com
Vice President Operations: Henry Savoy
Production Supervisor Benjamin Facility: Robert Barber
Estimated Sales: $7.6 Million
Number Employees: 10-19
Square Footage: 60000
Parent Co: International Whey Technics
Brands Exported: Desert Gold Dry; Kulactic; Kulsar
Regions Exported to: Europe, Asia
Percentage of Business in Exporting: 65

49746 Variety Glass Inc
201 Foster Ave
Cambridge, OH 43725-1219　　740-432-3643
　　　Fax: 740-432-8693　www.mosserglass.com
Manufacturer and exporter of drug and laboratory glassware
President: Thomas Mosser
VP: Tim Mosser
Estimated Sales: $ 2.5 - 5,000,000
Number Employees: 10-19
Regions Exported to: Canada

49747 Varimixer North America
14240 S Lakes Dr
Charlotte, NC 28273-6793　　980-333-0032
　　　Fax: 704-583-1703　800-221-1138
　mixer@varimixer.com　www.varimixer.com
Commercial mixers and food preparation equipment
President: Richard Aversa
Sales Manager: Gerald McGuffin
Operations: Charlie Strate
Plant Manager: Charlie Strate
Number Employees: 5-9
Square Footage: 400000
Parent Co: ENODIS
Type of Packaging: Food Service
Brands Exported: Varimixer
Regions Exported to: Central America, South America
Brands Imported: Varimixer
Regions Imported from: Europe

49748 Varitronic Systems
6835 Winnetka Cir
Brooklyn Park, MN 55428　　763-536-6400
　　　　　　Fax: 763-536-0769
Manufacturer and exporter of electronic lettering systems and labels
Manager: David Grey
President: Cathy Hudson
Estimated Sales: $ 20 - 30 Million
Number Employees: 5-9
Parent Co: W.H. Brady
Regions Exported to: Worldwide

49749 Varni Brothers/7-Up Bottling
400 Hosmer Avenue
Modesto, CA 95351-3920　　209-521-1777
　　　Fax: 209-521-0877　water@noahs7up.com
　　　　　　www.noahs7up.com
Manufacturer of soft drinks, spring water and other beverages.
President/CEO: Tony Varni
Contact: Deshawn Black
blackd@noahs7up.com
Estimated Sales: $17 Million
Number Employees: 60
Number of Brands: 4
Square Footage: 120000
Parent Co: Dr. Pepper/7-UP Bottling Companies
Type of Packaging: Food Service, Private Label
Regions Exported to: Asia, Guam

49750 Vasinee Food Corporation
1247 Grand Street
Brooklyn, NY 11211　　　718-349-6911
　　　Fax: 718-349-7002　800-878-5996
　　info@vasinee.com　vasineefoodcorp.com
Thai and Asian food: bamboo, juices, coconut milk, fruits and vegetables, curry and paste, noodles, preserves, rice, beans, sauces and spices.
Director of Business Development: Valaya Dipongam
Logistics & Orders Coordinator: Daniel Lee
Year Founded: 1978
Estimated Sales: $14.3 Million
Number Employees: 15
Type of Packaging: Food Service, Private Label, Bulk
Brands Imported: Wangderm, FOCO Pure Coconut Water, Chaokoh, Aroy-D, Pho Ga, Mama Cup, Smiling Fish and more.
Regions Imported from: Asia, Thailand

49751 Vaughn-Russell Candy Kitchen
401 Augusta Street
Greenville, SC 29601　　　864-271-7786
　　　Fax: 704-484-8326　info@vaughnrussell.com
　　　　　　www.vaughnrussell.com
Confectionary manufacturer; original makers of "Incredible Edibles™" and "Mint Pecans®."
Owner: Chris Beard
Plant Manager: Ashton Beard
Estimated Sales: 500,000
Number Employees: 4
Type of Packaging: Consumer, Food Service, Bulk
Regions Exported to: Worldwide
Regions Imported from: Worldwide

49752 Vauxhall Foods
PO Box 430
Vauxhall, AB T0K 2K0
Canada　　　　　　403-654-2771
　　　　　　Fax: 403-654-2211
Processor and exporter of dehydrated potato granules
President: Frank Gatto
CFO: Frank Inaba
Research & Development: Gordon Packer
General Manager: Ken Tamura
Production Manager: Ken Franz
Number Employees: 50-99
Square Footage: 200000
Type of Packaging: Food Service, Private Label, Bulk
Brands Exported: Gourmet; Aristocrat; Chipper; V.G. Blue
Regions Exported to: Central America, South America, Europe, Asia, USA
Percentage of Business in Exporting: 90

49753 (HQ)Vector Corp
675 44th St
Marion, IA 52302-3800　　　319-377-8263
　　　　　　Fax: 319-377-5574
　　　vector.sales@vectorcorporation.com
　　　　　　www.freund-vector.com
Designs, manufactures, and markets processing equipment for the processing of solid dosage form materials.
President: Max Kubota
max.kubota@vectorcorporation.com
CFO: Tatsuo Matsugaki
VP Marketing: Greg Smith
Sales: Greg Smith
Production: Mike Douglas
Purchasing Director: Keith Wenndt
Estimated Sales: $25-50 Million
Number Employees: 100-249
Square Footage: 75000
Other Locations:
　Vector Corp.
　　Huxley, IA
　Vector Corp.
Brands Exported: Vector
Regions Exported to: Central America, South America, Europe
Brands Imported: Freund
Regions Imported from: Asia

49754 Vector Technologies
6820 N 43rd St
Milwaukee, WI 53209　　　414-247-7100
　　　Fax: 414-247-7110　800-832-4010
　　　　　　sales@vector-vacuums.com
Manufacturer and exporter of dust collectors and vacuum cleaners and conveying systems
President: Stebe Schonberger
CFO: Chris Koe
Contact: Matthew Benson
mbenson@vector-vacuums.com
Operations Manager: Bruce Kolb
Estimated Sales: $ 5 - 10 Million
Number Employees: 20-49
Square Footage: 90000
Parent Co: Vector Technologies

Importers & Exporters / A-Z

Brands Exported: Vec Loader; Spartan; Titan; Hepavac; Invader; Klean Scrub
Regions Exported to: Central America, South America, Europe, Asia, Middle East
Percentage of Business in Exporting: 25

49755 Vega Americas Inc
4241 Allendorf Dr
Cincinnati, OH 45209-1501   513-272-0131
        Fax: 513-272-0133 800-367-5383
        www.vega-americas.com
Manufacturer and exporter of sensors and gauges
President: Ron Hegyesi
r.hegyesi@vega.com
CFO: Ken Seldmenn
Quality Control: Matt Phomas
Advertising Manager: Patrick Schreiber
r.hegyesi@vega.com
Estimated Sales: $ 20 - 50 Million
Number Employees: 100-249
Type of Packaging: Bulk
Regions Exported to: Worldwide

49756 Vega Trading Company
71 W 23rd St
New York, NY 10010-4102   212-741-8290
        Fax: 212-741-8855 www.rolandfood.com
Importer and exporter of snack foods, cookies, preserves, canned fruits, pate, fish, condiments and vegetables
President: Charles Scheidt
Marketing Director: Joanne Scheidt
Estimated Sales: $ .5 - 1 million
Number Employees: 1-4
Type of Packaging: Consumer, Food Service

49757 Vegetarian Resource Group
409 W Cold Spring Ln
Baltimore, MD 21210-2801   410-366-8343
        Fax: 410-366-8804 vrg@vrg.org
        www.vrg.org
Nonprofit specializing in marketing vegetarian products
CEO: Debra Wasserman
vrg@vrg.org
CFO: Suzanne Havala
vrg@vrg.org
Number Employees: 5-9

49758 Veggie Land
222 New Rd # 3
Parsippany, NJ 07054-5626   973-808-1540
        Fax: 973-882-3030 888-808-5540
        info@veggieland.com www.veggiburger.com
Processor and exporter of vegetarian foods including burgers, meat balls, frankfurters, sausage, sandwiches and chili
Executive VP: Len Torine
Estimated Sales: Below $ 5 Million
Number Employees: 20-49
Square Footage: 64000
Brands Exported: Veggieland
Regions Exported to: Asia, Canada
Percentage of Business in Exporting: 5

49759 Veggie Land
222 New Rd # 3
Parsippany, NJ 07054-5626   973-808-1540
        Fax: 973-882-3030 www.veggiburger.com
Manager: Len Torine
Contact: Paul Debello
info@veggieland.com
Estimated Sales: $ 10 - 20 Million
Number Employees: 20-49

49760 Vegi-Deli
17 Paul Dr Ste 104
San Rafael, CA 94903   415-883-6100
        Fax: 415-526-1453 888-473-3667
Vegetarian meat alternative deli products including pepperoni, cold cuts and pizza toppings and vegi-jerky, pepperoni snack sticks.
General Manager: Debra Ventura
Estimated Sales: $ 3-5 Million
Number Employees: 8
Square Footage: 24000
Type of Packaging: Consumer, Food Service, Private Label

49761 Vending Nut Co
2222 Montgomery St
Fort Worth, TX 76107-4519   817-737-3071
        Fax: 817-377-1316 800-429-9260
        www.vendingnutco.com
Nuts wholesaler
President: Johnny Minshew
Estimated Sales: $4 Million
Number Employees: 10-19

49762 Vendome Copper & Brass Works
729 Franklin St
Louisville, KY 40202-6007   502-587-1930
        Fax: 502-589-0639 888-384-5161
        office@vendomecopper.com
Manufacturer and exporter of copper and confectioners' kettles, distilling apparatus, vacuum pans, evaporators, coils, etc
President: Patricia Seale
pseale@cleansolutionspro.com
Estimated Sales: $5-10 Million
Number Employees: 50-99
Type of Packaging: Food Service
Regions Exported to: Worldwide
Percentage of Business in Exporting: 10

49763 Venetian Productions
6955 NW 52nd St
Miami, FL 33166-4844   786-464-4200
        Fax: 954-463-9466 yernest@bellsouth.net
        www.venetianproductions.com
Importer and exporter of Caribbean blue mountain green coffee beans
President: Olivier Caudron
Marketing Director: Marie Snizek
Purchasing Agent: Niki Fulgueira
Number Employees: 5-9
Parent Co: Century Export
Type of Packaging: Bulk
Regions Exported to: Africa, Latin America
Percentage of Business in Exporting: 10
Regions Imported from: Latin America
Percentage of Business in Importing: 90

49764 (HQ)Venner International Products
410 W Main St # 101
Mesquite, TX 75149-4263   972-289-4595
        Fax: 972-288-9926
Importer of scallops, shrimp, export multiline of materials, ingredients and surplus goods
President: George Venner Sr
VP: Shang Yuan Ding
Marketing: George Venner
Sales: George Venner
Estimated Sales: $2.5-5 Million
Number Employees: 5-9
Square Footage: 4000
Type of Packaging: Consumer, Private Label, Bulk
Other Locations:
    Venner International Products
    BeijingVenner International Products
Brands Exported: Generic, Private Label, Salvage
Regions Exported to: Central America, South America, Europe, Asia
Brands Imported: Private Label
Regions Imported from: Central America, South America, Europe, Asia, Middle East
Percentage of Business in Importing: 10

49765 Vent Master
1021 Brevik Place
Mississauga, ON L4W 3R7
Canada   905-624-0301
        Fax: 800-665-2438 800-565-2981
Manufacturer and exporter of exhaust fans, air filters, fire safety equipment, heat recovery units, hoods and utility distribution and ventilating systems
Vice President: Mark Meulenbeck
Sales Director: Dan O'Brien
Operations Manager: Barry Carter
Estimated Sales: $ 1 - 5 Million
Parent Co: ENODIS
Type of Packaging: Food Service
Regions Exported to: Worldwide

49766 (HQ)Vent-A-Hood Co
1000 N Greenville Ave
Richardson, TX 75081-2799   972-235-5201
        Fax: 972-231-0663 800-331-2492
        www.vahdistributing.com
Manufacturer and exporter of hoods
President: Miles Woodall Iii
CEO: Mileas Woodall
Quality Control: David Stiles
sjacobs@ventahood.com
HR Executive: Stewart Jacobs
sjacobs@ventahood.com
Limited Partner: Miles Woodall III
National Sales Manager: Ed Gober
Estimated Sales: $ 10 - 20 Million
Number Employees: 100-249

49767 Ventre Packing Company
P.O. Box 6487
Syracuse, NY 13217   315-463-2384
        Fax: 315-463-5897
Manufacturer and packager of spaghetti sauces and salsas; production plant bought by Giovanni Food Company Inc in 2010.
Chairman: Marty Ventre
President/CEO: Martin Ventre
Number of Brands: 1
Parent Co: Giovanni Food Company Inc.
Type of Packaging: Consumer, Food Service, Private Label
Brands Exported: Enrico's
Regions Exported to: Central America, Europe, Middle East, Canada, Caribbean, Mexico

49768 Ventura Coastal LLC
2325 Vista Del Mar Dr
Ventura, CA 93001-3700   805-653-7000
        Fax: 805-653-7777 sales@vcoastal.com
        www.venturacoastal.com
Manufacturer and exporter of citrus concentrates and single strength juices; contract packager of frozen pectin products
President: William Borgers
borgens@vcoastal.com
EVP, Sales & Marketing: Rick Torres
Estimated Sales: $44 Million
Number Employees: 50-99
Type of Packaging: Consumer, Food Service, Private Label, Bulk
Other Locations:
    Visalia, CA
    Tipton, CATipton
Regions Exported to: Europe, Asia
Percentage of Business in Exporting: 10

49769 (HQ)Venture Measurement Co LLC
150 Venture Blvd
Spartanburg, SC 29306-3805   864-574-8960
Fax: 864-574-8063 www.venturemeasurement.com
Manufacturer and exporter of level sensors
President: Mark Earl
CFO: Michael Hallinan
R&D: Roy Zielinski
Sales Manager: Rick Ayers
Contact: Russ Barnett
rbarnett@venturemeas.com
Estimated Sales: $30-50 Million
Number Employees: 50-99
Square Footage: 42000
Brands Exported: Roto-Bin-Dicator; Cap Level IIA; Bin-Dicators; Pulse Point
Regions Exported to: Central America, South America, Europe, Asia
Percentage of Business in Exporting: 20

49770 Venture Measurement Co LLC
150 Venture Blvd
Spartanburg, SC 29306-3805   864-574-8960
        Fax: 864-574-8063 800-426-9010
        sales@venturemeas.com
        www.venturemeasurement.com
Manufacturer and exporter of level measurement, weight and batching instrumentation for tanks, silos and hoppers; also, PC based bulk inventory monitoring software
President: Mark Earl
Quality Control: Bennett Connvlly
R&D: Joe Dejuzman
CFO: Mick Hallinan
Marketing: Jamie Ives
Contact: Jeff Baker
jeff.baker@kistlermorse.com
Estimated Sales: $ 5 - 10 Million
Number Employees: 50-99
Regions Exported to: Worldwide
Percentage of Business in Exporting: 40

Importers & Exporters / A-Z

49771 Venture Vineyards
8830 Upper Lake Rd
Lodi, NY 14860   607-582-6774
                              888-635-6277
                venturev@capital.net
Grower of asparagus, raspberries and grapes including concord, Niagara, Catawaba, and Delaware. Also a processor of grape juice and importer and exporter of concord grapes
President: Melvin Nass
VP: Phyllis Nass
Operations Manager: Andrew Nass
Number Employees: 5-9
Square Footage: 40000
Brands Exported: Venture For The Best
Regions Exported to: Canada
Regions Imported from: Canada
Percentage of Business in Importing: 20

49772 Venus Wafers Inc
100 Research Rd
Suite 3
Hingham, MA 02043-4345   781-740-1002
     Fax: 781-740-0791   800-545-4538
          www.venuswafers.com
Crackers
CFO: Edward Barmakian
Manager: James Anderko
jranderko@aol.com
Estimated Sales: $ 5 - 10 Million
Number Employees: 20-49
Type of Packaging: Consumer

49773 (HQ)Verax Chemical Co
20102 Broadway Ave
Snohomish, WA 98296-7937   360-668-2431
     Fax: 360-668-5186   800-637-7771
info@veraxproducts.com www.veraxproducts.com
Maintenance chemicals and supplies including hand and toilet bowl cleaners, disinfectants, mops, soap and floor polish; importer of cocoa mats
President: Julie Curkendall
Secretary/Treasurer: Sue Copeland
Contact: Brent Casteel
brent@veraxproducts.com
Estimated Sales: Less Than $500,000
Number Employees: 1-4
Square Footage: 30000
Regions Imported from: Asia
Percentage of Business in Importing: 15

49774 Verday
270 Lafayette St.
New York, NY 10012
                hello@drinkverday.com
                www.drinkverday.com
Flavored chlorophyll water
Founder/Chief Executive Officer: Randy Kohana
Number of Brands: 1
Number of Products: 4
Type of Packaging: Consumer, Private Label
Brands Exported: Verday
Regions Exported to: USA

49775 Verde Farms, LLC
300 Trade Center # 3540
Woburn, MA 01801   617-221-8922
     Fax: 617-221-8923 info@verdefarms.com
          www.verdefarms.com
Organic, free range, hormone-free and grass-fed beef for retail, wholesale, foodservice and ingredient customers
Co-Founder/Chief Executive Officer: Dana Ehrlich
Vice-President, Marketing: Pete Lewis
Co-Founder/Director of Operations: Pablo Garbarino
Year Founded: 2005
Number of Brands: 1
Type of Packaging: Food Service, Bulk
Brands Exported: Verde Farms
Regions Exported to: USA

49776 Verlasso
                              786-522-8418
                www.verlasso.com
Farm-raised sustainable salmon
Year Founded: 2011
Number of Brands: 1
Number of Products: 1
Brands Exported: Verlasso
Regions Exported to: USA

49777 Vermillion Flooring
1207 S Scenic Ave
Springfield, MO 65802-5199   417-862-3785
     Fax: 417-862-3789 www.vermillion-flooring.com
Manufacturer and exporter of serving trays, pantryware, wood-chopping blocks, cedar accessories and wall decor; also, racks including wine, cookbook and mug trees
President: Art Thomas
VP: Gary Robinson
Special Markets Manager: Steve Baker
Estimated Sales: Less Than $500,000
Number Employees: 1-4
Square Footage: 160000
Brands Exported: 10th St. Bakery; Chef's Select; Classic Images
Regions Exported to: Europe, Asia, Canada
Percentage of Business in Exporting: 10

49778 Vermont Tea & Trading Co Inc
43 Court St
43 Court Street
Middlebury, VT 05753-1454   802-388-4005
     Fax: 802-388-4005   888-255-9327
Loose leaf teas
Co-Owner: Curron Malhotra
Co-Owner: Bruce Malhotra
b.malhotra@vermonttea.com
Estimated Sales: $ 1 - 3 Million
Number Employees: 1-4

49779 Veroni USA
1110 Commerce Blvd
Suite 200
Logan Township, NJ 08085   609-970-0320
                www.veroni.it
Meat
CEO: Antonio Corsano
Operations Manager: Stefano Poldi
Estimated Sales: $130.8 Million
Number Employees: 28
Brands Imported: Veroni
Regions Imported from: Italy

49780 Veronica Foods Inc
1991 Dennison St
Oakland, CA 94606-5225   510-535-6833
     Fax: 510-532-2837   800-370-5554
     info@evoliveoil.com www.evoliveoil.com
Olive oil manufacturers and importers
President: Michael Bradley
CEO: Mike Bradley
mbradley@evoliveoil.com
CFO: Leah Bradley
VP: Veronica Bradley
Marketing: Arnie Kaufman
VP Retail Sales: Arnie Kaufman
Operations: Fred Johnson
Production: Myron Manown
Plant Manager: Dave Fitzgerald
Purchasing: Fred Johnson
Estimated Sales: $16,200,000
Number Employees: 50-99
Square Footage: 684000
Brands Exported: Delizia; Italia; Dainty-Pak
Brands Imported: Delizia; Italia; Dainty-Pak; Pure Life
Regions Imported from: South America, Europe

49781 Versa Conveyor
PO Box 899
London, OH 43140-0899   740-852-5609
     Fax: 740-869-2839 www.versaconveyor.com
Manufacturer and exporter of gravity and power conveyor
President: Andrew Petitt
Chief Executive Officer: Chris Cole
Vice President of Project Management: Alfred Rebello
Chief Technical Officer: Ray Neiser
Senior Vice President of Sales and Marke: Jim McKnight
Vice President of Operations: Chris Arnold
Estimated Sales: $20-50 Million
Number Employees: 100-249
Parent Co: Tomkins Industries
Regions Exported to: Worldwide

49782 (HQ)Versailles Lighting
1305 Poinsettia Dr Ste 6
Delray Beach, FL 33444   561-278-8758
     Fax: 561-278-8759   888-564-0240
Manufacturer, importer and exporter of lighting fixtures and metal tables
President: Max Guedj
CEO: Maurine Locke
CFO: Tung Nguyen
Quality Control: Rajendrauth James
Sales: Samantha Basdeo
Estimated Sales: $ 3 - 5 Million
Number Employees: 10-19
Square Footage: 40000
Other Locations:
   Versailles Lighting
   Delnay, FLVersailles Lighting
Regions Exported to: Central America, South America, Europe
Regions Imported from: Europe, Asia

49783 Vertex China
1793 W 2nd St
Pomona, CA 91766-1253   909-594-4800
     Fax: 909-595-1993   800-483-7839
info@vertexchina.com www.vertexchina.com
Manufacturer, importer and exporter of dinnerware, chinaware and tableware including lead-free, microwave/dishwasher safe, cups, saucers, bowls, dishes, platters and mugs; custom decoration available
President: Hoi Shum
info@vertexchina.com
Sales: Ken Joyce
Estimated Sales: $10-20 Million
Number Employees: 10-19
Square Footage: 50000

49784 Vertex Interactive
23 Carol Street
Clifton, NJ 07014-1490   973-777-3500
                Fax: 973-472-0814
Manufacturer and exporter of balances, weights, bar code and magnetic strip card readers, industrial scales and data collection software
Chairman: James Maloy
CEO/President: Ron Byer
Number Employees: 60
Parent Co: Vertex Industries
Brands Exported: Torbal; Identicon; Vertel

49785 Vertical Systems Intl
2126 Chamber Center Dr
Lakeside Park, KY 41017-1669 859-485-9650
     Fax: 859-485-9654 sales@vsilift.com
                www.vsilift.com
Manufacturer and exporter of vertical lifts, stackers, conveyors, dumpers, and autostore units
President: Daniel Quinn
dan.quinn@vsilift.com
Member: Daniel Quinn
VP Sales: Steve Templeton
Estimated Sales: $ 5 - 10 Million
Number Employees: 5-9
Square Footage: 88000
Regions Exported to: Worldwide
Percentage of Business in Exporting: 1

49786 Vescom America
2289 Ross Mill Rd
Henderson, NC 27537-5966   252-436-9067
     Fax: 252-436-9069 usacanada@vescom.com
Manufacturer, importer and exporter of recycling systems for food wastes including feeders, shredders, weight controllers, screeners, conveyors, packers and dust collection systems
Owner: Robert Vrabel
Contact: Lisa Brooks
l.brooks@vescom.com
Estimated Sales: $300,000-500,000
Number Employees: 1-4
Square Footage: 1000
Brands Exported: Food Recycling Systems; Shredding & Pulverizing; Screening Machinery
Brands Imported: Food Recycling Systems
Regions Imported from: Central America, Europe
Percentage of Business in Importing: 10

49787 Vessey & Co Inc
1605 Zenos Rd
P.O. Box 28
Holtville, CA 92250-9603   760-356-0130
     Fax: 760-356-0137 kevinolson@redshift.com
                www.vessey.com
Grower of cabbage including red, green, bok choy and napa; also, red and yellow onions, red and yukon potatoes, sweet corn, cantaloupes and garlic including fresh, whole, peeled, minced and chopped; importer and exporter of garlic

Importers & Exporters / A-Z

President: Jon Vessey
Partner: Jack Vessey
jack@vessey.com
Sales Manager: David Grimes
Sales: Eric Pompa
Estimated Sales: $3100000
Number Employees: 10-19
Type of Packaging: Food Service, Bulk
Brands Exported: Vessey; Spice Queen
Regions Exported to: South America, Europe, Canada, Mexico
Percentage of Business in Exporting: 10
Regions Imported from: South America, Mexico
Percentage of Business in Importing: 10

49788 Vesture Corp
120 E Pritchard St
Asheboro, NC 27203-4761   336-629-3000
Fax: 336-629-3100 www.vesture.com
President: Byron Owens
bowens@vesture.com
Estimated Sales: $ 5 - 10 Million
Number Employees: 10-19

49789 Vetrerie Bruni USA
2750 Maxwell Way
Fairfield, CA 94534   707-752-6200
Fax: 707-752-6201 877-278-6445
info@bruniglass.com
Importer of specialty green and clear glass bottles and jars for oil, vinegar, wine, spirits etc.; also, cork, screw cap and glass top closures
President: Roberto Del Bon
CFO: Raef Israel
Vice President: Annie Reyes
Estimated Sales: $10-20 Million
Number Employees: 10-19
Square Footage: 100000
Parent Co: Vetrerie Bruni SRL
Brands Imported: Fido Jar; Cobalt; Classic Jars; Pallet Program; Le Source; Le Gourmet
Regions Imported from: Europe, Asia, Middle East
Percentage of Business in Importing: 100

49790 VetriTech Laboratories
PO Box 2365
Pasco, WA 99302-2365   509-542-0523
Fax: 509-547-8095 800-564-8964
Wholesaler/distributor and importer of food supplements
Estimated Sales: $2.5-5 Million
Number Employees: 1-4
Regions Imported from: Asia

49791 Viatec
777 Fort Street
Victoria, BC V8W 1G9
Canada   250-483-3214
Fax: 269-945-2357 800-942-4702
sales@viatec.ca www.viatec.ca
Manufacturer and exporter of dairy processors, cookers, coolers, stainless and fiberglass tanks, mixers and valves
CEO: Dan Gunn
Marketing & Communications Coordinator: Robbie Aylesworth
Sales (Stainless): Bob Johnson
Manager of Operations & Finance: Michelle Gaetz
Estimated Sales: $10-20 Million
Number Employees: 50-99
Square Footage: 104000
Brands Exported: Chemtek; Duratek; Permasan; Resinfab
Regions Exported to: Central America, South America, Asia
Percentage of Business in Exporting: 10

49792 Viatec Process Storage System
500 Reed St
PO Box 99
Belding, MI 48809-1532   616-794-1230
Fax: 616-794-2487 klk@viatec.com
Manufacturer and exporter of dairy processors, cookers, coolers, stainless and fiberglass tanks, mixers and valves
Sales Director: Bob Johnson
Plant Manager: Ron Timmer
Estimated Sales: $5,000,000 - $9,900,000
Number Employees: 20-49
Square Footage: 52000
Parent Co: Viatec

49793 Vichy Springs Mineral Water
2605 Vichy Springs Rd
Ukiah, CA 95482-3507   707-462-9515
Fax: 707-462-9516 vichy@vichysprings.com
www.vichysprings.com
Processor and exporter of naturally carbonated bottled mineral water
President: Gilbert Ashoff
VP: Marjorie Ashoff
Estimated Sales: $500,000 appx.
Number Employees: 10-19
Square Footage: 28000
Type of Packaging: Private Label
Regions Exported to: Asia
Percentage of Business in Exporting: 10

49794 Vicksburg Chemical Company
5100 Poplar Ave Fl 24
Memphis, TN 38137-4000   901-747-0234
Fax: 901-747-4031 800-227-2798
jhreeves@aol.com
Processor, importer and exporter of potassium nitrates, potassium carbonates, monammonium phosphates and monopotassium phosphates
Sales Manager/Distributor: John Reeves
Estimated Sales: $ 1 - 5 Million
Number Employees: 100-250
Type of Packaging: Private Label
Regions Exported to: Worldwide
Percentage of Business in Exporting: 15
Regions Imported from: Middle East
Percentage of Business in Importing: 5

49795 Vicmore Manufacturing Company
20 Grand Avenue
Brooklyn, NY 11205-1317   718-855-7758
Fax: 718-852-3768 800-458-8663
Manufacturer and exporter of double polished clear tablecloths, and vinyl and chemical aprons
President: Morris Steinberg
Estimated Sales: $5-10 Million
Number Employees: 50-99
Regions Exported to: Worldwide
Percentage of Business in Exporting: 20

49796 Victor International
3111 E Via Mondo
Compton, CA 90221-5414   323-979-6730
Fax: 310-637-0490 sales@victorgroup.com
Exporter of gummy bears, aluminum foil, cookies, fruit juices, potato chips, etc
President: Alan Huang
Export Coordinator: Leona Liu
VP: Jack Hsu
Number Employees: 5-9
Square Footage: 240000
Brands Exported: Flyers; Diamond; Texsun; Gamesa; Pringles
Regions Exported to: Asia
Percentage of Business in Exporting: 100

49797 Victor Joseph Son Inc
2 University Plz # 410
Hackensack, NJ 07601-6210   201-996-1801
Fax: 201-592-1722
Importer of fruits
Owner: Joey Joseph
joey@victorjoseph.com
Estimated Sales: $ 5 - 10 Million
Number Employees: 5-9
Regions Imported from: Central America, South America, Australia

49798 Victor Packing
11687 Road 27 1/2
Madera, CA 93637-9440   559-673-5908
Fax: 559-673-4225 www.victorpacking.com
Manufacturer, and exporter of currants and raisins including organic, natural, golden and seedless; also, raisin juice concentrate and raisin paste available
Owner: Victor Sahatjian
victor@victorpacking.com
VP: Margaret Sahatjian
Domestic Sales: Kristina Surabian
International Sales: Richard Burright
Year Founded: 1928
Estimated Sales: $10 Million
Number Employees: 50-99
Square Footage: 150000
Type of Packaging: Consumer, Food Service, Private Label, Bulk
Brands Exported: Madera; Liberty Bell; Natural Thompson
Regions Exported to: Worldwide
Percentage of Business in Exporting: 70

49799 (HQ)Victoria Fine Foods
443 E 100th St
Brooklyn, NY 11236-2103   718-927-3000
Fax: 718-649-7069
victoria@victoriafinefoods.com
www.victoriafinefoods.com
Pasta and specialty sauces, condiments and gourmet spreads.
President: Brian Dean
CEO: Gerald Aquilina
Vice President, Finance: Robert Haberman
Executive VP, Sales: William Paskowski
Number Employees: 100-249
Type of Packaging: Consumer, Food Service, Private Label, Bulk
Brands Exported: Victoria
Regions Exported to: Central America, South America, Europe, Asia, Middle East
Percentage of Business in Exporting: 10
Regions Imported from: Central America, South America, Europe, Asia
Percentage of Business in Importing: 20

49800 Victoria Porcelain
7790 NW 67th St
Miami, FL 33166-2702   305-593-2353
Fax: 305-593-8363 888-593-2353
sales@victoriaporcelain.com
www.victoriaporcelain.com
Porcelain cups, bowls, plates, gravy boats, saucers, mugs, ovenware, teapots, etc.; importer and exporter of flatware and knives
President: Jose Espejo
jespejo@victoriaporcelain.com
VP Sales: David Yablin
Customer Service Manager: Phyllis Halpern
Estimated Sales: $ 2.5 - 5 Million
Number Employees: 1-4
Square Footage: 40000
Regions Exported to: Central America, South America, Caribbean, Mexico
Brands Imported: Dalia; Victoria Porcelain
Regions Imported from: South America, Europe
Percentage of Business in Importing: 15

49801 Videojet Technologies Inc
1500 N Mittel Blvd
Wood Dale, IL 60191-1073
800-843-3610
vti.domesticcs@videojet.com www.videojet.com
Manufacturer and exporter of coding and labeling equipment, printing inks and printing equipment; also, material handling equipment.
Chief Technology Officer/VP of R&D: John Folkers
Principal Software Engineer: Eric Amy
Mechanical Engineer Manager: Kevin Kuester
Number Employees: 4,000
Parent Co: Donaher Corporation
Brands Exported: Excel; Cheshire, Videojet, Marsh, Willette
Regions Exported to: Central America, South America, Europe, Asia, Middle East
Percentage of Business in Exporting: 40

49802 Vie-Del Co
11903 S Chestnut Ave
Fresno, CA 93725-9618   559-834-2525
Fax: 559-834-1348
Processor and exporter of fruit concentrates including grape; also, wine and brandy
President: Dianne Nury
dnury@vie-del.com
Vice President: Richard Watson
Customer Service: Janel Cook
Purchasing Manager: Robert Reiter
Estimated Sales: $18,800,000
Number Employees: 100-249
Regions Exported to: Central America, Asia

49803 Vienna Beef LTD
6033 Malburg Way
Vernon, CA 90058-3947   323-583-8951
Fax: 323-585-7580 800-733-6063
www.viennabeef.com
Pickles, cured meat, soups, kosher specialties and desserts.
CEO: James Eisenberg
CFO: Richard Steele
Vice President of Marketing: Keith Smith
SVP/Sales & Marketing: Thomas McGlade
VP/Human Resources: Jane Lustig
VP/Purchasing: Richard Ewert

Number Employees: 10-19
Type of Packaging: Consumer, Food Service, Private Label
Brands Exported: Pie Piper; Vienna; Central Park
Regions Exported to: Europe, Asia, Mexico, Canada
Percentage of Business in Exporting: 10

49804 Vienna Meat Products
170 Nugget Avenue
Scarborough, ON M1S 3A7
Canada　　　　　　　　　　　416-297-1062
　　　　　Fax: 416-297-0836　800-588-1931
Processor and importer of ham, sausage, cold cuts, turkey products, roast beef, corned beef and pastrami.
President: Michael Latifi
Director Retail Sales: Vince Romano
Estimated Sales: $9.5 Million
Number Employees: 100
Regions Imported from: Europe, USA
Percentage of Business in Importing: 10

49805 View-Rite Manufacturing
455 Allan St
Daly City, CA 94014-1627　　　415-468-3856
　　　　　　　　　　Fax: 415-468-4784
Manufacturer and exporter of store fixtures
President: Nha Nguyen
nnguyen@viewrite.com
VP: Nha Nguyen
Number Employees: 20-49
Square Footage: 160000
Regions Exported to: Worldwide

49806 Vigneri Chocolate Inc.
810 Emerson St
Rochester, NY 14613-1804　　585-254-6160
　　Fax: 585-254-6872　877-844-6374
　　info@vigneri.com　www.vigneri.com
chocolate tablets, filled chocolates, chocolate dipped products, novelty chocolates, chocolate covered products, drinking chocolate and wellness chocolate in the gifting, snacking, entertaining and decorating categories for our VigneriChocolate bran
CEO: Alexander Vigneri
Number Employees: 10+
Square Footage: 60000
Type of Packaging: Consumer, Food Service, Private Label, Bulk
Regions Exported to: Central America, Canada
Percentage of Business in Exporting: 10
Regions Imported from: Europe
Percentage of Business in Importing: 5

49807 Vigo Importing Co
4701 W Comanche Ave
P.O. Box 15584
Tampa, FL 33614
　　　　　　　　　　　　　800-282-4130
　　　　　　　　　　www.vigo-alessi.com
Processor and exporter of seasoned rice dinners, paella and bread crumbs; importer of olives, peppers, sundried tomatoes, olive oil, cheese, pasta, balsamic vinegar, bread sticks, pine nuts, coffee, vegetable pates, porcini mushroomsartichokes, etc.
General Manager: Sam Ciccarello
sam@vigo-alessi.com
Marketing Director: Laura De Lucia
VP, Sales: Alfred Alessi
Year Founded: 1947
Estimated Sales: $21.1 Million
Number Employees: 100-249
Square Footage: 165000
Type of Packaging: Consumer, Food Service, Private Label, Bulk
Brands Exported: Vigo; Alessi
Regions Exported to: Central America, South America, Canada, Latin America, Mexico
Percentage of Business in Exporting: 5
Brands Imported: Vigo; Alessi
Regions Imported from: South America, Europe, Asia
Percentage of Business in Importing: 50

49808 Viking Corp
210 Industrial Park Dr
Hastings, MI 49058-9631　　　269-945-9501
　　Fax: 269-945-4495　800-968-9501
　　　　　techsvcs@vikingcorp.com
Manufacturer and exporter of fire protection systems including wet and dry pipe, deluge and fire cycle; also, valves, sprinklers, spray nozzles and alarm devices
CEO: Tomdra Groos
CEO: Kevin Ortyl
Marketing Director: Sandra Wake
Sales Director: Bill Phair
Contact: Will Allgood
wallgood@supplynet.com
Purchasing Manager: Jerry Dinges
Estimated Sales: $ 20 - 30 Million
Number Employees: 100-249
Parent Co: Tyden Seal Company
Regions Exported to: Worldwide
Percentage of Business in Exporting: 45

49809 Viking Industries
489 Tumbull Bay Rd
New Smyma Beach, FL 32168　386-428-9800
　　Fax: 386-409-0360　888-605-5560
Manufacturer and exporter of hot melt adhesive application equipment for carton and case sealings; also, hot wax dispensing systems for wine bottle seals, cheese products and hot candy
Owner: Walter Warning Jr
VP Sales/Marketing: Douglas White
Estimated Sales: $2.5-5,000,000
Number Employees: 10-19
Square Footage: 40000
Brands Exported: Titan
Regions Exported to: Worldwide
Percentage of Business in Exporting: 15

49810 Villa Mt. Eden Winery
8711 Silverado Trl S
Saint Helena, CA 94574　　　866-931-1624
　　　　　　　　　　Fax: 707-963-7840
Processor and exporter of wines
Manager: Jeff Mc Bride
j.mcbride@villamteden.com
Estimated Sales: $ 10 - 20 Million
Number Employees: 10-19
Parent Co: Stimson Lane
Type of Packaging: Consumer
Percentage of Business in Exporting: 10

49811 Vilore Foods Co Inc
8220 San Lorenzo Dr
Laredo, TX 78045-8704　　　956-722-7190
　　Fax: 956-728-8383　info@vilore.com
　　　　　　　　　　　www.vilore.com
Jalapeno peppers
President: Suzanna Almanza
salmanza@vilore.com
Estimated Sales: $200 Million
Number Employees: 20-49

49812 Vilore Foods Company
3838 Medical Dr
San Antonio, TX 78229　　　210-509-9496
　　Fax: 210-616-9934　877-609-9496
　　　　　　　　　　　www.vilore.com
Wholesaler/distributor, importer and exporter of Hispanic foods including jalapeno peppers, fruit nectars, hot sauce, chicken bouillon, powdered drinks and nopalitos.
President: Marco Mena
Director of Finance: Walter Chapman
National Sales Director: Andrew Boyer
aboyer@vilore.com
Director, Operations & Logistics: Jose Murillo
Year Founded: 1983
Estimated Sales: $219 Million
Number Employees: 103
Square Footage: 470000
Type of Packaging: Consumer, Food Service, Private Label
Other Locations:
　Imperial, CA
　Santa Fe Springs, CA
　Stafford, TX
　San Ramon, CA
　Glen Ellyn, IL
　Laredo, TXSanta Fe Springs
Brands Exported: Cal-Co-Tose; Proctor & Gamble
Regions Exported to: Central America, Canada
Percentage of Business in Exporting: 5
Brands Imported: La Costna; Jumex; ChocoMilk; Congelli; Pronto
Regions Imported from: Mexico
Percentage of Business in Importing: 90

49813 Vilter Manufacturing Corporation
5555 S Packard Ave
Cudahy, WI 53110　　　　　414-744-0111
　　　　　Fax: 414-744-3483　www.vilter.com
Compressors, condensors, air untis and custom packaged systems
President/CEO/COO: Ron Prebish
VP Business Development: Wayne Wehber
VP Sales/Marketing: Mark Stencel
Contact: Mark Stencel
mark.stencel@emersonclimate.com
VP Operations: John Barry
Estimated Sales: $43 Million
Number Employees: 100-249
Number of Brands: 4
Number of Products: 7
Square Footage: 400000
Brands Exported: Vilter
Regions Exported to: Central America, South America, Europe, Asia

49814 Vince's Seafoods
1105 Lafayette St
Gretna, LA 70053-6345　　　504-368-1544
　　　　　　　　　　Fax: 504-368-1545
Processor and exporter of frozen and boiled seafood; shrimp, crabs, oysters, crawfish, catfish, tuna, trout, flounder and tilapia. Also gumbo and soups
President: Barbara Jimenez
vdesalvojr@yahoo.com
Estimated Sales: $500,000-$1 Million
Number Employees: 1-4
Square Footage: 32000
Regions Exported to: Europe
Percentage of Business in Exporting: 10

49815 Vincent B Zaninovich & Sons
20715 Avenue 8
Richgrove, CA 93261　　　　661-725-2497
　　Fax: 661-725-5153　www.vbzgrapes.com
Processor and exporter of grapes
Owner: Antone Zaninovich
Owner/President: Vincent Zaninovich
vincentz@vbzgrapes.com
VP: Andrew Zaninovich
Sales Team Member: Joe Butkiewicz
Human Resources Director: Mark Boyer
Estimated Sales: $11 Million
Number Employees: 10-19
Square Footage: 30900
Type of Packaging: Bulk
Regions Exported to: Worldwide
Percentage of Business in Exporting: 55

49816 Vincent Corp
2810 E 5th Ave
Tampa, FL 33605-5638　　　813-248-2650
　　Fax: 813-247-7557　vincent@vincentcorp.com
　　　　　　　　　　www.vincentcorp.com
Manufacturer and exporter of screw presses for dewatering; also, pectin peel and citrus by-product machinery for liquids separation/solids concentration
President: Robert Johnston
spj110@msn.com
Project Engineer: Bob Johnston
Estimated Sales: $2.5-5 Million
Number Employees: 50-99
Square Footage: 160000
Brands Exported: Vincent

49817 Vincent Formusa Company
2150 Oxford Road
Des Plaines, IL 60018　　　　847-813-6040
　　Fax: 312-421-1286　sales@marconi-foods.com
　　　　　　　　　　www.marconi-foods.com
Beans, salad dressings, giardiniera & peppers, olives, olive oils, pasta, Italian style salads, spices, tomatoes, vinegars
President: Robert Johnson
bob@marconi-foods.com
Estimated Sales: $830,000
Number Employees: 10
Square Footage: 100000
Type of Packaging: Consumer, Food Service, Bulk
Brands Exported: DiGiovanni; Marconi
Percentage of Business in Exporting: 5
Brands Imported: Marconi
Regions Imported from: Central America, Europe
Percentage of Business in Importing: 5

49818 Vincor Canada
441 Courtneypark Drive E
Mississauga, ON L5T 2V3
Canada　　　　　　　　　　　905-564-6900
　　Fax: 905-564-6909　800-265-9463
　　　　　　　　　　　www.cbrands.com

Importers & Exporters / A-Z

Wine and vodka cooler importer, marketer and distributor.
President & CEO: Eric Morham
CFO: Don Dychuck
SVP Marketing, Canadian Portfolio: Steve Bolliger
Director Sales & Marketing, RJ Spagnols: Ellen Johnson
SVP Operations: Martin van der Merwe
Square Footage: 60655
Type of Packaging: Consumer, Food Service
Other Locations:
   Vincor Quebec
   Rougemont, QCVincor Quebec
Regions Exported to: Worldwide

49819 Vineco International Products
27 Scott Street W
St Catharines, ON L2R 1E1
Canada   905-685-9342
    Fax: 905-685-9551
Manufacturer and wholesaler/distributor of wine and beer making kits
President: Rob Van Wely
CFO: Jason Hough
R&D: Sandra Sartor
Quality Control: Sandra Sartor
Marketing: Michael Hind
Estimated Sales: $ 5 - 10 Million
Number Employees: 45
Parent Co: Andres Wines
Type of Packaging: Consumer
Regions Exported to: Middle East, Iceland, Australia
Regions Imported from: Asia, Middle East, USA
Percentage of Business in Importing: 1

49820 Vingcard/Elsafe
931 Wekiva Springs Road
Longwood, FL 32779-2501   407-389-3400
    Fax: 407-423-8820
Importer and exporter of electronic safes
Sales Director: John Foley
Number Employees: 20-49
Parent Co: Vingcard
Type of Packaging: Food Service
Regions Exported to: Worldwide
Brands Imported: Elsafe
Regions Imported from: Norway

49821 Vinh Hoan USA, Inc.
2522 Chambers Rd
Suitr 200
Tustin, CA 92780   714-573-3458
    info@vinhhoan.com
    www.vinhhoan.com
Importer of Vietnam-based Pangasius/basa fish and other basa fish value added products.
President: Sang Phan
Chief Executive Officer: Vi Tam
Estimated Sales: $148.4 Million
Number Employees: 3000
Regions Imported from: Asia

49822 Vinos USA
44 Church Street
Waynesville, NC 28786-5709   828-452-3060
    Fax: 828-456-4352
Importer of Argentinian wines including Cabernet Sauvignon, Pinot Noir, aperitif, Chardonnay and Merlot
President: Suzanne Fernandez
VP/Marketing Director/Buyer: Ricardo Fernandez
Estimated Sales: $1-2.5 Million
Number Employees: 1-4
Regions Imported from: South America

49823 Vintage Food Corp
849 Newark Tpke
Kearny, NJ 07032-4308   201-955-1505
    Fax: 201-955-2906 info@vintagefood.com
    www.vintagefood.com
Confectionary, cookies, coffe, tea, edible oil, dairy products, dried fruits, nuts, olives, beverages, pasta, pickles, preserves, sweets, Turkish delights, bakery, pastry, as well as organic and dietary goods.
Contact: Ebru Arslan
ebru@vintagefood.com

49824 Viobin USA
226 W Livingston St
Monticello, IL 61856-1673   217-762-2561
    Fax: 217-762-2489 888-473-9645
    info@viobinusa.com www.viobinusa.com
Manufacturer of nutritional extract, defatted wheatgerm, and wheat germ oil.
CEO: Monte White
Marketing/Sales: Geni Heider
Manager: Bart Allen
sales@viobinusa.com
General Manager: Roger Mohr
Production: Kevin Stevens
Estimated Sales: $10-20 Million
Number Employees: 20-49
Number of Brands: 1
Parent Co: McShares, Inc.
Type of Packaging: Consumer, Bulk

49825 Violife
Thessaloniki,
Greece
    info@violifefoods.com
    www.violifefoods.com
Vegan, lactose-free, non-GMO, gluten-free dairy and meat alternatives in various flavors
Number of Brands: 1
Number of Products: 43
Type of Packaging: Consumer, Private Label
Brands Exported: Violife
Regions Exported to: Europe, USA

49826 Virgin Raw Foods LLC
11645 Wilshire Blvd.
Los Angeles, CA 90025   424-322-0535
    800-830-7047
cs@virginrawfoods.com www.virginrawfoods.com
Royal honey infused with herbs and superfoods
Founder/Owner: Monika Kozdrowiecka
Number of Brands: 1
Number of Products: 1
Type of Packaging: Consumer, Private Label
Brands Exported: Bee Panacea
Regions Exported to: USA

49827 Virginia Dare Extract Co
882 3rd Ave # 2
Brooklyn, NY 11232-1902   718-788-1776
    Fax: 718-768-3978 flavorinfo@virginiadare.com
    www.virginiadare.com
Flavor and extract company founded in 1835.
President: Howard Smith
hsmith@virginiadare.com
Number Employees: 100-249
Type of Packaging: Bulk
Regions Exported to: Central America, South America, Europe, Asia, Middle East

49828 Virginia Industrial Services
P.O.Box 532
Waynesboro, VA 22980-391
    Fax: 540-943-7192 800-825-3050
Manufacturer and exporter of food processing equipment; also, repair and modification available
President: William Merrill
Estimated Sales: Below $ 5,000,000
Number Employees: 10-19
Square Footage: 20000
Regions Exported to: Europe
Percentage of Business in Exporting: 5

49829 Virginia Plastics Co
3453 Aerial Way Dr SW
Roanoke, VA 24018-1503   540-981-9700
    Fax: 540-375-0135 800-777-8541
    sales@vaplastics.com www.vaplastics.com
Manufacturer and exporter of packaging materials including polyethylene film and tubing
President: Mike Callister
Estimated Sales: $5-10 Million
Number Employees: 20-49

49830 Visalia Fruit Exchange
500 N Santa Fe St
Visalia, CA 93292-5065   559-635-3000
    Fax: 559-734-0947 800-366-8238
    vcpg@vcpg.com
A packer of citrus fruits including oranges, grapefruits and limes, Visalia Citrus Packing Group (VCPG) is a licensed commercial shipper of Sunkist Growers, Inc.
President: Randy Veeh
randy@vcpg.com
Sales Representative: Greg Romanazzi
Sales Representative: Kathy Dodge
Number Employees: 5-9
Type of Packaging: Consumer
Regions Exported to: Worldwide

49831 Visiplex
100 N Fairway Dr # 120
Vernon Hills, IL 60061-1859   847-918-0250
    Fax: 847-918-0259 www.visiplex.com
Manager: Ben Agam
Contact: Sam Agam
s.agam@visiplex.com
Estimated Sales: $ 10 - 20 Million
Number Employees: 10-19

49832 Viskase Co Inc
8205 Cass Ave # 115
Darien, IL 60561-5319   630-874-0700
    Fax: 630-874-0178 800-323-8562
    www.viskase.com
Manufacturer and exporter of nonedible, fibrous and cellulosic food casings and film including barrier, polypropylene and cook-in
President/CEO: Robert Weisman
VP/COO: Henry Palacci
VP/CFO/Secretary/Treasurer: Charles Pullin
VP Sales, North America: Maurice Ryan
Contact: Eric Wynveen
eric.wynveen@viskase.com
VP Worldwide Operations: Bernard Lemoine
Estimated Sales: $20 Million
Number Employees: 1,000-4,999
Other Locations:
   Viskase Manufacturing Plant
   Kentland, IN
   Viskase Manufacturing Plant
   Loudon, TN
   Viskase Manufacturing Plant
   Osceola, ARViskase Manufacturing PlantLoudon

49833 Vista Food Exchange
1700 W. 40 Hwy
Suite 206
Blue Springs, MO 64015   816-228-7090
    Fax: 816-228-9214 vistafood.com
Wholesaler/distributor and exporter of meat, meat products, seafood, poultry, frozen foods and dairy/deli items; importer of lamb, mutton and beef; serving the food service and retail markets
Office Manager: D Martin
Executive Vice President: Phil Stephens
Sales/Transportation: J Dickey
Estimated Sales: $2.5-5 Million
Number Employees: 1-4
Parent Co: Vista Food Exchange
Type of Packaging: Consumer, Food Service, Bulk
Regions Exported to: Worldwide
Percentage of Business in Exporting: 15
Regions Imported from: Central America, South America, New Zealand, Australia
Percentage of Business in Importing: 5

49834 Vista Food Exchange Inc.
B101 Center Arcade
Hunts Point Co-op Market
Bronx, NY 10474   718-542-4401
    Fax: 718-542-0042 vlp27@aol.com
    www.vistafood.com
Exporter and wholesaler/distributor of fresh and frozen poultry, beef, pork and fish products; serving the food service market
President: Vincent Pacifico
Controller: Alan Butterfass
VP: Phil Stephens
Estimated Sales: $ 10 - 20 Million
Number Employees: 10-19
Type of Packaging: Food Service

49835 Visual Graphics Systems
330 Washington Ave
Carlstadt, NJ 07072-2806   201-528-2700
    Fax: 201-528-0890 800-203-0301
    sales@vgs-inc.com www.vgsonline.com
In-store communication systems in the foodservice industry with value engineering practices, multi-site installation capabilities and full service in-house design agency. Products include; menu boards, digital menu boards and digitalsignage, wall & ceiling displays, branding & design, wall murals, eco-friendly signage, freestanding displays, poster holders, diplay fixtures, countertop displays, interior and exterior signage
VP: Patrick Benasillo
Contact: Darsia Abreu
dabreu@vgs-inc.com
Estimated Sales: $25-40 Million
Number Employees: 1-4
Square Footage: 72000

Importers & Exporters / A-Z

49836 Visual Planning Corp
1320 Route 9 #3314
Champlain, NY 12919   518-298-8404
Fax: 518-298-2368   800-361-1192
info@visualplanning.com
www.visualplanning.com
Scheduling boards-magnetic, perforated, T-card, boardmaster, fixed, rotating, planner sheets, PC software & accessories, AV equipment & supplies-easels, pads, lecterns, bulletin boards, conference cabinets, electronic boardsprojectors, screens, markers, Graphic Arts materials-templates, portfolios, filing systems, precision knives; Signs-labels, badges, nameplates, directory boards, magnetic, etc; office supplies.
President: Joseph Josephson
Marketing: Boris Polanski
Plant Manager: Stefan Neciorek
Purchasing Manager: Paul Harrison
Estimated Sales: $ 1 - 3 Million
Number Employees: 20-49
Type of Packaging: Private Label
Regions Exported to: South America, Europe, Asia, Middle East
Percentage of Business in Exporting: 10
Regions Imported from: Europe
Percentage of Business in Importing: 5

49837 Vita Craft Corp
11100 W 58th St
Shawnee, KS 66203-2299   913-631-6265
Fax: 913-631-1143   800-359-3444
info@vitacraft.com
Manufacturer and exporter of stainless steel and multi-ply cooking utensils
President: Gary Martin
garymartin@vitacraft.com
CEO: Mamoru Imura
VP: John Ratigan
Estimated Sales: $10-20 Million
Number Employees: 20-49
Parent Co: Rena-Ware Distributors
Type of Packaging: Consumer, Food Service
Regions Exported to: Asia, Japan

49838 Vita Food Products Inc
2222 W Lake St
Chicago, IL 60612
   800-989-8482
www.vitafoodproducts.com
Pickled herring, lox & nova salmon, cream cheese with salmon, horseradish, cocktail and tarter sauces; gourmet sauces, marinades, salad dressings, dessert toppers, syrups & honey, salsa, drinks.
President & CEO: Clifford Bolen
Chief Financial Officer: R. Anthony Nelson
Vice President: William Zaikos
Production Manager: Henry Williams
Purchasing Manager: Doug Clark
Estimated Sales: $32 Million
Number Employees: 100-249
Square Footage: 82200
Type of Packaging: Consumer, Food Service
Regions Exported to: Worldwide
Percentage of Business in Exporting: 5

49839 Vita-Pakt Citrus Products Co
203 E Badillo St
Covina, CA 91723-2116   626-332-1101
Fax: 626-966-8196   888-684-8272
www.vita-pakt.com
Citrus and kiwi processor.
Chairman & CEO: James Boyles
james.boyle@vita-paktcitrus.com
Number Employees: 50-99
Type of Packaging: Consumer, Food Service, Bulk
Regions Exported to: Central America, Europe, Asia, Australia, Canada, Caribbean
Percentage of Business in Exporting: 65

49840 VitaMinder Company
23 Acorn St
Providence, RI 02903-1066   401-273-0444
Fax: 401-273-0630   800-858-8440
sales@vitaminder.com
www.medportllc.com
Manufacturer and exporter of multi-compartment vitamin containers, portable blenders for powdered drink mixes and food scales; importer of scales, tablet splitters/crushers and blenders
President: Larry Wesson
CFO: Larry Weffon
Quality Control: Vanessa Honwybhan
VP Sales: James Shuster
Sales Manager: Ken Michaels
Number Employees: 10-19
Parent Co: Ocean Group
Regions Exported to: Europe, Canada
Percentage of Business in Exporting: 10
Regions Imported from: Asia
Percentage of Business in Importing: 10

49841 Vital Proteins LLC
545 Busse Rd.
Elk Grove Village, IL 60007   224-544-9110
info@vitalproteins.com
www.vitalproteins.com
Collagen supplements in various flavors
Co-Founder/Chief Executive Officer: Kurt Seidensticker
Number of Brands: 1
Type of Packaging: Consumer, Private Label
Brands Exported: Vital Proteins
Regions Exported to: USA

49842 Vitality Works
8500 Bluewater Rd. NW
Albuquerque, NM 87121   505-268-9950
Fax: 505-268-9952   www.vitalityworks.com
Herbal, vitamin and nutraceutical supplements
Chief Executive Officer: Mitch Coven
Production Manager: Jackie Keepers
Year Founded: 1982
Number of Brands: 1
Type of Packaging: Private Label
Brands Exported: Vitality Works
Regions Exported to: USA

49843 (HQ)Vitaminerals
1815 Flower St
Glendale, CA 91201-2024   818-500-8718
Fax: 818-240-2785   800-432-1856
www.cryogel.tv
Processor and exporter of food supplements and vitamins
Owner: Michael Gorman
jgorman@vitamineralsinc.com
President: John Gorman
jgorman@vitamineralsinc.com
VP: Mike Gorman
National Sales Director: Charles DesVos
Estimated Sales: $ 5 - 10 Million
Number Employees: 20-49
Square Footage: 70000
Regions Exported to: Worldwide

49844 Vitamix
8615 Usher Rd
Olmsted Twp, OH 44138-2199   440-235-4840
Fax: 440-235-3726   800-437-4654
foodservice@vitamix.com   www.vitamix.com
Manufactures highly engineered, high performance commercial food blenders and drink mixers built for outstanding durability and versatility
President: John Barnard
CEO: Jodi Berg
international@vitamix.com
Marketing Director: D Scott Hinckley
Estimated Sales: $ 20 - 50 Million
Number Employees: 250-499
Regions Exported to: Worldwide

49845 Vitarich Ice Cream
572 Highway 1
Fortuna, CA 95540-9711   707-725-6182
Fax: 707-725-6186   info@humboldtcreamery.com
www.humboldtcreamery.com
Ice cream, sherbet, frozen yogurt and ice cream mixes and novelties
President: Rich Ghilarducci
Number Employees: 20-49
Type of Packaging: Consumer, Food Service, Private Label, Bulk
Other Locations:
   Vitarich Ice Cream Co.
   Seattle, WAVitarich Ice Cream Co.
Brands Exported: Vitarich; Welcome; Russian Label
Regions Exported to: Asia, Russia
Percentage of Business in Exporting: 3

49846 (HQ)Vitarich Laboratories
4365 Arnold Ave
Naples, FL 34104   239-430-2266
Fax: 239-430-4930   800-817-9999
Processor, importer and exporter of vitamins, nutraceuticals and food supplements including herbal, whole leaf wheat, barley and algae
President: Kevin Thomas
Marketing: Bill Foley
Sales Director: Frank Guzzo
Contact: Steve Colligan
colligans@vitarichlabs.com
Estimated Sales: $ .5 - 1 million
Number Employees: 5-9
Square Footage: 80000
Type of Packaging: Consumer, Private Label, Bulk
Other Locations:
   Vitarich Laboratories
   Bainbridge, GAVitarich Laboratories

49847 Vitasoy USA
57 Russell Street
Woburn, MA 01801   781-430-8988
Fax: 978-772-6881   800-848-2769
info@vitasoy-usa.com   www.vitasoy-usa.com
Tofu, asian noodles, fresh pasta wraps, vegan sandwich spreads, soymilks, juices and teas
President/Chief Executive Officer: Walter Riglian
Contact: Terry Arkinstall
terry.arkinstall@vitasoy-usa.com
Chief Executive Officer: Tom Perry
Research & Development: Fred Jewett
Quality Assurance Manager: Rick Baum
Vice President, Marketing: Tim Kenny
Sales Executive: Eugene Lye
Public Relations: Stella Lung
Vice President, Operations: John Wareham
Production Supervisor: Edgar Bonilla
Facility Manager: Peter Breed
Purchasing Manager: Heidi Bonasoro
Estimated Sales: $20 Million
Number Employees: 160
Number of Brands: 4
Square Footage: 21227
Type of Packaging: Consumer, Food Service, Private Label
Brands Imported: Vitasoy
Regions Imported from: Asia

49848 Viterra, Inc
2625 Victoria Ave.
Regina, SK S4T 7T9
Canada   306-569-4411
Fax: 306-569-4708   866-647-4090
www.viterra.com
Grain and oilseeds.
President/CEO: Kyle Jeworski
Estimated Sales: $2.4 Billion
Number Employees: 190,000
Parent Co: Glencore plc
Type of Packaging: Consumer, Food Service, Private Label, Bulk

49849 Vitro Seating Products
201 Madison St
St Louis, MO 63102-1329   314-241-2265
Fax: 314-241-8723   800-325-7093
mail@vitroseating.com   www.vitroseating.com
Manufacturer and exporter of hotel, restaurant and bar furniture including fountain and bar stools, booths, chairs and tables
CEO: Rose Crofford
rcrofford@ccstl.org
CEO: Stephen Scott
VP of Administration: Mike Scott
Senior Designer: Kim Luce
National Sales Manager: Matt Schliecher
Accounts Receivable Manager: Lauren Rush
VP of Manufacturing: Steve Scott Jr.
Purchasing Mngr./CSR: Matt Schleicher
Estimated Sales: $5-10 Million
Number Employees: 50-99
Square Footage: 450000
Type of Packaging: Food Service
Regions Exported to: Europe

49850 Vivolac Cultures Corporation
3862 E Washington St
Indianapolis, IN 46201   317-356-8460
Fax: 317-356-8450   sales@vivolac.com
www.vivolac.com
Manufacturer and exporter of dairy, meat and bread starter cultures in pelletized, frozen and freeze-dried form
President: Wesley Sing
Technical Sales Manager: Rossana Reyle
Chief Marketing Officer: Philip Reinhardt
Technical Sales: David Winters
Estimated Sales: $1.4 Million
Number Employees: 20-49
Type of Packaging: Private Label, Bulk

Importers & Exporters / A-Z

49851 Vivoo
Via del Commercio 16
Verona, 37066
Italy
info@vivoo.it
www.vivoo-re-evolution.com
Organic raw chocolate bars, energy bites, energy bars; raw cacao powder, cacao butter and cacao beans
Founder: Giorgio Sergio
Number of Brands: 1
Type of Packaging: Consumer, Private Label
Brands Exported: Vivoo
Regions Exported to: Europe, USA

49852 Vogel
Stamford Industrial Park
Stamford, CT 06902   203-973-0740
Fax: 203-973-0068
Wholesaler/distributor and exporter of advertising specialties; hot stamping services available
Owner/President: Peter Blais
Number Employees: 5-9
Square Footage: 4800
Regions Exported to: Worldwide
Percentage of Business in Exporting: 15

49853 Vogt Tube Ice
1000 W Ormsby Ave # 19
Louisville, KY 40210-1549   502-635-3000
Fax: 502-634-0479   800-853-8648
info@vogtice.com   www.vogtice.com
Manufacturer and exporter ice machines including cubers and crushers
Chairman/ Managing Member: J.T. Sims
President: Tobi Ferguson
CEO: Mark Barter
VP, Business Development & Engineering: Charles Holwerk
Manager of Quality & Manufacturing: Vince Stewart
Commercial Marketing Manager: Tim Burke
International Sales Manager: Ivan Villalba
Estimated Sales: $ 5 - 10 Million
Number Employees: 50-99
Type of Packaging: Food Service
Regions Exported to: Worldwide
Percentage of Business in Exporting: 40

49854 Vogt Tube Ice
1000 W Ormsby Ave # 19
Louisville, KY 40210-1549   502-635-3000
Fax: 502-634-0479   info@vogtice.com
www.vogtice.com
CEO: Paul Saville
psaville@vogtice.com
CEO: Mark Barter
Estimated Sales: $ 1 - 3 Million
Number Employees: 50-99

49855 Volckening Inc
6700 3rd Ave
Brooklyn, NY 11220-5296   718-836-4000
Fax: 718-748-2811   800-221-0276
info@volckening.com   www.volckening.com
Manufacturer and exporter of replacement parts for beverage filling machinery; also, industrial brushes
Chairman: William Schneider
wschneider@volckeninginc.com
CEO: F Schneider
Estimated Sales: $ 10-20 Million
Number Employees: 20-49
Square Footage: 50000
Regions Exported to: Central America, South America
Percentage of Business in Exporting: 30

49856 (HQ)Volk Corp
23936 Industrial Park Dr
Farmington Hills, MI 48335-2861   248-477-6700
Fax: 248-478-6884   800-521-6799
sales@volkcorp.com   www.volkcorp.com
Manufacturer and exporter of signs, rubber stamps, markers, name badges, envelopes, tapes, tape dispensers, advertising novelties, printing dies, zinc plates, steel stamps, ink cartridges, etc
President: Bill Woolfall
billw@volkcorp.com
Marketing Director: Todd Cruthfield
Sales Director: Ron Harper
Plant Manager: Donald Schultz
Purchasing Manager: Scott Szumanski
Estimated Sales: $5-10 Million
Number Employees: 50-99
Other Locations:
 Volk Corp.
 Grand Rapids, MI Volk Corp.
Regions Exported to: Central America, Europe, Middle East
Percentage of Business in Exporting: 2

49857 Volk Packaging Corp
11 Morin St
Biddeford, ME 04005   207-282-6151
Fax: 207-283-1165   vpc@volkboxes.com
www.volkboxes.com
Manufacturer and exporter of packaging and containerizing supplies including corrugated, fiber and wooden boxes, cartons and containers.
President/Owner: Derek Volk
Chief Executive Officer: Douglas Volk
Chief Financial Officer: Douglas Hellsfrom
Production Manager: Richard Wills
Purchasing Manager: Glorijane Winslow
Estimated Sales: $25-35 Million
Number Employees: 85
Square Footage: 140000

49858 Vollrath Co LLC
1236 N 18th St
Sheboygan, WI 53081-3201   920-457-4851
800-624-2051
vollrathcompany.com
Frozen treat equipment, contract manufacturing, industrial washers and electronic cleaning equipment, and wholesale/retail consumer cookware and bakeware.
President & CEO: Paul Bartlet
pbartlet@vollrathco.com
VP, Human Resources: Jeff Madson
Marketing & Communications Director: Cathy Fitzgerald
SVP, Operations: Dennis Heaney
Year Founded: 1874
Estimated Sales: $100-500 Million
Number Employees: 1000-4999
Type of Packaging: Food Service
Regions Exported to: Central America, South America, Europe, Asia, Worldwide
Percentage of Business in Exporting: 12
Regions Imported from: Asia
Percentage of Business in Importing: 18

49859 Volta Belting Technology, Inc.
11 Chapin Road
Pine Brook, NJ 07058   973-276-7905
Fax: 973-276-7908   sales@voltabelting.com
www.voltabelting.com
Food conveyor belts, power transmission & timing belts and belt welding tools.
Contact: Denise Buongiorno
denise@voltabelting.com
Regions Exported to: Central America, North America

49860 Voorhees Rubber Mfg Co
6846 Basket Switch Rd
Newark, MD 21841-2214   410-632-1582
Fax: 410-632-1522   info@voorheesrubber.com
www.voorheesrubber.com
Manufacturer, exporter and wholesaler/distributor of rubber candy molds
President: Richard Jackson
info@voorheesrubber.com
Vice President: Teresa Jackson
Estimated Sales: Below $ 5 Million
Number Employees: 5-9
Brands Exported: Vorhees
Regions Exported to: Canada
Percentage of Business in Exporting: 10

49861 Vorti-Siv
36165 Salem GangaRoad
PO Box 720
Salem, OH 44460-0720   330-332-4958
Fax: 330-332-1543   800-227-7487
info@vorti-siv.com   www.vorti-siv.com
Manufacturer and exporter of gyrating sieves and tanks; self-cleaning filters
President: Barbara Maroscher
CFO: Barb Groppe
VP: Vic Maroscher
Sales: Dennis Ulrich
Plant Manager: Kevin Penner
Estimated Sales: $ 3 - 5,000,000
Number Employees: 10-19
Square Footage: 35000
Parent Co: MM Industries
Brands Exported: Vorti-Siv
Regions Exported to: Central America, South America, Europe, Asia, Middle East
Percentage of Business in Exporting: 10
Brands Imported: Airpel
Regions Imported from: Europe
Percentage of Business in Importing: 5

49862 Vortron Smokehouse/Ovens
120 South Main Street
Iron Ridge, WI 53035   608-362-0862
Fax: 608-362-9012   800-874-1949
sales@vortronsmokehouses.com
www.vortronsmokehouses.com
Manufacturer and exporter of food processing machinery, ovens, smokehouses, drying rooms and smoke generators
VP: Dan Mertes
Plant Manager: Dan Mertes
Estimated Sales: $2.5-5 Million
Number Employees: 10-19
Parent Co: Apache Stainless Equipment
Other Locations:
 Vortron Smokehouse/Ovens
 Beaver Dam, WI Vortron Smokehouse/Ovens
Brands Exported: Vortron
Regions Exported to: Central America, South America, Canada
Percentage of Business in Exporting: 25

49863 Voyageur Trading Division
PO Box 428
Bemidji, MN 56619-0428   763-595-0051
Fax: 763-595-0078
Wholesaler/distributor and exporter of bulk and packaged wild rice
General Manager: Dwight Erickson
Estimated Sales: $10-20 Million
Number Employees: 10-19
Square Footage: 40000
Parent Co: Indian Harvest Specialty Foods
Type of Packaging: Bulk
Brands Exported: Voyageur
Regions Exported to: Asia
Percentage of Business in Exporting: 3

49864 Vresso International Corporation
14 Ward Street
Hackensack, NJ 07601-4410   201-342-9747
Fax: 201-342-9747   vressony@cs.com
Exporter of food equipment and machinery
President: Vrej Sabounjian
Manager: Daisy Nunez
VP: Maureen Parisi
Number Employees: 5-9
Square Footage: 14400
Type of Packaging: Food Service
Brands Exported: Alto-Shaam; Taylor; Blodgett; Henny Penny; Nieco

49865 Vulcan Electric Co
28 Endfield St
Porter, ME 04068-3502   207-625-3231
Fax: 207-625-8938   800-922-3027
sales@vulcanelectric.com
www.vulcanelectric.com
Manufacturer and exporter of heaters including immersion, strip and fin strip, radiant cartridge, band and flexible; also, tubular elements, thermocouples, programmable/mechanical temperature controls and sensors
President: Michael Quick
General Manager: Stan Haupt
CFO: Jenet Floyd
Quality Control: Bob Doglus
Estimated Sales: $ 20 - 30 Million
Number Employees: 50-99
Square Footage: 50000
Brands Exported: Cal-Stats
Regions Exported to: Worldwide
Percentage of Business in Exporting: 5

49866 Vulcan Food Equipment Group
3600 North Point Blvd
Baltimore, MD 21222-2726   410-284-0662
Fax: 410-288-3662   800-814-2028
www.vulcanequipment.com
Manufacturer and exporter of broilers, steam cookers, ranges, fryers and warmers; also, bakery, food processing, hotel, restaurant and pizza ovens

Vice President: Wally Beal
beal@vulcanequipment.com
VP Sales National Accounts: Tom Cassin
VP: Jim Cullinane
Director Sales: Dennis Ball
National Accounts Manager: Jim Thompson
Estimated Sales: $ 10 - 20 Million
Number Employees: 250-499
Parent Co: ITW Food Equipment Group LLC
Type of Packaging: Food Service
Regions Exported to: Worldwide
Percentage of Business in Exporting: 10

49867 Vulcan Industries
300 Display Dr
Moody, AL 35004-2100   205-640-2400
       Fax: 205-640-2412   888-444-4417
       hello@vulcanind.com www.vulcanind.com
Manufacturer and exporter of point of purchase display fixtures and products including tubular, sheet metal, hard board, plastic and wire
VP: J Whitley
Quality Control: Steve Brugge
Manager Sales/Marketing: Douglas Stockham
Accountant: Virgil Wells
Plant Manager: James Raynor
Number Employees: 10-19
Square Footage: 330000
Parent Co: Ebsco Industries
Regions Exported to: Central America, South America, Canada, Mexico, Caribbean
Percentage of Business in Exporting: 5

49868 Vyse Gelatin Co
5010 Rose St
Schiller Park, IL 60176-1023   847-678-4780
       Fax: 847-678-0329   800-533-2152
              sales@vyse.com www.vyse.com
Manufacturer, exporter and importer of food grade gelatins.
President: Gary Brunet
gbrunet@vyse.com
Estimated Sales: $2.5-5 Million
Number Employees: 10-19
Type of Packaging: Food Service, Private Label, Bulk
Regions Exported to: Central America, South America, Europe, Asia
Percentage of Business in Exporting: 5
Regions Imported from: South America, Europe, Asia
Percentage of Business in Importing: 25

49869 W & G Marketing Company
413 Kellogg Avenue
PO Box 1742
Ames, IA 50010   515-233-4774
       Fax: 515-233-4773 www.wgmarketing.com
Processor and exporter of roasting pigs including whole and frozen; also, meat and poultry by-products and fully cooked barbecue turkey, beef and pork
President/Sales and Marketing: Darren Dies
ddies@wgmarketing.com
VP Operations: Robert Olinger
Estimated Sales: $ 5 - 10 Million
Number Employees: 5
Square Footage: 21928
Type of Packaging: Consumer, Food Service, Private Label
Brands Exported: W&G's
Regions Exported to: Central America, Europe, Asia, Mexico, Canada
Percentage of Business in Exporting: 15

49870 W H Laboratories
8450 Rayson Rd
Houston, TX 77080-3623   713-895-7504
       Fax: 713-895-8906 info@whlabs.com
                  www.whlabs.com
Importer of German beer
President & CEO: Howard E. Heinsohn
hheinsohn@whlabs.com
Chem Lab Manager: Hassan Kabirzadeh
Quality Assurance Manager: Marilyn Duty
Estimated Sales: $ 5 - 10 Million
Number Employees: 20-49
Brands Imported: Bitburger Pils; Pils; Maisel's Weisse
Regions Imported from: Europe

49871 W J Egli & Co
205 E Columbia St
Alliance, OH 44601-2563   330-823-3666
       Fax: 330-823-0011 info@wjegli.com
Manufacturer and exporter of wire, wood and tube display racks
President: Jeff Egli
VP: Mike Egli
Marketing Director: Jeff Egli
Estimated Sales: $ 2.5 - 5 Million
Number Employees: 20-49
Square Footage: 200000

49872 W L Jenkins Co
1445 Whipple Ave SW
Canton, OH 44710-1321   330-477-3407
       Fax: 330-477-8404 info@wljenkinsco.com
                  www.wljenkinsco.com
Manufacturer and exporter of mechanically operated fire alarm systems; also, bells and gongs
Owner: Susan Jenkins
info@wljenkinsco.com
Estimated Sales: $2.5-5 Million
Number Employees: 5-9
Parent Co: W.L. Jenkins Company

49873 W R Grace & Co
7500 Grace Dr
Columbia, MD 21044   410-531-4000
       Fax: 410-531-4367 www.grace.com
Processor and exporter of silica gel absorbents; also, clarifying and anticaking agents.
President & Chief Executive Officer: Hudson La Force
Senior VP & Chief Financial Officer: William Dockman
Senior VP, Human Resources: Elizabeth Brown
Year Founded: 1832
Estimated Sales: $1.72 Billion
Number Employees: 3,900

49874 W.A. Schmidt Company
99 Brower Ave
Oaks, PA 19456   215-721-8300
       Fax: 215-721-5890 800-523-6719
                  www.pencoproducts.com
Manufacturer and exporter of storage systems and racks
President: Greg Grogan
Estimated Sales: $ 20-50 Million
Number Employees: 100-249
Square Footage: 246000
Brands Exported: H.F. Cradle System
Regions Exported to: Worldwide

49875 W.G. Durant Corporation
9825 Painter Ave # A-E
Whittier, CA 90605-2700   562-946-5555
       Fax: 562-946-5577
Manufacturer and exporter of palletizers, bag packers, conveyors and system electrical controls
Owner: Zara Badalian
Sales Manager: Jack Schreyer
Estimated Sales: $ 3 - 5 Million
Number Employees: 5-9
Square Footage: 600000
Parent Co: Westmont Industries
Brands Exported: HY-AC IV
Regions Exported to: Central America, South America, Europe, Asia, Middle East
Percentage of Business in Exporting: 15

49876 W.H. Moseley Co.
4090 W State St
Suite 1
Boise, ID 83703   208-342-2621
       Fax: 208-336-1611 www.whmoseley.com
Importer and exporter of frozen, dehydrated and fresh potatoes. Broker of frozen foods
President: Bill Moseley
VP/Sales: Tom Reeb
Estimated Sales: $5-10 Million
Number Employees: 1-4

49877 W.Y. International
2000 S. Garfield Ave.
Los Angeles, CA 90040   323-726-8733
       Fax: 323-726-9409 info@wyintl.com
                  www.wyintl.com
Asian sauces, canned goods, grains, and snacks; European and Californian wine and oils; machinery & tools.
President: David N. Wong
Vice President: Henry P. Wong
Year Founded: 1982
Estimated Sales: $2-5 Million
Number Employees: 2-10
Brands Exported: Pearl River Bridge, Grand Harvest, Huy Fong Foods Inc., Gold Plum, Yuet Heung Yuen, MaLing, and more.
Regions Exported to: China, Mexico, Spain, Italy, Malaysia and Thailand
Brands Imported: Pearl River Bridge, Grand Harvest, Huy Fong Foods Inc., Gold Plum, Yuet Heung Yuen, MaLing and more.
Regions Imported from: China, Mexico, Spain, Italy, Malaysia and Thailand

49878 WA Brown & Son
209 Long Meadow Dr
Salisbury, NC 28147   704-636-5131
       Fax: 704-637-0919
Manufacturer, importer and exporter of walk-in coolers, freezers, and structural insulated panels
President: Ed Brown
Vice President: Paul Brown
Sales Director: Dave Morris
Contact: Frank Preolette
kellerrd@appstate.edu
Operations Manager: Deric Skeen
Estimated Sales: $25-50 Million
Number Employees: 100-249
Square Footage: 250000
Type of Packaging: Food Service, Private Label
Regions Exported to: Caribbean
Regions Imported from: Europe, Canada

49879 WA Imports
8121 Ogden Ave
Lyons, IL 60534   708-443-5100
       Fax: 708-447-0530 888-204-4044
                  info@waimports.com www.waimports.com
Juices and marmalades
President: David Vohaska
Contact: Casey Felling
casey@waimports.com

49880 WACO Beef & Pork Processors
523 Precision Dr
Waco, TX 76710-6972   254-772-4669
       Fax: 254-772-4579 www.holysmokedsausage.com
Fresh portion controlled beef, chicken and pork including sausage, chorizo and bratwurst; importer of beef skirts; wholesaler/distributor of meat and general merchandise; serving the food service market
Manager: Sara Jones
Estimated Sales: $2.2 Million
Number Employees: 5-9
Square Footage: 28000
Type of Packaging: Food Service
Regions Imported from: Australia
Percentage of Business in Importing: 10

49881 WCB Ice Cream
1108 Frankford Ave
Philadelphia, PA 19125-4118   215-425-4320
       Fax: 215-426-2034 www.gram-equipment.com
Manufacturer and exporter of fillers, sealers, fittings, freezers, homogenizers, pumps, tanks and frozen novelty equipment
Manager: John Dorety
jdorety@wcbicecream.com
Office Manager: Susie Margolis
Plant Manager: Vince Somers
Estimated Sales: $2.5-5 Million
Number Employees: 10-19
Regions Exported to: Worldwide

49882 (HQ)WCC Honey Marketing
636 Turnbull Canyon Rd # A
City Of Industry, CA 91745-1107   626-855-3086
       Fax: 626-855-3087
Processor and exporter of natural sweeteners, syrups and nutritional supplements including honey, comb honey, molasses, blackstrap molasses, corn syrup, agave nectar and royal jelly; importer of honey, barley malt sweetener, rice syrup and juice concentrate
Owner: Anthony Li
info@wcchoney.com
General Manager: Chuck Burkholder
National Sales Manager: Norma Robinson
info@wcchoney.com
Purchasing Manager: James Littlejohn
Estimated Sales: $ 5 - 10 Million
Number Employees: 5-9
Square Footage: 118800
Type of Packaging: Consumer, Food Service, Private Label, Bulk
Other Locations:
   Western Commerce Corp.
   Kansas City, MO Western Commerce Corp.

Importers & Exporters / A-Z

Brands Exported: Cucamonga; Pot O'Gold
Regions Exported to: Europe, Asia, Middle East, Worldwide
Percentage of Business in Exporting: 5
Regions Imported from: Central America, South America, Asia, Canada, Mexico, Latin America

49883 WE Killam Enterprises
PO Box 741
Waterford, ON N0E 1Y0
Canada   519-443-7421
          Fax: 519-443-6922
Manufacturer, importer and exporter of packaging equipment including inkjet printers, case coding, full wrap and spot labelers, case and tray packing and sealing machinery and can ejectors, standard knapp, burt, fmc, ace/kore, ualcosystems.
President: Roger Elliott
Number Employees: 1-4
Square Footage: 5000
Brands Exported: Sauven; Standard Knapp; Mateer-Burt; F.M.C - Ace/Icore; UALCO Systems; FMC PTS, Sales & Service
Regions Exported to: Caribbean
Percentage of Business in Exporting: 2
Brands Imported: Sauven; Standard Knapp; Mateer-Burt
Regions Imported from: USA
Percentage of Business in Importing: 25

49884 (HQ)WEBB-Stiles Co
675 Liverpool Dr
PO Box 464
Valley City, OH 44280-9717   330-273-9222
    Fax: 330-225-5532 webb-stiles@webb-stiles.com
www.webb-stiles.com
Manufacturer and exporter of custom designed conveyor systems for custom package and pallet handling
CEO: Donald Stiles Jr
Vice President: Larry Birchler
Sales Director: Matthew Weisman
Estimated Sales: $10-20 Million
Number Employees: 100-249
Square Footage: 600000
Other Locations:
  Webb-Stiles Co.
  Gadsden, ALWebb-Stiles Co.
Regions Exported to: Central America, South America, Asia, Middle East
Percentage of Business in Exporting: 5

49885 WG Thompson & Sons
2 Hyland Dr.
Blenheim, ON N0P 1A0
Canada   519-676-5411
          Fax: 519-676-3185 800-265-5225
Agricultural products including soybeans, edible beans, and commercial grains to domestic and export markets.
President: Wes Thompson
Estimated Sales: $100 Million
Number Employees: 350
Type of Packaging: Consumer, Food Service, Private Label, Bulk
Brands Exported: C&G; Hyland
Regions Exported to: Central America, Europe, Asia, Middle East
Percentage of Business in Exporting: 30

49886 WILD Flavors (Canada)
7315 Pacific Circle
Mississauga, ON L5T 1V1
Canada   905-670-1108
          Fax: 905-670-0076 800-263-5286
www.wildflavors.com
Flavors, colors, seasonings, spray-dried ingredients, sauces, batters, coatings, marinades; also, custom blending; exporter of cheese powders
Acting Director: Tim Husted
Director Finance: Tamara Robichaud
R & D: Allison Berridge
Chief Operating Officer: Erik Donhowe
Plant Manager: Dave Oldroyd
Purchasing Manager: Leigh Bailey
Number Employees: 30-50
Number of Products: 200
Square Footage: 240000
Parent Co: WILD Flavors
Type of Packaging: Food Service, Bulk
Regions Exported to: Asia, Australia
Percentage of Business in Exporting: 35

49887 WITT Industries Inc
4600 N Mason Montgomery Rd
Mason, OH 45040-9176   513-923-5821
    Fax: 877-891-8200 800-543-7417
sales@witt.com www.witt.com
Manufacturer and exporter of wastebaskets and firesafe steel, outside, torpedo and fiberglass waste receptacles; importer of structural foam lockers
President: Tim Harris
Chairman: Marcy Wydman
Director Sales/Marketing: Chris Adams
Purchasing Manager: Rick Royce
Estimated Sales: $10-20 Million
Number Employees: 20-49
Square Footage: 150000
Type of Packaging: Food Service
Regions Exported to: Europe, Middle East
Percentage of Business in Exporting: 5
Regions Imported from: Europe
Percentage of Business in Importing: 4

49888 WNA
2155 W Longhorn Dr
Lancaster, TX 75134-2916
          Fax: 972-224-3067 800-334-2877
www.wna.biz
Manufacturer and importer of plastic fabrications, containers and cups.
Number Employees: 100-249
Regions Imported from: Canada

49889 WNA
5930 Quintus Loop
Chattanooga, TN 37421-2216
          Fax: 800-762-4753 800-404-9318
www.wna.biz
Manufacturer and exporter of injection molded plastic disposables including platters, bowls, utensils and specialty items.
Number Employees: 100-249
Regions Exported to: Worldwide

49890 WORC Slitting & Mfg Co
50 Suffolk St # 1
Worcester, MA 01604-3792   508-754-9112
    Fax: 508-754-9117 800-356-2961
info@coverallcovers.com
Duty vinyl Rack Covers, Velcro Strip Doors, PVC Display Rack, Quality Controlled Anti-Bacterial Covers for Health Care Industry, Carts, Transport Bins, Racks & Equipment, Food Service Equipment, Covers for Slicers, Utility Carts, DishDollies, Mixers
CEO: George Najemy
najemy@aol.com
Estimated Sales: $1 Million
Number Employees: 10-19
Square Footage: 60000
Type of Packaging: Bulk
Regions Exported to: Central America, Australia

49891 WOW! Nutrition
120 N Central Ave
Suite 2S
Ramsey, NJ 07446-1442   201-962-9241
Iced tea
Managing Partner: Bill Sipper
Brands Imported: Feel Good
Regions Imported from: Brazil

49892 WR Key
4770 Sheppard Avenue E
Scarborough, ON M1S 3V6
Canada   416-291-6246
          Fax: 416-291-4882 www.wrkey.com
Manufacturer and exporter of stainless steel serving carts, cash boxes, desk trays and card cabinets
President and CEO: Gw Key
R&D and QC: Lisa Key
Sales Manager: Lisa Key
Estimated Sales: $ 5 - 10 Million
Number Employees: 40
Type of Packaging: Consumer, Food Service, Private Label
Regions Exported to: USA
Percentage of Business in Exporting: 2

49893 (HQ)WS Packaging Group Inc
2571 S Hemlock Rd
Green Bay, WI 54229   877-977-5177
info@wspackaging.com
www.wspackaging.com
Manufacturer and exporter of labels, tags, folded cartons, instant redeemable coupons, F.D.A. packaging and tape; also, offset printing available.
President & Chief Financial Officer: Jay Tomcheck
Senior Vice Presient of Sales: Becky Smith
Year Founded: 1966
Estimated Sales: $400 Million
Number Employees: 1000-4999
Square Footage: 110000
Type of Packaging: Private Label
Other Locations:
  WL Group-Wisconsin Label
  Tulsa, OKWL Group-Wisconsin Label
Regions Exported to: Worldwide
Percentage of Business in Exporting: 5

49894 WS Packaging Group Inc
950 Breezewood Ln
Neenah, WI 54956
                     888-532-3334
www.wspackaging.com
Manufacturer and exporter of labels, tags, folded cartons, instant redeemable coupons, F.D.A. packaging and tape; also, offset printing available.

49895 WS Packaging Group Inc
1102 Jefferson St
Algoma, WI 54201
                     800-236-3424
www.wspackaging.com
Manufacturer and exporter of labels, tags, folded cartons, instant redeemable coupons, F.D.A. packaging and tape; also, offset printing available.

49896 WS Packaging Group Inc
3530 Pipestone Rd
Dallas, TX 75212   214-330-7770
www.wspackaging.com
Manufacturer and exporter of labels, tags, folded cartons, instant redeemable coupons, F.D.A. packaging and tape; also, offset printing available.

49897 WS Packaging Group Inc
303 W Marquette Ave
Oak Creek, WI 53154
                     800-837-3838
www.wspackaging.com
Manufacturer and exporter of labels, tags, folded cartons, instant redeemable coupons, F.D.A. packaging and tape; also, offset printing available.
Square Footage: 84000

49898 WS Packaging Group Inc
29 Jet View Dr
Rochester, NY 14624
                     800-836-8186
www.wspackaging.com
Manufacturer and exporter of labels, tags, folded cartons, instant redeemable coupons, F.D.A. packaging and tape; also, offset printing available.
Type of Packaging: Consumer, Food Service, Private Label

49899 WS Packaging Group Inc
1217 Rabas St
Algoma, WI 54201
                     800-323-6026
www.wspackaging.com
Labeling solutions, ranging from prime label and equipment to promotional coupons, screen labels and unsupported film labels for the beverage industry

49900 WS Packaging Group Inc
1642 DeBence Dr
Franklin, PA 16323
                     800-372-1313
www.wspackaging.com
Manufacturer and exporter of labels, tags, folded cartons, instant redeemable coupons, F.D.A. packaging and tape; also, offset printing available.

49901 WS Packaging Group Inc
7400 Industrial Row Dr
Mason, OH 45040-1302
                     800-877-9596
www.wspackaging.com
Manufacturer and exporter of labels, tags, folded cartons, instant redeemable coupons, F.D.A. packaging and tape; also, offset printing available.

Importers & Exporters / A-Z

49902 WS Packaging Group Inc
2222 Beebee St
San Luis Obispo, CA 93401
800-234-3320
www.wspackaging.com
Manufacturer and exporter of labels, tags, folded cartons, instant redeemable coupons, F.D.A. packaging and tape; also, offset printing available.

49903 WS Packaging Group Inc
7500 Industrial Row Dr
Mason, OH 45040-1302
800-877-3795
www.wspackaging.com
Manufacturer and exporter of labels, tags, folded cartons, instant redeemable coupons, F.D.A. packaging and tape; also, offset printing available.

49904 WS Packaging Group Inc
1720 James Pkwy
Heath, OH 43056
740-929-2210
www.wspackaging.com
Manufacturer and exporter of labels, tags, folded cartons, instant redeemable coupons, F.D.A. packaging and tape; also, offset printing available.

49905 WS Packaging Group Inc
202 Galewski Dr
Winona, MN 55987
507-452-2315
www.wspackaging.com
Manufacturer and exporter of labels, tags, folded cartons, instant redeemable coupons, F.D.A. packaging and tape; also, offset printing available.

49906 WS Packaging Group Inc
1 Riverside Way
Wilton, NH 03086
800-258-1050
www.wspackaging.com
Manufacturer and exporter of labels, tags, folded cartons, instant redeemable coupons, F.D.A. packaging and tape; also, offset printing available.

49907 WS Packaging Group Inc
10215 Caneel Dr
Knoxville, TN 37931
865-437-3400
www.wspackaging.com
Manufacturer and exporter of labels, tags, folded cartons, instant redeemable coupons, F.D.A. packaging and tape; also, offset printing available.

49908 WS Packaging Group Inc
531 Airpark Dr
Fullerton, CA 92833
714-992-2574
www.wspackaging.com
Manufacturer and exporter of labels, tags, folded cartons, instant redeemable coupons, F.D.A. packaging and tape; also, offset printing available.

49909 WS Packaging Group Inc
11 Col. La Leona
Garcia, NL
Mexico
www.wspackaging.com
Manufacturer and exporter of labels, tags, folded cartons, instant redeemable coupons, F.D.A. packaging and tape; also, offset printing available.

49910 Wabash Valley Mfg Inc
505 E Main St
Silver Lake, IN 46982-8943
260-352-2102
Fax: 260-352-2160 800-253-8619
wvmsales@wabashvalley.com
www.wabashvalley.com
CFO: Bob Austin
baustin@brownjordan.com
Vice President: Jim Haney
Sales/Marketing: Leslie Blouyette
Estimated Sales: $ 10 - 20 Million
Number Employees: 100-249

49911 Wadden Systems
5674 Sherbrooke Street W
Montreal, QC H4A 1W7
Canada
514-481-1189
Fax: 514-488-2567 800-392-3336
www.wadden.ca
Exporter and wholesaler/distributor of general merchandise including soft serve makers and flavoring systems; serving the food service market
President: Hugh Kane
Number Employees: 20-49
Regions Exported to: Worldwide
Percentage of Business in Exporting: 20

49912 Waddington North America
6 Stuart Rd
Chelmsford, MA 01824-4108
978-256-6553
Fax: 978-256-1614 888-962-2877
Manufacturer and exporter of disposable plastic dinnerware, drinkware, servingware, cutlery, cutlery packets, straws and stirrers
President: Mike Evans
CEO: Dave Gordon
CFO: Steve Morehouse
Quality Control: Tom Whitcumb
Marketing Director: Al Madonna
Contact: Russell Allen
rallen@mswalker.com
Operations Manager: Jim Messeder
Estimated Sales: $25-100 Million
Number Employees: 250-499
Square Footage: 12000
Parent Co: Waddington PLC
Brands Exported: Classicware; Classic Crystal; Designerware; Frost Flex
Regions Exported to: South America, Europe, Middle East, Canada, Latin America
Percentage of Business in Exporting: 1

49913 Wade Manufacturing Company
PO Box 23666
Tigard, OR 97281-3666
503-692-5353
Fax: 503-692-5358 800-222-7246
sales@waderain.com www.waderain.com
Manufacturer and exporter of agricultural irrigation systems including handrove, poweroll and center pivot; also, micro irrigation products and aluminum casters
President: Ed Newbegin
VP: Cliff Warner
Contact: Pierre Lameh
plameh@waderain.com
Estimated Sales: $20-50 Million
Number Employees: 50-99
Parent Co: R.M. Wade & Company
Brands Exported: Wade Rain
Regions Exported to: Central America, South America, Europe, Asia, Middle East
Percentage of Business in Exporting: 33

49914 Wag Industries
4117 Grove Street
Skokie, IL 60076-1713
773-638-7007
Fax: 773-533-6951 800-621-3305
blunt232@aol.com
Manufacturer and exporter of mobile catering truck units including bar and hot dog carts
President: Gail Gilbert
CEO: Doris Gilbert
CFO: George Gilbert
Quality Control: Gavin London
Purchasing Manager: Gavin Lendan
Estimated Sales: $5-10 Million
Number Employees: 10
Regions Exported to: Central America, Europe

49915 Wagner Gourmet Foods
10618 Summit St
Lenexa, KS 66215
913-469-5411
Fax: 913-469-1367
customerservice@wagner-gourmet.com
www.hicks-ashby.com
Spices, preserves, jams, ice cream sauces, seasoned rice and gift pack assortments; importer of tea; wholesaler/distributor of snack foods including cookies
President: James T Baldwin
Estimated Sales: $ 3 - 5 Million
Number Employees: 5-9
Square Footage: 480000
Parent Co: Wagner Gourmet Foods
Type of Packaging: Consumer, Private Label
Regions Imported from: Europe, Asia

49916 Wagner Vineyards
9322 State Route 414
Lodi, NY 14860-9641
607-582-6450
Fax: 607-582-6446 866-924-6378
d.wagner@wagnervineyards.com
www.wagnervineyards.com
Wines and beer; exporter of wines
President: Stanley A Wagner
s.wagner@wagnervineyards.com
Retail Manager: Carol Voorhees
COO: John Wagner
Director of PR & Marketing: Katie Roller
Operations: John Wagner
Estimated Sales: $2,762,368
Number Employees: 50-99
Square Footage: 144000
Type of Packaging: Consumer
Brands Exported: Wagner
Regions Exported to: Europe, Asia, Canada
Percentage of Business in Exporting: 5

49917 Wagshal's Imports
4845 Massachusetts Ave NW
Washington, DC 20016-2065
202-363-5698
Fax: 202-363-0893 feedback@wagshals.com
www.wagshals.com
Beef, seafood, produce, sauces & condiments, dairy, wines, iberico pork
Principal: Aaron Fuchs
Director of Sales: Ann Sayre
Estimated Sales: Under $500,000
Number Employees: 1-4
Brands Imported: Fermin Iberico de Bellota, Can Bech
Regions Imported from: Spain

49918 Wah Yet Group
28301 Industrial Blvd Ste C
Hayward, CA 94545-4429
510-887-3801
Fax: 510-887-3803 800-229-3392
Processor and exporter of diet and ginseng teas; importer of health drinks
President: Ying Lau
Manager: Judy Lau
Estimated Sales: $ 1 - 3 Million
Number Employees: 1 to 4
Square Footage: 4000
Type of Packaging: Consumer
Brands Exported: Dieters' Enjoy; Superb ""D""; Chinese Ginseng; Green Leaf Brand
Regions Exported to: Worldwide
Percentage of Business in Exporting: 40
Brands Imported: Dynamite
Regions Imported from: Asia
Percentage of Business in Importing: 2

49919 Wainani Kai Seafood
2126 Eluwene St
Suite A
Honolulu, HI 96819
808-847-7435
Fax: 808-841-7536 lpang00@yahoo.com
Seafood
President: Lance Pang
lpang00@yahoo.com
Estimated Sales: $ 3 - 5 Million
Number Employees: 5-9

49920 Wakunaga Of America Co LTD
23501 Madero
Mission Viejo, CA 92691-2764
949-855-2776
Fax: 949-458-2764 800-421-2998
info@wakunaga.com www.kyolic.com
Nutritional supplements
President: Kenro Nakamura
CEO: Kazuhiko Nomura
Research & Development Manager: Justin Oshima
Quality Control: Vithia Monica Lee
Manager: Jay Levy
jlevy@wakunaga.com
Estimated Sales: $24 Million
Number Employees: 50-99
Number of Brands: 5
Number of Products: 70
Square Footage: 42000
Parent Co: Wakunaga Pharmaceutical
Brands Exported: Kyolic; Kyodophilus; Kyogreen

49921 Wal-Vac
900 47th St SW # A
Suite A
Wyoming, MI 49509-5142
616-241-6717
Fax: 616-241-1771 info@walvac.com
www.walvac.com
Manufacturer and exporter of built-in central vacuum cleaning systems
President: David Mol
walvac@walvac.com
VP Operations: David Mol
Estimated Sales: Less Than $500,000
Number Employees: 1-4
Square Footage: 19200
Brands Exported: Wal-Vac
Percentage of Business in Exporting: 2

655

Importers & Exporters / A-Z

49922 Walco
820 Noyes St
PO Box 10527
Utica, NY 13502-5053   315-733-4663
              Fax: 315-733-6602 800-879-2526
                    sales@walcostainless.com
                    www.walcostainless.com
Manufacturer, importer and exporter of stainless steel flatware, steak knives, hollow ware, buffetware, and chafers
President: David S Allen
Sales/Marketing: Philip Benbenek
Contact: Phil Bembenek
phil@walcostainless.com
Estimated Sales: $ 10 - 20 Million
Number Employees: 100-249
Square Footage: 225000
Parent Co: Utica Cutlery Company
Type of Packaging: Food Service
Regions Exported to: Central America, South America, Asia, Canada, Caribbean, Latin America, Mexico
Regions Imported from: Asia

49923 Walco-Linck Company
PO Box 5643
Bellingham, WA 98227-5643   845-353-7600
              Fax: 845-353-8056 800-338-2329
Manufacturer and exporter of aerosol insecticides, ant and roach baits and fly paper
President: William Burge
Executive VP: Richard Bozzo
CFO and QC: Richard Bozzo
Estimated Sales: $ 5 - 10 Million
Number Employees: 15

49924 Walden Farms
1209 W Saint Georges Ave
Linden, NJ 07036-6117   908-925-6020
              Fax: 908-925-9537 800-229-1706
              info@waldenfarms.com www.waldenfarms.com
Processor and exporter of salad dressings, dips, bbq sauces, pancake syrups, fruit spread jams and jellies, fruit syrups, ketchup and seafood sauces, bruschetta and chocolate syrup.
President: Mitchell Berko
mitchellburko@waldenfarms.com
Vice President: Paul Berko
Operations: Brian Sherwood
mitchellburko@waldenfarms.com
Number Employees: 50-99
Square Footage: 64000
Type of Packaging: Consumer, Food Service
Regions Exported to: Caribbean
Percentage of Business in Exporting: 1

49925 Walker Bag Mfg Co
11198 Ampere Ct
Louisville, KY 40299-3879   502-266-5696
              Fax: 502-266-9823 800-642-4949
              bagmann@aol.com www.printex-usa.com
Custom designed burlap, canvas, cotton, jute, paper, tote and polypropylene bags; importer of polypropylene bags
CEO: Steve Dutton
steved@printex-usa.com
VP: Steve Dutton
Estimated Sales: $5-10 Million
Number Employees: 20-49

49926 Walker Foods
237 N Mission Rd
Los Angeles, CA 90033-2103   323-268-5191
              Fax: 323-268-7812 800-966-5199
              info@walkerfoods.net www.walkerfoods.net
Producers of hot spicy tomato sauce and other tomato products
President: Robert Walker
Cmo: Fernando Montano
elpatowfi@aol.com
Director, Retail Sales: Andy Zahra
Production Manager: Alfred Heredia
Plant Manager: Fernando Montano
Estimated Sales: $10-20 Million
Number Employees: 50-99
Square Footage: 360000
Type of Packaging: Consumer, Food Service, Private Label, Bulk
Brands Exported: El Pato, Private Label
Regions Exported to: Asia

49927 Walker Magnetics Group Inc
20 Rockdale St
Worcester, MA 01606-1922   508-853-3232
              Fax: 508-852-8649 800-962-4638
                    sales@walkermagnet.com
                    www.walkermagnet.com
Designer and manufacturer of magnetic workholding chucks, lifting, material handling, and separation applications.
Owner: Eric Englested
Plant Manager: Dick Isabell
Estimated Sales: Below $ 5 Million
Number Employees: 100-249
Regions Exported to: Worldwide

49928 Walker Stainless Equipment Co
625 W State St
New Lisbon, WI 53950   608-562-7500
                    www.walkerep.com
Manufacturer and exporter of stainless steel transportation and plant equipment tanks for the dairy industry.
Chief Executive Officer: Richard Giromini
President & Chief Operating Officer: Brent Yeagy
SVP & Chief Financial Officer: Jeffery Taylor
SVP, Human Resources: Bill Pitchford
Year Founded: 1943
Estimated Sales: $250-500 Million
Number Employees: 1000-4999
Square Footage: 200000
Parent Co: Wabash National Corporation
Regions Exported to: Central America, South America, Europe, Canada, Caribbean, Latin America, Mexico
Percentage of Business in Exporting: 10

49929 Walkers Shortbread
170 Commerce Dr
Hauppauge, NY 11788-3944   631-273-0014
              Fax: 631-273-0438 800-521-0141
                    cs@walkersshortbread.com
                    us.walkersshortbread.com
Shortbread and cookies
President: Steve Dawson
CEO: Neil Apple
cs@walkersshortbread.com
CFO: Joseph Gadaleta
Marketing: Lisa Sherman
Estimated Sales: $2800000
Number Employees: 20-49
Parent Co: Walkers Shortbread
Type of Packaging: Consumer, Bulk
Brands Imported: Walkers; Duchy Originals; Kambly
Regions Imported from: Europe
Percentage of Business in Importing: 100

49930 Wallace & Hinz
100 Taylor Way
P.O.Box 708
Blue Lake, CA 95525   707-668-1825
              Fax: 707-826-0224 800-831-8282
                    info@wallaceandhinz.com
                    www.wallaceandhinz.com
Manufacturer and exporter of bars including portable and modular
Owner: Tom Tellez
Sales Manager: Richard Cook
Estimated Sales: $10-20 Million
Number Employees: 20-49
Square Footage: 30000
Regions Exported to: Worldwide
Percentage of Business in Exporting: 27

49931 Wallace Fisheries
PO Box 2046
Gulf Shores, AL 36547-2046   251-986-7211
                       Fax: 251-987-5127
Seafood

49932 Wallace Grain & Pea Company
4932 State Route 27
Pullman, WA 99163   509-878-1561
                       Fax: 509-878-1671
Processor and exporter of chickpeas, barley, lentils and peas
President: Joe Hulett
Assistant Manager: Gary Heaton
Estimated Sales: $500,000-$1 Million
Number Employees: 1-4
Type of Packaging: Consumer, Food Service, Private Label, Bulk
Regions Exported to: Brazil, Germany, Greece, Italy, Spain, Venezuela
Percentage of Business in Exporting: 60

49933 Walle Corp
600 Elmwood Park Blvd
New Orleans, LA 70123-3350   504-734-8000
              Fax: 504-733-2513 800-942-6761
                    www.walle.com
Manufacturer and exporter of labels for cans, bottles, plastics, etc.; also, lithographic and flexographic printing available
Vice President: Allen Dummitt
allen_dummitt@walle.com
Vice Chairman/CEO: Michael Keeney
VP: Colleen Rottmann
Estimated Sales: $20-50 Million
Number Employees: 100-249
Square Footage: 300000
Regions Exported to: Central America, South America, Canada, Caribbean, Latin America, Mexico

49934 Walnut Packaging Inc
450 Smith St
Farmingdale, NY 11735-1105   631-293-3836
              Fax: 631-293-3878 info@wpiplasticbags.com
                    www.wpiplasticbags.com
Manufacturer and exporter of polyethylene bags; also, print designers
Owner: Jose Alvarado
Estimated Sales: $2.5-5 Million
Number Employees: 10-19
Regions Exported to: Puerto Rico

49935 Walong Marketing
6281 Regio Ave.
Buena Park, CA 90620-1040   714-670-8899
              Fax: 714-670-6668 www.asianfoodsonline.com
Asian foods: rice, cereal and grains, baking mixes, soups, vegetables, fruits, snacks, confections, condiments, sauces, drinks, deli, seafood, meats, kitchenware and canned foods.
Merchadiser: Tony Chiu
Chief Operating Officer: Coo Chen
Product Manager: Nancy Hsu
Estimated Sales: $73.2 Million
Number Employees: 130
Other Locations:
   Beuena Park, CA
   Bolingbrook, IL
   Duluth, GA
   Jersey City, NJ
   Stafford, TXBolingbrook
Brands Imported: AGV, Aroy-D, Bai Jia, ChiMei, Chin-Chi, Cici, Cremo, Datu Puti, E-Fa and Eulong.
Regions Imported from: Taiwan, China, Korea, Japan, Thailand, Vietnam, Malaysia

49936 Walsh & Simmons Seating
2511 Iowa Ave
Saint Louis, MO 63104   314-664-1215
              Fax: 314-664-0703 800-727-0364
                    sales@walshsimmons.com
                    www.walshsimmons.com
Manufacturer and exporter of benches, booths, chairs and cushion pads, stools and tables including legs and bases
President: Bill Simmons
Contact: Tony Pezzo
tonyp@walshsimmons.com
Estimated Sales: $ 10 - 20 Million
Number Employees: 100-249
Square Footage: 400000
Type of Packaging. Food Service
Regions Exported to: Canada
Percentage of Business in Exporting: 2

49937 Walsh Tropical Fruit Sales
721 Walsh Ave
Mission, TX 78572-4955   956-585-4887
                       Fax: 956-585-2558
Wholesaler/distributor and importer of mangos, pineapples, seedless limes, coconuts and white onions
Owner: Buddy Walsh
Plant Manager: Noe Elizondo
Estimated Sales: $2.5-5 Million
Number Employees: 100-249

49938 Walter E Jacques & Sons
17 Ewen Road
Hamilton, ON L8S 3C3
Canada
                              905-318-1543
                       Fax: 905-318-1543

Importers & Exporters / A-Z

Importer and wholesaler/distributor of biscuits and confectionery products
President: Bob Jacques
VP: Bob Baynton
Number Employees: 20-49
Brands Imported: Cadbury; Bassetts; Simmers; Fox's; Anthon Berg; Callard & Bowser; Aguila; Wilkinsons
Regions Imported from: South America, Europe, USA

49939 Waltkoch Limited
1990 Lakeside Pkwy
Suite 240
Tucker, GA 30084   404-378-3666
       Fax: 404-378-8492 www.waltkoch.com
Poultry frozen foods, meats, seafood.
Owner: Walter Koch
Partner: Sam Stanford
Chief Executive Officer: Keith Steinberg
Year Founded: 1950
Estimated Sales: $43 Million
Number Employees: 54
Type of Packaging: Consumer, Food Service
Regions Exported to: Central America, South America, Caribbean
Percentage of Business in Exporting: 100

49940 Walton & Post
8105 NW 77th St
Medley, FL 33166   305-591-1111
       Fax: 305-593-7070 mailcenter@waltonpost.com
       www.waltonpost.com
Wholesaler/distributor, importer and exporter of candy, canned fruits and vegetables, cookies, cereals, aluminum foil, plastic cups, film paper, paper napkins, juice, cooking oil, etc
VP: Jose Garrido Jr
VP: Alfredo Cuadrado
CEO: Jose A Garrido Jr
Estimated Sales: $20-50 Million
Number Employees: 20-49
Regions Exported to: Europe
Percentage of Business in Exporting: 97
Regions Imported from: Latin America
Percentage of Business in Importing: 15

49941 Walton's Inc
3639 N Comotara St
Wichita, KS 67226-1304   316-262-0651
       Fax: 316-262-5136   800-835-2832
       www.waltonsinc.com
Manufacturer and exporter of brine pumps; wholesaler/distributor of meat processing equipment and butchers' supplies including saws, slicers and tenderizers, vacuum machines and bags and smokehouses
Owner: Don Walton
CEO: Brett Walton
brett@waltonsinc.com
Sales Director: Kurt Carter
Sales: Mark Schrag
Operations Manager: Brett Walton
Production Manager: Tim Fox
Purchasing Manager: Brett Walton
Estimated Sales: $1.8 Million
Number Employees: 20-49
Number of Brands: 25
Number of Products: 200
Square Footage: 71000
Type of Packaging: Food Service
Regions Exported to: Caribbean, Mexico, Canada

49942 Wampler's Farm Sausage Company
781 U.S. 70
Lenoir City, TN 37771   865-986-2056
       Fax: 865-988-3280   800-728-7243
       sales@wamplersfarm.com
       www.wamplersfarm.com
Established in 1953. Processor, packer, and exporter of sausage.
Vice President: John Ed Wampler
Sales Manager: Doug Young
Operations Manager: Darrell Griffis
Plant Supervisor: Mike Marney
Plant Manager: Jim Wampler
Estimated Sales: $24000000
Number Employees: 100-249
Type of Packaging: Consumer, Food Service, Private Label, Bulk

49943 Wanchese Fish Co Inc
2000 Northgate Commerce Pkwy
Suffolk, VA 23435-2142   757-673-4500
       Fax: 757-653-4550 www.wanchese.com
Processor and exporter of fresh and frozen seafood including flounder, bass, scallops, tuna, scallops and shrimp.
President: Sam Daniels
sam@wanchese.com
CFO: Mark Palmer
VP: Kenny Daniels
Sales Manager: Gordon Craddock
Plant Manager: Chris Daniels
Estimated Sales: $6400000
Number Employees: 20-49
Square Footage: 1000000
Parent Co: Daniels Enterprises
Type of Packaging: Consumer, Food Service, Private Label, Bulk
Other Locations:
    Wanchese Fish Co.
    Hampton, VA Wanchese Fish Co.
Brands Exported: Captain Malc's; Ocean Choice
Regions Exported to: Europe, Asia
Percentage of Business in Exporting: 35
Brands Imported: Erin Bruce; Mr. Big
Regions Imported from: South America
Percentage of Business in Importing: 50

49944 Wanda's Nature Farm
1700 Cushman Dr
Lincoln, NE 68512-1238   402-423-1234
       Fax: 402-423-4586   800-735-6828
       heartlandgourmet.com
Processor and exporter of natural mixes including bread, cake, muffin, pancake, pasta, pizza, bagels, etc
President: Susan Zink
Vice President: David Eisner
Marketing Director: Shari Rogge-Fidler
Estimated Sales: $2311332
Number Employees: 20-49
Type of Packaging: Consumer, Food Service
Regions Exported to: Worldwide
Percentage of Business in Exporting: 1

49945 Wapsie Creamery
300 10th St NE
Independence, IA 50644-1220   319-334-7193
       Fax: 319-334-4914 markn@wapsievalley.com
       www.wapsievalley.com
Monterey and marble pepper jack, cheddar and colby cheese; processor and exporter of kosher reduced lactose whey, edible dried delactose and lactose.
President: Mark Nielsen
VP: Wilbur Nielsen
Estimated Sales: $20-50 Million
Number Employees: 50-99
Square Footage: 78000
Type of Packaging: Consumer, Private Label, Bulk
Regions Exported to: Central America, South America, Asia
Percentage of Business in Exporting: 10

49946 Wapsie Produce
702 E Water St
Decorah, IA 52101   563-382-4271
       Fax: 563-382-8210 info@capons.com
       www.capons.com
Processor and exporter of frozen capons and fowl
President: Marc Nichols
Vice President: Paul Nichols
paul.nichols@capons.com
Estimated Sales: $9 Million
Number Employees: 100
Type of Packaging: Consumer, Private Label
Regions Exported to: Canada
Percentage of Business in Exporting: 2

49947 Warbac Sales Co
722 Martin Behrman Ave
P.O. Box 9279
Metairie, LA 70005-2124   504-834-1395
       Fax: 504-684-8499   800-335-7425
       custsvc@pickapeppa.com www.pickapeppa.com
Importer of sauces and condiments.
Owner: Warren Backer
custsvc@pickapeppa.com
Year Founded: 1921
Estimated Sales: Under $500,000
Number Employees: 1-4
Square Footage: 12000
Brands Imported: Pickapeppa Sauce

Regions Imported from: Jamaica, Caribbean
Percentage of Business in Importing: 100

49948 Ward Ironworks
2 Broadway Avenue
Welland, ON L3B 5G4
Canada   905-732-7591
       Fax: 905-732-3310   888-441-9273
Manufacturer, importer and exporter of material handling machinery including bucket elevators, regular and vibrating conveyors, empty bag compactors, vibrating feeders and screens
President: Guy Nelson
Estimated Sales: $5-10 Million
Number Employees: 10
Square Footage: 200000
Parent Co: Ward Automation
Regions Exported to: Central America, Asia, Canada, Caribbean, Mexico
Percentage of Business in Exporting: 20
Regions Imported from: Europe
Percentage of Business in Importing: 10

49949 Wardcraft Conveyor & Quick Die
1 Wardcraft Dr
Spring Arbor, MI 49283-9757   517-750-9100
       Fax: 517-750-2244   800-782-2779
       info@wardcraft.net www.wardcraftconveyor.com
Manufacturer and exporter of pneumatic conveyors and quick die change systems
President: Pat Sprague
psprague@wardcraft.net
VP: Pat Sprague
National Sales: Paul Miner
Estimated Sales: $ 5 - 10 Million
Number Employees: 20-49
Square Footage: 72000

49950 Waring Products
314 Ella Grasso Ave
Torrington, CT 06790-2345   860-496-3100
       Fax: 860-496-9008   800-492-7464
       waring@conair.com www.waringproducts.com
Manufacturer, exporter and importer of commercial food processors, blenders, juice extractors, bar glass washers, rod mixers, food choppers, slicers, ice crushers and glass and can crushers
Manager: Richard Dombroski
HR Executive: James Mc Closkey
james_mccloskey@conair.com
CFO: James McCooskey
Consultant: Larry Casalino
Estimated Sales: $ 5 - 10 Million
Number Employees: 20
Parent Co: Dynamics Corporation of America
Type of Packaging: Food Service
Brands Exported: Waring, Acme, Qualheim
Regions Exported to: Central America, South America, Europe, Asia, Middle East
Percentage of Business in Exporting: 20
Brands Imported: Waring, Qualheim; Private Label
Regions Imported from: Europe, Asia
Percentage of Business in Importing: 20

49951 Warrell Corp
1250 Slate Hill Rd
Camp Hill, PA 17011-8011   717-761-5440
       Fax: 717-761-2206   844-234-3217
       sales@warrellcorp.com www.warrellcorp.com
Processor, importer and exporter of confectionery products.
President: Kevin Silva
Executive VP, Sales & Marketing: Richard Warrell
Vice President, Operations: Robert Bard
Number Employees: 250-499
Type of Packaging: Consumer, Food Service, Private Label, Bulk
Regions Exported to: Worldwide
Regions Imported from: Worldwide

49952 Warsaw Chemical Co Inc
390 Argonne Rd
Warsaw, IN 46580-3884   574-267-3251
       Fax: 574-267-3884   800-548-3396
       wcc@warsaw-chem.com www.warsaw-chem.com
Manufacturer and exporter of sanitary chemicals and compounds
President: Ken Bucher
ken-bucher@warsaw-chem.com
R & D: Jeff Rufner
Quality Control: Scott Ware
Estimated Sales: $10-20 Million
Number Employees: 50-99

Importers & Exporters / A-Z

49953 Warsteiner Importers Agency
9359 Allen Rd
West Chester, OH 45069-3846   513-942-9872
      Fax: 513-942-9874 www.warsteiner.us
Importer of German beer
President: Albert Cramer
acramer@warsteiner.de
Estimated Sales: $ 5 - 10 Million
Number Employees: 10-19
Parent Co: Warsteiner Importers Agency
Brands Imported: Isenbeck; Warsteiner
Regions Imported from: Europe

49954 Warwick Manufacturing &Equip
1112 12th St
North Brunswick, NJ 08902-1869   732-729-0400
      Fax: 732-729-1235 sales@warwickequipment.com
Manufacturer and exporter of new, used and rebuilt packaging and bakery food processing equipment
Managing Director: Gregory Pantchenko
Estimated Sales: Below $ 500,000
Number Employees: 1-4
Square Footage: 25000
Regions Exported to: Central America, South America, Europe, Africa, Canada
Percentage of Business in Exporting: 30

49955 Warwick Valley Winery & Distillery
114 Little York Rd.
Warwick, NY 10990   845-258-4858
      www.wvwinery.com
Fruit liqueurs, hard fruit ciders, gin, red and white wines
Owner: Jason Grizzanti
Year Founded: 2001
Number of Brands: 2
Number of Products: 23
Type of Packaging: Consumer, Private Label
Brands Exported: Warwick Winery, Doc's Draft Hard Cider, Warwick Distillery, American Fruits
Regions Exported to: USA

49956 Washington Frontier
PO Box 249
Grandview, WA 98930-0249   509-469-7662
      Fax: 509-469-7739
Used process equipment sales and fruit and vegetable juice sales
Manager General Operations: Joe Stoops
Estimated Sales: $ 10 - 15 Million
Number Employees: 50-100

49957 Washington Fruit & Produce Company
401 N 1st Ave
P.O.Box 1588
Yakima, WA 98907-1588   509-457-6177
      Fax: 509-452-8520 information@washfruit.com
      www.washfruit.com
Processor and exporter of fresh fruits including apples, pears, and cherries.
Manager: Tom Hanses
Contact: Lorri Denison
ldenison@neptunesociety.com
Estimated Sales: Less than $500,000
Number Employees: 1-4
Type of Packaging: Consumer, Bulk
Regions Exported to: Worldwide

49958 Washington Potato Company
1900 1st Ave West
PO Box 3110
Pasco, WA 99302   509-545-4545
      Fax: 509-545-4804 800-897-2526
      customerservice@oregonpotato.com
      www.oregonpotato.com
Processor and exporter of frozen and dehydrated potatoes
President/CEO: Frank Tiegs
Director of Sales: Barry Stice
Sales: Don Smith
Plant Manager: Bob Bernard
Estimated Sales: $16.6 Million
Number Employees: 100
Square Footage: 10000
Parent Co: Oregon Potato
Type of Packaging: Food Service, Bulk
Regions Exported to: Worldwide
Percentage of Business in Exporting: 50

49959 Washington State PotatoCmsn
108 S Interlake Rd
Moses Lake, WA 98837-2950   509-765-8845
      Fax: 509-765-4853 office@potatoes.com
Promotion of potato products including fresh frozen and dehydrated
Executive Director: Chris Voigt
cvoigt@potatoes.com
Marketing: Shannon Bornsen
Public Relations: Karen Bonaudi
Estimated Sales: $ 1 - 3 Million
Number Employees: 5-9
Regions Exported to: Central America, Asia
Percentage of Business in Exporting: 30

49960 Waste King Commercial
PO Box 4146
Anaheim, CA 92803-4146   714-524-7770
      Fax: 714-996-7073 800-767-6293
      www.anaheimmfg.com
President: Thomas P Dugan
Number Employees: 100-249

49961 Waste Minimization/Containment
2140 Scranton Rd
Cleveland, OH 44113-3544   216-696-8797
      Fax: 216-696-8794 jbecker@cryogenesis-usa.com
      www.cryogenesis-usa.com
Manufacturer and exporter of dry ice blast cleaning equipment
President: Jim Becker
jbecker@cryogenesis-usa.com
Sales Manager: John Whalen
Estimated Sales: Less Than $500,000
Number Employees: 1-4
Regions Exported to: Central America, Europe, Asia, Middle East, Africa, Caribbean
Percentage of Business in Exporting: 50

49962 Wastequip Inc
6525 Morrison Blvd # 300
Suite 300
Charlotte, NC 28211-0500   704-366-7140
      sales@wastequip.com
      www.wastequip.com
Manufacturer and exporter of waste handling equipment including compactors, hoists, balers, etc
Manager: Bram Chappell
CEO: Christine Anastasio
canastasio@wastequip.com
VP Sales/Marketing: Donald Sharp
Owner: Roy Holt
Estimated Sales: $ 5 - 10 Million
Number Employees: 1000-4999
Square Footage: 308000
Type of Packaging: Bulk
Regions Exported to: Central America
Percentage of Business in Exporting: 5

49963 Wastequip Teem
6526 Morrison Blvd
Suite 300
Charlotte, NC 28211   605-336-1333
      Fax: 605-334-8704 877-468-9278
      sales@wastequip.com www.wastequip.com
Manufacturer and exporter of rear-end loading refuse containers
Manager: Val Bochenek
Estimated Sales: $2.5-5 Million
Number Employees: 20-49
Parent Co: Wastequip
Regions Exported to: Canada, Mexico

49964 (HQ)Water & Power Technologies
P.O.Box 27836
Salt Lake City, UT 84127   801-974-5500
      Fax: 801-973-9733 888-271-3295
Manufacturer and exporter of custom designed skid-mounted and mobile water purification systems including reverse osmosis, demineralization, electrodeionization, ultrafiltration, manganese, greensand filters, softners, carbon towersand in-line filtration, etc.
General Manager: Jim Laraway
Controller: Tom Kirkland
Sales: Bryan Schillar
Purchase Manager: Chuck Gendre
Sales/Marketing: James Laraway
Contact: Alan Acker
alan.acker@a-wpt.com
Operations: Fred Farmer
Plant/Production Manager: Emma Anderson
Purchasing: Lee Courtney
Estimated Sales: $ 10 - 20 Million
Number Employees: 50-99
Square Footage: 84000
Type of Packaging: Consumer
Other Locations:
   Water & Power Technologies
   Portland, OR
   Water & Power Technologies
   Denver, CO
   Water & Power Technologies
   Dallas, TX
   Water & Power Technologies
   Columbia, SC
   Water & Power Technologies
   Houston, TXWater & Power TechnologiesDenver
Brands Exported: Water & Power Technologies
Regions Exported to: South America, Asia, Canada, Mexico
Percentage of Business in Exporting: 10

49965 Water Furnace RenewableEnergy
9000 Conservation Way
Fort Wayne, IN 46809-9794   260-478-5667
      Fax: 260-747-2828 bill_dean@waterfurnace.com
      www.waterfurnace.com
Manufacturer and exporter of geothermal heating and cooling systems
CEO: Tom Huntington
CEO: Bruce Ritchey
Director Sales: Mike Murphy
Estimated Sales: G
Number Employees: 500-999
Type of Packaging: Food Service
Regions Exported to: Worldwide
Percentage of Business in Exporting: 5

49966 Water Sciences Services, Inc.
280 Emmans Road
PO Box 5000-364
Jackson, TN 38302   973-584-4131
      Fax: 731-660-4115
Manufacturer and exporter of ice cubing/bagging machinery, bottled water sanitizers, bottled spring water, descaling equipment and water filters
President: Elizabeth Reed
Vice President: Paul Reed
Estimated Sales: $ 1-2.5 Million
Number Employees: 15
Square Footage: 36000
Brands Exported: Crystal Clean
Regions Exported to: South America, Asia, Middle East, Caribbean
Percentage of Business in Exporting: 20
Regions Imported from: Asia, Canada
Percentage of Business in Importing: 10

49967 Waterlink/Sanborn Technologies
4100 Holiday Street NW
Canton, OH 44718-2556   330-649-4000
      Fax: 330-649-4008 800-343-3381
      www.waterlink.com
Manufacturer and exporter of liquid/solid separation equipment and systems, wastewater pretreatment and food waste dewatering systems
VP Operations: Steve Friedman
Estimated Sales: Below $ 500,000
Number Employees: 4
Square Footage: 180000
Regions Exported to: Canada, Mexico

49968 (HQ)Watlow Electric
12001 Lackland Rd
St Louis, MO 63146   314-878-4600
      Fax: 314-878-6814 info@watlow.com
      www.watlow.com
Designer and manufacturer of heaters, sensors, controllers and software.
SVP & Chief Financial Officer: Steve Desloge
Welder: Elias Alanis
Year Founded: 1922
Estimated Sales: $330 Million
Number Employees: 2,000
Type of Packaging: Food Service
Regions Exported to: Worldwide

49969 Watlow Electric
5710 Kenosha St
Richmond, IL 60071
      info@watlow.com
      www.watlow.com
Designer and manufacturer of heaters, sensors, controllers and software.
Estimated Sales: $330 Million
Number Employees: 2,000
Parent Co: Watlow

Importers & Exporters / A-Z

Type of Packaging: Food Service
Other Locations:
  Watlow
  Columbia, MO
  Watlow
  Winona, MNWatlowWinona
Regions Exported to: Worldwide

49970 (HQ)Watson Inc
301 Heffernan Dr
West Haven, CT 06516-4139   203-932-3000
       Fax: 203-932-8266   800-388-3481
                    www.watson-inc.com
Ingredients manufacturer for the food and supplement industries.
President: James Watson
james.watson@watson-inc.com
Number Employees: 100-249
Type of Packaging: Bulk
Other Locations:
  Watson Foods Co.
  Rockville, CTWatson Foods Co.
Regions Exported to: Worldwide
Regions Imported from: Worldwide

49971 Watts Premier Inc
8716 W Ludlow Dr # 1
Peoria, AZ 85381-4918   480-675-7995
       Fax: 602-866-5666   800-752-5582
       mail@premierh2o.com www.premierh2o.com
Manufacturer and exporter of water purification equipment
Vice President: Shannon Murphy
VP: Shannon Murphy
Estimated Sales: $ 5-10 Million
Number Employees: 20-49
Parent Co: Watts Water Technologies Co.
Regions Exported to: Worldwide
Percentage of Business in Exporting: 30

49972 Waukesha Cherry-Burrell
2025 S Hurstbourne Pkwy
Louisville, KY 40220-1623   502-491-4310
       Fax: 502-491-4312 www.gowcb.com
Manufacturer and exporter of aseptic processing equipment, colloid mills, coopers/kettles, fittings, freezers, ingredient feeders, pumps and tanks
Manager: Jeff Comara
National Sales Manager: Tony Mazza
Sales Manager (Process Prod.): Paul Duddleson
Estimated Sales: $20-50 Million
Number Employees: 10-19
Parent Co: United Dominion Company
Regions Exported to: Worldwide

49973 Waukesha Specialty Company
N3355 Us Highway 14
PO Box 160
Darien, WI 53114-5014   262-724-3700
             Fax: 262-724-5120
Manufacturer and exporter of fittings, stainless steel hinges and sanitary valves
President: Stephen Miller
VP: Malcom Miller
Estimated Sales: $ 1 - 2.5 Million
Number Employees: 2
Regions Exported to: Mexico, Canada
Percentage of Business in Exporting: 5

49974 Wawona Frozen Foods Inc
100 W Alluvial Ave
Clovis, CA 93611-9176   559-299-2901
       Fax: 559-299-1921 info@wawona.com
                   www.wawona.com
Processor and exporter of IQF and syrup packed frozen fruits including peaches, strawberries and mixed fruit; also a variety of fruit-based portion controlled products; importer of frozen fruits including melons, grapes andpineapple
President: Jose Barajas
joseb@wawona.com
CFO: Julie Olsen
Director Quality Assurance: Duncan Donaldbe
VP Sales & Marketing: Willian Astin
Director of Sales: Toni Lindeleaf
VP Operations: Pete Peterson
Production Supervisor: Jose Valdez
Purchasing Manager: Ken Cole
Estimated Sales: $23.3 Million
Number Employees: 250-499
Square Footage: 125000
Type of Packaging: Consumer, Food Service, Private Label, Bulk
Regions Exported to: Canada, Mexico

Regions Imported from: Europe

49975 Waymar Industries
14400 Southcross Dr W
Burnsville, MN 55306   952-435-7100
       Fax: 952-435-2900   888-474-1112
                    www.plymold.com
Manufacturer and exporter of restaurant, cafeteria and industrial seating, table tops and trash containers
President: Dick Koehring
CFO: Greg Klingler
Director Manufacturing: Bill Smith
Marketing/Sales: Bill Ziegler
Contact: Jodie Anderson
j.anderson@waymar.com
Operations Manager: Bob Haugen
Plant Manager: Mike Boegeman
Purchasing Manager: Doug Schultz
Estimated Sales: $ 10 - 20 Million
Number Employees: 50-99
Square Footage: 280000
Parent Co: Foldcraft Co
Regions Imported from: Europe, Canada
Percentage of Business in Importing: 30

49976 Wayne Automation Corp
605 General Washington Ave
Eagleville, PA 19403-3695   610-630-8900
       Fax: 610-630-6116 www.wayneautomation.com
Automatic packaging equipment including partition inserters, case erectors, case packers and tray formers; exporter of partition inserters and case erectors
President: Jay L Bachman, Jr.
CFO: Dorothy Schlosser
dschlosser@wayneautomation.com
VP & General Manager: Jay L Bachman, III
VP, Sales and Marketing: Harry M. Dudley
Estimated Sales: $5-10 Million
Number Employees: 50-99
Square Footage: 60000
Regions Exported to: Central America
Percentage of Business in Exporting: 2

49977 Wayne Combustion Systems
801 Glasgow Ave
Fort Wayne, IN 46803-1344   260-425-9200
       Fax: 260-424-0904   800-443-4625
                    clagemann@waynecs.com
Manufacturer and exporter of custom gas and oil burners; also, oven, fryer and griddle design analysis available
Manager: Karen Myrice
R & D: Dan Voorhis
Marketing: Karen Wygant
Sales: Dennis Parda
Manager: Paul Wert
pwert@waynecs.com
Purchasing: Phil Fenker
Estimated Sales: $ 10 - 20 Million
Number Employees: 50-99
Square Footage: 560000
Parent Co: Scott Fetzer Company
Brands Exported: Blue Angel; Wayne
Regions Exported to: Central America, South America, Europe, Asia

49978 Wayne Engineering
701 Performance Dr
Cedar Falls, IA 50613-6952   319-266-1721
       Fax: 319-266-8207 info@wayneusa.com
Manufacturer and exporter of mobile material handling equipment and refuse equipment
CEO: Jim Marks
jimmarks@wayneusa.com
CEO: Kevin Watje
Sales Manager: Dave Severson
Sales Coordinator: Sherry Berak
Estimated Sales: $ 20-50 Million
Number Employees: 100-249
Square Footage: 60000
Regions Exported to: Central America, South America, Europe, Asia, Middle East
Percentage of Business in Exporting: 30

49979 Wayne Farms LLC.
4110 Continental Dr.
Oakwood, GA 30566
                          800-392-0844
                    www.waynefarms.com
Poultry producer.

President/CEO: J. Clinton Rivers
CFO/Treasurer: Courtney Fazekas
VP/General Manager, Prepared Foods: Tom Bell
VP, Quality Assurance & Food Safety: Bryan Miller
VP, Fresh Sales: Steve Clever
Year Founded: 1965
Estimated Sales: $2.2 Billion
Number Employees: 9,000
Number of Brands: 6
Parent Co: Continental Grain Company
Type of Packaging: Consumer, Food Service, Private Label
Other Locations:
  Albertville, AL
  Danville, AR
  Decatur, AL
  Dobson, NC
  Dothan, AL
  Enterprise, ALDanville
Regions Exported to: South America, Asia, Middle East
Percentage of Business in Exporting: 6

49980 Weaver Nut Co. Inc.
1925 W Main St
Ephrata, PA 17522-1112   717-738-3781
       Fax: 717-733-2226   800-473-2688
       info@weavernut.com www.weavergourmet.com
Processor importer and distributor of nuts, dried fruits, candies, confectionery items, snack mixes, gourmet coffees and teas, beans and spices; custom roasting and contract packaging available
President: E Paul Weaver III
Vice President: Michael Reis
Sales Director: Tom Flynn
Manager: Lisa Weaver
retail@weavernut.com
Estimated Sales: $18,000,000
Number Employees: 20-49
Number of Products: 3500
Square Footage: 116000
Type of Packaging: Consumer, Private Label, Bulk
Brands Imported: Dried fruit, nuts, candy
Regions Imported from: Central America, South America, Europe, Asia
Percentage of Business in Importing: 5

49981 Weaver Popcorn Co Inc
408 W Landess St
Van Buren, IN 46991
              concessionsales@popweaver.com
                    www.popweaver.com
Regular and microwave popcorn; also, caramel popcorn specialties including caramel with almonds and pecans and fat-free
CFO: Brian Hamilton
National Sales Manager: Jim Labas
Year Founded: 1928
Estimated Sales: $20-50 Million
Number Employees: 100-249
Type of Packaging: Consumer, Food Service, Private Label, Bulk
Brands Exported: Bonnie Lee; Weaver
Regions Exported to: Central America, South America, Europe, Asia, Middle East, Africa
Percentage of Business in Exporting: 20

49982 Weavewood, Inc.
7520 Wayzata Blvd
Golden Valley, MN 55426-1622   763-544-3136
       Fax: 763-544-3137   800-367-6460
Manufacturer and exporter of woodenware including bowls, plates, trays, coasters, tongs, susans, fork, spoon and magnetic server sets, etc.; also, aluminum and stainless steel steak platters
President: Howard Thompson
Quality Control: Tim Zanor
R&D: Tim Zanor
CFO: Howard Thompson Jr
Marketing Director: Peter Meyer
Estimated Sales: Below $ 5 Million
Number Employees: 20-49
Square Footage: 120000
Type of Packaging: Consumer, Food Service, Private Label, Bulk
Regions Exported to: Central America, South America, Europe, Asia, Middle East, Worldwide
Percentage of Business in Exporting: 5
Regions Imported from: Africa

Importers & Exporters / A-Z

49983 Web Label
600 Hoover St NE
Suite 500
Minneapolis, MN 55413   612-588-0737
         Fax: 612-706-3757 www.weblabel.com
Manufacturer and exporter of pressure sensitive labels
Owner: John Coldwell
Sales Manager: Dave Olson
Contact: James Bullert
jim.bullert@liesch.com
Estimated Sales: $ 5 - 10 Million
Number Employees: 20-49
Type of Packaging: Consumer, Bulk
Regions Exported to: Worldwide

49984 Webb-Triax Company
34375 W 12 Mile Rd
Farmington Hills, MI 48331   248-553-1000
         Fax: 440-285-1878 info@jervswebb.com
Manufacturer and exporter of automated storage and retrieval systems, including cooler and freezer storage systems and deep lane flow rack systems
Sales Director: Fred Cirino
Estimated Sales: $ 1 - 5,000,000
Number Employees: 20-49
Parent Co: Jervis B. Webb Company
Type of Packaging: Bulk
Regions Exported to: Worldwide

49985 Webeco Foods
PO Box 228764
Miami, FL 33222   305-635-0000
                         Fax: 305-639-6052
Wholesaler/distributor, importer and exporter of cheese, cream cheese and butter
Owner: Luis Teijeiro
luis@webecofoods.com
Treasurer: Jose Teijeiro
VP: Luis Teijeiro
Estimated Sales: $10-20 Million
Number Employees: 20-49
Square Footage: 135000
Brands Exported: Boursin; Jarlsberg
Regions Exported to: Central America, South America
Percentage of Business in Exporting: 25
Brands Imported: Gayo Azul; Hollandammer
Regions Imported from: Central America, Europe
Percentage of Business in Importing: 85

49986 Weber Packaging Solutions Inc
711 W Algonquin Rd
Arlington Heights, IL 60005-4457
                              800-843-4242
                      www.webermarking.com
Manufacturer and exporter of pressure-sensitive labels, labeling systems and continuous ink jet systems.
President & CEO: Doug Weber
Vice President, Finance & CFO: Chris Shealy
Year Founded: 1932
Estimated Sales: $100-500 Million
Number Employees: 200-500
Square Footage: 320000
Type of Packaging: Consumer, Food Service, Private Label, Bulk
Other Locations:
   Tape & Label Engineering
   St. Petersburg, FLTape & Label Engineering
Brands Exported: Legitrmic; Legijet
Regions Exported to: Central America, South America, Europe, Asia, Worldwide
Percentage of Business in Exporting: 15

49987 Wechsler Coffee Corporation
250 Central Avenue
Teterboro, NJ 07608-1861   201-994-1861
                              800-800-2633
Gourmet coffee, tea and drink bases; importer of green coffee; wholesaler/distributor of general merchandise and groceries including coffee and tea; serving the food service market
President: Mike O'Donnell
VP Finance: Jim Pypen
Estimated Sales: $300,000-500,000
Number Employees: 10-19
Square Footage: 200000
Parent Co: Superior Coffee & Foods
Type of Packaging: Food Service, Private Label
Regions Imported from: Central America, South America

49988 Wedgwood USA
1330 Campus Pkwy
Wall Township, NJ 07753-6811   732-938-5800
         Fax: 732-938-7108 800-999-9936
Manufacturer and importer of fine bone china tableware
Sales Manager: Michael Durao
Director Hotel/Restaurant Sales: Kathy Santangelo
Estimated Sales: $20-50 Million
Number Employees: 250-499
Square Footage: 368000
Parent Co: Waterford Wedgwood USA
Regions Imported from: Europe
Percentage of Business in Importing: 100

49989 Wedlock Paper ConvertersLtd.
2327 Stanfield Road
Mississauga, ON L4Y 1R6
Canada   905-277-9461
         Fax: 905-272-1108 800-388-0447
info@wedlockpaper.com www.wedlockpaper.com
Manufacturer and exporter of paper bags
Customer Service: Scott Wedlock
Number Employees: 100
Type of Packaging: Consumer

49990 Weetabix Canada
751 D'Arcy St.
Cobourg, ON K9A 4B1
Canada   800-343-0590
         Fax: 905-372-7261 888-933-8249
                           www.weetabix.com
Breakfast cereals and ingredients.
President/CEO, Post Consumer Brands: Howard Friedman
Year Founded: 1975
Estimated Sales: $300 Million
Number Employees: 250+
Number of Brands: 4
Parent Co: Post Holdings, Inc.
Type of Packaging: Consumer, Food Service, Private Label, Bulk
Other Locations:
   Weetabix Food Company
   Burton LatimerWeetabix Food Company
Brands Exported: Weetabix, Alpen, GrainShop, Barbara's
Regions Exported to: Central America

49991 Wega USA
524 North York Road
Bensenville, IL 60106-1607   630-350-0066
         Fax: 630-350-0005 info@expressoshoppe.com
                        www.expressoshoppe.com
Manufacturer, exporter and importer of coffee grinders and espresso equipment
President: David Dimbert
Estimated Sales: $500,000-$1 Million
Number Employees: 1-4
Square Footage: 20000
Type of Packaging: Food Service
Regions Exported to: Worldwide
Percentage of Business in Exporting: 70
Regions Imported from: Europe
Percentage of Business in Importing: 90

49992 Wehrfritz & Associates
PO Box 6618
Big Bear Lake, CA 92315-6618   909-584-7667
                         Fax: 909-584-7669
Import broker of general merchandise, groceries, private label products, seafood, etc
President: Alex Wehrfritz
CEO: Rita Wehrfritz
CFO: T Hughes
Estimated Sales: $4 Million
Number Employees: 5-9
Square Footage: 1600
Type of Packaging: Food Service, Private Label

49993 Wei-Chuan USA Inc
6655 Garfield Ave
Bell Gardens, CA 90201-1807   562-372-2020
         Fax: 562-927-0780 info@weichuanusa.com
                          www.weichuanusa.com
Manufacturer and distributor of frozen Chinese foods.
President, Wei-Chuan USA: Steve Lin
stevel@weichuanusa.com
Year Founded: 1972
Number Employees: 250-499
Type of Packaging: Consumer, Food Service, Private Label

Other Locations:
   Manufacturing Facility
   Los Angeles, CA
   Manufacturing Facility
   Murfreesboro, TNManufacturing
   FacilityMurfreesboro
Regions Exported to: Canada
Regions Imported from: Asia
Percentage of Business in Importing: 50

49994 WeighPack Systems/Paxiom Group
2525 Louis Amos
Montreal, QC H8T 1C3
Canada   514-422-0808
         Fax: 514-932-8118 888-934-4472
info@weighpack.com www.weighpack.com
Manufacturer and exporter of net-weighing systems; also, micro-processors and bagging systems
National Sales Manager: Anthony Delviscio
Number Employees: 30
Square Footage: 400000
Regions Exported to: Worldwide
Percentage of Business in Exporting: 90

49995 Weil's Food Processing
483 Erie Street N
PO Box 130
Wheatley, ON N0P 2P0
Canada   519-825-4572
         Fax: 519-825-7437 email@weilsfood.ca
                           www.weilsfood.ca
Asparagus, canned tomatoes and potatoes
President: Henry Weil
Vice President/Board Member: Robert Weil
Sales: Mark Weil
Estimated Sales: $1-2.5 Million
Number Employees: 10-19
Type of Packaging: Consumer, Food Service, Private Label
Regions Exported to: Europe, USA, Trinidad

49996 (HQ)Weiler & Company
1116 E Main St
Whitewater, WI 53190   262-473-5254
         Fax: 262-473-5867 800-558-9507
weilerinfo@provisur.com www.provisur.com
Manufacturer and exporter of meat, poultry and seafood processing equipment including grinders, mixers, screw and belt conveyors, portioning systems, meat/bone separators and mixers/grinders; also, special equipment and designservices available
CEO: Nick Lesar
Corporate Director Equipment Sales: Jim Schumacher
International Sales Manager: Dave Schumacher
Contact: Walter Jackson
wjackson@idcnet.com
General Manager: John Allred
Estimated Sales: $10-20 Million
Number Employees: 100-249
Square Footage: 144000
Other Locations:
   Weiler & Co.
   Sandy, UTWeiler & Co.
Brands Exported: Weiler; Beehive
Regions Exported to: Worldwide
Percentage of Business in Exporting: 35

49997 Weinberg Foods
11410 NE 124th Street
Suite 264
Kirkland, WA 98034-4305   800-866-3447
Fax: 310-230-9057 weinberg@weinbergfoods.com
                       www.bakingredients.com
Kosher egg products, dry milk and vegetable powders; importer of kosher vegetable powders; exporter of kosher egg products
President: W Weinberg
Sales: Ashley Hester
Estimated Sales: $930,000
Number Employees: 4
Square Footage: 12000
Type of Packaging: Bulk
Regions Exported to: Central America, South America, Europe, Asia, Middle East
Percentage of Business in Exporting: 2
Brands Imported: Cham Foods
Regions Imported from: Middle East

Importers & Exporters / A-Z

49998 Weinbrenner Shoe Co
108 S Polk St
Merrill, WI 54452-2348   715-536-5521
       Fax: 715-536-1172 800-826-0002
                www.weinbrennerusa.com
Manufacturer, importer and exporter of slip resisting safety shoes
President: L Nienow
CFO: David Giffleman
VP Sales/Marketing: Fred Girsky
Manager Sales: Shane Baganz
Manager: John Chezel
jschenzel@weinbrennerusa.com
Estimated Sales: $ 20 - 50 Million
Number Employees: 50-99
Parent Co: Weinbrenner Shoe Company
Brands Exported: Thorogood; ThoroGard; Mainstream
Regions Exported to: Worldwide
Percentage of Business in Exporting: 5
Regions Imported from: Asia
Percentage of Business in Importing: 5

49999 Weinstein International
810 Lilac Dr N Ste 114
Golden Valley, MN 55422   612-521-9590
       Fax: 612-521-9626 800-328-0959
                weinintl@aol.com
Importer of seafood including shrimp
General Manager: Louis Lipshultz
Estimated Sales: $ 3 - 5 Million
Number Employees: 1-4
Square Footage: 14000
Type of Packaging: Consumer, Food Service
Regions Imported from: Worldwide
Percentage of Business in Importing: 100

50000 Weisenberger Mills
2545 Weisenberger Mill Rd
Midway, KY 40347-9791   859-254-5282
       Fax: 859-254-0294 800-643-8678
       flourusa@te.net www.weisenberger.com
Processor and exporter of wheat flour, cornmeal and baking mixes including biscuit, pancake, pizza dough, cornbread and hush puppies; exporter of fish batter breading
President: Ernest Weisenberger
sales@weisenberger.com
Vice President: Philip Weisenberger
Estimated Sales: $900000
Number Employees: 5-9
Square Footage: 64000
Type of Packaging: Consumer, Food Service, Private Label

50001 Weiser River Packing
531 Unity Lane
Weiser, ID 83672-5372   208-549-0200
              Fax: 208-549-0503
Processor and exporter of onions
President: Calvin Hickey
Estimated Sales: $1,000,000
Number Employees: 20
Type of Packaging: Consumer, Food Service, Private Label, Bulk
Regions Exported to: Asia, Mexico, Canada

50002 Weiss Instruments Inc
905 Waverly Ave
Holtsville, NY 11742-1109   631-207-1200
       Fax: 631-207-0900 sales@weissinstruments.com
                www.weissinstrument.com
Manufacturer and exporter of thermometers and pressure gauges
President: John Weiss
johnw@weissinstruments.com
OEM Sales Manager: Stephen Weiss
Industrial Sales Manager: Thomas Keefe
Number Employees: 100-249
Square Footage: 200000
Regions Exported to: Central America, South America, Asia, Middle East, Australia
Percentage of Business in Exporting: 10

50003 (HQ)Welbilt Corporation
500 Summer St # 4
Stamford, CT 06901-4301   203-325-8300
       Fax: 203-323-4550 www.aquent.com
Manufacturer and exporter of ventilators, ice machines and commercial cooking, warming and refrigeration equipment including broilers, fryers, ovens, toasters, rotisseries, mixers, etc
Manager: Maggie Patterson
Vice President of Services: Deb McCusker
Account Director: Damien Rocherolle
Estimated Sales: $ 5 - 10 Million
Number Employees: 1-4
Square Footage: 7200000
Other Locations:
   Welbilt Corp.
   Shreveport, LA Welbilt Corp.
Regions Exported to: Worldwide

50004 Welbilt Inc.
2227 Welbilt Blvd.
New Port Richey, FL 34655   727-375-7010
       Fax: 727-375-0472 877-375-9300
                www.welbilt.com
Food and beverage equipment for commercial foodservice, including refrigerators, freezers, ovens, grills, fryers and more.
President/CEO: William Johnson
Executive VP/CFO: Martin Agard
Executive VP/General Counsel: Joel Horn
Executive VP/COO: Josef Matosevic
Year Founded: 1902
Estimated Sales: $138 Million
Number Employees: 5,500
Number of Brands: 13
Square Footage: 14120
Other Locations:
   Manitowoc Ice
   Franklin, TN
   Manitowoc Company
   Manitowoc, WI Manitowoc Ice Manitowoc
Brands Exported: Manitowoc; Kolpak; McCall
Regions Exported to: Worldwide
Percentage of Business in Exporting: 20

50005 Welch Foods Inc
300 Baker Ave # 101
Suite 101
Concord, MA 01742-2731   978-371-1000
       Fax: 978-371-3855 800-340-6870
                www.welchs.com
Juice, jellies and jams and frozen concentrates
President & CEO: Brad Irwin
birwin@welchs.com
CMO: Tom Dixon
Number Employees: 1000-4999
Square Footage: 2120000
Type of Packaging: Consumer, Food Service
Brands Exported: Welch's
Regions Exported to: Worldwide

50006 Welch Holme & Clark Co
7 Avenue L
Newark, NJ 07105-3805   973-465-1200
       Fax: 973-465-3486 www.welch-holme-clark.com
Sells and distributes: refined, USP/NF, crude and kosher vegetable oils.
President: William Dugan
bill@whcsales.com
Estimated Sales: $ 10 - 20 Million
Number Employees: 10-19
Type of Packaging: Bulk
Regions Exported to: Central America, South America, Europe, Middle East, Canada, Caribbean, Latin America, Mexico
Percentage of Business in Exporting: 5
Regions Imported from: South America, Europe, Asia
Percentage of Business in Importing: 5

50007 Well Luck
104 Harbor Dr
Jersey City, NJ 07305-4500   201-434-1177
                welluck.com
Rice, beans, nuts and grains, flour, canned foods, spices, sauces, seasonings, meat, vegetables, noodles, candy, drinks and frozen foods.
President: Chris Li
Chief Financial Officer: Ming Blinn
Number Employees: 11-50
Type of Packaging: Food Service
Other Locations:
   Atlanta, GA
   Houston, TX
   Chicago, IL
   Los Angeles, CA
   San Francisco, CA Houston
Brands Exported: ChaCha Sunflower Seeds, Cofoco Fulinmen Rice, Grand Earth Barn, Heng Shun Vinegar, Lucky Rice, Rice King, Wan Ja Shan and Hunsty.
Regions Exported to: Dominican Rep, Bahamas, Antigua, Guatemala, Panama, Brazil, Peru and more.

50008 Well-Pict Inc
209 Riverside Rd
PO Box 973
Watsonville, CA 95076-3656   831-722-3871
       Fax: 831-722-6041 sales@wellpict.com
                www.wellpict.com
Strawberries, raspberries
Owner: Keith Bungo
kbungo@wellpict.com
CFO: George Schaaf
General Manager: Eric Miyasaka
Quality Control: Keith Bungo
Estimated Sales: $ 30-50 Million
Number Employees: 20-49

50009 WellSet Tableware Manufacturing Company
201 Water Street
Brooklyn, NY 11201-1111   718-624-4490
              Fax: 718-596-3959

50010 (HQ)Wellesse
1441 W Smith Rd
Ferndale, WA 98248-8933   800-232-4005
       Fax: 360-384-1140 800-232-4005
       info@wellesse.com www.wellesse.com
Processor, exporter and contract packager of herbal and homeopathic food supplements in liquid form
President & CEO: Jim Thornton
COO & CFO: Shri Iyengar
Manager Research & Development: Mary Galloway
Quality Control Director: John Knight
VP Marketing/Product Management: Greg Andrews
VP Sales: Marc Kubota
Director Operations: Tim Schaafsma
Purchasing Manager: Scott Sticklin
Estimated Sales: $6 Million
Number Employees: 10-19
Square Footage: 181000
Type of Packaging: Consumer, Private Label
Brands Exported: Symtec
Regions Exported to: Worldwide

50011 Welliver Metal Products Corporation
672 Murlark Ave NW
Salem, OR 97304   503-362-1568
              Fax: 503-585-3374
Manufacturer and exporter of case packagers, size graders, steam kettles, tanks, size sorters, etc
President: Glenn Welliver
CEO/General Manager: Del Starr
Engineer Manager: Gray Johnson
Quality Control: John Hell
CEO: Del Starr
Estimated Sales: $ 3 - 5 Million
Number Employees: 20-49
Square Footage: 54000
Regions Exported to: South America, Europe, Asia, Canada, Mexico, Latin America
Percentage of Business in Exporting: 20

50012 Wells Enterprises Inc.
1 Blue Bunny Dr.
Le Mars, IA 51031   712-546-4000
       Fax: 712-548-3800 www.wellsenterprisesinc.com
Ice cream and frozen novelty manufacturer.
President/CEO: Michael Wells
Executive VP/CFO: Jeremy Pinkerman
Senior VP/General Counsel: Erick Opsahl
Executive VP/COO: Liam Killeen
Year Founded: 1913
Estimated Sales: Over $1 Billion
Number Employees: 2,500+
Number of Brands: 4
Type of Packaging: Consumer, Food Service, Bulk
Other Locations:
   Ice Cream Plant
   St. George, UT Ice Cream Plant
Brands Exported: Blue Bunny®
Regions Exported to: Central America, South America

50013 Wells Manufacturing Company
10 Sunnen Drive
P.O.Box 280
St. Louis, MO 63143-3800   775-345-0444
       Fax: 314-781-5445 888-356-5362
                www.wellsbloomfield.com

Importers & Exporters / A-Z

Manufacturer and exporter of commercial griddles, fryers, broilers, warmers, coffee and tea brewers, espresso machines and accessories, dispensers, decanters, etc
President: Paul Angrick
Quality Control: Terry Mees
Sales Manager: Jeanine Blue
Number Employees: 250-499
Square Footage: 308000
Parent Co: Specialty Equipment Companies
Type of Packaging: Food Service
Regions Exported to: Central America, South America, Europe, Asia, Middle East

50014 Wemas Metal Products
636 36th Avenue NE
Calgary, AB T2E 2L7
Canada
403-276-4451
Fax: 403-277-0725 sales@wemas.com
Manufacturer and exporter of custom stainless steel, aluminum and exotic metal food processing machinery
General Manager: Dave Swedak
Sales: Enno Ziemann
Sales: Joanne McCaughey
Number Employees: 44
Square Footage: 180000
Regions Exported to: Central America, Europe

50015 Wenix International Corporation
800 South Figueroa Street
Suite 641
Los Angeles, CA 90017-2521
213-627-0745
Fax: 213-627-0843
Exporter of frozen, dried and canned seafood
President: Walter Wu
Manager: Douglas Chang
Assistant Manager: Mike Liu
Estimated Sales: $ 3 - 5 Million
Number Employees: 5-9
Regions Exported to: Europe, Asia, Middle East

50016 Wenk Foods Inc
PO Box 368
Madison, SD 57042
605-256-4569
Fax: 605-256-3204 wfi@hcpd.com
Processor and exporter of frozen and dried egg products; also, frozen whole geese
President: William Wenk
Sales Director: Norbert Moldan
Number Employees: 50-99
Square Footage: 120000
Type of Packaging: Consumer, Food Service, Private Label, Bulk
Brands Exported: Wenk
Regions Exported to: Asia
Percentage of Business in Exporting: 2

50017 Wepackit
1-16 Tideman Drive
Orangeville, ON L9W 4N6
Canada
519-942-1700
Fax: 519-942-1702
Manufacturer and exporter of case packers, erectors, sealers, de-casers and tray formers
President: David Wiggins
Number Employees: 55-60
Number of Products: 7
Square Footage: 80000
Regions Exported to: Canada, Mexico, USA
Percentage of Business in Exporting: 60

50018 Wescor
370 W 1700 S
Logan, UT 84321-5294
435-752-6011
Fax: 435-752-4127 800-453-2725
biomed@wescor.com
Manufacturer and exporter of osmometers and thermometers
President: Wayne K Barlow
Estimated Sales: $5-10,000,000
Number Employees: 50-99
Regions Exported to: Worldwide

50019 Wescotek Inc
700 Tuna St
San Pedro, CA 90731-7340
310-831-3624
Fax: 310-831-8735 wescotek@wescotek.com
www.wescotek.com
Wholesaler/distributor, importer and exporter of tuna, seafood and foaming agents, pet food and food ingredients
President: Richard Harpe
dick@wescotek.com
Technical Manager: Mayra Olivera
Marketing Manager: Lee Anderson
Estimated Sales: Less Than $500,000
Number Employees: 1-4
Regions Exported to: Africa
Regions Imported from: Africa

50020 Wesley International Corp
3680 Chestnut St
Scottdale, GA 30079-1206
404-792-7441
Fax: 404-292-8469 800-241-8649
sales@wesleyintl.com
Manufacturer and exporter of electric vehicles, burden and personnel carriers and trucks including hand hydraulic pallets, skids and straddles
Sales/Marketing: Lee Gatins
Manager: Jeremy Driver
jeremy.driver@wesleyintl.com
Manager: Vanessa Holiday
Estimated Sales: $ 5 - 10 Million
Number Employees: 50-99
Square Footage: 50000
Regions Exported to: Central America
Percentage of Business in Exporting: 2

50021 West Agro
11100 N Congress Ave
Kansas City, MO 64153
816-891-7700
Fax: 816-891-1606 www.universaldairy.com
Manufacturer and exporter of cleaning and sanitation supplies including clean-in-place systems; also, sanitation control system consultant
President: Walt Maharay
VP: Thomas Fahey
Contact: Mark Curtis
dan.brookhart@delaval.com
Number Employees: 100-249
Parent Co: Tetra Laval Group
Regions Exported to: Worldwide

50022 West Bay Sales
351 Rancho Camino
Fallbrook, CA 92028-8488
760-731-3317
Fax: 760-731-3221 800-607-0495
ala@westbaysales.com
Importer of ginger, brewers' yeast spread and glace fruits including apricots, orange slices and peels, pineapple, peaches, pears, figs and kiwifruit. Also diced, dehydrated, and low sugar pineapple, papaya, mango, strawberry, peachpear, and banana, caramel, chocolate ganache, fruit variegates, dried apricots, figs, and tomatoes.
Owner: Alan Sipole
alan@westbaysales.com
Estimated Sales: $2.5-5 Million
Number Employees: 1-4
Square Footage: 8000
Type of Packaging: Consumer, Food Service, Bulk
Brands Imported: Vegemite; Robern Fruits
Regions Imported from: Fiji, Australia
Percentage of Business in Importing: 85

50023 (HQ)West Carrollton Parchment Company
PO Box 49098
West Carrollton, OH 45449
937-859-3621
Fax: 937-859-7610
Manufacturer and exporter of paper including printing, rewinding, sheeting, die cutting, creping and coating
President: Cameron Lonergan
CEO: Pierce Lonergan
VP Finance: Alan Berens
Quality Control: Brandon Carpenter
Sales/Marketing: Larry Teague
Operations: Bob Scancella
Production: Tom Bray
Purchasing Director: Jerry Lienesch
Estimated Sales: $30 Million
Number Employees: 100-249
Number of Products: 150
Square Footage: 260000
Parent Co: Friend Group
Type of Packaging: Food Service
Brands Exported: GVP-100; Parchment Paper
Regions Exported to: South America, Europe, Asia
Percentage of Business in Exporting: 1
Brands Imported: Greaseproof
Regions Imported from: Europe
Percentage of Business in Importing: 10

50024 (HQ)West Chemical Products
1000 Herrontown Rd Ste 2
Princeton, NJ 08540
609-921-0501
Fax: 609-924-4308
Manufacturer and exporter of sanitizing agents including detergents and disinfectants; also, insecticides including liquid and fly killing
President: Elwood Phares
CEO: Elwood W Phares Ii
Contact: Bruce Muretta
bmuretta@westchemicalproducts.com
Estimated Sales: G
Number Employees: 100-249
Other Locations:
West Chemical Products
Tenefly, NJ West Chemical Products
Regions Exported to: Worldwide

50025 West Coast Products
717 Tehama St
Orland, CA 95963-1248
530-865-3379
Fax: 530-865-1581 800-382-3072
www.westcoastproducts.net
Manufacturer and exporter of specialty olives and olive oil
President: Estelle Krackov
Manager: Dan Vecere
dan.vecere@westcoastproducts.net
Estimated Sales: $380,000
Number Employees: 10-19
Square Footage: 18608
Type of Packaging: Food Service, Bulk
Regions Exported to: Canada
Percentage of Business in Exporting: 5

50026 West Coast Seafood Processors Association
650 NE Holladay St
Suite 1600
Portland, OR 97232
503-227-5076
www.wcspa.com
Processor and exporter of frozen Pacific whiting
Manager: Tom Libby
Executive Director: Rod Moore
Contact: Rod Moore
tuna_1@charter.net
Estimated Sales: $ 10-20 Million
Number Employees: 100-249
Parent Co: California Shellfish
Type of Packaging: Bulk
Regions Exported to: Asia
Percentage of Business in Exporting: 100

50027 West Coast Specialty Coffee
71 Lost Lake Lane
Campbell, CA 95008
650-259-9308
Fax: 650-259-8024 rh@specialtycoffee.com
www.specialtycoffee.com
Coffee and coffee equipment and supplies
President: Robert Hensley
rh@specialtycoffee.com
Estimated Sales: $500,000
Number Employees: 2
Type of Packaging: Consumer, Food Service, Bulk
Brands Exported: Duran Estate Coffee
Brands Imported: Probat Roasters

50028 West Hawk Industries
1717 S State St Frnt
Ann Arbor, MI 48104-4684
734-761-3100
Fax: 734-761-8430 800-678-1286
sales@westhawkpromo.com
www.westhawkind.com
Manufacturer and exporter of advertising novelties, decals, signs, banners, calendars, imprinted matches, bags and custom printed cups; also, imprinted mints and chocolates
President: Jan Hawkins
CEO: Harry Hawkins
Vice President: Sarah Spratt
Sales Director: Harry Hawkins
Estimated Sales: $2.5-5 Million
Number Employees: 5-9
Number of Products: 800
Square Footage: 30000
Type of Packaging: Private Label

50029 West India Trading Company
505-300 Du Saint Sacrament Street
Montreal, QC H2Y 1X4
Canada
514-849-6031
Fax: 514-499-8449
Exporter of smoked cured herring and herring fillets, dried beans and peas; also, meat products

President: Aurelio de Vasconcelos
Office Manager: Brian Bourne
VP: Anthony de Montbrun
Number Employees: 10-19
Regions Exported to: Central America, South America, Caribbean
Percentage of Business in Exporting: 100

50030 West Liberty Foods LLC
207 W 2nd St
P.O. Box 318
West Liberty, IA 52776
888-511-4500
www.wlfoods.com
Ready-to-eat sliced processed meat, poultry and protein products.
CEO: Edward Garrett
President: Michael Quint
VP & CFO: Allen Hansen
VP & COO: Gerald Lessard
Quality Assurance: Chasity Abel
chasity.abel@wlfoods.com
Operations Manager: Chad Schnepper
Year Founded: 1996
Estimated Sales: $200-500 Million
Number Employees: 1,900
Square Footage: 175000
Parent Co: Iowa Turkey Growers Cooperative
Type of Packaging: Consumer, Food Service, Private Label
Other Locations:
West Liberty Foods Plant
Mt Pleasant, IA
West Liberty Foods Plant
Sigourney, IAWest Liberty Foods PlantSigourney
Regions Exported to: Worldwide

50031 West Oregon Wood Products Inc
2305 2nd St
Columbia City, OR 97018-9504   503-397-6707
Fax: 503-397-6887 mross@wowpellets.com
A manufacturer of premium wood fuel pellet, all 100 percent wood fire logs, animal bedding, firestarter, and BBQ pellets. The quality products combined with a strong value proposition has provided us the platform to build categoryleading products. We continue to lead the industry in innovation, product development, and service.
Owner: Christopher Sharron
csharron@wowpellets.com
General Manager: Mike Knobel
Director Marketing/Sales: Mark Ross
Estimated Sales: $1-2.5 Million
Number Employees: 20-49
Square Footage: 560000
Brands Exported: Lil' Devils
Regions Exported to: Asia, Canada, Caribbean
Percentage of Business in Exporting: 5

50032 West Pak Avocado Inc
38655 Sky Canyon Dr
Murrieta, CA 92563-2536   951-696-5845
Fax: 951-296-5744 800-266-4414
www.westpakavocado.com
Importer, exporter and packer of avocados; importer of Mexican and Chilean fruits; processor of persimmons and kumquats
President: Randy Shoup
randy.shoup@westpakavocado.com
Import Export Director: Dave Culpeper
VP/General Manager: Galen Newhouse
Estimated Sales: $ 3 - 5 Million
Number Employees: 50-99
Square Footage: 88000
Type of Packaging: Consumer, Food Service, Bulk
Percentage of Business in Exporting: 20
Regions Imported from: Central America, South America
Percentage of Business in Importing: 20

50033 West Rock
1000 Abernathy Road NE
Atlanta, GA 30328   770-448-2193
www.westrock.com
Produces containerboard and paperboard packaging for food, hardware, apparel and other consumer goods.
Chief Executive Officer: Steven Voohees
EVP/Chief Financial Officer: Ward Dickson
President, Business Development: Jim Porter
President, Consumer Packaging: Patrick Lindner
President, Corrugated Packaging: Jeff Chalovich
President, Multi Packaging Solutions: Marc Shore
Chief Transformation Officer: Shan Cooper
EVP/General Counsel/Secretary: Bob McIntosh
Chief Human Resources Officer: Vicki Lostetter
Chief Environmental Officer: Nina Butler
Chief Communications Officer: Donna Owens Cox
Year Founded: 2015
Estimated Sales: $14.8 Billion
Number Employees: 45,000
Type of Packaging: Consumer, Food Service, Private Label, Bulk
Regions Exported to: Central America, South America
Percentage of Business in Exporting: 5

50034 West Thomas Partners, LLC
4053 Brockton SE
Grand Rapids, MI 49512   616-755-8432
info@theglutenfreebar.com
www.theglutenfreebar.com
Gluten-free, non-GMO, soy-free and nut-free snack bars, energy bites and oats in various flavors
Co-Founder: Marshall Rader
Co-Founder: Elliott Rader
Year Founded: 2010
Number of Brands: 1
Number of Products: 17
Type of Packaging: Consumer, Private Label
Brands Exported: GFB: The Gluten Free Bar
Regions Exported to: USA, Canada

50035 (HQ)Westbrae Natural Foods
58 S Service Rd
Melville, NY 11747   631-730-2200
Fax: 631-730-2550 800-434-4246
www.westbrae.com
Processor, importer and exporter of natural and organic soy and rice beverages, tortilla and potato chips, soups, beans, chili, condiments, sauces, rice cakes, popcorn, pretzels, licorice, cookies, spreads and Asian foods
President/CEO: Irwin Simon
CFO/EVP: Ira Lamel
Number Employees: 1,000-4,999
Square Footage: 156000
Parent Co: The Hain Celestial Group, Inc.
Type of Packaging: Consumer, Private Label
Brands Exported: Little Bear; Westbrae Natural
Regions Exported to: Europe, Asia
Percentage of Business in Exporting: 2
Brands Imported: Westbrae Natural
Regions Imported from: Asia
Percentage of Business in Importing: 5

50036 Westbrook Trading Company
3410b Ogden Road SE
Calgary, AB T2G 4N5
Canada   403-290-0860
Fax: 403-264-3017 800-563-5785
Processor and exporter of fresh, frozen and boxed beef and pork
President: Michael Nutik
Sales Manager: Daren Uens
Number Employees: 100-249
Type of Packaging: Consumer, Food Service, Bulk
Regions Exported to: Worldwide
Percentage of Business in Exporting: 2

50037 Westco-BakeMark
7351 Crider Avenue
Pico Rivera, CA 90660-3705   562-949-1054
Fax: 562-948-5506 www.yourbakemark.com
Processor, importer and exporter of baking ingredients and supplies, including mixes, fillings, icings and frozen products.
Chief Supply Chain Officer: Jim Parker
CFO/VP of Finance: Refugio Reynoso
Marketing Director: David Roccio
EVP of Sales: William Day
VP of Human Resources: Kenneth Sparks
Estimated Sales: $20-50 Million
Number Employees: 500-999
Number of Brands: 1
Parent Co: CSM Bakery Solutions
Type of Packaging: Food Service, Bulk
Other Locations:
Union City, CA
Reno, NV
Phoenix, AZ
Seattle, WAReno
Regions Exported to: Worldwide
Percentage of Business in Exporting: 15
Regions Imported from: Europe

50038 Western Bagel Baking Corp
7814 Sepulveda Blvd
Van Nuys, CA 91405-1062   818-786-5847
Fax: 818-787-3221 wbinfo@westernbagel.com
www.westernbagel.com
Processor and exporter of fresh and frozen bagels.
President: Steve Ustin
Cmo: Corrie Ustin
custin@westernbagel.com
Vice President: Skip Scheidt
Operations Manager: Jim Schultz
Estimated Sales: $29280131
Number Employees: 250-499
Square Footage: 30000
Regions Exported to: Asia, Middle East
Percentage of Business in Exporting: 5

50039 Western Combustion Engineering
640 E Realty St
Carson, CA 90745-6016   310-834-9389
Fax: 310-834-4795 info@westerncombustion.com
www.westerncombustion.com
Manufacturer, exporter of ovens, oil fryers and food processing equipment
President: Marcia Paul
mpaul@westerncombustion.com
Vice President: Marcia Paul
Estimated Sales: $ 1-2,500,000
Number Employees: 10-19
Square Footage: 10000
Regions Exported to: Asia
Percentage of Business in Exporting: 20

50040 (HQ)Western Container Company
4323 Clary Blvd
Kansas City, MO 64130   816-924-5700
Fax: 816-924-7032
Manufacturer and exporter of cartons including folding, cellophane window and plastic coated
President: Richard Horton
CFO: Allen Booe
Quality Control: Charlie Palmer
Contact: Kyle Adams
kylea@westerncontainer.com
Estimated Sales: $ 20 - 50 Million
Number Employees: 100-249
Regions Exported to: Canada

50041 Western Pacific Produce
36 W Gutierrez
Santa Barbara, CA 93101   805-568-1550
Fax: 805-884-9181 800-963-4451
sales@western-pacific.com
www.western-pacific.com
Grower and packer of broccoli and other fresh produce.
President & CEO: Mark Vestal
mark@western-pacific.com
VP & Chief Financial Officer: Diana Vestal
Sales Manager: Steve Bellandi
Chief Operating Officer: Bob Cordova
Year Founded: 1990
Estimated Sales: $20-50 Million
Number Employees: 250-499
Type of Packaging: Consumer, Food Service, Private Label, Bulk
Regions Exported to: Canada and Mexico

50042 Western Pacific Stge Solutions
300 E Arrow Hwy
San Dimas, CA 91773-3339   909-305-9526
Fax: 909-451-0311 800-888-5707
trogers@wpss.com
Manufacturer and exporter of steel and boltless shelving, carton flow racks and mezzanine systems
President: Tom Rogers
trogers@wpss.com
Marketing Manager: Diane Gowgill
Estimated Sales: $5-10,000,000
Number Employees: 100-249
Regions Exported to: Worldwide

50043 Western Plastics
105 Western Dr
Portland, TN 37148-2018   615-325-7331
Fax: 615-325-4924 sales@wplastic.com

Importers & Exporters / A-Z

Manufacturer, importer and exporter of aluminum foil rolls, PVC film cutter-boxes, pallet stretch wrap, perforated food wrap and shrink film
President: Tommy Mcclean
tcmmy@westernplastics.ie
VP: Gene Ketter
Sales Manager: David Sullender
Estimated Sales: $5-10 Million
Number Employees: 100-249
Square Footage: 120000
Brands Exported: WP Foil; WP FoodFilm; WP Handywrap
Regions Exported to: Central America, Europe, Asia, Pacific Rim, Canada, Mexico
Percentage of Business in Exporting: 17
Regions Imported from: Worldwide
Percentage of Business in Importing: 15

50044 (HQ)Western Plastics
2399 Highway 41 South SW
Calhoun, GA 30701-3346   706-625-5260
    Fax: 706-625-0003 800-752-4106
    calhoun@wplastics.com www.wplastics.com
Manufacturer and exporter of packaging materials including plastic film and aluminum foil
President: Tom Cunningham
tcunningham@wplastics.com
CEO: Frederick Young
CFO: George Schultz
Vice President: Frederick Young
Marketing Director: Paul O'Loghlen
Operations Manager: Bobby Hyde
Purchasing Manager: Jeff Silvers
Estimated Sales: $ 40 Million
Number Employees: 50-99
Square Footage: 100000
Type of Packaging: Food Service, Private Label, Bulk
Other Locations: Western Plastics
Brands Exported: Eldorado
Regions Exported to: Worldwide

50045 Western Polymer Corp
32 Road R SE
Moses Lake, WA 98837-9303   509-765-1803
    Fax: 509-765-0327 800-362-6845
    www.westernpolymer.com
Processor, exporter and importer of starch; manufacturer of starch recovery systems
CEO: Sheldon Townsend
Marketing: Mike Markillie
Estimated Sales: $20-50 Million
Number Employees: 50-99
Parent Co: Moses Lake
Type of Packaging: Bulk
Regions Exported to: Mexico
Regions Imported from: Europe, Asia
Percentage of Business in Importing: 5

50046 Western Stoneware
521 W 6th Ave
Monmouth, IL 61462   309-734-2161
    Fax: 309-734-5942 www.westernstoneware.com
Manufacturer and exporter of stoneware bean pots, cheese crocks, canister sets, cups, mugs, soup bowls and steins
Owner: Jack Horner
CFO: Jean Wiseman
VP: Gene Wiseman
Estimated Sales: Below $5 Million
Number Employees: 20-49

50047 Western Syrup Company
13766 Milroy Pl
Santa Fe Springs, CA 90670   562-921-4485
    Fax: 562-921-5170
Processor and exporter of custom formulated beverage bases, concentrates, flavors and flavor emulsions for carbonated beverages, slushes, sno-cones, etc.; also, dessert toppings including chocolate syrup, fudge and fruit
President: Pushpa Sastry
Sales Director: Ken Molder
Plant Manager: Marlon King
Estimated Sales: $ 3 - 5 Million
Number Employees: 5-9
Square Footage: 110000
Parent Co: Western Syrup Company

50048 (HQ)Western Textile & Manufacturing Inc.
1750 Bridgeaway
Suite B207
Sausalito, CA 94965   415-431-1458
    Fax: 415-431-5980 800-734-8683
    westex@bagmakers.com www.bagmakers.com
Manufacturer and exporter of leather goods including menu covers
Owner: Craig Storek
Contact: David Hanson
david@bagmakers.com
Office Manager: Lorraine Storek
Estimated Sales: $2.5-5 Million
Number Employees: 1-4
Regions Exported to: Worldwide
Percentage of Business in Exporting: 5

50049 Westfalia Separator
100 Fairway Ct
Northvale, NJ 07647   201-767-3900
    Fax: 201-784-4313 800-722-6622
Equipment for clarifying suspensions, separating liquids with removal of solids, separating liquid mixtures of differing densities of viscosities, extracting of active substances, classifying substances, and concentrating anddewatering of solids.
President: Michael Vick
COO: Hanno Lehmann
CFO: Norbert Breuer
Lab Director: Pete Malanchuk
Quality Control Director: Bill Taylor
Marketing Manager: Frank Kennedy
Sales: Michael Rohr
Contact: Samuel Barcenas
samuel.barcenas@gea.com
VP Operations: Joseph Pavlosky
Purchasing Manager: John Nayancsik
Estimated Sales: $36.7 Million
Number Employees: 530
Square Footage: 105000

50050 (HQ)Westin Foods
11808 W Center Rd # 1
Omaha, NE 68144-4435   402-691-8800
    Fax: 402-691-7920 800-228-6098
    jweese@westinfoods.com www.westinfoods.com
Bacon bits, imitation bacon bits, lecithin, onion rings, breaded cheese, sunflower seeds, soy products, corn starch, salad dressings, sauces, etc.; importer of olives; exporter of frozen breaded vegetables
Chairman/Ceo: Richard Westin Sr
CEO/President: Scott Carlson
scarlson@westinfoods.com
Number Employees: 250-499
Type of Packaging: Consumer, Food Service, Private Label, Bulk
Other Locations:
    Westin
    Wahoo, NEWestin
Regions Exported to: Worldwide
Percentage of Business in Exporting: 5
Brands Imported: Mario
Regions Imported from: Europe
Percentage of Business in Importing: 35

50051 Weston Emergency Light Co
10 Sibley Rd
Weston, MA 02493-2550   781-894-1585
    Fax: 781-894-1590 800-649-3756
    sales@westonemergencylights.com
    www.westonemergencylights.com
Manufacturer and importer of exit signs, lamps and lighting fixtures; also, emergency light batteries, portable rechargeable hand lights and flashlights
President: Michelle Flynn
Manager: Thomas Silveira
Clerk: Paul Amsden
Estimated Sales: $5-10 Million
Number Employees: 1-4
Square Footage: 10000
Regions Imported from: Asia, Canada
Percentage of Business in Importing: 10

50052 Westvaco Corporation
2000 Ogletown Road
Newark, DE 19711-5439   302-453-7200
    Fax: 302-453-7280
Folding cartons and MAP packaging; exporter of ovenware packaging
Business Development Manager: Rufus Miller
Manager (Frozen Foods): Shelly Dicken
National Account Manager: Richard De Ruiter
Estimated Sales: $1-2.5 Million
Number Employees: 9
Square Footage: 120000
Regions Exported to: South America, Europe
Percentage of Business in Exporting: 10

50053 Westway Trading Corporation
365 Canal Street
Suite 2900
New Orleans, LA 70130   701-282-5010
    Fax: 701-281-2695 www.westway.com
Processor and exporter of molasses
CEO: Gene McClain
CFO: Thomas Masilla
Estimated Sales: $ 5 - 10 Million
Number Employees: 10-19
Type of Packaging: Bulk
Regions Exported to: Canada
Percentage of Business in Exporting: 10

50054 Westwind Resources
11733 9th Ave NW
Seattle, WA 98177   206-281-9262
    Fax: 206-283-1244 westwindresource@aol.com
Wholesaler/distributor, importer and exporter of fresh and frozen seafood
President: Gail Rowland
Estimated Sales: $5 Million
Number Employees: 1-4
Type of Packaging: Food Service, Bulk
Regions Exported to: Europe
Brands Imported: Westwind
Regions Imported from: South America, Asia
Percentage of Business in Importing: 25

50055 Westwood International
15469 Dupont Ave
Chino, CA 91710-7605   909-606-7310
    Fax: 909-606-6416 sguimond1@yahoo.com
Importer of kitchenware
Manager: Shih Tai
Contact: David Mi
sales@westwoodinternational.com
Estimated Sales: $ 5 - 10 Million
Number Employees: 5-9
Type of Packaging: Consumer, Food Service
Regions Imported from: Asia
Percentage of Business in Importing: 100

50056 Westwood International
265 Washington Street
Westwood, MA 02090-1339   781-329-0001
    Fax: 781-326-0056
Importer of pilchard
President: Frank Giovino
Estimated Sales: $300,000-500,000
Number Employees: 1-4

50057 Wet Towel International
1680 Midland Avenue
Suite 14
Scarborough, ON M1P 3C6
Canada   416-422-2888
    Fax: 416-446-7784 inghampeng@aol.com

50058 Wetoska Packaging Distributors
1099 Lunt Ave
Elk Grove Vlg, IL 60007-5021   847-437-6100
    Fax: 847-437-8991 www.wetoska.com
Wholesaler/distributor and importer of packaging supplies and vacuum packaging machines; serving the food service market
Owner: John Murray
Controller: S Lombardo
Sales Director: S Wetoska
jmurray@wetoska.com
Purchasing Manager: J Newham
Estimated Sales: $20-50 Million
Number Employees: 10-19
Square Footage: 27000
Type of Packaging: Food Service
Brands Imported: Supervac; Hajek (Dynavac)
Regions Imported from: Europe, Canada
Percentage of Business in Importing: 60

50059 Wexxar Corporation
3851 W Devon Avenue
Chicago, IL 60659-1024   630-983-6666
    Fax: 630-983-6948 sales@wexxar.com
    www.wexxar.com
Manufacturer and exporter of packaging equipment including tray and case formers and sealers
Vice President of Sales: Jim Stoddard

Estimated Sales: Less than $500,000
Number Employees: 4
Square Footage: 200000
Parent Co: Wexxar Packaging Machinery
Brands Exported: Wexxar
Regions Exported to: Central America, South America, Europe, Asia, Middle East
Percentage of Business in Exporting: 30

50060 Whaley Pecan Co Inc
1113 S Brundidge Blvd
Troy, AL 36081 334-566-3504
Fax: 334-566-9336 800-824-6827
info@whaleypecan.com www.whaleypecan.com
Processors of shelled pecans and some exports
Owner: Bob Whaley
whaleypecan@bellsouth.net
Estimated Sales: $5,000,000
Number Employees: 10-19
Square Footage: 160000
Type of Packaging: Consumer, Food Service, Bulk
Brands Exported: Whaley's Fancy Shelled
Regions Exported to: Europe, Canada
Percentage of Business in Exporting: 1

50061 Whallon Machinery Inc
205 N Chicago St
PO Box 429
Royal Center, IN 46978-2101 574-643-9561
Fax: 574-643-9218 info@whallon.com
www.whallon.net
Manufacturer and exporter of palletizers and depalletizers for cans, cases and pails
Owner: Leslie Smith
Engineering Manager: Jeff Tevis
Sales Manager: Bruce Ide
lsmith1@whallon.com
Purchasing Manager: Judy Roudebush
Estimated Sales: $10-20 Million
Number Employees: 50-99
Square Footage: 70000
Brands Exported: Whallon Machinery
Regions Exported to: Central America, South America, Asia, Canada, Latin America, New Zealand, Mexico, England, Australia
Percentage of Business in Exporting: 15

50062 Wharton Seafood Sales
43505 Belt Highway
PO Box 440
Paauilo, HI 96776-0440 808-776-1087
Fax: 877-591-8944 800-352-8507
Seafood
Owner/President: Bailey Wharton
wharton@aloha.net
Estimated Sales: Less than $100,000
Number Employees: 1-4

50063 Whatman
PO Box 8223
Haverhill, MA 01835-0723 978-374-7400
Fax: 978-374-7070
Manufacturer and exporter of filters, analytical instruments and laboratory equipment and supplies
VP Sales/Marketing: David Largesse
Estimated Sales: $ 500,000-$ 1 Million
Number Employees: 50-99
Type of Packaging: Bulk
Regions Exported to: Worldwide

50064 Wheel Tough Company
1597 E Industrial Drive
Terre Haute, IN 47802-9265 812-298-8606
Fax: 812-298-1166 888-765-8833
Manufacturer and exporter of aluminum bar and restaurant furniture including stools, chairs and tables; also, gas and charcoal grills, deep fryers and steamers
President: Rudolph J Stakeman Jr
Estimated Sales: $1 Million
Number Employees: 5
Square Footage: 272000
Brands Exported: The Driver's Seat; Casual Furniture; Trackside Cookery; Outdoor Cooking Appliances
Regions Exported to: Europe, Asia
Percentage of Business in Exporting: 1
Regions Imported from: Canada, Caribbean, Mexico
Percentage of Business in Importing: 1

50065 Whirley Drink Works
618 4th Ave
Warren, PA 16365-4947 814-723-7600
Fax: 814-723-3245 800-825-5575
www.whirleydrinkworks.com
President: Harry W Conarro
hconarro@whirley.com
Estimated Sales: $ 5 - 10 Million
Number Employees: 250-499

50066 Whirley Industries Inc
140 W Harmar St
Warren, PA 16365-2184 814-723-8696
Fax: 814-723-3245 800-825-5575
klabarbera@whirley.com
www.whirleydrinkworks.com
As the world's leading manufacturer of plastic promotional drink containers, Whirley Industries offers a diverse line of products ranging from 12-128 oz
Owner/CEO: Lincoln Sokolski
CFO: Greg Aross
Marketing: Andrew Solkoski
Sales: William Turner
Manager: Kitty Cerra
kcerra@whirleydrinkworks.com
Estimated Sales: $20-50 Million
Number Employees: 250-499
Type of Packaging: Bulk
Brands Exported: Whirley
Regions Exported to: Worldwide
Percentage of Business in Exporting: 8

50067 (HQ)Whisk Products Inc
130 Enterprise Dr
Wentzville, MO 63385-5544 636-327-6262
Fax: 636-327-6288 800-204-7627
whisk@whiskproducts.com
www.whiskproducts.com
Manufacturer and exporter of hand cleaners, germicidal hand soap and dishwashing detergents; also, soap dispensers
Owner: Raymond Lamantia
Sales: Brad LaMantia
ray@whiskproducts.com
Plant Manager: Scott Berg
Purchasing: Lisa Thess
Estimated Sales: $ 3 - 5 Million
Number Employees: 10-19
Number of Brands: 1
Number of Products: 32
Square Footage: 46000
Regions Exported to: Central America
Percentage of Business in Exporting: 5

50068 Whistler Brewing Company
1045 Miller Creek Road
Whistler, BC V0N 1B1
Canada 604-731-2900
Fax: 604-932-7293 tours@whistlerbeer.com
http://www.whistlerbeer.com
Processor and exporter of ale and lager
President: Trevor Khoe
Estimated Sales: F
Number Employees: 100-249
Type of Packaging: Consumer, Food Service
Regions Exported to: Europe, USA

50069 Whit-Log Trailers Inc
PO Box 668
Wilbur, OR 97494 541-673-0651
Fax: 541-673-1166 800-452-1234
brett@whitlogtrailers.com
www.whitlogtrailers.com
Manufacturer and exporter of hydraulic material handling equipment including truck mounted and pedestal electric stationary cranes
Owner: Gene Whitaker
gene@whitlogtrailers.com
Sales Manager: Jim Davidson
Estimated Sales: $300,000-500,000
Number Employees: 1-4
Brands Exported: Ramey
Regions Exported to: Worldwide

50070 White Coffee Corporation
18-35 38th Street
Long Island City, NY 11105 718-204-7900
Fax: 718-956-8504 800-221-0140
info@whitecoffee.com www.whitecoffee.com
Cocoa, coffee, tea, gelatin, soup mixes and bases
President: Carole White
Executive Vice President: Jonathan White
Vice President: Gregory White
Plant Manager: Tom Tolfree
Estimated Sales: $18,800,000
Number Employees: 100-249
Regions Exported to: Worldwide
Regions Imported from: Worldwide

50071 White House Foods
701 Fairmont Avenue
Winchester, VA 22601 540-662-3401
Fax: 540-665-4671 tbastas@nfpc.com
www.whitehousefoods.com
Apple products including apple juice, apple sauce, vinegar and apple slices.
Chairman & CEO: David Gum
VP of Food Service Div.: Mark Thomas
Brand Sales: Dave Durden
Director Private Label Retail: Charlie Wollbrinck
Type of Packaging: Consumer, Food Service, Private Label, Bulk
Other Locations:
National Fruit Product Plant
Winchester, NC
National Fruit Product Plant
Lincolnton, NCNational Fruit Product PlantLincolnton
Brands Exported: White House
Regions Exported to: Central America, South America
Percentage of Business in Exporting: 2
Regions Imported from: South America, Europe
Percentage of Business in Importing: 1

50072 White Mop Wringer Company
P.O. Box 16647
Tampa, FL 33687-6647 813-971-2223
Fax: 813-971-6090 800-237-7582
Manufacturer and exporter of janitorial equipment including burnishers, carts, floor and carpet care products and waste baskets and receptacles
Chief Financial Officer: Thomas Halluska
Estimated Sales: $ 50 - 100 Million
Number Employees: 100-249
Type of Packaging: Food Service
Regions Exported to: Worldwide

50073 White Mountain Freezer
800 E 101st Terrace
Kansas City, MO 64131-5322 816-943-4100
Fax: 816-943-4123
Manufacturer and exporter of ice cream and fruit processing machinery including freezers, parers and pitters
VP Marketing: Phil Gyori
Marketing Manager: Lori Baker
Production Manager: Melea Burghart
Parent Co: Rival Company

50074 White Oaks Frozen Foods
2525 Cooper Ave
Merced, CA 95348-4313 209-725-9492
Fax: 209-725-9441
www.whiteoakfrozenfoods.com
Reduced Moisture (RM) vegetable ingredients processor.
President: Jack Sollazzo
CEO: Suvan Sharma
Vice President, Sales: Dan Wilkinson
Number Employees: 1-4
Parent Co: Cascade Specialties, Inc.
Regions Exported to: South America, Europe, Asia, Canada, Mexico, Australia

50075 White Rabbit Dye Inc
4265 Meramec St
St Louis, MO 63116-2615 314-664-6563
Fax: 314-664-5563 800-466-6588
info@whiterabbitdye.com
www.whiterabbitdye.com
Easter egg dyes, kits and food colors; also, wire dippers; exporter of dry food colors
Co-Owner: Julie Consolino
Co-Owner: Jeff Petroski
Estimated Sales: $5-10 Million
Number Employees: 10-19
Square Footage: 32000
Parent Co: Premier Packaging
Type of Packaging: Consumer
Brands Exported: White Rabbit
Regions Exported to: Europe
Percentage of Business in Exporting: 25

Importers & Exporters / A-Z

50076 White Rock Products Corp
14107 20th Ave # 403
Flushing, NY 11357-3045   718-746-3400
       Fax: 718-767-0413 800-969-7625
               info@whiterockbev.com
               www.whiterockbeverages.com
Processor and exporter of carbonated and noncarbonated soft drinks; also, mixes, iced teas, fruit drinks and spring water
President: Larry Bodkin
lbodkin@whiterockbev.com
Marketing Director: Larry Bodkin
Estimated Sales: Less Than $500,000
Number Employees: 5-9
Number of Brands: 6
Type of Packaging: Consumer, Food Service
Brands Exported: White Rock
Regions Exported to: Central America, South America, Asia, Middle East, Carribean
Percentage of Business in Exporting: 2

50077 White Toque
11 Enterprise Ave N
Secaucus, NJ 07094-2505   201-863-6699
       Fax: 201-863-2886 800-237-6936
               www.whitetoque.com
Frozen desserts, mushrooms, frozen vegetables, fruit purees, Preserves, Dijon mustard and canned escargot; importer of frozen fruits, hors d'oevres and baked goods, bakery products
CEO: Didier Amiel
d.amiel@whitetoque.com
CFO: Christian Schmurr
Marketing Director: Michele Adams
Sales Director: Bernard Dueles
Estimated Sales: $30-35 Million
Number Employees: 10-19
Number of Brands: 9
Number of Products: 150+
Square Footage: 35000
Type of Packaging: Food Service, Private Label, Bulk
Regions Exported to: South America, Europe
Percentage of Business in Exporting: 5
Brands Imported: Maille, Bonne Maman, LaFruitiere, Toque d'Alsace, Prolounat, Marie, Delifrance, Elevages Perigord
Regions Imported from: South America, Europe
Percentage of Business in Importing: 95

50078 White Way Sign & Maintenance
451 Kingston Ct
Mt Prospect, IL 60056   847-391-0200
       Fax: 847-642-0272 800-621-4122
Manufacturer and exporter of electronic message displays
President: Robert B Flannery Jr
VP of Sales: Robert Flannery
kcooper@amfam.net
Contact: Keisha Cooper
kcooper@amfam.net
Plant Mgr: Pete Tomaselli
Estimated Sales: $ 20 - 50 Million
Number Employees: 100-249
Regions Exported to: Central America, Europe
Percentage of Business in Exporting: 5

50079 Whitecliff Vineyard & Winery
331 McKinstry Rd.
Gardiner, NY 12525   845-255-4613
               www.whitecliffwine.com
Chardonnay, Riesling, Merlot, Malbec, Traminette, Ros,, other wine blends
Co-Founder/Co-Owner: Michael Migliore
Co-Founder/Co-Owner: Yancey Stanforth-Migliore
Year Founded: 1979
Number of Brands: 1
Number of Products: 19
Type of Packaging: Consumer, Private Label
Brands Exported: Whitecliff
Regions Exported to: USA

50080 Whitewave Foods Company
12002 Airport Way
Broomfield, CO 80021   303-635-4000
       Fax: 303-635-5504 www.whitewave.com
Dairy products
President: Blaine McPeak
SVP: Roger Theodoredis
Contact: James Blumberg
melissa.gillespie@gsk.com
Number Employees: 350

50081 Whitfield Olive
18 E Goepp Street
Bethlehem, PA 18018-2818   610-865-8245
       Fax: 610-865-8246 800-645-5637
Importer, exporter and wholesaler/distributor of capers, olives, peppercorn, giardiniera, pickles, peppers, olive oil and spices
President: Giel Millner
Number Employees: 10-19
Square Footage: 600000
Type of Packaging: Consumer, Food Service, Private Label, Bulk
Brands Imported: Whitfield; Perfecto; Falcon; Mount Rose; Country Day; Little Elves
Regions Imported from: Central America, South America, Europe, Middle East

50082 Whitfield Olive
18 W Goepp Street
Bethlehem, PA 18018-2706   610-865-8245
       Fax: 610-865-8246 800-645-5637
Importer, exporter and wholesaler/distributor of capers, olives, pepperoncini, giardiniera, pickles, peppers, olive oil and spices
President: Giel Millner
Sales/Marketing Executive: Danielle George
Estimated Sales: $3-5 Million
Number Employees: 10-19
Square Footage: 400000
Type of Packaging: Consumer, Food Service, Private Label, Bulk
Regions Exported to: Middle East
Percentage of Business in Exporting: 1
Brands Imported: Amico; Whitfield; Perfecto; Falcon; Mount Rose; Little Elves; Country Day
Regions Imported from: Central America, South America, Europe, Middle East, Australia, Canada, Mexico
Percentage of Business in Importing: 90

50083 (HQ)Whitford Corporation
33 Sproul Rd
Frazer, PA 19355   610-296-3200
       Fax: 610-647-4849 sales@whitfordww.com
               www.whitfordww.com
Manufacturer and exporter of nonstick coatings designed for food contact and food associated applications
President: David Willis Jr
Chief Administrative Officer: Joan Eberhardt
CFO: Brian Kilty
Marketing Director: John Badner
Contact: Daniel Brim
daniel.brim@whitfordww.com
Plant Manager: Scott De Bourke
Purchasing Manager: Jill Schultz
Estimated Sales: $ 30 - 50 Million
Number Employees: 100
Square Footage: 60000
Brands Exported: Xylan; Ultralon; Excalibur; Xylac; Eclipse
Regions Exported to: Worldwide
Percentage of Business in Exporting: 50

50084 Whiting & Davis
PO Box 1270
Attleboro Falls, MA 02763-0270   508-699-0214
       Fax: 508-643-9303 800-876-6374
               www.whitinganddavis.com/
Manufacturer, exporter and importer of stainless steel ring mesh safety protective clothing including gloves, aprons, arm and body gear
Director Sales/Marketing: Ron DiMarzio
Contact: David Youngerman
david.youngerman@whitingdavis.com
Estimated Sales: $ 5-10 Million
Number Employees: 100
Square Footage: 400000
Parent Co: WDC Holdings
Brands Exported: Whiting & Davis Safety
Regions Exported to: Worldwide
Percentage of Business in Exporting: 15
Regions Imported from: Worldwide
Percentage of Business in Importing: 15

50085 Whitley Manufacturing Company
PO Box 112
Midland, NC 28107   704-888-2625
       Fax: 704-888-3023 www.whitleyhandle.com
Mop, broom and shovel handles; importer of dowels
President: Arlene Whitley
CEO: A Whitley
Quality Control: Arlene Whitley
Estimated Sales: $ 20 - 50 Million
Number Employees: 20-49
Square Footage: 35000
Regions Imported from: Central America, Asia
Percentage of Business in Importing: 80

50086 Whitley Peanut Factory Inc
2371 Hayes Rd
Hayes, VA 23072-3516   804-642-7688
       Fax: 804-642-7658 800-470-2244
               customercare@whitleyspeanut.com
               www.whitleyspeanut.com
Peanuts, almonds, cashews, mixed nuts, pecans and honey-roasted, brazil nuts and filberts; Virginia hams.
President: Craig Smith
VP Sales: James Scannell
Estimated Sales: $590000
Number Employees: 20-49
Type of Packaging: Consumer, Food Service, Private Label, Bulk
Brands Exported: The Peanut Factory; Flavor Crunch
Regions Exported to: Worldwide
Percentage of Business in Exporting: 10
Regions Imported from: Central America, South America, Asia
Percentage of Business in Importing: 20

50087 Whole Herb Co
19800 8th St E
Sonoma, CA 95476-3805   707-935-1077
       Fax: 707-935-3447 sales@wholeherbcompany.com
               www.berjeinc.com
Raw material supplier of herbs, spices, botanicals, spice blends, extracts and essential oils.
Manager: Holly Sherwood
Number Employees: 20-49
Square Footage: 50000
Parent Co: Berj, Inc.
Type of Packaging: Food Service, Bulk
Regions Exported to: Central America, Asia, Canada, Mexico
Regions Imported from: South America, Europe, Asia

50088 Wholesome!
14141 Southwest Freeway
Suite 160
Sugar Land, TX 77478
                    800-680-1896
               wholesomesweet.com
Fair trade, organic sweeteners.
CEO: Nigel Willerton
Contact: Dawn Archer
dawn.archer@wholesomesweet.com
Number Employees: 50
Parent Co: Arlon Group
Type of Packaging: Food Service, Bulk
Brands Exported: Sucanat
Regions Exported to: South America
Percentage of Business in Exporting: 25

50089 Wick's Packaging Service
7545 S State Road 75
Cutler, IN 46920   574-967-3104
       Fax: 765-268-2729 info@wickspackaging.com
               www.wickspackaging.com
Manufacturer and exporter of rebuilt vertical form/fill/seal packaging machinery. Distribute plastic pouch making machinery: T-shirt, standup zip lock pouch, and wicketed bags
Owner: Steven Wickersham
Vice President: Barb Wickersham
Research & Development: Craig Wickersham
Contact: Shawn Wickersham
shawn@wickspackaging.com
Packaging Engineer: Shawn Wickersham
Production Manager: Jerry Reef Jr
Estimated Sales: $2.5-5 Million
Number Employees: 1-4
Square Footage: 28000
Type of Packaging: Consumer, Food Service, Private Label, Bulk
Regions Exported to: Canada
Percentage of Business in Exporting: 5

50090 Wicklund Farms
3959 Maple Island Farm Rd
Springfield, OR 97477   541-747-5998
       Fax: 541-747-7299
Processor and exporter of spiced green beans and bean relish
President: Larry Wicklund

Estimated Sales: $1600000
Number Employees: 6
Type of Packaging: Consumer, Food Service, Private Label, Bulk
Regions Exported to: Canada

50091 Wiegardt Brothers
3215 273rd Street
Nahcotta, WA 98637
360-665-4111
Fax: 360-665-4950
Manufacturer and exporter of fresh oysters
President: Fritz Wiegardt
Estimated Sales: $10-20 Million
Number Employees: 50-99
Type of Packaging: Consumer
Brands Exported: Jolly Roger
Regions Exported to: Canada

50092 Wika Instrument LP
1000 Wiegand Blvd
Lawrenceville, GA 30043-5868
770-513-8200
Fax: 770-338-5118 800-645-0606
info@wika.us www.wika.us
Full line of mechanical and electronic pressure instruments, temperature instruments and diaphram seals manufactured to stric ISO 9001 standards
President: Dave Wannamaker
Estimated Sales: $ 20 - 50 Million
Number Employees: 500-999
Square Footage: 225000
Parent Co: Wika Instrument Corporation
Brands Exported: Trend
Regions Exported to: Worldwide
Percentage of Business in Exporting: 25

50093 Wilbur Curtis Co
6913 W Acco St
Montebello, CA 90640-5403
323-837-2300
Fax: 323-837-2406 800-421-6150
info@wilburcurtis.com www.wilburcurtis.com
Manufacturer and exporter of coffee and tea brewing equipment
CEO: Kevin Curtis
krcurtis@wilburcurtis.com
COO: Joe Laws
Estimated Sales: $ 30 - 50 Million
Number Employees: 100-249
Square Footage: 105000
Regions Exported to: Worldwide
Percentage of Business in Exporting: 5

50094 Wilch Manufacturing
1345 SW 42nd Street
Topeka, KS 66609-1267
785-267-2762
Fax: 785-267-6825
Manufacturer and exporter of ice cream blenders, cooking grills, freezers and dispensers including slush, cocktail, yogurt and soft serve
President: Bill Young
Sales: Dave White
Purchasing Manager: Dee Kuhn
Number Employees: 45
Square Footage: 102000
Brands Exported: Wilch
Regions Exported to: Central America, South America, Europe, Asia, Middle East
Brands Imported: GBG
Regions Imported from: Europe

50095 Wild Bill's Foods
200 Knauss Ave
Martinsville, VA 24112
276-656-3500
Fax: 717-295-9722 800-848-3236
www.wildbillsfoods.com
Beef jerky
General Manager/Public Relations: Michael Kane
CFO: Steve Woelkers
CEO: Phil Clemmens
R&D/Quality Control: Greg Rhinier
Marketing Director: John Connell
Sales Manager: Teresa Musser
Operations/Plant Manager: Steve Groff
Production Manager: Armando Torres
Estimated Sales: $10-15 Million
Number Employees: 20-49
Parent Co: Clemens Family Coporation
Type of Packaging: Consumer, Bulk
Brands Exported: Wild Bill's Foods Jerky
Regions Exported to: Canada
Percentage of Business in Exporting: 5

50096 (HQ)Wild Rice Exchange
1277 Santa Anita Ct
Woodland, CA 95776
530-669-0150
Fax: 530-668-9317 800-223-7423
thewildriceexch@aol.com www.wildrice.org
Processor, importer and exporter of wild rice, products and blends including basmati, arborio, red gourmet rices, organic, brown and polished white; also, quick-cook, frozen and pre-mixed pilaf; large line of specialty beans
Manager: Carlos Zambello
Sales: Carlos Zambello
Production: Golnar Emam
Type of Packaging: Consumer, Food Service, Private Label, Bulk
Brands Exported: Gourmet Valley/Great Valley
Regions Exported to: Central America, South America, Europe, Asia, Middle East
Regions Imported from: South America

50097 Wild Thyme Cottage Products
127-B Donegani
Pointe Claire, QC H9R 5E9
Canada
514-695-3602
Fax: 514-695-3602
Processor and exporter of jams, jellies, marmalades, relishes and chutneys
President: David Ranlings
Number Employees: 1-4
Number of Brands: 1
Number of Products: 50
Square Footage: 2800
Type of Packaging: Consumer, Food Service
Brands Exported: Wild Thyme Cottage Products
Regions Exported to: Asia, USA
Percentage of Business in Exporting: 1

50098 Wilder Manufacturing Company
41 Mechanic St
Port Jervis, NY 12771
845-856-5188
Fax: 845-856-1950 800-832-1319
Manufacturer and exporter of holding, warming and transporting equipment including proofing cabinets, bins, racks, utility tables, etc
VP Sales/Marketing: Ray Addington
Estimated Sales: $ 1 - 5 Million
Parent Co: Win-Holt Equipment Group
Type of Packaging: Food Service
Regions Exported to: Central America, South America, Asia, Middle East, Canada, Mexico
Percentage of Business in Exporting: 5

50099 Wileman Brothers & Elliott Inc
40232 Road 128
Cutler, CA 93615-2104
559-528-4772
Fax: 559-528-2456 info@mr-sunshine.com
Offers a full line of California citrus products
President: Frank Elliott III
CEO: Tommy Elliott
CFO: Brian Johnson
brian@mr-sunshine.com
Research & Development: Brad McCord
Quality Control: Raul Lopez
Sales Manager: Andrew Felts
Public Relations: Truman McGuire
Operations Manager: Manuel Guillen
Production Manager: Mark Savage
Plant Manager: Jon Hornburg
Estimated Sales: $930,000
Number Employees: 100-249
Square Footage: 16110
Type of Packaging: Consumer, Food Service, Private Label, Bulk
Brands Exported: Mr. Sunshine; BlueBird; Look; Stop
Regions Exported to: Central America, South America, Europe, Asia, Middle East, Australia/New Zealand
Percentage of Business in Exporting: 40

50100 Wilen Professional Cleaning Products
3760 Southside Industrial Pkwy
Atlanta, GA 30354-3219
404-366-2111
Fax: 404-361-8832 800-241-7371
www.wilen.com
Manufacturer and exporter of cleaning equipment and supplies including brushes, scouring and hand pads and floor/carpet products
President: Vance Perry
Quality Control: Rachael Alexander
VP Marketing/Customer Relations: Rhonda Lassiter
Production Manager: John Akin
Purchasing Manager: Norris Minnis
Estimated Sales: $ 75 - 100 Million
Number Employees: 100-249
Square Footage: 150000
Regions Exported to: Central America, Canada, Mexico
Percentage of Business in Exporting: 5

50101 Wilevco Inc
10 Fortune Dr
Billerica, MA 01821-3996
978-667-0400
Fax: 978-670-9191 sales@wilevco.com
www.wilevco.com
Manufacturer and exporter of automatic batter control systems, rotary atomization spray applicators and swept surface heat exchangers for process chilling systems
President: Leverett P Flint
Chairman/Founder: Putnam Flint
Vice President: John Whitmore
Estimated Sales: Below $ 5 Million
Number Employees: 10-19
Square Footage: 32000
Brands Exported: Wilevco Batter Systems; Cryolator; RAS Applicator
Regions Exported to: Worldwide
Percentage of Business in Exporting: 15

50102 Wilke International Inc
14321 W 96th Ter
Lenexa, KS 66215-4709
913-438-5544
Fax: 913-438-5554 800-779-5545
whw@wilkeinternational.com
www.wilkeinternational.com
Processor, importer, exporter and wholesaler/distributor of lactic acid, lactates, sports nutrition and dietary supplements
President: Wayne Wilke
wwilke@wilkeinternational.com
Director Administration: John Veazey
General Manager: James France
Estimated Sales: $ 5 - 10 Million
Number Employees: 10-19
Type of Packaging: Bulk
Brands Exported: NutraSense
Regions Exported to: Worldwide
Regions Imported from: Asia

50103 Wilkens-Anderson Co
4525 W Division St
Chicago, IL 60651-1674
773-384-4433
Fax: 773-384-6260 800-847-2222
waco@wacolab.com www.wacolab.com
Laboratory and quality control equipment, supplies instruments and chemicals can testing equipment, can seam evaluation equipment
President/CEO: Bruce Wilkens
info@waco-lab-supply.com
Marketing Director: Peter Thomases
Sales Director: Don Hartman
Operations Manager: Eric Jensen
Production Manager: Don Lamonica
Estimated Sales: $6-8 Million
Number Employees: 20-49
Square Footage: 220000
Regions Exported to: Worldwide
Percentage of Business in Exporting: 25

50104 (HQ)Wilkie Brothers Conveyor Inc
1765 Michigan Ave # 2
PO Box 219
Marysville, MI 48040-2046
810-364-4820
Fax: 810-364-4824 www.wilkiebros.com
Manufacturer and exporter of new and reconditioned overhead conveyor systems and equipment including chains, trolleys, attachments and structural components
Owner: Paul Naz
pnaz@wilkiebros.com
Sales Manager: Robert Wilkie
Sales: John Moews
Estimated Sales: $2.5-5 Million
Number Employees: 20-49
Square Footage: 240000
Type of Packaging: Bulk
Regions Exported to: Worldwide
Percentage of Business in Exporting: 10

Importers & Exporters / A-Z

50105 (HQ)Wilkins Rogers Inc
27 Frederick Rd
Ellicott City, MD 21043-4759   410-465-5800
Fax: 410-750-0163 consumer@wrmills.com
www.wrmills.com
Processor and exporter of flour, corn meal, baking mixes, breading and batters
President: Samuel Rogers
Joint CEO: Samuel Rogers
Joint CEO: Tom Rogers
black@wrmills.com
CEO: Sam Rogers Jr
General Manager: James Koehnlein
Director Sales/Marketing: Steve Friesner
Director/Operations: Aaron Black
Estimated Sales: $27,900,000
Number Employees: 100-249
Square Footage: 180000
Type of Packaging: Consumer, Food Service, Private Label, Bulk
Brands Exported: Indian Head; Washington; Raga Muffins
Regions Exported to: South America, Europe, Asia, Canada

50106 (HQ)Wilkinson ManufacturingCompany
PO Box 490
Fort Calhoun, NE 68023   402-468-5511
Fax: 402-468-5521 info@wilkmfg.com
Manufacturer and exporter of aluminum foil pans
President: Bob Dalziel
R&D: Ray Massey Jr
Quality Control: Claude Weimcr
Director Marketing: Ray Salinas
Contact: Joseph Richardson
j.richardson@wilkinsonindustries.com
Estimated Sales: $ 30 - 50 Million
Number Employees: 250-499
Type of Packaging: Consumer, Food Service
Regions Exported to: Worldwide

50107 Will-Pak Foods
3350 Shelby Street
Suite 200
Ontario, CA 91764-5556   909-945-4554
Fax: 909-899-7822   800-874-0883
taste_adv@earthlink.net www.tasteadventure.com
All-natural foods including soups, beans, chilies, and side dishes
President: Gary Morris
Estimated Sales: $990,000
Number Employees: 10
Square Footage: 40000
Type of Packaging: Food Service, Private Label, Bulk
Brands Exported: Taste Adventure
Regions Exported to: Canada
Percentage of Business in Exporting: 10

50108 Willamette Industries
PO Box 666
Beaverton, OR 97075-0666   503-641-1131
Fax: 503-526-8830 www.weyerhaeuser.com
Manufacturer and exporter of corrugated boxes and folding cartons
Plant Manager: David Dickey
Sales Manager: Brent Wagner
Estimated Sales: $20-50 Million
Number Employees: 100-249
Parent Co: Willamette Industries
Regions Exported to: Worldwide

50109 Willamette Industries
2300 Greene Way
Louisville, KY 40220-4040   502-753-0264
Fax: 502-753-0276   800-465-3065
Manufacturer and exporter of liquid bulk one-way disposable containers
Manager: Jim Woolums
General Manager: Larry Ogle
Sales Manager (Liquid Systems): H Edwin Cross
Estimated Sales: $ 50-100 Million
Number Employees: 5-9
Regions Exported to: Central America, Canada

50110 Willamette Valley Walnuts
475 NE 17th Street
PO Box 1007
McMinnville, OR 97128-3326   503-472-3215
Fax: 503-472-3294
wine@walnutcitywineworks.com
www.walnutcitywineworks.com
Processor and exporter of shelled walnuts and English walnut meats
Owner: Zac Spence
VP: Todd Heidgerken
Brand Manager: Andrew Minor
General Manager: John Gilpin
Winemakers: John Davidson
Estimated Sales: $500,000-$1 Million
Number Employees: 1-4
Type of Packaging: Consumer, Food Service, Private Label, Bulk
Brands Exported: Oregon Full Flavor; Select Orchard
Regions Exported to: South America, Europe, Canada
Percentage of Business in Exporting: 55

50111 William Bernstein Company
155 W 72nd St Rm 301
New York, NY 10023   212-799-3200
Fax: 212-799-3209
Importer and exporter of gums/incense including frankincense, olibanum, myrrh, benzoin and shellac, apricot kernels, tonka beans and camphor tablets
Owner: E Bernstein
Contact: Daisy Renigan
wbernsteinco@aol.com
Operations: Daisy Renigan
Estimated Sales: $ 1 - 3 Million
Number Employees: 1-4
Brands Imported: Dragon Fly; Gum Olibanum/Frankincense; Gum Myrrh
Regions Imported from: Asia
Percentage of Business in Importing: 75

50112 William E. Martin & Sons Company
55 Bryant Avenue
Suite 300
Roslyn, NY 11576   516-605-2444
Fax: 516-605-2442 mail@martinspices.com
www.martinspices.com
Processor, wholesaler/distributor, exporter and importer of spices, seasonings, salts, herbs and herbal supplements, seeds, powders and raisins. Wholesaler/distributor of dehydrated onion and garlic products, full line of ground spicesand bakery seeds
Owner: William Martin Jr
Contact: Martin Spencer
spencer@martinspices.com
Estimated Sales: $ 10 - 20 Million
Number Employees: 22
Number of Brands: 1
Square Footage: 60000
Type of Packaging: Bulk
Regions Exported to: Worldwide
Percentage of Business in Exporting: 10
Regions Imported from: Worldwide
Percentage of Business in Importing: 70

50113 Williams Refrigeration
65 Park Ave
Hillsdale, NJ 07642-2109   201-358-6005
Fax: 201-358-0401   800-445-9979
williamsref@msn.com
www.williams-refrigeration.co.uk
Manufacturer and exporter of commercial refrigeration equipment including blast chillers and reach-in, roll-in and counter refrigerators
Owner: William Gesner
william@williams-refrigeration.co.uk
VP: Nicholas Williams
Engineering Director: Steve Bernard
Marketing Director: Malcolm Harling
Sales Manager: Andy Ward
Purchasing Manager: Lynette Wixey
Number Employees: 250-499
Square Footage: 1400000
Parent Co: Williams Refrigeration
Type of Packaging: Food Service
Brands Exported: Williams
Regions Exported to: Europe, Asia, Middle East
Percentage of Business in Exporting: 25

50114 Williams Resource & Associates
1200 California Street
Suite 255
Redlands, CA 92374   909-748-7671
Fax: 909-748-7621
Dairy products for industrial food processors, milk powder, butter, cheese
CEO: H. G. Richard Williams
Operations Manager: Breanna Lucier
Estimated Sales: $2.5-5 Million
Number Employees: 1-4
Type of Packaging: Food Service, Bulk

50115 Williamson & Co
9 Shelter Dr
Greer, SC 29650-4818   864-848-1011
Fax: 864-848-4310   800-849-3263
www.williamsonandcompany.com
Manufacturer and exporter of automated packaging, data collection and material handling systems, transport trucks and jacks.
President: Dan Williamson
dwilliamson@williamsonandcompany.com
Chief Financial Officer: Larry Williamson
VP: Lester Collins
Operations: Gene Settles
Estimated Sales: $ 5 - 10 Million
Number Employees: 50-99
Regions Exported to: Central America, South America, Asia
Percentage of Business in Exporting: 2

50116 Willing Group
222 Saint Johns Avenue
Yonkers, NY 10704-2717   914-964-5800
Fax: 914-964-5293 cgctradingintl@aol.com
President: Louis J Goldstein
CEO: Carmela P Goldstein
CFO: Peter L Gallucci
Estimated Sales: $ 10 - 20 Million
Number Employees: 20
Square Footage: 15000
Type of Packaging: Consumer, Food Service, Private Label, Bulk
Regions Exported to: Central America, South America, Europe, Asia, Middle East
Percentage of Business in Exporting: 70
Regions Imported from: Central America, South America, Europe, Middle East
Percentage of Business in Importing: 20

50117 Willmark Sales Company
33 Nassau Ave
Brooklyn, NY 11222-3132   718-388-7141
Fax: 718-963-3924
Processor and exporter of bakery ingredients
President: Robert Leibowitz
willmark01@aol.com
VP: Edward Leibowitz
Estimated Sales: $5-10 Million
Number Employees: 50-99
Regions Exported to: Caribbean, Middle East
Regions Imported from: Mexico

50118 Willow Group LTD
34 Clinton St
Batavia, NY 14020   585-344-2900
Fax: 585-344-0044   800-724-7300
www.willowgroupltd.com
Wicker baskets.
Co-Owner: Bernard Skalny
bernards@willowgroupltd.com
Co-Owner: James Walsh
Year Founded: 1928
Estimated Sales: $20-50 Million
Number Employees: 1-4
Regions Imported from: Europe, Asia, Middle East, Worldwide

50119 (HQ)Wilson AL Chemical Co
1050 Harrison Ave
Kearny, NJ 07032-5941   201-997-3300
Fax: 201-997-5122   800-526-1188
help@alwilson.com www.alwilson.com
Manufacturer and exporter of laundry and dry cleaning stain removers
President: Bob Edwards
bob@alwilson.com
Estimated Sales: $ 10 - 20 Million
Number Employees: 10-19

50120 Wilton Armetale
903 Square St
Mt Joy, PA 17552-1911   717-653-4444
Fax: 717-653-6573   800-779-4586
kadams@armetale.com www.armetale.com
Manufacturer and exporter of metal tabletop ware and salad bar accessories
President: Ed Leibensperger
eleibensperger@armetale.com
Estimated Sales: $ 1 - 5 Million
Number Employees: 50-99

Importers & Exporters / A-Z

Regions Exported to: Central America, South America, Europe, Asia, Middle East

50121 (HQ)Wilton Brands LLC
2240 75th St
Woodridge, IL 60517-2333   630-963-7100
Fax: 630-810-2712 info@wilton.com
www.wilton.com
Manufacturer and exporter of kitchenware including bakeware, cake decorating supplies, tools and gadgets; also, picture frames
President: Danielle Detten
CEO: Sue Buchta
sbuchta@wilton.com
Chief Financial Officer: Tom Kasvin
Chief Operating Officer: Mary Merfeld
Estimated Sales: $ 50 Million
Number Employees: 500-999
Square Footage: 1000000
Brands Exported: Wilton; Copco; Rowoco; Weston Gallery
Regions Exported to: Worldwide

50122 Win-Holt Equipment Group
141 Eileen Way
Syosset, NY 11791   516-222-0335
Fax: 516-921-0538 800-444-3595
sales@winholt.com www.winholt.com
Material and food handling equipment, food service equipment and heating, holding and transporting equipment
President/ COO: Dominic Scarfogliero
Chairman, Chief Executive Officer: Jonathan J Holtz
R&D: Nancy Korista
Marketing Director: Bruce Schwartz
Sales Director: Jeff Herbert
Sales: Tim Sullivan
President, Chief Operating Officer: Dominick Scarfogliero
VP Operations: John Jameson
Purchasing Manager: Glen Stein
Estimated Sales: $ 10 - 20 Million
Number Employees: 300-500
Number of Brands: 4
Number of Products: 200
Regions Exported to: Worldwide
Percentage of Business in Exporting: 1

50123 Windsor Industries Inc
1351 W Stanford Ave
Englewood, CO 80110-5545   303-781-4833
Fax: 866-271-0520 800-444-7654
Manufacturer and exporter of carpet and floor maintenance equipment including wet/dry vacuums, automatic scrubbers, carpet extractors, pressure washers and polishers
CEO: Elliot Younessian
elliot.younessian@windsorind.com
Financial Services Manager: Pete Dewlaney
Technical Support Manager: Joel Yourzek
Distribution Manager: Mary Millibrandt
Estimated Sales: $ 75-100 Million
Number Employees: 250-499
Parent Co: Alfred Karcher GmbH & Co. KG
Type of Packaging: Food Service
Brands Exported: Versamatic; Fastraction; Powertree Scrubbers; Mr. Steam; Lightening Polishers
Regions Exported to: Central America, South America, Europe, Asia, Middle East
Percentage of Business in Exporting: 12

50124 (HQ)Windsor Wax Co Inc
510 Carolina Back Rd
Charlestown, RI 02813-3809   401-364-5941
Fax: 401-364-3729 800-243-8929
Manufacturer and exporter of floor care products including wax, polymer finishes, cleaning compounds, carpet cleaner and concrete coatings; importer of natural wax and paraffin
Office Manager: M Wojcik
CEO: D Kahn
CEO: David Kahn
Number Employees: 1-4
Brands Exported: CAB; Woodee; Konkrete; Winsom
Regions Exported to: Central America, South America, Europe, Asia, Australia, Latin America, Canada, Mexico, Caribbean
Percentage of Business in Exporting: 12
Regions Imported from: Central America, South America, Australia
Percentage of Business in Importing: 5

50125 Wine Chillers of California
1104 E 17th St Ste F
Santa Ana, CA 92701   714-541-5795
Fax: 714-541-3139 800-331-4274
Custom builder and provider of wine chilling equipment.
President: Robert Sizemore
CEO: D Sizemore
Estimated Sales: $ .5 - 1,000,000
Number Employees: 1-4
Square Footage: 4000000
Brands Exported: Vinotheque; Vinotemp; Wine Keeper; Vinocave; Wine Well; Marvelu - Line; Breezaire
Regions Exported to: Central America, South America, Europe, Asia

50126 Wine Well Chiller Co
301 Brewster Rd # 3c
Milford, CT 06460-3700   203-878-2465
Fax: 203-878-2466 winewellchiller@aol.com
www.epichead.com
Manufacturer and exporter of high-speed beverage chillers including wine
Owner: Tyrone Petr
CEO/President: Anabel Fisher
Sales: Melissa Lawless
winewellchiller@aol.com
Production: Tyrone P
Estimated Sales: $ 1 - 3 Million
Number Employees: 5-9
Square Footage: 4000
Brands Exported: Wine Well; Microchiller
Regions Exported to: South America, Europe, Middle East
Percentage of Business in Exporting: 2

50127 Wine World Wide
PO Box 1161
New Paltz, NY 12561-7161   845-255-1955
Fax: 845-255-3516 info@mediterraneanwine.com
www.mediterraneanwine.com
Wine
Director of Sales: Sam Ramic
Controller: Jessica Rumsey
Estimated Sales: $2.4 Million
Number Employees: 11-50
Brands Imported: Barbaresco, Dolcetto D'Alba, Barolo, Gavi, Lugana, Valpolicella Ripasso, Chateau Lagrange Monbadon, La Fleur Grand Cru 1999 and more.
Regions Imported from: Italy, Mediterranean, Macedona

50128 Winekeeper
625 E Haley St
Santa Barbara, CA 93103   805-963-3451
Fax: 805-965-5393 www.winekeeper.com
Wome dispensing and wine cellaring equipment
President: Norman Grant
Contact: Connie Grant
connie@winaire.com
Number Employees: 5-9
Parent Co: Winekeeper
Brands Exported: Winekeeper
Regions Exported to: Central America, South America, Europe, Asia, Middle East

50129 Wineracks by Marcus
PO Box 2713
Costa Mesa, CA 92628-2713   714-546-4922
Fax: 714-549-8238
Wineracks By Marcus; a strong, accessible, space-efficient aluminum racks with a sharp, clean look for restaurants, serious collectors and retail. Manufactured to order, custom sizes and layout drawings available
President: Steve Marcus
Estimated Sales: $300,000-500,000
Number Employees: 1-4

50130 Wing Nien Food
30560 San Antonio St
Hayward, CA 94544-7102   510-487-8877
Fax: 510-489-6666 ghall@wnfoods.com
www.wnfoods.com
Processor and packager of sauces, oils, salsa, mustard and syrups; exporter of organic oils and sauces; also, custom blending and packaging in portion packs, glass bottles and plastic containers available
Manager: Linda Lee
Manager: Margaret Liang
mliang@wnfoods.com
Plant Superintendent: Jon Choy
Estimated Sales: $ 10 - 20 Million
Number Employees: 20-49
Square Footage: 135000
Parent Co: US Enterprise Corporation
Type of Packaging: Consumer, Food Service, Private Label
Other Locations:
  Wing Nien Co.
  Vancouver, BCWing Nien Co.
Regions Exported to: Asia
Percentage of Business in Exporting: 5

50131 (HQ)Wing Sing Chong Company
152 Utah Avenue
Suite 140
S San Francisco, CA 94080-6718   415-552-1234
Fax: 415-552-3812
Manufacturer, importer and wholesaler/distributor of Asian foods
Owner: Roberta Woo
Estimated Sales: $15 Million
Number Employees: 1-4
Square Footage: 150000
Regions Imported from: Asia
Percentage of Business in Importing: 70

50132 (HQ)Winmix/Natural Care Products
7466 Cape Girardeau Street
Englewood, FL 34224-8004   941-475-7432
Fax: 941-475-7432
Processor and exporter of soft serve ice cream and sorbets, meat analogs, fruit juice and beverage bases, low-fat replacers and nonfat mixes. Importer of juice and coffee bases.
Board of Directors: Winsor Eveland
Owner: Martha Efird
Estimated Sales: $100000
Number Employees: 2
Number of Products: 350
Square Footage: 8000
Type of Packaging: Consumer, Food Service, Private Label, Bulk
Brands Exported: Winmix; Multy Grain Foods; SoyFlax 5000; Citrussoy 5000; Prostalgin
Regions Exported to: Central America, South America, Europe, Asia
Percentage of Business in Exporting: 15
Brands Imported: Ingredients Only
Regions Imported from: South America, Asia
Percentage of Business in Importing: 10

50133 (HQ)Winning Solutions Inc
3810 Conflans Rd
Irving, TX 75061-3915   972-986-5355
Fax: 972-986-5337 800-899-2563
info@miracleofaloe.com www.miracleofaloe.com
Processor and exporter of aloe vera gel drinks, juice blends, etc
Owner: Jess Clarke
winninginc@aol.com
Estimated Sales: $500,000-$1 Million
Number Employees: 10-19
Square Footage: 8000
Type of Packaging: Consumer, Food Service
Other Locations:
  Winning Solutions
  Westport, CTWinning Solutions
Brands Exported: Miracle of Aloe
Regions Exported to: South America, Europe, Middle East, Australia
Percentage of Business in Exporting: 20

50134 Winpak Portion Packaging
998 South Sierra Way
San Bernardino, CA 92408   909-885-0715
Fax: 909-381-1934 800-804-4224
www.winpak.com
Manufacturer and exporter of pre-formed portion controlled plastic packaging. Diecut for lidding and filling equipment
President: Thomas Herlihy
Vice President: Jim McMacken
Marketing Director: Debbie Calvarese
Contact: Kathy Boynton
kathy.boynton@winpak.com
Number Employees: 225
Parent Co: Winpak
Type of Packaging: Consumer, Food Service, Private Label
Regions Exported to: Europe

Importers & Exporters / A-Z

50135 Winpak Technologies
85 Laird Drive
Toronto, ON M4G 3T8
Canada
416-421-1700
Fax: 416-421-7957
Packaging
Director Sales & Marketing: L de Bellefeuille
Manufacturing: J Millwrad
Estimated Sales: $ 1 - 5 Million
Number Employees: 250
Square Footage: 600000
Parent Co: Winpak
Regions Exported to: Central America, Europe, USA
Percentage of Business in Exporting: 35

50136 Winston Industries
2345 Carton Dr
Louisville, KY 40299-2513
502-495-5500
Fax: 502-495-5458 800-234-5286
information@winstonind.com
www.winstonind.com
Manufacturer and exporter of stainless steel ovens, pressure cookers and holding cabinets
President/ CEO: Valerie Shelton
vshelton@winstonind.com
Quality Control: Tina Thompson
CFO: Bob Leavitt
VP Global Sales: Shaun Tanner
COO: Paul Haviland
VP Manufacturing: Leo Gutgsell
Estimated Sales: $ 10 - 20 Million
Number Employees: 100-249
Type of Packaging: Food Service
Brands Exported: CVAP, COLLECTRAMATIC
Regions Exported to: Worldwide

50137 Winzen Film
P.O.Box 677
407 West 2nd Street
Taylor, TX 76574
903-885-7595
Fax: 903-885-4702 800-779-7595
www.winzen.com
Manufacturer and exporter of plastic container materials
Manager: Frank Neidhart
CEO: Robert Williamson
Estimated Sales: $ 10 - 20 Million
Number Employees: 20-49
Parent Co: BAG Corporation

50138 Wire Belt Co Of America
154 Harvey Rd
Londonderry, NH 03053-7473
603-644-2500
Fax: 603-644-3600 sales@wirebelt.com
Stainless steel open-mesh conveyor belting
President: David Greer
dgreer@wirebelt.com
Marketing Director: Richard Spiak
Sales: Richard Spiak
Operations: Scott Monk
Estimated Sales: $20-50 Million
Number Employees: 100-249
Brands Exported: Flat-Flex; Flat-Flex XT; Eye-Flex; CompactGrid; EZSlice; C-CureEdge; TC-327; Carry Smart Conveyors; Flex-Turn Conveyors
Regions Exported to: Central America, South America, Europe

50139 Wire Products Mfg
1000 Mathews St
Merrill, WI 54452-2837
715-536-7884
Fax: 715-536-1476
Manufacturer and exporter of wire racks including display and fryer
President: Roger C Dupke
Manager: Jim Dupke
Estimated Sales: $20-50 Million
Number Employees: 20-49
Type of Packaging: Consumer, Food Service, Bulk
Regions Exported to: Europe

50140 Wirefab Inc
75 Blackstone River Rd
Worcester, MA 01607-1493
508-754-5359
Fax: 508-797-3620 877-877-4445
info@wirefab.com www.wirefab.com
Manufacturer and exporter of wire baskets, shelving and racks including doughnut and bagel baskets and deep-fry crumb screens
Owner: A B Zakarian
wirefab@gis.net
CEO: A Zakarian
VP: M M Zakarian
R & D: Larry Clough
Sales: William Binson
wirefab@gis.net
Public Relations: Michael Murdock
Operations: John Michaels
Production: Christopher Bousbouras
Plant Manager: James Hall
Purchasing: Barbara Vasdagalis
Estimated Sales: $5-10 Million
Number Employees: 50-99
Square Footage: 160000
Type of Packaging: Bulk
Regions Exported to: Europe, Canada, Mexico
Percentage of Business in Exporting: 5

50141 Wiremaid Products Div
11711 W Sample Rd
Coral Springs, FL 33065-3155
954-545-9000
Fax: 954-545-9011 800-770-4700
info@vutec.com www.vutec.com
Manufacturer and exporter of wire and metal products including displays, racks, shelves, etc
Manager: Bryan Sciullo
CEO: Howard L Sinkoff
howardsinkoff@vutec.com
CFO: Jeff Chanoff
VP: Allen Axman
R&D: Hai Nguyen
Marketing: John Cavanaugh
Sales: Allen Axman
Production: Raul Passalaqua
Plant Manager: Raul Passalaqua
Purchasing: Robert Ciarletto
Estimated Sales: $20-50 Million
Number Employees: 1-4
Square Footage: 100000
Parent Co: Vutec Corporation
Brands Exported: Wiremaid USA; Fluorescent Liteguard

50142 Wisco Industries Assembly
955 Market St
Oregon, WI 53575-1009
608-835-3300
Fax: 608-835-7399 800-999-4726
info@wiscoind.com www.wiscoind.com
Counter top ovens and warmers for pizza, pretzels and cookies; exporter of pizza ovens, food warmers, toasters and sandwich grills
CEO: Elving Kjellstrom
Marketing Director: Donald Porkner
Sales Director: Randy Kjellstrom
Estimated Sales: $ 20 - 30 Million
Number Employees: 5-9
Square Footage: 200000
Regions Exported to: Worldwide
Percentage of Business in Exporting: 5

50143 Wisconsin Aluminum Foundry Co
838 S 16th St
Manitowoc, WI 54220-5004
920-682-8286
Fax: 920-682-7285 inquiries@wafco.com
www.wafco.com
Manufacturer and exporter of griddles,grills, can sealers, sterilizers, pressure cookers,cookware, etc... importer of cookware.
President: Jim Hatt
jhatt@wafco.com
CEO: Philip Jacobs
Quality Control: Don Noworatsky
Estimated Sales: $ 5 - 10 Million
Number Employees: 250-499
Number of Brands: 1
Type of Packaging: Consumer
Brands Exported: All-American; Chef's Design
Regions Exported to: Central America, South America, Europe, Asia, Middle East
Percentage of Business in Exporting: 20
Brands Imported: Cookware

50144 Wisconsin Box Co
929 Townline Rd
PO Box 718
Wausau, WI 54403-6681
715-842-2248
Fax: 715-842-2240 www.wisconsinbox.com
Manufacturer and exporter of wooden shipping containers and crates
Owner: Jeff Davis
CFO: Michael Shipway
Vice President of Sales: Gene Davis
jdavis@wisconsinbox.com
Customer Service: Jim Geise
Plant Manager: Bob Schultz
Plant Manager: Charley Ewell
Estimated Sales: $ 5 - 10 Million
Number Employees: 20-49
Type of Packaging: Bulk
Regions Exported to: Canada

50145 Wisconsin Box Co
929 Townline Rd
PO Box 718
Wausau, WI 54403-6681
715-842-2248
Fax: 715-842-2240 800-876-6658
garyl@tcrllc.com www.wisconsinbox.com
Manufacturer and exporter of wirebound and collapsible pallet boxes and crates
Owner: Jeff Davis
jdavis@wisconsinbox.com
CEO: Gary LeMaster
Sales Manager: Dennis Maxson
jdavis@wisconsinbox.com
Controller / Human Resources: Michael Shipway
Estimated Sales: $ 10 - 20 Million
Number Employees: 20-49
Square Footage: 150000
Regions Exported to: Europe, Middle East, Canada
Percentage of Business in Exporting: 2

50146 Wisconsin Cheeseman
3650 Milwaukee Street
Madison, WI 53714-2399
608-837-5166
Fax: 608-837-5493 800-693-0834
customerservice@wisconsincheeseman.com
www.wisconsincheeseman.com
Food gifts company, products include; cheese, sausage, chocolates, fruitcakes, candy, nuts & snacks, sugar free items
CFO: Jay Singer
VP: Francis Cremer
VP Sales & Marketing: Bret Jenkin
Type of Packaging: Consumer, Food Service, Private Label, Bulk
Regions Exported to: Asia, Canada, Mexico, Latin America

50147 Wisconsin Specialty Protein
222 West Washington Ave. # 250
Madison, WI 53703
info@teraswhey.com
Organic flavored whey protein powder; flavored fatty acid health oil
Founder: Tera Johnson
Number of Brands: 1
Type of Packaging: Consumer, Private Label
Brands Exported: tera's
Regions Exported to: USA, Canada

50148 Wisconsin Spice Inc
478 S Industrial Park Rd
PO Box 190
Berlin, WI 54923-2241
920-361-3555
Fax: 920-361-0818 info@wisconsinspice.com
www.unclephilsmustard.com
Manufacturer and exporter of gourmet spices and herbs, seasoning blends, dry mustard products and prepared liquid mustards
President: Phillip Sass
wispice@wisconsinspice.com
VP Marketing: John Clausen
VP Sales: Phillips Sass
Estimated Sales: $7 Million
Number Employees: 20-49
Type of Packaging: Consumer, Food Service, Private Label, Bulk
Regions Exported to: Worldwide
Percentage of Business in Exporting: 1

50149 Wisconsin Whey International
N2689 County Road South
Juda, WI 53550-9714
608-233-5101
Fax: 608-934-1044
Processor and exporter of kosher and HALAL approved whey products including edible lactose and whey protein concentrate
President/CEO: Nicolas Hanson
Sales Manager: Doug Clairday
Number Employees: 50-99
Square Footage: 95600
Type of Packaging: Bulk

Brands Exported: Wisconsin Whey International, Inc.
Regions Exported to: Central America, South America, Europe, Asia, Canada, Pacific Rim, Mexico, China, Taiwan, Indonesia, Malaysia
Percentage of Business in Exporting: 50

50150 Wishbone Utensil Tableware Line
15 Paramount Pkwy
Wheat Ridge, CO 80215-6615   303-238-8088
       Fax: 253-595-7673   866-266-5928
Forever replaces chopsticks. One piece tong, skewer & ergonomic utensil. Child safe. Dishwasher friendly. Assisted living compatible. Solution for the chopstick challenged. Popular among hotel/resorts, restaurateur and occupationalhealth. Ten motif-friendly colors. FDA approved. Stylish, durable, reusable, fun. Sanitized and individually wrapped. Gourmet quality Feng Shui tableware
CEO: R Farlan Krieger Sr
Estimated Sales: Under $300,000
Number Employees: 9
Number of Brands: 4
Number of Products: 8
Square Footage: 50000
Parent Co: RF Krieger, LLC
Type of Packaging: Consumer, Food Service, Private Label, Bulk
Brands Exported: Wishbone Utensil
Regions Exported to: Central America, South America, Europe, Asia
Percentage of Business in Exporting: 15

50151 Wittco Foodservice Equipment
7737 N 81st St
Milwaukee, WI 53223-3839   414-365-4400
       Fax: 414-354-2821   800-821-3912
       www.wittco.com
Manufacturer and exporter of carts including hot/cold food delivery and insulated tray; also, cook/chill equipment
Cmo: Jim Sherman
jsherman@wittco.com
Estimated Sales: $ 5 Million
Number Employees: 20-49
Square Footage: 180000
Parent Co: Nichols Industries
Type of Packaging: Food Service
Regions Exported to: South America, Asia, Middle East
Percentage of Business in Exporting: 10

50152 Wittco Foodservice Equipment
7737 N 81st St
Milwaukee, WI 53223-3839   414-365-4400
       Fax: 414-354-2821   800-367-8413
       www.wittco.com
Manufacturer and exporter of heated food holding equipment and cook/hold ovens
General Manager: Steve Jensen
CEO: Tim Murray
VP: Jeff Smith
Marketing: Joe Burns
Operations Manager: Dave Braun
Estimated Sales: $5-10 Million
Number Employees: 20-49
Regions Exported to: Worldwide
Percentage of Business in Exporting: 25

50153 Witte Co Inc
507 Route 31 S
Washington, NJ 7882   908-689-6500
       Fax: 908-537-6806   info@witte.com
       www.witte.com
Manufacturer and exporter of vibrating screens, conveyors, fluid bed dryers and coolers
President: Tyson Witte
Sales/Marketing: Jim Schak
Engineering Manager: Larry Stoma
Purchasing Manager: Marilyn March
Estimated Sales: $ 10 - 20,000,000
Number Employees: 1-4
Square Footage: 60000
Type of Packaging: Private Label
Brands Exported: Witte
Regions Exported to: Worldwide
Percentage of Business in Exporting: 45

50154 Wittemann Company
1 Industry Dr
Palm Coast, FL 32137   386-445-4200
       Fax: 386-445-7042   us@union.dk
       www.wittemann.com
Manufacturer and exporter of carbon dioxide generation and recovery systems; also, dryers, cylinder filling units and dry ice systems
President: William Geiger
General Manager: Bill Gieyer
CFO: Cara Brammer
Sales Manager: Gabreil Dominguez
Regional Sales Manager: Daniel Gruber
Contact: Donna Grabowski
donnag@wittemann.com
Product Manager: Jay Soto
Estimated Sales: $ 3 - 5 Million
Number Employees: 10-19
Square Footage: 120000
Regions Exported to: Central America, South America, Europe, Asia, Middle East, Australia
Percentage of Business in Exporting: 85

50155 (HQ)Wittern Group
8040 University Blvd
Clive, IA 50325-1171   515-274-3641
       Fax: 515-271-8530   855-712-8729
contact@vending.com   www.witternfin.com
Manufacturer and exporter of vending machines for snacks, canned and hot beverages, refrigerated and frozen foods, desserts, etc
Chairman of the Board: Francis Wittern
President/CEO/Secretary/Treasurer: John Bruntz
jbruntz@wittern.com
Chief Financial Officer: Craig Mile
Vice President, Data Processing: Dave Twedale
Chief Marketing Officer: Mike McGillis
Vice President, Sales: Mike Frye
Purchasing Manager: Ron Harter
Estimated Sales: $ 9 Million
Number Employees: 250-499
Square Footage: 420000
Parent Co: 8040 Holdings, Inc.
Brands Exported: Servomatic
Regions Exported to: Worldwide

50156 Wixson Honey Inc
4937 Lakemont Himrod Rd
Dundee, NY 14837-8820   607-243-7301
       Fax: 607-243-7143   800-363-8209
       www.wixsonhoney.com
Manufacturer and importer of honey including clover, buckwheat, orange, beeswax and fall flower
Owner: Jerald Howell
jerry@wixsonhoney.com
Estimated Sales: $3-5 Million
Number Employees: 5-9
Type of Packaging: Consumer, Food Service, Private Label, Bulk
Regions Imported from: Central America, South America, China

50157 Wizards Cauldron, LTD
878 Firetower Road
Yanceyville, NC 27379   336-694-5665
       Fax: 336-664-5284
Manufacturer and exporter of natural and organic salad dressing and sauces including barbecue, steak, soy, poultry, stir-fry, hot, table and vegetable
President: Sean Kearney
CEO: John Troy
Administration: Glenda Smith
Research & Development: Tina Toney
Quality Control: Jason Dawson
VP Sales and Marketing: Ron Rash
Contact: Steve Bailey
steve@wizardscauldron.com
Purchasing Manager: Sean Kearney
Number Employees: 5-9
Square Footage: 40000
Parent Co: Wizard's Cauldron
Type of Packaging: Consumer, Food Service, Private Label, Bulk
Brands Exported: Simply Delicious; Troy; Harbor-Lites; Flavors of the Rainforest; Mr. Spice
Regions Exported to: Europe, Canada
Percentage of Business in Exporting: 15

50158 Wolens Company
PO Box 560964
Dallas, TX 75356-0964   214-634-0800
       Fax: 214-634-0880
Manufacturer and exporter of plastic letters and signs
President: Steve Schwartz
Estimated Sales: $ 1-2.5 Million
Number Employees: 1-4
Regions Exported to: Worldwide

50159 Wolf Canyon Foods
27880 Dorris Dr Ste 200
Carmel, CA 93923   831-626-1323
       Fax: 831-626-1325   info@wolfcanyon.com
       www.wolfcanyon.com
Processor and exporter of freeze-dried fruits, vegetables, meat, seafood and dairy products
Founder: James Mercer
VP: Marybeth Frearson
Sales Manager: Carlos Forte
Estimated Sales: Under $500,000
Number Employees: 3
Square Footage: 320000
Type of Packaging: Bulk
Regions Exported to: Worldwide
Percentage of Business in Exporting: 25

50160 Wolf Company
3101 S 2nd St
Louisville, KY 40208-1446
       800-814-2028
       www.wolfequipment.com
Manufacturer and exporter of commercial gas broilers, fryers, griddles, ranges and ovens; also, household ranges and slide-ins.
Chairman & CEO, ITW: E. Scott Santi
Estimated Sales: $100-500 Million
Parent Co: ITW Food Equipment
Regions Exported to: Central America, South America, Europe, Asia, Middle East
Percentage of Business in Exporting: 10

50161 Wolfson Casing Corp
700 S Fulton Ave
Mt Vernon, NY 10550-5014   914-668-5754
       Fax: 914-668-6900   800-221-8042
Processor, exporter and importer of sausage casings.
CEO: Phiil Schartz
tschartz@dccasing.com
Executive VP: David Gordon
Estimated Sales: $26300000
Number Employees: 50-99
Square Footage: 40000
Regions Exported to: Central America, South America, Europe, Asia, Middle East
Percentage of Business in Exporting: 50
Regions Imported from: South America, Europe, Asia

50162 Womack International Inc
451 Azuar Ave
Vallejo, CA 94592-1148   707-647-2370
       Fax: 707-562-1010   www.womack.com
Manufacturer and exporter of food processing filters including multiple plate, vertical stack and pressure
President: Thomas H. Womack
CEO: Michael Oakes
oakes@womack.com
VP Engineer: Michael Oakes
VP Sales: Stanley Jennings
Estimated Sales: $ 3 - 5 Million
Number Employees: 20-49
Square Footage: 100000
Brands Exported: Micron One; Filter-Max
Regions Exported to: Worldwide
Percentage of Business in Exporting: 70

50163 (HQ)Wonderful Pistachios & Almonds
13646 Hwy 33
Lost Hills, CA 93249   661-797-6500
       www.wonderfulpistachiosandalmonds.com
Grower and processor of almonds and pistachios.
President: Stewart Resnick
Co-Founder: Lynda Resnick
CFO: Mike Hohmann
VP, Domestic Sales: Michael Celani
Media Contact: Steven Bram
steven.bram@Wonderful.Com
Estimated Sales: $111 Million
Number Employees: 20-49
Square Footage: 15000
Other Locations:
    Plant and Farming Facility
    Lost Hills, CAPlant and Farming Facility
Brands Exported: Sunkist and Everybody's Nuts
Regions Exported to: Worldwide
Percentage of Business in Exporting: 50

Importers & Exporters / A-Z

50164 Wonton Food
220-222 Moore St
Brooklyn, NY 11206-3744   718-628-6868
       Fax: 718-628-1028   800-776-8889
goldenbowl@wontonfood.com
www.wontonfood.com
Producer of fortune cookies, eggroll and wonton skins, dry and fresh noodles including chow mein, lo mein, spinach and wonton; Importer of oriental canned and dry goods
President: Sing Lee
CEO: Norman Wong
CFO: Weilik Chan
Sales/Marketing Manager: Danny Zeng
Year Founded: 1984
Estimated Sales: $ 20 - 50 Million
Number Employees: 100-249
Type of Packaging: Consumer, Food Service, Private Label

50165 Wonton Food
1045 Firestone Parkway
La Vergne, TN 97086   615-501-8898
www.wontonfood.com
Producer of fortune cookies, eggroll and wonton skins, dry and fresh noodles including chow mein, lo mein, spinach and wonton; Importer of oriental canned and dry goods
Type of Packaging: Consumer, Food Service, Private Label

50166 Wonton Food
2902 Caroline St.
Houston, TX 77004   832-366-1280
www.wontonfood.com
Producer of fortune cookies, eggroll and wonton skins, dry and fresh noodles including chow mein, lo mein, spinach and wonton; Importer of oriental canned and dry goods
Type of Packaging: Consumer, Food Service, Private Label

50167 Wood Stone Corp
1801 W Bakerview Rd
Bellingham, WA 98226-9105   360-650-1111
       Fax: 360-650-1166   800-988-8103
info@woodstone.net www.woodstone-corp.com
Manufacturer and exporter of broilers, stone hearth ovens, pizza equipment and rotisseries; cast ceramic available
President: Kurt Eickmeyer
kurte@woodstone.net
CEO: Keith R. Carpenter
COO: Harry E. Hegarty
VP Sales: K Carpneter
President Manufacturing: Harry Hegarty
Estimated Sales: $ 5 - 10 Million
Number Employees: 100-249
Square Footage: 100000
Regions Exported to: Central America, South America, Europe, Asia, Middle East, Canada
Percentage of Business in Exporting: 5

50168 Woodfold-Marco Manufacturing
1811 18th Ave
PO Box 346
Forest Grove, OR 97116   503-357-7181
       Fax: 503-357-7185   info@woodfold.com
www.woodfold.com
Manufacturer and exporter of wood roll up and accordion doors and custom shutters; also, laminated kitchen and machined hardwood products
President: Mark Lewis
Vice President: Randall Roedl
Estimated Sales: $ 10-20 Million
Number Employees: 100-249
Square Footage: 320000
Brands Exported: Woodfold
Regions Exported to: Worldwide

50169 Woodland Foods
1200 Northwestern Ave
Gurnee, IL 60031-2365   847-625-8500
       Fax: 847-625-5050 www.woodlandfoods.com
Dried ingredients: mushrooms, chile pods, pastes and powders, herbs, spices, seasonings and rubs, grains and rices, tomatoes, beans, lentils, couscous and orzo, Asian noodles and flavor bases, flours and meals, corns and polentaspecialty salts, peppercorns and sugars, nuts and seeds, dried fruit, truffle products and snack mixes.
President & CEO: David Moore
davidmoore@woodlandfoods.com
Executive Vice President: Mike Brundidge
Vice President, Operations: Ely Suhre
Number Employees: 50-99
Square Footage: 300000
Type of Packaging: Consumer, Food Service, Private Label, Bulk
Regions Imported from: Central America, South America, Europe, Asia, Middle East

50170 Woodstock Farms Manufacturing
96 Executive Ave
Edison, NJ 08817
       800-526-4349
www.woodstockfarmsmfg.com
Importer, processor, packager, and wholesale distributor of nuts, dried fruit, seeds, trail mixes, natural and organic products, and confections.
President: Bob Kaufman
VP, Sales & Customer Service: Matt Mellet
Square Footage: 100000
Parent Co: United Natural Foods
Type of Packaging: Consumer, Food Service, Private Label, Bulk

50171 Woodstock Line Co
83 Canal St
Putnam, CT 06260-1909   860-928-6557
       Fax: 860-928-1096   info@woodstockline.com
www.woodstockline.com
Manufacturer and exporter of braided cordage and twine
Owner: Burney Phaneuf
info@woodstockline.com
Estimated Sales: $2.5-5 Million
Number Employees: 10-19
Square Footage: 50000
Regions Exported to: Europe, Canada, Australia, New Zealand
Percentage of Business in Exporting: 15

50172 Woodstock Plastics Co Inc
22511 W Grant Hwy
Marengo, IL 60152-9660   815-568-5281
       Fax: 815-568-5339   sales@woodstockplastics.com
www.woodstockplastics.com
Manufacturer and exporter of fabricated plastic displays, dump bins, containers, clamshell and vinyl pouches including sealed, vacuum formed, molded and blow molded
Owner: Brian Jenkner
brianj@woodstockplastics.com
CFO: Matthew Jenkner
Vice President: John Jenkner
Quality Control: Jude Jons
Estimated Sales: $ 10 - 20 Million
Number Employees: 20-49
Square Footage: 90000
Regions Exported to: South America, Europe, Asia
Percentage of Business in Exporting: 20

50173 Woody Associates Inc
844 E South St
York, PA 17403-2849   717-843-3975
       Fax: 717-843-5829   info@woody-decorators.com
www.woody-decorators.com
Manufacturer and exporter of automatic confectionery and bakery decorating machinery
President: Harry Reinke
woody@woody-decorators.com
VP: Kerrie Reinke
Sales: Harry Reinke
Estimated Sales: $ 1 - 3 Million
Number Employees: 5-9
Square Footage: 2000
Brands Exported: Woody
Regions Exported to: Worldwide
Percentage of Business in Exporting: 65

50174 Woolwich Dairy
425 Richardson Road
Orangeville, ON L9W 4Z4
Canada
       519-941-9206
       Fax: 519-941-9349   877-438-3499
gerhard@woolwichnova.com
www.woolwichdairy.com
Goat's milk cheeses including cheddar, whole and crumbled feta, mozzarella, gouda, cream and brie
CEO: Tony Dutra
VP Marketing: Michael Domingues
VP Sales: Liz Long
Year Founded: 1983
Estimated Sales: $24 Million
Number Employees: 97
Number of Brands: 7
Number of Products: 109
Square Footage: 4000
Parent Co: Saputo
Type of Packaging: Consumer, Food Service, Private Label, Bulk
Brands Exported: Chevrai; Madame Chevre; Gourmet Goat
Regions Exported to: Central America
Percentage of Business in Exporting: 75

50175 Worden
7217 W Westbow Boulevard
Spokane, WA 99224-5668   509-455-7835
       Fax: 509-838-4723   wordenwine@aol.com
Wine
President: Ken Barrett
CEO: Rebecca Chateaubriand
Estimated Sales: $ 1 000,000+
Number Employees: 10
Square Footage: 13000
Type of Packaging: Private Label, Bulk
Brands Exported: Wyvern
Regions Exported to: Asia, Australasia
Percentage of Business in Exporting: 20
Brands Imported: Raw Wine
Regions Imported from: South America, Europe, South Africa
Percentage of Business in Importing: 20

50176 Work Well Company
861 Taylor Road
Unit C
Gahanna, OH 43230-6275   614-759-8003
       Fax: 614-759-8013
Manufacturer and exporter of safety gloves and oven mitts
Contact: Bill Balentine
bbalentine@workwell.com
Estimated Sales: $ 1 - 5 Million
Regions Exported to: Worldwide

50177 Workman Packaging Inc.
345 Montee de Liesse
Saint-Laurent, QC H4T 1P5
Canada
       514-344-7227
       Fax: 514-737-4288   800-252-5208
info@multisac.com www.multisac.com
Manufacturer and exporter of woven and laminated polyethylene and polypropylene bags, covers and wraps
President: Mark Kraminer
CFO: Luc Dumont
Quality Control: Bryan Morton
Director Marketing: Mark Kraminer
Number Employees: 100
Regions Exported to: Europe, USA
Percentage of Business in Exporting: 22

50178 Worksafe Industries
130t W 10th Street
Huntington Station, NY 11746-1616   516-427-1802
       Fax: 516-427-1840   800-929-9000
Manufacturer and exporter of protective clothing including gloves, respirators, goggles and industrial safety equipment
President: Larry Densen
Number Employees: 300
Regions Exported to: Europe, Asia, Middle East, Africa, Latin America

50179 Worksman 800 Buy Cart
9415 100th St
Ozone Park, NY 11416-1707   718-322-2003
       Fax: 718-529-4803   800-289-2278
vending@worksman.com www.worksman.com
Manufacturer and exporter of vending carts, trucks, trailers and kiosks.
President: Wayne Sosin
Mobile Food Equity, VP: Jack Beller
Estimated Sales: $5-10 Million
Number Employees: 50-99
Square Footage: 360000
Type of Packaging: Food Service
Regions Exported to: Central America, South America, Europe, Middle East, Canada, Caribbean
Percentage of Business in Exporting: 10

50180 Workstead Industries
PO Box 1083
Greenfield, MA 01302-1083   413-772-6816
www.workstead.com

Distributor, packager and exporter of low methoxyl citrus pectin for low and sugar-free jam and jelly processing
Owner: Connie Sumberg
conniesumberg@pomonapectin.com
Estimated Sales: Less Than $500,000
Number Employees: 1-4
Number of Brands: 1
Number of Products: 2
Square Footage: 4000
Type of Packaging: Consumer, Bulk
Brands Exported: Pomona's Universal
Regions Exported to: Canada, Caribbean

50181 World Cheese Inc
178 28th St
Brooklyn, NY 11232-1604   718-965-1700
Fax: 718-965-0979
customerservice@worldcheeseco.com
www.worldcheeseco.com
World Cheese Company is the largest kosher cheese manufacturer in the United States.
Owner: Leo Thurm
lthurm@allkoshercheese.com
Year Founded: 1937
Number Employees: 20-49
Type of Packaging: Consumer, Food Service, Bulk
Regions Exported to: South America, Europe
Brands Imported: Schmerling Koser Cheese And Chocolate
Regions Imported from: South America

50182 World Class Beer Imports
P.O.Box 39588
Fort Lauderdale, FL 33339   954-564-2337
Fax: 954-564-3854 support@worldclassbeer.com
www.worldclassbeer.com
Importer and wholesaler/distributor of beer, wine, cordials and ciders
President: Reubin Share
Estimated Sales: $1-2.5 Million
Number Employees: 5-9
Square Footage: 28800
Parent Co: REU-DOM Investments & Holdings
Regions Imported from: South America, Europe, Asia, Canada, Worldwide

50183 World Confections Inc
14 S Orange Ave # A
South Orange, NJ 07079-1754   718-768-8100
Fax: 718-499-4918 Info@worldconfections.com
www.worldconfections.com
Manufacturer and exporter of confectionery products including gum, bagged, bars, boxed chocolates, caramels, lollypops, jaw breakers, peppermint and lemon twists, seasonal, etc
President: Mathew Cohen
Contact: Devin Abbott
devina@worldconfections.com
Estimated Sales: $10 Million
Number Employees: 50-99
Type of Packaging: Consumer, Private Label, Bulk

50184 World Cup Coffee & Tea
1740 NW Glisan St
Portland, OR 97209-2225   503-228-5453
Fax: 503-228-3489 www.worldcupcoffee.com
Processor and exporter of coffee and teas; also, roasting and water filltration services available
Owner: Dan Welch
info@worldcupcoffee.com
Number Employees: 20-49
Square Footage: 50000
Type of Packaging: Consumer, Food Service, Bulk
Regions Exported to: Canada

50185 World Division
12023 Denton Dr
Dallas, TX 75234   972-241-2612
Fax: 972-247-8807 800-433-9843
info@worlddivision.com www.worlddivision.com
Manufacturer and exporter of banners, pennants, streamers and signs
President: John Adams
Sr. VP: Francois Louis
Operations Director: David Fry
Estimated Sales: $5-10,000,000
Number Employees: 1-4
Regions Exported to: Worldwide
Percentage of Business in Exporting: 6

50186 World Dryer Corp
5700 Mcdermott Dr
Berkeley, IL 60163-1196   708-449-6950
Fax: 708-449-6958 800-323-0701
sales@worlddryer.com www.worlddryer.com
Warm air push button and automatic hand dryers, baby changing tables, automatic soap dispensers, 3-in-1 towel dispenser/hand dryer systems and ADA compliant/handicapped approved hand dryers.
President: Tom Vic
CFO: Tom Bic
Vice President: Chris Berl
Marketing Director: Stacey Hefford
Sales Director: Erin Eddy
Estimated Sales: $ 10 - 20 Million
Number Employees: 20-49
Square Footage: 100000
Parent Co: Specialty Equipment Companies
Brands Exported: World; Electric Aire
Regions Exported to: Worldwide
Percentage of Business in Exporting: 50

50187 (HQ)World Finer Foods Inc
1455 Broad St
4th Floor
Bloomfield, NJ 07003-3039   973-338-0300
Fax: 973-338-0382 800-225-1449
info@worldfiner.com www.worldfiner.com
Importer and wholesaler/distributor of specialty foods including canned vegetables and fish, cooking wines, vinegars, pastas, sauces, seasonings, croutons, soups, olives, olive oils, beans, rice mixes, preserves, cereals, cookiescrispbreads, etc
President: John Affel
affel@worldfiner.com
Chairman: John Beers
CFO: Barry O'Brien
VP & Controller: Neal Kaskel
VP Marketing: Todd Newstadt
VP Sales: Kevin Hubbard
Public Relations Director: Tom Barnes
Manager: Lisa Accunzo-Cheplic
VP Purchasing: Barbara Harloe
Estimated Sales: $13.9 Million
Number Employees: 1-4
Square Footage: 48000

50188 World Ginseng Ctr Inc
825 Kearny St
San Francisco, CA 94108-1303   415-362-2255
Fax: 415-362-0801 800-747-8808
info@worldginsengcenter.com
www.worldginsengcenter.com
Manufacturer and exporter of ginseng and frozen seafood
President: Raymond Chao
Manager: William Nghe
Treasurer: Jane Chao
Estimated Sales: Less Than $500,000
Number Employees: 1-4
Type of Packaging: Consumer, Food Service, Private Label, Bulk
Regions Exported to: Asia
Percentage of Business in Exporting: 80

50189 World Kitchen
PO Box 1555
Elmira, NY 14902-1555   607-377-8000
Fax: 607-377-8962 800-999-3436
www.worldkitchen.com
Manufacturer and exporter of glassware including bottles, jars, cookware, trays, urns, etc
President/ CEO: Carl Warschausky
CFO: Stephen Earhart
SVP, Human Resources & Chief Legal Offic: Ed Flowers
VP Marketing: Clark Kinlin
Contact: David Livingston
livingstond@worldkitchen.com
SVP/ General Manager, Global Business: Lee Mui
Estimated Sales: $ 5 - 10 Million
Number Employees: 10-19
Regions Exported to: Worldwide

50190 World Kitchen
5500 Pearl St Ste 400
Rosemont, IL 60018   847-678-8600
Fax: 847-678-9424
Manufacturer and exporter of plastic containers; wholesaler/distributor and exporter of bakery racks and food trays; serving the food service market
President: Jim Sharman
CEO: Joe Mallof
Contact: Michael Cwiertniakm
cwiertniakm@worldkitchen.com
Estimated Sales: $ 20 - 50 Million
Number Employees: 100-249
Parent Co: Borden Inc.
Type of Packaging: Food Service
Regions Exported to: Europe

50191 World Nutrition, Inc.
Scottsdale Seville
7001 N Scottsdale Rd
Scottsdale, AZ 85253-3666   480-921-1188
Fax: 480-921-1471 800-548-2710
customerservice@worldnutrition.info
www.worldnutrition.info
Processor and importer of vitamins, minerals, organic grains, fruits, vegetables and dehydrated fruits and vegetable juices
President: Ryuji Hirooka
CEO: Chuck Eberhardt
Marketing Manager: Robert Nisenfeld
Operations Executive: Andy Rodriguez
Plant Manager: Tony Negrete
Purchasing Agent: Rhonda Poe
Estimated Sales: $1.9 Million
Number Employees: 18
Square Footage: 34000
Regions Imported from: Worldwide

50192 World Spice
223-235 Highland Parkway
Roselle, NJ 07203   908-245-0600
Fax: 908-245-0696 800-234-1060
sales@wsispice.com www.wsispice.com
Spices, seasonings, herbs and dehydrated vegetables
President: Bela Lowy
Vice President: J Lefbowitz
Estimated Sales: $2 Million
Number Employees: 5-9
Square Footage: 60000
Type of Packaging: Food Service, Bulk
Brands Exported: WSI
Regions Exported to: Central America, South America
Percentage of Business in Exporting: 5
Brands Imported: WSI
Regions Imported from: Central America, South America, Europe, Asia, Middle East
Percentage of Business in Importing: 75

50193 World Tableware Inc
300 Madison Ave
Toledo, OH 43604-1561   419-325-2608
Fax: 419-325-2749 800-678-9849
stock@libbey.com www.libbey.com
Importer, exporter and wholesaler/distributor of tabletop supplies including flatware, dinnerware and holloware; serving the food service market
President: John Myer
CEO: Jay Achenbach
achenbachj@libbey.com
Quality Control: Allwyn Cahoun
CEO: John Meier
R & D: Bill Herp
Number Employees: 5-9
Parent Co: Libbey
Type of Packaging: Food Service
Brands Exported: Ultima; World Porcelain; Brandward; World
Regions Exported to: Asia, Canada
Brands Imported: Ultima; World Porcelain; Brandward; World
Regions Imported from: Europe, Asia, Canada, Mexico, China, Japan,Korea
Percentage of Business in Importing: 95

50194 World Variety Produce
5325 S Soto St
Vernon, CA 90058-3624   323-588-0151
Fax: 323-588-7841 800-468-7111
hotline@melissas.com
Wholesaler/distributor, importer and exporter of produce
President: Joe Hernandez
Director Marketing: Bill Schneider
Manager: Luis Sanchez
luiss@melissas.com
Plant Manager: Mike Stephens
Procurement: Jim Hernandez
Estimated Sales: $ 20 - 50 Million
Number Employees: 250-499
Square Footage: 125000

Importers & Exporters / A-Z

Regions Exported to: Worldwide
Regions Imported from: Worldwide

50195 World Water Works
4000 SW 113th St
Oklahoma City, OK 73173-8322   405-943-9000
  Fax: 405-943-9006   800-607-7973
Wastewater treatment.
Contact: Kyle Booth
kyle.booth@worldwaterworks.com
Number Employees: 50-99
Regions Exported to: Central America, South America, Europe, Asia, Middle East, Worldwide

50196 World Wide Hospitality Furn
7311 Madison St # D
Paramount, CA 90723-4038   562-630-2700
  Fax: 562-630-2227   800-728-8262
wrldwideh@aol.com   www.wwhfurniture.com
Manufacturer and importer of tables, chairs and booths
CEO: Isaac Gonshor
wrldwideh@aol.com
Estimated Sales: $ 1 - 5,000,000
Number Employees: 10-19
Type of Packaging: Food Service

50197 World Wide Safe Brokers
112 Cromwell Court
Woodbury, NJ 08096   856-863-1225
  Fax: 856-845-2266   800-593-2893
info@worldwidesafebrokers.com
www.worldwidesafebrokers.com
Fire safes, electronic safes, gun safes, safe deposit boxes, hotel room safes, insulated files, burglary safe, vaults, vault doors, in-floor safes, depository safes, custom designed and manufactured safes.
President: Edward Dornisch
VP: Mildred Dornisch
Estimated Sales: $ .5 - 1 million
Number Employees: 3
Square Footage: 16000
Regions Exported to: Central America, South America, Europe, Asia, Middle East
Percentage of Business in Exporting: 20
Regions Imported from: Europe, Asia

50198 World's Best Cheeses
111 Business Park Dr
Armonk, NY 10504-1708   914-273-1400
  Fax: 914-273-2052   914-273-7954
Cheese
President: Joseph Gellert
Vice President, Business Development: Stephen Gellert
Estimated Sales: $35-40 Million
Type of Packaging: Private Label
Brands Imported: Beechers, Bellwethar, Cora, Cow Girl Creamery, Guffanti, Jasper Hill, Laura Chenel, Meadow Creek Dairy, Nettle Meadow, Normandie Brie and World's Best Cheese
Regions Imported from: France, U.K., Italy, Spain, Germany, Switzerland, Portugal, Denmark, Holland, Norway and Canada

50199 World's Finest Chocolate Inc
4801 S Lawndale Ave
Chicago, IL 60632-3062   773-847-4600
  Fax: 773-847-4006   888-821-8452
www.worldsfinestchocolate.com
Chocolate manufacturer serving the North American fundraising and promotional/gift markets.
Owner: Rodney Amison
rodney.amison@worldsfinestchocolates.com
CEO: Eddie Opler
Number Employees: 500-999
Type of Packaging: Consumer
Regions Imported from: Caribbean

50200 Worldwide Food Imports
525 Fashion Ave # 914
New York, NY 10018-0446   212-869-0777
  Fax: 212-575-2373
Importer and exporter of meat and meat products including hams.
Owner: Joni Breschel
Managing Director: Adam Bachowski
VP: Lee Zimmerman
Estimated Sales: $2.5-5 Million
Number Employees: 1-4
Brands Imported: Krakus; Danskol; Bohemia
Regions Imported from: Europe
Percentage of Business in Importing: 75

50201 Worldwide Specialties In
2421 E 16th St Unit 1
Los Angeles, CA 90021   323-587-2200
  Fax: 323-587-0050   800-437-2702
Gourmet specialty produce; importer and exporter of baby squash, French beans and fresh herbs
President: Horacio Belloflore
Treasurer: Nora Belloflore
Contact: Bruce Hoffman
bruce@californiaspecialtyfarms.com
Estimated Sales: $10,000,000
Number Employees: 126
Regions Imported from: South America, Mexico
Percentage of Business in Importing: 5

50202 Wornick Company
4700 Creek Rd.
Cincinnati, OH 45242
  800-860-4555
  www.wornick.com
Convenience foods and military rations to restaurant chains, consumer product goods companies, and the U.S. government, including kids meals, sides, sauces, and breakfast.
President/Chief Executive Officer: John Kowalchik
VP Marketing/Business Development: Randy Newbold
Year Founded: 1970
Estimated Sales: $100-500 Million
Number Employees: 500-999
Square Footage: 600000
Type of Packaging: Food Service, Private Label
Other Locations:
  Wornick Co.
  McAllen, TX Wornick Co.
Regions Exported to: South America, Canada
Percentage of Business in Exporting: 10

50203 (HQ)Worthen Industries Inc
3 E Spit Brook Rd
Nashua, NH 03060-5783   603-888-5443
  Fax: 603-888-7945   info@worthenind.com
  www.upacofootwear.com
Manufacturer and exporter of labels and adhesive tapes
President: Robert Worthen
CEO: Eileen Morin
emorin@worthenind.com
CEO: Eileen Morin
Estimated Sales: $ 1 - 3 Million
Number Employees: 100-249

50204 Wrapade Packaging Systems
27 Law Dr # B
Suite B/C
Fairfield, NJ 07004-3206   973-787-1788
  Fax: 973-773-6010   888-815-8564
sales@wrapade.com   www.wrapade.com
Manufacturer and exporter of vertical, horizontal and stand-up pouch packaging machinery
President: Bill Beattie
bill.b@wrapade.com
Estimated Sales: $2.5-5 Million
Number Employees: 10-19
Square Footage: 88000

50205 Wraps
810 Springdale Avenue
East Orange, NJ 07017-1298   973-673-7873
  Fax: 973-673-2240
Manufacturer and exporter of flexible packaging materials, heat sealers and packaging machinery
President: Ralph Barone
General Manager: Michael Mikulis
Sales Manager: Brian Guidera
Contact: Chad Carpenter
chad.carpenter@wrapsforless.com
Estimated Sales: $2.5-5 Million
Number Employees: 20-49
Square Footage: 192000
Regions Exported to: Worldwide
Percentage of Business in Exporting: 10

50206 Wright Enrichment Inc
6428 Airport Rd
PO Box 821
Crowley, LA 70526-1604   337-783-3096
  Fax: 337-783-0724   800-201-3096
chris@wenrich.com   www.thewrightgroup.net
Processor and exporter of custom vitamin, mineral and amino acid premixes, microencapsulates and direct compressed granulations

Owner: Grant Bergstrom
Marketing Manager: Chris Hebert
Regional Sales Manager: John Miller
grant@wenrich.com
Estimated Sales: $ 10 - 20 Million
Number Employees: 100-249
Type of Packaging: Bulk

50207 (HQ)Wright Metal Products Crates
100 Ben Hamby Dr
Greenville, SC 29615-5700   864-297-6610
  Fax: 864-281-0594   www.wrightmetalproducts.com
Machine parts for food handling equipment
Vice President: Marty Hyatt
mhyatt@wrightmetalsinc.com
VP: Jim Camden
General Manager: Jim Camden
Estimated Sales: $ 10-20 Million
Number Employees: 20-49
Square Footage: 80000
Other Locations:
  Wright Metal Products
  Greenville, SC Wright Metal Products
Regions Exported to: Canada
Percentage of Business in Exporting: 1

50208 Wunder-Bar
2060 Cessna Dr
Vacaville, CA 95688   707-448-5151
  Fax: 707-448-1521   800-722-6738
sales@wunderbar.com   www.wunderbar.com
Food and beverage dispensing systems for; condiments, heated cheese, oils, salad dressings, refrigerated & non-refrigerated toppings, pizza toppings, sodas, juices, and liquors.
President & CEO: Rick Martindale
Vice President: Bret Baker
bret.baker@wunderbar.com
Vice President: Jim Tuyls
Estimated Sales: $50-100 Million

50209 Wusthoff Trident Cutlery
344 Taft Street NE
Minneapolis, MN 55413   612-379-1300
  866-797-0555
  www.eversharpknives.com
Importer and wholesaler/distributor of kitchen cutlery; serving the food service market
VP Sales: Scott Severinson
Estimated Sales: $5-10 Million
Number Employees: 10-19
Type of Packaging: Food Service
Regions Imported from: Germany

50210 (HQ)Wyandot Inc
135 Wyandot Ave
Marion, OH 43302-1595   740-383-4031
  Fax: 740-382-5584   800-992-6368
  www.wyandotsnacks.com
Private label snack foods including baked cheese puffs and chips including potato, tortilla, nacho and corn.
President & CEO: Rob Sarlls
CEO: Nick Chilton
nick.chilton@wyandotsnacks.com
CFO: Bob Wentz
Number Employees: 250-499
Type of Packaging: Consumer, Food Service, Private Label, Bulk
Brands Exported: Mexicali; MunchMates; Wyandot; American Classics
Regions Exported to: Europe
Percentage of Business in Exporting: 5

50211 Wylie Systems
1190 Fewster Drive
Mississauga, ON L4W 1A1
Canada   905-238-1619
  Fax: 905-238-5623   800-525-6609
info@wyliemetals.com   www.wyliemetals.com
Manufacturer and exporter of railings and partitions for hotels, restaurants, etc.; also, sneeze guards
President: Michael Wylie
Regions Exported to: Europe

50212 Wyssmont Co Inc
1470 Bergen Blvd
Fort Lee, NJ 07024-2197   201-947-4600
  Fax: 201-947-0324   www.wyssmont.com
Manufacturer, designer and exporter of food processing equipment including rotating tray dryers, lumpbreakers, fixed and rotating bars and self-cleaning airlock feeders; also, solid handling equipment

Importers & Exporters / A-Z

President: Edward Weisselberg
ebw@wyssmont.com
VP: Joseph Bevacqua
R&D: J Ulrich
VP Sales: Joseph Henderson
Estimated Sales: $2.5-5 Million
Number Employees: 20-49
Square Footage: 40000
Brands Exported: Turbo-Dryer, A Continous Toray Dryer
Regions Exported to: Central America, South America, Europe, Asia

50213 X-Press Manufacturing
271 Fm 306
New Braunfels, TX 78130-2557 830-629-2651
Fax: 830-620-4727 800-365-9440
sales@x-pressmfg.com www.x-pressmfg.com
Display tortilla cookers, pressers and warmers
Owner: Charles Smith
President/Owner: Rex Wilson
Customer Service: Anne Sowell
Shop Manager: Charlie Smith
Estimated Sales: $ .5 - 1 million
Number Employees: 1-4
Square Footage: 7500
Parent Co: Copprex
Brands Exported: X-Press
Regions Exported to: Europe, Asia, Middle East, Mexico
Percentage of Business in Exporting: 5

50214 X-R-I Testing Inc
1961 Thunderbird
Troy, MI 48084-5467 248-362-5050
Fax: 248-362-4422 800-973-4800
foodx@aol.com www.xritesting.com
Manufacturer and exporter of in-line and off-line X-ray inspection equipment; also, X-ray inspection services available
President: Scott Thams
Manager: Kurt Andrews
kurta@xrayindustries.com
Estimated Sales: $ 30 - 50 Million
Number Employees: 50-99
Square Footage: 30000
Parent Co: X-Ray Industries
Regions Exported to: Europe, Asia, Australia
Percentage of Business in Exporting: 5

50215 XDX Innovative Refrigeration
3176 N Kennicott Ave
Arlington Hts, IL 60004-1426 847-398-0250
Fax: 847-398-1365 sales@xdxusa.com
www.xdxusa.com
CEO: Brian Jones
brian@dewberryjones.com
CEO: David Wightman
CEO: David Wightman
Estimated Sales: $ 1 - 3 Million
Number Employees: 10-19

50216 Xango LLC
2889 W Ashton Blvd # 1
Lehi, UT 84043-4968 801-766-3050
Fax: 801-816-8001 877-469-2646
Markets daily dietary supplemental juice beverage made from the mangosteen fruit.
President/Chief Executive Officer: Aaron Garrity
Chairman: Gary Hollister
President Intnl Distributor Relations: Joe Morton
EVP International Relations: Bryan Davis
Quality Assurance Manufacturing: Wayne Davis
Chief Marketing Officer: Gordon Morton
President Operations: Ken Wood
Number Employees: 500-999

50217 Xcel Tower Controls
1600 W 6th St
PO Box 187
Gilbertsville, NY 13776 574-259-7804
Fax: 574-259-5769 800-288-7362
info@xcel.com www.xcel.com
Manufacturer and exporter of control and process control systems, universal programmers, programmable control systems and industrial computers, tower light controllers and monitoring systems
President: Bruce Shepard
CEO: John Brickley
Sales Director: Bruce Shepard
Estimated Sales: $2.5-5 Million
Number Employees: 10-19
Square Footage: 30000

Regions Exported to: South America, Europe, Canada, Carribean, Worldwide

50218 Xena International
910 S Division Avenue
Polo, IL 61064 815-946-2626
Fax: 815-946-2752
customerservice@xenainternational.com
www.xenainternational.com
Importer and manufacturer of dry and liquid ingredients.
President: Richard Sikorski
Contact: Nick Livingston
nick@xena.biz

50219 Xpresso
5195 Southridge Parkway
Atlanta, GA 30349-5966 770-996-9992
Fax: 770-996-8352
Importer and exporter of self-grinding espresso and cappuccino equipment
General Manager: Ben Leuenberger
Manager Logistics: Jay Moebus
Estimated Sales: $500,000-$1 Million
Number Employees: 5-9
Square Footage: 20000
Parent Co: Jura A.G.
Brands Exported: Impressa; Jura
Regions Exported to: Central America, Canada, Mexico, Caribbean
Percentage of Business in Exporting: 30
Brands Imported: Xpresso
Regions Imported from: Europe

50220 Xtreme Beverages, LLC
32565-B Golden Lantern
#282
Dana Point, CA 92629
Canada 949-495-7929
Fax: 949-495-8015 xtremebeverages@cox.net
Wood and bamboo box; wood and bamboo tea chest; wine box; baskets; tea and coffee accessories; wine accessories; MDF box; cardboard box; wooded tea dispenser; wrought iron tea can rack; wood and bamboo products, candles; candleholders; gourmet gift packaging and food and beverage gift packaging
President: William Quinley
VP: James Moffitt
Estimated Sales: $5 Million
Number Employees: 4
Type of Packaging: Consumer, Food Service, Private Label, Bulk
Regions Exported to: Central America, South America, Europe, Middle East, North America
Regions Imported from: Asia

50221 Y Z Enterprises Inc
1930 Indian Wood Cir # 100
Maumee, OH 43537-4001 419-893-8777
Fax: 419-893-8825 800-736-8779
info@almondina.com www.almondina.com
Processor and exporter of natural almond cookies including low-calorie, no-cholesterol, no-salt, kosher and parve
Owner: Yuval Zaliouk
CFO: Susan Zaliouk
Contact: Niwedita Bakshi
niwedita.bakshi@macys.com
Estimated Sales: Less Than $500,000
Number Employees: 5-9
Square Footage: 66000
Type of Packaging: Consumer
Brands Exported: Almondina Brand Biscuits
Regions Exported to: Europe, Asia, Middle East

50222 Y-Pers Inc
5622 Tulip St
PO Box 9559
Philadelphia, PA 19124-1698 215-743-1500
Fax: 215-289-6811 800-421-0242
www.ypers.com
Manufacturer and exporter of cheesecloths and uniforms including disposable clothing, hairnets and gloves
President: David Blum
ypers@aol.com
CFO: David Blum
R&D: David Blum
Estimated Sales: Below $ 5 Million
Number Employees: 10-19
Regions Exported to: Panama

50223 YESCO
1605 S Gramercy Rd
Salt Lake City, UT 84104-4888 801-487-8481
Fax: 801-762-0036 800-444-3847
info@yesco.com www.yesco.com
Manufacturer and exporter of electric signs
President: Michael Young
Cmo: Wes Van Dyke
wvandyke@yesco.com
CFO: Duane Wardle
Sales Manager: Susan Ward
Estimated Sales: $ 30 - 50 Million
Number Employees: 250-499

50224 Ya-Hoo Baking Co
5302 Texoma Pkwy
Sherman, TX 75090-2112 903-893-8151
Fax: 903-893-5036 888-869-2466
customerservice@yahoocake.com
www.yahoocake.com
Dessert cakes, cobblers, cookies, cake and pie fillings, bread, frozen dough; custom work is our specialty
President: Chelsea Lanehart
clanehart@boongroup.com
R&D: Monette Wible
Director Sales/Marketing: David Millican
Sales Administrator: Tanda Wall
Purchasing Manager: Becky Roberts
Number Employees: 50-99
Square Footage: 180000
Type of Packaging: Consumer, Food Service, Private Label, Bulk
Brands Exported: Original Ya-hoo! Baking Company
Regions Exported to: Worldwide

50225 Yakima Chief-Hopunion LLC
306 Division St.
Yakima, WA 98902 509-453-4792
Fax: 509-453-1551 hops@ychhops.com
www.yakimachief.com
Processor and exporter of hops and hops products.
Contact: Stephen Carpenter
stephen.carpenter@hopunion.com
Year Founded: 1869
Estimated Sales: $140 Million
Number Employees: 20
Square Footage: 75000
Type of Packaging: Bulk
Regions Exported to: Worldwide
Percentage of Business in Exporting: 50
Regions Imported from: Europe

50226 Yakima Craft Brewing Company
2920 River Rd
Suite 6
Yakima, WA 98902-7332 509-654-7357
www.yakimacraftbrewing.com
Processor and exporter of ales, stout and porter
President: Jeff Winn
CEO/Founder: Chris McCoy
Director of Marketing: Sheldon Weddle
Contact: Chris Swedin
chris@yakimacraftbrewing.com
Estimated Sales: $500,000-999,999
Number Employees: 5-9
Square Footage: 162000
Type of Packaging: Consumer
Brands Exported: Bert Grant's Ales
Regions Exported to: Asia, Canada

50227 Yakima Fresh
111 University Pkwy # 101
P.O. Box 1709
Yakima, WA 98901-1471 509-248-5770
Fax: 509-457-6137 steve.smith@yakimafresh.com
www.yakimafresh.com
Manufacturer and exporter of apples, cherries and pears
Quality Control Manager: Brian Mortimer
VP Marketing & Business Development: Tom Papke
Sales Manager: Randy Eckert
Manager: Steve Smith
steve.smith@yakimafresh.com
General Manager: Steve Smith
Estimated Sales: $2 Million
Number Employees: 20-49
Square Footage: 16452
Type of Packaging: Consumer, Food Service, Bulk
Other Locations:
  Yakima Fresh Warehouse
  Wapato, WA

Importers & Exporters / A-Z

Yakima Fresh Warehouse
Zillah, WA
Yakima Fresh Warehouse
Hood River, ORYakima Fresh WarehouseZillah

50228 Yakima Wire Works
1949 E. Manning Avenue
Reedley, CA 93654   559-638-8484
Fax: 559-638-7478 800-344-8951
info@swfcompanies.com www.swfcompanies.com
Manufacturer and exporter of fully and semi-automatic bagging, weighing and batching, modular net dispensers, check-weighers, dual-belt conveyors and blowers
President: Gary Germunson
Chairman/VP: Tim Main
Estimated Sales: $ .5 - 1 million
Number Employees: 1-4
Regions Exported to: South America, Canada
Percentage of Business in Exporting: 1

50229 Yamasho Inc
750 Touhy Ave
Elk Grove Village, IL 60007-4916   847-981-9342
Fax: 847-981-9347 info@yamashoinc.com
www.yamashoinc.com
Japanese products
President: Kunio Iwadate
Estimated Sales: $ 20 - 50 Million
Number Employees: 5-9

50230 Yamato Corporation
1775 S. Murray Blvd.
Colorado Springs, CO 80916-4513   719-591-1500
Fax: 719-591-1045 800-538-1762
www.yamatocorp.com
Manufacturer and exporter of electronic and mechanical scales, electronic weight printers and computerized weighing systems
President: Sadao Nakamura
CEO: Sado Nakamura
Marketing Director: Gary Mendenhall
Sales Director: Prague Mehta
Contact: Lula Babb
babb@yamatocorp.com
Estimated Sales: $ 2.5 - 5 Million
Number Employees: 20-49
Square Footage: 96000
Regions Exported to: Central America, South America, Canada, Latin America, Mexico
Percentage of Business in Exporting: 20

50231 Yankee Specialty Foods
22 Fish Pier St W
Boston, MA 02210-2008   617-951-0740
Fax: 617-951-9907 800-688-9904
info@bayshorechowders.com
www.yankeespecialtyfoods.com
Processor and exporter of chili, soup, gumbo and chowder
Owner: Sara Giargiari
saragiargiari@yankeespecialtyfoods.com
Estimated Sales: $300000
Number Employees: 5-9
Type of Packaging: Consumer, Private Label
Regions Exported to: Europe

50232 Yardney Water Management Syst
6666 Box Springs Blvd
Riverside, CA 92507-0736   951-656-6716
Fax: 951-656-3867 800-854-4788
www.yardneyfilters.com
Manufacturer and exporter of water quality improvement and filtration systems
President: Kenneth Phillips
kennethphillips@yardneyfilters.com
CFO: Kenneth Phillips
Quality Control: Janie Weissberg
Industrial Field Sales Manager: Ron Gamble
Estimated Sales: $ 5 - 10 Million
Number Employees: 20-49
Square Footage: 200000
Regions Exported to: Central America, South America, Asia, Middle East, Canada, Caribbean, Mexico, Latin America
Percentage of Business in Exporting: 20

50233 Yargus Manufacturing Inc
12285 E Main St
Marshall, IL 62441-4127   217-826-8059
Fax: 217-826-8551 layco@yargus.com
www.laycoproautomation.com
Stainless steel equipment including conveyors, hopper scales, blenders and bucket elevators; exporter of conveyor and blender systems
Owner: Jose Aguayo
Vice President US Sales: Mark Anderson
Sales: Lyle Yargus
jaguayo@bigwsales.com
Estimated Sales: $5-10 Million
Number Employees: 100-249
Square Footage: 102000
Brands Exported: Layco
Regions Exported to: South America, Europe
Percentage of Business in Exporting: 25

50234 Yaya Imports
530 Boulder Ct # 105
Pleasanton, CA 94566-8318   925-249-9292
Fax: 925-249-9293 www.yayaimports.com
Gourmet foods from spain. Almonds, beans and legumes, bonito tuna, chocolate, chorizo and sausages, coffee and tea, cookies and desserts, fruits and preserves, honey, gourmet meals, jamon serrano, mediterranean sea salt, olive oilolives, pimenton, puquillo peppers, paella rice, saffron, sauces and spreads, sherry vinegar, turron candy and vegetables
Owner: Dolores Hernandez
Number Employees: 5-9

50235 Yeager & Associates
79158 Buff Bay Court
Bermuda Dunes, CA 92203-1567   760-345-7404
Fax: 760-345-8816 pjyeager@gmail.com
Experts in developing new products using chicken, beef and pork for private labels. We have the ability to cook your meat/poultry product to final specification for further processing or packaging for retail sales. We haverepresentation in all major retail markets and food service.
President: Paula Yeager
VP: Robert Carian
Quality Control: Jason Carian
Sales: Paula Yeager
Sales: Lauren Hagadorn
Estimated Sales: $6 Million
Number Employees: 5
Square Footage: 16000
Parent Co: P&R Sales, Inc.
Type of Packaging: Consumer, Food Service, Private Label, Bulk

50236 Yemat Foods
2400 Camino Ramon
Suite 177
San Ramon, CA 94583-4373   925-415-9170
Fax: 925-361-5018 kimnara.com
Seaweed snack
Vice President, Business Development: Steve Oh
Sales Associate: Nate Han
Brands Imported: Yemat 1004, C-Weed Snack
Regions Imported from: Korea

50237 Yerba Prima
740 Jefferson Ave
Ashland, OR 97520-3743   541-488-2228
Fax: 541-488-2443 800-488-4339
yerba@yerba.com www.yerbaprima.com
Processor and exporter of high quality dietary supplements, specializing in dietary fiber, internal cleansing aids and herbal products.
CEO: John Jung
yerba@yerba.com
Marketing Manager: Shelley Matteson
Estimated Sales: $ 5 - 10 Million
Number Employees: 10-19
Type of Packaging: Consumer, Private Label
Brands Exported: Yerba Prima
Regions Exported to: Europe, Asia, Canada
Percentage of Business in Exporting: 10

50238 (HQ)Yergat Packing Co
5451 W Mission Ave
Fresno, CA 93722-5074   559-276-9180
Fax: 559-276-2841 info@yergatpacking.com
www.yergatpacking.com
Processor and exporter of grapevine leaves
President: Kirk Yergat
Contact: Thao Duong
thaod@yergatpacking.com
Number Employees: 5-9
Parent Co: Yergat Packing Company
Type of Packaging: Consumer, Private Label
Brands Exported: Yergat
Regions Exported to: Middle East

50239 YoFiit
167 Applewood Cr
Vaughan, ON L4K 4K7
Canada   647-997-7846
info@yofiit.com
yofiit.com
Fiber and energy bars; cereal; milk substitutes; quinoa; nutritional shakes.
Co-Founder: Marie Amazan
Year Founded: 2015
Number Employees: 5-9
Type of Packaging: Private Label
Brands Exported: YoFiit
Regions Exported to: Central America

50240 Yogi® Tea
950 International Way
Springfield, OR 97477
800-964-4832
yogitea.customerservice@yogiproducts.com
www.yogiproducts.com
Tea
Square Footage: 200000
Parent Co: Yogi Tea
Type of Packaging: Consumer, Food Service, Private Label, Bulk
Other Locations:
 Tea Business Sales
 Portland, ORTea Business Sales
Regions Exported to: Europe, Asia, Middle East, Canada
Percentage of Business in Exporting: 5
Regions Imported from: Europe, Asia
Percentage of Business in Importing: 5

50241 (HQ)Yohay Baking Co
146 Albany Ave
Lindenhurst, NY 11757-3628   631-225-0300
Fax: 631-225-4277
Processor, importer and exporter of wafer rolls, specialty cookies, biscotti, and fudge mix, kosher and all natural products. Retail packaging available
Owner: Michael Soloman
solomanyohay@aol.com
Number Employees: 20-49
Type of Packaging: Consumer, Food Service, Private Label, Bulk
Regions Exported to: South America

50242 York Saw & Knife
295 Emig Rd
P.O.Box 733
York, PA 17406-9734   717-767-6402
Fax: 717-764-2768 800-233-1969
info@yorksaw.com www.yorksaw.com
Manufacturer and exporter of circular and straight knives for food processing; custom and standard specifications available
President: Mike Pickard
mpickard@yorksaw.com
CFO: Todd Gladfeltzer
Quality Control: Tim Wentz
Estimated Sales: $ 10 Million
Number Employees: 50-99
Square Footage: 130000
Regions Exported to: Central America, South America, Europe

50243 Yorkraft
2675a Eastern Boulevard
York, PA 17402-2905   717-845-3666
Fax: 717-846-3213 800-872-2044
Food service equipment including cabinetry products, salad bars, buffet lines and merchandising carts; also, decorative lighting panels available
President: David Imhoff
dimhoff@yorkraft.com
VP Operations: Jack Smith
VP: William Imhoff
Estimated Sales: $5-10 Million
Number Employees: 10
Square Footage: 360000

50244 Yoshida Food Products Co
8338 NE Alderwood Rd
Suite A
Portland, OR 97220-6809   503-284-1114
Fax: 503-284-0004 800-653-1114
info@yfintl.com www.yfintl.com
Non MSG, nonfat and cholesterol-free sauces, marinades, drippings and coatings

President: Matt Guthrie
CFO: Tim Sether
CEO: Junki Yoshida
Quality Control: John Hunter
VP Sales/Marketing: John Moran
Sales Director: Andy Moberg
Public Relations: Marti Lucich
Operations Manager: Eric Rinearson
Production Manager: Frank Heuschkel
Purchasing Manager: Ken Hamilton
Estimated Sales: $8 Million
Number Employees: 5-9
Square Footage: 260000
Parent Co: Heinz
Type of Packaging: Consumer, Food Service, Private Label, Bulk
Regions Exported to: Europe, Asia, Canada
Percentage of Business in Exporting: 10

50245 Yost Candy Co Inc
51 S Cochran St
Dalton, OH 44618-9602   330-828-2777
Fax: 330-828-8296 800-750-1976
info@yostcandy.com
Processor and exporter of lollypops and Halloween candy
President: Earl Yost
Vice President: Joe Yost
Sales Director: Earl Yost
Estimated Sales: $2000000
Number Employees: 10-19
Type of Packaging: Consumer, Private Label, Bulk
Regions Exported to: Worldwide
Percentage of Business in Exporting: 25

50246 (HQ)Young Winfield
1700 Brampton Street
Hamilton, ON L8H 3S1
Canada   905-893-2536
Fax: 416-544-4390 youngwinfield.com
Onion oil, cajun spice, salt and vinegar seasonings
President/Contact: Amirali Sunderji
Estimated Sales: $3-5 Million
Number Employees: 12
Square Footage: 108000
Type of Packaging: Consumer, Food Service, Private Label, Bulk
Regions Imported from: South America, Europe, Asia, Middle East, East Africa
Percentage of Business in Importing: 60

50247 Young's Lobster Pound
4 Mitchell Street
Belfast, ME 04915   207-338-1160
Fax: 207-338-3498
Processor, exporter and importer of fresh and frozen seafood including crabs, lobster, live and shucked clams and mussels, scallops and shrimp; wholesaler/distributor of fresh and frozen seafood
Owner: Raymond Young
Co-Owner: Claire Young
Manager; Owner: Raymond Young
Estimated Sales: $ 3 - 5 Million
Number Employees: 20-49
Square Footage: 10944
Type of Packaging: Consumer, Food Service
Brands Exported: Young's
Regions Exported to: Europe, Asia, Canada
Percentage of Business in Exporting: 20
Regions Imported from: Canada
Percentage of Business in Importing: 15

50248 Your Place Menu Systems
2600 Lockheed Way
Carson City, NV 89706-0717   775-882-7834
Fax: 775-882-5210 800-321-8105
Manufacturer and exporter of outdoor and indoor illuminated and nonilluminated menu boards
President, Sales Manager: John O Neil
Operations Manager, Product Design: Matt Stutsman
Number Employees: 20-49
Square Footage: 280000
Parent Co: Impact International
Regions Exported to: Central America, South America, Worldwide

50249 Yum Yum Potato Chips
40 Du Moulin
Warwick, QC J0A 1M0
Canada   819-358-3600
Fax: 819-358-3687 800-567-5792
yumyum@yum-yum.com www.yum-yum.com
Snack foods including potato chips, cheese sticks, onion rings and fries
President: Pierre Riverd
Director Production: Guy Trudel
Number Employees: 200
Type of Packaging: Consumer, Private Label
Brands Exported: Yum Yum
Regions Exported to: Caribbean
Percentage of Business in Exporting: 1

50250 Z 2000 The Pick of the Millenium
819 S Madison Boulevard
Bartlesville, OK 74006-8534   918-335-2030
Fax: 918-335-1789 800-654-7311
Manufacturer and exporter of 45 degree angled dental cleaners
President: Mack Blevins
VP: Pamela Blevins
Estimated Sales: $ 1 - 5 Million
Number Employees: 1-4
Square Footage: 15000
Parent Co: Mack Blevins Enterprises
Type of Packaging: Consumer, Food Service, Private Label, Bulk
Brands Exported: Angled Pro Picks
Regions Exported to: Europe
Percentage of Business in Exporting: 20

50251 Z Specialty Food, LLC
1250 Harter Ave # A
Woodland, CA 95776-6106   530-668-0660
Fax: 530-668-6061 800-678-1226
tasty@zspecialtyfood.com
www.ZSpecialtyfood.com
Processor and exporter of gourmet chocolate and vanilla nut butters cremes, honey and honey products including fruit spreads and honey straws, bee pollen, bees wax, royal jelly and propolis; also, gift packs
Co-Owner: Ishai Zeldner
Square Footage: 16000
Type of Packaging: Consumer, Food Service, Private Label, Bulk
Percentage of Business in Exporting: 2

50252 Z-Loda Systems Engineering Inc
1010 Summer St # 101
Suite 101
Stamford, CT 06905-5533   203-325-8001
Fax: 203-978-0104 www.hugedomains.com
Manufacturer and exporter of vertical lift systems
President: Clifford Mollo
Estimated Sales: Less Than $500,000
Number Employees: 1-4
Regions Exported to: Asia, Mexico
Percentage of Business in Exporting: 1

50253 ZAK Designs Inc
1604 S Garfield Rd
Airway Heights, WA 99001-9705   509-244-0555
Fax: 509-244-0704 800-331-1089
www.zak.com
Importer, exporter and wholesaler/distributor of children's dinnerware, adult servingware, acrylic drinkware and oven mitts
President: Irv Zakheim
CEO: Thomas Pauley
thewd@st-lukes.org
VP (International): Michelle Jou
National Sales Manager: Ken Long
Estimated Sales: $20-50 Million
Number Employees: 100-249
Square Footage: 100000
Regions Exported to: Central America, South America, Europe, Asia, Middle East
Percentage of Business in Exporting: 15
Regions Imported from: Asia
Percentage of Business in Importing: 85

50254 Zachary Confections Inc
2130 W State Road 28
Frankfort, IN 46041-8771   765-659-4751
Fax: 765-659-1491 800-445-4222
www.zacharyconfections.com
Processor and exporter of confectionery products including caramels, boxed chocolates, marshmallows, mints, nougats and holiday novelties
President: Jack Zachary
Number Employees: 250-499
Type of Packaging: Consumer, Private Label, Bulk
Regions Exported to: Central America, South America
Percentage of Business in Exporting: 5
Percentage of Business in Importing: 3

50255 Zafari Art & Decor Design
PO Box 446
Terra Ceia, FL 34250-0446   941-729-4195

50256 Zaloom Marketing Corp
51 James St
South Hackensack, NJ 07606-1438   201-488-3535
Fax: 201-488-8056 800-878-7609
jzzmc@aol.com www.zaloommarketing.com
Consultant specializing in marketing, promotion and food technology; importer of seafood products including imitation crab meat
President: Roy Zaloom
jzzmc@aol.com
Estimated Sales: $10-20 Million
Number Employees: 10-19

50257 Zamilco International
135 Mineola Ave
Roslyn Heights, NY 11577   516-621-6364
Fax: 516-621-4370 zamrald@aol.com
Importer and exporter of coffee, honey, spices and corn oil and vanilla
President: Simon Zareh
VP: Edward Zareh
Treasurer: Shahin Zareh
Estimated Sales: $5-10 Million
Number Employees: 5-9
Regions Exported to: Worldwide
Percentage of Business in Exporting: 60
Regions Imported from: Asia, Madagascar
Percentage of Business in Importing: 40

50258 Zarda King LTD
33 E 35th Pl
Steger, IL 60475-1714   708-755-1007
Fax: 708-755-2445 Sales@zardaking.com
Importer and wholesaler/distributor of saffron incense, candle, spices, dvd, tabacco, henna
President: Bhim Hans
zardakings@aol.com
Estimated Sales: $1-2.5 Million
Number Employees: 1-4
Square Footage: 24000
Brands Imported: Incense, Candles, Tabacco, Saffron, Decauter, Spices, Henna
Regions Imported from: South America, Asia
Percentage of Business in Importing: 100

50259 Zd Wines
8383 Silverado Trl
Napa, CA 94558-9436   707-963-5188
Fax: 707-963-2640 800-487-7757
info@zdwines.com www.zdwines.com
Processor and exporter of wines including chardonnay, pinot noir and cabernet sauvignon
President/Partner: Brett DeLeuze
CEO/Partner: Robert DeLeuze
CFO: Julie De Leuze
Marketing Coordinator: Elyse Chambers
VP Sales: Teresa d'Aurizio
Winemaker: Chris Pisani
Estimated Sales: $5-10 Million
Number Employees: 20-49
Number of Brands: 2
Number of Products: 8
Square Footage: 90928
Type of Packaging: Consumer, Food Service
Brands Exported: Z.D. Wines
Regions Exported to: Europe, Asia
Percentage of Business in Exporting: 1

50260 Zealco Industries
PO Box 809
Calvert City, KY 42029-0809   800-759-5531
Fax: 270-395-9522
Manufacturer and exporter of high pressure commercial and industrial washing equipment
Parent Co: Purlanco
Regions Exported to: Worldwide
Percentage of Business in Exporting: 1

50261 Zebra Technologies Corporation
3 Overlook Point
Lincolnshire, IL 60069   847-634-6700
Fax: 847-913-8766 866-230-9494
www.zebra.com
Bar code equipment including printers, supplies and software for point-of-application labeling and performance thermal transferring.

Importers & Exporters / A-Z

Chief Executive Officer: Anders Gustafsson
Chief Financial Officer: Olivier Leonetti
Senior VP, Corporate Development: Michael Cho
Senior VP/General Counsel/Secretary: Cristen Kogl
Chief Marketing Officer: Jeff Schmitz
Senior VP, Global Sales: Joachim Heel
Year Founded: 1969
Estimated Sales: $3.7 Billion
Number Employees: 7,400
Square Footage: 167600
Regions Exported to: Central America, South America, Europe, Asia, Middle East

50262 Zed Industries
3580 Lightner Rd
PO Box 458
Vandalia, OH 45377-9735   937-667-8407
           Fax: 937-667-3340 info@zedindustries.com
                              www.zedindustries.com
Manufacturer and exporter of vacuum and pressure thermoforming equipment, heat sealers, formers/fillers/sealers, blister packers and custom engineered plastic packaging systems
President: Mark Zelnick
czelnick@zedindustries.com
CFO: Helen Zelnick
VP: Peter Zelnick
Sales: Leonard Loomis
Estimated Sales: $10-20 Million
Number Employees: 50-99
Type of Packaging: Consumer, Food Service, Bulk
Regions Exported to: Central America, South America, Europe, Asia

50263 Zeeco Inc
22151 E 91st St S
Broken Arrow, OK 74014-3250   918-258-8551
           Fax: 918-251-5519 sales@zeeco.com
                              www.zeeco.com
Manufacturer and exporter of gas and oil food burners used for heating and drying; also, fume/liquid incinerators used for hazardous waste disposal
President: Jason Abbott
jason.abbott@zeeco.com
Chairman: John Zink
Sales Manager: D Caho
Purchasing Manager: D Updike
Estimated Sales: Less Than $500,000
Number Employees: 1-4
Square Footage: 42000
Regions Exported to: Worldwide
Percentage of Business in Exporting: 40

50264 Zeier Plastic & Mfg Inc
2203 Leo Cir
Madison, WI 53704-2615   608-244-5782
           Fax: 608-244-1810 DZ@Zeierplastic.com
Manufacturer and exporter of thermoplastic injection molded trays and funnels; also, custom injection molded parts available
Owner: Dennis Zeier
dz@zeierplastic.com
VP: Dennis Zeier
Estimated Sales: $2.5-5 Million
Number Employees: 10-19

50265 Zel R. Kahn & Sons
2 Fifer Ave Ste 220
Corte Madera, CA 94925   415-924-9600
           Fax: 415-924-9690
Wholesaler/distributor and exporter of surplus, salvage and closeout merchandise including dried and canned fruits, vegetables, crackers, cereals, etc
President: Scott Kahn
Executive VP: Joel Jutovsky
Estimated Sales: $300,000-500,000
Number Employees: 5-9
Square Footage: 160000
Regions Exported to: Central America, South America, Europe, Middle East
Percentage of Business in Exporting: 10

50266 Zeltex
130 Western Maryland Parkway
Hagerstown, MD 21740   301-791-7080
           Fax: 301-733-9398 800-732-1950
                canders@zeltex.com www.zeltex.com
Manufacturer and exporter of near-infrared analyzers for the food, grain and patrochemical industries
President: Todd Rosenthal
Director of Sales: Chris Anders
Number Employees: 20
Brands Exported: Zeltex
Regions Exported to: Worldwide
Percentage of Business in Exporting: 50

50267 Zenar Corp
7301 S 6th St
Oak Creek, WI 53154-2047   414-764-1800
           Fax: 414-764-1267 mail@zenarcrane.com
                              www.zenarcrane.com
Manufacturer and exporter of electric overhead cranes and hoist units
President: John Maiwald
CEO: John A Maiwald
jmaiwald@zenarcrane.com
Estimated Sales: $10 - 20 Million
Number Employees: 100-249
Regions Exported to: Canada

50268 Zener America
170 Fort Path Rd Ste 22
Madison, CT 06443   203-245-3807
           Fax: 203-245-3813
Importer and exporter of AC motor speed controls in water tight enclosures
President: Thomas Burke
Estimated Sales: $500,000-$1 Million
Number Employees: 1-4
Regions Exported to: South America

50269 Zengine
4750 Hempstead Drive
Dayton, OH 45429   937-291-8270
           Fax: 509-275-0223

50270 Zenith Cutter
5200 Zenith Pkwy
Loves Park, IL 61111-2735   815-282-5200
           Fax: 815-282-5232   815-282-5202
           toddg@zenithcutter.com www.zenithcutter.com
Manufacturer and exporter of machine knives and cutters; also, custom manufacturing and duplicating available
President: Cedric Blazer
cedricb@zenithcutter.com
Personnel: Bob Yocum
VP: Robert Yocum
Quality Control: Tim Greve
Director Sales/Marketing: Tim Schoenecker
Production Manager: Terry Willis
Estimated Sales: $ 20 - 50 Million
Number Employees: 100-249
Square Footage: 140000
Type of Packaging: Bulk
Regions Exported to: Worldwide
Percentage of Business in Exporting: 1

50271 Zenith Specialty Bag Co
17625 Railroad St
PO Box 8445
City Of Industry, CA 91748-1195   626-912-2481
           Fax: 626-810-5136   800-962-2247
           cust.serv@zenithbag.com www.zbags.com
Manufacturer and exporter of paper products including custom print, pan liners, wax paper bags and grease resistant sheets
President: Marco Alcala
m.alcala@zenithbag.com
CEO: Betty Anderson
CFO: Jack Grave
Vice President: Ron Anderson
VP: Ron Anderson
Marketing Director: Susan Washle
Sales Director: Scott Apperson
Operations Manager: Jeff Behrends
Estimated Sales: $ 10 - 20 Million
Number Employees: 100-249
Square Footage: 170000
Brands Exported: Zenith
Regions Exported to: Central America, South America, Europe
Percentage of Business in Exporting: 5

50272 (HQ)Zenobia Co
5774 Mosholu Ave # B
Bronx, NY 10471-2200   347-843-8080
           Fax: 718-548-2313   866-936-6242
Processor, importer and exporter of pistachios, cashews, pumpkin and sunflower seeds, organic dried fruits, etc
President: Kenneth Bobker
National Sales Manager: Donald DiMatteo
Estimated Sales: $5-10 Million
Number Employees: 1-4
Square Footage: 100000
Type of Packaging: Consumer, Food Service, Private Label, Bulk
Other Locations:
   Zenobia Co.
   Bronx, NY Zenobia Co.
Brands Exported: Zenobia
Regions Exported to: Central America, South America, Asia
Percentage of Business in Exporting: 20
Regions Imported from: South America, Middle East
Percentage of Business in Importing: 20

50273 Zentis Sweet Ovations
1741 Tomlinson Rd
Philadelphia, PA 19116-3847   215-676-3900
           Fax: 215-613-2115   800-223-7073
Processor and exporter of fruit preparations
CEO: Kevin Daugherty
Plant Manager: Corey Arrick
Number Employees: 100-249
Parent Co: Systems Bio-Industries
Regions Exported to: Canada

50274 Zepa Trade
415 Beverley Road
Apt Ld
Brooklyn, NY 11218-3124   718-633-0456
           Fax: 718-633-0456 zepa@altavista.net
Importer and exporter of cereals, oils, seeds, grains, beverages, etc
Owner: Joel Oshri
Number Employees: 1-4
Regions Exported to: Europe, Asia, Middle East, Africa, Australia, Latin America
Percentage of Business in Exporting: 5
Percentage of Business in Importing: 60

50275 Zepf Technologies
5320 140th Ave N
Clearwater, FL 33760-3743   727-535-4100
           Fax: 727-539-8944 sales@zepf.com
                              www.pneumaticscale.com
Manufacturer and exporter of shrink wrappers, case packers, bundlers, tray formers, straw applicators, rotary uncasers, combiners and laners
President: Michael Mc Laughlin
Contact: Doug Dougherty
doug.dougherty@hayssen.com
Estimated Sales: $ 20-50 Million
Number Employees: 50-99
Square Footage: 45000
Regions Exported to: Central America, South America, Europe, Asia, Middle East
Percentage of Business in Exporting: 45

50276 Zephyr Manufacturing Co
200 Mitchell Rd
Sedalia, MO 65301-2114   660-827-0352
           Fax: 660-827-0713 info@zephyrmfg.com
                              www.zephyrmfg.com
Processor and exporter of brushes, floor and carpet cleaners, wet mops, handles, mopsticks, sponges, frames, squeegees
President: Charles Close
cclose@zephyrtool.com
Estimated Sales: $20-50 Million
Number Employees: 50-99
Regions Exported to: Worldwide
Percentage of Business in Exporting: 1

50277 Zerand Corp
15800 W Overland Dr
New Berlin, WI 53151-2882   262-827-3800
           Fax: 262-827-3911 www.zerand.com
Manufacturer and exporter of paper board printing and packaging machinery
VP: Paul Capper
Director Sales/Marketing/Administration: Bill Dennis
Estimated Sales: $ 10 - 20 Million
Number Employees: 50-99

50278 Zero Temp
2510 N Grand Ave # 112
Suite 112
Santa Ana, CA 92705-8753   714-538-3177
           Fax: 714-538-1531 gflassoc@aol.com
                              www.zerotempcoldstorage.com
Manufacturer and exporter of turn key refrigerated warehouses, walk-in freezers, walk-in coolers, controlled environment rooms and clean rooms

Importers & Exporters / A-Z

Owner: Gary F Lyons
gflassoc@aol.com
CEO: Michael Lyons
CFO: Donna Lyons
R&D: David Pinillos
Operations: Pat McBride
Production: Gary Lyons
Estimated Sales: $6 Million
Number Employees: 10-19
Square Footage: 6000
Parent Co: Garry F Lyons & Associates

50279 Zeroll Company
PO Box 999
Fort Pierce, FL 34954   772-461-3811
Fax: 772-461-1061   800-872-5000
sales@zeroll.com   www.zeroll.com
Manufacturer and exporter of scoops, dishers and spades
Plant Manager: Thomas Funka Sr
General Manager/CEO: Lenny Van Valkenburg
Plant Manager: Thomas Funka, Jr.
Estimated Sales: $10 Million
Number Employees: 20-49
Number of Brands: 5
Number of Products: 40
Square Footage: 60000
Type of Packaging: Consumer, Food Service, Private Label, Bulk

50280 Zesto Food Equipment Manufacturing
6450 Hutchison Street
Montreal, QC H2V 4C8
Canada   514-278-4621
Fax: 514-278-4622   info@zesto.ca
President: George Moshonas
Number Employees: 20

50281 Ziba Nut Inc
180 Main St
Port Washington, NY 11050-3212   516-944-5112
Fax: 516-767-1689   info@zibanut.com
www.zibanut.com
Wholesaler/distributor, exporter and importer of nuts, organic and natural dried fruits, seeds, cumin seeds, red chilies, ric crackers, and savory snacks, coated peanuts, vegetable chips, plantain chips, and sun dried tomatos
President: Massoud Morshee
CEO: Mehdi Kazemi
mkazemi@zibanut.com
Number Employees: 1-4
Type of Packaging: Bulk
Regions Exported to: Central America, Asia, Middle East
Percentage of Business in Exporting: 30
Regions Imported from: South America, Europe, Asia, Middle East, Australia
Percentage of Business in Importing: 70

50282 Zimmer Custom-Made Packaging
1450 E 20th St
Indianapolis, IN 46218   317-263-3436
Fax: 317-263-3427
A leading supplier in the worldwide flexible packaging industry. ZCMP has focused on frozen novelty, butter/margarine, candy, confectionary and other food markets and is currently beginning to supply die cut cone sleeves and die cutlids.
President: Mark Lastovich
CFO: Chuck Bollard
Quality Assurance Manager: Herbert Henson
VP Marketing/Sales: Mike DoBosh
Contact: Mark Murphy
mmurphy@zcmp.com
VP Operations: David Brown
Estimated Sales: $20-50 Million
Number Employees: 20-49
Square Footage: 60000
Other Locations:
Zimmer Custom-Made Packaging
Indianapolis, IN Zimmer Custom-Made Packaging
Brands Exported: Sherlock Premium III
Regions Exported to: Worldwide
Percentage of Business in Exporting: 10
Regions Imported from: Asia, Mexico
Percentage of Business in Importing: 5

50283 Zimmerman Handling Systems
29555 Stephenson Hwy
Madison Heights, MI 48071-2332   248-398-6200
Fax: 248-398-1374   800-347-7047
seekinfo@irco.com   www.irhoist.com
Manufacturer and exporter of ergonomic lifting systems
President: Gerard Geraghty
National Accounts Manager: Stephen Klostermeyer
Estimated Sales: $ 10 Million
Number Employees: 20-49
Parent Co: Ingersol-Rand
Regions Exported to: Worldwide

50284 Ziniz
3955 E Blue Lick Road
Louisville, KY 40229-6047   502-955-6573
Fax: 502-955-6960
Manufacturer and exporter of package handling conveyors including chain, gravity belt live roller and overhead trolley; also, installation available
President: Ronny Grant
Marketing/Sales: Paul McDonald
Estimated Sales: $50-100 Million
Number Employees: 250-499
Square Footage: 50000
Brands Exported: Ziniz
Regions Exported to: Europe, Asia

50285 Zoia Banquetier Co
4700 Lorain Ave
Cleveland, OH 44102-3443   216-631-6414
Fax: 216-961-5119
www.artisticmetalspinning.com
Food banquet covers, brushes, dollies and carts; exporter of food banquet covers
Owner: Lorraine Hangauer
artistic1@ameritech.net
Secretary: Donald Hangauer
Estimated Sales: $ 500,000-$ 1 Million
Number Employees: 1-4
Square Footage: 50000
Regions Exported to: Central America, Europe, Asia, Middle East
Percentage of Business in Exporting: 5

50286 Zoom Communications
1325 Capital Cir
Suite C
Lawrenceville, GA 30043-5892   770-277-0414
Fax: 770-338-9331

50287 Zumtobel Staff Lighting
3300 US Highway 9w
Highland, NY 12528-2630   845-691-6262
Fax: 973-340-9898   www.zumtobelstaff.com
Manufacturer, importer and exporter of lighting fixtures
President: Wolfgang Egger
Sales: Allison Craig
Estimated Sales: $ 50 - 100 Million
Number Employees: 5-9
Regions Exported to: Worldwide
Regions Imported from: Europe

50288 Zwilling J.A. Henckels
171 Saw Mill River Rd
Hawthorne, NY 10532   914-747-0300
Fax: 914-747-1850   800-777-4308
info@zwillingus.com   www.j-a-henckels.com
Importer of kitchen utensils including knives, graters, whisks, spoons, slicers, dicers, etc
President: Guido Weishaup
CFO: John Henkel
Vice President, Marketing: Joanna Rosenberg
Marketing Director: Kathleen McDonnell
Contact: Patrick Accorsi
paccorsi@zwillingus.com
Number Employees: 50-99
Brands Imported: Four Star; Professional S'; Gourmet; Twin Master; Twin Gadgets; Twin Select; Twinstar Plus; Five Star; Henckels International; Eversharp Pro; FineEdge Pro; EverEdge
Regions Imported from: Europe, Asia
Percentage of Business in Importing: 100

Export Region / Africa

Africa

A&A International, 41488
Abunda Life, 41617
ALPI Food Preparation Equipment, 41560
Arnold Equipment Co, 42058
Atlantic Rubber Products, 42116
Automated Food Systems, 42151
Basketfull, 42299
Beach Filter Products, 42318
Belshaw Adamatic Bakery Group, 42368
Blanver USA, 42472
C&P Additives, 42678
Capmatic, Ltd., 42801
Clabber Girl Corporation, 43056
Classic Flavors & Fragrances, 43065
Conquest International LLC, 43204
Currie Machinery Co, 43409
DairyAmerica, 43475
Darisil, 43502
Diazteca Inc, 43622
Dresco Belting Co Inc, 43704
Electro Freeze, 43887
Ensemble Beverages, 43955
Enviro-Clear Co, 43962
Evonik Corporation North America, 44033
Filling Equipment Co Inc, 44164
Flakice Corporation, 44202
Flexicon, 44230
Garden Row Foods, 44473
Ginseng Up Corp, 44582
Global Impex, 44607
Groupe Paul Masson, 44761
Healing Garden, 44945
Howell Brothers Chemical Laboratories, 45104
Inox Tech, 45295
Lifestyle Health Guide, 46030
Luxor California Exports Corp., 46166
Markwell Manufacturing Company, 46351
Mother Parker's Tea & Coffee, 46746
National Distributor Services, 46866
Natural Flavors, 46904
Nieco Corporation, 47023
Nielsen-Massey Vanillas Inc, 47025
Niutang Chemical, Inc., 47038
NOW Foods, 46828
Nutritional Counselors of America, 47155
Nutriwest, 47159
Packaging & Processing Equipment, 47382
Pan Pacific Plastics Inc, 47422
Peco Controls Corporation, 47512
Phelps Industries, 47585
Preferred Machining Corporation, 47709
Prima Foods International, 47741
Pronatura Inc, 47811
Pucel Enterprises Inc, 47827
PureCircle USA, 47846
Rio Syrup Co, 48107
San Joaquin Vly Concentrates, 48356
Saratoga Food Specialties, 48390
Sazerac Company, Inc., 48409
Serr-Edge Machine Company, 48529
Setterstix Corp, 48546
Setton International Foods, 48547
Shivji Enterprises, 48600
Smitty's Snowballs, 48707
Synthite USA Inc., 49108
Texas Traditions Gourmet, 49269
Textile Buff & Wheel, 49270
Tootsi Impex, 49391
Traex, 49425
Tranter INC, 49439
Turbo Refrigerating Company, 49531
United Industries Group Inc, 49638
United Textile Distribution, 49655
US Distilled Products Co, 49565
Venetian Productions, 49763
Warwick Manufacturing & Equip, 49954
Waste Minimization/Containment, 49961
Weaver Popcorn Co Inc, 49981
Wescotek Inc, 50019
Worksafe Industries, 50178
Zepa Trade, 50274

Antartica

Fax Foods, 44124
Stearnswood Inc, 48911

Antilles

Florart Flock Process, 44239

Argentina

Eclipse Systems Inc, 43829

Asia

3V Company, 41472
A C Horn & Co Sheet Metal, 41478
A G Russell Knives, 41480
A Legacy Food Svc, 41484
A&A International, 41488
A&B Safe Corporation, 41491
A&M Industries, 41497
A&M Thermometer Corporation, 41499
A-1 Refrigeration Co, 41501
A-B-C Packaging Machine Corp, 41503
A/R Packaging Corporation, 41519
Aabbitt Adhesives, 41596
Abbotsford Growers Ltd., 41605
ABCO Industries Limited, 41527
Abel Manufacturing Co, 41609
ABM Marking, 41531
Abunda Life, 41617
Accuflex Industrial Hose LTD, 41624
Accutek Packaging Equipment, 41626
Ace Specialty Mfg Co Inc, 41631
Aceto Corporation, 41634
Acme Engineering & Mfg Corp, 41637
Acme Scale Co, 41640
Acorto, 41646
Acp Inc, 41647
Acraloc Corp, 41649
Acta Health Products, 41652
Actron, 41658
Adamation, 41664
Adams & Brooks Inc, 41666
ADCO Manufacturing Inc, 41539
ADH Health Products Inc, 41540
Adhesive Technologies Inc, 41672
Admatch Corporation, 41673
Adrienne's Gourmet Foods, 41680
Advanced Detection Systems, 41688
Advanced Equipment, 41690
Advanced Ingredients, Inc., 41692
Adventure Foods, 41700
AEP Colloids, 41544
Aero Manufacturing Co, 41702
Aeromat Plastics Inc, 41704
Aeromix Systems, 41705
Agger Fish Corp, 41714
Agri-Dairy Products, 41719
Agri-Mark Inc, 41721
Agricor Inc, 41722
Agropur, 41728
Agvest, 41731
AIDP Inc, 41554
Air Quality Engineering, 41735
Air-Scent International, 41737
Ajinomoto Foods North America, Inc., 41744
Ajinomoto Frozen Foods USA, Inc., 41745
Alaskan Gourmet Seafoods, 41762
Albion Machine & Tool Co, 41767
Alconox Inc, 41771
Alderfer Inc, 41772
Alfa Laval Inc, 41778
Algood Food Co, 41784
Alkar Rapid Pak, 41790
Alkota Cleaning Systems Inc, 41792
All A Cart Custom Mfg, 41793
All American Container, 41794
All Fill Inc, 41796
Allen Harim Foods LLC, 41813
Alliance Rubber Co, 41818
Alloy Hardfacing & Engineering, 41828
Aloe Farms Inc, 41833
Aloe Laboratories, 41834
Alpha Packaging, 41841
Alternative Health & Herbs, 41847
Alto-Shaam, 41850
Alvarado Street Bakery, 41854
AM Todd Co, 41561
Amark Packaging Systems, 41857
Ameri-Kal Inc, 41866
America's Classic Foods, 41867
American Botanicals, 41870
American Brush Company, 41871
American Glass Research, 41890
American Importing Co., 41894
American Laboratories, 41900
American Louver Co, 41903
American Metalcraft Inc, 41907
American Pasien Co, 41912
American Range, 41915
American Store Fixtures, 41924
American Time & Signal Co, 41926
American Ultraviolet Co, 41928
American Water Broom, 41929
American Wax Co Inc, 41930
Americana Marketing, 41932
Ameripak Packaging Equipment, 41935
Ames International Inc, 41940
AMF Bakery Systems Corp, 41566
AMI, 41568
AMSOIL Inc, 41570
Amy's Kitchen Inc, 41962
Anabol Naturals, 41964
Analite, 41965
Anchor Brewing Company, 41968
Anchor Packaging, 41971
Andersen 2000, 41973
Anderson International Corp, 41977
Anderson-Crane Company, 41981
Andrew Peller Limited, 41984
Anguil Environmental Systems, 41989
Anhydro Inc, 41990
Animal Pak, 41991
Apple & Eve LLC, 42009
Appleton Produce Company, 42011
Applied Robotics Inc, 42016
Aqua Measure, 42019
Architecture Plus Intl Inc, 42028
Arctic Industries, 42033
Arde Inc, 42035
Arden Companies, 42037
Argo & Company, 42038
Ariel Vineyards, 42042
Arista Industries Inc, 42044
Arizona Instrument LLC, 42047
Armaly Brands, 42052
Arnold Equipment Co, 42058
Aroma Vera, 42060
Aroma-Life, 42061
Aromachem, 42062
Aromatech USA, 42063
Arpac LP, 42066
ASI Data Myte, 41584
ASI/Restaurant Manager, 41587
Assembled Products Corp, 42087
Assembly Technology & Test, 42088
Astor Chocolate Corp, 42092
Astral Extracts, 42095
At Last Naturals Inc, 42097
Athea Laboratories, 42100
ATI, 41589
Atkins Elegant Desserts, 42103
Atlanta SharpTech, 42106
Atlantic Chemicals Trading, 42110
Atlantic Rubber Products, 42116
Atlantic Ultraviolet Corp, 42118
Atlantic Veal & Lamb Inc, 42119
Atlantis Plastics Linear Film, 42121
Atlas Pacific Engineering, 42128
Atoka Cranberries, Inc., 42130
Atrium Biotech, 42131
Audion Automation, 42135
August Thomsen Corp, 42137
Aurora Packing Co Inc, 42141
Autio Co, 42144
Automated Flexible Conveyors, 42150
Automated Food Systems, 42151
Automatic Bar Controls Inc, 42152
Automatic Products/Crane, 42155
Automatic Specialties Inc, 42156
Automatic Timing & Controls, 42157
Autotron, 42161
Avery Weigh-Tronix, 42167
Avestin, 42169
Ayush Herbs Inc, 42181
B.C. Tree Fruits Limited, 42197
B.M. Lawrence & Company, 42198
Bacchus Wine Cellars, 42224
Baker Hughes, 42228
Bakers Pride Oven Company, 42244
Bakery Things, 42246
Bal Seal Engineering Inc, 42248
Baldewein Company, 42251
Baldor Electric Co, 42252
Ballantyne Food Service Equipment, 42255
Ballas Egg Products Corp, 42256
Bally Block Co, 42257
Bally Refrigerated Boxes Inc, 42258
Baltimore Aircoil Co, 42261
Bama Sea Products Inc, 42265
Bar Keepers Friend Cleanser, 42270
Bardo Abrasives, 42277
Barlean's Fisheries, 42282
Barliant & Company, 42283
Barrette Outdoor Living, 42285
Barrie House Gourmet Coffee, 42286
Barry Group, 42289
Basic American Foods, 42295
Basic Food Flavors, 42296
Basic Food Intl Inc, 42297
Batavia Wine Cellars, 42300
Baumer Foods Inc, 42305
BBCA USA, 42201
Be & Sco, 42317
Beach Filter Products, 42318
Bean Machines, 42321
Bear Creek Country Kitchens, 42322
Beaumont Products, 42327
Beck Flavors, 42332
Bedford Enterprises Inc, 42339
Beehive Botanicals, 42343
Bel-Art Products, 42353
Bell & Evans, 42356
Bell-Mark Corporation, 42360
Bells Foods International, 42365
Belshaw Adamatic Bakery Group, 42368
Beltram Foodservice Group, 42371
Bematek Systems Inc, 42374
Berg Chilling Systems, 42382
Berg Co, 42383
Berkshire Dairy, 42388
Bernal Technology, 42392
Bessamaire Sales Inc, 42401
Best & Donovan, 42403
Beta Screen Corp, 42414
Bete Fog Nozzle Inc, 42415
Bette's Oceanview Diner, 42418
Better Packages, 42421
BEVCO, 42206
Beverly International, 42426
Bevles Company, 42428
Biagio's Banquets, 42430
Bianchi Winery, 42431
Bijur Lubricating Corporation, 42435
Binks Industries Inc, 42439
Bio Cide Intl Inc, 42441
Bio-Foods, 42443
BioAmber, 42444
Bioclimatic Air Systems LLC, 42446
Biocontrol Systems Inc, 42447
Birchwood Foods Inc, 42454
Birdsong Corp., 42455
Biro Manufacturing Co, 42458
Black's Products of HighPoint, 42466
Blackhawk Molding Co Inc, 42467
Blair's Sauces & Snacks, 42468
Blanver USA, 42472
Blaze Products Corp, 42474
Blossom Farm Products, 42482
Blue Crab Bay, 42485
Blue Cross Laboratories, 42486

681

Export Region / Asia

Blue Giant Equipment Corporation, 42489
Blue Harvest Foods, 42490
Blue Mountain Enterprise Inc, 42491
Blue Pacific Flavors & Fragrances, 42492
Blue Sky Beverage Company, 42496
Blue Star Food Products, 42497
Bluffton Slaw Cutter Company, 42500
BluMetric Environmental Inc., 42484
Boca Bons East, 42507
Bonduelle North America, 42518
Bonnot Co, 42520
Bosch Packaging Technology, 42525
Boston Retail, 42530
Boston's Best Coffee Roasters, 42533
Botanical Products, 42534
Boxes.com, 42542
Boyd Lighting Company, 42544
Bradman Lake Inc, 42549
Brandmeyer Popcorn Co, 42555
Brandt Farms Inc, 42557
Braun Brush Co, 42564
Breakwater Fisheries, 42567
Breddo Likwifier, 42571
Brenton Engineering Co, 42574
Brewmatic Company, 42575
Broaster Co LLC, 42588
Brogdex Company, 42590
Brolite Products Inc, 42591
Brooks Instrument LLC, 42597
Brotherhood Winery, 42600
Brothers Metal Products, 42602
Brower, 42603
Brown & Haley, 42604
Brown Fired Heater, 42605
Brown International Corp LLC, 42606
Brown Machine LLC, 42607
Brown-Forman Corp, 42611
Brucia Plant Extracts, 42613
Bry-Air Inc, 42618
Bubbies Homemade Ice Cream, 42621
Buck Knives, 42622
Buena Vista Historic Tstng Rm, 42629
Buffalo Technologies Corporation, 42630
Buffalo Trace Distillery, 42631
Buffalo Wire Works Co Inc, 42632
Bullet Guard Corporation, 42636
Bunn-O-Matic Corp, 42640
Burke Corp, 42645
Burrows Paper Corp, 42650
Busse/SJI Corp, 42654
BW Container Systems, 42214
C C Pollen, 42664
C Nelson Mfg Co, 42670
C P Industries, 42671
C W Cole & Co, 42676
C&P Additives, 42678
C. Cretors & Company, 42680
C.E. Fish Company, 42683
Cabot Corp, 42720
Cadie Products Corp, 42726
Cafe Altura, 42727
Cafe Du Monde Coffee Stand, 42728
Caffe Luca Coffee Roaste, 42731
CAI International, 42687
Cal Harvest Marketing Inc, 42736
Cal-Mil Plastic Products Inc, 42741
Calgrain Corporation, 42747
California Cereal Products, 42749
California Custom Fruits, 42751
California Natural Products, 42754
California Olive Oil Council, 42756
California World Trade and Marketing Company, 42758
Calpro Ingredients, 42763
Cambridge Viscosity, Inc., 42766
Cambro Manufacturing Co, 42767
Campagana Winery, 42774
Can Lines Engineering Inc, 42778
Candy & Company/Peck's Products Company, 42787
Candy Manufacturing Co, 42789
Cantech Industries Inc, 42795
Capay Canyon Ranch, 42796
Capmatic, Ltd., 42801
Caraustar Industries, Inc., 42811

Caristrap International, 42827
Carle & Montanari-O P M, 42829
Carleton Technologies Inc, 42831
Carlin Manufacturing, 42832
Carlisle Food Svc Products Inc, 42833
Carlisle Sanitary Mntnc Prods, 42834
Carolina Pride Foods, 42842
Carrageenan Company, 42847
Carrier Vibrating Equip Inc, 42850
Cascade Mountain Winery, 42867
Casella Lighting, 42869
Caspian Trading Company, 42873
Casso-Solar Corporation, 42875
Castle Cheese, 42876
Cat Pumps, 42877
Cates Addis Company, 42880
Catskill Craftsmen Inc, 42883
Cedar Lake Foods, 42894
Centennial Food Corporation, 42902
Century Industries Inc, 42914
Champion Chemical Co, 42919
Charles Ross & Son Co, 42934
Chase Industries Inc, 42940
Chase-Doors, 42941
Chase-Logeman Corp, 42942
Chef Revival, 42952
Chef Specialties, 42953
Chefwear, 42957
Chemclean Corp, 42963
Chemex Division/International Housewares Corporation, 42965
Chemicolloid Laboratories, Inc., 42966
Chemifax, 42967
Cherokee Trading Co, 42972
Cherry Central Cooperative, Inc., 42973
Cherry's Industrial Eqpt Corp, 42974
Chico Nut Company, 42993
Chief Wenatchee, 42995
China Mist Brands, 43002
Chipmaker Tooling Supply, 43006
Chocolate Concepts, 43012
Chocolates a La Carte, 43017
Choice Organic Teas, 43019
Chong Imports, 43021
Chooljian Bros Packing Co, 43022
CHS Sunflower, 42697
Church & Dwight Co., Inc., 43031
Cincinnati Industrial Machry, 43035
Cincinnati Preserving Co, 43036
Cintex of America, 43039
Cipriani's Spaghetti & Sauce Company, 43041
Citadelle Maple Syrup Producers' Cooperative, 43046
Citrosuco North America Inc, 43049
Citrus Service, 43050
CJ America, 42699
Clabber Girl Corporation, 43056
Clarendon Flavor Engineering, 43059
Clark-Cooper Division Magnatrol Valve Corporation, 43061
Clarkson Grain Co Inc, 43063
Classic Flavors & Fragrances, 43065
Classic Tea, 43066
Classico Seating, 43067
Clawson Machine Co Inc, 43068
Clayton Corp., 43071
Clayton Industries, 43072
Clean Water Systems, 43073
Clean Water Technology, 43074
Clearwater Fine Foods, 43077
Cleaver-Brooks Inc, 43080
Climax Packaging Machinery, 43092
Clipper Belt Lacer Company, 43093
Clofine Dairy Products Inc, 43095
Clos Du Val Co LTD, 43096
Cloverdale Foods, 43099
Co-Rect Products Inc, 43103
Coburn Company, 43111
Cold Hollow Cider Mill, 43125
Coldmatic Refrigeration, 43128
Coleman Natural, 43131
Columbian TecTank, 43150
Columbus Instruments, 43151
Commercial Creamery Co, 43160
Commercial Dehydrator Systems, 43161

Commercial Furniture Group Inc, 43162
Compacker Systems LLC, 43172
Compactors Inc, 43174
Composition Materials Co Inc, 43179
Compris Technologies, 43180
Computype Inc, 43184
Comstock Castle Stove Co, 43185
Comtec Industries, 43186
Con Agra Snack Foods, 43188
Conax Buffalo Technologies, 43193
Concannon Vineyard, 43195
Conimar Corp, 43200
Conquest International LLC, 43204
Consolidated Baling Machine Company, 43205
Consolidated Commercial Controls, 43207
Consolidated Commerical Controls, 43208
Consolidated Container Co LLC, 43209
Constellation Brands Inc, 43214
Container Machinery Corporation, 43216
Contech Enterprises Inc, 43218
Continental Equipment Corporation, 43223
Control & Metering, 43234
Convay Systems, 43242
Conveyor Accessories, 43246
Cookie Tree Bakeries, 43256
Cooking Systems International, 43258
CookTek, 43254
Cool Care, 43259
Corenco, 43271
Cork Specialties, 43275
Cornelius Inc., 43278
Cornell Machine Co, 43279
Corona College Heights, 43281
Corson Rubber Products Inc, 43286
Coss Engineering Sales Company, 43292
Costa Deano's Gourmet Foods, 43294
Costco Wholesale Corporation, 43295
Cotton Goods Mfg Co, 43296
Country Save Products Corp, 43304
Country Smoked Meats, 43305
Courtright Companies, 43307
Couture Farms, 43309
Cozzoli Machine Co, 43314
CP Kelco, 42707
CPM Century Extrusion, 42708
Cramer Company, 43317
Crane & Crane Inc, 43320
Crane Environmental, 43322
Cres Cor, 43338
Cresset Chemical Company, 43343
Crestware, 43345
Cribari Vineyard Inc, 43347
Critzas Industries Inc, 43351
Crockett Honey, 43352
Croll Reynolds Inc, 43354
CROPP Cooperative, 42711
Crosby Molasses Company, 43356
Crowley Sales & Export Co, 43360
Crown Closures Machinery, 43363
Crown Controls Inc., 43364
Crown Iron Works Company, 43369
Crown Packing Company, 43372
Crown Processing Company, 43374
Cruvinet Winebar Co LLC, 43380
Cryochem, 43381
Crystal Creamery, 43382
Crystal-Vision Packaging Systems, 43390
CSC Scientific Co Inc, 42712
CSC Worldwide, 42713
CSS International Corp, 42714
Culligan Company, 43398
Culture Systems Inc, 43400
Cup Pac Packaging Inc, 43406
Currie Machinery Co, 43409
Cutler Industries, 43426
CVP Systems Inc, 42718
Cyanotech Corp, 43428
Cyclonaire Corp, 43431
D & L Manufacturing, 43435
D D Williamson & Co Inc, 43439
D R Technology Inc, 43440
D.F. International, 43448

Daily Printing Inc, 43468
DairyAmerica, 43475
DairyChem Inc., 43476
Daisy Brand, 43479
Dakota Specialty Milling, Inc., 43480
Dalemark Industries, 43482
Damp Rid, 43488
Daniele Inc, 43495
Darisil, 43502
Dark Tickle Company, 43503
Darnell-Rose Inc, 43504
Dart Container Corp., 43505
Davenport Machine, 43508
Davis Strait Fisheries, 43514
Davis Trade & Commodities, 43515
Dawes Hill Honey Company, 43518
DCL Solutions LLC, 43452
Dealers Food Products Co, 43538
Deep Creek Custom Packing, 43546
Defranco Co, 43553
Del Rey Packing, 43560
Del Rio Nut Company, 43561
Delavau LLC, 43564
Delicato Family Vineyards, 43569
Delta Machine & Maufacturing, 43575
Delta Pure Filtration Corp, 43576
DeltaTrak, 43578
Deluxe Equipment Company, 43580
Desert King International, 43590
Designed Nutritional Products, 43595
Detecto Scale Co, 43598
Di Mare Fresh Inc, 43606
Diamond Bakery Co LTD, 43612
Diamond Foods, 43616
Diamond Fruit Growers, 43617
Diamond Nutrition, 43619
Die Cut Specialties Inc, 43626
Dietzco, 43629
Dipix Technologies, 43635
DMC-David Manufacturing Company, 43458
DNE World Fruit Sales, 43459
Doran Scales Inc, 43671
Double Wrap Cup & Container, 43677
Douglas Machines Corp., 43680
Dovex Export Co, 43684
Doyon, 43689
Dr Konstantin Frank's Vinifera, 43691
Dresco Belting Co Inc, 43704
Driscoll Strawberry Assoc Inc, 43708
Dry Creek Vineyard, 43712
DSM Fortitech Premixes, 43461
Dunbar Manufacturing Co, 43719
Dunkley International Inc, 43723
DuPont Nutrition & Biosciences, 43713
Dura-Flex, 43728
Dura-Ware Company of America, 43730
Dyna-Veyor Inc, 43748
Dynamic Air Inc, 43754
E & E Process Instrumentation, 43755
E Waldo Ward & Son Marmalades, 43758
E-J Industries Inc, 43761
Eagle Products Company, 43797
East Bay International, 43803
East Coast Sea Port Corporation, 43804
East Coast Seafood Inc, 43805
Eatec Corporation, 43817
Eaton Corporation, 43819
Eckhart Corporation, 43825
Eckroat Seed Company, 43827
Eclipse Systems Inc, 43829
Eco-Air Products, 43831
Ecodyne Water Treatment, LLC, 43834
Econofrost Night Covers, 43840
Economy Paper & Restaurant Co, 43844
Ecoval Dairy Trade, 43846
EDA International Corp, 43772
Eden, 43850
Edge Manufacturing, 43854
Edgecraft Corp, 43856
Edison Price Lighting, 43858
Edlong Corporation, 43860
Edom Labs Inc, 43865
Edson Packaging Machinery, 43866
Einson Freeman, 43871
Elberta Crate & Box Company, 43881

Export Region / Asia

Eldorado Coffee Distributors, 43884
Electro Freeze, 43887
Eliason Corp, 43892
Ellingers Agatized Wood Inc, 43900
Elliott Manufacturing Co Inc, 43902
Ellison Milling Company, 43904
Elmar Worldwide, 43905
Elmer Hansen Produce Inc, 43907
Emblem & Badge, 43916
Emerald City Closets Inc, 43918
Emerald Kalama Chemical, LLC, 43919
Emerling International Foods, 43921
Emery Winslow Scale Co, 43926
Emtrol, 43935
Ener-G Foods, 43941
Energen Products Inc, 43942
Engineered Products Corp, 43947
Enjoy Foods International, 43952
ENM Co, 43784
Ensemble Beverages, 43955
Enterprise Company, 43959
Enviro-Clear Co, 43962
Enzyme Development Corporation, 43965
EP International, 43785
Equipment Specialists Inc, 43974
Erickson Industries, 43977
Erie Foods Intl Inc, 43978
Eriez Magnetics, 43979
Ermanco, 43981
ERO/Goodrich Forest Products, 43788
Erwyn Products Inc, 43983
Esselte Meto, 43990
Essential Industries Inc, 43991
Essential Products of America, 43992
Essiac Canada International, 43993
Esteem Products, 43994
Ettore, 43997
Euclid Coffee Co, 43998
Eurex International, 44000
EVAPCO Inc, 43792
Evaporator Dryer Technologies, 44021
Everbrite LLC, 44025
Evergreen Packaging, 44030
Everpure, LLC, 44031
Evonik Corporation   North America, 44033
Excalibur Miretti Group LLC, 44038
Exhibitron Co, 44047
Eximcan Canada, 44048
Eximco Manufacturing Company, 44049
Export Contract Corporation, 44051
F I L T E C-Inspection Systems, 44062
F&Y Enterprises, 44065
Fabohio Inc, 44086
Fabreeka International, 44087
Fabricated Components Inc, 44088
Fairbanks Scales, 44094
Fallas Automation Inc., 44104
Famarco Limited, 44106
Fantasy Chocolates, 44111
Far West Meats, 44113
Farmington Foods Inc, 44118
Fast Industries, 44120
Fax Foods, 44124
FECO/MOCO, 44074
Felbro Food Products, 44133
Felins USA Inc, 44136
Fernholtz Engineering, 44142
Ferntrade Corporation, 44143
Ferrell-Ross, 44146
Ferris Organic Farms, 44148
Fibre Leather Manufacturing Company, 44156
Fiesta Farms, 44159
Figaro Company, 44162
Filler Specialties, 44163
Filling Equipment Co Inc, 44164
Fillmore Piru Citrus, 44166
Fiorucci Foods USA Inc, 44181
First Colony Coffee & Tea Company, 44186
First District Association, 44187
Fish Oven & Equipment Co, 44189
Fishmore, 44194
Fitec International Inc, 44196

Flakice Corporation, 44202
Flanigan Farms, 44206
Flavor Dynamics Two, 44209
Flavor Wear, 44213
Flavormatic Industries, 44217
Fleischer's Bagels, 44222
Fleurchem Inc, 44226
Flex Products, 44227
Flexicon, 44230
Fluid Air Inc, 44250
Fluid Energy Processing & Eqpt, 44251
Fluid Metering Inc, 44252
Flying Dog Brewery, 44255
Flyover International Corporation, 44256
Fold-Pak South, 44266
Folklore Foods, 44271
Follett Corp, 44272
Food & Agrosystems, 44276
Food Technology Corporation, 44287
Foodscience Corp, 44295
Foppiano Vineyards, 44300
Forbes Industries, 44302
Ford Gum & Mach Co Inc, 44303
Forever Foods, 44308
Forte Technology, 44313
Fortune Products Inc, 44315
Foss Nirsystems, 44318
Foster Farms Inc., 44320
FPEC Corporation, 44079
Framarx Corp, 44331
France Delices, 44332
Franklin Trading Company, 44339
Fred D Pfening Co, 44344
Freeman Industries, 44350
Freemark Abbey Winery, 44351
French Oil Mill Machinery Co, 44362
Friedrich Metal Products, 44370
Friskem Infinetics, 44372
Front Range Snacks Inc, 44377
Frontline Inc, 44379
Frutex Group, 44389
Fry Foods Inc, 44390
Frye's Measure Mill, 44391
Fuji Foods Corp, 44393
Fuller Industries LLC, 44394
Fuller Packaging Inc, 44395
Fuller Weighing Systems, 44396
Fullway International, 44397
Fun Foods, 44400
Fun-Time International, 44401
Future Commodities Intl Inc, 44405
Galbreath LLC, 44454
Gamajet Cleaning Systems, 44460
Garcoa Laboratories Inc, 44469
Garden Row Foods, 44473
Gardner Manufacturing Inc, 44475
Garver Manufacturing Inc, 44484
Garvey Corp, 44485
Gasser Chair Co Inc, 44491
Gastro-Gnomes, 44493
Gch Internatonal, 44501
GCI Nutrients, 44419
Gea Intec, Llc, 44503
GEA North America, 44421
Gea Us, 44504
Gehnrich Oven Sales Company, 44509
GEM Berry Products, 44426
GEM Cultures, 44427
Gems Sensors & Controls, 44513
Genarom International, 44514
General Processing Systems, 44527
Genpak LLC, 44536
Gensaco Marketing, 44537
George A Jeffreys & Company, 44539
Georgia Spice Company, 44551
Georgia-Pacific LLC, 44552
GePolymershapes Cadillac, 44502
GERM-O-RAY, 44429
Gessner Products, 44562
Geyser Peak Winery, 44563
GH Ford Tea Company, 44431
GHM Industries Inc, 44432
Giles Enterprises Inc, 44573
Gilly Galoo, 44576
Gilster-Mary Lee Corp, 44578
Ginco International, 44579

Ginseng Up Corp, 44582
Girard's Food Service Dressings, 44585
Girton Manufacturing Co, 44586
Glacier Fish Company, 44589
Glacier Foods, 44590
Glass Pro, 44593
Glastender, 44594
Glenmarc Manufacturing, 44597
Glit Microtron, 44599
Glo-Quartz Electric Heater, 44600
Global Egg Corporation, 44602
Global Manufacturing, 44608
Globe Food Equipment Co, 44614
Goetze's Candy Co, 44620
Goldco Industries, 44625
Golden Moon Tea, 44635
Golden River Fruit Company, 44640
Golden Specialty Foods Inc, 44641
Golden Star, 44642
Golden State Foods Corp, 44643
Golden Walnut Specialty Foods, 44647
Good For You America, 44652
Governair Corp, 44678
Grain Machinery Mfg Corp, 44685
Grainaissance, 44687
Grande Custom Ingredients Group, 44693
Grandview Farms, 44694
Graphite Metalizing Corp, 44701
Grayco Products Sales, 44705
Great Glacier Salmon, 44710
Great Lakes Designs, 44713
Great Lakes International Trading, 44715
Great Northern Products Inc, 44717
Great Valley Mills, 44720
Great Western Co LLC, 44721
Great Western Manufacturing Company, 44724
Greater Omaha Packing Co Inc., 44725
Green Belt Industries Inc, 44731
Green Grown Products Inc, 44735
Green Spot Packaging, 44736
Greene Brothers, 44740
Greig Filters Inc, 44744
Grgich Hills Estates, 44747
Grocers Supply Co, 44757
Grow Co, 44762
GS Dunn & Company, 44438
GTCO CalComp, 44441
Guerra Nut Shelling Co Inc, 44768
Guglielmo Winery, 44769
Gulf Food Products Co Inc, 44776
Gum Technology Corporation, 44780
Guth Lighting, 44786
GWB Foods Corporation, 44443
H A Phillips & Co, 44789
H C Duke & Son Inc, 44793
H G Weber & Co, 44797
H R Nicholson Co, 44799
H T I Filtration, 44800
H. Interdonati, 44804
H20 Technology, 44813
Hackney Brothers, 44828
Hadley Fruit Orchards, 44829
Hadley's Date Gardens, 44830
Hagensborg Chocolates LTD., 44831
Haitai Inc, 44835
Haldin International, 44836
Hall Manufacturing Co, 44839
Hall-Woolford Wood Tank Co Inc, 44841
Halton Packaging Systems, 44844
Hamilton Beach Brands, 44847
Hamilton Caster, 44849
Hampton Associates & Sons, 44852
Hamrick Manufacturing & Svc, 44854
Handy International Inc, 44859
Hanif's International Foods, 44863
Hanimex Company, 44864
Hank Rivera Associates, 44865
Hanna Instruments, 44868
Hanson Brass Rewd Co, 44877, 44878
Harborlite Corporation, 44887
Hardwood Products Co LP, 44893
Hardy Systems Corporation, 44894
Harlan Bakeries, 44896
Harpak-ULMA Packaging LLC, 44902

Hart Design & Mfg, 44912
Hartness International, 44915
Hatfield Quality Meats, 44926
Haumiller Engineering Co, 44927
Hawaii Candy Inc, 44933
Haynes Manufacturing Co, 44938
Hcs Enterprises, 44943
Healing Garden, 44945
Health Plus, 44951
Healthy N Fit International, 44957
Heatcraft Worldwide Refrig, 44965
Heaven Hill Distilleries Inc., 44967
Heidi's Gourmet Desserts, 44971
Heise Wausau Farms, 44975
Heitz Wine Cellars, 44976
Heller Estates, 44980
Hemisphere Group, 44984
Henry Troemner LLC, 44992
Heterochemical Corp, 45005
Hewitt Soap Company, 45007
HFI Foods, 45008
Hialeah Products Co, 45010
Highlight Industries, 45018
Hillside Candy Co, 45024
Hirzel Canning Co & Farms, 45036
Hitec Food Equipment, 45037
HMG Worldwide In-Store Marketing, 44823
Hobe Laboratories Inc, 45038
Hoffer Flow Controls Inc, 45040
Hoffmaster Group Inc, 45042
Holistic Horizons/Halcyon Pacific Corporation, 45044
Holland Beef International Corporation, 45047
Hollowick Inc, 45051
Hollymatic Corp, 45052
Homarus Inc, 45057
Honee Bear Canning, 45064
Honey Acres, 45065
Honeywood Winery, 45068
Hood River Distillers Inc, 45071
Hoppmann Corporation, 45076
Horix Manufacturing Co, 45077
Hormann Flexan Llc, 45079
Hospitality Mints LLC, 45087
Houdini Inc, 45090
Hovair Systems Inc, 45098
Hsu's Ginseng Enterprises Inc, 45110
Hubbell Lighting Inc, 45115
Hudson Valley Coffee Company, 45119
Hudson-Sharp Machine Company, 45123
Hughes Co, 45124
Hungerford & Terry, 45128
Huskey Specialty Lubricants, 45135
Huther Brothers, 45138
Hybrinetics Inc, 45139
Hydrel Corporation, 45140
Hydropure Water Treatment Co, 45143
Hygrade Gloves, 45148
I-Health Inc, 45155
ICB Greenline, 45163
Iceomatic, 45194
Iconics Inc, 45195
Idaho Pacific Holdings Inc, 45196
Idaho Steel Products Inc, 45197
Idaho Supreme Potatoes Inc, 45198
Ideal Stencil Machine & Tape Company, 45200
Idesco Corp, 45205
ILHWA American Corporation, 45171
Imaging Technologies, 45214
IMECO Inc, 45172
IMI Cornelius, 45173
IMI Precision Engineering, 45174
Impact Confections, 45219
Imperial Salmon House, 45224
Improved Blow Molding, 45231
In A Bind Inc, 45233
Indel Food Products Inc, 45242
Indemax Inc, 45243
India Tree, Inc., 45246
Indian Bay Frozen Foods, 45247
Indian Valley Meats, 45250
Indiana Glass Company, 45252
Industrial Contracting & Rggng, 45260

Export Region / Asia

Industrial Product Corp, 45265
Inniskillin Wines, 45282
Innovative Components, 45286
Inovatech USA, 45294
Inox Tech, 45295
Insect-O-Cutor Inc, 45296
Inshore Fisheries, 45298
Insinger Co, 45300
Insulair, 45305
Interamerican Quality Foods, 45315
Intercomp, 45317
Interlab, 45320
Interlake Mecalux, 45321
International Coconut Corp, 45332
International Cooling Systems, 45335
International Dehydrated Foods, 45337
International Food Packers Corporation, 45342
International Home Foods, 45347
International Industries Corporation, 45348
International Packaging Machinery, 45358
International Paper Box Machine Company, 45359
International Patterns, Inc., 45361
International Reserve Equipment Corporation, 45362
International Sourcing, 45366
International Tank & Pipe Co, 45368
International Telcom Inc, 45369
International Tray Pads, 45371
ISF Trading, 45181
Island Marine Products, 45391
Island Oasis Frozen Cocktail, 45392
Island Sweetwater Beverage Company, 45394
Itac Label & Tag Corp, 45397
Italian Quality Products, 45403
Ito Cariani Sausage Company, 45407
ITW Angleboard, 45184
Ives-Way Products, 45411
Izabel Lam International, 45416
J C Watson Co, 45424
J G Van Holten & Son Inc, 45427
J R Carlson Laboratories Inc, 45432
J. Crocker Exports, 45436
JAAMA World Trade, 45449
Jakeman's Maple Products, 45481
James L. Mood Fisheries, 45484
Janta International Company, Inc, 45493
Jantec, 45494
Jay-Bee Manufacturing Inc, 45507
JD Sweid Foods, 45454
Jelly Belly Candy Co., 45512
Jessie's Ilwaco Fish Company, 45522
Jet Set Sam, 45524
Jewel Date Co, 45527
Jilasco Food Exports, 45529
Jim Did It Sign Company, 45531
Joe Tea and Joe Chips, 45537
Joey's Fine Foods, 45538
John Boos & Co, 45540
John E. Ruggles & Company, 45544
John J. Adams Die Corporation, 45547
John R Nalbach Engineering Co, 45548
Johns Cove Fisheries, 45551
Johnson Foods, Inc., 45553
Johnson Refrigerated Truck, 45556
Johnston Equipment, 45558
Johnston Farms, 45559
Jordon Commercial Refrigerator, 45568
Joseph Adams Corp, 45570
Juanita's Foods, 45581
Judel Products, 45582
Juice Tree, 45584
K Trader Inc., 45600
K-Way Products, 45605
K.F. Logistics, 45606
Kal Pac Corp, 45640
Kalsec, 45642
KAPS All Packaging, 45610
KASE Equipment, 45613
Kashi Company, 45654
Kay Home Products Inc, 45660
Kaye Instruments, 45662

Keeper Thermal Bag Co, 45685
Kelley Company, 45688
Kelly Gourmet Foods Inc, 45692
Kent Precision Foods Group Inc, 45706
Kenwood Vineyards, 45709
Keto Foods, 45715
Key Packaging Co, 45718
Key Technology Inc., 45719
Key-Pak Machines, 45721
KH McClure & Company, 45616
Khong Guan Corp, 45726
Kiefer Brushes, Inc, 45728
Kim Lighting, 45730
Kincaid Enterprises, 45732
Kinergy Corp, 45734
King B Meat Snacks, 45738
King Nut Co, 45744
Kings River Casting, 45750
Kiss International/Di-tech Systems, 45759
Kisters Kayat, 45760
Kittling Ridge Estate Wines & Spirits, 45763
Klaire Laboratories, 45764
Kleen Products Inc, 45765
KMT Aqua-Dyne Inc, 45625
Knight Seed Company, 45773
Knott Slicers, 45776
Koehler Instrument Co Inc, 45783
Kola, 45788
Kold-Hold, 45790
Kolpak Walk-ins, 45793
Kona Joe Coffee LLC, 45795
Korab Engineering Company, 45801
Kornylak Corp, 45803
Kosto Food Products Co, 45804
KP USA Trading, 45627
Krogh Pump Co, 45817
Kruger Foods, 45821
KTG, 45629
Kubla Khan Food Company, 45822
Kuhl Corporation, 45825
KWIK Lok Corp, 45631
Kyowa Hakko, 45833
Kysor Panel Systems, 45834
L F Lambert Spawn Co, 45837
L G I Intl Inc, 45838
L&A Process Systems, 45840
La Crosse, 45872
La Flor Spices, 45873
LA Monica Fine Foods, 45851
Lactalis American Group Inc, 45892
Laetitia Vineyard & Winery, 45894
Lakeside Foods Inc., 45905
Lakeside Manufacturing Inc, 45906
Lakeside-Aris Manufacturing, 45909
Lallemand, 45911
Lambent Technologies, 45913
Land O'Lakes Inc, 45926
Langen Packaging, 45935
Lanly Co, 45939
Latendorf Corporation, 45947
Laub-Hunt Packaging Systems, 45949
Lawrence Metal Products Inc, 45956
Lazzari Fuel Co LLC, 45960
Leader Candies, 45966
Least Cost Formulations LTD, 45967
Leavitt Corp., The, 45968
Lebermuth Company, 45969
Leland Limited Inc, 45986
Les Viandes du Breton, 46005
Letrah International Corp, 46010
Lewis M Carter Mfg Co Inc, 46014
Libido Funk Circus, 46028
Lifestar Millennium, 46029
Lifestyle Health Guide, 46030
Light Technology Ind, 46035
Lightlife, 46037
Liguria Foods Inc, 46039
Linvar, 46056
Lion Raisins Inc, 46059
Little Crow Foods, 46071
LMK Containers, 45865
Load King Mfg, 46081
Lodge Manufacturing Company, 46089
Lodi Metal Tech, 46090

Lone Pine Enterprise Inc, 46096
Longview Farms Emu Oil, 46104
Longview Fibre Company, 46105
Loriva Culinary Oils, 46112
Louis Baldinger & Sons, 46119
Love Controls Division, 46130
Love Quiches Desserts, 46131
Loveshaw Corp, 46133
Lovion International, 46134
Low Humidity Systems, 46135
Low Temp Industries Inc, 46136
Ltg Inc, 46139
Ludell Manufacturing Co, 46145
Lukas Confections, 46151
Lumber & Things, 46155
Luseaux Labs Inc, 46160
Luthi Machinery Company, Inc., 46162
Luxury Crab, 46167
Luyties Pharmacal Company, 46168
Lyco Manufacturing, 46169
Lyo-San, 46173
M-C McLane International, 46189
M-Vac Systems Inc, 46192
Mac Farms Of Hawaii Inc, 46220
Machine Ice Co, 46228
Madera Enterprises Inc, 46233
MAFCO Worldwide, 46198
Magic Valley Growers, 46245
Magnetic Products Inc, 46249
Magnolia Citrus Assn, 46251
Magnotta Winery Corporation, 46252
Maine Wild Blueberry Company, 46262
Maker's Mark Distillery Inc, 46270
Malo Inc, 46275
Mancuso Cheese Co, 46288
Mane Inc., 46291
Manischewitz Co, 46298
Manitowoc Foodservice, 46299
Maple Leaf Foods International, 46307
Mar-Con Wire Belt, 46311
Marantha Natural Foods, 46316
Marathon Equipment Co, 46318
Marcus Food Co, 46323
Mariani Nut Co, 46330
Marin Food Specialties, 46333
Mario's Gelati, 46338
Markham Industries, 46345
Marking Methods Inc, 46347
Markwell Manufacturing Company, 46351
Marlen, 46353
Marlen International, 46354
Marlyn Nutraceuticals, 46357
Marsan Foods, 46364
Marsh Company, 46365
Marshall Air Systems Inc, 46366
Martin Engineering, 46373
Martin Laboratories, 46374
Martin/Baron, 46375
Marubeni America Corp., 46376
Maryland China, 46383
Maselli Measurements Inc, 46389
Master Mix, 46395
Mastercraft Industries Inc, 46397
Mastex Industries, 46400
Materials Transportation Co, 46406
Matfer Inc, 46407, 46408
Mathews Packing, 46409
Matot - Commercial GradeLift Solutions, 46411
Matrix Health Products, 46413
Matrix Packaging Machinery, 46414
Matthiesen Equipment, 46418
Maui Gold Pineapple Company, 46420
Maxfield Candy, 46424
Maxi-Vac Inc., 46425
Maxim's Import Corporation, 46426
Mayacamas Vineyards & Winery, 46430
Mc Steven's Coca Factory Store, 46437
McAnally Enterprises, 46438
Mcbrady Engineering Co, 46454
McCabe's Quality Foods, 46439
McCormack Manufacturing Company, 46443
MCD Technologies, 46202
McDaniel Fruit, 46446

Mcfadden Farm, 46458
Mclaughlin Gormley King Co, 46461
Meadows Mills Inc, 46465
Meduri Farms, 46475
Mega Pro Intl, 46476
Mepsco, 46493
Merchandising Inventives, 46496
Merco/Savory, 46502
Mercury Equipment Company, 46504
Merix Chemical Company, 46509
Merrill's Blueberry Farms, 46515
Metaline Products Co Inc, 46524
Mettler-Toledo, LLC, 46531
Metzger Popcorn Co, 46534
Mexi-Frost Specialties Company, 46535
Mexican Accent, 46536
Meyenberg Goat Milk, 46539
MFI Food Canada, 46206
Michael Foods, Inc., 46550
Michael's Cookies, 46552
Michigan Desserts, 46567
Michigan Maple Block Co, 46569
Micro-Brush Pro Soap, 46573
Microbest Inc, 46577
Microfluidics International, 46580
Micropure Filtration Inc, 46585
MicroSoy Corporation, 46575
Mid-Atlantic Foods Inc, 46589
Midas Foods Intl, 46596
Middleby Marshall Inc, 46599
Mies Products, 46610
Miguel's Stowe Away, 46615
Mil-Du-Gas Company/Star Brite, 46617
Miljoco Corp, 46623
Milk Specialties Global, 46624
Mille Lacs Wild Rice Corp, 46628
Millerbernd Systems, 46632
Mills Brothers Intl, 46636
Milne Fruit Products Inc, 46639
Milwhite Inc, 46645
Mimi et Cie, 46646
Minn-Dak Growers LTD, 46650
Minuteman Power Boss, 46655
Miracapo Pizza, 46658
Miss Mary, 46665
Mixon Fruit Farms Inc, 46673
MLG Enterprises Ltd., 46214
MMR Technologies, 46216
Mo Hotta Mo Betta, 46677
Mocon Inc, 46678
MODAGRAPHICS, 46217
Modar, 46679
Moen Industries, 46686
Mold-Rite Plastics LLC, 46690
Moli-International, 46693
Momar, 46699
Mondial Foods Company, 46704
Money's Mushrooms, 46705
Monin Inc., 46706
Monitor Technologies LLC, 46708
Monroe Environmental Corp, 46709
Montana Naturals, 46714
Moore Production Tool Spec Inc, 46722
Morre-Tec Ind Inc, 46731
Morris & Associates, 46732
Morse Manufacturing Co Inc, 46738
Morton Salt Inc., 46741
Mosher Products Inc, 46743
Mountain Safety Research, 46753
Mountain Valley Products Inc, 46754
Mr Ice Bucket, 46761
Mrs. Leeper's Pasta, 46769
Muckler Industries, Inc, 46775
Muellermist Irrigation Company, 46776
Muir Copper Canyon Farms, 46778
Mulligan Associates, 46780
Multi-Pak, 46782
Multiflex Company, 46787
Multisorb Technologies Inc, 46790
Munson Machinery Co, 46794
Murakami Farms, 46797
Murzan Inc. Sanitary Sys, 46801
Musco Family Olive Co, 46802
Mushroom Wisdom, Inc, 46805
Muth Associates, 46807
Mutual Trading Co Inc, 46809

Export Region / Asia

Myers Container, 46815
N S I Sweeteners, 46816
Naltex, 46837
Namco Controls Corporation, 46838
Nancy's Specialty Foods, 46840
Napoleon Co., 46846
NaraKom, 46847
Natco Worldwide Representative, 46859
National Food Corporation, 46871
National Fruit Flavor Co Inc, 46875
National Hotpack, 46876
National Instruments, 46878
National Printing Converters, 46887
National Shippng Supply Co, 46891
National Tape Corporation, 46893
Nationwide Pennant & Flag Mfg, 46896
Natra US, 46898
Natur Sweeteners, Inc., 46901
Natural Flavors, 46904
Natural Group, 46909
Natural Oils International, 46910
Nature Most Laboratories, 46914
Nature Quality, 46915
Nature's Plus, 46924
Nature's Products Inc, 46925
Natures Sungrown Foods Inc, 46927
Navarro Pecan Co, 46929
Naya, 46931
Nebraska Bean, 46937
Nelson Crab Inc, 46947
Neogen Corp, 46951
Neon Design-a-Sign, 46952
NEPA Pallet & Container Co, 46825
Nepco Egg Of Ga, 46955
Neptune Foods, 46957
Nevo Corporation, 46964
New Attitude Beverage Corporation, 46966
New Earth, 46970
New England Machinery Inc, 46973
New England Natural Bakers, 46974
New Horizon Foods, 46979
New Klix Corporation, 46980
New Organics, 46981
New Season Foods Inc, 46983
New York Apple Sales Inc, 46986
Newell Brands, 46997
Newly Weds Foods Inc, 47001
Newman Sanitary Gasket Co, 47002
Newman's Own, 47003
NewStar Fresh Foods LLC, 46993
Nexel Industries Inc, 47009
Niagara Blower Company, 47011
Niagara Foods, 47012
Nice-Pak Products Inc, 47013
Nichem Co, 47015
Nieco Corporation, 47023
Nielsen Citrus Products Inc, 47024
Nielsen-Massey Vanillas Inc, 47025
Nikki's Cookies, 47028
Niro, 47031
Niroflex, USA, 47032
Nitech, 47036
Niutang Chemical, Inc., 47038
Noh Foods of Hawaii, 47041
Nor-Cliff Farms, 47047
Norback Ley & Assoc, 47052
Nordson Sealant Equipment, 47057
Noren Products Inc, 47058
North American Provisioners, 47065
North Bay Produce Inc, 47069
North River Roasters, 47076
North Star Ice EquipmentCorporation, 47078
North Taste Flavourings, 47079
Northeast Group Exporters Inc, 47081
Northeastern Products Corp, 47084
Northfield Freezing Systems, 47090
Northwest Analytical Inc, 47095
Northwest Chocolate Factory, 47097
Northwestern Coffee Mills, 47101
Norvell Co, 47104
Novelty Crystal, 47115
NOW Foods, 46828
Nu-World Amaranth Inc, 47126
Nuance Solutions Inc, 47128

Nuchief Sales Inc, 47129
Nulaid Foods Inc, 47132
Nustef Foods, 47137
Nutra Food Ingredients, LLC, 47140
Nutraceutical International, 47142
Nutri-Cell, 47146
Nutribiotic, 47147
Nutricepts, 47148
Nutritional Counselors of America, 47155
Nutritional Research Associates, 47157
Nutritional Specialties, 47158
O'Dell Corp, 47163
Oceanfood Sales, 47187
Oerlikon Leybold Vacuum, 47189
Ogden Manufacturing Company, 47192
Ohaus Corp, 47193
Ohio Magnetics Inc, 47194
Ok Industries, 47196
Old Sacramento Popcorn Company, 47203
Olde Country Reproductions Inc, 47204
Olivier's Candies, 47209
Olney Machinery, 47210
Omega Produce Company, 47222
Omega Products Inc, 47223
Omega Protein, 47224
Omicron Steel Products Company, 47225
Omni Pacific Company, 47230
Omnitech International, 47233
Once Again Nut Butter, 47237
Onevision Corp, 47240
Ontario Produce Company, 47245
OnTrack Automation Inc, 47236
Opie Brush Company, 47249
Orange Cove-Sanger Citrus, 47257
Oregon Freeze Dry, Inc., 47268
Oregon Hill Farms, 47270
Oregon Potato Co, 47271
Organic Milling, 47275
Orion Research, 47284
Orioxi International Corporation, 47286
Overlake Foods, 47304
Oxford Frozen Foods, 47309
OXO International, 47173
Oyang America, 47311
P J Rhodes Corporation, 47316
P R Farms Inc, 47317
Pacer Pumps, 47352
Pacific Choice Brands, 47354
Pacific Coast Fruit Co, 47355
Pacific Commerce Company, 47356
Pacific Salmon Company, 47364
Pacific Scientific Instrument, 47365
Pacific Seafoods International, 47366
Pacific World Enterprises, 47373
Package Systems Corporation, 47381
Packaging & Processing Equipment, 47382
Packaging Dynamics, 47384
Packaging Equipment & Conveyors, Inc, 47389
Packaging Machinery International, 47392
Packaging Systems Intl, 47395
Pacur, 47399
PAFCO Importing Co, 47322
Palms & Co, 47418
Paltier, 47419
Pangaea Sciences, 47428
Panoche Creek Packing, 47430
Paoli Properties, 47432
Paper Box & Specialty Co, 47433
Paper Systems Inc, 47437
Papertech, 47438
PAR-Way Tryson Co, 47325
Parachem Corporation, 47442
Paraclipse, 47443
Paradise Products Corporation, 47447
Paragon Group USA, 47450
Paramount Industries, 47454
Paratherm Corporation, 47455
Parducci Wine Cellars, 47456
Parish Manufacturing Inc, 47459
Parkson Corp, 47465, 47466
Parrish's Cake Decorating, 47470

Particle Dynamics, 47472
Partnership Resources, 47474
Parvin Manufacturing Company, 47477
Pasquini Espresso Co, 47479
Passport Food Group, 47480
Pastorelli Food Products, 47486
Patterson Industries, 47491
Paul N. Gardner Company, 47495
Paul O. Abbe, 47496
PC/Poll Systems, 47330
PDE Technology Corp, 47332
Peace River Citrus Products, 47504
Peace Village Organic Foods, 47505
Peacock Crate Factory, 47506
Pearson Packaging Systems, 47509
Pecan Deluxe Candy Co, 47511
Peco Controls Corporation, 47512
Peco Foods Inc., 47513
Peerless of America, 47521
Peking Noodle Co Inc, 47524
Pelican Products Inc, 47526
Pelouze Scale Company, 47528
Penauta Products, 47530
Penta Manufacturing Company, 47541
Pepperell Paper Company, 47546
Perry Videx LLC, 47559
Peter Pan Seafoods Inc., 47564
Petschl's Quality Meats, 47574
Pharmaceutical & Food Special, 47580
Pharmachem Labs, 47582
Phelps Industries, 47585
Philadelphia Macaroni Co, 47588
Phoenix Closures Inc, 47594
Phoenix Industries Corp, 47595
Piazza's Seafood World LLC, 47597
Pick Heaters, 47599
Pickard China, 47600
Pictsweet Co, 47603
Pie Piper Products, 47604
Pines International, 47613
Piper Products Inc, 47620, 47621
Pitco Frialator Inc, 47623
Plasti-Clip Corp, 47632
Plastic Suppliers Inc, 47635
Pleasant Grove Farms, 47641
PlexPack Corp, 47642
Pluto Corporation, 47644
PMC Specialties Group Inc, 47336
Pneumatic Scale Angelus, 47648
Pocino Foods, 47649
Pokanoket Ostrich Farm, 47653
Polycon Industries, 47664
Polypack Inc, 47665
Polyscience, 47668
POM Wonderful LLC, 47339
Popcorn Connection, 47673
Porcelain Metals Corporation, 47677
Portion-Pac Chemical Corp., 47682
Power Brushes, 47688
Powertex Inc, 47691
PPI Technologies Group, 47342
Prairie Cajun Wholesale, 47695
Prawnto Systems, 47699
Preferred Machining Corporation, 47709
Preferred Meal Systems Inc, 47710
Preferred Packaging Systems, 47711
Preferred Popcorn, 47712
Preiser Scientific Inc, 47714
Premier Skirting Products, 47720
Presence From Innovation LLC, 47727
Prestige Proteins, 47731
Preston Scientific, 47735
Prime Smoked Meats Inc, 47748
Primo Water Corporation, 47751
Prince Castle Inc, 47753
Prince of Peace, 47756
Printpack Inc., 47757
Priority One Packaging, 47759
Pro Form Labs, 47761
Pro Scientific Inc, 47763
Pro-Flo Products, 47764
Process Displays, 47771
Production Systems, 47785
Produits Belle Baie, 47790
Proffitt Manufacturing Company, 47796
Progenix Corporation, 47799

Progressive International/Mr. Dudley, 47801
Pronatura Inc, 47811
Pronova Biopolymer, 47812
Protein Research, 47816
Protica Inc, 47818
Psc Floturn Inc, 47825
Psyllium Labs, 47826
PTC International, 47344
PTR Baler & Compactor Co, 47346
Pucel Enterprises Inc, 47827
Pulse Systems, 47831
Pure Foods, 47841
Pure Sales, 47843
PureCircle USA, 47846
Puritan Manufacturing Inc, 47847
Puritan/Churchill Chemical Company, 47848
Purolator Facet Inc, 47851
Pyro-Chem, 47854
Q-Matic Technologies, 47859
Quadrel Labeling Systems, 47869
Quaker Chemical Company, 47870
Quality Industries Inc, 47882
Quality Naturally Foods, 47884
Quality Sausage Company, 47885
Quelle Quiche, 47892
Quest Corp, 47893
Quigley Industries Inc, 47896
R A Jones & Co Inc, 47902
R Torre & Co, 47910
R X Honing Machine Corp, 47911
R&J Farms, 47913
R.B. Morriss Company, 47917
R.L. Zeigler Company, 47920
Radlo Foods, 47945
Ragtime, 47949
Railex Corp, 47952
Rainbow Valley Frozen Yogurt, 47956
Rainforest Company, 47957
RainSoft Water Treatment System, 47953
Ram Equipment Co, 47961
Ramoneda Bros Stave Mill, 47964
Ramsey Popcorn Co Inc, 47966
RAO Contract Sales Inc, 47925
Rapid Industries Inc, 47971
RAS Process Equipment Inc, 47926
Ray Cosgrove Brokerage Company, 47978
Raymond Corp, 47980
RDM International, 47928
Real Aloe Company, 47989
Real Kosher Sausage Company, 47992
Real Soda, 47993
Red River Foods Inc, 48003
Red River Lumber Company, 48004
Redi-Call Inc, 48008
Reed Oven Co, 48012
Reede International Seafood Corporation, 48013
Reese Enterprises Inc, 48017
Reeve Store Equipment Co, 48018
Refractron Technologies Corp, 48020
Refresco Beverages US Inc., 48021
Regal Ware Inc, 48030
Rego China Corporation, 48034
Reheis Co, 48036
Reinhart Foods, 48042
Remcraft Lighting Products, 48053
Renold Products, 48061
Renovator's Supply, 48062
Reotemp Instrument Corp, 48063
Republic Foil, 48066
Resina, 48069
Rexcraft Fine Chafers, 48077
Rexford Paper Company, 48078
Reyco Systems Inc, 48082
Ribus Inc., 48088
Rice Company, 48089
Richardson International, 48098
Richland Beverage Association, 48099
Rieke Packaging Systems, 48104
Rio Syrup Co, 48107
Robar International Inc, 48124
Roberts Seed, 48133
Robinson's No 1 Ribs, 48138

685

Export Region / Asia

Rollprint Packaging Prods Inc, 48165
Roosevelt Dairy Trade, Inc, 48175
Rooto Corp, 48176
Roto-Flex Oven Co, 48198
Roxide International, 48207
Royal Accoutrements, 48209
Royal Label Co, 48220
Royal Welding & Fabricating, 48226
Royal Wine Corp, 48227
RPA Process Technologies, 47934
RPM Total Vitality, 47936
Rubbermaid, 48234
Rudolph Foods Co, 48239
Ruiz Food Products Inc., 48243
Rumiano Cheese Co., 48245
Rutherford Engineering, 48248
S & S Indl Maintenance, 48256
S L Sarderson & Co, 48259
S&P Marketing, Inc., 48261
S&P USA Ventilation Systems, LLC, 48262
S&R Imports, 48263
S.V. Dice Designers, 48270
Sabel Engineering Corporation, 48307
Sales & Marketing Dev, 48332
Sampco, 48345
San Jamar, 48355
San Joaquin Vly Concentrates, 48356
San-Ei Gen FFI, 48359
Sandco International, 48364
Sanden Vendo America Inc, 48365
SANGARIA USA, 48271
Sani-Matic, 48373
Sanitech Inc, 48376
Santa Barbara Olive Company, 48378
Santa Clara Nut Co, 48379
Sardee Industries Inc, 48391
Sasib Beverage & Food North America, 48393
Satake USA, 48395
Saunder Brothers, 48398
Saunders Manufacturing Co., 48399
Savoury Systems Inc, 48406
Sazerac Company, Inc., 48409
Scandia Packaging Machinery Co, 48414
Scandinavian Laboratories, 48418
Schenck Process, 48423
Schiff Food Products Co Inc, 48425
Schillinger Genetics Inc, 48426
Schlagel Inc, 48428
Schlueter Company, 48429
Schneider Foods, 48432
Scientech, Inc, 48440
Scientific Process & Research, 48441
Sconza Candy Co, 48442
SDIX, 48274
Se Kure Controls Inc, 48457
Sea Breeze Fruit Flavors, 48459
Seaboard Foods, 48466
Seafood Producers Co-Op, 48474
Seald Sweet, 48476
Sealstrip Corporation, 48477
Seattle Menu Specialists, 48486
Seattle-Tacoma Box Co, 48488
See's Candies, 48492
Seed Enterprises Inc, 48493
Select Food Products, 48497
Select Meat Company, 48498
Sellers Engineering Division, 48502
Semco Manufacturing Company, 48503
Seneca Foods Corp, 48508
Sensidyne, 48511
Sensient Colors Inc, 48512
Sensient Flavors and Fragrances, 48513
Sentinel Lubricants Inc, 48516
Sentry Equipment Corp, 48517
Serendipitea, 48525
Serfilco, 48526
Serpa Packaging Solutions, 48528
Serr-Edge Machine Company, 48529
Server Products Inc, 48535
Sesaco Corp, 48541
Sesinco Foods, 48542
Setterstix Corp, 48546
Setton International Foods, 48547
Severn Trent Svc, 48551

SEW Friel, 48276
SFP Food Products, 48277
SGS International Rice Inc, 48278
Shady Maple Farm, 48559
Shafer-Haggart, 48561
Shanker Industries, 48567
Shaw-Clayton Corporation, 48573
Shawano Specialty Papers, 48574
Shawnee Milling Co, 48575
Shenandoah Vineyards, 48581
Shepherd Farms Inc, 48584
Shick Esteve, 48589
Shields Bag & Printing Co, 48590
Shipley Sales, 48596
Shoei Foods USA Inc, 48602
SHURflo, 48279
Shuttleworth North America, 48610
Si-Lodec, 48611
Sico Inc, 48612
Sidney Manufacturing Co, 48616
Siena Foods, 48619
Sierra Dawn Products, 48620
SIG Combibloc USA, Inc., 48280
Sig Pack, 48621
Sigma Engineering Corporation, 48622
Signature Brands LLC, 48627
Signet Marking Devices, 48628
Signode Industrial Group LLC, 48629
Signs & Shapes Intl, 48630
Silesia Grill Machines Inc, 48634
Silgan Plastics Canada, 48638
Sillcocks Plastics International, 48642
Silver King Refrigeration Inc, 48645
Silver Weibull, 48650
Simmons Engineering Corporation, 48656
Simonds International, 48660
Simplex Filler Co, 48663
Simplimatic Automation, 48666
Sinbad Sweets, 48670
Sioux Corp, 48676
Skd Distribution Corp, 48684
SKW Nature Products, 48286
Skylark Meats, 48687
Slade Gorton & Co Inc, 48689
Slicechief Co, 48692
Smico Manufacturing Co Inc, 48698
Smith Frozen Foods Inc, 48700
Smurfit Stone Container, 48709
Snak King Corp, 48712
Sogelco International, 48733
Solvaira Specialties, 48739
Somerset Industries, 48743
Sonoco Paperboard Specialties, 48749
Sonoco ThermoSafe, 48750
Soodhalter Plastics, 48752
Soofer Co, 48753
South Valley Farms, 48765
Southbend, 48766
Southern Heritage Coffee Company, 48775
Southern Pride Distributing, 48779
Spangler Candy Co, 48792
Sparboe Foods Corp, 48793
Sparkler Filters Inc, 48794
Specialty Blades, 48805
Specialty Commodities Inc, 48807
Specialty Minerals Inc, 48812
Specialty Wood Products, 48816
Specific Mechanical Systems, 48817
Spectro, 48819
Spee-Dee Packaging Machinery, 48821
Spencer Turbine Co, 48825
Sperling Industries, 48827
Spinco Metal Products Inc, 48833
Spray Dynamics LTD, 48842
Spraying Systems Company, 48843
St John's Botanicals, 48859
Stahlbush Island Farms Inc, 48867
Stainless Specialists Inc, 48871
Standard Casing Company, 48875
Standard Terry Mills, 48882
Stanley Access Technologies, 48884
Stanley Orchards Sales, Inc., 48885
Stapleton Spence Packing Co, 48887
Staplex Co Inc, 48888

Star Filters, 48890
Star Industries, Inc., 48891
Star Manufacturing Intl Inc, 48893
Starwest Botanicals Inc, 48903
State Products, 48904
Stauber Performance Ingrdients, 48905
Stavis Seafoods, 48907
Steel City Corporation, 48913
Steiner Company, 48922
Steiner Industries Inc, 48923
Stepan Co., 48926
Sterling Ball & Jewel, 48931
Stevens Linen Association, 48945
Stewart's Private Blend Foods, 48951
STI Certified Products Inc, 48298
STI International, 48299
Stirling Foods, 48956
Stock Popcorn Ind Inc, 48957
Stogsdill Tile Co, 48961
Stone Soap Co Inc, 48965
Storm Industrial, 48972
Straub Designs Co, 48978
Stricklin Co, 48985
Sun Glo Of Idaho, 49008
Sun Harvest Foods Inc, 49010
Sun Pac Foods, 49013
Sunkist Growers, 49024
Sunny Avocado, 49026
Sunrich LLC, 49028
Sunrise Growers, 49032
Sunroc Corporation, 49033
Sunset Specialty Foods, 49035
Suntec Power, 49040
SunWest Foods, Inc., 49019
Supelco Inc, 49043
Superior Foods, 49053
Superior Paper & Plastic Co, 49057
SupHerb Farms, 49042
Supreme Chocolatier, 49061
Surco Products, 49063
Sure-Fresh Produce Inc, 49070
Surekap Inc, 49071
Sussman Electric Boilers, 49074
Suzanne's Specialties, 49076
Svedala Industries, 49078
Sweet Corn Products Co, 49083
Sweet Dried Fruit, 49084
SWF Co, 48303
SWF McDowell, 48304
Swirl Freeze Corp, 49092
Swiss-American Sausage Company, 49096
Swissh Commercial Equipment, 49098
Symms Fruit Ranch Inc, 49102
Symons Frozen Foods, 49103
Synergy Flavors Inc, 49107
Synthite USA Inc., 49108
T Hasegawa USA Inc, 49117
T.C. Food Export/Import Company, 49121
Tabco Enterprises, 49147
Tablecraft Products Co Inc, 49153
Taconic, 49155
Taku Smokehouse, 49160
Taste Teasers, 49191
Taste Traditions Inc, 49192
Tastepoint, 49194
Tate Western, 49196
Taylor Products Co, 49203
TDF Automation, 49127
TDH, 49128
Tech Lighting LLC, 49208
Tech Sales Inc, 49209
Technibilt/Cari-All, 49211
TechnipFMC, 49212
Technistar Corporation, 49213
Techno USA, 49215
Teelee Popcorn, 49224
Teledyne Benthos Inc, 49231
Telwar International Inc, 49236
Tema Systems Inc, 49237
TEMP-TECH Company, 49129
Tempco Electric Heater Corporation, 49239
Templar Food Products, 49240
Templock Corporation, 49241

Tenneco Inc, 49243
Texas Halal Corporation, 49266
Texas Traditions Gourmet, 49269
Tharo Systems Inc, 49274
The Scoular Company/TSC Container Freight, 49300
Therm-Tec Inc, 49306
Therma Kleen, 49307
Thermo Detection, 49310
Thermo-KOOL/Mid-South Ind Inc, 49311
Thermodyne International LTD, 49315
Theta Sciences, 49318
Thiele Engineering Company, 49320
Thirs-Tea Corp, 49322
Thomas L. Green & Company, 49324
Thorn Smith Laboratories, 49333
Tier-Rack Corp, 49344
Tillamook County Creamery Association, 49351
Tindall Packaging, 49357
Tipper Tie Inc, 49361
TLB Corporation, 49134
Todd's, 49369, 49370
Toddy Products Inc, 49371
Tolan Machinery Company, 49377
Tolas Health Care Packaging, 49378
Tomsed Corporation, 49384
Tooterville Trolley Company, 49390
Tootsi Impex, 49391
Toroid Corp, 49399
Toromont Process Systems, 49400
Toshoku America, 49407
Trader Vic's Food Products, 49423
Traex, 49425
Transmunday Company, 49436
Travelon, 49441
TRC, 49140
Treehouse Farms, 49445
Trefethen Family Vineyards, 49446
Trevor Industries, 49448
TREX Corp Inc., 49141
Tri-Pak Machinery Inc, 49452
Tri-Seal, 49453
Tribest Corp, 49463
Tribology Tech Lube, 49464
Trico Converting Inc, 49465
Trident Seafoods Corp, 49467
Tridyne Process Systems, 49469
Trilogy Essential Ingredients, 49470
Triple Leaf Tea Inc, 49482
Triple S Dynamics Inc, 49483
Triple-A Manufacturing Company, 49484
TRITEN Corporation, 49142
Triton International, 49486
Trojan Inc, 49489
Tropical Illusions, 49494
Tropical Link Canada Ltd., 49495
Tropical Preserving Co Inc, 49496
Trout Lake Farm, 49499
True Food Service Equipment, Inc., 49507
TruHeat Corporation, 49504
Tsar Nicoulai Caviar LLC, 49517
Turbo Refrigerating Company, 49531
TURBOCHEF Technologies, 49144
Turkey Hill Sugarbush, 49533
Turlock Fruit Co, 49534
Tuthill Vacuum & Blower Systems, 49539
Tyco Fire Protection Products, 49550
TyRy Inc, 49549
Tyson Foods Inc., 49554
Unarco Industries LLC, 49591
Ungerer & Co, 49599
Union Confectionery Machinery, 49609
Union Fish Co, 49611
United Canadian Malt, 49629
United Citrus, 49631
United Desiccants, 49632
United Electric Controls Co, 49633
United Industries Group Inc, 49638
United Meat Company, 49641
United Performance Metals, 49644
United Ribtype Co, 49646
United Textile Distribution, 49655

Export Region / Australasia

UniTrak Corporation, 49600
Universal Die & Stampings, 49664
Universal Jet Industries, 49668
Universal Paper Box, 49671
Universal Security Instrs Inc, 49672
Urbani Truffles, 49680
Urschel Laboratories, 49682
US Chemical, 49563
US Distilled Products Co, 49565
US Filter Dewatering Systems, 49566
US Food Products, 49567
US Mills, 49572
V C 999 Packaging Systems, 49689
V-Ram Solids, 49690
V.W. Joyner & Company, 49693
Vacuum Barrier Corp, 49709
Valentine Enterprises Inc, 49713
Valley Craft Inc, 49718
Valley Fig Growers, 49719
Van Air Systems, 49726
Van Drunen Farms, 49730
Vanmark Equipment, 49740
Varied Industries Corp, 49745
Varni Brothers/7-Up Bottling, 49749
Vauxhall Foods, 49752
Vector Technologies, 49754
Veggie Land, 49758
Venner International Products, 49764
Ventura Coastal LLC, 49768
Venture Measurement Co LLC, 49769
Vermillion Flooring, 49777
Viatec, 49791
Vichy Springs Mineral Water, 49793
Victor International, 49796
Victoria Fine Foods, 49799
Videojet Technologies Inc, 49801
Vie-Del Co, 49802
Vienna Beef LTD, 49803
Vilter Manufacturing Corporation, 49813
VIP Foods, 49698
Virginia Dare Extract Co, 49827
Visual Planning Corp, 49836
Vita Craft Corp, 49837
Vita-Pakt Citrus Products Co, 49839
Vitarich Ice Cream, 49845
VMC Corp, 49701
Vollrath Co LLC, 49858
Vorti-Siv, 49861
Voyageur Trading Division, 49863
VT Industries Inc, 49703
Vyse Gelatin Co, 49868
W & G Marketing Company, 49869
W.G. Durant Corporation, 49875
Wade Manufacturing Company, 49913
Wagner Vineyards, 49916
Walco, 49922
Walker Foods, 49926
Wanchese Fish Co Inc, 49943
Wapsie Creamery, 49945
Ward Ironworks, 49948
Waring Products, 49950
Washington State Potato Cmsn, 49959
Waste Minimization/Containment, 49961
Water & Power Technologies, 49964
Water Sciences Services, Inc., 49966
Wayne Combustion Systems, 49977
Wayne Engineering, 49978
Wayne Farms LLC., 49979
WCC Honey Marketing, 49882
Weaver Popcorn Co Inc, 49981
Weavewood, Inc., 49982
WEBB-Stiles Co, 49884
Weber Packaging Solutions Inc, 49986
Weinberg Foods, 49997
Weiser River Packing, 50001
Weiss Instruments Inc, 50002
Welliver Metal Products Corporation, 50011
Wells Manufacturing Company, 50013
Wenix International Corporation, 50015
Wenk Foods Inc, 50016
West Carrollton Parchment Company, 50023
West Coast Seafood Processors Association, 50026
West Oregon Wood Products Inc, 50031
Westbrae Natural Foods, 50035
Western Bagel Baking Corp, 50038
Western Combustion Engineering, 50039
Western Plastics, 50043
Wexxar Corporation, 50059
WG Thompson & Sons, 49885
Whallon Machinery Inc, 50061
Wheel Tough Company, 50064
White Oaks Frozen Foods, 50074
White Rock Products Corp, 50076
Whole Herb Co, 50087
Wilch Manufacturing, 50094
WILD Flavors (Canada), 49886
Wild Rice Exchange, 50096
Wild Thyme Cottage Products, 50097
Wilder Manufacturing Company, 50098
Wileman Brothers & Elliott Inc, 50099
Wilkins Rogers Inc, 50105
Williams Refrigeration, 50113
Williamson & Co, 50115
Willing Group, 50116
Wilton Armetale, 50120
Windsor Industries Inc, 50123
Windsor Wax Co Inc, 50124
Wine Chillers of California, 50125
Winekeeper, 50128
Wing Nien Food, 50130
Winmix/Natural Care Products, 50132
Wisconsin Aluminum Foundry Co, 50143
Wisconsin Cheeseman, 50146
Wisconsin Whey International, 50149
Wishbone Utensil Tableware Line, 50150
Wittco Foodservice Equipment, 50151
Wittemann Company, 50154
Wolf Company, 50160
Wolfson Casing Corp, 50161
Wood Stone Corp, 50167
Woodstock Plastics Co Inc, 50172
Worden, 50175
Worksafe Industries, 50178
World Ginseng Ctr Inc, 50188
World Tableware Inc, 50193
World Water Works, 50195
World Wide Safe Brokers, 50197
Wyssmont Co Inc, 50212
X-Press Manufacturing, 50213
X-R-I Testing Inc, 50214
Y Z Enterprises Inc, 50221
Yakima Craft Brewing Company, 50226
Yardney Water Management Syst, 50232
Yerba Prima, 50237
Yogi® Tea, 50240
Yoshida Food Products Co, 50244
Young's Lobster Pound, 50247
Z-Loda Systems Engineering Inc, 50252
ZAK Designs Inc, 50253
Zd Wines, 50259
Zebra Technologies Corporation, 50261
Zed Industries, 50262
Zenobia Co, 50272
Zepa Trade, 50274
Zepf Technologies, 50275
Ziba Nut Inc, 50281
Ziniz, 50284
Zoia Banquetier Co, 50285

Australasia

Worden, 50175

Australia

A Legacy Food Svc, 41484
Abbotsford Growers Ltd., 41605
ABCO Industries Limited, 41527
Actron, 41658
Adamation, 41664
Adams & Brooks Inc, 41666
Advanced Ingredients, Inc., 41692
Agrocan, 41727
Alfa Laval Inc, 41778
All Fill Inc, 41796
Allied International Corp, 41822
Aloe Laboratories, 41834
Amber Glo, 41861
American Lifts, 41902
American Store Fixtures, 41924
American Wax Co Inc, 41930
Aqua-Aerobic Systems Inc, 42021
Arcobaleno Pasta Machines, 42031
Argo & Company, 42038
Arizona Natural Products, 42048
Arnold Equipment Co, 42058
ASCENT Technics Corporation, 41583
Ashlock Co, 42081
ASI Data Myte, 41584
Atlas Pacific Engineering, 42128
Atrium Biotech, 42131
Automated Flexible Conveyors, 42150
Automated Food Systems, 42151
Bagcraft Papercon, 42232
Bakon Yeast, 42247
Baldor Electric Co, 42252
Barlean's Fisheries, 42282
Barrette Outdoor Living, 42285
Baycliff Co Inc, 42312
Beaumont Products, 42327
Bel-Art Products, 42353
Bete Fog Nozzle Inc, 42415
BEVCO, 42206
BioAmber, 42444
Biro Manufacturing Co, 42458
Blair's Sauces & Snacks, 42468
Blanver USA, 42472
Blue Crab Bay, 42485
Boehringer Mfg. Co. Inc., 42509
Brolite Products Inc, 42591
Brown-Forman Corp, 42611
Brucia Plant Extracts, 42613
Bryant Products Inc, 42620
Burgess Mfg. - Oklahoma, 42643
Cafe Altura, 42727
Cajun Boy's Louisiana Products, 42732
Cambridge Viscosity, Inc., 42766
Carrageenan Company, 42847
Charles Mayer Studios, 42933
Chase-Logeman Corp, 42942
Chefwear, 42957
Chipmaker Tooling Supply, 43006
Chocolates a La Carte, 43017
Cintex of America, 43039
Citadelle Maple Syrup Producers' Cooperative, 43046
Classic Flavors & Fragrances, 43065
Clean Water Systems, 43073
Clos Du Val Co LTD, 43096
Concannon Vineyard, 43195
Consolidated Baling Machine Company, 43205
Container Machinery Corporation, 43216
Contech Enterprises Inc, 43218
Cookie Tree Bakeries, 43256
Copper Brite, 43264
Cork Specialties, 43275
Creative Cookie, 43328
Currie Machinery Co, 43409
Damp Rid, 43488
Daymark Safety Systems, 43522
DeltaTrak, 43578
Desert King International, 43590
Di Mare Fresh Inc, 43606
DNE World Fruit Sales, 43459
Dunkley International Inc, 43723
Durkee-Mower, 43741
E F Bavis & Assoc Inc, 43757
Eastern Machine, 43809
Eatec Corporation, 43817
Edson Packaging Machinery, 43866
Ennio International, 43953
Ensemble Beverages, 43955
Ermanco, 43981
Essential Industries Inc, 43991
Everpure, LLC, 44031
Fast Industries, 44120
Feather Duster Corporation, 44126
Fenton Art Glass Company, 44139
First Colony Coffee & Tea Company, 44186
Fluid Energy Processing & Eqpt, 44251
Forever Foods, 44308
Fuller Industries LLC, 44394
Future Commodities Intl Inc, 44405
Gamajet Cleaning Systems, 44460
GEM Cultures, 44427
Gems Sensors & Controls, 44513
George Gordon Assoc, 44545
Giles Enterprises Inc, 44573
Globe Food Equipment Co, 44614
Goetze's Candy Co, 44620
Golden State Foods Corp, 44643
Good For You America, 44652
Great Western Manufacturing Company, 44724
Guerra Nut Shelling Co Inc, 44768
Hamilton Kettles, 44850
Hartness International, 44915
Hospitality Mints LLC, 45087
Huther Brothers, 45138
Ideal Stencil Machine & Tape Company, 45200
IMI Cornelius, 45173
Insignia Systems Inc, 45299
Insulair, 45305
International Environmental Solutions, 45340
International Patterns, Inc., 45361
Island Sweetwater Beverage Company, 45394
JAAMA World Trade, 45449
Jantec, 45494
Jarrow Formulas Inc, 45499
Jelly Belly Candy Co., 45512
Justman Brush Co, 45592
Keto Foods, 45715
KWS Manufacturing Co LTD, 45632
L F Lambert Spawn Co, 45837
Lamson & Goodnow, 45918
Langen Packaging, 45935
Lee Financial Corporation, 45970
Lion Raisins Inc, 46059
Lodi Metal Tech, 46090
Louisiana Packing Company, 46123
Love Controls Division, 46130
Magnolia Citrus Assn, 46251
Mariani Nut Co, 46330
Marking Methods Inc, 46347
Markwell Manufacturing Company, 46351
Marlen, 46353
Materials Transportation Co, 46406
Matfer Inc, 46407, 46408
Mayacamas Fine Foods, 46429
Mba Suppliers Inc., 46436
McCabe's Quality Foods, 46439
Merix Chemical Company, 46509
Messermeister, 46518
Midas Foods Intl, 46596
Miller Group Multiplex, 46629
Mimi et Cie, 46646
Momar, 46699
Morre-Tec Ind Inc, 46731
National Instruments, 46878
Natural Flavors, 46904
Natural Oils International, 46910
Nature Quality, 46915
New England Machinery Inc, 46973
Nexel Industries Inc, 47009
Nielsen-Massey Vanillas Inc, 47025
Niro, 47031
North Taste Flavourings, 47079
Novelty Crystal, 47115
Nu-World Amaranth Inc, 47126
Nuance Solutions Inc, 47128
Nutritional Research Associates, 47157
Nutriwest, 47159
OCS Process Systems, 47167
Ogden Manufacturing Company, 47192
Ole Hickory Pits, 47206
Omega Nutrition, 47221
Ottens Flavors, 47298
P J Rhodes Corporation, 47316
Pacific Choice Brands, 47354
Pacific Commerce Company, 47356
Pacific Scientific Instrument, 47365
Paraclipse, 47443
Paragon Group USA, 47450
Parvin Manufacturing Company, 47477
PDE Technology Corp, 47332
Peerless of America, 47521

687

Export Region / Bahamas

Philadelphia Macaroni Co, 47588
Pneumatic Conveying Inc, 47647
Pneumatic Scale Angelus, 47648
POM Wonderful LLC, 47339
Premier Skirting Products, 47720
Presence From Innovation LLC, 47727
Preston Scientific, 47735
Proffitt Manufacturing Company, 47796
Psyllium Labs, 47826
Pure Life Organic Foods, 47842
PureCircle USA, 47846
Pyro-Chem, 47854
RDM International, 47928
Real Soda, 47993
Reyco Systems Inc, 48082
Rio Syrup Co, 48107
Saeplast Canada, 48313
San Jamar, 48355
San Joaquin Vly Concentrates, 48356
San-J International Inc, 48360
Santa Barbara Olive Company, 48378
Santa Clara Nut Co, 48379
Savoury Systems Inc, 48406
Sayco Yo-Yo Molding Company, 48408
Scaltrol Inc, 48410
Scandinavian Laboratories, 48418
Schenck Process, 48423
Shivji Enterprises, 48600
Somerset Industries, 48743
Soodhalter Plastics, 48752
Sperling Industries, 48827
Spirit Foodservice, Inc., 48837
St John's Botanicals, 48859
Steiner Company, 48922
Stone Soap Co Inc, 48965
Strub Pickles, 48989
SunWest Foods, Inc., 49019
Superior Food Machinery Inc, 49052
Superior Packaging Equipment Corporation, 49056
Supreme Chocolatier, 49061
Surtec Inc, 49073
SWF Co, 48303
Swirl Freeze Corp, 49092
Synthite USA Inc., 49108
Technistar Corporation, 49213
Technology Flavors & Fragrances, 49216
Tecweigh, 49219
Texas Traditions Gourmet, 49269
The Good Crisp Company, 49287
Theta Sciences, 49318
Thomas Precision, Inc., 49326
Thorn Smith Laboratories, 49333
Tooterville Trolley Company, 49390
Tootsi Impex, 49391
Toromont Process Systems, 49400
Traex, 49425
Trans-Chemco Inc, 49432
Trident Seafoods Corp, 49467
TRITEN Corporation, 49142
True Food Service Equipment, Inc., 49507
TruHeat Corporation, 49504
Turbo Refrigerating Company, 49531
Turkey Hill Sugarbush, 49533
Tyco Fire Protection Products, 49550
TyRy Inc, 49549
Union Confectionery Machinery, 49609
Union Fish Co, 49611
United Industries Group Inc, 49638
US Industrial Lubricants, 49568
Vacuum Barrier Corp, 49709
Vineco International Products, 49819
Vita-Pakt Citrus Products Co, 49839
Weiss Instruments Inc, 50002
Whallon Machinery Inc, 50061
White Oaks Frozen Foods, 50074
WILD Flavors (Canada), 49886
Windsor Wax Co Inc, 50124
Winning Solutions Inc, 50133
Wittemann Company, 50154
Woodstock Line Co, 50171
WORC Slitting & Mfg Co, 49890
X-R-I Testing Inc, 50214
Zepa Trade, 50274

Bahamas

American Fire Sprinkler Services, Inc, 41883
Cool Care, 43259
Foppiano Vineyards, 44300
Snyder's-Lance Inc., 48729
Swisher Hygiene, 49093
Well Luck, 50007

Baltic

ITW Angleboard, 45184

Belgium

Foppiano Vineyards, 44300

Bermuda

Benner China & Glassware Inc, 42377
Best Provision Co Inc, 42411
Bindi-Dessert Service,Inc, 42437
Bittersweet Pastries, 42463
Conway Import Co Inc, 43251
D Waybret & Sons Fisher ies, 43442
Foppiano Vineyards, 44300
Freemark Abbey Winery, 44351
Gaspar's Linguica Co Inc, 44490
Innova Envelopes, 45284
Just Plastics Inc, 45591
Miguel's Stowe Away, 46615
Monument Industries Inc, 46720
United Showcase Company, 49650

Brazil

Bragard Professional Uniforms, 42551
Davron Technologies Inc, 43517
Mosaic Co, 46742
Radiation Processing Division, 47942
Wallace Grain & Pea Company, 49932
Well Luck, 50007

Brussels

Golden Harvest Pecans, 44633

Canada

A La Carte, 41483
A T Ferrell Co Inc, 41485
A&A Line & Wire Corporation, 41489
A&D Weighing, 41493
A-A1 Aaction Bag, 41502
A-Z Factory Supply, 41505
Aak USA Inc, 41598
Acatris USA, 41619
ACCO Systems, 41533
Ace Development, 41628
Acme Engineering & Mfg Corp, 41637
Action Lighting, 41654
Adams & Brooks Inc, 41666
Admatch Corporation, 41673
Adobe Creek Packing Co Inc, 41675
Adrienne's Gourmet Foods, 41680
Advance Pierre Foods, 41684
Advanced Ingredients, Inc., 41692
Advanced Labelworx Inc, 41695
Adventure Foods, 41700
Agricor Inc, 41722
Ajinomoto Foods North America, Inc., 41744
Ajinomoto Frozen Foods USA, Inc., 41745
AKC Commodities Inc, 41556
Al Pete Meats, 41750
Alacer Corp, 41754
Alconox Inc, 41771
Alderfer Inc, 41772
Algood Food Co, 41784
Allegheny Bradford Corp, 41808
Alliance Industrial Corp, 41817
Allied Glove Corporation, 41821
Alpha Packaging, 41841
Alsum Farms & Produce, 41844
Alternative Health & Herbs, 41847
Alumin-Nu Corporation, 41853
Alvarado Street Bakery, 41854
Amano Enzyme USA Company, Ltd, 41855
Ameri-Kal Inc, 41866
American Culinary Garden, 41876
American Eagle Food Machinery, 41878
American European Systems, 41879
American Hotel Register Co, 41891
American LEWA, 41898
American Lifts, 41902
American Material Handling Inc, 41906
American National Rubber, 41908
American Production Co Inc, 41914
American Roland Food Corporation, 41917
American Solving Inc., 41921
American Water Broom, 41929
American Wax Co Inc, 41930
Americana Marketing, 41932
Ameripak Packaging Equipment, 41935
Ameristamp/Sign-A-Rama, 41936
AMI, 41568
Amigos Canning Company, 41946
Ammeraal Beltech Inc, 41949
Ample Industries, 41956
Amrita Snacks, 41957
Amtab Manufacturing Corp, 41959
Amy's Kitchen Inc, 41962
Analite, 41965
Angry Orchard Cider Company, LLC, 41988
Anguil Environmental Systems, 41989
API Heat Transfer Inc, 41577
Appleton Produce Company, 42011
Applied Chemical Technology, 42014
Aqua-Aerobic Systems Inc, 42021
Archie Moore's, 42027
Architecture Plus Intl Inc, 42028
Arguimbau & Co, 42040
Arkfeld Mfg & Distributing Co, 42050
Armbrust Paper,Tubes Inc, 42054
ASI Electronics Inc, 41585
Aspen Mulling Company   Inc., 42086
Assembled Products Corp, 42087
Astor Chocolate Corp, 42092
Astral Extracts, 42095
ATD-American Co, 41588
Atkins Elegant Desserts, 42103
Atwater Foods, 42134
Auromere Inc, 42139
Austrade, 42143
Autio Co, 42144
Autobar Systems, 42146
Automated Food Systems, 42151
Automatic Bar Controls Inc, 42152
Automatic Timing & Controls, 42157
Axelrod, Norman N, 42177
B G Smith & Sons Oyster Co, 42189
Baja Foods LLC, 42234
Bakers Choice Products, 42243
Bar Keepers Friend Cleanser, 42270
Barbeque Wood Flavors Enterprises, 42274
Barber Foods, 42275
Barlean's Fisheries, 42282
Barliant & Company, 42283
Batching Systems, 42301
Bauducco Foods Inc., 42304
Baycliff Co Inc, 42312
Bayhead Products Corp., 42313
Bear Creek Country Kitchens, 42322
Beatrice Bakery Co, 42325
Beaumont Products, 42327
Beaver Street Fisheries, 42329
Beaverton Foods Inc, 42330
Beetroot Delights, 42348
Bella Sun Luci, 42362
Benner China & Glassware Inc, 42377
Berlin Foundry & Mach Co, 42390
Berry Global, 42396
Best Diversified Products, 42409
Best Value Textiles, 42412
Better Made Snack Foods, 42420
Better Packages, 42421
Betty Lou's, 42422
BEUMER Corp, 42205
BEVCO, 42206
Beverage Express, 42425
Bijol & Spices Inc, 42434
Bio Cide Intl Inc, 42441
Biocontrol Systems Inc, 42447
Biothane Corporation, 42452
Bissett Produce Company, 42461
Black's Products of HighPoint, 42466
Blair's Sauces & Snacks, 42468
Blanver USA, 42472
Blau Oyster Co Inc, 42473
Blue Crab Bay, 42485
Blue Feather Products Inc, 42488
Blue Mountain Enterprise Inc, 42491
Blue Planet Foods, 42493
Blue Sky Beverage Company, 42496
Bluffton Slaw Cutter Company, 42500
Boca Bons East, 42507
Boehringer Mfg. Co. Inc., 42509
Bolzoni Auramo, 42513
Bon Appetit International, 42515
Bonneau Company, 42519
Borroughs Corp, 42523
Bosch Packaging Technology, 42525
Boskovich Farms Inc, 42526
Boss Manufacturing Co, 42527
Bowman Hollis Mfg Corp, 42540
Boyd Lighting Company, 42544
Bragard Professional Uniforms, 42551
Branford Vibrator Company, 42558
Brecoflex Co LLC, 42570
Bremner Biscuit Company, 42572
Brewster Dairy Inc, 42576
Brogdex Company, 42590
Brothers Metal Products, 42602
Brown Produce Company, 42609
Bry-Air Inc, 42618
Bryant Products Inc, 42620
Buddy Squirrel LLC, 42627
Budget Blinds Inc, 42628
Buffalo Trace Distillery, 42631
Burrows Paper Corp, 42650
BVL Controls, 42213
Bylada Foods, 42657
C C Pollen, 42664
C R Daniels Inc, 42674
C W Cole & Co, 42676
C&P Additives, 42678
C&T Refinery, 42679
Cafe Altura, 42727
Caffe Luca Coffee Roaste, 42731
Cajun Boy's Louisiana Products, 42732
Caldwell Group, 42746
California Custom Fruits, 42751
Cameron Birch Syrup & Confections, 42771
Campbell Soup Co., 42775
Can & Bottle Systems, Inc., 42777
Candy & Company/Peck's Products Company, 42787
Canelake's Candy, 42792
Cannoli Factory, 42794
Capitol Hardware, Inc.,, 42800
Capway Conveyor Systems Inc, 42809
Carbis Inc, 42814
Carleton Helical Technologies, 42830
Carlson Products, 42836
Carolina Knife, 42840
Carothers Olive Oil, 42844
Carrageenan Company, 42847
Castle Cheese, 42876
Cates Addis Company, 42880
CBORD Group Inc, 42688
CCS Stone, Inc., 42690
Cedar Lake Foods, 42894
Cellofoam North America, 42899
Cellox Corp, 42900
Central Decal, 42906
Century Blends LLC, 42910
Charles E. Roberts Company, 42931
Charles Mayer Studios, 42933
Chas Boggini Co., 42939
Checker Bag Co, 42945
Chef Specialties, 42953
Chefwear, 42957
Chelten House Products, 42959
Chemdet Inc, 42964

Export Region / Canada

ChemTreat, Inc., 42962
Chincoteague Seafood Co Inc, 43005
Chocolate House, 43013
Choice Organic Teas, 43019
Choklit Molds LTD, 43020
Christy Wild Blueberry Farms, 43028
Church & Dwight Co., Inc., 43031
Cincinnati Preserving Co, 43036
Ciro Foods, 43044
City Grafx, 43055
Clabber Girl Corporation, 43056
Clarendon Flavor Engineering, 43059
Clarkson Grain Co Inc, 43063
Classic Tea, 43066
Clawson Machine Co Inc, 43068
Clayton & Lambert Manufacturing, 43070
Clear Springs Foods Inc., 43075
Cleaver-Brooks Inc, 43080
Climax Packaging Machinery, 43092
Clos Du Val Co LTD, 43096
Coating Place Inc, 43108
Coloma Frozen Foods Inc, 43137
Color Box, 43142
Columbia Labeling Machinery, 43148
Columbia Lighting, 43149
Commencement Bay Corrugated, 43159
Commercial Dehydrator Systems, 43161
Commodity Traders International, 43168
Compacker Systems LLC, 43172
Compris Technologies, 43180
Computerized Machinery Systs, 43182
Computrition, 43183
Comstock Castle Stove Co, 43185
Comus Restaurant Systems, 43187
Conductive Containers Inc, 43197
Conquest International LLC, 43204
Consolidated Can Co, 43206
Container Supply Co, 43217
Contrex Inc, 43233
Control Beverage, 43235
Conveyance Technologies LLC, 43245
Conway Import Co Inc, 43251
Cook & Beals Inc, 43253
Cool Care, 43259
Copper Brite, 43264
Corfu Foods Inc, 43272
Corson Manufacturing Company, 43285
Coss Engineering Sales Company, 43292
Country Pure Foods Inc, 43303
Country Save Products Corp, 43304
Crane Environmental, 43322
Creative Cookie, 43328
Cres Cor, 43338
Crespac Incorporated, 43342
Crestware, 43345
Cribari Vineyard Inc, 43347
Crouzet Corporation, 43359
Crown Candy Corp, 43362
Crown Closures Machinery, 43363
Crown Processing Company, 43374
Cruvinet Winebar Co LLC, 43380
Cryochem, 43381
Crystal Star Herbal Nutrition, 43388
CSC Worldwide, 42713
Cumberland Dairy, 43402
Currie Machinery Co, 43409
Curry King Corporation, 43410
Custom Packaging Inc, 43418
Cutler Industries, 43426
Dahl-Tech Inc, 43467
Dairy Fresh Foods Inc, 43471
Dairy Specialties, 43472
Dakota Specialty Milling, Inc., 43480
Dal-Don Produce, 43481
Daniele Inc, 43495
Dark Tickle Company, 43503
David's Goodbatter, 43511
Davidson's Organics, 43512
Davlynne International, 43516
Dawes Hill Honey Company, 43518
Day Spring Enterprises, 43520
De Ster Corporation, 43533
Delavau LLC, 43564
Delfield Co, 43566
Delta Wire And Mfg., 43577

Design Packaging Company, 43592
Desserts by David Glass, 43596
Detroit Forming, 43600
Diamond Crystal Brands Inc, 43615
Diamond Foods, 43616
Diamond Fruit Growers, 43617
Diamond Wipes Intl Inc, 43621
DIC International, 43456
Dipwell Co, 43636
Dismat Corporation, 43640
Dito Dean Food Prep, 43647
DMC-David Manufacturing Company, 43458
DNE World Fruit Sales, 43459
Dolphin Natural Chocolates, 43661
Dong Us I, 43667
Doosan Industrial Vehicle America Corp, 43669
Doran Scales Inc, 43671
Douglas Machines Corp., 43680
Downs Crane & Hoist Co Inc, 43688
Dr Konstantin Frank's Vinifera, 43691
Dr. John's Candies, 43693
Drake Co, 43697
Dream Confectioners LTD, 43702
Drum Rock Specialty Co Inc, 43710
Dry Creek Vineyard, 43712
Duke Manufacturing Co, 43717
Dunkley International Inc, 43723
Dura-Ware Company of America, 43730
Durable Engravers, 43731
DWL Industries Company, 43464
Dyco, 43746
Dynapro International, 43752
E-Z Lift Conveyors, 43764
E.L. Nickell Company, 43769
E.W. Knauss & Son, 43770
Eagle Products Company, 43797
Eastern Fish Company, 43808
Eatec Corporation, 43817
Eaton Manufacturing Co, 43821
Eckroat Seed Company, 43827
Eclipse Systems Inc, 43829
EcoNatural Solutions, 43833
Economy Folding Box Corporation, 43841
EGW Bradbury Enterprises, 43778
El Milagro, 43876
El Toro Food Products, 43879
Elmer Hansen Produce Inc, 43907
Emblem & Badge, 43916
Emc Solutions, 43917
Emerling International Foods, 43921
Emery Winslow Scale Co, 43926
Emmy's Organics, 43928
Empresas La Famosa, 43933
Ener-G Foods, 43941
Engineered Products Group, 43948
Enjoy Foods International, 43952
Ensinger Inc, 43956
Enzyme Development Corporation, 43965
Epi De France Bakery, 43967
Equipex Limited, 43972
Equipment Distributor Div, 43973
Erba Food Products, 43975
ERC Parts Inc, 43787
Erickson Industries, 43977
Erlab, Inc, 43980
Ermanco, 43981
Erwyn Products Inc, 43983
ESS Technologies, 43790
Essential Industries Inc, 43991
Esteem Products, 43994
Evonik Corporation North America, 44033
Excellence Commercial Products, 44041
Exel, 44043
Exhibitron Co, 44047
F B Washburn Candy Corp, 44057
F&Y Enterprises, 44065
Fabricon Products Inc, 44089
Fabwright Inc, 44091
Faciltec Corporation, 44092
Fair Publishing House, 44093
Fairborn USA Inc, 44095

Fairhaven Cooperative Flour Mill, 44099
Fallas Automation Inc, 44104
Fantasy Chocolates, 44111
Farmington Foods Inc, 44118
Fay Paper Products, 44125
FCD Tabletops, 44071
Fee Brothers, 44132
FEI Inc, 44075
Fenton Art Glass Company, 44139
FIB-R-DOR, 44077
Fibre Leather Manufacturing Company, 44156
Fieldbrook Foods Corp., 44158
Fillmore Piru Citrus, 44166
First Colony Coffee & Tea Company, 44186
Fixtur World, 44199
Flakice Corporation, 44202
Flavor Dynamics Two, 44209
Flavor House, Inc., 44210
Flex-Hose Co Inc, 44228
Flexicell Inc, 44229
Fluid Energy Processing & Eqpt, 44251
Flying Dog Brewery, 44255
Foam Concepts Inc, 44258
Foley-Belsaw Institute, 44269
Folgers Coffee Co, 44270
Food Equipment Manufacturing Company, 44278
Foppiano Vineyards, 44300
Ford Gum & Mach Co Inc, 44303
Formflex, 44309
Foster Family Farm, 44319
Foster Farms Inc., 44320
Foxon Co, 44330
Fredrick Ramond Company, 44346
Freeland Bean & Grain Inc, 44348
Freemark Abbey Winery, 44351
FreesTech, 44352
Friedman Bag Company, 44368
Friedrich Metal Products, 44370
Frontier Bag, 44378
Frontline Inc, 44379
Fry Foods Inc, 44390
Frye's Measure Mill, 44391
Fuller Industries LLC, 44394
FX-Lab Products, 44083
G K Skaggs Inc, 44409
Gadoua Bakery, 44446
Gallimore Industries, 44458
Gallo, 44459
Garber Farms, 44468
Garden Row Foods, 44473
Gardner's Gourmet, 44476
Garlic Valley Farms Inc, 44480
Garvey Corp, 44485
Gastro-Gnomes, 44493
Gateway Food Products Co, 44495
GEM Cultures, 44427
GEM Equipment Of Oregon Inc, 44428
General Press Corp, 44526
General Processing Systems, 44527
Genesee Brewing Company, 44533
Geo. Olcott Company, 44538
George Gordon Assoc, 44545
Georgia Spice Company, 44551
GERM-O-RAY, 44429
GHM Industries Inc, 44432
Gielow Pickles Inc, 44568
Gilster-Mary Lee Corp, 44578
Ginseng Up Corp, 44582
Girard's Food Service Dressings, 44585
Glass Industries America LLC, 44592
Glass Pro, 44593
Glastender, 44594
Glowmaster Corporation, 44618
Golden Fluff Popcorn Co, 44629
Golden State Herbs, 44644
Golden Walnut Specialty Foods, 44647
Goldenwest Sales, 44649
Gonterman & Associates, 44651
Goodell Tools, 44657
Gosselin Gourmet Beverages, 44666
Graphic Calculator Company, 44698
Great American Appetizers, 44706
Great Western Juice Co, 44722

Green Bay Packaging Inc., 44730
Green Foods Corp., 44733
Grimaud Farms-California Inc, 44754
GSW Jackes-Evans Manufacturing Company, 44440
Guerra Nut Shelling Co Inc, 44768
Guglielmo Winery, 44769
Guiltless Gourmet, 44771
Gulf Food Products Co Inc, 44776
Gulf Packing Company, 44778
Gulf Pride Enterprises, 44779
Gum Technology Corporation, 44780
H A Sparke Co, 44790
H B Taylor Co, 44792
H.K. Canning, 44810
H.L. Diehl Company, 44811
H.P. Neun, 44812
Hairnet Corporation of America, 44834
Hall Manufacturing Co, 44839
Halton Company, 44843
Hamilton Kettles, 44850
Handy Manufacturing Co Inc, 44860
Hanna Instruments, 44868
Hanson Lab Furniture Inc, 44879
Happy's Potato Chip Co, 44884
Hardy Systems Corporation, 44894
Harvard Folding Box Company, 44918
Hauser Chocolates, 44929
Healing Garden, 44945
Health Concerns, 44947
Heartland Gourmet LLC, 44961
Heaven Hill Distilleries Inc., 44967
Heck Cellars, 44968
Hectronic, 44969
Helken Equipment Co, 44977
Heller Estates, 44980
Heluva Good Cheese, 44982
Henry Troemner LLC, 44992
Herbs Etc, 44996
Herz Meat Company, 45003
HH Dobbins Inc, 44819
HHP Inc, 44820
Hillside Metal Ware Company, 45025
Hinchcliff Products Company, 45031
Hinckley Springs Bottled Water, 45032
Hobe Laboratories Inc, 45038
Hodell International, 45039
Holistic Horizons/Halcyon Pacific Corporation, 45044
Hollywood Banners, 45053
Holmco Container Manufacturing, LTD, 45055
Home Rubber Co, 45060
Home Style Foods Inc, 45062
Honee Bear Canning, 45064
Hood River Distillers Inc, 45071
Hoppmann Corporation, 45076
Hoshizaki America Inc, 45085
Hospitality Mints LLC, 45087
Hsin Tung Yang Foods Inc, 45109
Hunt Country Vineyards, 45129
Huntsman Packaging, 45133
Huther Brothers, 45138
I.W. Tremont Company, 45158
Icco Cheese Co, 45190
Ice-Cap, 45191
Idaho Steel Products Inc, 45197
Idaho Trout Company, 45199
Ideal of America/Valley Rio Enterprise, 45203
Ideal Wire Works, 45201
Ilapak Inc, 45208
Illuma Display, 45211
Image Experts Uniforms, 45212
Imperial Sensus, 45225
Improved Blow Molding, 45231
Indel Food Products Inc, 45242
Indian Ridge Shrimp Co, 45248
Indiana Vac Form Inc, 45253
Industrial Ceramic Products, 45258
Industrial Product Corp, 45265
Infitec Inc, 45270
Innovative Molding, 45291
Insignia Systems Inc, 45299
Instant Products of America, 45303
Instrumart, 45304

Export Region / Canada

Insulair, 45305
Intedge Manufacturing, 45306
Intermold Corporation, 45323
Intermountain Specialty Food Group, 45324
International Cold Storage, 45333
International Environmental Solutions, 45340
International Foodcraft Corp, 45344
International Packaging Machinery, 45358
International Tank & Pipe Co, 45368
Interplast, 45376
Isernio Sausage Company, 45389
ITW United Silicone, 45186
Ives-Way Products, 45411
J M Packaging Co, 45431
J W Outfitters, 45434
J.A. Thurston Company, 45439
J.F. Breun & Sons, 45441
J.V. Reed & Company, 45448
Jacob Holtz Co., 45478
JANA Worldwide, 45450
Jantec, 45494
Jarden Home Brands, 45496
Jelly Belly Candy Co., 45512
Jescorp, 45520
John E. Ruggles & Company, 45544
John Henry Packaging, 45545
Johnson Foods, Inc., 45553
Johnston Farms, 45559
Joneca Corp, 45562
Jones-Zylon Co, 45566
Judel Products, 45582
Judy's Cream Caramels, 45583
Juice Tree, 45584
Just Plastics Inc, 45591
JW Aluminum, 45469
Jyoti Cuisine India, 45593
K-Way Products, 45605
Kamflex Corp, 45644
Kashi Company, 45654
Keen Kutter, 45683
Kehr-Buffalo Wire Frame Co Inc, 45686
Kelman Bottles LLC, 45693
Kemex Meat Brands, 45696
Kennedy Group, 45702
Kenwood Vineyards, 45709
Keto Foods, 45715
Keystone Coffee Co, 45723
Kim Lighting, 45730
King Bag & Mfg Co, 45739
King Packaging Co, 45745
Kinsley Inc, 45756
Kirin Brewery Of America LLC, 45757
Kiss International/Di-tech Systems, 45759
Kisters Kayat, 45760
Kleen Products Inc, 45765
Klockner Pentaplast of America, 45768
Koehler-Gibson Marking, 45784
Kola, 45788
Kolpak Walk-ins, 45793
Kona Joe Coffee LLC, 45795
Kozlowski Farms, 45806
KOZY Shack Enterprises Inc, 45626
Krones, 45818
Kuepper Favor Company, Celebrate Line, 45823
KWS Manufacturing Co LTD, 45632
L F Lambert Spawn Co, 45837
L&A Process Systems, 45840
L. Cherrick Horseradish Company, 45842
La Belle Suisse Corporation, 45870
La Crosse, 45872
Labelette Company, 45888
Labelquest Inc, 45889
Lagorio Enterprises, 45895
Lake Shore Industries Inc, 45901
Lakeside Manufacturing Inc, 45906
Lakeside-Aris Manufacturing, 45909
Lamb Cooperative Inc, 45912
Lamports Filter Media, 45917
Lancer, 45921
Larien Products, 45941

Laros Equipment Co Inc, 45942
Lassonde Pappas & Company, Inc., 45946
Laub-Hunt Packaging Systems, 45949
LBP Manufacturing LLC, 45856
LDI Manufacturing Co, 45857
Le Fiell Co, 45964
Leader Candies, 45966
Lee Financial Corporation, 45970
Leelanau Fruit Co, 45974
Leon's Bakery, 45997
Les Industries Bernard et Fils, 46003
Lewisburg Printing, 46015
Liberty Engineering Co, 46021
Lifeway, 46032
Liguria Foods Inc, 46039
Lillsun Manufacturing Co, 46041
Limpert Bros Inc, 46047
Line-Master Products, 46053
Lion Labels Inc, 46058
Lite-Weight Tool & Mfg Co, 46067
Little Crow Foods, 46071
Livingston Farmers Assn, 46074
LoadBank International, 46082
Locknane, 46085
Lodge Manufacturing Company, 46089
Lodi Metal Tech, 46090
Lone Pine Enterprise Inc, 46096
Longview Fibre Company, 46105
Loriva Culinary Oils, 46112
Louisiana Packing Company, 46123
LPI Information Systems, 45866
LTI Printing Inc, 45869
Lutz Pumps Inc, 46163
M & E Mfg Co Inc, 46176
M O Industries Inc, 46181
M Phil Yen Company, 46182
M S Willett Inc, 46185
M.E. Heuck Company, 46194
Mac Farms Of Hawaii Inc, 46220
MAF Industries Inc, 46197
Magic Valley Growers, 46245
Magna Foods Corporation, 46246
Magnetool Inc, 46250
Maid-Rite Steak Company, 46259
Maier Sign Systems, 46260
Majestic Industries Inc, 46267
Mali's All Natural Barbecue Supply Company, 46273
Malthus Diagnostics, 46280
Manchester Tool & Die Inc, 46286
Manning Lighting Inc, 46301
Manufacturers Wood Supply Company, 46304
Maple Leaf Cheesemakers, 46306
Marcus Food Co, 46323
Marel Stork Poultry Processing, 46325
Mark Container Corporation, 46340
Markham Vineyards, 46345
Marnap Industries, 46358
Marshall Plastic Film Inc, 46367
Mastercraft Industries Inc, 46397
Mastercraft International, 46398
Matador Processors, 46402
Materials Transportation Co, 46406
Matfer Inc, 46408
Maui Gold Pineapple Company, 46420
Maxfield Candy, 46424
Maxi-Vac Inc., 46425
Mayacamas Fine Foods, 46429
Mc Steven's Coca Factory Store, 46437
McCarter Corporation, 46440
Mccullagh Coffee Roasters, 46456
Mcfadden Farm, 46458
McGunn Safe Company, 46448
Mckey Perforating Co Inc, 46460
Mele-Koi Farms, 46483
Mercado Latino, 46494
Merchandising Inventives, 46496
Merix Chemical Company, 46509
Merlin Candies, 46510
Mermaid Seafoods, 46513
Messermeister, 46518
Metal Equipment Company, 46522
Metaline Products Co Inc, 46524
Metzger Popcorn Co, 46534

Meyenberg Goat Milk, 46539
Meyer Machine & Garroutte Products, 46541
Micelli Chocolate Mold Company, 46549
Michiana Box & Crate, 46555
Michigan Agricultural Commdty, 46556
Michigan Agricultural Commodities Inc, 46557
Michigan Agriculture Commodities, 46558, 46559, 46560, 46561, 46562, 46563, 46564
Michigan Box Co, 46565
Michigan Freeze Pack, 46568
Micro-Brush Pro Soap, 46573
Micropoint, 46583
Micropure Filtration Inc, 46585
MicroSoy Corporation, 46575
Mid-Atlantic Foods Inc, 46589
Mid-West Wire Products, 46593
Midwest Stainless, 46609
MIFAB, 46210
Mild Bill's Spices, 46621
Mille Lacs Wild Rice Corp, 46628
Milmar Food Group, 46638
Milne Fruit Products Inc, 46639
Minuteman Power Boss, 46655
Mitsubishi Polyester Film, Inc., 46669
Mixon Fruit Farms Inc, 46673
Miyako Oriental Foods Inc, 46674
Mlp Seating, 46675
Mmi Engineered Soultions Inc, 46676
MMR Technologies, 46216
Modern Products Inc, 46682
Modular Packaging, 46683
Moen Industries, 46686
Molding Automation Concepts, 46691
Moli-International, 46693
Molins/Sandiacre Richmond, 46697
Montana Naturals, 46714
Morey's Seafood Intl LLC, 46726
Morris & Associates, 46732
Mouli Manufacturing Corporation, 46751
Mountain Safety Research, 46753
Mr Dell Foods, 46760
Mr Ice Bucket, 46761
Mrs. Denson's Cookie Company, 46767
MSSH, 46218
Muir Copper Canyon Farms, 46778
Mulholland-Harper Company, 46779
Multi-Panel Display Corporation, 46783
Multiflex Company, 46787
Multivac Inc, 46791
Murakami Farms, 46797
Murotech, 46798
Musco Family Olive Co, 46802
Mushroom Co, 46804
Mushroom Wisdom, Inc, 46805
Naltex, 46837
Namco Controls Corporation, 46838
Nancy's Specialty Foods, 46840
Napa Valley Kitchens, 46842
Natale Machine & Tool Co Inc, 46857
National Band Saw Co, 46861
National Distributor Services, 46866
National Foods, 46873
National Plastics Co, 46886
National Shippng Supply Co, 46891
Native Scents, 46897
Natra US, 46898
Natrol Inc, 46900
Natural Flavors, 46904
Natural Fruit Corp, 46908
Nature's Legacy Inc., 46921
Navarro Pecan Co, 46929
Naylor Candies Inc, 46932
Ne-Mo's Bakery Inc, 46934
Neal Walters Poster Corporation, 46935
Nelson Crab Inc, 46947
Neogen Corp, 46951
Neptune Foods, 46957
Nercon Engineering & Manufacturing, 46958
New Age Industrial, 46965
New Attitude Beverage Corporation, 46966
New England Wooden Ware, 46976

New Era Canning Company, 46977
New Season Foods Inc, 46983
New Zealand Lamb Co, 46992
Newly Weds Foods Inc, 47001
Newman's Own, 47003
NewStar Fresh Foods LLC, 46993
Newton OA & Son Co, 47006
Nexel Industries Inc, 47009
Niagara Blower Company, 47011
Nigrelli Systems Purchasing, 47026
Nikken Foods, 47027
Nikki's Cookies, 47028
Niro, 47031
Nitsch Tool Co Inc, 47037
Nonpareil Farms, 47044
Norpak Corp, 47061
Northeast Packaging Co, 47082
Northeastern Products Corp, 47084
Northwestern Coffee Mills, 47101
Novelty Advertising, 47114
Novelty Crystal, 47115
Now Plastics Inc, 47119
Noyes, P J, 47120
Nrd LLC, 47121
Nutraceutical International, 47142
Nutribiotic, 47147
Nutricepts, 47148
Nutritional Research Associates, 47157
Nutritional Specialties, 47158
Nutriwest, 47159
Ocean Cliff Corp, 47180
OCS Process Systems, 47167
Odenberg Engineering, 47188
Ole Hickory Pits, 47206
Olive Can Company, 47207
Olney Machinery, 47210
Olympic Foods, 47213
Omega Industrial Products Inc, 47220
Omega Nutrition, 47221
Omega Produce Company, 47222
Omega Products Inc, 47223
Omega Protein, 47224
Omni Metalcraft Corporation, 47229
Once Again Nut Butter, 47237
Onevision Corp, 47240
Open Date Systems, 47248
Optex, 47251
Orange Bakery, 47256
Oregon Chai, 47264
Outotec USA Inc, 47302
Paar Physica USA, 47349
Pacer Pumps, 47352
Pacific Salmon Company, 47364
Package Concepts & Materials Inc, 47378
Package Machinery Co Inc, 47380
Packaging Dynamics International, 47386
Packaging Equipment & Conveyors, Inc, 47389
Packaging Products Corp, 47393
Pacur, 47399
Pakmark, 47405
Paktronics Controls, 47406
Pamela's Products, 47420
Paper Systems Inc, 47437
Pappy's Sassafras Tea, 47440
PAR-Way Tryson Co, 47325
Parachem Corporation, 47442
Paradise Products Corporation, 47447
Park Cheese Company Inc, 47462
Parkway Plastic Inc, 47467
Parlor City Paper Box Co Inc, 47468
Parrish's Cake Decorating, 47470
Parvin Manufacturing Company, 47477
Paxton Corp, 47499
Peco Foods Inc., 47513
Penguin Frozen Foods Inc, 47534
Penley Corporation, 47535
Peregrine Inc, 47549
Performance Labs, 47553
Petschl's Quality Meats, 47574
Pez Candy Inc, 47575
Pfankuch Machinery Corporation, 47576
Phase II Pasta Machine Inc, 47584
Phytotherapy Research Laboratory, 47596

Export Region / Canada

Pilant Corp, 47608
Pioneer Plastics Inc, 47619
Plastech, 47631
Plastic Suppliers Inc, 47635
Plastic Supply Inc, 47636
Pluto Corporation, 47644
Pneumatic Conveying Inc, 47647
Podnar Plastics Inc, 47650
Polar Beer Systems, 47655
Polean Foods, 47660
PolyConversions, Inc., 47662
POM Wonderful LLC, 47339
Porinos Gourmet Food, 47678
Potlatch Corp, 47687
Precision Temp Inc, 47706
Preferred Meal Systems Inc, 47710
Premier, 47715
Preston Scientific, 47735
Pretium Packaging, LLC., 47737
Pretzels Inc, 47738
Prima Foods, 47740
Primo Water Corporation, 47751
Priority Plastics Inc, 47760
Process Solutions, 47776
Proffitt Manufacturing Company, 47796
Profire Stainless Steel Barbecue, 47797
Progenix Corporation, 47799
Prototype Equipment Corporation, 47819
Psc Floturn Inc, 47825
PTR Baler & Compactor Co, 47346
Purac America, 47834
Purchase Order Co Of Miami Inc, 47837
Pure Source LLC, 47844
PureCircle USA, 47846
Q.E. Tea, 47861
QBI, 47863
Qsx Labels, 47868
Qualifresh Michel St. Arneault, 47875
Quantum Performance Films, 47887
Queen Bee Gardens, 47889
R K Electric Co Inc, 47905
R Torre & Co, 47910
R&R Mill Company, 47914
Rahmann Belting & Industrial Rubber Products, 47951
RainSoft Water Treatment System, 47953
Ralphs Pugh Conveyor Rollers, 47960
RAM Center, 47923
Rapid Industries Inc, 47971
Rapid Rack Industries, 47973
Rational Cooking Systems, 47976
Real Aloe Company, 47989
Red River Commodities Inc, 48002
Redi-Call Inc, 48008
Redmond Minerals Inc, 48010
Rees Inc, 48016
Reese Enterprises Inc, 48017
Refractron Technologies Corp, 48020
Regina USA, 48033
Rene Produce Dist, 48058
Reter Fruit, 48074
Revent Inc, 48075
Rexcraft Fine Chafers, 48077
Rexford Paper Company, 48078
Reyco Systems Inc, 48082
Rice Company, 48089
Richards Packaging, 48096
Ripon Pickle Co Inc, 48110
RMI-C/Rotonics Manaufacturing, 47932
Robby Vapor Systems, 48125
Robinson's No 1 Ribs, 48138
Robot Coupe, 48139
Rogue Ales Brewery, 48158
Ron Son Foods Inc, 48169
Ronnie's Ceramic Company, 48173
Roquette America Inc., 48179
Roto-Flex Oven Co, 48198
Rowena, 48204
Rowland Coffee Roasters Inc., 48205
Royal Doulton, 48215
Royal Label Co, 48220
Royal Wine Corp, 48227
Rubschlager Baking Corp, 48237
Ruiz Food Products Inc., 48243
S&P Marketing, Inc., 48261

S&P USA Ventilation Systems, LLC, 48262
Sabel Engineering Corporation, 48307
Sable Technology Solution, 48309
Safe-T-Cut Inc, 48315
Sagawa's Savory Sauces, 48317
Saint-Gobain Corporation, 48325
Sales King International, 48333
Sampco, 48345
San Fab Conveyor, 48351
San Francisco Herb Co, 48353
San Joaquin Vly Concentrates, 48356
San-J International Inc, 48360
Sani-Matic, 48373
Sanitary Couplers, 48375
Santa Barbara Olive Company, 48378
Sargento Foods Inc, 48392
Satin Fine Foods, 48396
Sato America, 48397
Savoia Foods, 48403
Savory Foods, 48405
Savoury Systems Inc, 48406
SBK Preserves, 48272
Scaltrol Inc, 48410
Schaefer Machine Co Inc, 48419
Schenck Process, 48423
Schlueter Company, 48429
Schroeder Machine, 48436
Schwab Paper Products Co, 48438
Sconza Candy Co, 48442
Scott Hams, 48448
Sea Snack Foods Inc, 48462
Seafood Producers Co-Op, 48474
Seasons 4 Inc, 48481
Seneca Foods Corp, 48508
Separators Inc, 48520
Serendipitea, 48525
Seven Keys Co Of Florida, 48549
Seviroli Foods, 48554
SFP Food Products, 48277
Shank's Extracts Inc, 48566
Shanker Industries, 48567
Shat R Shield Inc, 48572
Shaw-Clayton Corporation, 48573
Shenandoah Vineyards, 48581
Shepard Brothers Co, 48582
Shine Companies, 48593
Shipley Basket Mfg Co, 48595
Shipley Sales, 48596
Shoes for Crews/Mighty Mat, 48603
Sigma Industries, 48623
Sign Systems, Inc., 48626
Silver Spring Foods, 48648
Simmons Engineering Corporation, 48656
Simolex Rubber Corp, 48658
Sinbad Sweets, 48670
Sine Pump, 48673
Sini Fulvi U.S.A., 48675
Sipco Products, 48678
Sisu Group Inc, 48682
Skylark Meats, 48687
Slicechief Co, 48692
Slip-Not Belting Corporation, 48694
Snack Factory, 48711
Sneaky Chef Foods, The, 48717
Snyder Crown, 48725
Solvay, 48740
Sonoco ThermoSafe, 48750
Soodhalter Plastics, 48752
Soofer Co, 48753
South Mill, 48763
Spanco Crane & Monorail Systems, 48791
Specialty Bakers, 48804
Spee-Dee Packaging Machinery, 48821
Sperling Industries, 48827
Spice & Spice, 48828
Spinco Metal Products Inc, 48833
Springfield Creamery Inc, 48848
Springport Steel Wire Products, 48849
SSW Holding Co Inc, 48294
St. Clair Pakwell, 48863
Stainless One DispensingSystem, 48869
Standard Folding Cartons Inc, 48876
Stanley Orchards Sales, Inc., 48885

STD Precision Gear, 48296
Stearnswood Inc, 48911
Steel King Industries, 48915
Steel Storage Systems Inc, 48917
Steel's Gourmet Foods, Ltd., 48918
Sterling Net & Twine Company, 48933
Sterling Novelty Products, 48934
STI International, 48299
Stickney & Poor Company, 48954
Stimo-O-Stam, Ltd., 48955
Stirling Foods, 48956
StoneHammer Brewing, 48966
Storage Unlimited, 48970
Straub Designs Co, 48978
Stretch Island Fruit, 48983
Stripper Bags, 48986
Stronghaven Containers Co, 48988
Sugar Foods Corp, 48995
Sun Chlorella USA, 49007
Sun Harvest Foods Inc, 49010
Sunrise Growers, 49032
Superior Foods, 49053
Superior Packaging Equipment Corporation, 49056
Supreme Corporation, 49062
Sure Torque, 49069
Surekap Inc, 49071
Suzanne's Specialties, 49076
Sweet Corn Products Co, 49083
Sweet Life Enterprises, 49087
Sweet Sue Kitchens, 49089
SWF Co, 48303
Swiss Food Products, 49095
Synergy Flavors Inc, 49107
Synthite USA Inc., 49108
Systems IV, 49111
T.O. Plastics, 49124
Tabco Enterprises, 49147
Tablecheck Technologies, Inc, 49151
Tablet & Ticket Co, 49154
Taj Gourmet Foods, 49158
Taku Smokehouse, 49160
Talbott Farms, 49161
Tamarind Tree, 49165
Tampa Bay Fisheries Inc, 49166
Tampa Maid Foods Inc, 49168
Tate Western, 49196
Taylor Orchards, 49201
Taylor Products Co, 49203
Tecweigh, 49219
Tee-Jay Corporation, 49223
Teelee Popcorn, 49224
Tema Systems Inc, 49237
Temco, 49238
Tempco Electric Heater Corporation, 49239
Templar Food Products, 49240
Templock Corporation, 49241
Tenth & M Seafoods, 49247
Terphane Inc, 49250
Terra Origin, Inc., 49252
Tew Manufacturing Corp, 49263
THARCO, 49131
The Amazing Chickpea, 49276
The Good Crisp Company, 49287
The Honest Stand, 49288
The Little Kernel, 49292
Thermodyne Foodservice Prods, 49314
This Bar Saves Lives, LLC, 49323
Thomas L. Green & Company, 49324
Thomas Precision, Inc., 49326
Thomas Tape & Supply Co Inc, 49327
Thorco Industries LLC, 49331
ThreeWorks Snacks, 49338
Thunderbird Real Food Bar, 49341
Tieco-Unadilla Corporation, 49343
Tier-Rack Corp, 49344
Titan Industries Inc, 49364
TNA Packaging Solutions, 49136
Tni Packaging Inc, 49365
Tolas Health Care Packaging, 49378
Tony Downs Foods, 49388
Touch Menus, 49412
Townsend Farms Inc, 49417
Trade Diversified, 49418
Traeger Industries, 49424

Traitech Industries, 49426
Tranter INC, 49439
TRC, 49140
TREX Corp Inc., 49141
Tri-Tronics, 49458
Trident Seafoods Corp, 49467
Tridyne Process Systems, 49469
Trilogy Essential Ingredients, 49470
Trio Packaging Corp, 49478
Trio Products, 49479
Triton International, 49486
Trojan Inc, 49489
Tropical Link Canada Ltd., 49495
Trout Lake Farm, 49499
TruHeat Corporation, 49504
Tucel Industries, Inc., 49521
TyRy Inc, 49549
UDEC Corp, 49560
Ultima Health Products Inc., 49582
Unarco Material Handling Inc, 49592
Uncle Dougie's, 49593
Uncle Matt's Organic, 49596
Union Confectionery Machinery, 49609
Uniplast Films, 49614
United Ad Label, 49623
United Salt Corp, 49647
United Showcase Company, 49650
United States Systems Inc, 49652
UniTrak Corporation, 49600
Universal Paper Box, 49671
Upright, 49677
US Chemical, 49563
US Chocolate Corp, 49564
US Industrial Lubricants, 49568
V.W. Joyner & Company, 49693
Vacuum Barrier Corp, 49709
Van de Kamps, 49733
Vance's Foods, 49735
Vanguard Technology Inc, 49737
Variety Glass Inc, 49746
Veggie Land, 49758
Ventre Packing Company, 49767
Venture Vineyards, 49771
Vermillion Flooring, 49777
Vessey & Co Inc, 49787
Vienna Beef LTD, 49803
Vigneri Chocolate Inc., 49806
Vigo Importing Co, 49807
Vilore Foods Company, 49812
VIP Foods, 49698
VIP Real Estate LTD, 49699
Vita-Pakt Citrus Products Co, 49839
VitaMinder Company, 49840
Voorhees Rubber Mfg Co, 49860
Vortron Smokehouse/Ovens, 49862
VT Industries Inc, 49703
Vulcan Industries, 49867
W & G Marketing Company, 49869
Waddington North America, 49912
Wagner Vineyards, 49916
Walco, 49922
Walker Stainless Equipment Co, 49928
Walle Corp, 49933
Walsh & Simmons Seating, 49936
Walton's Inc, 49941
Wapsie Produce, 49946
Ward Ironworks, 49948
Warwick Manufacturing & Equip, 49954
Wastequip Teem, 49963
Water & Power Technologies, 49964
Waterlink/Sanborn Technologies, 49967
Waukesha Specialty Company, 49973
Wawona Frozen Foods Inc, 49974
Wei-Chuan USA Inc, 49993
Weiser River Packing, 50001
Welch Holme & Clark Co, 50006
Welliver Metal Products Corporation, 50011
Wepackit, 50017
West Coast Products, 50025
West Oregon Wood Products Inc, 50031
West Thomas Partners, LLC, 50034
Western Container Company, 50040
Western Plastics, 50043
Westway Trading Corporation, 50053
Whaley Pecan Co Inc, 50060

691

Export Region / Caribbean

Whallon Machinery Inc, 50061
White Oaks Frozen Foods, 50074
Whole Herb Co, 50087
Wick's Packaging Service, 50089
Wicklund Farms, 50090
Wiegardt Brothers, 50091
Wild Bill's Foods, 50095
Wilder Manufacturing Company, 50098
Wilen Professional Cleaning Products, 50100
Wilkins Rogers Inc, 50105
Will-Pak Foods, 50107
Willamette Industries, 50109
Willamette Valley Walnuts, 50110
Windsor Wax Co Inc, 50124
Wirefab Inc, 50140
Wisconsin Box Co, 50144, 50145
Wisconsin Cheeseman, 50146
Wisconsin Specialty Protein, 50147
Wisconsin Whey International, 50149
Wizards Cauldron, LTD, 50157
Wood Stone Corp, 50167
Woodstock Line Co, 50171
Worksman 800 Buy Cart, 50179
Workstead Industries, 50180
World Cup Coffee & Tea, 50184
World Tableware Inc, 50193
Wornick Company, 50202
Wright Metal Products Crates, 50207
Xcel Tower Controls, 50217
Xpresso, 50219
Yakima Craft Brewing Company, 50226
Yakima Wire Works, 50228
Yamato Corporation, 50230
Yardney Water Management Syst, 50232
Yerba Prima, 50237
Yogi® Tea, 50240
Yoshida Food Products Co, 50244
Young's Lobster Pound, 50247
Zenar Corp, 50267
Zentis Sweet Ovations, 50273

Caribbean

A&A Line & Wire Corporation, 41489
A-Z Factory Supply, 41505
A. Suarez & Company, 41508
Abimar Foods Inc, 41610
Able Sales Company, 41612
Acme Engineering & Mfg Corp, 41637
Adams Fisheries Ltd, 41667
Adrienne's Gourmet Foods, 41680
Advance Storage Products, 41685
Agri-Mark Inc, 41721
Agricor Inc, 41722
Al-Rite Fruits & Syrups Co, 41752
Algood Food Co, 41784
Allegheny Bradford Corp, 41808
Amano Enzyme USA Company, Ltd, 41855
American Eagle Food Machinery, 41878
American Food Traders, 41888
American Hotel Register Co, 41891
American Lifts, 41902
American Roland Food Corporation, 41917
American Water Broom, 41929
American Wax Co Inc, 41930
Ameripak Packaging Equipment, 41935
Ammeraal Beltech Inc, 41949
Armbrust Paper Tubes Inc, 42054
Arnold Equipment Co, 42058
Astor Chocolate Corp, 42092
ATD-American Co, 41588
Atlantic Rubber Products, 42116
Atlas Packaging Inc, 42129
Automatic Bar Controls Inc, 42152
B. Terfloth & Company, 42195
Baldewein Company, 42251
Bally Refrigerated Boxes Inc, 42258
Bar Keepers Friend Cleanser, 42270
Barrie House Gourmet Coffee, 42286
Barry Group, 42289
Bauducco Foods Inc., 42304
Baycliff Co Inc, 42312
Beaver Street Fisheries, 42329

Berg Chilling Systems, 42382
Bericap North America, Inc., 42385
BEUMER Corp, 42205
BEVCO, 42206
Biocontrol Systems Inc, 42447
Birchwood Foods Inc, 42454
BluMetric Environmental Inc., 42484
Borroughs Corp, 42523
Boston Sausage & Provision, 42531
Botsford Fisheries, 42535
Boyd Lighting Company, 42544
Brandmeyer Popcorn Co, 42555
Bush Brothers Provision Co, 42651
C & E Canners Inc, 42661
C Nelson Mfg Co, 42670
C W Cole & Co, 42676
Canadian Fish Exporters, 42782
Capitol Foods, 42799
Capitol Hardware, Inc.,, 42800
Caribbean Produce Exchange, 42825
Carolina Mop, 42841
Carriere Foods Inc, 42851
Cawy Bottling Co, 42891
CCS Stone, Inc., 42690
Cedar Lake Foods, 42894
Cellofoam North America, 42899
Century Blends LLC, 42910
Charcuterie LaTour Eiffel, 42928
Chef Specialties, 42953
ChemTreat, Inc., 42962
CHS Inc., 42696
Church & Dwight Co., Inc., 43031
Ciro Foods, 43044
City Grafx, 43055
Clabber Girl Corporation, 43056
Classic Tea, 43066
Cleaver-Brooks Inc, 43080
Clos Du Val Co LTD, 43096
Comstock Castle Stove Co, 43185
Concannon Vineyard, 43195
Conductive Containers Inc, 43197
Conquest International LLC, 43204
Continental Seasoning, 43229
Cool Care, 43259
Cork Specialties, 43275
Cosgrove Enterprises Inc, 43289
Cres Cor, 43338
Crespac Incorporated, 43342
Crestware, 43345
Cribari Vineyard Inc, 43347
Crown Verity, 43377
Cruvinet Winebar Co LLC, 43380
Crystal Star Herbal Nutrition, 43388
CSC Worldwide, 42713
Culinary Masters Corporation, 43396
Cumberland Dairy, 43402
Curry King Corporation, 43410
Custom Diamond Intl., 43415
DairyAmerica, 43475
Dal-Don Produce, 43481
Damas Corporation, 43487
Danafilms Inc, 43492
Dart Container Corp., 43505
De Ster Corporation, 43533
Delfield Co, 43566
Diamond Fruit Growers, 43617
DNE World Fruit Sales, 43459
Dream Confectioners LTD, 43702
Dry Creek Vineyard, 43712
Dunhill Food Equipment Corporation, 43722
Dura-Ware Company of America, 43730
DWL Industries Company, 43464
Dyna-Veyor Inc, 43748
Dynaric Inc, 43753
E.W. Knauss & Son, 43770
Eastern Sea Products, 43811
Economy Folding Box Corporation, 43841
Economy Tent Intl, 43845
Eirich Machines, 43872
Emblem & Badge, 43916
Epi De France Bakery, 43967
Erickson Industries, 43977
Erwyn Products Inc, 43983
Euro-Bake, 44006

Ex-Cell KAISER LLC, 44035
Exaxol Chemical Corp, 44037
Excellence Commercial Products, 44041
Exel, 44043
Exeter Produce, 44045
Falcon Rice Mill Inc, 44101
Fantasy Chocolates, 44111
FCD Tabletops, 44071
Fee Brothers, 44132
Ferrer Corporation, 44147
Fieldbrook Foods Corp., 44158
Filling Equipment Co Inc, 44164
Fiori Bruna Pasta Products, 44180
Flex-Hose Co Inc, 44228
Florida Choice Foods, 44240
Flowers Baking Co, 44249
Foxon Co, 44330
Fry Foods Inc, 44390
G&R Graphics, 44412
Garden Row Foods, 44473
Gastro-Gnomes, 44493
Georgia Spice Company, 44551
GERM-O-RAY, 44429
Gilster-Mary Lee Corp, 44578
Ginseng Up Corp, 44582
Golden 100, 44626
Gonterman & Associates, 44651
Governair Corp, 44678
Grain Machinery Mfg Corp, 44685
Grayco Products Sales, 44705
Guiltless Gourmet, 44771
H A Sparke Co, 44790
H Fox & Co Inc, 44796
Habasit America, 44825
Hamersmith, Inc., 44846
Handy Wacks Corp, 44861
Hausbeck Pickle Co, 44928
Hcs Enterprises, 44943
Heaven Hill Distilleries Inc., 44967
Herbs Etc, 44996
Hodell International, 45039
Homarus Inc, 45057
Home Rubber Co, 45060
Horix Manufacturing Co, 45077
Hospitality Mints LLC, 45087
Hudson Commercial Foods, 45117
Humco Holding Group Inc, 45127
Hunter Walton & Co Inc, 45132
Huther Brothers, 45138
Ideal of America/Valley Rio Enterprise, 45203
Ilapak Inc, 45208
ILHWA American Corporation, 45171
Insignia Systems Inc, 45299
International Cooling Systems, 45335
International Environmental Solutions, 45340
International Food Packers Corporation, 45342
International Pack & Ship, 45357
International Packaging Machinery, 45358
International Patterns, Inc., 45361
Interstate Packaging, 45380
Jarden Home Brands, 45496
Jason Marketing Corporation, 45503
John Henry Packaging, 45545
Johnson-Rose Corporation, 45557
Judel Products, 45582
Kal Pac Corp, 45640
Kamflex Corp, 45644
KH McClure & Company, 45616
KHL Flavors Inc, 45617
Kinsley Inc, 45756
Kisters Kayat, 45760
Kloss Manufacturing Co Inc, 45769
Kola, 45788
Kuepper Favor Company, Celebrate Line, 45823
KWS Manufacturing Co LTD, 45632
Label Systems, 45886
Lancer, 45921
Laub-Hunt Packaging Systems, 45949
Leavitt Corp., The, 45968
Lee Kum Kee, 45971
Les Viandes du Breton, 46005

Lewisburg Printing, 46015
Limpert Bros Inc, 46047
Livingston-Wilbor Corporation, 46075
LMG Group, 45864
Mali's All Natural Barbecue Supply Company, 46273
Manhattan Truck Lines, 46294
Manufacturing Warehouse, 46305
Marel Stork Poultry Processing, 46325
Marina Foods, 46334
Materials Transportation Co, 46406
Maxi-Vac Inc., 46425
Maxim's Import Corporation, 46426
Merchants Export Inc, 46499
Merritt Estate Winery Inc, 46516
Meyenberg Goat Milk, 46539
Miami Beef Co, 46543
MLG Enterprises Ltd., 46214
Moen Industries, 46686
Molinaro's Fine Italian Foods Ltd., 46694
Molinera International, 46696
Momar, 46699
Moyer Diebel, 46756
Mr Ice Bucket, 46761
Murakami Farms, 46797
Murotech, 46798
NaceCare Solutions, 46833
National Foods, 46873
National Plastics Co, 46886
Native Scents, 46897
Natural Fruit Corp, 46908
Navarro Pecan Co, 46929
Nikken Foods, 47027
Norbest, LLC, 47053
Norpak Corp, 47061
Noyes, P J, 47120
Nutraceutical International, 47142
Nutri-Cell, 47146
Nutritional Research Associates, 47157
O-At-Ka Milk Prods Co-Op Inc., 47165
OCS Process Systems, 47167
Ole Hickory Pits, 47206
Olive Can Company, 47207
Omaha Steaks Inc, 47216
Omega Industrial Products Inc, 47220
Omni Pacific Company, 47230
Ono International, 47242
Open Date Systems, 47248
Optex, 47251
Orwak, 47290
P.F. Harris Manufacturing Company, 47320
Pacer Pumps, 47352
Packaging Equipment & Conveyors, Inc, 47389
Packaging Service Co Inc, 47394
Pacur, 47399
Pappy's Sassafras Tea, 47440
Paradise Products Corporation, 47447
Paramount Industries, 47454
Paxton Corp, 47499
Pecoraro Dairy Products, 47514
Phelps Industries, 47585
Pluto Corporation, 47644
Porinos Gourmet Food, 47678
Prawn Seafoods Inc, 47698
Presentations South, 47728
Prima Foods International, 47741
Produce Trading Corp, 47778
Productos Familia, 47786
Pruden Packing Company, 47824
PTR Baler & Compactor Co, 47346
Pucel Enterprises Inc, 47827
Purchase Order Co Of Miami Inc, 47837
Pure Source LLC, 47844
Qualifresh Michel St. Arneault, 47875
Quipco Products Inc, 47900
R M Felts' Packing Co, 47906
Rairdon Dodge Chrysler Jeep, 47959
RAM Center, 47923
Rational Cooking Systems, 47976
Raymond-Hadley Corporation, 47981
Rector Foods, 47995
Red Smith Foods Inc, 48006
Refrigerator Manufacturers LLC, 48023

Export Region / Caribbean Basin

Regina USA, 48033
Reilly Dairy & Food Company, 48039
Revent Inc, 48075
Rice Company, 48089
Richards Packaging, 48096
Rixie Paper Products Inc, 48119
Robby Vapor Systems, 48125
Robin Shepherd Group, 48135
Robot Coupe, 48139
Rowland Coffee Roasters Inc., 48205
Royal Doulton, 48215
S & L Store Fixture, 48255
S&P USA Ventilation Systems, LLC, 48262
Sato America, 48397
Scaltrol Inc, 48410
Sconza Candy Co, 48442
Select Food Products, 48497
Semco Manufacturing Company, 48503
Sesinco Foods, 48542
Shat R Shield Inc, 48572
Shine Companies, 48593
Shoes for Crews/Mighty Mat, 48603
Sid Wainer & Son Specialty, 48614
Silesia Grill Machines Inc, 48633
Slicechief Co, 48692
SPG International, 48290
Spice House International Specialties, 48829
Stainless One DispensingSystem, 48869
Stanley Orchards Sales, Inc., 48885
Steel's Gourmet Foods, Ltd., 48918
Stimo-O-Stam, Ltd., 48955
Storage Unlimited, 48970
Stripper Bags, 48986
Sun Pac Foods, 49013
Sunlike Juice, 49025
Superior Uniform Group, 49059
Sure Torque, 49069
Surekap Inc, 49071
Sweet Endings Inc, 49085
SWF Co, 48303
Swiss Food Products, 49095
Synergy Flavors Inc, 49107
Talbott Farms, 49161
Tampa Bay Fisheries Inc, 49166
Tampa Pallet Co, 49169
Tate Western, 49196
Taylor Products Co, 49203
Technium, 49214
Tecweigh, 49219
Thirs-Tea Corp, 49322
Thomas L. Green & Company, 49324
Thomas Tape & Supply Co Inc, 49327
Tieco-Unadilla Corporation, 49343
Tier-Rack Corp, 49344
Tradelink, 49422
Tri-Tronics, 49458
Triple Leaf Tea Inc, 49482
Ultimate International, 49583
Uniplast Films, 49614
United Industries Group Inc, 49638
United Marketing Exchange, 49640
United Showcase Company, 49650
Universal Handling Equipment, 49666
US Chemical, 49563
Vance's Foods, 49735
Vanguard Technology Inc, 49737
Ventre Packing Company, 49767
Victoria Porcelain, 49800
Vita-Pakt Citrus Products Co, 49839
VT Industries Inc, 49703
Vulcan Industries, 49867
WA Brown & Son, 49878
Walco, 49922
Walden Farms, 49924
Walker Stainless Equipment Co, 49928
Walle Corp, 49933
Waltkoch Limited, 49939
Walton's Inc, 49941
Ward Ironworks, 49948
Waste Minimization/Containment, 49961
Water Sciences Services, Inc., 49966
WE Killam Enterprises, 49883
Welch Holme & Clark Co, 50006
West India Trading Company, 50029

West Oregon Wood Products Inc, 50031
Willmark Sales Company, 50117
Windsor Wax Co Inc, 50124
Worksman 800 Buy Cart, 50179
Workstead Industries, 50180
Xpresso, 50219
Yardney Water Management Syst, 50232
Yum Yum Potato Chips, 50249

Caribbean Basin

Joey's Fine Foods, 45538

Cayman Islands

Premium Water, 47722

Central America

3V Company, 41472
A & B Process Systems Corp, 41476
A C Horn & Co Sheet Metal, 41478
A G Russell Knives, 41480
A La Carte, 41483
A Legacy Food Svc, 41484
A&B Safe Corporation, 41491
A&D Weighing, 41493
A&J Mixing International, 41495
A&L Laboratories, 41496
A&M Industries, 41497
A&M Thermometer Corporation, 41499
A-1 Refrigeration Co, 41501
A-A1 Aaction Bag, 41502
A-B-C Packaging Machine Corp, 41503
A-Z Factory Supply, 41505
A.C. Legg, 41510
Aabbitt Adhesives, 41596
Abbott & Cobb Inc, 41606
Abel Manufacturing Co, 41609
Abimar Foods Inc, 41610
ABM Marking, 41531
ABO Industries, 41532
Absorbco, 41615
Abuelita Mexican Foods, 41616
Accuflex Industrial Hose LTD, 41624
Accutek Packaging Equipment, 41626
Ace Specialty Mfg Co Inc, 41631
Aceto Corporation, 41634
ACLAUSA Inc, 41535
Acme Engineering & Mfg Corp, 41637
Acme Scale Co, 41640
Acorto, 41646
Acp Inc, 41647
Acraloc Corp, 41649
Acta Health Products, 41652
Actron, 41658
ADCO Manufacturing Inc, 41539
Adhesive Technologies Inc, 41672
Admatch Corporation, 41673
Advance Storage Products, 41685
Advanced Detection Systems, 41688
Advanced Food Systems, 41691
Advanced Labelworx Inc, 41695
Aero Manufacturing Co, 41702
Aeromix Systems, 41705
Affiliated Rice Milling, 41711
AFT Advanced Fiber Technologies, 41549
Agri-Dairy Products, 41719
Agricor Inc, 41722
AHD International, LLC, 41553
Air Quality Engineering, 41735
Al Safa Halal, 41751
Al-Rite Fruits & Syrups Co, 41752
Alabama Bag Co Inc, 41753
Alaska Sausage & Seafood, 41760
Albion Machine & Tool Co, 41767
ALCO Designs, 41558
Alfa International Corp, 41776
Alfa Laval Inc, 41778
Alfa Systems Inc, 41779
Alkar Rapid Pak, 41790
Alkota Cleaning Systems Inc, 41792
All A Cart Custom Mfg, 41793
All American Container, 41794
All American Seasonings, 41795
All Fill Inc, 41796
All Foils Inc, 41797

Alliance Industrial Corp, 41817
Alliance Rubber Co, 41818
Allied Glove Corporation, 41821
Alloy Hardfacing & Engineering, 41828
Allstrong Restaurant Eqpt Inc, 41830
Alsum Farms & Produce, 41844
Alternative Health & Herbs, 41847
Altman Industries, 41849
Alto-Shaam, 41850
Alumin-Nu Corporation, 41853
Amano Enzyme USA Company, Ltd, 41855
Amark Packaging Systems, 41857
America's Classic Foods, 41867
American Brush Company, 41871
American Eagle Food Machinery, 41878
American Food Traders, 41888
American Glass Research, 41890
American Hotel Register Co, 41891
American Housewares, 41892
American Importing Co., 41894
American Laboratories, 41900
American Lifts, 41902
American Louver Co, 41903
American Manufacturing-Engrng, 41904
American Metalcraft Inc, 41907
American Range, 41915
American Roland Food Corporation, 41917
American Seafood Imports Inc., 41919
American Store Fixtures, 41924
American Time & Signal Co, 41926
American Trading Company, 41927
American Ultraviolet Co, 41928
American Water Broom, 41929
Ameripak Packaging Equipment, 41935
AMF Bakery Systems Corp, 41566
AMI, 41568
Ammeraal Beltech Inc, 41949
AMSOIL Inc, 41570
Analite, 41965
Anchor Packaging, 41971
Andersen 2000, 41973
Anderson International Corp, 41977
Anderson-Crane Company, 41981
Anguil Environmental Systems, 41989
Anhydro Inc, 41990
Animal Pak, 41991
Anritsu Industrial Solutions, 41998
API Heat Transfer Inc, 41577
Apple Acres, 42010
Appleton Produce Company, 42011
Applied Chemical Technology, 42014
Applied Robotics Inc, 42016
Aqua Measure, 42019
Archie Moore's, 42027
Architecture Plus Intl Inc, 42028
Arctic Industries, 42033
Arde Inc, 42035
Arden Companies, 42037
Ariel Vineyards, 42042
Arista Industries Inc, 42044
Arizona Instrument LLC, 42047
Arkfeld Mfg & Distributing Co, 42050
Armaly Brands, 42052
Aroma Vera, 42060
Arpac LP, 42066
Arrow Tank Co, 42069
ASCENT Technics Corporation, 41583
ASI Data Myte, 41584
ASI/Restaurant Manager, 41587
Assembled Products Corp, 42087
Assembly Technology & Test, 42088
At Last Naturals Inc, 42097
ATD-American Co, 41588
Athea Laboratories, 42100
ATI, 41589
Atlanta SharpTech, 42106
Atlantic Rubber Company, 42116
Atlantic Ultraviolet Corp, 42118
Atlantis Plastics Linear Film, 42121
Atlas Match Company, 42125
Atlas Pacific Engineering, 42128
Atlas Packaging Inc, 42129
Audion Automation, 42135
August Thomsen Corp, 42137

Austrade, 42143
Autio Co, 42144
Auto Labe, 42145
Autobar Systems, 42146
Automated Flexible Conveyors, 42150
Automated Food Systems, 42151
Automatic Bar Controls Inc, 42152
Automatic Products/Crane, 42155
Automatic Specialties Inc, 42156
Automatic Timing & Controls, 42157
Autotron, 42161
Avalon Manufacturer, 42162
Avery Weigh-Tronix, 42167
Avestin, 42169
Azz/R-A-L, 42187
B H Bunn Co, 42190
B. Terfloth & Company, 42194, 42195
B.C. Tree Fruits Limited, 42197
Badger Meter Inc, 42229
Bagcraft Papercon, 42232
Baker Hughes, 42238
Bakers Pride Oven Company, 42244
Bal Seal Engineering Inc, 42248
Baldor Electric Co, 42252
Ballantyne Food Service Equipment, 42255
Ballas Egg Products Corp, 42256
Bally Refrigerated Boxes Inc, 42258
Baltimore Aircoil Co, 42261
Bar Keepers Friend Cleanser, 42270
Barliant & Company, 42283
Barrette Outdoor Living, 42285
Basic American Foods, 42295
Basic Food Flavors, 42296
Basic Food Intl Inc, 42297
Bauducco Foods Inc., 42304
Baumer Foods Inc, 42305
Baur Tape & Label Co, 42306
Baycliff Co Inc, 42312
Be & Sco, 42317
Beach Filter Products, 42318
Bean Machines, 42321
Bear Stewart Corp, 42324
Beaufurn, 42326
Beaver Street Fisheries, 42329
Beaverton Foods Inc, 42330
Beck Flavors, 42332
Bedford Enterprises Inc, 42339
Beemak-IDL Display, 42345
Bel-Art Products, 42353
Bell-Mark Corporation, 42360
Belleharvest Sales Inc, 42364
Belshaw Adamatic Bakery Group, 42368
Beltram Foodservice Group, 42371
Bematek Systems Inc, 42374
Berg Chilling Systems, 42382
Berg Co, 42383
Berkshire Dairy, 42388
Bernal Technology, 42392
Berns Co, 42395
Bessamaire Sales Inc, 42401
Best & Donovan, 42403
Best Brands Home Products, 42404
Beta Screen Corp, 42414
Bettcher Industries Inc, 42417
BEUMER Corp, 42205
BEVCO, 42206
Beverage Capital Corporation, 42424
Bevles Company, 42428
BFM Equipment Sales, 42208
Biazzo Dairy Products Inc, 42432
Bijur Lubricating Corporation, 42435
Bilt-Rite Conveyors, 42436
Biner Ellison Packaging Systs, 42438
Binks Industries Inc, 42439
Birdsong Corp., 42455
Birko Corporation, 42457
Biro Manufacturing Co, 42458
Bishamon Industry Corp, 42460
Blackhawk Molding Co Inc, 42467
Blair's Sauces & Snacks, 42468
Blaze Products Corp, 42474
Blossom Farm Products, 42482
Blue Cross Laboratories, 42486
Blue Giant Equipment Corporation, 42489

693

Export Region / Central America

Blue Sky Beverage Company, 42496
Bluff Manufacturing Inc, 42499
BluMetric Environmental Inc., 42484
Body Breakthrough Inc, 42508
Boehringer Mfg. Co. Inc., 42509
Bolzoni Auramo, 42513
Bon Appetit International, 42515
Bonnot Co, 42520
Borroughs Corp, 42523
Bosch Packaging Technology, 42525
Boston Retail, 42530
Bowman Hollis Mfg Corp, 42540
Boxes.com, 42542
Boyd Lighting Company, 42544
Bradman Lake Inc, 42549
Brandt Farms Inc, 42557
Braun Brush Co, 42564
Brecoflex Co LLC, 42570
Breddo Likwifier, 42571
Brewmatic Company, 42575
Brisker Dry Food Crisper, 42582
Broadleaf Venison USA Inc, 42587
Broaster Co LLC, 42588
Brogdex Company, 42590
Brooks Instrument LLC, 42597
Brothers Metal Products, 42602
Brower, 42603
Brown & Haley, 42604
Brown Fired Heater, 42605
Brown International Corp LLC, 42606
Brown Machine LLC, 42607
Brown-Forman Corp, 42611
Bry-Air Inc, 42618
Bryant Products Inc, 42620
Buck Knives, 42622
Buckhorn Canada, 42625
Buffalo Technologies Corporation, 42630
Buffalo Wire Works Co Inc, 42632
Bullet Guard Corporation, 42636
Bunn-O-Matic Corp, 42640
Burgess Mfg. - Oklahoma, 42643
Burke Corp, 42645
Bushman Equipment Inc, 42653
Busse/SJI Corp, 42654
BVL Controls, 42213
BW Container Systems, 42214
Byrnes & Kiefer Company, 42659
C Nelson Mfg Co, 42670
C R Daniels Inc, 42674
C. Cretors & Company, 42680
Cabot Corp, 42720
Cal Controls, 42735
Cal Harvest Marketing Inc, 42736
Cal-Mil Plastic Products Inc, 42741
California Cereal Products, 42749
California World Trade and Marketing Company, 42758
Cambridge Viscosity, Inc., 42766
Cambro Manufacturing Co, 42767
Campbell Soup Co., 42775
Can Lines Engineering Inc, 42778
Canadian Fish Exporters, 42782
Candy Manufacturing Co, 42789
Cantech Industries Inc, 42795
Cape Cod Potato Chips, 42797
Capmatic, Ltd., 42801
Caraustar Industries, Inc., 42811
Caristrap International, 42827
Carle & Montanari-O P M, 42829
Carleton Helical Technologies, 42830
Carlin Manufacturing, 42832
Carlisle Food Svc Products Inc, 42833
Carlisle Sanitary Mntnc Prods, 42834
Carlson Products, 42836
Carolina Knife, 42840
Carpigiani Corporation of America, 42846
Carrageenan Company, 42847
Casa Di Lisio Products Inc, 42863
Casella Lighting, 42869
Casso-Solar Corporation, 42875
Cat Pumps, 42877
Catskill Craftsmen Inc, 42883
Catty Inc, 42886
Cawy Bottling Co, 42891
CCL Container, 42689

Cedar Lake Foods, 42894
Cellofoam North America, 42899
Central Fabricators Inc, 42907
Century Industries Inc, 42914
Charles Beseler Company, 42930
Charles Mayer Studios, 42933
Charles Ross & Son Co, 42934
Chase Industries Inc, 42940
Chase-Doors, 42941
Chase-Logeman Corp, 42942
Chef Hans' Gourmet Foods, 42950
Chef Revival, 42952
Chef Specialties, 42953
Chefwear, 42957
Chem-Tainer Industries Inc, 42960
Chemdet Inc, 42964
Chemicolloid Laboratories, Inc., 42966
ChemTreat, Inc., 42962
Cherokee Trading Co, 42972
Chicago Scale & Slicer Company, 42989
Chief Wenatchee, 42995
China Mist Brands, 43002
Chocolate Concepts, 43012
Chooljian Bros Packing Co, 43022
CHS Inc., 42696
Cibao Meat Products Inc, 43033
Cincinnati Industrial Machry, 43035
Cintex of America, 43039
Circuits & Systems Inc, 43043
City Foods Inc, 43054
Clabber Girl Corporation, 43056
Clamp Swing Pricing Co Inc, 43058
Classic Flavors & Fragrances, 43065
Classic Tea, 43066
Classico Seating, 43067
Clawson Machine Co Inc, 43068
Clayton Industries, 43072
Clean Water Systems, 43073
Clean Water Technology, 43074
Cleaver-Brooks Inc, 43080
Clements Foods Co, 43083
Clextral USA, 43090
Climax Packaging Machinery, 43092
Clipper Belt Lacer Company, 43093
Co-Rect Products Inc, 43103
Coburn Company, 43111
Coldmatic Refrigeration, 43128
ColdZone, 43127
Coleman Natural, 43131
Colonial Coffee Roasters Inc, 43141
Columbia Labeling Machinery, 43148
Columbian TecTank, 43150
Columbus Instruments, 43151
Comark Instruments, 43153
Combi Packaging Systems LLC, 43155
Commercial Dehydrator Systems, 43161
Commercial Furniture Group Inc, 43162
Compactors Inc, 43174
Composition Materials Co Inc, 43179
Computype Inc, 43184
Comstock Castle Stove Co, 43185
Con Agra Snack Foods, 43188
Con-tech/Conservation Technology, 43189
Concannon Vineyard, 43195
Conimar Corp, 43200
Connecticut Laminating Co Inc, 43201
Conquest International LLC, 43204
Consolidated Baling Machine Company, 43205
Consolidated Commercial Controls, 43207
Consolidated Commerical Controls, 43208
Consolidated Label Company, 43210
Constar International, 43213
Constellation Brands Inc, 43214
Container Machinery Corporation, 43216
Container Supply Co, 43217
Contech Enterprises Inc, 43218
Continental Equipment Corporation, 43223
Continental Marketing, 43227
Continental Seasoning, 43229
Control & Metering, 43234
Control Beverage, 43235

Control Instruments Corp, 43238
Convay Systems, 43242
Convectronics, 43243
Conveyor Accessories, 43246
Cookie Tree Bakeries, 43256
CookTek, 43254
Cool Care, 43259
Cooperheat/MQS, 43263
Core Products Co, 43270
Corenco, 43271
Cork Specialties, 43275
Cornelius Inc., 43278
Cornell Machine Co, 43279
Corson Rubber Products Inc, 43286
Cosgrove Enterprises Inc, 43289
Costco Wholesale Corporation, 43295
Cotton Goods Mfg Co, 43296
Coulter Giufre & Co Inc, 43299
Country Save Products Corp, 43304
Country Smoked Meats, 43305
Cozzoli Machine Co, 43314
CP Kelco, 42707
CPM Century Extrusion, 42708
Crane & Crane Inc, 43320
Crane Environmental, 43322
Cres Cor, 43338
Crespac Incorporated, 43342
Cresset Chemical Company, 43343
Crestware, 43345
Critzas Industries Inc, 43351
Croll Reynolds Inc, 43354
Crown Foods International, 43367
Crown Iron Works Company, 43369
Cruvinet Winebar Co LLC, 43380
Cryochem, 43381
Crystal Creamery, 43382
CSC Scientific Co Inc, 42712
CSC Worldwide, 42713
CSS International Corp, 42714
Culligan Company, 43398
Culver Duck Farms Inc, 43401
Cumberland Dairy, 43402
Cup Pac Packaging Inc, 43406
Custom Diamond Intl., 43415
Custom Stamp Company, 43423
Customized Equipment SE, 43424
Cutrite Company, 43427
CVP Systems Inc, 42718
Cyclonaire Corp, 43431
D & L Manufacturing, 43435
D D Bean & Sons Co, 43438
D D Williamson & Co Inc, 43439
D R Technology Inc, 43440
Dacam Corporation, 43465
Daily Printing Inc, 43468
Dairy Conveyor Corp, 43470
Dairy Specialties, 43472
Dairy-Mix Inc, 43474
DairyAmerica, 43475
DairyChem Inc., 43476
Damas Corporation, 43487
Damp Rid, 43488
Danafilms Inc, 43492
Darisil, 43502
Darnell-Rose Inc, 43504
Dart Container Corp., 43505
Datapaq, 43507
Davenport Machine, 43508
Davis Trade & Commodities, 43515
Daymark Safety Systems, 43522
DBE Inc, 43451
DCL Solutions LLC, 43452
De Ster Corporation, 43533
Dealers Food Products Co, 43538
Defranco Co, 43553
Deiss Sales Co. Inc., 43556
Del Rey Packing, 43560
Delavau LLC, 43564
Delmonaco Winery & Vineyards, 43572
Delta Pure Filtration Corp, 43576
DeltaTrak, 43578
Deluxe Equipment Company, 43580
Demaco, 43582
Dependable Machine, Inc., 43586
Detecto Scale Co, 43598
Di Mare Fresh Inc, 43606

Diamond Foods, 43616
Diamond Fruit Growers, 43617
Diamond Wipes Intl Inc, 43621
DIC International, 43456
Dietzco, 43629
Dings Co Magnetic Group, 43632
Dixie Egg Co, 43653
DNE World Fruit Sales, 43459
Doran Scales Inc, 43671
Dorton Incorporated, 43674
Double Wrap Cup & Container, 43677
Dovex Export Co, 43684
Dow Industries, 43686
Dr. John's Candies, 43693
Drake Co, 43697
Dream Confectioners LTD, 43702
Dresco Belting Co Inc, 43704
Dri Mark Products, 43706
Driscoll Strawberry Assoc Inc, 43708
DSM Fortitech Premixes, 43461
Duke Manufacturing Co, 43717
Dunbar Manufacturing Co, 43719
Dundee Groves, 43720
DuPont Nutrition & Biosciences, 43713
Dura-Flex, 43728
Dura-Ware Company of America, 43730
Duralite Inc, 43733
DWL Industries Company, 43464
Dyna-Veyor Inc, 43748
Dynamic Air Inc, 43749
Dynaric Inc, 43753
E & E Process Instrumentation, 43755
E-J Industries Inc, 43761
Eagle Home Products, 43796
Eagle Products Company, 43797
Earth Saver, 43799
Easterday Fluid Technologies, 43806
Eastern Machine, 43809
Eaton Corporation, 43819
Eckels Bilt, 43824
Eckhart Corporation, 43825
Eco-Air Products, 43831
Ecodyne Water Treatment, LLC, 43834
Econofrost Night Covers, 43840
Economy Folding Box Corporation, 43841
Economy Paper & Restaurant Co, 43844
Ecoval Dairy Trade, 43846
EDA International Corp, 43772
Eda's Sugar Free, 43849
Eden, 43850
Edge Manufacturing, 43854
Edgecraft Corp, 43856
Edison Price Lighting, 43858
Edlong Corporation, 43860
Edom Labs Inc, 43865
Edson Packaging Machinery, 43866
EGW Bradbury Enterprises, 43778
Eirich Machines, 43872
El Charro Mexican Food Ind, 43874
Electro Freeze, 43887
Elliott Manufacturing Co Inc, 43902
Elmar Worldwide, 43905
Elmer Hansen Produce Inc, 43907
Emc Solutions, 43917
EMCO, 43782
Emerald City Closets Inc, 43918
Emerald Kalama Chemical, LLC, 43919
Emerling International Foods, 43921
Emery Winslow Scale Co, 43926
Encore Fruit Marketing Inc, 43937
Ener-G Foods, 43941
Energen Products Inc, 43942
Engineered Products Corp, 43947
Engineered Security System Inc, 43949
Ennio International, 43953
Enterprise Company, 43959
Enviro-Clear Co, 43962
Environmental Products Company, 43963
EP International, 43785
Epsen Hillmer Graphics Co, 43971
Equipex Limited, 43972
Equipment Specialists Inc, 43974
Erell Manufacturing Co, 43976
Erickson Industries, 43977
Eriez Magnetics, 43979

Export Region / Central America

ERO/Goodrich Forest Products, 43788
Erwyn Products Inc, 43983
Esquire Mechanical Corp., 43989
Esselte Meto, 43990
Essiac Canada International, 43993
Esteem Products, 43994
Ettore, 43997
Euclid Coffee Co, 43998
Evans Food Group LTD, 44020
EVAPCO Inc, 43792
Evaporator Dryer Technologies, 44021
Everbrite LLC, 44025
Everedy Automation, 44026
Evergreen Packaging, 44030
Everpure, LLC, 44031
Ex-Cell KAISER LLC, 44035
Excellence Commercial Products, 44041
Exel, 44043
Exhausto, 44046
Eximcan Canada, 44048
Eximco Manufacturing Company, 44049
Export Contract Corporation, 44051
F I L T E C-Inspection Systems, 44062
F N Smith Corp, 44064
F.H. Taussig Company, 44067
Fabreeka International, 44087
Fabricon Products Inc, 44089
Fairbanks Scales, 44094
Fairfield Line Inc, 44098
Falcon Rice Mill Inc, 44101
Fast Industries, 44120
Fax Foods, 44124
FECO/MOCO, 44074
FEI Inc, 44075
Felins USA Inc, 44136
Fernholtz Engineering, 44142
Ferrell-Ross, 44146
FIB-R-DOR, 44077
Fiesta Farms, 44159
Filler Specialties, 44163
Fine Cocoa Products, 44175
First Colony Coffee & Tea Company, 44186
Fish Oven & Equipment Co, 44189
Fitec International Inc, 44196
Flakice Corporation, 44202
Flavor Dynamics Two, 44209
Flavor Sciences Inc, 44211
Flavor Wear, 44213
Flavormatic Industries, 44217
Flex Products, 44227
Flexicell Inc, 44229
Flexicon, 44230
Flippin-Seaman Inc, 44233
Florart Flock Process, 44239
Florida Choice Foods, 44240
Fluid Air Inc, 44250
Fluid Energy Processing & Eqpt, 44251
Fluid Metering Inc, 44252
Flux Pumps Corporation, 44254
Foam Packaging Inc, 44259
Foell Packing Company, 44260
Fold-Pak Corporation, 44264
Foley-Belsaw Institute, 44269
Folgers Coffee Co, 44270
Folklore Foods, 44271
Follett Corp, 44272
Food Instrument Corp, 44279
Food Technology Corporation, 44287
Foodscience Corp, 44295
Forbes Industries, 44302
Foremost Machine Builders Inc, 44304
Formflex, 44309
Forte Technology, 44313
Forum Lighting, 44317
Foss Nirsystems, 44318
Foster Farms Inc., 44320
Fowler Products Co LLC, 44328
FPEC Corporation, 44079
Framarx Corp, 44331
Franklin Trading Company, 44339
FRC Systems International, 44081
Fred D Pfening Co, 44344
Fredrick Ramond Company, 44346
FreesTech, 44352
Freiria & Company, 44354

French Oil Mill Machinery Co, 44362
Friedrich Metal Products, 44370
Friskem Infinetics, 44372
Front Range Snacks Inc, 44377
Frontier Bag, 44378
Frozfruit Corporation, 44383
Fry Foods Inc, 44390
Fuller Industries LLC, 44394
Fun Foods, 44400
Fun-Time International, 44401
Furnace Belt Company, 44403
Future Commodities Intl Inc, 44405
Galbreath LLC, 44454
Gallimore Industries, 44458
Gamajet Cleaning Systems, 44460
Gar Products, 44466
Garcoa Laboratories Inc, 44469
Garland Commercial Ranges Ltd., 44478
Garroutte, 44482
Garver Manufacturing Inc, 44484
Garvey Corp, 44485
Gary Manufacturing Company, 44486
Gasser Chair Co Inc, 44491
Gch Internatonal, 44501
Gea Intec, Llc, 44503
Gea Us, 44504
Gebo Conveyors, Consultants & Systems, 44505
Gehnrich Oven Sales Company, 44509
GEM Cultures, 44427
Gems Sensors & Controls, 44513
General Films Inc, 44520
General Packaging Equipment Co, 44525
General Processing Systems, 44527
General, Inc, 44531
Genpak LLC, 44536
Gensaco Marketing, 44537
Georgia Spice Company, 44551
Gerlau Sales, 44558
GERM-O-RAY, 44429
Gessner Products, 44562
GHM Industries Inc, 44432
Gilson Co Inc, 44577
Gilster-Mary Lee Corp, 44578
Ginseng Up Corp, 44582
Girton Manufacturing Co, 44586
Glass Pro, 44593
Glastender, 44594
Glo-Quartz Electric Heater, 44600
Global Equipment Co Inc, 44603
Global Manufacturing, 44608
Global Sticks, Inc., 44612
Globe Food Equipment Co, 44614
Glowmaster Corporation, 44618
Goetze's Candy Co, 44620
Gold Pure Food Products Co. Inc., 44624
Goldco Industries, 44625
Golden 100, 44626
Golden Moon Tea, 44635
Golden Star, 44642
Golden Walnut Specialty Foods, 44647
Goldenwest Sales, 44649
Goodwrappers Inc, 44663
Grain Machinery Mfg Corp, 44685
Grande Custom Ingredients Group, 44693
Graphite Metalizing Corp, 44701
Grassland Dairy Products Inc, 44702
Grayco Products Sales, 44705
Great Western Co LLC, 44721
Great Western Manufacturing Company, 44724
Greater Omaha Packing Co Inc., 44725
Green Belt Industries Inc, 44731
Green Foods Corp., 44733
Greig Filters Inc, 44744
Grgich Hills Estates, 44747
Grimaud Farms-California Inc, 44754
Grocers Supply Co, 44757
GS Dunn & Company, 44438
GTCO CalComp, 44441
Guiltless Gourmet, 44771
Guth Lighting, 44786
GWB Foods Corporation, 44443
H A Phillips & Co, 44789
H A Sparke Co, 44790

H C Duke & Son Inc, 44793
H G Weber & Co, 44797
H Nagel & Son Co, 44798
Habasit America, 44825
Hackney Brothers, 44828
Hadley's Date Gardens, 44830
Hagensborg Chocolates LTD., 44831
Hairnet Corporation of America, 44834
Haldin International, 44836
Hall Safety Apparel, 44840
Hall-Woolford Wood Tank Co Inc, 44841
Hallberg Manufacturing Corporation, 44842
Halton Company, 44843
Halton Packaging Systems, 44844
Hamersmith, Inc., 44846
Hamilton Beach Brands, 44847
Hamilton Caster, 44849
Hamilton Kettles, 44850
Hampton Associates & Sons, 44852
Hamrick Manufacturing & Svc, 44854
Handy Manufacturing Co Inc, 44860
Handy Wacks Corp, 44861
Hank Rivera Associates, 44865
Hanson Brass Rewd Co, 44877, 44878
Harborlite Corporation, 44887
Harco Enterprises, 44890
Hardwood Products Co LP, 44893
Harpak-ULMA Packaging LLC, 44902
Hart Design & Mfg, 44912
Hartness International, 44915
Hatfield Quality Meats, 44926
Haumiller Engineering Co, 44927
Haynes Manufacturing Co, 44938
Hcs Enterprises, 44943
Health King Enterprise, 44950
Health Plus, 44951
HealthBest, 44954
Healthy N Fit International, 44957
Heatcraft Worldwide Refrig, 44965
Heaven Hill Distilleries Inc., 44967
Helken Equipment Co, 44977
Hemisphere Group, 44984
Hermann Laue Spice Company, 45001
Hess Machine Intl, 45004
Heterochemical Corp, 45005
HFI Products, 44818
Hi-Country Foods Corporation, 45009
Hialeah Products Co, 45010
Highlight Industries, 45018
Hill Manufacturing Co Inc, 45023
Hillside Candy Co, 45024
Hillside Metal Ware Company, 45025
Hinckley Springs Bottled Water, 45032
Hodell International, 45039
Hoffer Flow Controls Inc, 45040
Hoffmaster Group Inc, 45042
Holland Beef International Corporation, 45047
Hollowick Inc, 45051
Hollymatic Corp, 45052
Holman Boiler Works, 45054
Holmco Container Manufacturing, LTD, 45055
Home Plastics Inc, 45059
Home Rubber Co, 45060
Honeyville Grain Inc, 45066
Horix Manufacturing Co, 45077
Hormann Flexan Llc, 45079
Hose Master Inc, 45083
Hoshizaki America Inc, 45085
Hospitality Mints LLC, 45087
House of Spices, 45094
Houston Label, 45095
Howard-Mccray, 45101
Hubbell Lighting Inc, 45115
Hudson-Sharp Machine Company, 45123
Hughes Co, 45125
Hungerford & Terry, 45128
Hunter Walton & Co Inc, 45132
Hurst Labeling Systems, 45134
Huskey Specialty Lubricants, 45135
Huther Brothers, 45138
Hydrel Corporation, 45140
Hydropure Water Treatment Co, 45143
I Rice & Co Inc, 45152

I-Health Inc, 45155
ICB Greenline, 45163
Iceomatic, 45194
Iconics Inc, 45195
Idaho Pacific Holdings Inc, 45196
Ideal of America/Valley Rio Enterprise, 45203
Ideal Stencil Machine & Tape Company, 45200
Ideal Wire Works, 45201
Ideas Etc Inc, 45204
Idesco Corp, 45205
Ilapak Inc, 45208
ILHWA American Corporation, 45171
Illuma Display, 45211
Imaging Technologies, 45214
IMI Cornelius, 45173
IMI Precision Engineering, 45174
Imperial Industries Inc, 45221
Improved Blow Molding, 45231
In A Bind Inc, 45233
Indemax Inc, 45243
Independent Can Co, 45244
Indiana Glass Company, 45252
Industrial Contracting & Rggng, 45260
Industrial Kinetics, 45261
Industrial Laboratory Eqpt Co, 45262
Industrial Magnetics, 45263
Industrial Piping Inc, 45264
Inline Filling Systems, 45280
Insect-O-Cutor Inc, 45296
Insinger Co, 45300
Instrumart, 45304
Intercomp, 45317
Interlab, 45320
Interlake Mecalux, 45321
International Casings Group, 45328
International Coconut Corp, 45332
International Dehydrated Foods, 45337
International Food Packers Corporation, 45342
International Food Products, 45343
International Home Foods, 45347
International Industries Corporation, 45348
International Machinery Xchnge, 45351
International Market Brands, 45352
International Oils & Concentrates, 45354
International Pack & Ship, 45357
International Packaging Machinery, 45358
International Paper Box Machine Company, 45359
International Patterns, Inc., 45361
International Reserve Equipment Corporation, 45362
International Sourcing, 45366
International Specialty Supply, 45367
International Tank & Pipe Co, 45368
International Telcom Inc, 45369
International Tray Pads, 45371
Interstate Packaging, 45380
Invictus Systems Corporation, 45384
Island Oasis Frozen Cocktail, 45392
Island Sweetwater Beverage Company, 45394
Italian Quality Products, 45403
Item Products, 45405
J C Whitlam Mfg Co, 45425
J T Gibbons Inc, 45433
J W Outfitters, 45434
J.V. Reed & Company, 45448
Jarrow Formulas Inc, 45499
Jay-Bee Manufacturing Inc, 45507
Jayhawk Manufacturing Co Inc, 45508
Jeco Plastic Products LLC, 45510
Jet Set Sam, 45524
JET Tools, 45457
Jewel Case Corp, 45526
Joey's Fine Foods, 45538
John Boos & Co, 45540
John J. Adams Die Corporation, 45547
John R Nalbach Engineering Co, 45548
Johns Cove Fisheries, 45551
Johnson Refrigerated Truck, 45556
Johnson-Rose Corporation, 45557

695

Export Region / Central America

Jordon Commercial Refrigerator, 45568
Joseph Adams Corp, 45570
Joseph Struhl Co Inc, 45574
Juanita's Foods, 45581
Juice Tree, 45584
Justman Brush Co, 45592
K Trader Inc., 45600
K-Way Products, 45605
KaiRak, 45637
Kalsec, 45642
Kamflex Corp, 45644
KAPCO, 45609
KAPS All Packaging, 45610
KASE Equipment, 45613
Kason Central, 45656
Katagiri & Company, 45658
Kay Home Products Inc, 45660
Kemach Food Products, 45695
Kemutec Group Inc, 45699
Kent Corp, 45705
Kent Precision Foods Group Inc, 45706
Keto Foods, 45715
Key Technology Inc., 45719
Key-Pak Machines, 45721
Kiefer Brushes, Inc, 45728
Kim Lighting, 45730
Kincaid Enterprises, 45732
Kinergy Corp, 45734
King Company, 45741
King Engineering - King-Gage, 45742
King Nut Co, 45744
Kingston McKnight, 45753
Kinsley Inc, 45756
Kiss International/Di-tech Systems, 45759
KISS Packaging Systems, 45619
Kisters Kayat, 45760
Klockner Pentaplast of America, 45768
Kloss Manufacturing Co Inc, 45769
KMT Aqua-Dyne Inc, 45625
Knight Seed Company, 45773
Knott Slicers, 45776
Kodex Inc, 45782
Koehler Instrument Co Inc, 45783
Kohler Industries Inc, 45787
Kola, 45788
Kold-Hold, 45790
Kolpak Walk-ins, 45793
Kornylak Corp, 45803
Kosto Food Products Co, 45804
KOZY Shack Enterprises Inc, 45626
Krones, 45818
Kruger Foods, 45821
KTG, 45629
Kuhl Corporation, 45825
KWS Manufacturing Co LTD, 45632
Kysor Panel Systems, 45834
L&A Process Systems, 45840
La Belle Suisse Corporation, 45870
La Crosse, 45872
La Flor Spices, 45873
LA Monica Fine Foods, 45851
Label Systems, 45886
Labelette Company, 45888
Lactalis American Group Inc, 45892
Lakeside-Aris Manufacturing, 45909
Lallemand, 45911
Lambent Technologies, 45913
Lamports Filter Media, 45917
Lamson & Goodnow, 45918
Lancer, 45921
Land O'Lakes Inc, 45926
Langen Packaging, 45935
Langer Manufacturing Company, 45936
Langsenkamp Manufacturing, 45937
Lanly Co, 45939
Latendorf Corporation, 45947
Laub-Hunt Packaging Systems, 45949
Laughlin Sales Corp, 45950
Lawrence Metal Products Inc, 45956
Layflat Products, 45959
Le Smoker, 45965
Leader Candies, 45966
Least Cost Formulations LTD, 45967
Leavitt Corp., The, 45968
Lee Kum Kee, 45971

Leer Inc, 45975
Legion Export & Import Company, 45980
Legion Lighting Co Inc, 45981
Les Industries Touch Inc, 46004
Les Viandes du Breton, 46005
Letrah International Corp, 46010
Lewis M Carter Mfg Co Inc, 46014
Lexington Logistics LLC, 46018
Liberty Engineering Co, 46021
Liberty Machine Company, 46023
Lifeway, 46032
Light Technology Ind, 46035
Lilly Co Inc, 46042
Lin Pac Plastics, 46048
LinPac, 46049
Linvar, 46056
Lion Raisins Inc, 46059
Lista International Corp, 46065
Listo Pencil Corp, 46066
Lite-Weight Tool & Mfg Co, 46067
Little Crow Foods, 46071
Livingston-Wilbor Corporation, 46075
LMG Group, 45864
Load King Mfg, 46081
Lockwood Packaging, 46087
Loma International, 46092
Lonestar Banners & Flags, 46099
Longhorn Packaging Inc, 46103
Longview Fibre Company, 46105
Lord Label Group, 46108
Louis Baldinger & Sons, 46119
Louis Caric & Sons, 46120
Love Controls Division, 46130
Loveshaw Corp, 46133
Low Humidity Systems, 46135
Low Temp Industries Inc, 46136
Luban International, 46140
Ludell Manufacturing Co, 46145
Luetzow Industries, 46148
Lukas Confections, 46151
Lumax Industries, 46154
Lumber & Things, 46155
Lumenite Control Tech Inc, 46156
Luthi Machinery Company, Inc., 46162
Luxury Crab, 46167
Luyties Pharmacal Company, 46168
Lyco Manufacturing, 46169
M S Willett Inc, 46185
M&L Plastics, 46187
M-C McLane International, 46189
Machine Ice Co, 46228
MAF Industries Inc, 46197
MAFCO Worldwide, 46198
Magic Valley Growers, 46245
Magna Foods Corporation, 46246
Magnetic Products Inc, 46249
Magnetool Inc, 46250
Magsys Inc, 46257
Mainline Industries Inc, 46263
Maker's Mark Distillery Inc, 46270
Malgor & Company, 46272
Malnove Of Nebraska, 46274
Malo Inc, 46275
Mane Inc., 46291
Manischewitz Co, 46298
Manitowoc Foodservice, 46299
Manning Lighting Inc, 46301
Manufacturing Warehouse, 46305
Maple Leaf Foods International, 46307
Marathon Equipment Co, 46318
Marel Stork Poultry Processing, 46325
Maren Engineering Corp, 46327
Marina Foods, 46334
Marking Methods Inc, 46347
Markson Lab Sales, 46350
Marlen, 46353
Marlen International, 46354
Marlyn Nutraceuticals, 46357
Marsh Company, 46365
Marshall Air Systems Inc, 46366
Martin Engineering, 46373
Martin/Baron, 46375
Maryland China, 46383
Maselli Measurements Inc, 46389, 46390
Master Mix, 46395

Mastercraft Industries Inc, 46397
Matador Processors, 46402
Materials Transportation Co, 46406
Matfer Inc, 46407, 46408
Matrix Engineering, 46412
Matrix Health Products, 46413
Matrix Packaging Machinery, 46414
Matthiesen Equipment, 46418
Maxi-Vac Inc., 46425
Maxim's Import Corporation, 46426
Mayacamas Fine Foods, 46429
Mba Suppliers Inc., 46436
McAnally Enterprises, 46438
Mcbrady Engineering Co, 46454
McCormack Manufacturing Company, 46443
MCD Technologies, 46202
Mclaughlin Gormley King Co, 46461
Meadows Mills Inc, 46465
Mecco Marking & Traceability, 46469
Medallion International Inc, 46470
Mega Pro Intl, 46476
Melitta USA Inc, 46484
Mello Smello LLC, 46485
Mepsco, 46493
Merchandising Inventives, 46496
Merci Spring Water, 46501
Merco/Savory, 46502
Mercury Equipment Company, 46504
Merlin Candies, 46510
Messermeister, 46518
Metal Master Sales Corp, 46523
Mettler-Toledo Safeline Inc, 46530
Mettler-Toledo, LLC, 46531
Metzgar Conveyors, 46533
Metzger Popcorn Co, 46534
Meyenberg Goat Milk, 46539
Meyer Machine & Garroutte Products, 46541
Miami Beef Co, 46543
Miami Depot Inc, 46545
Miami Purveyors Inc, 46548
Michael Foods, Inc., 46550
Michigan Desserts, 46567
Michigan Maple Block Co, 46569
Micro-Brush Pro Soap, 46573
Microbest Inc, 46577
Micropure Filtration Inc, 46585
Mid-Atlantic Foods Inc, 46589
Middleby Marshall Inc, 46599
Midwest Badge & Novelty Co, 46604
Midwest Stainless, 46609
Mies Products, 46610
Migali Industries, 46611
Mil-Du-Gas Company/Star Brite, 46617
Miljoco Corp, 46623
Miller Group Multiplex, 46629
Millerbernd Systems, 46632
Mills Brothers Intl, 46636
Milwhite Inc, 46645
Min Tong Herbs, 46647
Minn-Dak Growers LTD, 46650
MIRA International Foods, 46211
Mitsubishi Polyester Film, Inc., 46669
ML Catania Company, 46213
Mmi Engineered Soultions Inc, 46676
Mocon Inc, 46678
MODAGRAPHICS, 46217
Modern Products Inc, 46682
Modular Panel Company, 46684
Moen Industries, 46686
Mold-Rite Plastics LLC, 46690
Molinaro's Fine Italian Foods Ltd., 46694
Molinera International, 46696
Molins/Sandiacre Richmond, 46697
Momar, 46699
Monitor Technologies LLC, 46708
Monroe Environmental Corp, 46709
Moore Production Tool Spec Inc, 46722
Morre-Tec Ind Inc, 46731
Morris & Associates, 46732
Morse Manufacturing Co Inc, 46738
Morton Salt Inc., 46741
Mosher Products Inc, 46743
Mountain Safety Research, 46753

Mountain Valley Water Company, 46755
Moyer Diebel, 46756
Mr Ice Bucket, 46761
MSSH, 46218
Muellermist Irrigation Company, 46776
Mulligan Associates, 46780
Multi-Fill Inc, 46781
Multi-Panel Display Corporation, 46783
Multisorb Technologies Inc, 46790
Multivac Inc, 46791
Munson Machinery Co, 46794
Murotech, 46798
Murray Envelope Corporation, 46799
Murzan Inc. Sanitary Sys, 46801
Muth Associates, 46807
My Daddy's Cheesecake, 46811
My Quality Trading Corp, 46813
Myers Container, 46815
N S I Sweeteners, 46816
Naltex, 46837
National Foods, 46873
National Fruit Flavor Co Inc, 46875
National Hotpack, 46876
National Instruments, 46878
National Plastics Co, 46886
National Printing Converters, 46887
National Tape Corporation, 46893
Nationwide Pennant & Flag Mfg, 46896
Native Scents, 46897
Natra US, 46898
Natural Food Holdings, 46905
Natural Oils International, 46910
Nature's Products Inc, 46925
Natures Sungrown Foods Inc, 46927
Naya, 46931
NCC, 46822
NDC Infrared EngineeringInc, 46823
Nebraska Bean, 46937
Neon Design-a-Sign, 46952
Nepco Egg Of Ga, 46955
Nercon Engineering & Manufacturing, 46958
Nevlen Co. 2, Inc., 46963
Nevo Corporation, 46964
New England Machinery Inc, 46973
New Horizon Foods, 46979
New York Export Co, 46989
Newcastle Co Inc, 46995
Newell Brands, 46997
Newly Weds Foods Inc, 47001
Newman Sanitary Gasket Co, 47002
Newman's Own, 47003
Newton OA & Son Co, 47006
Niagara Blower Company, 47011
Niagara Foods, 47012
Nice-Pak Products Inc, 47013
Nieco Corporation, 47023
Nielsen-Massey Vanillas Inc, 47025
Nigrelli Systems Purchasing, 47026
Nikken Foods, 47027
Niro, 47031
Niroflex, USA, 47032
Nitech, 47036
Noh Foods of Hawaii, 47041
Noral, 47050
Norback Ley & Assoc, 47052
Nordson Sealant Equipment, 47057
Noren Products Inc, 47058
Norimoor Company, 47060
North River Roasters, 47076
North Star Ice EquipmentCorporation, 47078
Northeast Group Exporters Inc, 47081
Northeastern Products Corp, 47084
Northfield Freezing Systems, 47090
Northwest Analytical Inc, 47095
Northwestern Corp, 47102
Norvell Co Inc, 47104
Norwood Marking Systems, 47105
Novelty Crystal, 47115
NOW Foods, 46828
Now Plastics Inc, 47119
NST Metals, 46830
NTN Wireless, 46831
Nuance Solutions Inc, 47128
Nuchief Sales Inc, 47129

Export Region / Central America

Nucon Corporation, 47130
Nulaid Foods Inc, 47132
Nutraceutical International, 47142
Nutribiotic, 47147
O-At-Ka Milk Prods Co-Op Inc., 47165
Occidental Foods International, LLC, 47178
Oerlikon Leybold Vacuum, 47189
Ogden Manufacturing Company, 47192
Ohaus Corp, 47193
Olcott Plastics, 47199
Ole Hickory Pits, 47206
Olney Machinery, 47210
Olymel, 47211
Omega Products Inc, 47223
Omega Protein, 47224
Omicron Steel Products Company, 47225
Omni Controls Inc, 47226
Omni Pacific Company, 47230
Omnitech International, 47233
OnTrack Automation Inc, 47236
Opie Brush Company, 47249
Optex, 47251
Oregon Freeze Dry, Inc., 47268
Oregon Potato Co, 47271
Orion Research, 47284
Orwak, 47290
Otis McAllister Inc., 47297
OTP Industrial Solutions, 47171
Oxbo International Corp, 47308
OXO International, 47173
P.F. Harris Manufacturing Company, 47320
Paar Physica USA, 47349
Pacer Pumps, 47352
Pacific Scientific Instrument, 47365
Package Concepts & Materials Inc, 47378
Package Machinery Co Inc, 47380
Package Systems Corporation, 47381
Packaging & Processing Equipment, 47382
Packaging Dynamics, 47384
Packaging Service Co Inc, 47394
Packaging Systems Intl, 47395
Pacur, 47399
Padinox, 47401
Paget Equipment Co, 47403
Paltier, 47419
Pangaea Sciences, 47428
Panoche Creek Packing, 47430
Paoli Properties, 47432
Paper Box & Specialty Co, 47433
Paper Service, 47436
Paper Systems Inc, 47437
Pappy's Sassafras Tea, 47440
Par-Pak, 47441
PAR-Way Tryson Co, 47325
Paraclipse, 47443
Paradise Products Corporation, 47447
Paramount Industries, 47454
Paratherm Corporation, 47455
Parish Manufacturing Inc, 47459
Parkson Corp, 47465, 47466
Parrish's Cake Decorating, 47470
Particle Dynamics, 47472
Pasquini Espresso Co, 47479
Pastorelli Food Products, 47486
Patrick Cudahy LLC, 47489
Paul G. Gallin Company, 47494
Paul N. Gardner Company, 47495
Paul O. Abbe, 47496
Paxton Corp, 47499
PC/Poll Systems, 47330
PDE Technology Corp, 47332
Peco Controls Corporation, 47512
Peerless of America, 47521
Peerless Ovens, 47520
Pelouze Scale Company, 47528
Penda Form Corp, 47532
Penley Corporation, 47535
Penta Manufacturing Company, 47541
Pepperell Paper Company, 47546
Perky's Pizza, 47554
Perma-Vault Safe Co Inc, 47558
Perry Videx LLC, 47559

Petra International, 47569
Pez Candy Inc, 47575
Pharmaceutical & Food Special, 47580
Phase II Pasta Machine Inc, 47584
Phoenix Closures Inc, 47594
Phoenix Industries Corp, 47595
Pick Heaters, 47599
Pines International, 47613
Pioneer Packing Co, 47618
Pioneer Plastics Inc, 47619
Piper Products Inc, 47621
Pitco Frialator Inc, 47623
Pittsburgh Brewing Co, 47624
Planet Products Corp, 47628
Plasti-Clip Corp, 47632
Plastic Suppliers Inc, 47635
PlexPack Corp, 47642
PMC Specialties Group Inc, 47336
Pneumatic Scale Angelus, 47648
Pocino Foods, 47649
Podnar Plastics Inc, 47650
PolyConversions, Inc., 47662
Polypack Inc, 47665
Polyplastics, 47666
Polyscience, 47668
Portion-Pac Chemical Corp., 47682
Powertex Inc, 47691
PPI Technologies Group, 47342
Prawnto Systems, 47699
Preferred Machining Corporation, 47709
Preferred Packaging Systems, 47711
Preferred Popcorn, 47712
Preiser Scientific Inc, 47714
Premier Brass, 47717
Premium Water, 47722
Presence From Innovation LLC, 47727
Presentations South, 47728
Pressure King Inc, 47729
Prestige Proteins, 47731
Prestige Skirting & Tablecloths, 47732
Prima Foods International, 47741
Prince Castle Inc, 47753
Priority One Packaging, 47759
Pro Form Labs, 47761
Pro Scientific Inc, 47763
Pro-Flo Products, 47764
ProBar Systems Inc., 47766
Process Displays, 47771
Process Engineering & Fabrication, 47772
Process Solutions, 47776
Productos Familia, 47786
Produits Ronald, 47791
Progressive International/Mr. Dudley, 47801
Pronova Biopolymer, 47812
ProTeam, 47768
Pruden Packing Company, 47824
PTR Baler & Compactor Co, 47346
Pulse Systems, 47831
Purchase Order Co Of Miami Inc, 47837
Pure Source LLC, 47844
Puritan Manufacturing Inc, 47847
Purity Products, 47850
Pyromation Inc, 47855
Quadrel Labeling Systems, 47869
Quaker Chemical Company, 47870
Qualifresh Michel St. Arneault, 47875
Quality Fabrication & Design, 47881
Quality Industries Inc, 47882
Quantum Storage Systems Inc, 47888
Quelle Quiche, 47892
Quest Corp, 47893
Quipco Products Inc, 47900
R A Jones & Co Inc, 47902
R H Saw Corp, 47904
R X Honing Machine Corp, 47911
R&R Mill Company, 47914
R.B. Morriss Company, 47917
R.L. Zeigler Company, 47920
Radlo Foods, 47945
Rahco International, 47950
Rahmann Belting & Industrial Rubber Products, 47951
Railex Corp, 47952
RainSoft Water Treatment System, 47953

Rainsweet Inc, 47958
Rairdon Dodge Chrysler Jeep, 47959
Ram Equipment Co, 47961
Ramsey Popcorn Co Inc, 47966
Rapid Rack Industries, 47973
Ray Cosgrove Brokerage Company, 47978
Raymond Corp, 47980
RDM International, 47928
Real Aloe Company, 47989
Real Kosher Sausage Company, 47992
Red Chamber Co, 47996
Reed Oven Co, 48012
Reeve Store Equipment Co, 48018
Refractron Technologies Corp, 48020
Refresco Beverages US Inc., 48021
Refrigerator Manufacturers LLC, 48023
Regal Ware Inc, 48030
Regina USA, 48033
Reheis Co, 48036
Remco Industries International, 48050
Remco Products Corp, 48051
Remcraft Lighting Products, 48053
Renard Machine Company, 48056
Renold Products, 48061
Reotemp Instrument Corp, 48063
Resina, 48069
Revent Inc, 48075
Rexford Paper Company, 48078
Rheon USA, 48084
Rheon, U.S.A., 48085
Ribus Inc., 48088
Rice Company, 48089
Rice Lake Weighing Systems, 48092
Richards Packaging, 48096
Richardson International, 48098
Richland Beverage Association, 48099
Rieke Packaging Systems, 48104
Rio Syrup Co, 48107
Ripon Pickle Co Inc, 48110
Riverside Manufacturing Company, 48116
Rixie Paper Products Inc, 48119
Robar International Inc, 48124
Robby Vapor Systems, 48125
Roechling Engineered Plastics, 48153
Ron Son Foods Inc, 48169
Roosevelt Dairy Trade, Inc, 48175
Rooto Corp, 48176
Roquette America Inc., 48179
Ross Industries Inc, 48191
Ross Technology Company, 48192
Roto-Flex Oven Co, 48198
Royal Accoutrements, 48209
Royal Welding & Fabricating, 48226
Royal Wine Corp, 48227
RPA Process Technologies, 47934
Rubbermaid, 48234
Rudolph Foods Co, 48239
Rudolph Industries, 48240
Ruggiero Seafood, 48242
Ruiz Food Products Inc., 48243
Rutherford Engineering, 48248
Rv Industries, 48249
S & L Store Fixture, 48255
S & S Indl Maintenance, 48256
S&P USA Ventilation Systems, LLC, 48262
S.V. Dice Designers, 48270
Sabel Engineering Corporation, 48307
Sadler Conveyor Systems, 48311
Saeplast Canada, 48313
Sales & Marketing Dev, 48332
Salmolux Inc, 48336
San Fab Conveyor, 48351
San Jamar, 48355
San-Ei Gen FFI, 48359
Sanchelima International, 48362
Sandco International, 48364
Sanden Vendo America Inc, 48365
Sanderson Farms, 48366
Sani-Matic, 48373
Sanitary Couplers, 48375
Sanitech Inc, 48376
Santa Barbara Olive Company, 48378
Santa Monica Seafood Co., 48380

Saratoga Food Specialties, 48390
Sardee Industries Inc, 48391
Sasib Beverage & Food North America, 48393
Satake USA, 48395
Sato America, 48397
Saunder Brothers, 48398
Saunders Manufacturing Co., 48399
Scaltrol Inc, 48410
Scandia Packaging Machinery Co, 48414
Scandinavian Formulas Inc, 48417
Schaefer Machine Co Inc, 48419
Schiff Food Products Co Inc, 48425
Schlagel Inc, 48428
Schlueter Company, 48429
Schroeder Machine, 48436
Scientech, Inc, 48440
Scientific Process & Research, 48441
SDIX, 48274
Se Kure Controls Inc, 48457
Sea Snack Foods Inc, 48462
Seaboard Foods, 48466
Sealstrip Corporation, 48477
Seatech Corporation, 48482
Seatex Ltd, 48483
Seattle Menu Specialists, 48486
Seepex Inc, 48495
Selecto Scientific, 48501
Sellers Engineering Division, 48502
Semco Manufacturing Company, 48503
Sensidyne, 48511
Sentinel Lubricants Inc, 48516
Sentry Equipment Corp, 48517
Separators Inc, 48520
Serfilco, 48526
Serpa Packaging Solutions, 48528
Serr-Edge Machine Company, 48529
Sertapak Packaging Corporation, 48530
Server Products Inc, 48535
Service Manufacturing, 48537
Setterstix Corp, 48546
Severn Trent Svc, 48551
SEW Friel, 48276
Shady Maple Farm, 48559
Sharon Manufacturing Inc, 48569
Sharp Brothers, 48570
Shat R Shield Inc, 48572
Shawano Specialty Papers, 48574
Shawnee Milling Co, 48575
Shick Esteve, 48589
Shields Bag & Printing Co, 48590
Shoes for Crews/Mighty Mat, 48603
SHURflo, 48279
Shuttleworth North America, 48610
Si-Lodec, 48611
Sico Inc, 48615
Siena Foods, 48619
SIG Combibloc USA, Inc., 48280
Signature Brands LLC, 48627
Signode Industrial Group LLC, 48629
Signs & Shapes Intl, 48630
Silesia Grill Machines Inc, 48633, 48634
Sillcocks Plastics International, 48642
Silver King Refrigeration Inc, 48645
Silver Weibull, 48650
Simkar Corp, 48655
Simmons Engineering Corporation, 48656
Simonds International, 48660
Simplimatic Automation, 48666
Sinbad Sweets, 48670
Sinclair Trading, 48671
Sine Pump, 48673
Sioux Corp, 48676
Sirocco Enterprises Inc, 48680
Skd Distribution Corp, 48684
SKW Nature Products, 48286
Smico Manufacturing Co Inc, 48698
Smith Frozen Foods Inc, 48700
Sogelco International, 48733
Solbern Corp, 48734
Solvaira Specialties, 48739
Somerset Industries, 48742, 48743
Sonoco Paperboard Specialties, 48749
South Valley Farms, 48765
Southbend, 48766

697

Export Region / China

Southern Automatics, 48770
Southern Champion Tray LP, 48771
Southern Pride Distributing, 48779
Southern Snow, 48782
Spangler Candy Co, 48792
Sparkler Filters Inc, 48794
Specialty Blades, 48805
Specialty Commodities Inc, 48807
Specialty Minerals Inc, 48812
Specialty Rice Inc, 48815
Spectro, 48819
Spee-Dee Packaging Machinery, 48821
Speedways Conveyors, 48823
Spencer Turbine Co, 48825
Sperling Industries, 48827
SPG International, 48290
Spinco Metal Products Inc, 48833
Spir-It/Zoo Piks, 48834
Spirit Foodservice, Inc., 48837
Spray Dynamics LTD, 48842
Spraying Systems Company, 48843
SSW Holding Co Inc, 48294
St John's Botanicals, 48859
St. Clair Industries, 48862
Stainless One DispensingSystem, 48869
Standard Casing Company, 48875
Standard Paper Box Mach Co Inc, 48880
Stanley Access Technologies, 48884
Stanpac, Inc., 48886
Stapleton Spence Packing Co, 48887
Staplex Co Inc, 48888
Star Filters, 48890
Star Manufacturing Intl Inc, 48893
Starkey Chemical Process Company, 48900
Starview Packaging Machinery, 48902
Starwest Botanicals Inc, 48903
State Products, 48904
Stauber Performance Ingrdients, 48905
Stavis Seafoods, 48907
Stay Tuned Industries, 48908
Steel City Corporation, 48913
Stepan Co., 48926
Steri Technologies Inc, 48929
Sterling Ball & Jewel, 48931
Sterling Rubber, 48936
Sterling Scale Co, 48937
Stogsdill Tile Co, 48961
Stone Soap Co Inc, 48965
Storm Industrial, 48972
Straub Designs Co, 48978, 48979
Stricklin Co, 48985
Summit Import Corp, 49005
Sun Harvest Foods Inc, 49010
Sun Pac Foods, 49013
Sunroc Corporation, 49033
Sunset Specialty Foods, 49035
Suntec Power, 49040
Supelco Inc, 49043
Superior Food Machinery Inc, 49052
Superior Foods, 49053
Superior Packaging Equipment Corporation, 49056
Superior Paper & Plastic Co, 49057
Sure Torque, 49069
Surekap Inc, 49071
Suzanne's Specialties, 49076
Svedala Industries, 49078
Sweet Corn Products Co, 49083
Sweet Dried Fruit, 49084
SWF Co, 48303
Swirl Freeze Corp, 49092
Swissh Commercial Equipment, 49098
Symms Fruit Ranch Inc, 49102
Synergy Flavors Inc, 49107
Tablecraft Products Co Inc, 49153
Tallygenicom, 49163
Tantos Foods International, 49176
Tapatio Hot Sauce, 49179
Taste Traditions Inc, 49192
Tastepoint, 49194
Taylor Orchards, 49201
Taylor Products Co, 49203
TDF Automation, 49127
Tech Lighting LLC, 49208
Tech Sales Inc, 49209

Technibilt/Cari-All, 49211
TechnipFMC, 49212
Technium, 49214
Technology Flavors & Fragrances, 49216
Tecweigh, 49219
Teilhaber Manufacturing Corp, 49225
Teledyne Benthos Inc, 49231
Telwar International Inc, 49236
Tema Systems Inc, 49237
Temco, 49238
Tempco Electric Heater Corporation, 49239
Templar Food Products, 49240
Templock Corporation, 49241
Tenneco Specialty Packaging, 49244
Tew Manufacturing Corp, 49263
Texas Halal Corporation, 49266
Textile Buff & Wheel, 49270
THARCO, 49131
Tharo Systems Inc, 49274
THE Corporation, 49132
The Long Life Beverage Company, 49293
The National Provisioner, 49296
The Scoular Company/TSC Container Freight, 49300
Theochem Laboratories Inc, 49304
Therm-Tec Inc, 49306
Therma Kleen, 49307
Thermo Detection, 49310
Thermodyne International LTD, 49315
Thiele Engineering Company, 49320
Thirs-Tea Corp, 49322
Thomas L. Green & Company, 49324
Thomas Precision, Inc., 49326
Thomas Tape & Supply Co Inc, 49327
Thorn Smith Laboratories, 49333
Tieco-Unadilla Corporation, 49343
Tier-Rack Corp, 49344
Timely Signs Inc, 49354
Tindall Packaging, 49357
Tipper Tie Inc, 49361
TLB Corporation, 49134
TNA Packaging Solutions, 49136
Tni Packaging Inc, 49365
Todd's, 49369
Todhunter Foods, 49373
Tofutti Brands Inc, 49374
Tomsed Corporation, 49384
Tooterville Trolley Company, 49390
Torre Products Co Inc, 49403
Townfood Equipment Corp, 49416
Tradelink, 49422
Traex, 49425
Traitech Industries, 49426
Trans Pecos Foods, 49430
Travelon, 49441
Tree Ripe Products, 49444
Treehouse Farms, 49445
Trefethen Family Vineyards, 49446
Tri-Pak Machinery Inc, 49452
Tri-Seal, 49453
Tri-Tronics, 49458
Tribest Corp, 49463
Tribology Tech Lube, 49464
Trico Converting Inc, 49465
Trident Seafoods Corp, 49467
Tridyne Process Systems, 49469
Trinity Packaging, 49476
Triple Leaf Tea Inc, 49482
Triple-A Manufacturing Company, 49484
TRITEN Corporation, 49142
Trojan Inc, 49489
Tropical Cheese, 49491
Tropical Illusions, 49494
Tropical Link Canada Ltd., 49495
Troy Lighting, 49500
True Food Service Equipment, Inc., 49507
TruHeat Corporation, 49504
Turbo Refrigerating Company, 49531
Tuthill Vacuum & Blower Systems, 49539
Tyco Fire Protection Products, 49550
Tyson Foods Inc., 49554
Ultrafilter, 49587

Unarco Industries LLC, 49591
Ungerer & Co, 49599
Union, 49608
Union Confectionery Machinery, 49609
Uniplast Films, 49614
United Ad Label, 49623
United Canadian Malt, 49629
United Desiccants, 49632
United Electric Controls Co, 49633
United Industries Group Inc, 49638
United International Indstrs, 49639
United Performance Metals, 49644
United Ribtype Co, 49646
United Salt Corp, 49647
United Steel Products Company, 49653
United Textile Distribution, 49655
UniTrak Corporation, 49600
Universal Die & Stampings, 49664
Universal Jet Industries, 49668
Universal Marketing, 49669
Update International, 49675
Urschel Laboratories, 49682
US Chemical, 49563
US Distilled Products Co, 49565
US Filter Dewatering Systems, 49566
US Food Products, 49567
US Marketing Company, 49571
US Mills, 49572
Utica Cutlery Co, 49686
V C 999 Packaging Systems, 49689
V-Ram Solids, 49690
Vacuum Barrier Corp, 49709
Valentine Enterprises Inc, 49713
Valley Craft Inc, 49718
Van Air Systems, 49726
Vanguard Technology Inc, 49737
Vanmark Equipment, 49740
Variant, 49744
Varimixer North America, 49747
Vauxhall Foods, 49752
Vector Corp, 49753
Vector Technologies, 49754
Venner International Products, 49764
Ventre Packing Company, 49767
Venture Measurement Co LLC, 49769
Versailles Lighting, 49782
Viatec, 49791
Victoria Fine Foods, 49799
Victoria Porcelain, 49800
Videojet Technologies Inc, 49801
Vie-Del Co, 49802
VIFAN Canada, 49697
Vigneri Chocolate Inc., 49806
Vigo Importing Co, 49807
Vilore Foods Company, 49812
Vilter Manufacturing Corporation, 49813
Virginia Dare Extract Co, 49827
Vita-Pakt Citrus Products Co, 49839
VMC Corp, 49701
Volckening Inc, 49855
Volk Corp, 49856
Vollrath Co LLC, 49858
Volta Belting Technology, Inc., 49859
Vorti-Siv, 49861
Vortron Smokehouse/Ovens, 49862
VT Industries Inc, 49703
VT Kidron, 49704
Vulcan Industries, 49867
Vyse Gelatin Co, 49868
W & G Marketing Company, 49869
W.G. Durant Corporation, 49875
Wade Manufacturing Company, 49913
Wag Industries, 49914
Walco, 49922
Walker Stainless Equipment Co, 49928
Walle Corp, 49933
Waltkoch Limited, 49939
Wapsie Creamery, 49945
Ward Ironworks, 49948
Waring Products, 49950
Warwick Manufacturing & Equip, 49954
Washington State Potato Cmsn, 49959
Waste Minimization/Containment, 49961
Wastequip Inc, 49962
Wayne Automation Corp, 49976
Wayne Combustion Systems, 49977

Wayne Engineering, 49978
Weaver Popcorn Co Inc, 49981
Weavewood, Inc., 49982
WEBB-Stiles Co, 49884
Webeco Foods, 49985
Weber Packaging Solutions Inc, 49986
Weetabix Canada, 49990
Weinberg Foods, 49997
Weiss Instruments Inc, 50002
Welch Holme & Clark Co, 50006
Wells Enterprises Inc., 50012
Wells Manufacturing Company, 50013
Wemas Metal Products, 50014
Wesley International Corp, 50020
West India Trading Company, 50029
West Rock, 50033
Western Plastics, 50043
Wexxar Corporation, 50059
WG Thompson & Sons, 49885
Whallon Machinery Inc, 50061
Whisk Products Inc, 50067
White House Foods, 50071
White Rock Products Corp, 50076
White Way Sign & Maintenance, 50078
Wilch Manufacturing, 50094
Wild Rice Exchange, 50096
Wilder Manufacturing Company, 50098
Wileman Brothers & Elliott Inc, 50099
Wilen Professional Cleaning Products, 50100
Willamette Industries, 50109
Williamson & Co, 50115
Willing Group, 50116
Wilton Armetale, 50120
Windsor Industries Inc, 50123
Windsor Wax Co Inc, 50124
Wine Chillers of California, 50125
Winekeeper, 50128
Winmix/Natural Care Products, 50132
Winpak Technologies, 50135
Wire Belt Co Of America, 50138
Wisconsin Aluminum Foundry Co, 50143
Wisconsin Whey International, 50149
Wishbone Utensil Tableware Line, 50150
Wittemann Company, 50154
Wolf Company, 50160
Wolfson Casing Corp, 50161
Wood Stone Corp, 50167
Woolwich Dairy, 50174
WORC Slitting & Mfg Co, 49890
Worksman 800 Buy Cart, 50179
World Spice, 50192
World Water Works, 50195
World Wide Safe Brokers, 50197
Wyssmont Co Inc, 50212
Xpresso, 50219
Xtreme Beverages, LLC, 50220
Yamato Corporation, 50230
Yardney Water Management Syst, 50232
YoFiit, 50239
York Saw & Knife, 50242
Your Place Menu Systems, 50248
Zachary Confections Inc, 50254
ZAK Designs Inc, 50253
Zebra Technologies Corporation, 50261
Zed Industries, 50262
Zel R. Kahn & Sons, 50265
Zenith Specialty Bag Co, 50271
Zenobia Co, 50272
Zepf Technologies, 50275
Ziba Nut Inc, 50281
Zoia Banquetier Co, 50285

China

Biro Manufacturing Co, 42458
Eastern Fish Company, 43808
Golden Harvest Pecans, 44633
Microtechnologies, 46586
Peace Mountain Natural Beverages, 47503
W.Y. International, 49877
Wisconsin Whey International, 50149

Columbia

Bijol & Spices Inc, 42434

Export Region / Cuba

Humboldt Creamery, 45126

Cuba
Roll-O-Sheets Canada, 48164

Curacao
Archie Moore's, 42027

Denmark
Foppiano Vineyards, 44300

Dominican Republic
Harris Ranch Beef Co, 44908

Eastern Europe
Demaco, 43582
Food Pak Corp, 44283
Palms & Co, 47418
Select Meat Company, 48498

Egypt
Goodell Tools, 44657

Europe
3V Company, 41472
A & B Process Systems Corp, 41476
A C Horn & Co Sheet Metal, 41478
A G Russell Knives, 41480
A Legacy Food Svc, 41484
A&A International, 41488
A&B Safe Corporation, 41491
A&J Mixing International, 41495
A&L Laboratories, 41496
A&M Thermometer Corporation, 41499
Aabbitt Adhesives, 41596
AAK, 41521
AANTEC, 41523
Abbotsford Growers Ltd., 41605
Abbott & Cobb Inc, 41606
ABCO Industries Limited, 41527
Abel Manufacturing Co, 41609
ABI Limited, 41529
Abimco USA, Inc., 41611
ABM International, 41531
ACCO Systems, 41533
Accuflex Industrial Hose LTD, 41624
Accutek Packaging Equipment, 41626
Ace Specialty Mfg Co Inc, 41631
Aceto Corporation, 41634
ACH Food Co Inc, 41534
Acme Scale Co, 41640
Acorto, 41646
Acp Inc, 41647
Acra Electric Corporation, 41648
Acraloc Corp, 41649
Acta Health Products, 41652
Actron, 41658
Adamation, 41664
Adams & Brooks Inc, 41666
ADCO Manufacturing Inc, 41539
Adex Medical Inc, 41670
ADH Health Products Inc, 41540
Adhesive Technologies Inc, 41672
Adonis Health Products, 41677
Adrienne's Gourmet Foods, 41680
Advanced Detection Systems, 41688
Advanced Equipment, 41690
Advanced Food Systems, 41691
Advanced Ingredients, Inc., 41692
Advanced Labelworx Inc, 41695
AEP Colloids, 41544
Aeromat Plastics Inc, 41704
Aeromix Systems, 41705
Agger Fish Corp, 41714
Agri-Mark Inc, 41721
Agro Foods, Inc., 41725
Agrocan, 41727
Agropur, 41728
Agvest, 41731
AHD International, LLC, 41553
Aidi International Hotels of America, 41733
AIDP Inc, 41554

Air Quality Engineering, 41735
Air-Scent International, 41737
Airsan Corp, 41742
AKC Commodities Inc, 41556
Alabama Bag Co Inc, 41753
Alacer Corp, 41754
Alaska Sausage & Seafood, 41760
Alaskan Gourmet Seafoods, 41762
Albion Machine & Tool Co, 41767
ALCO Designs, 41558
Alconox Inc, 41771
Alexander Machinery, 41773
Alfa International Corp, 41776
Alfa Laval Inc, 41778
Alfa Systems Inc, 41779
Algood Food Co, 41784
Alkar Rapid Pak, 41790
Alkota Cleaning Systems Inc, 41792
All A Cart Custom Mfg, 41793
All American Container, 41794
All Fill Inc, 41796
All Foils Inc, 41797
Allegheny Bradford Corp, 41808
Allen Harim Foods LLC, 41813
Alliance Rubber Co, 41818
Allied Engineering, 41820
Allied Glove Corporation, 41821
Allied International Corp, 41822
Allied Wine Corporation, 41827
Alloy Hardfacing & Engineering, 41828
Aloe Farms Inc, 41833
Alpha Packaging, 41841
Alternative Health & Herbs, 41847
Altman Industries, 41849
Alto-Shaam, 41850
Alumin-Nu Corporation, 41853
Alvarado Street Bakery, 41854
AM Todd Co, 41561
Amber Glo, 41861
America's Classic Foods, 41867
American Botanicals, 41870
American Brush Company, 41871
American Foods Group LLC, 41889
American Glass Research, 41890
American Housewares, 41892
American Importing Co., 41894
American Laboratories, 41900
American Lecithin Company, 41901
American Lifts, 41902
American Louver Co, 41903
American Metalcraft Inc, 41907
American National Rubber, 41908
American Range, 41915
American Seafood Imports Inc., 41919
American Store Fixtures, 41924
American Time & Signal Co, 41926
American Ultraviolet Co, 41928
American Water Broom, 41929
American Wax Co Inc, 41930
Americana Art China Company, 41931
Ameripak Packaging Equipment, 41935
AMF Bakery Systems Corp, 41566
AMI, 41568
Amigos Canning Company, 41946
Ammeraal Beltech Inc, 41949
AMSOIL Inc, 41570
Amtab Manufacturing Corp, 41959
Amy's Kitchen Inc, 41962
Anabol Naturals, 41964
Analite, 41965
Analytical Measurements, 41967
Anchor Brewing Company, 41968
Anchor Packaging, 41971
Andersen 2000, 41973
Anderson International Corp, 41977
Anderson-Crane Company, 41981
Anetsberger, 41986
Anguil Environmental Systems, 41989
Anhydro Inc, 41990
Animal Pak, 41991
Annie's Naturals, 41997
AP Dataweigh Inc, 41575
Apex Fountain Sales Inc, 42004
Apex Machine Company, 42005
Apple Acres, 42010
Applied Chemical Technology, 42014

Applied Robotics Inc, 42016
Aqua Measure, 42019
Architecture Plus Intl Inc, 42028
Arctic Industries, 42033
Arde Inc, 42035
Arden Companies, 42037
Argo & Company, 42038
Arguimbau & Co, 42040
Ariel Vineyards, 42042
Arista Industries Inc, 42044
Arizona Instrument LLC, 42047
Arizona Natural Products, 42048
Arkfeld Mfg & Distributing Co, 42050
Arnold Equipment Co, 42058
Aroma Vera, 42060
Aroma-Life, 42061
Aromachem, 42062
Aromatech USA, 42063
Arpac LP, 42066
Arrow Tank Co, 42069
ASCENT Technics Corporation, 41583
Ashlock Co, 42081
ASI Data Myte, 41584
ASI/Restaurant Manager, 41587
Aspen Mulling Company Inc., 42086
Assembled Products Corp, 42087
Assembly Technology & Test, 42088
Astral Extracts, 42095
Astro Pure Water, 42096
At Last Naturals Inc, 42097
Athea Laboratories, 42100
Atkins Elegant Desserts, 42103
Atkins Ginseng Farms, 42104
Atlanta SharpTech, 42106
Atlantic Blueberry, 42108
Atlantic Chemicals Trading, 42110
Atlantic Rubber Products, 42116
Atlantic Ultraviolet Corp, 42118
Atlantic Veal & Lamb Inc, 42119
Atlantis Plastics Linear Film, 42121
Atlas Match Corporation, 42126
Atlas Pacific Engineering, 42128
Atoka Cranberries, Inc., 42130
Atrium Biotech, 42131
Atwater Foods, 42134
Audion Automation, 42135
August Thomsen Corp, 42137
Auromere Inc, 42139
Aurora Design Associates, Inc., 42140
Autio Co, 42144
Autobar Systems, 42146
Automated Flexible Conveyors, 42150
Automated Food Systems, 42151
Automatic Bar Controls Inc, 42152
Automatic Products/Crane, 42155
Automatic Specialties Inc, 42156
Automatic Timing & Controls, 42157
Autotron, 42161
Avery Weigh-Tronix, 42167
Avestin, 42169
Avoca, 42171
Axelrod, Norman N, 42177
Ayush Herbs Inc, 42181
Aztec Grill, 42183
B H Bunn Co, 42190
B. Terfloth & Company, 42194
B.C. Tree Fruits Limited, 42197
Bacchus Wine Cellars, 42224
Badger Meter Inc, 42229
Bagcraft Papercon, 42232
Baker Hughes, 42238
Bakers Pride Oven Company, 42244
Bakon Yeast, 42247
Bal Seal Engineering Inc, 42248
Baldor Electric Co, 42252
Ballantyne Food Service Equipment, 42255
Ballas Egg Products Corp, 42256
Bally Block Co, 42257
Bally Refrigerated Boxes Inc, 42258
Baltimore Aircoil Co, 42261
Bama Sea Products Inc, 42265
Banner Chemical Co, 42267
Banner Equipment Co, 42268
Bar Keepers Friend Cleanser, 42270

Bardo Abrasives, 42277
Barlean's Fisheries, 42282
Barliant & Company, 42283
Barrette Outdoor Living, 42285
Barry Group, 42289
Basic American Foods, 42295
Basic Food Flavors, 42296
Basic Food Intl Inc, 42297
Batavia Wine Cellars, 42300
Batching Systems, 42301
Baumer Foods Inc, 42305
Baycliff Co Inc, 42312
Be & Sco, 42317
Beach Filter Products, 42318
Bean Machines, 42321
Bear Creek Operations, 42323
Bear Stewart Corp, 42324
Beatrice Bakery Co, 42325
Beaumont Products, 42327
Beaverton Foods Inc, 42330
Beck Flavors, 42332
Becker Brothers Graphite Co, 42333
Bedemco Inc, 42337
Bedford Enterprises Inc, 42339
Beehive Botanicals, 42343
Bel-Art Products, 42353
Bell-Mark Corporation, 42360
Bella Sun Luci, 42362
Belleharvest Sales Inc, 42364
Belshaw Adamatic Bakery Group, 42368
Beltram Foodservice Group, 42371
Belxport, 42373
Bematek Systems Inc, 42374
Berg Chilling Systems, 42382
Berg Co, 42383
Bericap North America, Inc., 42385
Berlin Foundry & Mach Co, 42390
Bernal Technology, 42392
Berns Co, 42395
Best & Donovan, 42403
Best Cooking Pulses, Inc., 42408
Beta Screen Corp, 42414
Bete Fog Nozzle Inc, 42415
Bettcher Industries Inc, 42417
Bette's Oceanview Diner, 42418
Better Packages, 42421
Beverly International, 42426
BEX Inc, 42207
Bianchi Winery, 42431
Biazzo Dairy Products Inc, 42432
Bijur Lubricating Corporation, 42435
Bilt-Rite Conveyors, 42436
Bio Cide Intl Inc, 42441
Bio-Foods, 42443
BioAmber, 42444
Bioclimatic Air Systems LLC, 42446
Biocontrol Systems Inc, 42447
BioExx Specialty Proteins, 42445
Birchwood Foods Inc, 42454
Birdsong Corp., 42455
Biro Manufacturing Co, 42458
Bishamon Industry Corp, 42460
Bissett Produce Company, 42461
Blackhawk Molding Co Inc, 42467
Blair's Sauces & Snacks, 42468
Blaze Products Corp, 42474
Blend Pak Inc, 42475
Blessed Herbs, 42477
Blue Crab Bay, 42485
Blue Feather Products Inc, 42488
Blue Giant Equipment Corporation, 42489
Blue Harvest Foods, 42490
Blue Ridge Converting, 42495
Blue Sky Beverage Company, 42496
Blue Star Food Products, 42497
Bluff Manufacturing Inc, 42499
BMT Commodity Corporation, 42211
Boca Bons East, 42507
Body Breakthrough Inc, 42508
Boehringer Mfg. Co. Inc., 42509
Bonduelle North America, 42518
Bonneau Company, 42519
Bonnot Co, 42520
Bos Smoked Fish Inc, 42524
Bosch Packaging Technology, 42525

699

Export Region / Europe

Boss Manufacturing Co, 42527
Boston Retail, 42530
Boston Sausage & Provision, 42531
Botanical Products, 42534
Botsford Fisheries, 42535
Boxes.com, 42542
Boyd Lighting Company, 42544
Bradman Lake Inc, 42549
Brandmeyer Popcorn Co, 42555
Brandt Farms Inc, 42557
Branford Vibrator Company, 42558
Brasserie Brasel Brewery, 42561
Braun Brush Co, 42564
Breakwater Fisheries, 42567
Breddo Likwifier, 42571
Brenton Engineering Co, 42574
Brewmatic Company, 42575
Broaster Co LLC, 42588
Brooks Instrument LLC, 42597
Brotherhood Winery, 42600
Brower, 42603
Brown & Haley, 42604
Brown International Corp LLC, 42606
Brown Machine LLC, 42607
Brown-Forman Corp, 42611
Brucia Plant Extracts, 42613
Bryant Products Inc, 42620
Buck Knives, 42622
Budget Blinds Inc, 42628
Buena Vista Historic Tstng Rm, 42629
Buffalo Technologies Corporation, 42630
Buffalo Trace Distillery, 42631
Bullet Guard Corporation, 42636
Bunn-O-Matic Corp, 42640
Burling Instrument Inc, 42646
Busse/SJI Corp, 42654
BVL Controls, 42213
BW Container Systems, 42214
Byrnes & Kiefer Company, 42659
C C Pollen, 42664
C E Elantech Inc, 42665
C Nelson Mfg Co, 42670
C P Industries, 42671
C&P Additives, 42678
C&T Refinery, 42679
C. Cretors & Company, 42680
C.M. Goettsche & Company, Inc., 42686
Cabot Corp, 42720
Cabot Creamery Co-Op, 42721
Cadie Products Corp, 42726
Cal-Mil Plastic Products Inc, 42741
California Natural Products, 42754
California Olive Oil Council, 42756
Calpro Ingredients, 42763
Cambridge Viscosity, Inc., 42766
Cambro Manufacturing Co, 42767
Cameron Birch Syrup & Confections, 42771
Can & Bottle Systems, Inc., 42777
Can Lines Engineering Inc, 42778
Candy Manufacturing Co, 42789
Cantech Industries Inc, 42795
Capay Canyon Ranch, 42796
Cape Cod Potato Chips, 42797
Capmatic, Ltd., 42801
Capway Conveyor Systems Inc, 42809
Caraustar Industries, Inc., 42811
Cardinal Packaging Prod LLC, 42816
Caristrap International, 42827
Carle & Montanari-O P M, 42829
Carleton Technologies Inc, 42831
Carlin Manufacturing, 42832
Carlisle Food Svc Products Inc, 42833
Carlisle Sanitary Mntnc Prods, 42834
Carlson Products, 42836
Carrageenan Company, 42847
Carrier Vibrating Equip Inc, 42850
Carriere Foods Inc, 42851
Casella Lighting, 42869
Caspian Trading Company, 42873
Casso-Solar Corporation, 42875
Cat Pumps, 42877
Cates Addis Company, 42880
Catskill Craftsmen Inc, 42883
Cawy Bottling Co, 42891
CCL Container, 42689

Century Blends LLC, 42910
Century Industries Inc, 42914
Chad Co Inc, 42917
Channel Fish Processing, 42925
Charles E. Roberts Company, 42931
Charles Mayer Studios, 42933
Charles Ross & Son Co, 42934
Chase Industries Inc, 42940
Chase-Doors, 42941
Chases Lobster Pound, 42943
Chef Hans' Gourmet Foods, 42950
Chef Merito Inc, 42951
Chef Revival, 42952
Chef Specialties, 42953
Chefwear, 42957
Chelten House Products, 42959
Chem-Tainer Industries Inc, 42960
Chemclean Corp, 42963
Chemicolloid Laboratories, Inc., 42966
Cherith Valley Gardens, 42971
Cherokee Trading Co, 42972
Cherry Central Cooperative, Inc., 42973
Chico Nut Company, 42993
Chief Wenatchee, 42995
Chilean Seafood Exchange, 42998
Chill & Moore, 42999
Chincoteague Seafood Co Inc, 43005
Chipmaker Tooling Supply, 43006
Chocolate Concepts, 43012
Chocolate Street of Hartville, 43015
Chocolates a La Carte, 43017
Choice Organic Teas, 43019
Choklit Molds LTD, 43020
Chooljian Bros Packing Co, 43022
Christy Wild Blueberry Farms, 43028
Church & Dwight Co., Inc., 43031
Cincinnati Industrial Machry, 43035
Cintex of America, 43039
Cisco Brewers, 43045
Citadelle Maple Syrup Producers' Cooperative, 43046
Citrosuco North America Inc, 43049
Citrus Service, 43050
Clarendon Flavor Engineering, 43059
Clarkson Grain Co Inc, 43063
Classic Flavors & Fragrances, 43065
Classic Tea, 43066
Classico Seating, 43067
Clawson Machine Co Inc, 43068
Clayton Corp., 43071
Clayton Industries, 43072
Clean Water Systems, 43073
Clean Water Technology, 43074
Clements Foods Co, 43083
Climax Packaging Machinery, 43092
Clipper Belt Lacer Company, 43093
Clos Du Val Co LTD, 43096
Cloud Nine, 43098
Co-Rect Products Inc, 43103
Coating Place Inc, 43108
Coburn Company, 43111
Cold Chain Technologies, 43124
Coloma Frozen Foods Inc, 43137
Columbian TecTank, 43150
Columbus Instruments, 43151
Comasec Safety, Inc., 43154
Commercial Furniture Group Inc, 43162
Commodities Marketing Inc, 43167
Comobar LLC, 43171
Compact Industries Inc, 43173
Compactors Inc, 43174
Composition Materials Co Inc, 43179
Compris Technologies, 43180
Computype Inc, 43184
Comtec Industries, 43186
Con Agra Snack Foods, 43188
Conax Buffalo Technologies, 43193
Concannon Vineyard, 43195
Conductive Containers Inc, 43197
Connecticut Laminating Co Inc, 43201
Conquest International LLC, 43204
Consolidated Baling Machine Company, 43205
Consolidated Commercial Controls, 43207

Consolidated Commerical Controls, 43208
Constar International, 43213
Constellation Brands Inc, 43214
Containair Packaging Corporation, 43215
Container Machinery Corporation, 43216
Contech Enterprises Inc, 43218
Continental Marketing, 43227
Continental Seasoning, 43229
Contrex Inc, 43233
Control & Metering, 43234
Control Instruments Corp, 43238
Convectronics, 43243
Conveyor Accessories, 43246
Conveyor Dynamics Corp, 43249
Conway Import Co Inc, 43251
Cook & Beals Inc, 43253
Cookie Tree Bakeries, 43256
Cooking Systems International, 43258
CookTek, 43254
Cool Care, 43259
Corbin Foods-Edibowls, 43266
Core Products Co, 43270
Corenco, 43271
Cork Specialties, 43275
Cornelius Inc., 43278
Cornell Machine Co, 43279
Corson Rubber Products Inc, 43286
Costa Deano's Gourmet Foods, 43294
Costco Wholesale Corporation, 43295
Cotton Goods Mfg Co, 43296
Coulter Giufre & Co Inc, 43299
Courtright Companies, 43307
Couture Farms, 43309
Cozzoli Machine Co, 43314
CP Kelco, 42707
CPM Century Extrusion, 42708
Cramer Company, 43317
Crane & Crane Inc, 43320
Crane Environmental, 43322
Creative Automation, 43326
Creative Cookie, 43328
Cresset Chemical Company, 43343
Crevettes Du Nord, 43346
Cribari Vineyard Inc, 43347
Critzas Industries Inc, 43351
Croll Reynolds Inc, 43354
CROPP Cooperative, 42711
Crowley Sales & Export Co, 43360
Crown Controls Inc., 43364
Crown Custom Metal Spinning, 43365
Crown Foods International, 43367
Crown Iron Works Company, 43369
Cruvinet Winebar Co LLC, 43380
Cryochem, 43381
Crystal Lake Farms, 43386
Crystal Star Herbal Nutrition, 43388
CSC Scientific Co Inc, 42712
CSC Worldwide, 42713
CSS International Corp, 42714
Culinary Masters Corporation, 43396
Culligan Company, 43398
Cummings, 43404
Cup Pac Packaging Inc, 43406
Cupper's Coffee Company, 43407
Currie Machinery Co, 43409
Curry King Corporation, 43410
Custom Rubber Stamp Co, 43420
Cutrite Company, 43427
CVP Systems Inc, 42718
Cyanotech Corp, 43428
Cyclonaire Corp, 43431
D & L Manufacturing, 43435
D D Bean & Sons Co, 43438
D D Williamson & Co Inc, 43439
D R Technology Inc, 43440
Dacam Corporation, 43465
Daily Printing Inc, 43468
Dairy Specialties, 43472
DairyChem Inc., 43476
Daisy Brand, 43479
Dalemark Industries, 43482
Danbury Plastics, 43493
Darisil, 43502
Dark Tickle Company, 43503
Darnell-Rose Inc, 43504

Dart Container Corp., 43505
Davenport Machine, 43508
Davis Strait Fisheries, 43514
Davis Trade & Commodities, 43515
Day Spring Enterprises, 43520
Daydots, 43521
Daymark Safety Systems, 43522
DCL Solutions LLC, 43452
De Ster Corporation, 43533
Dealers Food Products Co, 43538
Decartes Systems Group, 43543
Decko Products Inc, 43544
Defranco Co, 43553
Deiss Sales Co. Inc., 43556
Del Rey Packing, 43560
Del Rio Nut Company, 43561
Delavau LLC, 43564
Delicato Family Vineyards, 43569
Delta Machine & Maufacturing, 43575
DeltaTrak, 43578
Demaco, 43582
Descon EDM, 43589
Desert King International, 43590
Design Technology Corporation, 43593
Desserts by David Glass, 43596
Detecto Scale Co, 43598
Di Mare Fresh Inc, 43606
Diab International, 43608
Diamond Fruit Growers, 43617
Diamond Wipes Intl Inc, 43621
Dietzco, 43629
Dipix Technologies, 43635
Dixie Flag Mfg Co, 43654
DMC-David Manufacturing Company, 43458
DNE World Fruit Sales, 43459
Doering Machines Inc, 43657
Dominex, 43663
Dong Us I, 43667
Doran Scales Inc, 43671
Double Wrap Cup & Container, 43677
Douglas Machines Corp., 43680
Dovex Export Co, 43684
Doyon, 43689
Dr. John's Candies, 43693
Drake Co, 43697
Dream Confectioners LTD, 43702
Drehmann Paving & Flooring Company, 43703
Dri Mark Products, 43706
Driscoll Strawberry Assoc Inc, 43708
Dry Creek Vineyard, 43712
DSM Fortitech Premixes, 43461
Dunbar Manufacturing Co, 43719
Dundee Groves, 43720
Dunkley International Inc, 43723
DuPont Nutrition & Biosciences, 43713
Dura-Flex, 43728
Dura-Ware Company of America, 43730
Durable Engravers, 43731
Duralite Inc, 43733
Durkee-Mower, 43741
DWL Industries Company, 43464
Dyna-Veyor Inc, 43748
Dynamic Air Inc, 43749
Dynamic Cooking Systems, 43750
Dynapro International, 43752
E-Cooler, 43759
E-J Industries Inc, 43761
Eagle Home Products, 43796
Eagle Products Company, 43797
Earth Saver, 43799
East Bay International, 43803
East Coast Sea Port Corporation, 43804
East Coast Seafood Co Inc, 43805
Easterday Fluid Technologies, 43806
Eastern Fish Company, 43808
Eastern Sea Products, 43811
Eatec Corporation, 43817
Eaton Corporation, 43819
Eckels Bilt, 43824
Eckhart Corporation, 43825
Eclipse Systems Inc, 43829
Eco-Air Products, 43831
Ecodyne Water Treatment, LLC, 43834
Econofrost Night Covers, 43840

Export Region / Europe

Economy Paper & Restaurant Co, 43844
Ecoval Dairy Trade, 43846
Eda's Sugar Free, 43849
Eden, 43850
Edge Manufacturing, 43854
Edgecraft Corp, 43856
Edlong Corporation, 43860
Edom Labs Inc, 43865
Edson Packaging Machinery, 43866
EGW Bradbury Enterprises, 43778
Einson Freeman, 43871
El Charro Mexican Food Ind, 43874
Elberta Crate & Box Company, 43881
Eldorado Coffee Distributors, 43884
Electro Freeze, 43887
Eliason Corp, 43892
Elliott Manufacturing Co Inc, 43902
Elmar Worldwide, 43905
Elmer Hansen Produce Inc, 43907
Emblem & Badge, 43916
EMCO, 43782
Emerald City Closets Inc, 43918
Emerald Kalama Chemical, LLC, 43919
Emerling International Foods, 43921
Empress Chocolate Company, 43934
Ener-G Foods, 43941
Engineered Products Corp, 43947
Engineered Security System Inc, 43949
ENM Co, 43784
Ennio International, 43953
Ensemble Beverages, 43955
Enting Water Conditioning Inc, 43961
Enviro-Clear Co, 43962
Environmental Products Company, 43963
EP International, 43785
Erba Food Products, 43975
Erie Foods Intl Inc, 43978
Eriez Magnetics, 43979
Ermanco, 43981
ERO/Goodrich Forest Products, 43788
Erwyn Products Inc, 43983
Esselte Meto, 43990
Essential Industries Inc, 43991
Essiac Canada International, 43993
Ettore, 43997
Eurex International, 44000
EVAPCO Inc, 43792
Evaporator Dryer Technologies, 44021
Everbrite LLC, 44025
Everedy Automation, 44026
Evergreen Packaging, 44030
Everpure, LLC, 44031
Evonik Corporation   North America, 44033
Exaxol Chemical Corp, 44037
Excalibur Miretti Group LLC, 44038
Exel, 44043
Exeter Produce, 44045
Eximcan Canada, 44048
Eximco Manufacturing Company, 44049
Export Contract Corporation, 44051
F I L T E C-Inspection Systems, 44062
F N Sheppard & Co, 44063
F N Smith Corp, 44064
F&Y Enterprises, 44065
F.H. Taussig Company, 44067
Fabohio Inc, 44086
Fabreeka International, 44087
Fabwright Inc, 44091
Faciltec Corporation, 44092
Fairbanks Scales, 44094
Fallas Automation Inc., 44104
Famarco Limited, 44106
Farmington Foods Inc, 44118
Fast Industries, 44120
Fawema Packaging Machinery, 44123
Fax Foods, 44124
FDC Corporation, 44072
FECO/MOCO, 44074
Fee Brothers, 44132
Felbro Food Products, 44133
Felins USA Inc, 44136
Fenton Art Glass Company, 44139
Fernholtz Engineering, 44142
Ferrell-Ross, 44146
Ferris Organic Farms, 44148

Ferroclad Fishery, 44150
Festive Foods, 44151
Fibre Leather Manufacturing Company, 44156
Fieldbrook Foods Corp., 44158
Figaro Company, 44162
Filling Equipment Co Inc, 44164
Fillmore Piru Citrus, 44166
Filtercorp, 44170
Fine Chemicals, 44174
First Colony Coffee & Tea Company, 44186
First District Association, 44187
Fish Oven & Equipment Co, 44189
Fishmore, 44194
Fitec International Inc, 44196
Fitzpatrick Brothers, 44197
Flakice Corporation, 44202
Flamingo Food Service Products, 44205
Flavor Dynamics Two, 44209
Flavor Sciences Inc, 44211
Flavor Wear, 44213
Flavormatic Industries, 44217
Fleurchem Inc, 44226
Flex Products, 44227
Flexicell Inc, 44229
Flexicon, 44230
Flippin-Seaman Inc, 44233
Florart Flock Process, 44239
Florida Choice Foods, 44240
Florida European Export-Import, 44241
Florida Natural Flavors, 44244
Fluid Air Inc, 44250
Fluid Energy Processing & Eqpt, 44251
Fluid Metering Inc, 44252
Flying Dog Brewery, 44255
Fold-Pak Corporation, 44264
Fold-Pak South, 44266
Foley-Belsaw Institute, 44269
Folklore Foods, 44271
Follett Corp, 44272
Food Equipment Manufacturing Company, 44278
Food Instrument Corp, 44279
Food Pak Corp, 44283
Food Source Company, 44286
Food Technology Corporation, 44287
Food Tools, 44288
Foodscience Corp, 44295
Foppiano Vineyards, 44300
Forbes Industries, 44302
Ford Gum & Mach Co Inc, 44303
Foremost Machine Builders Inc, 44304
Forever Foods, 44308
Forte Technology, 44313
Fortune Products Inc, 44315
Foss Nirsystems, 44318
Foxon Co, 44330
Framarx Corp, 44331
Franco's Cocktail Mixes, 44335
Franklin Trading Company, 44339
Frazier Nut Farms Inc, 44342
FRC Systems International, 44081
Freeman Industries, 44350
Freemark Abbey Winery, 44351
FreesTech, 44352
Freixenet USA Inc, 44355
French Oil Mill Machinery Co, 44362
Friedrich Metal Products, 44370
Friskem Infinetics, 44372
Front Range Snacks Inc, 44377
Frozfruit Corporation, 44383
Fruit Belt Canning Inc, 44384
Frutex Group, 44389
Fry Foods Inc, 44390
Frye's Measure Mill, 44391
Fuller Industries LLC, 44394
Fuller Packaging Inc, 44395
Fuller Weighing Systems, 44396
Fun Foods, 44400
Fun-Time International, 44401
Furgale Industries Ltd., 44402
Furnace Belt Company, 44403
Future Commodities Intl Inc, 44405
FX-Lab Company, 44083
G.G. Greene Enterprises, 44416

Galbreath LLC, 44454
Garber Farms, 44468
Garcoa Laboratories Inc, 44469
Garden Row Foods, 44473
Gardner Manufacturing Inc, 44475
Garlic Valley Farms Inc, 44480
Garroutte, 44482
Garvey Corp, 44485
Gary Manufacturing Company, 44486
Gary Plastic Packaging Corporation, 44488
Gasser Chair Co Inc, 44491
Gastro-Gnomes, 44493
Gch Internatonal, 44501
GCI Nutrients, 44419
Gea Intec, Llc, 44503
GEA North America, 44421
Gea Us, 44504
Gehnrich Oven Sales Company, 44509
GEM Cultures, 44427
GEM Equipment Of Oregon Inc, 44428
Genarom International, 44514
General Processing Systems, 44527
General, Inc, 44531
Genpak, 44535
Genpak LLC, 44536
George A Jeffreys & Company, 44539
George Glove Company, Inc, 44544
George Gordon Assoc, 44545
GePolymershapes Cadillac, 44502
Gessner Products, 44562
Geyser Peak Winery, 44563
GH Ford Tea Company, 44431
GHM Industries Inc, 44432
Giles Enterprises Inc, 44573
Gilly Galoo, 44576
Gilson Co Inc, 44577
Gilster-Mary Lee Corp, 44578
Ginseng Up Corp, 44582
Girard's Food Service Dressings, 44585
Girton Manufacturing Co, 44586
Glacier Fish Company, 44589
Glastender, 44594
Glenmarc Manufacturing, 44597
Glit Microtron, 44599
Glo-Quartz Electric Heater, 44600
Global Equipment Co Inc, 44603
Global Manufacturing, 44608
Global Sticks, Inc., 44612
Globe Food Equipment Co, 44614
Glowmaster Corporation, 44618
Goetze's Candy Co, 44620
Gold Pure Food Products Co. Inc., 44624
Goldco Industries, 44625
Golden Fluff Popcorn Co, 44629
Golden Kernel Pecan Co, 44634
Golden Moon Tea, 44635
Golden Specialty Foods Inc, 44641
Golden Star, 44642
Golden State Herbs, 44644
Goldenwest Sales, 44649
Good Idea, 44655
Goodnature Products, 44659
Goodwrappers Inc, 44663
Grain Machinery Mfg Corp, 44685
Grande Custom Ingredients Group, 44693
Grandview Farms, 44694
Graphite Metalizing Corp, 44701
Grassland Dairy Products Inc, 44702
Grayco Products Sales, 44705
Great Lakes International Trading, 44715
Great Northern Products Inc, 44717
Great Valley Mills, 44720
Great Western Co LLC, 44721
Greater Omaha Packing Co Inc., 44725
Green Spot Packaging, 44736
Greene Brothers, 44740
Greig Filters Inc, 44744
Grey Owl Foods, 44746
Grgich Hills Estates, 44747
Grocers Supply Co, 44757
Grow Co, 44762
Grower Shipper Potato Company, 44763
GS Dunn & Company, 44438

GSW Jackes-Evans Manufacturing Company, 44440
GTCO CalComp, 44441
Guerra Nut Shelling Co Inc, 44768
Guglielmo Winery, 44769
Guido's International Foods, 44770
Guiltless Gourmet, 44771
GWB Foods Corporation, 44443
H A Phillips & Co, 44789
H A Sparke Co, 44790
H B Taylor Co, 44792
H C Duke & Son Inc, 44793
H Fox & Co Inc, 44796
H G Weber & Co, 44797
H R Nicholson Co, 44799
H T I Filtration, 44800
H.K. Canning, 44810
H.L. Diehl Company, 44811
Hackney Brothers, 44828
Hadley's Date Gardens, 44830
Hagensborg Chocolates LTD., 44831
Haldin International, 44836
Hall Manufacturing Co, 44839
Hall Safety Apparel, 44840
Hall-Woolford Wood Tank Co Inc, 44841
Halton Company, 44843
Halton Packaging Systems, 44844
Hamilton Beach Brands, 44847
Hamilton Kettles, 44850
Hammons Products Co, 44851
Hampton Associates & Sons, 44852
Hampton Roads Box Company, 44853
Hamrick Manufacturing & Svc, 44854
Handy International Inc, 44859
Handy Wacks Corp, 44861
Hank Rivera Associates, 44865
Hanna Instruments, 44868
Hanson Brass Rewd Co, 44877, 44878
Harborlite Corporation, 44887
Harco Enterprises, 44890
Hardwood Products Co LP, 44893
Hardy Systems Corporation, 44894
Harlan Bakeries, 44896
Harney & Sons Tea Co., 44899
Harpak-ULMA Packaging LLC, 44902
Hart Design & Mfg, 44912
Hartness International, 44915
Haumiller Engineering Co, 44927
Haynes Manufacturing Co, 44938
Hcs Enterprises, 44943
Health Concerns, 44947
Health Plus, 44951
Healthy N Fit International, 44957
Heartland Gourmet LLC, 44961
Heartland Mills Shipping, 44962
Heatcraft Worldwide Refrig, 44965
Heaven Hill Distilleries Inc., 44967
Heidi's Gourmet Desserts, 44971
Heitz Wine Cellars, 44976
Helken Equipment Co, 44977
Heller Estates, 44980
Herbs Etc, 44996
Hermann Laue Spice Company, 45001
Herz Meat Company, 45003
Hess Machine Intl, 45004
Hewitt Soap Company, 45007
HFI Foods, 44818
HH Dobbins Inc, 44819
Hialeah Products Co, 45010
High Liner Foods Inc., 45015
Highlight Industries, 45018
Hillside Candy Co, 45024
Hitec Food Equipment, 45037
HMC Corp, 44822
HMG Worldwide In-Store Marketing, 44823
Hobe Laboratories Inc, 45038
Hoffer Flow Controls Inc, 45040
Holistic Horizons/Halcyon Pacific Corporation, 45044
Holland Beef International Corporation, 45047
Hollowick Inc, 45051
Hollymatic Corp, 45052
Hollywood Banners, 45053
Holman Boiler Works, 45054

701

Export Region / Europe

Homarus Inc, 45057
Home Plastics Inc, 45059
Homestead Mills, 45063
Honee Bear Canning, 45064
Honey Acres, 45065
Hoppmann Corporation, 45076
Hormann Flexan Llc, 45079
Houdini Inc, 45090
Hovair Systems Inc, 45098
Howell Brothers Chemical Laboratories, 45104
Hub Pen Company, 45112
Hubbell Lighting Inc, 45115
Hudson Control Group Inc, 45118
Hudson-Sharp Machine Company, 45123
Hughes Co, 45124
Hughes Manufacturing Company, 45125
Hungerford & Terry, 45128
Hunt Country Vineyards, 45129
Hybrinetics Inc, 45139
Hydrel Corporation, 45140
Hydropure Water Treatment Co, 45143
I Rice & Co Inc, 45152
I-Health Inc, 45155
I.W. Tremont Company, 45158
ICB Greenline, 45163
Iceomatic, 45194
Iconics Inc, 45195
Idaho Pacific Holdings Inc, 45196
Idaho Steel Products Inc, 45197
Ideal of America/Valley Rio Enterprise, 45203
Ideal Stencil Machine & Tape Company, 45200
Ideal Wire Works, 45201
Ideas Etc Inc, 45204
Idesco Corp, 45205
ILHWA American Corporation, 45171
Illuma Display, 45211
Imaging Technologies, 45214
IMECO Inc, 45172
IMI Cornelius, 45173
IMI Precision Engineering, 45174
Impact Confections, 45219
Imperial Industries Inc, 45221
Imperial Salmon House, 45224
Improved Blow Molding, 45231
In A Bind Inc, 45233
Indel Food Products Inc, 45242
Indemax Inc, 45243
Independent Can Co, 45244
Indian Bay Frozen Foods, 45247
Indian Valley Meats, 45250
Indiana Glass Company, 45252
Industrial Contracting & Rggng, 45260
Industrial Kinetics, 45261
Industrial Laboratory Eqpt Co, 45262
Industrial Magnetics, 45263
Industrial Piping Inc, 45264
Infitec Inc, 45270
Inline Filling Systems, 45280
Inniskillin Wines, 45282
Innovative Components, 45286
Innovative Food Processors Inc, 45288
Inovatech USA, 45294
Insect-O-Cutor Inc, 45296
Inshore Fisheries, 45298
Insignia Systems Inc, 45299
Insinger Co, 45300
Insulair, 45305
Interamerican Quality Foods, 45315
Intercard Inc, 45316
Intercomp, 45317
Interlab, 45320
Interlake Mecalux, 45321
International Casings Group, 45328
International Coconut Corp, 45332
International Cooling Systems, 45335
International Environmental Solutions, 45340
International Food Packers Corporation, 45342
International Industries Corporation, 45348
International Machinery Xchnge, 45351
International Market Brands, 45352
International Oils & Concentrates, 45354
International Paper Box Machine Company, 45359
International Patterns, Inc., 45361
International Reserve Equipment Corporation, 45362
International Sourcing, 45366
International Tank & Pipe Co, 45368
International Telcom Inc, 45369
International Tray Pads, 45371
International Ventures, 45372
Interstate Packaging, 45380
Invictus Systems Corporation, 45384
Island Oasis Frozen Cocktail, 45392
Island Sweetwater Beverage Company, 45394
Italian Quality Products, 45403
ITW Angleboard, 45184
Ives-Way Products, 45411
Izabel Lam International, 45416
J & B Sausage Co, 45417
J A Heilferty & Co, 45422
J C Watson Co, 45424
J C Whitlam Mfg Co, 45425
J L Clark Corp, 45429
J R Carlson Laboratories Inc, 45432
J T Gibbons Inc, 45433
J.M. Smucker Co., 45445
JAAMA World Trade, 45449
Jakeman's Maple Products, 45481
James L. Mood Fisheries, 45484
James Skinner Company, 45486
Jarrow Formulas Inc, 45499
JD Sweid Foods, 45454
Jeco Plastic Products LLC, 45510
Jelly Belly Candy Co., 45512
Jescorp, 45520
Jessie's Ilwaco Fish Company, 45522
Jet Set Sam, 45524
Jewel Date Co, 45527
Jim Did It Sign Company, 45531
Joey's Fine Foods, 45538
John Boos & Co, 45540
John J. Adams Die Corporation, 45547
John R Nalbach Engineering Co, 45548
Johns Cove Fisheries, 45551
Johnson Foods, Inc., 45553
Johnson International Materials, 45555
Johnson Refrigerated Truck, 45556
Johnston Farms, 45559
Jones-Zylon Co, 45566
Jordon Commercial Refrigerator, 45568
Joseph Adams Corp, 45570
Joseph Struhl Co Inc, 45574
Judel Products, 45582
Juice Tree, 45584
Just Delicious Gourmet Foods, 45590
Justman Brush Co, 45592
K Trader Inc., 45600
K-Way Products, 45605
K.F. Logistics, 45606
KaiRak, 45637
Kal Pac Corp, 45640
Kalsec, 45642
KAPS All Packaging, 45610
KASE Equipment, 45613
Kashi Company, 45654
Kason Central, 45656
Katagiri & Company, 45658
Kay Home Products Inc, 45660
Kaye Instruments, 45662
Keeper Thermal Bag Co, 45685
Kemach Food Products, 45695
Kennedy Group, 45702
Kent Corp, 45705
Kent Precision Foods Group Inc, 45706
Kenwood Vineyards, 45709
Kerry Foodservice, 45713
Keto Foods, 45715
Key Packaging Co, 45718
Key Technology Inc., 45719
KH McClure & Company, 45616
Kiefer Brushes, Inc, 45728
Kim Lighting, 45730
Kincaid Enterprises, 45732
Kinergy Corp, 45734
King Nut Co, 45744
Kings River Casting, 45750
Kingston McKnight, 45753
Kinsley Inc, 45756
Kiss International/Di-tech Systems, 45759
KISS Packaging Systems, 45619
Klaire Laboratories, 45764
KMT Aqua-Dyne Inc, 45625
Knight Seed Company, 45773
Knott Slicers, 45776
Kodex Inc, 45782
Koehler Instrument Co Inc, 45783
Kola, 45788
Kold-Hold, 45790
Kona Joe Coffee LLC, 45795
Korab Engineering Company, 45801
Kornylak Corp, 45803
Kosto Food Products Co, 45804
Kozlowski Farms, 45806
KOZY Shack Enterprises Inc, 45626
Kraus & Sons, 45810
Krogh Pump Co, 45817
KSW Corp, 45628
KTG, 45629
Kuhl Corporation, 45825
KWIK Lok Corp, 45631
KWS Manufacturing Co LTD, 45632
L F Lambert Spawn Co, 45837
L G I Intl Inc, 45838
La Belle Suisse Corporation, 45870
La Brasserie McAuslan Brewing, 45871
La Crosse, 45872
La Flor Spices, 45873
LA Monica Fine Foods, 45851
La Pine Scientific Company, 45876
Labatt Brewing Company, 45881
Labelette Company, 45888
Labelquest Inc, 45889
Laetitia Vineyard & Winery, 45894
Lakeside Foods Inc., 45905
Lallemand, 45911
Lambent Technologies, 45913
Lamports Filter Media, 45917
Lamson & Goodnow, 45918
Lancaster Colony Corporation, 45920
Land O'Lakes Inc, 45926
Landis Plastics, 45928
Langen Packaging, 45935
Langsenkamp Manufacturing, 45937
Lanly Co, 45939
Laros Equipment Co Inc, 45942
Latendorf Corporation, 45947
Lawrence Schiff Silk Mills, 45957
LBP Manufacturing LLC, 45856
Le Creuset of America, 45963
Le Smoker, 45965
Least Cost Formulations LTD, 45967
Leavitt Corp., The, 45968
Lee Financial Corporation, 45970
Leer Inc, 45975
LEF McLean Brothers International, 45860
Legion Lighting Co Inc, 45981
Leland Limited Inc, 45986
Lenchner Bakery, 45992
Lentia Enterprises Ltd., 45995
Les Industries Touch Inc, 46004
Letrah International Corp, 46010
Lewis M Carter Mfg Co Inc, 46014
Leyman Manufacturing Corporation, 46019
Liberty Engineering Co, 46021
Libido Funk Circus, 46028
Lifestyle Health Guide, 46030
Lifeway, 46032
Light Technology Ind, 46035
Liguria Foods Inc, 46039
Limpert Bros Inc, 46047
Linvar, 46056
Lion Labels Inc, 46058
Lion Raisins Inc, 46059
Liqui-Box Corp, 46062
Listo Pencil Corp, 46066
Little Crow Foods, 46071
Livingston-Wilbor Corporation, 46075
Load King Mfg, 46081
LoadBank International, 46082
Lodge Manufacturing Company, 46089
Lone Pine Enterprise Inc, 46096
Longview Farms Emu Oil, 46104
Longview Fibre Company, 46105
Loriva Culinary Oils, 46112
Louis Baldinger & Sons, 46119
Louis Caric & Sons, 46120
Love Controls Division, 46130
Love Quiches Desserts, 46131
Loveshaw Corp, 46133
Low Humidity Systems, 46135
Ltg Inc, 46139
Ludwig Mueller Co Inc, 46147
Lukas Confections, 46151
Lumber & Things, 46155
Lumenite Control Tech Inc, 46156
Luthi Machinery Company, Inc., 46162
Luxury Crab, 46167
Luyties Pharmacal Company, 46168
Lyco Manufacturing, 46169
M Phil Yen Company, 46182
M S Willett Inc, 46185
M-C McLane International, 46189
M-Vac Systems Inc, 46192
M. Licht & Son, 46193
M.E. Heuck Company, 46194
M.H. Rhodes Cramer, 46195
Mac Farms Of Hawaii Inc, 46220
Machine Ice Co, 46228
Madelaine Chocolate Company, 46232
MAFCO Worldwide, 46198
Magic Valley Growers, 46245
Magnetic Products Inc, 46249
Magnetool Inc, 46250
Maier Sign Systems, 46260
Maine Wild Blueberry Company, 46262
Majestic Industries Inc, 46267
Maker's Mark Distillery Inc, 46270
Malo Inc, 46275
Mane Inc., 46291
Manischewitz Co, 46298
Manitowoc Foodservice, 46299
Maple Leaf Foods International, 46307
Maramor Chocolates, 46315
Marathon Equipment Co, 46318
Maren Engineering Corp, 46327
Mariani Nut Co, 46330
Mark NYS, 46341
Marking Devices Inc, 46346
Marking Methods Inc, 46347
Markwell Manufacturing Company, 46351
Marlen, 46353
Marlen International, 46354
Marlyn Nutraceuticals, 46357
Marsh Company, 46365
Marshall Air Systems Inc, 46366
Martin Engineering, 46373
Maryland China, 46383
Maselli Measurements Inc, 46389
Master Mix, 46395
Mastercraft Industries Inc, 46397
Mastercraft International, 46398
Matacor Processors, 46402
Materials Transportation Co, 46406
Matfer Inc, 46408
Mathews Packing, 46409
Matrix Engineering, 46412
Matrix Health Products, 46413
Matrix Packaging Machinery, 46414
Matthiesen Equipment, 46418
Maui Gold Pineapple Company, 46420
Maxim's Import Corporation, 46426
Mayacamas Fine Foods, 46429
Mayacamas Vineyards & Winery, 46430
MBC Food Machinery Corp, 46199
Mc Steven's Coca Factory Store, 46437
McAnally Enterprises, 46438
Mcbrady Engineering Co, 46454
Mccourt Manufacturing Co, 46455
MCD Technologies, 46202
McDaniel Fruit, 46446
Mcfadden Farm, 46458
McGunn Safe Company, 46448

Export Region / Europe

Mclaughlin Gormley King Co, 46461
Mecco Marking & Traceability, 46469
Medallion International Inc, 46470
Meduri Farms, 46475
Mega Pro Intl, 46476
Melitta USA Inc, 46484
Merci Spring Water, 46501
Merco/Savory, 46502
Mercury Equipment Company, 46504
Merix Chemical Company, 46509
Merrill's Blueberry Farms, 46515
Messermeister, 46518
Metabolic Nutrition, 46520
Metaline Products Co Inc, 46524
Mettler-Toledo, LLC, 46531
Metzgar Conveyors, 46533
Metzger Popcorn Co, 46534
Mexi-Frost Specialties Company, 46535
Mexican Accent, 46536
Meyer Machine & Garroutte Products, 46541
Mia Rose Products, 46542
Micelli Chocolate Mold Company, 46549
Michael Foods, Inc., 46550
Michael's Cookies, 46552
Michigan Maple Block Co, 46569
Micro-Brush Pro Soap, 46573
Microbest Inc, 46577
Microfluidics International, 46580
Micropure Filtration Inc, 46585
MicroSoy Corporation, 46575
Middleby Marshall Inc, 46599
Midwest Stainless, 46609
Mies Products, 46610
MIFAB Inc, 46210
Miguel's Stowe Away, 46615
Mil-Du-Gas Company/Star Brite, 46617
Milan Box Corporation, 46618
Miljoco Corp, 46623
Mill-Rose Co, 46627
Mille Lacs Wild Rice Corp, 46628
Miller Group Multiplex, 46629
Millerbernd Systems, 46632
Milne Fruit Products Inc, 46639
Milwhite Inc, 46645
Mimi et Cie, 46646
Min Tong Herbs, 46647
Minn-Dak Growers LTD, 46650
Minuteman Power Boss, 46655
Mister Label, Inc, 46668
Mitsubishi Polyester Film, Inc., 46669
Mixon Fruit Farms Inc, 46673
ML Catania Company, 46213
MLG Enterprises Ltd., 46214
Mmi Engineered Soultions Inc, 46676
MMR Technologies, 46216
Mo Hotta Mo Betta, 46677
Mocon Inc, 46678
MODAGRAPHICS, 46217
Modern Products Inc, 46682
Mold-Rite Plastics LLC, 46690
Moli-International, 46693
Momar, 46699
Monadnock Paper Mills Inc, 46700
Monin Inc., 46706
Monitor Technologies LLC, 46708
Morey's Seafood Intl LLC, 46726
Morre-Tec Ind Inc, 46731
Morris & Associates, 46732
Morse Manufacturing Co Inc, 46738
Mosher Products Inc, 46743
Mother Parker's Tea & Coffee, 46746
Motivatit Seafoods Inc, 46748
Mountain Safety Research, 46753
Mrs. Leeper's Pasta, 46769
Mt. Olympus Specialty Foods, 46773
Muellermist Irrigation Company, 46776
Mulholland-Harper Company, 46779
Mulligan Associates, 46780
Multi-Fill Inc, 46781
Multi-Pak, 46782
Multi-Panel Display Corporation, 46783
Multiflex Company, 46787
Multikem Corp, 46788
Multisorb Technologies Inc, 46790
Munson Machinery Co, 46794

Murzan Inc. Sanitary Sys, 46801
Mushroom Wisdom, Inc, 46805
Muth Associates, 46807
My Quality Trading Corp, 46813
N S I Sweeteners, 46816
Naltex, 46837
Namco Controls Corporation, 46838
Naraghi Group, 46848
NaraKom, 46847
Natco Worldwide Representative, 46859
National Band Saw Co, 46861
National Distributor Services, 46866
National Food Corporation, 46871
National Fruit Flavor Co Inc, 46875
National Hotpack, 46876
National Instruments, 46878
National Plastics Co, 46886
National Printing Converters, 46887
National Shippng Supply Co, 46891
National Tape Corporation, 46893
Nationwide Pennant & Flag Mfg, 46896
Native Scents, 46897
Natra US, 46898
Natural Flavors, 46904
Natural Fruit Corp, 46908
Natural Oils International, 46910
Natural Way Mills Inc, 46913
Nature Most Laboratories, 46914
Nature Quality, 46915
Nature's Best Inc, 46917
Nature's Legacy Inc., 46921
Nature's Path Foods, 46923
Nature's Plus, 46924
Nature's Products Inc, 46925
Natures Sungrown Foods Inc, 46927
Navarro Pecan Co, 46929
Naya, 46931
NCC, 46822
Nebraska Bean, 46937
NECO/Nebraska Engineering, 46824
Nellson Candies Inc, 46945
Neogen Corp, 46951
Neon Design-a-Sign, 46952
Nepco Egg Of Ga, 46955
Nevo Corporation, 46964
New Attitude Beverage Corporation, 46966
New Earth, 46970
New England Cranberry, 46971
New England Machinery Inc, 46973
New Horizon Foods, 46979
New Organics, 46981
New Season Foods Inc, 46983
New York Apple Sales Inc, 46986
New York Export Co, 46989
Newcastle Co Inc, 46995
Newell Brands, 46997
Newman Sanitary Gasket Co, 47002
Newman's Own, 47003
NewStar Fresh Foods LLC, 46993
Niagara Blower Company, 47011
Niagara Foods, 47012
Nice-Pak Products Inc, 47013
Nieco Corporation, 47023
Nielsen Citrus Products Inc, 47024
Nielsen-Massey Vanillas Inc, 47025
Nigrelli Systems Purchasing, 47026
Nikki's Cookies, 47028
Niro, 47031
Niroflex, USA, 47032
Nitech, 47036
Niutang Chemical, Inc., 47038
Noble Harvest, 47039
Noh Foods of Hawaii, 47041
Nor-Cliff Farms, 47047
Noral, 47050
Norback Ley & Assoc, 47052
Nordson Sealant Equipment, 47057
Noren Products Inc, 47058
Norimoor Company, 47060
North American Provisioners, 47065
North Bay Produce Inc, 47069
North Bay Trading Co, 47070
North Peace Apiaries, 47075
North River Roasters, 47076

North Star Ice EquipmentCorporation, 47078
North Taste Flavourings, 47079
Northeast Group Exporters Inc, 47081
Northeastern Products Corp, 47084
Northern Orchard Co Inc, 47086
Northwest Analytical Inc, 47095
Northwest Naturals Company, 47099
Northwestern Coffee Mills, 47101
Northwestern Corp, 47102
Norvell Co Inc, 47104
Nova Industries, 47110
Novelty Crystal, 47115
NOW Foods, 46828
Now Plastics Inc, 47119
Noyes, P J, 47120
NTN Wireless, 46831
Nu-World Amaranth Inc, 47126
Nucon Corporation, 47130
Nutra Food Ingredients, LLC, 47140
Nutraceutical International, 47142
Nutribiotic, 47147
Nutricepts, 47148
Nutritech Corporation, 47152
Nutritional Counselors of America, 47155
Nutritional Research Associates, 47157
Nutriwest, 47159
Nydree Flooring, 47160
O'Dell Corp, 47163
O-At-Ka Milk Prods Co-Op Inc., 47165
Oak Leaf Confections, 47176
Occidental Foods International, LLC, 47178
Ocean Cliff Corp, 47180
OCS Process Systems, 47167
Oerlikon Leybold Vacuum, 47189
Ogden Manufacturing Company, 47192
Ohaus Corp, 47193
Old Sacramento Popcorn Company, 47203
Olde Country Reproductions Inc, 47204
Ole Hickory Pits, 47206
Olney Machinery, 47210
Omega Produce Company, 47222
Omega Products Inc, 47223
Omega Protein, 47224
Omicron Steel Products Company, 47225
Omni Pacific Company, 47230
Omnitech International, 47233
Once Again Nut Butter, 47237
Ontario International, 47244
OnTrack Automation Inc, 47236
Opie Brush Company, 47249
Oregon Freeze Dry, Inc., 47268
Oregon Hill Farms, 47270
Oregon Potato Co, 47271
Organic Milling, 47275
Organic Products Trading Co, 47276
Orion Research, 47284
OTP Industrial Solutions, 47171
Ottens Flavors, 47298
Outotec USA Inc, 47302
Overlake Foods, 47304
Oxbo International Corp, 47308
Oxford Frozen Foods, 47309
OXO International, 47173
P J Rhodes Corporation, 47316
P R Farms Inc, 47317
Pacer Pumps, 47352
Pacific Choice Brands, 47354
Pacific Coast Fruit Co, 47355
Pacific Oasis Enterprise Inc, 47360
Pacific Salmon Company, 47364
Pacific Scientific Instrument, 47365
Pacific Seafoods International, 47366
Pack Line Corporation, 47374
Package Systems Corporation, 47381
Packaging & Processing Equipment, 47382
Packaging Systems Intl, 47395
Padinox, 47401
Palamatic Handling USA, 47407
Palme d'Or, 47412
Palms & Co, 47418
Pamela's Products, 47420

Pangaea Sciences, 47428
Panhandler, Inc., 47429
Panoche Creek Packing, 47430
Pantry Shelf Food Corporation, 47431
Paoli Properties, 47432
Paper Systems Inc, 47437
Papertech, 47438
Par-Pak, 47441
PAR-Way Tryson Co, 47325
Parachem Corporation, 47442
Paraclipse, 47443
Paradise Products Corporation, 47447
Paragon Group USA, 47450
Paragon Labeling, 47452
Paratherm Corporation, 47455
Parducci Wine Cellars, 47456
Parkson Corp, 47466
Parrish's Cake Decorating, 47470
Particle Dynamics, 47472
Partnership Resources, 47474
Parvin Manufacturing Company, 47477
Pastorelli Food Products, 47486
Patrick Cudahy LLC, 47489
Paul G. Gallin Company, 47494
Paul N. Gardner Company, 47495
Paul O. Abbe, 47496
PC/Poll Systems, 47330
PDC International, 47331
PDE Technology Corp, 47332
Peace River Citrus Products, 47504
Peacock Crate Factory, 47506
Pearson Packaging Systems, 47509
Pecan Deluxe Candy Co, 47511
Peco Controls Corporation, 47512
Peco Foods Inc., 47513
Peerless of America, 47521
Peking Noodle Co Inc, 47524
Pelican Bay Ltd., 47525
Pelican Products Inc, 47526
Pelouze Scale Company, 47528
Penda Form Corp, 47532
Penta Manufacturing Company, 47541
Pepe's Inc, 47542
Pepperell Paper Company, 47546
Perma-Vault Safe Co Inc, 47558
Perry Videx LLC, 47559
Perten Instruments, 47561
Peter Pan Seafoods Inc., 47564
Petra International, 47569
Pharmachem Labs, 47582
Phelps Industries, 47585
Phenix Label Co, 47586
Philadelphia Macaroni Co, 47588
Phoenix Closures Inc, 47594
Phoenix Industries Corp, 47595
Phytotherapy Research Laboratory, 47596
Piazza's Seafood World LLC, 47597
Pick Heaters, 47599
Pie Piper Products, 47604
Pilant Corp, 47608
Pines International, 47613
Pioneer Plastics Inc, 47619
Piper Products Inc, 47620, 47621
Pitco Frialator Inc, 47623
Planet Products Corp, 47628
Plasti-Clip Corp, 47632
Plastic Suppliers Inc, 47635
Pleasant Grove Farms, 47641
PlexPack Corp, 47642
Pluto Corporation, 47644
PMC Specialties Group Inc, 47336
Pneumatic Scale Angelus, 47648
Polean Foods, 47660
Polycon Industries, 47664
PolyConversions, Inc., 47662
Polypack Inc, 47665
Polyscience, 47668
POM Wonderful LLC, 47339
Popcorn Popper, 47674
Porcelain Metals Corporation, 47677
Portion-Pac Chemical Corp, 47682
Power Brushes, 47688
Powertex Inc, 47691
PPI Technologies Group, 47342
Praim Co, 47694

703

Export Region / Europe

Prairie Cajun Wholesale, 47695
Preferred Machining Corporation, 47709
Preferred Packaging Systems, 47711
Preferred Popcorn, 47712
Preiser Scientific Inc, 47714
Premier Brass, 47717
Premier Skirting Products, 47720
Presence From Innovation LLC, 47727
Presentations South, 47728
Pressure King Inc, 47729
Prestige Proteins, 47731
Prestige Skirting & Tablecloths, 47732
Preston Scientific, 47735
Prima Foods, 47740
Primo Water Corporation, 47751
Prince Castle Inc, 47753
Prince of Peace, 47756
Printpack Inc., 47757
Priority One Packaging, 47759
Pro Form Labs, 47761
Pro Scientific Inc, 47763
Pro-Flo Products, 47764
ProBar Systems Inc., 47766
Process Displays, 47771
Produits Belle Baie, 47790
Produits Ronald, 47791
Proffitt Manufacturing Company, 47796
Progenix Corporation, 47799
Progressive International/Mr. Dudley, 47801
Pronova Biopolymer, 47812
ProTeam, 47768
Protein Research, 47816
Protica Inc, 47818
Prototype Equipment Corporation, 47819
Psyllium Labs, 47826
PTR Baler & Compactor Co, 47346
Pucel Enterprises Inc, 47827
Pulse Systems, 47831
Purchase Order Co Of Miami Inc, 47837
Pure Foods, 47841
Pure Life Organic Foods, 47842
Pure Sales, 47843
Pure Source LLC, 47844
PureCircle USA, 47846
Puritan Manufacturing Inc, 47847
Purolator Facet Inc, 47851
Pyro-Chem, 47854
Pyromation Inc, 47855
Q-Matic Technologies, 47859
QBI, 47863
Qosina Corporation, 47867
Quaker Chemical Company, 47870
Qualicaps Inc, 47873
Quality Fabrication & Design, 47881
Quality Industries Inc, 47882
Quality Sausage Company, 47885
Quantum Storage Systems Inc, 47888
Quelle Quiche, 47892
R A Jones & Co Inc, 47902
R Torre & Co, 47910
R X Honing Machine Corp, 47911
R&J Farms, 47913
R&R Mill Company, 47914
R.W. Garcia, 47922
Ragtime, 47949
Rahco International, 47950
Railex Corp, 47952
Rainforest Company, 47957
RainSoft Water Treatment System, 47953
Rainsweet Inc, 47958
Ram Equipment Co, 47961
Ramoneda Bros Stave Mill, 47964
Ramos Orchards, 47965
Ramsey Popcorn Co Inc, 47966
RAO Contract Sales Inc, 47925
Rapid Industries Inc, 47971
Rapid Rack Industries, 47973
RDM International, 47928
Real Aloe Company, 47989
Real Kosher Sausage Company, 47992
Real Soda, 47993
Recco International, 47994
Red River Commodities Inc, 48002
Redi-Call Inc, 48008
Redmond Minerals Inc, 48010

Reed Oven Co, 48012
Reede International Seafood Corporation, 48013
Reeno Detergent & Soap Company, 48015
Refractron Technologies Corp, 48020
Refresco Beverages US Inc., 48021
Regal Ware Inc, 48030
Reheis Co, 48036
Remco Products Corp, 48051
Renard Machine Company, 48056
RENFRO Foods Inc, 47929
Renold Products, 48061
Renovator's Supply, 48062
Reotemp Instrument Corp, 48063
Republic Foil, 48066
Resina, 48069
Rexford Paper Company, 48078
Reyco Systems Inc, 48082
Ribus Inc., 48088
Rice Company, 48089
Richards Packaging, 48096
Richardson Brands Co, 48097
Richardson International, 48098
Rieke Packaging Systems, 48104
Rixie Paper Products Inc, 48119
Robar International Inc, 48124
Roberts Poly Pro Inc, 48132
Roberts Seed, 48133
Robin Shepherd Group, 48135
Robinson Canning Company, 48136
Robinson's No 1 Ribs, 48138
Rogue Ales Brewery, 48158
Roll-O-Sheets Canada, 48164
Rollprint Packaging Prods Inc, 48165
Romanow Container, 48167
Ross Industries Inc, 48191
Roto-Flex Oven Co, 48198
Roxide International, 48207
Royal Accoutrements, 48209
Royal Foods Inc, 48217
Royal Medjool Date Gardens, 48221
Royal Oak Enterprises, 48222
Royal Welding & Fabricating, 48226
Royal Wine Corp, 48227
RPA Process Technologies, 47934
RPM Total Vitality, 47936
Rubbermaid, 48234
Rudolph Foods Co, 48239
Rudolph Industries, 48240
Ruggiero Seafood, 48242
Ruiz Food Products Inc., 48243
Rutherford Engineering, 48248
S & S Indl Maintenance, 48256
S L Sanderson & Co, 48259
S&P Marketing, Inc., 48261
S&R Imports, 48263
Sabel Engineering Corporation, 48307
Sable Technology Solution, 48309
Safe-T-Cut Inc, 48315
Sales & Marketing Dev, 48332
Sampco, 48345
San Francisco Herb Co, 48353
San Jamar, 48355
San Joaquin Vly Concentrates, 48356
San-Ei Gen FFI, 48359
San-J International Inc, 48360
Sancoa International, 48363
Sandco International, 48364
Sanden Vendo America Inc, 48365
Sanderson Farms, 48366
Sands Brands International Food, 48369
Sani-Matic, 48373
Sanitary Couplers, 48375
Sanitech Inc, 48376
Sanitek Products Inc, 48377
Santa Barbara Olive Company, 48378
Santa Clara Nut Co, 48379
Sardee Industries Inc, 48391
Sargento Foods Inc, 48392
Satake USA, 48395
Saunder Brothers, 48398
Saunders Manufacturing Co., 48399
Savoury Systems Inc, 48406
Saxby Foods, 48407
Sazerac Company, Inc., 48409

SBK Preserves, 48272
Scaltrol Inc, 48410
Scandia Packaging Machinery Co, 48414
Scandinavian Formulas Inc, 48417
Scandinavian Laboratories, 48418
Schenck Process, 48423
Schiltz Foods Inc, 48427
Schlueter Company, 48429
Scientech, Inc, 48440
Scientific Process & Research, 48441
SDIX, 48274
Se Kure Controls Inc, 48457
Sea Breeze Fruit Flavors, 48459
Sea Safari, 48461
Seafood Producers Co-Op, 48474
Seald Sweet, 48476
Sealstrip Corporation, 48477
Seed Enterprises Inc, 48493
Selecto Scientific, 48501
Semco Manufacturing Company, 48503
Sensidyne, 48511
Sensient Colors Inc, 48512
Sensient Flavors and Fragrances, 48513
Sentinel Lubricants Inc, 48516
Sentry Equipment Corp, 48517
Serfilco, 48526
Serpa Packaging Solutions, 48528
Serr-Edge Machine Company, 48529
Sertapak Packaging Corporation, 48530
Server Products Inc, 48535
Service Packing Company, 48538
Sesaco Corp, 48541
Sesinco Foods, 48542
Severn Trent Svc, 48551
SEW Friel, 48276
Sfb Plastics Inc, 48557
Shady Maple Farm, 48559
Shafer-Haggart, 48561
Shanker Industries, 48567
Shaw-Clayton Corporation, 48573
Shawano Specialty Papers, 48574
Shenandoah Vineyards, 48581
Shine Companies, 48593
Shoes for Crews/Mighty Mat, 48603
Showeray Corporation, 48608
SHURflo, 48279
Shuttleworth North America, 48610
Si-Lodec, 48611
Sico Inc, 48612
Sid Wainer & Son Specialty, 48614
Sigma Engineering Corporation, 48622
Signature Brands LLC, 48627
Signode Industrial Group LLC, 48629
Signs & Shapes Intl, 48630
Silesia Grill Machines Inc, 48634
Sillcocks Plastics International, 48642
Silver King Refrigeration Inc, 48645
Silver Palate Kitchens, 48647
Silver Springs Citrus Inc, 48649
Silver Weibull, 48650
Simmons Engineering Corporation, 48656
Simonds International, 48660
Simplimatic Automation, 48666
Sioux Corp, 48676
Sipco Products, 48678
Skylark Meats, 48687
Slade Gorton & Co Inc, 48689
Slicechief Co, 48692
Smico Manufacturing Co Inc, 48698
Smith Frozen Foods Inc, 48700
Smith-Lee Company, 48704
Snak King Corp, 48712
Sogelco International, 48733
Solvaira Specialties, 48739
Somerset Industries, 48743
Sonoco Paperboard Specialties, 48749
Sonoco ThermoSafe, 48750
Soofer Co, 48753
South Valley Farms, 48765
Southbend, 48766
Southern Heritage Coffee Company, 48775
Southern Pride Catfish Company, 48778
Southern Pride Distributing, 48779
Spangler Candy Co, 48792

Sparkler Filters Inc, 48794
Specialty Blades, 48805
Specialty Commodities Inc, 48807
Specialty Minerals Inc, 48812
Spectro, 48819
Spee-Dee Packaging Machinery, 48821
Speedways Conveyors, 48823
Spencer Turbine Co, 48825
Sperling Industries, 48827
Spice House International Specialties, 48829
Spinco Metal Products Inc, 48833
Spir-It/Zoo Piks, 48834
Spirit Foodservice, Inc., 48837
Spray Dynamics LTD, 48842
Spraying Systems Company, 48843
Spreda Group, 48845
Spudnik Equipment Co, 48852
St John's Botanicals, 48859
St. Clair Industries, 48862
Stahlbush Island Farms Inc, 48867
Stainless One DispensingSystem, 48869
Stainless Specialists Inc, 48871
Standard Casing Company, 48875
Standard Paper Box Mach Co Inc, 48880
Standard Terry Mills, 48882
Stanley Access Technologies, 48884
Stanley Orchards Sales, Inc., 48885
Stapleton Spence Packing Co, 48887
Staplex Co Inc, 48888
Star Filters, 48890
Star Industries, Inc., 48891
Star Manufacturing Intl Inc, 48893
Starkey Chemical Process Company, 48900
Starwest Botanicals Inc, 48903
State Products, 48904
Stauber Performance Ingrdients, 48905
Stavis Seafoods, 48907
Stay Tuned Industries, 48908
STD Precision Gear, 48296
Stearnswood Inc, 48911
Steel Products, 48916
Steiner Industries Inc, 48923
Stengel Seed & Grain Co, 48925
Stepan Co., 48926
Steri Technologies Inc, 48929
Steril-Sil Company, 48930
Sterling Ball & Jewel, 48931
Sterling Rubber, 48936
Stevens Linen Association, 48945
Stevens Point Brewery, 48946
Stimo-O-Stam, Ltd., 48955
Stirling Foods, 48956
Stogsdill Tile Co, 48961
Stone Soap Co Inc, 48965
Storm Industrial, 48972
Straub Designs Co, 48978, 48979
Stretch Island Fruit, 48983
Stricklin Co, 48985
Stripper Bags, 48986
Suity Confections Co, 48998
Summit Import Corp, 49005
Sun Harvest Foods Inc, 49010
Sun Pac Foods, 49013
Sunkist Growers, 49024
Sunlike Juice, 49025
Sunny Avocado, 49026
Sunrich LLC, 49028
Sunrise Growers, 49032
Sunroc Corporation, 49033
Sunset Specialty Foods, 49035
Suntec Power, 49040
SunWest Foods, Inc., 49019
Supelco Inc, 49043
Super Seal ManufacturingLimited, 49046
Superior Food Machinery Inc, 49052
Superior Foods, 49053
Superior Packaging Equipment Corporation, 49056
Superior Uniform Group, 49059
SupHerb Farms, 49042
Surco Products, 49067
Sure Torque, 49069
Surtec Inc, 49073
Suzanne's Specialties, 49076

Export Region / Far East

Svedala Industries, 49078
Sweet Corn Products Co, 49083
Sweet Dried Fruit, 49084
Sweet Sue Kitchens, 49089
SWF Co, 48303
SWF McDowell, 48304
Swirl Freeze Corp, 49092
Swisscorp, 49097
Swisslog Logistics Inc, 49099
Symms Fruit Ranch Inc, 49102
Symons Frozen Foods, 49103
Synergee Foods Corporation, 49106
Synergy Flavors Inc, 49107
Synthite USA Inc., 49108
Systems Technology Inc, 49112
T Hasegawa USA Inc, 49117
Tablecraft Products Co Inc, 49153
Taconic, 49155
Taku Smokehouse, 49160
Tallygenicom, 49163
Tamarind Tree, 49165
Tampa Maid Foods Inc, 49168
Tantos Foods International, 49176
Tapatio Hot Sauce, 49179
Tape & Label Converters, 49180
Taste Teasers, 49191
Taste Traditions Inc, 49192
Tastepoint, 49194
Tate Western, 49196
TDF Automation, 49127
Tech Lighting LLC, 49208
Tech Sales Inc, 49209
Technibilt/Cari-All, 49211
TechnipFMC, 49212
Technistar Corporation, 49213
Technium, 49214
Technology Flavors & Fragrances, 49216
Tecweigh, 49219
Teelee Popcorn, 49224
Teledyne Benthos Inc, 49231
Televend, 49234
Telwar International Inc, 49236
Tema Systems Inc, 49237
TEMP-TECH Company, 49129
Tempco Electric Heater Corporation, 49239
Templar Food Products, 49240
Templock Corporation, 49241
Tenneco Inc, 49243
Tenneco Specialty Packaging, 49244
Texas Halal Corporation, 49266
Texas Toffee, 49268
Texas Traditions Gourmet, 49269
Textile Buff & Wheel, 49270
THARCO, 49131
Tharo Systems Inc, 49274
THE Corporation, 49132
The Long Life Beverage Company, 49293
The National Provisioner, 49296
The Scoular Company/TSC Container Freight, 49300
Theochem Laboratories Inc, 49304
Therma Kleen, 49307
Thermo Detection, 49310
Thermo-KOOL/Mid-South Ind Inc, 49311
Thermodyne International LTD, 49315
Theta Sciences, 49318
Thiele Engineering Company, 49320
Thirs-Tea Corp, 49322
Thomas L. Green & Company, 49324
Thomas Precision, Inc., 49326
Thompson Bagel Machine Mfg, 49328
Thorn Smith Laboratories, 49333
Tieco-Unadilla Corporation, 49343
Timely Signs Inc, 49354
Tindall Packaging, 49357
Tipper Tie, 49361
TLB Corporation, 49134
Tni Packaging Inc, 49365
TNT Crust, 49137
Todhunter Foods, 49373
Tolas Health Care Packaging, 49378
Tomsed Corporation, 49384
Tooterville Trolley Company, 49390

Tootsi Impex, 49391
Toromont Process Systems, 49400
Torrefazione Barzula & Import, 49404
Toscarora, 49406
Townfood Equipment Corp, 49416
Tradelink, 49422
Trader Vic's Food Products, 49423
Traex, 49425
Trans World Services, 49431
Trans-Chemco Inc, 49432
Travelon, 49441
TRC, 49140
Tree Ripe Products, 49444
Treehouse Farms, 49445
Trefethen Family Vineyards, 49446
Trevor Industries, 49448
Tri-Pak Machinery Inc, 49452
Tri-Seal, 49453
Tri-Tronics, 49458
Tribest Corp, 49463
Tribology Tech Lube, 49464
Trident Seafoods Corp, 49467
Tridyne Process Systems, 49469
Trilogy Essential Ingredients, 49470
Trinity Packaging, 49476
Trio Packaging Corp, 49478
Triple D Orchards Inc, 49480
Triple Leaf Tea Inc, 49482
Triple S Dynamics Inc, 49483
Triple-A Manufacturing Company, 49484
TRITEN Corporation, 49142
Triton International, 49486
Trojan Inc, 49489
Tropical Cheese, 49491
Tropical Illusions, 49494
Trout Lake Farm, 49499
True Food Service Equipment, Inc., 49507
TruHeat Corporation, 49504
TSA Griddle Systems, 49143
Tsar Nicoulai Caviar LLC, 49517
Tucel Industries, Inc., 49521
Turbo Refrigerating Company, 49531
TURBOCHEF Technologies, 49144
Turkey Hill Sugarbush, 49533
Turtle Island Foods, 49535
Tuthill Vacuum & Blower Systems, 49539
Twenty-First Century Foods, 49544
Tyco Fire Protection Products, 49550
TyRy Inc, 49549
Tyson Foods Inc., 49554
UDEC Corp, 49560
Ultimate International, 49583
Unarco Industries LLC, 49591
Ungerer & Co, 49599
Unified Food Ingredients, 49602
Unimove LLC, 49607
Union, 49608
Union Confectionery Machinery, 49609
Union Industries, 49612
Uniplast Films, 49614
Unique Vitality Products, 49621
United Ad Label, 49623
United Apple Sales, 49625
United Canadian Malt, 49629
United Citrus, 49631
United Desiccants, 49632
United Electric Controls Co, 49633
United Floor Machine Co, 49636
United Industries Group Inc, 49638
United International Indstrs, 49639
United Performance Metals, 49644
United Ribtype Co, 49646
United Showcase Company, 49650
United Textile Distribution, 49655
Unitherm Food System, 49659
UniTrak Corporation, 49600
Universal Die & Stampings, 49664
Universal Jet Industries, 49668
Universal Marketing, 49669
Universal Paper Box, 49671
Update International, 49675
Urbani Truffles, 49680
Urschel Laboratories, 49682
US Chemical, 49563

US Chocolate Corp, 49564
US Distilled Products Co, 49565
US Filter Dewatering Systems, 49566
US Food Products, 49567
US Marketing Company, 49571
US Mills, 49572
USA Laboratories Inc, 49574
V C 999 Packaging Systems, 49689
V-Ram Solids, 49690
Vacuum Barrier Corp, 49709
Valad Electric Heating Corporation, 49711
Valentine Enterprises Inc, 49713
Valley Craft Inc, 49718
Valley Fig Growers, 49719
Valley Fixtures, 49720
Valley Packaging Supply Co, 49721
Van Air Systems, 49726
Van Drunen Farms, 49730
Vance's Foods, 49735
Vanmark Equipment, 49740
Vapor Power Intl LLC, 49743
Varied Industries Corp, 49745
Vauxhall Foods, 49752
Vector Corp, 49753
Vector Technologies, 49754
Venner International Products, 49764
Ventre Packing Company, 49767
Ventura Coastal LLC, 49768
Venture Measurement Co LLC, 49769
Vermillion Flooring, 49777
Versailles Lighting, 49782
Vessey & Co Inc, 49787
Victoria Fine Foods, 49799
Videojet Technologies Inc, 49801
Vienna Beef LTD, 49803
Vilter Manufacturing Corporation, 49813
Vince's Seafoods, 49814
Violife, 49825
VIP Foods, 49698
Virginia Dare Extract Co, 49827
Virginia Industrial Services, 49828
Visual Planning Corp, 49836
Vita-Pakt Citrus Products Co, 49839
VitaMinder Company, 49840
Vitro Seating Products, 49849
Vivoo, 49851
VMC Corp, 49701
Volk Corp, 49856
Vollrath Co LLC, 49858
Vorti-Siv, 49861
VT Industries Inc, 49703
Vyse Gelatin Co, 49868
W & G Marketing Company, 49869
W.G. Durant Corporation, 49875
Waddington North America, 49912
Wade Manufacturing Company, 49913
Wag Industries, 49914
Wagner Vineyards, 49916
Walker Stainless Equipment Co, 49928
Walton & Post, 49940
Wanchese Fish Co Inc, 49943
Waring Products, 49950
Warwick Manufacturing & Equip, 49954
Waste Minimization/Containment, 49961
Wayne Combustion Systems, 49977
Wayne Engineering, 49978
WCC Honey Marketing, 49882
Weaver Popcorn Co Inc, 49981
Weavewood, Inc., 49982
Weber Packaging Solutions Inc, 49986
Weil's Food Processing, 49995
Weinberg Foods, 49997
Welch Holme & Clark Co, 50006
Welliver Metal Products Corporation, 50011
Wells Manufacturing Company, 50013
Wemas Metal Products, 50014
Wenix International Corporation, 50015
West Carrollton Parchment Company, 50023
Westbrae Natural Foods, 50035
Western Plastics, 50043
Westvaco Corporation, 50052
Westwind Resources, 50054
Wexxar Corporation, 50059

WG Thompson & Sons, 49885
Whaley Pecan Co Inc, 50060
Wheel Tough Company, 50064
Whistler Brewing Company, 50068
White Oaks Frozen Foods, 50074
White Rabbit Dye Inc, 50075
White Toque, 50077
White Way Sign & Maintenance, 50078
Wilch Manufacturing, 50094
Wild Rice Exchange, 50096
Wileman Brothers & Elliott Inc, 50099
Wilkins Rogers Inc, 50105
Willamette Valley Walnuts, 50110
Williams Refrigeration, 50113
Willing Group, 50116
Wilton Armetale, 50120
Windsor Industries Inc, 50123
Windsor Wax Co Inc, 50124
Wine Chillers of California, 50125
Wine Well Chiller Co, 50126
Winekeeper, 50128
Winmix/Natural Care Products, 50132
Winning Solutions Inc, 50133
Winpak Portion Packaging, 50134
Winpak Technologies, 50135
Wire Belt Co Of America, 50138
Wire Products Mfg, 50139
Wirefab Inc, 50140
Wisconsin Aluminum Foundry Co, 50143
Wisconsin Box Co, 50145
Wisconsin Whey International, 50149
Wishbone Utensil Tableware Line, 50150
WITT Industries Inc, 49887
Wittemann Company, 50154
Wizards Cauldron, LTD, 50157
Wolf Company, 50160
Wolfson Casing Corp, 50161
Wood Stone Corp, 50167
Woodstock Line Co, 50171
Woodstock Plastics Co Inc, 50172
Workman Packaging Inc., 50177
Worksafe Industries, 50178
Worksman 800 Buy Cart, 50179
World Cheese Inc, 50181
World Kitchen, 50190
World Water Works, 50195
World Wide Safe Brokers, 50197
Wyandot Inc, 50210
Wylie Systems, 50211
Wyssmont Co Inc, 50212
X-Press Manufacturing, 50213
X-R-I Testing Inc, 50214
Xcel Tower Controls, 50217
Xtreme Beverages, LLC, 50220
Y Z Enterprises Inc, 50221
Yankee Specialty Foods, 50231
Yargus Manufacturing Inc, 50233
Yerba Prima, 50237
Yogi® Tea, 50240
York Saw & Knife, 50242
Yoshida Food Products Co, 50244
Young's Lobster Pound, 50247
Z 2000 The Pick of the Millenium, 50250
ZAK Designs Inc, 50253
Zd Wines, 50259
Zebra Technologies Corporation, 50261
Zed Industries, 50262
Zel R. Kahn & Sons, 50265
Zenith Specialty Bag Co, 50271
Zepa Trade, 50274
Zepf Technologies, 50275
Ziniz, 50284
Zoia Banquetier Co, 50285

Far East

Compact Industries Inc, 43173
Enviro-Clear Co, 43962
Sable Technology Solution, 48309

France

Alleghany's Fish Farm, 41807
Fumoir Grizzly, 44398

Germany

Advance Pierre Foods, 41684

Export Region / Greece

Alleghany's Fish Farm, 41807
Ayush Herbs Inc, 42181
Foppiano Vineyards, 44300
Golden Harvest Pecans, 44633
Oskaloosa Food Products, 47293
Tenth & M Seafoods, 49247
Wallace Grain & Pea Company, 49932

Greece

Kleen Products Inc, 45765
Leslie Leger & Sons, 46008
Wallace Grain & Pea Company, 49932

Guam

Charlie's Pride, 42935
Lodi Metal Tech, 46090
San Francisco French Bread, 48352
Varni Brothers/7-Up Bottling, 49749

Guatemala

Well Luck, 50007

Haiti

Leslie Leger & Sons, 46008
Ultimate International, 49583

Holland

Foppiano Vineyards, 44300

Hong Kong

Babe Farms Inc, 42220
Calbee America Inc, 42744
Colchester Foods, 43123
Sales King International, 48333

Iceland

Vineco International Products, 49819

India

BluMetric Environmental Inc., 42484
GCI Nutrients, 44419
Gea Intec, Llc, 44503
Global Impex, 44607

Indonesia

Kerry Foodservice, 45713
Wisconsin Whey International, 50149

Ireland

Odenberg Engineering, 47188

Israel

Ex-Cell KAISER LLC, 44035
Maple Leaf Cheesemakers, 46306
Milan Box Corporation, 46618
Pure Life Organic Foods, 47842

Italy

Ayush Herbs Inc, 42181
Odenberg Engineering, 47188
W.Y. International, 49877
Wallace Grain & Pea Company, 49932

Jamaica

Golden 100, 44626
House of Flavors Inc, 45092
La Have Seafoods, 45874

Japan

Airomat Corp, 41740
Babe Farms Inc, 42220
Berghoff Brewery, 42384
Bering Sea Fisheries, 42386
Brown Produce Company, 42609
Calbee America Inc, 42744
Ceilidh Fisherman's Cooperative, 42897
Crown Processing Company, 43374
Diamond Bakery Co LTD, 43612
Eastern Fish Company, 43808
Fabwright Inc, 44091

Fluid-O-Tech International Inc, 44253
Fogo Island Cooperative Society, 44263
Gerber Agri, 44553
Goetze's Candy Co, 44620
Heartland Gourmet LLC, 44961
House of Flavors Inc, 45092
I. Deveau Fisheries LTD, 45156
Kuhlmann's Market Gardens & Greenhouses, 45826
Mid-Pacific Hawaii Fishery, 46591
Molinaro's Fine Italian Foods Ltd., 46694
Motivatit Seafoods Inc, 46748
Nature's Path Foods, 46923
Norac Technologies, 47049
North Bay Fisherman's Cooperative, 47068
O'Hara Corp, 47164
Redmond Minerals Inc, 48010
Rogue Ales Brewery, 48158
Sugar Creek, 48994
Tenth & M Seafoods, 49247
TRC, 49140
Tufty Ceramics Inc, 49528
Vita Craft Corp, 49837

Korea

La Crosse, 45872
M&L Gourmet Ice Cream, 46186
RAM Center, 47923

Latin America

A&D Weighing, 41493
A. Suarez & Company, 41508
ACCO Systems, 41533
Acme Engineering & Mfg Corp, 41637
Actron, 41658
Advanced Equipment, 41690
AFT Advanced Fiber Technologies, 41549
Agrocan, 41727
Alfa Systems Inc, 41779
Allied Glove Corporation, 41821
Amano Enzyme USA Company, Ltd, 41855
American Hotel Register Co, 41891
American Material Handling Inc, 41906
American Pasien Co, 41912
American Roland Food Corporation, 41917
American Water Broom, 41929
Ammeraal Beltech Inc, 41949
Applied Chemical Technology, 42014
Aqua-Aerobic Systems Inc, 42021
Arguimbau & Co, 42040
Arnold Equipment Co, 42058
ATD-American Co, 41588
Atlantic Rubber Products, 42116
Autobar Systems, 42146
Automatic Bar Controls Inc, 42152
Baycliff Co Inc, 42312
Bells Foods International, 42365
BEUMER Corp, 42205
Biscotti & Co., 42459
Boehringer Mfg. Co. Inc., 42509
Bon Appetit International, 42515
Bonduelle North America, 42518
Bosch Packaging Technology, 42525
Boyd Lighting Company, 42544
Brogdex Company, 42590
Carleton Helical Technologies, 42830
Carolina Pride Foods, 42842
Chase-Logeman Corp, 42942
Chemclean Corp, 42963
Chemdet Inc, 42964
ChemTreat, Inc., 42962
Clabber Girl Corporation, 43056
Clarkson Grain Co Inc, 43063
Cleaver-Brooks Inc, 43080
Clements Foods Co, 43083
Compris Technologies, 43180
Comstock Castle Stove Co, 43185
Conductive Containers Inc, 43197
Contrex Inc, 43233
Cool Care, 43259

Cres Cor, 43338
Crespac Incorporated, 43342
Crestware, 43345
CSC Worldwide, 42713
Culinary Institute Lenotre, 43395
Custom Diamond Intl., 43415
Cutler Industries, 43426
Dart Container Corp., 43505
De Ster Corporation, 43533
Delfield Co, 43566
Diamond Foods, 43616
Diamond Fruit Growers, 43617
DIC International, 43456
Doran Scales Inc, 43671
Dunkley International Inc, 43723
Dura-Ware Company of America, 43730
DWL Industries Company, 43464
Dynaric Inc, 43753
Eagle Products Company, 43797
Emblem & Badge, 43916
Emtrol, 43935
Ener-G Foods, 43941
Ensemble Beverages, 43955
Everbrite LLC, 44025
Ex-Cell KAISER LLC, 44035
Excellence Commercial Products, 44041
Fabricated Components Inc, 44088
Filling Equipment Co Inc, 44164
Flakice Corporation, 44202
Florida Natural Flavors, 44244
Fowler Products Co LLC, 44328
Garden Row Foods, 44473
General, Inc, 44531
Georgia Spice Company, 44551
GERM-O-RAY, 44429
Gilster-Mary Lee Corp, 44578
Glass Pro, 44593
Golden State Foods Corp, 44643
Gosselin Gourmet Beverages, 44666
Grain Machinery Mfg Corp, 44685
Green Bay Packaging Inc., 44730
Guerra Nut Shelling Co Inc, 44768
Habasit America, 44825
Halton Company, 44843
Hamersmith, Inc., 44846
Harvard Folding Box Company, 44918
Have Our Plastic Inc, 44932
Holland Co Inc, 45048
Hollymatic Corp, 45052
Hollywood Banners, 45053
Home Rubber Co, 45060
Honeyville Grain Inc, 45066
Hoppmann Corporation, 45076
Horix Manufacturing Co, 45077
Hoshizaki America Inc, 45085
Houdini Inc, 45090
Ilapak Inc, 45208
Insignia Systems Inc, 45299
Instrumart, 45304
International Cooling Systems, 45335
International Foodcraft Corp, 45344
International Market Brands, 45352
International Pack & Ship, 45357
International Packaging Machinery, 45358
J. Crocker Exports, 45436
JAAMA World Trade, 45449
Jantec, 45494
JMS, 45465
Juanita's Foods, 45581
Kamflex Corp, 45644
Keto Foods, 45715
Kings Choice Food, 45749
Kisters Kayat, 45760
Kloss Manufacturing Co Inc, 45769
Kola, 45788
Kolpak Walk-ins, 45793
KWS Manufacturing Co LTD, 45632
Labelquest Inc, 45889
Lancer, 45921
Laub-Hunt Packaging Systems, 45949
Laughlin Sales Corp, 45950
Libido Funk Circus, 46028
Lifestyle Health Guide, 46030
Liguria Foods Inc, 46039
Limpert Bros Inc, 46047

Longview Fibre Company, 46105
Marel Stork Poultry Processing, 46325
Marshall Plastic Film Inc, 46367
Material Storage Systems, 46404
Materials Transportation Co, 46406
Matfer Inc, 46408
Maxi-Vac Inc., 46425
Merchandising Inventives, 46496
Meximex Texas Corporation, 46537
Meyer Machine & Garroutte Products, 46541
Mitsubishi Polyester Film, Inc., 46669
ML Catania Company, 46213
MMR Technologies, 46216
Moen Industries, 46686
Moyer Diebel, 46756
Murotech, 46798
National Plastics Co, 46886
New Season Foods Inc, 46983
Newly Weds Foods Inc, 47001
Nikken Foods, 47027
Noyes, P J, 47120
Nutraceutical International, 47142
Nutritional Research Associates, 47157
Omni Pacific Company, 47230
Open Date Systems, 47248
Optex, 47251
Orwak, 47290
Pacer Pumps, 47352
Pacific Oasis Enterprise Inc, 47360
Pack-A-Drum, 47377
Package Concepts & Materials Inc, 47378
Package Machinery Co Inc, 47380
Packaging Service Co Inc, 47394
Pacur, 47399
Paper Systems Inc, 47437
Paradise Products Corporation, 47447
Paramount Industries, 47454
Paxton Corp, 47499
Plastic Suppliers Inc, 47635
Prima Foods International, 47741
Pucel Enterprises Inc, 47827
Recco International, 47994
Refractron Technologies Corp, 48020
Regina USA, 48033
Rexcraft Fine Chafers, 48077
Rice Company, 48089
Rice Lake Weighing Systems, 48092
Richards Packaging, 48096
Robby Vapor Systems, 48125
Royal Doulton, 48215
S & L Store Fixture, 48255
S&P USA Ventilation Systems, LLC, 48262
Sanitary Couplers, 48375
Sato America, 48397
Scaltrol Inc, 48410
Schaefer Machine Co Inc, 48419
Schenck Process, 48423
Schlueter Company, 48429
Select Meat Company, 48498
Semco Manufacturing Company, 48503
Servitrade, 48539
Sid Wainer & Son Specialty, 48614
Sig Pack, 48621
Silesia Grill Machines Inc, 48633
Sine Pump, 48673
Slicechief Co, 48692
Sonoco ThermoSafe, 48750
Spee-Dee Packaging Machinery, 48821
Spinco Metal Products Inc, 48833
ST Restaurant Supplies, 48295
Stainless One DispensingSystem, 48869
Starview Packaging Machinery, 48902
Sugar Creek, 48994
Sun Harvest Foods Inc, 49010
Sure Torque, 49069
Surekap Inc, 49071
SWF Co, 48303
Swiss Food Products, 49095
Talbott Farms, 49161
Tate Western, 49196
Taylor Products Co, 49203
Tecweigh, 49219
Tenneco Inc, 49243

Export Region / Malaysia

Texas Traditions Gourmet, 49269
Thomas L. Green & Company, 49324
Thomas Tape & Supply Co Inc, 49327
TNA Packaging Solutions, 49136
Traitech Industries, 49426
TruHeat Corporation, 49504
UDEC Corp, 49560
Ultrafilter, 49587
Union Confectionery Machinery, 49609
Uniplast Films, 49614
United Steel Products Company, 49653
Univar USA, 49661
Universal Marketing, 49669
Unlimited Exports & Imports, 49674
Vacuum Barrier Corp, 49709
Venetian Productions, 49763
Vigo Importing Co, 49807
Waddington North America, 49912
Walco, 49922
Walker Stainless Equipment Co, 49928
Walle Corp, 49933
Welch Holme & Clark Co, 50006
Welliver Metal Products Corporation, 50011
Whallon Machinery Inc, 50061
Windsor Wax Co Inc, 50124
Wisconsin Cheeseman, 50146
Worksafe Industries, 50178
Yamato Corporation, 50230
Yardney Water Management Syst, 50232
Zepa Trade, 50274

Malaysia

Wisconsin Whey International, 50149

Mediterranean

ITW Angleboard, 45184

Mexico

A&D Weighing, 41493
A-Z Factory Supply, 41505
Aak USA Inc, 41598
Abbott & Cobb Inc, 41606
ABCO Industries Limited, 41527
Abimar Foods Inc, 41610
ACCO Systems, 41533
Acme Engineering & Mfg Corp, 41637
Action Lighting, 41654
Actron, 41658
Adams & Brooks Inc, 41666
Admatch Corporation, 41673
Adobe Creek Packing Co Inc, 41675
Adrienne's Gourmet Foods, 41680
Advance Pierre Foods, 41684
Advance Storage Products, 41685
Advanced Labelworx Inc, 41695
AFT Advanced Fiber Technologies, 41549
Agri-Mark Inc, 41721
Agricor Inc, 41722
Airomat Corp, 41740
AL Systems, 41557
Alfa Systems Inc, 41779
Algood Food Co, 41784
Allied Glove Corporation, 41821
Altman Industries, 41849
Amano Enzyme USA Company, Ltd, 41855
American Eagle Food Machinery, 41878
American European Systems, 41879
American Hotel Register Co, 41891
American Lifts, 41902
American Roland Food Corporation, 41917
American Water Broom, 41929
Americana Marketing, 41932
Ameripak Packaging Equipment, 41935
Amigos Canning Company, 41946
Ammeraal Beltech Inc, 41949
Ample Industries, 41956
Anguil Environmental Systems, 41989
Annie's Frozen Yogurt, 41996
API Heat Transfer Inc, 41577
Aqua-Aerobic Systems Inc, 42021
Archie Moore's, 42027
Architecture Plus Intl Inc, 42028
Armbrust Paper Tubes Inc, 42054
Aromachem, 42062
ASI Data Myte, 41584
Astral Extracts, 42095
Atlantic Rubber Products, 42116
Austrade, 42143
Auto Labe, 42145
Autobar Systems, 42146
Automatic Bar Controls Inc, 42152
Automatic Timing & Controls, 42157
Aztec Grill, 42183
Baldewein Company, 42251
Banner Chemical Co, 42267
Barliant & Company, 42283
Batching Systems, 42301
Bauducco Foods Inc., 42304
Baur Tape & Label Co, 42306
Baycliff Co Inc, 42312
Bayhead Products Corp., 42313
Berg Chilling Systems, 42382
Berry Global, 42396
BEUMER Corp, 42205
BEVCO, 42206
Bio Cide Intl Inc, 42441
Biocontrol Systems Inc, 42447
Biscotti & Co., 42459
Blanver USA, 42472
BluMetric Environmental Inc., 42484
Boehringer Mfg. Co. Inc., 42509
Borroughs Corp, 42523
Bosch Packaging Technology, 42525
Bowman Hollis Mfg Corp, 42540
Boyd Lighting Company, 42544
Bragard Professional Uniforms, 42551
Bran & Luebbe, 42554
Brogdex Company, 42590
Bryant Products Inc, 42620
Budget Blinds Inc, 42628
Burgess Mfg. - Oklahoma, 42643
Bushman Equipment Inc, 42653
C&P Additives, 42678
Cajun Boy's Louisiana Products, 42732
California Custom Fruits, 42751
Calpro Ingredients, 42763
Candy & Company/Peck's Products Company, 42787
Capmatic, Ltd., 42801
Capway Conveyor Systems Inc, 42809
Carleton Helical Technologies, 42830
Carlson Products, 42836
Carolina Mop, 42841
Carolina Pride Foods, 42842
Casso Guerra & Company, 42874
Castle Cheese, 42876
CCS Stone, Inc., 42690
Cedar Lake Foods, 42894
Cellofoam North America, 42899
Central Decal, 42906
Charles Mayer Studios, 42933
Chef Specialties, 42953
Chefwear, 42957
Chemdet Inc, 42964
Chemifax, 42967
ChemTreat, Inc., 42962
Cher-Make Sausage Co, 42969
Chill & Moore, 42999
Church & Dwight Co., Inc., 43031
City Grafx, 43055
Clabber Girl Corporation, 43056
Clarkson Grain Co Inc, 43063
Classic Tea, 43066
Cleaver-Brooks Inc, 43080
Clements Foods Co, 43083
Color Box, 43142
Columbia Labeling Machinery, 43148
Columbia Lighting, 43149
Commercial Dehydrator Systems, 43161
Commodity Traders International, 43168
Comstock Castle Stove Co, 43185
Concannon Vineyard, 43195
Conductive Containers Inc, 43197
Conquest International LLC, 43204
Container Supply Co, 43217
Control Beverage, 43235
Conveyor Dynamics Corp, 43249
Conway Import Co Inc, 43251
Cool Care, 43259
Cres Cor, 43338
Crespac Incorporated, 43342
Crestware, 43345
Crown Closures Machinery, 43363
Crown Iron Works Company, 43369
Cruvinet Winebar Co LLC, 43380
Crystal Creamery, 43382
Crystal Star Herbal Nutrition, 43388
CSC Worldwide, 42713
Cumberland Dairy, 43402
Currie Machinery Co, 43409
Curry King Corporation, 43410
Custom Diamond Intl., 43415
Daisy Brand, 43479
Dakota Specialty Milling, Inc., 43480
Dart Container Corp., 43505
Davlynne International, 43516
Davron Technologies Inc, 43517
De Ster Corporation, 43533
Defranco Co, 43553
Delfield Co, 43566
Delta International, 43574
Delta Machine & Maufacturing, 43575
Delta Wire And Mfg., 43577
Diamond Foods, 43616
Diamond Fruit Growers, 43617
Diamond Wipes Intl Inc, 43621
DIC International, 43456
Dong Us I, 43667
Doran Scales Inc, 43671
Douglas Machines Corp., 43680
Downs Crane & Hoist Co Inc, 43688
Dura-Ware Company of America, 43730
Dyco, 43746
Dynaric Inc, 43753
E-Z Edge Inc, 43763
E-Z Lift Conveyors, 43764
Eagle Products Company, 43797
Eaton Manufacturing Co, 43821
Eclipse Systems Inc, 43829
EcoNatural Solutions, 43833
Edmonton Potato Growers, 43863
Edson Packaging Machinery, 43866
EGW Bradbury Enterprises, 43778
Einson Freeman, 43871
Eirich Machines, 43872
Elmer Hansen Produce Inc, 43907
Emc Solutions, 43917
Emmy's Organics, 43928
Engineered Products Group, 43948
Enzyme Development Corporation, 43965
Erba Food Products, 43975
ERC Parts Inc, 43787
Erickson Industries, 43977
ESS Technologies, 43790
Essential Industries Inc, 43991
Everbrite LLC, 44025
Evonik Corporation North America, 44033
Ex-Cell KAISER LLC, 44035
Excellence Commercial Products, 44041
Exel, 44043
Fabricated Components Inc, 44088
Faciltec Corporation, 44092
Falcon Rice Mill Inc, 44101
Far West Meats, 44113
Farmington Foods Inc, 44118
FCD Tabletops, 44071
FEI Inc, 44075
Fillmore Piru Citrus, 44166
Fixtur World, 44199
Flex Products, 44227
Flowers Baking Co, 44249
Fluid Energy Processing & Eqpt, 44251
Food Equipment Manufacturing Company, 44278
Foster Farms Inc., 44320
Fowler Products Co LLC, 44328
Friedman Bag Company, 44368
Front Range Snacks Inc, 44377
Frontier Bag, 44378
Frontline Inc, 44379
Fuller Packaging Inc, 44395
Garden Row Foods, 44473
Garvey Corp, 44485
Gary Manufacturing Company, 44486
Gastro-Gnomes, 44493
General Press Corp, 44526
General Processing Systems, 44527
George Gordon Assoc, 44545
GERM-O-RAY, 44429
Gilster-Mary Lee Corp, 44578
Girard's Food Service Dressings, 44585
Givaudan Fragrances Corp, 44588
Glass Pro, 44593
Goldco Industries, 44625
Goldenwest Sales, 44649
Goodell Tools, 44657
Gosselin Gourmet Beverages, 44666
Governair Corp, 44678
Grain Machinery Mfg Corp, 44685
Great Western Juice Co, 44722
Green Bay Packaging Inc., 44730
Grimaud Farms-California Inc, 44754
Gulf Packing Company, 44778
Gum Technology Corporation, 44780
GWB Foods Corporation, 44443
H.K. Canning, 44810
Hagensborg Chocolates LTD., 44831
Hairnet Corporation of America, 44834
Hall Manufacturing Co, 44839
Halton Company, 44843
Hamilton Kettles, 44850
Hardy Systems Corporation, 44894
Harvard Folding Box Company, 44918
Haumiller Engineering Co, 44927
Hausman Foods LLC, 44930
Healing Garden, 44945
Henry Troemner LLC, 44992
Hodell International, 45039
Hollywood Banners, 45053
Home Rubber Co, 45060
Honeyville Grain Inc, 45066
Hoppmann Corporation, 45076
Horix Manufacturing Co, 45077
Hoshizaki America Inc, 45085
Hospitality Mints LLC, 45087
Huther Brothers, 45138
Hygeia Dairy Company, 45146
Ice-Cap, 45191
Icee-USA Corporation, 45193
Idaho Steel Products Inc, 45197
Ideal of America/Valley Rio Enterprise, 45203
Ilapak Inc, 45208
Illuma Display, 45211
Imperial Sensus, 45225
Indel Food Products Inc, 45242
Industrial Ceramic Products, 45258
Infitec Inc, 45270
Innovative Molding, 45291
Insignia Systems Inc, 45299
Instrumart, 45304
Insulair, 45305
International Cold Storage, 45333
International Foodcraft Corp, 45344
International Pack & Ship, 45357
International Packaging Machinery, 45358
Interplast, 45376
Interstate Packaging, 45380
Item Products, 45405
ITW United Silicone, 45186
IWS Scales, 45188
J.F. Braun & Sons, 45441
J.H. Thornton Company, 45442
Jantec, 45494
Jarden Home Brands, 45496
Jelly Belly Candy Co., 45512
Jensen Meat Company, 45517
Jescorp, 45520
John Henry Packaging, 45545
John Rohrer Contracting Co, 45549
Johnson Foods, Inc., 45553
Johnson-Rose Corporation, 45557
Johnston Farms, 45559
Juanita's Foods, 45581
Judel Products, 45582
Just Plastics Inc, 45591

Export Region / Middle East

JW Aluminum, 45469
Kamflex Corp, 45644
Kenwood Vineyards, 45709
Keto Foods, 45715
Kinsley Inc, 45756
Kiss International/Di-tech Systems, 45759
Kisters Kayat, 45760
Klockner Pentaplast of America, 45768
Kloss Manufacturing Co Inc, 45769
Kolpak Walk-ins, 45793
Krones, 45818
Kuepper Favor Company, Celebrate Line, 45823
KWS Manufacturing Co LTD, 45632
L&A Process Systems, 45840
La Belle Suisse Corporation, 45870
LaCrosse Milling Company, 45879
Lagorio Enterprises, 45895
Lakeside Manufacturing Inc, 45906
Lancer, 45921
Lane's Dairy, 45933
Langer Packaging, 45935
Laub-Hunt Packaging Systems, 45949
Laughlin Sales Corp, 45950
LBP Manufacturing LLC, 45856
Le Fiell Co, 45964
Lee Kum Kee, 45971
Les Industries Touch Inc, 46004
Les Viandes du Breton, 46005
Line-Master Products, 46053
Lodi Metal Tech, 46090
Lone Star Container Corp, 46098
Lutz Pumps Inc, 46163
M.E. Heuck Company, 46194
Machine Ice Co, 46228
MAF Industries Inc, 46197
Magnetool Inc, 46250
Majestic Industries Inc, 46267
Malthus Diagnostics, 46280
Marel Stork Poultry Processing, 46325
Marshall Plastic Film Inc, 46367
Matador Processors, 46402
Materials Transportation Co, 46406
Matfer Inc, 46408
Matthiesen Equipment, 46418
Maui Gold Pineapple Company, 46420
Maxfield Candy, 46424
Maxi-Vac Inc., 46425
Mele-Koi Farms, 46483
Merix Chemical Company, 46509
Merlin Candies, 46510
Meyer Machine & Garroutte Products, 46541
Michael's Cookies, 46552
Michigan Box Co, 46565
Micropure Filtration Inc, 46585
Microtechnologies, 46586
Midwest Stainless, 46609
Minn-Dak Growers LTD, 46650
Mitsubishi Polyester Film, Inc., 46669
Miyako Oriental Foods Inc, 46674
ML Catania Company, 46213
Mmi Engineered Soultions Inc, 46676
MMR Technologies, 46216
Moen Industries, 46686
Molinaro's Fine Italian Foods Ltd., 46694
Molins/Sandiacre Richmond, 46697
Monroe Environmental Corp, 46709
Mouli Manufacturing Corporation, 46751
Moyer Diebel, 46756
MSSH, 46218
Muir Copper Canyon Farms, 46778
Mulholland-Harper Company, 46779
Multivac Inc, 46791
Murakami Farms, 46797
Murotech, 46798
NaceCare Solutions, 46833
Namco Controls Corporation, 46838
National Band Saw Co, 46861
National Plastics Co, 46886
Native Scents, 46897
Natural Flavors, 46904
Ne-Mo's Bakery Inc, 46934
Neptune Foods, 46957

Nercon Engineering & Manufacturing, 46958
New Age Industrial, 46965
Newman's Own, 47003
Nigrelli Systems Purchasing, 47026
Nikken Packaging, 47027
Niro, 47031
NJM/CLI, 46826
Norbest, LLC, 47053
Norpak Corp, 47061
North Taste Flavourings, 47079
Northeastern Products Corp, 47084
Noyes, P J, 47120
Nutraceutical International, 47142
Nutribiotic, 47147
Nutritional Research Associates, 47157
Nutritional Specialties, 47158
Ohio Magnetics Inc, 47194
Ok Industries, 47196
Ole Hickory Pits, 47206
Omega Industrial Products Inc, 47220
Omega Products Inc, 47223
Open Date Systems, 47248
Optex, 47251
Orwak, 47290
Oskaloosa Food Products, 47293
Oskri Corporation, 47294
P.F. Harris Manufacturing Company, 47320
Pacer Pumps, 47352
Pacific Choice Brands, 47354
Package Concepts & Materials Inc, 47378
Package Conveyor Co, 47379
Package Machinery Co Inc, 47380
Packaging & Processing Equipment, 47382
Packaging Service Co Inc, 47394
Pacur, 47399
Pakmark, 47405
Paktronics Controls, 47406
Paper Systems Inc, 47437
Pappy's Sassafras Tea, 47440
Paradise Products Corporation, 47447
Park Cheese Company Inc, 47462
Parlor City Paper Box Co Inc, 47468
Parrish's Cake Decorating, 47470
Pastorelli Food Products, 47486
Paxton Corp, 47499
Peco Foods Inc., 47513
Penguin Frozen Foods Inc, 47534
Peregrine Inc, 47549
Perley-Halladay Assoc, 47556
Pez Candy Inc, 47575
Phase II Pasta Machine Inc, 47584
Pie Piper Products, 47604
Plastic Suppliers Inc, 47635
Podnar Plastics Inc, 47650
Pokanoket Ostrich Farm, 47653
POM Wonderful LLC, 47339
Priority Plastics Inc, 47760
Process Solutions, 47776
Producers Cooperative, 47779
Proffitt Manufacturing Company, 47796
Protein Research, 47816
Prototype Equipment Corporation, 47819
Psc Floturn Inc, 47825
PTR Baler & Compactor Co, 47346
Purac America, 47834
Purchase Order Co Of Miami Inc, 47837
Pure Source LLC, 47844
PureCircle USA, 47846
Qualifresh Michel St. Arneault, 47875
Quality Naturally Foods, 47884
Quantum Performance Films, 47887
Quipco Products Inc, 47900
R Torre & Co, 47910
R&R Sales Company, 47915
R.B. Morriss Company, 47917
Rapid Industries Inc, 47971
Recco International, 47994
Red River Commodities Inc, 48002
Redi-Call Inc, 48008
Refractron Technologies Corp, 48020
Refrigerator Manufacturers LLC, 48023
Regina USA, 48033

Reliable Container Corporation, 48047
Revent Inc, 48075
Reyco Systems Inc, 48082
Rice Company, 48089
Rice Lake Weighing Systems, 48092
Richards Packaging, 48096
Ripon Pickle Co Inc, 48110
Robby Vapor Systems, 48125
Robot Coupe, 48139
Roquette America Inc., 48179
Roto-Flex Oven Co, 48198
Royal Doulton, 48215
Royal Label Co, 48220
Rubschlager Baking Corp, 48237
S & L Store Fixture, 48255
S&P Marketing, Inc., 48261
S&P USA Ventilation Systems, LLC, 48262
Sadler Conveyor Systems, 48311
Safe-T-Cut Inc, 48315
Sam KANE Beef Processors Inc, 48340
Sampco, 48345
San Joaquin Vly Concentrates, 48356
Sani-Matic, 48373
Sanitary Couplers, 48375
Saratoga Food Specialties, 48390
Sargento Foods Inc, 48392
Sato America, 48397
Savoury Systems Inc, 48406
Scaltrol Inc, 48410
Schenck Process, 48423
Schillinger Genetics Inc, 48426
Schlueter Company, 48429
Schwab Paper Products Co, 48438
Seatex Ltd, 48483
Select Food Products, 48497
Semco Manufacturing Company, 48503
Sertapak Packaging Corporation, 48530
Server Products Inc, 48535
Shanker Industries, 48567
Shat R Shield Inc, 48572
Shine Companies, 48593
Sigma Engineering Corporation, 48622
Sigma Industries, 48623
Sign Systems, Inc., 48626
Silesia Grill Machines Inc, 48633
Simolex Rubber Corp, 48658
Sine Pump, 48673
Skylark Meats, 48687
Slicechief Co, 48692
Smurfit Stone Container, 48709
Snack Factory, 48711
Snyder Crown, 48725
Solvay, 48740
Spanco Crane & Monorail Systems, 48791
Spee-Dee Packaging Machinery, 48821
Sperling Industries, 48827
SPG International, 48290
Springport Steel Wire Products, 48849
ST Restaurant Supplies, 48295
Stainless One DispensingSystem, 48869
Stainless Specialists Inc, 48871
Starview Packaging Machinery, 48902
Stay Tuned Industries, 48908
Steel King Industries, 48915
STI International, 48299
Stirling Foods, 48956
Storage Unlimited, 48970
Straub Designs Co, 48978
Stronghaven Containers Co, 48988
Sugar Creek, 48994
Sugar Foods Corp, 48995
Sun Harvest Foods Inc, 49010
Superior Foods, 49053
Superior Packaging Equipment Corporation, 49056
Sure Torque, 49069
Surekap Inc, 49071
Suzanne's Specialties, 49076
SWF Co, 48303
Swiss Food Products, 49095
Swisslog Logistics Inc, 49099
Synergy Flavors Inc, 49107
Synthite USA Inc., 49108
Systems IV, 49111

T.O. Plastics, 49124
Tampa Maid Foods Inc, 49168
Tape & Label Converters, 49180
Tate Western, 49196
Taylor Products Co, 49203
Technibilt/Cari-All, 49211
Technium, 49214
Tecweigh, 49219
Tema Systems Inc, 49237
Temco, 49238
Tempco Electric Heater Corporation, 49239
Templar Food Products, 49240
Thomas L. Green & Company, 49324
Thomas Tape & Supply Co Inc, 49327
Thompson Packers, 49329
Tieco-Unadilla Corporation, 49343
Tier-Rack Corp, 49344
Titan Industries Inc, 49364
TNA Packaging Solutions, 49136
Trade Diversified, 49418
Traitech Industries, 49426
TREX Corp Inc., 49141
Tri-Tronics, 49458
Trident Seafoods Corp, 49467
Tridyne Process Systems, 49469
Trio Packaging Corp, 49478
Trojan Inc, 49489
TruHeat Corporation, 49504
Tucel Industries, Inc., 49521
Tucson Container Corp, 49524
Ultrafilter, 49587
Unified Food Ingredients, 49602
Union Confectionery Machinery, 49609
United Seal & Tag Corporation, 49649
United States Systems Inc, 49652
United Textile Distribution, 49655
UniTrak Corporation, 49600
Universal Marketing, 49669
US Industrial Lubricants, 49568
Vacuum Barrier Corp, 49709
Valley Craft Inc, 49718
Ventre Packing Company, 49767
Vessey & Co Inc, 49787
Victoria Porcelain, 49800
Vienna Beef LTD, 49803
Vigo Importing Co, 49807
Vulcan Industries, 49867
W & G Marketing Company, 49869
W.Y. International, 49877
Walco, 49922
Walker Stainless Equipment Co, 49928
Walle Corp, 49933
Walton's Inc, 49941
Ward Ironworks, 49948
Wastequip Teem, 49963
Water & Power Technologies, 49964
Waterlink/Sanborn Technologies, 49967
Waukesha Specialty Company, 49973
Wawona Frozen Foods Inc, 49974
Weiser River Packing, 50001
Welch Holme & Clark Co, 50006
Welliver Metal Products Corporation, 50011
Wepackit, 50017
Western Plastics, 50043
Western Polymer Corp, 50045
Whallon Machinery Inc, 50061
White Oaks Frozen Foods, 50074
Whole Herb Co, 50087
Wilder Manufacturing Company, 50098
Wilen Professional Cleaning Products, 50100
Windsor Wax Co Inc, 50124
Wirefab Inc, 50140
Wisconsin Cheeseman, 50146
Wisconsin Whey International, 50149
X-Press Manufacturing, 50213
Xpresso, 50219
Yamato Corporation, 50230
Yardney Water Management Syst, 50232
Z-Loda Systems Engineering Inc, 50252

Middle East

3V Company, 41472

Export Region / Middle East

A C Horn & Co Sheet Metal, 41478
A Legacy Food Svc, 41484
A&A International, 41488
A&B Safe Corporation, 41491
A&M Thermometer Corporation, 41499
Aabbitt Adhesives, 41596
AAK, 41521
Abel Manufacturing Co, 41609
Absorbco, 41615
Accutek Packaging Equipment, 41626
Aceto Corporation, 41634
ACH Food Co Inc, 41534
Acme Engineering & Mfg Corp, 41637
Acorto, 41646
Acp Inc, 41647
Acra Electric Corporation, 41648
Acraloc Corp, 41649
Acta Health Products, 41652
Actron, 41658
ACTS, 41538
Adams & Brooks Inc, 41666
ADCO Manufacturing Inc, 41539
ADH Health Products Inc, 41540
Adhesive Technologies Inc, 41672
Advanced Detection Systems, 41688
Adventure Foods, 41700
Aero Manufacturing Co, 41702
Aeromix Systems, 41705
Affiliated Rice Milling, 41711
Agri-Dairy Products, 41719
Agri-Mark Inc, 41721
Agricor Inc, 41722
Agrocan, 41727
Aidi International Hotels of America, 41733
Air Quality Engineering, 41735
Airsan Corp, 41742
Alconox Inc, 41771
Alderfer Inc, 41772
Alfa International Corp, 41776
Alfa Laval Inc, 41778
Algood Food Co, 41784
Alkar Rapid Pak, 41790
Alkota Cleaning Systems Inc, 41792
All A Cart Custom Mfg, 41793
All American Container, 41794
All Foils Inc, 41797
Allen Harim Foods LLC, 41813
Alliance Rubber Co, 41818
Allied Glove Corporation, 41821
Alto-Shaam, 41850
Amark Packaging Systems, 41857
Amber Glo, 41861
America's Classic Foods, 41867
American Commodity & Shipping, 41873
American Glass Research, 41890
American Hotel Register Co, 41891
American Importing Co., 41894
American Laboratories, 41900
American Manufacturing-Engrng, 41904
American Metalcraft Inc, 41907
American Range, 41915
American Seafood Imports Inc., 41919
American Store Fixtures, 41924
American Time & Signal Co, 41926
American Ultraviolet Co, 41928
American Water Broom, 41929
American Wax Co Inc, 41930
Americana Art China Company, 41931
AMF Bakery Systems Corp, 41566
AMI, 41568
Amigos Canning Company, 41946
AMSOIL Inc, 41570
Amtab Manufacturing Corp, 41959
Anabol Naturals, 41964
Analytical Measurements, 41967
Anchor Packaging, 41971
Andersen 2000, 41973
Anderson International Corp, 41977
Anetsberger, 41986
Anhydro Inc, 41990
Animal Pak, 41991
Apple & Eve LLC, 42009
Applied Chemical Technology, 42014
Aqua Measure, 42019
Arctic Industries, 42033

Arde Inc, 42035
Ariel Vineyards, 42042
Arizona Instrument LLC, 42047
Armaly Brands, 42052
Arnold Equipment Co, 42058
Aroma-Life, 42061
Arpac LP, 42066
Arrow Tank Co, 42069
Ashlock Co, 42081
ASI Data Myte, 41584
ASI/Restaurant Manager, 41587
Assembled Products Corp, 42087
Astor Chocolate Corp, 42092
At Last Naturals Inc, 42097
Athea Laboratories, 42100
ATI, 41589
Atlanta SharpTech, 42106
Atlantic Ultraviolet Corp, 42118
Atlantic Veal & Lamb Inc, 42119
Atlas Pacific Engineering, 42128
Atrium Biotech, 42131
Attias Oven Corp, 42132
Autobar Systems, 42146
Automated Flexible Conveyors, 42150
Automated Food Systems, 42151
Automatic Bar Controls Inc, 42152
Automatic Products/Crane, 42155
Automatic Specialties Inc, 42156
Autotron, 42161
Avalon Manufacturer, 42162
Avery Weigh-Tronix, 42167
Avestin, 42169
B H Bunn Co, 42190
B.M. Lawrence & Company, 42198
Bacchus Wine Cellars, 42224
Badger Meter Inc, 42229
Bagcraft Papercon, 42232
Baker Hughes, 42238
Bakers Pride Oven Company, 42244
Baldor Electric Co, 42252
Ballantyne Food Service Equipment, 42255
Ballas Egg Products Corp, 42256
Bally Block Co, 42257
Bally Refrigerated Boxes Inc, 42258
Baltimore Aircoil Co, 42261
Bar Keepers Friend Cleanser, 42270
Barrette Outdoor Living, 42285
Basic American Foods, 42295
Basic Food Flavors, 42296
Basic Food Intl Inc, 42297
Baumer Foods Inc, 42305
Baycliff Co Inc, 42312
Bazzini Holdings LLC, 42316
Be & Sco, 42317
Beach Filter Products, 42318
Bear Creek Country Kitchens, 42322
Bear Stewart Corp, 42324
Becker Brothers Graphite Co, 42333
Bedemco Inc, 42337
Bedford Enterprises Inc, 42339
Beehive Botanicals, 42343
Bel-Art Products, 42353
Bell-Mark Corporation, 42360
Bells Foods International, 42365
Belshaw Adamatic Bakery Group, 42368
Beltram Foodservice Group, 42371
Berg Chilling Systems, 42382
Berg Co, 42383
Bericap North America, Inc., 42385
Berkshire Dairy, 42394
Bessamaire Sales Inc, 42401
Best & Donovan, 42403
Beta Screen Corp, 42414
Bete Fog Nozzle Inc, 42415
Bettcher Industries Inc, 42417
BEVCO, 42206
Beverly International, 42426
Bevles Company, 42428
Bilt-Rite Conveyors, 42436
Binks Industries Inc, 42439
Birchwood Foods Inc, 42454
Birdsong Corp., 42455
Biro Manufacturing Co, 42458
Bishamon Industry Corp, 42460
Blackhawk Molding Co Inc, 42467

Blaze Products Corp, 42474
Blue Cross Laboratories, 42486
Blue Giant Equipment Corporation, 42489
Body Breakthrough Inc, 42508
Bonnot Co, 42520
Borroughs Corp, 42523
Bosch Packaging Technology, 42525
Boston Retail, 42530
Boston's Best Coffee Roasters, 42533
Botsford Fisheries, 42535
Boxes.com, 42542
Boyd Lighting Company, 42544
Bradman Lake Inc, 42549
Breddo Likwifier, 42571
Broaster Co LLC, 42588
Brogdex Company, 42590
Brooks Instrument LLC, 42597
Brothers Metal Products, 42602
Brower, 42603
Brown & Haley, 42604
Brown International Corp LLC, 42606
Brown Machine LLC, 42607
Brown-Forman Corp, 42611
Brucia Plant Extracts, 42613
Buck Knives, 42622
Budget Blinds Inc, 42628
Busse/SJI Corp, 42654
BW Container Systems, 42214
C C Pollen, 42664
C Nelson Mfg Co, 42670
C. Cretors & Company, 42680
Cambridge Viscosity, Inc., 42766
Cambro Manufacturing Co, 42767
Can & Bottle Systems, Inc., 42777
Candy & Company/Peck's Products Company, 42787
Cantech Industries Inc, 42795
Capay Canyon Ranch, 42796
Capmatic, Ltd., 42801
Carle & Montanari-O P M, 42829
Carlin Manufacturing, 42832
Carlisle Food Svc Products Inc, 42833
Carlisle Sanitary Mntnc Prods, 42834
Carolina Pride Foods, 42842
Casa Di Lisio Products Inc, 42863
Casa Visco, 42866
Casella Lighting, 42869
Caspian Trading Company, 42873
Casso-Solar Corporation, 42875
Cat Pumps, 42877
Century Industries Inc, 42914
Channel Fish Processing, 42925
Charles Ross & Son Co, 42934
Chase Industries Inc, 42940
Chase-Doors, 42941
Chase-Logeman Corp, 42942
Chefwear, 42957
Chemicolloid Laboratories, Inc., 42966
Chief Wenatchee, 42995
Choolijan Bros Packing Co, 43022
CHS Sunflower, 42697
Church & Dwight Co., Inc., 43031
Cincinnati Industrial Machry, 43035
Cintex of America, 43039
City Foods Inc, 43054
Clabber Girl Corporation, 43056
Classic Flavors & Fragrances, 43065
Classic Tea, 43066
Classico Seating, 43067
Clawson Machine Co Inc, 43068
Clayton Corp., 43071
Clayton Industries, 43072
Clean Water Systems, 43073
Cleaver-Brooks Inc, 43080
Clements Foods Co, 43083
Climax Packaging Machinery, 43092
Clipper Belt Lacer Company, 43093
Clofine Dairy Products Inc, 43095
Cloud Nine, 43098
Co-Rect Products Inc, 43103
Coating Place Inc, 43108
Coburn Company, 43111
Coldmatic Refrigeration, 43128
Columbian TecTank, 43150
Columbus Instruments, 43151

Commercial Creamery Co, 43160
Commercial Furniture Group Inc, 43162
Commodities Marketing Inc, 43167
Compactors Inc, 43174
Composition Materials Co Inc, 43179
Compris Technologies, 43180
Computype Inc, 43184
Comstock Castle Stove Co, 43185
Comtec Industries, 43186
Con Agra Snack Foods, 43188
Conax Buffalo Technologies, 43193
Concannon Vineyard, 43195
Connecticut Laminating Co Inc, 43201
Conquest International LLC, 43204
Consolidated Baling Machine Company, 43205
Consolidated Commercial Controls, 43207
Consolidated Commerical Controls, 43208
Container Machinery Corporation, 43216
Contech Enterprises Inc, 43218
Continental Equipment Corporation, 43223
Convay Systems, 43242
Conveyor Accessories, 43246
Cookie Tree Bakeries, 43256
CookTek, 43254
Cool Care, 43259
Corenco, 43271
Cornelius Inc., 43278
Coss Engineering Sales Company, 43292
Costa Deano's Gourmet Foods, 43294
Costco Wholesale Corporation, 43295
Cotton Goods Mfg Co, 43296
Courtright Companies, 43307
Cozzoli Machine Co, 43314
CP Kelco, 42707
Crane & Crane Inc, 43320
Crane Environmental, 43322
Cres Cor, 43338
Cresset Chemical Company, 43343
Critzas Industries Inc, 43351
Croll Reynolds Inc, 43354
Crown Iron Works Company, 43369
Cruvinet Winebar Co LLC, 43380
Cryochem, 43381
Crystal Lake Farms, 43386
Crystal Lake Mfg Inc, 43387
Crystal Star Herbal Nutrition, 43388
CSC Scientific Co Inc, 42712
CSS International Corp, 42714
Culligan Company, 43398
Culver Duck Farms Inc, 43401
Cup Pac Packaging Inc, 43406
Currie Machinery Co, 43409
Curry King Corporation, 43410
Custom Diamond Intl., 43415
Cutler Industries, 43426
CVP Systems Inc, 42718
D D Bean & Sons Inc, 43438
D D Williamson & Co Inc, 43439
D R Technology Inc, 43440
Daily Printing Inc, 43468
DairyAmerica, 43475
Damp Rid, 43488
Danbury Plastics, 43493
Darisil, 43502
Darnell-Rose Inc, 43504
Dart Container Corp., 43505
Davis Trade & Commodities, 43515
Davlynne International, 43516
DBE Inc, 43451
DCL Solutions LLC, 43452
Dealers Food Products Co, 43538
Defranco Co, 43553
Del Rey Packing, 43560
Del Rio Nut Company, 43561
Delta Machine & Maufacturing, 43575
Delta Pure Filtration Corp, 43576
DeltaTrak, 43578
Demaco, 43582
Detecto Scale Co, 43598
Diamond Fruit Growers, 43617
Diamond Wipes Intl Inc, 43621
DNE World Fruit Sales, 43459

709

Export Region / Middle East

Doering Machines Inc, 43657
Dominex, 43663
Doran Scales Inc, 43671
Double Wrap Cup & Container, 43677
Dovex Export Co, 43684
Dresco Belting Co Inc, 43704
Dri Mark Products, 43706
Driscoll Strawberry Assoc Inc, 43708
Dunbar Manufacturing Co, 43719
Dunhill Food Equipment Corporation, 43722
Dunkley International Inc, 43723
DuPont Nutrition & Biosciences, 43713
Dura-Flex, 43728
Dura-Ware Company of America, 43730
Durkee-Mower, 43741
Dutch Gold Honey Inc, 43742
Dyna-Veyor Inc, 43748
Dynamic Cooking Systems, 43750
E & E Process Instrumentation, 43755
E F Bavis & Assoc Inc, 43757
E-J Industries Inc, 43761
Eagle Home Products, 43796
Eagle Products Company, 43797
East Bay International, 43803
Eastern Machine, 43809
Eaton Corporation, 43819
Eckhart Corporation, 43825
Eclipse Systems Inc, 43829
Eco-Air Products, 43831
Ecodyne Water Treatment, LLC, 43834
Ecoval Dairy Trade, 43846
EDA International Corp, 43772
Edgecraft Corp, 43856
Edison Price Lighting, 43858
Edlong Corporation, 43860
Edom Labs Inc, 43865
Edson Packaging Machinery, 43866
EGW Bradbury Enterprises, 43778
Einson Freeman, 43871
Electro Freeze, 43887
Elliott Manufacturing Co Inc, 43902
Elmar Worldwide, 43905
Emblem & Badge, 43916
EMCO, 43782
Emery Winslow Scale Co, 43926
Empress Chocolate Company, 43934
Energen Products Inc, 43942
Engineered Products Corp, 43947
Engineered Security System Inc, 43949
Ensemble Beverages, 43955
Enterprise Company, 43959
Enting Water Conditioning Inc, 43961
Enviro-Clear Co, 43962
Equipment Specialists Inc, 43974
Erickson Industries, 43977
Eriez Magnetics, 43979
Erwyn Products Inc, 43983
Essiac Canada International, 43993
Ettore, 43997
Eurex International, 44000
Evergreen Packaging, 44030
Everpure, LLC, 44031
Excalibur Miretti Group LLC, 44038
Export Contract Corporation, 44051
F H Overseas Export Inc, 44061
F I L T E C-Inspection Systems, 44062
Fabreeka International, 44087
Fabwright Inc, 44091
Fairbanks Scales, 44094
Fairfield Line Inc, 44098
Fax Foods, 44124
FDC Corporation, 44072
FECO/MOCO, 44074
Felbro Food Products, 44133
Felins USA Inc, 44136
Fernholtz Engineering, 44142
Ferrell-Ross, 44146
Fibre Leather Manufacturing Company, 44156
Filler Specialties, 44163
Filling Equipment Co Inc, 44164
Fillmore Piru Citrus, 44166
First Colony Coffee & Tea Company, 44186
Fish Oven & Equipment Co, 44189
Fisher Honey Co, 44190
Flakice Corporation, 44202
Flamingo Food Service Products, 44205
Flavor Dynamics Two, 44209
Flavor Sciences Inc, 44211
Flavor Wear, 44213
Fleischer's Bagels, 44222
Fleurchem Inc, 44226
Flex Products, 44227
Flex-Hose Co Inc, 44228
Flexicon, 44230
Fluid Energy Processing & Eqpt, 44251
Fluid Metering Inc, 44252
Foley-Belsaw Institute, 44269
Follett Corp, 44272
Food Instrument Corp, 44279
Food Source Company, 44286
Food Technology Corporation, 44287
Foodscience Corp, 44295
Forbes Industries, 44302
Foremost Machine Builders Inc, 44304
Fortune Products Inc, 44315
Forum Lighting, 44317
Foss Nirsystems, 44318
Foster Refrigerator Corporation, 44323
Framarx Corp, 44331
Franklin Trading Company, 44339
Fred D Pfening Co, 44344
Freeman Industries, 44350
French Oil Mill Machinery Co, 44362
Friskem Infinetics, 44372
Frozfruit Corporation, 44383
Fuller Industries LLC, 44394
Fuller Weighing Systems, 44396
Fun Foods, 44400
Fun-Time International, 44401
Furnace Belt Company, 44403
Future Commodities Intl Inc, 44405
FX-Lab Company, 44083
Galbreath LLC, 44454
Gar Products, 44466
Garcoa Laboratories Inc, 44469
Garden Row Foods, 44473
Gasser Chair Co Inc, 44491
GCI Nutrients, 44419
Gea Intec, Llc, 44503
Gea Us, 44504
Gehnrich Oven Sales Company, 44509
Gems Sensors & Controls, 44513
Genpak LLC, 44536
Georgia Spice Company, 44551
GERM-O-RAY, 44429
Gessner Products, 44562
Geyser Peak Winery, 44563
GH Ford Tea Company, 44431
Giles Enterprises Inc, 44573
Gilly Galoo, 44576
Gilster-Mary Lee Corp, 44578
Giovanni Food Co Inc, 44583
Glastender, 44594
Glit Microtron, 44599
Global Equipment Co Inc, 44603
Global Manufacturing, 44608
Globe Food Equipment Co, 44614
Gold Pure Food Products Co. Inc., 44624
Goldco Industries, 44625
Golden Kernel Pecan Co, 44634
Golden Moon Tea, 44635
Golden Star, 44642
Golden State Foods Corp, 44643
Golden Walnut Specialty Foods, 44647
Goodell Tools, 44657
Grande Custom Ingredients Group, 44693
Graphite Metalizing Corp, 44701
Grassland Dairy Products Inc, 44702
Grayco Products Sales, 44705
Great Northern Products Inc, 44717
Great Valley Mills, 44720
Great Western Co LLC, 44721
Great Western Manufacturing Company, 44724
Greater Omaha Packing Co Inc., 44725
Grocers Supply Co, 44757
GS Dunn & Company, 44438
Guth Lighting, 44786
GWB Foods Corporation, 44443
H C Duke & Son Inc, 44793
H G Weber & Co, 44797
H Nagel & Son Co, 44798
H.K. Canning, 44810
Hackney Brothers, 44828
Haldin International, 44836
Hall-Woolford Wood Tank Co Inc, 44841
Hallberg Manufacturing Corporation, 44842
Halton Packaging Systems, 44844
Hamilton Beach Brands, 44847
Hamilton Caster, 44849
Hampton Associates & Sons, 44852
Hamrick Manufacturing & Svc, 44854
Hanson Brass Rewd Co, 44877, 44878
Harborlite Corporation, 44887
Hardwood Products Co LP, 44893
Harpak-ULMA Packaging LLC, 44902
Hartness International, 44915
Hcs Enterprises, 44943
Health Concerns, 44947
Health Plus, 44951
Health Products Corp, 44952
Healthy N Fit International, 44957
Herbs Etc, 44996
Hess Machine Intl, 45004
Highlight Industries, 45018
Hillside Candy Co, 45024
Hobe Laboratories Inc, 45038
Hoffer Flow Controls Inc, 45040
Holland Beef International Corporation, 45047
Hollowick Inc, 45051
Hollymatic Corp, 45052
Holman Boiler Works, 45054
Honey Acres, 45065
Hood River Distillers Inc, 45071
Horix Manufacturing Co, 45077
Hormann Flexan Llc, 45079
Houston Label, 45095
Howard-Mccray, 45101
Hubbell Lighting Inc, 45115
Hudson-Sharp Machine Company, 45123
Hughes Co, 45124
Humco Holding Group Inc, 45127
Hungerford & Terry, 45128
Huntsman Packaging, 45133
Hybrinetics Inc, 45139
Hydrel Corporation, 45140
Hydropure Water Treatment Co, 45143
Hye Cuisine, 45144
I-Health Inc, 45155
ICB Greenline, 45163
Iceomatic, 45194
Iconics Inc, 45195
Idaho Pacific Holdings Inc, 45196
Ideal Stencil Machine & Tape Company, 45200
Idesco Corp, 45205
IMECO Inc, 45172
IMI Precision Engineering, 45174
Imperial Industries Inc, 45221
Improved Blow Molding, 45231
In A Bind Inc, 45233
Indemax Inc, 45243
India Tree, Inc., 45246
Indiana Glass Company, 45252
Industrial Laboratory Eqpt Co, 45262
Infitec Inc, 45270
Inovatech USA, 45294
Insect-O-Cutor Inc, 45296
Insinger Co, 45300
Insulair, 45305
Intercomp, 45317
International Cooling Systems, 45335
International Industries Corporation, 45348
International Market Brands, 45352
International Pack & Ship, 45357
International Packaging Machinery, 45358
International Patterns, Inc., 45361
International Reserve Equipment Corporation, 45362
International Sourcing, 45366
International Telcom Inc, 45369
International Tray Pads, 45371
Island Sweetwater Beverage Company, 45394
Izabel Lam International, 45416
J C Watson Co, 45424
J C Whitlam Mfg Co, 45425
J R Carlson Laboratories Inc, 45432
J T Gibbons Inc, 45433
JAAMA World Trade, 45449
Jay-Bee Manufacturing Inc, 45507
Jelly Belly Candy Co., 45512
John Boos & Co, 45540
John J. Adams Die Corporation, 45547
John R Nalbach Engineering Co, 45548
Johnson International Materials, 45555
Johnson Refrigerated Truck, 45556
Jordon Commercial Refrigerator, 45568
Juice Tree, 45584
Justman Brush Co, 45592
K Trader Inc., 45600
K-Way Products, 45605
KaiRak, 45637
Kalsec, 45642
KAPS All Packaging, 45610
KASE Equipment, 45613
Kason Central, 45656
Kay Home Products Inc, 45660
Kaye Instruments, 45662
Kemach Food Products, 45695
Kent Corp, 45705
Kent Precision Foods Group Inc, 45706
KERN Ridge Growers LLC, 45615
Keto Foods, 45715
Kim Lighting, 45730
Kincaid Enterprises, 45732
Kinergy Corp, 45734
Kinsley Inc, 45756
Kiss International/Di-tech Systems, 45759
KMT Aqua-Dyne Inc, 45625
Knight Seed Company, 45773
Knott Slicers, 45776
Kodex Inc, 45782
Koehler Instrument Co Inc, 45783
Kohler Industries Inc, 45787
Kold-Hold, 45790
Kolpak Walk-ins, 45793
Kona Joe Coffee LLC, 45795
Kornylak Corp, 45803
Kosto Food Products Co, 45804
Kozlowski Farms, 45806
Kruger Foods, 45821
KTG, 45629
KWIK Lok Corp, 45631
Kysor Panel Systems, 45834
L F Lambert Spawn Co, 45837
La Belle Suisse Corporation, 45870
La Flor Spices, 45873
Lakeside Foods Inc., 45905
Lakeside-Aris Manufacturing, 45909
Lambent Technologies, 45913
Lancaster Colony Corporation, 45920
Land O'Lakes Inc, 45926
Landry's Pepper Co, 45931
Langen Packaging, 45935
Lanly Co, 45939
Lawrence Metal Products Inc, 45956
Le Smoker, 45965
Leavitt Corp., The, 45968
Leer Inc, 45975
Legion Lighting Co Inc, 45981
Lenchner Bakery, 45992
Les Viandes du Breton, 46005
Lewis M Carter Mfg Co Inc, 46014
Liberty Engineering Co, 46021
Light Technology Ind, 46035
Limpert Bros Inc, 46047
Linvar, 46056
Lion Raisins Inc, 46059
Load King Mfg, 46081
Louis Baldinger & Sons, 46119
Love Quiches Desserts, 46131
Loveshaw Corp, 46133
Low Humidity Systems, 46135
Low Temp Industries Inc, 46136

Export Region / Middle East

Ltg Inc, 46139
Ludell Manufacturing Co, 46145
Lukas Confections, 46151
Lumax Industries, 46154
Lumenite Control Tech Inc, 46156
Luxor California Exports Corp., 46166
Luyties Pharmacal Company, 46168
M-C McLane International, 46189
Machine Ice Co, 46228
Magnetool Inc, 46250
Mainline Industries Inc, 46263
Maker's Mark Distillery Inc, 46270
Mane Inc., 46291
Manger Packing Corp, 46292
Manischewitz Co, 46298
Manitowoc Foodservice, 46299
Manufacturing Warehouse, 46305
Maple Leaf Foods International, 46307
Maramor Chocolates, 46315
Marathon Equipment Co, 46318
Mark NYS, 46341
Marking Methods Inc, 46347
Markson Lab Sales, 46350
Marlen, 46353
Marlen International, 46354
Marsh Company, 46365
Marshall Air Systems Inc, 46366
Martin Engineering, 46373
Maryland China, 46383
Maselli Measurements Inc, 46389
Master Mix, 46395
Mastercraft Industries Inc, 46397
Mastex Industries, 46400
Matfer Inc, 46407, 46408
Matot - Commercial GradeLift Solutions, 46411
Matrix Engineering, 46412
Matrix Health Products, 46413
Matrix Packaging Machinery, 46414
Matthiesen Equipment, 46418
Maxi-Vac Inc., 46425
McAnally Enterprises, 46438
Mcbrady Engineering Co, 46454
MCD Technologies, 46202
Mclaughlin Gormley King Co, 46461
Medallion International Inc, 46470
Mega Pro Intl, 46476
Merci Spring Water, 46501
Merco/Savory, 46502
Mercury Equipment Company, 46504
Merix Chemical Company, 46509
Mermaid Spice Corporation, 46514
Merrill's Blueberry Farms, 46515
Metal Master Sales Corp, 46523
Metzger Popcorn Co, 46534
Mexi-Frost Specialties Company, 46535
Mexican Accent, 46536
Meyer Machine & Garroutte Products, 46541
Michigan Desserts, 46567
Michigan Maple Block Co, 46569
Microfluidics International, 46580
Midas Foods Intl, 46596
Middleby Marshall Inc, 46599
MIFAB Inc, 46210
Mil-Du-Gas Company/Star Brite, 46617
Miller Group Multiplex, 46629
Milwhite Inc, 46645
Minn-Dak Growers LTD, 46650
Minuteman Power Boss, 46655
Mocon Inc, 46678
Mold-Rite Plastics LLC, 46690
Montana Naturals, 46714
Morre-Tec Ind Inc, 46731
Morris & Associates, 46732
Morse Manufacturing Co Inc, 46738
Morton Salt Inc., 46741
Mosher Products Inc, 46743
Mountain Safety Research, 46753
Muckler Industries, Inc, 46775
Muellermist Irrigation Company, 46776
Mulligan Associates, 46780
Multi-Pak, 46782
Multisorb Technologies Inc, 46790
Murotech, 46798
Murzan Inc. Sanitary Sys, 46801
Muth Associates, 46807
My Quality Trading Corp, 46813
Naltex, 46837
National Hotpack, 46876
National Instruments, 46878
National Tape Corporation, 46893
Nationwide Pennant & Flag Mfg, 46896
Natra US, 46898
Natural Group, 46909
Natural Oils International, 46910
Nature's Legacy Inc., 46921
Nature's Products Inc, 46925
Navarro Pecan Co, 46929
Naya, 46931
Nebraska Bean, 46937
NECO/Nebraska Engineering, 46824
Nellson Candies Inc, 46945
Neon Design-a-Sign, 46952
Nevlen Co. 2, Inc., 46963
Nevo Corporation, 46964
New Organics, 46981
New York Apple Sales Inc, 46986
Newell Brands, 46997
Newly Weds Foods Inc, 47001
Newman Sanitary Gasket Co, 47002
Newman's Own, 47003
Nexel Industries Inc, 47009
Niagara Blower Company, 47011
Nice-Pak Products Inc, 47013
Nieco Corporation, 47023
Nielsen-Massey Vanillas Inc, 47025
Norback Ley & Assoc, 47052
Norbest, LLC, 47053
Noren Products Inc, 47058
North River Roasters, 47076
North Star Ice EquipmentCorporation, 47078
Northeast Group Exporters Inc, 47081
Northeastern Products Corp, 47084
Northfield Freezing Systems, 47090
Northwest Analytical Inc, 47095
Northwestern Corp, 47102
Nova Industries, 47110
Novelty Crystal, 47115
NOW Foods, 46828
Noyes, P J, 47120
NTN Wireless, 46831
Nu-Trend Plastics Thermoformer, 47125
Nuchief Sales Inc, 47129
Nulaid Foods Inc, 47132
Nutraceutical International, 47142
Nutri-Cell, 47146
O-At-Ka Milk Prods Co-Op Inc., 47165
Ohaus Corp, 47193
Old Sacramento Popcorn Company, 47203
Olde Country Reproductions Inc, 47204
Olney Machinery, 47210
Omega Nutrition, 47221
Omega Products Inc, 47223
Omicron Steel Products Company, 47225
Omnitech International, 47233
Once Again Nut Butter, 47237
Ontario International, 47244
Opie Brush Company, 47249
Oregon Potato Co, 47271
Orion Research, 47284
Orwak, 47290
OWD, 47172
P R Farms Inc, 47317
Pacer Pumps, 47352
Pacific Commerce Company, 47356
Pacific Scientific Instrument, 47365
Packaging & Processing Equipment, 47382
Packaging Service Co Inc, 47394
Packaging Systems Intl, 47395
Pacur, 47399
Paget Equipment Co, 47403
Panoche Creek Packing, 47430
Paoli Properties, 47432
Paraclipse, 47443
Paradise Products Corporation, 47447
Paragon Group USA, 47450
Parish Manufacturing Inc, 47459
Parkson Corp, 47466
Particle Dynamics, 47472
Patrick Cudahy LLC, 47489
Paul G. Gallin Company, 47494
Paul N. Gardner Company, 47495
Paul O. Abbe, 47496
PDE Technology Corp, 47332
Peace River Citrus Products, 47504
Peace Village Organic Foods, 47505
Peco Controls Corporation, 47512
Pecoraro Dairy Products, 47514
Peerless of America, 47521
Peerless Ovens, 47520
Pelouze Scale Company, 47528
Penauta Products, 47530
Pepper Creek Farms, 47544
Pepperell Paper Company, 47546
Perky's Pizza, 47554
Perley-Halladay Assoc, 47556
Perry Videx LLC, 47559
Petra International, 47569
Pharaoh Trading Company, 47579
Phelps Industries, 47585
Philadelphia Macaroni Co, 47588
Phoenix Closures Inc, 47594
Pick Heaters, 47599
Pickard China, 47600
Pines International, 47613
Pioneer Plastics Inc, 47619
Piper Products Inc, 47620
Pitco Frialator Inc, 47623
Pittsburgh Brewing Co, 47624
Plasti-Clip Corp, 47632
Pluto Corporation, 47644
PMC Specialties Group Inc, 47336
Pneumatic Conveying Inc, 47647
Polypack Inc, 47665
Polyscience, 47668
Portion-Pac Chemical Corp., 47682
Powertex Inc, 47691
PPI Technologies Group, 47342
Prawnto Systems, 47699
Preferred Packaging Systems, 47711
Preferred Popcorn, 47712
Preiser Scientific Inc, 47714
Presence From Innovation LLC, 47727
Prestige Proteins, 47731
Preston Scientific, 47735
Prima Foods International, 47741
Prince Castle Inc, 47753
Prince of Peace, 47756
Printpack Inc, 47757
Pro Form Labs, 47761
Pro Scientific Inc, 47763
Pro-Flo Products, 47764
Process Solutions, 47776
Production Systems, 47785
Progressive International/Mr. Dudley, 47801
Pronova Biopolymer, 47812
Protica Inc, 47818
Prototype Equipment Corporation, 47819
PTC International, 47344
PTR Baler & Compactor Co, 47346
Pucel Enterprises Inc, 47827
Pulse Systems, 47831
Puritan Manufacturing Inc, 47847
Purity Products, 47850
Pyro-Chem, 47854
Q-Matic Technologies, 47859
Quaker Chemical Company, 47870
Qualifresh Michel St. Arneault, 47875
Quality Sausage Company, 47885
R A Jones & Co Inc, 47902
R X Honing Machine Corp, 47911
Radlo Foods, 47945
Rahco International, 47950
Railex Corp, 47952
Rainbow Valley Frozen Yogurt, 47956
RainSoft Water Treatment System, 47953
Ram Equipment Co, 47961
Ramsey Popcorn Co Inc, 47966
Rapid Industries Inc, 47971
Raymond Corp, 47980
RDM International, 47928
Reed Oven Co, 48012
Reese Enterprises Inc, 48017
Refresco Beverages US Inc., 48021
Regal Ware Inc, 48030
Reheis Co, 48036
Renard Machine Company, 48056
Renold Products, 48061
Reotemp Instrument Corp, 48063
Resina, 48069
Rexcraft Fine Chafers, 48077
Rexford Paper Company, 48078
Ribus Inc., 48088
Rice Company, 48089
Rice Lake Weighing Systems, 48092
Richardson International, 48098
Richland Beverage Association, 48099
Rieke Packaging Systems, 48104
Rio Syrup Co, 48107
Riverside Manufacturing Company, 48116
Rixie Paper Products Inc, 48119
Robar International Inc, 48124
Rooto Corp, 48176
Roto-Flex Oven Co, 48198
Roxide International, 48207
Royal Accoutrements, 48209
Royal Welding & Fabricating, 48226
Royal Wine Corp, 48227
Royce Rolls Ringer Co, 48230
RPA Process Technologies, 47934
Rubbermaid, 48234
S&P USA Ventilation Systems, LLC, 48262
Sabel Engineering Corporation, 48307
Saeplast Canada, 48313
Sales & Marketing Dev, 48332
San Fab Conveyor, 48351
San Jamar, 48355
San-Ei Gen FFI, 48359
Sandco International, 48364
Sanderson Farms, 48366
Sands African Imports, 48368
Sanitech Inc, 48376
Santa Monica Seafood Co., 48380
Sardee Industries Inc, 48391
Sasib Beverage & Food North America, 48393
Satake USA, 48395
Saunders Manufacturing Co., 48399
Sayco Yo-Yo Molding Company, 48408
Scandinavian Formulas Inc, 48417
Schlagel Inc, 48428
Schlueter Company, 48429
Scientech, Inc, 48440
Sconza Candy Co, 48442
Se Kure Controls Inc, 48457
Seatex Ltd, 48483
Sellers Engineering Division, 48502
SEMCO, 48275
Semco Manufacturing Company, 48503
Sensidyne, 48511
Sensient Colors Inc, 48512
Sentinel Lubricants Inc, 48516
Sentry Equipment Corp, 48517
Serr-Edge Machine Company, 48529
Server Products Inc, 48535
Setterstix Corp, 48546
Severn Trent Svc, 48551
SEW Friel, 48276
SGS International Rice Inc, 48278
Shady Maple Farm, 48559
Shepherd Farms Inc, 48584
Showeray Corporation, 48608
SHURflo, 48279
Shuttleworth North America, 48610
Si-Lodec, 48611
Sico Inc, 48612
Signature Brands LLC, 48627
Signode Industrial Group LLC, 48629
Silesia Grill Machines Inc, 48633, 48634
Sillcocks Plastics International, 48642
Silver King Refrigeration Inc, 48645
Simkar Corp, 48655
Simmons Engineering Corporation, 48656
Simplex Filler Co, 48663
Simplimatic Automation, 48666
Sinbad Sweets, 48670

711

Export Region / Netherlands

Sioux Corp, 48676
Slicechief Co, 48692
Smith Frozen Foods Inc, 48700
Smith-Lee Company, 48704
Sogelco International, 48733
Solvaira Specialties, 48739
Somerset Industries, 48742, 48743
Sonoco Paperboard Specialties, 48749
South Valley Farms, 48765
Southbend, 48766
Southern Automatics, 48770
Southern Gold Honey Co, 48774
Southern Heritage Coffee Company, 48775
Southern Pride Distributing, 48779
Southern Snow, 48782
Spangler Candy Co, 48792
Sparboe Foods Corp, 48793
Sparkler Filters Inc, 48794
Specialty Commodities Inc, 48807
Specialty Minerals Inc, 48812
Specialty Rice Inc, 48815
Spectro, 48819
Spencer Turbine Co, 48825
Spinco Metal Products Inc, 48833
Spray Dynamics LTD, 48842
Spraying Systems Company, 48843
St John's Botanicals, 48859
Stahlbush Island Farms Inc, 48867
Stainless One DispensingSystem, 48869
Standard Paper Box Mach Co Inc, 48880
Stanley Access Technologies, 48884
Stanley Orchards Sales, Inc., 48885
Stapleton Spence Packing Co, 48887
Staplex Co Inc, 48888
Star Filters, 48890
Star Manufacturing Intl Inc, 48893
Starkey Chemical Process Company, 48900
Starwest Botanicals Inc, 48903
State Products, 48904
Stepan Co., 48926
Sterling Ball & Jewel, 48931
STI International, 48299
Stock Popcorn Ind Inc, 48957
Stone Soap Co Inc, 48965
Storm Industrial, 48972
Straub Designs Co, 48979
Strub Pickles, 48989
Sunrise Growers, 49032
Sunroc Corporation, 49033
SunWest Foods, Inc., 49019
Supelco Inc, 49043
Superior Food Machinery Inc, 49052
Surekap Inc, 49071
Sussman Electric Boilers, 49074
Svedala Industries, 49078
Sweet Dried Fruit, 49084
Swirl Freeze Corp, 49092
Swisslog Logistics Inc, 49099
Tablecraft Products Co Inc, 49153
Taste Traditions Inc, 49192
Tastepoint, 49194
Tate Western, 49196
Taylor Products Co, 49203
TDF Automation, 49127
TDH, 49128
Tech Lighting LLC, 49208
Technibilt/Cari-All, 49211
TechnipFMC, 49212
Technium, 49214
Teelee Popcorn, 49224
Teledyne Benthos Inc, 49231
Televend, 49234
Telwar International Inc, 49236
Tema Systems Inc, 49237
Templar Food Products, 49240
Templock Corporation, 49241
Terneco Specialty Packaging, 49244
Texas Halal Corporation, 49266
Texas Traditions Gourmet, 49269
Tharo Systems Inc, 49274
THE Corporation, 49132
Theochem Laboratories Inc 49304
Therm-Tec Inc, 49306
Therma Kleen, 49307

Thermo Detection, 49310
Thermo-KOOL/Mid-South Ind Inc, 49311
Thiele Engineering Company, 49320
Thirs-Tea Corp, 49322
Tipper Tie Inc, 49361
TLB Corporation, 49134
Todhunter Foods, 49373
Tofutti Brands Inc, 49374
Tomsed Corporation, 49384
Tooterville Trolley Company, 49390
Tootsi Impex, 49391
Toroid Corp, 49399
Toromont Process Systems, 49400
Townfood Equipment Corp, 49416
Trader Vic's Food Products, 49423
Traex, 49425
Travelon, 49441
Treehouse Farms, 49445
Tri-Pak Machinery Inc, 49452
Tri-Seal, 49453
Trident Seafoods Corp, 49467
Tridyne Process Systems, 49469
Trio Packaging Corp, 49478
Triple Leaf Tea Inc, 49482
TRITEN Corporation, 49142
Trojan Inc, 49489
Tropical Illusions, 49494
True Food Service Equipment, Inc., 49507
True Organic Product Inc, 49510
TruHeat Corporation, 49504
Tundra Wild Rice, 49529
Turbo Refrigerating Company, 49531
Tuthill Vacuum & Blower Systems, 49539
Tyco Fire Protection Products, 49550
Tyson Foods Inc., 49554
Unarco Industries LLC, 49591
Ungerer & Co, 49599
Union Confectionery Machinery, 49609
Unique Vitality Products, 49621
United Apple Sales, 49625
United Electric Controls Co, 49633
United Industries Group Inc, 49638
United International Indstrs, 49639
United Performance Metals, 49644
United Ribtype Co, 49646
United Salt Corp, 49647
United Steel Products Company, 49653
United Textile Distribution, 49655
Universal Die & Stampings, 49664
Universal Jet Industries, 49668
Universal Marketing, 49669
Urschel Laboratories, 49682
US Chocolate Corp, 49564
US Distilled Products Co, 49565
US Filter Dewatering Systems, 49566
US Food Products, 49567
US Industrial Lubricants, 49568
V-Ram Solids, 49690
Vacuum Barrier Corp, 49709
Valley Fig Growers, 49719
Van Air Systems, 49726
Vanmark Equipment, 49740
Vector Technologies, 49754
Ventre Packing Company, 49767
Victoria Fine Foods, 49799
Videojet Technologies Inc, 49801
Vineco International Products, 49819
Virginia Dare Extract Co, 49827
Visual Planning Corp, 49836
Volk Corp, 49856
Vorti-Siv, 49861
VT Industries Inc, 49703
W.G. Durant Corporation, 49875
Waddington North America, 49912
Wade Manufacturing Company, 49913
Waring Products, 49950
Waste Minimization/Containment, 49961
Water Sciences Services, Inc., 49966
Wayne Engineering, 49978
Wayne Farms LLC., 49979
WCC Honey Marketing, 49882
Weaver Popcorn Co Inc, 49981
Weavewood, Inc., 49982

WEBB-Stiles Co, 49884
Weinberg Foods, 49997
Weiss Instruments Inc, 50002
Welch Holme & Clark Co, 50006
Wells Manufacturing Company, 50013
Wenix International Corporation, 50015
Western Bagel Baking Corp, 50038
Wexxar Corporation, 50059
WG Thompson & Sons, 49885
White Rock Products Corp, 50076
Whitfield Olive, 50082
Wilch Manufacturing, 50094
Wild Rice Exchange, 50096
Wilder Manufacturing Company, 50098
Wileman Brothers & Elliott Inc, 50099
Williams Refrigeration, 50113
Willing Group, 50116
Willmark Sales Company, 50117
Wilton Armetale, 50120
Windsor Industries Inc, 50123
Wine Well Chiller Co, 50126
Winekeeper, 50128
Winning Solutions Inc, 50133
Wisconsin Aluminum Foundry Co, 50143
Wisconsin Box Co, 50145
WITT Industries Inc, 49887
Wittco Foodservice Equipment, 50151
Wittemann Company, 50154
Wolf Company, 50160
Wolfson Casing Corp, 50161
Wood Stone Corp, 50167
Worksafe Industries, 50178
Worksman 800 Buy Cart, 50179
World Water Works, 50195
World Wide Safe Brokers, 50197
X-Press Manufacturing, 50213
Xtreme Beverages, LLC, 50220
Y Z Enterprises Inc, 50221
Yardney Water Management Syst, 50232
Yergat Packing Co, 50238
Yogi® Tea, 50240
ZAK Designs Inc, 50253
Zebra Technologies Corporation, 50261
Zel R. Kahn & Sons, 50265
Zepa Trade, 50274
Zepf Technologies, 50275
Ziba Nut Inc, 50281
Zoia Banquetier Co, 50285

Netherlands
Golden Harvest Pecans, 44633

New Zealand
Advanced Ingredients, Inc., 41692
Bakon Yeast, 42247
Blair's Sauces & Snacks, 42468
Burgess Mfg. - Oklahoma, 42643
Clean Water Systems, 43073
Dry Creek Vineyard, 43712
Ennio International, 43953
Foodscience Corp, 44295
Insignia Systems Inc, 45299
Marlen, 46353
Martin Laboratories, 46374
Mba Suppliers Inc., 46436
Minn-Dak Growers LTD, 46650
Nielsen-Massey Vanillas Inc, 47025
Orange Cove-Sanger Citrus, 47257
Otis McAllister Inc., 47297
Psyllium Labs, 47826
RDM International, 47928
Redmond Minerals Inc, 48010
Whallon Machinery Inc, 50061
Woodstock Line Co, 50171

North Africa
American Commodity & Shipping, 41873

North America
Anritsu Industrial Solutions, 41998
AOI Tea Company, 41574
Aromatech USA, 42063
Atoka Cranberries, Inc., 42130
Axiflow Technologies, Inc., 42179

Azz/R-A-L, 42187
Baader-Linco, 42216
BEX Inc, 42207
Clean Water Technology, 43074
CPM Century Extrusion, 42708
De Laval, 43530
Design Technology Corporation, 43593
Dona Yiya Foods, 43664
E-Cooler, 43759
Econofrost Night Covers, 43840
Edge Manufacturing, 43854
Elite Forming Design Solutions, 43893
Ennio International, 43953
Fa Lu Cioli, 44084
Filling Equipment Co Inc, 44164
FRC Systems International, 44081
Fristam Pumps USA LLP, 44374
Gates Mectrol Inc, 44494
Gea Intec, Llc, 44503
Gridpath, Inc., 44748
Handtmann Inc, 44858
Harpak-ULMA Packaging LLC, 44902
Harrison Electropolishing, 44909
Hcs Enterprises, 44943
Hitec Food Equipment, 45037
Kelley Company, 45688
Kingspan Insulated Panels, Ltd., 45751
KL Products, Ltd., 45620
Kohler Industries Inc, 45787
M-Vac Systems Inc, 46192
Marlen, 46353
Maselli Measurements Inc, 46390
Mayekawa USA, Inc., 46431
Mba Suppliers Inc., 46436
Natur Sweeteners, Inc., 46901
Nielsen-Massey Vanillas Inc, 47025
NJM/CLI, 46826
Nutra Food Ingredients, LLC, 47140
Onguard Industries LLC, 47241
Paramount Industries, 47454
Phelps Industries, 47585
Rheon, 48085
Stanpac, Inc., 48886
Tapp Technologies, 49182
Tech-Roll Inc, 49210
Unitherm Food System, 49659
Univar USA, 49661
Volta Belting Technology, Inc., 49859
Xtreme Beverages, LLC, 50220

Pacific Rim
Appleton Produce Company, 42011
Dickerson & Quinn, 43623
Food Pak Corp, 44283
Goodell Tools, 44657
Hi-Country Foods Corporation, 45009
Kisco Manufacturing, 45758
Royal Vista Marketing Inc, 48225
Sconza Candy Co, 48442
Server Products Inc, 48535
Spudnik Equipment Co, 48852
Sun Glo Of Idaho, 49008
Western Plastics, 50043
Wisconsin Whey International, 50149

Panama
Well Luck, 50007
Y-Pers Inc, 50222

Phillipines
Drehmann Paving & Flooring Company, 43703
Eclipse Systems Inc, 43829
Steve's Authentic Key Lime Pies, 48944

Puerto Rico
Andex Corp, 41983
Davron Technologies Inc, 43517
Eatec Corporation, 43817
Tolan Machinery Company, 49377
Walnut Packaging Inc, 49934

Export Region / Russia

Russia
Aidi International Hotels of America, 41733
Attias Oven Corp, 42132
Clofine Dairy Products Inc, 43095
Cool Care, 43259
Cousins D&N, 43308
Letrah International Corp, 46010
Ok Industries, 47196
Palms & Co, 47418
Prime Smoked Meats Inc, 47748
R.L. Zeigler Company, 47920
STI International, 48299
Sugar Creek, 48994
Vitarich Ice Cream, 49845

Samoa
Far West Meats, 44113

Saudi Arabia
M&L Gourmet Ice Cream, 46186

Scandinavia
Dura Electric Lamp Company, 43727

Singapore
Hanan Products Co, 44855

South Africa
Altman Industries, 41849
Composition Materials Co Inc, 43179
Cooking Systems International, 43258
Crown Foods International, 43367
El Peto Products, 43877
Ermanco, 43981
Foley-Belsaw Institute, 44269
Genpak, 44535
Inovatech USA, 45294
Insulair, 45305
KWIK Lok Corp, 45631
Ltg Inc, 46139
Marie F, 46332
Momar, 46699
Nigrelli Systems Purchasing, 47026
Psyllium Labs, 47826
Refractron Technologies Corp, 48020
Robinson Canning Company, 48136
Royal Wine Corp, 48227
Southern Snow, 48782

South America
3V Company, 41472
A & B Process Systems Corp, 41476
A C Horn & Co Sheet Metal, 41478
A Legacy Food Svc, 41484
A&A International, 41488
A&B Safe Corporation, 41491
A&D Weighing, 41493
A&J Mixing International, 41495
A&L Laboratories, 41496
A&M Industries, 41497
A&M Thermometer Corporation, 41499
A-1 Refrigeration Co, 41501
A-B-C Packaging Machine Corp, 41503
A.C. Legg, 41510
A/R Packaging Corporation, 41519
Aabbitt Adhesives, 41596
Aak USA Inc, 41598
Abbott & Cobb Inc, 41606
ABCO Industries Limited, 41527
Abel Manufacturing Co, 41609
ABM Marking, 41531
ABO Industries, 41532
Absorbco, 41615
ACCO Industries, 41533
Accuflex Industrial Hose LTD, 41624
Accutek Packaging Equipment, 41626
Ace Specialty Mfg Co Inc, 41631
Aceto Corporation, 41634
ACLAUSA Inc, 41535
Acme Engineering & Mfg Corp, 41637
Acorto, 41646
Acp Inc, 41647
Acraloc Corp, 41649
Actron, 41658
ADCO Manufacturing Inc, 41539
Adex Medical Inc, 41670
Adhesive Technologies Inc, 41672
Adonis Health Products, 41677
Advance Storage Products, 41685
Advanced Detection Systems, 41688
Advanced Insulation Concepts, 41694
Advanced Labelworx Inc, 41695
AEP Colloids, 41544
Aero Manufacturing Co, 41702
Aeromat Plastics Inc, 41704
Aeromix Systems, 41705
AFT Advanced Fiber Technologies, 41549
Agri-Dairy Products, 41719
Agricor Inc, 41722
Agropur, 41728
AHD International, LLC, 41553
AIDP Inc, 41554
Air Quality Engineering, 41735
Airomat Corp, 41740
Airsan Corp, 41742
Ajinomoto Heartland Inc, 41746
Al Gelato Bornay, 41749
Al-Rite Fruits & Syrups Co, 41752
Alabama Bag Co Inc, 41753
Alaskan Gourmet Seafoods, 41762
Albion Machine & Tool Co, 41767
ALCO Designs, 41558
Alexander Machinery, 41773
Alfa International Corp, 41776
Alfa Laval Inc, 41778
Alkar Rapid Pak, 41790
Alkota Cleaning Systems Inc, 41792
All A Cart Custom Mfg, 41793
All American Container, 41794
All Fill Inc, 41796
Allegheny Bradford Corp, 41808
Alliance Industrial Corp, 41817
Alliance Rubber Co, 41818
Allied Glove Corporation, 41821
Alloy Hardfacing & Engineering, 41828
Alternative Health & Herbs, 41847
Altman Industries, 41849
Alto-Shaam, 41850
Alumin-Nu Corporation, 41853
Amano Enzyme USA Company, Ltd, 41855
America's Classic Foods, 41867
American Eagle Food Machinery, 41878
American European Systems, 41879
American Food Traders, 41888
American Foods Group LLC, 41889
American Glass Research, 41890
American Hotel Register Co, 41891
American Housewares, 41892
American Importing Co., 41894
American Laboratories, 41900
American Lecithin Company, 41901
American LEWA, 41898
American Lifts, 41902
American Manufacturing-Engrng, 41904
American Metalcraft Inc, 41907
American Range, 41915
American Roland Food Corporation, 41917
American Solving Inc., 41921
American Time & Signal Co, 41926
American Ultraviolet Co, 41928
American Water Broom, 41929
American Wax Co Inc, 41930
AMF Bakery Systems Corp, 41566
AMI, 41568
Ammeraal Beltech Inc, 41949
AMSOIL Inc, 41570
Anabol Naturals, 41964
Analite, 41965
Anchor Packaging, 41971
Andersen 2000, 41973
Anderson International Corp, 41977
Anderson-Crane Company, 41981
Anguil Environmental Systems, 41989
Anhydro Inc, 41990
Animal Pak, 41991
Anritsu Industrial Solutions, 41998
AP Dataweigh Inc, 41575
Apex Fountain Sales Inc, 42004
Applied Chemical Technology, 42014
Applied Robotics Inc, 42016
Aqua Measure, 42019
Architecture Plus Intl Inc, 42028
Arctic Industries, 42033
Arde Inc, 42035
Arista Industries Inc, 42044
Arizona Instrument LLC, 42047
Arizona Natural Products, 42048
Arkfeld Mfg & Distributing Co, 42050
Armaly Brands, 42052
Aroma Vera, 42060
Aromachem, 42062
Aromatech USA, 42063
Arpac LP, 42066
Arrow Tank Co, 42069
ASCENT Technics Corporation, 41583
Ashlock Co, 42081
ASI Data Myte, 41584
ASI/Restaurant Manager, 41587
Assembled Products Corp, 42087
Assembly Technology & Test, 42088
Astor Chocolate Corp, 42092
Astral Extracts, 42095
At Last Naturals Inc, 42097
ATI, 41589
Atlanta SharpTech, 42106
Atlantic Blueberry, 42108
Atlantic Rubber Products, 42116
Atlantic Ultraviolet Corp, 42118
Atlas Match Company, 42125
Atlas Pacific Engineering, 42128
Atlas Packaging Inc, 42129
Atrium Biotech, 42131
Audion Automation, 42135
August Thomsen Corp, 42137
Austrade, 42143
Auto Labe, 42145
Automated Flexible Conveyors, 42150
Automatic Bar Controls Inc, 42152
Automatic Products/Crane, 42155
Automatic Specialties Inc, 42156
Autotron, 42161
Avery Weigh-Tronix, 42167
Avestin, 42169
B H Bunn Co, 42190
B. Terfloth & Company, 42194, 42195
B.C. Tree Fruits Limited, 42197
Badger Meter Inc, 42229
Bagcraft Papercon, 42232
BakeMark Ingredients Canada, 42236
Baker Hughes, 42238
Bakers Pride Oven Company, 42244
Bal Seal Engineering Inc, 42248
Baldewein Company, 42251
Baldor Electric Co, 42252
Ballantyne Food Service Equipment, 42255
Ballas Egg Products Corp, 42256
Bally Refrigerated Boxes Inc, 42258
Baltimore Aircoil Co, 42261
Banner Equipment Co, 42268
Bar Keepers Friend Cleanser, 42270
Barliant & Company, 42283
Barrette Outdoor Living, 42285
Basic American Foods, 42295
Basic Food Flavors Company, 42296
Basic Food Intl Inc, 42297
Batavia Wine Cellars, 42300
Baumer Foods Inc, 42305
Baycliff Co Inc, 42312
Be & Sco, 42317
Beach Filter Products, 42318
Bean Machines, 42321
Beaufurn, 42326
Beaverton Foods Inc, 42330
Beck Flavors, 42332
Bedford Enterprises Inc, 42339
Bel-Art Products, 42353
Bell-Mark Corporation, 42360
Bella Sun Luci, 42362
Belleharvest Sales Inc, 42364
Belshaw Adamatic Bakery Group, 42368
Beltram Foodservice Group, 42371
Bematek Systems Inc, 42374
Bericap North America, Inc., 42385
Berkshire Dairy, 42388
Berlin Foundry & Mach Co, 42390
Bernal Technology, 42392
Berns Co, 42395
Bessamaire Sales Inc, 42401
Best & Donovan, 42403
Best Cooking Pulses, Inc., 42408
Beta Screen Corp, 42414
Bete Fog Nozzle Inc, 42415
Bettcher Industries Inc, 42417
BEUMER Corp, 42205
BEVCO, 42206
Beverage Capital Corporation, 42424
Beverly International, 42426
Bevles Company, 42428
BFM Equipment Sales, 42208
Bijur Lubricating Corporation, 42435
Bilt-Rite Conveyors, 42436
Biner Ellison Packaging Systs, 42438
Binks Industries Inc, 42439
Biocontrol Systems Inc, 42447
Birdsong Corp., 42455
Birko Corporation, 42457
Biro Manufacturing Co, 42458
Bishamon Industry Corp, 42460
Black's Products of HighPoint, 42466
Blackhawk Molding Co Inc, 42467
Blair's Sauces & Snacks, 42468
Blanver USA, 42472
Blaze Products Corp, 42474
Blossom Farm Products, 42482
Blue Cross Laboratories, 42486
Blue Giant Equipment Corporation, 42489
Blue Pacific Flavors & Fragrances, 42492
Blue Ridge Converting, 42495
Bluff Manufacturing Inc, 42499
BluMetric Environmental Inc., 42484
Body Breakthrough Inc, 42508
Boehringer Mfg. Co. Inc., 42509
Bolzoni Auramo, 42513
Bon Appetit International, 42515
Bonduelle North America, 42518
Bonnot Co, 42520
Bosch Packaging Technology, 42525
Boston Retail, 42530
Bowman Hollis Mfg Corp, 42540
Boxes.com, 42542
Bradman Lake Inc, 42549
Brandmeyer Popcorn Co, 42555
Brandt Farms Inc, 42557
Braun Brush Co, 42564
Brecoflex Co LLC, 42570
Breddo Likwifier, 42571
Brenton Engineering Co, 42574
Brewmatic Company, 42575
Brisker Dry Food Crisper, 42582
Broadleaf Venison USA Inc, 42587
Broaster Co LLC, 42588
Brogdex Company, 42590
Brooks Instrument LLC, 42597
Brower, 42603
Brown & Haley, 42604
Brown Fired Heater, 42605
Brown International Corp LLC, 42606
Brown Machine LLC, 42607
Brown-Forman Corp, 42611
Bry-Air Inc, 42618
Bryant Products Inc, 42620
Buck Knives, 42622
Buckhorn Canada, 42625
Budget Blinds Inc, 42628
Buffalo Technologies Corporation, 42630
Buffalo Trace Distillery, 42631
Buffalo Wire Works Co Inc, 42632
Bullet Guard Corporation, 42636
Bunn-O-Matic Corp, 42640
Burgess Mfg. - Oklahoma, 42643
Bushman Equipment Inc, 42653
Busse/SJI Corp, 42654
BW Container Systems, 42214
Byrnes & Kiefer Company, 42659

713

Export Region / South America

C Nelson Mfg Co, 42670
C P Industries, 42671
C R Daniels Inc, 42674
C&P Additives, 42678
C. Cretors & Company, 42680
Cabot Corp, 42720
Cadie Products Corp, 42726
CAI International, 42687
Cal Controls, 42735
Cal Harvest Marketing Inc, 42736
Cambridge Viscosity, Inc., 42766
Cambro Manufacturing Co, 42767
Campbell Soup Co., 42775
Can Lines Engineering Inc, 42778
Canadian Fish Exporters, 42782
Candy Manufacturing Co, 42789
Cantech Industries Inc, 42795
Capmatic, Ltd., 42801
Capway Conveyor Systems Inc, 42809
Caraustar Industries, Inc., 42811
Caristrap International, 42827
Carle & Montanari-O P M, 42829
Carleton Helical Technologies, 42830
Carlin Manufacturing, 42832
Carlisle Food Svc Products Inc, 42833
Carlisle Sanitary Mntnc Prods, 42834
Carlson Products, 42836
Carpigiani Corporation of America, 42846
Carrageenan Company, 42847
Carrier Vibrating Equip Inc, 42850
Casella Lighting, 42869
Casso-Solar Corporation, 42875
Cat Pumps, 42877
Catskill Craftsmen Inc, 42883
Cawy Bottling Co, 42891
Cedar Lake Foods, 42894
Cellofoam North America, 42899
Central Fabricators Inc, 42907
Century Industries Inc, 42914
Chad Co Inc, 42917
Charles Beseler Company, 42930
Charles Mayer Studios, 42933
Charles Ross & Son Co, 42934
Chase Industries Inc, 42940
Chase-Doors, 42941
Chase-Logeman Corp, 42942
Chef Revival, 42952
Chef Specialties, 42953
Chefwear, 42957
Chem-Tainer Industries Inc, 42960
Chemclean Corp, 42963
Chemdet Inc, 42964
Chemicolloid Laboratories, Inc., 42966
ChemTreat, Inc., 42962
Cherokee Trading Co, 42972
Chico Nut Company, 42993
Chief Wenatchee, 42995
Chocolate Concepts, 43012
Chooljian Bros Packing Co, 43022
Cincinnati Industrial Machry, 43035
Cintex of America, 43039
Circuits & Systems Inc, 43043
Ciro Foods, 43044
City Foods Inc, 43054
Clamp Swing Pricing Co Inc, 43058
Clarendon Flavor Engineering, 43059
Clark-Cooper Division Magnatrol Valve Corporation, 43061
Clarkson Grain Co Inc, 43063
Classic Flavors & Fragrances, 43065
Classic Tea, 43066
Classico Seating, 43067
Clawson Machine Co Inc, 43068
Clayton Corp., 43071
Clayton Industries, 43072
Clean Water Systems, 43073
Clean Water Technology, 43074
Cleaver-Brooks Inc, 43080
Clements Foods Co, 43083
Clextral USA, 43090
Climax Packaging Machinery, 43092
Clipper Belt Lacer Company, 43093
Clofine Dairy Products Inc, 43095
Co-Rect Products Inc, 43103
Coburn Company, 43111
Coldmatic Refrigeration, 43128
ColdZone, 43127
Colonial Coffee Roasters Inc, 43141
Columbia Labeling Machinery, 43148
Columbian TecTank, 43150
Columbus Instruments, 43151
Comark Instruments, 43153
Combi Packaging Systems LLC, 43155
Commercial Dehydrator Systems, 43161
Commercial Furniture Group Inc, 43162
Compactors Inc, 43174
Composition Materials Co Inc, 43179
Computype Inc, 43184
Comstock Castle Stove Co, 43185
Comtec Industries, 43186
Con Agra Snack Foods, 43188
Con-tech/Conservation Technology, 43189
Conax Buffalo Technologies, 43193
Concannon Vineyard, 43195
Conflex, Inc., 43198
Conimar Corp, 43200
Connecticut Laminating Co Inc, 43201
Conquest International LLC, 43204
Consolidated Baling Machine Company, 43205
Consolidated Commercial Controls, 43207
Consolidated Label Company, 43210
Constar International, 43213
Constellation Brands Inc, 43214
Containair Packaging Corporation, 43215
Container Machinery Corporation, 43216
Container Supply Co, 43217
Contech Enterprises Inc, 43218
Continental Equipment Corporation, 43223
Continental Marketing, 43227
Continental Seasoning, 43229
Contract & Leisure, 43232
Control Instruments Corp, 43238
Convay Systems, 43242
Convergent Label Technology, 43244
Conveyor Accessories, 43246
CookTek, 43254
Cool Care, 43259
Cooperheat/MQS, 43263
Corenco, 43271
Cornelius Inc., 43278
Cornell Machine Co, 43279
Corson Rubber Products Inc, 43286
Cosgrove Enterprises Inc, 43289
Coss Engineering Sales Company, 43292
Costco Wholesale Corporation, 43295
Cotton Goods Mfg Co, 43296
Country Smoked Meats, 43305
Couture Farms, 43309
Cozzoli Machine Co, 43314
CP Kelco, 42707
CPM Century Extrusion, 42708
Crane & Crane Inc, 43320
Crane Environmental, 43322
Creative Automation, 43326
Cres Cor, 43338
Crespac Incorporated, 43342
Cresset Chemical Company, 43343
Crestware, 43345
Critzas Industries Inc, 43351
Croll Reynolds Inc, 43354
Crowley Sales & Export Co, 43360
Crown Controls Inc, 43364
Crown Custom Metal Spinning, 43365
Crown Foods International, 43367
Crown Iron Works Company, 43369
Cruvinet Winebar Co LLC, 43380
Cryochem, 43381
CSC Scientific Co Inc, 42712
CSS International Corp, 42714
Culligan Company, 43398
Cup Pac Packaging Inc, 43406
Currie Machinery Co, 43409
Custom Diamond Intl., 43415
Customized Equipment SE, 43424
Cutrite Company, 43427
CVP Systems Inc, 42718
Cyanotech Corp, 43428
Cyclonaire Corp, 43431
D & L Manufacturing, 43435
D D Bean & Sons Co, 43438
D D Williamson & Co Inc, 43439
D R Technology Inc, 43440
Dacam Corporation, 43465
Daily Printing Inc, 43468
Dairy Conveyor Corp, 43470
Dairy Specialties, 43472
DairyAmerica, 43475
Damp Rid, 43488
Daniele Inc, 43495
Darisil, 43502
Dart Container Corp., 43505
Datapaq, 43507
Davenport Machine, 43508
Davis Trade & Commodities, 43515
Daymark Safety Systems, 43522
DBE Inc, 43451
DCL Solutions LLC, 43452
De Ster Corporation, 43533
Dealers Food Products Co, 43538
Defranco Co, 43553
Deiss Sales Co. Inc., 43556
Del Rey Packing, 43560
Delavau LLC, 43564
Delmonaco Winery & Vineyards, 43572
Delta Machine & Maufacturing, 43575
Delta Pure Filtration Corp, 43576
DeltaTrak, 43578
Deluxe Equipment Company, 43580
Demaco, 43582
Dependable Machine, Inc., 43586
Desert King International, 43590
Designed Nutritional Products, 43595
Detecto Scale Co, 43598
Diamond Foods, 43616
Diamond Fruit Growers, 43617
Dietzco, 43629
Dings Co Magnetic Group, 43632
Dipasa USA Inc, 43634
Dipix Technologies, 43635
Dishaka Imports, 43639
DMC-David Manufacturing Company, 43458
DNE World Fruit Sales, 43459
Doran Scales Inc, 43671
Dorton Incorporated, 43674
Double Wrap Cup & Container, 43677
Douglas Machines Corp., 43680
Dovex Export Co, 43684
Dr. John's Candies, 43693
Dream Confectioners LTD, 43702
Drehmann Paving & Flooring Company, 43703
Dresco Belting Co Inc, 43704
Dri Mark Products, 43706
Driscoll Strawberry Assoc Inc, 43708
DSM Fortitech Premixes, 43461
Dunbar Manufacturing Co, 43719
Dundee Groves, 43720
Dunkley International Inc, 43723
DuPont Nutrition & Biosciences, 43713
Dura-Flex, 43728
Dura-Ware Company of America, 43730
Duralite Inc, 43733
DWL Industries Company, 43464
Dyco, 43746
Dyna-Veyor Inc, 43748
Dynamic Air Inc, 43749
Dynaric Inc, 43753
E & E Process Instrumentation, 43755
E F Bavis & Assoc Inc, 43757
E-J Industries Inc, 43761
E-Z Edge Inc, 43763
Eagle Home Products, 43796
Eagle Products Company, 43797
Earth Saver, 43799
East Bay International, 43803
Easterday Fluid Technologies, 43806
Eastern Machine, 43809
Eaton Corporation, 43819
Eckhart Corporation, 43825
Eclipse Systems Inc, 43829
Eco-Air Products, 43831
Ecodyne Water Treatment, LLC, 43834
Econofrost Night Covers, 43840
Economy Paper & Restaurant Co, 43844
Ecoval Dairy Trade, 43846
EDA International Corp, 43772
Eda's Sugar Free, 43849
Eden, 43850
Edge Manufacturing, 43854
Edgecraft Corp, 43856
Edison Price Lighting, 43858
Edl Packaging Engineers, 43859
Edlong Corporation, 43860
Edom Labs Inc, 43865
Eirich Machines, 43872
Elberta Crate & Box Company, 43881
Electro Freeze, 43887
Eliason Corp, 43892
Elliott Manufacturing Co Inc, 43902
Ellison Milling Company, 43904
Elmar Worldwide, 43905
Emc Solutions, 43917
EMCO, 43782
Emerald Kalama Chemical, LLC, 43919
Emerling International Foods, 43921
Emery Winslow Scale Co, 43926
Empress Chocolate Company, 43934
Ener-G Foods, 43941
Engineered Products Corp, 43947
Engineered Security System Inc, 43949
Ennio International, 43953
Enterprise Company, 43959
Enting Water Conditioning Inc, 43961
Enviro-Clear Co, 43962
Environmental Products Company, 43963
Enzyme Development Corporation, 43965
EP International, 43785
Equipex Limited, 43972
Equipment Specialists Inc, 43974
Erba Food Products, 43975
ERC Parts, 43787
Erickson Industries, 43977
Eriez Magnetics, 43979
Ermanco, 43981
ERO/Goodrich Forest Products, 43788
Esquire Mechanical Corp., 43989
Esselte Meto, 43990
Essential Industries Inc, 43991
Essiac Canada International, 43993
Ettore, 43997
Euclid Coffee Co, 43998
Eurex International, 44000
Evans Food Group LTD, 44020
EVAPCO Inc, 43792
Evaporator Dryer Technologies, 44021
Everbrite LLC, 44025
Everedy Automation, 44026
Evergreen Packaging, 44030
Everpure, LLC, 44031
Evonik Corporation North America, 44033
Exaxol Chemical Corp, 44037
Excellence Commercial Products, 44041
Exel, 44043
Eximco Manufacturing Company, 44049
Export Contract Corporation, 44051
F I L T E C-Inspection Systems, 44062
F N Smith Corp, 44064
Fabreeka International, 44087
Fabwright Inc, 44091
Fairbanks Scales, 44094
Fairfield Line Inc, 44098
Farmington Foods Inc, 44118
Fast Industries, 44120
Fax Foods, 44124
FECO/MOCO, 44074
Felbro Food Products, 44133
Felins USA Inc, 44136
Felix Storch Inc, 44137
Fernholtz Engineering, 44142
Ferrell-Ross, 44146
Filler Specialties, 44163
Filtercorp, 44170
Fiorucci Foods USA Inc, 44181
First Colony Coffee & Tea Company, 44186
First District Association, 44187

Export Region / South America

Fish Oven & Equipment Co, 44189
Fishmore, 44194
Fitec International Inc, 44196
Flakice Corporation, 44202
Flamingo Food Service Products, 44205
Flavor Dynamics Two, 44209
Flavor Wear, 44213
Flavouressence Products, 44218
Flex Products, 44227
Flexicell Inc, 44229
Flexicon, 44230
Flippin-Seaman Inc, 44233
Florart Flock Process, 44239
Florida Choice Foods, 44240
Fluid Air Inc, 44250
Fluid Energy Processing & Eqpt, 44251
Fluid Metering Inc, 44252
Flux Pumps Corporation, 44254
Fold-Pak Corporation, 44264
Fold-Pak South, 44266
Foley-Belsaw Institute, 44269
Folklore Foods, 44271
Follett Corp, 44272
Food Instrument Corp, 44279
Food Technology Corporation, 44287
Food Tools, 44288
Foodscience Corp, 44295
Foppiano Vineyards, 44300
Forbes Industries, 44302
Foremost Machine Builders Inc, 44304
Forte Technology, 44313
Fortune Products Inc, 44315
Forum Lighting, 44317
Foss Nirsystems, 44318
Fowler Products Co LLC, 44328
FPEC Corporation, 44079
Framarx Corp, 44331
Franklin Trading Company, 44339
Frazier Nut Farms Inc, 44342
FRC Systems International, 44081
Fred D Pfening Co, 44344
Fredrick Ramond Company, 44346
Freeman Industries, 44350
FreesTech, 44352
French Oil Mill Machinery Co, 44362
Friedman Bag Company, 44368
Friskem Infinetics, 44372
Front Range Snacks Inc, 44377
Fruit Growers Package Company, 44385
Fuller Industries LLC, 44394
Fuller Packaging Inc, 44395
Fuller Weighing Systems, 44396
Fun Foods, 44400
Fun-Time International, 44401
Furnace Belt Company, 44403
Future Commodities Intl Inc, 44405
G.G. Greene Enterprises, 44416
Galbreath LLC, 44454
Gamajet Cleaning Systems, 44460
Garcoa Laboratories Inc, 44469
Garroutte, 44482
Garver Manufacturing Inc, 44484
Gary Manufacturing Company, 44486
Gasser Chair Co Inc, 44491
Gastro-Gnomes, 44493
Gch Internatonal, 44501
GCI Nutrients, 44419
Gea Intec, Llc, 44503
GEA North America, 44421
Gea Us, 44504
Gebo Conveyors, Consultants & Systems, 44505
Gehnrich Oven Sales Company, 44509
GEM Cultures, 44427
GEM Equipment Of Oregon Inc, 44428
Gems Sensors & Controls, 44513
General Films Inc, 44520
General Packaging Equipment Co, 44525
General Processing Systems, 44527
General, Inc, 44531
Genpak LLC, 44536
Gensaco Marketing, 44537
George A Jeffreys & Company, 44539
Georgia Spice Company, 44551
GERM-O-RAY, 44429
Gessner Products, 44562

Giant Gumball Machine Company, 44567
Giles Enterprises Inc, 44573
Gilson Co Inc, 44577
Gilster-Mary Lee Corp, 44578
Ginseng Up Corp, 44582
Giovanni's Appetizing Food Co, 44584
Girard's Food Service Dressings, 44585
Girton Manufacturing Co, 44586
Glass Pro, 44593
Glastender, 44594
Glit Microtron, 44599
Glo-Quartz Electric Heater, 44600
Global Equipment Co Inc, 44603
Global Manufacturing, 44608
Globe Food Equipment Co, 44614
Glowmaster Corporation, 44618
Goetze's Candy Co, 44620
Gold Pure Food Products Co. Inc., 44624
Goldco Industries, 44625
Golden 100, 44626
Golden Moon Tea, 44635
Golden Star, 44642
Golden Walnut Specialty Foods, 44647
Goodell Tools, 44657
Goodwrappers Inc, 44663
Governair Corp, 44678
Grain Machinery Mfg Corp, 44685
Grande Custom Ingredients Group, 44693
Graphic Technology, 44700
Graphite Metalizing Corp, 44701
Grassland Dairy Products Inc, 44702
Grayco Products Sales, 44705
Great Western Co LLC, 44721
Great Western Manufacturing Company, 44724
Green Belt Industries Inc, 44731
Green Grown Products Inc, 44735
Green Spot Packaging, 44736
Greenbush Tape & Label Inc, 44739
Greig Filters Inc, 44744
Grgich Hills Estates, 44747
Grocers Supply Co, 44757
Groupe Paul Masson, 44761
GS Dunn & Company, 44438
GSW Jackes-Evans Manufacturing Company, 44440
GTCO CalComp, 44441
Gum Technology Corporation, 44780
Guth Lighting, 44786
GWB Foods Corporation, 44443
H A Phillips & Co, 44789
H C Duke & Son Inc, 44793
H G Weber & Co, 44797
Habasit America, 44825
Hackney Brothers, 44828
Hagensborg Chocolates LTD., 44831
Haldin International, 44836
Hall-Woolford Wood Tank Co Inc, 44841
Hallberg Manufacturing Corporation, 44842
Halton Packaging Systems, 44844
Hamersmith, Inc., 44846
Hamilton Beach Brands, 44847
Hamilton Caster, 44849
Hampton Associates & Sons, 44852
Hampton Roads Box Company, 44853
Hamrick Manufacturing & Svc, 44854
Handy Manufacturing Co Inc, 44860
Hanif's International Foods, 44863
Hank Rivera Associates, 44865
Hanna Instruments, 44868
Hanson Brass Rewd Co, 44877, 44878
Harborlite Corporation, 44887
Hardwood Products Co LP, 44893
Harpak-ULMA Packaging LLC, 44902
Hart Design & Mfg, 44912
Hartness International, 44915
Harvard Folding Box Company, 44918
Haumiller Engineering Co, 44927
Have Our Plastic Inc, 44932
Hcs Enterprises, 44943
Health Plus, 44951
Health Products Corp, 44952
HealthBest, 44954
Healthy N Fit International, 44957

Heatcraft Worldwide Refrig, 44965
Heaven Hill Distilleries Inc., 44967
Heitz Wine Cellars, 44976
Hess Machine Intl, 45004
Heterochemical Corp, 45005
Hialeah Products Co, 45010
Highlight Industries, 45018
Hill Manufacturing Co Inc, 45023
Hillside Candy Co, 45024
Hillside Metal Ware Company, 45025
HMG Worldwide In-Store Marketing, 44823
Hobe Laboratories Inc, 45038
Hodell International, 45039
Hoffer Flow Controls Inc, 45040
Hoffmaster Group Inc, 45042
Holland Beef International Corporation, 45047
Holland Co Inc, 45048
Hollowick Inc, 45051
Hollymatic Corp, 45052
Holman Boiler Works, 45054
Holmco Container Manufacturing, LTD, 45055
Homarus Inc, 45057
Home Plastics Inc, 45059
Home Rubber Co, 45060
Honeyville Grain Inc, 45066
Hoppmann Corporation, 45076
Horix Manufacturing Co, 45077
Hormann Flexan Llc, 45079
Hose Master Inc, 45083
Hoshizaki America Inc, 45085
Hot Springs Packing Co Inc, 45089
House of Spices, 45094
Houston Label, 45095
Hubbell Lighting, 45115
Hudson-Sharp Machine Company, 45123
Hughes Co, 45124
Hungerford & Terry, 45128
Hurst Labeling Systems, 45134
Huskey Specialty Lubricants, 45135
Huther Brothers, 45138
Hybrinetics Inc, 45139
Hydrel Corporation, 45140
Hydropure Water Treatment Co, 45143
I-Health Inc, 45155
ICB Greenline, 45163
Iceomatic, 45194
Iconics Inc, 45195
Idaho Pacific Holdings Inc, 45196
Ideal of America/Valley Rio Enterprise, 45203
Ideal Stencil Machine & Tape Company, 45200
Idesco Corp, 45205
Ilapak Inc, 45208
ILHWA American Corporation, 45171
Illuma Display, 45211
IMI Cornelius, 45173
IMI Precision Engineering, 45174
Impact Confections, 45219
Imperial Industries Inc, 45221
Improved Blow Molding, 45231
In A Bind Inc, 45233
Indemax Inc, 45243
Independent Can Co, 45244
Indiana Glass Company, 45252
Industrial Ceramic Products, 45258
Industrial Contracting & Rggng, 45260
Industrial Kinetics, 45261
Industrial Laboratory Eqpt Co, 45262
Industrial Magnetics, 45263
Industrial Piping Inc, 45264
Industrial Product Corp, 45265
Inline Filling Systems, 45280
Inovatech USA, 45294
Insect-O-Cutor Inc, 45296
Insignia Systems Inc, 45299
Insinger Co, 45300
Instrumart, 45304
Intelligent Controls, 45308
Intercomp, 45317
Interlab, 45320
Interlake Mecalux, 45321
International Casings Group, 45328

International Dehydrated Foods, 45337
International Food Packers Corporation, 45342
International Food Products, 45343
International Home Foods, 45347
International Industries Corporation, 45348
International Machinery Xchnge, 45351
International Oils & Concentrates, 45354
International Pack & Ship, 45357
International Packaging Machinery, 45358
International Paper Box Machine Company, 45359
International Patterns, Inc., 45361
International Reserve Equipment Corporation, 45362
International Sourcing, 45366
International Specialty Supply, 45367
International Tank & Pipe Co, 45368
International Telcom Inc, 45369
International Tray Pads, 45371
Invictus Systems Corporation, 45384
Island Sweetwater Beverage Company, 45394
Item Products, 45405
ITW Angleboard, 45184
Izabel Lam International, 45416
J W Outfitters, 45433
J&S Export & Trading Company, 45435
Jantec, 45494
Jarrow Formulas Inc, 45499
Jay-Bee Manufacturing Inc, 45507
Jayhawk Manufacturing Co Inc, 45508
JE Bergeron & Sons, 45456
Jeco Plastic Products LLC, 45510
Jelly Belly Candy Co., 45512
Jessie's Ilwaco Fish Company, 45522
Jet Set Sam, 45524
JET Tools, 45457
Jewel Case Corp, 45526
Joe Tea and Joe Chips, 45537
John Boos & Co, 45540
John Henry Packaging, 45545
John J. Adams Die Corporation, 45547
John R Nalbach Engineering Co, 45548
Johnson Refrigerated Truck, 45556
Johnson-Rose Corporation, 45557
Jordon Commercial Refrigerator, 45568
Joseph Adams Corp, 45570
Joseph Struhl Co Inc, 45574
Juice Tree, 45584
Justman Brush Co, 45592
K Trader Inc., 45600
Kalsec, 45642
Kamflex Corp, 45644
KAPCO, 45609
KAPS All Packaging, 45610
KASE Equipment, 45613
Katagiri & Company, 45658
Kay Home Products Inc, 45660
Kaye Instruments, 45662
Kemach Food Products, 45695
Kemutec Group Inc, 45699
Kent Corp, 45705
Kent Precision Foods Group Inc, 45706
Kerry Foodservice, 45713
Keto Foods, 45715
Key Technology Inc., 45719
Key-Pak Machines, 45721
Kiefer Brushes, Inc, 45728
Kim Lighting, 45730
Kincaid Enterprises, 45732
Kinergy Corp, 45734
King Engineering - King-Gage, 45742
Kinsley Inc, 45756
Kirin Brewery Of America LLC, 45757
Kiss International/Di-tech Systems, 45759
KISS Packaging Systems, 45619
Kisters Kayat, 45760
Klaire Laboratories, 45764
Kleen Products Inc, 45765
Klockner Pentaplast of America, 45768
KMT Aqua-Dyne Inc, 45625
Knight Equipment International, 45772

715

Export Region / South America

Knight Seed Company, 45773
Knott Slicers, 45776
Kodex Inc, 45782
Koehler Instrument Co Inc, 45783
Kohler Industries Inc, 45787
Kola, 45788
Kold-Hold, 45790
Kolpak Walk-ins, 45793
Konica Minolta Corp, 45796
Korab Engineering Company, 45801
Kornylak Corp, 45803
Kosto Food Products Co, 45804
Kozlowski Farms, 45806
KTG, 45629
Kuhl Corporation, 45825
KWIK Lok Corp, 45631
KWS Manufacturing Co LTD, 45632
Kysor Panel Systems, 45834
L&A Process Systems, 45840
La Belle Suisse Corporation, 45870
La Crosse, 45872
La Flor Spices, 45873
LA Monica Fine Foods, 45851
Labatt Brewing Company, 45881
Label Systems, 45886
Lactalis American Group Inc, 45892
Lakeside Manufacturing Inc, 45906
Lakeside-Aris Manufacturing, 45909
Lallemand, 45911
Lambent Technologies, 45913
Lamson & Goodnow, 45918
Lancer, 45921
Land O'Lakes Inc, 45926
Langen Packaging, 45935
Langsenkamp Manufacturing, 45937
Lanly Co, 45939
Latendorf Corporation, 45947
Laughlin Sales Corp, 45950
Lawrence Metal Products Inc, 45956
Le Fiell Co, 45964
Leader Candies, 45966
Least Cost Formulations LTD, 45967
Leavitt Corp., The, 45968
Lee Financial Corporation, 45970
Lee Kum Kee, 45971
Leer Inc, 45975
Legion Export & Import Company, 45980
Les Viandes du Breton, 46005
Letrah International Corp, 46010
Lewis M Carter Mfg Co Inc, 46014
Leyman Manufacturing Corporation, 46019
Liberty Engineering Co, 46021
Light Technology Ind, 46035
Lilly Co Inc, 46042
Lin Pac Plastics, 46048
Linvar, 46056
Lion Raisins Inc, 46059
Liqui-Box Corp, 46062
Lista International Corp, 46065
Little Crow Foods, 46071
Livingston-Wilbor Corporation, 46075
LMK Containers, 45865
Load King Mfg, 46081
Loma International, 46092
Longhorn Packaging Inc, 46103
Longview Fibre Company, 46105
Lord Label Group, 46108
Louis Baldinger & Sons, 46119
Love Controls Division, 46130
Loveshaw Corp, 46133
Low Humidity Systems, 46135
Low Temp Industries Inc, 46136
Ltg Inc, 46139
Ludell Manufacturing Co, 46145
Ludwig Mueller Co Inc, 46147
Luetzow Industries, 46148
Lukas Confections, 46151
Lumax Industries, 46154
Lumber & Things, 46155
Lumenite Control Tech Inc, 46156
Luthi Machinery Company, Inc., 46162
Luyties Pharmacal Company, 46168
M Phil Yen Company, 46182
M-C McLane International, 46189

M.H. Rhodes Cramer, 46195
Machem Industries, 46226
Machine Ice Co, 46228
Madelaine Chocolate Company, 46232
MAFCO Worldwide, 46198
Magna Foods Corporation, 46246
Magnetic Products Inc, 46249
Magnetool Inc, 46250
Magsys Inc, 46257
Mainline Industries Inc, 46263
Maker's Mark Distillery Inc, 46270
Mane Inc., 46291
Manischewitz Co, 46298
Manitowoc Foodservice, 46299
Manning Lighting Inc, 46301
Manufacturing Warehouse, 46305
Maple Leaf Foods International, 46307
Mar-Con Wire Belt, 46311
Marathon Equipment Co, 46318
Marel Stork Poultry Processing, 46325
Maren Engineering Corp, 46327
Marie F, 46332
Marina Foods, 46334
Marking Devices Inc, 46346
Marking Methods Inc, 46347
Markson Lab Sales, 46350
Marlen, 46353
Marlen International, 46354
Marlyn Nutraceuticals, 46357
Marsh Company, 46365
Marshall Air Systems Inc, 46366
Martin Engineering, 46373
Martin/Baron, 46375
Maryland China, 46383
Maselli Measurements Inc, 46389
Master Mix, 46395
Mastercraft Industries Inc, 46397
Mastercraft International, 46398
Materials Transportation Co, 46406
Matfer Inc, 46407, 46408
Matrix Engineering, 46412
Matrix Health Products, 46413
Matrix Packaging Machinery, 46414
Matthiesen Equipment, 46418
Maxi-Vac Inc., 46425
Maxim's Import Corporation, 46426
Mba Suppliers Inc., 46436
Mcbrady Engineering Co, 46454
McCormack Manufacturing Company, 46443
MCD Technologies, 46202
Mclaughlin Gormley King Co, 46461
Meadowbrook Meat Company, 46464
Meadows Mills Inc, 46465
Mecco Marking & Traceability, 46469
Mega Pro Intl, 46476
Melitta USA Inc, 46484
Mepsco, 46493
Merchandising Inventives, 46496
Merco/Savory, 46502
Mercury Equipment Company, 46504
Merlin Candies, 46510
Metal Master Sales Corp, 46523
Mettler-Toledo Safeline Inc, 46530
Mettler-Toledo, LLC, 46531
Metzgar Conveyors, 46533
Metzger Popcorn Co, 46534
Mexi-Frost Specialties Company, 46535
Meyenberg Goat Milk, 46539
Meyer Machine & Garroutte Products, 46541
Miami Depot Inc, 46545
Miami Purveyors Inc, 46548
Micelli Chocolate Mold Company, 46549
Michael Foods, Inc., 46550
Michael's Cookies, 46552
Michigan Desserts, 46567
Microbest Inc, 46577
Microfluidics International, 46580
Micropure Filtration Inc, 46585
Middleby Marshall Inc, 46599
Midwest Badge & Novelty Co, 46604
Mil-Du-Gas Company/Star Brite, 46617
Milan Box Corporation, 46618
Miljoco Corp, 46623
Millerbernd Systems, 46632

Milwhite Inc, 46645
Minn-Dak Growers LTD, 46650
Minuteman Power Boss, 46655
MIRA International Foods, 46211
Mitsubishi Polyester Film, Inc., 46669
Miyako Oriental Foods Inc, 46674
ML Catania Company, 46213
MMR Technologies, 46216
Mocon Inc, 46678
MODAGRAPHICS, 46217
Modern Products Inc, 46682
Modular Packaging, 46683
Moen Industries, 46686
Mold-Rite Plastics LLC, 46690
Molinaro's Fine Italian Foods Ltd., 46694
Molinera International, 46696
Molins/Sandiacre Richmond, 46697
Monitor Technologies LLC, 46708
Moore Production Tool Spec Inc, 46722
Morre-Tec Ind Inc, 46731
Morris & Associates, 46732
Morse Manufacturing Co Inc, 46738
Morton Salt Inc., 46741
Mosher Products Inc, 46743
Mouli Manufacturing Corporation, 46751
Mountain Safety Research, 46753
Moyer Diebel, 46756
Mr Ice Bucket, 46761
Muellermist Irrigation Company, 46776
Mulligan Associates, 46780
Multi-Panel Display Corporation, 46783
Multiflex Company, 46787
Multisorb Technologies Inc, 46790
Munson Machinery Co, 46794
Murotech, 46798
Murzan Inc. Sanitary Sys, 46801
Muth Associates, 46807
My Quality Trading Corp, 46813
N S I Sweeteners, 46816
Naltex, 46837
National Food Corporation, 46871
National Foods, 46873
National Fruit Flavor Co Inc, 46875
National Hotpack, 46876
National Instruments, 46878
National Plastics Co, 46886
National Printing Converters, 46887
National Tape Corporation, 46893
Nationwide Pennant & Flag Mfg, 46896
Native Scents, 46897
Natra US, 46898
Natur Sweeteners, Inc., 46901
Natural Flavors, 46904
Natural Food Holdings, 46905
Natural Oils International, 46910
Nature's Best Inc, 46917
Nature's Legacy Inc., 46921
Nature's Plus, 46924
Nature's Products Inc, 46925
Natures Sungrown Foods Inc, 46927
Naya, 46931
NCC, 46822
NDC Infrared Engineering Inc, 46823
Nebraska Bean, 46937
Neogen Corp, 46951
Neon Design-a-Sign, 46952
Nepco Egg Of Ga, 46955
Nercon Engineering & Manufacturing, 46958
Nevlen Co. 2, Inc., 46963
Nevo Corporation, 46964
New Earth, 46970
New England Machinery Inc, 46973
New Horizon Foods, 46979
New Organics, 46981
New York Export Co, 46989
Newcastle Co Inc, 46995
Newell Brands, 46997
Newly Weds Foods Inc, 47001
Newman's Own, 47003
Nexel Industries Inc, 47009
Niagara Foods, 47012
Nice-Pak Products Inc, 47013
Nichem Co, 47015
Nieco Corporation, 47023

Nielsen-Massey Vanillas Inc, 47025
Nigrelli Systems Purchasing, 47026
Nikken Foods, 47027
Nikki's Cookies, 47028
Niro, 47031
Niroflex, USA, 47032
Nitech, 47036
Niutang Chemical, Inc., 47038
Norback Ley & Assoc, 47052
Norbest, LLC, 47053
Nordson Sealant Equipment, 47057
Noren Products Inc, 47058
North Coast Processing, 47071
North River Roasters, 47076
North Star Ice Equipment Corporation, 47078
Northeastern Products Corp, 47084
Northfield Freezing Systems, 47090
Northwest Analytical Inc, 47095
Northwestern Corp, 47102
Norvell Co Inc, 47104
Norwood Marking Systems, 47105
Novelty Crystal, 47115
NOW Foods, 46828
Noyes, P J, 47120
NST Metals, 46830
NTN Wireless, 46831
Nu-Trend Plastics Thermoformer, 47125
Nucon Corporation, 47130
Nutra Food Ingredients, LLC, 47140
Nutraceutical International, 47142
Nutribiotic, 47147
O-At-Ka Milk Prods Co-Op Inc., 47165
Occidental Foods International, LLC, 47178
OCS Process Systems, 47167
Oerlikon Leybold Vacuum, 47189
Ogden Manufacturing Company, 47192
Ohaus Corp, 47193
Ohio Magnetics Inc, 47194
Olney Machinery, 47210
Olymel, 47211
Omega Products Inc, 47223
Omega Protein, 47224
Omicron Steel Products Company, 47225
Omni Controls Inc, 47226
Omni Pacific Company, 47230
Omnitech International, 47233
OnTrack Automation Inc, 47236
Opie Brush Company, 47249
Optex, 47251
Oregon Freeze Dry, Inc., 47268
Oregon Potato Co, 47271
Orion Research, 47284
Orwak, 47290
Otis McAllister Inc., 47297
OTP Industrial Solutions, 47171
Ottens Flavors, 47298
Outotec USA Inc, 47302
OWD, 47172
Oxbo International Corp, 47308
OXO International, 47173
P J Rhodes Corporation, 47316
P.F. Harris Manufacturing Company, 47320
Paar Physica USA, 47349
Pacer Pumps, 47352
Pacific Commerce Company, 47356
Pacific Scientific Instrument, 47365
Pacific Seafoods International, 47366
Package Machinery Co Inc, 47380
Packaging & Processing Equipment, 47382
Packaging Dynamics, 47384
Packaging Machinery International, 47392
Packaging Systems Intl, 47395
Paget Equipment Co, 47403
Paltier, 47419
Pangaea Sciences, 47428
Panoche Creek Packing, 47430
Pantry Shelf Food Corporation, 47431
Paoli Properties, 47432
Paper Systems Inc, 47437
PAR-Way Tryson Co, 47325
Paraclipse, 47443

716

Export Region / South America

Paradise Products Corporation, 47447
Paragon Films Inc, 47449
Paratherm Corporation, 47455
Parish Manufacturing Inc, 47459
Parkson Corp, 47465, 47466
Particle Dynamics, 47472
Pasquini Espresso Co, 47479
Pastorelli Food Products, 47486
Patrick Cudahy LLC, 47489
Patterson Industries, 47491
Paul G. Gallin Company, 47494
Paul N. Gardner Company, 47495
Paul O. Abbe, 47496
Paxton Corp, 47499
PC/Poll Systems, 47330
PDC International, 47331
PDE Technology Corp, 47332
Pearson Packaging Systems, 47509
Pecan Deluxe Candy Co, 47511
Peco Controls Corporation, 47512
Peco Foods Inc., 47513
Peerless of America, 47521
Pelouze Scale Company, 47528
Penta Manufacturing Company, 47541
Pepe's Mexican Restaurant, 47543
Pepper Creek Farms, 47544
Pepperell Paper Company, 47546
Perky's Pizza, 47554
Perry Videx LLC, 47559
Petra International, 47569
Pez Candy Inc, 47575
PFI Displays Inc, 47333
Pharaoh Trading Company, 47579
Phase II Pasta Machine Inc, 47584
Phoenix Closures Inc, 47594
Pick Heaters, 47599
Pines International, 47613
Pioneer Plastics Inc, 47619
Piper Products Inc, 47621
Pitco Frialator Inc, 47623
Planet Products Corp, 47628
Plasti-Clip Corp, 47632
Plastic Suppliers Inc, 47635
PlexPack Corp, 47642
PMC Specialties Group Inc, 47336
Pneumatic Conveying Inc, 47647
Pneumatic Scale Angelus, 47648
PolyConversions, Inc., 47662
Polypack Inc, 47665
Polyscience, 47668
POM Wonderful LLC, 47339
Porcelain Metals Corporation, 47677
Portion-Pac Chemical Corp., 47682
Powertex Inc, 47691
PPI Technologies Group, 47342
Prawnto Systems, 47699
Preferred Packaging Systems, 47711
Preferred Popcorn, 47712
Preiser Scientific, 47714
Premier Brass, 47717
Premium Water, 47722
Pressure King Inc, 47729
Prestige Proteins, 47731
Prima Foods International, 47741
Prime Ostrich International, 47746
Prince Castle Inc, 47753
Printpack Inc., 47757
Priority One Packaging, 47759
Pro Form Labs, 47761
Pro Scientific Inc, 47763
Pro-Flo Products, 47764
ProBar Systems Inc., 47766
Process Displays, 47771
Process Engineering & Fabrication, 47772
Process Solutions, 47776
Produce Trading Corp, 47778
Profire Stainless Steel Barbecue, 47797
Progressive International/Mr. Dudley, 47801
Pronatura Inc, 47811
Pronova Biopolymer, 47812
Prototype Equipment Corporation, 47819
Psc Floturn Inc, 47825
Pulse Systems, 47831
Purchase Order Co Of Miami Inc, 47837

Pure Source LLC, 47844
PureCircle USA, 47846
Puritan Manufacturing Inc, 47847
Purity Products, 47850
Purolator Facet Inc, 47851
Pyromation Inc, 47855
Q-Matic Technologies, 47859
Quadrel Labeling Systems, 47869
Qualifresh Michel St. Arneault, 47875
Quality Fabrication & Design, 47881
Quantum Storage Systems Inc, 47888
Quelle Quiche, 47892
Quest Corp, 47893
Quipco Products Inc, 47900
R A Jones & Co Inc, 47902
R X Honing Machine Corp, 47911
R.L. Zeigler Company, 47920
R.W. Garcia, 47922
Ragtime, 47949
Rahco International, 47950
Rahmann Belting & Industrial Rubber Products, 47951
Railex Corp, 47952
RainSoft Water Treatment System, 47953
Rainsweet Inc, 47958
Rairdon Dodge Chrysler Jeep, 47959
Ram Equipment Co, 47961
Rapid Industries Inc, 47971
Raymond Corp, 47980
RDM International, 47928
Real Aloe Company, 47989
Real Kosher Sausage Company, 47992
Reed Oven Co, 48012
Reeve Store Equipment Co, 48018
Refractron Technologies Corp, 48020
Refresco Beverages US Inc., 48021
Regal Ware Inc, 48030
Reheis Co, 48036
Reilly Dairy & Food Company, 48039
Remco Industries International, 48050
Remco Products Corp, 48051
Renard Machine Company, 48056
RENFRO Foods Inc, 47929
Renold Products, 48061
Reotemp Instrument Corp, 48063
Resina, 48069
Revent Inc, 48075
Rexcraft Fine Chafers, 48077
Rexford Paper Company, 48078
Reyco Systems Inc, 48082
Rheon USA, 48084
Rheon, U.S.A., 48085
Ribus Inc., 48088
Rice Company, 48089
Rice Lake Weighing Systems, 48092
Richards Packaging, 48096
Richardson International, 48098
Rieke Packaging Systems, 48104
Ripon Pickle Co Inc, 48110
Rixie Paper Products Inc, 48119
Robar International Inc, 48124
Roberts Poly Pro Inc, 48132
Robin Shepherd Group, 48135
Roechling Engineered Plastics, 48153
Rollprint Packaging Prods Inc, 48165
Ron Son Foods Inc, 48169
Roosevelt Dairy Trade, Inc, 48175
Rooto Corp, 48176
Roquette America Inc., 48179
Ross Industries Inc, 48191
Roto-Flex Oven Co, 48198
Roxide International, 48207
Royal Accoutrements, 48209
Royal Welding & Fabricating, 48226
Royal Wine Corp, 48227
RPA Process Technologies, 47934
Rubbermaid, 48234
Rudolph Foods Co, 48239
Ruggiero Seafood, 48242
Rutherford Engineering, 48248
Rv Industries, 48249
S & L Store Fixture, 48255
S & S Indl Maintenance, 48256
S&R Imports, 48263
Sabel Engineering Corporation, 48307
Saeplast Canada, 48313

Safe-T-Cut Inc, 48315
Sales & Marketing Dev, 48332
San Diego Products, 48350
San Francisco Herb Co, 48353
San Jamar, 48355
San-Ei Gen FFI, 48359
Sanchelima International, 48362
Sancoa International, 48363
Sandco International, 48364
Sani-Matic, 48373
Sanitary Couplers, 48375
Sanitech Inc, 48376
Santa Clara Nut Co, 48379
Santa Monica Seafood Co., 48380
Sardee Industries Inc, 48391
Sasib Beverage & Food North America, 48393
Satake USA, 48395
Sato America, 48397
Saunders Manufacturing Co., 48399
Savoury Systems Inc, 48406
Scaltrol Inc, 48410
Scandia Packaging Machinery Co, 48414
Scandinavian Formulas Inc, 48417
Schaefer Machine Co Inc, 48419
Schillinger Genetics Inc, 48426
Schlagel Inc, 48428
Schlueter Company, 48429
Schmidt Progressive, 48430
Schroeder Machine, 48436
Schwab Paper Products Co, 48438
Scientech, Inc, 48440
Scientific Process & Research, 48441
SDIX, 48274
Se Kure Controls Inc, 48457
Seald Sweet, 48476
Sealstrip Corporation, 48477
Seepex Inc, 48495
Selecto Scientific, 48501
Sellers Engineering Division, 48502
SEMCO, 48275
Semco Manufacturing Company, 48503
Sensidyne, 48511
Sentinel Lubricants Inc, 48516
Sentry Equipment Corp, 48517
Separators Inc, 48520
Serfilco, 48526
Serpa Packaging Solutions, 48528
Serr-Edge Machine Company, 48529
Sertapak Packaging Corporation, 48530
Server Products Inc, 48535
Servitrade, 48539
Sesinco Foods, 48542
Setton International Foods, 48547
Severn Trent Svc, 48551
SEW Friel, 48276
Shady Maple Farm, 48559
Sharon Manufacturing Inc, 48569
Sharp Brothers, 48570
Shawano Specialty Papers, 48574
Shick Esteve, 48589
Shoes for Crews/Mighty Mat, 48603
Showeray Corporation, 48608
SHURflo, 48279
Shuttleworth North America, 48610
Si-Lodec, 48611
Sico Inc, 48612
Sid Wainer & Son Specialty, 48614
Sidney Manufacturing Co, 48616
Sieco USA Corporation, 48618
SIG Combibloc USA, Inc., 48280
Signode Industrial Group LLC, 48629
Signs & Shapes Intl, 48630
Silesia Grill Machines Inc, 48633, 48634
Sillcocks Plastics International, 48642
Silver King Refrigeration Inc, 48645
Silver Weibull, 48650
Simkar Corp, 48655
Simmons Engineering Corporation, 48656
Simonds International, 48660
Simplex Filler Co, 48663
Simplimatic Automation, 48666
Sinbad Sweets, 48670
Sinclair Trading, 48671
Sine Pump, 48673

Sioux Corp, 48676
Skd Distribution Corp, 48684
Skim Delux Mendenhall Laboratories, 48685
SKW Nature Products, 48286
Slicechief Co, 48692
Smico Manufacturing Co Inc, 48698
Smith Frozen Foods Inc, 48700
Snyder Crown, 48725
Solbern Corp, 48734
Solvaira Specialties, 48739
Somerset Industries, 48743
Sonoco Paperboard Specialties, 48749
Sonoco ThermoSafe, 48750
Soodhalter Plastics, 48752
Soofer Co, 48753
Southbend, 48766
Southern Automatics, 48770
Southern Champion Tray LP, 48771
Southern Pride Distributing, 48779
Spangler Candy Co, 48792
Sparkler Filters Inc, 48794
Spartech Plastics, 48799
Specialty Blades, 48805
Specialty Commodities Inc, 48807
Specialty Minerals Inc, 48812
Specialty Rice Inc, 48815
Specific Mechanical Systems, 48817
Spectro, 48819
Spee-Dee Packaging Machinery, 48821
Speedways Conveyors, 48823
Spencer Turbine Co, 48825
Sperling Industries, 48827
Spice & Spice, 48828
Spinco Metal Products Inc, 48833
Spir-It/Zoo Piks, 48834
Spirit Foodservice, Inc., 48837
Spray Dynamics LTD, 48842
Spraying Systems Company, 48843
Spudnik Equipment Co, 48852
St John's Botanicals, 48859
Stainless One DispensingSystem, 48869
Standard Casing Company, 48875
Standard Paper Box Mach Co Inc, 48880
Standard Terry Mills, 48882
Stanley Access Technologies, 48884
Stanpac, Inc., 48886
Stapleton Spence Packing Co, 48887
Staplex Co Inc, 48888
Star Filters, 48890
Star Manufacturing Intl Inc, 48893
Starkey Chemical Process Company, 48900
Starview Packaging Machinery, 48902
Starwest Botanicals Inc, 48903
State Products, 48904
Stauber Performance Ingrdients, 48905
Stavis Seafoods, 48907
Stepan Co., 48926
Steri Technologies Inc, 48929
Sterling Ball & Jewel, 48931
Sterling Rubber, 48936
Stevens Linen Association, 48945
Stimo-O-Stam, Ltd., 48955
Stogsdill Tile Co, 48961
Stone Soap Co Inc, 48965
Storm Industrial, 48972
Straub Designs Co, 48978, 48979
Stricklin Co, 48985
Summit Import Corp, 49005
Sun Harvest Foods Inc, 49010
Sun Noodle New Jersey, 49012
Sun Pac Foods, 49013
Sunroc Corporation, 49033
Suntec Power, 49040
Supelco Inc, 49043
Superior Food Machinery Inc, 49052
Superior Foods, 49053
Superior Packaging Equipment Corporation, 49056
Superior Paper & Plastic Co, 49057
Sure Torque, 49069
Surekap Inc, 49071
Surtec Inc, 49073
Sussman Electric Boilers, 49074
Svedala Industries, 49078

Export Region / South Pacific

Sweet Dried Fruit, 49084
SWF Co, 48303
SWF McDowell, 48304
Swirl Freeze Corp, 49092
Swissh Commercial Equipment, 49098
Swisslog Logistics Inc, 49099
Synthite USA Inc., 49108
Tabco Enterprises, 49147
Tablecraft Products Co Inc, 49153
Taku Smokehouse, 49160
Tallygenicom, 49163
Taste Traditions Inc, 49192
Tastepoint, 49194
Tate Western, 49196
TDF Automation, 49127
Tech Lighting LLC, 49208
Tech Sales Inc, 49209
Technibilt/Cari-All, 49211
TechnipFMC, 49212
Technium, 49214
Technology Flavors & Fragrances, 49216
Tecweigh, 49219
Teelee Popcorn, 49224
Teledyne Benthos Inc, 49231
Televend, 49234
Telman Incorporated, 49235
Tema Systems Inc, 49237
Temco, 49238
Tempco Electric Heater Corporation, 49239
Templar Food Products, 49240
Templock Corporation, 49241
Tenneco Specialty Packaging, 49244
Terphane Inc, 49250
Tew Manufacturing Corp, 49263
Texas Halal Corporation, 49266
Textile Buff & Wheel, 49270
Tharo Systems Inc, 49274
THE Corporation, 49132
The Long Life Beverage Company, 49293
The Scoular Company/TSC Container Freight, 49300
Theochem Laboratories Inc, 49304
Therm-Tec Inc, 49306
Therma Kleen, 49307
Thermo Detection, 49310
Thermodyne International LTD, 49315
Theta Sciences, 49318
Thiel Cheese & Ingredients, 49319
Thiele Engineering Company, 49320
Thirs-Tea Corp, 49322
Thomas L. Green & Company, 49324
Thomas Precision, Inc., 49326
Thorn Smith Laboratories, 49333
Tieco-Unadilla Corporation, 49343
Timely Signs Inc, 49354
Tindall Packaging, 49357
Tipper Tie Inc, 49361
TLB Corporation, 49134
TNA Packaging Solutions, 49136
Tni Packaging Inc, 49365
Todd's, 49369
Todhunter Foods, 49373
Tomsed Corporation, 49384
Tooterville Trolley Company, 49390
Toromont Process Systems, 49400
Torre Products Co Inc, 49403
Toscarora, 49406
Townfood Equipment Corp, 49416
Tradelink 49422
Traex, 49425
Traitech Industries, 49426
Transmundo Company, 49436
Tranter INC, 49439
Travelon, 49441
TRC, 49140
Tree Ripe Products, 49444
Treehouse Farms, 49445
Trefethen Family Vineyards, 49446
Tri-Pak Machinery Inc, 49452
Tri-Seal, 49453
Tri-Tronics, 49458
Tribest Corp, 49463
Tribology Tech Lube, 49464
Trident Seafoods Corp, 49467

Tridyne Process Systems, 49469
Trilogy Essential Ingredients, 49470
Triple Leaf Tea Inc, 49482
TRITEN Corporation, 49142
Trojan Inc, 49489
Tropical Cheese, 49491
Tropical Illusions, 49494
Troy Lighting, 49500
True Food Service Equipment, Inc., 49507
TruHeat Corporation, 49504
TSA Griddle Systems, 49143
Tundra Wild Rice, 49529
Turbo Refrigerating Company, 49531
Tuthill Vacuum & Blower Systems, 49539
Tyco Fire Protection Products, 49550
Tyson Foods Inc., 49554
Ultrafilter, 49587
Unarco Industries LLC, 49591
Ungerer & Co, 49599
Unimove LLC, 49607
Union, 49608
Union Confectionery Machinery, 49609
Union Industries, 49612
Uniplast Films, 49718
United Canadian Malt, 49629
United Electric Controls Co, 49633
United Floor Machine Co, 49636
United International Indstrs, 49639
United Performance Metals, 49644
United Ribtype Co, 49646
United Salt Corp, 49647
United Steel Products Company, 49653
United Textile Distribution, 49655
Unitherm Food System, 49659
UniTrak Corporation, 49600
Universal Die & Stampings, 49664
Universal Jet Industries, 49668
Universal Marketing, 49669
Urbani Truffles, 49680
Urschel Laboratories, 49682
US Distilled Products Co, 49565
US Filter Dewatering Systems, 49566
US Food Products, 49567
US Marketing Company, 49571
Utica Cutlery Co, 49686
V C 999 Packaging Systems, 49689
V-Ram Solids, 49690
Vacuum Barrier Corp, 49709
Valentine Enterprises Inc, 49713
Valley Craft Inc, 49718
Valley Fig Growers, 49719
Van Air Systems, 49726
Vanderburgh & Company, 49736
Vanguard Technology Inc, 49737
Vanmark Equipment, 49740
Variant, 49744
Varimixer North America, 49747
Vauxhall Foods, 49752
Vector Corp, 49753
Vector Technologies, 49754
Venner International Products, 49764
Venture Measurement Co LLC, 49769
Versailles Lighting, 49782
Vessey & Co Inc, 49787
Viatec, 49791
Victoria Fine Foods, 49799
Victoria Porcelain, 49800
Videojet Technologies Inc, 49801
VIFAN Canada, 49697
Vigo Importing Co, 49807
Vilter Manufacturing Corporation, 49813
VIP Foods, 49698
Virginia Dare Extract Co, 49827
Visual Planning Corp, 49836
Volckening Inc, 49855
Vollrath Co LLC, 49858
Vorti-Siv, 49861
Vortron Smokehouse/Ovens, 49862
VT Industries Inc, 49703
VT Kidron, 49704
Vulcan Industries, 49867
Vyse Gelatin Co, 49868
W.G. Durant Corporation, 49875
Waddington North America, 49912

Wade Manufacturing Company, 49913
Walco, 49922
Walker Stainless Equipment Co, 49928
Walle Corp, 49933
Waltkoch Limited, 49939
Wapsie Creamery, 49945
Waring Products, 49950
Warwick Manufacturing & Equip, 49954
Water & Power Technologies, 49964
Water Sciences Services, Inc., 49966
Wayne Combustion Systems, 49977
Wayne Engineering, 49978
Wayne Farms LLC., 49979
Weaver Popcorn Co Inc, 49981
Weavewood, Inc., 49982
WEBB-Stiles Co, 49884
Webeco Foods, 49985
Weber Packaging Solutions Inc, 49986
Weinberg Foods, 49997
Weiss Instruments Inc, 50002
Welch Holme & Clark Co, 50006
Welliver Metal Products Corporation, 50011
Wells Enterprises Inc., 50012
Wells Manufacturing Company, 50013
West Carrollton Parchment Company, 50023
West India Trading Company, 50029
West Rock, 50033
Westvaco Corporation, 50052
Wexxar Corporation, 50059
Whallon Machinery Inc, 50061
White House Foods, 50071
White Oaks Frozen Foods, 50074
White Rock Products Corp, 50076
White Toque, 50077
Whole Herb Co, 50087
Wholesome!, 50088
Wilch Manufacturing, 50094
Wild Rice Exchange, 50096
Wilder Manufacturing Company, 50098
Wileman Brothers & Elliott Inc, 50099
Wilkins Rogers Inc, 50105
Willamette Valley Walnuts, 50110
Williamson & Co, 50115
Willing Group, 50116
Wilton Armetale, 50120
Windsor Industries Inc, 50123
Windsor Wax Co Inc, 50124
Wine Chillers of California, 50125
Wine Well Chiller Co, 50126
Winekeeper, 50128
Winmix/Natural Care Products, 50132
Winning Solutions Inc, 50133
Wire Belt Co Of America, 50138
Wisconsin Aluminum Foundry Co, 50143
Wisconsin Whey International, 50149
Wishbone Utensil Tableware Line, 50150
Wittco Foodservice Equipment, 50151
Wittemann Company, 50154
Wolf Company, 50160
Wolfson Casing Corp, 50161
Wood Stone Corp, 50167
Woodstock Plastics Co Inc, 50172
Worksman 800 Buy Cart, 50179
World Cheese Inc, 50181
World Spice, 50192
World Water Works, 50195
World Wide Safe Brokers, 50197
Wornick Company, 50202
Wyssmont Co Inc, 50212
Xcel Tower Controls, 50217
Xtreme Beverages, LLC, 50220
Yakima Wire Works, 50228
Yamato Corporation, 50230
Yardney Water Management Syst, 50232
Yargus Manufacturing Inc, 50233
Yohay Baking Co, 50241
York Saw & Knife, 50242
Your Place Menu Systems, 50248
Zachary Confections Inc, 50254
ZAK Designs Inc, 50253
Zebra Technologies Corporation, 50261
Zed Industries, 50262
Zel R. Kahn & Sons, 50265
Zener America, 50268

Zenith Specialty Bag Co, 50271
Zenobia Co, 50272
Zepf Technologies, 50275

South Pacific

A-1 Refrigeration Co, 41501
Diamond Bakery Co LTD, 43612
Reotemp Instrument Corp, 48063

Spain

Brown Produce Company, 42609
Davron Technologies Inc, 43517
W.Y. International, 49877
Wallace Grain & Pea Company, 49932

Switzerland

Ayush Herbs Inc, 42181
Gesco ENR, 44561
Mild Bill's Spices, 46621

Tahiti

Crane & Crane Inc, 43320

Taiwan

Wisconsin Whey International, 50149

Trinidad

Weil's Food Processing, 49995

USA

A&A Marine & Drydock Company, 41490
A&M Process Equipment, 41498
Advanced Equipment, 41690
Aerowerks, 41707
Agrocan, 41727
Agropur, 41728
Alati-Caserta Desserts, 41763
Alimentaire Whyte's Inc, 41786
American LEWA, 41898
Amrita Snacks, 41957
Angry Orchard Cider Company, LLC, 41988
Applewood Winery, 42013
Arcobaleno Pasta Machines, 42031
Atlantic Chemicals Trading, 42110
Atlantic Fish Specialties, 42112
Atlas Match Company, 42125
Avestin, 42169
Bad Seed Cider Company, LLC, 42228
Baker's Point Fisheries, 42242
Barber's Farm Distillery LLC, 42276
Beetroot Delights, 42348
Bericap North America, Inc., 42385
Birch Street Seafoods, 42453
Bonduelle North America, 42518
Brasserie Brasel Brewery, 42561
Brom Food Group, 42592
Brooklyn Cider House, 42595
Bull and Barrel Brewpub, 42635
Calkins & Burke, 42760
Canada Bread Co, Ltd, 42779
Canada Cutlery Inc., 42780
Canadian Mist Distillers, 42784
Cardinal Meat Specialists, 42815
Carrie's Chocolates, 42848
Carriere Foods Inc, 42851
Casey Fisheries, 42870
Catskill Brewery, 42882
Cattle Boyz Foods, 42885
Centennial Food Corporation, 42902
Chases Lobster Pound, 42943
Chocolaterie Bernard Callebaut, 43016
Christy Wild Blueberry Farms, 43028
CHS Sunprairie, 42698
Citadelle Maple Syrup Producers' Cooperative, 43046
Coby's Cookies, 43112
Convay Systems, 43242
Cordon Bleu International, 43269
Crevettes Du Nord, 43346
Crosby Molasses Company, 43356
Crown Custom Metal Spinning, 43365

Crown Verity, 43377
CTC Manufacturing, 42715
CTK Plastics, 42716
Culinary Depot, 43394
Cupper's Coffee Company, 43407
Custom Diamond Intl., 43415
D Waybret & Sons Fisheries, 43442
Davis Strait Fisheries, 43514
DB Kenney Fisheries, 43450
Decartes Systems Group, 43543
Dieffenbach's Potato Chips, 43627
Dimpflmeier Bakery, 43631
Dipix Technologies, 43635
Eastern Sea Products, 43811
Edmonton Potato Growers, 43863
Edson Packaging Machinery, 43866
El Peto Products, 43877
Eleanor's Best LLC, 43885
Elite Forming Design Solutions, 43893
Ellehammer Industries, 43897
Ellett Industries, 43899
Ellison Milling Company, 43904
Elmo Rietschle - A Gardner Denver Product, 43908
Enterprises Pates et Croutes, 43960
Enzamar, 43964
Exeter Produce, 44045
Extrutech Plastics Inc, 44054
Famco Automatic Sausage Linkers, 44107
Favorite Foods, 44122
Feature Foods, 44127
Finding Home Farms, 44173
Flavouressence Products, 44218
France Delices, 44332
FRC Systems International, 44081
Frobisher Industries, 44376
Furgale Industries Ltd., 44402
Gardner Denver Inc., 44474
Gea Intec, Llc, 44503
Gebo Conveyors, Consultants & Systems, 44505
Glopak, 44616
Golden Town Apple Products, 44645
Grain Process Enterprises Ltd., 44686
Grandview Farms, 44694
Graphic Apparel, 44697
Great Glacier Salmon, 44710
Greaves Jams & Marmalades, 44726
GS Dunn & Company, 44438
Gumpert's Canada, 44782
H&K Packers Company, 44802
H.J. Jones & Sons, 44809
Handtmann Inc, 44858
Harpak-ULMA Packaging LLC, 44902
High Liner Foods Inc., 45015
Highland Fisheries, 45017
Highwood Distillers, 45019
Howson Mills, 45106
Hudson Valley Malt, 45121
I. Deveau Fisheries LTD, 45156
Imperial Salmon House, 45224
Innova Envelopes, 45284
Inshore Fisheries, 45298
International Enterprises, 45339
IPL Plastics, 45178
J.E. Roy, 45440
J.P. Sunrise Bakery, 45446
Jakeman's Maple Products, 45481
Jet Set Sam, 45524
Jim Scharf Holdings, 45532
Keegan Ales, 45682
Kelley Company, 45688
King Cole Ducks Limited, 45740
Kisco Manufacturing, 45758
Kohler Industries Inc, 45787
Kuhlmann's Market Gardens & Greenhouses, 45826
Kurtz Orchards Farms, 45828
L&C Fisheries, 45841
La Brasserie McAuslan Brewing, 45871
La Societe, 45878
Label Systems, 45886
Lakeport Brewing Corporation, 45903
Lallemand, 45911
Laval Paper Box, 45951

Lenchner Bakery, 45992
Lentia Enterprises Ltd., 45995
Les Aliments Livabec Foods, 46001
Les Aliments Ramico Foods, 46002
Les Industries Touch Inc, 46004
Les Viandes du Breton, 46005
Lift Rite, 46033
Limberis Seafood Processing, 46046
Lovebiotics LLC, 46132
Lyo-San, 46173
Machem Industries, 46226
Mama Amy's Quality Foods, 46281
Mar-Con Wire Belt, 46311
Marie F, 46312
Maselli Measurements Inc, 46390
Matiss, 46410
Mayekawa USA, Inc., 46431
Mba Suppliers Inc., 46436
Millerbernd Systems, 46632
MLG Enterprises Ltd., 46214
Money's Mushrooms, 46705
Monster Core, 46711
Moosehead Breweries Ltd., 46724
Mortimer's Fine Foods, 46740
Mother Parker's Tea & Coffee, 46746
Nahmias et Fils, 46834
Naleway Foods, 46835
Newell Lobsters, 46998
Nor-Cliff Farms, 47047
Norac Technologies, 47049
North Bay Fisherman's Cooperative, 47068
North Taste Flavourings, 47079
Nustef Foods, 47137
O'Brien Installations, 47162
Ontario Glove and Safety Products, 47243
Osso Good, LLC, 47295
Overseas Food Trading, 47306
Palme d'Or, 47412
Papertech, 47438
Par-Pak, 47441
Pasta Quistini, 47483
Patty Palace Foods, 47492
Pearson's Berry Farm, 47510
Pepe's Mexican Restaurant, 47543
Pestano Foods, 47562
Piller's Fine Foods, 47612
Polytainers, 47669
Priority One Packaging, 47759
Produits Alimentaire, 47789
Produits Belle Baie, 47790
Pure Life Organic Foods, 47842
Purity Factories, 47849
QMS International, Inc., 47865
QualiGourmet, 47872
Quality Containers, 47878
Real Coconut Co. Inc., The, 47990
Red Hat Cooperative, 47998
Reinhart Foods, 48042
Rito Mints, 48112
Rogers' Chocolates Ltd, 48157
Ropak, 48177
Royce Corp, 48229
Rudolph's Specialty Bakery, 48241
Satin Fine Foods, 48396
Saxby Foods, 48407
Select Food Products, 48497
Service Packing Company, 48538
Shippers Supply, 48598
Smith Packaging, 48701
Sneaky Chef Foods, The, 48717
Snyder Foods, 48726
Sobaya, 48731
ST Restaurant Supplies, 48295
Stanpac, Inc., 48886
Starview Packaging Machinery, 48902
Strathroy Foods, 48977
Strub Pickles, 48989
Sun-Brite Canning, 49017
Sunlike Juice, 49025
T&S Blow Molding, 49119
Tantos Foods International, 49176
Tech-Roll Inc, 49210
Terra Ingredients LLC, 49251
Terra Origin, Inc., 49252

Teti Bakery, 49260
Teton Waters Ranch LLC, 49262
That's How We Roll, 49275
The Amazing Chickpea, 49276
The Ardent Homesteader, 49277
The Art of Broth, LLC, 49278
The Coconut Cooperative, LLC, 49284
The Coromega Company, 49285
The Good Crisp Company, 49287
The Honest Stand, 49288
The Lancaster Food Company, 49291
The Little Kernel, 49292
The Naked Edge, LLC, 49295
The Real Co, 49299
The Sola Company, 49301
The Tea Spot, Inc., 49302
This Bar Saves Lives, LLC, 49323
Thoughtful Food, 49335
Three Trees Almondmilk, 49337
ThreeWorks Snacks, 49338
Thunderbird Real Food Bar, 49341
Tierra Farm, 49345
Tiesta Tea, 49346
Tillamook Country Smoker, 49350
Tilly Industries, 49352
Toom Dips, 49389
Top Tier Foods Inc., 49394
Trevor Owen Limited, 49449
Tribali Foods, 49461
Trimen Foodservice Equipment, 49471
Trojan Commercial Furniture Inc., 49488
Tropical Acai LLC, 49490
Tropical Link Canada Ltd., 49495
Tru Fru, LLC, 49501
Truth Bar LLC, 49515
Tu Me Beverage Company, 49519
Tucson Tamale Company, 49525
Turveda, 49537
Ultima Health Products Inc., 49582
Uncle Dougie's, 49593
Uncle Matt's Organic, 49596
Unique Beverage Company, 49615
United With Earth, 49658
UnReal Brands, 49590
Uptime Energy, Inc., 49678
V C 999 Packaging Systems, 49689
Valvinox, 49725
Vana Life Foods, 49734
Vauxhall Foods, 49752
Verday, 49774
Verde Farms, LLC, 49775
Verlasso, 49776
VIFAN Canada, 49697
Violife, 49825
Virgin Raw Foods LLC, 49826
Vital Proteins LLC, 49841
Vitality Works, 49842
Vivoo, 49851
Warwick Valley Winery & Distillery, 49955
Weil's Food Processing, 49995
Wepackit, 50017
West Thomas Partners, LLC, 50034
Whistler Brewing Company, 50068
Whitecliff Vineyard & Winery, 50079
Wild Thyme Cottage Products, 50097
Winpak Technologies, 50135
Wisconsin Specialty Protein, 50147
Workman Packaging Inc., 50177
WR Key, 49892

United Kingdom

Curry King Corporation, 43410
Heartland Gourmet LLC, 44961
HH Dobbins Inc, 44819
Labatt Brewing Company, 45881
Omcan Manufacturing & Distributing Company, 47218
Pete's Brewing Company, 47563
Priority Plastics Inc, 47760
Shipyard Brewing Co, 48599

Venezuela

Wallace Grain & Pea Company, 49932

Virgin Islands

Conway Import Co Inc, 43251
Empresas La Famosa, 43933
Good-O-Beverages Inc, 44656
Schmidt Progressive, 48430

West Indies

B. Terfloth & Company, 42194
Gaudet & Ouellette, 44496
Nutritech Corporation, 47152
Sinclair Trading, 48671

Western Europe

Peace Mountain Natural Beverages, 47503
Univar USA, 49661

Worldwide

21st Century Products, Inc., 41471
A J Antunes & Co, 41482
A T Ferrell Co Inc, 41486
A-1 Booth Manufacturing, 41500
A.B. Sealer, Inc., 41509
A.D. Joslin Manufacturing Company, 41511
A.K. Robins, 41514
A.O. Smith Water Products Company, 41517
A1 Tablecloth Co, 41520
Aaburco Inc, 41597
Aaladin Industries Inc, 41599
AAMD, 41522
Aaron Equipment Co Div Areco, 41600
AB InBev, 41524
Abanaki Corp, 41602
ABB, 41525
Abco International, 41607
Abco Products, 41608
Acadian Seaplants, 41618
Access Solutions, 41620
Accu-Sort Systems, 41623
Ace Co Precision Mfg, 41627
Ace Engineering Company, 41629
Ace Technical Plastics Inc, 41632
ACMA/GD, 41536
Acme Sponge & Chamois Co Inc, 41642
Acorto, 41646
Acrison Inc, 41650
Acromag Inc., 41651
Action Technology, 41656
Actionpac Scales Automation, 41657
Acumen Data Systems Inc, 41659
Adamatic, 41663
Adhesive Applications, 41671
ADM Wild Flavors & Specialty, 41542
ADSI Inc, 41543
Advance Energy Technologies, 41682
Advance Fittings Corp, 41683
Advance Technology Corp, 41686
Advanced Control Technologies, 41687
Advantage Puck Technologies, 41698
Aerovent Co, 41706
AFF International, 41547
AFL Industries, 41548
Age International Inc, 41713
Agrana Fruit US Inc, 41717
AgraWest Foods, 41716
Agricore United, 41723
Agtron Inc, 41730
Air Savers Inc, 41736
Airfloat LLC, 41738
Airosol Co Inc, 41741
Airsan Corp, 41742
Alabama Bag Co Inc, 41753
Aladdin Bakers, 41755
Alaska Smokehouse, 41761
Alcoa - Massena Operations, 41770
Alfa Laval Ashbrook Simon-Hartley, 41777
Alfonso Gourmet Pasta, 41780
Algene Marking Equipment Company, 41782
Alger Creations, 41783

Export Region / Worldwide

Ali Group, 41785
Aline Heat Seal Corporation, 41787
Aliotti Wholesale Fish Company, 41788
Alkazone/Better Health Lab, 41791
All Packaging Machinery Corp, 41798
All Star Carts & Vehicles, 41802
Alldrin Brothers, 41806
Allen Signs Co, 41815
Allendale Cork Company, 41816
Alloyd Brands, 41825
Aloe'Ha Drink Products, 41835
Aloha Distillers, 41837
Alouf Plastics, 41839
ALP Lighting & Ceiling Products, 41559
Altech Packaging Company, 41845
Altek Co, 41846
Alumaworks, 41852
AM-Mac, 41562
Amco Metals Indl, 41863
Ameri Candy, 41865
American Containers Inc, 41874
American Coolair Corp, 41875
American Extrusion Intl, 41881
American Food Equipment, 41886
American Food Equipment Company, 41887
American Foods Group LLC, 41889
American Identity, 41893
American Packaging Machinery, 41910
American Panel Corp, 41911
American Pop Corn Co, 41913
American Renolit Corp LA, 41916
American Seafoods, 41920
American Star Cork Company, 41923
Amerivacs, 41937
Ametek, 41943
AMETEK National Controls Corp, 41565
AMF Bakery Systems Corp, 41566
Amick Farms LLC, 41944
Amoretti, 41951
Ampak, 41952
Ampco Pumps Co Inc, 41954
AMSECO, 41569
AMT Labs Inc, 41571
Amtekco, 41960
Analytical Development, 41966
Anchor Crane & Hoist Service Company, 41969
Anchor Hocking Operating Co, 41970
Andco Environmental Processes, 41972
Anderson Erickson Dairy, 41975, 41976
Anderson Machine Sales, 41978
Anderson Tool & Engineering Company, 41980
Andrew Peller Limited, 41984
Anita's Mexican Foods Corporation, 41992
Ann Arbor Computer, 41995
Anton Caratan & Son, 41999
ANVER Corporation, 41573
Apache Stainless Equipment, 42003
Apex Machine Company, 42005
Apex Packing & Rubber Co, 42006
APM, 41578
Apogee Translite Inc, 42007
Applewood Orchards Inc, 42012
Applied Thermal Technologies, 42017
APV Americas, 41580
Aquathin Corporation, 42023
Archon Industries Inc, 42029
Arctic Air, 42032
Arise & Shine Herbal Products, 42043
Armanino Foods of Distinction, 42053
Armstrong Hot Water, 42056
Arrow Plastic Mfg Co, 42068
Arrowac Fisheries, 42070
Art-Phyl Creations, 42073
Artex International, 42075
Arthur G Russell Co Inc, 42076
Artkraft Strauss LLC, 42080
Ashworth Bros Inc, 42082
Assembly Technology & Test, 42088
Associated Fruit Company, 42089
Associated Packaging Equipment Corporation, 42090
Associated Products Inc, 42091

Astoria General Espresso, 42093
Astra Manufacturing Inc, 42094
At-Your-Svc Software Inc, 42098
Athena Controls Inc, 42101
ATI, 41589
Atlantic Capes Fisheries, 42109
Atlantis Industries Inc, 42120
Atlas Minerals & Chemicals Inc, 42127
ATM Corporation, 41590
ATOFINA Chemicals, 41591
Auger Fab, 42136
Automated Business Products, 42149
Automatic Handling Int, 42153
Automatic Products, 42154
Automatic Specialties Inc, 42156
Autoprod, 42159
Autoquip Corp, 42160
Avery Weigh-Tronix LLC, 42168
Avon Tape, 42172
Aw Sheepscot Holding Co Inc, 42173
Axiohm USA, 42180
Azuma Foods Intl Inc USA, 42185
Azz/R-A-L, 42187
B & P Process Equipment, 42188
B.A.G. Corporation, 42194
B.C. Tree Fruits Limited, 42197
Babcock & Wilcox Power Generation Group, 42218
Bacon America, 42227
Badia Spices Inc., 42230
Bag Company, 42231
Baker's Coconut, 42241
Balboa Dessert Co Inc, 42250
Ballantine Produce Company, 42254
Banner Equipment Co, 42268
Bar Maid Corp, 42271
Barn Furniture Mart, 42284
Bartek Ingredients, Inc., 42290
Bascom Family Farms Inc, 42293
Baublys Control Laser, 42303
Bay Valley Foods, 42310
Bayard Kurth Company, 42311
BBQ Pits by Klose, 42202
Beam Industries, 42319
Beaumont Rice Mills, 42328
Bedemco Inc, 42337
Beehive/Provisur Technologies, 42344
Behnke Lubricants/JAX, 42349
Bella Coola Fisheries, 42361
Belly Treats, Inc., 42366
Belt Technologies Inc, 42370
Benko Products, 42376
Bentley Instruments Inc, 42379
Berberian Nut Company, 42380
Berg Chilling Systems, 42381
Berje, 42387
Berlekamp Plastics Inc, 42389
Bernard Food Industries Inc, 42393
Berner International Corp, 42394
Bert Manufacturing, 42397
Bertek Systems Inc, 42398
Bestech Inc, 42413
Bethel Engineering & Equipment Inc, 42416
Better Living Products, 42419
Beverage Air, 42423
Bio Zapp Laboratories, 42442
Biolog Inc, 42448
Biomerieux Inc, 42449
Bionova Produce, 42450
Biotest Diagnostics Corporation, 42451
Birkholm's Solvang Bakery, 42456
Black Brothers, 42465
Blakeslee, Inc., 42469
Blancett, 42470
Blanche P. Field, LLC, 42471
BLH Electronics, 42210
Blodgett Co, 42478
Blodgett Corp, 42479
Blodgett Oven Co, 42480
Blommer Chocolate Co, 42481
Blower Application Co Inc, 42483
Blundell Seafoods, 42501
Bmh Equipment Inc, 42502
BNW Industries, 42212
Boardman Molded Products Inc, 42503

Boca Bagelworks, 42506
Bohn & Dawson, 42510
Bolzoni Auramo, 42514
Boston Beer Co Inc., 42528
Boston Seafarms, 42532
Boston's Best Coffee Roasters, 42533
Botanical Products, 42534
Botsford Fisheries, 42535
Bouchard Family Farm, 42536
Boundary Fish Company, 42537
Bouras Mop Manufacturing Company, 42538
Bowers Process Equipment, 42539
Bradley Lifting, 42548
Brady Enterprises Inc, 42550
Brakebush Brothers, 42553
Branson Ultrasonics Corp, 42559
Brass Smith, 42560
Bridge Machine Company, 42579
Brooklace, 42594
Brooks Instrument LLC, 42597
Brookside Foods, 42599
Brown Manufacturing Company, 42608
Brown's Sign & Screen Printing, 42610
Brulin & Company, 42614
Brush Research Mfg Co Inc, 42616
Brute Fabricators, 42617
Bryan Boilers, 42619
Buckeye International, 42623
Buckhorn Inc, 42626
Bullet Guard Corporation, 42636
Bunge North America Inc., 42638
Bunn-O-Matic Corp, 42640
Burnette Foods, 42649
Bush Refrigeration Inc, 42652
Butter Buds Food Ingredients, 42655
C & F Foods Inc, 42662
C & K Machine Co, 42663
C E Rogers Co, 42666
C H Babb Co Inc, 42669
C&H Store Equipment Company, 42677
C.L. Deveau & Son, 42685
Caddy Corporation of America, 42725
Cal Trading Company, 42738
Cal-Grown Nut Company, 42739
California Custom Foods, 42750
California Independent Almond Growers, 42753
California Saw & Knife Works, 42757
Calmar, 42761
Caloritech, 42762
Cam Spray, 42764
Cambro Manufacturing Co, 42767
Camellia Beans, 42768
Cameron Intl. Corp., 42772
Camerons Brewing Co., 42773
Candy Flowers, 42788
Candy Mountain Sweets & Treats, 42790
Cantech Industries Inc, 42795
Capital Plastics, 42798
Cappo Drinks, 42802
Cappola Foods, 42803
Capriccio, 42806
Caravan Packaging Inc, 42812
Cardinal Scale Mfg Co, 42818
Care Controls, Inc., 42819
Carhoff Company, 42823
Carlota Foods International, 42835
Carnes Company, 42837
Carrier Corp, 42849
Carroll Co, 42852
Carroll Manufacturing International, 42853
Carron Net Co Inc, 42854
Carson Manufacturing Company, 42856
Carter Products, 42857
Carter-Day International Inc, 42858
Carter-Hoffmann LLC, 42859
Casa Herrera, 42864
Cascadian Farm Inc, 42868
Casey's Seafood Inc, 42871
Catalyst International, 42878
Catfish Wholesale, 42881
Cawley Co, 42890
Cayne Industrial Sales Corp, 42892
CDI Service & Mfg Inc, 42692

CEA Instrument Inc, 42693
Ceilcote Air Pollution Control, 42896
Cellucap Manufacturing Co, 42901
CEM Corporation, 42694
Centflor Manufacturing Co, 42904
Cereal Food Processors Inc, 42916
Challenge Dairy Products, Inc., 42918
Champion Industries Inc, 42920
Champion Nutrition Inc, 42921
Champion Plastics, 42922
Champion Trading Corporation, 42923
Charles Beck Machine Corporation, 42929
Charles H Baldwin & Sons, 42932
Charm Sciences Inc, 42936
Chart Industries Inc, 42938
Checker Machine, 42946
Chem-Tainer Industries Inc, 42961
Cherbogue Fisheries, 42970
Chester Hoist, 42976
Chester Inc Information, 42977
Chester-Jensen Co., Inc., 42980
Chicago Meat Authority Inc, 42988
Chickasaw Trading Company, 42991
Chief Industries, 42994
Chil-Con Products, 42996
Chile Guy, 42997
China Lenox Incorporated, 43001
Chiquita Brands LLC., 43008
Christy Industries Inc, 43026
Christy Machine Co, 43027
Chromalox, 43029
Chuppa Knife Manufacturing, 43030
Cin-Made Packaging Group, 43034
Cinelli Esperia, 43037
Cinnabar Specialty Foods Inc, 43038
Citra-Tech, 43047
City Brewing Company, 43053
CL&D Graphics, 42703
Clamco Corporation, 43057
Clearly Canadian Beverage Corporation, 43075
Clearwater Paper Corporation, 43079
Cleland Manufacturing Company, 43081
Cleland Sales Corp, 43082
Cleveland Menu Printing, 43084
Cleveland Range, 43086
Cleveland Wire Cloth & Mfg Co, 43088
Climate Master Inc, 43091
Cloud Inc, 43097
Cma Dishmachines, 43102
CMT, 42704
Coast Scientific, 43104
Coast Seafoods Company, 43105
Cobatco, 43109
Cober Electronics, Inc., 43110
Coco Lopez Inc, 43114
Codema, 43115
Cold Jet, LLC, 43126
Colin Ingram, 43133
Collins & Aikman, 43135
Colorcon, 43145
Columbus McKinnon Corporation, 43152
Comeau's Seafoods, 43156
Command Communications, 43157
Commercial Furniture Group Inc, 43162
Commercial Lighting Design, 43163
Commercial Manufacturing, 43164
Commercial Refrigeration Service, Inc., 43165
Common Folk Farm, 43169
Compactors Inc, 43174
Complete Packaging & Shipping, 43176
Compliance Control Inc, 43177
Component Hardware Group Inc, 43178
Computer Controlled Machines, 43181
Conagra Foodservice, 43192
Conflex, Inc., 43198
Connell International Company, 43203
Constantia Colmar, 43212
Continental Grain Company, 43225
Continental Identification, 43226
Continental Mills Inc, 43228
Control Module, 43239
Control Pak Intl, 43240
Conveyor Accessories, 43246

Export Region / Worldwide

Convoy, 43250
Conwed Global Netting Sltns, 43252
CookTek, 43254
Cooling Products Inc, 43260
Corby Hall, 43268
Cornelius, 43277
Cosco Home & Office Products, 43288
Costco Wholesale Corporation, 43295
Couch & Philippi, 43298
Country Butcher Shop, 43301
Cove Four, 43310
COVERIS, 42706
Cozzini LLC, 43313
CP Kelco, 42707
CPM Roskamp Champion, 42709
CPM Wolverine Proctor LLC, 42710
Crain Ranch, 43316
Crandall Filling Machinery, 43319
Crc Industries Inc, 43324
Crea Fill Fibers Corp, 43325
Creative Essentials, 43329
Creative Foam Corp, 43330
Creative Forming, 43331
Creative Packaging Corporation, 43333
Creative Techniques, 43334
Creegan Animation Company, 43337
Cresthill Industries, 43344
Criders Poultry, 43348
Crispy Lite, 43349
Croda Inc, 43353
Crookston Bean, 43355
Crown Battery Mfg, 43361
Crown Equipment Corp., 43366
Crown Holdings, Inc., 43368
Crown Metal Manufacturing Company, 43370
Crown Metal Mfg Co, 43371
Crown Tonka Walk-Ins, 43376
Crystal Creative Products, 43383
Crystal-Flex Packaging Corporation, 43389
Cube Plastics, 43391
Cumberland Packing Corp, 43403
Curtis Packaging, 43411
Curtis Ward Company, 43412
Curwood Specialty Films, 43413
Custom Food Machinery, 43416
Custom Sales & Svc Inc, 43421
CUTCO Corp, 42717
Cutrite Company, 43427
Cyanotech Corp, 43428
Cyclamen Collection, 43430
Cyrk, 43433
D & W Fine Pack, 43437
D D Williamson & Co Inc, 43439
D'Lights, 43446
Dade Engineering, 43466
Dairy State Foods Inc, 43473
Daley Brothers ltd., 43483
Dallas Group of America Inc, 43484
Darcor Casters, 43499
Dare Foods, 43500
Dashco, 43506
David's Cookies, 43510
Davis & Small Decor, 43513
Day & Ross Transportation Group, 43519
Dayton Bag & Burlap Co, 43525
De Bruyn Produce Company, 43527
De Leone Corp, 43531
Dedert Corporation, 43545
Del Monte Foods Inc., 43558
Del Monte Fresh Produce Inc., 43559
Delavan Spray Technologies, 43562
Delavan-Delta, 43563
Delfin Design & Mfg, 43567
Dema Engineering Co, 43581
Demag Cranes & Components Corp, 43583
Dempster Systems, 43584
Derco Foods Intl, 43587
Deshazo Crane Company, 43591
Destileria Serralles Inc, 43597
Dewied International Inc, 43603
Dexter Russell Inc, 43604
DH/Sureflow, 43455
Diablo Chemical, 43609

Diageo Canada Inc., 43610
Diamond Automation, 43611
Diamond Chemical Co Inc, 43614
Diamond Machining Technology, 43618
Dickey Manufacturing Company, 43624
DiLeo Brothers, 43607
Direct Fire Technical, 43637
Dispense Rite, 43641
Display Studios Inc, 43642
Diversified Capping Equipment, 43649
Diversified Lighting Diffusers Inc, 43650
Diversified Metal Engineering, 43651
Dixie Canner Machine Shop, 43652
DLX Industries, 43457
DNE World Fruit Sales, 43459
Do-It Corp, 43656
Dole Refrigerating Co, 43660
Donaldson Co Inc, 43666
Donoco Industries, 43668
Dorina So-Good Inc, 43672
Dorset Fisheries, 43673
Doucette Industries, 43678
Dove Screen Printing Co, 43681
Dover Chemical Corp, 43682
Dow Packaging, 43687
Doyon Equipment, 43690
Dr. Christopher's Herbal Supplements, 43692
Draper Valley Farms, 43699
Dreaco Products, 43701
Drehmann Paving & Flooring Company, 43703
Driall Inc, 43707
Drum-Mates Inc., 43711
DSW Converting Knives, 43462
DT Industrials, 43463
Duplex Mill & Mfg Co, 43724
DuPont Nutrition & Biosciences, 43713
Dupps Co, 43725
Dur-Able Aluminum Corporation, 43726
Durastill Export Inc, 43737
Dutchess Bakers' Machinery Co, 43743
Dutro Co, 43744
Dwyer Instruments Inc, 43745
Dynynstyl, 43754
E-Lite Technologies, 43762
E. Gagnon & Fils, 43766
E.F. Lane & Son, 43768
Eagle Foodservice Equipment, 43794
Eagle Group, 43795
Eagleware Manufacturing, 43798
Eastman Chemical Co, 43816
Eatem Foods Co, 43818
Eaton Filtration, LLC, 43820
EB Eddy Paper, 43771
Eclipse Innovative Ther mal Solutions, 43828
Eco-Bag Products, 43832
Ecolo Odor Control Systems Worldwide, 43835
Ecological Technologies, 43837
Econo Frost Night Covers, 43838
Econocorp Inc, 43839
Ederback Corporation, 43852
Edgar A Weber & Co, 43853
Edge Manufacturing, 43854
Edlong Corporation, 43860
Edlund Co, 43861
EGS Electrical Group, 43777
Eisenmann Corp USA, 43873
EIT, 43779
EKATO Corporation, 43780
El Dorado Packaging Inc, 43875
Elan Vanilla Co, 43880
Electrodex, 43889
Electronic Weighing Systems, 43890
ELF Machinery, 43781
Elliott-Williams Company, 43903
Elmer Chocolate®, 43906
Elmo Rietschle - A Gardner Denver Product, 43908
Elmwood Sensors, 43909
Elopak Americas, 43911
Elwell Parker, 43912
Elwood International Inc, 43913
Elwood Safety Company, 43914

Embassy Flavours Ltd., 43915
Emery Smith Fisheries Limited, 43923
Emery Thompson Machine &Supply Company, 43925
Emkay Trading Corporation, 43927
Encore Plastics, 43938
Energy Sciences Inc, 43944
Energymaster, 43945
Engraving Services Co., 43951
Enstrom Candies, Inc., 43957
EPCO, 43786
Epcon Industrial Systems, 43966
Ertelalsop, 43703
ESD Waste2water Inc, 43789
Esha Research, 43985
ET International Technologies, 43791
Eurex International, 44000
Evergreen Packaging, 44030
Exceldor Cooperative, 44040
Excello Machine Co Inc, 44042
Exeter Ivanhoe Citrus Assn, 44044
Extrutech Plastics Inc, 44054
F & A Fabricating Inc, 44056
F B Wright Co, 44058
F C C, 44060
F.B. Pease Company, 44066
F.M. Corporation, 44068
F.P. Smith Wire Cloth Company, 44069
Faber Foods and Aeronautics, 44085
Fairchild Industrial Products, 44096
Fairco Foods, 44097
Falcon Trading Intl Corp, 44102
Famco Automatic Sausage Linkers, 44107
Faraday, 44114
Farmers Rice Milling Co, 44117
Fas-Co Coders, 44119
Federal Heath Sign Co LLC, 44128
Ferrara Candy Co Inc, 44145
Ferrell-Ross, 44146
Ferro Corporation, 44149
Fetzer Vineyards, 44153
FFI Corporation, 44076
Fiesta Gourmet of Tejas, 44160
Fig Garden Packing Inc, 44161
Fillit, 44165
Filtrine Manufacturing, 44171
Firestone Farms, 44183
Fischbein LLC, 44188
Fisher Manufacturing Company, 44191
Fishers Investment, 44193
Fitzpatrick Co, 44198
Fizzle Flat Farm, L.L.C., 44200
Flaghouse, 44201
Flat Plate Inc, 44207
Flavor Wear, 44213
Flavorchem Corp, 44215
Flavorganics, 44216
FleetwoodGoldcoWyard, 44220
Fleig Commodities, 44221
Fleischer's Bagels, 44222
Fleischmann's Yeast, 44223
Fletcher's Fine Foods, 44224
FLEXcon Company, 44078
Flo-Matic Corporation, 44234
Flojet, 44236
Flomatic International, 44237
Florida Knife Co, 44243
Florida Plastics Intl, 44245
Florida's Natural Growers, 44246
Flow Aerospace, 44247
Flow International Corp., 44248
Fogg Filler Co, 44262
Folding Guard Co, 44267
Foley Sign Co, 44268
Follett Corp, 44272
Food Machinery Sales, 44281
Food Processing Equipment Co, 44284
Food Resources International, 44285
Food Warming Equipment Co, 44289
Formula Espresso, 44311
Fortune Plastics, Inc, 44314
Fountainhead, 44325
Foxboro Company, 44329
Franciscan Estate, 44334
Franrica Systems, 44340

FRC Environmental, 44080
Frelco, 44356
French Creek Seafood, 44360
French Oil Mill Machinery Co, 44362
Fresh Juice Delivery, 44364
Friskem Infinetics, 44372
Fristam Pumps USA LLP, 44374
Frito-Lay Inc., 44375
Frost ET Inc, 44380
Frost Food Handling Products, 44381
Frosty Factory Of America Inc, 44382
Fruitcrown Products Corp, 44386
Frutarom Meer Corporation, 44387
Furniturelab, 44404
G & F Systems Inc, 44406
G Scaccianoce & Co, 44411
G-M Super Sales Company, 44413
Gabila's Knishes, 44444
Gabriella Imports, 44445
Gaetano America, 44447
Gainco Inc, 44451
Gaiser's European Style, 44452
Galaxy Chemical Corp, 44453
Galley, 44457
Gamewell Corporation, 44461
Ganeden, Inc, 44462
Ganz Brothers, 44465
Garb-El Products Co, 44467
Garden & Valley Isle Seafood, 44470
Garuda International, 44483
Gary Plastic Packaging Corporation, 44487
Gasketman Inc, 44489
Gates Mectrol Inc, 44494
Gaylord Industries, 44498
Gbn Machine & Engineering, 44499
Gebo Corporation, 44506
GEI Autowrappers, 44423
GEI PPM, 44424
GEI Turbo, 44425
Geiger Bros, 44510
Gemini Bakery Equipment, 44512
General Floor Craft, 44521
General Formulations, 44522
General Machinery Corp, 44523
General Trade Mark Labelcraft, 44529
General Wax & Candle Co, 44530
General, Inc, 44531
Genesee Corrugated, 44534
Georgia Duck & Cordage Mill, 44550
Gerber Innovations, 44555
Giesecke & Devrient America, 44569
Gilbert Insect Light Traps, 44571
Gilchrist Bag Co Inc, 44572
Gillies Coffee, 44575
Giovanni Food Co Inc, 44583
Glaro Inc, 44591
Glo-Quartz Electric Heater, 44600
Global Marketing Assoc, 44609
Globe Fire Sprinkler Corp, 44613
Globe Machine, 44615
Glucona America, 44619
Goex Corporation, 44621
GOJO Industries Inc, 44436
Golden Needles Knitting & Glove Company, 44636
Golden Peanut and Tree Nuts, 44638
Golden Star, 44642
Goldenberg's Peanut Chews, 44648
Good Humor-Breyers Ice Cream, 44654
Goodheart Brand Specialty Food, 44658
Goodway Industries Inc, 44660
Goodway Technologies Corp, 44661
Gorbel Inc, 44664
Gorton's Inc., 44665
Grace Instrument Co, 44680
Graco Inc, 44682, 44683
Graham Engineering Corp, 44684
Granco Manufacturing Inc, 44688
Granville Gates & Sons, 44696
Graphic Packaging Intl, 44699
Gravymaster, Inc., 44703
Gray & Company, 44704
Great Northern Corp., 44716
Great Spice Company, 44719
Great Western Malting Co, 44723

Export Region / Worldwide

Green Gold Group LLC, 44734
Gregor Jonsson Inc, 44743
Gridpath, Inc., 44748
Griffin Bros Inc, 44750
Grills to Go, 44753
Grimm's Fine Food, 44755
Grindmaster-Cecilware Corp, 44756
Groeb Farms, 44758
Grote Co, 44760
Growers Cooperative Juice Co, 44764
Gruenewald ManufacturingCompany, 44765
GSB & Assoc, 44439
GTI, 44442
Gulf Coast Plastics, 44774
Gumix International Inc, 44781
Gusmer Enterprises Inc, 44784
H C Duke & Son Inc, 44793
H Cantin, 44794
H F Staples & Co Inc, 44795
H&H Fisheries Limited, 44801
H. Reisman Corporation, 44805
H.B. Dawe, 44806
H.D. Sheldon & Company, 44807
H.F. Coors China Company, 44808
Habasit America Plastic Div, 44826
Hach Co., 44827
Hain Celestial Group Inc, 44833
Halton Company, 44843
Hamilton Caster, 44849
Handgards Inc, 44857
Hanel Storage Systems, 44862
Hanover Uniform Co, 44872
Hansaloy Corp, 44874
Hansen Beverage Co, 44875
Hantover Inc, 44880
Hapman Conveyors, 44882
Harbour House Bar Crafting, 44888
Harbour Lobster Ltd, 44889
Hardt Equipment Manufacturing, 44891
Hardwood Products Co LP, 44893
Harford Systems Inc, 44895
Harland Simon Control Systems USA, 44897
Harmony Enterprises, 44898
Harper Trucks Inc, 44904
Harsco Industrial IKG, 44911
Hartstone Pottery Inc, 44916
Harwil Corp, 44921
Hatco Corp, 44924
Hawkhaven Greenhouse International, 44936
Hayes & Stolz Indl Mfg LTD, 44937
Hayon Manufacturing, 44939
Hayssen Flexible Systems, 44940
Hayward Industries Inc, 44941
Hazelnut Growers Of Oregon, 44942
Health Guardians, 44949
Health Valley Company, 44953
Healthy N Fit International, 44957
Hearthside Food Solutions, 44958
Heat-It Manufacturing, 44963
Heatcraft Refrigeration Prods, 44964
Hedwin Division, 44970
Heinz Portion Control, 44973
Heller Brothers Packing Corp, 44979
Henggeler Packing Company, 44986
Henkel Consumer Adhesive, 44987
Henry Hanger & Fixture Corporation of America, 44990
Heritage Packaging, 44999
Heritage Salmon Company, 45000
Hevi-Haul International LTD, 45006
Hi Roller Enclosed Belt Conveyors, 45008
Hickory Industries, 45012
High-Purity Standards, 45016
Hilden Halifax, 45021
Hillyard Inc, 45026
Hilmar Cheese Company, 45027
Himalayan Heritage, 45030
Hinds-Bock Corp, 45033
Hiram Walker & Sons, 45035
Hoffman & Levy Inc Tasseldepot, 45041
Hollingsworth Custom Wood Products, 45050
Honiron Corp, 45069
Hope Industrial Systems, 45074
House of Raeford Farms Inc., 45093
Houston Wire Works, Inc., 45097
Howard Turner & Son, 45100
Howard-Mccray, 45101
Howe Corp, 45102
Howes S Co Inc, 45105
Hoyt Corporation, 45107
Hubbard Peanut Co Inc, 45113
Hubbell Electric Heater Co, 45114
Hudson Commercial Foods, 45117
Hudson-Sharp Machine Co, 45122
Hunter Lab, 45131
Hydro-Miser, 45141
Hydromax Inc, 45142
Hyer Industries, 45145
Hygiene-Technik, 45147
Hyster Company, 45149
Idaho Pacific Holdings Inc, 45196
Ideal Wrapping Machine Company, 45202
Image National Inc, 45213
Imaje, 45215
Imar, 45217
Immu Dyne Inc, 45218
IMO Foods, 45175
Imperial Plastics Inc, 45223
Impulse Signs, 45232
Incinerator International Inc, 45238
INDEECO, 45177
Independent Ink, 45245
Indian Valley Industries, 45249
Indiana Carton Co Inc, 45251
Industries For The Blind, 45266
Infanti International, 45268
Ingersoll Rand Inc, 45272
Ingredion Inc., 45278
Inksolv 30, LLC., 45279
Innovation Moving Systems, 45285
Innovative Fishery Products, 45287
Innovative Space Management, 45293
Insects Limited Inc, 45297
Insta-Pro International, 45302
Integrated Restaurant Software/RMS Touch, 45307
Intercomp, 45317
InterMetro Industries, 45312
International Adhesive Coating, 45325
International Chemical Corp, 45330
International Environmental Solutions, 45340
International Market Brands, 45352
International Molasses Corp, 45353
International Omni-Pac Corporation, 45356
International Tray Pads, 45371
International Wood Industries, 45374
Interroll Corp, 45377
Interstate Monroe Machinery, 45379
Intertape Polymer Group, 45381
Intervest Trading Company Inc., 45382
IQ Scientific Instruments, 45180
Isadore A. Rapasadi & Son, 45388
ITC Systems, 45182, 45183
IVEX Packaging Corporation, 45187
J & J Snack Foods Corp, 45418
J & M Wholesale Meat Inc, 45420
J & R Mfg Inc, 45421
J C Ford Co, 45423
J F O'Neill & Packing Co, 45426
J L Becker Co, 45428
J M Canty Inc E1200 Engineers, 45430
Jaccard Corporation, 45471
Jack & Jill Ice Cream, 45472
Jack Brown Produce, 45473
Jack Daniel Distillery, 45474
Jack the Ripper Table Skirting, 45476
James Thompson, 45487
Jamieson Laboratories, 45488
Jamison Door Co, 45489
Jardine Ranch, 45497
Jarvis Caster Company, 45500
Jarvis Products Corp, 45501
Jasmine Vineyards, Inc., 45502
Java Jacket, 45504
Jb Prince, 45509
JBS USA LLC, 45452
JCH International, 45453
Jemolo Enterprises, 45513
Jennie-O Turkey Store, 45515
Jervis B WEBB Co, 45518
Jesco Industries, 45519
Jetstream Systems, 45525
JFC International Inc, 45458
JH Display & Fixture, 45459
Jif-Pak Manufacturing, 45528
JJI Lighting Group, Inc., 45460
JL Industries Inc, 45461
JMC Packaging Equipment, 45464
Jo Mar Laboratories, 45533
Joe Hutson Foods, 45536
John D Walsh Co, 45543
John I. Haas, 45546
John R Nalbach Engineering Co, 45548
Jomar Corp, 45561
Jones Dairy Farm, 45564
Jordan Paper Box Co, 45567
Jr Mats, 45579
Jus-Made, 45588
JW Leser Company, 45470
K C Booth Co, 45596
K Trader Inc., 45600
K&N Fisheries, 45601
K+S Windsor Salt Ltd., 45602
K.R. International, 45607
Kadon Corporation, 45635
Kady International, 45636
Kalle USA Inc, 45641
Kalustyan, 45643
KASE Equipment, 45613
Kasel Industries Inc, 45653
Kayco, 45661
KD Kanopy, 45614
Keating Of Chicago Inc, 45679
Kedem, 45681
Keenline Conveyor Systems, 45684
Kellogg Co., 45689
Kelly Dock Systems, 45690
Kemin Industries Inc, 45697
Ken Coat, 45700
Key Largo Fisheries, 45717
Keystone Adjustable Cap Co Inc, 45722
Keystone Fruit Marketing Inc, 45724
Kidde Residential & Commercial, 45727
Kimberly-Clark Corporation, 45731
Kinematics & Controls Corporation, 45733
Kinetico, 45736
King Arthur, 45737
King Plastic Corp, 45746
King Products, 45747
Kings River Casting, 45750
Kliklok-Woodman, 45767
KM International Corp, 45622
KMS Inc, 45624
Knight's Appleden Fruit LTD, 45774
Koch Bag & Supply Co, 45780
Kochman Consultants LTD, 45781
Kolpak, 45792
Kopykake, 45800
Koza's Inc, 45805
Kraft Heinz Canada, 45808
Kraissl Co Inc, 45809
Krewson Enterprises, 45812
Krinos Foods, 45813
Krispy Kist Company, 45815
Krowne Metal Corp, 45819
Krueger International Holding, 45820
Kwikprint Manufacturing Inc, 45831
L T Hampel Corp, 45839
L.C. Thompson Company, 45844
LA Marche Mfg Co, 45849
Labconco Corp, 45882
Laboratory Devices, 45890
Ladder Works, 45893
Laidig Inc, 45897
Laird & Company, 45898
Lakeside Foods Inc., 45904
Lakewood Juice Company, 45910
Lambert Company, 45914
Lancer Corp, 45922, 45923
Landau Uniforms Inc, 45927
Landoo Corporation, 45929
Landreth Wild Rice, 45930
Lane Labs, 45932
Lang Manufacturing Co, 45934
Langston Co Inc, 45938
Lanly Co, 45939
Larco, 45940
Lasertechnics Marking Corporation, 45945
Lavi Industries, 45953
Lawrence Equipment Inc, 45955
Least Cost Formulations LTD, 45967
Leedal Inc, 45973
LEESON Electric Corp, 45859
Leeward Winery, 45976
Lef Bleuges Marinor, 45977
Leggett & Platt Storage, 45979
Leland Limited Inc, 45987
Lematic Inc, 45989
Leo G. Atkinson Fisheries, 45996
Leroy Smith Inc, 46000
Les Viandes or Fil, 46006
Letica Corp, 46009
Lewtan Industries Corporation, 46016
Libbey Inc., 46020
Liberty Gold Fruit Co Inc, 46022
Liberty Natural Products Inc, 46024
Liberty Orchards Co Inc, 46025
Liberty Ware LLC, 46027
Liftomatic Material Handling, 46034
Light Waves Concept, 46036
Lights On, 46038
Lily of the Desert, 46043
Lilydale Foods, 46044
Lima Grain Cereal Seeds LLC, 46045
Lincoln Foodservice, 46051
Linda's Lollies Company, 46052
Linear Lighting Corp, 46054
Linker Machines, 46055
Liquid Solids Control Inc, 46064
Little Giant Pump Company, 46072
Lixi Inc, 46076
Lixi, Inc., 46077
Lloyd Disher Company, 46078
Lo Temp Sales, 46079
Lochhead Mfg. Co., 46083
Locknetics, 46086
Long Reach ManufacturingCompany, 46100
Loos Machine, 46106
Lorac Union Tool Co, 46107
Lord Label Machine Systems, 46109
Lorenz Couplings, 46111
Louis Dreyfus Company Citrus Inc, 46121
Louis Dreyfus Corporation, 46122
Louisiana Rice Mill, 46124
Louisiana Seafood Exchange, 46125, 46126, 46127
Louisville Dryer Company, 46128
Loveshaw Corp, 46133
Lozier Corp, 46138
LPS Technology, 45867
Lubriplate Lubricants, 46141
Luckner Steel Shelving, 46144
Ludfords, 46146
Luma Sense Technologies Inc, 46152
Lumacurve Airfield Signs, 46153
Lumsden Flexx Flow, 46158
Lyco Manufacturing, 46169
Lynch Corp, 46171
Lyoferm & Vivolac Cultures, 46174
Lyon LLC, 46175
M&R Flexible Packaging, 46188
M-E-C Co, 46191
Macco Organiques, 46224
Machine Builders & Design Inc, 46227
Machine Ice Co, 46229
MadgeTech, Inc., 46234
Madix Inc, 46237
Madys Company, 46239
Magi Kitch'n, 46241
Magic American Corporation, 46243
Magna Power Controls, 46247
Magnatech Corp, 46248

Export Region / Worldwide

Magnuson, 46254
Magnuson Industries, 46255
Mainstreet Menu Systems, 46264
Majestic, 46266
Malo Inc, 46275
Malteurop North America, 46279
Management Tech of America, 46283
Manitowoc Ice Machine, 46300
Maple Leaf Pork, 46308
Maple Products, 46309
Mar-Jac Poultry Inc., 46312
Marburg Industries Inc, 46319
Marel Food Systems, Inc., 46324
Marineland Commercial Aquariums, 46335
Marion Paper Box Co, 46339
Mark Products Company, 46342
Market Forge Industries Inc, 46344
Marky's Caviar, 46352
Marriott Walker Corporation, 46360
Mars Air Products, 46362
Mars Inc., 46363
Mart CART-Smt, 46370
Martin Engineering, 46373
Maruchan Inc, 46377
Maryland Packaging Corporation, 46384
Mason Candlelight Company, 46391
Massimo Zanetti Beverage USA, 46393
Master Air, 46394
Mastercraft Manufacturing Co, 46399
Mat Logo Company, 46401
Mateer Burt, 46403
Material Storage Systems, 46405
Matson Fruit Co, 46415
Matthews Marking Systems Div, 46417
Maximicer, 46427
Maytag Corporation, 46433
McCleskey Mills, 46441
McCormick & Company, 46444
Mccullough Industries Inc, 46457
Mcintyre Metals Inc, 46459
McNichols Conveyor Company, 46453
MDS-Vet Inc, 46204
Meadwestvaco Corp, 46466
MeGa Industries, 46463
Meguiar's Inc, 46478
Melco Steel Inc, 46482
Melvina Can Machinery Company, 46488
Membrane System Specialist Inc, 46489
Merchandising Frontiers Inc, 46495
Merchants Publishing Company, 46500
Meridian Nut Growers, 46506
Meritech, 46508
Merlin Process Equipment, 46511
Mermaid Spice Corporation, 46514
MERRICK Industries Inc, 46205
Metlar Us, 46526
Mettler-Toledo Process Analytics, Inc, 46529
Meyer Label Company, 46540
Miami Metal, 46547
Michael Leson Dinnerware, 46551
Michelle Chocolatiers, 46554
Microdry, 46579
Micromeritics, 46581
Micropub Systems International, 46584
MicroThermics, Inc., 46576
Mid West Quality Gloves Inc, 46588
Mid-Lands Chemical Company, 46590
Mid-States Mfg & Engr Co Inc, 46592
Midbrook Inc, 46597
Middleby Marshall Inc, 46599
Midwest Aircraft Products Co, 46603
Midwest Folding Products, 46605
Migatron Corp, 46612
Mikasa Hotelware, 46616
Milburn Company, 46620
Milligan & Higgins, 46634
Milton A. Klein Company, 46641
Milwaukee Dustless Brush Co, 46642
Milwaukee Sign Company, 46643
Mingo Bay Beverages, 46649
Minterbrook Oyster Co, 46653
Miroil, 46661
Mirro Company, 46662
MISCO Refractometer, 46212

Mission Produce Inc, 46667
Modern Brewing & Design, 46680
Mogen David Wine Corp, 46688
Moisture Register Products, 46689
Moline Machinery LLC, 46695
Molson Coors Beverage Company, 46698
Monitor Company, 46707
Monster Beverage Corp., 46710
Montague Co, 46712
Montalbano Development Inc, 46713
Montana Specialty Mills LLC, 46715
Monte Vista Farming Co, 46717
Moore Paper Boxes Inc, 46721
Morehouse Foods Inc, 46725
Morgan Winery, 46729
Morris Okun, 46734
Morrison Timing Screw Co, 46735
Mosuki, 46745
Motherland International Inc, 46747
Motom Corporation, 46749
Moyer Packing Co., 46757
Moyno, 46758
Mrs. Dog's Products, 46768
Mt Capra Products, 46770
Mt Valley Farms & Lumber Prods, 46771
Mt. Konocti Growers, 46772
Mts Seating, 46774
Multibulk Systems International, 46786
MultiMedia Electronic Displays, 46785
Murzan Inc, 46800
N.G. Slater Corporation, 46818
NACCO Materials HandlingGroup, 46819
Nalge Process Technologies Group, 46836
Namco Machinery, 46839
Napoleon Appliance Corporation, 46845
Nash-DeCamp Company, 46851
Nashua Corporation, 46853
Natalie's Orchid Island Juice Co., 46858
Natco Worldwide Representative, 46859
National Bar Systems, 46862
National Cart Co, 46863
National Computer Corporation, 46864
National Conveyor Corp, 46865
National Drying Machry Co Inc, 46867
National Equipment Corporation, 46868
National Frozen Foods Corp, 46874
National Label Co, 46880
National Metal Industries, 46882
National Package SealingCompany, 46884
National Packaging, 46885
National Raisin Co., 46888
Nature Most Laboratories, 46914
Nature's Apothecary, 46916
Nature's Bounty Co., 46918
Nature's Herbs, 46920
Naturex Inc, 46928
Navco, 46930
NDC Infrared EngineeringInc, 46823
Nemco Food Equipment, 46948
Neo-Ray Products, 46950
Neonetics Inc, 46953
New Chief Fashion, 46967
New City Packing Company, 46969
Newark Wire Cloth Co, 46994
Newco Enterprises Inc, 46996
Newell Brands, 46997
Newfound Resources, 46999
Newlands Systems, 47000
Newman Sanitary Gasket Co, 47002
Newstamp Lighting Factory, 47005
Nichols Specialty Products, 47017
Nimbus Water Systems, 47030
Niroflex, USA, 47032
Nissho Iwai American Corporation, 47035
Nolon Industries, 47042
Norandal, 47051
Nordson Corp, 47056
NORPAC Foods Inc, 46827
North American Reishi/Nammex, 47066
North Star Ice EquipmentCorporation, 47078
Northeast Packaging Materials, 47083

Northern Products Corporation, 47087
Northern Stainless Fabricating, 47088
Northern Wind Inc, 47089
Northridge Laboratories, 47093
Northwest Fisheries, 47098
Northwest Naturals LLC, 47100
Northwestern Extract, 47103
Nothum Food Processing Systems, 47107
Notre Dame Seafoods Inc., 47108
Nova Hand Dryers, 47109
Novozymes North America Inc, 47116
Nu-Star Inc, 47123
Nu-Tex Styles, Inc., 47124
Nunes Co Inc, 47133
Nunes Farms Marketing, 47134
NuTone, 47127
Nutraceutics Corp, 47143
Nutranique Labs, 47144
Nutrex Hawaii Inc, 47145
Nutrifaster Inc, 47149
Nutrisoya Foods, 47151
Nutrition & Food Associates, 47153
Nutrition Supply Corp, 47154
Nutritional Labs Intl, 47156
Oak International, 47175
Oakrun Farm Bakery, 47177
Ocean Garden Products Inc, 47182
Ocean Spray International, 47185
Ohlson Packaging, 47195
Old Dominion Wood Products, 47201
Omega Design Corp, 47219
Omni Craft Inc, 47227
Omni International, 47228
Omnion, 47232
Omnitemp Refrigeration, 47234
Oneida Food Service, 47239
Onguard Industries LLC, 47241
Opal Manufacturing Ltd, 47247
Oracle Hospitality, 47254
Orange Peel Enterprises, 47258
Ore-Cal Corp, 47262
Ore-Ida Foods, 47263
Oregon Cherry Growers Inc, 47265, 47266
Oregon Fruit Products Co, 47269
Orelube Corp, 47272
OSF, 47169
OTD Corporation, 47170
Oyster Bay Pump Works Inc, 47312
P. Janes & Sons, 47319
Pa R Systems Inc, 47348
Pace Packaging Corp, 47351
Pacific American Fish Co Inc, 47353
Pacific Foods, 47357
Pacific Nutritional, 47359
Pacific Refrigerator Company, 47362
Pacific Salmon Company, 47364
Pacific Spice Co, 47367
Pacific Steam Equipment, Inc., 47369
Pacific Valley Foods Inc, 47372
Pack Rite Machine Mettler, 47375
Pack West Machinery, 47376
Packaging Aids Corporation, 47383
Packaging Dynamics Corp, 47385
Packaging Enterprises, 47388
Packaging Machinery, 47390
Packaging Machinery & Equipment, 47391
Pacmac Inc, 47396
Pactiv LLC, 47398
Pall Filtron, 47409
Palmer Distributors, 47414
Palmer Fixture Company, 47415
Palmer Snyder, 47416
Paoli Properties, 47432
Paper Converting Machine Company, 47435
Paper Converting MachineCompany, 47434
Paperweights Plus, 47439
Paragon International, 47451
Paramount Export Co., 47453
Parish Chemical Company, 47458
Parisi Inc, 47460
Parity Corp, 47461
Party Yards, 47476

PASCO, 47326
Patterson Frozen Foods, 47490
Patty Paper Inc, 47493
Paul N. Gardner Company, 47495
Paul O. Abbe, 47496
Payne Controls Co, 47501
PB Leiner USA, 47328
PBC, 47329
Peace Industries, 47502
Peanut Patch Gift Shop, 47507
Peerless Food Equipment, 47516, 47517
Peerless Machinery Corporation, 47519
Peerless-Winsmith Inc, 47523
Pemberton & Associates, 47529
Penco Products, 47531
Pendery's, 47533
Penn Refrigeration Service Corporation, 47537
Per-Fil Industries Inc, 47547
Perdue Farms Inc., 47548
Perfect Equipment Inc, 47550
Perfect Fry Company, 47551
Perl Packaging Systems, 47555
Perlick Corp, 47557
Perry Videx LLC, 47559
Peter Rabbit Farms, 47565
Petrofsky's Bakery Products, 47572
Petroleum Analyzer Co LP, 47573
Pfanstiehl Inc, 47577
Pfeil & Holding Inc, 47578
Phoenician Herbals, 47592
Phoenix Agro-Industrial Corporation, 47593
Pick Heaters, 47599
Pickwick Manufacturing Svc, 47602
Piknik Products Company, 47607
Pilgrim's Pride Corp., 47610
Piller Sausages & Delicatessens, 47611
Pinnacle Furnishing, 47614
Pintys Delicious Foods, 47615
Pioneer Growers, 47616
Pizzey's Milling & Baking Company, 47627
Plantation Candies, 47629
Plasti-Mach Corporation, 47634
Plastipak Packaging, 47637
Plaza Sweets Bakery, 47639
PM Chemical Company, 47335
PMP Fermentation Products, 47337
Point Group, 47651
Polar Hospitality Products, 47656
Polar Plastics, 47658
Polar Ware Company, 47659
Poly Processing Co, 47661
PolyMaid Company, 47663
Polypro International Inc, 47667
Pomona Service & Pkgng Co LA, 47671
Porter Bowers Signs, 47680
Portland Shellfish Company, 47683
Power Electronics Intl Inc, 47689
Prairie Malt, 47696
Prawnto Systems, 47699
Praxair Inc, 47701
Precision Brush, 47703
Precision Component Industries, 47704
Precision Pours, 47705
Premier Meat Co, 47718
Premium Foil Products Company, 47721
Prentiss, 47723
Pres-Air-Trol Corporation, 47724
Prestige Plastics Corporation, 47730
Prevor Marketing International, 47739
Prime Ingredients Inc, 47744
Prince Industries Inc, 47754
Priority One America, 47758
Pro Line Co, 47762
Pro Scientific Inc, 47763
ProAmpac, 47765
ProBar Systems Inc., 47766
Procedyne Corp, 47770
Process Heating Corp, 47774
Process Sensors Corp, 47775
PROCON Products, 47343
Producers Cooperative Oil Mill, 47780
Producers Peanut Company, 47781
Producers Rice Mill Inc., 47782

723

Export Region / Worldwide

Production Equipment Co, 47783
Products A Curtron Div, 47787
Professional Marketing Group, 47794
Proheatco Manufacturing, 47803
Promarks, 47805
Promens, 47806
ProRestore Products, 47767
Protectowire Co Inc, 47815
Protexall, 47817
Provimi Foods, 47822
Provisur Technologies, 47823
Pulva Corp, 47832
PURA, 47347
Pure & Secure LLC-Cust Svc, 47838
Pure Fit Nutrition Bars, 47839
Q A Supplies LLC, 47858
QBD Modular Systems, 47862
QMI, 47864
Quaker Oats Company, 47871
Quality Cabinet & Fixture Co, 47876
Quality Container Company, 47877
Quality Control Equipment Co, 47879
Quality Corporation, 47880
Quality Seating Co, 47886
Quickcraft, 47895
QUIKSERV Corp, 47866
Quinault Pride, 47897
R F Hunter Co Inc, 47903
R T C, 47908
R X Honing Machine Corp, 47911
R.E. Meyer Company, 47918
Racine Paper Box Manufacturing, 47940
Radio Frequency Co Inc, 47943
Radius Display Products, 47944
Rainbow Valley Frozen Yogurt, 47956
Ramona's Mexican Foods, 47963
Randall Manufacturing Inc, 47967
Ranger Tool Co Inc, 47969
Rapid Pallet, 47972
Rapids Wholesale Equipment, 47974
Rath Manufacturing Company, 47975
Raypak Inc, 47982
Raytheon Co, 47983
Read Products Inc, 47984
Readco Kurimoto LLC, 47985
Reading Bakery Systems Inc, 47986
Ready Access, 47988
Redi-Print, 48009
Refcon, 48019
Refresco Beverages US Inc, 48021
Refrigeration Research, 48022
Refrigiwear, 48024
Regal Custom Fixture Company, 48027
Reichert Analytical Instruments, 48037
Reiner Products, 48041
Reinke & Schomann, 48043
Relco Unisystems Corp, 48046
Remel, 48054
Renato Specialty Product, 48057
Replacements LTD, 48064
Rer Services, 48067
Resina, 48069
Resource Trading Company, 48070
Respirometry Plus, LLC, 48071
Retalix, 48073
Rexnord Corporation, 48079
Reyco Systems Inc, 48081
Rhodes Bakery Equipment, 48086
Rhodes Machinery International, 48087
Rice Fruit Co, 48090
Rice Innovations, 48091
Ricetec, 48094
Rich Products Corp, 48095
Richardson International, 48098
Rico Packaging Company, 48102
Rieke Packaging Systems, 48104
Riverside Manufacturing Company, 48115
Riverside Wire & Metal Co., 48117
Riviana Foods Inc, 48118
Rjr Technologies, 48120
Rjs Carter Co Inc, 48121
RMF Companies, 47931
Robert Mondavi Winery, 48127
Robert-James Sales, 48129
Robertet Flavors, 48130

Roberts Ferry Nut Co, 48131
Robinson Industries Inc, 48137
Rochester Midland Corp, 48141
Rock-Tenn Company, 48144
Rocket Man, 48145
Rockford-Midland Corporation, 48146
Rockline Industries, 48147
Rod Golden Hatchery Inc, 48150
Roddy Products Pkgng Co Inc, 48151
Rohrer Corp., 48159
Rolfs @ Boone, 48163
Rome Machine & Foundry Co, 48168
Ronzoni, 48174
Ropak Manufacturing Co Inc, 48178
Rose Forgrove, 48181
Rose Packing Co Inc, 48183
Roseville Charcoal & Mfg Co, 48185
Ross & Wallace Inc, 48188
Ross Computer Systems, 48189
Ross Engineering Inc, 48190
Roth Sign Systems, 48195
Rotisol France Inc, 48197
Rotteveel Orchards, 48199
Rowe International, 48203
Royal Ecoproducts, 48216
Royale Brands, 48228
Rpac LLC, 48232
RTI Shelving Systems, 47937
Rubbermaid Commercial Products, 48235
Ruby Manufacturing & Sales, 48238
Rudolph Industries, 48240
RXI Silgan Specialty Plastics, 47938
Rytec Corporation, 48252
S J Controls Inc, 48257
S S Steiner Inc, 48260
Sabert Corp, 48308
Safe-Stride Southern, 48314
Sage V Foods, 48319
Sahagian & Associates, 48322
Salem-Republic Rubber Co, 48331
Salvajor Co, 48339
Sampac Enterprises, 48344
Samson Controls, 48346
Samuel Strapping Systems Inc, 48348
San Aire Industries, 48349
Sandler Seating, 48367
Sandvik Process Systems, 48370
Sanford Redmond Company, 48371
Sani-Fit, 48372
SaniServ, 48374
Saputo Cheese USA Inc., 48386
Saranac Brewery, 48388
Scan Corporation, 48413
Scheidegger, 48422
Schneider Electric, 48431
Scienco Systems, 48439
SCK Direct Inc, 48273
Scope Packaging, 48443
Scorpio Apparel, 48444
Scot Young Research LTD, 48445
Scotsman Ice Systems, 48447
Scott Sign Systems, 48449
Scott Turbon Mixer, 48450
Scott's Candy, 48451
Screen Print Etc, 48454
Scroll Compressors LLC, 48456
Sea Bear Smokehouse, 48458
Seal-O-Matic Corp, 48475
Seating Concepts Inc, 48484
Seattle Refrigeration & Manufacturing, 48487
Semi-Bulk Systems Inc, 48505
Seneca Foods Corp, 48509
Sensitech Inc, 48514
Sentry Seasonings, 48518
Sentry/Bevcon North America, 48519
Sepragen Corp, 48521
Serenade Foods, 48523
Serfilco, 48526
Sermia International, 48527
Serpa Packaging Solutions, 48528
Servco Equipment Co, 48533
SerVend International, 48522
Service Ideas, 48536
Sessions Co Inc, 48543

Setco, 48544
Sethness Caramel Color, 48545
Setton Pistachio, 48548
Sew-Eurodrive Inc, 48555
Seydel Co, 48556
Shafer Commercial Seating, 48560
Shaklee Corp, 48563
Shammi Industries, 48564
Shanzer Grain Dryer, 48568
Sharon Manufacturing Inc, 48569
Shekou Chemicals, 48576
Shen Manufacturing Co Inc, 48580
Shepard Niles Parts, 48583
Sherwood Tool, 48587
Shippers Paper Products Co, 48597
Showa-Best Glove, 48607
Sico Inc, 48612
SIGHTech Vision Systems, 48281
Sign Classics, 48624
Silgan Containers LLC, 48635
Silgan Plastic Closure Sltns, 48636, 48637
Silgan White Cap LLC, 48639
Silver Lining Seafood, 48646
Silverson Machines Inc, 48653
Simmons Foods Inc, 48657
Simonds International, 48659
Simonian Fruit Company, 48661
Simplex Time Recorder Company, 48664, 48665
Simpson & Vail, 48667
Sims Machinery Co Inc, 48669
Sinco, 48672
Sioux Honey Assn., 48677
Skrmetta Machinery Corporation, 48686
Slautterback Corporation, 48690
Slip Not, 48693
Smetco, 48697
Smirk's, 48699
Smith Packing Regional Meat, 48702
Smith-Lustig Paper Box Manufacturing, 48705
Smithfield Foods Inc., 48706
Smyth Co LLC, 48710
Snap Drape Inc, 48713
Snelgrove Ice Cream Company, 48719
Sno Shack Inc, 48721
Sno Wizard Inc, 48722
Something Different Linen, 48744
Sommers Plastic Product Co Inc, 48746
Sonics & Materials Inc, 48748
Sortex, 48756
Sossner Steel Stamps, 48757
Source for Packaging, 48760
South Georgia Pecan Co, 48762
Southbend, 48766
Southern Ag Co Inc, 48768
Southern Imperial Inc, 48776
Southern Rubber Stamp, 48780
Southern Store Fixtures Inc, 48783
Southern Tool, 48784
Sowden Brothers Farm, 48788
SP Industries, 48288
Spartec Plastics, 48798
Specialty Coffee Roasters, 48806
Specialty Commodities Inc, 48807
Specialty Equipment Company, 48808, 48809
Specialty Products, 48814
Specific Mechanical Systems, 48817
Speco Inc, 48818
Sperling Industries, 48826
Spice King Corporation, 48830
Spin-Tech Corporation, 48832
Spiral Biotech Inc, 48835
Spiral Manufacturing Co Inc, 48836
Sportabs International, 48840
Spray Drying, 48841
Sprayway Inc, 48844
SPX Flow Inc, 48291, 48292
Squab Producers of California, 48854
Squar-Buff, 48855
Squirrel Systems, 48857
St Charles Trading Inc, 48858
Stadelman Fruit LLC, 48866
Stainless, 48868

Stainless Products, 48870
Stainless Steel Coatings, 48872
Stampendous, 48873
Stanfos, 48883
Stapling Machines Co, 48889
Star Filters, 48890
Star Pacific Inc, 48894
Starkel Poultry, 48899
Stearns Technical Textiles Company, 48910
Stegall Mechanical INC, 48921
Steiner Company, 48922
Stella D'oro, 48924
Stephan Machinery GmbH, 48927
Sterling Systems & Controls, 48938
Sterner Lighting Systems, 48940
Sterno, 48941
Stevenson-Cooper Inc, 48948
Stewart Assembly & Machining, 48949
Stewart Systems Baking LLC, 48950
Stock Yards Packing Company, 48958
Stoffel Seals Corp, 48959
Stogsdill Tile Co, 48961
Stoller Fisheries, 48962
Stone Container, 48963
Stone Enterprises Inc., 48964
Stonewall Kitchen, 48968
Stoneway Carton Company, 48969
Stork Townsend Inc., 48971
Stormax International, 48973
Stout Sign Company, 48974
Strahman Valves Inc, 48975
Strand Lighting, 48976
Stremick's Heritage Foods, 48982
Stretch-Vent Packaging System, 48984
Sturm Foods Inc, 48990
Suffolk Iron Works Inc, 48993
Sugarman of Vermont, 48997
Summerfield Foods, 49001
Summit Hill Flavors, 49004
Summit Machine Builders Corporation, 49006
Sun-Maid Growers of California, 49018
Sunridge Farms, 49029
Sunshine Farm & Garden, 49036
Sunsweet Growers Inc., 49039
Sunterra Meats, 49041
Super Cooker, 49044
Super Radiator Coils, 49045
Super Vision International, 49047
Superflex Limited, 49049
Superior Industries, 49054
Supreme Metal, 49065
Sutter Home Winery, 49075
SWELL Philadelphia Chewing Gum Corporation, 48302
Swing-A-Way Manufacturing Company, 49091
Sympak, Inc., 49104
Systems Comtrex, 49110
T & S Brass & Bronze Work, 49113
T M Duche Nut Co, 49118
T.K. Products, 49123
T.S. Smith & Sons, 49125
Tampa Corrugated Carton Company, 49167
Tampico Beverages Inc, 49170
Tangent Systems, 49171
Tanimura Antle Inc, 49174
Tara Linens, 49183
Target Flavors Inc, 49185
Tartaric Chemicals, 49189
Taste of Gourmet, 49193
TC/American Monorail, 49126
Tecumseh Products Co., 49218
Tejon Ranch Co, 49226
Tek Visions, 49227
Tel-Tru Manufacturing Co, 49229
Teledyne TEKMAR, 49232
Telesonic Packaging, 49233
Tennant Co., 49242
Tennsco Corp, 49245
Terminix, 49249
Tesa Tape Inc, 49255
Tessenderlo Kerley Inc, 49257
Testing Machines Inc, 49259

Export Region / Worldwide

Tharo Systems Inc, 49274
The Bruss Company, 49280
The Carriage Works, 49281
Thermaco Inc, 49308
Thermal Bags By Ingrid Inc, 49309
Thermoil Corporation, 49316
Thermoquest, 49317
Thiele Technologies-Reedley, 49321
Thomas Lighting Residential, 49325
Thomson-Leeds Company, 49330
Thoreson Mc Cosh Inc, 49332
Tim's Cascade Snacks, 49353
Timemed Labeling Systems, 49355
Tisma Machinery Corporation, 49363
TKF Inc, 49133
Toastmaster, 49367
TODDS Enterprises Inc, 49138
Token Factory, 49375
Tokheim Co, 49376
Toledo Ticket Co, 49379
Tom's Snacks Company, 49380
Tomlinson Industries, 49382
Tonex, 49386
Tootsie Roll Industries Inc., 49392
Top Line Process Equipment Company, 49393
Tops Manufacturing Co, 49397
Torpac Capsules, 49402
Toter Inc, 49411
Trade Fixtures, 49420
Trane Inc, 49428
Transbotics Corp, 49434
Transnorm System Inc, 49437
Traulsen & Co, 49440
Traycon Manufacturing Co, 49442
Tri-Sterling, 49457
Triad Scientific, 49459
Triangle Package Machinery Co, 49460
Trident Seafoods Corp, 49468
Triner Scale & Mfg Co, 49473
Trinidad Benham Corporation, 49474
Trinkle Sign & Display, 49477
Triple S Dynamics Inc, 49483
Tropicana Products Inc., 49497
Tru Hone Corp, 49502, 49503
Trumark, 49514
Tualatin Estate Vineyards, 49520
Tuchenhagen, 49522
Tucker Industries, 49523
Tuway American Group, 49541
Twi Laq, 49545
Tyco Fire Protection Products, 49551
Tyco Plastics, 49552
Tyco Retail Solutions, 49553
Tyson Foods Inc., 49554
Uas Laboratories, 49578

Ulcra Dynamics, 49580
Ullman, Shapiro & UllmanLLP, 49581
Ultimate Nutrition, 49584
Ultra Enterprises, 49585
Ultra Seal, 49586
Ultrafryer Systems Inc, 49588
Umpqua Dairy, 49589
Uncle Lee's Tea Inc, 49595
Une-Viandi, 49597
Unibroue/Unibrew, 49601
Unilever US, 49606
Union Process, 49613
Unirak Storage Systems, 49622
United Bakery Equipment Company, 49627
United Filters Intl, 49634
United Flexible, 49635
United Universal Enterprises Corporation, 49656
Universal Beverages Inc, 49662
Universal Dynamics Technologies, 49665
Universal Packaging Inc, 49670
Univex Corp, 49673
Urnex Brands Inc, 49681
Us Rubber, 49684
US Seating Products, 49573
USECO, 49576
Utility Refrigerator Company, 49687
V & E Kohnstamm Inc, 49688
Vacumet Corp, 49708
Vacuum Barrier Corp, 49709
Val-Pak Direct Market Systems, 49710
Valco Melton, 49712
Valeo, 49715
Valley Container Inc, 49717
Valley View Packing Co, 49723
Van Blarcom Closures Inc, 49727
Vanilla Saffron Imports, 49739
Vanmark Equipment LLC, 49741
Vantage Performance Materials, 49742
Varitronic Systems, 49748
Vaughn-Russell Candy Kitchen, 49751
VC Menus, 49694
Vega Americas Inc, 49755
Vendome Copper & Brass Works, 49762
Vent Master, 49765
Venture Measurement Co LLC, 49770
Versa Conveyor, 49781
Vertical Systems Intl, 49785
Vicksburg Chemical Company, 49794
Vicmore Manufacturing Company, 49795
Victor Packing, 49798
View-Rite Manufacturing, 49805
Viking Corp, 49808
Viking Industries, 49809
Vincent B Zaninovich & Sons, 49815

Vincor Canada, 49818
Vingcard/Elsafe, 49820
VIP Sales Company, 49700
Visalia Fruit Exchange, 49830
Vista Food Exchange, 49833
Vita Food Products Inc, 49838
Vitaminerals, 49843
Vitamix, 49844
Vivolac Cultures Corporation, 49850
Vogel, 49852
Vogt Tube Ice, 49853
Vollrath Co LLC, 49858
Vulcan Electric Co, 49865
Vulcan Food Equipment Group, 49866
W.A. Schmidt Company, 49874
Wadden Systems, 49911
Wah Yet Group, 49918
Walker Magnetics Group Inc, 49927
Wallace & Hinz, 49930
Wanda's Nature Farm, 49944
Warrell Corp, 49951
Washington Fruit & Produce Company, 49957
Washington Potato Company, 49958
Water Furnace Renewable Energy, 49965
Watlow Electric, 49968, 49969
Watson Inc, 49970
Watts Premier Inc, 49971
Waukesha Cherry-Burrell, 49972
WCB Ice Cream, 49881
WCC Honey Marketing, 49882
Weavewood, Inc., 49982
Web Label, 49983
Webb-Triax Company, 49984
Weber Packaging Solutions Inc, 49986
Wega USA, 49991
WeighPack Systems/Paxiom Group, 49994
Weiler & Company, 49996
Weinbrenner Shoe Co, 49998
Welbilt Corporation, 50003
Welbilt Inc., 50004
Welch Foods Inc, 50005
Wellesse, 50010
Wescor, 50018
West Agro, 50021
West Chemical Products, 50024
West Liberty Foods LLC, 50030
Westbrook Trading Company, 50036
Westco-BakeMark, 50037
Western Pacific Stge Solutions, 50042
Western Plastics, 50044
Western Textile & Manufacturing Inc., 50048
Westin Foods, 50050
Whatman, 50063

Whirley Industries Inc, 50066
Whit-Log Trailers Inc, 50069
White Coffee Corporation, 50070
White Mop Wringer Company, 50072
Whitford Corporation, 50083
Whiting & Davis, 50084
Whitley Peanut Factory Inc, 50086
Wika Instrument LP, 50092
Wilbur Curtis Co, 50093
Wilevco Inc, 50101
Wilke International Inc, 50102
Wilkens-Anderson Co, 50103
Wilkie Brothers Conveyor Inc, 50104
Wilkinson Manufacturing Company, 50106
Willamette Industries, 50108
William E. Martin & Sons Company, 50112
Wilton Brands LLC, 50121
Win-Holt Equipment Group, 50122
Winston Industries, 50136
Wisco Industries Assembly, 50142
Wisconsin Spice Inc, 50148
Wittco Foodservice Equipment, 50152
Witte Co Inc, 50153
Wittern Group, 50155
WNA, 49889
Wolens Company, 50158
Wolf Canyon Foods, 50159
Womack International Inc, 50162
Wonderful Pistachios & Almonds, 50163
Woodfold-Marco Manufacturing, 50168
Woody Associates Inc, 50173
Work Well Company, 50176
World Division, 50185
World Dryer Corp, 50186
World Kitchen, 50189
World Variety Produce, 50194
World Water Works, 50195
Wraps, 50205
WS Packaging Group Inc, 49893
Xcel Tower Controls, 50217
Ya-Hoo Baking Co, 50224
Yakima Chief-Hopunion LLC, 50225
Yost Candy Co Inc, 50245
Your Place Menu Systems, 50248
Zamilco International, 50257
Zealco Industries, 50260
Zeeco Inc, 50263
Zeltex, 50266
Zenith Cutter, 50270
Zephyr Manufacturing Co, 50276
Zimmer Custom-Made Packaging, 50282
Zimmerman Handling Systems, 50283
Zumtobel Staff Lighting, 50287

Import Region / Africa

Africa

A&A International, 41488
Allegro Coffee Co, 41809
Aroma-Life, 42061
Beach Filter Products, 42318
Classic Flavors & Fragrances, 43065
Coffee Exchange, 43118
Cupper's Coffee Company, 43407
Elite Spice Inc, 43895
Enzyme Development Corporation, 43965
Garlic and Spice, Inc., 44481
Givaudan Fragrances Corp, 44588
Herz Meat Company, 45003
Kentea, 45707
Maxim's Import Corporation, 46426
Nexira, 47010
Occidental Foods International, LLC, 47178
Once Again Nut Butter, 47237
Organic Products Trading Co, 47276
Pendery's, 47533
Prentiss, 47723
Sands Brands International Food, 48369
Sesaco Corp, 48541
Sinclair Trading, 48671
Starbucks, 48897
Tea Importers Inc, 49205
Toddy Products Inc, 49371
Tootsi Impex, 49391
Torrefazione Barzula & Import, 49404
Weavewood, Inc., 49982
Wescotek Inc, 50019

Arabia

Starbucks, 48897

Argentina

American Agrotrading, 41868

Armenia

Eco Wine & Spirits, 43830

Asia

3V Company, 41472
A&A International, 41488
A&B Safe Corporation, 41491
A-A1 Aaction Bag, 41502
Aak USA Inc, 41598
AB InBev, 41524
Abimco USA, Inc., 41611
Able Sales Company, 41612
Aceto Corporation, 41634
Acta Health Products, 41652
Adex Medical Inc, 41670
Adhesive Technologies Inc, 41672
Admatch Corporation, 41673
Admiral Craft, 41674
Advanced Food Systems, 41691
AEP Colloids, 41544
Afec Commodities, 41709
AHD International, LLC, 41553
AIDP Inc, 41554
Ajinomoto Foods North America, Inc., 41744
Ajinomoto Frozen Foods USA, Inc., 41745
AKC Commodities Inc, 41556
Alchemie USA Inc., 41769
Alfa Chem, 41775
Alfa International Corp, 41776
Alfred L. Wolff, Inc., 41781
Algene Marking Equipment Company, 41782
Alger Creations, 41783
Alimentaire Whyte's Inc, 41786
All American Container, 41794
Allied Glove Corporation, 41821
Alnor Oil Co Inc, 41832
Alternative Health & Herbs, 41847
Amano Enzyme USA Company, Ltd, 41855
America's Classic Foods, 41867
American Bag & Burlap Company, 41869
American Design Studios, 41877
American Eagle Food Machinery, 41878
American Food Traders, 41888
American Hotel Register Co, 41891
American Importing Co., 41894
American Key Food Products Inc, 41897
American Laboratories, 41900
American Lifts, 41902
American Metalcraft Inc, 41907
American Seafood Imports Inc., 41919
American Trading Company, 41927
Americana Art China Company, 41931
Ampak Seafoods Corporation, 41953
ANVER Corporation, 41573
AP Dataweigh Inc, 41575
Apex Machine Company, 42005
Arista Industries Inc, 42044
Aroma Vera, 42060
Aroma-Life, 42061
Aromachem, 42062
Arrow Chemical Inc, 42067
Arrowac Fisheries, 42070
Astral Extracts, 42095
Atkins Ginseng Farms, 42104
Atlantic Capes Fisheries, 42109
Atlas Match Corporation, 42126
August Thomsen Corp, 42137
Auromere Inc, 42139
Aurora Design Associates, Inc., 42140
Aust & Hachmann, 42142
Austrade, 42143
Autocon Mixing Systems, 42147
Avery Weigh-Tronix LLC, 42168
Ayush Herbs Inc, 42181
Bakery Things, 42246
Balzac Brothers & Co Inc, 42262
Barhyte Specialty Foods Inc, 42278
Barrows Tea Company, 42287
Barry Group, 42289
Barton Beers, 42291
Bascom Food Products, 42294
Basic Food Intl Inc, 42297
Basic Leasing Corporation, 42298
Baycliff Co Inc, 42312
Bazzini Holdings LLC, 42316
BBCA USA, 42201
Beach Filter Products, 42318
Bean Machines, 42321
Beaufurn, 42326
Beaver Street Fisheries, 42329
Beayl Weiner/Pak, 42331
Bedemco Inc, 42337
Bee International, 42342
Benner China & Glassware Inc, 42377
Berti Produce Co, 42400
Best Buy Uniforms, 42405
Best Value Textiles, 42412
Better Living Products, 42419
Bijur Lubricating Corporation, 42435
Binks Industries Inc, 42439
Bishamon Industry Corp, 42460
Blue Cross Laboratories, 42486
Blue Giant Equipment Corporation, 42489
Blue Harvest Foods, 42490
Blue Star Food Products, 42497
Bluebird Manufacturing, 42498
BMT Commodity Corporation, 42211
Boehringer Mfg. Co. Inc., 42509
Bolner's Fiesta Spices, 42512
Bonduelle North America, 42518
Bonneau Company, 42519
Boricua Empaque, 42521
Boss Manufacturing Co, 42527
Boyd Lighting Company, 42544
Bradford A Ducon Company, 42546
Bratt-Foster-Advantage Sales, 42562
Braun Brush Co, 42564
Brewmatic Company, 42575
Brothers International Food Corporation, 42601
Brucia Plant Extracts, 42613
Bulk Sak Intl Inc, 42634
C Pacific Foods Inc, 42673
C R Daniels Inc, 42674
Cadie Products Corp, 42726
CAI International, 42687
Cajun Original Foods Inc, 42734
Cal Trading Company, 42738
Cal-Mil Plastic Products Inc, 42741
California Cereal Products, 42749
California Olive Oil Council, 42756
California World Trade and Marketing Company, 42758
Camerican International, 42770
Campbell Soup Co., 42775
Canada Cutlery Inc., 42780
Canadian Fish Exporters, 42782
Canarm, Ltd., 42785
Candy Tech LLC, 42791
Cash Register Sales, 42872
Caspian Trading Company, 42873
Catskill Craftsmen Inc, 42883
Caudill Seed Co Inc, 42887
CCi Scale Company, 42691
CCS Stone, Inc., 42690
CEA Instrument Inc, 42693
Celite Corporation, 42898
Centennial Food Corporation, 42902
Charmel Enterprises, 42937
Chef Merito Inc, 42951
Chef Revival, 42952
Chef Specialties, 42953
Chemicolloid Laboratories, Inc., 42966
Chesapeake Spice Company, 42975
Chia I Foods Company, 42984
Chicago Food Corporation, 42986
China Products, 43004
Chong Imports, 43021
CJ America, 42699
CJ Omni, 42700
CK Products, 42702
Classic Flavors & Fragrances, 43065
Classic Tea, 43066
Clipper Seafood, 43094
Clofine Dairy Products Inc, 43095
Coburn Company, 43111
Codema, 43115
Coffee Exchange, 43118
Comark Instruments, 43153
Commercial Furniture Group Inc, 43162
Commissariat Imports, 43166
Commodities Marketing Inc, 43167
Component Hardware Group Inc, 43178
Comstock Castle Stove Co, 43185
Con-tech/Conservation Technology, 43189
Conimar Corp, 43200
Connection Chemical LP, 43202
Consolidated Commercial Controls, 43207
Container Machinery Corporation, 43216
Continental Seasoning, 43229
Coronet Chandelier Originals, 43282
Crestware, 43345
Crystal-Vision Packaging Systems, 43390
CSC Scientific Co, Inc., 42712
Custom Food Machinery, 43416
D.F. International, 43448
Dairy Fresh Foods Inc, 43471
Dalemark Industries, 43482
Daprano & Co, 43498
Darik Enterprises Inc, 43501
Davidson's Organics, 43512
Davis Strait Fisheries, 43514
Davis Trade & Commodities, 43515
De Choix Specialty Foods Company, 43528
De Ster Corporation, 43533
Deep Foods Inc, 43547
Delavau LLC, 43564
Derco Foods Intl, 43587
Design Packaging Company, 43592
DeVries Imports, 43537
Dewied International Inc, 43603
DIC International, 43456
Dillanos Coffee Roasters, 43630
Dipasa USA Inc, 43634
Dishaka Imports, 43639
Doosan Industrial Vehicle America Corp, 43669
Douglas Homs Corporation, 43679
Dove Screen Printing Co, 43681
DSM Fortitech Premixes, 43461
Ducktrap River Of Maine, 43715
Dura-Ware Company of America, 43730
Dynamic Packaging, 43751
Dynynstyl, 43754
Eagle Home Products, 43796
Earth Saver, 43799
East Bay International, 43803
Eastern Tea Corp, 43813
Eckhart Corporation, 43825
Economy Novelty & Printing Co, 43843
Edoko Food Importers, 43864
Edward & Sons Trading Co, 43868
Elco Fine Foods, 43882
Elite Spice Inc, 43895
Elliot Lee, 43901
Elopak Americas, 43911
Emblem & Badge, 43916
Emerald City Closets Inc, 43918
Emerling International Foods, 43921
Empire Spice Mills, 43931
Empire Tea Svc, 43932
Ener-G Foods, 43941
Enzyme Development Corporation, 43965
Erie Foods Intl Inc, 43978
Erwyn Products Inc, 43983
Essential Products of America, 43992
Ettlinger Corp, 43996
Euroam Importers Inc, 44009
Excellence Commercial Products, 44041
Eximcan Canada, 44048
Eximco Manufacturing Company, 44049
F.H. Taussig Company, 44067
Fairfield Line Inc, 44098
Famarco Limited, 44106
Fantastic World Foods, 44110
Farm 2 Market, 44115
FDC Corporation, 44072
Feather Duster Corporation, 44126
Felbro Food Products, 44133
Felco Packaging Specialist, 44134
Felins USA Inc, 44136
Fernandez Chili Co, 44141
Ferntrade Corporation, 44143
Finest Foods, 44178
First Colony Coffee & Tea Company, 44186
Fitec International Inc, 44196
Flamingo Flats, 44204
Flavor Consultants, 44208
Flavormatic Industries, 44217
Fleurchem Inc, 44226
Flojet, 44236
Florida Food Products Inc, 44242
Flyover International Corporation, 44256
Food Resources International, 44285
Ford Gum & Mach Co Inc, 44303
Francis & Lusky Company, 44333
Franklin Trading Company, 44339
Freeda Vitamins Inc, 44347
Freeman Industries, 44350
Fruitcrown Products Corp, 44386
Fuller Packaging Inc, 44395
Fullway International, 44397
Furgale Industries Ltd., 44402
G K Skaggs Inc, 44409
G.P. de Silva Spices Inc, 44417
Gar Products, 44466
Garlic and Spice, Inc., 44481
Garuda International, 44483
GCI Nutrients, 44431
GEM Cultures, 44427
General Bag Corporation, 44515
George Degen & Co, 44542
George Glove Company, Inc, 44544
Georgia Spice Company, 44551
Gerber Products Co, 44557
Germack Pistachio Co, 44559
GH Ford Tea Company, 44431
Gillies Coffee, 44575
Ginco International, 44579
Glo-Quartz Electric Heater, 44600
Global Equipment Co Inc, 44603

727

Import Region / Asia

Globe Fire Sprinkler Corp, 44613
Glowmaster Corporation, 44618
Gold Pure Food Products Co. Inc., 44624
Golden Beach Inc, 44627
Golden Bridge Enterprises Inc, 44628
Golden Moon Tea, 44635
Goldmax Industries, 44650
Gourmet Club Corporation, 44671
Grace Instrument Co, 44680
Grace Tea Co, 44681
Grain Machinery Mfg Corp, 44685
Grande Chef Company, 44692
Graphic Technology, 44700
Great American Appetizers, 44706
Great Eastern Sun Trading Co, 44709
Great Lakes Brush, 44711
Great Lakes Designs, 44713
Great Lakes International Trading, 44715
Great Southern Corp, 44718
Greek Gourmet Limited, 44729
Green Foods Corp., 44733
Grindmaster-Cecilware Corp, 44756
GSW Jackes-Evans Manufacturing Company, 44440
Guans Mushroom Co, 44766
Gulf Food Products Co Inc, 44776
GWB Foods Corporation, 44443
H. Arnold Wood Turning, 44803
H. Interdonati, 44804
H. Reisman Corporation, 44805
Hadley Fruit Orchards, 44829
Haitai Inc, 44835
Haldin International, 44836
Hale Tea Co, 44837
Handgards Inc, 44857
Hanif's International Foods, 44863
Hanimex Company, 44864
Hansen Distribution Group, 44876
Hanson Brass Rewd Co, 44878
Harlan Bakeries, 44896
Harney & Sons Tea Co., 44899
Harold Leonard Southwest Corporation, 44901
Harvest Food Products Co Inc, 44919
Health & Wholeness Store, 44946
Health Flavors, 44948
Health King Enterprise, 44950
Health Plus, 44951
Heartland Mills Shipping, 44962
Hemisphere Group, 44984
Hermann Laue Spice Company, 45001
Herz Meat Company, 45003
HFI Foods, 44818
High Liner Foods Inc., 45015
Hodell International, 45039
Holland Beef International Corporation, 45047
Hoshizaki America Inc, 45085
Houdini Inc, 45090
House Foods America Corp, 45091
House of Spices, 45094
Houston Tea & Beverage, 45096
Howe Corp, 45102
Hoyt's Honey Farm, 45108
Hubco Inc, 45116
Hygrade Gloves, 45148
Ideas Etc Inc, 45204
ILHWA American Corporation, 45171
INA Co, 45176
Incasa Instant Soluble Coffee, 45237
Ind-Us Enterprises/Spice'n Flavor, 45240
Indianapolis Fruit Company, 45254
Indo-European Foods, 45256
Ingredient Inc, 45275
Insects Limited Inc, 45297
Instrumart, 45304
Intedge Manufacturing, 45306
Intercomp, 45317
International Business Trading, 45327
International Coconut Corp, 45332
International Food Packers Corporation, 45342
International Glace, 45346
International Paper Box Machine Company, 45359
International Reserve Equipment Corporation, 45362
International Resources Corporation, 45363
International Sourcing, 45366
International Telcom Inc, 45369
InterNatural Foods, 45313
Island Sweetwater Beverage Company, 45394
Iwatani International Corporation of America, 45415
IWS Scales, 45188
J A Heilferty & Co, 45422
J. Crocker Exports, 45436
Jam Group of Company, 45482
Jarden Home Brands, 45496
Jason Marketing Corporation, 45503
JET Tools, 45457
JFC International Inc, 45458
JH Display & Fixture, 45459
Jilson Group, 45530
Johnson-Rose Corporation, 45557
JW Leser Company, 45470
K & L Intl, 45595
K Katen & Company, 45598
Kal Pac Corp, 45640
KARI-Out Co, 45611
Katagiri & Company, 45658
KeHE Distributors, 45663
Kentea, 45707
Kerekes Bakery & Rstrnt Equip, 45710
KHL Flavors Inc, 45617
Khong Guan Corp, 45726
Kiefer Brushes, Inc, 45728
Kinergy Corp, 45734
Kingston McKnight, 45753
Kinnikinnick Foods, 45755
KM International Corp, 45622
KMT Aqua-Dyne Inc, 45625
Knight Seed Company, 45773
Knutsen Coffees, 45778
Korab Engineering Company, 45801
Kornylak Corp, 45803
Kosto Food Products Co, 45804
KP USA Trading, 45627
Kubla Khan Food Company, 45822
Kyowa Hakko, 45833
L.C. Thompson Company, 45844
L.N. White & Company, 45846
La Flor Spices, 45873
La Societe, 45878
LaCrosse Safety and Industrial, 45880
Lactalis American Group Inc, 45892
Le Fiell Co, 45964
Leavitt Corp., The, 45968
Lee Kum Kee, 45971
Lee's Food Products, 45972
Leedal Inc, 45973
Legion Export & Import Company, 45980
Les Industries Touch Inc, 46004
Letrah International Corp, 46010
Liberty Natural Products Inc, 46024
Liberty Ware LLC, 46027
Libido Funk Circus, 46028
LMK Containers, 45865
Lodge Manufacturing Company, 46089
Louisiana Packing Company, 46123
Lovion International, 46134
Ludwig Mueller Co Inc, 46147
Lumber & Things, 46155
Luminiere Corporation, 46157
Luseaux Labs Inc, 46160
M Phil Yen Company, 46182
M S Plastics & Packaging Inc, 46183
M.E. Heuck Company, 46194
M.H. Rhodes Cramer, 46195
Madys Company, 46239
Magnuson Industries, 46255
Majestic, 46266
Maloney Seafood Corporation, 46276
Mandalay Food Products Corporation, 46289
Manitowoc Foodservice, 46299
Maple Leaf Foods International, 46307
Marin Food Specialties, 46333
Mark NYS, 46341
Mark Products Company, 46342
Markson Lab Sales, 46350
Markwell Manufacturing Company, 46351
Marky's Caviar, 46352
Marsh Company, 46365
Maryland China, 46383
Masala Chai Company, 46388
Mason Transparent Package Company, 46392
Mastercraft Manufacturing Co, 46399
Matrix Packaging Machinery, 46414
McDowell Industries, 46447
Medallion International Inc, 46470
Meduri Farms, 46475
Mello Smello LLC, 46485
Mercado Latino, 46494
Mermaid Seafoods, 46513
Mermaid Spice Corporation, 46514
Messermeister, 46518
Metropolitan Lighting Fixture Company, 46528
Metz Premiums, 46532
Micro Wire Products Inc, 46572
Microplas Industries, 46582
Micropoint, 46583
Midland, 46600
Midwest Badge & Novelty Co, 46604
MIFAB Inc, 46210
Mincing Overseas Spice Company, 46648
Minn-Dak Growers LTD, 46650
Minuteman Trading, 46656
Miracle Exclusives, 46659
Mishima Foods USA, 46664
Mitsui & Co Commodity Risk Management Limited, 46670
Mitsui Foods Inc, 46671
Modern Macaroni Co LTD, 46681
Monarch Import Company, 46702
Montello Inc, 46718
Morris J Golombeck Inc, 46733
Motry International, 46750
Mountain Safety Research, 46753
Mr. Bar-B-Q, 46762
Mrs Auld's Gourmet Foods Inc, 46764
Multikem Corp, 46788
Multisorb Technologies Inc, 46790
Mundial, 46793
Murotech, 46798
Music City Metals Inc, 46806
Mutual Trading Co Inc, 46809
Napco Marketing Corp, 46843
Napoleon Co., 46846
National Scoop & Equipment Company, 46890
Natrol Inc, 46900
Natural Foods Inc, 46907
Natural Oils International, 46910
Nature's Legacy Inc., 46921
Nature's Products Inc, 46925
Near East Importing Corporation, 46936
Neonetics Inc, 46953
Neptune Fisheries, 46956
New England Natural Bakers, 46974
New Organics, 46981
New Orleans Food Co-op, 46982
New York Export Co, 46989
Nexel Industries Inc, 47009
Nexira, 47010
Nichem Co, 47015
Nichimen America, 47016
Nikken Foods, 47027
Northeast Packaging Co, 47082
Northwest Art Glass, 47096
Northwestern Coffee Mills, 47101
Nuchief Sales Inc, 47129
Nuherbs Company, 47131
Nutritional Specialties, 47158
NYP, 46832
Occidental Foods International, LLC, 47178
Okura USA Inc, 47198
Old Dominion Wood Products, 47201
Old Mansion Inc, 47202
Olympia International, 47212
Once Again Nut Butter, 47237
Oneida Food Service, 47239
Ontario Glove and Safety Products, 47243
Ontario International, 47244
OnTrack Automation Inc, 47236
Optimal Nutrients, 47253
Oregon Coffee Roaster, 47267
Organic Products Trading Co, 47276
Orioxi International Corporation, 47286
Ottens Flavors, 47298
Outlook Packaging, 47301
Overlake Foods, 47304
OXO International, 47173
Pacific American Fish Co Inc, 47353
Pacific Nutritional, 47359
Pacific Oasis Enterprise Inc, 47360
Pacific Valley Foods Inc, 47372
Packaging Dynamics, 47384
Padinox, 47401
PAFCO Importing Co, 47322
Pagatech, 47402
Paktronics Controls, 47406
Paleewong Trading Corporation, 47408
Palms & Co, 47418
Pan Pacific Plastics Inc, 47422
Panasonic Commercial Food Service, 47424
Pangaea Sciences, 47428
Pantry Shelf Food Corporation, 47431
Paradise Inc, 47444
Paradise Products, 47446
Paradise Products Corporation, 47447
Parrish's Cake Decorating, 47470
Party Yards, 47476
Parvin Manufacturing Company, 47477
Passport Food Group, 47480
Pastorelli Food Products, 47486
PDE Technology Corp, 47332
Peace Village Organic Foods, 47505
Pelican Bay Ltd., 47525
Pendery's, 47533
Penley Corporation, 47535
Penta Manufacturing Company, 47541
Petra International, 47569
Pharaoh Trading Company, 47579
Pharmachem Labs, 47582
Piazza's Seafood World LLC, 47597
Pictsweet Co, 47603
PMP Fermentation Products, 47337
Polar Ware Company, 47659
Port Royal Sales LTD, 47679
PPI Technologies Group, 47342
Preferred Packaging Systems, 47711
Premier Brass, 47717
Prima Foods, 47740
Primarque Products Inc, 47743
Prime Ingredients Inc, 47744
Primo Water Corporation, 47751
Primrose Candy Co, 47752
Prince of Peace, 47756
Pro-Flo Products, 47764
Producers Peanut Company, 47781
Progressive International/Mr. Dudley, 47801
Pronova Biopolymer, 47812
Purcell International, 47836
Purchase Order Co Of Miami Inc, 47837
Pure Food Ingredients, 47840
Pure Foods, 47841
Pure Sweet Honey Farms Inc, 47845
Putnam Group, 47853
Q.E. Tea, 47861
QBI, 47863
Qualicaps Inc, 47873
Queensway Foods Company, 47890
Queensway Foods Inc., 47891
R&R Sales Company, 47915
R.B. Morriss Company, 47917
Ragtime, 47949
Rahco International, 47950
Rapid Industries Inc, 47971
Rapid Rack Industries, 47973
Raymond-Hadley Corporation, 47981
RDM International, 47928
Red Diamond Coffee & Tea, 47997

728

Import Region / Australia

Redi-Call Inc, 48008
Reed Oven Co, 48012
Reede International Seafood Corporation, 48013
Rego China Corporation, 48034
Reiner Products, 48041
Reinhart Foods, 48042
Resource Trading Company, 48070
Rheon USA, 48084
Rice Company, 48089
Richards Packaging, 48096
Richport International Inc, 48100
Rl Alber T & Son Inc, 48122
Robert Wholey & Co Inc, 48128
Robinson Canning Company, 48136
Roland Foods, LLC, 48161
Roll-O-Sheets Canada, 48164
Rollprint Packaging Prods Inc, 48165
Ron Son Foods Inc, 48169
Ronnie's Ceramic Company, 48173
Roxy Trading Inc, 48208
Royal Baltic LTD, 48210
Royal Crown Enterprises, 48214
Royal Doulton, 48215
Royal Foods Inc, 48217
Royal Industries Inc, 48219
Royal Paper Products, 48224
Ruggiero Seafood, 48242
Russian Chef, 48247
Rv Industries, 48249
S & D Coffee Inc, 48253
S & S Indl Maintenance, 48256
S&R Imports, 48263
S. Ferens & Company, 48266
Sales & Marketing Dev, 48332
Sampac Enterprises, 48344
San Diego Products, 48350
San Fab Conveyor, 48351
San Francisco Herb Co, 48353
San-Ei Gen FFI, 48359
San-J International Inc, 48360
SANGARIA USA, 48271
Sanyo Corporation of America, 48382
Sapporo USA, Inc., 48385
Saratoga Food Specialties, 48390
Scan Coin, 48412
Schiff Food Products Co Inc, 48425
Seal-O-Matic Corp, 48475
Seattle Refrigeration & Manufacturing, 48487
Seawind Foods, 48490
Sentinel Lubricants Inc, 48516
Serendipitea, 48525
Service Ideas, 48536
Service Manufacturing, 48537
Service Packing Company, 48538
Sesaco Corp, 48541
SEW Friel, 48276
Seydel Co, 48556
SGS International Rice Inc, 48278
Shafer-Haggart, 48561
Shank's Extracts Inc, 48566
Sharp Electronics Corporation, 48571
Shekou Chemicals, 48576
Shibuya International, 48588
Shingle Belting, 48594
Shivji Enterprises, 48600
Showeray Corporation, 48608
Signature Brands LLC, 48627
Silver Springs Citrus Inc, 48649
Simco Foods, 48654
Simpson & Vail, 48667
Sinclair Trading, 48671
Slade Gorton & Co Inc, 48689
Snapdragon Foods, 48715
Sobaya, 48731
Sogelco International, 48733
Solutions, 48738
Somerset Industries, 48742
Soodhalter Plastics, 48752
Soofer Co, 48753
Southern Heritage Coffee Company, 48775
Southwestern Porcelain Steel, 48785
Sparkler Filters Inc, 48794
Sparrow Enterprises LTD, 48796

Specialty Blades, 48805
Specialty Commodities Inc, 48807
Spice & Spice, 48828
Spice House International Specialties, 48829
Spir-It/Zoo Piks, 48834
Standard Casing Company, 48875
Standard Paper Box Mach Co Inc, 48880
Standard Terry Mills, 48882
Stanley Orchards Sales, Inc., 48885
Starbruck Foods Corporation, 48896
Starwest Botanicals Inc, 48903
Stauber Performance Ingrdients, 48905
Stavis Seafoods, 48907
Steel City Corporation, 48913
Stichler Products Inc, 48952
Stone Soap Co Inc, 48965
Strohmeyer & Arpe Co Inc, 48987
Summit Import Corp, 49005
Sun Chlorella USA, 49007
Sun Harvest Foods Inc, 49010
Sun Pac Foods, 49013
Sun West Trading, 49016
Sunnyland Farms, 49027
Suntec Power, 49040
Superior Foods, 49053
Suram Trading Corporation, 49066
Sure-Fresh Produce Inc, 49070
Surtec Inc, 49074
Suzhou-Chem Inc, 49077
Sweet Dried Fruit, 49084
T Hasegawa USA Inc, 49117
T.C. Food Export/Import Company, 49121
Tablecraft Products Co Inc, 49153
Tai Foong USA Inc, 49156
Tampa Maid Foods Inc, 49168
Tape Tools, 49181
Taroco Food Corporation, 49187
Tata Tea, 49195
Tate Western, 49196
Taurus Spice, 49198
Tea Importers Inc, 49205
Tech Lighting LLC, 49208
Tecumseh Products Co., 49218
Tek Visions, 49227
Televend, 49234
Telman Incorporated, 49235
Templar Food Products, 49240
The Long Life Beverage Company, 49293
Theta Sciences, 49318
Thomson-Leeds Company, 49330
Tootsi Impex, 49391
Torpac Capsules, 49402
Toshoku America, 49407
Townfood Equipment Corp, 49416
Trade Diversified, 49418
Traex, 49425
Travelon, 49441
TREX Corp Inc., 49141
Tribest Corp, 49463
Triple Dot Corp, 49481
Tripper Inc, 49485
Trout Lake Farm, 49499
Tsar Nicoulai Caviar LLC, 49517
Tuthill Vacuum & Blower Systems, 49539
Twin Marquis, 49546
U L Wholesale Lighting Fixture, 49555
U.C. Import & Company, 49557
UDEC Corp, 49560
Unger Co, 49598
Ungerer & Co, 49599
Union Fish Co, 49611
Unique Manufacturing, 49617
United International Indstrs, 49639
United Meat Company, 49641
United Mineral & Chemical Corporation, 49642
United Performance Metals, 49644
United Seafood Imports, 49648
Universal Security Instrs Inc, 49672
Update International, 49675
Upham & Walsh Lumber, 49676
US Food Products, 49567

Utica Cutlery Co, 49686
Vacuform Inc., 49707
Valley Craft Inc, 49718
Variant, 49744
Vasinee Food Corporation, 49750
Vector Corp, 49753
Venner International Products, 49764
Verax Chemical Co, 49773
Versailles Lighting, 49782
Vetrerie Bruni USA, 49789
VetriTech Laboratories, 49790
Victoria Fine Foods, 49799
Vigo Importing Co, 49807
Vineco International Products, 49819
Vinh Hoan USA, Inc., 49821
VitaMinder Company, 49840
Vitasoy USA, 49847
VMC Corp, 49701
Vollrath Co LLC, 49858
Vyse Gelatin Co, 49868
Wagner Gourmet Foods, 49915
Wah Yet Group, 49918
Walco, 49922
Waring Products, 49950
Water Sciences Services, Inc., 49966
WCC Honey Marketing, 49882
Weaver Nut Co. Inc., 49980
Wei-Chuan USA Inc, 49993
Weinbrenner Shoe Co, 49998
Welch Holme & Clark Co, 50006
Westbrae Natural Foods, 50035
Western Polymer Corp, 50045
Weston Emergency Light Co, 50051
Westwind Resources, 50054
Westwood International, 50055
Whitley Manufacturing Company, 50085
Whitley Peanut Factory Inc, 50086
Whole Herb Co, 50087
Wilke International Inc, 50102
William Bernstein Company, 50111
Willow Group LTD, 50118
Wing Sing Chong Company, 50131
Winmix/Natural Care Products, 50132
Wolfson Casing Corp, 50161
Woodland Foods, 50169
World Class Beer Imports, 50182
World Spice, 50192
World Tableware Inc, 50193
World Wide Safe Brokers, 50197
Xtreme Beverages, LLC, 50220
Yogi® Tea, 50240
Young Winfield, 50246
ZAK Designs Inc, 50253
Zamilco International, 50257
Zarda King LTD, 50258
Ziba Nut Inc, 50281
Zimmer Custom-Made Packaging, 50282
Zwilling J.A. Henckels, 50288

Australia

Algene Marking Equipment Company, 41782
Automatic Bar Controls Inc, 42152
Berkshire Dairy, 42388
Birchwood Foods Inc, 42454
Breakwater Fisheries, 42567
Broadleaf Venison USA Inc, 42587
Campbell Soup Co., 42775
Classic Flavors & Fragrances, 43065
Continental Seasoning, 43229
Dewied International Inc, 43603
DNE World Fruit Sales, 43459
Farm 2 Market, 44115
Flavor Consultants, 44208
Freixenet USA Inc, 44355
Glazier Packing Co, 44595
Houdini Inc, 45090
House of Spices, 45094
Inniskillin Wines, 45282
International Glace, 45346
Island Sweetwater Beverage Company, 45394
J. Crocker Exports, 45436
JAAMA World Trade, 45449
JBS USA LLC, 45452

John I. Haas, 45546
Lamb Cooperative Inc, 45912
Louisiana Packing Company, 46123
Ludwig Mueller Co Inc, 46147
Manildra Milling Corporation, 46297
Natural Oils International, 46910
New England Natural Bakers, 46974
New Zealand Lamb Co, 46992
Nexira, 47010
Pantry Shelf Food Corporation, 47431
Peterson, 47567
Producers Peanut Company, 47781
Purcell International, 47836
RDM International, 47928
Real Soda, 47993
Royal Foods Inc, 48217
Seattle-Tacoma Box Co, 48488
Shivji Enterprises, 48600
Taormina Sales Company, 49178
Tapp Technologies, 49182
Tootsi Impex, 49391
Union Fish Co, 49611
United International Indstrs, 49639
Victor Joseph Son Inc, 49797
Vista Food Exchange, 49833
WACO Beef & Pork Processors, 49880
West Bay Sales, 50022
Whitfield Olive, 50082
Windsor Wax Co Inc, 50124
Ziba Nut Inc, 50281

Austria

Euro Mart/Stolzle Cberg las, 44002

Bahamas

Sunrise Fruit Company, 49031

Bangladesh

Jam Group of Company, 45482

Belgium

Neuhaus, 46962
R&R Sales Company, 47915

Bermuda

Outerbridge Peppers Limited, 47300

Brazil

Compact Industries Inc, 43173
Glazier Packing Co, 44595
Nat-Trop, 46856
Sales King International, 48333
WOW! Nutrition, 49891

Canada

A. Suarez & Company, 41508
AB InBev, 41524
Acatris USA, 41619
Ajinomoto Foods North America, Inc., 41744
Ajinomoto Frozen Foods USA, Inc., 41745
Alsum Farms & Produce, 41844
Altech Packaging Company, 41845
American Lifts, 41902
American Solving Inc., 41921
Ankeny Lake Wild Rice, 41994
Aromachem, 42062
Automatic Bar Controls Inc, 42152
Bakers Choice Products, 42243
Banner Equipment Co, 42268
Barker Company, 42281
Barlean's Fisheries, 42282
Bascom Family Farms Inc, 42293
Beaver Street Fisheries, 42329
Beer Magic Devices, 42347
Blue Cross Laboratories, 42486
Blue Harvest Foods, 42490
Canadian Fish Exporters, 42782
Caravell, 42813
Carolina Mop, 42841
Cascadian Farm Inc, 42868
Cavallini Coffee & Tea, 42888

Import Region / Caribbean

CCS Stone, Inc., 42690
Chesapeake Spice Company, 42975
Chicago Food Corporation, 42986
Ciro Foods, 43044
Complete Packaging & Shipping, 43176
Component Hardware Group Inc, 43178
Conveyance Technologies LLC, 43245
Crown Processing Company, 43374
Crystal Food Import Corporation, 43385
Custom Poly Packaging, 43419
Cybros, 43429
David's Goodbatter, 43511
Dawes Hill Honey Company, 43518
De Choix Specialty Foods Company, 43528
Delgrosso Foods Inc., 43568
Ducktrap River Of Maine, 43715
Dutch Gold Honey Inc, 43742
DWL Industries Company, 43464
East Coast Seafood Inc, 43805
Elopak Americas, 43911
Emerling International Foods, 43921
Ener-G Foods, 43941
Epi De France Bakery, 43967
Fabricon Products Inc, 44089
Feather Duster Corporation, 44126
Fillo Factory, The, 44167
Frontier Bag, 44378
George Degen & Co, 44542
Gerber Cheese Company, 44554
Giovanni's Appetizing Food Co, 44584
Globe Fire Sprinkler Corp, 44613
Good For You America, 44652
Gosselin Gourmet Beverages, 44666
Great Northern Products Inc, 44717
Green Valley Food Corp, 44738
H. Arnold Wood Turning, 44803
Hagensborg Chocolates LTD., 44831
Handy Wacks Corp, 44861
Harold Leonard Southwest Corporation, 44901
Heaven Hill Distilleries Inc., 44967
Henry Gonsalves Co, 44989
Hill 'N' Dale Meat, 45022
Hodell International, 45039
Ingredion Inc., 45278
Interamerican Quality Foods, 45315
International Tank & Pipe Co, 45368
Jilson Group, 45530
John E. Ruggles & Company, 45544
Johnson-Rose Corporation, 45557
Joseph Antognoli & Co, 45571
Lo Temp Sales, 46079
Lumber & Things, 46155
Mason Transparent Package Company, 46392
Mastercraft Industries Inc, 46397
Medallion International Inc, 46470
Medina & Medina, 46471
Merlin Candies, 46510
Merrill's Blueberry Farms, 46515
Metal Equipment Company, 46522
Micro Wire Products Inc, 46572
Minn-Dak Growers LTD, 46650
Miracle Exclusives, 46659
Montana Specialty Mills LLC, 46715
Morey's Seafood Intl LLC, 46726
Mountain Safety Research, 46753
Native Scents, 46897
Nature's Legacy Inc., 46921
Nelson Crab Inc, 46947
New England Natural Bakers, 46974
New England Pallets & Skids, 46975
New England Wooden Ware, 46976
Noon Hour Food Products Inc, 47045
Norpak Corp, 47061
North Bay Trading Co, 47070
North Country Natural Spring Water, 47072
Northwestern Coffee Mills, 47101
Nu-Tex Styles, Inc., 47124
Nutribiotic, 47147
Oneida Food Service, 47239
Oogolow Enterprises, 47246
Outlook Packaging, 47301
Packaging Aids Corporation, 47383
Paradise Products Corporation, 47447
Party Yards, 47476
PDE Technology Corp, 47332
Polean Foods, 47660
Portland Shellfish Company, 47683
Prestige Plastics Corporation, 47730
Priority One America, 47758
Prototype Equipment Corporation, 47819
Quality Sausage Company, 47885
Ragold, 47947
Reese Enterprises Inc, 48017
Rego Smoked Fish Company, 48035
Richards Packaging, 48096
Rigidized Metal Corp, 48106
Ripon Pickle Co Inc, 48110
Royal Palate Foods, 48223
Russian Chef, 48247
Sampco, 48345
San-Ei Gen FFI, 48359
Seatex Ltd, 48483
Seating Concepts Inc, 48484
Shine Companies, 48593
Sid Wainer & Son Specialty, 48614
Simpson & Vail, 48667
Snowcrest Packer, 48724
Sonora Seafood Company, 48751
Soofer Co, 48753
Specialty Meats & Gourmet, 48811
Sun Harvest Foods Inc, 49010
Sundial Herb Garden, 49021
Superior Food Machinery Inc, 49052
Superior Foods, 49053
Tarazi Specialty Foods, 49184
Tate Western, 49196
The Premium Beer Company, 49297
Thomson-Leeds Company, 49330
Trout Lake Farm, 49499
Universal Marketing, 49669
Venture Vineyards, 49771
VMC Corp, 49701
WA Brown & Son, 49878
Water Sciences Services, Inc., 49966
Waymar Industries, 49975
WCC Honey Marketing, 49882
Weston Emergency Light Co, 50051
Wetoska Packaging Distributors, 50058
Wheel Tough Company, 50064
Whitfield Olive, 50082
WNA, 49888
World Class Beer Imports, 50182
World Tableware Inc, 50193
Young's Lobster Pound, 50247

Caribbean

Anjo's Imports, 41993
Balzac Brothers & Co Inc, 42262
Beaver Street Fisheries, 42329
Catskill Mountain Specialties, 42884
Chesapeake Spice Company, 42975
Couture Farms, 43309
Crosby Molasses Company, 43356
DNE World Fruit Sales, 43459
DWL Industries Company, 43464
Eco Wine & Spirits, 43830
Flamingo Flats, 44204
Gillies Coffee, 44575
Hamersmith, Inc., 44846
Heaven Hill Distilleries Inc., 44967
International Pack & Ship, 45357
M Phil Yen Company, 46182
Molinaro's Fine Italian Foods Ltd., 46694
Neptune Fisheries, 46956
Northwestern Coffee Mills, 47101
Paradise Products Corporation, 47447
Portuguese United Grocer Co-Op, 47685
Prima Foods International, 47741
Producers Peanut Company, 47781
Raymond-Hadley Corporation, 47981
Refrigerator Manufacturers LLC, 48023
Rice Company, 48089
Rosenthal & Kline, 48184
Rowland Coffee Roasters Inc., 48205
Sampco, 48345
Saratoga Food Specialties, 48390
Sid Wainer & Son Specialty, 48614
Specialty Coffee Roasters, 48806
Tropical Commodities, 49492
Warbac Sales Co, 49947
Wheel Tough Company, 50064
World's Finest Chocolate Inc, 50199

Caribbean Islands

D Steengrafe Co Inc, 43441

Central America

3V Company, 41472
4M Fruit Distribution, 41474
Abarbanel Wine Company, 41603
Abbott & Cobb Inc, 41606
Able Sales Company, 41612
Agger Fish Corp, 41714
Agri-Dairy Products, 41719
Alfa Chem, 41775
Alfred L. Wolff, Inc., 41781
Allegro Coffee Co, 41809
Allied Glove Corporation, 41821
Allied International Corp, 41822
Alsum Farms & Produce, 41844
Alternative Health & Herbs, 41847
American Food Traders, 41888
American Importing Co., 41894
American Key Food Products Inc, 41897
American Seafood Imports Inc., 41919
Arista Industries Inc, 42044
Atrium Biotech, 42131
Avatar Corp, 42164
Awe Sum Organics, 42175
B. Terfloth & Company, 42194, 42195
Balzac Brothers & Co Inc, 42262
Bascom Food Products, 42294
Basic Food Intl Inc, 42297
Bayou Food Distributors, 42314
Beach Filter Products, 42318
Beaver Street Fisheries, 42329
Bedemco Inc, 42337
Ben-Bud Growers Inc., 42375
Best Value Textiles, 42412
Bolner's Fiesta Spices, 42512
Boston Sausage & Provision, 42531
Boston Seafarms, 42532
Boston's Best Coffee Roasters, 42533
Brooks Instrument LLC, 42597
Brooks Tropicals Inc, 42598
BVL Controls, 42213
BWI, Inc., 42215
Cabo Rojo Enterprises, 42719
Caffe Luca Coffee Roaste, 42731
Cal Trading Company, 42738
Cal-Tex Citrus Juice LP, 42742
California Cereal Products, 42749
California Olive Oil Council, 42756
California World Trade and Marketing Company, 42758
Campbell Soup Co., 42775
Candy Tech LLC, 42791
Carlota Foods International, 42835
Cascadian Farm Inc, 42868
Caspian Trading Company, 42873
Catskill Mountain Specialties, 42884
Caudill Seed Co Inc, 42887
CCS Stone, Inc., 42690
Celite Corporation, 42898
Cheeseland, Inc., 42948
Chef Merito Inc, 42951
Chef Revival, 42952
Chemicolloid Laboratories, Inc., 42966
Cherith Valley Gardens, 42971
Chesapeake Spice Company, 42975
Chiquita Brands LLC., 43008
Citrico, 43048
Classic Flavors & Fragrances, 43065
Coffee Express Roasting Co, 43119
Coffeeco, 43121
Community Coffee Co., 43170
Container Machinery Corporation, 43216
Continental Marketing, 43227
Continental Seasoning, 43229
Corby Distilleries, 43267
Cosgrove Enterprises Inc, 43289
Couture Farms, 43309
Crown Foods International, 43367
Custom Source LLC, 43422
D.F. International, 43448
Dairy Fresh Foods Inc, 43471
Dal-Don Produce, 43481
Darik Enterprises Inc, 43501
Davis Trade & Commodities, 43515
Dawes Hill Honey Company, 43518
Deep Sea Products, 43550
Defranco Co, 43553
Deiss Sales Co. Inc., 43556
Di Lusso & Be Bop Baskote LLC, 43605
Di Mare Fresh Inc, 43606
Dillanos Coffee Roasters, 43630
Dipasa USA Inc, 43634
Dishaka Imports, 43639
DSM Fortitech Premixes, 43461
Ducktrap River Of Maine, 43715
Dundee Groves, 43720
Dura-Ware Company of America, 43730
DWL Industries Company, 43464
Eastern Tea Corp, 43813
Eckhart Corporation, 43825
EDCO Food Products Inc, 43774
Elco Fine Foods, 43882
Elite Spice Inc, 43895
Emerling International Foods, 43921
Encore Fruit Marketing Inc, 43937
Ener-G Foods, 43941
Essential Products of America, 43992
Euclid Coffee Co, 43998
Eximcan Canada, 44048
Eximco Manufacturing Company, 44049
Felbro Food Products, 44133
Felins USA Inc, 44136
Fernandez Chili Co, 44141
Finest Foods, 44178
First Colony Coffee & Tea Company, 44186
Fitec International Inc, 44196
Flamingo Flats, 44204
Fleurchem Inc, 44226
Florida European Export-Import, 44241
Florida Food Products Inc, 44242
Franklin Trading Company, 44339
Freeman Industries, 44350
Fruit Belt Canning Inc, 44384
Fruitcrown Products Corp, 44386
Fry Foods Inc, 44390
G K Skaggs Inc, 44409
G-M Super Sales Company, 44413
Galil Importing Corp, 44455
Garuda International, 44483
General Bag Corporation, 44515
Gerber Products Co, 44557
Gillies Coffee, 44575
Glacier Foods, 44590
Gold Pure Food Products Co. Inc., 44624
Grain Machinery Mfg Corp, 44685
Great American Appetizers, 44706
Great Lakes International Trading, 44715
Gulf Pride Enterprises, 44779
H. Arnold Wood Turning, 44803
Haldin International, 44836
Hamersmith, Inc., 44846
Hanif's International Foods, 44863
Hanover Foods Corp, 44871
HealthBest, 44954
Heaven Hill Distilleries Inc., 44967
Hemisphere Group, 44984
HFI Foods, 44818
Hill 'N' Dale Meat, 45022
Holland Beef International Corporation, 45047
House of Spices, 45094
Howell Associates, 45103
Hoyt's Honey Farm, 45108
Hudson Valley Coffee Company, 45119
Incasa Instant Soluble Coffee, 45237
Indian Ridge Shrimp Co, 45248
Indianapolis Fruit Company, 45254
Ingersoll Rand Inc, 45272
Ingredient Inc, 45275
Ingredion Inc., 45278
Interamerican Quality Foods, 45315

730

Import Region / Chile

Intercomp, 45317
International Beverages, 45326
International Business Trading, 45327
International Oils & Concentrates, 45354
International Pack & Ship, 45357
International Reserve Equipment Corporation, 45362
International Sourcing, 45366
International Telcom Inc, 45369
InterNatural Foods, 45313
Island Sweetwater Beverage Company, 45394
JBS USA LLC, 45452
Jordon Commercial Refrigerator, 45568
KHL Flavors Inc, 45617
Khong Guan Corp, 45726
Kinergy Corp, 45734
Knutsen Coffees, 45778
Kosto Food Products Co, 45804
Kurtz Orchards Farms, 45828
L.N. White & Company, 45846
LA Cena Fine Foods LTD, 45848
La Flor Spices, 45873
Lemberger Candy Corporation, 45990
Letrah International Corp, 46010
Liberty Natural Products Inc, 46024
LMK Containers, 45865
Louisiana Packing Company, 46123
Ludwig Mueller Co Inc, 46147
Lukas Confections, 46151
Lumber & Things, 46155
MacGregors Meat & Seafood, 46222
Malgor & Company, 46272
Maple Leaf Foods International, 46307
Marantha Natural Foods, 46316
Marin Food Specialties, 46333
Marubeni America Corp., 46376
Maxim's Import Corporation, 46426
Melitta USA Inc, 46484
Mercado Latino, 46494
Messermeister, 46518
Messina Brothers Manufacturing Company, 46519
Milligan & Higgins, 46634
Mincing Overseas Spice Company, 46648
Mitsui Foods Inc, 46671
ML Catania Company, 46213
Molinaro's Fine Italian Foods Ltd., 46694
Morris J Golombeck Inc, 46733
Motivatit Seafoods Inc, 46748
My Quality Trading Corp, 46813
Napoleon Co, 46846
Natural Oils International, 46910
Neptune Fisheries, 46956
New Organics, 46981
North Bay Produce Inc, 47069
Northwest Naturals Company, 47099
Northwestern Coffee Mills, 47101
O'Dell Corp, 47163
Occidental Foods International, LLC, 47178
Old Mansion Inc, 47202
Once Again Nut Butter, 47237
Ontario International, 47244
Oregon Coffee Roaster, 47267
Organic Products Trading Co, 47276
Organics Unlimited, 47279
Orioxi International Corporation, 47286
Otis McAllister Inc., 47297
Ottens Flavors, 47298
Outlook Packaging, 47301
Overlake Foods, 47304
Oxygen Import LLC, 47310
Padinox, 47401
Pangaea Sciences, 47428
Pantry Shelf Food Corporation, 47431
Paradise Island Foods, 47445
Paradise Products, 47446
Paradise Products Corporation, 47447
Pastorelli Food Products, 47486
Pearl Coffee Co, 47508
Pendery's, 47533
Penta Manufacturing Company, 47541
Peter Pan Seafoods Inc., 47564
Piazza's Seafood World LLC, 47597

PPI Technologies Group, 47342
Prima Foods, 47740
Prima Foods International, 47741
Puratos Canada, 47835
Purcell International, 47836
Purchase Order Co Of Miami Inc, 47837
Pure Foods, 47841
R H Saw Corp, 47904
R.A.V. Colombia, 47916
R.B. Morriss Company, 47917
R.H. Chandler Company, 47919
Ray Cosgrove Brokerage Company, 47978
Raymond-Hadley Corporation, 47981
RDM International, 47928
Red Diamond Coffee & Tea, 47997
Regal Crown Foods Inc, 48026
Rice Company, 48089
Ripon Pickle Co Inc, 48110
Robin Shepherd Group, 48135
Roland Foods, LLC, 48161
Rowland Coffee Roasters Inc., 48205
Royal Crown Enterprises, 48214
Ruggiero Seafood, 48242
S & D Coffee Inc, 48253
S & S Indl Maintenance, 48256
S. Ferens & Company, 48266
Sands Brands International Food, 48369
Sassone Wholesale Groceries Co, 48394
Schiff Food Products Co Inc, 48425
Seawind Foods, 48490
Sentinel Lubricants Inc, 48516
Sesaco Corp, 48541
SEW Friel, 48276
Shekou Chemicals, 48576
Shipley Sales, 48596
Shivji Enterprises, 48600
Sid Wainer & Son Specialty, 48614
Sinclair Trading, 48671
Slade Gorton & Co Inc, 48689
Sogelco International, 48733
Somerset Industries, 48742
Southern Heritage Coffee Company, 48775
Sparrow Enterprises LTD, 48796
Specialty Coffee Roasters, 48806
Spice & Spice, 48828
Starbruck Foods Corporation, 48896
Starwest Botanicals Inc, 48903
Stauber Performance Ingrdients, 48905
Stavis Seafoods, 48907
Steelite International USA, 48919
Sterling Paper Company, 48935
Stewart's Private Blend Foods, 48951
Stone Soap Co Inc, 48965
Sun Harvest Foods Inc, 49010
Sun Pac Foods, 49013
Sunnyland Farms, 49027
Superior Foods, 49053
Surface Banana Company, 49072
Sweet Dried Fruit, 49084
Tai Foong USA Inc, 49156
Tampa Maid Foods Inc, 49168
Tantos Foods International, 49176
Tarazi Specialty Foods, 49184
Tea Importers Inc, 49205
Texas Coffee Co, 49264
The Long Life Beverage Company, 49293
Todhunter Foods, 49373
Torrefazione Barzula & Import, 49404
Trans Pecos Foods, 49430
Transit Trading Corporation, 49435
Tri Car Sales, 49450
Trout Lake Farm, 49499
Turbana Corp., 49530
Uncle Fred's Fine Foods, 49594
Ungerer & Co, 49599
United Banana Company, 49628
United International Indstrs, 49639
US Food Products, 49567
V-Ram Solids, 49690
V-Suarez Provisions, 49691
Venner International Products, 49764
Vescom America, 49786
Victor Joseph Son Inc, 49797

Victoria Fine Foods, 49799
Vincent Formusa Company, 49817
Vista Food Exchange, 49833
VMC Corp, 49701
WCC Honey Marketing, 49882
Weaver Nut Co. Inc., 49980
Webeco Foods, 49985
Wechsler Coffee Corporation, 49987
West Pak Avocado Inc, 50032
Whitfield Olive, 50081, 50082
Whitley Manufacturing Company, 50085
Whitley Peanut Factory Inc, 50086
Willing Group, 50116
Windsor Wax Co Inc, 50124
Wixson Honey Inc, 50156
Woodland Foods, 50169
World Spice, 50192

Chile

American Agrotrading, 41868
Ballantine Produce Company, 42254
Royal Vista Marketing Inc, 48225
Santini Foods, 48381
Sarant International Cmmdts, 48389
Unique Ingredients LLC, 49616

China

China Pharmaceutical Enterprises, 43003
DWL Industries Company, 43464
Everfresh Food Corporation, 44028
Fabriko, 44090
Garlic and Spice, Inc., 44481
GET Enterprises LLC, 44430
Hardware Components Inc, 44892
Harten Corporation, 44913
Kal Pac Corp, 45640
Kwok Shing Hong, 45832
Lights On, 46038
Metz Premiums, 46532
Mexspice, 46538
National Band Saw Co, 46861
R&R Sales Company, 47915
Spice & Spice, 48828
Sunflower Restaurant Supply, 49022
Taurus Spice, 49198
Thorpe & Associates, 49334
Tradeco International Corp, 49421
United Mineral & Chemical Corporation, 49642
W.Y. International, 49877
Walong Marketing, 49935
Wixson Honey Inc, 50156
World Tableware Inc, 50193

Columbia

Compact Industries Inc, 43173
Mani Imports, 46295

Costa Rica

Flamingo Flats, 44204

Cyprus

Athenee Imports Distributors, 42102

Denmark

Exhausto, 44046
World's Best Cheeses, 50198

Dominican Republic

Coco Lopez Inc, 43114
Prima Foods International, 47741

East Africa

Gillies Coffee, 44575
Young Winfield, 50246

Ecquador

Kitchens Seafood, 45762

Ecuador

Fine Cocoa Products, 44175
Unique Ingredients LLC, 49616

Egypt

Allied International Corp, 41822

Europe

3V Company, 41472
A Gift Basket by Carmela, 41481
A&A International, 41488
A&B Safe Corporation, 41491
A. Suarez & Company, 41508
A.J. Trucco, 41513
AAMD, 41522
AANTEC, 41523
Abbeon Cal Inc, 41604
Abbott & Cobb Inc, 41606
ABC Coffee & Pasta, 41526
Abimco USA, Inc., 41611
ABM Marking, 41531
ABO Industries, 41532
Aceto Corporation, 41634
ACH Food Co Inc, 41534
Acme Scale Co, 41640
Acta Health Products, 41652
ACTS, 41538
Adamba Imports Intl, 41665
Adams Fisheries Ltd, 41667
Admatch Corporation, 41673
Adolf's Meats & Sausage Kitchen, 41676
Adrienne's Gourmet Foods, 41680
Advance Fittings Corp, 41683
Advanced Food Systems, 41691
Advantage Gourmet Importers, 41697
AEP Colloids, 41544
Agger Fish Corp, 41714
Agri-Dairy Products, 41719
Agro Foods, Inc., 41725
Agropur, 41728
Agrusa, 41729
AHD International, LLC, 41553
AIDP Inc, 41554
Ajinomoto Heartland Inc, 41746
Al Gelato Bornay, 41749
Albert A Russo Inc, 41765
Albert Uster Imports Inc, 41766
Alfa Chem, 41775
Alfa International Corp, 41776
Alfred L. Wolff, Inc., 41781
Alimentaire Whyte's Inc, 41786
Allemagnia Imports Inc, 41811
Allied Glove Corporation, 41821
Allied International Corp, 41822
Amark Packaging Systems, 41857
Ambassador Fine Foods, 41860
Ambriola Co, 41862
American Bag & Burlap Company, 41869
American European Systems, 41879
American Key Food Products Inc, 41897
American Lecithin Company, 41901
American Specialty Coffee & Culinary, 41922
American Trading Company, 41927
Ameripak Packaging Equipment, 41935
Ames Company, Inc, 41939
Ammeraal Beltech Inc, 41949
Amphora International, 41955
ANVER Corporation, 41573
AP Dataweigh Inc, 41575
API Heat Transfer Inc, 41577
Apple & Eve LLC, 42009
Arla Foods Inc, 42051
Aroma Vera, 42060
Aroma-Life, 42061
Aromachem, 42062
Arrow Chemical Inc, 42067
Arrowac Fisheries, 42070
Astor Chocolate Corp, 42092
Astoria General Espresso, 42093
Astral Extracts, 42095
Atlantis Smoked Foods, 42122
Atwater Block Brewing Company, 42133
August Thomsen Corp, 42137
Aust & Hachmann, 42142
Austrade, 42143
Autocon Mixing Systems, 42147
Automatic Bar Controls Inc, 42152

731

Import Region / Europe

AV Olsson Trading Company, 41594
Awe Sum Organics, 42175
B T Engineering Inc, 42191
B. Terfloth & Company, 42194
Bacardi Canada, Inc., 42222
BakeMark Ingredients Canada, 42236
Bakers Choice Products, 42243
Banner Equipment Co, 42268
Barilla USA, 42280
Barker Company, 42281
Barrows Tea Company, 42287
Barry Group, 42289
Barton Beers, 42291
Bascom Food Products, 42294
Basic Leasing Corporation, 42298
Battaglia Distributing Corp, 42302
Bazzini Holdings LLC, 42316
Beach Filter Products, 42318
Beaufurn, 42326
Beaver Street Fisheries, 42329
Beer Import Co, 42346
Bel Brands USA, 42351
Bell'Amore Imports, 42359
Belt Technologies Inc, 42370
Belukus Marketing, 42372
Belxport, 42373
Benner China & Glassware Inc, 42377
Bericap North America, Inc., 42385
Best Chicago Meat, 42407
BEUMER Corp, 42205
Bewley Irish Imports, 42429
BFM Equipment Sales, 42208
Bijur Lubricating Corporation, 42435
Binks Industries Inc, 42439
Blachere Group, 42464
Blessed Herbs, 42477
Blossom Farm Products, 42482
Blue Feather Products Inc, 42488
Blue Giant Equipment Corporation, 42489
Bluebird Manufacturing, 42498
BMT Commodity Corporation, 42211
Bob Gordon & Associates, 42505
Boehringer Mfg. Co. Inc., 42509
Bolzoni Auramo, 42513
Bon Appetit International, 42515
Bonduelle North America, 42518
Boston's Best Coffee Roasters, 42533
Boyd Lighting Company, 42544
Bradford A Ducon Company, 42546
Brady Enterprises Inc, 42550
Brasserie Brasel Brewery, 42561
Bratt-Foster-Advantage Sales, 42562
Brechtesen, 42569
Brewmatic Company, 42575
British Depot, 42584
British Shoppe LLC, 42585
Brooks Instrument LLC, 42597
Brown-Forman Corp, 42611
Brucia Plant Extracts, 42613
Buckhorn Canada, 42625
Buena Vista Historic Tstng Rm, 42629
Buffalo Trace Distillery, 42631
Bulk Pack, 42633
Buonitalia, 42641
Burling Instrument Inc, 42646
BVL Controls, 42213
C Pacific Foods Inc, 42673
Cadie Products Corp, 42726
CAI International, 42687
Cal-Tex Citrus Juice LP, 42742
California Olive Oil Council, 42756
Camerican International, 42770
Campbell Soup Co., 42775
Canada Cutlery Inc., 42780
Candy Tech LLC, 42791
Carl Brandt Inc, 42828
Carle & Montanari-O P M, 42829
Carothers Olive Oil, 42844
Carpigiani Corporation of America, 42846
Carriere Foods Inc, 42851
Casa Pons USA, 42865
Cavallini Coffee & Tea, 42888
CCS Stone, Inc., 42690
CEA Instrument Inc, 42693

Celite Corporation, 42898
Charmel Enterprises, 42937
Cheese Merchants of America, 42947
Chef Merito Inc, 42951
Chef Revival, 42952
Chemicolloid Laboratories, Inc., 42966
Cher-Make Sausage Co, 42969
Chesapeake Spice Company, 42975
Chester Plastics, 42978
Chicago Scale & Slicer Company, 42989
Chipurnoi Inc, 43007
Chocolate Concepts, 43012
Chocolates a La Carte, 43017
Church & Dwight Co., Inc., 43031
Cipriani, 43040
Ciro Foods, 43044
Citterio USA, 43052
CK Products, 42702
Clarkson Scottish Bakery, 43064
Classic Flavors & Fragrances, 43065
Clown Global Brands, 43101
Coburn Company, 43111
Codema, 43115
Coffee Brothers Inc, 43117
Coffee Express Roasting Co, 43119
Collins International, 43136
Colonial Coffee Roasters Inc, 43141
Comark Instruments, 43153
Comasec Safety, Inc., 43154
Combi Packaging Systems LLC, 43155
Commercial Furniture Group Inc, 43162
Commodities Marketing Inc, 43167
Compact Industries Inc, 43173
Component Hardware Group Inc, 43178
Con-tech/Conservation Technology, 43189
Conca D'Oro Importers, 43194
Conflow Technologies, Inc., 43199
Connection Chemical LP, 43202
Container Machinery Corporation, 43216
Contemporary Product Inc, 43219
Continental Marketing, 43227
Continental Seasoning, 43229
Contract & Leisure, 43232
Cool Care, 43259
Corby Distilleries, 43267
Corby Hall, 43268
Coriell Associates, 43273
Cork Specialties, 43275
Coronet Chandelier Originals, 43282
Cosmopolitan Wine Agents, 43291
Cotton Goods Mfg Co, 43296
Craft Distillers, 43315
Creative Coatings Corporation, 43327
Crestware, 43345
Crown Custom Metal Spinning, 43365
Crown Foods International, 43367
Crystal Food Import Corporation, 43385
Crystal-Vision Packaging Systems, 43390
CSC Scientific Co Inc, 42712
Culinary Institute Lenotre, 43395
Culinary Masters Corporation, 43396
Culinary Specialties, 43397
Custom Rubber Stamp Co, 43420
Cutrite Company, 43427
Dairy Fresh Foods Inc, 43471
Dairy Specialties, 43472
Dairygold, 43477
Dairyland USA Corp, 43478
Dalemark Industries, 43482
Dana-Lu Imports, 43491
Danbury Plastics, 43493
Daniele International, 43496
Daprano & Co, 43498
David's Goodbatter, 43511
Davis Strait Fisheries, 43514
DBE Inc, 43451
De Choix Specialty Foods Company, 43528
De Ster Corporation, 43533
Dedert Corporation, 43545
Defranco Co, 43553
Dehydrates Inc, 43555
Deiss Sales Co. Inc., 43556
Delavau LLC, 43564
Delicious Desserts, 43570

Dependable Machine, Inc., 43586
Desco USA, 43588
Destileria Serralles Inc, 43597
DeVries Imports, 43537
Dewied International Inc, 43603
Dipasa USA Inc, 43634
Dishaka Imports, 43639
Ditting USA, 43648
DNE World Fruit Sales, 43459
Dorton Incorporated, 43674
Douglas Homs Corporation, 43679
Doyon, 43689
Drehmann Paving & Flooring Company, 43703
DSM Fortitech Premixes, 43461
Ducktrap River Of Maine, 43715
Dundee Groves, 43720
DuPont Nutrition & Biosciences, 43713
Dura-Ware Company of America, 43730
DWL Industries Company, 43464
E & E Process Instrumentation, 43755
E Waldo Ward & Son Marmalades, 43758
E-Z Edge Inc, 43763
East Coast Seafood Inc, 43805
Eastern Tea Corp, 43813
Ebonex Corporation, 43822
Eckhart Corporation, 43825
Economy Paper & Restaurant Co, 43844
Ecoval Dairy Trade, 43846
Eden, 43850
Edoko Food Importers, 43864
Edward & Sons Trading Co, 43868
El Peto Products, 43877
Elco Fine Foods, 43882
Elite Spice Inc, 43895
Elliot Lee, 43901
Elopak Americas, 43911
Emblem & Badge, 43916
Emerling International Foods, 43921
Empire Spice Mills, 43931
Emtrol, 43935
Emuamericas, 43936
Enzyme Development Corporation, 43965
Epi De France Bakery, 43967
Espresso Specialists, 43987
Essential Products of America, 43992
Euro-Excellence, 44007
Euroam Importers Inc, 44009
Eurobubblies, 44010
Eurodib, 44011
European Foods, 44015
European Imports, 44017
Excellence Commercial Products, 44041
Eximcan Canada, 44048
Eximco Manufacturing Company, 44049
F & A Dairy Products Inc, 44055
F.H. Taussig Company, 44067
Fabricon Products Inc, 44089
Famarco Limited, 44106
Fantastic World Foods, 44110
Fantis Foods Inc, 44112
Fawema Packaging Machinery, 44123
Felbro Food Products, 44133
Felins USA Inc, 44136
Ferrara Bakery & Cafe, 44144
Ferroclad Fishery, 44150
Filtercorp, 44170
Fiorucci Foods USA Inc, 44181
Flamingo Flats, 44204
Flavor Consultants, 44208
Flavor Dynamics Two, 44209
Flavormatic Industries, 44217
Fleurchem Inc, 44226
Florida Food Products Inc, 44242
Food Ireland, Inc., 44280
Food Resources International, 44285
FoodMatch, Inc., 44291
Foodworks International, 44297
FPEC Corporation, 44079
Franklin Trading Company, 44339
Franrica Systems, 44340
Frederick Wildman & Sons LTD, 44345
Fredrick Ramond Company, 44346
Freeda Vitamins Inc, 44347
Freeman Industries, 44350

Freixenet USA Inc, 44355
Freudenberg Nonwovens, 44367
Fruit Belt Canning Inc, 44384
Fruitcrown Products Corp, 44386
Furgale Industries Ltd., 44402
G K Skaggs Inc, 44409
G Nino Bragelli Inc, 44410
Gabriella Imports, 44445
Gar Products, 44466
GCI Nutrients, 44419
Gea Us, 44504
General Bag Corporation, 44515
General Commodities International, 44517
General, Inc, 44531
Gensaco Marketing, 44537
George Degen & Co, 44542
Gerber Cheese Company, 44554
Gerber Products Co, 44557
Gerlau Sales, 44558
Germack Pistachio Co, 44559
Giesser, 44570
Gilly Galoo, 44576
Giovanni's Appetizing Food Co, 44584
GLAC Seat Inc, 44433
Glo-Quartz Electric Heater, 44600
Global Manufacturing, 44608
Globe Fire Sprinkler Corp, 44613
Glowmaster Corporation, 44618
Glucona America, 44619
Gold Pure Food Products Co. Inc., 44624
Golden Beach Inc, 44627
Golden Bridge Enterprises Inc, 44628
Goodway Industries Inc, 44660
Gourm-E-Company Imports, 44669
Gourmet Club Corporation, 44671
Gourmet International Inc, 44675
Grace Tea Co, 44681
Grain Machinery Mfg Corp, 44685
Great American Appetizers, 44706
Great Eastern Sun Trading Co, 44709
Great Lakes International Trading, 44715
Greek Gourmet Limited, 44729
Green Valley Food Corp, 44738
Grgich Hills Estates, 44747
Griesedieck Imports, 44749
Grindmaster-Cecilware Corp, 44756
Groupe Paul Masson, 44761
Guans Mushroom Co, 44766
Guinness Import Co, 44772
Gumpert's Canada, 44782
GWB Foods Corporation, 44443
H A Phillips & Co, 44789
H R Nicholson Co, 44799
H. Interdonati, 44804
H. Reisman Corporation, 44805
Habasit America, 44825
Hagensborg Chocolates LTD., 44831
Haitai Inc, 44835
Hale Tea Co, 44837
Halton Company, 44843
Hampton Associates & Sons, 44852
Handy Wacks Corp, 44861
Hanif's International Foods, 44863
Hans Holterbosch Inc, 44873
Haram-Christensen Corp, 44885
Harold Leonard Southwest Corporation, 44901
Hart Design & Mfg, 44912
Hartstone Pottery Inc, 44916
Hassia, 44922
Health Flavors, 44948
HealthBest, 44954
Healthmate Products, 44955
Heaven Hill Distilleries Inc., 44967
Henry Gonsalves Co, 44989
Hermann Laue Spice Company, 45001
Herz Meat Company, 45003
HFI Foods, 44818
High Liner Foods Inc., 45015
Hilden Halifax, 45021
Hillside Candy Co, 45024
Hodell International, 45039
Holistic Products Corporation, 45045
Holland Beef International Corporation, 45047

Import Region / Europe

Holland-American International Specialties, 45049
Hollymatic Corp, 45052
Hood River Distillers Inc, 45071
Horix Manufacturing Co, 45077
Houdini Inc, 45090
House of Spices, 45094
Howell Associates, 45103
Hoyt's Honey Farm, 45108
Hudson-Sharp Machine Company, 45123
Hunter Walton & Co Inc, 45132
Hydropure Water Treatment Co, 45143
Ibertrade Commercial Corporation, 45189
IBF, 45161
Imperial Sensus, 45225
Important Wines, 45226
Indianapolis Fruit Company, 45254
Indo-European Foods, 45256
Ingersoll & Assoc, 45271
Ingersoll Rand Inc, 45272
Ingredient Exchange Co, 45274
Ingredient Inc, 45275
Inniskillin Wines, 45282
Inno-Vite, 45283
Inox Tech, 45295
Insects Limited Inc, 45297
Insinger Co, 45300
Instant Products of America, 45303
Intedge Manufacturing, 45306
Inter-Continental Imports Company, 45310
Intercomp, 45317
Intermix Beverage, 45322
International Beverages, 45326
International Enterprises Unlimited, 45338
International Foods & Confections, 45345
International Oils & Concentrates, 45354
International Reserve Equipment Corporation, 45362
International Sourcing, 45366
International Trading Company, 45370
International Ventures, 45372
InterNatural Foods, 45313
Irish Tea Sales, 45387
Island Sweetwater Beverage Company, 45394
Islander Import, 45395
Italian Quality Products, 45403
Italica Imports, 45404
J A Heilferty & Co, 45422
J. Crocker Exports, 45436
J. Rutigliano & Sons, 45438
JAAMA World Trade, 45449
Jack Stack, 45475
Jamaican Teas Limited C/O Eve Sales Corporation, 45483
Jamieson Laboratories, 45488
JET Tools, 45457
Jilson Group, 45530
JLS Foods International, 45462
Joe Clark Fund Raising Candies, 45535
John E. Ruggles & Company, 45544
John I. Haas, 45546
Johnson-Rose Corporation, 45557
Joseph Antognoli & Co, 45571
Joseph Gies Import, 45572
Josheph Gies Import, 45575
Jp Tropical Foods, 45578
Judel Products, 45582
JW Leser Company, 45470
K Katen & Company, 45598
Karoun Dairies Inc, 45652
Kedco Wine Storage Systems, 45680
KeHE Distributors, 45663
Kemach Food Products, 45695
Kemutec Group Inc, 45699
Kentea, 45707
Kerekes Bakery & Rstrnt Equip, 45710
KHL Flavors Inc, 45617
Kinergy Corp, 45734
Kinnikinnick Foods, 45755
Kisters Kayat, 45760
Knall Beverage, 45770

Kobrand Corporation, 45779
Kodex Inc, 45782
Korab Engineering Company, 45801
Kreiner Imports, 45811
Krinos Foods, 45813
KUKA Robotics Corp, 45630
L.C. Thompson Company, 45844
L.N. White & Company, 45846
La Belle Suisse Corporation, 45870
LA Cena Fine Foods LTD, 45848
La Flor Spices, 45873
La Pine Scientific Company, 45876
Lactalis American Group Inc, 45892
Larose & Fils Lte, 45943
Latendorf Corporation, 45947
Le Cordon Bleu, 45962
Lee's Food Products, 45972
Leedal Inc, 45973
Legion Export & Import Company, 45980
Leland Limited Inc, 45987
Leonidas, 45998
Letrah International Corp, 46010
Leyman Manufacturing Corporation, 46019
Liberty Natural Products Inc, 46024
Liberty Richter, 46026
Lifestar Millennium, 46029
Lodge Manufacturing Company, 46089
Longhorn Liquors, 46102
Ludwig Mueller Co Inc, 46147
Lukas Confections, 46151
Lumber & Things, 46155
Luminiere Corporation, 46157
Lutz Pumps Inc, 46163
M O Industries Inc, 46181
M Phil Yen Company, 46182
Mac Knight Smoke House Inc, 46221
MAF Industries Inc, 46197
Magnotta Winery Corporation, 46252
Magnuson Industries, 46255
Majestic Inc, 46266
Majesty, 46268
Malgor & Company, 46272
Malthus Diagnostics, 46280
Mancuso Cheese Co, 46288
Manicaretti Italian Food Importers, 46296
Maple Leaf Foods International, 46307
Margate Wine & Spirit Co, 46328
Marglo Products Corporation, 46329
Marin Food Specialties, 46333
Mario's Gelati, 46338
Mark NYS, 46341
Market Forge Industries Inc, 46344
Markson Lab Sales, 46350
Marky's Caviar, 46352
Marsh Company, 46365
Maryland China, 46383
MarySue.com, 46382
Mastercraft Industries Inc, 46397
Mastercraft Manufacturing Co, 46399
Matfer Inc, 46407, 46408
Max Landau & Company, 46423
Maxim's Import Corporation, 46426
Mecco Marking & Traceability, 46469
Medallion International Inc, 46470
Medina & Medina, 46471
Meduri Farms, 46475
MeGa Industries, 46463
Mehu-Liisa Products, 46479
Melitta USA Inc, 46484
Mercado Latino, 46494
Mermaid Seafoods, 46513
Mermaid Spice Corporation, 46514
Messermeister, 46518
Messina Brothers Manufacturing Company, 46519
Metropolitan Lighting Fixture Company, 46528
Mettler-Toledo Process Analytics, Inc, 46529
MFI Food Canada, 46206
Micelli Chocolate Mold Company, 46549
Micropure Filtration Inc, 46585
Midland, 46600

Midwest Imports LTD, 46607
Milligan & Higgins, 46634
Milwaukee Dustless Brush Co, 46642
Mincing Overseas Spice Company, 46648
Minuteman Trading, 46656
Miracle Exclusives, 46659
Mitsui Foods Inc, 46671
ML Catania Company, 46213
Mocon Inc, 46678
Modern Macaroni Co LTD, 46681
Modular Packaging, 46683
Molinera International, 46696
Molins/Sandiacre Richmond, 46697
Monarch-McLaren, 46703
Moorhead & Company, 46723
Morey's Seafood Intl LLC, 46726
Morris J Golombeck Inc, 46733
Mosuki, 46745
Mouli Manufacturing Corporation, 46751
Mountain Safety Research, 46753
Mulligan Associates, 46780
Multikem Corp, 46788
Multisorb Technologies Inc, 46790
Multivac Inc, 46791
Musco Food Corp, 46803
Mutual Wholesale Liquor, 46810
Napco Marketing Corp, 46843
Napoleon Co., 46846
National Band Saw Co, 46861
National Computer Corporation, 46864
Native Scents, 46897
Natra US, 46898
Natrol Inc, 46900
Natural Casing Co, 46903
Natural Group, 46909
Natural Oils International, 46910
Nature's Legacy Inc., 46921
Nature's Products Inc, 46925
Natures Sungrown Foods Inc, 46927
Near East Importing Corporation, 46936
Nederman, 46940
Nestor Imports Inc, 46960
New Organics, 46981
Newtown Foods, 47007
Nexira, 47010
Niagara Foods, 47012
Nick Sciabica & Sons, 47018
Nicky USA Inc, 47019
Noble Harvest, 47039
Noon Hour Food Products Inc, 47045
Nordic Group Inc, 47054
Norimoor Company, 47060
Norpak Corp, 47061
Norseland Foods Inc, 47062
North American Enterprises, 47063
North American Packaging Corp, 47064
Northwest Art Glass, 47096
Northwest Naturals Company, 47099
Nuova Distribution Centre, 47135
Nydree Flooring, 47160
O'Dell Corp, 47163
O-At-Ka Milk Prods Co-Op Inc., 47165
Oak Barrel Winecraft, 47174
Occidental Foods International, LLC, 47178
Ocean Cliff Corp, 47180
Oerlikon Leybold Vacuum, 47189
Old Dominion Wood Products, 47201
Old Mansion Inc, 47202
Olympia International, 47212
Omcan Inc., 47217
Omega Design Corp, 47219
Oneida Food Service, 47239
Ono International, 47242
Ontario Glove and Safety Products, 47243
OnTrack Automation Inc, 47236
Organic Gourmet, 47273
Organic Vintages, 47277
Original Swiss Aromatics, 47282
Orlando Food Corp, 47287
Ottens Flavors, 47298
Overlake Foods, 47304
Paar Physica USA, 47349
Pacific Coast Fruit Co, 47355
Pacific Nutritional, 47359

Pacific Valley Foods Inc, 47372
Package Systems Corporation, 47381
Packaging Aids Corporation, 47383
Packaging Dynamics, 47384
Pacmatic/Ritmica, 47397
Padinox, 47401
PAFCO Importing Co, 47322
Palms & Co, 47418
Pangaea Sciences, 47428
Pantry Shelf Food Corporation, 47431
Paper Systems Inc, 47437
Paradise Inc, 47444
Paradise Island Foods, 47445
Paradise Products, 47446
Paradise Products Corporation, 47447
Paris Gourmet, 47457
Parkson Corp, 47465
Pastene Co LTD, 47485
Pastorelli Food Products, 47486
Pavailler Distribution Company, 47497
Paxton Corp, 47499
PDE Technology Corp, 47332
Peace Village Organic Foods, 47505
Pendery's, 47533
Penn Herb Co, 47536
Pennsylvania Macaroni Company Inc., 47539
Penta Manufacturing Company, 47541
Perten Instruments, 47561
Peter Pan Seafoods Inc., 47564
Peterson, 47567
Petrini Foods International, DBA Foodworld Sales, 47570
Pfankuch Machinery Corporation, 47576
Pharmaceutical & Food Special, 47580
Pharmachem Labs, 47582
Phase II Pasta Machine Inc, 47584
Piazza's Seafood World LLC, 47597
Pittsburgh Casing Company, 47625
Plastic Suppliers Inc, 47635
Plaza de Espana Gourmet, 47640
Poiret International, 47652
Polean Foods, 47660
Polypro International Inc, 47667
Pompeian Inc, 47672
Porinos Gourmet Food, 47678
Port Royal Sales LTD, 47679
Portuguese United Grocer Co-Op, 47685
PPI Technologies Group, 47342
Praga Food Products, 47693
Preferred Packaging Systems, 47711
Preiser Scientific Inc, 47714
Premier Brand Imports, 47716
Premier Brass, 47717
Prentiss, 47723
Pressure King Inc, 47729
Prestige Technology, 47733
Prima Foods, 47740
Primarque Products Inc, 47743
Prime Ingredients Inc, 47744
Primo Water Corporation, 47751
Prince of Peace, 47756
Pro Scientific Inc, 47763
Pro-Flo Products, 47764
Proacema USA, 47769
Process Solutions, 47776
Producers Peanut Company, 47781
Produits Alimentaire, 47788
Promofood International, 47808
Pronatura Inc, 47811
Pronova Biopolymer, 47812
Protica Inc, 47818
Prototype Equipment Corporation, 47819
Provender International, 47820
Purac America, 47834
Purcell International, 47836
Purchase Order Co Of Miami Inc, 47837
Pure Food Ingredients, 47840
Purity Products, 47850
Pyrometer Instrument Co Inc, 47856
QBI, 47863
Qosina Corporation, 47867
Qualicaps Inc, 47873
Qzina Specialty Foods, 47901
R&J Farms, 47913
R&R Sales Company, 47915

733

Import Region / Far East

Ragold, 47947
Rahco International, 47950
Rational Cooking Systems, 47976
RDM International, 47928
Real Soda, 47993
Red Diamond Coffee & Tea, 47997
Red Pelican Food Products, 48001
Redi-Call Inc, 48008
Reede International Seafood Corporation, 48013
Reeno Detergent & Soap Company, 48015
Refractron Technologies Corp, 48020
Reiner Products, 48041
Reinhart Foods, 48042
Reis Robotics, 48044
Remco Products Corp, 48051
Revent Inc, 48075
Rexroth Corporation, 48080
Rice Company, 48089
Richards Packaging, 48096
Richardson Brands Co, 48097
Richport International Inc, 48100
RI Alber T & Son Inc, 48122
Robby Vapor Systems, 48125
Robertson Furniture Co Inc, 48134
Rogers International Inc, 48155, 48156
Roland Foods, LLC, 48161
Roll-O-Sheets Canada, 48164
Rollprint Packaging Prods Inc, 48165
Roman Sausage Company, 48166
Ron Son Foods Inc, 48169
Ron-Son Mushroom Products, 48170
Rondo Inc, 48171
Rosenthal & Kline, 48184
Rosito & Bisani Imports Inc, 48187
Routin America, 48201
Rowland Coffee Roasters Inc., 48205
Roxide International, 48207
Roxy Trading Inc, 48208
Royal Accoutrements, 48209
Royal Baltic LTD, 48210
Royal Crown Enterprises, 48214
Royal Doulton, 48215
Royal Industries Inc, 48219
Royal Paper Products, 48224
Royal Wine Corp, 48227
Rudolph Industries, 48240
Russian Chef, 48247
S & D Coffee Inc, 48253
S & S Indl Maintenance, 48256
S S Steiner Inc, 48260
S&R Imports, 48263
S. Ferens & Company, 48266
S.L. Kaye Company, 48269
Sainsbury & Company, 48324
Salad Oils Intl Corp, 48326
Salmolux Inc, 48336
San Francisco Herb Co, 48353
Sancoa International, 48363
Sands Brands International Food, 48369
SaniServ, 48374
Santa Barbara Olive Company, 48378
Saratoga Food Specialties, 48390
Sargento Foods Inc, 48392
Sazerac Company, Inc., 48409
Scan Coin, 48412
Scandinavian Laboratories, 48418
Scheidegger, 48422
Schiff Food Products Co Inc, 48425
Schuman Cheese, 48437
Seafood Merchants LTD, 48473
Seatex Ltd, 48483
Seattle Refrigeration & Manufacturing, 48487
Seawind Foods, 48490
Select Food Products, 48497
Sensient Colors Inc, 48512
Sentinel Lubricants Inc, 48516
Separators Inc, 48520
Serendipitea, 48525
Service Ideas, 48536
Service Packing Company, 48538
SEW Friel, 48276
Shady Maple Farm, 48559
Shafer-Haggart, 48561

Shank's Extracts Inc, 48566
Shekou Chemicals, 48576
Shivji Enterprises, 48600
Shuttleworth North America, 48610
Sid Wainer & Son Specialty, 48614
Sieb Distributor, 48617
Sieco USA Corporation, 48618
Siena Foods, 48619
Signature Brands LLC, 48627
Simco Foods, 48654
Simpson & Vail, 48667
Sinclair Trading, 48671
Sini Fulvi U.S.A., 48675
SIT Indeva Inc, 48282
Slade Gorton & Co Inc, 48689
Smarties, 48695
Smith Restaurant Supply Co, 48703
Solo Foods, 48736
Solutions, 48738
Solvaira Specialties, 48739
Somerset Industries, 48742
Soofer Co, 48753
Source Atlantique Inc, 48758
South Mill, 48763
Sovena USA Inc, 48786
Sovrana Trading Corp, 48787
Sparkler Filters Inc, 48794
Sparks Belting Co, 48795
Sparrow Enterprises LTD, 48796
Spaten West, Inc, 48802
Specialities Importers & Distributers, 48803
Specialty Blades, 48805
Specialty Coffee Roasters, 48806
Specialty Equipment Company, 48808
Spence & Company, 48824
Spice House International Specialties, 48829
Spiral Biotech Inc, 48835
Spruce Foods, 48851
Spurgeon Co, 48853
SPX Flow Inc, 48291
Stan-Mark Food Products Inc, 48874
Standard Casing Company, 48875
Standard Paper Box Mach Co Inc, 48880
Starwest Botanicals Inc, 48903
Stauber Performance Ingrdients, 48905
Stavis Seafoods, 48907
Steelite International USA, 48919
Stephan Machinery Inc, 48928
Steri Technologies Inc, 48929
Stone Soap Co Inc, 48965
Stormax International, 48973
Strohmeyer & Arpe Co Inc, 48987
Sucesores de Pedro Cortes, 48992
Sun Harvest Foods Inc, 49010
Sun Pac Foods, 49013
Sunnyland Farms, 49027
Superior Foods, 49053
Supramatic, 49060
Swing-A-Way Manufacturing Company, 49091
Swissh Commercial Equipment, 49098
Symrise Inc., 49105
Tablecraft Products Co Inc, 49153
Taconic, 49155
Taormina Sales Company, 49178
Tape Tools, 49181
Target Industries, 49186
Tatra Sheep Cheese Company, 49197
Tech Lighting LLC, 49208
Technium, 49214
Tecnicam Inc, 49217
Tecumseh Products Co., 49218
Tee Pee Olives, Inc., 49221
Televend, 49234
Telman Incorporated, 49235
Texture Technologies Corporation, 49272
Tharo Systems Inc, 49274
The Chefs' Warehouse, 49282
The Long Life Beverage Company, 49293
The Premium Beer Company, 49297
Theta Sciences, 49318
Thomson-Leeds Company, 49330
Tirawisu, 49362

Toastmasters International, 49368
Todhunter Foods, 49373
Tonex, 49386
Tootsi Impex, 49391
Torpac Capsules, 49402
Torre Products Co Inc, 49403
Torter Corporation, 49405
Tosi & Company, 49408
Tosi Trading Company, 49409
Trans-Chemco Inc, 49432
Transit Trading Corporation, 49435
Trevor Industries, 49448
Tri-State Logistics Inc, 49454
Tribest Corp, 49463
Trio Packaging Corp, 49478
Tripper Inc, 49485
Trout Lake Farm, 49499
Troy Lighting, 49500
Tsar Nicoulai Caviar LLC, 49517
Tudor Pulp & Paper Corporation, 49526
Turkana Food, 49532
Tuthill Vacuum & Blower Systems, 49539
Tuway American Group, 49541
UBC Food Distributors, 49559
UDEC Corp, 49560
Ultrafilter, 49587
Unger Co, 49598
Unique Vitality Products, 49621
United Canadian Malt, 49629
United Foods & Fitness, 49637
United International Indstrs, 49639
United Mineral & Chemical Corporation, 49642
United Performance Metals, 49644
Universal Marketing, 49669
Update International, 49675
Urbani Truffles, 49680
US Food Products, 49567
UVA Packaging, 49577
V-Ram Solids, 49690
V-Suarez Provisions, 49691
V.M. Calderon, 49692
Vacuum Barrier Corp, 49709
Van Air Systems, 49726
Varimixer North America, 49747
Venner International Products, 49764
Veronica Foods Inc, 49780
Versailles Lighting, 49782
Vescom America, 49786
Vetrerie Bruni USA, 49789
Victoria Fine Foods, 49799
Victoria Porcelain, 49800
Vienna Meat Products, 49804
Vigneri Chocolate Inc., 49806
Vigo Importing Co, 49807
Vincent Formusa Company, 49817
Visual Planning Corp, 49836
Vorti-Siv, 49861
Vyse Gelatin Co, 49868
W H Laboratories, 49870
WA Brown & Son, 49878
Wagner Gourmet Foods, 49915
Walkers Shortbread, 49929
Walter E Jacques & Sons, 49938
Ward Ironworks, 49944
Waring Products, 49950
Warsteiner Importers Agency, 49953
Wawona Frozen Foods Inc, 49974
Waymar Industries, 49975
Weaver Nut Co. Inc., 49980
Webeco Foods, 49985
Wedgwood USA, 49988
Wega USA, 49991
Welch Holme & Clark Co, 50006
West Carrollton Parchment Company, 50023
Westco-BakeMark, 50037
Western Polymer Corp, 50045
Westin Foods, 50050
Wetoska Packaging Distributors, 50058
White House Foods, 50071
White Toque, 50077
Whitfield Olive, 50081, 50082
Whole Herb Co, 50087
Wilch Manufacturing, 50094

Willing Group, 50116
Willow Group LTD, 50118
WITT Industries Inc, 49887
Wolfson Casing Corp, 50161
Woodland Foods, 50169
Worden, 50175
World Class Beer Imports, 50182
World Spice, 50192
World Tableware Inc, 50193
World Wide Safe Brokers, 50197
Worldwide Food Imports, 50200
Xpresso, 50219
Yakima Chief-Hopunion LLC, 50225
Yogi® Tea, 50240
Young Winfield, 50246
Ziba Nut Co, 50281
Zumtobel Staff Lighting, 50287
Zwilling J.A. Henckels, 50288

Far East

Oregon Coffee Roaster, 47267
Schiff Food Products Co Inc, 48425

Fiji

Ayush Herbs Inc, 42181
International Glace, 45346
West Bay Sales, 50022

France

Abarbanel Wine Company, 41603
Alouette Cheese USA, 41838
Alpha MOS America, 41840
Bragard Professional Uniforms, 42551
FoodMatch, Inc., 44291
Glen Raven Custom Fabrics LLC, 44596
Lights On, 46038
Norseland Foods Inc, 47062
Professional Home Kitchens, 47793
Rotisol France Inc, 48197
Sisson Imports, 48681
World's Best Cheeses, 50198

Germany

Automated Food Systems, 42151
Bermar America, 42391
Euro-Bake, 44006
Frelco, 44356
JJI Lighting Group, Inc., 45460
Lumenite Control Tech Inc, 46156
Marie F, 46332
Maurer North America, 46422
Metlar Us, 46526
Pfankuch Machinery Corporation, 47576
World's Best Cheeses, 50198
Wusthoff Trident Cutlery, 50209

Greece

Arguimbau & Co, 42040
Athenee Imports Distributors, 42102
Corfu Foods Inc, 43272
Cosmo Food Products, 43290
FoodMatch, Inc., 44291
Mani Imports, 46295
Nestor Imports Inc, 46960
San Marzano Imports, 48358
Valesco Trading, 49716

Grenada

Flamingo Flats, 44204

Holland

Akzo Nobel Functional Chemicals, 41748
Compact Industries Inc, 43173
De Boer Food Importers, 43526
The Brand Passport, 49279
VCPB Transportation, 49696
World's Best Cheeses, 50198

Honduras

Landau Uniforms Inc, 45927
Unique Ingredients LLC, 49616

Hungary
Sarant International Cmmdts, 48389

Iceland
International Enterprises Unlimited, 45338
Sands Brands International Food, 48369

India
Aust & Hachmann, 42142
Ayush Herbs Inc, 42181
Carry-All Canvas Bag Co., 42855
Crown Custom Metal Spinning, 43365
Eco-Bag Products, 43832
Erie Foods Intl Inc, 43978
GCI Nutrients, 44419
Harold Leonard Southwest Corporation, 44901
Himalayan Heritage, 45030
J.F. Braun & Sons, 45441
Jam Group of Company, 45482
L.T. Overseas, 45847
Liberty Ware LLC, 46027
Lights On, 46038
National Band Saw Co, 46861
Polypro International Inc, 47667
Prima Foods International, 47741
S.D. Mushrooms, 48268
SLT Group, 48287
Spice & Spice, 48828

Indonesia
GET Enterprises LLC, 44430
H. Arnold Wood Turning, 44803
My Style, 46814
Royal Paper Products, 48224
Starbucks, 48897

Israel
Aromor Flavors & Fragrances, 42065
Now Plastics Inc, 47119
Pack Line Corporation, 47374

Italy
Alfa Cappuccino Import LTD, 41774
ALPI Food Preparation Equipment, 41560
Ametco Manufacturing Corp, 41942
Ammirati Inc, 41950
Armanino Foods of Distinction, 42053
Artemis International, 42074
Bindi-Dessert Service,Inc, 42437
Buonitalia, 42641
C E Elantech Inc, 42665
Cafe Moak, 42729
Calio Groves, 42759
Cam Spray, 42764
Cappuccino Express Company, 42804
Cavallini Coffee & Tea, 42888
Cottura Commerciale, 43297
D'Ac Lighting, 43443
Espresso Coffee Machine Co, 43986
Fluid-O-Tech International Inc, 44253
FoodMatch, Inc., 44291
Italgi, 45399
JoDaSa Group International, 45534
L. Della Cella Company, 45843
Lavazza Premium Coffees, 45952
Les Aliments Livabec Foods, 46001
Lights On, 46038
Luigi Bormioli Corporation, 46150
Martin Engineering, 46373
Michaelo Espresso, 46553
NaceCare Solutions, 46833
Paperweights Plus, 47439
PBC, 47329
Pier 1 Imports, 47606
Professional Marketing Group, 47794
R&A Imports, 47912
Royal Vista Marketing Inc, 48225
Saeco, 48312
Sambonet USA, 48342
Santini Foods, 48381
Sapore della Vita, 48384
Saquella U.S.A., 48387
Savello USA, 48402
Scotsman Ice Systems, 48447
Sitma USA, 48683
Sopralco, 48754
The N Beverage Group, 49294
Tuscan Eat/Perdinci, 49538
United Olive Oil Import, 49643
Valentino USA, 49714
Valesco Trading, 49716
Veroni USA, 49779
W.Y. International, 49877
Wine World Wide, 50127
World's Best Cheeses, 50198

Jamaica
Flamingo Flats, 44204
Warbac Sales Co, 49947

Japan
ALP Lighting & Ceiling Products, 41559
Automated Business Products, 42149
Eden Foods Inc, 43851
ERC Parts Inc, 43787
Infinite Peripherals, 45269
Mexspice, 46538
Paperweights Plus, 47439
Senba USA, 48506
Sterling Corp, 48932
Sunflower Restaurant Supply, 49022
T.K. Products, 49123
Taiko Enterprise Corp, 49157
Walong Marketing, 49935
World Tableware Inc, 50193

Kenya
Tantos Foods International, 49176

Korea
DWL Industries Company, 43464
Hardware Components Inc, 44892
Walong Marketing, 49935
World Tableware Inc, 50193
Yemat Foods, 50236

Latin America
Allied Glove Corporation, 41821
American Food Equipment, 41886
Arla Foods Inc, 42051
Arrowac Fisheries, 42070
Austrade, 42143
Balzac Brothers & Co Inc, 42262
Bazzini Holdings LLC, 42316
Blue Harvest Foods, 42490
Boricua Empaque, 42521
Boston Seafarms, 42532
Caffe Luca Coffee Roaste, 42731
Carlota Foods International, 42835
Chesapeake Spice Company, 42975
China Products, 43004
Coco Lopez Inc, 43114
Coffee Exchange, 43118
Cupper's Coffee Company, 43407
Di Lusso & Be Bop Baskote LLC, 43605
Ducktrap River Of Maine, 43715
DWL Industries Company, 43464
Eagle Home Products, 43796
Eastern Tea Corp, 43813
Felbro Food Products, 44133
Flavor Consultants, 44208
Florida Natural Flavors, 44244
Frontier Bag, 44378
Georgia Spice Company, 44551
Gillies Coffee, 44575
Gosselin Gourmet Beverages, 44666
Harold Leonard Southwest Corporation, 44901
Hodell International, 45039
Houdini Inc, 45090
Houston Tea & Beverage, 45096
Indian Ridge Shrimp Co, 45248
Ingredion Inc., 45278
J A Heilferty & Co, 45422
J. Crocker Exports, 45436
JAAMA World Trade, 45449
Land O'Frost Inc, 45924
Mermaid Seafoods, 46513
Meximex Texas Corporation, 46537
Molinaro's Fine Italian Foods Ltd., 46694
Natco Worldwide Representative, 46859
Northwestern Coffee Mills, 47101
Olcott Plastics, 47199
Old Mansion Inc, 47202
Paradise Products Corporation, 47447
PB Leiner USA, 47328
Prima Foods International, 47741
Priority One America, 47758
Producers Peanut Company, 47781
Productos Familia, 47786
Real Soda, 47993
Rice Company, 48089
San-Ei Gen FFI, 48359
Shekou Chemicals, 48576
Sid Wainer & Son Specialty, 48614
Specialty Coffee Roasters, 48806
Starbucks, 48897
Suity Confections Co, 48998
Sun Harvest Foods Inc, 49010
Swisscorp, 49097
Tampa Maid Foods Inc, 49168
Tampico Beverages Inc, 49170
Tantos Foods International, 49176
Tecumseh Products Co., 49218
Tootsi Impex, 49391
Triton International, 49486
United Mineral & Chemical Corporation, 49642
Venetian Productions, 49763
Walton & Post, 49940
WCC Honey Marketing, 49882

Madagascar
Gourmet Club Corporation, 44671
Mimi et Cie, 46646
Zamilco International, 50257

Malaysia
Bentan Corporation, 42378
H. Arnold Wood Turning, 44803
Royal Paper Products, 48224
Walong Marketing, 49935

Mediterranean
Gilly Galoo, 44576
Turkana Food, 49532
Wine World Wide, 50127

Mexico
AB InBev, 41524
Abbott & Cobb Inc, 41606
Abimco USA, Inc., 41611
Advance Storage Products, 41685
Arrowac Fisheries, 42070
Azumex Corp., 42186
Babe Farms Inc, 42220
Balzac Brothers & Co Inc, 42262
Barker Company, 42281
Barton Beers, 42291
Beaver Street Fisheries, 42329
Bionova Produce, 42450
Blue Harvest Foods, 42490
Boricua Empaque, 42521
Boss Manufacturing Co, 42527
Boston Seafarms, 42532
Boston's Best Coffee Roasters, 42533
Cafe Altura, 42727
Caffe Luca Coffee Roaste, 42731
Carlota Foods International, 42835
Casa Amador, 42862
Casso Guerra & Company, 42874
Chef's Choice Mesquite Charcoal, 42955
Chesapeake Spice Company, 42975
Citrico, 43048
Compact Industries Inc, 43173
Comstock Castle Stove Co, 43185
Couture Farms, 43309
Crestware, 43345
Custom Food Machinery, 43416
Cyclone Enterprises Inc, 43432
Dal-Don Produce, 43481
Delta International, 43574
Di Lusso & Be Bop Baskote LLC, 43605
Di Mare Fresh Inc, 43606
Dipasa USA Inc, 43634
Eagle Home Products, 43796
EDCO Food Products Inc, 43773, 43774
Elopak Americas, 43911
Emery Thompson Machine &Supply Company, 43925
Fabricon Products Inc, 44089
Fabriko, 44090
Felbro Food Products, 44133
Frontier Bag, 44378
Gedney Foods Co, 44507
Gielow Pickles Inc, 44568
Gillies Coffee, 44575
Gosselin Gourmet Beverages, 44666
Hardware Components Inc, 44892
Heaven Hill Distilleries Inc., 44967
Honee Bear Canning, 45064
Ingredion Inc., 45278
Interamerican Quality Foods, 45315
Island Sweetwater Beverage Company, 45394
JH Display & Fixture, 45459
Jso Associates Inc, 45580
La Belle Suisse Corporation, 45870
Lazzari Fuel Co LLC, 45960
Le Fiell Co, 45964
Limpert Bros Inc, 46047
London Fruit Inc, 46095
Malena Produce Inc, 46271
Mali's All Natural Barbecue Supply Company, 46273
Margate Wine & Spirit Co, 46328
Mastercraft Industries Inc, 46397
McDaniel Fruit, 46446
Mercado Latino, 46494
Mexspice, 46538
Midland, 46600
Milwhite Inc, 46645
Molinaro's Fine Italian Foods Ltd., 46694
Nash-DeCamp Company, 46851
Natco Worldwide Representative, 46859
Native Scents, 46897
New England Natural Bakers, 46974
NewStar Fresh Foods LLC, 46993
Northwestern Coffee Mills, 47101
OFI Markesa Intl, 47168
Olcott Plastics, 47199
Ontario Glove and Safety Products, 47243
Oregon Coffee Roaster, 47267
P.F. Harris Manufacturing Company, 47320
Pacific American Fish Co Inc, 47353
Paradise Island Foods, 47445
Paradise Products Corporation, 47447
Priority One America, 47758
Producers Peanut Company, 47781
Prototype Equipment Corporation, 47819
Pure Sweet Honey Farms Inc, 47845
Putnam Group, 47853
R&A Imports, 47912
R&R Sales Company, 47915
Reese Enterprises Inc, 48017
Refrigerator Manufacturers LLC, 48023
Rice Company, 48089
Richards Packaging, 48096
Ripon Pickle Co Inc, 48110
Roll-O-Sheets Canada, 48164
Rowland Coffee Roasters Inc., 48205
Sales King International, 48333
Sales USA, 48334
San Jose Imports, 48357
Sarant International Cmmdts, 48389
Seatex Ltd, 48483
Shekou Chemicals, 48576
Shine Companies, 48593
Sid Wainer & Son Specialty, 48614
Snowcrest Packer, 48724

Import Region / Middle East

Sonora Seafood Company, 48751
Sun Harvest Foods Inc, 49010
Sun Harvest Salt, LLC, 49011
Sun Pac Foods, 49013
Sunny Avocado, 49026
Sunshine Food Sales, 49037
Superior Foods, 49053
Tantos Foods International, 49176
Tate Western, 49196
Thomson-Leeds Company, 49330
Tri Car Sales, 49450
Tripper Inc, 49485
Triton International, 49486
Unique Manufacturing, 49617
Valley Seafoods, 49722
Vessey & Co Inc, 49787
Vilore Foods Company, 49812
VIP Sales Company, 49700
W.Y. International, 49877
WCC Honey Marketing, 49882
Wheel Tough Company, 50064
Whitfield Olive, 50082
Willmark Sales Company, 50117
World Tableware Inc, 50193
Worldwide Specialties In, 50201
Zimmer Custom-Made Packaging, 50282

Middle East

3V Company, 41472
A&A International, 41488
Acme Scale Co, 41640
AKC Commodities Inc, 41556
Allied International Corp, 41822
Alnor Oil Co Inc, 41832
Alternative Health & Herbs, 41847
American Importing Co., 41894
American Key Food Products Inc, 41897
American Seafood Imports Inc., 41919
American Trading Company, 41927
Aroma-Life, 42061
Banner Chemical Co, 42267
Bascom Food Products, 42294
Bazzini Holdings LLC, 42316
Beach Filter Products, 42318
Beaver Street Fisheries, 42329
Bedemco Inc, 42337
Berkshire Dairy, 42388
Best Value Textiles, 42412
Binks Industries Inc, 42439
BMT Commodity Corporation, 42211
Bolner's Fiesta Spices, 42512
Brucia Plant Extracts, 42613
Cal Trading Company, 42738
Camerican International, 42770
Carriere Foods Inc, 42851
Caspian Trading Company, 42873
Celite Corporation, 42898
Chemicolloid Laboratories, Inc., 42966
Chesapeake Spice Company, 42975
Classic Flavors & Fragrances, 43065
Continental Marketing, 43227
Continental Seasoning, 43229
Defranco Co, 43553
Dehydrates Inc, 43555
Derco Foods Intl, 43587
Dewied International Inc, 43603
Dipasa USA Inc, 43634
Dishaka Imports, 43639
Eckhart Corporation, 43825
Elite Spice Inc, 43895
Elopak Americas, 43911
Empire Spice Mills, 43931
Ener-G Foods, 43941
Essential Products of America, 43992
Eximcan Canada, 44048
Fairfield Line Inc, 44098
Fantastic World Foods, 44110
Feather Duster Corporation, 44126
First Colony Coffee & Tea Company, 44186
Flamingo Flats, 44204
Flavor Consultants, 44208
Flavormatic Industries, 44217
Fleurchem Inc, 44226
Freeda Vitamins Inc, 44347

Freeman Industries, 44350
GCI Nutrients, 44419
Georgia Spice Company, 44551
Gerber Products Co, 44557
Germack Pistachio Co, 44559
Gilly Galoo, 44576
Golden Bridge Enterprises Inc, 44628
Great Eastern Sun Trading Co, 44709
GWB Foods Corporation, 44443
Hanif's International Foods, 44863
HealthBest, 44954
Herz Meat Company, 45003
Holland Beef International Corporation, 45047
House of Spices, 45094
Houston Tea & Beverage, 45096
Indianapolis Fruit Company, 45254
Indo-European Foods, 45256
International Business Trading, 45327
International Pack & Ship, 45357
International Reserve Equipment Corporation, 45362
International Sourcing, 45366
InterNatural Foods, 45313
Island Sweetwater Beverage Company, 45394
KeHE Distributors, 45663
Kemach Food Products, 45695
KHL Flavors Inc, 45617
Kinergy Corp, 45734
Kusha Inc., 45830
LA Cena Fine Foods LTD, 45848
La Flor Spices, 45873
Lawnelson Corporation, 45954
Liberty Natural Products Inc, 46024
Ludwig Mueller Co Inc, 46147
Luminiere Corporation, 46157
Luseaux Labs Inc, 46160
Mars Air Products, 46362
Medallion International Inc, 46470
Meduri Farms, 46475
Mincing Overseas Spice Company, 46648
MIRA International Foods, 46211
Mitsui Foods Inc, 46671
Morris J Golombeck Inc, 46733
My Quality Trading Corp, 46813
Napoleon Co., 46846
Natural Oils International, 46910
Near East Importing Corporation, 46936
New Organics, 46981
Northwestern Coffee Mills, 47101
NYP, 46832
Old Mansion Inc, 47202
Ontario Glove and Safety Products, 47243
Ottens Flavors, 47298
Outlook Packaging, 47301
Padinox, 47401
Paradise Products Corporation, 47447
Paskesz Candy Co, 47478
Pendery's, 47533
Pharaoh Trading Company, 47579
Plastic Suppliers Inc, 47635
Port Royal Sales LTD, 47679
Prince of Peace, 47756
Prototype Equipment Corporation, 47819
Purchase Order Co Of Miami Inc, 47837
RDM International, 47928
Reese Enterprises Inc, 48017
Rice Company, 48089
Roman Sausage Company, 48166
Royal Industries Inc, 48219
Royal Palate Foods, 48223
Royal Wine Corp, 48227
Russian Chef, 48247
Sahadi Importing Company, 48321
San Francisco Herb Co, 48353
Saratoga Food Specialties, 48390
Schiff Food Products Co Inc, 48425
Sensient Colors Inc, 48512
Sentinel Lubricants Inc, 48516
Service Manufacturing, 48537
Service Packing Company, 48538
SEW Friel, 48276
Simco Foods, 48654
Slade Gorton & Co Inc, 48689

Soofer Co, 48753
Sparrow Enterprises LTD, 48796
Specialty Commodities Inc, 48807
Spice & Spice, 48828
Stan-Mark Food Products Inc, 48874
Starwest Botanicals Inc, 48903
Taormina Sales Company, 49178
Tara Linens, 49183
Tee Pee Olives, Inc., 49221
Telman Incorporated, 49235
The Long Life Beverage Company, 49293
Thomson-Leeds Company, 49330
Todd's, 49370
Tootsi Impex, 49391
Transit Trading Corporation, 49435
Tripper Inc, 49485
Trout Lake Farm, 49499
Turkana Food, 49532
UBC Food Distributors, 49559
Ungerer & Co, 49599
United International Indstrs, 49639
United Textile Distribution, 49655
Update International, 49675
US Food Products, 49567
Variant, 49744
Venner International Products, 49764
Vetrerie Bruni USA, 49789
Vicksburg Chemical Company, 49794
Vineco International Products, 49819
Weinberg Foods, 49997
Whitfield Olive, 50081, 50082
Willing Group, 50116
Willow Group LTD, 50118
Woodland Foods, 50169
World Spice, 50192
Young Winfield, 50246
Zenobia Co, 50272
Ziba Nut Inc, 50281

Morocco

Arguimbau & Co, 42040
Cosmo Food Products, 43290
Orlando Food Corp, 47287
San Marzano Imports, 48358

New Zealand

Bear Creek Operations, 42323
Berkshire Dairy, 42388
Birchwood Foods Inc, 42454
Broadleaf Venison USA Inc, 42587
Cal Harvest Marketing Inc, 42736
Eternal Marketing Group, 43995
Glazier Packing Co, 44595
Hill 'N' Dale Meat, 45022
JBS USA LLC, 45452
Lamb Cooperative Inc, 45912
New Zealand Lamb Co, 46992
O-At-Ka Milk Prods Co-Op Inc., 47165
Orleans International, 47288
Pacific Resources, 47363
RDM International, 47928
Royal Wine Corp, 48227
Sapac International, 48383
Stanley Orchards Sales, Inc., 48885
United International Indstrs, 49639
Vista Food Exchange, 49833

North Africa

Caffe Luca Coffee Roaste, 42731
Crown Foods International, 43367
Rogers International Inc, 48156
Sovena USA Inc, 48786

North America

BMT Commodity Corporation, 42211
Dona Yiya Foods, 43664
Great Northern Products Inc, 44717

Norway

Norseland Foods Inc, 47062
Vingcard/Elsafe, 49820

Pacific Rim

Erie Foods Intl Inc, 43978
Gillies Coffee, 44575
MacGregors Meat & Seafood, 46222
Scandinavian Laboratories, 48418

Pakistan

Jam Group of Company, 45482
Messina Brothers Manufacturing Company, 46519
Polypro International Inc, 47667

Phillipines

J.F. Braun & Sons, 45441
Nature's Legacy Inc., 46921
RDM International, 47928

Portugal

Allendale Cork Company, 41816
American Star Cork Company, 41923
Socafe, 48732
World's Best Cheeses, 50198

Russia

Eco Wine & Spirits, 43830
Jet Set Sam, 45524
Letrah International Corp, 46010
Pacific Standard Distributors, 47368
QualiGourmet, 47872
The Frank Pesce International Group, L.L.C., 49286

South Africa

Bear Creek Operations, 42323
CAI International, 42687
CK Products, 42702
Globe Fire Sprinkler Corp, 44613
My Style, 46814
Pantry Shelf Food Corporation, 47431
PPI Technologies Group, 47342
Prima Foods International, 47741
RDM International, 47928
Service Packing Company, 48538
Vacaville Fruit Co, 49706
Worden, 50175

South America

3V Company, 41472
4M Fruit Distribution, 41474
A&A International, 41488
A-A1 Aaction Bag, 41502
AB InBev, 41524
Abbott & Cobb Inc, 41606
Abimco USA, Inc., 41611
Able Sales Company, 41612
Acme Smoked Fish Corporation, 41641
Adonis Health Products, 41677
Advanced Food Systems, 41691
Agger Fish Corp, 41714
Agri-Dairy Products, 41719
AHD International, LLC, 41553
Albert A Russo Inc, 41765
Alfa Chem, 41775
Alfred L. Wolff, Inc., 41781
Alimentaire Whyte's Inc, 41786
All American Container, 41794
Allegro Coffee Co, 41809
Allied Glove Corporation, 41821
Allied International Corp, 41822
Alnor Oil Co Inc, 41832
Alternative Health & Herbs, 41847
American Bag & Burlap Company, 41869
American Food Traders, 41888
American Importing Co., 41894
American Key Food Products Inc, 41897
American Laboratories, 41900
American Seafood Imports Inc., 41919
American Solving Inc., 41921
American Trading Company, 41927
Apple & Eve LLC, 42009
Arista Industries Inc, 42044
Arla Foods Inc, 42051

Import Region / South America

Aroma Vera, 42060
Aroma-Life, 42061
Aromachem, 42062
Astral Extracts, 42095
Atlantis Smoked Foods, 42122
Autocon Mixing Systems, 42147
Avatar Corp, 42164
Awe Sum Organics, 42175
B. Terfloth & Company, 42194, 42195
Bacchus Wine Cellars, 42224
BakeMark Ingredients Canada, 42236
Balzac Brothers & Co Inc, 42262
Bascom Food Products, 42294
Basic Food Intl Inc, 42297
Bauducco Inc., 42304
Bayou Food Distributors, 42314
Bazzini Holdings LLC, 42316
Beach Filter Products, 42318
Bear Creek Operations, 42323
Beaufurn, 42326
Beaver Street Fisheries, 42329
Bedemco Inc, 42337
Bell Amore Imports Inc, 42357
Ben-Bud Growers Inc., 42375
Birchwood Foods Inc, 42454
Blessed Herbs, 42477
Blossom Farm Products, 42482
Blue Harvest Foods, 42490
Blue Ribbon Fish Co, 42494
BMT Commodity Corporation, 42211
Bob Gordon & Associates, 42505
Boricua Empaque, 42521
Boston Seafarms, 42532
Boston's Best Coffee Roasters, 42533
Braun Brush Co, 42564
Breakwater Fisheries, 42567
Brooks Tropicals Inc, 42598
Brotherhood Winery, 42600
Brothers International Food Corporation, 42601
Brown-Forman Corp, 42611
Brucia Plant Extracts, 42613
Bunker Foods Corp., 42639
C F Gollott & Son Seafood, 42668
Cadie Products Corp, 42726
Caffe Luca Coffee Roaste, 42731
CAI International, 42687
Cal Trading Company, 42738
California Cereal Products, 42749
California Olive Oil Council, 42756
Camerican International, 42770
Campbell Soup Co., 42775
Candy Tech LLC, 42791
Carlota Foods International, 42835
Caudill Seed Co Inc, 42887
CCS Stone, Inc., 42690
Celite Corporation, 42898
Charmel Enterprises, 42937
Chef Merito Inc, 42951
Chemicolloid Laboratories, Inc., 42966
Chesapeake Spice Company, 42975
Chia Corp USA, 42983
Chicago Food Corporation, 42986
Chipurnoi Inc, 43007
Citrico, 43048
Citrosuco North America Inc, 43049
Classic Flavors & Fragrances, 43065
Clipper Seafood, 43094
Coastal Seafoods, 43106
Community Coffee Co., 43170
Compact Industries Inc, 43173
Con Agra Snack Foods, 43188
Conchita Foods Inc, 43196
Connection Chemical LP, 43202
Consolidated Commercial Controls, 43207
Continental Seasoning, 43229
Corby Distilleries, 43267
Cosgrove Enterprises Inc, 43289
Couture Farms, 43309
CROPP Cooperative, 42711
Crown Foods International, 43367
D.F. International, 43448
Dairy Fresh Foods Inc, 43471
Dairyland USA Corp, 43478
Darik Enterprises Inc, 43501

Davis Trade & Commodities, 43515
Dawes Hill Honey Company, 43518
Defranco Co, 43553
Dehydrates Inc, 43555
Deiss Sales Co. Inc., 43556
Dependable Machine, Inc., 43586
Derco Foods Intl, 43587
Dewied International Inc, 43603
Di Mare Fresh Inc, 43606
Dipasa USA Inc, 43634
DNE World Fruit Sales, 43459
DSM Fortitech Premixes, 43461
Ducktrap River Of Maine, 43715
Dutch Gold Honey Inc, 43742
DWL Industries Company, 43464
Dynamic Packaging, 43751
Dynynstyl, 43754
Earth Saver, 43799
East Coast Seafood Inc, 43805
Eastern Tea Corp, 43813
Eckhart Corporation, 43825
Eco Wine & Spirits, 43830
Edoko Food Importers, 43864
Edward & Sons Trading Co, 43868
Elliot Lee, 43901
Emerling International Foods, 43921
Empire Spice Mills, 43931
Essential Products of America, 43992
Euclid Coffee Co, 43998
Europaeus USA, 44013
Eximcan Canada, 44048
Eximco Manufacturing Company, 44049
F.H. Taussig Company, 44067
FDC Corporation, 44072
Feather Duster Corporation, 44126
Finest Foods, 44178
First Colony Coffee & Tea Company, 44186
Fitec International Inc, 44196
Flamingo Flats, 44204
Flavormatic Industries, 44217
Fleurchem Inc, 44226
Florida European Export-Import, 44241
Florida Food Products Inc, 44242
Franklin Trading Company, 44339
Frederick Wildman & Sons LTD, 44345
Freeman Industries, 44350
Fruitcrown Products Corp, 44386
Garuda International, 44483
GCI Nutrients, 44419
General Bag Corporation, 44515
George Degen & Co, 44542
Gerber Products Co, 44557
Germack Pistachio Co, 44559
Gillies Coffee, 44575
Givaudan Fragrances Corp, 44588
Gold Pure Food Products Co. Inc., 44624
Golden Beach Inc, 44627
Golden Bridge Enterprises Inc, 44628
Goodheart Brand Specialty Food, 44658
Grain Machinery Mfg Corp, 44685
Great Lakes Gourmet Food Service, 44714
Great Lakes International Trading, 44715
Green Grown Products Inc, 44735
Groupe Paul Masson, 44761
Gulf Pride Enterprises, 44779
GWB Foods Corporation, 44443
H. Arnold Wood Turning, 44803
H. Interdonati, 44804
H. Reisman Corporation, 44805
Hadley Fruit Orchards, 44829
Haitai, 44835
Hamersmith, Inc., 44846
Hanif's International Foods, 44863
Harco Enterprises, 44890
Hassia, 44922
Health Flavors, 44948
HealthBest, 44954
Hemisphere Group, 44984
Hermann Laue Spice Company, 45001
Herz Meat Company, 45003
High Liner Foods Inc, 45015
Holland Beef International Corporation, 45047
House of Spices, 45094

Hoyt's Honey Farm, 45108
Hudson Valley Coffee Company, 45119
Ibertrade Commercial Corporation, 45189
Incasa Instant Soluble Coffee, 45237
Indian Ridge Shrimp Co, 45248
Indianapolis Fruit Company, 45254
International Business Trading, 45327
International Food Packers Corporation, 45342
International Oils & Concentrates, 45354
International Pack & Ship, 45357
International Reserve Equipment Corporation, 45362
International Sourcing, 45366
InterNatural Foods, 45313
Island Sweetwater Beverage Company, 45394
J A Heilferty & Co, 45422
J.F. Braun & Sons, 45441
Jamaican Teas Limited C/O Eve Sales Corporation, 45483
Jason Marketing Corporation, 45503
JBS USA LLC, 45452
John I. Haas, 45546
Johnson & Sbrocco Associates, 45552
Jp Tropical Foods, 45578
KeHE Distributors, 45663
Kelly Foods, 45691
Kentea, 45707
KHL Flavors Inc, 45617
Khong Guan Corp, 45726
Kinergy Corp, 45734
Kinnikinnick Foods, 45755
Knight's Appleden Fruit LTD, 45774
Knutsen Coffees, 45778
Kobrand Corporation, 45779
Kopke, William H, 45798
Kosto Food Products Co, 45804
Kurtz Orchards Farms, 45828
L.N. White & Company, 45846
La Belle Suisse Corporation, 45870
LA Cena Fine Foods LTD, 45848
La Flor Spices, 45873
LA Wholesale Produce Market, 45853
Lakeside Mills, 45907
Leavitt Corp., The, 45968
Lemberger Candy Corporation, 45990
Letrah International Corp, 46010
Liberty Natural Products Inc, 46024
LMK Containers, 45865
Louisiana Packing Company, 46123
Ludwig Mueller Co Inc, 46147
Lumber & Things, 46155
MacGregors Meat & Seafood, 46222
Magnotta Winery Corporation, 46252
Malgor & Company, 46272
Maple Leaf Foods International, 46307
Marcus Food Co, 46323
Marglo Products Corporation, 46329
Markwell Manufacturing Company, 46351
Marubeni America Corp., 46376
MarySue.com, 46382
Mason Transparent Package Company, 46392
Maxim's Import Corporation, 46426
McDaniel Fruit, 46446
McDowell Industries, 46447
Medallion International Inc, 46470
Mercado Latino, 46494
Mermaid Seafoods, 46513
Messina Brothers Manufacturing Company, 46519
Milligan & Higgins, 46634
Mincing Overseas Spice Company, 46648
MIRA International Foods, 46211
Mitsui Foods Inc, 46671
ML Catania Company, 46213
Modular Packaging, 46683
Molinera International, 46696
Moorhead & Company, 46723
Morris J Golombeck Inc, 46733
Mundial, 46793
My Quality Trading Corp, 46813
Napoleon Co., 46846

Nash-DeCamp Company, 46851
Natco Worldwide Representative, 46859
Native Scents, 46897
Natrol Inc, 46900
Natural Casing Co, 46903
Natural Oils International, 46910
Nature's Products Inc, 46925
Naylor Candies Inc, 46932
Near East Importing Corporation, 46936
Neptune Fisheries, 46956
New England Natural Bakers, 46974
New Era Canning Company, 46977
New Organics, 46981
New Orleans Food Co-op, 46982
New York Export Co, 46989
NewStar Fresh Foods LLC, 46993
Newtown Foods, 47007
Nexira, 47010
Niagara Foods, 47012
NJM/CLI, 46826
Norpak Corp, 47061
North Bay Produce Inc, 47069
Northwest Naturals Company, 47099
Northwestern Coffee Mills, 47101
Nossack Fine Meats, 47106
Nuchief Sales Inc, 47129
O'Dell Corp, 47163
Occidental Foods International, LLC, 47178
Olcott Plastics, 47199
Old Mansion Inc, 47202
Once Again Nut Butter, 47237
Ontario Glove and Safety Products, 47243
Optimal Nutrients, 47253
Oregon Coffee Roaster, 47267
Organic Products Trading Co, 47276
Organically Grown Co, 47278
Otis McAllister Inc., 47297
Overlake Foods, 47304
Oxygen Import LLC, 47310
P.F. Harris Manufacturing Company, 47320
Pacific Coast Fruit Co, 47355
Packaging Dynamics, 47384
Padinox, 47401
PAFCO Importing Co, 47322
Palmer Candy Co, 47413
Pandol Brothers Inc, 47425, 47426, 47427
Pangaea Sciences, 47428
Pantry Shelf Food Corporation, 47431
Paradise Products Corporation, 47447
Pastorelli Food Products, 47486
PB Leiner USA, 47328
Pearl Coffee Co, 47508
Pelican Bay Ltd., 47525
Pendery's, 47533
Penta Manufacturing Company, 47541
Peter Pan Seafoods Inc., 47564
Pharaoh Trading Company, 47579
Piazza's Seafood World LLC, 47597
Polean Foods, 47660
Porinos Gourmet Food, 47678
Port Royal Sales LTD, 47679
PPI Technologies Group, 47342
Praga Food Products, 47693
Preiser Scientific Inc, 47714
Prentiss, 47723
Prima Foods, 47740
Prima Foods International, 47741
Primo Water Corporation, 47751
Priority One America, 47758
Producers Peanut Company, 47781
Productos Familia, 47786
Protica Inc, 47818
Prototype Equipment Corporation, 47819
Purcell International, 47836
Purchase Order Co Of Miami Inc, 47837
Pure Foods, 47841
Pure Sweet Honey Farms Inc, 47845
Purity Products, 47850
QBI, 47863
R&R Mill Company, 47914
R.B. Morriss Company, 47917

737

Import Region / Spain

Ray Cosgrove Brokerage Company, 47978
Raymond-Hadley Corporation, 47981
RDM International, 47928
Red Diamond Coffee & Tea, 47997
Reede International Seafood Corporation, 48013
Rice Company, 48089
Richardson Brands Co, 48097
Rl Alber T & Son Inc, 48122
Robert Wholey & Co Inc, 48128
Roland Foods, LLC, 48161
Rosenthal & Kline, 48184
Rowland Coffee Roasters Inc., 48205
Royal Banquet, 48211
Royal Crown Enterprises, 48214
Royal Palate Foods, 48223
Royal Wine Corp, 48227
Ruggiero Seafood, 48242
S & D Coffee Inc, 48253
S & S Indl Maintenance, 48256
S&R Imports, 48263
S. Ferens & Company, 48266
S.L. Kaye Company, 48269
Sales USA, 48334
Sampco, 48345
Sands Brands International Food, 48369
Scandinavian Formulas Inc, 48417
Schuman Cheese, 48437
SeaPerfect Atlantic Farms, 48464
Seatech Corporation, 48482
Seawind Foods, 48490
Sentinel Lubricants Inc, 48516
Service Packing Company, 48538
Servitrade, 48539
Sesaco Corp, 48541
SEW Friel, 48276
Seydel Co, 48556
Shawano Specialty Papers, 48574
Shekou Chemicals, 48576
Shingle Belting, 48594
Sid Wainer & Son Specialty, 48614
Simco Foods, 48654
Slade Gorton & Co Inc, 48689
Somerset Industries, 48742
Southern Gardens Citrus, 48773
Southern Heritage Coffee Company, 48775
Sparkler Filters Inc, 48794
Specialty Coffee Roasters, 48806
Specialty Commodities Inc, 48807
Springer-Penguin, 48847
Spruce Foods, 48851
Standard Casing Company, 48875
Stanley Orchards Sales, Inc., 48885
Starbruck Foods Corporation, 48896
Starwest Botanicals Inc, 48903
Stauber Performance Ingrdients, 48905
Stavis Seafoods, 48907
Stevens Tropical Plantation, 48947
Stewart's Private Blend Foods, 48951
Stone Soap Co Inc, 48965
Strohmeyer & Arpe Co Inc, 48987
Sucesores de Pedro Cortes, 48992
Sun Grove Foods Inc, 49009
Sun Harvest Foods Inc, 49010
Sun Pac Foods, 49013
Sunnyland Farms, 49027
Suntec Power, 49040
Superior Foods, 49053
Suram Trading Corporation, 49066
Surface Banana Company, 49072
Sweet Dried Fruit, 49084
Synergee Foods Corporation, 49106
Tai Foong USA Inc, 49156
Tampa Maid Foods Inc, 49168
Tangra Trading, 49173
Tantos Foods International, 49176
Taormina Sales Company, 49178
Tea Importers Inc, 49205
Tecumseh Products Co., 49218
Telman Incorporated, 49235
Templar Food Products, 49240
Terphone Inc, 49250
Texas Coffee Co, 49264
The Chefs' Warehouse, 49282
The Long Life Beverage Company, 49293
Todd's, 49370
Todhunter Foods, 49373
Tonex, 49386
Torrefazione Barzula & Import, 49404
Torter Corporation, 49405
Transit Trading Corporation, 49435
Transmundo Company, 49436
Triton International, 49486
Trout Lake Farm, 49499
Turbana Corp., 49530
Tuthill Vacuum & Blower Systems, 49539
Ungerer & Co, 49599
Union Fish Co, 49611
Unique Ingredients LLC, 49616
United International Indstrs, 49639
United Seafood Imports, 49648
Universal Marketing, 49669
Update International, 49675
US Food Products, 49567
V-Ram Solids, 49690
V-Suarez Provisions, 49691
Vacaville Fruit Co, 49706
Venner International Products, 49764
Veronica Foods Inc, 49780
Vessey & Co Inc, 49787
Victor Joseph Son Inc, 49797
Victoria Fine Foods, 49799
Victoria Porcelain, 49800
Vigo Importing Co, 49807
Vinos USA, 49822
VIP Sales Company, 49700
Vista Food Exchange, 49833
Vyse Gelatin Co, 49868
Walter E Jacques & Sons, 49938
Wanchese Fish Co Inc, 49943
WCC Honey Marketing, 49882
Weaver Nut Co. Inc., 49980
Wechsler Coffee Corporation, 49987
Welch Holme & Clark Co, 50006
West Pak Avocado Inc, 50032
Westwind Resources, 50054
White House Foods, 50071
White Toque, 50077
Whitfield Olive, 50081, 50082
Whitley Peanut Factory Inc, 50086
Whole Herb Co, 50087
Wild Rice Exchange, 50096
Willing Group, 50116
Windsor Wax Co Inc, 50124
Winmix/Natural Care Products, 50132
Wixson Honey Inc, 50156
Wolfson Casing Corp, 50161
Woodland Foods, 50169
Worden, 50175
World Cheese Inc, 50181
World Class Beer Imports, 50182
World Spice, 50192
Worldwide Specialties In, 50201
Young Winfield, 50246
Zarda King LTD, 50258
Zenobia Co, 50272
Ziba Nut Inc, 50281

Spain

Arguimbau & Co, 42040
Calio Groves, 42759
Cosmo Food Products, 43290
D'Ac Lighting, 43443
FoodMatch, Inc., 44291
Frelco, 44356
Imar, 45217
JBG International, 45451
L. Della Cella Company, 45843
Lights On, 46038
San Marzano Imports, 48358
Valesco Trading, 49716
W.Y. International, 49877
Wagshal's Imports, 49917
World's Best Cheeses, 50198

Sri-Lanka

Mexspice, 46538

Sudan

Mexspice, 46538

Sweden

Composition Materials Co Inc, 43179
Kristian Regale, 45816

Switzerland

Euro Mart/Stolzle Cberg las, 44002
Michaelo Espresso, 46553
World's Best Cheeses, 50198

Taiwan

GET Enterprises LLC, 44430
Hardware Components Inc, 44892
Lights On, 46038
Min Tong Herbs, 46647
Sterling Corp, 48932
Trade Diversified, 49418
Walong Marketing, 49935

Thailand

Kal Pac Corp, 45640
Kitchens Seafood, 45762
Vasinee Food Corporation, 49750
Walong Marketing, 49935

Turkey

Arguimbau & Co, 42040
Balsu, 42259
Cosmo Food Products, 43290
Great Lakes International Trading, 44715
J.F. Braun & Sons, 45441
San Marzano Imports, 48358
Sarant International Cmmdts, 48389
Teksem LLC, 49228

USA

Atlas Match Company, 42125
Bonduelle North America, 42518
Brum's Dairy, 42615
Canada Cutlery Inc., 42780
Carriere Foods Inc, 42851
Centennial Food Corporation, 42902
Exeter Produce, 44045
Fishmore, 44194
Food Source Company, 44286
Gouw Quality Onions, 44677
Grande Chef Company, 44692
Horizon Poultry, 45078
Inniskillin Wines, 45282
Inno-Vite, 45283
Inovatech USA, 45294
ITC Systems, 45182, 45183
J.R. Short Canadian Mills, 45447
Marie F, 46332
Olymel, 47211
Pepe's Mexican Restaurant, 47543
Roll-O-Sheets Canada, 48164
Select Food Products, 48497
Shafer-Haggart, 48561
Shippers Supply, 48598
Toastmasters International, 49368
Une-Viandi, 49597
Vienna Meat Products, 49804
Vineco International Products, 49819
Walter E Jacques & Sons, 49938
WE Killam Enterprises, 49883

United Kingdom

British Aisles, 42583
Dudson USA Inc, 43716
The Premium Beer Company, 49297
Twinings North America Inc, 49547
VCPB Transportation, 49696

Venezuela

Mimi et Cie, 46646

Vietnam

Walong Marketing, 49935

Virgin Islands

Flamingo Flats, 44204

West Africa

D Steengrafe Co Inc, 43441
Tiger Botanicals   1, 49347

Western Europe

Petra International, 47569

Worldwide

A&A Line & Wire Corporation, 41489
A. Gagliano Co Inc, 41506
Ace Technical Plastics Inc, 41632
Adpro, 41678
Advanced Equipment, 41689
American Identity, 41893
American Roland Food Corporation, 41917
Amsterdam Printing & Litho Inc, 41958
Aqua Star, 42020
Archon Industries Inc, 42029
Associated Products Inc, 42091
Astral Extracts, 42095
ATOFINA Chemicals, 41591
Avanti Products Inc, 42163
Azuma Foods Intl Inc USA, 42185
BBQ Pits by Klose, 42202
Bedemco Inc, 42337
Belly Treats, Inc., 42366
Berje, 42387
Best Brands Home Products, 42404
Blue Ridge Converting, 42495
Brookside Foods, 42599
C E Rogers Co, 42666
California Custom Foods, 42750
Caribbean Produce Exchange, 42825
Carolina Treet, 42843
Channel Fish Processing, 42925
Chester Hoist, 42976
Chester-Jensen Co., Inc., 42980
Chex Finer Foods Inc, 42982
Chile Guy, 42997
Chilean Seafood Exchange, 42998
Citrico, 43048
Cleland Sales Corp, 43082
Cleveland Wire Cloth & Mfg Co, 43088
Cma Dishmachines, 43102
Coffee Bean Intl, 43116
Colin Ingram, 43133
Connell International Company, 43203
Crystal Creative Products, 43383
Curry King Corporation, 43410
De Coty Coffee Co, 43529
Donaldson Co Inc, 43666
East Coast Sea Port Corporation, 43804
Econo Frost Night Covers, 43838
Edge Resources, 43855
Elco Fine Foods, 43883
Electro Freeze, 43887
Elwood International Inc, 43913
Euro American Brands, 44001
Ever Fresh Fruit Co, 44024
Falcon Trading Intl Corp, 44102
Felix Storch Inc, 44137
Flavorchem Corp, 44215
Fruitcrown Products Corp, 44386
Frutarom Meer Corporation, 44387
Frutex Group, 44389
Garden & Valley Isle Seafood, 44470
Gebo Corporation, 44506
Global Marketing Assoc, 44609
Gorton's Inc., 44665
Green Spot Packaging, 44736
Groeb Farms, 44758
Gruenewald Manufacturing Company, 44765
Gum Technology Corporation, 44780
Hanel Storage Systems, 44862
Harbor Seafood, 44886
Health Concerns, 44947
Hudson Commercial Foods, 45117
I Magid, 45150
Icco Cheese Co, 45190

Import Region / Worldwide

Imaje, 45215
Iman Pack, 45216
Incinerator International Inc, 45238
Infitec Inc, 45270
International Chemical Corp, 45330
InterNatural Foods, 45313
Interocean, 45375
Jarvis Products Corp, 45501
Jb Prince, 45509
JCH International, 45453
Jesco Industries, 45519
JL Industries Inc, 45461
John D Walsh Co, 45543
Kalustyan, 45643
King Bag & Mfg Co, 45739
Laird & Company, 45898
Lawrence Equipment Inc, 45955
Leedal Inc, 45973
Light Waves Concept, 46036
Longbottom Coffee & Tea Inc, 46101
Ludfords, 46146
M&R Flexible Packaging, 46188
Melvina Can Machinery Company, 46488
Mermaid Spice Corporation, 46514
Michelle Chocolatiers, 46554
Mid Valley Nut Co, 46587
Middleby Corp, 46598
Migatron Corp, 46612
MLG Enterprises Ltd., 46214
Moisture Register Products, 46689
Morehouse Foods Inc, 46725
Morre-Tec Ind Inc, 46731
Morris Okun, 46734
Mother Parker's Tea & Coffee, 46746
National Equipment Corporation, 46868
National Importers, 46877
Naturex Inc, 46928
Neogen Corp, 46951
Neptune Foods, 46957
New Hope Imports, 46978
Newark Wire Cloth Co, 46994
Nissho Iwai American Corporation, 47035
Northwest Naturals LLC, 47100
Nutraceutics Corp, 47143
Oregon Chai, 47264
Oskri Corporation, 47294
Oyang America, 47311
Pacific Foods, 47357
Pacific Spice Co, 47367
Palmer Fixture Company, 47415
Performance Labs, 47553
Perry Videx LLC, 47559
Prevor Marketing International, 47739
Pure Source LLC, 47844
Quality Cabinet & Fixture Co, 47876
Rader Company, 47941
Regal Health Food, 48028
Reliable Mercantile Company, 48048
Rexnord Corporation, 48079
RFi Ingredients, 47930
Rob Salamida Co Inc, 48123
Rocket Man, 48145
Rogers Collection, 48154
Roland Foods, 48160
Rudolph Industries, 48240
S L D Commodities Inc, 48258
Sagaya Corp, 48318
Salem-Republic Rubber Co, 48331
Sands African Imports, 48368
Sentry Seasonings, 48518
Sethness Caramel Color, 48545
Shen Manufacturing Co Inc, 48580
Simonds International, 48659
Smirk's, 48699
Spice King Corporation, 48830
Spreda Group, 48845
St Charles Trading Inc, 48858
St. Killian Importing, 48864
STE Michelle Wine Estates, 48297
Sterling Systems & Controls, 48938
Stretch-Vent Packaging System, 48984
Summit Commercial, 49003
Sunco & Frenchie, 49020
Sunridge Farms, 49029
Sunrise Growers, 49032
Sunshine Farm & Garden, 49036
Tampa Bay Fisheries Inc, 49166
Tartaric Chemicals, 49189
Templar Food Products, 49240
Tenth & M Seafoods, 49247
The Carriage Works, 49281
The Scoular Company/TSC Container Freight, 49300
TLB Corporation, 49134
TNA Packaging Solutions, 49136
Toromont Process Systems, 49400
Townsend Farms Inc, 49417
TRITEN Corporation, 49142
Try The World, 49516
Twinlab Corporation, 49548
United Universal Enterprises Corporation, 49656
Vacuum Barrier Corp, 49709
Vaughn-Russell Candy Kitchen, 49751
Warrell Corp, 49951
Watson Inc, 49970
Weinstein International, 49999
Western Plastics, 50043
White Coffee Corporation, 50070
Whiting & Davis, 50084
William E. Martin & Sons Company, 50112
Willow Group LTD, 50118
World Class Beer Imports, 50182
World Nutrition, Inc., 50191
World Variety Produce, 50194

TRANSPORTATION FIRMS

User Guide
Company Profiles
Transportation Region Index
Transportation Type Index

Transportation Firms User Guide

The **Transportation Firms Chapter** of *Food & Beverage Market Place* includes companies that transportation services to the food and beverage industry. The descriptive listings are organized alphabetically. Following the A-Z Transportation listings are two indexes: Transportation Region, organized by regions that the company transports to; and Transportation Type, that includes type of transportation services offered. These Indexes refer to listing numbers, not page numbers.

Below is a sample listing illustrating the kind of information that is or might be included in a Transportation Firm listing. Each numbered item of information is described in the User Key on the following page.

---

1 → 239239

2 → **(HQ) Always Freight Company**

3 → 12 Avion Drive

Fayetteville, AR 72702

4 → 001-444-6301

5 → 001-444-6302

6 → 888-001-6303

7 → info@Always.com

8 → www.Always.com

9 → Transportation firm providing domestic and international air shipping.

10 → President: Dan Coddle
CFO: Kenneth Center
COO: David Wood
Vice President: Shanna Twain
Marketing: Valerie Alamo

11 → *Estimated Sales*: $20-50 Million

12 → *Number Employees*: 75

13 → *Sq. Footage*: 19000

14 → *Parent Co.*: Airline Cargo Company

15 → *Company is also listed in the following section(s)*: Warehousing

16 → *Other Locations*: Always Freight Company, Washington, D.C.

17 → *Services*: Freight Forwarding, domestic and international air freight

18 → *Regions Served*: Worldwide

Transportation Firms User Key

1 → **Record Number:** Entries are listed alphabetically within each category and numbered sequentially. The entry number, rather than the page number, is used in the indexes to refer to listings.

2 → **Company Name:** Formal name of company. HQ indicates headquarter location. If names are completely capitalized, the listing will appear at the beginning of the alphabetized section.

3 → **Address:** Location or permanent address of the company. If the mailing address differs from the street address, it will appear second. Companies are indexed by state.

4 → **Phone Number:** The listed phone number is usually for the main office, but may also be for the sales, marketing, or public relations office as provided.

5 → **Fax Number:** This is listed when provided by the company.

6 → **Toll-Free Number:** This is listed when provided by the company.

7 → **E-Mail:** This is listed when provided, and is generally the main office e-mail.

8 → **Web Site:** This is listed when provided by the company and is also referred to as an URL address. These web sites are accessed through the Internet by typing http:// before the URL address.

9 → **Description**: This paragraph contains a brief description of the type of transportation available.

10 → **Key Personnel:** Names and titles of company executives.

11 → **Estimated Sales:** This is listed when provided by the company.

12 → **Number of Employees:** Total number of employees within the company.

13 → **Sq. Footage:** Size of facility.

14 → **Parent Co.:** If the listing is a division of another company, the parent is listed here.

15 → Indicates what other section in *Food & Beverage Market Place* this company is listed: Volume 1: Manufacturers. Volume 2: Equipment, Supplies & Services; Transportation; Warehouse; Wholesalers/Distributors. Volume 3: Brokers; Importers/Exporters.

16 → **Other locations:** Indicates other company locations.

17 → **Services Provided:** Types of related services that are available. Companies are indexed by type of service.

18 → **Regions Served:** This list states of region that the company transports to. Companies are indexed by regions served.

Transportation Firms / A-Z

51501 A Arnold Logistics
5200 Interchange Way
Louisville, KY 40229-2190   502-327-1369
Fax: 502-327-1378   800-626-5371
logisticsvp@a-arnold.com
www.aarnoldmovingcompany.com
Is a full-service logistics company providing turnkey solutions to customers' challenges, including fulfillment, contract packaging/kitting, call center, reverse logistics, print, direct mail, and transportation. In our CentralPennsylvania Campus we operate 3.6 million sq. ft., with 15 facilities and employ over 1000 associates. Arnold Logistics also has operations in Columbus, OH and Southwest Regional Campus in Dallas, TX. The company has been in operation for 26years
President: Rick Russell
rick.russell@a-arnold.com
Number Employees: 50-99
Services: Long & short haul trucking
Regions Served:
    Northeast, Southeast & Southwest

51502 A N Deringer Inc
64 N Main St
St Albans, VT 05478-1682   802-524-8110
Fax: 802-524-8236 www.anderinger.com
A full-service international and domestic freight forwarding, warehousing and distribution services, cargo insurance, and logistics consulting.
CEO: Jake Holzschieter
Number Employees: 500-999
Square Footage: 132000
Parent Co: A.N. Deringer
Services: Customs house & transportation broker providing freight forwarding & export packing
Regions Served:
    International: nationwide, Canada, Far East, Australia, Europe, Middle East, Africa & Near East

51503 A N Deringer Inc
64 N Main St
St Albans, VT 05478-1682   802-524-8110
Fax: 802-524-8236   888-612-6239
marketing@anderinger.com www.anderinger.com
A full-service international and domestic freight forwarding, warehousing and distribution services, cargo insurance, and logistics consulting.
President and CEO: Jake Holzschieter
Senior VP: John Holzschieter
Number Employees: 500-999
Parent Co: A.N. Deringer
Services: Air & ocean freight forwarding
Regions Served:
    Worldwide

51504 A W Sisk & Son
3601 Choptank Rd
P.O. Box 70
Preston, MD 21655   410-673-7111
Fax: 410-673-7360   sales@awsisk.com
www.awsisk.com
Broker of general merchandise and private label items including milk and dairy related products, bread, rolls, bagels and sweet good, and vegetables.
Chief Executive Officer: Al Turner
alturn@awsisk.com
Canned Food Sales: Leon Kanner
Protein Sales: Brenan Roser
Administrative Assistant: Melissa Corbin
Year Founded: 1891
Estimated Sales: $30-40 Million
Number Employees: 5-9
Square Footage: 100000
Type of Packaging: Consumer, Food Service, Private Label
Regions Served:
    East Coast

51505 A to Z Wineworks
30835 N Hwy 99 W
Newburg, OR 97132
    800-739-4455
info@AtoZwineworks.com
www.AtoZwineworks.com
Wine
Founder, CEO: Bill Hatcher
Founder, Chief Marketing & Sales Officer: Deb Hatcher
Founder, Consulting Winemaker: Cheryl Francis
Founder, Director of Winemaking: Sam Tannahill
Year Founded: 2002
Number Employees: 20-49

51506 (HQ)A-P-A Truck Leasing
1207 Tonnelle
North Bergen, NJ 07047-4721   201-553-7824
Transportation firm providing trucking services
Number Employees: 1-4

51507 AADF Warehouse Corporation
P.O.Box 26928
Albuquerque, NM 87125-6928   505-842-6563
Fax: 505-243-6097
Warehouse providing dry storage for canned and packaged foods, etc.; transportation broker providing long haul trucking; also, pick/pack, computer inventory bookkeeping, EDI terminals, UPS overpack and zone and rail siding available
Owner: Al Saloka
Number Employees: 20-49
Services: Broker providing long haul trucking via tractors, vans & step vans with lift gates
Regions Served:
    Southwest: NM

51508 (HQ)AFS Traffic Consulants
330 Marshall St.
Suite 400
Shreveport, LA 71101-3015   318-798-2111
Fax: 318-797-3628 info@afslogistics.com
Third party logistics firm with EDI capabilities that assesses plans, and implements logistics processes, also assisting manufacturers, distributors, and retailers
President: Jeff Harper
Chief Executive Officer: Brian J. Barker
Chief Financial Officer: Brigette Rose
Vice President of Operations: Randy Hollifield
Vice President of Marketing: Brian P. Barker
Contact: Nancy Gross
ngross@afs.net
Chief Operating Officer: Pete Zanmiller
Estimated Sales: $2.5-5 Million
Number Employees: 20-49
Other Locations:
    Dallas, TX
    Tulsa, OKTulsa
Services: Brokerage
Regions Served:
    48 States

51509 APL Logistics
1301 Riverplace Blvd # 1100
Jacksonville, FL 32207-9029   904-396-2517
Fax: 904-396-3984   800-331-4289
www.apllogistics.com
Key Services include: Contract warehousing; cross-docking; deconsolidation; distribution warehousing; freight management; inbound logistics; just-in-time delivery; parcel consolidation; reverse logistics; warehouse managementsystem.
President APL/APL Logistics Americas: Beat Simon
Senior Vice President: William Villalon
Markets Analyst: Paolo Hardtke
International Sales Support: Christine Goodwin
Corporate Communications Director: Michael Zampa
Number Employees: 1,000-4,999
Parent Co: NOL Group (Neptune Orient Lines Limited)

51510 ASAP Freight Systems
11252 E Hardy Rd
Houston, TX 77093-2368   281-442-1755
Fax: 713-272-7468   800-272-7468
www.asapfrt.com
Warehouse providing dry storage for nonperishable items; transportation services include long and short haul trucking and freight forwarding
Manager: Isabelle Mc Ibney
Manager: Linda Dicanio
asap3@asapfrt.net
Number Employees: 50-99
Services: Long & short haul trucking & freight forwarding
Regions Served:
    Worldwide

51511 ASW Supply Chain Svc
3375 Gilchrist Rd
Mogadore, OH 44260-1253   330-733-6291
Fax: 330-733-5196   888-363-8492
www.aswglobal.com
Warehouse providing dry storage for non-perishable foods; transportation firm providing long and short haul trucking, cross docking, rail car, and foreign trade zone services; also, distribution, pick/pack, display assemblyrelabeling, etc.
Owner: Andre Thornton
athornton@aswservices.com
Business Development: Nick Mihiylov
Number Employees: 10-19
Services: Rail car and long & short haul trucking

51512 (HQ)Aberdeen & Rockfish Railroad
101 E Main St
Aberdeen, NC 28315-2717   910-944-2341
Fax: 910-944-9738 info@aberdeen-rockfish.com
www.aberdeen-rockfish.com
Transportation firm offering railroad services
President: Edward Lewis
elewis@ac.net
Number Employees: 20-49
Services: Railroad
Regions Served:
    Regional/local: NC & SC

51513 (HQ)Ability/Tri-Modal Trnsprtn Svc
2011 E Carson St
Carson, CA 90810-1223   310-522-5506
Fax: 310-518-8982 sales@trimodal.com
www.abilitytrimodal.com
Transportation firm providing long and short haul trucking; warehouse offering dry storage for general commodities; also, rail siding available
President: Greg Owen
gowen@trimodal.com
Executive VP: Eldon Hatfield
VP Operations: Mike Kelso
Number Employees: 100-249
Other Locations:
    TRI Modal Distribution Servic
    CarsonTRI Modal Distribution Servic
Services: Long & short haul trucking
Regions Served:
    Nationwide

51514 Abler Transfer
2905 Dover Dr
Norfolk, NE 68701   402-371-0815
Fax: 402-371-0817
Warehouse providing storage for dry commodities; transportation services include local, short and long haul trucking and distribution
Owner: Leon Abler
Number Employees: 10-19
Regions Served:
    AR; CO; IA; IL; IN; KS; MI; MN; MO; NE; OK; SD; TX; WI; WY

51515 (HQ)Acme Distribution Ctr Inc
18101 E Colfax Ave
Aurora, CO 80011-5107   303-340-2100
Fax: 303-340-2424 info@acmd.com
www.acmedistribution.com
Warehouse providing cooler, dry and humidity-controlled storage; transportation firm providing freight consolidation and short haul trucking; rail siding, pick/pack, shrink wrapping, module building and display assembly servicesavailable
President: Joe Stam
stam@acmedistribution.com
Chief Financial Officer: Nancy Manilla
Sr Vice President: Doug Sampson
Estimated Sales: $2.5 Million
Number Employees: 100-249
Type of Packaging: Consumer, Food Service, Private Label, Bulk
Services: Short haul trucking & freight consolidation
Regions Served:
    Nationwide

51516 Acme Farms + Kitchen
3926 Irongate Road
Unit D
Bellingham, WA 98226   360-325-1903
    800-542-8309
info@acmefarmsandkitchen.com
www.acmefarmsandkitchen.com
A local delivery service that works in partnership with local farmers, fishers, ranchers and produces to create 'Locavore Boxes' containing fresh foods, recipes and meal plans.

745

Transportation Firms / A-Z

Contact: Maggie Stafford
maggie@acmefarmsandkitchen.com
Estimated Sales: 100 Thousand
Number Employees: 1-4
Type of Packaging: Consumer

51517 Adams Vegetable Oils Inc
P.O. Box 956
Arbuckle, CA 95912   530-668-2005
Fax: 530-476-2315 info@adamsgrp.com
www.adamsvegetableoils.com
Vegetable oils, grain and seeds.
Sales Manager: David Hoffsten
Estimated Sales: $100+ Million
Number Employees: 50-99
Square Footage: 5889
Type of Packaging: Bulk

51518 Adams Warehouse & Delivery
3701 Yale St
Houston, TX 77018-6563   713-699-3515
Fax: 713-694-7510 888-977-0502
www.adamsdist.com
Warehouse providing dry storage, re-packing and labeling for nonperishable foods; transportation firm providing short haul trucking, local delivery, shrink wrap, cross-dock, pick/pack, order fulfillment and storage; rail siding available.
President: Fred Adams
fredadams@adamsdist.com
Number Employees: 50-99
Services: Short haul trucking, local delivery, pick/pack & order fulfillment, storage
Regions Served:
Houston, TX

51519 Adcom Worldwide
P.O. Box 3627
Bellevue, WA 98009   425-462-1094
800-843-4784
www.adcomworldwide.com
Transportation services include air freight forwarding and long and short haul trucking of general line items. An import/export service with no specific brands of food products.
Contact: David Britnell
dbritnell@adcomworldwide.com
Number Employees: 10-19
Services: Air freight forwarding & long and short haul trucking
Regions Served:
Worldwide

51520 Air Land Transport Inc
11100 Calaska Cir.
Anchorage, AK 99515-2933   907-248-0362
Fax: 907-248-2695 800-478-2040
ar@airlandak.com www.airlandak.com
Transportation services include local and instate hauling.
President: John Snead
jsnead@airlandak.com
Number Employees: 50-99

51521 Air New Zealand LTD
1960 E Grand Ave # 900
El Segundo, CA 90245-5092   310-648-7000
Fax: 310-648-7017 800-223-9494
www.airnztravelagent.com
Transportation firm providing air cargo service to Australia, New Zealand, London and Frankfurt
CFO: Lynair Beilenson
lynair.beilenson@airnz.com
VP: Wayne Borland
Number Employees: 100-249
Parent Co: Air New Zealand
Services: Airline cargo
Regions Served:
Australia, New Zealand, London & Frankfurt

51522 (HQ)Airschott Inc
PO Box 17373
Washington, DC 20041-7373   703-471-7444
Fax: 703-471-4026 sales@airschott.com
www.airschott.com
Import and export broker of seafood, alcoholic beverages, produce, etc.; warehouse providing cooler and dry storage for seafood; transportation firm providing customs brokerage, freight forwarding, domestic and international airfreight and long haul trucking
President: Robert Schott
EVP: Tony Sequeira
Marketing Director: Andrew Shotwell
Contact: Carlos Balta
carlos@airschott.com
Director Operations: Hing Buon
Estimated Sales: $20-50 Million
Number Employees: 5-9
Square Footage: 4000
Other Locations:
Airschott
Baltimore, MD Airschott
Services: Customs brokerage, freight forwarding, domestic & international air freight & long haul trucking
Regions Served:
Worldwide

51523 Airways Freight Corp
3849 W Wedington Dr
Fayetteville, AR 72704-5734   479-442-6301
Fax: 479-442-6522 800-643-3525
dalec@airwaysfreight.com
www.airwaysfreight.com
Transportation firm providing domestic and international air shipping, freight forwarding and next and same day service; also, international and nationwide service available
President: Ken Center
CEO: Dale Caudle
Director Marketing Division: Mike Nimmo
VP Operations: Dave Hood
Number Employees: 100-249
Services: Domestic & international air & ocean shipping, freight forwarding, same day, next day, second day & 3 to 5 day service
Regions Served:
Nationwide & International

51524 Alaska Direct Transport
125 Oklahoma St
Anchorage, AK 99504-1210   651-982-9907
Transportation firm providing LTL, local and long haul trucking of dry freight
Number Employees: 1-4
Services: LTL, local & long haul trucking of dry freight
Regions Served:
AK & MN

51525 Alaska Railroad Corp
327 W Ship Creek Ave
Anchorage, AK 99501-1671   907-265-2300
Fax: 907-265-2416 800-321-6518
public_comment@akrr.com
www.alaskarailroadgiftshop.com
Warehouse providing dry storage for perishable goods; transportation services includes railroad; rail siding available
CEO: William O'Leary
olearyw@akrr.com
Number Employees: 500-999
Services: Railroad transportation
Regions Served:
Alaska & Canada

51526 Alaska Traffic Consultants
2214 4th Ave S
P.O. Box 3837
Seattle, WA 98134-1590   206-682-6804
Fax: 206-682-6804 info@alaskatraffic.com
www.alaskatraffic.com
Transportation services include freight forwarding, consolidation and shippers' agent
Contact: Cindy Christopherson
cindyc@alaskatraffic.com
Estimated Sales: Less Than $500,000
Number Employees: 1-4
Services: Shippers' agent, freight forwarding & consolidation to Alaska
Regions Served:
Alaska

51527 (HQ)Allied Cold Storage Corporation
28 Kondelin Rd # 1
Gloucester, MA 01930-5192   978-281-0800
Fax: 978-281-6642 www.alliedcoldstorage.com
Warehouse providing cooler and freezer storage for frozen foods; transportation firm providing local haul trucking; also, blast/plate freezing and rail siding available
Owner: Peter Maggio
Number Employees: 20-49
Square Footage: 1100000
Other Locations:
Gloucester, MA
Services: Local haul trucking
Regions Served:
Northeast corridor

51528 Allied Frozen Storage Inc
2501 Broadway St
Buffalo, NY 14227-1042   716-894-4000
Fax: 716-894-2403 dblum@alliedgrp.com
www.alliedfrozenstorage.com
Warehouse providing cooler, humidity-controlled, freezer and dry storage; transportation broker providing freight consolidation, cross docking, store door delivery and Canadian distribution; rail siding available
CEO: Drew Blum
VP: Terrance J. Collister
COO: Stephen Kincanon
Number Employees: 20-49
Services: Broker providing freight consolidation, cross docking, store door delivery & Canadian distribution
Regions Served:
Continental U.S. & Canada

51529 Allied Logistics
20 26th St
Huntington, WV 25703-1242   304-523-2131
Fax: 304-523-9531 800-218-4246
sales@alliedlogistics.com
www.alliedlogistics.com
Warehouse providing dry, freezer and cooler storage for food products, chemicals, general merchandise; also toll services, pick and pack, repackaging and just-in-time services available
President: Jeff Smith
CEO: Lake Polan III
VP: Ed Canterbury
Number Employees: 100-249
Parent Co: Allied Realty Company
Other Locations:
Allied Warehousing Services
Kenova, WV
Allied Warehousing Services
Nitro, WV Allied Warehousing Services Nitro
Services: toll services
Regions Served:
Nationwide

51530 Allround Forwarding Co
134 W 26th St # 1000
New York, NY 10001-6803   212-255-8444
Fax: 212-645-0138 www.allroundforwarding.com
Transportation firm providing freight forwarding services
Owner: Hatto Dachgruber
all@allroundusa.com
Number Employees: 10-19
Services: Freight forwarding
Regions Served:
International

51531 (HQ)Alpha International
510 Thornall St # 390
Suite 390
Edison, NJ 08837-2204   732-692-5300
Fax: 732-692-5307 sales@alpha-international.eu
www.alpha-pcl.eu
Transportation firm providing international freight forwarding and customs house services
Manager: Mark Baker
markbaker@simplexgrinnell.com
Number Employees: 10-19
Services: Customs house broker & freight forwarding services
Regions Served:
International

51532 Alton & Southern Railway Co
1000 S 22nd St
East St Louis, IL 62207-1943   618-482-7758
Fax: 618-482-7775 www.altonsouthern.com
Transportation services include rail deliveries; serving nationwide and regional areas
Manager: Michael McCarthy
Estimated Sales: $2.5-5 Million
Number Employees: 500-999
Parent Co: Union Pacific
Services: Rail
Regions Served:
Nationwide & regional

Transportation Firms / A-Z

51533 Alvan Motor Freight
PO Box 757
Ortonville, MI 48462-757
800-632-4172
www.alvanmotor.com
Transportation broker providing freight forwarding, rail car service, ocean freight and local and short haul trucking; also, shippers' association
Number Employees: 20-49
Parent Co: Alvan Motor Freigh
Services: Freight forwarding, rail car service, ocean freight & local & short haul trucking
Regions Served:
  Northeast, Central U.S.

51534 Amarillo Warehouse Co
620 N Fairfield St
PO Box 829
Amarillo, TX 79107-7911   806-381-0107
Fax: 806-383-1625 info@amarillowarehouse.com
www.amarillowarehouse.com
Warehouse providing freezer and dry storage for frozen and dry foods; transportation services include slip sheets, loading and unloading, local and short haul trucking, drayage and intrastate and interstate connections; rail siding available
Manager: Esther Bustos
Number Employees: 10-19
Services: Local & short haul trucking, drayage and intrastate & interstate connections
Regions Served:
  AR, CO, KS, LA, NM & TX

51535 Amax Nutrasource Inc
1770 Prairie Rd
Eugene, OR 97402-9734   541-688-4944
Fax: 541-688-4866 800-893-5306
www.amaxnutrasource.com
Manufacturer and distributor of herbal extracts and nutritional ingredients.
President: Larry Martinez
lm@amaxnutrasource.com
CFO: Daniel Rothwell
Business Development Manager: Steve Light
Production Manager: Charles Lofton
Number Employees: 10-19

51536 AmeriCold Logistics LLC
10 Glenlake Parkway
Suite 600, South Tower
Atlanta, GA 30328   678-441-6824
    888-808-4877
info@americold.com www.americold.com
Over 175 temperature-controlled warehouses around the world; Also transportation and logistics
President/CEO: Fred Boehler
EVP/CFO: Marc Smernoff
EVP/Chief Investment Officer: Jay Harron
EVP, Supply Chain Solutions: David Stuver
EVP/Chief Legal Officer: Jim Snyder
EVP/COO: Carlos Rodriguez
Year Founded: 1903
Estimated Sales: $1 Billion+
Number Employees: 10,000+
Services: Temperature-controlled transportation; Port facilities

51537 America's Service Line
1814 Elizabeth St
Green Bay, WI 54302   920-430-8427
    855-967-5275
www.americasserviceline.com
Private fleet for American Foods Group.
President: Scott Willert
Parent Co: American Foods Group LLC
Services: Refrigerated trailers

51538 American Airlines Inc
4333 Amon Carter Blvd
Fort Worth, TX 76155-2664   817-963-1234
Fax: 817-963-2523   800-227-4622
www.aa.com
Transportation firm providing cooler facilities and freight forwarding
Executive VP: Elise R Eberwein
elise.eberwein@aa.com
Estimated Sales: Over $1 Billion
Number Employees: 10000+
Services: Airline: freight forwarding & cooler facilities
Regions Served:
  Canada, Europe, Mexico, Bermuda, Caribbean, South & Central America & Far East

51539 American Cargo Services
222 Camp McDonald Rd # A
Wheeling, IL 60090-6529   847-394-4250
Owner: Gregory S Wisniewski
greg.wisniewski@amecar.com

51540 (HQ)American Cold Storage
607 Industry Rd
Louisville, KY 40208-1635   502-634-4753
Fax: 502-634-4757 www.americancold.com
Warehouse providing a total of 13,994,356 cu. ft of warehouse space throughout all five warehouses; also provides cooler and freezer storage for food and nonfood products; transportation firm providing local, long and short haul refrigerated trucking and rail car services; also, rail siding, USDA inspections, pork certification, etc. services available
Vice President: Dan Brittain
danb@americancoldtulsa.com
CEO and Chairman: Sam C. Bradshaw
Vice President Finance: Patty Bronaugh
Vice President: Dan Brittain
danb@americancoldtulsa.com
Sales & Marketing: Charles Cheatham
Office Manager: Lisa Blackburn
Warehouse Manager: Christy Ward
Number Employees: 50-99
Other Locations:
  American Cold Storage
  Louisville, KY
  Boonville, IN
  Jackson, TN
  Tulsa, OK
  Humboldt, TN American Cold Storage Boonville
Services: Local, long & short haul refrigerated trucking & rail car
Regions Served:
  Midwestern, Southeastern & Eastern states

51541 American Distribution Centers
P.O. Box 27404
Salt Lake City, UT 84127   801-972-3404
Fax: 801-972-9445 www.americandis.com
Warehouse providing cooler, dry and humidity-controlled storage for general merchandise and food products; transportation firm providing local haul trucking and freight consolidation services; rail siding available
President: David Pettit
Evp Sales/Marketing: Lenny Goodwin
Evp Operations: Jason Walker
Estimated Sales: $8.3 Million
Number Employees: 50-99
Square Footage: 1960000
Services: Freight consolidation & local haul trucking
Regions Served:
  Western states

51542 American Fast Freight
7400 45th Street Ct E
Fife, WA 98424-3775   253-926-5000
Fax: 253-926-5100   800-642-6664
www.americanfast.com
Provides quality transportation, warehousing, and distribution throughout Alaska.
CEO: Tim Jacobson
Number Employees: 100-249
Regions Served:
  Alaska, Hawaii, Guam, Peurto Rico, USVI

51543 American Port Services
PO Box 193
Savannah, GA 31402-0193   912-966-2198
Fax: 912-966-2791
Public warehouse providing dry storage; transportation firm providing local, long and short haul trucking; also, rail siding, LTL, TL, TOFC, COFC, M.I.D. meat inspections and U.S. custom bonded storage services available
VP: John Fergerson
Number Employees: 501-1000
Parent Co: Schneider Logistics
Services: Local, long & short haul trucking: LTL, TL, vans, flatbeds & containers; also, TOFC & COFC
Regions Served:
  Nationwide

51544 American Shipping Co
250 Moonachie Rd # 5
Moonachie, NJ 07074-1378   201-478-4600
Fax: 201-478-4601 www.shipamerican.com
Transportation and customs house broker providing services including U.S. Customs clearing, export freight forwarding, domestic and international air freight and shippers' associations
President: Connor Dromey
connord@shipamerican.com
CEO: Ralph Natale
Number Employees: 5-9
Services: Customs house & transportation broker providing air freight, freight forwarding, U.S. Customs clearing, etc.
Regions Served:
  International

51545 American Truck Dispatch
4186 W Swift Ave # 108
Fresno, CA 93722-6322   559-277-7555
Fax: 559-277-7561
Transportation broker providing interstate and local haul trucking
Owner: Tom Kourafas
Estimated Sales: $1-2.5 Million
Number Employees: 5-9
Services: Broker providing local haul trucking
Regions Served:
  Mid-Atlantic, West Coast, 48 States

51546 American Warehouse Co
5150 Colorado Blvd
Denver, CO 80216-3120   303-388-4521
Fax: 303-394-4514 sales@awc-denver.com
www.wsi.com
Warehouse providing dry storage of general merchandise; transportation firm offering truckload and LTL services
Manager: Scott Myhaver
smyhaver@wsi.com
Number Employees: 20-49
Parent Co: Warehouse Specialists Inc.
Services: Truckload & LTL
Regions Served:
  Colorado & the Rocky Mountain region

51547 American West
8181 Jetstar Dr
Suite 110
Irving, TX 75063-2806   972-915-3800
Fax: 972-915-3810
Transportation broker offering freight forwarding
President: Raymond Peak
Contact: Alfredo Barajas
alfredo.barajas@awest.com
Number Employees: 20-49
Parent Co: American West
Services: Brokerage & freight forwarding
Regions Served:
  Nationwide

51548 Amobelge Shipping Corporation
934 Broadway
Bayonne, NJ 07002   201-436-3036
Fax: 201-436-3057 www.amobelge.com
Transportation firm providing international freight forwarding services
President: Al Visone
Number Employees: 1-4
Type of Packaging: Bulk
Services: International freight forwarding
Regions Served:
  International

51549 Amware Distribution Warehouse
19801 Holland Rd
Cleveland, OH 44142   440-234-8888
Fax: 440-234-8055
Warehouse providing dry storage for nonperishable foods; transportation firm providing long and short haul trucking
President: Brad Maloof
Contact: Michael Liu
michael.liu@amwarelogistics.com
Number Employees: 10-19
Square Footage: 408000
Services: Long & short haul trucking
Regions Served:
  Nationwide

51550 Anadon Logistics
Po Box 271
Campbellville, CA L0P 1B0
Canada   905-854-5630
Freight forwarder and logistics provider specializing in the food and beverage industry. Provide prior notice service to comply with FDA requirements.

Transportation Firms / A-Z

Estimated Sales: 1 Million
Number Employees: 20-49
Square Footage: 20000
Other Locations:
   Anadon Logistics
   Ontario, CanadaAnadon Logistics

51551 Anchor Distribution Services
2950 Merced St
San Leandro, CA 94577-5635 510-483-9120
   Fax: 510-483-1826 877-640-0268
   http://www.anchordistribution.com/index.html
Food grade warehouse providing dry and cold storage; transportation firm providing local, long and short haul trucking; also, rail siding, re-packing, container de-vanning, export management, etc
Owner: Charles Callaghan
President: Chad Callaghan
Contact: Chad Anchor
chad@anchordistributinginc.com
Operations: Greg Zamira
Number Employees: 17
Square Footage: 720000
Services: Local, long & short haul trucking
Regions Served:
   West Coast

51552 Angelina & Neches River Railroad
PO Box 1328
Lufkin, TX 75902-1328 936-634-4403
   Fax: 936-639-3879 dperkins@anrrr.com
   www.anrrr.com
Transportation firm providing rail car services
President: David Perkins
Manager, Sales & Marketing: Tommy Swearingen
Number Employees: 20-49
Services: Rail car
Regions Served:
   Southwest Region

51553 Apl Logistics
222 westt Adams Street
Chicago, IL 60606 312-621-2000
   Fax: 311-62- 800-428-8161
   contactgatx@gatx.com www.gatx.com
Warehouse providing cooler and dry storage for refrigerated and nonperishable foods; transportation firm providing long, short and local haul trucking; also, re-packing and labeling available
CEO: Brian A Kenney
Number Employees: 250-499
Parent Co: GATX Logistics
Services: Long, short & local haul trucking
Regions Served:
   Nationwide

51554 (HQ)Archer Daniels Midland Company
77 West Wacker Dr.
Suite 4600
Chicago, IL 60601 312-634-8100
   www.adm.com
Food and feed ingredients, industrial chemicals and biofuels.
Chairman/CEO: Juan Luciano
Executive VP/CFO: Ray Young
Senior VP/General Counsel: D. Cameron Findlay
Year Founded: 1902
Estimated Sales: $64.3 Billion
Number Employees: 32,000
Services: Barge, Rail, Truck, Oceangoing Vessel
Regions Served:
   Global

51555 Arco Warehouse Co
1810 E Jasper St
Tulsa, OK 74110-4921 918-585-8191
   Fax: 918-587-9649 www.arco1.com
Warehouse offering dry food storage; transportation firm offering freight consolidation and trucking; also, distribution, repackaging, inventory control and rail siding available
President: John Blaine
jblaine@arco1.com
Estimated Sales: Less Than $500,000
Number Employees: 1-4
Square Footage: 1080000
Services: Freight consolidation & trucking
Regions Served:
   Nationwide

51556 (HQ)Arctic Beverages
107 Mountainview Road
Unit 2
Winnipeg, MB R3C 2E6
Can 204-633-8686
   866-503-1270
   winnipeg@arcticbev.com www.arcticbev.com
Soft drinks, juices, snack foods, bread, frozen food, chocolate.
Year Founded: 1991
Estimated Sales: $6 Million
Number Employees: 44
Number of Products: 68
Square Footage: 68000
Parent Co: Tribal Councils Investment Group of Manitoba Ltd.
Other Locations:
   Arctic Beverages Ltd.
   The Pas, MB
   Arctic Beverages Ltd.
   Thompson, MB
   Arctic Beverages Ltd.
   Winnipeg, MBArctic Beverages Ltd.Thompson
Services: Land, sea, air, rail
Regions Served:
   Northern Manitoba, Northern Saskatchewan, North-Western Ontario, Nunavut

51557 Arnhalt Transportation Brkrg
3701 38th St S # B
Fargo, ND 58104-6914 701-282-9211
   Fax: 701-282-9266 800-962-5877
Transportation firm providing international and domestic services for food products
President: D Anderson
Estimated Sales: $1-2.5 Million
Number Employees: 10-19
Square Footage: 7200
Services: Broker providing services for foods products
Regions Served:
   National, and Canada

51558 Aspen Distribution
21111 E. 36th Dr
P.O.Box 39108
Aurora, CO 80011 303-371-2511
   Fax: 303-576-9254 info@aspendistribution.com
   www.aspendistribution.com
Warehouse providing dry storage for food, re-packing and labeling for nonperishable and refrigerated foods; transportation services include local and short haul trucking throughout Colorado.
President: Bob Scott
Sales & Customer Service Manager: Jennifer Kirk
Estimated Sales: $12 Million
Number Employees: 120
Square Footage: 846720
Services: Local & short haul trucking
Regions Served:
   Colorado

51559 Aspen Distribution Inc
10875 E 40th Ave
PO Box 39108
Denver, CO 80239-3210 720-974-7366
   Fax: 303-373-9850 Info@aspendistribution.com
   www.aspendistribution.com
Warehouse providing dry storage for food, paper and medical supplies; transportation services include local and short haul trucking; rail siding available
IT: Deborah Killion
dkillion@aspendistribution.com
Number Employees: 50-99
Services: Local & short haul trucking
Regions Served:
   CO

51560 Associated Global Systems
3333 New Hyde Park Rd
New Hyde Park, NY 11042 516-627-8910
   Fax: 516-627-6051 800-645-8300
   nwcs@agsystems.com www.agsystems.com
Transportation firm offering air freight services; also, packing and repacking of perishables available.
President & CEO: James Tucci
VP, Global Supply Chain Solutions: Scott Richter
Year Founded: 1958
Estimated Sales: $100-500 Million
Number Employees: 200-499
Parent Co: Nippon Express
Services: Air freight; also, packing & repacking of perishables

Regions Served:
   International

51561 Associated Trucking Co Inc
477 Shoup Ave # 101
Idaho Falls, ID 83402-3658 208-524-0404
   Fax: 208-524-4093 800-762-6262
   www.associatedtrucking.com
Transportation broker providing local, long and short haul trucking services; also, reefers and flatbeds available
President: Charles Howard
choward@associatedtrucking.com
Fleet Supervisor: Randy White
Number Employees: 5-9
Services: Broker providing local, long & short haul trucking; also, reefers & flatbeds
Regions Served:
   Nationwide

51562 Atir Transportation Services
7123 Pearl Rd Ste 305
Cleveland, OH 44130 440-845-5055
   Fax: 440-845-6238
Transportation agent providing long haul trucking services; also, TL, temperature control service via contract and common motor carriers available
President: Richard Hessler
Number Employees: 5-9
Services: Broker providing long haul trucking, TL & temperature control services via contract & common carriers
Regions Served:
   Nationwide

51563 Atkins Bob Lin Inc
775 Rudolph Way
Greendale, IN 47025-8378 812-537-5618
   Fax: 812-537-5618
Transportation services include short and local haul trucking
Owner: Travis Chrisman
travis@dcitrucking.com
Number Employees: 10-19
Parent Co: Drue Chrisman
Services: Short & local haul trucking
Regions Served:
   Regional & local: IN, KY & OH

51564 Atlanta Bonded Warehouse Corporation
3000 Cobb International Blvd
Kennesaw, GA 30152-4383 770-425-3000
   Fax: 770-424-1440 info@atlantabonded.com
   www.atlantabonded.com
Provider of public and contract food-grade, temperature-controlled distribution services for over 60 years.
President: Joe Keith
VP, Sales & Operations: Hal Justice
Number Employees: 650
Services: LTL & TL transportation, refrigerated, local & long-haul trucking
Regions Served:
   Southeastern U.S.

51565 Atlantic Container
50 Cardinal Dr
Westfield, NJ 07090 908-518-5300
   info@aclcargo.com
   www.aclcargo.com
Transportation firm providing transatlantic and intermodal carrying of containerized and roll on/off cargo.
Chief Executive Officer: Andy Abbott
Year Founded: 1965
Estimated Sales: $267 Million
Number Employees: 100-249
Services: Ocean & intermodal carrier of containerized & roll on/off cargo.
Regions Served:
   Transatlantic

51566 Austin Transportation
P.O.Box D
Twin Falls, ID 83303-0019 208-733-3965
   Fax: 208-733-1094
Transportation broker providing common/contract carriers
Manager: Allen Hall
Number Employees: 20-49
Services: Broker providing common/contract carrier & export/import shipping management

Transportation Firms / A-Z

51567 B & H Railcorp
76 Maple Ave
Cohocton, NY 14826-9711   585-346-2090
    Fax: 585-346-6454   www.lalrr.com
Transportation company providing rail car service; serving nationwide and internationally with multiple class 1 rail connections, and a 282 mile system
President: William D Burt
Vice President: Raymond Martel
rmartel@lalrr.com
Number Employees: 5-9
Services: Rail car service
Regions Served:
    Western NY, and Northwestern PA

51568 B.R. Williams Trucking & Warehouse
23369 Hwy 21 South
P O Box 3310
Oxford, AL 36203   256-831-5580
    Fax: 256-831-8059   800-523-7963
dee.brown@brwilliams.com   www.brwilliams.com
Warehouse providing dry storage of nonperishable goods; transportation services include long haul trucking services nationwide and in Canada
President: Dee Brown
Communications and PR: Misty Kowatana
VP Operations: Jack Brim
Number Employees: 100-249
Parent Co: Bill Williams Trucking
Services: Long haul trucking
Regions Served:
    Nationwide & Canada

51569 BDP International Inc
510 Walnut St # 1400
Philadelphia, PA 19106-3690   215-629-0643
    Fax: 215-629-8940   www.bdpinternational.com
Warehouse providing cooler, freezer and dry storage for frozen food, meat, seafood and dry goods; transportation services include air and ocean freight forwarding, importing, exporting and long and short haul trucking
President & CEO: Richard Bolte
Cmo: Arnie Bornstein
abornstein@bdpnet.com
CEO: Richard Bolte Jr
Sales Administrator: Vanessa Spero
Number Employees: 250-499
Services: Air & ocean freight forwarding, importing, exporting and long & short haul trucking
Regions Served:
    Worldwide

51570 BLC Trucking Inc
3401 Lincoln Ave # C
Tacoma, WA 98421-4017   253-272-6191
    blctrucking@lbu.com
Warehouse providing dry storage for grocery products and general merchandise; transportation firm providing local container haul trucking; rail siding services available
President: Bernard Bordova
b.bordova@maplex.com
Estimated Sales: Less Than $500,000
Number Employees: 1-4
Services: Local container haul trucking
Regions Served:
    Local

51571 Baker Transfer & Storage
P.O.Box 21479
Billings, MT 59104-1479   406-245-3417
    Fax: 406-245-6608
Warehouse providing cooler, freezer and dry storage for frozen, refrigerated and nonperishable foods; transportation firm providing short and local haul trucking; rail siding services available
Owner: Richard Hunt
General Manager: David Krueger
Number Employees: 20-49
Services: Local & short haul trucking
Regions Served:
    Billings & Bozeman, MT

51572 Baldwin Distribution Services
P.O.Box 51618
Amarillo, TX 79159   806-383-7650
    Fax: 806-383-0528   800-692-1333
Transportation firm providing refrigerated local, short and long haul trucking, liftgate service
President: Shannon Baldwin Dowis
CEO: Dudley Baldwin
Operations Manager: Lacye Comer
Number Employees: 100-249
Services: Refrigerated local, short and long haul trucking
Regions Served:
    Nationwide, Canada and Mexico

51573 Baltimore International Warehousing
7646 Canton Center Dr
Baltimore, MD 21224-2027   410-633-3500
    Fax: 410-633-4147   800-562-5517
suemonaghan@biwt.com   www.biwt.com
Warehouse providing dry storage for canned foods; transportation services include local haul trucking, piers, piggy ramps and container hauling; rail siding available
President/CEO: Sue Monaghan
Vice President: James Miller
Manager: Darryl Bryant
darrylbryant@biwt.com
Warehouse Supervisor: William Turner
Estimated Sales: $5-10 Million
Number Employees: 20-49
Square Footage: 800000
Services: Container hauling & local haul trucking
Regions Served:
    Mid-Atlantic

51574 Barrett Distribution Ctr
15 Freedom Way
Franklin, MA 02038-2586   508-553-8800
    Fax: 508-553-2929   800-279-1801
    sales@barrettdistribution.com
    www.barrettdistribution.com
Warehouse offering humidity-controlled, dry, freezer and cooler storage for groceries, general merchandise, etc.; transportation firm providing freight consolidation via TL and LTL local and short haul trucking; distribution and railsiding services available
President: Arthur Barrett
abarrett@barrettdistribution.com
Senior VP: Mike O'Donnell
Director Customer Relations: Mark Sotir
COO: Timothy Barrett
Number Employees: 50-99
Parent Co: Barrett Warehouse & Transport
Services: Freight consolidation via TL & LTL local & short haul trucking
Regions Served:
    Northeast

51575 Barrett Trucking Co Inc
16 Austin Dr # 2
Burlington, VT 05401-5498   802-863-1311
    Fax: 802-863-4579   www.barretttruckingco.com
Transportation firm providing local and short haul trucking
Owner: Joe Barrett
VP of Sales: G Barrett
joe@barretttruckingco.com
Number Employees: 20-49
Services: Long & local haul trucking
Regions Served:
    MA, ME, NH, NY & VT

51576 Bay Cities Warehouse
31474 Hayman St
Hayward, CA 94544-7195   510-471-9770
    Fax: 510-471-1968   www.baycitieswarehouse.com
Warehouse providing storage for dry products; transportation services include local, short, long haul and common carrier trucking; also, rail siding available
President: Bob Bozek
bbozek@baycitieswarehouse.com
Number Employees: 5-9
Services: Local, long & short haul trucking & common carrier
Regions Served:
    CA

51577 Beacon Distribution Services
PO Box 40
Aliquippa, PA 15001-0040   724-857-0722
    Fax: 724-857-2659
Warehouse providing dry storage for grocery products; transportation services include local, short and long haul trucking; also, rail siding and distribution available
Owner: Ron Benson
Number Employees: 10-19
Services: Local, short & long haul trucking
Regions Served:
    PA, OH, VA, MD & Southwestern NY

51578 Beaver Express Svc LLC
4310 Oklahoma Ave
Woodward, OK 73801-3841   580-256-6460
    Fax: 580-256-6239   800-593-2328
    thoward@beaverexpress.com
    www.beaverexpress.com
Transportation firm offering LTL, freight forwarding and local and short haul trucking; also, Saturday morning delivery and warehousing available
Vice President: Ricky Frech
rfrech@beaverexpress.com
VP Operations: Mike Kirtley
Estimated Sales: G
Number Employees: 250-499
Services: Freight forwarding, LTL & local & short haul trucking
Regions Served:
    Regional: Southwest

51579 Belleharvest Sales Inc
11900 Fisk Road
Belding, MI 48809-9413
    800-452-7753
    sales@belleharvest.com   www.belleharvest.com
Manufacturer, wholesaler/distributor, exporter, and packer of fresh apples.
President/CEO: Mike Rothwell
bellehar@iserv.net
Controller: Tony Kramer
Director of Marketing: Chris Sandwick
Director of Field Operations: Tony Blattner
Plant Manager: Brad Pitsch
Number Employees: 50-99
Parent Co: Belding Fruit Storage
Type of Packaging: Private Label, Bulk

51580 Belts Logistics Services
949 Fell St
Baltimore, MD 21231-3505   410-342-1111
    Fax: 410-675-2399   info@beltslogistics.com
    www.beltslogistics.com
Belts Logistics Services is a warehouse providing dry storage, and separate transportation brokerage providing local, long and short haul trucking.
President: S Allen Brown
shunsicker@beltslogistics.com
Chairman: S.A. Brown
shunsicker@beltslogistics.com
Executive Vice President, Legal Councel: Scott Hunsicker
Vice President, Business Development: Larry Smith
Vice President, Logistics: Jim Woolfrey
Number Employees: 48
Square Footage: 2400000
Other Locations:
    Baltimore, MD
    Elkridge, MDElkridge
Services: Local, long & short haul trucking
Regions Served:
    Mid-Atlantic

51581 (HQ)Ben-Lee Motor Service Company
3344 S Lawndale Ave
Chicago, IL 60623-5006   773-247-1234
    Fax: 773-247-0521
Transportation firm providing foreign freight forwarding and short and local trucking services in the Ohio, Illinois, Indiana and Wisconsin and Michigan areas
Owner: David Zilligen Sr
Number Employees: 20-49
Other Locations:
    Ben-Lee Motor Service Co.
    Chicago, ILBen-Lee Motor Service Co.
Services: Foreign freight forwarding and local & short haul trucking
Regions Served:
    Regional/Local: OH, IL, IN, MI & WI

51582 Bender Warehouse Co
345 Parr Cir
Reno, NV 89512-1005   775-788-8800
    Fax: 775-788-8811   800-621-9402
    salesinfo@benderwhs.com
    www.bendergroup.com

Transportation Firms / A-Z

Warehouse providing dry, air conditioned and humidity-controlled storage for confectionery products, groceries, etc.; transportation firm providing freight consolidation and long haul trucking; also, rail siding, shrink wrapping pick/pack, etc
President: Brian Classen
brianclassen@bendergroup.com
CEO: Frank Bender
Estimated Sales: Less Than $500,000
Number Employees: 1-4
Services: Freight forwarding & long haul trucking
Regions Served:
48 States

51583 (HQ)Benlin Freight Forwarding Inc
2769 Broadway St
Buffalo, NY 14227-1004   716-891-4040
Fax: 716-891-4715 www.benlin.com
Warehouse providing dry storage; transportation firm providing freight consolidation, local, long and short haul trucking; also, rail siding, display modules and distribution services available
Vice President: Robert Bennett
bbennett@benlin.com
Office Manager/Controller: Randy Cole
Vice President, Distribution Services: Bob Bennett
Sales Manager: David Geiger
International Operations Manager: Mark Cramer
Number Employees: 20-49
Services: Freight consolidation & local, short & long haul trucking
Regions Served:
Northeast & Canada

51584 Bermuda Agencies Inc
1 Gateway Ctr # 2408
Newark, NJ 07102-5324   973-242-6890
Fax: 973-242-6286
Transportation firm providing ocean services for refrigerated and dry containers
Vice President: Marva Noel
VP: Marva Noel
Number Employees: 5-9
Parent Co: Container Ship Management
Services: Shipping via ocean
Regions Served:
Bermuda

51585 Better Trucking
5849 E Orange Blossom Ln
Phoenix, AZ 85018   480-970-5678
Transportation company providing long haul trucking.
President/CEO: Robin Zenner
Number Employees: 2
Regions Served:
Nationwide

51586 Biehl & Co
5200 Hollister St # 300
Houston, TX 77040-6298   713-690-7200
Fax: 713-895-3153 www.pctowing.com
Nationwide and international steamship transportation service
President: Lee Phillips
CEO: John Springer
Vice President: Thomas Springer
Number Employees: 250-499
Regions Served:
Nationwide; International

51587 Bilkays Express/Distribution Warehouse
400 S 2nd St
Elizabeth, NJ 07206   908-289-2400
Fax: 908-289-0290 sales@bilkays.com
www.bilkays.com
Warehousing & trucking company providing food-grade public warehousing, cross-docking, container storage, distribution, consolidation, and value-added services.
President: Robert Kortenhaus
Contact: W Hocart
w@bilkays.com
Services: Short haul, warehousing
Regions Served:
Regional/Local: CT, DE, MA, NJ, NY, PA

51588 Bill Clark Truck Line Inc
311 6th St
Alamosa, CO 81101-2696   303-288-1701
Fax: 719-589-6074

Transportation firm providing local and short haul trucking
President: Brad Flavin
brad@bctl.us
Number Employees: 10-19
Services: Local & short haul trucking
Regions Served:
Nationwide

51589 Biscontini DistributionCenters
232 Division Street
Po Box 1857
Kingston/Wilkes-Barre, PA   570-288-6683
Fax: 570-288-6601
Warehouse providing dry storage; transportation firm providing local, short and long haul trucking; rail siding and cross docking available
President: Richard Biscontini
Executive VP: Rudi Biscontini, Jr.
Number Employees: 50-99
Services: Local, long & short haul trucking
Regions Served:
New England & the Mid-Atlantic states

51590 Blendco Inc
8 J M Tatum Industrial Dr
Hattiesburg, MS 39401-8341   601-544-9800
Fax: 601-544-5634 888-253-6326
csr@blendcoinc.com www.blendcoinc.com
Dry food manufacturer. Provide custom blending and packaging, as well as private labeling and contract packaging services.
President: Charles McCaffrey
Chief Financial Officer: Ken Hrdlica
Estimated Sales: $8 Million
Number Employees: 20-49
Number of Brands: 2
Type of Packaging: Food Service, Private Label, Bulk

51591 Blue Line Cold Storage Chicago
1556 W 43rd St
Chicago, IL 60609-3328   773-579-1594
Fax: 773-254-0790 www.ashlandcoldstorage.com
Warehouse offering cooler and freezer storage; rail siding available; transportation firm providing trucking in the midwest
Manager: Pat Lombard
Vice President/General Manager: Alex Olejniczak
Sales and Logistics Manager: Alex Rosenbeck
Estimated Sales: Less Than $500,000
Number Employees: 1-4
Regions Served:
Midwest

51592 Blue Line Moving & Storage
5614 Nordic Dr
Cedar Falls, IA 50613-6949   319-266-3591
Fax: 319-266-0408 800-728-3591
www.unitedvanlines.com
Warehouse providing storage for dry goods; transportation firm providing local delivery in Iowa
Owner: Bob Mahncke
bluelinemoving@cfu.net
Estimated Sales: $1-2.5 Million
Number Employees: 10-19
Square Footage: 48000
Services: Local delivery
Regions Served:
Iowa

51593 Bob's Transport & Stge Co Inc
7980 Tarbay Dr
Jessup, MD 20794-9416   410-799-7524
Fax: 410-799-0951 www.bobstransport.com
Warehouse offering dry storage for groceries, general commodities and paper goods; transportation firm providing third party logistics, rail and intermodal trucking services; also, rail siding, pallet exchange, container drayage, crossdocking, packaging, etc
President: Bob Hightower
bob@bobstransport.com
Estimated Sales: $10-20 Million
Number Employees: 20-49
Services: Intermodal trucking, rail & 3rd party logistics
Regions Served:
Mid-Atlantic

51594 Bootz Distribution
4860 Joliet Street
Denver, CO 80239   303-371-6833
Fax: 303-371-6833

Public warehouse offering dry and cooler storage for food and nonfood items; also, rail siding available; transportation firm providing local and short haul trucking
President: Hank Bootz
Number Employees: 20-49
Services: Local & short haul trucking

51595 (HQ)Brauner International Corp
66 York St # 100
Jersey City, NJ 07302-3838   201-333-5400
Fax: 201-333-4030 import@braunerintl.com
www.braunerintl.com
Customs house broker providing international air freight forwarding, importing, and exporting
President: Matthew Brauner
mbrauner@braunerintl.com
Estimated Sales: $1-2.5 Million
Number Employees: 10-19
Type of Packaging: Bulk
Other Locations:
Brauner International Corp.
Jamaica, NY
Miami, FL Brauner International Corp. Miami
Services: Customs house brokerage providing international air freight forwarding
Regions Served:
International

51596 Bridge Terminal, Inc.
12 Fish Is
New Bedford, MA 02740   508-994-4300
Fax: 508-992-6267
HarryG@MaritimeInternational.org
www.maritimeinternational.org/bridge-details.html
Customs bonded warehouse providing freezer storage for fish; transportation firm providing freight forwarding services; also, ocean vessel loading/unloading and container stuffing/unstuffing services available
Warehouse Manager: Harry Gifford
Number Employees: 10-19
Square Footage: 168000
Parent Co: Maritime International
Regions Served:
Nationwide

51597 Britton Storage Trailers
1119 N 42nd St
Grand Forks, ND 58203-1915   701-772-6681
Fax: 701-746-6493 800-437-5306
dave@brittontransport.com
www.brittontransport.com
Transportation services include freight forwarding, long and short haul trucking nationwide, internationally and regionally
President: David Britton
dave@brittontransport.com
Operations Manager: Scott Burkel
Number Employees: 10-19
Services: Freight forwarding
Regions Served:
Nationwide, Regional & International including Canada

51598 (HQ)Brokers Logistics LTD
1000 Hawkins Blvd
El Paso, TX 79915-1205   915-778-7751
Fax: 915-778-1358 jwright@brokerslogistics.com
Warehouse providing cooler, humidity-controlled and dry storage; re-packing, labeling and rail siding available; transportation services include long and short haul trucking in the Southwest
President: Michelle Wright
CEO/Owner: Jerry Wright
jwright@brokerslogistics.com
COO: Mike Blough
Number Employees: 100-249
Other Locations:
Los Angeles: 100,000 Sq ft, CA
Laredo, TX
Del Rio: 60,000 Sq Ft, TX Laredo
Services: Long & short haul trucking
Regions Served:
National, and Internationally

51599 Brookshire Grocery Company
PO Box 1411
Tyler, TX 75710-1411   903-534-3000
888-937-3776
www.brookshires.com
Regional supermarket chain in Texas, Louisiana and Arkansas.

Transportation Firms / A-Z

Chairman/CEO: Bradley Brookshire
Year Founded: 1928
Estimated Sales: $2.5 Billion
Number Employees: 14,000+
Services: Trucking

51600 Bulldog Hiway Express
3390 Buffalo Ave
North Charleston, SC 29418-5927   843-744-1651
Fax: 843-747-3539   800-331-9515
wshell@bulldoghiway.com
www.bulldoghiway.com
Transportation firm providing short, local and long haul trucking
Owner: R D Moseley Sr
President and CEO: Phil Byrd
IT: Louann Adams
ladams@bulldoghiway.com
Number Employees: 250-499
Regions Served:
 AL, FL, GA, NC, SC, TN, VA; Nationwide

51601 Burlington Northern Santa Fe, LLC
2650 Lou Menk Dr
Fort Worth, TX 76131
800-832-5452
www.bnsf.com
Transportation firm providing railroad and logistics services.
President & CEO: Carl Ice
EVP & Chief Financial Officer: Julie Piggott
EVP, Operations: Kathryn Farmer
EVP, Law & Corporate Affairs: Roger Nober
EVP & Chief Marketing Officer: Stevan Bobb
Year Founded: 1996
Estimated Sales: $18 Billion
Number Employees: 42,000
Parent Co: Birkshire Hathaway, Inc
Services: Railroad & logistics

51602 Buske Lines
7 Gateway Commerce Center Dr W
Edwardsville, IL 62025   618-931-6091
Fax: 618-931-6387   800-879-2411
johnbabington@buske.com   www.buske.com
Transportation services include TL, long haul trucking, regional refrigeration carrier, dry van, full logistics and warehousing
President: John Babington
Number Employees: 50-99
Services: TL, long haul trucking, regional refrigeration carrier, dry van & warehousing
Regions Served:
 National, Global

51603 Byers Transport
2840-76 Avenue
P.O. Box 157
Edmonton, AB T5J 2J1
Canada
780-440-1000
Fax: 780-440-2083   800-661-6953
Warehouse providing cooler, dry, freezer and humidity-controlled storage for nonperishable items; transportation broker
Operations Manager: Janet Strom
Square Footage: 600000
Services: Broker providing LTL & TL local, long & short haul trucking, cross docking, freight forwarding, etc.
Regions Served:
 Northwest Territories: BC, & AB

51604 C H Robinson Worldwide Inc
14701 Charlson Rd
Eden Prairie, MN 55347-5076   952-937-8500
Fax: 952-937-6714   800-411-3596
www.chrobinson.com
Freight transportation services using trains, trucks, ships and airplanes
CEO: John P Wiehoff
john.wiehoff@chrobinson.com
VP: Jim Butts
CFO: Chad Lindbloom
VP: Ben Champbell
VP: Molly M DuBois
Estimated Sales: Over $1 Billion
Number Employees: 10000+

51605 C R England Inc
4701 W 2100 S
Salt Lake City, UT 84120-1223   801-972-2712
Fax: 801-977-5795   www.crengland.com
Transportation firm providing refrigerated long, short and local haul trucking services in North America
Chairman of the Board/ President: Dan England
CEO: Dean England
COO: Wayne Cederholm
Chief Sales Officer: Mike Bunnell
Number Employees: 1000-4999
Services: Refrigerated long, short & local haul trucking
Regions Served:
 U.S., Canada, and Mexico

51606 C.H. Robinson Co.
14701 Charlson Rd
Eden Prairie, MN 55347-5076   952-683-2800
Fax: 952-933-4747   855-229-6128
solutions@chrobinson.com   www.chrobinson.com
Provides: freight transportation (TL, intermodal, ocean, and air freight), cross docking, LTL, customs brokerage, freight forwarding and trucking services, fresh produce sourcing, and information services.
CEO: Bob Biesterfeld
President, NA Surface Transportation: Mac Pinkerton
CFO: Mike Zechmeister
President, Global Freight Forwarding: Michael Short
Year Founded: 1905
Estimated Sales: $14.87 Billion
Number Employees: 15,074
Type of Packaging: Consumer, Food Service, Bulk
Services: Truckload, intermodal, ocean & air freight, customs brokerage, freight forwarding, cross docking, LTL & TL
Regions Served:
 Worldwide

51607 C.J. Figone Cold Storage
420 17th Street
San Francisco, CA 94107   415-495-8040
Fax: 415-495-5026
Warehouse providing freezer storage for food; freight consolidation for overseas shipment
VP: Steve Figone
Number Employees: 10-19
Regions Served:
 San Francisco bay area

51608 C.P. Rail System
425 Etna St # 38
St Paul, MN 55106-5847   651-495-9500
Transportation firm providing railroad service in Minnesota and Canada
Number Employees: 250-499
Services: Railroad
Regions Served:
 Minnesota & Canada

51609 CHS Inc.
5500 Cenex Dr.
Inver Grove Hts., MN 55077   651-355-6000
800-328-6539
www.chsinc.com
Agriculture, energy, transportation and business services company, with food products through subsidiary Ventura Foods.
President/CEO: Jay Debertin
Executive VP/CFO: Olivia Nelligan
Executive VP/General Counsel: Jim Zappa
Estimated Sales: $32.6 Billion
Number Employees: 10000+
Type of Packaging: Consumer, Food Service, Private Label, Bulk
Services: Trucking, rail, barge and ocean vessel.
Regions Served:
 North America, Brazil, Eastern Europe and China.

51610 CMT Packaging & Designs, Inc.
312 Amboy Avenue
Metuchen, NJ 08840   732-321-4029
Fax: 732-549-3615   www.cmtpackaging.com
A custom packaging company for the food and perfume industry.
President: Priya Iyar
Vice President: Pat Archary
VP Sales: Preshal Almore
Estimated Sales: $5,000
Square Footage: 10000

51611 (HQ)COX Transportation Svc Inc
10448 Dow Gil Rd
Ashland, VA 23005-7639   804-798-1477
Fax: 804-798-1299   800-288-8118
info@truckingforamerica.com
www.truckingforamerica.com
Transportation broker providing long, short and local haul trucking services
President: John Cox
President: Jay Smith
Number Employees: 100-249
Services: Local, long & short haul trucking; also, brokerage
Regions Served:
 Nationwide & International

51612 CRST International Inc
3930 16th Ave SW
Cedar Rapids, IA 52404-2332   319-396-4400
Fax: 319-390-2649   800-736-2778
info@crst.com   www.crst.com
Transportation firm providing long and short haul trucking; team drivers provided on all loads
Chairman of the Board: John Smith
President and CEO: David Rusch
CFO: Wes Brackey
Manager: Tracy Lipcomb
Number Employees: 1000-4999
Services: Dry freight
Regions Served:
 Nationwide

51613 CSI Logistics
2741 Foundation Dr
South Bend, IN 46628   574-233-1047
Fax: 574-232-8461
Warehouse providing dry and humidity-controlled storage; transportation firm providing TL, LTL and long haul trucking
President: Leonard A Kanczuzewski
Number Employees: 20-49
Services: TL & LTL local & long haul trucking, intermodal, import/export, crating, etc.
Regions Served:
 National

51614 CSX Transportation
500 Water St
Jacksonville, FL 32202   904-359-3200
www.csx.com
Warehouse offering cooler and freezer storage of frozen and refrigerated foods; transportation firm providing rail and local.
President & CEO: James Foote
EVP/Chief Legal Officer/Secretary: Nathan Goldman
EVP: Edmond Harris
EVP/Chief Financial Officer: Kevin Boone
EVP/Chief Administrative Officer: Diana Sorfleet
SVP/Chief Information Officer: Kathleen Brandt
SVP, Operations South: Robert (Bob) Frulla, Jr.
Estimated Sales: Over $1 Billion
Number Employees: 10000+
Parent Co: CSX Corporation
Type of Packaging: Private Label
Services: Long, short & local haul trucking; also, rail
Regions Served:
 East of MS

51615 CT Logistics
12487 Plaza Dr
Cleveland, OH 44130   216-267-2000
Fax: 216-267-5945   sales@ctlogistics.com
www.ctlogistics.com
Transportation firm providing dry freight hauling, freight auditing, 3 PL services, local, long and short haul trucking, third party logistics and ICC broker nonasset based carrier services and T.M.S. software
CEO: Jack Miner
Contact: Pete Bodnar
pbodnar@ctlogistics.com
Purchasing Agent: Debra Rose
Number Employees: 5-9
Parent Co: Commercial Traffic Company
Services: Freight auditing, third party logistics, brokerage services, local, long and short haul trucking, etc.
Regions Served:
 Nationwide and Canada

751

Transportation Firms / A-Z

51616 Caldic USA Inc
2425 Alft Ln
Elgin, IL 60124-7864
847-468-0001
customerservice@caldic.us
Sourcing, R&D, processing, warehousing and distribution of ingredients.
Owner: Bob Leonard
bleonard@nealanders.com
Number Employees: 10-19
Parent Co: Caldic

51617 Caldwell Trucking Inc
45454 Adams Rd
Pendleton, OR 97801-9595   541-276-0695
Fax: 541-276-8179 www.pendletonchamber.com
Transportation firm providing short haul trucking
Owner: Bernie Caldwell
Estimated Sales: Less Than $500,000
Number Employees: 1-4
Services: Short haul trucking
Regions Served:
   West Coast

51618 (HQ)California Cartage Co
2931 Redondo Ave
Long Beach, CA 90806-2445   310-537-1432
Fax: 562-988-1351 www.calcartage.com
Transportation broker providing local, short and long haul trucking nationwide and regional in the CA area; warehouse providing dry storage for nonperishable items; also, rail siding available
President: Robert Curry
rcurry@cmimail.com
Number Employees: 5-9
Other Locations:
   California Cartage Co.
   Carson, CA California Cartage Co.
Services: Short, local & long haul trucking & brokerage
Regions Served:
   Nationwide; regional/local: CA

51619 Can-Am LTL
101 Doney Crescent
Concord, ON L4K 1P6
Canada   416-665-1702
Fax: 416-665-5699
Transportation firm providing long haul trucking including LTL and TL; cross docking available
Number Employees: 10-19
Square Footage: 60000
Parent Co: Vitran Corporation
Services: Long haul trucking: LTL & TL; also, cross docking
Regions Served:
   International & nationwide

51620 Canaan Logistics
101 1st Ave NE # 200
Cullman, AL 35056   256-734-4031
Fax: 256-737-0202 800-330-5749
www.canaanlogistics.com
Transportation brokers; serving nationwide
President: Eddie Hart
Manager: Chad Hart
Estimated Sales: $ 1 - 3 Million
Number Employees: 10-19
Services: Transportation broker
Regions Served:
   Nationwide

51621 Canada Distribution Centres
87 Wallbridge Crescent
Belleville, ON K8P 1Z5
Canada   613-967-2900
Fax: 613-967-2912 tim@rentxtrans.com
Warehouse providing dry storage of general merchandise and groceries; transportation firm providing short haul trucking; also, re-packaging, order assembly and rail siding available
Number Employees: 10-19
Square Footage: 800000
Parent Co: Rentx Transportation Sevices Corp.
Services: Short haul trucking
Regions Served:
   Eastern Ontario

51622 Canada Maritime Agencies
4 Refinery Road
Come-By-Chance, NF A0B 1N0   709-463-8735
Fax: 709-463-8737
opscbc@canadianmaritime.nf.ca
www.canadianmaritime.com
Transportation firm providing steamship service for coffee, rice, dried fruit and nuts
Number Employees: 1-4
Services: Steamship
Regions Served:
   Nationwide & International

51623 Canadian National Railway
935 De La Gauchetiere Street W
Montreal, QC H3B 2M9
Canada
888-888-5909
cscsvcom@cn.ca www.cn.ca
Transportation firm providing door to door intermodal transportation, logistics and rail car services throughout North America
Account Manager: Yves Guillemette
Number Employees: 10,000
Services: Door to door international transportation, logistics & rail car service
Regions Served:
   North America

51624 Canton Railroad Co
1841 S Newkirk St
Baltimore, MD 21224-6009   410-633-3064
Fax: 410-633-8720 jmagness@cantonrr.com
www.cantonrr.com
Transportation firm providing short line railroad services
President: John C Magness
jmagness@cantonrr.com
CFO: Valerie Kolman
VP: Diane Abate
Number Employees: 20-49
Services: Short line railroad
Regions Served:
   MD

51625 Cardinal Logistics Management
5333 Davidson Hwy
Concord, NC 28027-8478   704-789-2000
Fax: 704-788-6618 800-800-8293
www.cardlog.com
Transportation firm providing long haul trucking nationwide
President and COO: Jerry Bowman
CEO: Tom Hostetler
thostetler@cardlog.com
CFO: Carl Texter
Number Employees: 100-249
Parent Co: Carolina Freight Carriers Corporation
Services: Long haul trucking
Regions Served:
   CT, DE, GA, MD, NC, NH, NJ, NY, PA, RI, SC, TN, VA & VT

51626 Cargo
220 Thorndale Avenue
Bensenville, IL 60106-1113   847-956-7500
Fax: 630-766-2250 800-323-3294
Warehouse providing dry storage of nonperishable food products; transportation broker offering freight forwarding services
VP Corporate Development: Robert Imhof
Estimated Sales: $20-50 Million
Number Employees: 100-249
Square Footage: 70000
Services: Brokerage & freight forwarding
Regions Served:
   Worldwide

51627 Cargo Transporters Inc
3390 N Oxford St
Claremont, NC 28610   828-459-3282
www.cargotransporters.com
Transportation firm providing local, long and short haul trucking and TL services for dry grocery products.
President: P. Dennis Dellinger
Executive Vice President: Jerry Signmon
Vice President: Jerry Signmon, Jr.
VP, Safety & Recruiting: Shawn Brown
Estimated Sales: $50-100 Million
Number Employees: 250-499
Parent Co: CT Group
Services: Local, long & short haul trucking of dry grocery products; also, TL services
Regions Served:
   Midwest & the East Coast

51628 Cargo-Master Inc
12404 Park Central Dr Ste 300
Suite 201
Dallas, TX 75251-1803
Fax: 972-681-2027 800-683-7898
Transportation company that provides shipper and carrier services for the food and beverage industry.

51629 Carmichael International Svc
533 Glendale Blvd # 2
Los Angeles, CA 90026-5013   213-353-0800
Fax: 213-250-0710 info@carmnet.com
www.carmnet.com
Transportation firm providing international freight forwarding services
Founder: Enrico Salvo
enricos@carmnet.com
Number Employees: 100-249
Services: Freight forwarding
Regions Served:
   International

51630 Carolina Bonded StorageCo
1349 Old Dairy Dr
Columbia, SC 29201-4840   803-252-4703
Fax: 803-252-0517
Warehouse providing dry storage for food products, paper and other nonfood items; local and short trucking; rail siding available
Manager: Allen Mason
cbsc@bellsouth.net
Number Employees: 5-9
Services: Trucking
Regions Served:
   Regional

51631 Carolina Transfer & Stge Inc
2207 Kimball Rd SE
P O Box 20109
Canton, OH 44707-3631   330-453-3709
Fax: 330-453-5170 www.peoplesservices.com
Warehouse providing dry and cooler storage for nonperishable food; transportation firm providing local haul trucking
CEO: Ronald Sibila
VP Finance: Larry P Kelley
VP: Phil McCollum
Human Resources Manager: Jim Wickiser
Vice President of Marketing: John Matheos
Vice President of Sales: John Motheos
Vice President of Operations: Gregory J Hughes
Purchasing Manager: Jim Ehret
Estimated Sales: Less Than $500,000
Number Employees: 1-4
Parent Co: People's Services
Services: Local haul trucking
Regions Served:
   Southeast

51632 Castell Interlocks Inc
150 N Michigan Ave # 800
Sutie 800
Chicago, IL 60601-7585   312-360-1516
Fax: 312-268-5174 ussales@castell.com
www.castell.com
Dock locks
President: Bryan Gregory
bgregory@castell.com
Number Employees: 10-19

51633 (HQ)Castellini Group
PO Box 721610
Newport, KY 41072-1610
800-233-8560
info@castellinicompany.com
www.castellinicompany.com
Produce; private labeling and custom packaging; also, transportation company offering a 48 state authority of transporting
CEO: Brian Kocher
Number Employees: 250-499
Type of Packaging: Consumer, Food Service, Private Label, Bulk
Services: Local, long and short haul
Regions Served:
   48 States

51634 Cedar Rapids & Iowa City Railway Company
3150 12th St SW
Cedar Rapids, IA 52404   319-786-3610
www.crandic.com
Transportation company providing railroad service

Transportation Firms / A-Z

VP: Kevin Burke
Number Employees: 10-19
Parent Co: IES Transportation
Services: Railroad
Regions Served:
Regional; the Plains States

51635 Centra Worldwide
815 South Main Street
Jacksonville, FL 32207   714-903-3520
Fax: 714-373-0867 888-697-4079
suddathlogistics.com
Warehouse providing storage for nonperishable items; transportation broker providing international and domestic freight forwarding services via air and ocean freight; also, re-packing and sorting services available
President: Michael Kranisky
Vice President, International: Bob Gordon
Vice President, Sales: Tom Ruede
VP, North American Operations: Bob Thomas
Number Employees: 10-19
Parent Co: Suddath Companies
Services: Broker providing international & domestic freight forwarding via ocean & air freight
Regions Served:
Worldwide

51636 (HQ)Central American Warehouse Co
10320 Werch Dr
Woodridge, IL 60517-4935   630-972-0707
sales@centralamericangroup.com
www.centralamericangroup.com
A network of six warehouses providing cooler, dry and humidity-controlled storage and nationwide transportation provider. Third party logistics, contract packaging, custom distribution programs and RFID inventory control.
Vice President: Ed Augustyn
VP: Ed Augustyn
Estimated Sales: Less Than $500,000
Number Employees: 1-4
Square Footage: 2800000
Type of Packaging: Consumer, Food Service, Private Label, Bulk
Other Locations:
Central American Transportati
Northlake, ILCentral American Transportati
Services: Freight brokerage
Regions Served:
Nationwide

51637 Central Freight Lines Inc
5601 W Waco Dr
Waco, TX 76710-5753   254-772-2120
Fax: 254-741-5370 800-782-503
www.centralfreight.com
Transportation company providing local, and short haul trucking
Manager: Tony Osburn
CEO: Robert V Fasso
rfasso@centralfreight.com
Number Employees: 1000-4999
Services: Local & short haul trucking
Regions Served:
AR; OK; & TX

51638 Central Global Express
12755 E Nine Mile Road
Warren, MI 48089   734-955-2555
Fax: 734-729-8120 800-982-3924
contact@gocge.com
Transportation broker offering freight forwarding services
President: Alan Samouelian
Vice President: Jeffrey Miller
Contact: Terry Bastow
tbastow@gocge.com
Parent Co: Centra
Services: Transportation brokerage & freight forwarding
Regions Served:
Nationwide

51639 Central Maine & Quebec Railway
15 Iron Rd # 2
Hermon, ME 04401-1180   207-848-4200
Fax: 207-848-4346 www.cmqrailway.com
Transportation firm providing rail car services
President: Robert C Grindrod
CEO: John Giles

Estimated Sales: $10 - 25 Million
Number Employees: 250-499
Parent Co: Iron Road Railways
Services: Railroad
Regions Served:
Northeast Corridor & Canada

51640 Central States Distribution
3401 Lynch Creek Dr
Danville, IL 61834-9388   217-431-3325
info@cs-dist.com
www.centralillinoiswarehouse.com
Warehouse providing dry storage for paper products, household goods, dry foods and cans; transportation broker providing long, local and regional haul trucking; also, rail siding and packaging services available
President: Ted Osborn
ted@cs-dist.com
Number Employees: 10-19
Square Footage: 1587000
Services: Broker providing long, local & regional haul trucking
Regions Served:
Nationwide

51641 Central Transport Intl
2401 N 13th St
Norfolk, NE 68701-2271   402-371-9517
Fax: 402-371-7373 800-228-8206
www.centraltransportint.com
Transportation firm providing long and short haul trucking using food and nonfood tankers
President: Thomas Abler
Human Resources: David Schipporeit
Manager: Tom Abler
toma@telebeep.com
Estimated Sales: $5-10 Million
Number Employees: 50-99
Square Footage: 800000
Services: Long & short haul trucking using food & non-food tankers
Regions Served:
Continental U.S.: the Midwest

51642 Central Transportation System
4105 Rio Bravo
Suite 100
El Paso, TX 79902
800-283-3106
info@centralsystems.com
www.centralsystems.com
Warehouse providing dry storage for appliances, household goods, heavy machinery and nonperishable food items; transportation services include short, local and long haul trucking and freight forwarding; also, break bulk consolidation and crating
Owner: Bill Appleton
Contact: Eric Barker
barkereric@scobeymoving.com
Operations Manager: Jay Spoon
Estimated Sales: $2.5-5 Million
Number Employees: 20-49
Square Footage: 320000
Services: Short, local & long haul trucking & freight forwarding
Regions Served:
Continental U.S.

51643 Central Warehouse Operations, Inc.
1825 Rust Ave
Saginaw, MI 48601   989-752-4191
Fax: 989-752-0955 sales@peoplesservices.com
www.peoplesservices.com
Warehouse offering dry storage for general merchandise and food items; transportation firm providing local and long haul trucking
President/CEO: Douglas J. Sibla
CFO-Vice President of Finance: Larry P. Kelly
Vice President of Sales & Marketing: John Matheos
COO & Executive Vice President: Bill Hanlon
Estimated Sales: $500,000-$1 Million
Number Employees: 20-49
Square Footage: 200000
Services: Local & long haul trucking
Regions Served:
Midwest

51644 Central-Cumberland Corp
3287 Franklin Limestone # 320
Antioch, TN 37013-2765   615-333-0101
Fax: 615-333-6709 lcowan@cencum.com
www.cencum.com

Warehouse providing dry storage for general merchandise; transportation firm providing local haul trucking; also, order picking, re-packaging, shrink and stretch wrapping services; rail siding available
President & General Manager: Leland Cowan
Number Employees: 5-9
Square Footage: 700000
Services: Local haul trucking
Regions Served:
TN

51645 Charles M. Schayer & Company
7901 Somerset Blvd. #B
Paramount, CA 90723   310-641-3060
Fax: 310-641-5134 denver@schayer.com
www.schayer.com
Customs house broker providing foreign freight forwarding services via air and ocean freight
Owner: Charles M Schayer
Number Employees: 20-49
Square Footage: 280000
Services: Customs house broker providing foreign freight forwarding via air & ocean freight

51646 (HQ)Chase, Leavitt & Company
72 Commercial St Ste 4
Portland, ME 04101   207-772-6383
Fax: 207-774-8270 charrison@chaseleavitt.com
www.chaseleavitt.com
Customs house broker providing international and domestic freight forwarding services for fresh and frozen seafood
President: Jon Leavitt
Corp. Accts. Mgr.: W. Michael Walsh
Number Employees: 20-49
Other Locations:
Boston, MA
Miami, FL
Newark, NJ
Los Angeles, CAMiami
Services: Air & ocean freight for fresh & frozen seafood
Regions Served:
National, International

51647 Chattanooga Freight Bureau
118 Lee Parkway Dr Ste 205
Chattanooga, TN 37421   423-894-4622
Fax: 423-894-4665
Transportation broker providing consultations, freight bill audit and payment services
President: Turney Thompson
Number Employees: 5-9
Services: Broker providing consultations, freight bill audits & payments
Regions Served:
Nationwide & Canada

51648 Chester Transfer
1515 Oak St
Chester, IL 62233   618-826-2610
Fax: 618-282-2304 800-448-8871
hayesroberts@msn.com
Transportation firm providing regional local and short haul trucking
President: Gale Stellhorn
Number Employees: 1-4
Services: Local & short haul trucking
Regions Served:
Local

51649 Chilled Solutions LLC
470 West Crossroads Parkway
Unit B
Bolingbrook, IL 60440   630-863-7750
Fax: 630-863-7750 brett@chilledsolutions.net
www.chilledsolutions.net
We are a temperature controlled warehouse with a small fleet of temperature controlled trucks. We make local deliveries in the Chicagoland area.
President: Dean Osborn
Vice President: Ted Chan
Operations Manager: Brett Koch
Square Footage: 68000

51650 Choctaw Transportation Co Inc
16020 Highway 104 W
Dyersburg, TN 38024   731-285-4664
Fax: 731-285-4668 www.choctawtrans.com
Transportation company providing local and short haul trucking; serving nationwide
Owner: Fred Percy
Manager: Greg Ford
gregmford@earthlink.net

Transportation Firms / A-Z

Number Employees: 20-49
Services: Local & short haul trucking
Regions Served:
Nationwide

51651 Choice Reefer Systems
PO Box 340
Stirling, ON K0K 3E0
Canada
800-267-2820
www.crstrucking.com
Warehouse offering cooler and freezer storage; transportation firm providing short, local and long haul trucking
President: Stan Morrow
VP Operations: Diane Wilson
V.P. of Operations: Dianne Wilson
Services: Short, long & local haul trucking
Regions Served:
Canada & northern U.S.

51652 Cincinnati PackagingAnd Distribution
12000 Mosteller Rd Unit 2
Cincinnati, OH 45241   513-771-1860
Fax: 513-772-4854 800-543-7147
Info@CincinnatiGlassBlock.com
www.cincinnatiglassblock.com
Transportation firm providing TL, LTL local and long haul trucking; also, cartage, flats, vans and double drops
Manager: Greg Pierce
Contact: Bob Monley
bmonley@cincydist.com
Dispatcher: Mick Wagoner
Number Employees: 20-49
Services: Local TL & LTL cartage, long haul trucking, cross docking, flats, vans & double drops
Regions Served:
AL, TN, GA, IL, KY, FL, GA, NC, OH, SC, VA & Canada

51653 Circle Delivery
PO Box 100595
Nashville, TN 37224   615-256-1394
Fax: 615-254-5933 800-251-1834
info@circledelivery.com www.circledelivery.com
Transportation company providing long and short haul trucking
CEO: Gregory Brown
Number Employees: 50-99
Services: Long & short haul trucking
Regions Served:
Nationwide & International

51654 Clarden Trucking
3914 S Memorial Drive
Racine, WI 53403
Transportation firm providing long and local haul trucking
Number Employees: 10-19
Services: Local & long haul trucking
Regions Served:
Midwest

51655 Coastal Cold Storage Inc
306 N Nordic Dr
Petersburg, AK 99833   907-772-4177
Fax: 907-772-4176
A warehouse facility providing cold storage.
Owner: Greg Einerson
coastal@alaska.com
Number Employees: 10-19

51656 Cockrell Distribution System
2700 Deepwater Terminal Rd
Richmond, VA 23234   804-232-8941
Fax: 804-233-3215 info@clsrva.com
http://clsrva.com/
Warehouse providing cooler and dry storage, re-packing and labeling for nonperishable and refrigerated foods; transportation services include short haul trucking nationwide
President: H Clark Cockrell
Office Manager: Beverly Schnarrs
General Manager: Billy Jones
Vice President: P.M. Neal, Jr.
Number Employees: 20-49
Square Footage: 6000000
Services: Short haul trucking
Regions Served:
Nationwide

51657 Colombo Services
4000 Airline Drive
Suite A
Houston, TX 77022   713-691-3513
Fax: 713-691-5887
Transportation company providing domestic and international freight forwarding services
President: Earnest Alfaro
Number Employees: 5-9
Services: Freight forwarding
Regions Served:
International & nationwide

51658 Colonial Freight Systems
10924 Mcbride Ln
P. O. Box 22168
Knoxville, TN 37932-3221   865-966-9711
Fax: 865-966-3649 800-251-9734
cfsinfo@cfsi.com www.cfsi.com
Transportation firm providing TL and LTL long haul trucking, providing reefer, dry van trucking
President: Thomas W McBride
CEO: Lura McBride
CEO: Tom Mc Bride
VP Sales: Phyllis Keesee
Estimated Sales: $20-50 Million
Number Employees: 50-99
Services: TL & LTL long haul trucking
Regions Served:
Nationwide

51659 Columbian Logistics Network
900 Hall St SW
Grand Rapids, MI 49503-4821   616-514-6000
Fax: 616-514-5990 888-609-8542
donran@columbian.us www.columbian.us
Warehouse offering cooler, dry and humidity-controlled storage for general merchandise, groceries, health/beauty aids and candy; transportation firm providing LTL, TL and pool distribution; also, rail siding, and special handlingdistribution available
President: Dick Wickard
CEO: John Zevalkink
COO: Robert Christian
Marketing: Donna Randall
Sales: Jim Doorn
Operations: Bill Ekberg
Estimated Sales: $40-50 Million
Number Employees: 100-249
Square Footage: 1400000
Type of Packaging: Food Service
Services: LTL, TL & pool distribution services
Regions Served:
MI, N. IN, Chicago & N Ohio

51660 Commerce Express Inc
2945 Buckley Way
Inver Grove Hts, MN 55076-2019   651-451-7332
Fax: 651-451-2312 800-333-7731
info@commerceexpressinc.com
www.commerceexpressinc.com
Transportation broker providing intermodal carrier services
Owner: Joe O'Shunessey
joe@commerceexpressinc.com
Number Employees: 10-19
Services: Broker providing intermodal carrier services
Regions Served:
International

51661 Commercial Cold Storage
4300 Pleasantdale Road
Atlanta, GA 30340   770-448-7400
Public warehouse providing cooler, freezer, dry and humidity-controlled storage for refrigerated and frozen foods; transportation firm providing local and short haul trucking, bi-modal and consolidated pool distribution in theSoutheast
Estimated Sales: $10-25 Million
Number Employees: 100-249
Square Footage: 2700000
Parent Co: Stone & Webster
Other Locations:
Commercial Cold Storage
Wilmington, NCCommercial Cold Storage
Services: Freight consolidation, LTL, bi-modal, rail car, & local & short haul trucking
Regions Served:
Southeast: AL, FL, GA, LA, MS, TN, VA, WV, NC, OH & SC

51662 Commercial DistributionCtr
16500 E Truman Rd
P.O.Box 350
Independence, MO 64050-4169   816-836-1500
Fax: 816-836-0643 www.cdcinc.com
Warehouse providing storage for dry, refrigerated and frozen foods and nonfood items; also, freight consolidation, import/export, sqeeze packing, labeling, bulk storage, pool program and rail siding available
President: Doris Jones
Contact: Lori Barker
lbarker@stlcc.edu
Purchasing Manager: Gay Martin
Number Employees: 10-19
Services: Freight consolidation & pool program
Regions Served:
Midwest & South

51663 (HQ)Commercial Transport Inc
121 Premier Dr
Belleville, IL 62220-3424   618-233-5260
Fax: 618-233-5263 800-851-7541
www.cti-bulk.com
Transportation services include local, short and long haul trucking of food grade dry bulk products
Owner: Robert A White
rawhite@cti-bulk.com
Number Employees: 10-19
Type of Packaging: Bulk
Other Locations:
Commercial Transport
Belleville, ILCommercial Transport
Services: Dry bulk, pneumatic transportation
Regions Served:
Continental U.S. & Canada

51664 Commercial Warehouse Co
1340 Broadway Blvd NE
Albuquerque, NM 87102-1544   505-247-4246
Fax: 505-247-0739
www.commercialwarehouseabq.com
Warehouse providing dry storage for general merchandise; transportation firm providing local haul trucking and freight consolidation; also, pick/pack, free port work and importing services available
Owner: James Morris
cwcabq1@qwestoffice.net
Number Employees: 10-19
Square Footage: 224000
Services: Local haul trucking & freight consolidation
Regions Served:
Albuquerque & Burleo County

51665 Commonwealth Inc
11013 Kenwood Rd # 4
Blue Ash, OH 45242-1843   513-791-1966
Fax: 513-791-0880 sales@commonwealthinc.com
www.commonwealthinc.com
Warehouse providing dry and cold storage for refrigerated and nonperishable foods; transportation firm providing short haul trucking
President: Brent L Collins
Executive Vice President: Karen Hamm
Sales Manager: Donny Bray
Manager: Collins Brent
collins.brent@commonwealthinc.com
Opeartions Vice President: Andy Deardoff
Number Employees: 20-49
Services: Short haul trucking
Regions Served:
OH

51666 Compass Consolidators
47 Stephen St
Lemont, IL 60439   630-243-0200
Fax: 630-243-0250 800-845-5588
www.cpqs.com
Transportation firm offering FTL and intermodal (truck-rail-truck) logistical services and short, local and long haul trucking
President/Founder: Emile John Buteau
Contact: Mike Compagno
mjc@cras.com
VP Operations: Amy Buteau
Number Employees: 20-49
Services: FTL & intermodal (truck-rail-truck) logistics and short, long & local haul trucking
Regions Served:
North America

Transportation Firms / A-Z

51667 Compass Forwarding Co Inc
15915 Rockaway Blvd
Jamaica, NY 11434-4837
718-528-8038
Fax: 718-528-6751 www.compassfwd.com
Transportation and customs house broker providing freight forwarding services
President: Richard Shelala
Cio/Cto: Peter Wang
pwang@compassfwd.com
CFO: Robert Shelala
Human Resources Mgr: Janine Shelala
Number Employees: 50-99
Square Footage: 58000
Other Locations:
Compass Forwarding
East Boston, MA
Compass Forwarding
Los Angeles, CACompass ForwardingLos Angeles
Services: Transportation & customs house broker providing freight forwarding
Regions Served:
Nationwide, Far East, Australia, Europe, Middle East & Africa

51668 Consolidated Rail Corporation
1717 Arch Street
13th Floor
Philadelphia, PA 19103
215-209-2000
800-456-7509
www.conrail.com
Transportation firm providing railroad service.
President & Chief Operating Officer: Timothy Tierney
VP Corporate Development/Legal Officer: Jonathan Broder
VP/CAO/Treasurer: Anthony Carlini
Superintendent, Operations: Joseph Soto
Superintendent, Service Delivery/Support: Rodney Gordon
Year Founded: 1976
Estimated Sales: K
Number Employees: 1,000-4,999
Parent Co: CSX Corporation
Services: Railroad

51669 Consolidated Transfer Co Inc
1251 Taney St
Kansas City, MO 64116-4485
816-221-1503
Fax: 816-472-7235 800-279-3411
www.ctw-co.com
Warehouse providing dry storage for nonperishable foods, machinery, paper products, etc.; transportation broker providing local, long and short haul trucking; also, rail siding, EDI, cross docking, intermodal drayage, local cartageavailable
Owner: R Winsky
rtaylor@ctw-co.com
Number Employees: 50-99
Services: Broker providing local, long & short haul trucking; also, BN Spur with reciprocal switching
Regions Served:
Nationwide & Canada

51670 Continental Express Inc
10450 State Route 47 W
Sidney, OH 45365-9009
937-497-2100
Fax: 937-498-2155
www.continentalexpressinc.com
Transportation firm providing local, short and long haul trucking; warehouse providing storage for frozen foods, groceries and produce
President: Russell Gottemoeller
russ@ceioh.com
Maintenance Supervisor: Doug Subler
Sales: Susan Shaffer
Recruiting: David Caig
Operations Director: David Treadway
Number Employees: 100-249
Services: Local, long & short haul trucking
Regions Served:
Mid-West

51671 Cool Cargo
5324 Georgia Highway 85
Forest Park, GA 30297-2475
770-994-0338
Temperature control systems.
President: Burt Pedowitz

51672 Coppersmith
525 S Douglas St
El Segundo, CA 90245-4826
310-607-8000
Fax: 310-607-8001 www.coppersmith.com
Transportation broker providing international freight forwarding via ocean and air
President: Jeff Coppersmith
Contact: Dion Cheong
dion.cheong@coppersmith.com
Number Employees: 100-249
Square Footage: 300000
Services: Freight forwarding via ocean & air
Regions Served:
Nationwide - Specializing in fresh produce

51673 Corcoran International Corporation
14904 Guy R Brewer Blvd Ste 2
Jamaica, NY 11434
718-244-6063
Fax: 718-244-6203 Cicintcorp@aol.com
http://www.corcoranintl.com/
Customs house broker providing freight forwarding services
President: Ernesto Zapata
Number Employees: 5-9
Services: Customs house broker providing freight forwarding services
Regions Served:
International

51674 Craig Transportation Co
26699 Eckel Rd
Perrysburg, OH 43551-1209
419-872-3333
Fax: 419-874-3094 800-521-9119
www.craigtransport.com
Warehouse providing dry storage; transportation firm providing short, local and long haul trucking ; also, TL, J.I.T. deliveries, pallet exchanges, satellite communications and drop trailers available
President: Lance Craig
lance.graig@craigtransport.com
Marketing: Chris Simmons
Number Employees: 20-49
Services: Short, local & long haul trucking, J.I.T. deliveries, TL, pallet exchange, satellite communications & drop trailers
Regions Served:
Mid-Atlantic, Northeast Corridor & Midwest, Regional

51675 Cranston Air
5800 Tunnel Road
Charlotte, NC 28208
704-359-8282
Warehouse providing dry storage of nonperishable food items; transportation broker offering freight forwarding
Estimated Sales: $2.5-5 Million
Number Employees: 10-19
Parent Co: Cranston Printworks
Services: Brokerage & freight forwarding
Regions Served:
Worldwide

51676 Crate & Fly
26986 Trolley Industrial Drive
Taylor, MI 48180
313-295-3390
800-777-1070
Warehouse providing dry storage of nonperishable food items; transportation broker offering freight forwarding
Number Employees: 50-99
Services: Brokerage & freight forwarding
Regions Served:
Worldwide

51677 Crete Carrier Corp
400 NW 56th Street
Lincoln, NE 68528
402-475-9521
Fax: 402-479-2073 800-998-4095
www.cretecarrier.com
Warehouse providing cooler, dry and humidity-controlled storage for dry and refrigerated goods; transportation firm offering long and short haul trucking and equipment leasing services.
CEO & Chairman: Tonn Ostergard
President & COO: Tim Aschoff
President, Shaffer Trucking: Erick Kutter
Estimated Sales: Over $1 Billion
Number Employees: 1000-4999
Other Locations:
Crete Carrier Corporation
Phoenix, AZ
Deland, FL
Marietta, GA
Indianapolis, IN
Kansas City, MO
Omaha, NE
Crete Carrier CorporationDeland
Services: Short & long haul trucking; also, equipment leasing
Regions Served:
U.S.A., Canada & Mexico

51678 Crossroads DistributionLTD
701 E Avenue K
Temple, TX 76504-5978
254-773-2684
Fax: 254-773-1899 800-626-8813
www.kiaccess.com
Warehouse providing storage for canned goods, soft drinks, etc.; transportation firm providing local haul trucking; also, re-packing, labeling and rail siding available
Owner: Melvin Maddux
Number Employees: 10-19
Services: Local haul trucking
Regions Served:
Southwest

51679 Crowley Liner Services
9487 Regency Square Blvd
Jacksonville, FL 32225
904-727-2200
Fax: 904-727-2501 800-276-9539
www.crowley.com
Transportation firm providing ocean freight services and local, short and long haul trucking.
Chairman & CEO: Tom Crowley, Jr.
Vice COB & EVP: William Pennella
SVP/General Counsel/Corporate Secretary: Michael Roberts
SVP, Controller: John Calvin, Jr.
SVP, Corporate Services: Carl Fox
SVP, Treasurer: Daniel Warner
Estimated Sales: $211 Million
Number Employees: 1,200
Parent Co: Crowley Maritime Corporation
Services: Ocean freight & local, short & long haul trucking
Regions Served:
U.S., Canada, Mexico, Cental & South America, Puerto Rico, the Bahamas & Caribbean

51680 Crystal Cold Storage
23 Sycamore Ave
Medford, MA 02155-4943
781-391-6500
Fax: 781-391-1465
Public warehouse providing cooler and freezer storage for frozen and chilled products; transportation firm providing rail car services and local, long and short haul trucking; also, rail siding and delivery services available
Manager: Michelle Milano
General Manager: Dennis Martel
Estimated Sales: $1-2.5 Million
Number Employees: 10-19
Parent Co: Crystal Cold Storage
Services: Rail car & local, long & short haul trucking; also, delivery
Regions Served:
Nationwide

51681 Cumberland DistributionServices
4500 Westport Dr
Mechanicsburg, PA 17055
717-697-5770
Warehouse providing cooler, freezer and dry storage; transportation firm providing local, long and short haul trucking; rail siding available
Number Employees: 250-499
Services: Local, long & short haul trucking
Regions Served:
East Coast & Northeast Corridor

51682 D & D Distribution Svc
789 Kings Mill Rd
York, PA 17403-3472
717-845-1646
Fax: 717-846-0414 877-683-3358
info@dd-dist.com www.dd-dist.com
Warehouse providing cooler, dry and humidity-controlled storage for groceries and general commodities; transportation firm providing long and short haul trucking; also, rail siding, packaging, pick and pack, assembly, consolidation andstripping available
President: Tanja Gray
tgray@dd-dist.com
Number Employees: 20-49
Services: truck leasing
Regions Served:
Mid-Atlantic & Northeast

51683 (HQ)D & S Warehouse Inc
104 Alan Dr
Newark, DE 19711-8027
302-731-7440
Fax: 302-731-8017 www.wedistribute.com

Transportation Firms / A-Z

Warehouse providing heated and dry storage for general merchandise and food ingredients; transportation firm providing dry bulk and short haul trucking; also, rail siding available
CEO: John Schneider
Number Employees: 50-99
Services: Dry bulk & short haul trucking
Regions Served:
Northeast

51684 D W Air
1120 Yew Ave
Blaine, WA 98230-9222   360-332-6413
Fax: 360-332-6106   www.dwair.com
Warehouse providing dry storage of nonperishable goods; transportation services include freight forwarding via ground and air and local, long and short haul trucking nationwide
President: Tom Wilford
tom@dwair.com
Number Employees: 5-9
Services: Freight forwarding via ground & air and local, short & long haul trucking
Regions Served:
Worldwide

51685 D.J. Powers Company
5000 Business Dr
Ste 1000
Savannah, GA 31405   912-234-7241
Fax: 912-236-5230   www.djpowers.com
Transportation company providing brokerage and international and domestic freight forwarding services
Owner: Richard Carter
CFO: Roy Austin
VP: Carol Hendrickson
Number Employees: 20-49
Regions Served:
Nationwide & International

51686 DAV Transportation Services
374 Morrison Rd # C
Columbus, OH 43213-1446   614-759-1000
Fax: 614-759-9776   800-373-1996
Transportation broker providing long haul trucking throughout 48 states
Manager: Steve Faris
Number Employees: 5-9

51687 DCI Logistics
6085 Duquesne Dr SW
Atlanta, GA 30336   404-349-1824
Fax: 404-346-7206   www.dcilog.com
Warehouse providing dry storage for general commodities and food products; transportation broker providing local, short and long haul trucking; also, rail siding, consolidation and pool distribution services
Owner: Brenda Elwell
Chief Executive Officer: Larry Elwell
CFO/President Packaging: Joel Chase
Contact: Craig Bingham
craig@dcilogistics.net
Vice President Operations: Pat Keefe
President Warehousing: Brian West
Estimated Sales: $3-5 Million
Number Employees: 50-99
Square Footage: 1400000
Services: Broker providing local, long & short haul trucking
Regions Served:
National & International

51688 DFC Transportation Company
12007 Smith Drive
Huntley, IL 60142   847-669-3066
Transportation firm providing freight forwarding, TL, LTL, long and short haul trucking
Number Employees: 50-99
Parent Co: Dean Foods Company
Services: Freight forwarding via TL & LTL long & short haul trucking
Regions Served:
East Coast, Midwest & West Coast

51689 DHL Danzas
1200 South Pine Island Rd
Suite 140-145
Plantation, FL 33324
http://www.dhl-dgf.com/
Transportation firm providing domestic and international freight forwarding services
Contact: Samah Ahmed
soulsta@hotmail.com
Number Employees: 5-9
Parent Co: A.G. Danzas
Services: Freight forwarding
Regions Served:
Nationwide & International

51690 DSW Distribution Ctr Inc
8858 Rochester Ave
Rancho Cucamonga, CA 91730-4909   909-483-5841
Fax: 909-466-9684   www.dswdist.com
Warehouse offering cooler, ambient storage for refrigerated and dry food and food related products; also, rail siding, logistics planning/management and public and contract distribution services available
President: Brad Thayer
brad@dswdist.com
Vice President/General Manager: Chris Thier
Administrator: Liz Penrose
Quality Control: Don Munlon
Operations Manager: Ray Lopez
Plant Manager: Ray Lopez
Estimated Sales: $5-10 Million
Number Employees: 10-19
Square Footage: 200000
Parent Co: Thayer, Inc
Other Locations:
Rancho Cucamonga Facility
Rancho Cucamonga, CA Rancho Cucamonga Facility
Regions Served:
Western USA

51691 Darras Freight
2050 S Baker Ave
Ontario, CA 91761   909-930-5471
Fax: 909-930-5483   800-892-7447
Warehouse providing storage for dry freight and groceries; transportation broker providing local, long and short haul trucking; also, rail siding, freight forwarding, re-packing, distribution and trucking services available
Owner: Rena Darras
rdarras@darrasfreight.com
Number Employees: 10-19
Services: Broker providing local, long & short haul trucking; also freight forwarding services
Regions Served:
International & nationwide

51692 Dart Transit Co
800 Lone Oak Rd
St Paul, MN 55121-2212   651-686-2874
Fax: 651-688-2015   800-366-9000
tlundberg@dart.net   www.superstartransport.com
Transportation services including local, long and short haul trucking nationwide
President: Dave Oren
doren@darttransit.com
Number Employees: 250-499
Services: Local, long & short haul trucking
Regions Served:
Nationwide

51693 Day & Ross Transportation Group
398 Main Street
Hartland, NB E7P 1C6
Canada   506-375-4401
800-561-0013
custservice@dayandrossinc.ca   www.dayross.com
National transportation with 40 terminals across 10 Canadian provinces; Provides LTL, TL, temperature-controlled, specialized transportation, flatbed, and cross-border services
President, Day & Ross Freight: Doug Tingley
President/CEO: Bill Doherty
VP Pricing & Administration: Tony Crann
SVP Sales & Marketing: Bruce Morin
Director Human Resources: Janet Fidgen
VP Linehaul Operations: Frank MacIntyre
VP Terminals: Shawn Browne
Number Employees: 1000-4999
Parent Co: McCain Foods Ltd.

51694 Days Corporation
P.O. Box 668
Elkhart, IN 46515   574-262-9525
Fax: 574-264-2276   866-847-8330
www.dayscorp.com
Warehouse providing dry storage; transportation firm providing long and short haul trucking; rail siding available
President: James Spoatt
Days Machinery Movers: Bill Halt
Sales: Randy Bicard
General Manager: Tom Ridenour
Machinery Manager: Steve Crumo
Number Employees: 50-99
Parent Co: Days Distribution Services
Services: Long & short haul trucking
Regions Served:
Nationwide

51695 Decker Truck Line Inc
4000 5th Ave S
Fort Dodge, IA 50501-6450   515-576-4141
Fax: 515-576-7431   info@dtlinc.com
www.deckertruckline.com
Transportation firm providing TL, reefers, vans and flatbeds
President: Donald Decker
Estimated Sales: $20-50 Million
Number Employees: 50-99
Square Footage: 500000
Services: TL, reefers, vans & flatbeds
Regions Served:
Midwest & West Coast

51696 Deep South Freight
2221 17th St N
Birmingham, AL 35204-1708   205-326-0601
Fax: 205-326-0601   800-824-3515
info@deepsouthfreight.com
www.deepsouthfreight.com
Transportation broker providing insulated van trailers and local, long and short haul trucking
Owner: Jill Cox
jcox@deepsouthfreight.com
Number Employees: 5-9
Services: Broker providing insulated van trailers & local, long & short haul trucking
Regions Served:
Nationwide

51697 Del Corona & ScardigliUSA, Inc.
1 Washington Street
Suite 1301
Newark, NJ 07102   905-862-7333
Fax: 905-867-3133   info@us.dcsfreight.com
www.dcsfreight.com
Food transportation
Marketing: Marco Busanelli

51698 Dependable Distribution Services
1301 Union Ave
Pennsauken, NJ 8110   856-665-1762
Fax: 856-488-6332
Warehouse offering dry storage for food groceries, paper products, containers, pick-pack and displays; transportation firm providing TL, LTL and CFS local and long haul trucking; also, rail siding and import/export services available
President: Harvey Weiner
Sales Director: Dick Daniels
Contact: Richard Perrone
p.richard@taggroup.net
VP Operations: Richard Goodman
Estimated Sales: $15 Million
Number Employees: 20-49
Square Footage: 500000
Services: LTL, TL & CFS local & long haul trucking
Regions Served:
Mid-Atlantic & New England

51699 Des Moines Truck Brokers
1505 North Ave
Norwalk, IA 50211   515-981-5115
Fax: 515-981-0923   800-247-2514
info@dmtb.com   www.dmtb.com
Warehouse providing storage; transportation broker providing LTL local, long and short haul trucking
Owner: Jim Dematteis
Contact: Ben Batten
ben@dmtb.com
Number Employees: 5-9
Services: Transportation broker providing local, long & short haul trucking
Regions Served:
48 States, Mexico & Canada

51700 Detroit Warehouse Company
12885 Eaton Street
Detroit, MI 48227   313-491-1505

Transportation Firms / A-Z

Warehouse providing dry storage for alcoholic beverages, food products and general merchandise; transportation firm providing local, long and short haul trucking and freight consolidation; also, cross docking and store door deliveryservices available
Number Employees: 10-19
Services: Local, long & short haul trucking
Regions Served:
48 States

51701 Dhx-Dependable HawaiianExpress
23803 S. Wilmington Ave
Carson, CA 90745   310-522-4111
Fax: 310-522-4141 www.godependable.com
Warehouse providing dry storage of nonperishable foods; transportation firm offering freight forwarding
Manager: Paul Curry
CEO: Ronald Massman
CFO: Michael Dougan
VP: Bob Massman
Number Employees: 20-49
Services: Freight forwarding
Regions Served:
AK & HI

51702 Dist Tech
1701 Continental Blvd
Charlotte, NC 28273-6374   704-588-2867
Fax: 704-588-5846
mmiralia@distributiontechnology.com
www.distributiontechnology.com
Warehouse providing cooler, dry and humidity-controlled storage for groceries, candy, appliances, etc.; transportation broker providing long haul trucking, rail siding, assembling, pick/pack, inventory records, freight consolidationand forwarding, EDI capabilities, etc
CEO/President: Tom Miralia
tmiralia@distributiontechnology.com
VP of Operations: John Moss
Estimated Sales: $20-50 Million
Number Employees: 100-249
Square Footage: 1000000
Parent Co: Distribution Technology
Type of Packaging: Consumer, Food Service, Private Label, Bulk
Services: Pooling, cross docking, freight brokerage, piggyback drayage, push pull, reciprocal switching, etc.
Regions Served:
AL, FL, GA, NC, SC, TN, & VA

51703 (HQ)Distribution Services-America
208 North St
Foxboro, MA 02035-1099   508-543-3313
Fax: 508-543-7408 info@dsa-inc.com
Warehouse providing cooler, humidity controlled and dry storage; transportation firm providing long and short haul trucking, TL and LTL; also, re-packing and rail siding services available, fulfillment capabilities, software wmscompany
CEO: Paul Lestan
plestan@dsa-inc.com
CEO: David Petri
DSA - Software: Lee Petri
VP Sales/Marketing: Mark Slattery
VP of Transportation /Ops: Joe Gualtieri
Number Employees: 100-249
Services: LTL & TL, Local, National
Regions Served:
New England & Upstate New York

51704 (HQ)Distribution Unlimited
PO Box 98
Guilderland Center
Albany, NY 12085   518-355-3112
Fax: 518-355-3636 Adutcher@disunlt.com
distributionunlimited.com
Warehouse offering cooler, freezer and dry storage space handling forest products, machinery, food products and general merchandise; also, re-packaging, E.D.I., distribution, LTL and TL transportation services available
Number Employees: 100-249
Square Footage: 24000000
Services: TLT & TL

51705 Diversified Transfer & Storage
1640 Monad Rd
Billings, MT 59101-3200   406-245-4695
800-755-5855
dtsb@dtsb.com www.dtsb.com
Warehouse providing cooler, freezer and dry storage; transportation firm providing freight forwarding and local and long haul trucking including frozen/refrigerated LTL; TL; pool consolidation and distribution; cross docking; railsiding available
President: Jeremy Deardurff
jeremyd@dtsb.com
Estimated Sales: Less Than $500,000
Number Employees: 1-4
Services: Freight forwarding & local and long haul trucking: frozen/refrigerated LTL; also, intermodal available
Regions Served:
Midwest & Northwest

51706 Doc's Transfer & Warehouse
2620 13th Street Ensley
Birmingham, AL 35208-1106   205-783-6060
Fax: 205-783-6090 www.givens.com
Warehouse providing dry and humidity-controlled storage for dry goods, etc.; transportation services include local cartage, freight consolidation, local and short haul trucking; rail siding available
Owner: Ed Willis
docstransfer@aol.com
Director Operations: John Carroll
Estimated Sales: $3-5 Million
Number Employees: 10-19
Square Footage: 800000
Services: Freight consolidation, local cartage & local and short haul trucking
Regions Served:
Southeast

51707 Dolliff & Co Inc
395 Maverick St # 208
East Boston, MA 02128-2241   617-561-0900
Fax: 617-561-0181
Customs house broker providing international freight forwarding services for frozen and fresh seafood, canned goods and exported food stuffs, with EDI capabilities
Owner: Stuart Eldridge
stuart@dolliffco.com
Number Employees: 10-19
Services: Customs house broker providing freight forwarding for frozen & fresh seafood, canned goods & exported food stuffs
Regions Served:
Worldwide

51708 Doosan Industrial Vehicle America Corp
2475 Mill Center Parkway
Suite 400
Buford, GA 30518   678-745-2200
Fax: 678-745-2250 www.doosanlift.com
Manufacturer, importer and exporter of industrial trucks.
VP & CEO: Tony Jones
National Sales Director: Jeff Powell
Year Founded: 1962
Estimated Sales: $7 Billion
Number Employees: 7,728
Square Footage: 150000
Parent Co: Doosan Group

51709 Dot Foods Inc
1 Dot Way
P.O. Box 192
Mt. Sterling, IL 62353   217-773-4411
800-366-3687
www.dotfoods.com
Food redistributor of general grocery products.
Chief Executive Officer: Joe Tracy
Executive Chairman: John Tracy
President: Dick Tracy
EVP, Retail & Business Development: George Eversman
Chief Financial Officer: Anita Montgomery
Year Founded: 1960
Estimated Sales: $6.2 Billion
Number Employees: 4,500
Other Locations:
Dot Foods Distributor Center
Modesto, CA
Dot Foods Distributor Center
Williamsport, MD
Dot Foods Distributor Center
Liverpool, NY
Dot Foods Distributor Center
Ardmore, OK
Dot Foods Distributor Center
Vidalia, GADot Foods Distributor CenterWilliamsport

51710 Dreisbach Enterprises Inc
2530 E 11th St
P O Box 7509
Oakland, CA 94601-1425   510-533-6600
Fax: 510-533-7468 info@dreisbach.com
www.dreisbach.com
Warehouse offering cooler and freezer storage of refrigerated and frozen foods; transportation broker providing trucking services
President: Jason Dreisbach
jason@dreisbach.com
Chief Financial Officer: Doretta Carrion
General Manager: John Pienta
Vice President of Sales: Val Nunes
Vice President of Operations: John Swinnerton
Estimated Sales: $1-2.5 Million
Number Employees: 250-499
Services: Brokerage
Regions Served:
West Coast

51711 Dunagan Warehouse Corp
1507 Webber St
P.O. Box 151607
Lufkin, TX 75904-2698   936-637-6277
Fax: 936-639-1371 ronnie@dunagan.net
www.dunagan.net
Warehouse providing cooler, freezer and dry storage of perishable and nonperishable food items; transportation firm providing short haul trucking; rail siding, re-packing and labeling available
President and General Manager: Ronnie Robinson
Number Employees: 10-19
Square Footage: 400000
Services: Short haul trucking
Regions Served:
East TX

51712 Dunsmith International
5230 South Service Road
2nd Floor
Burlington, ON L7L 5K2
Canada   905-681-6162
Fax: 905-681-1944 800-263-3866
Transportation broker providing domestic and international services via rail car and air freight; also, LTL and TL services available
President: Deborah Dunn
Estimated Sales: $5-10 Million
Number Employees: 15
Square Footage: 17200
Services: Broker providing domestic & international services via rail car & air freight; also, LTL & FL available
Regions Served:
Nationwide & international

51713 (HQ)EPT Warehouses
PO Box 9248
El Paso, TX 79995-9248   915-772-2758
Fax: 915-772-9791
Public warehouse providing cooler, freezer and dry storage for nonfood and food items, ice cream, epoxy and food supplements; transportation firm providing local haul trucking; also, rail siding services are available
CEO: Angle Jackuac
Estimated Sales: $10-20 Million
Number Employees: 50-99
Services: Local haul trucking
Regions Served:
Local: El Paso

51714 Earl J Henderson Trucking Company
206 w Main Street
Salem, IL 62881   618-548-4667
Fax: 618-548-6204 800-447-8084
www.hendersontrucking.com
Transportation firm providing refrigerated trucking services including short, local and long haul
President: John Kaburick
Chief Operating Officer: Josh Kaburick
Number Employees: 500-999
Services: Refrigerated trucking: local, short & long haul

Transportation Firms / A-Z

51715 East Coast Warehouse & Distr
1140 Polaris St
Elizabeth, NJ 07201-2905　　　908-351-2800
　　Fax: 908-838-9068　www.eastcoastwarehouse.com
Warehouse providing cooler, dry and humidity-controlled storage; transportation firm providing LTL and TL local haul trucking; also, rail siding, pier drayage, break-bulk, co-manufacturing, cross dock and reefers available; U.S.customs exam site
President: Marc Lebovitz
Contact: Beth Lebovitz
Estimated Sales: $20-50 Million
Number Employees: 1-4
Square Footage: 3000000
Parent Co: Romark Logistics
Services: LTL & TL local haul trucking, pier drayage, reefers, etc.
Regions Served:
　　United States & Canada

51716 Eastern Distribution Inc
1502 Antioch Church Rd
Greenville, SC 29605-6108　　　864-277-2800
　　　　　　　　　　　　　Fax: 864-277-0372
　　　　　　info@easterndistributioninc.com
　　　　　　www.easterndistributioninc.com
Warehouse providing dry storage for food and general commodities; transportation firm providing LTL and TL local haul trucking; also, rail siding and loose cartage services available
President: Terry Smith
Estimated Sales: $20-50 Million
Number Employees: 5-9
Square Footage: 750000
Services: LTL & TL local haul trucking: loose cartage
Regions Served:
　　SC

51717 Eastern Refrigerater ExpRess
336 W Us Highway 30
Suite 201
Valparaiso, IN 46385-5345　　　773-847-5555
　　　　　　　　　　　　　Fax: 773-847-5632
Provides long and short haul trucking, serving the East coast and the Mid-Atlantic
President: Joi Lavery

51718 Eastern Shore Railroad
P.O.Box 212
Cape Charles, VA 23310-0312　　　757-331-1094
　　　　　　　　　　　　　Fax: 757-331-2772
Transportation firm providing rail car service and short haul trucking; serving the East Coast
VP: Larry Le Mond
Number Employees: 20-49
Services: Rail car service & short haul trucking
Regions Served:
　　East Coast

51719 Eastport Customs Brokers
732 Thimble Shls Blvd Ste 302a
Newport News, VA 23606　　　757-873-2215
Transportation firm providing customs house brokerage and freight fowarding services; also, arrangement and coordination of door to door movement and warehousing for importing and exporting shipments available
Owner: Linda Jennings
Estimated Sales: 2.5-5 Million
Number Employees: 5-9
Services: Customs house brokerage & freight forwarding
Regions Served:
　　International

51720 Ecs Warehouse
2381 Fillmore Ave
Buffalo, NY 14214-2129　　　716-833-7380
　　Fax: 716-833-7386　permerling@emerfood.com
　　　　　www.ecswarehouse.com
A warehouse that understands your needs. Frozen, dry, refrigerated warehouse on Canadian border, within 500 miles of 70% of the entire Canadian population and 55% of the entire USA population. Services include: pick & pack, crossdocking, express service, repacking, distribution, TL & LTL, rail, consolidation, salvage, quick access to NYC, Boston, D.C., Cleveland, Buffalo, Toronto, Rockland, Syracuse, Detroit and Cincinnati. If you have special product needs, call us.

CEO: Peter Emerling
pemerling@emerfood.com
Number Employees: 10-19
Square Footage: 500000
Type of Packaging: Bulk
Services: Express Service
Regions Served:
　　USA, Canada, NYC, Toronto, D.C., Cleveland, Detroit, Buffalo, Rockland, Syracuse, Boston

51721 Eimskip
460 Commercial St
Portland, ME 04101　　　207-619-5884
　　　　　　　　info@eimskipusa.com
　　　　　　　　www.eimskip.com
Transportation firm providing ocean freight service; serving nationwide and internationally
CEO: Vilhelm Mar Portsteinsson
President/CEO, North America: Gylfi Sigfuson
CFO: Egill Orn Petersen
VP Sales & Marketing: Matthias Matthiasson
VP Human Resources: Elin Hjalmsdottir
COO: Hilmar Petur Valgardsson
Year Founded: 1914
Estimated Sales: $744.2 Million
Number Employees: 1640
Parent Co: Avion Group
Services: Ocean freight
Regions Served:
　　Nationwide & International: North America, Europe & Iceland

51722 Ellis KARR & Co Inc
1975 Linden Blvd # 205
Elmont, NY 11003-4004　　　347-632-1500
　　Fax: 516-285-4131　www.karrellis.com
Warehouse providng cooler, freezer and dry storage; transportation firm providing international and domestic freight forwarding services via air and ocean freight, long, local and short haul trucking
President: Raymond J Walsh
rwalsh@karrellis.com
VP: Timothy R Marshall
VP Sales: Tim Marshall
Estimated Sales: $10-20 Million
Number Employees: 5-9
Services: International & domestic freight forwarding via air & ocean freight, local, long & short haul trucking
Regions Served:
　　Worldwide: national & local

51723 Emerling International Foods
2381 Fillmore Ave
Suite 1
Buffalo, NY 14214-2197　　　716-833-7381
　　Fax: 716-833-7386　pemerling@emerfood.com
　　　　　www.emerlinginternational.com
Bulk ingredients including: Fruits & Vegetables; Juice Concentrates; Herbs & Spices; Oils & Vinegars; Flavors & Colors; Honey & Molasses. Also produces pure maple syrup.
President: J Emerling
jemerling@emerfood.com
Sales: Peter Emerling
Public Relations: Jenn Burke
Year Founded: 1988
Estimated Sales: $10-20 Million
Number Employees: 20-49
Square Footage: 500000

51724 England Logistics
4701 West 2100 South
Salt Lake City, UT 84120　　　801-972-2712
　　Fax: 801-977-5795　800-887-0764
　　　　　info@englandlogistics.com
　　　　　www.englandlogistics.com
Transportation firm providing local, short and long haul trucking; also, contract warehousing available
President: Dan England
CEO: Dean England
Senior Vice President Chief Financial Of: Keith Wallace
Vice President: Brandon Harrison
Executive Vice President of Corporate Sa: David Kramer
Contact: Rolina Camello
rolina.camello@crengland.com
Services: Local, short & long haul trucking

51725 Englund Equipment Co
11498 W Buckeye Rd
Avondale, AZ 85323-6911　　　623-936-3365
　　Fax: 623-936-6216　800-528-4075
　　　　　englunddispatch@qwestoffice.net
Transportation, contract company and broker providing local, long and shorthaul trucking; serving regionally/locally and nationwide
Owner: Bill Englund
benglund1@qwestoffice.net
Number Employees: 5-9
Services: Brokerage: local, long & short haul trucking
Regions Served:
　　Nationwide; Regional/Local

51726 (HQ)Erdner Brothers
PO Box 68
Swedesboro, NJ 08085　　　856-467-0900
　　Fax: 856-467-5593　800-257-8143
　　info@erdnerbros.com　www.erdnerbros.com
Warehouse providing dry storage for food products; transportation firm providing local, long and short haul trucking in the Mid-Atlantic region; also, rail siding available
President: Richard Erdner
Number Employees: 50-99
Square Footage: 600000
Other Locations:
　　Erdner Brothers
　　Woodstown, NJErdner Brothers
Services: Local, long & short haul trucking
Regions Served:
　　United States

51727 Estes Express Lines Inc
3901 W Broad St
Richmond, VA 23230　　　804-353-1900
　　Fax: 804-353-8001　866-378-3748
　　　　　　www.estes-express.com
Transportation service providing common carrier, LTL, truckload, pool distribution, import/export shipments and long, local and short haul trucking.
President & CEO: Rob Estes
EVP/Chief Operating Officer: William Hupp
whupp@estes-express.com
Year Founded: 1931
Estimated Sales: Over $1 Billion
Number Employees: 18,000+
Services: Long, short & local haul trucking, LTL, truckload, pool distribution & import/export shipments
Regions Served:
　　AL; AR; CT; DE; FL; GA; IL; KS; KY; LA; MA; MD; ME; MO; MS; NC; HH; NJ; NY; OH; OK; PA; RI; SC; TN; TX; VA

51728 Evans Delivery Company
PO Box 268
Pottsville, PA 17901　　　570-385-9048
　　Fax: 570-385-9058　www.evansdelivery.com
Warehouse providing dry storage for frozen foods and dried milk products; transportation firm providing local, short and long haul trucking and shipping; also, re-packing and loading available
Owner: Albert L Evans Jr
Contact: Mike Beatty
mike.beatty@evansdelivery.com
Number Employees: 10-19
Services: Local, long & short haul trucking & shipping
Regions Served:
　　Mid-Atlantic & New England States

51729 Evergreen InternationalAirlines
3850 NE Three Mile Ln
McMinnville, OR 97128-9402　　　503-472-9361
　　Fax: 503-472-1048　www.evergreenaviation.com
Transportation firm providing international and domestic air freight services
CEO: Delford M Smith
Contact: Wayland Joe
waylandjoe@evergreenproduce.com
Number Employees: 500-999
Parent Co: Evergreen International Aviation
Services: Air freight
Regions Served:
　　International: nationwide

51730 Evergreen Sweeteners, Inc
1936 Hollywood Blvd
Suite 200
Hollywood, FL 33020　　　954-381-7776
　　Fax: 954-458-5793　www.esweeteners.com

Transportation Firms / A-Z

Bulk liquid sweeteners and bagged sweeteners
President: Arthur Green
Year Founded: 1925
Estimated Sales: $55 Million
Number Employees: 50+
Number of Products: 40
Square Footage: 150000
Type of Packaging: Food Service, Bulk
Other Locations:
　Evergreen Sweeteners, Inc.
　Atlanta, GA
　Evergreen Sweeteners, Inc.
　Sanford, FL
　Evergreen Sweeteners, Inc.
　Miami, FLEvergreen Sweeteners, Inc.Sanford

51731 Exel Inc
570 Polaris Pkwy
Westerville, OH 43082-7900　　614-865-8500
　　Fax: 614-865-8875　877-272-1054
　　www.exel.com
A global supply chain management company offering contract logistics and freight management solutions. Warehousing services include: dedicated and shared user operations; automation and sortation; temperature controlled facilities; specialized product storage and handling; cross docking and merge-in-transit; retail mixing center operations; on-site assembly and packaging services.
CEO: Lynn Anderson
lynn@securityinsuranceagency.com
Chief Executive Officer: William Meahl
Chief Financial Officer: Scot Hofacker
CEO: Bruce Edwards
Chief Development Officer: Michael Gardner
Chief Information Officer: Domenic Dilalla
Public Relations: Aaron Brown
SVP Human Resources: Rob Rosenberg
Estimated Sales: Over $1 Billion
Number Employees: 10000+
Services: TL & LTL, brokerage
Regions Served:
　International & National

51732 Express Air Cargo
14910 S. Figueroa
Gardena, CA 90248　　310-380-6733
　　Fax: 310-380- 676　800-521-5134
　　www.eacargo.com
Warehouse providing dry storage for perishables and nonperishable goods; transportation firm providing international freight forwarding via air freight and local, long and short haul trucking; also, re-packing available
President: Tom Aoyagi
Estimated Sales: $500,000-$1 Million
Number Employees: 5-9
Square Footage: 20000
Services: Trucking & freight forwarding via air
Regions Served:
　Worldwide

51733 (HQ)F B Washburn Candy Corp
137 Perkins Ave
P.O. Box 3277
Brockton, MA 02302-3891　　508-588-0820
　　Fax: 508-588-2205　www.fbwashburncandy.com
Manufactured and distributor of hard candies, specializing in ribbon candies; offer rebagging, private label and wrapping services.
President: James Gilson
jamesgilson@fbwashburncandy.com
Treasurer: Douglas Gilson
Estimated Sales: $10 Million
Number Employees: 20-49
Number of Brands: 2
Square Footage: 150000
Type of Packaging: Consumer, Private Label

51734 (HQ)FFE Transportation Services
P.O.Box 655888
Dallas, TX 75265-5888
　　Fax: 214-819-5625　800-569-9200
　　ir@ffex.net　www.ffex.net
To get to any information for the other FFE sites please visit the web address in this listing, transportation firm providing refrigerated local, long and short haul trucking and van service, LTL, and TL
CEO: Stoney M Stubbs Jr
Contact: Leonard Bartholomew
lbartholmew@ffex.net
Estimated Sales: D
Number Employees: 250-499

Other Locations:
　FFE Transportation Services
　Oakland, CAFFE Transportation Services
Services: Refrigerated local, long & short haul trucking & van
Regions Served:
　Nationwide, Canada & Mexico

51735 Farmers Distributing
PO Box 910399
St George, UT 84791-0399　　435-628-0846
　　Fax: 435-673-1146
Transportation firm providing refrigerated van and trucking services including local, long and short haul
Number Employees: 20-49
Services: Refrigerated van & trucking: local, short & long haul
Regions Served:
　13 western states

51736 Farmrail Corp
1601 W Gary Blvd
Clinton, OK 73601-3261　　580-323-4567
　　Fax: 580-323-4568　georgebetke@farmrail.com
　　www.farmrail.com
Transportation firm providing common rail services
Manager: Judy Petry
judypetry@farmrail.com
CEO: George Betke, Jr.
Manager: Judy Petry
judypetry@farmrail.com
Number Employees: 5-9
Parent Co: Farmrail
Services: Common carrier rail
Regions Served:
　Western OK

51737 Farrell Lines
1 Meadowlands Plaza
12th Floor
E Rutherford, NJ 07073　　212-440-4200
Transportation firm providing container vessels/ships adapted to handle specialized equipment cargo including break bulk and heavy lift
Number Employees: 100-249
Services: Specialized ships for cargo transport
Regions Served:
　Nationwide & international

51738 Farruggio Express
1419 Radcliffe St
Bristol, PA 19007-5422　　215-788-5596
　　Fax: 215-788-9230　Dispatch@farruggio.com
　　www.farruggio.com
Transportation services include intermodal, long haul, local haul and short haul trucking
President: Nancy Bono
nancy@farruggio.com
VP Ops & Business Development: Joe Green
Safety Manager: George Winberg Jr.
Sales Manager: Joseph Farruggio
Truck Manager: Kelvin Johnson
nancy@farruggio.com
Computer Programmer: Jim Hammer
Number Employees: 10-19
Other Locations:
　Farruggio's Express
　Baltimore, MD
　Farruggio's Express
　Norfolk, VA
　Farruggio's Express
　Harrisburg, PA
　Farruggio's Express
　Allentown, PAFarruggio's ExpressNorfolk
Services: Intermodal, long haul, local haul & short haul trucking
Regions Served:
　CT, IN, KY, MD, MI, NJ, OH, PA & VA

51739 Farwest Freight Systems
P.O.Box 439
Kapowsin, WA 98344　　253-826-4565
　　Fax: 253-826-0350　800-999-7581
Transportation broker providing freight forwarding services via air freight and local, long and short haul trucking
President/Owner: Robert Geddes
COO: Becki Wolford
Number Employees: 50-99
Services: Broker providing freight forwarding via air freight & local, long & short haul trucking
Regions Served:
　Nationwide, Canada

51740 FasTrans
5610 Highway 70 West
Waverly, TN 37185　　931-296-4275
　　Fax: 931-296-7123
Transportation firm providing nonrefrigerated TL, local and long haul trucking of grocery items
Number Employees: 20-49
Services: Non-refrigerated TL, local & long haul trucking of grocery items
Regions Served:
　TN & surrounding states, Northeast, Gulf Coast & Canada

51741 Faure Brothers Inc
700 State St
Calumet City, IL 60409-2044　　708-868-0816
　　www.faurebros.com
Warehouse providing cooler, dry, humidity-controlled and freezer storage for general merchandise and chemicals; also, rail siding available; transportation services include national brokerage
President: Craig Crohan
CEO/Owner: Amy Faure-Crohan
Sales/Marketing: Dianna Gill
Vice President Sales: William C Burnson
Operations Manager: Bill Crohan
Warehouse Manager: William Franker
Number Employees: 50-99
Services: Transportation brokerage
Regions Served:
　National

51742 Federal Companies
200 National Rd
East Peoria, IL 61611-2030　　309-244-4292
　　888-483-7117
　　www.federalcos.com
Local and long distance trucking; Warehousing
Chairman/CEO: Bill Cirone
EVP/CFO: Randall Schrock
VP Transportation: Kyle Gorden
VP Warehousing: Jim Flannelly
Director of Safety: Nicholas Baker
Director of Safety: Steve Flick
Purchasing Manager: Tom Morss
Year Founded: 1913
Estimated Sales: $ 20 - 50 Million
Number Employees: 250-499
Square Footage: 65000
Other Locations:
　Federal Logistics
　Dallas, TXFederal Logistics
Services: Local, short & long haul trucking; also, in & out of food distribution center services available
Regions Served:
　Nationwide

51743 Fiesta Warehousing & Distribution Company
302 Tayman
San Antonio, TX 78226　　210-337-9101
　　Fax: 210-333-1537　www.fiestawarehousing.com
Warehouse providing dry storage; transportation firm providing short and long haul trucking; rail siding and cross docking available
President: Thomas Delgado
Contact: Jerry Wright
jwright@fiestawarehousing.com
Number Employees: 10-19
Services: Long & short haul trucking

51744 Finch Companies
1505 Telegraph Rd
Mobile, AL 36610　　251-457-6671
　　Fax: 251-452-7220　800-844-5381
Warehouse providing storage of industrial paper and nonhazardous chemicals; transportation services include local and long haul trucking in Alabama, Florida, Georgia, Mississippi and Louisiana
President/CEO: Tommy Fulton
VP: Danny Fulton
Contact: Andrew Godfrey
acesrvpark@aol.com
Number Employees: 50-99
Services: Local & long haul trucking
Regions Served:
　AL, FL, GA, MS & LA

51745 Five Star Transport Service
P O Box 1936
President: Betty Reeves
Wsb/2071
Gainesville, GA 30504-0936

759

Transportation Firms / A-Z

51746 Florida Freezer LP
7952 Interstate Ct
North Fort Myers, FL 33917-2112   239-543-5154
Fax: 239-543-2335 rfay@flfreezer.com
www.flfreezer.com
Warehouse providing cooler, freezer and dry storage for frozen foods, etc.; transportation firm providing freight forwarding, local and long haul trucking, railroad, domestic and international air freight; also, U.S. customs bondedand rail siding available
President: Robert Fay
Founder, Senior Advisor: Gordon Fay
Transportation Manager: Julie Lemens
VP: Michael Curly
Manager: Laura Fay
lfay@flfreezer.com
Operations Manager: Dean Newman
Estimated Sales: Less Than $500,000
Number Employees: 5-9
Type of Packaging: Consumer, Food Service, Private Label, Bulk
Services: Local & long haul trucking, freight forwarding, domestic & international airfreight & railroad
Regions Served:
FL

51747 Footner & Co Inc
6510 Tributary St # 300
PO Box 9973
Baltimore, MD 21224-6514   410-631-7711
Fax: 410-631-7716 info@footner.com
www.footner.com
Transportation broker of international freight forwarding
Owner: Roberto Gutierrez
roberto@footner.com
Manager: John Ryan
Number Employees: 10-19
Services: Customs house brokerage & international freight forwarding
Regions Served:
Domestic & international

51748 Footprint Retail Svc
2200 Western Ct # 150
Lisle, IL 60532-1843   630-324-3400
Fax: 630-324-3432 800-747-2257
info@fprs.com
Transportation and logistics firm providing freight forwarding, long, short and local haul trucking, direct store delivery, assembly, placement, merchandising and detailing of P.O.P. displays, in-store advertising placements, etc
Number Employees: 50-99
Parent Co: US Delivery Systems
Services: Freight forwarding, long, local & short haul trucking, direct store delivery, assembly, etc. of P.O.P. displays, etc.
Regions Served:
International & nationwide

51749 Fort Transportation & Svc Co
1600 Janesville Ave
Fort Atkinson, WI 53538-2726   920-563-0800
Fax: 920-563-0801 800-242-0128
www.shipwithfort.com
Transportation firm providing local, long and short haul trucking
President: Robert Leslie
r.leslie@shipwithfort.com
Number Employees: 50-99
Services: Local, long & short haul trucking
Regions Served:
IA, IL, IN, MI, MN, OH & WI

51750 Fox Transportation Inc
135 Tide Rd
Tamaqua, PA 18252-4331   570-668-4189
Fax: 570-668-2099 800-922-9807
www.foxtransportation.com
Transportation firm providing refrigerated LTL, local haul and long haul trucking to eastern coastal states; warehouse offering cooler and dry storage for refrigerated products
President: Robert Fox
Number Employees: 50-99
Services: Refrigerated LTL, local haul & long haul trucking
Regions Served:
NY, NJ, VA, FL, GA, NC, SC, DE, MD & PA

51751 Franklin Express Co Inc
31 W North
Franklin, KY 42134   270-586-3296
Fax: 270-586-3298 800-467-0897
Warehouse providing dry storage for nonperishable foods; transportation services include local and short haul trucking; also, distribution services available
President: Wayne Dean
dean@franklinexp.com
Number Employees: 20-49
Services: Local & short haul trucking
Regions Served:
Local & Regional: KY, TN, IN & OH

51752 Franklin Storage Inc
900 Kriner Rd # 1
Suite 1
Chambersburg, PA 17202-7741   717-264-3700
Fax: 717-264-4049 dmartin@franklinstorage.com
www.franklinlogistics.com
Warehouse providing dry storage for nonperishable foods; transportation firm providing long and short haul trucking with EDI capabilities
President: Craig Nitterhouse
craignit@franklinstorage.com
Vice President: Ryan Johnston
Office Manager: Sherry Miller
General Manager: DelRay Martin
Number Employees: 20-49
Services: Long & short haul trucking
Regions Served:
Nationwide

51753 Freeway Warehouse Corp
30 Southard Ave
Farmingdale, NJ 07727-1213   732-938-2400
Fax: 732-938-9160 www.freewaywarehouse.com
Warehouse providing storage for food grade chemicals, preservatives, etc.; transportation services include trucking of food and food products
Owner: Fred Stern
Number Employees: 50-99
Services: Long & short haul
Regions Served:
National

51754 Freshway Distributors
50 Ludy St
Hicksville, NY 11801-5115   516-870-3333
www.freshway.com
Refrigerating company and also offers transportation services
Regions Served:
Northeast

51755 Fst Logistics Inc
2040 Atlas St
Columbus, OH 43228-9645   614-529-7900
Fax: 614-529-7912 800-758-4599
sales@fstlogistics.com www.fstlogistics.com
Warehouse providing cooler and dry storage for confectionery products, paper goods, etc.; transportation firm providing refrigerated short haul trucking; also, cross docking, pool distribution and temperature-controlled trailersavailable
President: Art Decrane
CFO: Dave Kent
Contact: Brandon Anderson
anderson.brandon@fstlogistics.com
Estimated Sales: Less Than $500,000
Number Employees: 1-4
Services: regional, long haul
Regions Served:
Nationwide

51756 GAMPAC Express
16100 N 71st St
Suite 400
Scottsdale, AZ 85254   480-927-4759
800-772-3721
info@gampac.com www.gampac.com
Logistics and transportation.
President: Ray Kredell
Parent Co: US Foods Inc
Services: Managed transportation; FTL and LTL dry and temperature-controlled; Intermodal; Drop trailer

51757 GATX Corp
222 W Adams St
Chicago, IL 60606   312-621-6200
Fax: 312-621-6648 800-428-8161
contactgatx@gatx.com www.gatx.com
Transportation firm providing rail car leasing including tank and covered hopper cars.
Chairman/President/CEO: Brian Kenney
bakenney@gatx.com
EVP/President, Rail North Ameica: Robert Lyons
EVP/CFO: Thomas Ellman
SVP/Chief Commercial Officer: Robert Zmudka
SVP/COO: Paul Titterton
Year Founded: 1898
Estimated Sales: $1.36 Billion
Number Employees: 2,200
Services: Rail car leasing & logistics
Regions Served:
North America

51758 GMW Freight Services Ltd
Suite 2225-4871 Shell Road
Richmond, BC V6X 3Z6
Canada   604-278-9880
Fax: 604-273-4800 877-469-9880
info@gmwfrt.com www.gmwfrt.com
Warehouse providing dry storage for nonperishable foods; rail siding services available; transportation firm providing freight forwarding, ocean and air freight services
President: Paul Leung
Parent Co: GMW Freight Services
Services: Freight forwarding, ocean & air freight

51759 Gabler Trucking Inc
5195 Technology Ave
Chambersburg, PA 17201-7876   717-261-1492
Fax: 717-709-0017 888-889-6978
bobsummers@hcgabler.com www.hcgabler.com
Warehouse providing storage for refrigerated and nonrefrigerated foods and food production materials; transportation broker providing short haul trucking, intermodal and equipment leasing services available
Cio/Cto: Chip Gabler
chipgabler@hcgabler.com
Contact: Robert Summers
VP: Harmon Piper
Number Employees: 100-249
Parent Co: H.C. Gabler
Services: Broker providing short haul trucking, intermodal & equipment leasing
Regions Served:
U.S.A. & Canada

51760 Gadsden Cartage Co
600 Rodney Austin Blvd SE
P.O.Box 567
Attalla, AL 35954-3377   256-570-0051
Fax: 256-538-1831
mledbetter@gadsdenwarehousing.com
www.gadsdenida.org
Warehouse providing dry storage for groceries, dry goods and general merchandise; transportation firm providing local, long and short haul trucking and rail car services
Owner: Larry Foster
gadsden.eso@dir.alabama.gov
Founder: Billy Austin
Number Employees: 20-49
Services: Local, long & short haul trucking & rail car
Regions Served:
Nationwide

51761 Garman Routing Systems Inc
1612 Barthel Road
PO Box 1126
Taylor, TX 76574   410-561-8085
Fax: 410-561-8086 512-535-0178
www.garmanrouting.com
Route accounting and distribution software for all route distribution applications including that of sales order entry; sales analysis; inventory control; full service vending; truck dispatch. Food industry uses include soft drinkbotllers, bottled water delivery, snack food distributors, dairy delivery, and coffee delivery services.
Sales Manager: Chip Sturm

51762 (HQ)Gatewood Products LLC
814 Jeanette St
3001 Gateman Drive
Parkersburg, WV 26101   304-422-5461
Fax: 304-485-2714 800-827-5461
Wood and wood-and-metal containers, pallets, skid shocks and wire-bounds; also, dry warehousing and transportation service available
President/CEO/Vice Chairman: Perry Smith

Transportation Firms / A-Z

Estimated Sales: $ 20-50 Million
Number Employees: 20-49
Square Footage: 1150000
Services: Trucking
Regions Served:
  East of the Mississippi

51763 Gay Truck Line
18361 Highway 15
Falkner, MS 38629-9513   662-837-8474
        Fax: 662-837-4090
Tranportation firm providing short and local haul trucking; serving MS and TN
Owner: Jerry Gay
Manager: Jerry Gay
Number Employees: 10-19
Services: Short & local haul trucking
Regions Served:
  Regional & local: MS & TN

51764 Gemini Data Systems
2855 N University Drive
Suite 410
Coral Springs, FL 33065   954-340-7978
                           877-281-1410
    sales@gemdat.com www.gemdat.com
We are an Appgen dealer and have customized software to specifically target the needs of the food industry
Marketing Director: Tony Repole

51765 Gemini Traffic Sales
41 Distribution Blvd
Edison, NJ 08817-6005   732-287-5477
    Fax: 732-287-6159 800-613-1287
Warehouse providing dry storage for food ingredients, flavorings, confectionery and pharmaceutical items; transportation firm offering local, long and short haul and refrigerated/temperature controlled LTL trucking of food and foodingredients
Manager: Ron Williams
Contact: John Biblis
jbiblis@geminitrafficsales.com
Services: Refrigerated/temperature controlled LTL, local, long & short haul trucking & frozen truckload service
Regions Served:
  Nationwide

51766 General Bonded Warehouses Inc
4001 Raleigh St
Po Box 790035
Charlotte, NC 28206-2046   704-333-0737
  Fax: 704-333-8159 michelle@generalbonded.com
              www.generalbonded.com
Warehouse offering cold and dry storage for grocery products, general commodities, industrial products and nonhazardous chemicals; transportation broker providing local haul trucking; rail siding available; freight brokerage; andtrans-loading. Masonry and sprinklered; monitored security systems; 260,000 square feet of dry, refrigerated, and air conditioned space; food grade space throughout.
Owner: Michelle Wellmon
Vice President of Sales: Brenda Wellmon
Number Employees: 10-19
Services: Brokerage & local haul trucking
Regions Served:
  Southeast

51767 General Warehouse & Transportation Company
7330 Santa Fe Dr
Hodgkins, IL 60525-5044   708-352-0754
Warehouse providing cooler storage for refrigerated and nonperishable foods; transportation firm providing local, long and short haul trucking
Number Employees: 20-49
Services: Local, long & short haul trucking
Regions Served:
  National

51768 Geneva Lakes Cold Storage
PO Box 39
Darien, WI 53114-0039   262-724-3295
        Fax: 262-724-4200
Warehouse offering cooler, freezer and dry storage for frozen, refrigerated and nonperishable food items; transportation firm providing refrigerated truck and van services including local, short and long haul
Number Employees: 1-4
Services: Refrigerated trucking & van: local, short & long haul

Regions Served:
  48 states, Canada & Mexico

51769 Gentzkow Trucking Svc Inc
10247 Highway 13
Lamoure, ND 58458-9433   701-883-5276
        www.americanheart.org
Transportation services include short and local haul trucking of livestock, furniture and freight
Owner: Susan Warcken
susanwarcken@caringbridge.org
Number Employees: 5-9
Services: Local & short haul trucking
Regions Served:
  Nationwide

51770 (HQ)George S. Bush & Company
825 NE Multnomah St.,
Suite 910
Portland, OR 97232   503-228-6501
    Fax: 503-294-0432 info@geosbush.com
              www.geosbush.com
Transportation broker offering freight forwarding
President: Brian Welsh
Contact: Sabina Raghubansh
sabina.raghubansh@geosbush.com
Number Employees: 50-99
Services: Freight forwarding & transportation brokerage
Regions Served:
  International

51771 Gilbert International
6219 Gilbert Rd
Laredo, TX 78041-2594   956-723-4308
    Fax: 956-724-3897 866-523-4308
    info@gilbertintl.com www.gilbertintl.com
Provides full service food grade warehousing, food product distribution services to/from Mexico, importer/exorter services available. Fully computerized state of the art distribution center
President: Joe Gilbert
jlg@gilbertintl.com
Number Employees: 20-49
Other Locations:
  Gilbert International
  Monterrey, N.L.Gilbert International
Services: Long & short haul trucking
Regions Served:
  North America

51772 (HQ)Giumarra Companies
P.O. Box 861449
Los Angeles, CA 90086   213-627-2900
        Fax: 213-628-4878 www.giumarra.com
Produce marketing
Senior VP, Strategic Development: Hillary Brick
Director of Quality Control: Jim Heil
Manager: Donald Corsaro

Number Employees: 50-99
Other Locations: Giumarra Agricom
Services: Trucking

51773 Glacier Cold Storage LTD
6820 Wilson Ave
Los Angeles, CA 90001-2159   323-583-2464
    Fax: 323-586-9121 glacierrog@aol.com
              www.glaciercold.com
Warehouse offering cooler and freezer storage for food products; transportation firm providing local and short haul trucking; blast freezing available
Vice President: Rick Mc Cutcheon
glaciervp@aol.com
VP: Rick Mc Cutcheon
Public Relations: Roger Hatfield
Operations: Ernest Mogelivesky
Plant Manager: Ricardo Dinz
Purchasing: Emy Magipeal
Number Employees: 20-49
Services: Local & short haul trucking
Regions Served:
  Los Angeles

51774 Glass Trucking LLC
200 E 6th St # 2
Newkirk, OK 74647-2213   580-362-6221
        Fax: 580-362-6225
Warehouse providing dry storage for food products; transportation firm providing local and long haul trucking; rail siding available
President: Marlan Glass Jr
Vice President: Bob Canaan

Number Employees: 5-9
Parent Co: Glass Wholesale
Services: Local & long haul trucking
Regions Served:
  Midwest

51775 Gleeson Construct & Engineers
2015 7th St
P.O.Box 625
Sioux City, IA 51101-2003   712-258-9300
    Fax: 712-277-5300 www.gleesonllc.com
Specializes in the construction of food processing facilities, freezers, cold storage facilities and distribution centers.
President: Harlan Vandezandschul
h.vandezandschul@gleesonllc.com
Number Employees: 1-4

51776 (HQ)Glen Rose Transportation Mgmt
1601 Texas Dr
Glen Rose, TX 76043-4325   254-897-7695
    Fax: 254-897-3537 800-223-9387
              www.grtminc.com
Transportation broker providing export management and freight consolidation
Owner: Byron Stinson
bstinson@grtminc.com
Number Employees: 20-49
Services: Brokerage
Regions Served:
  Nationwide

51777 Global Package
PO Box 634
Napa, CA 94559   707-224-5670
    Fax: 707-224-8170 info@globalpackage.net
              www.globalpackage.net
International packaging solutions for wine, spirits and food
CEO: Erica Harrop
Sales: Kathy Feder
Estimated Sales: $5 Million
Number Employees: 3
Type of Packaging: Food Service

51778 Goodpack USA Inc
550 N Commons Dr # 106
Suite 106
Aurora, IL 60504-8172   630-270-1250
    Fax: 630-898-1888 matt.orbell@goodpack.com
              www.goodpack.com
Leasing all-steel bins and bags for shipping juice concentrates, purees and processing fruit.
Vice President: David Hampton
david.hampton@goodpack.com
Accounting Manager: Lecy Cortez
EVP: Michael Liew
Information Technology Manager: Venkat Krishnan
Account Manager: Mitch Forsberg
Human Resources Compliance/Regulatory: Destiny Thurman
Manager: Maureen Lyons
Estimated Sales: $2.9 Million
Number Employees: 20-49

51779 Gourmet's Finest
704 Garden Station Rd
PO Box 160
Avondale, PA 19311   610-268-6910
    Fax: 610-268-2298 info@gourmetsfinest.com
Mushrooms
Owner: Richard Pia
Type of Packaging: Food Service, Private Label

51780 Graham Transfer & Storage
2108 A St
Meridian, MS 39301-5909   601-693-4933
    Fax: 601-693-4931 www.mayflower.com
Warehouse providing dry and humidity-controlled storage for general merchandise, household goods, cookware, etc.; transportation services include local, short and long haul trucking
President: Roger Burke
graham1@bellsouth.net
Operations Manager: Roger Burke
Estimated Sales: $1-2.5 Million
Number Employees: 10-19
Square Footage: 200000
Parent Co: Mayflower Transit
Services: Local, short & long haul trucking
Regions Served:
  Local & worldwide

Transportation Firms / A-Z

51781 Grane Warehousing & Distribution
1011 S Laramie Ave
Chicago, IL 60644-5506 773-379-9700
Fax: 773-854-2265 www.granetransportation.com
Warehouse providing dry storage for dry goods; transportation services include local and short haul trucking, freight forwarding, assembly and distribution, piggy-back and LTL; also, rail siding available
Co-Owner: Allan Grane
Co-Owner: Paul Grane
Data Processing: Joe Garza
Number Employees: 20-49
Services: Local & short haul trucking, freight forwarding, assembly & distribution, piggy-back & LTL

51782 Gray Transportation
2459 Gt Dr
Waterloo, IA 50703-9434 319-233-1011
Fax: 319-234-8841 800-234-3930
www.graytran.com
Transportation broker providing dry vans and flatbeds
Owner: Leroy Gray
lgray@graytran.com
Number Employees: 100-249
Services: Broker providing dry vans & flatbeds
Regions Served:
U.S., Canada & Mexico

51783 Greater Omaha Express, LLC
4626 Dahlman Ave.
Omaha, NE 68107 402-502-2600
Fax: 402-884-0065 goesafety@greateromaha.com
www.greateromahaexpress.com
Refrigerated products and dry goods.
President: Brenton Falgione
Operations Manager: Bill Crismon
Warehouse Manager: Trevor Storovich
Year Founded: 2006
Parent Co: Greater Omaha Packing Co Inc.
Regions Served:
48 States

51784 (HQ)Greenstein Trucking Company
1257 W Atlantic Blvd
Pompano Beach, FL 33069-2946 954-784-4045
Transportation firm providing long haul refrigerated trucking for produce and dairy products including cheese
President & CEO: Charles Greenstein
Number Employees: 10-19
Services: Long haul refrigerated trucking for produce & dairy products: cheese

51785 Greenway TransportationServices
14300 N Northsight Blvd
Suite 120
Scottsdale, AZ 85260 480-443-8500
Fax: 480-998-9440 800-528-4025
craig@shipgreenway.com
www.shipgreenway.com
Transportation broker providing local, long and short haul trucking of commodities, dry goods, etc.; refrigerated trucking, dry van, flatbed intermodal, rail and special equip services available.
President/Owner: Craig Skillicorn
CFO: Marsha Skillicorn
Estimated Sales: $12 Million
Number Employees: 10
Square Footage: 5200
Services: Transportation broker providing local, long & short haul trucking; refrigerated trucking, dry van & flatbeds
Regions Served:
Continental U.S., Canada & Mexico

51786 Gress Refrigerated Services & Logisitics
922 North South Road
Scranton, PA 18504 570-504-0191
Fax: 570-347-6922 www.gresscold.com
Warehouse offering cooler and freezer storage for food products; transportation firm providing local, short and long haul TL trucking services; also, blast freezing, re-packing and labeling available
Manager: Rich Charles
Warehouse Manager: Angelo Valvano
Number Employees: 10-19
Services: Local, short & long haul TL trucking

Regions Served:
Nationwide

51787 Grey Eagle Distributors
2340 Millpark Dr
Maryland Heights, MO 63043 314-429-9100
www.greyeagle.com
Distributor of beers and malt beverages.
President & CEO: David Stokes
jpjasiek@greyeagle.com
VP, Sales & Marketing: Scott Drysdale
Chief Operating Officer: Neil Komadoski
Year Founded: 1963
Estimated Sales: $110 Million
Number Employees: 250-499

51788 Greylawn Foods
2032 Plainfield Pike
Cranston, RI 02921-2059 401-223-3520
Fax: 401-223-3520 800-556-6490
www.greylawn.com
Warehouse providing frozen and refrigerated storage for food products; also, consignment and distribution services available; transportation firm providing LTL refrigeration services
Owner: Matt Leonard
mattl@patriotcompanies.com
Number Employees: 20-49
Services: LTL refrigeration, rail & ocean services
Regions Served:
48 States

51789 Grimes Co
600 Ellis Rd N
Jacksonville, FL 32254-2801 904-786-5711
Fax: 904-786-7805 800-881-9505
HR@grimescompanies.com
www.grimescompanies.com
Transportation firm providing freight consolidation; warehouse providing cooler, dry and humidity-controlled storage; rail siding and pick/pack available
Owner: Thomas Grimes
Number Employees: 20-49
Services: U.S. customs bonded freight consolidation
Regions Served:
FL & Southeast

51790 Groendyke Transport Inc
2510 Rock Island Blvd
Enid, OK 73701-1342 580-234-4663
Fax: 580-234-1216 www.groendyke.com
Transportation firm providing long, local and short haul trucking through flatbed and tank transport
Chairman & CEO: John Groendyke
CEO: Don Querciagrossa
kmcgahey@bowdenandwood.com
Number Employees: 1000-4999
Services: Long, short & local haul trucking
Regions Served:
Nationwide & international: Canada

51791 Gulf Central Distribution Ctr
4535 S Dale Mabry Hwy
Tampa, FL 33611-1425 813-837-5602
Fax: 813-831-4327
Warehouse providing cooler storage for food, paper, candy, appliances and general merchandise; also, rail siding and distribution to the Southeast available; transportation firm providing LTL and long haul trucking
Owner: Jimmy Sanmartin
jsanmartin@tampabay.rr.com
Number Employees: 10-19
Services: Trucking: LTL & long haul
Regions Served:
48 states

51792 H & M Bay Inc
1600 Industrial Park Rd
Federalsburg, MD 21632 410-754-5167
Fax: 410-754-3495 800-932-7521
information@hmbayinc.net www.hmbayinc.net
Warehouse offering cooler and freezer storage of seafood; transportation firm providing refrigerated trucking services including local, short and long haul
Co-Owner: Walter Messick
CFO: Al Nulph
Marketing And Sales Manager: Scott Steinhardt
Manager: Randy Hind
rhind@hmbayinc.com
COO: Michael Ryan
Number Employees: 100-249

Services: Refrigerated trucking: local, long & short haul
Regions Served:
Nationwide

51793 H&R Transport
3601 2nd Avenue N
Lethbridge, AB T1H 5K7
Canada 403-328-2345
Fax: 403-328-2877 www.hrtrans.com
Transportation firm providing local, long and short haul trucking for temperature controlled products
Chairman: Al Foder
President/CEO: D'Arcy Foder
Svp Finance/CFO: David Westwood
Svp Operations: Mark Foder
Number Employees: 500-999
Services: Local, long & short haul trucking for temperature controlled products
Regions Served:
USA & Canada

51794 (HQ)Hall's Warehouse Corp
501 Kentile Rd
P.O. Box 378
South Plainfield, NJ 07080-4800 908-756-6242
Fax: 908-757-2667 info@hallscorp.com
www.hallscorp.com
Temperature-controlled warehousing and transportation servicing the Northeast; 1.6 million sq. ft. and 75 trucks over 8 facilities
President: Bill Jayne
COO: Tom Brennan
CFO: Warren Tamaroff
Director of Sales: Salvatore LaBruno
Director of Operations: Nick Pizzo
Year Founded: 1966
Number Employees: 50-99
Services: Export packing services, freight consolidation, local & long haul trucking
Regions Served:
Northeast U.S.

51795 Hanjin Shipping Company
80 E State Rt 4 # 490
Paramus, NJ 07652-2655 201-291-4500
Fax: 201-291-9393 www.hanjin.com
Transportation firm providing containerized ocean freight services including reefer and other specialized cargos
Number Employees: 250-499
Parent Co: Hanjin Group
Services: Containerized ocean freight services: reefers & other specialized cargo
Regions Served:
North, South & Central America, Far East, Europe & the Middle East

51796 Hanover Terminal Inc
201 Center St
Hanover, PA 17331-2054 717-698-1392
Fax: 717-637-6835
Warehouse providing cooler and dry storage; transportation services including LTL freight consolidation, long and short haul trucking, cross docking, CSX railroad, container stripping and bonded U.S. customs; also, shrink wrapping andrail siding available
Manager: Jerry Livelsberger
COO: Tim Nicholas
timn@hanoverterminal.com
Number Employees: 50-99
Services: Long & short haul trucking, container stripping, CSX rail & bonded U.S. customs, etc.
Regions Served:
Northeast

51797 (HQ)Hanover Warehouses Inc
100 Central Ave
Building 17
Kearny, NJ 07032-4640 973-491-9204
Fax: 973-589-1794 www.hanoverwhse.com
Warehouse providing cooler and dry storage for wines, cheeses, pasta, nuts, oils and specialty foods; transportation firm offering local haul trucking in NY and NJ
President: Dave Telesco
Number Employees: 10-19
Square Footage: 3000000
Services: Local haul trucking
Regions Served:
NY & NJ

Transportation Firms / A-Z

51798 Hansen Co
611 4th St
Griswold, IA 51535-8092   712-778-2426
Fax: 712-778-2150
Transportation company providing local, long and short haul trucking; warehouse providing dry and refrigerated storage for general commodities
President: Craig Hansen
hanseng@netins.net
VP: chris Foote
Distribution Operations Manager: Mae Brunk
Sales Manager: Chris Foote
Estimated Sales: $3-5 Million
Number Employees: 20-49
Square Footage: 34000
Services: Local, long & short haul trucking
Regions Served:
  Nationwide

51799 Hansen Storage Co
2880 N 112th St
Milwaukee, WI 53222-4220   414-476-9221
Fax: 414-476-0646
information@hansenstorage.com
www.hansenstorage.com
Warehouse providing cooler, dry, freezer and humidity-controlled storage for alcoholic beverages, candy and confetti, food and grocery products, and paper products; transportation firm providing freight consolidation and local haultrucking; also, rail siding, distribution, re-packaging, shrink wrapping and labeling services available
President: Peter J. Hansen
CEO: William C. Hansen
Vice President Sales: Steven N. Draeger
General Manager Operations: Keith Peterson
IT: Signe Schmit
sschmit@hansenstorage.com
Number Employees: 20-49
Services: Freight consolidation & local haul trucking

51800 Hansen Trucking
96 Curtis St
Jerseyville, IL 62052-2202   618-498-4306
Fax: 618-498-4879   800-844-2984
mo@hansentrucking.net
www.hansentrucking.com
Transportation firm providing refrigerated and dry long and short haul trucking services
Owner: Phillip Hansen
balv@hansentrucking.net
Number Employees: 5-9
Services: Refrigerated & dry short & long haul trucking
Regions Served:
  Nationwide

51801 (HQ)Hanson Logistics
2900 S State St
St Joseph, MI 49085   269-982-1390
Fax: 269-982-1506   888-772-1197
blarkin@hansonlogistics.com
www.hansonlogistics.com
Temperature-controlled supply chain services including warehousing and transportation; 8 facilities in Michigan and Indiana with a total capacity of 34,000,000 cubic feet of deep frozen, refrigerated and dry warehousing space
President/CEO: Ken Whah
Vice President/CFO: Jack White
VP Business Development: Blake Larkin
VP Supply Chain Services: Matt Luckas
SVP Warehouse Operations: Jeff Frazier
Year Founded: 1954
Estimated Sales: $10-20 Million
Number Employees: 250-499
Other Locations:
  Zoschke Road
  Benton Harbor, MI
  Napier Avenue
  Benton Harbor, MI
  Hart, MI
  South Bend, IN
  Decatur, MI
  Logansport, IN
  Zoschke RoadBenton Harbor
Services: Dry and refrigerated moves
Regions Served:
  National

51802 Hapag-Lloyd America
399 HOES LANE
Piscataway Township, NJ 08854   732-562-1800
Fax: 732-885-6210   888-851-4083
www.hapag-lloyd.com
International transportation, cold storage, box cars
President: Wolfgang Freese
Senior VP: Hercules Angelatos
Director Sales: Stuart Sandlin
Director Operations: John Palmer
Number Employees: 100-249
Services: local, long, short haul trucking

51803 (HQ)Harry E. Hills & Associates
4340 N Brush College Rd
Decatur, IL 62524   217-875-3880
Transportation firm providing local, long and short haul trucking and brokerage services
President: Thomas Hills
Number Employees: 5-9
Services: Transportation brokerage & local, long & short haul trucking
Regions Served:
  Nationwide & international

51804 Heding Truck Services
PO Box 97
Union Center, WI 53962-0097   608-462-8441
Fax: 608-462-5009   800-236-8441
www.heding.com
Transportation firm providing EDI capabilities, special loads, brokerage, LTL, and local, long and short haul trucking services
President: H Heding
Contact: Sara Gorn
sara@heding.com
Number Employees: 50-99
Services: Local, long & short haul trucking
Regions Served:
  Nationwide

51805 Heiter Truck Line Inc
1835 340th St
1835 340th Street
Spencer, IA 51301-7447   712-262-2845
Fax: 712-262-3856   800-245-1966
mikeheiter@smunet.net   www.heitertruckline.com
Owner: Jeff Heiter
Number Employees: 20-49

51806 (HQ)Henningsen Cold Storage Co
21435 NW Cherry Ln
Hillsboro, OR 97124-6630   503-531-5400
Fax: 503-531-5410   800-791-2653
info@henningsen.com   www.henningsen.com
Warehousing and logistics services
President: Paul Henningsen
Vice President: Chris Henningsen
Chief Financial Officer: Eric Mauss
Director of Business Development: Chad Freeman
Food Safety Manager: Sripriya Agaram
EVP Sales & Marketing: Tony Lucarelli
Director of Sales: Phil Potter
Director of Human Resources: Craig Cude
EVP Warehouse Operations: Todd Larson
Director of Transportation: Todd Lanter
Year Founded: 1923
Number Employees: 250-499
Other Locations:
  Grand Forks, ND
  Forest Grove, OR
  Portland, OR
  Scranton, PA
  Richland, WA
  Twin Falls, IDForest Grove
Services: Cryogenic rail car & consolidated shipping; also, trucking, LTL & TL
Regions Served:
  National & International

51807 Henry L Taylor Trucking LLC
1280 Nawakwa Rd
Biglerville, PA 17307-9727   717-677-6138
Fax: 717-677-6514   www.mtvalleyfarms.com
Warehouse offering storage for groceries; transportation firm providing long and short haul trucking serving intra-state PA and fourty eight states; also, vans and flats available
Owner: Henry L Taylor
henry.l.taylor@henrytaylor.com
Number Employees: 10-19
Services: Vans, flats and long & short haul trucking
Regions Served:
  Intra-state PA & 48 states

51808 Hermann Services Inc
83 Stults Rd # 1
Dayton, NJ 08810-3001   609-860-5810
Fax: 609-409-9442   800-524-0067
sales@HermannTDS.com   www.hermanntds.com
Warehouse providing cooler and dry storage for groceries, general merchandise, etc.; transportation services include dedicated local regional, and short haul trucking; also packaging, re-packing EDI capabilities, assembly,distribution, and rail siding available
President: Richard Hermann
Vice President: Lisa Burke
lburke@hermanntds.com
Number Employees: 10-19
Other Locations:
  Hermann Warehouse Corp.
  Milltown, NJHermann Warehouse Corp.
Services: Local, Regional& short haul trucking
Regions Served:
  Nationwide

51809 (HQ)Hess Trucking Co
5737 Grayson Rd
Harrisburg, PA 17111-3381   717-561-8344
Fax: 717-561-8310   800-733-2509
wnelson@hesstrucking.com   www.hesstrucking.com
Warehouse providing dry, cooler and humidity-controlled storage; transportation firm providing freight consolidation, local and short haul trucking
President: Don Confer
dconfer@hesstrucking.com
VP Operations: Joseph Underkoffler
Number Employees: 100-249
Other Locations:
  Hess Trucking Company
  Harrisburg, PAHess Trucking Company
Services: Freight consolidation & local & short haul trucking
Regions Served:
  PA, Southern NJ, MD, Northern DE, Northern VA & DC

51810 Highland Transport
2815 14th Avenue
Markham, ON L3R 0H9
Canada
Fax: 905-477-0940   800-263-3356
www.highlandtransport.com
Transportation firm providing heated, dry van, local, long and short haul trucking in the continental U.S
President: Norm Sneyd
Controller: Simon Seupaul
Director, Systems: Don Maynard
Director of Sales: Mike King
VP Operations: Terry Gardiner
General Manager, Intermodel: John Hutton
Number Employees: 500-999
Parent Co: 3846113 Canada
Services: Heated, dry van, local, long & short haul trucking
Regions Served:
  Continental U.S.

51811 Highroad Warehouse, Inc
5452 Oceanus Dr
Huntington Beach, CA 92649   714-890-6110
Transportation company providing short, local, and long haul trucking

51812 Hillsboro Transportation Company
6256 Us Highway 50
Hillsboro, OH 45133   937-393-4213
Transportation company providing long and short haul trucking; serving around the Ohio area
Owner: Jim Duckwall
Contact: S Duckwall
mike.duckwall@hillsborotransportation.com
Number Employees: 5-9
Services: Long & short haul trucking
Regions Served:
  OH, IL, KY, IN, MI

51813 (HQ)Hirschbach Motor Lines
18355 US Highway 20 W
East Dubuque, IL 61025-8514   815-747-3850
Fax: 800-772-2500   800-554-2969
hr@hirschbach.com   www.hirschbach.com

Transportation Firms / A-Z

Trucking company providing specialized, economical, on-time truck transportation service
President & COO: Brad Pinchuk
Executive VP: Andrea Borowicz
andrea.borowicz@hirschbach.com
Number Employees: 1-4
Other Locations:
  Shanno Transportation
  Dubuque, IA Shanno Transportation
Regions Served:
  Upper Midwest, Southeast, Southwest, West Coast

51814 Hodges Co
4401 S 72nd East Ave
Tulsa, OK 74145-4610   918-622-3028
  Fax: 918-664-4625   888-622-3028
  sales@hodgesco.com   www.hodgesco.com
Warehouse providing dry storage for general merchandise and groceries; transportation firm providing LTL, TL and regional haul trucking; also, outdoor storage, slip sheet, push/pull, repackaging, reselecting, lift gate and rail sidingservices available
Vice President: Sherry Wallis
VP: Sherry Wallis
Number Employees: 5-9
Parent Co: Port City Property
Services: Regional haul trucking, LTL & TL, slip sheet, push/pull, repackaging, reselecting, lift gate, etc.
Regions Served:
  OK, TX, KS, MO & AR

51815 Holeman Distribution Ctr
22430 76th Ave S
Kent, WA 98032-2406   253-872-7140
  Fax: 253-395-0335   m_hobbs@holmanusa.com
  www.holmanusa.com
Warehouse providing dry storage for paper, appliances, groceries and raw materials; transportation firm providing local haul trucking; also, distribution, re-packing, value added, pick/pack and rail siding available
Marketing: Mitchell Hobbs
Number Employees: 100-249
Services: Local haul trucking
Regions Served:
  Northwest

51816 Holman Distribution Center
2300 SE Beta Street
Portland, OR 97222-7330   503-652-1912
  Fax: 503-652-1970   m_hobbs@holmanusa.com
  www.holmanusa.com
Warehouse offering cooler, dry and humidity-controlled storage for groceries, paper goods and industrial products; transportation firm providing local haul trucking and freight consolidation; also, rail siding, re-packing and labelingservices available
President: Robert Downie
Number Employees: 20-49
Services: Local haul trucking & freight consolidation
Regions Served:
  Pacific Northwest: Portland, OR & Seattle, WA

51817 Holt Logistics Corporation
101 South King Street
Gloucester City, NJ 08030   215-742-3000
  Fax: 856-742-3102   www.holtoversight.com
Warehouse offering cooler, dry storage, freezer and humidity controlled food storage; transportation services include re-packing and short and long haul trucking. Holt Cargo Systems provides cargo handling services such asstevedoring, warehousing, trucking and total distribution. Holt specializes in handling fresh fruits and all types of perishable commodities requiring temperature-controlled ambient care
Manager: Bill Mc Dermitt
Contact: Jb Burleson
jburleson@holtoversight.com
Number Employees: 1-4
Services: Re-packing, long & short haul
Regions Served:
  National & International

51818 Honolulu Freight Svc
1400 Date St
Montebello, CA 90640-6323   323-887-6777
  Fax: 323-887-6776   800-777-4963
  jginoza@hfsnet.com   www.hfsnet.com
Transportation firm providing Air, Rail, Barge, and Steamship services, warehousing and freight forwarding of refrigerated and dry goods nationwide and locally
Manager: Bob Green
Manager: Mary Agnew
maryagnew@honolulufreight.com
Number Employees: 50-99
Parent Co: Inter City Trucking
Services: Refrigerated & dry, door-to-door & warehousing
Regions Served:
  Nationwide & local

51819 Hoonah Cold Storage
303 1st St
Hoonah, AK 99829   907-945-3264
  Fax: 907-945-3441
Manager: Terrence Barry
Estimated Sales: Less Than $500,000
Number Employees: 1-4

51820 (HQ)Houston Central Industries, Ltd.
7080 Express Ln
Houston, TX 77078   713-491-0444
     800-856-3218
Warehouse providing cooler, freezer and dry storage of food; transportation firm providing local, short and long haul trucking; also, blast freezing, distribution, re-packaging, transloading, computer interfacing and rail sidingservices available
President: Micheal M. Feld
Sales: Michael M. Feld
Office Manager/Billing: Lori Weesner
Warehouse Manager: Sean Hebert
Number Employees: 20-49
Type of Packaging: Food Service
Services: Local, short & long haul trucking
Regions Served:
  Continental U.S., Canada, Mexico

51821 Icelandair
1900 Crown Colony Dr # 1
Quincy, MA 02169-0979   857-403-1790
  Fax: 410-715-3547   800- 22- 55
  www.icelandair.us
Transportation firm providing domestic and international air freight services
Manager: Kerstin Ockens
Contact: Petur Agustsson
peturagustsson@icelandair.com
Number Employees: 1-4
Parent Co: Flugleidir/Icelandair
Services: Air freight
Regions Served:
  U.S. & Europe

51822 Ideal Warehouse
150 Montreal-Toronto Blvd
Montreal, QC H8S 4L8
Canada   514-634-8886
     800-304-1816
  info@ideal.qc.ca   www.ideal.qc.ca
Warehouse offering dry storage for groceries and food products, rail siding available, transportation services include local and long haul trucking and local pick-up and full service of distribution
President: Bernard Pettigrew
Finance Controller: Carl Perron
Director of Operations: Nadia Pettigrew
Number Employees: 20-49
Services: Local & long haul trucking & local pick-up & delivery
Regions Served:
  Canada

51823 Idealease Inc
430 N Rand Rd
North Barrington, IL 60010-1496   847-304-6000
  Fax: 847-304-0076   info@idealease.com
  www.idealease.com
Transportation firm providing full-service truck leasing, maintenance and rentals
President and CEO: Dan Murphy
danmurphy@idealease.com
COO: Keric Kennedy
Number Employees: 20-49
Services: Transportation firm providing full-service truck leasing, maintenance and rentals
Regions Served:
  North America

51824 Imperal Freight Broker
2287 NW 102nd Pl
Doral, FL 33172-2523   305-592-6910
  Fax: 305-593-1781   sales@imperialfreight.com
  www.imperialfreight.com
Transportation firm providing freight forwarding and customs clearance of goods for the food industry in Florida
President: Ralph Delarosa
ralph.delarosa@imperialfreight.com
Number Employees: 10-19
Services: Freight forwarding, trucking and container loading & unloading
Regions Served:
  Fl, Caribbean, Central & South America

51825 Importers
420 5th Ave S # 203
Edmonds, WA 98020-3632   425-977-2364
  Fax: 425-977-2495   800-346-0389
Transportation firm providing freight forwarding of dry freight, expedited trucking, LTL and FTL services nationwide
President: Rich Rebenstorf
Number Employees: 1-4
Services: Expedited trucking, LTL, full truckloads and freight forwarding
Regions Served:
  Nationwide

51826 Indiana Harbor Belt Railroad
2721 161st St
Hammond, IN 46323-1099   219-989-4703
  Fax: 219-989-4707   jim.sheppard@ihbrr.com
  www.ihbrr.com
Transportation company providing 54 miles of mainline track, 24 double main tracks, 266 miles of additional and siding track
Assistant Director Business Development: Tony Kazakevicius
Director Sales/Marketing: Jim Sheppard
Director Labor Relations & Human Resourc: MaryKay Conley
Operations GM: Pat Daly
Plant Manager: Dan Kelley
Manager Purchasing: Mike Nicoletti
Number Employees: 100-249
Parent Co: Consolidated Rail Corporation
Services: Switching railroad
Regions Served:
  Local & regional

51827 Inland Empire Distribution
3808 N Sullivan Rd # 32d
Building 32
Spokane Valley, WA 99216-1615   509-922-0944
  Fax: 509-927-8593   mattewers@ieds.net
  www.ieds.net
Public warehouse providing dry for nonperishable foods; transportation services providing local, long and short haul trucking; also, rail siding, drayage, freight consolidation, freight management and forwarding services available
President and CEO: James P. Ewers
VP/General Manager: Daniel C. Ewers
VP, Business Development: Matthew P. Ewers
VP/Operations: Dan Ewers
Number Employees: 50-99
Square Footage: 3550000
Services: intermodal, drayage
Regions Served:
  Pacific Northwest: WA, OR, ID & MT

51828 Inland Star Distribution Ctr
3146 S Chestnut Ave
PO Box 2396
Fresno, CA 93725-2606   559-470-6826
  Fax: 559-237-9468   rsmith@inlandstar.com
  www.inlandstar.com
Warehouse offering dry storage for nonperishable food products; rail siding available; transportation division providing TL, LTL and overnight service in Western U.S.
President: Yvonne Adams
yadams@inlandstar.com
Sales/Marketing: Richard Smith
Number Employees: 50-99
Services: TL, LTL & overnight service
Regions Served:
  Western U.S.

Transportation Firms / A-Z

51829 InsulTote
10653 W 181st Ave
Lowell, IN 46356
219-696-3639
Fax: 219-696-5220   800-776-3645
www.insultote.net
Insulated shipping products
Parent Co: Innovative Energy

51830 Inter State Cold Storage
2400 Setterlin Dr
Columbus, OH 43228-9794
614-771-6700
Fax: 614-771-6925
info@interstatecoldstorage.com
www.interstatecoldstorage.com
Public warehouse providing cooler and freezer storage for refrigerated and frozen foods; transportation firm providing local and short haul trucking; also, custom packaging, USDA inspection and rail siding available. Refrigerated docks with 35 doors; 7,310,000 cubic feet; CSX with 10-car private siding; At I-270, near I-70.
Manager: Kevin Tackett
kevin.tackett@interstatecoldstorage.com
Chief Executive Officer: Vincent Tippmann
Manager: Kevin Tackett
kevin.tackett@interstatecoldstorage.com
General Manager: Ron Halm
Estimated Sales: $2.5-5 Million
Number Employees: 20-49
Parent Co: Interstate Cold Storage, Inc.
Services: Local & short haul trucking
Regions Served:
OH, IN, MI, KY, WV & PA

51831 Intercontinental Warehouses
135 Bethridge Rd
Etobicoke, ON M9W 1N4
Canada
416-743-5471
Fax: 416-743-8582
Custom bonded warehouse providing cooler, freezer and dry storage for frozen and refrigerated foods and groceries; transportation services include courier, LTL, TL, specialty hazardous carriers and consolidated transportation program; rail siding available
Number Employees: 45
Square Footage: 2400000
Parent Co: Valleydene Corporation
Services: Courier, LTL, truckload, specialty hazardous carriers & consolidated transportation program
Regions Served:
Canada & Northeast

51832 Intermodal Express
3449 Peripheral South, 4th Floor
Mexico DF, MX 34102
55- 68- 150
55- 59- 745
www.intermodalexpress.com.mx
Transportation firm providing intermodal services; transportation broker providing local, long and short haul trucking services
Number Employees: 5-9
Services: Intermodal; broker providing local, long & short haul trucking
Regions Served:
Nationwide excluding FL

51833 Interport Storage & Distribution Service
105-A Rocket Avenue
Opelika, AL 36804
334-745-0880
Fax: 334-745-6537   800-447-7094
Warehouse providing cooler and dry storage for nonperishable foods; transportation firm providing short and local haul trucking; also, railsiding and intermodal available
President: Dean Matheson
Operations Manager: Allen Barks
Number Employees: 20-49
Services: Short & local haul trucking
Regions Served:
Southeast

51834 (HQ)Interstate Cold StorageInc
4410 New Haven Ave
Fort Wayne, IN 46803-1650
260-428-2505
Fax: 260-428-2503   www.interstatecoldstorage.com
Public warehouse providing cooler and freezer storage for refrigerated and frozen goods; transportation firm providing local and short haul trucking, freight consolidation and rail car services; also, LTL, blast freezing, EDI/WINS andcontract services available. Each location has temperature ranges from -20F to 60F, providing flexibility needed to accommodate your needs. Strategic locations with easy highway and rail access assure cost effective inbound and outbound delivery ofproducts.
Chief Executive Officer: Vincent Tippmann
General Manager: Ron Halm
Facility Manager - Fort Wayne, IN - East: Gary Benson
Number Employees: 20-49
Other Locations:
Roberts Road
Columbus, OH
Interstate Drive
Napoleon, OH
Nelson Road
Fort Wayne, IN
Lincoln Parkway
Fort Wayne, IN
Setterlin Drive
Columbus, OHRoberts RoadNapoleon
Regions Served:
Regional Midwest

51835 Interstate Cold Storage
6606 Lincoln Pkwy
Fort Wayne, IN 46804-5684
260-432-3494
Fax: 260-432-0221
info@interstatecoldstorage.com
www.interstatecoldstorage.com
Public warehouse offering cooler and freezer storage; transportation firm providing freight consolidation via TL and LTL refrigerated short haul trucking; also, rail siding, custom packaging, USDA inspection, exporting andcertification services available. Refrigerated docks with 26 doors; 5,400,000 cubic feet; CSX and Rail America with 8-car private siding; US Highways 14 & I-69, near I-469.
Manager: Phil Garlinger
Chief Executive Officer: Vincent Tippmann
Manager: Nick Burnham
nick.burnham@interstatecoldstorage.com
General Manager: Ron Halm
Estimated Sales: $1-2.5 Million
Number Employees: 10-19
Parent Co: Interstate Cold Storage, Inc.
Services: Freight consolidation via refrigerated TL & LTL short haul trucking

51836 Iowa Interstate Railroad LTD
5900 6th St SW
Cedar Rapids, IA 52404-4804
319-298-5400
Fax: 319-298-5458   dhmiller@iaisrr.com
www.iaisrr.com
Transportation firm providing rail car services, industrial switching, transload, intermodal capabilities; operates over 500 miles between Omaha, Nebraska and Chicago, Illinois with a branch line from Bureau to Peoria in Illinois
President & CEO: Dennis Miller
CEO: Travis Tinken
travis.tinken@dot.iowa.gov
Estimated Sales: G
Number Employees: 100-249
Services: Rail car
Regions Served:
IL & IA connecting Chicago with Omaha, NE

51837 J & J Trucking
N4661 Oak Grove Rd
Brandon, WI 53919-9716
920-346-2880
Fax: 920-346-8589
A full-service truck line with brokerage authority.
Manager: Joe Sullivan
Number Employees: 20-49

51838 J B Hunt Transport Inc
615 J B Hunt Dr
Lowell, AR 72745-9142
800-452-4868
Customer.Experience@jbhunt.com
www.jbhunt.com
Transportation firm providing long and short haul trucking; services include intermodal transport, contract, TL and dry van services.
President & Chief Executive Officer: John Roberts III
Chairman: Kirk Thompson
Interim CFO: John Kuhlow
EVP, Operations/COO: Craig Harper
Year Founded: 1961
Estimated Sales: $7.19 Billion
Number Employees: 27,600
Services: Intermodal transport, logistics, TL & dry van
Regions Served:
International

51839 J D Double M Trucking
1125 Lew Ross Rd
Council Bluffs, IA 51501-8086
712-325-1160
Fax: 712-325-1182   mickey@jdmmtrucking.com
www.jdmmtrucking.com
Transportation company provifing long, short, and local haul trucking
Owner: Mickey Stogdill
Number Employees: 5-9

51840 J M Swank Co
395 Herky St
North Liberty, IA 52317-8523
319-626-3683
Fax: 319-626-3662   800-593-6375
www.jmswank.com
Food ingredients for the dairy, beverage, meat, bakery, snack, confection, ethnic and prepared foods industries
CEO: Shawn Meaney
Chief Financial Officer: Philip Garton
Senior Vice President: Paul Hillen
Vice President, Sales & Customer Service: Linda Loucks
Vice President, Operations: Reggie Hastings
Estimated Sales: $6 Million
Number Employees: 100-249
Parent Co: Conagra Brands
Other Locations:
Swank Great Lakes
Carol Stream, IL
Swank South
Dallas, TX
Swank West
Denver, CO
Tolleson, AZ
Buena Park, CA
Modesto, CA
Swank Great LakesDallas
Services: Delivery by truck (JRRW Transport)
Regions Served:
North America

51841 J&B Cold Storage Inc
13200 43rd Street North East
Saint Michael, MN 55376-8420
763-497-3700
Fax: 763-497-9481   800-872-4642
info@jbcold.com   www.jbgroup.com
Warehouse offering cooler, freezer and dry storage for food products; transportation firm providing local, short and long haul trucking; also, re-packing, labeling and blast freezing available
President: Robert Hageman
Contact: Stefano Bilich
stefano.bilich@jbgroup.com
Number Employees: 10-19
Parent Co: J&B Wholesale Distributing Inc
Services: Local, short & long haul trucking
Regions Served:
Upper Midwest, 27 States

51842 J.A. Tucker Company
900 Dudley Avenue
Cherry Hill, NJ 08002
856-317-9600
Fax: 856-317-9699   800-229-7780
info@tuckerco.com   www.tuckerco.com
Transportation broker providing freight forwarding, management, and consultation, also with EDI capabilities; and trucking including local, short and long haul
President & COO: Jim Tucker
CEO: Jeff Tucker
VP Operations: Gene Wherrity
Contact: William Tucker
william.tucker@tuckerco.com
Estimated Sales: $2.5-5 Million
Number Employees: 20-49
Square Footage: 11520
Services: Transportation brokerage, trucking & freight forwarding
Regions Served:
Nationwide & International

Transportation Firms / A-Z

51843 J.D. Smith & Sons
180 Basaltic Road
Concord, ON L4K 1G8
Canada
905-669-8980
Fax: 905-669-8981 866-669-8980
info@jdsmith.com www.jdsmith.com
Warehouse providing dry storage for general merchandise and groceries; transportation firm providing local contract trucking and daily service to major chains in metro Toronto and Ontario; also, re-packing and pallet control available
Number Employees: 250-499
Services: Local haul contract trucking
Regions Served:
Metro Toronto & Ontario

51844 Jacmar Foodservice
300 N Baldwin Park Blvd.
City of Industry, CA 91746
Fax: 626-430-2342 800-834-8806
contact@jacmar.com www.jacmar.com
Distributor of dry foods, cheese and dairy products, canned foods, meats and seafood, frozen products, and general groceries.
President & CFO: Jim Hliboki
CEO: James Dal Pozzo
Year Founded: 1959
Square Footage: 232000
Services: Multi-temperature, late-model vehicles

51845 Jacobson Warehouse Company
P.O. Box 224
Des Moines, IA
515-265-6171
Fax: 515-265-8927 800-636-6171
Warehouse providing dry storage for nonperishable items; transportation firm providing long and short haul trucking; also, re-packing services available, packaging
President: Scott Temple
CFO: Gordon Smith
Vice President: john Bartnick
Vice President of Business Development: Stan Schrader
Contact: John Barker
j_barker@jacobsonco.com
Executive Vice President of Operations: Patrick Coughlin
Number Employees: 20-49
Parent Co: Jacobson Companies
Other Locations:
Jacobson Warehouse Company
Phoenix, AR Jacobson Warehouse Company
Services: Long & short haul trucking
Regions Served:
48 States & Canada

51846 James H Clark & Son Inc
4100 S 500 W
Salt Lake City, UT 84123-1334
801-266-9322
Fax: 801-269-1553 800-523-9008
Transportation firm providing refrigerated long, short and local haul trucking services
President: Greg Mccandless
gr@jameshclark.com
Vice President: Craig j Clark
Number Employees: 100-249
Services: Refrigerated long, short & local haul trucking
Regions Served:
48 States

51847 Jantzen International
2100 E Devon Ave # 101
Elk Grove Vlg, IL 60007-6030
847-640-5200
Fax: 847-640-0155 info@jantzenweb.com
www.jantzenweb.com
Warehouse providing dry storage for goods; transportation company providing air and ocean freight services.
President: Marybeth Wilson
Accounting: Diane Keating
Operations & Air Import: Rhodora Sanguiped
Air Export Manager: Wolfgang Menke
Number Employees: 2 - 10
Services: Air & ocean freight
Regions Served:
Europe, South & Latin America & the Far East

51848 Jim Palmer Trucking
9730 Derby Dr
Missoula, MT 59808
406-721-5151
Fax: 406-728-7376 800-548-3110
www.jimpalmertrucking.com
Transportation firm providing refrigerated short and long haul trucking
President: Joe Kalaft
VP Sales: Matt Garrett
Number Employees: 50-99
Services: Refrigerated short & long haul trucking
Regions Served:
Nationwide

51849 Johanson TransportationSvc
5583 E Olive Ave
Fresno, CA 93727-2559
559-458-2200
Fax: 559-458-2234 800-742-2053
LJohanson@johansontrans.com
www.johansontrans.com
Transporters of dry and temperature controlled freight.
President: Larry Johanson
ljohanson@johansontrans.com
CFO: Janice Spicer
Vice President: Craig Johanson
Chief Operations Officer: Jerry Beckstead
Corporate Accounting & Administration Ma: Becky Martin
Number Employees: 20-49

51850 Johanson TransportationServices
PO Box 20617
Baltimore, MD 21223
443-398-4907
866-400-4453
boss@johansontrans.com www.johansontrans.com
Transportation broker providing services for perishable, nonperishable and agricultural finished goods including dry and temperature controlled vans, piggybacks, flatbeds and tankers
Chairman: Richard Johanson
President/CEO: Larry Johanson
CFO: Janice Spicer
VP of Perishable Goods: Rick Rattazzi
VP of Non-Perishable Goods: Bruce Negri
Operations Manager: Darryl Johnson
Number Employees: 20-49
Services: Dry & temperature-controlled vans, piggybacks, flatbeds & tankers
Regions Served:
Nationwide & international: Canada & Mexico

51851 John Cassidy Intl Inc
3680 NW 73rd St
Miami, FL 33147-5850
305-836-6216
Fax: 305-691-7614 paul@johncassidyintl.com
www.johncassidyintl.com
International freight forwarder and customs house broker; warehouse providing dry storage for general merchandise; rail siding available
President: Paul Cassidy
paul@internationaldistributioncenter.com
CEO: John Cassidy
Number Employees: 10-19
Services: Dry storage
Regions Served:
Caribbean, South America

51852 John Christner TruckingInc
19007 W Highway 33
Sapulpa, OK 74066-7545
918-512-8600
Fax: 918-227-6685 800-324-1900
chrda@johnchristner.com www.johnchristner.com
Warehouse offering cooler and freezer storage for frozen and refrigerated foods; transportation firm providing refrigerated local, short and long haul trucking services; also, distribution and logistics available
President: John Christner
chrj@johnchristner.com
VP/COO: Daniel Christner
Number Employees: 250-499
Services: Refrigerated local, long & short haul trucking
Regions Served:
48 states

51853 John S James Co
6002 Commerce Blvd # 115
Savannah, GA 31408-9760
912-201-1346
Fax: 912-233-2150 savannah@johnsjames.com
www.johnsjames.com
Warehouse providing dry storage for general cargo; customs house broker providing freight forwarding via domestic and international airline service
President: Thomas James
thomas.james@johnsjames.com
Number Employees: 20-49
Services: Customs house broker providing freight forwarding via domestic & international airline service
Regions Served:
Nationwide & international

51854 John-Jeffrey Corporation
PO Box 697
Bellmawr, NJ 08099-0697
856-456-0284
Fax: 856-456-4078
Warehouse providing dry storage for food, groceries and general merchandise; transportation firm providing consolidation delivery program to all food related accounts in VA, OH and New England; rail siding available
Chariman & Founder: John Juzaitis
Number Employees: 20-49
Services: Freight consolidation delivery programs
Regions Served:
East Coast, Some Nationwide available

51855 Judge & Sons P Inc
201a Export St
Newark, NJ 07114-3242
973-491-0500
Fax: 973-491-0066 sales@judgeorg.com
www.judgeorg.com
Transportation firm providing local, long and short haul trucking for citric acid, gelatin, beer and paper
President: Patrick Judge
pjudge@judgeorg.com
Safety Director: Doug Freese
Ross Logistics: Thomas Shattuck
Number Employees: 100-249
Services: Local, long & short haul trucking for citric acid, gelatin, beer & paper

51856 K&J Logistics
1800 E 50th St N
Sioux Falls, SD 57104
605-332-6782
Fax: 605-332-6016 800-843-5624
info@kandjtrucking.com www.kandjtrucking.com
Transportation brokerage firm providing dry, refrigerated and frozen TL services
President: Shelley Koch
bboese@kandjtrucking.com
Contact: Brenda Boese
bboese@kandjtrucking.com
Number Employees: 20-49
Parent Co: K&J Trucking
Services: Dry, refrigerated & frozen TL
Regions Served:
48 States

51857 K&K Express
2980 Commers Drive
Suite 100
Eagan, MN 55121
651-209-8771
Fax: 651-209-8774 800-445-7213
Warehouse providing dry storage of nonperishable items; transportation firm providing international and domestic freight forwarding services via air freight and local, long and short haul trucking, LTL, TL, Flatbed, and oversized also available
Owner, CEO: Chris Walhof
Owner, CEO: Bettina Walhof
VP, Finance: Ryan Blazei
VP, Operations: Cheri Donovan
Business Development: Dan Bruton
Contact: Alycn Bjergo-Justen
abjergo-justen@k2logistics.com
VP, Operations: Dion Anderson
Number Employees: 10-19
Parent Co: K&K Express
Services: International & domestic freight forwarding via air freight & local, long & short haul trucking
Regions Served:
Worldwide

51858 KANE Freight Lines Inc
3 Stauffer Industrial Park # 1
Taylor, PA 18517-9630
570-344-9801
Fax: 570-207-9781 888-356-5263
info@kaneisable.com www.kaneisable.com
Warehouse providing cold, frozen, humidity-controlled and dry storage for food products; transportation firm providing trucking, LTL and consolidation in the Northeast corridor
CEO: Michael J Gardner
CEO: Richard Kane
Number Employees: 10-19
Services: Trucking, LTL & consolidation
Regions Served:
Northeast corridor

Transportation Firms / A-Z

51859 KLLM Transport Svc LLC
135 Riverview Dr
Richland, MS 39218-4401   601-939-2545
            Fax: 601-936-7151 800-925-1000
                    www.kllm.com
Transportation firm providing TL local, short and long trucking of temperature-controlled and dry commodities; truck and trailer leasing services available
President/CEO: James M Richards Jr
CFO: Kevin Adams
VP Operations: Greg Carpenter
Number Employees: 1000-4999
Services: TL local, short & long haul trucking
Regions Served:
  Continental U.S., Canada & Mexico

51860 KW Transportation Services
496 Fricks Lock Rd
Pottstown, PA 19464   610-323-1691
Transportation broker providing TL and LTL services for dry and frozen goods
Owner: Elizabeth Wilson
Number Employees: 5-9
Services: TL & LTL for dry & frozen goods
Regions Served:
  Nationwide, Canada & Mexico

51861 Kak LLC
1507 S Olive St
PO Box 3559
South Bend, IN 46619-4213   574-232-9357
        Fax: 574-282-1377 ken@kakllc.com
                    www.kakllc.com
Warehouse providing dry storage for nonperishable items; transportation firm providing ocean freight services; also, rail siding, importing/exporting, labeling, blocking and bracing, container stuffing, crating and consolidation and FTZ services available
Owner/Managing Member: Kenneth Kanczuzewski
bob@kakllc.com
Site Manager: Bob Fitzpatrick
bob@kakllc.com
Plant Manager: Robert Fitzpatrick
Number Employees: 5-9
Services: Ocean freight

51862 Kedem
72 New Hook Rd
Bayonne, NJ 07002   718-369-4600
               customercare@kayco.com
                    www.kayco.com
Kosher, gluten free and all natural products. Kosher grape juice, non-alcoholic wines, jams and, cooking products and biscuits.
President: Ilan Ron
CEO: Mordy Herzog
Financial Manager: Dov Levi
Executive Vice President: Harold Weiss
Year Founded: 1948
Estimated Sales: $50-90 Million
Number of Brands: 23
Parent Co: Kayco
Type of Packaging: Consumer

51863 Kenco Group Inc
2001 Riverside Dr # 3000
Chattanooga, TN 37406-4303   423-756-5552
        Fax: 423-756-1529 800-758-3289
     info@kencogroup.com www.kencogroup.com
Warehouse providing cooler, humidity controlled and dry storage for groceries, confectionery items and general merchandise; transportation broker providing trucking, carrier selection, etc.; also, rail siding, re-packing and labeling available
President: James Kennedy Jr
kennedy.kennedy@kencogroup.com
Number Employees: 100-249
Services: Broker: dedicated fleet, routing, carrier selection, drayage, etc.
Regions Served:
  U.S.A. & Canada

51864 Kenco Logistic Svc LLC
2001 Riverside Dr # 3000
Chattanooga, TN 37406-4303   423-756-5552
                             800-758-3289
               info@kencogroup.com
            www.kencologisticservices.com
Warehouse providing cooler and dry storage, re-packing and labeling for nonperishable and refrigerated foods; transportation firm providing long haul trucking
CEO: Gary Mayfield
gary.mayfield@kencogroup.com
Number Employees: 1-4
Parent Co: Kenco Group
Services: Long haul trucking
Regions Served:
  Nationwide

51865 Kennesaw Transportation
3794 Highway 411 NE
Rydal, GA 30171-1501   678-792-0001
        Fax: 770-382-3011 800-624-2024
             patrick@kennesawtrans.com
                www.kennesawtrans.com
Transportation firm providing refrigerated long haul trucking
President: Charles Patrick
cwp@kennesawtrans.com
VP/General Manager: Chuck Patrick
Sales Manager: Coy Parker
Director of Maintenance: Taylor Wilson
Number Employees: 20-49
Other Locations:
  KTI Logistics
  Atlanta, GA KTI Logistics
Services: Refrigerated long haul trucking
Regions Served:
  Southeast, West Coast

51866 Kentucky Container Svc
4300 Fern Valley Rd
Louisville, KY 40219-1985   502-810-9979
        Fax: 502-810-9973 don_farris@kyfi.com
                    www.kyfi.com
Transportation firm providing international ocean and air freight forwarding services
President/CEO: Don Farris
Cio/Cto: Mack Thompson
mack_thompson@kyfi.com
VP Sales/Operations: Kurt Terhar
Number Employees: 100-249
Services: Ocean & air freight forwarding
Regions Served:
  International

51867 Keokuk Junction Railway
1318 S Johanson Rd
Peoria, IL 61607-1162   309-697-1400
        Fax: 309-697-5387 www.pioneer-railcorp.com
Transportation company providing railroad service
CEO: J Michael Carr
Contact: Robert Athen
athen@pioneer-railcorp.com
Estimated Sales: F
Number Employees: 100-249
Services: Railroad
Regions Served:
  Nationwide, Canada

51868 Keys Fisheries Market & Marina
3502 Gulfview Ave
Marathon, FL 33050-2362   305-743-4353
        Fax: 305-743-3562 866-743-4353
             keys.fisheries@comcast.net
                www.keysfisheries.com
Processor and wholesaler of seafood products.
Owner: Gary Graves
keysfisheries@comcast.net
Vice President: Gary Graves
Estimated Sales: $1-2.5 Million
Number Employees: 20-49
Type of Packaging: Consumer, Food Service

51869 Kimball & Thompson Produce
305 S Lincoln St
Lowell, AR 72745   479-872-0200
        Fax: 479-872-2786 chris@ktproduce.com
                    ktproduce.com
Wholesaler/distributor of produce and frozen food.
Owner: Chris Thompson
Chief Financial Officer: Giina Brown
Purchasing: Octavio Galindo
Estimated Sales: $27 Million
Number Employees: 23

51870 Kingston Fresh
477 Shoup Ave
Suite 207
Idaho Falls, ID 83402-3658   208-522-2365
        Fax: 208-552-7488 www.kingstonfresh.com
Potatoes; onions; broccoli; sweet pineapples; and lettuce.
President: Mike Kingston
CEO: Dave Kingston
Number Employees: 5-9
Type of Packaging: Consumer, Food Service
Services: Trucking

51871 Kline Transportation
504 Rogers Road
New Castle, DE 19720   302-655-5184
        Fax: 610-582-4404 888-720-5195
                www.kleintransportation.com
Transportation firm providing local, short and long haul trucking
CEO/Pres.: Joseph Kline
Number Employees: 20-49
Services: Local, short & long haul trucking
Regions Served:
  DC, DE, MD, NJ, NY & PA

51872 Klomar Ship Supplies Inc
PO BOX 1118
Mobile, AL 36633   251-471-1153
              Fax: 504-243-9301
         www.klomarshipsupplies.samsbiz.com/
Transportation company providing ocean transport
Owner: Mike Kloumassis

51873 Konoike Pacific California
1420 Coil Ave
Wilmington, CA 90744-2205   310-830-2326
        Fax: 310-518-3900 rburke@kpaccoldstorage.com
                www.kpaccoldstorage.com
Warehouse offering cooler, dry and freezer storage of frozen, refrigerated and nonperishable food products; transportation firm providing refrigerated trucking services including short and local haul
Vice President: Yutaka Kohara
ykohara@konoike-usa.com
Vice President Administration: Kane Urabe
Vice President of Sales: Doug Lopez
Vice President of Operations: Jeff Waite
Number Employees: 100-249
Services: Refrigerated trucking: local & short haul
Regions Served:
  CA

51874 L & L Truck Broker Inc
607 E 2nd St
Stuttgart, AR 72160-3739   870-673-2641
                www.leetruckbroker.com
Transportation services include brokering
Owner: Teresa Fischer
lltruck@centurytel.net
Number Employees: 1-4
Services: Transportation brokering
Regions Served:
  Nationwide

51875 L B Transport Inc
615 1st Ave NE
PO Box 10
Buffalo Center, IA 50424-7687 641-562-2048
        Fax: 641-562-2137 800-458-2048
                www.lbtransportinc.com
Transportation firm providing local, short and long haul trucking
Owner: Terry Kiewiet
terry.kiewiet@kiewiet.com
Owner: Sue Kiewiet
Safety Director: Sher Blomster
Sales: Todd Corporon
terry.kiewiet@kiewiet.com
Number Employees: 20-49
Services: Local, short & long haul trucking
Regions Served:
  Nationwide & Canada

51876 LCL Bulk Transport Inc
2100 Riverside Dr
Green Bay, WI 54301-2375   920-431-3500
        Fax: 920-431-3501 800-284-4321
         info@lclbulk.com www.lclbulk.com
Transportation firm providing long and short haul trucking of liquid and dry bulk food products liquid food transporter
Manager: Paul Denissen
paul.denissen@lclbulk.com
Number Employees: 20-49
Services: Long & short haul trucking of liquid & dry bulk food products
Regions Served:
  Continental U.S., Canada & Mexico

Transportation Firms / A-Z

51877 LMD Integrated Logistic Services
3136 E Victoria St
Compton, CA 90221-5618 310-605-5100
Fax: 310-605-5337 www.lmdlogistics.com
Warehouse providing dry and cooler storage for nonperishable and refrigerated foods; transportation services include short haul trucking in the Southwest
CEO: Louis Diblosi
CFO: Marilyn Zakis
VP Sales: Bill Sampson
Contact: Robert Spilabotte
rspilabotte@lmdlogistics.com
COO: Lou Diblosi
Number Employees: 5-9
Parent Co: LMD Integrated Logistics Services
Services: Short haul trucking
Regions Served:
Southwest

51878 LT's Brokerage
P.O.Box 415
Broken Arrow, OK 74013-0415 918-251-2044
Transportation broker for refrigerated and frozen foods, as well as dry. All types of equipment
President: Lyle Tracy
Number Employees: 5-9
Services: Van transportation for refrigerated & frozen foods
Regions Served:
Domestic & International

51879 La Grou Cold Storage
4300 S Halsted St
Chicago, IL 60609 773-523-2449
Warehouse offering cold, frozen, dry and humidity-controlled storage for food products; rail siding available; transportation firm providing local, long and short haul trucking
Number Employees: 50-99
Square Footage: 2000000
Parent Co: La Grou Distribution System
Services: Local, long & short haul
Regions Served:
Midwest

51880 Lake Erie Warehouse & Distribution Center
5650 Wattsburg Rd
Erie, PA 16509-4066 814-824-6077
Fax: 814-825-5914
Warehouse providing dry storage for nonperishable items; transportation firm providing LTL, local, long and short haul trucking; also, air freight, expediting and truck rentals, leasing and maintenance available
Manager: Mike Mc Leod
Number Employees: 100-249
Parent Co: TWL Corporation
Services: LTL, local, long & short haul trucking; also, air freight, expediting & truck rentals, leasing & maintenance
Regions Served:
Continental U.S. & Canada

51881 Land Span
1120 Griffin Rd
Lakeland, FL 33805 863-688-1102
Fax: 863-688-8875 www.landspan.com
Transportation company providing refrigerated trucking including local, long and short haul; serving nationwide
President: Roger Reed
VP Sales: Mike McSwain
Contact: Debbie Craft
debbie.craft@landspan.com
Estimated Sales: G
Number Employees: 50-99
Parent Co: Watkins Associated Industries
Services: Refrigerated trucking: local, long & short
Regions Served:
Eastern U.S., Canada, Mexico

51882 Landstar System, Inc
13410 Sutton Park Dr S
Jacksonville, FL 32224 904-398-9400
800-872-9400
www.landstar.com
Warehouse providing storage space, and a transportation firm providing long haul trucking.
President & CEO: Jim Gattoni
Vice President & CFO: Kevin Stout
Vice President & CIO: Rick Coro
VP/Chief Commercial Officer: Rob Brasher
VP/General Counsel/Secretary: Michael Kneller
VP/Chief Safety & Operations Officer: Joe Beacom
Year Founded: 1991
Estimated Sales: $3.6 Billion
Number Employees: 1,273
Other Locations:
Landstar Express America
Charlotte, SC
Landstar Ligon
Madisonville, KY
Landstar Logistics
Dublin, CALandstar Express
AmericaMadisonville
Services: Long haul trucking
Regions Served:
Nationwide, Canada & Mexico

51883 Laney & Duke Terminal Wrhse Co
1560 Jessie St
Jacksonville, FL 32206-6008 904-798-3500
Fax: 904-356-2605 info@laneyduke.com
www.laneyduke.com
Warehouse providing cooler, dry and humidity-controlled storage; transportation firm providing local haul trucking; also, consolidation, refrigeration and rail siding available
President: Thomas Duke
thomas@laneyduke.com
Number Employees: 50-99
Services: Local haul trucking
Regions Served:
FL & GA

51884 Langham Logistics
5335 W 74th St
Indianapolis, IN 46268-4180 317-290-0227
Fax: 317-290-0321 855-214-2844
info@elangham.com www.elangham.com
Warehouse providing dry storage; transportation firm providing LTL, TL, international and domestic freight forwarding services via air freight and expedited local, long and short haul trucking; logistics company providing freightmanagement, warehousing, distribution, tracking, and inventory
Owner: Trent Adams
trentadams@elangham.com
Vice President, Finance: John Langham
Vice President, Operations: Margaret Langham
Number Employees: 50-99
Services: International & domestic freight forwarding via air freight and expedited local, long & short haul trucking
Regions Served:
Worldwide: domestic and international

51885 Laub International
1051 Clinton St
Buffalo, NY 14206-2823 716-853-3703
Fax: 716-852-0136 laub@laubinternational.com
www.laubinternational.com
Transportation firm providing freight forwarding in North America; warehouse providing storage for dry goods, alcoholic beverages, machinery, paper products, etc.; also, re-packing, heated facilities, pick/pack, rail siding, crossdocking, distribtuion, assembly, consolidation, bulk, and light assembly services available
President: James Dusel
cczajka@laubinternational.com
Site Manager: Camille Czaka
cczajka@laubinternational.com
Number Employees: 10-19
Square Footage: 1440000
Services: Freight forwarding
Regions Served:
North America, Canada

51886 Lee Truck Broker Inc
2302 S Main St
Stuttgart, AR 72160-7003 870-673-6921
Fax: 870-673-7980 info@leetruckbroker.com
www.leetruckbroker.com
Contract transportation broker handling paper, canned goods, fresh and frozen seafood, produce, etc.; also, refrigerated vans and reefers available
President: Randall Lee
randylee@leetruckbroker.com
Number Employees: 10-19
Services: Broker handling paper, canned goods, fresh & frozen seafood, produce & vegetables; also, refrigerated vans & reefers
Regions Served:
Nationwide & Canada

51887 Lehigh-Pocono WarehouseInc
723 Bangor Rd
Nazareth, PA 18064-9389 610-759-7177
Warehouse providing dry storage for packaging and corrugated materials, food products, glass bottles, yarn, etc.; transportation firm providing local haul trucking; re-packing, picking/distribution and cross docking available
Owner: Merlin Tucker
Estimated Sales: Less Than $500,000
Number Employees: 1-4
Services: Local haul trucking
Regions Served:
PA

51888 Lester Coggins Trucking
P.O.Box 55
Okahumpka, FL 34762-0055 352-326-8900
Fax: 352-365-1181 800-874-3344
Transportation firm providing long haul, LTL and TL trucking, hauling orange juice, milk, frozen foods, fresh produce, plastics, grocery, paper goods, etc.
President: Dan Denhof
Estimated Sales: G
Number Employees: 100-249
Parent Co: Gainey Corporation
Services: Long haul, LTL & TL trucking
Regions Served:
National

51889 Lewis Storage
2751 Patterson St # 5
Greensboro, NC 27407-2335 336-275-8458
Fax: 336-370-9303 blewis@lewisstorage.com
www.lewisstorage.com
Warehouse providing storage for dry foods and general merchandise; transportation firm providing TL and LTL services; also rail siding available
President: Buster Lewis
blewis@lewisstorage.com
Number Employees: 5-9
Square Footage: 1400000
Services: LTL & TL
Regions Served:
NC, SC & VA

51890 Lincoln Cold Storage
1700 S Folsom St # A
Lincoln, NE 68522-1648 402-474-2653
Fax: 402-474-1605 www.lincolncoldstorage.com
Warehouse offering 2.2 million cubic feet of cooler and freezer storage; also, blast freezing available
Owner: Barry Nelson
susanlics@aol.com
Estimated Sales: Less Than $500,000
Number Employees: 5-9
Services: Short haul trucking
Regions Served:
Midwest

51891 Linden Warehouse & Dstrbtn Co
11 Distribution Blvd
Edison, NJ 08817-6005 732-287-5500
Fax: 908-662-7539 www.lindenwarehouse.com
Warehouse providing cooler and dry storage for refrigerated and nonperishable foods; transportation firm providing long and short haul trucking; also, re-packing, labeling, etc. services available
President: Debbie Salz
d.salz@lindenwarehouse.com
VP Finance: Michael Dotro
VP: Michael Salz
Operations Manager: Joe Adornetto
Number Employees: 10-19
Square Footage: 3600000
Parent Co: Linden Warehouse & Distribution Company
Type of Packaging: Bulk
Services: Long & short haul trucking
Regions Served:
Nationwide

51892 Live Oak Warehouse
17478 Texas 62
Orange, TX 77630 409-735-8193
Fax: 409-735-9462

Transportation Firms / A-Z

Warehouse providing dry storage of nonperishable food items; transportation firm offering long and short haul trucking; also, re-packing and labeling available
Manager: Paul Bertrand
Number Employees: 20-49
Services: Long & short haul trucking
Regions Served:
  Nationwide

51893 Logisco
1600 Gregory St
N Little Rock, AR 72114-4360   501-375-3755
                           Fax: 501-375-8834
Warehouse providing cooler and freezer storage for frozen goods; transportation firm providing short and local haul trucking
President: Cliff Jones
VP: Phillip Webb
General Manager: Mike Snow
Estimated Sales: $2.5-5 Million
Number Employees: 100-249
Services: Local & short haul trucking
Regions Served:
  AR

51894 Logistics Amber Worldwide
14760 175th St
Jamaica, NY 11434-5415   718-244-8923
  Fax: 718-244-8665 keith@amberworldwide.com
Warehouse providing dry storage for nonperishable foods; transportation services include ocean freight forwarding, long and short haul trucking, ocean, air and rail freight forwarding
Owner: Elaine Rosendorff
elaine@amberworldwide.com
VP: Keith Milliner
Number Employees: 10-19
Parent Co: AWLI Group
Services: Ocean freight forwarding, long & short haul trucking, rail & air
Regions Served:
  Worldwide

51895 Lone Elm Sales Inc
N9695 Van Dyne Rd
Van Dyne, WI 54979-9799   920-688-2338
  Fax: 920-688-5233   800-950-8275
                 www.loneelm.com
Transportatoin services
President: Glen Dedow
Vice President: Matthew Dedow
Manager: Matt Dedow
mdedow@loneelm.com
Estimated Sales: Below $ 5 Million
Number Employees: 20-49
Type of Packaging: Private Label

51896 (HQ)Los Angeles Cold Storage Co
400 S Central Ave
Los Angeles, CA 90013-1785   213-624-1831
               Fax: 213-680-4723 central@lacold.com
                              www.lacold.com
Warehouse providing a total of 6,694,000 Cu Ft. of cooler and freezer storage; also, rail siding, blast freezing, cross docking, repacking; transportation firm offering nationwide and local service
President: Larry Rauch
Warehouse Manager: Terry Miller
Number Employees: 100-249
Parent Co: Standard-Southern Southern Corporation
Type of Packaging: Private Label
Other Locations:
  Total: 1,148,000 Cu Ft
  410 South CentralTotal: 1,148,000 Cu Ft440 South Central
Services: Trucload, and less than truckload
Regions Served:
  Local, and Nationwide

51897 Louisiana Fresh Express
18120 Old Covington Highway
Suite B
Hammond, LA 70403-0652   985-542-1256
                           Fax: 985-898-5993
Transportation services
President: Mark Malkemus

51898 Lucca Freezer & Cold Storage
2321 Industrial Way
Vineland, NJ 08360-1551   856-690-9000
    Fax: 856-690-0700 info@luccacoldstorage.com
Bonded warehouse providing cooler, freezer, dry and humidity-controlled storage for produce, frozen and fresh foods, fish, etc.; transportation broker providing short and long haul trucking; also, re-packing, cold treatment and railsiding available
President: J Michael Lucca
Manager: Rusty Lucca
Repacking Manager: John Carillo
Number Employees: 250-499
Services: Long & short haul trucking & brokerage
Regions Served:
  Continental U.S., Canada

51899 Ludtke Pacific TruckingInc
4059 Bakerview Valley Rd
Bellingham, WA 98226-7729   360-733-6670
         Fax: 360-733-6835 info@ludtke.com
                              www.ludtke.com
Transportation firm providing refrigerated local, short and long haul trucking services
President: Lloyd A Ludtke
lloa@ludtke.com
VP: Lex A Ludtke
Secretary: Lance Ludtke
Office Manager: Charity Ventresca
Number Employees: 50-99
Services: Refrigerated local, short & long haul trucking
Regions Served:
  48 States, British Columbia

51900 Lufthansa Cargo
3400 Peachtree Rd NE # 1225
Atlanta, GA 30326-1170   404-814-5310
                           800-542-2746
                 lhcargo-northamerica@dlh.de
                 www.lufthansa-cargo.com
Transportation company providing international air shipping and air express cargo services
Chairman and CEO: Peter Gerber
Finance and Human Resources: Dr. Martin Schmitt
VP: Klaus Holler
Product and Sales: Dr. Andreas Otto
Operations: Dr. Karl-Rudolf Rupprecht
Number Employees: 500-999
Parent Co: Lufthansa German Airlines
Services: Air shipping & air express cargo services
Regions Served:
  International

51901 Lumber & Things
PO Box 386
Keyser, WV 26726   304-788-5600
       Fax: 304-788-7823   800-296-5656
                 www.lumberandthings.com
We have been in business for over 30 years. Our customers depend on the standards that we build on: Honesty-Quality-Service. We produce: Reconditioned, Remanufactured and New pallets; Reconditioned, Remanufactured and Recycled tier/slipsheets; Reconditioned, Remanufactured and New top frames; Reconditioned and New can and glass bulk pallets. With an attendant standing by our 24 hour hotline we can provide your company with delivery within 24 hours of your phone call.
President: Jack Amoruso
National Accounts Manager: Victor Knight
Customer Service Specialist: Patricia Davis
Plant Manager: Jack Amoruso
Purchasing Director: Ken Winter
Number Employees: 100-249
Square Footage: 150000
Type of Packaging: Consumer, Food Service, Private Label, Bulk
Services: Freight
Regions Served:
  West Virginia, Maryland, Delaware, Virginia, Ohio, Pennsylvania, Puerto Rico, Columbia, Venezuela, China

51902 Lykes Lines
401 E Jackson St Ste 3300
Tampa, FL 33602   813-276-4600
       Fax: 813-276-4619   800-834-6314
       USFLAG@HLAG.COM www.lykeslines.com
Transportation brokers; for other state listings visit the web
President and CEO: John Murray
CEO: John Murray
Contact: Ross Stemmler
ross.stemmler@hlag.com
Number Employees: 250-499
Regions Served:
  Nationwide & Internationally

51903 Lynden Transport Inc
18000 International Blvd
Suite 800
Seattle, WA 98188   206-241-8778
    Fax: 206-243-8415   888-596-3361
                 www.lynden.com
Transportation firm providing local, long and short haul trucking, freight consolidation and forwarding, barge and steamship service, reefers and heated vans for perishables and KFF.
Estimated Sales: $50-100 Million
Number Employees: 100-249
Services: Local, long & short haul trucking, steamships & barges, freight forwarding & consolidation, reefers & heated vans
Regions Served:
  AK

51904 M & W Logistics Group
1110 Pumping Station Rd
Nashville, TN 37210-2219   615-256-5755
       Fax: 615-726-3568   800-251-4209
            info@mwlginc.com www.mwlginc.com
Contractor of public warehouse services providing dry storage, re-packing and labeling for nonperishable foods; truckload services include long and short haul trucking in Tennessee and the Midwest
President: Mike Mcfarlin
mmcfarlin@mwtrans.com
Executive Vice President: Mark Boyette
Director of Business Development: Jason Pitt
Executive Vice President: Mark Boyette
Estimated Sales: $5-10 Million
Number Employees: 5-9
Square Footage: 800000
Services: Short & long haul trucking
Regions Served:
  TN & Midwest, East Coast

51905 MBX Logistics, LLC
6990 Creditview Rd
Suite 5
Mississauga, ON L5N 8R9
Canada   905-363-7000
    Fax: 905-363-6905 MBXSales@mbxlogistics.com
Supply chain and 3rd party logistic specialist in the food and beverage industry
Parent Co: Reyes Holdings, LLC

51906 (HQ)MCT Terminal & Transport Inc.
2555 Dollard Avenue
Lasalle, QC H8N 3A9
Canada   514-363-3100
       Fax: 514-363-3303   800-363-6493
            info@mct.ca www.mct.ca
Warehouse providing dry storage; transportation firm providing local, long and short haul trucking in Canada
Number Employees: 10-19
Services: Trucking: local, long & short haul
Regions Served:
  Canada

51907 MO Air International
183 Madison Avenue
Suite 1202
New York, NY 10016   212-792-9400
       Fax: 212-490-1763   800-247-3131
                 www.moair-usa.com
Manager: Sherry Kawabe
Parent Co: Mitsui & Co.

51908 (HQ)MTE Logistix
14627 128th Avenue NW
Edmonton, AB T5L 3H3
Canada   780-944-9009
    Fax: 780-451-3340 mteinfo@mtelogistix.com
                 www.mtelogistix.com
Warehouse providing cooler and dry storage for general merchandise, groceries and refrigerated foods; transportation services include local haul trucking; rail siding, consolidation, freight forwarding and crossdock available
President: Michael Haas
Chairman/CEO: Dennis Nolin
VP Finance: Gloria Morhun
Number Employees: 70
Square Footage: 4400000
Other Locations:
  MTE Logistix
  Delta, BCMTE Logistix
Services: Local haul trucking, freight forwarding

Transportation Firms / A-Z

51909 MacCosham Van Lines
1240 Sherwin Rd
Winnipeg, MB R3H 0V3
Canada 204-633-9225
www.maccosham.com
Warehouse providing cooler, freezer and dry storage for dry goods, groceries, appliances and chemicals; transportation firm providing local haul trucking and freight consolidation; also, rail siding, EDI bar coding, pick/pack, palletexchange, etc
President: Jay Lilge
Square Footage: 4000000
Services: Freight consolidation, local haul trucking & express service
Regions Served:
   Canada: coast to coast & U.S. points

51910 Maersk Sealand
P.O.Box 880
Madison, NJ 07940-0880 973-514-5000
Fax: 973-514-5410   www.maerskline.com
Transportation firm providing ocean freight nationwide and internationally
CEO: J Russell Bruner
Contact: Timothy Oconnell
timothy.oconnell@maersk.com
Number Employees: 10,000
Parent Co: A.P. Moller
Services: Ocean freight
Regions Served:
   Nationwide & Internationally

51911 Magic Valley Truck Brokers Inc
2906 S Featherly Way
Boise, ID 83709-2985 208-375-5677
Fax: 208-377-0956   800-635-3053
wes@magicvalleytruckbrokers.com
www.magicvalleytruckbrokers.com
Transportation broker providing reefer, vans and flatbed loads for fresh produce and frozen foods, and other products
Owner: Wes Blazer
wes@magicvalleytruckbrokers.com
Vice President: Debbie Blaser
Number Employees: 5-9
Services: Transportation brokers providing reefers, vans & flatbed loads for fresh produce & frozen foods other products
Regions Served:
   Nationwide, Canada & Mexico

51912 Majors Transit Inc
502 N Main St
Caneyville, KY 42721-9003 270-879-3010
Fax: 270-879-6401   800-732-4487
Transportation company providing local and short haul trucking
President: Jeff Majors
jeff.majors@majorstransit.com
Number Employees: 20-49
Services: Local & short haul trucking
Regions Served:
   IL, IN, KY, OH, TN, MO, VA, NC, SC, GA, AL, & MS

51913 Mallory Alexander Intl
4294 Swinnea Rd
Memphis, TN 38118-6620 901-367-9400
Fax: 901-370-4288   www.mallorygroup.com
Transportation firm providing international and domestic freight forwarding and local and short haul trucking
CEO: Neely Mallory
CFO: Geoff Collins
geoffcollins@mallorygroup.com
COO: Tina Sauter
Number Employees: 100-249
Parent Co: Mallory Group
Services: International & domestic freight forwarding and local & short haul trucking
Regions Served:
   Nationwide & international: Canada

51914 Mallory Alexander Intl
4294 Swinnea Rd
Memphis, TN 38118-6620 901-367-9400
Fax: 901-370-4288   800-257-8464
www.mallorygroup.com
Warehouse providing dry storage and labeling for nonperishable foods; transportation services include long haul trucking nationwide

Chairman & CEO: Neely Mallory
CFO: Geoff Collins
geoffcollins@mallorygroup.com
Estimated Sales: $ 10 - 20 Million
Number Employees: 100-249
Square Footage: 4000000
Services: Long haul trucking
Regions Served:
   Nationwide

51915 Manitoulin Group of Companies
9500 Venture Ave. S.E
Calgary, AB T3S 0A1
Canada Fax: 403-216-0880 888-640-9649
www.manitoulintransport.com
Warehouse providing cooler and dry storage for fresh and frozen foods, groceries and confectionery products; transportation firm providing local haul trucking; cross docking and temperature controlled LTL and TL shipment servicesavailable
Chief Executive Officer: Gord Smith
Number Employees: 100-249
Services: Local haul trucking: temperature controlled LTL & TL shipments
Regions Served:
   Western Canada

51916 Marten Transport LTD
129 Marten St.
Mondovi, WI 54755 855-336-1734
Fax: 715-926-5609   www.marten.com
Transportation firm providing short, long and local haul refrigerated trucking services.
President: Timothy Kohl
Chaiman/CEO: Randolph Marten
Executive VP/CFO: James Hinnendael
Executive VP, Sales & Marketing: Timothy Nash
Year Founded: 1946
Estimated Sales: $787.5 Million
Number Employees: 1000-4999
Other Locations:
   Forest Park, GA
   Ontario, CA
   Wilsonville, OR
   Indianapolis, INOntario
Services: Local, short & long haul refrigerated trucking
Regions Served:
   48 states & Canada

51917 Martin Warehousing & Distribution
1122 Mikole St
Honolulu, HI 96819 808-831-0405
Warehouse providing dry, cooler and humidity-controlled storage for groceries, health and beauty aids, soap and detergent, etc.; transportation firm providing local haul trucking and freight forwarding; also, re-packing and heat shrinkwrap
President: Jerry Anches
VP: Jan Brookshier
Number Employees: 20-49
Services: Local haul trucking & freight forwarding
Regions Served:
   HI

51918 (HQ)Massachusetts Central Railroad Corporation
2 Wilbraham St
Palmer, MA 01069-9649 413-283-5900
www.masscentralrr.com
Warehouse providing storage for dry products; customs house broker providing rail, intermodal and drayage services
VP: Gary Hoeppner
Number Employees: 10-19
Services: Customs house broker providing long & short haul trucking & rail, intermodal & drayage services
Regions Served:
   New England, NY, NJ & Montreal, Canada

51919 Match Maker
2736 Tv Rd
Florence, SC 29501-0705 843-665-4968
Fax: 843-665-5073   800-226-3696
Transportation broker providing services including freight forwarding, expedited air, LTL, TL, broker bonds and truck fuel tax bonds
Owner: Bert Belk
bert@mhmk.com

Estimated Sales: Less Than $500,000
Number Employees: 1-4
Parent Co: Sun Belt Line
Services: Broker providing freight forwarding, expedited air, LTL, TL, broker bonds & truck fuel tax bonds
Regions Served:
   U.S.A., Canada & Mexico

51920 Matchmaker Transportation Services
PO Box 3005
Wilmington, NC 28406-5 800-849-0197
Transportation broker providing rail car services and local, long and short haul trucking
Number Employees: 10-19
Services: Brokerage: rail car & local, long & short haul trucking
Regions Served:
   U.S. Canada & Mexico

51921 (HQ)Mauser Packaging Solutions
1515 W 22nd St
Suite 1100
Oak Brook, IL 60523 800-527-2267
www.mauserpackaging.com
Recyclable bulk packaging, bulk handling and shipping, and warehouse storage of both liquids and solids.
President & CEO: Kenneth Roessler
Chief Financial Officer: Tom De Weerdt
EVP, Procurement & Logistics: Leslie Bradshaw
Chief Information Officer: Ed DePrimo
EVP/General Counsel/CCO: Patrick Sheller
Year Founded: 2018
Estimated Sales: Over $1 Billion
Number Employees: 11,000
Type of Packaging: Bulk

51922 Mayberry RFD
P.O.Box 1108
Mount Airy, NC 27030 336-786-2388
Transportation broker providing services nationwide
Owner: Tom Webb
Number Employees: 1-4
Regions Served:
   Nationwide

51923 McCann's Piggyback Consolidation
575 Rudder Rd # 109
Fenton, MO 63026-2005 636-343-5222
Fax: 636-343-7559   800-533-6243
Transportation firm providing long and short haul trucking; also, piggyback drayage services available
Owner: Donna Mc Cann
CEO: Bill McCann
CFO: Donna McCann
Gen. Mgr./Dir. Sales & Mrktg: Bernie Gala
Operations: Michele Meyer
Services: Long & short haul trucking; also, piggyback drayage

51924 (HQ)McLean Cargo Specialists
16680 Central Green Blvd
Houston, TX 77032-5131 281-443-2777
Fax: 281-443-3777
Transportation firm providing freight consolidation for dry products via international air and ocean services; also, export packaging available
Number Employees: 50-99
Other Locations:
   McLean Cargo Specialists
   Miami, FLMcLean Cargo Specialists
Services: Freight forwarding for dry products via air & ocean services
Regions Served:
   International

51925 Mccracken Motor Freight
2155 W Broadway
Eugene, OR 97402-2796 541-484-6400
Fax: 541-484-6408   800-452-8995
www.mccrackenmotorfreight.com
Warehouse offering dry, cold and frozen storage for food products, commodities and household goods; transportation firm providing local trucking; also, re-packing, break bulk and rail siding available
Division Manager: Al Green
Manager: Mike Fox

Transportation Firms / A-Z

Estimated Sales: Less Than $500,000
Number Employees: 1-4
Square Footage: 108000
Parent Co: McCracken Brothers Motor Freight
Services: Local distribution: dry box & refrigerated
Regions Served:
  Pacific N.W.

51926 Melvin L. Jones Transportation Broker
2414 S Patterson St
Valdosta, GA 31601   229-245-1246
                Fax: 229-245-0382
Transportation broker specializing in long, short, local haul trucking, using reefers, flatbeds and vans
President: Melvin Jones
Number Employees: 5-9
Services: Brokerage
Regions Served:
  Nationwide

51927 (HQ)Merchandise Warehouse
1414 S West St
Indianapolis, IN 46225-1548   317-632-2525
     Fax: 317-266-0784   800-433-7107
           info@mwindy.com   www.mwindy.com
Warehouse providing cooler, freezer and dry storage for food and nonfood items; transportation services include TL short and long haul trucking; also, warehouse and office lease space and rail siding available
Chairman/CEO: Tim Siddiq
Sales Exec: Joe Daily
Number Employees: 20-49
Services: Full truckload
Regions Served:
  Midwest/Indiana

51928 Merchants Distribution Svc
1420 11th Ave NE
Altoona, IA 50009-1659   515-967-1194
     Fax: 515-244-7748   800-228-5009
           sales@merchantsdsm.com
           www.merchantsdsm.com
Warehouse providing dry and humidity-controlled storage for foods and paper; transportation services include LTL local and short haul trucking and freight consolidation; distribution, piggybacking and rail siding available
President: Greg Dickinson
Vice President: Randy Worth
Manager: Randy Worth
Number Employees: 20-49
Services: LTL local & short haul trucking
Regions Served:
  Midwest

51929 Mesa Cold Storage
9602 W Buckeye Rd
Tolleson, AZ 85353-9101   623-478-9392
           dcouryjr@mesacold.com
           www.mesacold.com
Warehouse providing coooler, freezer and dry storage; wholesaler/distributor of groceries; transportation firm providing local, long and short haul trucking
Owner: Dan Coury
Number Employees: 50-99
Square Footage: 200000
Services: In-house trucking
Regions Served:
  AZ, NV, UT, CO, NM & CA

51930 (HQ)Metro Park Warehouses Inc
6920 Executive Dr
Kansas City, MO 64120-2111   816-231-0777
                Fax: 816-231-7797
           metroparkwarehouses@mpwus.com
           www.metroparkwarehouses.com
Warehouse offering cooler, dry and temperature-controlled storage; also, rail siding, shrink wrapping, repacking and pallet display services available. Transportation firm providing local and long haul trucking, consolidation anddirect store delivery.
President: Robert Banach
bbanach@mpw-inc.com
Chairman: John Malinee
VP/Marketing: Steve Wedlan
Estimated Sales: $5 Million+
Number Employees: 50-99
Square Footage: 3790000
Type of Packaging: Consumer, Bulk
Services: Regional & local delivery

Regions Served:
  Mid-West

51931 Metropolitan Trucking Inc
299 Market St # 300
Saddle Brook, NJ 07663-5312   973-742-3000
     Fax: 201-843-6179   800-967-3278
           cs@mtrk.com   www.mtrk.com
Transportation company providing long and short haul trucking; warehouse providing dry storage for paper and food items
Owner: Ronald Gordy
rgordy@metrosoft-us.com
Chief Financial Officer: Matt Sullivan
EVP: Michael A. Maiore
Vice President of Maintenance: Wayne Beaudry
Number Employees: 1-4
Services: Long & short haul trucking
Regions Served:
  Nationwide

51932 Mid States Express Inc
540 W Galena Blvd Ste 1
Aurora, IL 60506   317-244-9995
                Fax: 630-820-4639
Transportation company providing local and short haul trucking
Owner: Bruce Hartman
Number Employees: 10-19
Services: Local & short haul trucking
Regions Served:
  IA, IL, IN, MI, MN, MO, WI & OH

51933 Mid-West Traffic
Hwy 7Rr Stn Main
Peterborough, ON K9J 6X3
Canada   705-743-5050
                Fax: 705-743-0782
Transportation broker providing long haul trucking for nonperishable foods and canned goods
Estimated Sales: $5-10 Million
Number Employees: 14
Services: Broker providing long haul trucking for non-perishable foods & canned goods
Regions Served:
  U.S., Canada & Mexico

51934 Midnite Express
1075 South Inner Loop Rd
Ste 201
Atlanta, GA 30337   770-933-9496
     Fax: 310-330-2358   800-643-6483
           nick.vincent@mnx.com   www.mnx.com
Warehouse providing dry storage; transportation firm providing international and domestic freight forwarding services via air freight, local, long and short haul trucking; also, re-packing services available
CEO: Scott Cannon
VP Operations: Nick Vincent
Number Employees: 1-4
Services: International & domestic freight forwarding via air freight, local, long & short haul trucking
Regions Served:
  Worldwide

51935 Midwest Coast Logistics LLC
1600 E Benson Rd
Sioux Falls, SD 57104-0871   605-339-8400
     Fax: 605-339-8407   800-843-9904
Transportation firm providing 48 state common and contract carrier services for general commodities with refrigerated and dry van equipment
President: Doug Sandvig
dsandvig@mctlog.com
Number Employees: 20-49
Parent Co: Comcar Industries
Other Locations:
  West Chicago, IL
  Sanford, FL
  Fridley, MNSanford
Services: Common & contract carrier of general commodities with refrigerated & dry van equipment
Regions Served:
  Nationwide

51936 Midwest Continental Inc
33941 Frelon Dr
Sioux City, IA 51108-8737   712-239-1613
     Fax: 712-239-1616   800-373-0810
           debi@midwestcontinental.com
           www.midwestcontinental.com

Transportation company providing superior logistics and services for the shippers and receivers for the frozen food industry
President: Deborah Weaver
debi@midwestcontinental.com
VP: Dave Frank
Number Employees: 50-99
Regions Served:
  Midwest

51937 Milan Supply Chain Solutions
1091 Kefauver Dr
Milan, TN 38358-3412   731-686-7428
     Fax: 731-686-8829   800-231-7303
           www.milanexpress.com
Warehouse providing short, and long term storage; transportation firm providing local and short haul trucking, and specializing in LTL, TL, and logistics
President: John Ross
jross@milanexpress.com
Number Employees: 100-249
Services: Short & local haul trucking
Regions Served:
  South

51938 Miller Container Corp
3402 78th Ave W
Rock Island, IL 61201-7331   309-787-6161
     Fax: 309-787-1213   www.millercontainer.com
Warehouse providing dry storage for corrugated sheets and boxes; transportation firm providing local and short haul trucking
President: Mike Vonderhaar
VP Sales: Jeff Peterson
Estimated Sales: $20-50 Million
Number Employees: 100-249
Square Footage: 300000
Services: Local & short haul trucking
Regions Served:
  Upper Midwest

51939 Minn-Dak Transport Inc
Highway 59 S
Pelican Rapids, MN 56572   218-863-5450
           www.minndak.com
Transportation services include brokerage and local haul trucking;produce and nursery goods included
President: Jeanne Hovland
anne@minndak.com
Estimated Sales: Less Than $500,000
Number Employees: 1-4
Services: Transportation brokers & local trucking
Regions Served:
  Nationwide, International & Canada

51940 Mo-Ark Truck Services
P.O.Box 16922
Kansas City, MO 64133   816-356-1250
                            877-290-2520
           info@truckingregister.com
           www.truckingregister.com
Transportation broker providing nationwide back haul services; ICC licensed
Number Employees: 1-4
Services: Back haul services
Regions Served:
  Nationwide, Regional & Local

51941 Modesto & Empire Traction Co
530 11th St
P.O.Box 1606
Modesto, CA 95354-3518   209-524-4631
     Fax: 209-529-0336   metblico@metrr.com
           www.metrr.com
Transportation services include line railroad
Manager: Butch Pirrone
Number Employees: 20-49
Services: Line Railroad
Regions Served:
  Nationwide, Canada, Mexico

51942 Moody Dunbar Inc
2000 Waters Edge Dr # 21
Johnson City, TN 37604-8312 423-952-0100
                Fax: 423-952-0289
           customerservice@moodydunbar.com
           www.moodydunbar.com
Processor of bell peppers, pimientos and sweet potatoes, products are certified Kosher
CEO: Stanley Dunbar
CFO: Christy Dunbar
R&D/Quality Assurance Manager: Katie Rohrbacher Nixa
Vice President of Sales & Marketing: Ed Simerly

Transportation Firms / A-Z

Estimated Sales: $37,000,000
Number Employees: 20-49
Number of Brands: 11
Type of Packaging: Consumer, Food Service, Private Label
Other Locations:
Saticoy Foods Corporation
Santa Paula, CA
Dunbar Foods Corporation
Dunn, NCSaticoy Foods CorporationDunn

51943 Moody's Quick
54 N. 48th Avenue
Ste. B
Phoenix, AZ 85043   602-861-2121
    Fax: 602-861-3852   800-528-0668
customerservice@moodysquick.com
www.moodysquick.com
Transportation company hauling dry and refrigerated freight, also domestic air is available
President: Mark Doughty
Contact: Darryl Herman
darryl.herman@moodysquick.com
Number Employees: 10-19
Services: Local
Regions Served:
Southwest (AZ; NM; NV; CA)

51944 (HQ)Moran Distribution Centers
1000 Estes Ave
Elk Grove Vlg, IL 60007-4908   847-439-0000
    Fax: 847-439-0047   webmaster@morandist.com
www.morantransportation.com
Warehouse providing dry, cooler and humidity-controlled storage for nonperishable goods; transportation firm providing local and short haul trucking; rail siding available
President: Michael Moran Sr
VP Sales: Michael Moran
Director Operations: Michael Mahler
Number Employees: 100-249
Type of Packaging: Consumer, Food Service
Regions Served:
Regional: Midwest & Northern IL

51945 Moran Logistics
202 East 7th street
P O Box 295
Watsontown, PA 17777-0295   570-538-5558
    Fax: 570-538-1432   800-223-1093
info@moranlogistics.com
www.moranlogistics.com
Warehouse providing dry storage for nonperishable foods; transportation firm providing local haul trucking
President: John Moran
Vice President: Joyce Arcarese
National Accounts Manager: Sharon Wilson
Customer Service: Dwuana Brown
VP Operations: Jeff Stroehmann
Number Employees: 20-49
Regions Served:
48 States

51946 Morristown & Erie Railway Inc
49 Abbett Ave
Morristown, NJ 07960-4334   973-267-4300
    Fax: 973-267-3138   sfriedland@merail.com
www.merail.com
Transportation firm providing local and regional rail car service
President: Wesley R Weis
wweis@merail.com
Number Employees: 20-49
Services: Railroad
Regions Served:
North East

51947 Mountain America Shippers
1125 E 13200 S
Draper, UT 84020-9063
    Fax: 801-973-0161   kimashippers@qwest.net
Transportation firm providing LTL distribution and freight forwarding services of general merchandise; also, van-container freight services available
General Manager: Kim Lamoreaux
Number Employees: 1-4
Services: LTL distribution & freight forwarding of general commodities; also, van-container freight services
Regions Served:
Western States

51948 Murphy Bonded Warehouse
2391 Levy St
Shreveport, LA 71103-3657   318-636-9000
    Fax: 318-636-6752   800-252-7467
www.mbwinc.com
Transportation firm providing TL and LTL local haul trucking, piggyback and freight consolidation; warehouse providing dry storage for general merchandise, food products, liquor, etc.; also, rail siding, inventory and managementservices available
President: Wade Sample
wsample@mbwinc.com
Operations Manager: Brian Lapsley
Warehouse Supervisor: David Ashlock
Estimated Sales: Less Than $500,000
Number Employees: 1-4
Services: LTL & TL local haul trucking, piggyback delivery & freight consolidation
Regions Served:
AK, LA & TX

51949 Murphy Warehouse Co
701 24th Ave SE
Minneapolis, MN 55414-2691   612-623-1200
    Fax: 612-623-9108   sales@murphywarehouse.com
www.murphywarehouse.com
Warehouse offering logistic support and dry and cooler storage for plastics, food products, etc.; transportation firm providing freight consolidation and local haul trucking; also, rail siding, packaging, re-packing, pick/packlabeling, etc
President/CEO: Richard Murphy, Jr.
richard@murphywarehouse.com
Number Employees: 250-499
Services: Freight consolidation, local haul trucking, cross docking, pool distribution, etc.
Regions Served:
National, International

51950 (HQ)Murray's Transfer Inc
1011 Floral Ln
Davenport, IA 52802   563-333-4570
    Fax: 563-333-4577   800-333-1011
www.murraystransfer.com
Transportation firm providing local and short haul trucking; TL and LTL; distribution and rail siding available
Founder & Owner: Marion Murray
Owners: Robert & Patty Powell
CFO: Patty Powell
General Manager: Steve Markham
Number Employees: 20-49
Services: Local & short haul trucking
Regions Served:
Midwest

51951 N.Y.K. Line (North America)
377 E Butterfield Rd
Lombard, IL 60148-5615   630-435-7800
    Fax: 630-435-3110   888-695-7447
Contact: Kathleen Sarullo
kathy.sarullo@na.nykline.com
Estimated Sales: $ .5 - 1 million
Number Employees: 5-9

51952 NFI Industries Inc
1515 Burnt Mill Rd
Cherry Hill, NJ 08003-3637   856-691-7000
    Fax: 856-507-4488   800-922-5088
info@natlfreight.com   www.nfiindustries.com
Warehouse providing rail siding services; transportation company providing long and short haul trucking
CEO: Nick Brummer
nick.brummer@investmentresearch.citi.com
CEO: Sidney Brown
Estimated Sales: Over $1 Billion
Number Employees: 5000-9999
Other Locations:
National Distribution Centers
Pensauken, NJ
National Distribution Centers
Edison, NJ
National Distribution Centers
Dayton, NJ
National Distribution Centers
Tampa, FL
National Distribution Centers
Orlando, FL
National Distribution Centers
Bensenville, IL
National Distribution CentersEdison
Services: Long & short haul trucking
Regions Served:
Nationwide

51953 NYK Line North America Inc
300 Lighting Way # 5
Secaucus, NJ 07094-3647   201-330-3000
www.nykline.com
Transportation firm providing ocean freight services
President: Yasumi Kudo
Executive VP: Peter Keller
peter.keller@na.nykline.com
Number Employees: 100-249
Parent Co: Nippon Yusen Kaisha
Services: Ocean freight
Regions Served:
International

51954 Nashua Motor Express
270 Amherst St
Nashua, NH 03063   603-882-6941
    Fax: 603-595-7634   800- 25- 15
Transportation company providing airline and local haul trucking services
President: Diana Juris
Number Employees: 50-99
Regions Served:
New England

51955 National Air Cargo Inc
350 Windward Dr
Orchard Park, NY 14127-1596   716-631-0011
    Fax: 716-631-9186   800-635-0022
www.nationalaircargo.com
Warehouse providing cooler, freezer and dry storage; transportation firm providing international and domestic freight forwarding services via local, long and short haul trucking
CEO: Christopher Alf
calf@nationalaircargo.com
CEO: Christopher Alf
Number Employees: 20-49
Services: International & domestic air freight forwarding
Regions Served:
Worldwide

51956 National Beef Packing Co LLC
12200 N. Ambassador Dr.
Suite 500
Kansas City, MO 64163
    800-449-2333
www.nationalbeef.com
Fresh, chilled and processed beef products.
CEO: Timothy Klein
tklein@nationalbeef.com
Year Founded: 1992
Estimated Sales: $7.3 Billion
Number Employees: 8,200
Number of Brands: 5
Type of Packaging: Consumer, Food Service, Private Label, Bulk
Other Locations:
HQ
Kansas City, MO
Dodge City, KS
Liberal, KS
Hummels Wharf, PA
Moultrie, GA
National Beef Leathers
St. Joseph, MO
HQDodge City

51957 National Carriers Inc
3925 Carbon Rd
Irving, TX 75038
    800-835-2097
ekentner@nationalcarriers.com
www.nationalcarriers.com
Transportation broker providing long and short haul trucking
President: Jim Franck
VP Sales: Loren Bridge
Year Founded: 1968
Estimated Sales: $100-$500 Million
Number Employees: 100-249
Parent Co: Farmland Industries
Services: Broker providing long & short haul trucking
Regions Served:
Nationwide & Canada

51958 National Distribution Centers
1515 Burnt Hill Road
Cherry Hill, NJ 08003   732-417-2276
    Fax: 732-417-0915   877-634-3777
www.ndc-nfi.com

Warehouse providing dry storage for nonperishable foods; transportation firm providing local, long and short haul trucking
Contact: Irwin Brown
irwin@sourcelogistics.net
Number Employees: 20-49
Parent Co: National Distribution Centers
Services: Local, long & short haul trucking
Regions Served:
  Northeast

51959 (HQ)Nature's Products Inc
1301 Sawgrass Corporate Pkwy
Sunrise, FL 33323-2813 954-233-3300
  Fax: 954-233-3301 800-752-7873
  info@natures-products.com
Manufacturer and supplier of raw materials specializing in gelatin, flavors, active pharmaceuticals, botanicals and pharmaceutical additives. Providing import/export services, warehousing and freight forwarding to and from the UnitedStates and worldwide
President: Jose Minski
josem@npi-gmi.com
Number Employees: 100-249
Type of Packaging: Private Label, Bulk

51960 (HQ)Nebraska Warehouse Co
10064 S 134th St
Omaha, NE 68138-3708 402-896-2200
  Fax: 402-896-2201 www.nebraskawarehouse.com
Warehouse providing cooler and dry storage of general merchandise; also, rail siding, daily local deliveries for Omaha and Lincoln metro area, piggyback drayage, re-packing, labeling, etc. services available
President: Jon Meyers
jmeyers@nebraskawarehouse.com
VP: Bruce Meyers
Director of Sales: Jeff Ziegler
Number Employees: 50-99
Square Footage: 1400000
Services: Piggyback drayage
Regions Served:
  Lincoln & Omaha, NE

51961 Network FOB
2980 Commers Drive
Suite 850
Eagan, MN 55121 651-256-1000
  Fax: 651-256-1010 800-325-7886
  www.networkfob.com
Transportation firm providing LTL and TL, freight forwarding and long, short and local haul
President: Timothy Taylor
CFO: Mark Applebaum
Vice President: Joseph Tutino
Contact: Joe Tutino
joseph.tutino@networkfob.com
Number Employees: 10-19
Services: TL and LTL, freight forwarding and long, short and local haul
Regions Served:
  Continental U.S.

51962 New Hampton Transfer & Storage
1970 N Linn Ave
New Hampton, IA 50659-9405 641-394-3191
  Fax: 641-394-3190 800-237-9098
  www.nhwarehouse.com
Warehouse providing dry and humidity-controlled storage of nonperishable food items; transportation firm offering LTL, short haul trucking, pick/pack, railcar loading and unloading, rental and rail siding
Owner: Chip Schwickerath
nhtf2@iowatelecom.net
Marketing Specialist: Megan Chip
Assistant Manager: William Chip
Number Employees: 5-9
Services: Short haul trucking, pick/pack, LTL shipping, railcar loading & unloading, rentals, etc.
Regions Served:
  Midwest Region

51963 New Orleans Cold Storage-Wrhse
3411 Jourdan Rd
New Orleans, LA 70126-5049 504-944-4400
  Fax: 504-948-0957 504-782-2653
  info@nocs.com www.nocs.com
Warehouse providing cooler and freezer storage for refrigerated and frozen food; transportation firm providing local, short and long haul trucking and ocean and rail car services
President: Mark Blanchard
markb@nocs.com
Vice President, Sales & Market: Jim Henderson
Number Employees: 20-49
Other Locations:
  NOCS
  New Orleans, LA
  NOCS
  Charleston, SC
  NOCS
  Houston, TXNOCSCharleston
Services: Local, short & long haul trucking & ocean and rail car
Regions Served:
  Worldwide

51964 New York
1 Railroad Ave
Cooperstown, NY 13326-1110 607-547-8582
  Fax: 607-547-9834 www.nysw.com
Transportation firm providing rail car services
President: Nathan Fenno
nathan.fenno@nysw.com
CEO: Tabetha Rathbone
Number Employees: 5-9
Services: Rail car
Regions Served:
  New York State & NY/NJ Metro

51965 Newport St Paul Cold Storage
2233 Maxwell Ave
Newport, MN 55055-7714 651-459-5555
  Fax: 651-459-5951 drew@newportcold.com
  www.newportcold.com
Warehouse providing cooler and freezer storage for perishables and frozen foods; transportation broker providing local, long and short haul trucking; also, rail siding, distribution, blast freezing, TL and refrigerated LTL truckingetc. services available
President: Andrew Greenberg
CEO: Dean Greenberg
deang@newportcold.com
Warehouse Supervisor: Michael King
Executive VP: Robert Franklin
Director Operations: Randy Lewis
Number Employees: 20-49
Square Footage: 12
Services: Broker providing local, long & short haul trucking; also, TL & LTL refrigerated trucking
Regions Served:
  Continental U.S.

51966 Nippon Cargo Airlines Co LTD
111 8th Ave
New York, NY 10011-5201 212-989-0146
Warehouse providing cooler and humidity-controlled storage; transportation firm providing air freight services for dangerous goods, perishables, computer equipment, live animals, oversized cargoes, etc.; also, LTL and exclusivetrucking services available
Number Employees: 5-9
Parent Co: NCA
Services: Air freight services for dangerous goods, perishables, computer equipment, etc.; also, LTL & exclusive trucking
Regions Served:
  Nationwide, Far East & Europe

51967 (HQ)Norfolk Southern Corp
3 Commercial Pl # 1a
Norfolk, VA 23510-2108 757-629-2680
  Fax: 757-629-2361 contactus@nscorp.com
  www.nscorp.com
Transportation firm providing railcar services
President and CEO: Charles Woorman
CEO: James A Squires
jasquires@nscorp.com
Overall Operations: Frank Brown
Estimated Sales: Over $1 Billion
Number Employees: 10000+
Other Locations:
  Norfolk Southern Corporation
  Roanoke, VANorfolk Southern Corporation
Services: Railcar
Regions Served:
  Plains States, Great Lakes, East & Southeast

51968 Norjo Distribution Services
4410 N Ravenswood Avenue
Suite 1
Chicago, IL 60640 773-481-0400
Nationwide transportation broker; also, logistic consulting services available
Number Employees: 5-9
Services: Logistic consulting
Regions Served:
  Nationwide

51969 Norman G. Jensen
9325 E Highway 61
Grand Portage, MN 55605 218-475-2229
  custserv.west@ngjensen.com
  www.ngjensen.com
Warehouse providing dry storage; transportation firm providing international and domestic freight forwarding services via local, long and short haul trucking, air and ocean freight
Contact: Vicky Bach
vbach@ngjensen.com
Manager: Bonnie Carlson
Number Employees: 20-49
Services: International & domestic freight forwarding services via local, long & short haul trucking, air & ocean freight
Regions Served:
  Worldwide

51970 North Park Transportation Co
5150 Columbine St
Denver, CO 80216-2305 303-295-0300
  Fax: 303-295-6244 www.nopk.com
Transportation services include LTL, local and short haul trucking
President: Peter Kooi
peter@nopk.com
Estimated Sales: G
Number Employees: 250-499
Services: Local & short haul trucking
Regions Served:
  Regional & local: CO, SD, NE, UT, WY & MT

51971 North Star World Trade Svc
1060 Lone Oak Rd # 112
St Paul, MN 55121-2252 651-379-5030
  Fax: 651-379-5031 mail@shipnorthstar.com
Transportation firm providing international and domestic freight forwarding services; also, software services available
Owner: Joe Pelliter
joep@shipnorthstar.com
Number Employees: 20-49
Parent Co: North Star International
Other Locations:
  North Star
  Oklahoma City, OKNorth Star
Services: Freight forwarding
Regions Served:
  International: nationwide

51972 Northeast Refrigerated
1650 Shawsheen St # 1
Tewksbury, MA 01876-1599 978-851-4747
  Fax: 978-851-0383 800-874-9642
  msancartier@neref.com www.neref.com
Warehousing and transportation services include long, short and local haul trucking of frozen and perishable foods; serving the New England area
Owner: James Monoxelos
jmonoxelos@neref.com
Owner: Mike Sancartier
Number Employees: 50-99
Services: Local, long & short haul trucking
Regions Served:
  New England

51973 Northern Air Cargo
4510 Old International Airport Road
Anchorage, AK 99502 907-243-3331
  Fax: 907-249-5194 800-727-2141
  customercare@nac.aero www.nacargo.com
Transportation company providing air transportation in Alaska
CEO: David Karp
Number Employees: 250-499

51974 Northland Cold Storage Inc
2490 S Broadway
Green Bay, WI 54304-5255 920-431-4600
  Fax: 920-431-4613 cpokel@ncold.com
  www.ncold.com
Warehouse providing cooler, freezer and dry storage; transportation firm providing refrigerated, LTL, short and long haul trucking

Transportation Firms / A-Z

President: Kathleen Pokel
kpokel@ncold.com
Manager - Information Technology: Ben Bergeron
Manager - Maintenance & Refrigeration: Martin Demeny
Manager - Customer Service: Caitlin Pokel
General Manager - Warehouse Operations: David Pokel
Number Employees: 20-49
Other Locations:
  Troutdale, OR
  McMinnville, TNMcMinnville
Services: Refrigerated, LTL, short & long haul trucking
Regions Served:
  WI

51975 Northland Express Transport
11288 US-31
Grand Haven, MI 49417-9665   616-846-8450
        Fax: 616-846-5300   800-748-0550
        ewiers@northlandexpresstransport.com
        www.northlandexpresstransport.com
Transportation broker providing long haul and short haul trucking
Owner: Richard Brolick
President, CEO: Todd Bustard
VP, Finance: Edward Wiers
Sales Director: Michelle Voss
General Manager: Matt Nease
Number Employees: 20-49
Parent Co: Spectral Enter
Services: Broker providing long haul trucking
Regions Served:
  Continental U.S. & Canada

51976 Nova Transportation Inc
9 Business Park Dr # 4
Unit 1
Branford, CT 06405-2931   203-488-2006
      Fax: 203-481-2774   800-229-6682
              info@novatransportation.com
Transportation broker providing local, long and short haul trucking; serving nationwide
Number Employees: 5-9
Services: Broker providing local, long & short haul trucking
Regions Served:
  Nationwide

51977 Nu-Lane Cargo Services
Po Box 7360
Visalia, CA 93290
        Fax: 559-625-9700   800-310-6506
Company moves refrigerated truck loads from the shipper to consignee.
Sales Rep.: Steve Brasiel

51978 (HQ)O'Byrne Distribution Ctr Inc
5855 N 94th St
Milwaukee, WI 53225-2652   414-463-9090
      Fax: 414-463-4662 info@obyrnedc.com
              www.obyrnedc.com
Warehouse providing cold, dry and humidity-controlled storage for groceries and general merchandise; rail siding, pick/pack, re-packing/re-couping, EDI, etc. available; transportation firm providing local haul trucking and consolidatedshipping
Owner: Rosemary O'Bryne
ro@obyrnedc.com
Number Employees: 20-49
Services: Local haul trucking & consolidated shipping
Regions Served:
  MI, WI, IL & IN

51979 ODW Logistics Inc
1530 Williams Rd
Columbus, OH 43207-5183   614-497-1660
      Fax: 614-491-1461 800-743-7062
        jclark@odwlogistics.com www.odwlogistics.com
Warehouse providing cooler and dry storage for beverages, cereal, health and beauty aids and general commodities; transportation firm providing TL and LTL trucking and contract and freight brokerage; also, rail siding, labelingkitting and point of sale packaging
President: John Ness
ness@odwlogistics.com
CEO: Robert Ness
CFO: David Hill
VP: Jeff Clark
VP Sales & Marketing: Jeff Clark
VP Operations: Jon Petticrew
Number Employees: 20-49
Other Locations:
  ODW Logistics
  Columbus, OHODW Logistics
Services: LTL & TL trucking & contract and freight brokerage
Regions Served:
  Midwest, northeast & southeast

51980 Oak Harbor Freight Lines
1225 37th St NW
Auburn, WA 98001-2417   206-244-3230
        Fax: 253-931-5137 www.oakh.com
Transportation firm providing LTL, freight consolidation, EDI capabilities, local and short haul trucking
Owner & Co-President: Edward Vander Pol
Owner & Co-President: David Vander Pol
Contact: Angela Albin
angela.albin@oakh.com
VP Operations: Ron Kieswether
Number Employees: 250-499
Services: Local & short haul trucking
Regions Served:
  OR, WA, CA, ID & NV

51981 Oborn Transfer & Stge Co Inc
Freeport Ctr # A13n
Clearfield, UT 84015   801-773-4902
      Fax: 801-773-4993 800-358-0646
              www.oborn.com
Public warehouse offering dry storage for bagged products and barrels; rail siding available; transportation services including local pickup and delivery
Owner: Kent Oborn
bret@oborn.com
Number Employees: 10-19
Services: Local pickup & delivery
Regions Served:
  UT

51982 Ocean World Lines
1981 Marcus Ave Ste E100
New Hyde Park, NY 11042-1038   516-616-2424
        Fax: 516-616-2400
Warehouse providing storage for frozen foods; transportation firm providing international and domestic freight forwarding via air and ocean freight and long and short haul trucking
President: Alan Baer
abaer@kellogg.com
Executive Assistant: Denise Steinberg
Number Employees: 1-4
Services: International & domestic freight forwarding via air & ocean freight, local & short haul trucking
Regions Served:
  Worldwide: nationwide

51983 Offshore Systems Inc
Mile 4 Captains Bay Rd
Dutch Harbor, AK 99692   907-581-1827
        Fax: 907-581-1630
        nreed@offshoresystemsinc.com
        www.offshoresystemsinc.com
President: Daniel Roseta
Executive VP: Joey Willis
Director of Marketing: Wayne Bouck
Business Development Manager: Rick Wilson
Manager: Nick Reed
nreed@offshoresystemsinc.com
Operations Manager: Mike Peek
Number Employees: 20-49

51984 Ohio Commerce Center
24 University Avenue NE
Suite 200
Minneapolis, MN 55413   651-855-9700
        Fax: 651-855-9701 www.meritex.com
Warehouse providing dry storage for nonperishable foods; transportation firm providing local, long and short haul trucking
Manager: Frank Sutliff
CEO: Paddy McNeely
CFO: Tom Hotover
Chief Operating Officer: Arvid Povilaitis
Number Employees: 10-19
Parent Co: Meritex Logistics
Services: Local, long & short haul trucking
Regions Served:
  Nationwide

51985 (HQ)Ohio Valley Shippers Assn
4950 Para Dr
Cincinnati, OH 45237-5012   513-242-7900
      Fax: 513-242-7932 800-837-2616
              ovsa@ovsa.cc www.ovsa.cc
Transportation services include full TL, TOFC and volume LTL of dry freight nationwide and internationally; also, warehouse storage of dry goods
Vice President: Ron Sickmeier
VP: Ron Sickmeier
Number Employees: 5-9
Services: Full TL, TOFC & volume LTL
Regions Served:
  Nationwide & International

51986 Olson Co
1717 Pearl St
Waukesha, WI 53186-5626   262-548-1220
      Fax: 262-548-1212 888-657-6611
              www.odwlogistics.com
Warehouse providing dry storage for nonperishable foods; transportation services include long and short haul trucking in the Midwest
President: Steve Jacobus
steve.jacobus@olsoncompany.com
Chairman: Jack Jacobus
General Manager-Logistics: Modupe Taylor-Pearce
Number Employees: 100-249
Services: Long & short haul trucking
Regions Served:
  Midwest/Nationwide

51987 Olymel
2200 Pratte Ave.
Suite 400
Saint-Hyacinthe, QC J2S 4B6
Canada   450-771-0400
        Fax: 450-773-6436 www.olymel.com
Pork and poultry.
President/CEO: Rejean Nadeau
First VP: Paul Beauchamp
Senior VP, Sales/Marketing: Richard Davies
Year Founded: 1991
Estimated Sales: $3.6 Billion
Number Employees: 13,000
Number of Brands: 3
Type of Packaging: Private Label, Bulk

51988 Omni North America
1500 County Road 517
Hackettstown, NJ 07840-2717   908-850-4490
      Fax: 908-850-4376 800-222-4285
Transportation firm providing freight forwarding and traffic management services for liquid and dry bulk goods including commodities, vegetable oil and potato flakes
President: Lou Trillo
Quality Control: Donna Vyniski
Traffic Manager: Dan Trillo
Business Development: Art Valetta
Estimated Sales: $ 1 - 3 Million
Number Employees: 10-19
Square Footage: 12800
Services: Freight forwarding & traffic management of liquid & dry bulk goods
Regions Served:
  National

51989 Orange County Cold Storage
1301 S Sunkist Avenue
Anaheim, CA 92806-5614   714-502-9763
        Fax: 714-502-9770
Warehouse providing storage for frozen foods; transportation firm offering short haul trucking; also re-packing services available
President: George Gamar
Number Employees: 20-49
Services: refrigerate
Regions Served:
  CA

51990 Oregon Transfer Co
5910 N Cutter Cir
Portland, OR 97217-3939   503-943-3500
        Fax: 503-659-0741 www.oregontransfer.com
Warehouse offering cooler, dry and humidity controlled storage for nonperishable foods, alcoholic beverages, etc.; rail siding available; transportation firm providing freight consolidation and local and short haul trucking

President: Gary C Eichman
garyeichman@oregontransfer.com
Chairman: Gary C Eitchman
CFO: Gary Hunt
Director of Human Resource: Victoria Masengale
Director Of Operations: Mike Delaney
Number Employees: 50-99
Services: Freight consolidation & local & short haul trucking
Regions Served:
Pacific Northwest: OR, WA, ID & MT

51991 Outerbridge Peppers Limited
20 Harry Shupe Blvd
Wharton, NJ 07885   626-296-2400
peppers@logic.bm
www.outerbridge.com
Packaging facility for Outerbridge Peppers LTD, specializing in sherry peppers and a variety of other sauces.
Managing Director: Norma Cross
Number of Brands: 1
Parent Co: Outerbridge Peppers Limited
Type of Packaging: Consumer, Food Service, Bulk
Regions Served:
Nationwide

51992 (HQ)Overflo
3010 Nieman Ave
Baltimore, MD 21230-2742   410-646-5200
Fax: 410-644-2224 800-626-0616
www.overflo.com
Warehouse offering dry storage; rail siding available
CEO: Gary Timme
Number Employees: 100-249
Regions Served:
Northeast Corridor

51993 Ozark Truck Brokers
3106 Service Road
ADA, OK 74820   918-436-7800
Transportation broker providing nationwide service
Owner: Jay Walker
Services: Transportation brokerage
Regions Served:
Nationwide

51994 Ozark Trucking
4916 Dudley Blvd
Mcclellan, CA 95652-2521   916-561-5400
Fax: 916-925-2838
Transportation firm providing refrigerated trucking
President: Jeff Cummings
jcummings@ozarkinc.com
Fleet Safety: Ed Gamache
Operations: Tom Ricci
Number Employees: 250-499
Parent Co: Ozark Trucking
Services: Refrigerated short haul trucking
Regions Served:
Northern NV & CA

51995 Ozburn-Hessey Logistics LLC
7101 Executive Ctr Dr Ste 333
Brentwood, TN 37027   615-401-6400
Fax: 615-377-3977 877-401-6400
recruiting@ohl.com www.ohl.com
Warehouse providing dry storage for general merchandise and food products; transportation service providing TL and local haul trucking; rail siding, pick and pack, intermodal, customs bonded, food grade logistic service available
President and COO: Bert Irigoyen
CEO: Scott McWilliams
CFO: Thomas Wilkas
Number Employees: 1,000-4,999
Other Locations:
ODC Integrated Logistics
Plainfield, IN
ODC Integrated Logistics
Chambersburg, PA
ODC Integrated Logistics
Sparks, NV
Ozburn-Hessey Logistics
Memphis, TNODC Integrated
LogisticsChambersburg
Services: TL & local haul trucking, intrastate, intermodal, customs bonded carrier, common & contract carrier
Regions Served:
Southeast & Midwest

51996 PBB Global Logistics
P.O.Box 950
Buffalo, NY 14213-0950   716-692-3100
Fax: 716-692-3103 www.livingstonintl.com
Transportation firm providing domestic and international freight forwarding services via local, long and short haul trucking, rail car, air and ocean freight; also, cooler, freezer and dry storage available by arrangement
Manager: Bill Conrad
Contact: Chirs Mcmullen
chirsm@pbb.com
Number Employees: 50-99
Services: International & domestic freight forwarding via trucking, rail car, ocean & air freight
Regions Served:
National & International

51997 PFS Transportation
225 Sharrow Vale Rd
Delran, NJ 08075-1916   856-764-1006
www.pfstransportation.com
Transportation broker providing TL, long and short haul trucking and load stop-offs for frozen, fresh and dry products
Owner: Pete Sudol
Estimated Sales: Less Than $500,000
Number Employees: 1-4
Services: Long & short haul, TL & load stop-offs for frozen, fresh & dry products
Regions Served:
Nationwide

51998 PM&O Line
353 Sacramento Street
Suite 740
San Francisco, CA 94111   415-421-5400
Fax: 415-421-6994
Transportation firm providing ocean freight services
Number Employees: 20-49
Services: Ocean freight
Regions Served:
Micronesia Islands, Hong Kong, & West Coast

51999 PRISM Team Services
1675 Overland Court
West Sacramento, CA 95691 925-838-1691
Fax: 925-838-1694 info@prismlogistics.com
www.prismlogistics.com
Warehouse facility for storage of grocery products, packaged goods, etc.; re-packing and labeling available; transportation services include JIT scheduling, common carrier, freight brokerage, long, local and short haul; rail sidingavailable, fullfillment.
President: Jere van Puffelen
VP: Paul Van de Roovaart
Contact: Dotty Martin
dmartin@prismlogistics.com
Number Employees: 20-49
Services: JIT scheduling, common carrier (intrastate), contract carrier (inter & intrastate), long, local & short haul
Regions Served:
CA, NV, WA, OR & AZ

52000 Pacific Cartage & Warehousing
33001 Dowe Ave
Union City, CA 94587   510-487-6026
Fax: 510-487-6064
Warehouse providing dry storage for food products and general merchandise; transportation services include freight consolidation; distribution; also, distribution, import distribution, fulfillment and rail siding available
Manager: John Costa
john@pcnw.com
Number Employees: 100-249
Services: Freight consolidation
Regions Served:
CA, NV, WA & OR

52001 Pacific Coast WarehouseCo
3601 Jurupa St
Ontario, CA 91761-2905   909-545-8100
cma@pcwc.com
www.pcwc.com
Warehouse providing dry storage; transportation firm providing freight consolidation services; also, cartage, pool distribution and cross docking services available; rail siding available
President: Jim Marcoly
Manager: Mark Burk
VP Operations & Customer Development: Michael Waring
Number Employees: 5-9
Other Locations:
Union City, CA
Services: Freight consolidation & cartage
Regions Served:
Western U.S.

52002 Page & Jones Inc
52 N Jackson St
PO Box 2167
Mobile, AL 36602-2810   251-432-1646
Fax: 251-433-1402 www.pageandjones.com
Customs house broker providing domestic and international freight fowarding and local, long and short haul trucking
President: Mike Lee Sr
Number Employees: 20-49
Services: Air, ocean & trucking services
Regions Served:
Domestic & International

52003 Pak Technologies
7025 W Marcia Rd
Milwaukee, WI 53223   414-438-8600
Fax: 414-977-1458
Packager and distributer
Owner: Kevin Scheule
Contact: Jim Barringer
jbarringer@paktech.com

52004 Palmer Logistics
13001 Bay Area Blvd
Pasadena, TX 77507-1322   281-291-7366
Fax: 713-671-6825 800-237-0370
www.palmerlogistics.com
Warehouse providing dry storage, re-packaging and labeling for nonperishable foods; transportation services include long and short haul trucking nationwide
President: Brett M Mears
Number Employees: 5-9
Services: Long & short haul trucking
Regions Served:
Nationwide

52005 Paschall Truck Lines Inc
3443 US Highway 641 S
PO Box 1080
Murray, KY 42071-7139   270-753-1717
Fax: 270-753-1904 www.ptl-inc.com
Transportation firm providing long and short haul trucking
President: Randall Waller
rwaller@ptl-inc.com
Number Employees: 250-499
Services: Long & short haul trucking
Regions Served:
Nationwide

52006 Pasquale Trucking Co
960 W County Road 250 S
Logansport, IN 46947-8271   574-722-4055
Fax: 574-722-5194
President: Tom Pasquale
tom@pasqualetrucking.com
Estimated Sales: $ 5 - 10 Million
Number Employees: 50-99
Regions Served:
Midwest

52007 Paul L. Broussard & Associate
4600 Gulf Fwy
Suite 200
Houston, TX 77023-3559   713-926-9053
Fax: 713-926-9641 www.broussardtrans.com
Transportation broker providing freight auditing and contract negotiation services
President/Founder: Paul Broussard
VP: Steve Broussard
Number Employees: 20-49
Services: Freight auditing & contract negotiation

52008 Peasley Transfer & Storage
111 N Curtis Rd
Boise, ID 83706-1433   208-901-8396
Fax: 208-376-3447 800-657-5390
www.allied.com
Warehouse providing storage for general commodities; also rail siding and delivery within a 50 mile radius available
Owner: Emmet Herndon
peasleyts@mindspring.com
VP: Dean Price
Sales: Kit Herndon

Transportation Firms / A-Z

Number Employees: 20-49
Parent Co: Nampa
Other Locations:
  Nampa, ID

52009 (HQ)Peerless Trucking Company
P.O.Box 54554
Los Angeles, CA 90054   310-637-3603
              Fax: 310-635-6739
Warehouse providing dry storage; transportation firm providing local and short haul trucking; rail siding available
President: Bill Hart
VP: John Hart
Number Employees: 20-49
Other Locations:
  Peerless Trucking Co.
  City of Commerce, CAPeerless Trucking Co.
Services: Local & short haul trucking
Regions Served:
  AZ & CA

52010 Peninsula Airways Inc
6100 Boeing Ave
Anchorage, AK 99502-1026   907-243-2323
    Fax: 907-243-6848 800-448-4226
         info@penair.com www.penair.com
LArgest commuter airline in Alaska, providing scheduled services to 36 communities throughout Southern Alaska, also provides cargo shipping, small package, and express delivery
President: Danny Seybert
CEO: Orin Siebert
orin.siebert@peninsulaairways.com
VP Finance: Mike Cerkovnik
VP/Director Operations: Bryan Carricaburu
VP Sales: Scott Bloomquist
Number Employees: 250-499
Regions Served:
  Alaska

52011 (HQ)Penser SC
11001 Pritchard Rd
Jacksonville, FL 32219-4803   904-786-1811
    Fax: 904-783-9953 www.pensersc.com
Warehouse providing cooler, dry and humidity-controlled storage for groceries, candy, packaging, etc.; transportation services include consolidation, dry and protected LTL and TL deliveries, pool distribution, etc.; rail sidingavailable
President: Russell O'Dell
CEO: Shawn Barnett
COO: Russell O'Dell
IT: Ash Harper
ashharper@pensersc.com
General Manager-Warehouse: Lawrence Starling
Number Employees: 50-99
Other Locations:
  Peninsular Warehouse Company
  Miami, FL
  Peninsular Warehouse Company
  Orlando, FLPeninsular Warehouse
  CompanyOrlando
Services: Dry & protected LTL & TL deliveries, pool distribution, container & piggy back moves, brokerage, etc.
Regions Served:
  FL, GA

52012 Penske Logistics
Route 10 Green Hills
Reading, PA 19603
        Fax: 610-775-2449 800-529-6531
              www.penskelogistics.com
Freezer and cold Storage Facility.
President: Marc Althen
SVP, Finance: Paul Ott
SVP, Global Sales: Joe Carlier
SVP, International Operations: Bill Scroggie
SVP, Operations: Jeff Bullard
SVP, Operations: Jeff Jackson
SVP, Operations: Steve Beverly
Estimated Sales: $100-500 Million
Number Employees: 500-999
Parent Co: Penske Truck Leasing
Type of Packaging: Food Service

52013 Peoples Cartage Inc
8045 Navarre Rd SE
Massillon, OH 44646-9653   330-833-8571
              Fax: 330-833-2035
         jmatheos@peoplesservices.com
              www.mayflower.com
Warehouse providing storage for general merchandise; transportation firm providing common and contract carrier and local haul trucking; rail siding available
Chairman of the Board: Ronald Sibila
President and CEO: Douglas Sibila
VP: Dan Stemple
Manager: Jim Ehret
jehret@peoplesservices.com
Number Employees: 20-49
Other Locations:
  Peoples Cartage
  Metro, WVPeoples Cartage
Services: Local haul trucking & common & contract carrier
Regions Served:
  OH, WV & VA

52014 Peterson Farms Inc
3104 W Baseline Rd
Shelby, MI 49455-9633   231-861-0119
    Fax: 231-861-2274 sarah@petersonfarmsinc.com
              www.petersonfarmsinc.com
Fruit
CEO: Aaron Peterson
aaron@petersonfarmsinc.com
Chief Sales & Marketing Officer: Sarah Schlukebir
Director of Sales: Larry Hicks
Number Employees: 500-999
Services: Trucking

52015 Philip P Massad Movers
100 Grand St # 3
Worcester, MA 01610-1647   508-752-0100
    Fax: 508-752-6645 massadmovers2@aol.com
              massadmovers.com
Transportation firm providing local haul trucking
Owner: Philip P Massad
Number Employees: 10-19
Services: Local haul trucking
Regions Served:
  Central MA

52016 Phoenix Industries LLC
621 Snively Ave
Eloise, FL 33880-5544   863-293-1151
    Fax: 863-299-2080 www.phoenixfl.com
Warehouse providing frozen, refrigerated, dry and humidity-controlled storage of frozen, chilled and dry food products; transportation company providing rail siding and distribution available
President: John Fleming
john@phoenixfl.com
Operations Manager: Mike Porter
Number Employees: 20-49
Regions Served:
  Florida

52017 Piedmont Distribution Centers
6100 Wheaton Drive SW
Atlanta, GA 30336   404-349-9578
Warehouse providing storage for appliances, candy, groceries, etc.; transportation services include local and long haul trucking, piggyback drayage, freight brokerage and freight forwarding; also, rail siding, assembling, poolingconsolidating, etc
Contact: David Ridgeway
dridgeway@piedmontdistrib.com
Number Employees: 50-99
Square Footage: 1140000
Parent Co: Distribution Technology
Services: Piggyback drayage, freight brokerage, long haul trucking & local delivery
Regions Served:
  Southeast: AL, FL, GA, LA, NC, SC, TN, VA & WV

52018 Pilot Freight Svc
3860 Broadway St # 4
Cheektowaga, NY 14227-1174   716-683-0600
    Fax: 716-683-8492 buf@pilotdelivers.com
              www.pilotair.com
Transportation firm providing international and domestic freight forwarding and local, long and short haul trucking; warehouse providing cooler, freezer and dry storage
Manager: Charlene Matie
buff@pilotdelivers.com
Number Employees: 5-9
Services: Freight forwarding via air & ocean and local, long & short haul trucking
Regions Served:
  Domestic, International, & Canada

52019 Pioneer Freight SystemsInc
144 Parsippany Rd
Whippany, NJ 07981-1127   973-887-0543
    Fax: 973-887-3890 800-221-0293
         DRKitchell@pioneerfreight.com
              www.pioneerfreight.com
Transportation broker providing freight forwarding via local and short haul trucking; refrigerated and temperature controlled transporation services available
Manager: David R Kitchell
drkitchell@pioneerfreight.com
Number Employees: 5-9
Parent Co: Richbar
Services: Brokerage: freight forwarding, local & short haul trucks and refrigerated & temperature controlled transporation
Regions Served:
  Northeast Corridor

52020 Pioneer Valley Refrigerated Warehouse
149 Plainfield St
Chicopee, MA 1013   413-736-1976
    Fax: 413-731-7978 888-376-9361
         sales@pioneercold.com
Warehouse providing dry cooler, freezer and humidity-controlled storage; transportation firm providing local haul trucking; rail siding available
President: Clement J Deliso Jr
Contact: Jason Adams
jadams@pioneercold.com
COO: Bryan Hedge
Number Employees: 50-99
Regions Served:
  Northeast Corridor

52021 Pitt Ohio
15 27th St
Pittsburgh, PA 15222-4729   412-232-3015
    Fax: 412-232-3392 800-366-7488
Transportation firm offering local, long and short haul trucking
President: Charles L Hammel Iii
chammel@pittohio.com
Number Employees: 1000-4999
Parent Co: Hammel Enterprises
Regions Served:
  OH; PA; MD; NJ; IL;IN; MI; KY; WV; VA; NY; DE

52022 Pitzer Transfer & Storage Corp.
2050 Cook Dr
Salem, VA 24153   540-769-2090
    Fax: 540-769-2097 800-334-0064
              www.peoplesservices.com
Warehouse providing dry storage for dry, liquid bulk and hazardous materials; bulk transfer facility providing freight consolidation, local and short haul trucking; rail siding and transloading services available
President: Vance Pitzer
Number Employees: 20-49
Square Footage: 12000000
Parent Co: Peoples Services
Other Locations:
  Pitzer Transfer & Storage Cor
  Charlotte, NCPitzer Transfer & Storage Cor
Services: Local, pneumatic & short haul trucking, freight consolidation, dry vans & bulk transfers
Regions Served:
  NC, SC, OH, WV, VA & GA

52023 Plymouth Rock Transportation
76 Maple St Ste 100
Stoneham, MA 02180   781-438-8200
Transportation firm providing local haul trucking
Number Employees: 50-99
Services: Local haul trucking
Regions Served:
  CT, DC, MA, MD, NH, NJ, NY, PA, RI & VA

52024 Port Canaveral Authority
445 Challenger Rd # 301
Suite 301
Cape Canaveral, FL 32920-4100   321-783-7831
    Fax: 321-783-4651 www.portcanaveral.com
Transportation

776

Transportation Firms / A-Z

Chief Executive Officer: John Walsh
jwalsh@portcanaveral.org
Deputy Executive Director, Chief Financi: Roger Rees
CEO: Stanley Payne
Sr. Director, Information Systems: Mark Lorusso
Chief of Police & Public Safety: Joe Hellebrand
Sr. Director of Business Development: Robert Giangrisostomi
Deputy Director, Human Resources: Brenda Morrish
Sr. Director, Cruise and Port Operations: Mike Meekins
Number Employees: 100-249

52025 Port Elizabeth TerminalCorp
201a Export St
Newark, NJ 07114-3242   973-491-6324
Fax: 973-491-0055 sales@judgeorg.com
www.judgeorg.com
Warehouse providing dry storage; transportation firm providing local and long haul trucking, also rail siding
Owner: Patrick Judge
Sales: Mike Morrow
pjudge@judgeorg.com
Number Employees: 100-249
Parent Co: The Judge Organization
Services: Local & long haul trucking
Regions Served:
 Nationwide

52026 (HQ)Port Jersey Logistics
4 Avenue E
Monroe Township, NJ 08831   609-860-1010
Fax: 609-860-1885 sales@portjersey.com
www.portjersey.com
Warehouse providing cooler and dry storage for dry groceries; transportation firm providing local, short and long haul trucking; freight consolidation, labeling, shrink wrapping and rail siding available
President: Robert Russo
Executive Vice President: Louis Keating
Marketing Manager: Stephanie Jauch
VP Sales: John Emelo
Services: Freight consolidation and short, local & long haul trucking
Regions Served:
 Northeast

52027 Port Terminal Railroad
8934 Manchester St
Houston, TX 77012-2149   713-393-6500
Fax: 713-393-6580 support@ptra.com
www.ptra.com
Transportation firm providing rail car service nationwide
Manager: Marvin Wells
Manager: Brenda Appelt
bappelt@ptra.com
Number Employees: 1-4
Parent Co: All Member Line Railroads
Services: Rail car
Regions Served:
 Nationwide

52028 (HQ)Preferred Freezer Services
1 Main St
3rd Floor
Chatham, NJ 07928   973-820-4040
Fax: 973-820-4004
marketing@preferredfreezer.com
www.preferredfreezer.com
Cold storage warehousing and temperature-controlled logistics
CEO: John Galiher
CFO: Sam Hensley
VP Intermodal: Chris Kelly
East Coast Sales Manager: David Aschenbrand
West Coast & Central Sales Manager: Chris Skraba
VP Operations: Marc Vendome
Year Founded: 1989
Estimated Sales: $300 Million
Number Employees: 2400
Type of Packaging: Food Service
Services: Long-haul, short-haul, intermodal, LTL

52029 Price Truck Lines Inc
4931 S Victoria St
Wichita, KS 67216-2004   316-945-6915
Fax: 316-945-3178 800-748-7397
rates@pricetruckline.com
www.pricetruckline.com
Transportation firm providing LTL and TL for wholesalers/distributors
President: Ed Toon
edtoon@pricetruckline.com
Number Employees: 100-249
Services: LTL & TL for wholesalers/distributors
Regions Served:
 KS

52030 Price's Creameries
600 N Piedras St
El Paso, TX 79903-4023   915-565-2711
Fax: 915-562-8232 www.pricescreameries.com
Milk, ice cream, sherbet, mellorine, cream and ice milk mixes.
Director of Export & ESL Expansion: Gene Carrejo
Cmo: Irene Pistella
irene.pistella@deanfoods.com
Year Founded: 1906
Number Employees: 100-249
Parent Co: Dean Foods Company
Type of Packaging: Consumer

52031 Priority Air Express
11 Technology Dr # A
Swedesboro, NJ 08085-1849   856-832-1500
Fax: 856-832-1987 800-257-4777
Warehouse providing dry storage for nonperishable and frozen foods; transportation firm providing international and domestic freight forwarding services via local, long and short haul trucking, air and ocean freight; also, dry icepacking services available
CFO: Jim Manion
CEO: David Matthia
Contact: Homar Alvarado
premiumbm@msn.com
Number Employees: 100-249
Services: International & domestic freight forwarders providing local, long & short haul trucking, air & ocean freight
Regions Served:
 Mid-Atlantic

52032 Prism Team Services, Inc
3656 Perlman Drive
Stockton, CA 95206   209-983-9915
www.prismlogistics.com
Warehouse providing dry storage for non-perishable goods; transportation firm providing TL and LTL trucking; also, cross-docking, distribution, machinery moving and rail siding services available.
President: Jere Van Puffelen
Executive Vice President: Paul Van de Roovaart
Contact: Mike Mayo
mmayo@prismlogistics.com
Number Employees: 20-49
Square Footage: 828000
Parent Co: PRISM Team Services
Services: TL & LTL and flat & low beds
Regions Served:
 Northern CA

52033 (HQ)Professional Transportation Brokers
604 Rico Way
Grand Junction, CO 81506-8221
Fax: 303-329-6298 800-735-4567
Domestic and international transportation broker service providing full and partial loads, dry, refrigerated, air-ride, blanket wrap and flatbed freights
President: Tom Paradis
Assistant Office Manager: Julie Warneke
Contact: Stuart Appleton
sappleton@mtn-creek.com
Number Employees: 20-49
Services: Full & partial loads, dry, refrigerated, air-ride, blanket wrap & flatbed freights
Regions Served:
 Domestic & International

52034 Providence & Worcester RR Company
P.O.Box 1188
Worcester, MA 01613   508-755-4000
Fax: 508-795-5548 frank@pwrr.com
Transportation firm providing rail car services for frozen foods, produce and canned goods
CEO: Robert H Eder
Manager Marketing Services: Larry Connor
Estimated Sales: G
Number Employees: 100-249
Services: Rail freight for frozen foods, produce & canned goods
Regions Served:
 RI, NY, VT, NH, ME, CT, & MA

52035 Pure Flo Water Co
7737 Mission Gorge Rd
Santee, CA 92071-3399   619-448-5120
Fax: 619-596-4154 800-787-3356
www.pureflo.com
Bottled water: purified, fluoridated and spring; water filtration system services
CEO: Brian Grant
bgrant@pureflo.com
General Manager: Leslie Alstad
Director of Marketing & Technology: Damon Grant
Accounting Manager: Bernadette Meyer
Estimated Sales: $13 Million
Number Employees: 100-249
Number of Brands: 1
Square Footage: 9000
Type of Packaging: Consumer, Bulk
Services: Product delivery
Regions Served:
 San Diego, CA

52036 Quality Logistics Systems
3801 Pinnacle Point Dr # 100
Dallas, TX 75211-1578   214-231-0446
Fax: 214-623-9644 info@qualitylogistics.com
www.qualitylogistics.com
Warehouse providing dry and cooler storage, re-packing and labeling for nonperishable foods; transportation services include long and short haul trucking nationwide
President: Jeff Ballard
Cmo: William Mcneil
william.mcneil@qualitylogistics.com
Number Employees: 50-99
Parent Co: Quality Logistics Services
Other Locations:
 Chicago, IL
 Green Bay, WI
 Meridian, MSGreen Bay
Services: Long & short haul trucking
Regions Served:
 Nationwide

52037 (HQ)Quast & Company
332 S Michigan Avenue
Suite 20
Chicago, IL 60604   312-435-3870
Fax: 312-435-1135
Transportation firm providing international and domestic freight forwarding via air freight
Number Employees: 20-49
Other Locations:
 Elk Grove Village, IL
 New Orleans, LANew Orleans
Services: Freight forwarding via air freight
Regions Served:
 International: nationwide

52038 Queen City Warehouse Corporation
PO Box 10008
Springfield, MO 65808-0008   417-869-4455
Fax: 417-864-6524
edeck@queencitywarehouse.com
Public and contract warehouse providing dry storage; transportation firm providing local and short trucking; rail siding, order filling, cross docking, freight consolidation and pool distribution services available. Food grade and rollpaper.
President: Ed Deck Jr
Estimated Sales: $ 3 - 5 Million
Square Footage: 600000
Regions Served:
 Midwestern states

52039 Quick Delivery
1700 W 29th St
Kansas City, MO 64108   816-931-7800
Fax: 816-931-6633 800-383-8388
www.quickdeliveryinc.com
Warehouse providing dry and humidity-controlled storage for nonrefrigerated and nonhazardous products; transportation firm providing local and short haul trucking and regional ground messenger services including break bulk, crossdocking, etc
President: John Reynolds
Number Employees: 10-19
Services: Local & short haul trucking; ground rush messenger services, break bulk, same day & next day distribution services
Regions Served:
 Regional: Kansas City metropolitan area, Northeastern KS, Springfield, MO area & Southern, Central & Western MO

Transportation Firms / A-Z

52040 R L Swearer Co Inc
115 Mclaughlin Rd
Coraopolis, PA 15108-3819   412-269-1919
    Fax: 412-269-1997 Imports@rlswearer.com
        www.rlswearer.com
Transportation broker offering worldwide freight forwarding
President: Charles Watson
cmwatson@rlswearer.com
Number Employees: 20-49
Services: Freight forwarding
Regions Served:
    Worldwide

52041 (HQ)R W Bozel Transfer Inc
500 Advantage Ave
Aberdeen, MD 21001-1146   443-327-6919
    Fax: 443-327-6925 800-927-9055
        www.bozelt.com
Transportation firm providing local, long and short haul trucking, TL and LTL consolidation, LTL cartage, refrigeration and pool distribution services; warehouse providing refrigerated storage
President: Patrick Bozel
patb@bozelt.com
Number Employees: 1-4
Services: TL & LTL consolidation, LTL cartage, local, long & short haul trucking & pool distribution
Regions Served:
    East Coast

52042 (HQ)R.F.K. Transportation Service
6414 Hampton Ave
St Louis, MO 63109-3662   314-776-1000
    Fax: 314-353-2267 800-225-6718
Transportation broker providing freight forwarding services
Number Employees: 5-9
Services: Broker providing freight forwarding
Regions Served:
    Nationwide & Canada

52043 (HQ)RGL Headquarters
1401 State St
Green Bay, WI 54304   920-432-8632
        www.rgllogistics.com
Warehouse providing cooler and dry storage for general merchandise; transportation services include local trucking; consolidation, cross-dock, rail siding and distribution services available
President/CEO: Bob Johnson
VP Marketing: Roger Whitton
Sales Contact: Rebecca Usiak
Contact: Ken Garwood
kgarwood@rgllogistics.com
Number Employees: 100-249
Services: Local trucking
Regions Served:
    Midwest

52044 RLS Logistics
Rosario Leo Building
2185 Main Road
Newfield, NJ 08344   856-694-2500
        800-579-9900
    info@rlslogistics.com www.rlslogistics.com
Transportation, warehousing and fulfillment to the frozen and refrigerated food industry.
Chief Executive Officer, President: Anthony Leo
Vice President of Development: John Gaudet
Director of Operations: Greg Deitz

52045 Ralph Moyle Inc
23599 Freedom Ln
Mattawan, MI 49071-8904   269-668-4531
    Fax: 269-668-4677
    http://www.ralphmoyle.com/index.php
Warehouse providing dry and refrigerated storage for nonperishable foods; transportation firm providing local haul and OTR trucking
President: Ralph Moyle
ralphmoyle@ralphmoyle.com
Owner/Manager: Mike Moyle
Sales/Marketing Executive: Jon Moyle
Number Employees: 50-99
Services: Local haul & OTR trucking
Regions Served:
    Southwest MI

52046 Ralph's Packing Co
500 W Freeman Ave
Perkins, OK 74059   405-547-2464
    Fax: 405-547-2364 800-522-3979
    comments@ralphspacking.com
        www.ralphspacking.com
Fresh and smoked meat products available to consumers and wholesalers.
President: Gary Crane
garycrane@ralphspacking.com
Year Founded: 1959
Estimated Sales: $4 Million
Number Employees: 20-49
Square Footage: 39200
Type of Packaging: Consumer, Food Service, Private Label
Regions Served:
    Cleveland and surrounding areas

52047 Ray West Warehouses/Transport
4801 Baldwin Blvd Ste 104
Corpus Christi, TX 78408   361-884-5595
    Fax: 361-884-0309
    johnm@raywestwarehouses.com
Warehouse providing dry and cooler storage for nonperishable foods; transporation, rail siding, re-packing and labeling available
President & CEO: Peter Anderson
pete@raywestwarehouses.com
Number Employees: 10-19
Services: Short haul trucking
Regions Served:
    Corpus Christi, TX

52048 Reed Trucking Co
522 Chestnut St
Milton, DE 19968-1320   302-684-8585
    Fax: 302-684-8590 800-441-8347
        www.reed-trucking.com
Transportation for refrigerated and dry goods
Owner: Rick Brady
rickb@reed-trucking.com
Number Employees: 50-99
Other Locations:
    LTL Division
    Newark, DELTL Division

52049 Reefco Logistics
314 W Millbrook Rd # 21
Raleigh, NC 27609-4380   919-845-0771
    Fax: 919-845-8558
Freight forwarder/NVOCC specializing in perishable food products, Reefer Logistics provides transportation/container shipments, checking for ports of departure and routing and booking to final destination and will have containersdelivered to loading facilities and monitor the arrival and departure from facilities. In addition, Reefco Logistics also arranges the trucking of cargo to cold storage loading facilities for transloading into export containers.
Owner: Ernie Beauregard
Services: Specializes in transportation of perishable food products.

52050 Reynolds Transfer & Storage
725 E Mifflin St
Madison, WI 53703-2391   608-257-3914
    Fax: 608-258-3692 800-430-4333
        www.unitedvanlines.com
Warehouse providing dry storage for general merchandise; transportation firm providing local haul trucking; rail siding available
President: Karen Michel
karen.michel@aonhewitt.com
Number Employees: 20-49
Services: Local haul trucking
Regions Served:
    WI

52051 Richwill Enterprises
1443 W 41st St
Chicago, IL 60609-2414   773-927-5757
    Fax: 773-927-7206 800-334-5757
        www.richwillcs.com
Warehouse providing cooler and freezer storage for perishable and nonperishable food items; transportation firm offering long and short haul trucking
President: Karen Reinschreiber
Contact: Karen Mccurrie
karen@richwillcs.com
Operations Manager: Gregory Principato
Estimated Sales: $2.5-5 Million
Number Employees: 20-49
Services: Long & short haul trucking

52052 River Terminal Distribution & Warehouse
3 Distribution Ave # 139
Suite 639
Kearny, NJ 07032   973-465-1084
    Fax: 973-465-0089 info@riverterminal.com
Warehouse handling dry foods and general commodities; transportation firm offering freight consolidation; also, re-packing, assembly and rail siding available
Manager: Svetin Govic
Contact: Phil Catelo
pcatelo@rtdwco.com
Number Employees: 20-49
Parent Co: River Terminal Development
Services: Freight consolidation

52053 Rivers Transportation
3319 Northbrook Dr
Sioux City, IA 51105-2400   712-293-1200
Transportation broker providing load reefers, dry vans and flat-bed equipment
Manager: Cris Kalkman
Services: Broker providing load reefers, dry-vans & flat-bed equipment
Regions Served:
    International

52054 Roads West Transportation
100 Beechboro Road
Bayswater, WA 6053   089-272-7500
    Fax: 089-271-5402 www.roadwest.com.au
Transportation firm providing local and long haul trucking for refrigerated, frozen and dry foods
Number Employees: 100-249
Services: Local and long haul trucking for refrigerated, frozen and dry freight
Regions Served:
    Nationwide

52055 Robert J. Preble & Sons
5 Westvale Road
Kennebunkport, ME 04046-6750   207-967-3477
    Fax: 207-967-8690
Providing trucking services to the food industry.
President: Duane Preble

52056 Robertson-Johnson Warehouses
2600 Shader Rd
P.O.Box 547900
Orlando, FL 32854-7900   407-293-3121
    Fax: 407-290-5371
Warehouse offering dry storage; transportation firm providing freight consolidation; pick/pack, cross docking, pool car and truck distribution, EDI, computerized inventory control and rail siding available
President: Thomas Johnson
VP: Whit Kendall
Number Employees: 10-19
Services: Freight consolidation
Regions Served:
    Southern U.S.

52057 (HQ)Rockwell Truck Line
28463 Highland Rd
Romulus, MI 48174   734-992-6078
    Fax: 734-992-6084 baljit@rockwelltrucks.com
        www.rockwelltrucks.com
Transportation firm providing rail car services and long haul trucking including TL and LTL; also, reefer, pallet exchange and handling services available.
Estimated Sales: $50-100 Million
Number Employees: 50-99
Other Locations:
    Tecumseh, Canada
Services: TL, TL, rail car services & long haul trucking; also, reefers, pallet exchange & handling services available
Regions Served:
    U.S.A., Canada & Mexico

52058 Ronnie Dowdy
1839 Batesville Blvd
Batesville, AR 72501   870-251-3222
    Fax: 870-251-3763 800-743-5611
Transportation firm providing refrigerated trucking services including local, long and short haul

Transportation Firms / A-Z

Owner: Ronnie Dowdy
Owner: Sandra Dowdy
Contact: David Bergan
dbergan@ronniedowdy.com
Number Employees: 250-499
Services: Refrigerated trucking: local, short & long haul
Regions Served:
Nationwide

52059 Rosen's Diversified Inc.
1120 Lake Ave.
PO Box 933
Fairmont, MN 56031   507-238-6001
                  Fax: 507-238-9966
ContactUs@RosensDiversified.com
www.rosensdiversifiedinc.com
Agribusiness, beef processing, pet foods and carrier services.
CEO: Tom Rosen
trosen@riw2000.com
Year Founded: 1946
Estimated Sales: $3.2 Billion
Number of Brands: 7

52060 (HQ)Ross Express Inc
195 N Main St
PO Box 8908
Boscawen, NH 03303-1106   603-753-4176
        Fax: 603-753-8614 800-762-5966
info@rossexpress.com www.rossexpress.com
Transportation services include short haul trucking throughout northern New England
President: Stephen Brown
sbrown@rossexpress.com
VP: Jack Laflamme
Sales: Lou Guertin
Number Employees: 50-99
Other Locations:
Sutton, MA
White River Jct, VT
Auburn, ME
Brewer, ME
Endfield, CT White River Jct
Regions Served:
Northern New England

52061 Royal Baltic LTD
9829 Ditmas Ave
Brooklyn, NY 11236-1925   718-385-8300
                  Fax: 718-385-4757
Manufactures smoked fish products; distributes gourmet foods, such as seafood delicacies, cheese, juice, feta, coffee, chocolate candy and sauces.
President: Alex Kaganovsky
alexkaganovsky@royalbaltic.com
Finance Manager: Alex Kaganovsky
Estimated Sales: $10-20 Million
Number Employees: 50-99
Type of Packaging: Consumer

52062 Royal Jordanian
21b N Service Rd
Jamaica, NY 11430-1616   718-656-0220
        Fax: 718-244-1821 www.rj.com
Warehouse providing dry and freezer storage for frozen foods and general merchandise; transportation firm providing air cargo services
Manager: Ziyad Atiyat
Number Employees: 10-19
Services: Warehousing & airline cargo services
Regions Served:
International

52063 Ryder
284 E 48 St
Holland, MI 49423   616-392-7011
                  www.ryder.com
Transportation firm providing leasing and transportation management services; also, vehicle maintenance and inventory deployment services available.
Type of Packaging: Food Service

52064 Ryder Integrated Logistics
11690 NW 105th St
Miami, FL 33178
                    888-793-3702
ryder.com/supply-chain-management
Offers a complete line of supply chain solutions
President, Global Supply Chain Solutions: J. Steven Sensing
Estimated Sales: K

52065 (HQ)Ryder System, Inc
11690 NW 105th St
Miami, FL 33178   305-500-3726
                    800-467-9337
                  www.ryder.com
Transportation firm providing leasing and transportation management services; also, vehicle maintenance and inventory deployment services available
Chairman & CEO: Robert Sanchez
EVP/Chief Legal Officer/Secretary: Robert Fatovic
EVP/Chief Financial Officer: Scott Parker
EVP/Chief Sales Officer: John Gleason
EVP/Chief Marketing Officer: Karen Jones
SVP/Chief Human Resources Officer: Frank Lopez
SVP/Chief Information Officer: Rajeev Ravindran
SVP/Chief Procurement Officer: Tim Fiore
Estimated Sales: $7.3 Billion
Number Employees: 39,600
Square Footage: 440000
Other Locations:
Ryder Integrated Logistics
Birmingham, AL Ryder Integrated Logistics
Services: Transportation management & leasing; also, inventory deployment & vehicle maintenance available
Regions Served:
International: nationwide, Canada, Europe, South Africa & Mexico

52066 (HQ)SAS Cargo
1 Newark Airport
Newark, NJ 07114-3401   973-648-0814
        Fax: 973-849-3366 larry.katz@sas.dk
                  www.sascargo.com
Transportation company providing domestic and international air freight services; warehouse providing cooler, freezer, dry and humidity-controlled storage
President & CEO: Kenneth Marx
Terminal Management: Larry Katz
Number Employees: 50-99
Services: Air freight
Regions Served:
Nationwide & International

52067 SDS Global Logistics, Inc.
37-18 57th Street
Woodside, NY 11377   718-784-5586
        Fax: 718-472-3474 888-737-3977
                  insidesales@sdsgl.com
Warehouse providing dry storage for nonperishable items; transportation firm providing international and domestic freight forwarding services via air freight, long and short haul trucking
Founder: Anthony Racioppo
Founder: John Racioppo
Contact: Alli Alvarado
aalvarado@sdsgl.com
Number Employees: 10-19
Services: International & domestic freight forwarding via air freight, long & short haul trucking
Regions Served:
Worldwide

52068 SEKO Worldwide Inc
1100 N Arlington Heights # 600
Itasca, IL 60143-3111   630-919-4800
        Fax: 630-773-9179 800-228-2711
                  sales@sekoworldwide.com
                  www.sekologistics.com
Warehouse providing dry storage of nonperishable food items; transportation firm offering air freight forwarding
President/CEO: William J Wascher
Chief Commercial Officer: Mark L White
CFO: Don Sarna
Evp/COO: Steven Goldberg
Vice President Marketing: Brian Bourke
Vice President Sales: David Emerson
Chief Operating Officer: Randy Sinker
Number Employees: 1000-4999
Services: Air freight forwarding
Regions Served:
Worldwide

52069 SOS Global Express Inc
2803 Trent Rd
New Bern, NC 28562-2029   252-635-1400
        Fax: 252-635-1920 800-628-6363
                  www.sosglobal.com
Warehouse providing dry storage for nonperishable items; transportation firm providing international and domestic freight forwarding services via air freight and long and short haul trucking
President: Fernando Soler
fsoler@sosglobal.com
Number Employees: 50-99
Services: International & domestic freight forwarding via air freight & long and short haul trucking
Regions Served:
Worldwide

52070 SPC Transport Co
224 W Hardscrabble Rd
P.O.Box 1718
Auburn, ME 04210-8343   207-783-4200
        Fax: 207-783-4288 866-376-0064
ttaylor@spctran.com www.spctran.com
Transportation firm providing local and long haul trucking
President: Todd Prawer
tprawer@spctran.com
Number Employees: 50-99
Services: Local & long haul trucking
Regions Served:
48 States, Canada, & Mexico

52071 (HQ)Sack Storage Corporation
66 Atlas St
Worcester, MA 01604   508-754-6802
                  Fax: 508-792-2550
Warehouse providing dry storage for groceries, chemicals, containers, paper and plastics; transportation broker providing freight consolidation and local and long haul trucking; also, rail siding, bulk transfers and packaging services available
Owner: Norman Sirk
Number Employees: 10-19
Services: Broker providing freight consolidation and local & long haul trucking
Regions Served:
Nationwide

52072 (HQ)Saddle Creek Logistics Svc
3010 Saddle Creek Rd
Lakeland, FL 33801-9638   863-665-0966
        Fax: 863-668-8711 888-878-1177
info@saddlecrk.com www.sclogistics.com
A leading nationwide distribution services company that provides warehousing, transportation, contract packaging, and integrated logistics services.
President/Owner: Cliff Otto
cliff.otto@saddlecrk.com
CEO: David Lyons
CFO: Mark Cabrera
Sales: Stephen Cook
Operations: Butch Riggleman
Number Employees: 500-999
Type of Packaging: Consumer
Other Locations:
Saddle Creek Corporation
Charlotte, NC
Waco, TX
Dallas/Fort Worth, TX
Oklahoma City, OK
Atlanta, GA
Orlando, FL
Saddle Creek Corporation Waco
Services: Consolidation services, cross docking, pool delivery, direct store delivery, multi vendor programs
Regions Served:
Nationwide

52073 Saddle Creek Logistics Svc
3010 Saddle Creek Rd
Lakeland, FL 33801-9638   863-665-0966
        Fax: 863-668-8711 866-668-0966
sales@sclogistics.com www.sclogistics.com
Warehouse providing dry storage of nonperishable food; transportation firm offering long and short haul trucking; also, pick-up and delivery services available
Chairman/Founder: David Lyons
President: Cliff Otto
cliff.otto@saddlecrk.com
Senior VP/ CFO: Mark Cabrera
VP Real Estate: Scott Thornton
VP of Marketing and Business Development: Duane Sizemore
Director Business Development: Greg Payne
Number Employees: 500-999
Services: Long & short haul trucking
Regions Served:
Florida

Transportation Firms / A-Z

52074 Safeway Freezer Storage Inc
97 N Mill Rd
Vineland, NJ 08360-3436   856-691-9696
                             Fax: 856-691-3399
                www.safewayfreezerstorage.com
Warehouse providing a total of 3,500,000 CF of cooler and freezer storage for frozen and refrigerated foods; transportation company providing local, long and short haul trucking; rail siding available
President: Eleanor Pepper
epepper@sjfreezergroup.com
Number Employees: 20-49
Parent Co: Safeway Stores
Services: Local, long & short haul trucking
Regions Served:
  Northeast

52075 Saia, Inc.
11465 Johns Creek Pkwy
Suite 400
Johns Creek, GA 30097
                             800-765-7242
        customerservice@saia.com   www.saia.com
Transportation company providing TL and LTL, local and short haul trucking; also, overnight and second day delivery services available.
President & CEO: Rick O'Dell
EVP, Finance & Chief Financial Officer: Frederick Holzgrefe
EVP & Chief Customer Officer: Raymond Ramu
EVP, Operations: Paul Peck
Year Founded: 1924
Estimated Sales: $1.7 Billion
Number Employees: 10,500
Parent Co: SCS Transportation
Services: LTL, local & short haul trucking; also, overnight & 2nd day delivery
Regions Served:
  Midwest, West, Puerto Rico, Canada, and Mexico

52076 Samuel Shapiro & Company
100 N Charles St
Ste 1200
Baltimore, MD 21201-3895   410-539-0540
          Fax: 410-547-6935   800-695-9465
                             www.shapiro.com
Transportation services include brokerage and freight forwarding; serving nationwide and international areas
President & CEO: Marjorie Shapiro
Contact: Jason Brown
jbrown@shapiro.com
Number Employees: 50-99
Services: Brokerage & freight forwarding
Regions Served:
  Nationwide & international

52077 San Diego & Imperial Valley Rr
1501 National Ave # 200
San Diego, CA 92113-1039   619-961-8038
                             Fax: 619-239-7128
          pete.jespersen@railamerica.com
                             www.gwrr.com
Railroad transportation service company
General Manager: Donald Seil
Marketing/Sales: Jose Ramos
Number Employees: 10-19
Parent Co: Railtex
Services: Railroad
Regions Served:
  CA: San Diego, El Cajon, National City, Chula Vista & San Ysidro; also, Mexico: Tijuana & Tecate

52078 San Jose Distribution Service
2055 S 7th St
Suite A
San Jose, CA 95112-6141   408-292-9100
          Fax: 408-292-7173 inquiry@sjdist.com
                             www.sjdist.com
San Jose Distribution Services is a third party warehousing company providing rail siding, pick/pack, assembly, re-pack, labeling, local, regional, and nationwide distribution services for over forty years.
President: Gary Minardi
CEO: Joe Caston
VP Operations: Richard Vega
Contact: Richard Vega
richard@sjdist.com
Number Employees: 50-99
Services: Local haul trucking

52079 Saturn Freight Systems
P.O. Box 680308
Marietta, GA 30068   770-952-3490
        Fax: 770-693-5749 www.saturnfreight.com
Warehouse providing dry storage for nonperishable items; transportation firm providing international and domestic freight forwarding services via air freight and local, long and short haul trucking
President: Guy Stark
Vice President: Bill Handley
Marketing: Justin Stark
VP, Business Development: Michael Moore
Operations: Christopher Lair
Number Employees: 10-19
Services: International & domestic freight forwarding via air freight, local, long & short haul trucking
Regions Served:
  Worldwide: U.S.

52080 Saudi Arabian Airlines
8002 Kew Gardens Rd # 401
Jamaica, NY 11415-3604   718-793-0500
          Fax: 718-551-3030 800-472-8342
                             www.saudiairlines.com
Transportation services including international air
Contact: Mohsen Talal
tmohsen@saudiairlines.com
Number Employees: 10-19
Parent Co: Saudi Arabian Airlines
Services: Air
Regions Served:
  International

52081 Sav Enterprises
11325 Xeon St NW
Coon Rapids, MN 55448-3148   763-278-3340
          Fax: 763-278-3354 866-868-3230
          erik@savtrans.com www.savtrans.com
Transportation broker providing international and domestic freight forwarding via air freight and local and short haul trucking; also, NVOCC, warehousing, distribution, private fleets and complete logistics services available
Owner: Dylan Abbott
dylan@savtrans.com
Co-Founder: Joe Speltz
Co-Founder: Don Divine
Number Employees: 20-49
Services: Broker providing freight forwarding via air freight and long & short haul trucking; also, NVOCC, warehousing, etc.
Regions Served:
  International: nationwide

52082 Savannah Distributing
2425 W Gwinnett St
Garden City, GA 31415-9602   912-233-1167
          Fax: 912-233-1157 800-551-0177
          info@gawine.com www.savdist.com
Distributor of liquor, craft beers, wines and sparkling wines.
Owner: Henri Gabriel
President: Henry Monsees
Estimated Sales: $10-20 Million
Number Employees: 50-99
Type of Packaging: Food Service
Other Locations:
  Atlanta Warehouse
  Atlanta, GA Atlanta Warehouse
Regions Served:
  Georgia

52083 (HQ)Schenker International
150 Albany Ave
Freeport, NY 11520-4702   516-377-3000
          Fax: 516-377-3133 info@schenker.com
                             www.dbschenkerusa.com
Providing a complete range of international air and sea freight forwarding, and all related logistics services as well as global supply chain management from a single source, also providing expertise and solutions for integrated logistics management—for more information on other companies belonging to Schenker, Inc. visit the website
Executive VP: Malcolm Heath
malcolm.heath@schenker.com
Number Employees: 1000-4999
Services: Broker providing local, long & short haul trucking and air & ocean freight
Regions Served:
  International

52084 (HQ)Schilli Transportation Services
1560 Kepner Dr
Lafayette, IN 47905   765-448-3400
          Fax: 765-449-9976 800-688-2101
          sales@schilli.com www.schilli.com
Transportation firm providing local, long and short haul trucking; warehouse providing dry storage
President: Thomas Schilli
Number Employees: 1,000-4,999
Services: Local, long & short haul trucking
Regions Served:
  Nationwide

52085 Schneider National Inc
3101 S Packerland Drive
Green Bay, WI 54313-2545
                             800-558-6767
                             www.schneider.com
Transportation firm providing van, rail, flatbed, heavy haul, long haul trucking, TL and logistics services in North America.
President & Chief Executive Officer: Mark Rourke
EVP/Chief Financial Officer: Stephen Bruffett
EVP/Chief Information Officer: Shaleen Devgun
EVP/General Counsel: Thom Jackson
EVP/Chief Administrative Officer: Rob Reich
Year Founded: 1935
Estimated Sales: Over $1 Billion
Number Employees: 17,450
Services: Van, rail, flatbed, heavy haul, long haul trucking, TL & logistics services
Regions Served:
  North America, Canada, Mexico

52086 Schugel J & R Trucking Inc
2026 N Broadway St
New Ulm, MN 56073-1030   507-359-2037
          Fax: 507-354-4366 800-359-2900
                             www.jrschugel.com
Transportation firm offering TL refrigerated transportation services; trailer spotting services and equipment maintenance available; dry vans and flatbeds also available; EDI capabilities
President: Jim Lamecker
jlamecker@newulmtel.net
Number Employees: 250-499
Services: TL refrigerated transportation, trailer spotting & equipment maintenance
Regions Served:
  Nationwide

52087 Schwebel Baking Co.
965 E. Midlothian Blvd.
P.O. Box 6018
Youngstown, OH 44502   330-783-2860
          Fax: 330-782-1774 800-860-2867
                             www.schwebels.com
White, wheat, whole and multigrain breads; deli buns, rolls and subs; bagels, light breads, pitas, flat bread and tortillas; cinnamon, italian, sour dough, potato, high fiber and raisin breads.
President/CEO: Steven Cooper
VP Marketing & Corporate Communications: Lee Schwebel
Senior VP, Sales: Alyson Winick
Year Founded: 1906
Estimated Sales: $130 Million
Number Employees: 1000-4999
Number of Brands: 6
Square Footage: 125000
Type of Packaging: Consumer, Food Service, Private Label, Bulk
Other Locations:
  Akron, OH
  Saybrook, OH
  Austintown, OH
  Canton, OH
  Cleveland, OH
  Hilliard, OH Saybrook

52088 Seaboard Warehouse Terminals
5400 NW 32 Court
Miami, FL 33147   305-633-8587
          Fax: 305-633-9621 800-273-8587
          info@seaboardwarehouse.com
                             www.seaboardwarehouse.com
Public warehouse providing cooler and dry storage for beverages, food, paper products, plastic bags, aluminum foil, etc.; transportation firm providing short and local haul trucking; also, dry and reefer services and rail siding available

Owner: Bob Fischer
VP/General Manager: Leon Hammond
Contact: Juan Policem
jpolicem@seaboardwarehouse.com
Estimated Sales: $ 10 - 20 Million
Number Employees: 100-249
Square Footage: 920000
Parent Co: Seaboard Warehouse Terminals
Services: Short & local haul trucking; also, dry & reefer available
Regions Served:
FL, CA, MA

52089 Seagate Transportation
555 F St
Perrysburg, OH 43551-4313   419-666-9919
Fax: 419-666-7324   800-833-8250
brad@seagatetrans.com   www.seagatetrans.com
Warehouse providing dry storage; transportation firm providing long haul trucking
President: Andrea Barta
abarta@seagatetrans.com
Recruiter: Bradley Gasser
Dispatch: Jackie Lasits
VP: Andrea Barta
Number Employees: 5-9
Services: Long haul trucking, vans & refrigerated trailers; also, dry storage for dry food & merchandise and frozen food
Regions Served:
U.S. & Canada

52090 (HQ)Seaonus
10060 Skinner Lake Dr
Jacksonville, FL 32246-8495   904-786-8038
Fax: 904-781-3256   info@seaonus.com
www.seaonus.com
Warehouse offering cooler and freezer storage; transportation firm providing local, short and long haul TL and LTL trucking; import/export inspections, blast freezing, break bulk, dockside ship loading and rail siding available
President: Terry Brown
VP Operations: Mark Gier
Number Employees: 100-249
Other Locations:
ICS Logistics
Jacksonville, FLICS Logistics
Services: Local, short & long haul TL & LTL trucking
Regions Served:
Continental U.S.

52091 Seaschott
2609 Cabover Dr # 9
Hanover, MD 21076-1662   410-863-1444
Fax: 410-863-1444   info@seaschott.com
www.seaschott.com
Warehouse providing dry storage for dry canned and imported foods; customs house and transportation broker providing freight forwarding services via local, long and short haul trucking; also, distribution, re-packing, export and importservices available
President/Founder: Robert Schott
Secretary/Treasurer: Joanne Schott
Executive VP: Tony Sequeira
Sales/Marketing: Andrew Shotwell
Manager: Jay Williamson
balimport@seaschott.com
Director Operations: Hing Buon
Number Employees: 5-9
Parent Co: Airschott
Other Locations:
Seaschott
Washington, DCSeaschott
Services: Customs house & transportation broker providing freight forwarding via local, long & short haul trucking
Regions Served:
International: Nationwide

52092 Service By Air Inc
5148 Kennedy Rd # 100
Forest Park, GA 30297-2048   404-762-1500
Fax: 404-762-0119   800-653-6488
sbaatl@servicebyair.com   www.sbaglobal.com
Domestic and International freight forwarder
Manager: Roy Russ
Number Employees: 10-19

52093 Service Craft Distribution Systems
6565 Knott Ave
Buena Park, CA 90620-1139   714-994-0827
Fax: 714-690-6545

Warehouse providing cooler, freezer and dry storage for groceries, refrigerated and frozen items; transportation firm providing local, long and short haul trucking; rail siding available
President: Peter McLoughlin
CFO: Erick Garcia
COO: Peter McLoughlin
Number Employees: 250-499
Services: Local, long & short haul trucking
Regions Served:
Southern CA

52094 Shaffer Trucking
49 E Main St
New Kingstown, PA 17072   717-766-4708
Fax: 717-795-5550   800-742-3337
www.shaffertrucking.com
Transportation services include refrigerated local, long and short haul trucking nationwide
CEO: Raymond Dunn
Manager: Han Goh
hgoh@sembcorp.com
Number Employees: 100-249
Services: Refrigerated local, short & long haul trucking
Regions Served:
Nationwide, Regional

52095 Shaw Montgomery Warehouse Company
1305 Wilbanks Street
Montgomery, AL 36108   334-269-1415
Public bonded warehouse providing dry storage for general merchandise and nonperishable foods; transportation firm providing local haul trucking; rail siding available
Contact: David Cultrera
dave@spwg.com
Office Manager: Connie Cauthen
Number Employees: 10-19
Services: Local haul trucking
Regions Served:
AL

52096 Shepard's Moving & Storage
32 Henry St # 3
Bethel, CT 06801-2406   203-830-8300
Fax: 203-744-6775   800-243-0993
www.mayflower.com
Warehouse offering dry storage for groceries; catalog fulfillment and rail siding available; transportation firm providing agent allied van lines
Owner: Michael Goodman
CEO/CFO: David Albin
Vice President of Sales: Michael Leahy
Warehouse Manager: Robert Badgley
Number Employees: 50-99
Services: Agent allied van lines
Regions Served:
Nationwide

52097 Shoreline Freezers
6 N Industrial Blvd
Bridgeton, NJ 08302-3414   856-451-8300
Fax: 856-451-5284   www.shorelinefreezers.com
Warehouse providing freezer storage; transportation company providing local trucking; rail siding services available
Manager: Eric Scheller
Number Employees: 10-19
Services: Local trucking

52098 Short Freight Lines Inc
459 S River Rd
Po Box 357
Bay City, MI 48708-9601   989-893-3505
Fax: 989-893-3151   llp@shortfreightlines.com
www.shortfreightlines.com
Transportation firm providing long haul trucking
Owner: Bob Short
shortbilling@shortfreightlines.com
Number Employees: 20-49
Services: Long haul trucking
Regions Served:
Nationwide & international: Canada

52099 Sierra Madre Mushrooms
92 McDonald Ln
Bayside, CA 95524   707-445-1420
Fax: 707-445-1424   tlinguini@hotmail.com
We are a 3rd party logistics provider that specializes in coast to coast refrigerate transportation.
President: Trenton Valvo

Estimated Sales: $1 Million
Square Footage: 2000
Regions Served:
Nationwide

52100 Sierra Meat & Seafood Co
1330 Capital Blvd.
Suite A
Reno, NV 89502   775-322-4073
   800-444-5687
sales@sierrameat.com   sierrameat.com
Meat and seafood.
President/CEO: Chris Flocchini
Executive Vice President: Bernadette Flocchini
Year Founded: 1934
Estimated Sales: $101 Million
Number Employees: 100-249
Square Footage: 25000
Type of Packaging: Food Service
Other Locations:
Santa Clara, CA
Monterey, CA
Reno, NVMonterey

52101 (HQ)Simard Warehouses
1212 32nd Avenue
Lachine, QC H8T 3K7
Canada   514-636-9411
Fax: 514-633-8078   888-282-9321
pabraham@simard.ca   www.simard.ca
Warehouse providing dry storage for canned goods and general merchandise; transportation services include LTL, TL, local trucking, container, distribution, hourly and contract serving Montreal and Toronto metropolitan areas
President: Peter Abraham
Chairman: Michael Abraham
Number Employees: 250-499
Services: LTL, TL, container, local trucking, distribution, hourly & contract
Regions Served:
Montreal & Toronto metropolitan areas

52102 Sky West Airlines Inc
444 S River Rd
St George, UT 84790-2085   435-634-3000
Fax: 435-634-3105   www.skywest.com
Transportation firm providing international and nationwide air shipping service for perishable goods
President and COO: Russell Childs
Chairman and CEO: Jerry Atkin
jatkin@skywest.com
CFO: Bradford Rich
Number Employees: 250-499
Services: Air shipping
Regions Served:
International & nationwide

52103 Smith Cartage
10800 NW 97th St Ste 102
Medley, FL 33178   305-953-4100
Fax: 305-688-1075
Transportation firm providing, local, long and short haul trucking; also, COFC, TOFC, etc
President: Jeff Futernick
jeff@smithcartage.com
Numer Employees: 50-99
Parent Co: Smith Terminal Distribution Systems
Services: TL local, long & short haul trucking; also, COFC, TOFC, etc.
Regions Served:
Port Everglades, Palm Beach & Miami; Miami & Ft. Lauderdale rail ramps; Atlanta to Miami freight lane; Southeastern states

52104 (HQ)Smith Terminal Distribution
10800 NW 97th St # 102
Medley, FL 33178-2527   305-685-0325
Fax: 305-688-0081
Warehouse providing cooler and dry storage for groceries and temperature-controlled and general commodities; transportation services include long and short haul trucking and freight consolidation, etc.; also, cross docking, localcartage and rail siding available
Owner: Frank Futernick
frank@smithterminal.com
Number Employees: 100-249
Services: Local, long & short haul trucking, local pick-up & delivery, pool car, freight consolidation, etc.
Regions Served:
International: nationwide; southern FL

Transportation Firms / A-Z

52105 Somerset Industries
901 North Bethlehem Pike
Spring House, PA 19477-0927
215-619-0480
Fax: 215-619-0489 800-883-8728
www.somersetindustries.com
Wholesaler/distributor, importer and exporter of closeout items bought and sold. The correctional food specialist. Warehouse and transportation services provided
President: Jay Shrager
CFO: Carole Shrager
VP: Alan Breslow
Marketing Director: Candace Shrager
Sales Manager: Kevin Murray Jr
General Manager: Ben Caldwell
Number Employees: 20-49
Type of Packaging: Food Service, Private Label, Bulk
Services: Trucking fleet
Regions Served:
  47 states

52106 Sonwil Distribution Center
100 Sonwil Dr
PO Box 126
Buffalo, NY 14225
716-684-0555
Fax: 716-684-6996
Public warehouse providing dry storage for food and medical supplies and general merchandise; transportation broker providing freight consolidation services; also, rail siding, controlled sanitation programs, pick and pack, shrinktunnel and EDI available
President and CEO: Peter Wilson
Vice President of Sales & Marketing: James Manno Jr.
darchilla@sonwil.com
Contact: Dennis Archilla
darchilla@sonwil.com
Chief Operations Officer: Richard Becker Jr
Services: Broker providing freight consolidation
Regions Served:
  US & Canada

52107 (HQ)Sopak Co Inc
118 S Cypress St
Mullins, SC 29574-3004
843-464-6001
www.sopakco.com
Warehouse providing dry storage, re-packing and labeling for nonperishable foods; transportation services include short haul trucking in the Southeast
Manager: Wesley Keller
Estimated Sales: Less Than $500,000
Number Employees: 1-4
Other Locations:
  Bennettsville, SC
  Mullins, SCMullins
Services: Short haul trucking
Regions Served:
  Southeast

52108 South Atlantic Warehouse Corporation
2020 E Market St
Greensboro, NC 27401
336-272-4163
Fax: 336-274-7660
Warehouse facility offering dry storage space for food, appliances, textile products, furniture and cans; transportation firm providing short haul trucking; also, uncrating, rail siding and sit-in services available
Owner: Jim Rucker
jim.rucker@southatlanticcompanies.com
Number Employees: 50-99
Services: Short haul trucking
Regions Served:
  NC, SC & TN

52109 South Bend Warehousing & Distribution
PO Box 1228
South Bend, IN 46624-1228
574-239-1310
Fax: 574-239-7695 storage@sbwd.com
Warehouse providing storage for industrial goods; transportation firm providing short haul trucking
Owner: Abraham Marcus
Number Employees: 10-19
Services: Short haul trucking
Regions Served:
  Regional

52110 (HQ)South Mill
649 West South Street
Kennett Square, PA 19348
610-444-4800
Fax: 610-444-1338 info@southmill.com
www.southmill.com
National mushroom supplier.
Contact: Iris Ayala
iayala@southmill.com
Year Founded: 1978
Number Employees: 1,000
Type of Packaging: Consumer, Food Service, Private Label, Bulk
Other Locations:
  Distribution
  Atlanta, GA
  Distribution
  New Orleans, LA
  Distribution
  Houston, TX
  Distribution
  Dallas, TXDistributionNew Orleans
Services: Long haul trucking
Regions Served:
  U.S. & Canada

52111 (HQ)Southshore Enterprises
3515 Lakeshore Drive
St Joseph, MI 49085-2977
269-983-2080
Fax: 269-983-7307
sales@southshorecompanies.com
www.southshorecompanies.com
Warehouse providing dry storage for nonperishable foods; transportation firm providing short haul trucking
President: Ted Kirshenbaum
Treasurer, CFO: Philip Maki
VP: Jordan Kirshenbaum
Contact: David Butler
dbutler@southshorecompanies.com
Senior Operations Manager: Robert Oberheu
Number Employees: 5-9
Other Locations:
  Southshore Enterprises
  East Hartford, CT
  Elkhart, IN
  Dayton, OHSouthshore EnterprisesElkhart
Services: Short haul trucking
Regions Served:
  Southwest MI

52112 Southwest Truck Service
50 Pine Street
P.O.Box 1810
Watsonville, CA 95076
831-724-1041
Fax: 831-724-0523 800-999-3680
order@swtrucking.com
Transportation firm providing local, long and short haul refrigerated trucking
Owner/President: Robert J. Spare
General Manager: Noe LeGaspi
Contact: Noe Legaspi
nlegaspi@swtrucking.com
Operations: Joel Ailes
Number Employees: 10-19
Services: Local, long & short haul refrigerated trucking

52113 Southwestern Motor Transport
4600 Goldfield
San Antonio, TX 78218-4601
210-662-2390
Fax: 210-662-3295 800-531-1071
info@smtl.com www.smtl.com
Transportation company providing TL and LTL trucking
CEO: Roy Gilbert
rgilbert@smtl.com
Number Employees: 500-999
Services: TL & LTL trucking
Regions Served:
  East Coast, Mexico, & Canada

52114 Space Center Inc
2501 Rosegate
Roseville, MN 55113-2717
651-604-4200
Fax: 651-604-4222 info@spacecenterinc.com
Warehouse providing dry and humidy-controlled storage for nonperishable items and paper products; transportation firm providing local haul trucking; also, re-packing, labeling services and rail siding available
President: Anthony Kraus
CEO: Charles Arend
carend@spacecenterinc.com
Estimated Sales: Less Than $500,000
Number Employees: 1-4
Parent Co: Space Center
Services: Local short haul trucking
Regions Served:
  Kansas City & Independence, MO

52115 Spartan Logistics
4140 Lockbourne Rd
Columbus, OH 43207-4221
614-497-1777
Fax: 614-497-1808 sales@spartanwarehouse.com
www.spartanwarehouse.com
Warehouse providing dry storage of cans, cereal, plastic materials, canned food and KD cartons; rail siding, distribution and packaging services available; transportation firm providing local haul trucking
President: Ed Harmon
CFO: Steve Harmon
Vice President: Jim Ranney
Number Employees: 5-9
Parent Co: Spartan Warehouse & Distribution
Services: Local haul trucking
Regions Served:
  Local

52116 St Charles Trading Inc
650 N Raddant Rd
Batavia, IL 60510-4207
630-377-0608
Fax: 630-406-1936
customerservice@stcharlestrading.com
Distributor,importer/exporter of food ingredients, specializing in beans and seeds; oar products; batters, coatins & breadcrumbs; dairy, potato, wheat, corn and protein products; cocoa and chcolate; dehydrated onion and garlic;spices;food chemicals and sweeteners; dehydrated vegetables and fruits; and rice.
CEO: William Manns
williammanns@stcharlestrading.com
Executive Vice President: Dave Nolan
Director, Manufacturing & Quality Contro: Andrew Rumshas
Vice President of Operations: Janet Matthews
Purchasing Manager: Novita Rahim
Estimated Sales: $64.4 Million
Number Employees: 20-49
Number of Brands: 49
Type of Packaging: Bulk

52117 St Onge Ruff & Associates
2400 Pershing Road
Ste 400
Kansas City, MO 64108
816-329-8700
Fax: 816-329-8701 800-800-5261
marketing@transystems.com
Engineering firm specializing in the planning, design and construction of processing and distribution facilities
Number Employees: 5-9

52118 St. John Brothers
20 Crofton Road
Kenner, LA 70062
504-469-9483
Customs house and transportation broker specializing in freight forwarding of imported and exported goods
Number Employees: 5-9
Services: Customs house & transportation broker specializing in freight forwarding of imported & exported goods
Regions Served:
  International

52119 Standard TransportationSvc
1801 Roosevelt Ave
Joplin, MO 64801-3753
417-782-1990
Fax: 417-782-5098 lbryant@stdtrans.com
Transportation broker providing freight forwarding and local haul trucking; warehouse providing dry storage
Owner: Geoff Roberts
Sales: Morris Glaze
Contact: Jeremy Hunsaker
jhunsaker@vinylren.com
Operations: Larry Bryant
Estimated Sales: Less Than $500,000
Number Employees: 1-4
Square Footage: 976000
Services: Brokerage; local haul trucking & freight forwarding; also, warehousing
Regions Served:
  Nationwide & Canada

Transportation Firms / A-Z

52120 Standard Warehouse
8501 River Rd
Pennsauken, NJ 08110-3325   856-488-0430
                                  www.stechgroup.com
Warehouse providing dry storage for nonperishable items; transportation firm providing local, long and short haul trucking
President: Marge Smith
msmith@stechgroup.com
Sales Manager: Tim Fox
General Manager: Jim Donelly III
Number Employees: 10-19
Services: Local, long & short haul trucking
Regions Served:
  48 States

52121 Stanley Orchards Sales, Inc.
2044 State Route 32
#6
Modena, NY 12548   845-883-7351
  Fax: 845-883-5077 sales@stanleyorchards.com
                    www.stanleyorchards.com
Apple growing and storage/packing facility; importer of apples and pears; cold storage facility.
President/CEO: Ronald Cohn
Sales & Marketing: Jordan Cohn
Sales Manager: Anthony Maresca
Domestic Sales: Janine Skurnick
Controller: Susan Surprise
Import/Export Liason: Lorrie Hazzard
Estimated Sales: $293 Thousand
Number Employees: 8
Type of Packaging: Consumer, Food Service, Private Label, Bulk

52122 Star Distribution Systems
2302 Henderson Way
Plant City, FL 33563-7904   813-659-1002
  Fax: 813-757-9666 info@stardistribution.us
                    www.stardistribution.us
Warehouse providing dry and cooler storage for refrigerated and nonperishable food; transportation firm providing local and short haul trucking
President/CEO: Larry Jimenez
ljimenez@stardistribution.us
Executive Vice President: David Mattioli
Number Employees: 100-249
Services: Local & short haul trucking
Regions Served:
  Florida

52123 Star Shipping
Fortunen 1
Po Box 1088 Sentrum
Bergen, NW N-5809   475-523-9600
Transportation firm offering steamship services to Canada, Japan, Korea, Europe and Brazil
Number Employees: 20-49
Parent Co: Star Shipping A/S
Services: Steamships
Regions Served:
  Canada, Europe, Japan, Korea & Brazil

52124 Starr Distribution Services Company
235 S 56th St
Chandler, AZ 85226-3304   480-961-0536
                          Fax: 480-961-0453
Warehouse providing cooler and dry storage; transportation firm providing local haul trucking
Owner: James Young
Number Employees: 20-49
Services: Local haul trucking
Regions Served:
  Arizona, Southwest

52125 Stemm Transfer & Storage
PO Box 397
St Cloud, MN 56302-0397   320-251-4080
                          Fax: 320-251-7741
Warehouse providing dry storage for paper products and dry foods; transportation firm providing local and long haul trucking; rail siding services available
President: Kathie Jordahl
Number Employees: 20-49
Services: Local & long haul trucking
Regions Served:
  Midwest

52126 Sterling Transportation
1927 SW 1st St
PO Box 176
Redmond, OR 97756-7119   541-923-8785
  Fax: 541-548-5139 800-627-5123
                    keving@sterlingtransport.net
                    www.sterlingtransport.net
Transportation broker providing long haul trucking
President: Kevin Groshong
keving@sterlingtransport.net
Operations Manager: Richard Kirk
Number Employees: 10-19
Services: Long haul trucking
Regions Served:
  Nationwide

52127 Stevens Transport
9757 Military Pkwy
Dallas, TX 75227-4805   972-216-9254
  Fax: 972-289-8545 800-823-9369
                    www.stevenstransport.com
Transportation firm providing refrigerated and dry rail and long haul TL and LTL services
President: Clay Aaron
Chairman and CEO: Steven Aaron
Executive Vice President: Michael Richey
mrichey@stevenstransport.com
Estimated Sales: Over $1 Billion
Number Employees: 5000-9999
Services: Refrigerated & dry rail and long haul TL & LTL
Regions Served:
  U.S. & Canada

52128 Stone Forwarding Company
P.O. Box 118
Galveston, TX 77553-0118   409-740-0420
Transportation firm providing freight forwarding for rice, flour and wheat
President: Frank Mendel
Number Employees: 1-4
Services: Freight forwarding
Regions Served:
  Regional: Gulf Coast

52129 Stonepath Logistics
1930 6th Ave S Ste 401
Seattle, WA 98134   206-624-4354
Warehouse providing dry storage for groceries and dry goods; transportation firm providing freight forwarding services via ocean freight, local, long and short haul trucking; also, re-packing services available
Number Employees: 50-99
Services: Freight forwarding via ocean freight, local, long & short haul trucking
Regions Served:
  U.S.

52130 Streamline Shippers-Affiliates
6279 E Slauson Ave # 303
Suite 303
Commerce, CA 90040-3040   323-271-3800
  Fax: 323-271-3888 www.streamlineshippers.com
Warehouse providing storage for dry foods; shippers' association providing LTL, FTL, LCL, FCL and logistical services; also, labeling, bar coding and sorting services available
President: Sarah Barriger
sarah@streamlineshippers.com
Number Employees: 50-99
Services: Shippers' association providing LTL, FTL, LCL, FCL & logistical services
Regions Served:
  Continental U.S., Mexico, Canada, HI, Peurto Rico

52131 Supreme Lobster
220 E North Ave
Villa Park, IL 60181-1207   630-832-6700
  Fax: 630-832-6688 www.supremelobster.com
Wholesaler/distributor of fresh and frozen seafood; serving the food service and retail markets; transportation firm providing refrigerated trucking
President/CEO: Dominic Stramaglia
Chief Financial Officer: Greg Shuda
VP: Mike Sakshaug
Sales: Tim Stramaglia
Purchasing Manager: Tim Fasshaur
Number Employees: 250-499
Square Footage: 400000
Type of Packaging: Food Service
Services: Refrigerated trucking

52132 Swan Transportation
1820 Shiloh Rd
Suite 1303
Tyler, TX 75703   903-705-0441
  Fax: 903-617-6887 903-705-0441
                    www.swantrans.com
Transportation agent with over 7,000 trucks available in any type.
Manager: Kimberly Smotherman
Corporate Manager: Kimberly Smotherman

52133 Sweeteners Plus Inc
5768 Sweeteners Blvd
Lakeville, NY 14480-9741   585-346-3193
  Fax: 585-346-2310 www.sweetenersplus.com
Manufacturer and distributor of liquid and dry sweeteners including white and brown sugar, organic and kosher products, fructose, maltitol, corn syrup, and invert syrups. Also bottling, custom blending, and liquid fondants. Shipped regionally long haul by rail and short haul by trucks and nationally by distribution products
President & CEO: Carlton Myers
Quality Assurance Manager: Mark Rudolph
VP Sales: Mark Whitford
Operation Manager: Bill Devine
Estimated Sales: $14.7 Million
Number Employees: 1-4
Type of Packaging: Food Service, Bulk

52134 T P Freight Lines Inc
2703 3rd St # A
Tillamook, OR 97141-2539   503-842-2574
  Fax: 503-842-6156 800-558-8217
                    www.tpfreight.net
Transportation firm offering short haul trucking for perishable and nonperishable goods
Owner: Buck Colleknon
bcolleknon@tpfreight.net
Number Employees: 10-19
Services: Short haul trucking for perishable & non-perishable goods
Regions Served:
  Regional/Local: OR

52135 TW Transport Inc
7405 S Hayford Rd
Cheney, WA 99004-9633   509-623-4004
  Fax: 509-623-4069 800-356-4070
                    twtcsr@twtrans.com www.trans-system.com
Transportation firm providing refrigerated van services
President: James J Williams
jwilliams@trans-system.com
CEO: James J Williams
Estimated Sales: Over 245
Number Employees: 100-249
Services: Refrigerated vans
Regions Served:
  West Coast, Northwest

52136 (HQ)TWL Corporation
5650 Wattsburg Rd
Erie, PA 16509-4066   814-825-1881
                          Fax: 814-825-9428
Warehouse providing dry storage of food and paper products, containers, plastics and machinery; transportation firm providing LTL, TL and just-in-time long haul trucking; also, air freight, expediting and truck rental, leasing and maintenance
President: Ray Benacci
CEO: Joe Benacci
Vice President: Chuck Sites
Contact: Kristina Benacci
kristinab@twl-erie.com
Number Employees: 100-249
Services: LTL, TL & just-in-time long haul trucking; also, air freight, expediting & truck rental, leasing & maintenance
Regions Served:
  Northeast, South, Mid-Atlantic, Canada

52137 Tazmanian Freight Forwarding
P.O. Box 11090
Cleveland, OH 44181-1090   216-265-7881
  Fax: 216-265-7888 800-426-6709
                    hr@tazmanian.com www.tazmanian.com
Warehouse providing dry storage for nonperishable and dry ice packed perishable items; transportation firm providing freight forwarding, air freight services, long haul and expedited trucking services available

Transportation Firms / A-Z

CEO: Rob Rossbach
Contact: Don Cotone
melanie@luvmytriplets.com
Number Employees: 50-99
Services: Freight forwarding, air freight, long haul & expedited trucking
Regions Served:
Nationwide

52138 Teal's Express Inc
22411 Teal Dr
Watertown, NY 13601   315-788-6437
Fax: 315-788-5060   800-836-0369
www.teals.com
Transportation services include regional TL and LTL
President: John Teal
CEO: Gordon Bush
gbush@teals.com
Secretary: Bob Teal
Number Employees: 20-49
Services: Regional LTL & TL
Regions Served:
NY, NJ & New England

52139 Team Hardinger
1314 W 18th St
Erie, PA 16502-1517   814-453-6587
Fax: 814-453-4919   800-877-6587
sales@team-h.com   www.team-h.com
Warehouse offering dry storage for general merchandise; also, transportation firm offering vans, storage trailers and flat beds
President: Jerry Allshouse
jerrya@team-h.com
VP: William Schaal Jr.
General Manager: H. Bender
Number Employees: 100-249
Services: Flat beds, vans & storage trailers
Regions Served:
48 states

52140 (HQ)Ted L. Rausch Company
875 Mahler Rd
Ste 168
Burlingame, CA 94010-1606   650-348-2211
Fax: 650-348-8811   rauschco@ix.netcom.com
www.rauschtrans.com
Customs house and transportation broker providing international and domestic freight forwarding via air and ocean freight; also, freight consolidation, local delivery and re-warehousing of products services available
President: Ted Rausch
VP: Helmut Boeck
General Manager: Tony Yee
Number Employees: 20-49
Other Locations:
Rausch, Ted L., Co.
Chicago, ILRausch, Ted L., Co.
Services: Customs house broker providing freight forwarding services via air & ocean freight; also, consolidation, etc.
Regions Served:
International

52141 Tejas Logistics System
301 Pleasant St
Waco, TX 76704-2536   254-753-0301
Fax: 254-752-4452   800-535-9786
info@tejaswarehouse.com
www.tejaswarehouse.com
Warehouse providing dry storage for dried milk, canned foods, glass bottles, health care products, etc.; transportation firm providing local, long and short haul trucking; rail siding, re-packing, cross docking and inventory controlavailable
CEO: Tom Greene
tom@tejaswarehouse.com
CFO: Rapture Hill
Number Employees: 50-99
Services: Trucking: local, short & long haul; also, contract calling
Regions Served:
Continental U.S.

52142 Texas Cartage WarehouseInc
12344 E Northwest Hwy
Dallas, TX 75228-8004   214-320-3200
Fax: 214-320-9103   sales@texcar.com
Public and contract warehouse providing dry storage; transportation division providing local and short haul trucking; rail siding, LTL, labeling, pick/pack, custom handling, pool cross docking, re-furbishing, pick-up and deliveryservices available

President: Jim Jouvenat
jjouvenat@texcar.com
Number Employees: 10-19
Services: Local & long haul trucking, LTL, TL pick-up & delivery in commercial zone & interstate regional market, etc.
Regions Served:
AR, KS, LA, MO, MS, NM, OK, TX, & TN

52143 Texas N Western RailwayCompany
6647 Road G
Sunray, TX 79086-2015   806-935-7474
Fax: 806-935-8152   www.tnwcorp.com
Transportation company providing rail car services
Manager: Norman Bottger
Number Employees: 10-19
Parent Co: TNW Corporation
Services: Rail car
Regions Served:
Regional & Locally: TX

52144 The Scoular Company/TSCContainer Freight
2027 Dodge Street
Omaha, NE 68102
food@scoular.com
www.scoular.com
Merchandise a full range of agricultural products: traditional and specialty crops, food and feed ingredients, and freight.
Chairman: David Faith
Chief Executive Officer: Paul Maass
Chief Financial Officer: Andrew Kenny
Chief Human Resources Officer: Kurt Peterson
Chief Information Officer: Jeff Schreiner
SVP & General Counsel: Megan Belcher
SVP & Division General Manager: Bob Ludington
SVP & Division General Manager: John Messerich
SVP & Division General Manager: Bryan Wurscher
Year Founded: 1892
Estimated Sales: $4.3 Billion
Number Employees: 1,000+
Number of Products: 100+
Other Locations:
Overland Park, KS
Minneapolis, MNMinneapolis
Services: Freight forwarding; also, truck, rail & ocean freight
Regions Served:
U.S.A., Central America, South America, Asia, Europe, Middle East, Europe & Africa

52145 (HQ)The Terminal Corporation
6610-B Tributary Street
Suite 212
Baltimore, MD 21224   410-276-3490
Fax: 410-276-3495   opsbal@termship.com
www.termship.com
Warehouse offering dry storage of groceries, beverages, paper products, etc.; transportation broker providing just-in-time delivery; also, specialty packing available available nationally
Owner, President: Robert A. Herb
Chairman: John Menzies
CFO: Craig Kershaw
VP: Michael Buckley
Accounting: Jennifer Miller
Contact: Betty Browne
b_browne@termship.com
Operations Manager: Joseph Lis
Number Employees: 100-249
Other Locations:
Jessup, MD
Timonium, MD
Baltimore, MDTimonium
Services: Brokerage
Regions Served:
Nationwide

52146 Three D Brokers
N7440 Osborn Way
Fond Du Lac, WI 54937-8903   920-922-0230
Fax: 920-922-0670   800-776-3587
dean@osborntrucking.com
www.osborntrucking.com
Warehouse offering cold and dry storage; transportation broker providing long haul trucking
President: Dean Osborn
dean@osborntrucking.com
Dispatcher: Charley Osborn
Number Employees: 10-19
Square Footage: 30000
Services: Broker & long haul trucking

Regions Served:
East Coast

52147 (HQ)Tighe Warehousing-Distribution
481 Wildwood Ave
Woburn, MA 01801-2027   781-939-0925
Fax: 781-721-1965   www.tts-logistics.com
Warehouse providing cooler, dry and humidity-controlled storage for canned goods, candy, etc.; transportation firm providing LTL, TL, freight brokerage, etc., rail siding available
President: John Tighe Sr
j.tighesr@tighe.com
VP: John F. Tighe II
Number Employees: 20-49
Other Locations:
T. Tighe & Sons
Woburn, MA
Tighe Warehousing & Distribution
Mansfield, MAT. Tighe & SonsMansfield
Services: LTL, TL brokerage & dedicated transportation
Regions Served:
Northeast & Mid-Atlantic

52148 Tolteca Foodservice
4305 Steve Reynolds Boulevard
Norcross, GA 30093   770-263-0490
800-541-6835
www.toltecafoods.com
A self-proclaimed one-stop shop for Mexican restaurants. A manufacturer of every kind of supplies a Mexican restaurant may need, including tortillas, spices, meats, dairy, oils, grains, fruit and vegetables, beverages, etc.
Estimated Sales: $1700000
Number Employees: 10-19
Number of Products: 2000
Square Footage: 50000
Type of Packaging: Consumer, Food Service, Private Label

52149 Totem Ocean Trailer Express
32001 32nd Ave S
Ste 200
Federal Way, WA 98001   253-449-8100
Fax: 253-449-8225   800-426-0074
generalinfo@totemocean.com
Transportation firm providing freight forwarding to and from Alaska via roll-on/roll-off steamship, rail and highway connections; serving WA and AK
President: John Parrott
CEO: Robert P Magee
Sales Manager: Curt Stoner
Contact: Ed Abram
eabram@saltchuk.com
Chief Operating Officer: Michael Noone
General Manager: Grace Greene
Number Employees: 100-249
Parent Co: Saltchuk Resources
Services: Cargo to & from Alaska via roll-on/roll-off steamship, rail & highway connections
Regions Served:
AK; WA; Lower 48 States; & Canada

52150 Trademark Transportation
739 Vandalia St
St Paul, MN 55114-1302   651-646-2500
Fax: 651-645-8135   800-646-2550
details@trademarktrans.com
www.trademarktrans.com
Transportation firm providing freight forwarding and long and short haul trucking; consolidation and distribution available
President: Justin Bratnober
VP: Steve Becker
Estimated Sales: $10 Million
Number Employees: 20-49
Square Footage: 30000
Services: Freight forwarding and long & short haul trucking
Regions Served:
IA, IL, IN, MI, MN, MO, ND, OH, SD, WI & Canada

52151 Trailwood Warehouse LLC
4825 Mustang Cir
Mounds View, MN 55112-1552   763-783-9999
Fax: 763-783-2058   877-897-6668

Warehouse providing cooler, dry and humidity-controlled storage for food products, confectionery items, health/beauty aids and paper-related items; also, rail siding and temperature-controlled T.L. and regional L.T.L. protectiveservice available
CEO: Larry Tyson
VP Operations/Sales: Gary Miller
Contact: Larry Tyson
mvsf@isd.net
Number Employees: 20-49
Parent Co: Tyson Foods
Services: Temperature-controlled T.L. & regional L.T.L protective service
Regions Served:
Northeast Quadrant of U.S.

52152 Tri County Citrus Packers
12143 Avenue 456
Orange Cove, CA 93646-9504   559-626-5010
Fax: 559-626-7951 vcpg@vcpg.com
Packinghouse and licensed shipper of citrus products for Sunkist Growers, Inc.
Manager: John Kalendar
Assistant Manager: Eric Fultz
Manager: John Clower
jclower@vcpg.com
Number Employees: 50-99
Parent Co: Visalia Citrus Packing Group

52153 Trinity Transport & Distribution Services
50 Fallon Avenue
P.O.Box 1620
Seaford, DE 19973-8920   800-846-3400
Fax: 302-337-3919 866-874-6489
jeff.banning@trinitytransport.com
Transportation broker providing local, LTL and short haul trucking; serving the continental U.S. and Canada
President/CEO: Jeff Banning
CFO: Doug Potvin
VP Operations: Doug Potvin
Number Employees: 5-9
Parent Co: Trinity Transport
Services: Brokerage & long, LTL & short haul trucking
Regions Served:
Continental U.S. & Canada

52154 Twin City Wholesale
519 Walker St
Opelika, AL 36801-5999   334-745-4564
Fax: 334-749-5125 800-344-6935
johanna@tcwholesale.com
Wholesaler and distributor of products and supplies for convenience stores and grocery chains; offers business floor plan design services.
Owner: Johanna Bottoms
twincity@mindspring.com
Estimated Sales: $76 Million
Number Employees: 50-99
Regions Served:
Alabama, Georgia

52155 Twin Modal
2699 Patton Rd
St Paul, MN 55113-1137   651-697-8800
Fax: 651-697-8895 800-366-8946
Transportation broker offering freight forwarding, pool distribution, freight management, trucking, rail shipping, etc
President: Chip Smith
VP & CFO: Ted Hansen
Contact: Char Hepburn
chepburn@twinmodal.com
Number Employees: 20-49
Services: Boxcar, TOFC/COFC, stacktrains, truckload brokerage, partial co-loading, pool distribution/assembly, etc.
Regions Served:
Nationwide, Canada & Mexico

52156 UPS Freight
1000 Semmes Ave
Richmond, VA 23224-2246   804-231-8000
Fax: 804-231-8723 www.ltl.upsfreight.com
Transportation company providing long and short haul trucking; serving the continental U.S. and internationally
President: Jack Holmes
Senior VP: David Birkmeyer
dbirkmeyer@upsfreight.com
Number Employees: 1000-4999
Parent Co: Union Pacific

Services: Long & short haul trucking
Regions Served:
Regional, National, & International

52157 USAir
2345 Crystal Drive
Arlington, VA 22227   800-428-4322
Transportation firm providing air freight services
Contact: Richard Till
richard.till@usairways.com
Number Employees: 500-999
Parent Co: USAir Group
Services: Air freight
Regions Served:
International: nationwide

52158 UTZ Quality Foods Inc
860 Gitts Run Rd
Hanover, PA 17331-8123   717-633-1710
Fax: 717-633-7445 800-669-8912
www.utzsnacks.com
Warehouse providing dry and humidity-controlled storage for general commodities and appliances; transportation services include short and long haul trucking in the continental U.S., LTL, container, and flatbed, along with EDIcapabilities
President: Glenn Longstreth
Sales Manager: Candee Waite
Number Employees: 100-249
Services: General commodities
Regions Served:
Continental U.S.

52159 Ultimate Foods
P.O. Box 1008
Linden, NJ 07036   908-486-0800
Fax: 908-486-2999 www.ultimatefoodsservice.com
Offer a full line of fresh and frozen seafood, produce, meats, oils, pastas, canned tomatoes, and other grocery and specialty items.
General Manager: Scott Greisman
Seafood Buyer/Quality Control: John Parisi
Produce Buyer/Quality Control: Albert Sindoni
Road Sales Manager: Al Ferrentino
Operations Manager: Anthony Stropoli
Dry Goods Buyer: James Boniface
Estimated Sales: $3.6 Million
Number of Brands: 1
Type of Packaging: Food Service, Bulk

52160 (HQ)Unicold Corp
3140 Ualena St # 101
Honolulu, HI 96819-1965   808-836-2931
Fax: 808-833-7296 sales@unicoldcorp.com
www.unicoldcorp.com
Warehouse with 3.4 million cubic feet of space providing frozen, chilled and temperature controlled storage for foods including chocolates; transportation firm providing freight consolidation and forwarding; also, rail sidingavailable
Manager: Darryl Kawano
dkawano@unicoldcorp.com
Number Employees: 50-99
Other Locations:
Los Angeles, CA
Oakland, CA
Seattle, WAOakland
Services: Freight consolidation & forwarding

52161 Union Pacific Railroad Co
1400 Douglas St
Omaha, NE 68179-0002   402-544-5000
888-870-8777
www.up.com
Transportation firm providing rail car service; serving nationwide.
Chairman/President/CEO: Lance Fritz
lancefritz@up.com
EVP/Chief Legal Officer/Secretary: Rhonda Ferguson
EVP/Chief Financial Officer: Jennifer Hamann
EVP/Chief Human Resources Officer: Beth Whited
Chief Operating Officer: Jim Vena
Year Founded: 1862
Estimated Sales: $22.8 Billion
Number Employees: 37,000
Parent Co: Union Pacific Corporation
Other Locations:
Hinkle, OR
Roseville, CA
N. Little Rock, AR
Rochelle, ILRoseville
Services: Rail car service
Regions Served:
Nationwide & international: Canada

52162 Union Storage & Transfer Co
4275 Main Ave
Fargo, ND 58103-1127   701-282-4321
Fax: 701-277-1244
Warehouse offering cold, dry and frozen storage for frozen foods, groceries, heated products and appliances; transportation firm providing local haul trucking; distribution and rail siding services available
President: David B Bertel
office@unionstorage.com
Number Employees: 20-49
Services: Local haul trucking

52163 United Express
W6390 Challenger Dr # 203
Appleton, WI 54914-9119   920-739-5123
Fax: 920-739-9722 www.airwis.com
Transportation firm providing domestic and international air freight services
Manager: Beverly Luetschwager
CEO: Jeff Crowley
Number Employees: 5-9
Parent Co: Air Wisconsin Airlines Corporation
Services: Domestic & international air freight
Regions Served:
IL, IN, MI, MN, PA, WI, KY, WV, AR, CO & CA

52164 Valley Distributors & Storage Company
1 Passan Dr
Wilkes Barre, PA 18702   570-654-2403
Fax: 570-654-4206 www.valleydist.com
Warehouse providing cooler, freezer and dry storage for general merchandise; transportation services include short and local haul in the Northeast and Mid-Atlantic areas; rail siding available
President: John Passan
Chief Financial Officer: Karen Haller
Director of Sales: Kyle Dickinson
Chief Operating Officer: Carol Keup
Number Employees: 50-99
Type of Packaging: Consumer, Private Label
Services: Short & local haul trucking
Regions Served:
Northeast & Mid-Atlantic

52165 (HQ)Van Brunt Port Jersey Warehouse
580 Division St
Elizabeth, NJ 07201-2003   908-282-7080
Fax: 908-282-7097 www.vanbruntwarehouse.com
Warehouse providing dry storage for general merchandise and imported dry foods; transportation firm providing local and long haul trucking; also, rail siding, re-packing and shrink wrapping services available
Owner: Ken Gross
Number Employees: 20-49
Services: Local & long haul trucking
Regions Served:
48 states, piers & local areas

52166 Van Wyk Freight Lines
619 East St S
Grinnell, IA 50112-8079   641-236-7551
Fax: 641-236-4247 800-362-2595
Transportation firm providing short and local haul trucking
Owner: Vernon Van Wyk
pinky@vanwykfreight.com
Number Employees: 50-99
Services: Short & local haul trucking
Regions Served:
Regional & local: IA; 2 to 3 day service to CA

52167 Vantage USA
4740 S Whipple St
Chicago, IL 60632   773-247-1086
Fax: 708-401-1565 www.VantageUSA.net
Organic/natural & commodity wholesale consolidator/supplier and logistics provider. Specializing in natural and private label products planning & development.
Owner: Dan Gash
dan@vantageusa.net
Type of Packaging: Food Service, Private Label, Bulk

Transportation Firms / A-Z

52168 Vermont Railway Inc
1 Railway Ln
Burlington, VT 05401-5290   802-862-2503
Fax: 802-658-2553   800-639-3088
dwulfson@vermontrailway.com
www.vermontrailway.com
Railroad transportation services for the New England area
President: David Wulfson
dwulfson@vrs.us.com
Executive VP: Lisa Wulfson
Number Employees: 100-249
Parent Co: Clarendon & Pittsford Railroad
Services: Railroad
Regions Served:
New England

52169 (HQ)Versacold Logistics Services
3371 No 6 Rd
Richmond, BC V6V 1P6
Canada   604-258-0350
Fax: 604-207-1971   877-207-1950
info@versacold.com   www.versacold.com
Temperature-sensitive products; 31 facilities across Canada
Chief Executive Officer: Paul Campbell
Chief Financial Officer: Jennifer Postelnik
Chief Commercial Officer: Mark Dienesch
Chief Operating Officer: Michele Arcamone
Year Founded: 1946
Estimated Sales: $500 Million
Number Employees: 1000-4999
Services: LTL & TL; Long-haul
Regions Served:
Canada & US

52170 (HQ)Verst Group Logistics Inc
300 Shorland Dr
Walton, KY 41094-9328   859-485-1212
Fax: 859-485-1428   sales@verstgroup.com
www.verstgroup.com
Family owned company provides fully integrated warehousing transportation and packaging services.
President & CEO: Paul Verst
pverst@verstgroup.com
CFO: Jim Stadtmiller
VP Transportation: Chris Cusick
COO: Bob Jackson
Number Employees: 50-99
Services: Local & long haul trucking
Regions Served:
Midwest

52171 Viterra, Inc
2625 Victoria Ave.
Regina, SK S4T 7T9
Canada   306-569-4411
Fax: 306-569-4708   866-647-4090
www.viterra.com
Grain and oilseeds.
President/CEO: Kyle Jeworski
Estimated Sales: $2.4 Billion
Number Employees: 190,000
Parent Co: Glencore plc
Type of Packaging: Consumer, Food Service, Private Label, Bulk

52172 Volunteer Express
565 Hollow Rd
Phoenixville, PA 19460-1136   610-630-0700
Fax: 610-630-0838   800-523-0596
Transportation firm providing local and short haul trucking service
President: Dan Volpe Sr.
danv@volpexp.com
Estimated Sales: Less Than $500,000
Number Employees: 1-4
Regions Served:
DE; MD; NJ; CT; PA; MA; RI

52173 (HQ)Volunteer Express
1116 Polk Ave
Nashville, TN 37210-4299   615-244-8636
Fax: 615-256-1039   800-251-1015
www.volunteerexpress.com
Transportation firm providing local and short haul trucking
President: Ken Hickman
VP of Operations: Dan Johnson
Sales Representative: Eric Bond
Manager: Brad Wilson
bwilson@volunteerexpress.com
Terminal Manager: Jeremy Williamson
Number Employees: 100-249

Other Locations:
Volunteer Express
Madison, TN Volunteer Express
Services: Local & short haul trucking
Regions Served:
East coast

52174 (HQ)W J Beitler Co & Beitler Truck
3379 Stafford St
Pittsburgh, PA 15204-1441   412-771-4204
Fax: 412-771-5066   800-771-4207
email@wjbeitler.com   www.wjbeitler.com
Warehouse providing humidity-controlled, dry and cooler storage for refrigerated and nonperishable foods; transportation firm providing local and short haul trucking; also, re-couping and rail car services available
Owner: W J Beitler
VP: William A Beitler
Warehouse Manager: Myke Flyn
Dispatcher: Kurt Beitler
qjb@wjbeitler.com
Fleet Manager: Dennis Coyne
Number Employees: 50-99
Square Footage: 600000
Services: Local & short haul trucking
Regions Served:
Regional

52175 W J Byrnes & Co
455 Hickey Blvd # 330
Daly City, CA 94015-2630   415-421-2068
Fax: 650-692-8498   800-733-1142
Warehouse providing dry storage for herbs, spices, dry and liquid goods and bailed products; custom house broker providing freight forwarding via air express and international and domestic air freight
President: John Leitner
VP/CFO: Lynsie Temple
VP/COO: Steve R. Enderson
Manager: Steve Besler
tus@byrnesglobal.com
Number Employees: 10-19
Services: Customs house broker providing freight forwarding via air express & international & domestic air freight
Regions Served:
International: nationwide

52176 W N Daul Transfer Lines
1521 Ellis St
Kewaunee, WI 54216-1805   920-388-0795
Transportation firm offering local and regional haul trucking
Owner: Gary Paul
Number Employees: 10-19
Services: Regional and local haul trucking
Regions Served:
WI

52177 (HQ)W T Young Storage Co
2225 Young Dr
P.O.Box 1110
Lexington, KY 40505-4218   859-266-1136
Fax: 859-266-8939   www.wtyoung.com
Public, private and contract warehouse providing cooler, freezer, dry and humidity-controlled storage; transportation firm providing local and long haul trucking; also, re-packing, piece picking, order assembly and rail siding available
President: William Young Jr
CFO: Bob Warren
bwarren@wtyoung.com
Vice President and COO: C. James Pierce
Number Employees: 50-99
Other Locations:
Young, W.T., Storage Co.
Lexington, KY Young, W.T., Storage Co.
Services: Local and long haul trucking; also, trailer load delivery
Regions Served:
National, Regional

52178 W. M. Stone & Company
1158 Lee Westfield Road
PO Box 278
East Otis, MA 01029-0278   413-269-4544
Fax: 413-269-6148   800-832-2052
info@WilliamsStone.com
www.williamsstone.com
Transportation broker providing freight forwarding services; serving nationwide and internationally

Owner: Meade Stone Jr
Number Employees: 20-49
Services: Broker: freight forwarding
Regions Served:
Nationwide & International

52179 (HQ)WOW Logistics
3040 W Wisconsin Avenue
Appleton, WI 54914   920-734-9924
Fax: 920-734-2697   800-236-3565
sherylle@wowlogistics.com
www.wowlogistics.com
Warehouse providing dry storage, re-packing and labeling for nonperishable foods; transportation services include short haul trucking; EDI capabilities; and cross-dock
President & CEO: Howard Kamerer
CFO: Lynda Peters
VP & General Counsel: Ben LaFrombois
Director Marketing: Randy Radtke
VP Sales: Jamie Walley
COO: Scott Gleason
Number Employees: 5-9
Square Footage: 2560 0000
Parent Co: Warehousing of Wisconsin
Other Locations:
Warehousing of Wisconsin
Schofield, WI
Wisconsin Rapids, WI
Appleton, WI Warehousing of Wisconsin Wisconsin Rapids
Services: Short haul trucking
Regions Served:
Midwest

52180 WR Zanes & Company of Louisiana
223 Tchoupitoulas St
New Orleans, LA 70130-2473   504-524-1301
Fax: 504-524-1309   norleans@wrzanes.com
www.wrzanes.com
Transportation broker providing freight forwarding and local haul trucking for exporters and importers
President: Diane Schexnayder
Sr. Vice President: William H. Lusk
Export Supervisor: Anthony Cassard
Other Locations:
New Orleans Air
Kenner, LA
Mobile Air & Ocean
Mobile, AL
Houston, TX
Dallas, TX New Orleans Air Mobile
Services: Brokers: freight forwarding & local haul trucking for exporters & importers
Regions Served:
Nationwide & international

52181 Walsh Transportation Group
140 Epping Rd
Exeter, NH 03833-4516   603-778-6202
Fax: 603-772-0259   800-797-6202
info@wtgnh.com
Warehouse providing cooler and dry storage for general commodities; also, transportation services including TL and local and long haul trucking; rail siding available
President: W Walsh
Contact: Larry Cuddy
lcuddy@wtgnh.com
Number Employees: 20-49
Services: Local & long haul
Regions Served:
National

52182 (HQ)Warehouse Associates LP
1200 E Kibby St
Lima, OH 45804-3163   419-228-6225
Fax: 419-228-8025   info@whalp.com
www.whalp.com
Warehouse offering dry storage; transportation firm providing local haul trucking; re-packing and rail siding available
Manager: Mark Schmieder
Manager: Ray Hughes
rhughes@whalp.com
Number Employees: 20-49
Other Locations:
Warehouse Associates, L.P.
Maple Heights, OH Warehouse Associates, L.P.
Services: Local haul trucking
Regions Served:
OH; IL; KY; IN; MI; TN; Western PA; Wv;

Transportation Firms / A-Z

52183 (HQ)Warehouse Service Inc
1501 Admiral Wilson Blvd
PO Box 1529
Pennsauken, NJ 08109-3905   856-365-0333
Fax: 856-365-0888   800-974-4968
sales@warehouseservice.com
www.warehouseservice.com
U.S. custom bonded warehouse providing dry storage for machinery and chemicals; transportation firm providing local, long and short haul trucking; also, common carrier, freight forwarding, pick-pack and rigging services available
Owner: Gilbert Benjamin
gbenjamin@warehouseservice.com
Number Employees: 10-19
Other Locations:
  Columbus, OH
  Jackson, MSJackson
Services: Local, long & short trucking; also, freight forwarding & common carrier
Regions Served:
  Mid-Atlantic & Regional

52184 (HQ)Warehouse Specialists Inc
1160 N Mayflower Dr
Appleton, WI 54913-9656   920-830-5000
Fax: 920-830-5199   800-999-2545
www.wsinc.com
Warehouse providing dry storage for nonperishable items; also, local, long and short haul trucking and rail car services available by arrangement
CEO: Robert Schroeder
CEO: Robert J Schroeder
Sales Associate: Frank Tomars
Estimated Sales: $500,000-$1 Million
Number Employees: 1000-4999
Square Footage: 52000000
Other Locations:
  Portland, OR
  Menasha, WI
  Green Bay, WI
  Wisconsin Rapids, WI
  Stevens Point, WI
  Glendale, AZMenasha
Services: Local, long & short haul trucking & rail car
Regions Served:
  Southwest U.S.

52185 (HQ)Weber Logistics
13530 Rosecrans Ave
Santa Fe Springs, CA 90670
    855-469-3237
info@weberlogistics.com
www.weberlogistics.com
Dry, refrigerated, and frozen transportation and storage
SVP & Chief Financial Officer: Margaret Movius
Chief Operating Officer: Bob Lilja
Sr Director Human Resources: Derick Quintana-Hooker
VP Transportation Operations: Jerry Critchfield
VP Warehouse Operations: Todd Naramore
Year Founded: 1924
Estimated Sales: $52 Million
Number Employees: 250-499
Services: Temperature-controlled; LTL
Regions Served:
  Western US

52186 Welling Company
100 James Dr # 200
St Rose, LA 70087   504-736-0965
Fax: 504-736-0324   800-256-3887
Warehouse providing cooler and dry storage for groceries and confectionery products; transportation services include brokerage, consolidation, LTL and nationwide TL
Owner: Bill Gist
Number Employees: 50-99
Services: Transportation broker, LTL & TL
Regions Served:
  LTL: LA, MI, AL, FL, TN, AR & TX; TL: Nationwide

52187 Werner Enterprises Inc
14507 Frontier Rd
Omaha, NE 68138-3875   402-895-6640
    800-228-2240
    www.werner.com
Transportation firm providing long, short and local haul trucking; also, contract carrier, dry van and temperature controlled services available.
Executive Chairman: Clarence Werner
President & Chief Executive Officer: Derek J Leathers
derek.leathers@werner.com
Senior EVP & Chief Operating Officer: H. Marty Nordlund
EVP/Treasurer/Chief Financial Officer: John Steele
EVP/Chief Administrative Officer: Jim Schelble
EVP/Chief Accounting Officer/Secretary: James Johnson
EVP/Chief Commercial Officer: Craig Callahan
EVP/Chief Legal Officer: Nathan Meisgeier
Year Founded: 1956
Estimated Sales: $2 Billion
Number Employees: 12,784
Services: Long, short & local haul trucking; also, dry van & temperature controlled
Regions Served:
  Nationwide, Canada & Mexico

52188 West Brothers Trailer Rental
8800 Westgate Park Dr # 100
Raleigh, NC 27617-4833   919-821-2557
Fax: 919-821-4602   800-743- 937
www.westbrotherstrailerrental.com
Warehouse providing dry storage of general commodities, food products and equipment; transportation broker offering LTL and TL services; rail siding available
Vice President: Rick Grannan
rgrannan@wetrailers.com
Executive VP, Sales and Marketing: Douglas Ostanek
Estimated Sales: Less Than $500,000
Number Employees: 1-4
Services: Broker providing LTL & TL
Regions Served:
  48 states

52189 West Logistics
1775 Westgate Pkwy SW
P.O.Box 43004
Atlanta, GA 30336-2847   404-344-8902
Fax: 404-346-5184   www.westlogisticsinc.com
Warehouse providing dry and humidity-controlled storage for groceries, confectionery products and general merchandise; transportation company providing freight consolidation, local and long haul trucking; LTL, TL; rail siding servicesavailable
President: Paula Finley
pfinley@mwdist.com
VP/General Manager: Joe Garger
Executive Vice President: Judy Shore
Number Employees: 100-249
Type of Packaging: Consumer, Private Label, Bulk
Services: Freight consolidation, local & long haul trucking
Regions Served:
  Southeast

52190 Western Ag Enterprises Inc
8121 W Harrison St
Tolleson, AZ 85353-3328   623-907-4034
Fax: 623-907-4100   800-347-8274
www.westernag.com
Transportation broker providing local, long and short haul trucking for refrigerated and dry foods
President: William Barnes
williamaverybarnes@gmail.com
Number Employees: 50-99
Services: Local, long & short haul trucking for dry & refrigerated foods
Regions Served:
  Nationwide

52191 Western Overseas Corp
10731 Walker St # B
Cypress, CA 90630-4757   714-226-9185
Fax: 562-986-1345
contactus@westernoverseas.com
www.westernoverseas.com
Transportation firm providing customs house brokerage, air and ocean freight forwarding and consolidation
President: Lizette Aguila
lizetteh@westernoverseas.com
Number Employees: 50-99
Services: Customs house brokerage, air & ocean freight forwarding & consolidation & drawback
Regions Served:
  Domestic & international

52192 Western Refrigerated Freight Systems
8238 W Harrison Street
Phoenix, AZ 85043   602-254-9922
www.westernrefrigerated.com
Handles all temperature sensitive shipping and distribution needs throughout California, Arizona & Nevada
President: Jeff Boley
Estimated Sales: $6 Million
Number Employees: 50
Other Locations:
  Las Vegas, NV

52193 (HQ)Whiting Distribution Services
26211 Groesbeck Hwy
Warren, MI 48089-4150   586-447-3117
Warehouse providing cooler and dry storage; transportation broker providing freight forwarding services and local, long and short haul trucking; also, rail siding, distribution, lumber re-loading and computerized inventory servicesavailable
Owner: Robert Whiting
Number Employees: 50-99
Other Locations:
  Whiting Distribution Services
  Hamtramck, MIWhiting Distribution Services
Services: Broker providing freight forwarding & local, long & short haul trucking
Regions Served:
  International

52194 Wikel Bulk Express
10216 Mudbrook Rd
Huron, OH 44839   419-668-4318
Transportation firm providing local and long haul trucking for liquid and dry bulk commodities
Contact: Mark Wikel
mark@wikelinc.com
Number Employees: 20-49
Services: Local & long haul trucking
Regions Served:
  East of Rockies, PQ, ON, SK & AB

52195 Wilhelm Machinery Movers
3250 NW Saint Helens Rd
Portland, OR 97210-1308   503-227-0561
Fax: 503-241-4913
Transportation firm providing local, short and long haul trucking
Owner: Bob Wilhelm
bobwilhelm@wilhelmtruck.com
General Manager: Dwayne Downs
Number Employees: 20-49
Services: Local, long & short haul trucking
Regions Served:
  Nationwide

52196 William B Meyer Inc
255 Long Beach Blvd
Stratford, CT 06615-7117   203-375-5801
Fax: 203-375-9820   800-727-5985
information@williambmeyer.com
www.meyermovers.com
Warehouse providing dry storage of groceries and nonfood items; also, transportation firm providing cross docking, trucking, regional and local delivery and courier services in the Northeast; also, rail available
President/Owner: Tom Gillon
CEO: Mike Racette
mracette@williambmeyer.com
Number Employees: 500-999
Services: Trucking, courier & regional and local delivery
Regions Served:
  Northeast

52197 Willis Day Storage
4100 Bennett Rd # 1
Toledo, OH 43612-1970   419-476-8000
Fax: 419-476-1087   wdinfo@willisday.com
www.willisday.com
Warehouse providing dry storage for general merchandise; transportation services include freight consolidation; rail siding available
President: Willis Day
Number Employees: 5-9
Square Footage: 3520000
Parent Co: Willis Day Storage Company
Services: Freight consolidation

Transportation Firms / A-Z

52198 Wilson Trucking Corp
137 Wilson Blvd
Fishersville, VA 22939   540-949-3299
        Fax: 540-949-3205 csd@wilsontrucking.com
Transportation firm providing LTL, TL, local, long and short haul trucking; also, appointment deliveries, lift-gate, pick-up, container and delivery services available
President: Charles L Wilson
CFO: J Herndon
EVP: T Wilson
VP Sales/Marketing: D Collier
VP Operations: J Kidd
Number Employees: 100-249
Services: LTL, TL, local, long & short haul trucking; also, appointment deliveries, lift-gate, pick-up, container & deliv
Regions Served:
  DC, GA, NC, SC, TN, VA, WV, MD, FL, AL

52199 Winpak Technologies
85 Laird Drive
Toronto, ON M4G 3T8
Canada   416-421-1700
        Fax: 416-421-7957
Packaging
Director Sales & Marketing: L de Bellefeuille
Manufacturing: J Millwrad
Estimated Sales: $ 1 - 5 Million
Number Employees: 250
Square Footage: 600000
Parent Co: Winpak

52200 Wisconsin & Southern Railroad
PO Box 090229
Milwaukee, WI 53209   414-438-8820
        Fax: 414-438-8826
Transportation firm providing rail car services; also, intermodal, air-pack RBLS, transloading, washout and point facility and mobile repair services available
CEO/President: William Gardner
Number Employees: 1-4
Services: Rail car, intermodal, dual air-pack RBLS, mobile repairs, etc.
Regions Served:
  Local

52201 Witte Brothers ExchangeInc
575 Witte Industrial
Troy, MO 63379-3964   636-462-8402
        Fax: 636-528-6139 800-325-8151
        info@wittebros.com www.wittebros.com
Warehousing, transportation and distribution for refrigerated and frozen products including LTL, TL (also dry), consolidation, freight pooling, rail service, and full freight management capabilities. Full inventory management. Temprange to -15ºF 2,000,000 cubic feet warehouse with 34 doors and 20,000 square feet refrigerated cross dock.
President: Brent Witte
Sr. Director of Business Development: Laura Wort
Director Of Operations: Shane Carter
Number Employees: 100-249
Regions Served:
  Nationwide

52202 Wootton Transportation Services
1400 E Geer St Ste 6
Durham, NC 27704   800-222-4751
        Fax: 603-688-6196
Transportation broker; warehouse providing dry storage
President/Founder: Frank Wootton
Transportation Manager: Chris Rahm
Number Employees: 10-19
Regions Served:
  International

52203 Worldwide Express Inc
70 Jansen Ave # 202
Essington, PA 19029-1541   610-521-5450
        Fax: 610-521-5740 info@worldwideexpress.com
        www.worldwideexpress.com
Transportation broker providing freight forwarding, customs house and express package services
President: Al Hendri
ahendri@wwex.com
Number Employees: 5-9
Parent Co: Worldwide Express
Services: Customs house, freight forwarding & express services

52204 XPO Logistics
1 N 59th Ave
Phoenix, AZ 85043-3502   602-233-3296
        Fax: 602-269-1742 800-695-0614
        www.southweststorage.com
Public warehouse providing cooler, freezer and dry storage; transportation firm providing local, long and short haul trucking; rail siding available
President/CEO: Fred Gretsch
CEO: Michael Wittman
michaelwittman@jacobsonco.com
CEO: Michael Wittman
VP Sales/Marketing: William Curling
VP Operations: Mike Wittman
Number Employees: 100-249
Services: Local, long & short haul trucking
Regions Served:
  Southwest: AZ, NM, NV & CA

52205 YRC Worldwide Inc
10990 Roe Ave
Overland Park, KS 66211   913-696-6100
        800-846-4300
        webcorp@yrcw.com www.yrcw.com
Provides shipping and transportation services including temperature controlled transport services for shipment of freezable products.
Chief Executive Officer: Darren Hawkins
Chief Financial Officer: Jamie Pierson
Chief Customer Officer: Jason Bergman
Chief Information Officer: Jason Ringgenberg
Chief Network Officer: Scott Ware
Chief Operating Officer: Thomas O'Connor
Year Founded: 1929
Estimated Sales: $4.8 Billion
Number Employees: 19,000

52206 Yang Ming Line Holding Co
525 Washington Blvd
Jersey City, NJ 07310-1606   201-420-5804
        Fax: 201-420-1476 www.yangming.com
Transportation firm providing ocean freight services
Contact: Angel Chang
angelchang@yangming.com
Number Employees: 5-9
Services: Steamships
Regions Served:
  Nationwide & International: Canada, Far East, Australia, Europe, Middle East, Near East

52207 York Rail Logistics
2790 W Market St
York, PA 17404   717-792-3119
        Fax: 717-792-1816 aabauzzese@gwrr.com
        www.gwrr.com
Warehouse providing dry storage for canned foods, beverages, perishable goods, etc; transportation broker serving the Mid-Atlantic, Northeast Corridor and New England areas; rail siding available
Manager: Pat Boland
Sales & Marketing Manager: Al Abruzzese
Estimated Sales: $500,000-$1 Million
Square Footage: 60000
Parent Co: Emons Transportation Group
Services: Truck brokerage
Regions Served:
  Mid-Atlantic, Northeast Corridor & New England

52208 Yowell Transportation
1840 Cardington Rd
Moraine, OH 45409-1503   937-294-5933
        Fax: 937-294-4132 800-543-4320
        info@yowellonline.com www.yowellonline.com
Transportation broker providing freight forwarding, local, long and short haul trucking, barges, domestic and international air forwarding and steam ships
President: Vic Yowell
CEO: Bob Yowell
yowelltran@donet.com
VP: Joe Ford
Operations Manager: Mike Subler
Number Employees: 50-99
Services: Transportation broker: domestic & international air freight, local, long & short haul trucking, etc.
Regions Served:
  Nationwide & International

Alabama
Finch Companies, 51744
Shaw Montgomery Warehouse Company, 52095
Twin City Wholesale, 52154

Alaska
Alaska Railroad Corp, 51525
Alaska Traffic Consultants, 51526
Dhx-Dependable Hawaiian Express, 51701
Lynden Transport Inc, 51903
Murphy Bonded Warehouse, 51948

Arizona
A-P-A Truck Leasing, 51506
Mesa Cold Storage, 51929
Peerless Trucking Company, 52009

Arkansas
Alaska Direct Transport, 51524
Amarillo Warehouse Co, 51534
Logisco, 51893
Texas Cartage Warehouse Inc, 52142

California
Bay Cities Warehouse, 51576
C.J. Figone Cold Storage, 51607
Dreisbach Enterprises Inc, 51710
DSW Distribution Ctr Inc, 51690
Konoike Pacific California, 51873
Ludtke Pacific Trucking Inc, 51899
Orange County Cold Storage, 51989
Pacific Cartage & Warehousing, 52000
PRISM Team Services, 51999
Prism Team Services, Inc, 52032
Pure Flo Water Co, 52035
San Diego & Imperial Valley Rr, 52077
Service Craft Distribution Systems, 52093
Western Refrigerated Freight Systems, 52192

Canada
Byers Transport, 51603
Canada Distribution Centres, 51621
Choice Reefer Systems, 51651
Ideal Warehouse, 51822
Intercontinental Warehouses, 51831
J.D. Smith & Sons, 51843
Manitoulin Group of Companies, 51915
Matchmaker Transportation Services, 51920
MCT Terminal & Transport Inc., 51906
Mid-West Traffic, 51933
MTE Logistix, 51908
Simard Warehouses, 52101
Wikel Bulk Express, 52194

Caribbean
Bermuda Agencies Inc, 51584

Colorado
American Warehouse Co, 51546
Aspen Distribution Inc, 51559
Bootz Distribution, 51594
North Park Transportation Co, 51970

Connecticut
Bilkays Express/Distribution Warehouse, 51587
Farruggio Express, 51738

Florida
Imperial Freight Broker, 51824
Keys Fisheries Market & Marina, 51868
Laney & Duke Terminal Wrhse Co, 51883
Phoenix Industries LLC, 52016
Saddle Creek Logistics Svc, 52073

Seaboard Warehouse Terminals, 52088
Smith Cartage, 52103
Star Distribution Systems, 52122

Georgia
Savannah Distributing, 52082

Hawaii
Martin Warehousing & Distribution, 51917
PM&O Line, 51998
Unicold Corp, 52160

Idaho
Peasley Transfer & Storage, 52008

Illinois
Chester Transfer, 51648
Grane Warehousing & Distribution, 51781
Iowa Interstate Railroad LTD, 51836
Majors Transit Inc, 51912
Miller Container Corp, 51938
Supreme Lobster, 52131

Indiana
Atkins Bob Lin Inc, 51563
Ben-Lee Motor Service Company, 51581
Interstate Cold Storage, 51835

Iowa
Fort Transportation & Svc Co, 51749

Kansas
Price Truck Lines Inc, 52029
Quick Delivery, 52039

Kentucky
Franklin Express Co Inc, 51751

Louisiana
Stone Forwarding Company, 52128

Maine
Barrett Trucking Co Inc, 51575

Maryland
Canton Railroad Co, 51624

Massachusetts
Bridge Terminal, Inc., 51596
Philip P Massad Movers, 52015

Mexico
Des Moines Truck Brokers, 51699

Michigan
Columbian Logistics Network, 51659
O'Byrne Distribution Ctr Inc, 51978
Ralph Moyle Inc, 52045
Southshore Enterprises, 52111

Mid-Atlantic
AFS Traffic Consulants, 51508
Allied Logistics, 51529
American Port Services, 51543
American Truck Dispatch, 51545
Belts Logistics Services, 51580
Buske Lines, 51602
Distribution Unlimited, 51704
Erdner Brothers, 51726
Fox Transportation Inc, 51750
Greenstein Trucking Company, 51784
Hess Trucking Co, 51809
Kline Transportation, 51871
Morristown & Erie Railway Inc, 51946
Reed Trucking Co, 52048
Standard Warehouse, 52120
The Terminal Corporation, 52145

Volunteer Express, 52172
W J Beitler Co & Beitler Truck, 52174
York Rail Logistics, 52207

Midwest
American West, 51547
Blue Line Cold Storage Chicago, 51591
Cedar Rapids & Iowa City Railway Company, 51634
Central Warehouse Operations, Inc., 51643
Continental Express Inc, 51670
Days Corporation, 51694
Diversified Transfer & Storage, 51705
Indiana Harbor Belt Railroad, 51826
Interstate Cold Storage Inc, 51834
Jacobson Warehouse Company, 51845
Judge & Sons P Inc, 51855
La Grou Cold Storage, 51879
Lincoln Cold Storage, 51890
M & W Logistics Group, 51904
McCann's Piggyback Consolidation, 51923
Merchants Distribution Svc, 51928
Metro Park Warehouses Inc, 51930
Mid States Express Inc, 51932
Moran Distribution Centers, 51944
Murray's Transfer Inc, 51950
New Hampton Transfer & Storage, 51962
Norfolk Southern Corp, 51967
ODW Logistics Inc, 51979
Queen City Warehouse Corporation, 52038
RGL Headquarters, 52043
Schugel J & R Trucking Inc, 52086
South Bend Warehousing & Distribution, 52109
Stemm Transfer & Storage, 52125
Trademark Transportation, 52150
United Express, 52163
Van Wyk Freight Lines, 52166
Verst Group Logistics Inc, 52170

Minnesota
C.P. Rail System, 51608

Mississippi
Gay Truck Line, 51763

Missouri
Space Center Inc, 52114

Montana
Baker Transfer & Storage, 51571

Nationwide
Ability/Tri-Modal Trnsprtn Svc, 51513
Airways Freight Corp, 51523
Allied Frozen Storage Inc, 51528
Alton & Southern Railway Co, 51532
Alvan Motor Freight, 51533
America's Service Line, 51537
AmeriCold Logistics LLC, 51536
Amware Distribution Warehouse, 51549
APL Logistics, 51509
Apl Logistics, 51553
Arco Warehouse Co, 51555
Associated Trucking Co Inc, 51561
Atir Transportation Services, 51562
Atlantic Container, 51565
Austin Transportation, 51566
B & H Railcorp, 51567
B.R. Williams Trucking & Warehouse, 51568
Baldwin Distribution Services, 51572
Baltimore International Warehousing, 51573
Biehl & Co, 51586
Bill Clark Truck Line Inc, 51588
Blendco Inc, 51590
Britton Storage Trailers, 51597
C R England Inc, 51605

Can-Am LTL, 51619
Canaan Logistics, 51620
Canada Maritime Agencies, 51622
Canadian National Railway, 51623
Central American Warehouse Co, 51636
Central States Distribution, 51640
Central Transport Intl, 51641
Central Transportation System, 51642
Chattanooga Freight Bureau, 51647
Choctaw Transportation Co Inc, 51650
Circle Delivery, 51653
Clarden Trucking, 51654
Cockrell Distribution System, 51656
Colombo Services, 51657
Colonial Freight Systems, 51658
Commercial Transport Inc, 51663
Compass Consolidators, 51666
Compass Forwarding Co Inc, 51667
Consolidated Transfer Co Inc, 51669
Coppersmith, 51672
COX Transportation Svc Inc, 51611
Crete Carrier Corp, 51677
Crowley Liner Services, 51679
CRST International Inc, 51612
Crystal Cold Storage, 51680
CT Logistics, 51615
D W Air, 51684
D.J. Powers Company, 51685
Darras Freight, 51691
Dart Transit Co, 51692
DAV Transportation Services, 51686
Deep South Freight, 51696
Detroit Warehouse Company, 51700
DHL Danzas, 51689
Dunsmith International, 51712
Earl J Henderson Trucking Company, 51714
Ecs Warehouse, 51720
Eimskip, 51721
Englund Equipment Co, 51725
Evergreen International Airlines, 51729
F B Washburn Candy Corp, 51733
Farrell Lines, 51737
Farwest Freight Systems, 51739
Faure Brothers Inc, 51741
Federal Companies, 51742
FFE Transportation Services, 51734
Footner & Co Inc, 51747
Footprint Retail Svc, 51748
Franklin Storage Inc, 51752
Freeway Warehouse Corp, 51753
Gabler Trucking Inc, 51759
Gadsden Cartage Co, 51760
GATX Corp, 51757
Gemini Traffic Sales, 51765
General Warehouse & Transportation Company, 51767
Geneva Lakes Cold Storage, 51768
Gentzkow Trucking Svc Inc, 51769
Gilbert International, 51771
Giumarra Companies, 51772
Glen Rose Transportation Mgmt, 51776
Gray Transportation, 51782
Greenway Transportation Services, 51785
Greylawn Foods, 51788
Groendyke Transport Inc, 51790
Gulf Central Distribution Ctr, 51791
H & M Bay Inc, 51792
H&R Transport, 51793
Hall's Warehouse Corp, 51794
Hanjin Shipping Company, 51795
Hansen Co, 51798
Hansen Trucking, 51800
Harry E. Hills & Associates, 51803
Heding Truck Services, 51804
Henry L Taylor Trucking LLC, 51807
Highland Transport, 51810
Hirschbach Motor Lines, 51813
Holt Logistics Corporation, 51817
Honolulu Freight Svc, 51818
Houston Central Industries, Ltd., 51820
Icelandair, 51821
Idealease Inc, 51823
Importers, 51825
Intermodal Express, 51832

789

Transportation Region / Nebraska

J M Swank Co, 51840
J&B Cold Storage Inc, 51841
J.A. Tucker Company, 51842
James H Clark & Son Inc, 51846
Jim Palmer Trucking, 51848
Johanson Transportation Services, 51850
John Christner Trucking Inc, 51852
John S James Co, 51853
K&J Logistics, 51856
Kedem, 51862
Kenco Group Inc, 51863
Kenco Logistic Svc LLC, 51864
Keokuk Junction Railway, 51867
KLLM Transport Svc LLC, 51859
KW Transportation Services, 51860
L & L Truck Broker Inc, 51874
L B Transport Inc, 51875
Lake Erie Warehouse & Distribution Center, 51880
Land Span, 51881
Landstar System, Inc, 51882
Langham Logistics, 51884
LCL Bulk Transport Inc, 51876
Lee Truck Broker Inc, 51886
Lester Coggins Trucking, 51888
Linden Warehouse & Dstrbtn Co, 51891
Live Oak Warehouse, 51892
LT's Brokerage, 51878
Lucca Freezer & Cold Storage, 51898
Lykes Lines, 51902
Maersk Sealand, 51910
Magic Valley Truck Brokers Inc, 51911
Mallory Alexander Intl, 51913, 51914
Marten Transport LTD, 51916
Match Maker, 51919
Mayberry RFD, 51922
Melvin L. Jones Transportation Broker, 51926
Merchandise Warehouse, 51927
Metropolitan Trucking Inc, 51931
Midwest Coast Logistics LLC, 51935
Milan Supply Chain Solutions, 51937
Minn-Dak Transport Inc, 51939
Mo-Ark Truck Services, 51940
Modesto & Empire Traction Co, 51941
Moody Dunbar Inc, 51942
National Carriers Inc, 51957
Network FOB, 51961
Newport St Paul Cold Storage, 51965
NFI Industries Inc, 51952
Nippon Cargo Airlines Co LTD, 51966
North Star World Trade Svc, 51971
Northland Express Transport, 51975
Nova Transportation Inc, 51976
Ocean World Lines, 51982
Ohio Commerce Center, 51984
Ohio Valley Shippers Assn, 51985
Olson Co, 51986
Omni North America, 51988
Outerbridge Peppers Limited, 51991
Ozark Truck Brokers, 51993
Page & Jones Inc, 52002
Palmer Logistics, 52004
Paschall Truck Lines Inc, 52005
PFS Transportation, 51997
Pilot Freight Svc, 52018
Port Elizabeth Terminal Corp, 52025
Port Terminal Railroad, 52027
Preferred Freezer Services, 52028
Professional Transportation Brokers, 52033
Quality Logistics Systems, 52036
Quast & Company, 52037
R W Bozel Transfer Inc, 52041
R.F.K. Transportation Service, 52042
Richwill Enterprises, 52051
Roads West Transportation, 52054
Rockwell Truck Line, 52057
Ronnie Dowdy, 52058
Ryder System, Inc, 52065
Sack Storage Corporation, 52071
Safeway Freezer Storage Inc, 52074
Samuel Shapiro & Company, 52076
SAS Cargo, 52066
Saturn Freight Systems, 52079

Sav Enterprises, 52081
Schilli Transportation Services, 52084
Schneider National Inc, 52085
Seagate Transportation, 52089
Seaonus, 52090
Seaschott, 52091
Shaffer Trucking, 52094
Shepard's Moving & Storage, 52096
Short Freight Lines Inc, 52098
Sky West Airlines Inc, 52102
Smith Terminal Distribution, 52104
Somerset Industries, 52105
Standard Transportation Svc, 52119
Sterling Transportation, 52126
Stevens Transport, 52127
Stonepath Logistics, 52129
Streamline Shippers-Affiliates, 52130
Team Hardinger, 52139
Tejas Logistics System, 52141
The Scoular Company/TSC Container Freight, 52144
Totem Ocean Trailer Express, 52149
Trinity Transport & Distribution Services, 52153
Twin Modal, 52155
Ultimate Foods, 52159
Union Pacific Railroad Co, 52161
UPS Freight, 52156
USAir, 52157
UTZ Quality Foods Inc, 52158
Van Brunt Port Jersey Warehouse, 52165
Versacold Logistics Services, 52169
W J Byrnes Inc, 52175
W T Young Storage Co, 52177
W. M. Stone & Company, 52178
Warehouse Specialists Inc, 52184
Welling Company, 52186
Werner Enterprises Inc, 52187
West Brothers Trailer Rental, 52188
Western Ag Enterprises Inc, 52190
Western Overseas Corp, 52191
Wilhelm Machinery Movers, 52195
WR Zanes & Company of Louisiana, 52180
Yang Ming Line Holding Co, 52206
Yowell Transportation, 52208

Nebraska

Nebraska Warehouse Co, 51960

Nevada

Ozark Trucking, 51994

New England

A W Sisk & Son, 51504
Allied Cold Storage Corporation, 51527
American Cold Storage, 51540
Barrett Distribution Ctr, 51574
Benlin Freight Forwarding Inc, 51583
Biscontini Distribution Centers, 51589
Bob's Transport & Stge Co Inc, 51593
California Cartage Co, 51618
Cardinal Logistics Management, 51625
Cargo Transporters Inc, 51627
Central Maine & Quebec Railway, 51639
Consolidated Rail Corporation, 51668
Craig Transportation Co, 51674
CSX Transportation, 51614
Cumberland Distribution Services, 51681
D & D Distribution Svc, 51682
D & S Warehouse Inc, 51683
Dependable Distribution Services, 51698
DFC Transportation Company, 51688
East Coast Warehouse & Distr, 51715
Eastern Shore Railroad, 51718
Evans Delivery Company, 51728
Gatewood Products LLC, 51762
Hanover Terminal Inc, 51796
Hermann Services Inc, 51808
John-Jeffrey Corporation, 51854
KANE Freight Lines Inc, 51858
Massachusetts Central Railroad Corporation, 51918
Nashua Motor Express, 51954

National Distribution Centers, 51958
Overflo, 51992
Pioneer Freight Systems Inc, 52019
Pioneer Valley Refrigerated Warehouse, 52020
Plymouth Rock Transportation, 52023
Port Jersey Logistics, 52026
Providence & Worcester RR Company, 52034
Ross Express Inc, 52060
Sonwil Distribution Center, 52106
South Mill, 52110
SPC Transport Co, 52070
Teal's Express Inc, 52138
Three D Brokers, 52146
Tighe Warehousing-Distribution, 52147
Trailwood Warehouse LLC, 52151
TWL Corporation, 52136
Valley Distributors & Storage Company, 52164
Vermont Railway Inc, 52168
Volunteer Express, 52173
William B Meyer Inc, 52196

New Hampshire

Walsh Transportation Group, 52181

New Jersey

River Terminal Distribution & Warehouse, 52052
Shoreline Freezers, 52097

New Mexico

AADF Warehouse Corporation, 51507
Commercial Warehouse Co, 51664

New York

Hanover Warehouses Inc, 51797
Stanley Orchards Sales, Inc., 52121

North Carolina

Aberdeen & Rockfish Railroad, 51512
Lewis Storage, 51889
Pitzer Transfer & Storage Corp., 52022
South Atlantic Warehouse Corporation, 52108

North Dakota

Union Storage & Transfer Co, 52162

Ohio

ASW Supply Chain Svc, 51511
Commonwealth Inc, 51665
Fst Logistics Inc, 51755
Hillsboro Transportation Company, 51812
Inter State Cold Storage, 51830
Peoples Cartage Inc, 52013
Pitt Ohio, 52021
Schwebel Baking Co., 52087
Spartan Logistics, 52115
Warehouse Associates LP, 52182
Willis Day Storage, 52197

Oklahoma

Farmrail Corp, 51736

Oregon

Holeman Distribution Ctr, 51815
Holman Distribution Center, 51816
Oak Harbor Freight Lines, 51980
Oregon Transfer Co, 51990
T P Freight Lines Inc, 52134

Pennsylvania

Beacon Distribution Services, 51577
Lehigh-Pocono Warehouse Inc, 51887
Moran Logistics, 51945
Worldwide Express Inc, 52203

South

A Arnold Logistics, 51501
Atlanta Bonded Warehouse Corporation, 51564
Bulldog Hiway Express, 51600
Carolina Transfer & Stge Inc, 51631
Cincinnati Packaging And Distribution, 51652
Commercial Cold Storage, 51661
Commercial Distribution Ctr, 51662
DCI Logistics, 51687
Dist Tech, 51702
Doc's Transfer & Warehouse, 51706
FasTrans, 51740
Florida Freezer LP, 51746
General Bonded Warehouses Inc, 51766
Grimes Co, 51789
Interport Storage & Distribution Service, 51833
Kennesaw Transportation, 51865
Ozburn-Hessey Logistics LLC, 51995
Penser SC, 52011
Piedmont Distribution Centers, 52017
Robertson-Johnson Warehouses, 52056
Saddle Creek Logistics Svc, 52072
Saia, Inc., 52075
Sopak Co Inc, 52107
West Logistics, 52189
Wilson Trucking Corp, 52198

South Carolina

Carolina Bonded Storage Co, 51630
Eastern Distribution Inc, 51716

Southwest

Abler Transfer, 51514
Angelina & Neches River Railroad, 51552
Beaver Express Svc LLC, 51578
Brokers Logistics LTD, 51598
Central Freight Lines Inc, 51637
Fiesta Warehousing & Distribution Company, 51743
Hodges Co, 51814
LMD Integrated Logistic Services, 51877
Southwest Truck Service, 52112
Southwestern Motor Transport, 52113
Starr Distribution Services Company, 52124
XPO Logistics, 52204

Tennessee

Central-Cumberland Corp, 51644

Texas

Adams Warehouse & Delivery, 51518
Dunagan Warehouse Corp, 51711
EPT Warehouses, 51713
Paul L. Broussard & Associate, 52007
Price's Creameries, 52030
Ray West Warehouses/Transport, 52047
Texas N Western Railway Company, 52143

Utah

Oborn Transfer & Stge Co Inc, 51981

Virginia

Estes Express Lines Inc, 51727

Washington

Acme Farms + Kitchen, 51516
BLC Trucking Inc, 51570
Mccracken Motor Freight, 51925

West

Acme Distribution Ctr Inc, 51515
American Distribution Centers, 51541
Anchor Distribution Services, 51551
Aspen Distribution, 51558

Transportation Region / Wisconsin

Bender Warehouse Co, 51582
Burlington Northern Santa Fe, LLC, 51601
Caldwell Trucking Inc, 51617
Decker Truck Line Inc, 51695
England Logistics, 51724
Farmers Distributing, 51735
Inland Star Distribution Ctr, 51828
Mountain America Shippers, 51947
Pacific Coast Warehouse Co, 52001
San Jose Distribution Service, 52078
TW Transport Inc, 52135

Wisconsin

Hansen Storage Co, 51799
Northland Cold Storage Inc, 51974
Reynolds Transfer & Storage, 52050
W N Daul Transfer Lines, 52176
Wisconsin & Southern Railroad, 52200

Worldwide

A N Deringer Inc, 51503
Adcom Worldwide, 51519
Airschott Inc, 51522
ASAP Freight Systems, 51510
BDP International Inc, 51569
C.H. Robinson Co., 51606
Cargo, 51626
Centra Worldwide, 51635
Central Global Express, 51638
Cranston Air, 51675
Crate & Fly, 51676
Dolliff & Co Inc, 51707
Ellis KARR & Co Inc, 51722
Express Air Cargo, 51732
Graham Transfer & Storage, 51780
K&K Express, 51857
Logistics Amber Worldwide, 51894
Midnite Express, 51934
National Air Cargo Inc, 51955
New Orleans Cold Storage-Wrhse, 51963
Norman G. Jensen, 51969
PBB Global Logistics, 51996
Priority Air Express, 52031
R L Swearer Co Inc, 52040
Rivers Transportation, 52053
SDS Global Logistics, Inc., 52067
SEKO Worldwide Inc, 52068
SOS Global Express Inc, 52069
Tazmanian Freight Forwarding, 52137

Transportation Type / Air Express/Expedited Package Services

Air Express/Expedited Package Services
Acme Distribution Ctr Inc, 51515
Allied Logistics, 51529
Anadon Logistics, 51550
Arco Warehouse Co, 51555
Associated Global Systems, 51560
Bay Cities Warehouse, 51576
Benlin Freight Forwarding Inc, 51583
Brokers Logistics LTD, 51598
Commercial Distribution Ctr, 51662
D & D Distribution Svc, 51682
Day & Ross Transportation Group, 51693
Laub International, 51885
Network FOB, 51961
Peninsula Airways Inc, 52010
Sonwil Distribution Center, 52106
W J Byrnes & Co, 52175
Walsh Transportation Group, 52181
Worldwide Express Inc, 52203

Airlines: Domestic & International
Adcom Worldwide, 51519
Air New Zealand LTD, 51521
Airways Freight Corp, 51523
American Fast Freight, 51542
American Shipping Co, 51544
BDP International Inc, 51569
Charles M. Schayer & Company, 51645
Ellis KARR & Co Inc, 51722
Evergreen International Airlines, 51729
Express Air Cargo, 51732
Florida Freezer LP, 51746
Footner & Co Inc, 51747
Icelandair, 51821
Jantzen International, 51847
John S James Co, 51853
Lufthansa Cargo, 51900
Nashua Motor Express, 51954
Nippon Cargo Airlines Co LTD, 51966
Northern Air Cargo, 51973
Page & Jones Inc, 52002
Quast & Company, 52037
Royal Jordanian, 52062
SAS Cargo, 52066
Saturn Freight Systems, 52079
Saudi Arabian Airlines, 52080
SDS Global Logistics, Inc., 52067
Sky West Airlines Inc, 52102
Ted L. Rausch Company, 52140
United Express, 52163
USAir, 52157
Yowell Transportation, 52208

Barges
Lynden Transport Inc, 51903

Bulk Transfer Facilities
A W Sisk & Son, 51504
ASW Supply Chain Svc, 51511
Central Transport Intl, 51641
Distribution Services-America, 51703
Glass Trucking LLC, 51774
Inland Empire Distribution, 51827
Morristown & Erie Railway Inc, 51946
Pitzer Transfer & Storage Corp., 52022
York Rail Logistics, 52207

Crating Services
Biscontini Distribution Centers, 51589
Gilbert International, 51771
Kak LLC, 51861
Overflo, 51992

Cross-Decking
Adams Warehouse & Delivery, 51518
Anchor Distribution Services, 51551
Aspen Distribution, 51558
Bender Warehouse Co, 51582
Blue Line Cold Storage Chicago, 51591
Bob's Transport & Stge Co Inc, 51593
Central States Distribution, 51640
Darras Freight, 51691
Doc's Transfer & Warehouse, 51706
DSW Distribution Ctr Inc, 51690
Ecs Warehouse, 51720
Farruggio Express, 51738
Fiesta Warehousing & Distribution Company, 51743
Freshway Distributors, 51754
Hermann Services Inc, 51808
Highroad Warehouse, Inc, 51811
Importers, 51825
Kenco Logistic Svc LLC, 51864
Lewis Storage, 51889
Metro Park Warehouses Inc, 51930
Orange County Cold Storage, 51989
Penser SC, 52011
Port Jersey Logistics, 52026
Queen City Warehouse Corporation, 52038
Ray West Warehouses/Transport, 52047
Seaboard Warehouse Terminals, 52088
Smith Terminal Distribution, 52104
Standard Transportation Svc, 52119
Tejas Logistics System, 52141
Texas Cartage Warehouse Inc, 52142
Union Storage & Transfer Co, 52162
Welling Company, $2186
William B Meyer Inc, 52196

Customs House Brokers
Airschott Inc, 51522
Alpha International, 51531
Compass Forwarding Co Inc, 51667
Coppersmith, 51672
Corcoran International Corporation, 51673
Eastport Customs Brokers, 51719
Massachusetts Central Railroad Corporation, 51918
WR Zanes & Company of Louisiana, 52180

Export Management
Austin Transportation, 51566
Murphy Warehouse Co, 51949
Schilli Transportation Services, 52084

Export Packing Services
McLean Cargo Specialists, 51924

Freight Auditing Services
Clarden Trucking, 51654
Columbian Logistics Network, 51659
CT Logistics, 51615
Paul L. Broussard & Associate, 52007

Freight Consolidation
Alaska Traffic Consultants, 51526
Allied Frozen Storage Inc, 51528
American Warehouse Co, 51546
Barrett Distribution Ctr, 51574
C.J. Figone Cold Storage, 51607
Commercial Cold Storage, 51661
Grimes Co, 51789
Hall's Warehouse Corp, 51794
Hansen Storage Co, 51799
Hess Trucking Co, 51809
Inland Star Distribution Ctr, 51828
Intercontinental Warehouses, 51831
Interstate Cold Storage, 51835
Interstate Cold Storage Inc, 51834
John-Jeffrey Corporation, 51854
KANE Freight Lines Inc, 51858
Murphy Bonded Warehouse, 51948
Northland Cold Storage Inc, 51974
O'Byrne Distribution Ctr Inc, 51978
Oregon Transfer Co, 51990
Pacific Cartage & Warehousing, 52000
Pacific Coast Warehouse Co, 52001
PRISM Team Services, 51999
River Terminal Distribution & Warehouse, 52052
Robertson-Johnson Warehouses, 52056
Saddle Creek Logistics Svc, 52072
Unicold Corp, 52160
West Logistics, 52189
Willis Day Storage, 52197

Freight Forwarding
A N Deringer Inc, 51502
Allround Forwarding Co, 51530
Alvan Motor Freight, 51533
American Airlines Inc, 51538
American West, 51547
Amobelge Shipping Corporation, 51548
Beaver Express Svc LLC, 51578
Brauner International Corp, 51595
C.H. Robinson Co., 51606
Cargo, 51626
Carmichael International Svc, 51629
Central Global Express, 51638
Central Transportation System, 51642
Chase, Leavitt & Company, 51646
Colombo Services, 51657
Cranston Air, 51675
Crate & Fly, 51676
D W Air, 51684
D.J. Powers Company, 51685
DFC Transportation Company, 51688
DHL Danzas, 51689
Dhx-Dependable Hawaiian Express, 51701
Dolliff & Co Inc, 51707
Farwest Freight Systems, 51739
Footprint Retail Svc, 51748
H&R Transport, 51793
Honolulu Freight Svc, 51818
Imperal Freight Broker, 51824
J.A. Tucker Company, 51842
K&K Express, 51857
Kentucky Container Svc, 51866
Mallory Alexander Intl, 51913
Mountain America Shippers, 51947
National Air Cargo Inc, 51955
Nature's Products Inc, 51959
Norman G. Jensen, 51969
North Star World Trade Svc, 51971
Omni North America, 51988
PBB Global Logistics, 51996
Piedmont Distribution Centers, 52017
Pioneer Freight Systems Inc, 52019
Priority Air Express, 52031
R L Swearer Co Inc, 52040
R.F.K. Transportation Service, 52042
Samuel Shapiro & Company, 52076
Seaschott, 52091
SEKO Worldwide Inc, 52068
Service By Air Inc, 52092
Sierra Madre Mushrooms, 52099
SOS Global Express Inc, 52069
St. John Brothers, 52118
Stone Forwarding Company, 52128
Stonepath Logistics, 52129
The Scoular Company/TSC Container Freight, 52144
Trademark Transportation, 52150
Twin Modal, 52155
Warehouse Service Inc, 52183
Western Overseas Corp, 52191
Whiting Distribution Services, 52193

Freight Forwarding: Foreign
A N Deringer Inc, 51503
American Cargo Services, 51539
ASAP Freight Systems, 51510
Ben-Lee Motor Service Company, 51581
John Cassidy Intl Inc, 51851
Logistics Amber Worldwide, 51894

Piggy-Back
Compass Consolidators, 51666

Railroads
Aberdeen & Rockfish Railroad, 51512
Alaska Railroad Corp, 51525
Alton & Southern Railway Co, 51532
American Cold Storage, 51540
Angelina & Neches River Railroad, 51552
B & H Railcorp, 51567
Burlington Northern Santa Fe, LLC, 51601
C.P. Rail System, 51608
Canadian National Railway, 51623
Canton Railroad Co, 51624
Cedar Rapids & Iowa City Railway Company, 51634
Central Maine & Quebec Railway, 51639
Consolidated Rail Corporation, 51668
CSX Transportation, 51614
Eastern Shore Railroad, 51718
Farmrail Corp, 51736
Faure Brothers Inc, 51741
Gadsden Cartage Co, 51760
Hanover Terminal Inc, 51796
Indiana Harbor Belt Railroad, 51826
Iowa Interstate Railroad LTD, 51836
Keokuk Junction Railway, 51867
Modesto & Empire Traction Co, 51941
New York, 51964
Norfolk Southern Corp, 51967
Peasley Transfer & Storage, 52008
Port Terminal Railroad, 52027
Providence & Worcester RR Company, 52034
San Diego & Imperial Valley Rr, 52077
San Jose Distribution Service, 52078
Stevens Transport, 52127
Texas N Western Railway Company, 52143
Union Pacific Railroad Co, 52161
Vermont Railway Inc, 52168
Warehouse Specialists Inc, 52184
Wisconsin & Southern Railroad, 52200

Special Equipment Carriers
Kenco Group Inc, 51863

Steamships
Atlantic Container, 51565
Bermuda Agencies Inc, 51584
Biehl & Co, 51586
Canada Maritime Agencies, 51622
Crowley Liner Services, 51679
Eimskip, 51721
Farrell Lines, 51737
GMW Freight Services Ltd, 51758
Hanjin Shipping Company, 51795
Klomar Ship Supplies Inc, 51872
Lykes Lines, 51902
Maersk Sealand, 51910
NYK Line North America Inc, 51953
Ohio Valley Shippers Assn, 51985
PM&O Line, 51998
Star Shipping, 52123
Streamline Shippers-Affiliates, 52130
Totem Ocean Trailer Express, 52149
Yang Ming Line Holding Co, 52206

Transportation Brokers
AADF Warehouse Corporation, 51507
AFS Traffic Consulants, 51508
American Truck Dispatch, 51545
Arnhalt Transportation Brkrg, 51557
Associated Trucking Co Inc, 51561
Atir Transportation Services, 51562
Britton Storage Trailers, 51597
C R England Inc, 51605
California Cartage Co, 51618
Canaan Logistics, 51620
Centra Worldwide, 51635
Chattanooga Freight Bureau, 51647
Commerce Express Inc, 51660
COX Transportation Svc Inc, 51611
D & S Warehouse Inc, 51683

793

Transportation Type / Truck & Trailer Leasing

Deep South Freight, 51696
Des Moines Truck Brokers, 51699
Dreisbach Enterprises Inc, 51710
Dunsmith International, 51712
Earl J Henderson Trucking Company, 51714
Englund Equipment Co, 51725
Gemini Traffic Sales, 51765
George S. Bush & Company, 51770
Glen Rose Transportation Mgmt, 51776
Gray Transportation, 51782
Greenway Transportation Services, 51785
Harry E. Hills & Associates, 51803
Intermodal Express, 51832
Johanson Transportation Services, 51850
K&J Logistics, 51856
KW Transportation Services, 51860
L & L Truck Broker Inc, 51874
Lee Truck Broker Inc, 51886
LT's Brokerage, 51878
Lucca Freezer & Cold Storage, 51898
Magic Valley Truck Brokers Inc, 51911
Match Maker, 51919
Matchmaker Transportation Services, 51920
Mayberry RFD, 51922
Melvin L. Jones Transportation Broker, 51926
Mid-West Traffic, 51933
Minn-Dak Transport Inc, 51939
National Carriers Inc, 51957
Norjo Distribution Services, 51968
Northland Express Transport, 51975
Ozark Truck Brokers, 51993
PFS Transportation, 51997
Professional Transportation Brokers, 52033
Richwill Enterprises, 52051
Rivers Transportation, 52053
Schenker International, 52083
Sterling Transportation, 52126
The Terminal Corporation, 52145
Three D Brokers, 52146
Tighe Warehousing-Distribution, 52147
Ultimate Foods, 52159
W. M. Stone & Company, 52178
Warehouse Associates LP, 52182
West Brothers Trailer Rental, 52188
Western Ag Enterprises Inc, 52190
Wootton Transportation Services, 52202

Truck & Trailer Leasing

GATX Corp, 51757
Idealease Inc, 51823
Ryder System, Inc, 52065
Team Hardinger, 52139

Trucking: Local Haul

A Arnold Logistics, 51501
Abler Transfer, 51514
Air Land Transport Inc, 51520
Alaska Direct Transport, 51524
Allied Cold Storage Corporation, 51527
Amarillo Warehouse Co, 51534
American Distribution Centers, 51541
American Port Services, 51543
Apl Logistics, 51553
Aspen Distribution Inc, 51559
Atlanta Bonded Warehouse Corporation, 51564
Baker Transfer & Storage, 51571
Baldwin Distribution Services, 51572
Baltimore International Warehousing, 51573
Barrett Trucking Co Inc, 51575
Beacon Distribution Services, 51577
Belts Logistics Services, 51580
Bill Clark Truck Line Inc, 51588
BLC Trucking Inc, 51570
Blue Line Moving & Storage, 51592
Bootz Distribution, 51594
Bulldog Hiway Express, 51600
Buske Lines, 51602
Byers Transport, 51603

Cargo Transporters Inc, 51627
Carolina Bonded Storage Co, 51630
Carolina Transfer & Stge Inc, 51631
Castellini Group, 51633
Central American Warehouse Co, 51636
Central Freight Lines Inc, 51637
Central Warehouse Operations, Inc., 51643
Central-Cumberland Corp, 51644
Chester Transfer, 51648
Choctaw Transportation Co Inc, 51650
Choice Reefer Systems, 51651
Cincinnati Packaging And Distribution, 51652
Commercial Transport Inc, 51663
Commercial Warehouse Co, 51664
Continental Express Inc, 51670
Crete Carrier Corp, 51677
Crossroads Distribution LTD, 51678
Crystal Cold Storage, 51680
Cumberland Distribution Services, 51681
DCI Logistics, 51687
Dependable Distribution Services, 51698
Detroit Warehouse Company, 51700
East Coast Warehouse & Distr, 51715
Eastern Distribution Inc, 51716
England Logistics, 51724
EPT Warehouses, 51713
Erdner Brothers, 51726
Estes Express Lines Inc, 51727
Evans Delivery Company, 51728
FasTrans, 51740
Federal Companies, 51742
FFE Transportation Services, 51734
Finch Companies, 51744
Fort Transportation & Svc Co, 51749
Fox Transportation Inc, 51750
Franklin Express Co Inc, 51751
Gay Truck Line, 51763
General Bonded Warehouses Inc, 51766
General Warehouse & Transportation Company, 51767
Geneva Lakes Cold Storage, 51768
Gentzkow Trucking Svc Inc, 51769
Glacier Cold Storage LTD, 51773
Graham Transfer & Storage, 51780
Grane Warehousing & Distribution, 51781
Gress Refrigerated Services & Logisitics, 51786
H & M Bay Inc, 51792
Hanover Warehouses Inc, 51797
Hansen Co, 51798
Heding Truck Services, 51804
Henningsen Cold Storage Co, 51806
Hirschbach Motor Lines, 51813
Hodges Co, 51814
Holeman Distribution Ctr, 51815
Holman Distribution Center, 51816
Houston Central Industries, Ltd., 51820
Ideal Warehouse, 51822
Inter State Cold Storage, 51830
Interport Storage & Distribution Service, 51833
J D Double M Trucking, 51839
J&B Cold Storage Inc, 51841
J.D. Smith & Sons, 51843
James H Clark & Son Inc, 51846
John Christner Trucking Inc, 51852
Judge & Sons P Inc, 51855
Kline Transportation, 51871
KLLM Transportation Svc LLC, 51859
Konoike Pacific California, 51873
L B Transport Inc, 51875
La Grou Cold Storage, 51879
Lake Erie Warehouse & Distribution Center, 51880
Land Span, 51881
Laney & Duke Terminal Wrhse Co, 51883
Langham Logistics, 51884
LCL Bulk Transport Inc, 51876
Lehigh-Pocono Warehouse Inc, 51887
Logisco, 51893
Los Angeles Cold Storage Co, 51896

Ludtke Pacific Trucking Inc, 51899
Lumber & Things, 51901
MacCosham Van Lines, 51909
Majors Transit Inc, 51912
Manitoulin Group of Companies, 51915
Marten Transport LTD, 51916
Martin Warehousing & Distribution, 51917
Mccracken Motor Freight, 51925
MCT Terminal & Transport Inc., 51906
Merchants Distribution Svc, 51928
Mesa Cold Storage, 51929
Mid States Express Inc, 51932
Midnite Express, 51934
Milan Supply Chain Solutions, 51937
Miller Container Corp, 51938
Mo-Ark Truck Services, 51940
Moody's Quick, 51943
Moran Distribution Centers, 51944
Moran Logistics, 51945
MTE Logistix, 51908
Murray's Transfer Inc, 51950
National Distribution Centers, 51958
Nebraska Warehouse Co, 51960
New Orleans Cold Storage-Wrhse, 51963
North Park Transportation Co, 51970
Northeast Refrigerated, 51972
Nova Transportation Inc, 51976
Oak Harbor Freight Lines, 51980
Oborn Transfer & Stge Co Inc, 51981
ODW Logistics Inc, 51979
Ohio Commerce Center, 51984
Ozburn-Hessey Logistics LLC, 51995
Pasquale Trucking Co, 52006
Peerless Trucking Company, 52009
Peoples Cartage Inc, 52013
Philip P Massad Movers, 52015
Phoenix Industries LLC, 52016
Pilot Freight Svc, 52018
Pioneer Valley Refrigerated Warehouse, 52020
Pitt Ohio, 52021
Plymouth Rock Transportation, 52023
Port Elizabeth Terminal Corp, 52025
Price Truck Lines Inc, 52029
Pure Flo Water Co, 52035
Quick Delivery, 52039
Ralph Moyle Inc, 52045
Reynolds Transfer & Storage, 52050
RGL Headquarters, 52043
Roads West Transportation, 52054
Ronnie Dowdy, 52058
Sack Storage Corporation, 52071
Safeway Freezer Storage Inc, 52074
Seaonus, 52090
Service Craft Distribution Systems, 52093
Shaffer Trucking, 52094
Shaw Montgomery Warehouse Company, 52095
Shoreline Freezers, 52097
Simard Warehouses, 52101
Smith Cartage, 52103
Southwest Truck Service, 52112
Southwestern Motor Transport, 52113
Space Center Inc, 52114
Spartan Logistics, 52115
SPC Transport Co, 52070
Standard Warehouse, 52120
Star Distribution Systems, 52122
Starr Distribution Services Company, 52124
Supreme Lobster, 52131
Teal's Express Inc, 52138
Trailwood Warehouse LLC, 52151
TW Transport Inc, 52135
Twin City Wholesale, 52154
Valley Distributors & Storage Company, 52164
Van Brunt Port Jersey Warehouse, 52165
Versacold Logistics Services, 52169
Verst Group Logistics Inc, 52170
Volunteer Express, 52172, 52173
W J Beitler Co & Beitler Truck, 52174
W N Daul Transfer Lines, 52176

W T Young Storage Co, 52177
Wikel Bulk Express, 52194
Wilhelm Machinery Movers, 52195
Witte Brothers Exchange Inc, 52201
XPO Logistics, 52204

Trucking: Long Haul

Ability/Tri-Modal Trnsprtn Svc, 51513
Amware Distribution Warehouse, 51549
APL Logistics, 51509
B.R. Williams Trucking & Warehouse, 51568
Better Trucking, 51585
Can-Am LTL, 51619
Cardinal Logistics Management, 51625
Colonial Freight Systems, 51658
CRST International Inc, 51612
CSI Logistics, 51613
Dart Transit Co, 51692
DAV Transportation Services, 51686
Days Corporation, 51694
Dist Tech, 51702
Distribution Unlimited, 51704
Diversified Transfer & Storage, 51705
Eastern Refrigerater ExpRess, 51717
Farmers Distributing, 51735
Franklin Storage Inc, 51752
Freeway Warehouse Corp, 51753
Greenstein Trucking Company, 51784
Groendyke Transport Inc, 51790
Gulf Central Distribution Ctr, 51791
Hansen Trucking, 51800
Hanson Logistics, 51801
Henry L Taylor Trucking LLC, 51807
Highland Transport, 51810
Hillsboro Transportation Company, 51812
Holt Logistics Corporation, 51817
J B Hunt Transport Inc, 51838
J M Swank Co, 51840
Jacobson Warehouse Company, 51845
Jim Palmer Trucking, 51848
Kennesaw Transportation, 51865
Landstar System, Inc, 51882
Lester Coggins Trucking, 51888
Lincoln Cold Storage, 51890
Linden Warehouse & Dstrbtn Co, 51891
Live Oak Warehouse, 51892
Mallory Alexander Intl, 51914
McCann's Piggyback Consolidation, 51923
Merchandise Warehouse, 51927
Metropolitan Trucking Inc, 51931
Midwest Coast Logistics LLC, 51935
Newport St Paul Cold Storage, 51965
NFI Industries Inc, 51952
Ocean World Lines, 51982
Olson Co, 51986
Palmer Logistics, 52004
Paschall Truck Lines Co, 52005
Quality Logistics Systems, 52036
R W Bozel Transfer Inc, 52041
Reed Trucking Co, 52048
Rockwell Truck Line, 52057
Saddle Creek Logistics Svc, 52073
Sav Enterprises, 52081
Schneider National Inc, 52085
Schugel J & R Trucking Inc, 52086
Seagate Transportation, 52089
Short Freight Lines Inc, 52098
South Mill, 52110
Tazmanian Freight Forwarding, 52137
TWL Corporation, 52136
UPS Freight, 52156
UTZ Quality Foods Inc, 52158

Trucking: Short Haul

A-P-A Truck Leasing, 51506
Atkins Bob Lin Inc, 51563
Bilkays Express/Distribution Warehouse, 51587
Caldwell Trucking Inc, 51617
Canada Distribution Centres, 51621
Circle Delivery, 51653

Transportation Type / Trucking: TL & LTL

Cockrell Distribution System, 51656
Commonwealth Inc, 51665
Consolidated Transfer Co Inc, 51669
Craig Transportation Co, 51674
Dunagan Warehouse Corp, 51711
Fst Logistics Inc, 51755
Gabler Trucking Inc, 51759
Gatewood Products LLC, 51762
Hapag-Lloyd America, 51802
LMD Integrated Logistic Services, 51877
M & W Logistics Group, 51904
Midwest Continental Inc, 51936
New Hampton Transfer & Storage, 51962
Ozark Trucking, 51994
Ross Express Inc, 52060
Sopak Co Inc, 52107
South Atlantic Warehouse Corporation, 52108
South Bend Warehousing & Distribution, 52109
Southshore Enterprises, 52111
T P Freight Lines Inc, 52134
Trinity Transport & Distribution Services, 52153
Van Wyk Freight Lines, 52166
WOW Logistics, 52179

Trucking: TL & LTL

AmeriCold Logistics LLC, 51536
Belleharvest Sales Inc, 51579
Bridge Terminal, Inc., 51596
Decker Truck Line Inc, 51695
Dot Foods Inc, 51709
Exel Inc, 51731
GAMPAC Express, 51756
Greylawn Foods, 51788
Saia, Inc., 52075
Weber Logistics, 52185
Werner Enterprises Inc, 52187
Wilson Trucking Corp, 52198

WAREHOUSE COMPANIES

User Guide
Company Profiles
Warehouse Region Index
Warehouse Type & Service Index

Warehouse Companies User Guide

The **Warehousing Chapter** of *Food & Beverage Market Place* includes companies that offer warehouse services to the food and beverage industry. The descriptive listings are organized alphabetically. Following the A-Z Warehouse listings are two indexes: **Warehouse Region**, organized by region in which the warehouse is located; and **Warehouse Type**, that includes type of warehousing available. These Indexes refer to listing numbers, not page numbers.

Below is a sample listing illustrating the kind of information that is or might be included in a Warehouse listing. Each numbered item of information is described in the User Key on the following page.

---

1 → 245678

2 → **(HQ) Another Worldwide Logistics**

3 → 1278 Old Missouri Road

Springdale, AK 72765

4 → 756-204-5011

5 → 756-204-5012

6 → 888-756-5013

7 → info@AWL.com

8 → www.AWL.com

9 → Public warehouse providing storage of frozen and refrigerated foods.

10 → President: Michael Milinger
CFO: Elaine Rosendale
COO: Barbara Dingee
Vice President: Ben Campbell
Marketing: Nina Lathem

11 → *Estimated Sales*: $10-20 Million

12 → *Number Employees*: 34

13 → *Sq. Footage*: 27100

14 → *Parent Co.*: AWL Group

15 → *Company is also listed in the following section(s)*: Transportation

16 → *Other Locations*: Another Worldwide Logistics, Oklahoma City, OK

17 → *Types of products warehoused*: Frozen Foods: chicken

18 → *Services Provided*: Local haul trucking.

19 → *Storage Facility Data*: Freezer Size: 10,000 Sq. Ft.

Warehouse Companies User Key

1 → **Record Number:** Entries are listed alphabetically within each category and numbered sequentially. The entry number, rather than the page number, is used in the indexes to refer to listings.

2 → **Company Name:** Formal name of company. HQ indicates headquarter location. If names are completely capitalized, the listing will appear at the beginning of the alphabetized section.

3 → **Address:** Location or permanent address of the company. If the mailing address differs from the street address, it will appear second.

4 → **Phone Number:** The listed phone number is usually for the main office, but may also be for the sales, marketing, or public relations office as provided.

5 → **Fax Number:** This is listed when provided by the company.

6 → **Toll-Free Number:** This is listed when provided by the company.

7 → **E-Mail:** This is listed when provided, and is generally the main office e-mail.

8 → **Web Site:** This is listed when provided by the company and is also referred to as an URL address. These web sites are accessed through the Internet by typing http:// before the URL address.

9 → **Description:** This paragraph contains a brief description of the type of warehousing available and food category warehoused.

10 → **Key Personnel:** Names and titles of company executives.

11 → **Estimated Sales:** This is listed when provided by the company.

12 → **Number of Employees:** Total number of employees within the company.

13 → **Square Footage:** Size of facility.

14 → **Parent Co.:** If the listing is a division of another company, the parent is listed here.

15 → Indicates what other section in *Food & Beverage Market Place* this company is listed: Volume 1: Manufacturers. Volume 2: Equipment, Supplies & Services; Transportation; Warehouse; Wholesalers/Distributors. Volume 3: Brokers; Importers/Exporters.

16 → **Other locations:** Indicates other company locations.

17 → **Types of products warehoused:** What type of food and beverages are warehoused. Companies are indexed by product type.

18 → **Services Provided:** Types of related services that are available. Companies are indexed by type of service.

19 → **Storage Facility Data:** Specifications of various storage capability, i.e. freezer and refrigerator sizes.

Warehousing / A-Z

52601 A Arnold Logistics
5200 Interchange Way
Louisville, KY 40229-2190   502-327-1369
         Fax: 502-327-1378 800-626-5371
         logisticsvp@a-arnold.com
         www.aarnoldmovingcompany.com
Is a full-service logistics company providing turnkey solutions to customers' challenges, including fulfillment, contract packaging/kitting, call center, reverse logistics, print, direct mail, and transportation. In our CentralPennsylvania Campus we operate 3.6 million sq. ft., with 15 facilities and employ over 1000 associates. Arnold Logistics also has operations in Columbus, OH and Southwest Regional Campus in Dallas, TX. The company has been in operation for 26years
President: Rick Russell
rick.russell@a-arnold.com
Number Employees: 50-99
Types of products warehoused:
  Frozen, refrigerated & non-perishable foods, dry goods, non-perishables, canned foods, general merchandise, sofware & publications
Services Provided:
  Re-packing, labeling, long & short haul trucking, rail siding, trucking, labeling, packaging, pick and pack, repackaging, reverse logistics
Storage Facility Data:
  Cooler Size 130000 Sq. Ft.
  Dry Storage Size: 2800000 Sq. Ft.

52602 A W Sisk & Son
3601 Choptank Rd
P.O. Box 70
Preston, MD 21655   410-673-7111
     Fax: 410-673-7360 sales@awsisk.com
         www.awsisk.com
Broker of general merchandise and private label items including milk and dairy related products, bread, rolls, bagels and sweet good, and vegetables.
Chief Executive Officer: Al Turner
alturn@awsisk.com
Canned Food Sales: Leon Kanner
Protein Sales: Brenan Roser
Administrative Assistant: Melissa Corbin
Year Founded: 1891
Estimated Sales: $30-40 Million
Number Employees: 5-9
Square Footage: 100000
Type of Packaging: Consumer, Food Service, Private Label
Types of products warehoused:
  Canned-goods, seeds, flour, detergents, cleaners, boxes and cartons, spices, paper products, dry goods, non-perishables, canned foods, general merchandise, packaging supplies
Services Provided:
  Re-label, re-palletize, cross-dock shipments, etc., rail siding, trucking
Storage Facility Data:
  Dry Storage Size: 80000 Sq. Ft.

52603 A to Z Nutrition International Inc
14359 Miramar Pkwy
#218
Miramar, FL 33027   954-885-3997
     Fax: 954-885-5592 info@atoznutritioninc.com
         www.atoznutritioninc.com
Supplier of raw materials to the nutritional, food, feed, cosmetic and pharmaceutical industries.
Other Locations:
  Warehouse
  Hacienda Heights, CAWarehouseBeijing, China

52604 A&M Warehouse & Distribution
9821 Fallard Court
Upper Marlboro, ML 20772   703-256-5800
     Fax: 709-642-0032 800-733-8480
         www.a-msupply.com
Warehouse providing dry storage for nonperishable foods; transportation broker providing local trucking; re-packing and rail siding available
Number Employees: 10-19
Types of products warehoused:
  Non-perishable foods, non-perishables
Services Provided:
  Re-packing, trucking, assembly & distribution, rail siding

52605 A. Gagliano Co Inc
300 N Jefferson St # 1
PO Box 511382
Milwaukee, WI 53202-5920   414-272-1515
     Fax: 414-272-7215 800-272-1516
         info@agagliano.com
Fresh fruits and vegetables
Owner: Anthony Gagliano
tony@agagliano.com
Owner: Nick Gagliano
Owner: Mike Gagliano
Warehouse Manager: Rick Alsum
Estimated Sales: $20 Million
Number Employees: 50-99
Number of Brands: 1
Number of Products: 500
Square Footage: 200000
Type of Packaging: Consumer, Food Service, Private Label, Bulk
Types of products warehoused:
  Produce, dry goods, non-perishables, produce
Services Provided:
  Re-packing & gassing, trucking, labeling, packaging, repackaging
Storage Facility Data:
  Cooler Size 200000 Sq. Ft.
  Humidity-Controlled Size: 200000 Sq. Ft.

52606 AADF Warehouse Corporation
P.O.Box 26928
Albuquerque, NM 87125-6928   505-842-6563
         Fax: 505-243-6097
Warehouse providing dry storage for canned and packaged foods, etc.; transportation broker providing long haul trucking; also, pick/pack, computer inventory bookkeeping, EDI terminals, UPS overpack and zone and rail siding available
Owner: Al Saloka
Number Employees: 20-49
Types of products warehoused:
  Packaging materials, drums & foods: canned, packaged & cartoned, dry goods, non-perishables, frozen goods, canned foods, general merchandise
Services Provided:
  Pick/pack, computer inventory, EDI, etc., rail siding, trucking
Storage Facility Data:
  Cooler Size 12000 Sq. Ft.
  Dry Storage Size: 275000 Sq. Ft.
  Freezer Size: 12000 Sq. Ft.

52607 AM-C Warehouses Inc
1475 Post N Paddock St
Grand Prairie, TX 75050-1233   972-988-0333
     Fax: 972-602-9936 www.amcwhse.com
Warehouse providing cooler, freezer, dry and humidity-controlled storage for dry, frozen and refrigerated foods; rail siding available
President: William Barnett
Estimated Sales: $1-2.5 Million
Number Employees: 100-249
Square Footage: 250000
Types of products warehoused:
  Dry, frozen & refrigerated foods, dry goods, frozen goods
Services Provided:
  rail siding
Storage Facility Data:
  Cooler Size 800000 Cubic Ft.
  Dry Storage Size: 4400000 Cubic Ft.
  Freezer Size: 540000 Cubic Ft.
  Humidity-Controlled Size: 200000 Cubic Ft.

52608 AME Nutrition
545 Metro Place S
Suite 100
Dublin, OH 43017   614-766-3638
         sales@amenutrition.com
         www.amenutrition.com
Plant- and dairy-based ingredients manufacturer
Director of Sales & Marketing: Bill Brickson

52609 APL Logistics
16220 N Scottsdale Rd # 300
Suite 300
Scottsdale, AZ 85254-1798   602-586-4800
     Fax: 602-586-4861 www.apllogistics.com
Key Services include: Contract warehousing; cross-docking; deconsolidation; distribution warehousing; freight management; inbound logistics; just-in-time delivery; parcel consolidation; reverse logistics; warehouse managementsystem.

President: Beat Simon
CEO: Thad Bedard
thad_bedard@apllogistics.com
Senior Vice President, Operations: Danny Goh
Estimated Sales: Over $1 Billion
Number Employees: 1000-4999

52610 APL Logistics
1301 Riverplace Blvd # 1100
Jacksonville, FL 32207-9029   904-396-2517
     Fax: 904-396-3984 800-331-4289
         www.apllogistics.com
Key Services include: Contract warehousing; cross-docking; deconsolidation; distribution warehousing; freight management; inbound logistics; just-in-time delivery; parcel consolidation; reverse logistics; warehouse managementsystem.
President APL/APL Logistics Americas: Beat Simon
Senior Vice President: William Villalon
Markets Analyst: Paolo Hardtke
International Sales Support: Christine Goodwin
Corporate Communications Director: Michael Zampa
Number Employees: 1,000-4,999
Parent Co: NOL Group (Neptune Orient Lines Limited)

52611 ASAP Freight Systems
11252 E Hardy Rd
Houston, TX 77093-2368   281-442-1755
     Fax: 713-272-7468 800-272-7468
         www.asapfrt.com
Warehouse providing dry storage for nonperishable items; transportation services include long and short haul trucking and freight forwarding
Manager: Isabelle Mc Ibney
Manager: Linda Dicanio
asap3@asapfrt.net
Number Employees: 50-99
Types of products warehoused:
  Non-perishable items, non-perishables
Services Provided:
  Trucking & shipping

52612 ASW Supply Chain Svc
3375 Gilchrist Rd
Mogadore, OH 44260-1253   330-733-6291
     Fax: 330-733-5196 888-363-8492
         www.aswglobal.com
Warehouse providing dry storage for non-perishable foods; transportation firm providing long and short haul trucking, cross docking, rail car, and foreign trade zone services; also, distribution, pick/pack, display assemblyrelabeling, etc.
Owner: Andre Thornton
athornton@aswservices.com
Business Development: Nick Mihiylov
Number Employees: 10-19
Types of products warehoused:
  dry goods, non-perishables, canned foods, general merchandise
Services Provided:
  rail siding, trucking, labeling, packaging, pick and pack, repackaging
Storage Facility Data:
  Dry Storage Size: 350,000 Sq. Ft.

52613 (HQ)Ability/Tri-Modal Trnsprtn Svc
2011 E Carson St
Carson, CA 90810-1223   310-522-5506
     Fax: 310-518-8982 sales@trimodal.com
         www.abilitytrimodal.com
Transportation firm providing long and short haul trucking; warehouse offering dry storage for general commodities; also, rail siding available
President: Greg Owen
gowen@trimodal.com
Executive VP: Eldon Hatfield
VP Operations: Mike Kelso
Number Employees: 100-249
Other Locations:
  TRI Modal Distribution Servic
  CarsonTRI Modal Distribution Servic
Types of products warehoused:
  General commodities, general merchandise
Services Provided:
  cross dock, transload, bar coding, shrink wrap, sort, rail siding, trucking, labeling, packaging, pick and pack

801

Warehousing / A-Z

52614 Abler Transfer
2905 Dover Dr
Norfolk, NE 68701   402-371-0815
                Fax: 402-371-0817
Warehouse providing storage for dry commodities; transportation services include local, short and long haul trucking and distribution
Owner: Leon Abler
Number Employees: 10-19
Types of products warehoused:
  Dry commodities, dry goods
Services Provided:
  Distribution & transportation

52615 (HQ)Acme Distribution Ctr Inc
18101 E Colfax Ave
Aurora, CO 80011-5107   303-340-2100
        Fax: 303-340-2424 info@acmd.com
        www.acmedistribution.com
Warehouse providing cooler, dry and humidity-controlled storage; transportation firm providing freight consolidation and short haul trucking; rail siding, pick/pack, shrink wrapping, module building and display assembly services available
President: Joe Stam
stam@acmedistribution.com
Chief Financial Officer: Nancy Manilla
Sr Vice President: Doug Sampson
Estimated Sales: $2.5 Million
Number Employees: 100-249
Type of Packaging: Consumer, Food Service, Private Label, Bulk
Types of products warehoused:
  dry goods, non-perishables, canned foods, general merchandise
Services Provided:
  rail siding, trucking, labeling, packaging, pick and pack, repackaging

52616 Adams Warehouse & Delivery
3701 Yale St
Houston, TX 77018-6563   713-699-3515
        Fax: 713-694-7510 888-977-0502
                www.adamsdist.com
Warehouse providing dry storage, re-packing and labeling for nonperishable foods; transportation firm providing short haul trucking, local delivery, shrink wrap, cross-dock, pick/pack, order fulfillment and storage; rail siding available
President: Fred Adams
fredadams@adamsdist.com
Number Employees: 50-99
Types of products warehoused:
  dry goods, non-perishables, canned foods, general merchandise, paper
Services Provided:
  rail siding, trucking, labeling, packaging, pick and pack, repackaging
Storage Facility Data:
  Dry Storage Size: 243000 Sq. Ft.

52617 Advance Distribution Svc
2349 Millers Ln
Louisville, KY 40216-5329   502-449-1720
  Fax: 502-778-1718 www.advancedistribution.com
Warehouse providing dry storage of nonperishable food items, as well as wine and spirits
President: Brian Johnson
bjohnson@advancedistribution.com
Estimated Sales: $5-10 Million
Number Employees: 50-99
Types of products warehoused:
  Wine & Spirits, non-perishables

52618 Advance Distribution Svc
2349 Millers Ln
Louisville, KY 40216-5329   502-449-1720
        Fax: 502-778-1718
        contactADS@advancedistribution.com
                www.advancedistribution.com
A packaging, warehouse and distributor company for the food industry
President: Brian Johnson
bjohnson@advancedistribution.com
R&D: J Perrier
Quality Control: L Defaint
Sales: Judy Jaedine
Operations: Aldo Dagnino
Plant Manager: Jorge Monge
Estimated Sales: $300,000-500,000
Number Employees: 50-99
Square Footage: 2400000
Type of Packaging: Consumer, Food Service

52619 Advanced Warehouses
241 Francis Ave
Mansfield, MA 02048-1548   508-339-8995
                Fax: 508-339-8994
                www.advancedwarehouses.com
Warehouse providing storage for boxed and canned goods, paper products and alcoholic and nonalcoholic drinks; also, re-packing, trucking, outside storage of lumber, consolidation and distribution services available
Manager: Chris De Perro
chris@advancedwarehouses.com
VP: Charles Canali
Warehouse Manager: Chris DePierro
Account Executive: Mark Giroux
Estimated Sales: $1-2.5 Million
Number Employees: 5-9
Square Footage: 1440000
Types of products warehoused:
  Boxed & canned goods, paper products, alcoholic & non-alcoholic drinks, canned foods
Services Provided:
  Re-packing, trucking, outside lumber storage & consolidation, rail siding

52620 Affiliated Warehouse CoInc
54 Village Ct
Hazlet, NJ 07730-1536   732-739-2323
        Fax: 732-739-4154 www.awco.com
Vice President: Patrick Mcbride
sales@awco.com
Vice President: Patrick Mcbride
sales@awco.com
VP Sales: Robert Nemeth
Number Employees: 5-9

52621 Affiliated Warehouse CoInc
P.O. Box 295
Hazlet, NJ 07730-0295   732-739-2323
                www.awco.com
Dry, air-conditioned, cooler, freezer and chemical HazMat space and services.
President: Patrick McBride
sales@awco.com
Estimated Sales: $50-100 Million
Type of Packaging: Food Service

52622 (HQ)Airschott Inc
PO Box 17373
Washington, DC 20041-7373   703-471-7444
        Fax: 703-471-4026 sales@airschott.com
                www.airschott.com
Import and export broker of seafood, alcoholic beverages, produce, etc.; warehouse providing cooler and dry storage for seafood; transportation firm providing customs brokerage, freight forwarding, domestic and international airfreight and long haul trucking
President: Robert Schott
EVP: Tony Sequeira
Marketing Director: Andrew Shotwell
Contact: Carlos Balta
carlos@airschott.com
Director Operations: Hing Buon
Estimated Sales: $20-50 Million
Number Employees: 5-9
Square Footage: 4000
Other Locations:
  Airschott
  Baltimore, MDAirschott
Types of products warehoused:
  Seafood, confectionery items & produce, produce
Storage Facility Data:
  Cooler Size 640 Sq. Ft.
  Dry Storage Size: 36000 Sq. Ft.

52623 Alaska Railroad Corp
327 W Ship Creek Ave
Anchorage, AK 99501-1671   907-265-2300
        Fax: 907-265-2416 800-321-6518
                public_comment@akrr.com
                www.alaskarailroadgiftshop.com
Warehouse providing dry storage for perishable goods; transportation services includes railroad; rail siding available
CEO: William O'Leary
olearyw@akrr.com
Number Employees: 500-999
Types of products warehoused:
  Perishables
Services Provided:
  Railroad transportation, rail siding

Storage Facility Data:
  Dry Storage Size: 15000 Cubic Ft.

52624 Alcor Corp
2100 Pittsburgh Ave
Erie, PA 16502-1946   814-453-6911
        Fax: 814-454-2670 800-48A-COR
                sales@alcorcoldstorage.com
                www.alcorcoldstorage.com
Warehouse providing cooler, dry and freezer storage for frozen and dry food products; also, rail siding and trucking available
President: James J. Alberico, Sr.
alcor2100@aol.com
VP: James J. Alberico, Jr.
General Manager: Jeffrey J. Alberico
Estimated Sales: $1-2.5 Million
Number Employees: 10-19
Square Footage: 340000
Types of products warehoused:
  Frozen & dry food products, dry goods, frozen goods
Services Provided:
  Trucking, rail siding, trucking
Storage Facility Data:
  Cooler Size 120000 Cubic Ft.
  Dry Storage Size: 300000 Cubic Ft.
  Freezer Size: 1500000 Cubic Ft.

52625 Alger Warehouse Company
1640 Clay St Ste 410
Detroit, MI 48211   313-872-3737
                Fax: 313-872-4620
Warehouse offering dry and humidity-controlled storage for food products
Manager: Lee Niedzwiecki
Manager: Lee Niedzwiecki
Estimated Sales: $500,000-$1 Million
Number Employees: 5 to 9
Parent Co: Kobylas Corporation
Types of products warehoused:
  Food products

52626 All Freight Distribution Co
6201 Seaforth St
Baltimore, MD 21224-6597   410-633-3200
        Fax: 410-633-7186 800-787-0105
                www.allfreightdistribution.com
Warehouse providing cooler and dry storage for canned foods, confectionery items, grocery products, paper and fiber products, packaging materials, etc.; also, rail siding delivery and distribution services available
President: Mark Eisenberg
aftbalt@aol.com
General Manager: Buzz McDougle
Estimated Sales: Less Than $500,000
Number Employees: 10-19
Square Footage: 1200000
Type of Packaging: Consumer, Private Label
Types of products warehoused:
  Canned foods, confectionery products, grocery items, paper & fiber products, packaging materials, etc., canned foods
Services Provided:
  Distribution & delivery, rail siding
Storage Facility Data:
  Cooler Size 4000 Sq. Ft.
  Dry Storage Size: 300000 Sq. Ft.
  Humidity-Controlled Size: 4000 Sq. Ft.

52627 All Freight Systems
P.O.Box 5279
1134 S 12th St
Kansas City, KS 66105-1615   913-281-1087
                Fax: 913-281-5741
Warehouse providing dry, freezer and refrigerated storage for nonperishable, refrigerated and frozen foods; also, re-packing and labeling available
Owner: Bob Smith
Operations Manager: Greg Smith
Estimated Sales: $20-50 Million
Number Employees: 100 to 249
Types of products warehoused:
  Non-perishable, refrigerated & frozen foods, non-perishables, frozen goods
Services Provided:
  Re-packing & labeling

52628 All South Warehouse
1775 Continental Way SE
Atlanta, GA 30316-4708   404-243-2062
        Fax: 404-241-5822 www.allsouthwarehouse.com

Warehousing / A-Z

Public warehouse handling dry food grade, chemicals and paper; also, railroad siding available
Vice President: Rob Roark
CFO: Turny Finance Executive
Vice President: Rob Roark
Sales Manager: Don Powell
Operations Manager: Rick Maltbie
Warehouse Manager: Ryan Roark
Estimated Sales: Less Than $500,000
Number Employees: 1-4
Square Footage: 1500000
Types of products warehoused:
  Dry food grade, chemicals & paper, dry goods
Services Provided:
  rail siding
Storage Facility Data:
  Cooler Size 5000 Sq. Ft.
  Dry Storage Size: 745000 Sq. Ft.

52629 All-Temp
5400 NE Main St
Fridley
Minneapolis, MN 55421   763-571-0215
         Fax: 763-502-2459 sales@all-storage.com
Warehouse providing freezer, cooler and dry storage for food products; rail siding available
Chairman/CEO: John Holman
VP of Sales and Operations: Gerry Mrosla
VP of Sales: Gerry Mrosla
Contact: Brad Carlson
bcarlson@copelandtruc-king.com
Customer Service Manager: Josie Holman
Controller: Margaret Siluk
Estimated Sales: $5 Million
Number Employees: 20-49
Square Footage: 2400000
Other Locations:
  Minneapolis, MN
Types of products warehoused:
  Food products, business records, dry goods, non-perishables, frozen goods, produce, canned foods, general merchandise
Services Provided:
  barcoding, cross-docking, rail siding, pick and pack
Storage Facility Data:
  Cooler Size 40000 Sq. Ft.
  Dry Storage Size: 300000 Sq. Ft.
  Freezer Size: 18000 Sq. Ft.

52630 Allegheny Cold Storage Co
16 57th St
Pittsburgh, PA 15201-2395   412-782-3670
         Fax: 412-782-0181
         www.alleghenycoldstorage.com
Warehouse providing cooler and freezer storage for refrigerated and frozen foods including ice cream; also, rail siding and cross dock delivery services available
President: Chuck Longsdorf
cjlongsdorf@alleghenycoldstorage.com
Accounting: Jean Snoke
VP: Kenneth Wagner
Office Manager: Dorothy Grainy
Engineering: Joe Ortlieb
Estimated Sales: $1-2.5 Million
Number Employees: 20-49
Square Footage: 400000
Types of products warehoused:
  Refrigerated & frozen foods including ice cream, frozen goods
Services Provided:
  Cross dock delivery, rail siding
Storage Facility Data:
  Cooler Size 20000 Sq. Ft.
  Freezer Size: 80000 Sq. Ft.

52631 Allegheny Valley
270 Alpha Drive
Pittsburgh, PA 15238-2906   412-967-9656
         Fax: 412-967-9654
Warehouse providing stoarge space for dry, and refrigerated goods
President: Barry Miller
CEO: Eddie DiPasquale
Director Sales: James Shipe
Estimated Sales: $ 20 - 50 Million
Number Employees: 20-49
Square Footage: 5000
Type of Packaging: Food Service
Types of products warehoused:
  refrigerated goods, dry goods
Storage Facility Data:
  Dry Storage Size: 200 sq ft

52632 Allentown Refrigerated Trmnls
125 Seneca Trl
Boyertown, PA 19512-8661   610-367-2174
         Fax: 610-367-9168 800-833-2174
         www.artcoldstorage.com
Warehouse providing cooler, dry and freezer storage for frozen and refrigerated foods; also, delivery services available
CEO: Neil Eichelberger
vorteil1@aol.com
Chief Operating Officer: Mark Azemar
Estimated Sales: $5-10 Million
Number Employees: 50-99
Square Footage: 448000
Types of products warehoused:
  Frozen & refrigerated foods, frozen goods
Services Provided:
  Delivery
Storage Facility Data:
  Cooler Size 16000 Sq. Ft.
  Freezer Size: 96000 Sq. Ft.

52633 (HQ)Allied Cold Storage Corporation
28 Kondelin Rd # 1
Gloucester, MA 01930-5192   978-281-0800
         Fax: 978-281-6642 www.alliedcoldstorage.com
Warehouse providing cooler and freezer storage for frozen foods; transportation firm providing local haul trucking; also, blast/plate freezing and rail siding available
Owner: Peter Maggio
Number Employees: 20-49
Square Footage: 1100000
Other Locations:
  Gloucester, MA
Types of products warehoused:
  Frozen foods, frozen goods
Services Provided:
  Blast/plate freezing, local haul trucking, etc., rail siding, trucking, blast freezing
Storage Facility Data:
  Cooler Size 100000 Cubic Ft.
  Freezer Size: 4,300,000 Cubic Ft.

52634 Allied Frozen Storage Inc
2501 Broadway St
Buffalo, NY 14227-1042   716-894-4000
         Fax: 716-894-2403 dblum@alliedgrp.com
         www.alliedfrozenstorage.com
Warehouse providing cooler, humidity-controlled, freezer and dry storage; transportation broker providing freight consolidation, cross docking, store door delivery and Canadian distribution; rail siding available
CEO: Drew Blum
VP: Terrance J. Collister
COO: Stephen Kincanon
Number Employees: 20-49
Types of products warehoused:
  Frozen, refrigerated & ambient foods, dry goods, frozen goods
Services Provided:
  Labeling, re-packing, custom clearance, distribution, etc., rail siding
Storage Facility Data:
  Cooler Size 750000 Cubic Ft.
  Dry Storage Size: 3600000 Cubic Ft.
  Freezer Size: 7300000 Cubic Ft.
  Humidity-Controlled Size: 4350000 Cubic Ft.

52635 Allied Logistics
20 26th St
Huntington, WV 25703-1242   304-523-2131
         Fax: 304-523-9531 800-218-4246
sales@alliedlogistics.com www.alliedlogistics.com
Warehouse providing dry, freezer and cooler storage for food products, chemicals, general merchandise; also toll services, pick and pack, repackaging and just-in-time services available
President: Jeff Smith
CEO: Lake Polan III
VP: Ed Canterbury
Number Employees: 100-249
Parent Co: Allied Realty Company
Other Locations:
  Allied Warehousing Services
  Kenova, WV
  Allied Warehousing Services
  Nitro, WVAllied Warehousing ServicesNitro
Types of products warehoused:
  dry goods, non-perishables, canned foods, general merchandise
Services Provided:
  rail siding, trucking, labeling, packaging, pick and pack, repackaging
Storage Facility Data:
  Cooler Size 80000 Sq. Ft.
  Dry Storage Size: 1120000 Sq. Ft.

52636 Amarillo Warehouse Co
620 N Fairfield St
PO Box 829
Amarillo, TX 79107-7911   806-381-0107
         Fax: 806-383-1625 info@amarillowarehouse.com
         www.amarillowarehouse.com
Warehouse providing freezer and dry storage for frozen and dry foods; transportation services include slip sheets, loading and unloading, local and short haul trucking, drayage and intrastate and interstate connections; rail sidingavailable
Manager: Esther Bustos
Number Employees: 10-19
Types of products warehoused:
  Dry & frozen foods, dry goods, frozen goods
Services Provided:
  Trucking, drayage & intrastate & interstate connections, rail siding
Storage Facility Data:
  Dry Storage Size: 100000 Sq. Ft.
  Freezer Size: 3000 Sq. Ft.

52637 AmeriCold Logistics LLC
10 Glenlake Parkway
Suite 600, South Tower
Atlanta, GA 30328   678-441-6824
                           888-808-4877
info@americold.com www.americold.com
Over 175 temperature-controlled warehouses around the world; Also transportation and logistics
President/CEO: Fred Boehler
EVP/CFO: Marc Smernoff
EVP/Chief Investment Officer: Jay Harron
EVP, Supply Chain Solutions: David Stuver
EVP/Chief Legal Officer: Jim Snyder
EVP/COO: Carlos Rodriguez
Year Founded: 1903
Estimated Sales: $1 Billion+
Number Employees: 10,000+
Types of products warehoused:
  frozen goods
Services Provided:
  trucking, labeling, blast freezing, pick and pack, repackaging, Kitting, Display Configuration, Tempering

52638 American Cold Storage
100 Lee St
Jackson, TN 38301-5326   731-422-7100
         Fax: 731-422-7119 800-344-5963
         samcbradshaw@yahoo.com
         www.americancold.com
Warehouse providing rail service, USDA inspections, computerized inventory, export services and distribution
CEO and Chairman: Sam C. Bradshaw
Vice President Finance: Patty Bronaugh
Sales & Marketing: Charles Cheatham
Manager: Steven Watlington
swatlington@uscold.com
Office Manager: Lisa Blackburn
Warehouse Manager: Christy Ward
Estimated Sales: $1-2.5 Million
Number Employees: 10-19
Types of products warehoused:
  Frozen & refrigerated foods, frozen goods
Services Provided:
  USDA inspection, export services, distribution, rail siding
Storage Facility Data:
  Cooler Size 2941000 Cubic Ft.
  Dry Storage Size: 100000 Sq. Ft.
  Freezer Size: 3500000 Cubic Ft.
  Humidity-Controlled Size: 15000 Sq. Ft.

52639 (HQ)American Cold Storage
607 Industry Rd
Louisville, KY 40208-1635   502-634-4753
         Fax: 502-634-4757 www.americancold.com
Warehouse providing a total of 13,994,356 cu. ft of warehouse space throughout all five warehouses; also provides cooler and freezer storage for food and nonfood products; transportation firm providing local, long and short haulrefrigerated trucking and rail car services; also, rail siding, USDA inspections, pork certification, etc. services available

803

Warehousing / A-Z

Vice President: Dan Brittain
danb@americancoldtulsa.com
CEO and Chairman: Sam C. Bradshaw
Vice President Finance: Patty Bronaugh
Vice President: Dan Brittain
danb@americancoldtulsa.com
Sales & Marketing: Charles Cheatham
Office Manager: Lisa Blackburn
Warehouse Manager: Christy Ward
Number Employees: 50-99
Other Locations:
  American Cold Storage
  Louisville, KY
  Boonville, IN
  Jackson, TN
  Tulsa, OK
  Humboldt, TNAmerican Cold StorageBoonville
Types of products warehoused:
  Food & non-food products, general merchandise
Services Provided:
  Blast freezing, trucking, USDA inspections, etc., rail siding, labeling, blast freezing
Storage Facility Data:
  Cooler Size 321915 Cubic Ft.
  Freezer Size: 3641471 Cubic Ft.

52640 American Cold Storage
P.O.Box 306
888 American Way
Boonville, IN 47601-8600   812-897-4713
    Fax: 812-897-1687 888-888-6931
            www.americancold.com
Cold storage - warehouse is 2,552,570 cubic feet fully racked refrigerated space
Manager: John Simpson
Warehouse Manager: John Simpson
Estimated Sales: $ 1 - 3 Million
Number Employees: 10 to 19

52641 American Cold Storage
100 Lee St
Jackson, TN 38301-5326   731-422-7100
    Fax: 731-784-6621 800-344-5963
    ACSNA_newbiz@americancold.com
            www.americancold.com
The Humboldt warehouse is a one-story brick, concrete, and panel warehouse with total refrigerated space of 2,151,000 cubic feet including total cooler space of 530,000 cubic feet.
Administrator: Charles Cheatham
Manager: Steven Watlington
swatlington@uscold.com
Warehouse Manager: Charles Cheatham
Estimated Sales: $ .5 - 1 million
Number Employees: 10-19
Type of Packaging: Food Service

52642 American Distribution Centers
P.O Box 27404
Salt Lake City, UT 84127   801-972-3404
    Fax: 801-972-9445 www.americandis.com
Warehouse providing cooler, dry and humidity-controlled storage for general merchandise and food products; transportation firm providing local haul trucking and freight consolidation services; rail siding available
President: David Pettit
Evp Sales/Marketing: Lenny Goodwin
Evp Operations: Jason Walker
Estimated Sales: $8.3 Million
Number Employees: 50-99
Square Footage: 1960000
Types of products warehoused:
  Food products & general merchandise, general merchandise
Services Provided:
  freight consolidation, assembly, cross-dock, rail siding, trucking, pick and pack, repackaging
Storage Facility Data:
  Cooler Size 30000 Sq. Ft.
  Dry Storage Size: 460000 Sq. Ft.
  Humidity-Controlled Size: 17000 Sq. Ft.

52643 American Port Services
PO Box 193
Savannah, GA 31402-0193   912-966-2198
            Fax: 912-966-2791
Public warehouse providing dry storage; transportation firm providing local, long and short haul trucking; also, rail siding, LTL, TL, TOFC, COFC, M.I.D. meat inspections and U.S. custom bonded storage services available
VP: John Fergerson

Number Employees: 501-1000
Parent Co: Schneider Logistics
Types of products warehoused:
  General merchandise, groceries & imports, dry goods, non-perishables, canned foods, general merchandise
Services Provided:
  Trucking, M.I.D. meat inspection & U.S. custom bonded storage, rail siding, trucking, labeling, packaging, pick and pack, repackaging
Storage Facility Data:
  Dry Storage Size: 160000 Sq. Ft.

52644 American Warehouse Co
5150 Colorado Blvd
Denver, CO 80216-3120   303-388-4521
    Fax: 303-394-4514 sales@awc-denver.com
            www.wsi.com
Warehouse providing dry storage of general merchandise; transportation firm offering truckload and LTL services
Manager: Scott Myhaver
smyhaver@wsi.com
Number Employees: 20-49
Parent Co: Warehouse Specialists Inc.
Types of products warehoused:
  General merchandise, dry goods, non-perishables, canned foods, general merchandise
Services Provided:
  rail siding, trucking, labeling, pick and pack, repackaging, stretch wrap
Storage Facility Data:
  Dry Storage Size: 200000 Cubic Ft.

52645 Ampoint Distribution Centers
PO Box 9040
Toledo, OH 419-666-32   419-666-0004
    Fax: 419-666-3207 jgunn@ampoint.com
            www.ampoint.com
Warehouse providing dry storage for nonperishable foods; also, rail siding, cross docking, packaging and quality control inspection services available
Contact: Mike Willinger
mwillinger@ampoint.com
Director Operations: John Gun
Estimated Sales: $2.5-5 Million
Number Employees: 20-49
Square Footage: 10600000
Types of products warehoused:
  non-perishables
Services Provided:
  Cross docking, packaging, quality control inspecions, etc., rail siding
Storage Facility Data:
  Dry Storage Size: 2750000 Sq. Ft.

52646 Amware Distribution Warehouse
19801 Holland Rd
Cleveland, OH 44142   440-234-8888
            Fax: 440-234-8055
Warehouse providing dry storage for nonperishable foods; transportation firm providing long and short haul trucking
President: Brad Maloof
Contact: Michael Liu
michael.liu@amwarelogistics.com
Number Employees: 10-19
Square Footage: 408000
Types of products warehoused:
  Non-perishable foods, non-perishables
Services Provided:
  Long & short haul trucking

52647 Anadon Logistics
Po Box 271
Campbellville, CA L0P 1B0
Canada   905-854-5630
Freight forwarder and logistics provider specializing in the food and beverage industry. Provide prior notice service to comply with FDA requirements.
Estimated Sales: 1 Million
Number Employees: 20-49
Square Footage: 20000
Other Locations:
  Anadon Logistics
  Ontario, CanadaAnadon Logistics

52648 Anchor Distribution Services
2950 Merced St
San Leandro, CA 94577-5635   510-483-9120
    Fax: 510-483-1826 877-640-0268
    http://www.anchordistribution.com/index.html

Food grade warehouse providing dry and cold storage; transportation firm providing local, long and short haul trucking; also, rail siding, re-packing, container de-vanning, export management, etc
Owner: Charles Callaghan
President: Chad Callaghan
Contact: Chad Anchor
chad@anchordistributinginc.com
Operations: Greg Zamira
Number Employees: 17
Square Footage: 720000
Types of products warehoused:
  Food products & general commodities, general merchandise
Services Provided:
  Re-packing, trcking, USDA meat inspection, consolidation, etc., rail siding
Storage Facility Data:
  Dry Storage Size: 120000 Sq. Ft.

52649 Apl Logistics
222 westt Adams Street
Chicago, IL 60606   312-621-2000
    Fax: 311- 62- 800-428-8161
    contactgatx@gatx.com www.gatx.com
Warehouse providing cooler and dry storage for refrigerated and nonperishable foods; transportation firm providing long, short and local haul trucking; also, re-packing and labeling available
CEO: Brian A Kenney
Number Employees: 250-499
Parent Co: GATX Logistics
Types of products warehoused:
  Refrigerated & non-perishable foods, non-perishables
Services Provided:
  Trucking, re-packing & labeling

52650 Arbre Farms Inc
6362 N 192nd Ave
Walkerville, MI 49459-8601   231-873-3337
    Fax: 231-873-5699 www.arbrefarms.com
Provides food service and frozen food manufacturing industries with the finest quality frozen fruits and vegetables.
President: C O Johnson
cjohnson@arbrefarms.com
Quality Control: Robert Anderson
Marketing: Tripper Showell
Sales: Jean Hovey
Plant Manager: Vince Miskosky
Number Employees: 250-499
Type of Packaging: Food Service, Bulk
Other Locations:
  Willow Cold Storage
  Walkerville, MIWillow Cold Storage

52651 (HQ)Archer Daniels Midland Company
77 West Wacker Dr.
Suite 4600
Chicago, IL 60601   312-634-8100
            www.adm.com
Food and feed ingredients, industrial chemicals and biofuels.
Chairman/CEO: Juan Luciano
Executive VP/CFO: Ray Young
Senior VP/General Counsel: D. Cameron Findlay
Year Founded: 1902
Estimated Sales: $64.3 Billion
Number Employees: 32,000

52652 Arco Warehouse Co
1810 E Jasper St
Tulsa, OK 74110-4921   918-585-8191
    Fax: 918-587-9649 www.arco1.com
Warehouse offering dry food storage; transportation firm offering freight consolidation and trucking; also, distribution, repackaging, inventory control and rail siding available
President: John Blaine
jblaine@arco1.com
Estimated Sales: Less Than $500,000
Number Employees: 1-4
Square Footage: 1080000
Types of products warehoused:
  Food products, dry goods, non-perishables, canned foods, general merchandise
Services Provided:
  Inventory, distribution & trucking, rail siding, trucking, pick and pack, repackaging
Storage Facility Data:
  Dry Storage Size: 70000 Sq. Ft.

Warehousing / A-Z

52653 Arctic Cold Storage
420 Currant Rd
Fall River, MA 02720-4711   508-672-1212
  Fax: 508-672-5987 David@arcticcoldstorage.com
  www.arcticcoldstorage.com
Warehouse for cold storage, plate freezing, refrigerated storage, container services, logistics services, and reboxing / relabeling / atrapping of cartons
Owner: David Demello
david@arcticcoldstorage.com
Operations Manager: Derek Parker
Number Employees: 10-19
Type of Packaging: Food Service

52654 Arctic Cold Storage Inc
4139 Roosevelt Rd # 1
St Cloud, MN 56301-9532   320-253-9979
  Fax: 320-253-8025 www.arcticcold.com
Warehouse providing cooler and freezer storage for food products.
Owner: Jeff Condom
jeff@arcticcold.com
Estimated Sales: $ .5 - 1 million
Number Employees: 10-19
Type of Packaging: Food Service

52655 Arctic Frozen Foods
4981 Commercial Dr # 3
Yorkville, NY 13495-1100   315-736-3026
  Fax: 315-736-5131 jme57@aol.com
  www.arcticfrozenfoods.com
Warehouse providing freezer storage
President: Wesley Smith
Manager: Nick Salerno
Operations: J Mark Evans
Estimated Sales: Less Than $500,000
Number Employees: 1-4
Square Footage: 112000
Types of products warehoused:
  frozen goods
Services Provided:
  labeling, pick and pack
Storage Facility Data:
  Freezer Size: 450000 Cubic Ft.

52656 Arctic Logistics
4360 S Haggerty Rd
Canton, MI 48188   734-397-9880
  arcticlogisticsmi.com
Temperature-controlled food distributor in the Midwest.
President & Principal: John Connor
Estimated Sales: $1 Million
Services Provided:
  trucking, blast freezing

52657 Arizona Cold Storage LLC
2100 W Mcdowell Rd
Phoenix, AZ 85009-3011   602-253-3186
  Fax: 602-258-5089
Warehouse offering cooler and freezer storage for food products; rail siding, ice manufacturing and sharp freezing available
Owner: Bob Campbell
Estimated Sales: Less Than $500,000
Number Employees: 1-4
Square Footage: 140000
Types of products warehoused:
  frozen goods
Services Provided:
  Ice manufacturing: wholesale & retail; also, sharp freezing, rail siding

52658 Arkansas Refrigerated Services
24 D Street N
Fort Smith, AR 72901   479-783-1006
  Fax: 479-783-1008
  support@arkansasrefrigerated.com
  www.arkansasrefrigerated.com
Warehouse providing frozen storage for food products; also, rail siding available
President: Ray Boatright
rayboatright@arkansasrefrigerated.com
Number Employees: 10-19
Types of products warehoused:
  Frozen products, frozen goods
Services Provided:
  rail siding

52659 Arro Corp
7440 Santa Fe Dr # A
Hodgkins, IL 60525-5076   708-639-9063
  Fax: 708-352-5293 877-929-2776
  Sales@arro.com www.arro.com
Corn, peanut, salad, soybean and vegetable oils.
Owner: Pat Gaughn
arrosales@aol.com
Sales Exec: Timothy Mcnicholas
Estimated Sales: $500,000-1 Million
Number Employees: 50-99
Type of Packaging: Food Service, Private Label, Bulk
Other Locations:
  Chicago, IL
  Hodgkins, ILHodgkins
Types of products warehoused:
  Food & food related products
Services Provided:
  rail siding

52660 (HQ)Artesian Ice
2700 Stockyards Expressway
Saint Joseph, MO 64501   816-232-6715
  Fax: 816-232-4585 mmodlin@nor-am.com
  nor-am.com
Warehouse providing cooler, dry, freezer and humidity controlled storage for perishables and non-food products; also, rail siding, pork certification and blast freezing services available
President & CEO: Greg Brandt
Secretary / Treasurer: Janna Brandt
Sales Managers: Mike Francis
Contact: Scott Albers
salbers@nor-am.com
Vice President Operations: Scott Albers
Plant Manager: Justin Brandt
Estimated Sales: Less than $500,000
Number Employees: 1 to 4
Square Footage: 800000
Parent Co: Nor-Am Corporate
Types of products warehoused:
  Non-food products & perishables, dry goods, non-perishables, frozen goods, canned foods, general merchandise
Services Provided:
  Blast freezing & Chicago Mercantile Exchange pork certification, rail siding, trucking, labeling, blast freezing
Storage Facility Data:
  Cooler Size 125000 Cubic Ft.
  Dry Storage Size: 131000 Sq. Ft.
  Freezer Size: 1750000 Cubic Ft.
  Humidity-Controlled Size: 13980 Sq. Ft.

52661 Ashland Cold Storage
1556 W 43rd St
Chicago, IL 60609-3389   773-847-2700
  Fax: 773-254-0790 www.ashlandcoldstorage.com
Warehouse providing frozen storage for foods; also, computerized inventory
Executive VP: Paul Michalak
pmichalak@ashlandcoldstorage.com
Chief Operating Officer: Jim Bradtke
VP, General Manager: Alex Olejniczak
Sales & Logistics Manager: A;ex Rosenbeck
VP Operations: Gary Scherer
Estimated Sales: $10-20 Million
Number Employees: 50-99
Types of products warehoused:
  Frozen food, frozen goods
Services Provided:
  Computerized inventory

52662 Aspen Distribution
21111 E. 36th Dr
P.O.Box 39108
Aurora, CO 80011   303-371-2511
  Fax: 303-576-9254 info@aspendistribution.com
  www.aspendistribution.com
Warehouse providing dry storage for food, re-packing and labeling for nonperishable and refrigerated foods; transportation services include local and short haul trucking throughout Colorado.
President: Bob Scott
Sales & Customer Service Manager: Jennifer Kirk
Estimated Sales: $12 Million
Number Employees: 120
Square Footage: 846720
Types of products warehoused:
  Non-perishable & refrigerated foods, dry goods, non-perishables, canned foods, general merchandise
Services Provided:
  Re-packing & labeling, rail siding, trucking, labeling, packaging, pick and pack, repackaging
Storage Facility Data:
  Cooler Size 650000 Sq. Ft.
  Dry Storage Size: 150000 Sq. Ft.
  Humidity-Controlled Size: 650000 Sq. Ft.

52663 Aspen Distribution Inc
10875 E 40th Ave
PO Box 39108
Denver, CO 80239-3210   720-974-7366
  Fax: 303-373-9850 Info@aspendistribution.com
  www.aspendistribution.com
Warehouse providing dry storage for food, paper and medical supplies; transportation services include local and short haul trucking; rail siding available
IT: Deborah Killion
dkillion@aspendistribution.com
Number Employees: 50-99
Services Provided:
  rail siding, pick and pack
Storage Facility Data:
  Dry Storage Size: 260000 Sq. Ft.

52664 Associated Global Systems
3333 New Hyde Park Rd
New Hyde Park, NY 11042   516-627-8910
  Fax: 516-627-6051 800-645-8300
  nwcs@agsystems.com www.agsystems.com
Transportation firm offering air freight services; also, packing and repacking of perishables available.
President & CEO: James Tucci
VP, Global Supply Chain Solutions: Scott Richter
Year Founded: 1958
Estimated Sales: $100-500 Million
Number Employees: 200-499
Parent Co: Nippon Express
Types of products warehoused:
  general merchandise
Services Provided:
  trucking, pick and pack

52665 Atlanta Bonded Warehouse Corporation
3000 Cobb International Blvd
Kennesaw, GA 30152-4383   770-425-3000
  Fax: 770-424-1440 info@atlantabonded.com
  www.atlantabonded.com
Provider of public and contract food-grade, temperature-controlled distribution services for over 60 years.
President: Joe Keith
VP, Sales & Operations: Hal Justice
Number Employees: 650
Types of products warehoused:
  Confections, candy & food products, general merchandise
Services Provided:
  Refrigerated trucking & co-packing/re-packing, rail siding
Storage Facility Data:
  Cooler Size 16220000 Cubic Ft.
  Dry Storage Size: 150000 Sq. Ft.

52666 Atlanta Service Warehouse Inc
PO Box 44197
Atlanta, GA 30336   404-699-5999
  Fax: 404-699-9165 www.aswdl.com
Warehouse providing dry storage for general merchandise; rail siding services available
CEO: Glen Turner
Contact: Patty Melton
patty.melton@aswdl.com
Estimated Sales: $1-2.5 Million
Number Employees: 10 to 19
Square Footage: 500000
Types of products warehoused:
  general merchandise
Services Provided:
  rail siding
Storage Facility Data:
  Dry Storage Size: 201800 Sq. Ft.

52667 Atlantic Coast Freezers
2192 N West Blvd
P.O. Box 863
Vineland, NJ 08360-2052   856-696-1770
  Fax: 856-794-8796 sam@mullicahg.com
Warehouse providing freezer storage for frozen foods; also, 12 truck platforms, blast freezing and rail siding available
Manager: Debbie Lebb
General Manager: J Bellusci
Secretary/Treasurer: J Taormina
Manager: Rahila Mughal
rahila.mughal@ricoh-usa.com

Warehousing / A-Z

Estimated Sales: $1-2.5 Million
Number Employees: 10-19
Square Footage: 320000
Types of products warehoused:
  Frozen foods, frozen goods
Services Provided:
  Blast freezing & 12 truck platforms, rail siding
Storage Facility Data:
  Freezer Size: 2160000 Cubic Ft.

52668 Atlantic Reefer Terminals Inc
8 Pond Rd
Gloucester, MA 01930-1833   978-281-4251
          Fax: 978-283-7647 fwbryce@fwbryce.com
                www.fwbryce.com
Services distributors, retail, food service, direct national accounts, Asian Products, and Fresh customers
President: Keith Moores
Founder: Carl Moores
Chief Financial Officer: Paul Cantrell
Vice President of Sales and Marketing: Mike Cusack
Quality Assurance: Justin Moores
Contact: Ian Moores
imoores@fwbryce.com
Operations Manager: Frank Souza
Estimated Sales: Less Than $500,000
Number Employees: 5-9
Square Footage: 12
Parent Co: FW Bryce, Inc.
Type of Packaging: Food Service, Private Label

52669 Aurora Storage & Distribution Center
30700 Aurora Rd
Suite 4
Cleveland, OH 44139   440-349-0085
      Fax: 440-349-1282 aurorastorage@aol.com
Warehouse offering dry storage for general merchandise; light assembly, packing, re-packing, labeling and distribution available
Owner/VP: Joshua Gamzeh
Sales: Cordell Ingman
Estimated Sales: $500,000-$1 Million
Number Employees: 10
Square Footage: 320000
Types of products warehoused:
  General merchandise, dry goods, general merchandise
Services Provided:
  Light assembly, packing, re-packing, labeling & distribution, trucking, labeling, packaging, pick and pack, repackaging
Storage Facility Data:
  Dry Storage Size: 80000 Sq. Ft.

52670 B. Barks & Sons
2550 Rear Grant Ave
Philadelphia, PA 19114-0948   215-671-9314
                Fax: 215-671-9330
Warehouse providing storage for frozen foods; rail siding available
Manager: Linda Mc Nulty
Estimated Sales: $2.1 Million
Number Employees: 10
Square Footage: 308000
Types of products warehoused:
  Frozen foods, frozen goods
Services Provided:
  rail siding
Storage Facility Data:
  Freezer Size: 2310000 Sq. Ft.

52671 B.R. Williams Trucking & Warehouse
23369 Hwy 21 South
P O Box 3203
Oxford, AL 36203   256-831-5580
      Fax: 256-831-8059 800-523-7963
dee.brown@brwilliams.com www.brwilliams.com
Warehouse providing dry storage of nonperishable goods; transportation services include long haul trucking services nationwide and in Canada
President: Dee Brown
Communications and PR: Misty Kowatana
VP Operations: Jack Brim
Number Employees: 100-249
Parent Co: Bill Williams Trucking
Types of products warehoused:
  Non-perishable goods, non-perishables

Services Provided:
  Transportation firm providing long haul trucking
Storage Facility Data:
  Dry Storage Size: 340000 Sq. Ft.

52672 BDP International Inc
510 Walnut St # 1400
Philadelphia, PA 19106-3690   215-629-0643
      Fax: 215-629-8940 www.bdpinternational.com
Warehouse providing cooler, freezer and dry storage for frozen food, meat, seafood and dry goods; transportation services include air and ocean freight forwarding, importing, exporting and long and short haul trucking
President & CEO: Richard Bolte
Cmo: Arnie Bornstein
abornstein@bdpnet.com
CEO: Richard Bolte Jr
Sales Administrator: Vanessa Spero
Number Employees: 250-499
Types of products warehoused:
  Frozen food, meat, seafood & dry goods, dry goods, frozen goods
Services Provided:
  Air & ocean freight forwarding, trucking, etc.

52673 BLC Trucking Inc
3401 Lincoln Ave # C
Tacoma, WA 98421-4017   253-272-6191
                blctrucking@lbu.com
Warehouse providing dry storage for grocery products and general merchandise; transportation firm providing local container haul trucking; rail siding services available
President: Bernard Bordova
b.bordova@mapletex.com
Estimated Sales: Less Than $500,000
Number Employees: 1-4
Types of products warehoused:
  Grocery products & general merchandise, general merchandise
Services Provided:
  Trucking, rail siding
Storage Facility Data:
  Dry Storage Size: 15000 Sq. Ft.

52674 Baker Transfer & Storage
P.O.Box 21479
Billings, MT 59104-1479   406-245-3147
                Fax: 406-245-6608
Warehouse providing cooler, freezer and dry storage for frozen, refrigerated and nonperishable foods; transportation firm providing short and local haul trucking; rail siding services available
Owner: Richard Hunt
General Manager: David Krueger
Number Employees: 20-49
Types of products warehoused:
  Frozen, refrigerated & non-perishable foods, dry goods, non-perishables, frozen goods, produce, canned foods, general merchandise, hazardous
Services Provided:
  Local & short haul trucking, rail siding, trucking, pick and pack, repackaging
Storage Facility Data:
  Cooler Size 8,000
  Dry Storage Size: 115,000
  Freezer Size: 12,000

52675 Baltimore International Warehousing
7646 Canton Center Dr
Baltimore, MD 21224-2027   410-633-3500
      Fax: 410-633-4147 800-562-5517
suemonaghan@biwt.com www.biwt.com
Warehouse providing dry storage for canned foods; transportation services include local haul trucking, piers, piggy ramps and container hauling; rail siding available
President/CEO: Sue Monaghan
Vice President: James Miller
Manager: Darryl Bryant
darrylbryant@biwt.com
Warehouse Supervisor: William Turner
Estimated Sales: $5-10 Million
Number Employees: 20-49
Square Footage: 800000
Types of products warehoused:
  Canned foods, canned foods
Services Provided:
  Trucking, piers & piggy back ramps; 48 state authority, rail siding

52676 Bama Sea Products Inc
756 28th St S
St Petersburg, FL 33712-1907   727-327-3474
      Fax: 727-322-0580 www.bamasea.com
Wholesaler/distributor and exporter of frozen fish and seafood; warehouse providing cooler and freezer storage for frozen food items
Owner: Hillary Hubble-Flinn
Director Quality Control: Fred Stengard
Marketing & Product Development: Dottie Stephens Guy
VP Sales: Jon Philbrick
hillary.hubbleflinn@leememorial.org
VP of Operations and Plant GM: John Jackson
VP Purchasing: Adam Zewen
Estimated Sales: $2.5-5 Million
Number Employees: 100-249
Square Footage: 360000
Types of products warehoused:
  Frozen food items, frozen goods
Services Provided:
  Wholesaling/distributing & exporting

52677 Barber's Poultry Inc
810 E 50th Ave
Denver, CO 80216-2009   303-466-7338
      Fax: 303-466-6960 www.barberspoultry.com
Wholesaler/distributor of frozen and canned food products; also, warehouse providing cold storage for frozen and canned food products
President: David Barber
dave@barberspoultry.com
Vice President: Mike Barber
Estimated Sales: $5- 10 Million
Number Employees: 5-9
Type of Packaging: Bulk
Types of products warehoused:
  Frozen & canned food products, frozen goods, canned foods

52678 Barrett Distribution Ctr
15 Freedom Way
Franklin, MA 02038-2586   508-553-8800
      Fax: 508-553-2929 800-279-1801
          sales@barrettdistribution.com
                www.barrettdistribution.com
Warehouse offering humidity-controlled, dry, freezer and cooler storage for groceries, general merchandise, etc.; transportation firm providing freight consolidation via TL and LTL local and short haul trucking; distribution and railsiding services available
President: Arthur Barrett
abarrett@barrettdistribution.com
Senior VP: Mike O'Donnell
Director Customer Relations: Mark Sotir
COO: Timothy Barrett
Number Employees: 50-99
Parent Co: Barrett Warehouse & Transport
Types of products warehoused:
  Grocery products, alcoholic beverages & general merchandise, dry goods, non-perishables, produce, canned foods, general merchandise
Services Provided:
  Trucking, storage, distribution & freight consolidation, rail siding, trucking, labeling, packaging, pick and pack, repackaging
Storage Facility Data:
  Cooler Size 15000 Sq. Ft.
  Dry Storage Size: 500000 Sq. Ft.
  Freezer Size: 11000 Sq. Ft.
  Humidity-Controlled Size: 10000 Sq. Ft.

52679 Batesville Cold Storage
3054 E Main St
Batesville, AR 72501-7360   870-698-2288
      Fax: 870-698-0339 www.frostyaire.com
CEO: Steve Thomas
Estimated Sales: $ 3 - 5 Million
Number Employees: 20-49

52680 Bay Cities Warehouse
31474 Hayman St
Hayward, CA 94544-7195   510-471-9770
      Fax: 510-471-1968 www.baycitieswarehouse.com
Warehouse providing storage for dry products; transportation services include local, short, long haul and common carrier trucking; also, rail siding available
President: Bob Bozek
bbozek@baycitieswarehouse.com
Number Employees: 5-9
Types of products warehoused:
  packaging, plastics, food ingredients, dry goods,

Warehousing / A-Z

non-perishables, canned foods, general merchandise
Services Provided:
  Trucking, rail siding, trucking, labeling, repackaging, shrink wrap, assembly
Storage Facility Data:
  Dry Storage Size: 77,000 Sq. Ft.

52681 Beacon Distribution Services
PO Box 40
Aliquippa, PA 15001-0040   724-857-0722
                       Fax: 724-857-2659
Warehouse providing dry storage for grocery products; transportation services include local, short and long haul trucking; also, rail siding and distribution available
Owner: Ron Benson
Number Employees: 10-19
Types of products warehoused:
  Groceries
Services Provided:
  rail siding
Storage Facility Data:
  Dry Storage Size: 500000 Sq. Ft.

52682 Beaver Dam Cold Storage
N6366 Jackson Rd
Beaver Dam, WI 53916-9617   920-887-1672
                    Fax: 920-887-0402 www.ggbarnett.com
Warehouse providing dry, cooler and freezer storage
Owner: Dawn Spranger
Co-Owner: Jean Barnett
Sales/Marketing: Rick Rost
Manager: Ryan Flinger
Estimated Sales: Less Than $500,000
Number Employees: 1-4
Square Footage: 380000
Types of products warehoused:
  Frozen foods, dairy products & dry goods, dry goods, frozen goods
Services Provided:
  Packing, inspection & labeling
Storage Facility Data:
  Cooler Size 273600 Cubic Ft.
  Dry Storage Size: 237600 Cubic Ft.
  Freezer Size: 200000 Cubic Ft.

52683 (HQ)Belt Route Warehouse & Storage
160 W Brookmont Blvd
Kankakee, IL 60901-2020   815-939-0257
Fax: 815-939-0257 info@beltroutewarehouse.com
          www.beltroutewarehouse.com
Warehouse providing dry storage for nonperishable foods and dry goods; rail siding and cross-docking are availabale
President: A Amiano
Manager: Barry Amiano
Manager: Bryan Amiano
Estimated Sales: $1-2.5 Million
Number Employees: 5-9
Square Footage: 400000
Types of products warehoused:
  Refrigerated, frozen & non-perishable foods & dry goods, dry goods, non-perishables, frozen goods, produce, canned foods, general merchandise
Services Provided:
  rail siding, trucking, labeling, packaging, pick and pack, repackaging

52684 Belt's Corp
949 Fell St
Baltimore, MD 21231-3505   410-342-1110
       Fax: 410-675-2399 www.beltslogistics.com
Warehouse providing cooler, dry and humidity-controlled storage for grocery products and general merchandise; also, pick/pack and rail siding available
President/Owner: Allen Brown
Manager: Anthony Gilman
Plant Manager: Tony Gilman
Estimated Sales: $2.5-5 Million
Number Employees: 20-49
Square Footage: 2400000
Types of products warehoused:
  Grocery products & general merchandise, general merchandise
Services Provided:
  Pick/pack, rail siding
Storage Facility Data:
  Cooler Size 7500 Sq. Ft.
  Dry Storage Size: 592500 Sq. Ft.
  Humidity-Controlled Size: 7500 Sq. Ft.

52685 Belts Logistics Services
949 Fell St
Baltimore, MD 21231-3505   410-342-1111
       Fax: 410-675-2399 info@beltslogistics.com
               www.beltslogistics.com
Belts Logistics Services is a warehouse providing dry storage, and separate transportation brokerage providing local, long and short haul trucking.
President: S Allen Brown
shunsicker@beltslogistics.com
Chairman: S.A. Brown
shunsicker@beltslogistics.com
Executive Vice President, Legal Councel: Scott Hunsicker
Vice President, Business Development: Larry Smith
Vice President, Logistics: Jim Woolfrey
Number Employees: 48
Square Footage: 2400000
Other Locations:
  Baltimore, MD
  Elkridge, MDElkridge
Types of products warehoused:
  Non-perishable items, non-perishables
Services Provided:
  Local, long & short haul trucking

52686 Bender Warehouse Co
345 Parr Cir
Reno, NV 89512-1005   775-788-8800
           Fax: 775-788-8811 800-621-9402
   salesinfo@benderwhs.com www.bendergroup.com
Warehouse providing dry, air conditioned and humidity-controlled storage for confectionery products, groceries, etc.; transportation firm providing freight consolidation and long haul trucking; also, rail siding, shrink wrappingpick/pack, etc
President: Brian Classen
brianclassen@bendergroup.com
CEO: Frank Bender
Estimated Sales: Less Than $500,000
Number Employees: 1-4
Types of products warehoused:
  Confectionery products, health & beauty aids, groceries & pharmaceuticals, dry goods, non-perishables, general merchandise
Services Provided:
  Assembly, shrink wrapping, pick/pack & overnight distribution, rail siding, trucking, pick and pack, repackaging, fulfillment
Storage Facility Data:
  Dry Storage Size: 700000 Sq. Ft.
  Freezer Size: 20000 Cubic Ft.
  Humidity-Controlled Size: 85000 Sq. Ft.

52687 (HQ)Benlin Freight Forwarding Inc
2769 Broadway St
Buffalo, NY 14227-1004   716-891-4040
       Fax: 716-891-4715 www.benlin.com
Warehouse providing dry storage; transportation firm providing freight consolidation, local, long and short haul trucking; also, rail siding, display modules and distribution services available
Vice President: Robert Bennett
bbennett@benlin.com
Office Manager/Controller: Randy Cole
Vice President, Distribution Services: Bob Bennett
Sales Manager: David Geiger
International Operations Manager: Mark Cramer
Number Employees: 20-49
Types of products warehoused:
  Groceries, food products & chemicals, dry goods, non-perishables, canned foods, general merchandise
Services Provided:
  Pool distribution, trucking & display modules, rail siding, trucking, labeling, packaging, pick and pack, repackaging
Storage Facility Data:
  Dry Storage Size: 400000 Sq. Ft.

52688 Bensussen Duetsch & Associates
15525 Woodinville Red Rd NE
Woodinville, WA 98072-6977   425-492-6111
           Fax: 425-492-7222 800-451-4764
                     www.bdainc.com
Marketing
CEO: Jay Deutsch
Marketing Communications Manager: Renee Hercules
Estimated Sales: $ 10 - 20 Million
Number Employees: 250-499
Type of Packaging: Food Service

52689 Berkshire Transportation Inc
PO Box 421206
Plymouth, MN 55442   612-529-8883
           Fax: 763-535-9163 888-537-5779
Warehouse providing cooler and freezer storage; also, labeling for refrigerated and frozen foods, import and export capabilities available bulk storage: furniture storage, general goods,farm product warehousing, foodsecurity services,and frozen meats.
President: Thaddeus Grzywacz
Contact: Kelly Dawson
kellydawson@berkshiretransportation.com
Estimated Sales: $10-20 Million
Number Employees: 40
Square Footage: 980000
Parent Co: Berkshire Refrigerated Warehouse LLC
Type of Packaging: Consumer, Food Service, Bulk
Types of products warehoused:
  Refrigerated & frozen foods, frozen goods
Services Provided:
  Labeling & import/export capabilities

52690 Berry's Arctic Ice
200 N Kansas Ave
Topeka, KS 66603-3682   785-357-4466
                       Fax: 785-357-1332
Warehouse services include cold and frozen storage of foods; also, ice manufacturing available
Owner: Walter Berry
Plant Manager: Walter Berry
Estimated Sales: $1-2.5 Million
Number Employees: 20-49
Types of products warehoused:
  Frozen foods, frozen goods
Services Provided:
  Ice manufacturing: wholesale & retail
Storage Facility Data:
  Cooler Size 386462 Cubic Ft.
  Freezer Size: 907124 Cubic Ft.

52691 Biscontini DistributionCenters
232 Division Street
Po Box 1857
Kingston/Wilkes-Barre, PA   570-288-6683
                       Fax: 570-288-6601
Warehouse providing dry storage; transportation firm providing local, short and long haul trucking; rail siding and cross docking available
President: Richard Biscontini
Executive VP: Rudi Biscontini, Jr.
Number Employees: 50-99
Types of products warehoused:
  Dry foods & general merchandise, dry goods, non-perishables, canned foods, general merchandise, lumber products
Services Provided:
  Stretch wrapping, pick/pack & cross docking, rail siding, trucking, labeling, packaging, pick and pack, repackaging
Storage Facility Data:
  Dry Storage Size: 1800000 Sq. Ft.

52692 Blast It Clean
7800 E 12th St
Suite 7
Kansas City, MO 64126-2370   816-241-9199
           Fax: 913-440-4725 877-379-4233
    info@blast-it-clean.com www.blastitclean.com
Industrial cleaning solutions
Owner: Rick Dillon
rdillon@blast-it-clean.com
Owner: Rick Salgado
Marketing Director: Erica Chen
Estimated Sales: $1.7 Million
Number Employees: 23
Square Footage: 160000
Types of products warehoused:
  Grocery products
Services Provided:
  Distribution, delivery & refrigerated space, rail siding

52693 Blendco Inc
8 J M Tatum Industrial Dr
Hattiesburg, MS 39401-8341   601-544-9800
           Fax: 601-544-5634 888-253-6326
      csr@blendcoinc.com www.blendcoinc.com
Dry food manufacturer. Provide custom blending and packaging, as well as private labeling and contract packaging services.
President: Charles McCaffrey
Chief Financial Officer: Ken Hrdlica

Warehousing / A-Z

Estimated Sales: $8 Million
Number Employees: 20-49
Number of Brands: 2
Type of Packaging: Food Service, Private Label, Bulk
Types of products warehoused:
  dry goods
Services Provided:
  labeling, packaging, Custom Blending, Contract Packaging

52694 Blendex Co
11208 Electron Dr
Louisville, KY 40299-3875
502-267-1003
Fax: 502-267-1024 800-626-6325
www.blendex.com
Dry ingredients blending company specializing in batters, breadings, seasonings, seasonings and marinades. 12 distribution warehouses located across the US.
President: Jacquelyn Bailey
CEO: Ronald Pottinger
rpottinger@blendex.com
Director: Olin Cook
Executive Vice President: Tony Jessee
Vice President Research/Development: Jordan Stivers
Vice President of Sales: Ron Carr
Estimated Sales: $28.5 Million
Number Employees: 50-99
Type of Packaging: Food Service, Private Label, Bulk
Types of products warehoused:
  dry goods
Services Provided:
  Blending

52695 Blue Line Cold Storage Chicago
1556 W 43rd St
Chicago, IL 60609-3328
773-579-1594
Fax: 773-254-0790 www.ashlandcoldstorage.com
Warehouse offering cooler and freezer storage; rail siding available; transportation firm providing trucking in the midwest
Manager: Pat Lombard
Vice President/General Manager: Alex Olejniczak
Sales and Logistics Manager: Alex Rosenbeck
Estimated Sales: Less Than $500,000
Number Employees: 1-4
Types of products warehoused:
  dry goods, non-perishables, frozen goods, canned foods, general merchandise
Services Provided:
  rail siding, trucking, labeling, pick and pack, re-packaging
Storage Facility Data:
  Cooler Size 100000 Sq. Ft.
  Dry Storage Size: 4000000
  Freezer Size: 50000 Sq. Ft.
  Humidity-Controlled Size: 50000 Sq. Ft.

52696 Blue Line Moving & Storage
5614 Nordic Dr
Cedar Falls, IA 50613-6949
319-266-3591
Fax: 319-266-0408 800-728-3591
www.unitedvanlines.com
Warehouse providing storage for dry goods; transportation firm providing local delivery in Iowa
Owner: Bob Mahncke
bluelinemoving@cfu.net
Estimated Sales: $1-2.5 Million
Number Employees: 10-19
Square Footage: 48000
Types of products warehoused:
  Dry goods, dry goods
Services Provided:
  Local delivery, rail siding

52697 Bob's Transport & Stge Co Inc
7980 Tarbay Dr
Jessup, MD 20794-9416
410-799-7524
Fax: 410-799-0951 www.bobstransport.com
Warehouse offering dry storage for groceries, general commodities and paper goods; transportation firm providing third party logistics, rail and intermodal trucking services; also, rail siding, pallet exchange, container drayage, crossdocking, packaging, etc
President: Bob Hightower
bob@bobstransport.com
Estimated Sales: $10-20 Million
Number Employees: 20-49
Types of products warehoused:
  Dry groceries & paper goods, dry goods, non-perishables, canned foods, general merchandise
Services Provided:
  Pallet exchange, trucking, clamp, slip sheet, cross docking, etc, rail siding, trucking
Storage Facility Data:
  Dry Storage Size: 15356000 Cubic Ft.

52698 Boise Cold Storage Co
495 S 15th St
Boise, ID 83702-6846
208-344-8477
Fax: 208-344-8598 www.boisecoldstorage.com
Warehouse providing freezer and cooler storage; also, blast freezing, USDA export facilities and distribution available
Owner: Tim Johnson
tfj@boisecold.com
CEO: Todd Spengenberg
Owner: Tim Johnson
Estimated Sales: $2.5-5 Million
Number Employees: 20-49
Square Footage: 400000
Types of products warehoused:
  dry goods, frozen goods
Services Provided:
  USDA inspection, rail siding, trucking, blast freezing, Order Picking
Storage Facility Data:
  Cooler Size 340815000 Cubic Ft.
  Freezer Size: 208255300 Cubic Ft.

52699 Boise Cold Storage Co
495 S 15th St
Boise, ID 83702-6846
208-344-8477
Fax: 208-344-8598 www.boisecoldstorage.com
Ice; warehouse providing cold, dry and freezer storage; also, distribution available
Owner: Tim Johnson
tfj@boisecold.com
Office Manager: B Grover
General Manager: M Tallent
Estimated Sales: $1-2,500,000
Number Employees: 20-49
Square Footage: 100000
Services Provided:
  Distribution, trucking
Storage Facility Data:
  Cooler Size 15390 Cubic Ft.
  Dry Storage Size: 20000 Cubic Ft.
  Freezer Size: 414148 Cubic Ft.

52700 Bonded Service Warehouse
1805 Watergate Parkway
Atlanta, GA 30336-2851
404-349-1466
Fax: 404-349-1637 www.bondedservice.com
Warehouse providing storage for general merchandise; also, transportation, packaging, distribution and rail siding available
President: Thomas Ghegan
Estimated Sales: $1-2.5 Million
Number Employees: 10-19
Square Footage: 2800000
Types of products warehoused:
  General merchandise, general merchandise
Services Provided:
  Transportation, barcoding & distribution, rail siding, labeling, packaging, pick and pack, re-packaging

52701 Bootz Distribution
4860 Joliet Street
Denver, CO 80239
303-371-6833
Fax: 303-371-6833
Public warehouse offering dry and cooler storage for food and nonfood items; also, rail siding available; transportation firm providing local and short haul trucking
President: Hank Bootz
Number Employees: 20-49
Types of products warehoused:
  Food & non-food, general merchandise
Services Provided:
  Trucking, rail siding
Storage Facility Data:
  Cooler Size 8000 Sq. Ft.
  Dry Storage Size: 80000 Sq. Ft.

52702 Bridge Terminal, Inc.
12 Fish Is
New Bedford, MA 02740
508-994-4300
Fax: 508-992-6267
HarryG@MaritimeInternational.org
www.maritimeinternational.org/bridge-details.html
Customs bonded warehouse providing freezer storage for fish; transportation firm providing freight forwarding services; also, ocean vessel loading/unloading and container stuffing/unstuffing services available
Warehouse Manager: Harry Gifford
Number Employees: 10-19
Square Footage: 168000
Parent Co: Maritime International
Types of products warehoused:
  Fish, dry goods, frozen goods
Services Provided:
  Ocean vessel loading/unloading & container stuffing/unstuffing, rail siding, trucking, blast freezing
Storage Facility Data:
  Freezer Size: 500000 Cubic Ft.

52703 Bristol Van & Storage Corporation
PO Box 743
Bristol, VA 24203-0743
540-669-5125
Fax: 540-669-4034
Warehouse offering dry storage for nonperishables; also, rail siding, local pick-up and delivery available
President: R Rutherford, Jr.
Estimated Sales: $500,000-$1 Million
Number Employees: 9
Square Footage: 200000
Types of products warehoused:
  Non-perishables, dry goods, non-perishables, canned foods, general merchandise
Services Provided:
  Heated & sprinkler space, local pick-up & delivery, rail siding
Storage Facility Data:
  Dry Storage Size: 50000 Sq. Ft.

52704 (HQ)Brokers Logistics LTD
1000 Hawkins Blvd
El Paso, TX 79915-1205
915-778-7751
Fax: 915-778-1358 jwright@brokerslogistics.com
Warehouse providing cooler, humidity-controlled and dry storage; re-packing, labeling and rail siding available; transportation services include long and short haul trucking in the Southwest
President: Michelle Wright
CEO/Owner: Jerry Wright
jwright@brokerslogistics.com
COO: Mike Blough
Number Employees: 100-249
Other Locations:
  Los Angeles:100,000 Sq ft, CA
  Laredo, TX
  Del Rio:60,000 Sq Ft, TXLaredo
Types of products warehoused:
  canned foods, general merchandise, document management
Services Provided:
  rail siding, trucking, labeling, blast freezing, packaging, pick and pack, repackaging
Storage Facility Data:
  Cooler Size 5000 Sq. Ft.
  Dry Storage Size: 400000 Sq. Ft.
  Humidity-Controlled Size: 5000 Sq. Ft.

52705 (HQ)Burris Logistics
501 SE 5th St
Milford, DE 19963
302-422-4531
Fax: 302-839-5175 800-805-8135
info@burrislogistics.com www.burrislogistics.com
Provides services at all points of the temperature-controlled supply chain including cold storage, freight management, consolidation & redistribution
Chairman: Jeffrey Swain
President/CEO: Donnie Burris
dburris@burrislogistics.com
EVP/CFO: Don McEntaffer
Director of Marketing: Maggie Owens
Buyer: Nancy Salo
Year Founded: 1925
Estimated Sales: $100-500 Million
Number Employees: 1000-4999
Square Footage: 25000
Types of products warehoused:
  frozen goods

52706 Burris Logistics
4501 Dignan St
Jacksonville, FL 32254
904-265-5990
Fax: 904-389-2199 www.burrislogistics.com

Warehouse providing freezer storage for frozen foods; rail siding and distribution services available. Total storage space 226,000 square feet; refrigerated space 197,000 square feet. Pallet positions 20,500; clearance height: dock 14feet, freezer 25 feet. 4 Refrigerated rooms, 2 freezers, 2 convertible room (-10F to 35F). Dock doors 28; dock width 40 feet; refrigerated dock space 18,000 square feet/252,000 cubic feet.
General Manager: Maurice Grier
Year Founded: 2001
Square Footage: 226160
Parent Co: Burris Foods
Types of products warehoused:
    Frozen foods, frozen goods
Services Provided:
    Distribution, transportation, export, rail siding, blast freezing
Storage Facility Data:
    Cooler Size 197000 Sq. Ft.

52707 Burris Logistics
383 Mt. Torrey Rd
Lyndhurst, VA 22952   540-712-2960
    Fax: 540-943-4680 www.burrislogistics.com
Facility offers access from 38 dock doors with 28,000 pallet positions. Clearance height is 25 feet on the dock and 33 feet/36 feet in the freezers. Facility is divided into seven refrigerated rooms. Seven freezers, six blast cellsand dry storage. Overall refrigeration capacity 1,158 tons per hour with 22,165 refrigerated pallet positions and 4,484 dry pallet positions. Blast capacity is 65 loads per week.
General Manager: Michael Ryan
mikeryan@burrislogistics.com
Year Founded: 1987
Square Footage: 223607
Parent Co: Burris Foods
Types of products warehoused:
    Frozen foods, dry goods, frozen goods
Services Provided:
    Export, dry storage, trailer spotting, rail siding, blast freezing

52708 Burris Logistics
1000 Centerpoint Blvd
New Castle, DE 19720   302-221-4100
    Fax: 302-221-0536 www.burrislogistics.com
The facility is fully equipped with data scanning equipment throughout the multiple temperature rooms. The facility has 10,484 pallet positions throughout the freezer areas. The 317,900 cubic feet of refrigerated dock is accessible by24 dock doors and has a width of 40 feet. The Burris-New Castle facility is fully protected with a facility wide sprinkler system.
General Manager: Chris Robbins
Year Founded: 1991
Square Footage: 135000
Parent Co: Burris Foods
Types of products warehoused:
    Dairy, meat, frozen goods
Services Provided:
    Transportation and order pick distribution, trucking

52709 Burris Logistics
100 Railroad Ave
Haines City, FL 33844   863-422-4911
    Fax: 863-422-1674 www.burrislogistics.com
Warehouse providing cooler and freezer for frozen foods; 2 million cubic feet of convertible freezer and cooler space, along with blast freezing and export capabilities. The facility is accessible through 11 dock doors along the fulllength of the 40 foot wide dock. The overall refrigeration capacity is 1,350 tons per hour with 14,437 refrigerated pallet positions. The blast capacity of the facility is 95 loads per week. Temperature range of -10F to 45F.
General Manager: James Wells
Year Founded: 2001
Square Footage: 168600
Parent Co: Burris Foods
Type of Packaging: Food Service
Types of products warehoused:
    Frozen foods, frozen goods
Services Provided:
    Import/export, case pick distribution, rail siding, blast freezing

52710 Burris Logistics
1801 N 5th St
Philadelphia, PA 19122   215-236-1700
    Fax: 215-235-2020 www.burrislogistics.com
3-temperature warehouse.
General Manager: Walt Tullis
Type of Packaging: Food Service
Types of products warehoused:
    frozen goods

52711 Burris Logistics
490 Brook St
Rocky Hill, CT 06067   860-757-3100
    Fax: 860-513-1370 www.burrislogistics.com
Refrigerated dock space of 46,000sq. ft., 29 dock doors, 30,000 pallet positions, 6 temperature-controlled rooms
General Manager: Michael de la Rocha
Year Founded: 2008
Square Footage: 263937
Parent Co: Burris Foods
Type of Packaging: Food Service
Types of products warehoused:
    frozen goods

52712 Burris Logistics
1110 County Line Rd
Lakeland, FL 33815   863-682-1442
    Fax: 863-686-9490 www.burrislogistics.com
Warehouse providing cooler and freezer storage. Services include importing/exporting and cross-docking capabilities. Private rail siding, for easy access served by CSX; fully-insulated rail and truck docks. Total pallet positions is17,000 (temperature controlled); 4 refrigerated rooms (1 convertible room); 10 dock doors. Total storage space of 117,247 square feet; total refrigerated space of 90,750 square feet.
General Manager: Jim Nestle
Year Founded: 2003
Square Footage: 117247
Parent Co: Burris Foods
Type of Packaging: Food Service
Types of products warehoused:
    frozen goods
Services Provided:
    Import/export, cross docking, rail siding
Storage Facility Data:
    Cooler Size 90750 Sq. Ft.

52713 Burris Logistics
10900 Central Port Dr
Orlando, FL 32824   407-812-7200
    Fax: 407-816-4123 www.burrislogistics.com
The facility offers access from 23 dock doors with 24,000 refrigerated pallet positions. Clearance height is 42 feet on the dock and in the freezers. Services include potential blast freezing, freezers, cooler, transportation, andexports. Refrigeration capacity is 7,400,000 cubic feet.
General Manager: Nick Falk
nfalk@burrislogistics.com
Year Founded: 2001
Square Footage: 210000
Parent Co: Burris Foods
Type of Packaging: Food Service
Types of products warehoused:
    frozen goods
Services Provided:
    Transportation, exports, trucking, blast freezing
Storage Facility Data:
    Cooler Size 7400000 Cubic Ft.

52714 Burris Logistics
350 King Mill Rd
McDonough, GA 30252   770-515-8950
    www.burrislogistics.com
Refrigerated warehouse facility with 28,000 pallet positions, 4 temperature-controlled rooms, 4 temperature-variable rooms, and 28 dock doors.
General Manager: Alan Perry
Year Founded: 2018
Square Footage: 250000
Parent Co: Burris Logistics
Type of Packaging: Food Service
Types of products warehoused:
    frozen goods

52715 Burris Logistics
451 Fletchwood Rd
Elkton, MD 21921
        443-245-1000
        Fax: 410-620-9497
        maggie.owens@burrislogistics.com
        www.burrislogistics.com
Offers access to 26 dock doors with 26,000 refrigerated pallet positions. Clearance height is not a problem with 42.5 feet on the dock and in the freezers. Sprinkler system over entire building; 4 refrigerated rooms. The ElktonDistribution Center is the newest addition to the Burris Refrigerated Logistics warehouse system. It has the potential for Blast Freezing and offers easy access to Interstate 95.
General Manager: Scott Burton
Year Founded: 2004
Square Footage: 227000
Parent Co: Burris Logistics
Type of Packaging: Food Service
Storage Facility Data:
    Cooler Size 8000000 Cubic Ft.

52716 Burris Logistics
3946 Federalsburg Hwy
Federalsburg, MD 21632   410-820-6930
    Fax: 410-754-7220 www.burrislogistics.com
Refrigerated facility is 3,526,970 cubic foot. Accessible through 30 dock doors along full length 40 foot wide dock. Clearance is 22 feet to 25 feet on the dock and 25 feet and 34 feet in the freezers. 4 refrigerated rooms: twofreezers (one operated as a cooler for meat and produce); four blast cells; 2 convertible rooms (-10F to 35F) and the main freezer space. The overall refrigeration capacity is 890 tons per hour with 11,268 refrigerated pallet positions. Blastcapacity 36 loads per week.
General Manager: Jennifer Gallagher
Square Footage: 137727
Parent Co: Burris Logistics
Type of Packaging: Food Service
Types of products warehoused:
    frozen goods

52717 Burris Logistics
111 Reese Ave
Harrington, DE 19952   302-398-5050
    Fax: 302-398-5063 www.burrislogistics.com
The 8 million cubic feet facility provides for a central location to serve major retail chains in the northeast and mid-Atlantic area of the United States. Transportation provided by Burris Express Company with: 21 tractors and 2553-foot trailers. State-of-the-art routing management technology; refrigerated docks/warehouse temperatures at -12F to -15°F; 30,027 pallet positions supported by 5 radio-controlled stacker cranes.
General Manager: Tina Hawkins
Year Founded: 1973
Parent Co: Burris Logistics
Type of Packaging: Food Service
Types of products warehoused:
    frozen goods
Storage Facility Data:
    Freezer Size: 8000000 Cubic Ft.

52718 Burris Logistics
2401 Se Tones Dr
Suite 1
Ankeny, IA 50021   515-207-1401
    Fax: 515-207-1404 www.burrislogistics.com
Temperature-controlled warehouse facility
General Manager: Jared Auten
Parent Co: Burris Logistics
Type of Packaging: Food Service
Types of products warehoused:
    frozen goods

52719 Burris Logistics
14343 N Kelley Ave
Oklahoma City, OK 73114   405-652-9065
    www.burrislogistics.com
Temperature-controlled warehouse facility
General Manager: Linda Roadcap
Parent Co: Burris Logistics
Type of Packaging: Food Service
Types of products warehoused:
    frozen goods

52720 Byers Transport
2840-76 Avenue
P.O. Box 157
Edmonton, AB T5J 2J1
Canada   780-440-1000
    Fax: 780-440-2083 800-661-6953
Warehouse providing cooler, dry, freezer and humidity-controlled storage for nonperishable items; transportation broker
Operations Manager: Janet Strom
Square Footage: 600000

Warehousing / A-Z

Types of products warehoused:
 Non-perishable items, non-perishables
Services Provided:
 Distribution, sorting, bar coding, trucking, etc., rail siding
Storage Facility Data:
 Cooler Size 2000 Sq. Ft.
 Dry Storage Size: 80000 Sq. Ft.
 Freezer Size: 1000 Sq. Ft.
 Humidity-Controlled Size: 750 Sq. Ft.

52721 C Summers Inc
112 Spruce St
Elizabethville, PA 17023-8775   717-362-8117
 Fax: 717-362-4434   800-752-1902
 www.csummersinc.com
Warehouse providing cooler and freezer storage; specializing in temperature-controlled, and freight shipments
Owner: Steve Summers
Service Manager: Tom Tonoff
Estimated Sales: $2.5-5 Million
Number Employees: 10-19
Types of products warehoused:
 frozen goods
Services Provided:
 trucking
Storage Facility Data:
 Cooler Size 16000 Cubic Ft.
 Freezer Size: 46000 Cubic Ft.

52722 C&M Warehouse, Inc.
95 Leggett St.
East Hartford, CT 06108   860-289-8211
 Fax: 860-528-1513   877-726-9473
 fgiordano@cmwarehouse.com
 www.cmwarehouse.com
Warehouse providing dry storage; rail siding available
Owner: Frank Giordano
VP: Frank Giordano
VP: Carl Giordano
Contact: Ben Baugh
ben.baugh@cmwarehouse.com
Estimated Sales: $2.5-5 Million
Number Employees: 20-49
Square Footage: 800000
Types of products warehoused:
 dry goods, non-perishables, general merchandise
Services Provided:
 Barcode, EDI transmission, temperature-controlled, rail siding, pick and pack
Storage Facility Data:
 Dry Storage Size: 200000 Sq. Ft.

52723 C.J. Figone Cold Storage
420 17th Street
San Francisco, CA 94107   415-495-8040
 Fax: 415-495-5026
Warehouse providing freezer storage for food; freight consolidation for overseas shipment
VP: Steve Figone
Number Employees: 10-19
Types of products warehoused:
 Food, frozen goods
Services Provided:
 blast freezing
Storage Facility Data:
 Freezer Size: 600000 Cubic Ft.

52724 CFC Logistics
4000 Am Dr
Quakertown, PA 18951-2197   215-529-1500
 Fax: 215-529-6514   bdrygas@pvtransco.com
Warehouse providing cooler/freezer space, shuttle services, blast freezing, exporting, and transportation/distribution
President: Joe Marchant
VP Sales/Operations: Joe Marchant
Contact: Nina Mazer
nmazer@metalsusa.com
Warehouse Supervisor: Dale Rush
Estimated Sales: $ 20 - 50 Million
Number Employees: 50-99
Square Footage: 153780
Type of Packaging: Food Service
Services Provided:
 shuttle services, temp-controlled, trucking, blast freezing

52725 CS Integrated LLC
1 Enterprise Avenue N
Secaucus, NJ 07094-2530   908-542-2000
 Fax: 908-604-2558   www.csicold.com

52726 CS Intergrated Retail Services LLC
500 S 99th Avenue
Tolleson, AZ 85353-9700   623-936-2255
 Fax: 623-936-2256   www.csicold.com

52727 CS Intergrated Retail Services
3800 Garman Road
Salem, VA 24153-8822   540-380-5260
 Fax: 540-380-5232

52728 CS Intergrated-Texas Limited Partnership
1313 Samuels Ave
Fort Worth, TX 76102-1130   817-338-9671
 Fax: 817-877-1927   marc.evans@versacold.com
 www.versacold.com
Freezer and Cold Storage Facility
Manager: Marc Evans
Estimated Sales: $ 10 - 20 Million
Number Employees: 100-249
Type of Packaging: Food Service

52729 CSI Logistics
2741 Foundation Dr
South Bend, IN 46628   574-233-1047
 Fax: 574-232-8461
Warehouse providing dry and humidity-controlled storage; transportation firm providing TL, LTL and long haul trucking
President: Leonard A Kanczuzewski
Number Employees: 20-49
Types of products warehoused:
 Food products
Services Provided:
 Trucking, handling, assembling, packaging, crating, etc.
Storage Facility Data:
 Dry Storage Size: 430000 Cubic Ft.
 Humidity-Controlled Size: 430000 Cubic Ft.

52730 CSRA Bonded Terminal
1261 New Savannah Rd
Augusta, GA 30906   706-722-1093
 Fax: 706-724-6138   866-466-4647
 www.augustagominis.com
Warehouse providing dry storage for food products and packing materials
President/CEO: Brian Ellefson
VP: E Murray
Estimated Sales: $150,000
Number Employees: 4
Square Footage: 360000
Parent Co: United Brokerage Company
Types of products warehoused:
 Food products & packing materials
Storage Facility Data:
 Dry Storage Size: 90000 Sq. Ft.

52731 CSX Transportation
500 Water St
Jacksonville, FL 32202   904-359-3200
 www.csx.com
Warehouse offering cooler and freezer storage of frozen and refrigerated foods; transportation firm providing rail and local.
President & CEO: James Foote
EVP/Chief Legal Officer/Secretary: Nathan Goldman
EVP: Edmond Harris
EVP/Chief Financial Officer: Kevin Boone
EVP/Chief Administrative Officer: Diana Sorfleet
SVP/Chief Information Officer: Kathleen Brandt
SVP, Operations South: Robert (Bob) Frulla, Jr.
Estimated Sales: Over $1 Billion
Number Employees: 10000+
Parent Co: CSX Corporation
Type of Packaging: Private Label
Types of products warehoused:
 Frozen & refrigerated goods, frozen goods
Services Provided:
 Transportation

52732 Caldic USA Inc
2425 Alft Ln
Elgin, IL 60124-7864
 847-468-0001
 customerservice@caldic.us
Sourcing, R&D, proccessing, warehousing and distribution of ingredients.
Owner: Bob Leonard
bleonard@nealanders.com
Number Employees: 10-19
Parent Co: Caldic

52733 (HQ)California Cartage Co
2931 Redondo Ave
Long Beach, CA 90806-2445   310-537-1432
 Fax: 562-988-1351   www.calcartage.com
Transportation broker providing local, short and long haul trucking nationwide and regional in the CA area; warehouse providing dry storage for non-perishable items; also, rail siding available
President: Robert Curry
rcurry@cmimail.com
Number Employees: 5-9
Other Locations:
 California Cartage Co.
 Carson, CA California Cartage Co.
Types of products warehoused:
 Non-perishable, non-perishables
Services Provided:
 rail siding

52734 Canada Distribution Centres
87 Wallbridge Crescent
Belleville, ON K8P 1Z5
Canada   613-967-2900
 Fax: 613-967-2912   tim@rentxtrans.com
Warehouse providing dry storage of general merchandise and groceries; transportation firm providing short haul trucking; also, re-packaging, order assembly and rail siding available
Number Employees: 10-19
Square Footage: 800000
Parent Co: Rentx Transportation Sevices Corp.
Types of products warehoused:
 General merchandise & groceries, general merchandise
Services Provided:
 Repackaging, trucking & order assembly, rail siding
Storage Facility Data:
 Dry Storage Size: 200000 Sq. Ft.

52735 Cannon Cold Storage
8141 Seashore Highway
P.O.Box 550
Bridgeville, DE 19933   302-337-5500
 Fax: 302-337-5505   paul@cannoncold.com
 www.cannoncold.com
Warehouse providing freezer, refrigerated and dry storage
General Manager: Paul Wolpert
Estimated Sales: $2.5-5 Million
Number Employees: 20-49
Parent Co: Pet Poultry
Storage Facility Data:
 Cooler Size 15000 Cubic Ft.
 Dry Storage Size: 250000 Cubic Ft.
 Freezer Size: 1500000 Cubic Ft.

52736 Canon Potato Company
P.O.Box 880
Center, CO 81125   719-754-3445
 Fax: 719-754-2227   sales@canonpotato.com
 www.canonpotato.com
Potatoes including Centennials, McClures, Norkotahs, Nuggets, Reds, Russets, Sangres and Yukon Gold.
Manager: Jim Tonso
Sales Representative: Matt Glowczewski
Sales Manager: David Tonso
d.tonso@canonpotato.com
General Manager: Jim Tonso
Office Manager: Sandy Tonso
Estimated Sales: $10-20 Million
Number Employees: 50-99
Square Footage: 865020
Type of Packaging: Consumer, Food Service, Bulk
Types of products warehoused:
 Potatoes, produce
Storage Facility Data:
 Dry Storage Size: 1500000 Sq. Ft.

52737 Capitol Station 65 ColdStorage
640 Bercut Dr # C
Sacramento, CA 95811-131
 Fax: 916-447-1381
Office Manager: Inez Ramsey
Estimated Sales: $ 1 - 3 Million
Number Employees: 10-19

Warehousing / A-Z

52738 Cargo
220 Thorndale Avenue
Bensenville, IL 60106-1113 847-956-7500
Fax: 630-766-2250 800-323-3294
Warehouse providing dry storage of nonperishable food products; transportation broker offering freight forwarding services
VP Corporate Development: Robert Imhof
Estimated Sales: $20-50 Million
Number Employees: 100-249
Square Footage: 70000
Types of products warehoused:
  Non-perishable food items, non-perishables
Services Provided:
  Brokerage & freight forwarding

52739 Carolina Bonded StorageCo
1349 Old Dairy Dr
Columbia, SC 29201-4840 803-252-4703
Fax: 803-252-0517
Warehouse providing dry storage for food products, paper and other nonfood items; local and short trucking; rail siding available
Manager: Allen Mason
cbsc@bellsouth.net
Number Employees: 5-9
Types of products warehoused:
  Food items, paper & other non-food items
Services Provided:
  Local & statewide trucking, rail siding
Storage Facility Data:
  Dry Storage Size: 40000 Sq. Ft.

52740 Carolina Cold Storage
P.O.Box 268
Tar Heel, NC 28392 910-862-7494
Fax: 910-862-7496 www.richmondcold.com
Warehouse providing cooler and freezer storage for perishable products along with web enabled customer access.
Manager: Marty Gaddy
mgaddy@richmondcold.com
Director Operations: Tom Bryant
Division Manager: Marty Gaddy
Warehouse Manager: Mark Dow
Estimated Sales: $ 10 - 20 Million
Number Employees: 100-249
Square Footage: 165000
Parent Co: Richmond Cold Storage
Type of Packaging: Food Service
Types of products warehoused:
  frozen goods
Services Provided:
  labeling, blast freezing, pick and pack

52741 Carolina Transfer & Stge Inc
2207 Kimball Rd SE
P O Box 20109
Canton, OH 44707-3631 330-453-3709
Fax: 330-453-5170 www.peoplesservices.com
Warehouse providing dry and cooler storage for nonperishable food; transportation firm providing local haul trucking
CEO: Ronald Sibila
VP Finance: Larry P Kelley
VP: Phil McCollum
Human Resources Manager: Jim Wickiser
Vice President of Marketing: John Matheos
Vice President of Sales: John Motheos
Vice President of Operations: Gregory J Hughes
Purchasing Manager: Jim Ehret
Estimated Sales: Less Than $500,000
Number Employees: 1-4
Parent Co: People's Services
Types of products warehoused:
  Refrigerated & non-perishable food, non-perishables
Services Provided:
  Trucking

52742 Cascade Properties
555 Walker Street
Watsonville, CA 95076 831-728-1468
Fax: 831-763-4610 leor@terminalfreezers.com
www.terminalfreezers.com
Cascade Properties of Watsonville features two separate warehouses with over 5 million cubic feet of cold storage space. Automated inventory control with EDI capability; Bulk program storage and distribution; office and laboratoryspace; fully sprinklered with automatic alarm; Bar code/RF inventory tracking; 12 door enclosed loading dock; 5 car private rail spur.
President/Chief Executive Officer: Lowell Dayton
Chief Financial Officer: Todd Nelson
Vice President/General Manager: David Dayton
Information Systems Manager: Kevin Jett
Warehouse Manager: Leo Rocha
Estimated Sales: $2.5-5 Million
Number Employees: 20-49
Parent Co: Terminal Freezers, Inc.
Type of Packaging: Food Service
Types of products warehoused:
  Frozen fruits & vegetables, frozen goods
Services Provided:
  rail siding

52743 Cascade Specialties, Inc.
1 Cascade Way
Boardman, OR 97818 541-481-2522
Fax: 541-481-2640 www.cascadespec.com
Dehydrated onion products.
Owner: Fraser Hawley
CEO: Suvan Sharma
Director of Quality: Tina Kovscek
General Manager: Carl Hearn
Production Manager: Jerry Dyer
Estimated Sales: $5-10 Million
Number Employees: 20-49
Parent Co: JAIN
Other Locations:
  Port Warehouse
  Boardman, ORPort Warehouse

52744 Cassco Refrigerated Services
W. Moler Ave. @ Factory St.
Martinsburg, WV 25401 304-263-3330
Fax: 304-267-4415 information@reddyice.com
www.reddyice.com
Distribution center for ice and ice products
Plant Manager: Rich Parsons
Estimated Sales: $300,000-500,000
Number Employees: 5-9
Type of Packaging: Bulk

52745 Castle Distribution SvcInc
16505 Avenue 24 1/2
P.O. Box 995
Chowchilla, CA 93610-9564 559-665-3716
Fax: 559-665-2848 888-665-3716
www.castledistribution.com
Public warehouse,dry storage
Owner: Brenda Zubeck
brendazubeck@castledistribution.com
General Manager: Craig Wood
Estimated Sales: $1-2.5 Million
Number Employees: 5-9
Square Footage: 880000
Types of products warehoused:
  Food products
Services Provided:
  rail siding
Storage Facility Data:
  Dry Storage Size: 140000 Sq. Ft.

52746 Celebrity Refrigerated Warehouse
1 Atalanta Plz
Elizabeth, NJ 07206-2120 908-351-8000
Fax: 908-351-0176
Packaging or Contract Packaging Services, Freight Brokers, Freight Container Loading Contractors, Packaging Shrink Wrapping Services, Bonded Warehousing, Order Picking Systems, Pallet Storage, Repacking Services, On Line InventoryWarehouse Management Systems, Meat Warehousing, Seafood Warehousing, Meat Inspection Warehousing, Consolidated Warehousing, Cross Docking Services, Poultry Warehousing
Chairman of the Board: George Gellert
General Manager: Matt Barany

52747 Centennial Warehousing Corp
10400 Hickman Rd # A
Clive, IA 50325-3703 515-278-9517
Fax: 515-278-8280
jmiddendorf@centennialwarehouse.com
www.centennialwarehouse.com
Warehouse services include dry and humidity-controlled storage
Vice President: Jason Middendorf
jmiddendorf@centennialwarehouse.com
VP: Jason Middendorf
Estimated Sales: $2.5-5 Million
Number Employees: 20-49
Square Footage: 320000
Storage Facility Data:
  Dry Storage Size: 80000

52748 Centra Worldwide
815 South Main Street
Jacksonville, FL 32207 714-903-3520
Fax: 714-373-0867 888-697-4079
suddathlogistics.com
Warehouse providing storage for nonperishable items; transportation broker providing international and domestic freight forwarding services via air and ocean freight; also, re-packing and sorting services available
President: Michael Kranisky
Vice President, International: Bob Gordon
Vice President, Sales: Tom Ruede
VP, North American Operations: Bob Thomas
Number Employees: 10-19
Parent Co: Suddath Companies
Types of products warehoused:
  Non-perishable items, non-perishables
Services Provided:
  Re-packing & sorting

52749 (HQ)Central American Warehouse Co
10320 Werch Dr
Woodridge, IL 60517-4935 630-972-0707
sales@centralamericangroup.com
www.centralamericangroup.com
A network of six warehouses providing cooler, dry and humidity-controlled storage and nationwide transportation provider. Third party logistics, contract packaging, custom distribution programs and RFID inventory control.
Vice President: Ed Augustyn
VP: Ed Augustyn
Estimated Sales: Less Than $500,000
Number Employees: 1-4
Square Footage: 2800000
Type of Packaging: Consumer, Food Service, Private Label, Bulk
Other Locations:
  Central American Transportati
  Northlake, ILCentral American Transportati
Types of products warehoused:
  dry goods, non-perishables, canned foods, general merchandise
Services Provided:
  Barcoding, work, re-work, AIB food grade, rail siding, trucking, labeling, packaging, pick and pack, repackaging
Storage Facility Data:
  Cooler Size 1000000 Cubic Ft.
  Dry Storage Size: 20000000 Cubic Ft.
  Humidity-Controlled Size: 1000000 Cubic Ft.

52750 Central Global Express
12755 E Nine Mile Road
Warren, MI 48089 734-955-2555
Fax: 734-729-8120 800-982-3924
contact@gocge.com
Transportation broker offering freight forwarding services
President: Alan Samouelian
Vice President: Jeffrey Miller
Contact: Terry Bastow
tbastow@gocge.com
Parent Co: Centra

52751 Central States Distribution
3401 Lynch Creek Dr
Danville, IL 61834-9388 217-431-3325
info@cs-dist.com
www.centralillinoiswarehouse.com
Warehouse providing dry storage for paper products, household goods, dry foods and cans; transportation broker providing long, local and regional haul trucking; also, rail siding and packaging services available
President: Ted Osborn
ted@cs-dist.com
Number Employees: 10-19
Square Footage: 1587000
Types of products warehoused:
  dry goods, non-perishables, canned foods, general merchandise
Services Provided:
  rail siding, trucking, labeling, packaging, pick and pack, repackaging
Storage Facility Data:
  Dry Storage Size: 687000 Sq. Ft.

Warehousing / A-Z

52752 Central States Warehouse
1629 Caledonia St # 110
La Crosse, WI 54603-3602   608-781-2818
Fax: 608-781-2964 solutions@csw-warehouse.com
www.csw-warehouse.com
Warehouse providing dry storage, re-packing and labeling for nonperishable foods. Providing business incubator sections for small businesses. Also providing warehou8se space of 375,000 SF in three other locations. CSW also leases out70,000SF of office space in several locations.
Owner & CEO: Cliff Le Cleir
General Manager: James Gullickson
Estimated Sales: $1-2.5 Million
Number Employees: 10-19
Square Footage: 1600000
Types of products warehoused:
   dry goods, non-perishables, canned foods, general merchandise
Services Provided:
   Arranging for local trucking, trucking, repackaging
Storage Facility Data:
   Dry Storage Size: 400000

52753 (HQ)Central Storage & Warehouse Co
4309 Cottage Grove Rd
Madison, WI 53716-1201   608-221-7600
Fax: 608-221-7603 steves@csw-wi.com
www.csw-wi.com
Wisconsin warehouse company providing refrigerated, frozen, humidity-controlled and dry storage for foods, food-grade materials, packaging, and dry goods; also, intrastate trucking, order filling and distribution service, blastfreezing, import/export services, individually temp controlled rooms, rail sidings; USDA and CME establishments
CEO: John Winegarden
johnwinegarden@csw-wi.com
Vice President Sales & Marketing: Steve Sharratt
Estimated Sales: $7 Million
Number Employees: 10-19
Square Footage: 1900000
Other Locations:
   Eau Claire, WI
   Madison, WI
   Menomonie, WI
   Pleasant Prairie, WI
   Wausau, WIMadison
Types of products warehoused:
   Food grade products, packaging, dry goods, dry goods, frozen goods
Services Provided:
   Intrastate trucking, order filling & distribution, tempering, rail siding, labeling, blast freezing, packaging, import/export service, EDI capabilities
Storage Facility Data:
   Cooler Size 135000
   Dry Storage Size: 2100000
   Freezer Size: 7000000
   Humidity-Controlled Size: 100000

52754 Central Storage & WrhseCo Inc
2650 Fortune Dr
Eau Claire, WI 54703-3909   715-874-2951
Fax: 715-834-0428 steves@csw-wi.com
Warehouse providing cooler, freezer, humidity-controlled and dry storage for food products; also, exporting, USDA inspection, blast freezing and rail siding available
Vice President Sales & Marketing: Steve Sharratt
Manager: John Wingarden
johnw@csw-wi.com
Estimated Sales: Less Than $500,000
Number Employees: 5-9
Square Footage: 480000
Types of products warehoused:
   Food products, dry goods, non-perishables, frozen goods, produce, canned foods
Services Provided:
   Exporting, USDA inspection & blast freezing, rail siding, trucking, labeling, blast freezing, packaging
Storage Facility Data:
   Cooler Size 300000 Cubic Ft.
   Dry Storage Size: 500000 Cubic Ft.
   Freezer Size: 2100000 Cubic Ft.

52755 Central Transport Intl
2401 N 13th St
Norfolk, NE 68701-2271   402-371-9517
Fax: 402-371-7373 800-228-8206
www.centraltransportint.com
Transportation firm providing long and short haul trucking using food and nonfood tankers
President: Thomas Abler
Human Resources: David Schipporeit
Manager: Tom Abler
toma@telebeep.com
Estimated Sales: $5-10 Million
Number Employees: 50-99
Square Footage: 800000
Types of products warehoused:
   dry goods, general merchandise
Services Provided:
   trucking
Storage Facility Data:
   Dry Storage Size: 200000 Sq. Ft.

52756 Central Transportation System
4105 Rio Bravo
Suite 100
El Paso, TX 79902   800-283-3106
info@centralsystems.com
www.centralsystems.com
Warehouse providing dry storage for appliances, household goods, heavy machinery and nonperishable food items; transportation services include short, local and long haul trucking and freight forwarding; also, break bulk consolidationand crating
Owner: Bill Appleton
Contact: Eric Barker
barkereric@scobeymoving.com
Operations Manager: Jay Spoon
Estimated Sales: $2.5-5 Million
Number Employees: 20-49
Square Footage: 320000
Types of products warehoused:
   Non-perishable food items, appliances, household goods, heavy machinery, etc., non-perishables
Services Provided:
   Break bulk, consolidation, crating, freight forwarding, etc.
Storage Facility Data:
   Dry Storage Size: 80000 Sq. Ft.

52757 Central Warehouse Operations, Inc.
1825 Rust Ave
Saginaw, MI 48601   989-752-4191
Fax: 989-752-0955 sales@peoplesservices.com
www.peoplesservices.com
Warehouse offering dry storage for general merchandise and food items; transportation firm providing local and long haul trucking
President/CEO: Douglas J. Sibla
CFO-Vice President of Finance: Larry P. Kelly
Vice President of Sales & Marketing: John Matheos
COO & Executive Vice President: Bill Hanlon
Estimated Sales: $500,000-$1 Million
Number Employees: 20-49
Square Footage: 200000
Types of products warehoused:
   Dry foods, plastic resin & general merchandise, dry goods, general merchandise
Services Provided:
   Pick & pack, bulk trucking & re-packing, rail siding
Storage Facility Data:
   Dry Storage Size: 50000 Sq. Ft.

52758 Central-Cumberland Corp
3287 Franklin Limestone # 320
Antioch, TN 37013-2765   615-333-0101
Fax: 615-333-6709 lcowan@cencum.com
www.cencum.com
Warehouse providing dry storage for general merchandise; transportation firm providing local haul trucking; also, order picking, re-packaging, shrink and stretch wrapping services; rail siding available
President & General Manager: Leland Cowan
Number Employees: 5-9
Square Footage: 700000
Types of products warehoused:
   General merchandise, general merchandise
Services Provided:
   Local haul trucking, order picking, shrink & stretch wrapping, rail siding

Storage Facility Data:
   Dry Storage Size: 175000 Sq. Ft.

52759 Central/Terminal Distribution Centers
1600 Gregory St
N Little Rock, AR 72114   501-375-3205
logisco.com
Warehouse offering dry and humidity-controlled storage for food products and general commodities; also, rail siding, pick and pack, trucking and transloading services available
Manager: Jeff Bone
Data Processing Executive: Cliff Jones
Sales Executive: Ed Linck
Estimated Sales: $5-10 Million
Number Employees: 50 to 99
Parent Co: Logisco
Types of products warehoused:
   Food products & general commodities, general merchandise
Services Provided:
   Pick & pack, trucking & transloading, rail siding
Storage Facility Data:
   Dry Storage Size: 443000 Sq. Ft.
   Humidity-Controlled Size: 12000 Sq. Ft.

52760 Chambersburg Cold Storage Inc
1480 Nitterhouse Dr
Chambersburg, PA 17201-4824   717-261-1288
Fax: 717-261-1399 fdeleo@mhwgroup.com
www.mhwgroup.com
Provides rail, truck, and warehousing cold chain services.
President: Tyrone Myers
Manager: Angela Gladfelder
agladfelder@mhwgroup.com
Estimated Sales: $ 3 - 5 Million
Number Employees: 20-49
Type of Packaging: Food Service
Storage Facility Data:
   Cooler Size 9000000

52761 Charles Walker North America
2901 Stanley Ave
Fort Worth, TX 76110   817-922-9834
Fax: 817-922-9854 cissy@charlesalaninc.com
www.charlesalanfurniture.com
Furniture manufacturer
Owner: Margaret Sevadjian
Vice President: Jim Boston
Operations Manager: Steve McDonald
Square Footage: 120

52762 Chicagoland Quad CitiesExpress
7715 S 78th Ave
Bridgeview, IL 60455-7305   708-594-6200
Fax: 708-594-6247
info@chicagolandquadcities.com
Warehouse providing dry and humidity-controlled storage for canned goods, food products and general merchandise; also, rail siding available; providing a total of 551,105 Sq Ft of warehouse space
President: Terri Wintermute
VP: Hans Bauer
Contact: James Koleff
james.koleff@chicagolandquadcities.com
Estimated Sales: $5-10 Million
Number Employees: 50-99
Square Footage: 1628420
Types of products warehoused:
   canned foods, general merchandise
Services Provided:
   Temperature controlled, EDI capabilities, pool distribution, rail siding, labeling, repackaging

52763 Chilled Solutions LLC
470 West Crossroads Parkway
Unit B
Bolingbrook, IL 60440   630-863-7750
Fax: 630-863-7750 brett@chilledsolutions.net
www.chilledsolutions.net
We are a temperature controlled warehouse with a small fleet of temperature controlled trucks. We make local deliveries in the Chicagoland area.
President: Dean Osborn
Vice President: Ted Chan
Operations Manager: Brett Koch
Square Footage: 68000

Warehousing / A-Z

52764 Cincinnati Freezer Corp
2881 E Sharon Rd
Cincinnati, OH 45241-1923   513-771-3573
Fax: 513-771-4717 shortwait@aol.com
www.cincinnatifreezer.com
Warehouse offering freezer storage of refrigerated products; rail siding available
Manager: Don Lucas
Manager: Tanya Duffy
tanya@brownlawohio.com
Estimated Sales: $500,000-$1 Million
Number Employees: 5-9
Types of products warehoused:
  Frozen/Refrigerated, frozen goods
Services Provided:
  rail siding, trucking, pick and pack
Storage Facility Data:
  Freezer Size: 1330000 Cubic Ft.

52765 Ciranda Inc.
221 Vine St
Hudson, WI 54016   715-386-1737
Fax: 715-386-3277 www.ciranda.com
Global supplier of organic, non-GMO and fair trade ingredients, specializing in tapioca syrups; starches and derivatives; honey and agave; cocoa and chocolates; coconut; soy and sunflower lecithin; and various oils and fats.
Contact: Patty Gfrerer
pgfrerer@gmail.com
Chief Financial Officer: Mark Cross
Marketing Manager: Tonya Lofgren
Human Resources Manager: Karen Brabec
Director of Commerical Operations: Joe Rouleau

52766 City Brewing Company
925 S 3rd St
La Crosse, WI 54601   608-785-4200
inquiries@citybrewery.com
www.citybrewery.com
Manufacturer/processor of beer for major and private label brands.
VP & Chief Financial Officer: Gregory Inda
Director, Supply Chain: Jeff Glynn
Year Founded: 1939
Estimated Sales: $38 Million
Number Employees: 400
Type of Packaging: Consumer
Other Locations:
  Latrobe, PA
  Memphis, TNMemphis
Storage Facility Data:
  Cooler Size 8,000 x

52767 City Packing Company
117 Newmarket Sq
Boston, MA 02118   617-442-8100
    800-654-5405
citypacking@gmail.com citypackingcompany.com
Wholesaler/distributor of meats; serving the food service market.
President: Alan Stearn
Year Founded: 1946
Estimated Sales: $20-50 Million
Number Employees: 20-49
Types of products warehoused:
  frozen goods, Boxed Beef

52768 Clauson Cold & Cooler
2423 2nd Avenue SE
Calgary, AB T2E 6K1
Canada   403-248-9808
Fax: 403-273-3691 www.clausoncoldstorage.com
Warehouse providing cold storage for perishable goods
President: Norman H Clauson
Account/Office Manager: Cathy Coels
Square Footage: 250000
Type of Packaging: Food Service

52769 Claxton Cold Storage
Highway 301 south
Claxton, GA 30417   912-739-9800
Fax: 912-739-3271 info@claxtoncoldstorage.com
www.claxtoncoldstorage.com
Warehouse providing freezer storage and labeling for frozen foods
Owner: Norman Fries, Jr.
CEO: Doris Fries
General Manager: Kirk Welch
Receptionist: Michelle Plyler
Operations Manager: Jeff Willoughby
Estimated Sales: Under $500,000
Number Employees: 1-4

Types of products warehoused:
  Frozen foods, frozen goods
Services Provided:
  Labeling

52770 Cleanfreak
3900 N Providence Ave
Appleton, WI 54913-8017   920-380-0777
Fax: 920-380-0878 888-722-5508
info@cleanfreak.com www.cleanfreak.com
Maufacturer and supplier of cleaning equipment and supplies
Vice President: Steve Menzner
smenzner@pti-1.com
Number Employees: 10-19
Parent Co: Packaging Tape Inc.
Services Provided:
  packaging, cleaning equipment

52771 (HQ)Cloverleaf Cold Storage
401 Douglas St
Suite 406
Sioux City, IA 51101   712-279-8000
Fax: 712-279-8015 info@cloverleaf.com
www.cloverleaf.com
Warehouses with dry storage, coolers, freezers, and blast freezing; Meat processing and packaging services provided through Farmers Produce division
President: Curtis Mastbergen
Co-CEO: Bill Feiges
Co-CEO: Daniel Kaplan
CFO: Matthew Bremer
VP Operations: Ken Smith
National Sales: Vern Rose
National Sales: Greg Shimonek
Business Development: Roger Rau
Farmers Produce: Scott Ebel
Number Employees: 1000-4999
Type of Packaging: Consumer
Other Locations:
  LeMars, IA
  Fairfield, OH
  Sioux City, IA
  Fairmont, MN
  Napoleon, OH
  Cherokee, IAFairfield
Types of products warehoused:
  dry goods, frozen goods
Services Provided:
  rail siding, trucking, labeling, blast freezing, packaging

52772 Cloverleaf Cold Storage
8425 Highway 45
Fort Smith, AR 72916   479-646-7757
www.cloverleaf.com
15.6 million cubic foot facility providing cold storage and dry storage; 45,700 pallet positions; Blast capacity 430 pallets; Convertible rooms; Temperature ranges from -10 to ambienet; 31 truck and 9 rail loading doors; USDAinspections; Import/export services
Types of products warehoused:
  dry goods, frozen goods
Services Provided:
  rail siding, trucking, blast freezing

52773 Cloverleaf Cold Storage
6403 S Ball
Johnson, AR 72704   479-521-1400
www.cloverleaf.com
5.6 million cubic foot facility providing cold storage; 29,000 pallet positions; Blast capacity 300 pallets; Convertible rooms; Temperature ranges from -10 to ambienet; 10 truck and 3 rail loading doors; USDA inspections; Import/exportservices
Types of products warehoused:
  frozen goods, produce
Services Provided:
  rail siding, trucking, blast freezing

52774 Cloverleaf Cold Storage
1400 Gregory St
North Little Rock, AR 72114   501-435-3900
www.cloverleaf.com
6.5 million cubic foot facility providing cold storage; 27,000 pallet positions; Blast capacity 180 pallets; Convertible rooms; Temperature ranges from -10 to 38F; 20 truck loading doors; USDA inspections; Import/export services
Types of products warehoused:
  frozen goods
Services Provided:
  trucking, blast freezing

52775 Cloverleaf Cold Storage
515 N Bloomington
Lowell, AR 72745   479-659-3000
www.cloverleaf.com
5.3 million cubic foot facility providing cold storage; 31,000 pallet positions; Blast capacity 350 pallets; Convertible rooms; Temperature ranges from -10 to 40F; 22 truck and 2 rail loading doors; USDA inspections; Import/exportservices
Types of products warehoused:
  frozen goods
Services Provided:
  rail siding, trucking, blast freezing

52776 Cloverleaf Cold Storage
500 SR 324 South
Russellville, AR 72802   479-967-3898
www.cloverleaf.com
8.1 million cubic foot facility providing cold storage; 29,000 pallet positions; Blast capacity 480 pallets; Convertible rooms; Temperature ranges from -10 to 38F; 34 truck and 2 rail loading doors; USDA inspections; Import/exportservices
Types of products warehoused:
  frozen goods
Services Provided:
  rail siding, trucking, blast freezing

52777 Cloverleaf Cold Storage
2900 Murray St
Sioux City, IA 51111   712-279-0918
www.cloverleaf.com
5 million cubic foot facility providing cold storage; 30,231 pallet positions; Blast capacity 543 pallets; 3 convertible rooms; Temperature ranges from -20 to 40F; 13 truck and 3 rail loading doors; USDA inspections; Export services
Types of products warehoused:
  frozen goods
Services Provided:
  rail siding, trucking, blast freezing

52778 Cloverleaf Cold Storage
2640 Murray St
Sioux City, IA 51111   712-279-8022
www.cloverleaf.com
4 million cubic foot facility providing cold storage; 20,602 pallet positions; Blast capacity 1330 pallets; 2 convertible rooms; Temperature ranges from -20 to 40F; 26 truck and 7 rail loading doors; USDA inspections; Exportservices
Types of products warehoused:
  frozen goods
Services Provided:
  rail siding, trucking, blast freezing

52779 Cloverleaf Cold Storage
1530 S 2nd St
Cherokee, IA 51012   712-225-5151
www.cloverleaf.com
2 million cubic foot facility providing cold storage; 10,227 pallet positions; Blast capacity 384 pallets; 3 convertible rooms; Temperature ranges from -20 to 40F; 10 truck and 4 rail loading doors; USDA inspections; Export services
Types of products warehoused:
  frozen goods
Services Provided:
  rail siding, trucking, blast freezing

52780 Cloverleaf Cold Storage
1609 18th St SW
LeMars, IA 51031   712-546-6121
www.cloverleaf.com
3 million cubic foot facility providing cold storage; 12,658 pallet positions; Blast capacity 400 pallets; 3 convertible rooms; Temperature ranges from -20 to 40F; 12 truck and 1 rail loading doors; USDA inspections
Types of products warehoused:
  frozen goods
Services Provided:
  rail siding, trucking, blast freezing

52781 Cloverleaf Cold Storage
16820 Churnovic Lane
Crest Hill, IL 60403   815-730-1250
www.cloverleaf.com
8.1 million cubic foot facility providing cold storage; 22,886 pallet positions; 27 truck loading doors
Types of products warehoused:
  frozen goods
Services Provided:
  trucking

Warehousing / A-Z

52782 Cloverleaf Cold Storage
1 Cloverleaf Dr
Monmouth, IL 61462   309-457-1400
                    www.cloverleaf.com
7.5 million cubic foot facility providing cold storage; 28,000 pallet positions; Blast capacity 340 pallets; Temperature ranges from -20 to 38F; 35 truck loading doors; USDA inspections; Export services
Types of products warehoused:
    frozen goods
Services Provided:
    rail siding, trucking, blast freezing

52783 Cloverleaf Cold Storage
2864 Eagandale Blvd
Eagan, MN 55121   651-454-5180
                    www.cloverleaf.com
3 million cubic foot facility providing cold storage; 25,000 pallet positions; Temperature ranges from -20 to 38F; 40 truck loading doors; USDA inspections; Export services
Types of products warehoused:
    frozen goods
Services Provided:
    rail siding, trucking

52784 Cloverleaf Cold Storage
21755 Cedar Ave
Lakeville, MN 55044   952-469-1221
         Fax: 952-469-1774 www.cloverleaf.com
5 million cubic foot facility providing cold storage and dry storage; 120,000 square feet of dry storage; 26,305 pallet positions; Blast capacity 840 pallets; 3 convertible rooms; Temperature ranges from -20 to 40F; 16 truck and 3 rail loading doors; Refrigerated docks; USDA inspections; Export services
Types of products warehoused:
    dry goods, frozen goods
Services Provided:
    rail siding, trucking, blast freezing
Storage Facility Data:
    Dry Storage Size: 120000 Sq. Ft.

52785 Cloverleaf Cold Storage
1400 E 8th St
Fairmont, MN 56031-3898   507-238-4211
         Fax: 507-238-9579 fairmont@cloverleaf.com
                    www.cloverleaf.com
2 million cubic foot facility providing cold storage; 13,108 pallet positions; Blast capacity 726 pallets; 2 convertible rooms; Temperature ranges from -20 to 40F; 14 truck and 6 rail loading doors; Refrigerated docks; USDA inspections; Export services
Types of products warehoused:
    dry goods, frozen goods
Services Provided:
    rail siding, trucking, blast freezing

52786 Cloverleaf Cold Storage
500 Corporate Dr
Chillicothe, MO 64601-3727 660-646-6939
         Fax: 660-646-2094 www.cloverleaf.com
18 million cubic foot facility providing cold storage; 36,711 pallet positions; Blast capacity 320 pallets; 6 convertible rooms; Temperature ranges from -20 to 40F; 27 truck and 2 rail loading doors; USDA inspections; Export services
Types of products warehoused:
    frozen goods
Services Provided:
    rail siding, trucking, blast freezing

52787 Cloverleaf Cold Storage
2350 New World Dr
Columbus, OH 43207   614-491-3890
                    www.cloverleaf.com
4 million cubic foot facility providing cold storage; 23,897 pallet positions; Blast capacity 280 pallets; 6 convertible rooms; Temperature ranges from -20 to 40F; 22 truck and 2 rail loading doors; Refrigerated docks; USDA inspections; Export services
Types of products warehoused:
    frozen goods
Services Provided:
    rail siding, trucking, blast freezing

52788 Cloverleaf Cold Storage
3110 Homeward Way
Fairfield, OH 45014-4254   513-860-5992
         Fax: 513-870-5232 www.cloverleaf.com
5 million cubic foot facility providing cold storage; 18,073 pallet positions; Blast capacity 105 pallets; 6 convertible rooms; Temperature ranges -20 to 40F; 15 truck and 2 rail loading doors; Refrigerated docks; USDA inspections; Export services
Types of products warehoused:
    frozen goods
Services Provided:
    rail siding, trucking, blast freezing

52789 Cloverleaf Cold Storage
1165 Independence Dr
Napoleon, OH 43545-9718   419-599-5015
         Fax: 419-592-5183 www.cloverleaf.com
4 million cubic foot facility providing cold storage and dry storage; 22,769 cold storage pallet positions, 30,794 dry storage pallet positions; Blast capacity 561 pallets; 6 convertible rooms; Temperature ranges from -20 to 40F, -50to 95F for dry storage; 42 truck and 5 rail loading doors; USDA inspections; Export services
Types of products warehoused:
    dry goods, frozen goods
Services Provided:
    rail siding, trucking, blast freezing
Storage Facility Data:
    Dry Storage Size: 6000000 Cubic Ft.

52790 Cloverleaf Cold Storage
444 Gilbert Rd
Benson, NC 27504   919-207-4420
                    www.cloverleaf.com
8 million cubic foot facility providing cold storage; 28,840 pallet positions; Blast capacity of 984 pallets; 7 convertible rooms; Temperature ranges from -20 to 38F; 30 truck and 1 rail loading doors; Refrigerated docks; USDA inspections
Types of products warehoused:
    frozen goods
Services Provided:
    rail siding, trucking, blast freezing

52791 Cloverleaf Cold Storage
111 Imperial Dr
Sanford, NC 27330-8610   919-775-4474
         Fax: 919-775-4459 www.cloverleaf.com
6 million cubic foot facility providing cold storage; 27,864 pallet positions; Blast capacity 528 pallets; 4 convertible rooms; Temperature ranges from -20 to 40F; 23 truck and 2 rail loading doors; USDA inspections; Export services
Types of products warehoused:
    frozen goods
Services Provided:
    rail siding, trucking, blast freezing

52792 Cloverleaf Cold Storage
1900 Corporate Way
Sumter, SC 29154   803-481-4745
                    www.cloverleaf.com
2 million cubic foot facility providing cold storage; 12,208 pallet positions; Blast capacity of 968 pallets; 3 convertible rooms; Temperature ranges from -20 to 40F; 16 truck and 2 rail loading doors; Refrigerated docks; USDA inspections; Export services
Types of products warehoused:
    frozen goods
Services Provided:
    rail siding, trucking, blast freezing

52793 Cloverleaf Cold Storage
1229 Fleetway Dr
Chesapeake, VA 23323   757-487-7847
                    www.cloverleaf.com
3 million cubic foot facility providing cold storage; 12,720 pallet positions; Blast capacity of 797 pallets; 4 convertible rooms; Temperature ranges from -20 to 40F; 27 truck and 3 rail loading doors; Refrigerated docks; USDA inspections; Import/Export services
Types of products warehoused:
    frozen goods
Services Provided:
    rail siding, trucking, blast freezing

52794 Coastal Cold Storage Inc
306 N Nordic Dr
Petersburg, AK 99833   907-772-4177
                     Fax: 907-772-4176
A warehouse facility providing cold storage.
Owner: Greg Einerson
coastal@alaska.com
Number Employees: 10-19

52795 Cockrell Distribution System
2700 Deepwater Terminal Rd
Richmond, VA 23234   804-232-8941
         Fax: 804-233-3215 info@clsrva.com
                    http://clsrva.com/
Warehouse providing cooler and dry storage, re-packing and labeling for nonperishable and refrigerated foods; transportation services include short haul trucking nationwide
President: H Clark Cockrell
Office Manager: Beverly Schnarrs
General Manager: Billy Jones
Vice President: P.M. Neal, Jr.
Number Employees: 20-49
Square Footage: 6000000
Types of products warehoused:
    Non-perishable & refrigerated foods, non-perishables
Services Provided:
    Re-packing & labeling

52796 Cold Storage
500 NE 185th St
Miami, FL 33179-4547   305-653-6678
         Fax: 305-653-9546 info@coldstorageassoc.com
                    www.coldstorageassoc.com
Owner: Tal Levenson
Operations: Julian Kriesberg
Estimated Sales: $ .5 - 1 million
Number Employees: 5-9

52797 ColdStor LLC
8525 Page Avenue
Saint Louis, MO 63114-6014 314-592-2007
                     Fax: 314-429-8651

52798 Colony Brands Inc
1112 7th Ave
Monroe, WI 53566-1364   608-328-8400
         Fax: 608-328-8457 800-544-9036
                    www.colonybrands.com
Cakes, tortes & pies; cookies & bars; pastries; petits fours; candy & chocolate; boxed assortments of all kinds; cheeses; sausage, ham and other meats; nuts & pre-mixed snacks; home furniture; home d,cor; electronics; jewelry; fitness equipment; unisex apparel; small appliances
CEO: John Baumann
Chairman: Pat Kubly
VP/CIO: Steve Cretney
Content Marketing Manager: Matt Stetler
Director of Strategic Planning: Ryan Kubly
Number Employees: 1000-4999
Square Footage: 13236
Parent Co: Colony Brands, Inc.

52799 Colorado Cold Storage
1600 W Colfax Ave
Denver, CO 80204   303-573-0555
                     Fax: 303-573-0554
Warehouse providing freezer storage for frozen foods
Manager: Jim Johnson
Manager: James Johnson
Plant Manager: James Johnson
Estimated Sales: $300,000-500,000
Number Employees: 1-4
Square Footage: 60400
Parent Co: Frozen Pet Ingredients
Types of products warehoused:
    Frozen foods, frozen goods
Storage Facility Data:
    Freezer Size: 1066000 Cubic Ft.

52800 Columbia Cheese
47-55 27th Street
Long Island City, NY 11101 718-937-7452
                    www.columbiacheese.com
Warehouse providing storage for frozen and dry food products
President: Joseph Moskowitz
Marketing: Sarah Zaborowski
Estimated Sales: $ .5 - 1 million
Number Employees: 1-4

52801 Columbia Valley Wine Warehouse
614 W Wine Country Rd
Grandview, WA 98930   509-882-6070
                     Fax: 509-586-2481

Warehousing / A-Z

Columbia Valley Wine Warehouse, operated by Columbia Colstor, Inc., offers 25,000 square feet of bonded refrigerated space (50-65 degrees). The facility offers computerized inventory control management, a secure temperature controlled environment and quality service to meet your needs. Rail access is available via transloading at the distribution center in Kennewick on both the BNSF and the UP. This is a bonded wine warehouse, available for both case and barrel storage.
Manager: Missy Tomjack
Director of Administrative Services: Mike Bolander
Controller: Missy Tomjack
Corporate Engineer: Joel Sandberg
Compliance Manager: Deb Langshaw
Director of Information Services: David Weston
Manager: Dan Kline
Parent Co: Columbia Colstor, Inc.
Type of Packaging: Food Service

52802 Columbian Logistics Network
900 Hall St SW
Grand Rapids, MI 49503-4821   616-514-6000
Fax: 616-514-5990   888-609-8542
donran@columbian.us   www.columbian.us
Warehouse offering cooler, dry and humidity-controlled storage for general merchandise, groceries, health/beauty aids and candy; transportation firm providing LTL, TL and pool distribution; also, rail siding, and special handling distribution available
President: Dick Wickard
CEO: John Zevalkink
COO: Robert Christian
Marketing: Donna Randall
Sales: Jim Doorn
Operations: Bill Ekberg
Estimated Sales: $40-50 Million
Number Employees: 100-249
Square Footage: 1400000
Type of Packaging: Food Service
Types of products warehoused:
   General merchandise, groceries, candy & health & beauty aids, dry goods, non-perishables, canned foods, general merchandise
Services Provided:
   Trucking, pool distribution, electronic security, etc., rail siding, trucking, labeling, packaging, pick and pack, repackaging
Storage Facility Data:
   Cooler Size 90000 Sq. Ft.
   Dry Storage Size: 1000000 Sq. Ft.
   Humidity-Controlled Size: 140000 Sq. Ft.

52803 Columbian Logistics Network
2900 Dixie Ave SW # 1
Grandville, MI 49418-1280   616-538-7738
Fax: 616-514-5990   888-609-8542
www.columbianlogistics.com
Warehouse offering cooler and dry storage for general commodities; rail siding available
President: Richard Wickard
CEO: John Zevalkink
john@columbianlogistics.com
CFO: Robert Christian
Marketing Director: Donna Randall
Director, Business Development: Stephanie Haight
Director, Customer Care: Blair Thomas
COO: Bob Christian
Estimated Sales: $ 10 - 20 Million
Number Employees: 100-249
Square Footage: 500000
Other Locations:
   Columbian Express Service
   Detroit, MI
   Columbian Interstate Services
   Gransville, MI
   Central Logistics
   Kentwood, MI Columbian Express Service Gransville
Types of products warehoused:
   General commodities, general merchandise
Services Provided:
   rail siding

52804 Columbus Cold Storage Inc.
4410 New Haven Ave.
Fort Wayne, IN 46803   260-428-2505
Fax: 260-428-2503
contactus@interstatecoldstorage.com
www.interstatecoldstorage.com
Warehouse providing storage for general merchandise, and food, and food grade products
Director of Operations: Scott Parker
General Manger: Kevin Tackett
Facility Manager East: Gary Benson
Facility Manager: Russell Borstelman
Facility Manager: Mike Browning
Facility Manager West: John Stone
Estimated Sales: $ 1 - 3 Million
Number Employees: 18
Type of Packaging: Food Service
Other Locations:
   Storage Facility
   Napolean, OH
   Storage Facility
   Columbus, OH
   Storage Facilty East
   Fort Wayne, IN
   Storage Facilty West
   Fort Wayne, IN Storage Facility Columbus

52805 Commercial Cold Storage
4300 Pleasantdale Road
Atlanta, GA 30340   770-448-7400
Public warehouse providing cooler, freezer, dry and humidity-controlled storage for refrigerated and frozen foods; transportation firm providing local and short haul trucking, bi-modal and consolidated pool distribution in the Southeast
Estimated Sales: $10-25 Million
Number Employees: 100-249
Square Footage: 2700000
Parent Co: Stone & Webster
Other Locations:
   Commercial Cold Storage
   Wilmington, NC Commercial Cold Storage
Types of products warehoused:
   Refrigerated & frozen foods, frozen goods
Services Provided:
   Consolidated distribution, blast freezing, space leasing, etc., rail siding
Storage Facility Data:
   Cooler Size 4000000 Cubic Ft.
   Dry Storage Size: 344660 Cubic Ft.
   Freezer Size: 43657000 Cubic Ft.

52806 Commercial Distribution Ctr
16500 E Truman Rd
P.O.Box 350
Independence, MO 64050-4169   816-836-1500
Fax: 816-836-0643   www.cdcinc.com
Warehouse providing storage for dry, refrigerated and frozen foods and nonfood items; also, freight consolidation, import/export, sqeeze packing, labeling, bulk storage, pool program and rail siding available
President: Doris Jones
Contact: Lori Barker
lbarker@stlcc.edu
Purchasing Manager: Gay Martin
Number Employees: 10-19
Types of products warehoused:
   Dry, refrigerated & frozen foods & non-food items, dry goods, non-perishables, frozen goods, produce, canned foods, general merchandise, Fresh Meats
Services Provided:
   Freight consolidation, year-round underground storage, etc., rail siding, trucking, labeling, packaging, pick and pack, repackaging, Boxing Fresh Meats
Storage Facility Data:
   Cooler Size 123000 Sq. Ft.
   Dry Storage Size: 500000 Sq. Ft.
   Freezer Size: 807000 Sq. Ft.
   Humidity-Controlled Size: 284000 Sq. Ft.

52807 Commercial Warehouse Co
1340 Broadway Blvd NE
Albuquerque, NM 87102-1544   505-247-4246
Fax: 505-247-0739
www.commercialwarehouseabq.com
Warehouse providing dry storage for general merchandise; transportation firm providing local haul trucking and freight consolidation; also, pick/pack, free port work and importing services available
Owner: James Morris
cwcabq1@qwestoffice.net
Number Employees: 10-19
Square Footage: 224000
Types of products warehoused:
   General merchandise, dry goods, non-perishables, canned foods, general merchandise
Services Provided:
   Pick/pack, free port work, consolidation, etc., trucking, pick and pack
Storage Facility Data:
   Dry Storage Size: 96000 Sq. Ft.

52808 Commonwealth Inc
11013 Kenwood Rd # 4
Blue Ash, OH 45242-1843   513-791-1966
Fax: 513-791-0880   sales@commonwealthinc.com
www.commonwealthinc.com
Warehouse providing dry and cold storage for refrigerated and nonperishable foods; transportation firm providing short haul trucking
President: Brent L Collins
Executive Vice President: Karen Hamm
Sales Manager: Donny Bray
Manager: Collins Brent
collins.brent@commonwealthinc.com
Opeartions Vice President: Andy Deardoff
Number Employees: 20-49
Types of products warehoused:
   Refrigerated & non-perishable foods, non-perishables
Services Provided:
   Short haul trucking

52809 Commonwealth Warehouse & Storage
123 36th St
Pittsburgh, PA 15142   412-687-6600
Fax: 412-687-6514
Warehouse offering dry and humidity controlled storage for general commodities; rail siding available
Owner: Ross Aiello
Contact: Chuck Costanza
chuckcostanza@commonwealthwarehouse.com
Estimated Sales: $500,000-$1 Million
Number Employees: 5-9
Square Footage: 800000
Types of products warehoused:
   General commodities, general merchandise
Services Provided:
   rail siding
Storage Facility Data:
   Dry Storage Size: 180000 Sq. Ft.
   Humidity-Controlled Size: 12000 Sq. Ft.

52810 Compton Transfer Storage Co
4302 S Industrial St
Boise, ID 83705-5319   208-331-3800
Fax: 208-331-3998   800-238-3452
Info@ComptonTransfer.com
www.comptontransfer.com
Commercial warehouse offering dry storage for general commodities; also, rail siding, local cartage and pool car distribution available
President: Brett Compton
info@comptontransfer.com
Secretary: MaryKay Sprague
Vice President: Scott Compton
Estimated Sales: $1-2.5 Million
Number Employees: 10-19
Square Footage: 240000
Types of products warehoused:
   General commodities, general merchandise
Services Provided:
   Local cartage & pool car distribution, rail siding
Storage Facility Data:
   Dry Storage Size: 60000 Sq. Ft.

52811 Concord Import
3151 Fruitland Ave
Vernon, CA 90058   323-588-8888
www.dollaritem.com
Supplier of food closeouts.
Owner: Ted Shayan
Estimated Sales: $100-500 Million
Type of Packaging: Bulk

52812 Conestoga Cold Storage
4767 27th Street SE
Calgary, AB T2B 3M5
Canada   403-207-6766
Fax: 403-248-1518   akerslake@coldstorage.com
www.coldstorage.com
Warehouse providing cooler and freezer storage.
Warehouse Manager: Jim Guthrie
Square Footage: 80000
Type of Packaging: Food Service
Types of products warehoused:
   frozen goods
Services Provided:
   Order picking and distribution
Storage Facility Data:
   Freezer Size: 1200000 Cubic Ft.

Warehousing / A-Z

52813 Conestoga Cold Storage
2660 Meadowpine Blvd
Mississauga, ON L5N 7E6
Canada 905-567-1144
Fax: 905-567-1040 dmunro@coldstorage.com
www.coldstorage.com
Freezer and Cold Storage
President: Greg Laurin
Chairman of the Board: Larry Laurin
Vice-President Finance: Denise St. Croix
Vice-President Automation: Gavin Sargeant
SVP Sales & Administration: Ed Shantz
Warehouse Manager: Greg Laurin
Square Footage: 56
Type of Packaging: Food Service
Types of products warehoused:
   frozen goods
Services Provided:
   Order picking and distribution, import/export, blast freezing
Storage Facility Data:
   Freezer Size: 11242596 Cubic Ft.

52814 (HQ)Conestoga Cold Storage
299 Trillium Drive
Kitchener, ON N2E 1W9
Canada 519-748-5415
Fax: 519-748-9852 koconnell@coldstorage.com
www.coldstorage.com
Warehouse providing cold storage for refrigerated and frozen foods; three additional locations in Canada.
President: Greg Laurin
SVP Sales & Administration: Ed Shantz
Warehouse Manager: Kevin O'Connell
Number Employees: 50-99
Square Footage: 1200000
Types of products warehoused:
   Refrigerated & frozen foods, frozen goods
Services Provided:
   Import/export capabilities, 24-hour service, blast freezing, pick and pack
Storage Facility Data:
   Cooler Size 400000 Cubic Ft.
   Freezer Size: 2900000 Cubic Ft.

52815 Confederation Freezers
240 Nuggett Court
Brampton, ON L6T 5H4
Canada 905-799-3609
Fax: 905-799-2223 sales_inquiries@gocold.ca
www.confederationfreezers.com
Multi-Temp Warehousing Confederation Freezers' multi-temp storage facilities are equipped with state-of-the-art refrigeration systems capable of providing temperatures ranging from -29C (-20F) to 2C (36F). Ambient storage is also available and customers can rest assured that each facility is monitored 24-hours/ day, guaranteeing safety and security for your products.
President/CEO Corporate Office: Harry Greenspan
Facility Manager: Jeff Brown
Type of Packaging: Food Service
Types of products warehoused:
   frozen goods
Services Provided:
   Cross docking, import/export, CFIA certified, rail siding, trucking, repackaging

52816 (HQ)Confederation Freezers
21 York Rd
Brantford, ON N3T 6H2
Canada 519-752-1177
Fax: 519-752-3013 general_inquiries@gocold.ca
www.confederationfreezers.com/contact.php
Head office and distribution warehouse providing cooler and freezer storage for frozen foods.
Multi-Temp Warehousing Confederation Freezers' multi-temp storage facilities are equipped with state-of-the-art refrigeration systems capable of providing temperatures ranging from -29C (-20F) to 2C (36F). Ambient storage is also available and customers can rest assured that each facility is monitored 24-hours/ day, guaranteeing safety and security for your products.
President/CEO: Harry Greenspan
Executive Vice President: John Greenspan
Executive Vice President: Alan Greenspan
Sales/Marketing: Kathie Krolicki
Number Employees: 50
Square Footage: 1400000
Other Locations:
   21 York Road
   Brantford, Ontario21 York RoadBrampton, Ontario
Types of products warehoused:
   frozen goods
Services Provided:
   Cross docking, import/export, transportation, rail siding, trucking, repackaging

52817 Connecticut Freezers
1 Brewery St
New Haven, CT 06511-5935 203-776-8989
Fax: 203-776-9655 maritimeinternational.org
Public warehouse providing freezer and cooler storage for frozen poultry, meat, seafood and desserts; also, convertible cooler and freezer storage available
Manager: John Ciardi
COO: Tim Ray
Sales/Marketing Executive: Frank Pallone
Manager, Freight Forwarding Division: Pierre Bernier
Estimated Sales: $2 Million
Number Employees: 10 to 19
Square Footage: 4000000
Parent Co: Maritime International
Types of products warehoused:
   Frozen poultry, meat, seafood & desserts, frozen goods
Services Provided:
   Convertible cooler & freezer storage, blast freezing, pick and pack
Storage Facility Data:
   Cooler Size 1200000 Cubic Ft.
   Freezer Size: 1637000 Cubic Ft.

52818 Consolidated Bonded Warehouse
PO Box 20407
2510 Magnet St
Houston, TX 77054-4507 713-799-1910
Fax: 713-799-1913
Public and US customs bonded warehouse providing climate-controlled storage to the food industry
President: Michael Slavin
Warehouse Manager: Jeffrey Cyr
Estimated Sales: $500,000-$1 Million
Number Employees: 10-19

52819 Consolidated Transfer Co Inc
1251 Taney St
Kansas City, MO 64116-4485 816-221-1503
Fax: 816-472-7235 800-279-3411
www.ctw-co.com
Warehouse providing dry storage for nonperishable foods, machinery, paper products, etc.; transportation broker providing local, long and short haul trucking; also, rail siding, EDI, cross docking, intermodal drayage, local cartageavailable
Owner: R Winsky
rtaylor@ctw-co.com
Number Employees: 50-99
Types of products warehoused:
   Non-perishable food items, machinery, paper products, etc., non-perishables
Services Provided:
   Computerized inventory, EDI, cross docking, etc., rail siding
Storage Facility Data:
   Dry Storage Size: 154000 Sq. Ft.

52820 Continental Express Inc
10450 State Route 47 W
Sidney, OH 45365-9009 937-497-2100
Fax: 937-498-2155
www.continentalexpressinc.com
Transportation firm providing local, short and long haul trucking; warehouse providing storage for frozen foods, groceries and produce
President: Russell Gottemoeller
russ@ceioh.com
Maintenance Supervisor: Doug Subler
Sales: Susan Shaffer
Recruiting: David Caig
Operations Director: David Treadway
Number Employees: 100-249
Types of products warehoused:
   frozen goods, canned foods, general merchandise
Services Provided:
   trucking

52821 Cornwall Warehousing
PO Box 894
Cornwall, ON K6H 5T7
Canada 613-933-1003
Fax: 613-938-9772
denis@cornwallwarehousing.com
Warehouse providing dry storage for general merchandise and groceries; rail siding services available
President: William Kaneb
Marketing Director: Denis Lemiewe
Number Employees: 19
Square Footage: 4000000
Type of Packaging: Bulk
Types of products warehoused:
   Groceries, dry goods, non-perishables, general merchandise
Services Provided:
   import/export, cross-dock,, rail siding, trucking, labeling, pick and pack, repackaging
Storage Facility Data:
   Dry Storage Size: 500000 Sq. Ft.

52822 Cotter Merchandise Storage Co
1564 Firestone Pkwy
1564 Firestone Pkwy
Akron, OH 44301-1626 330-773-9177
Fax: 330-773-8034
Warehouse providing dry storage for general commodities, plastics, chemicals, etc.; other services include liquid and dry bulk transfer and packaging of plastic pallets
President: Chris Geib
Finance Executive: Tonya Bridgeland
Controller: John White
Manager: Gary Medvetz
gmedvetz@cotterwhse.com
Estimated Sales: $5-10 Million
Number Employees: 20-49
Type of Packaging: Bulk
Types of products warehoused:
   General commodities, plastics, chemicals, etc., general merchandise
Services Provided:
   Liquid & dry bulk transfer, packaging of plastic pallets
Storage Facility Data:
   Dry Storage Size: 530000 Sq. Ft.

52823 Cranston Air
5800 Tunnel Road
Charlotte, NC 28208 704-359-8282
Warehouse providing dry storage of nonperishable food items; transportation broker offering freight forwarding
Estimated Sales: $2.5-5 Million
Number Employees: 10-19
Parent Co: Cranston Printworks
Types of products warehoused:
   Non-perishable food items, non-perishables
Services Provided:
   Transportation brokerage & freight forwarding
Storage Facility Data:
   Dry Storage Size: 7500 Sq. Ft.

52824 Crate & Fly
26986 Trolley Industrial Drive
Taylor, MI 48180 313-295-3390
  800-777-1070
Warehouse providing dry storage of nonperishable food items; transportation broker offering freight forwarding
Number Employees: 50-99
Types of products warehoused:
   Non-perishable food items, non-perishables
Services Provided:
   Transportation brokerage & freight forwarding

52825 Crescent
9817 Crescent Park Dr
West Chester, OH 45069-4870 513-759-7000
Fax: 513-759-7001 info@crescentpark.com
www.crescentpark.com
Warehouse providing storage for household goods, and general merchandise
President & CEO: Chris Taylor
ctaylor@crescentpark.com
Number Employees: 250-499
Square Footage: 4000000
Parent Co: Taylor Warehouse Corporation
Type of Packaging: Food Service
Other Locations:
   North Aurora, IL
   Mason City, IA
   Cincinnati, OHMason City

Warehousing / A-Z

52826 Crocker Moving & Storage Co
817 Brewster St
Corpus Christi, TX 78401-1030 361-884-3511
Fax: 361-887-6018
Warehouse providing dry storage for general merchandise and household goods; also, records storage management
Owner: Andy Crocker
acrocker@crockermoving.com
VP: A Crocker
Estimated Sales: $1-2.5 Million
Number Employees: 10-19
Square Footage: 190000
Types of products warehoused:
General merchandise & household goods, general merchandise
Services Provided:
Records storage management, rail siding
Storage Facility Data:
Dry Storage Size: 47500 Sq. Ft.

52827 Crossroads DistributionLTD
701 E Avenue K
Temple, TX 76504-5978 254-773-2684
Fax: 254-773-1899 800-626-8813
www.kiaccess.com
Warehouse providing storage for canned goods, soft drinks, etc.; transportation firm providing local haul trucking; also, re-packing, labeling and rail siding available
Owner: Melvin Maddux
Number Employees: 10-19
Types of products warehoused:
Canned goods & soft drinks, canned foods
Services Provided:
Re-packing & labeling, rail siding

52828 Crystal Cold Storage
23 Sycamore Ave
Medford, MA 02155-4943 781-391-6500
Fax: 781-391-1465
wcataldo@crystalcoldstorage.com
www.crystalcoldstorage.com
Warehouse with 2.5 million cubic feet of space providing cold storage for frozen foods; also, racked pallet positions, rail siding, rail car loading and container loading and unloading available
Manager: Michelle Milano
General Manager: Dennis Martel
Estimated Sales: $1-2.5 Million
Number Employees: 10-19
Types of products warehoused:
frozen goods
Services Provided:
rail siding

52829 Crystal Cold Storage
23 Sycamore Ave
Medford, MA 02155-4943 781-391-6500
Fax: 781-391-1465
Public warehouse providing cooler and freezer storage for frozen and chilled products; transportation firm providing rail car services and local, long and short haul trucking; also, rail siding and delivery services available
Manager: Michelle Milano
General Manager: Dennis Martel
Estimated Sales: $1-2.5 Million
Number Employees: 10-19
Parent Co: Crystal Cold Storage
Types of products warehoused:
Frozen & chilled products, frozen goods
Services Provided:
Delivery, rail car & local, long & short haul trucking, rail siding

52830 Crystal Distribution Svc
1656 Sycamore St
P.O. Box 1744
Waterloo, IA 50703-4926 319-234-6606
Fax: 319-233-9464 tpoe@crystaldist.com
Warehouse providing cooler, dry, freezer and humidity-controlled storage facilities for food products; also, LTL trucking and blast freezing services available; a total of 5,000,000 cu.ft. of freezer/cooler space, and 250,000 sq.ft. of dry storage
President: Tom Poe
tpoe@crystaldist.com
VP Operations: Don Johnston
Estimated Sales: $10-20 Million
Number Employees: 50-99
Parent Co: Standard Distribution Company
Types of products warehoused:
Refrigerated, general merchandise
Services Provided:
Shrink wrap, cross-dock, transload, rail siding, trucking, labeling, blast freezing, repackaging

52831 Cumberland DistributionServices
4500 Westport Dr
Mechanicsburg, PA 17055 717-697-5770
Warehouse providing cooler, freezer and dry storage; transportation firm providing local, long and short haul trucking; rail siding available
Number Employees: 250-499
Types of products warehoused:
Refrigerated, frozen & non-perishable foods, dry goods, non-perishables, frozen goods
Services Provided:
Local, long & short haul trucking, rail siding, pick and pack
Storage Facility Data:
Cooler Size 30000 Sq. Ft.
Dry Storage Size: 1500000 Sq. Ft.
Freezer Size: 70000 Sq. Ft.

52832 Cwo Distribution
9345 Santa Anita Ave
Rancho Cucamonga, CA 91730-6126 909-481-1600
Fax: 909-481-2213 www.weberdistribution.com
Warehouse providing dry and refrigerated storage for food products; transportation firm providing local and long haul trucking; also, rail siding, distribution, freight consolidation and cross docking services available. Warehouseservices include: 24-hour temperature and humidity controlled storage; lot and expiration date code tracking throughout the facility (inbound, storage, delivery); and perpetual cycle counting and stock rotation.
Manager: Herb Ng
President/Chief Executive Officer: William Butler
Senior Vice President: Bob Lilia
Director Client Solutions/Transportation: Dave Silver
VP Client Solutions & Marketing: Carl Neverman
Contact: Kevin Anderson
kanderson@weberlogistics.com
Chief Operating Officer: John Nutt
Estimated Sales: Less Than $500,000
Number Employees: 1-4
Parent Co: Weber Distribution
Types of products warehoused:
Dry, frozen & chilled, dry goods, frozen goods

52833 D & D Distribution Svc
789 Kings Mill Rd
York, PA 17403-3472 717-845-1646
Fax: 717-846-0414 877-683-3358
info@dd-dist.com www.dd-dist.com
Warehouse providing cooler, dry and humidity-controlled storage for groceries and general commodities; transportation firm providing long and short haul trucking; also, rail siding, packaging, pick and pack, assembly, consolidation andstripping available
President: Tanja Gray
tgray@dd-dist.com
Number Employees: 20-49
Types of products warehoused:
Groceries & general commodities, dry goods, non-perishables, canned foods, general merchandise, paper
Services Provided:
Packaging, pick & pack, assembly, consolidation & stripping, rail siding, trucking, labeling, packaging, pick and pack, repackaging, fulfillment
Storage Facility Data:
Cooler Size 150000
Dry Storage Size: 2000000
Humidity-Controlled Size: 150000

52834 (HQ)D & S Warehouse Inc
104 Alan Dr
Newark, DE 19711-8027 302-731-7440
Fax: 302-731-8017 www.wedistribute.com
Warehouse providing heated and dry storage for general merchandise and food ingredients; transportation firm providing dry bulk and short haul trucking; also, rail siding available
CEO: John Schneider
Number Employees: 50-99
Types of products warehoused:
General merchandise & food ingredients, dry goods, general merchandise
Services Provided:
Heated storage: 40,000 sq. ft., rail siding, trucking, labeling, packaging, repackaging
Storage Facility Data:
Dry Storage Size: 500000 Sq. Ft.

52835 D W Air
1120 Yew Ave
Blaine, WA 98230-9222 360-332-6413
Fax: 360-332-6106 www.dwair.com
Warehouse providing dry storage of nonperishable goods; transportation services include freight forwarding via ground and air and local, long and short haul trucking nationwide
President: Tom Wilford
tom@dwair.com
Number Employees: 5-9
Types of products warehoused:
Non-perishable goods, non-perishables
Services Provided:
Freight forwarding via ground & air

52836 D.D. Jones Transfer & Warehousing
2626 Indian River Rd
Chesapeake, VA 23325 757-545-6085
Warehouse providing storage of nonperishable and dry goods; rail siding services available.
Estimated Sales: $52 Million
Number Employees: 100-249
Square Footage: 1150000
Types of products warehoused:
Non-perishable & dry goods, dry goods, non-perishables
Services Provided:
rail siding
Storage Facility Data:
Dry Storage Size: 1000000 Sq. Ft.

52837 D.J. Powers Company
5000 Business Dr
Ste 1000
Savannah, GA 31405 912-234-7241
Fax: 912-236-5230 www.djpowers.com
Transportation company providing brokerage and international and domestic freight forwarding services
Owner: Richard Carter
CFO: Roy Austin
VP: Carol Hendrickson
Number Employees: 20-49
Services Provided:
import/export, labeling, pick and pack

52838 DCI Logistics
6085 Duquesne Dr SW
Atlanta, GA 30336 404-349-1824
Fax: 404-346-7206 www.dcilog.com
Warehouse providing dry storage for general commodities and food products; transportation broker providing local, short and long haul trucking; also, rail siding, consolidation and pool distribution services
Owner: Brenda Elwell
Chief Executive Officer: Larry Elwell
CFO/President Packaging: Joel Chase
Contact: Craig Bingham
craig@dcilogistics.net
Vice President Operations: Pat Keefe
President Warehousing: Brian West
Estimated Sales: $3-5 Million
Number Employees: 50-99
Square Footage: 1400000
Types of products warehoused:
General commodities & food products, general merchandise
Services Provided:
Freight consolidatinon, trucking, re-packing, etc., rail siding
Storage Facility Data:
Dry Storage Size: 170000 Sq. Ft.

52839 DFI Organics Inc.
711 Bay Area Blvd
Suite 321
Webster, TX 77598
888-970-9993
sales@dfiorganics.com us.dfiorganics.com
Importer & exporter of organic food and feed ingredients.

Warehousing / A-Z

Founder/CEO: Paul Magnotto
Commerical Director: Dennis Minnaard
Chief Commerical Officer: Richard Bellas
Parent Co: Doens Food Ingredients
Types of products warehoused:
   Ingredients, dry goods

52840 (HQ)DSC Logistics Inc
1750 S Wolf Rd
Des Plaines, IL 60018-1924   847-390-6800
  Fax: 847-390-7276 info@dsclogistics.com
        www.dsclogistics.com
Supply chain management company that develops strategies and solutions to help with distribution needs. National third party logistics provider with 31 facilities nationwide servicing companies in the following industries: foodconsumer package goods, health care, and electronics. Also provides: warehousing, transportation, consolidation, rail siding, packaging, consulting, integrated solutions, information technology, fulfillment, supply chain management and more.
President: Ed Bowersox
Chief Executive Officer: Ann Drake
drake@dsclogistics.com
Chief Financial Officer: David Copeland
Supply Chain Transformation Officer: Michelle Dilley
Chief Information Officer: Kevin Glynn
Chief Customer Officer: Kevin Coleman
Senior Vice President, Operations: Ken Heller
Vice President, Human Resources: Kate Daly
Year Founded: 1960
Estimated Sales: $141.5 Million
Number Employees: 1000-4999
Square Footage: 700000
Other Locations:
  DSC Logistics
  Allentown, PA
  DSC Logistics
  Mechanicsburg, PA
  DSC Logistics
  Chicago, IL
  DSC Logistics
  Columbus, OH
  DSC Logistics
  Munster, IN
  DSC Logistics
  Mira Loma, CA
  DSC LogisticsMechanicsburg
Types of products warehoused:
   Consumer packaged goods, frozen goods, Healthcare, Electronics
Storage Facility Data:
   Cooler Size 1200000 Sq. Ft.
   Dry Storage Size: 8800000 Sq. Ft.
   Humidity-Controlled Size: 1200000 Sq. Ft.

52841 DSW Distribution Ctr Inc
8858 Rochester Ave
Rancho Cucamonga, CA 91730-4909 909-483-5841
  Fax: 909-466-9684 www.dswdist.com
Warehouse offering cooler, ambient storage for refrigerated and dry food and food related products; also, rail siding, logistics planning/management and public and contract distribution services available
President: Brad Thayer
brad@dswdist.com
Vice President/General Manager: Chris Thier
Administrator: Liz Penrose
Quality Control: Don Munlon
Operations Manager: Ray Lopez
Plant Manager: Ray Lopez
Estimated Sales: $5-10 Million
Number Employees: 10-19
Square Footage: 200000
Parent Co: Thayer, Inc
Other Locations:
  Rancho Cucamonga Facility
  Rancho Cucamonga, CARancho Cucamonga Facility
Types of products warehoused:
   Refrigerated & dry groceries, canned foods, general merchandise, organic, drugs, alcohol
Services Provided:
   rail siding, trucking, labeling, packaging, pick and pack, repackaging
Storage Facility Data:
   Cooler Size 100000 Sq. Ft.
   Dry Storage Size: 100000 Sq. Ft.
   Humidity-Controlled Size: 100000 Sq. Ft.

52842 Dallas Transfer & Terminal
2424 N Westmoreland Rd
P O Box 224301
Dallas, TX 75212-4819   214-631-5047
  Fax: 214-631-2634 infodt@dallastransfer.com
        www.dallastransfer.com
Warehouse providing cooler and dry storage; transportation firm providing short haul trucking; re-packing, labeling and rail siding available
President & CEO: E John Ward
Vice President: Tracy Shawn
Estimated Sales: $2.5-5 Million
Number Employees: 10-19
Square Footage: 1008000
Types of products warehoused:
   dry goods, non-perishables
Services Provided:
   Cross-dock, EDI capabilities, rail siding, labeling, repackaging

52843 Darras Freight
2050 S Baker Ave
Ontario, CA 91761   909-930-5471
  Fax: 909-930-5483 800-892-7447
Warehouse providing storage for dry freight and groceries; transportation broker providing local, long and short haul trucking; also, rail siding, freight forwarding, re-packing, distribution and trucking services available
Owner: Rena Darras
rdarras@darrasfreight.com
Number Employees: 10-19
Types of products warehoused:
   Dry freight & groceries, dry goods, canned foods, general merchandise
Services Provided:
   Trucking, re-packing, distribution & freight forwarding, trucking, labeling, blast freezing, packaging, pick and pack, repackaging
Storage Facility Data:
   Dry Storage Size: 85000

52844 Days Corporation
P.O. Box 668
Elkhart, IN 46515   574-262-9525
  Fax: 574-264-2276 866-847-8330
        www.dayscorp.com
Warehouse providing dry storage; transportation firm providing long and short haul trucking; rail siding available
President: James Spoatt
Days Machinery Movers: Bill Halt
Sales: Randy Bicard
General Manager: Tom Ridenour
Machinery Manager: Steve Crumo
Number Employees: 50-99
Parent Co: Days Distribution Services
Services Provided:
   rail siding
Storage Facility Data:
   Dry Storage Size: 250000 Sq. Ft.

52845 Delavan Center, Inc.
509 W Fayette St
Syracuse, NY 13204   315-476-9001
  Fax: 315-474-3609 delavancenter.com
Warehouse providing dry storage of paper, food and point of purchase materials; also, distribution, re-packaging and local delivery services available
President: William Delavan
Estimated Sales: $500,000-$1 Million
Number Employees: 1-4
Square Footage: 800000
Types of products warehoused:
   Paper, food & point of purchase materials, dry goods, non-perishables, general merchandise
Services Provided:
   Distribution, repackaging & local delivery
Storage Facility Data:
   Dry Storage Size: 60000 Sq. Ft.
   Freezer Size: 70000

52846 Delivery Network
1000 Access Rd
Madison, IL 62060-1085   618-452-2611
  Fax: 618-452-8919 800-219-9248
        www.thedeliverynetwork.com
Warehouse providing dry and heated storage
President: Richard Kearns
rkearns@iwon.net
Estimated Sales: $2.5 Million
Number Employees: 10-19
Types of products warehoused:
   Dry goods, dry goods
Services Provided:
   Heated storage

52847 Delmonte Fresh
3151 Regatta Ave
Suite E
Richmond, CA 94804-6411   510-236-8968
        Fax: 510-236-2029
contact-us-executive-office@freshdelmonte.com
        www.freshdelmonte.com
Distribution center providing a variety of services including ripening, sorting, re-packing, fresh cut processing, and delivery of fruits and vegetables.
President/Chief Operating Officer: Hani El-Naffy
Chief Executive Officer/Chairman: Mohammad Abu-Ghazaleh
SVP/Chief Financial Officer: Richard Contreras
SVP/General Counsel & Secretary: Bruce Jordan
VP/Research-Development Agricultural Svs: Thomas Young
efiroozabady@freshdelmonte.com
SVP/North American Sales & Product Mgmt: Emanuel Lazopoulos
VP/Human Resources: Marissa Tenazas
SVP/North American Operations: Paul Rice
Number Employees: 10-19
Parent Co: Del Monte Fresh Produce Company
Type of Packaging: Consumer, Food Service

52848 Delmonte Fresh Produce Co
118 Forest Pkwy
Forest Park, GA 30297-2008   404-366-2112
        Fax: 404-366-3996
contact-us-executive-office@freshdelmonte.com
        www.freshdelmonte.com
Distribution center providing a variety of services including ripening, sorting, re-packing, fresh cut processing, and delivery of fruits and vegetables.
President: Mike Ford
mford@freshdelmonte.com
Chief Executive Officer/Chairman: Mohammad Abu-Ghazaleh
mford@freshdelmonte.com
SVP/Chief Financial Officer: Richard Contreras
SVP/General Counsel & Secretary: Bruce Jordan
VP/Research-Development Agricultural Svs: Thomas Young
mford@freshdelmonte.com
SVP/North American Sales & Product Mgmt: Emanuel Lazopoulos
VP/Human Resources: Marissa Tenazas
SVP/North American Operations: Paul Rice
Site Manager: Mike Ford
Number Employees: 10-19
Parent Co: Del Monte Fresh Produce Company
Type of Packaging: Consumer, Food Service

52849 Dematic USA
507 Plymouth Ave NE
Grand Rapids, MI 49505-6029   616-451-6200
  Fax: 616-913-7701 877-725-7500
logisticsresults@dematic.com www.dematic.com
Material handling, systems and management.
President/ CEO: Ulf Henricksson
CEO: David Abbey
david.abbey@dematic.com
CFO: Richard Paradise
EVP/ General Counsel: Ben Clark
EVP R&D: Jim Strollberg
EVP Human Resources: Dutch Burfield
EVP Global Operations: Robert Arguelles
Number Employees: 20-49
Parent Co: Siemens Dematic AG

52850 Denver Cold Storage
555 Sandy Hill Rd # A
Denver, PA 17517-9453   717-336-3900
  Fax: 717-336-5552 info@denvercoldstorage.com
        www.denvercold.com
Warehouse providing freezer and cooler storage for frozen foods; also, blast freezing and order picking services available
Owner: Moses Stoltzfus
President, CEO: Dave Fisher
davef@denvercold.com
Director, Technology & Compliance: Andrew Weiss
Director, Maintenance Operations: Jonathan Burkholder
Estimated Sales: $2.5-5 Million
Number Employees: 20-49
Types of products warehoused:
   frozen goods
Services Provided:
   Order picking, blast freezing

Warehousing / A-Z

Storage Facility Data:
  Cooler Size 663000 Cubic Ft.
  Dry Storage Size: 94000 Sq. Ft.
  Freezer Size: 2610328 Cubic Ft.

52851 Dependable Distribution Services
1301 Union Ave
Pennsauken, NJ 8110   856-665-1762
                        Fax: 856-488-6332
Warehouse offering dry storage for food groceries, paper products, containers, pick-pack and displays; transportation firm providing TL, LTL and CFS local and long haul trucking; also, rail siding and import/export services available
President: Harvey Weiner
Sales Director: Dick Daniels
Contact: Richard Petrone
p.richard@taggroup.net
VP Operations: Richard Goodman
Estimated Sales: $15 Million
Number Employees: 20-49
Square Footage: 5000000
Types of products warehoused:
  Food grocery, paper products, containers, pick-pack & displays, dry goods, non-perishables, canned foods, general merchandise
Services Provided:
  rail siding, trucking, labeling, pick and pack, re-packaging
Storage Facility Data:
  Dry Storage Size: 2000000 Sq. Ft.

52852 Dependable Distributors
1301 Union Ave
Pennsauken, NJ 08110   856-665-1762
                        Fax: 856-488-6332
Importer and exporter of cocoa beans; also, warehouse providing storage for cocoa beans
Owner: Harvey Weiner
VP: Harvey Weiner
Contact: Richard Petrone
p.richard@taggroup.net
Estimated Sales: $2.5-5 Million
Number Employees: 20 to 49
Square Footage: 560000
Types of products warehoused:
  Cocoa beans, dry goods
Services Provided:
  Import & export

52853 (HQ)Des Moines Cold StorageCo
800 New York Ave # 1
Des Moines, IA 50313-5500   515-283-8050
                        Fax: 515-283-8061
DMCold01@DMColdStorage.com
www.dmcoldstorage.com
Warehouse providing cold, frozen and dry storage; also, rail siding and humidity-controlled storage available
President: Deb Harmon
deb@dmcoldstorage.com
VP: Chad Witte
Sales Director: Deb Harmon
Estimated Sales: $5-10 Million
Number Employees: 50-99
Other Locations:
  Des Moines Cold StorageCo.
  Mason City, IA Des Moines Cold StorageCo.
Types of products warehoused:
  frozen goods
Services Provided:
  rail siding

52854 Des Moines Truck Brokers
1505 North Ave
Norwalk, IA 50211   515-981-5115
            Fax: 515-981-0923 800-247-2514
            info@dmtb.com www.dmtb.com
Warehouse providing storage; transportation broker providing LTL local, long and short haul trucking
Owner: Jim Dematteis
Contact: Ben Batten
ben@dmtb.com
Number Employees: 5-9

52855 Detroit Warehouse Company
12885 Eaton Street
Detroit, MI 48227   313-491-1505
Warehouse providing dry storage for alcoholic beverages, food products and general merchandise; transportation firm providing local, long and short haul trucking and freight consolidation; also, cross docking and store door delivery services available
Number Employees: 10-19
Types of products warehoused:
  Alcoholic beverages, general merchandise & food products, general merchandise
Services Provided:
  Freight consolidation, trucking, cross dock distribution, etc.
Storage Facility Data:
  Dry Storage Size: 125000 Sq. Ft.

52856 Dhx-Dependable HawaiianExpress
23803 S. Wilmington Ave
Carson, CA 90745   310-522-4111
    Fax: 310-522-4141 www.godependable.com
Warehouse providing dry storage of nonperishable foods; transportation firm offering freight forwarding
Manager: Paul Curry
CEO: Ronald Massman
CFO: Michael Dougan
VP: Bob Massman
Number Employees: 20-49
Types of products warehoused:
  Non-perishables, non-perishables
Services Provided:
  Freight forwarding

52857 Dick Cold Storage
3080 Valleyview Dr
Columbus, OH 43204-2011   614-272-6567
    Fax: 614-279-0099 dcs@dickcoldstorage.com
                       www.dickcoldstorage.com
President: Daniel Dick
CEO: Don Dick
don@capitalcityice.com
Estimated Sales: $ 5 - 10 Million
Number Employees: 50-99

52858 Dist Tech
1701 Continental Blvd
Charlotte, NC 28273-6374   704-588-2867
                        Fax: 704-588-5846
mmiralia@distributiontechnology.com
www.distributiontechnology.com
Warehouse providing cooler, dry and humidity-controlled storage for groceries, candy, appliances, etc.; transportation broker providing long haul trucking, rail siding, assembling, pick/pack, inventory records, freight consolidation and forwarding, EDI capabilities, etc
CEO/President: Tom Miralia
tmiralia@distributiontechnology.com
VP of Operations: John Moss
Estimated Sales: $20-50 Million
Number Employees: 100-249
Square Footage: 1000000
Parent Co: Distribution Technology
Type of Packaging: Consumer, Food Service, Private Label, Bulk
Types of products warehoused:
  Groceries, candy, appliances, etc., dry goods, non-perishables, canned foods, general merchandise
Services Provided:
  Trucking, assembling, pick/pack, inventory record, etc., rail siding, trucking, labeling, packaging, pick and pack, repackaging
Storage Facility Data:
  Cooler Size 104000 Sq. Ft.
  Dry Storage Size: 678000 Cubic Ft.
  Humidity-Controlled Size: 104000 Cubic Ft.

52859 (HQ)Distribution Services-America
208 North St
Foxboro, MA 02035-1099   508-543-3313
    Fax: 508-543-7408 info@dsa-inc.com
Warehouse providing cooler, humidity controlled and dry storage; transportation firm providing long and short haul trucking, TL and LTL; also, re-packing and rail siding services available, fulfillment capabilities, software wmscompany
CEO: Paul Lestan
plestan@dsa-inc.com
CEO: David Petri
DSA - Software: Lee Petri
VP Sales/Marketing: Mark Slattery
VP of Transportation /Ops: Joe Gualtieri
Number Employees: 100-249
Types of products warehoused:
  dry goods, non-perishables, frozen goods, canned foods, general merchandise, alcohol

Storage Facility Data:
  Cooler Size 45000 Cubic Ft.
  Dry Storage Size: 60000 Cubic Ft.
  Humidity-Controlled Size: 60000 Cubic Ft.

52860 (HQ)Distribution Unlimited
PO Box 98
Guilderland Center
Albany, NY 12085   518-355-3112
    Fax: 518-355-3636 Adutcher@disunlt.com
                       distributionunlimited.com
Warehouse offering cooler, freezer and dry storage space handling forest products, machinery, food products and general merchandise; also, re-packaging, E.D.I., distribution, LTL and TL transportation services available
Number Employees: 100-249
Square Footage: 24000000
Types of products warehoused:
  Forest products, machinery, food products & general merchandise, general merchandise
Services Provided:
  Re-packaging, E.D.I. & distribution, rail siding
Storage Facility Data:
  Cooler Size 400000 Cubic Ft.
  Dry Storage Size: 8000000 Sq. Ft.
  Freezer Size: 4500000 Cubic Ft.

52861 Distributors Terminal Corp
1441 Aberdeen St
Terre Haute, IN 47804-4204 812-466-2225
    Fax: 812-466-5586 disterm@aol.com
Warehouse providing storage
Owner: Dale Hendricks
dale@distributorsterminal.com
Estimated Sales: $1-2.5 Million
Number Employees: 5-9
Square Footage: 1200000

52862 Diversified Transfer & Storage
1640 Monad Rd
Billings, MT 59101-3200   406-245-4695
                            800-755-5855
    dtsb@dtsb.com www.dtsb.com
Warehouse providing cooler, freezer and dry storage; transportation firm providing freight forwarding and local and long haul trucking including frozen/refrigerated LTL; TL; pool consolidation and distribution; cross docking; railsiding available
President: Jeremy Deardurff
jeremyd@dtsb.com
Estimated Sales: Less Than $500,000
Number Employees: 1-4
Types of products warehoused:
  Frozen & refrigerated foods, dry goods & confectionery products, dry goods, frozen goods
Services Provided:
  Trucking, distribution, freight forwarding & intermodal, rail siding
Storage Facility Data:
  Cooler Size 96000 Cubic Ft.
  Dry Storage Size: 235200 Cubic Ft.
  Freezer Size: 116000 Cubic Ft.

52863 Diversified Transfer & Storage
1640 Monad Rd
Billings, MT 59101-3200   406-245-4695
    Fax: 303-298-9804   800-755-5855
                        www.dtsb.com
President: Jeremy Deardurff
jeremyd@dtsb.com
Manager: Dave Wood
Estimated Sales: Less Than $500,000
Number Employees: 1-4

52864 Dixie Warehouse Services
PO Box 36158
Louisville, KY 40233-6158   502-368-6564
                        Fax: 502-366-6133
Warehouse providing cooler, dry, heated and humidity-controlled storage for groceries and industrial products; rail siding, trucking and pooling services available; freight consolidation; bar coding and scanning; inventory management.
President: Don Smith
VP/Marketing: Rick Staab
Estimated Sales: $10-20 Million
Number Employees: 250-499
Square Footage: 6000000
Types of products warehoused:
  Groceries & industrial products
Services Provided:
  Freight consolidation, pool distribution, bar code, scan, EDI, rail siding

Warehousing / A-Z

52865 Doc's Transfer & Warehouse
2620 13th Street Ensley
Birmingham, AL 35208-1106   205-783-6060
   Fax: 205-783-6090 www.givens.com
Warehouse providing dry and humidity-controlled storage for dry goods, etc.; transportation services include local cartage, freight consolidation, local and short haul trucking; rail siding available
Owner: Ed Willis
docstransfer@aol.com
Director Operations: John Carroll
Estimated Sales: $3-5 Million
Number Employees: 10-19
Square Footage: 800000
Types of products warehoused:
   Dry goods & business forms, dry goods, non-perishables, canned foods, general merchandise
Services Provided:
   Freight consolidation, local cartage & trucking, rail siding, trucking, packaging, pick and pack, repackaging, paper
Storage Facility Data:
   Dry Storage Size: 244000 Sq. Ft.
   Humidity-Controlled Size: 13000 Sq. Ft.

52866 Dominex
P.O.Box 5069
St Augustine, FL 32085   904-810-2132
   Fax: 904-810-9852 sales@dominexeggplant.com
   www.dominexeggplant.com
Eggplant cutlets and appetizers; including peeled, breaded, battered, deep fried and IQF. All natural fully cooked breaded in italian crumbs, eggplant appetizers and cutlets
President: John McGarvey
Director- Sales and Marketing: Miranda Chalke
chalke@dominexeggplant.com
Estimated Sales: 10-19
Number Employees: 50-99
Number of Brands: 10
Number of Products: 145
Type of Packaging: Food Service, Private Label, Bulk

52867 Dreisbach Enterprises
500 34th St
Richmond, CA 94805   510-233-9970
   Fax: 510-233-9982 info@dreisbach.com
   www.dreisbach.com
Chief Executive Officer: Lance Larsen
Chief Financial Officer: BRIAN VINCHUR
Senior Vice President - Sales & Marketin: TIM SMITH
Estimated Sales: $ 5 - 10 Million
Number Employees: 10-19
Square Footage: 1200
Parent Co: Millard Refrigerated Services

52868 Dreisbach Enterprises Inc
2530 E 11th St
P O Box 7509
Oakland, CA 94601-1425   510-533-6600
   Fax: 510-533-7468 info@dreisbach.com
   www.dreisbach.com
Warehouse offering cooler and freezer storage of refrigerated and frozen foods; transportation broker providing trucking services
President: Jason Dreisbach
jason@dreisbach.com
Chief Financial Officer: Doretta Carrion
General Manager: John Pienta
Vice President of Sales: Val Nunes
Vice President of Operations: John Swinnerton
Estimated Sales: $1-2.5 Million
Number Employees: 250-499
Types of products warehoused:
   Refrigerated & frozen foods, non-perishables
Services Provided:
   Transportation brokerage

52869 Dreisbach Enterprises Inc
2530 E 11th St
P.O. Box 7509
Oakland, CA 94601-1425   510-533-6600
   Fax: 510-533-7468 info@dreisbach.com
   www.dreisbach.com
President: Jason Dreisbach
jason@dreisbach.com
Chief Financial Officer: BRIAN VINCHUR
Senior Vice President - Sales & Marketin: TIM SMITH
Estimated Sales: $ 1 - 3 Million
Number Employees: 250-499
Square Footage: 2037
Parent Co: Millard Refrigerated Services

52870 Dreisbach-Hilltop
2530 East 11th Street
P.O. Box 7509
Oakland, CA 94601   510-533-6600
   Fax: 510-534-2316 info@dreisbach.com
   www.dreisbach.com
President: Jason Dreisbach
Chief Financial Officer: Doretta Carrion
Vice President of Sales: Val Nunes
VP of Operations and Logistics: John Swinnerton
Estimated Sales: $ 1 - 3 Million
Number Employees: 20-49

52871 (HQ)Dri View Mfg Co
3214 E Blue Lick Rd
Shepherdsville, KY 40165-7459   502-957-2700
   Fax: 502-957-2720 www.driview.com
Warehouse handling promotional material; fulfillment and special packaging services available
Owner: Williaml Roederer
VP: Paul Andriot
Sales: Jeff Durbin
wroederer@johnstonplants.com
Estimated Sales: $5-10 Million
Number Employees: 20-49
Square Footage: 2000000
Types of products warehoused:
   Promotional material
Services Provided:
   Fulfillment & special packaging

52872 Dried Ingredients, LLC.
9010 NW 105th Way
Miami, FL 33178   786-999-8499
   Fax: 888-893-6595 info@driedingredients.com
   www.driedingredients.com
Maufacturer of organic, precooked pulses (beans, lentils, peas); also teas, tea ingredients, herbs, spices, essential oils & dried vegetables. Provide product development & logistics services.
President: Armin Dilles
armin.dilles@driedingredients.com
Sales Manager: Maria Rosello
Parent Co: Dried Ingredients GmbH
Type of Packaging: Food Service, Bulk

52873 Dunagan Warehouse Corp
1507 Webber St
P.O. Box 151607
Lufkin, TX 75904-2698   936-637-6277
   Fax: 936-639-1371 ronnie@dunagan.net
   www.dunagan.net
Warehouse providing cooler, freezer and dry storage of perishable and nonperishable food items; transportation firm providing short haul trucking; rail siding, re-packing and labeling available
President and General Manager: Ronnie Robinson
Number Employees: 10-19
Square Footage: 400000
Types of products warehoused:
   Perishable & non-perishable food items, non-perishables
Services Provided:
   Trucking, re-packing & labeling, rail siding
Storage Facility Data:
   Cooler Size 40000 Cubic Ft.
   Dry Storage Size: 70000 Cubic Ft.
   Freezer Size: 555000 Cubic Ft.

52874 (HQ)EPT Warehouses
PO Box 9248
El Paso, TX 79995-9248   915-772-2758
   Fax: 915-772-9791
Public warehouse provinding cooler, freezer and dry storage for nonfood and food items, ice cream, epoxy and food supplements; transportation firm providing local haul trucking; also, rail siding services are available
CEO: Angle Jackuac
Estimated Sales: $10-20 Million
Number Employees: 50-99
Types of products warehoused:
   Non-foods & food items, epoxy & food supplements, frozen goods
Services Provided:
   Local haul trucking, rail siding, trucking

52875 Earth Science
475 N Sheridan St
Corona, CA 92880   951-371-7565
   Fax: 909-371-0509
Vitamin C products
President: Kristine Schoenauer
VP: Michael Rutledge
Contract Sales Manager: Diane Smart
Contact: Sergio Aguirre
saguirre@cosmedxscience.com
Number Employees: 100-249
Square Footage: 160000
Type of Packaging: Consumer, Bulk

52876 East Coast Warehouse & Distr
1140 Polaris St
Elizabeth, NJ 07201-2905   908-351-2800
   Fax: 908-838-9068 www.eastcoastwarehouse.com
Warehouse providing cooler, dry and humidity-controlled storage; transportation firm providing LTL and TL local haul trucking; also, rail siding, pier drayage, break-bulk, co-manufacturing, cross dock and reefers available; U.S.customs exam site
President: Marc Lebovitz
Contact: Beth Lebovitz
Estimated Sales: $20-50 Million
Number Employees: 1-4
Square Footage: 3000000
Parent Co: Romark Logistics
Types of products warehoused:
   Confectionery, beverages, pharmaceuticals & groceries
Services Provided:
   Trucking, bulk-break, co-manufacturing, cross dock, etc., rail siding
Storage Facility Data:
   Cooler Size 500000 Sq. Ft.
   Dry Storage Size: 500000 Sq. Ft.
   Humidity-Controlled Size: 2000000 Sq. Ft.

52877 Eastern Distribution Inc
1502 Antioch Church Rd
Greenville, SC 29605-6108   864-277-2800
   Fax: 864-277-0372
   info@easterndistributioninc.com
   www.easterndistributioninc.com
Warehouse providing dry storage for food and general commodities; transportation firm providing LTL and TL local haul trucking; also, rail siding and loose cartage services available
President: Terry Smith
Estimated Sales: $20-50 Million
Number Employees: 5-9
Square Footage: 750000
Types of products warehoused:
   Food & general commodities, general merchandise
Services Provided:
   Local haul trucking: loose cartage, rail siding
Storage Facility Data:
   Dry Storage Size: 750000 Sq. Ft.

52878 Ecs Warehouse
2381 Fillmore Ave
Buffalo, NY 14214-2129   716-833-7380
   Fax: 716-833-7386 permerling@emerfood.com
   www.ecswarehouse.com
A warehouse that understands your needs. Frozen, dry, refrigerated warehouse on Canadian border, within 500 miles of 70% of the entire Canadian population and 55% of the entire USA population. Services include: pick & pack, crossdocking, express service, repacking, distribution, TL & LTL, rail, consolidation, salvage, quick access to NYC, Boston, D.C., Cleveland, Buffalo, Toronto, Rockland, Syracuse, Detroit and Cincinnati. If you have special product needs, call us.
CEO: Peter Emerling
pemerling@emerfood.com
Number Employees: 10-19
Square Footage: 500000
Type of Packaging: Bulk
Types of products warehoused:
   dry goods, non-perishables, frozen goods, produce, canned foods, general merchandise
Services Provided:
   labeling, packaging, pick and pack, repackaging
Storage Facility Data:
   Cooler Size 200000 c
   Dry Storage Size: 3000000 c
   Freezer Size: 300000 c

Warehousing / A-Z

52879 Ellis KARR & Co Inc
1975 Linden Blvd # 205
Elmont, NY 11003-4004
347-632-1500
Fax: 516-285-4131 www.karrellis.com
Warehouse providng cooler, freezer and dry storage; transportation firm providing international and domestic freight forwarding services via air and ocean freight, long, local and short haul trucking
President: Raymond J Walsh
rwalsh@karrellis.com
VP: Timothy R Marshall
VP Sales: Tim Marshall
Estimated Sales: $10-20 Million
Number Employees: 5-9
Types of products warehoused:
   Dry, frozen & refrigerated foods, dry goods, frozen goods
Services Provided:
   International & domestic freight forwarding

52880 Elmwood Warehousing Co
1800 Elmwood Ave
Buffalo, NY 14207-2410
716-874-2765
Fax: 716-874-4273
www.elmwoodwarehousing.com
Warehouse providing cooler, freezer and dry storage
President: Glenn Bailey
elmwoodwhse@aol.com
Estimated Sales: Less Than $500,000
Number Employees: 5-9
Square Footage: 500000
Types of products warehoused:
   dry goods, non-perishables, frozen goods, canned foods, general merchandise
Storage Facility Data:
   Cooler Size 8000
   Dry Storage Size: 100000
   Freezer Size: 8000 Cubic Ft.

52881 Elston Richards Warehouse
3733 Patterson Ave SE
Grand Rapids, MI 49512-4024
616-942-2130
Fax: 616-942-7457
Contract and public warehouse offering dry storage for food products, general commodities and appliances; rail siding available
President: J Holmes
VP Operations: Mark Anderson
Estimated Sales: Less Than $500,000
Number Employees: 1-4
Square Footage: 1960000
Other Locations:
   Anderson 388,000 Sq Ft, IN
   Starr 163,600 Sq Ft, SC
   Kent 128,000 Sq Ft, WAStarr 163,600 Sq Ft
Types of products warehoused:
   Food products, general commodities & appliances, general merchandise
Services Provided:
   Contract & public warehousing, transportation management, etc., rail siding, labeling, repackaging
Storage Facility Data:
   Dry Storage Size: 980000 Sq. Ft.

52882 Emerling International Foods
2381 Fillmore Ave
Suite 1
Buffalo, NY 14214-2197
716-833-7381
Fax: 716-833-7386 pemerling@emerfood.com
www.emerlinginternational.com
Bulk ingredients including: Fruits & Vegetables; Juice Concentrates; Herbs & Spices; Oils & Vinegars; Flavors & Colors; Honey & Molasses. Also produces pure maple syrup.
President: J Emerling
jemerling@emerfood.com
Sales: Peter Emerling
Public Relations: Jenn Burke
Year Founded: 1988
Estimated Sales: $10-20 Million
Number Employees: 20-49
Square Footage: 500000

52883 Empire Cold Storage
1327 N Oak St
Spokane, WA 99201-2892
509-328-2070
Fax: 509-328-7164
empirecoldstorage@comcast.net
Warehouse providing cooler, freezer and dry storage for food and packaged ice; also, rail siding, quick freezing and local delivery available
Owner: Ron F Plummer
empirecoldstorage@comcast.net
Warehouse Manager: B Figy
Estimated Sales: Less Than $500,000
Number Employees: 1-4
Square Footage: 260000
Types of products warehoused:
   Refrigerated food & packaged ice, frozen goods
Services Provided:
   Local delivery, rail siding, blast freezing
Storage Facility Data:
   Cooler Size 60000 Cubic Ft.
   Dry Storage Size: 4800 Sq. Ft.
   Freezer Size: 710000 Cubic Ft.

52884 Emporia Cold Storage Co
2601 W 6th Ave
Emporia, KS 66801-6333
620-343-8010
Fax: 620-342-7368
Warehouse providing freezer storage; rail siding available
Manager: Ken Howell
Manager: Greg Davis
davisg@tyson.com
Manager (Freezer): Ken Howell
Estimated Sales: $2.5-5 Million
Number Employees: 20-49
Square Footage: 140000
Parent Co: IBP
Types of products warehoused:
   Refrigerated
Services Provided:
   rail siding
Storage Facility Data:
   Freezer Size: 800000 Cubic Ft.

52885 Englund Equipment Co
11498 W Buckeye Rd
Avondale, AZ 85323-6911
623-936-3365
Fax: 623-936-6216 800-528-4075
englunddispatch@qwestoffice.net
Transportation, contract company and broker providing local, long and shorthaul trucking; serving regionally/locally and nationwide
Owner: Bill Englund
benglund1@qwestoffice.net
Number Employees: 5-9
Types of products warehoused:
   dry goods, non-perishables, general merchandise
Services Provided:
   trucking
Storage Facility Data:
   Dry Storage Size: 25000 Sq. Ft.

52886 Equity Cooperative Exchange
2186 Railroad Ave
Burlington, CO 80807
719-346-0212
Fax: 719-346-9307
http://burlingtonequitycoopexchange.com/index.cfm
Warehouse providing storage for grains
General Manager: Jon Francis
Estimated Sales: $5-10 Million
Number Employees: 7
Types of products warehoused:
   Grains, feedmill, dry goods

52887 (HQ)Erdner Brothers
PO Box 68
Swedesboro, NJ 08085
856-467-0900
Fax: 856-467-5593 800-257-8143
info@erdnerbros.com www.erdnerbros.com
Warehouse providing dry storage for food products; transportation firm providing local, long and short haul trucking in the Mid-Atlantic region; also, rail siding available
President: Richard Erdner
Number Employees: 50-99
Square Footage: 600000
Other Locations:
   Erdner Brothers
   Woodstown, NJErdner Brothers
Types of products warehoused:
   dry goods, non-perishables, canned foods, general merchandise
Services Provided:
   Trucking, rail siding, trucking
Storage Facility Data:
   Dry Storage Size: 150000 Sq. Ft.

52888 Etobicold
10 Shorncliffe Road
Etobicoke, ON M9B 3S3
Canada
416-231-7239
Fax: 416-231-0968
Public warehouse providing cooler, freezer and refrigerated storage for cheese, frozen fish, meat, poultry, fruits, vegetables and nuts
President: B Comfort
Branch Manager: Tom Hayes
Sales/Service: D Newton
Estimated Sales: $500,000-1 Million
Number Employees: 1-4
Square Footage: 460000
Types of products warehoused:
   Cheese, frozen fish, meat, poultry, fruits, vegetables & nuts, frozen goods
Storage Facility Data:
   Cooler Size 15000 Sq. Ft.
   Freezer Size: 100000 Sq. Ft.

52889 (HQ)Eugene Freezing & Storage Company
310 Seneca Rd
Eugene, OR 97402
541-343-1694
Fax: 541-343-9243
Warehouse offering cooler and freezer storage for fruits and vegetables; rail siding available. Refrigerated space: 200,000 cubic feet; Frozen space: 3,800,000 cubic feet; Convertible space: 400,000 cubic feet; Total space: 4,100,000cubic feet; 10 car capacity, private rail siding (Union Pacific & Burlington Northern Santa Fe); 16 enclosed truck bays; 2 outside truck bays. Temperature range of -18F to 40F.
President: Peter Lafferty
Contact: Marc Bickley
marc@snotemp.com
Plant Manager: Jerry Honea
Estimated Sales: $1-2.5 Million
Number Employees: 10-19
Other Locations:
   Albany 7 Million Cu Ft, OR
Types of products warehoused:
   Frozen fruits & vegetables, frozen goods
Services Provided:
   rail siding, blast freezing

52890 Eureka Ice & Cold Storage Company
12 Waterfront Dr
Eureka, CA 95501-0368
707-443-5663
Fax: 707-443-6481
http://eurekaice.com/index.html
Warehouse providing freezer and cooler storage and a manufacturer of ice. Eureka Ice also offers Blast Freezing, a quick freezing of up to 80 tons of product in a short time.
Manager: Tom Devere
Manager: Tom Devero
Estimated Sales: $2.5-5 Million
Number Employees: 5-9
Square Footage: 140000
Services Provided:
   rail siding
Storage Facility Data:
   Freezer Size: 372000

52891 Evans Delivery Company
PO Box 268
Pottsville, PA 17901
570-385-9048
Fax: 570-385-9058 www.evansdelivery.com
Warehouse providing dry storage for frozen foods and dried milk products; transportation firm providing local, short and long haul trucking and shipping; also, re-packing and loading available
Owner: Albert L Evans Jr
Contact: Mike Beatty
mike.beatty@evansdelivery.com
Number Employees: 10-19
Types of products warehoused:
   Frozen foods & dried milk products, dry goods, frozen goods
Services Provided:
   Re-packing, loading & trucking
Storage Facility Data:
   Dry Storage Size: 200000 Sq. Ft.

52892 (HQ)Evans Distribution Systems
18765 Seaway Dr
Melvindale, MI 48122-1954
313-388-3200
Fax: 313-388-0136 www.evansdist.com

Warehousing / A-Z

Warehouse providing 1,459,600 Sq Ft of dry, cooler and freezer storage; transportation firm providing long and short haul trucking
President: John A Evans
jevans@evansdist.com
VP Finance: Patrick LaFave
Estimated Sales: $20-50 Million
Number Employees: 500-999
Square Footage: 409600
Parent Co: Evans Distribution Systems
Type of Packaging: Consumer, Food Service, Private Label, Bulk
Other Locations:
  Mt. Elliott
  Detroit 60,000 Sq Ft, MI
  Fort Street
  Detroit 600,000 Sq Ft, MI
  Howell 118,000 Sq Ft, MI
  Norfolk 90,000 Sq Ft, VA
  Boston 182,000 Sq Ft, MAMt. ElliottDetroit 600,000 Sq Ft
Types of products warehoused:
  dry goods, non-perishables, canned foods, general merchandise
Services Provided:
  Long & short haul trucking, rail siding, trucking, labeling, packaging, pick and pack, repackaging

52893 Evergreen Sweeteners, Inc
1936 Hollywood Blvd
Suite 200
Hollywood, FL 33020   954-381-7776
          Fax: 954-458-5793 www.esweeteners.com
Bulk liquid sweeteners and bagged sweeteners
President: Arthur Green
Year Founded: 1925
Estimated Sales: $55 Million
Number Employees: 50+
Number of Products: 40
Square Footage: 150000
Type of Packaging: Food Service, Bulk
Other Locations:
  Evergreen Sweeteners, Inc.
  Atlanta, GA
  Evergreen Sweeteners, Inc.
  Sanford, FL
  Evergreen Sweeteners, Inc.
  Miami, FLEvergreen Sweeteners, Inc.Sanford

52894 Exel Inc
570 Polaris Pkwy
Westerville, OH 43082-7900   614-865-8500
          Fax: 614-865-8875 877-272-1054
                    www.exel.com
A global supply chain management company offering contract logistics and freight management solutions. Warehousing services include: dedicated and shared user operations; automation and sortation; temperature controlled facilities;specialized product storage and handling; cross docking and merge-in-transit; retail mixing center operations; on-site assembly and packaging services.
CEO: Lynn Anderson
lynn@securityinsuranceagency.com
Chief Executive Officer: William Meahl
Chief Financial Officer: Scot Hofacker
CEO: Bruce Edwards
Chief Development Officer: Michael Gardner
Chief Information Officer: Domenic Dilalla
Public Relations: Aaron Brown
SVP Human Resources: Rob Rosenberg
Estimated Sales: Over $1 Billion
Number Employees: 10000+

52895 Eximcan Canada
481 University Avenue
Suite 301
Toronto, ON M5G 259
Canada   416-979-7967
          Fax: 416-979-8866 export@eximcan.com
                    eximcan.com
Beans; seeds; dairy products; rice; salt; juice; spices; oil; sparkling wine; dry fruits and nuts.
CEO: Mike Mehta
Import Export Coordinator: Roxana Fotouhi
Year Founded: 1992
Number Employees: 11-50

52896 Express Air Cargo
14910 S. Figueroa
Gardena, CA 90248   310-380-6733
          Fax: 310-380- 676 800-521-5134
                    www.eacargo.com

Warehouse providing dry storage for perishables and nonperishable goods; transportation firm providing international freight forwarding via air freight and local, long and short haul trucking; also, re-packing available
President: Tom Aoyagi
Estimated Sales: $500,000-$1 Million
Number Employees: 5-9
Square Footage: 20000
Types of products warehoused:
  Perishables & non-perishable goods, non-perishables
Services Provided:
  Re-packing, trucking & freight forwarding via air

52897 FDI Inc
5440 Saint Charles Rd
Suite 201
Berkeley, IL 60163-1231   708-544-1880
          Fax: 708-544-4117 info@fdiusa.net
                    www.fdiusa.net
Canned and frozen foods; uses freeze-drying to preserve herbs, fruits, vegetables, spices, meat, pasta and fish
President: Joseph Lucas
National Sales Manager: Barbara Laffey
Manager: Terry Bliudzius
info@fdiusa.net
Estimated Sales: $1.3 Million
Number Employees: 10-19
Parent Co: Groneweg Group
Type of Packaging: Consumer

52898 FEI Co
1125 Berryhill St # 2
Harrisburg, PA 17104-1704   717-232-2310
                    Fax: 888-381-6910
Warehouse providing cooler, freezer, humidity-controlled and dry storage
Manager: Greg Shipe
Estimated Sales: Less Than $500,000
Number Employees: 5-9
Square Footage: 160000
Type of Packaging: Consumer, Food Service
Types of products warehoused:
  Dry, frozen, refrigerated & humidity-controlled foods, dry goods, frozen goods, canned foods
Services Provided:
  Import/export, meat inspection & ocean going containers, rail siding, trucking, blast freezing, pick and pack, repackaging
Storage Facility Data:
  Cooler Size 30,000
  Dry Storage Size: 50,000
  Freezer Size: 50,000

52899 Fanelli's Warehousing-Distrbtn
300 Peacock St
Pottsville, PA 17901-1122   570-622-3300
                    Fax: 570-628-4701
Warehouse providing dry storage for packaged products, nonfrozen foods, empty glass and plastic containers, film products and packaging; also, re-packing, pick and pack, trucking and consolidation available
Owner: Dan Fanelli
dfanelli@fanelliwarehousing.com
General Manager: James Stokes
Estimated Sales: Less Than $500,000
Number Employees: 1-4
Square Footage: 840000
Types of products warehoused:
  Canned & packaged products, non-frozen foods, empty glass & plastic containers, film products & packaging, canned foods
Services Provided:
  Re-packing, trucking, consolidation & pick & pack
Storage Facility Data:
  Dry Storage Size: 210000 Sq. Ft.

52900 (HQ)Farbest-Tallman Foods Corp
160 Summit Ave # 2
#3101
Montvale, NJ 07645-1721   201-573-4900
          Fax: 201-573-0404 www.farbest.com
Manufacturer of dairy and soy proteins, carotenoids, vitamins, sweeteners and nutraceuticals.

President/Chairman: Daniel Meloro
dmeloro@farbest.com
Senior Vice President: Bob Claire
Senior Vice President: Chip Jackson
Vice President: Brent Lambert
Vice President: Paul Guzman
Quality Assurance & Compliance Manager: Shakirul Alom
Sales Director: Michael Sepela
Human Resources Manager: Teresa Lauricella
Director of Operations: Frank Volpe
Dir. Product Management & Supply Chain: Kevin Burke
Estimated Sales: $20-50 Million
Number Employees: 20-49
Number of Brands: 1
Type of Packaging: Consumer, Bulk
Other Locations:
  Kentucky Office
  Louisville, KY
  California Office
  Huntington Beach, CA
  Farbest Brands Warehousing Center
  Edison, NJ
  Farbest Brands Warehousing Center
  Columbus, OH
  Farbest Brands Warehousing Center
  Carson, CAKentucky OfficeHuntington Beach
Types of products warehoused:
  Organic products
Services Provided:
  labeling, repackaging

52901 Faribault Foods, Inc.
3401 Park Ave. NW
Faribault, MN 55021   507-331-1400
          ConsumeResponse@faribaultfoods.com
                    www.faribaultfoods.com
Canned vegetables, sauced beans, refried beans, baked beans, pasta, soup, chili, and organic and Mexican specialties.
President/CEO: Reid MacDonald
CFO: Mike Weber
Executive VP, Sales/Marketing: Frank Lynch
Year Founded: 1888
Estimated Sales: $164 Million
Number Employees: 5
Number of Brands: 8
Parent Co: Arizona Canning Company, LLC
Type of Packaging: Consumer, Private Label, Bulk
Other Locations:
  Faribault Foods Distribution
  Faribault, MN
  Faribault Foods Plant
  Cokato, MNFaribault Foods DistributionCokato

52902 Farmers Cooperative-Dorchester
208 W Depot St
Dorchester, NE 68343-2375   402-946-2211
          Fax: 402-266-2101 800-642-6439
                    www.farmersco-operative.com
Warehouse offering grain storage
Manager: Ronald Velder
Cmo: Jeff Jensby
jjensby@farmersco-operative.com
Merchandiser: Mike Briggs
General Manager: Ron Velder
Department Manager (Feed): Dan Pernicek
Estimated Sales: $1-2.5 Million
Number Employees: 10-19
Parent Co: Dorchester Cooperative
Types of products warehoused:
  Grain, dry goods

52903 Farwest Freight Systems
P.O.Box 439
Kapowsin, WA 98344   253-826-4565
          Fax: 253-826-0350 800-999-7581
Transportation broker providing freight forwarding services via air freight and local, long and short haul trucking
President/Owner: Robert Geddes
COO: Becki Wolford
Number Employees: 50-99
Types of products warehoused:
  dry goods, non-perishables, canned foods, general merchandise
Services Provided:
  trucking
Storage Facility Data:
  Dry Storage Size: 50000 Sq. Ft.

Warehousing / A-Z

52904 Faulk-Collier Bonded Warehouses
502 N 2nd St
Monroe, LA 71201 318-323-2254
Fax: 318-361-9315 800-334-5176
Warehouse providing dry storage of canned goods, cereals, appliances and detergents; also, truck load handling and distribution, delivery service and household and commercial moving available.
Owner: Robert A Breithaupt
Quality Assistance Representative: Melinda Winn
Sales Consultant: Jerry Collins
Operations Manager: Donnie Foster
Estimated Sales: $1-2.5 Million
Number Employees: 10-19
Types of products warehoused:
    Canned goods, cereals, appliances & detergents, canned foods
Services Provided:
    Truck load handling & distribution, delivery & moving

52905 Faure Brothers Inc
700 State St
Calumet City, IL 60409-2044 708-868-0816
www.faurebros.com
Warehouse providing cooler, dry, humidity-controlled and freezer storage for general merchandise and chemicals; also, rail siding available; transportation services include national brokerage
President: Craig Crohan
CEO/Owner: Amy Faure-Crohan
Sales/Marketing: Dianna Gill
Vice President Sales: William C Burnson
Operations Manager: Bill Crohan
Warehouse Manager: William Franker
Number Employees: 50-99
Types of products warehoused:
    General merchandise & approved food grade (ASI inspected) chemicals, dry goods, non-perishables, canned foods, general merchandise
Services Provided:
    Transportation brokerage, rail siding, labeling, packaging, pick and pack, repackaging
Storage Facility Data:
    Cooler Size 48000 Cubic Ft.
    Dry Storage Size: 650000 Sq. Ft.
    Freezer Size: 6600 Cubic Ft.
    Humidity-Controlled Size: 32000 Sq. Ft.

52906 (HQ)Federal Business Ctr Inc
300 Raritan Center Pkwy
Edison, NJ 08837-3609 732-225-2201
Fax: 732-225-0812
arispoli@federalbusinesscenters.net
www.federalbusinesscenters.com
Warehouse providing cooler, dry and humidity-controlled storage for food products; rail siding and warehouse space rental services available.
President: Peter Visceglia
Director Marketing/Sales/Real Esate: Anthony Rispoli
Human Resources Executive: Dawn White
Estimated Sales: $5- 10 Million
Number Employees: 50-99
Square Footage: 16980000
Types of products warehoused:
    Food products
Services Provided:
    Rental space, rail siding
Storage Facility Data:
    Cooler Size 2500 Sq. Ft.
    Dry Storage Size: 4242500 Sq. Ft.
    Humidity-Controlled Size: 10000 Sq. Ft.

52907 Federal Companies
200 National Rd
East Peoria, IL 61611-2030 309-244-4292
888-483-7117
www.federalcos.com
Local and long distance trucking; Warehousing
Chairman/CEO: Bill Cirone
EVP/CFO: Randall Schrock
VP Transportation: Kyle Gorden
VP Warehousing: Jim Flannelly
Director of Safety: Nicholas Baker
Director of Safety: Steve Flick
Purchasing Manager: Tom Morss
Year Founded: 1913
Estimated Sales: $ 20 - 50 Million
Number Employees: 250-499
Square Footage: 65000
Other Locations:
    Federal Logistics
    Dallas, TXFederal Logistics

Types of products warehoused:
    dry goods, non-perishables, canned foods, general merchandise, Food Adatives, Tobacco Product
Services Provided:
    rail siding, trucking, pick and pack, repackaging
Storage Facility Data:
    Dry Storage Size: 400000 Sq. Ft.

52908 Federal Warehouse Company
3033 E Clear Lake Ave
Springfield, IL 62702-6012 217-744-3401
Fax: 217-744-3423 800-728-5123
www.alliedvanlines.com
Warehouse: 14,000 square feet; 24 foot ceiling; 4 dock doors; ground-level ramp; alarmed, climate controlled.
Manager: Frank Reed
Chairman: Don Ullman
VP Finance & Administration: Randall Schrock
VP Sales & Marketing: Jeffrey Bogdan
Type of Packaging: Food Service

52909 Fiesta Warehousing & Distribution Company
302 Tayman
San Antonio, TX 78226 210-337-9101
Fax: 210-333-1537 www.fiestawarehousing.com
Warehouse providing dry storage; transportation firm providing short and long haul trucking; rail siding and cross docking available
President: Thomas Delgado
Contact: Jerry Wright
jwright@fiestawarehousing.com
Number Employees: 10-19
Services Provided:
    short and long haul trucking, rail siding, trucking

52910 Finch Companies
1505 Telegraph Rd
Mobile, AL 36610 251-457-6671
Fax: 251-452-7220 800-844-5381
Warehouse providing storage of industrial paper and nonhazardous chemicals; transportation services include local and long haul trucking in Alabama, Florida, Georgia, Mississippi and Louisiana
President/CEO: Tommy Fulton
VP: Danny Fulton
Contact: Andrew Godfrey
acesrvpark@aol.com
Number Employees: 50-99
Types of products warehoused:
    Industrial paper & non-hazardous chemicals, dry goods, non-perishables, general merchandise
Services Provided:
    Re-packing & trucking, rail siding, trucking, labeling, packaging, pick and pack, repackaging

52911 Finkbiner Transfer & Storage
2215 N Burton Ave
Springfield, MO 65803-5292 417-866-5033
Fax: 417-866-1796 www.atlasvanlines.com
Warehouse providing dry storage for grocery products
President & Sales Manager: Terry Hayes
Estimated Sales: Less Than $500,000
Number Employees: 1-4
Square Footage: 80000
Types of products warehoused:
    Grocery products
Storage Facility Data:
    Dry Storage Size: 16400 Sq. Ft.

52912 Florida Freezer LP
7952 Interstate Ct
North Fort Myers, FL 33917-2112 239-543-5154
Fax: 239-543-2335 rfay@flfreezer.com
www.flfreezer.com
Warehouse providing cooler, freezer and dry storage for frozen foods, etc.; transportation firm providing freight forwarding, local and long haul trucking, railroad, domestic and international air freight; also, U.S. customs bondedand rail siding available
President: Robert Fay
Founder, Senior Advisor: Gordon Fay
Transportation Manager: Julie Lemens
VP: Michael Curly
Manager: Laura Fay
lfay@flfreezer.com
Operations Manager: Dean Newman
Estimated Sales: Less Than $500,000
Number Employees: 5-9

Type of Packaging: Consumer, Food Service, Private Label, Bulk
Types of products warehoused:
    Frozen foods, refrigerated foods & dry goods, dry goods, non-perishables, frozen goods, produce, canned foods, general merchandise, Refrigerated Products; Dairy
Services Provided:
    U.S. Customs bonded; local & regional truck distribution, rail siding, trucking, labeling, packaging, pick and pack, repackaging, Each Picking
Storage Facility Data:
    Cooler Size 180,000 Cubic Ft.
    Dry Storage Size: 5,000 Cubic Ft.
    Freezer Size: 1,320,000 Cubic Ft.

52913 Florida Freezer LP
7952 Interstate Ct
North Fort Myers, FL 33917-2112 239-543-5154
Fax: 239-543-2335 rfay@flfreezer.com
www.flfreezer.com
President: Robert Fay
Accounts Receivable: Gretchen Harper
Customer Service Manager: Lora Warren
Operations Manager: Dean Newman
Estimated Sales: Less Than $500,000
Number Employees: 5-9

52914 Food Link Inc
14809 Granada Rd
Overland Park, KS 66224-9724 913-851-2985
Fax: 913-851-2946 888-327-4696
info@foodlinkusa.com www.foodlinkusa.com
Dry warehouse space of 2.2 million cubic feet with land for future expansion.
President: Joe Arkabauer
joearkabauer@foodlinkusa.com
VP: Greg Huesgen
Estimated Sales: $5.0 Million
Number Employees: 5-9
Type of Packaging: Food Service
Types of products warehoused:
    dry goods, general merchandise
Services Provided:
    Cross docking/transloading, import/export, local trucking, trucking
Storage Facility Data:
    Dry Storage Size: 2200000 Cubic Ft.

52915 Foodservice Center Inc
2301 S 3rd St
St Louis, MO 63104-4227 314-773-9300
Fax: 314-773-0383 sales@fsc.us
www.fscstl.com
Warehouse providing cooler, freezer, dry and humidity-controlled storage
Owner: Marci Dornhoff
mdornhoff@fscstl.com
Director of Sales and Marketing: Debbie Gebhardt-Weissflug
Operations Manager: Brian Volansky
Purchasing: Lisa Straub
Number Employees: 20-49

52916 Fox Transportation Inc
135 Tide Rd
Tamaqua, PA 18252-4331 570-668-4189
Fax: 570-668-2099 800-922-9807
www.foxtransportation.com
Transportation firm providing refrigerated LTL, local haul and long haul trucking to eastern coastal states; warehouse offering cooler and dry storage for refrigerated products
President: Robert Fox
Number Employees: 50-99
Types of products warehoused:
    Refrigerated foods
Services Provided:
    Local & long distance trucking
Storage Facility Data:
    Cooler Size 15000 Sq. Ft.
    Dry Storage Size: 65000 Sq. Ft.

52917 Franklin Express Co Inc
31 W North
Franklin, KY 42134 270-586-3296
Fax: 270-586-3298 800-467-0897
Warehouse providing dry storage for candy; transportation services include local and short haul trucking; also, distribution services available
President: Wayne Dean
dean@franklinexp.com
Number Employees: 20-49

Warehousing / A-Z

Types of products warehoused:
  Candy, non-perishables
Services Provided:
  Distribution, long & short haul trucking

52918 Franklin Storage Inc
900 Kriner Rd # 1
Suite 1
Chambersburg, PA 17202-7741   717-264-3700
  Fax: 717-264-4049 dmartin@franklinstorage.com
  www.franklinstorage.com
Warehouse providing dry storage for nonperishable foods; transportation firm providing long and short haul trucking with EDI capabilities
President: Craig Nitterhouse
craignit@franklinstorage.com
Vice President: Ryan Johnston
Office Manager: Sherry Miller
General Manager: DelRay Martin
Number Employees: 20-49
Types of products warehoused:
  Non-perishable foods, non-perishables
Services Provided:
  Long & short haul trucking

52919 Freeport Cold Storage Inc
440 S Main St
Clearfield, UT 84015-1721   801-773-5911
  Fax: 801-773-5912 freeportcoldinc@aol.com
Public warehouse offering freezer storage for vegetables, poultry, meats and dairy products; also, rail siding, re-packing and EDI services available
President: Michelle Smith
Vice President: Stuart Smith
freeportcold@aol.com
Vice President: Stuart Smith
Operations Manager: Wayne Aladas
Estimated Sales: $ .5 - 1 million
Number Employees: 5-9
Square Footage: 640000
Types of products warehoused:
  Frozen vegetables, poultry, meats, dairy products, etc., frozen goods
Services Provided:
  Re-packing & EDI, rail siding, trucking, packaging, repackaging
Storage Facility Data:
  Freezer Size: 2300000 Cubic Ft.

52920 Freeport Logistics Inc
431 N 47th Ave
Phoenix, AZ 85043-2805   602-233-3891
  Fax: 602-352-2985 sales@freeport-logistics.com
  www.freeport-logistics.com
Food grade warehouse offering dry and temperature-controlled storage, rail siding, pallet building, recouping, pickpack, re-packing and trucking available
CEO: John F Bauermeister
CFO/ VP: Bill Olson
VP: Sharon Bauermeister
Information Technology: Chas Moore
Manager, Business Development: Trudy McCleary
Customer Service Manager: Sammi Pryer
Operations Manager: Mike Krause
Estimated Sales: Less than $500,000
Number Employees: 100-249
Square Footage: 1500000
Types of products warehoused:
  Groceries
Services Provided:
  Shrink wrap, rail siding, trucking, pick and pack, repackaging

52921 Freeway Warehouse Corp
30 Southard Ave
Farmingdale, NJ 07727-1213   732-938-2400
  Fax: 732-938-9160 www.freewaywarehouse.com
Warehouse providing storage for food grade chemicals, preservatives, etc.; transportation services include trucking of food and food products
Owner: Fred Stern
Number Employees: 50-99
Types of products warehoused:
  Food grade chemicals, preservatives, etc.
Services Provided:
  Trucking, rail siding

52922 Freeze-Dry Foods Inc
111 West Ave # 4
Albion, NY 14411-1500   585-589-6399
  Fax: 585-589-6402 info@freeze-dry.com
  www.freeze-dry.com
Freeze dried ingredients specializing in meat, seafood and protein items
President: Karen Richardson
krichardson@freeze-dry.com
Business Development: Lisa Horvath
Estimated Sales: $4.5 Million
Number Employees: 20-49
Type of Packaging: Consumer

52923 (HQ)Frostar Corporation
12 Brookside Rd
Westford, MA 01886   978-692-7410
  Fax: 617-445-1608
Warehouse providing cooler and freezer storage for frozen foods
President: C Maggio
Estimated Sales: Less than $500,000
Number Employees: 1 to 4
Other Locations:
  Frostar Corp.
  Salem, NH Frostar Corp.
Types of products warehoused:
  Frozen foods, frozen goods
Services Provided:
  rail siding

52924 Frostyaire for Frozen Foods
11100 Louis Nelson Dr
Maumelle, AR 72113-7040   501-734-0039
  Fax: 501-734-0043 kdunlap@frostyaire.com
  www.frostyaire.com
Warehouse providing freezer storage for frozen foods; also, rail siding, blast freezing of fresh products. 1,700,000 cubic feet of space; modern single story; fully racked and palletized facility; -10F to -40F degree capabilities; truck dock with 8 fully functional bays; rail dock with 2 fully functional bays.
Manager: Luke Thomas
Director of Warehousing: Kenny Dunlap
Number Employees: 20-49
Type of Packaging: Food Service
Types of products warehoused:
  Frozen foods, frozen goods

52925 Frostyaire for Frozen Foods
P.O.Box 2946
Batesville, AR 72503   501-268-5888
  Fax: 870-698-0339 kdunlap@frostyaire.com
Warehouse providing freezer storage for frozen foods; also, rail siding, blast freezing of fresh products. 2,900,000 cubic feet of space; modern single story; fully racked and palletized facility; -10F to -40F degree capabilities; truck dock with 8 fully functional bays; rail dock with 3 fully functional bays.
CEO: Steve Thomas
Director of Warehousing: Kenny Dunlap
Number Employees: 20-49
Type of Packaging: Food Service
Types of products warehoused:
  Frozen foods, frozen goods

52926 Frostyaire of Arkansas, Inc.
3504 E Main
Batesville, AR 72501   870-698-2288
  Fax: 501-268-5889 kdunlap@frostyaire.com
  www.frostyaire.com
Warehouse providing freezer storage for frozen foods; also, rail siding, blast freezing of fresh products. 1,800,000 cubic feet of space; modern single story; 90% racked and palletized facility; -10F to -40F degree capabilities; truckdock with 11 fully functional bays.
President: James Thomas Jr
Director of Warehousing: Kenny Dunlap
Estimated Sales: $2.5-5 Million
Number Employees: 20-49
Types of products warehoused:
  Frozen foods, frozen goods

52927 Frozen Storage Company
4239 Highway 52 N
Rochester, MN 55901-4168   507-285-9550
  Fax: 507-289-7327
President/Owner: Wayne Wesela

52928 Fst Logistics Inc
2040 Atlas St
Columbus, OH 43228-9645   614-529-7900
  Fax: 614-529-7912   800-758-4599
  sales@fstlogistics.com www.fstlogistics.com
Warehouse providing cooler and dry storage for confectionery products, paper goods, etc.; transportation firm providing refrigerated short haul trucking; also, cross docking, pool distribution and temperature-controlled trailers available
President: Art Decrane
CFO: Dave Kent
Contact: Brandon Anderson
anderson.brandon@fstlogistics.com
Estimated Sales: Less Than $500,000
Number Employees: 1-4
Types of products warehoused:
  Confectionery products, paper goods, foodstuffs, plastic film & general commodities, etc., general merchandise
Services Provided:
  Cross docking, trucking & pool distribution

52929 G&A Warehouses
2919 Samuel Dr
Bensalem, PA 19020   215-639-9410
  Fax: 215-639-9410
Warehouse providing dry storage for nonperishable foods
President: Manuel Avino
VP: Mary Avino
Estimated Sales: $5-10 Million
Number Employees: 12
Types of products warehoused:
  Non-perishable foods, non-perishables

52930 GMW Freight Services Ltd
Suite 2225-4871 Shell Road
Richmond, BC V6X 3Z6
Canada   604-278-9880
  Fax: 604-273-4800   877-469-9880
  info@gmwfrt.com www.gmwfrt.com
Warehouse providing dry storage for nonperishable foods; rail siding services available; transportation firm providing freight forwarding, ocean and air freight services
President: Paul Leung
Parent Co: GMW Freight Services
Types of products warehoused:
  Non-perishable foods, non-perishables
Services Provided:
  Freight forwarding, ocean & air freight, rail siding
Storage Facility Data:
  Dry Storage Size: 300000 Sq. Ft.

52931 Gabler Trucking Inc
5195 Technology Ave
Chambersburg, PA 17201-7876   717-261-1492
  Fax: 717-709-0017   888-889-6978
  bobsummers@hcgabler.com www.hcgabler.com
Warehouse providing storage for refrigerated and nonrefrigerated foods and food production materials; transportation broker providing short haul trucking, intermodal and equipment leasing services available
Cio/Cto: Chip Gabler
chipgabler@hcgabler.com
Contact: Robert Summers
VP: Harmon Piper
Number Employees: 100-249
Parent Co: H.C. Gabler
Types of products warehoused:
  Refrigerated & non-refrigerated foods & food production materials
Services Provided:
  Short haul trucking, intermodal & equipment leasing, labeling, pick and pack, import/export, shrink wrap, bar coding, bulk
Storage Facility Data:
  Dry Storage Size: 205000 Sq. Ft.

52932 Gadsden Cartage Co
600 Rodney Austin Blvd SE
P.O.Box 567
Attalla, AL 35954-3377   256-570-0051
  Fax: 256-538-1831
  mledbetter@gadsdenwarehousing.com
  www.gadsdenida.com
Warehouse providing dry storage for groceries, dry goods and general merchandise; transportation firm providing local, long and short haul trucking and rail car services
Owner: Larry Foster
gadsden.eso@dir.alabama.gov
Founder: Billy Austin
Number Employees: 20-49
Types of products warehoused:
  Groceries, dry goods & general merchandise, dry goods, general merchandise

Warehousing / A-Z

Services Provided:
  Local, long & short haul trucking & rail car

52933 Garvey Public Warehouse
5755 S Hoover Rd # 5
Wichita, KS 67215-9300   316-522-4745
                    Fax: 316-522-2213
www.garveypublicwarehouse.com
Warehouse providing dry storage; also, re-packing, pick/pack and rail siding available
Manager: Jack Brooks
Office Manager: Merv Maxwell
General Manager: Jack Brooks
Foreman: Albert Spencer
Estimated Sales: $500,000-$1 Million
Number Employees: 5-9
Square Footage: 2000000
Types of products warehoused:
  Food products, general merchandise, lumber & steel, dry goods, non-perishables, canned foods, general merchandise
Services Provided:
  Re-packing & pick/pack, rail siding, pick and pack
Storage Facility Data:
  Dry Storage Size: 500000 Sq. Ft.

52934 (HQ)Gatewood Products LLC
814 Jeanette St
3001 Gateman Drive
Parkersburg, WV 26101   304-422-5461
       Fax: 304-485-2714 800-827-5461
Wood and wood-and-metal containers, pallets, skid shocks and wire-bounds; also, dry warehousing and transportation service available
President/CEO/Vice Chairman: Perry Smith
Estimated Sales: $ 20-50 Million
Number Employees: 20-49
Square Footage: 1150000
Types of products warehoused:
  Dry, dry goods

52935 Gemini Traffic Sales
41 Distribution Blvd
Edison, NJ 08817-6005   732-287-5477
       Fax: 732-287-6159 800-613-1287
Warehouse providing dry storage for food ingredients, flavorings, confectionery and pharmaceutical items; transportation firm offering local, long and short haul and refrigerated/temperature controlled LTL trucking of food and foodingredients
Manager: Ron Williams
Contact: John Biblis
jbiblis@geminitrafficsales.com
Types of products warehoused:
  dry goods, non-perishables, canned foods
Services Provided:
  cross docking

52936 General Bonded Warehouses Inc
4001 Raleigh St
Po Box 790035
Charlotte, NC 28206-2046   704-333-0737
  Fax: 704-333-8159 michelle@generalbonded.com
                    www.generalbonded.com
Warehouse offering cold and dry storage for grocery products, general commodities, industrial products and nonhazardous chemicals; transportation broker providing local haul trucking; rail siding available; freight brokerage; andtrans-loading. Masonry and sprinklered; monitored security systems; 260,000 square feet of dry, refrigerated, and air conditioned space; food grade space throughout.
Owner: Michelle Wellmon
Vice President of Sales: Brenda Wellmon
Number Employees: 10-19
Types of products warehoused:
  Grocery products, general commodities, industrial products & non-hazardous chemicals, general merchandise
Services Provided:
  Trucking, rail siding

52937 General Cold Storage
8457 S.Eastern Avenue
Blvd B-C
Bell Gardens, CA 90201   562-806-2445
       Fax: 562-927-1755 rceballos@generalcold.com
Warehouse providing frozen and refrigerated storage
President: Ron Ceballos
General Manager: Ronnie Ceballos
VP: Kathy Carrillo
Customer Service Supervisor: Pat Landa

Estimated Sales: $ 3 - 5 Million
Number Employees: 20 to 49
Types of products warehoused:
  frozen goods

52938 General Warehouse & Transportation Company
7330 Santa Fe Dr
Hodgkins, IL 60525-5044   708-352-0754
Warehouse providing cooler storage for refrigerated and nonperishable foods; transportation firm providing local, long and short haul trucking
Number Employees: 20-49
Types of products warehoused:
  Refrigerated & non-perishable foods, non-perishables
Services Provided:
  Local, long & short haul trucking

52939 General Warehouse & Transportation Company
970 N Oaklawn Avenue
Elmhurst, IL 60126-1059   630-941-0400
                    Fax: 630-941-3557
Warehouse providing cooler and dry storage for refrigerated and nonperishable foods; transportation firm providing long and short haul trucking; import/export and real estate services available
President: James Conley
CFO: Patrick Horan
Marketing Director: Mark Ferzacca
COO: John Rouan
Estimated Sales: Less than $500,000
Number Employees: 4
Square Footage: 24000000
Parent Co: C&L
Types of products warehoused:
  Non-perishable & refrigerated food, non-perishables
Services Provided:
  Long & short haul trucking; import/export & real estate services

52940 Genesee Valley Rural Preservation Council, Inc.
Route 63 Hampton Corners
5861 Groveland Station Road
Mount Morris, NY 14510   585-658-4860
       Fax: 585-658-4874 800-662-1220
          jalcorn@gvrpc.com gvrpc.com
Warehouse providing freezer storage for food products; rail siding available
President and CEO: Jill A. Alcorn
Production Coordinator: Adam Backus
Estimated Sales: $500,000-$1 Million
Number Employees: 15
Square Footage: 220000
Types of products warehoused:
  dry goods, non-perishables, frozen goods
Services Provided:
  rail siding
Storage Facility Data:
  Freezer Size: 1000000 Cubic Ft.

52941 Geneva Lakes Cold Storage
PO Box 39
Darien, WI 53114-0039   262-724-3295
                    Fax: 262-724-4200
Warehouse offering cooler, freezer and dry storage for frozen, refrigerated and nonperishable food items; transportation firm providing refrigerated truck and van services including local, short and long haul
Number Employees: 1-4
Types of products warehoused:
  Frozen, refrigerated & non-perishable foods, non-perishables, frozen goods
Services Provided:
  Refrigerated transportation

52942 Georgia Cold Storage
503 Ship St
Tifton, GA 31794-9617   229-382-5800
                    Fax: 912-382-5803
Cold Storage
Estimated Sales: $300,000-500,000
Number Employees: 1-4

52943 Georgia Cold Storage Inc
193 Basket Factory Dr
Americus, GA 31709-8115   229-924-6136
       Fax: 229-928-2018 www.gacold.com

Warehouse providing cooler, freezer, dry and humidity-controlled storage; re-packing, shrink wrapping, bulk loading and rail siding available
President: John L Crisp
jcrisp@gacold.com
Manager (Freezer): John Crisp
Secretary: Deb Daniel
Estimated Sales: $ 1 - 3 Million
Number Employees: 20-49
Square Footage: 1800000
Types of products warehoused:
  Refrigerated & frozen foods, dry goods, non-perishables, frozen goods
Services Provided:
  Re-packing, shrink wrapping & bulk loading, rail siding
Storage Facility Data:
  Cooler Size 5200000 Cubic Ft.
  Dry Storage Size: 800000 Cubic Ft.
  Freezer Size: 500000 Cubic Ft.

52944 Giant Warehousing Inc
3090 Pennington Dr
Orlando, FL 32804-3334   407-293-1154
                    Fax: 407-293-5431
Warehouse providing dry storage of food products including baby food; rail siding services available
President: Larry Dimit
larryd@giantwarehouseinc.com
Estimated Sales: $1-2.5 Million
Number Employees: 1-4
Square Footage: 272640
Types of products warehoused:
  Medical Supplies, Grocery, Ingredients, Raw Plastics, Chemicals, general merchandise
Services Provided:
  rail siding, trucking

52945 Gilbert International
6219 Gilbert Rd
Laredo, TX 78041-2594   956-723-4308
       Fax: 956-724-3897 866-523-4308
       info@gilbertintl.com www.gilbertintl.com
Provides full service food grade warehousing, food product distribution services to/from Mexico, importer/exorter services available. Fully computerized state of the art distribution center
President: Joe Gilbert
jlg@gilbertintl.com
Number Employees: 20-49
Other Locations:
  Gilbert International
  Monterrey, N.L.Gilbert International
Types of products warehoused:
  dry goods, non-perishables, canned foods, general merchandise
Services Provided:
  import/export, rail siding, labeling, pick and pack, repackaging

52946 Gillette Creamery
47 Steve's Lane
Gardiner, NY 12525
       Fax: 845-419-0901 800-522-2507
                 www.gillettecreamery.com
Packaged food products, ice cream and frozen novelties, refrigerated foods and other frozen desserts
President: J.B. Gillette
Vice-President/General Manager: Rich Gillette
Type of Packaging: Consumer, Food Service, Bulk
Types of products warehoused:
  frozen goods

52947 Glacier Cold Storage LTD
6820 Wilson Ave
Los Angeles, CA 90001-2159   323-583-2464
       Fax: 323-586-9121 glacierog@aol.com
                 www.glaciercold.com
Warehouse offering cooler and freezer storage for food products; transportation firm providing local and short haul trucking; blast freezing available
Vice President: Rick Mc Cutcheon
glaciervp@aol.com
VP: Rick Mc Cutcheon
Public Relations: Roger Hatfield
Operations: Ernest Mogelivesky
Plant Manager: Ricardo Dinz
Purchasing: Emy Magipeal
Number Employees: 20-49
Types of products warehoused:
  Refrigerated & frozen foods, frozen goods
Services Provided:
  Blast freezing & trucking

Warehousing / A-Z

Storage Facility Data:
   Cooler Size 300000 Sq. Ft.
   Freezer Size: 1800000 Sq. Ft.

52948 Glacier Transit & Storage Inc
404 Schwartz St
P.O. Box 378
Plymouth, WI 53073-1522   920-893-6811
   Fax: 920-892-4116 866-329-0159
   knothem@glacier-gts.com www.glacier-gts.com
Warehouse providing a total of 55,000 sq ft of freezer space; 265,000 sq ft of cooler space; and 193,500 sq ft of dry space
President: Kyle Nothem
CEO: Jeff Goelzer
jgoelzer@glacier-gts.com
VP Logistics: Krautkramer Krautkramer
IT Manager: Kevin Karas
Warehouse OPS: John Ziegler
Estimated Sales: $ 3 - 5 Million
Number Employees: 20-49
Square Footage: 110000
Type of Packaging: Food Service
Other Locations:
   Clifford Street
   Plymouth, WI
   Cold Storage Street
   Plymouth, WI
   Depot Street
   Plymouth, WI
   Schwartz Street
   Plymouth, WI
   Laack Street
   Plymouth, WI
   Factory Street
   Plymouth, WI
   Clifford StreetPlymouth
Types of products warehoused:
   Food ingredients, meats & cheese, dry goods, frozen goods, canned foods, general merchandise

52949 Global Stevedoring
2035 Talleyrand Avenue
Jacksonville, FL 32206   904-355-6669
   Fax: 904-861-0392 info@seaonus.com
   www.seaonus.com
Warehouse providing cooler, freezer, and dry storage space
Manager: Cindy Hollums
General Manager: Dave Alberts
Contact: Jay Chavers
jchavers@icslogistics.com
Estimated Sales: $ 1 - 3 Million
Number Employees: 10-19
Square Footage: 640000
Parent Co: Seaonus
Storage Facility Data:
   Cooler Size 40000 Sq. Ft.
   Dry Storage Size: 40000 Sq. Ft.
   Freezer Size: 80000 Sq. Ft.

52950 Goff Distribution
1801 E Roosevelt Rd
Little Rock, AR 72206-2545   501-376-6616
   Fax: 501-376-0851 rgoff@cei.net
   www.goffdist.com
Warehouse providing dry storage of appliances, general commodities, dry goods and nonperishable foods; also, re-packaging, rail siding and cross dock distribution available
President: Richard Goff
rgoff@goffdist.com
VP Sales: Tom Hollis
General Manager: Joe Ramer
Estimated Sales: $600,000-$1 Million
Number Employees: 5-9
Square Footage: 1200000
Types of products warehoused:
   Appliances, raw materials, finished goods, dry goods, non-perishables, canned foods, general merchandise
Services Provided:
   Cross dock distribution, rail siding, trucking, labeling, packaging, pick and pack, repackaging

52951 Graham Transfer & Storage
2108 A St
Meridian, MS 39301-5909   601-693-4933
   Fax: 601-693-4931 www.mayflower.com
Warehouse providing dry and humidity-controlled storage for general merchandise, household goods, cookware, etc.; transportation services include local, short and long haul trucking
President: Roger Burke
graham1@bellsouth.net
Operations Manager: Roger Burke
Estimated Sales: $1-2.5 Million
Number Employees: 10-19
Square Footage: 200000
Parent Co: Mayflower Transit
Types of products warehoused:
   General merchandise, household goods, cookware, etc., general merchandise
Services Provided:
   Local, short & long haul trucking
Storage Facility Data:
   Dry Storage Size: 115000 Sq. Ft.
   Humidity-Controlled Size: 20000 Sq. Ft.

52952 Grane Warehousing & Distribution
1011 S Laramie Ave
Chicago, IL 60644-5506   773-379-9700
   Fax: 773-854-2265 www.granetransportation.com
Warehouse providing dry storage for dry goods; transportation services include local and short haul trucking, freight forwarding, assembly and distribution, piggy-back and LTL; also, rail siding available
Co-Owner: Allan Grane
Co-Owner: Paul Grane
Data Processing: Joe Garza
Number Employees: 20-49
Types of products warehoused:
   Dry goods, dry goods
Services Provided:
   Local & short haul trucking, freight forwarding, piggy-back, etc, rail siding, expidited services, pool distribution

52953 Gratton Warehouse Co
9995 I St
Omaha, NE 68127-1107   402-339-9993
   Fax: 402-339-0854 800-411-5877
   www.grattonwarehouse.com
Warehouse providing storage for food and nonfood items, groceries, chemical products, soap and cleaning products; also, inventory management and turnkey warehouse office set up
President: William Gratton
gratton100@aol.com
Operations Manager: Mike Bressman
Warehouse Manager: Bill Rhoades
Estimated Sales: $1-2.5 Million
Number Employees: 10-19
Square Footage: 600000
Types of products warehoused:
   Grocery, chemical products, soap & cleaning products, dry goods, non-perishables, canned foods, general merchandise
Services Provided:
   Inventory management & turnkey warehouse office set up, rail siding, trucking, pick and pack, repackaging

52954 Great Lakes Cold Storage
6531 Cochran Rd
Cleveland, OH 44139-3959   440-248-3950
   Fax: 440-248-4315 888-248-9600
   solon-info@glcsinc.com www.glcsinc.com
Cold Storage Facility
President: Pat Gorbett
pgorbett@glcsinc.com
Accounts Payable and Receivable: Daphne Bengough
Chief Engineer: Phil Watson
VP National Sales and Marketing: Ken Mossgrove
IT/HR Manager: Regina Twining
pgorbett@glcsinc.com
Director of Operations: Tom Johnson
Estimated Sales: $ 3 - 5 Million
Number Employees: 50-99
Type of Packaging: Food Service
Storage Facility Data:
   Cooler Size 4500000 Cubic Ft.

52955 Great Lakes Cold Storage
6531 Cochran Rd
Cleveland, OH 44139-3959   440-248-3950
   Fax: 440-248-4315 888-248-9600
   info@glcsinc.com www.glcsinc.com
Cold Storage Facility
President: Pat Gorbett
pgorbett@glcsinc.com
Accounts Payable and Receivable: Daphne Bengough
Chief Engineer: Phil Watson
VP National Sales and Marketing: Ken Mossgrove
IT/HR Manager: Regina Twining
pgorbett@glcsinc.com
Director of Operations: Tom Johnson
Estimated Sales: $ 3 - 5 Million
Number Employees: 50-99
Type of Packaging: Food Service

52956 Great Lakes Cold Storage
6531 Cochran Rd
Cleveland, OH 44139-3959   440-248-3950
   Fax: 440-248-4315 888-248-9600
   info@glcsinc.com www.glcsinc.com
Terminal
President: Pat Gorbett
pgorbett@glcsinc.com
Accounts Payable and Receivable: Daphne Bengough
Chief Engineer: Phil Watson
VP National Sales and Marketing: Ken Mossgrove
IT/HR Manager: Regina Twining
pgorbett@glcsinc.com
Director of Operations: Tom Johnson
Estimated Sales: $ 3 - 5 Million
Number Employees: 50-99

52957 Great Lakes Cold Storage
263 W Kensinger Dr
Cranberry Twp, PA 16066-3423   724-742-0201
   Fax: 724-742-0213 877-742-0200
   cranberry-info@glcsinc.com www.glcsinc.com
Storage and distribution for supermarket, food service, industrial, seasonal pick, commodities and ingredients
CEO and President: Patrik Gorbett
Accounts Payable and Receivable: Daphne Bengough
Chief Engineer: Phil Watson
VP National Sales and Marketing: Ken Mossgrove
IT/HR Manager: Regina Twining
Director of Operations: Tom Johnson
Estimated Sales: $ 5 - 10 Million
Number Employees: 20-49
Type of Packaging: Food Service

52958 (HQ)Great Lakes Warehouse Corp
1334 Field St
Hammond, IN 46320-2663   219-937-4395
   Fax: 773-932-0024
Warehouse providing dry, refrigerated and humidity-controlled storage; also, rail siding distribution, pick/pack and re-pack services available
President: Amy Faute
VP: Craig Crohan
VP Sales: William Burnson
Contact: Ivan Mcintosh
imcintosh@aerotek.com
Number Employees: 1-4
Square Footage: 1084000
Other Locations:
   Great Lakes Warehouse
   Calumet City, ILGreat Lakes Warehouse
Types of products warehoused:
   dry goods, general merchandise, Food Grade
Services Provided:
   Distribution, pick/pack & re-packing, rail siding, labeling, pick and pack, repackaging
Storage Facility Data:
   Cooler Size 80000 Sq. Ft.
   Dry Storage Size: 712000 Sq. Ft.
   Humidity-Controlled Size: 33000 Sq. Ft.

52959 (HQ)Green Valley Packers LLC
14322 Di Giorgio Rd
Arvin, CA 93203-9519   661-854-4436
   Fax: 661-854-0810
   webmaster@greenvalleypackers.com
   www.greenvalleypackers.com
Year round cold storage for grapes, melons, and other fruits and vegetables
Owner: Bruce Goren
CAO: Linda Leary
linda.leary@greenvalleypackers.com
General Manager: Jim Carlisle
Estimated Sales: $ 20 - 50 Million
Number Employees: 10-19
Type of Packaging: Private Label

Warehousing / A-Z

52960 Gress Enterprises
992 N South Rd
Scranton, PA 18504-1412   570-561-0150
Fax: 570-341-1299 www.gresscold.com
Warehouse providing frozen storage
Owner: Edward Gress
gnnss@aol.com
Estimated Sales: $1 to 2.5 million
Number Employees: 10-19
Type of Packaging: Food Service

52961 Gress Public Refrigerated Services
102 Hudson Avenue (#2)
Scranton, PA 18504   570-341-0970
Fax: 570-341-1299 www.gresscold.com
Warehouse providing frozen storage
President: Glenn Gress
Estimated Sales: $ 1 - 3 Million
Number Employees: 19
Type of Packaging: Food Service

52962 Gress Refrigerated Services & Logisitics
922 North South Road
Scranton, PA 18504   570-504-0191
Fax: 570-347-6922 www.gresscold.com
Warehouse offering cooler and freezer storage for food products; transportation firm providing local, short and long haul TL trucking services; also, blast freezing, re-packing and labeling available
Manager: Rich Charles
Warehouse Manager: Angelo Valvano
Number Employees: 10-19
Types of products warehoused:
  Frozen & refrigerated foods, frozen goods
Services Provided:
  Re-packing, labeling, blast freezing & trucking

52963 Grey Eagle Distributors
2340 Millpark Dr
Maryland Heights, MO 63043   314-429-9100
www.greyeagle.com
Distributor of beers and malt beverages.
President & CEO: David Stokes
jpjasiek@greyeagle.com
VP, Sales & Marketing: Scott Drysdale
Chief Operating Officer: Neil Komadoski
Year Founded: 1963
Estimated Sales: $110 Million
Number Employees: 250-499

52964 Greylawn Foods
2032 Plainfield Pike
Cranston, RI 02921-2059   401-223-3520
Fax: 401-223-3520 800-556-6490
www.greylawn.com
Warehouse providing frozen and refrigerated storage for food products; also, consignment and distribution services available; transportation firm providing LTL refrigeration services
Owner: Matt Leonard
mattl@patriotcompanies.com
Number Employees: 20-49
Types of products warehoused:
  Frozen & refrigerated food products, frozen goods
Services Provided:
  Distribution, consignment & LTL refrigeration
Storage Facility Data:
  Cooler Size 89000 Sq. Ft.
  Freezer Size: 35000

52965 Grimes Co
600 Ellis Rd N
Jacksonville, FL 32254-2801   904-786-5711
Fax: 904-786-7805 800-881-9505
HR@grimescompanies.com
www.grimescompanies.com
Transportation firm providing freight consolidation; warehouse providing cooler, dry and humidity-controlled storage; rail siding and pick/pack available
Owner: Thomas Grimes
Number Employees: 20-49
Types of products warehoused:
  Food (dry); consumer products; hospital supplies; specialty chemicals, dry goods, non-perishables, canned foods, general merchandise
Services Provided:
  Trucking, bar coding, pick/pack & value added services, rail siding, trucking, labeling, packaging, pick and pack, repackaging, Reverse logistics

Storage Facility Data:
  Cooler Size 232000 Cubic Ft.
  Dry Storage Size: 800000 Sq. Ft.
  Humidity-Controlled Size: 300000 Cubic Ft.

52966 Group Warehouse
3550 S Willow Ave
3550 S Willow Ave
Fresno, CA 93725-9350   559-265-4200
Fax: 559-265-4205 www.groupwarehouse.com
Warehouse providing cooler, humidity-controlled and dry storage for dry and refrigerated goods; also, re-packing, contract packaging, sub-assembly, trucking and rail siding available
President: Michael Goosev
mkg@americanwarehouse.com
General Manager: Michael Goosey
Estimated Sales: $1-3 Million
Number Employees: 10-19
Square Footage: 1692000
Types of products warehoused:
  Dry & refrigerated goods, dry goods
Services Provided:
  Repacking, club store packaging, sub-assembly, trucking, etc.
Storage Facility Data:
  Cooler Size 8000 Sq. Ft.
  Dry Storage Size: 415000 Sq. Ft.
  Humidity-Controlled Size: 4000 Sq. Ft.

52967 Gulf Atlantic Cold Storage
PO Box 2493
New Orleans, LA 70176-2493   504- 73- 963
Fax: 504-392-3443 800-343-6736
General Manager: Al Smith

52968 Gulf Central Distribution Ctr
4535 S Dale Mabry Hwy
Tampa, FL 33611-1425   813-837-5602
Fax: 813-831-4327
Warehouse providing cooler storage for food, paper, candy, appliances and general merchandise; also, rail siding and distribution to the Southeast available; transportation firm providing LTL and long haul trucking
Owner: Jimmy Sanmartin
jsanmartin@tampabay.rr.com
Number Employees: 10-19
Types of products warehoused:
  Food, paper, candy, appliances & general merchandise, general merchandise
Services Provided:
  Distribution to 48 states, rail siding
Storage Facility Data:
  Cooler Size 10000 Sq. Ft.
  Dry Storage Size: 120000 Sq. Ft.

52969 Gulf Cold Storage
P.O.Box 1365
Pascagoula, MS 39568   228-769-1061
Fax: 228-762-1551
Refrigeration Warehouse/Storage
Manager: Patrick McClain
Contact: Boyd Hammond
bh@jkgroup.com
Operations Manager: Patrick McClain
Number Employees: 50 - 99
Type of Packaging: Food Service

52970 H & M Bay Inc
1600 Industrial Park Rd
Federalsburg, MD 21632   410-754-5167
Fax: 410-754-3495 800-932-7521
information@hmbayinc.com www.hmbayinc.net
Warehouse offering cooler and freezer storage of seafood; transportation firm providing refrigerated trucking services including local, short and long haul
Co-Owner: Walter Messick
CFO: Al Nulph
Marketing And Sales Manager: Scott Steinhardt
Manager: Randy Hind
rhind@hmbayinc.com
COO: Michael Ryan
Number Employees: 100-249
Types of products warehoused:
  Seafood
Services Provided:
  Refrigerated trucking

52971 H&M Warehouse
485B Route 1 South
Iselin, NJ 08830   732-510-4640
Fax: 732-510-4697 800-446-4685
www.hmit.net
Warehouse offering dry storage for raw coffee; rail siding available
Owner: Charles Connors
Manager: Vince Kraus
Estimated Sales: $63,000
Number Employees: 1
Square Footage: 1400000
Types of products warehoused:
  Raw coffee, dry goods
Services Provided:
  rail siding
Storage Facility Data:
  Dry Storage Size: 350000 Sq. Ft.

52972 Hall Street Storage LLC
12 Hall St
Suite 200
Brooklyn, NY 11205-1379   718-855-3636
Fax: 718-855-0470 info@hallstreetstorage.com
www.hallstreetstorage.com
Warehouse providing cooler and freezer storage for frozen and refrigerated foods. Also dry storage, blast freezing, computerized inventory control and USDA import inspection.
Warehouse Manager: Ezra Mavorah
Estimated Sales: $2.5-5 Million
Number Employees: 20-49
Types of products warehoused:
  frozen goods
Services Provided:
  USDA import inspection, & inventory control, blast freezing
Storage Facility Data:
  Cooler Size 400000 Cubic Ft.
  Freezer Size: 1600000 Cubic Ft.

52973 (HQ)Hall's Warehouse Corp
501 Kentile Rd
P.O. Box 378
South Plainfield, NJ 07080-4800   908-756-6242
Fax: 908-757-2667 info@hallscorp.com
www.hallscorp.com
Temperature-controlled warehousing and transportation servicing the Northeast; 1.6 million sq. ft. and 75 trucks over 8 facilities
President: Bill Jayne
COO: Tom Brennan
CFO: Warren Tamaroff
Director of Sales: Salvatore LaBruno
Director of Operations: Nick Pizzo
Year Founded: 1966
Number Employees: 50-99
Types of products warehoused:
  Refrigerated & frozen foods & general merchandise, dry goods, frozen goods, produce, general merchandise
Services Provided:
  Export packing services, freight consolidation & trucking, rail siding, trucking
Storage Facility Data:
  Cooler Size 300000 Cubic Ft.
  Dry Storage Size: 1400000 Sq. Ft.
  Freezer Size: 750000 Cubic Ft.

52974 Hamco Warehouses LTD
101 Poplar St
Scranton, PA 18509-2745   570-346-5776
Fax: 570-343-6361
Warehouse providing dry storage
Manager/President/CEO: Patrick McMahon
Estimated Sales: Less Than $500,000
Number Employees: 1-4

52975 Hanover Cold Storage
52 Industrial Rd
Elizabethtown, PA 17022-9425   717-361-7359
Fax: 717-361-7815
bmartel@hanovercoldstorage.net
Freezer and Cold Storage Facility
Owner: Bill Martel
bmartel@hanovercoldstorage.net
Estimated Sales: $ .5 - 1 million
Number Employees: 10-19
Type of Packaging: Food Service

52976 Hanover Terminal Inc
201 Center St
Hanover, PA 17331-2054   717-698-1392
Fax: 717-637-6835

Warehousing / A-Z

Warehouse providing cooler and dry storage; transportation services including LTL freight consolidation, long and short haul trucking, cross docking, CSX railroad, container stripping and bonded U.S. customs; also, shrink wrapping and rail siding available
Manager: Jerry Livelsberger
COO: Tim Nicholas
timn@hanoverterminal.com
Number Employees: 50-99
Types of products warehoused:
  Groceries & paper products
Services Provided:
  Shrink wrapping, trucking, consolidation, etc., rail siding, labeling, import/export, pool consolidation
Storage Facility Data:
  Cooler Size 13000 Sq. Ft.
  Dry Storage Size: 455000 Sq. Ft.

52977 (HQ)Hanover Warehouses Inc
100 Central Ave
Building 17
Kearny, NJ 07032-4640   973-491-9204
       Fax: 973-589-1794 www.hanoverwhse.com
Warehouse providing cooler and dry storage for wines, cheeses, pasta, nuts, oils and specialty foods; transportation firm offering local haul trucking in NY and NJ
President: Dave Telesco
Number Employees: 10-19
Square Footage: 3000000
Types of products warehoused:
  Wines, cheeses, pasta, nuts, oils & specialty foods, dry goods
Services Provided:
  Trucking
Storage Facility Data:
  Cooler Size 72000 Cubic Ft.
  Dry Storage Size: 728000 Cubic Ft.

52978 Hansen Co
611 4th St
Griswold, IA 51535-8092   712-778-2426
       Fax: 712-778-2150
Transportation company providing local, long and short haul trucking; warehouse providing dry and refrigerated storage for general commodities
President: Craig Hansen
hanseneg@netins.net
VP: chris Foote
Distribution Operations Manager: Mae Brunk
Sales Manager: Chris Foote
Estimated Sales: $3-5 Million
Number Employees: 20-49
Square Footage: 34000
Types of products warehoused:
  Shelled eggs, juice & cheese
Services Provided:
  Trucking & distribution

52979 Hansen Storage Co
2880 N 112th St
Milwaukee, WI 53222-4220   414-476-9221
       Fax: 414-476-0646
information@hansenstorage.com
       www.hansenstorage.com
Warehouse providing cooler, dry, freezer and humidity-controlled storage for alcoholic beverages, candy and confetti, food and grocery products, and paper products; transportation firm providing freight consolidation and local haul trucking; also, rail siding, distribution, re-packaging, shrink wrapping and labeling services available
President: Peter J. Hansen
CEO: William C. Hansen
Vice President Sales: Steven N. Draeger
General Manager Operations: Keith Peterson
IT: Signe Schmit
sschmit@hansenstorage.com
Number Employees: 20-49
Types of products warehoused:
  Groceries & general merchandise, general merchandise
Services Provided:
  Freight consolidation, distribution, etc., rail siding, labeling, pick and pack, repackaging
Storage Facility Data:
  Cooler Size 2477000 Cubic Ft.
  Dry Storage Size: 12000000 Cubic Ft.
  Freezer Size: 373000 Cubic Ft.
  Humidity-Controlled Size: 2477000 Cubic Ft.

52980 (HQ)Hanson Logistics
2900 S State St
St Joseph, MI 49085   269-982-1390
       Fax: 269-982-1506 888-772-1197
       blarkin@hansonlogistics.com
       www.hansonlogistics.com
Temperature-controlled supply chain services including warehousing and transportation; 8 facilities in Michigan and Indiana with a total capacity of 34,000,000 cubic feet of deep frozen, refrigerated and dry warehousing space
President/CEO: Ken Whah
Vice President/CFO: Jack White
VP Business Development: Blake Larkin
VP Supply Chain Services: Matt Luckas
SVP Warehouse Operations: Jeff Frazier
Year Founded: 1954
Estimated Sales: $10-20 Million
Number Employees: 250-499
Other Locations:
  Zoschke Road
  Benton Harbor, MI
  Napier Avenue
  Benton Harbor, MI
  Hart, MI
  South Bend, IN
  Decatur, MI
  Logansport, IN
  Zoschke RoadBenton Harbor
Types of products warehoused:
  Frozen, cooler-fresh, dry, dry goods, frozen goods, general merchandise
Services Provided:
  Ice production, USDA inspection, hydro cooling, blast freezing

52981 Hanson Logistics
101 Bronson Street
P.O. Box 35
Decatur, MI 49045   269-423-7076
       Fax: 269-423-7270 blarkin@hansonlogistics.com
       www.hansonlogistics.com
Warehouse providing cooler, freezer and dry storage
Contact: Blake Larkin
Types of products warehoused:
  dry goods, frozen goods, produce, general merchandise
Services Provided:
  USDA inpsection facilities, pick and pack
Storage Facility Data:
  Cooler Size 652000 Cubic Ft.
  Dry Storage Size: 96800 Cubic Ft.
  Freezer Size: 1337600 Cubic Ft.

52982 Hanson Logistics
2150 S County Rd 125 W
Logansport, IN 46947-8477   574-753-0424
       Fax: 574-722-5107 jhamm@hansonlogistics.com
       www.hansonlogistics.com
Warehouse providing cooler and freezer storage
Contact: Justin Hamm
Other Locations:
  Hanson Cold Storage Co.of In
  Lafayette, INHanson Cold Storage Co.of In
Types of products warehoused:
  frozen goods, produce
Services Provided:
  rail siding, blast freezing, pick and pack, USDA inspection facilities
Storage Facility Data:
  Cooler Size 334121 Cubic Ft.
  Freezer Size: 2322310 Cubic Ft.

52983 Hanson Logistics
61834 Red Arrow Hwy E
P.O.Box 98
Hartford, MI 49057-8766   269-621-3118
       Fax: 269-621-2789 kcraig@hansonlogistics.com
       www.hansonlogistics.com
Warehouse providing cooler, freezer and dry storage
Contact: Kris Craig
Types of products warehoused:
  dry goods, frozen goods, general merchandise
Services Provided:
  USDA inspection facilities, rail siding, blast freezing, pick and pack
Storage Facility Data:
  Cooler Size 212952 Cubic Ft.
  Dry Storage Size: 2892540 Cubic Ft.
  Freezer Size: 3877284 Cubic Ft.

52984 Hanson Logistics
2201 Northwind Pkwy
Hobart, IN 46342   219-947-7200
       Fax: 219-947-7260
       jandersen@hansonlogistics.com
       www.hansonlogistics.com
Warehouse providing cooler and freezer storage
Contact: Jeff Andersen
Square Footage: 362685
Types of products warehoused:
  frozen goods, produce
Services Provided:
  rail siding, trucking

52985 Hanson Logistics
2875 S Pipestone Rd
Sodus, MI 49126   269-925-0091
       Fax: 269-925-6325 abutler@hansonlogistics.com
       www.hansonlogistics.com
Warehouse providing cooler, freezer and dry storage
Contact: Ashley Butler
Types of products warehoused:
  dry goods, frozen goods, produce, general merchandise
Services Provided:
  pick and pack, USDA inspection facilities
Storage Facility Data:
  Cooler Size 652000 Cubic Ft.
  Dry Storage Size: 133920 Cubic Ft.
  Freezer Size: 4555432 Cubic Ft.

52986 Hanson Logistics
1151 S Griswold
Hart, MI 49420   231-873-2178
       Fax: 231-873-3230 jkinahan@hansonlogistics.com
       www.hansonlogistics.com
Warehouse providing cooler, freezer and dry storage
Contact: John Kinahan
Types of products warehoused:
  dry goods, frozen goods, produce, general merchandise
Services Provided:
  pick and pack, USDA inspection facilities
Storage Facility Data:
  Cooler Size 488448 Cubic Ft.
  Dry Storage Size: 96800 Cubic Ft.
  Freezer Size: 5643456 Cubic Ft.

52987 Hanson Logistics
1476 Zoschke Rd
Benton Harbor, MI 49022   269-849-3336
       Fax: 269-849-3414 blarkin@hansonlogistics.com
       www.hansonlogistics.com
Warehouse providing heated and dry storage
Contact: Blake Larkin
Types of products warehoused:
  dry goods, general merchandise
Services Provided:
  rail siding, pick and pack
Storage Facility Data:
  Dry Storage Size: 12000000 Cubic Ft.

52988 Hanson Logistics
3440 Concord Rd
Lafayette, IN 47909   765-477-1666
       Fax: 765-477-6526 kheadley@hansonlogistics.com
       www.hansonlogistics.com
Warehouse providing cooler and freezer storage
Contact: Kent Headley
Types of products warehoused:
  frozen goods, produce
Services Provided:
  rail siding, blast freezing, pick and pack, USDA inspection facilities
Storage Facility Data:
  Cooler Size 7091980 Cubic Ft.

52989 (HQ)Harbor International
154 Water Street
PO Box 808
Bay Roberts, NL A0A 1G0
Canada
                  709-786-9093
       Fax: 709-786-9096
       moorsholm@hil-moorfrost-adm.ca
       www.moorfrost.ca
Warehouse providing cold storage for seafood; also, stevedoring services available
President: David Moores
Managing Director: R David Moores
Number Employees: 20-49
Parent Co: CX
Other Locations:
  Harbor International
  Holy Rod, NFHarbor International

Warehousing / A-Z

52990 Harborside RefrigeratedSvc
802 Terminal St
San Diego, CA 92101-7813   619-702-9334
          Fax: 619-702-9337 800-822-1591
fplant@hrs-sdrs.com www.harborsidesd.com
Warehouse providing public refrigeration services including blast freezing and delivery
General Manager: Frank Plant III
Estimated Sales: $ 3 - 5 Million
Number Employees: 50-99
Square Footage: 400000
Types of products warehoused:
  Frozen & refrigerated foods, frozen goods
Services Provided:
  Blast freezing, trucking, rail siding
Storage Facility Data:
  Cooler Size 60000
  Dry Storage Size: 60000
  Freezer Size: 1100000

52991 Harborside RefrigeratedSvc
802 Terminal St
San Diego, CA 92101-7813   619-702-9334
          Fax: 619-702-9337 www.harborsidesd.com
Freezer and Cold Storage Facility
President: Adriana De
ade@harborsidesd.com
Estimated Sales: $ 3 - 5 Million
Number Employees: 50-99
Type of Packaging: Food Service

52992 Harborside RefrigeratorServices
2900 Guy N Verger Boulevard
Tampa, FL 33605-6818   813-248-6996
          Fax: 813-248-5669
Warehouse offering cold, frozen, dry and humidity-controlled storage for food products; rail siding, trucking and re-cooping services available
Sr. VP: Richard Grenzilla
Contact: John Cokley
jcoakley@harborsidesd.com
Estimated Sales: $1-2.5 Million
Number Employees: 19
Square Footage: 800000
Types of products warehoused:
  Food products
Services Provided:
  Trucking & re-cooping, rail siding
Storage Facility Data:
  Cooler Size 100000 Sq. Ft.
  Dry Storage Size: 100000 Sq. Ft.
  Freezer Size: 100000 Sq. Ft.
  Humidity-Controlled Size: 200000 Sq. Ft.

52993 Harman Ice & Cold Storage
724 W Walnut St
Johnson City, TN 37604-6982   423-926-9164
          Fax: 423-926-9165 www.harmanice.com
Warehouse providing freezer storage of frozen foods
President: Harry Harman
bkeh1@aol.com
Estimated Sales: $500,000-$1 Million
Number Employees: 10-19
Types of products warehoused:
  frozen goods
Storage Facility Data:
  Freezer Size: 256000 Cubic Ft.

52994 Hartford Despatch Mvg &Stor
225 Prospect St
East Hartford, CT 06108-1687   860-528-9551
          Fax: 860-289-2295 www.hartforddespatch.com
Warehouse offering storage space and local and long distance moving services
President: Anson Mooney
amooney@hartforddespatch.com
Estimated Sales: $5-10 Million
Number Employees: 50-99
Services Provided:
  Local & long distance moving

52995 Hartford Freezers
241 Park Ave
East Hartford, CT 06108-1795   860-282-8000
          Fax: 860-282-3456
georgec@maritimeinternational.org
          www.maritimeinternational.org
Warehouse providing cooler and freezer storage for ice cream, meat, fish, groceries and cranberries; rail siding available
CEO: Tim Ray
Sales: Rosanne Medeiros
Manager: George Cote
Operations: George Cote
Estimated Sales: $2.5-5 Million
Number Employees: 20-49
Square Footage: 420000
Parent Co: Maritime International
Types of products warehoused:
  Ice cream, meat, fish, groceries & cranberries, dry goods, frozen goods
Services Provided:
  rail siding, labeling
Storage Facility Data:
  Cooler Size 25000
  Dry Storage Size: 5000
  Freezer Size: 75000 Sq. Ft.

52996 Hayes/Dockside Inc.
500 Louisiana Avenue
New Orleans, LA 70115   504-415-2664
          Fax: 504-895-4412 jbertel@hayesdock.com
          www.hayesdock.com
Warehouse providing dry storage of general merchandise, confectionery products and imported food products; rail siding and inside and outside steel storage available
VP: Jim Magee
Estimated Sales: $ 3 - 5 Million
Number Employees: 20
Square Footage: 220000
Types of products warehoused:
  Confectionery procucts & imported food products, general merchandise
Services Provided:
  Inside & outside steel storage, rail siding
Storage Facility Data:
  Dry Storage Size: 850000 Sq. Ft.

52997 (HQ)Henningsen Cold Storage Co
21435 NW Cherry Ln
Hillsboro, OR 97124-6630   503-531-5400
          Fax: 503-531-5410 800-791-2653
info@henningsen.com www.henningsen.com
Warehousing and logistics services
President: Paul Henningsen
Vice President: Chris Henningsen
Chief Financial Officer: Eric Mauss
Director of Business Development: Chad Freeman
Food Safety Manager: Sripriya Agaram
EVP Sales & Marketing: Tony Lucarelli
Director of Sales: Phil Potter
Director of Human Resources: Craig Cude
EVP Warehouse Operations: Todd Larson
Director of Transportation: Todd Lanter
Year Founded: 1923
Number Employees: 250-499
Other Locations:
  Grand Forks, ND
  Forest Grove, OR
  Portland, OR
  Scranton, PA
  Richland, WA
  Twin Falls, IDForest Grove
Types of products warehoused:
  Frozen, refrigerated & dry food products, dry goods, frozen goods, produce
Services Provided:
  Room & blast freezing, distribution, special handling, etc., rail siding, blast freezing, pick and pack

52998 Henningsen Cold Storage Co
2025 Saint St
Richland, WA 99354-5302   509-375-0463
          Fax: 509-375-1515 www.henningsen.com
Freezer storage facility
Square Footage: 720000
Types of products warehoused:
  Processed potatoes, fruits & vegetables, frozen goods, produce
Services Provided:
  USDA approved, transloading, rail siding, trucking, blast freezing
Storage Facility Data:
  Freezer Size: 4865404 Cubic Ft.

52999 Henningsen Cold Storage Co
432 S Park Ave W
P.O. Box 1659
Twin Falls, ID 83301   208-733-4140
          Fax: 208-736-8661 www.henningsen.com
Freezer storage facility
Square Footage: 1560000
Types of products warehoused:
  frozen goods
Services Provided:
  rail siding, trucking
Storage Facility Data:
  Freezer Size: 12016086 Cubic Ft.

53000 Henningsen Cold Storage Co
5200 11th Ave S
Grand Forks, ND 58201-8034   701-335-5000
          Fax: 701-335-5005 www.henningsen.com
Freezer storage facility
Types of products warehoused:
  frozen goods
Services Provided:
  Import/export capabilities, USDA approved, transloading, rail siding, trucking
Storage Facility Data:
  Freezer Size: 3958825 Cubic Ft.

53001 Henningsen Cold Storage Co
4124 24th Ave
Forest Grove, OR 97116-2256   503-359-1100
          Fax: 503-359-1109 www.henningsen.com
Cooler, freezer, and dry storage facility
Types of products warehoused:
  Fruit & vegetables, dry goods, frozen goods, produce
Services Provided:
  USDA approved meat and poultry, import/export, transloading, rail siding, trucking

53002 Henningsen Cold Storage Co
19450 NE San Rafael St
Portland, OR 97230-5944   503-489-2995
          www.henningsen.com
Cooler, freezer, and dry storage facility
Types of products warehoused:
  dry goods, frozen goods, produce
Services Provided:
  Transloading, import/export, USDA approved, rail siding, trucking

53003 Henningsen Cold Storage Co
229 Maple St
Scranton, PA 18505-1231   570-207-0219
          Fax: 570-207-0225 www.henningsen.com
Cooler and dry storage facility
Types of products warehoused:
  dry goods, produce
Services Provided:
  Transloading, import/export, USDA approved, distribution, rail siding, trucking

53004 Henningsen Cold Storage Co
1000 Paul Mead Rd
Stilwell, OK 74960   918-696-4642
          www.henningsen.com
Freezer storage facility
Types of products warehoused:
  frozen goods
Services Provided:
  Import/export capabilities, USDA approved, transloading, rail siding, trucking, blast freezing
Storage Facility Data:
  Freezer Size: 4033538 Cubic Ft.

53005 Henningsen Cold Storage Co
17400 NE Sacramento St
Portland, OR 97230-5944   503-256-2525
          www.henningsen.com
Cooler, freezer, and dry storage facility
Types of products warehoused:
  dry goods, frozen goods, produce
Services Provided:
  Transloading, import/export, USDA approved, rail siding, trucking

53006 Henningsen Cold Storage Co
2320 Madrona Ave SE
Salem, OR 97302   503-485-0720
          www.henningsen.com
Freezer storage facility
Types of products warehoused:
  frozen goods
Services Provided:
  rail siding, trucking

Warehousing / A-Z

Storage Facility Data:
  Freezer Size: 8299255 Cubic Ft.

53007 Henningsen Cold Storage Co
7629 S 188th St
Kent, WA 98032   253-867-1320
                        www.henningsen.com
Cooler, freezer and dry storage facility
Square Footage: 720000
Types of products warehoused:
  dry goods, frozen goods, produce
Services Provided:
  Import/Export, trucking

53008 Henry L Taylor Trucking LLC
1280 Nawakwa Rd
Biglerville, PA 17307-9727   717-677-6138
  Fax: 717-677-6514 www.mtvalleyfarms.com
Warehouse offering storage for groceries; transportation firm providing long and short haul trucking serving intra-state PA and fourty eight states; also, vans and flats available
Owner: Henry L Taylor
henry.l.taylor@henryltaylor.com
Number Employees: 10-19
Types of products warehoused:
  Groceries
Services Provided:
  Trucking

53009 Hermann Services Inc
83 Stults Rd # 1
Dayton, NJ 08810-3001   609-860-5810
  Fax: 609-409-9442   800-524-0067
  sales@HermannTDS.com www.hermanntds.com
Warehouse providing cooler and dry storage for groceries, general merchandise, etc.; transportation services include dedicated local regional, and short haul trucking; also packaging, re-packing EDI capabilities, assembly, distribution, and rail siding available
President: Richard Hermann
Vice President: Lisa Burke
lburke@hermanntds.com
Number Employees: 10-19
Other Locations:
  Hermann Warehouse Corp.
  Milltown, NJHermann Warehouse Corp.
Types of products warehoused:
  dry goods, canned foods, general merchandise
Services Provided:
  rail siding, trucking, labeling, packaging, pick and pack, repackaging
Storage Facility Data:
  Dry Storage Size: 750000 Sq. Ft.

53010 Hermann Services Warehouse Corporation
P.O. Box 7144
North Brunswick, NJ 08902   732-274-1794
  Fax: 732-274-1796   800-524-0067
  sales@hermanntds.com www.hermanntds.com
Array of supply chain management assets
Manager: Jeff Petersen
Contact: Dennis Hermann
dwhermann@hermanntds.com
Facility Manager: Jeff Petersen
Estimated Sales: $ 1 - 3 Million
Number Employees: 10-19
Type of Packaging: Food Service

53011 High Plains Freezer
575 Snowy Range Road
Bldg 43
Laramie, WY 82072-2461   307-742-6649
                Fax: 307-742-4856
Warehouse providing cooler, dry and freezer storage for frozen, chilled and dry foods; rail siding available
Estimated Sales: $ .5 - 1 million
Number Employees: 19
Types of products warehoused:
  frozen goods
Services Provided:
  rail siding
Storage Facility Data:
  Freezer Size: 4403232 Cubic Ft.

53012 Hillier Storage & Moving
2728 S 11th St
Springfield, IL 62703-3902   217-525-8550
  Fax: 217-525-8557   800-500-6683
  hsmhhg@hillierstg.com www.allied.com
Warehouse providing dry storage for general merchandise; also, cartage, re-shipping, palletizing, distribution and break bulk trailer services available
President: Tom Swift
tswift@hillierstg.com
Estimated Sales: $1-2.5 Million
Number Employees: 20-49
Square Footage: 80000
Types of products warehoused:
  General merchandise, general merchandise
Services Provided:
  Cartage, re-shipping, palletizing, distribution, etc.
Storage Facility Data:
  Dry Storage Size: 60000 Sq. Ft.

53013 Hodge Transit Warehouse
7465 Chavenelle Rd
Dubuque, IA 52002   563-583-9781
  Fax: 563-556-1805   800-397-8464
                www.hodgecompany.com
Warehouse providing dry storage for nonfood items; rail siding available
President: Tim Hodge
Contact: Lisa Boyd
lboyd@hehodge.com
General Manager: Michael Hodge
Estimated Sales: Less than $500,000
Number Employees: 1-4
Square Footage: 1200000
Types of products warehoused:
  Non-food items, general merchandise
Services Provided:
  rail siding
Storage Facility Data:
  Dry Storage Size: 220000 Sq. Ft.

53014 Hodges Co
4401 S 72nd East Ave
Tulsa, OK 74145-4610   918-622-3028
  Fax: 918-664-4625   888-622-3028
  sales@hodgesco.com www.hodgesco.com
Warehouse providing dry storage for general merchandise and groceries; transportation firm providing LTL, TL and regional haul trucking; also, outdoor storage, slip sheet, push/pull, repackaging, reselecting, lift gate and rail sidingservices available
Vice President: Sherry Wallis
VP: Sherry Wallis
Number Employees: 5-9
Parent Co: Port City Property
Types of products warehoused:
  General merchandise & groceries, general merchandise
Services Provided:
  Outside yard storage, trucking, etc., rail siding
Storage Facility Data:
  Dry Storage Size: 500000 Sq. Ft.

53015 Holeman Distribution Ctr
22430 76th Ave S
Kent, WA 98032-2406   253-872-7140
  Fax: 253-395-0335 m_hobbs@holmanusa.com
                www.holmanusa.com
Warehouse providing dry storage for paper, appliances, groceries and raw materials; transportation firm providing local haul trucking; also, distribution, re-packing, value added, pick/pack and rail siding available
Marketing: Mitchell Hobbs
Number Employees: 100-249
Types of products warehoused:
  Paper, appliances, groceries & raw materials
Services Provided:
  Distribution, trucking, re-packing, value added & pick/pack, rail siding, pick and pack, repackaging
Storage Facility Data:
  Dry Storage Size: 1000000 Sq. Ft.

53016 (HQ)Holley Cold Storage Fruit Co
16677 State Route 31
Holley, NY 14470-9074   585-638-6393
                Fax: 585-638-6730
Warehouse providing cooler, freezer, dry and humidity-controlled storage for produce and frozen meats, fruits and vegetables; also, IQF poly re-packing and rail siding available
Manager: Jeff Shampine
Estimated Sales: $1-2.5 Million
Number Employees: 10-19
Square Footage: 8000000
Types of products warehoused:
  Produce & frozen meats, fruits & vegetables, frozen goods, produce
Services Provided:
  IQF poly re-packing, rail siding
Storage Facility Data:
  Cooler Size 600000 Cubic Ft.
  Freezer Size: 190000 Cubic Ft.

53017 Holman Distribution Center
2300 SE Beta Street
Portland, OR 97222-7330   503-652-1912
  Fax: 503-652-1970 m_hobbs@holmanusa.com
                www.holmanusa.com
Warehouse offering cooler, dry and humidity-controlled storage for groceries, paper goods and industrial products; transportation firm providing local haul trucking and freight consolidation; also, rail siding, re-packing and labelingservices available
President: Robert Downie
Number Employees: 20-49
Types of products warehoused:
  Groceries, paper goods & industrial products
Services Provided:
  Freight consolidation, trucking, re-packing & labeling, rail siding, labeling, repackaging
Storage Facility Data:
  Cooler Size 35000 Sq. Ft.
  Dry Storage Size: 515000 Sq. Ft.
  Humidity-Controlled Size: 5000 Sq. Ft.

53018 Holt Logistics Corporation
101 South King Street
Gloucester City, NJ 08030   215-742-3000
  Fax: 856-742-3102 www.holtoversight.com
Warehouse offering cooler, dry storage, freezer and humidity controlled food storage; transportation services include re-packing and short and long haul trucking. Holt Cargo Systems provides cargo handling services such asstevedoring, warehousing, trucking and total distribution. Holt specializes in handling fresh fruits and all types of perishable commodities requiring temperature-controlled ambient care
Manager: Bill Mc Dermitt
Contact: Jb Burleson
jburleson@holtoversight.com
Number Employees: 1-4

53019 Hoosier Warehouses Inc
245 S Franklin Road
Indianapolis, IN 46219   317-897-1726
                Fax: 317-897-1742
President: Kevin Molloy
Estimated Sales: $ 1 - 3 Million
Number Employees: 20 to 49

53020 (HQ)Houston Central Industries, Ltd.
7080 Express Ln
Houston, TX 77078   713-491-0444
                              800-856-3218
Warehouse providing cooler, freezer and dry storage of food; transportation firm providing local, short and long haul trucking; also, blast freezing, distribution, re-packaging, transloading, computer interfacing and rail sidingservices available
President: Micheal M. Feld
Sales: Michael M. Feld
Office Manager/Billing: Lori Weesner
Warehouse Manager: Sean Hebert
Number Employees: 20-49
Type of Packaging: Food Service
Types of products warehoused:
  Dry & frozen foods, dry goods, frozen goods, produce, canned foods
Services Provided:
  Distribution, re-packaging, trans loading, blast freezing, etc., rail siding, trucking, labeling, blast freezing, packaging, pick and pack, repackaging
Storage Facility Data:
  Cooler Size 100000 Sq. Ft.
  Dry Storage Size: 300000 Sq. Ft.
  Freezer Size: 1100000 Sq. Ft.

53021 Howell Logistics Services
514 Carlingview Drive
Toronto, ON M9W 5R3
Canada
                              416-675-6090
  Fax: 415-674-2987   888-649-3278

Warehouse providing dry storage of nonrefrigerated items; also, E.D.I. distribution, pick and pack, computerized inventory control, logistic services and rail siding available
President: Adrian Donnelly
Number Employees: 30
Square Footage: 920000
Parent Co: Howell Warehouses Company
Types of products warehoused:
  Non-refrigerated
Services Provided:
  Distribution, computerized inventory control, rail siding, pick and pack
Storage Facility Data:
  Dry Storage Size: 230000 Sq. Ft.

53022 Ice Cold Storage
3336 Fruitland Avenue
Los Angeles, CA 90058-3714   323-584-0313
                              Fax: 323-584-9107
CEO: Marty Evanson
Contact: Benjamin Asoulin
benasoulin@gmail.com
Number Employees: 12

53023 Ice King & Cold Storage Inc
4045 State Route 33
Neptune, NJ 07753-7401   732-922-0852
        Fax: 732-922-3445   800-848-0272
             fred@icekingandcoldstorage.com
             www.icekingandcoldstorage.com
Ice Manufacturing
Owner: Frank P Lomangino
ikcsinc@aol.com
Estimated Sales: $ 5 - 10 Million
Number Employees: 20-49
Type of Packaging: Bulk

53024 Ideal Warehouse
150 Montreal-Toronto Blvd
Montreal, QC H8S 4L8
Canada   514-634-8886
                                800-304-1816
                             info@ideal.qc.ca
                             www.ideal.qc.ca
Warehouse offering dry storage for groceries and food products, rail siding available, transportation services include local and long haul trucking and local pick-up and full service of distribution
President: Bernard Pettigrew
Finance Controller: Carl Perron
Director of Operations: Nadia Pettigrew
Number Employees: 20-49
Types of products warehoused:
  Groceries & Food products, dry goods, non-perishables, canned foods, general merchandise, Paper Products
Services Provided:
  Trucking, rail siding, trucking, pick and pack, repackaging
Storage Facility Data:
  Dry Storage Size: 2400000 Cubic Ft.

53025 Imperal Freight Broker
2287 NW 102nd Pl
Doral, FL 33172-2523   305-592-6910
   Fax: 305-593-1781 sales@imperialfreight.com
                     www.imperialfreight.com
Transportation firm providing freight forwarding and customs clearance of goods for the food industry in Florida
President: Ralph Delarosa
ralph.delarosa@imperialfreight.com
Number Employees: 10-19
Types of products warehoused:
  Dry food products, dry goods
Services Provided:
  Re-packing, trucking & exporting, trucking, repackaging
Storage Facility Data:
  Dry Storage Size: 10000 Sq. Ft.

53026 Imperial Cold Storage And Distribution
7570 Torbram Road
Mississauga, ON L5W 0A5
Canada   905-672-6582
                           Fax: 905-672-6584
Warehouse providing frozen storage
General Manager: Ken Chin
Operations Manager: John Collison
Number Employees: 10
Type of Packaging: Food Service

53027 Importers
420 5th Ave S # 203
Edmonds, WA 98020-3632   425-977-2364
        Fax: 425-977-2495   800-346-0389
Transportation firm providing freight forwarding of dry freight, expedited trucking, LTL and FTL services nationwide
President: Rich Rebenstorf
Number Employees: 1-4
Types of products warehoused:
  Dry Freight, dry goods
Services Provided:
  trucking, labeling

53028 (HQ)Inland Cold Storage
2356 Fleetwood Dr
Riverside, CA 92509-2409   951-787-1936
                           Fax: 951-369-0232
Warehouse providing a total of 34 Million Cubic Feet of warehouse space between all seven locations, for freezer and cooler space
President: Paul Hendricksen
CEO: Bill Hendrickson
CFO: Randy Plotkin
VP/General Manager: Ken Evans
VP/Sales & Marketing: Len Anderson
Estimated Sales: $ 20 - 50 Million
Number Employees: 10-19
Other Locations:
  Fontana, CA
  Bloomington, CABloomington
Types of products warehoused:
  frozen goods
Services Provided:
  Cross-docking, freight consolidation, labeling, blast freezing, repackaging

53029 Inland Empire Distribution
3808 N Sullivan Rd # 32d
Building 32
Spokane Valley, WA 99216-1615 509-922-0944
     Fax: 509-927-8593 mattewers@ieds.net
                              www.ieds.net
Public warehouse providing dry for nonperishable foods; transportation services providing local, long and short haul trucking; also, rail siding, drayage, freight consolidation, freight management and forwarding services available
President and CEO: James P. Ewers
VP/General Manager: Daniel C. Ewers
VP, Business Development: Matthew P. Ewers
VP/Operations: Dan Ewers
Number Employees: 50-99
Square Footage: 3550000
Types of products warehoused:
  dry goods, non-perishables, canned foods, general merchandise, paper
Services Provided:
  rail siding, trucking, labeling, packaging, pick and pack, repackaging
Storage Facility Data:
  Dry Storage Size: 500000 Sq. Ft.

53030 Inland Star Distribution Ctr
3146 S Chestnut Ave
PO Box 2396
Fresno, CA 93725-2606   559-470-6826
     Fax: 559-237-9468 rsmith@inlandstar.com
                             www.inlandstar.com
Warehouse offering dry storage for nonperishable food products; rail siding available; transportation division providing TL, LTL and overnight service in Western U.S.
President: Yvonne Adams
yadams@inlandstar.com
Sales/Marketing: Richard Smith
Number Employees: 50-99
Types of products warehoused:
  Non-perishable food products, dry goods, non-perishables, canned foods, general merchandise
Services Provided:
  temperature-controlled, and barcode capabilities, rail siding, trucking, labeling, pick and pack, repackaging
Storage Facility Data:
  Dry Storage Size: 698000

53031 Innovative Cold StorageEnterprises
7850 Waterville Road
San Diego, CA 92154   619-671-9933
     Fax: 619-671-2435 www.innovativecold.com
Warehouse providing frozen storage space
President: Doug Gadker
Contact: Monika Baumann
mbaumann@innovativecold.com
General Manager: Doug Gadker
Estimated Sales: $ 1 - 3 Million
Number Employees: 20 to 49
Storage Facility Data:
  Freezer Size: 3700000 Cubic Ft.

53032 Inter State Cold Storage
2400 Setterlin Dr
Columbus, OH 43228-9794   614-771-6700
                           Fax: 614-771-6925
                    info@interstatecoldstorage.com
                    www.interstatecoldstorage.com
Public warehouse providing storage for frozen and cooler products; also, rail siding, distribution, freezing of fresh meats, custom packaging, USDA inspection, export and certification services available. Temperature ranges from -20F to 60F; 4,2000,000 Cubic Feet; refrigerated docks with 20 doors; Norfolk Southern with 5-car private siding; at I-270, near I-70.
President: Russell Borstelman
Chief Executive Officer: Vincent Tippmann
Manager: Kevin Tackett
kevin.tackett@interstatecoldstorage.com
Facility Manager: Mike Browning
Estimated Sales: $2.5-5 Million
Number Employees: 20-49
Parent Co: Interstate Cold Storage, Inc.
Types of products warehoused:
  Frozen & cooler products, frozen goods
Services Provided:
  rail siding

53033 Inter State Cold Storage
2400 Setterlin Dr
Columbus, OH 43228-9794   614-771-6700
                           Fax: 614-771-6925
                    info@interstatecoldstorage.com
                    www.interstatecoldstorage.com
Public warehouse providing cooler and freezer storage for refrigerated and frozen foods; transportation firm providing local and short haul trucking; also, custom packaging, USDA inspection and rail siding available. Refrigerated docks with 35 doors; 7,310,000 cubic feet; CSX with 10-car private siding; At I-270, near I-70.
Manager: Kevin Tackett
kevin.tackett@interstatecoldstorage.com
Chief Executive Officer: Vincent Tippmann
Manager: Kevin Tackett
kevin.tackett@interstatecoldstorage.com
General Manager: Ron Halm
Estimated Sales: $2.5-5 Million
Number Employees: 20-49
Parent Co: Interstate Cold Storage, Inc.
Services Provided:
  rail siding

53034 Inter-Cities Cold Storage
1075 Oak St
Pittston, PA 18640-3773   570-654-6971
        Fax: 570-655-5573 intercities@epix.net
Warehouse providing storage; rail siding and blast freezing are available
Owner: James O Brown
Estimated Sales: $ 1 - 3 Million
Number Employees: 10-19
Type of Packaging: Food Service
Services Provided:
  Cross-dock, order picking, humidity-controlled, & USDA approved, rail siding, blast freezing

53035 Inter-County Bakers Inc
1095 Long Island Ave # A
Deer Park, NY 11729-3800   631-957-1350
        Fax: 631-957-1013   800-696-1350
                                www.icbakers.com
Warehouse providing freezer and dry storage; also, rail siding, distribution and shipping services available
CEO: Ted Heim Jr.
sales Executive: Andy Hislop
Estimated Sales: $20-50 Million
Number Employees: 10-19
Square Footage: 70000
Types of products warehoused:
  Frozen perishables, dry grocery items, all commodities, and pharmaceuticals, dry goods, frozen goods
Services Provided:
  Distribution & shipping, rail siding

Warehousing / A-Z

Storage Facility Data:
    Dry Storage Size: 255000 Cubic Ft.
    Freezer Size: 200000 Cubic Ft.

53036 Intercontinental Warehouses
135 Bethridge Rd
Etobicoke, ON M9W 1N4
Canada
416-743-5471
Fax: 416-743-8582
Custom bonded warehouse providing cooler, freezer and dry storage for frozen and refrigerated foods and groceries; transportation services include courier, LTL, TL, specialty hazardous carriers and consolidated transportation program; rail siding available
Number Employees: 45
Square Footage: 2400000
Parent Co: Valleydene Corporation
Types of products warehoused:
    Frozen & refrigerated foods, groceries, dry goods, non-perishables, frozen goods, canned foods, general merchandise
Services Provided:
    Slow freezing, meat inspection room, customs bond, etc., rail siding, trucking, labeling, pick and pack, repackaging, shrink wrap
Storage Facility Data:
    Cooler Size 35000 Sq. Ft.
    Dry Storage Size: 465000 Sq. Ft.
    Freezer Size: 100000 Sq. Ft.

53037 International Packaging
420 W Jones St
Millersburg, OH 44654-1087
330-674-0824
Fax: 330-674-3289 info@intlpack.com
Packaging of food products for club stores and private label
President: David Bird
General Manager: Robert Haines
Manager: Pam Cabe
rhaines@intlpack.com
Number Employees: 20-49
Type of Packaging: Consumer, Private Label, Bulk

53038 International Refrigerated
8791 Hampton Blvd
Norfolk, VA 23505-1026
757-451-3211
Fax: 757-451-3171
Warehouse located on Virginia International Terminal IRPS specializing in import and export of perishable products.
President: Mike Hobson
mhobson@lineagelogistics.com
Director Operations: Jimmy Rutledge
Division Manager: Mike Hobson
Estimated Sales: $ 3 - 5 Million
Number Employees: 50-99
Square Footage: 200000
Parent Co: Richmond Cold Storage
Type of Packaging: Food Service
Types of products warehoused:
    frozen goods
Services Provided:
    Cross docking, web enabled customer access, import/export, rail siding, trucking, labeling, blast freezing, pick and pack

53039 International Refrigerated Facility
700 Edwards Ave
New Orleans, LA 70123-3187
504-733-7030
Fax: 504-733-3212
Warehouse providing cooler, freezer and dry storage
Manager: Jim Longo
Estimated Sales: $1-2.5 Million
Number Employees: 10 to 19

53040 Interport Storage & Distribution Service
105-A Rocket Avenue
Opelika, AL 36804
334-745-0880
Fax: 334-745-6537 800-447-7094
Warehouse providing cooler and dry storage for nonperishable foods; transportation firm providing short and local haul trucking; also, railsiding and intermodal available
President: Dean Matheson
Operations Manager: Allen Barks
Number Employees: 20-49
Types of products warehoused:
    Non-perishable food products, paper, plastics & general merchandise, non-perishables, general merchandise
Services Provided:
    Re-packing, pick & pack, cross dock & stretch wrapping, rail siding, packaging, repackaging

Storage Facility Data:
    Cooler Size 12000 Sq. Ft.
    Dry Storage Size: 103000 Sq. Ft.

53041 (HQ)Interstate Cold StorageInc
4410 New Haven Ave
Fort Wayne, IN 46803-1650
260-428-2505
Fax: 260-428-2503 www.interstatecoldstorage.com
Public warehouse providing cooler and freezer storage for refrigerated and frozen goods; transportation firm providing local and short haul trucking, freight consolidation and rail car services; also, LTL, blast freezing, EDI/WINS and contract services available. Each location has temperature ranges from -20F to 60F, providing flexibility needed to accommodate your needs. Strategic locations with easy highway and rail access assure cost effective inbound and outbound delivery of products.
Chief Executive Officer: Vincent Tippmann
General Manager: Ron Halm
Facility Manager - Fort Wayne, IN - East: Gary Benson
Number Employees: 20-49
Other Locations:
    Roberts Road
    Columbus, OH
    Interstate Drive
    Napoleon, OH
    Nelson Road
    Fort Wayne, IN
    Lincoln Parkway
    Fort Wayne, IN
    Setterlin Drive
    Columbus, OHRoberts RoadNapoleon
Types of products warehoused:
    Refrigerated & frozen goods, frozen goods
Services Provided:
    rail siding, labeling, blast freezing

53042 Interstate Cold StorageCo
1 Interstate Dr
Napoleon, OH 43545-9714
419-599-0510
Fax: 419-599-1665
info@interstatecoldstorage.com
www.interstatecoldstorage.com
Public warehouse providing storage for refrigerated and frozen foods; also, distribution, consolidation, transportation, custom packaging, USDA inspection, export, certification and rail siding available. Maumee and Western and CSX with 5-car private siding; refrigerated docks with 8 doors; temperature ranges from -20F to 60F; 3,175,000 Cubic Feet; US Highways 6 & 24, near I-80/90 & I-75.
President: Russell Borstelman
russb@interstatecoldstorage.com
Chief Executive Officer: Vincent Tippmann
Manager: Russell Borstelman
russb@interstatecoldstorage.com
Facility Manager: Russell Borstelman
Estimated Sales: $1-3 Million
Number Employees: 10-19
Parent Co: Interstate Cold Storage, Inc.
Types of products warehoused:
    Refrigerated & frozen, frozen goods
Services Provided:
    Distribution, consolidation, packaging, inspection, export, etc., rail siding
Storage Facility Data:
    Cooler Size 475000 Cubic Ft.
    Freezer Size: 2700000 Cubic Ft.

53043 Interstate Cold Storage
7725 Nelson Rd
Fort Wayne, IN 46803-1999
260-493-2541
Fax: 260-493-2470
info@interstatecoldstorage.com
www.interstatecoldstorage.com
Public warehouse offering cooler and freezer storage; rail siding, re-packing, distribution, transportation, inspection, certification, exporting and ice manufacturing available. Refrigerated docks with 12 doors; 1,728,000 cubic feet; US Highways 24 & 30, near I-469.
Chief Executive Officer: Vincent Tippmann
Manager: Ron Mays
ronm@interstatecoldstorage.com
Facility Manager: John Stone
Estimated Sales: $1-2.5 Million
Number Employees: 5-9
Parent Co: Interstate Cold Storage, Inc.
Services Provided:
    rail siding
Storage Facility Data:
    Cooler Size 432000 Cubic Ft.
    Freezer Size: 1296000 Cubic Ft.

53044 Interstate Cold Storage
6606 Lincoln Pkwy
Fort Wayne, IN 46804-5684
260-432-3494
Fax: 260-432-0221
info@interstatecoldstorage.com
www.interstatecoldstorage.com
Public warehouse offering cooler and freezer storage; transportation firm providing freight consolidation via TL and LTL refrigerated short haul trucking; also, rail siding, custom packaging, USDA inspection, exporting and certification services available. Refrigerated docks with 26 doors; 5,400,000 cubic feet; CSX and Rail America with 8-car private siding; US Highways 14 & I-69, near I-469.
Manager: Phil Garlinger
Chief Executive Officer: Vincent Tippmann
Manager: Nick Burnham
nick.burnham@interstatecoldstorage.com
General Manager: Ron Halm
Estimated Sales: $1-2.5 Million
Number Employees: 10-19
Parent Co: Interstate Cold Storage, Inc.
Services Provided:
    Trucking, custom packaging, exporting, etc., rail siding

53045 Interstate Merchandise Warehose
117 Park Street
Union, MS 39365-2130
601-482-4689
Fax: 662-483-4356 interstatemdse1@aol.com
Warehouse offering dry and humidity-controlled storage for paper products and groceries; rail siding and space rental available
President: Bill Cassel
Secretary/Treasurer: James Farmer
Vice President: Walker Jones
Estimated Sales: $1 Million
Number Employees: 22
Square Footage: 1760000
Types of products warehoused:
    Paper products & groceries
Services Provided:
    Space rental, rail siding
Storage Facility Data:
    Dry Storage Size: 440000 Sq. Ft.
    Humidity-Controlled Size: 37500 Sq. Ft.

53046 Interstate Underground Wrhse
8201 E 23rd St
Kansas City, MO 64129-1387
816-833-0000
Fax: 816-833-2085 info@kcinterstate.com
www.webselfstorage.com
Warehouse handling food and nonfood products, paper goods, ice cream, soda, candy, raw goods and machinery; also, rail siding, repackaging, export and stencilling
Owner/President: Sammy Jo Reeder
CEO: Stacy Robinson
Controller: John Cobb
VP: Ed Gilmore
Manager: Tamie Carter
tamie@kcinterstate.com
VP Operations: Ed Gilmore
Estimated Sales: $2.5-5 Million
Number Employees: 20-49
Types of products warehoused:
    Food & non-foods products, paper, general merchandise, ice cream, soda, candy & raw goods, non-perishables, frozen goods, general merchandise
Services Provided:
    Repackaging, export & stencilling, rail siding
Storage Facility Data:
    Cooler Size 145000 Sq. Ft.
    Dry Storage Size: 310000 Sq. Ft.
    Freezer Size: 533000 Sq. Ft.

53047 J M Swank Co
395 Herky St
North Liberty, IA 52317-8523
319-626-3683
Fax: 319-626-3662 800-593-6375
www.jmswank.com
Food ingredients for the dairy, beverage, meat, bakery, snack, confection, ethnic and prepared foods industries
CEO: Shawn Meaney
Chief Financial Officer: Philip Garton
Senior Vice President: Paul Hillen
Vice President, Sales & Customer Service: Linda Loucks
Vice President, Operations: Reggie Hastings
Estimated Sales: $6 Million
Number Employees: 100-249
Parent Co: Conagra Brands

Warehousing / A-Z

Other Locations:
  Swank Great Lakes
  Carol Stream, IL
  Swank South
  Dallas, TX
  Swank West
  Denver, CO
  Tolleson, AZ
  Buena Park, CA
  Modesto, CA
  Swank Great LakesDallas
Types of products warehoused:
  dry goods, produce, raw ingredients
Services Provided:
  trucking

53048 J W Mitchell Investment
2 Corporate Park # 108
Suite108
Irvine, CA 92606-5103   949-975-1999
    Fax: 949-975-1919 800-777-9772
Real Estate Company
Owner: Josalynn Weaver
jweaver@jwmitchellco-inc.com
CEO: J.W. Mitchell
Project Manager: Tony Rigdon
Estimated Sales: $ 1 - 3 Million
Number Employees: 1-4
Type of Packaging: Food Service

53049 J&B Cold Storage Inc
13200 43rd Street North East
Saint Michael, MN 55376-8420   763-497-3700
    Fax: 763-497-9481 800-872-4642
info@jbcold.com www.jbgroup.com
Warehouse offering cooler, freezer and dry storage for food products; transportation firm providing local, short and long haul trucking; also, re-packing, labeling and blast freezing available
President: Robert Hageman
Contact: Stefano Bilich
stefano.bilich@jbgroup.com
Number Employees: 10-19
Parent Co: J&B Wholesale Distributing Inc
Types of products warehoused:
  Non-perishable, refrigerated & frozen foods, non-perishables, frozen goods
Services Provided:
  Trucking, re-packing, labeling & blast freezing, labeling, blast freezing, repackaging

53050 J.D. Smith & Sons
180 Basaltic Road
Concord, ON L4K 1G8
Canada
        905-669-8980
    Fax: 905-669-8981 866-669-8980
info@jdsmith.com www.jdsmith.com
Warehouse providing dry storage for general merchandise and groceries; transportation firm providing local contract trucking and daily service to major chains in metro Toronto and Ontario; also, re-packing and pallet controlavailable
Number Employees: 250-499
Types of products warehoused:
  General merchandise & groceries, general merchandise
Services Provided:
  Distribution, delivery, contract trucking, re-packing, etc.
Storage Facility Data:
  Dry Storage Size: 500000 Sq. Ft.

53051 Jacintoport International LLC
16398 Jacintoport Blvd
Houston, TX 77015-6586   281-457-2415
    Fax: 713-673-7300 www.jacintoport.com
Cargo handling and stevedoring firm that offers the latest in computerized inventory control, electronic reporting, and full service terminal and stevedoring.
President: David Labbe
Accounting: Diane Bounds
Vice President: Alicia Menchaca
alicia.menchaca@cscisd.net
Sales/Marketing Manager: Frank Pizzitola
Human Resources: Blanca Alvarez
Operations: Jackie Reece
Facilities Manager: Capt. Don Kwon
Number Employees: 250-499
Square Footage: 1380000
Parent Co: Seaboard Corporation
Type of Packaging: Food Service
Services Provided:
  Cross-docking

53052 Jacmar Foodservice
300 N Baldwin Park Blvd.
City of Industry, CA 91746
    Fax: 626-430-2342 800-834-8806
contact@jacmar.com jacmar.com
Distributor of dry foods, cheese and dairy products, canned foods, meats and seafood, frozen products, and general groceries.
President & CFO: Jim Hliboki
CEO: James Dal Pozzo
Year Founded: 1959
Square Footage: 232000
Types of products warehoused:
  dry goods, frozen goods, produce, canned foods, general merchandise, Dairy, seafood, meats, etc.
Storage Facility Data:
  Cooler Size 75,000 x
  Dry Storage Size: 132,000 x
  Freezer Size: 75,000 x

53053 Jacobson Warehouse Company
P.O.Box 224
Des Moines, IA   515-265-6171
    Fax: 515-265-8927 800-636-6171
Warehouse providing dry storage for nonperishable items; transportation firm providing long and short haul trucking; also, re-packing services available, packaging
President: Scott Temple
CFO: Gordon Smith
Vice President: john Bartnick
Vice President of Business Development: Stan Schrader
Contact: John Barker
j.barker@jacobsonco.com
Executive Vice President of Operations: Patrick Coughlin
Number Employees: 20-49
Parent Co: Jacobson Companies
Other Locations:
  Jacobson Warehouse Company
  Phoenix, ARJacobson Warehouse Company
Types of products warehoused:
  Non-perishable items, dry goods, non-perishables, frozen goods, produce, canned foods, general merchandise
Services Provided:
  Re-packing, packaging & trucking, bar-coding, shrink wrapping, rail siding, trucking, labeling, packaging, pick and pack, repackaging

53054 Jantzen International
2100 E Devon Ave # 101
Elk Grove Vlg, IL 60007-6030 847-640-5200
    Fax: 847-640-0155 info@jantzenweb.com
        www.jantzenweb.com
Warehouse providing dry storage for goods; transportation company providing air and ocean freight services.
President: Marybeth Wilson
Accounting: Diane Keating
Operations & Air Import: Rhodora Sanguiped
Air Export Manager: Wolfgang Menke
Number Employees: 2 - 10
Types of products warehoused:
  Goods
Services Provided:
  Air & ocean freight

53055 Jaxport Refrigerated
10060 Skinner Lake Dr.
Jacksonville, FL 32246   904-786-8038
    Fax: 904-781-3256 info@seaonus.com
        www.icslogistics.com
Public warehouse providing freezer storage for poultry, pork, beef and seafood; also, custom-bonded space, import/export refrigeration and transportation services available
Manager: Cindy Hollums
CEO: Jeff Spence
CFO: Mark Gier
CIO: Dennis Rhodes
Director Sales/Marketing: Brenda Goble
General Manager: Dave Alberts
Dir Warehouse Operations: Ben Campbell
Estimated Sales: $1-2.5 Million
Number Employees: 10 to 19
Square Footage: 640000
Parent Co: ICS Logistics
Types of products warehoused:
  Poultry, pork, beef & seafood
Services Provided:
  Custom bonded space, import/export refrigeration services, etc., rail siding

Storage Facility Data:
  Cooler Size 40000 Sq. Ft.
  Dry Storage Size: 40000 Sq. Ft.
  Freezer Size: 80000 Sq. Ft.

53056 Jel Sert
501 Conde St
West Chicago, IL 60185   630-876-4838
        800-323-2592
        www.jelsert.com
Frozen juice pops, juice beverages and mixes
President: Kenneth Wegner
Research & Development Director: John Dobrozsi
Senior Quality Engineer: Erika Scherer
Director of Human Resources: Juan Chavez
Engineer & Plant Manager: Simon Richards
Square Footage: 1600000
Type of Packaging: Consumer, Food Service, Bulk

53057 Jody's Gourmet Popcorn
1160 Millers Ln
Virginia Beach, VA 23451-5716   757-422-8646
    customerservice@jodyspopcorn.com
        www.jodyspopcorn.com
Popcorn and fudge
Founder: Jody Wagner
Number Employees: 20-49
Other Locations:
  Retail Store , Laskin Road
  Virginia Beach, VARetail Store , Laskin Road

53058 John Cassidy Intl Inc
3680 NW 73rd St
Miami, FL 33147-5850   305-836-6216
    Fax: 305-691-7614 paul@johncassidyintl.com
        www.johncassidyintl.com
International freight forwarder and customs house broker; warehouse providing dry storage for general merchandise; rail siding available
President: Paul Cassidy
paul@internationaldistributioncenter.com
CEO: John Cassidy
Number Employees: 10-19
Types of products warehoused:
  General merchandise, general merchandise
Services Provided:
  Consolidation, import & export, rail siding
Storage Facility Data:
  Dry Storage Size: 50000

53059 John Christner TruckingInc
19007 W Highway 33
Sapulpa, OK 74066-7545   918-512-8600
    Fax: 918-227-6685 800-324-1900
chrda@johnchristner.com www.johnchristner.com
Warehouse offering cooler and freezer storage for frozen and refrigerated foods; transportation firm providing refrigerated local, short and long haul trucking services; also, distribution and logistics available
President: John Christner
chrj@johnchristner.com
VP/COO: Daniel Christner
Number Employees: 250-499
Types of products warehoused:
  Frozen & refrigerated foods, frozen goods
Services Provided:
  Transportation, distribution & logistics

53060 John S James Co
6002 Commerce Blvd # 115
Savannah, GA 31408-9760   912-201-1346
    Fax: 912-233-2150 savannah@johnsjames.com
        www.johnsjames.com
Warehouse providing dry storage for general cargo; customs house broker providing freight forwarding via domestic and international airline service
President: Thomas James
thomas.james@johnsjames.com
Number Employees: 20-49
Types of products warehoused:
  General cargo
Services Provided:
  Airlines, freight forwarding, customs house brokerage, etc.
Storage Facility Data:
  Dry Storage Size: 10000 Sq. Ft.

53061 John-Jeffrey Corporation
PO Box 697
Bellmawr, NJ 08099-0697
        856-456-0284
    Fax: 856-456-4078

833

Warehousing / A-Z

Warehouse providing dry storage for food, groceries and general merchandise; transportation firm providing consolidation delivery program to all food related accounts in VA, OH and New England; rail siding available
Chariman & Founder: John Juzaitis
Number Employees: 20-49
Types of products warehoused:
  Food, groceries & general merchandise, general merchandise
Services Provided:
  Special packaging for wholesale clubs, rail siding
Storage Facility Data:
  Dry Storage Size: 205000 Sq. Ft.

53062 John-Jeffrey Corporation
P.O.Box 697
850 Charles St
Gloucester City, NJ 08030-2450 856-456-0284
    Fax: 856-456-4078 johnjcorp@aol.com
Warehouse providing cooler and dry storage for groceries and confectionery products; labeling, packaging and consolidation delivery programs for companies mid-Atlantic and Northeast; rail siding available
President: John A Juzaitis
President: John Juzaitis, Sr.
CFO: Bill Thompson
Administration: Janet Forcinito
Operations Manager: Joe Vito
Estimated Sales: $20-50 Million
Number Employees: 50 to 99
Square Footage: 312000
Types of products warehoused:
  Groceries & confectionery products, dry goods, non-perishables, canned foods, general merchandise
Services Provided:
  Labeling, packaging & consolidation delivery program, rail siding, trucking, labeling, packaging, pick and pack, repackaging
Storage Facility Data:
  Cooler Size 30000 Sq. Ft.
  Dry Storage Size: 312000 Sq. Ft.

53063 Johnston Training Group, Inc.
2821 Second Avenue
Suite 903
Seattle, WA 98121-1248 206-948-0074
    karen@jtgroup.com
    www.jtgroup.com
Warehouse handling frozen and refrigerated products; other services include export/import facilities, meat inspection and blast freezing
Manager: Patrick McClain
Department Manager: Pat McClair
Warehouse Manager: Pat McClair
Human Resources Executive: Mike Lauland
Operations Manager: Joe Lacoste
Estimated Sales: $5-10 Million
Number Employees: 50 to 99
Square Footage: 320000
Types of products warehoused:
  Frozen & refrigerated products, frozen goods
Services Provided:
  Export/import facilities, meat inspection & blast freezing, rail siding
Storage Facility Data:
  Cooler Size 500000 Cubic Ft.
  Dry Storage Size: 20000 Sq. Ft.
  Freezer Size 1500000 Cubic Ft.

53064 Jones Moving & Storage Co
2404 Wilson Rd
Harlingen, TX 78552-5009 956-423-6030
    Fax: 956-423-4328 800-684-3894
    jones@jonesmoving.com www.mayflower.com
Warehouse providing dry storage for general goods and food; also, local delivery available
Owner: Martha Crouch
martha@jonesmoving.com
President/Finance executive: Mark Groves
Vice President: David Groves
Sales Director: Jack McNally
martha@jonesmoving.com
Production Manager: Martha Crouch
Estimated Sales: $2.5- 5 Million
Number Employees: 20-49
Square Footage: 120000
Types of products warehoused:
  General goods & food, dry goods, non-perishables, canned foods, general merchandise

Services Provided:
  Local delivery, trucking, pick and pack, repackaging
Storage Facility Data:
  Dry Storage Size: 30000 Sq. Ft.

53065 K M Davies Co
6509 Lake Ave
Williamson, NY 14589-9504 315-589-4811
    Fax: 315-589-9272 www.kmdavies.com
Warehouse offering cold, dry, and humidity controlled storage for fresh apples; rail siding available
President: Lloyd Verbridge
CEO: Jim Verbridge
jverbridge@kmdavies.com
Estimated Sales: $500,000 - 1 Million
Number Employees: 10-19
Square Footage: 1460000
Types of products warehoused:
  Fresh apples, produce
Services Provided:
  Trucking, rail siding
Storage Facility Data:
  Cooler Size 9000000 Cubic Ft.
  Dry Storage Size: 450000 Cubic Ft.
  Freezer Size: 600000 Cubic Ft.
  Humidity-Controlled Size: 6000000 Cubic Ft.

53066 K&K Express
2980 Commers Drive
Suite 100
Eagan, MN 55121 651-209-8771
    Fax: 651-209-8774 800-445-7213
Warehouse providing dry storage of nonperishable items; transportation firm providing international and domestic freight forwarding services via air freight and local, long and short haul trucking, LTL, TL, Flatbed, and oversized also available
Owner, CEO: Chris Walhof
Owner, CEO: Bettina Walhof
VP, Finance: Ryan Blazei
VP: Cheri Donovan
Business Development: Dan Bruton
Contact: Alycn Bjergo-Justen
abjergo-justen@k2logistics.com
VP, Operations: Dion Anderson
Number Employees: 10-19
Parent Co: K&K Express
Types of products warehoused:
  Non-perishable items, non-perishables
Services Provided:
  Freight forwarding via truck & air freight

53067 KANE Freight Lines Inc
3 Stauffer Industrial Park # 1
Taylor, PA 18517-9630 570-344-9801
    Fax: 570-207-9781 888-356-5263
    info@kaneisable.com www.kaneisable.com
Warehouse providing cold, humidity-controlled and dry storage for food products; transportation firm providing trucking, LTL and consolidation in the Northeast corridor
CEO: Michael J Gardner
CEO: Richard Kane
Number Employees: 10-19
Types of products warehoused:
  Frozen foods, frozen goods
Services Provided:
  Packaging
Storage Facility Data:
  Cooler Size 3600000 Cubic Ft.
  Dry Storage Size: 1000000 Cubic Ft.
  Freezer Size: 1200000 Cubic Ft.
  Humidity-Controlled Size: 3600000 Cubic Ft.

53068 Kak LLC
1507 S Olive St
PO Box 3559
South Bend, IN 46619-4213 574-232-9357
    Fax: 574-282-1377 ken@kakllc.com
    www.kakllc.com
Warehouse providing dry storage for nonperishable items; transportation firm providing ocean freight services; also, rail siding, importing/exporting, labeling, blocking and bracing, container stuffing, crating and consolidation and FTZ services available
Owner/Managing Member: Kenneth Kanczuzewski
bob@kakllc.com
Site Manager: Bob Fitzpatrick
bob@kakllc.com
Plant Manager: Robert Fitzpatrick
Number Employees: 5-9

Types of products warehoused:
  Non-perishable items, dry goods, non-perishables, canned foods, general merchandise
Services Provided:
  Import/export, labeling, blocking/bracing, etc., rail siding, trucking, labeling, packaging, pick and pack, repackaging
Storage Facility Data:
  Dry Storage Size: 355000 Sq. Ft.

53069 Kasseler Food Products Inc.
1031 Brevik Place
Mississauga, ON L4W 3R7
Canada 905-629-2142
    Fax: 905-629-1699 sales@kasselerfoods.com
    www.kasselerfoods.com
Bread and biscuits.
President: Erich Lamshoeft
Types of products warehoused:
  dry goods, non-perishables, Refrigerated products

53070 Kayco
72 New Hook Rd
Bayonne, NJ 07002 718-369-4600
    customercare@kayco.com
    kayco.com
Kosher, all natural, gluten free, vegan, and fair trade products; also specializes in grape juice.
President: Ilan Ron
CEO: Mordy Herzog
Financial Manager: Dov Levi
Executive Vice President: Harold Weiss
Year Founded: 1948
Estimated Sales: $86 Million
Number Employees: 500-999
Number of Brands: 76
Type of Packaging: Consumer, Food Service, Bulk
Types of products warehoused:
  dry goods, non-perishables, frozen goods, canned foods, general merchandise

53071 Kedney Warehouse Co Inc
4700 Demers Ave
Grand Forks, ND 58201-3801 701-772-6683
    Fax: 701-746-7050 www.atlasvanlines.com
Warehouse providing storage for nonfood items
Owner: Todd Berge
mberge@gfwireless.com
General Manager: Todd Berge
Estimated Sales: $ .5 - 1 million
Number Employees: 10-19
Square Footage: 48000
Types of products warehoused:
  Non-food items

53072 Kenco Group Inc
2001 Riverside Dr # 3000
Chattanooga, TN 37406-4303 423-756-5552
    Fax: 423-756-1529 800-758-3289
    info@kencogroup.com www.kencogroup.com
Warehouse providing cooler, humidity controlled and dry storage for groceries, confectionery items and general merchandise; transportation broker providing trucking, carrier selection, etc.; also, rail siding, re-packing and labeling available
President: James Kennedy Jr
kennedy.kennedy@kencogroup.com
Number Employees: 100-249
Types of products warehoused:
  Groceries, confectionery items & general merchandise, general merchandise
Services Provided:
  Freight brokerage, pick & pack, trucking, re-packing, etc., rail siding
Storage Facility Data:
  Cooler Size 75000 Sq. Ft.
  Dry Storage Size: 14000000 Sq. Ft.
  Humidity-Controlled Size: 75000 Sq. Ft.

53073 Kenco Logistic Svc LLC
2001 Riverside Dr # 3000
Chattanooga, TN 37406-4303 423-756-5552
    800-758-3289
    info@kencogroup.com
    www.kencologisticservices.com
Warehouse providing cooler and dry storage, re-packing and labeling for nonperishable and refrigerated foods; transportation firm providing long haul trucking
CEO: Gary Mayfield
gary.mayfield@kencogroup.com
Number Employees: 1-4
Parent Co: Kenco Group

Warehousing / A-Z

Types of products warehoused:
   dry goods, non-perishables, produce, canned foods, general merchandise
Services Provided:
   rail siding, trucking, labeling, packaging, pick and pack, repackaging

53074 Kenyon Zero Storage
250 Grandridge Rd
P.O. Box 604
Grandview, WA 98930-1554   509-882-1103
   Fax: 509-882-1926 www.kenyonzero.com
Warehouse providing cooler storage within twelve different buildings
President: Scott Wingert
scott@kenyonzero.com
Chief Engineer: Russ Mears
Operations Manager: Ken Aker
Office/Warehouse Manager: Peggy Brewer
Estimated Sales: $ 1 - 3 Million
Number Employees: 20-49
Square Footage: 925454
Type of Packaging: Food Service
Other Locations:
   Building C-1 16,000 Sq FtBuilding C-2 50,400 Sq FtBuilding C-3 38,696 Sq FtBuilding C-6 57,600 Sq FtBuilding C-7 49,839 Sq FtBuilding C-8 110,000 SqFtBuilding C-2 50,400 Sq Ft

53075 Klamath Cold Storage
661 S Spring St
Klamath Falls, OR 97601-0148   541-884-5158
   Fax: 541-884-6560
Public refrigerated warehouse providing cooler and freezer storage for cranberries, fish, butter, algae, ice and frozen foods including vegetables; also, rail siding available
President: Marta Kollman
Mgr.: Michael Wilson
Office Mgr.: April Sandoe
Estimated Sales: $1,5 Million
Number Employees: 15
Square Footage: 640000
Types of products warehoused:
   Cranberries, fish, U.S.D.A. butter, algae, frozen foods & ice, frozen goods, produce
Services Provided:
   rail siding
Storage Facility Data:
   Cooler Size 1000000 Cubic Ft.
   Freezer Size 2300000 Cubic Ft.

53076 Klondike Foods
14804-119th Avenue
Edmonton, AB T5L 2P2
Canada   780-451-6677
   Fax: 780-451-7733 info@klondikefoods.com
   www.klondikefoods.com/
Wholesaler/distributor and import broker of confectionery and dairy/deli products, frozen foods, general merchandise, groceries, private label items, etc. Warehouse providing dry storage for cheese and dry food products alsoavailable
President: Jacob Trach
CEO: Wayne Slosky
CFO: Neville Crawford
Office Manager: Charmaine Slosky
Number Employees: 5
Square Footage: 24000
Parent Co: Klondike Foods Import Export Division
Types of products warehoused:
   Dry food products & cheese, dry goods
Services Provided:
   Import broker & wholesaler/distributor
Storage Facility Data:
   Dry Storage Size: 6000 Sq. Ft.

53077 Konoike Pacific California
1420 Coil Ave
Wilmington, CA 90744-2205   310-830-2326
   Fax: 310-518-3900 rburke@kpaccoldstorage.com
   www.kpaccoldstorage.com
Warehouse offering cooler, dry and freezer storage of frozen, refrigerated and nonperishable food products; transportation firm providing refrigerated trucking services including short and local haul
Vice President: Yutaka Kohara
ykohara@konoike-usa.com
Vice President Administration: Kane Urabe
Vice President of Sales: Doug Lopez
Vice President of Operations: Jeff Waite
Number Employees: 100-249

Types of products warehoused:
   Refrigerated foods, non-perishables, frozen goods
Services Provided:
   Refrigerated trucking
Storage Facility Data:
   Cooler Size 28,935 Sq. Ft.
   Freezer Size: 92,005 Sq. Ft.

53078 Kuehne & Nagel Inc.
6700 Boul. Pierre Bertrand
Suite 301
Quebec, QC G2J 0B4
Canada   418-263-0009
   Fax: 418-263-0294 www.kn-portal.com
Warehouse providing dry storage for nonperishable food products; bonded storage area also available
CEO: Dr. Detlef Trefzger
Chief Financial Officer: Gerard van Kesteren
Executive Vice President Overland: Stefan Paul
Number Employees: 15
Square Footage: 632000
Parent Co: Kuehne & Nagel International
Types of products warehoused:
   General merchandise, general merchandise
Services Provided:
   Bonded storage area, rail siding

53079 Kyrie Global Inc.
P.O. Box 36139
Greensboro, NC 27416   336-458-0157
   Fax: 336-458-0203 office@kyrieglobal.com
   www.kyrieglobal.com
Cold storage/distribution services and contract packaging
Manager: Michael Wares
Sales: Mike Wares
Operations: Norm Hemberg
Production: Norm Hemberg
Plant Manager: Charles Davis
Estimated Sales: $ 3 - 5 Million
Number Employees: 15
Square Footage: 300000
Type of Packaging: Food Service
Types of products warehoused:
   dry goods, non-perishables, frozen goods, produce, canned foods, general merchandise
Services Provided:
   trucking, labeling, blast freezing, packaging, pick and pack, repackaging, distribution
Storage Facility Data:
   Cooler Size 18000
   Dry Storage Size: 165000
   Freezer Size: 25000

53080 L A Hearne Co
512 Metz Rd
King City, CA 93930   831-385-4841
   Fax: 831-385-4377 info@hearneco.com
   www.hearneco.com
Conditioner and warehouser of dried beanss.
Manager: Brad Hearne
brad@herneco.com
Year Founded: 1938
Estimated Sales: $26 Million
Number Employees: 100-249
Number of Brands: 1
Number of Products: 50
Square Footage: 200000
Type of Packaging: Food Service, Private Label, Bulk

53081 L.C. Entreposage Storage
160 Rue King
Montreal, QC H3C 2P3
Canada   514-871-1178
   Fax: 514-871-8001
Warehouse providing cooler and freezer storage
President: Joe Wineck
Number Employees: 8
Square Footage: 177200
Types of products warehoused:
   Refrigerated & frozen foods, frozen goods
Storage Facility Data:
   Cooler Size 9300 Sq. Ft.
   Freezer Size 35000 Sq. Ft.

53082 LMD Integrated Logistic Services
3136 E Victoria St
Compton, CA 90221-5618   310-605-5100
   Fax: 310-605-5337 www.lmdlogistics.com
Warehouse providing dry and cooler storage for nonperishable and refrigerated foods; transportation services include short haul trucking in the Southwest

CEO: Louis Diblosi
CFO: Marilyn Zakis
VP Sales: Bill Sampson
Contact: Robert Spilabotte
rspilabotte@lmdlogistics.com
COO: Lou Diblosi
Number Employees: 5-9
Parent Co: LMD Integrated Logistics Services
Types of products warehoused:
   Non-perishable & refrigerated foods, non-perishables
Services Provided:
   Re-packing & labeling

53083 La Grou Cold Storage
4300 S Halsted St
Chicago, IL 60609   773-523-2449
Warehouse offering cold, frozen, dry and humidity-controlled storage for food products; rail siding available; transportation firm providing local, long and short haul trucking
Number Employees: 50-99
Square Footage: 2000000
Parent Co: La Grou Distribution System
Types of products warehoused:
   Food products
Services Provided:
   rail siding
Storage Facility Data:
   Cooler Size 100000 Sq. Ft.
   Freezer Size: 500000 Sq. Ft.

53084 Lagrou Distribution Inc
3534 S Kostner Ave
Chicago, IL 60632   773-843-3200
   www.lagrou.com
Warehouse providing freezer, cooler, dry and humidity-controlled storage; transportation firm providing local, long and short haul trucking; rail siding available.
Director, Information Technology: Michael McInerney
Sales & Marketing Department: Timothy Kelly
Estimated Sales: $50-100 Million
Number Employees: 250-499
Parent Co: La Grou Distribution Systems
Other Locations:
   La Grou Distribution System
   Rochelle, ILLa Grou Distribution System
Types of products warehoused:
   dry goods, non-perishables, frozen goods, canned foods, general merchandise, confection
Services Provided:
   rail siding, trucking, labeling, pick and pack, re-packaging

53085 Lagrou Distribution Inc
551 St James Gate
Bolingbrook, IL 60440   630-972-2203
   www.lagrou.com
Warehouse providing freezer, cooler, dry and humidity-controlled storage; transportation firm providing local, long and short haul trucking; rail siding available.
Vice President, Operations: Dale Stang
Estimated Sales: $0.5 - 1 million
Number Employees: 250-499

53086 Lagrou Warehouse
1800 S Wolf Rd
Des Plaines, IL 60018   847-298-8195
   www.lagrou.com
Warehouse providing freezer, cooler, dry and humidity-controlled storage; transportation firm providing local, long and short haul trucking; rail siding available.
Accounting Department: Richard Gerbatsch
Sales & Marketing Department: Jack Stewart
Estimated Sales: $50-100 Million
Number Employees: 50-99

53087 Lake Erie Warehouse & Distribution Center
5650 Wattsburg Rd
Erie, PA 16509-4066   814-824-6077
   Fax: 814-825-5914
Warehouse providing dry storage for nonperishable items; transportation firm providing LTL, local, long and short haul trucking; also, air freight, expediting and truck rentals, leasing and maintenance available
Manager: Mike Mc Leod
Number Employees: 100-249
Parent Co: TWL Corporation

Warehousing / A-Z

Types of products warehoused:
Food, General Merchandise, Industrial Non-perishable items, dry goods, non-perishables, canned foods, general merchandise, Food Quality to Industrial
Services Provided:
Local, long & short haul trucking, trucking
Storage Facility Data:
Dry Storage Size: 850,000 Sq. Ft.

53088 Lancaster Company
5105 W Nob Hill Boulevard
Yakima, WA 98908-3748   509-966-4020
                          Fax: 509-966-1109
Warehouse for apples
Owner: Lowell Lancaster
Contact: Kevin Broom
kbroom@lancastercountymarine.com
Estimated Sales: $1-2.5 Million
Number Employees: 4
Types of products warehoused:
Apples, produce

53089 Landstar System, Inc
13410 Sutton Park Dr S
Jacksonville, FL 32224   904-398-9400
                          800-872-9400
                          www.landstar.com
Warehouse providing storage space, and a transportation firm providing long haul trucking.
President & CEO: Jim Gattoni
Vice President & CFO: Kevin Stout
Vice President & CIO: Rick Coro
VP/Chief Commercial Officer: Rob Brasher
VP/General Counsel/Secretary: Michael Kneller
VP/Chief Safety & Operations Officer: Joe Beacom
Year Founded: 1991
Estimated Sales: $3.6 Billion
Number Employees: 1,273
Other Locations:
Landstar Express America
Charlotte, SC
Landstar Ligon
Madisonville, KY
Landstar Logistics
Dublin, CALandstar Express
AmericaMadisonville
Services Provided:
general freight

53090 Laney & Duke Terminal Wrhse Co
1560 Jessie St
Jacksonville, FL 32206-6008   904-798-3500
       Fax: 904-356-2605 info@laneyduke.com
                          www.laneyduke.com
Warehouse providing cooler, dry and humidity-controlled storage; transportation firm providing local haul trucking; also, consolidation, refrigeration and rail siding available
President: Thomas Duke
thomas@laneyduke.com
Number Employees: 50-99
Types of products warehoused:
Food, groceries, general commodities & textiles, general merchandise
Services Provided:
Refrigeration, trucking, consolidation, etc., rail siding
Storage Facility Data:
Cooler Size 59000 Sq. Ft.
Dry Storage Size: 900000 Sq. Ft.
Humidity-Controlled Size: 59000 Sq. Ft.

53091 Langham Logistics
5335 W 74th St
Indianapolis, IN 46268-4180   317-290-0227
        Fax: 317-290-0321 855-214-2844
        info@elangham.com www.elangham.com
Warehouse providing dry storage; transportation firm providing LTL, TL, international and domestic freight forwarding services via air freight and expedited local, long and short haul trucking; logistics company providing freightmanagement, warehousing, distribution, tracking, and inventory
Owner: Trent Adams
trentadams@elangham.com
Vice President, Finance: John Langham
Vice President, Operations: Margaret Langham
Number Employees: 50-99
Types of products warehoused:
dry goods, general merchandise
Storage Facility Data:
Dry Storage Size: 300000

53092 Lanier Cold Storage LLC
3801 Cornelia Hwy
Lula, GA 30554-2524   770-869-7100
      Fax: 770-869-1373 www.laniercoldstorage.com
Warehouse providing storage as well as providing customers with knowledge, and reliable service by creating new efficient ways of doing business.
Owner: Preston Bowen
pbowen@laniercoldstorage.com
Human Resources Manager: Vaughan Smith
Plant Manager: Jody Cooper
Estimated Sales: $ 1 - 3 Million
Number Employees: 20-49
Type of Packaging: Food Service
Services Provided:
Cross-dock, distribution, blast freezing

53093 Lanter Distribution LLC
3 Caine Dr
Madison, IL 62060-1574   618-452-4759
      Fax: 618-452-6928 888-861-9662
                        www.lanterdist.com
Warehouse providing dry and humidity and temperature controlled storage of general merchandise; rail siding services available
President/ CEO: Bill Behrmann
bbehrmann@ohl.com
VP: Eric Behrmann
Info Systems (EDI): Rhonda Chilton
Sales/Marketing Executive: Chris Davis
Administrative Director: Joni Buck
VP/Warehousing: Tim Lanter
Regional Sales Manager: Chris Davis
Estimated Sales: $10-20 Million
Number Employees: 100-249
Square Footage: 231000
Parent Co: Logistics, Inc
Other Locations:
St. Louis, MO
Madison, IL
Knsas City, KS
Knoxville, TN
Memphis, TN
Omaha, NEMadison
Types of products warehoused:
dry goods, non-perishables, canned foods, general merchandise
Services Provided:
Shrink wrap, barcode, EDI capabilities, cross-dock, rail siding, trucking, labeling, pick and pack, repackaging
Storage Facility Data:
Dry Storage Size: 840000 Sq. Ft.
Humidity-Controlled Size: 232000 Sq. Ft.

53094 Las Vegas Ice & Cold Storage
8750 North Central Expressway
Suite 1800
Dallas, TX 75231   214-526-6740
      Fax: 702-649-7456 800-683-4423
      information@reddyice.com www.reddyice.com
Manufacturer and distributor of pakaged ice products
Manager: Jim Sisco
Warehouse Manager: Craig Call
Estimated Sales: $ .5 - 1 million
Number Employees: 5-9
Type of Packaging: Bulk

53095 Laub International
1051 Clinton St
Buffalo, NY 14206-2823   716-853-3703
      Fax: 716-852-0136 laub@laubinternational.com
                        www.laubinternational.com
Transportation firm providing freight forwarding in North America; warehouse providing storage for dry goods, alcoholic beverages, machinery, paper products, etc.; also, re-packing, heated facilities, pick/pack, rail siding, crossdocking, distribuion, assembly, consolidation, bulk, and light assembly services available
President: James Dusel
cczajka@laubinternational.com
Site Manager: Camille Czaka
cczajka@laubinternational.com
Number Employees: 10-19
Square Footage: 1440000
Types of products warehoused:
Dry foods, machines, alcoholic beverages, paper products, electronics, etc., dry goods, non-perishables, canned foods, general merchandise
Services Provided:
Heated facilities, re-packing, pick & pack, light assembly, etc, rail siding, trucking, labeling, packaging, pick and pack, repackaging
Storage Facility Data:
Dry Storage Size: 360,0000 Sq. Ft.

53096 Laval Cold Storage Ltd.
110 Montee Du Moulin
Laval, QC H7N 3Y6
Canada   450-669-2638
      Fax: 450-669-1131 www.frigolaval.ca
Warehouse providing cooler, freezer and dry storage for produce, confectionery products, general merchandise, etc.; rail siding available
President: Claude Prud'homme
Number Employees: 6
Square Footage: 260000
Types of products warehoused:
Fresh produce, frozen foods, confectionery products, pharmaceutical items & general merchandise, frozen goods, produce, general merchandise
Services Provided:
rail siding
Storage Facility Data:
Cooler Size 309216 Cubic Ft.
Dry Storage Size: 11200 Sq. Ft.
Freezer Size: 260304 Cubic Ft.

53097 Lawrence Freezer Corporation
2439 Byron Center Ave.,
Wyoming, MI 49519   616-531-8425
                    Fax: 616-531-7584
Frozen meat, poultry and produce
President/General Manager: Mike Carpp
Estimated Sales: $ .5 - 1 million
Number Employees: 5-9
Square Footage: 263120

53098 Lehigh-Pocono WarehouseInc
723 Bangor Rd
Nazareth, PA 18064-9389   610-759-7177
Warehouse providing dry storage for packaging and corrugated materials, food products, glass bottles, yarn, etc.; transportation firm providing local haul trucking; re-packing, picking/distribution and cross docking available
Owner: Merlin Tucker
Estimated Sales: Less Than $500,000
Number Employees: 1-4
Types of products warehoused:
Packaging & corrugated materials, food products, glass bottles, yarn, etc.
Services Provided:
Re-packing, trucking, picking, distribution & cross docking, pick and pack, repackaging
Storage Facility Data:
Dry Storage Size: 70000 Sq. Ft.

53099 Lewis Storage
2751 Patterson St # 5
Greensboro, NC 27407-2335   336-275-8458
      Fax: 336-370-9303 blewis@lewisstorage.com
                        www.lewisstorage.com
Warehouse providing storage for dry foods and general merchandise; transportation firm providing TL and LTL services; also rail siding available
President: Buster Lewis
blewis@lewisstorage.com
Number Employees: 5-9
Square Footage: 1400000
Types of products warehoused:
dry goods, canned foods, general merchandise
Services Provided:
Trucking, rail siding, trucking, labeling, packaging, pick and pack, repackaging
Storage Facility Data:
Dry Storage Size: 280000 Sq. Ft.

53100 Lieb Cold Storage LLC
2550 23rd Ave
PO Box 329
Forest Grove, OR 97116-1777   503-359-5413
      Fax: 503-359-5413 800-919-2289
                        info@liebcoldstorage.com
Warehouse providing cooler, dry and freezer storage; rail siding available
Owner: Jim Lieb
jim@jliebfoods.com
General Manager: Jerry Simmons
Estimated Sales: $1-2.5 Million
Number Employees: 10-19
Square Footage: 880000
Types of products warehoused:
Frozen, chilled & dry goods, dry goods,

non-perishables, frozen goods, produce, canned foods, general merchandise
Services Provided:
rail siding
Storage Facility Data:
Cooler Size 20000 Sq. Ft.
Dry Storage Size: 150,000 Sq. Ft.
Freezer Size: 56000 Sq. Ft.

53101 Lincoln Cold Storage
1700 S Folsom St # A
Lincoln, NE 68522-1648 402-474-2653
Fax: 402-474-1605 www.lincolncoldstorage.com
Warehouse offering 2.2 million cubic feet of cooler and freezer storage; also, blast freezing available
Owner: Barry Nelson
susanlics@aol.com
Estimated Sales: Less Than $500,000
Number Employees: 5-9
Types of products warehoused:
Refrigerated & frozen foods, frozen goods
Services Provided:
Trucking & blast freezing

53102 Linden Warehouse & Dstrbtn Co
11 Distribution Blvd
Edison, NJ 08817-6005 732-287-5500
Fax: 908-862-7539 www.lindenwarehouse.com
Warehouse providing cooler and dry storage for refrigerated and nonperishable foods; transportation firm providing long and short haul trucking; also, re-packing, labeling, etc. services available
President: Debbie Salz
d.salz@lindenwarehouse.com
VP Finance: Michael Dotro
VP: Michael Salz
Operations Manager: Joe Adornetto
Number Employees: 10-19
Square Footage: 3600000
Parent Co: Linden Warehouse & Distribution Company
Type of Packaging: Bulk
Types of products warehoused:
Refrigerated & non-perishable foods, non-perishables
Services Provided:
Re-packing, labeling, trucking, etc.

53103 (HQ)Lineage Logistics
46500 Humboldt Dr
Novi, MI 48377
800-678-7271
www.lineagelogistics.com
Warehouse services including cooler and freezer storage, blast freezing and boxing. Additional services are product handling, logistics support, exporting and product tempering, storage and distribution.
President & CEO: Greg Lehmkuhl
glehmkuhl@millardref.com
EVP, Optimization & Integration: Mike McClendon
Chief Financial Officer: Matthew Hardt
SVP & General Counsel: Jason Burnett
Chief Information Officer: Sudarsan Thattai
Chief Human Resources Officer: Sean Vanderelzen
EVP, Logistics: Greg Bryan
EVP, Sales & Business Development: Tim Smith
Chief Operating Officer: Jeff Rivera
EVP, Continuous Improvement: Brian McGowan
Estimated Sales: $90 Million
Number Employees: 10,000+
Square Footage: 15600
Types of products warehoused:
Refrigerated & frozen foods, frozen goods
Services Provided:
Freezing, blast freezing, boxing, etc.

53104 Live Oak Warehouse
17478 Texas 62
Orange, TX 77630 409-735-8193
Fax: 409-735-9462
Warehouse providing dry storage of nonperishable food items; transportation firm offering long and short haul trucking; also, re-packing and labeling available
Manager: Paul Bertrand
Number Employees: 20-49
Types of products warehoused:
Non-perishable food items, non-perishables
Services Provided:
Trucking, re-packing & labeling

53105 Lloyd A Gray Co Inc
5132 Shawland Rd
Jacksonville, FL 32254-1651 904-786-2080
Fax: 904-786-1007 www.lagwarehouse.biz
Broker of general merchandise and groceries, with a warehouse providing dry storage
President/Owner: Tom Watkins
info@lagwarehouse.biz
Estimated Sales: $500,000-$1 million
Number Employees: 5-9
Square Footage: 100000
Other Locations:
Dry: 22,000 Sq Ft, Cool: 30,000 SF
Jacksonville, FLDry: 22,000 Sq Ft, Cool: 30,000 SF
Services Provided:
Barcode, cross-dock, import/export, EDI, & stretch wrap
Storage Facility Data:
Dry Storage Size: 25000 Sq. Ft.

53106 Logisco
1600 Gregory St
N Little Rock, AR 72114-4360 501-375-3755
Fax: 501-375-8834
Warehouse providing cooler and freezer storage for frozen goods; transportation firm providing short and local haul trucking
President: Cliff Jones
General Manager: Mike Snow
Estimated Sales: $2.5-5 Million
Number Employees: 100-249
Types of products warehoused:
Frozen goods, frozen goods
Services Provided:
Local & short haul trucking
Storage Facility Data:
Cooler Size 4300 Cubic Ft.
Freezer Size: 6500000 Cubic Ft.

53107 Logistics Amber Worldwide
14760 175th St
Jamaica, NY 11434-5415 718-244-8923
Fax: 718-244-8665 keith@amberworldwide.com
Warehouse providing dry storage for nonperishable foods; transportation services include ocean freight forwarding, long and short haul trucking, ocean, air and rail freight forwarding
Owner: Elaine Rosendorff
elaine@amberworldwide.com
VP: Keith Milliner
Number Employees: 10-19
Parent Co: AWLI Group
Types of products warehoused:
Non-perishable items, dry goods, non-perishables, general merchandise
Services Provided:
Trucking, railroad and air & ocean freight forwarding, trucking, labeling, pick and pack
Storage Facility Data:
Dry Storage Size: 10000 Sq. Ft.

53108 Loop Cold Storage
4000 W Military Hwy
McAllen, TX 78503-8840 956-687-9501
Fax: 956-687-1643
Warehouse providing cooler and freezer storage for fruit, and vegetables
President: Anthan Fuller
Data Processing Executive: Joe Rodriguez
Estimated Sales: $20-50 Million
Number Employees: 250-499
Types of products warehoused:
Fruit, & vegetables, produce

53109 (HQ)Los Angeles Cold Storage Co
400 S Central Ave
Los Angeles, CA 90013-1785 213-624-1831
Fax: 213-680-4723 central@lacold.com
www.lacold.com
Warehouse providing a total of 6,694,000 Cu Ft. of cooler and freezer storage; also, rail siding, blast freezing, cross docking, repacking; transportation firm offering nationwide and local service
President: Larry Rauch
Warehouse Manager: Terry Miller
Number Employees: 100-249
Parent Co: Standard-Southern Southern Corporation
Type of Packaging: Private Label
Other Locations:
Total: 1,148,000 Cu Ft
410 South CentralTotal: 1,148,000 Cu Ft440 South Central
Types of products warehoused:
Refrigerated & frozen foods, frozen goods
Services Provided:
Blast freezing, cross docking, repacking, local delivery, etc., rail siding

53110 Lucca Freezer & Cold Storage
2321 Industrial Way
Vineland, NJ 08360-1551 856-690-9000
Fax: 856-690-0700 info@luccacoldstorage.com
Bonded warehouse providing cooler, freezer, dry and humidity-controlled storage for produce, frozen and fresh foods, fish, etc.; transportation broker providing short and long haul trucking; also, re-packing, cold treatment and railsiding available
President: J Michael Lucca
Manager: Rusty Lucca
Repacking Manager: John Carillo
Number Employees: 250-499
Types of products warehoused:
Produce, frozen & fresh foods, frozen meat, fish, etc., frozen goods, produce
Services Provided:
Re-packing, trucking & cold treatment
Storage Facility Data:
Cooler Size 1000000 Cubic Ft.
Dry Storage Size: 1000000 Cubic Ft.
Freezer Size: 201600 Cubic Ft.
Humidity-Controlled Size: 1000000 Cubic Ft.

53111 Lucerne Elevator
PO Box 36
Lucerne, IN 46950 574-889-2475
Warehouse offering storage of corn and beans
Manager: Art Burrough
Estimated Sales: $500,000-$1 Million
Number Employees: 1-4
Types of products warehoused:
Corn & beans, dry goods

53112 Lynchburg Public Warehouse
4630 Murray Pl
Lynchburg, VA 24502-2236 434-847-5556
Fax: 804-528-3068 www.lpwstorage.com
Warehouse providing heated and dry storage for general merchandise; rail siding available
Owner: L Davis
lpw5556@aol.com
Office Manager: Lois Ferguson
Warehouse Manager: Steve Ritzer
Estimated Sales: $1-2.5 Million
Number Employees: 5-9
Square Footage: 320000
Types of products warehoused:
General merchandise, general merchandise
Services Provided:
Heated storage: 40,000 sq. ft., rail siding
Storage Facility Data:
Dry Storage Size: 80000 Sq. Ft.

53113 Lynden Incorporated
6441 S Airpark Pl
Anchorage, AK 99502 907-245-1544
Fax: 904-245-1744 www.lynden.com
Warehouse providing cooler and dry storage for general merchandise and groceries; also, rail siding and food packaging services available.
Estimated Sales: $50-100 Million
Number Employees: 100-249
Types of products warehoused:
General merchandise & groceries, general merchandise
Services Provided:
Food packaging service, rail siding
Storage Facility Data:
Cooler Size 20000 Sq. Ft.
Dry Storage Size: 258379 Sq. Ft.

53114 M & W Logistics Group
1110 Pumping Station Rd
Nashville, TN 37210-2219 615-256-5755
Fax: 615-726-3568 800-251-4209
info@mwlginc.com www.mwlginc.com
Contractor of public warehouse services providing dry storage, re-packing and labeling for nonperishable foods; truckload services include long and short haul trucking in Tennessee and the Midwest
President: Mike Mcfarlin
mmcfarlin@mwtrans.com
Executive Vice President: Mark Boyette
Director of Business Development: Jason Pitt
Executive Vice President: Mark Boyette

Warehousing / A-Z

Estimated Sales: $5-10 Million
Number Employees: 5-9
Square Footage: 800000
Types of products warehoused:
 Non-perishable foods, dry goods, non-perishables, canned foods, general merchandise
Services Provided:
 Re-packing & labeling, rail siding, trucking, labeling, packaging, pick and pack, repackaging
Storage Facility Data:
 Dry Storage Size: 272000

53115 (HQ)M T C Logistics Corp
4851 Holabird Ave
Baltimore, MD 21224-6020 410-631-2734
 Fax: 410-522-1163 info@mtccold.com
Warehouse providing cooler and freezer storage for refrigerated and frozen foods; also, computerized inventory control and rail siding available
President: Harry Halpert
Director of Admin.: Cal Franklin
Contact: Mike Barisse
mbarisse@mtccold.com
Warehouse Manager: Patrick Vitek
Estimated Sales: $ 3 - 5 Million
Number Employees: 5-9
Square Footage: 440000
Other Locations:
 Total: 241,000 Sq Ft
 Jessup, MD
 Total: 223,000 Sq Ft
 Landover, MDTotal: 241,000 Sq FtLandover
Types of products warehoused:
 Refrigerated foods, frozen goods
Services Provided:
 Computerized inventory control, import/export, rail siding, blast freezing

53116 M T C Logistics Corp
4851 Holabird Ave
Baltimore, MD 21224-6020 410-631-2734
 Fax: 410-522-1163 info@mtccold.com
Public warehouse providing cooler and freezer storage for frozen and chilled foods; also, blast freezing, distribution, import and export services available
President: Harry Halpert
VP Sales: Ernest Ferguson
Contact: Mike Barisse
mbarisse@mtccold.com
VP Operations: Kenneth Johnson
Estimated Sales: $2.5-5 Million
Number Employees: 5-9
Types of products warehoused:
 Frozen & chilled foods, frozen goods
Services Provided:
 Blast freezing, distribution, import & export services, rail siding
Storage Facility Data:
 Cooler Size 1500000 Cubic Ft.
 Freezer Size: 12000000 Cubic Ft.

53117 MCS Merchants Cold Storage
240 Shorland Dr # 100
Walton, KY 41094-9388 859-485-4474
 Fax: 859-485-4475 cold@mcstorage.com
 www.mcstorage.com
Warehouse providing cooler and freezer storage for frozen and refrigerated foods; blast freezing, leasing and rail siding services available
President: Phillip Castellini
phillipc@mcstorage.com
Finance Executive: Mike Kubler
VP Marketing: V Hawk
General Manager: Skip Hawk
Estimated Sales: $2.5-5 Million
Number Employees: 20-49
Square Footage: 800000
Types of products warehoused:
 Frozen & refrigerated foods, frozen goods
Services Provided:
 Blast freezing & leasing, rail siding

53118 (HQ)MCT Terminal & Transport Inc.
2555 Dollard Avenue
Lasalle, QC H8N 3A9
Canada 514-363-3100
 Fax: 514-363-3303 800-363-6493
 info@mct.ca www.mct.ca
Warehouse providing dry storage; transportation firm providing local, long and short haul trucking in Canada
Number Employees: 10-19
Types of products warehoused:
 Groceries
Services Provided:
 On site Canada customs personnel/office

53119 MTC Delaware LLC
4851 Holabird Avenue
Baltimore, MD 21224 410-342-9300
 Fax: 410-522-1163 info@mtccold.com
 www.merchantsterminal.com
Public warehouse providing freezer storage of frozen foods, poultry, seafood, chilled vegetables and fruit, bread, etc.; also, convertible freezer space, cartage, and re-packing services are available
President: Harry Halpert
VP, Sales: Ernie Ferguson
VP, Operations: Ken Johnson
Plant Manager: Dan Poarch
Estimated Sales: $2.5-5 Million
Parent Co: Rosenberger Companies
Types of products warehoused:
 Frozen & cooled meat, poultry, seafood, frozen dinners & desserts, breads, candy, juice concentrate & fruits, frozen goods
Services Provided:
 Convertible freezer space, cartage, rail siding, trucking, labeling, blast freezing
Storage Facility Data:
 Cooler Size 6400000 Cubic Ft.

53120 (HQ)MTE Logistix
14627 128th Avenue NW
Edmonton, AB T5L 3H3
Canada 780-944-9009
 Fax: 780-451-3340 mteinfo@mtelogistix.com
 www.mtelogistix.com
Warehouse providing cooler and dry storage for general merchandise, groceries and refrigerated foods; transportation services include local haul trucking; rail siding, consolidation, freight forwarding and crossdock available
President: Michael Haas
Chairman/CEO: Dennis Nolin
VP Finance: Gloria Morhun
Number Employees: 70
Square Footage: 4400000
Other Locations:
 MTE Logistix
 Delta, BCMTE Logistix
Types of products warehoused:
 General merchandise, groceries, refrigerated foods, lumber & paper products, general merchandise
Services Provided:
 Crossdock, consolidation, freight forwarding, water access, etc., rail siding
Storage Facility Data:
 Cooler Size 34070 Sq. Ft.
 Dry Storage Size: 1018965 Sq. Ft.

53121 MacCosham Van Lines
1240 Sherwin Rd
Winnipeg, MB R3H 0V3
Canada 204-633-9225
 www.maccosham.com
Warehouse providing cooler, freezer and dry storage for dry goods, groceries, appliances and chemicals; transportation firm providing local haul trucking and freight consolidation; also, rail siding, EDI bar coding, pick/pack, palletexchange, etc
President: Jay Lilge
Square Footage: 4000000
Types of products warehoused:
 Dry goods, groceries, appliances & chemicals, dry goods
Services Provided:
 EDI bar coding, pick/pack, local cartage, consolidation, etc., rail siding

53122 (HQ)Madison Warehouse Corporation
4300 Planned Industrial Dr
St Louis, MO 63120-1716 314-383-4300
 Fax: 314-383-2828 866-243-9834
Warehouse providing cooler and dry storage of grocery and confectionery products; rail siding services available
President: Jack Lipin
Contact: Sandy Beckman
sandybeckman@madisonwarehouse.com
Estimated Sales: $5-10 Million
Number Employees: 100-249
Square Footage: 1200000
Other Locations:
 Total: 970,000 Sq Ft
 Fort Worth, TX
 Total: 267,000 Sq Ft
 Joliet (Crossroads Dr), IL
 Total: 300,000 Sq Ft
 Baltimore (Carbridge Rd), MD
 Total: 190,000 Sq Ft
 Baltimore (Chesapeaker), MD
 Total: 179,000 Sq Ft
 Decatur, IL
 Total: 200,000 Sq Ft
 Pacific, MO
 Total: 970,000 Sq FtJoliet (Crossroads Dr)
Types of products warehoused:
 Grocery & confectionery products
Services Provided:
 rail siding

53123 Maines Paper & Food SvcInc
650 Conklin Rd
Conklin, NY 13748 607-772-0055
 Fax: 607-722-3161 www.maines.net
Warehouse providing freezer, cooler and dry storage; rail siding services available
Manager: John Current
CEO: Chris Mellon
Manager: John Current
Logistics Manager: Jamie Kimmel
Estimated Sales: $500,000-$1 Million
Number Employees: 50-99
Square Footage: 200000
Parent Co: Maines Paper & Foodservice
Services Provided:
 rail siding
Storage Facility Data:
 Cooler Size 3000 Sq. Ft.
 Dry Storage Size: 17000 Sq. Ft.
 Freezer Size: 30000 Sq. Ft.

53124 Mallory Alexander Intl
4294 Swinnea Rd
Memphis, TN 38118-6620 901-367-9400
 Fax: 901-370-4288 800-257-8464
 www.mallorygroup.com
Warehouse providing dry storage and labeling for nonperishable foods; transportation services include long haul trucking nationwide
Chairman & CEO: Neely Mallory
CFO: Geoff Collins
geoffcollins@mallorygroup.com
Estimated Sales: $ 10 - 20 Million
Number Employees: 100-249
Square Footage: 4000000
Types of products warehoused:
 Non-perishable foods, non-perishables
Services Provided:
 trucking, labeling

53125 Malteurop North America
3830 W Grant St
Milwaukee, WI 53215 414-671-1166
 www.malteurop.com
Processor and exporter of malt, also offers several modes of commercial collaboration, as well as consulting, engineering, and training services.
CEO: Olivier Parent
President, North America: Kevin Eikerman
Chief Commercial & Innovation Officer: Alain Caekaert
Year Founded: 1984
Estimated Sales: $31.5 Million
Number Employees: 100-249
Parent Co: Malteurop
Type of Packaging: Food Service, Bulk

53126 Manfredi Cold Storage
290 Chambers Rd
Toughkenamon, PA 19374-1025 610-444-5832
 Fax: 610-444-3390
 info@manfredicoldstorage.com
 www.manfredicoldstorage.com
Warehouse providing temperature controlled storage for food products
President: Frank Manfredi
eileen@manfredicoldstorage.com
Sales Exec: Eileen Kelly
Operations Director: Rob Wharry
Estimated Sales: $ 3 - 5 Million
Number Employees: 20-49
Square Footage: 450000
Type of Packaging: Food Service
Types of products warehoused:
 dry goods, frozen goods, produce

Warehousing / A-Z

53127 Manitoulin Group of Companies
9500 Venture Ave. S.E
Calgary, AB T3S 0A1
Canada
Fax: 403-216-0880 888-640-9649
www.manitoulintransport.com
Warehouse providing cooler and dry storage for fresh and frozen foods, groceries and confectionery products; transportation firm providing local haul trucking; cross docking and temperature controlled LTL and TL shipment servicesavailable
Chief Executive Officer: Gord Smith
Number Employees: 100-249
Types of products warehoused:
   Fresh & frozen products, groceries & confectionery products, frozen goods
Services Provided:
   Cross docking & trucking: temperature controlled LTL & TL
Storage Facility Data:
   Cooler Size 350 Sq. Ft.
   Dry Storage Size: 6500 Sq. Ft.

53128 Maritime International
276 Macarthur Dr
New Bedford, MA 02740-7303   508-996-8500
Fax: 508-991-3431 www.maritimeinternational.org
Customs bonded warehouse providing cooler, freezer and dry storage for frozen foods, fish, meat, bulk cranberries and chilled produce; also, rail siding, ship loading and unloading, in-house freight forwarding and USDA coldtreatment
Owner: David Wechsler
davidw@maritimeinternational.org
COO: Tim Ray
Sales Executive: Steve Murphy
davidw@maritimeinternational.org
Warehouse Manager: Carlos Rita
Estimated Sales: $5-10 Million
Number Employees: 50-99
Square Footage: 200000
Parent Co: Maritime International
Types of products warehoused:
   Frozen foods, fish, meat, bulk cranberries & chilled produce, frozen goods
Services Provided:
   Ship loading & unloading, in-house freight forwarding, etc., rail siding, trucking, blast freezing
Storage Facility Data:
   Cooler Size 1500000 Cubic Ft.

53129 Marshall Cold Storage
816 Union St
Marshalltown, IA 50158-2056   641-752-1419
Fax: 641-752-8289 www.dmcoldstorage.com
Warehouse providing storage for beef, pork, poultry, and any other food that needs to be frozen
Manager: Chad Witte
Estimated Sales: Less Than $500,000
Number Employees: 5-9

53130 Martin Warehousing & Distribution
1122 Mikole St
Honolulu, HI 96819   808-831-0405
Warehouse providing dry, cooler and humidity-controlled storage for groceries, health and beauty aids, soap and detergent, etc.; transportation firm providing local haul trucking and freight forwarding; also, re-packing and heat shrinkwrap
President: Jerry Anches
VP: Jan Brookshier
Number Employees: 20-49
Types of products warehoused:
   Dry groceries, health & beauty aids, soaps & detergents and candy & confectionery, dry goods
Services Provided:
   Trucking, re-pack & heat shrink wrap, freight forwarding, etc.
Storage Facility Data:
   Cooler Size 17500 Sq. Ft.
   Dry Storage Size: 2412500 Cubic Ft.
   Humidity-Controlled Size: 812500 Cubic Ft.

53131 Mason City Cold Storage
633 15th St SE
Mason City, IA 50401   641-424-8369
Fax: 641-424-8279
www.des.moines.diningchannel.com
Warehouse providing cooler, freezer, humidity-controlled and dry storage; also, rail siding available
Manager: Eldon Reinhardt
Estimated Sales: $500,000-1 Million
Number Employees: 5 to 9

53132 (HQ)Massachusetts Central Railroad Corporation
2 Wilbraham St
Palmer, MA 01069-9649   413-283-5900
www.masscentralrr.com
Warehouse providing storage for dry products; customs house broker providing rail, intermodal and drayage services
VP: Gary Hoeppner
Number Employees: 10-19
Types of products warehoused:
   Panel products, wood, lumber & building products
Services Provided:
   rail siding
Storage Facility Data:
   Dry Storage Size: 45000 Cubic Ft.

53133 (HQ)Mauser Packaging Solutions
1515 W 22nd St
Suite 1100
Oak Brook, IL 60523
   800-527-2267
www.mauserpackaging.com
Recyclable bulk packaging, bulk handling and shipping, and warehouse storage of both liquids and solids.
President & CEO: Kenneth Roessler
Chief Financial Officer: Tom De Weerdt
EVP, Procurement & Logistics: Leslie Bradshaw
Chief Information Officer: Ed DePrimo
EVP/General Counsel/CCO: Patrick Sheller
Year Founded: 2018
Estimated Sales: Over $1 Billion
Number Employees: 11,000
Type of Packaging: Bulk

53134 McKenna Logistic Centres
1260 Lakeshore Road E
Mississauga, ON L5E 3B8
Canada   905-274-1234
Fax: 905-274-6151 800-561-4997
sales@mckennalogistics.ca
www.mckennalogistics.ca
Warehouse providing dry storage for general merchandise including nonperishable foods; C.P.C. pallet exchange, computerized services, freight consolidation services available
President: John McKenna
VP Sales/Marketing: Nevil Corbeth
VP Operations: John McKenna
Estimated Sales: $1-3 Million
Number Employees: 20
Square Footage: 350000
Types of products warehoused:
   General merchandise, general merchandise
Services Provided:
   C.P.C. pallet exchange, freight consolidation, etc.
Storage Facility Data:
   Dry Storage Size: 2400000 Sq. Ft.

53135 Mccracken Motor Freight
2155 W Broadway
Eugene, OR 97402-2796   541-484-6400
Fax: 541-484-6408 800-452-8995
www.mccrackenmotorfreight.com
Warehouse offering dry, cold and frozen storage for food products, commodities and household goods; transportation firm providing local trucking; also, re-packing, break bulk and rail siding available
Division Manager: Al Green
Manager: Mike Fox
Estimated Sales: Less Than $500,000
Number Employees: 1-4
Square Footage: 108000
Parent Co: McCracken Brothers Motor Freight
Types of products warehoused:
   Frozen, chilled & dry foods, commodities & household goods, dry goods, non-perishables, frozen goods, canned foods, general merchandise
Services Provided:
   Re-packing, break bulk & local distribution, trucking
Storage Facility Data:
   Cooler Size 3000 Cubic Ft.
   Dry Storage Size: 54000 Cubic Ft.
   Freezer Size: 3000 Cubic Ft.

53136 Meador Warehousing-Dstrbtn
1750 N Dr Martin L King Jr Dr
Mobile, AL 36610-1845   251-457-4376
Fax: 251-456-9684 www.meadorwarehouse.com
Warehouse providing dry storage of food products and general merchandise; rail siding available
President: Michael Meador
michael@meadorwarehouse.com
VP: Sam Meador
Estimated Sales: $1-3 Million
Number Employees: 20-49
Square Footage: 2000000
Types of products warehoused:
   Food products & general merchandise, general merchandise
Services Provided:
   rail siding
Storage Facility Data:
   Dry Storage Size: 500000 Sq. Ft.

53137 Medina Cold Storage Co Inc
106 North Ave
Medina, NY 14103-1522   585-798-3811
Fax: 585-798-4785
contact@medinacoldstorage.com
www.medinacoldstorage.com
Public warehouse providing cooler, freezer and dry storage for frozen meats, fruits and vegetables; pallet exchange and stretch wrapping services available
President: James Grinnell
jgrinnel@rochester.rr.com
Vice President: ED Grinnell
Estimated Sales: Less Than $500,000
Number Employees: 5-9
Square Footage: 260000
Types of products warehoused:
   Frozen meats, fruits & vegetables, dry goods, non-perishables, frozen goods
Services Provided:
   Pallet exchange & stretch wrapping, labeling, repackaging
Storage Facility Data:
   Cooler Size 70000 Cubic Ft.
   Dry Storage Size: 40000 Cubic Ft.
   Freezer Size: 400000 Cubic Ft.

53138 Melissa's
PO Box 514599
Los Angeles, CA 90051
   800-588-0151
www.melissas.com
Fruits and vegetables
Founder: Joe Hernandez
Founder: Sharon Hernandez

53139 Mercantile Refrigerated Warehouses
2055 W Pershing Rd
Chicago, IL 60609-2201   773-579-1919
Fax: 773-650-1801
Warehouse offering cooler and freezer storage; rail siding and leased storage, office and processing space available; serving the food service market
President: Donald Schimmeck
Estimated Sales: $ 3 - 5 Million
Number Employees: 330
Square Footage: 2000000
Parent Co: La Grou Distribution
Types of products warehoused:
   Frozen foods & groceries, frozen goods
Services Provided:
   Leased storage, office & processing space, rail siding
Storage Facility Data:
   Cooler Size 100000 Sq. Ft.
   Freezer Size: 40000 Sq. Ft.

53140 Merchandise Multi-Temp Warehouse
1414 S. West St.
P.O.Box 575
Indianapolis, IN 46225   317-632-2525
Fax: 317-266-0784 800-433-7107
info@mwindy.com www.mwindy.com
Freezer and cold Storage Facility
Owner: Don Foley Jr
Chairman/CEO: Tim Siddiq
Estimated Sales: $ 3 - 5 Million
Number Employees: 20-49
Type of Packaging: Food Service

Warehousing / A-Z

53141 (HQ)Merchandise Warehouse
1414 S West St
Indianapolis, IN 46225-1548   317-632-2525
Fax: 317-266-0784   800-433-7107
info@mwindy.com   www.mwindy.com
Warehouse providing cooler, freezer and dry storage for food and nonfood items; transportation services include TL short and long haul trucking; also, warehouse and office lease space and rail siding available
Chairman/CEO: Tim Siddiq
Sales Exec: Joe Daily
Number Employees: 20-49
Types of products warehoused:
  Food & non-food items, dry goods, non-perishables, frozen goods, produce, canned foods, general merchandise
Services Provided:
  Warehouse & office lease space & intra/interstate transportation, trucking, labeling, blast freezing, packaging, pick and pack, repackaging, barcoding

53142 Merchants Distribution Svc
1420 11th Ave NE
Altoona, IA 50009-1659   515-967-1194
Fax: 515-244-7748   800-228-5009
sales@merchantsdsm.com
www.merchantsdsm.com
Warehouse providing dry and humidity-controlled storage for foods and paper; transportation services include LTL local and short haul trucking and freight consolidation; distribution, piggybacking and rail siding available
President: Greg Dickinson
Vice President: Randy Worth
Manager: Randy Worth
Number Employees: 20-49
Types of products warehoused:
  Foods & paper
Services Provided:
  Pool distribution, piggyback services & consolidation, rail siding
Storage Facility Data:
  Dry Storage Size: 600000 Sq. Ft.
  Humidity-Controlled Size: 1500 Sq. Ft.

53143 Merchants Export Inc
200 Dr Mlk Jr Blvd
Riviera Beach, FL 33404   561-844-7000
www.merchantsmarket.com
Exporter of juices, poultry, meats, seafood, cleaning supplies and fresh, canned and frozen fruits and vegetables; warehouse offering dry, cooler, humidity-controlled and freezer storage for produce, dairy items, meat products.
President & CEO: Terry Collier
terry.collier@merchantexport.com
Director, Accounting & Finance: Tom Homberger
Director, Sales: Steve Shoupp
Year Founded: 1967
Estimated Sales: $73.7 Million
Number Employees: 50-99
Number of Brands: 1000
Number of Products: 4000
Square Footage: 100000
Parent Co: Clare Holdings
Type of Packaging: Food Service
Types of products warehoused:
  Produce, poultry, seafood, vegetables, french fries, breads, juices, prepared foods & dairy; eggs, butter & cheese, frozen goods, produce
Services Provided:
  Foreign trade zone; USDA commodity storage approved, rail siding, USDA meat export inspection; APHIS/PPQ
Storage Facility Data:
  Cooler Size 1000000 Cubic Ft.
  Dry Storage Size: 800000 Cubic Ft.
  Freezer Size: 300000 Cubic Ft.
  Humidity-Controlled Size: 45000 Cubic Ft.

53144 Merchants Transfer Company
1201 Papermill Road
Mobile, AL 36610   251-457-8691
Fax: 251-452-6707
Public and contract warehouse providing dry storage for general merchandise; rail siding available
President: Tom Taul Iii
Operations Manager: Michael McFarland
Estimated Sales: $10-20 Million
Number Employees: 20-49
Square Footage: 1600000
Types of products warehoused:
  General merchandise, general merchandise

Services Provided:
  rail siding
Storage Facility Data:
  Dry Storage Size: 800000 Sq. Ft.

53145 Meritex Logistics
24 University Ave NE
Minneapolis, MN 55413   651-855-9700
Fax: 651-855-9701   888-855-9709
www.meritexlogistics.com
Warehouse providing storage for groceries, paper products, general merchandise including paper products; also, air-conditioned storage available
Chairman/ CEO: Paddy McNeely
CFO: Tom Hotovec
COO: Arvid Povilaitis
General Manager: C.E. (Smitty) Smith
Estimated Sales: $10-20 Million
Number Employees: 50-99
Square Footage: 1300000
Parent Co: Enterprise, Inc.
Other Locations:
  Total: 1,500,000 Sq Ft
  Warren, OH
  Total: 250,000 Sq Ft
  Lenexa, KS
  Total: 120,000 Sq Ft
  St. Paul, MN
  Total: 440,000 Sq Ft
  Matteson, IL
  Total: 500,000 Sq Ft
  Cumberland Furnace, TN
  Total: 2,500,000 Sq Ft
  Wampum, PA
  Total: 1,500,000 Sq FtLenexa
Types of products warehoused:
  Groceries, paper products, and drugs, dry goods, non-perishables, canned foods, general merchandise
Services Provided:
  Cross-dock, EDI capabilities, barcoding, rail siding, labeling, pick and pack, repackaging
Storage Facility Data:
  Dry Storage Size: 535,000 Sq. Ft.
  Humidity-Controlled Size: 200,000 Sq. Ft.

53146 Mesa Cold Storage
9602 W Buckeye Rd
Tolleson, AZ 85353-9101   623-478-9392
dcouryjr@mesacold.com
www.mesacold.com
Warehouse providing coooler, freezer and dry storage; wholesaler/distributor of groceries; transportation firm providing local, long and short haul trucking
Owner: Dan Coury
Number Employees: 50-99
Square Footage: 200000
Types of products warehoused:
  General line
Services Provided:
  In-house trucking
Storage Facility Data:
  Cooler Size 400000 Cubic Ft.
  Dry Storage Size: 100000 Cubic Ft.
  Freezer Size: 500000 Cubic Ft.

53147 Mesa Cold Storage
9602 W Buckeye Rd
Tolleson, AZ 85353-9101   623-478-9392
Fax: 480-834-1017   dcouryjr@mesacold.com
www.mesacold.com
Freezer and Cold Storage Facility
Owner: Dan Coury
Number Employees: 50-99
Type of Packaging: Food Service

53148 Metro Freezer & Storage
5 Chrysler Rd
Natick, MA 01760-1502   508-647-9296
Fax: 508-647-9299
VP Operations: Todd Lewis
Type of Packaging: Food Service

53149 (HQ)Metro Park Warehouses Inc
6920 Executive Dr
Kansas City, MO 64120-2111   816-231-0777
Fax: 816-231-7797
metroparkwarehouses@mpwus.com
www.metroparkwarehouses.com
Warehouse offering cooler, dry and temperature-controlled storage; also, rail siding, shrink wrapping, repacking and pallet display services available. Transportation firm providing local and long haul trucking, consolidation anddirect store delivery.

President: Robert Banach
bbanach@mpw-inc.com
Chairman: John Malinee
VP/Marketing: Steve Wedlan
Estimated Sales: $5 Million+
Number Employees: 50-99
Square Footage: 3790000
Type of Packaging: Consumer, Bulk
Types of products warehoused:
  dry goods, non-perishables, canned foods, general merchandise, Pharmaceutical
Services Provided:
  shrink wrap, cross-dock, EDI, rail siding, trucking, labeling, packaging, pick and pack, repackaging

53150 Metropolitan Trucking Inc
299 Market St # 300
Saddle Brook, NJ 07663-5312   973-742-3000
Fax: 201-843-6179   800-967-3278
cs@mtrk.com   www.mtrk.com
Transportation company providing long and short haul trucking; warehouse providing dry storage for paper and food items
Owner: Ronald Gordy
rgordy@metrosoft-us.com
Chief Financial Officer: Matt Sullivan
EVP: Michael A. Maiore
Vice President of Maintenance: Wayne Beaudry
Number Employees: 1-4
Types of products warehoused:
  Paper products & food items
Services Provided:
  Trucking
Storage Facility Data:
  Dry Storage Size: 110000 Cubic Ft.

53151 (HQ)Michel Distribution Service
600 Hickory Dr
Aberdeen, MD 21001   410-297-8077
Fax: 410-994-1241   800-829-6826
Warehouse providing cooler, dry and humidity-controlled storage for general merchandise, groceries and paper; also, consolidated deliveries, pool car distribution, pick/pack, re-packing and rail siding available
Co-Principal: J Michel
Co-Principal: C Michel
Marketing Director: Mike Geppi
Sales Director: Joe Dabbs
Estimated Sales: $20-50 Million
Number Employees: 250
Square Footage: 1000000
Types of products warehoused:
  Groceries & paper, general merchandise
Services Provided:
  Consolidated deliveries, pool car distribution, etc., rail siding, pick and pack

53152 Michigan Cold Storage Facilities
PO Box 668
Taylor, MI 48180-0668   313-295-1310
Fax: 313-295-0448   800-878-1800
Warehouse providing cooler, dry, freezer and humidity-controlled storage for packaged products; rail siding and limited delivery available
President: Marshall Loewenstein
VP: Claire Boie
Estimated Sales: $1-2.5 Million
Number Employees: 19
Types of products warehoused:
  Packaged products
Services Provided:
  Limited delivery, rail siding
Storage Facility Data:
  Cooler Size 621620 Cubic Ft.
  Dry Storage Size: 2734704 Cubic Ft.
  Freezer Size: 1612800 Cubic Ft.
  Humidity-Controlled Size: 576000 Cubic Ft.

53153 Mid Columbia Warehouse Inc
1810 E Ainsworth St
PO Box 1050
Pasco, WA 99301-5850   509-547-7761
Fax: 509-547-2194
Public warehouse offering dry storage for canned and packaged dry foods, honey, canned juices, jams and jellies; rail siding and distribution services available
President: Mike Paris
mparis@mcwhse.com
Controller: Chris Zadow
Customer Support: Mike Paris

Warehousing / A-Z

Estimated Sales: Less Than $500,000
Number Employees: 5-9
Square Footage: 344000
Types of products warehoused:
  canned foods, packaged dry foods, honey, canned juices, jams & jellies
Services Provided:
  Distribution, rail siding
Storage Facility Data:
  Dry Storage Size: 86000

53154 Mid Continent Indl Insultation
5200 E 45th St
Kansas City, MO 64130-2336   816-921-4300
Fax: 816-861-0931
Storage facility providing space for refrigeration equipment and insulation panels
Owner: Michael Lillig
mikel@m-cii.com
Director Operations: Jack Zimmerman
Estimated Sales: $1 to 2.5 million
Number Employees: 10-19
Square Footage: 80000
Type of Packaging: Private Label

53155 Mid Eastern Cold Storage LLC
198 N Orchard Rd
PO Box 489
Vineland, NJ 08360-3402   856-691-3700
Fax: 856-691-3399
www.mideasterncoldstorage.com
Warehouse providing freezer and cooler storage; blast freezing and rail siding available
President: Eleonor Pepper
Director Sales: Mark Pepper
Manager: Eleanor Pepper
Director Operations: William Carrol
Estimated Sales: Less Than $500,000
Number Employees: 1-4
Parent Co: Safeway Stores
Type of Packaging: Food Service
Services Provided:
  rail siding, blast freezing
Storage Facility Data:
  Freezer Size: 1037550 Cubic Ft.

53156 Mid-Continent WarehouseCompany
1325 Port Terminal Rd
Duluth, MN 55802   218-722-1427
Fax: 218-722-0246 jlandwehr@michelinas.com
Storage of frozen and dry goods
Manager: Aaron Hansen
General Manager: Jeanne Landwehr
Estimated Sales: Less than $500,000
Number Employees: 5 to 9
Square Footage: 240000
Parent Co: Luiginos
Types of products warehoused:
  General merchandise & dockside cargo handling, non-perishables, produce, general merchandise
Services Provided:
  truck loading, unloading, order picking, rail siding, trucking
Storage Facility Data:
  Dry Storage Size: 40000 Sq. Ft.
  Freezer Size: 20000 Sq. Ft.

53157 Mid-Florida Freezer Warehouse
P.O.Box 429
Plymouth, FL 32768   407-886-1971
Fax: 407-880-1993
Warehouse providing freezer, cooler, humidity-controlled and dry storage; also, rail siding, pool distribution and stevedoring facilities available.
Manager: Bill Koeditz
General Partner: Patrick Lee
Sales Director: Betty Gause
Estimated Sales: $2.5-5 Million
Number Employees: 20
Types of products warehoused:
  Food & related merchandise
Services Provided:
  Pool distribution, stevedoring facilities, etc., rail siding
Storage Facility Data:
  Cooler Size 7000000 Sq. Ft.
  Dry Storage Size: 7000000 Sq. Ft.
  Freezer Size: 7000000 Sq. Ft.
  Humidity-Controlled Size: 7000000 Sq. Ft.

53158 Midland Terminals
2520 Schuette Rd
Midland, MI 48642-6951   989-496-0880
Fax: 517-496-0131
Warehouse providing dry storage for nonfood and food items
Manager: John Riffel
Sales Manager: Patrick Ruffels
Manager: Angie Laur
Estimated Sales: $ .5 - 1 million
Number Employees: 1-4
Square Footage: 324000
Parent Co: Central Warehouse Company
Types of products warehoused:
  Non-food & food items
Storage Facility Data:
  Dry Storage Size: 67000 Sq. Ft.

53159 Midnite Express
1075 South Inner Loop Rd
Ste 201
Atlanta, GA 30337   770-933-9496
Fax: 310-330-2358 800-643-6483
nick.vincent@mnx.com www.mnx.com
Warehouse providing dry storage; transportation firm providing international and domestic freight forwarding services via air freight, local, long and short haul trucking; also, re-packing services available
CEO: Scott Cannon
VP Operations: Nick Vincent
Number Employees: 1-4
Types of products warehoused:
  Dry goods, dry goods
Services Provided:
  Re-packing and international & domestic freight forwarding

53160 Midwest Assembly Warehouse
5001 County Road G
West Bend, WI 53095   262-335-1980
Fax: 262-335-2768 www.midwestawd.com
Warehouse providing dry storage, re-packing and labeling for nonperishable foods
General Manager: George Bichanich
george.bichanich@midwest-awd.com
Estimated Sales: $ 1 - 3 Million
Number Employees: 10-19
Square Footage: 800000
Types of products warehoused:
  Non-perishable foods, non-perishables
Services Provided:
  Re-packing & labeling

53161 Midwest Cold Storage & Ice Company
1101 S 5th St Ste A
Kansas City, KS 66105   913-281-2771
Fax: 913-281-5519
Warehouse offering cooler, freezer
President: Paul Mies
Plant Manager: Farley Hill
Estimated Sales: Less than $500,000
Number Employees: 1-4
Types of products warehoused:
  Cooler & freezer merchandise, frozen goods
Services Provided:
  rail siding
Storage Facility Data:
  Cooler Size 212500 Cubic Ft.
  Dry Storage Size: 135000 Cubic Ft.
  Freezer Size: 753500 Cubic Ft.

53162 Midwest Distribution Systems
6555 West mill Road
Milwaukee, WI 53218-1219   414-760-2100
Fax: 414-760-0480 800-317-0214
www.mdsfulfillment.com
Warehouse providing dry storage for nonperishable foods
President: Brad Felker
VP: Susan Allen
Estimated Sales: $500,000-$1 Million
Number Employees: 20 to 49
Parent Co: Allen Management
Types of products warehoused:
  Non-perishable, non-perishables

53163 Milan Supply Chain Solutions
1091 Kefauver Dr
Milan, TN 38358-3412   731-686-7428
Fax: 731-686-8829 800-231-7303
www.milanexpress.com
Warehouse providing short, and long term storage; transportation firm providing local and short haul trucking, and specializing in LTL, TL, and logistics
President: John Ross
jross@milanexpress.com
Number Employees: 100-249

53164 Millbrook Lofts
9 Medford St
Somerville, MA 02143-4248   617-209-4222
Fax: 617-661-4131 medford@aol.com
www.millbrooklofts.com
Warehouse providing cooler and freezer storage of frozen meat, fish and poultry; also, blast freezing services available
Owner: Charles Petri
VP: Thomas Mazzone
Estimated Sales: $1 - 2.5 Million
Number Employees: 1-4
Types of products warehoused:
  Frozen meat, fish & poultry, frozen goods
Services Provided:
  Blast freezing - 25 Degrees below 0
Storage Facility Data:
  Cooler Size 89220 Sq. Ft.
  Freezer Size: 746180 Sq. Ft.

53165 Millbrook Lofts
9 Medford St
P.O. Box 564
Somerville, MA 02143-4248   617-209-4222
Fax: 617-661-4131 www.millbrooklofts.com
Cold storage and distribution services for commercial and industrial customers throughout the United States and Canada
President: Charles Petri
Estimated Sales: $ 1 - 3 Million
Number Employees: 1-4
Type of Packaging: Food Service

53166 Miller Container Corp
3402 78th Ave W
Rock Island, IL 61201-7331   309-787-6161
Fax: 309-787-1213 www.millercontainer.com
Warehouse providing dry storage for corrugated sheets and boxes; transportation firm providing local and short haul trucking
President: Mike Vonderhaar
VP Sales: Jeff Peterson
Estimated Sales: $20-50 Million
Number Employees: 100-249
Square Footage: 300000
Types of products warehoused:
  Corrugated sheets & boxes
Services Provided:
  Local & short haul trucking

53167 Minnesota Freezer Warehouse Co
820 E 13th St
PO Box 86
Albert Lea, MN 56007-5213   507-373-1477
Fax: 507-373-2174 info@mfwc-cold.com
www.mfwc-cold.com
Warehouse providing refrigerated and freezer storage
President: Thomas Newell
tnewell@mfwc-cold.com
Plant Manager: Randy Skophammer
Estimated Sales: $1-2.5 Million
Number Employees: 20-49
Square Footage: 248000
Types of products warehoused:
  Refrigerated & frozen foods, dry goods, non-perishables, frozen goods, produce, canned foods, general merchandise
Services Provided:
  rail siding, labeling, blast freezing, packaging, pick and pack, repackaging
Storage Facility Data:
  Cooler Size 15000 Sq. Ft.
  Freezer Size: 42000 Sq. Ft.

53168 Miramar Cold Storage
8385 Miramar Mall
San Diego, CA 92121   858-452-6420
Fax: 858-452-6819 info@miramarcoldstorage.com
Manager: Tibor Nemeth
Operations Manager: Carol Chang
Estimated Sales: $300,000-500,000
Number Employees: 5 to 9

841

Warehousing / A-Z

53169 Mississippi Cold and Dry Storage
PO Box 660
Forest, MS 39074-0660
501-469-9996
Fax: 501-469-9958
President/CEO: Schoenl Don

53170 Modern Packaging
3245 N Berkeley Lake Rd NW
Duluth, GA 30096
770-622-1500
Fax: 770-814-0046
www.modernpackaginginc.com
Contract packager of condiments and liquid food items; warehouse providing dry, cooler and humidity-controlled storage of foodstuffs, liquid packaging products and seasonal sales items; also, pick and pack and rail siding available
President: Herb Sodel
VP: Nancy Sodel
Estimated Sales: $3.6 Million
Number Employees: 50-99
Square Footage: 400000
Types of products warehoused:
    Foodstuffs, liquid packaging & seasonal sales items
Services Provided:
    Pick & pack, rail siding

53171 (HQ)Moran Distribution Centers
1000 Estes Ave
Elk Grove Vlg, IL 60007-4908
847-439-0000
Fax: 847-439-0047 webmaster@morandist.com
www.morantransportation.com
Warehouse providing dry, cooler and humidity-controlled storage for nonperishable goods; transportation firm providing local and short haul trucking; rail siding available
President: Michael Moran Sr
VP Sales: Michael Moran
Director Operations: Michael Mahler
Number Employees: 100-249
Type of Packaging: Consumer, Food Service
Services Provided:
    Local & Short Haul Trucking, Regional Trucking, rail siding, trucking, labeling, packaging, pick and pack

53172 Moran Logistics
202 East 7th streeet
P O Box 295
Watsontown, PA 17777-0295
570-538-5558
Fax: 570-538-1432 800-223-1093
info@moranlogistics.com
www.moranlogistics.com
Warehouse providing dry storage for nonperishable foods; transportation firm providing local haul trucking
President: John Moran
Vice President: Joyce Arcarese
National Accounts Manager: Sharon Wilson
Customer Service: Dwuana Brown
VP Operations: Jeff Stroehmann
Number Employees: 20-49
Types of products warehoused:
    Non-perishable foods, non-perishables
Services Provided:
    Local, Long, and Short haul trucking, pick and pack

53173 Morrison Storage & Homes
34 Township Road 1421
South Point, OH 45680-7272
740-894-3000
Fax: 231-264-8415
www.morrisonstorageandhomes.com
Warehouse services include frozen and dry storage of products
Owner: Gary Morrison
Owner: Garry Morrison
Estimated Sales: Less Than $500,000
Number Employees: 1-4
Types of products warehoused:
    Refrigerated
Storage Facility Data:
    Dry Storage Size: 500000 Cubic Ft.
    Freezer Size: 1300000 Cubic Ft.

53174 Morrow Cold Storage LLC
730 NE Columbia Ave
Boardman, OR 97818
541-481-6900
Fax: 541-481-6902
Cold Storage Facility
President: Jim Barnes
Estimated Sales: $ 3 - 5 Million
Number Employees: 50-99
Type of Packaging: Food Service

53175 Mosinee Cold Storage
751 Maple Ridge Rd
Mosinee, WI 54455-9272
715-693-2130
Fax: 715-693-3006
Warehouse providing cooler storage for cheese and other food products; rail siding available
CEO: Marie Rondeau
CFO: Paul Rondeau
Accounts Manager: Gary Janz
Estimated Sales: $1-2.5 Million
Number Employees: 10-19
Square Footage: 596888
Types of products warehoused:
    Cheese & other food products
Services Provided:
    rail siding
Storage Facility Data:
    Cooler Size 2306400 Cubic Ft.

53176 Mount Airy Cold Storage
500 Redland Court
Suite 305
Owings Mills, MD 21117-0487
410-654-6700
Fax: 410-654-2234 www.mhwgroup.com
Warehouse providing freezer storage for frozen foods; rail siding and refrigerated dock services available
Owner: Marvin Weiner
Estimated Sales: $300,000
Number Employees: 6
Square Footage: 380000
Types of products warehoused:
    Frozen foods, frozen goods
Services Provided:
    Refrigerated docks, rail siding
Storage Facility Data:
    Freezer Size: 2200000 Cubic Ft.

53177 Mullica Hill Cold Storage
554 Franklinville Rd
Mullica Hill, NJ 08062-4706
856-478-4200
Warehouse providing temperature-controlled, computer-monitored storage for frozen foods and fresh fruits; also, re-packing and trucking service from port to cold storage
CEO: Fred Sorbello
fred@mullicahg.com
V.P. Finance: Anthony Kimsal
QC Manager: Alex Sorbello
President Operations: Dan Sorbello
Estimated Sales: $1-2.5 Million
Number Employees: 5-9
Square Footage: 200000
Parent Co: The Mullica Hill Group
Types of products warehoused:
    Frozen foods & fresh fruits, frozen goods, produce
Services Provided:
    Re-packing, trucking from port to cold storage
Storage Facility Data:
    Cooler Size 492000 Cubic Ft.
    Dry Storage Size: 7000 Cubic Ft.
    Freezer Size: 800000 Cubic Ft.

53178 MultiSystems Barcode Solutions
3900 NW 79th Ave # 216
Doral, FL 33166-6546
787-751-2720
Fax: 787-751-0155 877-746-0678
sales@multisystems.com
TLC's VanBuren Dedicated Facility handles product for a top food manufacturer. This frozen food distribution center is attached to a processing plant, designed for import/export services, blast freezing capabilities, as well asefficient cross-docking and high-turn requirements. Van Buren Dedicated Warehouse is located adjacent to I-540 at Twin Circle Drive.
President: Leo Puerbo
Vice President: Radames del Mazo
Sales Director: Alexander Mackenzie
Estimated Sales: $3 Million
Square Footage: 98929
Parent Co: MultiSystems
Type of Packaging: Food Service
Types of products warehoused:
    Poultry, frozen goods, general merchandise
Services Provided:
    Export, trucking, blast freezing, pick and pack

53179 Murphy Bonded Warehouse
2391 Levy St
Shreveport, LA 71103-3657
318-636-9000
Fax: 318-636-6752 800-252-7467
www.mbwinc.com
Transportation firm providing TL and LTL local haul trucking, piggyback and freight consolidation; warehouse providing dry storage for general merchandise, food products, liquor, etc.; also, rail siding, inventory and managementservices available
President: Wade Sample
wsample@mbwinc.com
Operations Manager: Brian Lapsley
Warehouse Supervisor: David Ashlock
Estimated Sales: Less Than $500,000
Number Employees: 1-4
Types of products warehoused:
    Plastics, roll paper, lumber, glass containers, rubber, corrugated boxes, food products, liquor, etc.
Services Provided:
    Inventory & management services, rail siding
Storage Facility Data:
    Cooler Size 5000 Sq. Ft.
    Dry Storage Size: 500000 Sq. Ft.

53180 Murphy Warehouse
500 S Independence Ave # 6
Rockford, IL 61102-1977
815-987-4860
Fax: 815-987-4862
Warehouse offering cooler, dry and freezer storage for general merchandise and refrigerated and frozen items; rail siding, complete distribution service for foreign trade zone, re-packing and trucking
Manager: Nancy Nance
VP: Mike Meyero
VP: Allen Murphy
Contact: Allen Murphy
amurphy@murphywarehouse.com
Estimated Sales: $2.5-5 Million
Number Employees: 5-9
Square Footage: 7200000
Parent Co: Murphy Transfer & Storage
Types of products warehoused:
    General merchandise and refrigerated & frozen items, frozen goods, general merchandise
Services Provided:
    Re-packing, trucking & distribution for foreign trade zone, rail siding
Storage Facility Data:
    Cooler Size 50000
    Dry Storage Size: 200000
    Freezer Size: 20000

53181 Murphy Warehouse Co
701 24th Ave SE
Minneapolis, MN 55414-2691
612-623-1200
Fax: 612-623-9108 sales@murphywarehouse.com
www.murphywarehouse.com
Warehouse offering logistic support and dry and cooler storage for plastics, food products, etc.; transportation firm providing freight consolidation and local haul trucking; also, rail siding, packaging, re-packing, pick/packlabeling, etc
President/CEO: Richard Murphy, Jr.
richard@murphywarehouse.com
Number Employees: 250-499
Types of products warehoused:
    Food products, confections, beverages, plastics & paper products, medical supplies, dry goods, non-perishables, canned foods, general merchandise
Services Provided:
    Trucking, packaging, re-pack, pick-pack, labeling & distribution, rail siding, trucking, labeling, packaging, pick and pack, repackaging, Foreign trade zone CES/CFS/GO
Storage Facility Data:
    Cooler Size 60000 Sq. Ft.
    Dry Storage Size: 1800000 Sq. Ft.

53182 (HQ)Murray's Transfer Inc
1011 Floral Ln
Davenport, IA 52802
563-333-4570
Fax: 563-333-4577 800-333-1011
www.murraytransfer.com
Transportation firm providing local and short haul trucking; TL and LTL; distribution and rail siding available
Founder & Owner: Marion Murray
Owners: Robert & Patty Powell
CFO: Patty Powell
General Manager: Steve Markham
Number Employees: 20-49
Types of products warehoused:
    General commodities & food stuff, general merchandise
Services Provided:
    Distribution & refrigerated deliveries, rail siding

Warehousing / A-Z

Storage Facility Data:
 Dry Storage Size: 230000 Sq. Ft.

53183 NAPA Distribution Ctr
250 Osage Ave
Kansas City, KS 66105-1488   913-281-2000
 Fax: 913-281-2614 www.napaonline.com
Warehouse providing dry, cold and frozen storage; also, rail siding available
Manager: Doug Black
HR Executive: Alan Bell
alan_bell@genpt.com
Estimated Sales: $ 10 - 20 Million
Number Employees: 100-249
Services Provided:
 rail siding

53184 NFI Industries Inc
1515 Burnt Mill Rd
Cherry Hill, NJ 08003-3637   856-691-7000
 Fax: 856-507-4488 800-922-5088
info@natlfreight.com www.nfiindustries.com
Warehouse providing rail siding services; transportation company providing long and short haul trucking
CEO: Nick Brummer
nick.brummer@investmentresearch.citi.com
CEO: Sidney Brown
Estimated Sales: Over $1 Billion
Number Employees: 5000-9999
Other Locations:
 National Distribution Centers
  Pensauken, NJ
 National Distribution Centers
  Edison, NJ
 National Distribution Centers
  Dayton, NJ
 National Distribution Centers
  Tampa, FL
 National Distribution Centers
  Orlando, FL
 National Distribution Centers
  Bensenville, IL
 National Distribution CentersEdison
Services Provided:
 rail siding

53185 NOCS West Gulf
9223 Highway 225
La Porte, TX 77571   281-930-8002
 Fax: 281-930-8135 800-782-2653
 info@nocs.com www.nocs.com
Freezer and Cold Storage Facility
Manager: John Chapman
Vice President, Sales & Marketing: Jim Henderson
Contact: Laurie Ballard
laurieb@nocs.com
Estimated Sales: $ 1 - 3 Million
Number Employees: 20-49
Square Footage: 140
Type of Packaging: Food Service

53186 Napa Barrel Care
1075 Golden Gate Dr
Napa, CA 94558-6187   707-254-1985
 Fax: 707-254-2092 info@barrelcare.com
  www.barrelcare.com
Manufacturing and storage of wine barrels
President/Winemaker: Mike Blom
mike@barrelcare.com
Warehouse Manager: Jorge Vargas
Estimated Sales: Less Than $500,000
Number Employees: 1-4

53187 National Air Cargo Inc
350 Windward Dr
Orchard Park, NY 14127-1596   716-631-0011
 Fax: 716-631-9186 800-635-0022
  www.nationalaircargo.com
Warehouse providing cooler, freezer and dry storage; transportation firm providing international and domestic freight forwarding services via local, long and short haul trucking
CEO: Christopher Alf
calf@nationalaircargo.com
CEO: Christopher Alf
Number Employees: 20-49
Services Provided:
 International & domestic freight forwarding

53188 National Cold Storage Inc
12755 Loring Dr
Bonner Springs, KS 66012   913-422-4050
 Fax: 913-422-5807 www.coldkc.com
Temperature controlled storage: cooler, freezer and dry

President: Amir Minoofar
Warehouse Manager: Roger Fullington
Estimated Sales: $5-10 Million
Number Employees: 5-9
Square Footage: 3700000
Types of products warehoused:
 dry goods, frozen goods, produce
Services Provided:
 Transloading from rail to truck & truck to rail (cross dock), rail siding, blast freezing, USDA approved; Import/export services
Storage Facility Data:
 Cooler Size 876750 Cubic Ft.
 Freezer Size: 5541570 Cubic Ft.
 Humidity-Controlled Size: 2438100 Cubic Ft.

53189 National Distribution Centers
1515 Burnt Hill Road
Cherry Hill, NJ 08003   732-417-2276
 Fax: 732-417-0915 877-634-3777
  www.ndc-nfi.com
Warehouse providing dry storage for nonperishable foods; transportation firm providing local, long and short haul trucking
Contact: Irwin Brown
irwin@sourcelogistics.net
Number Employees: 20-49
Parent Co: National Distribution Centers
Types of products warehoused:
 Non-perishable foods, non-perishables
Services Provided:
 Local, long & short haul trucking

53190 National Distribution Centers
250 Johnson Lake Rd SE
Adairsville, GA 30103   706-624-0662
 Fax: 706-624-0664 www.ndc-nfi.com
Warehouse providing dry storage for nonperishable food
Regional Manager: Mike Bryden
mbryden@ndc-nfi.com
Estimated Sales: $ 1 - 3 Million
Number Employees: 10 to 19
Parent Co: National Distribution Centers
Types of products warehoused:
 Non-perishable food, non-perishables

53191 National Warehouse Corporation
531 S Water St
Milwaukee, WI 53204-1663   414-291-4400
 Fax: 414-291-4410
Warehouse providing dry storage for appliances, chemicals, candy, paper and cleaning products and nonperishable food; also, rail siding available
Owner: Robert Feind
Estimated Sales: $500,000-$1 Million
Number Employees: 5 to 9
Square Footage: 600000
Types of products warehoused:
 Appliances, candy, paper, cleaning products & non-perishable foods, non-perishables
Services Provided:
 rail siding
Storage Facility Data:
 Dry Storage Size: 3000000 Cubic Ft.

53192 (HQ)Nebraska Warehouse Co
10064 S 134th St
Omaha, NE 68138-3708   402-896-2200
 Fax: 402-896-2201 www.nebraskawarehouse.com
Warehouse providing cooler and dry storage of general merchandise; also, rail siding, daily local deliveries for Omaha and Lincoln metro area, piggyback drayage, re-packing, labeling, etc. services available
President: Jon Meyers
jmeyers@nebraskawarehouse.com
VP: Bruce Meyers
Director of Sales: Jeff Ziegler
Number Employees: 50-99
Square Footage: 1400000
Types of products warehoused:
 General merchandise, general merchandise
Services Provided:
 Re-packing, labeling, piggyback drayage, etc., rail siding
Storage Facility Data:
 Cooler Size 20000 Sq. Ft.
 Dry Storage Size: 285000 Sq. Ft.

53193 Needham Inc
1204 Jones St
Omaha, NE 68102-3209   402-344-3820
 Fax: 402-342-5567

Warehouse providing cooler and freezer storage of meat and poultry; also, distribution and re-packing services available
President: Bill Needham
bneedham@needhaminc.net
Vice President: Rich Needham
Research & Development: Jerry Owens
Estimated Sales: $5-10 Million
Number Employees: 20-49
Types of products warehoused:
 Meat & poultry
Services Provided:
 Distribution & re-packing

53194 Nevada Cold Storage
1515 Silver St
P.O. BOX 670
Elko, NV 89803-0670   775-738-8799
 Fax: 775-753-5213
President: Doug Passmore
Estimated Sales: $300,000-500,000
Number Employees: 1-4
Type of Packaging: Private Label

53195 New Federal Cold Storage
1501 Penn Ave
Pittsburgh, PA 15222-4324   412-471-5161
 Fax: 412-471-8920
Warehouse offering cooler, freezer, dry and humidity controlled storage; rail siding available
Manager: Jim Perko
General Manager: Jerry Peri
Estimated Sales: $500,000-$1 Million
Number Employees: 5 to 9
Services Provided:
 rail siding

53196 New Hampton Transfer & Storage
1970 N Linn Ave
New Hampton, IA 50659-9405   641-394-3191
 Fax: 641-394-3190 800-237-9098
  www.nhwarehouse.com
Warehouse providing dry and humidity-controlled storage of nonperishable food items; transportation firm offering LTL, short haul trucking, pick/pack, railcar loading and unloading, rental and rail siding
Owner: Chip Schwickerath
nhtf2@iowatelecom.net
Marketing Specialist: Megan Chip
Assistant Manager: William Chip
Number Employees: 5-9
Types of products warehoused:
 Non-perishable food items, non-perishables
Services Provided:
 Trucking, railcar loading & unloading, rentals, pick/pack, etc., rail siding
Storage Facility Data:
 Dry Storage Size: 100000 Sq. Ft.
 Humidity-Controlled Size: 20000 Sq. Ft.

53197 New Orleans Cold Storage-Wrhse
3411 Jourdan Rd
New Orleans, LA 70126-5049   504-944-4400
 Fax: 504-948-0957 800-782-2653
  info@nocs.com www.nocs.com
Warehouse providing cooler and freezer storage for refrigerated and frozen food; transportation firm providing local, short and long haul trucking and ocean and rail car services
President: Mark Blanchard
markb@nocs.com
Vice President, Sales & Market: Jim Henderson
Number Employees: 20-49
Other Locations:
 NOCS
  New Orleans, LA
 NOCS
  Charleston, SC
 NOCS
  Houston, TXNOCSCharleston
Types of products warehoused:
 Frozen & refrigerated food, dry goods, frozen goods
Services Provided:
 rail siding, trucking, blast freezing
Storage Facility Data:
 Cooler Size 1,000,000

53198 New Orleans Cold Storage & Warehouse
6300 Terminal Drive
Henry Clay Wharf, LA 70115   504-837-9150
 Fax: 504-944-8539 800-782-2653
 info@nocs.com www.nocs.com

Warehousing / A-Z

President: Gary Escoffier
Vice President, Sales & Marketing: Jim Henderson
Estimated Sales: $300,000-500,000
Number Employees: 1-4
Square Footage: 381

53199 New Orleans Cold Storage-Wrhse
3411 Jourdan Rd
New Orleans, LA 70126-5049   504-944-4400
           Fax: 504-944-8539 800-782-2653
           info@nocs.com www.nocs.com
President: Mark Blanchard
markb@nocs.com
Vice President, Sales & Marketing: Jim Henderson
Estimated Sales: $ 5 - 10 Million
Number Employees: 20-49
Square Footage: 480

53200 (HQ)Newark Refrigerated Warehouse
104 Avenue C
Newark, NJ 07114-2487   973-508-1492
           Fax: 973-824-8130 www.pnrw.com
Warehouse providing cooler, refrigerator and humidity-controlled storage for frozen foods, nuts and juice concentrates.
President: Jerry Vonbohlen
Vice President: Michelle Mastroberardino
michelle@pnrw.com
Office Manager: Carolyn Gruetze
General Manager: Richard Signorelli
Estimated Sales: $ 20 - 50 Million
Number Employees: 10-19
Square Footage: 160000
Other Locations:
   Newark Refrigerated Warehouse
   Port Newark, NJ Newark Refrigerated Warehouse
Types of products warehoused:
   Frozen foods, nuts & juice concentrates, dry goods, frozen goods
Storage Facility Data:
   Cooler Size 600000 Cubic Ft.
   Freezer Size: 1000000 Cubic Ft.
   Humidity-Controlled Size: 800000 Cubic Ft.

53201 Newport St Paul Cold Storage
2233 Maxwell Ave
Newport, MN 55055-7714   651-459-5555
           Fax: 651-459-5951 drew@newportcold.com
                      www.newportcold.com
Warehouse providing cooler and freezer storage for perishables and frozen foods; transportation broker providing local, long and short haul trucking; also, rail siding, distribution, blast freezing, TL and refrigerated LTL trucking etc. services available
President: Andrew Greenberg
CEO: Dean Greenberg
deang@newportcold.com
Warehouse Supervisor: Michael King
Executive VP: Robert Franklin
Director Operations: Randy Lewis
Number Employees: 20-49
Square Footage: 12
Types of products warehoused:
   Perishables & frozen foods, frozen goods
Services Provided:
   Blast freezing, cross docking, re-packing, exporting, etc., rail siding
Storage Facility Data:
   Cooler Size 400000 Cubic Ft.
   Freezer Size: 2500000 Cubic Ft.

53202 Nippon Cargo Airlines Co LTD
111 8th Ave
New York, NY 10011-5201   212-989-0146
Warehouse providing cooler and humidity-controlled storage; transportation firm providing air freight services for dangerous goods, perishables, computer equipment, live animals, oversized cargoes, etc.; also, LTL and exclusive trucking services available.
Number Employees: 5-9
Parent Co: NCA
Storage Facility Data:
   Cooler Size 2000 Sq. Ft.

53203 Nocs South Atlantic
1091 Remount Rd
North Charleston, SC 29406-3529   843-747-4833
           Fax: 803-747-8164 800-782-2653
                      www.nocs.com
Refrigerated Cargo Industry
Manager: Russell Walters
Vice President, Sales & Marketing: Jim Henderson
Contact: Tom Tennant
info@nocs.com
Estimated Sales: $ 1 - 3 Million
Number Employees: 20-49
Square Footage: 55
Type of Packaging: Food Service

53204 Nocs South Atlantic
1091 Remount Rd
North Charleston, SC 29406-3529   843-747-4833
           Fax: 843-747-8164 800-782-2653
                      info@nocs.com www.nocs.com
Cold Storage and Warehouse
Manager: Russell Walters
Vice President, Sales & Marketing: Jim Henderson
Contact: Tom Tennant
info@nocs.com
Estimated Sales: $ 1 - 3 Million
Number Employees: 20-49
Square Footage: 55
Type of Packaging: Food Service

53205 Nocus West Gulf
9223 Highway 225
La Porte, TX 77571   281-930-8002
           Fax: 281-930-8135 www.nocs.com
Freezer and Cold Stoarage Facility
Manager: John Chapman
Contact: Laurie Ballard
laurieb@nocs.com
Estimated Sales: $ 1 - 3 Million
Number Employees: 20-49
Square Footage: 140
Type of Packaging: Food Service

53206 Nor-AM Cold Storage
801 6th St SW
Le Mars, IA 51031-1817   712-548-4433
           Fax: 712-548-4663 gbrandt@nor-am.com
                      www.nor-am.com
Freezer and cold Storage Facility
CEO: Greg Brandt
gbrandt@nor-am.com
CFO: Janna Brandt
Vice President Operations: Scott Albers
Estimated Sales: $ 3 - 5 Million
Number Employees: 20-49
Type of Packaging: Food Service

53207 Nor-Am Cold Storage
1555 21st Street Southwest
Le Mars, IA 51031   712-548-4433
           Fax: 712-548-4663 dcasey@nor-am.com
                      www.nor-am.com
President & CEO: Greg Brandt
Sales Manager: Mike Francis
Contact: Tom Duenow
tduenow@nor-am.com
Vice President Operations: Scott Albers
Plant Manager: Dan Casey
Estimated Sales: $ 3 - 5 Million
Number Employees: 20-49

53208 Nordic Logistics and Warehousing, LLC
670 Airport Road
Oxford, AL 36203   256-835-2211
           Fax: 256-831-9798 info@nordiccold.com
                      www.nordiccold.com
Warehouse providing cooler and freezer storage for food products.
President: Don Schoenl
Chief Executive Officer: Darrell McKinnon
Chief Financial Officer: David Apseloff
Sales/Alabama & Mississippi: Larry Robinson
Contact: Mark Bruns
mbruns@ventor-nordic.com
Transportation (GA/OH/AL/MS/NC/SC): Bill Crotty
Senior Vice-President of Production: Bill Austin
Estimated Sales: $ 1 - 3 Million
Number Employees: 20-49
Parent Co: Nordic Cold Storage
Type of Packaging: Food Service
Services Provided:
   Transportation, export, rail siding, trucking, blast freezing

53209 (HQ)Nordic Logistics and Warehousing, LLC
4300 Pleasantdale
Atlanta, GA 30340   770-448-7400
           Fax: 770-446-1861 www.nordiccold.com/
Corporate office for 14 warehouses throughout the Southeast US providing a total of 54 million cubic feet of temperature controlled storage; also transportation, distribution, rail siding, repacking and labeling.
President: Don Schoenl
Chief Engineering Officer: Darrell McKinnon
Chief Financial Officer: David Apseloff
Sales/Georgia & Ohio: Bill Croty
Contact: Roland Connell
roland.connell@nordiccold.com
Sales/North & South Carolina: Steve Smith
Senior Vice-President of Production: Chris Austin
Number Employees: 500-999
Type of Packaging: Food Service
Types of products warehoused:
   frozen goods, produce
Services Provided:
   Export, transportation, rail siding, trucking, blast freezing

53210 Nordica Warehouses Inc
2101 E 39th St N
Sioux Falls, SD 57104-7014   605-336-9152
           Fax: 605-332-8919 www.nordicawarehouses.com
Warehouse providing dry, cooler and freezer storage for general merchandise, meat, produce and dry and frozen foods; rail siding available. Foreign trade zone
President: Dan Afdahl
nordicawarehousesinc@aol.com
Vice President: Dave Lyng
Office Manager: Sue Linton
Estimated Sales: $3-5 Million
Number Employees: 20-49
Square Footage: 1400000
Types of products warehoused:
   Dry & frozen foods, meat, produce & general merchandise, dry goods, frozen goods, general merchandise
Services Provided:
   rail siding, labeling, blast freezing, packaging, pick and pack, repackaging
Storage Facility Data:
   Cooler Size 100000000 Cubic Ft.
   Dry Storage Size: 4500000 Cubic Ft.
   Freezer Size: 350000 Cubic Ft.

53211 Norfolk Warehouse Distribution Centers
6969 Tidewater Dr
Norfolk, VA 23509   757-853-5411
           Fax: 757-858-5376 800-296-6081
Warehouse providing dry storage for food and general food grade, specific commodities and hazardous materials; also, slip sheet, drum, paper box clamp services available; rail siding available
President: Robert Taylor
VP/General Manager: Fred Schultz
Operations Manager: Gary Telecsaw
Estimated Sales: $1-2 Million
Number Employees: 20-49
Square Footage: 1400000
Types of products warehoused:
   Food & general merchandise, dry goods, canned foods, general merchandise, food grade
Services Provided:
   Slip Sheet, drum, paper & box clamp, etc., rail siding
Storage Facility Data:
   Dry Storage Size: 350000

53212 Norman G. Jensen
9325 E Highway 61
Grand Portage, MN 55605   218-475-2229
           custserv.west@ngjensen.com
                      www.ngjensen.com
Warehouse providing dry storage; transportation firm providing international and domestic freight forwarding services via local, long and short haul trucking, air and ocean freight
Contact: Vicky Bach
vbach@ngjensen.com
Manager: Bonnie Carlson
Number Employees: 20-49
Types of products warehoused:
   Dry goods, dry goods

Warehousing / A-Z

Services Provided:
International & domestic freight forwarding

53213 North American Warehousing
6800 W 68th St
Bedford Park, IL 60638-4838 708-496-1549
Fax: 708-594-1091 www.nawarehouse.com
Warehouse handling food grade material and chemicals; other services include drumming, bulk liquid storage and specialty blending
Owner: Marc Chudy
chudy@nawarehouse.com
CFO: Marc Chudy
Estimated Sales: $ 3 - 5 Million
Number Employees: 20-49
Square Footage: 800000
Type of Packaging: Food Service, Private Label, Bulk
Types of products warehoused:
Food grade material, chemicals, general merchandise, Chemicals
Services Provided:
Drumming, bulk liquid drum storage & specialty blending, rail siding, trucking, labeling, packaging, repackaging

53214 North Bay Produce Inc
1771 N US Highway 31 S
Traverse City, MI 49685-8748 231-946-1941
Fax: 231-946-1902
marketing@northbayproduce.com
www.northbayproduce.com
Cooperative, importer and exporter of fresh produce including apples, asparagus, blueberries, cherries, peaches, plums, snow peas, sugar snaps, mangos, raspberries, blackberries, red currants, etc.; also, apple cider.
President: Mark Girardin
National Marketing Manager: Sharon Robb
Facilities & Compliance Manager: Jonathan Wall
Estimated Sales: $73 Million
Number Employees: 20-49
Number of Brands: 1
Square Footage: 15000
Type of Packaging: Consumer, Food Service, Private Label, Bulk
Other Locations:
North Bay Produce Warehouse
Miami, FL
North Bay Produce Warehouse
Mascoutah, ILNorth Bay Produce
WarehouseMascoutah
Types of products warehoused:
produce
Services Provided:
Cooling, handling, storage

53215 North Carolina State Ports Authority: Port of Wilmington
1 Shipyard Boulevard
Wilmington, NC 28401 910-763-1621
Fax: 910-763-6440 800-334-0682
www.ncports.com
CEO: Thomas J Eagar
Contact: Kevin Gaskill
kgaskill@ncports.com
Number Employees: 100-249
Type of Packaging: Food Service

53216 North Western WarehouseCo
417 Pine St
Rapid City, SD 57701-1676 605-342-1460
Fax: 605-342-1744
nww@northwesternwarehouse.com
www.allied.com
Warehouse providing cooler, freezer and dry storage for frozen and canned food
President: Douglas Koppmann
CEO: Doug Koppman
d.koppmann@northwesternwarehouse.com
Estimated Sales: $500,000-$1 Million
Number Employees: 10-19
Square Footage: 428000
Types of products warehoused:
Frozen & canned food, frozen goods, canned foods
Storage Facility Data:
Cooler Size 16000 Cubic Ft.
Dry Storage Size: 50000 Sq. Ft.
Freezer Size: 100000 Cubic Ft.

53217 Northeast Refrigerated
1650 Shawsheen St # 1
Tewksbury, MA 01876-1599 978-851-4747
Fax: 978-851-0383 800-874-9642
msancartier@neref.com www.neref.com
Warehousing and transportation services include long, short and local haul trucking of frozen and perishable foods; serving the New England area
Owner: James Monoxelos
jmonoxelos@neref.com
Owner: Mike Sancartier
Number Employees: 50-99
Types of products warehoused:
Frozen & perishable foods, frozen goods
Services Provided:
Trucking in the New England area, trucking, labeling, pick and pack
Storage Facility Data:
Cooler Size 200000 Cubic Ft.
Freezer Size: 350000 Cubic Ft.

53218 Northland Cold Storage Inc
2490 S Broadway
Green Bay, WI 54304-5255 920-431-4600
Fax: 920-431-4613 cpokel@ncold.com
www.ncold.com
Warehouse providing cooler, freezer and dry storage; transportation firm providing refrigerated, LTL, short and long haul trucking
President: Kathleen Pokel
kpokel@ncold.com
Manager - Information Technology: Ben Bergeron
Manager - Maintenance & Refrigeration: Martin Demeny
Manager - Customer Service: Caitlin Pokel
General Manager - Warehouse Operations: David Pokel
Number Employees: 20-49
Other Locations:
Troutdale, OR
McMinnville, TNMcMinnville
Types of products warehoused:
Frozen, refrigerated & non-perishable food, dry goods, non-perishables, frozen goods, canned foods, general merchandise
Services Provided:
rail siding, trucking, blast freezing
Storage Facility Data:
Cooler Size 17000 Sq. Ft.
Dry Storage Size: 200000 Sq. Ft.
Freezer Size: 200000 Sq. Ft.

53219 Northwestern Ice & ColdStorage
21435 NW Cherry Lane
Hillsboro, OR 97124-6630 503-531-5400
800-791-2653
www.henningsen.com
Estimated Sales: $300,000-500,000
Number Employees: 9

53220 Nu-Lane Cargo Services
Po Box 7360
Visalia, CA 93290
Fax: 559-625-9700 800-310-6506
Company moves refrigerated truck loads from the shipper to consignee.
Sales Rep.: Steve Brasiel

53221 Nutra Food Ingredients, LLC
4683 50th Street SE
Kentwood, MI 49512 616-656-9928
Fax: 419-730-3685
sales@nutrafoodingredients.com
www.nutrafoodingredients.com
Functional and nutritional ingredients supplier to the food, beverage, nutraceutical and cosmetics industries
President: Bryon Yang
Director of Business Development: Tim Wolffis
Quality Control: Monica Mylet
monica.mylet@nutrafoodingredients.com
Director of Sales and Marketing: Clarence Harvey
Year Founded: 2004
Estimated Sales: Under $500,000
Number Employees: 1-4
Other Locations:
Distribution Center
Edison, NJ
Distribution Center
Carson, CADistribution CenterCarson

53222 (HQ)O'Byrne Distribution Ctr Inc
5855 N 94th St
Milwaukee, WI 53225-2652 414-463-9090
Fax: 414-463-4662 info@obyrnedc.com
www.obyrnedc.com
Warehouse providing cold, dry and humidity-controlled storage for groceries and general merchandise; rail siding, pick/pack, re-packing/re-couping, EDI, etc. available; transportation firm providing local haul trucking and consolidatedshipping
Owner: Rosemary O'Bryne
ro@obyrnedc.com
Number Employees: 20-49
Types of products warehoused:
Groceries & general merchandise, general merchandise
Services Provided:
Trucking, inventory control, pool distribution, EDI, etc., rail siding
Storage Facility Data:
Cooler Size 500 Sq. Ft.
Dry Storage Size: 220000 Sq. Ft.
Humidity-Controlled Size: 26736 Sq. Ft.

53223 O-G Packing & Cold Storage Co
2097 Beyer Ln
Stockton, CA 95215-2009 209-931-4392
Fax: 209-931-5887 mail@ogpacking.com
www.ogpacking.com
Public warehouse providing cooler, freezer and humidity-controlled storage for refrigerated and frozen foods and cherries including fresh, sweet bing and maraschino; also, rail siding, packing and export services available.
Number Employees: 2,000
Types of products warehoused:
Refrigerated foods, fresh cherries & frozen foods, frozen goods, produce
Services Provided:
Packing & export services available, rail siding
Storage Facility Data:
Cooler Size 1200000 Cubic Ft.
Freezer Size: 500000 Cubic Ft.
Humidity-Controlled Size: 1200000 Cubic Ft.

53224 ODW Logistics Inc
1580 Williams Rd
Columbus, OH 43207-5183 614-497-1660
Fax: 614-491-1461 800-743-7062
jclark@odwlogistics.com www.odwlogistics.com
Warehouse providing cooler and dry storage for beverages, cereal, health and beauty aids and general commodities; transportation firm providing TL and LTL trucking and contract and freight brokerage; also, rail siding, labelingkitting and point of sale packaging
President: John Ness
ness@odwlogistics.com
CEO: Robert Ness
CFO: David Hill
VP: Jeff Clark
VP Sales & Marketing: Jeff Clark
VP Operations: Jon Petticrew
Number Employees: 20-49
Other Locations:
ODW Logistics
Columbus, OHODW Logistics
Types of products warehoused:
Beverages, cereal, health & beauty aids & general commodities, general merchandise
Services Provided:
LTL & TL trucking, labeling, kitting, etc., rail siding
Storage Facility Data:
Cooler Size 25000 Sq. Ft.
Dry Storage Size: 1500000 Sq. Ft.

53225 Oborn Transfer & Stge Co Inc
Freeport Ctr # A13n
Clearfield, UT 84015 801-773-4902
Fax: 801-773-4993 800-358-0646
www.oborn.com
Public warehouse offering dry storage for bagged products and barrels; rail siding available; transportation services including local pickup and delivery
Owner: Kent Oborn
bret@oborn.com
Number Employees: 10-19
Types of products warehoused:
Dry bagged products & barrels, dry goods
Services Provided:
rail siding

Warehousing / A-Z

53226 Occidental Foods International, LLC
4 Middlebury Blvd
Suite 3, Aspen Business Park
Randolph, NJ 07869   973-970-9220
    Fax: 973-970-9222 info@occidentalfoods.com
                    www.occidentalfoods.com
Representatives and importers of bulk spices and seeds, including paprika; pure mancha saffron; chilies dried, crushed and ground; turmeric; granulated garlic and garlic powder; cardamom; annatto, allspice and sesame seeds
President: Scott Hall
Chief Financial Officer: Denise Hall
Estimated Sales: $4.9 Million
Type of Packaging: Food Service, Bulk

53227 Ocean World Lines
1981 Marcus Ave Ste E100
New Hyde Park, NY 11042-1038   516-616-2424
                    Fax: 516-616-2400
Warehouse providing storage for frozen foods; transportation firm providing international and domestic freight forwarding via air and ocean freight and long and short haul trucking
President: Alan Baer
abaer@kellogg.com
Executive Assistant: Denise Steinberg
Number Employees: 1-4
Types of products warehoused:
    Frozen foods, frozen goods

53228 Oceana County Freezer Storage
4730 W Shelby Rd
Shelby, MI 49455-8683   231-861-6575
                    Fax: 231-861-6578
Warehouse offering cooler and freezer storage for food products; also, re-packing and labeling available
President: Earl Peterson
Contact: Randall Carlin
rcarlin@petersonfarmsinc.com
Estimated Sales: $2.5-5 Million
Number Employees: 10-19
Parent Co: Peterson Farms
Types of products warehoused:
    Refrigerated & frozen foods, frozen goods
Services Provided:
    Re-packing & labeling

53229 Ohio Commerce Center
24 University Avenue NE
Suite 200
Minneapolis, MN 55413   651-855-9700
            Fax: 651-855-9701 www.meritex.com
Warehouse providing dry storage for nonperishable foods; transportation firm providing local, long and short haul trucking
Manager: Frank Sutliff
CEO: Paddy McNeely
CFO: Tom Hotover
Chief Operating Officer: Arvid Povilaitis
Number Employees: 10-19
Parent Co: Meritex Logistics
Types of products warehoused:
    Non-perishable foods, non-perishables
Services Provided:
    Local, long & short haul trucking

53230 (HQ)Ohio Valley Shippers Assn
4950 Para Dr
Cincinnati, OH 45237-5012   513-242-7900
        Fax: 513-242-7932 800-837-2616
            ovsa@ovsa.cc www.ovsa.cc
Transportation services include full TL, TOFC and volume LTL of dry freight nationwide and internationally; also, warehouse storage of dry goods
Vice President: Ron Sickmeier
VP: Ron Sickmeier
Number Employees: 5-9
Types of products warehoused:
    Dry freight

53231 Olson Co
1717 Pearl St
Waukesha, WI 53186-5626   262-548-1220
        Fax: 262-548-1212 888-657-6511
                www.odwlogistics.com
Warehouse providing dry storage for nonperishable foods; transportation services include long and short haul trucking in the Midwest
President: Steve Jacobus
steve.jacobus@olsoncompany.com
Chairman: Jack Jacobus
General Manager-Logistics: Modupe Taylor-Pearce
Number Employees: 100-249
Types of products warehoused:
    Non-perishable foods, electronic equipment, steel, consumer goods, dry goods, non-perishables, canned foods, general merchandise, Telecommunications equipment
Services Provided:
    Third-party logistics provider throughout the Midwest, rail siding, trucking, labeling, packaging, pick and pack, repackaging, Catalog & internet fulfillment
Storage Facility Data:
    Dry Storage Size: 1200000 Sq. Ft.

53232 Olson Commercial Cold Storage
P.O.Box 332
1340 W High St
Defiance, OH 43512-5302   41 - 7 - 47
        Fax: 419-784-2026 800-886-5766
Warehouse providing freezer, cooler and dry storage for dairy and meat products, specialty foods, etc.; also, order picking, packaging, trucking and quality control services available
Owner: Scott Olson
Manager: Steve Olson
VP: Gail Olson
Estimated Sales: $ 3 - 5 Million
Number Employees: 20
Types of products warehoused:
    Frozen & specialty foods and dairy & meat products, frozen goods
Services Provided:
    Order picking, packaging, trucking, quality control, etc.
Storage Facility Data:
    Cooler Size 1300000 Cubic Ft.
    Dry Storage Size: 800000 Cubic Ft.

53233 Onieda Cold Storage AndWarehouse
8001 E 88th Ave
Henderson, CO 80640-8107   303-288-7211
        Fax: 303-287-7911 www.oneidacoldstorage.com
Cold Storage and Warehouse
Manager: Ben Gudorf
Estimated Sales: $ 1 - 3 Million
Number Employees: 20-49
Type of Packaging: Food Service

53234 Onieda Cold Storage AndWarehouse
8001 E 88th Ave
Henderson, CO 80640-8107   303-288-7211
                    Fax: 303-287-7911
Cold Storage and Warehouse
Manager: Ben Gudorf
Estimated Sales: $ 1 - 3 Million
Number Employees: 20-49
Type of Packaging: Food Service

53235 Onieta Cold Storage AndWarehouse
3825 Lafayette Street
Denver, CO 80205-3316   303-288-7211
                    Fax: 303-287-7911
Cold Storage and Warehouse
Type of Packaging: Food Service

53236 Ontario Produce Company
PO Box 880
Ontario, OR 97914   541-889-6485
                    Fax: 541-889-7823
Red, yellow and white onions; dry storage for onions
President and CEO: Robert A Komoto
Office Manager & Transportation: Janet Komoto
Shed Foreman: Arturo Rodriguez
Inspector: Alan Lovitt
Estimated Sales: $5-10 Million
Number Employees: 20 to 49
Square Footage: 160000
Type of Packaging: Consumer, Food Service, Private Label, Bulk
Types of products warehoused:
    Onions, produce
Services Provided:
    rail siding
Storage Facility Data:
    Dry Storage Size: 88400 Sq. Ft.

53237 Orange County Cold Storage
1301 S Sunkist Avenue
Anaheim, CA 92806-5614   714-502-9763
                    Fax: 714-502-9770
Warehouse providing storage for frozen foods; transportation firm offering short haul trucking; also re-packing services available
President: George Gamar
Number Employees: 20-49
Types of products warehoused:
    Frozen foods, frozen goods, produce, canned foods, general merchandise
Services Provided:
    Re-packing & trucking, pick and pack, repackaging
Storage Facility Data:
    Cooler Size 50000
    Freezer Size: 100000

53238 Orefield Cold Stge & Dstrbtng
3824 Route 309
Orefield, PA 18069-2007   610-395-8263
        Fax: 610-395-6074 www.ocslog.com
Wholesale frozen food and storage
President: Neil Eichelberger
ostorage@aol.com
Estimated Sales: $16,700,000
Number Employees: 100-249
Type of Packaging: Food Service, Bulk

53239 Oregon Transfer Co
5910 N Cutter Cir
Portland, OR 97217-3939   503-943-3500
        Fax: 503-659-0741 www.oregontransfer.com
Warehouse offering cooler, dry and humidity controlled storage for nonperishable foods, alcoholic beverages, etc.; rail siding available; transportation firm providing freight consolidation and local and short haul trucking
President: Gary C Eichman
garyeichman@oregontransfer.com
Chairman: Gary C Eitchman
CFO: Gary Hunt
Director of Human Resource: Victoria Masengale
Director Of Operations: Mike Delaney
Number Employees: 50-99
Types of products warehoused:
    Non-perishable food products, alcoholic beverages, general merchandise & groceries, dry goods, non-perishables, canned foods, general merchandise
Services Provided:
    Repacking, shrinkwrapping, trucking & freight consolidation, rail siding, trucking, labeling, pick and pack, repackaging
Storage Facility Data:
    Cooler Size 175000 Sq. Ft.
    Dry Storage Size: 525000 Sq. Ft.
    Humidity-Controlled Size: 175000 Sq. Ft.

53240 (HQ)Overflo
3010 Nieman Ave
Baltimore, MD 21230-2742   410-646-5200
        Fax: 410-644-2224 800-626-0616
                www.overflo.com
Warehouse offering dry storage; rail siding available
CEO: Gary Timme
Number Employees: 100-249
Types of products warehoused:
    Grocery, Paper, dry goods, non-perishables
Services Provided:
    rail siding, trucking, labeling, pick and pack, repackaging
Storage Facility Data:
    Dry Storage Size: 2000000 Sq. Ft.

53241 Ozburn-Hessey Logistics LLC
7101 Executive Ctr Dr Ste 333
Brentwood, TN 37027   615-401-6400
        Fax: 615-377-3977 877-401-6400
            recruiting@ohl.com www.ohl.com
Warehouse providing dry storage for general merchandise and food products; transportation service providing TL and local haul trucking; rail siding, pick and pack, intermodal, customs bonded, food grade logistic service available
President and COO: Bert Irigoyen
CEO: Scott McWilliams
CFO: Thomas Wilkas
Number Employees: 1,000-4,999
Other Locations:
    ODC Integrated Logistics
    Plainfield, IN
    ODC Integrated Logistics

Chambersburg, PA
ODC Integrated Logistics
Sparks, NV
Ozburn-Hessey Logistics
Memphis, TNODC Integrated
LogisticsChambersburg
Types of products warehoused:
General merchandise & food products, general merchandise
Services Provided:
Food grade logistics, distribution, pick & pack & transportation, rail siding, pick and pack
Storage Facility Data:
Dry Storage Size: 5000000 Sq. Ft.

53242 PBB Global Logistics
P.O.Box 950
Buffalo, NY 14213-0950   716-692-3100
Fax: 716-692-3103 www.livingstonintl.com
Transportation firm providing domestic and international freight forwarding services via local, long and short haul trucking, rail car, air and ocean freight; also, cooler, freezer and dry storage available by arrangement
Manager: Bill Conrad
Contact: Chirs Mcmullen
chirsm@pbb.com
Number Employees: 50-99

53243 PPC Perfect Packaging Co
26974 Eckel Rd
PO Box 286
Perrysburg, OH 43551-1214   419-874-3167
Fax: 419-874-8044
Manufacturer and exporter of custom wooden boxes for machinery and related equipment and domestic, export and military packaging; also, heated warehousing available
Owner: Anil Sharma
Estimated Sales: Less Than $500,000
Number Employees: 1-4
Square Footage: 28000

53244 PRISM Team Services
1675 Overland Court
West Sacramento, CA 95691   925-838-1691
Fax: 925-838-1694 info@prismlogistics.com
www.prismlogistics.com
Warehouse facility for storage of grocery products, packaged goods, etc.; re-packing and labeling available; transportation services include JIT scheduling, common carrier, freight brokerage, long, local and short haul; rail sidingavailable, fullfillment.
President: Jere van Puffelen
VP: Paul Van de Roovaart
Contact: Dotty Martin
dmartin@prismlogistics.com
Number Employees: 20-49
Types of products warehoused:
Grocery products, packaged materials, etc., dry goods, non-perishables, canned foods, general merchandise
Services Provided:
Re-packaging, freight consolidation, labeling, etc., rail siding, trucking, labeling, packaging, pick and pack
Storage Facility Data:
Dry Storage Size: 700000 Sq. Ft.

53245 Pacific Cartage & Warehousing
33001 Dowe Ave
Union City, CA 94587   510-487-6026
Fax: 510-487-6064
Warehouse providing dry storage for food products and general merchandise; transportation services include freight consolidation; distribution; also, distribution, import distribution, fulfillment and rail siding available
Manager: John Costa
john@pcnw.com
Number Employees: 100-249
Types of products warehoused:
Food products & general merchandise, general merchandise
Services Provided:
Distribution & import distribution, consolidation & fulfillment, rail siding, pick and pack, barcoding

53246 Pacific Coast WarehouseCo
3601 Jurupa St
Ontario, CA 91761-2905   909-545-8100
cma@pcwc.com
www.pcwc.com
Warehouse providing dry storage; transportation firm providing freight consolidation services; also, cartage, pool distribution and cross docking services available; rail siding available
President: Jim Marcoly
Manager: Mark Burk
VP Operations & Customer Development: Michael Waring
Number Employees: 5-9
Other Locations:
Union City, CA
Types of products warehoused:
Dry, institutional & industrial products, dry goods
Services Provided:
Pool distribution, cartage, cross-docking, etc., rail siding, labeling, packaging
Storage Facility Data:
Dry Storage Size: 975000 Sq. Ft.

53247 Pacific Cold Storage
2851 E 44th Street
Los Angeles, CA 90058-2401   323-581-6271
Fax: 323-581-3021
Warehouse providing cooler and freezer storage for frozen foods; also, rail siding available
President: Bill Duffy
Types of products warehoused:
Frozen foods, frozen goods
Services Provided:
rail siding

53248 Pacific Commerce Company
16320 Bake Parkway
Irvine, CA 92618   949-679-4700
Fax: 949-589-9002
Exporter of maraschino cherries, pie fillings, bakery items, mayonnaise, salad dressings, etc.; wholesaler/distributor of general line products; serving the food service market; warehouse offering dry storage for groceries
President: Bryan McCullough
VP: Mark Roberts
Contact: Mackay Ramsay
mramsay@pacificommerce.com
Estimated Sales: $2.5-5 Million
Number Employees: 1-4
Square Footage: 73728
Types of products warehoused:
Dry groceries & frozen foods, dry goods, frozen goods
Storage Facility Data:
Dry Storage Size: 18432 Sq. Ft.
Freezer Size: 2200 Cubic Ft.

53249 Pacific Harvest Products
13405 SE 30th Street
Bellevue, WA 98005-4454   425-401-7990
Dry blends, sauces, dressings, bases
Contact: Nicholas Ade
n.ade@pnb.org
Number Employees: 20-49
Type of Packaging: Consumer, Food Service, Private Label, Bulk

53250 Pacific Transload Systems
737 Bay St
Oakland, CA 94607-1118   510-893-5420
Fax: 510-893-8351 800-458-4788
www.pcc-cfs.com
Manager: Vivian Dewey
Manager: Samuel Johnson
General Manager: Sam Johnson
Estimated Sales: $ 1 - 3 Million
Number Employees: 5-9
Square Footage: 174

53251 Packaged Ice
PO Box 1143
Martinsburg, WV 25402-1143   304-263-3330
Fax: 304-267-4415

53252 Packaged Ice
610 Pleasant Valley Road
P.O.Box 548
Harrisonburg, VA 22801-0548   540-433-2751
Fax: 540-564-6855 www.reddyice.com
Ice Distribution
Manager: R O Deavers
Estimated Sales: $ 10 - 20 Million
Number Employees: 50-99
Type of Packaging: Food Service

53253 Palmer Logistics
13001 Bay Area Blvd
Pasadena, TX 77507-1322   281-291-7366
Fax: 713-671-6825 800-237-0370
www.palmerlogistics.com
Warehouse providing dry storage, re-packaging and labeling for nonperishable foods; transportation services include long and short haul trucking nationwide
President: Brett M Mears
Number Employees: 5-9
Types of products warehoused:
Non-perishable foods, non-perishables
Services Provided:
Re-packaging & lableing, labeling, repackaging

53254 Panalpina Inc.
1200 Avenue St. Jean-Baptiste
Suite 104
Quebec City, QC G2E 5E8
Canada   418-877-4774
Fax: 418-877-1248 info.canada@panalpina.com
www.panalpina.com
Warehouse providing storage for dry goods; also, order picking, invoicing, collection, EDI and rail siding available
President/CEO: Peter Ulber
CFO: Robert Erni
Number Employees: 20-49
Square Footage: 580000
Parent Co: Panalpina
Types of products warehoused:
Dry foods, dry goods
Services Provided:
Distribution, order picking, invoicing, collection & EDI, rail siding

53255 Panamerican Logistics
1270 Woolman Pl
Atlanta, GA 30354-1392   404-767-1700
Fax: 404-559-4380
Handling facitility
Owner: Camilo Bundia
operations@panamlogistics.com
Estimated Sales: $ 3 - 5 Million
Number Employees: 10-19

53256 Parkside Warehouse Inc
5940 Falcon Rd
Rockford, IL 61109-2916   815-397-9614
Fax: 815-397-6127
cshank@parksidewarehouse.com
www.parksidewarehouse.com
Warehouse providing dry storage for general merchandise; also, FI-FO rotation, lot/batch control, labeling, re-coop and re-packing, light assembly, pick and pack, order picking, stretch wrap, slip sheet, humidity checks and yardstorage available
Owner: C Carson
cc@methodmodels.com
CEO: Steve Tigner
General Manager: Chris Shank
Estimated Sales: $500,000-$1 Million
Number Employees: 5-9
Square Footage: 1400000
Types of products warehoused:
General merchandise: grocery products, packaging material, raw food material, paper, appliances, oils & lubricants, etc., dry goods, non-perishables, canned foods, general merchandise
Services Provided:
FI-FO rotation, lot/batch control, labeling, etc., rail siding, labeling, repackaging
Storage Facility Data:
Dry Storage Size: 350000 Sq. Ft.

53257 Partners Alliance Cold Storage
565 E California St
P.O.Box 850
Ontario, CA 91761-1735   909-986-4400
Fax: 909-986-8224 rj@partnersacs.com
www.partnersacs.com
GENERAL MANAGER: RJ NEU
Estimated Sales: $ .5 - 1 million
Number Employees: 10-19

53258 Patane Brothers FreezerWrhses
108 Densten Rd
Sewell, NJ 08080-1890   856-589-7256
Fax: 856-589-2543
Warehouse offering cooler and freezer storage
Owner: Mike Nolan
CEO: Michael Nolan

Warehousing / A-Z

Estimated Sales: Less Than $500,000
Number Employees: 1-4
Types of products warehoused:
  frozen goods, general merchandise
Services Provided:
  labeling, repackaging
Storage Facility Data:
  Freezer Size: 750000 Cubic Ft.

53259 Peasley Transfer & Storage
111 N Curtis Rd
Boise, ID 83706-1433   208-901-8396
           Fax: 208-376-3447 800-657-5390
                              www.allied.com
Warehouse providing storage for general commodities; also rail siding and delivery within a 50 mile radius available
Owner: Emmet Herndon
peasleyts@mindspring.com
VP: Dean Price
Sales: Kit Herndon
Number Employees: 20-49
Parent Co: Nampa
Other Locations:
  Nampa, ID
Types of products warehoused:
  dry goods, non-perishables, canned foods, general merchandise
Services Provided:
  rail siding, labeling
Storage Facility Data:
  Dry Storage Size: 60000 Sq. Ft.

53260 (HQ)Peerless Trucking Company
P.O.Box 54554
Los Angeles, CA 90054   310-637-3603
                         Fax: 310-635-6739
Warehouse providing dry storage; transportation firm providing local and short haul trucking; rail siding available
President: Bill Hart
VP: John Hart
Number Employees: 20-49
Other Locations:
  Peerless Trucking Co.
  City of Commerce, CAPeerless Trucking Co.
Services Provided:
  Short & local haul trucking, rail siding
Storage Facility Data:
  Dry Storage Size: 200000 Sq. Ft.

53261 Penguin Cold Storage
1619 S 31st Ave
Phoenix, AZ 85009-6246   602-233-1786
          info@penguincoldstorage.com
                  penguincoldstorage.com
Warehouse providing cooler and freezer storage for the food industry
Estimated Sales: $500,000-$1 Million
Number Employees: 1-4

53262 (HQ)Penser SC
11001 Pritchard Rd
Jacksonville, FL 32219-4803   904-786-1811
           Fax: 904-783-9953 www.pensersc.com
Warehouse providing cooler, dry and humidity-controlled storage for groceries, candy, packaging, etc.; transportation services include consolidation, dry and protected LTL and TL deliveries, pool distribution, etc.; rail sidingavailable
President: Russell O'Dell
CEO: Shawn Barnett
COO: Russell O'Dell
IT: Ash Harper
ashharper@pensersc.com
General Manager-Warehouse: Lawrence Starling
Number Employees: 50-99
Other Locations:
  Peninsular Warehouse Company
  Miami, FL
  Peninsular Warehouse Company
  Orlando, FLPeninsular Warehouse
  CompanyOrlando
Types of products warehoused:
  Grocery products, candy, packaging, etc., dry goods, non-perishables, canned foods, general merchandise, roller paper
Services Provided:
  Transportation & tunnel-wrapping, rail siding, trucking, labeling, packaging, pick and pack, re-packaging
Storage Facility Data:
  Cooler Size 70000 Sq. Ft.
  Dry Storage Size: 246000 Sq. Ft.
  Humidity-Controlled Size: 70000 Sq. Ft.

53263 Penske Logistics
Route 10 Green Hills
Reading, PA 19603
           Fax: 610-775-2449 800-529-6531
                              www.penskelogistics.com
Freezer and cold Storage Facility.
President: Marc Althen
SVP, Finance: Paul Ott
SVP, Global Sales: Joe Carlier
SVP, International Operations: Bill Scroggie
SVP, Operations: Jeff Bullard
SVP, Operations: Jeff Jackson
SVP, Operations: Steve Beverly
Estimated Sales: $100-500 Million
Number Employees: 500-999
Parent Co: Penske Truck Leasing
Type of Packaging: Food Service

53264 Peoples Cartage Inc
8045 Navarre Rd SE
Massillon, OH 44646-9653   330-833-8571
                         Fax: 330-833-2035
                  jmatheos@peoplesservices.com
                              www.mayflower.com
Warehouse providing storage for general merchandise; transportation firm providing common and contract carrier and local haul trucking; rail siding available
Chairman of the Board: Ronald Sibila
President and CEO: Douglas Sibila
VP: Dan Stemple
Manager: Jim Ehret
jehret@peoplesservices.com
Number Employees: 20-49
Other Locations:
  Peoples Cartage
  Metro, WVPeoples Cartage
Types of products warehoused:
  General merchandise, general merchandise
Services Provided:
  Trucking, rail siding

53265 Peter Johansky Studio
152 W 25th St
New York, NY 10001-7402   212-242-7013
                  peter@johansky.com
                              www.johansky.com
Total food ingredient source with technical support. Dry, canned, refrigerated and frozen ingredients
Owner: Peter Johansky
pjohansky@michaelhowardstudios.com
Estimated Sales: Less Than $500,000
Number Employees: 1-4
Square Footage: 202800
Type of Packaging: Bulk

53266 Philadelphia Warehousing & Cold Storage Company
500 N Columbus Blvd
Philadelphia, PA 19123   215-627-8181
           Fax: 215-627-0846 info@phillycold.com
                  philadelphiacoldstorage.com
Warehouse providing dry, cooler and freezer storage for frozen foods
President: Ray Tarnowski
VP Administration: Maria Koleda
Customer Service: Teresa Wloczynska
Estimated Sales: $ 1 - 3 Million
Number Employees: 10-19
Square Footage: 5135000
Types of products warehoused:
  Frozen foods, frozen goods
Storage Facility Data:
  Cooler Size 200000 Cubic Ft.
  Dry Storage Size: 200000 Cubic Ft.
  Freezer Size: 1200000 Cubic Ft.

53267 Phoenix Industries LLC
621 Snively Ave
Eloise, FL 33880-5544   863-293-1151
           Fax: 863-299-2080 www.phoenixfl.com
Warehouse providing frozen, refrigerated, dry and humidity-controlled storage of frozen, chilled and dry food products; transportation company providing rail siding and distribution available
President: John Fleming
john@phoenixfl.com
Operations Manager: Mike Porter
Number Employees: 20-49
Types of products warehoused:
  dry goods, non-perishables, frozen goods, produce, canned foods, general merchandise, packaging
Services Provided:
  rail siding, trucking, labeling, packaging, pick and pack, repackaging
Storage Facility Data:
  Cooler Size 67,000
  Dry Storage Size: 50,000
  Freezer Size: 142,500
  Humidity-Controlled Size: 32,000

53268 Phoenix Industries LLC
621 Snively Ave
Eloise, FL 33880-5544   863-293-1151
           Fax: 863-299-2080 www.phoenixfl.com
Frozen, Chilled, Dry Storage
President: John Fleming
john@phoenixfl.com
Operations Manager: Mike Porter
Estimated Sales: $ 3 - 5 Million
Number Employees: 20-49
Type of Packaging: Food Service

53269 Physical Distribution
3610 N Suttle Rd
Portland, OR 97217-7773   503-289-4888
           Fax: 503-289-5102 pdi1@pcez.com
Warehouse providing dry storage for paper products, packaging materials, etc.; also, rail siding, U.S. customs foreign trade zone, re-packing, appliance installation, home delivery, pick and pack and third party logistics servicesavailable
President: Tecla Tipton
Executive Assistant: Tonina Brunz-Dautzenberg
Manager: Leo Norkus
Estimated Sales: $2.5-5 Million
Number Employees: 45
Square Footage: 720000
Types of products warehoused:
  Paper products, food related packaging materials, bottled & powdered products, etc.
Services Provided:
  U.S. Customs foreign trade zone, re-packing, pick & pack, etc., rail siding
Storage Facility Data:
  Dry Storage Size: 180000 Sq. Ft.

53270 Piedmont Distribution Centers
6100 Wheaton Drive SW
Atlanta, GA 30336   404-349-9578
Warehouse providing storage for appliances, candy, groceries, etc.; transportation services include local and long haul trucking, piggyback drayage, freight brokerage and freight forwarding; also, rail siding, assembling, poolingconsolidating, etc
Contact: David Ridgeway
dridgeway@piedmontdistrib.com
Number Employees: 50-99
Square Footage: 1140000
Parent Co: Distribution Technology
Types of products warehoused:
  Appliances, candy, health/beauty aids, groceries & foodservice items
Services Provided:
  Transportation, assembling, cross docking, pick/pack, etc., rail siding
Storage Facility Data:
  Dry Storage Size: 285000 Sq. Ft.

53271 Piedmont Distribution Services
2819 Wade Hampton Blvd
#100
Taylors, SC 29687-2788   864-244-8787
                         Fax: 864-244-8788
                  bwallace@piedmontdistrib.com
                  www.piedmontdistribution.com
Warehouse providing cooler, dry and freezer storage for dry palletized groceries and frozen foods; also, re-packing, slip sheet and carton clamps available
President: Bill Wallace
bwallace@piedmontdistrib.com
Office Manager: Harolyn Callaham
Human Resources Director: Chuck Gentry
Estimated Sales: $340,000
Number Employees: 5
Square Footage: 13980
Types of products warehoused:
  Dry palletized groceries & frozen foods, dry goods, frozen goods
Services Provided:
  Re-packing, slip sheet & carton clamps
Storage Facility Data:
  Cooler Size 40000 Cubic Ft.
  Dry Storage Size: 350000 Cubic Ft.
  Freezer Size: 350000 Cubic Ft.

Warehousing / A-Z

53272 Pilot Freight Svc
3860 Broadway St # 4
Cheektowaga, NY 14227-1174   716-683-0600
Fax: 716-683-8492 buf@pilotdelivers.com
www.pilotair.com
Transportation firm providing international and domestic freight forwarding and local, long and short haul trucking; warehouse providing cooler, freezer and dry storage
Manager: Charlene Matie
buff@pilotdelivers.com
Number Employees: 5-9
Types of products warehoused:
  Refrigerated, frozen & dry goods, dry goods, frozen goods

53273 Pioneer Cold Logistics
149 Plainfield St
Chicopee, MA 01013   413-736-1976
Fax: 413-731-7978 888-376-9361
sales@pioneercold.com www.pioneercold.com
Warehouse providing dry and cold storage for meat products; also, blast freezing, re-packing, shipping and rail siding available
President: Bryan Hedge
Customer Service Manager: Michael Carr
mcarr@pioneercold.com
Human Resource Manager: Janice Casillas
Operations Director: Susanne Gagnon
Year Founded: 1947
Estimated Sales: $11.7 Million
Number Employees: 85
Types of products warehoused:
  Meat: beef, pork & poultry
Services Provided:
  Blast freezing, re-packing & shipping, rail siding

53274 Pioneer Valley Refrigerated Warehouse
149 Plainfield St
Chicopee, MA 1013   413-736-1976
Fax: 413-731-7978 888-376-9361
sales@pioneercold.com
Warehouse providing dry cooler, freezer and humidity-controlled storage; transportation firm providing local haul trucking; rail siding available
President: Clement J Deliso Jr
Contact: Jason Adams
jadams@pioneercold.com
COO: Bryan Hedge
Number Employees: 50-99
Types of products warehoused:
  Frozen food, cheese, ice cream, dry goods, frozen goods, produce, canned foods, Frozen foods & dairy
Services Provided:
  Re-packing, cross docking, USDA inspection, distribution, etc., rail siding, trucking, labeling, blast freezing, pick and pack, repackaging
Storage Facility Data:
  Cooler Size 2000000 Cubic Ft.
  Dry Storage Size: 500000 Sq. Ft.
  Freezer Size: 5500000 Cubic Ft.

53275 Pioneer Warehouse Corporation
7640 Edgecomb Drive
Liverpool, NY 13088   315-451-3101
Fax: 315-451-1290 info@pioneerwhs.com
www.pioneerwhs.com
Warehouse offering cooler and dry storage for food, pharmaceuticals, appliances, household goods and general commodities; re-packing, UPS, pallet exchange, rail siding and specialized handling available
Manager: Rich Laigaie
Vice President: Michael Bown
Estimated Sales: $500,000-$1 Million
Number Employees: 5 to 9
Square Footage: 840000
Types of products warehoused:
  Foods, pharmaceuticals, appliances, household goods & general commodities, general merchandise
Services Provided:
  Pallet exchange, specialized handling, etc., rail siding
Storage Facility Data:
  Cooler Size 10000 Sq. Ft.
  Dry Storage Size: 200000 Sq. Ft.

53276 Pitzer Transfer & Storage Corp.
2050 Cook Dr
Salem, VA 24153   540-769-2090
Fax: 540-769-2097 800-334-0064
www.peoplesservices.com
Warehouse providing dry storage for dry, liquid bulk and hazardous materials; bulk transfer facility providing freight consolidation, local and short haul trucking; rail siding and transloading services available
President: Vance Pitzer
Number Employees: 20-49
Square Footage: 12000000
Parent Co: Peoples Services
Other Locations:
  Pitzer Transfer & Storage Cor
  Charlotte, NCPitzer Transfer & Storage Cor
Types of products warehoused:
  Dry, liquid bulk & hazardous materials, dry goods
Services Provided:
  Trucking, freight consolidation, etc., rail siding
Storage Facility Data:
  Dry Storage Size: 2000000 Sq. Ft.

53277 Planters Cooperative
701 S Lee St
Altus, OK 73521-4429   580-482-7100
Fax: 580-482-9436 www.planterscoop.org
Warehouse providing dry storage for wheat; rail siding available
President: Paul Kruska
Secretary: John Schaufele
Vice President: Stan Funkhouser
Manager: Seferino Perez
sperez@planterscoop.org
Manager: Geary James
Estimated Sales: $500,000 to $1 million
Number Employees: 50-99
Square Footage: 5200000
Types of products warehoused:
  Wheat, dry goods
Services Provided:
  rail siding
Storage Facility Data:
  Dry Storage Size: 1300000 Sq. Ft.

53278 Polar Cold Storage
1317 E Main St
Dillon, SC 29536   843-774-5706
Fax: 843-841-2445 800-353-9886
Warehouse providing refrigerated and frozen storage; also, re-packing, labeling and blast freezing available
President: Joe Herring
Estimated Sales: $500,000-$1 Million
Number Employees: 5 to 9
Parent Co: Polar Cold Storage
Other Locations:
  Polar Cold Storage
  Statesville, NCPolar Cold Storage
Types of products warehoused:
  Refrigerated & frozen foods, frozen goods
Services Provided:
  Re-packing, labeling & blast freezing

53279 Polarville
30 Exchange Ave
Natl Stock Yards, IL 62071-1003   618-274-7000
Fax: 618-274-7004 www.coldcologistics.com
Manager: Bill Meister
Manager: David Macheca
dmacheca@aol.com
Estimated Sales: $300,000-500,000
Number Employees: 20-49

53280 Port Elizabeth TerminalCorp
201a Export St
Newark, NJ 07114-3242   973-491-6324
Fax: 973-491-0055 sales@judgeorg.com
www.judgeorg.com
Warehouse providing dry storage; transportation firm providing local and long haul trucking, also rail siding
Owner: Patrick Judge
Sales: Mike Morrow
pjudge@judgeorg.com
Number Employees: 100-249
Parent Co: The Judge Organization
Types of products warehoused:
  Non-perishable foods, non-perishables
Services Provided:
  Local & long haul trucking, barcoding

53281 (HQ)Port Jersey Logistics
4 Avenue E
Monroe Township, NJ 08831   609-860-1010
Fax: 609-860-1885 sales@portjersey.com
Warehouse providing cooler and dry storage for dry groceries; transportation firm providing local, short and long haul trucking; freight consolidation, labeling, shrink wrapping and rail siding available
President: Robert Russo
Executive Vice President: Louis Keating
Marketing Manager: Stephanie Jauch
VP Sales: John Emelo
Types of products warehoused:
  dry goods, non-perishables, canned foods, general merchandise, cooler freezer
Services Provided:
  temperature-controlled, rail siding, trucking, pick and pack
Storage Facility Data:
  Cooler Size 30000 Sq. Ft.

53282 Port Of Corpus Christi
222 Power St
P.O. Box 1541
Corpus Christi, TX 78401-1529   361-882-5633
Fax: 361-881-5157 800-580-7110
webmaster@pocca.com www.portofcc.com
Cold Storage
Managing Director: Frank C. Brogan
Executive Director: John P. LaRue
Director of Finance: Dennis J. DeVries
Director of Gov't Affairs: Nelda Olivo
Director of Engineering Services: David L. Krams
Environmental Compliance Manager: Sarah Garza
Director of Business Development: Ruben C. Medina
Director of Human Resources: Sandra Terrell-Davis
Director of Operations: Anthony Alejandro
Number Employees: 50-99
Type of Packaging: Food Service

53283 Port Of Miami Cold Storage Inc
1630 Port Blvd
Miami, FL 33132-2011   305-536-2644
Fax: 305-530-9627
Contact: Mario Velasquez
mario.velasquez@mountdorafarms.hn
Facilities Manager: Tom Emanuello
Estimated Sales: Less Than $500,000
Number Employees: 1-4

53284 Port of Palm Beach Cold
200 Martin Luther King Jr Blvd
Riviera Beach, FL 33404-7506   561-863-7171
Fax: 561-863-8448
Owner: Terry Collier
Operations: Terry Collier
Estimated Sales: $ 1 - 3 Million
Number Employees: 100 to 249

53285 Port of Virginia
600 World Trade Ctr
Norfolk, VA 23510   757-675-8087
jharris@portofvirginia.com
www.portofvirginia.com
Warehouse providing dry and freezer storage for frozen foods and general merchandise; rail siding available.
VP, Marketing & Communications: Jay Stecher
jstetcher@portofvirginia.com
Sr. Director, Communications/Spokesman: Joe Harris
Estimated Sales: $50-100 Million
Number Employees: 250-499
Square Footage: 1000000
Types of products warehoused:
  Frozen foods & general merchandise, frozen goods, general merchandise
Services Provided:
  rail siding
Storage Facility Data:
  Dry Storage Size: 1000000 Sq. Ft.
  Freezer Size: 300000 Cubic Ft.

53286 Post Consumer Brands
20802 Kensington Blvd.
Lakeville, MN 55044
800-431-7678
www.postconsumerbrands.com
Cereal and grain products.
CEO: William Stiritz
Year Founded: 2015
Estimated Sales: $750 Million

Warehousing / A-Z

Number Employees: 3,500
Number of Brands: 24
Parent Co: Post Holdings
Type of Packaging: Consumer, Food Service, Private Label, Bulk
Other Locations:
   Asheboro, NC
   Coppell, TX
   Grove City, OH
   Northfield, MN
   Salt Lake City, UT
   St. Ansgar, IACoppell
Types of products warehoused:
   cereal products

53287 Power Logistics
1260 W Sycamore Rd
Manteno, IL 60950   815-468-2030
   Fax: 815-468-2033 www.powergroup.com
Warehouse providing storage for ice cream
President: Chris Simms
VP Business Development: Ken Battista
Plant Manager: Todd Benton
Estimated Sales: $2.5-5 Million
Number Employees: 20-49
Parent Co: Power Group
Other Locations:
   Power Logistics
   Bourbonnais, ILPower Logistics
Types of products warehoused:
   Ice cream, frozen goods

53288 Power Logistics
1200 Internationale Pkwy
Suite 300
Woodridge, IL 60517-4976   815-936-1800
   Fax: 815-936-1970 www.powergroup.com
Warehouse offering cooler, freezer and dry storage for frozen, refrigerated and nonperishable food products
VP Business Development: Ken Battista
Director Operations: Drew Walker
Estimated Sales: $ 1-2.5 Million
Number Employees: 19
Parent Co: Power Group
Types of products warehoused:
   Frozen, refrigerated & non-perishable food products, non-perishables, frozen goods

53289 (HQ)Power Packaging Inc
525 Dunham Rd
St Charles, IL 60174   630-377-3838
   www.powerpackaging.com
Full-service contract manufacturer for dry foods, beverage mixes, bulk blending and filling, hot fill, organic, nutraceuticals, aseptic and commissary. Designs, owns and operates multi-customer and dedicated food manufacturingfacilities nationwide.
President: Gordon Gruszka
Senior Director, Quality Assurance: Keith Schafer
Executive Director, Sales & Marketing: Chuck Woods
Senior Director, Engineering: Gary Gross
Estimated Sales: $50-100 Million
Number Employees: 1000-4999

53290 (HQ)Preferred Freezer Services
1 Main St
3rd Floor
Chatham, NJ 07928   973-820-4040
   Fax: 973-820-4004
   marketing@preferredfreezer.com
   www.preferredfreezer.com
Cold storage warehousing and temperature-controlled logistics
CEO: John Galiher
CFO: Sam Hensley
VP Intermodal: Chris Kelly
East Coast Sales Manager: David Aschenbrand
West Coast & Central Sales Manager: Chris Skraba
VP Operations: Marc Vendome
Year Founded: 1989
Estimated Sales: $300 Million
Number Employees: 2400
Type of Packaging: Food Service
Types of products warehoused:
   frozen goods
Services Provided:
   labeling, blast freezing, repackaging

53291 Preferred Freezer Services
518 Forest Pkwy
College Park, GA 30349   404-767-2210
   Fax: 404-767-2218
   erodgers@preferredfreezer.com
   www.preferredfreezer.com/atlanta
Warehouse providing freezer storage
General Manager: Roland Burnett
Sales Manager: Ed Rodgers *Year Founded:* 2007
Types of products warehoused:
   frozen goods
Services Provided:
   labeling, repackaging
Storage Facility Data:
   Freezer Size: 5600000 Cubic Ft.

53292 Preferred Freezer Services
737 Douglas Hills Rd
Lithia Springs, GA 30122   470-632-4600
   www.preferredfreezer.com/atlanta-west
Warehouse providing freezer storage
General Manager: Garret Ekstrum
Sales Manager: Charles Betts *Year Founded:* 2018
Types of products warehoused:
   frozen goods
Services Provided:
   labeling, repackaging
Storage Facility Data:
   Freezer Size: 8400000 Cubic Ft.

53293 Preferred Freezer Services
2700 Trade St
Chesapeake, VA 23323   757-558-4700
   www.preferredfreezer.com/norfolk
Warehouse providing freezer storage
General Manager: Kevin Wallace
Sales Manager: Adam Mille *Year Founded:* 2007
Types of products warehoused:
   frozen goods
Services Provided:
   labeling, repackaging, USDA/FDA/USDC inspection
Storage Facility Data:
   Freezer Size: 7900000 Cubic Ft.

53294 Preferred Freezer Services
3101 S Third St
Philadelphia, PA 19148   215-271-5600
   Fax: 215-271-5601
   pchipman@preferredfreezer.com
   www.preferredfreezer.com/philadelphia
Warehouse providing freezer storage
General Manager: David Ryan
Sales Manager: PJ Chipman *Year Founded:* 2007
Types of products warehoused:
   frozen goods
Services Provided:
   labeling, repackaging, USDA/FDA/USDC inspection
Storage Facility Data:
   Freezer Size: 6700000 Cubic Ft.

53295 Preferred Freezer Services
2500 S Damen Ave
Chicago, IL 60608   773-847-1800
   Fax: 773-847-1300
   skaroubas@preferredfreezer.com
   www.preferredfreezer.com/chicago-1
Warehouse providing freezer storage
General Manager: Dan Johnson
Sales Manager: Soto Karoubas *Year Founded:* 2003
Types of products warehoused:
   frozen goods
Services Provided:
   labeling, repackaging, USDA/FDA/USDC inspection; Export services
Storage Facility Data:
   Freezer Size: 6600000 Cubic Ft.

53296 Preferred Freezer Services
4500 W Ann Lurie Place
Chicago, IL 60632   773-254-9500
   skaroubas@preferredfreezer.com
   www.preferredfreezer.com/chicago-2
Warehouse providing freezer and cooler storage
General Manager: Dan Johnson
Sales Manager: Soto Karoubas *Year Founded:* 2009
Types of products warehoused:
   frozen goods
Services Provided:
   labeling, blast freezing, repackaging, Export services

Storage Facility Data:
   Cooler Size 2300000 Cubic Ft.
   Freezer Size: 6600000 Cubic Ft.

53297 Preferred Freezer Services
2357 S Wood St
Chicago, IL 60608   773-268-3400
   www.preferredfreezer.com/chicago-3
Warehouse providing freezer storage
General Manager: Mark Teicher
Sales Manager: Kosta Aneziris *Year Founded:* 2017
Types of products warehoused:
   frozen goods
Services Provided:
   labeling, blast freezing, repackaging, Import/export services
Storage Facility Data:
   Freezer Size: 223000 Sq. Ft.

53298 Preferred Freezer Services
7080 Express Lane
Houston, TX 77078   832-708-2200
   www.preferredfreezer.com/houston-express
Warehouse providing freezer and cooler storage
General Manager: Adam Benson
Sales Manager: Greg Muse *Year Founded:* 2015
Types of products warehoused:
   frozen goods
Services Provided:
   labeling, repackaging, USDA inspection
Storage Facility Data:
   Freezer Size: 10000000 Cubic Ft.

53299 Preferred Freezer Services
10585 Red Bluff Rd
Pasadena, TX 77507   281-291-9100
   www.preferredfreezer.com/houston-gulf-coast
Warehouse providing freezer storage
General Manager: David Wilkinson
Sales Manager: Barrett Larkey *Year Founded:* 2017
Types of products warehoused:
   frozen goods
Services Provided:
   labeling, repackaging, USDA/FDA inspection; Import/export services
Storage Facility Data:
   Freezer Size: 9600000 Cubic Ft.

53300 Preferred Freezer Services
555 Aleen St
Houston, TX 77029   713-222-6300
   www.preferredfreezer.com/houston-metro
Warehouse providing freezer storage
General Manager: Adam Benson
Sales Manager: Greg Muse *Year Founded:* 2010
Types of products warehoused:
   frozen goods
Services Provided:
   labeling, repackaging
Storage Facility Data:
   Freezer Size: 4000000 Cubic Ft.

53301 Preferred Freezer Services
10060 Porter Rd
La Porte, TX 77571   281-867-4500
   www.preferredfreezer.com/houston-port
Warehouse providing freezer and cooler storage
General Manager: David Wilkinson
Sales Manager: Barrett Larkey *Year Founded:* 2007
Types of products warehoused:
   frozen goods
Services Provided:
   labeling, repackaging, USDA/FDA/USDC inspection
Storage Facility Data:
   Cooler Size 910000 Cubic Ft.
   Freezer Size: 6800000 Cubic Ft.

53302 Preferred Freezer Services
150 Bayway Ave
Elizabeth, NJ 07202   973-854-9400
   Fax: 973-854-9401 jharris@preferredfreezer.com
   www.preferredfreezer.com/elizabeth
Warehouse providing freezer storage
General Manager: Patrick Ternyila
Sales Manager: Justin Harris *Year Founded:* 2008
Types of products warehoused:
   frozen goods
Services Provided:
   labeling, USDA/FDA inspection; Export/import
Storage Facility Data:
   Freezer Size: 9400000 Cubic Ft.

Warehousing / A-Z

53303 Preferred Freezer Services
2710 Extension of Allen St
Linden, NJ 07036   908-282-6500
www.preferredfreezer.com/elizabeth-2
Warehouse providing freezer storage
General Manager: Dan Albretsen
Sales Manager: Joe Serritella *Year Founded:* 2011
Types of products warehoused:
  frozen goods
Services Provided:
  labeling
Storage Facility Data:
  Freezer Size: 10000000 Cubic Ft.

53304 Preferred Freezer Services
536 Fayette St
Perth Amboy, NJ 08861   732-324-2000
www.preferredfreezer.com/fayette-street
Warehouse providing freezer storage
General Manager: John Kennedy
Sales Manager: Peter Soto *Year Founded:* 1989
Types of products warehoused:
  frozen goods
Services Provided:
  labeling, blast freezing, repackaging
Storage Facility Data:
  Freezer Size: 10000000 Cubic Ft.

53305 Preferred Freezer Services
231 Elm St
Perth Amboy, NJ 08861   732-324-2000
Fax: 732-324-2709 psoto@preferredfreezer.com
www.preferredfreezer.com/frozen-food-division
Warehouse providing freezer and cooler storage
General Manager: John Kennedy
Sales Manager: Peter Soto *Year Founded:* 1999
Types of products warehoused:
  frozen goods
Services Provided:
  labeling
Storage Facility Data:
  Cooler Size 600000 Cubic Ft.
  Freezer Size: 3400000 Cubic Ft.

53306 Preferred Freezer Services
100 Polar Way
Jersey City, NJ 07305   201-915-3800
Fax: 201-915-5199 bkeen@preferredfreezer.com
www.preferredfreezer.com/jersey-city-1
Warehouse providing freezer storage
General Manager: Paul Pagnozzi
Sales Manager: Brett Keen *Year Founded:* 2001
Types of products warehoused:
  frozen goods
Services Provided:
  labeling, repackaging
Storage Facility Data:
  Freezer Size: 5000000 Cubic Ft.

53307 Preferred Freezer Services
200 Polar Way
Jersey City, NJ 07302   201-395-6400
www.preferredfreezer.com/jersey-city-2
Warehouse providing freezer storage
VP Logistics: Chris Kelly
VP Logistics: Marc Vendome *Year Founded:* 2001
Types of products warehoused:
  frozen goods
Services Provided:
  labeling, repackaging
Storage Facility Data:
  Freezer Size: 5000000 Cubic Ft.

53308 Preferred Freezer Services
435A Bergen Ave
Kearny, NJ 07032   201-955-3300
www.preferredfreezer.com/kearny
Warehouse providing freezer storage
General Manager: Dwayne Rivera
Sales Manager: Ben Lising
Sales Manager: Martin Barry *Year Founded:* 2018
Types of products warehoused:
  frozen goods
Services Provided:
  labeling, repackaging
Storage Facility Data:
  Freezer Size: 197000 Sq. Ft.

53309 Preferred Freezer Services
360 Avenue P
Newark, NJ 07105   973-820-4000
Fax: 973-820-4001 mbarry@preferredfreezer.com
www.preferredfreezer.com/newark
Warehouse providing freezer storage
General Manager: John Gerced
Sales Manager: Martin Barry *Year Founded:* 2006
Types of products warehoused:
  frozen goods
Services Provided:
  labeling, repackaging, USDA/FDA/USDC inspection
Storage Facility Data:
  Freezer Size: 9500000 Cubic Ft.

53310 Preferred Freezer Services
275 Blair Rd
Avenel, NJ 07001   732-340-1600
www.preferredfreezer.com/woodbridge
Warehouse providing freezer storage
General Manager: Dave Quinn
Sales Manager: Michael Bowman *Year Founded:* 2015
Types of products warehoused:
  frozen goods
Services Provided:
  labeling, repackaging, USDA/USDC/FDC inspection
Storage Facility Data:
  Freezer Size: 9500000 Cubic Ft.

53311 Preferred Freezer Services
55 Murphy Dr
Avon, MA 02322   508-521-6000
www.preferredfreezer.com/avon
Warehouse providing freezer storage
General Manager: Bill Casey
Sales Manager: Matthew Tenaglia *Year Founded:* 2012
Types of products warehoused:
  frozen goods
Services Provided:
  labeling, USDA/USDC/FDC inspection; Export services
Storage Facility Data:
  Freezer Size: 10000000 Cubic Ft.

53312 Preferred Freezer Services
1 Commercial Street
Sharon, MA 02067   781-784-8399
          Fax: 781-784-8699
mtenaglia@preferredfreezer.com
www.preferredfreezer.com/boston
Warehouse providing freezer storage
General Manager: Bill Casey
Sales Manager: Matthew Tenaglia *Year Founded:* 2002
Types of products warehoused:
  frozen goods
Services Provided:
  labeling, repackaging
Storage Facility Data:
  Freezer Size: 4700000 Cubic Ft.

53313 Preferred Freezer Services
60 Commercial St
Everett, MA 02149   617-387-2050
www.preferredfreezer.com/boston-harbor
Warehouse providing freezer storage
General Manager: Jim Walker
Sales Manager: Ryan Martin *Year Founded:* 2006
Types of products warehoused:
  frozen goods
Services Provided:
  rail siding, labeling, repackaging, USDA/FDA/USDC inspection; Export/import
Storage Facility Data:
  Freezer Size: 6400000 Cubic Ft.

53314 Preferred Freezer Services
571 Paramount Dr
Raynham, MA 02767   508-977-0333
          Fax: 508-977-0344
www.preferredfreezer.com/raynham
Warehouse providing freezer storage
General Manager: Bill Casey
Sales Manager: TJ McNeany *Year Founded:* 2003
Types of products warehoused:
  frozen goods
Services Provided:
  labeling, USDA/FDA/USDC inspection; Export services
Storage Facility Data:
  Freezer Size: 5300000 Cubic Ft.

53315 Preferred Freezer Services
45 Campanelli Dr
Westfield, MA 01085   413-562-0885
Fax: 413-562-0855 jadams@preferredfreezer.com
www.preferredfreezer.com/westfield
Warehouse providing freezer storage
General Manager: Nathan Maker
Sales Manager: Jason Adams *Year Founded:* 2006
Types of products warehoused:
  frozen goods
Services Provided:
  labeling, USDA/FDA/USDC inspection; Export services
Storage Facility Data:
  Freezer Size: 7500000 Cubic Ft.

53316 Preferred Freezer Services
604 Curt Maberry Rd
Lynden, WA 98264   360-354-3900
www.preferredfreezer.com/lynden
Warehouse providing freezer storage
General Manager: Dan Shuler
Sales Manager: Ron Viola *Year Founded:* 2015
Types of products warehoused:
  frozen goods
Services Provided:
  labeling
Storage Facility Data:
  Freezer Size: 12600000 Cubic Ft.

53317 Preferred Freezer Services
2800 Polar Way
Richland, WA 99354   509-371-2800
www.preferredfreezer.com/richland
Warehouse providing freezer storage
General Manager: Ed Gottschalk *Year Founded:* 2015
Types of products warehoused:
  frozen goods
Services Provided:
  rail siding, labeling, Export services
Storage Facility Data:
  Freezer Size: 455000 Sq. Ft.

53318 Preferred Freezer Services
1780 W Beaver St
Jacksonville, FL 32209   904-301-1400
Fax: 904-301-1401 bgoble@preferredfreezer.com
www.preferredfreezer.com/jacksonville
Warehouse providing freezer storage
General Manager: Mark Schultz
Sales Manager: Brenda Goble *Year Founded:* 2008
Types of products warehoused:
  frozen goods
Services Provided:
  labeling, repackaging, USDA/FDA/USDC inspection
Storage Facility Data:
  Freezer Size: 8700000 Cubic Ft.

53319 Preferred Freezer Services
13700 NW 115th Ave
Medley, FL 33178   305-885-7077
          Fax: 305-885-7377
www.preferredfreezer.com/medley
Warehouse providing freezer storage
General Manager: Paul Montero
Sales Manager: Jason Mulvihill *Year Founded:* 2003
Types of products warehoused:
  frozen goods
Services Provided:
  rail siding, labeling, repackaging, USDA/FDA/USDC inspection
Storage Facility Data:
  Freezer Size: 8900000 Cubic Ft.

53320 Preferred Freezer Services
13801 NW 112th Ave
Hialeah Gardens, FL 33018   786-845-8000
www.preferredfreezer.com/miami-3
Warehouse providing freezer storage
General Manager: Jason Szczutkowski
Sales Manager: Rod Armesto *Year Founded:* 2014
Types of products warehoused:
  frozen goods
Services Provided:
  labeling, USDA/FDA/USDC inspection; Export services
Storage Facility Data:
  Freezer Size: 7100000 Cubic Ft.

Warehousing / A-Z

53321 Preferred Freezer Services
12855 NW 113th Ct
Miami, FL 33178
305-885-2200
rarmesto@preferredfreezer.com
www.preferredfreezer.com/south-florida
Warehouse providing freezer storage
General Manager: Jason Szczutkowski
Sales Manager: Rod Armesto *Year Founded:* 1999
Types of products warehoused:
  frozen goods
Services Provided:
  labeling, blast freezing, repackaging
Storage Facility Data:
  Freezer Size: 6250000 Cubic Ft.

53322 Preferred Freezer Services
1400 Los Palos St
Los Angeles, CA 90023
323-430-8550
www.preferredfreezer.com/big-bear-la-7
Warehouse providing freezer and cooler storage
General Manager: Bret Summers
Sales Manager: Justin Ernest *Year Founded:* 2018
Types of products warehoused:
  frozen goods
Services Provided:
  labeling, USDA/FDA/USDC inspection
Storage Facility Data:
  Freezer Size: 491000 Sq. Ft.

53323 Preferred Freezer Services
4901 Bandini Blvd
Vernon, CA 90058
323-263-8811
www.preferredfreezer.com/long-beach-freeway
Warehouse providing freezer storage
General Manager: Adrian Sinay
Sales Manager: Stephen Hludzik *Year Founded:* 2007
Types of products warehoused:
  frozen goods
Services Provided:
  labeling, repackaging, USDA/FDA/USDC inspection
Storage Facility Data:
  Freezer Size: 10000000 Cubic Ft.

53324 Preferred Freezer Services
3100 E Washington Blvd
Los Angeles, CA 90023
323-526-4134
shludzik@preferredfreezer.com
www.preferredfreezer.com/los-angeles
Warehouse providing freezer storage
General Manager: David Love
Sales Manager: Stephen Hludzik *Year Founded:* 2001
Types of products warehoused:
  frozen goods
Services Provided:
  labeling, repackaging, USDA/FDA/USDC inspection; Export services
Storage Facility Data:
  Freezer Size: 4500000 Cubic Ft.

53325 Preferred Freezer Services
400 Polar Way
San Leandro, CA 94577
510-352-3900
www.preferredfreezer.com/san-leandro
Warehouse providing freezer storage
General Manager: Tom Alexander
Sales Manager: Mark Costello *Year Founded:* 2014
Types of products warehoused:
  frozen goods
Services Provided:
  labeling, repackaging, USDA/FDA/USDC inspection; Import/export svcs
Storage Facility Data:
  Freezer Size: 12332000 Cubic Ft.

53326 Preferred Freezer Services
2100 E 55th St
Vernon, CA 90058
323-582-6333
www.preferredfreezer.com/ultrafreeze
Warehouse providing freezer storage
General Manager: Jose Delgado
Sales Manager: Peter Lepe *Year Founded:* 2002
Types of products warehoused:
  frozen goods
Services Provided:
  labeling, blast freezing, repackaging, USDA/FDA/USDC inspection
Storage Facility Data:
  Freezer Size: 2900000 Cubic Ft.

53327 Preferred Freezer Services
2050 E 55th St
Vernon, CA 90058
323-587-4600
plepe@preferredfreezer.com
www.preferredfreezer.com/vernon
Warehouse providing freezer storage
General Manager: Jose Delgado
Sales Manager: Peter Lepe *Year Founded:* 2001
Types of products warehoused:
  frozen goods
Services Provided:
  labeling, repackaging, USDA/USDC/FDA inspection; Export services
Storage Facility Data:
  Freezer Size: 4100000 Cubic Ft.

53328 Preferred Freezer Services
3200 E Washington Blvd
Vernon, CA 90058
323-261-4500
www.preferredfreezer.com/washington-boulevard
Warehouse providing freezer and cooler storage
General Manager: Cuco Sanchez
Sales Manager: Lawrence Abbott *Year Founded:* 2007
Types of products warehoused:
  frozen goods
Services Provided:
  labeling, repackaging, USDA/FDA/USDC inspection
Storage Facility Data:
  Cooler Size 1000000 Cubic Ft.
  Freezer Size: 7400000 Cubic Ft.

53329 Preferred Freezer Services
900 E M St
Wilmington, CA 90744-2712
310-518-1800
Fax: 310-518-1870 jzarrella@preferredfreezer.com
www.preferredfreezer.com/wilmington
Warehouse providing freezer storage
General Manager: Adrian Sinay
Sales Manager: John Zarrella *Year Founded:* 2003
Types of products warehoused:
  frozen goods
Services Provided:
  labeling, USDA inspection
Storage Facility Data:
  Freezer Size: 4800000 Cubic Ft.

53330 Priority Air Express
11 Technology Dr # A
Swedesboro, NJ 08085-1849
856-832-1500
Fax: 856-832-1987 800-257-4777
Warehouse providing dry storage for nonperishable and frozen foods; transportation firm providing international and domestic freight forwarding services via local, long and short haul trucking, air and ocean freight; also, dry icepacking services available
CFO: Jim Manion
CEO: David Matthia
Contact: Homar Alvarado
premiumbm@msn.com
Number Employees: 100-249
Types of products warehoused:
  Non-perishable & frozen foods, non-perishables, frozen goods
Services Provided:
  Dry ice packing & freight forwarding
Storage Facility Data:
  Dry Storage Size: 50000 Sq. Ft.

53331 Prism Team Services, Inc
3656 Perlman Drive
Stockton, CA 95206
209-983-9915
www.prismlogistics.com
Warehouse providing dry storage for non-perishable goods; transportation firm providing TL and LTL trucking; also, cross-docking, distribution, machinery moving and rail siding services available.
President: Jere Van Puffelen
Executive Vice President: Paul Van de Roovaart
Contact: Mike Mayo
mmayo@prismlogistics.com
Number Employees: 20-49
Square Footage: 828000
Parent Co: PRISM Team Services
Types of products warehoused:
  Non-perishable goods, non-perishables
Services Provided:
  Cross-docking, distribution & machinery moving, rail siding
Storage Facility Data:
  Dry Storage Size: 207000 Sq. Ft.

53332 Procold Refrigarated Svc
1914 Pope Rd
Allentown, PA 18104-9308
610-395-1925
Fax: 610-391-1973 www.profruit.com
Warehouse providing temperature controlled storage for food products
Manager: Larry Mack
Manager: Jack Wehr
procold@rcn.com
Estimated Sales: Less Than $500,000
Number Employees: 5-9
Type of Packaging: Food Service

53333 Products Distribution
369 George St
New Brunswick, NJ 08901-2003
732-247-3000
Fax: 732-247-9088
Warehouse providing dry storage for nonperishable items; also, packaging and re-packing services available
President: William Bowie
Office Manager: Dun Par
Estimated Sales: $1-2.5 Million
Number Employees: 10-19
Square Footage: 520000
Types of products warehoused:
  Non-perishable items, non-perishables
Services Provided:
  Packaging & re-packing

53334 Profood International
670 W Fifth Ave
Suite 116
Naperville, IL 60563
630-428-2386
Fax: 630-527-9905 888-288-0081
support@profoodinternational.com
www.profoodinternational.com
Preservatives, emulsifiers, enzymes, texturizers and acids
Contact: Dave Shi
daves@profoodinternational.com

53335 Psyllium Labs
1701 E Woodfield Road
Suite 636
Schaumburg, IL 60173
888-851-6667
info@psyllium.com www.psylliumlabs.com
Psyllium, chia and quinoa
Operations Executive: Drew West
Other Locations:
  Manufacturing Facility
  North Gujarat, IndiaManufacturing FacilitySanta Cruz, Bolivia

53336 Puerto Rico Cold Storage
PO Box 13922
Santurce, PR 00908-3922
787-787-4050
Fax: 787-780-1102

53337 Pure Life Organic Foods
6625 W Sahara Ave
Suite 1
Las Vegas, NV 89146
708-990-5817
info@purelifeorganicfoods.com
www.purelifeorganicfoods.com
Organic sugars, coconut milk and coconut oil
Managing Director: Pradeep Mathur
Sales and Marketing Head: Sayida Bano
Parent Co: Pure Diets Intl. Ltd.
Type of Packaging: Bulk
Types of products warehoused:
  Sugar

53338 Purefect Ice
2900 South State Street
St. Joseph, MI 49085
888-772-1197
Fax: 269-982-1506 info@hansonlogistics.com
www.hansonlogisticsgroup.com
Warehouse for temperature-controlled foods, pharmaceuticals, chemicals, and confectioneries.
President: J. Daniel Bernson
Chairman and CEO: Gary Sarner
Executive Vice President of Supply Chain: John Sommavilla
Manager: Jordan Tatter
Estimated Sales: $ 10 - 20 Million
Number Employees: 20-49
Type of Packaging: Food Service

Warehousing / A-Z

53339 Quality Logistics Systems
3801 Pinnacle Point Dr # 100
Dallas, TX 75211-1578   214-231-0446
Fax: 214-623-9644 info@qualitylogistics.com
www.qualitylogistics.com
Warehouse providing dry and cooler storage, re-packing and labeling for nonperishable foods; transportation services include long and short haul trucking nationwide
President: Jeff Ballard
Cmo: William Mcneil
william.mcneil@qualitylogistics.com
Number Employees: 50-99
Parent Co: Quality Logistics Services
Other Locations:
   Chicago, IL
   Green Bay, WI
   Meridian, MSGreen Bay
Types of products warehoused:
   Non-perishable foods, general merchandise & chemicals
Services Provided:
   Re-packing & labeling
Storage Facility Data:
   Cooler Size 1800000 Cubic Ft.
   Dry Storage Size: 8000000 Cubic Ft.
   Humidity-Controlled Size: 40000 Cubic Ft.

53340 Quandt's Foodservice Distributors
P.O.Box 700
Amsterdam, NY 12010   518-842-1550
Fax: 518-770-1966 800-666-8443
Wholesaler/distributor of provisions/meats, produce, dairy products, frozen foods, baked goods, equipment and fixtures, seafood, etc.; serving the food service market; warehouse providing dry storage; rail siding available
President: Robert Quandt
Chairman: Thomas Quandt
Secretary/Treasurer: Thomas Quandt, Jr.
Contact: Betsy Niemczyk
bniemczyk@quandts.com
Estimated Sales: $ 20 - 50 Million
Number Employees: 100-249
Square Footage: 102001
Types of products warehoused:
   Dry goods, dry goods
Services Provided:
   rail siding

53341 Queen City Warehouse Corporation
PO Box 10008
Springfield, MO 65808-0008   417-869-4455
Fax: 417-864-6524
edeck@queencitywarehouse.com
Public and contract warehouse providing dry storage; transportation firm providing local and short trucking; rail siding, order filling, cross docking, freight consolidation and pool distribution services available. Food grade and rollpaper.
President: Ed Deck Jr
Estimated Sales: $ 3 - 5 Million
Square Footage: 600000
Types of products warehoused:
   dry goods, non-perishables, roll paper
Services Provided:
   rail siding, trucking, labeling, cross docki
Storage Facility Data:
   Dry Storage Size: 140000 Sq. Ft.

53342 Quick Delivery
1700 W 29th St
Kansas City, MO 64108   816-931-7800
Fax: 816-931-6633 800-383-8388
www.quickdeliveryinc.com
Warehouse providing dry and humidity-controlled storage for nonrefrigerated and nonhazardous products; transportation firm providing local and short haul trucking and regional ground messenger services including break bulk, crossdocking, etc
President: John Reynolds
Number Employees: 10-19
Types of products warehoused:
   General commodity dry goods & non-perishable, non-refrigerated & non-hazardous products, dry goods, non-perishables
Services Provided:
   Cross docking, re-packing & transportation
Storage Facility Data:
   Dry Storage Size: 10000 Sq. Ft.
   Humidity-Controlled Size: 5000 Sq. Ft.

53343 (HQ)R W Bozel Transfer Inc
500 Advantage Ave
Aberdeen, MD 21001-1146   443-327-6919
Fax: 443-327-6925 800-927-9055
www.bozelt.com
Transportation firm providing local, long and short haul trucking, TL and LTL consolidation, LTL cartage, refrigeration and pool distribution services; warehouse providing refrigerated storage
President: Patrick Bozel
patb@bozelt.com
Number Employees: 1-4

53344 R&A Imports
1439 El Bosque Ct
Pacific Palisades, CA 90272   310-454-2247
Fax: 310-459-3218 zonevdka@gte.net
Vodka
President: Veronica Pekarovic
Estimated Sales: $1-$2.5 Million
Number Employees: 1 to 4

53345 RBW Logistics
326 Prep Phillips Dr
Augusta, GA 30901-1758   706-724-0106
Fax: 706-722-7762 info@rbwlogistics.com
www.recordsmanagementcenter.com
Warehouse providing dry and humidity-controlled storage for nonfoods and food products; also, rail siding available
CEO: Charles Anderson
Vice President: Frank Anderson
Senior Operations Manager: John Albright
Estimated Sales: $230,000
Number Employees: 50-99
Square Footage: 580000
Types of products warehoused:
   Non-foods & foods, general merchandise
Services Provided:
   rail siding
Storage Facility Data:
   Dry Storage Size: 124000 Sq. Ft.
   Humidity-Controlled Size: 21000 Sq. Ft.

53346 RFDI
2701 Red Lion Rd
Philadelphia, PA 19114-1019   215-934-6000
Fax: 215-934-5717 www.nep.com
Manager: Dan Ryan
Estimated Sales: $ 5 - 10 Million
Number Employees: 50-99

53347 (HQ)RGL Headquarters
1401 State St
Green Bay, WI 54304   920-432-8632
www.rgllogistics.com
Warehouse providing cooler and dry storage for general merchandise; transportation services include local trucking; consolidation, cross-dock, rail siding and distribution services available
President/CEO: Bob Johnson
VP Marketing: Roger Whitton
Sales Contact: Rebecca Usiak
Contact: Ken Garwood
kgarwood@rgllogistics.com
Number Employees: 100-249
Types of products warehoused:
   General merchandise, general merchandise
Services Provided:
   Trucking & distribution, rail siding
Storage Facility Data:
   Cooler Size 5000 Sq. Ft.
   Dry Storage Size: 3000000 Sq. Ft.

53348 RLS Logistics
Rosario Leo Building
2185 Main Road
Newfield, NJ 08344   856-694-2500
800-579-9900
info@rlslogistics.com www.rlslogistics.com
Transportation, warehousing and fulfillment to the frozen and refrigerated food industry.
Chief Executive Officer, President: Anthony Leo
Vice President of Development: John Gaudet
Director of Operations: Greg Deitz

53349 RLS Logistics
Rosario Leo Building
2185 Main Road
Newfield, NJ 08344   856-694-2500
Fax: 856-694-2828 www.rlslogistics.com
Freezer and Cold Storage Facility
President Warehousing/Transportation: Anthony Leo
VP Warehousing: Anthony Leo
Estimated Sales: $ .5 - 1 million
Number Employees: 5-9
Type of Packaging: Food Service

53350 Rainier Cold Terminal
6004 Airport Way S
Seattle, WA 98108-2716   206-762-0287
Fax: 206-682-7068
Warehouse providing cooler, dry, freezer and humidity controlled storage for seafood; also, rail siding and re-packing services available
President: Robert King
VP: Mike Roberts
Warehouse Manager: Bill McCutcheon
Estimated Sales: $ 1 - 3 Million
Number Employees: 10-19
Parent Co: Rainier Cold Storage & Ice
Other Locations:
   Rainier Cold Terminal 25
   Seattle, WARainier Cold Terminal 25
Types of products warehoused:
   Seafood
Services Provided:
   Seafood re-packing, rail siding
Storage Facility Data:
   Freezer Size: 3000000 Cubic Ft.

53351 Rainier Cold-Storage & Ice
3625 1st Ave S
Seattle, WA 98134-2233   206-682-5646
Fax: 206-621-8661 info@rainiercold.com
www.rainiercold.com
Warehouse providing freezer storage for produce, seafood and refrigerated foods; also, blast freezing, processing, ice making, space rental and rail siding available
President: Greg Moore
Manager: Randy Klein
randy@rainiercold.com
Office Manager: Pat Godfrey
Warehouse Manager: Randy Klein
Estimated Sales: $2.5-5 Million
Number Employees: 5-9
Types of products warehoused:
   Produce, seafood & refrigerated foods, produce
Services Provided:
   Processing, blast freezing, ice making & space rental, rail siding
Storage Facility Data:
   Freezer Size: 4000000 Cubic Ft.

53352 Rainier Cold-Storage & Ice
3625 1st Ave S
Seattle, WA 98134-2233   206-682-5646
Fax: 206-621-8661 greg@rainiercold.com
www.rainiercold.com
Warehouse providing freezer storage for produce, seafood and refrigerated foods; also, blast freezing, processing, ice making, space rental and rail siding available
President: Greg Moore
VP: Mike Roberts
VP: Doug Watson
Manager: Randy Klein
randy@rainiercold.com
Number Employees: 5-9
Type of Packaging: Food Service
Types of products warehoused:
   Produce, seafood & refrigerated foods, produce
Services Provided:
   Processing, blast freezing, ice making & space rental, rail siding
Storage Facility Data:
   Freezer Size: 4000000 Cubic Ft.

53353 Ralph Moyle Inc
23599 Freedom Ln
Mattawan, MI 49071-8904   269-668-4531
Fax: 269-668-4677
http://www.ralphmoyle.com/index.php
Warehouse providing dry and refrigerated storage for nonperishable foods; transportation firm providing local haul and OTR trucking
President: Ralph Moyle
ralphmoyle@ralphmoyle.com
Owner/Manager: Mike Moyle
Sales/Marketing Executive: Jon Moyle
Number Employees: 50-99
Types of products warehoused:
   Non-perishable foods, dry goods, non-perishables, canned foods

Warehousing / A-Z

53354 Rancho Cold Storage
670 Mesquit St
Los Angeles, CA 90021-1306   213-624-8861
     Fax: 213-622-8256 www.ranchocoldstorage.com
Public warehouse offering cooler, dry, freezer and humidity controlled storage; rail siding available
Owner: Jeremy Corselli
jcorselli@ranchocoldstorage.com
Secretary/Treasurer: Theresa Gallo
Estimated Sales: $1-2.5 Million
Number Employees: 10-19
Square Footage: 400000
Services Provided:
     rail siding

Services Provided:
     Local haul & OTR trucking, rail siding, trucking, repackaging
Storage Facility Data:
     Dry Storage Size: 200,000 Sq. Ft.

53355 Ray West Warehouses/Transport
4801 Baldwin Blvd Ste 104
Corpus Christi, TX 78408   361-884-5595
     Fax: 361-884-0309
     johnm@raywestwarehouses.com
Warehouse providing dry and cooler storage for nonperishable foods; transportation, rail siding, re-packing and labeling available
President & CEO: Peter Anderson
pete@raywestwarehouses.com
Number Employees: 10-19
Types of products warehoused:
     dry goods, non-perishables, canned foods, general merchandise
Services Provided:
     rail siding, trucking, labeling, packaging, pick and pack, repackaging
Storage Facility Data:
     Cooler Size 2400 Sq. Ft.
     Dry Storage Size: 200000 Sq. Ft.
     Humidity-Controlled Size: 1200 Sq. Ft.

53356 (HQ)Reddy Ice
5720 LBJ Freeway
Suite 200
Dallas, TX 75240   214-526-6740
     800-683-4423
     information@reddyice.com www.reddyice.com
Packaged ice products including cubes, blocks, and dry; Cold storage warehouse
Chairman: Bill Corbin
CEO: Deborah Conklin
CFO: Steven Janusek
COO: Paul Smith
Contact: Karen Apperson
kapperson@reddyice.com
Year Founded: 1927
Estimated Sales: $300 Million
Number Employees: 1000-4999
Types of products warehoused:
     frozen goods

53357 Reddy Ice
1201 Searles Ave
Las Vegas, NV 89101   702-649-8002
     coldstorage@reddyice.com
     www.reddyice.com/las-vegas-cold-storage
Cold storage warehouse
Types of products warehoused:
     frozen goods
Storage Facility Data:
     Freezer Size: 2500000 Cubic Ft.

53358 Refrigerated Food Distributors
2701 Red Lion Rd
Philadelphia, PA 19114   215-934-6000
     Fax: 215-934-5717 www.nep.com
Wholesale Food Distribution
Manager: Dan Ryan
Estimated Sales: $ 5 - 10 Million
Number Employees: 50-99
Type of Packaging: Bulk

53359 Refrigerated Warehouse Marketing Group
PO Box 530
La Verne, CA 91750-0530   909-625-4512
     Fax: 909-625-4612

53360 Resource Alliance
1725 Windward Concourse
Suite 100
Alpharetta, GA 30005-1784   678-691-6600
     Fax: 678-691-6871 888-840-7325
     info@real-hr.com www.resourcealliance.com
Warehouse offering dry storage for food and nonfood products; rail siding available
Manager: Daniel Johnson
Estimated Sales: Less Than $500,000
Number Employees: 1-4
Square Footage: 600000
Types of products warehoused:
     Non-foods & food
Services Provided:
     rail siding
Storage Facility Data:
     Dry Storage Size: 142000 Sq. Ft.

53361 Rex & Company
2411 N American Street
Philadelphia, PA 19133-3431   215-739-2627
     Fax: 215-739-3832
Warehouse providing dry storage for canned, glass packed and bulk food products; also, heated space, re-packing, re-labeling, salvage work and inventory control available
President: Norman Bauman Jr
Operations Manager: Denise Bauman
Estimated Sales: $1-2.5 Million
Number Employees: 9
Square Footage: 600000
Type of Packaging: Consumer
Types of products warehoused:
     Canned & glass packed foods & bulk food products, dry goods, canned foods, general merchandise
Services Provided:
     Heated space, re-packing, re-labeling, salvage work & inventory, trucking, pick and pack, re-packaging
Storage Facility Data:
     Dry Storage Size: 150000 Sq. Ft.

53362 Reynolds Transfer & Storage
725 E Mifflin St
Madison, WI 53703-2391   608-257-3914
     Fax: 608-258-3692 800-430-4333
     www.unitedvanlines.com
Warehouse providing dry storage for general merchandise; transportation firm providing local haul trucking; rail siding available
President: Karen Michel
karen.michel@aonhewitt.com
Number Employees: 20-49
Types of products warehoused:
     General merchandise, general merchandise
Services Provided:
     Local haul trucking, rail siding

53363 Riceland Foods Inc.
PO Box 927
Stuttgart, AR 72160   870-673-5500
     855-742-3929
     riceland@riceland.com www.riceland.com
Rice and rice bran oils.
CEO: Danny Kennedy
Estimated Sales: $1.3 Billion
Number Employees: 1,500
Type of Packaging: Consumer, Food Service, Private Label, Bulk
Other Locations:
     Newport, AR
     Weiner, AR
     Knobel, AR
     Holly Grove, AR
     Tuckerman, AR
     Corning, ARWeiner
Types of products warehoused:
     Grains, dry goods
Services Provided:
     rail siding

53364 Richmond Cold Storage Smithfield
P.O.Box 906
Smithfield, VA 23431-0906   757-357-0434
     Fax: 757-357-0351 www.richmondcold.com
Warehouse providing cooler and freezer storage for perishable products.
Manager: Mark Dow
Director Operations: Tom Bryant
Division Manager: Calvin Austin
Warehouse Manager: Jeff Falls
Estimated Sales: $ 5 - 10 Million
Number Employees: 50-99
Square Footage: 520000
Parent Co: Richmond Cold Storage
Types of products warehoused:
     Frozen foods, meat & poultry, frozen goods
Services Provided:
     Web enabled customer service, labeling, blast freezing, pick and pack
Storage Facility Data:
     Cooler Size 2000000 Cubic Ft.

53365 Richwill Enterprises
1443 W 41st St
Chicago, IL 60609-2414   773-927-5757
     Fax: 773-927-7206 800-334-5757
     www.richwillcs.com
Warehouse providing cooler and freezer storage for perishable and nonperishable food items; transportation firm offering long and short haul trucking
President: Karen Reinschreiber
Contact: Karen Mccurrie
karen@richwillcs.com
Operations Manager: Gregory Principato
Estimated Sales: $2.5-5 Million
Number Employees: 20-49
Types of products warehoused:
     Perishable & non-perishable food items, dry goods, canned foods, cooler
Services Provided:
     Trucking, trucking
Storage Facility Data:
     Cooler Size 360000
     Dry Storage Size: 480000
     Freezer Size: 1080000

53366 River Terminal Distribution & Warehouse
3 Distribution Ave # 139
Suite 639
Kearny, NJ 07032   973-465-1084
     Fax: 973-465-0089 info@riverterminal.com
Warehouse handling dry foods and general commodities; transportation firm offering freight consolidation; also, re-packing, assembly and rail siding available
Manager: Svetin Govic
Contact: Phil Catelo
pcatelo@rtdwco.com
Number Employees: 20-49
Parent Co: River Terminal Development
Types of products warehoused:
     Dry foods & general commodities, dry goods, general merchandise
Services Provided:
     Re-packing, consolidation, assembly, rail siding

53367 Riverport Warehouse Company
P.O.Box 58098
Louisville, KY 40268-0098   502-933-0924
     Fax: 502-933-7149
Warehouse providing dry storage for nonperishable food items
CEO: Richard Boone
Estimated Sales: $1-2.5 Million
Number Employees: 1-4
Types of products warehoused:
     Non-perishable food items, non-perishables

53368 Robertson-Johnson Warehouses
2600 Shader Rd
P.O.Box 547900
Orlando, FL 32854-7900   407-293-3121
     Fax: 407-290-5371
Warehouse offering dry storage; transportation firm providing freight consolidation; pick/pack, cross docking, pool car and truck distribution, EDI, computerized inventory control and rail siding available
President: Thomas Johnson
VP: Whit Kendall
Number Employees: 10-19
Types of products warehoused:
     Food products, dry goods, general merchandise
Services Provided:
     Pick/pack, pool car & truck distribution, EDI, etc., rail siding, labeling, pick and pack, repackaging
Storage Facility Data:
     Cooler Size 2000
     Dry Storage Size: 226000 Sq. Ft.

Warehousing / A-Z

53369 Robinson & Co
PO Box 11142
Houston, TX 77293-1142 281-924-9213
Fax: 281-442-3408 800-444-0735
www.trane.com
Warehouse providing dry and humidity-controlled storage for candy, paper products, dry goods and general merchandise; local cartage, pool car segregation and distribution services available
Owner: Calvin Robinson Jr
CEO: C Robinson
Estimated Sales: $ .5 - 1 million
Number Employees: 5-9
Square Footage: 720000
Types of products warehoused:
  Dry goods, candy, paper products & general merchandise, dry goods, non-perishables, canned foods, general merchandise
Services Provided:
  Local cartage, pool car segregation & distribution
Storage Facility Data:
  Dry Storage Size: 150000 Sq. Ft.
  Humidity-Controlled Size: 30000 Sq. Ft.

53370 Robinson Cold Storage
24415 NE 10th Ave
Ridgefield, WA 98642 360-887-3501
Frozen foods storage
President/CEO: Allen Nirenstein
Chairman: Thomas Klein
Estimated Sales: Less than $500,000
Number Employees: 1-4

53371 Rochester RefrigeratingCorporation
8026 Coates Road
Naples, NY 14512-9107 716-473-4967
Fax: 716-473-1684
Warehouse providing cooler and freezer storage for perishable refrigerated and frozen foods
President: Jeffrey Berger
Number Employees: 5-9
Square Footage: 200000
Types of products warehoused:
  Perishable refrigerated & frozen foods, frozen goods, Refrigerated Items
Storage Facility Data:
  Cooler Size 87750 Cubic Ft.
  Freezer Size 227150 Cubic Ft.

53372 Roederer Transfer & Storage
513 Fillmore St
Davenport, IA 52802-1294 563-323-3631
Fax: 563-323-3634 800-553-1875
www.mayflower.com
Warehouse providing cooler, humidity-controlled and dry storage for foods and nonfoods; also, rail siding available
President: Thomas J Roederer
thomas.roederer@roederertransfer.com
Estimated Sales: $1-2.5 Million
Number Employees: 20-49
Types of products warehoused:
  Non-foods & foods
Services Provided:
  rail siding
Storage Facility Data:
  Cooler Size 5000 Sq. Ft.
  Dry Storage Size: 200000 Sq. Ft.
  Humidity-Controlled Size: 5000 Sq. Ft.

53373 Rosa Food Products
2750 Grays Ferry Ave
Philadelphia, PA 19146-3801 215-467-2214
Fax: 215-467-6850 rosa@rosafoods.com
Manufacturer and wholesaler of pastas, sauces, cooking ingredients, condiments, etc.
President: Jack Foti
CEO: Giacomo Foti
mfoti@rosafoods.com
Chief Financial Officer: Leonardo Foti
Manager: Mary Foti
Estimated Sales: $11 Million
Number Employees: 10-19
Number of Brands: 9
Square Footage: 68000
Type of Packaging: Consumer, Food Service, Private Label, Bulk
Types of products warehoused:
  dry goods, non-perishables, canned foods, general merchandise

53374 Rosenberger Cold Storage Company
P.O.Box 309
309 Colonial Drive
Akron, PA 17501 717-859-8900
Fax: 717-859-7044 info@rosenbergerna.com
www.rosenberger.com
Warehouse offering cooler and freezer storage for food products; also, blast freezing available
Contact: Tim Quigley
tquigley@rosenbergerna.com
Plant Manager: Larry Alderfer
Estimated Sales: $500,000-$1 Million
Number Employees: 9
Parent Co: Rosenberger Cold Storage Company
Types of products warehoused:
  Refrigerated & frozen foods, frozen goods
Services Provided:
  Blast freezing

53375 Royal Jordanian
21b N Service Rd
Jamaica, NY 11430-1616 718-656-0220
Fax: 718-244-1821 www.rj.com
Warehouse providing dry and freezer storage for frozen foods and general merchandise; transportation firm providing air cargo services
Manager: Ziyad Atiyat
Number Employees: 10-19
Types of products warehoused:
  Frozen foods & general merchandise, frozen goods, general merchandise
Services Provided:
  Containerized transportation & airline cargo services
Storage Facility Data:
  Dry Storage Size: 15000 Sq. Ft.

53376 Ryder Integrated Logistics
11690 NW 105th St
Miami, FL 33178
888-793-3702
ryder.com/supply-chain-management
Offers a complete line of supply chain solutions
President, Global Supply Chain Solutions: J. Steven Sensing
Estimated Sales: K

53377 (HQ)SAS Cargo
1 Newark Airport
Newark, NJ 07114-3401 973-648-0814
Fax: 973-849-3366 larry.katz@sas.dk
www.sascargo.com
Transportation company providing domestic and interantional air freight services; warehouse providing cooler, freezer, dry and humidity-controlled storage
President & CEO: Kenneth Marx
Terminal Management: Larry Katz
Number Employees: 50-99

53378 SCS Supply Chain Solutions LLC
502 10th Avenue North
Algona, WA 98001 253-272-0900
Fax: 253-333-2198 800-378-0901
Freezer and Cold Storage Facility
President/CEO: Hugh Carr
Parent Co: Lineage Logistics Holdings, LLC
Type of Packaging: Food Service

53379 SCS Supply Chain Solutions LLC
2302 Milwaukee Way
Tacoma, WA 98421 253-272-0900
Fax: 253-272-0211 JDaniel@lineagelogistics.com
Manager: Greg Tainatongo
Estimated Sales: $ 1 - 3 Million
Number Employees: 20-49
Parent Co: Lineage Logistics Holdings, LLC

53380 SDS Global Logistics, Inc.
37-18 57th Street
Woodside, NY 11377 718-784-5586
Fax: 718-472-3474 888-737-3977
insidesales@sdsgl.com
Warehouse providing dry storage for nonperishable items; transportation firm providing international and domestic freight forwarding services via air freight, long and short haul trucking
Founder: Anthony Racioppo
Founder: John Racioppo
Contact: Alli Alvarado
aalvarado@sdsgl.com
Number Employees: 10-19
Types of products warehoused:
  Non-perishable items, non-perishables
Services Provided:
  International & domestic freight forwarding

53381 SEKO Worldwide Inc
1100 N Arlington Heights # 600
Itasca, IL 60143-3111 630-919-4800
Fax: 630-773-9179 800-228-2711
sales@sekoworldwide.com
www.sekologistics.com
Warehouse providing dry storage of nonperishable food items; transportation firm offering air freight forwarding
President/CEO: William J Wascher
Chief Commercial Officer: Mark L White
CFO: Don Sarna
Evp/COO: Steven Goldberg
Vice President Marketing: Brian Bourke
Vice President Sales: David Emerson
Chief Operating Officer: Randy Sinker
Number Employees: 1000-4999
Types of products warehoused:
  Non-perishable food items, non-perishables
Services Provided:
  Air freight forwarding

53382 SOPAKCO Foods
215 S Mullins St
Mullins, SC 29574-3207 843-464-0121
Fax: 423-639-7270 800-276-9678
www.sopakco.com
Pasta sauces; also, retortable pouch manufacturer, canner and contract packager of poultry, meat, fish, pasta, vegetable, bean, fruit and dessert products, flexible, semi-rigid and glass containers
CEO: Al Reitzer
CFO: Steve Keight
R&D: Jim Dukes
Quality Control: Phyllis Calhoun
General Manager: Wynn Pettibone
Plant Manager: Carl Whitmore
Purchasing Director: Beverly Stacey
Estimated Sales: $5-10 Million
Number Employees: 100
Square Footage: 400000
Parent Co: Unaka Corporation
Type of Packaging: Consumer, Food Service, Private Label
Types of products warehoused:
  Meats, fruits, vegetables & general merchandise, dry goods, non-perishables, produce, canned foods, general merchandise
Services Provided:
  Government contract packaging, retort pouching & co-packing, rail siding, labeling, packaging, repackaging
Storage Facility Data:
  Dry Storage Size: 40000 Sq. Ft.

53383 SOS Global Express Inc
2803 Trent Rd
New Bern, NC 28562-2029 252-635-1400
Fax: 252-635-1920 800-628-6363
www.sosglobal.com
Warehouse providing dry storage for nonperishable items; transportation firm providing international and domestic freight forwarding services via air freight and long and short haul trucking
President: Fernando Soler
fsoler@sosglobal.com
Number Employees: 50-99
Types of products warehoused:
  Non-perishable items, non-perishables
Services Provided:
  International & domestic freight forwarding

53384 (HQ)Sack Storage Corporation
66 Atlas St
Worcester, MA 01604 508-754-6802
Fax: 508-792-2550
Warehouse providing dry storage for groceries, chemicals, containers, paper and plastics; transportation broker providing freight consolidation and local and long haul trucking; also, rail siding, bulk transfers and packaging servicesavailable
Owner: Norman Sirk
Number Employees: 10-19
Types of products warehoused:
  Groceries, chemicals, paper, containers & plastics
Services Provided:
  Trucking, freight consolidation, bulk transfer & packaging, rail siding

Warehousing / A-Z

Storage Facility Data:
Dry Storage Size: 180000 Sq. Ft.

53385 Saddle Creek Corp
440 Joe Tamplin Industrial Blv
Macon, GA 31217-7607   478-744-9712
Fax: 912-745-1304 info@sclogistics.com
www.sclogistics.com
Warehouse providing dry storage for nonperishable food
Manager: Ralph Skipper
Estimated Sales: $10-20 Million
Number Employees: 5-9
Parent Co: Saddle Creek Corporation
Types of products warehoused:
Non-perishable food, non-perishables

53386 (HQ)Saddle Creek Logistics Svc
3010 Saddle Creek Rd
Lakeland, FL 33801-9638   863-665-0966
Fax: 863-668-8711   888-878-1177
info@saddlecrk.com www.sclogistics.com
A leading nationwide distribution services company that provides warehousing, transportation, contract packaging, and integrated logistics services.
President/Owner: Cliff Otto
cliff.otto@saddlecrk.com
CEO: David Lyons
CFO: Mark Cabrera
Sales: Stephen Cook
Operations: Butch Riggleman
Number Employees: 500-999
Type of Packaging: Consumer
Other Locations:
Saddle Creek Corporation
Charlotte, NC
Waco, TX
Dallas/Fort Worth, TX
Oklahoma City, OK
Atlanta, GA
Orlando, FL
Saddle Creek CorporationWaco
Types of products warehoused:
Appliances, beverage, alcohol, tabacco, apparel, dry goods, non-perishables, canned foods, general merchandise, retail alcohol, beverages
Services Provided:
Contract/Public, Crossdock, rail siding, trucking, labeling, packaging, pick and pack, repackaging

53387 Saddle Creek Logistics Svc
105 Eagle Vista Pkwy SW
Atlanta, GA 30336-2864   404-346-6000
Fax: 404-346-6021 info@sclogistics.com
www.sclogistics.com
Warehouse providing dry storage for nonperishables; also, re-packing and labeling available
VP/General Manager: Don Cote
Manager: Charles Puzder
charles.puzder@sclogistics.com
Estimated Sales: $10-20 Million
Number Employees: 250-499
Parent Co: Saddle Creek Corporation
Types of products warehoused:
Non-perishables, non-perishables
Services Provided:
Re-packing & labeling

53388 Saddle Creek Logistics Svc
3010 Saddle Creek Rd
Lakeland, FL 33801-9638   863-665-0966
Fax: 863-668-8711   866-668-0966
sales@sclogistics.com www.sclogistics.com
Warehouse providing dry storage of nonperishable food; transportation firm offering long and short haul trucking; also, pick-up and delivery services available
Chairman/Founder: David Lyons
President: Cliff Otto
cliff.otto@saddlecrk.com
Senior VP/ CFO: Mark Cabrera
VP Real Estate: Scott Thornton
VP of Marketing and Business Development: Duane Sizemore
Director Business Development: Greg Payne
Number Employees: 500-999
Types of products warehoused:
Non-perishable, non-perishables
Services Provided:
Trucking, pick-up & delivery

53389 Safeway Freezer StorageInc
97 N Mill Rd
Vineland, NJ 08360-3436   856-691-9696
Fax: 856-691-3399
www.safewayfreezerstorage.com
Warehouse providing a total of 3,500,000 CF of cooler and freezer storage for frozen and refrigerated foods; transportation company providing local, long and short haul trucking; rail siding available
President: Eleanor Pepper
epepper@sjfreezergroup.com
Number Employees: 20-49
Parent Co: Safeway Stores
Types of products warehoused:
Frozen & refrigerated food, frozen goods, refrigerated
Services Provided:
Local, long & short haul trucking, rail siding, trucking, labeling, blast freezing, order pick

53390 (HQ)Safeway Inc.
5918 Stoneridge Mall Rd.
Pleasanton, CA 94588
877-723-3929
www.safeway.com
Supermarket products such as bakery items, dairy, deli meats, dry cleaning, frozen foods, fuel, grocery, pharmacy, produce, meants, snack foods, and more.
Executive Chairman/CEO: Robert Miller
robert.miller@safeway.com
Executive VP/CFO: Peter Bocian
Year Founded: 1915
Estimated Sales: Over $1 Billion
Number Employees: 10000+
Number of Brands: 12
Parent Co: Albertsons
Type of Packaging: Consumer

53391 San Antonio Cold Storage
510 Regal Row
Dallas, TX 75247-5208   214-630-2300
Fax: 214-630-6932 dallas@yumiicecream.com
www.yumiicecream.com
Ice Cream Distribution
Type of Packaging: Bulk

53392 San Diego Cold Storage Inspctn
1240 W 28th St # 6
National City, CA 91950-6319   619-474-6525
Fax: 619-474-6103   800-522-1591
INFO@SDCOLD.COM www.sdcold.com
Warehouse providing cooler, dry and freezer storage of frozen and chilled foods; re-packaging, re-marking, blast freezing, leased space, rail siding and office space available; also, transporter of ice products
Manager: Mike Jerde
mikej@sdcold.com
President: Edward Plant
Manager: Mike Jerde
mikej@sdcold.com
Estimated Sales: $1-2.5 Million
Number Employees: 20-49
Square Footage: 212000
Types of products warehoused:
Frozen & chilled foods, frozen goods
Services Provided:
Re-packing, blast freezing, re-marking of packages, etc., rail siding
Storage Facility Data:
Cooler Size 119853 Cubic Ft.
Dry Storage Size: 56000 Cubic Ft.
Freezer Size: 893460 Cubic Ft.

53393 San Diego Cold Storage Inspctn
1240 W 28th St # 6
National City, CA 91950-6319   619-474-6525
Fax: 619-474-6103 INFO@SDCOLD.COM
www.sdcold.com
Manager: Mike Jerde
mikej@sdcold.com
Operations Manager: Edward Plant
Number Employees: 20-49
Square Footage: 30

53394 San Jose Distribution Service
2055 S 7th St
Suite A
San Jose, CA 95112-6141   408-292-9100
Fax: 408-292-7173 inquiry@sjdist.com
www.sjdist.com
San Jose Distribution Services is a third party warehousing company providing rail siding, pick/pack, assembly, re-pack, labeling, local, regional, and nationwide distribution services for over forty years.
President: Gary Minardi
CEO: Joe Caston
VP Operations: Richard Vega
Contact: Richard Vega
richard@sjdist.com
Number Employees: 50-99
Types of products warehoused:
Groceries, wine, general merchandise & industrial products, dry goods, canned foods, general merchandise
Services Provided:
Local haul trucking, pick/pack & computerized inventory control, rail siding, trucking, labeling, packaging, pick and pack, repackaging
Storage Facility Data:
Dry Storage Size: 330,000 Sq. Ft.

53395 Sanmarc Liquidators Inc
13451 Damar Dr # E
Philadelphia, PA 19116-1819   215-969-6955
Fax: 215-969-5079
Liquidator of frozen and dry food products, selling to end users and the retail secondary market and correctional facilities. Meats, seafood, poultry, dairy, canned goods, baked goods, etc.
Vice President: Randy Stark
Estimated Sales: $5 Million
Number Employees: 20-49
Square Footage: 25000
Type of Packaging: Consumer, Food Service, Private Label, Bulk

53396 Santemp Co
1532 Adelaide St
P.O.Box 7189
Detroit, MI 48207-4513   313-259-4647
Fax: 313-259-1067
Warehouse providing freezer and cold storage for frozen food
President: Bill Sullivan
CEO: Timothy Sullivan
V.P. Exports: Heather Sullivan
Vice President of Sale: Terry Shook
Manager: Steve Sullivian
Estimated Sales: $500,000-$1 Million
Number Employees: 5-9
Types of products warehoused:
Freezer & cold storage
Services Provided:
rail siding

53397 Saroni Co
1301 26th St
Oakland, CA 94607-2442   510-465-6010
Fax: 510-465-6020 www.saronifoods.com
Freezer and Cold Storage Facility
Owner: Alford Saroni
nsx4u@aol.com
Sales: Al Saroni
Estimated Sales: Less Than $500,000
Number Employees: 1-4
Type of Packaging: Food Service

53398 Saturn Freight Systems
P.O.Box 680308
Marietta, GA 30068   770-952-3490
Fax: 770-693-5749 www.saturnfreight.com
Warehouse providing dry storage for nonperishable items; transportation firm providing international and domestic freight forwarding services via air freight and local, long and short haul trucking
President: Guy Stark
Vice President: Bill Handley
Marketing: Justin Stark
VP, Business Development: Michael Moore
Operations: Christopher Lair
Number Employees: 10-19
Types of products warehoused:
Non-perishable items, non-perishables
Services Provided:
International & domestic freight forwarding

53399 Sauce Crafters
3695 Interstate Park Way
#2
Riviera Beach, FL 33404   561-848-2335
Fax: 561-841-8666   888-477-2823
www.saucecrafters.com
Manufacturers of hot sauces and condiments

President: Charlie Schandelmayer
Estimated Sales: $700,000
Number Employees: 1-4
Number of Products: 105
Square Footage: 28000
Type of Packaging: Consumer, Food Service, Private Label

53400 Savannah Distributing
2425 W Gwinnett St
Garden City, GA 31415-9602   912-233-1167
Fax: 912-233-1157   800-551-0777
info@gawine.com   www.savdist.com
Distributor of liquor, craft beers, wines and sparkling wines.
Owner: Henri Gabriel
President: Henry Monsees
Estimated Sales: $10-20 Million
Number Employees: 50-99
Type of Packaging: Food Service
Other Locations:
 Atlanta Warehouse
 Atlanta, GAAtlanta Warehouse
Types of products warehoused:
 Alcoholic Beverages

53401 (HQ)Schaefers
9820 D St
Oakland, CA 94603-2439   510-632-5064
Fax: 510-632-2754   www.schaefersmeats.com
Warehouse providing freezer storage
President: Otto Schaefer
Manager: Adam Chan
schaefmeats@gmail.com
Estimated Sales: Less Than $500,000
Number Employees: 1-4
Square Footage: 80000
Types of products warehoused:
 Beef, lamb, pork & poultry
Storage Facility Data:
 Freezer Size: 250000 Cubic Ft.

53402 (HQ)Schenker Logistics Inc
PO Box 20107
Greensboro, NC 27420-0107   336-273-3465
Fax: 336-271-2084
Warehouse handling appliances, general commodities, packaging, candy and canned goods; also, re-packing, local cartage, poll distribution and pick-pack services available
Manager: Jerome Tillery
Vice President: Hans Stronck
Marketing Director: Brenda Kelly
Operations Manager: Les Peters
Estimated Sales: $2.5-5 Million
Number Employees: 20-49
Square Footage: 12000000
Type of Packaging: Consumer, Food Service, Private Label, Bulk
Types of products warehoused:
 General commodities, packaging, candy, canned goods, appliances, dry goods, non-perishables, canned foods, general merchandise
Services Provided:
 Re-packing, local cartage, pool distribution, pick-pack, rail siding, trucking, labeling, packaging, pick and pack, repackaging
Storage Facility Data:
 Dry Storage Size: 3000000 Sq. Ft.

53403 (HQ)Schilli Transportation Services
1560 Kepner Dr
Lafayette, IN 47905   765-448-3400
Fax: 765-449-9976   800-688-2101
sales@schilli.com   www.schilli.com
Transportation firm providing local, long and short haul trucking; warehouse providing dry storage
President: Thomas Schilli
Number Employees: 1,000-4,999
Types of products warehoused:
 dry goods, canned foods, general merchandise
Services Provided:
 trucking
Storage Facility Data:
 Dry Storage Size: 125000 Sq. Ft.

53404 Sea Snack Cold Storage
200 Mesnagers St
Los Angeles, CA 90012-1960   323-223-1955
Fax: 323-223-1970   jefk@ient.net
Manager: Jeff Kahn
Estimated Sales: $ 1 - 3 Million
Number Employees: 20-49
Type of Packaging: Food Service

53405 Seaboard Cold Storage
402 East Ohio Street
Plant City, FL 33566   813-887-5984
Fax: 813-887-3484   info@seaboardcs.com
www.seaboardcs.com
President: Elliot Greenbaum
elliot.greenbaum@seaboardcs.com
Estimated Sales: $300,000-500,000
Number Employees: 1-4

53406 Seaboard Cold Storage
402 E Ohio St
Plant City, FL 33566   813-887-5984
Fax: 813-887-3484   info@seaboardcs.com
www.seaboardcs.com
Freezer, Cooler, Dry Storage
President: Elliot Greenbaum
elliot.greenbaum@seaboardcs.com
Estimated Sales: $300,000-500,000
Number Employees: 1-4
Type of Packaging: Food Service

53407 Seaboard Cold Storage Inc
5601 Anderson Rd
Tampa, FL 33614-5313   813-887-5984
Fax: 813-887-3484   info@seaboardcs.com
www.seaboardcs.com
Warehouse providing freezer, cooler and humidity controlled storage for frozen foods; also, rail siding, freight consolidation, transloading, import/export, computerized warehouse management and USDA on-site inspection servicesavailable
President: Elliot Greenbaum
info@seaboardcs.com
Co-owner: Lois Greenbaum
Estimated Sales: $2.5-5 Million
Number Employees: 10-19
Square Footage: 1600000
Types of products warehoused:
 Frozen foods, frozen goods
Services Provided:
 Freight consolidation & computerized management, rail siding
Storage Facility Data:
 Cooler Size 1125000 Cubic Ft.
 Freezer Size: 8414475 Cubic Ft.
 Humidity-Controlled Size: 10756000 Cubic Ft.

53408 Seaboard Cold Storage Inc
5601 Anderson Rd
Tampa, FL 33614-5313   813-887-5984
Fax: 813-887-3484   info@seaboardcs.com
www.seaboardcs.com
President: Elliot Greenbaum
info@seaboardcs.com
Estimated Sales: $ 1 - 3 Million
Number Employees: 10-19

53409 Seaboard Foods
2801 Hurliman Rd
Guymon, OK 73942-6024   580-338-4900
Fax: 580-338-4900   877-562-7675
communitynetwork@seaboardfoods.com
www.seaboardfoods.com
Pork Product Producers
Manager: Stan Scott
Manager: Joe Locke
Estimated Sales: $ .5 - 1 million
Number Employees: 50-99
Type of Packaging: Bulk

53410 Seaboard Warehouse Terminals
5400 NW 32 Court
Miami, FL 33142   305-633-8587
Fax: 305-633-9621   800-273-8587
info@seaboardwarehouse.com
www.seaboardwarehouse.com
Public warehouse providing cooler and dry storage for beverages, food, paper products, plastic bags, aluminum foil, etc.; transportation firm providing short and local haul trucking; also, dry and reefer services and rail sidingavailable
Owner: Bob Fischer
VP/General Manager: Leon Hammond
Contact: Juan Policem
jpolicem@seaboardwarehouse.com
Estimated Sales: $ 10 - 20 Million
Number Employees: 100-249
Square Footage: 920000
Parent Co: Seaboard Warehouse Terminals
Types of products warehoused:
 Beverages, food, paper products, plastic bags, aluminum foil, general merchandise, etc., dry goods, non-perishables, canned foods, general merchandise, building materials
Services Provided:
 Short & local haul trucking and value added services, rail siding, trucking, Cooler Space, cross-dock
Storage Facility Data:
 Cooler Size 57000
 Dry Storage Size: 400000 Sq. Ft.
 Humidity-Controlled Size: 57000

53411 Seaborard Marine
8001 N.W.
79th Avenue
Miami, FL 33166-2154   305-863-4444
Fax: 305-579-9162   www.seabordcorp.com
Parent Co: SEABOARD CORPORATION

53412 Seafood Connection
841 Pohukaina St # I
Suite I
Honolulu, HI 96813-5332   808-591-8550
Fax: 808-591-8445   sales@seafood-connection.com
www.seafood-connection.com
Seafood and gourmet products
President: Stuart Simmons
Estimated Sales: $ 10 - 20 Million
Number Employees: 10-19

53413 (HQ)Seaonus
10060 Skinner Lake Dr
Jacksonville, FL 32246-8495   904-786-8038
Fax: 904-781-3256   info@seaonus.com
www.seaonus.com
Warehouse offering cooler and freezer storage; transportation firm providing local, short and long haul TL and LTL trucking; import/export inspections, blast freezing, break bulk, dockside ship loading and rail siding available
President: Terry Brown
VP Operations: Mark Gier
Number Employees: 100-249
Other Locations:
 ICS Logistics
 Jacksonville, FLICS Logistics
Types of products warehoused:
 frozen goods
Services Provided:
 Import/export inspections, break bulk, etc., rail siding, blast freezing
Storage Facility Data:
 Cooler Size 1000000 Cubic Ft.
 Freezer Size: 4000000 Cubic Ft.

53414 Seaschott
2609 Cabover Dr # 9
Hanover, MD 21076-1662   410-863-1444
Fax: 410-863-1444   info@seaschott.com
www.seaschott.com
Warehouse providing dry storage for dry canned and imported foods; customs house and transportation broker providing freight forwarding services via local, long and short haul trucking; also, distribution, re-packing, export and importservices available
President/Founder: Robert Schott
Secretary/Treasurer: Joanne Schott
Executive VP: Tony Sequeira
Sales/Marketing: Andrew Shotwell
Manager: Jay Williamson
balimport@seaschott.com
Director Operations: Hing Buon
Number Employees: 5-9
Parent Co: Airschott
Other Locations:
 Seaschott
 Washington, DCSeaschott
Types of products warehoused:
 Dry, canned & imported foods, dry goods, canned foods
Services Provided:
 Trucking, distribution, re-packaging, importing, exporting, etc.
Storage Facility Data:
 Dry Storage Size: 6000 Sq. Ft.

53415 Security Bonded Warehouse
1525 S Blount St
Raleigh, NC 27603-2507   919-834-1341
Fax: 919-834-5171   SBW@securitybonded.com
www.securitybondedwarehouse.com
Warehouse providing cooler, freezer and dry storage for nonperishable food
President: Mohamahad Gholizadeh

Warehousing / A-Z

Estimated Sales: $500,000-$1 Million
Number Employees: 5-9
Types of products warehoused:
Non-perishable food, non-perishables
Storage Facility Data:
Cooler Size 600 Sq. Ft.
Dry Storage Size: 150000 Sq. Ft.
Freezer Size: 800 Sq. Ft.

53416 Sedalia Cold Storage Company
320 W Main St
Sedalia, MO 65301   660-826-5540
Fax: 816-826-6419 sedcold@i-land.net
Warehouse providing cooler, freezer and dry storage of ice
President: Fred Branson
Contact: Ted Perkins
sedcold@i-land.net
Estimated Sales: $1-2.5 Million
Number Employees: 5-9
Types of products warehoused:
Ice, frozen goods

53417 Service Cold Storage Inc
3220 SW 2nd Ave
Fort Lauderdale, FL 33315-3382   954-761-7772
Fax: 954-761-3633 www.servicecold.com
Warehouse providing freezer and cooler storage; rail siding available
Owner: Mike Weber
mike@servicecold.com
Marketing Director: Kora Allen
Estimated Sales: $500,000-$1 Million
Number Employees: 5-9
Square Footage: 2640000
Types of products warehoused:
Seafood, meat, bait, frozen goods, Cooler products
Services Provided:
Cold Storage, rail siding
Storage Facility Data:
Cooler Size 330000 Cubic Ft.
Freezer Size: 660000 Cubic Ft.

53418 Service Cold Storage Inc
3220 SW 2nd Ave
Fort Lauderdale, FL 33315-3382   954-761-7772
Fax: 954-761-3633 keith@servicecold.com
www.servicecold.com
Owner: Mike Weber
mike@servicecold.com
Office Mgr: Lisa Fowler
Estimated Sales: $ 1 - 3 Million
Number Employees: 5-9

53419 Service Craft Distribution Systems
6565 Knott Ave
Buena Park, CA 90620-1139   714-994-0827
Fax: 714-690-6545
Warehouse providing cooler, freezer and dry storage for groceries, refrigerated and frozen items; transportation firm providing local, long and short haul trucking; rail siding available
President: Peter McLoughlin
CFO: Erick Garcia
COO: Peter McLoughlin
Number Employees: 250-499
Types of products warehoused:
Groceries, refrigerated & frozen items, frozen goods
Services Provided:
Local, long & short haul trucking, rail siding

53420 Service Warehouse & Distribution
PO Box 66290
Chicago, IL 60666-0290   630-775-1535
Fax: 630-775-1536
Warehouse providing dry storage for canned goods, potato flour, cereals, nonfood groceries and candy; also, rail siding and pick and pack services available
Owner: Thomas Kurgan
Director Operations: Tom Kurgan
Estimated Sales: $300,000-500,000
Number Employees: 1-4
Square Footage: 1048000
Types of products warehoused:
Canned goods, potato flour, cereals, non-food groceries & candy, dry goods, canned foods
Services Provided:
Pick & pack, rail siding
Storage Facility Data:
Dry Storage Size: 262000 Cubic Ft.

53421 Serviplast
1271 Lougar Street
Sarnia, ON N7S 5N5
Canada   519-336-4972
Fax: 519-344-0729
Warehouse providing dry storage for nonperishable foods and general merchandise
Manager: Joe Sharpe
Number Employees: 1-4
Square Footage: 728000
Types of products warehoused:
General merchandise & non-perishable foods, non-perishables, general merchandise

53422 Shamrock Warehouse
219 Virginia St
Gary, IN 46402-1390   219-882-6933
Fax: 219-883-6294
Warehouse offering dry storage for general merchandise; also, shipping, local cartage and container facilities services available
Owner: Richard LA Font
Estimated Sales: Less Than $500,000
Number Employees: 1-4
Square Footage: 1060000
Type of Packaging: Private Label
Types of products warehoused:
General merchandise, general merchandise
Services Provided:
Shipping, local cartage & container facilities
Storage Facility Data:
Dry Storage Size: 265000 Sq. Ft.

53423 Shaw Montgomery Warehouse Company
1305 Wilbanks Street
Montgomery, AL 36108   334-269-1415
Public bonded warehouse providing dry storage for general merchandise and nonperishable foods; transportation firm providing local haul trucking; rail siding available
Contact: David Cultrera
dave@spwg.com
Office Manager: Connie Cauthen
Number Employees: 10-19
Types of products warehoused:
Non-perishable food & general merchandise, dry goods, non-perishables, canned foods, general merchandise
Services Provided:
Local haul trucking, rail siding, trucking, pick and pack, repackaging
Storage Facility Data:
Dry Storage Size: 90000 Sq. Ft.

53424 Shaw Warehouse Company
305 26th Ave W
Birmingham, AL 35204   205-251-7188
Fax: 205-328-1865   800-467-7429
Warehouse providing cooler, dry and humidity-controlled storage for groceries and general merchandise; rail siding services available
President: Bill Crow
Secretary/Treasurer: Warren Crow
Contact: Sherry Franklin
sfranklin@shawwarehouse.com
Warehouse Manager: Wilburn Keith
Estimated Sales: $2.5-5 Million
Number Employees: 5-9
Square Footage: 560000
Types of products warehoused:
Groceries & general merchandise, grocery merchandise
Services Provided:
rail siding
Storage Facility Data:
Cooler Size 20000 Sq. Ft.
Dry Storage Size: 140000 Sq. Ft.
Humidity-Controlled Size: 140000 Sq. Ft.

53425 Shaw's Southern Belle Frozen
821 Virginia St
Jacksonville, FL 32208-4950   904-768-1591
Fax: 904-768-3663   888-742-9772
info@shawsouthernbelle.com
shawsouthernbelle.com
Cold storage warehouse facility.
Owner: Howard Shaw
hshaw@shawsouthernbelle.com
CEO: John Shaw
Shipping/Receiving: Steve Anderson
Shipping/Receiving: Chris Robinson
Number Employees: 100-249
Parent Co: Shaw's Southern Belle Frozen, Inc.
Types of products warehoused:
Frozen seafood, frozen goods

53426 Shawnee Trucking Co Inc
212 Washington Ave
Carlstadt, NJ 07072-3007   201-438-7060
Fax: 201-438-7175 www.shawneetrucking.com
Warehouse providing dry storage; also, full container drayage and LTL consolidation and distribution services available
Owner: Chris Lall
clall@shawneetrucking.com
Warehouse Manager: Tom Sabatino
Terminal Manager: Bob Jones
Number Employees: 20-49
Types of products warehoused:
Dry goods, dry goods
Services Provided:
Full container drayage & LTL consolidation & distribution

53427 Shepard's Moving & Storage
32 Henry St # 3
Bethel, CT 06801-2406   203-830-8300
Fax: 203-744-6775   800-243-0993
www.mayflower.com
Warehouse offering dry storage for groceries; catalog fulfillment and rail siding available; transportation firm providing agent allied van lines
Owner: Michael Goodman
CEO/CFO: David Albin
Vice President of Sales: Michael Leahy
Warehouse Manager: Robert Badgley
Number Employees: 50-99
Types of products warehoused:
Groceries, paper products, general merchandise, etc., general merchandise
Services Provided:
Catalog fulfillment, rail siding
Storage Facility Data:
Dry Storage Size: 350000 Sq. Ft.

53428 (HQ)Shippers Warehouse
8901 Forney Rd
Dallas, TX 75227-4506   214-381-5050
Fax: 214-275-1051
mstrickland@shipperswarehouse.com
www.shipperswarehouse.com
Warehouse providing cooler and humidity-controlled storage of groceries; rail siding, pool distribution, trucking, small package logistics, e-commerce catalog fulfillment and EDI services available
President: Ken Johnson
kjohnson@shipperswarehouse.com
Executive VP: Mark Strickland
Estimated Sales: $10-20 Million
Number Employees: 100-249
Square Footage: 1600000
Other Locations:
Shippers Warehouse
Garland, TXShippers Warehouse
Types of products warehoused:
Groceries
Services Provided:
Trucking, pool distribution, small package logistics, EDI, etc., rail siding
Storage Facility Data:
Cooler Size 10000 Cubic Ft.
Humidity-Controlled Size: 40000 Cubic Ft.

53429 Shoreham Cooperative Apple Producer
3442 Route 22a
Shoreham, VT 5770   802-897-7400
Fax: 802-897-7401
Warehouse providing cooler storage for apples
President: J Barney Hodges
Estimated Sales: $10-20 Million
Number Employees: 20-49
Square Footage: 200000
Types of products warehoused:
Apples, produce

53430 Shoreland Inc
3843 Devonshire Dr
Salisbury, MD 21804-2516   410-742-1128
Fax: 410-548-2742
Warehouse providing freezer and cooler storage; also, blast freezing, exporting and rail siding services available

President: Arthur Cooley
Vice President: D Dryden
Warehouse Manager: J Schrecongost
Estimated Sales: Less Than $500,000
Number Employees: 1-4
Square Footage: 548000
Parent Co: Shoreland
Types of products warehoused:
   frozen goods
Services Provided:
   Exporting, USDA inspection, computer access to inventory, rail siding, blast freezing
Storage Facility Data:
   Cooler Size 20000 Cubic Ft.
   Freezer Size: 1440000 Cubic Ft.

53431 Shoreline Freezers
6 N Industrial Blvd
Bridgeton, NJ 08302-3414   856-451-8300
  Fax: 856-451-5284 www.shorelinefreezers.com
Warehouse providing freezer storage; transportation company providing local trucking; rail siding services available
Manager: Eric Scheller
Number Employees: 10-19
Types of products warehoused:
   Frozen foods, frozen goods
Services Provided:
   Local trucking, rail siding

53432 Shoreline Freezers
6 N Industrial Blvd
Bridgeton, NJ 08302-3414   856-451-8300
  Fax: 856-451-5284 www.shorelinefreezers.com
Public Cold Storage Facility
Owner: June Hess
Manager: Eric Scheller
Estimated Sales: $ .5 - 1 million
Number Employees: 10-19
Type of Packaging: Food Service

53433 Shoreline Fruit
10850 E Traverse Hwy
Suite 4460
Traverse City, MI 49684-1365   231-941-4336
  Fax: 231-941-4525 800-836-3972
cs@shorelinefruit.com www.shorelinefruit.com
Dried fruits, fruit juice and fruit concentrate
CEO: John Sommavilla
cs@shorelinefruit.com
Marketing Manager: Kristen Moravcik
Director, Sales & Marketing: Brian Gerberding
Number Employees: 10-19
Other Locations:
   Headquarters
   Traverse City, MI
   Production & Storage
   Williamsburg, MIHeadquartersWilliamsburg

53434 Sierra Meat & Seafood Co
1330 Capital Blvd.
Suite A
Reno, NV 89502   775-322-4073
       800-444-5687
sales@sierrameat.com sierrameat.com
Meat and seafood.
President/CEO: Chris Flocchini
Executive Vice President: Bernadette Flocchini
Year Founded: 1934
Estimated Sales: $101 Million
Number Employees: 100-249
Square Footage: 25000
Type of Packaging: Food Service
Other Locations:
   Santa Clara, CA
   Monterey, CA
   Reno, NVMonterey

53435 Sierra Pacific Distribution
4300 Finch Rd
Modesto, CA 95357-4102   209-572-2882
  Fax: 209-572-2884 contact@spwg.com
       www.spwg.com
President: Mike Mc Nulty
modesto@spwg.com
V.P. Sales and Marketing: Chris Murphy
Customer Service Managers: Chantel Torres
General Manager: Merv Fikse
Estimated Sales: $ 3 - 5 Million
Number Employees: 20-49

53436 Sierra Pacific Distribution
4300 Finch Rd
Modesto, CA 95357-4102   209-572-2882
  Fax: 209-572-2884 www.spwg.com

Warehousing and distribution
President: Mike Mc Nulty
modesto@spwg.com
Estimated Sales: $ 3 - 5 Million
Number Employees: 20-49
Type of Packaging: Food Service

53437 Sierra Pacific Refrigerated
340 S 1st St
Patterson, CA 95363-2800   209-892-6700
  Fax: 209-892-5920 contact@spwg.com
       www.spwg.com
Warehouse providing cooler and freezer storage for frozen foods including dinners, pasta, produce, turkey meat, etc.; also, rail siding available
President: Michael J. McNulty
Chief Operating Officer: Gary Fox
CFO: Michelle Van Artsdalen
Executive Vice President: Roy Atkins
Vice President, General Manager: Ken Sauls
Vice President, Marketing: Chris Murphy
Vice President, Sales: Chirs Murphy
Manager: Birdie Rodriguez
birdie@spwg.com
Office Manager: Jennifer Marquez
Estimated Sales: $1-2.5 Million
Number Employees: 20-49
Types of products warehoused:
   Frozen foods, produce & turkey meat, frozen goods, produce
Services Provided:
   rail siding

53438 (HQ)Simard Warehouses
1212 32nd Avenue
Lachine, QC H8T 3K7
Canada   514-636-9411
  Fax: 514-633-8078 888-282-9321
pabraham@simard.ca www.simard.ca
Warehouse providing dry storage for canned goods and general merchandise; transportation services include LTL, TL, local trucking, container, distribution, hourly and contract serving Montreal and Toronto metropolitan areas
President: Peter Abraham
Chairman: Michael Abraham
Number Employees: 250-499
Types of products warehoused:
   Canned goods & general merchandise, dry goods, non-perishables, canned foods, general merchandise
Services Provided:
   Order picking, distribution, LTL & TL trans. & cross-docking, rail siding, trucking, labeling, pick and pack, repackaging
Storage Facility Data:
   Dry Storage Size: 300000 Cubic Ft.

53439 Smedley Company
40 Flax Mill Rd
Branford, CT 06405-2898   203-315-6066
  Fax: 203-315-6060 wrp4@smedleycrane.com
       www.smedleycrane.com
Warehouse providing dry storage; rail siding available
President/Treasurer: William Palmer
Marketing Manager: W Palmer
Estimated Sales: $2.6 Million
Number Employees: 25
Services Provided:
   rail siding
Storage Facility Data:
   Dry Storage Size: 120000 Sq. Ft.

53440 Smg Summit Cold Storage
5450 S Center Ave
Summit Argo, IL 60501-1025   708-458-8646
  Fax: 708-924-1142 Janice@summitcold.com
       www.summitcold.com
Office Manager: Janice Stang-Jensen
Account Manager: Pawel Mroczek
Vice President: Mike Kucharski
Director of Sales: Bryan Korda
Warehouse Manager: Chris Glaesner
Estimated Sales: Less Than $500,000
Number Employees: 1-4

53441 (HQ)Smith Terminal Distribution
10800 NW 97th St # 102
Medley, FL 33178-2527   305-685-0325
       Fax: 305-688-0081

Warehouse providing cooler and dry storage for groceries and temperature-controlled and general commodities; transportation services include long and short haul trucking and freight consolidation, etc.; also, cross docking, localcartage and rail siding available
Owner: Frank Futernick
frank@smithterminal.com
Number Employees: 100-249
Types of products warehoused:
   Groceries, paper, plastics & medical and general commodities, dry goods, non-perishables, canned foods, general merchandise
Services Provided:
   Cross docking, trucking, local cartage, pool car, etc., rail siding, trucking, labeling
Storage Facility Data:
   Cooler Size 25000 Sq. Ft.
   Dry Storage Size: 350000 Sq. Ft.

53442 Sno Temp Cold Storage
3815 Marion St SE
Albany, OR 97322-3877   541-928-5755
  Fax: 541-928-0888 www.snotemp.com
Warehouse offering freezer storage for meat, vegetables and seafood; rail siding available. Frozen space: 6,890,000 cubic feet; Convertible space: 400,000 cubic feet; 18 enclosed truck bays; 10 car capacity, private rail siding (UnionPacific & Burlington Northern Santa Fe); Fresh to frozen blast freezing; 18 enclosed truck bays; Temperature range of -18F to 40.
Manager: Rob Young
rob@snotemp.com
Operations: Michael Lafferty
Plant Manager: Charlie Kroeger
Estimated Sales: $1-2.5 Million
Number Employees: 10-19
Square Footage: 752000
Types of products warehoused:
   Meat, vegetables & seafood, produce
Services Provided:
   rail siding

53443 (HQ)Sodus Cold Storage Co
50 Maple Ave
P.O. Box 278
Sodus, NY 14551-1018   315-483-6966
  Fax: 315-483-6822 scs@sodus.com
Warehouse providing cooler, freezer and dry storage
President: William Bishop Jr
CEO: Sandra Bishop
VP: Sandra Bishop
Manager: M Creynolds
creynolds@sodus.com
Corporate Operations Manager: Joel Dougherty
Estimated Sales: $1-2.5 Million
Number Employees: 20-49
Types of products warehoused:
   Dry, cooler & frozen, dry goods, frozen goods
Storage Facility Data:
   Cooler Size 1500000 Cubic Ft.
   Dry Storage Size: 180000 Sq. Ft.
   Freezer Size: 2000000 Cubic Ft.

53444 Somerset Industries
901 North Bethlehem Pike
Spring House, PA 19477-0927   215-619-0480
  Fax: 215-619-0489 800-883-8728
       www.somersetindustries.com
Wholesaler/distributor, importer and exporter of closeout items bought and sold. The correctional food specialist. Warehouse and transportation services provided
President: Jay Shrager
CFO: Carole Shrager
VP: Alan Breslow
Marketing Director: Candace Shrager
Sales Manager: Kevin Murray Jr
General Manager: Ben Caldwell
Number Employees: 20-49
Type of Packaging: Food Service, Private Label, Bulk
Types of products warehoused:
   Portion control & pack foods, kosher, halal & frozen foods, canned & dry goods and closeout items, dry goods, non-perishables, frozen goods, canned foods
Services Provided:
   Trucking fleet & re-packing

Warehousing / A-Z

53445 Sonwil Distribution Center
100 Sonwil Dr
PO Box 126
Buffalo, NY 14225 716-684-0555
 Fax: 716-684-6996
Public warehouse providing dry storage for food and medical supplies and general merchandise; transportation broker providing freight consolidation services; also, rail siding, controlled sanitation programs, pick and pack, shrinktunnel and EDI available
President and CEO: Peter Wilson
Vice President of Sales & Marketing: James Manno Jr.
darchilla@sonwil.com
Contact: Dennis Archilla
darchilla@sonwil.com
Chief Operations Officer: Richard Becker Jr
Types of products warehoused:
 dry goods, canned foods, general merchandise, Paper roll
Services Provided:
 rail siding, trucking, labeling, packaging, pick and pack, repackaging
Storage Facility Data:
 Dry Storage Size: 700000 Sq. Ft.

53446 (HQ)Sopak Co Inc
118 S Cypress St
Mullins, SC 29574-3004 843-464-6001
 www.sopakco.com
Warehouse providing dry storage, re-packing and labeling for nonperishable foods; transportation services include short haul trucking in the Southeast
Manager: Wesley Keller
Estimated Sales: Less Than $500,000
Number Employees: 1-4
Other Locations:
 Bennettsville, SC
 Mullins, SCMullins
Types of products warehoused:
 Non-perishable foods, non-perishables
Services Provided:
 Re-packing & labeling, trucking, labeling, re-packaging

53447 South Atlantic Warehouse Corporation
2020 E Market St
Greensboro, NC 27401 336-272-4163
 Fax: 336-274-7660
Warehouse facility offering dry storage space for food, appliances, textile products, furniture and cans; transportation firm providing short haul trucking; also, uncrating, rail siding and sit-in services available
Owner: Jim Rucker
jim.rucker@southatlanticcompanies.com
Number Employees: 50-99
Types of products warehoused:
 Food, appliances, textile products, furniture & cans
Services Provided:
 LTL, TL, uncrating & sit-in, rail siding
Storage Facility Data:
 Dry Storage Size: 240000 Sq. Ft.

53448 South Bend Warehousing & Distribution
PO Box 1228
South Bend, IN 46624-1228 574-239-1310
 Fax: 574-239-7695 storage@sbwd.com
Warehouse providing storage for industrial goods; transportation firm providing short haul trucking
Owner: Abraham Marcus
Number Employees: 10-19
Types of products warehoused:
 Industrial goods
Services Provided:
 Short haul trucking

53449 (HQ)South Mill
649 West South Street
Kennett Square, PA 19348 610-444-4800
 Fax: 610-444-1338 info@southmill.com
 www.southmill.com
National mushroom supplier.
Contact: Iris Ayala
iayala@southmill.com
Year Founded: 1978
Number Employees: 1,000
Type of Packaging: Consumer, Food Service, Private Label, Bulk

Other Locations:
 Distribution
 Atlanta, GA
 Distribution
 New Orleans, LA
 Distribution
 Houston, TX
 Distribution
 Dallas, TXDistributionNew Orleans
Types of products warehoused:
 Produce, produce
Services Provided:
 Transportation
Storage Facility Data:
 Cooler Size 30000 Sq. Ft.

53450 South Texas Freezer Company
P.O.Box 2422
Corpus Christi, TX 78403-2422
 Fax: 361-289-2212
Warehouse Food Storage
President: Daniel Dettmer
Estimated Sales: $ .5 - 1 million
Number Employees: 5 to 9
Type of Packaging: Food Service

53451 Southeast Food Distribution
18770 N. E. 6th Ave
Miami, FL 33179 305-652-4622
 Fax: 305-651-8329 800-662-4622
 www.seff.com
Food Distribution
CEO: Rich Bauer
Operations Manager: Tony Antenelo
Estimated Sales: $300,000-500,000
Number Employees: 1-4
Square Footage: 470000
Type of Packaging: Bulk

53452 Southeastern Freezer
PO Box 6056wsb
Gainesville, GA 30504 770-536-4311
 Fax: 770-536-8488
President: Jan Cooley
Estimated Sales: $ 3 - 5 Million
Number Employees: 20-49

53453 Southern Belle Refrigerated
625 N Commerce St
Tupelo, MS 38804-4032 662-842-5778
 Fax: 662-842-4223
 jeremy.biggs@southernbelle.biz
 www.southernbelle.biz
Freezer and Cold Storage Facility
Manager: Danny Miles
Estimated Sales: $ 1 - 3 Million
Number Employees: 10-19
Type of Packaging: Food Service

53454 Southern Cold Storage Co
7150 S Choctaw Dr
Baton Rouge, LA 70806-1354 225-929-6400
 Fax: 225-924-6474 www.southerncold.com
Warehouse providing temperature controlled storage.
Owner: Fermin Deoca
fermin.deoca@southerncold.com
Operations Manager: Jon Aycock
Estimated Sales: $1-2.5 Million
Number Employees: 20-49
Square Footage: 360000
Parent Co: Southern Cold Storage, LLC.
Services Provided:
 Web enabled customer access, case picking and distribution, rail siding, trucking, labeling, pick and pack, -12F to +40F temperature range

53455 Southern Colorado CourtSvc
200 W B St # 226
Pueblo, CO 81003-3574 719-595-1634
 Fax: 719-595-1643
President: Anthony Estrada
Number Employees: 5-9

53456 Southern Packaging & Distribution
1550 Ellis Rd N
Jacksonville, FL 32254 904-783-0391
 Fax: 904-786-5627
Full service logistics company; rail siding available
CEO/President: Foster Sheperd
VP Operations: D Byrd
General Manager: John Sheperd

Estimated Sales: $ 3 - 5 Million
Number Employees: 20-49
Square Footage: 3700000
Types of products warehoused:
 Private label foods
Services Provided:
 rail siding
Storage Facility Data:
 Dry Storage Size: 925000

53457 Southern Warehousing & Distribution
3232 Ih 35 N
San Antonio, TX 78219 210-224-7771
 Fax: 210-226-9485 www.southernwd.com
Warehouse offering general storage and distribution including cold and dry storage, re-packaging and trucking for nonfood and grocery products; also, import and export services to Mexico available; served by Southern PacificRailroad
President: Jonathan Walker
Vice President: Johnathan Walker
Sales: Richard Pacheco
Operations Manager: Mark Weikel
Estimated Sales: $2.5-5 Million
Number Employees: 20-49
Square Footage: 960000
Types of products warehoused:
 Non-food & grocery products
Services Provided:
 Re-packaging, trucking, distribution, importing & exporting, rail siding
Storage Facility Data:
 Cooler Size 50000 Cubic Ft.
 Dry Storage Size: 230000 Sq. Ft.

53458 Southern Warehousing-Dstrbtn
3232 N Panam Expy
San Antonio, TX 78219-2310 210-224-7771
 Fax: 210-226-9409 jwalker@southernwd.com
 www.southernwd.com
Warehouse providing cooler, freezer and dry storage for nonperishable, refrigerated and frozen foods, general merchandise, etc.; rail siding available
Owner: Courtney Walker
Safety & Fleet Manager: Todd Miller
Sales: Richard Pacheco
jwalker@southernwd.com
Operations Manager: Mark Weikel
Estimated Sales: $1-2.5 Million
Number Employees: 10-19
Types of products warehoused:
 Non-perishable, refrigerated & frozen foods, general merchandise, etc., non-perishables, frozen goods, general merchandise
Services Provided:
 rail siding

53459 (HQ)Southshore Enterprises
3515 Lakeshore Drive
St Joseph, MI 49085-2977 269-983-2080
 Fax: 269-983-7307
 sales@southshorecompanies.com
 www.southshorecompanies.com
Warehouse providing dry storage for nonperishable foods; transportation firm providing short haul trucking
President: Ted Kirshenbaum
Treasurer, CFO: Philip Maki
VP: Jordan Kirshenbaum
Contact: David Butler
dbutler@southshorecompanies.com
Senior Operations Manager: Robert Oberheu
Number Employees: 5-9
Other Locations:
 Southshore Enterprises
 East Hartford, CT
 Elkhart, IN
 Dayton, OHSouthshore EnterprisesElkhart
Types of products warehoused:
 Non-perishable foods, non-perishables
Services Provided:
 Short haul trucking

53460 Southwest Logistics
2129 Hightower Drive
Garland, TX 75041-6103 972-271-5621
 Fax: 972-271-8568
Warehouse providing cooler and dry storage; rail siding services available
General Manager: Melvin LaBard
Estimated Sales: $1-2.5 Million
Number Employees: 19

Warehousing / A-Z

Square Footage: 648000
Parent Co: Shippers' Warehouse
Services Provided:
  rail siding
Storage Facility Data:
  Cooler Size 750000 Cubic Ft.
  Dry Storage Size: 122000 Sq. Ft.

53461 Space Center Inc
2501 Rosegate
Roseville, MN 55113-2717 651-604-4200
  Fax: 651-604-4222 info@spacecenterinc.com
Warehouse providing dry and humidy-controlled storage for nonperishable items and paper products; transportation firm providing local haul trucking; also, re-packing, labeling services and rail siding available
President: Anthony Kraus
CEO: Charles Arend
carend@spacecenterinc.com
Estimated Sales: Less Than $500,000
Number Employees: 1-4
Parent Co: Space Center
Types of products warehoused:
  Non-perishable food items & paper products, non-perishables
Services Provided:
  Re-packing, labeling & local short haul trucking, rail siding
Storage Facility Data:
  Dry Storage Size: 2200000 Cubic Ft.

53462 Spartan Logistics
4140 Lockbourne Rd
Columbus, OH 43207-4221 614-497-1777
  Fax: 614-497-1808 sales@spartanwarehouse.com
  www.spartanwarehouse.com
Warehouse providing dry storage of cans, cereal, plastic materials, canned food and KD cartons; rail siding, distribution and packaging services available; transportation firm providing local haul trucking
President: Ed Harmon
CFO: Steve Harmon
Vice President: Jim Ranney
Number Employees: 5-9
Parent Co: Spartan Warehouse & Distribution
Types of products warehoused:
  Cans, cereal, plastic materials, canned food & KD cartons, dry goods, canned foods
Services Provided:
  Distribution, packaging, crossdocking & local haul trucking, rail siding, labeling, pick and pack

53463 Spaten West, Inc
284 Harbor Way
South San Francisco, CA 94080 650-794-0800
  Fax: 650-794-9567 spaten@spatenusa.com
  www.spatenusa.com
Importer and distributor of Bavarian beer.
President: Chris Hildebrandt
Estimated Sales: $2.5 Million
Number Employees: 15
Number of Brands: 1
Parent Co: Spaten-Franziskaner-Brau
Type of Packaging: Consumer, Food Service, Bulk
Types of products warehoused:
  Alcoholic beverages

53464 Springfield Underground
2019 N Le Compte Rd
Springfield, MO 65802 417-874-1406
  Fax: 417-874-1450
  www.springfieldunderground.com
Controlled climate warehouses. Freezers, coolers, dry storage facilities
CEO: Louis Griesemer
CFO: Sam Cox
Manager: Dow Fabro
dofabro@springfieldunderground.com
Estimated Sales: $4.2 Million
Number Employees: 20-49
Square Footage: 10000000
Types of products warehoused:
  Refrigerated, frozen & dry foods, dry goods, frozen goods
Services Provided:
  Computer inventory control, end of month reports & distribution, rail siding
Storage Facility Data:
  Cooler Size 500000 Sq. Ft.
  Dry Storage Size: 1800000 Sq. Ft.

Freezer Size: 200000 Sq. Ft.
Humidity-Controlled Size: 10245000 Sq. Ft.

53465 Stage One Coldstorage
285 East Broad St
Ozark, AL 36360-2142 334-774-9361
  Fax: 334-774-7979
Warehouse providing cooler, freezer and dry storage of food products; rail siding available
Owner: H Jack Mizell
Number Employees: 10-19
Types of products warehoused:
  Food products
Services Provided:
  rail siding
Storage Facility Data:
  Cooler Size 2092963 Cubic Ft.
  Dry Storage Size: 10180 Sq. Ft.
  Freezer Size: 114480 Cubic Ft.

53466 Standard TransportationSvc
1801 Roosevelt Ave
Joplin, MO 64801-3753 417-782-1990
  Fax: 417-782-5098 lbryant@stdtrans.com
Transportation broker providing freight forwarding and local haul trucking; warehouse providing dry storage
Owner: Geoff Roberts
Sales: Morris Glaze
Contact: Jeremy Hunsaker
jhunsaker@vinylren.com
Operations: Larry Bryant
Estimated Sales: Less Than $500,000
Number Employees: 1-4
Square Footage: 976000
Types of products warehoused:
  Processed food products & dry goods, dry goods, canned foods, general merchandise
Services Provided:
  Local haul trucking, barcode, rail siding, trucking
Storage Facility Data:
  Dry Storage Size: 488000 Sq. Ft.

53467 Standard Warehouse
8501 River Rd
Pennsauken, NJ 08110-3325 856-488-0430
  www.stechgroup.com
Warehouse providing dry storage for nonperishable items; transportation firm providing local, long and short haul trucking
President: Marge Smith
msmith@stechgroup.com
Sales Manager: Tim Fox
General Manager: Jim Donelly III
Number Employees: 10-19
Types of products warehoused:
  Non-perishable items, dry goods, non-perishables, canned foods, general merchandise
Services Provided:
  Local, long & short haul trucking, rail siding, trucking, labeling, packaging, pick and pack, re-packaging
Storage Facility Data:
  Cooler Size 15,000 Sq. Ft.
  Dry Storage Size: 750,000 Cubic Ft.

53468 Stanford Refrigerated Warehouses
21700 Barton Road
Colton, CA 92324 478-781-6565
  Fax: 478-781-8309 800-678-7271
President: Brent Stanford
Chief Executive Officer: Bill Hendricksen
Corporate CFO: Todd Nelson
Operational CFO: Jeremy Breaux
Chief Information Officer: Sudarsan Thattai
EVP, Business Development and Strategy: Tim Smith
SVP, Sales and Marketing: Scott Chapman
VP, Human Resources: Patricia Gaudin
Chief Administration Officer: Allen Merrill
Estimated Sales: $ 1 - 3 Million
Number Employees: 20-49

53469 Stanford Refrigerated Warehouse
1945 Waterville Rd
Macon, GA 31206-1147 478-746-6623
  Fax: 912-743-7880
Warehouse offering cooler and freezer storage for refrigerated and frozen foods; also, rail siding, local area delivery, blast freezing and export services available
President: Brent Stanford

Estimated Sales: $ 1 - 3 Million
Number Employees: 10-19
Square Footage: 520000
Types of products warehoused:
  Refrigerated & frozen foods, frozen goods
Services Provided:
  Blast freezing, local area delivery & export services, rail siding
Storage Facility Data:
  Cooler Size 1500000 Cubic Ft.
  Freezer Size: 360000 Cubic Ft.

53470 Stanley Orchards Sales, Inc.
2044 State Route 32
#6
Modena, NY 12548 845-883-7351
  Fax: 845-883-5077 sales@stanleyorchards.com
  www.stanleyorchards.com
Apple growing and storage/packing facility; importer of apples and pears; cold storage facility.
President/CEO: Ronald Cohn
Sales & Marketing: Jordan Cohn
Sales Manager: Anthony Maresca
Domestic Sales: Janine Skurnick
Controller: Susan Surprise
Import/Export Liason: Lorrie Hazzard
Estimated Sales: $293 Thousand
Number Employees: 8
Type of Packaging: Consumer, Food Service, Private Label, Bulk
Types of products warehoused:
  produce

53471 Stanz Foodservice Inc
1840 Commerce Dr
South Bend, IN 46628-1563 574-232-6666
  Fax: 574-236-4169 800-342-5664
  www.stanz.com
Family owned food service distributer. Stanz offers services to regions such as Northern Indiana, Southwest Lower Michigan, Eastern and Central Illinois and Nothwest Ohio.
President: Mark Harman
CEO: Shirley Geraghty
Vice President: Wendy Harman
VP, Information Technology: Mark Gaddie
VP, Marketing & Merchandising: Jeff Nicholas
VP, Sales: Todd Stearns
VP, Operations: Dave Dausinas
Estimated Sales: $100+ Million
Number Employees: 100-249
Square Footage: 10000
Types of products warehoused:
  produce
Services Provided:
  trucking

53472 Star Distribution Systems
2302 Henderson Way
Plant City, FL 33563-7904 813-659-1002
  Fax: 813-757-9666 info@stardistribution.us
  www.stardistribution.us
Warehouse providing dry and cooler storage for refrigerated and nonperishable food; transportation firm providing local and short haul trucking
President/CEO: Larry Jimenez
ljimenez@stardistribution.us
Executive Vice President: David Mattioli
Number Employees: 100-249
Types of products warehoused:
  Refrigerated & non-perishable food, non-perishables
Services Provided:
  pool distribution, cross docking, stretch wrap, trans load, rail siding, trucking, pick and pack

53473 Starr Distribution Services Company
235 S 56th St
Chandler, AZ 85226-3304 480-961-0536
  Fax: 480-961-0453
Warehouse providing cooler and dry storage; transportation firm providing local haul trucking
Owner: James Young
Number Employees: 20-49
Types of products warehoused:
  Dry & refrigerated items, dry goods, non-perishables, canned foods, general merchandise
Services Provided:
  bar code, pool consolidation, rail siding, trucking, packaging, pick and pack, repackaging

Warehousing / A-Z

Storage Facility Data:
 Cooler Size 20000 Sq. Ft.
 Dry Storage Size: 105000 Sq. Ft.

53474 State Center Warehouse & Cold Storage
5621 W McKenzie Ave # D
Fresno, CA 93723-9240 559-445-1144
 Fax: 559-445-0702 stctrwhse@aol.com
Warehouse providing cool and dry storage for non-hazardous materials, animal and soil nutrients, food pharmaceuticals and food processing products
President: Steve Major
Manager: H McCullar
Office Manager: Susan Nelson
Estimated Sales: $500,000-1 Million
Number Employees: 5-9
Square Footage: 360000
Types of products warehoused:
 Non-hazardous materials, animal & soil nutrients, food pharmaceuticals & food processing products, liq. fertilizers, dry goods, non-perishables, canned foods, general merchandise, Animal feed supplements
Storage Facility Data:
 Cooler Size 10000 Sq. Ft.
 Dry Storage Size: 80000 Sq. Ft.

53475 Stemm Transfer & Storage
PO Box 397
St Cloud, MN 56302-0397 320-251-4080
 Fax: 320-251-7741
Warehouse providing dry storage for paper products and dry foods; transportation firm providing local and long haul trucking; rail siding services available
President: Kathie Jordahl
Number Employees: 20-49
Types of products warehoused:
 Paper products & dry foods, dry goods
Services Provided:
 Local & long haul trucking, rail siding
Storage Facility Data:
 Dry Storage Size: 40000 Sq. Ft.

53476 Stengel Seed & Grain Co
14698 SD Highway 15
Milbank, SD 57252-5452 605-432-6030
 Fax: 605-432-6064 gstengel@tnics.com
 www.tnics.com
Organic grains. Services include cleaning, dehulling, packaging, warehousing and shipping.
President: Doug Stengel
stengelseed@tnics.com
Estimated Sales: Less than $500,000
Number Employees: 5-9
Square Footage: 60000

53477 Sterling Bay Companies
1000 W Fulton Market
Chicago, IL 60607 312-466-4100
 INFO@1KFULTON.COM
 www.1kfulton.com
Warehouse providing cold and frozen storage; also, rail siding available
President/Owner: Amit Hasak
Chairman/Owner: Nehemiah Hasak
Vice President: Tom Grau
Estimated Sales: $5-10 Million
Number Employees: 50-99
Types of products warehoused:
 Refrigerated, frozen goods
Services Provided:
 trucking, labeling, blast freezing, packaging, pick and pack, repackaging

53478 Stockton Cold Storage
1320 W Weber Ave
Stockton, CA 95203-3132 209-948-0793
 Fax: 209-948-4269 contact@spwg.com
 www.spwg.com
Warehouse providing cooler, freezer and humidity-controlled storage for frozen foods; also, bulk packing and pick/pack; customized distribution processes available
President: Michael J. McNulty
CFO: Michelle Van Artsdalen
VP Sales/Marketing: Chris Murphy
Manager: Gary Fox
foxs@spwg.com
Chief Operating Officer: Gary Fox
Estimated Sales: $ .5 - 1 million
Number Employees: 10-19
Square Footage: 472000
Parent Co: Sierra Pacific Distribution Services

Other Locations:
 Sierra Pacific Distribution S
 Turlock, CA Sierra Pacific Distribution S
Types of products warehoused:
 Frozen foods, nuts, etc., dry goods, frozen goods
Services Provided:
 Re-packing
Storage Facility Data:
 Cooler Size 468226 Cubic Ft.
 Freezer Size: 1481000 Cubic Ft.
 Humidity-Controlled Size: 200000 Cubic Ft.

53479 Stonepath Logistics
1930 6th Ave S Ste 401
Seattle, WA 98134 206-624-4354
Warehouse providing dry storage for groceries and dry goods; transportation firm providing freight forwarding services via ocean freight, local, long and short haul trucking; also, re-packing services available
Number Employees: 50-99
Types of products warehoused:
 Groceries & dry goods, dry goods
Services Provided:
 Re-packing & freight forwarding, repackaging

53480 Strategic Development Concepts
1075 Central Park Avenue
Suite 410
Scarsdale, NY 10583-3232 914-723-5100
 Fax: 914-723-6207
Warehouse providing freezer storage
President: David Buntzman
Contact: Gary Stowe
glstowe@us.ibm.com
Estimated Sales: $2.5-5 Million
Number Employees: 19
Storage Facility Data:
 Freezer Size: 5000000 Cubic Ft.

53481 Streamline Shippers-Affiliates
6279 E Slauson Ave # 303
Suite 303
Commerce, CA 90040-3040 323-271-3800
 Fax: 323-271-3888 www.streamlineshippers.com
Warehouse providing storage for dry foods; shippers' association providing LTL, FTL, LCL, FCL and logistical services; also, labeling, bar coding and sorting services available
President: Sarah Barriger
sarah@streamlineshippers.com
Number Employees: 50-99
Types of products warehoused:
 Dry foods, dry goods
Services Provided:
 Labeling, bar coding & sorting
Storage Facility Data:
 Dry Storage Size: 118000 Sq. Ft.

53482 Suffolk Cold Storage
2000 Northgate Commerce Pkwy
Suffolk, VA 23435 757-465-3600
 Fax: 757-465-0298 info@suffolkcoldstorage.com
 www.suffolkcoldstorage.com
Freezer and Cold Storage
General Manager: Mike Group
Operations Manager: Ed Luskin
Estimated Sales: $ 1 - 3 Million
Number Employees: 20-49
Square Footage: 30
Type of Packaging: Food Service

53483 Sullivan TransportationInc
39 S Broad St
Westfield, MA 01085-4409 413-739-2558
 Fax: 413-642-3612 800-628-1067
 www.sulco.com
Warehouse providing dry and humidity-controlled storage
Vice President: Todd Douville
tdouville@sulco.com
President: Therese S Walch
VP/ Controller: Dick Casey
VP, Sales: Steve Conjar
VP, Operations: Todd Douville
Estimated Sales: $ 10 - 20 Million
Number Employees: 50-99

53484 Sunland Distribution
4401 Piggly Wiggly Dr
North Charleston, SC 29405-5606 843-744-7621
 Fax: 843-744-7624 800-295-0081
 www.acmedistribution.com

Warehouse offering dry storage for food products, chemicals, papers and general merchandise; also, computerized inventory control, rail siding and contract warehousing services available
President: Samuel Cole
Manager: Dave Manners
davem@sunlandls.com
Director Sales Development: Arch Thomason
VP Operations: Bob Kouvolo
Estimated Sales: $2.5-5 Million
Number Employees: 10-19
Square Footage: 840000
Types of products warehoused:
 Food, paper, chemicals & general merchandise, general merchandise
Services Provided:
 Computerized inventory control & contract warehousing, rail siding

53485 Superior Pack Group
2 Bailey Farm Rd.
Harriman, NY 10926 845-534-1015
 Fax: 845-534-1015 sales@superiorpackgroup.com
 www.superiorpackgroup.com
Contract food packaging, warehousing and inventory management
Director, Sales: Joel Hirsch *Year Founded:* 1995
Types of products warehoused:
 Food packaging
Services Provided:
 packaging
Storage Facility Data:
 Cooler Size 150000 Sq. Ft.

53486 Sutter Basin Growers Cooperative
21831 Knights Rd
Knights Landing, CA 95645 530-735-6295
 Fax: 530-735-6297
Warehouse providing storage for dried beans and rice
Manager: Ray Davis
Estimated Sales: $ .5 - 1 million
Number Employees: 5-9
Types of products warehoused:
 Dried beans & rice, dry goods

53487 Systems Online
1001 NW 62nd St
Fort Lauderdale, FL 33309-1900 954-840-3467
 Fax: 954-376-3338 support@sysonline.com
 www.sysonline.com
EZ Trade, the ultimate forms based e-trading solution/distribution management software DiMan for Windows95/98,2000; e-commerce, inventory, sales, purchasing, accounting
Estimated Sales: $1-2.5 Million
Number Employees: 1-4

53488 TCT Logistics
10920-178th Street NW
Edmonton, AB T5S 1R7
Canada 780-452-9880
 Fax: 780-484-1565
Warehouse providing dry storage for general merchandise and groceries; rail siding available
Branch Manager: Doug Bremness
Customer Service Representative: Lorna Kilworth
Number Employees: 50-99
Square Footage: 1280000
Types of products warehoused:
 General merchandise & groceries, general merchandise
Services Provided:
 rail siding
Storage Facility Data:
 Dry Storage Size: 130000 Sq. Ft.

53489 (HQ)TWL Corporation
5650 Wattsburg Rd
Erie, PA 16509-4066 814-825-1881
 Fax: 814-825-9428
Warehouse providing dry storage of food and paper products, containers, plastics and machinery; transportation firm providing LTL, TL and just-in-time long haul trucking; also, air freight, expediting and truck rental, leasing and maintenance
President: Ray Benacci
CEO: Joe Benacci
Vice President: Chuck Sites
Contact: Kristina Benacci
kristinab@twl-erie.com
Number Employees: 100-249
Types of products warehoused:
 Dry food, containers, cartons, plastics, machin-

ery & paper, dry goods, non-perishables, canned foods, general merchandise
Services Provided:
  LTL, TL, just-in-time long haul trucking, truck rental, etc., trucking
Storage Facility Data:
  Dry Storage Size: 850,000 Sq. Ft.

53490 Taylor Warehouse
2875 E Sharon Rd
Cincinnati, OH 45241-1976   513-771-1850
  Fax: 513-672-8549 www.taylordistributing.com
Cold Storage Facility
Owner: Rex Taylor
rextaylor@taylordistrubuting.com
Estimated Sales: $ 10 - 20 Million
Number Employees: 100-249
Type of Packaging: Food Service

53491 Tazmanian Freight Forwarding
P.O. Box 11090
Cleveland, OH 44181-1090   216-265-7881
  Fax: 216-265-7888 800-426-6709
hr@tazmanian.com www.tazmanian.com
Warehouse providing dry storage for nonperishable and dry ice packed perishable items; transportation firm providing freight forwarding, air freight services, long haul and expedited trucking services available
CEO: Rob Rossbach
Contact: Don Cotone
melanie@luvmytriplets.com
Number Employees: 50-99
Types of products warehoused:
  Non-perishable & dry ice packed perishable items, non-perishables
Services Provided:
  Freight forwarding, long haul trucking, air freight, etc., pick and pack

53492 Team Hardinger
1314 W 18th St
Erie, PA 16502-1517   814-453-6587
  Fax: 814-453-4919 800-877-6587
sales@team-h.com www.team-h.com
Warehouse offering dry storage for general merchandise; also, transportation firm offering vans, storage trailers and flat beds
President: Jerry Allshouse
jerrya@team-h.com
VP: William Schaal Jr.
General Manager: H. Bender
Number Employees: 100-249
Types of products warehoused:
  General merchandise, general merchandise
Services Provided:
  Trucking
Storage Facility Data:
  Dry Storage Size: 35000 Sq. Ft.

53493 Technical Food Sales Inc
1050 Mehring Way
Cincinnati, OH 45203-1832   513-621-0544
  Fax: 513-345-2222 800-622-1050
service@techfood.com www.techfood.com
Total food ingredients source with technical support. Dry, canned, refrigerated and frozen ingredients
President: Jane Makstell
jmakstell@techfood.com
Regional Sales Manager: Lloyd Makstell
Regional Sales Manager: Nadine Whitsett
Estimated Sales: $25-50 Million
Number Employees: 5-9
Square Footage: 200000
Type of Packaging: Bulk

53494 Tejas Logistics System
301 Pleasant St
Waco, TX 76704-2536   254-753-0301
  Fax: 254-752-4452 800-535-9786
info@tejaswarehouse.com
www.tejaswarehouse.com
Warehouse providing dry storage for dried milk, canned foods, glass bottles, health care products, etc.; transportation firm providing local, long and short haul trucking; rail siding, re-packing, cross docking and inventory controlavailable
CEO: Tom Greene
tom@tejaswarehouse.com
CFO: Rapture Hill
Number Employees: 50-99
Types of products warehoused:
  dry goods, non-perishables, general merchandise

Services Provided:
  rail siding, trucking, packaging, pick and pack, repackaging
Storage Facility Data:
  Dry Storage Size: 560000 Sq. Ft.
  Freezer Size: 850000

53495 Tennessee Cold & Dry Storage
P.O.Box 991
Chattanooga, TN 37401   423-265-1698
  Fax: 423-755-9044
Warehouse providing freezer and dry storage of food products and paper goods; also, rail siding, blast freezing, exporting, trucking and processing space available
Warehouse Manager: Stan Koby
Estimated Sales: $2.5-5 Million
Number Employees: 20-49
Square Footage: 480000
Parent Co: ConAgra Poultry
Types of products warehoused:
  Food products & paper goods
Services Provided:
  Blast freezing, exporting, trucking & processing space, rail siding
Storage Facility Data:
  Dry Storage Size: 82000 Sq. Ft.
  Freezer Size: 60500 Sq. Ft.

53496 Tennessee Commercial Wrhse Inc
22 Stanley St
Nashville, TN 37210-2189   615-780-3200
  Fax: 615-780-3246 800-452-8291
www.tcwonline.com
Warehouse providing consolidation, distribution and intermodal drayage
President: Dave Manning
CEO: Phillip Scott George
CEO: P Scott George
Operations Manager: Scott George
Estimated Sales: $35 Million
Number Employees: 250-499
Square Footage: 100000
Types of products warehoused:
  dry goods, general merchandise
Services Provided:
  Consolidation, distribution & intermodal drayage, trucking
Storage Facility Data:
  Dry Storage Size: 100000

53497 Terminal Cold Storage Co Inc
20 Eaker St # 60
Dayton, OH 45402-2550   937-223-3138
  Fax: 937-223-7870 888-223-3138
www.daytonfrozen.com
Warehouse offering cooler, dry and freezer storage for frozen foods; also, rail siding, product breakdown and refrigerated truck and trailer distribution
President: Brenda Neroni
brenda.neroni@terminalcold.com
Office Manager: Cindy Watkins
Estimated Sales: $3 Million
Number Employees: 20-49
Square Footage: 400000
Types of products warehoused:
  Frozen food, frozen goods
Services Provided:
  Product breakdown & refrigerated truck & trailer distribution, rail siding
Storage Facility Data:
  Cooler Size 15000 Sq. Ft.
  Dry Storage Size: 20000 Sq. Ft.
  Freezer Size: 100000 Sq. Ft.

53498 Tex-Mex Cold Storage
6665 Padre Island Hwy
Brownsville, TX 78521-5218   956-831-9433
  Fax: 956-831-9572
info@texmexcoldstorage.bzzp.net
www.texmexcoldstorage.bzzp.net
Seafood including shrimp; warehouse providing freezer and dry storage
President: Emilio Sanchez
VP: Norma Sanchez
Plant Manager: Nick Sato
Estimated Sales: $6,307,658
Number Employees: 225
Square Footage: 620000
Type of Packaging: Private Label, Bulk
Types of products warehoused:
  Frozen & dry seafood & food, dry goods, frozen goods

Services Provided:
  Brine freezing, re-packing, freezing, rail siding
Storage Facility Data:
  Dry Storage Size: 20000 Sq. Ft.
  Freezer Size: 3000000 Cubic Ft.

53499 Texas Cartage WarehouseInc
12344 E Northwest Hwy
Dallas, TX 75228-8004   214-320-3200
  Fax: 214-320-9103 sales@texcar.com
Public and contract warehouse providing dry storage; transportation division providing local and short haul trucking; rail siding, LTL, labeling, pick/pack, custom handling, pool cross docking, re-furbishing, pick-up and deliveryservices available
President: Jim Jouvenat
jjouvenat@texcar.com
Number Employees: 10-19
Types of products warehoused:
  Groceries, paper products, packaging, chemical products, appliances, automobile parts, etc., dry goods, non-perishables, canned foods, general merchandise
Services Provided:
  Re-furbishing, labeling, pick & pack, custom handling, etc., trucking, labeling, packaging, pick and pack, repackaging, pool distribution
Storage Facility Data:
  Dry Storage Size: 420000 Sq. Ft.

53500 The Commercial Exchange, Inc.
2301 E Michigan Ave
Jackson, MI 49202-3700   517-782-9305
  Fax: 517-782-9306
info@thecommercialexchange.com
www.thecommercialexchange.com
Warehouse providing dry and humidity-controlled storage for nonperishable foods and general merchandise; also, heated space, packing and inventory available
Manager: Earle Hopping
Contact: Joann Boeckermann
j.boeckermann@bluecrossmn.com
General Manager: T Hetu
Property Manager: E Hopping
Estimated Sales: $1-2.5 Million
Number Employees: 5 to 9
Square Footage: 2400000
Types of products warehoused:
  General merchandise & non-perishables, non-perishables, general merchandise
Services Provided:
  Packing & inventory
Storage Facility Data:
  Dry Storage Size: 600000 Sq. Ft.
  Humidity-Controlled Size: 100000

53501 The Jackson Kearney Group
1555 Poydras St # 1600
New Orleans, LA 70112   504-587-1100
  Fax: 504-587-1101
Warehouse providing dry storage for green coffee; rail siding and overnight delivery services available
President: Daniel Haeuser
Contact: Salvatore Anastasio
saa@jkgroup.com
Estimated Sales: $2.5-5 Million
Number Employees: 10-19
Square Footage: 476000
Parent Co: Jackson Kearney
Types of products warehoused:
  Green coffee, dry goods
Services Provided:
  Overnight delivery, rail siding
Storage Facility Data:
  Dry Storage Size: 119000 Sq. Ft.

53502 (HQ)The Terminal Corporation
6610-B Tributary Street
Suite 212
Baltimore, MD 21224   410-276-3490
  Fax: 410-276-3495 opsbal@termship.com
www.termship.com
Warehouse offering dry storage of groceries, beverages, paper products, etc.; transportation broker providing just-in-time delivery; also, specialty packing available available nationally

Warehousing / A-Z

Owner, President: Robert A. Herb
Chairman: John Menzies
CFO: Craig Kershaw
VP: Michael Buckley
Accounting: Jennifer Miller
Contact: Betty Browne
b_browne@termship.com
Operations Manager: Joseph Lis
Number Employees: 100-249
Other Locations:
  Jessup, MD
  Timonium, MD
  Baltimore, MDTimonium
Types of products warehoused:
  Groceries, dry goods, beverages & paper prducts, dry goods
Services Provided:
  Specialty packing, just-in-time delivery, contracting, etc., rail siding, trucking, labeling, packaging, pick and pack
Storage Facility Data:
  Dry Storage Size: 4500000 Cubic Ft.

53503 Three D Brokers
N7440 Osborn Way
Fond Du Lac, WI 54937-8903   920-922-0230
        Fax: 920-922-0670   800-776-3587
        dean@osborntrucking.com
Warehouse offering cold and dry storage; transportation broker providing long haul trucking
President: Dean Osborn
dean@osborntrucking.com
Dispatcher: Charley Osborn
Number Employees: 10-19
Square Footage: 30000
Types of products warehoused:
  Dry, refrigerated & frozen foods, ingredients & paper, dry goods, non-perishables, canned foods, 55 deg. temperature controlled
Services Provided:
  Container stripping & consolidation, trucking, labeling, pick and pack
Storage Facility Data:
  Cooler Size 21000 Sq. Ft.
  Dry Storage Size: 35000 Sq. Ft.
  Humidity-Controlled Size: 68000

53504 (HQ)Tighe Warehousing-Distribution
481 Wildwood Ave
Woburn, MA 01801-2027   781-939-0925
        Fax: 781-721-1965 www.tts-logistics.com
Warehouse providing cooler, dry and humidity-controlled storage for canned goods, candy, etc.; transportation firm providing LTL, TL, freight brokerage, etc., rail siding available
President: John Tighe Sr
j.tighesr@tighe.com
VP: John F. Tighe II
Number Employees: 20-49
Other Locations:
  T. Tighe & Sons
  Woburn, MA
  Tighe Warehousing & Distribution
  Mansfield, MAT. Tighe & SonsMansfield
Types of products warehoused:
  Food products, canned goods, consumer items & candy, canned foods
Services Provided:
  Re-packing, trucking, labeling, EDI, ASN & bar coding, rail siding
Storage Facility Data:
  Cooler Size 100000 Sq. Ft.
  Dry Storage Size: 680000 Sq. Ft.
  Humidity-Controlled Size: 100000 Sq. Ft.

53505 Timberline Cold StorageInc
55 Commerce Ave
Pitman, NJ 08071-1170   856-589-3130
        Fax: 856-589-3332
Freezer and Cold Storage Facility
President: Mike Nolan
Estimated Sales: $ .5 - 1 million
Number Employees: 5-9
Type of Packaging: Food Service

53506 Tippmann Group
9009 Coldwater Rd # 300
Fort Wayne, IN 46825-2072   260-490-3000
        Fax: 260-490-1362 www.tippmanngroup.com
Warehouse providing cooler, freezer and dry storage for frozen and dry foods; rail siding available

President: John Tippmann Jr.
Contact: Kyle Angelet
kangelet@tippmanngroup.com
Estimated Sales: $2.5-5 Million
Number Employees: 50-99
Square Footage: 1760000
Types of products warehoused:
  Frozen & dry, dry goods, frozen goods
Services Provided:
  rail siding
Storage Facility Data:
  Dry Storage Size: 440000 Sq. Ft.

53507 Tippmann Group
9009 Coldwater Rd # 300
Fort Wayne, IN 46825-2072   260-490-3000
        Fax: 260-490-1362 www.tippmanngroup.com
Warehouse offering cooler, freezer and humidity-controlled storage; also, blast freezing, railroad siding and cross docking services available
COO: Chuck Tippmann
Sr. VP/Operations: Milt Hamman
m.hamman@interstatewarehousing.com
Sr. VP/Corporate Development: Steven Tippmann
Estimated Sales: $ 1 - 3 Million
Number Employees: 50-99
Square Footage: 5680000
Parent Co: Tippmann Group
Types of products warehoused:
  Frozen & refrigerated foods, frozen goods
Services Provided:
  Blast freezing & cross docking, rail siding
Storage Facility Data:
  Cooler Size 1000000 Cubic Ft.
  Freezer Size: 18000000 Cubic Ft.
  Humidity-Controlled Size: 1000000 Cubic Ft.

53508 (HQ)Tippmann Group
9009 Coldwater Rd # 300
Fort Wayne, IN 46825-2072   260-490-3000
        Fax: 260-490-1362 www.tippmanngroup.com
Corporate office for a network of nine refrigerated and frozen storage warehouses with a total combined capacity of 50 million cubic feet.
President/CEO: John Tippmann
COO: Charles Tippmann
Contact: Kyle Angelet
kangelet@tippmanngroup.com
Number Employees: 50-99
Parent Co: Tippmann Group
Type of Packaging: Food Service
Other Locations:
  Franklin 4,816,000 Cu Ft, IN
  Denver 6,000,000 Cu Ft, CO
  Newport News 7,050,000cf, VA
  Grand Junction 2,042,000, CO
  Hudsonville 4,600,000 CF, MI
  Indianapolis 12,875,000cf, INDenver 6,000,000 Cu Ft

53509 Tolteca Foodservice
4305 Steve Reynolds Boulevard
Norcross, GA 30093   770-263-0490
        800-541-6835
        www.toltecafoods.com
A self-proclaimed one-stop shop for Mexican restaurants. A manufacturer of every kind of supplies a Mexican restaurant may need, including tortillas, spices, meats, dairy, oils, grains, fruit and vegetables, beverages, etc.
Estimated Sales: $1700000
Number Employees: 10-19
Number of Products: 2000
Square Footage: 50000
Type of Packaging: Consumer, Food Service, Private Label
Types of products warehoused:
  dry goods, non-perishables, canned foods

53510 Tomahawk Warehousing Services
3040 Avemore Square Place
Charlottesville, VA 22911   434-984-2700
        Fax: 434-978-1444 www.wwassociates.net
Warehouse providing dry storage for nonperishable and perishable food items; also, re-packing and labeling services available
President: Herert F White
Senior Associate: Richard T Mathews
Associate: Richard D Hartman
Vice President: Jason A Clark
Estimated Sales: $2.5-5 Million
Number Employees: 10-19
Square Footage: 1200000

Types of products warehoused:
  Non-perishable & perishable food items, non-perishables
Services Provided:
  Re-packing & labeling

53511 Topflight Grain Co-Op
400 E Bodman St
Bement, IL 61813-1299   217-678-2261
        Fax: 217-678-8113 www.topflightgrain.com
Stores and distributes corn and grains
Manager: Derrick Bruhn
Manager: Yoshi Hatanaka
hatanaka@us.astellas.com
Estimated Sales: $ 10 - 20 000,000
Number Employees: 50-99
Types of products warehoused:
  Grains, dry goods, Corn and grains
Services Provided:
  GRAIN ELEVATOR

53512 Torbit Dry Products Group
4350 S Taylor Dr
Sheboygan, WI 53081   920-457-7761
        Fax: 920-457-3899 www.subcofoods.com
Blending and packaging of dry products, development to warehousing and distribution
President: Brett Milligan
Director Quality Control: Cheryl Ellioff
Sales/Marketing: Mark Donlon
VP Operations: Maged Latif
Plant Manager: Lee Petersen
VP Purchasing: Mark Wagor
Estimated Sales: $20 Million
Number Employees: 250-499
Number of Products: 17+
Square Footage: 113000
Type of Packaging: Food Service, Private Label, Bulk

53513 Total Logistic Control
602 S 4th St
Van Buren, AR 72956   479-769-0308
        Fax: 479-524-6562   800-333-5599
Providing temperature controlled storage, the Tolleson Dedicated Facility is a refrigerated/frozen warehouse that was built in 2002. This location handles product for a leading food manufacturer, including items such as meats, bakedgoods, and coffee. The Tolleson facility ships product throughout California, Arizona, Nevada, New Mexico, Oregon and Utah with export to the Pacific Rim and Mexico.
Chief Operating Officer: Pete Westermann
VP Information Systems: Rick Brouwer
VP Supply Chain Solutions: Paul Lomas
VP Real Estate Assets: John Peters
EVP Business Development: Duanne Sizemore
EVP Business Development: Steve Thoke
Press/Media Inquiries: Rebekah Fawcett
VP Human Resources: Ron Witzke
Square Footage: 246004
Parent Co: Total Logistic Control
Type of Packaging: Food Service
Types of products warehoused:
  frozen goods, general merchandise
Services Provided:
  trucking, pick and pack

53514 Total Logistics Control
1251 N Schmidt Rd
Romeoville, IL 60446-1161   815-372-0375
        800-333-5599
The Romeoville Dedicated Facility is a dedicated facility responsible for the distribution and storage for a leading nutritional bars and supplements manufacturer. This location not only distributes product throughout the UnitedStates, but also to Australia as well, carrying 79 SKU's with an inventory of over 676,000 cases. The majority of orders coming into the Romeoville Dedicated Facility have less than a two day turnaround.
Manager: Dan Albin
VP Information Systems: Rick Brouwer
VP Supply Chain Solutions: Paul Lomas
VP Real Estate Assets: John Peters
EVP Business Development: Duanne Sizemore
EVP Business Development: Steve Thoke
Press/Media Inquiries: Rebekah Fawcett
VP Human Resources: Ron Witzke
Parent Co: Total Logistic Control
Type of Packaging: Food Service, Bulk

Warehousing / A-Z

53515 Tracy Cold Storage
PO Box 790026
Middle Village, NY 11379   718-894-9201
tpearlman@tracycoldstorage.com
www.tracycoldstorage.com
Warehouse providing cooler and freezer storage for frozen foods and fresh fruits and vegetables
President: T Passmore
Estimated Sales: $500,000-$1 Million
Number Employees: 4
Types of products warehoused:
   Frozen foods & fresh fruits & vegetables, frozen goods, produce
Storage Facility Data:
   Cooler Size 754800 Cubic Ft.
   Freezer Size 120960 Cubic Ft.

53516 Trailwood Warehouse LLC
4825 Mustang Cir
Mounds View, MN 55112-1552   763-783-9999
Fax: 763-783-2058   877-897-6668
Warehouse providing cooler, dry and humidity-controlled storage for food products, confectionery items, health/beauty aids and paper-related items; also, rail siding and temperature-controlled T.L. and regional L.T.L. protectiveservice available
CEO: Larry Tyson
VP Operations/Sales: Gary Miller
Contact: Larry Tyson
mvsf@isd.net
Number Employees: 20-49
Parent Co: Tyson Foods
Types of products warehoused:
   Food products, confectionery items, health/beauty aids, paper related products
Services Provided:
   Trucking, order assembly, pick & pack, data interchange, etc., rail siding
Storage Facility Data:
   Cooler Size 1500 Sq. Ft.
   Dry Storage Size: 300000 Sq. Ft.
   Humidity-Controlled Size: 40000 Sq. Ft.

53517 Transcor
4250 Wissahickon Ave
Philadelphia, PA 19129-1295   215-226-2222
Fax: 215-225-6479   800-255-6331
sales@transcor-usa.com   www.transcor-usa.com
Warehouse providing storage for food products and general commodities in Eastern PA and Southern FL; also, distribution services available
President: Howard Weiss
CEO: Nelson Henry
nelson@pcstechnologies.com
VP: Jeffrey Weiss
Sales Manager: Paul Siderio
Estimated Sales: $5-10 Million
Number Employees: 100-249
Types of products warehoused:
   Food products & general commodities, general merchandise
Services Provided:
   Distribution

53518 Trenton Cold Storage
178 Stockdale Rd
Trenton, ON K8V 5P6
Canada   613-394-3317
Fax: 613-394-3263   sales@trencold.com
www.trencold.com
Warehouse services include cold and frozen storage of foods; also, consolidated freight distribution available
VP/General Manager: R Borthwick
Square Footage: 1200000
Types of products warehoused:
   Frozen food, frozen goods
Services Provided:
   Consolidated freight distribution, rail siding
Storage Facility Data:
   Cooler Size 375000 Cubic Ft.
   Freezer Size: 9100000 Cubic Ft.

53519 Tri-Temp Distribution
P.O.Box 607
3203 Industrial Park Rd
Van Buren, AR 72956-6109   479-471-5115
Fax: 479-471-1711
Warehouse providing cooler, freezer and dry storage for fresh and frozen edible commodities; rail siding available
VP: Sue Salyars
Estimated Sales: $1-2.5 Million
Number Employees: 10 to 19
Square Footage: 11440000
Types of products warehoused:
   Fresh & frozen edible commodities, frozen goods
Services Provided:
   rail siding
Storage Facility Data:
   Cooler Size 30000 Sq. Ft.
   Dry Storage Size: 114000 Sq. Ft.
   Freezer Size: 10000 Sq. Ft.

53520 Tri-Waters Warehouse
19 35th Street
Pittsburgh, PA 15201-1917   412-688-9077
Fax: 412-391-1944
Warehouse providing dry storage for general merchandise; also, distribution and re-packing available
VP: Charles Stix
Number Employees: 10-19
Square Footage: 256000
Types of products warehoused:
   General merchandise, general merchandise
Services Provided:
   Delivery service within 120 mile radius, distribution, repacking
Storage Facility Data:
   Dry Storage Size: 58000 Sq. Ft.

53521 Tucson Frozen Storage
6964 E Century Park Dr
Tucson, AZ 85756-9188   520-623-1411
Fax: 520-624-2869
mail@tucsonfrozenstorage.com
www.tucsonfrozenstorage.com
Warehouse providing freezer storage, re-packing and labeling for frozen foods
Manager: Laura Levin
laura@tucsonfrozenstorage.com
Operations: Alan Levin
Estimated Sales: $500,000-$1 Million
Number Employees: 5-9
Types of products warehoused:
   Frozen foods, frozen goods
Services Provided:
   Re-packing & labeling

53522 Turlock Cold Storage
107 S Kilroy Rd
Turlock, CA 95380-9531   209-632-2599
Fax: 209-632-5199   www.spwg.com
Manager: Kenny Sauls
kenny@spwg.com
VP/General Manager: Ken Sauls
Estimated Sales: Less Than $500,000
Number Employees: 1-4

53523 Tusla Cold Storage
505 W 2nd St
Tulsa, OK 74103-3017   918-583-3151
Fax: 918-382-9382   bobd@americancold.com
www.americancold.com
Warehouse providing freezer and dry storage for red meat, juice concentrates, seafood, vegetables and prepared foods; rail siding available
Manager: Dan Brittain
Warehouse Manager: S Jamison
Foreman: D Cromer
Estimated Sales: $1-2.5 Million
Number Employees: 10-19
Square Footage: 180000
Parent Co: Trigen of Oklahoma
Types of products warehoused:
   Red meat, juice concentrate, seafood, vegetables & prepared foods, produce
Services Provided:
   rail siding
Storage Facility Data:
   Dry Storage Size: 5000 Sq. Ft.
   Freezer Size: 1200000 Cubic Ft.

53524 Twin Cities Dry StorageLtd.
335 Gage Ave.
Suite 3
Kitchener, ON N2M 5E1
Canada   519-743-1466
Fax: 519-743-1831   barry@kearnsstorage.ca
www.kearnsstorage.ca
Warehouse providing dry storage for groceries and nonfoods
President: B Kearns
Number Employees: 5-9
Square Footage: 320000
Types of products warehoused:
   Non-foods & groceries, general merchandise
Storage Facility Data:
   Dry Storage Size: 600000 Sq. Ft.

53525 URS Logistics
3801 E Princess Anne Rd
Norfolk, VA 23502-1539   757-857-1268
Fax: 757-855-5418
Warehouse providing freezer storage for frozen foods; rail siding available
Manager: Thil Lowman
Estimated Sales: $10-20 Million
Number Employees: 10-19
Parent Co: United Refrigerated Services
Types of products warehoused:
   Frozen foods, frozen goods
Services Provided:
   rail siding

53526 URS Logistics
700 W 9th Street
Charlotte, NC 28202   828-323-7708
Fax: 828-322-7932   bsmith@amclog.com
Warehouse offering cold, frozen and dry storage for food products; rail siding available
Director Regional Sales: Bart Smith
Parent Co: Amerigold Logistics
Types of products warehoused:
   Food products
Services Provided:
   rail siding

53527 US Growers Cold Storage
3141 E 44th St
Vernon, CA 90058-2405   323-583-3163
Fax: 323-583-2542   800-366-3163
info@usgrowers.com   usgrowers.com
Warehouser providing dry, cooler and freezer storage for frozen foods; rail siding available. Some of the services they offer include computerized inventory control, Pallet Exchange Program, import/export inspection, blast freezingWorldwide distribution and more.
Owner & President: Angelo Antoci
Vice President: Peter Corselli
General Manager: Ralph Newton
Estimated Sales: $20-25 Million
Number Employees: 100 to 249
Types of products warehoused:
   Dairy & deli products, frozen food, general merchandise, groceries, ingredients, meat, private label, produce, seafood.
Services Provided:
   EDI capabilities, order pick, and cross-dock, rail siding, blast freezing

53528 US Jet Logistical Warehouses
1301 Four Mile View Road
Butte, MT 59701-6973   888-328-7537
Fax: 406-494-4388
Operations Manager: Kenneth DeBree

53529 UTZ Quality Foods Inc
860 Gitts Run Rd
Hanover, PA 17331-8123   717-633-1710
Fax: 717-633-7445   800-669-8912
www.utzsnacks.com
Warehouse providing dry and humidity-controlled storage for general commodities and appliances; transportation services include short and long haul trucking in the continental U.S., LTL, container, and flatbed, along with EDIcapabilities
President: Glenn Longstreth
Sales Manager: Candee Waite
Number Employees: 100-249
Types of products warehoused:
   General commodities & appliances, general merchandise
Services Provided:
   Distribution & trucking
Storage Facility Data:
   Dry Storage Size: 50000 Sq. Ft.

53530 Ultimate Foods
P.O. Box 1008
Linden, NJ 07036   908-486-0800
Fax: 908-486-2999   www.ultimatefoodsservice.com
Offer a full line of fresh and frozen seafood, produce, meats, oils, pastas, canned tomatoes, and other grocery and specialty items.

Warehousing / A-Z

General Manager: Scott Greisman
Seafood Buyer/Quality Control: John Parisi
Produce Buyer/Quality Control: Albert Sindoni
Road Sales Manager: Al Ferrentino
Operations Manager: Anthony Stropoli
Dry Goods Buyer: James Boniface
Estimated Sales: $3.6 Million
Number of Brands: 1
Type of Packaging: Food Service, Bulk
Types of products warehoused:
  dry goods, frozen goods, produce, canned foods, general merchandise, Seafood

53531 Underground Warehouses
P.O.Box 529
Quincy, IL 62306   217-224-1124
  Fax: 217-222-1849 qibkc@huber.com
Warehouse providing dry, cooler, freezer and humidity-controlled storage for frozen foods, dairy products, etc.; distribution, commodity export, USDA pork certification, re-packing, cross docking and rail siding available
Manager: Ed Powell
Operations Coordinator: Paul Lewellen
Estimated Sales: $2.5-5 Million
Number Employees: 20-49
Square Footage: 2600000
Parent Co: J.M. Huber Corporation
Types of products warehoused:
  Frozen foods, dairy products, groceries & ingredients, dry goods, non-perishables, frozen goods, produce, canned foods, general merchandise
Services Provided:
  Commodity export, cross dock, USDA pork cert. & re-packing, rail siding, trucking, labeling, blast freezing, packaging, pick and pack, repackaging
Storage Facility Data:
  Cooler Size 2650000 Cubic Ft.
  Dry Storage Size: 8600000 Cubic Ft.
  Freezer Size: 1450000 Cubic Ft.
  Humidity-Controlled Size: 8600000 Cubic Ft.

53532 (HQ)Unicold Corp
3140 Ualena St # 101
Honolulu, HI 96819-1965   808-836-2931
  Fax: 808-833-7296 sales@unicoldcorp.com
  www.unicoldcorp.com
Warehouse with 3.4 million cubic feet of space providing frozen, chilled and temperature controlled storage for foods including chocolates; transportation firm providing freight consolidation and forwarding; also, rail sidingavailable
Manager: Darryl Kawano
dkawano@unicoldcorp.com
Number Employees: 50-99
Other Locations:
  Los Angeles, CA
  Oakland, CA
  Seattle, WAOakland
Types of products warehoused:
  Food products including chocolates
Services Provided:
  Freight consolidation & forwarding, rail siding
Storage Facility Data:
  Cooler Size 673000 Cubic Ft.
  Freezer Size: 2672000 Cubic Ft.

53533 Unicold Corp
4339 Fruitland Ave
Vernon, CA 90058-3119   323-585-5111
  Fax: 323-589-4132 LosAngeles@unicoldcorp.com
  www.unicoldcorp.com
Manager: Norma Ross
nross@unicoldcorp.com
General Manager: Darryl Kawano
Estimated Sales: $ 1 - 3 Million
Number Employees: 10-19

53534 Unicold Corp
1762 6th Ave S
Seattle, WA 98134-1609   206-447-9257
  Fax: 206-447-9404 888-808-4877
  info@americold.com www.unicoldcorp.com
Cold Storage
Manager: Travis Jobb
tjobb@macpiper.com
Estimated Sales: Less Than $500,000
Number Employees: 1-4
Type of Packaging: Food Service

53535 Union Ice Co
2970 E 50th St
Vernon, CA 90058-2920   323-826-1914
  Fax: 32 - 2 - 10 www.unionice.com
Warehouse providing cooler and freezer storage for frozen and refrigerated foods; also, rail siding available
President: Brent Larson
Vice President: Brett Willberg
Estimated Sales: $1-2.5 Million
Number Employees: 50-99
Types of products warehoused:
  Refrigerated foods
Services Provided:
  EDI capabilities, rail siding, blast freezing
Storage Facility Data:
  Freezer Size: 1300000 Cubic Ft.

53536 Union Storage & Transfer Co
4275 Main Ave
Fargo, ND 58103-1127   701-282-4321
  Fax: 701-277-1244
Warehouse offering cold, dry and frozen storage for frozen foods, groceries, heated products and appliances; transportation firm providing local haul trucking; distribution and rail siding services available
President: David B Bertel
office@unionstorage.com
Number Employees: 20-49
Types of products warehoused:
  Frozen foods, groceries, heated products & appliances, dry goods, non-perishables, frozen goods, canned foods, general merchandise
Services Provided:
  Local trucking & distribution, rail siding, blast freezing, pick and pack
Storage Facility Data:
  Cooler Size 4000 Sq. Ft.
  Dry Storage Size: 228000 Sq. Ft.
  Freezer Size: 60000 Sq. Ft.

53537 United Cold Storage
1600 Donner Ave
San Francisco, CA 94124-3220   415-822-8445
  Fax: 415-822-8456 orders@unitedcoldstorage.com
Warehouse providing freezer, cooler and humidity-controlled storage for food and technology products; also, quick freezing
President: Jim Morgan
Estimated Sales: $500,000-$1 Million
Number Employees: 10-19
Square Footage: 120000
Types of products warehoused:
  Food & technology products, frozen goods, Perishable
Services Provided:
  Quick freezing & office rental, EDI, import/export, blast freezing
Storage Facility Data:
  Cooler Size 90000 Cubic Ft.
  Freezer Size: 450000 Cubic Ft.

53538 United Facilities
P.O.Box 559
Peoria, IL 61651   309-699-7271
  Fax: 309-699-0228 866-699-7271
  salesinfo@unifac.com www.unifac.com
Warehouse providing cooler and dry storage of groceries, confectionery products, etc.; packing, pick/pack, EDI, display building, transportation management and rail siding available
VP: Daniel Altorfer
altorfer@unifac.com
VP: David Altorfer
VP: Robert Altorfer
Estimated Sales: $5-10 Million
Number Employees: 20-49
Square Footage: 1646000
Types of products warehoused:
  Groceries, confectionery products, etc.
Services Provided:
  EDI, in-store set up, etc., rail siding, packaging, pick and pack, repackaging

53539 United Refrigerations Svc
1355 Railroad Ave
Albertville, AL 35951-3764   256-891-4433
  Fax: 256-891-4402 888-808-4877
  info@americold.com www.americold.com
Services include air shipment capabilities, blast freezing, export services, small package express delivery, USDA Inspection Service, 4,634 cubic feet (usable).

President and Chief Operating Officer: Fred Boehler
Chief Executive Officer: Tony Schnug
EVP and Chief Financial Officer: Allison Aden
VP Supply Chain Solutions: Chris Hughes
EVP & Chief Information Officer: Thomas Musgrave
EVP & Chief Human Resources Officer: Jed Milstein
Estimated Sales: $ 3 - 5 Million
Number Employees: 20-49
Square Footage: 30
Parent Co: Americold
Type of Packaging: Food Service

53540 (HQ)United States Cold Storage
2 Aquarium Dr
Suite 400
Camden, NJ 08103   856-354-8181
  Fax: 856-772-1876 info@uscold.com
  www.uscold.com
Temperature-controlled warehousing and logistics
President & CEO: David Harlan
COO: Larry Alderfer
VP & CFO: Charles de Zoete
VP Logistics: Keith Mowery
VP Corporate Development: Mickey Hoffmann
VP Human Resources: Michelle Grimes
Year Founded: 1889
Number Employees: 2400
Types of products warehoused:
  frozen goods

53541 United States Cold Storage
419 Milford Harrington Hwy
Milford, DE 19963   302-422-7536
  Fax: 302-422-8420 rlonghany@uscold.com
  www.uscold.com
Cold storage facility
General Manager: Ron Longhany
Types of products warehoused:
  frozen goods
Services Provided:
  rail siding, blast freezing, Import/export; USDA meat/poultry inspection
Storage Facility Data:
  Freezer Size: 4300000 Cubic Ft.

53542 United States Cold Storage
4302 S 30th St
Omaha, NE 68107   402-731-9900
  Fax: 402-731-3955 dgoodhard@uscold.com
  www.uscold.com
Cold storage facility
General Manager: Daniel Goodhard
Types of products warehoused:
  frozen goods
Services Provided:
  rail siding, blast freezing, Import/export
Storage Facility Data:
  Freezer Size: 3500000 Cubic Ft.

53543 United States Cold Storage
6501 District Blvd
Bakersfield, CA 93313   661-832-2653
  Fax: 661-832-5846 rdorrell@uscold.com
  www.uscold.com
Cold storage facility
General Manager: Randy Dorrell
Types of products warehoused:
  frozen goods
Services Provided:
  rail siding, USDA inspection; Import/export
Storage Facility Data:
  Freezer Size: 9900000 Cubic Ft.

53544 United States Cold Storage
3100 52nd Ave
Sacramento, CA 95823   916-392-9160
  Fax: 915-392-5012 cbrumley@uscold.com
  www.uscold.com
Cold storage facility
General Manager: Coy Brumley
Types of products warehoused:
  frozen goods
Services Provided:
  rail siding
Storage Facility Data:
  Freezer Size: 2500000 Cubic Ft.

53545 United States Cold Storage
2901 Kenny Biggs Rd
Lumberton, NC 28358-6300   910-739-1992
  Fax: 910-739-1974 smusselwhite@uscold.com
Cold storage facility

Warehousing / A-Z

General Manager: Steve Musselwhite
Types of products warehoused:
  frozen goods
Services Provided:
  rail siding, blast freezing, Import/export
Storage Facility Data:
  Freezer Size: 7000000 Cubic Ft.

53546 United States Cold Storage
2525 E North Ave
Fresno, CA 93725   559-237-6145
Fax: 559-486-6040 ksali@uscold.com
www.uscold.com
Cold storage facility
General Manager: Kris Sali
Types of products warehoused:
  frozen goods
Services Provided:
  rail siding, blast freezing, Import/export
Storage Facility Data:
  Freezer Size: 14100000 Cubic Ft.

53547 United States Cold Storage
15 Emery St
Bethlehem, PA 18015   610-433-7378
Fax: 610-433-7380 therm@uscold.com
www.uscold.com
Cold storage facility
General Manager: Tim Herm
Types of products warehoused:
  frozen goods
Services Provided:
  Cross docking/transloading; Import/export, rail siding, labeling, repackaging
Storage Facility Data:
  Freezer Size: 13300000 Cubic Ft.

53548 United States Cold Storage
1050 Heller Rd
Quakertown, PA 18951   215-892-1541
Fax: 215-892-1542 fmarino@uscold.com
www.uscold.com
Cold storage facility
General Manager: Frank Marino
Types of products warehoused:
  frozen goods
Services Provided:
  rail siding, blast freezing, repackaging
Storage Facility Data:
  Freezer Size: 14600000 Cubic Ft.

53549 United States Cold Storage
1400 N Macarthur Dr
Tracy, CA 95376-2829   209-835-2653
Fax: 209-835-4117 dregnart@uscold.com
www.uscold.com
Cold storage facility
General Manager: Daniel Regnart
Types of products warehoused:
  frozen goods
Services Provided:
  rail siding, blast freezing, Import/export
Storage Facility Data:
  Freezer Size: 7500000 Cubic Ft.

53550 United States Cold Storage
810 E Continental Ave
Tulare, CA 93274-6816   559-686-1110
Fax: 559-686-3827 ccox@uscold.com
www.uscold.com
Cold storage facility
General Manager: Chad Cox
Types of products warehoused:
  frozen goods
Services Provided:
  rail siding, blast freezing, Import/export
Storage Facility Data:
  Freezer Size: 7300000 Cubic Ft.

53551 United States Cold Storage
211 NE McCloskey Ave
Lake City, FL 32055   386-438-2653
Fax: 386-438-2080 pboartfield@uscold.com
www.uscold.com
Cold storage facility
General Manager: Paul Boartfield
Types of products warehoused:
  frozen goods
Services Provided:
  labeling, Crossdocking
Storage Facility Data:
  Freezer Size: 8400000 Cubic Ft.

53552 United States Cold Storage
601 Twin Rail Dr
Minooka, IL 60447   815-467-0455
Fax: 815-467-0460 mreed@uscold.com
www.uscold.com
Cold storage facility
General Manager: Matt Reed
Types of products warehoused:
  frozen goods
Services Provided:
  rail siding, blast freezing, Import/export; Crossdocking
Storage Facility Data:
  Freezer Size: 12100000 Cubic Ft.

53553 United States Cold Storage
10711 Olive St
La Vista, NE 68128-2946   402-339-8855
Fax: 402-339-8856 rtech@uscold.com
www.uscold.com
Cold storage facility
Operations Manager: Randy Tech
Types of products warehoused:
  frozen goods
Services Provided:
  Import/export
Storage Facility Data:
  Freezer Size: 3000000 Cubic Ft.

53554 United States Cold Storage
240 Bruce Costin Rd
Warsaw, NC 28398   910-293-7400
Fax: 910-293-7090 csimendiner@uscold.com
www.uscold.com
Cold storage facility
General Manager: Chad Simendinger
Types of products warehoused:
  frozen goods
Services Provided:
  rail siding, blast freezing, Export
Storage Facility Data:
  Freezer Size: 8600000 Cubic Ft.

53555 United States Cold Storage
1727 JP Hennessy Dr
Lavergne, TN 37086   615-641-9800
Fax: 615-641-3150 jshepherd@uscold.com
www.uscold.com
Cold storage facility
General Manager: Jason Shepherd
Types of products warehoused:
  frozen goods
Services Provided:
  rail siding, blast freezing, Import/export
Storage Facility Data:
  Freezer Size: 6000000 Cubic Ft.

53556 United States Cold Storage
125 Threet Industrial Rd
Smyrna, TN 37167   615-355-0047
Fax: 615-355-9359 jshepherd@uscold.com
www.uscold.com
Cold storage facility
General Manager: Jason Shepherd
Types of products warehoused:
  frozen goods
Services Provided:
  blast freezing, Import/export
Storage Facility Data:
  Freezer Size: 2100000 Cubic Ft.

53557 United States Cold Storage
3300 E Park Row Dr
Arlington, TX 76010   817-633-3070
Fax: 817-649-3505 smckee@uscold.com
www.uscold.com
Cold storage facility
General Manager: Shawn McKee
Types of products warehoused:
  frozen goods
Services Provided:
  rail siding, USDA inspection; Import/export
Storage Facility Data:
  Freezer Size: 5000000 Cubic Ft.

53558 United States Cold Storage
2554 Downing Dr
Fort Worth, TX 76106   817-624-1900
Fax: 817-624-7190 fmonroe@uscold.com
www.uscold.com
Cold storage facility
General Manager: Frank Monroe
Types of products warehoused:
  frozen goods

Services Provided:
  rail siding, Import/export
Storage Facility Data:
  Freezer Size: 11400000 Cubic Ft.

53559 United States Cold Storage
1602 Island St
Laredo, TX 78041   956-722-3951
Fax: 956-723-8386 gpalencia@uscold.com
www.uscold.com
Cold storage facility
General Manager: Gerardo Palencia
Types of products warehoused:
  dry goods, frozen goods
Services Provided:
  rail siding, Import/export; Crossdocking
Storage Facility Data:
  Freezer Size: 8700000 Cubic Ft.

53560 United States Cold Storage
1600 W Calton Rd
Laredo, TX 78041   956-726-4181
Fax: 956-722-4325 gpalencia@uscold.com
www.uscold.com
Cold storage facility
General Manager: Gerardo Palencia
Types of products warehoused:
  dry goods, frozen goods
Services Provided:
  rail siding, repackaging, Import/export; Crossdocking
Storage Facility Data:
  Freezer Size: 1900000 Cubic Ft.

53561 United States Cold Storage
780 Pleasant Valley Rd
Harrisonburg, VA 22801   540-564-6800
Fax: 540-564-6890 lburkholder@uscold.com
www.uscold.com
Cold storage facility
General Manager: Leslie Burkholder
Types of products warehoused:
  frozen goods
Services Provided:
  blast freezing, Import/export
Storage Facility Data:
  Freezer Size: 4500000 Cubic Ft.

53562 United States Cold Storage
1102 N Park Dr
Hazleton, PA 18202   570-384-2319
Fax: 570-384-0994 rhorvath@uscold.com
www.uscold.com
Cold storage facility
General Manager: Ryan Horvath
Services Provided:
  rail siding, repackaging, Import/export; Crossdock/transloading
Storage Facility Data:
  Freezer Size: 13500000 Cubic Ft.

53563 United States Cold Storage
114 Cuddy Dr
P.O. Box 39
Marshville, NC 28103   704-624-3555
Fax: 704-624-6892 drobinson@uscold.com
www.uscold.com
Cold storage facility
Operations Manager: David Robinson
Types of products warehoused:
  frozen goods
Services Provided:
  blast freezing, Import/export
Storage Facility Data:
  Freezer Size: 2300000 Cubic Ft.

53564 United States Cold Storage
104 Witherington Dr
Covington, TN 38019   901-313-2653
Fax: 901-313-2037 mhughes@uscold.com
www.uscold.com
Cold storage facility
General Manager: Matthew Hughes
Types of products warehoused:
  frozen goods
Services Provided:
  repackaging, Import/export
Storage Facility Data:
  Freezer Size: 14000000 Cubic Ft.

Warehousing / A-Z

53565 United States Cold Storage
3404 Halifax St
Dallas, TX 75247   214-854-3100
     Fax: 214-854-3112 aduncan@uscold.com
                       www.uscold.com
Cold storage facility
General Manager: Althea Duncan
Types of products warehoused:
   frozen goods
Services Provided:
   Import/export
Storage Facility Data:
   Freezer Size: 1300000 Cubic Ft.

53566 United States Cold Storage
2225 N Cockrell Hill Rd
Dallas, TX 75212   214-854-3100
     Fax: 214-854-3112 tritchie@uscold.com
                       www.uscold.com
Cold storage facility
Operations Manager: Toby Ritchie
Types of products warehoused:
   frozen goods
Services Provided:
   rail siding, blast freezing, Import/export
Storage Facility Data:
   Freezer Size: 14800000 Cubic Ft.

53567 United States Cold Storage
3255 Jim Christal Rd
Denton, TX 76207   940-295-7050
                       jstephens@uscold.com
                       www.uscold.com
Cold storage facility
Operations Manager: Joseph Stephens
Types of products warehoused:
   frozen goods
Services Provided:
   rail siding, Import/export
Storage Facility Data:
   Freezer Size: 7700000 Cubic Ft.

53568 United States Cold Storage
2519 E North Ave
Fresno, CA 93725   559-753-5000
                       ksali@uscold.com
                       www.uscold.com
Cold storage facility
General Manager: Kris Sali
Types of products warehoused:
   frozen goods
Services Provided:
   rail siding, Import/export
Storage Facility Data:
   Freezer Size: 6400000 Cubic Ft.

53569 United States Cold Storage
18728 FM 1472
Laredo, TX 78045   956-267-2950
     Fax: 956-267-2969 atinoco@uscold.com
                       www.uscold.com
Cold storage facility
General Manager: Arnold Tinoco
Types of products warehoused:
   frozen goods
Services Provided:
   repackaging, Import/export
Storage Facility Data:
   Freezer Size: 7000000 Cubic Ft.

53570 United States Cold Storage
415 S Mt Zion Rd
Lebanon, IN 46052   765-482-2653
     Fax: 765-482-2652 aashley@uscold.com
                       www.uscold.com
Cold storage facility
General Manager: Adam Ashley
Types of products warehoused:
   frozen goods
Services Provided:
   Import/export; Crossdocking; USDA inspection
Storage Facility Data:
   Freezer Size: 6400000 Cubic Ft.

53571 United States Cold Storage
3936 Dudley Blvd
McClellan Park, CA 95652   916-640-2800
     Fax: 916-640-2802 spalefsky@uscold.com
                       www.uscold.com
Cold storage facility
General Manager: Steven Palefsky
Types of products warehoused:
   frozen goods

Services Provided:
   rail siding, Crossdocking
Storage Facility Data:
   Freezer Size: 6800000 Cubic Ft.

53572 United States Cold Storage
1420 Greenwood Rd
McDonough, GA 30253   678-544-2653
     Fax: 678-544-2654 mirvin@uscold.com
                       www.uscold.com
Cold storage facility
General Manager: Mike Irvin
Types of products warehoused:
   frozen goods
Services Provided:
   rail siding, Import/export
Storage Facility Data:
   Freezer Size: 7000000 Cubic Ft.

53573 United States Cold Storage
1275 Medline Pl
McDonough, GA 30253   678-544-2653
     Fax: 678-544-2654 dvolz@uscold.com
                       www.uscold.com
Cold storage facility
General Manager: David Volz
Types of products warehoused:
   frozen goods
Services Provided:
   rail siding, repackaging, Import/export; Crossdocking
Storage Facility Data:
   Freezer Size: 7100000 Cubic Ft.

53574 United States Cold Storage
11801 NW 102nd Rd
Medley, FL 33178   305-691-5391
     Fax: 305-884-9955 dfrank@uscold.com
                       www.uscold.com
Cold storage facility
General Manager: Dorian Frank
Types of products warehoused:
   frozen goods
Services Provided:
   Import/export
Storage Facility Data:
   Freezer Size: 4200000 Cubic Ft.

53575 United States Cold Storage
4000 Miller Circle N
Bethlehem, PA 18020   610-997-6100
     Fax: 610-997-6145 bissa@uscold.com
                       www.uscold.com
Cold storage facility
General Manager: Brian Issa
Types of products warehoused:
   frozen goods
Services Provided:
   Import/export
Storage Facility Data:
   Freezer Size: 4200000 Cubic Ft.

53576 United States Cold Storage
4000 Am Dr
Quakertown, PA 18951   267-875-6100
     Fax: 267-875-6125 mharper@uscold.com
                       www.uscold.com
Cold storage facility
General Manager: Mitch Harper
Types of products warehoused:
   frozen goods
Services Provided:
   blast freezing, Import/export
Storage Facility Data:
   Freezer Size: 6600000 Cubic Ft.

53577 United States Cold Storage
1093 W 450 S
Syracuse, UT 84075   801-776-2653
     Fax: 801-776-6360 rheywood@uscold.com
                       www.uscold.com
Cold storage facility
General Manager: Ryan Heywood
Types of products warehoused:
   dry goods, frozen goods
Services Provided:
   rail siding
Storage Facility Data:
   Dry Storage Size: 1000000 Cubic Ft.
   Freezer Size: 6000000 Cubic Ft.

53578 United States Cold Storage
1021 E Walnut Ave
Tulare, CA 93274   559-687-3320
     Fax: 559-687-3330 bford@uscold.com
                       www.uscold.com

Cold storage facility
General Manager: Brian Ford
Types of products warehoused:
   frozen goods
Services Provided:
   rail siding, blast freezing, Import/export
Storage Facility Data:
   Freezer Size: 12600000 Cubic Ft.

53579 United States Cold Storage
537 Fransil Ln
Turlock, CA 95380   209-668-1636
     Fax: 209-668-8609 rhernandez@uscold.com
                       www.uscold.com
Cold storage facility
General Manager: Robert Hernandez
Types of products warehoused:
   frozen goods
Services Provided:
   Import/export
Storage Facility Data:
   Freezer Size: 13200000 Cubic Ft.

53580 United States Cold Storage
800 E Kankakee River Dr
Wilmington, IL 60481   815-467-2653
     Fax: 815-467-9475 grohrbaugh@uscold.com
                       www.uscold.com
Cold storage facility
General Manager: Greg Rohrbaugh
Types of products warehoused:
   frozen goods
Services Provided:
   Import/export; Crossdocking
Storage Facility Data:
   Freezer Size: 13500000 Cubic Ft.

53581 United Warehouse Co
901 E 45th St N
Park City, KS 67219-3113   316-712-1000
     Fax: 316-838-8730 800-262-5458
                       sales@unitedwarehouse.com
                       www.unitedwarehouse.com
Public warehouse providing dry and humidity-controlled storage of salt and sugar; rail siding services available
President: Charles Schaefer
cschaefer@unitedwarehouse.com
Marketing Manager: Bob Kroblin
Estimated Sales: $5-10 Million
Number Employees: 20-49
Square Footage: 500000
Other Locations:
   Tulsa, OK
Types of products warehoused:
   Salt & sugar, dry goods
Services Provided:
   rail siding
Storage Facility Data:
   Dry Storage Size: 115000 Sq. Ft.
   Humidity-Controlled Size: 10000 Sq. Ft.

53582 Univar USA
17411 NE Union Hill Rd
Redmond, WA 98052-3375   425-889-3400
                          855-888-8648
                       www.univarusa.com
Distributor of specialty and basic food ingredients and chemicals used in the food manufacturing industry.
Director, Food Ingredients: Austin Nichols
Product Management: Denise McLaughlin
Number Employees: 10-19

53583 Valley Distributors & Storage Company
1 Passan Dr
Wilkes Barre, PA 18702   570-654-2403
     Fax: 570-654-4206 www.valleydist.com
Warehouse providing cooler, freezer and dry storage for general merchandise; transportation services include short and local haul in the Northeast and Mid-Atlantic areas; rail siding available
President: John Passan
Chief Financial Officer: Karen Haller
Director of Sales: Kyle Dickinson
Chief Operating Officer: Carol Keup
Number Employees: 50-99
Type of Packaging: Consumer, Private Label
Types of products warehoused:
   dry goods, non-perishables, frozen goods, canned foods, general merchandise
Services Provided:
   Private truck fleet serving Northeast & Mid-At-

lantic areas, rail siding, trucking, labeling, packaging, pick and pack, repackaging

53584 Valley International Cold Storage, Inc.
200 N Loop 509
P.O. Box 3547
Harlingen, TX 78550   956-423-7799
Fax: 956-423-0158 800-850-6288
www.valleycold.com
Warehouse providing cooler and freezer storage
CEO: Matt Gorges
CEO: Matt Gorges
Estimated Sales: $ 10 - 20 Million
Number Employees: 100-249
Square Footage: 190000
Type of Packaging: Food Service
Services Provided:
  EDI, stretch wrap, slip sheet, freight fwdng and consolidation, rail siding, labeling, packaging
Storage Facility Data:
  Cooler Size 250000 Cubic Ft.
  Freezer Size 4100000 Cubic Ft.

53585 Valley Storage Company
1911 S 900 W
Salt Lake City, UT 84104   801-972-3443
Fax: 801-972-3323 kaye@valleystorage.com
Warehouse providing cooler and freezer storage; intrastate trucking services available
Owner: Gary Mc Nally
Estimated Sales: $1-2.5 Million
Number Employees: 5-9
Services Provided:
  Intrastate trucking authority
Storage Facility Data:
  Cooler Size 1600 Sq. Ft.
  Freezer Size 27000 Sq. Ft.

53586 (HQ)Van Brunt Port Jersey Warehouse
580 Division St
Elizabeth, NJ 07201-2003   908-282-7080
Fax: 908-282-7097 www.vanbruntwarehouse.com
Warehouse providing dry storage for general merchandise and imported dry foods; transportation firm providing local and long haul trucking; also, rail siding, re-packing and shrink wrapping services available
Owner: Ken Gross
Number Employees: 20-49
Types of products warehoused:
  General merchandise & imported dry foods, dry goods, general merchandise
Services Provided:
  Re-packing, trucking & shrink wrapping, rail siding
Storage Facility Data:
  Dry Storage Size: 234000 Sq. Ft.

53587 Vanilla Corp Of America LLC
2273 N Penn Rd
Hatfield, PA 19440-1952   215-996-1978
Fax: 215-996-9867
Grain and field bean merchant wholesalers
President: Doug Daugherty
vanillacorp@aol.com
Estimated Sales: $500,000-1 Million
Number Employees: 5-9
Type of Packaging: Food Service, Bulk

53588 Vaughn-Russell Candy Kitchen
401 Augusta Street
Greenville, SC 29601   864-271-7786
Fax: 704-484-8326 info@vaughnrussell.com
www.vaughnrussell.com
Confectionary manufacturer; original makers of "Incredible Edibles™" and "Mint Pecans®."
Owner: Chris Beard
Plant Manager: Ashton Beard
Estimated Sales: 500,000
Number Employees: 4
Type of Packaging: Consumer, Food Service, Bulk

53589 Vermont Commercial Warehouse
166 Boyer Cir
Williston, VT 05495-9561   802-863-4104
Fax: 802-863-1867 kevin@vtcw.com
www.vtcw.com
Warehouse offering cooler, freezer and dry storage for general commodities and groceries; rail siding available
Owner: Debbie Bowtin
debbie@vtcw.com
Warehouse Manager: Hector Boutin
Financial Operations: Bonnie Day
Estimated Sales: $2.5-5 Million
Number Employees: 20-49
Square Footage: 500000
Type of Packaging: Bulk
Types of products warehoused:
  General commodities & groceries, general merchandise
Services Provided:
  rail siding
Storage Facility Data:
  Cooler Size 750 Sq. Ft.
  Dry Storage Size: 121250 Sq. Ft.
  Freezer Size: 3000 Sq. Ft.

53590 Versa Cold
2115 Commissioner Street
Vancouver, BC V5L1A6
Canada   604-255-4656
Fax: 573-471-7728 800-563-2653
sales@versacold.com www.versacold.com
Warehouse providing temperature controlled storage: freezer; as well as logistics and transportation solutions. Refrigerated Storage Space: 5.7 million Cubic Feet.
General Manager: Jeff Hartman
VP, Marketing and Business Development: Brian Ware
Plant Manager: Larry Jones
Estimated Sales: $ 3 - 5 Million
Number Employees: 20-49
Parent Co: Atlas Cold Storage
Type of Packaging: Private Label
Types of products warehoused:
  Poultry and pork, frozen goods
Services Provided:
  Room and slow freeze, cross docking, trucking, labeling, repackaging

53591 (HQ)Versacold Logistics Services
3371 No 6 Rd
Richmond, BC V6V 1P6
Canada   604-258-0350
Fax: 604-207-1971 877-207-1950
info@versacold.com www.versacold.com
Temperature-sensitive products; 31 facilities across Canada
Chief Executive Officer: Paul Campbell
Chief Financial Officer: Jennifer Postelnik
Chief Commercial Officer: Mark Dienesch
Chief Operating Officer: Michele Arcamone
Year Founded: 1946
Estimated Sales: $500 Million
Number Employees: 1000-4999
Types of products warehoused:
  frozen goods
Storage Facility Data:
  Freezer Size: 118000000 Cubic Ft.

53592 (HQ)Verst Group Logistics Inc
300 Shorland Dr
Walton, KY 41094-9328   859-485-1212
Fax: 859-485-1428 sales@verstgroup.com
www.verstgroup.com
Family owned company provides fully integrated warehousing transportation and packaging services.
President & CEO: Paul Verst
pverst@verstgroup.com
CFO: Jim Stadtmiller
VP Transportation: Chris Cusick
COO: Bob Jackson
Number Employees: 50-99
Types of products warehoused:
  Groceries, paper, confectionery goods & beverages
Services Provided:
  Re-packing, pallet exchange, trucking, security, EDI & WIMS, rail siding
Storage Facility Data:
  Cooler Size 50000 Cubic Ft.
  Dry Storage Size: 3000000 Sq. Ft.
  Humidity-Controlled Size: 50000 Cubic Ft.

53593 Vineland Ice & Storage
544 E Pear St
Vineland, NJ 08360   856-692-3990
Fax: 856-692-3992
Warehouse providing frozen storage; manufacturer of ice
Owner: Mark Di Meo
Estimated Sales: $ 1 - 3 Million
Number Employees: 5-9
Type of Packaging: Food Service, Bulk
Types of products warehoused:
  frozen goods
Storage Facility Data:
  Freezer Size: 650000 Cubic Ft.

53594 Vivion Inc
929 Bransten Rd
San Carlos, CA 94070-4073   650-595-3600
Fax: 650-595-2094 800-479-0997
www.vivioninc.com
Broker and distributor of food ingredients.
Founder: Edward Poleselli
President: Michael Poleselli
mpoleselli@vivioninc.com
General Manager: Patrick Rhodes
Estimated Sales: $28 Million
Number Employees: 10-19
Other Locations:
  Branch/Warehouse
  Vernon, CA
  Branch/
  Portland, OR
  Branch
  Ogden, UT
  Branch
  Pheonix/Warehouse, AZ
  Warehouse
  Salt Lake City, UT
  Warehouse
  San Carlos, CA
  Branch/WarehousePortland
Types of products warehoused:
  Ingredients

53595 (HQ)W J Beitler Co & Beitler Truck
3379 Stafford St
Pittsburgh, PA 15204-1441   412-771-4204
Fax: 412-771-5066 800-771-4207
email@wjbeitler.com www.wjbeitler.com
Warehouse providing humidity-controlled, dry and cooler storage for refrigerated and nonperishable foods; transportation firm providing local and short haul trucking; also, re-couping and rail car services available
Owner: W J Beitler
VP: William A Beitler
Warehouse Manager: Myke Flyn
Dispatcher: Kurt Beitler
qjb@wjbeitler.com
Fleet Manager: Dennis Coyne
Number Employees: 50-99
Square Footage: 600000
Types of products warehoused:
  Refrigerated & non-perishable foods, non-perishables
Services Provided:
  Re-couping, local & short haul trucking, rail siding
Storage Facility Data:
  Cooler Size 20000 Sq. Ft.
  Dry Storage Size: 150000 Sq. Ft.
  Humidity-Controlled Size: 20000 Sq. Ft.

53596 W J Byrnes & Co
455 Hickey Blvd # 330
Daly City, CA 94015-2630   415-421-2068
Fax: 650-692-8498 800-733-1142
www.byrnesglobal.com
Warehouse providing dry storage for herbs, spices, dry and liquid goods and bailed products; custom house broker providing freight forwarding via air express and international and domestic air freight
President: John Leitner
VP/CFO: Lynsie Temple
VP/COO: Steve R. Enderson
Manager: Steve Besler
tus@byrnesglobal.com
Number Employees: 10-19
Types of products warehoused:
  Herbs, spices, dry goods, liquid food & bailed products, dry goods
Storage Facility Data:
  Dry Storage Size: 360000

53597 (HQ)W T Young Storage Co
2225 Young Dr
P.O.Box 1110
Lexington, KY 40505-4218   859-266-1136
Fax: 859-266-8939 www.wtyoung.com

Warehousing / A-Z

Public, private and contract warehouse providing cooler, freezer, dry and humidity-controlled storage; transportation firm providing local and long haul trucking; also, re-packing, piece picking, order assembly and rail siding available
President: William Young Jr
CFO: Bob Warren
bwarren@wtyoung.com
Vice President and COO: C. James Pierce
Number Employees: 50-99
Other Locations:
   Young, W.T., Storage Co.
   Lexington, KYYoung, W.T., Storage Co.
Types of products warehoused:
   Rolled paper, food containers, automobile parts, dry goods, general merchandise
Services Provided:
   Trucking, re-packing, piece picking, order assembly, etc., rail siding, trucking, pick and pack, repackaging
Storage Facility Data:
   Cooler Size 330000 Cubic Ft.
   Dry Storage Size: 71670000 Cubic Ft.
   Freezer Size: 330000 Cubic Ft.
   Humidity-Controlled Size: 22400 Sq. Ft.

53598 (HQ)WOW Logistics
3040 W Wisconsin Avenue
Appleton, WI 54914   920-734-9924
   Fax: 920-734-2697   800-236-3565
sherylle@wowlogistics.com
www.wowlogistics.com
Warehouse providing dry and refrigerated storage for nonperishable foods and cheese
President & CEO: Hovard Kamerer
CFO: Lynda Peters
VP & General Counsel: Ben LaFrombois
Director of Engineering: Jamie Hess
Director of Marketing: Randy Radtke
VP Sales: Jamie Walley
COO: Scott Gleason
Estimated Sales: $3 Million
Number Employees: 20 to 49
Square Footage: 2227600
Parent Co: WoW Logistics
Types of products warehoused:
   Non-perishable foods, dry goods, non-perishables, canned foods, general merchandise, cheese
Services Provided:
   rail siding, trucking, labeling, packaging, pick and pack, repackaging
Storage Facility Data:
   Cooler Size 46,900 Sq. Ft.
   Dry Storage Size: 510,000 Sq. Ft.

53599 Wabash Heritage Mfg LLC
2525 N 6th St
Vincennes, IN 47591-2405   812-886-0147
   Fax: 812-895-0064 info@knoxcountyarc.com
www.knoxcountyarc.com
Spices, powders
President: Michael Carney
Vice President: Bobby Harbison
bharbison@knoxcountyarc.com
Research & Development: John TRUE
Quality Control: John TRUE
Plant Manager: Leroy Douffron
Number Employees: 20-49
Number of Brands: 1
Number of Products: 90
Square Footage: 480000
Type of Packaging: Consumer, Food Service, Private Label, Bulk

53600 Walsh TransportationGroup
140 Epping Rd
Exeter, NH 03833-4516   603-778-6202
   Fax: 603-772-0259   800-797-6202
info@wtgnh.com
Warehouse providing cooler and dry storage for general commodities; also, transportation services including TL and local and long haul trucking; rail siding available
President: W Walsh
Contact: Larry Cuddy
lcuddy@wtgnh.com
Number Employees: 20-49
Types of products warehoused:
   General commodities, dry goods, non-perishables, canned foods, general merchandise
Services Provided:
   Trucking services, rail siding, trucking, labeling

53601 Ward Trucking Corporation
1436 Ward Trucking Dr
Altoona, PA 16602   814-944-0803
   Fax: 814-944-5470   800-458-3625
CService@Wardtrucking.com
Warehouse providing dry storage for food and paper products; small package consolidation, rail siding, pick/pack and order fulfillment.
Chairman & CEO: William Ward
VP, Processes & Quality Assurance: Timothy Ward
VP, Marketing & Yield Manager: Thomas Reger
Director, Service Center Operations: Rick Fleischer
rafleischer@wardtrucking.com
Chief Operating Officer: Mike Moss
Year Founded: 1931
Estimated Sales: $50-100 Million
Square Footage: 400000
Types of products warehoused:
   Food & paper products
Services Provided:
   Small package consolidation, order fulfillment & pick/pack, rail siding
Storage Facility Data:
   Dry Storage Size: 400000 Sq. Ft.

53602 (HQ)Warehouse Associates LP
1200 E Kibby St
Lima, OH 45804-3163   419-228-6225
   Fax: 419-228-8025 info@whalp.com
www.whalp.com
Warehouse offering dry storage; transportation firm providing local haul trucking; re-packing and rail siding available
Manager: Mark Schmieder
Manager: Ray Hughes
rhughes@whalp.com
Number Employees: 20-49
Other Locations:
   Warehouse Associates, L.P.
   Maple Heights, OHWarehouse Associates, L.P.
Types of products warehoused:
   dry goods, non-perishables, canned foods, general merchandise
Services Provided:
   rail siding, trucking, labeling, packaging, pick and pack, repackaging
Storage Facility Data:
   Dry Storage Size: 100000 Sq. Ft.

53603 (HQ)Warehouse Service Inc
1501 Admiral Wilson Blvd
PO Box 1529
Pennsauken, NJ 08109-3905   856-365-0333
   Fax: 856-365-0888   800-974-4968
sales@warehouseservice.com
www.warehouseservice.com
U.S. custom bonded warehouse providing dry storage for machinery and chemicals; transportation firm providing local, long and short haul trucking; also, common carrier, freight forwarding, pick-pack and rigging services available
Owner: Gilbert Benjamin
gbenjamin@warehouseservice.com
Number Employees: 10-19
Other Locations:
   Columbus, OH
   Jackson, MSJackson
Types of products warehoused:
   Machinery & chemicals
Services Provided:
   freight forwarding & freight consolidation, trucking, pick and pack
Storage Facility Data:
   Dry Storage Size: 100000 Sq. Ft.

53604 Warehouse Specialists Inc
8530 Janssen Dr
Neenah, WI 54956-9395   920-830-5000
   Fax: 920-727-5167   800-999-2545
wisales@wsinc.com www.wsinc.com
Warehouse providing storage for food items, dry goods, paper, machinery, lumber and steel; rail siding and distribution services available
CEO: Robert J Schroeder
Manager: Andrew Berry
a.berry@wsinc.com
Estimated Sales: G
Number Employees: 10-19
Types of products warehoused:
   Food items, dry goods, paper, machinery, lumber & steel, dry goods
Services Provided:
   Distribution, rail siding

Storage Facility Data:
   Dry Storage Size: 8000000 Sq. Ft.

53605 (HQ)Warehouse Specialists Inc
1160 N Mayflower Dr
Appleton, WI 54913-9656   920-830-5000
   Fax: 920-830-5199   800-999-2545
www.wsinc.com
Warehouse providing dry storage for nonperishable items; also, local, long and short haul trucking and rail car services available by arrangement
CEO: Robert Schroeder
CEO: Robert J Schroeder
Sales Associate: Frank Tomars
Estimated Sales: $500,000-$1 Million
Number Employees: 1000-4999
Square Footage: 52000000
Other Locations:
   Portland, OR
   Menasha, WI
   Green Bay, WI
   Wisconsin Rapids, WI
   Stevens Point, WI
   Glendale, AZMenasha
Types of products warehoused:
   Non-perishable items, non-perishables
Services Provided:
   Trucking & rail car by arrangement

53606 Warehousing of Wisconsin
3040 W Wisconsin Ave
Appleton, WI 54914   920-380-9742
   Fax: 920-734-2697   800-236-3565
haroldsc@wowwhses.com
Warehouse providing cooler, dry and humidity-controlled storage for canned vegetables, bagged ingredients, powdered foods, cheese, seasonings, etc.; also, sampling, lot control, stretchwrapping, fulfillment services and rail siding available
President: Harold Schiferl
VP/CFO: Thomas Oswald
Director Sales/Marketing: Dennis Tweedle
Estimated Sales: $2.5-5 Million
Number Employees: 1 to 4
Square Footage: 20000000
Types of products warehoused:
   Canned vegetables, pulp & paper products, bagged ingredients, powdered foods, cheese, seasonings & furniture, dry goods, canned foods
Services Provided:
   Sampling, lot control, stretchwrapping & fulfillment services, rail siding
Storage Facility Data:
   Cooler Size 5750000 Cubic Ft.
   Dry Storage Size: 112500000 Cubic Ft.
   Humidity-Controlled Size: 2200000 Cubic Ft.

53607 Washington Cold Storage
240 15th St SE
Puyallup, WA 98372-3411   253-848-8511
   Fax: 253-845-8011   800-689-7955
customerservice@washingtoncoldstorage.com
www.washingtoncoldstorage.com
Warehouse providing cooler, freezer, and dry storage.
Manager: Mitch Brown
mitchb@washingtoncoldstorage.com
Estimated Sales: $ 1 - 3 Million
Number Employees: 10-19
Square Footage: 260000
Parent Co: Fischer Properties
Type of Packaging: Food Service
Other Locations:
   Kent 18,000 Sq Ft-Freezer, WA
Types of products warehoused:
   dry goods, frozen goods, general merchandise
Services Provided:
   blast freezing
Storage Facility Data:
   Cooler Size 25000 Sq. Ft.
   Dry Storage Size: 40000 Sq. Ft.
   Freezer Size: 65000 Sq. Ft.

53608 Washington Fruit & Produce Company
401 N 1st Ave
P.O.Box 1588
Yakima, WA 98907-1588   509-457-6177
   Fax: 509-452-8520 information@washfruit.com
www.washfruit.com
Processor and exporter of fresh fruits including apples, pears, and cherries.

Warehousing / A-Z

Manager: Tom Hanses
Contact: Lorri Denison
ldenison@neptunesociety.com
Estimated Sales: Less than $500,000
Number Employees: 1-4
Type of Packaging: Consumer, Bulk
Types of products warehoused:
   produce

53609 We Pack Logistics
222 East Hickory St.
P.O.Box 876
Paris, TX 75460   903-737-0522
   Fax: 903-737-0888 www.wepack.com
Warehouse providing storage space for non-perishables, and frozen goods.
Owner: Chip Harper
General Manager: David Owens
Estimated Sales: $ 20 - 50 Million
Number Employees: 100-249
Type of Packaging: Food Service
Types of products warehoused:
   dry goods, non-perishables, frozen goods

53610 Weber Distribution
13530 Rosecrans Avenue
Tolleson, AZ 85353-3203   623-936-3777
   Fax: 623-415-9115 www.weberdistribution.com
Warehouse providing dry and refrigerated storage for food products; transportation firm providing local and long haul trucking; also, rail siding, distribution, freight consolidation and cross docking services available. Warehouseservices include 24-hour temperature and humidity controlled storage; lot and expiration date code tracking throughout the facility (inbound, storage, delivery); and, perpetual cycle counting and stock rotation.
Manager: Tony Fontillia
President/Chief Executive Officer: William Butler
Senior Vice President: Bob Lilia
Director Client Solutions/Transportation: Dave Silver
VP Client Solutions & Marketing: Carl Neverman
Vice President Information Technology: Tom Wilkinson
Chief Operating Officer: John Nutt
Parent Co: Weber Distribution
Type of Packaging: Food Service

53611 (HQ)Weber Logistics
13530 Rosecrans Ave
Santa Fe Springs, CA 90670
                          855-469-3237
                info@weberlogistics.com
                www.weberlogistics.com
Dry, refrigerated, and frozen transportation and storage
SVP & Chief Financial Officer: Margaret Movius
Chief Operating Officer: Bob Lilja
Sr Director Human Resources: Derick Quintana-Hooker
VP Transportation Operations: Jerry Critchfield
VP Warehouse Operations: Todd Naramore
Year Founded: 1924
Estimated Sales: $52 Million
Number Employees: 250-499
Types of products warehoused:
   dry goods, frozen goods, produce

53612 Weber Logistics
13530 Rosencrans Ave
Santa Fe Springs, CA 90670-0568   562-802-8802
   Fax: 562-802-9792 www.weberlogistics.com
Dry and refrigerated products; Specializing in chemicals and hazardous materials
Year Founded: 1975
Square Footage: 219300
Other Locations:
   Weber Distribution Warehouse
   La Mirada, CA
   Weber Distribution
   San Diego, CA
   Weber Distribution
   Rancho Cucamonga, CAWeber Distribution
   WarehouseSan Diego
Types of products warehoused:
   dry goods, frozen goods, Chemicals
Services Provided:
   rail siding, trucking, labeling, packaging, pick and repackaging

53613 Weber Logistics
1366 30th St
San Diego, CA 92154-3434   619-423-8770
   Fax: 619-423-0035 www.weberlogistics.com
Groceries and beverages
Year Founded: 1980
Square Footage: 103000
Types of products warehoused:
   general merchandise, groceries
Services Provided:
   rail siding, transloading, crossdocking

53614 Weber Logistics
7199 Longe St
Stockton, CA 95206   209-333-1079
   Fax: 209-943-3520 www.weberlogistics.com
General merchandise
Year Founded: 1997
Square Footage: 50000
Types of products warehoused:
   non-perishables, general merchandise
Services Provided:
   labeling, repackaging

53615 Weber Logistics
15301 Showmaker Ave
Norwalk, CA 90650   562-404-9996
   Fax: 562-404-6566 www.weberlogistics.com
General merchandise
Year Founded: 1977
Square Footage: 179975
Types of products warehoused:
   dry goods, general merchandise

53616 Weber Logistics
9345 Santa Anita Ave
Rancho Cucamonga, CA 91730   909-481-1600
   Fax: 909-481-1612 www.weberlogistics.com
Dry, refrigerated, and frozen products
Year Founded: 1980
Square Footage: 275760
Types of products warehoused:
   dry goods, frozen goods, produce, general merchandise
Services Provided:
   trucking, repackaging, transloading

53617 Weber Logistics
13265 Valley Blvd
Fontana, CA 92335   909-355-2617
   Fax: 909-355-2767 www.weberlogistics.com
General merchandise
Year Founded: 2006
Square Footage: 303000
Types of products warehoused:
   general merchandise
Services Provided:
   labeling, repackaging

53618 Weber Logistics
13473 Santa Ana Ave
Fontana, CA 92337   909-428-1946
                www.weberlogistics.com
General merchandise
Year Founded: 2001
Square Footage: 334361
Types of products warehoused:
   general merchandise
Services Provided:
   labeling, repackaging

53619 Weber Logistics
14909 Summit Dr
Building 4
Eastvale, CA 92880
                www.weberlogistics.com
Consumer goods and food
Year Founded: 2018
Square Footage: 301388
Types of products warehoused:
   general merchandise
Services Provided:
   labeling, pick and pack

53620 Weber Logistics
4727 Fite Court
Stockton, CA 95215   209-467-4968
   Fax: 209-467-4385 www.weberlogistics.com
General merchandise, dry goods
Year Founded: 2004
Square Footage: 155000
Types of products warehoused:
   dry goods, general merchandise

Services Provided:
   labeling, repackaging

53621 Weber Logistics
30300 Whipple Rd
Union City, CA 94587
                www.weberlogistics.com
Chemicals, paints
Year Founded: 1987
Square Footage: 126456
Types of products warehoused:
   Chemicals, paints
Services Provided:
   labeling, pick and pack

53622 Wegmans Food Markets Inc.
1500 Brooks Ave.
PO Box 30844
Rochester, NY 14624-0844
                          800-934-6267
                www.wegmans.com
Grocery, bakery, dairy, deli, floral, meat, produce, seafood, alcoholic beverages, and more.
President/CEO: Colleen Wegman
Chairman: Danny Wegman
daniel.wegman@wegmans.com
Senior VP: Nicole Wegman
Year Founded: 1916
Estimated Sales: $9.7 Billion
Number Employees: 50,000

53623 Welling Company
100 James Dr # 200
St Rose, LA 70087   504-736-0965
   Fax: 504-736-0324   800-256-3887
Warehouse providing cooler and dry storage for groceries and confectionery products; transportation services include brokerage, consolidation, LTL and nationwide TL
Owner: Bill Gist
Number Employees: 50-99
Types of products warehoused:
   dry goods, non-perishables, canned foods
Services Provided:
   sort, trucking, labeling, packaging, pick and pack

53624 West Brothers Trailer Rental
8800 Westgate Park Dr # 100
Raleigh, NC 27617-4833   919-821-2557
   Fax: 919-821-4602   800-743- 937
         www.westbrotherstrailerrental.com
Warehouse providing dry storage of general commodities, food products and equipment; transportation broker offering LTL and TL services; rail siding available
Vice President: Rick Grannan
rgrannan@wetrailers.com
Executive VP, Sales and Marketing: Douglas Ostanek
Estimated Sales: Less Than $500,000
Number Employees: 1-4
Types of products warehoused:
   General commodities, food products & equipment, general merchandise
Services Provided:
   Transportation, rail siding
Storage Facility Data:
   Dry Storage Size: 5600000 Cubic Ft.

53625 West Logistics
1775 Westgate Pkwy SW
P.O.Box 43004
Atlanta, GA 30336-2847   404-344-8902
   Fax: 404-346-5184 www.westlogisticsinc.com
Warehouse providing dry and humidity-controlled storage for groceries, confectionery products and general merchandise; transportation company providing freight consolidation, local and long haul trucking; LTL, TL; rail siding servicesavailable
President: Paula Finley
pfinley@mwdist.com
VP/General Manager: Joe Garger
Executive Vice President: Judy Shore
Number Employees: 100-249
Type of Packaging: Consumer, Private Label, Bulk
Types of products warehoused:
   Groceries, confectionery products & general merchandise, dry goods, non-perishables, canned foods, general merchandise
Services Provided:
   Trucking & freight consolidation, rail siding, trucking, labeling, pick and pack, repackaging

Warehousing / A-Z

Storage Facility Data:
   Cooler Size 25000 Sq. Ft.
   Dry Storage Size: 550000 Sq. Ft.
   Humidity-Controlled Size: 45000 Sq. Ft.

53626 West Texas Warehouse Company
2511 Avenue C
Lubbock, TX 79404-1413   806-747-2929
              Fax: 806-747-2923
Warehouse providing dry and humidity-controlled storage of grocery store products; rail siding and air conditioned storage available
Manager: Bob Dobbins
Estimated Sales: $ 1 - 3 Million
Number Employees: 10-19
Parent Co: West Texas Industries
Types of products warehoused:
   Groceries
Services Provided:
   Air conditioned - 3,000 sq ft, rail siding
Storage Facility Data:
   Dry Storage Size: 160000 Sq. Ft.
   Humidity-Controlled Size: 35000 Sq. Ft.

53627 Western Carriers
2220 91st Street
North Bergen, NJ 07047-4713   800-631-7776
                       201-869-3300
                wine@westerncarriers.com
                www.westerncarriers.com
Warehouse providing storage for wines and spirits, and the alcoholic beverage industry.
President: Michael Hodes
Contact: Rick Albee
walter@itoasys.com
Estimated Sales: $5-10 Million
Number Employees: 50-99
Square Footage: 3600000
Other Locations:
   Vallejo 1,000,000 Sq Ft, CA

53628 Western Gateway StorageCo
130 W 28th St
Ogden, UT 84401-3533   801-394-7781
      Fax: 801-394-7784 800-542-2653
                       wgstorage.com
Warehouse providing freezer and cooler storage for frozen meats, cheese, juice, etc.; also, exporting, distribution and rail siding available
Owner: David Bornemeier
david@wgstorage.com
Estimated Sales: Less Than $500,000
Number Employees: 5-9
Square Footage: 200000
Types of products warehoused:
   Frozen foods: meats, cheese, juice, etc., frozen goods
Services Provided:
   Exporting & distribution, rail siding
Storage Facility Data:
   Cooler Size 346386 Cubic Ft.
   Freezer Size: 346436

53629 (HQ)Whiting Distribution Services
26211 Groesbeck Hwy
Warren, MI 48089-4150   586-447-3117
Warehouse providing cooler and dry storage; transportation broker providing freight forwarding services and local, long and short haul trucking; also, rail siding, distribution, lumber re-loading and computerized inventory servicesavailable
Owner: Robert Whiting
Number Employees: 50-99
Other Locations:
   Whiting Distribution Services
   Hamtramck, MIWhiting Distribution Services
Services Provided:
   Lumber re-loading, freight forwarding, trucking & distribution, rail siding
Storage Facility Data:
   Cooler Size 13000 Sq. Ft.
   Dry Storage Size: 1200000 Sq. Ft.

53630 William B Meyer Inc
255 Long Beach Blvd
Stratford, CT 06615-7117   203-375-5801
      Fax: 203-375-9820 800-727-5985
             information@williambmeyer.com
                   www.meyermovers.com

Warehouse providing dry storage of groceries and nonfood items; also, transportation firm providing cross docking, trucking, regional and local delivery and courier services in the Northeast; also, rail available
President/Owner: Tom Gillon
CEO: Mike Racette
mracette@williambmeyer.com
Number Employees: 500-999
Types of products warehoused:
   Groceries & non-foods, dry goods, non-perishables, general merchandise
Services Provided:
   Trucking, distributing, order fulfillments, etc., rail siding, trucking, labeling, packaging, pick and pack
Storage Facility Data:
   Dry Storage Size: 525000 Sq. Ft.
   Freezer Size: 1000 Sq. Ft.

53631 William R. Hill & Company
4500 E Main St
Richmond, VA 23231-1105   804-226-4464
      Fax: 804-226-0272 800-535-3719
                   www.wmrhill.com
Warehouse providing dry storage of nonfoods, glass and plastic containers with closures, canned goods, dried beans and sugar
President: William R Hill Iii
Contact: Joesph Davenport
jdavenport@hill-co.com
Estimated Sales: $ 10 - 20 Million
Number Employees: 5 to 9
Square Footage: 60000
Types of products warehoused:
   Non-foods, glass & plastic containers with closures, canned goods, dried beans & sugar, dry goods, canned foods

53632 Williamson Cold StorageInc
4009 State Route 104
Williamson, NY 14589-9325   315-589-5351
             Fax: 315-589-3921
Warehouse offering cold, dry and frozen storage for food products; rail siding available
Plant Manager: Kent Johnson
Estimated Sales: $500,000-$1 Million
Number Employees: 5-9
Types of products warehoused:
   Refrigerated, dry & frozen foods, dry goods, frozen goods
Services Provided:
   rail siding

53633 Willis Day Storage
4100 Bennett Rd # 1
Toledo, OH 43612-1970   419-476-8000
      Fax: 419-476-1087 wdinfo@willisday.com
                   www.willisday.com
Warehouse providing dry storage for general merchandise; transportation services include freight consolidation; rail siding available
President: Willis Day
Number Employees: 5-9
Square Footage: 3520000
Parent Co: Willis Day Storage Company
Types of products warehoused:
   General merchandise, dry goods, non-perishables, canned foods, general merchandise
Services Provided:
   Freight consolidation, rail siding, trucking, labeling, packaging, pick and pack, repackaging
Storage Facility Data:
   Dry Storage Size: 1500000 Sq. Ft.

53634 Wilmington Bonded Warehouse
810 Sunnyvale Dr
Wilmington, NC 28412-7031   910-791-6753
             Fax: 910-763-9873
Warehouse providing receipt, dry storage and palletization of imported foods, general merchandise, building materials, groceries, etc.; re-packing, and distribution available
Owner: Bill Stanfield
Estimated Sales: $1-2.5 Million
Number Employees: 10-19
Square Footage: 200000
Types of products warehoused:
   Imported foods, clothing, building materials, groceries, general merchandise & amino acids, general merchandise
Services Provided:
   Re-packing & distribution, rail siding

Storage Facility Data:
   Dry Storage Size: 50000 Sq. Ft.

53635 Wilmington Cold Storage
2 Industrial Way
Wilmington, MA 01887-3492   781-935-8670
      Fax: 978-657-6347 www.keepitcoldstorage.com
Warehouse providing cooler and freezer storage; rail siding services available
President: Peter Lewis
Vice President: Todd Lewis
Manager: Gail Delaure
gailwcs@aol.com
General Manager: Robert Ormond
Estimated Sales: $1-2.5 Million
Number Employees: 10-19
Services Provided:
   rail siding
Storage Facility Data:
   Cooler Size 210000 Cubic Ft.
   Freezer Size: 1056000 Cubic Ft.

53636 Winchester Cold Storage
605 N Loudoun St
Winchester, VA 22601-4833   540-662-4151
      Fax: 540-667-6181 www.wcslogistics.com
Warehouse providing dry, frozen and refrigerated storage.
Manager: Brian k. Beazer
bbeazer@winchestercold.com
General Manager: Brian Beazer
Sales & Marketing: Michelle Gordon
Estimated Sales: $ 5 - 10 Million
Number Employees: 20-49
Type of Packaging: Food Service
Other Locations:
   Front Royal, VA
   Charlestown, VA
   Barryville, VACharlestown
Types of products warehoused:
   dry goods, non-perishables, frozen goods, general merchandise
Storage Facility Data:
   Cooler Size 7900000 Cubic Ft.
   Dry Storage Size: 13700000 Cubic Ft.
   Freezer Size: 1200000 Cubic Ft.

53637 Wootton Transportation Services
1400 E Geer St Ste 6
Durham, NC 27704   800-222-4751
             Fax: 603-688-6196
Transportation broker; warehouse providing dry storage
President/Founder: Frank Wootton
Transportation Manager: Chris Rahm
Number Employees: 10-19
Storage Facility Data:
   Dry Storage Size: 41000 Cubic Ft.

53638 World Trade Distribution
PO Box 1577
2601 Main Street
Houston, TX 77002   713-371-3500
      Fax: 713-371-3702 800-275-0221
             jeffj@wtcfs.com www.thegreensheet.com
Warehouse providing dry storage
President: Kathy Douglass
Vice President: Nelik Ebrahim
Customer Relations: Carolyn Brumfield
Number Employees: 50-99

53639 Worley Warehousing Inc
423 Southgate Ct SW
Cedar Rapids, IA 52404-5423   319-365-5247
      Fax: 319-364-3426 800-475-5247
                   www.worleycompanies.com
Warehouse offering dry storage for nonperishable food products; also, contract distribution services available
President: Aaron Allred
aallred@worleywarehousing.com
CEO: Robert Worley
CFO: Dave Wilson
Executive VP: Blaine Worley
Estimated Sales: $10-20 Million
Number Employees: 100-249
Types of products warehoused:
   non-perishables
Services Provided:
   Cross-dock, EDI capabilities, Import/Export, labeling, repackaging

Warehousing / A-Z

53640 XPO Logistics
1 N 59th Ave
Phoenix, AZ 85043-3502   602-233-3296
Fax: 602-269-1742 800-695-0614
www.southweststorage.com
Public warehouse providing cooler, freezer and dry storage; transportation firm providing local, long and short haul trucking; rail siding available
President/CEO: Fred Gretsch
CEO: Michael Wittman
michaelwittman@jacobsonco.com
CEO: Michael Wittman
VP Sales/Marketing: William Curling
VP Operations: Mike Wittman
Number Employees: 100-249
Types of products warehoused:
  Frozen, chilled & dry foods, dry goods, non-perishables, frozen goods, produce, canned foods, general merchandise
Services Provided:
  Trucking & distribution, rail siding, trucking, labeling, pick and pack, repackaging
Storage Facility Data:
  Cooler Size 20000
  Dry Storage Size: 40000
  Freezer Size: 94000

53641 Yarnall Warehouse Inc
1590 N East Ave
Sarasota, FL 34237-2715   941-365-3060
Fax: 941-363-5109 800-527-5753
www.unitedvanlines.com
Warehouse providing air conditioned storage
President: Jay Vandroff
yarnall1@aol.com
Operations Manager: David Shay
Estimated Sales: $ 5 - 10 Million
Number Employees: 50-99
Parent Co: Allied Van Lines
Storage Facility Data:
  Cooler Size 2500000 Cubic Ft.

53642 York Cold Storage LLC
402 Commerce St
York, NE 68467-1739   402-362-5563
Fax: 402-362-7118 www.yorkcoldstorage.com
Warehouse offering cold, dry and frozen storage for food products, offering more than 125 companies
Manager: Adam Broughton
Manager: Matt Spanjers
mattycs@windstream.net
Estimated Sales: $2.5-5 Million
Number Employees: 20-49
Square Footage: 7000000
Types of products warehoused:
  frozen goods
Services Provided:
  Freight consolidation, Order picking

53643 York Rail Logistics
2790 W Market St
York, PA 17404   717-792-3119
Fax: 717-792-1816 aabauzzese@gwrr.com
www.gwrr.com
Warehouse providing dry storage for canned foods, beverages, perishable goods, etc; transportation broker serving the Mid-Atlantic, Northeast Corridor and New England areas; rail siding available
Manager: Pat Boland
Sales & Marketing Manager: Al Abruzzese
Estimated Sales: $500,000-$1 Million
Square Footage: 60000
Parent Co: Emons Transportation Group
Services Provided:
  rail siding, trucking
Storage Facility Data:
  Dry Storage Size: 15000 Sq. Ft.

53644 Yuba City RefrigeratingCompany
PO Box 626
Yuba City, CA 95992-0626   530-673-5627
Fax: 530-673-7889
Warehouse providing cooler, freezer, humidity controlled and dry storage for frozen, canned and dry foods including juices, meat, fish and dairy products
Manager: Dave Apling
General Manager: D Apling
Estimated Sales: $1-2.5 Million
Number Employees: 10-19
Square Footage: 6399440
Types of products warehoused:
  Juices, meat, fish & dairy products, dry goods, frozen goods, canned foods
Storage Facility Data:
  Cooler Size 1360000 Cubic Ft.
  Dry Storage Size: 593000 Cubic Ft.
  Freezer Size: 794000 Cubic Ft.

53645 (HQ)Zero Mountain, Inc.
8425 Hwy 45 S
Fort Smith, AR 72916   479-646-7757
800-691-1010
cindyparker@zeromtn.com www.zeromtn.com
Warehouse providing a total of 8.12 million cubic feet of frozen and refrigerated space for frozen dinners, frozen yogurt, poultry, beef, vegetables and other food ingredients.
Chairman: Mark Rumsey
President & CEO: Joseph Rumsey, Jr.
joerumsey@zeromtn.com
EVP & Information Officer: Andy Sudigala
VP & Chief Financial Officer: Toni Bell
VP & Maintenance Officer: John Young
Assistant Secretary: Kathy Karsten
Compliance Officer: Chris Beason
Safety & Environmental Manager: Joel Neisler
Plant Manager/Russellville Location: Cindy Parker
Year Founded: 1951
Estimated Sales: $50 Million
Number Employees: 50-99
Square Footage: 262500
Other Locations:
  Little Rock 434,400cf, AR
  Lowell 3,000,000cf, AR
  Johnson 280,000cf, AR
  Russellville 100,000cf, AR Lowell 3,000,000cf
Types of products warehoused:
  Frozen: dinners, turkeys & chickens, frozen goods
Services Provided:
  rail siding, blast freezing
Storage Facility Data:
  Cooler Size 225000 Cubic Ft.
  Freezer Size: 6000000 Cubic Ft.

Warehouse Region / Alabama

Alabama
B.R. Williams Trucking & Warehouse, 52671
Doc's Transfer & Warehouse, 52865
Finch Companies, 52910
Gadsden Cartage Co, 52932
Interport Storage & Distribution Service, 53040
Meador Warehousing-Dstrbtn, 53136
Merchants Transfer Company, 53144
Nordic Logistics and Warehousing, LLC, 53208
Shaw Montgomery Warehouse Company, 53423
Shaw Warehouse Company, 53424
Stage One Coldstorage, 53465
United Refrigerations Svc, 53539

Alaska
Alaska Railroad Corp, 52623
Coastal Cold Storage Inc, 52794
Lynden Incorporated, 53113

Alberta
Byers Transport, 52720
Clauson Cold & Cooler, 52768
Conestoga Cold Storage, 52812
Klondike Foods, 53076
Manitoulin Group of Companies, 53127
MTE Logistix, 53120
TCT Logistics, 53488

Arizona
APL Logistics, 52609
Arizona Cold Storage LLC, 52657
CS Intergrated Retail Services LLC, 52726
Englund Equipment Co, 52885
Freeport Logistics Inc, 52920
Mesa Cold Storage, 53146, 53147
Penguin Cold Storage, 53261
Starr Distribution Services Company, 53473
Tucson Frozen Storage, 53521
Weber Distribution, 53610
XPO Logistics, 53640

Arkansas
Arkansas Refrigerated Services, 52658
Batesville Cold Storage, 52679
Central/Terminal Distribution Centers, 52759
Cloverleaf Cold Storage, 52772, 52773, 52774, 52775, 52776
Frostyaire for Frozen Foods, 52924, 52925
Frostyaire of Arkansas,Inc., 52926
Goff Distribution, 52950
Logisco, 53106
Riceland Foods Inc., 53363
Total Logistic Control, 53513
Tri-Temp Distribution, 53519
Zero Mountain, Inc., 53645

British Columbia
GMW Freight Services Ltd, 52930
Versa Cold, 53590
Versacold Logistics Services, 53591

California
Ability/Tri-Modal Trnsprtn Svc, 52613
Anadon Logistics, 52647
Anchor Distribution Services, 52648
Bay Cities Warehouse, 52680
C.J. Figone Cold Storage, 52723
California Cartage Co, 52733
Capitol Station 65 ColdStorage, 52737
Cascade Properties, 52742
Castle Distribution SvcInc, 52745
Concord Import, 52811
Cwo Distribution, 52832
Darras Freight, 52843
Delmonte Fresh, 52847
Dhx-Dependable HawaiianExpress, 52856
Dreisbach Enterprises, 52867
Dreisbach Enterprises Inc, 52868, 52869
Dreisbach-Hilltop, 52870
DSW Distribution Ctr Inc, 52841
Earth Science, 52875
Eureka Ice & Cold Storage Company, 52890
Express Air Cargo, 52896
General Cold Storage, 52937
Glacier Cold Storage LTD, 52947
Green Valley Packers LLC, 52959
Group Warehouse, 52966
Harborside RefrigeratedSvc, 52990, 52991
Ice Cold Storage, 53022
Inland Cold Storage, 53028
Inland Star Distribution Ctr, 53030
Innovative Cold StorageEnterprises, 53031
J W Mitchell Investment, 53048
Jacmar Foodservice, 53052
Konoike Pacific California, 53077
L A Hearne Co, 53080
LMD Integrated Logistic Services, 53082
Los Angeles Cold Storage Co, 53109
Melissa's, 53138
Miramar Cold Storage, 53168
Napa Barrel Care, 53186
Nu-Lane Cargo Services, 53220
O-G Packing & Cold Storage Co, 53223
Orange County Cold Storage, 53237
Pacific Cartage & Warehousing, 53245
Pacific Coast WarehouseCo, 53246
Pacific Cold Storage, 53247
Pacific Commerce Company, 53248
Pacific Transload Systems, 53250
Partners Alliance Cold Storage, 53257
Peerless Trucking Company, 53260
Preferred Freezer Services, 53322, 53323, 53324, 53325, 53326, 53327, 53328, 53329
PRISM Team Services, 53244
Prism Team Services, Inc, 53331
R&A Imports, 53344
Rancho Cold Storage, 53354
Refrigerated Warehouse Marketing Group, 53359
Safeway Inc., 53390
San Diego Cold Storage Inspctn, 53392, 53393
San Jose Distribution Service, 53394
Saroni Co, 53397
Schaefers, 53401
Sea Snack Cold Storage, 53404
Service Craft Distribution Systems, 53419
Sierra Pacific Distribution, 53435, 53436
Sierra Pacific Refrigerated, 53437
Spaten West, Inc, 53463
Stanford Refrigerated Warehouses, 53468
State Center Warehouse & Cold Storage, 53474
Stockton Cold Storage, 53478
Streamline Shippers-Affiliates, 53481
Sutter Basin Growers Cooperative, 53486
Turlock Cold Storage, 53522
Unicold Corp, 53533
Union Ice Co, 53535
United Cold Storage, 53537
United States Cold Storage, 53543, 53544, 53546, 53549, 53550, 53568, 53571, 53578, 53579
US Growers Cold Storage, 53527
Vivion Inc, 53594
W J Byrnes & Co, 53596
Weber Logistics, 53611, 53612, 53613, 53614, 53615, 53616, 53617, 53618, 53619, 53620, 53621
Yuba City RefrigeratingCompany, 53644

Colorado
Acme Distribution Ctr Inc, 52615
American Warehouse Co, 52644
Aspen Distribution, 52662
Aspen Distribution Inc, 52663
Barber's Poultry Inc, 52677
Bootz Distribution, 52701
Canon Potato Company, 52736
Colorado Cold Storage, 52799
Equity Cooperative Exchange, 52886
Onieda Cold Storage AndWarehouse, 53233, 53234
Onieta Cold Storage AndWarehouse, 53235
Southern Colorado CourtSvc, 53455

Connecticut
Burris Logistics, 52711
C&M Warehouse, Inc., 52722
Connecticut Freezers, 52817
Hartford Despatch Mvg &Stor, 52994
Hartford Freezers, 52995
Shepard's Moving & Storage, 53427
Smedley Company, 53439
William B Meyer Inc, 53630

Delaware
Burris Logistics, 52705, 52708, 52717
Cannon Cold Storage, 52735
D & S Warehouse Inc, 52834
United States Cold Storage, 53541

District of Columbia
Airschott Inc, 52622

Florida
A to Z Nutrition International Inc, 52603
APL Logistics, 52610
Bama Sea Products Inc, 52676
Burris Logistics, 52706, 52709, 52712, 52713
Centra Worldwide, 52748
Cold Storage, 52796
CSX Transportation, 52731
Dominex, 52866
Dried Ingredients, LLC., 52872
Evergreen Sweeteners, Inc, 52893
Florida Freezer LP, 52912, 52913
Giant Warehousing Inc, 52944
Global Stevedoring, 52949
Grimes Co, 52965
Gulf Central Distribution Ctr, 52968
Harborside RefrigeratorServices, 52992
Imperial Freight Broker, 53025
Jaxport Refrigerated, 53055
John Cassidy Intl Inc, 53058
Landstar System, Inc, 53089
Laney & Duke Terminal Wrhse Co, 53090
Lloyd A Gray Co Inc, 53105
Merchants Export Inc, 53143
Mid-Florida Freezer Warehouse, 53157
MultiSystems Barcode Solutions, 53178
Penser SC, 53262
Phoenix Industries LLC, 53267, 53268
Port Of Miami Cold Storage Inc, 53283
Port of Palm Beach Cold, 53284
Preferred Freezer Services, 53318, 53319, 53320, 53321
Robertson-Johnson Warehouses, 53368
Ryder Integrated Logistics, 53376
Saddle Creek Logistics Svc, 53386, 53388
Sauce Crafters, 53399
Seaboard Cold Storage, 53405, 53406
Seaboard Cold Storage Inc, 53407, 53408
Seaboard Warehouse Terminals, 53410
Seaboard Marine, 53411
Seaonus, 53413
Service Cold Storage Inc, 53417, 53418
Shaw's Southern Belle Frozen, 53425
Smith Terminal Distribution, 53441
Southeast Food Distribution, 53451
Southern Packaging & Distribution, 53456
Star Distribution Systems, 53472
Systems Online, 53487
United States Cold Storage, 53551, 53574
Yarnall Warehouse Inc, 53641

Georgia
All South Warehouse, 52628
American Port Services, 52643
AmeriCold Logistics LLC, 52637
Atlanta Bonded Warehouse Corporation, 52665
Atlanta Service Warehouse Inc, 52666
Bonded Service Warehouse, 52700
Burris Logistics, 52714
Claxton Cold Storage, 52769
Commercial Cold Storage, 52805
CSRA Bonded Terminal, 52730
D.J. Powers Company, 52837
DCI Logistics, 52838
Delmonte Fresh Produce Co, 52848
Georgia Cold Storage, 52942
Georgia Cold Storage Inc, 52943
John S James Co, 53060
Lanier Cold Storage LLC, 53092
Midnite Express, 53159
Modern Packaging, 53170
National Distribution Centers, 53190
Nordic Logistics and Warehousing, LLC, 53209
Panamerican Logistics, 53255
Piedmont Distribution Centers, 53270
Preferred Freezer Services, 53291, 53292
RBW Logistics, 53345
Resource Alliance, 53360
Saddle Creek Logistics, 53385
Saddle Creek Logistics Svc, 53387
Saturn Freight Systems, 53398
Savannah Distributing, 53400
Southeastern Freezer, 53452
Stanford Refrigerated Warehouse, 53469
Tolteca Foodservice, 53509
United States Cold Storage, 53572, 53573
West Logistics, 53625

Hawaii
Martin Warehousing & Distribution, 53130
Seafood Connection, 53412
Unicold Corp, 53532

Idaho
Boise Cold Storage Co, 52698, 52699
Compton Transfer Storage Co, 52810
Henningsen Cold Storage Co, 52999
Peasley Transfer & Storage, 53259

Illinois
Apl Logistics, 52649
Archer Daniels Midland Company, 52651
Arro Corp, 52659
Ashland Cold Storage, 52661
Belt Route Warehouse & Storage, 52683
Blue Line Cold Storage Chicago, 52695
Caldic USA Inc, 52732
Cargo, 52738
Central American Warehouse Co, 52749
Central States Distribution, 52751
Chicagoland Quad CitiesExpress, 52762
Chilled Solutions LLC, 52763
Cloverleaf Cold Storage, 52781, 52782
Delivery Network, 52846
DSC Logistics Inc, 52840
Faure Brothers Inc, 52905
FDI Inc, 52897
Federal Companies, 52907
Federal Warehouse Company, 52908
General Warehouse & Transportation Company, 52938, 52939
Grane Warehousing & Distribution, 52952

Warehouse Region / Indiana

Hillier Storage & Moving, 53012
Jantzen International, 53054
Jel Sert, 53056
La Grou Cold Storage, 53083
Lagrou Distribution Inc, 53084, 53085
Lagrou Warehouse, 53086
Lanter Distribution LLC, 53093
Mauser Packaging Solutions, 53133
Mercantile Refrigerated Warehouses, 53139
Miller Container Corp, 53166
Moran Distribution Centers, 53171
Murphy Warehouse, 53180
North American Warehousing, 53213
Parkside Warehouse Inc, 53256
Polarville, 53279
Power Logistics, 53287, 53288
Power Packaging Inc, 53289
Preferred Freezer Services, 53295, 53296, 53297
Profood International, 53334
Psyllium Labs, 53335
Richwill Enterprises, 53365
SEKO Worldwide Inc, 53381
Service Warehouse & Distribution, 53420
Smg Summit Cold Storage, 53440
Sterling Bay Companies, 53477
Topflight Grain Co-Op, 53511
Total Logistics Control, 53514
Underground Warehouses, 53531
United Facilities, 53538
United States Cold Storage, 53552, 53580

Indiana

American Cold Storage, 52640
Columbus Cold Storage Inc., 52804
CSI Logistics, 52729
Days Corporation, 52844
Distributors Terminal Corp, 52861
Great Lakes Warehouse Corp, 52958
Hanson Logistics, 52982, 52984, 52988
Hoosier Warehouses Inc, 53019
Interstate Cold Storage, 53043, 53044
Interstate Cold StorageInc, 53041
Kak LLC, 53068
Langham Logistics, 53091
Lucerne Elevator, 53111
Merchandise Multi-Temp Warehouse, 53140
Merchandise Warehouse, 53141
Schilli Transportation Services, 53403
Shamrock Warehouse, 53422
South Bend Warehousing & Distribution, 53448
Stanz Foodservice Inc, 53471
Tippmann Group, 53506, 53507, 53508
United States Cold Storage, 53570
Wabash Heritage Mfg LLC, 53599

Iowa

Blue Line Moving & Storage, 52696
Burris Logistics, 52718
Centennial Warehousing Corp, 52747
Cloverleaf Cold Storage, 52771, 52777, 52778, 52779, 52780
Crystal Distribution Svc, 52830
Des Moines Cold StorageCo, 52853
Des Moines Truck Brokers, 52854
Hansen Co, 52978
Hodge Transit Warehouse, 53013
J M Swank Co, 53047
Jacobson Warehouse Company, 53053
Marshall Cold Storage, 53129
Mason City Cold Storage, 53131
Merchants Distribution Svc, 53142
Murray's Transfer Inc, 53182
New Hampton Transfer & Storage, 53196
Nor-AM Cold Storage, 53206
Nor-Am Cold Storage, 53207
Roederer Transfer & Storage, 53372
Worley Warehousing Inc, 53639

Kansas

All Freight Systems, 52627

Berry's Arctic Ice, 52690
Emporia Cold Storage Co, 52884
Food Link Inc, 52914
Garvey Public Warehouse, 52933
Midwest Cold Storage & Ice Company, 53161
NAPA Distribution Ctr, 53183
National Cold Storage Inc, 53188
United Warehouse Co, 53581

Kentucky

A Arnold Logistics, 52601
Advance Distribution Svc, 52617, 52618
American Cold Storage, 52639
Blendex Co, 52694
Dixie Warehouse Services, 52864
Dri View Mfg Co, 52871
Franklin Express Co Inc, 52917
MCS Merchants Cold Storage, 53117
Riverport Warehouse Company, 53367
Verst Group Logistics Inc, 53592
W T Young Storage Co, 53597

Louisiana

Faulk-Collier Bonded Warehouses, 52904
Gulf Atlantic Cold Storage, 52967
Hayes/Dockside Inc., 52996
International Refrigerated Facility, 53039
Murphy Bonded Warehouse, 53179
New Orleans Cold Storage& Warehouse, 53198
New Orleans Cold Storage-Wrhse, 53197, 53199
Southern Cold Storage Co, 53454
The Jackson Kearney Group, 53501
Welling Company, 53623

Manitoba

MacCosham Van Lines, 53121

Maryland

A W Sisk & Son, 52602
All Freight Distribution Co, 52626
Baltimore International Warehousing, 52675
Belt's Corp, 52684
Belts Logistics Services, 52685
Bob's Transport & Stge Co Inc, 52697
Burris Logistics, 52715, 52716
H & M Bay Inc, 52970
M T C Logistics Corp, 53115, 53116
Michel Distribution Service, 53151
Mount Airy Cold Storage, 53176
MTC Delaware LLC, 53119
Overflo, 53240
R W Bozel Transfer Inc, 53343
Seaschott, 53414
Shoreland Inc, 53430
The Terminal Corporation, 53502

Massachusetts

Advanced Warehouses, 52619
Allied Cold Storage Corporation, 52633
Arctic Cold Storage, 52653
Atlantic Reefer Terminals Inc, 52668
Barrett Distribution Ctr, 52678
Bridge Terminal, Inc., 52702
City Packing Company, 52767
Crystal Cold Storage, 52828, 52829
Distribution Services-America, 52859
Frostar Corporation, 52923
Maritime International, 53128
Massachusetts Central Railroad Corporation, 53132
Metro Freezer & Storage, 53148
Millbrook Lofts, 53164, 53165
Northeast Refrigerated, 53217
Pioneer Cold Logistics, 53273
Pioneer Valley Refrigerated Warehouse, 53274
Preferred Freezer Services, 53311, 53312, 53313, 53314, 53315
Sack Storage Corporation, 53384

Sullivan TransportationInc, 53483
Tighe Warehousing-Distribution, 53504
Wilmington Cold Storage, 53635

Michigan

Alger Warehouse Company, 52625
Arbre Farms Inc, 52650
Arctic Logistics, 52656
Central Global Express, 52750
Central Warehouse Operations, Inc., 52757
Columbian Logistics Network, 52802, 52803
Crate & Fly, 52824
Dematic USA, 52849
Detroit Warehouse Company, 52855
Elston Richards Warehouse, 52881
Evans Distribution Systems, 52892
Hanson Logistics, 52980, 52981, 52983, 52985, 52986, 52987
Lawrence Freezer Corporation, 53097
Lineage Logistics, 53103
Michigan Cold Storage Facilities, 53152
Midland Terminals, 53158
North Bay Produce Inc, 53214
Nutra Food Ingredients, LLC, 53221
Oceana County Freezer Storage, 53228
Purefect Ice, 53338
Ralph Moyle Inc, 53353
Santemp Co, 53396
Shoreline Fruit, 53433
Southshore Enterprises, 53459
The Commercial Exchange, Inc., 53500
Whiting Distribution Services, 53629

Minnesota

All-Temp, 52629
Arctic Cold Storage Inc, 52654
Berkshire Transportation Inc, 52689
Cloverleaf Cold Storage, 52783, 52784, 52785
Faribault Foods, Inc., 52901
Frozen Storage Company, 52927
J&B Cold Storage Inc, 53049
K&K Express, 53066
Meritex Logistics, 53145
Mid-Continent WarehouseCompany, 53156
Minnesota Freezer Warehouse Co, 53167
Murphy Warehouse Co, 53181
Newport St Paul Cold Storage, 53201
Norman G. Jensen, 53212
Ohio Commerce Center, 53229
Post Consumer Brands, 53286
Space Center Inc, 53461
Stemm Transfer & Storage, 53475
Trailwood Warehouse LLC, 53516

Mississippi

Blendco Inc, 52693
Graham Transfer & Storage, 52951
Gulf Cold Storage, 52969
Interstate Merchandise Warehose, 53045
Mississippi Cold and Dry Storage, 53169
Southern Belle Refrigerated, 53453

Missouri

Artesian Ice, 52660
Blast It Clean, 52692
Cloverleaf Cold Storage, 52786
ColdStor LLC, 52797
Commercial DistributionCtr, 52806
Consolidated Transfer Co Inc, 52819
Finkbiner Transfer & Storage, 52911
Foodservice Center Inc, 52915
Grey Eagle Distributors, 52963
Interstate Underground Wrhse, 53046
Madison Warehouse Corporation, 53122
Metro Park Warehouses Inc, 53149
Mid Continent Indl Insultation, 53154
Queen City Warehouse Corporation, 53341
Quick Delivery, 53342

Sedalia Cold Storage Company, 53416
Springfield Underground, 53464
Standard TransportationSvc, 53466

Montana

Baker Transfer & Storage, 52674
Diversified Transfer & Storage, 52862, 52863
US Jet Logistical Warehouses, 53528

Nebraska

Abler Transfer, 52614
Central Transport Intl, 52755
Farmers Cooperative-Dorchester, 52902
Gratton Warehouse Co, 52953
Lincoln Cold Storage, 53101
Nebraska Warehouse Co, 53192
Needham Inc, 53193
United States Cold Storage, 53542, 53553
York Cold Storage LLC, 53642

Nevada

Bender Warehouse Co, 52686
Nevada Cold Storage, 53194
Pure Life Organic Foods, 53337
Reddy Ice, 53357
Sierra Meat & Seafood Co, 53434

New Hampshire

Walsh TransportationGroup, 53600

New Jersey

Affiliated Warehouse CoInc, 52620, 52621
Atlantic Coast Freezers, 52667
Celebrity Refrigerated Warehouse, 52746
CS Integrated LLC, 52725
Dependable Distribution Services, 52851
Dependable Distributors, 52852
East Coast Warehouse & Distr, 52876
Erdner Brothers, 52887
Farbest-Tallman Foods Corp, 52900
Federal Business Ctr Inc, 52906
Freeway Warehouse Corp, 52921
Gemini Traffic Sales, 52935
H&M Warehouse, 52971
Hall's Warehouse Corp, 52973
Hanover Warehouses Inc, 52977
Hermann Services Inc, 53009
Hermann Services Warehouse Corporation, 53010
Holt Logistics Corporation, 53018
Ice King & Cold StorageInc, 53023
John-Jeffrey Corporation, 53061, 53062
Kayco, 53070
Linden Warehouse & Dstrbtn Co, 53102
Lucca Freezer & Cold Storage, 53110
Metropolitan Trucking Inc, 53150
Mid Eastern Cold Storage LLC, 53155
Mullica Hill Cold Storage, 53177
National Distribution Centers, 53189
Newark Refrigerated Warehouse, 53200
NFI Industries Inc, 53184
Occidental Foods International, LLC, 53226
Patane Brothers FreezerWrhses, 53258
Port Elizabeth TerminalCorp, 53280
Port Jersey Logistics, 53281
Preferred Freezer Services, 53290, 53302, 53303, 53304, 53305, 53306, 53307, 53308, 53309, 53310
Priority Air Express, 53330
Products Distribution, 53333
River Terminal Distribution & Warehouse, 53366
RLS Logistics, 53348, 53349
Safeway Freezer StorageInc, 53389
SAS Cargo, 53377
Shawnee Trucking Co Inc, 53426
Shoreline Freezers, 53431, 53432
Standard Warehouse, 53467
Timberline Cold StorageInc, 53505
Ultimate Foods, 53530

United States Cold Storage, 53540
Van Brunt Port Jersey Warehouse, 53586
Vineland Ice & Storage, 53593
Warehouse Service Inc, 53603
Western Carriers, 53627

New Mexico

AADF Warehouse Corporation, 52606
Commercial Warehouse Co, 52807

New York

Allied Frozen Storage Inc, 52634
Arctic Frozen Foods, 52655
Associated Global Systems, 52664
Benlin Freight Forwarding Inc, 52687
Columbia Cheese, 52800
Delavan Center, Inc., 52845
Distribution Unlimited, 52860
Ecs Warehouse, 52878
Ellis KARR & Co Inc, 52879
Elmwood Warehousing Co, 52880
Emerling International Foods, 52882
Freeze-Dry Foods Inc, 52922
Genesee Valley Rural Preservation Council, Inc., 52940
Gillette Creamery, 52946
Hall Street Storage LLC, 52972
Holley Cold Storage Fruit Co, 53016
Inter-County Bakers Inc, 53035
K M Davies Co, 53065
Laub International, 53095
Logistics Amber Worldwide, 53107
Maines Paper & Food SvcInc, 53123
Medina Cold Storage Co Inc, 53137
National Air Cargo Inc, 53187
Nippon Cargo Airlines Co LTD, 53202
Ocean World Lines, 53227
PBB Global Logistics, 53242
Peter Johansky Studio, 53265
Pilot Freight Svc, 53272
Pioneer Warehouse Corporation, 53275
Quandt's Foodservice Distributors, 53340
Rochester RefrigeratingCorporation, 53371
Royal Jordanian, 53375
SDS Global Logistics, Inc., 53380
Sodus Cold Storage Co, 53443
Sonwil Distribution Center, 53445
Stanley Orchards Sales,Inc., 53470
Strategic Development Concepts, 53480
Superior Pack Group, 53485
Tracy Cold Storage, 53515
Wegmans Food Markets Inc., 53622
Williamson Cold StorageInc, 53632

Newfoundland and Labrador

Harbor International, 52989

North Carolina

Carolina Cold Storage, 52740
Cloverleaf Cold Storage, 52790, 52791
Cranston Air, 52823
Dist Tech, 52858
General Bonded Warehouses Inc, 52936
Kyrie Global Inc., 53079
Lewis Storage, 53099
North Carolina State Ports Authority: Port of Wilmington, 53215
Schenker Logistics Inc, 53402
Security Bonded Warehouse, 53415
SOS Global Express Inc, 53383
South Atlantic Warehouse Corporation, 53447
United States Cold Storage, 53545, 53554, 53563
URS Logistics, 53526
West Brothers Trailer Rental, 53624
Wilmington Bonded Warehouse, 53634
Wootton Transportation Services, 53637

North Dakota

Henningsen Cold Storage Co, 53000
Kedney Warehouse Co Inc, 53071

Union Storage & Transfer Co, 53536

Ohio

AME Nutrition, 52608
Ampoint Distribution Centers, 52645
Amware Distribution Warehouse, 52646
ASW Supply Chain Svc, 52612
Aurora Storage & Distribution Center, 52669
Carolina Transfer & Stge Inc, 52741
Cincinnati Freezer Corp, 52764
Cloverleaf Cold Storage, 52787, 52788, 52789
Commonwealth Inc, 52808
Continental Express Inc, 52820
Cotter Merchandise Storage Co, 52822
Crescent, 52825
Dick Cold Storage, 52857
Exel Inc, 52894
Fst Logistics Inc, 52928
Great Lakes Cold Storage, 52954, 52955, 52956
Inter State Cold Storage, 53032, 53033
International Packaging, 53037
Interstate Cold StorageCo, 53042
Morrison Storage & Homes, 53173
ODW Logistics Inc, 53224
Ohio Valley Shippers Assn, 53230
Olson Commercial Cold Storage, 53232
Peoples Cartage Inc, 53264
PPC Perfect Packaging Co, 53243
Spartan Logistics, 53462
Taylor Warehouse, 53490
Tazmanian Freight Forwarding, 53491
Technical Food Sales Inc, 53493
Terminal Cold Storage Co Inc, 53497
Warehouse Associates LP, 53602
Willis Day Storage, 53633

Oklahoma

Arco Warehouse Co, 52652
Burris Logistics, 52719
Henningsen Cold Storage Co, 53004
Hodges Co, 53014
John Christner TruckingInc, 53059
Planters Cooperative, 53277
Seaboard Foods, 53409
Tusla Cold Storage, 53523

Ontario

Canada Distribution Centres, 52734
Conestoga Cold Storage, 52813, 52814
Confederation Freezers, 52815, 52816
Cornwall Warehousing, 52821
Etobicold, 52888
Eximcan Canada, 52895
Howell Logistics Services, 53021
Imperial Cold Storage And Distribution, 53026
Intercontinental Warehouses, 53036
J.D. Smith & Sons, 53050
Kasseler Food Products Inc., 53069
McKenna Logistic Centres, 53134
Serviplast, 53421
Trenton Cold Storage, 53518
Twin Cities Dry StorageLtd., 53524

Oregon

Cascade Specialties, Inc., 52743
Eugene Freezing & Storage Company, 52889
Henningsen Cold Storage Co, 52997, 53001, 53002, 53005, 53006
Holman Distribution Center, 53017
Klamath Cold Storage, 53075
Lieb Cold Storage LLC, 53100
Mccracken Motor Freight, 53135
Morrow Cold Storage LLC, 53174
Northwestern Ice & ColdStorage, 53219
Ontario Produce Company, 53236
Oregon Transfer Co, 53239
Physical Distribution, 53269
Sno Temp Cold Storage, 53442

Pennsylvania

Alcor Corp, 52624
Allegheny Cold Storage Co, 52630
Allegheny Valley, 52631
Allentown Refrigerated Trmnls, 52632
B. Barks & Sons, 52670
BDP International Inc, 52672
Beacon Distribution Services, 52681
Biscontini DistributionCenters, 52691
Burris Logistics, 52710
C Summers Inc, 52721
CFC Logistics, 52724
Chambersburg Cold Storage Inc, 52760
Commonwealth Warehouse & Storage, 52809
Cumberland DistributionServices, 52831
D & D Distribution Svc, 52833
Denver Cold Storage, 52850
Evans Delivery Company, 52891
Fanelli's Warehousing-Distrbtn, 52899
FEI Co, 52898
Fox Transportation Inc, 52916
Franklin Storage Inc, 52918
G&A Warehouses, 52929
Gabler Trucking Inc, 52931
Great Lakes Cold Storage, 52957
Gress Enterprises, 52960
Gress Public Refrigerated Services, 52961
Gress Refrigerated Services & Logisitics, 52962
Hamco Warehouses LTD, 52974
Hanover Cold Storage, 52975
Hanover Terminal Inc, 52976
Henningsen Cold Storage Co, 53003
Henry L Taylor Trucking LLC, 53008
Inter-Cities Cold Storage, 53034
KANE Freight Lines Inc, 53067
Lake Erie Warehouse & Distribution Center, 53087
Lehigh-Pocono WarehouseInc, 53098
Manfredi Cold Storage, 53126
Moran Logistics, 53172
New Federal Cold Storage, 53195
Orefield Cold Stge & Dstrbtng, 53238
Penske Logistics, 53263
Philadelphia Warehousing & Cold Storage Company, 53266
Preferred Freezer Services, 53294
Procold Refrigerated Svc, 53332
Refrigerated Food Distributors, 53358
Rex & Company, 53361
RFDI, 53346
Rosa Food Products, 53373
Rosenberger Cold Storage Company, 53374
Sanmarc Liquidators Inc, 53395
Somerset Industries, 53444
South Mill, 53449
Team Hardinger, 53492
Transcor, 53517
Tri-Waters Warehouse, 53520
TWL Corporation, 53489
United States Cold Storage, 53547, 53548, 53562, 53575, 53576
UTZ Quality Foods Inc, 53529
Valley Distributors & Storage Company, 53583
Vanilla Corp Of America LLC, 53587
W J Beitler Co & Beitler Truck, 53595
Ward Trucking Corporation, 53601
York Rail Logistics, 53643

Puerto Rico

Puerto Rico Cold Storage, 53336

Quebec

Ideal Warehouse, 53024
Kuehne & Nagel Inc., 53078
L.C. Entreposage Storage, 53081
Laval Cold Storage Ltd., 53096
MCT Terminal & Transport Inc., 53118
Panalpina Inc., 53254

Simard Warehouses, 53438

Rhode Island

Greylawn Foods, 52964

South Carolina

Carolina Bonded StorageCo, 52739
Cloverleaf Cold Storage, 52792
Eastern Distribution Inc, 52877
Nocs South Atlantic, 53203, 53204
Piedmont Distribution Services, 53271
Polar Cold Storage, 53278
Sopak Co Inc, 53446
SOPAKCO Foods, 53382
Sunland Distribution, 53484
Vaughn-Russell Candy Kitchen, 53588

South Dakota

Nordica Warehouses Inc, 53210
North Western WarehouseCo, 53216
Stengel Seed & Grain Co, 53476

Tennessee

American Cold Storage, 52638, 52641
Central-Cumberland Corp, 52758
Harman Ice & Cold Storage, 52993
Kenco Group Inc, 53072
Kenco Logistic Svc LLC, 53073
M & W Logistics Group, 53114
Mallory Alexander Intl, 53124
Milan Supply Chain Solutions, 53163
Ozburn-Hessey Logistics LLC, 53241
Tennessee Cold & Dry Storage, 53495
Tennessee Commercial Wrhse Inc, 53496
United States Cold Storage, 53555, 53556, 53564

Texas

Adams Warehouse & Delivery, 52616
AM-C Warehouses Inc, 52607
Amarillo Warehouse Co, 52636
ASAP Freight Systems, 52611
Brokers Logistics LTD, 52704
Central Transportation System, 52756
Charles Walker North America, 52761
Consolidated Bonded Warehouse, 52818
Crocker Moving & Storage Co, 52826
Crossroads DistributionLTD, 52827
CS Intergrated-Texas Limited Partnership, 52728
Dallas Transfer & Terminal, 52842
DFI Organics Inc., 52839
Dunagan Warehouse Corp, 52873
EPT Warehouses, 52874
Fiesta Warehousing & Distribution Company, 52909
Gilbert International, 52945
Houston Central Industries, Ltd., 53020
Jacintoport International LLC, 53051
Jones Moving & Storage Co, 53064
Las Vegas Ice & Cold Storage, 53094
Live Oak Warehouse, 53104
Loop Cold Storage, 53108
NOCS West Gulf, 53185
Nocus West Gulf, 53205
Palmer Logistics, 53253
Port Of Corpus Christi, 53282
Preferred Freezer Services, 53298, 53299, 53300, 53301
Quality Logistics Systems, 53339
Ray West Warehouses/Transport, 53355
Reddy Ice, 53356
Robinson & Co, 53369
San Antonio Cold Storage, 53391
Shippers Warehouse, 53428
South Texas Freezer Company, 53450
Southern Warehousing & Distribution, 53457
Southern Warehousing-Dstrbtn, 53458
Southwest Logistics, 53460
Tejas Logistics System, 53494
Tex-Mex Cold Storage, 53498
Texas Cartage WarehouseInc, 53499

877

Warehouse Region / Utah

United States Cold Storage, 53557, 53558, 53559, 53560, 53565, 53566, 53567, 53569
Valley International Cold Storage, Inc., 53584
We Pack Logistics, 53609
West Texas Warehouse Company, 53626
World Trade Distribution, 53638

Utah

American Distribution Centers, 52642
Freeport Cold Storage Inc, 52919
Oborn Transfer & Stge Co Inc, 53225
United States Cold Storage, 53577
Valley Storage Company, 53585
Western Gateway StorageCo, 53628

Vermont

Shoreham Cooperative Apple Producer, 53429
Vermont Commercial Warehouse, 53589

Virginia

Bristol Van & Storage Corporation, 52703
Burris Logistics, 52707
Cloverleaf Cold Storage, 52793
Cockrell Distribution System, 52795
CS Intergrated Retail Services, 52727
D.D. Jones Transfer & Warehousing, 52836
International Refrigerated, 53038
Jody's Gourmet Popcorn, 53057
Lynchburg Public Warehouse, 53112
Norfolk Warehouse Distribution Centers, 53211
Packaged Ice, 53252
Pitzer Transfer & Storage Corp., 53276
Port of Virgina, 53285
Preferred Freezer Services, 53293
Richmond Cold Storage Smithfield, 53364
Suffolk Cold Storage, 53482
Tomahawk Warehousing Services, 53510
United States Cold Storage, 53561
URS Logistics, 53525
William R. Hill & Company, 53631
Winchester Cold Storage, 53636

Washington

Bensussen Duetsch & Associates, 52688
BLC Trucking Inc, 52673
Columbia Valley Wine Warehouse, 52801
D W Air, 52835
Empire Cold Storage, 52883
Farwest Freight Systems, 52903
Henningsen Cold Storage Co, 52998, 53007
Holeman Distribution Ctr, 53015
Importers, 53027
Inland Empire Distribution, 53029
Johnston Training Group, Inc., 53063
Kenyon Zero Storage, 53074
Lancaster Company, 53088
Mid Columbia Warehouse Inc, 53153
Pacific Harvest Products, 53249
Preferred Freezer Services, 53316, 53317
Rainier Cold Terminal, 53350
Rainier Cold-Storage & Ice, 53351, 53352
Robinson Cold Storage, 53370
SCS Supply Chain Solutions LLC, 53378, 53379
Stonepath Logistics, 53479
Unicold Corp, 53534
Univar USA, 53582
Washington Cold Storage, 53607
Washington Fruit & Produce Company, 53608

West Virginia

Allied Logistics, 52635
Cassco Refrigerated Services, 52744
Gatewood Products LLC, 52934
Packaged Ice, 53251

Wisconsin

A. Gagliano Co Inc, 52605
Beaver Dam Cold Storage, 52682
Central States Warehouse, 52752
Central Storage & Warehouse Co, 52753
Central Storage & WrhseCo Inc, 52754
Ciranda Inc., 52765
City Brewing Company, 52766
Cleanfreak, 52770
Colony Brands Inc, 52798
Geneva Lakes Cold Storage, 52941
Glacier Transit & Storage Inc, 52948
Hansen Storage Co, 52979
Malteurop North America, 53125
Midwest Assembly Warehouse, 53160
Midwest Distribution Systems, 53162
Mosinee Cold Storage, 53175
National Warehouse Corporation, 53191
Northland Cold Storage Inc, 53218
O'Byrne Distribution Ctr Inc, 53222
Olson Co, 53231
Reynolds Transfer & Storage, 53362
RGL Headquarters, 53347
Three D Brokers, 53503
Torbit Dry Products Group, 53512
Warehouse Specialists Inc, 53604, 53605
Warehousing of Wisconsin, 53606
WOW Logistics, 53598

Wyoming

High Plains Freezer, 53011

Warehouse Type and Service / Blast Freezing

Blast Freezing

A Arnold Logistics, 52601
A. Gagliano Co Inc, 52605
Ability/Tri-Modal Trnsprtn Svc, 52613
Acme Distribution Ctr Inc, 52615
Adams Warehouse & Delivery, 52616
Allied Logistics, 52635
American Cold Storage, 52639
American Port Services, 52643
American Warehouse Co, 52644
AmeriCold Logistics LLC, 52637
Arctic Frozen Foods, 52655
Artesian Ice, 52660
Aspen Distribution, 52662
ASW Supply Chain Svc, 52612
Aurora Storage & Distribution Center, 52669
Barrett Distribution Ctr, 52678
Bay Cities Warehouse, 52680
Belt Route Warehouse & Storage, 52683
Benlin Freight Forwarding Inc, 52687
Biscontini Distribution Centers, 52691
Blendco Inc, 52693
Blue Line Cold Storage Chicago, 52695
Bonded Service Warehouse, 52700
Brokers Logistics LTD, 52704
Carolina Cold Storage, 52740
Central American Warehouse Co, 52749
Central States Distribution, 52751
Central Storage & Warehouse Co, 52753
Central Storage & Wrhse Co Inc, 52754
Chicagoland Quad Cities Express, 52762
Cloverleaf Cold Storage, 52771
Columbian Logistics Network, 52802
Commercial Distribution Ctr, 52806
Cornwall Warehousing, 52821
Crystal Distribution Svc, 52830
D & D Distribution Svc, 52833
D & S Warehouse Inc, 52834
D.J. Powers Company, 52837
Dallas Transfer & Terminal, 52842
Darras Freight, 52843
Dependable Distribution Services, 52851
Dist Tech, 52858
DSW Distribution Ctr Inc, 52841
Ecs Warehouse, 52878
Elston Richards Warehouse, 52881
Evans Distribution Systems, 52892
Farbest-Tallman Foods Corp, 52900
Faure Brothers Inc, 52905
Finch Companies, 52910
Florida Freezer LP, 52912
Gabler Trucking Inc, 52931
Gilbert International, 52945
Goff Distribution, 52950
Great Lakes Warehouse Corp, 52958
Grimes Co, 52965
Hanover Terminal Inc, 52976
Hansen Storage Co, 52979
Hartford Freezers, 52995
Hermann Services Inc, 53009
Holman Distribution Center, 53017
Houston Central Industries, Ltd., 53020
Importers, 53027
Inland Cold Storage, 53028
Inland Empire Distribution, 53029
Inland Star Distribution Ctr, 53030
Intercontinental Warehouses, 53036
International Refrigerated, 53038
Interstate Cold Storage Inc, 53041
J&B Cold Storage Inc, 53049
Jacobson Warehouse Company, 53053
John-Jeffrey Corporation, 53062
Kak LLC, 53068
Kenco Logistic Svc LLC, 53073
Kyrie Global Inc., 53079
Lagrou Distribution Inc, 53084
Lanter Distribution LLC, 53093
Laub International, 53095
Lewis Storage, 53099
Logistics Amber Worldwide, 53107
M & W Logistics Group, 53114
Mallory Alexander Intl, 53124
Manfredi Cold Storage, 53126
Medina Cold Storage Co Inc, 53137
Merchandise Warehouse, 53141
Meritex Logistics, 53145
Metro Park Warehouses Inc, 53149
Minnesota Freezer Warehouse Co, 53167
Moran Distribution Centers, 53171
MTC Delaware LLC, 53119
Murphy Warehouse Co, 53181
Nordica Warehouses Inc, 53210
North American Warehousing, 53213
Northeast Refrigerated, 53217
Olson Co, 53231
Oregon Transfer Co, 53239
Overflo, 53240
Pacific Coast Warehouse Co, 53246
Palmer Logistics, 53253
Parkside Warehouse Inc, 53256
Patane Brothers Freezer Wrhses, 53258
Peasley Transfer & Storage, 53259
Penser SC, 53262
Phoenix Industries LLC, 53267
Pioneer Valley Refrigerated Warehouse, 53274
Preferred Freezer Services, 53290, 53291, 53292, 53293, 53294, 53295, 53296, 53297, 53298, 53299, 53300, 53301, 53302, 53303, 53304, 53305, 53306, 53307, 53308, 53309, 53310, 53311, 53312, 53313, 53314, 53315, 53316, 53317, 53318, 53319, 53320, 53321, 53322, 53323, 53324, 53325, 53326, 53327, 53328, 53329
PRISM Team Services, 53244
Queen City Warehouse Corporation, 53341
Ray West Warehouses/Transport, 53355
Richmond Cold Storage Smithfield, 53364
Robertson-Johnson Warehouses, 53368
Saddle Creek Logistics Svc, 53386
Safeway Freezer Storage Inc, 53389
San Jose Distribution Service, 53394
Schenker Logistics Inc, 53402
Simard Warehouses, 53438
Smith Terminal Distribution, 53441
Sonwil Distribution Center, 53445
Sopak Co Inc, 53446
SOPAKCO Foods, 53382
Southern Cold Storage Co, 53454
Spartan Logistics, 53462
Standard Warehouse, 53467
Sterling Bay Companies, 53477
Texas Cartage Warehouse Inc, 53499
The Terminal Corporation, 53502
Three D Brokers, 53503
Underground Warehouses, 53531
United States Cold Storage, 53547, 53551
Valley Distributors & Storage Company, 53583
Valley International Cold Storage, Inc., 53584
Versa Cold, 53590
Walsh Transportation Group, 53600
Warehouse Associates LP, 53602
Weber Logistics, 53612, 53614, 53617, 53618, 53619, 53620, 53621
Welling Company, 53623
West Logistics, 53625
William B Meyer Inc, 53630
Willis Day Storage, 53633
Worley Warehousing Inc, 53639
WOW Logistics, 53598
XPO Logistics, 53640

Canned Foods

A Arnold Logistics, 52601
A W Sisk & Son, 52602
AADF Warehouse Corporation, 52606
Acme Distribution Ctr Inc, 52615
Adams Warehouse & Delivery, 52616
Advanced Warehouses, 52619
All Freight Distribution Co, 52626
All-Temp, 52629
Allied Logistics, 52635
American Port Services, 52643
American Warehouse Co, 52644
Arco Warehouse Co, 52652
Artesian Ice, 52660
Aspen Distribution, 52662
ASW Supply Chain Svc, 52612
Baker Transfer & Storage, 52674
Baltimore International Warehousing, 52675
Barber's Poultry Inc, 52677
Barrett Distribution Ctr, 52678
Bay Cities Warehouse, 52680
Belt Route Warehouse & Storage, 52683
Benlin Freight Forwarding Inc, 52687
Biscontini Distribution Centers, 52691
Blue Line Cold Storage Chicago, 52695
Bob's Transport & Stge Co Inc, 52697
Bristol Van & Storage Corporation, 52703
Brokers Logistics LTD, 52704
Central American Warehouse Co, 52749
Central States Distribution, 52751
Central States Warehouse, 52752
Central Storage & Wrhse Co Inc, 52754
Chicagoland Quad Cities Express, 52762
Columbian Logistics Network, 52802
Commercial Distribution Ctr, 52806
Commercial Warehouse Co, 52807
Continental Express Inc, 52820
Crossroads Distribution LTD, 52827
D & D Distribution Svc, 52833
Darras Freight, 52843
Dependable Distribution Services, 52851
Dist Tech, 52858
Distribution Services-America, 52859
Doc's Transfer & Warehouse, 52865
DSW Distribution Ctr Inc, 52841
Ecs Warehouse, 52878
Elmwood Warehousing Co, 52880
Erdner Brothers, 52887
Evans Distribution Systems, 52892
Fanelli's Warehousing-Distrbtn, 52899
Farwest Freight Systems, 52903
Faulk-Collier Bonded Warehouses, 52904
Faure Brothers Inc, 52905
Federal Companies, 52907
FEI Co, 52898
Florida Freezer LP, 52912
Garvey Public Warehouse, 52933
Gemini Traffic Sales, 52935
Gilbert International, 52945
Glacier Transit & Storage Inc, 52948
Goff Distribution, 52950
Gratton Warehouse Co, 52953
Grimes Co, 52965
Hermann Services Inc, 53009
Houston Central Industries, Ltd., 53020
Ideal Warehouse, 53024
Inland Empire Distribution, 53029
Inland Star Distribution Ctr, 53030
Intercontinental Warehouses, 53036
Jacmar Foodservice, 53052
Jacobson Warehouse Company, 53053
John-Jeffrey Corporation, 53062
Jones Moving & Storage Co, 53064
Kak LLC, 53068
Kayco, 53070
Kenco Logistic Svc LLC, 53073
Kyrie Global Inc., 53079
Lagrou Distribution Inc, 53084
Lake Erie Warehouse & Distribution Center, 53087
Lanter Distribution LLC, 53093
Laub International, 53095
Lewis Storage, 53099
Lieb Cold Storage LLC, 53100
M & W Logistics Group, 53114
Mccracken Motor Freight, 53135
Merchandise Warehouse, 53141
Meritex Logistics, 53145
Metro Park Warehouses Inc, 53149
Minnesota Freezer Warehouse Co, 53167
Murphy Warehouse Co, 53181
Norfolk Warehouse Distribution Centers, 53211
North Western Warehouse Co, 53216
Northland Cold Storage Inc, 53218
Olson Co, 53231
Orange County Cold Storage, 53237
Oregon Transfer Co, 53239
Parkside Warehouse Inc, 53256
Peasley Transfer & Storage, 53259
Penser SC, 53262
Phoenix Industries LLC, 53267
Pioneer Valley Refrigerated Warehouse, 53274
Port Jersey Logistics, 53281
PRISM Team Services, 53244
Ralph Moyle Inc, 53353
Ray West Warehouses/Transport, 53355
Rex & Company, 53361
Richwill Enterprises, 53365
Robinson & Co, 53369
Rosa Food Products, 53373
Saddle Creek Logistics Svc, 53386
San Jose Distribution Service, 53394
Schenker Logistics Inc, 53402
Schilli Transportation Services, 53403
Seaboard Warehouse Terminals, 53410
Seaschott, 53414
Service Warehouse & Distribution, 53420
Shaw Montgomery Warehouse Company, 53423
Simard Warehouses, 53438
Smith Terminal Distribution, 53441
Somerset Industries, 53444
Sonwil Distribution Center, 53445
SOPAKCO Foods, 53382
Spartan Logistics, 53462
Standard Transportation Svc, 53466
Standard Warehouse, 53467
Starr Distribution Services Company, 53473
State Center Warehouse & Cold Storage, 53474
Texas Cartage Warehouse Inc, 53499
Three D Brokers, 53503
Tighe Warehousing-Distribution, 53504
Tolteca Foodservice, 53509
TWL Corporation, 53489
Ultimate Foods, 53530
Underground Warehouses, 53531
Union Storage & Transfer Co, 53536
Valley Distributors & Storage Company, 53583
Walsh Transportation Group, 53600
Warehouse Associates LP, 53602
Warehousing of Wisconsin, 53606
Welling Company, 53623
West Logistics, 53625
William R. Hill & Company, 53631
Willis Day Storage, 53633
WOW Logistics, 53598
XPO Logistics, 53640
Yuba City Refrigerating Company, 53644

Dry Goods

A Arnold Logistics, 52601
A W Sisk & Son, 52602
A. Gagliano Co Inc, 52605
AADF Warehouse Corporation, 52606
Abler Transfer, 52614
Acme Distribution Ctr Inc, 52615
Adams Warehouse & Delivery, 52616
Alcor Corp, 52624
All South Warehouse, 52628
All-Temp, 52629
Allegheny Valley, 52631
Allied Frozen Storage Inc, 52634
Allied Logistics, 52635
AM-C Warehouses Inc, 52607
Amarillo Warehouse Co, 52636
American Port Services, 52643
American Warehouse Co, 52644
Arco Warehouse Co, 52652
Artesian Ice, 52660
Aspen Distribution, 52662
ASW Supply Chain Svc, 52612

Warehouse Type and Service / Frozen Foods

Aurora Storage & Distribution Center, 52669
Baker Transfer & Storage, 52674
Barrett Distribution Ctr, 52678
Bay Cities Warehouse, 52680
BDP International Inc, 52672
Beaver Dam Cold Storage, 52682
Belt Route Warehouse & Storage, 52683
Bender Warehouse Co, 52686
Benlin Freight Forwarding Inc, 52687
Biscontini Distribution Centers, 52691
Blendco Inc, 52693
Blendex Co, 52694
Blue Line Cold Storage Chicago, 52695
Blue Line Moving & Storage, 52696
Bob's Transport & Stge Co Inc, 52697
Boise Cold Storage Co, 52698
Bridge Terminal, Inc., 52702
Bristol Van & Storage Corporation, 52703
Burris Logistics, 52707
C&M Warehouse, Inc., 52722
Central American Warehouse Co, 52749
Central States Distribution, 52751
Central States Warehouse, 52752
Central Storage & Warehouse Co, 52753
Central Storage & Wrhse Co Inc, 52754
Central Transport Intl, 52755
Central Warehouse Operations, Inc., 52757
Cloverleaf Cold Storage, 52771, 52772, 52784, 52785, 52789
Columbian Logistics Network, 52802
Commercial Distribution Ctr, 52806
Commercial Warehouse Co, 52807
Cornwall Warehousing, 52821
Cumberland Distribution Services, 52831
Cwo Distribution, 52832
D & D Distribution Svc, 52833
D & S Warehouse Inc, 52834
D.D. Jones Transfer & Warehousing, 52836
Dallas Transfer & Terminal, 52842
Darras Freight, 52843
Delavan Center, Inc., 52845
Delivery Network, 52846
Dependable Distribution Services, 52851
Dependable Distributors, 52852
DFI Organics Inc., 52839
Dist Tech, 52858
Distribution Services-America, 52859
Diversified Transfer & Storage, 52862
Doc's Transfer & Warehouse, 52865
Ecs Warehouse, 52878
Ellis KARR & Co Inc, 52879
Elmwood Warehousing Co, 52880
Englund Equipment Co, 52885
Equity Cooperative Exchange, 52886
Erdner Brothers, 52887
Evans Delivery Company, 52891
Evans Distribution Systems, 52892
Farmers Cooperative-Dorchester, 52902
Farwest Freight Systems, 52903
Faure Brothers Inc, 52905
Federal Companies, 52907
FEI Co, 52898
Finch Companies, 52910
Florida Freezer LP, 52912
Food Link Inc, 52914
Gadsden Cartage Co, 52932
Garvey Public Warehouse, 52933
Gatewood Products LLC, 52934
Gemini Traffic Sales, 52935
Genesee Valley Rural Preservation Council, Inc., 52940
Georgia Cold Storage Inc, 52943
Gilbert International, 52945
Glacier Transit & Storage Inc, 52948
Goff Distribution, 52950
Grane Warehousing & Distribution, 52952
Gratton Warehouse Co, 52953
Great Lakes Warehouse Corp, 52958
Grimes Co, 52965
Group Warehouse, 52966

H&M Warehouse, 52971
Hall's Warehouse Corp, 52973
Hanover Warehouses Inc, 52977
Hanson Logistics, 52980, 52981, 52983, 52985, 52986, 52987
Hartford Freezers, 52995
Henningsen Cold Storage Co, 52997, 53001, 53002, 53003, 53005, 53007
Hermann Services Inc, 53009
Houston Central Industries, Ltd., 53020
Ideal Warehouse, 53024
Imperal Freight Broker, 53025
Importers, 53027
Inland Empire Distribution, 53029
Inland Star Distribution Ctr, 53030
Inter-County Bakers Inc, 53035
Intercontinental Warehouses, 53036
J M Swank Co, 53047
Jacmar Foodservice, 53052
Jacobson Warehouse Company, 53053
John-Jeffrey Corporation, 53062
Jones Moving & Storage Co, 53064
Kak LLC, 53068
Kasseler Food Products Inc., 53069
Kayco, 53070
Kenco Logistic Svc LLC, 53073
Klondike Foods, 53076
Kyrie Global Inc., 53079
Lagrou Distribution Inc, 53084
Lake Erie Warehouse & Distribution Center, 53087
Langham Logistics, 53091
Lanter Distribution LLC, 53093
Laub International, 53095
Lewis Storage, 53099
Lieb Cold Storage LLC, 53100
Logistics Amber Worldwide, 53107
Lucerne Elevator, 53111
M & W Logistics Group, 53114
MacCosham Van Lines, 53121
Manfredi Cold Storage, 53126
Martin Warehouse & Distribution, 53130
Mccracken Motor Freight, 53135
Medina Cold Storage Co Inc, 53137
Merchandise Warehouse, 53141
Meritex Logistics, 53145
Metro Park Warehouses Inc, 53149
Midnite Express, 53159
Minnesota Freezer Warehouse Co, 53167
Murphy Warehouse Co, 53181
National Cold Storage Inc, 53188
New Orleans Cold Storage-Wrhse, 53197
Newark Refrigerated Warehouse, 53200
Nordica Warehouses Inc, 53210
Norfolk Warehouse Distribution Centers, 53211
Norman G. Jensen, 53212
Northland Cold Storage Inc, 53218
Oborn Transfer & Stge Co Inc, 53225
Olson Co, 53231
Oregon Transfer Co, 53239
Overflo, 53240
Pacific Coast Warehouse Co, 53246
Pacific Commerce Company, 53248
Panalpina Inc., 53254
Parkside Warehouse Inc, 53256
Peasley Transfer & Storage, 53259
Penser SC, 53262
Phoenix Industries LLC, 53267
Piedmont Distribution Services, 53271
Pilot Freight Svc, 53272
Pioneer Valley Refrigerated Warehouse, 53274
Pitzer Transfer & Storage Corp., 53276
Planters Cooperative, 53277
Port Jersey Logistics, 53281
PRISM Team Services, 53244
Quandt's Foodservice Distributors, 53340
Queen City Warehouse Corporation, 53341
Quick Delivery, 53342
Ralph Moyle Inc, 53353
Ray West Warehouses/Transport, 53355
Rex & Company, 53361

Riceland Foods Inc., 53363
Richwill Enterprises, 53365
River Terminal Distribution & Warehouse, 53366
Robertson-Johnson Warehouses, 53368
Robinson & Co, 53369
Rosa Food Products, 53373
Saddle Creek Logistics Svc, 53386
San Jose Distribution Service, 53394
Schenker Logistics Inc, 53402
Schilli Transportation Services, 53403
Seaboard Warehouse Terminals, 53410
Seaschott, 53414
Service Warehouse & Distribution, 53420
Shaw Montgomery Warehouse Company, 53423
Shawnee Trucking Co Inc, 53426
Simard Warehouses, 53438
Smith Terminal Distribution, 53441
Sodus Cold Storage Co, 53443
Somerset Industries, 53444
Sonwil Distribution Center, 53445
SOPAKCO Foods, 53382
Spartan Logistics, 53462
Springfield Underground, 53464
Standard Transportation Svc, 53466
Standard Warehouse, 53467
Starr Distribution Services Company, 53473
State Center Warehouse & Cold Storage, 53474
Stemm Transfer & Storage, 53475
Stockton Cold Storage, 53478
Stonepath Logistics, 53479
Streamline Shippers-Affiliates, 53481
Sutter Basin Growers Cooperative, 53486
Tejas Logistics System, 53494
Tennessee Commercial Wrhse Inc, 53496
Tex-Mex Cold Storage, 53498
Texas Cartage Warehouse Inc, 53499
The Jackson Kearney Group, 53501
The Terminal Corporation, 53502
Three D Brokers, 53503
Tippmann Group, 53506
Tolteca Foodservice, 53509
Topflight Grain Co-Op, 53511
TWL Corporation, 53489
Ultimate Foods, 53530
Underground Warehouses, 53531
Union Storage & Transfer Co, 53536
United States Cold Storage, 53559, 53560, 53577
United Warehouse Co, 53581
Valley Distributors & Storage Company, 53583
Van Brunt Port Jersey Warehouse, 53586
W J Byrnes & Co, 53596
W T Young Storage Co, 53597
Walsh Transportation Group, 53600
Warehouse Associates LP, 53602
Warehouse Specialists Inc, 53604
Warehousing of Wisconsin, 53606
Washington Cold Storage, 53607
We Pack Logistics, 53609
Weber Logistics, 53611, 53612, 53615, 53616, 53620
Welling Company, 53623
West Logistics, 53625
William B Meyer Inc, 53630
William R. Hill & Company, 53631
Williamson Cold Storage Inc, 53632
Willis Day Storage, 53633
Winchester Cold Storage, 53636
WOW Logistics, 53598
XPO Logistics, 53640
Yuba City Refrigerating Company, 53644

Frozen Foods

AADF Warehouse Corporation, 52606
Alcor Corp, 52624
All Freight Systems, 52627
All-Temp, 52629
Allegheny Cold Storage Co, 52630
Allentown Refrigerated Trmnls, 52632

Allied Cold Storage Corporation, 52633
Allied Frozen Storage Inc, 52634
AM-C Warehouses Inc, 52607
Amarillo Warehouse Co, 52636
American Cold Storage, 52638
AmeriCold Logistics LLC, 52637
Arctic Frozen Foods, 52655
Arizona Cold Storage LLC, 52657
Arkansas Refrigerated Services, 52658
Artesian Ice, 52660
Ashland Cold Storage, 52661
Atlantic Coast Freezers, 52667
B. Barks & Sons, 52670
Baker Transfer & Storage, 52674
Bama Sea Products Inc, 52676
Barber's Poultry Inc, 52677
BDP International Inc, 52672
Beaver Dam Cold Storage, 52682
Belt Route Warehouse & Storage, 52683
Berkshire Transportation Inc, 52689
Berry's Arctic Ice, 52690
Blue Line Cold Storage Chicago, 52695
Boise Cold Storage Co, 52698
Bridge Terminal, Inc., 52702
Burris Logistics, 52705, 52706, 52707, 52708, 52709, 52710, 52711, 52712, 52713, 52714, 52716, 52717, 52718, 52719
C Summers Inc, 52721
C.J. Figone Cold Storage, 52723
Carolina Cold Storage, 52740
Cascade Properties, 52742
Central Storage & Warehouse Co, 52753
Central Storage & Wrhse Co Inc, 52754
Cincinnati Freezer Corp, 52764
City Packing Company, 52767
Claxton Cold Storage, 52769
Cloverleaf Cold Storage, 52771, 52772, 52773, 52774, 52775, 52776, 52777, 52778, 52779, 52780, 52781, 52782, 52783, 52784, 52785, 52786, 52787, 52788, 52789, 52790, 52791, 52792, 52793
Colorado Cold Storage, 52799
Commercial Cold Storage, 52805
Commercial Distribution Ctr, 52806
Conestoga Cold Storage, 52812, 52813, 52814
Confederation Freezers, 52815, 52816
Connecticut Freezers, 52817
Continental Express Inc, 52820
Crystal Cold Storage, 52828, 52829
CSX Transportation, 52731
Cumberland Distribution Services, 52831
Cwo Distribution, 52832
Denver Cold Storage, 52850
Des Moines Cold Storage Co, 52853
Distribution Services-America, 52859
Diversified Transfer & Storage, 52862
DSC Logistics Inc, 52840
Ecs Warehouse, 52878
Ellis KARR & Co Inc, 52879
Elmwood Warehousing Co, 52880
Empire Cold Storage, 52883
EPT Warehouses, 52874
Etobicold, 52888
Eugene Freezing & Storage Company, 52889
Evans Delivery Company, 52891
FEI Co, 52898
Florida Freezer LP, 52912
Freeport Cold Storage Inc, 52919
Frostar Corporation, 52923
Frostyaire for Frozen Foods, 52924, 52925
Frostyaire of Arkansas, Inc., 52926
General Cold Storage, 52937
Genesee Valley Rural Preservation Council, Inc., 52940
Geneva Lakes Cold Storage, 52941
Georgia Cold Storage Inc, 52943
Gillette Creamery, 52946
Glacier Cold Storage LTD, 52947
Glacier Transit & Storage Inc, 52948

Warehouse Type and Service / General Merchandise

Gress Refrigerated Services & Logisitics, 52962
Greylawn Foods, 52964
Hall Street Storage LLC, 52972
Hall's Warehouse Corp, 52973
Hanson Logistics, 52980, 52981, 52982, 52983, 52984, 52985, 52986, 52988
Harborside Refrigerated Svc, 52990
Harman Ice & Cold Storage, 52993
Hartford Freezers, 52995
Henningsen Cold Storage Co, 52997, 52998, 52999, 53000, 53001, 53002, 53004, 53005, 53006, 53007
High Plains Freezer, 53011
Holley Cold Storage Fruit Co, 53016
Houston Central Industries, Ltd., 53020
Inland Cold Storage, 53028
Inter State Cold Storage, 53032
Inter-County Bakers Inc, 53035
Intercontinental Warehouses, 53036
International Refrigerated, 53038
Interstate Cold Storage Co, 53042
Interstate Cold Storage Inc, 53041
Interstate Underground Wrhse, 53046
J&B Cold Storage Inc, 53049
Jacmar Foodservice, 53052
Jacobson Warehouse Company, 53053
John Christner Trucking Inc, 53059
Johnston Training Group, Inc., 53063
KANE Freight Lines Inc, 53067
Kayco, 53070
Klamath Cold Storage, 53075
Konoike Pacific California, 53077
Kyrie Global Inc., 53079
L.C. Entreposage Storage, 53081
Lagrou Distribution Inc, 53084
Laval Cold Storage Ltd., 53096
Lieb Cold Storage LLC, 53100
Lincoln Cold Storage, 53101
Lineage Logistics, 53103
Logisco, 53106
Los Angeles Cold Storage Co, 53109
Lucca Freezer & Cold Storage, 53110
M T C Logistics Corp, 53115, 53116
Manfredi Cold Storage, 53126
Manitoulin Group of Companies, 53127
Maritime International, 53128
Mccracken Motor Freight, 53135
MCS Merchants Cold Storage, 53117
Medina Cold Storage Co Inc, 53137
Mercantile Refrigerated Warehouses, 53139
Merchandise Warehouse, 53141
Merchants Export Inc, 53143
Midwest Cold Storage & Ice Company, 53161
Millbrook Lofts, 53164
Minnesota Freezer Warehouse Co, 53167
Mount Airy Cold Storage, 53176
MTC Delaware LLC, 53119
Mullica Hill Cold Storage, 53177
MultiSystems Barcode Solutions, 53178
Murphy Warehouse, 53180
National Cold Storage Inc, 53188
New Orleans Cold Storage-Wrhse, 53197
Newark Refrigerated Warehouse, 53200
Newport St Paul Cold Storage, 53201
Nordic Logistics and Warehousing, LLC, 53209
Nordica Warehouses Inc, 53210
North Western Warehouse Co, 53216
Northeast Refrigerated, 53217
Northland Cold Storage Inc, 53218
O-G Packing & Cold Storage Co, 53223
Ocean World Lines, 53227
Oceana County Freezer Storage, 53228
Olson Commercial Cold Storage, 53232
Orange County Cold Storage, 53237
Pacific Cold Storage, 53247
Pacific Commerce Company, 53248
Patane Brothers Freezer Wrhses, 53258
Philadelphia Warehousing & Cold Storage Company, 53266
Phoenix Industries LLC, 53267
Piedmont Distribution Services, 53271

Pilot Freight Svc, 53272
Pioneer Valley Refrigerated Warehouse, 53274
Polar Cold Storage, 53278
Port of Virgina, 53285
Power Logistics, 53287, 53288
Preferred Freezer Services, 53290, 53291, 53292, 53293, 53294, 53295, 53296, 53297, 53298, 53299, 53300, 53301, 53302, 53303, 53304, 53305, 53306, 53307, 53308, 53309, 53310, 53311, 53312, 53313, 53314, 53315, 53316, 53317, 53318, 53319, 53320, 53321, 53322, 53323, 53324, 53325, 53326, 53327, 53328, 53329
Priority Air Express, 53330
Reddy Ice, 53356, 53357
Richmond Cold Storage Smithfield, 53364
Rochester Refrigerating Corporation, 53371
Rosenberger Cold Storage Company, 53374
Royal Jordanian, 53375
Safeway Freezer Storage Inc, 53389
San Diego Cold Storage Inspctn, 53392
Seaboard Cold Storage Inc, 53407
Seaonus, 53413
Sedalia Cold Storage Company, 53416
Service Cold Storage Inc, 53417
Service Craft Distribution Systems, 53419
Shaw's Southern Belle Frozen, 53425
Shoreland Inc, 53430
Shoreline Freezers, 53431
Sierra Pacific Refrigerated, 53437
Sodus Cold Storage Co, 53443
Somerset Industries, 53444
Southern Warehousing-Dstrbtn, 53458
Springfield Underground, 53464
Stanford Refrigerated Warehouse, 53469
Sterling Bay Companies, 53477
Stockton Cold Storage, 53478
Terminal Cold Storage Co Inc, 53497
Tex-Mex Cold Storage, 53498
Tippmann Group, 53506, 53507
Total Logistic Control, 53513
Tracy Cold Storage, 53515
Trenton Cold Storage, 53518
Tri-Temp Distribution, 53519
Tucson Frozen Storage, 53521
Ultimate Foods, 53530
Underground Warehouses, 53531
Union Storage & Transfer Co, 53536
United Cold Storage, 53537
United States Cold Storage, 53540, 53541, 53542, 53543, 53544, 53545, 53546, 53547, 53548, 53549, 53550, 53551, 53552, 53553, 53554, 53555, 53556, 53557, 53558, 53559, 53560, 53561, 53563, 53564, 53565, 53566, 53567, 53568, 53569, 53570, 53571, 53572, 53573, 53574, 53575, 53576, 53577, 53578, 53579, 53580
URS Logistics, 53525
Valley Distributors & Storage Company, 53583
Versa Cold, 53590
Versacold Logistics Services, 53591
Vineland Ice & Storage, 53593
Washington Cold Storage, 53607
We Pack Logistics, 53609
Weber Logistics, 53611, 53612, 53616
Western Gateway Storage Co, 53628
Williamson Cold Storage Inc, 53632
Winchester Cold Storage, 53636
XPO Logistics, 53640

York Cold Storage LLC, 53642
Yuba City Refrigerating Company, 53644
Zero Mountain, Inc., 53645

General Merchandise

A Arnold Logistics, 52601
A W Sisk & Son, 52602
AADF Warehouse Corporation, 52606
Ability/Tri-Modal Trnsprtn Svc, 52613
Acme Distribution Ctr Inc, 52615
Adams Warehouse & Delivery, 52616
All-Temp, 52629
Allied Logistics, 52635
American Cold Storage, 52639
American Distribution Centers, 52642
American Port Services, 52643
American Warehouse Co, 52644
Anchor Distribution Services, 52648
Arco Warehouse Co, 52652
Artesian Ice, 52660
Aspen Distribution, 52662
Associated Global Systems, 52664
ASW Supply Chain Svc, 52612
Atlanta Bonded Warehouse Corporation, 52665
Atlanta Service Warehouse Inc, 52666
Aurora Storage & Distribution Center, 52669
Baker Transfer & Storage, 52674
Barrett Distribution Ctr, 52678
Bay Cities Warehouse, 52680
Belt Route Warehouse & Storage, 52683
Belt's Corp, 52684
Bender Warehouse Co, 52686
Benlin Freight Forwarding Inc, 52687
Biscontini Distribution Centers, 52691
BLC Trucking Inc, 52673
Blue Line Cold Storage Chicago, 52695
Bob's Transport & Stge Co Inc, 52697
Bonded Service Warehouse, 52700
Bootz Distribution, 52701
Bristol Van & Storage Corporation, 52703
Brokers Logistics LTD, 52704
C&M Warehouse, Inc., 52722
Canada Distribution Centres, 52734
Central American Warehouse Co, 52749
Central States Distribution, 52751
Central States Warehouse, 52752
Central Transport Intl, 52755
Central Warehouse Operations, Inc., 52757
Central-Cumberland Corp, 52758
Central/Terminal Distribution Centers, 52759
Chicagoland Quad Cities Express, 52762
Columbian Logistics Network, 52802, 52803
Commercial Distribution Ctr, 52806
Commercial Warehouse Co, 52807
Commonwealth Warehouse & Storage, 52809
Compton Transfer Storage Co, 52810
Continental Express Inc, 52820
Cornwall Warehousing, 52821
Cotter Merchandise Storage Co, 52822
Crescent, 52825
Crocker Moving & Storage Co, 52826
Crystal Distribution Svc, 52830
D & D Distribution Svc, 52833
D & S Warehouse Inc, 52834
Darras Freight, 52843
DCI Logistics, 52838
Delavan Center, Inc., 52845
Dependable Distribution Services, 52851
Detroit Warehouse Company, 52855
Dist Tech, 52858
Distribution Services-America, 52859
Distribution Unlimited, 52860
Doc's Transfer & Warehouse, 52865
DSW Distribution Ctr Inc, 52841
Eastern Distribution Inc, 52877
Ecs Warehouse, 52878
Elmwood Warehousing Co, 52880

Elston Richards Warehouse, 52881
Englund Equipment Co, 52885
Erdner Brothers, 52887
Evans Distribution Systems, 52892
Farwest Freight Systems, 52903
Faure Brothers Inc, 52905
Federal Companies, 52907
Finch Companies, 52910
Florida Freezer LP, 52912
Food Link Inc, 52914
Fst Logistics Inc, 52928
Gadsden Cartage Co, 52932
Garvey Public Warehouse, 52933
General Bonded Warehouses Inc, 52936
Giant Warehousing Inc, 52944
Gilbert International, 52945
Glacier Transit & Storage Inc, 52948
Goff Distribution, 52950
Graham Transfer & Storage, 52951
Gratton Warehouse Co, 52953
Great Lakes Warehouse Corp, 52958
Grimes Co, 52965
Gulf Central Distribution Ctr, 52968
Hall's Warehouse Corp, 52973
Hansen Storage Co, 52979
Hanson Logistics, 52980, 52981, 52983, 52985, 52986, 52987
Hayes/Dockside Inc., 52996
Hermann Services Inc, 53009
Hillier Storage & Moving, 53012
Hodge Transit Warehouse, 53013
Hodges Co, 53014
Ideal Warehouse, 53024
Inland Empire Distribution, 53029
Inland Star Distribution Ctr, 53030
Intercontinental Warehouses, 53036
Interport Storage & Distribution Service, 53040
Interstate Underground Wrhse, 53046
J.D. Smith & Sons, 53050
Jacmar Foodservice, 53052
Jacobson Warehouse Company, 53053
John Cassidy Intl Inc, 53058
John-Jeffrey Corporation, 53061, 53062
Jones Moving & Storage Co, 53064
Kak LLC, 53068
Kayco, 53070
Kenco Group Inc, 53072
Kenco Logistic Svc LLC, 53073
Kuehne & Nagel Inc., 53078
Kyrie Global Inc., 53079
Lagrou Distribution Inc, 53084
Lake Erie Warehouse & Distribution Center, 53087
Laney & Duke Terminal Wrhse Co, 53090
Langham Logistics, 53091
Lanter Distribution LLC, 53093
Laub International, 53095
Laval Cold Storage Ltd., 53096
Lewis Storage, 53099
Lieb Cold Storage LLC, 53100
Logistics Amber Worldwide, 53107
Lynchburg Public Warehouse, 53112
Lynden Incorporated, 53113
M & W Logistics Group, 53114
Mccracken Motor Freight, 53135
McKenna Logistic Centres, 53134
Meador Warehousing-Dstrbtn, 53136
Merchandise Warehouse, 53141
Merchants Transfer Company, 53144
Meritex Logistics, 53145
Metro Park Warehouses Inc, 53149
Michel Distribution Service, 53151
Mid-Continent Warehouse Company, 53156
Minnesota Freezer Warehouse Co, 53167
MTE Logistix, 53120
MultiSystems Barcode Solutions, 53178
Murphy Warehouse, 53180
Murphy Warehouse Co, 53181
Murray's Transfer Inc, 53182
Nebraska Warehouse Co, 53192
Nordica Warehouses Inc, 53210

881

Warehouse Type and Service / Labeling

Norfolk Warehouse Distribution Centers, 53211
North American Warehousing, 53213
Northland Cold Storage Inc, 53218
O'Byrne Distribution Ctr Inc, 53222
ODW Logistics Inc, 53224
Olson Co, 53231
Orange County Cold Storage, 53237
Oregon Transfer Co, 53239
Ozburn-Hessey Logistics LLC, 53241
Pacific Cartage & Warehousing, 53245
Parkside Warehouse Inc, 53256
Patane Brothers Freezer Wrhses, 53258
Peasley Transfer & Storage, 53259
Penser SC, 53262
Peoples Cartage Inc, 53264
Phoenix Industries LLC, 53267
Pioneer Warehouse Corporation, 53275
Port Jersey Logistics, 53281
Port of Virginia, 53285
PRISM Team Services, 53244
Ray West Warehouses/Transport, 53355
RBW Logistics, 53345
Rex & Company, 53361
Reynolds Transfer & Storage, 53362
RGL Headquarters, 53347
River Terminal Distribution & Warehouse, 53366
Robertson-Johnson Warehouses, 53368
Robinson & Co, 53369
Rosa Food Products, 53373
Royal Jordanian, 53375
Saddle Creek Logistics Svc, 53386
San Jose Distribution Service, 53394
Schenker Logistics Inc, 53402
Schilli Transportation Services, 53403
Seaboard Warehouse Terminals, 53410
Serviplast, 53421
Shamrock Warehouse, 53422
Shaw Montgomery Warehouse Company, 53423
Shaw Warehouse Company, 53424
Shepard's Moving & Storage, 53427
Simard Warehouses, 53438
Smith Terminal Distribution, 53441
Sonwil Distribution Center, 53445
SOPAKCO Foods, 53382
Southern Warehousing-Dstrbtn, 53458
Standard Transportation Svc, 53466
Standard Warehouse, 53467
Starr Distribution Services Company, 53473
State Center Warehouse & Cold Storage, 53474
Sunland Distribution, 53484
TCT Logistics, 53488
Team Hardinger, 53492
Tejas Logistics System, 53494
Tennessee Commercial Wrhse Inc, 53496
Texas Cartage Warehouse Inc, 53499
The Commercial Exchange, Inc., 53500
Total Logistic Control, 53513
Transcor, 53517
Tri-Waters Warehouse, 53520
Twin Cities Dry Storage Ltd., 53524
TWL Corporation, 53489
Ultimate Foods, 53530
Underground Warehouses, 53531
Union Storage & Transfer Co, 53536
UTZ Quality Foods Inc, 53529
Valley Distributors & Storage Company, 53583
Van Brunt Port Jersey Warehouse, 53586
Vermont Commercial Warehouse, 53589
W T Young Storage Co, 53597
Walsh Transportation Group, 53600
Warehouse Associates LP, 53602
Washington Cold Storage, 53607
Weber Logistics, 53613, 53614, 53615, 53616, 53617, 53618, 53619, 53620
West Brothers Trailer Rental, 53624
West Logistics, 53625
William B Meyer Inc, 53630
Willis Day Storage, 53633
Wilmington Bonded Warehouse, 53634
Winchester Cold Storage, 53636
WOW Logistics, 53598
XPO Logistics, 53640

Labeling

A Arnold Logistics, 52601
A W Sisk & Son, 52602
A. Gagliano Co Inc, 52605
AADF Warehouse Corporation, 52606
Ability/Tri-Modal Trnsprtn Svc, 52613
Acme Distribution Ctr Inc, 52615
Adams Warehouse & Delivery, 52616
Alcor Corp, 52624
Allied Cold Storage Corporation, 52633
Allied Logistics, 52635
American Distribution Centers, 52642
American Port Services, 52643
American Warehouse Co, 52644
AmeriCold Logistics LLC, 52637
Arco Warehouse Co, 52652
Arctic Logistics, 52656
Artesian Ice, 52660
Aspen Distribution, 52662
Associated Global Systems, 52664
ASW Supply Chain Svc, 52612
Aurora Storage & Distribution Center, 52669
Baker Transfer & Storage, 52674
Barrett Distribution Ctr, 52678
Bay Cities Warehouse, 52680
Belt Route Warehouse & Storage, 52683
Bender Warehouse Co, 52686
Benlin Freight Forwarding Inc, 52687
Biscontini Distribution Centers, 52691
Blue Line Cold Storage Chicago, 52695
Bob's Transport & Stge Co Inc, 52697
Boise Cold Storage Co, 52698, 52699
Bridge Terminal, Inc., 52702
Brokers Logistics LTD, 52704
Burris Logistics, 52708, 52713
C Summers Inc, 52721
Central American Warehouse Co, 52749
Central States Distribution, 52751
Central States Warehouse, 52752
Central Storage & Wrhse Co Inc, 52754
Central Transport Intl, 52755
CFC Logistics, 52724
Cincinnati Freezer Corp, 52764
Cloverleaf Cold Storage, 52771, 52772, 52773, 52774, 52775, 52776, 52777, 52778, 52779, 52780, 52781, 52782, 52783, 52784, 52785, 52786, 52787, 52788, 52789, 52790, 52791, 52792, 52793
Columbian Logistics Network, 52802
Commercial Distribution Ctr, 52806
Commercial Warehouse Co, 52807
Confederation Freezers, 52815, 52816
Continental Express Inc, 52820
Cornwall Warehousing, 52821
Crystal Distribution Svc, 52830
D & D Distribution Svc, 52833
D & S Warehouse Inc, 52834
Darras Freight, 52843
Dependable Distribution Services, 52851
Dist Tech, 52858
Doc's Transfer & Warehouse, 52865
DSW Distribution Ctr Inc, 52841
Englund Equipment Co, 52885
EPT Warehouses, 52874
Erdner Brothers, 52887
Evans Distribution Systems, 52892
Farwest Freight Systems, 52903
Federal Companies, 52907
FEI Co, 52898
Fiesta Warehousing & Distribution Company, 52909
Finch Companies, 52910
Florida Freezer LP, 52912
Food Link Inc, 52914
Freeport Cold Storage Inc, 52919
Freeport Logistics Inc, 52920
Giant Warehousing Inc, 52944
Goff Distribution, 52950
Gratton Warehouse Co, 52953
Grimes Co, 52965
Hall's Warehouse Corp, 52973
Hanson Logistics, 52984
Henningsen Cold Storage Co, 52998, 52999, 53000, 53001, 53002, 53003, 53004, 53005, 53006, 53007
Hermann Services Inc, 53009
Houston Central Industries, Ltd., 53020
Ideal Warehouse, 53024
Imperal Freight Broker, 53025
Importers, 53027
Inland Empire Distribution, 53029
Inland Star Distribution Ctr, 53030
Intercontinental Warehouses, 53036
International Refrigerated, 53038
J M Swank Co, 53047
Jacobson Warehouse Company, 53053
John-Jeffrey Corporation, 53062
Jones Moving & Storage Co, 53064
Kak LLC, 53068
Kenco Logistic Svc LLC, 53073
Kyrie Global Inc., 53079
Lagrou Distribution Inc, 53084
Lake Erie Warehouse & Distribution Center, 53087
Lanter Distribution LLC, 53093
Laub International, 53095
Lewis Storage, 53099
Logistics Amber Worldwide, 53107
M & W Logistics Group, 53114
Mallory Alexander Intl, 53124
Manfredi Cold Storage, 53126
Maritime International, 53128
Mccracken Motor Freight, 53135
Merchandise Warehouse, 53141
Metro Park Warehouses Inc, 53149
Mid-Continent Warehouse Company, 53156
Moran Distribution Centers, 53171
MTC Delaware LLC, 53119
MultiSystems Barcode Solutions, 53178
Murphy Warehouse Co, 53181
New Orleans Cold Storage-Wrhse, 53197
Nordic Logistics and Warehousing, LLC, 53208, 53209
North American Warehousing, 53213
Northeast Refrigerated, 53217
Northland Cold Storage Inc, 53218
Olson Co, 53231
Oregon Transfer Co, 53239
Overflo, 53240
Penser SC, 53262
Phoenix Industries LLC, 53267
Pioneer Valley Refrigerated Warehouse, 53274
Port Jersey Logistics, 53281
PRISM Team Services, 53244
Queen City Warehouse Corporation, 53341
Ralph Moyle Inc, 53353
Ray West Warehouses/Transport, 53355
Rex & Company, 53361
Richwill Enterprises, 53365
Saddle Creek Logistics Svc, 53386
Safeway Freezer Storage Inc, 53389
San Jose Distribution Service, 53394
Schenker Logistics Inc, 53402
Schilli Transportation Services, 53403
Seaboard Warehouse Terminals, 53410
Shaw Montgomery Warehouse Company, 53423
Simard Warehouses, 53438
Smith Terminal Distribution, 53441
Sonwil Distribution Center, 53445
Sopak Co Inc, 53446
Southern Cold Storage Co, 53454
Standard Transportation Svc, 53466
Standard Warehouse, 53467
Stanz Foodservice Inc, 53471
Star Distribution Systems, 53472
Starr Distribution Services Company, 53473
Sterling Bay Companies, 53477
Tejas Logistics System, 53494
Tennessee Commercial Wrhse Inc, 53496
Texas Cartage Warehouse Inc, 53499
The Terminal Corporation, 53502
Three D Brokers, 53503
Total Logistic Control, 53513
TWL Corporation, 53489
Underground Warehouses, 53531
Valley Distributors & Storage Company, 53583
Versa Cold, 53590
W T Young Storage Co, 53597
Walsh Transportation Group, 53600
Warehouse Associates LP, 53602
Warehouse Service Inc, 53603
Weber Logistics, 53612, 53616
Welling Company, 53623
West Logistics, 53625
William B Meyer Inc, 53630
Willis Day Storage, 53633
WOW Logistics, 53598
XPO Logistics, 53640
York Rail Logistics, 53643

Non-Perishables

A Arnold Logistics, 52601
A W Sisk & Son, 52602
A&M Warehouse & Distribution, 52604
A. Gagliano Co Inc, 52605
AADF Warehouse Corporation, 52606
Acme Distribution Ctr Inc, 52615
Adams Warehouse & Delivery, 52616
Advance Distribution Svc, 52617
All Freight Systems, 52627
All-Temp, 52629
Allied Logistics, 52635
American Port Services, 52643
American Warehouse Co, 52644
Ampoint Distribution Centers, 52645
Amware Distribution Warehouse, 52646
Apl Logistics, 52649
Arco Warehouse Co, 52652
Artesian Ice, 52660
ASAP Freight Systems, 52611
Aspen Distribution, 52662
ASW Supply Chain Svc, 52612
B.R. Williams Trucking & Warehouse, 52671
Baker Transfer & Storage, 52674
Barrett Distribution Ctr, 52678
Bay Cities Warehouse, 52680
Belt Route Warehouse & Storage, 52683
Belts Logistics Services, 52685
Bender Warehouse Co, 52686
Benlin Freight Forwarding Inc, 52687
Biscontini Distribution Centers, 52691
Blue Line Cold Storage Chicago, 52695
Bob's Transport & Stge Co Inc, 52697
Bristol Van & Storage Corporation, 52703
Byers Transport, 52720
C&M Warehouse, Inc., 52722
California Cartage Co, 52733
Cargo, 52738
Carolina Transfer & Stge Inc, 52741
Centra Worldwide, 52748
Central American Warehouse Co, 52749
Central States Distribution, 52751
Central States Warehouse, 52752
Central Storage & Wrhse Co Inc, 52754
Central Transportation System, 52756
Cockrell Distribution System, 52795
Columbian Logistics Network, 52802
Commercial Distribution Ctr, 52806
Commercial Warehouse Co, 52807
Commonwealth Inc, 52808
Consolidated Transfer Co Inc, 52819
Cornwall Warehousing, 52821
Cranston Air, 52823
Crate & Fly, 52824
Cumberland Distribution Services, 52831
D & D Distribution Svc, 52833
D W Air, 52835
D.D. Jones Transfer & Warehousing, 52836

Warehouse Type and Service / Packaging

Dallas Transfer & Terminal, 52842
Delavan Center, Inc., 52845
Dependable Distribution Services, 52851
Dhx-Dependable Hawaiian Express, 52856
Dist Tech, 52858
Distribution Services-America, 52859
Doc's Transfer & Warehouse, 52865
Dreisbach Enterprises Inc, 52868
Dunagan Warehouse Corp, 52873
Ecs Warehouse, 52878
Elmwood Warehousing Co, 52880
Englund Equipment Co, 52885
Erdner Brothers, 52887
Evans Distribution Systems, 52892
Express Air Cargo, 52896
Farwest Freight Systems, 52903
Faure Brothers Inc, 52905
Federal Companies, 52907
Finch Companies, 52910
Florida Freezer LP, 52912
Franklin Express Co Inc, 52917
Franklin Storage Inc, 52918
G&A Warehouses, 52929
Garvey Public Warehouse, 52933
Gemini Traffic Sales, 52935
General Warehouse & Transportation Company, 52938, 52939
Genesee Valley Rural Preservation Council, Inc., 52940
Geneva Lakes Cold Storage, 52941
Georgia Cold Storage Inc, 52943
Gilbert International, 52945
GMW Freight Services Ltd, 52930
Goff Distribution, 52950
Gratton Warehouse Co, 52953
Grimes Co, 52965
Ideal Warehouse, 53024
Inland Empire Distribution, 53029
Inland Star Distribution Ctr, 53030
Intercontinental Warehouses, 53036
Interport Storage & Distribution Service, 53040
Interstate Underground Wrhse, 53046
J&B Cold Storage Inc, 53049
Jacobson Warehouse Company, 53053
John-Jeffrey Corporation, 53062
Jones Moving & Storage Co, 53064
K&K Express, 53066
Kak LLC, 53068
Kasseleer Food Products Inc., 53069
Kayco, 53070
Kenco Logistic Svc LLC, 53073
Konoike Pacific California, 53077
Kyrie Global Inc., 53079
Lagrou Distribution, 53084
Lake Erie Warehouse & Distribution Center, 53087
Lanter Distribution LLC, 53093
Laub International, 53095
Lieb Cold Storage LLC, 53100
Linden Warehouse & Dstrbtn Co, 53102
Live Oak Warehouse, 53104
LMD Integrated Logistic Services, 53082
Logistics Amber Worldwide, 53107
M & W Logistics Group, 53114
Mallory Alexander Intl, 53124
Mccracken Motor Freight, 53135
Medina Cold Storage Co Inc, 53137
Merchandise Warehouse, 53141
Meritex Logistics, 53145
Metro Park Warehouses Inc, 53149
Mid-Continent Warehouse Company, 53156
Midwest Assembly Warehouse, 53160
Midwest Distribution Systems, 53162
Minnesota Freezer Warehouse Co, 53167
Moran Logistics, 53172
Murphy Warehouse Co, 53181
National Distribution Centers, 53189, 53190
National Warehouse Corporation, 53191
New Hampton Transfer & Storage, 53196
Northland Cold Storage Inc, 53218

Ohio Commerce Center, 53229
Olson Co, 53231
Oregon Transfer Co, 53239
Overflo, 53240
Palmer Logistics, 53253
Parkside Warehouse Inc, 53256
Peasley Transfer & Storage, 53259
Penser SC, 53262
Phoenix Industries LLC, 53267
Port Elizabeth Terminal Corp, 53280
Port Jersey Logistics, 53281
Power Logistics, 53288
Priority Air Express, 53330
PRISM Team Services, 53244
Prism Team Services, Inc, 53331
Products Distribution, 53333
Queen City Warehouse Corporation, 53341
Quick Delivery, 53342
Ralph Moyle Inc, 53353
Ray West Warehouses/Transport, 53355
Riverport Warehouse Company, 53367
Robinson & Co, 53369
Rosa Food Products, 53373
Saddle Creek Corp, 53385
Saddle Creek Logistics Svc, 53386, 53387, 53388
Saturn Freight Systems, 53398
Schenker Logistics Inc, 53402
SDS Global Logistics, Inc., 53380
Seaboard Warehouse Terminals, 53410
Security Bonded Warehouse, 53415
SEKO Worldwide Inc, 53381
Serviplast, 53421
Shaw Montgomery Warehouse Company, 53423
Simard Warehouses, 53438
Smith Terminal Distribution, 53441
Somerset Industries, 53444
Sopak Co Inc, 53446
SOPAKCO Foods, 53382
SOS Global Express Inc, 53383
Southern Warehousing-Dstrbtn, 53458
Southshore Enterprises, 53459
Space Center Inc, 53461
Standard Warehouse, 53467
Star Distribution Systems, 53472
Starr Distribution Services Company, 53473
State Center Warehouse & Cold Storage, 53474
Tazmanian Freight Forwarding, 53491
Tejas Logistics System, 53494
Texas Cartage Warehouse Inc, 53499
The Commercial Exchange, Inc., 53500
Three D Brokers, 53503
Tolteca Foodservice, 53509
Tomahawk Warehousing Services, 53510
TWL Corporation, 53489
Underground Warehouses, 53531
Union Storage & Transfer Co, 53536
Valley Distributors & Storage Company, 53583
W J Beitler Co & Beitler Truck, 53595
Walsh Transportation Group, 53600
Warehouse Associates LP, 53602
Warehouse Specialists Inc, 53605
We Pack Logistics, 53609
Weber Logistics, 53614
Welling Company, 53623
West Logistics, 53625
William B Meyer Inc, 53630
Willis Day Storage, 53633
Winchester Cold Storage, 53636
Worley Warehousing Inc, 53639
WOW Logistics, 53598
XPO Logistics, 53640

Packaging

Allied Cold Storage Corporation, 52633
American Cold Storage, 52639
AmeriCold Logistics LLC, 52637
Arctic Logistics, 52656
Artesian Ice, 52660
Boise Cold Storage Co, 52698
Bridge Terminal, Inc., 52702
Brokers Logistics LTD, 52704
Burris Logistics, 52706, 52707, 52709, 52713
C.J. Figone Cold Storage, 52723
Carolina Cold Storage, 52740
Central Storage & Warehouse Co, 52753
Central Storage & Wrhse Co Inc, 52754
CFC Logistics, 52724
Cloverleaf Cold Storage, 52771, 52772, 52773, 52774, 52775, 52776, 52777, 52778, 52779, 52780, 52782, 52784, 52785, 52786, 52787, 52788, 52789, 52790, 52791, 52792, 52793
Conestoga Cold Storage, 52813, 52814
Connecticut Freezers, 52817
Crystal Distribution Svc, 52830
Darras Freight, 52843
Denver Cold Storage, 52850
Empire Cold Storage, 52883
Eugene Freezing & Storage Company, 52889
FEI Co, 52898
Hall Street Storage LLC, 52972
Hanson Logistics, 52980, 52982, 52983, 52988
Henningsen Cold Storage Co, 52997, 52998, 53004
Houston Central Industries, Ltd., 53020
Inland Cold Storage, 53028
Inter-Cities Cold Storage, 53034
International Refrigerated, 53038
Interstate Cold Storage Inc, 53041
J&B Cold Storage Inc, 53049
Kyrie Global Inc., 53079
Lanier Cold Storage LLC, 53092
M T C Logistics Corp, 53115
Maritime International, 53128
Merchandise Warehouse, 53141
Mid Eastern Cold Storage LLC, 53155
Minnesota Freezer Warehouse Co, 53167
MTC Delaware LLC, 53119
MultiSystems Barcode Solutions, 53178
National Cold Storage Inc, 53188
New Orleans Cold Storage-Wrhse, 53197
Nordic Logistics and Warehousing, LLC, 53208, 53209
Nordica Warehouses Inc, 53210
Northland Cold Storage Inc, 53218
Pioneer Valley Refrigerated Warehouse, 53274
Preferred Freezer Services, 53290, 53296, 53297, 53304, 53321, 53326
Richmond Cold Storage Smithfield, 53364
Safeway Freezer Storage Inc, 53389
Seaonus, 53413
Shoreland Inc, 53430
Sterling Bay Companies, 53477
Underground Warehouses, 53531
Union Ice Co, 53535
Union Storage & Transfer Co, 53536
United Cold Storage, 53537
United States Cold Storage, 53541, 53542, 53545, 53546, 53548, 53549, 53550, 53552, 53554, 53555, 53556, 53561, 53563, 53566, 53576, 53578
US Growers Cold Storage, 53527
Washington Cold Storage, 53607
Zero Mountain, Inc., 53645

Pick & Pack

A Arnold Logistics, 52601
A. Gagliano Co Inc, 52605
Ability/Tri-Modal Trnsprtn Svc, 52613
Acme Distribution Ctr Inc, 52615
Adams Warehouse & Delivery, 52616
Allied Logistics, 52635
American Port Services, 52643
Aspen Distribution, 52662
ASW Supply Chain Svc, 52612
Aurora Storage & Distribution Center, 52669
Barrett Distribution Ctr, 52678
Belt Route Warehouse & Storage, 52683
Benlin Freight Forwarding Inc, 52687
Biscontini Distribution Centers, 52691
Blendco Inc, 52693
Bonded Service Warehouse, 52700
Brokers Logistics LTD, 52704
Central American Warehouse Co, 52749
Central States Distribution, 52751
Central Storage & Warehouse Co, 52753
Central Storage & Wrhse Co Inc, 52754
Cleanfreak, 52770
Cloverleaf Cold Storage, 52771
Columbian Logistics Network, 52802
Commercial Distribution Ctr, 52806
D & D Distribution Svc, 52833
D & S Warehouse Inc, 52834
Darras Freight, 52843
Dist Tech, 52858
Doc's Transfer & Warehouse, 52865
DSW Distribution Ctr Inc, 52841
Ecs Warehouse, 52878
Evans Distribution Systems, 52892
Faure Brothers Inc, 52905
Finch Companies, 52910
Florida Freezer LP, 52912
Freeport Cold Storage Inc, 52919
Goff Distribution, 52950
Grimes Co, 52965
Hermann Services Inc, 53009
Houston Central Industries, Ltd., 53020
Inland Empire Distribution, 53029
Interport Storage & Distribution Service, 53040
Jacobson Warehouse Company, 53053
John-Jeffrey Corporation, 53062
Kak LLC, 53068
Kenco Logistic Svc LLC, 53073
Kyrie Global Inc., 53079
Laub International, 53095
Lewis Storage, 53099
M & W Logistics Group, 53114
Manfredi Cold Storage, 53126
Merchandise Warehouse, 53141
Metro Park Warehouses Inc, 53149
Minnesota Freezer Warehouse Co, 53167
Moran Distribution Centers, 53171
Murphy Warehouse Co, 53181
Nordica Warehouses Inc, 53210
North American Warehousing, 53213
Olson Co, 53231
Pacific Coast Warehouse Co, 53246
Penser SC, 53262
Phoenix Industries LLC, 53267
PRISM Team Services, 53244
Ray West Warehouses/Transport, 53355
Saddle Creek Logistics Svc, 53386
San Jose Distribution Service, 53394
Schenker Logistics Inc, 53402
Sonwil Distribution Center, 53445
SOPAKCO Foods, 53382
Standard Warehouse, 53467
Starr Distribution Services Company, 53473
Sterling Bay Companies, 53477
Superior Pack Group, 53485
Tejas Logistics System, 53494
Texas Cartage Warehouse Inc, 53499
The Terminal Corporation, 53502
Underground Warehouses, 53531
United Facilities, 53538
Valley Distributors & Storage Company, 53583
Valley International Cold Storage, Inc., 53584
Warehouse Associates LP, 53602
Weber Logistics, 53612
Welling Company, 53623
William B Meyer Inc, 53630
Willis Day Storage, 53633
WOW Logistics, 53598

Produce

A. Gagliano Co Inc, 52605

Warehouse Type and Service / Railroad Siding

Airschott Inc, 52622
All-Temp, 52629
Baker Transfer & Storage, 52674
Barrett Distribution Ctr, 52678
Belt Route Warehouse & Storage, 52683
Canon Potato Company, 52736
Central Storage & Wrhse Co Inc, 52754
Cloverleaf Cold Storage, 52773
Commercial Distribution Ctr, 52806
Ecs Warehouse, 52878
Florida Freezer LP, 52912
Hall's Warehouse Corp, 52973
Hanson Logistics, 52981, 52982, 52984, 52985, 52986, 52988
Henningsen Cold Storage Co, 52997, 52998, 53001, 53002, 53003, 53005, 53007
Holley Cold Storage Fruit Co, 53016
Houston Central Industries, Ltd., 53020
J M Swank Co, 53047
Jacmar Foodservice, 53052
Jacobson Warehouse Company, 53053
K M Davies Co, 53065
Kenco Logistic Svc LLC, 53073
Klamath Cold Storage, 53075
Kyrie Global Inc., 53079
Lancaster Company, 53088
Laval Cold Storage Ltd., 53096
Lieb Cold Storage LLC, 53100
Loop Cold Storage, 53108
Lucca Freezer & Cold Storage, 53110
Manfredi Cold Storage, 53126
Merchandise Warehouse, 53141
Merchants Export Inc, 53143
Mid-Continent Warehouse Company, 53156
Minnesota Freezer Warehouse Co, 53167
Mullica Hill Cold Storage, 53177
National Cold Storage Inc, 53188
Nordic Logistics and Warehousing, LLC, 53209
North Bay Produce Inc, 53214
O-G Packing & Cold Storage Co, 53223
Ontario Produce Company, 53236
Orange County Cold Storage, 53237
Phoenix Industries LLC, 53267
Pioneer Valley Refrigerated Warehouse, 53274
Rainier Cold-Storage & Ice, 53351, 53352
Shoreham Cooperative Apple Producer, 53429
Sierra Pacific Refrigerated, 53437
Sno Temp Cold Storage, 53442
SOPAKCO Foods, 53382
South Mill, 53449
Stanley Orchards Sales, Inc., 53470
Stanz Foodservice Inc, 53471
Tracy Cold Storage, 53515
Tusla Cold Storage, 53523
Ultimate Foods, 53530
Underground Warehouses, 53531
Washington Fruit & Produce Company, 53608
Weber Logistics, 53611, 53616
XPO Logistics, 53640

Railroad Siding

A Arnold Logistics, 52601
A W Sisk & Son, 52602
Adams Warehouse & Delivery, 52616
Baker Transfer & Storage, 52674
Biscontini Distribution Centers, 52691
Brokers Logistics LTD, 52704
City Packing Company, 52767
Commercial Distribution Ctr, 52806
D & D Distribution Svc, 52833
Distribution Services-America, 52859
DSC Logistics Inc, 52840
DSW Distribution Ctr Inc, 52841
Federal Companies, 52907
Florida Freezer LP, 52912
Great Lakes Warehouse Corp, 52958
Ideal Warehouse, 53024

Inland Empire Distribution, 53029
J M Swank Co, 53047
Jacmar Foodservice, 53052
Kasseler Food Products Inc., 53069
Lagrou Distribution Inc, 53084
Lake Erie Warehouse & Distribution Center, 53087
Metro Park Warehouses Inc, 53149
Norfolk Warehouse Distribution Centers, 53211
North American Warehousing, 53213
Olson Co, 53231
Penser SC, 53262
Phoenix Industries LLC, 53267
Pioneer Valley Refrigerated Warehouse, 53274
Port Jersey Logistics, 53281
Post Consumer Brands, 53286
Queen City Warehouse Corporation, 53341
Richwill Enterprises, 53365
Rochester Refrigerating Corporation, 53371
Saddle Creek Logistics Svc, 53386
Safeway Freezer Storage Inc, 53389
Savannah Distributing, 53400
Seaboard Warehouse Terminals, 53410
Service Cold Storage Inc, 53417
Sonwil Distribution Center, 53445
State Center Warehouse & Cold Storage, 53474
Three D Brokers, 53503
Topflight Grain Co-Op, 53511
Ultimate Foods, 53530
United Cold Storage, 53537
Weber Logistics, 53612, 53613, 53621
WOW Logistics, 53598

Repacking

A Arnold Logistics, 52601
Ability/Tri-Modal Trnsprtn Svc, 52613
Acme Distribution Ctr Inc, 52615
Adams Warehouse & Delivery, 52616
All-Temp, 52629
Allied Logistics, 52635
American Distribution Centers, 52642
American Port Services, 52643
American Warehouse Co, 52644
AmeriCold Logistics LLC, 52637
Arco Warehouse Co, 52652
Arctic Frozen Foods, 52655
Aspen Distribution, 52662
Aspen Distribution Inc, 52663
Associated Global Systems, 52664
ASW Supply Chain Svc, 52612
Aurora Storage & Distribution Center, 52669
Baker Transfer & Storage, 52674
Barrett Distribution Ctr, 52678
Belt Route Warehouse & Storage, 52683
Bender Warehouse Co, 52686
Benlin Freight Forwarding Inc, 52687
Biscontini Distribution Centers, 52691
Blue Line Cold Storage Chicago, 52695
Bonded Service Warehouse, 52700
Brokers Logistics LTD, 52704
C&M Warehouse, Inc., 52722
Carolina Cold Storage, 52740
Central American Warehouse Co, 52749
Central States Distribution, 52751
Cincinnati Freezer Corp, 52764
Columbian Logistics Network, 52802
Commercial Distribution Ctr, 52806
Commercial Warehouse Co, 52807
Conestoga Cold Storage, 52814
Connecticut Freezers, 52817
Cornwall Warehousing, 52821
Cumberland Distribution Services, 52831
D & D Distribution Svc, 52833
D.J. Powers Company, 52837
Darras Freight, 52843
Dependable Distribution Services, 52851
Dist Tech, 52858
Doc's Transfer & Warehouse, 52865

DSW Distribution Ctr Inc, 52841
Ecs Warehouse, 52878
Evans Distribution Systems, 52892
Faure Brothers Inc, 52905
Federal Companies, 52907
FEI Co, 52898
Finch Companies, 52910
Florida Freezer LP, 52912
Freeport Logistics Inc, 52920
Gabler Trucking Inc, 52931
Garvey Public Warehouse, 52933
Gilbert International, 52945
Goff Distribution, 52950
Gratton Warehouse Co, 52953
Great Lakes Warehouse Corp, 52958
Grimes Co, 52965
Hansen Storage Co, 52979
Hanson Logistics, 52981, 52982, 52983, 52985, 52986, 52987, 52988
Henningsen Cold Storage Co, 52997
Hermann Services Inc, 53009
Holeman Distribution Ctr, 53015
Houston Central Industries, Ltd., 53020
Howell Logistics Services, 53021
Ideal Warehouse, 53024
Inland Empire Distribution, 53029
Inland Star Distribution Ctr, 53030
Intercontinental Warehouses, 53036
International Refrigerated, 53038
Jacobson Warehouse Company, 53053
John-Jeffrey Corporation, 53062
Jones Moving & Storage Co, 53064
Kak LLC, 53068
Kenco Logistic Svc LLC, 53073
Kyrie Global Inc., 53079
Lagrou Distribution Inc, 53084
Lanter Distribution LLC, 53093
Laub International, 53095
Lehigh-Pocono Warehouse Inc, 53098
Lewis Storage, 53099
Logistics Amber Worldwide, 53107
M & W Logistics Group, 53114
Merchandise Warehouse, 53141
Meritex Logistics, 53145
Metro Park Warehouses Inc, 53149
Michel Distribution Service, 53151
Minnesota Freezer Warehouse Co, 53167
Moran Distribution Centers, 53171
Moran Logistics, 53172
MultiSystems Barcode Solutions, 53178
Murphy Warehouse Co, 53181
Nordica Warehouses Inc, 53210
Northeast Refrigerated, 53217
Olson Co, 53231
Orange County Cold Storage, 53237
Oregon Transfer Co, 53239
Overflo, 53240
Ozburn-Hessey Logistics LLC, 53241
Pacific Cartage & Warehousing, 53245
Penser SC, 53262
Phoenix Industries LLC, 53267
Pioneer Valley Refrigerated Warehouse, 53274
Port Jersey Logistics, 53281
PRISM Team Services, 53244
Ray West Warehouses/Transport, 53355
Rex & Company, 53361
Richmond Cold Storage Smithfield, 53364
Robertson-Johnson Warehouses, 53368
Saddle Creek Logistics Svc, 53386
San Jose Distribution Service, 53394
Schenker Logistics Inc, 53402
Shaw Montgomery Warehouse Company, 53423
Simard Warehouses, 53438
Sonwil Distribution Center, 53445
Southern Cold Storage Co, 53454
Spartan Logistics, 53462
Standard Warehouse, 53467
Star Distribution Systems, 53472
Starr Distribution Services Company, 53473
Sterling Bay Companies, 53477
Tazmanian Freight Forwarding, 53491

Tejas Logistics System, 53494
Texas Cartage Warehouse Inc, 53499
The Terminal Corporation, 53502
Three D Brokers, 53503
Total Logistic Control, 53513
Underground Warehouses, 53531
Union Storage & Transfer Co, 53536
United Facilities, 53538
Valley Distributors & Storage Company, 53583
W T Young Storage Co, 53597
Warehouse Associates LP, 53602
Warehouse Service Inc, 53603
Weber Logistics, 53612, 53619, 53621
Welling Company, 53623
West Logistics, 53625
William B Meyer Inc, 53630
Willis Day Storage, 53633
WOW Logistics, 53598
XPO Logistics, 53640

Trucking

A Arnold Logistics, 52601
A W Sisk & Son, 52602
A&M Warehouse & Distribution, 52604
AADF Warehouse Corporation, 52606
Ability/Tri-Modal Trnsprtn Svc, 52613
Acme Distribution Ctr Inc, 52615
Adams Warehouse & Delivery, 52616
Advanced Warehouses, 52619
Alaska Railroad Corp, 52623
Alcor Corp, 52624
All Freight Distribution Co, 52626
All South Warehouse, 52628
All-Temp, 52629
Allegheny Cold Storage Co, 52630
Allied Cold Storage Corporation, 52633
Allied Frozen Storage Inc, 52634
Allied Logistics, 52635
AM-C Warehouses Inc, 52607
Amarillo Warehouse Co, 52636
American Cold Storage, 52638, 52639
American Distribution Centers, 52642
American Port Services, 52643
American Warehouse Co, 52644
Ampcint Distribution Centers, 52645
Anchor Distribution Services, 52648
Arco Warehouse Co, 52652
Arizona Cold Storage LLC, 52657
Arkansas Refrigerated Services, 52658
Arro Corp, 52659
Artesian Ice, 52660
Aspen Distribution, 52662
Aspen Distribution Inc, 52663
ASW Supply Chain Svc, 52612
Atlanta Bonded Warehouse Corporation, 52665
Atlanta Service Warehouse Inc, 52666
Atlantic Coast Freezers, 52667
B. Barks & Sons, 52670
Baker Transfer & Storage, 52674
Baltimore International Warehousing, 52675
Barrett Distribution Ctr, 52678
Bay Cities Warehouse, 52680
Beacon Distribution Services, 52681
Belt Route Warehouse & Storage, 52683
Belt's Corp, 52684
Bender Warehouse Co, 52686
Benlin Freight Forwarding Inc, 52687
Biscontini Distribution Centers, 52691
Blast It Clean, 52692
BLC Trucking Inc, 52673
Blue Line Cold Storage Chicago, 52695
Blue Line Moving & Storage, 52696
Bob's Transport & Stge Co Inc, 52697
Boise Cold Storage Co, 52698
Bonded Service Warehouse, 52700
Bootz Distribution, 52701
Bridge Terminal, Inc., 52702
Bristol Van & Storage Corporation, 52703
Brokers Logistics LTD, 52704

884

Warehouse Type and Service / Trucking

Burris Logistics, 52706, 52707, 52709, 52712
Byers Transport, 52720
C&M Warehouse, Inc., 52722
California Cartage Co, 52733
Canada Distribution Centres, 52734
Carolina Bonded Storage Co, 52739
Cascade Properties, 52742
Castle Distribution Svc Inc, 52745
Central American Warehouse Co, 52749
Central States Distribution, 52751
Central Storage & Warehouse Co, 52753
Central Storage & Wrhse Co Inc, 52754
Central Warehouse Operations, Inc., 52757
Central-Cumberland Corp, 52758
Central/Terminal Distribution Centers, 52759
Chicagoland Quad Cities Express, 52762
Cincinnati Freezer Corp, 52764
Cloverleaf Cold Storage, 52771, 52772, 52773, 52775, 52776, 52777, 52778, 52779, 52780, 52782, 52783, 52784, 52785, 52786, 52787, 52788, 52789, 52790, 52791, 52792, 52793
Columbian Logistics Network, 52802, 52803
Commercial Cold Storage, 52805
Commercial Distribution Ctr, 52806
Commonwealth Warehouse & Storage, 52809
Compton Transfer Storage Co, 52810
Confederation Freezers, 52815, 52816
Consolidated Transfer Co Inc, 52819
Cornwall Warehousing, 52821
Crocker Moving & Storage Co, 52826
Crossroads Distribution LTD, 52827
Crystal Cold Storage, 52828, 52829
Crystal Distribution Svc, 52830
Cumberland Distribution Services, 52831
D & D Distribution Svc, 52833
D & S Warehouse Inc, 52834
D.D. Jones Transfer & Warehousing, 52836
Dallas Transfer & Terminal, 52842
Days Corporation, 52844
DCI Logistics, 52838
Dependable Distribution Services, 52851
Des Moines Cold Storage Co, 52853
Dist Tech, 52858
Distribution Unlimited, 52860
Diversified Transfer & Storage, 52862
Dixie Warehouse Services, 52864
Doc's Transfer & Warehouse, 52865
DSW Distribution Ctr Inc, 52841
Dunagan Warehouse Corp, 52873
East Coast Warehouse & Distr, 52876
Eastern Distribution Inc, 52877
Elston Richards Warehouse, 52881
Empire Cold Storage, 52883
Emporia Cold Storage Co, 52884
EPT Warehouses, 52874
Erdner Brothers, 52887
Eugene Freezing & Storage Company, 52889
Eureka Ice & Cold Storage Company, 52890
Evans Distribution Systems, 52892
Faure Brothers Inc, 52905
Federal Business Ctr Inc, 52906
Federal Companies, 52907
FEI Co, 52898
Fiesta Warehousing & Distribution Company, 52909
Finch Companies, 52910
Florida Freezer LP, 52912
Freeport Cold Storage Inc, 52919
Freeport Logistics Inc, 52920
Freeway Warehouse Corp, 52921
Frostar Corporation, 52923
Garvey Public Warehouse, 52933
General Bonded Warehouses Inc, 52936
Genesee Valley Rural Preservation Council, Inc., 52940
Georgia Cold Storage Inc, 52943

Giant Warehousing Inc, 52944
Gilbert International, 52945
GMW Freight Services Ltd, 52930
Goff Distribution, 52950
Grane Warehousing & Distribution, 52952
Gratton Warehouse Co, 52953
Great Lakes Warehouse Corp, 52958
Grimes Co, 52965
Gulf Central Distribution Ctr, 52968
H&M Warehouse, 52971
Hall's Warehouse Corp, 52973
Hanover Terminal Inc, 52976
Hansen Storage Co, 52979
Hanson Logistics, 52982, 52983, 52984, 52987, 52988
Harborside Refrigerated Svc, 52990
Harborside Refrigerator Services, 52992
Hartford Freezers, 52995
Hayes/Dockside Inc., 52996
Henningsen Cold Storage Co, 52997, 52998, 52999, 53000, 53001, 53002, 53003, 53004, 53005, 53006
Hermann Services Inc, 53009
High Plains Freezer, 53011
Hodge Transit Warehouse, 53013
Hodges Co, 53014
Holeman Distribution Ctr, 53015
Holley Cold Storage Fruit Co, 53016
Holman Distribution Center, 53017
Houston Central Industries, Ltd., 53020
Howell Logistics Services, 53021
Ideal Warehouse, 53024
Inland Empire Distribution, 53029
Inland Star Distribution Ctr, 53030
Inter State Cold Storage, 53032, 53033
Inter-Cities Cold Storage, 53034
Inter-County Bakers Inc, 53035
Intercontinental Warehouses, 53036
International Refrigerated, 53038
Interport Storage & Distribution Service, 53040
Interstate Cold Storage, 53043, 53044
Interstate Cold Storage Co, 53042
Interstate Cold Storage Inc, 53041
Interstate Merchandise Warehose, 53045
Interstate Underground Wrhse, 53046
Jacobson Warehouse Company, 53053
Jaxport Refrigerated, 53055
John Cassidy Intl Inc, 53058
John-Jeffrey Corporation, 53061, 53062
Johnston Training Group, Inc., 53063
K M Davies Co, 53065
Kak LLC, 53068
Kenco Group Inc, 53072
Kenco Logistic Svc LLC, 53073
Klamath Cold Storage, 53075
Kuehne & Nagel Inc., 53078
La Grou Cold Storage, 53083
Lagrou Distribution Inc, 53084
Laney & Duke Terminal Wrhse Co, 53090
Lanter Distribution LLC, 53093
Laub International, 53095
Laval Cold Storage Ltd., 53096
Lewis Storage, 53099
Lieb Cold Storage LLC, 53100
Los Angeles Cold Storage Co, 53109
Lynchburg Public Warehouse, 53112
Lynden Incorporated, 53113
M & W Logistics Group, 53114
M T C Logistics Corp, 53115, 53116
MacCosham Van Lines, 53121
Madison Warehouse Corporation, 53122
Maines Paper & Food Svc Inc, 53123
Manfredi Cold Storage, 53126
Maritime International, 53128
Massachusetts Central Railroad Corporation, 53132
MCS Merchants Cold Storage, 53117
Meador Warehousing-Dstrbtn, 53136
Mercantile Refrigerated Warehouses, 53139
Merchants Distribution Svc, 53142
Merchants Export Inc, 53143

Merchants Transfer Company, 53144
Meritex Logistics, 53145
Metro Park Warehouses Inc, 53149
Michel Distribution Service, 53151
Michigan Cold Storage Facilities, 53152
Mid Columbia Warehouse Inc, 53153
Mid Eastern Cold Storage LLC, 53155
Mid-Continent Warehouse Company, 53156
Mid-Florida Freezer Warehouse, 53157
Midwest Cold Storage & Ice Company, 53161
Minnesota Freezer Warehouse Co, 53167
Modern Packaging, 53170
Moran Distribution Centers, 53171
Mosinee Cold Storage, 53175
Mount Airy Cold Storage, 53176
MTC Delaware LLC, 53119
MTE Logistix, 53120
Murphy Bonded Warehouse, 53179
Murphy Warehouse, 53180
Murphy Warehouse Co, 53181
Murray's Transfer Inc, 53182
NAPA Distribution Ctr, 53183
National Cold Storage Inc, 53188
National Warehouse Corporation, 53191
Nebraska Warehouse Co, 53192
New Federal Cold Storage, 53195
New Hampton Transfer & Storage, 53196
New Orleans Cold Storage-Wrhse, 53197
Newport St Paul Cold Storage, 53201
NFI Industries Inc, 53184
Nordic Logistics and Warehousing, LLC, 53208, 53209
Nordica Warehouses Inc, 53210
Norfolk Warehouse Distribution Centers, 53211
North American Warehousing, 53213
Northland Cold Storage Inc, 53218
O'Byrne Distribution Ctr Inc, 53222
O-G Packing & Cold Storage Co, 53223
Oborn Transfer & Stge Co Inc, 53225
ODW Logistics Inc, 53224
Olson Co, 53231
Ontario Produce Company, 53236
Oregon Transfer Co, 53239
Overflo, 53240
Ozburn-Hessey Logistics LLC, 53241
Pacific Cartage & Warehousing, 53245
Pacific Coast Warehouse Co, 53246
Pacific Cold Storage, 53247
Panalpina Inc., 53254
Parkside Warehouse Inc, 53256
Peasley Transfer & Storage, 53259
Peerless Trucking Company, 53260
Penser SC, 53262
Peoples Cartage Inc, 53264
Phoenix Industries LLC, 53267
Physical Distribution, 53269
Piedmont Distribution Centers, 53270
Pioneer Cold Logistics, 53273
Pioneer Valley Refrigerated Warehouse, 53274
Pioneer Warehouse Corporation, 53275
Pitzer Transfer & Storage Corp., 53276
Planters Cooperative, 53277
Port Jersey Logistics, 53281
Port of Virgina, 53285
Preferred Freezer Services, 53313, 53317, 53319
PRISM Team Services, 53244
Prism Team Services, Inc, 53331
Quandt's Foodservice Distributors, 53340
Queen City Warehouse Corporation, 53341
Rainier Cold Terminal, 53350
Rainier Cold-Storage & Ice, 53351, 53352
Ralph Moyle Inc, 53353
Rancho Cold Storage, 53354
Ray West Warehouses/Transport, 53355
RBW Logistics, 53345
Resource Alliance, 53360
Reynolds Transfer & Storage, 53362
RGL Headquarters, 53347

Riceland Foods Inc., 53363
River Terminal Distribution & Warehouse, 53366
Robertson-Johnson Warehouses, 53368
Roederer Transfer & Storage, 53372
Sack Storage Corporation, 53384
Saddle Creek Logistics Svc, 53386
Safeway Freezer Storage Inc, 53389
San Diego Cold Storage Inspctn, 53392
San Jose Distribution Service, 53394
Santemp Co, 53396
Schenker Logistics Inc, 53402
Seaboard Cold Storage Inc, 53407
Seaboard Warehouse Terminals, 53410
Seaonus, 53413
Service Cold Storage Inc, 53417
Service Craft Distribution Systems, 53419
Service Warehouse & Distribution, 53420
Shaw Montgomery Warehouse Company, 53423
Shaw Warehouse Company, 53424
Shepard's Moving & Storage, 53427
Shippers Warehouse, 53428
Shoreland Inc, 53430
Shoreline Freezers, 53431
Sierra Pacific Refrigerated, 53437
Simard Warehouses, 53438
Smedley Company, 53439
Smith Terminal Distribution, 53441
Sno Temp Cold Storage, 53442
Sonwil Distribution Center, 53445
SOPAKCO Foods, 53382
South Atlantic Warehouse Corporation, 53447
Southern Cold Storage Co, 53454
Southern Packaging & Distribution, 53456
Southern Warehousing & Distribution, 53457
Southern Warehousing-Dstrbtn, 53458
Southwest Logistics, 53460
Space Center Inc, 53461
Spartan Logistics, 53462
Springfield Underground, 53464
Stage One Coldstorage, 53465
Standard Transportation Svc, 53466
Standard Warehouse, 53467
Stanford Refrigerated Warehouse, 53469
Star Distribution Systems, 53472
Starr Distribution Services Company, 53473
Stemm Transfer & Storage, 53475
Sunland Distribution, 53484
TCT Logistics, 53488
Tejas Logistics System, 53494
Tennessee Cold & Dry Storage, 53495
Terminal Cold Storage Co Inc, 53497
Tex-Mex Cold Storage, 53498
The Jackson Kearney Group, 53501
The Terminal Corporation, 53502
Tighe Warehousing-Distribution, 53504
Tippmann Group, 53506, 53507
Trailwood Warehouse LLC, 53516
Trenton Cold Storage, 53518
Tri-Temp Distribution, 53519
Tusla Cold Storage, 53523
Underground Warehouses, 53531
Unicold Corp, 53532
Union Ice Co, 53535
Union Storage & Transfer Co, 53536
United Facilities, 53538
United States Cold Storage, 53541, 53542, 53543, 53544, 53545, 53546, 53547, 53548, 53549, 53550, 53552, 53554, 53555, 53557, 53558, 53559, 53560, 53562, 53566, 53567, 53568, 53571, 53572, 53573, 53577, 53578
United Warehouse Co, 53581
URS Logistics, 53525, 53526
US Growers Cold Storage, 53527
Valley Distributors & Storage Company, 53583
Valley International Cold Storage, Inc., 53584

885

Warehouse Type and Service / Trucking

Van Brunt Port Jersey Warehouse, 53586
Vermont Commercial Warehouse, 53589
Verst Group Logistics Inc, 53592
W J Beitler Co & Beitler Truck, 53595
W T Young Storage Co, 53597
Walsh Transportation Group, 53600
Ward Trucking Corporation, 53601

Warehouse Associates LP, 53602
Warehouse Specialists Inc, 53604
Warehousing of Wisconsin, 53606
Weber Logistics, 53612, 53613
West Brothers Trailer Rental, 53624
West Logistics, 53625
West Texas Warehouse Company, 53626

Western Gateway Storage Co, 53628
Whiting Distribution Services, 53629
William B Meyer Inc, 53630
Williamson Cold Storage Inc, 53632
Willis Day Storage, 53633
Wilmington Bonded Warehouse, 53634
Wilmington Cold Storage, 53635

WOW Logistics, 53598
XPO Logistics, 53640
York Rail Logistics, 53643
Zero Mountain, Inc., 53645

WHOLESALERS & DISTRIBUTORS

User Guide
Company Profiles
Wholesale Product Type Index

Wholesaler & Distributor User Guide

The **Wholesalers & Distributors Chapter** of *Food & Beverage Market Place* includes companies that offer products or services wholesale to the food and beverage industry, or offers distribution services. The descriptive listings are organized alphabetically. Following the A-Z Wholesalers & Distributors listings is a **Wholesale Product Type Index**, organized by type of product that is wholesaled of distributed. This Index refers to listing numbers, not page numbers.

Below is a sample listing illustrating the kind of information that is or might be included in a Wholesaler & Distributor listing. Each numbered item of information is described in the User Key on the following page.

---

1 → 320044

2 → **(HQ) A.W. Distribution Company**

3 → 43 South Water Street

Chicago, IL 60608

4 → 012-222-0808

5 → 012-222-0809

6 → 888-222-0810

7 → info@AWDist.com

8 → www.AWDist.com

9 → Wholesaler/distributor of dairy products; serving supermarkets and independent stores.

10 → Chairman: Martin Pearl
CFO: Tim Johnson
COO: Jessica Thompson
Vice President: Laura Tilly
Marketing: Sandy Bradshaw
Sales: Kathleen Morengo

11 → *Estimated Sales*: $10-25 Million

12 → *Number Employees*: 240

13 → *Sq. Footage*: 20000

14 → *Other Locations.*: A.W. Distribution Company, Sun Valley, CA

15 → *Private Brands Carried*: CalSium

16 → *Number of Customer Locations*: 250

17 → *Types of products Distributed:* Health Food

18 → *Storage Facility Data*: Freezer Size: 10,000 Sq. Ft.

Wholesaler & Distributor Companies User Key

1 → **Record Number:** Entries are listed alphabetically within each category and numbered sequentially. The entry number, rather than the page number, is used in the indexes to refer to listings.

2 → **Company Name:** Formal name of company. HQ indicates headquarter location. If names are completely capitalized, the listing will appear at the beginning of the alphabetized section.

3 → **Address:** Location or permanent address of the company. If the mailing address differs from the street address, it will appear second.

4 → **Phone Number:** The listed phone number is usually for the main office, but may also be for the sales, marketing, or public relations office as provided.

5 → **Fax Number:** This is listed when provided by the company.

6 → **Toll-Free Number:** This is listed when provided by the company.

7 → **E-Mail:** This is listed when provided, and is generally the main office e-mail.

8 → **Web Site:** This is listed when provided by the company and is also referred to as an URL address. These web sites are accessed through the Internet by typing http:// before the URL address.

9 → **Description:** This paragraph contains a brief description of products that the company wholesales and distributes.

10 → **Key Personnel:** Names and titles of company executives.

11 → **Estimated Sales:** This is listed when provided by the company.

12 → **Number of Employees:** Total number of employees within the company.

13 → **Square Footage:** Size of facility.

14 → **Other Locations:** Indicates other company locations.

15 → **Private Brands Carried:** Listing of brand names carried by the company.

16 → **Number of customer locations:** The number of locations that sell the company's products.

17 → **Types of products distributed:** This indicates food or beverage type. Companies are indexed by product type.

Wholesalers & Distributors / A-Z

54501 1000 Islands River Rat Cheese
242 James St
Clayton, NY 13624-1010   315-686-2480
       Fax: 315-686-4701 800-752-1341
       support@riverratcheese.net
       www.riverratcheese.net
Distributor: NYS Cheese, Adirondack Sausage
President: Mary Scudera
1000islandsriverratcheese@gmail.com
Estimated Sales: $2,500,000
Number Employees: 10-19
Type of Packaging: Consumer, Food Service, Private Label, Bulk
Private Brands Carried:
   River Rat Cheese; T.J. River Rat; Gold Cup, Adirondack Cheese
Number of Customer Locations: 3
Types of Products Distributed:
   Food Service, Provisions/Meat, Seafood, Specialty Foods

54502 1642
2025 rue Parthenais
Suite 318
Montreal, QC H2K 3T2
Canada
                                800-774-4907
         info@1642.ca www.1642.ca
Soft drinks
Types of Products Distributed:
   Soda

54503 (HQ)4M Fruit Distribution
34 Market St
Suite 18
Everett, MA 02149   617-387-7575
       Fax: 617-387-7272 maria@4mfruit.com
                              4mfruit.com
Importer and distributor of produce, including apples, appricots, berries, cherries, cantalopes, figs, grapefruit, grapes, kiwi, lemons, mixed melons, pears, oranges, peaches, plums, pomegranates, quince, tangelos, tangerines watermelon, nectarines, and more.
President & Principal: Mark DeFrancesco
mark@4mfruit.com
Officer Manager: Maria DeFrancesco *Year Founded:* 1996
Type of Packaging: Consumer, Food Service

54504 518 Corporation
518 Martin Luther King Jr.
Savannah, GA 31401-4881   912-232-1141
               Fax: 912-236-7969
President: Louis C Mathews III
Estimated Sales: $5-10 Million
Number Employees: 10-19

54505 5280 Produce
1890 E 58th Ave
Denver, CO 80216   303-292-1303
               www.5280produce.com
Wholesaler/distributor of produce.
Founder & Owner: Brad Jester
Founder & Owner: Michael Martelli, Jr.
Business Manager & Accountant: Megan Ficco
Year Founded: 2013
Estimated Sales: $20-50 Million
Number Employees: 50-99
Types of Products Distributed:
   Produce

54506 7 Seas Submarine
11216 S Michigan Ave
Chicago, IL 60628-4910   773-785-0550
               Fax: 312-942-0236
Owner: Natibad Cortez
natibadcortez@hrblock.com
Estimated Sales: Less Than $500,000
Number Employees: 1-4

54507 88 Acres
P.O. Box 79
Allston, MA 02121   617-208-8651
               hello@88acres.com
                         88acres.com
Seed bars, seed granola, and seed butters
Co-Founder: Rob Dalton
Co-Founder: Nicole Ledoux
Marketing Manager: Dayna Scandone
Director of Sales: J.D. Collins
Other Locations:
   Bakery
   Dorchester, MA Bakery

Types of Products Distributed:
   General Line

54508 A & A Global Industries Inc
17 Stenerson Ln
Cockeysville, MD 21030-2113   410-252-1020
      Fax: 410-252-7137 800-638-6000
       contact@aaglobal.com www.aaglobal.com
Wholesaler/distributor of candy vending machines
President: Edward B Kovens
ekovens@aaglobalind.com
Vice President: Brian Kovens
VP: Steve Kovens
Marketing Director: Italy McElroy
Sales Director: Gerry Clothier
Estimated Sales: $300,000-500,000
Number Employees: 100-249
Type of Packaging: Consumer, Private Label, Bulk
Types of Products Distributed:
   Candy, Gum

54509 A & B Distributing Co
107 Randolph St
Knoxville, TN 37915-1194   865-525-9000
       Fax: 865-525-7167 800-257-7644
                www.aandbdistributors.com
Wholesaler/distributor of specialty foods, groceries, meats, dairy products, frozen foods and bakery products; serving the food service market
President: Sam Pavlis
sam@aandbdistributing.com
Operations: S Pavlis
Estimated Sales: $10-20 Million
Number Employees: 10-19
Types of Products Distributed:
   Food Service, Frozen Food, General Line, Provisions/Meat, Specialty Foods, Bakery & dairy products, etc.

54510 A & D Seafood Corp
2501 Knapp St
Brooklyn, NY 11235-1007   718-769-9447
               Fax: 718-769-9448
Wholesaler/distributor of lobsters
Manager: William McCoy
Estimated Sales: Less Than $500,000
Number Employees: 1-4
Types of Products Distributed:
   Frozen Food, Seafood, Lobsters

54511 A & G Foods
6945 S State St
Chicago, IL 60637-4528   773-783-1672
               Fax: 773-994-9623
Owner: Sam Johnson
Estimated Sales: $3-5 Million
Number Employees: 10-19

54512 A & W Wholesale Co Inc
2525 Phillips Field Rd
Fairbanks, AK 99709-3942   907-452-2138
       Fax: 907-451-8411 888-236-4867
                www.awwholesale.com
Wholesaler/distributor of restaurant supplies and smallware; serving the food service industry
President: Wayne Walker
Estimated Sales: $2.5-5 Million
Number Employees: 10-19
Types of Products Distributed:
   Food Service, Frozen Food, General Merchandise, Restaurant supplies & smallware

54513 A Better Way
3233 Fee Fee Rd
Bridgeton, MO 63044-3208   314-739-1492
               www.a-better-way.com
Wholesaler/distributor of herbs, extracts, vitamins, minerals and weight management products including alfalfa, chamomile, garlic, damiana, etc
Owner: Duane Weed
drweed@a-better-way.com
Estimated Sales: $300,000-500,000
Number Employees: 1-4
Types of Products Distributed:
   Frozen Food, Health Food, Alfalfa, garlic, ginger, etc.

54514 A Couple of Squares, Inc
501-B Nightingale Avenue
London, ON N5W 4C4
Canada
                                519-672-6979
       Fax: 519-672-4487 866-672-6979
               info@acoupleofsquares.com
               www.acoupleofsquares.com

Cookie manufacturer and wholesaler.
Director of Marketing: Bernadette Erb
Sales Marketing: Carol Dobbin
Square Footage: 9000

54515 A Daigger & Co Inc
620 Lakeview Pkwy
Vernon Hills, IL 60061-1828   847-816-5060
       Fax: 847-816-5051 www.daigger.com
Distributor of laboratory equipment and supplies for food manufacturing research and development.
President: Jim Woldenberg
Owner: Lou Iannuzzelli
CFO: Mike Dost
Account Manager: Rebecca Earl
Human Resources: Sandra Mack
Marketing/Communications Manager: Amber Halteman
Sales Manager: Marc Friedman
International Sales: Armando Cardenas
Director of Operations: Mike Espinosa
Information Technology Manager: Tim Bruess
Purchasing Manager: Dan Churchill
Estimated Sales: $44 Million
Number Employees: 50-99

54516 A Dattilo Fruit Co
211 W Main St
Madison, IN 47250-3707   812-265-5431
               Fax: 812-265-5537
Wholesaler/distributor of produce
President: Anthony Dattilo
Estimated Sales: $5-10 Million
Number Employees: 5-9
Number of Customer Locations: 40
Types of Products Distributed:
   Frozen Food, Produce

54517 A J Linz Sons
2855 Henshaw Ave
Cincinnati, OH 45225-2207   513-541-3931
Wholesaler/distributor of pickles and sauerkraut; serving the food service market
Owner: Bill Linz
Estimated Sales: $500,000-$1 Million
Number Employees: 1-4
Number of Customer Locations: 400
Types of Products Distributed:
   Food Service, Frozen Food, General Line, Pickles & sauerkraut

54518 A J Oster Foils LLC
2081 Mccrea St
Alliance, OH 44601-2793   330-823-1700
       Fax: 330-823-1705 800-321-9750
       osteroh@ajoster.com www.ajoster.com
Wholesaler/distributor of coated and bare aluminum foil in coil or cut sheet sizes for food packaging applications
Manager: Beth Tirey
beth.tirey@ajoster.com
Sales Manager: Beth Tirey
General Sales Manager: Ed Schilling
Estimated Sales: $1-2.5 Million
Number Employees: 50-99
Square Footage: 312000
Parent Co: Olin Brass
Types of Products Distributed:
   Frozen Food, General Merchandise, Aluminum foil for food packaging

54519 A J Rinella Co Inc
381 Broadway # 6
Menands, NY 12204-2741   518-465-4581
       Fax: 518-465-0446 ajproduce@aol.com
Wholesaler/distributor of produce; serving the food service market
Owner: A J Rinella
ajproduce@aol.com
VP: A Rinella
General Manager: Paul Rinella
Estimated Sales: $10-20 Million
Number Employees: 10-19
Types of Products Distributed:
   Food Service, Produce

54520 A J Silberman & Co
838 Braddock Ave
Braddock, PA 15104-1747   412-271-3373
       Fax: 412-271-1987 www.silbermans.com
Wholesaler/distributor of groceries, frozen food, equipment and fixtures, general merchandise, health and beauty aids, snacks and general line products; serving the food service market

Wholesalers & Distributors / A-Z

President: Alfred Silberman
President: David Silberman
Contact: Amy Flanagan
amy.flanagan@silbermans.com
Buyer: Matt Silberman
Estimated Sales: $20-50 Million
Number Employees: 5-9
Number of Customer Locations: 2500
Types of Products Distributed:
   Food Service, Frozen Food, General Line, General Merchandise, Snacks, etc.

54521 A La Mode Distributors
105 Dempsey Road
Madison, WI 53714-3003   608-249-7413
                          Fax: 608-249-2648
Wholesaler/distributor of ice cream, desserts and specialty frozen and refrigerated foods; serving the food service market
President: Michael Olson
Estimated Sales: $1-2.5 Million
Number Employees: 10-19
Square Footage: 20000
Types of Products Distributed:
   Food Service, General Line, Specialty Foods, Desserts: ice cream

54522 A Plus Marketing
708 Viewpoint Drive
St. Charles, IL 60174   630-513-1300
            Fax: 630-443-5188 877-517-700
            francine@aplusmarketing.org
            www.aplusmarketing.org
Wholesaler/distributor of nutritional supplements including vitamins, herbs and herbal remedies
President: Francine Vienne
Vice President: Peter Vienne
Types of Products Distributed:
   Frozen Food, Health Food, Vitamins, herbs & herbal remedies

54523 A Tarantino & Sons Poultry
2275 Jennings St
San Francisco, CA 94124-3266   415-822-3366
                          Fax: 415-822-4463
Wholesaler/distributor of fresh and frozen chicken, turkey, shellfish and fillets; serving the food service market
Owner: Angela Tarantino
angela@atarantinoandsons.com
Secretary: Angela Lynn Tarantino
Estimated Sales: $20-50 Million
Number Employees: 20-49
Square Footage: 10000
Types of Products Distributed:
   Food Service, Frozen Food, Provisions/Meat, Seafood, Poultry

54524 A Taste for Life
11025 Carolina Place Pkwy
Pineville, NC 28134   908-591-1507
            ataste4life@gmail.com
            www.ataste.net
Gourmet Spanish foods

54525 A&A Halal Distributors
5165 Forsyth Commerce Rd
Orlando, FL 32807   407-282-3200
            www.aahalal.com
Halal meats, cold cuts, fish, beverages, groceries, pharmaceuticals
Owner: Mohamed Assim
Types of Products Distributed:
   Provisions/Meat

54526 A&A Spice and Food
8101 Presidents Dr
Orlando, FL 32809   407-851-9432
       Fax: 407-857-7171 www.spiceworldinc.com
President: Andrew Caneza
Estimated Sales: $5-10 Million
Number Employees: 100-249

54527 A&D Distributors
631 Tremont St
Boston, MA 02118-1256   617-859-0222
            Fax: 978-459-0071 866-289-2733
            thedoughball@aol.com
Wholesaler/distributor of bakery, pizza and pasta ingredients, frozen foods, produce, baked goods, dairy products, kosher, organic and specialty items. Distributor of ingredients to bakeries, bagel shops, patisseries and foodmanufacturers, large and small

Owner: Al Maroun
Marketing/Sales Executive: Brendan Hyatt
Office Manager: Carol Corriveau
Estimated Sales: $8-10 Million
Number Employees: 1-4
Square Footage: 240000
Private Brands Carried:
   Pillsbury; Fleischman's; Bax State Milling; North Dakota; Quality Ingredients Corporation
Number of Customer Locations: 175
Types of Products Distributed:
   Frozen Food, General Line, Health Food, Specialty Foods, Baked goods, ingredients, etc.

54528 A&H Seafood Market
4960 Bethesda Ave
Bethesda, MD 20814   301-986-9692
                          Fax: 301-986-5555
Owner: Santi Zabaleta
Sales Manager: Kalimar Maia
Contact: Herminio Martinez
martinez@anhmarket.com
Estimated Sales: $.5-1 million
Number Employees: 1-4

54529 A&J Food Wholesalers, Inc.
25 Brooklyn Terminal Market
Brooklyn, NY 11236   718-251-7144
                          Fax: 718-209-2511
Wholesaler/distributor of groceries and general merchandise
President: Steven Di Paola
VP: D Fischer
Estimated Sales: $5-10 Million
Number Employees: 5-9
Number of Customer Locations: 400
Types of Products Distributed:
   Frozen Food, General Line, General Merchandise, Groceries

54530 A&J Forklift & Equipment
11425 Woodside Ave
Santee, CA 92071-4718   619-562-6862
            Fax: 935-562-4054 888-805-5438
Wholesaler/distributor of automatic storage and handling systems
Estimated Sales: $3-5 Million
Number Employees: 5-9
Types of Products Distributed:
   Frozen Food, General Merchandise, Automatic storage & handling systems

54531 A&J Produce Corporation
138 Bronx Terminal Market
#144
Bronx, NY 10474   718-589-7877
            Fax: 718-378-1095 800-223-8054
            ajprodny@aol.com www.ajproduce.com
Wholesaler/distributor of produce; serving the food service market
VP: Al Weiler
Sales Manager: Thomas Tramutola
Contact: Frankie Rivera
frivera@ajproduce.com
Estimated Sales: $3-5 Million
Number Employees: 5-9
Types of Products Distributed:
   Food Service, Frozen Food, Produce

54532 A&M Enterprises
3424 1st St
Oceanside, NY 11572
                          Fax: 516-536-3635
Wholesaler/distributor of health products including vitamins; also, coffee, beef snacks, nutritional bars and nut mixes; serving food service operators; rack jobber services available, espresso machines
Owner: Larry Cohen
Type of Packaging: Food Service, Private Label, Bulk
Private Brands Carried:
   Pioneer Beef; Fresh Start Vitimay Co.; Coffee Roaster
Types of Products Distributed:
   Food Service, Health Food, Provisions/Meat, Rack Jobbers, Coffee, vitamins & snack foods

54533 A&M Seafood Company
207 Saint Peter Street
Houma, LA 70363-6751   985-876-4185
                          Fax: 504-868-6313

54534 A&S Crawfish
6960 Chataignier Rd
Eunice, LA 70535   337-885-5565
                          Fax: 318-885-2150
Owner: Aubry Brown

54535 A-1 Seafood Center
1627 Route 37 E
Toms River, NJ 08753-5755   732-929-1118
                          Fax: 732-929-1113
Wholesaler/distributor of seafood, general merchandise, equipment and fixtures
Owner: Virginia Sisler
Operations Manager: Donna Sisler
Estimated Sales: Less than $500,000
Number Employees: 1-4
Types of Products Distributed:
   Frozen Food, General Line, General Merchandise, Seafood, Equipment & fixtures

54536 A-A1 Aaction Bag
5601 Logan St
Denver, CO 80216-1301   303-297-9955
            Fax: 303-297-9960 800-783-1224
            www.centralbag.com
Manufacturer and wholesaler/distributor of packaging materials including paper and plastic bags, deli containers, cups and packaging for meats and seafood; also, custom printed and plain bags available
President: Esther Seaman
CEO: Elly Zussman
elly@centralbag.com
CFO: David Fine
Vice President: Morton Zussman
VP, Marketing: Morty Zussman
Sales: Chuck Fine
Operations Manager: David Zussman
Estimated Sales: $5 Million
Number Employees: 10-19
Square Footage: 70000
Parent Co: Al-AAction Bag Company
Type of Packaging: Consumer, Food Service, Private Label, Bulk
Types of Products Distributed:
   Frozen Food, General Merchandise, Paper & plastic bags, packaging, etc.

54537 A-B Products
PO Box 185
North Lima, OH 44452-0185   330-758-9382
                          Fax: 330-758-7772
Wholesaler/distributor of material handling equipment including conveyors, pallet rack, wire shelving, bins, hand trucks, storage shelving, work stations, win displays, insulated cabinets
President: John Hjerpe
Sales/Marketing Executive: Terri Hauser
Estimated Sales: $1-2.5 Million
Number Employees: 1-4
Private Brands Carried:
   Ridge-U-Rak; Inner Metro; Wesco
Types of Products Distributed:
   General Merchandise, Material handling equipment

54538 A-Line Electric Supply Inc
8704 Foster Ave
Brooklyn, NY 11236-3209   718-257-4100
            Fax: 718-257-5315 www.alineelectric.com
Wholesaler/distributor of electrical supplies including outlet boxes, lighting fixtures, electric and fluorescent lamps, light bulbs and emergency lights
Owner: John Rendo
aline996@aol.com
Operations Manager: Frank Rendo
Estimated Sales: $1-2.5 Million
Number Employees: 5-9
Square Footage: 12000
Private Brands Carried:
   Osram Sylvania; Thomas & Betts; Challenger
Number of Customer Locations: 200
Types of Products Distributed:
   Frozen Food, General Merchandise, Electrical supplies

54539 A. Berkowitz & Company
731 Pinehurst Lane
Buffalo Grove, IL 60089-1533   312-243-0808
                          Fax: 312-243-0811
Wholesaler/distributor of produce; serving the food service market
Co-Owner: Steve Berkowitz
Estimated Sales: $1-2.5 Million
Number Employees: 5-9

Wholesalers & Distributors / A-Z

Types of Products Distributed:
  Food Service, Produce

54540 A. Bohrer
50 Knickerbocker Road
Moonachie, NJ 07074-1613 201-935-3055
Fax: 201-935-3579 800-631-0086
Wholesaler/distributor of produce, frozen foods, groceries, dairy products and meats; serving the food service market
President: Arthur Bohrer
Contact: Anthony Battle
anthony_battle@lincolnelectric.com
Number Employees: 100-249
Private Brands Carried:
  Nugget; Wendy
Types of Products Distributed:
  Food Service, Frozen Food, General Line, Provisions/Meat, Produce, Groceries & dairy products

54541 A. De LaChevrotiere
Cp940
Rouyn-Noranda, QC J9X 2C5
Canada 819-797-1900
Fax: 819-797-1327
ebeaupre.adl@cablevision.qc.ca
Wholesaler/distributor of meat, frozen foods, general line products and produce; serving the food service market; also, rack jobber services available
President/CEO: R Cloutier
Marketing Director: J Dame
Head Buyer: R Robichaud
Number Employees: 250-499
Square Footage: 540000
Parent Co: J. Montemurro
Private Brands Carried:
  Metlo; Super C; Richelieu; Grad
Number of Customer Locations: 400
Types of Products Distributed:
  Food Service, Frozen Food, General Line, Provisions/Meat, Produce, Rack Jobbers

54542 A. Friscia Seafoods
483 Alameda De La Loma
Novato, CA 94949-5967 415-673-8650
Fax: 415-673-9972
Wholesaler/distributor of fresh and frozen seafood; serving the food service market
President: Anthony Friscia
Estimated Sales: $2.5-5 Million
Number Employees: 5-9
Types of Products Distributed:
  Food Service, Frozen Food, Seafood

54543 A. Gagliano Co Inc
300 N Jefferson St # 1
PO Box 511382
Milwaukee, WI 53202-5920 414-272-1515
Fax: 414-272-7215 800-272-1516
info@agagliano.com
Fresh fruits and vegetables
Owner: Anthony Gagliano
tony@agagliano.com
Owner: Nick Gagliano
Owner: Mike Gagliano
Warehouse Manager: Rick Alsum
Estimated Sales: $20 Million
Number Employees: 50-99
Number of Brands: 1
Number of Products: 500
Square Footage: 200000
Type of Packaging: Consumer, Food Service, Private Label, Bulk
Private Brands Carried:
  Gagliano
Types of Products Distributed:
  Produce

54544 A. Nonini Winery
2640 N Dickenson Ave
Fresno, CA 93723-9644 559-275-1936
Fax: 209-241-7119 noniniwinery@gmail.com
Wine
President & Wine Maker: James Jordan
noniniwinery@gmail.com
Estimated Sales: $1-2.5 Million
Number Employees: 1-4
Type of Packaging: Private Label

54545 (HQ)A. Sargenti Company
240 Food Center Drive
Bronx, NY 10474-7030 718-842-0630
Fax: 718-206-7343 800-464-6990
Wholesaler/distributor of specialty groceries and condiments
President: Philip Sargent
VP: Robert Sargent
Number Employees: 20-49
Types of Products Distributed:
  Frozen Food, General Line, Specialty Foods, Condiments

54546 A. Simos & Company
62 Avocado St
Springfield, MA 1104 413-734-8232
Fax: 413-734-8234 800-648-6008
businessfinder.masslive.com
Wholesaler/distributor of fresh fruits, vegetables, frozen foods and groceries; serving the food service market
President: Tony Delis
VP: William Delia
VP: Chris O'Leazy
Estimated Sales: $10-20 Million
Number Employees: 10-19
Square Footage: 40000
Types of Products Distributed:
  Food Service, Frozen Food, General Line, Produce

54547 A. Visconti Company
14 Brooklyn Terminal Market
Brooklyn, NY 11236 718-241-7777
Fax: 718-763-6838
Wholesaler/distributor of produce
Owner: A Visconti
Estimated Sales: Less than $500,000
Number Employees: 5-9
Types of Products Distributed:
  Frozen Food, Produce

54548 A.B. Wise & Sons
900 Albert Street
Youngstown, OH 44505-2968 513-874-9642
Fax: 513-874-1229 800-837-9642
hirschey@aol.com
Wholesaler/distributor of seafood, equipment and fixtures, groceries, produce, meats, dairy and baked products and health and frozen foods; serving the retail and food service markets
President: Hirsch Wise
Square Footage: 120000
Parent Co: Miller Buckeye Biscuit Company
Other Locations:
  Wise, A.B., & Sons
  Atlanta, GAWise, A.B., & Sons
Private Brands Carried:
  Queen Ester
Number of Customer Locations: 3000
Types of Products Distributed:
  Food Service, Frozen Food, General Line, Health Food, Provisions/Meat, Produce, Seafood, Specialty Foods, Groceries

54549 A.C. Covert
500 Thorne Ave
Dartmouth, NS B3B 1Y5
Canada 902-454-8688
Fax: 902-453-6249 800-565-7915
www.accovert.com
Wholesaler/distributor of fresh and frozen fish fillets
Managing Director: Bob Convert
Types of Products Distributed:
  Frozen Food, Seafood

54550 A.C. Inc.
125 Black Duck Cove Rd
Beals, ME 04611 207-497-2261
Fax: 207-497-2731
Seafood wholesaler
President, CEO & Co-Owner: Albert Carver
Vice President & Co-Owner: Patrick Robinson

54551 A.C. Kissling Company
161 E Allen St
Philadelphia, PA 19125-4194 215-423-4700
Fax: 215-425-0525 800-445-1943
Sauerkraut
President: R W Kissling Jr
Contact: R Kissling
kaultejk@yahoo.com
Estimated Sales: $2 Million
Number Employees: 10-19
Type of Packaging: Consumer
Types of Products Distributed:
  General Line, Provisions/Meat, Sauerkraut

54552 A.G. Lobster
78 Reach Road
Deer Isle, ME 04627-3344 207-367-2488
Fax: 207-367-2493

54553 A.J. Jersey
125 Saint Nicholas Ave
South Plainfield, NJ 07080 908-754-7333
Fax: 908-754-6188 800-675-7337
www.ajjersey.net
Wholesaler/distributor of material handling equipment including trucks
President: David Rizzo
VP Sales: John Robertson
Contact: Bryan Aller
bryana@ajjersey.net
Number Employees: 50-99
Square Footage: 80000
Private Brands Carried:
  Crown; Daewoo; Interlake
Types of Products Distributed:
  Frozen Food, General Merchandise, Material handling equipment & trucks

54554 A.L. Duck Jr Inc
26231 River Run Trail
Zuni, VA 23898-3215 757-562-2387
Smoked sausage
President: Brenda Redd
Estimated Sales: $1-2.5 Million
Number Employees: 5-9
Type of Packaging: Consumer, Food Service

54555 A.L. Verna Company
929 S 2nd Street
Philadelphia, PA 19147-4202 215-465-9840
Fax: 215-551-1762
Wholesaler/distributor of garlic, spices and nuts; serving the food service market
Owner/President: William Verna
Estimated Sales: $5-10 Million
Number Employees: 10-19
Types of Products Distributed:
  Food Service, Produce, Specialty Foods, Garlic, spices & nuts

54556 A.M.BRIGGS
2130 Queens Chapel Road
Washington, DC 20018-3608 202-832-2600
Fax: 202-269-0534 800-929-6655
Wholesaler/distributor of meats, seafood, orange and grapefruit juice and specialty foods; serving the food service market
President: Chuck Harris
CEO: Charles Harris Jr
Contact: Butch Baxter
gbaxter@ambriggs.com
Number Employees: 100-249
Square Footage: 100000
Parent Co: Sysco Corporation
Types of Products Distributed:
  Food Service, General Line, Provisions/Meat, Seafood, Specialty Foods, Orange & grapefruit juice

54557 A/R Packaging Corporation
PO Box 466
Brookfield, WI 53008-0466 262-549-1500
Fax: 262-549-3711 800-414-0125
wiorders@spectrumcorporation.com
www.arpackaging.com
Contract packager and exporter of specialty lubricants; wholesaler/distributor of industrial lubricants
Chairman: Alan Baumann
Executive Vice President: Craig Baumann
VP Sales: Bruce Davidson
Contact: Brian Leach
bleach@spectrumcorporation.com
Plant Manager: Greg Wrobbel
Estimated Sales: $1-2.5 Million
Number Employees: 20-49
Square Footage: 200000
Type of Packaging: Private Label
Types of Products Distributed:
  Frozen Food, General Merchandise, Industrial lubricants

54558 A2 Milk Company
P.O. Box 20651
Boulder, CO 80308 844-422-6455
hello@a2milk.com
www.a2milk.com
Milk
Chief Executive USA: Blake Waltrip

Wholesalers & Distributors / A-Z

Parent Co: Hain Celestial Group
Types of Products Distributed:
    Dairy

54559 A2Z Specialty Advertising
13 Eglin Pkwy NE
Fort Walton Bch, FL 32548-4914   850-654-3080
    Fax: 850-654-3070 Gabby@a2zDestin.com
    www.a2zspecialtyadv.com
Wholesaler/distributor of flags, pennants, banners and advertising specialties
Owner: Gabby Bruce
gabby@a2zdestin.com
Estimated Sales: Less Than $500,000
Number Employees: 1-4
Number of Customer Locations: 500
Types of Products Distributed:
    Frozen Food, General Merchandise, Flags, pennants, banners, etc.

54560 AA Specialty Advertising Products
24705 Silverwood Lane
Howey In the Hills, FL 34737-3702   407-869-4900
Wholesaler/distributor of advertising and promotional items including matchbooks, uniforms and chef hats; serving the food service market
President: Stephen Kane
Number Employees: 1-4
Number of Customer Locations: 400
Types of Products Distributed:
    Food Service, Frozen Food, General Merchandise, Advertising & promotional items

54561 AANTEC
3116 N Pointer Rd
Appleton, WI 54911   920-830-9723
    Fax: 920-830-9840
Packaging equipment; case packers, palletizers, tray packers/formers, case erectors/sealers, napkin folders, towel and tissue interfolders, tissue rewinders, napkin wrappers and bundlers, roll wrappers, conveyors, grip per elevators and lowerators, high-speed case-packers
President: Robert Schuh
VP: Corben Hoffman
Sales: Jeffrey Aissen
Public Relations: Julia Kirsch
Operations: Paul Tassoul
Estimated Sales: $5-10 Million
Number Employees: 10-19
Type of Packaging: Consumer, Food Service, Private Label, Bulk
Private Brands Carried:
    Involvo, TMC, Schneider, PackAir, Bretting, AANTEC
Types of Products Distributed:
    Frozen Food, General Merchandise

54562 ABC Country Club Coffee
2506 W Central Park Ave
Davenport, IA 52804-2503   563-386-4700
    Fax: 563-386-4337 www.countryclubcoffee.com
Wholesaler/distributor of coffee
Owner: Drake Bishop
Estimated Sales: $20-50 Million
Number Employees: 5-9
Private Brands Carried:
    Folgers; Superior
Types of Products Distributed:
    Frozen Food, General Line, Coffee

54563 ABCO HVACR Supply & Solutions
49-70 31st St
Long Island City, NY 11101   718-937-9000
    Fax: 718-937-9776 abcohvacr.com
Wholesaler/distributor of food service equipment including ice machines.
Manager: Vincent Riker
vriker@abco.co
Estimated Sales: $50-100 Million
Number Employees: 50-99
Private Brands Carried:
    Manitowoc
Number of Customer Locations: 50
Types of Products Distributed:
    Frozen Food, General Merchandise, Foodservice equipment

54564 ABI Limited
8900 Keele Street, Unit 1
Concord, ON L4K 2N2
Canada   905-738-6070
    Fax: 905-738-6085 800-297-8666
    info@abiltd.com
ABI Ltd. manufacturers automated food processing equipment with the emphasis on performance, durability, reliability and simplicity in maintenance.
President: Alex Kuperman
Marketing: Regine Kuperman
Production VP: Mike Kuperman
Number Employees: 20
Square Footage: 60000
Types of Products Distributed:
    Frozen Food

54565 ABM Industries
3424 Garfield Ave
Commerce, CA 90040-3104   323-767-4000
    Fax: 323-767-4037 www.2onesource.com
Wholesaler/distributor of janitorial supplies
Manager: Mark Olivas
Estimated Sales: $1-3 Million
Number Employees: 50-99
Square Footage: 1000000
Types of Products Distributed:
    Frozen Food, General Merchandise, Janitorial items

54566 AC Paper & Supply
P.O. Box 4466
Hayward, CA 94540   510-964-0600
    Fax: 510-964-9100 800-547-2737
Wholesaler/distributor of paper, plastic and styrofoam cups and plates, janitorial supplies and restaurant disposables; also, syrups and salt-free and sugar-free seasonings
President: Ted Robinson
CEO: Deanna Robinson
CFO: Jeff Robinson
Vice President: David Robinson
Sales/Marketing Executive: Jeff Robinson
Purchasing Agent: Antonio Spann
Estimated Sales: $5-10 Million
Number Employees: 10-19
Square Footage: 200000
Type of Packaging: Consumer, Food Service, Private Label
Types of Products Distributed:
    Food Service, General Line, Disposables, salt-free seasonings, etc.

54567 ACC Distributors Inc
300 Oakland Ct
Highway 82 West
Leesburg, GA 31763   229-432-9141
    Fax: 229-431-2307 800-476-9141
    meganrogers@accdistributors.com
    www.accdistributors.com
Wholesaler/distributor of produce, meats, dairy and frozen products, baked goods, equipment and fixtures, general merchandise, seafood, private label items, etc.; serving the food service market.
Owner: Martha McWhorter
Manager: Megan Rogers
Accounts Payable: Stacie McNamar
Vice President, Legal: Anthony Hawkins
Marketing: Mitch Logan
Director, Sales: Bernie Waters
marthamcwhorter@accdistributors.com
Receiving: Louie Goodwin
Purchasing: De Rogers
Estimated Sales: $13 Million
Number Employees: 50-99
Square Footage: 25000
Private Brands Carried:
    NIFDA
Types of Products Distributed:
    Food Service, Frozen Food, General Line, General Merchandise, Provisions/Meat, Produce, Seafood

54568 ACK Industrial Electronics
554 Deering Rd NW
Atlanta, GA 30309-2267   404-351-6340
    Fax: 404-351-1879 www.acksupply.com
Wholesaler/distributor of electrical supplies, lighting, tools and instruments
Owner: Steve Atkerson
gasales@acksupply.com
Number Employees: 1-4
Number of Customer Locations: 100

Types of Products Distributed:
    Frozen Food, General Merchandise, Electrical supplies, etc.

54569 ACME Sign Corp
3 Lakeland Park Dr
Peabody, MA 01960-3835   978-535-6600
    Fax: 978-536-5051 info@acmesigncorp.com
    www.acmesigncorp.com
Custom sign manufacturer and supplier
President: Darius Aleksas
darius@acmesigncorp.com
Estimated Sales: $1 Million
Number Employees: 1-4
Square Footage: 16000
Types of Products Distributed:
    Frozen Food

54570 ADE Restaurant Service
471 S Irmen Dr
Addison, IL 60101   630-628-0811
    Fax: 630-628-0825 www.adefoodservice.com
Wholesaler/distributor of food service equipment; serving the food service market
President: Steve Schoop
VP: Raymond Hickey
Contact: Dolores Chantos
dchantos@adefoodservice.com
Estimated Sales: $3-5 Million
Number Employees: 10-19
Private Brands Carried:
    Hobart; True; Vulcan
Types of Products Distributed:
    Food Service, Frozen Food, General Merchandise, Equipment

54571 ADI
263 Old Country Rd
Melville, NY 11747-2712   631-692-1508
    Fax: 714-283-9254 800-245-2498
    awebadmin@adi-dist.com www.adiglobal.us
Wholesaler/distributor of burglar and fire alarms; also, video/card access security
Manager: Andy Applegate
CEO: Dave Cote
dave.cote@honeywell.com
Sales Manager: Gary Gray
Estimated Sales: $2.5-5 Million
Number Employees: 5-9
Parent Co: Ademco
Types of Products Distributed:
    Frozen Food, General Merchandise, Burglar & fire alarms

54572 ADL Group
14631 Best Ave
Norwalk, CA 90650-5258   562-926-5522
    Fax: 562-921-0039 800-423-8837
Vitamins
Supervisor: Joe Bensler
VP: Patricia Heydlauff
National Sales Representative: Ron Coleman
Estimated Sales: $2.5-5 Million
Number Employees: 10-19
Type of Packaging: Private Label

54573 ADT Inc
1501 NW 51st St
Boca Raton, FL 33431-4438
    800-521-1734
    www.adt.com
Wholesaler/distributor of general merchandise including burglar and fire alarm systems, access control systems, security equipment and closed circuit TV.
Chief Executive Officer: Jim DeVries
Chief Financial Officer: Jeff Likosar
Chief Administration Officer: Dan Bresingham
Chief Legal Officer: P. Gray Finney
Chief Customer Officer: Jamie Rosand Haenggi
Chief Information Officer: Donald Young
Year Founded: 1874
Estimated Sales: Over $1 Billion
Number Employees: 18,000
Parent Co: Apollo Global Management
Private Brands Carried:
    ADT
Types of Products Distributed:
    Frozen Food, General Merchandise, Burglar & fire alarms, etc.

Wholesalers & Distributors / A-Z

54574 ADT Security Systems
1714 Bull Street
Savannah, GA 31401-7437   912-236-5539
                Fax: 912-238-0878
Wholesaler/distributor of access control systems including burglar and fire alarm systems and closed circuit TV
Instrument Service Manager: Billy Bonwaldner
Estimated Sales: $20-50 Million
Number Employees: 20-49
Private Brands Carried:
  ADT
Types of Products Distributed:
  Frozen Food, General Merchandise, Burglar & fire alarm systems

54575 AIDP Inc
19535 E Walnut Dr S
City Of Industry, CA 91748-2318   909-718-0124
       Fax: 626-964-6739   866-262-6699
       customercare@aidp.com www.aidp.com
Wholesaler/distributor, importer and exporter of vitamins, specialty chemicals and herbal extracts
President: Edward Lee
edward.lee@aidp.com
SVP: Dave Dannenhold
Director Business Development: Katherine Lund
VP, Business Development: Kathy Lund
Estimated Sales: $1-3 Million
Number Employees: 20-49
Type of Packaging: Bulk
Types of Products Distributed:
  Frozen Food, Health Food, Vitamins & herbal extracts

54576 AIN Plastics
249 E Sandford Boulevard
Mount Vernon, NY 10550-4637   914-668-6800
       Fax: 914-668-8820   800-431-2451
       tmxainad@aol.com
Wholesaler/distributor of plastic rod tube sheet material and accessories
President: Norman Drucker
VP: Alex Gabay
Sales Manager: John Colleluori
Contact: Steven Royer
steven.royer@ainplastic.com
Estimated Sales: $20-50 Million
Number Employees: 100-249
Square Footage: 70000
Types of Products Distributed:
  Frozen Food, General Merchandise, Plastics

54577 AJ Trucco, Inc
343-344 New York City
Terminal Market
Bronx, NY 10474   718-893-3060
       Fax: 718-617-9884 info@truccodirect.com
       www.truccodirect.com
Importer, Distributor and Wholesaler of Chestnuts, Kiwi, Tomatoes, Garlic, Grapes, Figs and Clementines, Hazelnuts, Dried Fruits and Nuts
President: Salvatore Vacca
Partner: Nick Pacia
Estimated Sales: $10-20 Million
Number Employees: 4
Types of Products Distributed:
  Frozen Food

54578 AJC International
1000 Abernathy Rd NE
Suite 600
Atlanta, GA 30328   404-252-6750
       Fax: 404-252-9340 www.ajcfood.com
Wholesaler/distributor of frozen pork, beef, tuna, juice, shellfish, vegetables and poultry; serving the food service market/
Chairman: Gerald Allison
Vice Chairman: Eric Joiner
Chief Executive Officer: Brad Allison
President & Chief Compliance Officer: Evan Davidman
SVP & Chief Financial Officer: John Partington
Secretary & Director, Global Credit: Tina Sorrels
Estimated Sales: $52 Million
Number Employees: 300
Square Footage: 14000
Other Locations:
  AJC International
  San Juan, PRAJC International
Number of Customer Locations: 1000
Types of Products Distributed:
  Food Service, Frozen Food, General Line, Provisions/Meat, Produce, Seafood, Juice

54579 AKC Commodities Inc
1086 Stelton Rd
Piscataway, NJ 08854-5201   732-339-0071
       Fax: 732-339-0073   800-252-1716
       info@akccommodities.com
Importer, exporter and wholesaler/distributor of dried fruits, nuts, spices, beans, basmati rice, seeds, apricots, cashews, dates, pistachio, raisins, organic product and cranberries
Owner: Azam Kadeer
VP: Azam Kadeer
Marketing: Kyas Nazir
Number Employees: 5-9
Type of Packaging: Food Service
Private Brands Carried:
  Arya
Types of Products Distributed:
  Importer & Distributor

54580 AM-Mac
311 US Highway 46 # C
Fairfield, NJ 07004-2419   973-575-7567
       Fax: 973-575-1956   800-829-2018
       ammac1@aol.com www.am-mac.com
Manufacturer and exporter of meat and bread slicers, mixers, vegetable cutters and meat grinders; wholesaler/distributor of food handling and storage equipment, wire shelving and ovens
President: Judith Spritzer
ammac1@aol.com
Vice President: Jon Spritzer
Estimated Sales: $10-20,000,000
Number Employees: 10-19
Types of Products Distributed:
  Frozen Food, General Merchandise, Food handling & storage equipment

54581 AMCON Distributing Co
7405 Irvington Rd
Omaha, NE 68122-1232   402-331-3727
       Fax: 402-331-4834 www.amcon.com
Wholesaler/distributor of confectionery products; serving the food service market
President: Kathleen M Evans
kevans@amcon.com
Chairman and Chief Executive Officer: Christopher Atayan
Vice President and CFO: Andrew Plummer
SVP of Planning and Compliance: Philip Campbell
Director, IT: Glenn Berger
Vice President, Marketing: Rick Vance
Vice President, Sales: Clem O'Donnell
Estimated Sales: Over $1 Billion
Number Employees: 500-999
Types of Products Distributed:
  Food Service, General Line, Confectionery products

54582 AMCON Distributing Co
3125 E Thayer Ave
Bismarck, ND 58501-5170   701-258-3618
       Fax: 701-258-0945   800-220-0176
       www.amcon.com
Wholesaler/distributor of frozen foods, meats, confectionery and general line items; serving the food service market
Manager: John Job
Sales/Marketing Executive: Bill MacKinnon
Manager: Bill Mackinnon
bmackinnon@amcon.com
General Manager: John Jobe
Purchasing Manager: Jim Bender
Estimated Sales: $20-50 Million
Number Employees: 50-99
Square Footage: 45000
Parent Co: Amcon Distributing Company
Private Brands Carried:
  Quality Chef
Number of Customer Locations: 2500
Types of Products Distributed:
  Food Service, Frozen Food, General Line, Provisions/Meat, Candy, etc.

54583 AME Nutrition
545 Metro Place S
Suite 100
Dublin, OH 43017   614-766-3638
       sales@amenutrition.com
       www.amenutrition.com
Plant- and dairy-based ingredients manufacturer
Director of Sales & Marketing: Bill Brickson

54584 AMN Distributors/Premium Blend
2661 W 81st St
Hialeah, FL 33016   305-557-1464
       Fax: 305-557-8454   800-899-0331
       cs@premiumblend.com www.premiumblend.com
Wholesaler/distributor of cocktail mixes, liquors, liquor substitutes and frozen cocktail machinery; serving the food service market
President: Orestes Santos
VP: Enrique Santos
Contact: Cindy House
cindy@premiumblend.com
Estimated Sales: $5-10 Million
Number Employees: 10-19
Square Footage: 20000
Private Brands Carried:
  Premium Blend Rhumbero; Vlast; Tequesta
Types of Products Distributed:
  Food Service, Frozen Food, General Line, General Merchandise, Cocktail mixes, liquors, etc.

54585 AP Fish & Produce
875 Main Street
Worcester, MA 01610-1456   508-756-0834
              Fax: 508-791-2072
Wholesaler/distributor of seafood; serving the food service market
President: Angelo Pizzarella
Types of Products Distributed:
  Food Service, Frozen Food, Seafood

54586 APM
1500 Hillcrest Rd
Norcross, GA 30093-2617   770-921-6300
       Fax: 770-925-7801   800-226-5557
              www.apminc.org
Wholesaler/distributor and importer of mesh bags, pallet netting, bulk containers and pressure sensitive labels
Owner: James Sabourin
Sales Manager: Joel Corner
Estimated Sales: $5-10 Million
Number Employees: 10-19
Parent Co: NNZ Beheer
Types of Products Distributed:
  Frozen Food, General Merchandise, Imported packaging supplies

54587 ATI
3415 S Sepulveda Blvd
Suite 610
Los Angeles, CA 90034-6060   310-397-9797
       Fax: 310-445-1411 ati@american-trading.com
              www.american-trading.com
California-based export trading company servicing the needs of food and beverage importers worldwide in four major categories: name-brand products, generic products, private label products, and raw ingredients. All sizes and packagingstyles are available. We work closely with the US Department of Agriculture, US Department of Commerce, the California Trade and Development Agency
President/CEO: Seth Wilen
CFO: Dan Wilen
Vice President: Matthew Good
Marketing Director: Nova Gatewood
Sales Director: Mike Davis
Estimated Sales: $10-20 Million
Number Employees: 5-9
Number of Brands: 500
Number of Products: 1000
Square Footage: 10000
Type of Packaging: Consumer, Food Service, Private Label, Bulk

54588 (HQ)Aaburco Inc
17745 Atwater Ln
Grass Valley, CA 95949-7416   530-268-2734
       Fax: 530-273-9312   800-533-7437
       support@piemaster.com www.piemaster.com
Manufacturer, exporter and wholesaler/distributor of food processing equipment including manually operated, semi-automatic and electro-pneumatic machines and dough rollers for calzones, empanadas and pierogies
President: Edward Downs
aaburco@piemaster.com
CFO: F Burgard
Estimated Sales: Less Than $500,000
Number Employees: 1-4
Square Footage: 40000
Type of Packaging: Consumer, Food Service
Types of Products Distributed:
  Food Service, Bakery Equipment

Wholesalers & Distributors / A-Z

54589 Aala Meat Market Inc
751 Waiakamilo Rd
Honolulu, HI 96817-4312   808-832-6650
                    Fax: 808-832-6659
Meats
President: Sandra Moribe
gmoribe5@hawaiiantel.net
Estimated Sales: $1-3 Million
Number Employees: 10-19

54590 Abal Material Handling Inc
1401 Plantation Rd NE
Roanoke, VA 24012-5714   540-982-2796
     Fax: 540-982-2798 800-296-2225
          www.abalmh.com
Wholesaler/distributor of material handling equipment including conveyors, shelving, jacks, etc
President: Scott Bauman
sb@abalmh.com
Sales: Dave Willa
Estimated Sales: $10-20 Million
Number Employees: 10-19
Square Footage: 76000
Private Brands Carried:
   Metro; Warewell; Rubbermaid
Types of Products Distributed:
   Frozen Food, General Merchandise, Material handling equipment

54591 Abatar Institutional Food Company
1133 May Street
Lansing, MI 48906-5508   517-322-2263
                    Fax: 517-322-2483
Wholesaler/distributor of dry goods and groceries; serving the prison market
President: Andrew Lukomski
Secretary: James Knowlton
Types of Products Distributed:
   Food Service, Frozen Food, General Line, Dry goods & groceries

54592 Abbot's Butcher
350 Clinton St.
Costa Mesa, CA 92626   949-726-2156
          hello@theabbotsbutcher.com
          www.abbotsbutcher.com
Plant-based meats including imitation ground beef, chicken, and chorizo
Founder, CEO: Kerry Song
Types of Products Distributed:
   Provisions/Meat

54593 Abbott's Candy Shop
48 E Walnut St
Hagerstown, IN 47346-1542   765-489-4442
     Fax: 765-489-5501 877-801-1200
          abbottscandy@abbottscandy.com
          www.abbottscandy.com
Gourmet chocolates and caramels
President: Suanna Goodnight
Vice President: Gordon Goodnight
Manager: Becky Diercks
abbottscandy@abbottscandy.com
Estimated Sales: $780,000
Number Employees: 20-49
Square Footage: 28
Type of Packaging: Private Label

54594 Abel IHS
1 International Way
Lawrence, MA 01843
                    800-554-2887
          solutions@abelwomack.com
          www.abelwomack.com
Wholesaler/distributor of material handling equipment including conveyors, shelving, and Raymond lift trucks.
President: Mike Petinge
Chief Executive Officer: John Croce
Chief Financial Officer: Gary Mell
Chief Operating Officer: Anthony Fedele
Engineering Manager: Joe Duquette
Estimated Sales: $50-100 Million
Number Employees: 100-249
Private Brands Carried:
   Raymond; Demag; Frazier
Types of Products Distributed:
   Frozen Food, General Merchandise, Material handling equipment

54595 Able Sales Company
Centro Distribucin Del Norte Edificio 1
Carr. 869 Bo. Palmas
Catano, PR 00962   787-620-4141
     Fax: 787-620-4100 info@ablesales.com
          www.ablesales.com
Import, wholesale and distribution of raw material for food and pharmaceutical industries, including sugar flour, salt, juice concentrates. Warehousing and logistic services.
President: Luis Silva
Chairman of the Board: Alvaro Silva
CFO/Treaturer: Jose Rodriguez
Estimated Sales: $16 Million
Number Employees: 120
Square Footage: 75000
Parent Co: Able Sales Company
Type of Packaging: Consumer, Food Service, Private Label, Bulk
Private Brands Carried:
   Pennant Products; National Starch; Cargill-Corn Wet Milling Division; Tate & Lyle North American Sugars
Types of Products Distributed:
   Food Service, Frozen Food, General Line, General Merchandise, Sugar, salt & juice concentrates

54596 Above All Health
7645 E Evans Rd # 3
Scottsdale, AZ 85260-2944   480-483-7000
                    Fax: 480-483-0215
Wholesaler/distributor of vitamins and minerals
Owner/President: Redgie Hansen
Secretary/Treasurer: Janelle Hansen
Estimated Sales: Less than $500,000
Number Employees: 1-4
Types of Products Distributed:
   Frozen Food, General Line, Vitamins & minerals

54597 Academy Packing Co Inc
2881 Wyoming St
Dearborn, MI 48120-1599   313-841-4900
     Fax: 313-841-9762 academypacking@gmail.com
          www.academypackingcompany.com
Wholesaler/distributor of frozen foods and provisions/meats
President: Donald Polk
Estimated Sales: $10-20 Million
Number Employees: 5-9
Types of Products Distributed:
   Provisions/Meat

54598 Acatris USA
3300 Edinborough Way
Suite 712
Edina, MN 55435-5963   952-920-7700
     Fax: 952-920-7704 www.acatris.com
Blended dough conditioners, antioxidant solutions, release agents and lubricants; wholesaler/distributor of soy flour, vitamin/mineral blends and oils including soybean and canola
President: Laurent Leduc
Manager: Joni Johnson
Sales Manager: Cherie Jones
Estimated Sales: $5-10 Million
Number Employees: 20-49
Number of Brands: 15
Square Footage: 64000
Parent Co: Royal Schouten Group
Type of Packaging: Bulk
Types of Products Distributed:
   Frozen Food, General Line, Health Food, Flour, vitamins & oil: soybean & canola

54599 Accord International
PO Box 925
Succ. B Station
Montreal, QC H3B 3K5
Canada
                    514-484-0380
                    Fax: 514-483-2905
Wholesaler/distributor of fish and seafood
President: John Dike
Number Employees: 10-19
Types of Products Distributed:
   Frozen Food, Seafood

54600 Accurate Forklift
85 Scenic Ave
Santa Rosa, CA 95407-8209   707-585-3675
                    Fax: 707-585-9734
          smchenry@accurateforklift.com
          www.accurateforklift.com
Material handling equipment
Owner: Sam McHenry
Year Founded: 1976
Estimated Sales: $10-20 Million
Number Employees: 20-49
Private Brands Carried:
   UniCarriers; Steinbock

54601 Ace Chemical
4 Georgetown Oval
New City, NY 10956-6804   800-301-4593
                    Fax: 845-639-6911
Wholesaler/distributor of cleaning and dishwashing chemicals; serving the food service market
President: Rich Sabater
Service Manager: Dwayne Bleise
Number Employees: 5-9
Parent Co: Women's World
Private Brands Carried:
   Envirochen
Types of Products Distributed:
   Food Service, Frozen Food, General Merchandise, Cleaning & dishwashing chemicals

54602 Ace Electric Supply
119 Hamilton Park Dr # 2
Tallahassee, FL 32304-0809   850-224-0188
                    Fax: 850-222-1329
Wholesaler/distributor of electrical supplies, lighting, etc
Manager: John Chapman
Branch Operations Manager: John Jenkins
Estimated Sales: $1-3 Million
Number Employees: 1-4
Parent Co: WESCO Distribution
Number of Customer Locations: 200
Types of Products Distributed:
   Frozen Food, General Merchandise, Electrical supplies, lighting, etc.

54603 Ace Endico Corp
80 International Blvd
Brewster, NY 10509   845-940-1501
     Fax: 845-940-1515 info@aceendico.com
Wholesaler/distributor of frozen foods, canned goods, fresh produce, refrigerated items and paper goods.
Chief Executive Officer: William Endico
william.endico@aceendico.com
President: Murray Hertzberg
Vice President: Michael Endico
Marketing Manager: Laura Endico-Verzello
Vice President, Operations: Matthew Hertzberg
Year Founded: 1982
Estimated Sales: $50-100 Million
Number Employees: 5-9
Square Footage: 30000
Private Brands Carried:
   Ace Endico; All Kitchen; Pallante
Number of Customer Locations: 1000
Types of Products Distributed:
   Frozen Food, General Line, General Merchandise, Produce, Paper goods

54604 Ace Fixture Company
7101 Lincoln Ave
Buena Park, CA 90620   714-226-9800
                    Fax: 714-226-9812
Wholesaler/distributor of restaurant fixtures; serving the food service market
Manager: John Lau
General Manager: John Lau
Estimated Sales: $20-50 Million
Number Employees: 10-19
Private Brands Carried:
   Wolf; Isomatic; Cambro
Types of Products Distributed:
   Food Service, Frozen Food, General Merchandise, Restaurant fixtures

54605 (HQ)Ace Mart Restaurant Supply
1220 S Saint Marys St
San Antonio, TX 78210-1246   210-224-0082
     Fax: 210-224-1629 888-898-8079
          custserv@acemart.com
Wholesaler/distributor of restaurant equipment and supplies; serving the food service market
President: Paul Gustafson
VP: Carl Gustafson
Contact: Norma Gustafson
n.gustafson@acemart.com
Secretary/Treasurer: Norma Gustafson
Estimated Sales: $2.5-5 Million
Number Employees: 5-9

Wholesalers & Distributors / A-Z

Other Locations:
Ace Mart
San Antonio, TXAce Mart
Types of Products Distributed:
Food Service, Frozen Food, General Merchandise, Restaurant equipment & supplies

54606 Ackerman Industrial Equipment
300 W Mill St
Curtice, OH 43412-7704   419-836-2100
Fax: 419-836-2040 800-589-5842
www.ackermantoledo.com
Wholesaler/distributor of forklifts; also, parts and service available
Owner: Sam Schwiefert
sam.schwiefert@ackermantoledo.com
General Manager: Paul Ackerman
Estimated Sales: $5-10 Million
Number Employees: 10-19
Private Brands Carried:
Nissan
Types of Products Distributed:
Frozen Food, General Merchandise, Forklifts

54607 Acme Bread Co
1601 San Pablo Ave
Berkeley, CA 94702-1317   510-524-1327
www.acmebread.com
Bread
Founder: Steven Sullivan
Contact: Hannah Jukovsky
hannah@acmebread.com
Estimated Sales: Less Than $500,000
Number Employees: 5-9

54608 Acme Food Sales Inc
5940 1st Ave S
Seattle, WA 98108-3248   206-762-5150
Fax: 206-762-8629 800-777-2263
www.acmefood.com
Wholesaler/distributor of frozen and fresh meats, produce and groceries; serving the food service market
President: Robert Janatschii
rjanatschii@ameristarmeats.com
CFO: Gary Hibma
EVP: Rob Polik
Operations Manager: Mike Fink
Estimated Sales: $10-20 Million
Number Employees: 20-49
Square Footage: 39000
Private Brands Carried:
Acme; Germaine; Old Timer; Wisconsin Maid
Number of Customer Locations: 450
Types of Products Distributed:
Food Service, Frozen Food, Provisions/Meat

54609 Acme Scale Co
1801 Adams Ave
P.O. Box 1922
San Leandro, CA 94577-1069   510-638-5040
Fax: 510-638-5619 888-638-5040
www.acmescales.com
Wholesaler/distributor of mechanical and electronic scales and force measurement products. We also service the products we sell
Manager: Jerry Anderson
janderson@acmescales.com
Estimated Sales: $2.5-5 Million
Number Employees: 20-49
Square Footage: 36000
Types of Products Distributed:
General Merchandise, Mechanical & electronic scales

54610 Acme Steak & Seafood
31 Bissell Ave
Youngstown, OH 44505-2707   330-270-8000
Fax: 330-270-8006 800-686-2263
support@acmesteak.com www.acmesteak.com
Fresh produce, seafood, sausage, hamburgers and portion controlled meat.
Owner/President: Michael Mike
mike@acmesteak.com
Year Founded: 1947
Estimated Sales: $2.40 Million
Number Employees: 10-19
Square Footage: 68000
Type of Packaging: Consumer, Food Service, Private Label
Types of Products Distributed:
General Line, Provisions/Meat, Seafood, Meatballs, shellfish, cabbage, etc.

54611 Acorn Distributors Inc
5820 Fortune Cir W
Indianapolis, IN 46241-5503   317-243-9234
Fax: 317-260-2289 800-783-2446
www.acorndistributors.com
Wholesaler/distributor of janitorial supplies including soaps, disinfectants, disposables, floor/carpet care products, etc; also, paper and restaurant supplies; serving the food service market
President: Jennifer Rosenberg
CEO: Al Wachter
awachter@acorndistributors.com
CEO: Al Wachter
General Manager: Gary Hegeman
Estimated Sales: $10-20 Million
Number Employees: 50-99
Square Footage: 120000
Types of Products Distributed:
Food Service, Frozen Food, General Merchandise, Janitorial, paper & restaurant supplies

54612 Action Advertising
8445 Bergen Dr
Cordova, TN 38018   901-737-3955
Fax: 901-737-4198
Wholesaler/distributor of advertising specialties
Owner: Joyce Echols
jcechols1@comcast.net
Estimated Sales: $500,000-$1 Million
Number Employees: 1-4
Number of Customer Locations: 400
Types of Products Distributed:
Frozen Food, General Merchandise, Advertising specialties

54613 Action Sales
415 S Atlantic Blvd
Monterey Park, CA 91754-3209   626-308-1988
Fax: 626-308-9780 800- 3-8 66
esales@actionsales.com www.actionsales.com
Wholesaler/distributor of restaurant equipment
President: Jack Chang
Cmo: Mona Lau
mona@actionsales.com
Estimated Sales: $5-10 Million
Number Employees: 50-99
Types of Products Distributed:
Frozen Food, General Merchandise, Restaurant equipment

54614 Acushnet Fish Corporation
46 Middle Street
Fairhaven, MA 02719-3086   508-997-7482
Fax: 508-999-6697
Fish
President: Ralph Parsons

54615 Ad Lib Advertising
109 White Oak Ln # 72-A
Old Bridge, NJ 08857-1981   800-622-3542
Fax: 732-679-9511 800-622-3542
info@adlibadvertising.com
Wholesaler/distributor of general merchandise including advertising specialties, badges, medals, calendars, marking and writing pens, logos and premiums
President: Ed Cogland
VP: Don Cogland
Estimated Sales: $500,000-$1 Million
Number Employees: 1-4
Square Footage: 5200
Private Brands Carried:
3-M; Hazel; Letts of London
Number of Customer Locations: 1000
Types of Products Distributed:
Frozen Food, General Merchandise, Advertising specialties

54616 Ad Specialty Plus
7125 Duncourtney Drive NE
Atlanta, GA 30328-1258   770-395-6174
Fax: 770-395-7201
Wholesaler/distributor of advertising specialties
President: Larry Wilson
VP: Karl Tulisalo
Estimated Sales: Less than $500,000
Number Employees: 1-4
Number of Customer Locations: 250
Types of Products Distributed:
Frozen Food, General Merchandise, Advertising specialties

54617 Ad-Centive Ideas
5053 Ocean Boulevard
Suite 25a
Sarasota, FL 34242-1607   941-349-9300
Fax: 941-346-3414
Distributor of merchandise including advertising specialties and calendars; graphic design and imprinting services available
President: Ken Graham
VP: Barry Graham
Number Employees: 5-9
Types of Products Distributed:
Frozen Food, General Merchandise, Advertising specialties & calendars

54618 Ad-Craft Products Compay
P.O.Box 38868
Germantown, TN 38183-0868   901-756-7767
adcraftpro@aol.com
Wholesaler/distributor of advertising specialties, calendars, decals, emblems, hand fans and imprinted items
President/National Sales Manager: Stuart Lavene
Estimated Sales: $5-10 Million
Number Employees: 5-9
Square Footage: 13200
Number of Customer Locations: 2500
Types of Products Distributed:
Frozen Food, General Merchandise, Advertising specialties

54619 Adams & Knickle
PO Box 699
Lunenburg, NS B0J 2C0
Canada   902-634-4349
Fax: 902-634-4529
Wholesaler/distributor of fresh scallops
President: Glen Geldert
Number Employees: 50-99
Types of Products Distributed:
Frozen Food, Seafood, Fresh scallops

54620 Adams Chapman Co
13 Food Mart Rd
Boston, MA 02118-2886   617-269-6363
Fax: 617-464-0100 sales@adamschapman.com
www.adamschapman.com
Wholesaler/distributor of poultry and dairy products; serving the foodserv ice market
President: Brad Benson
bbenson@adamschapman.com
Estimated Sales: $10-20 Million
Number Employees: 10-19
Types of Products Distributed:
Food Service, General Line, Provisions/Meat, Dairy products

54621 Adams Wholesale Co
101 Nashville Rd
PO Box 1988
Rocky Mount, NC 27803-3627   252-977-2185
Fax: 252-977-2075
service@adamswholesalecompany.com
www.fredsfoodclub.com
Wholesaler/distributor of groceries, meats, produce, dairy products, frozenfoods, baked goods, etc.; serving the food service market
CEO: Fred Adams
CFO: Fred Adams
VP: Roger Boles
IT: Van Baker
vbaker@adamswholesalecompany.com
Estimated Sales: $19.6 Million
Number Employees: 20-49
Square Footage: 250000
Number of Customer Locations: 600
Types of Products Distributed:
Food Service, Frozen Food, General Line, General Merchandise, Provisions/Meat, Produce

54622 Adams-Burch
1901 Stanford Ct
Landover, MD 20785   301-276-2000
800-347-8093
customerservice@adams-burch.com
www.adams-burch.com
Wholesaler/distributor of restaurant supplies.
President: Dan Blaylock Sr
Estimated Sales: $50-100 Million
Number Employees: 100-249
Parent Co: TriMark
Types of Products Distributed:
Frozen Food, General Merchandise, Restaurant supplies

Wholesalers & Distributors / A-Z

54623 Addison Foods Inc
16415 Addison Rd # 135
Addison, TX 75001-5404   972-381-7200
        Fax: 972-713-6700 www.addisonfoods.com
Wholesaler/distributor of beef, pork, chicken and seafood
President: Randy Burwell
jerry@addisonfoods.com
Assistant VP: Barry Sobol
Estimated Sales: $20-50 Million
Number Employees: 20-49
Types of Products Distributed:
  Frozen Food, Provisions/Meat, Seafood, Beef, pork, chicken, etc.

54624 Adel Grocery Company
395 Oyster Point Boulevard
South San Francisco, CA 94080-1928 229-896-7531
        Fax: 229-896-7492 800-289-2335
Wholesaler/distributor of candy, petroleum products, health/beauty aids and groceries; serving convenience stores
General Manager/VP: Mr. Pickett
Director Marketing: G Mashburn
Sales Manager: D Conley
Estimated Sales: $20-50 Million
Number Employees: 100-249
Parent Co: Head Distributing Company
Private Brands Carried:
  Slush Puppie
Number of Customer Locations: 900
Types of Products Distributed:
  Frozen Food, General Line, General Merchandise, Health & beauty aids, etc.

54625 Adelman Foods
803 E 92nd St
Brooklyn, NY 11236-1795   718-272-7373
        Fax: 718-272-1049
Wholesaler/distributor of dairy products including cheese, butter, yogurt and sour cream; also, juice
President: N Kross
Vice President: Jan Kross
Manager: Tamisha Harper
Estimated Sales: $3 Million
Number Employees: 1-4
Square Footage: 24000
Number of Customer Locations: 55

54626 Adex Medical Inc
6101 Quail Valley Ct # D
Riverside, CA 92507-0764   951-653-9122
        Fax: 951-653-9133 800-873-4776
info@adexmed.com www.adexmed.com
Manufacturer, wholesaler/distributor, importer and exporter of disposable apparel including gloves, goggles, aprons, hair nets, caps, masks, shoe covers, etc.; also, towels, industrial safety products, emergency preparednessproducts
President/CEO: Michael Ghafouri
mmg@adexmed.com
Estimated Sales: $5 Million
Number Employees: 20-49
Number of Brands: 3
Number of Products: 200
Square Footage: 44000
Type of Packaging: Consumer, Food Service, Private Label
Types of Products Distributed:
  Frozen Food, General Merchandise

54627 Adirondack Direct
3040 48th Ave
Long Island City, NY 11101   718-932-4003
        Fax: 718-204-4537 800-221-2444
        info@adirondackdirect.com
Wholesaler/distributor of furniture
Controller: Randy Mittasch
Advertising Manager: Andrea Ross
Contact: Greg Abraham
abraham@adirondackrents.com
Estimated Sales: $1-3 Million
Number Employees: 100-249
Types of Products Distributed:
  Frozen Food, General Merchandise, Furniture

54628 Adluh Flour
804 Gervais St
PO Box 1437
Columbia, SC 29201-3126   803-779-2460
        Fax: 803-252-0014 800-692-3584
        info@adluh.com www.adluh.com
Flour and corn meal
President: William Allen
info@adluh.com
Year Founded: 1900
Estimated Sales: $5 Million
Number Employees: 10-19
Type of Packaging: Food Service
Private Brands Carried:
  Morton
Types of Products Distributed:
  Food Service, General Line, Salt

54629 Admiral Craft
940 S Oyster Bay Rd
Hicksville, NY 11801-3518   516-433-2291
        Fax: 516-433-4453 info@admiralcraft.com
                www.admiralcraft.com
Importer and wholesaler/distributor of food service utensils includinng pails, scoops, funnels, pans, spatulas, etc.; also, containers, ingredient bins, processing drums, pumps and tanks; serving the food service market
President: Victor Caglioti
victor.caglioti@admiralcraft.com
VP of Finance: Robert Vogel
Executive VP: Rick Powers
Director Marketing: Kerri Frino
VP Procurement/Material Handling: Michael Lazco
Estimated Sales: $20-30 Million
Number Employees: 20-49
Square Footage: 120000
Types of Products Distributed:
  Food Service, Frozen Food, General Merchandise, Utensils

54630 Adolf Kusy & Company
89 5th Avenue
Suite 602
New York, NY 10003-3020   212-242-4755
        Fax: 212-627-0193 info@clubviplife.com
                www.clubviplife.com
Wholesaler/distributor of meats and frozen foods; serving the food service market
Founder/President: Lisa Clampitt
VP Marketing/Matching: Beth Mandell
Estimated Sales: $300,000-500,000
Number Employees: 1-4
Number of Customer Locations: 500
Types of Products Distributed:
  Food Service, Frozen Food, Provisions/Meat

54631 Adonis Health Products
810 E 1650th Rd
Baldwin City, KS 66006   785-594-2791
Wholesaler/distributor, importer and exporter of vitamins, etc
Owner: Mike Hiebert
CEO: Sue Nanninga
CFO: Linda Lynn
Estimated Sales: $300,000-500,000
Number Employees: 1-4
Square Footage: 40000
Type of Packaging: Bulk
Private Brands Carried:
  Adonis; Universal; Pines; Natures Purest; Adonis Sport Supplements
Types of Products Distributed:
  Health Food, Vitamins

54632 Adprint Specialties
1708 Loma St
Santa Barbara, CA 93103-1822 805-963-9181
        Fax: 805-683-6526 800-230-6052
Wholesaler/distributor of advertising specialties, matches, magnets, decals, labels, embroidered hats, etc
Owner: Roy Coleman
Estimated Sales: $3-5 Million
Number Employees: 1-4
Number of Customer Locations: 2000
Types of Products Distributed:
  Advertising & promotional specialties

54633 Adsmith
850 S Rancho Drive
Suite 2320
Las Vegas, NV 89106-3831   702-870-8494
        Fax: 702-320-1933
Wholesaler/distributer of advertising specialties
President: Douglas Cacciola
Estimated Sales: $20-50 Million
Number Employees: 100-249
Types of Products Distributed:
  Frozen Food, General Merchandise, Advertising specialties & drinkware

54634 Advanced Chemical
136 Excelsior Ave
P.O.Box 2125
Middletown, NY 10940-3314   845-342-2466
        Fax: 845-342-2557 800-244-2078
        info@advancedchemicalsystems.com
                www.advancedchemicalsystems.com
Wholesaler/distributor of kitchen equipment, chemicals and supplies; serving the food service market
Owner: Tim Mondello
adchem@frontiernet.net
Co-Owner: Anthony Mondello
Estimated Sales: $500,000-$1 Million
Number Employees: 1-4
Types of Products Distributed:
  Food Service, Frozen Food, General Merchandise, Kitchen equipment, chemicals & supplies

54635 Advanced Equipment Company
P.O. Box 11382
Charlotte, NC 28220   704-527-3141
        Fax: 704-522-7262 www.aec-carolina.com
Wholesaler/distributor of material handling equipment including conveyors
President: Daryle Ogburn
Contact: Darin Boik
darin@aec-carolina.com
Plant Manager: Steve Fergusson
Estimated Sales: $5-10 Million
Number Employees: 10-19
Square Footage: 64320
Types of Products Distributed:
  Frozen Food, General Merchandise, Material handling equipment: conveyors

54636 Advanced Handling Systems Inc
4861 Duck Creek Rd
Cincinnati, OH 45227-1421   513-351-6500
        Fax: 513-351-8583 800-891-5504
                ahs@fuse.net
Wholesaler/distributor of material handling equipment
President: Chuck Frank
Estimated Sales: $5-10 Million
Number Employees: 10-19
Private Brands Carried:
  Matthews; Ermanto
Types of Products Distributed:
  Frozen Food, General Merchandise, Material handling equipment

54637 Advantage Gourmet Importers
480 Main Ave
Wallington, NJ 07057   973-777-0007
        Fax: 973-591-5556 888-676-3663
                crfagi@gmail.com
        www.advantagegourmetimporters.com
Broker, importer and wholesaler/distributor of chestnut products including organic chestnut flour and Italian specialty foods
Owner: Nicholas Puzino
Vice President: Emile Boustani
Purchasing: V Lampariello
Estimated Sales: $2.5-5 Million
Number Employees: 1-4
Square Footage: 800
Types of Products Distributed:
  Frozen Food, Specialty Foods, Chestnut products, Italian foods

54638 Adventure Foods
481 Banjo Lane
Whittier, NC 28789-7999   828-497-4113
        Fax: 828-497-7529
CustomerService@adventurefoods.com
                www.adventurefoods.com
Freeze-dried; dehydrated; shelf stable foods and instant food; food storage programs; health food markets; baking mixes, bulk spices and ingredients; specialty foods and special packing for vegetarian, diabetics, gluten intolerance andother food or health restrictions.
President: Jean Spangenberg
jean@adventurefoods.com
CEO: Sam Spangenberg
Number Employees: 5-9
Parent Co: Jean's Garden Greats
Type of Packaging: Consumer, Food Service, Private Label, Bulk
Private Brands Carried:
  Baker Packers; Macayamas Soups; Mini Minute Coffee Filters; GSi; Open Country; Lumen/Heartline Soy

Wholesalers & Distributors / A-Z

Types of Products Distributed:
Food Service, Frozen Food, General Line, General Merchandise, Health Food, Provisions/Meat, Groceries, etc.

54639 Adventure Inn Food Trading Company
381 Broadway
PO Box 11610
Albany, NY 12211-0610   518-436-7603
Fax: 518-436-9035 store@adventureinfood.com
www.adventureinfood.com
Gourmet and exotic foods
General Manager: Eric Guenther
Purchasing Director: Eric Guenther
Estimated Sales: $1.3 Million
Number Employees: 5-9
Number of Products: 1500
Square Footage: 20000
Type of Packaging: Consumer, Food Service, Private Label, Bulk
Types of Products Distributed:
Food Service, Health Food, Provisions/Meat, Seafood, Specialty Foods

54640 Advertising Specialties
7263 Murdy Cir
Huntington Beach, CA 92647-3533   714-847-0496
Fax: 714-842-4134
Wholesaler/distributor of advertising calendars, promotional products and business and computer forms
Owner: Pat Mc Laughlin Jr
VP: Pat McLaughlin
Contact: Sheryl Wren
sheryl@mclent.com
Estimated Sales: $.5-1 million
Number Employees: 5-9
Number of Customer Locations: 200
Types of Products Distributed:
Frozen Food, General Merchandise, Promotional products, forms, etc.

54641 Advertising SpecialtiesImprinted
10 E Main St
Smithtown, NY 11787-2803   631-724-2011
Fax: 631-862-8100
Wholesaler/distributor of general merchandise including advertising specialties, badges, medals, calendars, decals, premiums, novelties, give-a-ways, glassware and sportsware
Owner: Del Berg
Estimated Sales: Less than $500,000
Number Employees: 1-4
Square Footage: 12000
Number of Customer Locations: 1000
Types of Products Distributed:
Frozen Food, General Merchandise, Advertising specialties

54642 Aerchem Inc
3935 W Roll Ave
Bloomington, IN 47403-3181   812-334-9996
Fax: 812-334-1960   800-523-0091
aerchem@aerchem.com www.aerchem.com
Wholesaler/distributor of ingredients
President: Richard Sikorski
Chairman: Judith Sikorski
CFO: Rick Sikorski
VP, New Business Development: Salvatore Ziccarelli
VP, Sales: Salvatore Ziccarelli
Contact: Cliff Chulos
chulos@aerchem.com
General Manager: Stuart White
Estimated Sales: $2.5-5 Million
Number Employees: 1-4
Types of Products Distributed:
Frozen Food, General Line, Ingredients

54643 AeroFarms
212 Rome St
Newark, NJ 07105   973-242-2495
info@aerofarms.com
www.aerofarms.com
Baby greens, microgreens, herbs; Aeroponic technology
Chief Executive Officer: David Rosenberg
Chief Financial Officer: Guy Blanchard
Chief Operating Officer: Roger Post
Chief Science Officer: Ed Harwood
Chief Technology Officer: Roger Buelow
Chief Marketing Officer: Marc Oshima
General Counsel: Ariel Lager
Year Founded: 2004
Number Employees: 50-99
Type of Packaging: Food Service
Types of Products Distributed:
Produce

54644 Aerolator Systems
2716 Chamber Dr
Monroe, NC 28110   704-289-9585
Fax: 704-289-9580   800-843-8286
Hood systems; wholesaler/distributor of exhaust fans; serving the food service market
President: Janet Griffen
Sales Manager: Steve Surratt
Estimated Sales: $10-20 Million
Number Employees: 50-99
Square Footage: 80000
Private Brands Carried:
Aerolator
Types of Products Distributed:
Food Service, Frozen Food, General Merchandise, Exhaust fans

54645 Aetna Plastics Corporation
4466 Orchard St.
Mantua, OH 44255   330-274-2855
Fax: 330-274-8984   800-634-3074
sales@aetnaplastics.com www.aetnaplastics.com
Wholesaler/distributor of industrial plastics, pipes and fittings; serving the food service market
President: Gary P Davis
Contact: Robin Ronchetti
robin.ronchetti@aetnaplastics.com
Operations Manager: Alicia Cornelius
Operations Supervisor-Akron: Don Hakola
Customer Service Manager: Chuck Ogrin
Estimated Sales: $2.5-5 Million
Number Employees: 20-49
Square Footage: 96000
Number of Customer Locations: 2
Types of Products Distributed:
Food Service, General Merchandise, Industrial plastics, pipes & fittings

54646 Afassco
2244 Park Pl # C
Suite C
Minden, NV 89423-8632   775-783-3555
Fax: 775-783-3555 www.afassco.com
CEO: Don Schumaker
afassco@intercomm.com
Number Employees: 10-19
Private Brands Carried:
Papenol, Buffinox, Aquaskin, Pain Free, Pain Free Plus, Cut Cleaners, Medlunpes, SunFree
Types of Products Distributed:
First Aid Kits/Supplies

54647 Affiliated Resource Inc
3839 N Western Ave
Chicago, IL 60618-3733   773-509-9300
Fax: 773-509-9929   800-366-9336
info@4ledsigns.com www.forledsigns.com
Manufacturer, wholesaler/distributor of indoor and outdoor electronic signs
President: Stephen Stillman
stephen@yledsigns.com
National Sales Manager: Rick Markle
Regional Sales Manager: Pam Zayas
Estimated Sales: $1-3 Million
Number Employees: 1-4
Square Footage: 4000
Types of Products Distributed:
Frozen Food, General Merchandise, Moving message & electronic signs

54648 (HQ)Afflink LLC
1400 Afflink Pl
Tuscaloosa, AL 35406-2289   205-345-4180
Fax: 205-345-0064   800-222-5521
info@afflink.com www.afflink.com
Wholesaler/distributor of paper, plastic and janitorial supplies, and packaging
President: Dennis Riffer
driffer@afflink.com
CFO: Chip Shields
Marketing Director: Michael Wilson
Estimated Sales: Over $1 Billion
Number Employees: 1000-4999
Square Footage: 520000
Type of Packaging: Food Service, Private Label
Private Brands Carried:
AFFEX; AFFLAR; AFFPRINT
Types of Products Distributed:
Food Service, Paper, plastic & janitorial supplies

54649 Afia Foods
P.O. Box 170651
Austin, TX 78717   512-698-8448
sales@afiafoods.com
www.afiafoods.com
Greek, Mediterranean, and Middle Eastern foods
President: Farrah Moussallati Sibai
Types of Products Distributed:
General Line

54650 Age International Inc
229 W Main St # 202
Suite 202
Frankfort, KY 40601-1879   502-223-9874
Fax: 502-223-9877 www.blantonsbourbon.com
Wholesaler/distributor and exporter of liquor, including bourbon
President: Yutaka Takano
Cio/Cto: Justin Williams
jwilliams@ageintl.com
CFO: Nancy Fulks
Treasurer: Nancy Fulks
Marketing/Sales: John Polo
Number Employees: 5-9
Parent Co: Buffalo Trace Distillery
Private Brands Carried:
Blanton's Single Barrel Bourbon
Types of Products Distributed:
Frozen Food

54651 Agri-Dairy Products
3020 Westchester Ave
Purchase, NY 10577   914-697-9580
Fax: 914-697-9586
customerservice@agridairy.com
www.agridairy.com
Dairy and food ingredients including whey and lactose, milkfat, milk powders, casein, milk proteins, cheese and butter.
President: Steven Bronfield
CEO: Frank Reeves III
CFO: Mary Ellen Storino
Year Founded: 1985
Estimated Sales: $52 Million
Number Employees: 10
Number of Products: 50+
Square Footage: 1600
Type of Packaging: Bulk
Types of Products Distributed:
Food Service, Ingredients

54652 Agri-Equipment International
493 Colonial Trace Dr
Longs, SC 29568   843-283-2583
Fax: 864-343-0076   877-550-4709
www.agri-equipmentonline.com
Manufacturer and wholesaler/distributor of release (interleaver) sheets, thermometers, temperature data loggers and probes
President: Tom Gaffney
VP Sales: Gary Gaffney
Estimated Sales: $1-2.5,000,000
Number Employees: 1-4
Types of Products Distributed:
Frozen Food, General Merchandise, Thermometers, probes, etc.

54653 Agrium Advanced Technologies
10 Craig Street
Brantford, ON N3J 7J1
Canada   519-757-0077
Fax: 519-757-0080
Wholesaler/distributor of insecticides
Marketing Coordinator: Brandon Lovegrove
Types of Products Distributed:
Frozen Food, General Merchandise, Insecticides

54654 Agro Foods, Inc.
3531 SW 13th St
Miami, FL 33145   786-552-9006
Fax: 305-361-7639 www.agrofoods.com
Spanish olives
Manager: Isa Knight
Estimated Sales: $1-2.5 Million
Number Employees: 5-9
Square Footage: 526000
Parent Co: Agro Aceitunera SA
Type of Packaging: Consumer, Food Service, Private Label, Bulk

Wholesalers & Distributors / A-Z

Types of Products Distributed:
  Frozen Food, General Line, Specialty Foods, Spanish olives: pitted, plain, etc.

54655 Aidi International Hotels of America
1050-17th Street NW
Suite 600
Washington, DC 20036-   202-331-9299
Fax: 202-478-0367 sales@royalregencyhotels.com
www.royalregencyhotels.com
Engineering and marketing consultant specializing in construction, management, decoration and operations in overseas hotels; wholesaler/distributor and exporter of equipment, furniture and food
President: Ghassane Aidi
Chairman: Adnan Aidi
VP: Samia Aidi
Number Employees: 200
Square Footage: 28000
Parent Co: Aidi Group
Types of Products Distributed:
  Frozen Food, General Line, General Merchandise, Equipment & furniture

54656 Aileen Quirk & Sons Inc
235 W 12th Ave
Kansas City, MO 64116-4178   816-471-4580
Fax: 816-842-8063 info@aileenquirkandsons.com
www.aileenquirkandsons.com
Dried edible beans for wholesalers and grocery stores.
Owner: Kelly Quirk
quirksons@aol.com
CEO: Larry Quirk
Traffic Manager: Leslie Quirk
Office Manager: Frances Kuhn
Estimated Sales: $3 Million
Number Employees: 10-19
Type of Packaging: Food Service, Private Label, Bulk

54657 Aim This Way
19 Pemberton Street
Cambridge, MA 02140   617-661-1518
   800-627-4689
info@aimthisway.com www.aimthisway.com
Wholesaler/distributor of nutritional supplements, garlic, ginkgo, bee pollen, etc
Owner: Larry Brogan
Number Employees: 1-4
Types of Products Distributed:
  Frozen Food, Health Food, Nutritional supplements, etc.

54658 Aimonetto and Sons
720 N 10th St
Renton, WA 98057   206-767-2777
Fax: 206-762-6792   866-823-2777
Milk, juice, cottage cheese, sour cream and yogurt; wholesaler/distributor of dairy products
Owner: Jim Aimonetto
Estimated Sales: $10-20 Million
Number Employees: 10-19
Type of Packaging: Consumer, Food Service
Types of Products Distributed:
  Food Service, Frozen Food, General Line, Dairy products

54659 (HQ)Air Savers Inc
4400 Lawndale Ave
Lyons, IL 60534-1726   708-447-4646
Fax: 708-447-6259   888-447-4643
www.air-savers.com
Wholesaler/distributor and exporter of air cleaning equipment; serving the food service market
President/CEO: Mark Olson
Estimated Sales: $5-10 Million
Number Employees: 10-19
Square Footage: 12000
Other Locations:
  Air Savers
  Lyons, ILAir Savers
Types of Products Distributed:
  Food Service, Frozen Food, General Merchandise, Air cleaning equipment

54660 Ajax Philadelphia
60 Tomlinson Road
Huntingdon Valley, PA 19006   215-947-8500
Fax: 215-947-6757   800-516-9916
sales@ajaxelectric.com www.ajaxelectric.com

Wholesaler/distributor of frozen beverage and dessert equipment, ice makers and dispensers, microwaves, water filters, etc
VP: Ellis Weiss
Sales Manager: Alan Baglwo
Estimated Sales: $10-20 Million
Number Employees: 20-49
Square Footage: 60000
Private Brands Carried:
  Crystal Tips; Cuno
Types of Products Distributed:
  Frozen Food, General Merchandise

54661 Akin & Porter Produce Inc
143 Airport Rd
Greenfield, TN 38230   731-235-2287
Fax: 731-235-9171   800-227-2253
jeffperkins@akin-porter.com
www.akin-porter.com
Wholesaler/distributor of produce.
President: Joe Porter
jporter@akin-porter.com
Treasurer: Jamie Prince
Vice President: Jeff Perkins
Year Founded: 1937
Estimated Sales: $38.08 Million
Number Employees: 50-99
Types of Products Distributed:
  Produce

54662 (HQ)Akron Cotton Products
437 W Cedar St
Akron, OH 44307-2321   330-434-7171
Fax: 330-434-7150   800-899-7173
akroncotton@akroncotton.com
www.akroncotton.com
Manufacturer filter bags: beer and winemaking
President: Michael L Zwick
mike@akroncotton.com
VP: Shawn Zwick
Estimated Sales: $1-3 Million
Number Employees: 10-19
Square Footage: 52000
Private Brands Carried:
  Multi-Clean; Proctor & Gamble; 3M
Types of Products Distributed:
  Food Service, Frozen Food, General Merchandise, Cheesecloths, degreasers, aprons, etc.

54663 Al Campisano Fruit Company
4601 Jennings Lane
Louisville, KY 40218-2910   502-458-5311
Wholesaler/distributor of produce
General Manager: Ken Winfield
Types of Products Distributed:
  General Line, Produce, Fresh

54664 Al Lehrhoff Sales
p o BOX 41
Wharton, NJ 07885   973-328-1448
Fax: 973-328-6858 juan@allehrhoffsales.com
Wholesaler/distributor of general merchandise
Owner: Terry Rucker
VP: Terry Rucker
Estimated Sales: $5-10 Million
Number Employees: 5-9
Square Footage: 12000
Types of Products Distributed:
  Frozen Food, General Merchandise

54665 Alabama Food Group
P.O.Box 442
Alexander City, AL 35011   256-234-5071
Fax: 256-215-7289
Wholesaler/distributor of general line products; serving the food service market
President: Hugh Neighbors
Sales Manager: Ronnie Milligan
Estimated Sales: $18 Million
Number Employees: 5-9
Types of Products Distributed:
  Food Service, Frozen Food, General Line

54666 Alabama Food Group
P.O.Box 442
Alexander City, AL 35011   256-234-5071
Fax: 256-215-7289
Wholesaler/distributor of grocery items, meat, produce and dairy items, frozen and baked goods, general merchandise, private label items, etc.; serving the food service market
President: Hugh Neighbors
Sales/General Manager: John Spain

Estimated Sales: $35 Million
Number Employees: 5-9
Square Footage: 98000
Private Brands Carried:
  Pocahontas
Number of Customer Locations: 987
Types of Products Distributed:
  Food Service, Frozen Food, General Line, General Merchandise, Provisions/Meat, Produce

54667 Alabama Gulf Seafood
9280 Seafood House Rd
Bayou La Batre, AL 36509   251-824-4396
Fax: 251-824-7579 eatalabamaseafood.com
Seafood
President: Richard Gazzier
Vice President: Donna Gazzier
Estimated Sales: $5-10 Million
Number Employees: 10-19

54668 Alabama Wholesale Company
P.O.Box 426
Pine Hill, AL 36769   334-963-4345
Fax: 334-963-4981
Wholesaler/distributor of general line products
President: Blanche Spinkes
Estimated Sales: $5-10 Million
Number Employees: 5-9
Types of Products Distributed:
  Frozen Food, General Line

54669 Alack Refrigeration Co Inc
17420 Highway 190 E
Hammond, LA 70401-9506   985-345-9476
Fax: 985-542-6560 www.alack.com
Wholesaler/distributor of equipment and furnishings; serving the food service market
President: Louis Alack
louis@alack.com
VP: Ruth Alack
Estimated Sales: $5-10 Million
Number Employees: 20-49
Square Footage: 48000
Types of Products Distributed:
  Food Service, Frozen Food, General Merchandise, Equipment & furnishings

54670 Alaska Sausage & Seafood
2914 Arctic Blvd
Anchorage, AK 99503-3811   907-562-3636
Fax: 907-562-7343   800-798-3636
aks@ak.net www.alaskasausage.com
Sausage, processed meats and smoked fish; exporter of smoked salmon
President: Herbert Eckmann
Secretary/Treasurer: Eva Eckmann
Quality Control Manager: Martin Eckmann
IT: Amanda Ingram
aks@ak.net
Estimated Sales: $10-20 Million
Number Employees: 20-49
Square Footage: 30000
Type of Packaging: Consumer, Food Service, Private Label, Bulk
Types of Products Distributed:
  Frozen Food

54671 Alaska Seafood Co
5731 Concrete Way
Juneau, AK 99801-9543   907-780-4808
Fax: 907-780-5140   800-451-1400
info@alaskaseafoodcompany.com
www.alaskaseafoodcompany.com
Fish.
President: Richard Hand
Year Founded: 1987
Estimated Sales: $800,000
Number Employees: 10-19
Types of Products Distributed:
  Seafood

54672 Alaskan Gourmet Seafoods
1020 International Airport Road
Anchorage, AK 99518
Fax: 907-563-2592   800-288-3740
www.akgourmet.com
Frozen and canned smoked halibut and salmon.
President: Paul Schilling
Estimated Sales: $5-10 Million
Number Employees: 18
Square Footage: 40000

Wholesalers & Distributors / A-Z

54673 Albanese Confectionery Group
5441 E Lincoln Hwy
Merrillville, IN 46410-5947 219-942-1877
Fax: 219-769-6897 800-536-0581
retail@albaneseconfectionery.com
www.albanesecandy.com
Chocolate covered nuts, candies, and gummies.
President: Scott Albanese
ciaoalbanese@albaneseconfectionary.com
Vice President: Richard Albanese
Purchasing: Alan Levinson
Estimated Sales: $5-10 Million
Number Employees: 5-9
Other Locations:
 Hobart Manufacturing Facility
 Hobart, INHobart Manufacturing Facility

54674 Albert Guarnieri & Co
1133 E Market St
Warren, OH 44483
800-686-2639
www.albertguarnieri.com
Wholesaler/distributor of grocery and food service products.
Grocery Coordinator: Larry Spano
School Coordinator: Laura Davy
Concessions Coordinator: Donna Pinkerton
Concession Sales Representative: John Jackson
Key Accounts Manager: Dave Donegan
Southern Division Manager: Jeff Goodwin
IT Department: Chris Sabol
School, Concession & Equipment Manager: Jim Carsten
Accounts Payable: Kitty Kassan
Midstates Fundraising: Donna Guarnieri
Purchasing Manager: Stacie Crane
Year Founded: 1888
Estimated Sales: $20-50 Million
Number Employees: 20-49
Type of Packaging: Food Service
Other Locations:
 New Philadelphia, OH
 Akron, OH
 Weirton, WVAkron
Types of Products Distributed:
 Frozen Food, General Line, Provisions/Meat, Produce, Seafood, Grocery & foodservice products

54675 Albert Uster Imports Inc
9211 Gaither Rd
Gaithersburg, MD 20877-1419 301-963-5074
Fax: 301-948-2601 800-231-8154
info@auiswiss.com
Wholesaler/distributor and importer of European chocolates, cookies, hors d'oeuvres, soups/soup bases, mixes, flavors, dehydrated fruits, cereals, liqueur concentrates, pistachios, glazes, knives, molds, etc.
President: Albert Uster
CEO: Philipp Braun
CEO: Philipp Braun
Branch Manager: Lisa Barrantes
Sales Coordinator: Joanna Peschin
Estimated Sales: $20-50 Million
Number Employees: 20-49
Private Brands Carried:
 Carma; Laderach; Flachsmann; Hug; Hugli; Bombasei
Types of Products Distributed:
 Frozen Food, General Line, General Merchandise, Specialty Foods, European foods

54676 Albert's Organics Inc
1155 Commerce Blvd
Swedesboro, NJ 08085-1763 856-241-9090
Fax: 856-241-9676 800-899-5944
www.albertsorganics.com
Distributor of quality organically grown products and perishables
President: Scott Dennis
sdennis@albertsorganics.com
Business Manager: Charles Nealis
Sales Director: Kim Moyer
Operations Manager: Keith Osga
Purchasing Manager: Donald Lusk
Estimated Sales: $3-5 Million
Number Employees: 10-19
Parent Co: United Natural Foods

54677 Albert's Organics: South
6272 McIntosh Road
Sarasota, FL 34238 863-291-6262
Fax: 863-291-4901 800-996-0004
www.albertsorganics.com
Distributor of quality organically grown products and perishables
President: Barclay Hope
Business Manager: James Day
james.day@albertsorganics.com
Sales/Operations: Shawn Butler
Operations Manager: Jeff Carr
Estimated Sales: $1-3 Million
Number Employees: 10-19
Parent Co: United Natural Foods

54678 Albert's Organics: West
3268 East Vernon Avenue
Vernon, CA 90058 323-587-6367
Fax: 323-587-6567 800-899-4595
www.albertsorganics.com
Distributor of quality organically grown products and perishables. The company acquired the assets of Roots & Fruits Cooperative
President: Kurt Lutteke
Business Manager: Andrew Weis
Sales Manager: Roger Niebolt
Contact: Jesse Aguilar
jaguilar@albertsorganics.com
Estimated Sales: $5-10 Million
Number Employees: 50-99
Parent Co: United Natural Foods

54679 Albion Enterprises
5577 Skylane Blvd Ste 5a
Santa Rosa, CA 95403 707-528-1473
Fax: 707-528-0608 800-248-1475
Wholesaler/distributor of vegetable juicers and small appliances including yogurt makers, kitchen mills and food dehydrators
Owner: Ann Hurst
Estimated Sales: $3-5 Million
Number Employees: 1-4
Types of Products Distributed:
 Frozen Food, General Merchandise, Vegetable juicers, yogurt makers, etc.

54680 Albion Fisheries
740 Tyee Road
Vancouver, BC V9A 6X3
Canada 250-382-8286
Fax: 250-381-1346 800-451-9776
albionVIC@albion.bc.ca www.albion.bc.ca
Wholesaler/distributor of seafood
President: Johnn Goodvin
CEO: Dave Athey
Manager: Mark Blouin
Number Employees: 100-249
Types of Products Distributed:
 Frozen Food, Seafood

54681 Alchemie USA Inc.
790 S Main
Suite 2C
Southington, CT 06489 860-621-2470
Fax: 860-621-9570 psavla@alchemieusa.com
www.alchemieusa.com
Wholesaler/distributor and importer of vitamin supplements including melatonin, ranitidine and niacin
President/CEO: Pete Savla
VP: Bhame Savla
Estimated Sales: $3-5 Million
Number Employees: 1-4
Type of Packaging: Bulk
Types of Products Distributed:
 Frozen Food, Health Food, Vitamin supplements

54682 Alderiso Brothers
Newark Farmers Market
Newark, NJ 07105 973-589-4386
Fax: 973-589-8288
Wholesaler/distributor of produce
President: Frank Travisano
VP: Richard Alderiso
Number Employees: 10-19
Types of Products Distributed:
 Frozen Food, Produce

54683 Aleias Gluten Free Foods
4 Pin Oak Dr
Branford, CT 06405-6506 203-488-5556
connect@aleias.com
www.aleias.com
Gluten-free cookies, bread crumbs, panko, croutons, breads and stuffing mixes.
Contact: Jim Snow
jims@aleias.com
Estimated Sales: Less Than $500,000
Number Employees: 1-4

54684 Alerta-Mat
7280 Sly Park Road
Placerville, CA 95667-8138 530-647-8535
Fax: 530-647-8536
Wholesaler/distributor of fatigue mats and alarm and door bell announcers; serving the food service market
Owner: Rod Avery
Types of Products Distributed:
 Food Service, Frozen Food, General Merchandise

54685 Alex & George
2 Rockwood St
Rochester, NY 14610-2611 585-323-2020
Fax: 585-473-1684 800-773-0475
www.a-gmeats.com
Wholesaler/distributor of pita bread and specialty foods; serving the food service market
Owner: George Tonas
Owner: Alex Stathopoulos
CEO, Director: Bill Stathopoulos
Packaging/Quality Control: John Pampoukidis
Marketing, Sales: Dino Marou
Sales: John Rozaklis
Contact: John Henchen
johnh@a-gmeats.com
Operations: George Haltses
Purchasing, Sales: John Henchen
Estimated Sales: $5-10 Million
Number Employees: 10-19
Types of Products Distributed:
 Food Service, Frozen Food, Specialty Foods, Pita bread

54686 Alfa Cappuccino Import LTD
231 Millway Avenue
Unit 7
Concord, ON L4K 3T7
Canada 905-660-2750
Fax: 905-660-2755 800-764-2532
info@expresso.com www.espresso.com
Importer of cappuccino machines
President: Ross Cammalleri
Number Employees: 10
Types of Products Distributed:
 Frozen Food

54687 Alfa Chem
2 Harbor Way
Kings Point, NY 11024-2117 516-504-0059
Fax: 516-504-0039 800-375-6869
alfachem@gmail.com www.alfachem1.com
Provides raw materials to industries such as manufacturing, repackaging, research, pharmaceutical, food and cosmetics, as well as Universities and Hospitals.
President: Alfred Khalily
alfredkhalily@yahoo.com
Estimated Sales: $2.5 000,000
Number Employees: 1-4
Number of Products: 300
Square Footage: 7500
Type of Packaging: Private Label, Bulk
Types of Products Distributed:
 Health Food

54688 Alfa International Corp
4 Kaysal Ct # 1
Armonk, NY 10504-1309 914-273-2222
Fax: 914-273-3666 800-327-2532
www.alfaco.com
Wholesaler/distributor, importer and exporter of replacement parts for food processing equipment including mixers, slicers, bandsaws, cutters, graters/shredders, etc.; also, aprons, gloves, metal mesh, blades and small food choppersand cheese graters

Wholesalers & Distributors / A-Z

President: Roger Madigan
rmadigan@alfaco.com
Controller: Joseph Valerio
R&D: Eric Stull
Quality Control: Jose Quintero
Marketing Director: Christar Cambriello
Sales Director: Charles Boccia
Public Relations: Jolita Meskauskaite
Operations: David Tate
Production: Ted Sumaski
Plant Manager: Greg Hintze
Purchasing Agent: Michael Henry
Estimated Sales: $5-10 Million
Number Employees: 10-19
Square Footage: 80000
Type of Packaging: Food Service
Private Brands Carried:
 Sosteel
Types of Products Distributed:
 General Merchandise, Replacement parts, aprons, gloves, etc.

54689 Alfred Louie Inc
4501 Shepard St
Bakersfield, CA 93313-2310   661-831-2520
            Fax: 661-833-9197
Fruits and vegetables, pasta, and Chinese canned goods and vegetables.
President: Susan Louie
Manager: Gordon Louie
peakdragon@yahoo.com
Estimated Sales: $5,115,628
Number Employees: 10-19

54690 Algen Scale Corp
390 Knickerbocker Ave # 13
Bohemia, NY 11716-3123   631-342-1975
    Fax: 631-342-1979 800-836-8445
info@algen.com www.algen.com
Sales, service and rental of all types of scales for all applications.
President: Randall D Aigen
raigen@algen.com
CEO: Jeffrey Aigen
CFO: Randall Aigen
Estimated Sales: $1-3 Million
Number Employees: 5-9
Square Footage: 12000
Type of Packaging: Consumer, Food Service
Types of Products Distributed:
 General Merchandise, Scales and Weighing Systems

54691 Alioto Lazio Fish Co
440 Jefferson St
San Francisco, CA 94109-1315   415-673-5868
    Fax: 415-922-8183 888-673-5868
aliotolazio@sbcglobal.net www.crabonline.com
Wholesaler/distributor of fresh Pacific fish and shellfish; also, equipment and fixtures
Owner: Tom Lazio
Contact: Angel Cincotta
Estimated Sales: $2.5-5 Million
Number Employees: 10-19
Square Footage: 40000
Types of Products Distributed:
 Frozen Food, General Merchandise, Seafood, Equipment & fixtures

54692 Aliquippa Fruit Market
1294 Meadow Dr
Aliquippa, PA 15001   724-378-8008
            Fax: 724-378-8733
Wholesaler/distributor of apples, grapefruit, lettuce, oranges, potatoes, etc.
President: Trefen Drostis
Co-Owner/VP: Thomas Drostis, Jr.
Estimated Sales: Less than $500,000
Number Employees: 1-4
Types of Products Distributed:
 Frozen Food, Produce, Apples, grapefruit, lettuce, etc.

54693 All American Specialty Corporation
8449 Arlington Expy
Jacksonville, FL 32211   904-739-2550
    Fax: 904-739-2789 800-852-1183
Wholesaler/distributor of advertising specialties; also, screen printing and embroidering available
Owner: Robert Talley
Sales Manager: Tim Miller
Manager: John Preacher

Estimated Sales: $1-2.5 Million
Number Employees: 10-19
Number of Customer Locations: 1200
Types of Products Distributed:
 Frozen Food, General Merchandise, Advertising specialties

54694 All Caribbean Food Service
6814 NW 12th Court
Plantation, FL 33313-6025   954-587-3051
    Fax: 954-587-4079 acfs97@aol.com
Wholesaler/distributor of frozen foods, meats, equipment, supplies and paper goods
President: Jerry Nemeth
VP: Fernando Perez
Types of Products Distributed:
 Frozen Food, General Line, General Merchandise, Provisions/Meat, Paper goods, supplies, etc.

54695 All Cinema Sales & Services
120 Laurel Road
East Northport, NY 11731   631-754-5655
    Fax: 631-754-2213 800-628-5788
            mail@allcinemasales.com
Wholesaler/distributor of lighting fixtures and electric lighting dimmers
President: Jim Kelly
Vice President: Tom Kelly
Contact: Steven Marvin
marvinsteven@exec.ny.gov
Estimated Sales: $1-3 Million
Number Employees: 1-4
Square Footage: 24000
Parent Co: East Coast Lamp Sales Inc
Private Brands Carried:
 Lightolier; Progress; Advance; Heviduty
Types of Products Distributed:
 General Merchandise, Lighting fixtures & electric dimmers

54696 All Fresh Products
40 20th St
San Diego, CA 92102-3896   619-232-1008
    Fax: 619-232-3740 www.allfreshproducts.com
Wholesaler/distributor of frozen foods and general line products; serving the food service market
President: Richard Goodwin
richgoodwin@gmail.com
Estimated Sales: $10-20 Million
Number Employees: 10-19
Types of Products Distributed:
 Food Service, Frozen Food, General Line

54697 All Lift Equipment
611 Manwell Blvd
Bakersfield, CA 93307-9492   661-364-0161
    Fax: 661-364-0163 wheelermachinery@att.net
            www.alwinc.com
Wholesaler/distributor of material handling equipment and automatic storage and handling systems
President: Ryan Wheeler
VP: Erin Wheeler
Estimated Sales: $2.5-5 Million
Number Employees: 5-9
Number of Customer Locations: 300
Types of Products Distributed:
 Frozen Food, General Merchandise, Automatic storage & handling systems

54698 All Pack Co Inc
718 Arrow Grand Cir
Covina, CA 91722-2147   626-966-3526
    Fax: 626-966-8101 800-669-7225
            www.all-pack.com
Wholesaler/distributor of packaging machinery and systems including baggers, bag sealers, weighers, formers, fillers and sealers, box tapers, bundle strappers, pallet wrappers, jet printers and shrink wrappers; also, parts, service and installation available
President: Ed Kissell
elvira.c@all-pack.com
Sales Director: John Underwood
Manager: Bill Kissell
Estimated Sales: $10-20 Million
Number Employees: 10-19
Square Footage: 30000
Types of Products Distributed:
 General Merchandise, Baggers, bag sealers, box tapers, etc.

54699 All Power Inc
2228 Murray St
Sioux City, IA 51111-1148   712-258-0681
    Fax: 712-258-6561 info@allpowerinc.com
            www.allpowerinc.com
Manufacturer and wholesaler/distributor of packing house equipment, trolleys, shackles and stainless steel conveyors; also, sludge pumps, pressure vessels, indexers, auto feeders and drives including electric motor, gear boxes hydraulics and line shafting
President: Eugene Anderson
General Manager: Gene Anderson, Jr.
Purchasing Manager: Jim Tucker
Estimated Sales: $10-20 Million
Number Employees: 50-99
Square Footage: 70000
Types of Products Distributed:
 Frozen Food, General Merchandise, Packing house equipment

54700 All QA Products
63 Mcadenville Rd
Belmont, NC 28012-2434   704-829-6600
    Fax: 704-829-6602 800-845-8818
            sales@allqa.com www.allqa.com
Wholesaler/distributor and importer of thermometers; also, HAACP plans and training materials available
Owner: Janet Cox
sales@allqa.com
Number Employees: 1-4
Types of Products Distributed:
 Frozen Food, General Merchandise, Thermometers

54701 All Seasons Fisheries
Unit 15
Scarborough, ON M8Z 5Z8
Canada   416-255-3474
            Fax: 416-752-8742
Wholesaler/distributor of fish
VP: Eddie Li
Number Employees: 50-99
Types of Products Distributed:
 Frozen Food, Seafood

54702 All Seasons International Distributors
650 Park East Blvd
New Albany, IN 47150   812-949-1898
General grocery
President: Michael Tao
Vice President: Richard Tao
Year Founded: 1989
Estimated Sales: $2.60 Million

54703 All Seasons Uniforms & Textile
3600 Hacienda Blvd # G
Davie, FL 33314-2822   954-583-5208
            Fax: 954-584-3169
Wholesaler/distributor of linen products including table cloths, skirting, napkins, uniforms, chef hats and place mats; serving the food service market
Owner: Bob Miller
Estimated Sales: $2.5-5 Million
Number Employees: 20-49
Types of Products Distributed:
 Food Service, Frozen Food, General Merchandise, Linen products: table cloths, etc.

54704 All Star Dairy Foods
620 New Ludlow Rd
South Hadley, MA 01075-2669   413-538-5240
    Fax: 413-532-4093 800-462-1129
            www.allstardairyfoods.com
Dairy products
Owner: Russ Sawyer
Inside Sales Manager: Lynne Sawyer
rsawyer@allstardairyfoods.com
Office Manager: Lynn Rivest
Estimated Sales: $7.5 Million
Number Employees: 20-49
Square Footage: 10400
Type of Packaging: Consumer
Other Locations:
 Schenkel's Dairy
 Fort Wayne, IN Schenkel's Dairy

54705 All Star Janitorial Supply
61 S Highway 602
Gallup, NM 87301   505-863-4496
    Fax: 505-863-4372 800-995-7392
            www.unisourceworldwide.com

Wholesaler/distributor of sanitary and janitorial supplies; serving the food service market
Manager: David Radosevich
Estimated Sales: $.5-1 million
Number Employees: 1-4
Parent Co: Georgia Pacific
Private Brands Carried:
  All-Star
Types of Products Distributed:
  Food Service, Frozen Food, General Merchandise, Sanitary & janitorial supplies

54706 All Star, Ltd.
PO Box 1445
Fond Du Lac, WI 54936-1445   920-921-0005
              Fax: 920-921-2287 800-854-0492
      sales@allstarcheese.com www.allstarcheese.com
Dairy products and cheeses
President: Bob Brandl
VP: Patricia Brandl
Marketing: Mary Sclavi
Customer Service: Lynne Kottke
Estimated Sales: $10 Million
Number Employees: 1-4
Type of Packaging: Consumer, Food Service, Private Label, Bulk
Private Brands Carried:
  All Star
Types of Products Distributed:
  Food Service, Food Processing/Dairy Products

54707 All State Restaurant Supply
PO Box 1267
Mansfield, OH 44901-1267   419-525-3373
                            Fax: 419-525-3375
              all-staterestaurantequipment.com
Wholesaler/distributor of tabletop, kitchen, cooking and food preparation equipment; serving the food service market
Co-Owner: Nora Guzzo
Co-Owner: Garry Guzzo
Estimated Sales: $1-3 Million
Number Employees: 1-4
Types of Products Distributed:
  Food Service, Frozen Food, General Merchandise, Tabletop supplies, etc.

54708 All Valley Packaging
PO Box 63201
Colorado Springs, CO 80962-3201
                            Fax: 425-650-5090
Printed boxes, labels, bags, pouches, food service containers, pallets, janitorial maintenance supply
President: Cheryl Mikel
VP/Sales: Steve Hobden
Purchasing Manager: Cheryl Mikel
Number Employees: 5
Number of Brands: 100+
Number of Products: 1000
Type of Packaging: Food Service, Private Label

54709 All-Redi Flour & Salt Company
99 Crescent Avenue
Chelsea, MA 02150-2516   617-884-5113
Wholesaler/distributor of bakery products
President: Eugene Monahan
Estimated Sales: $10-20 Million
Number Employees: 5-9
Types of Products Distributed:
  Frozen Food, General Line

54710 All-State Industries Inc
520 S 18th St
West Des Moines, IA 50265-6449   515-223-5843
              Fax: 515-223-8305 800-247-4178
              dsmsales@all-statebelting.com
                      www.all-stateind.com
Wholesaler/distributor of food handling belting for conveyors
President: Doug Berner
dberner@all-statebelting.com
Vice President: Casey Price
Research & Development: Doug Tibkin
Quality Control: Sherry Wilkinson
Estimated Sales: $20-50 Million
Number Employees: 10-19
Parent Co: All-State Industries
Types of Products Distributed:
  Frozen Food, General Merchandise, Food handling belting

54711 All-Tech Materials Handling
255 Centre Ave
Abington, MA 02351-2207   781-871-0943
              Fax: 781-871-5921 800-242-1360
                      www.all-techmaterials.com
Wholesaler/distributor of material handling equipment including conveyors, shelving, jacks, etc
President: Leo Parkes
alltech@gis.net
Estimated Sales: $5-10 Million
Number Employees: 10-19
Square Footage: 180000
Private Brands Carried:
  Hi Line; Amco/GAI; Hodge
Types of Products Distributed:
  Frozen Food, General Merchandise, Material handling equipment

54712 Allan Chemical Corp
2147 Hudson Ter
Fort Lee, NJ 07024-7729   973-962-4014
              Fax: 201-592-9298 800-633-0274
              allanchem@juno.com www.allanchem.com
Wholesaler/distributor of FCC/USP food grade nutritional supplements and flavors including triacetin, citric acid, sodium benzoate, manganese and magnesium sulphates, etc.; serving the food service market
President: Allan Raphael
allanchem@allanchem.com
Manager Flavors/Fragrances: Irma Campbell
Operations Manager: Rulu Perez
Estimated Sales: $5-10 Million
Number Employees: 5-9
Square Footage: 4000
Types of Products Distributed:
  Food Service, Frozen Food, General Line, Citric acid, sodium benzoate, etc.

54713 Allegheny Valley
270 Alpha Drive
Pittsburgh, PA 15238-2906   412-967-9656
                            Fax: 412-967-9654
Warehouse providing stoarge space for dry, and refrigerated goods
President: Barry Miller
CEO: Eddie DiPasquale
Director Sales: James Shipe
Estimated Sales: $20-50 Million
Number Employees: 20-49
Square Footage: 5000
Type of Packaging: Food Service

54714 Allegro Coffee Co
12799 Claude Ct
Suite B
Thornton, CO 80241-3828   303-444-4844
              Fax: 303-920-5468 800-666-4869
                      www.allegrocoffee.com
Roasted specialty coffees; importer of green coffee beans.
President/General Manager: Jeff Teter
jeff_teter@allegro-coffee.com
CFO: Clarence Peterson
VP: David Kubena
Marketing Director: Tara Cross
Sales Director: Glenda Chamberlain
Human Resources Director: Mimi Fins
Plant Operations Manager: Alejandro Rodolfo
Marketing/Purchasing Manager: Susan Drexel
Estimated Sales: $10 Million
Number Employees: 50-99
Square Footage: 50000
Parent Co: Whole Foods Market
Types of Products Distributed:
  General Line, Specialty Foods, Roasted specialty coffees

54715 Allemagnia Imports Inc
10731 Forest St
Santa Fe Springs, CA 90670-3927 562-941-7225
                            Fax: 562-941-4704
Wholesaler/distributor of baking products, candies, potato products, pickles, mustards, chocolates, cookies, cheeses, etc.; importer of pickles, red and white cabbage, mustards, canned vegetables and fruits, fish, dextrose productsjams, noodles, ketchup
President: Helmut Graef
allemania1@juno.com
Estimated Sales: $3-5 Million
Number Employees: 1-4
Square Footage: 21200
Type of Packaging: Consumer
Private Brands Carried:
  Panni; Champignon; Kaiserdom
Types of Products Distributed:
  Specialty Foods, Candy, cookies, cheese, pickles, etc.

54716 Allen Brothers Inc
3737 S Halsted St
Chicago, IL 60609-1689   773-890-5100
              Fax: 773-890-9146 800-548-7777
              foodservice@allenbrothers.com
                      www.allenbrothers.com
Wholesaler/distributor of meats and equipment; serving the food service market
President: Robert Hatoff
Chairman: Melvin Salomon
VP: Todd Alatoff
VP Sales: Michael Hicks
Estimated Sales: $10-20 Million
Number Employees: 100-249
Square Footage: 105000
Types of Products Distributed:
  Food Service, Frozen Food, General Merchandise, Provisions/Meat

54717 Allen Rosenthal Company
PO Box 24927
Fort Lauderdale, FL 33307-4927   305-824-9797
                            Fax: 305-824-1197
Wholesaler/distributor of hotel and restaurant supplies including contract furniture and food; serving the food service market
President: Allen Rosenthal
VP: Lee Rosenthal
Marketing Manager: Mauree Talman
Estimated Sales: $2.5-5 Million
Number Employees: 10-19
Types of Products Distributed:
  Food Service, Frozen Food, General Line, General Merchandise, Hotel & restaurant supplies

54718 Allendale Produce Plant
24241 Peckham Rd
Wilder, ID 83676   208-482-6221
                            Fax: 208-482-6222
Wholesaler/distributor of onions
President: Chris Inouye
Manager: Carey Inouye
Estimated Sales: $1-2.5 Million
Number Employees: 20-49
Types of Products Distributed:
  Frozen Food, Produce

54719 Alliance Supply Management
4551 Kenny Commerce Dr
Houston, TX 77032-3425   713-335-2500
              asm@asmlimited.com
                      www.asmlimited.com
Wholesaler/distributor of general line products; serving the food service market; also, ship chandler services to cruise ships available.
Sales Manager/President: John Lacey
Year Founded: 1906
Estimated Sales: $20-50 Million
Number Employees: 50-99
Types of Products Distributed:
  Food Service, Frozen Food, General Line

54720 Allie's GF Goodies
1B West Village Green
Hicksville, NY 11801   855-943-7330
                            alliesgfg.com
Gluten free, tree nut free, peanut free products

54721 Allied Blending & Ingredients
121 Royal Rd
Keokuk, IA 52632-2028   319-524-1235
              Fax: 319-524-9889 800-758-4080
              cs@alliedblending.com www.alliedblending.com
Cheese and tortilla products; also baked goods and ingredients.
President: Randy Schmelzel
rschmelzel@alliedblending.com
CFO: Charles Cross
VP Technical Services: John Fannon
Director, Sales & Marketing: Tara Perry
Operations: Matt Stelzer
Plant Manager: Jeff Brunenn
Purchasing: Stephanie Slattery
Number Employees: 50-99
Square Footage: 1200
Types of Products Distributed:
  Frozen Food, General Line, Starches, sweeteners, etc.

Wholesalers & Distributors / A-Z

54722 Allied Domecq Spirits USA
355 Riverside Avenue
Westport, CT 06880-4810 203-221-5400
Fax: 203-221-5444 www.adsw.com
/www.allieddomecqplc.com
Saler, marketer and wholesaler/distributor company for several premium spirits: Beefeater, Canadian Club, Sauza, Maker's mark, Couvoisier, Ballantine's and Hiram Walker liqueurs
President: Martin Jones
CFO: Alfredo Valdes
President, USA: Todd Martin
Contact: Antony Hales
antony.hales@adsw.com
Number Employees: 100-249
Parent Co: Pernod Ricard
Type of Packaging: Consumer, Food Service
Types of Products Distributed:
Frozen Food

54723 Allied Food Service
4500 Sheppard Avenue E
Unit 25
Scarborough, ON M1S 3R6
Canada 416-321-0422
Fax: 416-321-2258
Wholesaler/distributor of meats, groceries and cleaning supplies; serving the food service market
President: Gerard McKinnon
Number Employees: 10-19
Square Footage: 40000
Types of Products Distributed:
Food Service, Frozen Food, General Line, General Merchandise, Provisions/Meat, Groceries & cleaning supplies

54724 Allied Industrial Equipment
1640 Island Home Ave
Knoxville, TN 37920 865-573-0995
Fax: 865-579-1028 www.alliedtoyotalift.com
Wholesaler/distributor of material handling equipment including forklifts and conveyors
President: Jerry Hatmaker
jhatmaker@alliedtoyotalift.com
Estimated Sales: $20-50 Million
Number Employees: 20-49
Private Brands Carried:
Toyota; Linde-Baker; Taylor Dunn
Types of Products Distributed:
Frozen Food, General Merchandise, Material handling equipment

54725 (HQ)Allied International Corp
22570 Markey Ct # 108
Sterling, VA 20166-6915 703-444-5515
Fax: 703-444-6493 800-626-2623
allied@alliedint.com www.aicit.com
Wholesaler/distributor and importer of candy, chocolate, cookies, crackers, teas, coffee, preserves, dill pickles, gum, pasta, honey, oils, cereals, dried fruits etc. and exporter
President: Chad Akhavan
Chairman: Kelly Akhavan
CFO: Willy Gloriouso
CEO: Kelly Ackland
Quality Control: Heather Vincent
Marketing Director: Asad Kasini
Sales Director: Bob Kinothe
Public Relations: Paul Akhavan
Purchasing Manager: Chad Akhavan
Estimated Sales: $10-20 Million
Number Employees: 10-19
Number of Brands: 10
Square Footage: 200000
Type of Packaging: Consumer, Food Service, Private Label
Private Brands Carried:
Forrelli; Bon Sante; Smith & Johnson; McGuniss
Types of Products Distributed:
Food Service, Specialty Foods, Grocery Products

54726 Allied Packaging
5640 S 16th St
Phoenix, AZ 85040 602-437-3831
Fax: 602-437-3938 info@alliedonline.com
www.alliedonline.com
Manufactures labels, custom packaging, polyethylene, corrugated.
President: Darrel Bison
dbison@alliedonline.com
Year Founded: 1979
Estimated Sales: $50-100 Million
Number Employees: 50-99
Square Footage: 105000

54727 Allied Premium Company
1170 Broadway
New York, NY 10001-7507 212-532-7180
Fax: 212-683-5052
Wholesaler/distributor of general merchandise including advertising specialties, incentives, premiums and business gifts
Office Manager: Doris Becker
General Manager: Bernie Rosten
Estimated Sales: $2.5-5 Million
Number Employees: 100-249
Square Footage: 8000
Number of Customer Locations: 400
Types of Products Distributed:
Frozen Food, General Merchandise, Advertising specialties

54728 Allied Provision Company
PO Box 7158
Detroit, MI 48207-0158 313-568-2200
Fax: 313-568-0639
Wholesaler/distributor of packaged and processed meats including specialty sausages, smoked meat and fish, portion cut meat and poultry; serving the food service market
VP: Richard Lehmer
Manager (Specialty Food): Craig Berry
Estimated Sales: $10-20 Million
Number Employees: 10-19
Private Brands Carried:
Hormel; Oscar Meyer; Allied
Types of Products Distributed:
Food Service, Provisions/Meat, Seafood, Specialty sausages, smoked meat, etc.

54729 Allkind Container Co
4471 Dunham St
Los Angeles, CA 90023-4192 323-268-9111
Fax: 323-268-2491
Wholesaler/distributor of jars, bottles and containers
Owner: George Boyadjani
Estimated Sales: Less Than $500,000
Number Employees: 1-4
Types of Products Distributed:
Frozen Food, General Merchandise, Jars, bottles & containers

54730 Allstate Insurance Company
1819 Electric Rd. S.W.
P.O. Box 12055
Roanoke, VA 24018 773-268-2100
Fax: 773-268-6216 800-255-7828
www.allstate.com
Wholesaler/distributor of conveyor systems
Contact: Anita Reed
areed@allstate.com
Parent Co: Motion Industry
Types of Products Distributed:
Frozen Food, General Merchandise, Conveyor systems

54731 Alnor Oil Co Inc
70 E Sunrise Hwy
Suite 418
Valley Stream, NY 11581 516-561-6146
877-561-6146
www.alnoroil.com
Wholesaler/distributor of domestic and imported vegetable oils.
President: Marjorie Klayman
marge@alnoroil.com
Vice President & Treasurer: Gordon Kaplan
Vice President & Secretary: Nancy Kaplan
Sales: Joan Bassi
Year Founded: 1968
Estimated Sales: $20-50 Million
Square Footage: 3750
Types of Products Distributed:
Frozen Food, General Line, Oils: vegetable, castor, etc.

54732 (HQ)Alpha Baking Company
1910 Lincoln Way West
South Bend, IN 46628 773-261-6000
spowell@alphabaking.com
www.alphabaking.com
Fresh and frozen bread, buns, and bagels sold through wholesale or retail
CEO: Lawrence Marcucci
Vice President of Division: Gary Narcisi
VP of Sales & Marketing: Tim Gill
Estimated Sales: $7 Million
Number Employees: 1000
Square Footage: 600000
Type of Packaging: Consumer, Food Service
Types of Products Distributed:
Frozen Food, General Line

54733 Alpha Foods
2130 Beaver Rd
Landover, MD 20785 301-322-2222
Fax: 301-322-2224
Wholesaler/distributor serving the food service market
President: Angelo Magafan
Estimated Sales: $10-20 Million
Number Employees: 5-9
Types of Products Distributed:
Food Service, Frozen Food

54734 (HQ)Alpha Omega Technology
14 Ridgedale Avenue #110
Cedar Knolls, NJ 07927-1106 973-537-0073
Fax: 973-292-4999 800-442-1969
info@karibafarms.com www.karibafarms.com
Designer, builder and wholesaler/distributor of turn-key facilities; also, irradiation processing facility for the sanitation and sterilization of food ingredients
CEO: Martin Welt
Office Manager: Ruth Welt
Estimated Sales: $500,000-$1 Million
Number Employees: 5-9
Square Footage: 120000
Types of Products Distributed:
Frozen Food, General Merchandise, Turn-key facilities

54735 Alphin Brothers
2302 Us Highway 301 S
Dunn, NC 28334 910-892-8751
Fax: 910-892-2709 800-672-4502
alphin@alphinbrothers.com
www.alphinbrothers.com
Wholesaler/distributor of frozen seafood, beef and pork.
President: Jesse Alphin Jr
VP/Financial Officer: Ernest Alphin
Production Manager: John Hyland
Estimated Sales: $2 Million
Number Employees: 26
Type of Packaging: Consumer, Food Service
Types of Products Distributed:
Frozen Food, Seafood

54736 Alpine Food Distributing Inc
2400 SE Mailwell Dr
Milwaukie, OR 97222 503-905-5201
Fax: 503-905-5243 800-979-9643
www.alpinefoods.com
Wholesaler/distributor of frozen foods, general line and dairy products, provisions/meats and seafood.
Owner: Gregory Carlston
gcarlston@alpinefoods.com
Director, Finance: Dianne Sanders
Sales Manager: George Ware
Vice President, Marketing: Dave Kester
General Manager: Shawn Hood
Vice President, Purchasing: Michael Kamprath
Year Founded: 1983
Estimated Sales: $52 Million
Number Employees: 115
Square Footage: 280000
Number of Customer Locations: 333
Types of Products Distributed:
Frozen Food, General Line, Provisions/Meat, Seafood, Dairy products

54737 Alpine Gloves
41093 County Center Dr
Temecula, CA 92591 951-296-2521
Fax: 951-296-2541 800-888-4669
www.alpinegloves.com
Importer and wholesaler/distributor of protective clothing including disposable gloves, aprons and caps; serving the food service market
President/CEO: Patrick Schmidt
Estimated Sales: $5-10 Million
Number Employees: 10-19
Square Footage: 160000
Type of Packaging: Consumer, Food Service, Private Label, Bulk
Private Brands Carried:
Alpine

54738 Alpine Industries/Alpine Air Products
4546 American Way
Cottage Grove, WI 53527-9734   608-839-5447
Fax: 608-839-5628   800-659-5447
Wholesaler/distributor of air purification systems
Owner: Tom Laugen
National Sales Manager: Thomas Laugen
Estimated Sales: $.5-1 million
Number Employees: 1-4
Private Brands Carried:
  Alpine Air
Types of Products Distributed:
  Frozen Food, General Merchandise, Air purification systems

54739 Alpine Meats
7850 Lower Sacramento Rd
Stockton, CA 95210-3912   209-477-2691
Fax: 209-477-1994   800-399-6328
info@alpinemeats.com www.alpinemeats.com
Frankfurters, sausages and hams.
President: Jerry Singer
Quality Control: James Sturgeon
Controller: Cecil McKie
Production: Dennis Saragoza
Purchasing: Robby Jaynes
Estimated Sales: $8 Million
Number Employees: 50-99
Square Footage: 196000
Type of Packaging: Consumer, Food Service, Private Label, Bulk
Private Brands Carried:
  Aidells Sausage; Franks Foods; Martins Pure Foods; Niman Ranch; Rego's Purity Food; VIP Food Service
Number of Customer Locations: 120

54740 Alson Specialty Company
44 Maiden Ln
Kingston, NY 12401   845-331-8547
Fax: 845-331-1075
Wholesaler/distributor of general merchandise including advertising specialties, calendars, pens, decals, coffee mugs, placemats, napkins, etc
Owner: Marc Sonnenberg
Estimated Sales: $125,000
Number Employees: 1
Square Footage: 900
Parent Co: Impromoteu
Private Brands Carried:
  Spring Print/Medallion; Sorg's Paper Place
Number of Customer Locations: 300
Types of Products Distributed:
  Frozen Food, General Merchandise, Advertising specialties, etc.

54741 Alsum Farms & Produce
N9083 County Road E
Cambria, WI 53923-9668   920-348-5127
Fax: 920-348-5174   800-236-5127
www.alsum.com
Potatoes and onions; fresh fruits and vegetables.
President & CEO: Larry Alsum
CEO: Randy Fischer
randy.fischer@alsum.com
National Sales & Marketing Manager: Heidi Alsum-Randall
Year Founded: 1972
Number Employees: 100-249
Number of Brands: 4
Number of Products: 300
Type of Packaging: Consumer, Food Service, Private Label, Bulk
Types of Products Distributed:
  Food Service

54742 Alta Equipment Co
6327 Jomar Ct
Lansing, MI 48917-8549   517-272-5033
Fax: 517-272-7257   800-261-9642
www.alta.com
Wholesaler/distributor of forklifts; also, parts, service and rental available
President: Jeff Hodgkins
Manager: Lloyd Minto
lminto@sprinterservices.com
Estimated Sales: $10-20 Million
Number Employees: 20-49
Private Brands Carried:
  Cascade; P.C.M.
Types of Products Distributed:
  Frozen Food, General Merchandise, Forklifts

54743 Altech Packaging Company
330 Himrod St
Brooklyn, NY 11237   718-386-8800
Fax: 718-366-2398   800-362-2247
mitchell@altechpackaging.com
www.altechpackaging.com
Wholesaler/distributor, importer and exporter of shrink, skin, blister, sealing, stretch, bag closing, heat sealing and vacuum packaging systems; also, packaging materials including bags, films, boxes, labels, display board and vacuumpouches
President: Mitchell Lomazow
chicoman57@aol.com
Estimated Sales: $4 Million
Number Employees: 10-19
Number of Brands: 50
Number of Products: 300
Square Footage: 180000
Type of Packaging: Food Service, Private Label, Bulk
Types of Products Distributed:
  General Line, Specialty Foods, Packaging systems & materials

54744 Alter Eco
2339 3rd St
Suite 70
San Francisco, CA 94107-3100   415-701-1214
Fax: 415-701-1213 sales@alterecofoods.com
www.alterecofoods.com
Fair trade and organic quinoa, rice, sugar, cacao
Co-founder/Co-CEO: Edouard Rollet
Co-founder/Co-CEO: Mathieu Senard
President: Kate Tierney
Quality Assurance: Anissa Bouziane
Director, Marketing: Antoine Ambert
Director, Operations: Jeanne Cloutier
Number Employees: 1-4

54745 Alternative Health & Herbs
425 Jackson St SE
Albany, OR 97321   541-791-8400
Fax: 541-791-8401   800-345-4152
healthinfo@healthherbs.com
www.healthherbs.com
Liquid herbal formulations; herbal teas and vitamins.
Owner: Bishop Truman Berst
Estimated Sales: Less than $500,000
Number Employees: 1-4
Square Footage: 12000
Type of Packaging: Consumer, Private Label, Bulk
Private Brands Carried:
  American Health & Herbs; American Natural; Truman's
Types of Products Distributed:
  Frozen Food, General Merchandise, Health Food, Specialty Foods, Air & water filters

54746 Alto-Hartley
1313 Dolley Madison Blvd Ste 400
Mc Lean, VA 22101   703-883-1448
Fax: 703-883-0244
Wholesaler/distributor of turn key restaurant equipment
President: Jack Hartley
Sales Manager: Peter Huebner
Contact: John Brandenburg
john@altohartley.com
Estimated Sales: $1-2.5 Million
Number Employees: 10-19
Types of Products Distributed:
  Food Service Equipment

54747 Altrua Marketing & Design
3225 Hartsfield Rd
Tallahassee, FL 32303-3153   850-562-4564
Fax: 850-562-8511   800-443-6939
mfloyd@altrua.com www.wave94.com
Manufacturer and wholesaler/distributor of signs, banners, flags, pennants, table displays, decals and other printed promotional materials
President: Michael Floyd
msmelko@altrua.com
Sales Exec: Melode Smelko
Estimated Sales: $6 Million
Number Employees: 20-49
Square Footage: 160000
Types of Products Distributed:
  Frozen Food, General Merchandise, Signs, banners, flags, etc.

54748 Alwan & Sons
703 E War Memorial Dr
Peoria Heights, IL 61616-7547   309-688-8711
Fax: 309-688-8718 info@alwanandsons.com
www.alwanandsons.com
Wholesaler/distributor of general line products, produce, meats, seafood and specialty food products; serving the food service market
Owner: Brian Alwan
alwanandsons@ameritech.net
Estimated Sales: $5 Million
Number Employees: 20-49
Square Footage: 32000
Number of Customer Locations: 4
Types of Products Distributed:
  Food Service, Frozen Food, General Line, Provisions/Meat, Produce, Seafood, Specialty Foods

54749 AmTech Ingredients
573 County Route A
Suite 102
Hudson, WI 54016   715-381-5746
www.amtechingredients.com
Producer/distributor of specialty food ingredients, primarily in powder form.
Contact: Andrew Brudevold
abrudevold@amtechingredients.com
Estimated Sales: $330,000
Number Employees: 3
Square Footage: 6734

54750 Amana Meat Shop & SmokeHouse
4513 F St
Amana, IA 52203-8027   319-622-7586
Fax: 319-622-6245   800-373-6328
info@amanameatshop.com
Hickory-smoked meats including sausage, ham, bacon, pork tenderloin and bratwurst.
Manager: Greg Hergert
Director: Mike Shoup
Estimated Sales: Less than $500,000
Number Employees: 10-19
Parent Co: Amana Society Corporation
Type of Packaging: Consumer, Food Service
Types of Products Distributed:
  Provisions/Meat

54751 Ambassador Fine Foods
16625 Saticoy St
Van Nuys, CA 91406   818-787-2000
Fax: 818-778-6464 www.ambassadorfoods.com
Wholesaler/distributor and importer of baking ingredients including flour, decorative elements and colorings
Owner: Cory Vestal
VP: Kathy Schreiber
Contact: Peter Seeger
peter.seeger@qzina.com
Office Manager: Victoria Morfin
Estimated Sales: $10-20 Million
Number Employees: 20-49
Types of Products Distributed:
  Frozen Food, General Line, Baking ingredients

54752 Amcan Industries
570 Taxter Road
Elmsford, NY 10523-2356   914-347-4838
Fax: 914-347-4960
Meat, jam, jelly, preserves, health food, nutriceuticals, confectionery, fish, seafood, dairy, beverage and juices, bakery and cereal, natural and artificial sweeteners
President: Bowes Dempsey
VP: Benjamin Dempsey
Contact: Guylaine Boucher
guylaine@dempseycorporation.com
Estimated Sales: $5-10 Million
Number Employees: 7

54753 Amende & Schultz Co
1017 Fremont Ave
South Pasadena, CA 91030-3224   323-682-3806
Fax: 626-799-7572
Importer and wholesaler/distributor of fish including lobster, scallops, scampi, etc; serving the food service market
President: Terry Schultz
Vice President: Bruce Beagle

Wholesalers & Distributors / A-Z

Estimated Sales: $5-10 Million
Number Employees: 5-9
Types of Products Distributed:
 Seafood

54754 Amenity Services
110 W Dayton St # 201
Suite 3-201
Edmonds, WA 98020-7210 206-224-0393
 Fax: 206-224-9304 800-533-2619
 info@amenityservices.com
 www.amenityservices.com
Wholesaler/distributor of coffee and coffee makers; serving the food service market
CEO: Don Stoulil
dstoulil@wpcoffee.com
President/Co-Founder: Eric McCoy
Co-Founder: Richard Stoulil
VP, Design & Development: Sherri Scheck-Merrill
Director Sales/Marketing: Sherry Kurdziel
General Manager: Ryan Stoulil
Estimated Sales: $1-2.5 Million
Number Employees: 10-19
Parent Co: Starbrand Products
Other Locations:
 Amenity Service
 Orange, CAAmenity Service
Private Brands Carried:
 La Matina; Krups; Kitchen Aid; Hawaiian Kona; Bruto
Types of Products Distributed:
 Food Service, Frozen Food, General Line, General Merchandise, Coffee & coffee makers

54755 American Advertising Specialties Company
1623 Dutch Broadway
Elmont, NY 11003-5008 516-561-8080
 Fax: 516-561-0389 877-791-8080
Wholesaler/distributor of general merchandise including advertising specialties, badges, medals, calendars, emblems, flags, pennants, banners, pencils, marking and writing pens and measuring rules; premiums and custom imprintingavailable
Owner/General Manager: Art Silverman
art.silverman@americanspec.net
VP: Joel Streiter
Sales Manager: Sam Streiter
Estimated Sales: $5-10 Million
Number Employees: 10-19
Square Footage: 8800
Private Brands Carried:
 Bic; Cross; Paper Mate
Number of Customer Locations: 2500
Types of Products Distributed:
 Frozen Food, General Merchandise, Advertising specialties

54756 American Agrotrading
P.O.Box Am
P.O. Box 1141
Carmel, CA 93921 831-625-5603
  831-622-0936
 www.agrotrade.com
Raw, processed, gourmet and specialty food products. Dried bananas, dried apples, pears, prunes, peaches and raisins; almonds, walnuts, pistachios and hazelnuts
General Manager: Eugene Andruchowicz
VP: Eugene Andruchowicz
Estimated Sales: $2.5-5 Million
Number Employees: 1-4
Type of Packaging: Bulk
Types of Products Distributed:
 Specialty Foods

54757 American Bakers Association
1300 I Street NW
Suite 700W
Washington, DC 20005-7203 202-789-0300
 Fax: 202-898-1164 info@americanbakers.org
 www.americanbakers.org
Enhances the baking industry through public policy advocacy, education and networking opportunities.
President, CEO: Robb Mac Kie
Executive Assistant to the President & C: Christina Donnelly
Senior Vice President Government Relatio: Lee Sanders
Contact: John Blouch
j.blouch@americanbakers.org
Vice President, Operations: Christopher Clark, CAE
Number Employees: 10-19

54758 American Bakery Equipment Company
435 Johnston St # B
PO Box 3135
Half Moon Bay, CA 94019 650-560-9970
 Fax: 650-560-9971 800-341-5581
 www.americanbakeryequipment.biz
Wholesaler/distributor of new and used bakery equipment for pastries, muffins, cookies, cakes, breads, pizzas, bagels, etc.; installation services available
Manager: John Candelori Jr
CEO: Ken Skelton
CFO: Norman Gwinn
VP: John Candelori, Jr.
Research & Development: Polly Vandersyde
CFO: Sabatino Compi
Estimated Sales: Below $5,000,000
Number Employees: 5-9
Number of Brands: 200
Number of Products: 1000
Square Footage: 4750
Private Brands Carried:
 Winkler Oven; Adamatic; Win-Holt; Arctica Showcases; Wilder; Meadow Mills; A.M.Mfg.Adamatic; Cutler Reed Oven Company; Mimax; Erika; Icetec
Types of Products Distributed:
 Frozen Food, General Merchandise, New & used bakery equipment

54759 American Banana Company
250 Coster St
Bronx, NY 10474 718-842-4565
 Fax: 718-589-2703
Wholesaler/distributor of bananas, plantains and tropicals
President: Demetrios Contos
VP: George Mauyios
Secretary: George Contos
Estimated Sales: $5-10 Million
Number Employees: 10-19
Square Footage: 60000
Types of Products Distributed:
 Frozen Food, General Line, Produce, Bananas, plantains, etc.

54760 (HQ)American Classic Ice Cream Company
1146 Grand Avenue
South Hempstead, NY 11550-7904 516-489-8850
 Fax: 516-485-2636
Ice cream, toppings, frozen desserts and candy.
Owner: Steve Kronard
Manager: Edgar Williams
Estimated Sales: $20-50 Million
Number Employees: 20-49
Number of Customer Locations: 2000
Types of Products Distributed:
 Frozen Food, General Line, Ice cream, toppings, candy, etc.

54761 American Container Concepts
150 Remington Blvd
Ronkonkoma, NY 11779-6912 631-737-6300
 Fax: 631-737-6318 888-588-9187
 aconcep163@aol.com
 www.americancontainerconcepts.com
Wholesaler/distributor of retail food packaging including, boxes, cartons, bags, custom designing printing stock
President: Charles Blor
cblor@americancontainerconcepts.com
Account Executive: Catherine Hayes
Estimated Sales: $2.5-5 Million
Number Employees: 10-19
Types of Products Distributed:
 Frozen Food, General Merchandise, Bags, boxes, cartons, film & labels

54762 American European Systems
5456 Louie Lane
Reno, NV 89510-7061 775-852-1114
 Fax: 775-852-1163 info@aes-sorma.com
 www.aes-sorma.com
Importer and wholesaler/distributor of cutting, peeling, bagging and weighing equipment
President: Robert Sapeta
Sales/Marketing Executive: Don Bergin
Estimated Sales: $3-5 Million
Number Employees: 5-9
Square Footage: 32000

Private Brands Carried:
 Fam; Finis; Spang; Sorma
Types of Products Distributed:
 General Merchandise, Food processing & packaging equipment

54763 American Farms Produce
PO Box 268
Mineral Ridge, OH 44440-0268 330-783-1890
 Fax: 330-788-9642
Wholesaler/distributor of fresh produce; serving the food service market
President: Robert Zimmerman
Number Employees: 10-19
Square Footage: 8800
Types of Products Distributed:
 Food Service, Frozen Food, Produce

54764 American Fish & SeafoodInc
5501 Opportunity Ct
Hopkins, MN 55343-9697 952-935-3474
 Fax: 952-935-7861
Wholesaler/distributor of fresh and frozen seafood and poultry; serving the food service market
President: Lp Bialick
lbialick@americanfish.net
Director Food Service: L Braufman
Estimated Sales: $20-50 Million
Number Employees: 50-99
Square Footage: 40000
Types of Products Distributed:
 Food Service, Frozen Food, Seafood, Fresh & frozen poultry

54765 American Food & VendingCorporation
3606 John Glenn Blvd
Syracuse, NY 13209
 Fax: 315-457-0186
Wholesaler/distributor of vending machinery; also, service available
President: Henry Wells
Contact: John Edminster
jedminster@exec.afvusa.com
Estimated Sales: $20-50 Million
Number Employees: 100-249
Types of Products Distributed:
 Frozen Food, General Merchandise, Vending machinery

54766 American Food Equipment
1301 N Miami Ave
Miami, FL 33136-2815 305-377-8991
 Fax: 305-358-4328
 michael@americanfoodequipment.com
 www.americanfoodequipment.com
Wholesaler/distributor of restaurant equipment and supplies; serving the food service market
Owner: Michael Clements
americanfoodequipment@gmail.com
Manager: Robert Tom
Estimated Sales: $1-2.5 Million
Number Employees: 5-9
Types of Products Distributed:
 Food Service, Frozen Food, General Merchandise, Restaurant equipment & supplies

54767 (HQ)American Food Equipment& Supply
2400 Forsyth Road
Suite 106
Orlando, FL 32807 407-671-0689
 Fax: 407-671-5747 800-827-0681
Wholesaler/distributor of general merchandise, food packaging, portioning and processing equipment, etc
Owner: Randall St John
CFO: Randall St. John
VP: Deborah St. John
Quality Control: Gordon Smith
Marketing Director: Gordon Smith
Operations Manager: Randall St. John
Estimated Sales: $1-2.5 Million
Number Employees: 1-4
Square Footage: 22000
Type of Packaging: Food Service
Other Locations:
 American Food Equipment& Sup
 Fort Lauderdale, FLAmerican Food Equipment& Sup
Private Brands Carried:
 Juice Tree Products; Hollymatic Products; Sipromac Products; Enviro-Pack; Butcher Boy;

Daniels Food Equipment; Process Plus; Trirf USA; Biro Manufacturing; Parry-O-Matic
Number of Customer Locations: 200
Types of Products Distributed:
Frozen Food, General Merchandise, Food packaging & processing equipment

54768 American Food Systems
30 B St
Burlington, MA 01803-3488 781-273-3230
Fax: 781-273-0393 www.jimmysarlington.net
Wholesaler/distributor of general merchandise, general line and specialty food products and provisions/meats
Owner: Mark Miminos
jmurphey@americanfoodsystems.com
VP: James Mininos
Estimated Sales: $2.5-5 Million
Number Employees: 20-49
Square Footage: 60000
Types of Products Distributed:
Frozen Food, General Line, General Merchandise, Provisions/Meat, Specialty Foods, USDA inspected portion cut meat

54769 American Food Traders
10661 N Kendall Dr Ste 206A
Miami, FL 33176 305-273-7090
Fax: 305-670-6468 www.americanfoodtraders.com
Wholesaler/distributor, importer and exporter of corned beef, peanut butter, juices, foam, plastic and paper disposable goods and sodas
President: Freddy Olcese
Number Employees: 1-4
Type of Packaging: Consumer, Food Service, Private Label, Bulk
Types of Products Distributed:
Food Service, Frozen Food, General Line, Provisions/Meat, Peanut butter, juices, etc.

54770 American Forklifter
P.O.Box 3281
Spring Hill, FL 34611-3281 815-886-2200
Fax: 815-886-9511
Wholesaler/distributor of forklifts
Co-Owner: Charles Riedl
Co-Owner: James Leonard
Controller: Sharon Riedl
Estimated Sales: $5-10 Million
Number Employees: 10-19
Private Brands Carried:
TCM; Blue Giant
Types of Products Distributed:
General Merchandise, Forklifts

54771 American Frozen Foods
155 Hill St
Suite 4
Milford, CT 06460
800-233-5554
CustomerService@americanfoods.com
www.americanfoods.com
Wholesaler/distributor of frozen food, produce, provisions/meats, dairy and pastry products; serving the food service market.
President: Bill Rappaport
billyrapp@americanfoods.com
Secretary/General Counsel: William Corey
Year Founded: 1921
Estimated Sales: $63 Million
Number Employees: 10-19
Square Footage: 100000
Types of Products Distributed:
Food Service, Frozen Food, General Line, Provisions/Meat, Produce, Dairy & pastry products

54772 American Grocery & Beverage
184 Whitman Ave
Edison, NJ 8817 732-248-8080
Fax: 732-248-8404
Wholesaler/distributor of general merchandise, private label/generic items and beverages
Owner: Dj Ganpat
Contact: Govind Itwaru
gitwaru@gmail.com
General Manager: Carl Piegari
Estimated Sales: $10-20 Million
Number Employees: 10-19
Number of Customer Locations: 500
Types of Products Distributed:
Frozen Food, General Line, General Merchandise, Beverages

54773 American Health & Safety
3202 Progress Rd # 1
Madison, WI 53716-3345 608-273-4000
Fax: 608-273-3892 800-522-7554
www.ahsafety.com
Wholesaler/distributor of personal safety equipment including aprons, hair nets, gloves, footwear, earplugs, back and wrist supports, goggles, eyewash, etc
President: John Crnokrak
Marketing Manager: Pat Van De Wall
Estimated Sales: $2.5-5 Million
Number Employees: 5-9
Square Footage: 100000
Types of Products Distributed:
Frozen Food, General Merchandise, Hair nets, aprons, footwear, etc.

54774 American Hotel RegisterCo
100 S Milwaukee Ave
Vernon Hills, IL 60061-4035
Fax: 800-688-9108 800-323-5686
orderdpt@americanhotel.com
www.americanhotel.com
Wholesaler/distributor, importer and exporter of food preparation equipment for hotels/motels, restaurant chains, medical facilities and government and airline food service operators.
Chairman: James F Leahy, Jr.
Vice Chairman: Tom Leahy
President & CEO: Angela Koromopilas
akorompilas@americanhotel.com
Year Founded: 1865
Estimated Sales: $50-100 Million
Number Employees: 500-999
Square Footage: 250000
Type of Packaging: Food Service
Types of Products Distributed:
Food Service, Frozen Food, General Merchandise, Food preparation equipment

54775 American International Chemical
135 Newbury St
Framingham, MA 01701 508-270-1800
800-238-0001
info@aicma.com www.aicma.com
Supplier/Wholesaler of preservatives, minerals, acidulants, and chelates to the beverage industry.
EVP, Marketing: Mark Robertson
Year Founded: 1972
Estimated Sales: $20-50 Million
Number Employees: 20-49
Types of Products Distributed:
Frozen Food, General Line, Chemical food additives

54776 American Key Food Products Inc
1 Reuten Dr
Closter, NJ 07624-2115 201-767-8022
Fax: 201-767-9124 877-263-7539
contactus@akfponline.com www.akfponline.com
Bulk quantity starches, spices and ingredients.
Manager: Luis Mansueto
VP: Ivan Sarda
Sales: Mel Festejo
Manager: Foss Carter
cfoss@akfponline.com
Operations: Edwin Pacia
Purchasing: Connie Ponce de Leon
Number Employees: 1-4
Type of Packaging: Bulk
Private Brands Carried:
Emsland Starke Potato, King Lion
Types of Products Distributed:
Spices/ Starches/Baking Ingredients

54777 American Legion
2035 N Highland Ave
Los Angeles, CA 90068-3296 323-851-3030
Fax: 323-874-6785 800-446-5463
www.legion.org
Wholesaler/distributor of linens; serving the food service market
Administrator: Terance Duddy
Manager: Karl Risinger
crew@hollywoodpost43.org
Estimated Sales: $10-20 Million
Number Employees: 5-9
Parent Co: Steiner Corporation
Private Brands Carried:
Steiner
Number of Customer Locations: 2000

Types of Products Distributed:
Food Service, Frozen Food, General Merchandise, Linens

54778 American Lighting & Electric
3100 6th Ave S
Birmingham, AL 35233-3525 205-322-0570
Fax: 205-322-1054 800-510-5454
www.amlight.com
Wholesaler/distributor of lighting fixtures and supplies, ballasts, electric and fluorescent lamps and energy conservation equipment
President: Bruce Compton
bruce@amlight.com
Executive VP: Jay Boyd
General Manager: Bruce Compton
Estimated Sales: $1-2.5 Million
Number Employees: 10-19
Number of Customer Locations: 300
Types of Products Distributed:
Frozen Food, General Merchandise, Lighting fixtures, lamps, etc.

54779 American Lighting Supply
800 Indian Trail Road
Suite C 109
Lilburn, GA 30047 770-923-5426
Fax: 770-923-8137 800-332-9896
Wholesaler/distributor of lighting fixtures, electric and fluorescent lamps, light bulbs, etc
Owner: William Milligan
General Manager: William Milligan
Estimated Sales: $5-10 Million
Number Employees: 5-9
Types of Products Distributed:
Frozen Food, General Merchandise, Lighting fixtures, lamps, etc.

54780 American Material Handling Inc
9013 Highway 165
PO Box 17878
N Little Rock, AR 72117-9728 501-375-6611
Fax: 501-375-8931 800-482-5801
sales@amermaterial.com www.amermaterial.com
Wholesaler/distributor and exporter of material handling systems; also, design consultant
Owner: Jackie Lackie
General Manager: Jay Carman
VP of Marketing: Albert Redding
Sales Manager: Adam Dickens
Manager: Adam Dickens
adam.dickens@amermaterial.com
Estimated Sales: $5-10 Million
Number Employees: 10-19
Square Footage: 80000
Parent Co: Cetrum Industries
Private Brands Carried:
American Mezzanines
Number of Customer Locations: 1000
Types of Products Distributed:
Frozen Food, General Merchandise, Material handling systems

54781 American Meat & Seafood
RR 302
Naples, ME 4055 207-693-6255
Fax: 207-693-3995
Wholesaler/distributor of provisions/meats
Owner: Kris Klemik
chris-merrill@fairpoint.net
Estimated Sales: $10-20 Million
Number Employees: 5-9
Types of Products Distributed:
Frozen Food, Provisions/Meat

54782 American Metalcraft Inc
3708 River Rd
Suite 800
Franklin Park, IL 60131-2158 708-345-1177
Fax: 708-345-5758 info@amnow.com
www.amnow.com
Manufacturer, importer, exporter and wholesaler/distributor of stainless steel restaurant/bar tabletop supplies, funnels, pizza trays and food covers; serving the food service market
President: David Kahn
davidk@amnow.com
Sales Manager: Richard Packer
Estimated Sales: $10-20 Million
Number Employees: 50-99
Square Footage: 240000
Type of Packaging: Food Service

Wholesalers & Distributors / A-Z

Types of Products Distributed:
Food Service, Frozen Food, General Merchandise

54783 American Mussel Harvesters Inc
165 Tidal Dr
North Kingstown, RI 02852-8003   401-294-8999
Fax: 401-294-0449 www.americanmussel.com
Wholesaler/distributor of fresh and frozen oysters, clams and mussels
President: William Silkes
williams@americanmussel.com
CFO: Jane Bugbee
Marketing Director: Tom Ahern
Production Manager: Roberto Vazquez
Estimated Sales: $5-10 Million
Number Employees: 20-49
Private Brands Carried:
Golden Neck; Whitewater
Types of Products Distributed:
Frozen Food, Seafood, Oysters, clams & mussels

54784 American Osment
2923 5th Ave S
Birmingham, AL 35233-2916   205-326-3456
Fax: 205-325-8134 www.americanosment.com
Wholesaler/distributor of paper products, cleaning supplies, commercial vacuums and buffers
President: Stan Burt
stan.burt@american-osment.com
Estimated Sales: $5-10 Million
Number Employees: 50-99
Types of Products Distributed:
Frozen Food, General Merchandise, Paper, cleaning supplies, vacuums, etc.

54785 American Packaging Corporation
44562 Morley Dr
Clinton Twp, MI 48036-1358   586-468-8400
Fax: 586-468-2180
Wholesaler/distributor of packaging materials including FDA bags, tape, stretch wrap, pallets, corrugated boxes, foam products, bubble wrap and set-up boxes
President: Richard Rottier
Inside Sales: Dawn Armstrong
Contact: Jeff Koch
jkoch@ampkcorp.com
Estimated Sales: $2.5-5 Million
Number Employees: 20-49
Types of Products Distributed:
Frozen Food, General Merchandise, Packaging materials

54786 American Pie Council
28495 N Ballard Dr
Lake Forest, IL 60045-4510   847-724-5070
Fax: 847-371-0199 www.piecouncil.org
Owner: Richard Hoskins
Contact: Liviu Coman
lee@colborne.com
Estimated Sales: $5-10 Million
Number Employees: 100-249

54787 American Produce Company
1601 E Olympic Blvd Ste 500
Los Angeles, CA 90021   213-622-2358
Fax: 213-622-0256
Wholesaler/distributor of produce; serving the food service market
Contact: Bob Ailworth
bailworth@chiquita.com
Estimated Sales: $1-2.5 Million
Number Employees: 1-4
Types of Products Distributed:
Food Service, Frozen Food, Produce

54788 American Quality Foods
353 Banner Farm Rd
Mills River, NC 28759-8707   828-890-8344
www.americanqualityfoods.com
Gluten free and diet dessert mixes
Manager: Debbie Allison
debbie@americanqualityfoods.com
Number Employees: 20-49
Square Footage: 17000

54789 American Raisin Packers
2335 Chandler St
PO Box 30
Selma, CA 93662-2705   559-896-4760
Fax: 559-896-8942 americanraisin@sbcglobal.net
www.americanraisinpacking.com
Packers of raisins
Owner: John Paboojian
Estimated Sales: $2.5 Million
Number Employees: 20-49
Square Footage: 120000
Type of Packaging: Consumer, Bulk

54790 American Restaurant Supply
4395 Fl Ga Hwy
Havana, FL 32333   850-539-9103
Fax: 850-224-4516 800-833-2136
Wholesaler/distributor of equipment, paper products, cleaning supplies and steel, plastic and disposable dinnerware; serving the food service market
Owner: Dan Wohlrab
VP Sales: John Creamer
Purchasing Manager: Kim Brandon
Estimated Sales: $5-10 Million
Number Employees: 10-19
Square Footage: 72000
Private Brands Carried:
Hobart; Verimix; Rubbermaid
Types of Products Distributed:
Food Service, Frozen Food, General Merchandise, Dinnerware, equipment, etc.

54791 American Restaurant Supply
3083 Aukele St
Lihue, HI 96766-1465   808-246-4953
Fax: 808-246-8658
Wholesaler/distributor of restaurant equipment
Manager: Mark Dill
Estimated Sales: Less than $500,000
Number Employees: 1-4
Types of Products Distributed:
Frozen Food, General Merchandise, Restaurant equipment

54792 American Roland Food Corporation
71 W 23rd St
New York, NY 10010-4102   212-741-8290
800-221-4030
salessupport@rolandfood.com
www.rolandfood.com
Importer and exporter of vegetables, seafood, condiments, olive oil and specialty foods; wholesaler/distributor of general line items, canned fruit, seafood and specialty food; serving the food service market.
CEO: Charles Scheidt
Marketing Director: Joanne Scheidt
Contact: Tyrus Brailey
tyrus.r.brailey@jpmorgan.com
Estimated Sales: $.5-1 million
Number Employees: 50-99
Type of Packaging: Consumer, Food Service, Bulk
Private Brands Carried:
Roland; Costamar; Consul; McCann's; Twinings; Carr's
Types of Products Distributed:
Food Service, General Line, Seafood, Specialty Foods, Canned fruit, etc.

54793 American Sales & Marketing
PO Box 95
Bahama, NC 27503   919-471-2980
Fax: 919-471-2980
Broker, retail, wholesale, grocer of general merchandise.
Owner: Charles Roedel
Types of Products Distributed:
Frozen Food

54794 American Seafood Imports Inc.
560 Sylvan Ave
Suite 1010
Englewood Cliffs, NJ 07632-3124   201-568-2525
Fax: 201-568-7737 800-989-3939
charlie@americanseafoodimports.com
www.americanseafoodimports.com
Frozen seafood
Partner: Charlie Goldstein
charlie@americanseafoodimports.com
Partner: George Lemery
Partner: Brian Lemery
Estimated Sales: $20-50 Million
Number Employees: 10-19
Type of Packaging: Consumer, Food Service, Private Label, Bulk
Private Brands Carried:
Capt's Catch; Mayflower; Sea Jewel
Types of Products Distributed:
Food Service, Frozen Food, Seafood, Specialty Foods

54795 American Seaway Foods Inc
5300 Richmond Rd
Bedford, OH 44146-1335   216-292-7000
Fax: 216-591-2640 800-553-2324
www.gianteagle.com
Wholesaler/distributor of meats, general line items and frozen foods; serving the food service market
Manager: Anthony Rego
anthony.ergo@gianteagle.com
VP: John Koscielski
Estimated Sales: $300,000-500,000
Number Employees: 5-9
Parent Co: Riser Foods
Private Brands Carried:
Del Monte; Perdue; Bird's Eye
Types of Products Distributed:
Food Service, Frozen Food, General Line, Provisions/Meat

54796 American Select Foods
11940 Goldring Rd # D
Arcadia, CA 91006-6013   626-359-2220
Fax: 626-447-8233
Wholesaler/distributor of espresso machines, coffee and pastries
President: Harula Rigas
americanselectfoods@gmail.com
Estimated Sales: Less Than $500,000
Number Employees: 1-4
Number of Customer Locations: 250
Types of Products Distributed:
Frozen Food, General Line, General Merchandise, Espresso machines, coffee & pastries

54797 American Society of Baking
7809 N Chestnut Avenue
Kansas City, MO 64119   847-920-9885
Fax: 888-315-2612 800-713-0462
info@asbe.org www.asbe.org
Contact: Kent Amburg
kvanamburg@asbe.org

54798 American Softshell Crab
49676 Freemans Road
Dameron, MD 20628-3106   301-872-4444
Fax: 301-872-5831
Wholesaler/distributor of hard and softshell crabs including live, frozen and steamed
Owner: Dale Scheible
Owner: Mary Scheible
Estimated Sales: $1-2.5 Million
Number Employees: 1-4
Square Footage: 80000
Parent Co: Scheible & Son Maritime
Types of Products Distributed:
Frozen Food, Seafood, Hard & softshell crabs

54799 American Specialty Coffee & Culinary
1360 Union Hill Road
Suite E
Alpharetta, GA 30004   770-754-0092
Fax: 770-754-0093 800-472-5282
Wholesaler/distributor and importer of food service equipment including espresso/cappuccino machines, coffee grinders, granita machines, deli showcases, pasta machinery, pasta cookers, wood-fired pizza ovens and water filtration systems; also, espresso coffee
President: Ron Sciortino
r.sciortino@americanspecialtycoffee.com
Estimated Sales: 1-5 Million
Number Employees: 5-9
Square Footage: 20000
Parent Co: ASCC
Private Brands Carried:
Brasilia
Types of Products Distributed:
Food Service, Frozen Food, General Merchandise, Food service equipment

54800 American Trading Company
866 Americas Rm 901
New York, NY 10001   212-685-0081
Fax: 212-937-6839 800-275-0106
Wholesaler/distributor, importer and exporter of linens and uniforms
President/CEO: Henry Salem
Purchasing: Henry Salem
Estimated Sales: $1 Million
Number Employees: 10
Square Footage: 40000
Type of Packaging: Bulk

Wholesalers & Distributors / A-Z

54801 American Uniforms SalesInc
8342 State Rd # 6
Unit 6
Philadelphia, PA 19136-2939   215-333-5763
         Fax: 215-333-6640   800-394-5959
                 www.americanuniform.com
Wholesaler/distributor of uniforms and food handlers' clothing; serving the food service market
General Manager: Philip Endicott
Manager: Margie Leipert
mleipert@americanuniform.com
Estimated Sales: $1-2.5 Million
Number Employees: 10-19
Square Footage: 94000
Types of Products Distributed:
  Food Service, Frozen Food, General Merchandise, Uniforms

54802 American Wholesale Grocery
131 New Jersey Street
Mobile, AL 36603-2111   251-433-2528
         Fax: 251-432-7982
Groceries
President: Harold Owens
Secretary/Treasurer: James Statter
Vice President: John Carpenter

54803 American Yeast Sales
319 Commerce Way # 2
Pembroke, NH 03275   603-228-8454
         Fax: 603-228-6745 www.lallemand.com
Yeast products
Manager: Len Musick
Estimated Sales: $5-10 Million
Number Employees: 20-49
Parent Co: L'Allemand
Types of Products Distributed:
  Frozen Food, General Line, Yeast products

54804 (HQ)American/Brenner Wholesale
1636 Gilbreth Rd
Burlingame, CA 94010   650-259-7855
         Fax: 650-259-9630
Wholesaler/distributor of plastic food storage products, janitorial supplies and chemicals; serving the food service market
President: Ron Kahn
VP: Stacy Kahn
Inventory Control: Matt Dunlap
Estimated Sales: $1-2.5 Million
Number Employees: 5-9
Square Footage: 60000
Private Brands Carried:
  Rubbermaid
Types of Products Distributed:
  Food Service, Frozen Food, General Merchandise, Janitorial supplies

54805 Americhicken
1330 Copper Dr
Cape Girardeau, MO 63701-1730   573-651-6485
         Fax: 573-651-4669 www.americhicken.com
Frozen chicken and entrees
President: Taylor Bass
taylor@americhicken.com
Number Employees: 5-9

54806 Amerivap Systems Inc
31 Successful Way
Dawsonville, GA 30534-6841   706-531-1509
         Fax: 404-350-9214   800-763-7687
Dry steam cleaning and sanitizing systems.
President: Werner Diercks
werner.diercks@amerivap.com
CFO: Paula Marshal
VP Marketing: Dolly Diercks
VP Sales: Gabriel Perez
Estimated Sales: $3 Million
Number Employees: 10-19
Square Footage: 20000
Private Brands Carried:
  AmeriVap; DS3; DS7
Number of Customer Locations: 1000
Types of Products Distributed:
  Food Service, Frozen Food, General Merchandise, Cleaning & sanitizing equipment

54807 Amick Farms LLC
2079 Batesburg Hwy.
Batesburg, SC 29006   803-532-1400
         Fax: 803-532-1491   800-926-4257
                 www.amickfarms.com
Chicken products.
Chief Executive Officer: Ben Harrison
bharrison@amickfarms.com
Vice President, Sales & Marketing: Steve Kernen
Year Founded: 1941
Estimated Sales: $100-499 Million
Number Employees: 1000-4999
Number of Brands: 2
Square Footage: 10992
Parent Co: OSI Industries, LLC
Type of Packaging: Consumer, Food Service, Private Label, Bulk
Other Locations:
  Hurlock, MD
Types of Products Distributed:
  Food Service, Provisions/Meat

54808 Ammirati Inc
500 Fifth Ave
Pelham, NY 10803-1206   914-738-2500
         Fax: 914-738-2503   800-441-8101
                 www.ammiraticoffee.com
Importer and wholesaler/distributor of espresso machines; serving the food service market. La Cimbali espresso machines and La Vazza premium coffees
Owner: T J Taratetta
info@ammiraticoffee.com
Estimated Sales: $2.5-5 Million
Number Employees: 20-49
Type of Packaging: Food Service
Types of Products Distributed:
  Food Service, Frozen Food, General Merchandise, Espresso machines

54809 Amos's PA Wonder Products
2901 Plough Street
Pittsburgh, PA 15212-2542   412-734-0300
         Fax: 412-734-4636 www.amosdirect.com
Wholesaler/distributor of biodegradable cleaning chemicals for rugs, upholstery and furniture; serving the food service market
Sales: Sandra Fransica
Estimated Sales: Less than $500,000
Number Employees: 1-4
Types of Products Distributed:
  Food Service, Frozen Food, General Merchandise, Biodegradable cleaning products

54810 Ampak Seafoods Corporation
315 Whitney Ave
New Haven, CT 06511-3715   203-786-5121
         Fax: 203-786-5120
Importer and wholesaler/distributor of pasteurized crabmeat; serving the food service market
CEO: Barry White
Estimated Sales: $2.5-5 Million
Number Employees: 1-4
Square Footage: 2000
Type of Packaging: Consumer, Food Service, Private Label
Types of Products Distributed:
  Food Service, Frozen Food, Seafood, Pasteurized crabmeat

54811 Amrita Snacks

Hartsdale, NY 10530
                 888-728-7779
                 www.amritahealthfoods.com
Plant-based, vegan, all-natural protein bars, protein snack bites and energy bars in various flavors
Founder/CEO: Arshad Bahl
Number of Brands: 1
Number of Products: 21
Type of Packaging: Consumer, Private Label
Private Brands Carried:
  Amrita
Types of Products Distributed:
  Health Food

54812 Amster-Kirtz Co
2830 Cleveland Ave NW
Canton, OH 44709-3204   330-535-6021
         Fax: 330-437-2015   800-257-9338
                 www.amsterkirtz.com
Wholesaler/distributor of merchandise for convenience stores including; candy and grocery items
President: James Ulery
jimu@amsterkirtzco.net
General Manager: Larry H
Sales Manager: Everett M
Number Employees: 50-99
Type of Packaging: Consumer, Bulk
Number of Customer Locations: Ohio
Types of Products Distributed:
  Frozen Food, General Line, General Merchandise, Health Food, Provisions/Meat, Rack Jobbers, Specialty Foods, Candy

54813 Amtex Packaging
5865 E Rosedale St
Fort Worth, TX 76112   817-654-3341
         Fax: 817-457-0080
Wholesaler/distributor of corrugated paper boxes
President: Bill Morgan
Estimated Sales: $300,000-500,000
Number Employees: 1-4
Types of Products Distributed:
  Frozen Food, General Merchandise, Corrugated paper boxes

54814 Amy Food Inc
3324 S Richey St
Houston, TX 77017-6259   713-910-5860
         Fax: 713-910-4812 www.amyfood.com
Egg rolls, potstickers, empanadas and party platters, natural and organic foods.
Owner: Phyllis Hsu
amyfood@aol.com
Number Employees: 50-99
Square Footage: 40000
Type of Packaging: Consumer, Food Service, Private Label

54815 Ananda Hemp
PO Box 648
Cynthiana, KY 41031
                 hello@anandahemp.com
                 www.anandahemp.com
Hemp extract
Number of Brands: 1
Number of Products: 5
Type of Packaging: Consumer

54816 Ancient Organics
726 Allston Way
Berkeley, CA 94710   510-280-5043
                 morgyne@ancientorganics.com
                 www.ancientorganics.com
Organic ghee (clarified butter)
Founder: Peter Malakoff
Owner: Matteo Girard Maxon
CFO: Abinashi Khalsa
VP Sales & Marketing: Greg Glass
National Sales Manager: Tim Transon
Types of Products Distributed:
  General Line

54817 Ancora Coffee Roasters
3701 Orin Road
Madison, WI 53704   608-255-2900
         Fax: 608-255-2901   800-260-0217
service@ancoracoffee.com www.ancoracoffee.com
Coffees, whole bean and ground; loose leaf teas
President/CEO: George Krug
Quality Control/Production: Rob Jeffries
Marketing: Christy Gibbs
cgibbs@ancoracoffee.com
Estimated Sales: $1-5 Million
Number Employees: 10-19
Square Footage: 60000
Type of Packaging: Consumer, Food Service, Bulk
Private Brands Carried:
  Ancora Coffee
Types of Products Distributed:
  General Line, Specialty Foods

54818 Andalusia Distributing Co Inc
117 Allen Ave
Andalusia, AL 36420-2501   334-222-3671
                 www.adc1.com
Deli products
President: Ricky Jones
Vice President: Billy Jones
CFO: Chris Jones
General Manager: Ronnie Taylor
Year Founded: 1956
Estimated Sales: $50-100 Million
Number Employees: 50-99
Types of Products Distributed:
  Provisions/Meat

909

Wholesalers & Distributors / A-Z

54819 Anderson Dubose Company
5300 Tod Ave SW
Lordstown, OH 44481   440-248-8800
Fax: 330-824-2256 www.anderson-dubose.com
Wholesaler/distributor of frozen, refrigerated (produce & dairy), dry foods, paper, operating supplies, and promotional iteams for McDonald's and Chipotle restaurants.
President: Warren Anderson
Chief Financial Officer: Tony Wiglusz
Chief Sales & Marketing Officer: Mike Trua
Chief Operating Officer: Mike Boddy
Estimated Sales: $170 Million
Number Employees: 90
Square Footage: 158000
Type of Packaging: Food Service
Number of Customer Locations: 275
Types of Products Distributed:
Food Service, Frozen Food, General Line

54820 Anderson International Foods
193 Elm Place
Mineola, NY 11501   516-747-2210
Fax: 516-747-2520 anderson@aifoods.com
www.aifoods.com
Wholesaler of Kosher cheese (organic and natural)
President: Bridgette Mizihri
Contact: Elliot Budd
ebudd@aifoods.com
Estimated Sales: $1-2.5 Million
Number Employees: 10-19
Type of Packaging: Bulk

54821 Anderson Seafood
4780 E Bryson St
Anaheim, CA 92807-1901   714-777-7100
Fax: 714-777-7116
contactus@andersonseafoods.com
www.shopandersonseafoods.com
Fresh and frozen seafood
President: Dennis Anderson
CFO: Alberto Andrade
Vice President: Todd Anderson
VP, Procurement, Sales & Operations: Carl Oliphant
Year Founded: 1979
Number Employees: 20-49
Type of Packaging: Consumer, Food Service
Number of Customer Locations: 200
Types of Products Distributed:
Food Service, Frozen Food, Seafood

54822 Anderson Studio Inc
2609 Grissom Dr
Nashville, TN 37204-2820   615-255-4807
Fax: 615-255-4812 800-831-7062
www.andersonstudioinc.com
Wholesaler/distributor of advertising specialties; screen printing services available
Manager: Glenda Smith
glenda@andersonstudioinc.com
Estimated Sales: $5-10 Million
Number Employees: 10-19
Types of Products Distributed:
Frozen Food, General Merchandise, Advertising specialties

54823 Andre Tea & Coffee Company
PO Box 269
Grove City, PA 16127-0269   724-282-6341
Fax: 724-458-1134
Wholesaler/distributor of coffee, tea and related products; serving the food service market
President: Ernie May
Estimated Sales: Less than $500,000
Number Employees: 1-4
Private Brands Carried:
Andre's; Carnation Hot Chocolate
Types of Products Distributed:
Food Service, Frozen Food, General Line, Coffee, tea & related products

54824 Andrew & Williamson Sales Co
9940 Marconi Dr
San Diego, CA 92154-7270   619-661-6000
Fax: 619-661-6007 www.bajaclassic.com
Wholesaler/distributor of fresh produce including strawberries, tomatoes, cucumbers, etc.
President: Fred Williamson
fredwilliamson@andrew-williamson.com
Estimated Sales: $2.5-5 Million
Number Employees: 20-49
Private Brands Carried:
A&W
Number of Customer Locations: 150

Types of Products Distributed:
Frozen Food, Produce, Strawberries, tomatoes, cucumbers, etc.

54825 Andros Foods North America
10119 Old Valley Pike
Mount Jackson, VA 22842   540-217-4100
844-426-3767
sales@androsna.com www.androsna.com
Fruit based food and beverages, confectionary, preserves, frozen desserts
CEO/COO: Terry Stoehr
Estimated Sales: $52.3 Million
Number Employees: 500-999
Parent Co: Andros Group

54826 Angel Beltran Corporation
1630 E Paisano Drive
El Paso, TX 79901-3122   915-544-7070
Fax: 915-544-8326
Wholesaler/distributor serving the food service market
President: Angel Beltran, Sr.
Estimated Sales: $2.5-5 Million
Number Employees: 5-9
Types of Products Distributed:
Food Service, Frozen Food

54827 Angel's Produce
13331 Tobacco Rd
El Paso, TX 79938-8963   915-855-0422
Fax: 915-855-0594
Wholesaler/distributor of produce; serving the food service market
Owner: Miguel Angel
Estimated Sales: Less than $500,000
Number Employees: 10-19
Types of Products Distributed:
Food Service, Frozen Food, Produce

54828 Angelo M. Formosa Foods
1300 4th Ave N
Nashville, TN 37208   615-254-1416
Fax: 615-244-5914
Wholesaler/distributor of fresh and pre-cut produce and spices; serving the food service market
President: A Formosa
VP: A Formose
Estimated Sales: $20-50 Million
Number Employees: 20-49
Type of Packaging: Food Service
Types of Products Distributed:
Food Service, Frozen Food, General Line, Produce, Spices

54829 Angelo Refrigeration & Rstrnt
17 W Highland Blvd
San Angelo, TX 76903-7426   325-655-4148
Fax: 325-655-1001 800-592-4610
arrs4148@aol.com www.angelorefrigeration.com
Wholesaler/distributor of stainless steel fabrication and tabletop supplies and restaurant equipment; serving the food service industry
President: Rodney Brown
angelorefrigeration@gmail.com
Estimated Sales: $6-8 Million
Number Employees: 10-19
Square Footage: 240000
Number of Customer Locations: 600
Types of Products Distributed:
Food Service, Frozen Food, General Merchandise

54830 Angers Equipment Company
PO Box 703090
Plymouth, MI 48170   313-533-7960
Fax: 313-931-4970
Wholesaler/distributor of lockers, warehouse racks, benches, stools and shelving; rack jobber services available
President: Darrel Sanderson
Sales Director: Gary Lewis
Operations Manager: David Crans
Estimated Sales: $2.5-5 Million
Number Employees: 10-19
Square Footage: 68000
Private Brands Carried:
Edsal; Clymer; Palmer-Shile; Prest Rack
Types of Products Distributed:
Rack Jobbers, Lockers, racks, benches, stools, etc.

54831 Anixter Inc
146 Ridge Ave S
Tifton, GA 31794-4735   229-382-9670
Fax: 229-382-9670 www.hughessupply.com
Wholesaler/distributor of general merchandise including electrical supplies, fuses and lighting fixtures
Manager: Bill Mc Daniel
william.mcdaniel@hdsupply.com
Estimated Sales: $3-5 Million
Number Employees: 1-4
Parent Co: Hughes Supply
Types of Products Distributed:
Frozen Food, General Merchandise, Electrical supplies, fuses, etc.

54832 Anjo's Imports
PO Box 4031
Cerritos, CA 90703-4031   562-865-9544
Fax: 562-865-9544 anjosimports.com
Jamaican hot sauce
President: Lloyd Webster

54833 Ann Clark, LTD
112B Quality Lane
Rutland, VT 05701   802-773-7886
Fax: 802-775-6864 800-252-6798
info@annclark.com www.annclark.com
Shaped and holiday themed cookie cutters
President: Ann Clark
VP: John Clark Jr
Sales Manager: Elizabeth Clark
Contact: Pat Buchanan
pat@annclark.com

54834 Annapolis Produce & Restaurant
15 Lee St
Annapolis, MD 21401-3980   410-266-5211
Fax: 410-266-0568
Groceries, fish, meats and dairy products.
President: Charles Bassford
Chief Financial Officer: Bobby Goldbeck
Vice President: Elaine Bassford
Estimated Sales: $10-19.9 Million
Number Employees: 5-9
Types of Products Distributed:
Produce

54835 Annette's Donuts Ltd.
1965 Lawrence Ave W
Toronto, ON M9N 1H5
Canada   416-656-3444
Fax: 416-656-5400 888-839-7857
Bread, pastries and other bakery products
President: Nicolas Yannopoulos
Board Member: Ariadni Yannopoulos
Estimated Sales: $5.9 Million
Number Employees: 85
Square Footage: 124000
Type of Packaging: Consumer, Food Service, Bulk

54836 Anniston Paper & SupplyCompany
PO Box 220
Moody, AL 35004-0220   256-835-1331
Fax: 256-835-0085
Wholesaler/distributor of general merchandise; serving the food service market
Manager: Bob Keith
Estimated Sales: $20-50 Million
Number Employees: 20-49
Types of Products Distributed:
Food Service, Frozen Food, General Merchandise

54837 Anter Brothers Company
12501 Elmwood Avenue
Cleveland, OH 44111-5909   216-252-4555
Fax: 216-252-4566
Wholesaler/distributor of confectionery products; rack jobber services available; serving the food service market
President: Richard Anter
VP: George Anter
Estimated Sales: $15.9 Million
Number Employees: 45
Types of Products Distributed:
Food Service, Frozen Food, General Line, Rack Jobbers, Confectionery products

Wholesalers & Distributors / A-Z

54838 Anthony Marano Co Inc
3000 S Ashland Ave # 100
Suite 100
Chicago, IL 60608-5349   312-829-5055
Fax: 773-631-6528 www.anthonymarano.com
Wholesaler/distributor of produce
Owner: Anton Marano
amarano@anthonymaranotrucking.com
Estimated Sales: $300,000-500,000
Number Employees: 100-249
Types of Products Distributed:
  Frozen Food, Produce

54839 Anthony's Snack & Vending
8235 Leo Kidd Ave
Port Richey, FL 34668   727-848-4242
727-489-0685   800-247-0541
Wholesaler/distributor of snack foods and vending machines; serving the food service market
President: Anthony Donnaruma
Secretary/Treasurer: Barbara Bull
Estimated Sales: $1-2.5 Million
Number Employees: 10-19
Types of Products Distributed:
  Food Service, Frozen Food, General Line, General Merchandise, Snack foods & vending machines

54840 Anthracite Provision Co
510 S Pearl St
Coal Twp, PA 17866-6599   570-644-0405
Fax: 570-644-0516
Wholesaler/distributor of meats, cheeses, groceries, dressings, frozen foods, produce, etc.; serving the food service market
Owner: Patti Sheriff
Estimated Sales: $5-10 Million
Number Employees: 5-9
Types of Products Distributed:
  Food Service, General Line, Health Food, Provisions/Meat, Produce, Rack Jobbers, Seafood, Specialty Foods, Dressings

54841 Anton-Argires
12345 S Latrobe Ave
Alsip, IL 60803-3210   708-388-6250
Fax: 312-226-5154   800-837-0100
www.anuts.com
Wholesaler/distributor of fresh fruits and vegetables; also, packer and distributor of nuts including peanuts, tree nuts and pistachios
President: George Argires
george@argires.com
Secretary: Steve Argires
Estimated Sales: $5-10 Million
Number Employees: 5-9
Square Footage: 52000
Private Brands Carried:
  Argires
Types of Products Distributed:
  Frozen Food, Produce, Specialty Foods

54842 Antone's Import Company
2424 Dunstan Road
Suite 100
Houston, TX 77005-2569   713-521-2883
Fax: 713-521-1973
Wholesaler/distributor of imported specialty foods
Owner: Kay Nader
CEO: Randolph Clendenen
Manager: Laura Armstrong
Contact: Forrest Coppock
forrest@txmusicgroup.com
Estimated Sales: $20-50 Million
Number Employees: 2
Number of Customer Locations: 8
Types of Products Distributed:
  Food Service, Frozen Food, Specialty Foods

54843 Apache Inc
4805 Bowling St SW
Cedar Rapids, IA 52404-5021   319-365-0471
Fax: 319-365-2522   800-553-5455
info@apache-inc.com www.apache-inc.com
Wholesaler/distributor of hose and conveyor belting. Products for the food industry.
President/CEO: Tom Pientok
Chief Financial Officer: Randy Walter
Controller: Eric Hentges
Quality Engineer: Rick Coyle
Marketing & Communications Manager: Jill Miller
VP, Operations: Kyle Gingrich
VP, Business Development: John Shafer
VP, Product Management: Tom Weisenstine
Purchasing Manager: Randy James
Estimated Sales: $75-85 Million
Number Employees: 100-249
Square Footage: 125000
Types of Products Distributed:
  Frozen Food, General Merchandise, Hose & conveyor belting

54844 Apilico/Cuthbertson Imports
6 Hollyhock Lane
Wilton, CT 06897-4414   203-834-0506
Fax: 203-834-0610   800-607-7231
Wholesaler/distributor of high fired porcelain ovenware, bakeware and dinnerware
Director Sales: Jay Powell
Types of Products Distributed:
  Frozen Food, General Merchandise, Ovenware, bakeware & dinnerware

54845 Applewood Seed & Garden Group
5380 Vivian Street
Arvada, CO 80002-1959   303-431-7333
Fax: 303-467-7886   800-232-0666
sales@applewoodseed.com
www.applewoodseed.com
Wildflower and garden seed producers
President: Gene Milstein
General Manager: Norm Poppe
Contact: Kendall Holdrem
kholdren@applewoodseed.com
Estimated Sales: $5-10 Million
Parent Co: Applewood Seed & Garden Group

54846 Applied Handling Equipment Company
330 Leo Street
Dayton, OH 45404   937-449-8000
Fax: 937-449-7999   800-871-8971
www.aheco.com
Wholesaler/distributor of materials handling equipment, conveyors and shelving; also, parts and service available
President: Tim Colston
sales@aheco.com
Estimated Sales: $2.5-5 Million
Number Employees: 1-4
Private Brands Carried:
  Albion, Southworth, Prest Rack
Types of Products Distributed:
  Frozen Food, General Merchandise, Material handling equipment

54847 Applied Handling NW
8531 South 222nd St
Kent, WA 98031   253-395-8500
Fax: 253-395-8585   888-395-3943
ahnwi@aol.com www.appliednw.com
Wholesaler/distributor of material handling equipment including package conveyors and pallet racks; rack jobber services available
President: Michael Tucker
Contact: Richard Chaffee
richc@appliednw.com
Estimated Sales: $5-10 Million
Number Employees: 10-19
Private Brands Carried:
  Unarco, H.K. Systems
Types of Products Distributed:
  Frozen Food, General Merchandise, Rack Jobbers, Material handling equipment

54848 Applied Industrial TechInc
1 Applied Plz
Cleveland, OH 44115-2519   216-426-4000
Fax: 216-426-4845 www.applied.com
Wholesaler/distributor and exporter of electric motors, belting, packing and power transmission equipment for food processing machinery
Branch Operations Manager: Ronnie Moore
Branch Manager: Matt Loe
Estimated Sales: Over $1 Billion
Number Employees: 5000-9999
Types of Products Distributed:
  Frozen Food, General Merchandise, Electric motors, belting, etc.

54849 Aqua Solutions Inc
6913 Highway 225
Deer Park, TX 77536-2414   281-479-2569
Fax: 281-479-2790 www.aquasolutions.org
Wholesaler/distributor of bottled Canadian natural spring water
President: Jonathan Alexander
j.alexander@jesuitcp.org
Number Employees: 50-99
Private Brands Carried:
  Aqua Nature
Types of Products Distributed:
  Frozen Food, General Line, Bottled Canadian natural spring water

54850 Aqua Source
445 5th Ave
New York, NY 10016-0133   212-681-9142
Fax: 212-343-2548
Wholesaler/distributor of aquaculture-farmed seafood
Owner: Susan Rudman
Estimated Sales: $300,000-500,000
Number Employees: 1-4
Types of Products Distributed:
  Frozen Food, Seafood

54851 Aqua-Tec Co
12410 Clark St
Santa Fe Springs, CA 90670-3916   562-941-1203
Fax: 562-941-1202
Wholesaler/distributor of filtration supplies including bags, paper, cartridges, vessels, tubes and panels
Manager: Mark Mac Kenzie
mmackenzie@strainrite.com
Sales Director: Ed Earl
General Manager: Mark MacKenzie
Purchasing Manager: Robin Beilstein
Estimated Sales: Less Than $500,000
Number Employees: 1-4
Square Footage: 32000
Parent Co: Lapoint Industries
Types of Products Distributed:
  Frozen Food, General Merchandise, Filtration supplies, etc.

54852 Ar Line Promotions Inc
10520 Plainview Cir
Boca Raton, FL 33498-6359   561-477-6268
Fax: 561-477-0905 LoisInBoca@aol.com
www.ar-linepromotions.com
Wholesaler/distributor of general merchandise including advertising specialties, calendars, incentives, premiums and business gifts, wearables and trade show items
President: Lois Pathman
VP: Arline Taplitz
Estimated Sales: Less Than $500,000
Number Employees: 1-4
Square Footage: 4800
Number of Customer Locations: 300
Types of Products Distributed:
  Frozen Food, General Merchandise, Advertising specialties

54853 Aragadz Foods Corporation
PO Box 852832
Richardson, TX 75085-2832   214-306-3033
Fax: 972-680-1949 aragadz@aol.com
Wholesaler/distributor of health foods, groceries, salsas and salads
Chairman/CEO: Karren Gazian
Estimated Sales: $5-10 Million
Number Employees: 5-9
Private Brands Carried:
  Sunny Salsa
Number of Customer Locations: 500
Types of Products Distributed:
  Frozen Food, General Line, Health Food, Groceries, salsas & salads

54854 Aramark Uniform Svc
115 N First St # 203
Burbank, CA 91502-1857   818-973-3700
Fax: 818-973-3545   800-272-6275
www.aramarkuniform.com
Manufacturer and wholesaler/distributor of uniforms; serving the food service market
President: Brad Drummond
brad.drummond@uniform.aramark.com
CFO: David Solomon
VP Marketing: Judith Weiss

Wholesalers & Distributors / A-Z

Estimated Sales: Over $1 Billion
Number Employees: 10000+
Parent Co: Aramark Services
Types of Products Distributed:
  Food Service, Frozen Food, General Merchandise, Uniforms

54855 Arbre Farms Inc
6362 N 192nd Ave
Walkerville, MI 49459-8601 231-873-3337
  Fax: 231-873-5699 www.arbrefarms.com
Provides food service and frozen food manufacturing industries with the finest quality frozen fruits and vegetables.
President: C O Johnson
cjohnson@arbrefarms.com
Quality Control: Robert Anderson
Marketing: Tripper Showell
Sales: Jean Hovey
Plant Manager: Vince Miskosky
Number Employees: 250-499
Type of Packaging: Food Service, Bulk
Other Locations:
  Willow Cold Storage
  Walkerville, MIWillow Cold Storage
Types of Products Distributed:
  Food Service, Frozen Food

54856 (HQ)Arctic Beverages
107 Mountainview Road
Unit 2
Winnipeg, MB R3C 2E6
Can 204-633-8686
  866-503-1270
winnipeg@arcticbev.com www.arcticbev.com
Soft drinks, juices, snack foods, bread, frozen food, chocolate.
Year Founded: 1991
Estimated Sales: $6 Million
Number Employees: 44
Number of Products: 68
Square Footage: 68000
Parent Co: Tribal Councils Investment Group of Manitoba Ltd.
Other Locations:
  Arctic Beverages Ltd.
  The Pas, MB
  Arctic Beverages Ltd.
  Thompson, MB
  Arctic Beverages Ltd.
  Winnipeg, MBArctic Beverages Ltd.Thompson
Private Brands Carried:
  Pepsi; 7-Up; Crush; Dr. Pepper; Schweppes; Allen's Juices, Mug, Dole, Sunrype, Gatorade, Spitz, Parmalat; Oreo; Haagen Dazs; Kit Kat; Smarties; Dempster's; Lorissa's Kitchen; Nestle; Mars; Cadbury
Types of Products Distributed:
  Food Service, Frozen Food, General Line, Provisions/Meat, Specialty Foods

54857 Arctic Glacier Premium Ice
625 Henry Avenue
Winnepeg, MB R3A 0V1
Canada 204-772-2473
  Fax: 204-783-9857 888-783-9857
info@arcticglacier.com www.arcticglacier.com
Bagged ice.
Chief Financial Officer: Linda Davachi
Vice President: Jeremy Spencer
Year Founded: 1996
Estimated Sales: $100-500 Million
Number Employees: 650
Parent Co: H.I.G. Capital

54858 Arctic Logistics
4360 S Haggerty Rd
Canton, MI 48188 734-397-9880
  arcticlogisticsmi.com
Temperature-controlled food distributor in the Midwest.
President & Principal: John Connor
Estimated Sales: $1 Million
Number of Customer Locations: 425
Types of Products Distributed:
  Frozen Food

54859 Arctic Star Distributing
412 W 53rd Ave
Anchorage, AK 99518 907-563-3454
  Fax: 907-562-3548
Wholesaler/distributor, importer and exporter of snack foods, general merchandise, beverages, etc.; serving the food service market in Alaska and Washington; also, rack jobber services available

President/CEO: Jim Baumann
Sales Manager: Bob Capeletti
General Manager: George Derr
Estimated Sales: $5-10 Million
Number Employees: 5-9
Square Footage: 50000
Parent Co: Arctic Star Distribution
Type of Packaging: Food Service
Number of Customer Locations: 5363
Types of Products Distributed:
  Food Service, Frozen Food, General Line, General Merchandise, Provisions/Meat, Produce, Rack Jobbers, Snack foods, beverages, etc.

54860 Arctic Zero
4241 Jutland Drive
Suite 305
San Diego, CA 92117 888-272-1715
  www.arcticzero.com
Low glycemic, lactose free, gluten free and GMO free frozen desserts
Founder: Greg Holtman
Contact: Megan Abordo
megan@myarcticzero.com

54861 Arctica Showcase Company
88 Talbot St. E
P.O.Box 130
Cayuga, ON N0A 1E0
Canada 905-772-5214
  Fax: 905-772-3179 800-839-5536
info@cayugadisplays.com www.cayugadisplays.com
Supplier of Hot Food, Deli, Meat, Seafood, Bakery, Candy Cafeteria showcases and more.
President: Rick Schotsman
Project Coordinator: Jennifer Zuidema
Vice President, Sales & Marketing: Chris Schotsman
Sales Director: Kirk Bessey
Number Employees: 85
Square Footage: 188000
Parent Co: Cayuga Displays Inc.
Types of Products Distributed:
  Frozen Food, Display shelving

54862 Argus Protective Services
1 Riverchase Pkwy S
Birmingham, AL 35244-2008 205-987-5600
  Fax: 205-987-5568
Wholesaler/distributor of general merchandise including burglar and fire alarms, security guards and systems, closed circuit TV and gate openers
President/CEO: Charles Knight
Number Employees: 100-249
Private Brands Carried:
  Argus
Number of Customer Locations: 2000
Types of Products Distributed:
  Frozen Food, General Merchandise, Security equipment & systems

54863 Aries Paper & Chemical Company
501 N Enterprise Blvd
Lake Charles, LA 70601-2336 337-433-8794
  Fax: 337-433-8891
Wholesaler/distributor of food service equipment and cleaning supplies; serving the food service market
Manager: James Butler
Secy./Treas.: Charlotte Butler
Operations Manager: Scott Tayloy
Estimated Sales: $1-2.5 Million
Number Employees: 5-9
Square Footage: 80000
Private Brands Carried:
  Proctor & Gamble; Spartan; Reynolds
Number of Customer Locations: 20
Types of Products Distributed:
  Food Service, Frozen Food, General Merchandise, Equipment & cleaning supplies

54864 Arista Industries Inc
557 Danbury Rd
Wilton, CT 06897-2218 203-761-1009
  Fax: 203-761-4980 800-255-6457
  info@aristaindustries.com
  www.aristaindustries.com
Oils, frozen shrimp, lobster tails and octopus. Importer of octopus, shrimp, squid, lobster tails, oils and surimi products.
President: Alan Weitzer
CEO: Charles Hillyer
Chairman: Stephen Weitzer
steve@aristaindustries.com

Estimated Sales: $2.5-5 Million
Number Employees: 20-49
Type of Packaging: Consumer, Food Service
Types of Products Distributed:
  Food Service, Frozen Food, Seafood, Oils, frozen shrimp & lobster tails

54865 Arizona Storage & Retrieval Systems
6411 E Carolina Drive
Scottsdale, AZ 85254-2003 623-949-7616
  Fax: 480-994-5991
Wholesaler/distributor of filing equipment and supplies, store fixtures and steel and wood shelving
President: Terry Tops
Estimated Sales: $1-2.5 Million
Number Employees: 1-4
Types of Products Distributed:
  Frozen Food, General Merchandise, Store fixtures & shelving

54866 Arkansas Tomato Shippers
106 N John C Moss III St
Warren, AR 71671-2510 870-463-8258
  brooks@dakotacom.net
Distributor and processor of fresh produce
President: Charlie Sarcey
Estimated Sales: $1-5 Million
Number Employees: 6

54867 Arkansas Valley Wholesale Grocery Company
PO Box 380
Morrilton, AR 72110-0380 501-354-3451
  Fax: 501-354-1388
Wholesaler/distributor of general line items and general merchandise
President: Larry Gordon
Estimated Sales: $5-10 Million
Number Employees: 10-19
Square Footage: 220000
Private Brands Carried:
  W-R; Petit Jean
Number of Customer Locations: 300
Types of Products Distributed:
  Frozen Food, General Line, General Merchandise

54868 Arla Foods Inc
675 Rivermede Road
Concord, ON L4K 2G9
Canada 905-669-9393
  Fax: 905-669-5614 www.arlafoods.com
Cheese
President: Andrew Simpson
Estimated Sales: $19 Million
Number Employees: 120
Square Footage: 200000
Type of Packaging: Consumer, Food Service, Private Label, Bulk
Types of Products Distributed:
  Frozen Food, General Line, Cheese

54869 (HQ)Arleen Food Products Company
2500 E Ontario St
Philadelphia, PA 19134-5398 215-634-6410
  Fax: 215-634-9928
Wholesaler/distributor of general line products
President: Joseph Osendowski Jr
Treasurer: Arleen Patton
VP: Dennis Osendowski
Estimated Sales: $10-20 Million
Number Employees: 10-19
Square Footage: 80000
Number of Customer Locations: 400
Types of Products Distributed:
  Frozen Food, General Line

54870 Arlington Coffee Company
1519 Industrial Dr
Itasca, IL 60143 630-625-5141
Wholesaler/distributor of espresso machines and coffee; also, vending services available; serving the food service market
Owner: Bob Connelly
Estimated Sales: $1-2.5 Million
Number Employees: 1-4
Number of Customer Locations: 200
Types of Products Distributed:
  Food Service, Frozen Food, General Line, General Merchandise, Espresso machines & coffee

Wholesalers & Distributors / A-Z

54871 Armaday Paper
527 W 14th Street
New York, NY 10014-1006
212-242-5560
Fax: 212-924-3842
Wholesaler/distributor of paper and plastic disposables; serving the food service market
Traffic Mgr.: Keith O'Dwyer
Executive VP: Chris Skelley
Secretary/Treasurer: Joyce Malcolm
Number Employees: 10-19
Square Footage: 200000
Types of Products Distributed:
 Food Service, Frozen Food, General Merchandise, Disposables

54872 Armbrust Meats
224 S Main St
Medford, WI 54451
715-748-3102
Fax: 715-748-6399
Fresh and frozen sausage, beef, pork and poultry
President: Thomas Armbrust
Estimated Sales: $500,000-$1 Million
Square Footage: 132000
Type of Packaging: Consumer, Bulk

54873 Armstrong Jones
123 Sunrise Avenue
Toronto, ON M4A 2V9
Canada
416-751-2380
Fax: 416-751-5771 800-268-6570
Wholesaler/distributor of safety valves, filtration and vibration isolation equipment, spray nozzles, acoustic products and material handling products
Inside Sales: Malcolm McKaye
Parent Co: Masdom
Types of Products Distributed:
 Frozen Food, General Merchandise, Material handling products

54874 Arnall Grocery Co
32 E Washington St
Newnan, GA 30263-1984
770-253-4556
Fax: 770-253-4600 www.arnallgrocery.com
Wholesaler/distributor of general merchandise and general line products; serving the food service market
Owner: Shane Prophett
sprophett@arnallgrocery.com
CFO and Office Manager: Pam Beavers
Estimated Sales: $5-10 Million
Number Employees: 5-9
Number of Customer Locations: 50
Types of Products Distributed:
 Food Service, Frozen Food, General Line, General Merchandise

54875 (HQ)Arnett Brokerage Co
4010 82nd St # 115
Suite 115
Lubbock, TX 79423-1933
806-744-1477
Fax: 806-744-0119 www.arnettbrokerage.com
Export broker of confectionery products, frozen foods, private label items, produce, seafood, dairy/deli products, general merchandise, groceries, meat and meat products, etc.
President: Mike Poteet
CEO: Jeff Poteet
poteetj@arnettbrokerage.com
VP: Mike Couch
Estimated Sales: $7 Million
Number Employees: 20-49
Square Footage: 6600

54876 Arnold Machinery Co
2975 W 2100 S
Salt Lake City, UT 84119
801-972-4000
www.arnoldmachinery.com
Wholesaler/distributor of forklifts.
President: Kayden Bell
kaydenb@arnoldmachinery.com
Chairman: Arnie Richer
Chief Financial Officer: John Pugmire
COO & President, Mining Equipment: Tom O'Byrne
President, Construction Equipment: Mike Miles
President, Material Handling Equipment: Mike Brown
President, Material Handling Equipment: Kirk Reese
General Implement Distribution: Darrell Buttars
Year Founded: 1929
Estimated Sales: $100-500 Miillion
Number Employees: 250-499
Private Brands Carried:
 Hyster
Types of Products Distributed:
 Frozen Food, General Merchandise, Forklifts

54877 Aroma Coffee Roasters Inc
1601 Madison St
Hoboken, NJ 07030-2313
201-792-1730
Fax: 201-659-1883 www.aromacoffee.com
Coffee wholesaler
Manager: Ruth Santuccio
Estimated Sales: $1-2.5 Million
Number Employees: 20-49

54878 Aroma Foods
6470 Northam Drive
Mississauga, ON L4V 1H9
Canada
905-677-1313
Fax: 905-677-0200 800-765-3826
Wholesaler/distributor of Italian foods; serving the food service market
President: Mauro Marchettini
Number Employees: 10-19
Types of Products Distributed:
 Food Service, Frozen Food, General Merchandise, Specialty Foods, Italian foods

54879 Aron Corporation
PO Box 1408
Juana Diaz, PR 00795-1408
787-837-7030
Fax: 787-837-2043 www.gemasco.com
Wholesaler/distributor of forklifts; also, parts, service and rental available
VP of Sales: Jose Gonzales
Number Employees: 20-49
Private Brands Carried:
 Nissan; Drexel; Prime Mover
Types of Products Distributed:
 Frozen Food, General Merchandise, Forklifts

54880 Arrow Chemical Inc
41 W Putnam Ave
Third Floor
Greenwich, CT 06830-5300
203-769-1740
Fax: 203-769-1741
Wholesaler/distributor and importer of preservatives
Owner: Roger Trief
Estimated Sales: $1-3 Million
Number Employees: 10-19
Square Footage: 4000
Type of Packaging: Bulk
Types of Products Distributed:
 Frozen Food, General Line, Preservatives

54881 Arrow Distributing
800 N Cummings Rd
Covina, CA 91724-2505
626-967-3375
Fax: 626-967-5378
Wholesaler/distributor of provisions/meats
Owner: Abu Sama
arrowdistributing@gmail.com
Manager: Ken Higa
Estimated Sales: Less than $500,000
Number Employees: 1-4
Types of Products Distributed:
 Frozen Food, Provisions/Meat

54882 Arrow Restaurant Equipment
5061 Arrow Hwy
Montclair, CA 91763-1304
909-621-7428
Fax: 909-624-2453 www.arrowreste.com
Wholesaler/distributor of commercial kitchen and bakery equipment; serving the food service market; also, installation services available
President: Michael Serrao
mike@arrowreste.com
Estimated Sales: $5-7 Million
Number Employees: 10-19
Square Footage: 100000
Parent Co: Arrow Beca
Private Brands Carried:
 Hobart; Amana; Traulsen; Frymaster; Bunn; Hamilton Beach; Cambro; Univex; U.S. Range; Merco/Savory; Dean; Wells; Continental; Vollrath; Champion; Dormont; Eagle; Scotsman; Cleveland; Bevles;
Types of Products Distributed:
 Food Service, General Merchandise, Commerical kitchen equipment, etc.

54883 Art's Trading
830 7th St
San Francisco, CA 94107
415-863-7886
Fax: 415-863-2768
Wholesaler/distributor of Oriental and frozen foods
President: Art Chan
VP: Ann Chan
Estimated Sales: $10-20 Million
Number Employees: 10-19
Number of Customer Locations: 185
Types of Products Distributed:
 Frozen Food, General Line, Specialty Foods, Oriental foods

54884 Arthur G. Meier Company/Inland Products Company
1369 Clarke Avenue Sw
Roanoke, VA 24016-4901
540-345-7793
Fax: 540-344-6571
Broker of confectionery products, frozen foods, general merchandise, seafood, groceries, meats, etc.; serving all markets; wholesaler/distributor of salt, cookies, compactors and balers
Owner: May M Justice
VP: J Robert Justice
Estimated Sales: $1-2.5 Million
Number Employees: 4
Types of Products Distributed:
 General Line, General Merchandise

54885 Artique
PO Box 44
Midland Park, NJ 07432
201-444-8989
Wholesaler/distributor of specialty foods
Manager: Edward Reeman
Estimated Sales: $1-2.5 Million
Number Employees: 1-4
Types of Products Distributed:
 Frozen Food, Specialty Foods

54886 Artist Coffee
51 Harvey Road
Unit D
Londonderry, NH 03053-7414
603-434-9385
Fax: 603-216-8029 866-440-4511
Producer of gourmet coffee, tea and candy for promotional trade. Specializing in Custom Labeling with very special products.
President: Tom Rushton
Marketing Director: Dan Sewell
Estimated Sales: $3-5 Million
Number Employees: 1-4
Type of Packaging: Consumer, Private Label
Other Locations:
 Lambent Technologies
 Gurnee, ILLambent Technologies

54887 Asanti Distributors
4260 Dow Road
Melbourne, FL 32934-9223
321-255-1446
Fax: 321-255-7707 888-524-3663
Wholesaler/distributor of Caribbean grocery products, spices, beans, cured fish and meats, produce and snacks; serving the retail and food service markets
President: John Shirley
Accounts: Grace Shirley
Number Employees: 5-9
Square Footage: 12000
Private Brands Carried:
 Angel; Seastar; Cirale; DTC; St. Mark; Royal Caribbean; La Caye
Number of Customer Locations: 150
Types of Products Distributed:
 Food Service, Frozen Food, General Line, Provisions/Meat, Produce, Seafood, Specialty Foods, Caribbean foods, spices, snacks, etc.

54888 Asheboro Wholesale Grocery Inc
228 W Ward St
Asheboro, NC 27203-5486
336-625-5570
Fax: 336-629-4929 800-423-2134
www.michaelscigars.com
Wholesaler/distributor of candy
President: M Ayers
VP: Harold Ayers
Estimated Sales: $10-20 Million
Number Employees: 1-4
Number of Customer Locations: 500
Types of Products Distributed:
 Frozen Food, General Line, Candy

54889 Ashland Equipment
1324 Brass Mill Rd
Belcamp, MD 21017
410-273-1856
Wholesaler/distributor of restaurant equipment and supplies; serving the food service market.
Year Founded: 2000
Estimated Sales: $55 Million

Wholesalers & Distributors / A-Z

Number Employees: 50-99
Square Footage: 540000
Type of Packaging: Food Service

54890 Ashley Koffman Foods
6030 Freemont Boulevard
Mississauga, ON L5R 3X4
Canada
905-507-6161
Fax: 905-507-2727
Wholesaler/distributor of imported groceries including confectionery and dairy/deli product; serving the food service market and supermarket chains
General Manager: P Cook
Private Brands Carried:
  Oscar Meyer; Werther; Brown & Haley
Types of Products Distributed:
  Food Service, General Line, Groceries: confectionery items, etc.

54891 Asia Shipping & TradingCorporation
1117 Westminster Ave
Alhambra, CA 91803
626-576-8493
Fax: 626-576-1323
Wholesaler/distributor of general line products
President: Kenneth Chan
kenneth@netpath.net
Estimated Sales: $500,000-$1 Million
Number Employees: 1-4
Types of Products Distributed:
  Frozen Food, General Line

54892 Asiamerica Ingredients
245 Old Hood Rd #3
Westwood, NJ 07675-3174
201-497-5993
Fax: 201-497-5994 201-497-5531
info@asiamericaingredients.com
www.asiamericaingredients.com
Processor, importer, exporter and distributor of bulk vitamins, amino acids, nutraceuticals, aromatic chemicals, food additives, herbs, mineral nutrients and pharmaceuticals.
President/Owner: Mark Zhang
CFO: Lillian Yang
Quality Control: Michelle Naomi
Sales: Cari Pandero
Contact: Elizabeth Gysbers
egysbers@asiamericaingredients.com
Purchasing: Michelle N. Riley
Estimated Sales: $5-10 Million
Number Employees: 10
Type of Packaging: Bulk

54893 ASpecialtybox.Com
12437 E 60th St
Tulsa, OK 74146
918-461-0609
Fax: 918-249-2602 888-408-7269
aspecialtybox@calvertco.com
www.aspecialtybox.com
Wholesaler/distributor of advertising specialties
President: Cynthia Calvert
Marketing: Jennifer Giebel
Contact: Jan Obrien
jobrien@aspecialtybox.com
General Manager: Bob Bartels
Estimated Sales: $1-3 Million
Number Employees: 50-99
Square Footage: 8000
Types of Products Distributed:
  Frozen Food, General Merchandise, Advertising specialties

54894 Aspen Corporate Identity Group
1240 North Avenue
West Chicago, IL 60185
800-848-0212
Fax: 630-293-7584
Wholesaler/distributor of advertising specialties
President: Patrick Orahilly
VP of Sales: Dane Van Breene
Estimated Sales: $.5-1 million
Number Employees: 1-4
Parent Co: Aspen Marketing
Types of Products Distributed:
  Frozen Food, General Merchandise, Advertising specialties

54895 Assemblyonics Inc
89 Cabot Ct # H
Hauppauge, NY 11788-3719
631-231-4440
Fax: 631-434-1777 800-222-4583
assemblyon@aol.com www.assemblyonics.com
Wholesaler/distributor of dispensing, packaging and adhesive equipment; serving the food service market
President: Carl Cirilli
CEO: Jo Cirilli
CFO: Angela Cirilli
Vice President: Angela Cirilli
angela.cirilli@assemblyonics.com
Marketing Director: Maria Cirilli
Estimated Sales: $1-3 Million
Number Employees: 5-9
Square Footage: 40000
Type of Packaging: Bulk
Private Brands Carried:
  ITW Dynatec; 3M; Loctite; Borden Adhesive; HB Fuller Adhesives; Glue Fast Equipment; Hot Melt Adhesives
Types of Products Distributed:
  Food Service, General Merchandise, Dispensing & packaging equipment

54896 Associated Bag Co
400 W Boden St
Milwaukee, WI 53207-6276
414-769-1000
Fax: 414-769-1820 800-926-6100
customerservice@associatedbag.com
www.associatedbag.com
Wholesaler/distributor of food grade stretch wrap and bags, gloves and shipping and packaging products
President: Herbert Rubenstein
hrubenstein@associatedbag.com
CFO: Sue Zelga
Quality Control: Mary Samanski
Marketing/Sales Director: Scott Pietila
Customer Service Manager: Philip Roedel
hrubenstein@associatedbag.com
Purchasing Manager: Sue Zylka
Estimated Sales: $20-50 Million
Number Employees: 100-249
Square Footage: 300000
Private Brands Carried:
  Write-On
Types of Products Distributed:
  General Merchandise, Bags, shipping & packaging pdts., etc.

54897 Associated Food Equipment
10381 Express Dr
Gulfport, MS 39503-4611
228-896-0043
Fax: 228-896-9032 800-526-3201
contact@afesco.com www.afesco.com
Wholesaler/distributor of food service equipment and supplies; also, design and layout services available
Owner: James Watts
james@afesco.com
CEO: Barnes
VP: Robert Barnes
Secretary: Roberta Shelton
Estimated Sales: $1-2.5 Million
Number Employees: 10-19
Square Footage: 60000
Types of Products Distributed:
  Food Service, Frozen Food, General Merchandise, Foodservice equipment & supplies

54898 Associated Food Stores
11615 Metropolitan Ave
Jamaica, NY 11418
718-847-1010
Fax: 718-847-0953
Wholesaler/distributor of groceries
Manager: Silzia Almonte
Estimated Sales: Less than $500,000
Number Employees: 20-49
Private Brands Carried:
  Super A
Number of Customer Locations: 150
Types of Products Distributed:
  Frozen Food, General Line, Groceries

54899 Associated Food Stores Inc
1850 W 2100 S
Salt Lake City, UT 84119
801-973-4400
888-574-7100
www.afstores.com
Wholesaler/distributor of groceries, meats, produce, dairy products, frozen foods, baked goods, equipment and fixtures, general merchandise and private label items.
President & CEO: Neal Berube
Year Founded: 1940
Estimated Sales: $1.6 Billion
Number Employees: 1,400
Private Brands Carried:
  Western Family
Number of Customer Locations: 210
Types of Products Distributed:
  Frozen Food, General Line, General Merchandise, Provisions/Meat, Produce, Groceries, dairy products, etc.

54900 Associated Grocers
7100 44th Street SE
Calgary, AB T2C 2V7
Canada
800-242-3182
Fax: 800-461-8876 www.associated-grocers.com
Wholesaler/distributor of frozen foods, general merchandise, general line items, produce and meats; serving the food service market
President: Steve Vaneerlest
Director Sales/Operations: Larry Klassen
General Manager: Ron Klassen
Distribution Centre Manager: Scott Leask
Number Employees: 100-249
Parent Co: Buy-Low Foods
Types of Products Distributed:
  Food Service, Frozen Food, General Line, General Merchandise, Provisions/Meat, Produce

54901 Associated Material Handling
3106 Independence Dr
Fort Wayne, IN 46808-4501
260-373-1032
Fax: 260-482-7540 877-860-2225
www.associated-solutions.com
Wholesaler/distributor of material handling equipment including electric forklifts
Manager: James Yoquelet
Sales Engineer: Peter Nix
Sales Engineer: Jay Melcher
Estimated Sales: $5-10 Million
Number Employees: 1-4
Parent Co: Associated Material Handling
Types of Products Distributed:
  Frozen Food, General Merchandise, Material handling equipment

54902 Associated Wholesale Grocers
5000 Kansas Ave
Kansas City, KS 66106
913-288-1000
www.awginc.com
Nation's second largest wholesaler/distributor of general line products, groceries, meat, produce, dairy products, frozen food, baked goods and private label items.
President & CEO: David Smith
SVP, Finance: David Carl
Year Founded: 1924
Estimated Sales: $9.7 Billion
Number Employees: 1000-4999
Square Footage: 2500000
Private Brands Carried:
  Best Choice; Always Save
Number of Customer Locations: 883
Types of Products Distributed:
  Frozen Food, General Line, Provisions/Meat, Produce, Groceries, baked goods, etc.

54903 Associates Material Handling
12241 Montague St
Pacoima, CA 91331-2290
818-897-3055
Fax: 818-897-3546 800-427-5279
www.amhonline.com
Wholesaler/distributor of material handling equipment including conveyors, pallet jacks, etc
President: Barbara Bell
VP: William Bell
Manager: Steve Bell
steve@amhonline.com
Estimated Sales: $2.5-5 Million
Number Employees: 10-19
Private Brands Carried:
  Starrco; M.F.G.; Bio-Fit
Types of Products Distributed:
  Frozen Food, General Merchandise, Material handling equipment

54904 Astar Inc.
5 Everett St
Wellesley, MA 02481
781-235-8624
Fax: 781-235-2022 fbuchbind@aol.com
Gluten-free, bread/biscuits, cakes/pastries, cookies, olive oil, balsamic vinegar, other chocolate.
Marketing: Franco Buchbinder
Contact: Franco Buchbinder
fbuchbind@aol.com

Wholesalers & Distributors / A-Z

54905 Astoria General Espresso
7912 Industrial Village Rd
Greensboro, NC 27409   336-393-0224
Fax: 336-393-0295 info@geec.com
www.usa.astoria.com
Manufacturer, importer and exporter of espresso and cappuccino machines, coffee grinders, espresso equipment accessories and sandwich grills
Owner: Roberto Daltio
CEO: Umberto Terreni
Accounting/Office Manager: Linda Sizemore
Sales & Marketing: Courtney Baber
Managing/Sales Director: Scott Gordon
Technical Support Specialist: Jimmy Wardell
Number Employees: 5-9
Number of Brands: 2
Number of Products: 36
Square Footage: 50000
Parent Co: CMA
Type of Packaging: Private Label
Private Brands Carried:
  Astoria, Grillmaster

54906 Astral Extracts
50 Eileen Way
Unit 6
Syosset, NY 11791-5313   516-496-2505
Fax: 516-496-4248 info@astralextracts.com
www.astralextracts.com
Processor, wholesaler, distributor, importer and exporter of fruit juice concentrates, essential oils and citrus products
President: Cynthia Astrack
info@astralextracts.com
General Manager: Joan Pace
Estimated Sales: $5-10 Million
Number Employees: 5-9
Square Footage: 30000
Type of Packaging: Food Service, Private Label, Bulk

54907 Atchison Wholesale Grocery
100 S 3rd St
Atchison, KS 66002-2979   913-367-0043
Fax: 913-367-7531
Wholesaler/distributor of general line products, provisions/meats, specialty foods, canned goods, dairy products, seafood, frozen foods and groceries
Manager: Joe Warren
Estimated Sales: $3-5 Million
Number Employees: 1-4
Private Brands Carried:
  Lady B.; Sysco
Types of Products Distributed:
  Frozen Food, General Line, Provisions/Meat, Seafood, Specialty Foods, Groceries, etc.

54908 Atco Marine Service
28 NW North River Drive
Miami, FL 33128-1633   305-374-5070
Fax: 305-374-6637
Wholesaler/distributor of lobster
Owner: Indalacio Fernandez
Types of Products Distributed:
  Frozen Food, Seafood

54909 Atka Pride Seafoods Inc
302 Gold St
Suite 202
Juneau, AK 99801-1127   907-586-0161
Fax: 907-586-0165 888-927-4232
info@apicda.com www.apicda.com
Supplier of seafood
Chief Executive Officer: Larry Cotter
Chief Financial Officer: Robert Smith
Chief Operating Officer: John Sevier
Number Employees: 1-4
Parent Co: Aleutian Pribilof Island Community Development Association

54910 Atlanta Fixture & SalesCompany
3185 Northeast Expy NE
Chamblee, GA 30341   770-455-8844
Fax: 770-986-9202 800-282-1977
www.atlantafixture.com
Wholesaler/distributor of food service equipment, tabletop and janitorial supplies, paper products and chemicals; serving the food service market
President: Paul Klein
VP Marketing/Sales: Ken Kay
Regional Sales Manager: Tim Frykman
Estimated Sales: $20-50 Million
Number Employees: 100-249
Square Footage: 87000

Types of Products Distributed:
  Food Service, Frozen Food, General Merchandise, Foodservice equipment, etc.

54911 Atlantic Dominion Distributors
5400 Virginia Beach Blvd
Virginia Beach, VA 23462   757-497-1001
Fax: 757-499-0984 800-468-6612
www.atlanticdominiondistributors.com
Wholesaler/distributor of convenience and retail store products; including, candy, tobacco, general groceries and beverages.
President & Chief Executive Officer: Robin Ray
robin.ray@atlanticdominion.com
Year Founded: 1904
Estimated Sales: $487.30 Million
Number Employees: 100-249
Number of Products: 10K
Number of Customer Locations: 3500
Types of Products Distributed:
  Frozen Food, General Line, General Merchandise, Candy & groceries

54912 Atlantic Gem Scallop Co
8 South St
New Bedford, MA 02740-7221   508-999-5861
Fax: 508-999-5668
www.seatrade-international.com
Wholesaler/distributor of fresh and frozen scallops
President: Al Reitzer
Number Employees: 50-99
Private Brands Carried:
  Atlantic Gem
Types of Products Distributed:
  Frozen Food, Seafood, Fresh & frozen scallops

54913 Atlantic Industrial & Marine Supplies
17 Kyle Avenue
Mount Pearl, NL A1N 4R4
Canada   709-368-2467
Wholesaler/distributor of material handling equipment
Sales Manager: G Wayne Yetman
Number Employees: 10-19
Private Brands Carried:
  Blue Giant; Lift-Rite; Steelcraft Doors
Types of Products Distributed:
  Frozen Food, General Merchandise, Material handling equipment

54914 Atlantic Lift Systems
5736 Sellger Dr
Norfolk, VA 23502-5252   757-466-9280
Fax: 757-461-8337 www.atlanticliftsystems.com
Wholesaler/distributor of forklifts and racks; also, parts and service available
President: Allan Haynsworth
allan@atlanticliftsystems.com
Estimated Sales: $20-50 Million
Number Employees: 20-49
Private Brands Carried:
  Toyota; Clark; Daewoo
Types of Products Distributed:
  Frozen Food, General Merchandise, Material handling equipment

54915 Atlantic Rentals
Lockhart Mill Road
Woodstock, NB E0J 2B0
Canada   506-325-9341
Fax: 506-328-1229
Wholesaler/distributor of forklifts
Number Employees: 10-19
Private Brands Carried:
  Nissan
Types of Products Distributed:
  Frozen Food, General Merchandise, Forklifts

54916 Atlantic Salmon of Maine
57 Little River Dr
Belfast, ME 04915   207-338-9028
Fax: 207-338-6288
Fresh salmon and seafood manufacturer
CEO: Dave Peterson
CFO: John Thibaoou
Vice President: Stephen Young
Contact: Peter Christensen
pchristensen@majesticsalmon.com
Number Employees: 140
Parent Co: Fjord Seafood USA

54917 Atlantic Sea Pride
16 Fish Pier
Boston, MA 02210-2054   617-269-7700
Fax: 617-269-7766
Processor and wholesaler/distributor of fresh fish and fillets; serving the food service market
President: Anthony Correnti
VP: Frank Mazza
Estimated Sales: $4.30 Million
Number Employees: 20
Type of Packaging: Consumer, Food Service, Bulk
Types of Products Distributed:
  Food Service, Seafood, Fresh fish & fillets

54918 Atlantic Seacove Inc
20 Newmarket Sq
Boston, MA 02118-2601   617-442-6206
Fax: 617-482-7733
Wholesale dealers in fresh and frozen fish
President/CEO: John Wojitasinski
Owner: Andrew Bunten
Treasurer: Mitchell Wojitasinski
Estimated Sales: $3.3 Million
Number Employees: 10-19

54919 Atlantic Seafood Direct
12 A Portland Fish Pier
PO Box 682
Portland, ME 04104
          800-774-6025
Seafood fresh and frozen
President: Jerry Knecht
VP/General Manager: Mike Norton

54920 Atlantic Seafood Intl Group
8533 Terminal Rd
Lorton, VA 22079-1428   703-339-4550
Fax: 703-339-4555
Wholesaler/distributor of frozen shrimp and scallops
Owner: George Cheung
g8cheung@yahoo.com
Co-Ownr.: Linda Cheung
Estimated Sales: $3-5 Million
Number Employees: 5-9
Types of Products Distributed:
  Frozen Food, Seafood, Frozen shrimp & scallops

54921 Atlantic Spice Co
2 Shore Rd
North Truro, MA 2652   508-487-6100
Fax: 508-487-2550 800-316-7965
info@atlanticspice.com www.atlanticspice.com
Specializing in herbs, spices, teas and potpourri
Owner: Cory Chapman
cory@atlanticspice.com
Estimated Sales: $5-10 Million
Number Employees: 10-19
Type of Packaging: Bulk

54922 Atlantic Store Fixture Company
280 Mishawum Rd
Woburn, MA 01801   781-935-4300
Fax: 781-935-3326 800-852-3755
Wholesaler/distributor of food service equipment; serving supermarket chains and the food service market; also, design and installation services available
President: Elliott Stein
General Manager: David Smith
Purchasing Manager: Colin Woodfall
Estimated Sales: $2.5-5 Million
Number Employees: 5-9
Square Footage: 40000
Type of Packaging: Food Service
Number of Customer Locations: 1
Types of Products Distributed:
  Food Service, Foodservice equipment

54923 Atlantic Wholesalers
12 Dominion Crescent
Lakeside, NS B3T 1A1
Canada   902-876-8201
Fax: 902-876-7069
Wholesaler/distributor of general line items
Director: Matt Davidson
Distribution Manager: Craig Sutherland
Number Employees: 150
Square Footage: 520000
Parent Co: Loblaw Companies
Private Brands Carried:
  President's Choice
Number of Customer Locations: 200

Wholesalers & Distributors / A-Z

Types of Products Distributed:
  Frozen Food, General Line

54924 Atlantic Wholesalers
3-13 Premier Drive
Lewisporte, NL A0G 3A0
Canada   709-535-8641
                           Fax: 709-535-6208
Wholesaler/distributor of groceries
Sales Manager: Les Walton
Types of Products Distributed:
  Frozen Food, General Line, Groceries

54925 Atlas Equipment Company
3111 Wyandotte St # 102
Kansas City, MO 64111-1369   816-842-9188
         Fax: 816-842-9192   800-842-9188
            2info@atlasequipment.com
               www.atlasequipment.com
Wholesaler/distributor of storage and material handling systems, belt conveyors, steel shelving and pallet racks
President: Julie Duvall
Estimated Sales: $5-10 Million
Number Employees: 1-4
Square Footage: 600000
Types of Products Distributed:
  Frozen Food, General Merchandise, Automatic storage & handling systems

54926 Atlas Lift Truck Rentals & Sales
1815 Landmeier Rd
Elk Grove Village, IL 60007   847-678-3450
                    www.atlaslift.com
Wholesaler/distributor of material handling equipment including pallet trucks, racking and wire mesh decking.
President: Allen Rawson
Year Founded: 1951
Estimated Sales: $100-500 Million
Number Employees: 200-500
Private Brands Carried:
  Aatlas; Zenith
Types of Products Distributed:
  Frozen Food, General Merchandise, Material handling equipment

54927 Attar Herbs & Spices
5 Sargent Camp Road
Harrisville, NH 03450   603-924-2210
         Fax: 603-924-2211   800-541-6900
            info@attarherbs.com www.attarherbs.com
Wholesaler/distributor of essential oils, fragrances, spices, herbs, botanicals, gums and dried flowers
Owner: Dick Martin
Contact: Melissa Spencer
melissa@attarherbs.com
Estimated Sales: $500,000-$1 Million
Number Employees: 1-4
Square Footage: 24000
Types of Products Distributed:
  Frozen Food, General Line, Essential oils, fragrances, etc.

54928 Atwater Foods
10182 Roosevelt Hwy
Route 18
Lyndonville Orleans, NY 14098-9785 585-765-2639
         Fax: 585-765-9443 www.shorelinefruit.com
Manufacturer, exporter and wholesaler of many kinds of dried fruit, including apples, cherries, cranberries, blueberries and strawberries. Star-K Kosher. Our customer service support is responsive to timelines and responsible for keeping everything on track
Manager: Randy Atwater
Quality Control: Chris Fraser
Sales/Marketing: Jim Palmer
Contact: Fred Freeman
fred@atwaterfoods.com
Plant Manager: Steve Mohr
Purchasing Manager: Pat Glidden
Estimated Sales: 15-20 Million
Number Employees: 50-99
Number of Products: 50+
Square Footage: 180000
Type of Packaging: Private Label, Bulk
Types of Products Distributed:
  Frozen Food, Health Food, Produce

54929 Atwood Lobster Co
286 Island Ave
Spruce Head, ME 4859   207-596-6691
         Fax: 207-596-6958 www.atwoodlobster.com

Wholesaler/distributor of live, fresh and frozen lobsters
Owner: William Atwood
COO: Bill McGonagle
Sales Manager: Bob Graves
Manager: Corey Thompson
corey.thompson@atwoodlobster.com
Estimated Sales: $10-20 Million
Number Employees: 50-99
Types of Products Distributed:
  Frozen Food, Seafood, Live, fresh & frozen lobsters

54930 Aunt Heddy's Bakery
234 N 9th Street
Brooklyn, NY 11211-2012   718-782-0582
Food wholsaler and maufacturer of breads and babka
Owner: Rich Zablocki
Estimated Sales: $63 Thousand
Number Employees: 2
Types of Products Distributed:
  Baked Goods

54931 Aunt Sally's Praline Shops
750 Saint Charles Ave
New Orleans, LA 70130-3714   504-522-2126
         Fax: 504-944-5925   800-642-7257
            service@auntsallys.com www.auntsallys.com
New Orleans style creamy praline candies in four flavors, and other specialty food items.
Manager: Bethany Gex
CEO: Frank Simoncioni
Sales: Becky Hebert
Sales: Cherie Cunningham
Director Of Operations: Karl Schmidt
Estimated Sales: $5 Million+
Number Employees: 20-49
Square Footage: 20000
Type of Packaging: Consumer, Food Service, Private Label, Bulk

54932 Auromere Inc
2621 W Highway 12
Lodi, CA 95242-9200   209-339-3710
         Fax: 209-339-3715   800-735-4691
            info@auromere.com www.auromere.com
Wholesaler/distributor, importer and exporter of supplements and jams, also deals with natural body care
President: Dakshina Vanzetti
dakshina@auromere.com
VP: Vishnu Eschner
Estimated Sales: Less Than $500,000
Number Employees: 1-4
Square Footage: 28000
Type of Packaging: Consumer
Private Brands Carried:
  Auromere; Auromere-Ayurvedic; Chandrika; Herbomineral
Types of Products Distributed:
  General Merchandise, Health Food, HBA

54933 Aurora Alaska Premium Smoked Salmon & Seafood
PO Box 211376
Anchorage, AK 99521-1376   907-338-2229
         Fax: 907-338-2228   800-653-3474
Seafood products
Owner: Bill Dornberger
Owner: Gloria Dornberger

54934 Aust & Hachmann
1751 Richardson Street
Suite 4303
Montreal, Quebec, CN H3K 1G0
Canada   514-482-4615
                           Fax: 514-483-6183
Importer and wholesaler/distributor of vanilla beans and vanilla by-products
Director: David Van Der Walde
Fin.: Diane Lotosky
Sales Director: Patricia Raymond
Types of Products Distributed:
  Frozen Food, General Line, Vanilla beans & vanilla by-products

54935 Auster Company
2404 S Wolcott Ave
Unit 33
Chicago, IL 60608   312-829-6550
                           Fax: 312-666-0095
Wholesaler/distributor of produce
President: Thomas Bastounes

Estimated Sales: $9.90
Number Employees: 44
Square Footage: 150000
Types of Products Distributed:
  Produce

54936 Austin Special Foods Company
10000 Inshore Drive
Austin, TX 78730   512-372-8665
                           Fax: 512-652-2699
Wholesaler of all natural and kosher dairy biscotti, cookies and frozen cookie dough. Many biscotti flavors
Owner: Laura Logan
CEO: Gene Austin
Year Founded: 1994
Estimated Sales: $10-20 Million
Number Employees: 3

54937 Austrade
3309 Northlake Blvd
Suite 201
Palm Beach Gardens, FL 33403   561-586-7145
         Fax: 561-585-7164 info@austradeinc.com
                    www.austradeinc.com
Importer, wholesaler of non-GMO and organic ingredients
President: Gary Bartl
Finance Director: Schantl Joseph
VP: Stephen Barti
Vice President Business Development: Robert Rice
VP Operations: Josef Schantl
Estimated Sales: $380,000
Number Employees: 1-4
Square Footage: 8000
Parent Co: GBI Bartl Intertrading
Type of Packaging: Private Label, Bulk
Types of Products Distributed:
  Frozen Food, General Line, Health Food, Potato & tapioca starches, etc.

54938 Auth Brothers Food Service
2144 Queens Chapel Road N
Washington, DC 20018-3608   202-529-6900
                           Fax: 202-526-5053
Wholesaler/distributor of provisions/meats; serving the food service market
President: A Auth
VP: T Auth
Secretary: H Auth
Number Employees: 100-249
Types of Products Distributed:
  Food Service, Frozen Food, Provisions/Meat

54939 Auto City Candy Company
PO Box 427
Troy, MI 48099   248-689-3850
                           Fax: 248-689-4653
Wholesaler/distributor of confectionery items and frozen foods; rack jobber services available
CEO/Pres.: John Levy
Sales Manager: Richard Johnson
Estimated Sales: $5-10 Million
Number Employees: 5-9
Square Footage: 200000
Parent Co: L&L Concession
Private Brands Carried:
  Mars; Hershey; Leaf; Bazooka; Tops; Willy Wonka
Types of Products Distributed:
  General Line, Rack Jobbers, Confectionery items

54940 Automation Fastening Company
1138 W 9th St
Cleveland, OH 44113-1007   216-241-4487
         Fax: 216-241-5918   800-837-5939
            service@mailshipsolutions.com
               www.mailshipsolutions.com
Wholesaler/distributor of staples and staplers, tackers, scales, folders, inserters, blisters and other shipping and office supplies
Owner: Jim Johnson
Supv.: Patrick Burns
Executive VP: James Johnson
Manager: Robert Bush
Estimated Sales: $5-10 Million
Number Employees: 10-19
Square Footage: 54000
Types of Products Distributed:
  Frozen Food, General Merchandise, Shipping & office supplies

Wholesalers & Distributors / A-Z

54941 Automation Systems & Services
5710 W Manchester Ave Ste 102
Los Angeles, CA 90045   323-776-2424
        Fax: 323-649-1650 800-747-6309
Wholesaler/distributor of sensors and controls for counting, rate, temperature, labeling, color detection, safety, bar code readers and dimensional sensors
President: George Saghbazian
Estimated Sales: $1-2.5 Million
Number Employees: 1-4
Private Brands Carried:
  Sick; Red Lion; Photoswitch
Types of Products Distributed:
  Food Service, Frozen Food, General Line, General Merchandise, Health Food, Provisions/Meat, Produce, Rack Jobbers, Seafood

54942 Avalon Gourmet
1051 E Broadway Rd
Phoenix, AZ 85040-2301   602-253-0343
                Fax: 480-253-0432
Manufacturer of gourmet foods
President: Richard Du Pree
richdupree@fsiaz.com
Owner: Alan Parker
VP: Dolores DuPree
Year Founded: 1994
Estimated Sales: $5-10 Million
Number Employees: 5-9

54943 Avalon International Breads
422 W Willis St
Detroit, MI 48201-1702   313-832-0008
    Fax: 313-832-0018 www.avalonbreads.net
Organic breads and baked goods
CEO: Vanessa Blanchard
vanessablanchard@avalonbreads.net
Number Employees: 50-99

54944 Avalon Trade Company
PO Box 8454
Greensboro, NC 27419-0454   336-547-8277
                Fax: 336-292-8156
Wholesaler/distributor of bars, grills, etc
President: W Sherrill
Estimated Sales: $.5-1 million
Number Employees: 1-4
Private Brands Carried:
  Spring Garden
Types of Products Distributed:
  Frozen Food, General Line, General Merchandise, Bar, grills, etc.

54945 Avatar Corp
500 Central Ave
University Park, IL 60484-3147   708-534-5511
    Fax: 708-534-0123 800-255-3181
    inquiries@avatarcorp.com
Manufacture, refine and supply raw materials and ingredients for the food, drug and personal care industries.
Owner: Kari Boykin
k.boykin@avatarholdings.com
President: Michael Shamie
VP Marketing: David Darwin
Chief Operating Officer: Phil Ternes
Plant Manager: Kent Taylor
Purchasing: Kristina Gutyan
Year Founded: 1982
Estimated Sales: $9 Million
Number Employees: 10-19
Square Footage: 80000
Type of Packaging: Private Label, Bulk
Types of Products Distributed:
  Frozen Food

54946 Awe Sum Organics
123 Locust St
Santa Cruz, CA 95060   831-462-2244
        info@awesumorganics.com
        www.awesumorganics.com
Organic apples, grapes, citrus, pears, kiwis, and blueberries
General Manager: Matt Landi
Financial Controller: Michael Meschi
Sales Coordinator: Sara Pettit
Year Founded: 1985
Number Employees: 20-49
Types of Products Distributed:
  Produce

54947 Axelrod Foods
100 Thomas St
Paterson, NJ 07503-2315   973-684-0600
    Fax: 973-684-0943 www.axelrod.com
Wholesaler/distributor of dairy products including cheese, cottage cheese, sour cream, yogurt, etc.; serving the food service market
General Manager: Mitch Tuch
Estimated Sales: $20-50 Million
Number Employees: 20-49
Parent Co: Crowley Foods
Private Brands Carried:
  Axelrod
Types of Products Distributed:
  Food Service, Frozen Food, General Line, Dairy products

54948 Axia Distribution Corporation
247-2628 Granville Street
Vancouver, BC V6H 4B4
Canada   778-371-9885
    Fax: 778-371-9000 info@axiadistribution.com
        www.axiadistribution.com
Distributor & Manufacutuer of High Quality Rubber Mats. The Mats are molded with virgin rubber that offers durability, less odor, stability and anti-fatigue properties
Type of Packaging: Food Service

54949 Axium Foods
239 Oak Grove Ave
PO Box 187
South Beloit, IL 61080-1936   815-389-3053
                800-523-8644
                www.axiumfoods.com
Corn-based snack foods
President: Jerry Stokely
jstokely@axiumfoods.com
Number Employees: 100-249
Type of Packaging: Consumer, Food Service, Private Label

54950 Aydelotte & Engler Inc
15352 Merry Cat Ln
Belle Haven, VA 23306   757-442-2337
Wholesaler/distributor of beer
Owner: Harley Park
aeinc1@verizon.net
Estimated Sales: $2.5-5 Million
Number Employees: 10-19
Types of Products Distributed:
  Frozen Food, General Line, Beer

54951 Aylesworth's Fish & Bait
1295 28th St S
St Petersburg, FL 33712-1909   727-327-8608
    Fax: 727-323-6753 800-227-4577
    info@fishandbait.com www.fishandbait.com/
Wholesaler/distributor of seafood including black mullet, black mullet roe, ladyfish, Spanish sardines and squid
Owner: Dawn Aylesworth
dawn@fishandbait.com
Estimated Sales: $2.5-5 Million
Number Employees: 10-19
Types of Products Distributed:
  Frozen Food, General Merchandise, Seafood, Squid, ladyfish, etc.

54952 Ayush Herbs Inc
2239 152nd Ave NE
Redmond, WA 98052-5519   425-637-1400
    Fax: 425-451-2670 800-925-1371
    customerservice@ayush.com www.ayush.com
Wholesaler/distributor of general line items and health food including herbal and Ayurvedic extracts, standardized powder, raw herbs/spices, essential oils and Ayurvedic, herbal and green teas; importer and exporter of herbs
President: Shailinder Sodhi
shailinder@ayush.com
Sales Manager: Tarlok Kumar
Estimated Sales: $500,000-$1 Million
Number Employees: 5-9
Square Footage: 20000
Type of Packaging: Consumer, Bulk
Private Brands Carried:
  Ayush; R-UVed; Garcik; Memoren; Boswelya Plus; Livtone
Types of Products Distributed:
  Frozen Food, General Line, Health Food, Herbs, spices, oils & teas

54953 Aztec Secret Health & Beauty
951 W Wilson Rd
Pahrump, NV 89048-4533   775-727-8351
            Fax: 775-727-1882
Wholesaler/distributor of essential oils including vitamin E, tree tea, kukui nut, etc.; also, vitamin B12 and folic acid
Owner: Denise Roman
VP: Linda Roman
Estimated Sales: Less Than $500,000
Number Employees: 1-4
Private Brands Carried:
  Beamer's
Types of Products Distributed:
  Frozen Food, General Line, Health Food, Essential oils & vitamins

54954 Aztech Systems
40 Cindy Lane
Ocean, NJ 07712-7250   732-493-9373
    Fax: 732-493-9372 800-571-1182
            www.aztechsys.com
Wholesaler/distributor of material handling equipment including lifting andunitizing systems
President: Alan Zimmermann
Number Employees: 1-4
Square Footage: 3200
Parent Co: UNITECH Industries
Private Brands Carried:
  Unimove; Lift-O-Flex
Types of Products Distributed:
  Lifting Equipment

54955 B & B Beverages
3670 Sawmill Rd
Doylestown, PA 18902-9000   215-348-3318
            www.bandbbeverages.com
Wholesaler/distributor of beer
Owner: Andy Jarin
Estimated Sales: Less than $500,000
Number Employees: 5-9
Private Brands Carried:
  Budweiser; Coors; Yuengling
Number of Customer Locations: 2000
Types of Products Distributed:
  Frozen Food, General Line, Beer

54956 B & B Distributors Inc
1600 Porter Rd
Rock Hill, SC 29730-8608   803-366-8383
    Fax: 803-366-6909 www.bbdistributors.net
Wholesaler/distributor of beer
President: Kossi Agbeagogno
kossi.agbeagogno@bbdistributors.net
VP/COO: Rick Bridges
Executive VP: Linda Bridges
Sales Manager: Tommy Papas
General Manager: Mike Thomas
Estimated Sales: $5-10 Million
Number Employees: 20-49
Parent Co: Anheuser Busch
Private Brands Carried:
  Budweiser; Bud Light; Michelob
Types of Products Distributed:
  Frozen Food, General Line, Beer

54957 B & B Food Distributors Inc
724 S 13th St
Terre Haute, IN 47807-4997   812-238-1438
    Fax: 812-232-0670 800-264-1438
    sales@bandbfoods.net www.bandbfoods.net
Wholesaler/distributor of frozen food and seafood; serving the food service market
President: Scott Isles
scott@bandbfoods.net
Estimated Sales: $10-20 Million
Number Employees: 50-99
Number of Customer Locations: 400
Types of Products Distributed:
  Food Service, Frozen Food, Seafood

54958 B & G Restaurant Supply
48 Eagle St
Pittsfield, MA 01201-4715   413-442-0390
    Fax: 413-442-1559 800-696-4949
    bg@berkshire.net www.bgrestsupply.com
Wholesaler/distributor of restaurant equipment and supplies; serving the food service market

Wholesalers & Distributors / A-Z

President: Robert Powers
bob@bgrestsupply.com
Treasurer: Gloria J Powers
VP: Robert F Powers
Sales & Project Manager: Dennis Dominic
Operations Manager: Tricia Powers Dambrauskas
Project Management & Design: Herb Paige
Purchasing: Robert Powers
Estimated Sales: $5-10 Million
Number Employees: 10-19
Square Footage: 200000

54959 B & G Venegoni Distribution
850 W Egyptian Ave
Christopher, IL 62822-1531   618-724-2721
                        Fax: 618-724-4740
Wholesaler/distributor of beer
Owner: Bert Venegoni
bud1@bgvenegoni.com
Mgr.: Randy Venegoni
Estimated Sales: $3-5 Million
Number Employees: 10-19
Number of Customer Locations: 104
Types of Products Distributed:
    Frozen Food, General Line, Beer

54960 B & J Food Svc Inc
1616 Dielman Rd
St Louis, MO 63132-1516   314-428-1247
        Fax: 314-429-1035 800-255-3663
salesoverthenet@bjprls.com www.bjpeerless.com
Wholesaler/distributor of new and used food service equipment and supplies; also, 3-D and interior designs and installation services available; serving the food service market
Vice President: Scott Mosburg
s.mosburg@bjpeerless.com
CFO: Jeffery Schmidt
VP: Mike Shade
Sales Director: Josephine Tocco
Operations Manager: Terence Carmen
Purchasing Manager: Jennifer White
Estimated Sales: $6 Million
Number Employees: 20-49
Number of Brands: 2000
Number of Products: 3600
Square Footage: 292000
Parent Co: Peerless Industries
Type of Packaging: Food Service
Types of Products Distributed:
    Food Service, Frozen Food, General Merchandise, Foodservice equipment & supplies

54961 B & K Distributing Inc
1140 13th St
Steamboat Spgs, CO 80487   970-879-1906
    Fax: 970-879-0900 www.exploresteamboat.com
Wholesaler/distributor of beer
Owner: Kevin Kaminski
kkaminski@bkdistributing.com
Sales Manager: Chris Kaminski
Estimated Sales: $10-20 Million
Number Employees: 20-49
Private Brands Carried:
    Budweiser; Miller; Coors
Types of Products Distributed:
    Frozen Food, General Line, Beer

54962 B & M Provision Co
1040 N Graham St
Allentown, PA 18109-3217   610-434-9611
    Fax: 610-434-9988 info@bandmprovisions.com
                    bandmprovisions.com
Wholesaler/distributor serving the foodserv ice market
President/CEO: Richard Oravec
roravec@bandmprovisions.com
CFO: Jean Pacala
Vice President: Richard Oravec
Quality Control: Rodney Strobl
Marketing/Sales: Rodney Strobl
Purchasing Manager: John Pacala
Estimated Sales: $6 Million
Number Employees: 20-49
Number of Brands: 400
Number of Products: 2500
Type of Packaging: Food Service, Bulk
Private Brands Carried:
    Gold Bond National Buying Group
Types of Products Distributed:
    Food Service, Frozen Food, General Merchandise, Provisions/Meat, Produce, Seafood, Specialty Foods, Dairy

54963 B & R Quality Meats Inc
200 Park Rd
Waterloo, IA 50703   319-232-6328
                Fax: 319-232-8623
customerservice@b-rqualitymeats.com
        www.b-rqualitymeats.com
Processor and wholesaler/distributor of meat including beef, pork, veal and poultry; serving the foodservice market
Estimated Sales: $5-10 Million
Number Employees: 10-19
Square Footage: 24000
Type of Packaging: Consumer, Food Service, Bulk
Types of Products Distributed:
    Food Service, Provisions/Meat

54964 B & S Wasilko Distr
80 Main St
Mocanaqua, PA 18655-1506   570-542-4448
Wholesaler/distributor of beer
Owner: Syl Rutkoski
Assistant Manager: Syl Rutkoski
Estimated Sales: $2.5-5 Million
Number Employees: 5-9
Private Brands Carried:
    Budweiser; Genny; Coors
Types of Products Distributed:
    Frozen Food, General Line, Beer

54965 B & W Frozen Foods
4307 30th St W
Bradenton, FL 34205-2798   941-756-5575
                    www.bandwfoods.com
Wholesaler/distributor of frozen foods; serving foodserv ice operators in the Florida west coast
President: Robert B Mc Call
Treasurer: Wilbert Wichers, Jr.
Secretary: Bernard Bandra, Jr.
Estimated Sales: $10-20 Million
Number Employees: 10-19
Square Footage: 12000
Types of Products Distributed:
    Food Service, Frozen Food

54966 B & W Supply Co
510 3rd St
Ithaca, NY 14850-3209   607-273-5300
        Fax: 607-277-6293 800-433-0830
        customerservice@bwsupply.com
                www.bwsupply.com
Wholesaler/distributor of foodserv ice equipment and supplies including smallwares, glass, china, silverware, paper, etc.; also, complete commercial kitchen installations available
President: Becky Benjamin
becky@bwsupply.com
VP: Rebecca Benjamin
Sales Manager: Randy Lawrence
Estimated Sales: $10-20 Million
Number Employees: 5-9
Types of Products Distributed:
    Food Service, Frozen Food, General Merchandise, Smallwares, glass, china, etc.

54967 B Giambrone & Co
132 Mushroom Blvd
Rochester, NY 14623-3204   585-272-7070
        Fax: 585-272-9454 info@bgiambrone.com
                www.bgiambrone.com
Wholesaler/distributor of fresh fruits and vegetables; serving the foodserv ice market
President: Benedict Giambrone
Partner: Ben Giambrone
ben@bgiambrone.com
VP: Joseph Giambrone
Estimated Sales: $10-20 Million
Number Employees: 10-19
Types of Products Distributed:
    Food Service, Produce

54968 B&B Beer Distributing Company
505 Ball Ave NE
Grand Rapids, MI 49503   616-458-1177
        Fax: 616-458-0270 www.bbbeer.com
Wholesaler/distributor of beer
President: Sullivan
VP: Kevin Sullivan
Estimated Sales: $20-50 Million
Number Employees: 50-99
Private Brands Carried:
    T.G.I. Friday's; Miller; Stroh's
Number of Customer Locations: 1000
Types of Products Distributed:
    Frozen Food, General Line, Beer

54969 B&F Distributing Company
P.O.Box 1871
Idaho Falls, ID 83403-1871   208-524-0700
                    Fax: 208-524-0704
Wholesaler/distributor of beer
Owner: Tony Watkins
Estimated Sales: $20-50 Million
Number Employees: 20-49
Private Brands Carried:
    Budweiser; Michelob; Busch
Number of Customer Locations: 400
Types of Products Distributed:
    Frozen Food, General Line, Beer

54970 B&F Sales Corporation
Route 2
Fort Dodge, IA 50501   515-573-2940
                Fax: 515-576-7704
Frozen foods, general groceries
President: Nicholas Garst
Estimated Sales: $5-10 Million
Number Employees: 5-9

54971 B&M Fisheries
15 Pingree Farm Road
Georgetown, MA 01833   978-352-6663
                Fax: 978-352-7565
Manufacturer of seafood
Manager: Matt Lofton
Manager: Brad Zimmerman
Contact: Allan Robicheau
allan@houmardacadie.com

54972 B&O Beer Distributors
4731 N Front St
Philadelphia, PA 19120-4443   215-324-8211
Wholesaler/distributor of beer
Owner: Les Grycewicz
Estimated Sales: $1-3 Million
Number Employees: 1-4
Private Brands Carried:
    Budweiser; Miller
Types of Products Distributed:
    Frozen Food, General Line, Beer

54973 B&W Distributing Company
4140 Brew Master Dr
Ceres, CA 95307-7583   209-524-2477
                Fax: 209-524-4475
Wholesaler/distributor of beer
Owner: Don Miller
dmiller@cencalbev.com
Estimated Sales: $10-20 Million
Number Employees: 20-49
Types of Products Distributed:
    Frozen Food, General Line, Beer

54974 B. Calalani Produce Company
1500 S Zarzamora St # 326
San Antonio, TX 78207   210-227-2266
        Fax: 210-222-8741 sales@bcatalani.com
                    www.bcatalani.com
Wholesaler/distributor of produce
Owner: Dan Catalani
Estimated Sales: $10-20 Million
Number Employees: 6
Number of Customer Locations: 60
Types of Products Distributed:
    Produce

54975 B. Fernandez & Sons
Carr 5 #305 Urb. Industrial
Luchetti, Bayamon, PR 00961-7422 787-288-7272
                    info@bfernandez.com
                    www.bfernandez.com
Wholesaler/distributor of alcoholic beverages, dairy/deli items, grocery products and general merchandise; serving the foodserv ice market
President: Angel Vasquez
CEO: Jose Teixidor
VP Finance: Mildred Garcia
IT Director: Enrique Lopez
Marketing Director: Lara Rodriguez
VP Sales: Reinaldo Aponte
VP Operations: Jose Maldonado
Types of Products Distributed:
    Food Service, Frozen Food, General Line, General Merchandise, Alcoholic beverages, etc.

54976 B.C. Fisheries
P.O.Box 334
Hanckock Point Road
Hancock, ME 04640-0334   207-422-8205
                    Fax: 207-422-8206

Wholesalers & Distributors / A-Z

Seafood
Manager: Pete Daley

54977 B.M. Lawrence & Company
601 Montgomery St
Suite 1115
San Francisco, CA 94111-2614 415-981-2926
Fax: 415-981-2926 info@bmlawrence.com
Wholesaler/Processor and distributor of soft drinks, nonalcoholic beer, canned fruits, vegetables, juices and fish
President: B Lawrence
Purchasing Agent: Hugh Ditzler
info@bmlawrence.com
Estimated Sales: $5-10 Million
Number Employees: 5-9
Square Footage: 8000
Types of Products Distributed:
Frozen Food

54978 B.M. Sales Company
1221 E 2nd Ave SE
Rome, GA 30161-3397 706-234-9439
Wholesaler/distributor of general merchandise; rack jobber services available
Owner: Spencer Cantrell
VP: S Cantrell
Estimated Sales: $500,000-$1 Million
Number Employees: 1-4
Types of Products Distributed:
Frozen Food, General Merchandise, Rack Jobbers

54979 B.W. Clifford
90 Blachley Place (Elm Street)
Morristown, NJ 07960 973-539-1400
bwcliffordcandy@gmail.com
www.bwcliffordcandy.com
Wholesaler/distributor of general line merchandise including confectionery products
President: Ronald Bernstein
Secretary: Lila Bernstein
Sales Manager: Lisa Bernstein
Estimated Sales: $1-2.5 Million
Number Employees: 1-4
Types of Products Distributed:
Frozen Food, General Line, Confectionery

54980 B/R Sales Company
31308 Via Colinas Ste 109
Westlake Village, CA 91362 818-597-5727
Fax: 818-705-2935 brsclsout@aol.com
Exporter and wholesaler/distributor of closeout items including meats, fruit, vegetables, beverages, entrees, condiments, dry goods and frozen foods
President: Darrell Garnett
Estimated Sales: $2.5-5 Million
Number Employees: 1-4
Type of Packaging: Consumer, Food Service, Private Label, Bulk
Number of Customer Locations: 1000
Types of Products Distributed:
Food Service, Frozen Food, General Line, General Merchandise, Health Food, Provisions/Meat, Seafood

54981 BBCA USA
20825 E Rocky Point Ln
Walnut, CA 91789-4029
Fax: 626-581-3543 bbca1688@aol.com
Wholesaler/distributor, importer and exporter of citric acid, lactic acid; additive for food industry, potassium citrate, sodium citrate, calcium citrate
President: Walter Wang
Chairman: Kelvie Wen
Vice President: Wei Yang
Estimated Sales: $3-5 Million
Number Employees: 1-4
Square Footage: 60000
Parent Co: BBCA Biochemical Group
Types of Products Distributed:
Frozen Food, General Line, Citric acid

54982 BBQ Bunch
13100 Woodland Avenue
Kansas City, MO 64146-1801 816-941-4534
Fax: 816-941-0263 lewieb@aol.com
BBQ and mustard sauce; wholesaler/distrinutor of BBQ products; marketing consultant to the BBQ industry.
Owner: Lewis Bunch
Estimated Sales: $500,000-$1 Million
Number Employees: 1-4

Type of Packaging: Food Service, Private Label, Bulk
Types of Products Distributed:
Frozen Food, General Line, General Merchandise, Barbecue products

54983 BBS Lobster Co
141 Smalls Point Rd
Machiasport, ME 04655-3231 207-255-8888
Fax: 207-255-3987 info@lobstertrap.com
www.lobstertrap.com
Wholesaler of lobsters
Owner: Susan West
General Manager: Blair West
CFO: Greg Menzel
Assistant General Manager: Rosie Barrett
Domestic/International Sales: David Madden
Lobster Purchasing/Operations: Tom Platt
Estimated Sales: $1,600,000
Number Employees: 5-9
Parent Co: Lobster Trap Wholesale Seafood Dealers

54984 BCIS Inc
4700 Industry Dr
Fairfield, OH 45014-1971 513-829-2400
Fax: 513-829-1950 www.bcisinc.com
Wholesaler/distributor of material handling equipment including forklifts
Owner: Jasamine Driskell
jdriskell@vescomedical.com
Estimated Sales: $5-10 Million
Number Employees: 5-9
Private Brands Carried:
TCM; Mitsubishi; Yale
Types of Products Distributed:
Frozen Food, General Merchandise, Material handling equipment

54985 BFM Equipment Sales
209 Steel Road
P.O. Box 117
Fall River, WI 53932-0117 920-484-3341
Fax: 920-484-3077 info@bfmequip.com
www.bfmequip.com
Manufacturer, importer, exporter and wholesaler/distributor of food processing machinery, can end cleaners and dryers, replacement parts and supplies
Owner: Richard Bindley
Executive Manager: Russell Quandt
Contact: Leann Vick
lvick@bfmequip.com
Estimated Sales: Below $5 Million
Number Employees: 1-4
Square Footage: 40000
Types of Products Distributed:
Frozen Food, General Merchandise, Can end cleaners & dryers

54986 BI Nutraceuticals
2384 East Pacifica Pl
Rancho Dominquez, CA 90220-6214 310-669-2100
Fax: 310-637-3644 contact@botanicals.com
www.botanicals.com
Wholesaler/distributor of processed herbal raw materials including ginseng and other nutritional ingredients.
President/CEO: George Pontiakos
Financial Exective, Int. Business Dev.: Christoph Kirchner
Director, Fulfillment Services: Corey Leon
Quality Control Manager: Steve Smith
VP, Global Quality & Compliance: Rupa Das
Director of Marketing: Randy Kreienbrink
Contact: Patrisha Abergas
patrishaabergas@tmmc.com
Director, Extract Operations: William Meer
patrishaabergas@tmmc.com
Director, Procurement: Theresa Aranda
Estimated Sales: $19 Million
Number Employees: 105
Square Footage: 140000
Type of Packaging: Bulk
Other Locations:
Primary Milling Facility
McCarran, NV
Particle Engineering Facility
Islandia, NY
Extraction Facility
Boonton, NJPrimary Milling FacilityIslandia
Types of Products Distributed:
Frozen Food, Health Food, Herbal raw materials: ginseng

54987 BI-LO
P.O. Box B
Jacksonville, FL 32203-0297
844-745-0463
www.bi-lo.com
Wholesaler distributor of general groceries, dry foods, frozen foods, produce, meats, seafoods, and dairy products.
SVP, Operations: Bill Nasshan
Year Founded: 1961
Parent Co: Southeastern Grocers
Types of Products Distributed:
Frozen Food, General Line, General Merchandise, Provisions/Meat, Produce, Seafood

54988 (HQ)BJ'S Wholesale Club Inc
25 Research Dr
Westborough, MA 01581-3680 774-512-6799
Fax: 774-512-6859 800-257-2582
www.bjs.com
Wholesaler/distributor of general merchandise and general line items.
Executive Chairman: Christopher Baldwin
cbaldwin@bjs.com
President & CEO: Lee Delaney
Executive VP/CFO: Robert Eddy
Executive VP/CIO: Scott Kessler
Executive VP/Chief Membership Officer: Brian Poulliot
Executive VP/Club Operations Officer: Jeff Desroches
Year Founded: 1984
Estimated Sales: $12.7 Billion
Number Employees: 25,000
Parent Co: Beacon Holding Inc
Other Locations:
BJ's Wholesale Club
Bristol, PABJ's Wholesale Club
Private Brands Carried:
Berkley-Jensen; Wellsley Farms; Kerrygold; Amy's Kitchen; Kashi; Newman's Own; American Flatbread
Types of Products Distributed:
Frozen Food, General Line, General Merchandise

54989 BMT Commodity Corporation
950 3rd Ave
10th Floor
New York, NY 10022 212-302-4200
Fax: 212-302-0007 bmt@bmtny.com
www.bmtny.com
Importer and wholesaler/distributor of fruit purees and pastes, dehydrated foods, tomato powders, health foods, dried fruit, sun dried tomatoes, honey, garlic, etc.; serving the foodservice and retail markets.
President: Robert Ganz
Executive Vice President: Edward Siel
Year Founded: 1922
Estimated Sales: $30-60 Million
Number Employees: 20-49
Parent Co: A/T Products Corporation
Type of Packaging: Consumer, Bulk
Private Brands Carried:
Lion; Sunset
Types of Products Distributed:
Food Service, General Line, Health Food, Specialty Foods, Honey, garlic, etc.

54990 BNG Enterprises
1801 W 4th St
Tempe, AZ 85281 480-967-9115
Fax: 480-967-0798 www.bngprodx.com
Wholesaler/distributor of natural supplements
President: Bradley Grossman
VP: Russell Grossman
Sales Manager: Mike Reinman
Contact: Russell Grossman
rgrossman@bngprodx.com
Estimated Sales: $10-20 Million
Number Employees: 10-19
Private Brands Carried:
Natural Treasures; Herbal Clean
Types of Products Distributed:
Frozen Food, Health Food, Natural supplements

54991 BOSS
701 Hudson Ave
Scranton, PA 18504-9693 570-342-4984
Fax: 570-342-1368 800-666-8870
Wholesaler/distributor of sport nutrition products
COO: Joe Mies
General Manager: Bob O'Leary

919

Wholesalers & Distributors / A-Z

Number Employees: 50-99
Types of Products Distributed:
  Frozen Food, Health Food, Sports nutrition products

54992 BRINS
Brooklyn, NY
orders@staggjam.com
www.brinsjam.com
Jams and marmalades
Founder: Candice Ross *Year Founded:* 2015
Types of Products Distributed:
  General Line

54993 BS&R Equipment Company
198 Locust Street South
Twin Falls, ID 83301 208-733-4221
Fax: 208-733-4308 800-360-3181
sales@bsrequipment.com www.bsrequipment.com
Wholesaler/distributor of equipment; serving the foodserv ice market
Owner: Tim Carroll
tim@bsrequipment.com
Sales Director: Mike Littleton
Estimated Sales: $2-5 Million
Number Employees: 10-19
Square Footage: 48000
Parent Co: BS&R Equipment Company
Type of Packaging: Food Service
Private Brands Carried:
  Hobart; Vollrath; True; Cambro; Libby
Types of Products Distributed:
  Food Service, Equipment

54994 BW Acquisition
PO Box 37
Richfield, WI 53076-0037 262-375-9377
Wholesaler/distributor of bakery equipment; serving the foodserv ice market; also, service and re-building available
Co-Owner/President: Marvin Lesch
Co-Owner/VP: Kent Martin
Square Footage: 40000
Types of Products Distributed:
  Food Service, Frozen Food, General Merchandise, Bakery equipment

54995 Babush Conveyor Corporation
W222n5739 Miller Way
Sussex, WI 53089-3988 262-820-2500
Fax: 262-820-2599 www.babush.com
Wholesaler/distributor of custom made conveyors and package handling conveyor systems
Owner: Chris Shult
Estimated Sales: $10-20 Million
Number Employees: 50-99
Square Footage: 44000
Private Brands Carried:
  Hytrol Conveyor Co., Inc.; Richards Wilcox Carousel Co.
Types of Products Distributed:
  Frozen Food, General Merchandise, Conveyors, etc.

54996 Bachman Foods
41 Mercedes Way # 13
Edgewood, NY 11717-8334 631-586-4865
Fax: 631-586-1360 www.bachmanco.com
Wholesaler/distributor of specialty foods
Manager: Pat Mooney
Contact: Pat Mooy
pmooy@bachmanco.com
Branch Manager: Pat Moony
Estimated Sales: $3-5 Million
Number Employees: 1-4
Types of Products Distributed:
  Frozen Food, Specialty Foods, Snack food

54997 Back to the Roots
424 2nd St
Oakland, CA 94607 510-922-9758
www.backtotheroots.com
Organic cereal and windowsill gardens
Co-Founder: Nikhil Arora
Co-Founder: Alejandro Velez *Year Founded:* 2009

54998 Baden Baden Food Equipment
3947 W Columbus Ave
Chicago, IL 60652 773-284-9009
Fax: 773-284-9109 877-368-8375
Sales of food and bakery equipment and wares

President: Vernon Condon
Contact: David Uhl
d.uhl@badenfoodequip.com
Estimated Sales: $1,500,000
Number Employees: 5-9
Square Footage: 12000
Private Brands Carried:
  Traulsen, Edhard, American Metalcraft, Oliver, Rondo, Pitco, Otto Broun, Varimixer, Houpt Cutters.
Types of Products Distributed:
  General Merchandise, New & used bakery equipment

54999 Badger Island Shell-Fish & Lobster
2 Badgers Is W
Kittery, ME 03904-1601 207-703-0431
Fax: 207-703-0432 joe@herbertbrothers.com
www.herbertbrothers.com
Seafood, shellfish, lobster
Owner: Joe Herbert
Co-Owner: Dave Herbert
Estimated Sales: $.5-1 million
Number Employees: 1-4
Parent Co: Herbert Brothers Entertainment Inc

55000 Badger Material Handling
16805 W Victor Rd
New Berlin, WI 53151-4134 262-782-0220
Fax: 262-782-4703 800-242-0541
www.badgertl.com
Wholesaler/distributor of material handling equipment including forklifts
Manager: Patrick Stemper
pstemper@badgertl.com
VP: Patrick Stemper
Estimated Sales: $10-20 Million
Number Employees: 50-99
Private Brands Carried:
  Toyota; Big Joe; Barrett
Types of Products Distributed:
  Frozen Food, General Merchandise, Material handling equipment

55001 Badger Popcorn
2914 Latham Dr
Madison, WI 53713-3233 608-274-5058
Fax: 608-274-5408 800-962-6227
getpoppin@badgerpopcorn.com
www.badgerpopcorn.com
Wholesaler/distributor of concession supplies; serving the foodserv ice market
President: Tim Virnoche
tim@badgerpopcorn.com
VP: Tom Virnoche
Estimated Sales: $1-2.5 Million
Number Employees: 10-19
Private Brands Carried:
  Caramel Crunch Supreme; Copper Kettle Caramel Corn; Old Tyme Popcorn
Number of Customer Locations: 4200
Types of Products Distributed:
  Food Service, Frozen Food, General Line, General Merchandise, Concession supplies

55002 Badger Wholesale Company
PO Box 998
Green Bay, WI 54305-0998 920-437-7132
Fax: 920-437-1755 800-456-7869
Wholesaler/distributor of produce, frozen food, groceries, dairy products, baked goods, provisions/meats, general merchandise, etc.; serving the foodserv ice market
President: K Callahan
Estimated Sales: $20-50 Million
Number Employees: 20-49
Private Brands Carried:
  Badger Chemicals
Number of Customer Locations: 2250
Types of Products Distributed:
  Food Service, Frozen Food, General Line, General Merchandise, Provisions/Meat, Produce

55003 Badger Wholesale Meat & Provisions
505 W Juneau Ave
Milwaukee, WI 53203-1004 414-264-7500
Fax: 414-272-2386
Wholesaler/distributor of meats
Pres.: W Heimerl
Estimated Sales: $2.5-5 Million
Number Employees: 10-19

Types of Products Distributed:
  Frozen Food, Provisions/Meat

55004 Baensch Food Products Co
1025 E Locust St
Milwaukee, WI 53212 414-562-4643
Fax: 414-562-5525 www.mabaensch.com
Pickled & creamed herring
Owner/President: Kim Wall
kim@mabaensch.com
GM: David Jackson
Year Founded: 1932
Number Employees: 10-19
Square Footage: 120000
Parent Co: Wild Foods
Type of Packaging: Consumer, Food Service, Private Label, Bulk

55005 Baers Beverage of C.W.
P.O.Box 558
Schofield, WI 54476-0558 715-359-0448
Fax: 715-359-3028
Wholesaler/distributor of beer
Owner: Jerry Baer
Estimated Sales: $20-50 Million
Number Employees: 20-49
Private Brands Carried:
  Budweiser; Michelob; Bud Light
Types of Products Distributed:
  Frozen Food, General Line, Beer

55006 Bagel Factory
2320 S Robertson Blvd # 202
Boulevard
Los Angeles, CA 90034-2053 310-836-9865
www.bagelfactoryinc.com
Bagels
Owner: Sanford Brody
sanford@thebagelfactory.com
CEO/President: Jay Epstein
Estimated Sales: Less Than $500,000
Number Employees: 1-4
Square Footage: 10000

55007 Bagel Lites
240 51st Ave
Apt. 1F
Long Island City, NY 11101 844-678-5544
sales@bagellites.com
www.bagellites.com
Bite-size bagels
Owner: Raquel Salas
Estimated Sales: $100,000
Number Employees: 1-4
Type of Packaging: Private Label
Private Brands Carried:
  Big City Bagel Lites
Types of Products Distributed:
  General Merchandise

55008 Bagman
31 August Road
Simsbury, CT 06070-2824 860-651-3848
Fax: 860-651-7798 800-955-2247
bagmanltd@aol.com
Wholesaler/distributor of paper and plastic bags and boxes
President: Gary Swerling
Quality Control: Carol Jirdanhazy
Marketing Director: Ray Faneuf
Sales Director: Art Spivak
Public Relations: Becky Faneuf
Operations Manager: John Nunes
Plant Manager: Al Wendt
Purchasing Manager: Judy Digiorgio
Estimated Sales: $1-2.5 Million
Number Employees: 5-9
Square Footage: 30000
Parent Co: Packaging Specialties
Types of Products Distributed:
  Food Service, General Merchandise, Paper & plastic bags & boxes

55009 Bailey Co Inc
501 Cowan St
Nashville, TN 37207 615-242-0351
800-342-1665
bsweeney@baileycompany.com
www.baileycompany.com
Wholesaler/distributor of material handling equipment.
Chief Executive Officer: Bert Bailey
bbailey@baileycompany.com
General Manager: Bill Sweeney

Wholesalers & Distributors / A-Z

Year Founded: 1949
Estimated Sales: $50-100 Million
Number Employees: 300
Private Brands Carried:
  Crown; Mitsubishi; Caterpiller
Types of Products Distributed:
  Frozen Food, General Merchandise, Material handling equipment

55010 Bailey's Basin Seafood
1683 Front Street
Morgan City, LA 70380-3034   985-384-4926
       Fax: 985-384-4926
Fish and seafood
President: Nolton Bailey
Estimated Sales: $2.6 Million
Number Employees: 30
Type of Packaging: Consumer, Food Service

55011 Baily Tea USA Inc
2275 research blvd
Suite 720
Rockville, MD 20850   301-704-1739
       sales@bailytea.com
       www.bailytea.com
Tea
CEO: Sudath Munasinghe
s.munasinghe@bailytea.com

55012 Baja Trading Company
636 W Root St
Chicago, IL 60609   773-376-9030
       Fax: 773-376-9245
Wholesaler/distributor of Mexican foods including stone ground corn and flour tortillas
Owner: Art Velasquez
Chmn./Secy.: Dahmen Brown
Estimated Sales: $10-20 Million
Number Employees: 20-49
Types of Products Distributed:
  Frozen Food, General Line, Specialty Foods, Mexican foods

55013 Bake Star
1881 County Road C
Somerset, WI 54025-7508   763-427-7611
  Fax: 763-323-9821 www.bakestar.com
Manufacturer and wholesaler/distributor of chocolate spiral shavers, pre-depanners, semi-automatic strawberry cappers, surplus topping removers and UV surface sterilizers
CEO: Sherri Stumpl
President: Gary Hanson
R & D: Roger Hanson
Contact: Gary Hanson
grh230377@msn.com
General Manager: Laura Tuckner
Estimated Sales: Below $5 Million
Number Employees: 10
Square Footage: 36000
Types of Products Distributed:
  Frozen Food, General Merchandise, Chocolate spiral shavers, etc.

55014 BakeMark Ingredients Canada
2480 Viking Way
Richmond, BC V6V 1N2
Canada   604-303-1700
  Fax: 604-270-8002 800-665-9441
       www.yourbakemark.com
Baked goods, breads, baking mixes, cookies, pie filling, icing, frozen fruit
President: Larry Sullivan
Vice President: Michael Armstrong
Marketing: David Lopez
Sales Manager: Jeff Bligh
General Manager: Rick Barnes
Manufacturing: Ellen Tsang
Estimated Sales: $23 Million
Number Employees: 160
Number of Brands: 12
Number of Products: 2000
Type of Packaging: Private Label, Bulk
Private Brands Carried:
  Bakemark Caravan; Brill' Marquerite; Bib Ulmer Spatz; Diamalt; Meistermarken; DeGoede; DreiDoppel
Number of Customer Locations: 6
Types of Products Distributed:
  Bakery Ingredients

55015 BakeMark Ingredients West Inc
11350 Sunrise Park Dr
Rancho Cordova, CA 95742-6542   916-631-9642
       Fax: 916-631-9253
Wholesaler/distributor of ingredients, groceries, frozen foods, general merchandise, equipment and fixtures and baked goods including bread, cakes, muffins and pies; serving the food service market
Manager: Jim Balding
Controller: Mike Beairsto
Sales/Marketing: Jeff Denney
Estimated Sales: $10-20 Million
Number Employees: 20-49
Square Footage: 90000
Parent Co: Westco/Bakemark
Private Brands Carried:
  Westco
Number of Customer Locations: 800
Types of Products Distributed:
  Food Service, Frozen Food, General Line, General Merchandise, Baked goods, ingredients, etc.

55016 Baker Beverage
455 Kunzler Ranch Rd # A
Ukiah, CA 95482-3186   707-462-7528
       Fax: 707-462-6645
Wholesaler/distributor of beer
President: Susan Schlosser
Manager: Matt Miller
Estimated Sales: $10-20 Million
Number Employees: 20-49
Parent Co: Baker Beverage
Private Brands Carried:
  Coors; Keystone; Steinlager
Types of Products Distributed:
  Frozen Food, General Line, Beer

55017 Baker Bottling & Distributing Company
1241 Marilyn Drive
Cape Girardeau, MO 63701-3640   573-335-7863
Wholesaler/distributor of fountain syrup including cherry, root beer, grape, orange and strawberry; serving the foodserv ice market
President: Roy Baker
Estimated Sales: $1-2.5 Million
Number Employees: 1-4
Types of Products Distributed:
  Food Service, General Line, Fountain syrups

55018 Baker Boy Bake Shop Inc
170 Gta Dr
Dickinson, ND 58601-7200   701-225-4444
  Fax: 701-225-7981 800-437-2008
Processor of frozen dough products; wholesaler/distributor of bakery supplies including flour, sugar, etc.; serving the foodservice market.
CEO: Guy Moos
guym@bakerboy.com
Year Founded: 1955
Number Employees: 250-499
Square Footage: 135000
Type of Packaging: Consumer, Food Service, Private Label
Types of Products Distributed:
  Food Service, Frozen Food, General Line, Flour, sugar, etc.

55019 Baker Distributing Corp
130 Orion Dr
Colchester, VT 05446   802-665-5060
  Fax: 802-655-4028 www.bakerdistributing.com
Wholesaler/distributor of beer, wine and soft drinks.
Chief Executive Officer: Dave Baker
VP & General Manager: Al McPherson
South General Manager: Gerry Courture
Sales Director: Dave Romano
Estimated Sales: $50-100 Million
Number Employees: 50-99
Private Brands Carried:
  Miller; Coors; Robert Mondavi
Types of Products Distributed:
  Frozen Food, General Line, Beer, wine & soft drinks

55020 Baker's Candies Factory Store
831 S Baker St
PO Box 88
Greenwood, NE 68366-1000   402-789-2700
  Fax: 402-789-2013 800-804-7330
info@bakerscandies.com www.bakerscandies.com
Fine chocolates, including our chocolate meltaways in seven flavors

Owner: Todd Baker
todd@bakerscandies.com
VP: Patty Baker
Estimated Sales: $3-5 Million
Number Employees: 5-9
Type of Packaging: Consumer

55021 Baker's Cash & Carry Inc
44 W Vine St
Salt Lake City, UT 84107-4718   801-487-3300
  Fax: 801-487-3384 www.bakerscandc.com
Wholesaler/distributor of cake decorations and chocolate for bakeries
Owner: Steve Drost
Estimated Sales: $1-2.5 Million
Number Employees: 1-4
Private Brands Carried:
  Guittard; Wilton; Merckens
Types of Products Distributed:
  Frozen Food, General Line, Cake decorations & chocolate

55022 Bakery Barn Inc
111 Terence Dr
Pittsburgh, PA 15236-4133   412-655-1113
  Fax: 412-655-8566 888-322-BARN
       sales@bakery-barn.com
High-protein cookies
President/Owner: Sean Perich
frontoffice@bakery-barn.com
Number Employees: 100-249
Type of Packaging: Private Label

55023 Bakery Equipment Sales & Services
16532 Redland Road
Derwood, MD 20855-1945   301-948-3761
       Fax: 301-519-9564
Wholesaler/distributor of bakery equipment
President: Jon Tashiro
dmr12345@aol.com
Estimated Sales: $1-2.5 Million
Number Employees: 1-4
Number of Customer Locations: 400
Types of Products Distributed:
  Frozen Food, General Merchandise, Bakery equipment

55024 Bakery Services
400 Ernest W Barrett NW # 240
Kennesaw, GA 30144-4956   770-590-4449
  Fax: 770-590-4449 800-356-7591
       www.bakersshoes.com
Wholesaler/distributor of bakery ovens, oven parts and conveyors
Manager: Kim Radinlaw
Estimated Sales: Less than $500,000
Number Employees: 1-4
Number of Customer Locations: 150
Types of Products Distributed:
  Bakery equipment parts and conveyors

55025 Bakery Systems
7246 Beach Dr SW 1
Ocean Isle Beach, NC 28469   910-575-2253
  Fax: 910-575-5057 800-526-2253
Importer, exporter and wholesaler/distributor of bakery equipment nd supplies
President: Hayden O'Neil
patzcuaro@juno.com
Sales Manager: Lee Wagner
Estimated Sales: $2.5 Million
Number Employees: 5-9
Square Footage: 2000
Types of Products Distributed:
  Bakery equipment & Supplies

55026 Bakery Things
7142 East Condor Street
Commerce, CA 90040   323-888-0008
  Fax: 323-888-0003 800-242-4KGP
Importer, exporter and wholesaler/distributor of ginseng, herb teas, processed bean, portable gas range, etc
President: Chung Sup Song
CEO: Soon Song
VP: Thomas Lee
Marketing Director: Steve Ham
Sales Director: Kristin Kim
Estimated Sales: $5 Million
Number Employees: 5-9
Number of Brands: 80
Number of Products: 30
Square Footage: 20000

Wholesalers & Distributors / A-Z

Private Brands Carried:
  KGP; Dieter's Drink; Lotte; Taeguk; Green Nature; McKinly
Number of Customer Locations: 180
Types of Products Distributed:
  General Merchandise, Health Food, Specialty Foods, Ginseng & processed bean teas

55027 Bakkavor USA
2700 Westinghouse Blvd
Charlotte, NC 28273
                                              800-842-3025
              sales@bakkavor.us   www.bakkavor.com
Fresh soups, breads, sauces, hummus, burritos, dips, and ready meals
President & CEO: Ben Waldron
CFO: Mary Barnett
Quality Assurance Manager: Julie Morrison
Director of Marketing: Therese Griffin
VP Strategic Business Development: Stephen Young
Number Employees: 500-999
Parent Co: Bakkavor Group

55028 Bakker Produce
211 W Main St
Griffith, IN 46319   219-924-8950
         Fax: 219-922-3636   866-924-8950
Wholesaler/distributor of produce
President: Charles Bakker
CEO: Thomas Bakker
VP/Partner: Richard Bakker
Contact: Chuck Bakker
cbakker@bakerproduce.com
Operations Manager: Douglas Bakker
Estimated Sales: $11.42 Million
Number Employees: 60
Square Footage: 135000
Type of Packaging: Consumer
Types of Products Distributed:
  Food Service, Frozen Food, Produce, Specialty Foods

55029 Bakri Trading Inc
1241 W Side Ave
Jersey City, NJ 07306-6112   201-222-3448
                 Fax: 201-222-3747
Wholesaler/distributor of general merchandise and bags including fabric, produce, shopping and plastic; also, custom printing available
President: Marwan Bakri
Estimated Sales: Less Than $500,000
Number Employees: 1-4
Number of Customer Locations: 50
Types of Products Distributed:
  Frozen Food, General Merchandise, Bags

55030 Bald Eagle Beer Store Co
125 Hogan Blvd
Mill Hall, PA 17751-1903   570-748-4073
Wholesaler/distributor of beer
Manager: Joe Dicello
Estimated Sales: $2.5-5 Million
Number Employees: 1-4
Private Brands Carried:
  Rolling Rock; Budweiser; Coors Light
Types of Products Distributed:
  Frozen Food, General Line, Beer

55031 Baldwin Richardson Foods
#2390, One Tower Lane
Oakbrook Terrace, IL 60181   866-644-2732
                                www.brfoods.com
Liquid ingredient manufacturer specializing in signature sauces, dessert toppings, beverage and pancake syrups, specialty fruit fillings and condiments. The company also offers processing options such as hot-fill, cold-fillhomogenization, and emulsion.
President & CEO: Eric Johnson
Chief Financial Officer: Evelyn White
Sr. Director of Sales: Cara Hughes
Year Founded: 1916
Estimated Sales: $5-10,000,000
Number Employees: 200-500
Square Footage: 900000
Type of Packaging: Consumer, Food Service, Private Label, Bulk
Other Locations:
  Macedon Manufacturing Facility
  Macedon, NY
  Williamson Manufacturing
  East Williamson, NYMacedon Manufacturing FacilityEast Williamson
Types of Products Distributed:
  Food Service, Specialty Foods

55032 Balford Farms
4 Manhattan Dr
Burlington, NJ 08016   609-699-2630
         Fax: 609-699-2660   800-969-2691
                                   balford.com
Wholesaler/distributor of dairy and refrigerated products including specialty cheese.
Chairman & CEO: Larry Bowes
President: Laurance Walker
Vice President, Finance: Bob Venafra
VP, IT & Customer Service: Frank Ieradi
Director, Business Development: Chris Morris
Controller: Sue Remolde
Sales Coordinator: Michelle Leshner
Sales Coordinator: Laura Kelly
Estimated Sales: $20-50 Million
Number Employees: 100-249
Types of Products Distributed:
  Frozen Food, General Line, Specialty Foods, Dairy products

55033 Ballantine Industrial Truck Service
1250 Wood Ln
Langhorne, PA 19047   215-750-0823
                 Fax: 215-750-3230
Wholesaler/distributor of lift trucks; also, service available
President: Bill Ellis
Estimated Sales: $2.5-5 Million
Number Employees: 10-19
Private Brands Carried:
  Toyota; Clark; Nissan
Types of Products Distributed:
  Frozen Food, General Merchandise, Lift trucks

55034 Ballard Custom Meats
55 Myrtle St
Manchester, ME 04351-3251   207-622-9764
                 Fax: 207-621-0242
Meats and seafood
President: Kenneth Ballard
Year Founded: 1969
Estimated Sales: $2,000,000
Number Employees: 10-19

55035 Ballew Distributors
509 E 2nd Street
Roswell, NM 88201-6217   505-622-3761
                 Fax: 505-622-6909
Wholesaler/distributor of groceries; serving the foodserv ice market
Owner: Ray Bell
General Manager: Karl Matson
Estimated Sales: $10-20 Million
Number Employees: 10-19
Types of Products Distributed:
  Food Service, Frozen Food, General Line

55036 Balter Meat Co
12390 SW 128th St
Miami, FL 33186-5425   305-255-7230
         Fax: 305-254-1603 baltermeat@aol.com
                         www.baltermeatcompany.com
Wholesaler/distributor of meats including beef, pork and poultry; serving the foodserv ice market
President: Steve Balter
baltermeat@aol.com
VP: S Balter
Estimated Sales: $10-20 Million
Number Employees: 20-49
Types of Products Distributed:
  Food Service, Frozen Food, Provisions/Meat, Beef, pork, poultry, etc.

55037 Balter Sales Co
209 Bowery # A
New York, NY 10002-2887   212-674-2960
         Fax: 212-226-4463   info@baltersales.com
                                www.google.com
Wholesaler/distributor of restaurant equipment including chinaware, glassware, cutlery, etc.; serving the foodserv ice market
Owner: Lori Balter
lorib@baltersales.com
Estimated Sales: $5-10 Million
Number Employees: 20-49
Types of Products Distributed:
  Food Service, Frozen Food, General Merchandise, Chinaware, cutlery, glassware, etc.

55038 Baltimore Belting Co
766 E 25th St
Baltimore, MD 21218-5482   410-338-1230
         Fax: 410-889-2358   800-225-2358
                          mary@baltimorebelting.com
                          www.baltimorebelting.com
Wholesaler/distributor of V-belts and conveyor belts; serving the foodserv ice market
President: John Slingluff
Vice President: Richard Slingloff
Marketing Director: Russ Agnes
Sales/Marketing Executive: Brian Green
Public Relations: Mary Fitch
Purchasing Manager: Christie Crivelli
Estimated Sales: $1.6 Million
Number Employees: 5-9
Square Footage: 28000
Parent Co: Baltimore Belting Company
Types of Products Distributed:
  Food Service, Frozen Food, General Merchandise, V-belts

55039 Bama Budweiser Montgomery
400 N Perry Street
Montgomery, AL 36104-2647   334-263-2039
Wholesaler/distributor of beer
Manager: Butch Kraus
Estimated Sales: $20-50 Million
Number Employees: 50-99
Private Brands Carried:
  Budweiser; Bud Light; Michelob
Types of Products Distributed:
  Frozen Food, General Line, Beer

55040 Bama Budweiser of Anniston
P.O.Box 1601
Anniston, AL 36202   256-831-7754
                 Fax: 256-831-7751
Wholesaler/distributor of beer
Manager: Chuck Bussey
General Manager: Gary Haugens
Estimated Sales: $10-20 Million
Number Employees: 20-49
Private Brands Carried:
  Budweiser; Red Dog; Michelob
Number of Customer Locations: 500
Types of Products Distributed:
  Frozen Food, General Line, Beer

55041 Bama Fish Atlanta
3113 Main Street
East Point, GA 30344-4802   404-765-9896
                 Fax: 404-765-9874
Fresh and frozen fish

55042 Bama Sea Products Inc
756 28th St S
St Petersburg, FL 33712-1907   727-327-3474
         Fax: 727-322-0580   www.bamasea.com
Wholesaler/distributor and exporter of frozen fish and seafood; warehouse providing cooler and freezer storage for frozen food items
Owner: Hillary Hubble-Flinn
Director Quality Control: Fred Stengard
Marketing & Product Development: Dottie Stephens Guy
VP Sales: Jon Philbrick
hillary.hubbleflinn@leememorial.org
VP of Operations and Plant GM: John Jackson
VP Purchasing: Adam Zewen
Estimated Sales: $2.5-5 Million
Number Employees: 100-249
Square Footage: 360000
Types of Products Distributed:
  Seafood

55043 Banana Distributing Company
1500 S Zarzamora Street
Unit 405
San Antonio, TX 78207   210-227-8285
         Fax: 210-227-8285   www.banana-distributing.com
Bananas, plantains, hass avocados, oranges, apples, sugar cane
Owner/Manager: Jim Scarsdale
Year Founded: 2007
Estimated Sales: $5-10 Million
Number Employees: 10-19
Parent Co: Barshop Enterprises
Type of Packaging: Consumer, Food Service, Bulk
Private Brands Carried:
  Del Monte; Dole; Chiquita; Turbana
Types of Products Distributed:
  Food Service, Produce

Wholesalers & Distributors / A-Z

55044 Band Snacks
3801 37th Pl
Brentwood, MD 20722-1703
301-566-6125
Fax: 301-779-9826
Distributor of potato chips
Estimated Sales: $6.5 Million
Number Employees: 20-49

55045 Bandwagon Brokerage
2180 E 10th St
Los Angeles, CA 90021
213-622-5601
Fax: 213-622-5686
Wholesaler/distributor of produce and specialty fruits and vegetables; serving the food service market
President: Dennis Berman
dennis@bandwagoninc.com
Secretary: Ilene Berman
Director Operations: Shawn Guthrie
Estimated Sales: $5-10 Million
Number Employees: 10-19
Square Footage: 40000
Types of Products Distributed:
  Food Service, Frozen Food, Produce, Specialty Foods

55046 Bangkok Market
4757 Melrose Ave
Los Angeles, CA 90029-3344
323-662-9705
Fax: 323-210-1408
Wholesaler/distributor of frozen food
Manager: Jet Tila
bkm1972@aol.com
Estimated Sales: $5-10 Million
Number Employees: 20-49
Parent Co: Bangkok Markets
Number of Customer Locations: 1
Types of Products Distributed:
  Frozen Food

55047 Banner Wholesale Grocers
3000 S Ashland Ave # 30
Chicago, IL 60608-5348
312-421-2650
Fax: 312-421-5175 www.bannerwholesale.com
Wholesaler/distributor of groceries, general merchandise, frozen and Hispanic foods; serving the food service market
President: Martha Fisher
kirdona@yahoo.com
Sales: Mario Gomez
Operations: Irwin Friedman
Plant Manager: Aurelio Frutos
Purchasing: Scott Hilligoss
Estimated Sales: $20-50 Million
Number Employees: 50-99
Square Footage: 88000
Private Brands Carried:
  Durango
Number of Customer Locations: 1500
Types of Products Distributed:
  Food Service, Frozen Food, General Line, General Merchandise, Specialty Foods, Hispanic foods

55048 Bantam Bagels
283 Bleecker St
New York, NY 10014
646-852-6320
contact@bantambagels.com
www.bantambagels.com
Gourmet bagels
Co-Owner: Nick Oleksak
Co-Owner: Elyse Olesak
Year Founded: 2015
Estimated Sales: $500,000
Number Employees: 1-4
Type of Packaging: Consumer, Food Service
Private Brands Carried:
  Bantam Bagels

55049 Bar Boy Products Inc
250 Merritts Rd
Farmingdale, NY 11735-3292
516-293-7155
Fax: 516-293-7984 www.barboyproducts.com
Wholesaler/distributor of equipment and supplies; serving the food service market
Owner: Eddie DE Felice
barboyprod@aol.com
Estimated Sales: $5-10 Million
Number Employees: 20-49
Types of Products Distributed:
  Food Service, Frozen Food, General Merchandise, Equipment & supplies

55050 Bar Controls Of Florida
180 Lyman Rd # 112
Casselberry, FL 32707-2805
407-834-2569
Fax: 407-834-6333 800-872-5979
info@floridanaturalflavors.com
www.barcontrolsofflorida.com
Wholesaler/distributor of bar equipment and supplies including beverage mixers, frozen drink mixes, cocktail machines, etc.; serving the food service market
Owner: David A Erdman
derdman@floridanaturalflavors.com
Estimated Sales: $10-20 Million
Number Employees: 20-49
Types of Products Distributed:
  Food Service, Frozen Food, General Line, General Merchandise, Bar equipment & supplies

55051 Bar Harbor Foods
1112 Cutler Rd
Whiting, ME 04691-3436
207-259-3341
Fax: 207-259-3343 info@barharborfoods.com
www.barharborfoods.com
Seafood
Contact: Mike Sansing
msansing@barharborfoods.com

55052 Bar NA, Inc.
PO Box 6599
Champaign, IL 61826-6599
217-687-4810
Fax: 217-687-4830 www.baraninc.com
Manufacturer, distribution and installation of small to medium capacity equipment for soy foods and vegetable oilseeds production and processing
President: Ramlakhan Boodram
Estimated Sales: $1-2.5 Million
Number Employees: 10-19

55053 Bar-Plex
10 Jay Street
Suite 206
Brooklyn, NY 11201-1128
718-921-0565
Fax: 718-680-7057 800-201-5381
Wholesaler/distributor of food service equipment; serving the food service market
President: Steven Dubliver
VP: Louis Bernitt
Estimated Sales: $2.5-5 Million
Number Employees: 5-9
Square Footage: 51000
Types of Products Distributed:
  Food Service, Frozen Food, General Merchandise, Foodservice equipment

55054 Bar-S Foods Co
5090 N 40th St # 300
Phoenix, AZ 85018-2185
602-264-7272
Fax: 602-285-5252 800-699-4115
www.bar-s.com
Meat products
CEO: Delilah Aguilar
delilah.aguilar@bar-sfoods.com
Number Employees: 50-99

55055 Barber Pure Milk Company(HQ)
PO Box 586
Tupelo, MS 38802-0586
662-767-8187
Fax: 662-767-8190 800-264-6114
Wholesaler/distributor of milk, ice cream and fruit drinks
Sales Manager: Wayne Turner
District Manager: James Shelton
Estimated Sales: $1 Million
Number Employees: 0-25
Square Footage: 48000
Parent Co: Barber Dairy's
Types of Products Distributed:
  General Line, Milk, ice cream & fruit drinks

55056 Barber's Poultry Inc
810 E 50th Ave
Denver, CO 80216-2009
303-466-7338
Fax: 303-466-6960 www.barberspoultry.com
Wholesaler/distributor of frozen and canned food products; also, warehouse providing cold storage for frozen and canned food products
President: David Barber
dave@barberspoultry.com
Vice President: Mike Barber
Estimated Sales: $5- 10 Million
Number Employees: 5-9
Type of Packaging: Bulk
Types of Products Distributed:
  Frozen Food, General Line, Canned foods

55057 Bari Italian Foods
3875 Bengert St
Orlando, FL 32808-4659
407-298-0560
Fax: 407-293-2032 www.bellissimofoods.com
Wholesaler/distributor and importer of Italian foods; serving the food service market
President: Joe Paparella
Contact: Anthony Paparella
anthony@bellissimofoods.com
Estimated Sales: $20-50 Million
Number Employees: 50-99
Parent Co: Bellissimo Foods
Type of Packaging: Food Service
Types of Products Distributed:
  Food Service, Frozen Food, General Line, Specialty Foods, Italian foods

55058 Bari Olive Oil Co
40063 Road 56
Dinuba, CA 93618-9708
559-595-9260
877-638-3626
orders@barioliveoil.com www.barioliveoil.com
Olive oils
President: Robert Sawatzky
Contact: Breann Borges
borgesbreann@barioliveoil.com
Number Employees: 1-4

55059 Bari Produce
7567 Road 28
Madera, CA 93637
559-560-5600
Fax: 559-674-4911 www.bariproduce.com
Packer of peaches, plums, nectarines, apples, and grapes
Contact: Tj Andrews
tandrews@bariproduce.com

55060 Baring Industries
3249 SW 42nd St
Fort Lauderdale, FL 33312-6810
954-327-6700
Fax: 954-327-6781 sales@baring.com
www.baring.com
Wholesaler/distributor of food service equipment; serving the food service market; also, installation, after-sales services, project management, engineering and procurement services available
President: Charles Sperry
charles.sperry@baring.com
EVP: 0 Fitzgibbon
Regional VP-Nashville/Dallas: Mike Mackey
VP, Engineering: Michael Perez
Project Executive-Chicago: Michael Heim
Contract Administrations Manager: Helene Durocher
Purchasing Manager: Nancy Smith
Number Employees: 50-99
Square Footage: 80000
Parent Co: White Consolidated Industries
Types of Products Distributed:
  Food Service, Frozen Food, General Merchandise, Foodservice equipment

55061 Barkett Fruit Company
205 Deeds Dr
Dover, OH 44622
330-364-6645
Fax: 330-364-7683 www.barkettfruit.com
Wholesaler/distributor of produce, specialty foods, frozen and canned meats, chicken and dairy products; serving the food service market
President: Jim Barkett
Vice President: Tom Barkett
Sales Manager: Lee Stockon
Contact: Ronald Barkett
rbarkett@aol.com
VP Purchasing: Tom Barkett
Estimated Sales: $10-20 Million
Number Employees: 20-49
Square Footage: 72000
Private Brands Carried:
  Anchor; Tyson; Reiter Dairy
Number of Customer Locations: 400
Types of Products Distributed:
  Food Service, Frozen Food, General Line, Provisions/Meat, Produce, Specialty Foods, Chicken, dairy products, etc.

55062 Barlean's Fisheries
3660 Slater Rd
Ferndale, WA 98248-9518
360-384-0325
Fax: 360-384-1746 bfmain@barleansfishery.com
www.barleansfishery.com
Organic flaxseed oil, fish oil

Wholesalers & Distributors / A-Z

Owner/President: Cindy Smith
Vice President: Ronan Smith
Marketing Director: Andreas Koch
Manager: Yehya Ahmed
yahmed@barleans.com
Year Founded: 1972
Number Employees: 10-19
Number of Customer Locations: 4000
Types of Products Distributed:
  Frozen Food, General Line, Health Food, Organic flax & borage oil

55063 Barnana
1746 Berkeley St
Unit B
Santa Monica, CA 90404   858-480-1543
info@barnana.com
barnana.com
Dried banana snacks
Co-Founder/CEO: Caue Suplicy
CMO: Nik Ingersoll
COO: Matt Clifford *Year Founded:* 2012
Type of Packaging: Private Label

55064 Barnett Lighting Corporation
10801 Roosevelt Ave
Corona, NY 11368   718-565-6533
Fax: 718-565-6533   800-570-2852
www.barnettlighting.com
Wholesaler/distributor of lighting fixtures
Owner: Farroukh Hafeez
barnettlighting@hotmail.com
Estimated Sales: $1-2.5 Million
Number Employees: 5-9
Types of Products Distributed:
  Frozen Food, General Merchandise, Lighting fixtures

55065 Baron Spices Inc
1440 Kentucky Ave
St Louis, MO 63110-3817   314-535-9020
Fax: 314-535-7227   sales@baronspices.com
www.baronspices.com
Wholesaler/distributor and contract packager of spices, seasonings, herbs, flavors and extracts
President: Tim Weigers
tweigers@baronspices.com
Estimated Sales: $5-10 Million
Number Employees: 20-49
Number of Products: 300
Square Footage: 220000
Type of Packaging: Food Service, Private Label, Bulk
Types of Products Distributed:
  Frozen Food, General Line, Spices

55066 Barr Packing Company
661 L St
Sanger, CA 93657   559-875-2541
Fax: 559-875-6153
Wholesaler/distributor of citrus fruit, peaches, plums, nectarines and grapes
President: Kirt Barr
Estimated Sales: $3-5 Million
Number Employees: 6
Types of Products Distributed:
  Frozen Food, Produce, Peaches, plums, nectarines & grapes

55067 Barravox/Metrovox Snacks
6116 Walker Avenue
Maywood, CA 90270-3447   323-771-3221
Fax: 323-771-2429   800-428-0522
Gift boxes, gourmet popcorn and pretzel packages, snack foods
President: Paul Vofland
Contact: Carol Gregory
csnacks1@aol.com
Estimated Sales: $300,000-500,000
Number Employees: 1-4

55068 Barrel O'Fun of Milwaukee
N26w23880d Commerce Drive
Waukesha, WI 53188-1018   414-444-0200
Fax: 414-444-9777
Wholesaler/distributor of potato chips and snack foods; serving the food service market
President: Matt Chambers
Number Employees: 20-49
Types of Products Distributed:
  Food Service, Frozen Food, Potato chips/snack foods

55069 Bartlett Dairy & Food Service
90-04 161 St
Suite 609
Jamaica, NY 11435   718-658-2299
www.bartlettny.com
Dairy and general grocery products
President: Thomas Malave, Jr.
Senior Logistics Analyst: Gary Kwan
gkwan@bartlettny.com
Year Founded: 1990
Estimated Sales: $123.3 Million
Number Employees: 171
Number of Brands: 1

55070 Bartolini Ice Cream
967 E 167th St
Bronx, NY 10459-1951   718-589-5151
Fax: 718-893-3171
Ice cream, ices, cheese, eggs, and dairy products
Owner: Michael Bartolini
Year Founded: 1971
Estimated Sales: $3 Million
Number Employees: 10-19

55071 Baruvi Fresh LLC
535 Fifth Ave
27th Flr
New York, NY 10017   646-346-1074
info@baruvi.com
www.hummustir.com
Hummus
CEO/Co-Founder: Rakesh Barmecha
COO/Co-Founder: Alon Kruvi
Vice President of Sales: Brian Stuckleman
Operations Manager: Johnny Makkar
Year Founded: 2015
Number Employees: 1-10
Type of Packaging: Food Service, Private Label

55072 Barwell Food Sales
Suite 202
London, ON N6A 2S2
Canada   519-645-1070
Fax: 519-645-7249   veggies@bartlettfarms.com
www.bartlettfarms.com
Importer and wholesaler/distributor of frozen fruits and vegetables; serving supermarket chains and the food service market
Owner/President: Donald Bartlett
Private Brands Carried:
  Bartlett Farms
Types of Products Distributed:
  Food Service, Frozen Food, Frozen fruits & vegetables

55073 Bascom Food Products
36 E 13th St
Paterson, NJ 07524   973-569-1558
Fax: 973-684-6544   basfood@aol.com
Importer of gourmet and specialty foods
President: John Fressie
Research & Development: Guadalupe Fernandez
Sales Director: Brian Egan
Estimated Sales: $5-10 Million
Number Employees: 5-9
Square Footage: 600000
Type of Packaging: Consumer, Food Service, Private Label, Bulk
Private Brands Carried:
  Gemini; Coco Lopez; Queen Gate
Number of Customer Locations: 250
Types of Products Distributed:
  Specialty Foods

55074 Basic Food Intl Inc
901 S Federal Hwy
Suite 202
Fort Lauderdale, FL 33316   954-467-1700
Fax: 954-764-5110   info@basicfood.com
www.basicfood.com
Importer, exporter and wholesaler/distributor of produce, dairy products, frozen meats, poultry, fish, groceries, oils, etc.
Owner: John Bauer
Year Founded: 1968
Estimated Sales: $20-50 Million
Number Employees: 20-49
Square Footage: 20000
Type of Packaging: Food Service, Private Label, Bulk
Types of Products Distributed:
  Food Service, Frozen Food, Provisions/Meat, Seafood, Dairy products, groceries, etc.

55075 (HQ)Basic Leasing Corporation
12a Port Kearny
Kearny, NJ 07032-4612   973-817-7373
Consultant specializing in the design of industrial kitchens; exporter of ice makers, dishwashers, etc.; importer of ice machines; wholesaler/distributor of equipment and fixtures and frozen drink machines and coffee machines
President: Harold Weber
VP: Johnathan Weber
Estimated Sales: $20-50 Million
Number Employees: 50-99
Square Footage: 28500
Types of Products Distributed:
  Food Service, Frozen Food, General Merchandise, Coffee & frozen drink machines, etc.

55076 Basic Organics
885 Claycraft Rd # A
Columbus, OH 43230-6866   614-863-3004
Fax: 614-863-9007   800-334-9969
www.ushealthclub.net
Wholesaler/distributor of vitamins, food supplements, body building and diet products
President: Scott Johnson
letslivesj@aol.com
Sales: Holland Seymour
Estimated Sales: $5-10 Million
Number Employees: 5-9
Type of Packaging: Private Label
Types of Products Distributed:
  Frozen Food, Health Food, Vitamins, food supplements, etc.

55077 Basin Crawfish Processors
P.O.Box 25
522 Parkway Drive
Breaux Bridge, LA 70517-4306   337-332-6655
Fax: 337-332-5917   www.bbcrawfest.com
Crawfish, frozen fish and seafood
President: Brayon Blanchard
Estimated Sales: $300,000-500,000
Number Employees: 1-4

55078 Bassham Institutional Foods
5409 Hemphill St
Fort Worth, TX 76111-4411   817-921-1600
Fax: 817-921-0334   ron@basshamfoods.com
www.basshamfoods.com
Wholesaler/distributor of frozen foods, general merchandise, produce, meats, seafood and general line products; serving the food service market
President: Ronnie Bassham
VP: Randy Bassham
Sales/Marketing Executive: Todd Hoffman
Purchasing Agent: Wes Bassham
Estimated Sales: $40 Million
Number Employees: 50-99
Square Footage: 70000
Private Brands Carried:
  Broadline, Nugget
Types of Products Distributed:
  Food Service, Frozen Food, General Line, General Merchandise, Provisions/Meat, Produce, Seafood

55079 Bates Distributing
301 N Commerce Ave
Russellville, AR 72801-3730   479-968-4717
Fax: 479-890-5582
Wholesaler/distributor of nonperishable groceries, candy and paper products
President: Buck Bates
Estimated Sales: $10-20 Million
Number Employees: 10-19
Square Footage: 30000
Number of Customer Locations: 70
Types of Products Distributed:
  Frozen Food, General Line, General Merchandise, Candy, paper products & groceries

55080 Bathroom & Towel Systems
124 Enterprise Avenue S
Secaucus, NJ 07094-1902   201-392-1886
Fax: 201-392-3810   800-364-3377
Wholesaler/distributor of janitorial supplies and paper goods including hand towels, wipers, toilet tissue, soap and air fresheners; serving the food service market
President: Milton Wolfson
Sales Manager: Usha Wadhwani
Estimated Sales: $1-2.5 Million
Number Employees: 5-9
Parent Co: Patty Group

Wholesalers & Distributors / A-Z

Types of Products Distributed:
  Food Service, Frozen Food, General Merchandise, Janitorial supplies & disposable goods

55081 Battaglia Distributing Corp
2500 S Ashland Ave
Chicago, IL 60608   312-738-1111
        www.battagliafoods.com
Italian mozzarella, sausage, extra virgin olive oil, and wine.
President: Frank Battaglia
fbattaglia@battaglia.com
Year Founded: 1902
Estimated Sales: $100-500 Million
Number Employees: 50-200
Type of Packaging: Private Label

55082 Battistella's Sea Foods
3620 Tolmas Drive
Metairie, LA 70002-1843   504-949-2724
      Fax: 504-949-2799 800-375-2728
Wholesaler/distributor of fresh seafood; serving the food service market; also, direct air shipments available
CEO/President: Preston Battistella
VP: Frank Zuccarelli
Sales Manager: Val Sevin
Number Employees: 20-49
Types of Products Distributed:
  Food Service, Frozen Food, Seafood

55083 Batty & Hoyt
1444 Emerson Street
Rochester, NY 14606-3009   716-647-9400
      Fax: 716-458-4790 800-558-2874
Wholesaler/distributor of material handling equipment and office furniture
President: Gary Albanese
Estimated Sales: $10-20 Million
Number Employees: 20-49
Private Brands Carried:
  Eagle; A.C.S.I.
Types of Products Distributed:
  Frozen Food, General Merchandise, Material handling equipment

55084 Bauducco Foods Inc.
1705 NW 133 Ave
Suite 101
Miami, FL 33182   305-477-9270
  Fax: 305-477-4703 sales@bauduccofoods.com
        www.bauducco.com
Panettone, wafers, cookies, crackers and bars
President/General Manager: Stefano Mozzi
Manager: Fred Rodrigues
Contact: Alfredo Rivera
alfredor@bauduccofoods.com
Year Founded: 2004
Estimated Sales: $5 Million
Number Employees: 1-4

55085 Baumann Paper Company
P.O.Box 13022
Lexington, KY 40583   859-252-8891
      Fax: 859-254-0579 800-860-8891
        www.baumannpaper.com
Wholesaler/distributor of bags, boxes, trays, film, food service disposables, labels, label guns, sanitary products, tapes, plastic and paper goods, janitorial supplies and floor machines; serving the food service market
Owner: Fred Baumann
fbaumann@baumannpaper.com
VP: C Gray
VP of Purchasing: T Hodgson
Estimated Sales: $10-20 Million
Number Employees: 20-49
Square Footage: 170000
Private Brands Carried:
  Thoroughbred
Number of Customer Locations: 612
Types of Products Distributed:
  Food Service, Frozen Food, General Merchandise, Bags, boxes, trays, film, labels, etc.

55086 Bavarian Specialty Foods, LLC
22417 S Vermont St
Los Angeles, CA 90502-2449   626-856-3188
Bakery products
Number Employees: 100-249
Type of Packaging: Food Service, Private Label, Bulk

55087 Bay Area Trash Compactor
P.O.Box 1857
Byron, CA 94505   925-935-1113
  Fax: 925-935-1163 www.batc-compacts.com
Wholesaler/distributor of trash compactors and recycling equipment; serving the food service market
President: Tim McMurray
Estimated Sales: $1-2.5 Million
Number Employees: 5-9
Square Footage: 8000
Private Brands Carried:
  Power Packer; GPI; Hansen; Nedland
Number of Customer Locations: 1000
Types of Products Distributed:
  Food Service, Frozen Food, General Merchandise, Trash compactors & recycling equipment

55088 Bay Baby Produce
424 Greenleaf Ave
Burlington, WA 98233-1800   360-755-2299
  Fax: 360-755-8010 info@baybabyproduce.com
        www.baybabyproduce.com
Organic pie pumpkins, spaghetti squash, butternut squash, acorn squash, carnival squash, delicata squash, kabocha squash, and red kuri squash
Founder/President: Michele Youngquist
Sales: Tyann Schlimmer
Types of Products Distributed:
  Produce

55089 Bay Cities Produce Co Inc
2109 Williams St
San Leandro, CA 94577   510-346-4943
  Fax: 510-352-4704 www.baycitiesproduce.com
Frozen and prepared fruits and vegetables.
President: Steve Del Masso
Vice President: Vince Del Masso
Secretary/Treasurer/VP: Diana Del Masso
diana@baycitiesproduce.com
Office Manager/Accounts Payable: JoLynn Eala
Quality Control: Luis Vaca
General Manager: Jason Shipps
Sales Manager: Tony D'Amato
Frozen Foods Supervisor: Jeff Christensen
Senior Buyer: Mike Short
Year Founded: 1947
Estimated Sales: $20-50 Million
Number Employees: 20-49
Square Footage: 55000
Type of Packaging: Food Service
Private Brands Carried:
  Chef's Delight; West American Wood Work
Number of Customer Locations: 400
Types of Products Distributed:
  Food Service, General Line, General Merchandise, Produce, Salads, produce labels, fruits, etc.

55090 Bay Haven Lobster Pound
280 Chases Pond Rd
York, ME 3909   207-363-5265
        Fax: 907-486-6417
Lobster, fish, and seafood
Owner: Randy Small
President: Tim Small
Year Founded: 1998
Estimated Sales: $1-3 Million
Number Employees: 5-9

55091 Bay State Lobster Company
395 Commercial Street
Boston, MA 02109-1028   617-523-4588
        Fax: 978-378-9770
Wholesaler/distributor of fresh and frozen seafood
President: Richard Faro
Number Employees: 20-49
Types of Products Distributed:
  Seafood

55092 Bay State Restrnt Products Inc
9 Hervey St # 15
Brockton, MA 02301-5942   508-586-6692
        Fax: 508-586-6865
Wholesaler/distributor of restaurant and bar equipment and supplies including toasters, silverware, dishes, stoves, etc.; serving the food service market
President: Robert Owens
Purchasing Manager: Robert Owens
Estimated Sales: $1-2.5 Million
Number Employees: 1-4
Square Footage: 36000
Types of Products Distributed:
  Food Service, Frozen Food, General Merchandise, Restaurant & bar equipment & supplies

55093 Bay View Food Products
2606 N Huron Rd
Pinconning, MI 48650-9512   989-879-3555
    Fax: 989-879-2659 www.bayviewfoods.com
Wholesaler/distributor of fresh picklings and brine pickling cucumbers
President: Joseph Janicke
jjanicke@bayviewfoods.com
Vice President: Sharon Janicke
General Manager: Dave Schubert
Estimated Sales: $5-10 Million
Number Employees: 50-99
Types of Products Distributed:
  General Line, Fresh picklings & pickling cucumbers

55094 Bayley's Lobster Pound
9 Avenue Six
Pine Point
Scarborough, ME 04074-8838   207-883-4571
      Fax: 207-510-7317 800-932-6456
      bayleys@bayleys.com www.bayleys.com
Fresh and frozen shrimp, clams and lobster
Owner: William Bayley
bill@bayleys.com
Year Founded: 1915
Number Employees: 5-9

55095 Bayou Container & Supply Inc
14021 Hemley Rd
Coden, AL 36523-3146   251-824-2658
    Fax: 251-824-2670 www.bayoucontainer.com
Owner/President: Mike Frederick
Estimated Sales: Less Than $500,000
Number Employees: 1-4

55096 Bayou Crab
10380 Foots Rd
Grand Bay, AL 36541-6491   251-824-2076
        Fax: 251-824-1484
Cajum foods
Owner: Dan Viravong
Estimated Sales: $3-5 Million
Number Employees: 10-19

55097 Bayou Food Distributors
949 Industry Rd
Kenner, LA 70062-6848   504-469-1745
      Fax: 504-469-1852 800-516-8283
        bayoufoods@hughes.com
Fillet fish, crabs, shrimp; frozen foods, such as beef, pork, poultry and seafood
CEO: Arthur Mitchell
bayoufoods@hughes.net
Estimated Sales: $5-10 Million
Number Employees: 5-9
Square Footage: 54400
Type of Packaging: Food Service
Number of Customer Locations: 550
Types of Products Distributed:
  Food Service, Frozen Food, General Line, Provisions/Meat, Produce, Seafood, Specialty Foods

55098 Bayou Land Seafood
1108 Vincent Berard Rd
Breaux Bridge, LA 70517   337-667-6118
  Fax: 337-667-6059 bayoulandseafood@aol.com
Seafood, including fresh and frozen crawfish, fish, crabs and shrimp; also, alligator and turtle
Owner: Adam Johnson
bayoulandseafood@aol.com
VP: Sharon Difatta
Plant Manager: Jeff Guidry
Year Founded: 2000
Estimated Sales: $2 Million
Number Employees: 50-99
Number of Products: 100
Square Footage: 38400
Type of Packaging: Consumer, Food Service, Bulk
Types of Products Distributed:
  Frozen Food, Seafood, Fresh & frozen crawfish, crabs, etc.

55099 Bayou Packing
9155 Little River Rd
Bayou La Batre, AL 36509   251-824-7710
        Fax: 251-824-4061
Packages seafood
Owner: Richard Roush

925

Wholesalers & Distributors / A-Z

55100 Bayshore Equipment
1800 NW 93rd Ave
Doral, FL 33172-2915 305-594-0747
Fax: 305-477-8943 800-648-6177
dmills@bayshore-equipment.com
www.bayshore-equipment.com
Wholesaler/distributor of ice cream soft serve machines, ice makers, bins, dispensers, water conditioners, etc.; serving the food service market
President: Dale Mills
dmills@bayshore-equipment.com
Estimated Sales: $10-20 Million
Number Employees: 10-19
Types of Products Distributed:
Food Service, Frozen Food, General Merchandise, Bins, dispensers, ice makers, etc.

55101 Beal's Lobster Pier
186 Clark Point Rd
SW Harbor, ME 04679 207-244-3202
Fax: 207-244-9479 800-244-7178
orders@bealslobster.com www.bealslobster.com
Lobster
President/Owner: Sam Beal
Year Founded: 1930
Estimated Sales: $1-3 Million
Number Employees: 10-19

55102 Beans & Machines
5784 E Green Lake Way N
Seattle, WA 98103-5954 206-625-1482
Fax: 206-625-1484
Wholesaler/distributor of commercial espresso machines
President: Jennifer Alber
Executive VP: Donald Alber
Estimated Sales: $5-10 Million
Number Employees: 10-19
Types of Products Distributed:
Frozen Food, General Merchandise, Coffee roasters

55103 Bear Creek Operations
PO Box 9000
Medford, OR 97501-0303 541-779-5080
Fax: 541-864-2926 jroberts@bco.com
Importer and wholesaler/distributor of apples, pears and stonefruit; wholesaler/distributor of groceries, meats, produce, dairy and bakery products and seafood; exporter of fresh pears; mail order fruit gift packs available
CEO: Nancy Tait
CFO: Jane Emkes
Sr VP: John Roberts
Quality Control VP: Perry Higgins
Contact: Tiffany Swartz
tswartz@bco.com
Operations: Lawna Wyatt
Estimated Sales: $1-3 Million
Number Employees: 1,000-4,999
Square Footage: 1000000
Parent Co: Bear Creek Corporation
Type of Packaging: Bulk
Private Brands Carried:
Bear Creek; Harry & David
Number of Customer Locations: 70
Types of Products Distributed:
General Line, Provisions/Meat, Produce, Seafood, Fruit gift packs

55104 Bear Meadow Gourmet Foods
29337 Summit Road
Evergreen, CO 80439-7442 970-679-1949
Fax: 303-674-6971 800-255-6559
www.bearmeadowgourmet.com
Wholesaler/distributor of mixes including dip, baking, dessert and soup, also; cake and spice blends
President: Ann Holloway
ann@bearcreekplumbing.com
Types of Products Distributed:
General Line

55105 Bear Stewart Corp
1025 N Damen Avenue
Chicago, IL 60622 773-276-0400
Fax: 773-276-3512 800-697-2307
info@bearstewart.com www.bearstewart.com
Fillings, jams, jellies, and premade mixes for bakers and confectioners.
VP of Sales: Michael Hoffman
COO: Jason Brooks
Year Founded: 1966
Estimated Sales: $5-10 Million

Number Employees: 1-4
Square Footage: 200000
Type of Packaging: Food Service, Bulk
Types of Products Distributed:
Frozen Food, General Line, General Merchandise

55106 Bear's Distributing Company
303 Swan Ave
Centralia, IL 62801 618-532-1901
Fax: 618-532-6034
Foodservice
Owner: Mike Donnewald
Estimated Sales: $20-50 Million
Number Employees: 20-49

55107 Beaumont Products
1560 Big Shanty Dr NW
Kennesaw, GA 30144-7040 770-514-7400
Fax: 770-514-7400 800-451-7096
www.beaumontproducts.com
Cleaning supplies
President: Hank Picken
Vice President: Mark Woods
mwoods@beaumontproducts.com
Estimated Sales: $3-5 Million
Number Employees: 20-49

55108 Beaver Enterprises
29 Garden Avenue
Rockland, ME 04841 207-596-2900
Fax: 207-596-2922
Kitchen equipment
Owner: Wayne Stinson
Estimated Sales: $800,000
Number Employees: 5-9

55109 Becker Foods
15136 Goldenwest Cir
Westminster, CA 92683-5235 714-891-9474
www.beckerfoods.com
Custom processor and packager of; fresh and frozen poultry, beef, pork, lamb, veal, cheese products, and more
President: Stan Becker
stan@beckerfoods.com
Vice President: Dian Vendel
Number Employees: 5-9
Type of Packaging: Food Service, Private Label

55110 Bedessee Imports
2350 Midland Avenue
Scarborough, ON M1S 1P8
Canada 416-292-2400
www.bedessee.com
Importer, exporter and wholesaler/distributor of East/West Indian and Latin American foods including noodles, dried peas and beans, flour, coconut and mustard oils, meats, canned fish and spices
President: Lionel Bedessee
VP: Vernan Bedessee
VP: Rayman Bedessee
Number Employees: 10-19
Square Footage: 100000
Type of Packaging: Consumer, Food Service
Types of Products Distributed:
Frozen Food, Specialty Foods

55111 Bedford Enterprises Inc
1940 W Betteravia Rd
Santa Maria, CA 93455-5926 805-922-4977
Fax: 805-928-7241 800-242-8884
bedfordscrap@gmail.com www.beibedford.com
Manufacturer and exporter of stainless platforms, hand railing, stair treads, ladders and decking; wholesaler/distributor of fiberglass gratings; installation services available
Vice President: Hugh Bedford
bedford@tcsn.net
VP: David Thomas
Estimated Sales: $1-2.5 Million
Number Employees: 10-19
Types of Products Distributed:
Frozen Food, General Merchandise, Fiberglass gratings

55112 Bedre Fine Chocolate
37 N Colbert Rd
Davis, OK 73030-9338 580-369-4200
800-367-5390
bedre.chocolates@chickasaw.net
www.bedrechocolates.com
Chocolate

Contact: Brenda Cloud
brenda.cloud@chickasaw.net
Number Employees: 10-19
Type of Packaging: Consumer, Private Label

55113 Beecher's Handmade Cheese
1600 Pike Place
Seattle, WA 98101 206-956-1964
sales@beecherscheese.com
www.beechershandmadecheese.com
Cheese
Owner: Kurt Beecher Dammeier
Year Founded: 2003
Number Employees: 20-40

55114 Beer Bakers Inc.
5515 Edmondson Pike
Suite 121
Nashville, TN 37211 615-775-3329
soberdough.com
Baked goods made with beer.
Co-Owner: Jordan Mychal
Co-Owner: Veronic Mychal
Type of Packaging: Consumer, Private Label

55115 Beer Import Co
2536 Springfield Ave
Vauxhall, NJ 07088-1016 908-686-0800
Fax: 908-686-0609
Importer and wholesaler/distributor of European beer
Marketing Manager: Doug Oley
Estimated Sales: $20-50 Million
Number Employees: 1-4
Private Brands Carried:
Dab; Chimay; Hacker-Pschorr
Number of Customer Locations: 300
Types of Products Distributed:
Frozen Food, General Line, Specialty Foods, European beer

55116 Behm's Valley Creamery
9405 E Sprague Ave Ste A
Spokane Valley, WA 99206 509-926-1424
Wholesaler/distributor of ice cream, fruit juice and dairy products
President: Iva Behm
Estimated Sales: $2.5-5 Million
Number Employees: 1-4
Private Brands Carried:
Valley Maid
Types of Products Distributed:
Frozen Food, General Line, Ice cream, juice, dairy products

55117 Belair Produce Co Inc
7226 Parkway Dr
Hanover, MD 21076-1307 410-782-8000
Fax: 410-782-8009 www.belairproduce.com
Wholesaler/distributor of produce; serving the food service market
Owner: C N Berman
VP: Karen Wood
Estimated Sales: $10-20 Million
Number Employees: 50-99
Square Footage: 4500
Types of Products Distributed:
Food Service, Frozen Food, Produce

55118 Belco Packaging Systems
910 S Mountain Ave
Monrovia, CA 91016-3641 626-930-0366
Fax: 626-359-3440 800-833-1833
info@belcopackaging.com
www.belcopackaging.com
Manufacturer and wholesaler/distributor of shrink packaging equipment, carton sealers, shrink tunnels, conveyors and accumulating tables
President: Michael A. Misik
CEO: Helen Misik
R&D: Tom Bolby
Quality Control: Dave Macneil
National Sales Manager: Thomas Misik
Distributor Sales Manager: Bruce Miles
Estimated Sales: $10-20 Million
Number Employees: 20-49
Square Footage: 70000
Types of Products Distributed:
Frozen Food, General Merchandise, Packaging equipment & materials

Wholesalers & Distributors / A-Z

55119 Belew Sound & Visual
P.O.Box 3167
Bristol, TN 37625-3167 423-764-4116
  800-676-4116
Wholesaler/distributor of general merchandise including burglar and fire alarms, fire alarm and intercommunication systems, closed circuit televisions, etc
President: Sam Belew
Estimated Sales: $10-20 Million
Number Employees: 1-4
Number of Customer Locations: 500
Types of Products Distributed:
  Frozen Food, General Merchandise, Burglar & fire alarms, etc.

55120 Belin & Nye
611 Summit Ave
Columbia, SC 29203-4130 803-786-6589
  Fax: 803-786-0883 travisnye1@yahoo.com
  www.belinandnye.com
Wholesaler/distributor of provisions/meats; serving the food service market
President: Don Nye
Estimated Sales: $1-2.5 Million
Number Employees: 5
Types of Products Distributed:
  Food Service, Provisions/Meat

55121 Bell & Sons
26514 W 7 Mile Rd
Redford, MI 48240-1958 313-531-2119
  Fax: 313-531-5210 www.bellandsons.com
Wholesaler/distributor of general line items and general merchandise including canned foods, paper and plastic products, janitorial supplies and glassware, party favors, bar and restaurant supplies, etc.; serving the food servicemarket
President: Thomas Bell
VP: Greg Bell
Secretary: Christine Bell
Estimated Sales: $5-10 Million
Number Employees: 10-19
Square Footage: 60000
Types of Products Distributed:
  Food Service

55122 Bell Foods
134 Brookhollow Esplanade
New Orleans, LA 70123-5102 504-837-2355
  Fax: 504-837-2365 info@bellfoods.net
  www.bellfoods.net
Appetizers and prepared foods, USDA proteins, Louisiana seafood, chemicals, dairy, paper products
Owner: John Bellina
jb@bellfoods.net
Co-Owner/Dir., Sales: Shane Nicaud, Sr.
jb@bellfoods.net
Co-Owner/Dir., Operations: John Bellini III
Number Employees: 20-49

55123 Bell Foods International
3213 Waconda Rd.
Gervais, OR 97026 503-390-1451
  Fax: 503-390-9526 info@bellfoodsintl.com
  www.bellfoodsintl.com
Maraschino cherry manufacturers
Contact: Monica Guzman
monicag@bellfoodsintl.com
Type of Packaging: Consumer, Private Label

55124 Bell Fork Lift Inc
47 S Main St
Mt Clemens, MI 48043 586-296-2020
  Fax: 586-469-3592 888-404-2575
  bellforklift@c3net.net www.bellforklift.com
Wholesaler/distributor of material handling equipment including forklifts, pallet trucks and order pickers
CEO: Eric Lehman
Sales Coordinator: Lynn Bell
Contact: Ron Sabo
rsabo@bellforklift.com
Estimated Sales: $20-50 Million
Number Employees: 100-249
Square Footage: 53000
Private Brands Carried:
  Toyota; Schaeff
Types of Products Distributed:
  Frozen Food, General Merchandise, Material handling equipment

55125 Bell-View Brand Food Products
P.O. Box 358
N Railroad St
Penn, PA 15675 724-523-5406
  Fax: 724-523-3206 800-223-2848
  info@bellview.com www.bellview.com
wholesaler/distributors of non perishable specialty and main line food products packed in unique packaging with an old fashioned look. Services a wide range of customers from fortune 500 companies to mom & pop stores.
Co-Owner: Robert Fawcett
Year Founded: 1930
Estimated Sales: $50-100 Million
Number Employees: 50-99
Type of Packaging: Consumer, Food Service
Number of Customer Locations: 13
Types of Products Distributed:
  Specialty Foods

55126 Belleco Inc
414 Hill St
Biddeford, ME 04005-4334 207-283-8006
  Fax: 207-283-8080 sales@bellecocooking.com
  www.bellecocooking.com
Customized toasters, conveyor Pizza Ovens and Heat Lamps
President: Russ Bellerose
rbellerose@bellecocooking.com
CFO: Kevin Roche
Quality Control Manager: Gil Cole
Sales: Mike Clavet
Materials Manager: Ron Hevey
Number Employees: 10-19
Type of Packaging: Food Service

55127 Belleharvest Sales Inc
11900 Fisk Road
Belding, MI 48809-9413
  800-452-7753
  sales@belleharvest.com www.belleharvest.com
Manufacturer, wholesaler/distributor, exporter, and packer of fresh apples.
President/CEO: Mike Rothwell
bellehar@iserv.net
Controller: Tony Kramer
Director of Marketing: Chris Sandwick
Director of Field Operations: Tony Blattner
Plant Manager: Brad Pitsch
Number Employees: 50-99
Parent Co: Belding Fruit Storage
Type of Packaging: Private Label, Bulk
Private Brands Carried:
  BelleHarvest
Types of Products Distributed:
  Frozen Food, Produce

55128 Belli Produce Company
512 W Cowles Street
Long Beach, CA 90813-1517 562-437-7441
  Fax: 562-436-3151
Wholesaler/distributor of produce; serving the food service market
President: T Belli
Estimated Sales: $2.5-5 Million
Number Employees: 5-9
Types of Products Distributed:
  Food Service, Produce

55129 Bellin Advertising
PO Box 182
New York, NY 10032-0182 212-923-4844
Wholesaler/distributor of general merchandise including advertising specialties, calendars, marking and writing pens, t-shirts, premiums, mugs and key holders
President: Walter Bellin
Number Employees: 5-9
Number of Customer Locations: 100
Types of Products Distributed:
  Frozen Food, General Merchandise, Advertising specialties

55130 Belly Treats, Inc.
210-200 Wellington St W
Toronto, ON M5V 3C7
Canada 416-418-3285
  Fax: 905-479-4135 www.bellytreats.com
Candies and nuts
Owner/Sales & Marketing: George Tsioros
Estimated Sales: $1 Million
Number of Products: 500+
Type of Packaging: Bulk

55131 Belting Associates
145 Serpentine Ln
Islandia, NY 11749 631-234-0695
  Fax: 516-433-2030 800-223-6287
Wholesaler/distributor of floor mats and matting
Owner/President: Jack Bischoff
Estimated Sales: $1-2.5 Million
Number Employees: 1-4
Square Footage: 28000
Private Brands Carried:
  Teknor Apex; Belting Associates; USCOA; Niru; Biltrite; 3M
Types of Products Distributed:
  Frozen Food, General Merchandise, Mats & matting

55132 Beltram Foodservice Group
6800 N Florida Ave
Tampa, FL 33604-5558 813-239-1136
  Fax: 813-238-6673 800-940-1136
  bfgtampa@beltram.com www.beltram.com
Wholesaler/distributor of food service supplies and equipment; serving the food service market
President: Dan Beltram
dan@beltram.com
CFO: Hal Herdman
VP: Allen Cope
VP: Kathy McCain
Purchasing Manager: John Zloch
Estimated Sales: $20-50 Million
Number Employees: 50-99
Parent Co: Beltram Foodservice Group
Private Brands Carried:
  Vulcan Heart; Eagle Metal Master; True Manufacturing; APW; frymaster
Types of Products Distributed:
  Food Service, Frozen Food, General Merchandise, Foodservice equipment & supplies

55133 (HQ)Ben E. Keith
601 E 7th St
Fort Worth, TX 76102 817-877-5700
  www.benekeith.com
Wholesaler/distributor of frozen food, produce, groceries, dairy products, meats, beer, etc.; serving the food service market.
President & COO: Robert Hallam Jr
CEO: John Howard Hallam
CFO & Treasurer: Gordon Crow
Corporate Secretary & General Counsel: Craig Woodcook
VP Independent Sales & Marketing: David Werner
VP Corporate Strategy: Brian Lynch
Year Founded: 1906
Estimated Sales: $3.5 Billion
Number Employees: 3,500
Square Footage: 591000
Type of Packaging: Food Service, Private Label, Bulk
Types of Products Distributed:
  Food Service, Frozen Food, General Line, General Merchandise, Provisions/Meat, Produce, Beer

55134 Ben E. Keith
1 Ben E. Keith Way
North Little Rock, AR 72117 501-978-5000
  Fax: 501-978-5921 www.benekeith.com
Wholesaler/distributor of meat, dairy products, frozen foods, produce, groceries, etc.; serving the food service market.
General Manager: Rusty Mathis
Assistant General Manager: Rick Gammill
Assistant General Manager: George Knollmeyer
Types of Products Distributed:
  Food Service, Frozen Food, General Line, General Merchandise, Provisions/Meat, Produce, Groceries

55135 Ben E. Keith
7650 Will Rogers Blvd
Fort Worth, TX 76140 817-759-6000
  Fax: 817-759-6238 www.benekeith.com
Wholesaler/distributor of meat, dairy products, frozen foods, produce, groceries, etc.; serving the food service market.
General Manager: Doug Swick
Assistant General Manager: Steve McWilliams
Assistant General Manager: Mike Ferrell
Types of Products Distributed:
  Food Service, Frozen Food, General Line, General Merchandise, Provisions/Meat, Produce, Groceries

Wholesalers & Distributors / A-Z

55136 Ben E. Keith
1 Ben E. Keith Way
Missouri City, TX 77489   832-652-5888
www.benekeith.com
Wholesaler/distributor of meat, dairy products, frozen foods, produce, groceries, etc.; serving the food service market.
General Manager: Mike Needham
Assistant General Manager: Jerry Dubose
Assistant General Manager: Clint Weber
Types of Products Distributed:
Food Service, Frozen Food, General Line, General Merchandise, Provisions/Meat, Produce, Groceries

55137 Ben E. Keith
3205 Broadway Blvd
SE Albuquerque, NM 87105   505-843-7766
Fax: 505-842-8060 www.benekeith.com
Wholesaler/distributor of meat, dairy products, frozen foods, produce, groceries, etc.; serving the food service market.
General Manager: Todd Hickam
Assistant General Manager: Josh Collman
Types of Products Distributed:
Food Service, Frozen Food, General Line, General Merchandise, Provisions/Meat, Produce, Groceries

55138 Ben E. Keith
14200 North Santa Fe Ave
Edmond, OK 73013   405-753-7600
Fax: 405-753-7853 www.benekeith.com
Wholesaler/distributor of meat, dairy products, frozen foods, produce, groceries, etc.; serving the food service market.
General Manager: Kirk Purnell
Assistant General Manager: Nolen Cleaves
Assistant General Manager: Michael Powers
Types of Products Distributed:
Food Service, Frozen Food, General Line, General Merchandise, Provisions/Meat, Produce, Groceries

55139 Ben E. Keith
17635 Ben E. Keith Way
Selma, TX 78154   210-662-7997
Fax: 210-661-9815 www.benekeith.com
Wholesaler/distributor of meat, dairy products, frozen foods, produce, groceries, etc.; serving the food service market.
General Manager: Doak Pierce
Assistant General Manager: Keith Scudday
Assistant General Manager: Marco Digiosia
Types of Products Distributed:
Food Service, Frozen Food, General Line, General Merchandise, Provisions/Meat, Produce, Groceries

55140 Ben E. Keith
1697 Lower Curtis Rd
Elba, AL 36323   334-897-5761
www.benekeith.com
Wholesaler/distributor of meat, dairy products, frozen foods, produce, groceries, etc.; serving the food service market.
General Manager: Scott Davison
Assistant General Manager: Keith Swan
Types of Products Distributed:
Food Service, Frozen Food, General Line, General Merchandise, Provisions/Meat, Produce, Groceries

55141 Ben E. Keith
2300 North Lakeside Dr
Amarillo, TX 79108   806-376-6257
Fax: 806-677-2278 www.benekeith.com
Wholesaler/distributor of meat, dairy products, frozen foods, produce, groceries, etc.; serving the food service market.
General Manager: Jeff Yarber
Assistant General Manager: Duke Pepper
Assistant General Manager: Kevin Smith
Types of Products Distributed:
Food Service, Frozen Food, General Line, General Merchandise, Provisions/Meat, Produce, Groceries

55142 Ben E. Keith
2250 Lone Star Dr
Dallas, TX 75212   214-634-0456
Fax: 214-634-0474 www.benekeith.com
Wholesaler/distributor of meat, dairy products, frozen foods, produce, groceries, etc.; serving the food service market.
Plant Manager: Chris Jackson
Types of Products Distributed:
Food Service, Frozen Food, General Line, General Merchandise, Provisions/Meat, Produce, Groceries

55143 Ben E. Keith
1697 Lower Curtis Rd
Elba, AL 36323   334-897-5761
www.benekeith.com
Wholesaler/distributor of meat, dairy products, frozen foods, groceries, etc.; serving the food service market.
Plant Manager: Kenneth Hattaway
Types of Products Distributed:
Food Service, Frozen Food, General Line, General Merchandise, Provisions/Meat, Produce, Groceries

55144 Ben E. Keith
2141 Cottonwood
Abilene, TX 79601   325-676-5777
Fax: 325-676-5783 www.benekeith.com
Wholesaler/distributor of beer
General Manager: Michael Hernandez
Sales Manager: Craig Jackson
Types of Products Distributed:
Beer

55145 Ben E. Keith
4101 McKinney Falls Pkwy
Austin, TX 78744   512-444-2337
Fax: 512-444-3871 www.benekeith.com
Wholesaler/distributor of beer
General Manager: Kevin Nettleton
Division Manager: Ray Hanson
Off Premise Sales Manager: Brad McCabe
On Premise Sales Manager: Joe Burns
Types of Products Distributed:
Beer

55146 Ben E. Keith
104 E. Industrial Dr
Early, TX 76802   325-649-9321
Fax: 325-646-6863 www.benekeith.com
Wholesaler/distributor of beer
General Manager: Cody Fly
Sales Manager: Patrick Montoya
Types of Products Distributed:
Beer

55147 Ben E. Keith
512 Brookside Dr E
Bryan, TX 77801   713-849-9195
Fax: 713-937-8777 www.benekeith.com
Wholesaler/distributor of beer
General Manager: Kevin Nettleton
Division Manager: David Cordill
Sales Manager: Ryan Rothermel
Types of Products Distributed:
Beer

55148 Ben E. Keith
2248 Live Oak St
Commerce, TX 75428   903-886-2158
Fax: 903-886-4047 www.benekeith.com
Wholesaler/distributor of beer
General Manager: Michael Williams
Sales Manager: Dwayne Sears
Types of Products Distributed:
Beer

55149 Ben E. Keith
118 N Brownlee Blvd
Corpus Christi, TX 78401   888-448-7708
www.benekeith.com
Wholesaler/distributor of beer
General Manager: Kevin Nettleton
Division Manager: Roy Hanson
Types of Products Distributed:
Beer

55150 Ben E. Keith
1805 Record Crossing
Dallas, TX 75235   214-634-1500
Fax: 214-638-4418 www.benekeith.com
Wholesaler/distributor of beer
General Manager: Jason Bush
Assistant General Manager: Jeff Stillwell
On Premise Sales Manager: Brian Trice
Types of Products Distributed:
Beer

55151 Ben E. Keith
2801 North I-35
Denton, TX 76207   940-383-3502
Fax: 940-387-3623 www.benekeith.com
Wholesaler/distributor of beer
General Manager: Don Fischer
General Sales Manager: Joel Lipe
Types of Products Distributed:
Beer

55152 Ben E. Keith
12170 Rojas St
Suite A-B
El Paso, TX 79936   915-872-9606
www.benekeith.com
Wholesaler/distributor of beer
General Manager: Michael Hernandez
Sales Manager: Nick Mendoza
Types of Products Distributed:
Beer

55153 Ben E. Keith
7001 Will Rogers Blvd
Fort Worth, TX 76140   817-568-4000
Fax: 817-568-2652 www.benekeith.com
Wholesaler/distributor of beer
General Manager: Philip Ward
General Sales Manager: Derek Gonzales
On Premise Sales Manager: Bruce Beville
Types of Products Distributed:
Beer

55154 Ben E. Keith
3803 Parkwood Blvd
Suite 300
Frisco, TX 75034   214-618-5900
Fax: 214-618-5908 www.benekeith.com
Wholesaler/distributor of beer
General Manager: Don Fischer
General Sales Manager: Joel Lipe
Types of Products Distributed:
Beer

55155 Ben E. Keith
6720 Commerce Creek Dr
Houston, TX 77040   713-849-9195
Fax: 713-937-8771 www.benekeith.com
Wholesaler/distributor of beer
General Manager: Kevin Nettleton
Division Manager: David Cordill
Sales Manager: Ryan Rothermel
Types of Products Distributed:
Beer

55156 Ben E. Keith
3369 Fredericksburg Rd
Kerrville, TX 78028   830-792-1130
Fax: 830-792-1148 www.benekeith.com
Wholesaler/distributor of beer
General Manager: Cody Fly
Types of Products Distributed:
Beer

55157 Ben E. Keith
1604 Bessemer
Llano, TX 78643   325-247-4224
Fax: 325-247-5794 www.benekeith.com
Wholesaler/distributor of beer
General Manager: Cody Fly
Sales Manager: Patrick Montoya
Types of Products Distributed:
Beer

55158 Ben E. Keith
2019 W Oak
Palestine, TX 75801   903-729-1770
Fax: 903-729-1086 www.benekeith.com
Wholesaler/distributor of beer
General Manager: Andrew Gregory
Assistant General Manager: Greg Jones
Types of Products Distributed:
Beer

55159 Ben E. Keith
5108 Rittiman Rd
Suite 126
San Antonio, TX 78218   888-448-7708
www.benekeith.com
Wholesaler/distributor of beer

Wholesalers & Distributors / A-Z

General Manager: Kevin Nettleton
Division Manager: Ray Hanson
Sales Manager: Blake Loftin
Types of Products Distributed:
  Beer

55160 Ben E. Keith
320 S University Parks Dr
Waco, TX 76701   254-752-5574
    Fax: 254-752-3501 www.benekeith.com
Wholesaler/distributor of beer
General Manager: David Underwood
Sales Manager: Gary Holcomb
Types of Products Distributed:
  Beer

55161 Ben E. Keith
548 Sante Fe Dr
Weatherford, TX 76086   817-599-4009
    Fax: 817-594-2186 www.benekeith.com
Wholesaler/distributor of beer
General Manager: Philip Ward
Sales Manager: Terry Smith
Types of Products Distributed:
  Beer

55162 Ben H. Roberts Produce
PO Box 11039
Tampa, FL 33680-1039   813-239-1105
    Fax: 813-236-0431
Wholesaler/distributor of produce including fruits and vegetables
President: Tom Howell
VP: J Dombrosky
Number Employees: 10-19
Types of Products Distributed:
  Produce, Fruits & vegetables

55163 Bender Meat
175 Lewis St
Buffalo, NY 14206-2223   716-852-4422
    Fax: 716-852-6368 http://www.findlaymarket.org/
Wholesaler/distributor of fresh and frozen veal, lamb, pork, beef, chicken and turkey; also, frozen seafood
President: John Riffel
Estimated Sales: $10-20 Million
Number Employees: 10-19
Types of Products Distributed:
  Frozen Food, Provisions/Meat, Seafood

55164 Benfield Electric Supply Co
25 Lafayette Ave
White Plains, NY 10603-1613   914-948-6660
    Fax: 914-993-0558 www.benfieldelectric.com
Wholesaler/distributor of electrical supplies including wiring devices, motors, lighting fixtures and electric and fluorescent lamps
CEO: Leslie Alvarado
l.alvarado@benfieldelectric.com
CEO: Daniel J McLaughlin
Director Sales/Marketing: Patrick O'Brien
Estimated Sales: $20-50 Million
Number Employees: 100-249
Square Footage: 170000
Private Brands Carried:
  Hubbell; Allen-Bradley; U.S. Motors
Number of Customer Locations: 4000
Types of Products Distributed:
  Frozen Food, General Merchandise, Electrical supplies

55165 Benman Industries Inc
1870 E Main St
PO Box 5327
Bridgeport, CT 06610-2038   203-334-0376
    Fax: 203-579-7778 800-252-7222
    benservice@aol.com www.benmanind.com
Wholesaler/distributor of general merchandise including custodial supplies; also, cleaning equipment repair available
President: E J Benedetto
benservice@aol.com
CFO: P Hayman
Estimated Sales: $2.5-5 Million
Number Employees: 5-9
Square Footage: 72000
Private Brands Carried:
  Bensan; SSS; Vaportek; Big D; Butcher's; Drackett; Envirox; Eureka; Hoover; Mastercraft; NSS; Nobles; 3M; Proctor & Gamble; Rubbermaid; Unger
Types of Products Distributed:
  Food Service, General Merchandise, Custodial supplies

55166 Bennett Material Handling
1009 Hill St
Hopkins, MN 55343-2099   320-255-9545
    Fax: 952-933-5913 www.bmhmn.com
Wholesaler/distributor of material handling equipment including forklifts
President: Gregg Bennett
Sales Manager: Taylor Lucas
Estimated Sales: $20-50 Million
Number Employees: 20-49
Private Brands Carried:
  Komatsu; Baker; Hydromat
Types of Products Distributed:
  Frozen Food, General Merchandise, Material handling equipment

55167 Bensinger's
8543 Page Avenue
Saint Louis, MO 63114-6008   314-426-5100
Wholesaler/distributor of meats, seafood, pasta, produce, etc.; also, restaurant equipment
Estimated Sales: $10-20 Million
Number Employees: 20-49
Types of Products Distributed:
  Frozen Food, General Line, General Merchandise, Provisions/Meat, Produce, Seafood, Restaurant equipment, pasta, etc.

55168 Benson's Wholesale Fruit
303 Royall Avenue
Elroy, WI 53929-1044   608-462-8236
    Fax: 608-462-8764 800-762-0283
    bfruits@aol.com
Wholesaler/distributor of produce; serving the food service market
Owner: David Roalkvam
Estimated Sales: $5-10 Million
Number Employees: 15
Types of Products Distributed:
  Food Service, Produce

55169 Bentan Corporation
4555 196th Pl
Flushing, NY 11358   718-281-1978
    Fax: 718-793-2527 coffemix@aol.com
    members.aol.com/coffeemix/default.htm
Importer and wholesaler/distributor of instant beverages, biscuits, cookies, coffee, ginger tea, cereal, etc
Manager: Richard Tan
rtan@bentan.com
Estimated Sales: $5-10 Million
Number Employees: 5-9
Private Brands Carried:
  Coffeemix
Types of Products Distributed:
  Frozen Food, General Line, Specialty Foods, Cookies, ginger tea, coffee, etc.

55170 Benton's Seafood Ctr
711 Central Ave S
Tifton, GA 31794-5212   229-382-4976
    Fax: 229-382-0779
Seafood. Founded in 1987.
Owner: Tim Benton
Estimated Sales: $1-3 Million
Number Employees: 1-4

55171 Bergin Fruit & Nut Co.
2000 Energy Park Dr
St. Paul, MN 55108   651-642-1234
    Fax: 651-558-9702 800-486-6808
    www.berginfruit.com
Wholesaler/distributor of health foods including fresh fruits, vegetables and nut meats; serving the food service market.
President: Thomas Bergin
thomas.bergin@berginnut.com
Sales Director: Tom Bergin, Jr.
Year Founded: 1951
Estimated Sales: $50-100 Million
Number Employees: 100-249
Square Footage: 25000
Type of Packaging: Consumer, Food Service, Private Label, Bulk
Number of Customer Locations: 400
Types of Products Distributed:
  Food Service, General Merchandise, Health Food, Produce, Specialty Foods

55172 Berje
5 Lawrence St Ste 10
Bloomfield, NJ 07003   973-748-8980
    Fax: 973-680-9618 berje@berjeinc.com
    www.berjeinc.com
Importer, exporter and wholesaler/distributor of essential oils and aromatic chemicals for teas and fusion flavored juices
President: Kim Bleimann
VP: Marc Parrilli
Executive VP: Barry Dowles
Contact: Charlene Burkett
ombud@idoa.in.gov
Estimated Sales: $20-50 Million
Number Employees: 50-99
Square Footage: 180000
Types of Products Distributed:
  Frozen Food, General Line, Aromatic chemicals & essential oils

55173 Berkel Products Company
5169 Bradco Boulevard
Mississauga, ON L4W 2A6
Canada   905-625-4160
    Fax: 905-625-3166 800-465-0727
    contactus@berkelcompany.com www.berkel.com
Wholesaler/distributor of food service equipment including slicers and scales
Sales Manager: John Darragh
Parent Co: Avery Berkel Group
Private Brands Carried:
  Berkel
Types of Products Distributed:
  Food Service, Frozen Food, General Merchandise

55174 Berlin Packaging
1195 Washington Pike
Bridgeville, PA 15017   412-257-3000
    info@berlinpackaging.com
    www.berlinpackaging.com
Wholesaler/distributor of glass, plastic and metal containers and closures.
Type of Packaging: Consumer, Private Label
Types of Products Distributed:
  General Line, General Merchandise, Health Food, Specialty Foods, Containers, closures & labels

55175 Berlin Packaging
508 Angie Pl
Mullica Hill, NJ 08062   856-418-1092
    info@berlinpackaging.com
    www.berlinpackaging.com
Wholesaler/distributor of glass, plastic and metal containers and closures.
Parent Co: Berlin Packaging
Types of Products Distributed:
  Frozen Food, General Merchandise, Containers & closures

55176 (HQ)Berlin Packaging
525 W Monroe St
Chicago, IL 60661
    Fax: 312-876-9290 800-723-7546
    info@berlinpackaging.com
    www.berlinpackaging.com
Wholesaler/distributor of glass, plastic and metal containers and closures.
Chairman & CEO: Andrew Berlin
aberlin@berlinpackaging.com
Year Founded: 1898
Estimated Sales: $100-500 Million
Number Employees: 500-1000
Other Locations:
  Berlin Packaging
  Houston, TX Berlin Packaging
Types of Products Distributed:
  Frozen Food, General Merchandise, Containers & closures

55177 Berlin Packaging
2 Capital Dr
Suite 2
Cranbury, NJ 08512   609-395-7633
    info@berlinpackaging.com
    www.berlinpackaging.com
Wholesaler/distributor of glass, plastic and metal containers and closures.
Parent Co: Berlin Packaging
Types of Products Distributed:
  Frozen Food, General Merchandise, Containers & closures

Wholesalers & Distributors / A-Z

55178 Berlin Packaging
7400 W Campus Rd
Suite 140
New Albany, OH 43054   614-775-6193
www.berlinpackaging.com
Wholesaler/distributor of glass, plastic and metal containers and closures.

55179 Bernard & Sons
4011 Jewett Ave
Bakersfield, CA 93301   661-327-4431
Fax: 661-327-7461 www.bernardandsons.com
Meat Products. Founded in 1965.
Owner: Dennis Bernard
General Manager: Hal Ulmer
Estimated Sales: $11,100,000
Number Employees: 20-49

55180 Bernard Jensen Intl
1255 Linda Vista Dr
San Marcos, CA 92078-3827   760-471-9977
Fax: 858-755-2026
www.bernardjenseneducation.com
Wholesaler/distributor of health food products
President & Director: Art Jensen
ajensen@bernardjensen.com
General Manager: Frank Stolarczyk
Estimated Sales: Less Than $500,000
Number Employees: 1-4
Types of Products Distributed:
   Frozen Food, Health Food

55181 Bernard's Bakery
5017 Skillman Ave
Flushing, NY 11377-4155   718-651-0495
Fax: 718-651-0117
Wholesaler/distributor of specialty foods, bread, pastries and cookies; importer of French ham, pate, garlic sausage
Owner: Bernard Eglim
Estimated Sales: $500,000-$1 Million
Number Employees: 5-9
Square Footage: 12000
Types of Products Distributed:
   Frozen Food, General Line, Specialty Foods, Bread, pastries & cookies

55182 Bernatello's Foods
5625 W 78th St
Suite B
Edina, MN 55439-3153   952-831-6622
800-878-5001
www.bernatellos.com
Frozen pizza manufacturer in the Midwest.
Number Employees: 100-249

55183 Bernco Specialty Adverti
P.O.Box 250
Bethpage, NY 11714-0250   516-681-7676
Fax: 516-681-7685 800-877-3110
bernco4@banet.net
Wholesaler/distributor of general merchandise including advertising specialties
Owner: Sandy Kane
Administrator Assistant: Etta Smith
Estimated Sales: $2.5-5 Million
Number Employees: 1-4
Square Footage: 16000
Number of Customer Locations: 1000
Types of Products Distributed:
   Advertising Specialties Cutter&Buck

55184 (HQ)Berns Co
1250 W 17th St
Long Beach, CA 90813-1391   562-436-1074
Fax: 562-436-1074 800-421-3773
Gary@thebernscompany.com
www.thebernscompany.com
Wholesaler/distributor, importer and exporter of pallet trucks and forkliftparts
Owner: Steve Berns
Sales/Marketing Executive: Steve Berns
bernsco@aol.com
Estimated Sales: $5 Million
Number Employees: 20-49
Square Footage: 80000
Private Brands Carried:
   Bishamon; BT

55185 Berry Material Handling
P.O.Box 9288
Wichita, KS 67277   316-945-0101
Fax: 316-946-9627 800-323-6576
www.berrymaterial.com
Wholesaler/distributor of material handling equipment
President: Joe Wilson
General Manager: Joe Beason
Estimated Sales: $10-20 Million
Number Employees: 20-49
Square Footage: 24000
Parent Co: Berry Companies
Private Brands Carried:
   Yale; Drexel; Big Joe
Types of Products Distributed:
   Frozen Food, General Merchandise, Material handling equipment

55186 Berrywine Plantations
13601 Glissans Mill Rd
Mt Airy, MD 21771-8507   410-795-6432
Fax: 301-829-1970 info@linganore-wine.com
www.linganorewines.com
Estate bottled wines and cooking wines
President: Eric Aellen
info@linganorewines.com
Vice President: Lucille Aellen
Marketing Director: Lucia Simmons
Estimated Sales: $5-9.9 Million
Number Employees: 20-49
Type of Packaging: Private Label

55187 Bertolino Beef Co
45 Food Mart Rd
Boston, MA 02118-2801   617-269-5790
Fax: 617-269-7745
Wholesaler/distributor of provisions/meats
President: Frank Bertolino
Estimated Sales: $20-50 Million
Number Employees: 20-49
Types of Products Distributed:
   Frozen Food, Provisions/Meat

55188 Berton Company
7101 E Slauson Avenue
Cty of Cmmrce, CA 90040-3622   323-728-5080
Fax: 323-728-0036
Wholesaler/distributor of general merchandise; rack jobber services available
President: R Craig
VP Buying: Rob Primm
VP Marketing: Jim Prindiville
Estimated Sales: $20-50 Million
Number Employees: 250-499
Number of Customer Locations: 1600
Types of Products Distributed:
   Frozen Food, General Merchandise, Rack Jobbers

55189 Bertrand's
1500 Oliver St
Houston, TX 77007-6035   713-951-0956
Fax: 713-880-4222 www.bertrandsinc.com
Wholesaler/distributor of baked goods, frozen cakes, hors d'oeurvies, frozen vegetables, frozen danish, cavivar, fish salmon, artisan cheeses, tart's, pelite flours and specialty frozen
President: Bertrand Oriot
CFO: Bill Aulick
Contact: Brandie Ford
fordb@bertrandsinc.com
Plant Manager: Randy Delmastro
Purchasing Director: Gene Duke
Estimated Sales: $5-10 Million
Number Employees: 20-49
Square Footage: 120000
Number of Customer Locations: 500
Types of Products Distributed:
   Food Service, Frozen Food, Specialty Foods, Artisan Cheeses

55190 Bess Eaton
127 High St
Westerly, RI 02891-1821   401-596-5533
www.besseaton.com
Coffee and baked goods
Management: David Liguori
Estimated Sales: Less Than $500,000
Number Employees: 5-9

55191 Best Brands Incorporated
7337 Cockrill Bend Blvd
Nashville, TN 37209
Fax: 615-350-8500 800-966-9643
info@bestbrandsinc.com www.bestbrandsinc.com
Wholesale/Distributor of beer, wines, spirits, and non-alcholic beverages.
Chairman & CEO: Robert Moses
Year Founded: 1983
Estimated Sales: $100-500 Million
Number Employees: 50-200
Type of Packaging: Consumer, Food Service, Private Label
Types of Products Distributed:
   Wines; Beers; Spirits

55192 Best Buy Uniforms
500 E 8th Ave
Homestead, PA 15120-1904   412-461-4600
Fax: 412-461-4016 800-345-1924
customer-service@bestbuyuniforms.com
www.bestbuyuniforms.com
Manufacturer, wholesaler/distributor and importer of image apparel uniforms; also, custom T-shirts, table cloths, napkins and work uniforms; serving the food service market
Owner: David Frischman
davidf@bestbuyuniforms.com
CEO: Lester Frischman
Estimated Sales: $1-5 Million
Number Employees: 5-9
Square Footage: 24000
Type of Packaging: Food Service
Types of Products Distributed:
   Food Service, Frozen Food, Uniforms, tablecloths & napkins

55193 Best Chicago Meat
4649 W Armitage Ave
Chicago, IL 60639
www.bestchicagomeat.com
Meat products including frozen hamburger patties, sausages, spare ribs, chitterlings, bacon, ham, breakfast links, chicken nuggets, rib tips and kosher hot dogs
CFO: Paul Dwyer
Regional Sales Manager: Edward Allaway
Estimated Sales: $20-50 Million
Number Employees: 20-49
Number of Brands: 4
Square Footage: 20000
Parent Co: Beavers Holdings
Type of Packaging: Consumer, Food Service
Types of Products Distributed:
   Frozen Food

55194 Best Express Foods Inc
1458 E Grand River Rd
Williamston, MI 48895-9336   517-655-2288
Fax: 517-655-8568
Frozen pizza and pizza related items
Contact: Dave Spencer
dspencer@bestexpressfoods.com
Number Employees: 20-49
Type of Packaging: Consumer

55195 Best Foods
700 Sylvan Ave
Englewood Cliffs, NJ 07632   201-894-4000
Fax: 201-894-2186 www.bestfoods.com
Best Foods manufactures the best-selling mayonnaise in the United States. East of the Rockies, Best Foods is known as Hellman's.
President, Unilever Foods: Amanda Sourry
Contact: Cordell Price
cordell.price@unilever.com
Number Employees: 44,000
Number of Products: 13
Parent Co: Unilever
Type of Packaging: Consumer, Food Service

55196 Best Friends Cocoa
282 Bussey St
Dedham, MA 02026   781-329-8800
Fax: 781-329-8800
Wholesaler/distributor of gourmet flavored low-fat and cholesterol-free kosher cocoa mixes including traditional, cinnamon twist, raspberry truffle, amaretto, mocha, mint, malt, marshmallow, cherry and vanilla velvet; serving the foodservice market, gift basketers and retail gourmet/ gift shops
President: Sima Naomi Storm
Estimated Sales: $300,000
Number Employees: 1-4
Square Footage: 2880
Parent Co: Spare Parts
Private Brands Carried:
   Best Friends Cocoa
Number of Customer Locations: 200
Types of Products Distributed:
   Food Service, Frozen Food, General Line, Spe-

cialty Foods, Gourmet flavored & low-fat cocoa mixes

55197 Best Industries
PO Box 908
Woodstock, IL 60098-0908   815-338-7919
                Fax: 815-338-7954
Wholesaler/distributor of convex security mirrors
President: George Clifford
Secretary: Sally Nicholls
Secretary: Phyllis Kirchberg
Estimated Sales: Less than $500,000
Number Employees: 1-4
Types of Products Distributed:
  Frozen Food, General Merchandise, Convex security mirrors

55198 Best Market
1 Lexington Ave.
Bethpage, NY 11714   516-570-5300
                      bestmarket.com
Wholesaler/distributor of dairy products, frozen foods, general merchandise, private label items, groceries, and seafood.
Founder: Ben Raites *Year Founded:* 1994
Number of Customer Locations: 19
Types of Products Distributed:
  Frozen Food, General Line, General Merchandise, Provisions/Meat, Produce, Seafood, Groceries, dairy products, etc.

55199 Best Material Handling
7150 Oak Valley Dr
Colorado Springs, CO 80919-3409   719-599-9191
  Fax: 719-599-9193   800-933-5270
Wholesaler/distributor of conveyors, containers, racks and shelving
President: Barbara Harrington
bharrington@best-materials.com
Estimated Sales: $1-2.5 Million
Number Employees: 1-4
Private Brands Carried:
  Rapid; Intermetro; Speedway
Types of Products Distributed:
  Frozen Food, General Merchandise, Conveyors, containers, racks, etc.

55200 Best Restaurant Equip &Design
4020 Business Park Dr
Columbus, OH 43204-5023   614-488-2378
  Fax: 614-488-4732   800-837-2378
          www.bestrestaurant.com
Wholesaler/distributor of furniture, cookware and refrigeration, cooking and serving equipment; serving the food service market; installation and restaurant design services available
President: James Hanson
jhanson@betsrestaurant.com
CFO: Suzane Yosick
Estimated Sales: $10-20,000,000
Number Employees: 50-99
Private Brands Carried:
  Vollrath; Vulcan; Hobart; Rubbermaid
Types of Products Distributed:
  Food Service, Frozen Food, General Merchandise, Equipment & supplies

55201 Betsy's Best
                 888-483-2019
      info@betsysbest.com betsysbest.com
Nut and seed butters
Founder: Betsy Opyt
Number of Brands: 1
Number of Products: 4
Type of Packaging: Consumer

55202 Better Beverages Inc
10624 Midway Ave
Cerritos, CA 90703-1581   562-924-8321
  Fax: 562-924-6204   800-344-5219
    customercare@betbev.com www.betbev.com
Soft drinks, juices, energy drinks, coffee, punch syrups, bar mixes, beverage dispensers, and glass washer and sanitizer.
Owner: Harold Harris
haroldh@betbev.com
CEO: G Harris
Estimated Sales: $20-50 Million
Number Employees: 20-49
Type of Packaging: Consumer, Food Service
Private Brands Carried:
  Coca-Cola

Types of Products Distributed:
  Food Service, Frozen Food, General Line, Soft drinks & juices

55203 Better Health Products
101 Washington Ave
Grand Haven, MI 49417   616-846-4161
  Fax: 616-846-9470   800-638-4141
Wholesaler/distributor of allergy-free nutritional supplements and herbal weight control products; also, private label items available
President: Patrick Powers
Estimated Sales: $300,000-500,000
Number Employees: 1-4
Square Footage: 12000
Parent Co: Kelly Association
Private Brands Carried:
  Chondroitin Sulfate Plus; Executive Stress Formula; Ultra Arth Support; Joint Nutrition; Defense Plus
Number of Customer Locations: 500
Types of Products Distributed:
  Frozen Food, Health Food, Nutritional supplements

55204 Better Janitor Supplies
3434 Dalworth St
Arlington, TX 76011   817-640-8607
                Fax: 817-633-4009
Wholesaler/distributor of cleaning supplies and disposables; serving the food service market
Co-Owner: Gary Spikes
Co-Owner: Linda Spikes
Estimated Sales: $.5-1 million
Number Employees: 1-4
Types of Products Distributed:
  Food Service, Frozen Food, General Merchandise

55205 Better Meat
305 NW 82nd St
Seattle, WA 98117-4033   206-783-0570
                Fax: 206-783-2364
Wholesaler/distributor of beef including fresh and processed; serving the food service market
President: Micheal Evesen
Secretary: S Evensen
Estimated Sales: $5-10 Million
Number Employees: 1-4
Types of Products Distributed:
  Food Service, Frozen Food, Provisions/Meat

55206 (HQ)Betters International Food Corporation
60 Main St
Oakfield, NY 14125-1044   585-948-5242
                Fax: 585-948-5912
Wholesale Suppliers of Concentrates, Frozen Fruits, Frozen Vegetables and Frozen Seafood to the Food Industry
President/CEO: F Betters
CFO: P Betters
VP: B Betters
R&D: Floyd Betters
Quality Control: P Betters
Marketing: Floyd Better
Operations/Manufacturing: Becky Palmer
Production: Floyd Betters
Estimated Sales: $1.2 Million
Number Employees: 5
Type of Packaging: Consumer, Food Service, Private Label, Bulk
Types of Products Distributed:
  Frozen Food

55207 Beverage Express
4580 Fieldgate Rd
Oceanside, CA 92056   760-941-9114
                       800-923-8372
          www.beverageexpress.com
Wholesaler/distributor and exporter of post mix and Italian soda syrups, coffee and juice concentrates; also, portable carbonating appliances
Co-Owner: Gordon Mirrett
Co-Owner: Charlene Mirrett
Estimated Sales: Less than $500,000
Number Employees: 1-4
Square Footage: 2000
Type of Packaging: Consumer
Types of Products Distributed:
  Frozen Food, General Line, General Merchandise, Soda syrups, coffee concentrates, etc.

55208 Bevistar
615 Vista Drive
Oswego, IL 60543-8129   847-758-1581
  Fax: 847-758-1617   877-238-7827
Markets and distributes the newest technology in small-scale beverage dispensers and related consumable concentrate syrups. Specializes in systems comprised of patented technology ideal for the small volumeaccount/establishment/workplace
Marketing Director: Lynda Filicette
Sales Director: Saul Strankus
Plant Manager: Joe Rosado
Estimated Sales: $1-5 Million
Number of Brands: 1
Number of Products: 15
Square Footage: 18400
Parent Co: Isoworth Limited
Private Brands Carried:
  Bevstar, CH310, CHP 310, Enterprise EPOU 310, ERW 310, Voda Bay Concentrate Syrups
Number of Customer Locations: 25
Types of Products Distributed:
  Food Service

55209 Bewley Irish Imports
1130 Greenhill Rd
West Chester, PA 19380-4005   610-696-2682
  Fax: 610-344-7618   888-239-5397
        info@bewleyirishimports.com
        www.bewleyirishimports.com
Importer of Irish specialties
Owner: Bruce Flamm
info@bewleyirishimports.com
Sales/Marketing: Alison Watkins
Estimated Sales: $500,000-$1 Million
Number Employees: 1-4
Number of Brands: 15
Number of Products: 162
Square Footage: 14400
Type of Packaging: Food Service, Private Label
Types of Products Distributed:
  Specialty Foods

55210 Bi-O-Kleen Industry
PO Box 2679
Clackamas, OR 97015-2679   360-260-1587
                Fax: 503-557-7818
Cleaning products.

55211 Bickford Daniel LobsterCompany
Lanes Is
Vinalhaven, ME 04863   207-863-4688
                Fax: 207-863-4525
Lobster
Estimated Sales: $1-3 Million
Number Employees: 5-9

55212 Big Al's Seafood
7701 Quacker Neck Rd
PO Box 293
Bozman, MD 21612   410-745-2637
                Fax: 410-745-9046
Wholesaler/distributor of crabs, clams, fish and oysters. Founded in 1979.
President: Alan Poore
Estimated Sales: Less than $500,000
Number Employees: 5
Square Footage: 24000
Type of Packaging: Consumer
Types of Products Distributed:
  Frozen Food, Seafood

55213 Big Apple Tea Company
4215 81st St Apt 2p
Flushing, NY 11373   718-505-1242
Wholesaler/distributor of iced teas
President: Regina Kessler
Estimated Sales: $1-2.5 Million
Number Employees: 1-4
Other Locations:
  Big Apple Tea Co. Shangri-La
  Kingston, NYBig Apple Tea Co. Shangri-La
Private Brands Carried:
  Shangri-La
Types of Products Distributed:
  General Line, Iced teas

55214 Big Horn Co-Op Tire Shop
346 Greybull Ave
Greybull, WY 82426-2035   307-765-2051
  Fax: 307-765-2562 www.bighorncoop.com
Wholesaler/distributor of beans

Wholesalers & Distributors / A-Z

Manager: Larry Mead
Manager: Jared Dalton
General Manager: Louis Pistulka
Estimated Sales: Less Than $500,000
Number Employees: 1-4
Types of Products Distributed:
  Produce, Beans

55215 Big Island Seafood, LLC
1201 University Drive NE
Atlanta, GA 30306-2504   404-366-8943
                    Fax: 404-366-9129
Tuna, swordfish, snapper, grouper, sea bass, mahi-mahi, tilapia, seafood

55216 Big Shoulders Coffee
1105 W Chicago Ave
Chicago, IL 60642   312-846-1883
         information@bigshoulderscoffee.com
                www.bigshoulderscoffee.com
Coffee
Founder: Tim Coonan
General Manager: Abigail Helmus
VP Operations: Gregg Piazzi
Director of Sales: Dave Marsalek
Year Founded: 2012
Number Employees: 20-49
Types of Products Distributed:
  General Line

55217 Big Spoon Roasters
4517 Hillsborough Rd
#101-B
Durham, NC 27705   919-309-9100
         info@bigspoonroasters.com
             www.bigspoonroasters.com
Nut butters and nut butter snack bars
Founder: Mark Overbay
Marketing & Communications Manager: Mackenzie Props
Regional Sales Representative: Andrew Anderson
Director of Operations: Michael Silver
Year Founded: 2011
Number Employees: 10-19
Types of Products Distributed:
  General Line

55218 (HQ)Big State Vending Company
6201 Gulf Fwy
Houston, TX 77023-5602   713-923-5985
                    Fax: 713-923-9361
Wholesaler/distributor of vending equipment for coffee, tea, water, snacks, soups, hot chocolate; also, refrigerators, coolers, microwaves, etc
Owner/President: Don Camp
Sales Manager: Jean Dominik
General Manager: Jerry Riggs
Number Employees: 50-99
Types of Products Distributed:
  Frozen Food, General Merchandise, Vending equipment

55219 Big Valley Marketing Corporation
PO Box 14175
Fremont, CA 94539-1375   510-651-2270
                    Fax: 510-651-2436
Wholesaler/distributor of frozen fruits and vegetables; serving the food service market
President: Rod Bentley
Estimated Sales: $20-50 Million
Number Employees: 20-49
Types of Products Distributed:
  Food Service, Frozen Food, Frozen fruits & vegetables

55220 Bilas Distributing Company
32340 Arlington Drive
Beverly Hills, MI 48025-4218   248-646-1030
Wholesaler/distributor of portable drinking water treatment units and antiseptics
President: Michael Bilas
VP: Nancy Bilas
Estimated Sales: $.5-1 million
Number Employees: 1-4
Private Brands Carried:
  Hzok; Hike
Types of Products Distributed:
  Frozen Food, General Merchandise, Portable drinking water treatment units

55221 Bill's Seafood
9016 Belair Rd
Baltimore, MD 21236-2120   410-256-9520
                    Fax: 410-256-3491
              www.billsseafoodandcatering.net
Seafood
Owner: Bill Paulshock
bscrabs@aol.com
Estimated Sales: $5-10 Million
Number Employees: 20-49

55222 (HQ)Billingsgate Fish Company
1941 Uxbridge Drive NW
Calgary, AB T2N 2V2
Canada   403-571-7700
    Fax: 403-571-7717 www.billingsgate.com
Processor and packager of fish, meat and deli products; wholesaler/distributor of meats and seafood; serving the food service market. Founded in 1966.
President/Board Member: Bryan Fallwell
Sales Representative: Brenda Shreindorfer
Operations Manager: Mark Puffer
Estimated Sales: $2.8 Million
Number Employees: 20
Square Footage: 140000
Type of Packaging: Consumer, Food Service
Other Locations:
  Billingsgate Fish Company
  Edmonton, AlbertaBillingsgate Fish CompanySt. Albert, Alberta
Types of Products Distributed:
  Food Service, Frozen Food, Provisions/Meat, Seafood

55223 Billy's Seafood Inc
16780 River Rd
Bon Secour, AL 36511-3428   251-949-6288
    Fax: 251-949-6505   888-424-5597
    billys@gulftel.com www.billys-seafood.com
Seafood
Owner: Billy Parks
billys@gulftel.com
Estimated Sales: $2,000,000
Number Employees: 1-4

55224 Binghamton Material Handling
295 Court St # 2
Binghamton, NY 13904-3621   607-723-3456
         Fax: 607-723-6070   800-345-5271
                    sales@bmhinc.com
Wholesaler/distributor of containers, carts, hand trucks, conveyors, racks and shelving
President: John Foley
Controller: Jeff Lubs
Sales Director: Chris Burke
Estimated Sales: $5-10 Million
Number Employees: 10-19
Square Footage: 180000
Types of Products Distributed:
  Frozen Food, General Merchandise, Containers, racks, shelving, etc.

55225 Bintz Restaurant SupplyCompany
P.O.Box 1350
Salt Lake City, UT 84110-1350   801-463-1515
         Fax: 801-463-1693   800-443-4746
         sales@bintzsupply.com www.bintzsupply.com
Wholesaler/distributor and design consultant of hotel and restaurant equipment and supplies
President: Roger Brown
CFO: Troy Hanson
Vice President: Brad Garner
Sales Manager: Michael Bailey
Purchasing Manager: Christie Smith
Estimated Sales: $10-20 Million
Number Employees: 20-49
Square Footage: 40000
Number of Customer Locations: 4000
Types of Products Distributed:
  Frozen Food, General Merchandise, Restaurant equipment & supplies

55226 Bioriginal Food and Science Corp
102 Melville Street
Saskatoon, SK S7J 0R1
Canada   306-975-1166
    Fax: 306-242-3829 business@bioriginal.com
                    www.bioriginal.com
Essential fatty acids, omega 3, omega 6, and omega 9.
President/CEO: Joe Vidal
EVP Global Marketing/Sales: Johan Kamphuis
VP Operations: Cameron Kupper

55227 Bioscience International Inc
11333 Woodglen Dr
Rockville, MD 20852-3071   301-231-7400
    Fax: 301-231-7277 bioinfo@biosci-intl.com
                    www.biosci-intl.com
Manufacturer and wholesaler/distributor of microbial air samplers for the food and beverage industry.
President: Don Queen
VP: Marsha Pratt
Customer Service: Don Queen
Number Employees: 1-4
Square Footage: 140000
Types of Products Distributed:
  Frozen Food, General Merchandise, Testing & sampling instrumentation

55228 Biostim LLC
111 Staffel St
Boerne, TX 78006-2547   830-331-9878
         Fax: 210-822-7717   800-338-8812
                    www.biostim.com
Wholesaler/distributor of microbial plumbing products
Manager: Bonnie Andrews
sales@biostim.com
Managing Director: David Johnson
Estimated Sales: Less Than $500,000
Number Employees: 5-9
Private Brands Carried:
  Natural Recyclen
Number of Customer Locations: 3000
Types of Products Distributed:
  Frozen Food, General Merchandise, Microbial products

55229 Birchwood Meats
1821 Dividend Dr
Columbus, OH 43228-3848   614-771-1330
         Fax: 614-771-9590   800-541-1685
                    www.birchwood.com
Wholesaler/distributor of provisions/meats; serving the food service market
President: Charlie Vigneri
VP: Richard Baker
Contact: Lorena Holiday
lorenah@bwfoocs.com
Plant Manager: Troy Maynard
Estimated Sales: $20-50 Million
Number Employees: 100-249
Parent Co: Birchwood Meats
Number of Customer Locations: 1150
Types of Products Distributed:
  Food Service, Frozen Food, Provisions/Meat

55230 Birdie Pak Products
3925 W 31st St
Chicago, IL 60623-4934   773-247-5293
    Fax: 773-247-4280 www.birdiepak.com
Processor and distributor of frozen beef, poultry and fish
President: Thomas Krueger
VP: Kevin Krueger
Estimated Sales: $2.5-5 Million
Number Employees: 10-19
Type of Packaging: Consumer, Food Service, Private Label
Types of Products Distributed:
  Frozen Food

55231 Birdseye Dairy-Morning Glory
2325 Memorial Dr
Green Bay, WI 54303-6399   920-494-5388
    Fax: 920-494-4388 www.birdseyejuice.com
Apple and orange juice; wholesaler/distributor of dairy products including milk, ice cream, butter and sour cream; serving the food service market. Founded in 1925.
President: Steven Williams
steve.williamss@birdseye.com
Estimated Sales: $10-20 Million
Number Employees: 10-19
Type of Packaging: Consumer, Food Service, Private Label, Bulk
Types of Products Distributed:
  Food Service, General Line, Milk, ice cream, butter & sour cream

55232 Birdsong Peanuts
307 E Commerce St
Hartford, AL 36344-1712   334-588-2252
                    Fax: 334-588-0330
Wholesaler/distributor of raw and shelled peanuts

Wholesalers & Distributors / A-Z

Manager: Todd Smith
Manager: Alice Mowbray
Site Manager: Todd Smith
Estimated Sales: $1-2.5 Million
Number Employees: 5-9
Parent Co: Alabama Farmers Cooperative
Type of Packaging: Private Label
Private Brands Carried:
  Anderson's Peanuts
Types of Products Distributed:
  Frozen Food, Produce, Raw & shelled peanuts

55233 (HQ)Birmingham Vending Games
540 2nd Ave N
Birmingham, AL 35204-4715   850-234-3693
Fax: 205-322-6639   800-288-7635
www.funland-arcade.com
Wholesaler/distributor of coin-operated amusement and vending machines
Owner: Steven Toranto
VP: Jerry Speiegelman
VP: Steven Turanto
Contact: Danny Robinson
drobinson@bhmvending.com
General Manager: Gary Gouse
Estimated Sales: $20-50 Million
Number Employees: 10-19
Square Footage: 50000
Other Locations:
  Birmingham Vending Co.
  Orlando, FLBirmingham Vending Co.
Types of Products Distributed:
  Frozen Food, General Merchandise, Vending & amusement machines

55234 Birnn Chocolates of Vermont
102 Kimball Ave
Suite 4
South Burlington, VT 05403
Fax: 802-860-1256   800-338-3141
www.birnn.com
Premium wholesale truffles
President: H Birnn
bh@birnn.com
Co-Owner: Bill Birnn
VP: Bill Birnn
Estimated Sales: $2 Million
Number Employees: 20-49
Type of Packaging: Private Label

55235 Bisek & Co Inc
4873 S Oliver Dr # 200
Suite 200
Virginia Beach, VA 23455-2700   757-460-0968
Fax: 757-460-2185   craig@bisek.com
www.bisek.com
Bisek & Company is a distributing agent and broker to U.S. military commissary stores worldwide and handles all brand name grocery store products including such items as confectionery, dairy/deli products, frozen foods, spicesseafood, meats and meat products, etc.
President/CEO: Craig Bisek
bisek@bisek.com
Marketing: Laurie Cust
SVP Sales: Don Stickles
Operations: Jennifer Harrell
Estimated Sales: $2.9 Million
Number Employees: 10-19
Square Footage: 5000
Type of Packaging: Consumer
Types of Products Distributed:
  Frozen Food, General Line, Health Food, Seafood, Specialty Foods

55236 Bishop Brothers
113 W 5th Ave
Bristow, OK 74010-2824   918-367-2270
Fax: 918-367-2270   800-859-8304
info@bishoptaboli.com   www.bishoptaboli.com
Wholesaler/distributor of bulgur wheat including tabbouleh; custom packaging services available. Founded in 1962.
Owner: Eddie Bishop
ebishop07@aol.com
Estimated Sales: $2.5-5 Million
Number Employees: 1-4
Type of Packaging: Consumer, Food Service, Bulk
Private Brands Carried:
  Steakhouse Taboli Wheat/Steakhouse Salad Mix (Soft white bulgur wheat; Bishop Brothers
Types of Products Distributed:
  Food Service, General Merchandise, Health Food, Specialty Foods, Bulgur wheat: tabbouleh

55237 Bite Size Bakery
504 Frontage Rd NE
Rio Rancho, NM 87124   505-994-3093
www.bitesizebakery.com
Manufacturer of bite-sized cookies in a variety of flavours, including bizcochitos, pinon nut chocolate chip, lemon verde pistachio. ginger snap, and raisin oatmeal.
Owner: Lucia Deichmann
Parent Co: KDK Enterprises
Types of Products Distributed:
  Cookies

55238 Bizerba USA
5200 Anthony Rd # F
Suite F
Sandston, VA 23150-1929   804-649-2064
Fax: 804-649-2064   us.info@bizerba.com
www.bizerba.com
Packaging equipment
Vice President: Rainer Dallairosa
rainer.dallairosa@cporinc.com
CFO: Cheryll Ziemblicki
VP, Engineered Solutions: Rainer DallaRosa
Marketing Manager: Chuck Saje
Director Retail Systems: Robert Weisz
Operations Manager: Joanne Scuccimarri
Number Employees: 50-99

55239 Blachere Group
210 Holabird Ave
Winsted, CT 06098-1747   860-738-1100
Fax: 860-738-1103   800-641-4808
eva@blachere.com   www.blachere.com
Wholesaler/distributor and importer of stainless steel and French silverplated flatware, earthenware, holloware and china; serving the food service market
President: Eva Blachere
eva@blachere.com
Vice President: Jean Paul Blachere
Estimated Sales: Less than $500,000
Number Employees: 1-4
Types of Products Distributed:
  Food Service, Frozen Food, General Merchandise, Flatware, holloware & china

55240 Black Diamond Fruit & Produce
PO Box 386
Milton, WV 25541   304-525-8179
Fax: 304-781-6818   800-624-3579
www.supervalu.com
Wholesaler/distributor of produce
President/CEO: Sam Duncan
EVP/CFO: Bruce Besanko
EVP/Chief Information Officer: Randy Burdick
EVP, General Counsel, Corp. Secretary: Karla Robertson
EVP, Chief Strategy Officer: Rob Woseth
EVP, Merchandising, Marketing & Retail: Mark Van Buskirk
EVP, Human Resources & Corp. Comm,: Michele Murphy
General Manager: Jerry Love
Estimated Sales: $10-20 Million
Number Employees: 20-49
Parent Co: SUPERVALU
Types of Products Distributed:
  Produce

55241 Black's Barbecue
215 N Main St
Lockhart, TX 78644-2121   512-398-2712
Fax: 512-398-6000   888-632-8225
info@blacksbbq.com   www.blacksbbq.com
Barbequed sausage; wholesaler/distributor of meats including brisket, ribs, chicken, pork and loin. Established in 2009.
Manager: Steve Cloud
CEO: Terry Black
Owner: Norma Black
Co-Owner: Edgar Black
Manager: Barrett Black
barrett@blacksbbq.com
Estimated Sales: $300,000-500,000
Number Employees: 5-9
Type of Packaging: Bulk
Types of Products Distributed:
  General Line, Provisions/Meat, Produce, Salads, etc.

55242 Blackbur Bros Inc
440 Lake Park Blvd N
Carolina Beach, NC 28428-4803   910-458-9001
Fax: 910-458-9703   www.blackburnseafood.com
Wholesaler/distributor of fresh seafood
President: R Blackburn
VP: William Blackburn
Marketing Manager: Bret Blackburn
Contact: Rc Blackburn
info@blackburnseafood.com
Estimated Sales: $1-2.5 Million
Number Employees: 5-9
Number of Customer Locations: 200
Types of Products Distributed:
  Frozen Food, Seafood

55243 Blackburn-Russell Co
157 Railroad St
Bedford, PA 15522-1014   814-623-5181
Fax: 814-623-1216   800-325-2815
www.blackburnrussell.com
Wholesaler/distributor of frozen foods, general line items and candy; serving the food service and retail markets
Owner: Jeff Blackburn
blackburnrussellcl@yahoo.com
VP: William Blackburn
Estimated Sales: $20-50 Million
Number Employees: 20-49
Number of Customer Locations: 400
Types of Products Distributed:
  Food Service, Frozen Food, General Line, Candy, etc.

55244 Blackwing Ostrich MeatsInc.
19588 Il Route 173
Antioch, IL 60002-7206   847-838-4888
Fax: 847-838-4899   800-326-7874
roger@blackwing.com   www.blackwing.com
Organic beef, chicken, buffalo, ostrich and game meats
President/Owner: Roger Gerber
VP: Beth Kaplan
bak@blackwing.com
Estimated Sales: $12 Million
Number Employees: 26
Number of Brands: 5
Number of Products: 140
Square Footage: 32000
Type of Packaging: Consumer, Food Service, Private Label, Bulk
Private Brands Carried:
  Blackwing, Buffalo Valley Farms
Number of Customer Locations: 12000
Types of Products Distributed:
  Frozen Food, Provisions/Meat

55245 Blake's All Natural Foods
178 Silk Farm Rd
Concord, NH 03301-8411   603-225-3532
Fax: 603-225-3390   info@blakesallnatural.com
www.blakesallnatural.com
Frozen natural, organic and family-sized meals
CEO: Sean M Connolly
sean@blakesallnature.com
Number Employees: 20-49

55246 Blake's Creamery Inc
46 Milford St
Manchester, NH 03102-4799   603-623-7242
Fax: 603-623-7244   www.blakesicecream.com
Dairy distributor.
Owner: Ann Mirageas
jordan957@hotmail.com
Estimated Sales: $6.7 Million
Number Employees: 100-249
Number of Products: 80
Type of Packaging: Consumer, Food Service, Private Label, Bulk
Types of Products Distributed:
  Frozen Food

55247 Blalock Seafood & Specialty
24822 Canal Rd
Orange Beach, AL 36561-3894   251-974-5811
Fax: 251-974-5812
Manufacturer and wholesaler of seafood. Founded in 1992.
Owner: Pete Blalock
pblalock419@gmail.com
Estimated Sales: $4,000,000
Number Employees: 5-9
Type of Packaging: Consumer

Wholesalers & Distributors / A-Z

55248 Blanc Industries
88 King St # 1
Dover, NJ 07801-3655   973-537-0090
Fax: 973-537-0906 888-332-5262
email@blancind.com www.blancind.com
Manufacture, design and print point of sale promotional signage, displays and fixtures for the food and retail industry. Founded in 1997.
President: Didier Blanc
dblanc@blancind.com
Operations: Dorothy Vitiello
Number Employees: 20-49

55249 Blanke Bob Sales Inc
1549 Helton Dr
Florence, AL 35630-2400   256-764-5983
Wholesaler/distributor of frozen foods; serving the food service market
President: Henry T Blanke
Estimated Sales: $20-50 Million
Number Employees: 10-19
Private Brands Carried:
  Frosty Acres
Number of Customer Locations: 500
Types of Products Distributed:
  Food Service, Frozen Food

55250 Blazer Concepts
120 Fulton St
New York, NY 10038-2775   212-962-2517
Fax: 212-962-4049 800-841-7507
Wholesaler/distributor of uniforms
Owner: Brian Levinsohn
Estimated Sales: Less than $500,000
Number Employees: 1-4
Types of Products Distributed:
  Frozen Food, General Merchandise, Uniforms

55251 Blondie's
4601 Jennings Ln # 5
Louisville, KY 40218-2964   502-454-4626
Fax: 502-454-6115
Wholesaler/distributor of produce; serving the food service market
President: Alice Fink
Estimated Sales: $500,000-$1 Million
Number Employees: 1-4
Types of Products Distributed:
  Food Service, Produce

55252 Bloom Honey
          805-379-0040
          877-555-9300
www.bloomhoney.com
Raw honey
President/Owner: David Jefferson
Number of Brands: 1
Number of Products: 8
Type of Packaging: Consumer

55253 Bloomfield Farms
575 Spencer Mattingly Ln
Bardstown, KY 40004-9103   502-348-0012
Fax: 502-348-7711 www.thebloomfieldfarms.com
Gluten free mixes including brownies, pancakes, pizza dough and cake mixes
Manager: Davis Chesser
davisc@blendpak.com
Number Employees: 10-19

55254 Blue Bottle Coffee Co
300 Webster St
Oakland, CA 94607-4122   510-653-3394
support@bluebottlecoffee.com
www.bluebottlecoffee.com
Coffee, coffee grinders and brewers
Number Employees: 20-49

55255 Blue Buoy Foods
PO Box 1198
Lewisporte, NL A0G 3A0
Canada   709-535-6908
Fax: 709-535-2828
Wholesaler/distributor of frozen foods, groceries, provisions/meats and seafood; serving the food service market
Manager: Sid Manuel
Number Employees: 10-19
Parent Co: Blue Buoy Foods
Number of Customer Locations: 600
Types of Products Distributed:
  Food Service, Frozen Food, General Line, Provisions/Meat, Seafood, Groceries

55256 Blue Chip Cookies
5991 Meijer Dr
Suite 24
Milford, OH 45150-1531   513-697-6610
Fax: 513-297-9494 800-888-9866
www.bluechipcookiesdirect.com
Manufacturer and wholesaler of fresh baked cookies
President/Chief Cookie Officer: Donna Drury
Estimated Sales: Less Than $500,000
Number Employees: 1-4

55257 Blue Delft Supply
PO Box 211
Wausaukee, WI 54177-0211   715-856-6227
Wholesaler/distributor of bar and restaurant supplies including smallwares and paper products; serving the food service market
Owner: Shirley Hawley
Estimated Sales: Less than $500,000
Number Employees: 1-4
Types of Products Distributed:
  Food Service, Frozen Food, General Merchandise, Smallwares & paper products

55258 Blue Diamond Growers
1802 C St.
Sacramento, CA 95811
          800-987-2329
www.bluediamond.com
Processor, grower and exporter of almonds, macadamians, pistachios and hazelnuts. Two thousand almond products in many cuts, styles, sizes and shapes for use in confectionery, bakery, dairy and processed foods. In house R/D for customproducts.
President/Chief Executive Officer: Mark Jansen
Chairman of The Board: Clinton Shick
CFO: Dean LaVallee
Vice Chairman: Dale Van Groningen
Quality Assurance Lab Manager: Steven Phillips
Director, Marketing: Al Greenlee
Manager, Communications: Cassandra Keyse
Manager, Operations: Bruce Lisch
Manager, Product Development: Mike Stoddard
Senior Vice President, Procurement: David Hills
Year Founded: 1910
Estimated Sales: $709 Million
Number Employees: 1,100
Type of Packaging: Consumer, Food Service, Private Label, Bulk

55259 Blue Harbour Cheese
P.O. Box 46011 Novalea
Halifax, NS B3K 5V8
Canada   902-240-0305
info@blueharbourcheese.com
www.blueharbourcheese.com
Cheese
Cheese Maker: Lyndell Findlay
Types of Products Distributed:
  Cheese

55260 Blue Line Foodservice Distr
24120 Haggerty Rd
Farmington Hills, MI 48335-2645   248-478-6200
Fax: 248-442-4570 800-892-8272
www.bluelinedist.com
Wholesaler/distributor of equipment; serving the food service market
Owner: Michael Ilitch
militch@bluelinedist.com
Marketing: Lisa Davis
Estimated Sales: $500,000-$1 Million
Number Employees: 50-99
Types of Products Distributed:
  Food Service, Frozen Food, General Merchandise, Equipment

55261 Blue Mountain Meats Inc.
333 South 200 East
PO Box 279
Monticello, UT 84535-0279   435-587-2289
Fax: 435-587-2179 800-437-3448
scottfrost@bluemountainmeats.com
www.bluemountainmeats.com
Wholesaler/distributor of groceries, produce, frozen foods, dairy and bakery items, mutton, seafood, general merchandise, etc.; serving the food service market
President: Scott Frost
VP: Allen Frost
Marketing: Tom Tibbs
Sales Director: Troy Tibbs
General Manager: Doug Hall
Estimated Sales: $5-10 Million
Number Employees: 20-49
Square Footage: 80000
Type of Packaging: Consumer, Food Service, Private Label, Bulk
Private Brands Carried:
  Bar S; Hormel; Tyson; Commsource
Number of Customer Locations: 300
Types of Products Distributed:
  Food Service, Frozen Food, Provisions/Meat, Produce, Mutton, bakery & dairy items, etc.

55262 Blue Rhino Compaction Services
4711 E Falcon Drive
Suite 151
Mesa, AZ 85215-2593   800-894-1988
Fax: 623-218-1273
Wholesaler/distributor of compaction and recycling equipment and balers
President: John King
Marketing Director: Michael Gallob
Number Employees: 5-9
Private Brands Carried:
  Sanitac; JV
Types of Products Distributed:
  Frozen Food, General Merchandise, Recycling equipment

55263 Blue Ribbon Fish Co
800 Food Center Dr # 67
Unit 67
Bronx, NY 10474-0041   718-620-8580
www.blueribbonfish.com
Importer and wholesaler/distributor of seafood; serving the food service market
Partner/VP: Bob Samuels
Estimated Sales: $2.5-5 Million
Number Employees: 5-9
Types of Products Distributed:
  Food Service, Frozen Food, Seafood

55264 Blue Ribbon Meats
3316 W 67th Pl
Cleveland, OH 44102   216-631-8850
Fax: 216-631-8934 800-262-0395
www.blueribbonmeats.com
Meat and seafood.
President: Al Radis
Year Founded: 1948
Estimated Sales: $20-50 Million
Number Employees: 100-249
Number of Customer Locations: 13
Types of Products Distributed:
  Food Service, Frozen Food, Provisions/Meat

55265 Blue Ribbon Wholesale
14333 Diplomat Dr
Tampa, FL 33613-3100   813-966-4965
Fax: 813-247-5316
Wholesaler/distributor of provisions and meats, seafood and frozen food
Owner: Ralph Bobo
Estimated Sales: $300,000-500,000
Number Employees: 1-4
Types of Products Distributed:
  Frozen Food, Provisions/Meat, Seafood

55266 Blue Ridge Poultry
396 Foundry Street
Athens, GA 30601   706-546-6767
Fresh and frozen poultry including turkey; wholesaler/distributor of poultry and eggs
President: Robert Harris
Estimated Sales: $1-3 Million
Number Employees: 5-9
Square Footage: 18000
Type of Packaging: Consumer
Number of Customer Locations: 200
Types of Products Distributed:
  Frozen Food, General Line, Provisions/Meat, Poultry & eggs

55267 Bluefin Seafoods
617 E Washington St
Louisville, KY 40202-1048   502-587-1505
Fax: 502-561-0286 www.bluefinseafood.com
Owner: Ken Berry
kenberry@bluefinseafoods.com
Estimated Sales: $20-50 Million
Number Employees: 20-49

Wholesalers & Distributors / A-Z

55268 (HQ)Blum & Bergeron, Inc.
7016 Alma St
Houma, LA 70364-2696   985-868-3810
    Fax: 985-873-8884 blumbergeron@bellsouth.net
Packer and shipper of dried shrimp, whole and ground. Also fish bind and animal food
Owner: Joe Blum Jr
CEO: Thomas Cobb
Estimated Sales: $5-10 Million
Number Employees: 20-49
Number of Brands: 2
Number of Products: 1
Type of Packaging: Bulk

55269 Bmh Equipment Inc
1217 Blumenfeld Dr
P.O. Box 162109
Sacramento, CA 95815-3903   916-922-8828
    Fax: 916-922-8820 800-350-8828
    www.bmhe.com
Distributor/exporter of custom material handling equipment, hand trucks, casters, conveyor systems, dollies, pallet jacks and racks, aluminum ramps, dock boards, shelving and work tables; design and engineering for nonstandard materialhandling problems
President: Jack Alexander
jackalex@bmhequipment.com
VP: Jerry Berg
Conveyor Specialist: Richard Wales
Estimated Sales: $2.5-5 Million
Number Employees: 10-19
Square Footage: 20800
Private Brands Carried:
    Colson; Darnell; Dutro; Rubbermaid; Intermetro; Jilson; Tente
Types of Products Distributed:
    Frozen Food, General Merchandise, Shelving, hand trucks, carts, casters

55270 Bnutty
Merrillville, IN 46410   844-426-8889
    bnutty.com
Gourmet peanut butter
Number Employees: 1-4
Number of Products: 12
Type of Packaging: Consumer, Private Label

55271 Bode-Finn Company
2160 Karla Ave
Cincinnati, OH 45211-8167   513-661-2200
    Fax: 513-853-8458
Wholesaler/distributor of material handling equipment, aerial work platforms, waste reduction and recycling equipment and turn key systems
President: Charles Raterman
VP of Marketing: Bob Risheill
Estimated Sales: $.5-1 million
Number Employees: 1-4
Square Footage: 112000
Parent Co: Nations Rent
Private Brands Carried:
    Hyster; Gente
Types of Products Distributed:
    Frozen Food, General Merchandise, Material handling equipment

55272 Bodean Restaurant & Market
3376 E 51st St
Tulsa, OK 74135-3512   918-749-1407
    Fax: 918-747-9543 www.bodean.net
Wholesaler/distributor of seafood; serving the food service and retail markets
Owner: Kieron St Ledger
kieron@bodean.net
Estimated Sales: $1-2.5 Million
Number Employees: 50-99
Number of Customer Locations: 45
Types of Products Distributed:
    Food Service, Frozen Food, Seafood

55273 Boelter Companies
N22w23685 Ridgeview Pkwy W
Waukesha, WI 53188   414-535-4796
    800-392-3278
    www.boelter.com
Wholesaler/distributor of restaurant equipment supplies including chinaware, glassware, disposables, stoves, pizza ovens, utility carts, coffee urns, mats, etc
Owner: Bill Boelter
Estimated Sales: $20-50 Million
Number Employees: 100-249

Types of Products Distributed:
    Frozen Food, General Merchandise, Chinaware, glassware, ovens, mats, etc.

55274 Boeuf Merite
11701 Rue Albert-Hudon
Montreal Nord, QC H1G 3K6
Canada   514-328-8000
    Fax: 514-328-8033 800-361-5622
Wholesaler/distributor of meats and frozen foods
VP: Lawrence Timmons
Sales Manager: Richard Erbour
Purchasing Manager: Paul Renaud
Parent Co: Metro-Richelieu 2000
Number of Customer Locations: 900
Types of Products Distributed:
    Frozen Food, Provisions/Meat

55275 Bolton & Hay
2701 Delaware Ave
Des Moines, IA 50317-3590   515-265-2554
    Fax: 515-265-6090 800-362-1861
info@boltonhay.com www.boltonhay.com
Wholesaler/distributor of new and used food service equipment and supplies; installation services available
President: Lew Bolton
clarac@boltonhay.com
Vice President: John Speicher
Sales Director: Darrell Bower
Estimated Sales: $5-10 Million
Number Employees: 10-19
Square Footage: 120000
Types of Products Distributed:
    General Merchandise, New & used foodservice equipment, etc.

55276 Bon Appetit Gourmet Foods
7863 W Mossy Cup St # A
Boise, ID 83709-2987   208-345-0475
    Fax: 208-384-5461
Distributor of frozen food.
Owner: John Lee
Estimated Sales: $1-3 Million
Number Employees: 5-9

55277 Bon Appetit International
3737 Savannah Loop
Oviedo, FL 32765-9204   407-366-4973
    Fax: 407-359-8861 800-473-3513
info@bonappetit-int.com www.bonappetit-int.com
Wholesaler/distributor and importer of smoked, marinated and frozen portion control salmon; exporter of countertop display cases and smoked salmon
President: Mick Chandler
VP: Marcelle Simon
Number Employees: 1-4
Parent Co: Trade Europe
Type of Packaging: Consumer, Food Service
Types of Products Distributed:
    Frozen Food, Seafood, Salmon

55278 Bon Secour Fisheries Inc
17449 County Road 49 S
Bon Secour, AL 36511   251-949-7411
    Fax: 251-949-6478
bonsec@bonsecourfisheries.com
    www.bonsecourfisheries.com
Fresh and frozen flounder, whiting, snapper, shrimp, oysters, scallops, crawfish, snow, soft shell and king crab, lobster, cod, catfish, tuna, grouper, pollock, shark, mahi, talapia, etc.; also, alligator meat.
CFO: Melani Parker
Vice President: Chris Nelson
Director, Sales: Leon Russell
Procurement Manager: Robert Eckerle
Year Founded: 1896
Estimated Sales: $25.10 Million
Number Employees: 100-249
Square Footage: 60000
Type of Packaging: Consumer, Food Service, Bulk
Private Brands Carried:
    Bon Secour Brand; Nelson's Brand; Chef's Choice Brand; King O' Seas Brand
Types of Products Distributed:
    Frozen Food, Seafood

55279 Bon Ton Food Products
910 M St NW Apt 1130
Washington, DC 20001-6337
    Fax: 301-779-9826
Wholesaler/distributor of snack food; serving the food service market

President: Patrick Welch
VP: P Hollins
Estimated Sales: $20-50 Million
Number Employees: 20-49
Number of Customer Locations: 2500
Types of Products Distributed:
    Food Service, Frozen Food, General Line, Rack Jobbers, Specialty Foods, Snack food

55280 Bon Ton Products
275 E Hintz Rd
Wheeling, IL 60090-6002   847-520-8300
Meat buyer, boxed beef and pork cuts.
Owner: George Christie
Marketing Director: Dave Centino
Human Resources Executive: Leslie Baker
Manager: James Cristy
Estimated Sales: $17 Million
Number Employees: 5-9

55281 Bono Burns DistributingInc
3616 S Big Bend Blvd
St Louis, MO 63143-4092   314-644-6166
    Fax: 314-644-1401 800-873-2666
    www.bonoburns.com
Wholesaler/distributor of smallwares and baking equipment; also, cake mixes, pie fillings, frozen dough, etc
President: Jerry Burns
gburnes@bonoburns.com
Estimated Sales: $10-20 Million
Number Employees: 20-49
Types of Products Distributed:
    Frozen Food, General Line, General Merchandise, Bakery mixes & equipment

55282 Booker Promotions
1753 Tullie Cir NE
Atlanta, GA 30329-2305   404-321-5511
    Fax: 404-321-4902 800-226-9321
sales@bookerpromo.com www.bookerpromo.co
Wholesaler/distributor of advertising specialties
Owner: Neil Kalnitz
CSR Manager: Irwin Kelly
nkalnitz@bookerpromo.com
Estimated Sales: $1-2.5 Million
Number Employees: 5-9
Number of Customer Locations: 3000
Types of Products Distributed:
    Frozen Food, General Merchandise, Advertising specialties

55283 Boone's Wholesale
4695 Mountain Lakes Boulevard
Redding, CA 96003-1450   530-241-4631
    Fax: 530-241-6980
Wholesaler/distributor of groceries, paper, frozen foods, restaurant equipment and chemicals; serving the food service market
President: A Burker
Estimated Sales: $10-20 Million
Number Employees: 50-99
Square Footage: 106000
Number of Customer Locations: 1500
Types of Products Distributed:
    Food Service, Frozen Food, General Line, General Merchandise, Groceries, paper, etc.

55284 Boothbay Lobster Wharf
97 Atlantic Ave
Boothbay Harbor, ME 04538-2220   207-633-4900
    Fax: 207-633-4077
    sales@boothbaylobsterwharf.com
Lobster
Owner: Kim Simmons
ksimmons@boothbaylobsterwharf.com
Estimated Sales: Less Than $500,000
Number Employees: 1-4

55285 Boricua Empaque
S Puerta De Tierra
P.O. Box 9021741
San Juan, PR 00902-1741   787-723-5366
    Fax: 787-722-3567 bempaque@spiderlink.net
Wholesaler/distributor and importer of biscuits, cookies, groceries, canned seafood and general merchandise including bags and dinnerware
President/Chairman: J Llanos-Pinera
Treasurer/Secretary: A Llanos
Number Employees: 20-49
Square Footage: 120000
Type of Packaging: Consumer
Private Brands Carried:
    Orchids Paper Products, Inc.; Industrias

Wholesalers & Distributors / A-Z

Alimenticias Noel S.A.; Compania Nacional De Chocolates; Argo Industries Inca S.A.
Types of Products Distributed:
General Line, General Merchandise, Seafood, Biscuits, groceries, dinnerware, etc.

55286 Bosch Distributors
9415 Philadelphia Rd
Baltimore, MD 21237 410-391-7700
Fax: 410-682-5207
Wholesaler/distributor of janitorial and disposable paper supplies and dry groceries; serving the food service market
President: C Bosch
VP: Sharon Hershey
Estimated Sales: $10-20 Million
Number Employees: 5-9
Number of Customer Locations: 1000
Types of Products Distributed:
Food Service, Frozen Food, General Line, General Merchandise

55287 Bosco Food Service
P.O.Box 547
Bay City, MI 48707-0547 989-892-1052
Fax: 989-892-0010 800-892-6726
Wholesaler/distributor of meat, frozen food, produce and equipment and supplies; serving the food service market
President: Michael Bosco
VP: David Bosco
VP: Richard Bosco
Estimated Sales: $10-20 Million
Number Employees: 10-19
Private Brands Carried:
Nugget
Number of Customer Locations: 250
Types of Products Distributed:
Food Service, Frozen Food, General Merchandise, Provisions/Meat, Produce, Equipment & supplies

55288 Bosgraaf Sales Company
5501 40th Ave
Hudsonville, MI 49426-9467 616-669-8211
Fax: 616-669-3474
Wholesaler/distributor of produce
President: James Van Overloop
Contact: James Meyer
jmeyer@bosgraaf.com
Estimated Sales: $500,000-$1 Million
Number Employees: 20-49
Types of Products Distributed:
Frozen Food, Produce

55289 Boston Coffee Cake
351 Willow Street South
North Andover, MA 01845
800-434-0500
customerservice@bostoncoffeecake.com
www.bostoncoffeecake.com
Coffee cake
Founder: Mark Forman
customerservice@bostoncoffeecake.com

55290 Boston Direct Lobsters
207 Iris Ave
Jefferson, LA 70121-2807 504-834-6404
Fax: 504-834-6404
Lobsters
President/Owner: Earl Duke
directlobster@aol.com
Estimated Sales: $340,000
Number Employees: 1-4

55291 Boston Lobster Co
345 W 1st St # 1
Boston, MA 02127-1386 617-464-1500
Fax: 617-464-1131
www.bostonlobstercompany.com
Wholesaler/distributor of seafood including live and cooked lobster and fresh lobster meat
Owner/President: A Zarella
CEO/ Owner: Neil Zarella
nzarella@bostonlobstercompany.com
Sales: Lee Smith
Production: R Behrman
Estimated Sales: $10-20 Million
Number Employees: 20-49
Square Footage: 26000
Types of Products Distributed:
Frozen Food, Seafood, Live & cooked lobster & lobster meat

55292 Boston Sausage & Provision
7 Wells Avenue
Newton Center, MA 02459 508-647-0558
Wholesaler/distributor and exporter of eggs, seafood, fresh and frozen beef, poultry and pork; importer of beef
President/CEO: Arthur Weiss
arthur@bostonagrex.com
VP: Joe Valdivia
Manager International Sales: J Cochran
Estimated Sales: $20-50 Million
Number Employees: 12
Square Footage: 2000
Types of Products Distributed:
Frozen Food, General Line, Provisions/Meat, Seafood, Eggs & poultry

55293 Boston Seafarms
119 Marlborough Street
Boston, MA 2116 617-784-4777
Fax: 800-692-9907 bostonseafarms@gmail.com
www.bostonseafarm.com
Processor, wholesaler/distributor, importer and exporter of seafood including fish and shellfish
President/CEO: Adam Weinberg
bostonseafarms@gmail.com
Estimated Sales: $12-13,000,000
Number Employees: 5
Square Footage: 36000
Types of Products Distributed:
Frozen Food, Seafood, Fish & shellfish

55294 Boston Showcase Company
66 Winchester Road
Newton, MA 02461 617-965-1100
Fax: 617-965-6326 800-422-5290
info@bostonshowcase.com
www.bostonshowcase.com
Wholesaler/distributor of restaurant equipment and supplies; serving the food service market
President: Alan Starr
Co-Owner: Jack Starr
Co-Owner: Alan Starr
Purchasing Agent: Jeff Segal
Estimated Sales: $5-10 Million
Number Employees: 20-49
Private Brands Carried:
Magi Kitchen; Lakeside; Vollrath; Oneida; Hall China Co.
Types of Products Distributed:
Food Service, Frozen Food, General Merchandise, Equipment & supplies

55295 Botanical Bakery, LLC
PO Box 11083
Napa, CA 94581 707-344-8103
Fax: 707-863-8949
Shortbread cookies.
CEO: Sondra Wells

55296 Boteilho Hawaii Enterprises
PO Box 190
Hawi, HI 96719-0190 808-889-5838
Wholesaler/distributor of fresh milk
President: Edward Boteilho
Estimated Sales: $1-2.5 Million
Number Employees: 10-19
Types of Products Distributed:
Frozen Food, General Line, Fresh milk

55297 Bottom Line Foods
15757 Pines Blvd # 302
Suite 302
Pembroke Pines, FL 33027-1207 954-843-0562
Fax: 954-843-0568
Distributor and packer, exporter for frozen foods, meats, cheese, groceries, seafood, spices, etc.
President: Rein Bos
General Manager: Brandon Koppert
Estimated Sales: $1.1 Million
Number Employees: 1-4
Square Footage: 4000
Type of Packaging: Food Service, Private Label, Bulk
Private Brands Carried:
TopLine; IBP; Tyson; Edward's; Rymer Meats
Types of Products Distributed:
Food Service, Frozen Food, Health Food, Provisions/Meat, Seafood, Specialty Foods, Dairy

55298 Boulangerie Pelletier
126 Rue Maltais
Sept-Iles, QC G4R 3J5
Canada 418-962-7711
Fax: 418-962-1148
Wholesaler/distributor of bread
President: J Pellatier
Manager: M Fortin
Number Employees: 10-19
Types of Products Distributed:
Frozen Food, General Line, Bread

55299 Boulder Brands, Inc.
115 West Century Road
Suite 260
Paramus, NJ 07652-1432 201-421-3970
Ed.Bryson@fleishman.com
www.smartbalance.com
Buttery spreads
President/COO: Terrence Schulke
Chairman/CEO: Stephen Hughes
Chief Finacial Officer: Christine Sacco
EVP/General Counsel: Norman Matar
Chief Innovation Officer: Peter Dray
Contact: Michael Adamson
madamson@boulderbrands.com
Estimated Sales: $1.5 Million
Number Employees: 56

55300 Boulder Fruit Express
17901 E. 40th Avenue
Aurora, CO 80011 303-666-4242
Fax: 303-666-0323 800-671-0707
tdenio@albertsorganics.com
www.albertsorganics.com
Distributor of quality organically grown products and perishables
President: Barclay Hope
Business Manager: Wade Pruter
Sales Director: Steve Versoi
Operations Manager: Tom Denio
Purchasing Manager: Brian Wheeler
Parent Co: United Natural Foods

55301 Boulder Sausage Co
513 S Pierce Ave
Louisville, CO 80027-3019 303-665-6302
Fax: 303-665-3109 866-529-0595
www.bouldersausage.com
Meat
Vice President: Tom Griffiths
bouldersausage@webaccess.net
Secretary/Treasurer: James Burton
Vice President: Donald Gullickson
Saleman Manager: Ronda Haire
Office Manager;Operations Manager: Suzanne Richards
Estimated Sales: $2.4,000,000
Number Employees: 20-49
Number of Products: 14
Type of Packaging: Consumer, Food Service, Private Label, Bulk

55302 Boutique Seafood Brokers
1326 White St SW
Atlanta, GA 30310-1648 404-752-8852
Fax: 404-752-6634 www.buckheadrestaurants.com
Seafood, red snapper, sea bass, lobster meat, crabmeat, grouper
President/CEO: Pano Karatassos
CFO: Christo Makrides
Senior Director of Marketing: Jennifer Parker
Director of Operations: Niko Karatassos
Estimated Sales: $4.5 Million
Number Employees: 1-4

55303 Bowlin J P Co LLC
3450 Alemeda St # 343
Fort Worth, TX 76126-9724 817-332-8116
Fax: 817-332-2145 www.jpbowlin.com
Wholesaler/distributor of scales and measurement equipment. Scales & calibration.
Manager: Billy Vaughn
billy@jpbowlin.com
VP: Warner Phillips
Sales Manager: Billy Vaughn
Estimated Sales: $5-10 Million
Number Employees: 5-9
Other Locations:
J.P. Bowlin Co.
Houston, TX J.P. Bowlin Co.
Types of Products Distributed:
Food Service, Frozen Food, General Merchandise, Scales

Wholesalers & Distributors / A-Z

55304 Bowman Produce
PO Box 188
Marsing, ID 83639-0188 208-896-4343
Fax: 208-896-4034 bowmprod@cyberhighway.net
Wholesaler/distributor and packer of onions
President: Jerry Bowman
CEO: Laura Bowman
Number Employees: 20-49
Number of Brands: 4
Number of Products: 1
Type of Packaging: Private Label
Types of Products Distributed:
 Frozen Food, General Line, Dried onions

55305 Boxed Meat Revolution
383 York Road
Guelph, ON N1E 3H3
Canada 519-822-6661
Fax: 519-821-6815 bmrKymm@hotmail.com
Wholesaler/distributor of fresh and frozen beef, pork and lamb
President: Roy Illerbrun
Private Brands Carried:
 Elmont; Snyders
Types of Products Distributed:
 Frozen Food, Provisions/Meat, Fresh & frozen beef, pork & lamb

55306 Boxer-Northwest Company
438 NW Broadway
Portland, OR 97209 503-226-1186
Fax: 503-226-6725 800-547-5700
Wholesaler/distributor of restaurant supplies and equipment; serving the food service market
President: Don Clarke
Controller: Tom Slick
Marketing Manager: Jim Cook
Contact: Roger Myers
rrdmyers@gmail.com
Purchasing Manager: Dino Arditi
Estimated Sales: $10-20 Million
Number Employees: 20-49
Types of Products Distributed:
 Food Service, Frozen Food, General Merchandise, Restaurant supplies & equipment

55307 (HQ)Boykin & Southern Wholesale Grocers
P.O.Box 1549
Wilson, NC 27894-1549 252-243-2131
Fax: 252-243-7599
Wholesaler/distributor of groceries, canned meat, candy, paper and cleaning products, etc.; serving the food service market
President: S Windham
VP: W Windham, Jr
Estimated Sales: $10-20 Million
Number Employees: 1-4
Other Locations:
 Boykin & Southern Wholesale G
 Wilson, NCBoykin & Southern Wholesale G
Number of Customer Locations: 200
Types of Products Distributed:
 Food Service, Frozen Food, General Line, General Merchandise, Groceries, canned meat, etc.

55308 Boyle Meat Company
1638 Saint Louis Ave
Kansas City, MO 64101-1130 816-221-6283
Fax: 816-221-3888 800-821-3626
theresa@boylescornedbeef.com
Steaks, corn beef, pastrami and pot roast
President: Don Wendl
Special Project Manager: James Crouch
VP: Christy Chester
Estimated Sales: $20-50 Million
Number Employees: 20-49
Square Footage: 10000
Type of Packaging: Food Service, Private Label, Bulk
Private Brands Carried:
 Boyle Meat (Supply To pricehopperhyVee)
Types of Products Distributed:
 Provisions/Meat

55309 Boyton Shellfish
RR 2
Box 85a
Ellsworth, ME 04605 207-667-8580
Fax: 619-474-6103
Shellfish
Owner: Dean Smith

55310 Bozzano Olive Ranch
6880 East Navone Road
PO Box 5009
Stockton, CA 95215 209-451-3665
Fax: 209-467-8362 info@bozzanoranch.com
www.bozzanoranch.com
Olive oils
President: Joe Bozzano
Vice President: Jack Bozzano
jack@bozzanoranch.com
Number Employees: 15

55311 Bozzuto's Inc.
275 Schoolhouse Rd.
Cheshire, CT 06410 203-272-3511
800-243-9761
www.bozzutos.com
General merchandise and general line products.
Chairman/Perident/CEO: Michael Bozzuto
mbuzzuto@buzzutos.com
Vice President/General Counsel: Kevin Daly
Year Founded: 1945
Estimated Sales: $1.7 Billion
Number Employees: 1000-4999
Private Brands Carried:
 Freshline; IGA; Real Value
Number of Customer Locations: 280
Types of Products Distributed:
 Frozen Food, General Line, General Merchandise, Rack Jobbers

55312 Brace Frozen Foods
1220 Ortega Road
West Palm Beach, FL 33405-1049 561-832-7013
Fax: 561-832-9459
Wholesaler/distributor of frozen foods; serving the food service market
Owner: Charlie Neal
Number Employees: 1-4
Types of Products Distributed:
 Food Service, Frozen Food

55313 Bradley Kitchen Center
120 Albert Street
Regina, SK S4R 2N2
Canada 306-545-8066
Fax: 306-545-8110
Wholesaler/distributor of small appliances, cookware and organic grain
President: John Bradley
Number Employees: 5-9
Private Brands Carried:
 Fissler; Bosch; Flatlander Grain
Types of Products Distributed:
 Frozen Food, General Line, General Merchandise, Small appliances, organic grain, etc.

55314 Bradshaw Homenc
9409 Buffalo Ave
Rancho Cucamonga, CA 91730 909-476-3884
Fax: 909-476-3616 sales@bradshawhome.com
www.bradshawintl.com
Wholesaler/distributor of imported kitchenware products; serving retail outlets worldwide.
Co-President: Brett Bradshaw
Chief Executive Officer: Mike Rodrigue
Chief Financial Officer: Jerry Vigliotti
SVP, Product Development: Thomas Barber
SVP, Marketing: Scott Weaver
VP, Distribution: Scott Stephenson
Year Founded: 1905
Estimated Sales: $48.90 Million
Number Employees: 250-499
Private Brands Carried:
 GoodCook, Betty Crocker, Bonny, Pro Professionals, Oneida, Bialetti, Butler, Dawn, Mr Clean, Black & Decker
Types of Products Distributed:
 Frozen Food, General Merchandise, Kitchenware products

55315 Braman Fruit Company
P.O.Box 1377
Grand Rapids, MI 49501 616-784-0738
Fax: 616-784-8288
Wholesaler/distributor of fresh apples
President: Tom Braman
Types of Products Distributed:
 Produce, Apples

55316 Branton Industries
PO Box 10536
New Orleans, LA 70181-0536 504-733-7770
Fax: 504-734-7818 www.distributionintl.com
Wholesaler/distributor of fired rated products for commercial and industrial kitchens; serving the food service market
Manager: Jerry Malter
VP: Jerry Malter
Number Employees: 20-49
Square Footage: 240000
Types of Products Distributed:
 Food Service, Frozen Food, General Merchandise, Fire rated products

55317 Brasco
1400 E Washington Ave
Jonesboro, AR 72401-3259 870-932-7483
Fax: 870-932-3571 800-535-9166
Wholesaler/distributor of food service equipment and supplies; serving the food service market
President: Pete Barker
VP: Gladys Barker
Estimated Sales: $2.5-5 Million
Number Employees: 5-9
Types of Products Distributed:
 Food Service, Frozen Food, General Merchandise, Foodservice equipment & supplies

55318 Braswell Distributing Co
500 Albemarle Ave
Tarboro, NC 27886-4303 252-823-2344
Fax: 252-823-3332 www.braswells.com
Wholesaler/distributor of groceries and industrial ingredients; serving the food service market; also, retail packaging available
President: A Owens
a@braswells.com
Estimated Sales: $1-2.5 Million
Number Employees: 5-9
Type of Packaging: Bulk
Number of Customer Locations: 300
Types of Products Distributed:
 Food Service, Frozen Food, General Line, Groceries & industrial ingredients

55319 Braswell's Winery
7556 Bankhead Highway
Dora, AL 35062-2041 205-648-8335
Fax: 205-648-8335
Wines
President: Wayne Braswell
Owner: Ruth Braswell
Estimated Sales: $1-4.9,000,000
Number Employees: 1-4

55320 Brauer Material Handling Systs
226 Molly Walton Dr
Hendersonville, TN 37075-2154 615-859-2930
Fax: 615-859-2937 800-645-6083
www.braueronline.com
Wholesaler/distributor of material handling equipment
President: Jeff Brauer
jeff@braueronline.com
Estimated Sales: F
Number Employees: 50-99
Types of Products Distributed:
 Frozen Food, General Merchandise, Material handling equipment

55321 Brawner Paper Co Inc
5702 Armour Dr
Houston, TX 77020-8007 713-675-6584
Fax: 713-673-6923 800-962-9384
info@brawnerpaper.com www.brawnerpaper.com
Wholesaler/distributor of cleaning supplies, disposables and wraps; serving the food service market
Owner: Leonard Beasley
lbeasley@brawnerpaper.com
Number Employees: 20-49
Types of Products Distributed:
 Food Service, Frozen Food, General Merchandise, Cleaning supplies, disposables & wraps

55322 Breads from Anna
3007 Sierra Ct
Iowa City, IA 52240 319-354-3886
Fax: 319-358-9920 877-354-3886
info@breadsfromanna.com breadsfromanna.com
Gluten- and allergen-free baking mixes.

55323 Breakwater Seafoods & Chowder
306 S F St
Aberdeen, WA 98520-4144 360-532-5693
Fax: 360-533-6488
Seafoods

Wholesalers & Distributors / A-Z

Owner: Sonny Bridges
President: Lloyd Bridges
Treasurer: Jack Thompson
Vice President: Linda Mertz
Estimated Sales: Less Than $500,000
Number Employees: 5-9

55324 Brenham Wholesale Groc Co Inc
602 W First St
Brenham, TX 77833
800-392-4869
customer@brenhamwholesale.com
www.brenhamwholesale.com
Wholesaler/distributor of groceries, meat, produce, dairy products, frozen foods, baked goods, equipment and fixtures, general merchandise, health and beauty aids, private label items, general line products and seafood; serving the food service market
Director of Sales: Jeremy Woodruff
Estimated Sales: $100-500 Million
Number Employees: 100-249
Square Footage: 200000
Number of Customer Locations: 1200
Types of Products Distributed:
  Food Service, Frozen Food, General Line, General Merchandise, Provisions/Meat, Produce, Groceries, etc.

55325 Bresco
2428 6th Ave S
Birmingham, AL 35233-3322   205-252-0076
Fax: 205-323-8630 800-344-2455
www.brescoinc.com
Wholesaler/distributor of ranges, refrigerators, walk-in coolers/freezers, china, silverware, pans, etc.; serving the food service market
President: George Tobia
gtobia@brescoinc.com
VP Engineering: W Steven Burke
VP Operations: Sam Howell
Estimated Sales: $10-20 Million
Number Employees: 50-99
Square Footage: 66000
Types of Products Distributed:
  Food Service, Frozen Food, General Merchandise, Ranges, refrigerators, etc.

55326 Bresco
2428 6th Ave S
Birmingham, AL 35233-3322   205-252-0076
Fax: 205-323-8630 sales@brescoinc.com
www.brescoinc.com
Wholesaler/distributor of restaurant equipment and supplies; design services available
President: George Tobia
gtobia@brescoinc.com
Estimated Sales: $10-20 Million
Number Employees: 50-99
Types of Products Distributed:
  Frozen Food, General Merchandise, Equipment & supplies

55327 Brevard Restaurant Equipment
565 Gus Hipp Blvd.
Rockledge, FL 32955-48   321-631-0318
Fax: 321-631-6040
Wholesaler/distributor of new and used equipment; serving the food service market; also, design and layout plans
President: John Schneider
VP: Diana Schneider
General Manager: Glenn Pierson
Estimated Sales: $1-2.5 Million
Number Employees: 1-4
Square Footage: 30000
Types of Products Distributed:
  Food Service, Frozen Food, General Merchandise, New & used equipment

55328 Brew Dr. Kombucha
PO Box 42291
Portland, OR 97242   760-487-8895
info@brekki.com
www.brekki.com
Kombucha
Founder & CEO: Matt Thomas
Number of Brands: 1
Number of Products: 5
Type of Packaging: Consumer

55329 Brewer Meats Inc
2418 Sunset Rd
Des Moines, IA 50321-1143   515-244-7788
Fax: 515-244-0571
Wholesaler/distributor of meats; serving the food service market
Owner: Phil Barber
Estimated Sales: $1-2.5 Million
Number Employees: 10-19
Types of Products Distributed:
  Food Service, Provisions/Meat

55330 Brewers Outlet-Chestnut Hill
7401 Germantown Ave
Philadelphia, PA 19119-1605   215-247-1265
Fax: 215-247-1855 info@mybrewersoutlet.com
www.mybrewersoutlet.com
Craft and specialty beers
Owner: Paul Egonopoulos
Estimated Sales: $2.5-5 Million
Number Employees: 5-9
Square Footage: 15000
Parent Co: Brewers Outlet

55331 Bridgeport Wholesale Producs
2624 112th St S
Lakewood, WA 98499-8890   253-272-3063
Fax: 425-656-0462 800-845-6653
Private label, manufacture, repackage, wholesale and distributor vitamins, minerals and OTC's, full line pharmaceuticals wholesalers
Owner: Jeff Wells
CEO: Charel Fisher
Marketing Director: Dave Westin
Sales Director: Marc Taylor
Operations Manager: Mike Downing
Estimated Sales: $300,000-500,000
Number Employees: 1-4
Number of Products: 250
Type of Packaging: Private Label, Bulk

55332 Bridgetown Coffee
2101 NW York St
Portland, OR 97210-2108   503-224-3330
Fax: 503-224-9529 800-726-0320
orders@bridgetowncoffee.com
www.bridgetowncoffee.com
Processor and exporter of coffee; wholesaler/distributor and exporter of tea; serving the food service market
President: Kirk Jensen
kirkj@bridgetowncoffee.com
CEO: Timothy Timmins
Treasurer: Susan Jensen
Estimated Sales: $3,000,000
Number Employees: 20-49
Number of Brands: 6
Number of Products: 21
Square Footage: 80000
Type of Packaging: Consumer, Food Service, Private Label, Bulk
Private Brands Carried:
  Crown Point
Types of Products Distributed:
  Food Service, General Line, Tea

55333 Bridgford Foods Corp
1308 N Patt St
Anaheim, CA 92801   714-526-5533
800-527-2105
www.bridgford.com
Wholesaler/distributor of processed meats and dry sausage items.
Chairman & Vice President: Allan Bridgford
Vice President: Bruce Bridgford
Vice President & Assistant Secretary: Michael Bridgford
Vice President, Manufacturing: Joe deAlcuaz
Vice President, Information Technology: Bob Delong
EVP/CFO/Treasurer: Raymond Lancy
Corp Secretary & Controller: Cindy Matthews-Morales
Senior Vice President: Daniel Yost
Estimated Sales: $167 Million
Number Employees: 500-999
Number of Customer Locations: 5000
Types of Products Distributed:
  Frozen Food, Provisions/Meat, Processed meats & dry sausage items

55334 Briggs Co
5501 Fairpines Ct
Chesterfield, VA 23832-8283   804-233-0966
Fax: 804-233-1250 800-255-5125
Wholesaler/distributor of belting including endless, specialty, silicone glass supported, unsupported, hapalon urethane, stretch, mylar, kapton, melinex and feed round; also, hoses for brewery, dairy, etc
Sales: Frank Chamberlain
Manager: Frank Chamberlain
frankchamberlain@verizon.net
Estimated Sales: Less than $500,000
Number Employees: 1-4
Square Footage: 6000
Parent Co: Briggs Company
Types of Products Distributed:
  Frozen Food, General Merchandise, Belting, hoses, etc.

55335 Brilliant Lighting Fixture Corporation
137 W 24th St
New York, NY 10011   212-244-2345
Fax: 212-244-3975
Wholesaler/distributor of general merchandise and lighting fixtures including electric and fluorescent lamps
President: Moe Behar
Estimated Sales: $1-2.5 Million
Number Employees: 1-4
Types of Products Distributed:
  Frozen Food, General Merchandise, Electric & flourescent lamps, etc.

55336 Brimhall Foods
PO Box 34185
Bartlett, TN 38184-0185   901-377-9016
Fax: 901-377-0476 800-628-6559
brimsnacks.com
Snacks
President: Terry Brimhall
Contact: Dan Scoggin
dscoggin@brimsnacks.com
Estimated Sales: $5-10 Million
Number Employees: 100-249
Type of Packaging: Private Label

55337 Bringgold Wholesale Meats
1114 Zane Ave N
Golden Valley, MN 55422   763-545-0845
Fax: 763-546-0053
Wholesaler/distributor of meats and frozen foods; serving the food service market
President: John Schumacher
VP: Merold Mohni
Estimated Sales: $10-20 Million
Number Employees: 20-49
Parent Co: Schumacher Wholesale Meats
Types of Products Distributed:
  Food Service, Frozen Food, Provisions/Meat

55338 Brings Co
600 Lakeview Point Dr
St Paul, MN 55112-3494   651-484-2666
Fax: 651-484-8857
Wholesaler/distributor of onions and rutabagas
Owner: Patricia Coan
patricia.coan@bringsco.com
Estimated Sales: $10-20 Million
Number Employees: 20-49
Types of Products Distributed:
  Produce

55339 Brita Foods
20 Owens Rd
Hackensack, NJ 07601-3203   201-489-8101
Fax: 201-489-1523
Wholesaler/distributor of pizza products including mozzarella, tomato products and flour, frozen foods, general merchandise and provisions/meats; serving the Italian restaurant industry
President: Joseph Brita
VP: Bruno Brita
Estimated Sales: $5-10 Million
Number Employees: 5-9
Private Brands Carried:
  Bel-Capri, Bel-Bari, Divella
Number of Customer Locations: 120
Types of Products Distributed:
  Frozen Food, General Line, General Merchandise, Provisions/Meat, Pizza products, mozzarella, etc.

55340 British Aisles
1634 Greenland Road
Greenland, NH 03840   603-431-5075
Fax: 603-431-5079 800-520-UKOK
sales@britishaisles.com www.britishaisles.com

Wholesaler/distributor and importer of biscuits, jams, apple juice, condiments, mustards, cereals, tea and chocolate; wholesaler/distributor of health, specialty and private label items
President: Stephanie Pressinger
Co-Founder: Denise Pressinger
Co-Founder: Gerry Pressinger
VP: Gerald Pressinger
Estimated Sales: $1-2.5 Million
Number Employees: 5-9
Square Footage: 40000
Private Brands Carried:
  Thursday Cottage; Moore's Biscuits; Taylor's Original 1830 Mustard; Dorset Cereal; Cheshire Confectionery; St. James Tea
Types of Products Distributed:
  Frozen Food, General Line, Health Food, Specialty Foods, Biscuits, jams, condiments, etc.

55341 British Shoppe LLC
809 N Mills Ave
Orlando, FL 32803-4021   407-898-1634
       Fax: 203-245-3477 888-965-1700
       gourmet@thebritishshoppe.com
       www.thebritishshoppe.com
Importer and wholesaler/distributor of tea and tea accessories
Owner: John Hanson
VP: Fern Grace
Estimated Sales: Less Than $500,000
Number Employees: 1-4
Square Footage: 20000
Types of Products Distributed:
  Frozen Food, General Line, General Merchandise, Tea & tea accessories

55342 British Wholesale Imports
5711 Corsa Ave
Westlake Village, CA 91362-4001   818-991-6644
       Fax: 818-991-8829 info@bwi-imports.com
       www.bwi-imports.com
Importer and wholesaler/distributor of equipment and fixtures, general merchandise, groceries, provisions/meats and specialty and frozen foods and English tea
Owner: Kerry Bamberger
kerry@bwi-imports.com
VP: Susan Wells
Business Development Manager: Jim Owens
Marketing: James Schreiber
HR/ Customer Service Manager: Sue Harwood
Estimated Sales: $10-20 Million
Number Employees: 20-49
Private Brands Carried:
  Norfolk Manner; Whitworth's; Taylor of Harrogate
Types of Products Distributed:
  Frozen Food, General Line, General Merchandise, Provisions/Meat, Specialty Foods, Groceries

55343 Brittain Merchandising
310 E D4 Avenue
Lawton, OK 73501   580-355-4430
             Fax: 580-355-3135
Wholesaler/distributor of general merchandise and health/beauty aids; rack jobber services available
Treasurer: Scott Crumpton
VP: Scott Crumpton
Estimated Sales: $10-20 Million
Number Employees: 50-99
Number of Customer Locations: 600
Types of Products Distributed:
  Frozen Food, General Line, Rack Jobbers, Health & beauty aids

55344 Broadleaf Venison USA Inc
5600 S Alameda St
Vernon, CA 90058-3428   323-826-9890
       Fax: 323-826-9830
       support@broadleafgame.com
       www.broadleafgame.com
Specialty and exotic meats; Wagyu Beef, Buffalo, Cervena Venison, kurobuta Pork
Owner: Mark Mitchell
broadleaf@broadleafgame.com
CEO: Pat McGowan
CFO: Ara Temuryan
Vice President: Annie Mitchell
Sales Director: Nathan Cooney
broadleaf@broadleafgame.com
Operations Manager: Pierre La Breton
Production Manager: Randy Eves
Plant Manager: Jose Madera
Purchasing Manager: Edward Townsend
Estimated Sales: $20-30 Million
Number Employees: 50-99
Square Footage: 56000
Type of Packaging: Consumer, Food Service
Types of Products Distributed:
  Food Service, Frozen Food, Provisions/Meat

55345 Broaster Sales & Svc
2025 Wayne Haven St
Fort Wayne, IN 46803-3232   260-749-5408
             Fax: 219-749-7503
Wholesaler/distributor of food products and equipment; serving the food service market in Ohio and northern Indiana
Owner: Tom Reuille
Office Manager: Shari Tuttle
Estimated Sales: $1-2.5 Million
Number Employees: 5-9
Types of Products Distributed:
  Food Service, Frozen Food, General Line, General Merchandise, Equipment

55346 Brockman E W Co Inc
901 W 18th St
Connersville, IN 47331-1687   765-825-2146
             Fax: 765-825-5341
Wholesaler/distributor of confectionery items; serving the food service market
President: Michael Brockman
ewbrockman@cnz.com
VP: Kimberly Rose
Estimated Sales: $5.60 Million
Number Employees: 10-19
Number of Customer Locations: 400
Types of Products Distributed:
  Food Service, General Line, Confectionery items

55347 Brockman Forklift
15800 Tireman St
Detroit, MI 48228-3610   313-584-4550
             Fax: 313-584-2423
Wholesaler/distributor of material handling equipment including forklifts
President: Tim Riley
Number Employees: 50-99
Private Brands Carried:
  Taylor
Types of Products Distributed:
  Frozen Food, General Merchandise, Material handling equipment

55348 Brody Food Brokerage Corporation
780 Broadway Ave Ste 2
Holbrook, NY 11741   631-244-8900
             Fax: 631-244-8908
Broker of dairy/deli products, groceries, industrial ingredients, private label items, spices, etc.; serving food processors, food service operators and wholesalers/distributors
President: Philip S Brody
Estimated Sales: $1.3 Million
Number Employees: 8
Square Footage: 2000
Types of Products Distributed:
  Food Service, General Merchandise

55349 Bronx Butter & Egg Company
1191 Spofford Avenue
Bronx, NY 10474-5833   718-617-4867
       Fax: 718-617-4869 bbe1191@aol.com
Wholesaler/distributor of dairy products, meats, seafood, produce, paper goods, etc produce, deli products, frozen foods, candy and beverages
President: Michael Annuziata
VP: Joseph Troiano
Estimated Sales: $5-10 Million
Number Employees: 5-9
Square Footage: 20000
Types of Products Distributed:
  Food Service, Frozen Food, General Line, General Merchandise, Provisions/Meat, Produce, Rack Jobbers, Seafood, Specialty Foods, Dairy products, paper goods, etc.

55350 Brooklyn Biltong
314 Prospect Ave.
Brooklyn, NY 11215   407-538-8876
             info@brooklynbiltong.com
             www.brooklynbiltong.com
South African style beef jerky
Principal CEO: Ben van den Heever *Year Founded:* 2012
Types of Products Distributed:
  Provisions/Meat

55351 Brooklyn Boys Pizza & Pasta
9967 Glades Rd
Boca Raton, FL 33434-3920   561-477-3663
Manufacturer and wholesaler of knives, cutlery, china, dinnerware and related table-setting products
Owner: Carlos Sierra
Estimated Sales: $1-5 Million
Number Employees: 10-19
Number of Customer Locations: 10
Types of Products Distributed:
  Food Service, General Merchandise, Cutlery

55352 (HQ)Brooklyn Sugar Company
920 E 149th St
Bronx, NY 10455   718-401-1212
       Fax: 718-401-3111 800-711-2237
             solarwiz@aol.com
Wholesaler/distributor, exporter and importer of sugar and rice products; serving the food service market
Owner/President: Mel Glickman
VP: Mark Glickman
VP: Eric Glickman
Contact: Barbara Glickman
barbara@brooklynsugar.com
Estimated Sales: $20-50 Million
Number Employees: 20-49
Square Footage: 15000
Parent Co: Powerhouse Logistics, Inc.
Type of Packaging: Consumer, Food Service, Private Label, Bulk
Other Locations:
  Brooklyn Sugar Co.
  Bronx, NYBrooklyn Sugar Co.
Private Brands Carried:
  Domino; Jack Frost
Types of Products Distributed:
  Food Service, Frozen Food, General Line, Sugar & rice

55353 Brooks Barrel Company
8 W Hamilton St
Baltimore, MD 21201-5008   410-228-0790
       Fax: 410-221-1693 800-398-2766
       brooksbarrel@shorenet.net www.brooksbarrel.com
Wooden barrels, kegs, planters and buckets; wholesaler/distributor of bushel baskets and crates for shipping and display
President: Kenneth Knox
Office Manager: Tammy Doege
Estimated Sales: $500,000-$1 Million
Number Employees: 15
Square Footage: 40000
Types of Products Distributed:
  Frozen Food, General Merchandise, Bushel baskets & crates

55354 Brooks Industries
4420 SW 29th St
Oklahoma City, OK 73119-1004   405-685-1200
       Fax: 405-685-9529 www.brooksindustries.com
Wholesaler/distributor of food equipment; serving the food service market
Owner: Tony Brooks
tonybrooksokc@aol.com
Estimated Sales: $2.5-5 Million
Number Employees: 10-19
Other Locations:
  Tulsa, OK
  West Fork, ARWest Fork
Private Brands Carried:
  Henny-Penny; Hoshicake; True
Types of Products Distributed:
  Food Service, Frozen Food, General Merchandise, Food equipment

Wholesalers & Distributors / A-Z

55355 Brooks Tropicals Inc
18400 SW 256th St
Homestead, FL 33031-1892   305-247-3544
Fax: 305-242-7393   800-327-4833
maryo@brookstropicals.com
Grower, packer and shipper of papayas, avocados, starfruit, limes, passion fruit, mangos, guavas, uglyfruit and other tropical produce.
President: Pal Brooks
CEO: Greg Smith
Year Founded: 1928
Number Employees: 100-249
Type of Packaging: Bulk
Types of Products Distributed:
   Frozen Food, Produce

55356 Brotherhood Winery
100 Brotherhood Plaza Dr
P.O.Box 190
Washingtonville, NY 10992-2279   845-496-3661
Fax: 845-496-8720
contact@brotherhoodwinery.net
www.brotherhood-winery.com
wines.
President: Hernan Donoso
Co-Owner: Cesar Baeza
Vice President: Philip Dunsmore
Commercial Assistant, Marketing & Sales: Ren,e Schweizer
Production Manager: Mark Daigle
Plant Manager: Carol Tepper
Estimated Sales: $10 Million
Number Employees: 50
Type of Packaging: Consumer, Food Service, Private Label, Bulk
Private Brands Carried:
   Brotherhood Winery Varietal & Traditional Wines, NEW YORK Wines, Standard Cider Co. Ciders.

55357 Brothers Restaurant Supply
1125 N Cedar Road
Mason, MI 48854-8722   517-244-8000
Fax: 517-244-1031   800-242-4058
Wholesaler/distributor of equipment and supplies; serving the food service market
President: Tom Ziolkowski
VP: Russ Higgins
VP: Art Lopes
Estimated Sales: $500,000-$1 Million
Number Employees: 5-9
Square Footage: 140000
Parent Co: Brothers Restaurant Supply
Types of Products Distributed:
   Food Service, Frozen Food, General Merchandise, Equipment & supplies

55358 Brown Foods
3659 Atlanta Highway
PO Box 953
Dallas, GA 30132-5731   770-445-4358
Fax: 770-445-5349
Poultry, pork, seafood, produce, beef
Principal: William Brown
Owner: Graham Kirkman
Estimated Sales: $540,000
Number Employees: 4

55359 Brown's Dairy
P.O. Box 961447
El Paso, TX 79996
800-395-7004
deanfoods@casupport.com   www.brownsdairy.com
Wholesaler/distributor of milk, juice, sour cream, cottage cheese and yogurt; serving the food service market.
CEO, Dean Foods Company: Ralph Scozzafava
Estimated Sales: $50-100 Million
Number Employees: 250-499
Parent Co: Dean Foods Company
Private Brands Carried:
   Brown's Velvet
Types of Products Distributed:
   Food Service, Frozen Food, General Line, Dairy: milk, sour cream, cheese, etc.

55360 Brown's Ice Cream Co
3501 Marshall St NE # 150
Minneapolis, MN 55418-0073   612-378-1075
Fax: 612-331-9273   info@brownsicecream.com
www.brownsicecream.com
Wholesaler/distributor of frozen foods including ice cream; serving the food service market

Owner: Robert Nelson
browns@popp.net
Vice President: Bob Nelson
Estimated Sales: $5-10 Million
Number Employees: 20-49
Number of Customer Locations: 800
Types of Products Distributed:
   Food Service, Frozen Food, General Line, Ice cream

55361 Brown, R H
12 S Idaho St
Seattle, WA 98134-1119   206-682-7469
Fax: 206-682-7469   866-936-9410
info@rhbrown.com   www.rhbrown.com
Wholesaler/distributor of material handling equipment
President: Richard Larsen
Contact: Chelsea Abbott
c.abbott@rhbrown.com
Estimated Sales: $2.5-5 Million
Number Employees: 5-9
Private Brands Carried:
   Hytrol; Magliner; Colson
Types of Products Distributed:
   Frozen Food, General Merchandise, Material handling equipment

55362 Browne & Company
100 Esna Park Drive
Markham, ON L3R 1E3
Canada   905-475-6104
Fax: 866-849-4719   sales@browneco.com
www.browneco.com
A leading supplier of glassware, dinnerware and smallwares to the food service industry in Canada
President: Michael Browne
CFO: Alen Budish
Vice President: Brian Wood
Marketing Director: Katherine Dilk
Sales Director: Brian Wood
Number Employees: 10
Type of Packaging: Food Service
Types of Products Distributed:
   Food Service

55363 Browns' Ice Cream Company
3501 Marshall St. NE
Suite 150
Minneapolis, MN 55418   612-378-1075
info@brownsicecream.com
www.brownsicecream.com
Distributor of ice cream
President: Jerry Conder
Treasurer: William Brown
Contact: Bob Nelson
bnelson@brownsicecream.com
Estimated Sales: $8.3 Million
Number Employees: 60
Type of Packaging: Consumer, Food Service, Bulk
Types of Products Distributed:
   Frozen Food, Ice cream

55364 Bruce Edmeades Sales
235 Ardelt Avenue
Kitchener, ON N2C 2M3
Canada   519-745-7226
Wholesaler/distributor of general line items and merchandise including plastics and equipment
President: Bruce Edmeades, Sr.
Number Employees: 100-249
Number of Customer Locations: 2000
Types of Products Distributed:
   Frozen Food, General Line, General Merchandise, Plastics & equipment

55365 Brucken's
401 North West 4th Street
Evansville, IN 47708   812-423-4414
Fax: 812-422-8011   800-489-4414
www.bruckens.com
Wholesaler/distributor of equipment and supplies; serving the food service market
President/CEO: Roger Griffin
CEO: Roger Griffen
Contact: Greg Hillenbrand
gph@bruckens.com
General Manager: Greg Hillenbrand
Estimated Sales: $1-2.5 Million
Number Employees: 1-4
Parent Co: Brucken Company
Types of Products Distributed:
   Food Service, Frozen Food, General Merchandise, Equipment & supplies

55366 Bruegger's Bagels
496 Main St
Melrose, MA 02176-3841   781-665-1913
Fax: 781-665-4953   www.brueggers.com
Bagels
Co-Owner: Nord Brue
Co-Owner: Mike Dressel
Number Employees: 10-19

55367 Bryan Foods
PO Box 3901
Peoria, IL 61612   800-544-3870
www.bryanfoods.com
Bacon, sausage, hot dogs, ham, corn dogs and lunchmeat

55368 Bryant Products Inc
W1388 Elmwood Ave
Ixonia, WI 53036-9437   920-206-6920
Fax: 920-206-6929   800-825-3874
www.bryantpro.com
Manufacturer and exporter of tensioning devices for conveyors, straight and tapered rollers, machine grade conveyor pulleys
President: Fred Thimmel
Vice President: Dave Roessler
dave@bryantpro.com
Purchasing: Jody Mack
Estimated Sales: $20-50 Million
Number Employees: 20-49
Square Footage: 50000
Types of Products Distributed:
   Frozen Food

55369 Buak Fruit Company
1314 Green Valley Rd
Watsonville, CA 95076-8640   831-724-6375
Fax: 831-724-8194
Wholesaler/distributor of apples
General Partner: William Buak
Partner: Nick Buak
Partner: Martin Buak
Estimated Sales: $1.0 Million
Number Employees: 10
Types of Products Distributed:
   Produce, Apples

55370 Bubba's Fine Foods
225 42nd Street SW
Suite C
Loveland, CO 80537
bubbasfoods.com
Gourmet chips
Co-Founder & CEO: Jeff Schmidgall
COO: Jared Menzel
Number of Brands: 1
Number of Products: 9
Type of Packaging: Consumer

55371 Bublitz Machinery Company
703 E 14th Ave
Kansas City, MO 64116   816-221-7335
Fax: 816-221-7340
Wholesaler/distributor of material handling equipment including forklifts
President: Jeff Bublitz
bublitzj@bublitzco.com
Estimated Sales: $20-50 Million
Number Employees: 20-49
Private Brands Carried:
   Yale; American Lincoln
Types of Products Distributed:
   Frozen Food, General Merchandise, Material handling equipment

55372 Buckelew Hardware Co
8230 S Choctaw Dr
Baton Rouge, LA 70815-8082   225-926-3657
Fax: 225-927-9032
Wholesaler/distributor of cleaning supplies, disposables, tabletop needs and equipment; serving the food service market
Manager: Danny Butler
danny@buckfoodsvc.com
VP: John Hunsicker
Estimated Sales: $5-10 Million
Number Employees: 5-9
Parent Co: Buckelew Company
Types of Products Distributed:
   Food Service, Frozen Food, General Merchandise, Cleaning supplies, tabletop needs, etc.

55373 Buckelew's Food Svc Equipment
1715 Spring St
Shreveport, LA 71101-4058 318-424-6673
Fax: 318-424-6681 www.buckfoodsvc.com
Wholesaler/distributor of tabletop supplies and equipment; serving the food service market
Owner: Charles H Hunsicker
chenry@buckfoodsvc.com
Manager: Gary Spangler
Estimated Sales: $1-2.5 Million
Number Employees: 20-49
Parent Co: Buckelew's Food Service Equipment Company
Types of Products Distributed:
 Food Service, Frozen Food, General Merchandise, Tabletop supplies & equipment

55374 (HQ)Buckelew's Food Svc Equipment
1715 Spring St
Shreveport, LA 71101-4058 318-424-6673
Fax: 318-424-6681 www.buckfoodsvc.com
Wholesaler/distributor of cleaning supplies, table top needs, disposables and equipment; serving the food service market
Owner: Charles H Hunsicker
CEO: J Hunsicker, Jr.
Sales/Marketing Executive: William Hunsicker
chenry@buckfoodsvc.com
Estimated Sales: $10-20 Million
Number Employees: 20-49
Other Locations:
 Buckelew's Food ServiceEquip
 Baton Rouge, LABuckelew's Food ServiceEquip
Types of Products Distributed:
 Food Service, Frozen Food, General Merchandise, Cleaning supplies, disposables, etc.

55375 Buckeye Handling Equipment Company
21245 Lorain Road
Cleveland, OH 44126-2146 440-333-3939
Fax: 440-333-6975
Wholesaler/distributor of conveyors, containers, shelving and racks
President: Martin McCarthy
Estimated Sales: $2.5-5 Million
Number Employees: 5-9
Private Brands Carried:
 Jarke; Metro; Henges
Types of Products Distributed:
 Frozen Food, General Merchandise, Material handling equipment

55376 Buckhead Beef
4500 Wickersham Dr
Atlanta, GA 30337-5122 404-355-4400
Fax: 404-355-4541 800-888-5578
hf@buckheadbeef.com www.buckheadbeef.com
Fresh and frozen specialty cut meat products including beef, veal, lamb and pork
Founder/CEO: Howard Halpern
President: Chad Stine
CFO: Paul Mooring
frostypauly@yahoo.com
Vice President: Andrew Malcolm
Director of Marketing: Rick Morris
Vice President of Sales: Beverly Ham
Human Resources Executive: Sue Kozbiel
Manager: Chris Aloia
Director of Production: Raymond Morehouse
Director of Purchasing: Jason Lees
Number Employees: 500-999
Type of Packaging: Food Service
Private Brands Carried:
 Angus
Types of Products Distributed:
 Food Service, Frozen Food, Provisions/Meat, Fresh & frozen specialty cut meats

55377 Budd Foods
431 Somerville St
Manchester, NH 03103-5129 603-623-3528
Chicken pot-pies and all-in-one meals
Contact: Jenifer Bechtol
jenifer@mrsbudds.com
Number Employees: 1-4

55378 Buddha Teas
5130 Avenida Encinas
Carlsbad, CA 92008
 800-642-3754
service@buddhateas.com www.buddhateas.com
Loose leaf, herbal, green, black and specialty teas
Number of Brands: 1
Type of Packaging: Consumer

55379 Buddy Squirrel LLC
1801 E Bolivar Ave
St Francis, WI 53235-5317 414-483-4500
Fax: 414-483-4137 800-972-2658
www.buddysquirrel.com
Processor, exporter and packer of candy including regular and sugar-free boxed, chocolates, brittles, toffees, holiday, mints, molded novelties, etc.; also, nuts, nut mixes and gourmet popcorn
President: Margaret Gile
margaretg@qcbs.com
Number Employees: 100-249
Number of Brands: 2
Number of Products: 2000
Square Footage: 120000
Parent Co: Quality Candy Shoppes
Type of Packaging: Consumer, Food Service, Private Label, Bulk
Types of Products Distributed:
 Frozen Food

55380 Buffalo Bills Premium Snacks
1547 Joel Dr.
P.O. Box 866
Lebanon, PA 17042 717-273-7499
Fax: 717-273-7699
customerservice@choochoorsnacks.com
www.bbjerky.com
Jerky, meat sticks, meat snacks, pickled sausages, gifts
General Manager: Paul Squires
Sales Manager: Patrick Sherburne
Types of Products Distributed:
 Provisions/Meat

55381 Buffalo Hotel Supply CoInc
375 Commerce Dr
Amherst, NY 14228-2394 716-691-8080
Fax: 716-691-3255
www.bhsfoodservicesolutions.com
Wholesaler/distributor of equipment and supplies; serving the food service market
CEO: James Bedard Sr
Estimated Sales: $10-20 Million
Number Employees: 20-49
Types of Products Distributed:
 Food Service, Frozen Food, General Merchandise, Equipment & supplies

55382 Buffalo Paper & Detergent Co
182 Breckenridge St
Buffalo, NY 14213-1562 716-886-1114
Fax: 716-875-2871
Wholesaler/distributor of paper supplies including imprinted napkins, placemats, cups, boxes, etc.; also, janitorial supplies; serving the food service market
President: Joseph A Gigante
Sales Manager: Joseph Gigante
Office Manager: Donna Hahn
Estimated Sales: $5-10 Million
Number Employees: 5-9
Square Footage: 112000
Types of Products Distributed:
 Food Service, Frozen Food, General Merchandise, Paper napkins, cups, placemats, etc.

55383 Buffalo Rock Co.
111 Oxmoor Rd
Birmingham, AL 35209 205-942-3435
www.buffalorock.com
Ginger ale and grape drinks. Bottler of PepsiCo Products.
President/COO: Matthew Dent
Chairman/CEO: James Lee
Executive VP/CFO: Bruce Parsons
Year Founded: 1901
Estimated Sales: $550 Million
Number Employees: 2,100
Type of Packaging: Consumer, Food Service

55384 Bulk Bag Express
294 Phillips Rd.
Hardeeville, SC 29927 843-784-2990
Fax: 843-784-5290 800-645-3183
Wholesaler of recycled of bulk bags
Manager: Deborah Waldron
VP of Sales: Linda Medal
Public Relations Manager: Deborah Waldron

Estimated Sales: $5-10 Million
Number Employees: 10-19
Square Footage: 120000

55385 Bulk Food Marketplace
21514 Harper Ave
St Clair Shores, MI 48080-2211 586-779-0840
Fax: 586-779-4971
www.bulkfoodmarketplace.com
Wholesaler/distributor of candy, nuts and baking items
Owner: Ken Meldrum
Estimated Sales: $2.5-5 Million
Number Employees: 5-9
Types of Products Distributed:
 Frozen Food, General Line, Candy, nuts & baking items

55386 Bunn Capitol Company
1400 Stevenson Drive
Springfield, IL 62703 217-529-5401
Fax: 217-542-2827 800-325-2866
www.bunn.com
Wholesaler/distributor of frozen foods, meats, groceries and seafood; serving the food service market
President: Robert Bunn
Estimated Sales: $890 Thousand
Number Employees: 4
Number of Customer Locations: 5000
Types of Products Distributed:
 Food Service, Frozen Food, General Line, Provisions/Meat, Seafood, Groceries

55387 Bunzl Distribution USA
One CityPlace Dr
Suite 200
St. Louis, MO 63141 314-997-5959
Fax: 314-997-1405 888-997-5959
www.bunzldistribution.com
Outsourced food packaging, disposable supplies, and cleaning and safety products to food processors, supermarkets, retailers, convenience stores and other users.
President & CEO: Patrick Larmon
Executive Vice President: Jeff Earnhart
Year Founded: 1981
Estimated Sales: Over $1 Billion
Number Employees: 5,000
Parent Co: Bunzl PLC
Type of Packaging: Food Service, Private Label, Bulk
Other Locations:
 Bunzl Distribution
 West Valley City, UTBunzl Distribution
Private Brands Carried:
 Prime Source
Types of Products Distributed:
 Food Service, Frozen Food, General Line, General Merchandise

55388 Bur-Gra Meat & Grocery
516 S Anthony St
Burlington, NC 27215-6610 336-226-4183
Wholesaler/distributor of meat and groceries; serving the food service market
President: Gene Ray
Estimated Sales: $1-2.5 Million
Number Employees: 5-9
Number of Customer Locations: 20
Types of Products Distributed:
 Food Service, General Line, Provisions/Meat

55389 Burch-Lowe
2238 Pinson Valley Parkway
Birmingham, AL 35217 205-841-6666
Fax: 404-699-1679 800-239-2694
www.cowin.com
Wholesaler/distributor of forklifts
President: Jaime Cowin
VP: David Whitby
Estimated Sales: $3-5 Million
Number Employees: 20-49
Private Brands Carried:
 Ingersol-Rand; Kobelco
Types of Products Distributed:
 Frozen Food, General Merchandise, Forklifts

55390 Burdick Packing Company
163 Minges Cir
Battle Creek, MI 49015 269-962-5111
Fax: 616-962-3220 800-632-5424
Wholesaler/distributor of meat
President: M Burdick
Chairman: P Burdick

Wholesalers & Distributors / A-Z

Estimated Sales: $20-50 Million
Number Employees: 20-49
Private Brands Carried:
  Pick of the Pig
Types of Products Distributed:
  Frozen Food, Provisions/Meat

55391 Burgess Mfg.-Oklahoma
1250 Roundhouse Rd
P.O. Box 237
Guthrie, OK 73044-4700   405-282-1913
  Fax: 405-282-7132 800-804-1913
bmfg@sbcglobal.net www.burgesspallets.com
Manufacturer and exporter of pallets, boxes, crating and lumber; wholesaler/distributor of lumber, plywood, stretch film, plastic pallets, chipboard and plastic components
Plant Manager: Lee Williams
Estimated Sales: $3 Million
Number Employees: 20-49
Square Footage: 42000
Types of Products Distributed:
  Frozen Food, General Merchandise, Lumber, plywood & stretch film

55392 Burkhardt Sales & Svc
3935 Inman Rd
St Augustine, FL 32084-0534 904-829-3008
  Fax: 904-829-3207 800-749-1999
www.abwholesaler.com
Wholesaler/distributor of beer.
President: Burkhardt Brookes
dancebug87@aol.com
Sales Manager: Peter Burkhardt
Estimated Sales: $20-50 Million
Number Employees: 20-49
Parent Co: Anheuser Busch
Private Brands Carried:
  Budweiser; Michelob; Busch
Types of Products Distributed:
  Frozen Food, General Line, Beer

55393 Burklund Distributors Inc
2500 N Main St
Suite 3
East Peoria, IL 61611   309-694-1900
  800-322-2876
www.burklund.com
Wholesaler/distributor of tobacco, candy, groceries, frozen foods, baked goods and general merchandise.
President/Chief Operating Officer: Jonathan Burklund
VP, Finance & Administration: Paul Benes
Plant Manager: Randy Eckstein
Buyer: Steve Reinholdt, Sr.
Estimated Sales: $23 Million
Number Employees: 50-99
Square Footage: 104500
Other Locations:
  Burklund Distributors
  Peoria Heights, ILBurklund Distributors
Number of Customer Locations: 3500
Types of Products Distributed:
  Frozen Food, General Line, General Merchandise, Candy & baked goods

55394 Burlington Equipment Company
PO Box 2600
Burlington, NC 27216-2600 336-229-6671
  Fax: 336-229-5246
Wholesaler/distributor of ovens, grills and fryers; serving the food service market
C.P.M.: Dan Hotchkiss
CEO: Jerry Sparrow
Number Employees: 20-49
Parent Co: Bell
Private Brands Carried:
  Baker's Pride
Types of Products Distributed:
  Food Service, Frozen Food, General Merchandise, Ovens, grills, fryers

55395 Burnand & Company
PO Box 2180
Nogales, AZ 85628   520-281-0211
  Fax: 520-281-0083
Wholesaler/distributor of cherry tomatoes, bell peppers and squash
Owner: Kenneth Olmos
Estimated Sales: $2.5-5 Million
Number Employees: 10-19
Types of Products Distributed:
  Frozen Food, Produce, Cherry tomatoes, bell peppers & squash

55396 Bush Brothers ProvisionCo
1931 N Dixie Hwy
West Palm Beach, FL 33407-6084 561-832-6666
  Fax: 561-832-1460 800-327-1345
orders@bush-brothers.com
www.bush-brothers.com
Processor and exporter of fresh and frozen portion cut beef, veal, lamb, pork and poultry; wholesaler/distributor of dairy products; serving the food service market.
President: Harry Bush
sales@bushb-brothers.com
Vice President: Billy Bush
Sales Manager: Doug Bush
Operations Manager: John Bush
Estimated Sales: $13.3 Million
Number Employees: 20-49
Square Footage: 10000
Type of Packaging: Consumer, Food Service, Private Label, Bulk
Types of Products Distributed:
  Food Service, General Line, Dairy products

55397 Business Documents
129 W Southern Hills Rd
Phoenix, AZ 85023   727-581-2552
  800-678-9959
kurt@phoenixdocument.com
Wholesaler/distributor of custom advertising specialties, envelopes, business forms, labels, incentives, premiums and business gifts
President: Agena Ridenour
Estimated Sales: $1-2.5 Million
Number Employees: 1-4
Number of Customer Locations: 7000
Types of Products Distributed:
  Frozen Food, General Merchandise, Advertising specialties, etc.

55398 Business Services Alliance
PO Box 7815
Romeoville, IL 60446-0815 708-407-0231
  Fax: 708-407-2232 rogcern@excite.com
Wholesaler/distributor of spray sign-making kits, price labels, labeling guns, employee benefit plans, and employee evaluation and assessments
President: Roger Cernoch
Number Employees: 1-4
Square Footage: 2000
Types of Products Distributed:
  General Merchandise, Sign-making kits, message signs, etc.

55399 Business Systems & Conslnts
113 Little Valley Ct
Hoover, AL 35244-2001 205-988-3300
  Fax: 205-985-9510 skiptaylor@bscsolutions.com
  www.bscsolutions.com
Wholesaler/distributor of material handling equipment; rack jobber services available
President: Rick Romano
rickromano@bscsolutions.com
VP: O Taylor
Estimated Sales: $5-10 Million
Number Employees: 20-49
Types of Products Distributed:
  Rack Jobbers, Material handling equipment

55400 Buster Lind Produce Company
502 W Schunior St
Edinburg, TX 78541   956-383-1665
  Fax: 956-383-3934
Wholesaler/distributor of fresh fruits and vegetables; serving the food service market
President: Pat Lind
Estimated Sales: $10-20 Million
Number Employees: 20-49
Types of Products Distributed:
  Food Service, Produce

55401 Butler Foods LLC
P.O. Box 40
Grand Ronde, OR 97347   503-437-9133
info@butlerfoods.com
www.butlerfoods.com
Vegan products including soy curls, soy jerky, and taco crumbles
Owner: Dan Butler
Types of Products Distributed:
  General Line

55402 Butte Produce Company
605 Utah Ave
Butte, MT 59701-2694   406-782-2369
  Fax: 406-782-3929
Wholesaler/distributor of produce, meat, seafood, canned goods, paper goods, specialty goods, cleaning supplies and private label goods
Owner: William F Dewolf
Manager: William DeWolf
Estimated Sales: $20-50 Million
Number Employees: 20-49
Square Footage: 35000
Private Brands Carried:
  Nugget; Rykoff
Types of Products Distributed:
  Frozen Food, General Line, General Merchandise, Provisions/Meat, Produce, Seafood, Specialty Foods, Private label

55403 Butts Foods
432 N Royal St
Jackson, TN 38301
  800-972-8570
www.buttsfoods.com
Wholesaler/distributor of meats and poultry.
President & CEO: Ray Butts
EVP & Chief Operating Officer: R.E. Butts
Finance Director & Business Manager: Drew Shaub
Finance Director & Officer Manager: Frank Jordan
Director, National Business Development: Rick Delong
Inside Sales Director: Mark Thomas
Purchasing Director: Tim Roberts
Year Founded: 1935
Estimated Sales: $20-50 Million
Number Employees: 50-99
Other Locations:
  Distribution Center
  Hattiesburg, MS
  Distribution Center
  Nashville, TNDistribution CenterNashville
Types of Products Distributed:
  Provisions/Meat, Poultry

55404 Buz's Crab
2159 East St
Redding, CA 96001-2094   530-243-2120
  Fax: 530-243-4310 www.buzscrab.com
Wholesaler/distributor of produce, equipment and fresh and frozen seafood including dungeness crab; serving seafood markets and restaurants
President: G Santilena
Contact: Sue Desimas
sdesimas@buzscrab.com
Estimated Sales: $10-20 Million
Number Employees: 20-49
Types of Products Distributed:
  Food Service, Frozen Food, General Merchandise, Produce, Seafood, Fresh & frozen seafood

55405 Buzz Food Svc
4818 Kanawha Blvd E
Charleston, WV 25306-6328 304-925-4781
  Fax: 304-925-1502 info@buzzfoodsvc.com
  www.buzzbutteredsteaks.com
Distributor of; beef, lamb, veal, chicken, pork, seafood, cheese, dairy, produce, canned goods, flour & baking supplies, frozen entrees and appetizers, ethnic specialties, gourmet items, beverage service, concession supplies and equipment, cleaning products and smallwares
President: Dickinson Gould
dickinson@buzzfoodsvc.com
Sales Manager: Jason Jean
General Manager: John Haddy
Operations Manager: Jeramy Kidd
Purchasing: Dennis Benson
Estimated Sales: $10.22 Million
Number Employees: 50-99
Square Footage: 90000
Type of Packaging: Consumer, Food Service

55406 Byczek Enterprises
3924 W Devon Ave
Lincolnwood, IL 60712-1040 847-673-6050
  Fax: 847-673-6085 800-323-8072
Wholesaler/distributor of food service equipment including cooking, work tables, sinks, display cases and refrigerators; also, custom fabrication, replacement equipment and installation services available
President: J Byczek
Purchasing Agent: Fran Travis

Estimated Sales: $1-3 Million
Number Employees: 5-9
Square Footage: 120000
Types of Products Distributed:
   Food Service, Frozen Food, General Merchandise, Cooking equipment, tables, sinks, etc.

55407 Bykowski Equipment
12360 Eastend Ave
Chino, CA 91710-2009   909-902-9400
   Fax: 909-902-9339 ContactUs@GoBEECO.com
            www.bykowskiequipment.net
Wholesaler/distributor of food processing machinery, homogenizers and sanitary pumps
Owner: Jack Wiersma
VP: Jack Wiersma
IT: Myrna Garcia
mgarcia@gobeeco.com
Estimated Sales: $5-10 Million
Number Employees: 20-49
Types of Products Distributed:
   Frozen Food, General Merchandise, Food processing machinery

55408 Bynoe Printers
167 W 126th Street
New York, NY 10027-4412   212-662-5041
Manufacturer and wholesaler/distributor of advertising specialties including labels, raffle tickets and paper cups
President: Mark Bynoe
Estimated Sales: $1-2,500,000
Number Employees: 1-4
Types of Products Distributed:
   Frozen Food, General Merchandise, Advertising specialties

55409 Byrd Mill Co
14471 Washington Hwy
Ashland, VA 23005   804-798-3627
   Fax: 804-798-9357 888-897-3336
      sales@byrdmill.com www.byrdmill.com
Specialty mixes including bread, pound cake, cookie, fruit cobbler, biscuit, pancake, waffle, muffin, spoon bread, shortbread, corn bread, hushpuppy, stoneground grits, etc
President: Todd Attkisson
sales@byrdmill.com
Estimated Sales: $300,000-$500,000
Number Employees: 10-19
Square Footage: 3300
Type of Packaging: Consumer, Food Service, Private Label, Bulk

55410 Byrne Brothers Foods Inc
1021 E Dallas St
Mansfield, TX 76063-2052   817-473-9303
   Fax: 817-477-4214 www.byrnebrothers.com
Wholesaler/distributor of frozen foods; serving the food service market
Owner: John Byrne
service@byrnebrothers.com
Estimated Sales: $5-10 Million
Number Employees: 20-49
Types of Products Distributed:
   Food Service, Frozen Food

55411 C & J Tender Meat Co
324 E Intl Airport Rd
Anchorage, AK 99518-1215   907-562-2838
   Fax: 907-561-5846 www.cjtendermeat.com
Meats
Owner: Steve Jones
Treasurer: Arlita Jones
Estimated Sales: $1.1 Million
Number Employees: 5-9

55412 C & R Food Svc Inc
10 Van Dorn Ave
Mt Morris, NY 14510-1507   585-658-2810
         Fax: 585-658-3864
Wholesaler/distributor of meats, produce, cheese, seafood, groceries and paper and cleaning supplies; serving the food service market
Owner: Craig Bolesky
crfood@rochester.rr.com
Co-Owner: Harry Elliott
Estimated Sales: $10-20 Million
Number Employees: 10-19
Types of Products Distributed:
   Food Service, Frozen Food, General Line, General Merchandise, Provisions/Meat, Produce, Seafood, Groceries, etc.

55413 C & S Sales Inc
9265 Activity Rd # 106
San Diego, CA 92126-4444   858-566-4111
   Fax: 858-674-4848 sdsales@cssales.com
            www.cssales.com
Wholesaler/distributor of advertising specialties and packaging products
Manager: Barbara Walker
Estimated Sales: Less Than $500,000
Number Employees: 5-9
Number of Customer Locations: 1000
Types of Products Distributed:
   Frozen Food, General Merchandise, Advertising specialties & packaging

55414 C & S Wholesale GrocersInc
7 Corporate Dr
Keene, NH 03431-5042
                       www.cswg.com
Wholesaler/distributor of dairy products, frozen foods, general merchandise, private label items, groceries and seafood.
Executive Chairman: Rick Cohen
rcohen@cswg.com
Chief Executive Officer: Mike Duffy
Chief Financial Officer: Kevin McNamara
Chief Legal Officer: Bill Boyd
Chief Information Officer: George Dramalis
EVP, Procurement: Tracy Moore
Chief Human Resources Officer: Miriam Ort
Chief Commercial Officer: Joe Cavaliere
Chief Supply Chain Officer: Chris Smith
Year Founded: 1918
Estimated Sales: $30 Billion
Number Employees: 10000+
Number of Customer Locations: 6500
Types of Products Distributed:
   Frozen Food, General Line, General Merchandise, Seafood, Groceries, dairy products, etc.

55415 C & T Design & Equipment Co
2750 Tobey Dr
Indianapolis, IN 46219-1418   317-898-9602
   Fax: 317-899-8753 800-966-3374
      ctcincy@aol.com www.2c-tdesign.com
Wholesaler/distributor of restaurant equipment and furniture; serving the food service market
President: Mark Green
markg@c-tdesign.com
Estimated Sales: $1-3 Million
Number Employees: 20-49
Parent Co: C&T Design & Equipment Company
Private Brands Carried:
   Hobart; True; Frymaster
Types of Products Distributed:
   Food Service, Frozen Food, General Merchandise, Restaurant equipment

55416 C & T Design & Equipment Co
2750 Tobey Dr
Indianapolis, IN 46219-1418   317-898-9602
         Fax: 317-899-8753
Wholesaler/distributor of food service equipment through out the U.S
Manager: Mark Green
markg@c-tdesign.com
CFO: Michael Kennedy
Marketing: Gawain Guy
Sales: Gawain Guy
Operations: Mark Green
Estimated Sales: $35 Million
Number Employees: 20-49
Square Footage: 30000

55417 C A Curtze
1717 E 12th St
Erie, PA 16511   814-452-2281
   Fax: 814-459-1213 800-352-0940
            www.curtze.com
Wholesaler/distributor of groceries, meats, produce, dairy products, frozen foods, bakery items, etc.; serving the food service market.
President: Bruce Kern
Vice President & General Counsel: Scott Kern
Vice President, Sales: David Boyd
VP, Marketing & Procurement: Janet Dennen
Year Founded: 1878
Estimated Sales: $94 Million
Number Employees: 250-499
Square Footage: 100000
Private Brands Carried:
   Commodore; Gold Coast; San Marco
Types of Products Distributed:
   Food Service, Frozen Food, General Line, General Merchandise, Provisions/Meat, Produce, Seafood, Specialty Foods, Groceries, meats, produce, etc.

55418 (HQ)C D Hartnett Co
302 N Main St
Weatherford, TX 76086-3245   817-594-3813
   Fax: 817-594-9714 www.cd-hartnett.com
Wholesaler/distributor of groceries, meats, produce, frozen foods, bakery products, general merchandise, private label items, equipment and fixtures serving the food service market; also, rack jobber
President: Stephen E Milliken
smilliken@cd-hartnett.com
Chairman: C Milliken
Estimated Sales: $20-50 Million
Number Employees: 20-49
Square Footage: 120000
Number of Customer Locations: 1475
Types of Products Distributed:
   Food Service, Frozen Food, General Line, General Merchandise, Provisions/Meat, Produce, Rack Jobbers

55419 C H Robinson Worldwide Inc
14701 Charlson Rd
Eden Prairie, MN 55347-5076   952-937-8500
   Fax: 952-937-6714 855-229-6128
   solutions@chrobinson.com www.chrobinson.com
Wholesaler/distributor of food ingredients and fresh fruit and vegetables
President: John Weihoff
CEO: D Verdoorn
Manager: Mark Bogucki
Estimated Sales: Over $1 Billion
Number Employees: 10000+
Types of Products Distributed:
   Frozen Food, General Line, Produce

55420 C M Tanner Grocery Co
421 Maple St
Carrollton, GA 30117-3242   770-832-6381
         Fax: 770-834-2654
Wholesaler/distributor of general merchandise and general line products; serving the food service market
President: John W Tanner Iii
Estimated Sales: $20-50 Million
Number Employees: 20-49
Number of Customer Locations: 300
Types of Products Distributed:
   Food Service, Frozen Food, General Line, General Merchandise

55421 C Pacific Foods Inc
13503 Pumice St
Norwalk, CA 90650-5250   562-802-2199
   Fax: 562-802-3022 www.cpacificfoods.com
Wholesaler/distributor, importer and exporter of canned goods, seafood and food ingredients, paper products and specialty food; serving the food service market; also, warehouse for canned goods, specialty Asian cuisine
President: Eric Chan
Sales Manager: Ed Chan
Manager: Ed Chan
Operations Manager: Alice Shih
Estimated Sales: $1-2.5 Million
Number Employees: 10-19
Square Footage: 200000
Type of Packaging: Food Service
Private Brands Carried:
   Jack Pot; Sunpak; Sunrise
Types of Products Distributed:
   Food Service, Frozen Food, General Line, General Merchandise, Seafood, Specialty Foods

55422 C&C Lift Truck
Victory Bridge Plz
South Amboy, NJ 8879   732-727-4500
   Fax: 732-727-7597 866-770-5438
            www.cnclifttruck.com
Wholesaler/distributor of material handling equipment including lift trucks and forklifts
President: Ronald Casaletto
VP: Gary Casaletto
Estimated Sales: $10-20 Million
Number Employees: 50-99
Private Brands Carried:
   B.T. Lift; LPM Parts; Power-Flo Batteries
Types of Products Distributed:
   Frozen Food, General Merchandise, Material handling equipment

Wholesalers & Distributors / A-Z

55423 C&H Store Equipment Company
2530 S Broadway
Los Angeles, CA 90007 213-748-7165
Fax: 213-749-6135 800-648-4979
Manufacturer, wholesaler/distributor and exporter of store fixtures, office furniture, showcases, and metal shelving
CEO: Cheon Kim
Estimated Sales: $2.5-5,000,000
Number Employees: 10-19
Types of Products Distributed:
Frozen Food, General Merchandise, Store fixtures & office furniture

55424 (HQ)C&R Refrigeration Inc
PO Box 93
Center, TX 75935 936-598-2761
Fax: 936-598-7858 800-438-6182
www.crrefrig.com
Custom Metal Fabrication-3A tanks, process piping installation, platforms, flow panels, valve clusters, hoppers, skid systems, dryers, orbital welding. Distributor for Alfalaval, Ampco Pumps, Definix Valves.
President: Ronald Murphy
VP: Phillip McKitrick
Sales Manager: Jim McAnaul
Estimated Sales: $5-10 Million
Number Employees: 11
Square Footage: 160000
Other Locations:
C&R
Largo, FLC&R
Private Brands Carried:
Ampco
Types of Products Distributed:
Frozen Food, General Merchandise, Centrifugal pumps

55425 C&W Frozen Foods
950 Elm Avenue
Suite 355
San Bruno, CA 94066-3036 650-875-1902
Fax: 650-875-1646
Wholesaler/distributor of frozen vegetables
President: Bob Maier
Estimated Sales: $5-10 Million
Number Employees: 5-9
Private Brands Carried:
C&W
Types of Products Distributed:
Frozen Food, Vegetables

55426 C. Eberle Sons Company
3222 Beekman St
Cincinnati, OH 45223 513-542-7200
Fax: 513-542-8425
Wholesaler/distributor of frozen foods, produce, meats, seafood and specialty foods; serving the food service market
President: W Eberle
VP: J East
Sr. VP: J Eberle
Estimated Sales: $10-20 Million
Number Employees: 10-19
Number of Customer Locations: 2000
Types of Products Distributed:
Food Service, Frozen Food, General Line, Provisions/Meat, Produce, Seafood, Specialty Foods

55427 (HQ)C. Lloyd Johnson Company
8031 Hampton Blvd
Norfolk, VA 23505 757-423-2832
Fax: 757-423-0645 800-446-8089
Broker of frozen foods, general merchandise and groceries
CEO: C Llyod Johnson Jr
Sales Representative/Eastern-Northern: Rosa Geroca
Contact: Carol Vangilder
cvangilder@clloydjohnson.com
Number Employees: 1-4
Types of Products Distributed:
Frozen Food

55428 C.A. Flipse & Sons Company
1119 Pennsylvania Ave
Sheboygan, WI 53081-4319 920-452-5321
Fax: 920-452-4450 800-517-2414
Wholesaler/distributor of confectionery products, peanut roasters and plastic and paper products
Owner: John Rindfleisch
j.rindfleisch@flipseandsons.com
Estimated Sales: $1-2.5 Million
Number Employees: 6
Types of Products Distributed:
General Line, General Merchandise, Confectionery products, etc.

55429 C.B.S. Lobster Company
41 Union Wharf
Portland, ME 04101 207-775-2917
Fax: 207-772-0169 www.mainelobsterdirect.com
Lobster
Owner: Lee Kressbach
CEO: Joi Kressbach
Estimated Sales: $5-10 Million
Number Employees: 20-49

55430 C.G. Suarez Distributing Company
PO Box 1134
Tampa, FL 33601-1134 813-685-4701
Fax: 813-684-1929 3—
Wholesaler/distributor of specialty foods
President: C Dean
VP: C Dean, Jr.
Number Employees: 50-99
Square Footage: 80000
Number of Customer Locations: 575
Types of Products Distributed:
Frozen Food, Specialty Foods

55431 C.H. Robinson Co.
14701 Charlson Rd
Eden Prairie, MN 55347-5076 952-683-2800
Fax: 952-933-4747 855-229-6128
solutions@chrobinson.com www.chrobinson.com
Provides: freight transportation (TL, intermodal, ocean, and air freight), cross docking, LTL, customs brokerage, freight forwarding and trucking services, fresh produce sourcing, and information services.
CEO: Bob Biesterfeld
President, NA Surface Transportation: Mac Pinkerton
CFO: Mike Zechmeister
President, Global Freight Forwarding: Michael Short
Year Founded: 1905
Estimated Sales: $14.87 Billion
Number Employees: 15,074
Type of Packaging: Consumer, Food Service, Bulk
Types of Products Distributed:
Frozen Food

55432 C.S. Woods Company
91 Depot Rd
Manchester, NH 03103 603-623-4553
Fax: 603-627-7344 800-562-8207
Wholesaler/distributor serving the food service market
President: T Penner
Estimated Sales: $20-50 Million
Number Employees: 20-49
Types of Products Distributed:
Food Service, Frozen Food

55433 C.T. Grasso
705 Flittertown Road
Hammonton, NJ 08037-9014 609-561-0584
Fax: 609-567-3980
Wholesaler/distributor of produce
President: Carmen Grasso
Secretary: Dolores Grasso
Estimated Sales: $2.5-5 Million
Number Employees: 5-9
Types of Products Distributed:
Frozen Food, Produce

55434 C.W. Shasky & Associates Ltd.
2880 Portland Drive
Oakville, ON L4K 5P2
Canada 905-829-9414
Fax: 905-760-7715 www.shasky.com
Manufacturers' representative for foodservice, club and HMR segments
President: Michael Shasky
VP: James Shasky
Estimated Sales: $7.3 Million
Number Employees: 25
Types of Products Distributed:
Frozen Food

55435 CAI International
Steuart Tower
1 Market Plaza, Suite 900
San Francisco, CA 94105 415-788-0100
Fax: 415-788-3430 www.capps.com
Wholesaler/distributor, importer and exporter of groceries, wine, beer, sherry and port.
President & CEO: Victor Garza
VP, Information Technology: Matthew Easton
Chief Financial Officer: Timothy Page
VP, Finance & Corporate Controller: David Morris
SVP, Global Marketing: Daniel Hallahan
SVP, Logistics Sales & Marketing: Jason Miller
VP, Operations & Human Resources: Camille Cutino
Estimated Sales: $174 Million
Number Employees: 91
Type of Packaging: Consumer, Food Service
Types of Products Distributed:
General Line, Groceries, wine, beer, port & sherry

55436 (HQ)CB Mfg. & Sales Co.
4475 Infirmary Rd
Miamisburg, OH 45342 937-866-5986
Fax: 937-528-2006 800-543-6860
sales@cbmfg.com www.cbmfg.com
Manufacturer and distributor of industrial knives and blades
Chief Executive Officer: Chuck Biehn
CFO: Don Cain
VP Manufacturing: Roger Adams
Contact: Jess Ahern
jahern@cbmfg.com
Purchasing Manager: Angie Matheney
Estimated Sales: $10-20 Million
Number Employees: 10
Square Footage: 200000
Type of Packaging: Private Label, Bulk
Other Locations:
CB Manufacturing & Sales Company
Centerville, OHCB Manufacturing & Sales Company
Types of Products Distributed:
Frozen Food

55437 CB Pallet
14701 Proctor Ave
La Puente, CA 91746-3203 626-961-2783
Fax: 626-369-6908
Wholesaler/distributor of automatic storage and handling systems and pallets
Estimated Sales: $2.5-5 Million
Number Employees: 5-9
Types of Products Distributed:
Frozen Food, General Merchandise, Pallets & storage & handling systems

55438 CBN Advertising Sales Company
4614 Sunrise Highway
Oakdale, NY 11769-1001 631-563-3400
Fax: 631-563-3428 cbnady@yahoo.com
Wholesaler/distributor of general merchandise including advertising specialties, badges, medals, plastic bags, calendars, decals, emblems, labels, marking and writing pens, metal tags and promotional lollipops and candy
Owner: Charles Kosppen
Number Employees: 5-9
Square Footage: 4000
Parent Co: All Star Flag
Number of Customer Locations: 400

55439 CBS Food Equipment
841 Yosemite Way
Milpitas, CA 95035-6329 408-946-2820
Fax: 408-946-3247 800-662-6212
Wholesaler/distributor of food equipment, food handling equipment and spices
President: Edward Cambra
Estimated Sales: $2.5-5 Million
Number Employees: 10-19
Types of Products Distributed:
Frozen Food, General Line, General Merchandise, Food handling equipment & spices

55440 CF Equipment
9950 Washington Boulevard N
Laurel, MD 20723-1932 301-490-2500
800-772-9005
Wholesaler/distributor of material handling equipment
President: George Belo
Procurement: Mellisa Quessimberry
VP Marketing: Tony Sessa
Estimated Sales: $10-20 Million
Number Employees: 20-49
Private Brands Carried:
Bendi; Barrett; Nissan

944

Wholesalers & Distributors / A-Z

Types of Products Distributed:
  Frozen Food, General Merchandise, Material handling equipment

55441 CF Imperial Sales
PO Box 966
Watsonville, CA 95077-0966   831-728-1787
                           Fax: 831-728-2328
Wholesaler/distributor of frozen foods, groceries, seafood and spices; serving the food service market
President: Daniel Gibbs
Contact: Isabel Tovar
itovar@imperialsalescompany.com
Office Manager: E Gomez
Estimated Sales: $5-10 Million
Number Employees: 5
Parent Co: V.J. Catalano
Types of Products Distributed:
  Food Service, General Line, Seafood, Spices & groceries

55442 CFE Equipment Corp
818 Widgeon Rd
Norfolk, VA 23513-3050   757-858-2660
     Fax: 757-853-4280 www.cfeequipment.com
Wholesaler/distributor of material handling equipment including forklifts
President: Tony Sessa
tony.sessa@cseequipment.com
Sales Manager: Mark Mazonkey
Estimated Sales: $20-50 Million
Number Employees: 50-99
Private Brands Carried:
  Nissan; Crown; Taylor-Dunn
Types of Products Distributed:
  Frozen Food, General Merchandise, Material handling equipment

55443 CHLU International
P.O. Box 10027
Toronto, ON M2M 4K3
Canada   416-250-7098
Research and development of innovative nutraceutical ingredients
President: Richard Lu
Number of Brands: 7
Number of Products: 25
Square Footage: 15000
Type of Packaging: Bulk
Private Brands Carried:
  Avoflex ASU; Arthrocoll Chicken Collagen; Lactocalcium Essential Milk Minerals; Biovin Grape Extract; Biovinca Vinpocetine; Biocasanol Rice Policosanol
Types of Products Distributed:
  Nutraceuticals

55444 CHiKPRO
                                 417-708-0988
                           www.chikpro.com
Chicken protein powder
Number of Brands: 1
Number of Products: 26
Type of Packaging: Consumer

55445 CJI Process Systems
12000 Clark St
Santa Fe Springs, CA 90670-3709   562-907-1100
       Fax: 562-907-1105 800-322-7422
           sales@cjiprocesssystems.com
           www.cjiprocesssystems.com
Manufacturer and custom fabrication of food processing and manufacturing equipment, large and small, as well as lifetime equipment servicing and installation.
President: Archie Cholakian
Finance Manager: Michelle Hansen
VP: John Cholakian
Sales Manager: Jim Sutherland
Estimated Sales: $6.9 Million
Number Employees: 50-99
Square Footage: 100000

55446 CK Products
310 Racquet Dr
Fort Wayne, IN 46825-4229   260-484-2517
       Fax: 260-484-2510 888-484-2517
           mail@ckproducts.com
Wholesaler/distributor, importer and exporter of chocolate and chocolate coatings; also, candy making, bakery and cake decorating supplies
President: Orlie Brand
Contact: Steve Burdick
steve.burdick@ckproducts.com
Estimated Sales: $2.5-5 Million
Number Employees: 50-99
Square Footage: 220000
Private Brands Carried:
  Precise Plastic Tips; Pantastic Plastic Bakeware
Number of Customer Locations: 1500
Types of Products Distributed:
  Frozen Food, General Line, Chocolate, candy & bakery supplies

55447 COnut Butter
727 Lyons St
New Orleans, LA 70115
                        info@COnutButter.com
                        www.COnutButter.com
Nut butters
Owner: Alexandra Pericak *Year Founded:* 2015
Types of Products Distributed:
  General Line

55448 CRC Products
1703 N 13th Street
Terre Haute, IN 47804-4113   812-235-6058
         Fax: 812-232-4820 800-457-0515
Wholesaler/distributor serving the food service market
President: Scott Roeleder
CEO: Reid Zoll
Branch Manager: Michael Beachkofsky
Estimated Sales: $5-10 Million
Number Employees: 20-49
Types of Products Distributed:
  Food Service, Frozen Food

55449 CRS Marking Systems
3315 NW 26th Ave #1
Portland, OR 97210-1856   503-228-7624
         Fax: 503-228-2464 800-547-7158
              info@crsdatasolutions.com
Manufacturer and wholesaler/distributor of marking, coding, printing, labeling and bar code equipment
CEO: Julia Farrenkopf
Customer Service: Dwaine Brandson
COO: David Snmodgrass
Estimated Sales: $1-3 Million
Number Employees: 10 to 19
Types of Products Distributed:
  Frozen Food, General Merchandise

55450 CSI Material Handling
3075 Avenue B
Bethlehem, PA 18017
         Fax: 610-866-5115 866-942-1121
                        www.csiforklifts.com
Wholesaler/distributor of material handling equipment.
President: Raymond Robinson
Estimated Sales: $50-100 Million
Number Employees: 100-249
Private Brands Carried:
  Clark; Pay; Nissan
Types of Products Distributed:
  Frozen Food, General Merchandise, Material handling equipment

55451 CTS/Bulk Sales
PO Box 8318
Northfield, IL 60093   847-267-0837
Wholesaler/distributor of baked goods and potato flour and flakes; serving the food service market
President: C Brooks
Estimated Sales: $10-20 Million
Number Employees: 5-9
Types of Products Distributed:
  Food Service, Frozen Food, General Line, Baked goods, potato flour, etc.

55452 CUNICO
750, L,o-Lacombe
Suite 100
Laval, QC H7N 3Y6
Canada   514-947-7481
         Fax: 450-663-1130 877-663-7117
                        cunico@qc.aira.com
Wholesaler/distributor of air chilled rabbit, chicken and rock cornish game hen
Types of Products Distributed:
  Frozen Food, Provisions/Meat, Rabbit, chicken & rock cornish game hen

55453 CW Paper
8305 Stewart Ave
Wausau, WI 54401-9471   715-842-2241
         Fax: 715-842-8110 800-688-1872
                        www.midlandpaper.com
Wholesaler/distributor of disposables; serving the food service market
Manager: Wally Haglund
Sales Manager: R Bret Miller
Purchasing Manager: John Feldman
Estimated Sales: $20-50 Million
Number Employees: 20-49
Square Footage: 60000
Types of Products Distributed:
  Food Service, Frozen Food, General Merchandise, Disposables

55454 Cable Meat Center
1204 S Broadway St
Marlow, OK 73055   580-658-6646
                           Fax: 580-658-6648
Wholesaler/distributor of frozen foods and meats; serving the food service market
President: Tom Wheat
Plant Manager: Newt Moore
Estimated Sales: $20-50 Million
Number Employees: 20-49
Types of Products Distributed:
  Food Service, Frozen Food, Provisions/Meat

55455 Cactus Holdings Inc
4705 Metropolitan Ave
Ridgewood, NY 11385-1046   718-417-3770
         Fax: 718-628-2356 www.westernbeef.com
Wholesaler/distributor of produce and provisions/meats.chain of supermarkets
Manager: Richie Rodriguez
CEO: Peter Castellana Jr
CFO: Thomas Moranzoni
COO: Richard Frashilla
Marketing Manager: Richard Fraschilla
Estimated Sales: $10-20 Million
Number Employees: 1000-4999
Parent Co: Food Nation
Types of Products Distributed:
  Frozen Food, Provisions/Meat, Produce

55456 (HQ)Cadco Inc
145 Colebrook River Rd
Winsted, CT 06098-2203   860-738-2500
         Fax: 860-738-9772 info@cadco-ltd.com
                        www.cadco-ltd.com
Wholesaler/distributor, exporter and marketer of convection ovens, buffet ranges, waffle irons, juicers, toasters, can openers, soup kettles and cordless stick mixers; serving the food service market
President: Mike Shanahan
mike@cadco-ltd.com
Chairman: Neil Gerhardt
Finance & HR: Patricia Warner
Quality Control: Marc Faulkner
Marketing Director: Erin Shanahan
Sales/Culinary Manager: Christopher Kasik
Customer Service: Lisa Smith
Estimated Sales: $5-10 Million
Number Employees: 5-9
Square Footage: 120000
Other Locations:
  Cadco Ltd.
  Winsted, CTCadco Ltd.
Types of Products Distributed:
  Food Service

55457 Cadillac Meat Company
3853 Shellmarr Lane
Bloomfield Hills, MI 48302-4054   313-341-8900
Wholesaler/distributor of fresh and frozen beef, lamb, pork, chicken and turkey; serving the food service market
President: Arnold Greenbaum
VP: Ruth Greenbaum
Estimated Sales: $20-50 Million
Number Employees: 10-19
Types of Products Distributed:
  Food Service, Frozen Food, Provisions/Meat, Beef, lamb, pork & poultry

55458 Cadillac Packaging Corporation
5424 17th Ave
Brooklyn, NY 11204   718-851-0436
                           Fax: 718-851-3656
Wholesaler/distributor of poly and cellophane bags, corrugated boxes, tapes, stretch films, strapping, etc

Wholesalers & Distributors / A-Z

Vice President: Mordy Gross
Manager: Mordy Gross
Number Employees: 10-19
Number of Customer Locations: 1000
Types of Products Distributed:
  Frozen Food, General Merchandise, Poly & cellophane bags, film, etc.

55459 Caesar Electric Supply
10 John Davenport Drive NW
Rome, GA 30165-2536 706-232-4226
  Fax: 706-232-4117 800-234-2730
Wholesaler/distributor of electrical supplies, controls, lighting, switches, etc
President: Dan Caesar
Number Employees: 14
Types of Products Distributed:
  Food Service, Frozen Food, General Line, General Merchandise, Health Food, Provisions/Meat, Rack Jobbers, Seafood, Specialty Foods, Electrical supplies, lighting, etc.

55460 Cafe Grumpy
199 Diamond St
Brooklyn, NY 11222 718-383-0748
  info@cafegrumpy.com
  cafegrumpy.com
Coffee roasters
Co-Owner: Chris Timbrell
Co-Owner: Caroline Bell
Head Roaster: Chris Cross
Buyer: Cheryl Kingan *Year Founded:* 2005
Type of Packaging: Consumer, Private Label

55461 Cafe Jumbo
1070 2nd Ave (Btwn 56th & 57th st)
New York, NY 10022-2802 212-344-6185
  Fax: 212-355-6882
Wholesaler/distributor of bagels and bialys; serving the food service market
Owner: Kevin Murphy
Estimated Sales: $.5-1 million
Number Employees: 10-19
Types of Products Distributed:
  Food Service, Frozen Food, General Line, Bagels & bialys

55462 Cafe Kreyol
Manassas, VA 20109
  www.coffeehunterproject.com
Organic specialty coffee

55463 Caffe Darte
33926 9th Ave S
Federal Way, WA 98003-6708 253-252-7050
  Fax: 206-763-4665 800-999-5334
  sales@caffedarte.com www.caffedarte.com
Processor of coffee beans.
General Manager: Joe Mancuso
jmancuso@caffedarte.com
National Sales Manager: Tim Fleming
Director of Operations: John Virden
Estimated Sales: $5-10,000,000
Number Employees: 20-49
Other Locations:
  Boise Caff,
  Boise, ID
  Bonney Lake Caff,
  Tehaleh, WA
  Portland Caff,
  Portland, OR
  Seattle Caff,-1st & Yesler
  Seattle, WABoise Caff,Tehaleh
Types of Products Distributed:
  Coffee

55464 Cagles Appliance Center
Ontario, CA 91761 909-986-9789
  Fax: 909-988-3144 800-672-2453
  sales@cagles.com www.cagles.com
Wholesaler of washer and dryers.
Sales Manager: David Gotts
Year Founded: 1952
Estimated Sales: Less than $500,000
Number Employees: 10-19
Number of Brands: 19+
Number of Products: 300+
Type of Packaging: Consumer, Food Service
Private Brands Carried:
  Whirlpool; LG Appliances; KitchenAid; Brown Stove Works; Amana; Dandy; Fisher & Paykel; Everpure; PureWash; Speed Queen; U-Line; Jenn Air; Kobe Hoods; Roper; Sharp; Waste King Disposers; Maytag; Imperial Range Hoods; DCS; FiveStar; WindCrest; Asko
Types of Products Distributed:
  Appliances

55465 Cain's Coffee Company
208 NW Business Park Lane
Riverside, MO 64150-9696 816-587-8978
  Fax: 816-587-9061
Wholesaler/distributor of coffee
Sales Manager: Terry Baker
Estimated Sales: $3-5 Million
Number Employees: 20-49
Types of Products Distributed:
  Frozen Food, General Line, Coffee

55466 Cajun Brothers Seafood Company
P.O.Box 7503
Monroe, LA 71211-7503 318-325-1221
  Fax: 318-325-1881
Wholesaler/distributor of fresh and frozen seafood including breaded and stuffed shrimp and stuffed crabs
Owner: Larry Rhodes
Estimated Sales: $2.5-5 Million
Number Employees: 1-4
Types of Products Distributed:
  Frozen Food, Seafood, Stuffed crabs, etc.

55467 Cajun Crawfish Distributors
379 Industrial Blvd
PO Box 393
Branch, LA 70516
  Fax: 337-334-8477 888-254-8626
  boudreaux@cajuncrawfish.com
  www.cajuncrawfish.com
Live crawfish, cooked crawfish, gumbos, Cajun meats, turducken
Co-Owner: Mark Fruge
Co-Owner: Michael Fruge
Administration: Pam Estes
Marketing Director: Courtney Fruge
Sales Manager: Richard Hotard
Public Relations: Carol Schultz
Operations Manager: Ed Guidry
Year Founded: 1972
Estimated Sales: $30 Million
Number Employees: 4
Types of Products Distributed:
  Frozen Food, Seafood

55468 Cajun Seafood Enterprises
9650 Highway 52 E
Murrayville, GA 30564-6901 706-864-9688
  Fax: 706-864-9688
Seafood

55469 Cajun Sugar Company LLC
2711 Northside Rd
New Iberia, LA 70563 337-365-3401
  Fax: 337-365-7820 andrew@cajunsugar.net
  www.amscl.org
Wholesaler/distributor of sugar.
Estimated Sales: $20-50 Million
Number Employees: 50-99
Types of Products Distributed:
  Frozen Food, General Line, Sugar

55470 Cal Coast Promo-Products
1500 Callens Road
Ventura, CA 93003-5607 805-656-3394
  Fax: 805-644-4543 800-444-6436
Wholesaler/distributor of promotional products
Office Manager: Logan Jett
Number Employees: 5-9
Number of Customer Locations: 2000
Types of Products Distributed:
  Frozen Food, General Merchandise, Promotional products

55471 Cal-West Produce
PO Box 4318
Visalia, CA 93278-4318 559-627-5457
  Fax: 559-627-9047 800-444-9844
  calwestpro@aol.com
Wholesaler/distributor of vegetables
President: Joel Hayden
Sales: Doug Fisher
Number Employees: 1-4
Types of Products Distributed:
  Frozen Food, Produce, Vegetables

55472 Calico Cottage
210 New Hwy
Amityville, NY 11701-1116 631-841-2100
  Fax: 631-841-2401 800-645-5345
  www.calicocottage.com
Fudge mixes, flavors and colorings.
President & CEO: Mark Wurzel
m.wurzel@calicocottage.com
Chief Financial Officer: Michael Lobaccaro
Vice President: Larry Wurzel
Executive VP, Sales & Marketing: David Sank
Director, Human Resources & Admin: Barbara Stone-Carroll
Sr. VP, Operations & Technology: Thomas Montoya
Estimated Sales: $5 Million
Number Employees: 50-99
Square Footage: 45000
Type of Packaging: Consumer
Types of Products Distributed:
  Fudge

55473 Calico Industries Inc
9045 Junction Dr
Annapolis Jct, MD 20701-1149 301-490-1595
  Fax: 301-498-2056 800-638-0828
Wholesaler/distributor of institutional wiping rags, plastic bags, aprons, gloves, dish towels, shelving and pot holders; serving the food service market
Owner: Dirk Wiersma
dwiersma@calicoindustries.com
Director Marketing: Dirk Weirsma
Purchasing Agent: Lee Hirsch
Estimated Sales: $20-50 Million
Number Employees: 50-99
Number of Customer Locations: 4000
Types of Products Distributed:
  Food Service, Frozen Food, General Merchandise, Wiping rags, dish towels, etc.

55474 California Agriculture & Foodstuff
6220 Stanford Ranch Rd
Suite 200
Rocklin, CA 95765-4428 916-899-6183
  Fax: 916-889-6184 nature-expo.com
Nuts and dried fruit
President: D Ajami
president@Californiafoodstuff.com
Managing Director/Partner: M Safaie
Type of Packaging: Food Service, Bulk

55475 California Caster & Handtruck
1400 17th St
San Francisco, CA 94107-2412 415-552-6750
  Fax: 415-552-0463 800-950-8750
  customerservice@californiacaster.com
Stainless steel hand trucks and carts, dollies, casters, leveling pads and oven and bun pan racks; wholesaler/distributor of casters
Owner: Alan Mc Clure
alanm@californiacaster.com
VP: Terry Cavannaugh
Estimated Sales: $5-10 Million
Number Employees: 10-19
Square Footage: 33000
Private Brands Carried:
  Darcor; Jarvis & Jarvis; Faultless; RWM; Darnell; Shephard
Types of Products Distributed:
  Frozen Food, General Merchandise, Stainless steel casters

55476 California Fruit Market
580 W Main St
Watertown, NY 13601-1350 315-788-1390
  Fax: 315-788-1414 800-836-0952
Wholesaler/distributor of pita bread
Owner: Jerry Levos
Purchasing Manager: Jerry Levos
Estimated Sales: $20-50 Million
Number Employees: 20-49
Types of Products Distributed:
  Frozen Food, General Line, Pita bread

55477 California Independent Almond Growers
13000 Newport Road
Merced, CA 95303-9704 209-667-4855
  Fax: 209-667-4854
Growers, packers, processors and shippers worldwide. California grown whole natural almonds direct from the source. State-of-the-art equipment
President: Karen Barstow

Wholesalers & Distributors / A-Z

Estimated Sales: $2.5-5 Million
Number Employees: 50-99
Square Footage: 60000
Type of Packaging: Consumer, Food Service, Private Label, Bulk
Types of Products Distributed:
Frozen Food

55478 California Marketing Group Inc
10731 Walker St # A
Cypress, CA 90630-4757   714-895-1447
Fax: 714-894-3883 linda@calmktg.com
www.calmktg.com
Wholesaler/distributor of advertising specialties and awards
President: Linda Labar
Vice President: Ed Enriquez
ed.enriquez@exelisinc.com
Assistant Sales: Bill Labar, Jr.
Estimated Sales: $5-10 Million
Number Employees: 10-19
Number of Customer Locations: 3000
Types of Products Distributed:
Frozen Food, General Merchandise, Advertising specialties & awards

55479 California Sprout & Celery
21158 Birds Nest Terrace
Boca Raton, FL 33433-1943   312-226-7551
Fax: 312-226-4165
Wholesaler/distributor of produce
President: John De Arcangelis
Estimated Sales: $2.5-5 Million
Number Employees: 5-9
Number of Customer Locations: 250
Types of Products Distributed:
Produce

55480 California Tag & Label
882 N Poinsettia Avenue
Brea, CA 92821-2216   213-747-0131
Fax: 213-747-0091 caltnl@hotmail.com
Wholesaler/distributor of general merchandise including labels, tags, bar code printers and labeling machinery
Owner: Bill Hobart
Estimated Sales: Less than $500,000
Number Employees: 1-4
Types of Products Distributed:
Frozen Food, General Merchandise, Labels, tags, bar code printers, etc.

55481 California-Antilles Trading
3735 Adams Ave
San Diego, CA 92116-2220   619-283-4834
Fax: 619-283-4834 800-330-6450
www.calantilles.com
Hot sauces, salsas, barbecue sauces
President: Richard E Gardner
irina.profosovitskaya@kp.org
Operations: Tevor Dyer
Production: Robert Davis
Estimated Sales: $2.5-5,000,000
Number Employees: 1-4
Number of Brands: 2
Number of Products: 25
Type of Packaging: Consumer, Private Label
Private Brands Carried:
Tres Tropical and West Indies Creole

55482 Callahan Grocery Company
P.O.Box 725
Bainbridge, GA 39818   229-246-0849
Wholesaler/distributor of general line products; serving the food service market
President: D Bryan, Sr.
Number Employees: 1-4
Number of Customer Locations: 250
Types of Products Distributed:
Food Service, Frozen Food, General Line

55483 Callif Foods
4561 E 5th Avenue
Columbus, OH 43219-1896   614-238-7300
Wholesaler/distributor of produce; serving the food service market
President: Mike Callif
Number Employees: 10-19
Types of Products Distributed:
Food Service, Produce

55484 Cambridge Packing Company
41 Foodmart Road
Boston, MA 02118   617-269-6700
Fax: 617-269-0266 800-722-6726
salesinfo@cambridgepacking.com
www.cambridgepacking.com
Fine meats and seafoods including beef, lamb, pork, chicken, fish and shellfish
President/CEO: Bruce Rodman
Co-CEO: Alan Roberts
CFO: Wendy DeMonico
Operations: Paul Dias
Year Founded: 1923
Estimated Sales: $45 Million
Number Employees: 62
Square Footage: 30000
Types of Products Distributed:
Food Service, Frozen Food, Provisions/Meat, Seafood

55485 Cameo Metal Products Inc
127 12th St
Brooklyn, NY 11215-3891   718-788-1106
Fax: 718-788-3761 sales@cameometal.com
www.cameometal.com
Cameo Metal Products Manufactures metal closures for the food and beverage industry.
President: Vito Di Maio
cameosales@cameometals.com
Finance Manager: Adolspoll Cruz
Director of Sales/Plant Manager: Robert Geddis
Director of Operations: Anthony Di Maio
Estimated Sales: $5.8 Million
Number Employees: 20-49
Square Footage: 100000

55486 Cameron Seafood Processors
PO Box 1228
Cameron, LA 70631-1228   318-775-5510
Fax: 318-755-5529
Seafood
President: Bruce Bang

55487 Campbell's Food Service
1 Campbell Pl.
Camden, NJ 08103-1701
800-879-7687
www.campbellsfoodservice.com
Fresh, frozen, canned and dried foods.
President/CEO, Campbell Soup Co.: Mark Clouse
Estimated Sales: $656 Million
Number Employees: 1-4
Square Footage: 3000
Parent Co: Campbell Soup Company
Private Brands Carried:
Campbell's
Types of Products Distributed:
Food Service, Frozen Food, General Line, Fresh, frozen, canned & dried foods

55488 Campione Resturant Supply
844 Caledonia Road
Toronto, ON M6B 3Y1
Canada   416-789-7207
Fax: 416-789-1781
Wholesaler/distributor of food service supplies and equipment
Types of Products Distributed:
Food Service, Frozen Food, General Merchandise

55489 Can Am Seafood
972 County Road
Lubec, ME 04652   207-733-2267
Fax: 207-733-0927
Seafood
President: William Jackson
Estimated Sales: $200,000
Number Employees: 1

55490 Canada Cutlery Inc.
1964 Notion Road
Pickering, ON L1V 2G3
Canada
905-683-8480
Fax: 905-683-9184 800-698-8277
www.canadacutlery.com
Food service cutlery
Owner, President: Peter Huebner, HAAC
VP & Marketing Director: Mary Louise Huebner
Estimated Sales: $1-3 Million
Number Employees: 5-9
Square Footage: 20000
Type of Packaging: Consumer, Food Service, Private Label, Bulk
Private Brands Carried:
Superior Culinary Master
Types of Products Distributed:
Food Service, General Merchandise, Cutlery

55491 Canada Dry Bottling Co
5206 Pierson Hwy
Lansing, MI 48917-9589   517-322-2133
www.cdry.net
Wholesaler/distributor of soft drinks
Owner: Randy Shanker
randy@cdry.net
Estimated Sales: $20-50 Million
Number Employees: 20-49
Parent Co: Cadbury Schweppes
Private Brands Carried:
Hawaiian Punch; Crush; Faygo; Ecerfresh; Nantucket; Stewarts; Canada Dry; Jones Soda; Honest Tea; IBC; Orangina; Clearly Canadian; Gatorade; Glaceau Vitamin Water; Crystal Geyser
Number of Customer Locations: 800
Types of Products Distributed:
Food Service, General Line, Soft drinks

55492 Canada Pure Water Company Ltd
7 Kodiak Crescent
Toronto, ON M3J 3E5
Canada   416-631-5800
Fax: 416-635-1711 800-361-2369
info@canadapure.com www.canadapure.com
Wholesaler/distributor of flavored spring water and teas
President: David Tavares
Marketing Assistant: Sophia Ahmed
Director Purchasing: Tracy Tavares
Number Employees: 10-19
Types of Products Distributed:
Frozen Food, General Line, Health Food, Flavored spring water & teas

55493 Canada Safeway
1020 64th Avenue NE
Calgary, AB T2E 7V8
Canada
800-723-3929
customer.helpline@sobeys.com www.safeway.ca
Wholesaler/distributor of frozen food, general line items, general merchandise, produce, provisions/meats and seafood
President, Sobeys Inc. Western Canada: Jason Potter
Number Employees: 250-499
Parent Co: Sobeys
Number of Customer Locations: 215
Types of Products Distributed:
Frozen Food, General Line, General Merchandise, Provisions/Meat, Produce, Seafood

55494 Canadian Gold Seafood
209 Aerotech Drive
Unit 10B
Enfield, NS B2T 1K3
Canada   902-873-3766
Fax: 902-873-4535
Wholesaler/distributor of live, processed, cooked and frozen lobster, live crab, I.Q.F. scallops, fresh whiting, sea urchins and dogfish
President: Doug McRae
Controller: Carol Ennis
Quality Control: Pam Boyle
General Manager: Brent Davis
Buyer: Brian Thorbourne
Estimated Sales: $16 Million
Number Employees: 20-49
Square Footage: 20000
Types of Products Distributed:
General Line, Seafood, Lobster, scallops, crab, whiting, etc.

55495 Cannon/Tayloe
4230 Lyndon B Johnso Fwy # 360
Dallas, TX 75244-5820   972-663-3300
Fax: 214-357-4576 800-442-3061
wwcannon@wwcannon.com
www.cdirealestate.com
Wholesaler/distributor of material handling systems including conveyor storage and packaging systems with turnkey installation
Owner: Robert Cannon
Purchasing Manager: Jerry Lawrence
Estimated Sales: $15 Million
Number Employees: 50-99
Square Footage: 50000

Wholesalers & Distributors / A-Z

55496 Canoe Lagoon Oyster Company
118 Bayview Ave
Coffman Cove, AK 99918   907-329-2253
Fax: 425-643-7266
Oyster
Owner: Sharon Gray
Owner: Don Nicholson
Estimated Sales: $310,000
Number Employees: 2
Type of Packaging: Consumer, Food Service, Bulk

55497 Canon Potato Company
P.O.Box 880
Center, CO 81125-0880   719-754-3445
Potato packer and shipper
President: David Tonso
d.tonso@canonpotato.com
Estimated Sales: $2,689,000
Number Employees: 40
Parent Co: Woerner Holdings, L.P.
Type of Packaging: Private Label
Types of Products Distributed:
  Produce

55498 Cantab Industries
PO Box 54
Toronto, ON M9C 4V2
Canada   416-923-2288
Fax: 416-923-2277
Wholesaler/distributor of confectionery machinery, tablet coating systems and chocolate processing machinery
President: F Rose
Private Brands Carried:
  NID; Low & Duff; Driam
Types of Products Distributed:
  Frozen Food, General Merchandise, Confectionery machinery, etc.

55499 Canterbury's Crack & Peel
24 Crescent Street
Claremont, NH 03743-2279   603-542-2863
Fax: 603-543-1333   888-705-4779
Wholesaler/distributor of dressings including garlic and honey, balsamic Italian and honey dijon; serving the food service market
President: Bob Weaver
VP: Eileen Weaver
Number Employees: 1-4
Private Brands Carried:
  Delectable Dressings
Types of Products Distributed:
  Food Service, Frozen Food, General Line, Dressings

55500 Canton Foods
1840 East 38th Street
Minneapolis, MN 55407-2964   612-722-9501
Fax: 612-722-9502
Wholesaler/distributor of private label Chinese foods including pasta, chow mein noodles and wrappers including egg roll and wonton; serving the food service and retail markets
Pres.: Victor Wang
Estimated Sales: $3-5 Million
Number Employees: 5-9
Square Footage: 40000
Types of Products Distributed:
  Food Service, Frozen Food, General Line, Specialty Foods, Chinese foods: pasta, wrappers, etc.

55501 Canty Wiper & Supply Company
571 New York Avenue
164
Lyndhurst, NJ 07071-1506   201-438-7213
Fax: 201-438-7218
Wholesaler/distributor of cotton wiping rags, plastic bags and liners, paper towels and tissues; serving the food service market
President: Scott Wolf
CEO: Frank Wolf
Number Employees: 5-9
Square Footage: 32000
Private Brands Carried:
  Western Pacific; Roach Conveyors; Spacerak; Modular Drawer Storage; Packaging; Drive-In/Drive-Thru Storage Racks
Types of Products Distributed:
  Frozen Food, General Merchandise, Material handling equipment

55502 Canyon Bakehouse LLC
1510 E 11th St
Loveland, CO 80537-5049   970-461-3844
www.canyonglutenfree.com
Gluten free baked goods
Co-Founder: Christi Skow
Co-Founder: Josh Skow
jskow@canyonbakehouse.com
Co-Founder: Ed Miknevicius
Estimated Sales: Less Than $500,000
Number Employees: 1-4

55503 Capalbo's Fruit Baskets
350 Allwood Rd
Clifton, NJ 07012-1701   973-667-6262
Fax: 973-450-1199   800-252-6262
service@capalbosonline.com
www.capalbosonline.com
Produces gift baskets for the specialty food industry.
President: Frank Capalbo
Vice President: Susan Capalbo
Digital Marketing Manager: Joe Wilson
Estimated Sales: $4,8,000,000
Number Employees: 50-99
Type of Packaging: Food Service
Types of Products Distributed:
  Specialty Foods, Gift Baskets

55504 Cape Dairy LLC
44 Bodick Rd
Hyannis, MA 02601-2001   508-771-4700
Fax: 508-771-9770
Wholesaler/distributor of milk and ice cream; serving the food service market
Owner: Stephen Ward
capedairy@aol.com
General Manager: Paul Ritzman
Estimated Sales: $5-10 Million
Number Employees: 20-49
Parent Co: H.P. Hood
Types of Products Distributed:
  Food Service, Frozen Food, General Line, Dairy products

55505 Cape May Fishery Cooperative
788 W Montgomery Ave
Wildwood, NJ 08260-1727   609-522-2300
Wholesaler/distributor of fresh fish including porgy, whiting, flounder, etc; serving the food service market
Owner: Donna Tilsner
Estimated Sales: $300,000-500,000
Number Employees: 1-4
Types of Products Distributed:
  Food Service, Frozen Food, Seafood, Fresh fish

55506 Capital City Fruit
1850 Colonial Pkwy
P.O. Box 337
Norwalk, IA 50211   515-981-5111
Fax: 515-981-4564   800-535-6826
ccfsales@capitalcityfruit.com
www.capitalcityfruit.com
Wholesaler/distributor of produce.
President & CEO: Christian Comito
Chairman: Joe Comito
Business Development Manager: Mike Ireland
Director of Sales & Marketing: Brent Addison
Chief Operating Officer: Brendan Comito
Purchasing: Barb Van Gorder
Year Founded: 1949
Estimated Sales: $50-100 Million
Number Employees: 100-249
Types of Products Distributed:
  Frozen Food, Produce

55507 Capital Equipment & Handling
1100 Cottonwood Ave # 100
Hartland, WI 53029-8364   262-369-5500
Fax: 262-369-9700   800-813-0000
sales@cehnissan.com   www.cehwi.com
Wholesaler/distributor of material handling equipment including forklifts
President: Richard Muenster
Estimated Sales: $10-20 Million
Number Employees: 20-49
Types of Products Distributed:
  Frozen Food, General Merchandise, Material handling equipment

55508 Capital Produce II Inc
8005 Rappahanock Ave
Jessup, MD 20794-9438   443-755-1733
Fax: 443-755-0282   www.capitalseaboard.com
Seafood
Owner: Tom Alascio
tom@capitalseaboard.com
Vice President: Steve Hanson
Estimated Sales: $3.7 Million
Number Employees: 50-99

55509 Capitol City Produce
16550 Commercial Ave
Baton Rouge, LA 70816   225-272-8153
Fax: 225-272-8152   800-349-1583
www.capitolcityproduce.com
Wholesaler/distributor of frozen foods and produce; serving the food service market.
Owner & CEO: Paul Ferachi
Year Founded: 1947
Estimated Sales: $100+ Million
Number Employees: 175
Square Footage: 20000
Number of Customer Locations: 675
Types of Products Distributed:
  Food Service, Frozen Food, Produce

55510 Capitol Foods
PO Box 751541
Memphis, TN 38175-1541   662-781-9021
Fax: 662-781-0697
Canned vegetables, diced peaches, mixed fruits and edible oils; exporter of canned vegetables; wholesaler/distributor of bakery, dairy and grocery products, soups and bases, produce, syrups, oils, pasta, meats; serving the food servicemarkets
President: Kenneth Porter
CFO: Phillip Duncan
Number Employees: 134
Square Footage: 20000
Type of Packaging: Consumer, Food Service
Types of Products Distributed:
  Food Service, Frozen Food, General Line, General Merchandise, Health Food, Provisions/Meat, Produce, Seafood, Specialty Foods, Industrial ingredients, etc.

55511 Capone Foods
14 Bow St. Union Square
Somerville, MA 02143   617-629-2296
Fax: 617-776-0318   albert@caponefoods.com
www.caponefoods.com
Producer of pasta and sauces. Some of their products include fresh pasta, ravioli, tortellini, gnocchi, pizza, entr‚es, meatballs, sausage, empanadas and many more items. Their products can be found in several store locationsthroughout Massachusetts, such as Bedford, Boston, Brighton, Brookline, Cambridge, Concord, and other locations.
Owner: Albert Capone
Manager: Jennifer Capone
Estimated Sales: $320,000
Number Employees: 7
Types of Products Distributed:
  Specialty Foods, Pasta

55512 Cappello Foods
3320 N Hampton Road
Dallas, TX 75212-2405   214-638-4797
Fax: 214-638-4807
Wholesaler/distributor of provisions/meats and frozen foods; serving the food service market
President: John Cappello
Estimated Sales: Less than $500,000
Number Employees: 1-4
Square Footage: 112000
Private Brands Carried:
  Decker; Oscar Myer; Earl Campell
Types of Products Distributed:
  Food Service, Frozen Food, Provisions/Meat

55513 Cappuccino Express Company
1718 Waukegan Rd
Glenview, IL 60025   847-361-9776
Fax: 847-824-7103   800-824-8041
Wholesaler/distributor and importer of fully automatic espresso and cappuccino machines
CEO: Jim Morton
Estimated Sales: $.5-1 million
Number Employees: 1-4

Types of Products Distributed:
  Frozen Food, General Merchandise, Espresso & cappuccino machines

55514 Capriole Inc
10329 New Cut Rd
Greenville, IN 47124-9202   812-923-9408
       Fax: 812-923-8901
cheese@capriolegoatcheese.com
       www.capriolegoatcheese.com
Cheese
President: Judy Schad
judygoat@aol.com
Estimated Sales: Less Than $500,000
Number Employees: 5-9

55515 Capt Collier Seafood
14733 Tom Johnson Ave
Coden, AL 36523-3116   251-824-4925
       Fax: 251-824-2374
Seafood
Owner: Phil Brannon
brannonmerle@aol.com
Estimated Sales: $3-5 Million
Number Employees: 5-9

55516 Capt Joe & Sons Inc
95 E Main St
Gloucester, MA 01930-3860   978-283-1454
   Fax: 978-283-1466 captijoe06@yahoo.com
Seafood
President: Benjamin Ciaramitaro
Treasurer/Clerk: Charles Ciaramitaro
Vice President: Frank Ciaramitaro
Manager: Joe Ciaramitaro
Estimated Sales: Less Than $500,000
Number Employees: 1-4

55517 Captain Alex Seafoods
8874 N Milwaukee Ave
Niles, IL 60714-1752   847-803-8833
   Fax: 847-803-9854 www.fishandseafoodniles.com
Seafood
President/Secretary: Alex Malidis
Vice President: Matthew Mallidis
Office Manager: Ilir Veliu
Estimated Sales: $530,000
Number Employees: 5-9

55518 Captain Little Seafood
413 Central Port Mouton Td.
Queens County, NS B0T1T0
Canada   902-947-2087
   Fax: 902-947-2088 www.scotiafish.com
Lobster, Atlantic sea cucumber, red sea cucumber, sea urchin, snow crab, Jonah crab, salmon caviar, halibut, herring, capelin fish, whelk, cold water shrimp, tuna, scallops
Procurement: Steven Shi
Square Footage: 72500
Types of Products Distributed:
  Seafood

55519 Captain Morrills Inc
7 Baker Blvd
Brewer, ME 04412-2254   207-989-2277
       Fax: 207-989-1561 800-633-0800
       www.thelobsternet.com
President/CEO: Philip Morrill
pam@maine-web.com
CFO: Kelly Roberts
Quality Control: Steve Doughty
Director Sales/Marketing: Frank Plummer
Estimated Sales: $1-3 Million
Number Employees: 5-9
Square Footage: 32000
Type of Packaging: Bulk
Types of Products Distributed:
  Food Service, Frozen Food, Seafood

55520 Captree Clam
440 Falmouth Rd
West Babylon, NY 11704-5802   631-422-0517
   Fax: 631-422-0229 billzeller@CaptreeClam.com
       www.captreeclam.com
Wholesaler/distributor of hard clams, oysters and lobsters
President/Founder/Owner: Bill Zeller
sokie@halstead.com
VP: Maureen Zeller
General Manager: Kenny Murphy
Plant Engineer/Dock Buyer: Dan Brucceleri

Estimated Sales: $2.5-5 Million
Number Employees: 1-4
Square Footage: 20000
Types of Products Distributed:
  Frozen Food, Seafood, Hard clams, oysters & lobsters

55521 Caracolillo Coffee Mills
4419 N Hesperides St
Tampa, FL 33614-7618   813-876-0302
       Fax: 813-875-6407 800-682-0023
       info@ccmcoffee.com www.ccmcoffee.com
Coffee
President: Julian Faedo
info@ccmcoffee.com
Estimated Sales: $3-5 Million
Number Employees: 5-9
Type of Packaging: Consumer, Food Service, Private Label
Private Brands Carried:
  Cafe La Paloma; Cubita

55522 CarbRite Diet
3 Terminal Rd
New Brunswick, NJ 08901   732-545-3130
       Fax: 732-509-0458 732-872-0101
       info@carbritediet.com www.carbritediet.com
Low-carb snack bars and brownies
President: Danny Keller
VP: Robert Gluckin
Year Founded: 2000
Parent Co: Universal Nutrition
Types of Products Distributed:
  Health Food

55523 Carbonella & Desarbo Inc
307 Food Terminal Plz
New Haven, CT 06511-5980   203-624-5127
       Fax: 203-787-3130
Wholesaler/distributor of general merchandise, general line products, produce and seafood; serving the food service market
President & CEO: Joseph Desarbo
Estimated Sales: $10-20 Million
Number Employees: 50-99
Number of Customer Locations: 1000
Types of Products Distributed:
  Food Service, Frozen Food, General Line, General Merchandise, Produce, Seafood

55524 Carborator Rental Svc
6500 Eastwick Ave
PO Box 33327
Philadelphia, PA 19142-3399   215-726-8000
       Fax: 215-726-6367 800-220-3556
       info@carbonatorrental.com
       www.carbonatorrental.com
Soda water syrups and bar mixes; wholesaler/distributor of beverage dispensing equipment
President: Andy Pincus
andy@carbonatorrental.com
Chairman: Herbert Pincus
Corporate Secretary: Susan Pincus
Vice President: Leatrice Pincus
Manager: Thomas Moreno
Production: George Rossi
Estimated Sales: $3.7 Million
Number Employees: 20-49
Square Footage: 80000
Types of Products Distributed:
  Frozen Food, General Merchandise, Beverage dispensing equipment

55525 Carden Foods Inc
442 Wilson Rd
Griffin, GA 30224-4549   770-227-9421
       Fax: 770-227-9443 800-487-3530
       info@cardenfoods.com www.cardenfoods.com
Wholesaler/distributor of frozen food, general line products and produce; serving the food service market
Owner: Charles Carden
Secretary: C Carden
Estimated Sales: $5-10 Million
Number Employees: 20-49
Number of Customer Locations: 500
Types of Products Distributed:
  Food Service, Frozen Food, General Line, Produce

55526 Cardinal Carryor Inc
1055 Grade Ln
Louisville, KY 40213-2610   502-363-6641
       Fax: 270-363-6644 800-666-5600
       www.cardinalcarryor.com
Wholesaler/distributor of forklifts and personnel lifts
President: Brad Baker
bradb@cardinalcarryor.com
Estimated Sales: $5-10 Million
Number Employees: 50-99
Private Brands Carried:
  Clark; Crown; Mitsubishi
Types of Products Distributed:
  Frozen Food, General Merchandise, Forklifts & personnel lifts

55527 Cardinal International
P.O.Box 897
43 Route 46 East, Suite 709
Pine Brook, NJ 7058   973-628-0900
       Fax: 973-633-5555 cardinalsales@arc-intl.com
       www.cardinalglass.com
Wholesaler/distributor of crystal dishware and glassware; serving the food service market
President: Brian O'Rourke
Customer Service: Nancy Kamphausen
Estimated Sales: $10-20 Million
Number Employees: 50-99
Types of Products Distributed:
  Food Service, Frozen Food, General Merchandise, Crystal dishware & glassware

55528 Carefree Kanopy
915 Dolphin Drive
Malvern, PA 19355-3143   610-889-3299
       Fax: 610-889-3304 carekanopy@aol.com
       www.carefreekanopy.com
Wholesaler/distributor of pop-up temporary canopies
Co-Owner: Nick Giambri
Co-Owner: Bill Peck
Private Brands Carried:
  KD Kanopy
Types of Products Distributed:
  Frozen Food, General Merchandise, Canopies

55529 Caribbean Produce Exchange
4th St Bldg. D, Mrcado Cntl
P.O. Box 11990
San Juan, PR 00920-1990   787-793-0750
       Fax: 787-792-2617 888-783-2754
Wholesaler/distributor, exporter and importer of fresh fruits and vegetables
President: Gualberto Rodriguez
VP: Luis Rodriquez
VP: Marta Zanvela
Accounts Payable: Ivtte Rivera
Purchasing Coordinator: Felix Martinez
Purchasing Director: Manny Garcia
Number Employees: 100-249
Square Footage: 240000
Types of Products Distributed:
  Frozen Food, General Line, Produce

55530 Caribbean Restaurants
3 Camino Tabonucal
San Juan, PR 00926-9010   787-474-7777
       Fax: 787-782-4500
Wholesaler/distributor of frozen and dry foods
Purchasing Director: Juan Ogeunda
Estimated Sales: Less Than $500,000
Number Employees: 5-9
Square Footage: 20000
Private Brands Carried:
  Heinz; Solo Cups; Hams
Types of Products Distributed:
  Frozen Food, General Line, Dry foods

55531 Carl Stahl Amer Lifting LLC
21825 Doral Rd
Waukesha, WI 53186-1894   262-786-2710
       Fax: 262-786-8510 800-236-0729
       sales@amlift.com www.americanlifting.com
Wholesaler/distributor of ergonomic material handling equipment including hoists, light rail crane systems, fans, vacuum lifters, and manipulators
Manager: James Schmalle
jim@amlift.com
VP: Jim Schmale
Operations Manager: Russ Schmidt
Estimated Sales: $3 Million
Number Employees: 10-19
Square Footage: 34000

Wholesalers & Distributors / A-Z

Types of Products Distributed:
  Material handling equipment

55532 (HQ)Carle & Montanari-O P M
625 Hutton St # 107
Raleigh, NC 27606-6321　　919-664-7401
　　Fax: 919-664-7407　www.cm-opm.com
Importer and wholesaler/distributor of confectionery equipment and supplies including molding plants, wrapping equipment, pans, etc.; serving processors only
President: Moreno Roncato
Estimated Sales: $1-2.5 Million
Number Employees: 1-4
Square Footage: 40000
Types of Products Distributed:
  Frozen Food, General Merchandise, Confectionery equipment & supplies

55533 Carlisle Food Systems Inc
11020 Lakeridge Pkwy
Ashland, VA 23005-8127　　804-550-2169
　　Fax: 804-550-2829　800-626-8259
　　www.carlislefoodsystems.com
Wholesaler/distributor of general merchandise and pizza, cooking and heating equipment including pressure fryers, warmers, etc.; serving the food service market
President: Robert Carlisle
bcarlisle@carlislefoodsystems.com
Secretary: Carey Carlisle
Sales Manager: Jay Pence
Number Employees: 10-19
Square Footage: 36000
Private Brands Carried:
  Henny Penny; Perky's Pizza Concepts; Smokanoma
Number of Customer Locations: 500
Types of Products Distributed:
  Food Service, Frozen Food, General Merchandise, Pressure fryers, warmers, etc.

55534 Carlson Company
33 N Avenue NW At Spring Street
Atlanta, GA 30308　　404-881-8784
　　Fax: 404-874-6401
Wholesaler/distributor of lift trucks and castors
Chairman: Betty Carlson
Estimated Sales: $2.5-5 Million
Number Employees: 5-9
Private Brands Carried:
  Fairbanks; Faultless; Payson
Types of Products Distributed:
  Frozen Food, General Merchandise, Lift trucks & castors

55535 Carlton Company
P.O.Box 1018
Thomasville, GA 31799-1018　　229-228-8100
　　Fax: 912-431-3032　800-443-2640
　　www.carlco.com
Wholesaler/distributor of forklifts
President: Andy Gravitt
VP: Mark Stenberg
Estimated Sales: $10-20 Million
Number Employees: 20-49
Private Brands Carried:
  Caterpillar; Crown; Generac; Olympian
Types of Products Distributed:
  Frozen Food, General Merchandise, Forklifts

55536 Carnival Fruit
475 NE 185th St
Miami, FL 33179-4537　　786-279-2100
Wholesaler/distributor of fruit; serving the food service market
President: Alan Spriz
Controller: Eduardo Solana
Contact: Spritz Alan
alan.spritz@freshpoint.com
Estimated Sales: $20-50 Million
Number Employees: 5-9
Parent Co: Sysco Corporation
Types of Products Distributed:
  Frozen Food, Produce, Fruit

55537 Caro Foods
2324 Bayou Blue Rd
Houma, LA 70364　　985-872-1483
　　Fax: 985-876-0825　800-395-2276
Fresh meat and produce, canned and dry goods.
Parent Co: Performance Food Group Company

55538 Carole's Cheesecake Company
1275 Castlefield Ave
Toronto, ON M6B 1G3
Canada　　416-256-0000
　　Fax: 416-256-0001　www.carolescheesecake.com
cheesecakes including praline, lemon, blueberry, raspberry and strawberry; also, pies, low-fat salad dressings, pasta sauces and toppings for cakes and ice cream.
President: Edison Carbajal
CEO: Carole Ogus
Executive VP: Michael Ogus
Estimated Sales: $1-5 Million
Number Employees: 30
Number of Brands: 2
Number of Products: 160
Square Footage: 60000
Type of Packaging: Consumer, Food Service, Private Label
Types of Products Distributed:
  Food Service, Frozen Food

55539 Carolina Belting
3205 Rutherford Rd
Taylors, SC 29687-2129　　864-268-5946
　　Fax: 864-268-5672　www.carolinabelting.com
Wholesaler/distributor of belting fasteners including conveyor and transmission; also, belt installation service available
President: Bob Hammersla
bhammersla@carolinabelting.com
CEO: Denane Team
VP Sales: Jim Evatt
Estimated Sales: $5-10 Million
Number Employees: 10-19
Square Footage: 48000
Types of Products Distributed:
  Frozen Food, General Merchandise, Conveyor belting & transmission

55540 (HQ)Carolina Beverage Corp
1413 Jake Alexander Blvd S
Salisbury, NC 28146-8359　　704-633-4550
　　Fax: 704-633-7491　custserv@cheerwine.com
　　www.cheerwine.com
Syrups and beverage concentrates; exporter of soft drinks and concentrates; wholesaler/distributor of soft drinks and water
President: Clift Ritchie
critchie@carolinabottlingcompanyinc.com
CFO: Tommy Page
CIO: Bill Barten
VP Operations: David Swaim
Estimated Sales: $10-20 Million
Number Employees: 20-49
Square Footage: 75000
Parent Co: Cheerwine & Diet Cheerwine
Type of Packaging: Consumer
Other Locations:
  Carolina Beverage Corp.
  Hickory, NC
  Carolina Beverage Corp.
  Greenville, SCCarolina Beverage Corp.Greenville
Private Brands Carried:
  Cheerwine; Blue Mist
Types of Products Distributed:
  Soft drinks & water

55541 Carolina Canners Inc
300 Highway 1 S
P.O. Box 1628
Cheraw, SC 29520　　843-537-5281
　　Fax: 843-537-6743
　　amity.albridge@carolinacanners.com
　　www.carolinacanners.com
Wholesaler/distributor and exporter of beverages and fountain syrups.
President: Mark Avent
Chief Executive Officer: Jeff Stevens
Chief Financial Officer: Frank Cobia
Vice President: Lee Teeter
Secretary: Maughan Hull
Chief Information Officer: Tim Geddings
VP, Sales & Marketing: Sterling Whitley
VP, Human Resources: Jerry Tucker
VP, Manufacturing: David Rhine
Estimated Sales: $33.7 Million
Number Employees: 100-249
Private Brands Carried:
  Pepsi Cola
Types of Products Distributed:
  Frozen Food, General Line, Beverages & fountain syrups

55542 Carolina Handling LLC
3101 Piper Ln
Charlotte, NC 28208　　704-357-6273
　　Fax: 704-357-1911　800-688-8802
　　www.carolinahandling.com
Wholesaler/distributor of forklifts.
Year Founded: 1966
Estimated Sales: $100-500 Million
Number Employees: 250-499
Private Brands Carried:
  Raymond Forklifts
Types of Products Distributed:
  Frozen Food, General Merchandise, Forklifts

55543 Carolina Material Handling
151 Greenlawn Dr
Columbia, SC 29209-2504　　803-695-0149
　　Fax: 803-783-1659　marketing@cmhservices.com
　　www.cmhservices.net
Wholesaler/distributor of material handling equipment including forklifts and shelving
President: Buddy Smith
VP: Mike Smith
VP: Buddy Smith
Estimated Sales: $20-50 Million
Number Employees: 50-99
Private Brands Carried:
  Nissan; Crown
Types of Products Distributed:
  Frozen Food, General Merchandise, Material handling equipment

55544 Carolina Mountain
235 Milton Mashburn Dr
Andrews, NC 28901-8051　　828-321-3335
　　Fax: 828-321-4902　800-722-9477
　　www.carolinamountaintrout.com
Wholesaler/distributor of fish
President: Howard Brown
eatmoretrout@yahoo.com
Estimated Sales: $20-50 Million
Number Employees: 20-49
Types of Products Distributed:
  Frozen Food, Seafood

55545 Carolina Produce
121 W River St
Anderson, SC 29624-1556　　864-224-4376
　　Fax: 864-225-5996
　　service@carolinaproducecompany.com
　　www.carolinaproducecompany.com
Wholesaler/distributor of produce; serving the food service market
President / Sales: Jerry L. Welborn
Secretary, Treasurer, HR, QA, Sales: Donald A. Welborn
Vice President / Buyer: Kenneth Stone
Accounting / Billing / Customer Service: Pamela A. Mcleod
Estimated Sales: $5-10 Million
Number Employees: 10-19
Square Footage: 72000
Types of Products Distributed:
  Food Service, Produce

55546 Carolina Steel ShelvingCompany
3528 Gladehill Ln
Leland, NC 28451　　910-754-6048
　　Fax: 910-842-8191　800-245-3570
　　lvogt@infoave.net
Wholesaler/distributor of racks, shelving and lockers
President: John Vogt
VP Sales: John Vogt, Jr.
Number Employees: 1-4
Private Brands Carried:
  Dexco; Speed-Rak; Triboro
Types of Products Distributed:
  Frozen Food, General Merchandise, Racks, shelving & lockers

55547 Carolina Tractor and Equipment Company
P.O. Box 1095
Charlotte, NC 28201
　　800-277-1080
　　info@cte1926.com　cte1926.com
Wholesaler/distributor of forklifts and other large industrial equipment.
President & CEO: Ed Weisiger, Jr.
VP & Chief Financial Officer: Matt Nazzaro
VP, Human Resources & Secretary: Tom Bell

Wholesalers & Distributors / A-Z

Year Founded: 1926
Estimated Sales: $100-500 Million
Number Employees: 1000-4999
Private Brands Carried:
  Caterpiller; Ottawa; Shuttle Wagon; Atlets
Types of Products Distributed:
  Frozen Food, General Merchandise, Forklifts

55548 Carolyn Darden Enterprises
306 Pecan Ave
P.O. Box 38
Albertville, AL 35950-2732   256-878-6634
    Fax: 256-878-2604 800-316-7490
    darden@darden.net www.darden.net
Wholesaler/distributor of advertising specialties and awards
President: Carolyn Darden
VP/CEO: Allen Darden
Estimated Sales: Less Than $500,000
Number Employees: 1-4
Types of Products Distributed:
  Frozen Food, General Merchandise, Advertising specialties & awards

55549 Carpenter Snack Food Distribution Company
930 Mosler Avenue
Hamilton, OH 45011-4432   513-896-1115
Wholesaler/distributor of snack foods including potato and corn chips, pretzels, popcorn, pork rinds, tortillas, nuts, etc.; serving the food service and retail markets
President: K Carpenter
Treasurer: R Carpenter
Estimated Sales: $5-10 Million
Number Employees: 10-19
Number of Customer Locations: 1000
Types of Products Distributed:
  Food Service, General Line, Snack foods

55550 Carrabassett Coffee Roasters
2 Mountain View Rd
North Main St.
Kingfield, ME 4947   207-265-2326
    Fax: 207-265-3527 888-292-2326
    carrcoff@tdstelme.net
    www.carrabassettcoffee.com
Roaster and wholesaler of coffee
Owner: Tom Hildreth
carrcoff@tds.com
CEO: Steve Skaling
Estimated Sales: Less Than $500,000
Number Employees: 5-9
Number of Brands: 35
Number of Products: 1
Square Footage: 7200
Type of Packaging: Bulk
Types of Products Distributed:
  Coffee

55551 Carriage Foods
P.O. Box 267
Kenner, LA 70063-0267   504-466-9391
    Fax: 504-469-0864
Wholesaler/distributor of dairy products and meats; serving the food service market
President: John Abernathy
Estimated Sales: $20-50 Million
Number Employees: 10-19
Number of Customer Locations: 200
Types of Products Distributed:
  Food Service, Frozen Food, General Line, Provisions/Meat, Dairy products & wild game

55552 Carroll Distributing Co
1553 Chad Caroll Way
Melbourne, FL 32940   321-421-6283
    mdougherty@carrolldist.com
    www.carrolldist.com
Wholesaler/distributor of beer.
President: Mike Eubank
meubank@carrolldist.com
General Manager: Mike Dougherty
Sales Manager: Tom Joynes
IT Manager: Roger Osburn
Estimated Sales: $50-100 Million
Number Employees: 100-249
Parent Co: Anheuser Busch
Private Brands Carried:
  Budweiser; Michelob; Busch
Types of Products Distributed:
  Frozen Food, General Line, Alcoholic beverages

55553 Carrollton Products Company
PO Box 1314
Alexandria, VA 22313   703-548-2799
    Fax: 703-550-2464 800-260-3031
Wholesaler/distributor of vacuum sealers and shrink wrapping machinery for special sizes
President: Elliott Dimond
Estimated Sales: $1-2.5 Million
Number Employees: 1-4
Types of Products Distributed:
  Frozen Food, General Merchandise, Shrink wrapping machinery, etc.

55554 Carrot Top Pastries
3931 Broadway
New York, NY 10032-1538   212-927-4800
    Fax: 212-740-7470 www.carrottoppastries.com
Wholesaler/distributor of pastries, cakes, pies and muffins; serving the food service market
Manager: Guillermo Deralta
gderalta@carrottoppastries.com
Owner: Bob Mancino
Manager: Guillermo Deralta
gderalta@carrottoppastries.com
Purchasing Manager: Elmer Mathews
Estimated Sales: $1-3 Million
Number Employees: 10-19
Types of Products Distributed:
  Food Service, Frozen Food, Specialty Foods

55555 Carter Promotions
1216 Canton St
Roswell, GA 30075   770-640-0333
    Fax: 770-642-2255
Wholesaler/distributor of advertising specialties
VP: Matt Carter
VP: Tom Carter, Jr.
Estimated Sales: $500,000-$1 Million
Number Employees: 5-9
Private Brands Carried:
  Carter Promotions
Number of Customer Locations: 250
Types of Products Distributed:
  Frozen Food, General Merchandise, Advertising specialties

55556 Cartwright's Market
825 Union Ave
Grants Pass, OR 97527-5549   541-479-0321
    Fax: 541-474-7380 www.cartwrightsmarket.com
Wholesaler/distributor of meat
Owner: Sandy Cartwright
Estimated Sales: $10-20 Million
Number Employees: 20-49
Types of Products Distributed:
  Provisions/Meat

55557 Casa Amador
810 Texas Ave
El Paso, TX 79901   915-533-7861
    Fax: 915-533-8585 866-323-9649
    casa-amador@sbcglobal.net
Importer and distributor of pinatas and other mexican handcrafts
President/COO: Ann Pearson
Estimated Sales: $500,000-$1 Million
Number Employees: 1-4
Square Footage: 26240

55558 Casa Di Carfagna
408 N 6th St
Columbus, OH 43215   614-469-1103
    Fax: 614-469-1104
Owner: Sam Carfagna
Estimated Sales: $1-3 Million
Number Employees: 1-4

55559 Casa Herrera
2655 Pine St
Pomona, CA 91767-2115   909-392-3930
    Fax: 909-392-0231 800-624-3916
    www.casaherrera.com
Flat bread and tortilla making machines
President: Michael Herrera
michaelh@casaherrera.com
CEO: Alfred Herrera
Sales: Chris Herrera
Sales: Alfredo Juarez
Sales: Rudy Herrera
Number Employees: 100-249

55560 Casa Sanchez Foods
P.O. Box 12582
San Francisco, CA 94112   650-697-7525
    Fax: 650-697-1810 877-227-2726
    info@casasanchez.com
    www.casasanchez.com/index.html
Guacamole and salsas
Contact: Roger Esponilla
roger@casasanchez.com

55561 Cascade Glacier Ice Cream Company
865 Grant Street
Eugene, OR 97402-4345   541-484-9123
    Fax: 541-485-7653 www.cascadeglacier.com
Wholesaler/distributor of frozen food; serving the food service market
President: Gene Gustafson
Estimated Sales: $20-50 Million
Number Employees: 50-99
Types of Products Distributed:
  Food Service, Frozen Food

55562 Cash Grocery & Sales Company
211 Ogden Street
Alexandria, LA 71302-6449   318-443-6381
    Fax: 318-443-6370
Wholesaler/distributor serving the food service market
General Manager: Russell Roy
Estimated Sales: $20-50 Million
Number Employees: 20-49
Parent Co: Consolidated Companies
Types of Products Distributed:
  Food Service, Frozen Food

55563 Cash Register Sales
4851 White Bear Pkwy
St Paul, MN 55110-3325   651-294-2700
    Fax: 651-294-2900 800-333-4949
    moreinfo@crs-usa.com www.crs-usa.com
Wholesaler/distributor and importer of cash registers, calculators and small business machines; serving the food service market
President: David Sanders
Controller: Bill Oas
Direct Sales: James R. Sanders
Contact: Annette Borrelli
aborrelli@mmm.com
Estimated Sales: $10-20 Million
Number Employees: 1-4
Type of Packaging: Consumer, Food Service
Private Brands Carried:
  Samsung; CRS 3000
Types of Products Distributed:
  Food Service, Frozen Food, General Merchandise, Cash registers, calculators, etc.

55564 (HQ)Cash-Wa Distributing
401 W 4th St
Kearney, NE 68845-7825   308-237-3151
    customerservice@cashwa.com
    web.cashwa.com
Wholesaler/distributor of groceries, meats, produce, frozen foods, equipment and fixtures, general merchandise, etc.; serving the food service market.
CEO: Tom Henning
Senior VP, Sales: Jim Kindig
Estimated Sales: $20-50 Million
Number Employees: 250-499
Square Footage: 175000
Other Locations:
  Cash-Wa Distributing
  Lincoln, NECash-Wa Distributing
Number of Customer Locations: 1500
Types of Products Distributed:
  Food Service, Frozen Food, General Line, General Merchandise, Provisions/Meat, Produce, Equipment & fixtures, etc.

55565 Cash-Wa Distributing
810 3rd Ave SE
Aberdeen, SD 57401   605-225-1275
    web.cashwa.com
Parent Co: Cash-Wa Distributing Company
Types of Products Distributed:
  Food Service, Frozen Food, General Line, General Merchandise, Provisions/Meat, Produce

55566 Cash-Wa Distributing
4101 15th Ave NW
Fargo, ND 83642   701-282-8200
    web.cashwa

Wholesalers & Distributors / A-Z

55567 Casper Foodservice Company
310 N Green St
Chicago, IL 60607-1300 312-226-2265
Fax: 312-226-2686
President: Thomas Casper
Estimated Sales: $1-3 Million
Number Employees: 10-19

55568 Caspian Trading Company
3321 W. Gary Drive
P.O.Box 400
Tempe, AZ 85280 480-967-3454
Fax: 480-967-3482 800-227-7426
info@caspiantrading.net www.caspiantrading.net
Wholesaler/distributor, importer and exporter of fresh, frozen, dried and canned seafood
President: Mohammad Bozorgnia
CFO: Bruce Kochanck
VP: S Mehrostami
Estimated Sales: $1-2.5 Million
Number Employees: 1-4
Square Footage: 2000
Type of Packaging: Bulk
Private Brands Carried:
  Caspian Gulf
Types of Products Distributed:
  Frozen Food, Seafood, Canned & dried seafood

55569 Cass Hudson Company
28117 Charlotte Ave
Elkhart, IN 46517 574-970-2100
Fax: 574-970-3100 800-423-1511
www.casshudson.com
Wholesalers/distributors of material handling equipment including casters
President: Eric Larson
Estimated Sales: $10-20 Million
Number Employees: 10-19
Square Footage: 30000
Private Brands Carried:
  Bassick; Albion; Roach; Lewisystems; Lyon; Magline
Types of Products Distributed:
  Frozen Food, General Merchandise, Material handling equipment

55570 Casso Guerra & Company
215 Regal Drive
Suite 527
Laredo, TX 78041-2336 956-725-9185
cassoguerra@surfus.net
Wholesaler/distributor, importer and exporter of general line items, equipment and produce; serving the food service market
President: A Casso, Sr.
Estimated Sales: $20-50 Million
Number Employees: 20-49
Number of Customer Locations: 500
Types of Products Distributed:
  Food Service, Frozen Food, General Line, General Merchandise, Produce

55571 Castello di Borghese Vineyard
17150 Rte 48
Cutchogue, NY 11935 631-734-5111
Fax: 631-734-5485 info@castellodiborghese.com
castellodiborghese.com
Vineyard and winery
Owner: Marco Borghese
Owner: Ann Marie Borghese
Estimated Sales: $500-1 Million appx.
Number Employees: 10-19
Type of Packaging: Private Label

55572 Caster Wheels & Indl Handling
8 Engineers Ln
Farmingdale, NY 11735-1208 631-650-0500
Fax: 361-650-0501 800-672-2783
sales@cwih.com www.cwih.com
Wholesaler/distributor of stainless steel casters and wheels; serving the food service market
President: John Mayberger
johnm@cwih.com
VP Sales: Kevin McPartland
Marketing Director: George Ashford, Jr.
Sales/Marketing Executive: Lissa Wong
Operations Manager: Diana Yonthkins
Plant Manager: Frank Siplis
Estimated Sales: $5-10 Million
Number Employees: 20-49
Square Footage: 60000
Types of Products Distributed:
  Food Service, Frozen Food, General Merchandise, Casters, and wheels

55573 Castino Restaurant Equipment
50 Utility Ct
Rohnert Park, CA 94928-1659 800-238-0404
Fax: 707-585-7306 800-238-0404
solutions@castinosolutions.com
www.castinosolutions.com
Wholesaler/distributor of restaurant equipment, kitchen equipment, furniture, refrigeration hood systems, chinaware, glassware, pots, pans, etc
President/CEO: David Castino
david_castino@castinosolutions.com
Purchasing Manager: Ron Nasuti
Estimated Sales: $8 Million
Number Employees: 5-9
Square Footage: 60000
Parent Co: Castino Refrigeration Company
Types of Products Distributed:
  Food Service, Frozen Food, General Merchandise, Restaurant equipment, pots, pans, etc.

55574 Castle Hill Lobster
333 Linebrook Rd
Suite R
Ipswich, MA 01938-1146 978-356-3947
Fax: 978-356-9883
Whole seafoods; lobsters
Owner: Robert Marcaurelle
Contact: Dennis Wilke
dennis.wilke@castlehillco.com
Estimated Sales: $2 Million
Number Employees: 1-4
Type of Packaging: Food Service

55575 Castor Technology Corporation
11552 Markon Dr
Garden Grove, CA 92841-1809 866-547-8090
Fax: 714-897-6315 www.castertech.com
Wholesaler/distributor of material handling equipment including food handling conveyor belts; serving the food service market
President: Lynn Vandercook
CEO: David Elles
Contact: Kearson Albrecht
kalbrecht@castertech.com
Number Employees: 20-49
Parent Co: Oregon Handling Equipment
Types of Products Distributed:
  Food Service, Frozen Food, General Merchandise, Material handling equipment

55576 Cataract Foods
6873 Joanne Cir S
Niagara Falls, NY 14304 716-284-8817
Fax: 716-284-8810
Wholesaler/distributor of specialty baskets, frozen foods, produce, seafood and meats; serving the food service market
President: Greg Manarino
thecataract@multo.com
Estimated Sales: $2.5-5 Million
Number Employees: 1-4
Types of Products Distributed:
  Food Service, Frozen Food, Provisions/Meat, Produce, Seafood, Specialty Foods, Fruit & vegetable baskets

55577 Catering Co
24833 Commercial Ave
Orange Beach, AL 36561-3845 251-974-5000
Fax: 251-974-5640 www.catering.com
Owner: J Schenck
hazels@gulftel.com
Vice President: J Hall Schenck
Estimated Sales: Below 1 Million
Number Employees: 10-19

55578 Cauble & Field
421 S Middle St
Cape Girardeau, MO 63703-6865 573-335-6641
Fax: 573-335-6610
Wholesaler/distributor of frozen food, general line and specialty food products, produce and provisions/meats; serving the food service market
President: R Hagedorn
Estimated Sales: $10-20 Million
Number Employees: 10-19
Private Brands Carried:
  Show Me
Number of Customer Locations: 380
Types of Products Distributed:
  Food Service, Frozen Food, General Line, Provisions/Meat, Produce, Specialty Foods, Groceries

55579 Caudill Seed Co Inc
1402 W Main St
Louisville, KY 40203-1328 502-583-4402
Fax: 502-583-4405 800-626-5357
hf@caudillseed.com
Distributor of seeds and supplies
President: Dan Caudill
dcaudill@caudillseed.com
CFO: Iris Mudd
Vice President: Edgar Caudill
Branch Manager: Eugene Stratton
Sales Director: Jack Donahoe
Year Founded: 1947
Estimated Sales: $20 Million
Number Employees: 20-49
Number of Brands: 5
Number of Products: 400
Square Footage: 275000
Type of Packaging: Private Label, Bulk
Private Brands Carried:
  Whole Alternatives
Types of Products Distributed:
  Specialty Foods

55580 Cavanna Packaging USA Inc
2150 Northmont Pkwy # A
Suite A
Duluth, GA 30096-5835 770-688-1501
Fax: 973-383-0741 www.cavanna.com
Wholesaler/distributor of horizontal flow wrapping machinery
President: William Stoebling
Contact: Adam Caplan
a.caplan@cavannagroup.com
Estimated Sales: Below $5 Million
Number Employees: 10-19
Types of Products Distributed:
  Frozen Food, General Merchandise, Horizontal flow wrapping machinery

55581 Cavazos Candy, Produce & Groceries
P.O.Box 3320
Laredo, TX 78044 956-722-8226
Fax: 956-727-7674
Wholesaler/distributor of frozen food, general line items, candy, produce, meat, dairy products, etc.; serving the food service market
President: Ruben Cavazos
Purchasing Manager: Alma Cavazos
Estimated Sales: $20-50 Million
Number Employees: 20-49
Types of Products Distributed:
  Food Service, Frozen Food, General Line, Provisions/Meat, Produce, Candy & dairy & bakery products

55582 Cavens Meats
US Route 36
Conover, OH 45317-0400 937-368-3841
Fax: 937-368-3849
Processor and wholesaler/distributor of meat products; serving the food service market
President: Victor Caven
VP: Dean Caven
Estimated Sales: $10-20 Million
Number Employees: 10-19
Square Footage: 45000
Type of Packaging: Consumer, Food Service
Types of Products Distributed:
  Food Service, Frozen Food, Provisions/Meat

55583 Cayard's Inc
4215 Choctaw Dr
Baton Rouge, LA 70805-6797 225-356-3534
Fax: 225-356-3539 rudy@cayards.com
www.cayards.com
Wholesaler/distributor of cleaning supplies, disposables, wraps, table top needs and equipment; serving the institutional food service market
President: James Dellafiora
jdellafiora@cayards.com
Estimated Sales: $5-10 Million
Number Employees: 20-49

55584 Cb Equipment Co
12001 SE Jennifer St
Clackamas, OR 97015-9014 800-962-4491
Fax: 503-657-7281 cbtoyotacock@msn.com
www.toyotaliftnorthwest.com
Wholesaler/distributor of material handling equipment including forklifts and pallet jacks

Manager: Bill Hamilton
Contact: Mike Gerking
mgerking@cbtoyotalift.com
General Manager: Larry McCart
Estimated Sales: $10-20 Million
Number Employees: 20-49
Parent Co: C.B Toyata
Private Brands Carried:
   Toyota; Halla
Types of Products Distributed:
   Frozen Food, General Merchandise, Material handling equipment

55585 Cedar Valley Fish Market
218 Division St
Waterloo, IA 50703   319-236-2965
   Fax: 253-761-0504
Seafood
Owner: Marilyn Ruvino
Estimated Sales: $370,000
Number Employees: 5-9

55586 Cedarlane Natural FoodsToc
1135 E Artesia Blvd
Carson, CA 90746-1602   310-527-7833
   www.cedarlanefoods.com
Breakfast selections, tamales and vegetarian foods
CEO: Robert Atallah
ktorosyan@franklyfresh.com
Number Employees: 5-9
Type of Packaging: Private Label

55587 Centerchem, Inc.
20 Glover Ave # 4n
Norwalk, CT 06850-1234   203-822-9800
   Fax: 203-822-9820 orders@centerchem.com
   www.centerchem.com
Manufacturer & distributor of pectin, bittering agents, essential oils, polishing and glazing agents, waxes, release agents & encapsulated specialty ingredients.
President: Jon Packer
Chief Financial Officer & Treasurer: Mary Fcc
Vice President: John Dondero
Marketing Coordinator: Claude Dougherty
Vice President Sales: Ray Sourial
Tech. Sales Rep.: Jennifer Czerner
Estimated Sales: $6.7 Million
Private Brands Carried:
   Capol; Capolex
Types of Products Distributed:
   Frozen Food, General Line, Pectin, essential oils, waxes, etc.

55588 Central Baking Supplies
PO Box 2141
Northbrook, IL 60065-2141   847-480-0760
   Fax: 847-480-0044   800-359-2166
Wholesaler/distributor of bakery supplies including flour, shortening, sugar, salt, mixes, seeds, spices, raisins, etc
President: William Martin, Jr.
CEO: Jeanette Martin
Number Employees: 5-9
Square Footage: 28000
Type of Packaging: Food Service, Bulk
Number of Customer Locations: 100
Types of Products Distributed:
   General Line, Baking supplies: flour, sugar, etc.

55589 Central Carolina Farm &Mower
801 E Wendover Ave
Greensboro, NC 27405-6772   336-574-4400
   Fax: 336-574-2880   800-672-6103
Wholesaler/distributor of general line products
Manager: Greg James
General Manager: John Moore
Estimated Sales: $1-3 Million
Number Employees: 5-9
Number of Customer Locations: 250
Types of Products Distributed:
   Frozen Food, General Line

55590 (HQ)Central Coast Seafood
5495 Traffic Way
Atascadero, CA 93422-4246   805-462-3474
   Fax: 805-466-6613   800-273-4741
   www.ccseafood.com
Wholesaler/distributor and exporter of fresh seafood; serving the food service market in California
CEO: Giovanni Comin
VP Sales/Marketing: Nancy Osorio
Estimated Sales: $5.9 Million
Number Employees: 5-9
Square Footage: 40000
Other Locations:
   Central Coast Seafoods
   Morro Bay, CACentral Coast Seafoods
Private Brands Carried:
   Central Coast Seafood; Morro Bay Cypress
Number of Customer Locations: 300
Types of Products Distributed:
   Food Service, Frozen Food, Seafood

55591 Central Distributing Co
245 South Ave
245 South Avenue
Grand Junction, CO 81501-7807   970-243-0024
   Fax: 970-243-1568 info@centraldistributing.ws
   www.centraldistributing.ws
Wholesaler/distributor of groceries, cleaning supplies, disposables, wraps, table top needs and equipment; serving the food service market
Vice President: Howard Wilsey
VP: Howard Wilsey
Purchasing: Joleen Newlon
Estimated Sales: $10-20 Million
Number Employees: 100-249
Types of Products Distributed:
   Food Service, Frozen Food, General Merchandise

55592 Central Illinois Equipment Company
1803 W Washington Street
Bloomington, IL 61701-3703   309-828-6068
   Fax: 309-827-7033
Wholesaler/distributor of racks, shelving, fork lifts, pallet jacks and dock and door equipment
Owner: Rebecca Wright
Estimated Sales: $2.5-5 Million
Number Employees: 10-19
Square Footage: 40000
Types of Products Distributed:
   Frozen Food, General Merchandise, Material handling & distribution equip.

55593 Central Oklahoma Produce Services
PO Box 83165
Oklahoma City, OK 73148   405-236-0465
   Fax: 405-239-6741
Wholesaler/distributor of produce; serving the food service market
President: Mike Stout
Estimated Sales: $5-10 Million
Number Employees: 10-19
Types of Products Distributed:
   Food Service, Frozen Food, Produce

55594 Central Package & Display
3901 85th Ave N
Minneapolis, MN 55443-1907   763-425-7444
   Fax: 763-425-7917
customerservice@centralcontainer.com
   www.centralpackage.com
Manufacturer and wholesaler/distributor of corrugated boxes, cushion packaging, flexible films, litho labels and static control products
President: James E Haglund
CEO: Mike Haglund
mhaglund@centralpackage.com
Sales: Steve Braun
VP Sales/Marketing: Steve Braun
General Manager: Jerry Condon
Estimated Sales: $10-20 Million
Number Employees: 100-249
Square Footage: 300000
Types of Products Distributed:
   Frozen Food, General Merchandise, Packaging materials & supplies

55595 Central Restaurant Supply Inc
642 N Salina St
P.O.Box 11185
Syracuse, NY 13208-2527   315-474-6848
   Fax: 315-474-1737   800-244-6848
   www.centralrestaurantsupply.com
Wholesaler/distributor of food service equipment and supplies; serving the food service market
President: William Alciati
central@twcny.rr.com
Estimated Sales: $5-10 Million
Number Employees: 10-19
Private Brands Carried:
   BK Industries
Types of Products Distributed:
   Food Service, Frozen Food, General Merchandise, Foodservice equipment & supplies

55596 Central Sanitary Supply
10840 Mulberry Ave
Fontana, CA 92337   909-822-5449
   Fax: 909-822-709 sales@centralsanitary.com
   www.centralsanitary.com
Wholesaler/distributor of sanitorial/cleaning supplies and paper products
Sales Manager: David Patrick
Estimated Sales: $10-20 Million
Number Employees: 20-49
Square Footage: 50000
Types of Products Distributed:
   Food Service, Frozen Food, General Merchandise, Janitorial/cleaning supplies & paper

55597 (HQ)Central Security Service
P.O. Box 2527
Temecula, CA 92593-2527   951-676-7121
   Fax: 951-695-4379 www.centralssi.com
Wholesaler/distributor of fire alarms and security systems
President: William Joyce
Estimated Sales: $20-50 Million
Number Employees: 50-99
Other Locations:
   Central Security Service
   Corona, CACentral Security Service
Types of Products Distributed:
   Frozen Food, General Merchandise, Fire alarms & security systems

55598 Central Wholesale Grocery Corporation
275 Union Street N
Rochester, NY 14605-2446   716-454-4700
Wholesaler/distributor of general merchandise and general line products
President: G Cassorla
VP: J Cassorla
Estimated Sales: $10-20 Million
Number Employees: 5-9
Type of Packaging: Bulk
Number of Customer Locations: 250
Types of Products Distributed:
   Frozen Food, General Line, General Merchandise

55599 Centreside Dairy
61 Lorne Street North
Renfrew, ON K7V 1K8
Canada   613-432-2914
   Fax: 613-432-5157   800-889-9974
   info@traceysicecream.ca traceysicecream.ca
Ice cream; wholesaler/distributor of dairy products
President: Mark Tracey
General Manager: Melany Tracey
Estimated Sales: $2 Million
Number Employees: 15
Type of Packaging: Consumer, Food Service, Private Label
Types of Products Distributed:
   Frozen Food, General Line, Dairy products

55600 Century 21 Products
6671 Langford Rd
Mesa, WA 99343-9626
   Fax: 509-547-3681
Wholesalers/distributor of produce including potatoes
President: Jo Foglesong
Number Employees: 1-4
Number of Brands: 2
Number of Products: 1
Type of Packaging: Food Service, Bulk
Private Brands Carried:
   Best
Types of Products Distributed:
   Frozen Food, Produce

55601 Century Conveyor Svc
4 Gladys Ct
Edison, NJ 08817-2275   732-248-4900
   Fax: 732-248-4960   800-422-0224
   www.centuryconveyor.com
Wholesaler/distributor of conveyors, palletizers and carousel

Wholesalers & Distributors / A-Z

President: Ron Serrara
ronserrara@centuryconveyor.com
Vice President: Gary Wilder
Estimated Sales: $20-50 Million
Number Employees: 50-99
Square Footage: 40000
Private Brands Carried:
  Hytrol; Flexlink; Arrowhead; Remstar
Types of Products Distributed:
  Conveyors, pallet jacks, etc.

55602 Century Data Systems
6638 Old Wake Forest Road
Raleigh, NC 27616-1812 919-713-0301
      Fax: 919-713-0273
Wholesaler/distributor of computer software including hospitality cost control, accounting, payroll, etc.; also, cash registers and paging systems
President: Todd Barstow
CEO: Wayne Williams
Number Employees: 100-249
Parent Co: Century Data Systems
Types of Products Distributed:
  Frozen Food, General Merchandise, Software, cash registers, etc.

55603 Century Distributors Inc
15710 Crabbs Branch Way
Rockville, MD 20855 301-212-9100
  Fax: 301-212-9681 www.centurydist.com
Wholesaler/distributor of candy, groceries, dairy and frozen foods, general merchandise and bakery and convenience store items.
President: Debra Robins
Chief Financial Officer: Jim Mullen
Controller: Harold Fletcher
Vice President, Sales: Lori Rodman
Human Resources Director: Mary Solla
General Manager: Sheldon Sadugor
Vice President, Operations: David Sadugor
Warehouse Manager: Mike Wertz
Purchasing Manager: Ron Winson
Estimated Sales: $39 Million
Number Employees: 250-499
Square Footage: 65000
Types of Products Distributed:
  Frozen Food, General Line, General Merchandise, Candy & convenience store items

55604 Century Fournier Inc
4300 Simon Rd # 1
Youngstown, OH 44512-1348 330-783-0444
  Fax: 330-783-9710 800-708-0444
      www.century-fournierinc.com
Wholesaler/distributor of material handling and storage equipment
President: William Petro
wmpetro@century-fournierinc.com
Estimated Sales: $2.5-5 Million
Number Employees: 5-9
Private Brands Carried:
  Serco; Hamilton; Porta-Fab
Types of Products Distributed:
  Frozen Food, General Merchandise, Material handling & storage equipment

55605 Cerca Foodservice
4960 Walker Road
Windsor, ON N9A 6J3
Canada 519-737-6115
Wholesaler/distributor of dried products, meats and frozen foods; serving the food service market
Sales Manager: L Shepley
General Manager: D MacTavish
Number Employees: 50-99
Square Footage: 160000
Parent Co: Oshawa Holdings
Number of Customer Locations: 1500
Types of Products Distributed:
  Food Service, Frozen Food, General Line, Provisions/Meat, Dried products

55606 Cereal Byproducts
601 E Kensington Rd
Mount Prospect, IL 60056 847-818-1550
      800-369-1550
      www.cerealbyproducts.com
Wholesaler/distributor of grains, dairy powders and ingredients.
VP: Dale Danner
Year Founded: 1917
Estimated Sales: $20-50 Million
Number Employees: 6
Square Footage: 4000
Other Locations:
  Cereal Byproducts
  Mt. Prospect, IL Cereal Byproducts

55607 Ceres Solutions
1260 E 1450 N
Perrysville, IN 47974-8087 765-793-0063
      Fax: 765-294-4563
Wholesaler/distributor of grains
President: Jason Stonecipher
Estimated Sales: $1-3 Million
Number Employees: 10-19
Parent Co: Indiana Farm Bureau Cooperative Association
Types of Products Distributed:
  Frozen Food, General Line, Farm supplies & grains

55608 Cermack
2711 W Cermak Rd
Chicago, IL 60608-3509 773-376-1387
      Fax: 773-254-1953
Seafood
President: Jose Valez
Estimated Sales: $300,000-500,000
Number Employees: 1-4

55609 Certco Inc.
5321 Verona Rd.
Fitchburg, WI 53711 608-271-4500
  Fax: 608-278-2223 www.certcoinc.com
Frozen foods, meats, produce and private label and general line items.
President/CEO: Randall Simon
Executive VP/CFO: Amy Niemetscheck
VP, Sales/Marketing: David Ryman
Year Founded: 1930
Estimated Sales: $569.69 Million
Number Employees: 250-499
Private Brands Carried:
  Shur Fine
Number of Customer Locations: 150
Types of Products Distributed:
  Frozen Food, General Line, Provisions/Meat, Produce, Dairy products & groceries

55610 Certi-Fresh Foods, Inc
842 Flint Ave
Wilmington, CA 90744 910-221-6262
  Fax: 310-427-6060 www.certi-fresh.com
Seafood
CEO/Owner: Nino Palma
President/COO/Owner: Pete Palma
US Sales Manager: Mario Galaz
International And Domestic Procurement: Ramiro Ayala

55611 Certified Cleaning Supplies
1180 Kalamath St
Denver, CO 80204-3538 303-825-0103
      Fax: 303-893-2221
      www.certifiedjanitorialsupplies.com
Wholesaler/distributor of cleaning and janitorial supplies
Owner: Michael Kaplan
mskappy15@aol.com
Estimated Sales: $1-2.5 Million
Number Employees: 1-4
Types of Products Distributed:
  Frozen Food, General Merchandise, Cleaning & janitorial supplies

55612 Certified Food Service
22322 62nd Avenue E
Spanaway, WA 98387-5856 253-847-4179
Wholesaler/distributor of new and used bakery and deli equipment
Owner: Joan Resenauer
Contact: Joan Reisenauer
bpequip@msn.com
Estimated Sales: $1-3 Million
Number Employees: 1-4
Private Brands Carried:
  Baxter; Oliver; Revent
Types of Products Distributed:
  Frozen Food, General Merchandise

55613 Certified Food Services
2923 Old Tampa Highway
Lakeland, FL 33803-1674 407-851-8228
      Fax: 407-856-0275
Wholesaler/distributor of Greek spices, dairy products, salad dressings and egg products and substitutes
Number Employees: 20-49
Private Brands Carried:
  Renaissance; Conway; Pepita's; Grecian Delight; Kronos
Types of Products Distributed:
  Frozen Food, General Line, Specialty Foods, Greek spices, dairy products, etc.

55614 Certified Grocers Midwest
1 Certified Dr
Hodgkins, IL 60525 708-579-2100
  Fax: 708-354-7502 www.certisaver.com
Grocery supplier
President: James Bradley
CEO: Jim Denges
Number Employees: 100-249

55615 Certified Interior Systems
1125 S Redwood Rd
Salt Lake City, UT 84104 801-973-7474
  Fax: 801-973-6847 888-973-7474
      www.certifiedhandling.com
Wholesaler/distributor of conveyors, racks and shelving
President: Marilyn Tang
Contact: Jeff Thomas
jeff@certifiedhandling.com
Estimated Sales: $5-10 Million
Number Employees: 10-19
Number of Customer Locations: 1000
Types of Products Distributed:
  Frozen Food, General Merchandise, Conveyors, racks & shelving

55616 Chacewater Winery and Olive Mill
5625 Gabby Lane
Kelseyville, CA 95451 707-279-2995
  Fax: 707-279-1972 info@chacewaterwine.com
      www.chacewaterwine.com
Fine wines, olive oils, and soaps
Owner/General Manager: Paul Manuel
Mill Master: Emilio De La Cruz
Winemaker: Mark Burch
Number Employees: 10

55617 Challenge Dairy Products, Inc.
6701 Donion Way
Dublin, CA 94568 877-883-2479
  Fax: 925-551-7591 800-733-2479
      consumerinfo@challengedairy.com
      www.challengedairy.com
Processor and exporter of butter and dehydrated milk; wholesaler/distributor of butter and frozen foods.
President, CEO: Irv Holmes
Controller: Geoffrey Uy
SR VP Retail & Foodservice: Tim Anderson
EDI Coordinator: Michael Jenkins
Office Manager: Daisrea Smith
Estimated Sales: $500 Thousand
Number Employees: 175
Number of Brands: 2
Square Footage: 8500
Type of Packaging: Consumer, Food Service, Private Label, Bulk
Private Brands Carried:
  Danish
Number of Customer Locations: 5040
Types of Products Distributed:
  Food Service, General Line, Butter

55618 Chamberlain Wholesale Grocery
400 E Prospect Ave
Chamberlain, SD 57325 605-234-6513
  Fax: 605-234-5929 800-658-3093
Wholesaler/distributor of general line products, general merchandise, produce and specialty foods; serving the food service market
Manager: Jim Maxon
Grocery Manager: Ken Soulek
Manager: Jim Maxon
Operations Manager: Jim Maxon
Estimated Sales: $10-20 Million
Number Employees: 10-19
Square Footage: 40000
Private Brands Carried:
  Anheuser-Busch; Federated Foods Group
Number of Customer Locations: 50
Types of Products Distributed:
  Food Service, Frozen Food, General Line, General Merchandise, Produce, Specialty Foods

Wholesalers & Distributors / A-Z

55619 Chameleon Beverage Co Inc
6444 E 26th St
Commerce, CA 90040-3214 323-724-8223
Fax: 323-724-9048 800-989-2028
customerservice@chameleonbeverage.com
www.chameleonbeverage.com
Wholesaler/distributor of private label spring water; Custom labeling services available
Owner: Derek Reineman
derekreinwman@chameleonbeverage.com
Estimated Sales: $5-10 Million
Number Employees: 5-9
Types of Products Distributed:
 Food Service, Frozen Food, Health Food

55620 Champaign Plastics Company
PO Box 6413
Champaign, IL 61822 217-359-3664
Fax: 217-359-0091 800-575-0170
products@champaignplastics.com
www.champaignplastics.com
Manufacturer and wholesaler/distributor of disposable aprons, gloves, boots, shoe covers, hats, beard restraints, sleeves, children's and adult bibs and banquet rolls
President: Donna Williams
Contact: Joseph Bateman
joseph.bateman@champaignplastics.com
Estimated Sales: Below $5,000,000
Number Employees: 1-4
Types of Products Distributed:
 Frozen Food, General Merchandise, Disposable aprons, gloves, hats, etc.

55621 Chapman's Food Service
1108 W 8th St
Ashtabula, OH 44004-3316 440-964-3316
Fax: 440-964-2026
Wholesaler/distributor of frozen foods and meats; serving the food service market
President: R Burnett
Contact: Katherine Burnett
kburnett@jhchapman.com
Estimated Sales: $2.5-5 Million
Number Employees: 10-19
Type of Packaging: Private Label
Types of Products Distributed:
 Food Service, Frozen Food, Provisions/Meat

55622 Charissa
8595 Cox Ln
Unit 3
Cutchogue, NY 11935 631-734-8878
charissaspice.com
Morrocan seasonings
Co-Founder: Earl Fultz
Co-Founder: Gloria Fultz
Number Employees: 4
Type of Packaging: Private Label

55623 Charles C. Parks Company
388 N Belvedere Dr
Gallatin, TN 37066
 800-873-2406
info@charlescparks.com www.charlescparks.com
Wholesaler/distributor of meat, dairy products, frozen food, general merchandise and general line products.
Year Founded: 1934
Estimated Sales: $268.26 Million
Number Employees: 145
Number of Customer Locations: 700
Types of Products Distributed:
 Frozen Food, General Line, General Merchandise, Provisions/Meat, Dairy products

55624 Charles Rockel & Son
4303 Smith Rd
Cincinnati, OH 45212-4236 513-631-3009
Fax: 513-631-3083
Food brokers of dairy/deli products, frozen foods, general merchandise, groceries, industrial ingredients, etc
President: Charles Rockel
CFO: Don Rockel
Estimated Sales: $2.5-5 Million
Number Employees: 3

55625 Charles Wetgrove Company
Fm 1762
Raymondville, TX 78580 956-689-3443
Fax: 956-689-3017
Wholesaler/distributor of onions and cabbage
Manager: D Wetgrove

Estimated Sales: $5-10 Million
Number Employees: 10-19
Types of Products Distributed:
 Frozen Food, Produce, Onions & cabbage

55626 Charlie Beigg's Sauce Company
4 Heritage Lane
Windham, ME 04062-4984 888-502-8595
sales@charliebeiggs.com
BBQ sauce and salsa.
Head of Sales/Marketing: Paula Standley
Parent Co: Equitythink Holdings, LLC
Types of Products Distributed:
 Frozen Food

55627 Charlton & Hill
655 30th Street N
Lethbridge, AB T1H 5G5
Canada 403-328-3388
Fax: 403-328-3533 www.charltonandhill.com
Conveyors; wholesaler/distributor of ranges, coolers and hot plates; serving the food service market; also, metal fabrication available
Sales Manager: Dwayne Huber
Estimated Sales: $1-5 Million
Number Employees: 100-250
Private Brands Carried:
 Vulcan; Hobart
Types of Products Distributed:
 Frozen Food, General Merchandise, Ranges, coolers, hot plates, etc.

55628 (HQ)Charmel Enterprises
638 Lindero Canyon Rd # 363
Oak Park, CA 91377 818-991-8760
Fax: 818-889-6305 charmelent@aol.com
Dealer/wholesaler of foodservice equipment
President: Frank Abundis
CEO: Michael Bulmer
CFO: Irwin Parker
Sales: Frank Abundis
Contact: Martin Shea
martin_shea@wellsfargo.com
Estimated Sales: $1 Million
Number Employees: 4
Square Footage: 2000
Type of Packaging: Food Service
Types of Products Distributed:
 General Merchandise, China, glassware, flatware, etc.

55629 Chas. Wetterling & Sons
1244 W George St
Chicago, IL 60657 773-248-2910
Fax: 773-248-2919
Wholesaler/distributor of provisions/meats
President: Frank Wetterling
CEO: David Ries
CFO: Marian Wetterling
Estimated Sales: $1-3 Million
Number Employees: 5-9
Square Footage: 20000
Private Brands Carried:
 Jones Dairy Farm; Leon's Sausage; Plainville Farms Turkey Products
Types of Products Distributed:
 Health Food, Provisions/Meat

55630 Chatfield Dairy
311,Main St N
Chatfield, MN 55923 507-867-3649
www.dairyqueen.com
Wholesaler/distributor of dairy products including milk, cheese, eggs, yogurt, butter, cream and milk drinks
President: Howard Waldron
Estimated Sales: Less than $500,000
Number Employees: 1-4
Types of Products Distributed:
 Frozen Food, General Line, Dairy products

55631 Chatila's
254 N Broadway
Salem, NH 03079-2132 603-898-5459
Fax: 603-893-1586
customercare@chatilasbakery.com
www.chatilasbakery.com
All sugar-free items. Chatila's muffins, cookies, pastries, cheesecakes, donuts, bagels, pies, breads, chocolates and ice cream. All items sweetend with Splenda and/or Melltitol, low carb, low cal, low fat, low cholestrol, notrans-fat.

President: Mohamad Chatila
cutomercare@chatilas.com
Sales: Jennifer Marks
Estimated Sales: Less Than $500,000
Number Employees: 1-4
Number of Brands: 1
Number of Products: 100+
Square Footage: 24000
Type of Packaging: Consumer, Food Service, Private Label, Bulk

55632 Chattanooga Button & Badge Company
438 Frazier Avenue
Chattanooga, TN 37405-4169 423-267-4039
Fax: 423-267-4039
Wholesaler/distributor of advertising specialties, emblems and flags, pennants and banners
Owner: W Russell
Estimated Sales: Less than $500,000
Number Employees: 1-4
Types of Products Distributed:
 Frozen Food, General Merchandise, Flags, pennants, banners, etc.

55633 Chattanooga Restaurant Supl
822 E 11th St
Chattanooga, TN 37403-3201 423-266-8181
Fax: 423-267-7901 elwynv@chattrestsupply.com
www.chattrestsupply.com
Wholesaler/distributor of groceries, frozen foods, smallwares, equipment and fixtures; serving the food service market
General Manager: Elwyn Vincent
elwynv@chattrestsupply.com
Sales Exec: Elwyn Vincent
Warehouse Manager: Bob Sullivan
Estimated Sales: $5-10 Million
Number Employees: 10-19
Square Footage: 140000
Number of Customer Locations: 300
Types of Products Distributed:
 Food Service, Frozen Food, General Line, General Merchandise, Smallwares, equipment & fixtures

55634 Chebe Bread Products
1840 Lundberg Dr W
Spirit Lake, IA 51360-7661 712-336-4211
www.chebe.com
Gluten free dry mixes and frozen bread
Owner: Richard Reed
dreed@chebe.com
Number Employees: 5-9

55635 Cheese Shop
1219 Fulton St
Ottawa, IL 61350-2053 815-433-0478
Fax: 815-433-2075 info@thecheeseshop.biz
www.thecheeseshop.biz
Wholesaler/distributor of cheese and deli meats; serving the food service market
President: Martin D Ruhland
catering@thecheeseshop.biz
Cheesemaker: Matt Ruhland
Estimated Sales: $500,000-$1 Million
Number Employees: 10-19
Types of Products Distributed:
 Food Service, Frozen Food, General Line, Cheese & deli meats

55636 Cheeseland, Inc.
P.O. Box 22230
Seattle, WA 98122-0230 206-709-1220
cheeselandinc.com
Dutch cheese and cheese products
Owner & Founder: Jan Kos
Number Employees: 6
Types of Products Distributed:
 General Line

55637 Chef John Folse & Co
2517 S Philippe Ave
Gonzales, LA 70737 225-644-6000
Fax: 225-644-1295 folse@jfolse.com
Wholesaler/distributor of frozen foods, soups, vegetables, glazes, prepared bases, desserts, sauces and seafood
Owner: Dawn Delhommer
dawnd@agcenter.lsu.edu
Marketing/Sales Executive: Chris Landry
Purchasing Manager: Carroll Folse

Wholesalers & Distributors / A-Z

Estimated Sales: $50-100 Million
Number Employees: 20-49
Square Footage: 20000
Other Locations:
   Chef John Folse & Co.
   New Orleans, LAChef John Folse & Co.
Private Brands Carried:
   Louisana Premier Products
Types of Products Distributed:
   Food Service, Frozen Food, Produce, Seafood

55638 Chef's Choice Mesquite Charcoal
1729 Ocean Oaks Rd
PO Box 707
Carpinteria, CA 93014-0707   805-684-8284
                 Fax: 805-684-8284
Manufacturer and importer of mesquite charcoal
Owner: Bill Lord
Number of Products: 2
Type of Packaging: Food Service
Types of Products Distributed:
   Frozen Food

55639 Chef's Pride Gifts LLC
21740 Trolley Industrial # 1
Taylor, MI 48180-1875   313-295-1800
        Fax: 313-295-0448   800-878-1800
www.chefspride.com
Wholesaler/distributor of poultry and specialty foods; serving the food service market
President: M Loewenstein
Vice President: M Loewenstein
Manager: Mike Parks
mike@chefspride.com
Estimated Sales: Less Than $500,000
Number Employees: 1-4
Square Footage: 120000
Types of Products Distributed:
   Food Service, Frozen Food, Provisions/Meat, Specialty Foods, Poultry

55640 Chef's Supply & Design
485 N Hollywood St
Memphis, TN 38112-2548   901-458-2503
        Fax: 901-458-2505   800-489-0951
Wholesaler/distributor of general merchandise including restaurant equipment and supplies and table top needs; serving the food service market; also, restaurant designing services available
President: Greg Shahun
greg@chefs-supply.com
Corporate Secretary/Co-Owner: Scott Giles
Vice President: Greg Shahun
greg@chefs-supply.com
Marketing/Accounting: Ashley Murray
Service Manager: Eddie Vaughn
Buyer: Alan Williams
Estimated Sales: $2-3 Million
Number Employees: 10-19
Square Footage: 40000
Types of Products Distributed:
   Food Service, Frozen Food, General Merchandise, Restaurant equipment & supplies

55641 Chefwise
2200 NW 102nd Ave # 2
Unit 2
Doral, FL 33172-2225   786-845-3884
        Fax: 786-845-9997   866-254-CHEF
chefwise@hotmail.com   www.chefwise.com
Au jus, desserts, sauces, soups and stocks
Owner: Daniel Durand
ddurand@chefwise.com
Chef: Daniel Durand
Number Employees: 1-4

55642 Chellino Cheese Co
505 Bennett Ave
Joliet, IL 60433-2301   815-726-5969
                Fax: 815-726-6441
Wholesaler/distributor of Italian cheese; serving the food service market
President: Fred Cemeno
Estimated Sales: $10-20 Million
Number Employees: 10-19
Types of Products Distributed:
   Food Service, Frozen Food, Specialty Foods, Italian cheese

55643 Chelsea Market Baskets
75 9th Ave
New York, NY 10011-7006   212-727-0311
www.cmb-wholesale.com
cookies; snack chips; chocolate; relish; special food packaging; giftwrap; labels; containers
Owner: David Porat   *Year Founded:* 1993
Private Brands Carried:
   Tregroes; Cornish Sea Salt; Gran Luchito; Hasslacher's; Island Bakery; Lakrids; Melting Pots; Mighty Fine Kitchen; Peter's Yard Crispbread; Prestat Chocolate; Shortbread House Of Edinburgh; Summerdown Mint; Torres Chips; Broderick's; & LuscombeDrinks
Types of Products Distributed:
   General Line, General Merchandise, Specialty Foods, Specialty Food Packaging

55644 Chem Care
10206 Forest Ln
Dallas, TX 75243   972-233-9119
Wholesaler/distributor of cleaning supplies including deodorizers, floor finishes, mops, brooms, etc
President: Lou Polka
VP: Vivian Polka
Types of Products Distributed:
   Frozen Food, General Merchandise, Cleaning supplies

55645 (HQ)Chem-Mark of Buffalo
385 Heim Rd
Getzville, NY 14068   716-631-8416
        Fax: 716-631-8688   800-723-8416
Wholesaler/distributor of beverage equipment, dishwashers, ice makers, water softeners, coolers, freezers and cleaning chemicals; serving the food service market
President: Lawrence Read
Number Employees: 5-9
Square Footage: 24000
Private Brands Carried:
   Manitowoc; True; Beverage-Air; C.M.A.
Number of Customer Locations: 500
Types of Products Distributed:
   Food Service, Frozen Food, General Merchandise, Coolers, freezers, etc.

55646 Chemcraft Industries Inc
2345 W Roscoe St
Chicago, IL 60618-6200   773-929-6800
        Fax: 773-929-3925   877-907-5802
www.chemcraftind.com
Wholesaler/distributor of janitorial supplies
President: Martin Munvez
marty@chemcraftind.com
Vice President: Michelle Munvez
Inside Sales Coordinator: Angela Veronico
Office Manager: Bonita Taylor
Estimated Sales: $1-3 Million
Number Employees: 10-19
Square Footage: 41200
Private Brands Carried:
   Rubbermaid; 3M; Johnsons Wax
Types of Products Distributed:
   Frozen Food, General Merchandise, Janitorial supplies

55647 Chemroy Canada
2201 Drew Road
Mississauga, ON L5S 1S4
Canada   905-677-0701
                Fax: 905-677-8411
Wholesaler/distributor of gums, flavors, hydrolyzed vegetable proteins, free-flow agents and nondairy creamers
President: Joseph Bernardi
VP: John Graham
Types of Products Distributed:
   Frozen Food, General Line, Ingredients

55648 Cheney Brothers Inc
1 Cheney Way
Riviera Beach, FL 33404
                800-432-1341
webmaster@cheneybrothers.com
www.cheneybrothers.com
Wholesaler/distributor of food service equipment and supplies and general line products; serving the food service market.
President & CEO: Byron Russell
byron@cheneybrothers.com
Director of Marketing: Kinna Denowitz
Year Founded: 1925
Estimated Sales: Over $2 Billion
Number Employees: 3,000
Number of Products: 9999
Private Brands Carried:
   Hunts; Uncle Ben's; Hillshire
Number of Customer Locations: 2800
Types of Products Distributed:
   Food Service, Frozen Food, General Line, General Merchandise, Foodservice equipment & supplies

55649 (HQ)Chernoff Sales
3308 Park Central Blvd N
Pompano Beach, FL 33064   954-972-1414
        Fax: 954-972-4214   800-226-7600
sales@chernoffsales.com   www.chernoffsales.com
Manufacturers' representative and wholesaler/distributor for commercial cooking and refrigeration equipment, microwave ovens, ice machines, ice cream cabinets, stainless steel sinks and tables, can openers, scales, food warmers andsteamers
Principal: James Cox
Principal: Joe Andisman
Principal: Michael Turetzky
VP Sales/Marketing: Michael Turetzky
Sales: Barrie Spear
Customer Service: Tonya Smith
Estimated Sales: $15.5 Million
Number Employees: 10-19
Square Footage: 128000
Private Brands Carried:
   Silver King; Imperial; Ice-O-Matic; Edlund; Powers; Nexel
Number of Customer Locations: 1000
Types of Products Distributed:
   Food Service, Frozen Food, General Merchandise, Foodservice equipment & supplies

55650 Cherry Central Cooperative, Inc.
1771 N. US Highway 31 S.
Traverse City, MI 49684   231-946-1860
        Fax: 231-941-4167   info@cherrycentral.com
www.cherrycentral.com
Red tart cherries, apples and blueberries and also a major supplier of cranberries, strawberries, pomegranate arils and asparagus. Supplier to major manufacturers for dried, frozen, canned and custom products.
President/CEO: Steve Eisler
Director, Food Service: David Barger
Retail National Sales Manager: Vince Higgs
Director, Private/Custom Label: Frank Wolff
Year Founded: 1973
Estimated Sales: $154 Million
Number Employees: 100-249
Square Footage: 15500
Type of Packaging: Consumer, Food Service, Private Label, Bulk

55651 Cherry Moon Farms
4840 Eastgate Mall
San Diego, CA 92121   858-729-2800
                800-580-2913
wecare@customercare.cherrymoonfarms.com
Fruit baskets, gift baskets wth chocolates and treats, and spa baskets
President/COO: Abe Wynperle
VP Finance: Rex Bosen
VP/General Counsel: Blake Bilstad

55652 Cheryl's Cookies
646 Mccorkle Blvd
Westerville, OH 43082-8778   614-776-1500
        Fax: 614-891-8599   800-443-8124
www.cheryls.com
Cookies and baked goods
President: Cheryl Krueger
CFO/COO: Dennis Hicks
dhicks@cherylandco.com
Quality Assurance Director: Sara Reed
VP Creative Services: Lisa Henry
Estimated Sales: $25.5 Million
Number Employees: 250-499
Square Footage: 23103
Parent Co: 1-800-Flowers

55653 Chester River Clam Co
305 Roe Ingleside Rd
Centreville, MD 21617-2012   410-758-3810
                Fax: 410-758-4089
Clams
Owner: Mel Hickman
mhickman@chesterriverhealth.org
Estimated Sales: $2,100,000
Number Employees: 5-9

Wholesalers & Distributors / A-Z

55654 Chia I Foods Company
P.O.Box 670
La Puente, CA 91747-670
Fax: 626-401-9519
Wholesaler/distributor and importer of sliced, diced and granulated dehydrated fruits including pineapple, papaya, mango and coconut; also, crystallized ginger, dried red chili peppers, etc.; rack jobber services available; serving thefood service market
President: Ann Huang
VP: Steve Huang
Estimated Sales: $1-2.5 Million
Number Employees: 10-19
Square Footage: 36000
Type of Packaging: Bulk
Types of Products Distributed:
  Food Service, Frozen Food, General Line, General Merchandise, Rack Jobbers, Specialty Foods, Dried fruits, spices, etc.

55655 Chicago Bar & Restaurant Supply
1510 W Lawrence Avenue
Chicago, IL 60640-4703 773-271-3600
Fax: 773-271-3065 nadburn@hotmail.com
Wholesaler/distributor of china, paper products, cutlery, janitorial supplies and equipment; serving the food service market
President: L Nadborne
Number Employees: 5-9
Square Footage: 40000
Types of Products Distributed:
  Food Service, General Merchandise, China, paper, cutlery, equipment, etc.

55656 Chicago Coffee Roastery
11880 Smith Court
Huntley, IL 60142 847-669-1156
Fax: 847-669-1114 800-762-5402
sales@chicagocoffee.com www.chicagocoffee.com
Coffee, instant cocoa, instant cappuccio, tea
Owner: Sandra Knight
sknight@coffeemasters.com
Vice President: Brian Gosell
Purchasing Manager: Brian Gosell
Estimated Sales: $2 Million
Number Employees: 5-9
Square Footage: 32000
Type of Packaging: Consumer, Food Service, Private Label, Bulk
Private Brands Carried:
  Toreni Syrup; Monin Syrup; Stash Tea; Ahmad Tea
Types of Products Distributed:
  Specialty Foods

55657 Chicago Food Corporation
5800 N Pulaski Rd
Chicago, IL 60646 773-478-0007
Fax: 773-478-0084 chcgofood@aol.com
www.chicagofood.com
Wholesaler/distributor and exporter of produce, frozen items, seafood and Oriental foods; importer of frozen seafood
Owner: Kipyo Hong
Contact: Ki Hong
k_hong@chicagofood.com
Estimated Sales: $20-50 Million
Number Employees: 10-19
Type of Packaging: Private Label, Bulk
Private Brands Carried:
  Sasum; Deer
Number of Customer Locations: 2
Types of Products Distributed:
  Frozen Food, Produce, Seafood, Specialty Foods, Oriental foods

55658 Chicago Food Market
2245 S Wentworth Ave
Chicago, IL 60616-2011 312-842-4361
Fax: 312-842-6448
President: Matthew Chan
Estimated Sales: $2,500,000
Number Employees: 10-19

55659 Chicago Market Company
1101 W Fulton Market
Chicago, IL 60607-1253 773-733-6160
Wholesaler/distributor of groceries and meats
Estimated Sales: $.5-1 million
Number Employees: 1-4
Number of Customer Locations: 100
Types of Products Distributed:
  General Line, Provisions/Meat, Groceries

55660 Chicago Premier Meats
822 W Exchange Ave
Chicago, IL 60609-2507 773-847-3364
Fax: 773-847-3364 800-385-0661
tschicagosteak@aol.com www.chicagosteaks.com
Meat packing
President/CEO/Treasurer: Tom Summers
CEO/Principal: Thomas Campbell
Vice President: Rick Allison
Estimated Sales: $5.50 Million
Number Employees: 10-19

55661 Chicago Steaks
Chicago, IL 773-847-5400
www.chicagosteaks.com
Meat products, value added products, and gift steaks
Estimated Sales: $9 Million
Number Employees: 20-49
Number of Brands: 5
Square Footage: 6560
Type of Packaging: Food Service, Private Label
Private Brands Carried:
  Chicago Steak
Types of Products Distributed:
  Food Service, Frozen Food, Provisions/Meat

55662 Chicago Vendor Supply
7000 W 60th St
Chicago, IL 60638-3102 773-586-4300
Fax: 773-586-4336
Wholesale vend and office coffee service distributor. Also candy, snacks, cups, soda, juices paper, goods, frozen and refrigerated foods.
Owner: Len Mahler
cvsvend@aol.com
Number Employees: 50-99

55663 Chile Guy
168 Calle Don Francisco
Bernalillo, NM 87004-6519 505-867-4251
Fax: 505-867-4252 800-869-9218
www.thechileguy.com
Wholesaler/distributor, importer and exporter of exotic dried chiles including whole and powdered
Owner: Mark Sanchez
mark@thechileguy.com
Office Manager: Pam Harris
Estimated Sales: $5-10 Million
Number Employees: 5-9
Parent Co: Direct Marketing de Santa Fe
Type of Packaging: Bulk
Types of Products Distributed:
  General Line, Specialty Foods, Exotic dried chiles

55664 China D Food Service
2535 S Kessler Street
Wichita, KS 67217-1044 316-945-2323
Fax: 316-945-5557
Food service and management
Purchasing: Lisa Diez
Estimated Sales: $300,000-500,000
Number Employees: 1-4
Type of Packaging: Food Service

55665 Chinese Trading Company
2263 S Wentworth Avenue
Chicago, IL 60616-2011 312-842-2820
Wholesaler/distributor of Asian foods; serving the food service market
President: Ping Tom
Secretary: Eunice Tom Wong
Treasurer: Mary Tom
Estimated Sales: $2.5-5 Million
Number Employees: 1-4
Types of Products Distributed:
  Food Service, Asian

55666 Chip Steak & Provision Co
232 Dewey St
Mankato, MN 56001-2393 507-388-6277
Fax: 507-388-6279
Wholesales meat & meat products; wholesales packaged frozen foods
President: Michael Miller
ddi95@yahoo.com
Estimated Sales: $5-9.9 Million
Number Employees: 5-9
Square Footage: 16000
Type of Packaging: Consumer, Food Service, Bulk

55667 Chipurnoi Inc
3 Cemetery Hill Rd
P.O. Box 1708
Sharon, CT 06069-2073 860-364-0870
Fax: 860-364-5982 800-982-9002
www.checkmatescandy.com
Importer and wholesaler/distributor of confectionery products and specialty foods
President: Laurence Chipurnoi
lchipurnoi@chipurnoi.com
General Manager: J Schmidt
Estimated Sales: $3-5 Million
Number Employees: 5-9
Types of Products Distributed:
  Frozen Food, Specialty Foods, Confectionery

55668 ChocAlive
16 Mt Ebo Road South
Brewster, NY 10509 845-279-1715
orderchocalive@verizon.net
Gluten free, vegan and raw truffles

55669 Chocolate Maven
Chocolate Maven Bakery & Cafe 821
W. San Mateo Rd
Santa Fe, NM 87505 505-984-1980
www.chocolatemaven.com
Pastries and baked goods

55670 Chocolate Works
114 Church St
Freeport, NY 11520
info@chocolateworks.com
www.chocolateworks.com
Chocolate
Founder: Joe Whaley

55671 Chocolates by Mark
2100 Space Park Drive
Suite 102
Houston, TX 77058 832-736-2626
Fax: 603-925-8000 www.chocolatesbymark.com
Custom chocolate wedding/party favors, gifts
President: Mark Caffey
Number Employees: 1-4
Square Footage: 8800
Type of Packaging: Private Label, Bulk
Types of Products Distributed:
  Frozen Food

55672 Choice Food Group Inc
618 Church St # 220
Nashville, TN 37219-2453 615-248-9255
www.choicefood.com
Shelf-stable and prepared foods
Number Employees: 1-4
Type of Packaging: Consumer, Private Label

55673 Choice Restaurant Equipment
8011 S Dixie Highway
West Palm Beach, FL 33405-4823 561-586-4002
Fax: 561-586-5199 800-331-2255
Wholesaler/distributor of food service equipment, furniture and appliances; serving the food service market
Owner/President: Doug Shupe
Sales/Marketing Executive: Jerry Culbertson
Purchasing Agent: Nancy Esplen
Estimated Sales: $20-50 Million
Number Employees: 50-99
Parent Co: Clark Foodservice
Private Brands Carried:
  Vulcan-Hart; True; Cambro
Number of Customer Locations: 2200
Types of Products Distributed:
  Food Service, Frozen Food, General Merchandise, Foodservice equipment

55674 Chong Mei Trading
1130 Oakleigh Dr
East Point, GA 30344 404-768-3838
Fax: 404-768-0008
Pork, beef, seafood, chicken, dry goods, dairy, produce, Oriental grocery items
President: Kai Chen Wong
Estimated Sales: $1-3 Million
Number Employees: 10-19

55675 Choyce Produce
3140 Ualena St
Suite 206
Honolulu, HI 96819-1965 808-839-1502

Wholesalers & Distributors / A-Z

President: Edmund Choy
Contact: Annette Forness
aforness@choycehi.com
Estimated Sales: $5-10 Million
Number Employees: 5-9

55676 Chris Hansen Seafood
134 Chris Ln
Port Sulphur, LA 70083-2814   504-564-2888
Seafood
Owner: Chris Hansen
Estimated Sales: Less Than $500,000
Number Employees: 1-4

55677 Christian County Grain Inc
214 Duffy St
Pembroke, KY 42266   270-475-4216
Fax: 270-475-4216 www.christiancountygrain.com
Wholesaler/distributor of white and yellow whole kernel cleaned corn; serving corn chip processors
Owner: Pat Covington
patcov@apex.net
VP: Pat Covington
Estimated Sales: $10-20 Million
Number Employees: 5-9
Square Footage: 200000
Types of Products Distributed:
    Frozen Food, Produce, Whole kernel cleaned corn

55678 Christopher Wholesalers
70 Main St
Madison, ME 04950-1223   207-696-4402
Fax: 207-696-8007
Wholesaler/distributor of general merchandise
President: David Christopher
Estimated Sales: $10-20 Million
Number Employees: 10-19
Number of Customer Locations: 800
Types of Products Distributed:
    Frozen Food, General Merchandise

55679 Christopher's Herb Shop
188 S Main St
Springville, UT 84663-1849   801-489-4500
Fax: 801-489-4814 888-372-4372
www.drchristophersherbshop.com
Food supplements manufacturer, private label items, herbs and health foods
President: David Christopher
Vice President: Ruth Christopher Bacalla
Manager: Bobbie Henderson
manager@drchristophersherbshop.com
Production Manager: James Webster
Purchasing Manager: Josh Bruni
Estimated Sales: Less Than $500,000
Number Employees: 5-9
Square Footage: 15000
Type of Packaging: Private Label
Number of Customer Locations: 500
Types of Products Distributed:
    Health Food, Specialty Foods

55680 Christy Industries Inc
1812 Bath Ave # 1
Brooklyn, NY 11214-4690   718-236-0211
Fax: 718-259-3294 800-472-2078
www.christy-ind.com
Manufacturer and exporter of fire and burglar alarms; wholesaler/distributor of intercoms and television equipment including security and closed circuit
President: Statz Cheryl
s.cheryl@alarmdistributor.com
Estimated Sales: $1-3 Million
Number Employees: 5-9
Square Footage: 6000
Types of Products Distributed:
    General Merchandise, Security equipment

55681 Church & Dwight Co., Inc.
Princeton South Corporate Center
500 Charles Ewing Boulevard
Ewing, NJ 08628   609-806-1200
    800-833-9532
www.churchdwight.com
Personal care, household cleaning, fabric care, and health and well-being products for the consumer market. Manufacturer of Arm & Hammer brand sodium bicarbonate (baking soda), and other leavening products for the baking industry.

Chairman/President/CEO: Matthew Farrell
Executive VP/CFO: Rick Dierker
Executive VP/General Counsel/Secretary: Patrick de Maynadier
Executive V, Global R&D: Carlos Linares
Executive VP/CMO: Britta Bomhard
Executive VP, U.S. Sales: Paul Wood
Executive VP, Global Operations: Rick Spann
Year Founded: 1846
Estimated Sales: $4.15 Billion
Number Employees: 4,700
Number of Brands: 34
Type of Packaging: Consumer, Food Service, Bulk

55682 Church Point Wholesale Grocer
PO Box 40
Church Point, LA 70525-0040   337-684-5413
    Fax: 337-684-6666
Wholesaler/distributor of frozen foods, meats, groceries
Vice Preisdent/General Manager: George Casanova
Estimated Sales: $20-50 Million
Number Employees: 50-99
Square Footage: 130000
Private Brands Carried:
    Better Vall; Red & White
Number of Customer Locations: 450
Types of Products Distributed:
    Frozen Food, General Line, Provisions/Meat, Groceries

55683 Churro Corporation
127 Payne St
Dallas, TX 75207-7205   214-747-8677
    Fax: 214-748-0985 800-255-6254
Wholesaler/distributor of nacho and sesame snack thins, tostadas and jalapeno sticks; also, nacho and jalapeno bean dip and chalupa and tostada shells,; serving the food service market
Owner: Arnaldo Cavazos Sr
Secretary/Treasurer: Ila Cavazos
Estimated Sales: $500,000-$1 Million
Number Employees: 5-9
Types of Products Distributed:
    General Line, Nacho & sesame snack thins, etc.

55684 Cibaria International
705 Columbia Ave
Riverside, CA 92507   951-823-8490
    Fax: 951-823-8495 www.cibaria-intl.com
Oils, vinegars and accessories
Founder: Kathy Griset
Square Footage: 55000
Type of Packaging: Food Service, Private Label, Bulk

55685 Cielo Foods
9238 Bally Ct
Rancho Cucamonga, CA 91730-5313 909-945-2323
    Fax: 909-945-9090 877-652-4356
    www.cielousa.com
Frozen yogurt
Owner: Dan Kim
info@cielousa.com
Number Employees: 5-9

55686 Cilurzo Vineyards & Winery
41220 Calle Contento
Temecula, CA 92592   951-676-5250
    Fax: 909-676-7458 800-783-5250
    info@bellavistawinery.com
    www.bellavistawinery.com
Wines
Co-Owner: Vincenzo Cilurzo
Co-Owner: Audrey Cilurzo
Sales Director: J Richardson
Estimated Sales: $500-1 Million appx.
Number Employees: 1-4
Number of Products: 15
Type of Packaging: Private Label
Private Brands Carried:
    Cilurzo
Number of Customer Locations: 1

55687 Cipriani
30271 Tomas
Rancho Sta Marg, CA 92688-2123   949-589-3978
    Fax: 949-589-3979 www.ciprianicorp.com
Manufacturer, distributor and importer of hygienic stainless steel valves

President: Maria Carlo
mg@ciprianicorp.com
CEO: Robert Moreno
Vice President: Maria Grazia Cipriani
Marketing/Sales VP: Carlo Cipriani
Sales Manager: Chris P Winsek
Estimated Sales: $1,000,000
Number Employees: 5-9
Square Footage: 6000

55688 Circle B Ranch
RR2 Box 2824
Seymour, MO 65746   417-683-0271
    www.circlebranchpork.com
Pork products, bacon, meat sticks, sauces, chutneys, and gluten free Bloody Mary mix
Owner: Marina Backes
Owner: John Backes
Types of Products Distributed:
    Provisions/Meat

55689 Cirelli Foods
630 John Hancock Rd
Taunton, MA 02780-7380
    Fax: 508-947-8604 800-242-0939
Wholesaler/distributor of frozen and specialty foods, general merchandise, disposables, paper and warewashing products, produce, meats, groceries, dairy and private label items, baked goods and seafood; serving the food servicemarket
CEO/President: Chuck Dillon
VP/CFO: Ray LeBlanc
CEO: Raymond Le Blanc
Executive Director Sales/Marketing: Leon Tarentino
Contact: Ray Leblanc
jammyz@msn.com
Estimated Sales: $20-50 Million
Number Employees: 100-249
Number of Customer Locations: 4200
Types of Products Distributed:
    Food Service, Frozen Food, General Line, General Merchandise, Provisions/Meat, Produce, Seafood, Specialty Foods, Disposables, paper products, etc.

55690 Ciro Foods
PO Box 44096
Pittsburgh, PA 15205-0296   412-771-9018
    Fax: 412-771-9018 cirofoods@usa.net
Roasted red pepper spread, Italian salsa, sauces including pizza, barbecue and cooking and hot honey mustard; wholesaler/distributor of hot pepper sauce; serving the food service market; importer of vinegar; exporter of hot honeymustard
President: Robert Pasquarelli
VP: Josephine Proto
Marketing Executive: Armand Pasquarelli
Number Employees: 20
Type of Packaging: Consumer, Food Service, Private Label
Number of Customer Locations: 106
Types of Products Distributed:
    Food Service, Frozen Food, General Line, Hot pepper sauce

55691 Cisco-Eagle
10015 E 51st St
Tulsa, OK 74146-5730   918-622-9010
    Fax: 918-622-9059 888-887-3861
    www.cisco-eagle.com
Wholesaler/distributor of material handling equipment including pallet jacks, conveyors and shelving
President: Warren Gandall
warren.gandall@cisco-eagle.com
Advertising Manager: Scott Stone
Estimated Sales: $10-20 Million
Number Employees: 10-19
Private Brands Carried:
    Hytrol Conveyor; Steel King; Penco
Types of Products Distributed:
    Frozen Food, General Merchandise, Pallet jacks, conveyors, etc.

55692 Citrobio Inc
7614 15th St E
Sarasota, FL 34243-3248   941-359-1647
    Fax: 941-359-8279 800-332-1647
    mac@citrobio.com
Organic food washes used for the seafood, produce, retail, agriculture, milk and other applications.
Founder: Richard Maguire
mac@citrobio.com
Estimated Sales: $2 Million
Number Employees: 5-9

55693 City Deli Distributing
2200 Jerrold Ave Ste Y
San Francisco, CA 94124 415-648-8770
Fax: 415-648-6309
Wholesaler/distributor of meats; serving the food service market
Owner: George Elhihi
Estimated Sales: $2.5-5 Million
Number Employees: 1-4
Types of Products Distributed:
　Food Service, Frozen Food, Provisions/Meat

55694 City Espresso Roasting Company
76 Sunol Street
San Jose, CA 95126 408-248-4500
Fax: 408-248-4570 cityesp@aol.com
www.barefootcoffeeroasters.com
Wholesaler/distributor of roasted coffee beans including regular, decaffeinated, flavored and decaffeinated flavored
Owner: Andy Newbom
Estimated Sales: $5-10 Million
Number Employees: 5-9
Types of Products Distributed:
　Frozen Food, General Line, Roasted coffee beans

55695 City Fish Sales
Bay 8 3515-27 Street NE
Calgary, AB T1Y 5E4
Canada 403-250-8222
Fax: 403-250-7746 800-505-8505
info@cityfish.ca www.cityfish.ca
Wholesaler/distributor of fresh and frozen fish
Director: Nelson Leung
Quality Control/Production Manager: David Yip
Sales Representative: Sam Szeto
Estimated Sales: $8-17 Million
Number Employees: 10-19
Square Footage: 28000
Types of Products Distributed:
　Frozen Food, Seafood, Fresh & frozen fish

55696 City Line Food Distributors
20 Industry Dr
West Haven, CT 06516-1442 203-931-3707
Fax: 203-931-3706 www.citylinefoods.com
Wholesaler/distributor of general merchandise, meats/provisions, frozen and specialty foods, seafood, produce and groceries; serving the food service market
Owner: Robert Berkowitz
Food Service Sales: Jack Farkas
rberkowitz@citylinefoods.com
Estimated Sales: $20-50 Million
Number Employees: 100-249
Private Brands Carried:
　EMCO; CODE
Types of Products Distributed:
　Food Service, Frozen Food, General Line, Provisions/Meat, Produce, Seafood, Specialty Foods

55697 City Market
1508 Gloucester St
Brunswick, GA 31520-7143 912-265-4430
Fax: 912-261-2191 www.citymarketseafood.com
Fish and seafood
Owner: Michael Howell
m.howell@citymarket.com
Manager: Frank Owens
Estimated Sales: $3,500,000
Number Employees: 5-9

55698 City Packing Company
117 Newmarket Sq
Boston, MA 02118 617-442-8100
800-654-5405
citypacking@gmail.com citypackingcompany.com
Wholesaler/distributor of meats; serving the food service market.
President: Alan Stearn
Year Founded: 1946
Estimated Sales: $20-50 Million
Number Employees: 20-49
Types of Products Distributed:
　Food Service, Provisions/Meat, Kosher meats & frozen foods

55699 City Produce Co
202 Mill St SE
Ardmore, OK 73402 580-223-0257
Fax: 580-223-8023 877-244-0257
customerservice@cityproduceinc.com
www.cityproduceinc.com
Wholesaler/distributor of produce, frozen foods and general line items; serving the food service market.
President: Bob Bell
bob@cityproduceinc.com
Chief Financial Officer: Kim Bell
Sales Representative: Joe Caudle
Sales Manager: Charles Cathcart
Grocery Buyer: Mike Summers
Produce Buyer: Clay Bell
Year Founded: 1953
Estimated Sales: $12 Million
Number Employees: 50-99
Types of Products Distributed:
　Food Service, General Line, Produce

55700 City Wholesale Company
125 W Lakeview Dr NE
Milledgeville, GA 31061 478-452-3121
Fax: 478-452-9520
Wholesaler/distributor of general line products; serving the food service market
President: Gordon Giles
Estimated Sales: $5-10 Million
Number Employees: 5-9
Types of Products Distributed:
　Food Service, Frozen Food, General Line

55701 City Wide Produce Distributors
2404 S Wolcott Ave
Chicago, IL 60608-5300 312-666-6190
Fax: 312-666-8852 info@cipm.org
www.chicagoproducemarket.com
Wholesaler/distributor of vegetables including potatoes, onions and garlic
President: John Maentanis
Contact: Sam Gaglione
samgaglione@chicagoproducemarket.com
Estimated Sales: $10-20 Million
Number Employees: 20-49
Types of Products Distributed:
　Produce, Potatoes, onions & garlic

55702 Claremont Herbal Health
RR 3
Box 2g
Claremont, NH 03743-9804 603-542-7146
Wholesaler/distributor of vitamins, herbs and weight-loss supplements
Sales/Marketing Executive: Albert Stukas
Purchasing Agent: Susan Stukas
Number Employees: 1-4
Parent Co: Herbalife
Types of Products Distributed:
　Frozen Food, Health Food, Vitamins & herbs

55703 Clarence Mayfield Produce Company
Louisville Produce Terminal
Louisville, KY 40218 502-456-6900
Fax: 502-456-6903
Wholesaler/distributor of fresh produce; serving the food service market
President: Jim Schuengel
Number Employees: 10
Types of Products Distributed:
　Food Service, General Line, Produce, Fresh

55704 Clarion Fruit Co
1060 E Main St
Clarion, PA 16214 814-226-8070
clarionfruit@verizon.net
www.facebook.com/clarionfruitcompany
Wholesaler/distributor of produce and dry and frozen foods; serving the food service market.
Year Founded: 2011
Estimated Sales: $20-50 Million
Number Employees: 10-19
Types of Products Distributed:
　Food Service, General Line, Produce, Dry goods

55705 Clark Food Service Equipment
2207 Old Philadelphia Pike
Lancaster, PA 17602 717-392-7363
www.clarkfoodserviceequipment.biz
Wholesaler/distributor of equipment, chemicals and janitorial supplies; serving the food service market.
President: Gene Clark
Project Developer: Michael Fenske
Year Founded: 1971
Estimated Sales: $450 Million
Number Employees: 1,000
Square Footage: 70000
Other Locations:
　The Restaurant Store
　Lehigh Valley, PA
　The Restaurant Store
　Philadelphia, PA
　The Restaurant Store
　Wilmington, DEThe Restaurant StorePhiladelphia
Types of Products Distributed:
　Food Service

55706 (HQ)Clark Foodservice Equipment
2209 Old Philadelphia Pike
Lancaster, PA 17602 717-392-7363
www.clarkfoodserviceequipment.biz
Foodservice equipment including; design consultations and services, bidding & estimation, project management, full line of commercial equipment, custom stainless steel fabrication & millwork, delivery & installation, and equipmentservices
Other Locations:
　Sarasota, FL

55707 Clark Meat Servicing
3524 NE Stallings Dr
Nacogdoches, TX 75965-8732 936-564-5356
Fax: 936-564-2220
Wholesaler/distributor of meat including beef and pork
Partner: Kristi Mc Lain
Estimated Sales: $1-2.5 Million
Number Employees: 5-9
Types of Products Distributed:
　Provisions/Meat

55708 Clark Restaurant Svc
2803 Tamarack Rd
PO Box 1984
Owensboro, KY 42301-6566 270-684-1469
Fax: 270-685-5696 800-264-0710
info@crsonesource.com www.crsonesource.com
Wholesaler/distributor of groceries, general merchandise, produce, fresh meats, frozen foods, etc.; serving the food service market
President: Steve Clark
sclark@crsonesource.com
Estimated Sales: $10-20 Million
Number Employees: 50-99
Type of Packaging: Bulk
Number of Customer Locations: 750
Types of Products Distributed:
　Food Service, Frozen Food, General Line, General Merchandise, Provisions/Meat, Produce

55709 Clark's Wholesale Meats
6002 S State Highway 349
Midland, TX 79706-7637 432-570-8003
Wholesaler/distributor of fresh and frozen beef, lamb, pork and veal
Owner: Mark Dovel
Estimated Sales: $1-3 Million
Number Employees: 5
Parent Co: Clark & Winfords
Types of Products Distributed:
　Provisions/Meat

55710 (HQ)Clarkson Company
1945 Cliff Vly Way NE Ste 250b
Atlanta, GA 30329 404-320-0002
Fax: 404-320-0805 800-394-7044
eclarkco@aol.com
Wholesaler/distributor of advertising specialties, awards and promotional items
Accounting Manager: Edwina Hawes
Estimated Sales: Less than $500,000
Number Employees: 5-9
Other Locations:
　Clarkson Co.
　Cornelius, NCClarkson Co.
Number of Customer Locations: 100
Types of Products Distributed:
　Frozen Food, General Merchandise, Advertising novelties

Wholesalers & Distributors / A-Z

55711 Clarkson Grain Co Inc
320 E South St
P.O. Box 80
Cerro Gordo, IL 61818-4035   217-763-2861
    Fax: 217-763-2111   800-252-1638
    www.clarksongrain.com
Wholesaler/distributor and exporter of organic, raw and cleaned food grade white and yellow corn and soybeans. Also exporter of organic, nongmo, conrentional food grade corns and soybeans
President: Lynn Clarkson
lynn.clarkson@clarksongrain.com
VP/General Manager: Dick Widmer
VP Specialty Crop: Jim Traub
Estimated Sales: $20-50 Million
Number Employees: 10-19
Types of Products Distributed:
    Frozen Food, General Line, Produce, Soy beans & corn

55712 Class Produce Group LLC
8477 Dorsey Run Rd
P.O. Box 2003
Jessup, MD 20794   410-799-5700
    Fax: 410-799-6488 www.classproduce-test.com
Wholesaler/distributor of produce.
Sales: Matthew Moon
Year Founded: 1936
Estimated Sales: $50-100 Million
Number Employees: 250-499
Square Footage: 72000
Types of Products Distributed:
    Frozen Food, Produce

55713 Clayton's Crab Co
5775 US Highway 1
Rockledge, FL 32955-5729   321-636-6673
    Fax: 321-636-4631
    www.claytonscrabcompany.com
Crab meat; wholesaler/distributor of fresh, frozen and canned seafood and meat; serving the food service market
Owner: Janet Walker
claytoncrabjan@cfl.rr.com
Estimated Sales: $1-3 Million
Number Employees: 10-19
Number of Customer Locations: 80
Types of Products Distributed:
    Food Service, Frozen Food, Provisions/Meat, Seafood, Fresh, frozen & canned

55714 Clearbrook Farms
3015 E Kemper Rd
Cincinnati, OH 45241-1514   513-771-2000
    Fax: 513-771-8381   800-222-9566
    www.clearbrookfarm.com
Manufacturer and distributor of fruit fillings, preserves, spreads and sauces
President: Stanley Liscow
dan@clearbrookfarm.com
VP: Andy Liscow
Vice President: Dan Cohen
Sales Exec: Dan Cohen
Plant Manager: Scott Smith
Estimated Sales: $20-50 Million
Number Employees: 20-49
Parent Co: Rockview Dairies
Type of Packaging: Consumer, Food Service, Private Label, Bulk
Types of Products Distributed:
    Food Service, Frozen Food, General Line, Orange juice & dairy products

55715 Clem's Seafood & Specialties
4505 Mattingly Ct
Buckner, KY 40010-8830   502-222-7571
    Fax: 502-222-7598
Seafood
Owner: Michael McAlister
Estimated Sales: $3-5 Million
Number Employees: 1-4

55716 Clement's Pastry Shops Inc
3355 52nd Ave # B
Hyattsville, MD 20781-1033   301-277-6300
    Fax: 301-277-2897 office@clementspastry.com
    www.clementspastry.com
Custom manufacturing of specialty dessert and pastry items.
President: Richard Barrazotto
Co-Owner: Matthew Barrazotto
VP: John Barrazotto
Estimated Sales: $11 Million
Number Employees: 100-249

Number of Brands: 1
Number of Products: 200
Type of Packaging: Food Service, Private Label

55717 Clements Distribution Company
1 Thomas Cir
NW 8th Floor
Washington, DC 20005   202-872-0060
    Fax: 202-466-9064   800-872-0067
    www.clements.com
Wholesaler/distributor of frozen foods; serving the food service market
President: Chris Beck
Chairman & CEO: Jon B. Clements
VP of Finance: Tarun Chopra
SVP: Dan Tuman
Contact: Phyllis Abkin
pabkin@clements.com
Estimated Sales: $10-20 Million
Number Employees: 50-99
Types of Products Distributed:
    Food Service, Frozen Food

55718 Clif Bar & Co
1451 66th St
Emeryville, CA 94608-1004   510-547-1144
    Fax: 510-558-7872   802-254-3227
    www.clifbar.com
Energy bars, nutrition bars, protein bars, energy chews, energy granolas, energy gel, protein drink mixes, and electrolyte drink mixes
CEO: Kevin Cleary
Founder/Owner & Co-CVO: Gary Erickson
Owner & Co-CVO: Kit Crawford
EVP Food & Innovation: Michelle Ferguson
Marketing Director: Joey Steger
Year Founded: 1992
Estimated Sales: $500 Million-$1 Billion
Number Employees: 1200
Type of Packaging: Consumer, Private Label
Types of Products Distributed:
    General Line, Health Food

55719 Clifford D. Fite
908 West Ave
Cedartown, GA 30125   770-748-5315
    Fax: 770-748-4332   800-660-3483
Wholesaler/distributor of groceries
President: Dan Reid
Assistant Manager: Dan Reid
Number Employees: 20-49
Square Footage: 260000
Number of Customer Locations: 550
Types of Products Distributed:
    Frozen Food, General Line, Groceries

55720 Clifton Fruit & Produce
60 E End Avenue
Apt 11a
New York, NY 10028-7973   718-251-4200
    Fax: 718-251-8272
Wholesaler/distributor of fresh and frozen fruits and vegetables
President: Harry Levy
Warehouse Manager: Richard Young
Number Employees: 20-49
Types of Products Distributed:
    Produce, Fresh & frozen fruits & vegetables

55721 Clinton St Baking Co
4 Clinton St
New York, NY 10002-1703   646-602-6263
    dede@clintonstreetbaking.com
    www.clintonstreetbaking.com
Baked goods
Owner: Neal Kleinberg
graybiscuits@earthlink.net
Estimated Sales: Less Than $500,000
Number Employees: 1-4

55722 (HQ)Clipper Mill
404 Talbert St
Daly City, CA 94014-1623   415-330-2400
    Fax: 415-330-9640 info@clippermill.com
    www.frenchfryholders.com
Manufacturer and product converter which sells and distributes its products wholesale only
General Manager: Johnny Cheung
Estimated Sales: $10-20 Million
Number Employees: 10-19

55723 Clipper Seafood
209 NE 95th St # 2
Miami Shores, FL 33138-2745   305-759-5400
    Fax: 305-759-5050 clipperseafood@aol.com
Importer and wholesaler/distributor of frozen fish including mahi mahi, wahoo, tuna, shark, marlin, alaskan pollock, whiting and swordfish
President: Olga Serrano
VP: Estaban Serrano
Estimated Sales: $1-2.5 Million
Number Employees: 1-4
Types of Products Distributed:
    Frozen Food

55724 (HQ)Clofine Dairy Products Inc
1407 New Rd
P.O. Box 335
Linwood, NJ 08221   609-653-1000
    Fax: 609-653-0127 info@clofinedairy.com
    www.clofinedairy.com
Fluid and dried dairy products; proteins, cheeses, milk replacement blends, tofu and soymilk powders, vital wheat gluten, etc.
Chairman: Larry Clofine
lclofine@clofinedairy.com
President & CEO: Frederick Smith
CFO: Butch Harmon
Warehouse Coordinator: Pamela Gerety
Estimated Sales: $20-50 Million
Number Employees: 10-19
Number of Brands: 2
Number of Products: 100
Type of Packaging: Food Service, Private Label, Bulk
Other Locations:
    Midwest Officer
    Chicago, ILMidwest Officer
Number of Customer Locations: 8
Types of Products Distributed:
    Food Service, Ingredients

55725 Clogmaster
Mobile Boutique & Fitting Truck
Costa Mesa, CA 92626   714-707-5108
    Fax: 310-657-8090 clogs@clogmaster.com
    www.clogmaster.com
Wholesaler & distributor of clogs for the food service market.
Owner: Dave Welling
Estimated Sales: Less than $500,000
Number Employees: 1-4
Type of Packaging: Food Service
Private Brands Carried:
    Clog-Master
Types of Products Distributed:
    Food Service, Frozen Food, General Merchandise, Clogs

55726 Clover Leaf Cheese
1201 45th Avenue NE
Calgary, AB T2E 2P2
Canada   403-250-3780
    Fax: 888-835-0127   888-835-0126
    www.cloverleafcheese.ca
Packer and wholesaler/distributor of cheese
President: John Downey
Sales Manager: Chris Cameron
Plant Manager: Brad Lake
Estimated Sales: F
Number Employees: 50-99
Types of Products Distributed:
    Frozen Food, General Line, Cheese

55727 Clover Leaf Seafoods
80 Tiverton Court
Markham, ON L3R 5B7
Canada   403-254-4366
    877-893-9880
    www.cloverleaf.ca
Wholesaler/distributor of fresh, frozen, canned and farmed salmon, herring and salmon roe and canned tuna; also, fish meal and oil
President: Phil Fitzpatrick
Number Employees: 1-4
Parent Co: ConAgra Foods
Private Brands Carried:
    Maple Leaf; Red Rose; Universal
Types of Products Distributed:
    General Line, Seafood, Canned tuna, salmon, herring, etc.

Wholesalers & Distributors / A-Z

55728 (HQ)Cloverdale Foods
3015 34th St NW
Mandan, ND 58554
800-669-9511
www.cloverdalefoods.com
Manufacturer and wholesaler/distributor of meat products including hickory smoked franks, bacon, ham and sausages, along with other quality pork products.
President & CEO: Scott Russell

Estimated Sales: $49 Million
Number Employees: 250-499
Number of Brands: 2
Square Footage: 61000
Type of Packaging: Consumer, Food Service, Private Label, Bulk
Other Locations:
  Cloverdale Foods Plant
  Minot, NDCloverdale Foods Plant
Private Brands Carried:
  Schwan's
Types of Products Distributed:
  Food Service, Provisions/Meat, Ham & sausage: smoked

55729 Coast to Coast Foods Group
3890 Pleasant Hill Rd
Duluth, GA 30096-4807
678-205-5200
Fax: 770-205-5209 ctcfoods@hotmail.com
Wholesaler/distributor of meats, produce, frozen foods, general merchandise and seafood; serving the food service market
President: Matthew Aloia
VP: John Hogan
VP Sales: John Hogan
Number Employees: 5-9
Square Footage: 8000
Types of Products Distributed:
  Food Service, Frozen Food, Provisions/Meat, Seafood

55730 Coastal Beverage LTD
4747 Progress Ave
Naples, FL 34104-7032
239-643-4343
Fax: 941-643-6178 www.coastalbeverage.com
Wholesaler/distributor of alcoholic and nonalcoholic beverages including beer; serving the food service market
President: Mark Vroman
dstrmn8r@aol.com
Estimated Sales: $2.5-5 Million
Number Employees: 100-249
Parent Co: Anheuser Busch
Private Brands Carried:
  Budweiser; Michelob; O'Douls
Types of Products Distributed:
  Food Service, Frozen Food, General Line, Alcoholic/non-alcoholic beverages: beer

55731 Coastal Seafood Partners
2939 West Grand Avenue
Chicago, IL 60622
773-235-4000
Fax: 773-989-7799
Seafood
President: Chris Costello
Estimated Sales: $1-3 Million
Number Employees: 20-49

55732 Coastal Seafood Processors
134 Brookhollow Esplanade
Harahan, LA 70123
504-734-9444
Fax: 504-736-9447
Seafood
President: Brian Quartano

55733 Coastside Lobster Company
PO Box 151
Stonington, ME 04681-0151
207-367-2297
Fax: 207-367-5929
Lobster
President: Peter Collin
Purshing Director: Karen Rains
Number Employees: 5-9

55734 Cobscook Bay Seafood
PO Box 252
Perry, ME 04667-0252
207-853-2890
Fax: 208-459-3712
Seafood
President: Joyce Pottle

55735 Coca-Cola Beverages Northeast
1 Executive Park Drive
Suite 330
Bedford, NH 03110
603-627-7871
844-619-3388
www.cokenortheast.com
Sparkling soft drinks, still beverages, and emerging brands such as vitamin water
President: Mark Francoeur
VP, Sales Center Operations: Steve Perrelli
VP, Sales & Marketing: Andrew Marchesseault
VP, Operations: David Dumont
Year Founded: 1977
Number Employees: 3,500
Parent Co: Kirin Brewery Company, Ltd.
Type of Packaging: Consumer, Food Service, Bulk
Private Brands Carried:
  Coca-Cola, Keurig Dr Pepper, Monster Energy Corporation, and BODYARMOR
Types of Products Distributed:
  Frozen Food

55736 Coca-Cola Bottling Co. Consolidated
PO Box 31487
Charlotte, NC 28231
800-866-2653
www.cokeconsolidated.com
Bottled soft drinks and fountain syrup.
Chairman/CEO: J Frank Harrison, III
Year Founded: 1902
Estimated Sales: $4.3 Billion
Number Employees: 15,500
Number of Brands: 300
Type of Packaging: Consumer, Food Service, Bulk
Private Brands Carried:
  Coca-Cola brand products
Types of Products Distributed:
  Frozen Food, General Line, Soft drinks

55737 Coca-Cola Bottling Company UNITED, Inc.
46090 East Lake Boulevard
Birmingham, AB 35217
205-841-2653
800-844-2653
cocacolaunited.com
Bottled soft drinks and fountain syrup.
Chairman: Claude Nielsen
President & CEO: John Sherman, III
Executive VP/CAO/CFO: Hafiz Chandiwala
General Counsel/VP: Lucas Gambino
VP, Supply Chain & Operations: Stanley Ellington
VP/Controller/CIO: Eric Steadman
Year Founded: 1902
Estimated Sales: $2.81 Billion
Number Employees: 10,000
Type of Packaging: Consumer, Food Service, Bulk
Private Brands Carried:
  Coca-Cola brand products
Types of Products Distributed:
  General Line, Bottled soft drinks & fountain syrup

55738 Coca-Cola European Partners
Pemberton House
Bakers Road
Uxbridge, Middx, UB8 1EZ
UK
800-418-4223
comms@ccep.com www.cocacolaep.com
Coca-Cola brands products.
Chairman: Sol Daurella
CEO: Damian Gammell
CFO: Nik Jhangiani
Chief Public Affairs Officer: Lauren Sayeski
Estimated Sales: $10.9 Billion
Number Employees: 23,300
Number of Brands: 44
Type of Packaging: Consumer, Food Service, Bulk

55739 Cochran Brothers Company
P.O.Box 370
Dublin, GA 31040
478-272-5144
Fax: 478-272-4400
Wholesaler/distributor of general line products; serving the food service market
President/CEO: Wick Cochran
Operations Manager: Sonny Wirmock
Estimated Sales: $20-50 Million
Number Employees: 20-49
Types of Products Distributed:
  Food Service, Frozen Food, General Line

55740 Cockrell Banana
405 E Elizabeth St
Tupelo, MS 38804-4921
662-842-2638
Fax: 662-842-2087 www.cockrellbanana.com
Wholesaler/distributor of fruits and vegetables; serving the food service market
Owner: Eddy Taylor
eddyt@cockrellbanana.com
Vice President: Richard Cockrell
Office Manager: James Brown
Estimated Sales: $10-20 Million
Number Employees: 20-49
Square Footage: 48000
Number of Customer Locations: 1000
Types of Products Distributed:
  Food Service, Frozen Food, Produce

55741 Cockrell's Creek Seafood & Deli
567 Seaboard Road
Reedville, VA 22539
804-453-6326
Fax: 804-453-7305 www.smithpointseafood.com
Wholesaler/distributor of seafood
Owner: Ronnie Jets
Manager: Robert McKenny
Estimated Sales: $3-5 Million
Number Employees: 10-19
Types of Products Distributed:
  Frozen Food, Seafood

55742 Coffee Break Systems
RD45 Currant Road
Mishawaka, IN 46545-4801
574-674-9991
Fax: 219-674-9992
Wholesaler/distributor of coffee and water; serving the food service market
President: Dave Keck
Secretary: Karen Keck
VP: Doug Keck
Estimated Sales: $1-2.5 Million
Number Employees: 10-19
Square Footage: 27200
Parent Co: Keck's Koffee
Types of Products Distributed:
  Food Service, Frozen Food, General Line, Coffee & water

55743 Coffee Brothers Inc
1204 Via Roma
Colton, CA 92324-3909
909-370-1100
Fax: 909-370-1101 888-443-5282
info@coffeebrothers.com www.coffeebrothers.com
Coffee and espresso; importer and wholesaler/distributor of espresso machines
Owner: Cal Amodemo
cal@coffeebrothers.com
General Manager: Max Amodeo
Estimated Sales: $2.5-5 Million
Number Employees: 1-4
Square Footage: 44000
Type of Packaging: Private Label, Bulk
Private Brands Carried:
  Sigma; Il Caffe
Types of Products Distributed:
  Food Service, Coffee & Coffee Equipment

55744 Coffee Express RoastingCo
47722 Clipper St
Plymouth, MI 48170-2437
734-459-4900
Fax: 734-459-5511 800-466-9000
info@coffeeexpressco.com
www.coffeeexpressco.com
Wholesaler roaster of specialty coffees; distributors of associated products.
President: Tom Isaia
Office Manager: Joyce Novak
Contact: Genevieve Boss
g.boss@coffeeexpressco.com
Production: Scott Novak
Estimated Sales: Less Than $500,000
Number Employees: 1-4
Number of Brands: 8
Number of Products: 20
Square Footage: 32000
Type of Packaging: Consumer, Food Service, Private Label, Bulk
Private Brands Carried:
  Rancilio Machine Per Coffee; DaVinci Gourmet Syrups; Harvey & Sons Fine Teas; Oregon Chai; Ghirardelli: Chocolate; Avita Artesian Water
Types of Products Distributed:
  Specialty Foods, Espresso machines, syrups, teas, etc.

Wholesalers & Distributors / A-Z

55745 Coffee Expresso & Service
50 Jefferson Street
Newark, NJ 07105-2224   973-578-4991
Fax: 973-578-4991
Wholesaler/distributor of coffee and espresso machines
President: Mauro Bustos
Number Employees: 8
Number of Customer Locations: 500
Types of Products Distributed:
Frozen Food, General Merchandise, Coffee & expresso machines

55746 Coffee Heaven
PO Box 6755
Branson, MO 65615-6755   417-732-9217
888-432-7662
Wholesaler/distributor of custom-roasted coffee
President: Mark Silverthorn
Number Employees: 10-19
Types of Products Distributed:
Frozen Food, General Line, Custom-roasted coffee

55747 Cogent Technologies
11140 Luschek Drive
Cincinnati, OH 45241-2434   513-469-6800
Fax: 513-469-6811
Wholesaler/distributor of laboratory and quality control instrumentation
General Manager: Jim LeRoy
Estimated Sales: $2.5-5 Million
Number Employees: 5-9
Square Footage: 8000
Private Brands Carried:
Microbial Luminescence; IUL Instruments
Number of Customer Locations: 150
Types of Products Distributed:
Frozen Food, General Merchandise, Laboratory instrumentation

55748 Cohen Foods
2301 Illinois Ave
Granite City, IL 62040   618-452-3156
Fax: 618-452-6030   www.cohen-foods.com
Wholesaler/distributor of nonperishable groceries and equipment and fixtures
President: Harvey Cohen
VP: Wally Cohen
Secretary: Norman Cohen
Contact: Marc Allen
marca@cohen-foods.com
Estimated Sales: $10-20 Million
Number Employees: 10-19
Number of Customer Locations: 51
Types of Products Distributed:
Frozen Food, General Line, General Merchandise, Non-perishable groceries & equipment

55749 Cohokia Bake Mark
4919 Kingston St
Denver, CO 80239-2516   303-375-1041
Fax: 303-375-1135
Wholesaler/distributor of bakers' and confectioners' supplies including mixes, fillings, sugar, shortening and flour
Manager: Robert Alarcon
Manager: Joe Boland
Estimated Sales: $5-10 Million
Number Employees: 10-19
Square Footage: 48000
Parent Co: Adams Syrup
Types of Products Distributed:
General Line, Mixes, fillings, sugar, etc.

55750 Colavita USA
1 Runyons Ln
Edison, NJ 08817-2219   732-404-8300
Fax: 732-287-9401   888-265-2848
usa@colavita.com   www.colavita.com
Grains and oils including; extra virgin olive oil, vinegar, pasta, sauces, gnocchi, polenta, rice, marinated vegetables, and gift baskets and foodservice bulk supply
President: Sophia Aspromatis
sophiaa@colavita.com
CEO: Giovanni Colavita
VP Quality Control: Anthony Profaci
VP of Sales: Tom Marrone
VP Sales & Marketing: John Profaci
Director of Marketing: Nicole Jeannette
Plant Manager: Les Horowitz
VP Purchasing: Robert Profaci

Estimated Sales: $15 Million
Number Employees: 50-99
Types of Products Distributed:
Frozen Food, General Line, Olive & blended oils

55751 Colbourne Seafood
102 Main St
Secretary, MD 21664   410-943-3993
Wholesaler/distributor of shellfish, crabs and fish
Owner/President: Jack Colbourne
Estimated Sales: Less Than $500,000
Number Employees: 1-4
Square Footage: 12000
Parent Co: Colburne Seafood
Types of Products Distributed:
Seafood

55752 Cold Hollow Cider Mill
3600 Waterbury-Stowe Rd
PO Box 420
Waterbury Center, VT 05677-8020   802-244-8771
Fax: 802-244-7212   800-327-7537
info@coldhollow.com   www.coldhollow.com
Apple products including cider, cider jelly, butters, syrup, sauce, preserves and juices; exporter of cider jelly; wholesaler/distributor of health and specialty foods, general merchandise, private label items and produce
Owner: Paul Brown
Vice President: Gayle Brown
Estimated Sales: $5-10 Million
Number Employees: 20-49
Square Footage: 40000
Type of Packaging: Consumer, Food Service, Bulk
Types of Products Distributed:
Produce

55753 Cole Brothers & Fox Company
252 Yandell Ave
Canton, MS 39046   601-859-1414
Fax: 601-859-2739
Wholesaler/distributor of groceries, meats, produce, frozen and dairy products, general merchandise and equipment and fixtures
Chairman Board: C Fox, Sr.
President: William Fox
VP: C Fox, Jr.
Estimated Sales: $20-50 Million
Number Employees: 50-99
Square Footage: 100000
Type of Packaging: Bulk
Number of Customer Locations: 2000
Types of Products Distributed:
Frozen Food, General Line, General Merchandise, Provisions/Meat, Produce, Groceries, candy, etc.

55754 Collins & Company
880 N Addison Ave Ste 1
Elmhurst, IL 60126   630-530-5100
Fax: 630-530-3643   800-323-4528
www.collinsandcompany.net
Wholesaler/distributor of hot melt and cold glue equipment, food grade pumps and cleaning equipment
President: T Collins
Sales Manager: B Racine
Estimated Sales: $5-10 Million
Number Employees: 10-19
Square Footage: 20000
Private Brands Carried:
Graco, Inc.; ITW Dyntec; Gray Mills; Pyces Div.; Binks-Sames
Types of Products Distributed:
Frozen Food, General Merchandise, Food pumps, cleaning equipment, etc.

55755 Colonial Coffee Roasters Inc
3250 NW 60th St
Miami, FL 33142-2125   305-638-0885
Fax: 305-634-2538   info@colonialcoffee.com
Importer and wholesaler/distributor of coffee and espresso machinery including coffee roasters
Owner: Rafael Acevedo
main@colonialcoffee.com
CEO: Ava Acevedo
Number Employees: 10-19
Square Footage: 60000
Parent Co: Colonial Coffee Roasters
Private Brands Carried:
Bezzera Espresso Machines; Colonial Coffee
Number of Customer Locations: 50

Types of Products Distributed:
General Merchandise, Coffee & espresso machinery

55756 Colony Brands Inc
1112 7th Ave
Monroe, WI 53566-1364   608-328-8400
Fax: 608-328-8457   800-544-9036
www.colonybrands.com
Cakes, tortes & pies; cookies & bars; pastries; petits fours; candy & chocolate; boxed assortments of all kinds; cheeses; sausage, ham and other meats; nuts & pre-mixed snacks; home furniture; home d,cor; electronics; jewelry; fitnessequipment; unisex apparel; small appliances
CEO: John Baumann
Chairman: Pat Kubly
VP/CIO: Steve Cretney
Content Marketing Manager: Matt Stetler
Director of Strategic Planning: Ryan Kubly
Number Employees: 1000-4999
Square Footage: 13236
Parent Co: Colony Brands, Inc.

55757 Colony Foods
439 Haverhill St
Lawrence, MA 01841   978-682-9677
Fax: 978-687-8448
Frozen, fresh and special order food items.
President: Dereck Barbagallo
Contact: George Abdallah
georgeabdallah@colonyfoods.com
Estimated Sales: $10-20 Million
Number Employees: 20-49

55758 Colorado Boxed Beef Company
3205 SE 19th Ave
Ft. Lauderdale, FL 33316   954-764-1781
customerservice@cbbcorp.com
www.coloradoboxedbeef.com
Wholesaler/distributor of beef, pork, lamb, poultry, frozen fish and veal; also, smoked meats.
Types of Products Distributed:
Provisions/Meat, Beef, Veal, Pork, Lamb, Smoked Meats

55759 Colorado Boxed Beef Company
6150 Xavier Dr SW
Atlanta, GA 30336   404-799-0099
customerservice@cbbcorp.com
www.coloradoboxedbeef.com
Wholesaler/distributor of beef, pork, lamb, poultry, frozen fish and veal; also, smoked meats.
Type of Packaging: Consumer, Food Service, Private Label, Bulk
Other Locations:
Colorado Boxed Beef Co.
North Miami Beach, FLColorado Boxed Beef Co.
Types of Products Distributed:
Provisions/Meat, Beef, veal, pork & lamb

55760 (HQ)Colorado Boxed Beef Company
404 N Ingraham Rd
Lakeland, FL 33801   863-967-0636
Fax: 863-503-3288   800-955-0636
customerservice@cbbcorp.com
www.coloradoboxedbeef.com
Wholesaler/distributor of beef, pork, lamb, poultry, frozen fish and veal; also, smoked meats.
President & CEO: John Rattigan
Principal & Co-Chairman: John Saterbo
Principal & Co-Chairman: Bryan Saterbo
Chief Financial Officer: John Sullivan
Year Founded: 1975
Estimated Sales: $468 Million
Number Employees: 600
Types of Products Distributed:
Provisions/Meat, Beef, Veal, Pork, Lamb, Smoked Meats

55761 Colorado Boxed Beef Company
1190 W Loop N
Houston, TX 77055   713-880-0880
www.coloradoboxedbeef.com
Wholesaler/distributor of beef, pork, lamb, poultry, frozen fish and veal; also, smoked meats.
Types of Products Distributed:
Frozen Food, Provisions/Meat, Beef, Veal, Pork, Lamb & Smoked Meats

Wholesalers & Distributors / A-Z

55762 Colorado Chemical Company
3855 Forest Street
Denver, CO 80207-1152   303-388-9331
Fax: 303-388-0277   800-825-3267
Wholesaler/distributor of cleaning supplies and disposables; serving the food service market
President: Carl Larson
Estimated Sales: $5-10 Million
Number Employees: 20-49
Square Footage: 100000
Type of Packaging: Bulk
Types of Products Distributed:
  Food Service, Frozen Food, General Merchandise, Cleaning supplies & disposables

55763 Colorado Nut Co
2 Kalamath St
Denver, CO 80223-1550   303-733-7311
                           800-876-1625
sales@coloradonutco.com
www.coloradonutco.com
Manufactures and Imports candies, chocolates, unique trail mixes, snack mixes, dried fruits and gift baskets for any occasion. Also roast nuts on site. Also offer products with private labeling and customized logos for a variety of specialized events.
Owner: Mark Goodman
mgoodman@coloradonutco.com
Owner: Roger Renaud
Estimated Sales: Less Than $500,000
Number Employees: 5-9
Type of Packaging: Consumer, Private Label
Types of Products Distributed:
  Specialty Foods

55764 (HQ)Colorado Potato Growers Exchange
2401 Larimer Street
Denver, CO 80205-2122   303-292-0159
Fax: 303-298-8445
http://www.coloradopotato.org/
Wholesaler/distributor of potatoes and onions
President: Byron Kunugi
Estimated Sales: $10-20 Million
Number Employees: 1-4
Types of Products Distributed:
  Frozen Food, General Line, Potatoes & onions

55765 Colorado Restaurant Supply
6538 S Yosemite Cir
Greenwood Vlg, CO 80111-4969   303-790-9400
Fax: 303-790-2680
Wholesaler/distributor of cooking equipment, tabletop supplies, etc.; serving the food service market; rack jobber services available
President: B Melton
Estimated Sales: $3-5 Million
Number Employees: 5-9
Number of Customer Locations: 60
Types of Products Distributed:
  Food Service, Frozen Food, General Merchandise, Rack Jobbers, Cleaning & table supplies, wraps, etc.

55766 Colors Gourmet Pizza
2349 LA Mirada Dr
Vista, CA 92081-7863   760-597-1400
Fax: 760-431-0914 info@colorspizza.com
www.colorspizza.com
Gourmet pizza, handmade crusts, focaccia and panini bread
Chef, Owner: Martial Bricnet
martialb@colorspizza.com
Director of Sales/Distribution: James Tuckwell
Estimated Sales: $1-3 Million
Number Employees: 20-49
Square Footage: 30000
Private Brands Carried:
  Scholstad Danish Pastry, Galaxy Deserts, Polar Bakery Croissants, Checkmates Candy, Michael's Cookies, Sundown Foods Roasted Tomotoes
Number of Customer Locations: 250
Types of Products Distributed:
  Frozen Food

55767 Columbia Paper Company
P.O.Box 9599
Columbia, SC 29290-0599   803-783-2447
Fax: 803-783-2446   800-227-8860
Wholesaler/distributor of disposable food service supplies
Owner: Donald Cato
Estimated Sales: $5-10 Million
Number Employees: 20-49
Square Footage: 111200
Parent Co: Affiliated Paper Company
Types of Products Distributed:
  Frozen Food, General Merchandise, Disposables foodservice supplies

55768 Columbia Restaurant & Bar Supply Co.
401 W Intl Airport Rd Ste 5
Anchorage, AK 99518   907-561-1060
Fax: 907-562-0698   800-478-1060
Wholesaler/distributor of restaurant equipment and smallwares; serving the food service market
Owner: Amy Goggins
Estimated Sales: $1-2.5 Million
Number Employees: 5-9
Types of Products Distributed:
  Food Service, Frozen Food, General Merchandise, Restaurant equipment & smallwares

55769 Columbia Scale Company
333 W North Ave Ste E
Chicago, IL 60610   773-235-1800
Fax: 773-235-1876   800-834-2326
Wholesaler/distributor of scales including laboratory, portion control, gram, counting and bench
President: Martin Lawrence
laurence@columbiascale.com
Sales/Marketing Executive: Evelyn Zakeski
Estimated Sales: $1-2.5 Million
Number Employees: 5-9
Square Footage: 60000
Private Brands Carried:
  Cas; NCI/Weightronix; A.D. Cambridge; Ohaus; Nexus; Tanita
Types of Products Distributed:
  Frozen Food, General Merchandise, Scales

55770 Com-Pak International
11615 Cardinal Circle
Garden Grove, CA 92843-3814   714-537-5772
Fax: 714-537-4326
Wholesaler/distributor of food and chemical processing and packaging equipment
President: Billy Fielder
VP: David West
Estimated Sales: $1-3 Million
Number Employees: 7
Square Footage: 72000
Parent Co: Garden Grove
Other Locations:
  Com-Pak International
  Hemet, CACom-Pak International
Types of Products Distributed:
  Frozen Food, General Merchandise, Food & chemical processing equipment

55771 Comissos Cash & Carry
2436 Haines Road
Mississauga, ON L4Y 1Y6
Canada   905-566-8277
Fax: 905-566-0600
Wholesaler/distributor of groceries; serving the food service market
Manager: Ned Tassone
Number Employees: 20-49
Parent Co: Lanzarotta Wholesale Grocers
Private Brands Carried:
  Kellogg; Kraft; Campbell
Number of Customer Locations: 1500
Types of Products Distributed:
  Food Service, Frozen Food, General Line, Groceries

55772 Comissos Cash & Carry
434 Birchmount Road
Scarborough, ON M1K 1M6
Canada   416-691-4562
Fax: 416-691-4103
Wholesaler/distributor of cash and carry groceries; serving the food service market
Manager: Greg Tomlinson
Number Employees: 10-19
Parent Co: Lanzarotta Wholesale Grocers
Private Brands Carried:
  Christie's; Maple Leaf
Number of Customer Locations: 1700
Types of Products Distributed:
  Food Service, Frozen Food, General Line, Groceries

55773 Comissos Cash & Carry
485 Logan Avenue
Toronto, ON M4M 2R5
Canada   416-469-4056
Fax: 416-469-1651
Wholesaler/distributor of groceries; serving the food service market
Manager: Alan Riddell
Number Employees: 20-49
Parent Co: Lanzarotta Wholesale Grocers
Number of Customer Locations: 2000
Types of Products Distributed:
  Food Service, Frozen Food, General Line

55774 Comissos Cash & Carry
1453 Dupont Street
Toronto, ON M6P 3R9
Canada   416-532-1018
Fax: 416-532-7828
Wholesaler/distributor of groceries; serving the food service market
Manager: John Harrigan
Number Employees: 20-49
Parent Co: Lanzarotta Wholesale Grocers
Private Brands Carried:
  Christie's; Maple Leaf; Allen's
Number of Customer Locations: 1300
Types of Products Distributed:
  Food Service, Frozen Food, General Line

55775 Commercial Appliance Svc
8416 Laurel Fair Cir # 114
Tampa, FL 33610-7360   813-663-0313
Fax: 813-663-0212   800-282-4718
tampa.parts@nacps.com   www.comapp.com
Wholesaler/distributor of food service equipment parts; also, repair services available; serving the food service market
President: Tina M Reese
tina.reese@nacps.com
Estimated Sales: $5 Million
Number Employees: 20-49
Square Footage: 52000
Private Brands Carried:
  All manufacturings equipment parts.
Types of Products Distributed:
  Food Service, General Merchandise, Foodservice equipment parts

55776 Comissos Cash & Carry
671 Bayview Drive
Barrie, ON L4N 9A5
Canada   705-737-0727
Fax: 705-737-4722
Wholesaler/distributor of groceries; serving the food service market
Manager: Steve Morano
Number Employees: 10-19
Square Footage: 64000
Parent Co: Lanzarotta Wholesale Grocers
Private Brands Carried:
  Christie's; Maple Leaf; Allen's
Number of Customer Locations: 300
Types of Products Distributed:
  Food Service, Frozen Food, General Line, Groceries

55777 Commodities Assistance Corporation
13102 40th Road
Flushing, NY 11354-5107   718-939-8000
Fax: 718-939-0194 info@commast.com
Wholesaler/distributor of surplus food items including cookies, confectionery products and beverages: juice, soft drinks, water, etc
President: J Grossfeld
Vice President: L Grossfeld
Secretary/Treasurer: M DeLuca
Purchasing Manager: Frank Tamuccio
Estimated Sales: $10 Million
Number Employees: 50-99
Square Footage: 240000
Type of Packaging: Consumer
Types of Products Distributed:
  General Line, General Merchandise, Health Food

55778 Commodities Marketing Inc
6 Stone Tavern Dr
Clarksburg, NJ 08510   732-516-0700
Fax: 732-516-0600 weldonrice@usa.net
www.weldonfoods.com

Jasmine rice, Basmati rice, Coconut drinks, Coconut milk, Fruits, Beans, Guar gum, Fruit juices and Cashews, Almonds, Saffron (Spain) White Rice/Parboiled Rice.
President: Herbander Sahni
herbandersahni@weldonfoods.com
CEO: Gagandeep Sahni
CFO: Soena Sahni
VP: Avneet Sodhi
R&D: Manoj Hedge
Marketing: Harbinder Singh Sahni & Dee Mirchandai
Sales: Avneet Sodhi
Public Relations: Mr. Dough & Harshida Shaw
Operations: Harshida Shah
Production: Mr Nobpsaul
Plant Manager: Mr Chandej
Estimated Sales: $25 Million
Number Employees: 5-9
Number of Brands: 3
Number of Products: 6
Square Footage: 3000
Type of Packaging: Consumer, Food Service, Private Label, Bulk
Private Brands Carried:
 Weldon, Meher
Number of Customer Locations: 70
Types of Products Distributed:
 Food Service, General Line, General Merchandise, Specialty Foods, Private Label

55779 Community Coffee Co.
3332 Partridge Ln.
Building A
Baton Rouge, LA 70809   800-884-5282
                   Fax: 800-643-8199
customerservice@communitycoffee.com
           www.communitycoffee.com
Coffee and tea; importer of green coffee; and wholesaler/distributor of coffee creamer.
President/CEO: David Belanger
dbelanger@communitycoffee.com
Chairman: Matthew Saurage
CFO: Annette Vaccaro
Year Founded: 1919
Estimated Sales: $195 Million
Number Employees: 1000-4999
Type of Packaging: Consumer, Food Service, Private Label, Bulk
Types of Products Distributed:
 Food Service, General Line, Coffee creamer

55780 Compass Concepts
467 Forbes Blvd
S San Francisco, CA 94080-2017   650-583-4244
      Fax: 650-583-9564   800-356-7464
Wholesaler/distributor of commercial floorcovering, developed specifically for the hospitality industry
Manager: Elias Doss
Operations Manager: Elias Doiss
Estimated Sales: $10-20 Million
Number Employees: 50-99
Private Brands Carried:
 Altro Safety Flooring; Forbo Linoleum & Vinyl Floor Coverings; LG Chem Commercial Sheet Vinyl; Tarkett Speciality Homogeneous Flooring; Toli Luxury Tile & Sheet Vinyl; Quartz Tile; Statiflor Conductive & Static Dissipative Sheet Vinyl
Types of Products Distributed:
 Safety Flooring, Commercial Flooring

55781 Composition Materials Co Inc
249 Pepes Farm Rd
Milford, CT 06460-3671   203-874-6500
      Fax: 203-874-6505   800-262-7763
info@compomat.com   www.compomat.com
Plastic Blasting Media, a distributor of a multitude of filers and extenders, supplier of Walnut Shell grits and flours, and importer of birch wood flour from Sweden.
President: Alan Nudelman
nudelman@compomat.com
Chairman: Theodore Diamond
Sales Representative: Steven D. Essex
Product Operations Manager: David M. Elster
Estimated Sales: $2.5-5 Million
Number Employees: 10-19
Square Footage: 30000
Types of Products Distributed:
 General Merchandise

55782 (HQ)Comprehensive Lighting Svc
208 Blydenburg Rd # C
Islandia, NY 11749-5023   631-232-1057
      Fax: 631-232-1517   800-225-6113
molly@all-lights.com   www.all-lights.com
Wholesaler/distributor of lighting fixtures, light bulbs and lamps
Owner: Larry Rabinowitz
jawan.betts@flhealth.org
Vice President: Jeffrey Rabinowitz
VP: Larry Rabinowitz
Estimated Sales: $10-20 Million
Number Employees: 10-19
Other Locations:
 Comprehensive Lighting Servic
 Nishinomiya HyogoComprehensive Lighting Servic
Types of Products Distributed:
 Frozen Food, General Merchandise, Lighting fixtures, light bulbs, etc.

55783 (HQ)Computerized Machinery Systs
11733 95th Ave N
Maple Grove, MN 55369-5551   763-493-0099
      Fax: 763-493-0093   sales@cmsitechnologies.com
                    www.labelmart.com
Manufacturer and exporter of pressure sensitive labels; wholesaler/distributor and exporter of barcode printers, label scanners and applicators
Owner: Kate Jackson
Sales: Eric Sorensen
kate@labelmart.com
Estimated Sales: Below $5 Million
Number Employees: 20-49
Private Brands Carried:
 Symbol; Sato; Fargo; Datamay; Zebra-Tec
Types of Products Distributed:
 Frozen Food, General Merchandise, Barcode printers, label scanners, etc.

55784 Conagra Brands Canada
5055 Satellite Drive
Mississauga, ON L4W 5K7
Canada   416-679-4200
               800-461-4556
               www.conagrabrands.ca
Consumer brands.
VP/General Manager: Ian Roberts
Number Employees: 500
Square Footage: 20000
Parent Co: Conagra Brands
Type of Packaging: Consumer, Food Service
Other Locations:
 Boisbriand Office
 Boisbriand, QCBoisbriand Office
Types of Products Distributed:
 Food Service, Frozen Food, Prepared Meals

55785 Conca D'Oro Importers
72-02 51st Avenue
Woodside, NY 11377   718-446-0800
      Fax: 718-424-3300   psalviaconcadoro@aol.com
                    concadorofood.com
Importer and wholesaler/distributor of Italian and specialty gourmet foods including pasta, olive oil, coffee, tomatoes and confectionery products
President: Paul Salvia
Secretary: Ciro Salvia
Marketing: Paolo Salvia
Contact: Ciro Salvia
agriturismo@concadoro.com
Estimated Sales: $20-50 Million
Number Employees: 20-49
Square Footage: 20000
Types of Products Distributed:
 Frozen Food, General Line, Specialty Foods, Pasta, olive oil, coffee, etc.

55786 Concept Equipment Corporation
57 Bay State Road
Cambridge, MA 02138-1203   617-868-1147
      Fax: 617-868-2716   800-253-3431
Wholesaler/distributor of ice, frozen drink and soft serve ice cream and yogurt machines, commerical gas ranges and air conditioners
President: Jerry Clancy
VP: Paul Clancy
Estimated Sales: $2.5-5 Million
Number Employees: 10-19
Square Footage: 32000
Private Brands Carried:
 Crystal Tips; Sani-Serve; Vogt; Carrier; Friedrich
Types of Products Distributed:
 Frozen Food, General Merchandise, Gas ranges, air conditioners, etc.

55787 Concession & RestaurantSupply
PO Box 520550
Longwood, FL 32752-0550   407-834-6604
               Fax: 407-834-0686
Wholesaler/distributor of food service equipment and supplies
Director Purchasing: Steve Williams
Estimated Sales: $1-2.5 Million
Number Employees: 5-9
Private Brands Carried:
 Metel Masters; Troulson
Types of Products Distributed:
 Food Service, Frozen Food, General Merchandise, Equipment & supplies

55788 Conchita Foods Inc
9115 NW 105th Way
Medley, FL 33178-1221   305-888-9703
      Fax: 305-888-1020   www.conchita-foods.com
Wholesaler/distributor and importer of beans, fruits, vegetable oils, olives, pimientos, rice, etc
President: Sixto Ferro
Estimated Sales: $20-50 Million
Number Employees: 50-99
Types of Products Distributed:
 Frozen Food, General Line, Canned fruits, olives, rice, etc.

55789 Concho Valley Pecan Company
1700 N Bryant Blvd
San Angelo, TX 76903-4534   325-655-5318
      Fax: 325-657-2995   800-473-2267
            cupc@wcc.net   www.pecans.com
Wholesaler/distributor of pecans, syrup, salsa, BBQ sauce, fundraising candy, toffee, glazed and coated candy nuts, jams, jellies, marmalades and preserves, honey, brazilian nuts, trail mixes, cashews, filberts, hazelnuts, macadamiapeanuts, including granulated, raw and shelled, pine nuts, pistachios, walnuts and black walnuts, and coated yogurt nuts; serving the food service and retail markets
President: Dewayne McCasland
CEO: Philip Glass
Estimated Sales: $20-50 Million
Number Employees: 5-9
Parent Co: Pecan Producers
Types of Products Distributed:
 Food Service, Frozen Food, General Line, Pecans

55790 Concord Foods Co
4601 E Guasti Rd
Ontario, CA 91761-8105   909-975-2000
      Fax: 909-975-2007   800-439-5675
               www.concordfoodsinc.com
Wholesaler/distributor of Italian pizza products
Owner: Nick Sciortino
n.sciortino@concordfoodsinc.com
VP: John Sciortino
Estimated Sales: $20-50 Million
Number Employees: 20-49
Types of Products Distributed:
 Frozen Food, General Line, Specialty Foods, Italian pizza products

55791 Concord Foods, LLC
10 Minuteman Way
Brockton, MA 02301-7508   508-580-1700
      Fax: 508-584-9425   www.concordfoods.com
Supplier of retail food products and custom ingredients. The retail line includes companian items for fresh produce (juices, produce seasoning mixes, smoothie mixes, fresh desserts, dips, etc) and seasoning mixes for ground beefpoultry and seafood. The business ingredients division supplies beverage bases, fountain syrups, toppings, caramels, fruit purees and chocolate products, breadings and batters, and pancake and baking mixes. Recapitalized by Arbor Investments in2015.
President/CEO: Peter Neville
pneville@concordfoods.com
VP: Rich Renna
Marketing Manager: Samantha McCaul
Production Supervisor: Michelle Marvel
Warehouse Team Leader: Gabriel Alves
Estimated Sales: $38 Million
Number Employees: 100-249
Number of Brands: 4
Square Footage: 190000
Parent Co: Arbor Investments

Wholesalers & Distributors / A-Z

55792 Concord Import
3151 Fruitland Ave
Vernon, CA 90058   323-588-8888
www.dollaritem.com
Supplier of food closeouts.
Owner: Ted Shayan
Estimated Sales: $100-500 Million
Type of Packaging: Bulk
Types of Products Distributed:
 Frozen Food, General Line, General Merchandise, Provisions/Meat, Baking Supplies, Canned Food, Coffee

55793 Coney Island Classics
65 Roosevelt Ave
Suite 107
Valley Stream, NY 11581   516-823-3001
Fax: 516-823-3003 www.coneyislandclassics.com
Kettle corn, potato chips and cookies

55794 Confecco
7007 NW 53rd Ter
Miami, FL 33166-4803
Fax: 305-599-1325
Wholesaler/distributor of confectionery products
Owner: Jose Melo
Estimated Sales: $1-2.5 Million
Number Employees: 5-9
Private Brands Carried:
 M&M Mars, Mr.Peanuts, Nestle, Hersheys.
Types of Products Distributed:
 Frozen Food, General Line, Confectionery products

55795 Confoco USA, Inc.
1139 E Jersey St
Suite 415
Elizabeth, NJ 07201   908-659-0566
Fax: 908-659-9339 confocosales@confoco.com
www.confoco.com
Manufacturer and distributor of fruit and vegetable flakes, powder and essences as well as aseptic banana puree. Kosher & Halal Certified products
General Manager: Edwardo Chiriboga
Contact: Francisco Larrea
flarrea@confoco.com
Type of Packaging: Food Service, Bulk

55796 Conger Industries Inc
2290 S Ashland Ave
Green Bay, WI 54304-4859   920-499-5181
Fax: 920-498-6150 www.conger.com
Wholesaler/distributor of material handling equipment
President: Anika Conger
conger@conger.com
Estimated Sales: $20-50 Million
Number Employees: 10-19
Private Brands Carried:
 Toyota; Versa Conveyor; Prest Rack
Types of Products Distributed:
 Frozen Food, General Merchandise, Material handling equipment

55797 Connecticut Shellfish Co Inc
26 E Industrial Rd
Branford, CT 06405-6510   203-488-7705
Fax: 203-488-1787 800-743-5534
www.ipswichshellfish.com
Wholesaler/distributor of fresh and frozen seafood; serving the food service market
Sales Manager: Arnold Pappas
Contact: Doug Aikman
douga@ipswichshellfish.com
General Manager: David Taylor
Estimated Sales: $5-10 Million
Number Employees: 20-49
Types of Products Distributed:
 Food Service, Frozen Food, Seafood

55798 (HQ)Connection Chemical LP
126 S State St # 200
Suite 200
Newtown, PA 18940-3524   215-497-3063
www.connectionchemical.com
Wholesaler/distributor and importer of acidulants and humectants/solvents including citric acid, sodium citrate, glycerine and sodium benzoate
President & CEO: Frank Farish
CFO: Martin L. Pagliughi
Vice President-Eastern Region: Samuel J. McGinness
VP Sales Northeast Region: Steve Brewster
Contact: Frank Alari
falari@connectionchemical.com
Number Employees: 5-9
Square Footage: 120000
Types of Products Distributed:
 Frozen Food, General Line, Chemical ingredients for baking, etc.

55799 Connellsville Bottling Works
237 N 1st St
Connellsville, PA 15425   724-628-3030
Fax: 724-628-9306
Wholesaler/distributor of alcoholic and nonalcoholic beverages; serving the food service market
Owner: Delphine Bell
Estimated Sales: $3-5 Million
Number Employees: 6
Types of Products Distributed:
 Food Service, General Line, Alcoholic & non-alcoholic beverages

55800 Conner Produce Co
125 Oakley Ave # B
Lynchburg, VA 24501-3238   434-845-4583
Fax: 434-846-0304
Wholesaler/distributor of general line products and produce; serving the food service market
Manager: Donald Johns
Salesman: Randy Campbell
Estimated Sales: $5-10 Million
Number Employees: 10-19
Types of Products Distributed:
 Food Service, Frozen Food, General Line, Produce

55801 Consolidated Beverage Corporation
255 W 138th Street
New York, NY 10030-2102   212-926-3800
Fax: 212-491-5297
Wholesaler/distributor of beverages including alcoholic, water and soft drinks
CEO/President: Albert Thompson
Number Employees: 5-9
Square Footage: 16000
Types of Products Distributed:
 Frozen Food, General Line, Beverages

55802 (HQ)Consolidated Bottle Company
77 Union Street
Toronto, ON M6N 3N2
Canada   416-656-7777
Fax: 416-656-6394 800-561-1354
en.consbottle.com
Wholesaler/distributor of glass and plastic containers, closures and seals
Chairman: Harry Korolnek
President: Mark Korolnek
VP: Steve Korolnek
Number Employees: 50-99
Square Footage: 750000
Other Locations:
 Consolidated Bottle Co.
 Pointe Claire, PQConsolidated Bottle Co.
Types of Products Distributed:
 Frozen Food, General Merchandise, Containers, closures & seals

55803 Consolidated Fruit Distributor
941 S Ninth Ave
Alpena, MI 49707-2997   989-356-1276
Fax: 989-356-4540 800-589-2230
Wholesaler/distributor of fruits and vegetables
President: W Butch
VP: James Butch
Estimated Sales: $3-5 Million
Number Employees: 1-4
Number of Customer Locations: 50
Types of Products Distributed:
 Frozen Food, Produce

55804 Consolidated Poultry & Egg Company
2884 Walnut Grove Rd
Memphis, TN 38111-2714   901-324-0818
Fax: 901-324-7283
Wholesaler/distributor of dairy items, frozen foods, general merchandise, meats and specialty items, serving the institutional markets, and canned goods
President: James Skefos
Sales/Marketing Executive: Sam Escue
Executive Assistant: Beth Craig
Estimated Sales: $3-5 Million
Number Employees: 5-9
Types of Products Distributed:
 Food Service, Frozen Food, General Line, General Merchandise, Provisions/Meat, Specialty Foods, Dairy products, etc.

55805 Constellation Brands Inc
207 High Point Dr.
Suite 100
Victor, NY 14564   585-678-7100
                           888-724-2169
www.cbrands.com
Beer, champagne, table, sparkling and kosher wines, Scotch whiskey, spirits, etc.
Executive Chair: Robert Sands
robert.sands@cbrands.com
President/CEO: Bill Newlands
CFO: Garth Hankinson
Executive Vice Chair: Richard Sands
Chief Marketing Officer: Jim Sabia
Chief Human Resources Officer: Thomas Kane
Estimated Sales: $7.3 Billion
Number Employees: 10,000
Number of Brands: 100+
Type of Packaging: Consumer
Other Locations: Constellation Brands
Private Brands Carried:
 Corona, Esprit de Vie, St. Pauli Girl, Wild Irish Rose, Paul Mason, Inglenook
Types of Products Distributed:
 General Line, Beer, wine, champagne, etc.

55806 Consumers Fresh Produce
One 21st St
Pittsburgh, PA 15222   412-281-0722
marketing@consumersproduce.com
www.consumersproduce.com
Wholesaler/distributor of produce; serving the food service and retail markets.
President: Les Ainsman
Chief Executive Officer: Gregory Cessna
Business Manager: Linda Yinger
Director of Business Systems: Sean Neubauer
Professional Sales & Buyer: Pete Machi
Operations Manager: Regis Sullivan
General Manager: Ronald Casertano
Year Founded: 1952
Estimated Sales: $55 Million
Number Employees: 100-249
Square Footage: 100000
Types of Products Distributed:
 Food Service, Produce

55807 Consumers Packing Co
1301 Carson Dr
Melrose Park, IL 60160-2970   708-345-6780
Fax: 708-345-9052 800-356-9876
www.consumerspacking.com
Wholesaler/distributor of meat products
President: William Schutz
Estimated Sales: $10-20 Million
Number Employees: 100-249
Types of Products Distributed:
 Frozen Food, Provisions/Meat

55808 Consumers Packing Co
1301 Carson Dr
Melrose Park, IL 60160-2970   708-345-6780
Fax: 708-345-9052 800-356-9876
www.consumerspacking.com
Meat products
President: William Schutz
Finance Executive: Anthony Barone
VP Sales and Marketing: Mike Gale
Estimated Sales: $17 Million
Number Employees: 100-249

55809 Container Systems Inc
205 E Burlington Ave
P.O.Box 366
Westmont, IL 60559-1719   815-965-2800
Fax: 630-960-4176 877-712-1596
info@containersystems.com
www.containersystems.com
Wholesaler/distributor of material handling equipment including forklifts and conveyors

Wholesalers & Distributors / A-Z

President: Michael Wall
mike@containersystems.com
Chairman: Bob Wall
Office Manager: Roseann Hopkins
Sales: Rob Kruger
Estimated Sales: $5-10 Million
Number Employees: 20-49
Private Brands Carried:
  Intermetro; Speed Rack; Jarke
Types of Products Distributed:
  Frozen Food, General Merchandise, Material handling equipment

55810 Conti Group Company
100 N La Salle St # 1720
Chicago, IL 60602-8800   312-332-7800
          Fax: 312-332-7818
Wholesaler/distributor of produce including wheat and corn
Partner: Gregory Adamski
Product Manager: Peter Welge
Estimated Sales: $300,000-500,000
Number Employees: 1-4
Types of Products Distributed:
  Frozen Food, Produce, Wheat & corn

55811 Continental Glass & Plastic
218 N Jefferson St # 400
Chicago, IL 60661-1306   312-831-2100
          Fax: 312-831-1900
Wholesaler/distributor of food packaging products including glass and plastic jars, pouches, bottles, tubes, closures, sprayers, pumps and dispensing caps
Owner: Matthew J Conti
CEO: Dick Giesen
Senior VP: Alan Miretzky
Estimated Sales: $20-50 Million
Number Employees: 5-9
Types of Products Distributed:
  Frozen Food, General Merchandise, Packaging materials

55812 Continental Lift Truck Corp
16600 Johnson Memorial Dr
P.O.Box 26
Jordan, MN 55352-9503   952-492-3900
  Fax: 952-492-6218 sales@continental-lift.com
          www.continental-lift.com
Wholesaler/distributor of used forklifts
President: Mary Kay Tamasi
VP: Micheal Sibulkin
Office Manager: Kelsey Anderson
Vice President: Michael Sibulkin
mike@continental-lift.com
Estimated Sales: $5-10 Million
Number Employees: 10-19
Private Brands Carried:
  Hyster; Clark; Catterpillar
Types of Products Distributed:
  Frozen Food, General Merchandise, Used forklifts

55813 Continental Marketing
18 Lithgow St
Winslow, ME 04901   207-872-4938
          Fax: 207-872-2062
Exporter and wholesaler/distributor of closeout food items from overstocks, package changes, buy backs, downgrades, etc.; serving the food service market
CEO: Charles Ladd
Estimated Sales: $2 Milion
Number Employees: 1-4
Square Footage: 100000
Type of Packaging: Food Service
Types of Products Distributed:
  Food Service, Frozen Food, General Line, Closeout food items

55814 Contract & Leisure
20 Nassau Street
Suite 237
Princeton, NJ 08542-4505   609-860-6700
          Fax: 609-860-6701
Wholesaler/distributor and importer of stacking plastic chairs and tables for indoor and outdoor use and cantilevered umbrellas; exporter of cantilevered umbrellas
Manager: Jack Dessailly
Number Employees: 1-4
Type of Packaging: Food Service
Private Brands Carried:
  Tango; Mambo; Sirtaki
Types of Products Distributed:
  Frozen Food, General Merchandise, Plastic chairs & tables

55815 Controls Group International
P.O.Box 172001
Memphis, TN 38187   901-821-0960
          Fax: 901-821-0272
President: Webster Mc Donald
wmcdonald@controlsgroup.com
Estimated Sales: $1-3 Million
Number Employees: 5-9

55816 Convenience Food Systems
91 Wales Ave
Avon, MA 02322-1090   508-588-2600
          Fax: 508-588-1791
Wholesaler/distributor of food processing and packaging machinery
President: Ron Merrill
VP Technical Services: Tony Bayet
Administrative VP: Chris van Wandelen
Estimated Sales: $20-50 Million
Number Employees: 50-99
Square Footage: 50000
Parent Co: CFS
Types of Products Distributed:
  Frozen Food, General Merchandise, Food processing & packaging equipment

55817 Cook Associates Your CoStore
10 Fitch St
Norwalk, CT 06855-1309   203-838-0490
  Fax: 203-838-0762 sales@yourcompanystore.net
          www.yourcompanystore.net
Wholesaler/distributor of general merchandise including advertising specialties
President: Paul Cook
paulcook@yourcompanystore.net
VP: Karin Cook
Estimated Sales: $1-2.5 Million
Number Employees: 1-4
Square Footage: 16000
Private Brands Carried:
  Bic; Cross
Types of Products Distributed:
  Frozen Food, General Merchandise, Advertising specialties

55818 Cook Flavoring Company
3319 Pacific Ave
Tacoma, WA 98418   253-472-1361
          Fax: 253-472-1390 800-735-0545
Wholesaler/distributor of vanilla extract and powder and other natural flavors for ice cream and bakery products; also, mail order service for retail market available
President: Raymond Lochhead
CEO: Kimberly Bowman
Estimated Sales: $500,000-$1 Million
Number Employees: 1-4
Private Brands Carried:
  Cooks Choice; Cooks
Types of Products Distributed:
  Frozen Food, General Line, Vanilla exract & powder, etc.

55819 Cook's Mate Restaurant Equipment Supply
505 Ellesmere Road
Suite 1
Scarborough, ON M1R 4E5
Canada   416-759-8122
       Fax: 416-759-9198 info@cooksmate.com
Wholesaler/distributor of food service equipment and supplies
Sales Manager: Amelia Hui
Number Employees: 5-9
Private Brands Carried:
  Garland; Falcon; Berkel
Types of Products Distributed:
  Food Service, Frozen Food, General Merchandise, Equipment & supplies

55820 Cooker T. Corporation
5621 Brookline Drive
Orlando, FL 32819-4008   407-876-0982
          Fax: 407-876-0982
Wholesaler/distributor of uniforms and chefs' hats; also, advertising materials, electronic equipment and catalogs available; serving the food service market
President: Jim Whaples
Number Employees: 1-4

Types of Products Distributed:
  Food Service, Frozen Food, General Merchandise, Uniforms & chefs' hats

55821 Cookie Kingdom
1201 E Walnut St
Oglesby, IL 61348-1344   815-883-3331
  Fax: 815-883-3332 ckingdomoffice@gmail.com
          www.cookiekingdom.com
Manufacturer of cookies, ice cream wafers and dairy inclusions; co-packer for private label companies; and builder and upgrader of dairy equipment for lease or purchase.
President: Cliff Sheppard
ckingdom@ivnet.com
Director: Patty Smith
Estimated Sales: $13 Million
Number Employees: 100-249
Type of Packaging: Consumer, Private Label, Bulk
Types of Products Distributed:
  Frozen Food, Cookies

55822 CoolBrands International
4175 Veterans Memorial Highway
3rd Floor
Ronkonkoma, NY 11779-7639   631-737-9700
     Fax: 631-737-9792 www.eskimopie.com
Distributor of frozen desserts including ice cream, also flexible packaging
CFO: Gary Stevens
Estimated Sales: $35 Million
Number Employees: 35
Type of Packaging: Food Service, Bulk
Private Brands Carried:
  Disney, Yoplait, Crayola, Eskimo Pie, Snapple, Breyers, Godiva Ice Cream, No Pudge, Chipwich, Tropicana, Fruit a Freeze, Wholefruit, Care Bears, Trix
Types of Products Distributed:
  Frozen Food

55823 (HQ)Cooperative Atlantic
123 Halifax
Moncton, NB E1C 9R6
Canada   506-858-6000
          Fax: 506-858-6472
Wholesaler/distributor of general merchandise, meats, frozen foods and produce; serving cooperative stores
President: Bertha Campbell
1st VP: Adelair Cormier
2nd VP: Wayne Lee
Sales/Marketing Executive: Jennifer MacLeod
Number Employees: 250-499
Other Locations:
  Coop. Atlantic
  Gander, NFCoop. Atlantic
Private Brands Carried:
  Kraft; Harmony; Catelli
Number of Customer Locations: 160
Types of Products Distributed:
  Frozen Food, General Merchandise, Provisions/Meat, Produce

55824 Cooperative Country
205 W Eighth St
Palisade, CO 81526-8662   970-464-7277
     Fax: 970-464-7995 www.fruitacoop.org
Cooperative packer and seller of fresh peaches
Public Relations Officer: Ed Whitman
Manager: Doug Randall
drand@fruitacoop.com
Estimated Sales: $500,000-$1 Million
Number Employees: 5-9
Square Footage: 144000
Parent Co: Fruita Consumers Cooperative
Type of Packaging: Consumer, Private Label, Bulk

55825 Cooseman's D.C.
2144 Queens Chapel Rd NE
Washington, DC 20018-3608   202-832-9000
          Fax: 202-544-0777
Wholesaler/distributor of specialty and exotic produce; serving the food service market
Compt.: Alyx Damron
Sales: Denise Huffer
Contact: Diana Noboa
noboadiana@coosemansdc.com
General Manager: Lolo Mengel
Number Employees: 20-49
Square Footage: 28000
Private Brands Carried:
  Rock Garden; Cooseman's

Wholesalers & Distributors / A-Z

Types of Products Distributed:
Food Service, Frozen Food, Produce, Specialty Foods

55826 Copperwood InternationalInc
9249 S Broadway
Unit 200-238
Highland Ranch, CO 80129-5692 303-683-1234
Fax: 303-683-0933 800-411-7887
copperwoodfoods@aol.com
Broker of a wide variety of closeout, excess and discounted food items
Sales Director: Michael Casey
Estimated Sales: $5,000,000
Number Employees: 4
Number of Brands: 76
Number of Products: 127
Square Footage: 50000
Number of Customer Locations: 4
Types of Products Distributed:
Frozen Food, General Line, General Merchandise, Provisions/Meat, Seafood, Closeouts

55827 Coquitlam City Hall
3000 Guildford Way
Coquitlam, BC V3B 7N2
Canada 604-927-3000
Fax: 604-517-2152 www.coquitlam.ca
Wholesaler/distributor of frozen poultry, beef and pork; serving the food service market
General Manager: Danny Chan
Number Employees: 50-99
Parent Co: J.M. Schneider
Types of Products Distributed:
Food Service, Frozen Food, Provisions/Meat, Beef, pork & poultry products

55828 Cora Italian Specialties
9630 Joliet Rd
Countryside, IL 60525-4138 708-482-4660
Fax: 708-482-4663 800-696-2672
info@corainc.com www.corainc.com
Monin syrups, Oregon chai, Guitiard and Ghirardelli chocolates, Mocafe, Jet tea etc
President: John Cora
jcora@corainc.com
Sales: Paul Rekstad
Estimated Sales: 1.80 Million
Number Employees: 10-19
Square Footage: 60000
Type of Packaging: Food Service
Types of Products Distributed:
Frozen Food

55829 Corbo Restaurant Supply
150 Main St
Asbury Park, NJ 07712-7090 732-774-1341
Fax: 732-774-6627
Wholesaler/distributor of commercial restaurant furniture, smallwares and equipment; also, CAD consulting available
President: Lester Reiff
Estimated Sales: $1.5-2 Million
Number Employees: 1-4
Square Footage: 160000
Private Brands Carried:
Hobart; Blodgett
Types of Products Distributed:
Food Service

55830 (HQ)Core-Mark Holding Company, Inc
1500 Solana Blvd
Suite 3400
Westlake, TX 76262 940-293-8600
806-221-713
www.core-mark.com
Wholesaler/distributor of confectionery items, snack foods, general line products and general merchandise.
President & CEO: Scott McPherson
Chairman: Randolph Thornton
SVP/Chief Financial Officer: Christopher Miller
Year Founded: 1888
Estimated Sales: Over $1 Billion
Number Employees: 8,413
Other Locations:
Core-Mark International
Fort Worth, TXCore-Mark International
Types of Products Distributed:
Frozen Food, General Line, General Merchandise, Snack foods, confectionery & groceries

55831 Core-Mark Holding Company, Inc
7800 Riverfront Gate
Burnaby, BC V5J 5L3
Canada 604-430-2181
www.core-mark.com
Wholesaler/distributor of confectionery items, snack foods, general line products and general merchandise.
Number of Customer Locations: 500
Types of Products Distributed:
General Line, Rack Jobbers, Candy/confectionery

55832 Core-Mark Holding Company, Inc
99 Bannister Road
Winnipeg, MB R2R 0S2
Canada 204-633-9244
www.core-mark.com
Wholesaler/distributor of confectionery items, snack foods, general line products and general merchandise.
Number of Customer Locations: 2500
Types of Products Distributed:
Food Service, Frozen Food, General Line, Specialty Foods, Confectionery items, snacks, etc.

55833 Core-Mark Holding Company, Inc
200 Core-Mark Court
Bakersfield, CA 93307 661-366-2673
800-310-1392
www.core-mark.com
Wholesaler/distributor of confectionery items, snack foods, general line products and general merchandise.
Types of Products Distributed:
Frozen Food, General Line, General Merchandise, Rack Jobbers, Confectionery items, etc.

55834 Core-Mark Holding Company, Inc
9020 King Palm Dr
Tampa, FL 33619 813-664-0414
855-268-2672
www.core-mark.com
Wholesaler/distributor of confectionery items, snack foods, general line products and general merchandise.
Number of Customer Locations: 900
Types of Products Distributed:
Frozen Food, General Line, General Merchandise, Rack Jobbers, Confectionery products, groceries. etc.

55835 Core-Mark Holding Company, Inc
8225 30th St SE
Calgary, AB T2C 1H7
Canada 403-279-5581
www.core-mark.com
Wholesaler/distributor of confectionery items, snack foods, general line products and general merchandise.
Number of Customer Locations: 2900
Types of Products Distributed:
Frozen Food, General Line, General Merchandise, Rack Jobbers, Confectionery items, groceries, etc.

55836 Core-Mark Holding Company, Inc
1035 Nathan Ln N
Minneapolis, MN 55441 763-545-3700
800-742-5655
www.core-mark.com
Wholesaler/distributor of confectionery items, snack foods, general line products and general merchandise.

55837 Core-Mark Holding Company, Inc
Canada Region Headquarters
#207, 3445-114 Ave SE,
Calgary, AB T2Z 0K6
Canada 403-720-3848
www.core-mark.com
Wholesaler/distributor of confectionery items, snack foods, general line products and general merchandise.

55838 Core-Mark Holding Company, Inc
8030 Esquesing Line
Suite 1
Milton, ON L9T 6W3
Canada 403-720-3848
www.core-mark.com
Wholesaler/distributor of confectionery items, snack foods, general line products and general merchandise.

55839 Core-Mark Holding Company, Inc
1355 S.E. Johnson
Portland, OR 97222 503-652-0200
800-234-9994
www.core-mark.com
Wholesaler/distributor of confectionery items, snack foods, general line products and general merchandise.
Square Footage: 60000
Number of Customer Locations: 46,000
Types of Products Distributed:
Frozen Food, General Line, General Merchandise, Rack Jobbers, Confectionery items, etc.

55840 Core-Mark Holding Company, Inc
855 Wigwam Pkwy
Henderson, NV 89104 702-876-5220
800-451-1870
www.core-mark.com
Wholesaler/distributor of confectionery items, snack foods, general line products and general merchandise.
Private Brands Carried:
Shurfine
Number of Customer Locations: 520
Types of Products Distributed:
Frozen Food, General Line, General Merchandise, Rack Jobbers, Confectionery products, groceries, etc.

55841 Corea Lobster Cooperative
191 Crowley Island Rd
Corea, ME 04624 207-963-7936
Fax: 207-963-5952
Processors of lobsters
President: Michael Hunt
Treasurer: F.D. Rodgers
VP: Gary Moore
Estimated Sales: $1.5 Million
Number Employees: 4

55842 Corenco
3275 Dutton Ave
Santa Rosa, CA 95407-7891 707-824-9868
Fax: 707-528-3197 888-267-3626
ngorsuch@corenco.biz www.corenco.biz
Manufactures size reduction equipment for the food processing industry.
President/CEO: Chris Cory
ccory@corenco.biz
Corporate Secretary/Accounting: Saraj Cory
VP/COO: Jeff Boheim
Inside Machinery Sales: Neil Gorsuch
Production Manager: Matt Young
Estimated Sales: $1-2.5 Million
Number Employees: 5-9
Number of Brands: 1
Number of Products: 14
Square Footage: 14000
Types of Products Distributed:
Machinery

55843 Corey Bros Inc WHLS Produce
1410 Lewis St
Charleston, WV 25301-1407 304-344-3601
Fax: 304-345-8162 www.coreybrothers.com
Wholesaler/distributor of produce; serving the food service market
Owner: Bob Corey
cbisales@wvdsl.net
Secretary/Treasurer: K Denison
cbisales@wvdsl.net
VP: R Corey
Estimated Sales: $20-50 Million
Number Employees: 50-99
Number of Customer Locations: 750
Types of Products Distributed:
Food Service, Frozen Food, Produce

Wholesalers & Distributors / A-Z

55844 Corfu Foods Inc
755 Thomas Dr
Bensenville, IL 60106-1624 630-595-2510
Fax: 630-595-3884 800-874-9767
www.corfufoods.com
Gyros
President: Vasilios Memmos
vmemmos@corfufoods.com
Estimated Sales: $10-20 Million
Number Employees: 50-99

55845 Coriell Associates
149 Coriell Avenue
Fanwood, NJ 07023-1611 908-889-5537
Fax: 908-889-5535
Importer and distributor of specialty confections, gourmet candies and semi-liquid and paste coffee concentrates; also, new product development consulting and sourcing of ingredients for the food trade
President: Jane Chuffo
Director: Tony Chuffo
Number Employees: 1-4
Square Footage: 24000
Type of Packaging: Food Service, Private Label, Bulk
Types of Products Distributed:
  Frozen Food, Specialty Foods, Confections & gourmet candies

55846 Corim Industries Inc
1112 Industrial Pkwy
Brick, NJ 08724-2508 732-840-1640
Fax: 732-840-1608 800-942-4201
sales@corimindustries.com
www.corimindustries.com
Manufacturer, wholesaler and exporter of gourmet coffees, custom printed sugar packets, instant cappuccino, chai, and soluble milk for vending machines, custom blending and supplies, and also custom branding for private label suppliers.
President: Nathan Teren
nathan.teren@marinemax.com
CEO: Sam Teren
Treasurer/Controller: Nathan Teren
Estimated Sales: $2.1 Million
Number Employees: 20-49
Square Footage: 41672
Type of Packaging: Consumer, Food Service, Private Label, Bulk

55847 Corporate Display Specialty
50 Sage Ave # 60
Bridgeport, CT 06610-3060 203-366-8185
Fax: 203-366-6420 800-367-2531
www.cdsdisplays.com
Wholesaler/distributor of advertising specialties and promotional items
President: William Steeves
Contact: Matt Maguire
matt@cdsdisplays.com
Estimated Sales: $1-2.5 Million
Number Employees: 10-19
Private Brands Carried:
  Max-a-Trax; Featherlite; Channel-Kor
Types of Products Distributed:
  Frozen Food, General Merchandise, Advertising specialties

55848 Cosa Xentaur Corp
84 Horseblock Rd # F
Yaphank, NY 11980-9742 631-345-3434
Fax: 201-767-6804 cosa@cosaic.com
www.cosa-instrument.com
Importer and wholesaler/distributor of protein and moisture analyzers
President: Christopher Mueller
Contact: Bryan Flanagan
b.flanagan@cosaxentaur.com
Estimated Sales: $5-10 Million
Number Employees: 20-49
Private Brands Carried:
  Elementar; KF; Rapid N
Types of Products Distributed:
  Frozen Food, General Merchandise, Protein & moisture analyzers

55849 Cosgrove Distributors Inc
120 S Greenwood St
Spring Valley, IL 61362-2014 815-664-4121
Fax: 815-663-1433 800-347-3071
www.cosgrovedistributors.com
Wholesaler/distributor of general line products; serving the food service market.
President: Nora Cosgrove
cosgroves@insightbb.com
Estimated Sales: $2.5-5 Million
Number Employees: 20-49
Number of Customer Locations: 200
Types of Products Distributed:
  Food Service, Frozen Food, General Line

55850 Cost Plus
3447 S Lawrence St
Philadelphia, PA 19148-5615 215-336-1700
Fax: 215-389-8430
Wholesaler/distributor of seafood, provisions/meats and equipment and fixtures
Owner: Sal Davis
Estimated Sales: $5-10 Million
Number Employees: 10-19
Types of Products Distributed:
  Frozen Food, General Merchandise, Provisions/Meat, Seafood, Equipment & fixtures

55851 Costa Fruit & Produce
18 Bunker Hill Industrial Park
Boston, MA 02129 617-241-8007
Fax: 617-241-8718 www.freshideas.com
Wholesaler/distributor of produce including fresh fruit; serving the food service market, healthcare institutions, k-12 schools, and post-secondary institutions.
President & CEO: Manuel Costa
Chief Financial Officer: Kevin Linnehan
Vice President: Brad Woodgate
Director, Sales & Marketing: Barry Milanese
Estimated Sales: $20-50 Million
Number Employees: 250-499
Types of Products Distributed:
  Food Service, Produce

55852 Costco Wholesale Corporation
P.O. Box 34331
999 Lake Drive
Issaquah, WA 98027 425-313-8100
  800-955-2292
www.costco.net
Wholesaler/distributor/grocery store manufacturing and selling general merchandise, general line items, meats, confectionery, frozen foods, baked goods, produce, beer, wine, etc.
Chairman: Hamilton James
Chief Executive Officer: W. Craig Jelinek
VP/Chief Financial Officer: Richard Galanti
Chief Information Officer: Paul Moulton
Year Founded: 1976
Estimated Sales: $152.7 Billion
Number Employees: 254,000
Type of Packaging: Consumer, Food Service, Private Label, Bulk
Other Locations:
  Manufacturing Facility-Dairy
  Seattle, WA
  Manufacturing Facility-Meats
  Hillsboro, OR Manufacturing Facility-Dairy Hillsboro
Private Brands Carried:
  Kirkland Signature; Culinary Essentials; Clout; Court Classic; Jobmaster; Simply Soda; Funhouse Treats; Seattle Mountain; Traditions; Canine Club; Chocolates of the World
Number of Customer Locations: 385
Types of Products Distributed:
  Food Service, Frozen Food, General Line, General Merchandise, Health Food, Provisions/Meat, Produce, Rack Jobbers, Seafood, Specialty Foods, Bakery, Deli Foods, Pharmacy, Optical

55853 Cotati Brand Eggs & Food Svc
441 Houser St
Cotati, CA 94931-3034 707-795-4489
Fax: 707-795-2671 800-834-3447
www.cotatifoodservice.com
Wholesaler/distributor of frozen, specialty and health foods, groceries and seafood; serving the food service market
President: Mike Kenney
Estimated Sales: $20-50 Million
Number Employees: 20-49
Square Footage: 21000
Number of Customer Locations: 300
Types of Products Distributed:
  Food Service, Frozen Food, General Line, Health Food, Seafood, Specialty Foods

55854 (HQ)Couch's Rich Plan Foods
Us Route 30
Latrobe, PA 15650 724-539-2238
Fax: 724-539-0425
Wholesaler/distributor of meat products including beef, pork, poultry, frozen seafood, veal, lamb, etc.; also, cheese
President: Chris Couch
Estimated Sales: $3-5 Million
Number Employees: 10-19
Types of Products Distributed:
  General Line, Provisions/Meat, Seafood, Cheese & beef, pork, poultry, etc.

55855 Cougar Mountain Baking Co
4224 24th Ave W
Seattle, WA 98199-1216 206-467-5044
Fax: 206-467-0993 877-328-2622
comments@cougar-mountain.com
www.cookieman.com
Producers of bakery products.
Owner: David Saulnier
david@cougar-mountain.com
Customer Service: Dana Pantley
Estimated Sales: $300,000-500,000
Number Employees: 20-49

55856 Counter Culture Coffee
812 Mallard Ave
Durham, NC 27701 919-361-5282
  888-238-5282
counterculturecoffee.com
Coffee
Coffee Buyer: Chelsea Thoumsin *Year Founded:* 1995

55857 Country Butcher Shop
286 Mcallister Church Rd
Carlisle, PA 17015-9504 717-249-4691
Fax: 573-769-4652 800-272-9223
www.countrybutchershopinc.com
Processor and distributor of lamb, beef and pork.
Owner: Mary Finkenbinder
finkenbinder@socket.net
Estimated Sales: $10-20 Million
Number Employees: 5-9
Type of Packaging: Private Label
Types of Products Distributed:
  Provisions/Meat

55858 Country Cupboard
101 Hafer Rd
Lewisburg, PA 17837-7408 570-523-3211
Fax: 570-524-9299 info@countrycupboardinc.com
www.mattyssporthouse.com
Dehydrated soups, pastas, rices, sauces, relish, jams, beans, sugar-free chocolates, cornbread, honey and salsa, among other products.
Owner: Nicole Edinger
nicicci@dejazzd.com
CEO: Chris Baylor
General Manager: Steve Kulhavy
Events Coordinator: Melissa Swartz
Estimated Sales: $5-10 Million
Number Employees: 250-499
Types of Products Distributed:
  Frozen Food

55859 Country Life Foods
641 52nd St
Pullman, MI 49450-9200 269-236-5011
Fax: 269-236-8357 800-456-7694
mail@clnf.org www.clnf.org
Wholesaler/distributor of natural and organic bulk products; serving health food stores and coops
President: Mark LA Vanture
mlavanture@clnf.org
Warehouse Manager: Kevin Hug
Estimated Sales: $4.5 Million
Number Employees: 20-49
Square Footage: 128000
Parent Co. Oak Haven
Type of Packaging: Consumer, Bulk
Types of Products Distributed:
  Health Food, Specialty Foods, Natural & organic products

55860 Country Springs Hotel
2810 Golf Rd
Pewaukee, WI 53072-5499 262-547-0201
Fax: 262-547-0207 800-928-9266
www.countryspringshotel.com
Wholesaler/distributor of spring water

President: Russ Avery
Secretary: Christina Avery
HR Executive: Donna Johnson
donna@countryinnhotel.com
Estimated Sales: $1-2.5 Million
Number Employees: 250-499
Square Footage: 12800
Private Brands Carried:
  Sand Springs Water
Types of Products Distributed:
  Frozen Food, Spring water

55861 County Supply Co
711 Old County Rd
San Carlos, CA 94070-3295   650-591-8500
                   Fax: 650-598-0387
Wholesaler/distributor of food service equipment and supplies including pots and pans; serving the food service market
President: Scott Krampert
scott@crscatalog.com
VP: Mark Krampert
VP: Scott Krampert
Estimated Sales: $1-2.5 Million
Number Employees: 5-9
Types of Products Distributed:
  Food Service, Frozen Food, General Merchandise, Pots & pans

55862 Couprie Fenton
4282 Belair Frontage Rd
Suite 5
Augusta, GA 30909   706-650-7017
                   Fax: 706-868-1534
Crab, conch, crabmeat, dogfish, full line seafood, halibut, lobster, lobster meat
Manager: Yves Latremouille
Estimated Sales: $.5-1 million
Number Employees: 1-4

55863 Cousin's Uniform
360 Fairfield Ave
Stamford, CT 06902-7249   203-329-8603
              Fax: 203-323-7229 800-881-5343
              sales@concertattire.com www.concertattire.com
Wholesaler/distributor of aprons, chefs' apparel, tuxedos and tuxedo shirts, etc.; serving the food service market
President: Barry Chavkin
Estimated Sales: Less Than $500,000
Number Employees: 5-9
Types of Products Distributed:
  Food Service, Frozen Food, General Merchandise, Uniforms

55864 Cover The World
755 Il Route 83 # 219
Bensenville, IL 60106-1267   630-616-0010
                   Fax: 630-616-0655
Meats and meat products
President: Steve Lee
CEO/Operations Manager: Helen Lee
Estimated Sales: $11.9 Million
Number Employees: 1-4
Types of Products Distributed:
  Meat

55865 Coy's Bakery
411 W Broadway Street
Bradley, IL 60915-2254   815-932-3324
Wholesaler/distributor of baked goods
Co-Owner: Patrick Coy
Co-Owner: Elwin Coy
Estimated Sales: Less than $500,000
Number Employees: 1-4
Types of Products Distributed:
  Frozen Food, General Line, Baked goods

55866 Coyne Chemical Co Inc
3015 State Rd
Croydon, PA 19021-6997   215-785-4500
          Fax: 215-785-6030 www.coynechemical.net
Wholesaler/distributor of food grade phosphates, sodium nitrates and white mineral oils
President: Bradley Arnold
barnold@eqt.com
Marketing Manager: Thomas Coyne
Estimated Sales: $20-50 Million
Number Employees: 50-99
Types of Products Distributed:
  Frozen Food, General Merchandise, Phosphates, sodium nitrates, etc.

55867 Cozy Harbor Seafood Inc
75 Saint John St
Portland, ME 04102-3013   207-879-2665
              Fax: 207-879-2666 800-225-2586
              jnorton@cozyharbor.com www.cozyharbor.com
Buys, processes and distributes premium quality seafood products
Founder and President: John Norton
CEO: John S Norton
jnorton@cozyharbor.com
CFO: Mark Lannon
Co-founder and Technical Manager: Joe Donovan
Domestic and Intl Shrimp Lobster Sales: Tom Keegan
Operations VP: Joseph Donovan Norton
Plant/Production Manager: Roland Jacques
Estimated Sales: $.5-1 million
Number Employees: 100-249
Type of Packaging: Consumer, Food Service, Bulk
Types of Products Distributed:
  Seafood

55868 Crab
7692 Belair Rd
Baltimore, MD 21236-4088   410-665-5555
                   Fax: 410-663-9177
Wholesaler/distributor of shellfish, blue crabs, fresh and frozen fish, gulf shrimp, oysters, clams and mussels
Estimated Sales: $500,000-$1 Million
Number Employees: 1-4
Types of Products Distributed:
  Frozen Food, Seafood

55869 Crab Connection
6401 Highway 56
Chauvin, LA 70344-2604   985-466-5005
                   Fax: 985-594-5881
Wholesaler/distributor of fresh crabs and crab meat; serving the food service market
Owner: Nicholas Guidry
crabconnection@yahoo.com
Estimated Sales: Less Than $500,000
Number Employees: 5-9
Types of Products Distributed:
  Food Service, Frozen Food, Seafood, Fresh crabs & crab meat

55870 Crab Quarters
2909 Eastern Ave
Baltimore, MD 21224-3812   410-686-2222
                   Fax: 410-686-0343
Fresh crab
Owner: Jim Myrick
Estimated Sales: $1-3 Million
Number Employees: 20-49

55871 Cracker Jack Advertising Specialty Corporation
106 Arlington Ave
Port Jefferson, NY 11777   631-331-1587
              Fax: 631-331-1552 800-704-7155
              www.crackerjackadspec.com
Wholesaler/distributor of general merchandise including advertising specialties, custom imprinting and promotional items
Owner: Steven Oil
Estimated Sales: $2.5-5 Million
Number Employees: 1-4
Square Footage: 20000
Number of Customer Locations: 500
Types of Products Distributed:
  Frozen Food, General Merchandise, Advertising specialties

55872 Cranberry Isles Fisherman's
1 Water St
Islesford, ME 4646   207-244-5438
                   Fax: 207-244-9479
Manager: Mark Neighman
Estimated Sales: $.5-1 million
Number Employees: 1-4

55873 Craver Supply Company
7933 SW 34th Street
Oklahoma City, OK 73179-4419   405-942-6111
                   Fax: 405-236-3466
Wholesaler/distributor of cleaning supplies, disposables and wraps; serving the food service market
President: David Reese
Estimated Sales: $2.5-5 Million
Number Employees: 10-19
Types of Products Distributed:
  Food Service, Frozen Food, General Merchandise, Cleaning supplies, etc.

55874 Craveright
5902 Mount Eagle Dr
Alexandria, VA 22303-2513   703-888-3796
              info@craveright.com
              www.craveright.com
Gluten free treats.
Owner: Darioush Danaei
ddanaei@craveright.com
Estimated Sales: Less Than $500,000
Number Employees: 1-4

55875 Creager Mercantile Cash& Carry
4900 Acoma Street
Denver, CO 80216   303-293-0210
              Fax: 303-292-1612 www.creagermerc.com
Wholesaler/distributor of frozen food and candy; serving the food service market
Owner: D Creager
Contact: Donald Creager
dcreager@crb.com
Estimated Sales: $10-20 Million
Number Employees: 5-9
Number of Customer Locations: 380
Types of Products Distributed:
  Food Service, Frozen Food, General Line, Candy

55876 Cream Hill Estates
9633 rue Clement
LaSalle, QC H8R 4B4
Canada   514-363-2066
              Fax: 514-363-1614 866-727-3628
              info@creamhillestates.com
Producer and distributor of guaranteed pure oats

55877 Cream of Weeber
PO Box 50523
Idaho Falls, ID 83405-0523   208-522-2211
                   Fax: 208-529-1628
Wholesaler/distributor of butter, cheese and whey powder
Regional Sales Rep.: Vern Bowden
Estimated Sales: $10-20 Million
Number Employees: 20-49
Types of Products Distributed:
  Frozen Food, General Line, Dairy products

55878 Creative Foods of the Southwest
PO Box 6824
Las Cruces, NM 88006-6824   877-585-8032
Wholesaler/distributor of onion appetizers and garnishes
President: Scott Bannister
Types of Products Distributed:
  Frozen Food, General Line, Specialty Foods, Onion appetizers & garnishes

55879 Creative Lighting Fixture Company
998C Old Country Road
STE 336
Plainview, NY 11803   888-614-1698
              Fax: 877-532-0180 sales@creativelighting.com
              www.creativelighting.com
Wholesaler/distributor of lighting fixtures including indoor/outdoor, flourescent and incandescent
Owner: Bertram Friedman
VP: Mark Friedman
Sales Manager: Jim Donnelly
Estimated Sales: $1-2.5 Million
Number Employees: 10-19
Types of Products Distributed:
  Frozen Food, General Merchandise, Lighting fixtures

55880 Crescent Foods
4343 W 44th Place
Chicago, IL 60632
              800-939-6268
              communications@crescentfoods.com
              www.crescentfoods.com
Halal beef and poultry
President & CEO: Ahmad Adam
VP: Ibrahim Abed
Director of Sales & Marketing: Amna Haq
VP Human Resources: Muneeza Arjmand
Year Founded: 1995
Number Employees: 50-99
Types of Products Distributed:
  Provisions/Meat

Wholesalers & Distributors / A-Z

55881 Cresinco
PO Box 23725
Overland Park, KS 66283-3725   913-897-4220
Fax: 913-897-5820
General grocery
Director: Diane Devine

55882 Crest International Corporation
P.O. Box 83309
San Diego, CA 92138-3309   619-296-4300
Fax: 619-296-3624   800-548-1232
www.crestinternational.com
Fresh or frozen fish and seafoods, fresh and frozen packaged seafood
Owner/President: Stephen Willis
Corporate Secretary: Lourdes Garber
Estimated Sales: $2 Million
Number Employees: 10
Type of Packaging: Food Service, Bulk

55883 Crishawn Kitchen Equipment Company
4426 Baldwin Blvd
Corpus Christi, TX 78408   361-884-7353
Fax: 361-882-7854
Wholesaler/distributor of institutional equipment serving the food service market
President: G Terry
Estimated Sales: $1-2.5 Million
Number Employees: 1-4
Square Footage: 48000
Types of Products Distributed:
Food Service, Frozen Food, General Merchandise, Institutional equipment

55884 Crispy Bagel Co
230 N Franklintown Rd
Baltimore, MD 21223
800-533-7655
www.nefoods.com
Wholesaler/distributor of bread, cakes, pies and doughnuts
Plant Manager: Tom Richie
Estimated Sales: $10-20 Million
Number Employees: 50-99
Types of Products Distributed:
Frozen Food, General Line, Specialty Foods, Bread, cakes, pies & doughnuts

55885 Cristina Foods Inc
4555 S Racine Ave
Chicago, IL 60609-3371   312-829-0360
Fax: 312-829-0408   www.cristinafoods.com
Wholesaler/distributor of produce; and disposable paper and plastics serving the food service market
President: Cesar Bovalina
cbovalina@cristinafoodsinc.com
Sales/Marketing Manager: John Juarez, Jr.
Estimated Sales: $5-6 Million
Number Employees: 10-19
Square Footage: 60000
Number of Customer Locations: 200
Types of Products Distributed:
Food Service, Frozen Food, Produce

55886 Critelli Olive Oil
2445 South Watney Way, Ste D
Fairfield, CA 94533-6721   707-426-3400
Fax: 707-426-3423   800-865-4836
www.critelli.com
Manufacturer of organic olive oil and dipping oil. Importer of culinary oil, Balsamic, Varietal Wine, and flavored vinegars from around the world.
Director Food Service: Mike Brossier
Director Of Operations: Brian Witbracht
Type of Packaging: Food Service, Private Label

55887 Crocker & Winsor Seafoods
100 Widett Cir
Boston, MA 2118   617-269-3100
Fax: 617-269-3376   800-225-1597
fish@crockerwinsor.com   www.crockerwinsor.com
Importer and master distributor of 500 frozen seafood items
President: John Parker
VP: Dick Parker
Contact: Andy Arnold
aarnold@crockerwinsor.com
Estimated Sales: $10-20 Million
Number Employees: 20-49
Parent Co: Frozen Seafood Distributors
Private Brands Carried:
Captain Jeff; Skipper Sam; Winsor Bay; Jako
Types of Products Distributed:
Seafood

55888 Cross Automation
2001 Oaks Parkway
PO Box 1026
Belmont, NC 28012   704-523-2222
Fax: 704-523-6500   800-866-4568
www.cross-automation.com
Wholesaler/distributor of PLC systems, scada software, man machine interface, limit switches, counters, timers and controls including sensor, process/temperature and motion; also, training and seminars available
President: Steve Earley
CEO: Mike Grooms
COO: Joe Grooms
Contact: Charles Carver
charles.carver@crossco.com
Number Employees: 50-99
Types of Products Distributed:
Frozen Food, General Merchandise, Controls, counters, etc.

55889 (HQ)Crosset Co LLC
10295 Toebben Dr
Independence, KY 41051-9615   859-283-5830
Fax: 859-817-7634   800-347-4902
customersupport@crosset.com   www.crosset.com
Wholesaler/distributor of produce
Owner: Joe Crist
CEO: Dan Pardekooper
dpardekooper@crosset.com
Executive VP: Daniel Pardekooper
Sales Manager: Robert Lummis
Director Procurement: Tim Shepard
Estimated Sales: $300,000-500,000
Number Employees: 250-499
Square Footage: 216000
Private Brands Carried:
Salad Time
Number of Customer Locations: 600
Types of Products Distributed:
Frozen Food, Produce

55890 Crown Equipment Corp.
44 S. Washington St.
New Bremen, OH 45869   419-629-2311
Fax: 419-629-2900   www.crown.com
Lift trucks.
Chairman/Chief Executive Officer: James Dicke
President: James Dicke
VP: Keith Sinram
Senior Vice President: James Mozer
Senior Vice President: Timothy Quellhorst
Senior Vice President: John Tate
Vice President, Sales: Christopher Rahe
Vice President, Engineering: Steven Dues
Vice President, Design: Michael Gallagher
Vice President, Manufacturing Operations: David Beddow
Year Founded: 1945
Estimated Sales: $3.48 Billion
Number Employees: 16,100
Types of Products Distributed:
Lift trucks, shelving & forklifts

55891 Crown Lift Trucks
10685 Medallion Dr
Cincinnati, OH 45241-4827   513-874-2600
Fax: 513-874-8755   www.crown.com
Wholesaler/distributor of material handling equipment including forklifts
President: Dave Reder
Cmo: Dan Zinn
dan.zinn@okisys.com
COO/Executive VP: Dave Reder
Estimated Sales: $20-50 Million
Number Employees: 100-249
Private Brands Carried:
Crown; Interlake; Kelley
Types of Products Distributed:
Frozen Food, General Merchandise, Material handling equipment

55892 Crown O'Maine Organic Cooperative
PO Box 565
Madawaska, ME 04756-0565   207-895-5234
800-743-7783
Wholesaler/distributor of certified organic potatoes, carrots, beets, garlic, onions and grain products
Director Sales/Marketing: James Cook
Private Brands Carried:
Wood Prairie; Skylandia Organic Farm; French Chantenay Carrot
Number of Customer Locations: 40
Types of Products Distributed:
Frozen Food, Health Food, Produce, Potatoes, carrots, beets, garlic, etc.

55893 Crown Point
118 S Cypress St
Mullins, SC 29574-3004   843-464-8165
Fax: 843-464-8598   www.crownpt.com
Wholesaler/distributor and exporter of beans, peanuts, almonds, cashews, canned mushrooms, pizza products, popcorn, spices, tomato paste, frozen vegetables, military rations including meals and ready-to-eat, etc. Importer of mushrooms and olives
President: Kevin Gates
VP: Scott Copes
Export Sales: Virginia Harrelson
Contact: John Anderson
johna@crownpt.com
Estimated Sales: $3-5 Million
Number Employees: 1-4
Parent Co: Unaka Company
Type of Packaging: Consumer, Food Service, Bulk
Private Brands Carried:
Sopakco; Sure-Pak; M-Packed; Camp & Trail; Sportsman; Summit
Types of Products Distributed:
Frozen Food, General Line, Specialty Foods, Ready-to-eat meals, etc.

55894 Crown Restaurant Equipment
5307 4th Street SE
Calgary, AB T2H 1K6
Canada   403-253-4888
Fax: 403-258-2003   800-665-0413
info@crownfoodequipment.com
www.crownfoodequipment.com
Wholesaler/distributor of restaurant equipment and supplies; serving the food service market
President: Nick Poulos
Estimated Sales: $6 Million
Number Employees: 10-19
Square Footage: 180000
Private Brands Carried:
Vollrath; Avtec; Panasonic
Types of Products Distributed:
Food Service, General Merchandise, Restaurant equipment

55895 Crown Sanitary Supply
5553 Ravenswood Rd Ste 105
Ft Lauderdale, FL 33312   954-987-7546
Fax: 954-964-6828   800-564-6828
Wholesaler/distributor of private label items, cleaners, degreasers, disinfectants, warewashing chemicals and janitorial supplies
President: Mario Fernandez
CEO: Mark Finkelstein
CFO: Mike Lang
VP Sales: George Gross
Estimated Sales: $10-20 Million
Number Employees: 50-99
Square Footage: 78000
Private Brands Carried:
3M; Johnson Wax; Rubbermaid; Kimberly-Clark
Types of Products Distributed:
Frozen Food, General Merchandise, Cleaners, janitorial supplies, etc.

55896 Crown Valley Food Service
550 East First Street
PO Box 2101
Beaumont, CA 92223-1001   951-769-8786
Fax: 951-769-8788
Prepared specialty foods
President: Sheldon Zaritsky
CEO: Mike Cavanaugh
Estimated Sales: $1-3 Million
Number Employees: 10-19

55897 Crusader Tomato
215 N River Rd
Auburn, ME 04210   207-782-0922
Fax: 207-782-1248
Wholesaler/distributor and packer of tomatoes; serving chain store suppliers and operations and warehouses
Owner: John Mauro
Manager: Jon Cedergreen

Wholesalers & Distributors / A-Z

Estimated Sales: $1-2 Million
Number Employees: 6
Square Footage: 24000
Private Brands Carried:
  Crusader Brand Tomatoes
Types of Products Distributed:
  Frozen Food, Produce, Tomatoes

55898 Crystal Food Import Corporation
245 Sumner St
Boston, MA 02128   617-569-7500
                    Fax: 617-561-0397
Importer and distribuor of Italian cheeses

55899 Crystal-Vision Packaging Systems
23870 Hawthorne Blvd
Torrance, CA 90505-5908   310-373-6057
    Fax: 310-373-6157   800-331-3240
              don@crystalvisionpkg.com
              www.crystalvisionpkg.com
Shrink film; printed shrink labels; dry food weigh/fill machines; packaging machines and bag sealers; food bags; & printed stand-up food bags.
President/CEO/CFO: Donald Hilmer
Quality Control: Emilio Diaz
Sales: Karl Behrens
Contact: Mark Bayless
mbayless@drbayless.com
General Manager: Jeff Hilmer
Purchasing: Bernie Johnson
Estimated Sales: $5 Million
Number Employees: 11
Square Footage: 60000
Parent Co: AID Corporation
Types of Products Distributed:
  Frozen Food, General Merchandise, Packaging machinery & supplies

55900 Csra Advertising Specialties
608 Reynolds St
Augusta, GA 30901-1432   706-722-5344
    Fax: 706-722-5341   800-258-9564
              csraadspec@aol.com
              www.csraadvertisingspecialties.com
Wholesaler/distributor of general merchandise including advertising specialties
Owner: Bruce Parker
csraadspec@aol.com
Estimated Sales: Less Than $500,000
Number Employees: 1-4
Number of Customer Locations: 1000
Types of Products Distributed:
  Frozen Food, General Merchandise, Advertising specialties

55901 Cubberley's
PO Box 3114
Marion, IN 46953   765-674-7727
                    Fax: 765-674-7728
Wholesaler/distributor of confectionery products
President: Kim Linn
Estimated Sales: $10-20 Million
Number Employees: 10-19
Types of Products Distributed:
  Frozen Food, General Line, Confectionery products

55902 Cudlin's Meat Market
8 Cox Rd
Newfield, NY 14867-9420   607-564-3443
Meat products; also, slaughtering services available
President: Vince Distefano
Estimated Sales: Less Than $500,000
Number Employees: 1-4
Type of Packaging: Consumer
Types of Products Distributed:
  Frozen Food

55903 Cuisine International
1920 Swarthmore Ave
Suite 1
Lakewood, NJ 08701-4589   732-367-2145
    Fax: 732-730-9913 info@cuisinellc.com
              www.cuisinellc.com
Frozen hors d'oeuvres
Estimated Sales: Less Than $500,000
Number Employees: 5-9
Type of Packaging: Consumer, Food Service

55904 (HQ)Culinar Canada
2 Complex Desjardins
Montreal, QC H5B 1B2
Canada   514-288-3101
          Fax: 514-982-4220
Wholesaler/distributor of baked goods including snack cakes, cookies and breads
CEO/President: Gaetan Lussier
Number Employees: 50-99
Private Brands Carried:
  Drakes
Types of Products Distributed:
  Frozen Food, General Line, Baked goods: cakes, cookies & breads

55905 (HQ)Culinary Depot
2 Melnick Dr.
Monsey, NY 10952
    Fax: 845-352-2700   888-845-8200
              customerservice@culinarydepot.biz
              www.culinarydepotinc.com
Kitchen and restaurant equipment, janitorial supplies, restaurant furniture and food storage and transport materials
Founder/President: Sholem Potash
CEO: Michael Lichter
Number of Customer Locations: 1
Types of Products Distributed:
  General Merchandise, Restaurant and kitchen equipment

55906 Culinary Masters Corporation
69 Brandywine Trl
Suite 109
Alpharetta, GA 30005   770-667-1688
    Fax: 770-667-1682   800-261-5261
              www.culinarymasters.com
Wholesaler/distributor and importer of specialty foods, baked goods, equipment and tools; serving the food service market; exporter of spices, blends and specialty equipment
Master Chef/President: Helmut Holzer
Controller: Beth Ann Jackson
Vice President: Sara Jane Holzer
Sales: Michelle Brayley
Estimated Sales: $3-5 Million
Number Employees: 5-9
Square Footage: 16000
Type of Packaging: Food Service, Private Label
Types of Products Distributed:
  Food Service, Frozen Food, General Merchandise, Specialty Foods, Specialty equipment & fine foods

55907 Culinary Products Inc
160 E Morley Dr
Saginaw, MI 48601-9482   989-754-2457
    Fax: 989-754-5640   888-666-0738
              sales@cpi-mi.com www.cpi-mi.com
Wholesaler/distributor of food service equipment and supplies; serving the food service market; also, food service consulting services available
President: Scott Rahn
scott@cpi-mi.com
Manager: Kati Hutchenson
Estimated Sales: $500,000-$1 Million
Number Employees: 5-9
Square Footage: 42000
Types of Products Distributed:
  Food Service, Frozen Food, General Merchandise, Foodservice equipment & supplies

55908 Culinary Specialties
1231 Linda Vista Dr
San Marcos, CA 92078-3809   760-744-8220
    Fax: 760-744-1486 info@culinaryspecialties.net
              www.culinaryspecialties.net
Importer and wholesaler/distributor mousse and sponge cake mixes, pastry shells, couvertures, chocolate cups, pastes, compounds, marmalades, glazes and flavorings; wholesaler/distributor of frozen foods, general merchandise, generalline items, etc
President: Christian Schragner
cschragner@culinaryspecialties.net
VP: Tom Solomon
National Sales Manager: Vishka Rosenblum
Production Manager: Francois Resch
Director of Purchasing: Dwayne Ferris
Estimated Sales: $1-2.5 Million
Number Employees: 20-49
Square Footage: 300000
Private Brands Carried:
  Cacao Barry; Pruve; Dolba
Types of Products Distributed:
  Frozen Food, General Line, General Merchandise, Provisions/Meat, Produce, Seafood, Specialty Foods, Bakery supplies

55909 Culinary Specialties
1231 Linda Vista Dr
San Marcos, CA 92078-3809   760-744-8220
    Fax: 760-744-1486 vishka@culinaryspecialties.net
              www.culinaryspecialties.net
Wholesaler/distributor of specialty foods; serving the food service market
President: Christian Schragner
cschragner@culinaryspecialties.net
Gourmet Chef: Patrick O'Farrell
Accurate Inventory: Javier Sanchez
National Sales Manager: Vishka Rosenblum
Sales Director: Verdette Ibong-Konkol
Office Manager: Elizabeth Brown
Production Manager: Francois Resch
Director of Piurchase: Dwayne Terris
Estimated Sales: $2.5-5 Million
Number Employees: 20-49
Private Brands Carried:
  La Romaaiola; Hega Bases
Types of Products Distributed:
  Food Service, Frozen Food, Specialty Foods

55910 Culture Systems Inc
3224 N Home St
Mishawaka, IN 46545-4436   574-258-0602
    Fax: 574-258-1136 info@culturesystemsinc.com
              www.culturesystemsinc.com
Processor, exporter and wholesaler/distributor of dairy ingredients; also, researcher for the food industry
President: David Kim
dhyungkim@aol.com
Estimated Sales: $1-2.5 Million
Number Employees: 10-19
Square Footage: 16000
Types of Products Distributed:
  Frozen Food, General Line, Dairy ingredients

55911 Culver Fish Farm
1316 W Kansas Ave
Mcpherson, KS 67460-6053   620-241-5200
    Fax: 620-241-5202   800-241-5205
Fish
Owner: Brent Culver
culverfish@gmail.com
Estimated Sales: Less Than $500,000
Number Employees: 1-4

55912 Cumberland Farms
100 Crossing Blvd
Framingham, MA 01702   781-828-4900
    Fax: 781-828-9012 www.cumberlandfarms.com
Milk and ice cream
Chairman: Lily Bentas
VP: George Haseotes, Sr.
Senior VP: Don Holt
Sales Director: Barbara Paidy
Contact: Ahmed Ali
aali@cumberlandfarms.com
VP Manufacturing: Emanuel Cavaco
Number Employees: 250-499
Parent Co: Suiza Foods

55913 Cummings Restaurant Equipment
234 Ross Clark Cir
Dothan, AL 36303   334-792-9510
    Fax: 334-794-3393   800-239-9510
Wholesaler/distributor of restaurant equipment; serving the food service market
President: Deborah Breckenridge
Treasurer: Leo Breckenridge
Manager: Regina Tharpe
Estimated Sales: $1-2.5 Million
Number Employees: 5-9
Square Footage: 34000
Types of Products Distributed:
  Food Service, Frozen Food, General Merchandise, Restaurant equipment

55914 Curley Brothers
215 A Street
Suite 102
Boston, MA 02210-1302   617-227-5577
                         Fax: 617-269-2433
Wholesaler/distributor of produce
President: Peter Niosi
Estimated Sales: $5-10 Million
Number Employees: 10-19
Types of Products Distributed:
  Frozen Food, Produce

Wholesalers & Distributors / A-Z

55915 Curtis Packing Co
2416 Randolph Ave
Greensboro, NC 27406-2910   336-275-7684
                                Fax: 336-275-1901
www.curtispackingcompany.com
Wholesaler/distributor of meats including beef and pork; serving the food service market
President: Douglas B Curtis
douglas.curtis@curtispackingcompany.com
Sr Marketing Executive & Vice President: John Curtis
Sales Manager: Steve Henderson
Human Resources Manager: Douglas Curtis
douglas.curtis@curtispackingcompany.com
Estimated Sales: $18 Million
Number Employees: 50-99
Square Footage: 120000
Types of Products Distributed:
   Food Service, Provisions/Meat, Beef & pork

55916 Curtis Restaurant Equipment
742 Rossanley Dr
Medford, OR 97501-1707   541-779-8335
          Fax: 541-779-0300 800-422-7818
rodona@cosnet.net www.curtisresteq.com
Wholesaler/distributor of food service equipment; serving the food service market
Manager: Rod Manning
rodm@curtisresteq.com
Sales Representative: Scott Coupe
Manager: Rod Manning
Estimated Sales: $1-2.5 Million
Number Employees: 5-9
Parent Co: Curtis Restaurant Equipment
Private Brands Carried:
   Hobart; Wolf; Montague
Types of Products Distributed:
   Food Service, Frozen Food, General Merchandise, Equipment

55917 Curtis Restaurant Equipment
P.O.Box 7307
Springfield, OR 97401   541-746-7480
   Fax: 541-746-7384 sales@curtisresteq.com
www.curtisresteq.com
Consultant specializing in design for the food service market; wholesaler/distributor of equipment and supplies; serving the food service market
CEO: Daniel Curtis
Chief Financial Officer: Bill Kettas
Estimated Sales: $20-30 Million
Number Employees: 50-99
Square Footage: 38000
Number of Customer Locations: 2000
Types of Products Distributed:
   Food Service, Frozen Food, General Merchandise, Equipment & supplies

55918 Curtis Restaurant Supply
6577 E 40th St
Tulsa, OK 74145-4516   918-622-7390
       Fax: 918-665-0990 918-766-2878
       BennettK@curtisequipment.com
       www.curtisequipment.com
Wholesaler/distributor of cleaning supplies, wraps, tabletop supplies and restaurant equipment and supplies; serving the food service market; also, contract designing services available
Owner: David Hillin
Owner: Jay Gulick
gulickj@curtisequipment.com
Sales Representative: Kathy Bennett
Estimated Sales: Less than $500,000
Number Employees: 20-49
Square Footage: 140000
Number of Customer Locations: 3500
Types of Products Distributed:
   Food Service, Frozen Food, General Merchandise, Restaurant equipment, etc.

55919 Curtis Ward Company
3722 28th Street
Long Island City, NY 11101-2629   718-478-4900
                                    Fax: 718-478-1030
Wholesaler/distributor and exporter of general merchandise including commercial refrigerators, air conditioners and cooking equipment; serving the food service market
President: Jay Pachtman
Vice President: Stuart Ellison
Estimated Sales: $1-2.5 Million
Number Employees: 1-4
Square Footage: 24000

55920 Cushner Seafoods Inc
4141 Amos Ave
Baltimore, MD 21215-3309   410-358-5564
                              Fax: 410-358-5558
Fish & Seafood
Owner: Jack Deckelbaum
Estimated Sales: $1,600,000
Number Employees: 5-9

55921 (HQ)Custom Fabricating & Repair
1932 E 26th St
Marshfield, WI 54449-5500   715-387-6598
          Fax: 715-384-3768 800-236-8773
dawn.isenberg@gotocfr.com www.gotocfr.com
Stainless steel filtration and cheese processing equipment; wholesaler/distributor of fittings, valves and pumps
President: Kyle Balcom
kyle.balcom@gotocfr.com
VP: Dawn Isenberg
Sales Director: Jay Moore
Estimated Sales: $7 Million
Number Employees: 50-99
Square Footage: 130000
Other Locations:
   Custom Fabricating & Repair
   Fridley, MNCustom Fabricating & Repair
Private Brands Carried:
   Fristam; Thermaline; Waukesha Cherry Burrell
Types of Products Distributed:
   Frozen Food, General Merchandise, Fittings, valves & pumps

55922 Custom Food Svc Inc
719 E Jackson St
Phoenix, AZ 85034-2284   602-254-1876
   Fax: 602-256-6216 www.customfoodservice.com
President: Carl Schnitzer
smarsiglil@customfoodservice.com
VP: Nadine Schnitzer
Vice President: David Schnitzer
Sales Exec: Steve Marsiglil
Estimated Sales: $20-50 Million
Number Employees: 20-49

55923 Custom Foods Inc
9101 Commerce Dr
De Soto, KS 66018-8410   913-585-1900
       Fax: 913-585-1470 www.customfoodsinc.com
Frozen bakery products
Number Employees: 20-49

55924 Custom House Seafoods
PO Box 7112
Portland, ME 04112   207-773-2778
                              Fax: 207-761-9458
Fish and seafood.
President: Craig Johnson
Estimated Sales: $820,000
Number Employees: 1-4

55925 Custom Pools Inc
373 Shattuck Way
Portsmouth, NH 03801-2828   603-431-7800
          Fax: 603-431-5109 800-323-9509
info@custompools.com www.custompools.com
Manufacturer and wholesaler/distributor of ultraviolet disinfection equipment for opaque fluids, juices, etc
President: Kelsey Hemming
kelsey.hemming@gmail.com
Vice President: Darrel Short
VP: David Short
Estimated Sales: $3-5 Million
Number Employees: 20-49
Types of Products Distributed:
   Frozen Food, General Merchandise, Ultraviolet disinfection equipment

55926 Custom Produce Sales
13475 E Progress Dr
Parlier, CA 93648-9674   559-254-5800
                              Fax: 559-646-1003
Peaches, nectarines, blueberries, apricots, plums and grapes
Manager: Bob Melenbacker
Number Employees: 100-249

55927 Cutrufello's Creamery
1390 Barnum Avenue
Stratford, CT 06614-5491   203-378-2651
Wholesaler/distributor of Italian cheese
Estimated Sales: $1-2.5 Million
Number Employees: 10-19
Types of Products Distributed:
   Frozen Food, General Line, Italian cheese

55928 Cuyler Food Machinery &Appraisal
468 Salt Rd
Webster, NY 14580-9703   585-265-0715
   Fax: 585-265-1724 cuyler@foodmachinery.com
www.foodmachinery.com
Wholesaler/distributor of fruit and vegetable canning machinery, freezers, etc.; also, appraisal, liquidation and rebuilding services available
President: Otto Cuyler Jr
Estimated Sales: $1-2.5 Million
Number Employees: 1-4
Square Footage: 400000
Types of Products Distributed:
   Frozen Food, General Merchandise, Canning machinery, freezers, etc.

55929 Czimer's Game & Seafoods
13136 W 159th St
Homer Glen, IL 60491   708-301-0500
                              888-294-6377
                              www.czimers.com
Meat and fish
Owner: Richard Czimer Jr
Estimated Sales: $300,000
Number Employees: 1-4

55930 D A C Labels & Graphic
10491 Brockwood Rd
Dallas, TX 75238-1641   214-340-2055
          Fax: 214-340-2272 800-483-1700
daclbl@aol.com www.daclabels.com
Printed labels and tags; wholesaler/distributor of thermal transfer printers and ribbons
Vice President: Judy Benson
daclbl@aol.com
CEO: Jay Fair
R & D: Greg Swindle
VP: Judy Vinson
Marketing Manager: Greg Towers
Customer Support: Michelle Ywhite
Estimated Sales: $5-10 Million
Number Employees: 10-19
Types of Products Distributed:
   Frozen Food, General Merchandise, Thermal transfer printers & ribbons

55931 D E Shipp Belting Co
123 S Industrial Dr
Waco, TX 76710-6925   254-366-8216
          Fax: 254-776-2635 800-537-1429
www.shippbelting.com
Wholesaler/distributor of vulcanized endless belts, cleated conveyor belting and center guides on conveyor belting
President: Gregory A Ogden
gregogden@shippbelting.com
Vice President, Plant Operations: Chase Sligh
Vice President, Marketing: Troy Cobb
Estimated Sales: $5-10 Million
Number Employees: 10-19
Square Footage: 100000

55932 D J Enterprises
18345 Ventura Blvd # 314
Tarzana, CA 91356-4242   818-345-0820
                              Fax: 818-345-3249
Wholesaler/distributor of advertising specialties, calendars, pencils and pens
Owner: Deborah Newmark
dnewmark@loweenterprises.com
Estimated Sales: Less Than $500,000
Number Employees: 1-4
Types of Products Distributed:
   Frozen Food, General Merchandise, Advertising specialties

55933 D L Systems Inc
1801 Old Highway 8 NW # 122
P.O.Box 120649
New Brighton, MN 55112-2307   651-636-5177
       Fax: 651-636-8475 sales@dl-systems.com
       www.skarnes.com
Wholesaler/distributor of material handling equipment
President: Paul Wanous
Estimated Sales: $5-10 Million
Number Employees: 10-19

Types of Products Distributed:
Frozen Food, General Merchandise, Material handling equipment

55934 D Rosen Co Inc
350 Meserole St
Brooklyn, NY 11206-1733　　　718-381-0600
Fax: 718-456-7699　davidrosen3501@yahoo.com
Full service bakery supply company and wholesaler/distributor/importer of pie fillings, nuts, seeds, flavors, flours, raisins, glace fruit, mixes, shelf life extenders, etc.; serving bakeries and supermarkets
President: Stuart Rosen
CEO: Clare Rosen
Marketing/Sales: David Bikofsky
Operations Manager: Oswald Green
Plant Manager: Eddie Mendez
Purchasing Director: Issac Lermer
Estimated Sales: $20-50 Million
Number Employees: 50-99
Square Footage: 42000
Type of Packaging: Food Service
Private Brands Carried:
Fulafnute/Sayda
Types of Products Distributed:
Food Service, Frozen Food, General Merchandise, Bakery Supply

55935 D Seafood
2723 S Poplar Avenue
Chicago, IL 60608-5915　　　312-808-1086
Fax: 312-808-0869
Seafood
Owner: De Trinh

55936 (HQ)D&E Pharmaceuticals
710 Central Ave
Farmingdale, NJ 07727　　　877-838-0560
Fax: 973-838-0560　800-221-1833
Manufacturer and wholesaler/distributor of herbal energizers and nutritional food supplements and vitamins
CEO: Eric Organ
Vice President: Richard Quine
Sales Director: Todd Weller
Purchasing Manager: Ted Weller
Estimated Sales: $20-50 Million
Number Employees: 20-49
Square Footage: 32000
Private Brands Carried:
Steromax; Bolt Energy; Super Capacity
Number of Customer Locations: 1500
Types of Products Distributed:
Health Food, Herbal energizers, etc.

55937 D&M Seafood
135 N King St # 2b
Honolulu, HI 96817-5084　　　808-531-0687
Fax: 808-531-4947
Seafood
Owner: Hansen Chong

55938 D'Arrigo Brothers Company of New York, Inc
315 Hunts Point Terminal Market
Bronx, NY 10474　　　718-991-5900
Fax: 718-960-0544　gdarrigo@darrigony.com
www.darrigony.com
Wholesale/Distributor of produce.
President & Buyer Western Veg: Paul D'Arrigo
CFO: David Bub
Director of Marketing: Gabriela D'Arrigo
VP, Sales & Fruit Buyer: Michael D'Arrigo
Corp. Sales/Deliveries/Drop Shipments: Steve Grandquist
Human Resources/Facilities Manager: Joe Schneider
Year Founded: 1948
Estimated Sales: $71 Million
Number Employees: 100-249
Square Footage: 75000
Private Brands Carried:
Andy Boy; Green Head; Page Boy
Types of Products Distributed:
Frozen Food, Produce

55939 D'Eon Fisheries
P.O.Box 70 West Pubnico
Yarmouth County, NS B0W 2M0
Canada　　　902-762-2217
Fax: 902-762-3295　877-930-3366
info@vernondeon.com　www.vernondeon.com
Wholesaler/distributor of seafood specializing in silver hake
President: Sylvain D'Eon

Number Employees: 250-499
Types of Products Distributed:
Frozen Food, Seafood

55940 D. Brickman Produce Company
1664 Western Ave
Albany, NY 12203-4218　　　518-464-6464
Fax: 518-472-1240
Wholesaler/distributor of produce
Owner: N Brickman
Estimated Sales: $1-3 Million
Number Employees: 6
Private Brands Carried:
Dole
Types of Products Distributed:
Produce

55941 D. Deodati & Sons
PO Box 679
Conshohocken, PA 19428-0679　　　610-834-9300
Fax: 610-834-9150
Wholesaler/distributor of general merchandise; also, rack jobber
Owner: Ned Moore
Operations Mgr: George Cummins
Estimated Sales: $10-20 Million
Number Employees: 20-49
Types of Products Distributed:
Frozen Food, General Merchandise, Rack Jobbers

55942 D. Fillet & Company
38 Hassey St
New Bedford, MA 02740　　　508-997-0442
Fax: 508-997-0631
Wholesaler/distributor of seafood
Owner: Antone De Mello
Estimated Sales: $3-5 Million
Number Employees: 5-9
Types of Products Distributed:
Frozen Food, Seafood

55943 D.A. Colongeli & Sons
16 Pomeroy Street
Cortland, NY 13045-2241　　　607-753-0888
Fax: 607-756-2997　800-322-7687
Established in 1970; purveyors of fine foods.
President: Donald Colongeli
Number Employees: 1
Square Footage: 4000
Type of Packaging: Food Service
Private Brands Carried:
Knorr Food Products; Hacco Food Products; Wild Game Meats; Dietetic Foods; Specialty Foods
Number of Customer Locations: 1
Types of Products Distributed:
Food Service, General Line, Health Food, Provisions/Meat, Specialty Foods

55944 D.A. Foodservice
29 Olney Avenue
Cherry Hill, NJ 08003-1615　　　856-424-7788
Fax: 856-424-3588
Wholesaler/distributor of canned and dry grocery products; serving the food service market
President: Dennis Aslanian
Estimated Sales: $500,000-$1 Million
Number Employees: 1-4
Types of Products Distributed:
Food Service, Frozen Food, General Line, Canned & dry products

55945 D.M. Rothman Company
355 Food Center Dr # A109
Bronx, NY 10474-7000　　　718-991-5006
Fax: 718-542-2765
Wholesaler/distributor of produce
Owner: James J Hunt Jr
Estimated Sales: $10-20 Million
Number Employees: 20-49
Types of Products Distributed:
Frozen Food, Produce

55946 DAO Water Company
1040 Collier Center Way
Unit 10
Naples, FL 34110
Fax: 239-513-9364　800-841-1973
info@daowater.com　www.daowater.com
A portion of the profits from DAO are donated to the Dent Foundation for medical research.

President/CEO: Michael Dent
Quality Control: Tamra VanHaezebrouck
Marketing/Sales/Public Relations: Christine Rhodes
Type of Packaging: Consumer

55947 DC Media & Marketing
5524 S Fort Apache
Suite 110
Las Vegas, NV 89148　　　702-778-0211
Fax: 702-778-4086　800-278-8707
www.tabletopsusa.com
Wholesaler/distributor of large merchandise including vinyl advertisement wraps on buses and trucks
President: Dan Curtin
CFO: Tom Bloss
VP: Michael Curtin
Sales Manager: Alan Japely
Contact: Steve Niedzwiecke
steve@tabletopsusa.com
Estimated Sales: $1-2.5 Million
Number Employees: 1-4
Parent Co: DC Sales Co.
Types of Products Distributed:
Frozen Food, General Merchandise, Advertising specialties

55948 DIP Seafood Mudbugs
1870 Dauphin Island Pkwy
Mobile, AL 36605-3000　　　251-479-0123
Fax: 251-479-9869　info@dipseafoodmudbugs.com
www.dipseafoodmudbugs.com
Seafood
Owner: Phan Nguyen
Estimated Sales: Less Than $500,000
Number Employees: 1-4

55949 DKW International Nutrition Company
PO Box 18002
Knoxville, TN 37928-2002　　　865-688-3784
Fax: 865-688-1078　800-874-1288
Wholesaler/distributor of stimulants, diet aids, vitamins, encapsulated herbs, herbal extracts, general merchandise and private label items
President: Dan Webb
Estimated Sales: Less than $500,000
Number Employees: 1-4
Square Footage: 34000
Number of Customer Locations: 4000
Types of Products Distributed:
Frozen Food, Health Food, Stimulants, etc.

55950 DMI Distribution, Inc.
990 Industrial Park Dr.
Winchester, IN 47394　　　765-584-3234
Fax: 765-584-1551
Wholesaler/distributor of frozen foods, groceries, meats and dairy products; serving the food service market
Partner: Hank Richardson
Partner: Jerry Franke
Estimated Sales: $500,000-$1 Million
Number Employees: 5-9
Square Footage: 60000
Number of Customer Locations: 100
Types of Products Distributed:
Food Service, Frozen Food, General Line, Provisions/Meat, Groceries & dairy products

55951 DNO Inc
3650 E 5th Avenue
Columbus, OH 43219　　　614-231-3601
dno@dnoproduce.com
www.dnoinc.com
Pre-cut prepackaged fresh fruit and vegetables
Founder/Owner: Tony DiNovo
tdinovo@dnoproduce.com
President/COO: Alex DiNovo
Purchasing Manager: Tony DiNovo
Estimated Sales: $10-20 Million
Number Employees: 20-49
Square Footage: 10000
Type of Packaging: Consumer, Food Service, Private Label, Bulk
Private Brands Carried:
Fresheath
Number of Customer Locations: 75
Types of Products Distributed:
Produce

Wholesalers & Distributors / A-Z

55952 DNX Foods
120 S Houghton Rd
Suite 138-273
Tucson, AZ 85748
888-612-5037
info@dnxbar.com www.dnxbar.com
Nutrition bars made from meat and superfoods
Founder/CEO: John Rooney
CFO: Josh Nelson
VP Sales: Tim Larsen *Year Founded:* 2015
Types of Products Distributed:
    Provisions/Meat

55953 DPI Mid Atlantic
1000 Prince Georges Blvd
Upper Marlboro, MD 20774   301-430-2200
            Fax: 301-430-2204
MD-GeneralInquiries@dpispecialtyfoods.com
        www.dpispecialtyfoods.com
Wholesaler/distributor of groceries, meat, produce, dairy, bakery, frozen, specialty and perishable foods; serving the retail and food service markets.
Chief Executive Officer: Mike Rodrigue
Number Employees: 1-4
Square Footage: 82000
Parent Co: DPI Specialty Foods
Private Brands Carried:
    Double H
Types of Products Distributed:
    Food Service, Frozen Food, General Line, Provisions/Meat, Produce, Specialty Foods, Dairy & bakery items

55954 DPI Midwest
6800 Santa Fe Dr
Suite E
Hodgkins, IL 60525   708-698-5701
    Fax: 708-588-1326 www.dpispecialtyfoods.com
Distributor of specialty perishable foods from around the world, all natural and all organic, 6,000 items carried.
Chief Executive Officer: Mike Rodrigue
President, Chief Commercial Officer: Russ Blake
Chief Financial Officer: Conor Crowley
VP, Information Technology: Nadia Rosseels
VP, Human Resouces: Kristen Flynn
Chief Operating Officer: Jeff Steiner
Number Employees: 50-99
Parent Co: DPI Specialty Foods
Type of Packaging: Food Service, Private Label
Other Locations:
    DPI Corporate
    Wilmette, IL
    DPI Rock Mountain
    Henderson, CO
    DPI Northwest
    Tualatin, OR
    DPI West
    Ontario, CA
    DPI Southwest
    Albuquerque, NM
    DPI Arizona
    Mesa, AZ
    DPI CorporateHenderson

55955 DPI Rocky Mountain
8125 E 88th Ave
Henderson, CO 80640-8121   303-301-1226
        Fax: 303-301-6931 800-888-0812
Wholesaler/distributor of specialty, health and frozen foods, groceries, produce, meats and deli and dairy products; serving retail supermarkets and military commissaries within the Rocky Mountain region
President: Russ Blake
Sales: John Prinzi
Purchasing: Charlotte Romero
Estimated Sales: $20-50 Million
Number Employees: 100-249
Parent Co: Distribution Plus
Private Brands Carried:
    Code; Aspen Valley
Number of Customer Locations: 1000
Types of Products Distributed:
    Food Service, Frozen Food, General Line, Health Food, Provisions/Meat, Produce, Specialty Foods, Groceries, deli items, etc.

55956 DPI Specialty Foods Inc.
601 Rockefeller Ave.
Ontario, CA 91761   909-975-1019
    Fax: 909-975-7238 www.dpispecialtyfoods.com
Gourmet, natural, organic, gluten free, local and ethnic foods.
CEO: Russ Blake
Chief Financial Officer: Marc Barth
Chief Information Officer: Nadia Rosseels
Chief Operating Officer: Christopher Erklenz
Year Founded: 1963
Estimated Sales: Over $1 Billion
Number Employees: 1000-4999
Types of Products Distributed:
    Specialty Foods

55957 DS Services of America
200 Eagles Landing Blvd.
Lakeland, FL 33810
        800-728-5508
        www.water.com
Bottled water, water filtration coolers, spring water, purified drinking water, distilled drinking water, and more.
President: Dave Muscato
CEO: Tom Harrington
CFO: Jerry Hoyle
General Manager: Mike Garrity
Year Founded: 1985
Estimated Sales: $787 Million
Number Employees: 5300
Type of Packaging: Consumer, Food Service, Private Label, Bulk

55958 DW Montgomery & Company
1103 W Hibiscus Blvd
P.O. Box 177
Melbourne, FL 32901-2714   321-953-9860
        Fax: 866-648-3808 800-323-7154
        dwm@dwmco.com www.dwmco.com
Wholesaler/distributor and broker of industrial and grocery grade refined sugar including natural and specialty organic. Wholesaler/distributor of health foods
Owner: David Montgomery
Principal: Robert Wormley
Sales: Paul Montgomery
Contact: Andrew Montgomery
andrew@dwmco.com
Operations: David Montgomery
andrew@dwmco.com
Estimated Sales: $330,000
Number Employees: 5
Square Footage: 10428
Types of Products Distributed:
    General Line, Health Food, Natural sugars & sweeteners

55959 DWL Industries Company
65 Industrial Road
Lodi, NJ 07644   973-916-9958
        Fax: 973-916-9959 888-946-2682
        cs@wincous.com www.wincodwl.com
Wholesaler/distributor, importer and exporter of knives, utensils and tableware; serving the food service market
President: David Li
Officer: Jieyui Ding
VP Sales: Steve Chang
Contact: Steven Chu
1and1admin@wincous.com
Number Employees: 15
Square Footage: 40000
Private Brands Carried:
    Winco
Types of Products Distributed:
    Food Service, Frozen Food, General Merchandise, Knives, utensils, tableware, etc.

55960 DXP Enterprises Inc
7272 Pinemont Dr
Houston, TX 77040   713-597-7370
        Fax: 713-996-4701 800-830-3973
        www.dxpe.com
Professional distribution management company that provides products and services to a variety of industries through its Innovative Pumping Solutions (IPS), Supply Chain Services and MROP Products and Services.
President/Chairman/CEO: David Little
dlittle@dxpe.com
SVP & Chief Financial Officer: Kent Yee
SVP/Supply Chain Services & Marketing: John Jeffery
SVP, Information Technology: Chris Gregory
SVP, Sales/Service Centers: Todd Hamlin
SVP, Innovative Pumping Operations: David Vinson
Year Founded: 1908
Estimated Sales: $50-100 Million
Number Employees: 1000-4999
Square Footage: 48000
Types of Products Distributed:
    Frozen Food, General Merchandise, Conveyor belts

55961 Dacotah Paper Co
3940 15th Ave N
Fargo, ND 58102-2835   701-838-6458
        Fax: 701-281-0446 800-270-6352
        dacotah@dacotahpaper.com
        www.dacotahpaper.com
Wholesaler/distributor of paper and disposable products and janitorial supplies
Manager: Al Fwedmark
Cmo: Matthew Mohr
mmohr@dacotahpaper.com
Sales Director: Jim Mortensen
Manager: Allen Swedmark
Estimated Sales: $500,000-1 Million
Number Employees: 100-249
Square Footage: 16000
Number of Customer Locations: 750
Types of Products Distributed:
    Food Service, Paper & disposable products, etc.

55962 Dacotah Paper Co
3940 15th Ave N
Fargo, ND 58102-2835   701-838-6458
        Fax: 701-281-0446 www.dacotahpaper.com
Wholesaler/distributor of equipment and fixtures and general merchandise
President: Matthew Mohr
mmohr@dacotahpaper.com
Sales/Marketing Executive: Keith Bresin
Purchasing Manager: Norm Dufact
Estimated Sales: $20-50 Million
Number Employees: 100-249
Square Footage: 144000
Private Brands Carried:
    Network
Types of Products Distributed:
    Frozen Food, General Merchandise

55963 Dade Paper Co
30427a County Road 49
Loxley, AL 36551-2607   251-964-1500
        Fax: 251-964-6010 800-844-5601
        www.dadepaper.com
Wholesaler/distributor of general merchandise
President: Lenny Genet
Manager: Craig Huey
chuey@dadepaper.com
Branch Manager: Bob Worch
Estimated Sales: $5-10 Million
Number Employees: 50-99
Types of Products Distributed:
    Frozen Food, General Merchandise

55964 Daffin Mercantile Company
2867 Estes St
Marianna, FL 32448   850-482-4026
        Fax: 850-526-1961
Wholesaler/distributor of equipment and fixtures, dairy and frozen foods, seafood, produce and meats; serving the food service market
Chairman: J Milton
President: R Daffin, Jr.
VP/Secretary: R Gary Lee
Treasurer/Sales Manager: John Milton
Estimated Sales: $10-20 Million
Number Employees: 5-9
Parent Co: Marianna
Private Brands Carried:
    NIFDA
Types of Products Distributed:
    Food Service, Frozen Food, General Line, General Merchandise, Provisions/Meat, Produce, Seafood

55965 Dairy Fresh Corporation
PO Box 10457
Mobile, AL 36610   251-867-7406
        Fax: 251-452-7313 800-239-4481
Wholesaler/distributor of dairy products including cottage cheese, milk, cream, yogurt, sour cream, ice cream, etc
Manager: Steve Ripstein
Plant Manager: Darrel Duvall
Estimated Sales: $1-2.5 Million
Number Employees: 10-19
Parent Co: Dairy Fresh
Types of Products Distributed:
    General Line, Cottage cheese, milk, yogurt, etc.

Wholesalers & Distributors / A–Z

55966 Dairy Fresh Corporation
PO Box 289
Columbus, MS 39703-0289 662-329-8601
  Fax: 662-327-2495 800-239-5114
Wholesaler/distributor of ice cream and milk
Manager: Tommy Richardson
Branch Manager: Tommy Hardy
Estimated Sales: $2.5-5 Million
Number Employees: 10-19
Number of Customer Locations: 450
Types of Products Distributed:
  General Line, Ice cream & milk

55967 Dairy King Milk Farms/Foodservice
PO Box 1259
11954 East Washington Blvd
Whitter, CA 90606 818-243-6455
  Fax: 818-243-2455 800-900-6455
  www.dairyberries.com
Dairy products, frozen vegetables and dry goods; wholesaler/distributor of frozen foods, general merchandise, general line products, produce, meats and seafood; serving the food service market
VP: Joseph Goldstein
Number Employees: 50-99
Square Footage: 280000
Type of Packaging: Consumer
Types of Products Distributed:
  Food Service, Frozen Food, General Line, General Merchandise, Provisions/Meat, Produce, Seafood

55968 Dairy Maid Ravioli Mfg Co
216 Avenue U
Brooklyn, NY 11223-3825 718-449-2620
  Fax: 718-449-3206 866-777-3661
  dairymaid1@aol.com
Manufacturer and distributor of pasta products including ravioli and tortellini
President/Co-Owner: Louis Ballarino
  dairymaid1@aol.com
Co-Owner: Salvatore Ballarino
Vice President: Anthony Ballarino
Estimated Sales: $1-2.5 Million appx.
Number Employees: 5-9
Square Footage: 44000
Type of Packaging: Consumer, Private Label, Bulk
Types of Products Distributed:
  Frozen Food

55969 Dairy Source
433 Broad St
Lake Geneva, WI 53147-1813 262-348-3480
  Fax: 262-728-1901 cheese@dairysourceinc.com
Wholesaler/distributor of commodities, cheese and other dairy products for private label items; serving retail, food service, industrial sectors
Owner: Rose Mennella
  marie@rosesmarketlakegeneva.com
CEO/Operations Director: Rose Steinmann
Estimated Sales: $3-5 Million
Number Employees: 1-4
Square Footage: 120000
Private Brands Carried:
  Dairy Source
Types of Products Distributed:
  Food Service, Dairy & Deli

55970 Dairy Specialties
8536 Cartney Ct
Dublin, OH 43017 614-764-1216
  Fax: 614-855-3114 dsibrown@aol.com
Exporter, importer and wholesaler/distributor of milk proteins, flavor producing enzymes and dried dairy ingredients
President: David Brown
  d.brown@dsm.com
CEO: V Brown
Estimated Sales: $2 Million
Number Employees: 1-4
Square Footage: 6000
Type of Packaging: Bulk
Private Brands Carried:
  Miles Milk Protein
Types of Products Distributed:
  Dried Milk Proteins, Dairy Enzymes

55971 Dairyland USA Corp
1300 Viele Ave
Bronx, NY 10474-7134 626-465-4200
  Fax: 718-378-2234
Wholesaler/distributor and importer of groceries, tomatoes, cheeses, olive oil and butter; serving the food service market
President: Christopher Pappas
VP/Treasurer: Dean Facatselis
VP/Secretary: John Pappas
Contact: Brian Adair
  brianadair@chefswarehouse.com
Estimated Sales: $20-50 Million
Number Employees: 1-4
Types of Products Distributed:
  Food Service, Frozen Food, General Line, Produce, Cheeses, olive oil & butter

55972 Dal-Don Produce
PO Box 29
Oldsmar, FL 34677-0029 352-394-2161
  Fax: 352-394-0517 800-874-9059
Importer, exporter and wholesaler/distributor of watermelons
Types of Products Distributed:
  Frozen Food, Produce, Watermelons

55973 Dale's Meats
308 Walnut St
Brighton, CO 80601-1751 303-659-8796
  Fax: 303-659-1090
Wholesaler/distributor of frozen and canned specialty meats including buffalo, venison, elk, pheasant, duck and alligator
President: Dale Beier
Estimated Sales: $1-2.5 Million
Number Employees: 5-9
Types of Products Distributed:
  Frozen Food, Provisions/Meat, Specialty Foods, Specialty game meats

55974 (HQ)Dalmatian Bay Wine Company
1384 E 40th St
Cleveland, OH 44103-1102 216-391-1717
  Fax: 216-391-6315
Wholesaler/distributor and importer of wine, coffee, specialty foods, groceries, general merchandise and private label items
President: Barry Martinis
VP: Tina Martinis
Sales Manager: Pete Milicevic
Estimated Sales: USD $8,016,000
Number Employees: 10-19
Square Footage: 40000
Private Brands Carried:
  Bosna Cafe Coffees
Types of Products Distributed:
  Frozen Food, General Line, General Merchandise, Specialty Foods, Beverages-alcoholic & nonalcoholic

55975 Dalo Button & Emblem Company
1170 Broadway
New York, NY 10001-7507 212-679-1196
  Fax: 212-889-2982
Wholesaler/distributor of general merchandise including advertising specialities, custom-printed buttons, badges, medals and emblems
President: Lois Schneider
VP: David Schneider
Estimated Sales: $500,000-$1 Million
Number Employees: 1-4
Square Footage: 2000
Number of Customer Locations: 1000
Types of Products Distributed:
  Frozen Food, General Merchandise, Advertising specialties

55976 Damian's Enterprises Inc
5100 Sycamore Dr
Pensacola, FL 32503-7944 850-453-8811
  Fax: 850-453-8803 800-232-4929
  www.damiansicecream.com
Wholesaler/distributor of frozen fruit slush drinks; serving the food service market
President: Anthony Jacobs
  damians13@aol.com
VP: Sigurd Lee
Estimated Sales: Less than $500,000
Number Employees: 50-99
Types of Products Distributed:
  Food Service, Frozen Food, General Line, Frozen slush drinks

55977 Dana's Rush Equipment Company
3400 Highway 30 W
Pocatello, ID 83201-6071 208-232-1020
  Fax: 208-232-2730
Wholesaler/distributor of restaurant equipment including table top items; serving the food service market
Manager: Tiffany Thomsen
Manager: Julie Hardenbrook
Estimated Sales: $1-2.5 Million
Number Employees: 1-4
Number of Customer Locations: 200
Types of Products Distributed:
  Food Service, Frozen Food, General Merchandise, Restaurant equipment: table top items

55978 Dana-Lu Imports
280 N Midland Ave Ste 414
Saddle Brook, NJ 07663 201-791-2244
  Fax: 201-791-2288
Importer and wholesaler/distributor of CMA espresso machines and grinders
President: Dana Rafferty
Sales: Maryann Tomko
Sales: Elaine Molnar
Number Employees: 10-19
Square Footage: 70000
Private Brands Carried:
  Linea Scanno; Rancilio
Types of Products Distributed:
  Frozen Food, General Merchandise, CMA espresso machines & grinders

55979 Danish Cones
PO Box 530522
Miami, FL 33153 305-756-9500
  Fax: 305-756-1155 danishcones@aol.com
Wholesaler/distributor of pre-made Danish waffle sugar cones and toppings
CEO: Victoria Busch
Estimated Sales: $3-5 Million
Number Employees: 5-9
Types of Products Distributed:
  Frozen Food, Specialty Foods, Pre-made danish waffle sugar cones

55980 Danville Paper & Supply
118 E North St
Danville, IL 61832-5815 217-442-0851
  Fax: 217-442-1182
Wholesaler/distributor of sanitary paper, coffee and janitorial supplies; serving the food service market
Owner: Jim Christison
  jim@danvillepaper.com
VP/Sales Manager: Jim Christison
Manager: Kevin Wright
Estimated Sales: $20-50 Million
Number Employees: 10-19
Square Footage: 30000
Types of Products Distributed:
  Food Service, Frozen Food, General Merchandise, Janitorial, coffee & paper supplies

55981 Darisil
15 Campbell Avenue
Suffern, NY 10901-6301 845-357-2740
  Fax: 845-357-1966
Wholesaler/distributor and exporter of grain, rice, dairy products, dry beans, peas, potatoes, poultry, etc
President: Joseph Silver
VP: William Stewart
VP: Richard Silver
Estimated Sales: Less than $500,000
Number Employees: 1-4
Square Footage: 20000
Private Brands Carried:
  Atlas; Beauty Queen
Types of Products Distributed:
  Frozen Food, General Line, Provisions/Meat, Produce, Dairy products, rice, grain, etc.

55982 Darlington Packing Co
319 Society Hill Rd
Darlington, SC 29532-2351 843-393-5801
  Fax: 843-393-3433
Wholesaler/distributor of provisions/meats including beef, lamb and pork
Owner: Louie Irick
Estimated Sales: $5-10 Million
Number Employees: 10-19

Wholesalers & Distributors / A-Z

Types of Products Distributed:
 Frozen Food, Provisions/Meat, Beef, lamb & pork

55983 Dataflow Technologies
1513 York Road
Lutherville, MD 21093-5611   410-296-2630
         Fax: 410-321-6524 800-801-6992
Wholesaler/distributor of bar code devices; also, system integration and VAR for Auto-ID products available
President: Walter Cushman
Account Executive: Ray Lawson
Account Executive: Sandy Howell
Estimated Sales: $1-2.5 Million
Number Employees: 1-4
Square Footage: 10400
Types of Products Distributed:
 Frozen Food, General Merchandise, Bar code devices

55984 Datatech Enterprises
10 Clipper Rd
W Conshohocken, PA 19428-2721   610-825-2266
         Fax: 610-825-7659
Wholesaler/distributor of paper and computer printout shredders, shredder/baler combinations, balers and addressing/labeling equipment; serving the food service market
Owner: Sam Silverton
Director Marketing: Patricia Weston
Estimated Sales: $5-10 Million
Number Employees: 10-19
Types of Products Distributed:
 Food Service, Frozen Food, General Merchandise, Balers, shredders, etc.

55985 Dauito Produce
PO Box 279
Vineland, NJ 08362-0279   856-692-6054
 Fax: 856-691-4274 cherylbden@aol.com
Distributor of produce
President: Sharon Dauito
VP: Cheryl Densten
Estimated Sales: $5-10 Million
Number Employees: 10-19

55986 David Food Processing Equipment, Inc.
52 Carrier Drive
Unit 14
Rexdale, ON M9W 5R1
Canada   416-675-5566
 Fax: 416-675-7431 800-461-3058
 info@davidfoodprocessing.com
 www.davidfoodprocessing.com
Wholesaler/distributor and importer of food processing equipment including meat slicers, patty machines, sausage stuffers, etc
President: W Butcher
Number Employees: 5-9
Square Footage: 22400
Private Brands Carried:
 Hollymatic; Henkovac; Talsa; Globe; Old Hickory
Types of Products Distributed:
 Frozen Food, General Merchandise, Meat slicers, patty machines, etc.

55987 David Puccia & Company
200 Howk St
Watertown, NY 13601-2468   315-788-0072
         Fax: 315-788-4971
Wholesaler/distributor of produce; serving the food service market
Owner: David Puccia
Bookkeeper: Marion Capone
Estimated Sales: $2.5-5 Million
Number Employees: 5-9
Parent Co: David Puccia & Company
Types of Products Distributed:
 Food Service, Frozen Food, Produce

55988 David's Cookies
11 Cliffside Dr
Cedar Grove, NJ 07009
    800-500-2800
 custserv@davidscookies.com
 www.davidscookies.com
Thaw and serve tarts, layer cakes and single serve desserts, cookies, cookie dough, scones, crumbcake, ruggalach, butter cookies, brownies and mini-muffins
President: Ari Margulies
Vice President: Michael Zuckerman
Year Founded: 1979
Estimated Sales: $90 Million+
Number Employees: 350
Number of Brands: 2
Square Footage: 160000
Parent Co: Fairfield Gourmet Foods Corp.
Type of Packaging: Consumer, Food Service
Types of Products Distributed:
 Frozen Food, General Merchandise

55989 Davis Coffee Co
7608 Woodway Dr
Waco, TX 76712-3801   254-772-1361
         Fax: 254-772-1395
Wholesaler/distributor of groceries and dairy products; rack jobber services available; serving the food service market
President: Robert Gianella
Estimated Sales: Less Than $500,000
Number Employees: 1-4
Types of Products Distributed:
 Food Service, Frozen Food, General Line, Rack Jobbers, Groceries & dairy products

55990 Davis Distributors of Owensboro Company
2534 Lawrin Court
Owensboro, KY 42301-4104   270-926-1558
         Fax: 270-683-5385
Wholesaler/distributor of frozen and nonfrozen food; serving the food service market
Owner: George Wathen
Number Employees: 10-19
Square Footage: 60000
Parent Co: Frosty Acre
Type of Packaging: Food Service
Private Brands Carried:
 Frosty Acres
Types of Products Distributed:
 Food Service, Frozen Food, General Line, Seafood

55991 Davis Street Fish Market
501 Davis Street
Evanston, IL 60201   847-869-3474
 Fax: 847-869-6435 davisstreetfish@gmail.com
Seafood
Contact: Ed Huelke
ehuelke@cleanplate.net
Manager: Ed Heulke
Estimated Sales: $3-5 Million
Number Employees: 50-99

55992 Davis-Le Grand Company
1365 Obispo Ave
Long Beach, CA 90804   562-597-6681
         Fax: 562-597-6796
Wholesaler/distributor of paper products, groceries, equipment and fixtures, general merchandise and frozen foods; rack jobber services available
President: Marvin Davis
VP: Michael Davis
Sales Manager: Craig Seyb
Estimated Sales: $20-50 Million
Number Employees: 20-49
Square Footage: 49000
Parent Co: Nugget
Private Brands Carried:
 Dinner Hour; Nuggett
Number of Customer Locations: 2500
Types of Products Distributed:
 Food Service, Frozen Food, General Merchandise, Rack Jobbers, Paper products, etc.

55993 Dayco Distributing
933 Ritson Road S
Oshawa, ON L1H 0A5
Canada   905-436-5336
 Fax: 905-571-6571 800-565-2762
Wholesaler/distributor of food service equipment and supplies; serving the food service market
Secretary: Susan Sheppard
Number Employees: 5-9
Square Footage: 36000
Private Brands Carried:
 Vulcan; Hobart; Garland; Libbey
Types of Products Distributed:
 Food Service, Frozen Food, General Merchandise, Foodservice equipment & supplies

55994 De Bilio Food Distributors
605 E Commercial St
Anaheim, CA 92801   714-773-9323
         Fax: 714-738-0245
President: Joseph DeBilio
VP: Joseph DeBilio
Estimated Sales: $10-20 Million
Number Employees: 10-19

55995 De Choix Specialty Foods Company
5825 52nd Avenue
Woodside, NY 11377-7402   718-507-8080
 Fax: 718-335-9150 800-332-4649
 dechoix@dechoix.com
Wholesaler/distributor and importer of specialty cheeses, chocolates, vanilla, vinegar, spices, mustards, smoked fish, dried fruits, herring, coffees, teas, grains, salami, prosciutto, preserves, fruit purees, olives, olive oilcaviar, nuts and pate
President: Gene Kaplan
CEO: Henry Kaplan
Executive VP: Bob Bruno
Number Employees: 20-49
Square Footage: 142000
Private Brands Carried:
 Sicoly; Callebaut; Fabbri
Types of Products Distributed:
 Frozen Food, General Line, Provisions/Meat, Seafood, Specialty Foods, Cheeses, chocolates, caviar, nuts, etc.

55996 De Coty Coffee Co
1920 Austin St
San Angelo, TX 76903-8704   325-655-5607
 Fax: 325-655-6837 800-588-8001
 eric@decoty.com www.decoty.com
Importer, Roaster, & Distributor of coffe. Manufacturer of coffee, tea, spices & seasonings.
CEO/President: Michael Agan
agan@decoty.com
Sales/Marketing: Bryan Baker
Operations: Ronnie Wallace
Production Manager: Eric Fischer
Purchasing: Teresa Rocha
Estimated Sales: $12 Million
Number Employees: 50-99
Square Footage: 50000
Type of Packaging: Food Service, Private Label, Bulk
Types of Products Distributed:
 Frozen Food

55997 De Leone Corp
1258 SW Lake Rd
Redmond, OR 97756-8611   541-504-8311
 Fax: 541-504-8411 sam@deleone.com
         www.cascadelabel.com
Manufacturer and exporter of pressure sensitive and custom labels; wholesaler/distributor of label dispensers
President: Samuel A DE Leone
steve@deleone.com
General Manager: David Hawes
Sales Director: Diana Jibiden
Estimated Sales: $5-10 Million
Number Employees: 20-49
Types of Products Distributed:
 Frozen Food, General Merchandise, Label dispensers

55998 De Palo & Sons Inc
9101 Yellow Brick Rd # B
Suite B
Rosedale, MD 21237-4705   410-483-1900
 Fax: 410-485-0337 800-552-9588
 depalo@depalo.com www.depalo.com
Wholesaler/distributor of food service equipment, paper and chemicals
President: Jill Martin
jill@reportmill.com
Co-Owner: Nick DePalo
Estimated Sales: $10-20 Million
Number Employees: 20-49
Type of Packaging: Private Label, Bulk
Private Brands Carried:
 Perlich; Waring; Anchor Hocking
Types of Products Distributed:
 Food Service, Frozen Food, General Merchandise, Foodservice equipment

Wholesalers & Distributors / A-Z

55999 De Vara Designs
19519 Business Center Drive
Northridge, CA 91324-3402   818-886-8177
Fax: 818-886-8460   800-433-8272
Wholesaler/distributor of advertising specialties; also, engraving available
Operations Manager: Patrick Thaney
Estimated Sales: $10-20 Million
Number Employees: 20-49
Parent Co: Morris Rosenbloom
Types of Products Distributed:
  Frozen Food, General Merchandise, Advertising specialties

56000 DeVries Imports
16700 Schoenborn Street
North Hills, CA 91343-6108   818-893-6906
Fax: 818-893-9446
Wholesaler/distributor and importer of specialty foods and confectionery products including candy and chocolates; also, basket supplies including wrap, bows, etc
President/Owner: Hugh DeVries
VP/Owner: Louise DeVries
Estimated Sales: $2.5-5 Million
Number Employees: 10-19
Square Footage: 52000
Type of Packaging: Consumer, Private Label
Types of Products Distributed:
  Frozen Food, General Line, General Merchandise, Specialty Foods, Confectionery products, etc.

56001 Dealers Food Products Co
23800 Commerce Park # D
Cleveland, OH 44122-5828   216-292-6666
Fax: 216-292-4600   www.dealersfoods.com
Wholesaler/distributor, exporter and importer of milk powders, cheese powders, flavors, snack food seasonings, industrial ingredients, candy canes, lollypops, caramels, energy candy, cough drops, wrapped hard candy and dehydrated potato products
President: Bob Glaser
bob@dealersfoods.com
Export Manager: Dennis Krall
Estimated Sales: $2.5-5 Million
Number Employees: 1-4
Square Footage: 8000
Type of Packaging: Consumer, Food Service, Private Label, Bulk
Types of Products Distributed:
  Frozen Food, General Line, Industrial ingredients, etc.

56002 Dean & Company
PO Box 26934
Salt Lake City, UT 84126-0934   801-943-1296
Wholesaler/distributor of frozen foods, provisions/meats and general line products; serving the food service market
President: E Shelledy
Manager: C Todd
Estimated Sales: $10-20 Million
Number Employees: 20-49
Square Footage: 80000
Number of Customer Locations: 290
Types of Products Distributed:
  Food Service, Frozen Food, General Line, Provisions/Meat

56003 Dean Supply Co
3500 Woodland Ave
Cleveland, OH 44115-3421   216-771-3300
Fax: 216-781-5992   800-275-3326
info@shopatdean.com   www.shopatdean.com
Wholesaler/distributor of paperware, janitorial supplies and appliances; serving the food service market
President: Larry DE Satnik
larry@deansupplyco.com
CFO: Neal Desatnik
Sales Manager: Michael Gigliotti
Operations: Dave Desatnik
Purchasing Director: Mark Desatnik
Estimated Sales: $10 Million
Number Employees: 50-99
Square Footage: 170000
Private Brands Carried:
  Libbey Glass; Pitco; South Bend; Rubbermaid; Carlisle; Dart
Number of Customer Locations: 3000
Types of Products Distributed:
  Food Service, General Line, General Merchandise, Paperware, appliances, etc.

56004 Dean's Ice Cream Dstrbtn Ctr
1253 Kingsland Dr
Batavia, IL 60510-1324   630-879-0800
Fax: 630-879-9210   deandairy.com
Wholesaler/distributor of ice cream, frozen foods, etc
Vice President: John D'Alessandro
VP: John D'Alessandro
Purchasing Agent: Joe Thielen
Number Employees: 50-99
Parent Co: Dean Foods Company
Number of Customer Locations: 600
Types of Products Distributed:
  Frozen Food, General Line, General Merchandise, Ice cream, pizza, etc.

56005 Dearborn Cash & Carry Stores
2455 S Damen Ave
Unit 100
Chicago, IL 60608   773-254-4300
Fax: 773-847-3838
Wholsaler/distributor of frozen food, general line products and general merchandise; serving the food service market
Manager: Charles Krauchen
Contact: Sandra Nunez
snunez@dearbornwholesale.com
Manager: Chuck Krauchun
Estimated Sales: $5-10 Million
Number Employees: 5-9
Parent Co: Dearborn Wholesale Grocers
Private Brands Carried:
  Parade
Number of Customer Locations: 1400
Types of Products Distributed:
  Food Service, Frozen Food, General Line, General Merchandise

56006 Dearborn Wholesale Grocers LP
1849 W 79th St
Chicago, IL 60620-5241   773-487-5656
Fax: 773-487-8225   www.dearbornwholesale.com
Wholesaler/distributor of frozen foods, general line items and general merchandise
Manager: Larry Walsh
Manager: Alana Irving
alanai@dearbornwholesale.com
Manager: Larry Walsh
Estimated Sales: $5-10 Million
Number Employees: 10-19
Parent Co: Dearborn Wholesale Grocers
Private Brands Carried:
  Parade
Types of Products Distributed:
  Frozen Food, General Line, General Merchandise

56007 Dearborn Wholesale Grocers
4525 W Madison St
Chicago, IL 60624   773-378-5353
www.dearborn-wholesale.com
Wholesaler/distributor of groceries, bakery items, private label items, frozen foods, general merchandise, general line items and meat products; serving the food service market.
Executive Vice President: Martin Friedman
Director of Operations: Keith Stirrat
Estimated Sales: $100-500 Million
Other Locations:
  Dearborn Wholesale Grocers
  Chicago, IL Dearborn Wholesale Grocers
Number of Customer Locations: 6000
Types of Products Distributed:
  Food Service, Frozen Food, General Line, General Merchandise, Provisions/Meat, Bakery items, groceries, etc.

56008 Dearborn Wholesale Grocers
1601 S Ashland Ave
Chicago, IL 60608-2012   312-421-4411
Fax: 312-421-4415   www.remodeloan.com
Wholesaler/distributor of meats, general line items, candy and frozen foods; serving the food service market and convenience stores
President: Jim Lotz
Contact: Martin Friedman
mfriedman@dearbornwholesale.com
Manager: Jim Lotz
Estimated Sales: $10-20 Million
Number Employees: 10-19
Parent Co: Dearborn Wholesale Grocers
Private Brands Carried:
  Parade; Coca Cola; Del Monte
Number of Customer Locations: 2000
Types of Products Distributed:
  Food Service, Frozen Food, General Line, Provisions/Meat, Candy

56009 Dearborn Wholesale Grocers
4525 W Madison St
Chicago, IL 60624-2230   773-378-5353
Fax: 773-378-5356   www.dearbornwholesale.com
Wholesaler/distributor of general merchandise, meats, general line items and frozen foods; serving the food service market
Manager: James Kennedy
Contact: Dawn Chambers
dchambers@dearbornwholesale.com
Manager: Jim Kennedy
Assistant Manager: Bob White
Estimated Sales: $10-20 Million
Number Employees: 10-19
Parent Co: Dearborn Wholesale Grocers
Private Brands Carried:
  Parade
Number of Customer Locations: 1600
Types of Products Distributed:
  Food Service, Frozen Food, General Line, General Merchandise, Provisions/Meat

56010 Dearborn Wholesale Grocers
4525 W Madison St
Chicago, IL 60647-4046   773-772-3000
Fax: 773-772-0291
Wholesaler/distributor of general merchandise, general line items and frozen foods; serving the food service market
Contact: Dawn Chambers
dchambers@dearbornwholesale.com
Manager: Michael Baker
Assistant Manager: Humberto Mireles
Estimated Sales: $5-10 Million
Number Employees: 5-9
Parent Co: Dearborn Wholesale Grocers
Private Brands Carried:
  Parade
Types of Products Distributed:
  Food Service, Frozen Food, General Line, General Merchandise

56011 Debbie Wright Sales
5852 E Berry St
PO Box 15554
Fort Worth, TX 76119-1803   817-429-8282
Fax: 817-429-8882   800-935-7883
www.debbiewrightsales.net
Manufacturer and wholesaler/distributor of stud welding equipment and supplies
Owner: Debbie Wright
Sls. Rep.: Allan Yarber
Estimated Sales: $1-2.5 Million
Number Employees: 5-9
Types of Products Distributed:
  Frozen Food, General Merchandise, Stud welding equipment

56012 Debragga & Spitler
65-77 Amity St
Jersey City, NJ 07304-3509
info@debragga.com
www.debragga.com
Prime cuts of beef, lamb and pork; wholesaler/distributor of further processed beef, veal, lamb and pork.
President & CEO: Marc John Sarrazin
Year Founded: 1920
Estimated Sales: $20-50 Million
Number Employees: 50-99
Number of Brands: 1
Type of Packaging: Food Service, Bulk
Types of Products Distributed:
  Food Service, Provisions/Meat, Further processed beef, lamb, etc.

56013 Deen Meat & Cooked Foods
813 E Northside Dr
PO Box 4155
Fort Worth, TX 76102-1017   817-335-2257
Fax: 817-338-9256   800-333-3953
www.deenmeat.com
Meat

Wholesalers & Distributors / A-Z

President: Danny Deen
danny77@deenmeat.com
VP: Craig Deen
VP: Matthew Deen
Business Development Manager: Steve Dumas
Quality Assurance/ R&D: Marc de Plante
Director of Partner Development: Pat Harrington
VP Operations: Joe Cholopisa
VP, Purchase: Mike Pritchard
Number Employees: 100-249

56014 Deep Creek Custom Packing
Mile 137 Sterling Highway
PO Box 39752
Ninilchik, AK 99639   907-567-3395
    Fax: 907-567-3579 800-764-0078
                  dccp@ptialaska.net
Alaska smoked salmon, halibut, canned giftpacks, custom processing and gourmet seafood
CEO: Jeff Berger
Plant Manager: Chris Baobo
Estimated Sales: $7 Million
Number Employees: 20-49
Square Footage: 24000
Types of Products Distributed:
    Frozen Food

56015 Deep Foods Inc
1090 Springfield Rd
Suite 1
Union, NJ 07083-8147   908-810-7500
    Fax: 908-810-8482 www.deepfoods.com
Indian foods such as snacks, frozen meals, ice creams and others.
Vice President: Pravin Amin
deepfoods@aol.com
VP Marketing: Archit Amin
Sales Director: Chintam Trivedi
Estimated Sales: $5-10 Million
Number Employees: 50-99
Square Footage: 120000
Type of Packaging: Consumer, Food Service, Bulk
Other Locations:
    Deep Foods
    Mississagua, CANADA, ONDeep Foods
Number of Customer Locations: 2000
Types of Products Distributed:
    Food Service, Frozen Food, Health Food, Specialty Foods, Ethinic Stores

56016 Deep Sea Products
1735 NW 79th Avenue
Doral, FL 33126-1112   305-594-3816
                  Fax: 305-594-9705
Wholesaler/distributor and importer of shrimp
President: Robert Daglio, Jr.
Estimated Sales: $500,000-$1 Million
Number Employees: 1-4
Types of Products Distributed:
    Frozen Food, Seafood

56017 Deep South Equipment Co
4201 Michoud Blvd
New Orleans, LA 70129-2229   504-254-2700
                  Fax: 504-254-0858
Wholesaler/distributor of material handling equipment
President: Charles Smith
VP: Jim Johnson
Manager: Gerald Boudreaux
gerald.boudreaux@deepsouthequipment.com
Estimated Sales: $20-50 Million
Number Employees: 20-49
Types of Products Distributed:
    Frozen Food, General Merchandise, Material handling equipment

56018 Deer Park Spring Water
50 Commerce Way
Norton, MA 02766-3313   800-325-3337
    Fax: 201-955-4050 www.deerparkwater.com
Wholesaler/distributor of water
Retail Manager: Jim McGuire
Number Employees: 250-499
Parent Co: Perrier Group of America
Private Brands Carried:
    Deer Park; Poland Springs; Great Bear
Types of Products Distributed:
    Water

56019 Dees Paper Co
1551 Azalea Rd
Mobile, AL 36693-5219   251-666-4885
    Fax: 251-666-9206 800-467-3337
                  tonymadson@deespaperco.com
                  www.deespaperco.com
Wholesaler/distributor of general merchandise including paper and janitorial supplies; serving the food service market
President: Monty Dees
montydees@deespaperco.com
Estimated Sales: $15.97 Million
Number Employees: 50-99
Square Footage: 130000
Types of Products Distributed:
    Food Service, Frozen Food, General Merchandise, Paper & janitorial supplies

56020 Deiss Sales Co. Inc.
S. Chaparral Court
Suite 270
Anaheim, CA 92808-2282   714-974-9513
    Fax: 714-974-8136 jim@deisssales.com
                  www.deisssales.com
Importer/exporter, wholesaler/distributor of all frozen seafood, all natural beef, poultry and other quality food products
Owner: James Deiss
Quality Control: Annabelle Wright
Estimated Sales: $10 Million
Number Employees: 6
Square Footage: 3000
Type of Packaging: Food Service, Private Label, Bulk
Other Locations:
    Northern CA
    Walnut Creek, CANorthern CA
Private Brands Carried:
    Royal Greenland; Paradise P&D Shrimp; Rock Shrimp; Ocean Garden Products; Aleutian Light Surimi; Captain's Harvest Surimi
Types of Products Distributed:
    Seafood, Imitation crab meat, etc.

56021 Del Bene Meats
1500 Race Street
Manor, PA 15665   724-863-1540
                  Fax: 724-863-7389
Wholesaler/distributor of provisions/meats
President: Frank Del Bene
Number Employees: 5
Number of Customer Locations: 150
Types of Products Distributed:
    Provisions/Meat

56022 Del Mar Seafood's Inc
331 Ford St
Watsonville, CA 95076-4108   831-763-3000
    Fax: 831-763-2444 www.delmarseafoods.com
Wholesaler/distributor of fresh and frozen seafood including shrimp, oysters, octopus, squid, crab, clams, scallops, etc
CEO: Joseph Cappuccio
CFO: Joseph Roggio
Sales Manager: Mary Lou Gonzales
VP COO: Alexander Luchich
Estimated Sales: $1-2.5 Million
Number Employees: 50-99
Types of Products Distributed:
    Frozen Food, Seafood, Squid, octopus, clams, crab, etc.

56023 Del Valle Food Products
1401 NW 88th Ave
Doral, FL 33172   305-592-8865
    Fax: 305-599-5288 www.delvallebrands.com
Wholesaler/distributor of general line items, health and beauty aids, paper products and microwave popcorn
President: Israel Lapciuc
Vice President: Isaac Lapci
Estimated Sales: $20-50 Million
Number Employees: 20-49
Square Footage: 100000

56024 Delicious Popcorn
300 DE Lish US Ave
Waupaca, WI 54981-1260   715-258-7683
    Fax: 715-258-1514 www.wisnack.com
Potato chips and popcorn; wholesaler/distributor of pretzels, tostados, tortillas, baked and fried corn curls, party snack mix, corn chips, raw popcorn and popping oil and gourmet popcorn products

President/Co-Owner: James Hollnbacher
CEO/Co-Owner: Jeff Hollnbacher
Marketing/Sales: Jeff Hollnbacher
Production Manager: James Hollnbacher
Purchasing Manager: James Hollnbacher
Estimated Sales: $2-5 Million
Number Employees: 10-19
Type of Packaging: Consumer, Food Service, Private Label, Bulk
Types of Products Distributed:
    Snack Foods

56025 Delisa Pallet Corporation
91-97 Blanchard St
Newark, NJ 07105   973-344-8600
    Fax: 973-344-0689 866-308-8600
    info@delisapallet.com www.delisapallet.com
Wholesaler/distributor of wooden pallets; also, scrap wood removal services available
President: John Delisa
Secretary/Treasurer: James Chichelo
VP: James Chichelo
Estimated Sales: $2.5-5 Million
Number Employees: 10-19
Types of Products Distributed:
    Frozen Food, General Merchandise, Wooden pallets

56026 Dell Enterprises
7949 Broadway
Lemon Grove, CA 91945   619-469-2100
    Fax: 619-469-1266 877-355-495
                  www.dellawards.com
Wholesaler/distributor of advertising specialties and promotional items including medals, name plates, plaques, badges, buttons, etc.; also, engraving services available
Owner: Mike Telles
Contact: John Buffington
jb@ironfish.net
Estimated Sales: Less than $500,000
Number Employees: 1-4
Number of Customer Locations: 4000
Types of Products Distributed:
    Frozen Food, General Merchandise, Advertising specialties, medals, etc.

56027 Delta Bay
2273 S G Street
Fresno, CA 93721-3435   559-266-1355
    Fax: 559-266-1439 888-869-8500
Wholesaler/distributor of food service and material handling equipment and supplies; serving the food service market
VP Sales/Marketing: Y Castanon
Number Employees: 5-9
Square Footage: 28000
Private Brands Carried:
    Amana; MenuMaster; Sharp; True; Rubbermaid; Dito Dean
Types of Products Distributed:
    Food Service, Frozen Food, General Merchandise, Foodservice & material handling equip.

56028 Delta Catfish Products
602 E Lee St
PO Box 99
Eudora, AR 71640   870-355-4192
                  Fax: 714-778-0998
Catfish
President/CEO: Thomas Marshall

56029 Delta Materials Handling Inc
4676 Clarke Rd
Memphis, TN 38141-6719   901-795-7230
    Fax: 901-362-5721 800-228-0492
                  www.deltamat.com
Wholesaler/distributor of material handling equipment
President: Greg Costa
gcosta@deltamat.com
Estimated Sales: $10-20 Million
Number Employees: 100-249
Private Brands Carried:
    Komatsu; Clark; Daywood
Types of Products Distributed:
    Frozen Food, General Merchandise, Material handling equipment

56030 Delta Pride Catfish
1301 Industrial Parkway
Indianola, MS 38751   662-887-5401
    Fax: 662-887-5950 800-228-3474
    sales@deltapride.com www.deltapride.com

Manufacturer of farm-raised catfish and wholesaler/distributor of fresh and frozen farm raised catfish and hush puppies.
President and CEO: Steve Osso
Owner: Adrian Percy
Contact: Darry Adams
dadams@deltapride.com
Year Founded: 1981
Estimated Sales: $30 Million
Number Employees: 450
Parent Co: Delta Pride Catfish
Types of Products Distributed:
 Seafood, Fresh & frozen catfish & hush puppies

56031 Demak & Company
2002 Strand Street
Galveston, TX 77550-1631   409-765-5559
             Fax: 409-763-5752
Wholesaler/distributor of frozen food and produce; serving the food service market
President: Charles Demak
Number Employees: 10-19
Types of Products Distributed:
 Food Service, Frozen Food, Produce

56032 Demma Fruit Company
11404 W Dodge Road
Suite 300
Omaha, NE 68154-2576   402-592-4000
             Fax: 402-597-3481 800-264-6150
Wholesaler/distributor of fresh and processed produce; serving the food service market
President: John Kaplan, Jr.
Chairman: John Kaplan, Sr.
VP: Thomas King
Number Employees: 100-249
Square Footage: 200000
Parent Co: John Galt Holdings
Private Brands Carried:
 Juan Chico; Nino's
Types of Products Distributed:
 Food Service, Frozen Food, General Line, General Merchandise, Provisions/Meat, Produce, Specialty Foods, Groceries & ethnic foods

56033 Den-Tex Restaurant Supply
102 Maple St
Denton, TX 76201-6826   940-382-2229
             Fax: 940-565-1994
Wholesaler/distributor of restaurant and refrigeration equipment, ovens, smallwares, ice makers and dispensers and tables and chairs
President: Stephen Kniatt
Estimated Sales: $1-2.5 Million
Number Employees: 5-9
Types of Products Distributed:
 Frozen Food, General Merchandise, Ovens, tables, chairs, ice makers, etc.

56034 Deng's
35430 Jefferson Ave
Harrison Twp, MI 48045-3247   586-790-5939
             Fax: 810-463-8651 800-968-3364
Wholesaler/distributor of general line and dairy products and frozen and specialty foods, meat, baked goods, equipment and seafood; serving the food service market
Owner: Ming Psam
Controller: Robert Schoen
Sales Manager: Michael Klimer
Estimated Sales: $300,000-500,000
Number Employees: 1-4
Square Footage: 158800
Private Brands Carried:
 NIFDA; Deng's
Types of Products Distributed:
 Food Service, Frozen Food, General Line, General Merchandise, Provisions/Meat, Seafood, Specialty Foods, Baked goods, equipment, etc.

56035 Dent Electrical Supply Company
39 Newtown Rd
Danbury, CT 06810-6219   203-743-5578
             Fax: 203-798-7882 800-879-3368
             www.ew-inc.com
Wholesaler/distributor of electrical supplies, bulbs and lighting fixtures
Manager: Tony Piekarski
VP: Richard Godfrey
Sales Manager: Sal Cerminaro
Estimated Sales: $10-20 Million
Number Employees: 20-49
Square Footage: 29000
Private Brands Carried:
 Sylvania; Hubbell; ITE Siemans
Number of Customer Locations: 2200
Types of Products Distributed:
 Frozen Food, General Merchandise, Electrical supplies & lighting fixtures

56036 Dentici Produce
138 N McKean St
Kittanning, PA 16201   724-543-1982
Wholesaler/distributor of produce
President: Mark Dentici
Estimated Sales: $3-5 Million
Number Employees: 1-4
Types of Products Distributed:
 Produce

56037 Denton Dairy Products Inc
116 N Pearman Ave
Cleveland, MS 38732-2632   662-843-9451
             Fax: 662-843-9454
Wholesaler/distributor of dairy products including milk and ice cream
Owner: Butler Denton
Estimated Sales: $10-20 Million
Number Employees: 10-19
Types of Products Distributed:
 Frozen Food, General Line

56038 Denver Restaurant Equipment Company
6778 E NC 150 Hwy
Sherills Ford, NC 28037-0340   704-483-3213
             Fax: 704-483-5095 800-222-9746
             amvhaughn@denverequipment.com
Wholesaler/distributor of restaurant equipment designed and dealer supplies including silverware; serving the food service market
President/CEO: C. Scott Langham
CFO: Don King
Contact: Conor Owsley
conorowsley@denverequipment.com
General Manager: Todd Brown
Estimated Sales: $10,000,000
Number Employees: 30
Square Footage: 30000
Types of Products Distributed:
 Food Service, Frozen Food, General Merchandise, Restaurant equipment & supplies

56039 Dependable Food Corp
29 Executive Ave
Edison, NJ 08817-6007   732-287-8838
             Fax: 718-435-5538 877-488-7055
             www.dependablefood.com
Food distributor
President: Sam Blau
sa.b@dependablefood.com
Estimated Sales: $10-20 Million
Number Employees: 1-4

56040 Dependable Plastics & Supls
1215 38th St
Brooklyn, NY 11218-1928   718-437-5000
             Fax: 718-437-5044 info@dependableplastic.com
             www.dependableplastic.com
Wholesaler/distributor of plasticware; serving the food service market
Owner: A Budinski
ab@dependableplastic.com
Estimated Sales: Less Than $500,000
Number Employees: 1-4
Types of Products Distributed:
 Food Service, Frozen Food, General Merchandise, Plasticware

56041 Dere Street
5 Shelter Rock Road
Unit 5D
Danbury, CT 06810   203-797-9386
             Fax: 203-797-0714 www.derestreet.com
Scones and shortbread
President: David Dere
Vice President: Robin Dere

56042 Designs Furnishings & Eqpt Inc
889 Brentwood Dr
Daytona Beach, FL 32117-4704   386-252-4728
             Fax: 386-253-8059
Wholesaler/distributor of food service equipment; serving the food service market
President: Garrett Mc Kernan Jr
CEO: Garritt McKernan
Estimated Sales: $1-3 Million
Number Employees: 5-9
Private Brands Carried:
 Hobart; Market Forge; Thermo Kool
Number of Customer Locations: 500
Types of Products Distributed:
 Food Service, Frozen Food, General Merchandise, Foodservice equipment

56043 Destileria Serralles Inc
P.O. Box 198
Mercedita, PR 00715-0198   787-840-1000
             Fax: 787-840-1155
Rum, vodka, gin, cordials and wine; importer of scotch; exporter of rum; wholesaler/distributor of general merchandise
President & CEO: Felix Serralles, Jr.
Chief Financial Officer: Jorge Vazquez
Product Quality Director: Roberto Pantoja
Chief Marketing Officer: Gabriela Ripepi
State Manager: Vanessa Gehl
Human Resources Director: Daniel Beautista
Estimated Sales: $28.5 Million
Number Employees: 370
Square Footage: 18777
Type of Packaging: Consumer, Private Label, Bulk
Types of Products Distributed:
 Frozen Food, General Merchandise

56044 Detroit Popcorn
12843 Greenfield Road
Detroit, MI 48227-2163   313-835-3600
             800-642-2676
Wholesaler/distributor of specialty foods and equipment
President: R Jasgur
VP: R Jasgur
Contact: David Barber
david.barber@detroitpopcorn.com
Estimated Sales: $5-10 Million
Number Employees: 50-99
Number of Customer Locations: 6500
Types of Products Distributed:
 Frozen Food, General Merchandise, Specialty Foods, Equipment

56045 Deverell Equipment
P.O.Box 357
Leeds, AL 35094-0006   205-699-2562
             Fax: 205-699-3547 800-783-5933
Wholesaler/distributor of refurbished meat and poultry processing equipment
President: Don Deverell
Treasurer: Debra Watson
VP: Don Deverell, Jr.
Estimated Sales: $1-2.5 Million
Number Employees: 5-9
Types of Products Distributed:
 Frozen Food, General Merchandise, Refurbished meat & poultry equipment

56046 Deville Restaurant Equipment & Supply Company
1810 N Interstate 35 E
Lancaster, TX 75134-2610   972-296-9271
             Fax: 972-296-9337
Wholesaler/distributor of new and used restaurant equipment; serving the food service market
President: Sonny Gerard
VP: Dean Gerard
Estimated Sales: $5-10 Million
Number Employees: 10-19
Square Footage: 112000
Parent Co: DeVille Enterprises
Private Brands Carried:
 Hobart; Delfield; Dean; US Range; Star; Blodgett
Types of Products Distributed:
 Food Service, Frozen Food, General Merchandise, New & used restaurant equipment

56047 Dharma Bars
             sales@dharmabars.com
             www.dharmabars.com
Organic, gluten free, and vegan energy bars
Founder: James Ricciuti
Types of Products Distributed:
 General Line

Wholesalers & Distributors / A-Z

56048 Di Cola's Seafood
10754 S Western Ave
Chicago, IL 60643-3199   773-238-7071
Fax: 773-238-8337
www.dicolasseafoodbeverly.com
Seafood
Owner: Robert Di Cola
Estimated Sales: $5-10 Million
Number Employees: 20-49

56049 (HQ)Di Mare Fresh Inc
4629 Diplomacy Rd
Fort Worth, TX 76155-2621   817-385-3000
Fax: 817-385-3015 www.dimarefresh.com
Growers, packers and distributors of fresh fruits and vegetables.
President: Paul DiMare
CFO: Cheryl Taylor
cheryl.taylor@dimarefresh.com
Year Founded: 1930
Number Employees: 50-99
Type of Packaging: Consumer, Food Service, Private Label, Bulk
Types of Products Distributed:
  Frozen Food

56050 DiGregorio Food Products
5200 Daggett Ave
St Louis, MO 63110   314-776-1062
Fax: 314-776-3954 www.digregoriofoods.com
Sausage, meat balls and spaghetti sauce
President: Dora Di Gregorio
d.digregorio@digregoriofoods.com
CEO: John DiGregorio
Estimated Sales: $.5-1 million
Number Employees: 20-49
Square Footage: 200000
Type of Packaging: Food Service, Private Label
Types of Products Distributed:
  Food Service, Frozen Food, Provisions/Meat, Specialty Foods

56051 DiLeo Brothers
23 Commercial Street
Waterbury, CT 06702-1002   203-759-3600
Fax: 203-759-3606 800-441-4762
Wholesaler/distributor and exporter of sugar, butter, cheese, tea, groceries, meats, private label items, dairy products, frozen foods, general merchandise, etc.; serving independent retailers; rack jobber services available
President: J DiLeo J.
CEO: J C Lord
VP: John Dileo
Marketing: Christine Dileo
Operations: Rich Bellemarc
Estimated Sales: $14 Million
Number Employees: 20-49
Number of Products: 8500
Square Footage: 170000
Private Brands Carried:
  Arizona Tea; Hornell Brewing
Number of Customer Locations: 770
Types of Products Distributed:
  Frozen Food, General Line, General Merchandise, Provisions/Meat, Dollar Store Items

56052 DiNovo Produce Company
135 Wilson Street
Newark, OH 43055-4921   740-345-4025
Fax: 740-349-7209
Processor and wholesaler/distributor of produce and dairy; and some wholesaler/distributor of frozen foods
President: Mark DiNovo
Estimated Sales: $500,000
Number Employees: 4
Types of Products Distributed:
  Food Service, Frozen Food, General Line, Provisions/Meat, Produce, Spices

56053 Dial Industries Inc
31 Hamlet Dr
Plainview, NY 11803-1532   516-367-2037
Fax: 718-523-4259 www.dialindustries.com
Wholesaler/distributer of closeout items including groceries, frozen foods, general merchandise, potatoes, soups, ketchup, tomato paste, canned fruits and vegetables, condiments, juices, honey, sauces, etc
President: Steven Maller
CFO & Treasurer: Natasha Mayo
VP & Secretary: Janee Mallor
Executive Director & VP of Sales: Joanne Valentin
Number Employees: 5-9
Square Footage: 80000
Private Brands Carried:
  Palazzo
Number of Customer Locations: 300
Types of Products Distributed:
  Food Service, Frozen Food, General Line, General Merchandise, Specialty Foods, Soups, ketchup, tomato paste, etc.

56054 Diamond Chemical & Supply Co
524 S Walnut St # B
Wilmington, DE 19801-5243   302-656-7786
Fax: 302-656-3039 800-355-7786
sales@diamondchemical.com
www.diamondchemical.com
Wholesaler/distributor of paper products, commercial dishwashing and laundry chemicals, floor maintenance and janitorial equipment and insecticides
President: Susan Hartzel
susan@diamondchemical.com
CFO: Saeed Malik
VP: Richard Ventresca
Sales Manager: Gene Mirolli
Warehouse: Ryan Rynar
Estimated Sales: $5 Million
Number Employees: 20-49
Square Footage: 52000
Private Brands Carried:
  Airwick/Airkem (Odor control chemicals); Unikem (Dishwashing chemicals); Butchers (Floor maintenance chemicals); James River (Paper products); Kent (Floor maintenance equipment)
Types of Products Distributed:
  Food Service

56055 Diamond Herpanacine Assoc
1518 Grove Ave # 2b
Suite #2B, Dept. #WP9
Jenkintown, PA 19046-2302   215-885-6880
Fax: 215-885-6884 888-467-4200
herpana@aol.com www.diamondformulas.com
Wholesaler/distributor of nutritional and dietary supplements; custom formulations available
Director/Managing Partner: Leslie Anne Diamond
leslie@diamondformulas.com
Vice President: Jay Jacobs
Research & Development: Wayne Diamond, N.D.
Sales Director: Leslie Diamond
Public Relations: Laura Marcoux
Director Special Projects: Deborah Jacobs-Wagner
Estimated Sales: $1-3 Million
Number Employees: 10-19
Square Footage: 8000
Private Brands Carried:
  Herpanacine; Healthy Horizons; Diamond Mind; Diamond Etern-L Renewal Support System
Types of Products Distributed:
  Nutritional supplement combination

56056 Diamond Nutrition
2219 Lee Ave
South El Monte, CA 91733-2509   626-279-6999
Fax: 626-279-1699
Wholesaler/distributor, importer and exporter of health food and general line items including fish oil and lecithin
President: George Liu
Estimated Sales: $96,000
Number Employees: 1-4
Private Brands Carried:
  Diamond
Types of Products Distributed:
  Frozen Food, General Line, Health Food, Fish oil, lecithin, etc.

56057 Diamond Reef Seafood
24709 Louisiana Highway 333
Abbeville, LA 70510   337-893-5844
Wholesaler/distributor of shrimp
Owner: Johnny Scott
Estimated Sales: Less than $500,000
Number Employees: 1-4
Types of Products Distributed:
  Frozen Food, Seafood, Shrimp

56058 Diamond Seafood
204 N Edgewood Avenue
Wood Dale, IL 60191-1610   630-787-1100
Fax: 630-787-1309
Seafood
President: Thomas Hannagan
Contact: Thomas Hanigan
diamondseafood@yahoo.com
Estimated Sales: $5-10 Million
Number Employees: 10-19

56059 Dicarlo Distributors Inc
1630 N Ocean Ave
Holtsville, NY 11742
800-342-2756
www.dicarlofood.com
Wholesaler/distributor of groceries, dairy, private label and bakery items, general merchandise, meats, frozen foods, seafood and produce; serving the food service market.
President: John Di Carlo
Year Founded: 1963
Estimated Sales: $50-100 Million
Number Employees: 50-99
Types of Products Distributed:
  Food Service, Frozen Food, General Line, General Merchandise, Provisions/Meat, Produce, Seafood, Dairy & bakery products

56060 Dick Dunphy Advertising Specialties
189 Berdan Ave
#107
Wayne, NJ 07470   973-513-9393
Fax: 973-513-9391 dunphyadv@optimum.net
www.dunphyadv.com
Wholesaler/distributor of general merchandise including advertising specialties and wall calendars
President: Dick Dunphy
VP: Rich Dunphy
Number Employees: 5-9
Square Footage: 4800
Private Brands Carried:
  Cross; Lenox
Number of Customer Locations: 60
Types of Products Distributed:
  Frozen Food, General Merchandise, Advertising specialties

56061 Dickerson & Quinn
4000 Executive Parkway
Suite 160
San Ramon, CA 94583-4314   925-904-5300
Fax: 925-256-8880
Wholesaler/distributor and exporter of confectionery items, meats, private label items, groceries and general merchandise; serving the food service market
President: D Dickerson
VP: R Quinn
Estimated Sales: $20-50 Million
Number Employees: 5-9
Private Brands Carried:
  Proctor & Gamble; Hormel; Kellogg's; Campbell's; Real Fresh; Best Foods
Types of Products Distributed:
  Food Service, Frozen Food, General Line, General Merchandise, Provisions/Meat, Groceries, confectionery items, etc.

56062 Dickerson Foods
1550 Likens Road
Marion, OH 43302-8652   740-383-3630
Fax: 740-383-4199 800-451-3663
Wholesaler/distributor of frozen foods, general line items, produce, meats, seafood and specialty foods; serving the food service market
President: Kent Smith
Secretary: Joe Kraus
Estimated Sales: $5-10 Million
Number Employees: 20-49
Square Footage: 100000
Private Brands Carried:
  Pleezing; Dickerson Foods
Number of Customer Locations: 700
Types of Products Distributed:
  Food Service, Frozen Food, General Line, Provisions/Meat, Produce, Seafood, Specialty Foods

56063 Dickson Brothers
8170 E 46th St
Tulsa, OK 74145-4821   918-628-1285
Fax: 918-665-8326
Wholesaler/distributor, importer and exporter of water treatment systems including purification, reverse osmosis and ultra violet applications; also, portable systems

President: John Hambrick
Vice President: Jay Hambrick
jayhambrick@hfinctul.com
Sales: Jim Mangette
Estimated Sales: $2.5-5 Million
Number Employees: 5-9
Square Footage: 20000
Types of Products Distributed:
 Frozen Food, General Merchandise, Water treatment systems

56064 Dierks Foods
1616 Elmwood Road
Rockford, IL 61103-1239 815-877-7031
Fax: 815-877-0198
Wholesaler/distributor of groceries, meat, produce, dairy products, frozen food, baked goods, equipment and fixtures, general merchandise, private label items and seafood; serving the food service market
President: Ronald Dierks
VP Finance: Richard Tones
Estimated Sales: $10-20 Million
Number Employees: 1-4
Square Footage: 120000
Parent Co: Waukesha
Number of Customer Locations: 2000
Types of Products Distributed:
 Food Service, Frozen Food, General Line, General Merchandise, Provisions/Meat, Produce, Seafood, Groceries, etc.

56065 Difeo & Sons Poultry Inc
1075 Grant St
Akron, OH 44301 330-773-1927
www.jimdifeoscatering.com
Wholesaler/distributor of eggs and poultry.
Owner: Jim DiFeo
Year Founded: 1918
Estimated Sales: Less Than $500,000
Number Employees: 1-4
Square Footage: 40
Types of Products Distributed:
 Frozen Food, General Line, Provisions/Meat, Eggs & poultry

56066 (HQ)Diggs Packing Company
1207 Rogers St
Columbia, MO 65201-4796 573-449-2995
Fax: 573-449-3163
Beef, ham, sausage, meat packing services, distributes fresh meat, provides slaughtering
Owner: Dale Diggs
Public Relations: Dan Reynolds
Estimated Sales: $14.10 Million
Number Employees: 20-49
Type of Packaging: Consumer
Types of Products Distributed:
 Frozen Food

56067 Digital Monitoring Products
2500 N Partnership Blvd
Springfield, MO 65803-8877 417-831-9362
Fax: 417-831-1325 888-266-2826
info@dmp.com www.dmp.com
Wholesaler/distributor of general merchandise including fire alarms and systems
President: Rick Britton
rbritton@dmp.com
General Manager: David Parker
Number Employees: 100-249
Number of Customer Locations: 600
Types of Products Distributed:
 Frozen Food, General Merchandise, Fire alarms & systems

56068 Dilgard Frozen Foods
830 Hayden St
Fort Wayne, IN 46803-1142 260-422-7531
Fax: 260-426-0212 www.dilgardfoods.com
Wholesaler/distributor of produce, equipment/fixtures, general merchandise, provisions/meats, frozen foods, specialty foods and ice cream; serving the food service market
President: Kevin Geesman
kgeesman@dilgardfoods.com
VP Merchandising: K Geeasman
Estimated Sales: $20-50 Million
Number Employees: 20-49
Square Footage: 40000
Number of Customer Locations: 125
Types of Products Distributed:
 Food Service, Frozen Food, General Merchandise, Provisions/Meat, Produce, Specialty Foods

56069 (HQ)Dillon Provision Co
408 N 1st Ave
Dillon, SC 29536-2804 843-774-9491
Fax: 843-774-5161
Wholesaler/distributor of meat products including beef and pork; serving the food service and retail markets
President: Daniel D Bozard
danbozard@bellsouth.net
Estimated Sales: $11 Million
Number Employees: 20-49
Square Footage: 60000
Type of Packaging: Bulk
Other Locations:
 Dillon Provision Co.
 Manning, SC Dillon Provision Co.
Private Brands Carried:
 Lundy Pork; Excel Beef; Farmland; Carolina Turkeys
Number of Customer Locations: 350
Types of Products Distributed:
 Food Service, Provisions/Meat, Beef & pork

56070 Dillons Food Stores
2700 E 4th Ave
Hutchinson, KS 67501-1903 620-665-5511
Fax: 620-669-3167 www.dillons.com
Supermarket chain
President: Colleen Juergensen
colleen.juergensen@kroger.com
Plant Manager: Albert Garcia
Number Employees: 100-249
Parent Co: Kroger

56071 Dimond Tager Company Products
2801 E Hillsborough Ave
Tampa, FL 33610-4410 813-238-3111
Fax: 813-238-3114
Manufacturer and wholesaler/distributor of produce
President: Raymond Charlton
Estimated Sales: $1.7 Million
Number Employees: 10
Square Footage: 16000
Type of Packaging: Consumer, Food Service, Bulk
Types of Products Distributed:
 Frozen Food, Produce

56072 Dinetz Restaurant Equipment
844 Caledonia Road
Toronto, ON M6B 3Y1
Canada 416-368-8657
Fax: 416-368-3627 www.dinetz.ca
Wholesaler/distributor of restaurant equipment and supplies; serving the food service market
Number Employees: 10-19
Private Brands Carried:
 Garland; Hobart; Libbey
Types of Products Distributed:
 Food Service, Frozen Food, General Merchandise, Restaurant equipment & supplies

56073 Dino's Sausage & Meat Co Inc
722 Catherine St
Utica, NY 13501-1304 315-732-2661
Fax: 315-732-3094 www.dinossausage.com
Sausage and beef products; wholesaler/distributor of bacon, ham, pork, lamb, etc
President: Chris Houser
fchousercpa@yahoo.com
Vice President: Anthony Ferrucci
Estimated Sales: $10-20 Million
Number Employees: 10-19
Type of Packaging: Consumer
Types of Products Distributed:
 Frozen Food, Provisions/Meat, Bacon, ham, pork, lamb, etc.

56074 Dino-Meat Company
PO Box 95
White House, TN 37188-0095 615-643-1022
Fax: 615-643-1022 877-557-6493
Emu meat including steaks, ground, breakfast sausage, summer sausage, hot dogs, hot links, meat balls, snack sticks and jerky. Also emu oil and emu oil products
President: Neil Williams
Type of Packaging: Consumer, Food Service
Types of Products Distributed:
 Frozen Food

56075 Dipasa USA Inc
6600 Ruben Torres Sr Blvd # B
Brownsville, TX 78526-6954 956-831-4072
Fax: 956-831-5893 info@dipasausa.com
www.dipasausa.com
Tahini and sesame seeds, raisins, oil, flour and candy; wholesaler/distributor of onion and cheese breadsticks, baked snacks, halvah and confectionery items, natural colors, oleoresins
Vice President: Garry Lowder
garrysula@dipasausa.com
Vice President: Garry Lowder
garrysula@dipasausa.com
Vice President, Marketing: Garry Lowder
Estimated Sales: $8 Million
Number Employees: 10-19
Number of Brands: 2
Number of Products: 10
Square Footage: 80000
Type of Packaging: Consumer, Food Service, Private Label, Bulk
Private Brands Carried:
 Dipasa; Sesamin; Biladi
Types of Products Distributed:
 Frozen Food, General Line, Health Food, Specialty Foods, Baked snacks, confectionery items, etc.

56076 Direct Media
12431 Conquistador Way
San Diego, CA 92128-2152 858-485-8481
Fax: 858-485-8481 855-477-7200
john@directmediapromo.com
www.directmediapromo.com
Wholesaler/distributor of advertising specialties
President: John D Rauch
john@directmediapromo.com
Estimated Sales: Less Than $500,000
Number Employees: 1-4
Number of Customer Locations: 250
Types of Products Distributed:
 Frozen Food, General Merchandise, Advertising specialties

56077 Direct Promotions
29395 Agoura Rd # 207
Suite 207
Agoura Hills, CA 91301-2514 818-591-9010
Fax: 818-591-2071 800-444-7706
sales@directpromotions.net
www.directpromotions.net
Wholesaler/distributor of advertising specialties
Owner: Randy Perry
randy@directpromotions.net
Sales Director: Randy Perry
Estimated Sales: $2.5-5 Million
Number Employees: 1-4
Number of Customer Locations: 5000
Types of Products Distributed:
 Frozen Food, General Merchandise, Advertising specialties

56078 Direct Seafood
Unit 10-14 Ceder Way Industrial estate
Camley Street, LN N1C 4PD 120-658-4790
Fax: 727-398-1649 sales@directseafoods.co.uk
www.directseafoods.co.uk
Wholesaler/distributor of frozen seafood
Chief Executive: Stephen Oswald
Groups Operations officer: Brian Hall
COO: Paul Gower
Group Sales Director: Gary Apps
Estimated Sales: $3-5 Million
Number Employees: 5-9
Number of Customer Locations: 40
Types of Products Distributed:
 Frozen Food, Seafood

56079 Dirt Killer Pressure Washer
1708 Whitehead Rd # 103
Gwynn Oak, MD 21207-4021 410-944-9966
Fax: 410-944-8866 800-544-1188
info@dirtkiller.com www.dirtkiller.com
Manufacturer and wholesaler/distributor of pressure washers, accessories and cleaning soaps
President: Jeffrey Paulding
jpaulding@dirtkiller.com
Sales Director: Ken Rankin
Estimated Sales: $3-5 Million
Number Employees: 5-9
Square Footage: 60000
Types of Products Distributed:
 Frozen Food, General Merchandise

Wholesalers & Distributors / A-Z

56080 Discount Equipment Intl
3908 N 29th Ave
Hollywood, FL 33020-1010 954-920-9499
Fax: 954-920-9802 800-779-3028
Wholesaler/distributor of freezers, furniture, bakers' equipment, etc.; serving the food service market
President: Dennis Braff
Estimated Sales: $5-10 Million
Number Employees: 10-19
Square Footage: 28000
Private Brands Carried:
 Hobart; Vulcan; Metro
Number of Customer Locations: 500
Types of Products Distributed:
 Food Service, Frozen Food, General Merchandise, Freezers, bakers' equipment, etc.

56081 Dishaka Imports
11300 S Sam Houston Pkwy W
Houston, TX 77031-2350 832-831-3456
Fax: 713-988-2905 888-424-4724
www.zafaranirice.com
Importer and wholesaler/distributor of bismati rice, snacks, beverages-fruit juices, biscuits and cookies
Owner: Kawal Oberoi
Estimated Sales: $20 Million
Number Employees: 5-9
Square Footage: 100000
Type of Packaging: Consumer, Food Service, Private Label, Bulk
Private Brands Carried:
 Chirag; Maxaca, Chispas Manyou, Zaffarani, India Chef
Number of Customer Locations: 450
Types of Products Distributed:
 General Merchandise, Specialty Foods

56082 Dispenser Juice
4307 Vineland Road
Suite H-9
Orlando, FL 32811 510-346-2200
Fax: 510-357-9500 888-354-5525
www.dispenserbeverages.com
Wholesaler/distributor of frozen fruit juice concentrates and coffee; serving the food service market
President: Vince Vacolini
Estimated Sales: $10-20 Million
Number Employees: 50-99
Number of Customer Locations: 1820
Types of Products Distributed:
 Food Service, Frozen Food, General Line, Frozen fruit juice concentrates, etc.

56083 Dispenser Services
117 Beaver St
Waltham, MA 02452 781-891-6595
Fax: 781-891-7576
Wholesaler/distributor of fruit juice concentrate
Contact: Will Crosby
will.crosby@dispenserservices.com
Estimated Sales: $20-50 Million
Number Employees: 20-49
Types of Products Distributed:
 Frozen Food, Fruit juice

56084 Distribution Kowloon
1555 Boul Provencher
Brossard, QC J4W 1Z3
Canada 450-444-8384
Fax: 450-444-8254
Wholesaler/distributor of frozen and health foods, general merchandise, general line items, provisions/meats, produce, seafood, produce and specialty food items; serving the food service market
Owner: Florence Ma
Types of Products Distributed:
 Food Service, Frozen Food, General Line, General Merchandise, Health Food, Provisions/Meat, Produce, Seafood, Specialty Foods

56085 Distribution Plus
825 Green Bay Rd
Wilmette, IL 60091-2597 847-256-8289
Fax: 847-256-8299
Wholesaler/distributor of frozen food, general line items, specialty and health foods, ethnic foods, produce and seafood; serving the food service and retail markets
CEO/President: Daniel O'Connell
Number Employees: 10-19
Square Footage: 2800000
Parent Co: IDB Holdings

Other Locations:
 Distribution Plus
 Mesa, AZDistribution Plus
Types of Products Distributed:
 Food Service, Frozen Food, General Line, Health Food, Produce, Seafood, Specialty Foods

56086 Diverse Sales
5796 Ward Court
Virginia Beach, VA 23455-3323 757-460-2404
Fax: 757-363-8170
Wholesaler/distributor of groceries and general merchandise; serving the food service market
President: P Damalas
Treasurer: T Damalas
VP: Stella Damalas
Number Employees: 5-9
Square Footage: 140000
Number of Customer Locations: 150
Types of Products Distributed:
 Food Service, Frozen Food, General Line, General Merchandise, Groceries

56087 Diversified FoodserviceSupply, LLC
607 W Dempster St
Mt. Prospect, IL 60056
dfsupply.com
Maintenance repair and operation parts for the foodservice industry.
President & CEO: Jeff King
Year Founded: 2012
Estimated Sales: K

56088 Divine Ice Cream Company
311 E Clarendon Street
Arlington Hts, IL 60004-4706 847-398-0095
Wholesaler/distributor of ice cream; serving the food service market
President: Joe Martalini
Number Employees: 1-4
Private Brands Carried:
 Food for the Angels
Types of Products Distributed:
 Food Service, Frozen Food, General Line, Ice cream

56089 Dixie Advertising Company
1 Lamar St NW
Rome, GA 30165-2221 706-235-5252
Fax: 706-235-2544 dixieadvertising@comcast.net
dixielogomall.espwebsite.com
Wholesaler/distributor of advertising specialties including calendars, flags, pennants and banners
President: William Hooper
Estimated Sales: $.5-1 million
Number Employees: 1-4
Number of Customer Locations: 200
Types of Products Distributed:
 Frozen Food, General Merchandise, Advertising specialties

56090 Dixie Equipment Co
6918 Kinro Rd
Liberty, NC 27298-8528 336-622-4202
Fax: 336-622-6050 www.edu-env.com
Wholesaler/distributor of deli equipment; serving the food service market
President: Brian Gilbert
VP: Dennis Bollinger
Business Develpoment: Gary Davis
Manager: Donna Gordon
Office Manager: Donna Gordon
Number Employees: 5-9
Private Brands Carried:
 Alto-Shaam Hot Deli Equipment; Crispy Lite Fryer; Harot Rotisseries; Promolux Lights
Types of Products Distributed:
 Food Service, Frozen Food, General Merchandise, Deli equipment

56091 Dixie Lily Foods
251-457-7641
info@chinadollrice.com
www.dixielily.com
Wholesaler/distributor of corn meal products; serving the food service market.
President: Harris Morrissette
Vice President, Sales: Gerald Baggett
Estimated Sales: $20-50 Million
Number Employees: 20-49
Types of Products Distributed:
 Food Service, Frozen Food, General Line, Corn meal products

56092 Dixie Mart
P.O.Box 5040
Huntsville, AL 35814-5040 256-430-4356
Fax: 256-721-1893
Wholesaler/distributor of food service equipment
Owner: Ken Christian
Estimated Sales: $1-3 Million
Number Employees: 1-4
Parent Co: Dixie Store Fixtures
Private Brands Carried:
 Polar; Hobart; Frymaster
Types of Products Distributed:
 Food Service, Frozen Food, General Merchandise, Foodservice equipment

56093 (HQ)Dixie Store Fixtures & Sales
2425 1st Ave N
Birmingham, AL 35203-4395 205-322-2442
Fax: 205-322-2445 800-323-4943
www.dixiestorefixtures.com
Wholesaler/distributor of kitchen supplies and equipment, furniture, refrigeration equipment, etc.; serving the food service market; also, contracting services available
President: Marty Fonner
laurindaloggin11@yahoo.com
CEO: Frances Cypress
Estimated Sales: $5-10 Million
Number Employees: 20-49
Square Footage: 520000
Other Locations:
 Dixie Store Fixtures & Sales
 Birmingham, ALDixie Store Fixtures & Sales
Number of Customer Locations: 250
Types of Products Distributed:
 Food Service, Frozen Food, General Merchandise, Commercial kitchen equipment & supplies

56094 Dixon's Fisheries
1807 N Main St
East Peoria, IL 61611-2193 800-373-1457
Fax: 309-694-0539 800-373-1457
internetsales@dixonsseafood.com
www.dixonsseafood.com
Appetizers, caviar, squid, dips, spreads, marinades, sauces, fresh fish & shellfish, frozen fish & shellfish, smoked fish, exotic meats
President: Robert Dixon
Principal: James Dixon
Estimated Sales: $20-50 Million
Number Employees: 5-9

56095 Dobert's Dairy
68 3rd St
Glens Falls, NY 12801-4126 518-792-3415
Fax: 518-798-8595 800-727-2051
Wholesaler and distributor of ice cream; wholesaler/distributor of dairy products and nonfood items; serving the food service market
President: Norm Dobert
General Manager: Scott Dobert
Estimated Sales: $10-20,000,000
Number Employees: 10-19
Type of Packaging: Consumer, Food Service, Private Label
Types of Products Distributed:
 Food Service, Frozen Food, Dairy products & non-food items

56096 Dockmasters Inc
4436 Worth St
Los Angeles, CA 90063-2538 818-843-0808
Fax: 323-222-6381 800-439-9808
servcor@dockmasters.com
Wholesaler/distributor of general merchandise including docks, doors, lifts and material handling equipment
President: Nicholas Davis
nick@dockmasters.com
Sales: Mike Yaeger
Sales Director: Richard Yousko
Estimated Sales: $1-2.5 Million
Number Employees: 20-49
Parent Co: Eagle Material Handling
Private Brands Carried:
 Dockmasters; DLM; W.B. McGuire; Flexon
Types of Products Distributed:
 General Merchandise, Docks, doors, lifts, etc.

56097 Dockside Seafood & Specs Inc
1528 Highway 11 N
Picayune, MS 39466-2028 601-749-0400
Fax: 601-749-0402 800-516-9232
Wholesaler/distributor of seafood

Owner: Pat Carbone
sales@docksideseafood.net
Estimated Sales: Less than $500,000
Number Employees: 10-19
Types of Products Distributed:
  Frozen Food, Seafood

56098 Doerle Food Svc
4980 Flournoy Lucas Rd
Shreveport, LA 71129-5105   318-686-2186
   Fax: 318-688-2623 800-737-2484
   www.doerlefoods.com
Wholesaler/distributor of frozen foods, general merchandise, general line products, provisions/meats and seafood; serving the institutional food service market
Manager: David Whitener
david.whitener@doerlefoodservice.com
Sales Manager: Blaine Rabalis
Sales Manager: Blaine Rabalis
Manager: David Whitener
david.whitener@doerlefoodservice.com
Division Manager: R Whitener
Estimated Sales: $20-50 Million
Number Employees: 50-99
Square Footage: 22500
Parent Co: Doerele
Types of Products Distributed:
  Food Service, Frozen Food, General Line, General Merchandise, Provisions/Meat, Seafood, Groceries & cleaning supplies

56099 (HQ)Doerle Food Svc LLC
113 Kol Dr
Broussard, LA 70518-3825   337-252-8551
   Fax: 337-252-8558 800-256-1631
   www.doerlefoods.com
Fresh and frozen meats and poultry, a wide variety of beverages and chemical supplies, also includes seafood, gourmet foods, fresh produce, dry groceries, dairy products, disposables, small ware and table top items, specialtyhealthcare products and janitorial supplies
President & CEO: Allen Boudreaux
VP Operations & Transportation: John Romero
VP Sales & Marketing: Charlie Martin
VP Purchasing & Merchandising: Rick Blum
Year Founded: 1950
Estimated Sales: $20-50 Million
Number Employees: 100-249
Other Locations:
  Doerle Food Service
  Shreveport, LADoerle Food Service

56100 Doggett Equipment Services Group
9111 N Freeway
Houston, TX 77037   281-249-4600
   www.doggett.com
Wholesaler/distributor of material handling equipment.
Co-Head: Jim Flowers
Co-Head: Ken Townsend
Year Founded: 1993
Estimated Sales: $50-100 Million
Number Employees: 100-249
Private Brands Carried:
  Toyota
Types of Products Distributed:
  Frozen Food, General Merchandise, Material handling equipment

56101 Dol Cice' Gelato Company
PO Box 343
Yardley, PA 19067   215-499-5661
   Fax: 215-493-6348 Info@DolCice.com
   www.dolcice.com
Italian water ices
President: Laurence Dobelle
Type of Packaging: Food Service, Private Label
Types of Products Distributed:
  Frozen Food, Italian water ices

56102 (HQ)Dole & Bailey Inc
16 Conn St
Woburn, MA 01801-5699   781-935-1234
   Fax: 781-935-9085 sales@doleandbailey.com
   www.doleandbailey.com
Meats such as lamb, sheep, beef, poultry and pork, as well as maple syrups, cheeses, breads and desserts.

President/CEO: Nancy Matheson-Burns
nancymb@doleandbailey.com
Founder: Cyprus Dole
Co-Founder: Frank Bailey
Vice President: Bill Burns
General Manager/Corporate Chef: Ed Brylczyk
Year Founded: 1868
Estimated Sales: $25 Million
Number Employees: 100-249

56103 Dolly Madison Ice Cream
25 E Chestnut St
Massapequa, NY 11758-4754   631-585-0900
   Fax: 631-737-9792
Wholesaler/distributor of specialty food and ice cream; serving the food service market
President: Jerry Tucci
CEO: Joe Bucco
Estimated Sales: $1-2.5 Million
Number Employees: 20-49
Types of Products Distributed:
  Food Service, Frozen Food, General Line, Specialty Foods, Ice cream

56104 Dom's Sausage Co Inc
10 Riverside Park
Malden, MA 02148-6781   781-324-6390
   Fax: 781-322-6776 info@domsausage.com
   www.domsausage.com
Meats including beef, pork, chicken, lamb and sausages.
President: Angelo Botticelli
CEO: Dominic Botticelli
summerman9@aol.com
Estimated Sales: $15 Million
Number Employees: 20-49
Number of Brands: 1
Type of Packaging: Bulk
Types of Products Distributed:
  Provisions/Meat

56105 Domestic Casing Co
410 3rd Ave
Brooklyn, NY 11215-3179   718-522-1902
Wholesaler/distributor of meat casings
Owner: Harold Klagsbald
Estimated Sales: $1-2.5 Million
Number Employees: 5-9
Types of Products Distributed:
  Frozen Food, Provisions/Meat

56106 Dominion Equipment & Supply Co.
1414 Semmes Ave
Richmond, VA 23224   804-794-5700
   Fax: 804-794-6515
Wholesaler/distributor of conveyors, tote containers, carts, racks and shelving; also, parts and service available
President: William Adams
william.adams@dom.com
CFO: Roberta Cousins
Sales: Micheal Gutknecht
Sales Manager: Jr McGuinn
Secretary: Robert Giberson
Head Operations: Robert Giberson
Number Employees: 20-49
Private Brands Carried:
  Steel King; Lista; Intermetro
Types of Products Distributed:
  Frozen Food, General Merchandise, Material handling equipment

56107 Don Luis Garcia Fernandez
PO Box 1006
Saint Augustine, FL 32085-1006   904-829-3013
   Fax: 904-829-3013
Wholesaler/distributor of natural Spanish-style orange marmalade
CEO: Yolanda Garcia
CFO: Greer Edminston
Number Employees: 5-9
Type of Packaging: Private Label
Private Brands Carried:
  Seville; Orange; Marmalade
Types of Products Distributed:
  Frozen Food, General Line, Spanish-style orange marmalade

56108 Don McDonald & Sons
15 Maiden Ln Ste 200
New York, NY 10038   212-267-0970
   Fax: 212-964-6040 infoNY@altrum.com
   www.altrum.com/financial-deal

Wholesaler/distributor of advertising specialties, corporate gifts, promotions and premiums; also, imprinting available
President/CEO: Stephen Sokoler
VP: Patrick McDonald
Regional Sales Manager: Tony Chong
Contact: Susan Butler
sbutler@dmcdonald.com
Estimated Sales: $5-10 Million
Number Employees: 50-99
Types of Products Distributed:
  Frozen Food, General Merchandise, Advertising specialties

56109 Don Walters Company
11630 Western Ave
Stanton, CA 90680   714-892-0275
   Fax: 714-901-1852 donwaltersco@aol.com
   www.donwaltersinc.com
Wholesaler/distributor of restaurant equipment; also, design consulting available
President/CEO: Roger Criswell
CFO/VP: Mindy Criswell
Estimated Sales: $1-2,500,000
Number Employees: 5-9
Type of Packaging: Food Service
Private Brands Carried:
  Henny Penny; Berkel; Powersoak; Stoelting
Types of Products Distributed:
  Food Service, General Line, Specialty Foods, Restaurant equipment

56110 Don's Dock Seafood Market
1220 E Northwest Hwy
Des Plaines, IL 60016-3391   847-827-1817
   Fax: 847-827-1846 donsdockinc@yahoo.com
Fresh seafood
Owner: Andy Johnson
dkarr4604@yahoo.com
Co-Owner: George Johnson
Co-Owner: Don Johnson
Estimated Sales: $3-5 Million
Number Employees: 10-19

56111 Donut Farm
6037 San Pablo
Oakland, CA 94608   510-338-6319
   www.vegandonut.farm
Organic, vegan donuts
Founder: Josh Levine *Year Founded:* 2007
Types of Products Distributed:
  General Line

56112 Door County Fish Market
2831 Dundee Rd
Northbrook, IL 60062-2501   847-559-9229
   Fax: 847-559-9273
Seafood
President: Steven Messner
Secretary/Treasurer: Jeannie Lindwall
Estimated Sales: $1 Million
Number Employees: 6

56113 Dore Foods
44 W Jefryn Blvd Ste R
Deer Park, NY 11729   631-389-2269
   Fax: 631-586-2341
Food Service distributor to pizzeria and restaurant trade on Long Island, NY
Manager: Tom Domune
Estimated Sales: $5-10 Million
Number Employees: 5-9
Types of Products Distributed:
  Frozen Food, Specialty Foods, Italian foods

56114 Dornan Uniforms & Specialty Advertising
653 11th Avenue
New York, NY 10036-2007   212-247-0937
   Fax: 212-956-7672 800-223-0363
Wholesaler/distributor of general merchandise including uniforms and accessories and advertising specialties; also, screen printing available
President: Gabriel Piro
Sales Manager: Sebrina Johnson
Sales Manager: Elsa Johnson
Number Employees: 5-9
Square Footage: 12800
Number of Customer Locations: 5000
Types of Products Distributed:
  Frozen Food, General Merchandise, Uniforms, advertising specialties, etc.

Wholesalers & Distributors / A-Z

56115 Dorsel Distribution Company
1405 Jamike Avenue
222
Erlanger, KY 41018-3182   859-371-4244
Wholesaler/distributor of flour and corn meal
Manager: Warren True
Estimated Sales: $500,000-$1 Million
Number Employees: 1-4
Square Footage: 11800
Parent Co: Wilson's Corn Products
Private Brands Carried:
  Dorsel's
Types of Products Distributed:
  General Line, Flour & corn meal

56116 Dorsett & Jackson Inc
3800 Noakes St
Los Angeles, CA 90023-3224   323-268-1815
  Fax: 323-268-9082 www.dorsettandjackson.com
Wholesaler/distributor of food additives and containers
President: Donald Witteman
Executive VP: Romer Johnson
Sales: Pat Tostenson
Estimated Sales: $20-50 Million
Number Employees: 10-19
Square Footage: 25000
Types of Products Distributed:
  Frozen Food, General Merchandise, Specialty Foods, Food additives & containers

56117 Doscher's Candies Co.
24 W Court St
Cincinnati, OH 45244   513-381-8656
          greg@doscherscandies.com
          www.doscherscandies.com
Candy including bars, canes and taffy products. Founded in 1871.
Chairman: Chip Nielson
VP, Operations: Kevin Gilligan
Estimated Sales: $1-2.5 Million
Number Employees: 5-9
Square Footage: 33600
Type of Packaging: Consumer
Types of Products Distributed:
  General Merchandise

56118 Dot Foods Inc
1 Dot Way
P.O. Box 192
Mt. Sterling, IL 62353   217-773-4411
            800-366-3687
          www.dotfoods.com
Food redistributor of general grocery products.
Chief Executive Officer: Joe Tracy
Executive Chairman: John Tracy
President: Dick Tracy
EVP, Retail & Business Development: George Eversman
Chief Financial Officer: Anita Montgomery
Year Founded: 1960
Estimated Sales: $6.2 Billion
Number Employees: 4,500
Other Locations:
  Dot Foods Distributor Center
  Modesto, CA
  Dot Foods Distributor Center
  Williamsport, MD
  Dot Foods Distributor Center
  Liverpool, NY
  Dot Foods Distributor Center
  Ardmore, OK
  Dot Foods Distributor Center
  Vidalia, GADot Foods Distributor
  CenterWilliamsport

56119 Double B Distributors
1031 W New Circle Rd
Lexington, KY 40511-1843   859-255-8822
          Fax: 859-233-1241
Meat snack foods
Owner: Bob Heim
bbdis@aol.com
Estimated Sales: $5-10 Million
Number Employees: 10-19

56120 Doug Hardy Company
Mountainville Rd
Deer Isle, ME 04627   207-348-6604
          Fax: 207-348-6100
Seafood
Owner: Doug Hardy
Estimated Sales: $3-5 Million
Number Employees: 5-9

56121 Douglas Brothers Produce Company
648 W Cowles Street
Long Beach, CA 90813-1592   562-436-2213
          Fax: 562-435-4321
Wholesaler/distributor of equipment, produce and frozen foods including vegetables; serving the food service market
President: N Douglas
Estimated Sales: $5-10 Million
Number Employees: 10-19
Types of Products Distributed:
  Food Service, Frozen Food, General Merchandise, Produce

56122 Douglas Freight Salvage
3451 NW 48th Street
Miami, FL 33142-3367   305-637-5544
          Fax: 561-595-3444
Wholesaler/distributor of general merchandise
President: Tom Douglas
VP: Steven Douglas
Estimated Sales: $1-3 Million
Number Employees: 1-4
Square Footage: 268000
Types of Products Distributed:
  Frozen Food, General Merchandise

56123 Douglas Homs Corporation
295 Old County Road
Suite 12
San Carlos, CA 94070-6240   650-592-1616
  Fax: 650-592-1619 800-592-1616
Wholesaler/distributor and importer of scales
President: J Nielsen
Number Employees: 1-4
Types of Products Distributed:
  Frozen Food, General Merchandise, Scales

56124 Douglass Produce Company
474 Finley Avenue W
10692
Birmingham, AL 35204-1068   205-251-5104
Wholesaler/distributor of produce; serving the food service market
President: Gary Wallace
Secretary: Sherrie Wallace
VP: Paul Wallace
Estimated Sales: $2.5-5 Million
Number Employees: 5-9
Types of Products Distributed:
  Food Service, Produce

56125 Doumak Inc
2201 Touhy Avenue
Elk Grove Village, IL 60007
          800-323-0318
customerservice@doumak.com www.doumak.com
Manufacturer of marshmallows.
CFO: Tim Etzkorn
Director of Operations: Brent Lyons
Estimated Sales: $2.5-5 Million
Number Employees: 50-99
Square Footage: 160000
Type of Packaging: Consumer, Food Service, Private Label

56126 Down East Specialty Products/Cape Bald Packers
P.O. Box 9739
Suite 1200
Portland, ME 04103   207-878-9170
  Fax: 207-878-9104 800-369-6327
          www.capebaldpackers.com
Lobster, mussels, rock crab and red crab
Manager: Kathy Nally
Manager: Patrice Landry
Estimated Sales: $1-3 Million
Number Employees: 1-4
Parent Co: Cape Bald Packers
Type of Packaging: Private Label

56127 Down To Earth Distributors
3030 Judkins Rd
Eugene, OR 97403-2231   541-485-5932
  Fax: 541-485-7141 800-234-5932
          info@downtoearthdistributors.com
Wholesaler/distributor of kitchen utensils, glassware, baskets, cleaning equipment, ceramics and health/beauty care items
Owner: Brenda Black
Sales Manager: Brenda Black
Sales Manager: Jack Bates
brenda@downtoearthdistributors.com
Estimated Sales: $10-20 Million
Number Employees: 50-99
Square Footage: 52000
Types of Products Distributed:
  Frozen Food, General Merchandise, Kitchen utensils, glassware, etc.

56128 Downco Packaging Inc
50 Lake Latimer Dr NE
Kennesaw, GA 30144-1597   770-924-2015
  Fax: 770-924-8996 www.downcopackaging.com
Wholesaler/distributor of packaging materials and bags
President: Bob Downing
CEO: Jacqueline Downing
Vice President: Robert Downing
b.downing@downcopackaging.com
Sales Director: J Downing
Plant Manager: Tom Downing
Estimated Sales: Less Than $500,000
Number Employees: 1-4
Type of Packaging: Consumer, Food Service, Private Label, Bulk
Types of Products Distributed:
  Frozen Food, General Merchandise, Packaging materials

56129 Downeast Food Distributors Inc
94 Merrow Rd
Auburn, ME 04210-8318   207-786-0356
  Fax: 207-786-0358 800-639-5802
          Heather@downeastfood.com
Wholesaler/distributor of baking ingredients, specialty foods and frozen foods; serving the food service market
Owner: Linc Hayes
Outside Sales Representative: Peter Garrow
linc@downeastfood.com
Estimated Sales: $2.5-5 Million
Number Employees: 10-19
Square Footage: 60000
Number of Customer Locations: 200
Types of Products Distributed:
  Food Service, Frozen Food, General Line, Specialty Foods, Baking ingredients

56130 Downesville Foods
2920 Commerce St
Monroe, LA 71201-7204   318-361-0431
  Fax: 318-361-0433 800-277-1294
Wholesalers/distributors of meats
President: Brent Creel
Manager: Lornie Carter
lp02carter@hotmail.com
Estimated Sales: $5-10 Million
Number Employees: 5-9
Types of Products Distributed:
  Provisions/Meat, Sausage

56131 Dr. John's Candies
2201 Oak Industrial Dr NE
Grand Rapids, MI 49505   616-454-3707
  Fax: 616-459-3378 888-375-6462
          www.drjohns.com
Wholesaler/distributor of sugar-free candy including lollipops, sour balls, taffy, caramels, toffee, mints, etc
President/CEO: Debra Bruinsma
Estimated Sales: $500,000
Number Employees: 1-4
Number of Brands: 1
Number of Products: 10
Square Footage: 20000
Type of Packaging: Consumer, Private Label, Bulk
Private Brands Carried:
  Dr. John s Candies; Sugar Free Candies
Number of Customer Locations: 150
Types of Products Distributed:
  General Line, Health Food, Specialty Foods, Sugar-free lollipops, sour balls, etc.

56132 Dr. Smoothie Brands
1730 Raymer Avenue
Fullerton, CA 92833   714-449-9787
  Fax: 714-449-9474 888-466-9941
info@drsmoothie.com www.drsmoothie.com or
          www.cafeessentials.com

Dr. Smoothie Brands is a full line beverage company manufacturing shelf-stable, liquid natural fruit smoothies and powdered cocoa, mocha, latte, and chai blends. Manufactures nutritional blends ranging from raw, whole food nutritionbars to a full range of botanicals, including medically endorsed products like The Complete Meal, and Amino line.
Contact: Megan Wood
meganwood@inewsource.org
Number of Brands: 6
Number of Products: 93
Type of Packaging: Consumer, Food Service
Private Brands Carried:
  Dr. Smoothie, Cafe Essentials, Aminos, FreshFace, BioBar, Smothieceuticals
Types of Products Distributed:
  Food Service, Health Food, Specialty Foods

56133 Dr. Willy's Great American Seafood
23789 Garrett Hwy
Mc Henry, MD 21541-1338   301-387-7380
       Fax: 301-387-7380 800-296-8862
              www.drwillys.com
Wholesaler/distributor of fresh and frozen seafood; serving the food service market
Owner: Willy Hughes
Estimated Sales: Less than $500,000
Number Employees: 1-4
Types of Products Distributed:
  Food Service, Frozen Food, Seafood

56134 Draco Natural Products Inc
539 Parrott St
San Jose, CA 95112-4121   408-287-7871
       Fax: 408-287-8838 info@dracoherbs.com
              www.draconatural.com
Wholesales herbal extracts
CEO: Jerry Wu
Sales: Ed Schack
Estimated Sales: $3 Million
Number Employees: 10-19

56135 Dragnet Fisheries
4141 B St
Anchorage, AK 99503-5940   907-276-4551
       Fax: 907-274-3617
Fresh and frozen herring, black cod, halibut and salmon
President: Jay Cherrier
Estimated Sales: Less than $500,000
Number Employees: 1-4
Type of Packaging: Consumer, Food Service
Types of Products Distributed:
  Frozen Food

56136 Dragonfly Screen Graphics Inc
1630 State St
Nashville, TN 37203-2928   615-329-3776
       Fax: 615-320-5844 www.dragonflysg.com
Wholesaler/distributor of advertising specialties
Owner: Bruce Hackett
bruce@dragonflysg.com
Sales Director: David Hackett
Estimated Sales: $1-2.5 Million
Number Employees: 10-19
Number of Customer Locations: 350
Types of Products Distributed:
  Frozen Food, General Merchandise, Advertising specialties

56137 Drake Equipment Co
160 Presumpscot St # 1
Portland, ME 04103-5241   207-775-1832
       Fax: 207-775-7139
Wholesaler/distributor of conveyors, shelving and racks
President: Francis Drake
drakeqpt@aol.com
Estimated Sales: Less Than $500,000
Number Employees: 1-4
Private Brands Carried:
  Yale; Arrowhead; Blue Giant
Types of Products Distributed:
  Frozen Food, General Merchandise, Conveyors, shelving & racks

56138 Draper's Super Bee
914 S St
Auburn, NE 68305-1303   402-274-3725
       Fax: 402-274-3128
Wholesaler/distributor of honey and bee pollen
Owner: Larry Draper
Co-Owner: B Draper
Estimated Sales: Less Than $500,000
Number Employees: 1-4
Square Footage: 30000
Types of Products Distributed:
  Frozen Food, General Line, Honey & bee pollen

56139 Draught Services
2923 Portland Drive
Oakville, ON L6H 5S4
Canada   905-829-9015
       Fax: 905-829-9054 800-668-4718
draught@thebeerstore.ca www.draughtservices.ca
Wholesaler/distributor of draught equipment serving the food service market; also, installation services available
Supervisor: Doug Lytle
Supervisor: Tim Kontkanen
Manager: Peter George
Estimated Sales: $3-5 Million
Number Employees: 20-49
Square Footage: 23200
Parent Co: Brewers Retail
Types of Products Distributed:
  Frozen Food, General Merchandise, Draught equipment

56140 Dreyer's Grand Ice Cream Inc.
5929 College Ave.
Oakland, CA 94618
                             877-437-3937
              www.dreyers.com
Premium ice creams.
CEO: Kim Peddle Rguem
Year Founded: 1928
Estimated Sales: $1.5 Billion
Number Employees: 10,000
Number of Brands: 28
Parent Co: Nestl, USA
Type of Packaging: Consumer, Food Service
Other Locations:
  Dreyer's Grand Ice Cream
  Fort Wayne, INDreyer's Grand Ice Cream
Types of Products Distributed:
  Food Service, Frozen Food

56141 Droubi's Imports
2721 Hillcroft Street
Houston, TX 77057-5003   713-334-1829
       Fax: 713-988-9506
Manufacturer, importer and wholesaler/distributor of tea and coffee
President: A Droubi
VP: Sharon Droubi
Estimated Sales: $1-2.5 Million
Number Employees: 20-49
Square Footage: 48000
Parent Co: Droubi's Bakery & Delicatessen
Types of Products Distributed:
  Frozen Food, Specialty Foods, Coffee & tea

56142 Druid Fire Equipment Company
P.O.Box 2882
Tuscaloosa, AL 35403-2882   205-349-4216
       Fax: 205-759-2612 877-759-2632
Wholesaler/distributor of fire extinguishers and fire suppression systems
Owner: John Freeman
Sales/Marketing Executive: David Patrick, Sr.
Purchasing Manager: Brad Smith
Estimated Sales: $3-5 Million
Number Employees: 5-9
Private Brands Carried:
  Amerex; Ansul; Rarge Guard
Number of Customer Locations: 200
Types of Products Distributed:
  Fire extinguishers, etc.

56143 Dub Harris Corporation
2875 Metropolitan Place
Pomona, CA 91767   909-596-6300
       Fax: 909-596-6336 dubharris@dubharris.com
              www.dubharris.com
Plastic bags; wholesaler/distributor of corrugated boxes and packaging materials
President: Maurice Harris
Contact: Ming Yu
dubharris@dubharris.com
Estimated Sales: $2.5-5 Million
Number Employees: 5-9
Types of Products Distributed:
  Frozen Food, General Merchandise, corrugated boxes & packaging materials

56144 Dublin Produce Company
1 Brooklyn Terminal Market
Brooklyn, NY 11236   718-251-6910
       Fax: 718-251-7005
Wholesaler/distributor of fresh produce
Owner: Mel Schwartz
Estimated Sales: $5-10 Million
Number Employees: 10-19
Types of Products Distributed:
  Frozen Food, Produce

56145 Dubois Seafood
285 Saint Peter St
Houma, LA 70363   985-876-2514
       Fax: 985-851-6147
Seafood wholesalers
President: Kerry Dubois
Estimated Sales: $6 Million
Number Employees: 5

56146 Dudson USA Inc
5604 Departure Dr
Raleigh, NC 27616-1841   919-877-0200
       Fax: 919-877-0300 800-438-3766
              usasales@dudson.com
Importer and wholesaler/distributor of dinnerware including china; serving the food service market
President: Elmer Carr
VP: Lorraine Delois
VP Marketing/Sales: Joel DeNoble
VP Corporate Accounts: Maire-Anne Bassil
Manager: Steve Abourisk
Estimated Sales: $1-2.5 Million
Number Employees: 10-19
Square Footage: 180000
Parent Co: Dudson Company
Type of Packaging: Food Service
Types of Products Distributed:
  Food Service, General Merchandise, Dinnerware, china, etc.

56147 Dugdale Beef Company
4420 Stout Field North Dr.
Indianapolis, IN 46241   317-520-9981
       Fax: 317-298-7608 jeff@dugdalefoods.com
              www.dugdalefoods.com
Fine meats, seafood, poultry, cheese, salads, breads, desserts
President: Jean Deering
Founder: Eleanor Dugdale
Contact: Joe Dugdale
joe@dugdalefoods.com
Year Founded: 1975
Estimated Sales: $20-50 Million
Number Employees: 20-49
Type of Packaging: Consumer

56148 Dunham's Lobster Pot
60 Mt Blue Pond Rd
Avon, ME 04966-3301   207-639-2815
       Fax: 207-639-2815
Fresh seafood including fish, clams, haddock, scallops, crab meat, mussels, oysters, shrimp, lobster and rib-eye steaks
Owner: Bruce Dunham
Co-Owner: Mary Dunham
Estimated Sales: $220 Thousand
Number Employees: 2
Type of Packaging: Food Service, Bulk

56149 Dunlevy Food Equipment
60 West 7th Avenue
Vancouver, BC V5Y 1L6
Canada   604-873-2236
       Fax: 604-873-0899 800-879-8819
       email@dunlevyfoodequipment.com
              www.dunlevyfoodequipment.com
Wholesaler/distributor of new and used food equipment including glassware, kitchenware and chinaware; serving the food service market
President: Harry Jung
Sales Manager: Jim Forman
Purchasing: Alen Lew
Types of Products Distributed:
  Food Service, Frozen Food, General Merchandise

56150 Dura-Flex
95 Goodwin St
East Hartford, CT 06108-1146 860-528-9838
       Fax: 860-528-2802 877-251-5418
contact_us@dur-a-flex.com www.dur-a-flex.com

Wholesalers & Distributors / A-Z

Commercial and seemless industrial flooring systems and wall coatings and polymer components-epoxies, urethanes and methyl methacrylates (MMA) plus premium colored quartz aggregates.
CEO: Robert Smith
roberts@dur-a-flex.com
Marketing: Mark Paggioli
Number Employees: 50-99
Square Footage: 260000
Types of Products Distributed:
 Frozen Food

56151 Durable Textile Company
PO Box 5039
Wheaton, IL 60189-5039 630-766-8900
Fax: 630-766-9082
Wholesaler/distributor of institutional linens including polyester pillows, terry towel pieces, tablecloths, napkins, handi-wipes, etc. serving the food service market
President: Lane Trueblood
Sales Manager: Herbert Twery
Estimated Sales: $1-2.5 Million
Number Employees: 5-9
Square Footage: 24800
Private Brands Carried:
 Adagio; Clean-Ups; Handy Dandies; Permalux; Softee Wipers
Number of Customer Locations: 1000
Types of Products Distributed:
 Linen Textile Supplies

56152 Durbin
PO Box 87
Canton, MS 39046-0087 601-859-6164
Fax: 601-855-5031
Chickens
Plant Manager: Mike Moulder
Estimated Sales: $20-50 Million
Number Employees: 250-499
Parent Co: Marshall Durbin Industries

56153 Durey-Libby Edible Nuts
100 Industrial Rd
Carlstadt, NJ 07072 201-939-2775
Fax: 201-939-0386 800-332-6887
Custom roasted nuts
President: Wendy Dicker
CEO: Billy Dicker
Contact: William Dicker
billythenutman@msn.com
Estimated Sales: $1-2.5 Million
Number Employees: 20-49
Square Footage: 120000
Type of Packaging: Bulk

56154 Durham Flavor Rich
3000 Muldee Street
Durham, NC 27707 919-598-0063
Fax: 919-598-0102 800-672-0097
Wholesaler/distributor of dairy products; serving the food service market
Parent Co: Land of Sun
Types of Products Distributed:
 Food Service, Frozen Food, General Line, Dairy products

56155 Durham Ranch
1330 Capital Blvd
Suite A
Reno, NV 89502 775-322-4073
 800-444-5687
sales@sierrameat.com durhamranch.com
Wholesaler/distributor of beef, pork, lamb and veal; importer of venison; exporter of venison and buffalo.
President: John Flocchini
Year Founded: 1965
Estimated Sales: $20-50 Million
Number Employees: 50-99
Types of Products Distributed:
 Frozen Food, Provisions/Meat, Beef, pork, lamb & veal

56156 Dutch Creek Foods
1411 Old Route 39 NE
Sugarcreek, OH 44681 330-852-2631
Fax: 330-852-4990 800-852-2631
www.dutchcreekfoods.com
Wholesaler/distributor of grocery products, meat, frozen foods, equipment and fixtures, seafood, etc.; serving the food service market
Manager: Brian Stutzman
VP: Stephen Steiner
Contact: Lynn Dessecker
ldessecker@dutchcreekfoods.com
Estimated Sales: $8-10 Million
Number Employees: 20-49
Square Footage: 108000
Parent Co: Dutch Corporation
Private Brands Carried:
 Dutch Creek Foods; Yoder's Amish Country Meats; Dutch Valley
Types of Products Distributed:
 Food Service, Frozen Food, General Line, General Merchandise, Provisions/Meat, Seafood, Groceries, equipment & fixtures, etc.

56157 Dutch Valley Food Distributors
7615 Lancaster Ave
7615 Lancaster Ave
Myerstown, PA 17067-2004 717-933-4191
Fax: 717-933-5466 800-733-4191
customerservice@dutchvalleyfoods.com
www.dutchvalleyfoods.com
Wholesaler/distributor of general line products; serving the food service market
President: Matthew Burkholder
mburkholder@dutchvalleyfoods.com
Estimated Sales: $10-20 Million
Number Employees: 100-249
Types of Products Distributed:
 Food Service, Frozen Food, General Line

56158 Dutchess Restaurant Equipment
795 Dutchess Tpke
Poughkeepsie, NY 12603-2057 845-471-1240
Fax: 845-471-2148 www.drequipmentco.com
Wholesaler/distributor of food service equipment; serving the food service market
President: William H Donaldson Jr
VP: Keith Donaldson
Estimated Sales: $1-2.5 Million
Number Employees: 5-9
Types of Products Distributed:
 Food Service, Frozen Food, General Merchandise, Foodservice equipment

56159 Dutra Distributing
3500 Atwater Blvd
Atwater, CA 95301-9501 209-358-3249
Fax: 209-358-4930
Wholesaler/distributor of milk, cream, cottage cheese, yogurt and ice cream; serving the food service market
President: Frank Dutra
Manager: Barbara Dutra
Estimated Sales: $1-2.5 Million
Number Employees: 1-4
Parent Co: Crystal Dairy
Number of Customer Locations: 200
Types of Products Distributed:
 Food Service, Frozen Food, General Line, Health Food, Dairy products

56160 Duval Container Co
91 S Myrtle Ave
Jacksonville, FL 32204-2117 904-355-0711
Fax: 904-350-9709 800-342-8194
www.duvalcontainer.com
Corrugated boxes; wholesaler/distributor of containers and packaging materials
President: Richard L Gills
CFO: Mary Geller
Contact: William Erwin
william@duvalcontainer.com
Estimated Sales: $10-20 Million
Number Employees: 20-49
Types of Products Distributed:
 Frozen Food, General Merchandise, Containers & packaging materials

56161 Duxbury Mussel & Seafood Corporation
8 Joseph St # B
Kingston, MA 02364-1122 781-585-5517
Fax: 781-585-2976
Wholesale seafood
President: Robert Marconi

56162 Dwan & Company
142 Industrial Ln
Torrington, CT 06790 860-489-3149
Fax: 860-489-4805
Wholesaler/distributor of alcoholic beverages
Owner/President: W Sweetman
Contact: William Sweetman
bill7228@hotmail.com
Estimated Sales: $5-10 Million
Number Employees: 20-49
Types of Products Distributed:
 Frozen Food, General Line, Alcoholic beverages

56163 Dykes Restaurant Supply Inc
1217 Jordan Ln NW
Huntsville, AL 35816-3033 256-837-1107
Fax: 256-721-1365 800-221-0115
www.dykesrestsupply.com
Wholesaler/distributor of food service equipment and supplies; serving the food service market
Vice President: Mark Ance
mnance@dykesrestsupply.com
Executive VP/General Manager: Francis Spinelli
Estimated Sales: Less Than $500,000
Number Employees: 5-9
Square Footage: 200000
Types of Products Distributed:
 Food Service, Frozen Food, General Merchandise, Equipment & supplies

56164 Dyna Tabs LLC
1933 E 12th St
Brooklyn, NY 11229-2703 718-376-6084
sales@dynatabs.com
www.dynatabs.com
Health, wellness, beauty products including oral edible strips, aloe vera drinking gel and passion punch.
Executive Director: Harold Baum
hbaum@dynatabs.com
CFO: Setty Baum
Estimated Sales: $830,000
Number Employees: 10-19
Parent Co: Baum International, Inc
Type of Packaging: Consumer, Private Label
Types of Products Distributed:
 Frozen Food, General Line, General Merchandise, Janitorial supplies, dispensers, etc.

56165 Dyna-Lift Inc
184 West Blvd
Montgomery, AL 36108-1600 334-263-1600
Fax: 334-262-0420 800-222-6353
dabbott264@aol.com www.dyna-lift.com
Wholesaler/distributor of material handling equipment including forklifts, pallet racks, dock equipment, etc.; also, parts, service and rentals available
President: Craig Pinson
rayk@dyna-lift.com
Sales Exec: Ray King
Branch Manager: Craig Pinson
Estimated Sales: $10-20 Million
Number Employees: 20-49
Private Brands Carried:
 Nissan; Barrett; Bendi
Number of Customer Locations: 4000
Types of Products Distributed:
 Frozen Food, General Merchandise, Forklifts, pallet racks, etc.

56166 Dynalon Labware
175 Humboldt St
Suite 300
Rochester, NY 14610 585-334-2064
Fax: 585-334-0241 800-334-7585
dynaloninfo@dyna-labware.com
www.dynalabcorp.com
Wholesaler and distributor of plastic lab supplies
President & CEO: Martin Davies
Data Processing: Brian Genter
Product Manager: Steve Yudicky
Human Resources Director: Patti Zimmer
Engineering Manager: William Potter
Manager: Christine Leskovar
Plant Manager: Robert Pfeil
Estimated Sales: $6.7 Million
Number Employees: 35
Square Footage: 100000

56167 (HQ)Dynamic Marketing
40 Western Industrial Dr
Cranston, RI 02921-3403 401-946-3111
Fax: 401-946-7303 800-789-7711
Wholesaler and distributor of supplements for sports nutrition and bodybuilding, also offers sports drinks, and protein bars
CEO: Joe O'Brien
Number Employees: 50-99

Wholesalers & Distributors / A-Z

Other Locations:
Dynamic Marketing
Henderson, NVDynamic Marketing

56168 E A Sween Co
16101 W 78th St
Eden Prairie, MN 55344   866-787-8862
                                  800-328-8184
                                  easween.com
Prepackaged individual sandwiches.
President: Tom Sween
tom.sween@easween.com
Chairman: Tom Sween
Chief Financial Officer: John Davis
SVP, Strategic Business Development: Rob Linner
VP, Information Systems: Ron Myshka
SVP, Sales/Marketing/R&D: Bryan Virgin
VP, Human Resources: Kim Larish
VP, Operations: Aaron Scott
Year Founded: 1954
Estimated Sales: $100-500 Million
Number Employees: 250-499
Type of Packaging: Private Label
Private Brands Carried:
Deli Express; Market Sandwich; San Luis Burritos; Simply Delicious Bakery
Types of Products Distributed:
Food Service, Frozen Food

56169 E D Farrell Co Inc
105 Empire Dr
Buffalo, NY 14224-1319   716-668-2722
       Fax: 716-656-7967 buffalo@edfarrell.com
                                  www.edfarrell.com
Wholesaler/distributor of material handling equipment
President: Edward Otis
eotis@edfarrell.com
CFO: Dave Moran
Vice President: James Otis
Sales Manager: Matt Warne
Estimated Sales: $10-20 Million
Number Employees: 20-49
Square Footage: 73000
Private Brands Carried:
Yale; Ridg-U-Rak; Crown
Types of Products Distributed:
Frozen Food, General Merchandise, Material handling equipment

56170 E Friedman Assoc
2237 New York Ave
Brooklyn, NY 11234-2620   718-338-5800
       Fax: 718-338-5870 800-555-0666
       info@ckitchen.com www.ckitchen.com
Wholesaler/distributor of institutional food service equipment and supplies; serving the food service market; also, design and installation available
President: Elliot Friedman
elliot@efriedman.com
Contract Sales: Lenny Teller
General Manager: Joel Kaplan
Estimated Sales: $1-2.5 Million
Number Employees: 10-19
Square Footage: 8000
Private Brands Carried:
Hobart; Vulcan; Metro
Types of Products Distributed:
Food Service, General Merchandise, Institutional equipment & supplies

56171 E G Forrest Co Inc
1023 N Chestnut St
Winston Salem, NC 27101-1519   336-723-9151
                        Fax: 336-725-7674
Wholesaler/distributor of frozen foods, general line products, general merchandise, produce, meats and seafood; serving the food service market
President: J Holderfield
CEO: L Forrestield
Sales Manager: Olin Willis
Estimated Sales: $20-50 Million
Number Employees: 100-249
Square Footage: 104000
Private Brands Carried:
EGF; Nifda
Number of Customer Locations: 3500
Types of Products Distributed:
Food Service, Frozen Food, General Line, General Merchandise, Provisions/Meat, Produce, Seafood

56172 E Goodwin & Sons
7901 Oceano Ave # 36
Jessup, MD 20794-9407   410-799-5300
       Fax: 410-799-2754 800-462-9486
                       www.egoodwinseafood.com
Wholesaler/distributor of fresh and frozen seafood
President: Lou Goodwin
VP: Lou Goodwin
Sales: Ed Goodwin, Jr.
Estimated Sales: $10-20 Million
Number Employees: 50-99
Number of Customer Locations: 400
Types of Products Distributed:
Frozen Food, Seafood

56173 E M Trisler Sales Co FdProds
934 Fleming Rd
Maysville, KY 41056-9504   606-564-3257
Wholesaler/distributor of general line items, groceries and specialty food products
Owner: Forrest Jackson
Estimated Sales: $2.5-5 Million
Number Employees: 5-9
Number of Customer Locations: 300
Types of Products Distributed:
Frozen Food, General Line, Specialty Foods, Groceries

56174 E&A Hotel & Restaurant Epment And Supplies
140 E 5th St
Plainfield, NJ 07060   908-755-9333
       Fax: 908-755-1668 800-832-1369
       sales@easupply.com www.easupply.com
Wholesaler/distributor of food service equipment; serving food service market
President: Joel Green
Customer Service: Valerie Rojas
Contact: Ron Gisonna
ron@easupply.com
Estimated Sales: $5-10 Million
Number Employees: 20-49
Private Brands Carried:
Vulcan; Traulson; Magic Kitchen
Types of Products Distributed:
Food Service, Frozen Food, General Merchandise, Foodservice equipment

56175 E&M Fancy Foods
8411 Monticello Avenue
Apt 1
Skokie, IL 60076-2873   847-679-6950
                        Fax: 847-679-0345
Wholesaler/distributor of meat products; serving the retail market
President: Edward Figlewicz
Number Employees: 10-19
Types of Products Distributed:
Frozen Food, Provisions/Meat

56176 E&M Packaging
1116 N Bankerd Ave Ste A
Nogales, AZ 85621   520-287-9243
                        Fax: 520-287-7311
Wholesaler/distributor of packaging for produce
Owner: Ernest Legleu
Estimated Sales: $1-2.5 Million
Number Employees: 1-4
Types of Products Distributed:
Frozen Food, General Merchandise, Packaging for produce

56177 E. Armata Fruit & Produce, Inc.
114 NYC Terminal Market
Bronx, NY 10474-7303   718-991-5600
       Fax: 718-991-1599 800-223-8070
       carmata@aol.com www.earmata.com/
Wholesaler/distributor of produce
President: Chris Armata
Vice President: Paul Armata
Office Manager: Phyllis Rosenberg
Number Employees: 1-4
Types of Products Distributed:
Frozen Food, Produce

56178 E. De la Garza
P.O.Box 2045
Brownsville, TX 78522-2045   956-542-3576
       Fax: 956-542-4129 edelagarzainc@yahoo.com
Wholesaler/distributor of equipment and fixtures and general line items
President: Rudy De La Garza
Secretary: M Garcia
Vice President: G Buitron
Estimated Sales: $10-20 Million
Number Employees: 20-49
Square Footage: 78000
Number of Customer Locations: 600
Types of Products Distributed:
Frozen Food, General Line, General Merchandise

56179 E. LaRocque & Fils
265 Rue Lindsay
Drummondville, QC J2B 1G2
Canada   819-477-0313
                        Fax: 819-477-5058
Wholesaler/distributor of fruits and vegetables; serving the food service market
VP: Benoit Brodeur
Types of Products Distributed:
Food Service, Produce

56180 E. Oliver Zellner Company
4771 W Grant Street
Slatington, PA 18080-3644   610-767-3903
Wholesaler/distributor of potatoes
Ownr./Pres.: E Zellner
Number Employees: 5-9
Square Footage: 39200
Types of Products Distributed:
Produce, Potatoes

56181 E.A. Robinson & Company
PO Box 337
Maysville, KY 41056-0337   606-564-5595
Wholesaler/distributor of restaurant, deli, catering, paper and cleaning supplies; also, candy
Office Manager: Garnetta Applegate
Manager: John Denham
Purchasing Manager: Roger Rayborn
Estimated Sales: $5-10 Million
Number Employees: 10
Square Footage: 160000
Number of Customer Locations: 250 0
Types of Products Distributed:
General Line, General Merchandise, Rack Jobbers, Paper supplies, candy, etc.

56182 E.C. Phillips & Son
PO Box 7090
Ketchikan, AK 99901-3235   907-247-7975
       Fax: 907-225-7250 ecp@ecphillipsalaska.com
                       www.ecphillipsalaska.com
Buyers and processors of salmon
Owner: Colleen Picillo
CEO: Larry Elliot
VP: Michael Cusack
Estimated Sales: $10-20 Million
Number Employees: 60
Type of Packaging: Consumer

56183 E.H. Thompson Company
4655 Lenox Ave
Jacksonville, FL 32205   904-358-1555
       Fax: 904-354-4448 800-780-1555
                       info@ehthompson.com
Wholesaler/distributor of equipment and fixtures; serving the food service market
Manager: Bill Adkins
CEO: Walter Simon
wlsimon@ehthompson.com
General Manager: Lee Webber
Estimated Sales: $5-10 Million
Number Employees: 5-9
Square Footage: 180000
Private Brands Carried:
ABC; Prestige; Valueline
Types of Products Distributed:
Food Service, Frozen Food, General Merchandise

56184 EB Box Company
20 Pollard Street
Unit #3
Richmond Hill, ON L4B 1C3
Canada   905-889-5600
       Fax: 905-889-5602 800-513-2269
       sales@ebbox.com www.ebbox.com
Paper boxes for fish and chips, Chinese food, doughnuts andpatties, auto parts, computer parts, health products, cosmetics, garments, innerboxes, trays and custom boxes
Number Employees: 5-9

Wholesalers & Distributors / A-Z

56185 EFCO Products Inc
130 Smith St
Poughkeepsie, NY 12601
800-284-3326
info@efcoproducts.com www.efcoproducts.com
Leading supplier of mixes, fruit and creme style fillings, jellies, jams and concentrated icing fruits to the baking industry.
CEO: David Miller
Vice President: Andy Herzing
Senior Director of Sales & Marketing: Mark Lowman
Director of Manufacturing Operations: Veronica Miller
Year Founded: 1903
Estimated Sales: $2.5-5 Million
Number Employees: 50-99
Types of Products Distributed:
 Specialty Foods

56186 EMG Associates
645 N Michigan Ave
Chicago, IL 60611-2826
312-649-0062
Fax: 312-649-0787
Wholesaler/distributor of electronic locking systems to secure food storage, liquor storage, private offices and employee entrances
President: Joshua Alper
VP: Zalman Alper
Estimated Sales: $5-10 Million
Number Employees: 5-9
Square Footage: 10000
Parent Co: CSI Corporation
Types of Products Distributed:
 Frozen Food, General Merchandise, Electronic locking systems

56187 EMSCO Scientific Enterprises, Inc.
51st Street and Parkside Avenue
PO Box 28032
Philadelphia, PA 19131
215-477-5601
Fax: 215-477-2526 800-542-6026
info@emscoscientific.com
www.emscoscientific.com
Wholesaler/distributor of laboratory supplies and equipment including glassware, plastics and gloves
President: Evalind Minor
VP: Roderick Cliford
Estimated Sales: $5-10 Million
Number Employees: 10-19
Square Footage: 50000
Types of Products Distributed:
 Frozen Food, General Merchandise, Laboratory equipment & supplies

56188 ERC Parts Inc
4001 Cobb International Blvd N
Kennesaw, GA 30152-4374
770-984-0276
Fax: 770-951-1875 800-241-6880
marketing@erconline.com www.erconline.com
Drive-thru displays, recording devices and timers and battery chargers; importer of cash register parts; exporter of point of sale systems, parts and software; wholesaler/distributor of VAR products; serving the food service market
Owner: Chuck Rollins
cerollins@erconline.com
CFO: Stuart Dobson
Vice President: Charles Barnes
Research & Development: Timothy Adams
Marketing Director: Bryon Finkel
Parts/Manufacturing Division: Eric Hart
Purchasing Manager: Rob Haight
Estimated Sales: $1-2.5 Million
Number Employees: 50-99
Square Footage: 180000
Other Locations:
 ERC Parts
  Louisville, KY
 ERC Parts
  Lexington, KY
 ERC Parts
  Cleveland, OH
 ERC Parts
  Las Vegas, NV
 ERC Parts
  Baltimore, MD
 ERC Parts
  Greensboro, NC
 ERC PartsLexington
Private Brands Carried:
 Panasonic

Types of Products Distributed:
 Food Service, Frozen Food, General Merchandise, VAR products

56189 EZ Foods
1151 Grier Drive
Suite A
Las Vegas, NV 89119-3711
702-454-5000
Fax: 702-361-0861
Wholesaler/distributor of gourmet foods including spices, imported cheeses, nuts and chocolates
President: Earl Ziegel
CEO: Aaron Ziegel
Number Employees: 20-49
Square Footage: 56000
Type of Packaging: Food Service
Private Brands Carried:
 EZ Foods; Golden Harvest; Trader Bay
Types of Products Distributed:
 Frozen Food, Specialty Foods, Imported cheeses, chocolates, etc.

56190 (HQ)Eagle Coffee Co Inc
1027 Hillen St
Baltimore, MD 21202-4132
410-685-5893
Fax: 410-528-0369 contactus@eaglecoffee.com
www.eaglecoffee.com
Restaurant and gourmet coffees, coffee machines and grinders and coffee beans; serving the food service market
Owner: Nick Constantine
eaglecoffee@aol.com
Controller: Tom Brooks
VP: Jacqueline Parris
Estimated Sales: $1.6 Million
Number Employees: 10-19
Square Footage: 120000
Type of Packaging: Food Service, Private Label
Other Locations:
 Eagle Coffee Co.
  Baltimore, MDEagle Coffee Co.
Private Brands Carried:
 Eagle; Gourmet Blend Coffee; Harbor City Tea; Old Town Coffee & Tea; Bunn-O-Matic Coffee Machines
Types of Products Distributed:
 Food Service, General Line, General Merchandise, Coffee, coffee machines, etc.

56191 Eagle Industrial Distribution
1000 Chestnut St SE
Suite E
Gainesville, GA 30501-6909
770-538-0200
Fax: 770-538-0375 www.eagleindustrial.biz
Wholesaler/distributor of electrical supplies, lighting fixtures, fuses, switches, etc
President: Jerry Cain
jerry@eagleindustries.com
Estimated Sales: $5-10 Million
Number Employees: 5-9
Number of Customer Locations: 200
Types of Products Distributed:
 Frozen Food, General Merchandise, Electrical supplies, etc.

56192 Eagle Wholesale Drug Company
413 Coolidge St
Lafayette, LA 70501-8803
337-235-1148
Fax: 337-232-2623
Wholesaler/distributor of general merchandise and health and beauty aids; rack jobber services available
Owner: Chester Begnaud Jr
Estimated Sales: $1-2.5 Million
Number Employees: 10-19
Number of Customer Locations: 300
Types of Products Distributed:
 Frozen Food, General Merchandise, Rack Jobbers, HBA

56193 Eagle-Concordia Paper Corporation
1 Adams Blvd
Farmingdale, NY 11735-6611
212-255-3860
Fax: 212-249-4530 info@eaglebox.com
www.eaglebox.com
Wholesaler/distributor of boxes, cartons, packaging tape, bubble wrap, etc.; also, package design services available
Owner: Michael Hoffman
Estimated Sales: $10-20 Million
Number Employees: 20-49

Types of Products Distributed:
 Frozen Food, General Merchandise, Boxes, cartons, tape, bubble wrap, etc.

56194 Earl Gill Coffee Co
222 Castleberry St
Hot Springs, AR 71901-3704
501-624-5671
Wholesaler/distributor of food service equipment and supplies, groceries, dairy products, cleaning supplies, disposables, wraps and tabletop needs; serving the food service market
Owner: Earl Gill
Estimated Sales: $1-2.5 Million
Number Employees: 10-19
Number of Customer Locations: 500
Types of Products Distributed:
 Food Service, Frozen Food, General Line, General Merchandise, Foodservice equipment & supplies, etc.

56195 Earp Distribution
2730 S 98th St
Edwarsville, KS 56111
913-287-3311
Fax: 913-287-6029 800-866-3277
www.earpdistribution.com
Wholesaler/distributor of general merchandise, general line items, meats and frozen foods; serving the food service market. The plant consists of a 20,000 sq ft freezer, a 17,000 sq ft cooler, a 26,000 sq ft cold dock, 67,000 sq ft ofdry storage, 18,000 sq ft office area, and a 14,000 sq ft truck maintenance garage.
CEO & General Manager: Steve Hewlett
stevehewlett@earpdistribution.com
Chairman & Owner: Cliff Earp
COO & Assistant General Manager: Thom Bear
VP of Operations: Mike Hoyle
Warehouse Manager: Doug Hudson
Year Founded: 1954
Estimated Sales: $100-500 Million
Number Employees: 100-249
Square Footage: 184000
Number of Customer Locations: 415
Types of Products Distributed:
 Food Service, Frozen Food, General Line, General Merchandise, Provisions/Meat

56196 Earth Circle Organics
12745 Earhart Ave
Auburn, CA 95602
877-922-3663
earthcircleorganics.com
Organic ingredients
President & COO: Herb Heller
Founder & CEO: Eric Botner
Vice President, Sales & Marketing: Claire Modjeski
Type of Packaging: Consumer, Bulk

56197 Earth Grains Baking Co
1527 Crescent Dr
Augusta, GA 30909-2423
706-733-4492
Fax: 706-733-4491
Wholesaler/distributor of bread, rolls and soft cakes; serving the food service market
Sales Manager: Bruce Wheatley
bruce.wheatley@slbg.com
Sales Director: Wayne Gallups
Estimated Sales: Less Than $500,000
Number Employees: 5-9
Square Footage: 6000
Parent Co: Sara Lee Bakery Group
Types of Products Distributed:
 Food Service, General Line, Bread, rolls & soft cakes

56198 EarthGrains Banking Companies, Inc.
PO Box 976
Horsham, PA 19044
608-244-4747
Fax: 608-244-9440 866-613-2784
Wholesaler/distributor of baked goods including bread, buns and doughnuts
VP: Mike Krafft
Plant Manager: Steve Vial
Estimated Sales: $300,000-500,000
Number Employees: 1-4
Parent Co: Sara Lee Bakery Group
Types of Products Distributed:
 Frozen Food, General Line, Bread, buns & doughnuts

Wholesalers & Distributors / A-Z

56199 Earthbound Farm
1721 San Juan Hwy
San Jn Bautista, CA 95045-9780 831-623-7881
  800-690-3200
scabaluna@ebfarm.com www.earthboundfarm.com
Supplier of organic specialty salad mixes and organic produce
President: Bryan Aguirre
b.aguirre@ebfarm.com
Number Employees: 1000-4999
Type of Packaging: Consumer

56200 Earthgrains
PO Box 976
Horsham, PA 19044 256-837-1511
  Fax: 256-721-9887 866-613-2784
Wholesaler/distributor of bread, buns and rolls; serving the food service market
VP: Ron Whitehouse
Director Sales: Bill Bethune
Number Employees: 100-249
Parent Co: Sara Lee Bakery Group
Types of Products Distributed:
  Food Service, Frozen Food, General Line, Bread, buns & rolls

56201 East Bay International
2434 Research Drive
Livermore, CA 94550-3850 925-373-9547
  Fax: 925-373-1989 800-982-6167
wdrenik@eastbayusa.com
Importer of coconut milk powder; exporter of restaurant equipment and supplies to international franchises. Also offers consulting services
President: William Drenik
Estimated Sales: $5-10 Million
Number Employees: 10-19
Square Footage: 80000
Types of Products Distributed:
  Food Service, Frozen Food, General Line, General Merchandise, Grocery products

56202 East Coast Seafood Inc
448 Boston St
PO Box 790
Topsfield, MA 01983-1216 781-593-1737
  Fax: 781-593-9583 www.eastcoastseafood.com
Importer, exporter and wholesaler/distributor of live lobster, fresh skatewings, dogfish, monk tails, etc.; serving the food service market
President: Michael Tourkistas
CFO: James Bouras
VP: Spiros Tourkakis
Estimated Sales: $10-20 Million
Number Employees: 10-19
Square Footage: 120000
Parent Co: American Holdco
Type of Packaging: Food Service
Types of Products Distributed:
  Food Service, Frozen Food, Seafood, Lobster, skatewings, dogfish, etc.

56203 East Poultry Co
2615 E 6th St
Austin, TX 78702-3900 512-476-5367
  Fax: 512-476-5360 www.eastpoultry.com
Poultry and eggs
President: Ken Aune
eastpoultry@austin.rr.com
Estimated Sales: $4.10 Million
Number Employees: 10-19
Square Footage: 54000
Type of Packaging: Food Service, Bulk
Types of Products Distributed:
  Poultry, Eggs

56204 East Side Fisheries
Box 40 Lower E Pubnico
Yarmouth, NS B0W 2A0
Canada
  902-762-2170
  Fax: 902-762-2666
Wholesaler/distributor of lobster and groundfish
President: Louise LeBlanc
Number Employees: 20-49
Types of Products Distributed:
  Frozen Food, Seafood, Lobster & groundfish

56205 Eastern Bag & Paper Company
200 Research Dr
Milford, CT 06460
  Fax: 203-878-0438 800-972-9622
  marketing@EBPsupply.com
Wholesaler/distributor of paper/plastic disposables, food service equipment and smallwares, janitorial equipment, repair and supplies.
President: Matthew Sugarman
Chief Executive Officer: Meredith Reuben
Chief Financial Officer: William O'Donnell
Chief Information Officer: Jack Jurkowski
SVP, Human Resources: Joseph LoPresti
VP, Supply Chain: Joe Ondriezek
Year Founded: 1918
Estimated Sales: $177.98 Million
Number Employees: 285
Square Footage: 180000
Types of Products Distributed:
  Frozen Food, General Merchandise, Paper/plastic disposables, etc.

56206 Eastern Bakers Supply Co Inc
145 N Washington St
Boston, MA 02114-2150 617-742-0228
  Fax: 617-723-8835
Wholesaler/distributor of new and used food service equipment and supplies
President: Robert Kalustian
rkalust299@aol.com
Controller: Rita Murphy
VP: William Morrissey
Estimated Sales: $5-10 Million
Number Employees: 20-49
Square Footage: 119000
Types of Products Distributed:
  Food Service, Frozen Food, General Merchandise, New & used equipment

56207 Eastern Energy LightingSystems
PO Box 1543
Greenwood Lake, NY 10925-1543 914-674-0093
  Fax: 914-674-0433 800-794-0083
Wholesaler/distributor and exporter of lighting fixtures
President: Ted Siebert
VP: Lance Edwards
Estimated Sales: $5-10 Million
Number Employees: 10-19
Square Footage: 8000
Number of Customer Locations: 50
Types of Products Distributed:
  Frozen Food, General Merchandise, Lighting fixtures

56208 (HQ)Eastern Fish Company
Glennpointe Centre East
300 Frank W Burr Blvd Ste 30
Teaneck, NJ 07666 201-801-0800
  Fax: 201-801-0802 800-526-9066
  www.easternfish.com
Manufacturer and importer of farm raised shrimp and other seafood, bay and sea scallops, lobster, king crab legs and claws, snow crab clusters, yellow fin tuna
Founder: Bill Bloom
President: Eric Bloom
Secretary: Charna Bloom
Vice President: Lee Bloom
Estimated Sales: $6.7 Million
Number Employees: 30
Square Footage: 18000
Type of Packaging: Private Label
Other Locations:
  Norwestern Sales Office
  Kingston, WA
  Western Sales Office
  Anaheim, CA
  Northeastern Sales Office
  Gloucester, MA
  Southeastern Sales Office
  Coral Springs, FLNorwestern Sales OfficeAnaheim
Types of Products Distributed:
  Frozen Food

56209 Eastern Refrigeration &Restaurant Equipment
640 Harvard St Ste 4
Manchester, NH 03103 603-625-5920
  Fax: 603-622-8236
Wholesaler/distributor of refrigeration and equipment for restaurants, stores, schools, cafeterias, etc
Owner: Jason Smith
VP: Charles Tsiatsios
Estimated Sales: $1-2.5 Million
Number Employees: 5-9
Square Footage: 60000
Types of Products Distributed:
  Food Service, Frozen Food, General Merchandise, Refrigeration & equipment

56210 Eastern Seafood Co
1020 W Hubbard St
Chicago, IL 60642-6526 312-243-2090
  Fax: 312-243-9467
Seafood
President: Mario Falco
easternseafood@att.net
Estimated Sales: $730 Thousand
Number Employees: 5-9

56211 Eastern Shore Clam Company
304 Burns Street
St Michaels, MD 21663 410-745-2900
  info@thecrabclaw.com
  www.thecrabclaw.com
Wholesaler/distributor of shellfish.
Year Founded: 1965
Estimated Sales: $20-50 Million
Number Employees: 100-249
Types of Products Distributed:
  Seafood

56212 Eastimpex
500 Selby Street
San Francisco, CA 94124-1122 415-282-2000
  Fax: 415-282-1020
Wholesaler/distributor, importer and exporter of groceries including short-grain rice, oyster sauce and bamboo shoots
President: Don Chan
Number Employees: 20-49
Square Footage: 440000
Types of Products Distributed:
  Frozen Food, General Line, General Merchandise, Groceries & health/beauty aids

56213 Eatmore Fruit Company
1240 Sherman St
Allentown, PA 18109-1797 610-433-3188
  Fax: 610-776-0396 www.eatmore.net
Wholesaler/distributor of fruits and vegetables; serving the food service market
President: David Fine
Estimated Sales: $20-50 Million
Number Employees: 20-49
Type of Packaging: Private Label
Types of Products Distributed:
  Food Service, Frozen Food, Produce

56214 (HQ)Eaton Corporation
1000 Eaton Blvd
Beachwood, OH 44122
  800-386-1911
  www.eaton.com
Manufacturer and exporter of emergency, indoor and outdoor lighting
Chairman & CEO: Craig Arnold
Vice Chairman & CFO: Richard Fearon
Executive VP & General Counsel: April Miller Boise
Executive VP, Supply Chain Management: Rogerico Branco
Estimated Sales: $21.4 Billion
Number Employees: 97,000
Types of Products Distributed:
  Frozen Food

56215 Eaton Market
1343 S Mound Street
Grenada, MS 38901-4511 662-226-2525
  Fax: 662-226-2525
Wholesaler/distributor of provisions/meats; serving the food service market
President: Larry Eaton
Number Employees: 5-9
Types of Products Distributed:
  Food Service, Frozen Food, Provisions/Meat

56216 Eau de Source Boischatel
2165 Rue Lavoisier
Ste. Foy, QC G1N 4B2
Canada 418-687-3754
  Fax: 418-687-2428
Wholesaler/distributor of natural spring water; serving the food service market
President: Rene Coulombe
VP: Marc Coulombe
Number Employees: 50-99

Wholesalers & Distributors / A-Z

Types of Products Distributed:
Food Service, Frozen Food, General Line, Natural spring water

56217 Ebonex Corporation
2380 S. Wabash Street
Melvindale, MI 48122   313-388-0060
             Fax: 313-388-6495 ebonex@flash.net
                                    www.ebonex.com
Wholesaler/distributor and importer of ammonium carbonate
President: Michelle Toenniges
Pres.: Michael Szczepanik
Tech. Dir.: Michele Toenngies
Estimated Sales: $2.5-5 Million
Number Employees: 10-19
Square Footage: 32000
Types of Products Distributed:
Frozen Food, General Line, Ammonium carbonate

56218 Eby-Brown Company
1415 W Diehl Rd
Suite 300N
Naperville, IL 60563   630-778-2800
                                    800-553-8249
                             www.eby-brown.com
Wholesaler/distributor of general merchandise and candy; serving convenience stores.
Co-President/CEO: Dick Wake
Co-President/CEO: Tom Wake
Year Founded: 1887
Estimated Sales: $6 Billion
Number Employees: 2,300
Square Footage: 1933000
Parent Co: Performance Food Group
Types of Products Distributed:
Frozen Food, General Line, General Merchandise, Candy

56219 (HQ)Eckert Machines
2875 Portland Drive
Oakville, ON L6B 5S4
Canada   905-356-8356
    Fax: 905-356-1704 info@eckertmachines.com
                            www.eckertmachines.com
Wholesaler/distributor of food processing machinery
President: Paul Eckert
Sales Director: Warren Morgan
Estimated Sales: 1-3 Million
Number Employees: 8
Square Footage: 6000
Other Locations:
Eckert Machines
Lewiston, NYEckert Machines
Types of Products Distributed:
Food processing machinery

56220 Eco Wine & Spirits
3235 N San Fernando Road
Los Angeles, CA 90065-1443   323-257-9055
         Fax: 323-257-6997 ecows@aol.com
Importer and wholesaler/distributor of wine, beer and spirits
President: Vahan Plovzian
VP: Harry Apikian
Estimated Sales: $1 Million
Number Employees: 5-9
Square Footage: 20000
Type of Packaging: Consumer
Types of Products Distributed:
Alcoholic Beverages

56221 Ecological Formulas
1061 Shary Cir # B
Concord, CA 94518-2407   925-827-2636
         Fax: 925-676-9231 800-888-4585
Wholesaler/distributor of nutritional products
President: Jonathan Rothschild
Estimated Sales: $2.5-5 Million
Number Employees: 5-9
Types of Products Distributed:
Frozen Food, Health Food

56222 Ecological Technologies
PO Box 4733
Boynton Beach, FL 33324   561-585-2195
                Fax: 561-547-0993
Wholesaler/distributor and exporter of waste water treatment systems; serving the food service market
President: Dennis Paul
Estimated Sales: $1-2.5 Million
Number Employees: 10-19
Parent Co: DynynStyl

Types of Products Distributed:
Food Service, General Merchandise, Waste water treatment systems

56223 Economy Cash & Carry LP
1000 E Overland Ave
El Paso, TX 79901   915-532-2660
                Fax: 915-533-8240
Wholesaler/distributor of groceries and general merchandise; serving the food service market; rack jobber services available.
Owner: Paul Dipp
Estimated Sales: $50-100 Million
Number Employees: 50-99
Square Footage: 100000
Parent Co: Economy Wholesale Food Distributors
Private Brands Carried:
Red & White; Laziat Soda
Number of Customer Locations: 500
Types of Products Distributed:
Food Service, General Line, General Merchandise, Rack Jobbers, Groceries

56224 Economy Paper & Restaurant Co
180 Broad St
Clifton, NJ 07013-1299   973-279-5500
    Fax: 973-279-4140 sales@economysupply.com
                            www.economysupply.com
Soaps, degreasers and custom fabricated equipment; wholesaler/distributor and exporter of food service equipment, disposables, janitorial supplies, smallwares, glassware, flatware and china; installation and consulting available
President: L J Konzelman
CFO: Susan Majors
VP: Micheal Konzelman
R&D: Alex Nasarone
Public Relations: Susan Majors
Purchasing: Kevin Konzelman
Estimated Sales: $3-5 Million
Number Employees: 10-19
Square Footage: 50000
Type of Packaging: Food Service
Types of Products Distributed:
Specialty Foods

56225 Economy Restaurant Fixtures
1200 7th St
San Francisco, CA 94107   415-626-5611
                                    800-323-3384
                             www.trimarkusa.com
Wholesaler/distributor of equipment, furniture, smallwares, paper goods, china, glassware and cleaning supplies; serving the food service market.
President: Jeff Weinstock
Number Employees: 50-99
Square Footage: 120000
Private Brands Carried:
Wolf; Beverage Air; Anchor Hocking
Types of Products Distributed:
Food Service, Frozen Food, General Merchandise, Equipment, furniture, etc.

56226 Economy Wholesale Company
P.O.Box 3346
Cumberland, MD 21504-3346   301-724-0202
                Fax: 301-724-0213
Wholesaler/distributor of groceries, confectionery items, dairy products, equipment and fixtures, general merchandise, health and beauty aids, luncheon meats and frozen foods
President: George F Garlitz
Treasurer: Don Snyder
General Manager: David Snyder
Estimated Sales: $10-20 Million
Number Employees: 10-19
Square Footage: 60000
Number of Customer Locations: 50
Types of Products Distributed:
Frozen Food, General Line, General Merchandise, Provisions/Meat, Dairy items, equipment, etc.

56227 (HQ)Ecoval Dairy Trade
Takenhofplein 6
1st Floor
Nijmegen, 6538 SZ
Netherlands
                                    www.ecoval.com
Wholesaler/distributor, importer and exporter of dairy products including nonfat dry milk, whey powder, butter, oil, buttermilk powder and cheese; serving the food service market

President: Donald Street
Director Sales: Carolyn Spack
Number Employees: 20-49
Square Footage: 12000
Parent Co: Louis Dreyfus Commodities Suisse S.A.
Type of Packaging: Food Service
Other Locations:
M.E. Franks
Stillwater, MNM.E. Franks
Types of Products Distributed:
Food Service, Frozen Food, General Line, Dairy products, oil, butter, etc.

56228 Ecuadorian Rainforest LLC
25 Main St
Building 6
Belleville, NJ 07109   973-759-2002
    Fax: 973-759-3002 info@intotherainforest.com
                         www.intotherainforest.com
Wholsaler of bulk raw materials; nutraceutical ingredient supplier.
Owner: Marlene Siegel
Vice President: Steve Siegel
Types of Products Distributed:
Health Food, Specialty Foods, Ingredients

56229 Ed's Kasilof Seafoods
26085 Williamson Ln
Kasilof, AK 99610   907-262-7295
        Fax: 907-262-1617 800-982-2377
        eks@alaska.net www.kasilofseafoods.com
Seafood
President: James Trujillo
eks@alaska.net
Estimated Sales: $960 Thousand
Number Employees: 20-49

56230 Eden
PO Box 544
Utica, OH 43080-0544   740-745-2745
        Fax: 740-745-2748 800-831-9505
Importer, exporter and wholesaler/distributor of natural food supplements
President: Deborah Ruyan
Estimated Sales: $500,000-$1 Million
Number Employees: 5-9
Square Footage: 100000
Private Brands Carried:
Cernilton; Pollitabs; Ventrux; Cervital; Napolen Gold
Types of Products Distributed:
Frozen Food, Health Food, Nutritional supplements

56231 Eden Creamery
Los Angeles, CA
                                info@halotop.com
                                www.halotop.com
Low calorie ice cream
Co-Founder: Justin Woolverton
Co-Founder: Douglas Bouton
Types of Products Distributed:
Frozen Food

56232 Edinburg Citrus Assn
401 W Chapin St
Edinburg, TX 78541   956-383-2743
                Fax: 956-383-2435
                www.edinburgcitrusassociation.com
Non-profit organization representing citrus growers, harvest, pack and sell our grower members citrus
Sales & Marketing: Ashlynn Elliff
Sales manager: Jeffrey Arnold II
Manager: Bengie Garcia
bengie@txcitrus.com
Estimated Sales: $15 Million
Number Employees: 100-249
Number of Brands: 5
Number of Products: 2
Square Footage: 390000
Types of Products Distributed:
Produce

56233 Edmer Sanitary Supply Co Inc
519 E Meadow Ave
East Meadow, NY 11554-3999   516-794-2000
        Fax: 516-228-8759 edmer@optonline.net
                             www.edmersupply.com
Wholesaler/distributor of janitorial equipment, sanitary chemicals, cleaning supplies and paper products

President: Dominic Fragiorgi
dfragiorgi@edmersupply.com
CEO: Bill Zeitlin
Vice President: Randy Siegmann
Estimated Sales: $5-10 Million
Number Employees: 10-19
Number of Products: 6000
Square Footage: 60000
Private Brands Carried:
   Everything For Cleaning Anything
Types of Products Distributed:
   Frozen Food, General Merchandise, Cleaning & janitorial supplies, etc.

56234 Edner Corporation
1200 Zephyr Ave
Hayward, CA 94544   510-441-8504
   Fax: 510-441-9395
Breads (specialty), cakes, cookies, croissants (filled and unfilled), muffins, pastries, & scones (filled and unfilled)
President: Ed Kirschner
VP Technical Sales: Mark Aquilar
Manager: Sandy Caires
Estimated Sales: $2 Million
Number Employees: 30
Parent Co: Edner Corporation
Type of Packaging: Consumer, Food Service, Private Label, Bulk
Types of Products Distributed:
   Frozen Food

56235 (HQ)Edom Labs Inc
100 E Jefryn Blvd
Suite M
Deer Park, NY 11729-5729   631-586-2266
   Fax: 631-586-2385 800-723-3366
   info@edomlaboratories.com
   www.edomlaboratories.com
Vitamins and dietary supplements
Owner: Eric Pollack

Estimated Sales: Less Than $500,000
Number Employees: 1-4
Type of Packaging: Consumer, Private Label, Bulk
Types of Products Distributed:
   Frozen Food, Health Food, Dietary supplements & vitamins

56236 Edsung
1337 Mookaula St
Honolulu, HI 96817-4308   808-845-3931
   Fax: 808-842-4702
Wholesaler/distributor of bakery supplies and institutional foods
President: Edward Chio
VP: Dennis Choi
Contact: Diana Choi
diana.choi@cfcorporation.com
Estimated Sales: $20-50 Million
Number Employees: 20-49
Parent Co: Edsung
Number of Customer Locations: 490
Types of Products Distributed:
   Food Service, Frozen Food, General Line, Institutional foods & bakery supplies

56237 Edward Badeaux Company
311 Jackson St
Thibodaux, LA 70301   985-447-3338
   Fax: 985-447-1598
Wholesaler/distributor of confectionery items
President: Manuel Rodrigue
Estimated Sales: $5-10 Million
Number Employees: 10-19
Types of Products Distributed:
   Frozen Food, General Line, General Merchandise, Confectionery items

56238 Edward Don & Co
84 Stemmers Ln
Westampton, NJ 08060
   800-777-4366
   www.don.com
Wholesaler/distributor of general merchandise, equipment and fixtures and supplies, tabletop items, smallwares, disposables and janitorial products; serving the food service market.
President & CEO: Steve Don
Year Founded: 1921
Estimated Sales: $50-100 Million
Number Employees: 100-249
Square Footage: 147000
Types of Products Distributed:
   Food Service, Frozen Food, General Merchandise, Equipment & supplies

56239 Edward Don & Co
6255 Brook Hollow Pkwy
Norcross, GA 30071-4618   770-239-5098
   Fax: 404-297-7037 800-777-4DON
   www.edwarddon.com
Wholesaler/distributor of tabletop items, smallwares, disposables and janitorial products; serving the food service market
Manager: Paul Brown
paulbrown@don.com
Manager: Ron Ellsworth
Estimated Sales: $5-10 Million
Number Employees: 50-99
Parent Co: Edward Don & Company
Types of Products Distributed:
   Food Service, Frozen Food, General Merchandise, Equipment & supplies

56240 Edward Don & Co
11500 Miramar Pkwy
Suite 600
Miramar, FL 33025
   800-777-4366
   www.don.com
Wholesaler/distributor of general merchandise, equipment and fixtures and supplies, tabletop items, smallwares, disposables and janitorial products; serving the food service market.
President & CEO: Steve Don
Year Founded: 1921
Estimated Sales: $50-100 Million
Number Employees: 100-249
Square Footage: 161000
Types of Products Distributed:
   Food Service, Frozen Food, General Merchandise, Glassware, china dishware, etc.

56241 (HQ)Edward Don & Company
9801 Adam Don Pkwy
Woodridge, IL 60517
   800-777-4366
   www.don.com
Wholesaler/distributor of general merchandise, equipment and fixtures and supplies, tabletop items, smallwares, disposables and janitorial products; serving the food service market.
President & CEO: Steve Don
Year Founded: 1921
Estimated Sales: $50-100 Million
Number Employees: 100-249
Square Footage: 362500
Other Locations:
   Edward Don & Co.
   Norcross, GAEdward Don & Co.
Number of Customer Locations: 5000
Types of Products Distributed:
   Food Service, Frozen Food, General Merchandise, Equipment & supplies

56242 Edward Don & Company
3501 Plano Pkwy
The Colony, TX 75056
   800-388-4366
   www.don.com
Wholesaler/distributor of general merchandise, equipment and fixtures and supplies, tabletop items, smallwares, disposables and janitorial products; serving the food service market.
President & CEO: Steve Don
Year Founded: 1921
Estimated Sales: $50-100 Million
Number Employees: 100-249
Square Footage: 187000
Types of Products Distributed:
   Food Service, Frozen Food, General Merchandise, Equipment & supplies

56243 Edward G Rahll & Sons
7460 Conowingo Ave # 42
Units 30-52
Jessup, MD 20794-9434   410-799-3800
   Fax: 410-799-8063 info@rahllproduce.com
   www.rahllproduce.com
Wholesaler/distributor of produce and in business since 1951
President: Joe Rahll Sr
egrahll@juno.com
Sales Exec: Joe Rahll
Office Manager: T.J. Rahll

Estimated Sales: $5-10 Million
Number Employees: 20-49
Square Footage: 145376
Types of Products Distributed:
   Food Service, Produce

56244 Edward I. Friedland
3539 N 8th Street
Philadelphia, PA 19140-4498   215-226-3471
   Fax: 215-226-3474
Wholesaler/distributor of beer
Owner: Edith Friedland
Estimated Sales: $1-2.5 Million
Number Employees: 5-9
Types of Products Distributed:
   Frozen Food, Beer

56245 Edward Marc Brands
55 38th St
Pittsburgh, PA 15201   877-488-1808
   edwardmarc.com
Chocolate; confections; and milk shakes
CEO: Mark Edwards
VP of Operations: Steve Brown
Year Founded: 1914
Number Employees: 50-200
Type of Packaging: Food Service, Private Label

56246 (HQ)Edwards Distributing
125 Double E Dr
Hidalgo, TX 78557-4313   956-843-2716
   Fax: 956-843-8122
Wholesaler/distributor of produce; serving the food service market
Manager: Gary Wiener
Estimated Sales: $10-20 Million
Number Employees: 20-49
Types of Products Distributed:
   Food Service, Frozen Food, Produce

56247 Efficient Foodservice Response
201 Park Washington Court
Falls Church, VA 22046-4527   703-532-9400
   Fax: 703-538-4673
Number Employees: 10-19

56248 (HQ)Ehrlich Food Co
581 Austin Pl # 2
Bronx, NY 10455-3899   718-993-4800
   Fax: 718-993-4802 www.jcehrlich.com
Wholesaler/distributor of general line products, frozen foods, produce, meats, seafood, etc.; serving the food service market
President: Gloria Ehrlich
sehrlich@aol.com
CEO: Jarret Ehrlich
CFO: Greg Wallace
VP: G Ehrlich
Marketing: Karen Jackson
Sales: Scott Ehrlich
Estimated Sales: Less Than $500,000
Number Employees: 1-4
Type of Packaging: Food Service, Private Label, Bulk
Number of Customer Locations: 1500
Types of Products Distributed:
   Food Service, Frozen Food, General Line, General Merchandise, Health Food, Provisions/Meat, Produce, Rack Jobbers, Seafood

56249 Eklof & Company
157 Boone Trail
Severna Park, MD 21146-4503   410-539-5030
   Fax: 410-783-5642
Wholesaler/distributor of commercial kitchen equipment serving the food service market
President: R Meier
VP: L Meier
Manager: C Reddick
Estimated Sales: $1-2.5 Million
Number Employees: 1-4
Square Footage: 160000
Parent Co: RFM
Types of Products Distributed:
   Food Service, Frozen Food, General Merchandise, Commercial kitchen equipment

56250 El Molino Tamales
117 S 22nd Street
Phoenix, AZ 85034-2515   602-244-2536
Wholesaler/distributor of Mexican food products including pre-made tacos and enchiladas
Owner: Paul Carbajal
Number Employees: 5-9

Wholesalers & Distributors / A-Z

Types of Products Distributed:
   Frozen Food, Specialty Foods, Mexican foods: tacos & enchiladas

56251 El Popular Inc VF Garza
910 E Chicago Ave
East Chicago, IN 46312-3513   219-397-3728
   Fax: 219-398-1648 www.chorizo.us
Wholesaler/distributor of Mexican-style foods; rack jobber services available
Owner: Edward Garza
elpopular@usa.com
Estimated Sales: $10-20 Million
Number Employees: 10-19
Private Brands Carried:
   El Popular
Number of Customer Locations: 500
Types of Products Distributed:
   Frozen Food, Rack Jobbers, Specialty Foods, Mexican-style foods

56252 Elco Fine Foods
233 Alden Road
Markham, ON L4B 1G5
Canada   905-731-7337
   Fax: 905-731-2391 info@elcofinefoods.com
   www.elcofinefoods.com
Distributor of premium confectionery, food and beverage products
CEO: Moe Cussen
Number Employees: 100
Square Footage: 270000

56253 Elco Fine Foods
7660 Winston Street
Burnaby, BC V5A 4N2
Canada   604-944-2505
   Fax: 604-944-2569
Wholesaler/distributor and importer of Dutch and European cookies, crackers, rusk, honey and candy cake, sauces, jams, dressings, confectionary, smoked herring, soup and soup concentrates and other gourmet food items.
Branch Manager: Fred van Rijswijk
Number Employees: 5-9
Square Footage: 36000
Parent Co: Holtzheuser Brothers
Private Brands Carried:
   Ribenhus; Honig; Hille; Bella; Tantos; Loretta
Number of Customer Locations: 600
Types of Products Distributed:
   Frozen Food, General Line, Specialty Foods, Cookies, crackers, rusk, cakes, etc.

56254 Elco Fine Foods
233 Alden Road
Markham, OT L3R 3W6
Canada   905-474-2400
   Fax: 905-474-2499 800-421-ELCO
   info@elcofinefoods.com www.elcocanada.com
Importer and wholesaler/distributor of international specialty food products including confectionery items and cheeses; also, general merchandise and health foods; serving the food service market
Sales Manager: Brian Wright
Number Employees: 10-19
Parent Co: Elco Fine Foods
Type of Packaging: Consumer, Food Service, Private Label, Bulk
Private Brands Carried:
   Eoetker; Hille; Honig; Cardini
Number of Customer Locations: 300
Types of Products Distributed:
   Food Service, Frozen Food, General Line, General Merchandise, Health Food, Specialty Foods, International food products

56255 Eleanor's Best LLC
PO Box 9
Garrison, NY 10524   646-296-6870
   info@eleanorsbest.com
   www.eleanorsbest.com
Handmade, vegan, gluten jams and marmalades, maple syrup, wildflower honey
Founder/Owner: Jennifer Mercurio
Year Founded: 2013
Number Employees: 10
Number of Brands: 1
Number of Products: 16
Type of Packaging: Consumer, Private Label
Private Brands Carried:
   Eleanor's Own
Number of Customer Locations: 1

Types of Products Distributed:
   Preserves

56256 Electra Supply Co
331 Mill St
Poughkeepsie, NY 12601-3318   845-452-9000
   Fax: 845-452-4720
Wholesaler/distributor of electrical supplies including lighting fixtures
Manager: Randy Kelsey
rkelsey@wesco.com
Administration Manager: Lisa Conger
Estimated Sales: $10-20 Million
Number Employees: 10-19
Number of Customer Locations: 600
Types of Products Distributed:
   Frozen Food, General Merchandise, Electrical supplies: lighting fixtures

56257 Electric Forklift Repair
837 Somerset St
Somerset, NJ 08873-3526   732-249-7757
   Fax: 732-249-7068 866-249-7068
   forkliftpeople@msn.com
   www.theforkliftpeople.com
Supplier of forklift trucjs and pallets jacks, LPG, electric, diesel. Rentail, sales, service, transportation
Owner: Raul Pretto
CEO: Philip Pretto
CFO: Felix Mitchell
Vice President: Mavi Pretto
Marketing Director: Katherine Pretto
Sales Director: Skip Luise
Public Relations: Eileen Avci
Operations Manager: Carlos Saldana
Purchasing Manager: Priscilla Blue
Estimated Sales: $3 Million
Number Employees: 10-19
Number of Brands: 2
Number of Products: 5650
Square Footage: 70000
Private Brands Carried:
   Carer, Tailift
Types of Products Distributed:
   Material handling equipment

56258 Electro Freeze Distrs Inc
57 Mall Dr # A
Commack, NY 11725-5703   631-864-9090
   Fax: 631-864-9191 800-548-8800
   info@electrofreezetristate.com
   www.electrofreezetristate.com
Wholesaler/distributor of food service equipment; serving the food service market
Owner: John Agliato
johna@efdist.com
VP: John Agliato
Estimated Sales: $5-10 Million
Number Employees: 10-19
Private Brands Carried:
   Electro Freeze; Broaster
Number of Customer Locations: 3000
Types of Products Distributed:
   Food Service, Frozen Food, General Merchandise, Foodservice equipment

56259 Electroshield Inc
708 S High St
Yellow Springs, OH 45387-1530   937-767-1054
   Fax: 937-767-1354 800-662-1054
   sales@electroshield.com www.electroshield.com
Wholesaler/distributor of electronic components
Owner: Nick Eastman
nick@electroshield.com
Marketing Manager: Chuck Clevell
Estimated Sales: $5-10 Million
Number Employees: 10-19
Square Footage: 28000
Types of Products Distributed:
   Frozen Food, General Merchandise, Electronic components

56260 Elegant Desserts
275 Warren St
Lyndhurst, NJ 07071-2017   201-933-0770
   Fax: 201-933-7309 info@elegantdesserts.com
   www.elegantdesserts.com
Manufacturer and wholesaler/distributor of pastries including tarts and miniature grand viennas
President: John Mazur
jjmazur@bellatlantic.net
Estimated Sales: $2 Million
Number Employees: 20-49
Type of Packaging: Food Service, Private Label

Types of Products Distributed:
   Food Service, Frozen Food, General Line, Specialty Foods, Pastries: tarts, etc.

56261 Elemental Superfood
Torrance, CA 90501
   tryzen.com
Organic seedbars and crumble
Founder: Nicole Anderson

56262 Eliot's Adult Nut Butters
   503-847-9457
   info@eliotsadultnutbutters.com
   eliotsadultnutbutters.com
Nut butters
Founder: Michael Kanter
Number of Brands: 1
Number of Products: 7
Type of Packaging: Consumer

56263 Elizabeth Town Grain
PO Box 203
Elizabethtown, IN 47232-0203   812-579-5231
   Fax: 812-579-5916 800-464-5056
Wholesaler/distributor of grain
President: Jeff Trimpe
Estimated Sales: Less than $500,000
Number Employees: 1-4
Types of Products Distributed:
   Grain

56264 Elk Provision Co Inc
1260 Clinton St
Buffalo, NY 14206-2869   716-825-5555
   Fax: 716-825-0509
Wholesaler/distributor of beef and pork; serving the food service market
President: Ed Mangone
Estimated Sales: $10-20 Million
Number Employees: 5-9
Types of Products Distributed:
   Food Service, Produce

56265 Elkhorn Distributing Company
Hc 71 Box 152a
Meadow Bluff, WV 24977-9674   304-392-6311
   Fax: 304-392-6313 wvbud@inetone.net
Wholesaler/distributor of beer and general merchandise; warehouse providing cooler storage for beer
President: Don Runyon
Estimated Sales: $5-10 Million
Number Employees: 20-49
Square Footage: 220000
Private Brands Carried:
   Anheuser Busch; Heineken
Number of Customer Locations: 250
Types of Products Distributed:
   Frozen Food, General Line, General Merchandise, Beer

56266 Ella's Kitchen
1209 Orange St
New Castle, DE 19801
   800-685-7799
   www.ellaskitchen.com
Organic baby food and kids' food
Founder: Paul Lindley
CEO: Mark Cuddigan
Year Founded: 2009
Parent Co: Hain Celestial
Types of Products Distributed:
   General Line

56267 Elliot Horowitz & Co
675 3rd Ave
New York, NY 10017-5704   212-972-7500
   Fax: 212-972-7050 ehorowitz@elliothorowitz.com
   www.elliothorowitz.com
Manufacturers' representative for food service equipment and supplies including smallwares and heavy cooking and freezing equipment
Owner: Elliot Horowitz
Estimated Sales: $.5-1 million
Number Employees: 5-9
Type of Packaging: Food Service
Types of Products Distributed:
   Food Service

56268 Elliot Lee
445 Central Ave Unit 100
Cedarhurst, NY 11516   516-569-9595
   Fax: 516-569-8088 sales@misterpromotion.com
   www.misterpromotion.com

Manufacturer, importer and wholesaler/distributor of advertising specialties including sign holders, awards, badges, bags, cups, pens and plaques
President/CFO: Victor Deutsch
CFO: Elliot Deutsch
Marketing Director: Elliot Deutsch
Estimated Sales: Below $5 Million
Number Employees: 5-9
Private Brands Carried:
  Bic; Cross
Number of Customer Locations: 300
Types of Products Distributed:
  Frozen Food, General Merchandise, Advertising specialties

56269 Elliott Seafood Company
53 Stevens Ln
Cushing, ME 04563   207-354-2533
              Fax: 207-354-2533
Seafood
President: Stan Elliott

56270 Ellsworth Cooperative Creamery
232 N. Wallace St.
PO Box 610
Ellsworth, WI 54011   715-273-4311
  Fax: 715-273-5318 www.ellsworthcheese.com
Cheese curds, also available in flavors such as garlic, taco, cajun, natural, premium cheddar and ranch, also breaded and vacuum sealed/freezable.
President/Director: Albert Knegendorf
CEO/Manager: Paul Bauer
paulb@ellsworthcreamery.net
Vice President, Sales/Marketing: Jim Grande
Year Founded: 1910
Estimated Sales: $145 Million
Number Employees: 100-249
Number of Brands: 5
Square Footage: 120000
Type of Packaging: Consumer, Private Label, Bulk

56271 Ellsworth Foods
1510 Eastman Dr
Tifton, GA 31793-8228   229-386-8448
  Fax: 229-387-9749 www.ellsworthfoods.com
Grocery products
Owner: Ken Ellsworth Jr
kellsworth@ellsworthfoods.com
VP: Rebecca Ellsworth
Estimated Sales: $5 Million
Number Employees: 20-49

56272 Elm Electric Supply
PO Box 265
Stamford, CT 06904-0265   203-348-6278
              Fax: 203-961-8637
Wholesaler/distributor of electrical supplies including exhaust fans, bulbs and lighting fixtures
President: Joel Most
Estimated Sales: $1-3 Million
Number Employees: 6
Square Footage: 40000
Private Brands Carried:
  Nutone; Sylvania-Osram; Progress Lighting; Sea-Gull Lighting; Juno Lighting; Phillips Lamp; RAB Lighting; Klein Tool; Greenlee Tools; Raco Boxes; Lutron; Leviton; Eagle' Bryant; Wiremold' Trine; Intermatic; Murray Products
Number of Customer Locations: 395
Types of Products Distributed:
  Frozen Food, General Merchandise, Exhaust fans, bulbs, etc.

56273 Elmira Distributing Company
374 Upper Oakwood Ave
Elmira, NY 14903   607-734-6231
  Fax: 607-733-6989 toby41756@aol.com
Wholesaler/distributor of equipment and fixtures, general merchandise, wines, spirits, beverages and candies; serving the food service market, convenience stores and schools
President: Toby Lagonegro
toby41756@aol.com
Vice President: Richard Rinde
Sales Manager: Stefano Rinoes
Estimated Sales: $5-10 Million
Number Employees: 20-49
Square Footage: 112000

56274 Elon Products Company
10200 W 9 Mile Rd
Oak Park, MI 48237   248-548-1380
  Fax: 248-548-1380 elonproduc@aol.com

Seasoned ground beef and pork and poultry; ground and injected.
Owner: Jacob Friedman
Number of Products: 4
Square Footage: 12800
Type of Packaging: Food Service
Types of Products Distributed:
  Food Service

56275 Emco Industrial Plastics
99 Commerce Rd
Cedar Grove, NJ 07009   973-239-0202
  Fax: 973-239-1595 800-292-9906
          mailbox@emcoplastics.com
              www.emcoplastics.com
Supplier of plastic sheet, rod, tubing and films including plexiglass, cutting boards, and vinyl door strip. Manufacturer of plastic point of purchase displays including bulk food containers, bagel bins, pastry cases, candy binsframes, sign holders, and sneeze guards.
President: James Mc Namara
Vice President: Mark Mercadante
Sales Manager: Jim McNamara
Estimated Sales: $20-50 Million
Number Employees: 50-99
Square Footage: 50000
Type of Packaging: Food Service
Types of Products Distributed:
  Frozen Food, General Merchandise, Point of purchase displays & bins

56276 Emerling International Foods
2381 Fillmore Ave
Suite 1
Buffalo, NY 14214-2197   716-833-7381
  Fax: 716-833-7386 pemerling@emerfood.com
          www.emerlinginternational.com
Bulk ingredients including: Fruits & Vegetables; Juice Concentrates; Herbs & Spices; Oils & Vinegars; Flavors & Colors; Honey & Molasses. Also produces pure maple syrup.
President: J Emerling
jemerling@emerfood.com
Sales: Peter Emerling
Public Relations: Jenn Burke
Year Founded: 1988
Estimated Sales: $10-20 Million
Number Employees: 20-49
Square Footage: 500000
Types of Products Distributed:
  Food Service, Frozen Food

56277 Emiliomiti
219 9th St
San Francisco, CA 94103-3806   415-621-1909
  Fax: 415-621-4613 866-867-2782
          info@pastabiz.com www.pastabiz.com
Wholesaler/distributor of espresso coffee machines, pasta machines and wood burning brick pizza ovens; serving the food service market
CEO: Emilio Mitidieri
Estimated Sales: 900000
Number Employees: 10-19
Number of Brands: 5
Number of Products: 16
Square Footage: 12000
Types of Products Distributed:
  Food Service, Frozen Food, General Merchandise, Espresso, pasta machy/pizza brick ovens

56278 Emkay Confectionery Machinery Company
3313 Mill Grove Terrace
Dracula, GA 30019   770-614-1302
  Fax: 770-614-0515 info@emkaymachinery.com
              www.emkaymachinery.com
Wholesaler/distributor of packaging machinery for confections
President: Jason Kaderli
VP Sales: Jason Kaderli
Estimated Sales: $1-3 Million
Number Employees: 1-4
Number of Customer Locations: 50
Types of Products Distributed:
  General Merchandise, Packaging machinery for confections

56279 Emkay Trading Corporation
250 Clearbrook Road
PO Box 504
Elmsford, NY 10523   914-592-9000
  Fax: 914-347-3616 hkpilot@aol.com

Manufacturer and distributor of cheese including cream, bakers, neuchatel, lite, tvorog (Russian style soft cheese) and quark, also, bulk cream, custom fluid diary blends, bulk skim, sour cream, bulk cultured buttermilk and condensedskim milk
Owner: Howard Kravitz
tlindquistturner@limitedbrands.com
Vice President: Ruth Kravitz
Estimated Sales: $2 Million
Number Employees: 30
Square Footage: 800000
Type of Packaging: Consumer, Food Service, Private Label, Bulk
Types of Products Distributed:
  Frozen Food

56280 Empire Cash Register Systems
1738 E 2nd St
Scotch Plains, NJ 07076-1708   908-322-4900
  Fax: 908-322-4902 posman1@aol.com
Wholesaler/distributor of general merchandise including point of sale systems, cash registers and scales; serving the food service market
President: Phil Rubin
posman1@aol.com
Estimated Sales: $1-2.5 Million
Number Employees: 5-9
Parent Co: Phil Rubin Association
Private Brands Carried:
  Sanyo; Sharp; Samsung
Types of Products Distributed:
  Food Service, Frozen Food, General Merchandise, Point of sale systems, etc.

56281 Empire Comfort Systems
918 Freeburg Ave
Belleville, IL 62220-2623   618-233-7420
  Fax: 618-233-7097 800-851-3153
              www.empirezoneheat.com
Wholesaler/distributor of portable cooking stoves; serving the food service market
President: D Sahdev
Executive VP: Don Rigney
drigney@empirecomfort.com
VP Sales: Joseph Brueggemann
Sales Representative: Marisa Lucash
Estimated Sales: $20-50 Million
Number Employees: 100-249
Private Brands Carried:
  Superb
Types of Products Distributed:
  Food Service, Frozen Food, General Merchandise, Portable cooking stoves

56282 Empire Forklift Inc
376 Petticoat Ln
Bloomingburg, NY 12721-3055   845-733-4555
  Fax: 845-733-1129 www.empireforklift.com
Wholesaler/distributor of material handling equipment including forklifts
President: Larry Mc Dowell
jr@empireforklift.com
Vice President: Larry McDowell, Jr.
Sales Director: Geoffrey Gollub
Operations Manager: Larry McDowell, Jr.
Estimated Sales: $10-20 Million
Number Employees: 20-49
Private Brands Carried:
  Barrett; TCM; Scrubbers; PowerBose; Sweepers; BT Prime Movers
Types of Products Distributed:
  General Merchandise, Forklifts, etc.

56283 Empire Packing Co
8648 Fenkell St
Detroit, MI 48238-1796   313-345-6565
              Fax: 313-345-4841
Wholesaler/distributor of meats, dairy products, frozen foods, baked goods, seafood and private label items; serving the food service market
President: Karen Holder
holderkarenk@wix.com
President: Lou Popper
Estimated Sales: $20-50 Million
Number Employees: 10-19
Number of Customer Locations: 650
Types of Products Distributed:
  Food Service, Frozen Food, General Line, Provisions/Meat, Seafood, Dairy products, baked goods, etc.

Wholesalers & Distributors / A-Z

56284 Empire Tea Svc
1965 St James Pl
Columbus, IN 47201-2805   812-375-1937
    Fax: 812-376-7382   800-790-0246
    sales@empiretea.com   www.empiretea.com
Importer of tea in tins, black tea, green tea, herb tea bulk tea, tea bags in wood boxes and various forms of packing
President: Lalith Guy Paranavitana
info@empiretea.com
Plant Manager: Cheryl Paranavitana
Estimated Sales: $250,000
Number Employees: 1-4
Number of Brands: 3
Number of Products: 27
Square Footage: 8000
Type of Packaging: Consumer, Food Service, Private Label, Bulk
Private Brands Carried:
    Guy's Tea; Unicom; Tea Temptations
Types of Products Distributed:
    Food Service, General Merchandise, Specialty Foods

56285 Empress Food Prods Co Inc
10592 Taconic Ter
Cincinnati, OH 45215-1125   513-771-1441
    Fax: 513-771-1442
Wholesaler/distributor of frozen chili; serving the food service market
Owner: Kevin Tuchfarber
empress_chili@yahoo.com
VP: Carol Kiradjieff
Estimated Sales: Less Than $500,000
Number Employees: 1-4
Square Footage: 40000
Private Brands Carried:
    Empress (Chili)
Types of Products Distributed:
    Food Service, Frozen Food, General Line, Chili

56286 Emuamericas
1799 Pennsylvania St
4th Floor
Denver, CO 80203   303-733-3385
    Fax: 303-733-3384   800-726-0368
    info@emuamericas.com   www.emuamericas.com
Wholesaler/distributor and importer of indoor and outdoor chairs and tables; serving the food service market
President: Benjamin Fromgaglia
Private Brands Carried:
    .mu
Types of Products Distributed:
    Outdoor/Indoor Furniture.

56287 (HQ)Emulsol Egg Products Corporation
7101 N Cicero Avenue
Suite 102
Lincolnwood, IL 60712-2112   847-763-0500
Wholesaler/distributor of egg products
President: Mel Lipschultz
VP: Howard Lipschultz
VP: Mary Picker
Number Employees: 5-9
Types of Products Distributed:
    Frozen Food, General Line, Egg products

56288 Encore Sales
500 Bic Dr # 9
Ste 102
Milford, CT 06461-1777   203-301-4949
    Fax: 203-301-4947   800-653-6267
    encoresales@prodigy.net   www.encoresales.net
Wholesaler/distributor of general merchandise including advertising specialties, calendars, marking and writing pens, matchbooks, cocktail napkins and wearables
Owner: Paul Pennino
VP: Paul Pennino
Estimated Sales: $5-10 Million
Number Employees: 5-9
Private Brands Carried:
    Cross
Number of Customer Locations: 5000
Types of Products Distributed:
    Frozen Food, General Merchandise, Advertising specialties

56289 Ener-G Foods
5960 1st Ave S
Seattle, WA 98108   206-767-3928
    Fax: 206-764-3398   800-331-5222
    customerservice@ener-g.com   www.ener-g.com
Wholesaler/distributor of bakery ingredients; serving the food service market.
President: Sam Wylde III
National Sales Manager: Gerald Colburn
Year Founded: 1887
Estimated Sales: $20-50 Million
Number Employees: 20-49
Square Footage: 80000
Other Locations:
    Sam Wylde Flour Co.
    Portland, OR   Sam Wylde Flour Co.
Types of Products Distributed:
    Food Service, Frozen Food, Bakery ingredients

56290 (HQ)Ener-G Foods
5960 1st Ave S
Seattle, WA 98108-3248   206-767-3928
    Fax: 206-764-3398   800-331-5222
    samiii@ener-g.com
Manufacturer and exporter of wheat free and gluten free, dairy free, nut free; bread, hamburger buns, cereals, cookies, pasta, mixes, etc.; also allergy-free foods; importer of gluten-free pasta and starches, Medical and diet foods and low protein foods for PKU.
President: Sam Wylde III
cje@ener-g.com
Marketing/Sales: Jerry Colburn
Sales Exec: Jerry Colburn
Production Manager: Roger Traynor
Purchasing Manager: Sabina Milovic
Estimated Sales: $10 Milion
Number Employees: 20-49
Number of Brands: 2
Number of Products: 200
Square Footage: 40000
Type of Packaging: Consumer, Food Service, Private Label
Types of Products Distributed:
    Health Food

56291 Engineered Handling Products
38507 Cherry St
Newark, CA 94560   510-793-8000
    Fax: 510-793-9655
Wholesaler/distributor of material handling products including doors, dock equipment, rack, shelving, conveyors, levelers and compactors, pallet rack shellving; vertical-horizontal carousels, service and installation available
President: Michael Coletti
VP: Marc Coletti
Quality Control: Jeff Coletti
Public Relations: Mark Coletti
Operations: Belinda Runas
Purchasing: Adia Hamilton
Estimated Sales: $2.5-5 Million
Number Employees: 20-49
Square Footage: 52000
Other Locations:
    Engineered Handling Products
    Sacramento, CA
    Engineered Handling Products
    Fresno, CA
    Engineered Handlinh Products
    Reno, NV   Engineered Handling Products   Fresno
Private Brands Carried:
    Kelley Dock Truck Restraints and Shelters, McGuire, Southworth, Hanel, Automated Conveyor, Bishmon Lifts, Lyon, Interlake Rytec High Speed Doors, ITC, Bluff, Eagle
Types of Products Distributed:
    General Merchandise, Rack Jobbers, Specialty Foods

56292 Engineered Storage Products Company
9983 40th Ave S
Seattle, WA 98118   206-682-6596
    Fax: 206-682-4995   800-735-7153
    www.eppape.com
Wholesaler/distributor of material handling equipment
Manager: Ted Maroutsos
Estimated Sales: $300,000-500,000
Number Employees: 1-4
Private Brands Carried:
    Lyon Metal Products; Anderson Rack; Rivet Rack
Types of Products Distributed:
    Frozen Food, General Merchandise, Material handling equipment

56293 English Honey Farms
885 County Road 471
El Campo, TX 77437   979-543-8188
Wholesaler/distributor of unfiltered pure honey; serving fruit stands, grocery and health food stores and bakeries
President: A Fucik
VP: Barbara Fucik
Estimated Sales: $3-5 Million
Number Employees: 1-4
Square Footage: 5000
Private Brands Carried:
    English Honey Farms
Number of Customer Locations: 15
Types of Products Distributed:
    Food Service, Frozen Food, General Line, Health Food, Pure unfiltered honey

56294 Enprotech Corp
4259 E 49th St
Cleveland, OH 44125-1001   216-206-0081
    Fax: 216-206-0088   800-454-8600
    www.enprotech.com
Wholesaler/distributor of position sensors and controls
Controller: Christopher Pascarella
cpascarella@enprotech.com
Operations Manager: Jeff Edmisten
Estimated Sales: $5-10 Million
Number Employees: 500-999
Parent Co: Enprotech Corporation
Private Brands Carried:
    Sanyo Denki; N.S.D. for America; Toyota

56295 Enslin & Son Packing Company
2500 Glendale Ave
Hattiesburg, MS 39401   601-582-9300
    Fax: 601-544-2010   800-898-4687
Manufacturer, packer and wholesaler/distributor of sausage
President: August Enslin
Estimated Sales: $4 Million
Number Employees: 30
Square Footage: 32000
Type of Packaging: Consumer, Private Label, Bulk
Types of Products Distributed:
    Frozen Food, Provisions/Meat, Sausage

56296 Enterprise Company
P.O.Box 960702
Savannah, GA 30296-0702   912-958-8788
    Fax: 678-658-9100   866-991-7771
    fthompson214@yahoo.com
    www.frankiethompson.com
Wholesaler/distributor of general merchandise including pipes, valves, pumps, generators, motors and safety equipment
President: Frankie Thompson
Estimated Sales: $2.5-5 Million
Number Employees: 5-9
Parent Co: Frankie & Thompson Enterprises
Types of Products Distributed:
    Frozen Food, General Merchandise, Lighting fixtures, water heaters, etc.

56297 Enviro-Green Products
P.O.Box 620
Livingston, NJ 07039-0620   973-740-9800
    Fax: 973-535-6005   sales@aclequipment.com
    www.aclequipment.com
Wholesaler/distributor of general merchandise including crowd controls, bar fixtures, sneeze guards, food shields and displays, tray slides, wine and glass racks and bellman's carts
President: Martin Reinfeld
VP: Tara Lutkins
Estimated Sales: $1-3 Million
Number Employees: 1-4
Type of Packaging: Bulk
Types of Products Distributed:
    Frozen Food, General Merchandise, Bar fixtures, sneeze guards, etc.

56298 Environmental Express
2345 Charleston Regional Pkwy
Charleston, SC 29492-8405   843-881-6560
    Fax: 843-881-3964   800-343-5319
    suggestions@envexp.com   www.envexp.com

Supplier of environmentally safer laboratory equipment for the food and beverage research & developent industry.
CEO: Dennis Pope
CFO: Nikki Truman
nikkit@envexp.com
Vice President: Paul Strickler
Technical Sales Representative: Allison Ditullio
Manager: Paula Borgstedt
Estimated Sales: $5.2 Million
Number Employees: 50-99

56299 Environmental PackagingAssociates
8450 S Octavia Ave
Bridgeview, IL 60455   708-599-2944
Fax: 708-599-2889   800-372-2697
sales@epapkg.com
Wholesaler/distributor of corrugated boxes, folding cartons and wooden and plastic pallets
President: Thomas Porter
VP: Thomas Porter
Sales Manager: Martin Henner
Estimated Sales: $5-10 Million
Number Employees: 1-4
Types of Products Distributed:
  Frozen Food, General Merchandise, Boxes, cartons & pallets

56300 Enzamar
10060 London Avenue
Montreal, QC H1H 4H1
Canada   514-323-6068
Fax: 514-323-1989
Wholesaler/distributor, importer and exporter of gourmet Italian beverages, desserts, chocolates, cakes and Canadian spring water; serving the food service market; also, private label available
President: Enza Cappadoro
Vice President: Marilena Cappadoro
Director: Franco Cappadoro
Estimated Sales: $1-3 Million
Number Employees: 5-9
Type of Packaging: Consumer, Food Service
Private Brands Carried:
  Seibella; Rouge Royal; St. Remi
Number of Customer Locations: 2000
Types of Products Distributed:
  Food Service, Frozen Food, General Line, Specialty Foods, Spring water & Italian beverages

56301 Epic
280 Madison Ave Rm 1210
New York, NY 10016   212-308-7039
Fax: 212-308-7266
Wholesaler/distributor, importer and exporter of refractometers and polarimeters
President: Peter Letica
CEO: Florence Dan
CFO: Anna Volovik
Estimated Sales: $750,000
Number Employees: 3
Square Footage: 6000
Types of Products Distributed:
  General Merchandise, Measuring Instruments

56302 Epic Provisions
PO Box 684581
Austin, TX 78768   512-944-8502
Fax: 512-900-7982   eatepic@epicbar.com
epicprovisions.com
Protein bars and snacks; duck fat; cured meats; smoked seafood.
Co-Founder: Taylor Collins
Co-Founder: Katie Forrest
Sales Director: Martha Siskron
marth@epicbar.com
Year Founded: 2012
Estimated Sales: $4 Million
Number Employees: 11-50
Type of Packaging: Private Label

56303 Epicurean Foods
246 S Robson St
Mesa, AZ 85210   480-969-9333
Fax: 480-461-3645   info@epicurean-foods.com
www.epicurean-foods.com
Wholesaler/distributor of groceries, meats, general merchandise and bakery, frozen, imported cheeses, smoked seafood, caviar, dairy, deli and dry products; serving the food service market.
President: Chip Forster
chip@epicurean-foods.com
Chief Executive Officer: Fred Charley
Chief Financial Officer: Mark Dahm
National Accounts Manager: Carrie Levi
Director, Retail Sales: Diana Slonaker
Director, Operations: John Stevenson
Cheese Room Manager: Alan Singer
Director, Purchasing: Tammie Rice
Estimated Sales: $50-100 Million
Number Employees: 50-99
Number of Products: 3000
Square Footage: 60580
Parent Co: Distribution Plus
Type of Packaging: Food Service
Private Brands Carried:
  Code
Types of Products Distributed:
  Food Service, General Line, General Merchandise, Provisions/Meat, Produce, Seafood, Dairy, bakery, deli products, etc.

56304 (HQ)Equal Exchange Inc
50 United Dr
West Bridgewater, MA 02379-1026   774-776-7400
Fax: 508-587-0088   orders@equalexchange.coop
www.equalexchange.coop
Organic coffee, tea, chocolate, and nuts
Co-Executive Director: Rink Dickinson
Co-Executive Director: Rob Everts
dabbott@equalexchange.coop
Marketing: Bruce McKinnon
Sales: Mark Sweet
Director Operations: Denise Abbott
Estimated Sales: $20-50 Million
Number Employees: 50-99
Square Footage: 10000
Type of Packaging: Bulk
Types of Products Distributed:
  General Line

56305 Equipco
1889 Mayview Rd
Bridgeville, PA 15017-1518   412-221-2800
Fax: 412-257-3109   800-245-6484
equipco@equipco.com   www.equipco.com
Wholesaler/distributor of material handling equipment including lift trucks, fork lifts, conveyors, shelving, personal lifts and sweeper scrubbers
Owner: Carl H Swanson
VP: Tom Rush
Marketing Head: Charlie Adams
Sales Coordinator: Steve Kotula
cswanson@equipto.com
Estimated Sales: $20-50 Million
Number Employees: 100-249
Parent Co: Phillips Corporation
Private Brands Carried:
  Powerboss; Unarco Rack; Hyster Fork
Types of Products Distributed:
  Frozen Food, General Merchandise, Material handling equipment

56306 Equipment
P.O.Box 1987
Jackson, MS 39215-1987   601-948-3272
Fax: 601-948-3282   www.equipmentinc.com
Wholesaler/distributor of material handling equipment including conveyors, lift trucks, shelving and fork lifts
President: Joe Schmelzer Iii
Estimated Sales: $20-50 Million
Number Employees: 50-99
Private Brands Carried:
  Nissan; Bobcat; Steel King
Types of Products Distributed:
  Frozen Food, General Merchandise, Material handling equipment

56307 Equipment Distributor Div
1307 11th St SE
Jamestown, ND 58401-5909   701-252-3339
Fax: 701-252-3339
Wholesaler/distributor and exporter of high pressure cleaning equipment, meat grinders, slicers and choppers; serving the food service market
Owner: Paul Tahran
equipdis@daktel.com
General Manager: Dave Tahran
Estimated Sales: $500,000-$1 Million
Number Employees: 1-4
Type of Packaging: Food Service, Bulk
Types of Products Distributed:
  Food Service, Frozen Food, General Merchandise, Grinders, slicers & choppers

56308 Equipment Engineering Company
3952 Willow Lake Blvd # 5
Memphis, TN 38118-7042   901-396-7000
Fax: 901-396-7774   www.crown.com
Wholesaler/distributor of material handling equipment
Manager: Chris Webster
VP: Bernard Panchakal
Sales Manager: Ronnie Lambert
Estimated Sales: $10-20 Million
Number Employees: 5-9
Private Brands Carried:
  Toyota; Yale; Halla
Types of Products Distributed:
  Frozen Food, General Merchandise, Material handling equipment

56309 Equipment Inc.
7408 Hampton Road
Texarkana, TX 75503   903-838-4508
Fax: 903-832-3074   888-836-5537
www.equipmentinc.com
Wholesaler/distributor of material handling equipment including lift trucks
Owner: Scott Atkins
Estimated Sales: $10-20 Million
Number Employees: 20-49
Private Brands Carried:
  Nissan; Barrett; U.D. Trucks
Types of Products Distributed:
  Frozen Food, General Merchandise, Material handling equipment

56310 Equipment Picard
1307 Av Conway
Quebec, QC G1J 3S3
Canada   418-522-4014
Fax: 418-522-7743   800-361-9517
www.fpicard.com
Wholesaler/distributor of food service equipment and refrigeration; serving the food service market
Co-Owner/President: Frederick Picard
Co-Owner/VP: Marie-Claude Ipcard
Number Employees: 20-49
Square Footage: 40000
Private Brands Carried:
  Vulcan; Hobart; Sipromac
Types of Products Distributed:
  Food Service, Frozen Food, General Merchandise, Refrigeration & foodservice equipment

56311 Equipment Specialty Company
PO Box 273
South Milwaukee, WI 53172-0273   414-762-7997
Fax: 414-762-7899
Wholesaler/distributor of material handling equipment including conveyors, scissor lifts, monorails, etc
President: Paul Fruncek
Estimated Sales: $1-2.5 Million
Number Employees: 1-4
Private Brands Carried:
  ACCO-Louden; Mathews; American
Types of Products Distributed:
  Frozen Food, General Merchandise, Material handling equipment

56312 Equipment for Industry
2710 Woodhill Rd
Cleveland, OH 44104   216-721-7400
Fax: 216-721-4334   efi@mail.ohio.net
Wholesaler/distributor of material handling and loading dock equipment and cold storage and high speed doors
Owner/President: Richard Andrews
Sales/Marketing Director: Ted Rumbaugh
Contact: Rick Andrews
efi@mail.ohio.net
Estimated Sales: $5-10 Million
Number Employees: 10-19
Private Brands Carried:
  Stell King; Medart; Fairborn
Types of Products Distributed:
  Frozen Food, General Merchandise, Material handling equipment

56313 Equipment/Plus
102 Jackson St
Salem, MA 01970-3096   978-744-7525
Fax: 978-745-8040

Wholesalers & Distributors / A-Z

Wholesaler/distributor of restaurant equipment and smallwares; serving the food service market; also, service and consultation available
President: Suzanne Julien
VP: Ray Julien
Estimated Sales: $1-2.5 Million
Number Employees: 1-4
Square Footage: 100000
Private Brands Carried:
 Equipment Plus
Types of Products Distributed:
 Food Service, Frozen Food, General Merchandise, Restaurant equipment & smallwares

56314 (HQ)Erickson's Fork Lifts Inc
712 N Washington St
Albany, GA 31701-2351   229-883-3939
        Fax: 229-434-1567   800-727-2356
Wholesaler/distributor of material handling equipment including fork lifts, pallet jacks, hand trucks, casters, racking in addition to industrial sweepers and scrubbers. Services includes sales, service, parts and rentals.
President: Richard Erickson
derickson@ericksonforklifts.com
VP/CFO: Marianne Erickson
Sales Director: Jerry Delcambre
Estimated Sales: $4 Million
Number Employees: 10-19
Private Brands Carried:
 T.C.M.; Blue Giant; Kalmar AC
Types of Products Distributed:
 Frozen Food, General Merchandise, Material Handling equipment

56315 Erlab, Inc
388 Newburyport Turnpike
Rowley, MA 01969   978-948-2216
        Fax: 978-948-3354   800-964-4434
captairsales@erlab.com   www.erlab.com
Wholesaler/distributor and exporter of ductless filtering fume hoods, filtering storage cabinets, laminar flow hoods, balance enclosures and PCR workstations
Owner: George Hallatt
Marketing Director: Karen Ardinger
Product Specialist: Vicki Willett
Contact: Josh Bartholomew
jbartholomew@erlab.com
General Manager: Stephan Hauville
Production Manager: Brian Scanlon
Plant Manager: Jan Griffin
Estimated Sales: $2.5-5 Million
Number Employees: 10-19
Square Footage: 60320
Private Brands Carried:
 Filtair; Toxicap; Captair; Labx
Types of Products Distributed:
 Frozen Food, General Merchandise, Fume hoods, laboratory furniture, etc.

56316 Erman & Son
1210 E Whitcomb Avenue
Madison Heights, MI 48071-5615   586-493-9305
        Fax: 248-588-5189
Wholesaler/distributor of groceries, restaurant supplies and paper products; rack jobber services available; serving the food service market
President: D Erman
VP/Secretary/Treasurer: Jeff Erman
Estimated Sales: $1-2.5 Million
Number Employees: 5-9
Square Footage: 32000
Private Brands Carried:
 Heinz; Carnation; Kraft
Number of Customer Locations: 300
Types of Products Distributed:
 Food Service, Frozen Food, General Line, General Merchandise, Rack Jobbers, Restaurant supplies, groceries, etc.

56317 Erneston & Sons ProduceInc
1220 Ortega Rd # A
West Palm Beach, FL 33405-1099   561-832-2446
        Fax: 561-832-9459   eproduce@aol.com
        www.ernestonproducewpb.com
Wholesaler/distributor of produce
President: James Erneston
eproduce@aol.com
VP: J Erneston
Estimated Sales: $10-20 Million
Number Employees: 20-49
Number of Customer Locations: 400

Types of Products Distributed:
 Frozen Food, Produce

56318 Ervan Guttman Co
8208 Blue Ash Rd
Cincinnati, OH 45236-2188   513-791-0767
        Fax: 513-891-0559   800-203-9213
info@theervanguttmancompany.com
        www.theervanguttmancompany.com
Candy making equipment and supplies including release papers and flavorings
Owner: Harold Guttman
harold@guttmanfam.com
Estimated Sales: Less Than $500,000
Number Employees: 1-4
Square Footage: 4000
Type of Packaging: Bulk
Types of Products Distributed:
 Flavoring

56319 Eschete's Seafood
229 New Orleans Blvd
Houma, LA 70364-3345   985-872-4120
        Fax: 504-851-6147
Seafood
Owner: John Eschete
Estimated Sales: $300,000-500,000
Number Employees: 1-4

56320 Eskimo Candy Inc
2665 Wai Wai Pl
Kihei, HI 96753-8178   808-879-5686
        Fax: 808-874-0504   www.eskimocandy.com
Seafood and other fine foods.
Owner: Jeff Hansen
eskimo@maui.net
Estimated Sales: $10-20 Million
Number Employees: 20-49

56321 Espresso Buy the Cup
74 Green St
Hackensack, NJ 07601   201-342-6322
        Fax: 201-342-3692
Wholesaler/distributor of espresso and cappuccino machines with coffee included; also, rental service available; serving the food service market
President: Steven Knight
Estimated Sales: $1-3 Million
Number Employees: 1-4
Types of Products Distributed:
 Food Service, Frozen Food, General Merchandise, Espresso & cappuccino machines

56322 Espresso Coffee MachineCo
3709 1st Avenue
Burnaby, BC V5C 3V6
Canada   604-291-6363
        Fax: 604-291-6302   800-971-8833
Wholesaler/distributor and importer of Italian espresso and cappuccino machines; serving the food service market
Sales Manager: Tim Mercier
Number Employees: 10-19
Type of Packaging: Food Service
Types of Products Distributed:
 Food Service, Frozen Food, General Merchandise, Espresso & cappuccino machines

56323 Espresso Machine Experts
231 SE 102nd Ave
Portland, OR 97216-2705   503-255-9900
        Fax: 503-255-9845   888-909-0002
        www.espressomachineexperts.com
Wholesaler/distributor of beverage equipment including espresso. Broker of specialty foods
Owner: Scott Kellerman
scott@espressomachineexperts.com
General Manager: Bob Cox
Service Manager: Brian Conroy
Estimated Sales: $500,000-$1 Million
Number Employees: 5-9
Private Brands Carried:
 La Mazocco; Rio; Ambiente Wilch; Franke
Types of Products Distributed:
 Food Service, General Merchandise, Beverage equipment

56324 Espresso Magic
436 Hickson Avenue
London, ON N6C 2L5
Canada   519-432-7118
        Fax: 519-858-4337   achish4463@aol.com
Wholesaler/distributor of espresso machines and coffee equipment; serving the food service market

Co-Owner: Arch Chisholm
Co-Owner: Ann Chisholm
Number Employees: 1-4
Types of Products Distributed:
 Food Service, Frozen Food, General Merchandise, Espresso machines & coffee equipment

56325 Espresso Roma
1310 65th St
Emeryville, CA 94608-1119   510-420-8898
        Fax: 510-420-8980   800-437-1668
sandyboyd@aol.com
        www.sweetonyouberkeley.com
Processor and wholesaler/distributor of roast coffee; manufacturer and wholesaler/distributor of espresso machines and restaurant equipment
President: Sandy Boyd
VP: Pat Weigt
Sales Manager: Sandy Boyd
Estimated Sales: $1-2.5 Million
Number Employees: 10-19
Private Brands Carried:
 San Marco
Types of Products Distributed:
 Frozen Food, General Line, General Merchandise, Roasted coffee, espresso machines, etc.

56326 Essbar Equipment Company
P.O.Box 10885
Wilmington, DE 19850   302-323-0300
        Fax: 302-762-6285
Wholesaler/distributor of food service equipment
President: Michael Laurence
Estimated Sales: $2.5-5 Million
Number Employees: 5-9
Private Brands Carried:
 Hobart; Vulcan; Garland
Types of Products Distributed:
 Food Service, Frozen Food, General Merchandise, Foodservice equipment

56327 Essence of India
9 Fox Run Lane
Lexington, MA 02420-2338   781-861-1993
        Fax: 952-935-5933   www.essenceofindia.com
Wholesaler of tardoon spice, royal bumin spice, madreo blend, dal spice blend to the food service industry
President: Swati Elavia
Estimated Sales: Under $500,000
Number Employees: 1-4
Number of Products: 25
Type of Packaging: Food Service, Private Label

56328 Essex Food Ingredients
9 Lee Blvd
Frazier, PA 19355
                             800-441-1017
        www.essexfoodingredients.com
Wholesaler/distributor of salt, sugar, starch, corn, tapioca, potato dextrose corn syrup solids, maltodextrins, soy proteins and lecithin, textured and hydrolyzed vegetable protein, flour, soy, wheat, mustard, etc.
President: Luke Pallante
VP, Sales & Marketing: Matt Rita
VP, Customer Services: Candance Jumbo
Operations Manager: Justin Sohl
Year Founded: 1972
Estimated Sales: $50-70 Million
Number Employees: 50-99
Square Footage: 160000
Private Brands Carried:
 ADM; AG Processing Central Soya Protein Technologies International; Cargill/Azko Salt; Morton Salt; Domino Sugar
Types of Products Distributed:
 Food ingredients

56329 Esteem Products
1800 136th Pl NE
Ste 5
Bellevue, WA 98005   425-562-1281
        Fax: 425-562-1284   800-255-7631
customerservice@esteemproducts.com
        www.esteemproducts.com
Manufacturer, wholesaler/distributor and exporter of nutritional supplements and specialty vitamins. All combination formulas for consumer simplicity
CEO/President: John Sheaffer
VP: Linda Sheaffer
Marketing: Amy Braisford
Contact: Chana Madsen
chana@esteemproducts.com

Wholesalers & Distributors / A-Z

Estimated Sales: $500,000-$1 Million
Number Employees: 5-9
Square Footage: 20000
Types of Products Distributed:
   Frozen Food, Health Food, Vitamins & nutrient supplements

56330 Eternal Marketing Group
2003 Pewaukee Road
Suite 5
Waukesha, WI 53188-2469   262-549-1705
   Fax: 262-549-1555   877-854-5494
info@eternalwater.com www.eternalwater.com
Wholesaler/distributor and importer of bottled water; serving the food service market
President: Jim Klein
Number Employees: 5-9
Type of Packaging: Consumer, Food Service
Types of Products Distributed:
   Food Service, Frozen Food, General Line, Bottled water

56331 Ettline Foods Corp
525 N State St
York, PA 17403   717-848-1564
   Fax: 717-843-3091   800-632-1876
www.ettline.com
Wholesaler/distributor of frozen food, general merchandise, produce and meats; serving the food service market.
President & CEO: Joe Ayoub
jayoub@ettline.com
Year Founded: 1889
Estimated Sales: $55 Million
Number Employees: 100-249
Number of Products: 8500
Square Footage: 104000
Type of Packaging: Food Service, Private Label
Types of Products Distributed:
   Food Service, Frozen Food, General Line, General Merchandise, Provisions/Meat, Produce, Seafood

56332 Euclid Coffee Co
17230 S Waterloo Rd
Cleveland, OH 44110-3811   216-481-3330
   Fax: 216-383-7269
Wholesaler/distributor, exporter and importer of coffees and teas; wholesaler/distributor of groceries
President: James Repak
james.repak@euclidcoffee.com
Vice President: Andrew Repak
Estimated Sales: $5-10 Million
Number Employees: 10-19
Type of Packaging: Consumer, Food Service
Private Brands Carried:
   Old Master Mello Cup; Don-De
Types of Products Distributed:
   General Line, Coffees & teas

56333 Euclid Fish Co
7839 Enterprise Dr
Mentor, OH 44060-5386   440-951-6448
   Fax: 440-951-1817 www.euclidfish.com
Wholesaler/distributor of frozen foods, general merchandise, general line and specialty food products, health food, meats, etc.; serving the food service market
President: Charles Young
cyoung@euclidfish.com
VP: J Young
Estimated Sales: $20-50 Million
Number Employees: 20-49
Number of Customer Locations: 1000
Types of Products Distributed:
   Food Service, Frozen Food, General Line, General Merchandise, Health Food, Provisions/Meat, Seafood, Specialty Foods, Poultry & dairy products

56334 Eugene & Company
516 Warren Ave
Spring Lake, NJ 07762-1245   732-449-7090
   Fax: 732-842-5339
Wholesaler/distributor of general line items, meats, produce, dairy products, frozen foods and seafood; serving the food service market
Owner: Joseph Egan
VP: M Clayton
Estimated Sales: $1-2.5 Million
Number Employees: 1-4
Private Brands Carried:
   Eugene Quality Foods

Types of Products Distributed:
   Food Service, Frozen Food, General Line, Provisions/Meat, Produce, Seafood, Dairy products

56335 Euro Mart/Stolzle Cberglas
7219 Investment Dr
North Charleston, SC 29418-8304   843-767-1994
   Fax: 843-767-5953   877-786-5953
info@stolzle-usa.com www.stolzle-usa.com
Wholesaler/distributor and importer of china, porcelain dishes, crystal stemware and glassware, in addition to being a European (German) manufacturer of fine lead-free crystal for the food service and retail market.
President: Ed Artildello
VP: Jay Aule
Estimated Sales: $5-10 Million
Number Employees: 5-9
Square Footage: 60000
Types of Products Distributed:
   Food Service, General Merchandise, China, dishes, glassware, etc.

56336 Euro-Bake
1927 4th Ave S
Saint Petersburg, FL 33712   727-823-1113
   Fax: 727-823-1201   800-809-3876
info@eurobake.com www.eurobake.com
Wholesaler/distributor, exporter and importer of frozen par-baked bread, rolls, danishes; also, ready-baked pretzels, desserts and cakes
President: Harty Gerhard
mike@eurobake.com
Marketing Director: Ralph Hoffman
Purchasing Manager: Mike Gerhard
Estimated Sales: $10-20 Million
Number Employees: 50-99
Square Footage: 25000
Type of Packaging: Food Service, Private Label, Bulk
Private Brands Carried:
   Euro-Bake
Types of Products Distributed:
   Food Service, Frozen Food, Frozen par-baked bread, rolls, etc.

56337 Euro-Excellence
8559 Dalton
Mont-Royal, QC H4T 1V5
Canada   450-632-9440
   Fax: 450-600-5528   800-461-3876
info@euro-excellence.ca www.euro-excellence.ca
Wholesaler/distributor and importer of produce and genereal line items including candy, jam and cookies; serving the food service market
President: Andre Clemence
Controller: Sandra Romann
Purchasing Agent: Ibanne Puchuluteguy
Number Employees: 10-19
Square Footage: 12000
Type of Packaging: Consumer
Private Brands Carried:
   Barnier; Doucet; Cote D'Or
Number of Customer Locations: 800
Types of Products Distributed:
   Food Service, Frozen Food, General Line, Produce, Candy, jam & cookies

56338 Eurofood Distributors
PO Box 1381
Newport, RI 02840-0997   401-841-8238
   Fax: 401-841-8239
Importer and wholesaler/distributor of frozen desserts including ice cream
Private Brands Carried:
   Bornay
Types of Products Distributed:
   Frozen Food, Ice cream

56339 Europe's Finest Imports
733 Springtown Rd
Tillson, NY 12486   845-658-9258
   Fax: 845-658-8489
Food and non food products
President: Franziska Bornemann
f.bornemann@europesfinestimports.com
Estimated Sales: $2.5-5 Million
Number Employees: 5-9
Type of Packaging: Private Label

56340 European Foods
6 Farmhouse Lane
P O Box 14842
Panmure, AK NZ
Canada   649-551-7410
   Fax: 649-551-7411 info@europeanfood.co.nz
Importer and wholesaler/distributor of European jams, preserves and cheeses
President: Oliver Pokrandt
VP: George Pokrandt
Number Employees: 5-9
Types of Products Distributed:
   Frozen Food, General Line, Specialty Foods, European jams, preserves & cheeses

56341 European Hotel & Restaurant Imports
343 Horner Avenue
Etobicoke, ON M8W 1Z6
Canada   416-253-9449
   Fax: 416-253-9552
Wholesaler/distributor and importer of food service supplies and equipment including fixtures; serving the food service market
President: John Rainbow
Secretary: Gary Crawford
Number Employees: 10-19
Types of Products Distributed:
   Food Service, Frozen Food, General Merchandise, Foodservice equipment & supplies

56342 European Imports
2475 N Elston Ave
Chicago, IL 60647   773-227-0600
   Fax: 773-227-6775   800-323-3464
info@eiltd.com www.eiltd.com
Importer and wholesaler/distributor of olive oil, cheeses, gourmet foods and pastry products
President: Seymour Binstein
VP: Glenn Binstein
VP: Jeff Binstein
Marketing: Trish Pohanka
Contact: Caryn Burgess
caryn@asktt.com
Estimated Sales: $20-50 Million
Number Employees: 100-249
Private Brands Carried:
   Alta Cucina; Amber Valley
Types of Products Distributed:
   Frozen Food, General Line, Olive oil, cheeses, etc.

56343 Eurpac Warehouse Sales
1405 30th Street
Suite S
San Diego, CA 92154-3403   935-423-3409
   Fax: 935-423-8167
Wholesaler/distributor of general merchandise; also, rack jobber services available
VP: Jim Burgio
Estimated Sales: $20-50 Million
Number Employees: 20-49
Square Footage: 25000
Parent Co: Eurpac Service
Types of Products Distributed:
   Frozen Food, General Merchandise, Rack Jobbers

56344 Evan Peters & Company
85 Norman Ave
Brooklyn, NY 11222   718-383-2000
Wholesaler/distributor of specialty foods
Owner: Peter Laras
Estimated Sales: Less than $500,000
Number Employees: 1-4
Types of Products Distributed:
   Specialty Foods, Cheeses

56345 Evans BS&R
2772 S Cole Road
Suite 140
Boise, ID 83709   208-345-5755
   Fax: 208-343-3109   800-727-6389
Wholesaler/distributor of equipment; serving the food service market
Owner: Marty Evans
President: Martin Evans
Estimated Sales: $3-5 Million
Number Employees: 5-9
Parent Co: BS&R Equipment Company
Private Brands Carried:
   Taylor; Flavor Crisp; Astra

Wholesalers & Distributors / A-Z

Types of Products Distributed:
Food Service, Frozen Food, General Merchandise, Equipment

56346 Evans Foodservice Inc.
6460 Maple Avenue
PO Box 237
Swartz Creek, MI 48473-0237 810-635-2444
Fax: 810-635-2534 800-968-1520
Wholesaler/distributor of meat and poultry, frozen foods, groceries, beverages, dairy products, produce, and equipment; serving the food service market
President: Larry Ridge
Senior Vice President: Scott Solesby
Director of Business Development: Dan Cuppernoll
Vice President/Sales: Ken Durbal
Customer Service: Stephanie Chaney
Logistics Manager: Carman Munsell
Director of Purchasing: Ryan Solesby
Estimated Sales: $21.98 Million
Number Employees: 48
Square Footage: 56000
Types of Products Distributed:
Food Service, Frozen Food, General Line, General Merchandise, Provisions/Meat, Produce, Seafood, Dairy items, poultry, beverages, etc.

56347 Evco Wholesale Food Corp
309 Merchant St
Emporia, KS 66801-7207 620-343-7000
Fax: 620-343-6375
Wholesaler/distributor of groceries, meat, coffee, produce, frozen foods, baked goods, general merchandise and fixtures; serving the food service market
President: Charles Evans
Director Sales: Bob Wells
Director Purchasing: Steve Kephart
Estimated Sales: $20-50 Million
Number Employees: 50-99
Types of Products Distributed:
Food Service, Frozen Food, General Line, General Merchandise, Provisions/Meat, Produce, Baked goods, groceries, etc.

56348 Event Equipment Sales
9000 67th St
Hodgkins, IL 60525-7606 708-352-0662
Fax: 708-352-8267 800-337-0093
sales@eventequipment.com
www.eventequipment.com
Wholesaler/distributor of equipment and fixtures and general merchandise including tables, grills, china, wood folding chairs, etc
Owner: Mary Shipper
sales@eventequipment.com
CEO: Douglas Crowe
VP, Sales: Roberta Decillo
sales@eventequipment.com
Number Employees: 5-9
Private Brands Carried:
Bluecrate; Big Ben
Types of Products Distributed:
Frozen Food, General Merchandise, Tables, grills, folding chairs, etc.

56349 Everson District
280 New Ludlow Rd
Chicopee, MA 01020-4468 413-533-9261
Fax: 413-536-4564 bob@treasuretreats.com
Wholesaler/distributor, importer and contract packager of candy
President: Robert Everson
robert@treasuretreats.com
Director of Sales: Tami Sharrow-Gero
Office Manager: Diana Gaouette
Production Supervisor: Steve Harris
Estimated Sales: $7 Million
Number Employees: 20-49
Square Footage: 80000
Type of Packaging: Private Label
Number of Customer Locations: 100
Types of Products Distributed:
Candy

56350 Evonuk Oregon Hazelnuts
PO Box 7121
Eugene, OR 97401-0006 541-998-1848
800-992-6887
Wholesaler/distributor of hazelnuts including raw, roasted, in-shell and kernel
Owner: Phil Evonuk
Owner: Shannon Evonuk
Estimated Sales: Less than $500,000
Number Employees: 1-4
Types of Products Distributed:
Frozen Food, General Line, Hazelnuts

56351 Excel Food Distribution Company
PO Box 98
National Stock Yards, IL 62071-0098 618-288-1918
Fax: 618-288-5143 800-962-9129
Wholesaler/distributor of meats
Account Manager: Marcus Huddleston
Sales Manager: Tom Nenninger
General Manager: Mark Wolff
Estimated Sales: $20-50 Million
Number Employees: 10-19
Square Footage: 15000
Parent Co: Excel Corporation
Private Brands Carried:
Honeysuckle/Riverside; Emgee; Excel
Number of Customer Locations: 150
Types of Products Distributed:
Frozen Food, Provisions/Meat

56352 Excellence Commercial Products
1750 N University Dr
Pompano Beach, FL 33071-8903 954-752-0010
Fax: 954-752-0080 800-441-4014
howard@stajac.com www.stajac.com
Wholesaler/distributor, importer and exporter of coolers, freezers and ice cream cabinets
President: Howard Noskowicz
Quality Control: Catherina Derr
Number Employees: 1-4
Parent Co: Stajac Industries
Private Brands Carried:
Excellence Commercial Products
Types of Products Distributed:
Frozen Food, General Merchandise, Coolers, freezers & ice cream cabinets

56353 Excellent Food Products
1601 Prospect Avenue
Kansas City, MO 64127-2504 816-471-6030
Fax: 816-471-5999
Wholesaler/distributor serving the food service market
Chairman Board/President: Anthony Palmentere
Estimated Sales: $10-20 Million
Number Employees: 10-19
Types of Products Distributed:
Food Service, Frozen Food

56354 Excello Machine Co Inc
236 Stevens St SW
Grand Rapids, MI 49507-1566 616-949-1861
Fax: 616-949-2810 800-678-2409
sales@excellomachineco.com
www.excellomachineco.com
Wholesaler/distributor and exporter of folding carton equipment for box marking of cake mix, cereal, etc.; also, printing machinery repairing and rebuilding available
President: Mark Cassis
excellomac@aol.com
Purchasing Agent: Ronald Meschke
Estimated Sales: $500,000-$1 Million
Number Employees: 1-4
Square Footage: 19400
Private Brands Carried:
Miehle; Heidelberg
Types of Products Distributed:
Frozen Food, General Merchandise, Folding carton equipment

56355 Excelon
3312 N Summit Ave
Milwaukee, WI 53211 414-671-1181
Fax: 414-671-2499 excelon@execpc.com
excelon@execpc.com
Wholesaler/distributor of whey protein concentrates, fat replacers and extenders and fat/oil substitutes
President: Joe White
Estimated Sales: $300,000-500,000
Number Employees: 1-4
Number of Brands: 2
Number of Products: 5
Type of Packaging: Food Service, Bulk
Private Brands Carried:
Excelon; Superbase
Types of Products Distributed:
Frozen Food, General Line, Whey protein concentrates, etc.

56356 Express Point Technology Services
1109 Zane Ave N
Golden Valley, MN 55422 763-543-6000
Fax: 763-949-0750 800-328-7723
rburton@expresspoint.com www.expresspoint.com
Wholesaler/distributor of new and refurbished point of sale equipment
President: Mike Cibulka
CEO: David L Anderson
Estimated Sales: $10-20 Million
Number Employees: 250-499
Types of Products Distributed:
Frozen Food, General Merchandise, New & refurbished point of sale equip.

56357 Express Wholesale Grocers
7729 S State St
Chicago, IL 60619-2317 773-846-7400
Fax: 773-846-7403
Wholesaler/distributor of general line products
Owner: Mike Judeh
Estimated Sales: $5-10 Million
Number Employees: 5-9
Types of Products Distributed:
Frozen Food, General Line

56358 Ezy Trading International
6145 98th Street
Apt 10f
Rego Park, NY 11374-1465 718-271-1333
Wholesaler/distributor of disposable vinyl, latex and poly gloves
President: W Boctor
Types of Products Distributed:
Frozen Food, General Merchandise, Gloves

56359 F & A Food Sales Inc
2221 Lincoln St
Concordia, KS 66901 785-243-2301
info@fafoodsales.com
www.fafoodsales.com
Wholesaler/distributor of produce, meats, groceries and frozen foods; serving convenience stores, the food service market and grocery stores.
Sales Manager: Frank Headrick
Year Founded: 1970
Estimated Sales: $24 Million
Number Employees: 100-249
Square Footage: 20000000
Type of Packaging: Consumer, Food Service, Private Label, Bulk
Private Brands Carried:
First Choice; Garrett's Gold; Parade; Spencer's Pride
Number of Customer Locations: 3000
Types of Products Distributed:
Food Service, Frozen Food, Provisions/Meat, Produce, Seafood, Ice Cream

56360 F & C Sawaya Wholesale
516 W Main St
Trinidad, CO 81082-2626 719-846-2263
Fax: 719-846-3427 www.fconline.host-ed.me
Wholesaler/distributor of groceries, meats, produce, dairy products, baked goods, equipment and fixtures, general merchandise, health/beauty aids and specialty foods; serving the food service market; rack jobber services available
Owner: Charles D Sawaya Sr
Partner: H Sawaya
Estimated Sales: $5-10 Million
Number Employees: 5-9
Number of Customer Locations: 150
Types of Products Distributed:
Food Service, Frozen Food, General Line, General Merchandise, Provisions/Meat, Produce, Rack Jobbers, Specialty Foods, Groceries, dairy products, etc.

56361 F B Mc Fadden Wholesale Co
415 Railroad Ave
Rock Springs, WY 82901-5098 307-362-5441
Fax: 307-382-8466 877-720-9115
Wholesaler/distributor of groceries, meats, frozen foods, baked goods, equipment and fixtures, general merchandise, etc.; serving the food service market
President: D Mc Fadden
mcfaddenwholesale@gmail.com
CEO: John McFadden
CFO: P McFadden
Estimated Sales: $10-20 Million
Number Employees: 10-19
Square Footage: 36540
Number of Customer Locations: 150

Wholesalers & Distributors / A-Z

Types of Products Distributed:
Food Service, Frozen Food, General Line, General Merchandise, Health Food, Provisions/Meat, Seafood, Specialty Foods

56362 F B Wright Co
9999 Mercier St
Dearborn, MI 48120-1410   313-843-8250
Fax: 313-843-8450 fbw401@aol.com
www.fbwright.com
Wholesaler/distributor and exporter of gloves including plastic and rubber
President: Jack Doer
CEO: Jack Doerr
fbw401@aol.com
CEO: Wj Reno
Estimated Sales: $20-50 Million
Number Employees: 50-99
Private Brands Carried:
Granet; Pioneer
Types of Products Distributed:
Frozen Food, General Merchandise, Gloves: rubber & plastic

56363 F C Bloxom & Co
2250 Occidental Ave S
Seattle, WA 98134-1414   206-624-1000
Fax: 206-682-1435
Wholesaler/distributor, importer and exporter of produce
Owner: Robert Bloxom
robertb@fcbloxom.com
Estimated Sales: $10-20 Million
Number Employees: 20-49
Types of Products Distributed:
Frozen Food, Produce

56364 F Christiana & Co
7251 River Rd
Marrero, LA 70072-1145   504-348-3391
Fax: 504-341-2453 800-299-0740
www.fchristiana.com
Wholesaler/distributor of provisions/meats, dry goods and nonfood items; serving the food service market.
General Manager: Frank Christiana
Year Founded: 1934
Estimated Sales: $100-500 Million
Number Employees: 100-249
Parent Co: US Foods
Number of Customer Locations: 5000
Types of Products Distributed:
Food Service, Frozen Food, General Line, Provisions/Meat, Dry good & non-food items

56365 F McConnell & Sons
1102 E Lincoln Highway
P.O. Box 417
New Haven, IN 46774-0417   260-493-6607
Fax: 260-749-6116 800-552-0835
sales@fmcconnell.com www.fmcconnell.com
Wholesaler/distributor of confectionery items, groceries, general merchandise and specialty foods.
President: Martha Doan
Director of Purchasing: Jim Harrington
Year Founded: 1973
Estimated Sales: $50-100 Million
Number Employees: 50-99
Square Footage: 40000
Type of Packaging: Private Label
Types of Products Distributed:
Frozen Food, General Line, General Merchandise, Specialty Foods, Groceries & confectionery items

56366 F-M Forklift Sales & Svc Inc
4350 Main Ave
Fargo, ND 58103-1128   701-281-1660
Fax: 701-281-1887 866-364-6191
www.fmforklift.com
Wholesaler/distributor of material handling equipment including forklifts
President: Al Fosberg
al@fmforklift.com
Estimated Sales: $10-20 Million
Number Employees: 50-99
Private Brands Carried:
Crown; Toyota; A.P.V.
Types of Products Distributed:
Frozen Food, General Merchandise, Material handling equipment

56367 F. Gavina & Sons
2700 Fruitland Ave
Vernon, CA 90058
800-428-4627
hello@gavina.com www.gavina.com
Gourmet coffee
CEO: Pedro Gavina
VP, Marketing: Leonor Gavina-Valls
VP, Operations: Carlos Fandino

56368 F.A. Davis & Sons
PO Box 676
Pasadena, MD 21123-0676   410-360-6000
Fax: 410-360-1023
Wholesaler/distributor of groceries, general merchandise, confectionery products, fountain supplies, paper products and health and beauty aids; also, rack jobber services available
President: Lou Manzo
Number Employees: 100-249
Parent Co: F.A. Davis & Sons
Types of Products Distributed:
General Line, General Merchandise, Rack Jobbers, Confectionery, paper, etc.

56369 FCM
345 3rd St
Forest Park, GA 30297-2602   404-363-4888
Fax: 404-363-0898
Wholesaler/distributor of material handling equipment
President: Matthew Dougherty
Estimated Sales: $1-2.5 Million
Number Employees: 1-4
Types of Products Distributed:
Frozen Food, General Merchandise, Material handling equipment

56370 FDI Inc
5440 Saint Charles Rd
Suite 201
Berkeley, IL 60163-1231   708-544-1880
Fax: 708-544-4117 info@fdiusa.net
www.fdiusa.net
Canned and frozen foods; uses freeze-drying to preserve herbs, fruits, vegetables, spices, meat, pasta and fish
President: Joseph Lucas
National Sales Manager: Barbara Laffey
Manager: Terry Bliudzius
info@fdiusa.net
Estimated Sales: $1.3 Million
Number Employees: 10-19
Parent Co: Groneweg Group
Type of Packaging: Consumer

56371 FLAMEX Inc
4365 Federal Dr
Greensboro, NC 27410-8116   336-299-2933
Fax: 336-299-2944 flamex@sparkdetection.com
www.sparkdetection.com
Wholesaler/distributor of fire protection and detection equipment
President: Alan Wagoner
flamex@sparkdetection.com
Estimated Sales: $5-10 Million
Number Employees: 10-19
Square Footage: 28000

56372 (HQ)Fab Inc
1225 Old Alpharetta Rd # 235
Suite 235
Alpharetta, GA 30005-2903   678-341-9799
Fax: 678-356-0100 800-569-4821
Wholesaler/distributor cooperative of groceries, meats, produce, dairy products, frozen foods, baked goods, general merchandise, health and beauty aids; equipment and fixtures and specialty foods; serving the food service market
President/CEO: Timothy Carper
CEO: George T Watson
gwatson@frostyacres.com
CEO: George T Watson
Marketing VP: Bridgett Van Buzen
Operations Director: Ashley Waters
Operations VP: Earnest Livaditis Jr
VP Puchasing: Billy Elmore
Estimated Sales: $2.5-5 Million
Number Employees: 50-99
Square Footage: 70000
Other Locations:
FAB
Appleton, WIFAB

Private Brands Carried:
Frosty Acres; Frosty Seas; Frosty Lite; Frosty Springs
Types of Products Distributed:
Food Service, Frozen Food, General Line, General Merchandise, Health Food, Provisions/Meat, Produce, Seafood, Specialty Foods, Groceries, etc.

56373 Fab-X/Metals
PO Box 1903
Washington, NC 27889-1903   252-977-3229
Fax: 252-977-6605 800-677-3229
Manufacturer and wholesaler/distributor of chairs, ovens, sinks, spoons, tables, etc.; also, supermarket equipment including store fixtures and racks; serving the food service market
President: Jonathan Turner
COO: Cyrus Watson
Quality Control: Carol Causeway
Estimated Sales: $10-20 Million
Number Employees: 10
Square Footage: 200000
Types of Products Distributed:
Food Service, Frozen Food, General Merchandise, Ovens, sinks, spoons, tables, etc.

56374 Fadler Company
P.O.Box 472306
Tulsa, OK 74147-2306   918-627-0770
Fax: 918-641-5363
Wholesaler/distributor of groceries, meats, produce, frozen foods, baked goods, private label items, etc.; serving the food service market
President: Dan Fulps
Executive VP: Ed Hawkins
Marketing Executive: Mike Peer
Operations Manager: Rick Maxwell
Purchasing Manager: Gene Fry
Estimated Sales: $33 Million
Number Employees: 100-249
Square Footage: 98100
Parent Co: Hale-Halsell Company
Type of Packaging: Food Service
Other Locations:
Fadler Co.
Tulsa, OKFadler Co.
Private Brands Carried:
All Kitchens
Number of Customer Locations: 3500
Types of Products Distributed:
Food Service, Frozen Food, Health Food, Provisions/Meat, Produce, Seafood, Baked goods, groceries, etc.

56375 Faema
672 Dupont Street
Toronto, ON M6G 1Z6
Canada   416-535-1555
Fax: 416-535-3843 www.faema.net
Wholesaler/distributor serving the food service market
President: Mike Di Donato
Number Employees: 20-49
Private Brands Carried:
Faema; Rancilio; Eurostar
Types of Products Distributed:
Food Service, Frozen Food

56376 Fagerholt Brothers
7636 139th Ave NE
Hoople, ND 58243-9408   701-894-6447
Fax: 701-894-6447
Wholesaler/distributor of potatoes
Owner: Mark Fagerholt
Estimated Sales: $5-10 Million
Number Employees: 10-19
Types of Products Distributed:
Frozen Food, Produce, Potatoes

56377 Fairs Seafood
2105 Carlisle Rd
York, PA 17408-4060   717-764-9236
Fax: 717-848-4138 800-340-0556
Wholesaler/distributor of fresh and frozen seafood; also, meat, Greek items and frozen vegetables
Owner: Jack Fair
VP: John Fair
Estimated Sales: $10-20 Million
Number Employees: 5-9
Types of Products Distributed:
Frozen Food, Provisions/Meat, Seafood, Specialty Foods, Greek items & frozen vegetables

Wholesalers & Distributors / A-Z

56378 Fairview Dairy Inc
1562 Mission Rd
Latrobe, PA 15650-2845
724-537-7111
Fax: 724-537-7249 mblystone@valleydairy.net
www.valleydairy.net
Processor and wholesaler/distributor of ice cream; serving the food service market
President: Melissa Blystone
Vice President: Melissa Blystone
Marketing Director: Virgina Greubel
Contact: Lujean Wasnesky
lwasnesky@valleydairy.net
Director of Operations: Tom Webb
Plant Manager: Ray Sneets
Number Employees: 250-499
Square Footage: 24000
Parent Co: Fairview Dairy
Type of Packaging: Consumer, Food Service
Private Brands Carried:
  Ice Cream Joe
Types of Products Distributed:
  Food Service, General Line, Ice cream

56379 Fairway Foods
PO Box 52
Northfield, MN 55057-0052
507-645-9311
Fax: 952-830-8864
Wholesaler/distributor of frozen food, general merchandise, general line products, produce, meats, seafood, etc
CEO/President: W Farmer
Number Employees: 250-499
Parent Co: Fairway Foods
Private Brands Carried:
  Golden Treat; Homestead; Serv-Well; Super Select
Number of Customer Locations: 234
Types of Products Distributed:
  Frozen Food, General Line, General Merchandise, Provisions/Meat, Produce, Seafood, Dairy/deli

56380 Falcon Trading Intl Corp
4606 Fairfield Rd
East Fairfield, VT 05448-4917
802-849-2021
Fax: 877-790-7901 falconti@together.net
www.falconti.com
Wholesaler/distributor, importer and exporter of herbs, spices, oils, proteins, vitamins, amino acids, enzymes, fibers, gelatin capsules, desiccants and alcohol
President: Robert Adams
radams@together.net
Number Employees: 1-4
Type of Packaging: Bulk
Number of Customer Locations: 350
Types of Products Distributed:
  Frozen Food, General Line, Health Food, Spices, proteins, vitamins, oils, etc.

56381 Falls City Mercantile Co Inc
223 W 8th St
PO Box 68
Falls City, NE 68355-3241
402-245-2726
Fax: 402-245-2019 800-756-6372
info@fallscitymercantile.com
www.fallscityedge.com
Wholesaler/distributor of groceries, meat, produce, frozen foods, baked goods, equipment, etc.; serving the food service market
President: Dan Simon
dansimonfcmerc@hotmail.com
Secretary: C Simon
Estimated Sales: $10-20 Million
Number Employees: 10-19
Private Brands Carried:
  Lil Brave
Number of Customer Locations: 450
Types of Products Distributed:
  Food Service, Frozen Food, General Line, General Merchandise, Provisions/Meat, Produce, Baked goods, equipment, etc.

56382 Family Foods Home Service
5532 Douglas Road
Toledo, OH 43613-2086
419-474-0983
Fax: 419-474-0801 echalon@wbtv.com
Wholesaler/distributor of groceries, frozen foods, meats, vegetables, juices and margarine
President: Al Leal Estate
Plant Manager: Luis Leal
Estimated Sales: $500,000-$1 Million
Number Employees: 1-4
Square Footage: 14000

Types of Products Distributed:
  Food Service, Frozen Food, Health Food, Provisions/Meat, Produce, Seafood, Specialty Foods, Vegetables, juices & margarine

56383 Family Tree Farms
41646 Road 62
Reedley, CA 93654-9124
559-591-8394
Fax: 559-595-7795 866-352-8671
www.familytreefarms.com
Plumcots, white peaches and nectarines, donut peaches and nectarines, yellow peaches and nectarines, apricots, apriums, plums, blueberries, cherries, satsumas
President: David Jackson
djackson@familytreefarms.com
CFO: Dan Clenney
Executive Director of Global Development: Gerome Raco
Director of Research & Development: Eric Wuhl
Quality Control: Mary Ortiz
Director of Marketing: Don Goforth
Estimated Sales: $20-50 Million
Number Employees: 250-499

56384 Fancy Delights
110b Route 59
Airmont, NY 10952-3908
845-352-0203
Wholesaler/distributor of kosher gift baskets and platters including chocolates, dried fruits, nuts and coffee; serving the retail market
CEO: Dennis Greenberg
Estimated Sales: Less than $500,000
Number Employees: 1-4
Private Brands Carried:
  Empress; Shutra; Blooms
Types of Products Distributed:
  Frozen Food, General Line, Specialty Foods, Kosher chocolates, dried fruits, etc.

56385 Farallon Fisheries Co
207 S Maple Ave
S San Francisco, CA 94080-6305
650-583-3474
Fax: 650-583-0137
Seafood
Manager: Juan De Alva
Contact: Aiden Coburn
Manager: Juan De
juande@farallonfisheries.com
Estimated Sales: $500,000-$1,000,000
Number Employees: 5-9

56386 Fare Foods Corp
208 Cherry Lake Rd
Du Quoin, IL 62832-1248
618-542-2155
Fax: 618-542-2396 www.farefoods.com
Fresh fruits and vegetables
President: Ron Porter
rporter@farefoods.com
Estimated Sales: $10-20 Million
Number Employees: 20-49

56387 (HQ)Farm Boy Food Svc
2761 N Kentucky Ave
Evansville, IN 47711-6203
812-428-8436
Fax: 812-428-8432 800-852-3976
www.farmboy-foodservice.com
Established in 1952. Manufacturer of beef and pork; wholesaler/distributor of frozen, refrigerated and dry food products, meat, equipment and fixtures. Specializes in pizza toppings and equipment.
President/Co-Owner: Robert Bonenberger
VP/Co-Owner: Richard Bonenberger
Estimated Sales: $38 Million
Number Employees: 50-99
Type of Packaging: Consumer, Food Service, Private Label
Types of Products Distributed:
  General Line, General Merchandise, Provisions/Meat, Refrigerated & dry food products, etc.

56388 Farm Fish
11147 Carter Rd
Yazoo City, MS 39194-9440
662-836-5188
Fax: 662-836-5184
Wholesaler/distributor of raw live catfish
Owner: Debbie Hill
Manager: Ed Dew
Number Employees: 20-49
Types of Products Distributed:
  Frozen Food, Seafood

56389 Farm Stores
Grove Forest Plz
2937 Sw 27th Ave. Suite 203
Coconut Grove, FL 33133
800-726-3276
www.farmstores.com
Distributor/wholesaler of general grocery products to stores.
CEO & COO: Maurice Bared
CFO: Ade Batista
VP, Business Development: Victor Arechavaleta
Franchise Sales: Jim Cobban
Year Founded: 1935
Estimated Sales: $50-100 Million
Number Employees: 700

56390 Farmers Seafood Co Wholesale
1192 Hawn Ave
Shreveport, LA 71107-6699
318-222-9504
Fax: 318-424-2029 800-874-0203
farmersseafood@aol.com
www.farmersseafood.com
Wholesaler/distributor of groceries, dairy products and seafood; serving the food service market
Owner: Alex Mijalis
farmersseafood@aol.com
Estimated Sales: $5-10 Million
Number Employees: 50-99
Number of Customer Locations: 2000
Types of Products Distributed:
  Food Service, Frozen Food, General Line, Seafood, Groceries & dairy products

56391 Farmfresh
PO Box 2250
Virginia Beach, VA 23450-2250
757-479-5701
Fax: 757-306-2218 www.farmfreshmarkets.com
Wholesaler/distributor of general line items, produce, groceries, meat, dairy products, frozen foods, equipment and fixtures, general merchandise and seafood; serving supermarket chains
President: Ron Dennis
VP Human Resources: Linda Johnson
Manager: Joe Brown
jbrown@farmfreshsupermarkets.com
Number Employees: 1,000-4,999
Parent Co: Rich Foods Holdings
Types of Products Distributed:
  Frozen Food, General Line, General Merchandise, Provisions/Meat, Produce, Seafood

56392 Farmington Foods Inc
7419 West Franklin St
Forest Park, IL 60130-1016
708-771-3600
Fax: 708-771-4140 800-609-3276
info@farmingtonfoods.com
www.farmingtonfoods.com
Pork chops, boneless pork, baby back ribs, St. Louis-style spareribs, pre-packaged kabobs made with beef, chicken and pork, frenched pork racks, and seasoned port tenderloins and roasts
President: Tony Dijohn
tony.dijohn@farmingtonfoods.com
CFO: Albert LaValle
Quality Assurance: Marnie Adamski
Sales Manager: Tony DiJohn
Plant Manager/Director Operations: Dan Bernkopf
Warehouse Manager: Ram McKee
Estimated Sales: $30 Million
Number Employees: 100-249
Square Footage: 55000
Types of Products Distributed:
  Frozen Food, Provisions/Meat

56393 Farmstead At Long Meadow Ranch
738 Main St
St Helena, CA 94574-2005
707-963-4555
Fax: 707-963-1956 877-627-2645
info@longmeadowranch.com
www.longmeadowranch.com
Olive oils, fine wines, and grass fed beef
President/General Manager: Ted Hall
tedhall@longmeadowranch.com
Director/Chairman: Les Denend
Chief Financial Officer: Devonna Smith
VP/General Manager: Chris Hall
Director of Winemaking: Ashley Heisley
Cellarmaster-Red Wine: Hans Van Dale
Cellarmaster-White Wine: Jeff Restell
Operations Manager: Tony Fernandez
Estimated Sales: $20 Million
Number Employees: 100-249

Wholesalers & Distributors / A-Z

56394 Farner-Bocken Co
1751 E US Highway 30
P.O. Box 368
Carroll, IA 51401-2691 800-274-8692
Fax: 712-792-7351 800-644-6323
www.farner-bocken.com
Wholesaler/distributor of groceries, seafood, meats, produce, dairy products, frozen foods, general merchandise, confectionery items, paper, institutional foods, small equipment, cleaners, etc.; serving the food service market
President: Dean Onken
doncken@farner-bocken.com
VP: Dean Onken
General Manager: Denny Vetter
Number Employees: 500-999
Square Footage: 900000
Parent Co: Farner-Bocken
Private Brands Carried:
  Pocohontas
Types of Products Distributed:
  Food Service, General Line, General Merchandise, Provisions/Meat, Produce, Seafood, Confectionery, small equipment, etc.

56395 Fast Fixing Foods
1481 US Highway 431
Boaz, AL 35957-1552 256-593-7221
Fax: 256-593-7208 800-317-4232
www.fastfixinfoods.com
Fast foods
Owner: Eugene Davis
eugene.davis@fastfixin.com
Estimated Sales: $10-20 Million
Number Employees: 10-19

56396 Fayter Farms Produce
69400 Jolon Rd
Bradley, CA 93426-9676 831-385-8515
Fax: 831-385-0833
Fresh herbicide pesticide-free Kiss of Burgundy globe artichokes.
President: Thomas Fayter
Estimated Sales: $300,000-500,000
Number Employees: 1-4
Type of Packaging: Private Label, Bulk
Other Locations:
  Fayter Farms Produce
  Bradley, CAFayter Farms Produce

56397 Feather Crest Farms
9112 Sovereign Row
Dallas, TX 75247-4585 214-631-7752
Fax: 214-631-8373 www.feathercrest.com
Wholesaler/distributor of eggs; serving the food service market; rack jobber services available
Manager: Keith Webster
VP/General Manager: T Coleman
Manager: Marc Andreessen
marc.andreessen@bluecoat.com
Operations Manager: T Pitts
Estimated Sales: $10-20 Million
Number Employees: 5-9
Parent Co: Feather Crest Company
Types of Products Distributed:
  Food Service, Frozen Food, General Line, Rack Jobbers, Eggs

56398 Federal Supply USA
116 Washington St
Waukegan, IL 60085-5612 888-623-4499
Fax: 847-623-2425 888-623-4499
fsupplyco@aol.com www.federalsupply.com
Wholesaler/distributor of food service equipment; also, installation services available; serving the Midwest area
Owner: Demetrios Selevreds
VP: N Selevredes
Estimated Sales: $2.5-5 Million
Number Employees: 1-4
Square Footage: 96000
Types of Products Distributed:
  Food Service, General Merchandise, Foodservice equipment

56399 Federated Cooperative
2626 10th Avenue NE
Calgary, AB T2A 2M3
Canada 403-531-6600
Fax: 403-531-2275
Wholesaler/distributor of general line items
Regional Manager: Barry Manovich
Number Employees: 250-499
Parent Co: Federated Cooperative
Types of Products Distributed:
  Food Service, Frozen Food, General Line, General Merchandise, Health Food, Produce, Seafood

56400 (HQ)Federated Cooperative Lt
401 22nd Street E
Saskatoon, SK H2K 0
Canada 306-244-3311
Fax: 306-244-3403 inquiries@fcl.ca
www.coopconnection.ca
Wholesaler/distributor of groceries, meats, dairy products, produce, seafood, frozen foods, baked goods, equipment and fixtures and private label items
Owner/President: Dusty MacDonald
Vice-President Corporate Affairs: V. Huard
Number Employees: 500-999
Other Locations:
  Federated Coop. Ltd.
  Saskatoon, ABFederated Coop. Ltd.
Private Brands Carried:
  Co-Op; Harmonie; Country Morning
Number of Customer Locations: 350
Types of Products Distributed:
  Frozen Food, General Line, General Merchandise, Provisions/Meat, Produce, Seafood, Bakery products, etc.

56401 Federated Cooperative Lt
PO Box 1004
Winnipeg, MB R3C 2W6
Canada 204-633-8950
Fax: 204-631-4647 inquiries@fcl.ca
www.coopconnection.ca
Wholesaler/distributor of general line items
Owner/President: Dusty MacDonald
Vice-President Corporate Affairs: V. Huard
Parent Co: Federated Cooperative
Private Brands Carried:
  Country Morning; Harmony
Number of Customer Locations: 75
Types of Products Distributed:
  Frozen Food, General Line, Produce

56402 Federated Cooperative Lt
13232-170th Street
Edmonton, AB T5V 1M7
Canada 780-447-8500
Fax: 780-454-2153 inquiries@fcl.ca
www.coopconnection.ca
Wholesaler/distributor of frozen food and general line items
Owner/President: Dusty MacDonald
Vice-President Corporate Affairs: V. Huard
Parent Co: Federated Cooperative
Private Brands Carried:
  Co-op; Harmonie
Number of Customer Locations: 75
Types of Products Distributed:
  Frozen Food, General Line

56403 Feed The Party
2055 Nelson Miller Pkwy
Louisville, KY 40223
partyon@feedtheparty.com
feedtheparty.com
Supplier of the finest butcher shop quality meats, including steak, pork, chicken, and lamb.
President & Founder: Matt Kenney
Estimated Sales: $100+ Million
Number Employees: 2-10
Square Footage: 89000
Type of Packaging: Food Service, Bulk
Private Brands Carried:
  A. Thomas Meats, Berkwood Farms, Border Springs Farm Lamb, Shire Gate, Shuckman's Fish Co. & Smokery, Inc., Joyce Farms, Big Fork
Types of Products Distributed:
  Provisions/Meat

56404 Feesers
5561 Grayson Rd
Harrisburg, PA 17111
800-326-2828
www.feesers.com
Wholesaler/distributor of general merchandise, seafood, frozen foods and groceries.
Procurement: Denny Ball
dball@feesers.com
Year Founded: 1901
Estimated Sales: $30 Million
Number Employees: 300
Square Footage: 275000
Private Brands Carried:
  NIFDA; Chef Pak; Econo Pak
Number of Customer Locations: 4200
Types of Products Distributed:
  General Line, General Merchandise, Seafood, Groceries, etc.

56405 Fein Brothers
2007 N M L King Dr
Milwaukee, WI 53212 414-562-0220
Fax: 414-562-3346 800-222-8789
sales@feinbrothers.com www.feinbrothers.com
Wholesaler/distributor of equipment and supplies; serving the food service market
Owner: Todd Minkin
Outside Sales: Tammy Faanes
Administrative Assistant: Jackie Bordak
Estimated Sales: $1-2.5 Million
Number Employees: 5-9
Square Footage: 300000
Types of Products Distributed:
  Food Service, Frozen Food, General Merchandise, Equipment & supplies

56406 Feinkost Ingredients
103 Billman St
Lodi, OH 44254-1029 330-948-3006
Fax: 330-948-3016
Wholesaler/distributor of dry goods
Manager: Tim Warner
Estimated Sales: $.5-1 million
Number Employees: 5-9
Parent Co: Sandridge Corporation
Types of Products Distributed:
  Frozen Food, General Line, Dry goods

56407 Fendall Ice Cream Company
470 South 700 East
Salt Lake City, UT 84102 801-355-3583
Fax: 801-521-0133 sales@fendalls.com
Manufacturer and wholesaler/distributor of ice cream, sherbet, water ices, sorbets and frozen yogurt
Owner: Carol Radinger
Contact: Gunter Radinger
gunter@fendalls.com
Estimated Sales: $1-2.5 Million
Number Employees: 5-9
Type of Packaging: Consumer
Private Brands Carried:
  Gold Band; Bryer's; Good Humor; Heart to Heart
Types of Products Distributed:
  Frozen Food, General Line, Ice cream, sherbet, ices, sorbet, etc.

56408 Ferntrade Corporation
1010 S 3rd St
San Jose, CA 95112 408-971-0997
Fax: 408-286-1866 fcgferntrade@aol.com
Wholesaler/distributor and importer of Oriental specialty foods; exporter of canned fruits, vegetables and groceries, for American food products; also an importer for Philippine food products
President: Fernando Guevarra
CFO: Maria Guevarra
Marketing Director: Ramon Guevarra
Estimated Sales: $8 Million
Number Employees: 5-9
Square Footage: 40000
Type of Packaging: Consumer, Food Service, Private Label, Bulk
Private Brands Carried:
  Anahaw
Number of Customer Locations: 80
Types of Products Distributed:
  Food Service, Frozen Food, General Line, General Merchandise, Provisions/Meat, Seafood, Specialty Foods, Oriental foods

56409 Ferris Coffee & Nut Co
227 Winter Ave NW
Grand Rapids, MI 49504-6452 616-459-6257
Fax: 616-459-2146 www.ferriscoffee.com
Wholesaler/distributor of nuts and coffee; serving the food service market
President: John Vantongeren
john@ferriscoffee.com
Estimated Sales: $5-10 Million
Number Employees: 100-249
Types of Products Distributed:
  Food Service, Frozen Food, General Line, Nuts & coffee

1001

Wholesalers & Distributors / A-Z

56410 Ferris Organic Farms
3565 Onondaga Rd
Eaton Rapids, MI 48827-9608 517-628-2506
Fax: 517-628-8257 800-628-8736
ferrisorganicfarm@gmail.com
www.ferrisorganicfarm.com
Manufacturer, grower and exporter of organic beans including black, soy, black turtle and pinto; also, grains including wheat and barley; wholesaler/distributor of organic natural foods
Co-Owner: Richard Ferris
ferrisorganicfarm@excite.com
Estimated Sales: $1-2.5 Million
Number Employees: 1-4
Square Footage: 14000
Type of Packaging: Bulk
Private Brands Carried:
   Eden
Number of Customer Locations: 25
Types of Products Distributed:
   Frozen Food, General Line, Health Food, Organic natural foods

56411 Ferry-Morse Seed Company
PO Box 4938
Modesto, CA 95352
Fax: 209-527-8684 www.harrismoran.com
Wholesaler/distributor of vegetable seeds
Finance Executive: Angie Rooney
VP Domestic Sales: Antonio Neves
VP International Sales: Gil Hernandez
Sales Manager (Processing): Tom Harrison
Estimated Sales: $10-20 Million
Number Employees: 100-249
Parent Co: Limagrain Group
Types of Products Distributed:
   General Line, Vegetable seeds

56412 Festival Ice Cream
PO Box 389
Paterson, NJ 07543 973-684-8935
Fax: 973-684-3570
Wholesaler/distributor of ice cream
President: Mario Calbi
Number Employees: 20-49
Private Brands Carried:
   Festival Ice Cream; Richmond Ice Cream
Types of Products Distributed:
   Frozen Food, General Line, Ice cream

56413 Fetzer Vineyards
12901 Old River Rd
Hopland, CA 95449 707-744-1250
www.fetzer.com
Wines
CEO: Giancarlo Bianchetti
CFO: Jorge Lyng Benitez
COO: Cindy DeVries
SVP Sales & Distribution: Barry Marek
Year Founded: 1968
Estimated Sales: $20-50 Million
Number Employees: 100-249
Types of Products Distributed:
   Wine

56414 Fetzers'
3401 S 1400 W
West Valley City, UT 84119-4049 801-974-5400
Fax: 801-974-0492 800-825-2400
Wholesaler/distributor of ice machines, fryers, ovens, ice cream machinery, warmers, sinks, dishwashers, coolers and freezers, steamers, etc.; serving the food service market
Sales Manager (Southeast): Bud Bath
Sales Manager (Northeast): Rolland Wall
General Manager: Norman Stevens
Parent Co: Fetzers'
Private Brands Carried:
   Ice-O-Matic; Stoelting; FlashBake; Wilshire
Types of Products Distributed:
   Food Service, Frozen Food, General Merchandise, Fryers, ovens, etc.

56415 Fiber Foods Inc
2400 Florida Avenue
Norfolk, VA 23513-4520 757-853-2888
Fax: 757-853-4756
Gluten-free, organic/natural, otehr grains, cereal and pasta, pasta (dry).

56416 Fidelity Container Corporation
1601 Lunt Ave
Elk Grove Vlg, IL 60007-5642 847-364-2520
Fax: 847-364-0385

Wholesaler/distributor of custom packaging and displays
CEO: William Ross
Vice President: Larry Carlson
Sales Director: Rick Klare
Estimated Sales: $20-50 Million
Number Employees: 20-49
Types of Products Distributed:
   Frozen Food, General Merchandise, Custom packaging products

56417 Fidelity Fruit & Produce Co
16 Forest Pkwy # F11
Forest Park, GA 30297-2033 404-366-8445
Fax: 404-361-2279
Wholesaler/distributor of bananas, pineapples and lemons
Owner: Walter Hoch
fidelitybanana@aol.com
General Manager: Steve Roney
Estimated Sales: $5-10 Million
Number Employees: 10-19
Private Brands Carried:
   Dole; Del Monte; Chiquita
Types of Products Distributed:
   General Line, Produce, Bananas, pineapples & lemons

56418 Figi's Business Services
3200 S Central Avenue
Marshfield, WI 54449-8612 715-384-1183
Fax: 715-384-1468 www.figis.com
Other chocolate, other candy, cheese, other meat/game/pate. chips, other snacks.
Marketing: Melissa Larson
Contact: Jim Krueger
jim.krueger@figis.com

56419 Filler Paper Company
2906 William Penn Hwy # 506
Easton, PA 18045-5282 610-253-3591
Fax: 610-253-9870
Wholesaler/distributor of general merchandise
President: Charles W Fuller
Estimated Sales: $20-50 Million
Number Employees: 10-19
Types of Products Distributed:
   General Merchandise

56420 Findlay Foods Kingston
675 Progress Ave.
Kingston, ON K7M 0C7
Canada 613-384-5331
Fax: 613-384-9290 800-267-2596
http://findlayfoods.com/
Wholesaler/distributor serving the food service market
President: Ted Hood
Number Employees: 20-49
Types of Products Distributed:
   Food Service, Frozen Food

56421 Fine Cocoa Products
224 48th St
Brooklyn, NY 11220-1012 201-244-9210
Fax: 201-244-8555 info@cocoasupply.com
www.cocoasupply.com
Importers and distributors of conventional, organic, and kosher cocoa and other ingredients. Some of their products include Cocoa Powders, Cacao Nibs & Beans, Cocoa Butter, Cocoa Liquor/Mass, Chocolate Couvertures and more.
Estimated Sales: Less Than $500,000
Number Employees: 2-10
Type of Packaging: Consumer, Food Service, Private Label, Bulk

56422 Fine Distributing
3719 Corporex Park Drive
Suite 200
Tampa, FL 33619-1161 813-621-1222
Fax: 813-621-1167
Wholesaler/distributor of general line products and specialty foods
Account Executive: Terry Mull
Chain Account Executive: Robert Zambito
Estimated Sales: $500,000-$1 Million
Number Employees: 5-9
Parent Co: Fine Distributing
Number of Customer Locations: 500
Types of Products Distributed:
   Frozen Food, General Line, Specialty Foods

56423 Fine Foods Australia
5419 Hollywood Boulevard
C 133
Los Angeles, CA 90027 323-375-1777
Fax: 323-309-2208 info@finefoodsaustralia.com
Imports specialty foods from Australia
Estimated Sales: $500,000
Number Employees: 2
Number of Brands: 10
Number of Products: 49
Type of Packaging: Consumer

56424 Finesaler
161 North Water Street
1st Floor
Greenwich, CT 06830 914-732-3111
Fax: 914-732-3109 order@finesaler.com
www.finesaler.com
Wholesale fine foods: specialty gourmet
Marketing: Charlene Branchereau
Contact: Daniel Arnould
daniel@finesaler.com

56425 Finest Foods
355 Food Center Dr # B260
Bronx, NY 10474-7000 718-893-5410
Fax: 718-893-6645
Wholesaler/distributor and importer of produce including fruits and vegetables
Buyer: Aaron Bertell
Estimated Sales: $20-50 Million
Number Employees: 50-99
Private Brands Carried:
   Merenge
Types of Products Distributed:
   Frozen Food, Produce, Fruits & vegetables

56426 Finestkind Fish Market
855 US Route 1
York, ME 03909-5835 207-363-5000
Fax: 207-363-2664 800-288-8154
Manufacturer and Wholesaler full service seafood company.
Owner: Michael Goslin
Estimated Sales: $2.2 Million
Number Employees: 5

56427 Finger Lakes Organic Growers
PO Box 170
Rose, NY 14542-0170 607-387-3333
Fax: 607-257-2195 www.fingerlakesorganic.com
Cooperative wholesaler/distributor of certified organic produce
President: Carol Stull
Manager: Carolyn Twesten
Estimated Sales: $1-2.5 Million
Number Employees: 1-4
Types of Products Distributed:
   Frozen Food, Produce, Certified organic

56428 Finke Co
2226 Springboro Pike
Moraine, OH 45439-1795 937-294-0316
Fax: 937-294-0399 800-762-4822
Wholesaler/distributor of stationery products and general merchandise; rack jobber services available
Owner: Jim Finke Sr
tim@finkecompany.com
Secretary: Herb Finke
VP: Tim Finke
Sales Exec: Tim Finke
Estimated Sales: $20-50 Million
Number Employees: 20-49
Square Footage: 58000
Number of Customer Locations: 200
Types of Products Distributed:
   Frozen Food, General Merchandise, Rack Jobbers, Stationery products, etc.

56429 Fire Device Co
15835 Main St
La Puente, CA 91744-4716 626-968-5597
Fax: 626-330-5949 www.firedevice.com
Wholesaler/distributor of burglar and fire alarms, smoke detectors and security equipment
Owner: Steven Stolar
steven@firedevice.com
Manager: Steven Stolar
Estimated Sales: Less than $500,000
Number Employees: 1-4
Types of Products Distributed:
   Frozen Food, General Merchandise, Burglar & fire alarms, detectors, etc.

Wholesalers & Distributors / A-Z

56430 Fire Master
13050 Metro Pkwy # 1
Suite 1
Fort Myers, FL 33966-4800   239-896-1685
Fax: 239-896-1695   800-522-7150
www.firemasterweb.com
Wholesaler/distributor of fire suppression systems, heat and smoke alarms and extinguishers
Manager: Mary Vogt
mvogt@firemaster-mpc.com
Manager: Tom Forwood
Estimated Sales: $10-20 Million
Number Employees: 5-9
Parent Co: Fire Master/Master Protection Corporation
Types of Products Distributed:
   Frozen Food, General Merchandise, Fire suppression systems

56431 Fire Protection SystemsInc
99 Quaker Church Rd
Randolph, NJ 07869-1518   973-361-0640
Fax: 973-361-4777
Wholesaler/distributor of fire extinguishers, alarms, suppression systems and sprinklers
Owner: Robert Bretzger
robert@fireprotectionsys.com
Treasurer: Eleanor Bretzger
VP Marketing: Robert Bretzger, Jr.
Estimated Sales: $5-10 Million
Number Employees: 5-9
Square Footage: 16000
Types of Products Distributed:
   Frozen Food, General Merchandise, Fire extinguishers, alarm systems, etc.

56432 Fireline Corp
4506 Hollins Ferry Rd
Baltimore, MD 21227   410-247-1422
Fax: 410-247-4676   800-553-3405
www.fireline.com
Wholesaler/distributor of restaurant kitchen hood systems and fire extinguishers; serving the food service market.
President: Anna Waters Gavin
agavin@fireline.com
Executive Director: Cynthia Rueppel
Director, Business Development: Dave Taylor
Year Founded: 1947
Estimated Sales: $50-100 Million
Number Employees: 100-249
Types of Products Distributed:
   Food Service, Frozen Food, General Merchandise, Rest. kitchen hood equip., fire ext.

56433 Firemaster
430 N Canal St Ste 22
South San Francisco, CA 94080   650-588-3478
Fax: 650-873-7893
Wholesaler/distributor of fire alarms and security systems
Manager: Sue Rantanen
General Manager: Steve Muron
Estimated Sales: $20-50 Million
Number Employees: 20-49
Parent Co: Master Protection Corporation
Types of Products Distributed:
   Frozen Food, General Merchandise

56434 Firestone Farms
18400 N Highway 99 W
Dayton, OR 97114-7225   503-864-2672
Fax: 503-864-2816   www.seattlechinesepost.com
Wholesaler/distributor and exporter of hazelnuts
Owner: Joan Firestone
ffarms@nwlink.com
VP: Joan Firestone
Estimated Sales: Less Than $500,000
Number Employees: 1-4
Private Brands Carried:
   Firestone Farms Brand
Types of Products Distributed:
   Frozen Food, General Line, Hazelnuts

56435 First Choice Ingredients
N112 W19528 Mequon Rd
Germantown, WI 53022   262-251-4322
Fax: 262-251-3881   roddyt@fcingredients.com
www.fcingredients.com
Food flavor and ingredients manufacturers; including cheese powders & pasts, dairy powders, meat flavors, savory flavors, bakery flavors, and beverage liquids & powders
President: Jim Pekar
EVP: Roger Mullins
Sales Manager: Natalie Moore
Contact: Lucas Lieffring
llieffring@fcingredients.com
Estimated Sales: $3 Million
Number Employees: 20

56436 First Coast Promotions
3948 Sunbeam Rd # 5
Jacksonville, FL 32257-8931   904-262-9155
Fax: 904-262-2992   800-762-4653
promonorm@gmail.com   www.promonorm.com
Wholesaler/distributor of general merchandise including advertising specialties, pens, pencils, etc
Owner: Norm Blum
promonorm@aol.com
Estimated Sales: Less Than $500,000
Number Employees: 1-4
Number of Customer Locations: 100
Types of Products Distributed:
   Frozen Food, General Merchandise, Advertising specialties, pens, etc.

56437 First Fire Systems Company
6000 Venice Blvd
Los Angeles, CA 90034   323-965-9300
Fax: 323-965-2700   888-431-3473
ffs@firstfiresystems.com
www.firstfiresystems.com
Wholesaler/distributor of low voltage circuits, fire alarms and security systems
President: Robbie Kashani
VP: Hooshang Kashani
Contact: Lita De La Cruz
litac@firstfiresystems.com
Estimated Sales: $5-10 Million
Number Employees: 20-49
Types of Products Distributed:
   Frozen Food, General Merchandise, Fire alarms, paging & security systems

56438 First Oriental Market
2774 E Ponce DE Leon Ave
Decatur, GA 30030-2715   404-377-6950
Fax: 404-377-7505
Tilapia, flounder, catfish, mackerel, oriental food items
Owner: Diane Bounngaseng
Estimated Sales: $5-10 Million
Number Employees: 5-9

56439 First Source LLC
3612 LA Grange Pkwy
Toano, VA 23168-9347   757-566-5360
Fax: 757-566-5379   800-296-0273
www.wythewill.com
Distributor of specialty foods and fine confections across the US
President: Keith McDaniel
Owner: John McCurry
CFO & VP Finance: Rod Hogan
VP: Belton Joyner
Director of Sales & Marketing: David Mastricola
Director of Human Resources: Lisa Weakland
Operations Manager: Bill Hall
Purchasing Manager: Nanette Ross
Estimated Sales: $8.9 Million
Number Employees: 50-99
Square Footage: 200000
Type of Packaging: Consumer, Bulk

56440 Fish Breeders of Idaho
18374 Hwy 30
Hagerman, ID 83332   208-837-6114
Fax: 208-837-6254   fpi@fishbreedersofidaho.com
www.fishbreedersofidaho.com
Breeders of fish. Varieties include trout, sturgeon, catfish, tilapia, and tropical aquarium fish.
Owner: Leo Ray
Vice President: Tod Ray
Sales: Netty Marino
Contact: Judith Ay
judith.ray@alaskasbest.com
Production Manager: Starla Barnes
Estimated Sales: $5-10 Million
Number Employees: 2-10
Types of Products Distributed:
   Frozen Food, Seafood

56441 Fish Express
3343 Kuhio Hwy # 10
Suite 10
Lihue, HI 96766   808-245-9918
Fax: 808-246-9188
Seafood
Principal: David Wada
Estimated Sales: $3-5 Million
Number Employees: 10-19

56442 Fish Market Inc
1406 W Chestnut St
Louisville, KY 40203-1776   502-587-7474
Fax: 502-587-7503
Seafood
President: Steven Smith
sseafoods@aol.com
Estimated Sales: $10 Million
Number Employees: 20-49

56443 Fisher Mills
11167 White Birch Dr
Rancho Cucamonga, CA 91730-3820   951-278-9055
Fax: 909-484-1326   800-540-2253
Wholesaler/distributor of bakery ingredients and packaging; serving the food service market
President: Carlos Figueiredo
Sr. VP Distribution: Gene Erhardt
Manager: Joaquin Vergara
jvergara@puiratos.com
VP Food Distribution: Jana McLellan
Estimated Sales: $20-50 Million
Number Employees: 20-49
Parent Co: Fish Mills
Types of Products Distributed:
   Food Service, Frozen Food, General Line, General Merchandise, Bakery ingredients & packaging

56444 Fisherman's Seafood Market
3116 Main Street
P.O.Box 118
Grasonville, MD 21638   410-827-7323
Fax: 410-827-4227   www.crabdeck.com
Manufacturer/wholesaler/distributor of seafood
Manager: Danny Brown
Owner: Andy Schulz
Owner: Tracy Schulz
Estimated Sales: $500,000-$1 Million
Number Employees: 5-9
Parent Co: Fisherman Seafood Enterprises
Types of Products Distributed:
   Frozen Food, Seafood

56445 Fishermens Net
849 Forest Ave
Portland, ME 04103-4162   207-772-3565
Fax: 207-828-1726
Seafood
Owner: Benjamin Lindner
Estimated Sales: Less Than $500,000
Number Employees: 1-4

56446 Fitch Co
2201 Russell St
Baltimore, MD 21230-3198   410-539-1953
Fax: 410-727-2244   800-933-4824
www.fitchco.com
Wholesaler/distributor of general merchandise including sweeping compounds, hand soap and towels
President: Raymond Kirsner
raymond@fitchco.com
VP Sales: Cordt Goldeisen
Estimated Sales: $20-50 Million
Number Employees: 50-99
Square Footage: 30000
Types of Products Distributed:
   Frozen Food, General Merchandise, Sweeping compounds, soap & towels

56447 Fitness & Nutrition Center
2122 Blount Rd
Pompano Beach, FL 33069   954-968-1188
Fax: 954-968-5661   800-344-4967
Wholesaler/distributor of sports nutrition products
President: Richard Pallisso
CEO: Mark Devandara
Contact: Marappan Devandara
mdevandara@fitnessweb.com
Estimated Sales: $10-20 Million
Number Employees: 20-49
Square Footage: 16400
Number of Customer Locations: 1953

1003

Wholesalers & Distributors / A-Z

Types of Products Distributed:
Frozen Food, Health Food, Sports nutrition products

56448 Five Continents
P.O.Box 2134
Darien, IL 60561-7134   773-927-0100
                             Fax: 773-927-5113
Marketing Manager: Marilyn Mara
Estimated Sales: $30-35 Million
Number Employees: 100-250
Types of Products Distributed:
Food Service, Frozen Food, Health Food, Produce, Seafood, Specialty Foods, Ethnic Foods

56449 Five Ponds Farm
1933 E Mill Rd
Lineville, AL 36266   256-396-5217
                             Fax: 256-386-5899
Fruits and vegetables
President: Edward Donlon

56450 Fizz-O Water Co
809 N Lewis Ave
Tulsa, OK 74110-5365   918-834-3691
   Fax: 918-832-0899 water@fizzowater.com
                   www.fizzowater.com
Bottler and wholesaler/distributor of spring, drinking and distilled water
President: Harry R Doerner
fizzowater@att.net
Owner: Hency Doerner
Owner: Rick Doerner
Plant Manager: Rick Malkey
Estimated Sales: $1-3 Million
Number Employees: 20-49
Number of Brands: 4
Square Footage: 30000
Type of Packaging: Consumer
Types of Products Distributed:
General Line, Bottled spring, Drinking + Distilles Wa

56451 Flaghouse
601 Us Highway 46 W
Department 9009
Hasbrouck Hts, NJ 07604   201-288-7600
          Fax: 201-288-7887 800-793-7900
info@flaghouse.com www.flaghouse.com
Wholesaler/distributor and exporter of office furniture, cabinets, tables and chairs
President: George Cramel
Contact: Janet Alston
jalston@flaghouse.com
Estimated Sales: $20-50 Million
Number Employees: 100-249
Types of Products Distributed:
Frozen Food, General Merchandise, Office furniture

56452 Flags & Banners Unlimited
22114 Ventura Blvd
Woodland Hills, CA 91364-1648 818-348-9880
                               800-331-8458
              www.flagsbanners.net
Wholesaler/distributor of signs, flags, pennants and banners
Owner: Barbara Kaufman
flags2010@adelphia.net
Estimated Sales: Less Than $500,000
Number Employees: 1-4
Types of Products Distributed:
Frozen Food, General Merchandise, signs, flags, pennants & banners

56453 Flair Beverages
3857 9th Ave
New York, NY 10034-3739   212-569-8713
                             Fax: 212-567-8509
Wholesaler/distributor of beverages; serving the food service market
President: Matthew Gagliardi
Estimated Sales: $20-50 Million
Number Employees: 20-49
Types of Products Distributed:
Food Service, Frozen Food, General Line, Beverages

56454 Flamingo Flats
100 Talbot St
PO Box 441
St Michaels, MD 21663   410-745-2053
   Fax: 410-745-2402 800-468-8841
          bigbird@flamingoflats.com
          www.flamingoflats.com
Wholesaler/distributor and importer of garlic, mustards, olives, olive oils, hot sauces, peppers and vinegar; also, specialty Caribbean, Cajun, Southwest, Indian and Oriental products
Owner/President: Robert Deppe
bigbird@flamingoflats.com
Estimated Sales: Less than $500,000
Number Employees: 1-4
Square Footage: 3200
Types of Products Distributed:
Frozen Food, General Line, Specialty Foods, Garlic, mustards, olives, oils, etc.

56455 (HQ)Flanders
1104 Gilmore St
Waycross, GA 31501-1307   912-283-5191
     Fax: 912-283-6228 info@flandersburgers.com
                   www.flandersprovision.com
Manufacturer, distributor and packager of beef patties
President/CEO: Huey Dubberly
CEO: Chris Huff
chuff@flandersprovision.com
CEO/Chief Financial Officer: Chris Huff
Quality Assurance Manager: Michael Denton
Sales: Hollis Yarn
Operations Manager: Rusty Rainey
Year Founded: 1958
Estimated Sales: $36.80 Million
Number Employees: 100-249
Types of Products Distributed:
Frozen Food

56456 FlapJacked
960 W 124th Ave
Suite 100
Westminster, CO 80234   720-476-4758
              info@flapjacked.com
              www.flapjacked.com
Pancake, muffin and cookie mixes
Co-Founder: Jennifer Bacon
Co-Founder: Dave Bacon
Number of Brands: 1
Number of Products: 18
Type of Packaging: Consumer

56457 Flash Foods
215 Pendleton St
Waycross, GA 31501   912-285-4011
                             800-673-9397
         customerservice@flashfoods.com
                   www.flashfoods.com
Wholesaler/distributor of general line items.
Vice President/Chief Financial Officer: Kevin Sheehan
Year Founded: 1952
Estimated Sales: $11 Billion
Number Employees: 14,500
Number of Customer Locations: 3000
Types of Products Distributed:
Frozen Food, General Line

56458 Flatland Food Distributors
3930 W 29th St S # 90
Wichita, KS 67217-1070   316-945-5172
                             Fax: 316-945-9614
Wholesaler/distributor of groceries, frozen foods and meats; serving the food service market
Manager: Ken Blank
Branch Manager: F Blank
Estimated Sales: $10-20 Million
Number Employees: 10-19
Types of Products Distributed:
Food Service, Frozen Food, General Line, Provisions/Meat, Groceries

56459 Flatout Inc
1422 Woodland Dr
Saline, MI 48176-1633   734-944-5445
   Fax: 734-944-5115 866-944-5445
          feedback@flatoutbread.com
              www.flatoutbread.com
Flatbreads
Owner: Stacey Marsh
Co-Owner: Mike Marsh
Sales/Marketing: Bob Palotta
Number Employees: 100-249

56460 Flav-O-Rich
1735 Old Dean Forest Rd
Pooler, GA 31322   912-232-2116
                             Fax: 912-966-0505
Wholesaler/distributor of dairy products including milk and ice cream
Branch Manager: John Deal
Number Employees: 10-19
Square Footage: 5600
Parent Co: Suiza Dairy Group
Private Brands Carried:
Flav-O-Rich
Types of Products Distributed:
Food Service, General Line, Dairy products

56461 Flav-O-Rich
1105 N William St
Goldsboro, NC 27530-2123   919-734-0728
   Fax: 919-735-6344 800-209-3118
Wholesaler/distributor of milk and fruit drink concentrates
Manager: Dean Holmes
Estimated Sales: $10-20 Million
Number Employees: 20-49
Parent Co: Suiza Dairy Group
Types of Products Distributed:
General Line, Milk & fruit drink concentrates

56462 Flavor Savor
285 Fullerton Ave
Carol Stream, IL 60188-1886 630-868-0350
     Fax: 630-868-0310 sales@flavorsavor.com
                   www.prinovausa.com
Distributor of flavors used in food and beverages
President: Julie Kedzior
j.kedzior@greenfieldthorp.com
Marketing Director: Patricia Palmisano
Sales Director: Charles Turner
Operations Manager: Ricki Matz
Purchasing Manager: Sandra Powrozek
Estimated Sales: $20-50 Million
Number Employees: 50-99
Number of Brands: 1
Number of Products: 300
Square Footage: 132000
Private Brands Carried:
Firmenich Flavors
Number of Customer Locations: 4
Types of Products Distributed:
Ingredient, Flavors

56463 Flavor-Crisp of America
P.O.Box 488
Fort Calhoun, NE 68023-0488 402-453-4444
   Fax: 402-453-7238 800-262-5016
              www.flavor-crisp.com
Wholesaler/distributor and exporter of food service equipment including fryers, smokers, rotisseries and accessories; serving the food service market
Owner: Brad French
flavorcrisp@gmail.com
Executive VP Sales: Ray Boegner
VP Sales: Michael Nulty
Estimated Sales: $20-50 Million
Number Employees: 50-99
Square Footage: 280
Parent Co: Ballantyne of Omaha
Type of Packaging: Food Service
Private Brands Carried:
Flavor Crisp; Flavor Pit;
Types of Products Distributed:
Food Service, Frozen Food, General Merchandise, Foodservice equipment: smokers, etc.

56464 Flax Council of Canada
465-467 Lombard Avenue
Winnipeg, MB R3B 0T6
Canada   204-982-2115
     Fax: 204-942-1841 www.flaxcouncil.ca

56465 Fleet Fisheries Inc
20 Blackmer St
New Bedford, MA 02744-2614   508-910-2100
     Fax: 508-996-3785 www.fleetfisheries.com
Scallops
President: Lars Vinjerud
lars@oceansfleet.com
Vice President: Rick Miller
Quality Control: Rick Tavis
Operations: Shaun Souza
Accounts Receivable: Dan Pacheco
Plant Manager: Chris Brown
Estimated Sales: $5-10 Million
Number Employees: 10-19

Wholesalers & Distributors / A-Z

56466 Fleig Commodities
657 Sussex Drive
Janesville, WI 53546-1915   608-754-6457
Fax: 608-754-2899
Wholesaler/distributor and exporter of Wisconsin cheese
President: Michael Fleig
Number Employees: 1-4
Type of Packaging: Consumer, Food Service, Private Label, Bulk
Types of Products Distributed:
Frozen Food, General Line, Wisconsin cheese

56467 Flint Provision Inc Zalack's
2801 Lippincott Blvd
Flint, MI 48507-2064   810-742-4100
Fax: 810-742-5280 lizflintprovision@yahoo.com
www.flintprovision.com
Wholesaler/distributor of frozen foods, provisions/meats, general merchandise and seafood; serving the food service market
President: Thomas Zalack
VP: Liz Ostrander
Estimated Sales: $10-20 Million
Number Employees: 10-19
Square Footage: 16680
Types of Products Distributed:
Food Service, Frozen Food, General Merchandise, Provisions/Meat, Seafood

56468 Flora Foods Inc
11927 West Sample Road
Coral Springs, FL 33065   954-785-3100
Fax: 954-785-2353
customerservice@florafoods.com
www.florafoods.com
Wholesaler/distributor, importer and exporter of pasta, olive oil, tomatoes, grilled vegetables, spices, sauces, pastries, meats and granulated garlic; serving the food service and retail markets
CEO/President: John Flora
jflora@florafoods.com
CFO: Richard DeCario
Operations Manager: Guy Rizzo
Estimated Sales: $10-20 Million
Number Employees: 20-49
Square Footage: 160000
Type of Packaging: Food Service
Private Brands Carried:
Flora
Types of Products Distributed:
Food Service, Frozen Food, General Line, Provisions/Meat, Specialty Foods, Pasta, olive oil, etc.

56469 Florida Beverage Connection
1627 E Gary Rd
Lakeland, FL 33801   863-688-3357
Fax: 863-688-0273 800-741-3847
Wholesaler/distributor of yogurt, juices and specialty foods; serving the food service market
President: Marc Malone
Estimated Sales: Less than $500,000
Number Employees: 1-4
Private Brands Carried:
Hawaiian Julep; Columbo; Florida's Natural
Number of Customer Locations: 200
Types of Products Distributed:
Food Service, Frozen Food, General Line, Specialty Foods, Yogurt & juices

56470 Florida Carbonic Distributor
1610 S Division Ave
Orlando, FL 32805-4755   407-425-4645
Fax: 407-841-0330 www.flcarbonic.com
Wholesaler/distributor of beverage service and helium equipment, carbonic gas and dry ice; serving the food service market
President: Herb Hinely
fc52@aol.com
Manager: Brian Sullivan
Estimated Sales: $1-2.5 Million
Number Employees: 5-9
Types of Products Distributed:
Food Service, Frozen Food, General Merchandise, Beverage equipment, dry ice, etc.

56471 Florida Choice Foods
1413 N. State Road 7
Hollywood, FL 33023   954-989-7964
Fax: 954-987-0367 info@fcfpopcorn.com
www.fcfpopcorn.com
Wholesaler/distributor and exporter of concession equipment and supplies including popcorn machines, popcorn, ice cream and dry yogurt mixes, etc.; serving the food service market
Owner: Craig S Garber
craig@fcfpopcorn.com
VP: Sharon Martin
Estimated Sales: $1-2.5 Million
Number Employees: 5-9
Square Footage: 12000
Private Brands Carried:
Ricos; Gold Medal; FCF
Types of Products Distributed:
Food Service, Frozen Food, General Line, General Merchandise, Popcorn machines, popcorn, etc.

56472 Florida Distributing Source
14038 63rd Way N
Clearwater, FL 33760-3618   727-431-0444
Fax: 727-531-2906 800-838-1818
info@florida-distributing.com
www.florida-distributing.com
Wholesaler/distributor and broker of food service equipment
Owner/President: Kevin Eaton
CEO: Bob Eaton
bob@florida-distributing.com
Estimated Sales: $1.8 Million
Number Employees: 1-4
Private Brands Carried:
Sani Serv; Scottsman
Types of Products Distributed:
Food Service, Frozen Food, General Merchandise, Foodservice equipment

56473 Florida Fresh Stonecrab
6565 W Linden Drive
Homosassa, FL 34446-3012   352-628-5906
Fax: 954-925-5861
Wholesaler/distributor of frozen lobster, shrimp, stonecrab, etc,; serving the food service market
Buyer: Charlie Raines
Types of Products Distributed:
Food Service, Frozen Food, Seafood, Frozen lobster, shrimp, stonecrab, etc.

56474 Florida Gulf Packaging
7704 Industrial Ln Ste C
Tampa, FL 33637   813-983-9800
Fax: 813-983-9810 800-264-5014
Wholesaler/distributor of packaging equipment and materials for carton closing, bar code label printing, shrink bundling, neck banding, etc
Estimated Sales: $500,000-$1 Million
Number Employees: 10-19
Parent Co: Gulf Systems
Types of Products Distributed:
Frozen Food, General Merchandise, Packaging equipment

56475 Florida Smoked Fish Company
1111 NW 159th Drive
Miami, FL 33169-5883   954-735-4445
Fax: 954-735-4447 800-321-6516
Wholesaler/distributor of dairy products and poultry; serving the food service market
Sales Manager: Bob Sprigel
Number Employees: 100-249
Parent Co: Sun City Industries
Private Brands Carried:
Dorman; Bongard; Friendship
Types of Products Distributed:
Food Service, Frozen Food, General Line, Provisions/Meat, Dairy products & poultry

56476 Flostor Engineering
3366 Enterprise Ave
Hayward, CA 94545   510-887-7179
Fax: 510-785-7463 800-500-8256
information@flostor.com www.flostor.com
Wholesaler/distributor of conveyors and shelving; also, parts and service available
Owner: Robert Weeks
VP Operations: David Rebata
Estimated Sales: $5-10 Million
Number Employees: 20-49
Private Brands Carried:
Hytrol; Sanuc
Types of Products Distributed:
Frozen Food, General Merchandise, Material handling equipment

56477 Flowers Foods Inc.
1919 Flowers Circle
Thomasville, GA 31757   229-226-9110
Fax: 229-225-3823 www.flowersfoods.com
Packaged bakery foods.
President/CEO: A. Ryals McMullian
CFO/Chief Administrative Officer: R. Steve Kinsey
Senior VP/Chief Accounting Officer: Karyl Lauder
Chief Marketing Officer: Debo Mukherjee
Chief Sales Officer: D. Keith Wheeler
COO: Bradley Alexander
Year Founded: 1919
Estimated Sales: Over $1 Billion
Number Employees: 9,800
Number of Brands: 12
Type of Packaging: Consumer, Food Service
Types of Products Distributed:
Food Service

56478 Fluid-O-Tech International Inc
161 Atwater St
Plantsville, CT 06479-1644   860-276-9270
Fax: 860-620-0193 info@fluid-o-tech.com
www.fluidotech.it
Importer, exporter and wholesaler/distributor of rotary vane, oscillating piston and magnetic drive gear pumps
President: Mark Petrucci
fotint@aol.com
VP: Mark Petrucci
Number Employees: 5-9
Square Footage: 40000
Parent Co: Fluid O Tech
Private Brands Carried:
Fluid-O-Tech
Types of Products Distributed:
Frozen Food, General Merchandise, Pumps

56479 Flushing Lighting
13423 Northern Blvd # 1
Flushing, NY 11354-4082   718-353-2894
Fax: 718-445-9458 800-452-5937
questions@flushinglighting.com
Wholesaler/distributor of electrical supplies including light bulbs, decorative fixtures, lighting systems, ventilating equipment and fans; also, energy management services
Owner: Stuart Schneiderman
stuart@flushinglighting.com
VP: Stuart Schneiderman
Estimated Sales: $5-10 Million
Number Employees: 5-9
Square Footage: 20000
Private Brands Carried:
Nutone; Lutron; Lightolier
Types of Products Distributed:
Frozen Food, General Merchandise, Electrical supplies & lighting systems

56480 Flynt Wholesale Company
551 Eagle Day Ave
Columbia, MS 39429-3605   601-736-6137
Fax: 601-736-3496
Wholesaler/distributor of general line products; serving the food service market
President: F Griffith
VP: Eddie Sullivan
Estimated Sales: $20-50 Million
Number Employees: 1-4
Number of Customer Locations: 600
Types of Products Distributed:
Food Service, Frozen Food, General Line

56481 Focus Marketing
6860 108th Street
Forest Hills, NY 11375-2973   718-261-4881
Fax: 718-575-9780 800-532-4438
Wholesaler/distributor of general merchandise including advertising specialties
President: Eda Easton
Estimated Sales: $1 Million
Number Employees: 5-9
Types of Products Distributed:
Frozen Food, General Merchandise, Advertising specialties

56482 Fold-Pak LLC
33 Powell Dr
Hazleton, PA 18201-7360   570-454-0433
Fax: 570-454-0456 800-486-0490
www.fold-pak.com

1005

Wholesalers & Distributors / A-Z

Wire handled square paper food containers, round cup style closeable food and soup containers, square closeable paper food containers (microwaveable, carry out and storage capable)
Manager: Charlie Mattson
Director of Operations: Wes Gentles
Sales Director: Jim Keitges
Corporate Credit Manager: William Moon
Plant Manager: Lee King
Number Employees: 5000-9999
Number of Brands: 16
Number of Products: 66
Square Footage: 416000
Parent Co: Rock-Tenn Company
Type of Packaging: Consumer, Food Service, Private Label
Private Brands Carried:
  Fold-Pak, Bio-Pak, Smartserv
Types of Products Distributed:
  Carry out Food Containers (Paper)

56483 Foley-Belsaw Institute
1173 Benson St
River Falls, WI 54022-1594   715-426-2275
        Fax: 715-426-2198 800-821-3452
            www.foley-belsaw.com
Wholesaler/distributor and exporter of sharpening equipment, carbide saws, knives, scissors, shears, bandsaws, etc.; also, hog splitting, carcass and bandsaw machinery
Partner: Ron Bearl
rbearl@foley-belsaw.com
Number Employees: 20-49
Private Brands Carried:
  Foley-Belsaw; Tru-Hone
Types of Products Distributed:
  Frozen Food, General Merchandise, Food processing equipment

56484 (HQ)Folgers Coffee Co
1 Strawberry Ln
Orrville, OH 44667-0208
                800-937-9745
            www.folgerscoffee.com
Roasted, ground, regular and decaffeinated coffee. Also, Folgers is the licensed manufacturer and distributor of Dunkin' Donuts retail coffee brand.
Chief Executive Officer: Richard Smucker
SVP/Chief Financial Officer: Mark Belgya
Chief Operating Officer: Vincent Byrd
VP/Controller: John Denman
VP/General Counsel: Jeannette Knudsen
SVP/Corporate Communications: Christopher Resweber
Logistics Leader/Operations Manager: Shane Boddie
Number Employees: 100-249
Parent Co: J.M Smucker Company
Type of Packaging: Consumer
Types of Products Distributed:
  Coffee

56485 Follex Distributing Co Inc
1952 W Houghton Lake Dr
Prudenville, MI 48651-9329   989-366-8985
        Fax: 989-366-8992
Wholesaler/distributor of restaurant and janitorial equipment and supplies; serving the food service market
Owner: Rick Follrath
follexdistributing@freeway.net
Estimated Sales: $2.5-5 Million
Number Employees: 5-9
Square Footage: 40000
Types of Products Distributed:
  Food Service, Frozen Food, General Merchandise, Janitorial equipment & supplies

56486 Folmer Fruit & Produce Company
748 Guilford St
Lebanon, PA 17046-3532   717-272-8471
        Fax: 717-272-8677
Wholesaler/distributor of produce; serving the food service market
President: Thomas Folmer
Estimated Sales: $1-2.5 Million
Number Employees: 1-4
Types of Products Distributed:
  Food Service, Produce

56487 Foltz Meat Processors
12526 S Middle Rd
Edinburg, VA 22824-3201   540-984-8138
        Fax: 540-984-8139
Wholesaler of beef pork and lamb
Owner: Jeff Gore
Co-Owner: Joe Gore
Estimated Sales: $3-5 Million
Number Employees: 10-19
Type of Packaging: Consumer
Types of Products Distributed:
  Frozen Food

56488 Food Authority Inc
3400 Lawson Blvd
Oceanside, NY 11572-3708   516-887-0500
    Fax: 516-887-0573 www.foodauthority.com
Wholesaler/distributor of baked goods, dairy products, frozen and specialty foods, general merchandise, groceries, private label items, produce and seafood; serving the food service market
Manager: Dennis Rueter
VP: Tim Motley
Director Operations: Dennis Reutter
Estimated Sales: $5-10 Million
Number Employees: 1-4
Square Footage: 280000
Private Brands Carried:
  Pocahontas; Tropicana; Del Monte
Types of Products Distributed:
  Food Service, Frozen Food, General Line, General Merchandise, Produce, Seafood, Specialty Foods, Groceries, baked goods, etc.

56489 Food Buying Service
18805 80th Pl S, #A
Kent, WA 98032-1016   206-768-1283
    Fax: 206-768-1307 larry.jamieson@p-h-s.com
Wholesaler/distributor of groceries; serving the food service market
Marketing: Larry Jamieson
Number Employees: 1-4
Number of Customer Locations: 300
Types of Products Distributed:
  Food Service, Frozen Food, General Line, Groceries

56490 Food City
201 Trigg St
Abingdon, VA 24210   276-623-5100
            www.foodcity.com
Wholesaler of general line groceries.
President & CEO: Steve Smith
Year Founded: 1918
Estimated Sales: $2.3 Billion
Number Employees: 13,000
Square Footage: 10000000
Type of Packaging: Consumer
Private Brands Carried:

Types of Products Distributed:
  Frozen Food, General Line, Health Food, Provisions/Meat, Produce, Baking Supplies; Snack Foods

56491 Food Equipment Distributors
2920 NW 109th Avenue
Doral, FL 33172-5005   305-357-0271
    Fax: 305-592-2240 sales@fedmiami.com
Wholesaler/distributor of food service equipment and supplies including freezers, ice makers, dispensers, etc
President: Robin Anderson
Sales Manager: Mike Woodward
Parts Manager: Greg Matwijow
Number Employees: 5-9
Square Footage: 34400
Private Brands Carried:
  Manitowoc; True; Amana
Number of Customer Locations: 400
Types of Products Distributed:
  Food Service, Frozen Food, General Merchandise, Foodservice equipment & supplies

56492 Food Equipment Specialist
10460 S Sam Houston Pkwy W
Houston, TX 77071-3138   713-988-8700
        Fax: 713-988-5129 800-578-1519
Wholesaler/distributor of tabletop supplies and equipment; serving the food service market
President: Bill Bley
Treasurer: Ben Owen
Estimated Sales: $5-10 Million
Number Employees: 20-49
Types of Products Distributed:
  Food Service, Frozen Food, General Merchandise, Tabletop supplies & equipment

56493 Food Factory
875 Waimanu St
Suite 535
Honolulu, HI 96813   808-593-2633
        Fax: 808-591-2943
Frozen foods
President: David Phillips
Estimated Sales: $300,000-500,000
Number Employees: 5-9

56494 Food For Thought Inc
10704 Oviatt Rd
Honor, MI 49640-9546   231-326-5444
    Fax: 231-326-2649 sales@foodforthought.net
            www.foodforthought.net
Organic and fair trade preserves, salsa, maple syrup, hot sauce, and mustard.
President: Timothy Young
sales@foodforthought.net
Number Employees: 10-19
Type of Packaging: Consumer, Private Label

56495 Food Ingredient Solutions
10 Malcolm Ave
Suite 1
Teterboro, NJ 07608   917-449-9558
    Fax: 201-440-4211 jgreaves@foodcolor.com
            www.foodcolor.com
Manufacturer and distributor of ingredients for barbeque sauces, spices, seasonings, colors, flavors, gums
CEO: Jeff Greaves
jeffgreaves@earthlink.net
VP, Operations: Helen Greaves
Estimated Sales: $6 Million
Number Employees: 10-19
Number of Brands: 2
Number of Products: 80
Type of Packaging: Food Service, Private Label, Bulk
Other Locations:
  Food Ingredients Solutions
  Signal Hill, CA Food Ingredients Solutions

56496 Food Ingredients
2155 Drew Road
Mississauga, ON L5S 1T4
Canada   905-676-1090
        Fax: 905-676-9333
Wholesaler/distributor of food ingredients
VP/General Manager: David Grimshaw
Parent Co: McCormick Canada
Types of Products Distributed:
  Frozen Food, General Line, Food ingredients

56497 Food Instrument Corp
115 Academy Ave
Federalsburg, MD 21632-1202   410-754-8606
        Fax: 410-754-8796 800-542-5688
                kickout@verizon.net
            www.foodinstrumentcorporation.com
Manufacturer, wholesaler/distributor and exporter of microprocessor based quality control instrumentation including closure seal testers, rejectors, data analyzers, can orienters and diverters
President: Richard V Kudlich
Sales Director: James Boehm
Estimated Sales: $1-5 Million
Number Employees: 1-4
Number of Brands: 1
Number of Products: 6
Square Footage: 40000
Types of Products Distributed:
  General Merchandise, Quality control instrumentation

56498 Food Ireland, Inc.
230 East 3rd Street
New York, NY 10553   914-699-5000
    Fax: 914-665-4083 wholesale@foodireland.com
            www.foodirelandwholesale.com
Importer and wholesaler of baked goods, beverages, candy, canned vegetables, cereal, cookies, desserts, instant meals, jams, salads, sauces, seasonings and more.
Owner: Patrick Coleman
Estimated Sales: $1.1 Million
Number Employees: 6
Square Footage: 40000

56499 Food People Inc
268 Michelle Ct
S San Francisco, CA 94080-6201   650-952-1307
    Fax: 650-952-3547 www.foodpeopleinc.com

Wholesaler/distributor of gourmet specialty foods and health food including bars and cookies
Owner: Frank Antonelli
Operations Manager: Darrell Vannelli
Estimated Sales: $1 Million
Number Employees: 5-9
Square Footage: 16000
Private Brands Carried:
  Allegria Cookies; Clif Bars; Meeks Honey; Bellasunluci Tomato Sauce and Pesto Sauce; Dirty Chips; Lavache Crackers
Number of Customer Locations: 120

56500 Food Service Design & Furnishings
50 Barrett Pkwy # 1200 Pmb 403
Marietta, GA 30066-3332   770-419-0811
                              Fax: 770-422-9396
Wholesaler/distributor of cafeteria foodservice and restaurant equipment national, designing and consulting services available
President: Bill Wissing
Estimated Sales: $1-3 Million
Number Employees: 1-4

56501 Food Services Inc
17889 Mclean Rd
Mt Vernon, WA 98273   360-424-7147
  Fax: 360-416-5151   800-377-7147
                www.foodservicesinc.com
Wholesaler/distributor of restaurant equipment, frozen foods, produce, dairy products, meat products, etc.; serving the food service market; rack jobber services available.
Transportation & Compliance Manager: Tom Nasin
Director, Sales & Marketing: Sandy Cobbin
Customer Service: Deborah Stevens
Vice President, Operations: Bob Crawford
Estimated Sales: $18 Million
Number Employees: 50-99
Types of Products Distributed:
  Frozen Food, General Line, General Merchandise, Provisions/Meat, Produce, Rack Jobbers, Restaurant equipment

56502 Food Supply Inc
3100 S Ridgewood Ave
Unit 100
South Daytona, FL 32119   386-763-7500
                info@foodsupply.com
                www.foodsupply.com
Wholesaler/distributor of general line items, frozen foods, provisions/meats, general merchandise, groceries and baked goods; serving the food service market.
Chief Executive Officer: David Sacks
President: Steve Motzel
Director, Operations: Steve Stidham
Year Founded: 1905
Estimated Sales: $33 Million
Number Employees: 20-49
Square Footage: 100000
Parent Co: Daytona Beach Cold Storage Company
Types of Products Distributed:
  Food Service, Frozen Food, General Line, General Merchandise, Provisions/Meat, Baked goods

56503 Food Wholesalers Inc
701 46th St S
St Petersburg, FL 33711-1841   727-321-2514
  Fax: 727-896-4959 www.foodwholesalers.net
Wholesaler/distributor of general line food products; serving the food service market
Owner: Jim Anson
ansonj@foodwholesalers.net
Estimated Sales: $10-20 Million
Number Employees: 20-49
Private Brands Carried:
  Smith; Morrell; Excel
Types of Products Distributed:
  Food Service, Frozen Food, General Line

56504 Food for Life Baking
Corona, CA 92879
                              800-797-5090
                www.foodforlife.com
Breads, buns, cereals, pasta, tortillas and waffles
CFO: Scott Kraus
Marketing Manager: Gary Torres
Type of Packaging: Consumer

56505 Food-Products
410 SE Division Place
Portland, OR 97202-1020   503-236-2126
  Fax: 503-236-2171   800-248-3017
Wholesaler/distributor of frozen foods, general merchandise, general line products, produce, meats, seafood and specialty foods; serving the food service market; also, rack jobber services available
President: Dennis Updegraff
Number Employees: 20-49
Number of Customer Locations: 10
Types of Products Distributed:
  Food Service, Frozen Food, General Line, General Merchandise, Provisions/Meat, Produce, Rack Jobbers, Seafood, Specialty Foods

56506 Foods Etc.
690 Donald Drive
Hollister, CA 95023-6346   831-637-5700
                              Fax: 831-637-9172
Wholesaler/distributor of meats and dairy products; serving convenience stores and independent grocers
Partner: Max Sparrer
Partner: Alex Kennett
Estimated Sales: $2.5-5 Million
Number Employees: 1-4
Square Footage: 40000
Types of Products Distributed:
  Frozen Food, General Line, Provisions/Meat, Dairy products

56507 Foodtopia USA
11 Harristown Rd
Suite 101
Glen Rock, NJ 07452   201-444-8810
                info@foodtopiausa.com
                www.foodtopiausa.com
Distributor of ingredients to the food, nutraceutical, pharmaceutical, cosmetic, and feed industries. Offering creatine, specialty ingredients, food additives (such as aspartame and stevia), vitamins and amino acids
President: Young Yoon
General Manager: Tad Kim
Contact: Audri Yoon
asy@foodtopiausa.com
Estimated Sales: $1.1 Million
Number Employees: 6
Type of Packaging: Bulk

56508 Fora Foods
Brooklyn, NY 11206
                info@forafoods.com
                forafoods.com
Dairy-free butter
Co-Founder & CEO: Aidan Altman
Co-Founder & CFO: Andrew McClure

56509 Forbes Frozen Foods
438 Main St
Milford, OH 45150-1128   513-576-6660
  Fax: 513-576-6661   www.forbesfoods.com
Wholesaler/distributor and broker of food ingredients, fruit juice concentrates and essences, as well as frozen fruits and vegetables
President: David Winters
Estimated Sales: $2.5-5 million
Number Employees: 1-4
Types of Products Distributed:
  Frozen Food

56510 Ford Hotel Supply Co
2204 N Broadway
St Louis, MO 63102-1404   314-231-8400
  Fax: 314-231-8436   800-472-3673
                www.fordstl.com
Commercial foodservice equipment and supplies, kitchen layout and design, equipment consultation, interior design- all for commercial food industry.
Owner: Christy Schlafly
christyschlafly@fordstl.com
Estimated Sales: $20-50 Million
Number Employees: 50-99
Square Footage: 120000
Other Locations:
  Ford Restaurant Supply
  Columbia, MO Ford Restaurant Supply
Types of Products Distributed:
  Food Service, Frozen Food, General Merchandise, Equipment & supplies

56511 Ford Ice Cream
PO Box 518
Newton, MS 39345-0518   601-683-2055
  Fax: 601-683-6203   800-826-6159
Wholesaler/distributor of ice cream
President: James Briscoe
Estimated Sales: $5-10 Million
Number Employees: 5-9
Types of Products Distributed:
  Frozen Food

56512 Foreign Candy Company
1 Foreign Candy Dr
Hull, IA 51239-7499   712-439-1496
  Fax: 712-439-3207   800-831-8541
                www.foreigncandy.com
Developer and distributor of candy.
CEO, President & Owner: Peter De Yager
VP, Marketing & Sales: Bill Lange
HR Manager: Bethany Bosma
Estimated Sales: $5-10 Million
Number Employees: 11-50
Type of Packaging: Private Label
Types of Products Distributed:
  Candy

56513 Foreign Domestic Chemicals
3 Post Rd
Oakland, NJ 07436-1609   201-651-9700
                              Fax: 201-651-9703
Manufactures ingredients and additives
President: Heinrich Dieseldorff
Estimated Sales: $500,000-1 Million
Number Employees: 1-4

56514 Foremost Farms USA
E10889 Penny Lane
Baraboo, WI 53913-8115   608-355-8700
                              800-362-9196
                www.foremostfarms.com
Dairy products including cheeses, fresh milk, butter, and whey ingredients.
President/CEO: Greg Schlafer
Senior VP/CFO: Bob Bascom
VP, Milk Division & Risk Management: Darin Hanson
Manager: Wally Heil
Year Founded: 1994
Estimated Sales: Over $1 Billion
Number Employees: 1000-4999
Number of Brands: 2
Number of Products: 10
Type of Packaging: Consumer, Food Service, Private Label, Bulk
Types of Products Distributed:
  Food Service, General Line

56515 Foremost Foods Company
72 Suffolk Dr
Madison, CT 06443-8118   203-933-5407
                              Fax: 203-934-3728
Wholesaler/distributor of frozen food, general line products, meats, frozen seafood, grocery and dairy products; serving the food service market
President: Joseph DeLuca, Jr.
Secretary: Ron Arbour
Estimated Sales: $20-50 Million
Number Employees: 20-49
Private Brands Carried:
  Chef's Choice
Types of Products Distributed:
  Food Service, Frozen Food, General Line, Provisions/Meat, Seafood, Dairy & grocery products

56516 Forest City Weingart Produce
4000 Orange Ave # 23
Cleveland, OH 44115-3562   216-881-3232
  Fax: 216-881-3235 www.economyproduce.net
Wholesaler/distributor of produce
President: Jim Weingart
Estimated Sales: $5-10 Million
Number Employees: 5-9
Parent Co: Beatrice Foods
Types of Products Distributed:
  Frozen Food, Produce

56517 (HQ)Forever Foods
325 E Washington Street
137
Sequim, WA 98382-3488   360-582-3822
  Fax: 360-681-0186   888-407-6672
Wholesaler/distributor and exporter of freeze-dried and dehydrated foods

Wholesalers & Distributors / A-Z

President: Steve Sparkowich
VP: Crystal Sparkowich
Sales Manager: Debra Poe
Number Employees: 1-4
Types of Products Distributed:
 Frozen Food, General Line, Freeze dried & dehydrated foods

56518 Forklift Systems Inc-Parts Dpt
884 Elm Hill Pike
Nashville, TN 37210-2849 615-255-6321
 Fax: 615-255-8242 www.forkliftsystems.com
Wholesaler/distributor of material handling equipment
President: Duane Hardy
dhardy@forkliftsystems.com
VP: Kathy Kernell
VP: Duane Hardy
Estimated Sales: $20-50 Million
Number Employees: 50-99
Private Brands Carried:
 Nissan; Barrett; Star; Teledyne Princeton; Prime Mover
Types of Products Distributed:
 Frozen Food, General Merchandise, Material handling equipment

56519 Forklifts
741 Independence Ave
Mechanicsburg, PA 17055 717-761-8700
 Fax: 717-918-8729
Wholesaler/distributor of material handling equipment
President: Doug Gibson
Contact: Chris Campbell
chris.campbell@eqdepot.com
Estimated Sales: $1-2.5 Million
Number Employees: 10-19
Private Brands Carried:
 Niessan; Clark; Daewoo
Types of Products Distributed:
 Frozen Food, General Merchandise, Material handling equipment

56520 Fort Pitt Candy Co
1642 Penn Ave # 2
Pittsburgh, PA 15222-4389 412-281-9016
 info@fortpittcandy.com
 www.fortpittcandy.com
Wholesaler/distributor of candy and canned goods
Owner: Milton Eisenstat
Estimated Sales: $500,000-$1 Million
Number Employees: 1-4
Types of Products Distributed:
 General Line, Candy & canned goods

56521 Fort Smith Restaurant Supply
930 Phoenix Ave
Fort Smith, AR 72901-7898 479-646-1606
 Fax: 479-646-4871 800-542-1059
 accounts@foodservequip.com
 www.foodservequip.com
Wholesaler/distributor of equipment and supplies; serving the food service market
President: Robert R Marley Jr
CEO: Betty Marley
CFO: Harold Steward
Estimated Sales: $5-10 Million
Number Employees: 10-19
Types of Products Distributed:
 Food Service, Frozen Food, General Merchandise, Equipment & supplies

56522 Fort Wayne Door Inc
3203 Clearfield Ct
Fort Wayne, IN 46808-4517 260-483-5600
 Fax: 260-471-3667 info@fortwaynedoor.com
 www.fortwaynedoor.com
Wholesaler/distributor of doors and grillwork; serving the food service market
Owner: Gordon Murphy
ftwdoor@frontier.com
Sales Manager: Harold Albersmeyer
Estimated Sales: $1-2.5 Million
Number Employees: 5-9
Private Brands Carried:
 Wayne Dalton; North American/Kinnear
Types of Products Distributed:
 Food Service, Frozen Food, General Merchandise, Doors & grillwork

56523 Forte Industries
6037 Commerce Ct
Mason, OH 45040-8819 513-398-2800
 Fax: 513-398-2837 800-796-5566
 www.forte-industries.com
Wholesaler/distributor of material handling equipment including conveyors
CEO: Gene Forte
Vice President: Rachel Beohm
rachel@nonverbalforte.com
VP, Sales & Marketing: Tom Rentschler
Director, Sales & Marketing: Robyn Poe
Estimated Sales: $2.5-5 Million
Number Employees: 20-49
Types of Products Distributed:
 Frozen Food, General Merchandise, Material handling equipment

56524 Fortune Equipment Company
1260 Lakeshore Drive
Hensley, AR 72065-8046 501-565-2770
 Fax: 501-565-2918 800-447-3889
Wholesaler/distributor of specialty equipment, parts and supplies; warehouse providing storage of food service equipment; also, machine repair and delivery available
Accounting Manager: Eloise Worlow
VP: Ken Fortune
Sales Manager: Tim Tipton
Estimated Sales: $5-10 Million
Number Employees: 20-49
Square Footage: 74000
Types of Products Distributed:
 Frozen Food, General Merchandise, Specialty equipment, parts & supplies

56525 Fortville Produce
325 W Broadway St
Fortville, IN 46040-1408 317-485-5332
Wholesaler/distributor of poultry and eggs; serving the food service market
President: Robert Hiday
Estimated Sales: $1-2.5 Million
Number Employees: 1-4
Number of Customer Locations: 50
Types of Products Distributed:
 Food Service, General Line, Poultry & eggs

56526 Foss North America Inc
8091 Wallace Rd
Eden Prairie, MN 55344-2224 952-974-9892
 Fax: 952-974-9823 800-547-6275
 info@fossna.com www.foss.dk
Wholesaler/distributor of analysis instrumentation
President: Jan Elgarard
jelgarard@fossnorthamerica.com
Marketing: Jennifer Montville
Estimated Sales: $5-10 Million
Number Employees: 20-49

56527 Foster Dairy Farms Inc
529 Kansas Ave
Modesto, CA 95351-1515 209-576-3400
 Fax: 209-576-3437 866-225-4821
 www.crystalcreamery.com
Wholesaler/distributor of milk, butter, cottage cheese, cream and yogurt; serving the food service market
President: Jeff Foster
jeff.foster@fosterfarms.com
CFO: Tom Van Autreve
VP Business Development: Dan Conrad
Corporated Quality/Food Safety Director: Richard Earp
Vice President Sales: Richard Werhel
VP Human Resources: Luis Miranda
VP Operations & Transportation: Jeff Fowler
General Manager Dairy Operations: Ron Haile
Estimated Sales: $28.8 Million
Number Employees: 500-999
Square Footage: 11521
Parent Co: Foster Farms Dairy
Other Locations:
 Modesto, CA
 Hickman, CA
 Fresno, CA
 Bakersfield, CA
 Hayward, CA
 Fresno, CAHickman
Types of Products Distributed:
 Food Service, Frozen Food, General Line, Health Food, Dairy products

56528 Fought's Mill
250 Race St
Hughesville, PA 17737-1521 570-584-2764
Wholesaler/distributor of flour, feed and meal
Owner/President: Jerry Fought
Estimated Sales: $500,000-$1 Million
Number Employees: 1-4
Types of Products Distributed:
 Frozen Food, General Line, Flour, feed & meal

56529 (HQ)Fountain Valley Foods
2175 N Academy Circle # 201
PO Box 9882
Colorado Springs, CO 80932 719-573-6012
 Fax: 719-573-5192 www.fountainvalleyfoods.com
Salsa, ketchup, bean dip and specialty chili products; Importer/Distributor of cheese sauce, jalapeno peppers, banana peppers, chipotle peppers, green chile.
President: James Loyacono
Contact: Ginger Steineke
ginger@fountainvalleyfoods.com
Estimated Sales: $4.9 Million
Number Employees: 4
Square Footage: 20000
Type of Packaging: Consumer, Food Service, Private Label, Bulk
Other Locations:
 Den-Mar Products
 Trinidad, CODen-Mar Products
Types of Products Distributed:
 Food Service, Salsa & Bean Dip, Chip Sauces

56530 Four Oaks Farm
4856 Augusta Rd
Lexington, SC 29073-9198 803-356-3194
 Fax: 803-951-0843 800-858-5006
 www.fouroaksfarm.com
Retailer /country, frozen food, general merchandise, beef, pork and vegetables; serving the food service market
President: Fred Mathias
fred@fouroaksfarm.com
Secretary: Fred Mathias, Jr.
VP: Tillman Mathias
Estimated Sales: $1-2.5 Million
Number Employees: 5-9
Types of Products Distributed:
 Food Service, Frozen Food, General Line, General Merchandise, Provisions/Meat, Produce, Beef, pork, etc.

56531 Four Today
1905 W 4700 S
444
Salt Lake City, UT 84118-1105 801-281-2938
  877-448-6329
Wholesaler/distributor of nutritional supplements including vitamins, amino acids, herbs, antioxidants, minerals and phytonutrients
President: Jan Kerr
Estimated Sales: Less than $500,000
Number Employees: 1-4
Types of Products Distributed:
 Frozen Food, Health Food, Nutritional supplements

56532 Fournier R & Sons Seafood
14147 Old Highway 67
Biloxi, MS 39532-8803 228-392-4293
 Fax: 228-392-7130
Wholesaler/distributor of seafood including shucked oysters, green headless and peeled shrimp and crabmeat
Owner: Doty Fournier
Secretary: Jayne Fournier
Sales Assistant Manager: Doty Fournier
Estimated Sales: $1-3 Million
Number Employees: 20-49
Square Footage: 60000
Private Brands Carried:
 Waterfall
Types of Products Distributed:
 Seafood, Shucked oysters, crabmeat, etc.

56533 Foutch's Coffee and Spring Water
PO Box 21
Cookeville, TN 38503 931-537-6643
 Fax: 931-537-6647 info@foutchs.com
 foutchs.com
Wholesaler/distributor of frozen foods and general line items; serving the food service market
President: Martin Foutch
Estimated Sales: $500,000-$1 Million
Number Employees: 5-9

Private Brands Carried:
   Parade; Federated Foods
Types of Products Distributed:
   Food Service, Frozen Food, General Line

56534 Fox Brush Company
29 Tiger Hill Road
Oxford, ME 4270   207-539-2208
              Fax: 207-539-2208
Wholesaler/distributor of corn, road, push and street sweeper brooms and brushes; manufacturer of specialty brushes
Owner: Linda Cushman
Manager: Thomas Cushman
Estimated Sales: Below $5 Million
Number Employees: 1
Types of Products Distributed:
   Frozen Food, General Merchandise, Brooms & brushes

56535 Fox Deluxe Inc
370 N Morgan St
Chicago, IL 60607   312-421-3737
       Fax: 312-421-8067 www.foxdeluxefoods.com
Wholesale frozen meats
Owner: Sam Samano
Estimated Sales: $50-100 Million
Number Employees: 50-99
Types of Products Distributed:
   Provisions/Meat

56536 Foxtail Foods
6880 Fairfield Business Ctr
Fairfield, OH 45014-5476   513-881-7900
       Fax: 513-881-7910 800-487-2253
          customerservice@foxtailfoods.com
                www.foxtailfoods.com
Pies, cookies, muffin batter, mixes and syrups and specialty products
President: Lonnie Howard
VP: Matt Daniel
Director of R&D: Doug Snedden
VP Sales/Marketing: Athos Rostan
Manager: Joe Reinhardt
Purchasing Agent: Rich Frysinger
Estimated Sales: $10-20 Million
Number Employees: 100-249
Square Footage: 179055
Parent Co: Perkins
Type of Packaging: Consumer, Food Service, Private Label, Bulk
Other Locations:
   Foxtail Foods-Corporate
   MemphisFoxtail Foods-CorporateTennesse
Types of Products Distributed:
   Frozen Food

56537 Frabosk Magic Cappuccino
5642 N Vine Avenue
Chicago, IL 60631-2943   847-825-7239
              Fax: 773-804-0066
Wholesaler/distributor of cappuccino makers
Types of Products Distributed:
   Frozen Food, General Merchandise, Cappuccino makers

56538 Frain Industries
245 E North Ave
Carol Stream, IL 60188-2021   630-629-9900
       Fax: 630-629-6575 847-629-6575
          sales@fraingroup.com www.frainindustries.com
Wholesaler/distributor of used packaging and processing equipment; rental/leasing services
Owner: Richard Frain
rfrain@fraingroup.com
CEO: David Eggleston
Marketing Director: Suzanne Eaton
Estimated Sales: $14 Million
Number Employees: 50-99
Square Footage: 350000
Types of Products Distributed:
   Frozen Food, General Merchandise, Used packaging & processing machinery

56539 Francis Produce Company
3048 White Horse Rd
Greenville, SC 29611   864-295-2780
       Fax: 864-269-6687 800-848-6212
          Sales@francisproduce.com
                www.francisproduce.com
Wholesaler/distributor of produce

President: W Francis
Contact: Mcdaniel Freddie
freddie@francisproduce.com
Manager: S Francis
Estimated Sales: $10-20 Million
Number Employees: 50-99
Number of Customer Locations: 75
Types of Products Distributed:
   Frozen Food, General Line, Produce

56540 Franco Roma Foods
2700 E Hanna Avenue
Tampa, FL 33610-1434   813-237-2511
              888-782-9292
Wholesaler/distributor serving Subway sandwich shops
Types of Products Distributed:
   Food Service, Frozen Food, General Line

56541 Frank Beer
2115 Pleasant View Road
Middleton, WI 53562-5518   608-836-6000
       Fax: 608-836-1140 www.frankbeer.com
Wholesaler/distributor of beer
President: Steve Frank
Contact: Larissa Aunet
larissaaunet@frankbeer.com
Number Employees: 50-99
Private Brands Carried:
   Coors; Stroh; Heineken
Types of Products Distributed:
   Frozen Food, General Line, Beer

56542 Frank Brunckhorst Company
1819 Main St.
Suite 800
Sarasota, FL 34236   804-722-4100
       Fax: 804-863-1409 www.boarshead.com
Boar's Head brands of deli meats and cheeses.
Year Founded: 1905
Estimated Sales: $500+ Million
Number Employees: 250-500
Parent Co: Boar's Head
Types of Products Distributed:
   Provisions/Meat

56543 Frank G. Schmitt Company
213 N Main Street
258
Henderson, KY 42420-3182   270-826-2748
              Fax: 270-827-2308
Wholesaler/distributor of general merchandise and general line items; serving the food service market
President: H Chaney
VP: Darrel Chaney
Estimated Sales: $10-20 Million
Number Employees: 5-9
Number of Customer Locations: 500
Types of Products Distributed:
   Food Service, Frozen Food, General Line, General Merchandise, Equipment, fixtures, etc.

56544 Frank H Gill Co
2859 Bernice Rd
P.O.Box 703
Lansing, IL 60438-1207   708-474-9750
       Fax: 708-895-8871 sales@frankhgillco.com
                www.frankhgillco.com
Manufacturers' representative for material handling equipment
President: John Gill
john.gill@frankhgillco.com
VP/Treasurer/Secretary: John Gill
Estimated Sales: $2.5-5 Million
Number Employees: 5-9
Types of Products Distributed:
   Frozen Food

56545 Frank Mattes & Sons Reliable Seafood
2327 Edwards Lane
Bel Air, MD 21015-5001   410-879-5444
              Fax: 410-734-6061
Seafood

56546 Frank P. Corso
221 Caillavet St
Biloxi, MS 39530   228-436-4697
       Fax: 228-374-8627 www.fpcorso.com
Wholesaler/distributor of confectionery products, groceries, sundries, paper products and vending machines; also, rack jobber services available

President: Elizabeth Joachim
Sales Director: John Joachim
tj@fpcorso.com
Contact: Tj Corso
tj@fpcorso.com
Purchasing Manager: Wayne Ross
Estimated Sales: $10-20 Million
Number Employees: 20-49
Square Footage: 60000
Private Brands Carried:
   Welches; Bottled Water
Number of Customer Locations: 1500
Types of Products Distributed:
   Frozen Food, General Line, General Merchandise, Rack Jobbers, Confectionery, groceries, etc.

56547 Frank Pagano Company
1513 S State Street
Lockport, IL 60441-3550   815-838-0303
              Fax: 815-723-9861
Quality meats
President/CEO: Frank Pagano

56548 Frank Wardynski & Sons Inc
336 Peckham St
PO Box 336
Buffalo, NY 14206-1717   716-854-6083
       Fax: 716-854-4887 www.wardynski.com
Smoked polish sausage, italian sausage, natural casing wieners, tender casing weiners, skinless weiners, knockwurst, bologna, cooked salami, liver sausage, kiska, blood tongue, sweet or sour head cheese.
Chairman/President: Raymond Wardynski
rmwardynski@wardynski.com
Estimated Sales: $5-10 Million
Number Employees: 20-49
Square Footage: 105000
Types of Products Distributed:
   Provisions/Meat, Ham

56549 Frank's Produce
309 Court Ave NW
Canton, OH 44702-1531   330-455-9475
              Fax: 330-455-9477
Wholesaler/distributor of produce; serving retail stores
President: Phillip Frank
VP: Nancy Jo Frank
Contact: Aaron Luper
aaronluper@franksproduce.com
Estimated Sales: $2.5-5 Million
Number Employees: 1-4
Square Footage: 40000
Number of Customer Locations: 60
Types of Products Distributed:
   Produce

56550 Franklin Machine Products
PO Box 992
Marlton, NJ 08053-0992   856-983-2500
       Fax: 800-255-9866 800-257-7737
          sales@fmponline.com www.fmponline.com
Wholesaler/distributor of parts and accessories: serving the food service market
CEO: Carol Adams
Vice President: Michael Conte, Sr.
Estimated Sales: $20-50 Million
Number Employees: 100-249
Square Footage: 50000
Types of Products Distributed:
   Food Service, Frozen Food, General Merchandise

56551 Franklin Produce Company
3 Produce Row
Saint Louis, MO 63102   314-421-4580
              Fax: 314-421-5355
Wholesaler/distributor of produce
President: Frank Kusumano
Contact: Francis Cusumano
cusumano@franklinfarmseast.com
Estimated Sales: $5-10 Million
Number Employees: 10-19
Types of Products Distributed:
   Frozen Food, Produce

56552 Frankstown Fish Co Inc
8500 Frankstown Rd
Pittsburgh, PA 15235-1044   412-731-4545
              Fax: 412-731-5357
Wholesaler/distributor of fresh and frozen seafood and poultry

Wholesalers & Distributors / A-Z

Owner: Valine Rouse
VP: Kurt Rouse
Estimated Sales: $1-2.5 Million
Number Employees: 5-9
Types of Products Distributed:
Frozen Food, Provisions/Meat, Seafood, Poultry

56553 Fred Band & Associates
8366 Rovana Cir
Sacramento, CA 95828-2522 916-388-5500
Fax: 916-388-5501 hsgriswold@aol.com
Wholesaler/distributor of food processing equipment including pumps and heat exchangers
President: Fred Band
Marketing Manager: Scott Griswold
Estimated Sales: $5-10 Million
Number Employees: 10-19
Types of Products Distributed:
Frozen Food, General Merchandise, Pumps, heat exchangers, etc.

56554 Fred Hill & Son Co
2101 Hornig Rd # 1
Philadelphia, PA 19116-4298 215-464-0602
Fax: 215-698-4539 800-523-0112
fredhill@msn.com
Wholesaler/distributor of material handling equipment and rack storage systems
President: Kenneth Shaw, Jr.
HR Executive: Denise Moore
Graphics Advertising Manager: Joe Blannett
General Manager: Ken Shaw
Estimated Sales: $20-50 Million
Number Employees: 10-19
Types of Products Distributed:
Frozen Food, General Merchandise, Material handling systems

56555 (HQ)Fred W Albrecht GroceryCo
2700 Gilchrist Rd # A
Akron, OH 44305-4467 330-733-2263
Fax: 330-733-8782
Wholesaler/distributor of frozen foods, general merchandise and general line products, produce and provisions/meats; serving the food service market
Owner: Kim Adorni
kim_adorni@acmestores.com
CFO: Dave Hicks
VP Sales/Marketing: Rick Ryeland
Head of Marketing: Trout
Operations Manager: Rick Rylend
Estimated Sales: $500,000-$1 Million
Number Employees: 1-4
Private Brands Carried:
Food Club; Top Fresh; Top Frost
Number of Customer Locations: 28
Types of Products Distributed:
Food Service, Frozen Food, General Line, General Merchandise, Provisions/Meat, Produce, Rack Jobbers

56556 Frederick Produce Company
321 E 5th St
Frederick, MD 21701 301-663-3171
Fax: 301-662-8397 800-368-2556
Wholesaler/distributor of frozen food, produce and provisions/meats; serving the food service market
Manager: Marion Devereux
VP: J Dennis Easterday
Estimated Sales: $20-50 Million
Number Employees: 100-249
Number of Customer Locations: 750
Types of Products Distributed:
Food Service, Frozen Food, Provisions/Meat, Produce

56557 Frederick Wildman & Sons LTD
307 E 53rd St # 3
New York, NY 10022-4985 212-355-0700
Fax: 212-355-4719 800-733-9463
info@frederickwildman.com
www.frederickwildman.com
Manufacturer, importer and distributor of fine wines.
President: John Sellar
CEO: Davide Mascalzoni
d.mascalzoni@frederickwildman.com
VP, Finance: James DiCicco
VP/Director, Marketing: Martin Sinkoff
VP/National Sales Manager: Bill Seawrigth
Assistant VP/Director, Public Relations: Odila Galer-Noel
Year Founded: 1934
Estimated Sales: $20-50 Million

Number Employees: 100-249
Number of Brands: 26
Type of Packaging: Consumer, Food Service
Types of Products Distributed:
Frozen Food, Wine

56558 Fredon Handling Inc
3590 Scheele Dr
Jackson, MI 49202-1218 517-789-8157
Fax: 517-789-6894 800-952-0642
fredonmail@fredonhandling.com
Wholesaler/distributor of material handling equipment including conveyors, pallet racks and personnel lifts; also, shelving
President: Gregory Wait
gwait@fredonhandling.com
Estimated Sales: $2.5-5 Million
Number Employees: 5-9
Private Brands Carried:
Serco; Magline; Prest Rack
Types of Products Distributed:
Frozen Food, General Merchandise, Conveyors, pallet racks, shelving, etc.

56559 Freiria & Company
Mercado Central Plaza
Po Box 364165
Puerto Nuevo, PR 920 787-792-4460
Fax: 787-783-3945 888-792-0160
Import and export broker of confectionery products, frozen foods, general merchandise, corn meal, granulated garlic, dehydrated onions, paprika, adobo powder, garlic powder, apple cider and white distilled vinegar, groceries, spices etc.
President: Enrique Freiria
CEO: F Freiria
CFO: Juan Garcia
VP: H Freiria Jr
Quality Control: Elvis Diaz
Marketing: F Freiria
Sales: Angel Rosario
Public Relations: Jose Lopez
Estimated Sales: $19.5 Millionn
Number Employees: 52
Square Footage: 120000
Parent Co: Henframar Corporation
Type of Packaging: Food Service, Private Label
Private Brands Carried:
Bohio; La Choey
Types of Products Distributed:
General Merchandise, Provisions/Meat, Specialty Foods

56560 French Quarter Seafood
2933 Paris Road
Chalmette, LA 70043-3346 504-277-1679
Fax: 504-277-1679
Seafood
Owner: Philippe Despointes

56561 Fresco Y Mas
P.O. Box B
Jacksonville, FL 32203-0297 305-556-6588
866-946-6349
www.frescoymas.com
Wholesaler/distributor of general groceries, meats, and frozen foods.
SVP, Operations: Bill Nasshan
Parent Co: Southeastern Grocers
Types of Products Distributed:
Frozen Food, General Line, General Merchandise, Provisions/Meat, Produce

56562 Fresh Island Fish
312 Alamaha St
Unit G
Kahului, HI 96732-2430 808-871-1111
Fax: 808-871-6818 www.freshislandfish.com
Seafood
President: Mike Lee
Owner/Founder/C.E.O: Bruce Johnson
fif@maui.net
Estimated Sales: $10-20 Million
Number Employees: 50-99

56563 Fresh Pack Seafood
PO Box 1008
Waldoboro, ME 04572-1008 207-832-7720
Fax: 207-832-7795
Fresh seafood
President: Frank Minio
VP/General Manager: Roger Greene

56564 Fresh Point
711 N Orlando Ave
Suite 201
Maitland, FL 32751
800-367-5690
www.freshpoint.com
Wholesaler/distributor of produce; serving the food service market within a 50 mile radius of Nashville.
President & CEO: Robert Gordon
Chief Financial Officer: Mark Zucker
Vice President, Sales: Ted Beall
Vice President, Operations: Greg Musselwhite
Vice President, Procurement: Rich Dachman
Estimated Sales: $50-100 Million
Number Employees: 50-99
Square Footage: 50000
Types of Products Distributed:
Food Service, Frozen Food, Produce

56565 Fresh Point Dallas
4721 Simonton Rd
Dallas, TX 75244 972-385-5800
Fax: 972-239-2820 dallas.freshpoint.com
Wholesaler/distributor of frozen foods, general line products, general merchandise, dairy products, produce and meats; serving the food service market.
Square Footage: 480000
Types of Products Distributed:
Food Service, Frozen Food, General Line, General Merchandise, Provisions/Meat, Produce, Dairy products

56566 Fresh Seafood Distrib
9910 Milton Jones Rd
Daphne, AL 36526-6143 251-626-1106
Fax: 251-626-1109
Seafood
Co-Owner: Steve Miller
Estimated Sales: $3-5 Million
Number Employees: 5-9

56567 FreshPro Food Distributors
2 Dedrick Pl
West Caldwell, NJ 07007 973-575-9526
Fax: 973-575-1019 inquiries@freshprofood.com
www.freshprofood.com
Wholesaler/distributor of produce, floral, baked goods, private label items and deli and specialty food items.
President & Chief Operating Officer: Floyd Avillo
Year Founded: 1985
Estimated Sales: $100-150 Million
Number Employees: 100-249
Square Footage: 100000
Type of Packaging: Consumer, Food Service, Private Label, Bulk
Number of Customer Locations: 150
Types of Products Distributed:
Food Service, Provisions/Meat, Produce, Specialty Foods, Flowers & Plants

56568 Freskeeto Frozen Foods Inc
8019 Route 209
Ellenville, NY 12428-5615 845-647-5112
Fax: 845-647-5611 www.freskeeto.com
Wholesaler/distributor serving the food service market
President: Gary Dickman
fff4food@aol.com
Secretary/Treasurer: H Dickman
General Manager: G Dickman
Estimated Sales: $20-50 Million
Number Employees: 20-49
Private Brands Carried:
Freskeets
Number of Customer Locations: 2000
Types of Products Distributed:
Food Service, Frozen Food

56569 (HQ)Friedman Bag Company
865 Manhattan Beach Boulevard
Suite 204
Manhattan Beach, CA 90266-4955 213-628-2341
Fax: 213-687-9772
Manufacturer and exporter of burlap, cotton, polyethylene, open mesh bags; wholesaler/distributor of paper bags, cartons and packaging supplies
President: Al Lanfeld
VP/Operations Manager: David Friedman
Sales/Service: Diane Dal Porto
Estimated Sales: $20-50 Million
Number Employees: 250-499
Square Footage: 400000

Types of Products Distributed:
  Frozen Food, General Merchandise, paper bags, cartons, etc.

56570 Friedman Fixtures Co
2394 Riverside Dr
Danville, VA 24540-4298   434-792-7633
     Fax: 434-799-2551 friedjc@gamewood.net
Wholesaler/distributor of restaurant supplies; serving the food service market
Owner: J D Cook
friedjc@gamewood.net
CFO: Barbara Cook
Estimated Sales: $1-2.5 Million
Number Employees: 1-4
Square Footage: 208000

56571 Friendly Wholesale Co
655 Cushman St
Wooster, OH 44691-3677   330-264-8222
     Fax: 330-262-5408 www.fwholesale.net
Wholesaler/distributor of janiterial/cleaning products, food service disposables.
President/Owner: Joann Davidson
fwholesale@aol.com
Vice President: Mark Davidson
General Manager: Gary Schempp
Secretary/Treasurer: Cindy Maurer
Warehouse Manager: Dawn Baker
Estimated Sales: $2-5 Million
Number Employees: 20-49
Square Footage: 29000
Number of Customer Locations: 1200
Types of Products Distributed:
  Food Service, Frozen Food, General Line, General Merchandise, Candy, paper, fountains, etc.

56572 Fries Bros Eggs LLC
1455 Dalton Ave # 7
Cincinnati, OH 45214-2029   513-621-2366
                         Fax: 513-621-6979
Wholesaler/distributor of produce; serving the food service market
Owner: Don Goetz
friesbrothers@zoomtown.com
Sales Exec: Don Goetz
Estimated Sales: $5-10 Million
Number Employees: 10-19
Types of Products Distributed:
  Food Service, Produce

56573 Fritzie Fresh Products
25 West Cliff Road
Suite 115
Burnsville, MN 55337
         Fax: 952-882-4703 800-798-7481
              dfoster@trudeaudistributing.com
Wholesaler/distributor providing storage for candy, groceries and general merchandise; serving the food service market.
President: Jim Fritz
Owner: Doug Foster
Year Founded: 1940
Estimated Sales: $50-100 Million
Number Employees: 10-19
Parent Co: Trudeau Distributing
Private Brands Carried:
  Fritzie Fresh
Types of Products Distributed:
  Food Service, General Line, General Merchandise, Candy

56574 Front Line Safety
1643 Puddingstone Dr
La Verne, CA 91750-5810   909-593-9990
     Fax: 909-593-8995 800-538-4555
       mail@frontlinesales.com www.frontlinesales.com
Wholesaler/distributor of safety equipment including mats, first aid kits, spill response kits, containment equipment, etc
Owner: Al Smith
smitha@frontlinesales.com
Co-Owner: John Russo
Estimated Sales: $1-3 Million
Number Employees: 20-49
Square Footage: 20000
Parent Co: Front Line Saler
Private Brands Carried:
  Front Line Safety
Number of Customer Locations: 1000
Types of Products Distributed:
  Frozen Food, General Merchandise, Safety equipment

56575 (HQ)Front Range Snacks Inc
6547 S Racine Cir # 1800
Centennial, CO 80111-6463   303-744-8850
                         Fax: 303-389-6859
Processor and exporter of ready-to-eat popcorn
Owner: Tim Bradley
tim@openroadsnacks.com
Estimated Sales: Less Than $500,000
Number Employees: 1-4
Number of Brands: 1
Number of Products: 10
Square Footage: 80000
Type of Packaging: Consumer, Food Service, Private Label, Bulk
Types of Products Distributed:
  Frozen Food

56576 Frontier Bag Co Inc
2420 Grant St
Omaha, NE 68111-3825   402-342-0992
     Fax: 402-342-2107 800-278-2247
       customerservice@frontierbagco.com
              www.frontierbagco.com
Burlap and cotton bags; wholesaler/distributor of paper and plastic bags; serving the food service market
President: Judy Pearl-Lee
jplee@frontierbagco.com
Sales Manager: Judy Pearl-Lee
Estimated Sales: $1-2.5 Million
Number Employees: 10-19
Types of Products Distributed:
  Food Service, Frozen Food, General Merchandise, Paper & plastic bags

56577 Frontier Co-op
P.O. Box 299
3021 78th St.
Norway, IA 52318-9520   319-227-7996
     Fax: 800-717-4372 844-550-6200
       customercare@frontiercoop.com
              www.frontiercoop.com
Sustainably sourced and organic herbs, spices, seasonings, teas, sauces, mixes, dips, dressings, dried fruits and vegetables, indgredients, flavors and extracts.
CEO: Tony Bedard
VP Finance: Nicole Erickson
VP Technical Services: Ravin Donald
VP Marketing: Dave Karpick
SVP Business Development: Clint Landis
VP Human Resources: Megan Schulte
EVP Operations: Cole Daily
Year Founded: 1976
Estimated Sales: $100-499.9 Million
Number Employees: 100-249
Type of Packaging: Consumer, Private Label
Types of Products Distributed:
  General Line, Health Food

56578 Frontline Inc
3200a Danville Blvd # 101
Suite 101
Alamo, CA 94507-1971   925-362-8000
     Fax: 925-362-8078 800-562-7702
       frontline.jan@sbcglobal.net
              www.frontline-inc.com
Wholesaler/distributor of store and safety equipment including check stands, shopping carts, refrigeration cases and specialty lighting; also, gloves, mats and floor cones; exporter of floor cones, check stands and fluorescent lamps
President: Barry Nauroth
Comptroller: John Hudson
Estimated Sales: Less Than $500,000
Number Employees: 1-4
Square Footage: 4000
Types of Products Distributed:
  Frozen Food, General Merchandise, Mats, floor cones, safety gloves, etc.

56579 Frosty Products
41160 Joy Rd
Plymouth, MI 48170   734-454-0900
     Fax: 734-454-0910 800-442-0255
Wholesaler/distributor of yogurt smoothie mixes, frozen yogurt and custard, etc.; serving the food service market
Owner: John Becker
j.becker@frostyproducts.com
VP Sales/Marketing: Allen Bell
Estimated Sales: $5 Million
Number Employees: 1-4
Private Brands Carried:
  Frosty; Classic

Types of Products Distributed:
  Frozen Food, General Line, Frozen yogurt & custard, etc.

56580 Fru-Terra
4200 Boulevard Thimens
St. Laurent, QC H4R 2B9
Canada   514-337-8220
     Fax: 514-337-8228 inquiries@fru-terra.com
              www.fru-terra.com/
Wholesaler/distributor of fruit drinks, juices and nectars
President: Robert Cracower
Number Employees: 20-49
Square Footage: 280000
Private Brands Carried:
  Bennett's; Fruitkins; Fru-Terra
Types of Products Distributed:
  Frozen Food, General Line, Fruit drinks, juices & nectars

56581 Fru-V
Stouffville, ON
Canada
                         info@fruvsmoothie.com
                         www.fruvsmoothie.com
Frozen smoothie blends
Year Founded: 2016
Parent Co: Health Addict Inc
Types of Products Distributed:
  Frozen Food

56582 Fruge Aquafarms
7172 Church Point Hwy
Branch, LA 70516   337-334-8477
     Fax: 337-334-8477 888-254-8626
              www.cajuncrawfish.com
Wholesaler/distributor of crawfish and value-added seafood products
Owner: Michael Fruge
mike@cajuncrawfish.com
Co-Owner: Mark Fruge
Estimated Sales: Less Than $500,000
Number Employees: 5-9
Square Footage: 10000
Number of Customer Locations: 70
Types of Products Distributed:
  Frozen Food, Seafood, Value-added products

56583 Fruit Belt Canning Inc
54168 60th Ave
P.O. Box 81
Lawrence, MI 49064-9525   269-674-3939
     Fax: 269-674-8354 office@fruitbeltfoods.com
              www.fruitbeltfoods.com
Manufacturer, wholesaler/distributor of fruits and vegetables such as; asparagus, red tart cherries and strawberries
President: David Frank
davf@fruitbeltfoods.com
Vice President: Warren Frank
Sales Manager: Jim Armstrong
Estimated Sales: $5-9.9 Million
Number Employees: 100-249
Type of Packaging: Food Service, Private Label, Bulk
Types of Products Distributed:
  Food Service, Produce, Fruits & frozen vegetables

56584 Fruit Growers Supply Company
27770 N Entertainment Drive
Valencia, CA 91355
                         888-997-4855
     news@fruitgrowers.com www.fruitgrowers.com
Cooperative group for agricultural supplies. They manufacture pallets, irrigation systems, and boxes, and they sell other agricultural supplies such as outer wear and pesticides.
President: Bill Dodd
Estimated Sales: $3-5 Million
Number Employees: 1-4
Square Footage: 4800
Type of Packaging: Consumer, Private Label, Bulk
Types of Products Distributed:
  Agricultural Supplies

56585 Fruit Of The Vine Of DeValley
54 Conchester Rd
Glen Mills, PA 19342-1506   610-358-9250
     Fax: 610-361-7505 Nick@fruitofthevinedv.com
              www.fruitofthevinedv.com

Wholesaler/distributor of personalized candy, champagne, wine, soda and sparkling and spring water; also, uniforms
CEO/President: Jamie Burgess, Sr.
Assistant Manager: Franchette Dubose-Burgess
Number Employees: 5-9
Square Footage: 12000
Private Brands Carried:
   Martinelli's; Meier's; Bauser
Number of Customer Locations: 14
Types of Products Distributed:
   Food Service, Frozen Food, General Line, General Merchandise, Specialty Foods, Personalized candy, wine, soda, etc.

56586 Fruit Ranch Inc
6301 W Bluemound Rd
Milwaukee, WI 53213-4146   414-476-9600
       Fax: 414-258-9377 800-433-3289
              info@fruitranch.com
Fruit gift baskets. Wholesaler of baskets and supplies
Owner/President: Tanya Gearheart
Estimated Sales: Less Than $500,000
Number Employees: 5-9
Square Footage: 20000
Type of Packaging: Consumer, Private Label, Bulk
Number of Customer Locations: 1
Types of Products Distributed:
   Frozen Food, Baskets

56587 Fruit d'Or
306 Route 265
Villeroy, QC G0S 3K0
Canada   819-385-1126
    Fax: 819-715-0059 info@fruit-dor.ca
              www.fruit-dor.ca
Organic cranberries and blueberries in dried, pureed, concentrated, frozen, and powedered forms; neutraceuticals
Founder/President/CEO: Martin Le Moine
Year Founded: 1999
Estimated Sales: $20-50 Million
Number Employees: 50-99
Types of Products Distributed:
   Frozen Food, General Line, Health Food

56588 Fruitco Corp
B201 Hunts Point Term Mkt # 2
Bronx, NY 10474   718-893-4500
                    Fax: 718-893-4505
Wholesaler/distributor of domestic and imported fruit
Owner: Jeffery Kraiences
fruitco@aol.com
Estimated Sales: $10-20 Million
Number Employees: 20-49
Types of Products Distributed:
   Frozen Food, Produce

56589 Fuji Produce
13011 SE Jennifer St # 206
Clackamas, OR 97015-9042   503-656-3228
                    Fax: 503-236-4342
Wholesaler/distributor of produce
Owner: David Pienovi
dave@fujiiproduce.com
Estimated Sales: $2.5-5 Million
Number Employees: 5-9
Square Footage: 6400
Types of Products Distributed:
   Produce

56590 Full Harvest
560 Sutter St.
Ste. 200
San Francisco, CA 94102   415-523-0601
              info@fullharvest.com
              www.fullharvest.com
Wholesaler/distributor of surplus and/or imperfect produce. Offers a solution to reduce food waste on farms.
Founder & CEO: Christine Moseley
CFO: Russell Sprole
Head of Marketing: Keely Wachs
Head of Sales: Fernando Alvear
Head of Supply & Operations: Tyler Young
Director of Product: David Dewey
Year Founded: 2015
Number Employees: 40-60
Types of Products Distributed:
   Food Service, Produce

56591 Fullway International
1891 Peeler Road
Atlanta, GA 30338-5714   770-604-9299
                    Fax: 770-604-9296
Importer, exporter and wholesaler/distributor of soybean and fish oils; also, canned foods
President: Ralph Lai
Private Brands Carried:
   Fullway; Lucky Chef; Upstar; Big Tree
Types of Products Distributed:
   Frozen Food, General Line, Health Food, Soybean & fish oils

56592 Futurebiotics LLC
70 Commerce Dr
Hauppauge, NY 11788-3936   631-273-6300
    Fax: 631-273-1165 800-645-1721
              customerservice@futurebiotics.com
Manufacturer and distributor of natural health food supplements and vitamins
Owner: Saisul Kibria
skibria@aol.com
Manager: Ed Keenan
Director Operations: Wendy L Kauffman
Estimated Sales: $10-20 Million
Number Employees: 20-49
Type of Packaging: Consumer, Private Label, Bulk
Types of Products Distributed:
   Frozen Food

56593 (HQ)Futurity Products
114 W Atlantic Avenue
Clementon, NJ 08021-7194   609-267-3681
                    Fax: 856-783-7616
Wholesaler/distributor of custom flavors for beverages and soft drinks
President: Michael Fessler
Chairman: William Fessler
Number Employees: 1-4
Square Footage: 40000
Types of Products Distributed:
   Frozen Food, General Line, Custom flavors for beverages

56594 G & J Land & Marine Food Distr
506 Front St
Morgan City, LA 70380-3708   985-385-2251
    Fax: 985-385-3614 800-256-9187
          order@gjfood.com www.agbr.com
Full service food distributor dedicated to providing an extensive grocery and janitorial product line to the offshore oil and gas, commercial shipping and restaurant industry.
President/Owner: Mike Lind
mike@gjfood.com
Financial Controller: Christine DeHart
Vice President: Erik Lind
Operations: Adam Mayon
Purchasing: Jarrod Leonard
Estimated Sales: $10-20 Million
Number Employees: 100-249

56595 G & L Davis Meat Co
111 Gateway Park Dr
P.O. Box 5430
North Syracuse, NY 13212   315-471-9164
    Fax: 315-471-4474 866-471-9164
              www.gianellisausage.com
Wholesaler/distributor of sausage.
Owner & CEO: I. Stephen Davis
Chief Financial Officer: Jennifer Swindon
Controller & Quality Assurance: Lou Pilotti
Director, Sales: David Farina
Human Resources Manager: Tony Lauretti
Plant Manager: John Slafkosky
Year Founded: 1946
Estimated Sales: $20-50 Million
Number Employees: 20-49
Number of Customer Locations: 150
Types of Products Distributed:
   Provisions/Meat

56596 G & L Import Export Corp
4828 E 22nd St
Tucson, AZ 85711-4904   520-790-9016
Wholesaler/distributor, importer and exporter of Oriental and Hispanic food, frozen seafood, shrimp and produce; serving the food service market
Manager: Park Pang
Estimated Sales: Less Than $500,000
Number Employees: 1-4
Square Footage: 160000
Types of Products Distributed:
   Food Service, Frozen Food, Produce, Seafood, Specialty Foods, Oriental & Hispanic Foods

56597 G & W Equipment Inc
600 Lawton Rd
Charlotte, NC 28216-3437   704-394-6316
    Fax: 704-394-0912 800-768-6316
              www.gwequip.com
Wholesaler/distributor of material handling equipment including forklifts
Owner: Jackie Beck
jbeck@gwequip.net
Estimated Sales: $5-10 Million
Number Employees: 20-49
Private Brands Carried:
   Mitsubishi; Thomas; Sky Jack
Types of Products Distributed:
   Frozen Food, General Merchandise, Material handling equipment

56598 G & W Food Products
267 23rd St
Brooklyn, NY 11215-6595   718-788-7734
                    Fax: 718-788-2638
Wholesaler/distributor of provisions, frozen foods, general merchandise and general line products
President: Joe Wolf
Sales Manager: A Wolf
General Manager: P Scott
Estimated Sales: $10-20 Million
Number Employees: 10-19
Square Footage: 8000
Number of Customer Locations: 300
Types of Products Distributed:
   Frozen Food, General Line, General Merchandise, Provisions/Meat

56599 G A B Empacadora Inc
9330 San Mateo Dr
Laredo, TX 78045-8728   956-727-0100
                    Fax: 956-726-0079
Wholesaler/distributor, importer and exporter of fresh and frozen vegetables
President: Liz Martinez
liz@empgab.com
Sales Coordinator: Carmen Lopez
Traffic: Juan Ramirez
Manager: George Hughes
Estimated Sales: $10-20 Million
Number Employees: 10-19
Types of Products Distributed:
   Frozen Food, Produce, Vegetables

56600 G&G Distributing
P.O. Box 3001
Butte, MT 59702-3001   406-723-3626
                    Fax: 406-723-3608
Wholesaler/distributor of frozen pastries, cookies, crackers, dehydrated fruits and trail mix candies
Owner: Wayne Gabey
Partner: Michael Hocking
Estimated Sales: $.5-1 million
Number Employees: 1-4
Square Footage: 12800
Types of Products Distributed:
   Food Service, Frozen Food, Specialty Foods, Snack foods

56601 G&T Commodities
PO Box 1057
Rochester, MI 48308   248-656-1661
    Fax: 248-656-0513 800-524-7246
Wholesaler/distributor of close-out food products including canned and frozen foods
President: George Enders
Types of Products Distributed:
   Frozen Food, General Line, Close-out items including canned foods

56602 G&T Terminal Packaging Company
266 Hunts Point Term Mkt
Bronx, NY 10474-7402   718-893-1717
                    Fax: 718-991-9138
Wholesaler/distributor of potatoes and onions; serving the food service market
President: Peter Demytrk
Estimated Sales: $1-3 Million
Number Employees: 1-4
Types of Products Distributed:
   Food Service, Frozen Food, Produce

Wholesalers & Distributors / A-Z

56603 G.B. Sales & Service
39550 Schoolcraft Rd
Plymouth, MI 48170-2705 734-455-5150
  Fax: 734-455-7475 www.gbsalesservice.com
Wholesaler/distributor of material handling equipment including forklifts
President: Gregory Blackwood
Estimated Sales: $20-50 Million
Number Employees: 20-49
Private Brands Carried:
  Mitsubishi; Bakers
Types of Products Distributed:
  Frozen Food, General Merchandise

56604 G.D. Mathews & Sons
521 Medford St
Charlestown, MA 02129-1419 617-242-1770
  Fax: 617-242-1989
Wholesaler/distributor of gourmet and deli foods
President: David Matteosian
Contact: Joanne Savinen
jsavinen@comcast.net
Estimated Sales: $5-10 Million
Number Employees: 5-9
Types of Products Distributed:
  Frozen Food, Specialty Foods

56605 G.W. Market
672 N Spring St
Los Angeles, CA 90012-2835 213-624-0277
  Fax: 213-624-7925
Wholesaler/distributor of seafood and produce; serving the food service market
Owner: William Chan
Owner: Nelson Wang
Estimated Sales: $2.5-5 Million
Number Employees: 10-19
Types of Products Distributed:
  Food Service, Frozen Food, Produce, Seafood

56606 GAC Produce Company
1370 N Industrial Park Dr
Nogales, AZ 85621-4500 520-281-0052
  Fax: 520-281-2382
Wholesaler/distributor of fresh cucumbers, eggplant, peppers, squash, tomatoes and zucchini
Executive Director: Jose Vega
Manager: Bet Maldonado
Number Employees: 20-49
Types of Products Distributed:
  Frozen Food, Produce

56607 GAF Seelig Inc
5905 52nd Ave
Flushing, NY 11377-7480 718-899-5000
  Fax: 718-803-1198
Wholesaler and distributor of juice, milk, cheese, yogurt, sour cream, purees, raviolis and pastas, oils and vinegars, chocolate and many more food service items.
President: Rodney Seelig
rseelig@gafseelig.com
Executive Vice President: Gary Lavery Sr.
Director of Sales: John Arena
Estimated Sales: $5-10 Million
Number Employees: 100-249
Number of Customer Locations: 1000
Types of Products Distributed:
  General Line, Produce, Dairy products & juice

56608 GB Enterprises
411 W 90th Avenue
Anchorage, AK 99515-1724 907-349-5103
  Fax: 907-349-5355 888-359-5650
  www.2xtreme.com
Wholesaler/distributor of nutritional supplements and weight loss products
Owner/General Manager: Raymond Gulyas
Number Employees: 1-4
Types of Products Distributed:
  Frozen Food, Health Food, Weight loss products, etc.

56609 GCS Service
3902 Corporex Park Dr Ste 350
Tampa, FL 33619 813-626-6044
  Fax: 813-621-1174 800-282-3008
  www.gcsparts.com
Wholesaler/distributor of food service equipment; serving the food service market
Manager: Joe Bogen
Contact: Dery Wyne
dery.wyne@ecolab.com
Manager: Charles Rosete
Estimated Sales: $20-50 Million
Number Employees: 20-49
Parent Co: GCS Service
Private Brands Carried:
  Vulcan; Groen; Blodgett
Number of Customer Locations: 7000
Types of Products Distributed:
  Food Service, Frozen Food, General Merchandise, Foodservice equipment

56610 GET Enterprises LLC
1515 W Sam Houston Pkwy N
Houston, TX 77043-3112 713-467-9394
  Fax: 713-467-9396 800-727-4500
  info@get-melamine.com www.get-melamine.com
Importer and wholesaler/distributor of dinnerware, high chairs, tray stands, tumblers, platters and soup and coffee mugs; serving the food service market
President: Glen Hou
HR Executive: Joyce Liu
joyceliu@get-melamine.com
VP Sales/Marketing: Eve Hou
Estimated Sales: $5-10 Million
Number Employees: 50-99
Square Footage: 40000
Types of Products Distributed:
  Food Service

56611 GFS (Canada) Company
330 Nash Road N
Hamilton, ON L8H 7P5
Canada 905-561-8410
  Fax: 905-561-4248
Wholesaler/distributor of dairy products, fresh and frozen seafood, frozen dry produce, etc.; serving the food service market
President: J Greenwood
Buyer: H Goldhar
Number Employees: 50-99
Square Footage: 400000
Parent Co: GFS
Number of Customer Locations: 1500
Types of Products Distributed:
  Food Service, Frozen Food, General Line, Produce, Seafood, Dairy products

56612 GIANT Food Stores
1149 Harrisburg Pike
Carlisle, PA 17013
  president@giantfoodstores.com
  giantfoodstores.com
Wholesaler/distributor of general groceries, meats, produce, frozen foods, and seafood.
President: Nicholas Bertram
CFO: Julie Morales
Chief Merchandising Officer: John Ruane
Chief Strategy Officer: Manuel Haro
Chief Marketing Officer: Matt Simon
COO: John Ponnett
Year Founded: 1923
Number Employees: 22,000
Number of Customer Locations: 169
Types of Products Distributed:
  Frozen Food, General Line, General Merchandise, Provisions/Meat, Produce, Seafood

56613 GLAC Seat Inc
115 Bray Ave
Milford, CT 06460-5408 203-874-4513
  Fax: 203-874-4514 800-233-7381
  glacseat@aol.com www.glacseat.com
Wholesaler/distributor, importer and exporter of resin chairs, cantilevered umbrellas and rattan chairs and tables; serving the food service market
CEO: Annie Claude
glacseat@aol.com
CEO: Annie Claude
Operations Manager: Annie Claude
Estimated Sales: $1 Million
Number Employees: 1-4
Square Footage: 24000
Type of Packaging: Food Service
Private Brands Carried:
  Poitoux
Types of Products Distributed:
  Food Service, Frozen Food, General Merchandise, Chairs, tables & umbrellas

56614 GMT Dairy Products Inc
187 Florida St
Farmingdale, NY 11735-6308 631-752-7657
  Fax: 631-752-1724
Wholesaler/distributor of cheese and cheese products; serving the food service market
Owner: Gary Cornibert
gcornie1@aol.com
Secretary/Treasurer: Gary Connibett, Jr.
Estimated Sales: Less Than $500,000
Number Employees: 5-9
Types of Products Distributed:
  Food Service, Frozen Food, General Line, Cheese & cheese products

56615 GMZ Inc
5115 Excello Ct
West Chester, OH 45069-3091 513-860-9300
  Fax: 513-870-5210 800-543-1121
Wholesaler/distributor of plastic and steel containers; also, extender pigments, colors, additives, tall oil rosin and resin
President: Tom Wells
VP, Bus. Dev & Technology: Bill Buckley
Marketing Director: Steve Prodromo
4: John Luskinlusk
Manager: Kim Borke
kborke@gmzinc.com
Purchasing Agent: Kim Borke
Estimated Sales: $10-20 Million
Number Employees: 20-49
Square Footage: 100000
Private Brands Carried:
  Specialty Minerals; Cognis; Elements
Types of Products Distributed:
  Food Service, Frozen Food, General Line, General Merchandise, Health Food

56616 GNS Foods
2109 E Division St
Arlington, TX 76011-7817 817-795-4671
  Fax: 817-795-4673 sales@gnsfoods.com
  www.greatnuts.com
Raw and roasted nuts, packaged pecan candy and dried fruits including raisins, mango, pineapple, apple, banana chips, apricots and mixed; wholesaler/distributor of specialty foods; serving the food service market
President: Kim Peacock
Marketing: Carissa Mark
Contact: Lee Eggleston
sales@gnsfoods.com
Estimated Sales: $5-10 Million
Number Employees: 50-99
Square Footage: 25192
Type of Packaging: Consumer, Food Service, Private Label, Bulk

56617 GSC Enterprises Inc.
130 Hillcrest Dr.
Sulphur Springs, TX 75482 903-885-7621
  Fax: 903-439-1056
  customercare@grocerysupply.com
  www.grocerysupply.com
Frozen foods, groceries, general merchandise, produce and meats.
President/Chief Executive Officer: Michael Bain
mbain@gscenterprises.com
Chairman of the Board: Michael McKenzie
Vice President, Finance/CFO: Kerry Law
Vice President, Operations/COO: Ryan McKenzie
Year Founded: 1947
Estimated Sales: $1.7 Billion
Number Employees: 1,150
Square Footage: 2100000
Other Locations:
  GSC Enterprises
  El Paso, TXGSC Enterprises
Private Brands Carried:
  Parade
Number of Customer Locations: 15000
Types of Products Distributed:
  Food Service, Frozen Food, General Line, General Merchandise, Health Food, Produce, Specialty Foods

56618 GTM
7663 Broadway
Lemon Grove, CA 91945-1607 619-460-2990
  Fax: 619-460-9724
Wholesaler/distributor of general merchandise, general line products and specialty foods
President: Dana Cornell
Manager: Jacob Garza
jacob@m3h.com
Operations Manager: Dick Whalstrom
Purc. Manager: Jerry Crouch
Number Employees: 20-49
Square Footage: 180000
Parent Co: GTM Corporation

1013

Wholesalers & Distributors / A-Z

56619 GW Supply Company
PO Box 8265
Chattanooga, TN 37414-0265   423-517-0690
Fax: 423-622-3264
Wholesaler/distributor of electrical supplies and lighting fixtures
VP: John Williams
Estimated Sales: $5-10 Million
Number Employees: 10-19
Number of Customer Locations: 350
Types of Products Distributed:
Frozen Food, General Merchandise, Electrical supplies & lighting fixtures

Types of Products Distributed:
Frozen Food, General Line, General Merchandise, Specialty Foods, Salvage items

56620 GWB Foods Corporation
PO Box 228
Brooklyn, NY 11204-0228   718-686-6611
Fax: 718-686-6161   877-977-7610
info@gwbfoods.com   www.gwbfoods.com
Processor, exporter, importer and wholesaler/distributor of specialty and frozen foods including cookies, candies, crackers, rice cakes, vegetables in jars, bottled water, pickles and pimiento peppers
President: Joshua Weinstein
Export Manager: S Williams
Sales Manager: Jack Yumens
Estimated Sales: $2.5-5 Million
Number Employees: 10-19
Square Footage: 80000
Parent Co: President Baking Company
Type of Packaging: Consumer, Food Service, Private Label, Bulk
Types of Products Distributed:
Food Service, Frozen Food, General Line, Health Food, Specialty Foods

56621 (HQ)Gachot & Gachot
440 W 14th St
New York, NY 10014   212-929-5988
Fax: 212-929-5772 cgachot@aol.com
Wholesaler/distributor of meats and poultry including beef, veal, lamb, pork, game, etc
President: Chris Gachot
Chairman/CEO: Charles Gachot
General Manager: Harold Petrak
Estimated Sales: $20-50 Million
Number Employees: 20-49
Square Footage: 15000
Types of Products Distributed:
Frozen Food, General Line, Provisions/Meat, Poultry, game, etc.

56622 Gaggia Espresso MachineCompany
1335 Davenport Road
Toronto, ON M6H 2H4
Canada   416-537-3439
Fax: 416-588-9012
Importer and wholesaler/distributor of Italian espresso machines; serving the food service market
President: Karen Zuccarini
Sales Manager: Jackie Zuccarini
Number Employees: 5-9
Types of Products Distributed:
Frozen Food, General Merchandise, Italian espresso machines

56623 Gaiser's European Style
2019 Morris Ave
Union, NJ 07083-6013   908-686-3421
Fax: 908-686-7131
Processor, exporter and wholesaler/distributor of sausage, liverwurst and smoked ham
Owner: Efem Rablov
gaisers@verizon.net
Estimated Sales: $500,000-$1 Million
Number Employees: 10-19
Types of Products Distributed:
Frozen Food, Provisions/Meat, Sausage, liverwurst & smoked ham

56624 Galaxy Tea Company
13 NW Barry Road
202
Kansas City, MO 64155-2728   816-436-6651
Fax: 816-436-6651
Wholesaler/distributor of general merchandise, iced teas and brewing equipment
Owner: John Tyhurst

Number Employees: 1-4
Square Footage: 4000
Private Brands Carried:
Shangri-La
Types of Products Distributed:
Iced teas & brewing equipment

56625 Galerie Au Chocolat
8985 Henri Bourassa W
Montreal, QC H4S 1P7
Canada   514-331-8460
Fax: 514-331-8462 888-806-9840
support@galerieauchocolat.ca galerieauchocolat.ca
Wholesaler/distributor of packaged candy and private label items.
President: Noah Pinsky
Sales Manager: Jeremy Arthurs
Year Founded: 1985
Estimated Sales: $100-500 Million
Number Employees: 11-50
Types of Products Distributed:
Frozen Food, General Line, Confectionery

56626 Galilee Splendor
333 Sylvan Avenue
Englewd Clfs, NJ 07632-2724   201-871-4433
Fax: 201-871-8726 800-200-6736
galileespl@aol.com
Wholesaler/distributor and importer of crisp breads, bottled water and Israeli foods
President: Peter Shamir
Estimated Sales: $5-10 Million
Number Employees: 5-9
Parent Co: Sky is the Limited
Private Brands Carried:
Bible Bread; River Jordan Spring Water
Types of Products Distributed:
Frozen Food, General Line, Specialty Foods, Gourmet bread, bottled water, etc.

56627 Galland's Institutional Food
520 Kentucky St
PO Box 3007
Bakersfield, CA 93305-4344   661-631-5505
Fax: 661-631-5513
Distributors of a full service food line, exceptions produce and meat.
President: Joan Galland
Owner: Leonard Galland
CFO: Leonard Galland
Estimated Sales: $3-5 Million
Number Employees: 10-19

56628 Galleron Signature Wines
PO Box 2
Rutherford, CA 94573   707-265-6552
Fax: 707-265-6559
Ultra premium Napa Valley vineyard designated wines
President: Gary Galleron
Marketing Director: Paula Galleron
Public Relations: Joanne Van Kamper
Estimated Sales: $1-3 Million
Number Employees: 1-4

56629 Galli Produce Inc
1650 Old Bayshore Hwy
San Jose, CA 95112   408-436-6100
Fax: 408-436-6119 www.galliproduce.com
Wholesaler/distributor of fresh fruits, vegetables, specialty produce and imported items; serving the food service market.
President: Gerald Pieracci
galliproduce@yahoo.com
VP & Food Safety Director: Jeff Pieracci
Year Founded: 1957
Estimated Sales: $20-50 Million
Number Employees: 20-49
Square Footage: 11000
Number of Customer Locations: 600
Types of Products Distributed:
Food Service, Produce, Specialty Foods

56630 Galloway's Specialty Foods
7860 Alderbridge Way
Richmond, BC V6X 1W4
Canada   604-270-6363
Fax: 604-270-0452 www.gallowaysfoods.com
Wholesaler/distributor of specialty foods
President: Annie Muljiani
Number Employees: 20-49
Private Brands Carried:
Hi Taste

Types of Products Distributed:
Frozen Food, Specialty Foods

56631 Gamez Brothers Produce Co
1802 Marcella Ave
Laredo, TX 78040-3999   956-722-5136
Fax: 956-722-7048
Wholesaler/distributor of produce, poultry and meats
Owner: Juan Gamez
juan@gamezproduce.com
Manager: Juan Gamez
Estimated Sales: $1-2.5 Million
Number Employees: 10-19
Square Footage: 52000
Types of Products Distributed:
Provisions/Meat, Produce, Poultry

56632 Gandy's Dairies
P.O.Box 992
San Angelo, TX 76902-0992   325-655-6965
Fax: 325-655-5266
Wholesaler/distributor of dairy products
Manager: Randy Kucharski
Estimated Sales: $5-10 Million
Number Employees: 20-49
Private Brands Carried:
Field Crest; Country Charm; Gandy
Types of Products Distributed:
Frozen Food, General Line, Dairy products

56633 Garavaglia Meat Company
2857 Lafayette Avenue
Saint Louis, MO 63104-2015   314-776-7993
Wholesaler/distributor of canned goods including groceries, general merchandise, meats, seafood, specialty items and frozen foods; serving the food service market
Owner: Tony Garavaglia
Estimated Sales: Less than $500,000
Number Employees: 1-4
Types of Products Distributed:
Food Service, General Line, General Merchandise, Provisions/Meat, Seafood, Specialty Foods

56634 Garber Bros Inc
P.O. Box 815
Morgan City, LA 70381   985-384-4511
info@garberbrosinc.com
www.garberbrosinc.com
Wholesaler/distributor of frozen food, dairy items, baked goods, candy, groceries, produce and meats; rack jobber services available; serving convenience stores.
President: Harold Garber
Human Resources Manager: Frank Gaylor
Purchasing Agent: Jody Garber
Estimated Sales: $100-500 Million
Number Employees: 100-249
Types of Products Distributed:
Frozen Food, General Line, General Merchandise, Provisions/Meat, Produce, Rack Jobbers, Candy, groceries, etc.

56635 Garden & Valley Isle Seafood
225 N Nimitz Hwy # 3
Honolulu, HI 96817-5349   808-524-4847
Fax: 808-528-5590 800-689-2733
info@gvisfd.com www.gvisfd.com
Ahi, sashimi, swordfish and snapper; importer and exporter of fresh seafood; wholesaler/distributor of smoked fish and general merchandise
President: Robert Fram
info@gvisfd.com
CFO: Richard Jenks
Vice President: David Marabella
Operations: Cliff Yamauchi
Estimated Sales: $13,500,000
Number Employees: 20-49
Square Footage: 18000
Type of Packaging: Bulk
Private Brands Carried:
Ocean Trader; Hawaiian Shark Bites
Types of Products Distributed:
Frozen Food, General Merchandise, Seafood, Smoked fish

56636 Garden City Supply
PO Box 26618
San Jose, CA 95159-6618   408-292-0509
Fax: 408-292-4475   800-722-2400
www.gcssupply.com

Wholesaler/distributor of equipment and supplies including refrigerators, serving and buffet equipment, furniture, fixtures and utensils; serving the food service market; storage and handling services available
President: Roberta Sardell
VP: John Sardell
Office Manager: Jackie Alford
Estimated Sales: $1-2.5 Million
Number Employees: 10-19
Square Footage: 52000
Types of Products Distributed:
  Food Service, Frozen Food, General Merchandise, Foodservice equipment & supplies, etc.

56637 (HQ)Garden Spot Distributors
191 Commerce Dr
New Holland, PA 17557-9114   717-354-4936
        Fax: 717-354-4934 800-829-5100
Natural, organic and specialty foods. Whole grain flours, beans, raw nuts and dried fruits; frozen foods; cereals and granola; breads and baked goods; snack foods; free-range and natural meats and seafood; special-dietary foods andprepared meals including more than 400 gluten free products
President: John Clough
jclough@gardenspotfoods.com
Marketing Coordinator: Amanda Byrd
Sales Director: Jean O'Donnell
General Manager/Operations Director: Brad Crull
Purchasing Manager: Mark Drury
Estimated Sales: $8 Million
Number Employees: 20-49
Number of Brands: 100+
Square Footage: 40000
Type of Packaging: Consumer, Private Label, Bulk
Other Locations:
  Garden Spot Distributors
  Sulphur Springs, ARGarden Spot Distributors
Types of Products Distributed:
  Frozen Food, General Line, Health Food, Specialty Foods, Organic foods

56638 Garden Spot Produce Co
2203 W Main St
Farmington, NM 87401-3222   505-325-8888
        Fax: 505-325-7055
Wholesaler/distributor of frozen food, produce and meats; serving the food service market
Owner: Jamie Erickson
Estimated Sales: $5-10 Million
Number Employees: 1-4
Types of Products Distributed:
  Food Service, Frozen Food, Provisions/Meat, Produce

56639 Gardner & Benoit
11401 Granite St Ste A
Charlotte, NC 28273   704-504-1151
        Fax: 704-504-5529 800-467-6676
Wholesaler/distributor of food service equipment and supplies; serving the food service market; design and installation services available
President: Karlo Waataja
Secretary/Treasurer: Karlo Waataja
Vice President: Jack Mock, Sr.
Estimated Sales: $5-10 Million
Number Employees: 10-19
Square Footage: 104000
Types of Products Distributed:
  Food Service, General Merchandise, Foodservice equipment & supplies

56640 Garland C Norris Co
1101 Perry Rd
Apex, NC 27502   919-387-1059
        www.gcnorris.com
Wholesaler/distributor of paper and plastic items.
Chief Operating Officer: James King
Year Founded: 1904
Estimated Sales: $20-50 Million
Number Employees: 50-99
Square Footage: 125000
Types of Products Distributed:
  General Merchandise, Paper & plastic items

56641 Garuda International
PO Box 159
Exeter, CA 93221-0159   559-594-4380
        Fax: 559-594-4689 www.garudaint.com
Development and marketing of ingredients derived from natural sources
President/CEO: J Roger Matkin
Marketing/Sales: Bassam Faress
Contact: Liang Chen
lchen@garudaint.com
Estimated Sales: $500,000-$1 Million
Number Employees: 5-9
Square Footage: 30000
Type of Packaging: Private Label, Bulk
Private Brands Carried:
  Rice*Trin
Types of Products Distributed:
  Frozen Food, General Line, Health Food, Mushroom extracts, herbs, grains, etc.

56642 Garvey Nut & Candy
8825 Mercury Ln
Pico Rivera, CA 90660   562-942-3400
        Fax: 562-725-0879 www.garveycandy.com
Wholesaler/distributor of candy and natural foods
Owner: Steve Corri
Sales Representative: Srephen Clendenin
Sales Representative: Steven Corri
Contact: Scott Corri
scottcorri@yahoo.com
Estimated Sales: $20-50 Million
Number Employees: 20-49
Square Footage: 30000
Types of Products Distributed:
  Frozen Food, General Line, Health Food, Candy & natural foods

56643 Gasketman Inc
PO Box 78136
Corona, CA 92877-0137   951-870-7116
        Fax: 951-341-5117
Wholesaler/distributor and exporter of nonasbestos belting, cups, gaskets, hose, matting, O-rings, packing rod, packing sheet, plastics, protective clothing and tape
Sales: Mike Lucas
Estimated Sales: $2.5-5 Million
Number Employees: 1-4
Types of Products Distributed:
  Frozen Food, General Merchandise, Protective clothing & tape

56644 Gateway Food Products Co
1728 N Main St
Dupo, IL 62239-1045   618-286-4844
        Fax: 618-286-3444 877-220-1963
        traines@gatewayfoodproducts.com
        www.gatewayfoodproducts.com
Syrups, vegetable oils and shortenings; exporter of corn syrup; wholesaler/distributor of general line items; also shortening flakes, popcorn oils and butter toppings
President: John Crosley
jcrosley@gatewayfoodproducts.com
Vice President: Carroll Crosley
Quality Control: Jeremy Gray
Marketing Director: Teresa Raines
Sales Director: Teresa Raines
Operations Manager: Jeremy Gray
Production Manager: Jim Raines
Plant Manager: Jim Raines
Purchasing Manager: John Crosley
Estimated Sales: $10-20 Million
Number Employees: 10-19
Number of Products: 9
Square Footage: 75000
Type of Packaging: Food Service, Private Label, Bulk
Types of Products Distributed:
  General Line

56645 Gatto & Sons
PO Box 14367
Portland, OR 97293   503-235-5589
        Fax: 503-232-4144
Wholesaler/distributor of produce, frozen food and equipment and fixtures; serving the food service market
Owner/President: August Gatto
Secretary/Treasurer: Marian Moliser
VP: Joseph Gatto
Estimated Sales: $5-10 Million
Number Employees: 20-49
Square Footage: 56000
Types of Products Distributed:
  Food Service, General Merchandise, Produce

56646 Gatto Wholesale Produce
PO Box 22
Ebensburg, PA 15931-0022   814-472-8470
Wholesaler/distributor of produce; serving the food service market
President: August Gatto
Number Employees: 1-4
Types of Products Distributed:
  Food Service, Frozen Food, Produce

56647 Gaylord's Meat Co
1100 E Ash Ave # C
Fullerton, CA 92831-5004   714-526-2278
        Fax: 714-526-3439
Wholesaler/distributor of hamburger, fresh, frozen, cured beef, pork, lamb and poultry, frozen fish, fries, oils, etc.; serving the food service market
President: Vance Dixon
Estimated Sales: $5-10 Million
Number Employees: 20-49
Square Footage: 26000
Types of Products Distributed:
  Food Service, Frozen Food, General Line, Provisions/Meat, Seafood, Fries, oils, poultry, etc.

56648 GePolymershapes Cadillac
25900 Telegraph Road
Southfield, MI 48033-5222   248-603-8600
        Fax: 248-603-8693 800-488-1200
Wholesaler/distributor and exporter of plastic sheets, rods, tubes and films; also, replacement parts for food processing equipment
President: Kent Darragh
VP Marketing: Tom Taylor
Parent Co: M.A. Hanna
Private Brands Carried:
  Cadco; Trade-Mate; Foam-Cor; GatorFoam; Lexan; Sintra; MDO; Plexiglas
Types of Products Distributed:
  Frozen Food, General Merchandise

56649 Gelson's
16400 Ventura Blvd.
Ste. 240
Encino, CA 91436-2123   818-906-5700
        www.gelsons.com
Wholesaler/distributor of produce, meats, deli, and general groceries.
President & CEO: Rob McDougall
CFO: John Hammack
SVP, Warehouse & Distribution: Tom Frattali
Executive Director, Marketing: Yvonne Manganaro
Chief Merchandising Officer: John Bagan
VP, Team Development & Public Affairs: Hee-Sook Nelson
SVP, Operations: Donna Tyndall
Executive Director, Operations: Tim Mahoney *Year Founded:* 1951
Number of Customer Locations: 27
Types of Products Distributed:
  Frozen Food, General Line, General Merchandise, Provisions/Meat, Produce, Baked goods

56650 Gem Berry Products
733 Kaniksu Shores Rd
Sandpoint, ID 83864   208-790-2804
        Fax: 866-357-3505 800-231-1699
        gemberryproducts@gmail.com
        www.gemberry.com
Jams, jellies, syrups, gift packs.
President and Owner: Harry Menser
Sales and Marketing: Sandy Dell
Estimated Sales: $500,000-$1,000,000
Type of Packaging: Consumer, Food Service, Bulk
Types of Products Distributed:
  General Line, Confectionary, Huckleberry products

56651 Gemsy's Money Handling Systems
1108 South Service Road West
Oakville, ON L6L 5T7
Canada   905-823-4316
        Fax: 905-823-8563 800-465-0465
        info@gemsysinc.on.ca www.gemsysinc.on.ca
Wholesaler/distributor of money handling equipment including cash and coin couters and counterfeit detection systems
President: Jack Lord
Number Employees: 5-9
Types of Products Distributed:
  Frozen Food, General Merchandise, Money handling equipment

Wholesalers & Distributors / A-Z

56652 Gemtek Products LLC
3808 N 28th Ave
Phoenix, AZ 85017-4733   602-265-8586
     Fax: 602-265-7241 800-331-7022
info@gemtek.com www.gemtek.com
Manufacturer and supplier of safe solvents, cleaners, and lubrications
President: Sarah Kristoff
sarah.hunt@cdctn.org
Number Employees: 5-9
Other Locations:
   Manufacturing Plant
   Hayward, CA
   Manufacturing Plant
   Mecedonia, OHManufacturing PlantMecedonia

56653 (HQ)Gen Pac
1910 Hollywood Dr
Jackson, TN 38305-4381   731-424-1463
     Fax: 731-424-1490 800-489-1463
sales@genpac.net www.genpac.net
Wholesaler/distributor of general merchandise including packaging supplies
Manager: Larry Bell
larry@genpac.net
Customer Relations: Kim Shappley
Number Employees: 10-19
Other Locations:
   Gen Pac/General Packaging
   Tupolo, MSGen Pac/General Packaging
Number of Customer Locations: 500
Types of Products Distributed:
   Frozen Food, General Merchandise, Packaging supplies

56654 General Candy Co
4800 Oleatha Ave
St Louis, MO 63116-1722   314-353-1133
     Fax: 314-353-1134 gencdy@sbcglobal.net
www.generalcandycompany.com
Wholesaler/distributor of candy, snacks and paper supplies
Owner: Bill Hellwege
bhellwege@generalcandycompany.com
Buyer: Bill Hellwege
Estimated Sales: $5-10 Million
Number Employees: 10-19
Types of Products Distributed:
   Frozen Food, General Line, General Merchandise, Candy, snacks & paper supplies

56655 General Carriage & Supply Co
264 Roosevelt Trl
Windham, ME 04062-4353   207-892-2537
     Fax: 207-892-8926 800-462-6676
Wholesaler/distributor of food service equipment and supplies including bakery ovens, grinders, slicers, scales, proofers, shelving, sinks, tables and smallwares; serving the New England area
President: Terry Tait
gencarr@aol.com
VP: Catherine Tait
Estimated Sales: $2.5-5 Million
Number Employees: 5-9
Square Footage: 40000
Types of Products Distributed:
   Food Service, Frozen Food, General Merchandise, Machinery & smallwares

56656 General Cash & Carry
P.O.Box 2365
Greenville, NC 27836   252-752-3108
     Fax: 252-752-9452
Wholesaler/distributor of confections and produce; also general merchandise products including paper products and janitorial supplies; serving the food service market
Manager: Bobby Kittrell
Manager/Buyer: E Sullivan
Estimated Sales: $5-10 Million
Number Employees: 5-9
Square Footage: 28000
Number of Customer Locations: 300
Types of Products Distributed:
   Food Service, Frozen Food, General Line, General Merchandise, Produce

56657 General Sales
229 N Commerce Dr
Grayson, KY 41143-6110   606-928-3418
     Fax: 606-928-8382 800-467-2737
gsc@wwd.net www.gsales.com
Wholesaler/distributor of janitorial supplies and paper products including napkins, wipes, plates, bags, etc.; serving the food service market
Owner: Lee Kerley
VP: Don Magann
Director Operations: Dennis Rosencrance
IT: Barbara Blair
gscbarb@windstream.net
Estimated Sales: $20-50 Million
Number Employees: 20-49
Types of Products Distributed:
   Food Service, Frozen Food, General Merchandise, Janitorial supplies & paper products

56658 General Sales Associates
999 Old Country Rd
Westbury, NY 11590-5620   516-333-6900
     Fax: 516-333-1119 nrosen2111@aol.com
Wholesaler/distributor of general merchandise including advertising specialties for sales promotions and premiums
President: Norman Rosenberg
Estimated Sales: $1-2.5 Million
Number Employees: 1-4
Number of Customer Locations: 200
Types of Products Distributed:
   Frozen Food, General Merchandise, Advertising specialties

56659 General Sales Co
406 Huger St
Columbia, SC 29201-5224   803-776-0380
     Fax: 803-776-3417
Wholesaler/distributor of stainless steel general merchandise including furnishings, chairs, etc
President: Larry Polk
VP Marketing: Laura Scheeler
Sales Manager: Laura Carlson
Estimated Sales: $10-20 Million
Number Employees: 10-19
Square Footage: 32000
Types of Products Distributed:
   Frozen Food, General Merchandise, Stainless steel furnishings

56660 General Trading Co
455 16th St
Carlstadt, NJ 07072-1922   201-935-2219
     Fax: 201-438-6353
Wholesaler/distributor of meats, frozen food, equipment and fixtures, dry groceries and dairy products
President: George Abed
g_abad@yahoo.com
Sales/Marketing Executive: Phil Roland
Purchasing Agent: Mary Leonard
Estimated Sales: $5-10 Million
Number Employees: 250-499
Parent Co: Jiffy Trucking
Number of Customer Locations: 4000
Types of Products Distributed:
   Frozen Food, General Line, General Merchandise, Provisions/Meat, Dry groceries & dairy products

56661 Generichem Corporation
5 Taft Rd
Totowa, NJ 07512   973-256-9266
     Fax: 973-256-0069 info@generichem.com
www.generichem.com
Generichem is a supplier of active and inactive ingredients to the pharmaceutical and nutritional industries.
President: E. Oishi
Estimated Sales: $5-10 Million
Number Employees: 10-19
Square Footage: 30000
Types of Products Distributed:
   Frozen Food, Health Food, Calcium, iron, magnesium, zinc, etc.

56662 Genoa Wholesale Foods
261 S River St
Plains, PA 18705-1123   570-823-6142
     Fax: 570-823-6143 www.genoafoods.com
Wholesaler/distributor of pizza supplies including crushed tomatoes and sauce; serving the food service market
Owner: Joe Nardone
Chief Executive Officer: Jay Nardone Jr.
Sales: Jay Nardone, Jr.
Chief Operating Officer: Jay Nardone Sr.
Estimated Sales: $5-10 Million
Number Employees: 5-9
Square Footage: 29600
Private Brands Carried:
   Genoa Pizza Sauce; Helena Crushed Tomatoes; Cynthia Tomatoes
Number of Customer Locations: 200
Types of Products Distributed:
   Food Service, Frozen Food, General Line, Pizza supplies: tomatoes & sauce

56663 Geoghegan Brothers Company
8835 S Greenwood Ave
Chicago, IL 60619   773-731-6767
     Fax: 773-731-6763
Wholesaler/distributor serving the food service market
President: Francis Geoghegan
Estimated Sales: $20-50 Million
Number Employees: 20-49
Types of Products Distributed:
   Food Service, Frozen Food

56664 George A Heimos ProduceCo
34 Produce Row
St Louis, MO 63102-1419   314-231-3787
     Fax: 314-621-5156
Wholesaler/distributor of fresh fruits and vegetables
Owner/President: James Heimos
Estimated Sales: $10-20 Million
Number Employees: 20-49
Types of Products Distributed:
   Frozen Food, Produce

56665 George D. Spence & Sons
PO Box 147
Quinby, VA 23423-0147   757-442-9571
Wholesaler/distributor of seafood
Owner: George Spence Jr
Estimated Sales: $500,000-$1 Million
Number Employees: 1-4
Types of Products Distributed:
   Frozen Food, Seafood

56666 George Degen & Co
144 Woodbury Rd # 34
Woodbury, NY 11797-1418   516-692-6862
     Fax: 516-692-3140 sales@tungoil.com
www.tungoil.com
Wholesaler/distributor and importer of oils including dehydrated castor, rape seed, tung and oiticica
President: John Blake-Hanson
blakehanson@tungoil.com
Estimated Sales: $2.5-5 Million
Number Employees: 1-4
Type of Packaging: Bulk
Types of Products Distributed:
   Frozen Food, Specialty Foods, Vegetable oils

56667 George E. Kent Company
153 Morse St
Norwood, MA 02062   781-769-1100
     Fax: 781-769-6205
Wholesaler/distributor of material handling equipment including forklifts
President: Jonathan Dolan
Contact: Barbara Dolan
bdolan@kent.edu
Estimated Sales: $5-10 Million
Number Employees: 10-19
Private Brands Carried:
   Mitsubishi; Linde-Baker; Dexco; Blue-Giant; Cascade
Types of Products Distributed:
   General Merchandise, Material handling equipment

56668 George Greer Company
90 Kenwood St
Providence, RI 02907   401-942-2450
     Fax: 401-944-2660
Wholesaler/distributor of snack foods; rack jobber services available
President: Albert Greer
General Manager: A Greer
Estimated Sales: $20-50 Million
Number Employees: 20-49
Private Brands Carried:
   Wise; Cape Cod; Louise's Fat Free
Number of Customer Locations: 2000
Types of Products Distributed:
   Frozen Food, General Line, Rack Jobbers, Snack foods

Wholesalers & Distributors / A-Z

56669 George J Howe Co
629 W Main St
Grove City, PA 16127-1199
724-458-9410
Fax: 724-458-1134 800-367-4693
www.howewholesale.com
Wholesaler/distributor of candy, coffee and nuts; rack jobber services available
President: Hal Mcclure
hmcclure@malvernconsultinggroup.com
VP: Dick Beech
Director Sales: Rick Knepp
Estimated Sales: $10-20 Million
Number Employees: 100-249
Square Footage: 100000
Type of Packaging: Private Label
Number of Customer Locations: 3300
Types of Products Distributed:
  Frozen Food, General Line, Rack Jobbers, Coffee, candy & nuts

56670 George O Pasquel Company
1416 SW Adams St
Peoria, IL 61602
309-673-7467
Fax: 309-673-4249 gop@pasquel.com
www.pasquel.com
Wholesaler/distributor of groceries, canned/dried goods, smallwares, private label items, paper and janitorial products, etc.; serving the food service market.
Owner/Chairman: Pete Pasquel
Director, Purchasing: Brian Frank
Year Founded: 1946
Estimated Sales: $5 Million
Number Employees: 18
Number of Products: 2000
Square Footage: 215000
Private Brands Carried:
  Nugget; Campbell's
Number of Customer Locations: 1000
Types of Products Distributed:
  Food Service, Frozen Food, General Line, General Merchandise, Groceries, janitorial supplies, etc.

56671 George Uhe Company, Inc.
230 W. Parkway
Suite 5
Pompton Plains, NJ 07444
201-843-4000
Fax: 973-835-2321 global@uhe.com
www.uhe.com
General merchandise and industrial ingredients including food chemicals, dried fruits and vegetables, juices and essential oils; serving food processors.
Year Founded: 1921
Estimated Sales: $2.4 Million
Number Employees: 11
Square Footage: 5000
Types of Products Distributed:
  General Line, General Merchandise, Industrial ingredients

56672 Georgia Seafood Wholesale
5634 New Peachtree Rd
Chamblee, GA 30341
770-936-0483
Fax: 770-936-9332
Scallops, frozen seafood, shrimp
President: Liz Wang
Owner: Jack Wong
Estimated Sales: $3-5 Million
Number Employees: 5-9

56673 Gerlau Sales
5015 Cliff Drive
Delta, BC V4M 2C2
Canada
604-943-0961
Fax: 604-943-4799
Wholesaler/distributor, importer and exporter of ceiling/wall panels; food processing equipment & services, smokehouse installation, refurbishing, HACCP implemented, control & recording data acquisition, smokehouse & parts.
President: Sigrid Lauk
VP: Gerhard Lauk
Marketing: Irene Langlais
Private Brands Carried:
  Winkelplast; Maurer
Types of Products Distributed:
  Frozen Food, General Merchandise, Ceiling panels, smokehouses & cutters

56674 Gexpro
1920 W Green Dr
High Point, NC 27260-1666
336-884-4016
Fax: 336-884-1854 800-768-7619
www.gexpro.com
Wholesaler/distributor of stainless steel fasteners, cutting tools, food grade aerosol chemicals and special screw machine parts
President: Robbie Gilchrist
Director Sales: Ashley Graeber
Customer Service: Jim Gane
Estimated Sales: $20-50 Million
Number Employees: 10-19
Square Footage: 40000
Parent Co: Questron Technolgy
Types of Products Distributed:
  Frozen Food, General Merchandise, Cutting tools, fasteners, etc.

56675 Giambrocco Food Service
3755 Wazee St.
P.O. Box 16507
Denver, CO 80216
303-295-0802
info@giambrocco.com
www.giambrocco.com
Wholesaler/distributor of produce and canned, frozen and paper products.
Year Founded: 1933
Estimated Sales: $50-100 Million
Number Employees: 50-99
Square Footage: 101500
Types of Products Distributed:
  Frozen Food, General Line, General Merchandise, Produce, Canned & paper products

56676 Giancola Brothers, Inc.
1914 14th St
Santa Monica, CA 90404
310-450-1464
Fax: 310-450-6360
Wholesaler/distributor serving the food service market
President: M Giancola
giancolabrosinc@gmail.com
Estimated Sales: $5-10 Million
Number Employees: 5-9
Type of Packaging: Private Label, Bulk
Private Brands Carried:
  Angela Maria; Carmela
Number of Customer Locations: 600
Types of Products Distributed:
  Food Service, Frozen Food

56677 Giant Eagle American Seaway Foods
101 Kappa Dr.
Pittsburgh, PA 15238
800-553-2324
www.gianteagle.com
Provisions/meats, produce, dairy products, seafood, produce, frozen foods, general merchandise, private label items and health/beauty aids; serving the food service market.
Chairman: David Shapira
President/CEO: Laura Karet
Year Founded: 1931
Estimated Sales: $8.9 Billion
Number Employees: 37,000
Number of Brands: 4
Private Brands Carried:
  Seaway; ShureFine; Savers Choice
Types of Products Distributed:
  Food Service, Frozen Food, General Line, General Merchandise, Health Food, Provisions/Meat, Produce, Seafood, Dairy products & health/beauty aids

56678 Gibson Wholesale Co Inc
3108 W Central Ave
Wichita, KS 67203-4912
316-945-7700
Fax: 316-945-0055
www.barneysdiscountdrugs.com
Wholesaler of health and beauty aids and general merchandise
Owner: Vic Riffel Iii
barneysdrug@gmail.com
VP: V Riffel
Estimated Sales: $2.5-5 Million
Number Employees: 1-4
Number of Customer Locations: 150
Types of Products Distributed:
  Frozen Food, General Merchandise

56679 Gillco Ingredients
1701 LA Costa Meadows Dr
San Marcos, CA 92078-5105
760-759-7900
Fax: 760-599-5566 800-525-0732
sales@gillco.com www.gillco.com
Wholesaler/distributor of antioxidants, emulsifiers, preservatives, specialty and organic sugars, wheat gluten and starch, flavors, enzymes, essential oils and shortenings
President: Willard Gillies
VP: Mike Montgomery
Number Employees: 20-49
Types of Products Distributed:
  Frozen Food, General Line, Health Food, Specialty Foods, Sugars, wheat gluten, oils, etc.

56680 Gillette Creamery
47 Steve's Lane
Gardiner, NY 12525
Fax: 845-419-0901 800-522-2507
www.gillettecreamery.com
Packaged food products, ice cream and frozen novelties, refrigerated foods and other frozen desserts
President: J.B. Gillette
Vice-President/General Manager: Rich Gillette
Type of Packaging: Consumer, Food Service, Bulk
Number of Customer Locations: 1
Types of Products Distributed:
  Frozen Food

56681 Gillette Nebraska Dairies
PO Box 2553
Rapid City, SD 57709-2553
605-348-1500
Fax: 605-348-1903
Wholesaler/distributor of orange juice, equipment and fixtures and dairy products including sour cream, cottage cheese, milk and ice cream
Chairman: Les Chaffin
Estimated Sales: $20-50 Million
Number Employees: 100-249
Types of Products Distributed:
  Frozen Food, General Line, General Merchandise, Dairy products & orange juice

56682 Gillies Coffee
150 19th St
P.O. Box 320206
Brooklyn, NY 11232-1005
718-499-7766
Fax: 718-499-7771 800-344-5526
info@gilliescoffee.com www.gilliescoffee.com
Coffee
Owner: David Chabbott
davidhchabbott@gmail.com
Estimated Sales: $3.4 Million
Number Employees: 20-49
Square Footage: 28000
Type of Packaging: Food Service, Private Label, Bulk
Types of Products Distributed:
  Frozen Food, General Line, Specialty Foods, Coffee & tea

56683 Gilmore's Seafoods
129 Court St
Bath, ME 04530-2054
207-443-5231
Fax: 207-386-3271 800-849-9667
gilmore@gilmoreseafood.com gilmoreslobster.com
Seafood
Co-Owner: Kevin Gilmore
Co-Owner: Ben Gilmore
Contact: Danny Gilmore
danny@gilmoreseafood.com
Estimated Sales: $300,000-500,000
Number Employees: 1-4

56684 (HQ)Gilster-Mary Lee Corp
1037 State St
PO Box 227
Chester, IL 62233
618-826-2361
Fax: 618-826-2973
webmaster@gilstermarylee.com
www.gilstermarylee.com
Cake & bread mixes, pancake mixes, drink mixes, cereal, potatoes, frostings, muffin mixes, popcorn, stuffing, chocolate items, brownie mixes, pie shell, baking soda, soups, sauces, and gravies, pastas, cookie mixes, marshmallow items macaroni & cheese, coatings, biscuit mixes, puddings & gelatins, rice, dinners, and organic foods.
VP Sales/Marketing: Tom Welge
Number Employees: 1000-4999
Type of Packaging: Consumer, Food Service, Private Label, Bulk

1017

Other Locations:
Baking Mix/Shredded Wheat Plants
Chester, IL
Baking/Mac&Cheese & Pasta Plants
Steeleville, IL
Cocoa Plant
Momence, IL
Baking Mix Plant
Centralia, IL
Popcorn/Cereal Plant Dist, Ctr
McBride, MO
Corrugated Sheet Plant
McBride, MO
Baking Mix/Shredded Wheat PlantsSteeleville
Types of Products Distributed:
Frozen Food, General Line, General Merchandise

56685 Gimme Sum Mo Cajun Foods Corporation
4522 San Marco Road
New Orleans, LA 70129-2633   504-254-3593
Fax: 504-254-3790
Wholesaler/distributor of cajun foods including gumbo, jambalaya, shrimp creole, hot sauce and creole spices
President: Arthur Humphrey, Jr.
VP: Shawnette Sylvester
Number Employees: 1-4
Parent Co: W.F. N'Awlins Cajun & Creole Spices
Types of Products Distributed:
Frozen Food, General Line, Specialty Foods, Cajun foods & creole spices

56686 Gina Marie RefrigeratorDoor
910 Wellwood Ave
Lindenhurst, NY 11757-1226   631-789-1757
Fax: 631-789-2163 800-262-4462
www.ginamariedoors.com
Wholesaler/distributor of refrigerator door systems including glass reach-in, walk-in, swinging and sliding doors; serving the food service market; also, service and installation available
Owner: Peter Rizzo
Controller: John Rizzo
Marketing/Sales: Dan Rizzo
Operations Coordinator: Pete Rizzo
Estimated Sales: $3-5 Million
Number Employees: 10-19
Square Footage: 34000
Types of Products Distributed:
Food Service, Frozen Food, General Merchandise, Refrigerator door systems

56687 Ginsberg's Institutional Foods
29 Ginsbergs Ln
P.O. Box 17
Hudson, NY 12534   518-828-4004
800-999-6006
info@ginsbergsfoods.com www.ginsbergs.com
Wholesaler/distributor of groceries, meats, produce, dairy products, frozen foods, baked goods, equipment and fixtures, general merchandise, private label items and fresh and frozen seafood; serving the food service market.
President: David Ginsberg
dginsberg@ginsbergs.com
Executive Vice President: Nancy Ginsberg
Marektig Manager: Tracy Cantele
Chief Operating Officer: Suzanne Rajczi
Purchasing Manager: Patrick McCrudden
Year Founded: 1909
Estimated Sales: $131 Million
Number Employees: 270
Square Footage: 73000
Types of Products Distributed:
Food Service, General Merchandise, Provisions/Meat, Produce, Seafood, Groceries, etc.

56688 Giovanni Food Co Inc
6050 Court Street Rd
Syracuse, NY 13206-1711   315-457-2373
sales@giovannifoods.com
www.giovannifoods.com
Sauces
CEO: Louis DeMent
Chief Financial Officer: David Monahan
Vice President of Operations: Tim Budd
Director of Research & Development: Eric Lynch
National Sales Director: Joe Barbara
Production/Purchasing Manager: Katie Weber
Estimated Sales: $20-50 Million
Number Employees: 20-49

Number of Brands: 5
Square Footage: 67000
Type of Packaging: Consumer, Food Service, Private Label
Private Brands Carried:
DeMent's Italian Spaghetti Sauce, Greenview Kithcen, Tuscan Traditions, Jose Perdo Organic Salsa
Types of Products Distributed:
Food Service, General Merchandise, Health Food, Specialty Foods

56689 (HQ)Giumarra Companies
P.O. Box 861449
Los Angeles, CA 90086   213-627-2900
Fax: 213-628-4878 www.giumarra.com
Produce marketing
Senior VP, Strategic Development: Hillary Brick
Director of Quality Control: Jim Heil
Manager: Donald Corsaro

Number Employees: 50-99
Other Locations: Giumarra Agricom
Types of Products Distributed:
Frozen Food

56690 Glandt-Dahlke
P.O.Box 18689
Milwaukee, WI 53218   414-466-8884
Fax: 414-466-0834
Wholesaler/distributor of produce; also, rack jobber services available; serving the food service market
President: B Glandt
VP: C Glandt
Estimated Sales: $20-50 Million
Number Employees: 20-49
Number of Customer Locations: 800
Types of Products Distributed:
Food Service, Frozen Food, Produce, Rack Jobbers

56691 Glazier Packing Co
3140 State Route 11
Malone, NY 12953-4708   518-483-4990
Fax: 518-483-8300
Sausage and frankfurters; importer of other meat products
President/Owner: John Glazier
jglazier@glazierfoodservice.com
Vice President: Shawn Glazier
General Manager: Lynn Raymond
Estimated Sales: $10-11 Million
Number Employees: 50-99
Square Footage: 90000
Type of Packaging: Consumer, Food Service
Types of Products Distributed:
Food Service, Frozen Food, Provisions/Meat

56692 Global Botanical
545 Welham Road
Barrie, ON L4N 8Z6
Canada   705-733-2117
Fax: 705-733-2391 info@globalbotanical.com
Herbs, spices, oils
President: Sandra Thuna
Office Manager: Therese White
General Manager: Joel Thuna
Number Employees: 12
Square Footage: 40000
Type of Packaging: Private Label, Bulk
Types of Products Distributed:
Health Food, Herbs, spices, oils, etc.

56693 Global Harvest
13514 Glen Harwell Rd
Dover, FL 33527   813-752-8441
Fax: 813-754-1263
Wholesaler/distributor of produce, mushrooms, specialty foods, nuts and nut meats; serving the food service market
President: Jay Webster
Estimated Sales: $5-10 Million
Number Employees: 10-19
Private Brands Carried:
Del Monte
Types of Products Distributed:
Food Service, Frozen Food, General Line, Produce, Specialty Foods, Mushrooms, nuts & nut meats

56694 Global Marketing Assoc
3536 Arden Rd
Hayward, CA 94545-3908   510-887-2462
Fax: 510-887-1882 800-869-0763
global@gmaherbs.com www.gmaherbs.com
Wholesaler/distributor, importer and exporter of herbal extracts and nutritional supplements including garlic tablets and powders, ginkgo biloba, milk thistle and St. John's wort
President: Clement Yo
clement@gmaherbs.com
Chairman: Kenneth Yeung
Vice President: Lolita Lim
Estimated Sales: $500,000-$1 Million
Number Employees: 5-9
Square Footage: 280000
Type of Packaging: Bulk
Types of Products Distributed:
Health Food, Nutritional supplements, etc.

56695 Globe Equipment Co
300 Dewey St
Bridgeport, CT 06605-2143   203-367-6611
Fax: 203-366-7003 800-972-4972
www.globeman.com
Wholesaler/distributor of food service equipment
President: Jay Eingelheim
jay@globeequipment.com
VP: Bob Ginsberg
Estimated Sales: $5-10 Million
Number Employees: 20-49
Private Brands Carried:
Hobart; Vulcan; True
Types of Products Distributed:
Food Service, Frozen Food, General Merchandise, Foodservice equipment

56696 Globe-Monte-Metro Company
4702 Metropolitan Ave
Flushing, NY 11385-1047   718-366-5880
Fax: 718-366-0819
Wholesaler/distributor of food processing equipment and machinery, cash registers and cooking and material handling equipment; serving the food service market
Owner: Bill Rose
Estimated Sales: $20-50 Million
Number Employees: 50-99
Private Brands Carried:
Advance; Amana; Artofex; Ashley; Bally Block; Biro; Cecilware; Chatillon; Curtron; Dick; Edlund; Esquire; Fairbanks; Forschner; Heat Sealing; Henny Penny; Hickory; Hobart; Hookeye; Kason; Multiton; Patty-O-Matic; Robot Coupe; Rubbermaid; TEC
Types of Products Distributed:
Food Service, Frozen Food, General Merchandise

56697 Gloria Kay Uniforms
3720 N 124th St # G
Milwaukee, WI 53222-2100   414-464-1400
Fax: 262-790-0077 800-242-7454
info@gloriakay.com www.gkuscrubs.com
Distributor of uniforms, aprons, chef clothing and kitchen and waitstaff wear; serving the food service market
Owner: Mike Weinshel
mike@gloriakay.com
Vice President: Mike Weinshel
Estimated Sales: $1 Million+
Number Employees: 10-19
Square Footage: 29600

56698 GloryBee
PO Box 2744
Eugene, OR 97402   541-689-0913
800-456-7923
sales@glorybee.com glorybee.com
Honey, sweeteners, spices, dried fruits, nuts, oils and ingredients.
President: Richard Turanski
richard.turanski@glorybee.com
Vice President: Alan Turanski
Director of Sales and Marketing: Roger Plant
Purchasing Manager: Randy Djonne
Number Employees: 10-19
Type of Packaging: Consumer, Bulk

56699 Glosson Food Eqpt-Hobart Svc
6110 Bluffton Rd # 208
Fort Wayne, IN 46809-2200   260-478-1658
Fax: 260-478-2141

Wholesalers & Distributors / A-Z

Wholesaler/distributor of equipment including food processing, weighing, wrapping and food service; serving the food service market
President: John Glosson
Estimated Sales: $5-10 Million
Number Employees: 10-19
Private Brands Carried:
  Hobart; Adamatic; Vulcan
Types of Products Distributed:
  Food Service, Frozen Food, General Merchandise, Equipment

56700 Go Cocktails
98 4th Street
Suite 107
Brooklyn, NY 11231   347-853-7462
  Fax: 718-768-0932 nycorganic@aol.com
                www.goodgroceries.com
Gluten-free, lactose-free, other lifestyle, sugar-free, non-alcoholic beverages, RTD-ready to drink (coffee, tea, concentrates, powders).
Marketing: Marty Sokoloff

56701 Go Max Go Foods
        info@gomaxgofoods.com
        www.gomaxgofoods.com
Vegan candy bars free from dairy, eggs, hydrogenated oils, trans fats, artificial ingredients, and cholesterol; 6 gluten-free flavors available
Co-Owner: Scott Ostrander
Co-Owner: Jon Ostrander
Types of Products Distributed:
  General Line

56702 Goetz & Sons Western Meat
19210 144th Ave NE
Woodinville, WA 98072-8472   425-252-1151
              Fax: 425-252-1153
Wholesaler/distributor of provisions/meats, seafood and frozen foods
President: J Goetz
Secretary: A Goetz
General Manager: R Goetz
Estimated Sales: $5-10 Million
Number Employees: 20-49
Square Footage: 101068
Number of Customer Locations: 17
Types of Products Distributed:
  Frozen Food, Provisions/Meat, Seafood

56703 Goff's Seafood
525 Parker Street
Chester, PA 19013-4147   610-490-0100
Wholesaler/distributor of frozen food and seafood; serving the food service market
Owner/Manager: R Newman
Estimated Sales: $1-2.5 Million
Number Employees: 10-19
Types of Products Distributed:
  Food Service, Frozen Food, Seafood

56704 Goff's Seafood
120 W Merion Ave
Pleasantville, NJ 08232   609-641-3345
              Fax: 609-484-8411
Wholesaler/distributor of seafood including clams, oysters, lobsters, etc
Owner: Gregory Goff Sr
Secretary: Gregory Goff, Jr.
Sales: James Jones
Estimated Sales: $5-10 Million
Number Employees: 5-9
Square Footage: 16000
Parent Co: Casino Lobster
Number of Customer Locations: 20
Types of Products Distributed:
  Frozen Food, Seafood, Clams, oysters, lobsters, etc.

56705 Golbon
877 W Main St
Suite 700
Boise, ID 83702   208-342-7771
  Fax: 208-336-9212   800-657-6360
              www.golbon.com
Purchasing and marketing group for independent food service distributors.
Year Founded: 1963
Estimated Sales: $50-100 Million
Number Employees: 50-99

56706 Gold Coast Baking Co Inc
1590 E Saint Gertrude Pl
Santa Ana, CA 92705   714-545-2253
  Fax: 714-751-2253 orders@goldcoastbakery.com
                goldcoastbakery.com
Bakery products and breads
Production Supervisor: Armando Ramirez
Estimated Sales: $76 Million
Number Employees: 100-249
Type of Packaging: Private Label
Other Locations:
  Addison, IL
Private Brands Carried:
  Pioneer French Bakery, Breads of Venice, Gold Coast
Types of Products Distributed:
  Bakery items

56707 Gold Coast Ingredients
2429 Yates Ave
Commerce, CA 90040-1917   323-724-8935
  Fax: 323-724-9354   800-352-8673
  info@goldcoastinc.com   goldcoastinc.com
Flavor and color manufacturer
President: Jim Sgro
  jim@goldcoastinc.com
CEO: Chuck Brasher
Vice President: Laurie Goddard
Estimated Sales: $12 Million
Number Employees: 20-49
Type of Packaging: Private Label, Bulk

56708 Gold Star Foods
3781 E Airport Dr
P.O. Box 4328
Ontario, CA 91761   909-843-9600
  Fax: 909-843-9659   800-540-0215
        comments@goldstarfoods.com
            www.goldstarfoods.com
Wholesaler/distributor of frozen foods for Southern California school districts.
Chief Executive Officer: Sean Leer
Year Founded: 1978
Estimated Sales: $100-500 Million
Number Employees: 100-249
Types of Products Distributed:
  Frozen Food

56709 Gold Star Seafoods
2300 W 41st St
Chicago, IL 60609-2214   773-376-8080
  Fax: 773-376-9879 Vang@goldstarseafood.com
            www.goldstarseafood.com
Seafood
President: Van Giragosian
  vang@goldstarseafood.com
Estimated Sales: $10-20 Million
Number Employees: 10-19

56710 Goldberg & Solovy FoodsInc
5925 S Alcoa Ave
Vernon, CA 90058   323-581-6161
  Fax: 323-589-2106   800-273-6637
  marketing@gsfoods.com www.gsfoods.com
Wholesaler/distributor of dry goods, frozen foods, fresh poultry and meats, seafood, groceries, equipment and supplies; serving the food service market.
CEO/President: Earl Goldberg
Year Founded: 1974
Estimated Sales: $100-500 Million
Number Employees: 250-499
Number of Products: 9500
Square Footage: 75000
Private Brands Carried:
  Code
Number of Customer Locations: 2000
Types of Products Distributed:
  Food Service, Frozen Food, General Line, General Merchandise, Provisions/Meat, Seafood, Dry goods, groceries, etc.

56711 Golden Brown Bakery Inc
421 Phoenix St
South Haven, MI 49090-1309   269-637-3418
  Fax: 269-637-7822 www.goldenbrownbakery.com
Bakery products
Owner: David Braschi
  dave@goldenbrownbakery.com
Estimated Sales: $1-1,500,000
Number Employees: 20-49
Type of Packaging: Consumer, Food Service, Private Label, Bulk
Types of Products Distributed:
  Bakery Products

56712 Golden City Brewery
920-12th St
Golden, CO 80401   303-279-8092
  Fax: 303-279-8092   info@gcbrewery.com
                gcbrewery.com
Beer
President: Jennie Sturdavant
Wholesale Distribution Manager: Josh Norton
Contact: Calvin Cline
  ccline@gcbrewery.com
Assistant Brewer & Mad Scientist: Derek Sturdavant
Estimated Sales: $5-9.9 Million
Number Employees: 2-10
Type of Packaging: Private Label
Types of Products Distributed:
  Beer

56713 Golden Eye Seafood
17640 Clarke Rd
Tall Timbers, MD 20690-2055   301-994-2274
              Fax: 301-994-9960
Seafood
President: Robert Lumpkins
Estimated Sales: $1.2 Million
Number Employees: 5-9
Types of Products Distributed:
  Frozen Food, Seafood

56714 Golden Gate Co
390 Swift Ave # 19
S San Francisco, CA 94080-6221 650-588-3632
              Fax: 650-588-5912
        sales@goldengatecompany.com
          www.goldengatebridge.org
Importer of European james, jellies, candy, gourmet foods, crackers, teas, chocolate gourmet foods
Owner: Dieter Steindeck
  dieters@ix.netcom.com
Senior Project Manager: Kris Krause
Estimated Sales: $2.8 Million
Number Employees: 5-9
Square Footage: 28800

56715 Golden Harvest Pecans
348 Vereen Bell Road
Cairo, GA 39828-4910   229-377-5617
  Fax: 229-762-3335   800-597-0968
Pecans and preserves, cookies and jellies
President/CEO: J Van Ponder
Estimated Sales: $250,000
Number Employees: 500-999
Square Footage: 6218
Type of Packaging: Consumer, Food Service, Private Label, Bulk
Types of Products Distributed:
  Frozen Food

56716 Golden Lake Electric Supply
1761 Nostrand Avenue
Brooklyn, NY 11226-7133   718-469-1350
              Fax: 718-469-3063
Wholesaler/distributor of lighting fixtures
President: Kim Suk
Estimated Sales: $500,000-$1 Million
Number Employees: 1-4
Types of Products Distributed:
  Frozen Food, General Merchandise, Lighting fixtures

56717 Golden Light Equipment Co
1010 SW 6th Ave
Amarillo, TX 79101-1118   806-373-4277
  Fax: 806-373-4286 www.goldenlightequip.com
Wholesaler/distributor of food service equipment and supplies; serving the food service market
Chairman: T Donnell
  info@goldenlightequip.com
Sales Exec: Andy Donnell
Estimated Sales: $20-50 Million
Number Employees: 20-49
Types of Products Distributed:
  Food Service, Frozen Food, General Merchandise, Equipment & supplies

56718 Golden Moon Tea
PO Box 146
Bristow, VA 20136   425-820-2000
  Fax: 425-821-9700   877-327-5473
        service@goldenmoontea.com
            www.goldenmoontea.com
Tea and chocolates
President: Cynthia Knotts
Owner: Marcus Stout
Number of Products: 30

1019

Wholesalers & Distributors / A-Z

Type of Packaging: Consumer, Food Service, Private Label, Bulk
Types of Products Distributed:
Food Service, General Line, Health Food, Specialty Foods

56719 Golden Orchard
15253 NW Mason Hill Rd
North Plains, OR 97133 503-647-5769
Fax: 503-647-0186 800-769-0832
info@golden-orchard.com
www.golden-orchard.com
Gourmet preserves including peach butter, conserve and marmalade; also, seedless berry preserves, creamed honey, pepper jelly and jalapeno marinades
Owner: Pat Golden
CEO: John Golden
Contact: Candice Chavez
chavezc@golden-orchard.com
Estimated Sales: $500,000-$1 Million
Number Employees: 1-4
Number of Brands: 1
Number of Products: 11
Square Footage: 16400
Type of Packaging: Consumer, Food Service, Private Label, Bulk
Private Brands Carried:
Golden Orchard
Types of Products Distributed:
Food Service, Frozen Food, Specialty Foods, Kosher Preservatives; Creamed Honeys

56720 Golden Organics
4941 Allison St
Units 1-4
Arvada, CO 80002 303-456-5616
Fax: 303-456-5449 orders@goldenorganics.net
www.goldenorganics.org
Organic bulk ingredients
Owner: David Rickard
Sales Manager: Peter Clem
Operations Manager: Ralph Melcher
Types of Products Distributed:
General Line

56721 Golden Valley Popcorn Supply
3850 N Ann Ave # 102
Fresno, CA 93727-7453 559-292-9633
Fax: 559-292-9638 800-553-7677
Wholesaler/distributor of specialty food products and popcorn and concession supplies and machines
Owner: Jim Tomajan
Estimated Sales: $300,000-500,000
Number Employees: 1-4
Private Brands Carried:
Kernel Pops; Gold Metal; Star
Number of Customer Locations: 200
Types of Products Distributed:
Frozen Food, General Line, General Merchandise, Specialty Foods, Popcorn & concession supplies

56722 Golden West Food Group
4401 S Downey Rd
Vernon, CA 90058 888-807-3663
Fax: 323-585-8483 info@gwfg.com
www.gwfg.com
Beef, poultry and pork products
CEO: Erik Litmanovich
Chief Sales Officer: Tim White
Contact: Mak Abbasi
it@gwfg.com
Estimated Sales: $100-499 Million
Number Employees: 750
Number of Brands: 14
Type of Packaging: Consumer, Food Service, Private Label
Types of Products Distributed:
Provisions/Meat

56723 Goldy Food Sales Company
112 Grove St # B
Worcester, MA 01605-2629 508-756-1293
Fax: 508-791-9828 goldyfoods@aol.com
Wholesaler/distributor of snack foods; serving the retail market in central Massachusetts
Owner: Barry Goldy
CEO: B Goldy
Estimated Sales: $10-20 Million
Number Employees: 20-49
Private Brands Carried:
Wise Foods; Cape Cod; Snyder's; Boston; Keebler; Pringles

Types of Products Distributed:
Frozen Food, General Line, Specialty Foods, Snacks

56724 Gone Wild!!!
414 W Cedar Street
San Diego, CA 92101-2910 619-696-6677
Fax: 619-696-0244
Wholesaler/distributor of specialty meats; serving the food service and retail markets
General Manager: Tony Mendez
Estimated Sales: Less than $500,000
Number Employees: 1-4
Parent Co: Swift International Meat Company
Private Brands Carried:
Gone Wild!!!
Types of Products Distributed:
Food Service, Frozen Food, Provisions/Meat, Specialty Foods

56725 Good's Wholesale-BakerySupls
2117 Webb St
Williamsport, PA 17701-5521 570-322-0111
Fax: 570-322-2093
Wholesaler/ distributor of bakery and restaurant supplies and canned goods; serving the food service market
Owner: Kenneth Frey Jr
Secretary: Dean Brooks
Estimated Sales: $1-2.5 Million
Number Employees: 1-4
Types of Products Distributed:
Food Service, Frozen Food, General Line, General Merchandise, Bar/restaurant supplies & canned goods

56726 Gooding Rubber Company
3701 Tree Court Industrial Boulevard
Kirkwood, MO 63122-6623 636-861-2213
Fax: 636-861-2886
Wholesaler/distributor of conveyor, elevator and transmission belting, rubber and plastic hoses, sheet rubber, plastic urethane and UHMW, cutting tools, abrasives, etc
President: J Mork
VP Sales: R Wagner
VP Operations: D Goldbeck
Purchasing Manager: K Heis
Estimated Sales: $3-5 Million
Number Employees: 15
Square Footage: 88000
Parent Co: Gooding Rubber Company
Types of Products Distributed:
Frozen Food, General Merchandise, Equipment

56727 Goodman Wiper & Paper Co
120 Mill St
Auburn, ME 04210-5647 207-784-5779
Fax: 207-777-1717 ken@goodmanwiper.com
www.goodmanwiper.com
New and recycled wiping cloths; distributor of paper towels, towel systems, trash liners, linen and terry towels, cleaners, gloves, oil absorbent pads and compounds.
Owner: Ken Goodman
CFO: Ken Goodman
VP/Plant Manager: Steve Goodman
Sales/Purchasing Director: Ken Goodman
kengoodman@goodmanwiper.com
Plant Manager: Steven Goodman
Estimated Sales: $10-20 Million
Number Employees: 10-19
Square Footage: 12000
Type of Packaging: Consumer, Food Service, Private Label
Private Brands Carried:
Kimberly Clark; Lakeland Protective Clothing; North River/Cascade; Permatex; Scott Canada; Cello; Rubbermaid; PXG; Continental; Carolina Paper; Drackett; Chemtex; Brown
Types of Products Distributed:
Paper products, janitorial supplies

56728 Goodwin Brothers Inc
319 E Jefferson St
Montgomery, AL 36104-3656 334-834-3800
Fax: 334-834-3811 800-835-8030
www.goodwinbrothers.com
Wholesaler/distributor of general merchandise; serving the food service market
President: Buddy Goodwin
goodbrs@bellsouth.net
Owner: Cope Goodwin

Estimated Sales: $5-10 Million
Number Employees: 10-19
Types of Products Distributed:
Food Service, Frozen Food, General Merchandise, Restaurant supplies

56729 Gopal's Healthfoods
800 CR 125
Sidney, TX 76474
866-646-7257
customercare@gopalshealthfoods.com
www.gopalshealthfoods.com
Nut and seed mixes, nut and seed butters, vegan parmesan, nori-wrapped energy sticks, fruit and nut bars, brownies, crackers
Founder: Stefan Knueppel
Types of Products Distributed:
Health Food

56730 (HQ)Gordon Food Service
1300 Gezon Parkway SW
Wyoming, MI 49509 616-530-7000
Fax: 616-717-7600 800-968-4164
www.gfs.com
Wholesaler/distributor of produce, frozen food, meats, general line items and general merchandise; serving the food service market.
Chairman: Daniel Gordon
CEO: Jim Gordon
Year Founded: 1897
Estimated Sales: $7.7 Billion
Number Employees: 19,000
Square Footage: 750000
Other Locations:
Gordon Food Service
Mississauga, ONGordon Food Service
Private Brands Carried:
Gordon
Number of Customer Locations: 57
Types of Products Distributed:
Food Service, Frozen Food, General Line, General Merchandise, Provisions/Meat, Produce

56731 Gordon Food Service
342 Gordon Industrial Dr
Shepherdsville, KY 40165 502-215-1250
Fax: 502-215-1093 www.gfs.com
Wholesaler/distributor of frozen foods, produce, meats, seafood and general line products; serving the food service market. Distribution center location.
Other Locations:
Bridge Brand Food Services Lt
Winnipeg, MBBridge Brand Food Services Lt
Types of Products Distributed:
Food Service, Frozen Food, General Line, Provisions/Meat, Produce, Seafood

56732 Gordon Food Service
4900 Clay Ave SW
Wyoming, MI 49548 616-717-4164
www.gfs.com
Wholesaler/distributor of general merchandise, meats, general line items, frozen foods and produce; serving the food service market. Distribution center location.
Private Brands Carried:
Gordon
Types of Products Distributed:
Food Service, Frozen Food, General Line, General Merchandise, Provisions/Meat, Produce

56733 Gordon Food Service
7770 Kensington Ct
Brighton, MI 48116 248-446-8326
Fax: 248-486-3506 www.gfs.com
Wholesaler/distributor of general merchandise, general line items, meats, frozen foods and produce; serving the food service market. Distribution center location.
Types of Products Distributed:
Food Service, Frozen Food, General Line, General Merchandise, Provisions/Meat, Produce

56734 Gordon Food Service
6200 Gordon Food Service Dr
Kannapolis, NC 28027 704-652-3800
www.gfs.com
Wholesaler/distributor of general merchandise, meats, coffee, beverages, frozen foods, produce, etc.; serving the food service market. Distribution center location.
Private Brands Carried:
Gordon

Types of Products Distributed:
Food Service, Frozen Food, General Line, General Merchandise, Provisions/Meat, Produce, Coffee, disposables, etc.

56735 Gordon Food Service
10901 38th St
Kenosha, WI 53144 262-525-1475
Fax: 262-552-1523 www.gfs.com
Wholesaler/distributor of general merchandise, meats, general line items, frozen foods and produce; serving the food service market. Distribution center location.
Number of Customer Locations: 400
Types of Products Distributed:
Food Service, Frozen Food, General Line, General Merchandise, Provisions/Meat, Produce

56736 Gordon Food Service
3301 NW 125th St
Miami, FL 33167 305-507-2882
Fax: 305-685-1794 800-830-9767
www.gfs.com
Wholesaler/distributor of general merchandise, meats, general line items, frozen foods and produce; serving the food service market. Distribution center location.
Types of Products Distributed:
Food Service, Frozen Food, General Line, General Merchandise, Provisions/Meat, Produce

56737 Gordon Food Service
777 Freeport Parkway
Suite 100
Coppell, TX 75009 469-637-4100
www.gfs.com
Wholesaler/distributor of general merchandise, meats, general line items, frozen foods and produce; serving the food service market. Distribution center location.
Types of Products Distributed:
Food Service, Frozen Food, General Line, General Merchandise, Provisions/Meat, Produce

56738 Gordon Food Service
333 50th St SW
Wyoming, MI 49548
www.gfs.com
Wholesaler/distributor of general merchandise, meats, general line items, frozen foods and produce; serving the food service market. Distribution center location.
Private Brands Carried:
Gordon
Types of Products Distributed:
Food Service, Frozen Food, General Line, General Merchandise, Provisions/Meat, Produce

56739 Gordon Food Service
504 Advantage Way
Aberdeen, MD 21001 410-273-3406
www.gfs.com
Wholesaler/distributor of general merchandise, meats, general line items, frozen foods and produce; serving the food service market. Distribution center location.
Private Brands Carried:
Gordon
Types of Products Distributed:
Food Service, Frozen Food, General Line, General Merchandise, Provisions/Meat, Produce

56740 Gordon Food Service
2850 NW 120th Terrace
Miami, FL 33167 305-685-5851
www.gfs.com
Wholesaler/distributor of general merchandise, meats, general line items, frozen foods and produce; serving the food service market. Freezer facility location.
Types of Products Distributed:
Food Service, Frozen Food, General Line, General Merchandise, Provisions/Meat, Produce

56741 Gordon Food Service
1500 North River Rd
Lithia Springs, GA 30122 770-745-3901
www.gfs.com
Wholesaler/distributor of general merchandise, meats, general line items, frozen foods and produce; serving the food service market. Distribution center location.
Private Brands Carried:
Gordon
Types of Products Distributed:
Food Service, Frozen Food, General Line, General Merchandise, Provisions/Meat, Produce

56742 Gordon Food Service
1410 Gordon Food Service Dr
Plant City, FL 33563 813-703-6501
www.gfs.com
Wholesaler/distributor of general merchandise, meats, general line items, frozen foods and produce; serving the food service market. Distribution center location.
Private Brands Carried:
Gordon
Types of Products Distributed:
Food Service, Frozen Food, General Line, General Merchandise, Provisions/Meat, Produce

56743 Gordon Food Service
8152 Kensington Ct
Brighton, MI 48116 616-530-7000
www.gfs.com
Wholesaler/distributor of general merchandise, meats, general line items, frozen foods and produce; serving the food service market. Distribution center location.
Private Brands Carried:
Gordon
Types of Products Distributed:
Food Service, Frozen Food, General Line, General Merchandise, Provisions/Meat, Produce

56744 Gordon Food Service
11303 Antoine Dr
Houston, TX 77066
800-989-6411
www.gfs.com
Wholesaler/distributor of general merchandise, meats, general line items, frozen foods and produce; serving the food service market. Distribution center location.
Private Brands Carried:
Gordon
Types of Products Distributed:
Food Service, Frozen Food, General Line, General Merchandise, Provisions/Meat, Produce

56745 Gordon Food Service
4980 Gateway Blvd
Springfield, OH 45502 937-525-7240
www.gfs.com
Wholesaler/distributor of general merchandise, meats, general line items, frozen foods and produce; serving the food service market. Distribution center location.
Private Brands Carried:
Gordon
Types of Products Distributed:
Food Service, Frozen Food, General Line, General Merchandise, Provisions/Meat, Produce

56746 Gordon Food Service
225 Solar Dr
Imperial, PA 15126 724-899-5303
www.gfs.com
Wholesaler/distributor of general merchandise, meats, general line items, frozen foods and produce; serving the food service market. Distribution center location.
Private Brands Carried:
Gordon
Types of Products Distributed:
Food Service, Frozen Food, General Line, General Merchandise, Provisions/Meat, Produce

56747 Gordon Food Service
630 John Hancock Rd
Taunton, MA 02780 508-824-2800
www.gfs.com
Wholesaler/distributor of general merchandise, meats, general line items, frozen foods and produce; serving the food service market. Distribution center location.
Private Brands Carried:
Gordon
Types of Products Distributed:
Food Service, Frozen Food, General Line, General Merchandise, Provisions/Meat, Produce

56748 (HQ)Gosselin Gourmet Beverages
11203 Paloma Court
Louisville, KY 40229-2844 800-804-7831
Wholesaler/distributor, importer and exporter of gourmet coffee, teas and specialty flavorings; also, cafe equipment
President of Sales/Marketing: Craig Gosselin
Number Employees: 1-4
Private Brands Carried:
Arabica; Enter-Stuart; Monin; Divinci; La Temptesta; Ghirdelli
Types of Products Distributed:
Frozen Food, General Line, General Merchandise, Specialty Foods, Gourmet coffees, teas & flavorings

56749 Gourmet Award Foods
860 Vandalia Street
Saint Paul, MN 55114-1305 612-333-1505
Fax: 651-646-1816 800-366-3986
Wholesaler/distributor of groceries, specialty and ethnic foods, meats, confectionery products and cheeses; serving the food service market
President (Midwest Division): D Rotchadl
Director Finance: J Cline
Director Purchasing: L Johnson
Estimated Sales: $1-3 Million
Number Employees: 5-9
Square Footage: 460000
Parent Co: Tree of Life
Private Brands Carried:
Gourmet Award; Zapata; Venecia
Number of Customer Locations: 1400
Types of Products Distributed:
Frozen Food, General Line, Provisions/Meat, Specialty Foods, Ethnic foods, cheeses, etc.

56750 Gourmet Cafe Wholesale
PO Box 437
Plainsboro, NJ 08536-0437 856-799-7069
Fax: 856-799-4543 888-494-2233
cafestuff@aol.com
members.aol.com/cafestuff/cb.html
Wholesaler/distributor of confectionery items
Pres.: Marina Furey
VP: Jim Furey
Parent Co: Confection Boutique
Types of Products Distributed:
Frozen Food

56751 Gourmet Club Corporation
20 Potash Rd
Oakland, NJ 07436-3100 201-337-5882
Fax: 201-337-0479
Wholesaler/distributor and importer of freeze-dried seafood, mushrooms, seasonings and spices, seafood and vegetable powders, green and pink peppercorns, dehydrated tropical fruits and vegetables and dried vanilla beans
President: Warren Gaffery
Contact: James Magna
james@mpba.org
Estimated Sales: $3-5 Million
Number Employees: 1-4
Square Footage: 100000
Types of Products Distributed:
General Line, Seafood, Freeze-dried seafoods, mushrooms, etc.

56752 Gourmet Foods Intl
255 Ted Turner Dr SW
Atlanta, GA 30303-3705 404-954-7600
Fax: 404-954-7672 800-966-6172
www.afiaww.com
Wholesaler/distributor and importer of salmon, cheeses, caviar, truffles and foie gras
Owner: Russell Mc Call
rmccall@gfifoods.com
Estimated Sales: $300,000-500,000
Number Employees: 250-499
Number of Customer Locations: 250
Types of Products Distributed:
Frozen Food, General Line, Seafood, Salmon, cheeses, caviar, truffles, etc.

56753 Gourmet Products
PO Box 387
Thomaston, CT 06787-0387 860-283-5147
Fax: 860-283-6912
Sauces, mustards, relishes, salsas
Owner: A Yurgelun
Marketing Director: W Yurgelun
VP Operations: David Yurgelun
Production Manager: T Del Gadio
Purchasing Manager: T Curnell
Number Employees: 10-19
Square Footage: 12000

Type of Packaging: Consumer, Private Label, Bulk
Private Brands Carried:
Gourmet Products
Number of Customer Locations: 100
Types of Products Distributed:
Specialty Foods

56754 Gourmet Technologies Inc
35 Trade Zone Ct
Ronkonkoma, NY 11779-7368   631-981-2100
Fax: 631-981-3509   877-2GE-ATO
info@worldofgelato.com
Wholesaler/distributor of soft serve ice cream and yogurt equipment, batch freezers, gelato equipment and granita, slush and frozen drink machinery; serving the food service market
President: Andrew Seabury
a.seabury@worldofgelato.com
Service Manager: Samantha Albert
Estimated Sales: $5-10 Million
Number Employees: 20-49
Private Brands Carried:
Coldelite; Baskin Robbins; Douwe Egberts Coffee Systems; Louisiana Daiquiri Co.
Types of Products Distributed:
Food Service, Frozen Food, General Merchandise, Ice cream, yogurt & drink equipment

56755 Govadinas Fitness Foods
2651 Ariane Drive
San Diego, CA 92117-3422   858-270-0691
Fax: 858-270-0696   800-900-0108
Health food bars and natural snacks
CEO: Larry Gatpandan
Accountant: Alberto Hael
VP: Zenaida Gatpandan
Marketing: Michael Pugliese
Sales: Lisa Gatpandan
Production: Jose Marquez
Purchasing: Nila Morrill
Estimated Sales: $3 Million
Number Employees: 20-49
Number of Products: 25
Square Footage: 10000
Type of Packaging: Private Label
Types of Products Distributed:
Health Food, Snack Foods

56756 Grace Technologies
1040 Highway 87 S Apt 1522
Orange, TX 77630   281-873-8633
Fax: 281-873-9329   800-873-4247
mgrace3101@aol.com
Wholesaler/distributor of including air cylinders and tubing; also, valves, silicon vacuum cups, etc
VP: Mark Grace
Marketing Director: Mark Grace
Estimated Sales: $2.5-5 Million
Number Employees: 1-4
Private Brands Carried:
Schrader; Bellows; Parker; Hannifin
Number of Customer Locations: 2200
Types of Products Distributed:
General Merchandise, Air tubing, valves, cylinders, etc.

56757 Grafco
3644 Getwell
Memphis, TN 38181   901-362-0120
Fax: 901-362-0124   info@grafcoinc.com
www.grafcoinc.com
Wholesaler/distributor of material handling equipment including conveyors
President: Fred Graflund
Estimated Sales: $5-10 Million
Number Employees: 5-9
Types of Products Distributed:
Frozen Food, General Merchandise, Material handling equipment

56758 Graffam Brothers
211 Union St
Rockport, ME 04856-6107   207-236-3396
Fax: 207-236-2569   800-535-5358
sales@lobstersogo.com   www.lobstersogo.com
Lobsters and clams
Owner: Janice Graffam
sales@lobstertogo.com
Number Employees: 10-19

56759 Graham Fisheries
13890 Shell Belt Rd
Bayou La Batre, AL 36509-2304   251-824-7370
Fax: 251-824-7370   shrimp1951@aol.com
Seafood, shrimp
Owner: Darrell Graham
Estimated Sales: $.5-1 million
Number Employees: 1-4

56760 Graham Ice & Locker Plant
328 Elm Street
Graham, TX 76450-2514   940-549-1975
Ice; slaughterer, processor and wholesaler/distributor of deer
Owner: James Black
Estimated Sales: Less than $500,000
Number Employees: 1 to 4
Type of Packaging: Consumer
Types of Products Distributed:
Frozen Food, Provisions/Meat, Deer

56761 Grainger Industrial Supply
1657 Shermer Rd
Northbrook, IL 60062-5315   847-498-5900
Fax: 847-498-3402   www.grainger.com
Wholesaler/distributor of parts, accessories and smallware including front and back of the house equipment; serving the food service market
Business Manager: John Stride
Manager: Susan Strecker
strecker.s@grainger.com
Manager Specialty Markets: Ellen Albin
Equipment Specialist: Peter Pace
Number Employees: 250-499
Parent Co: W.W. Grainger
Types of Products Distributed:
Food Service, Frozen Food, General Merchandise, Equipment replacement parts

56762 Grainger Industrial Supply
5002 Speedway Dr
Fort Wayne, IN 46825-5245   260-444-2725
Fax: 260-483-0311   800-472-4643
www.grainger.com
Wholesaler/distributor of material handling equipment
Manager: Kelly Souder
Manager: Clinton Foor
clint.foor@grainger.com
Branch Manager: Mike Ferguson
Estimated Sales: $5-10 Million
Number Employees: 10-19
Parent Co: Grainger
Private Brands Carried:
G.E.; Dayton; Hubbell
Types of Products Distributed:
Frozen Food, General Merchandise, Material handling equipment

56763 (HQ)Gralab Instruments
900 Dimco Way
Centerville, OH 45458-2710   937-433-7600
Fax: 937-433-0520   800-876-8353
www.gralab.com
Electromechanical and electronic timing devices for commercial cooking and baking applications, food testing laboratories, process control systems and sanitation; also, thermoset and thermoplastic compression and injection moldedproducts.
President & CEO: Michael Sieron
msieron@dimcogray.com
Treasurer: Terry Tate
Quality Control: Lyle Crum
Sales & Marketing Manager: Linda Raisch
Production: James Daulton
Number Employees: 50-99
Number of Brands: 1
Number of Products: 20
Parent Co: Dimco-Gray Corporation
Types of Products Distributed:
Food Service, Frozen Food, General Line, Provisions/Meat, Produce

56764 Grande Cuisine Systems
20 Banigan Drive
Toronto, ON M4H 1E9
Canada   416-421-0421
Fax: 416-421-0334   888-233-2862
Wholesaler/distributor of equipment and fixtures; serving the food service market
President: Jean Pierre Boue
Hotel/Restaurant Division: Lynn Weaver
Number Employees: 20-49
Types of Products Distributed:
Food Service, Frozen Food, General Merchandise

56765 Grande Custom Ingredients Group
250 Camelot Dr
Fond du Lac, WI 54935   920-952-7200
Fax: 920-922-2921   800-772-3210
gcig@grande.com   www.grandecig.com
Processor and exporter of specialty whey products and lactose.
Group Vice President: Paul Graham
Research & Development: Rory McCarthy
Sales & Marketing: Brad Nielsen
Operations: Lary Turner
Purchasing Director: Chris Richards
Square Footage: 10000
Parent Co: Grande Cheese Company
Type of Packaging: Bulk
Types of Products Distributed:
Dairy Ingredients; Proteins

56766 Granite State Fruit
30 Auburn St
Manchester, NH 03103-6236   603-627-4131
Fax: 603-627-0480
Wholesaler/distributor of fruits and vegetables
President: Harry Theodosopoulos
Estimated Sales: $5-10 Million
Number Employees: 5-9
Square Footage: 20000
Types of Products Distributed:
Frozen Food, Produce, Fruits & vegetables

56767 Grantstone Supermarket
8 W Grant Rd
Tucson, AZ 85705-5529   520-628-7445
Fax: 520-628-1259
Chinese, Japanese, Korean, Thai and Vietnamese products; fresh Chinese fruit and produce
President: Janet Hom
grantstonemarket@aol.com
Estimated Sales: $3-5 Million
Number Employees: 20-49
Types of Products Distributed:
Produce, Specialty Foods

56768 Gray Lift
4646 E Jensen Ave
Fresno, CA 93725-1699   559-268-6621
Fax: 559-485-0110   800-464-3225
www.graylift.com
Wholesaler/distributor of material handling equipment; also, lift truck services available
CEO: Jay Waugh
jwaugh@graylift.com
CEO: J Waugh
Estimated Sales: $20-50 Million
Number Employees: 100-249
Types of Products Distributed:
Frozen Food, General Merchandise, Material handling equipment

56769 Grayco Products Sales
100 Tec Street
Hicksville, NY 11801-3650   516-997-9200
Fax: 516-870-0510
Wholesaler/distributor and exporter of paper and disposable products including tabletop and industrial equipment, packaging and printing supplies
Owner: Helen Kushner
CEO: Adrienne Kushner
Vice President: Alan Kushner
Operations Manager: D Pascale
Estimated Sales: $1-5 Million
Number Employees: 2
Square Footage: 10000
Parent Co: ASK Sales
Types of Products Distributed:
Frozen Food, General Merchandise, Disposable paper & packaging supplies

56770 Grayon Industrial Products
10 Planchet Road
Unit 15-18
Vaughan, ON L4K 2C8
Canada   905-660-3200
Fax: 905-660-4042   800-668-6350
Wholesaler/distributor of material handling equipment
President: Grace Pearson
Executive Assistant: Cari Meredith
Number Employees: 10-19
Private Brands Carried:
Chrysler; Clark; Hyster

Wholesalers & Distributors / A-Z

56771 Great Age Container
948 Whittier Street
952
Bronx, NY 10474-4925   203-932-8000
          Fax: 203-934-7172 greatage@aol.com
Wholesaler/distributor of closures, glass and plastic bottles, gloves, packaging, vacuum packing and laboratory equipment
President: Larry Stein
Estimated Sales: $1-2.5 Million
Number Employees: 10-19
Number of Customer Locations: 400
Types of Products Distributed:
  Frozen Food, General Merchandise, Bottles, gloves, closures, etc.

56772 Great American Health Bar
35 W 57th St # 1
New York, NY 10019-3494   212-355-5177
                Fax: 212-355-5466
          greatamericantogo@yahoo.com
Wholesaler/distributor of vitamins, food supplements, etc
Owner: Frank Ross
Division Director: Jessica Pitzel
Number Employees: 50-99
Parent Co: Swanson Health Products
Types of Products Distributed:
  Frozen Food, General Merchandise, Health Food, Mineral & food supplements

56773 Great American Popcorn Works of Pennsylvania
PO Box 214
Telford, PA 18969-0214   215-721-0414
        Fax: 215-721-6082 855-542-2676
               www.popcornworks.com
Gourmet popcorn
Manager: Alice Barnes
Vice President: Jack Egner
Sales Director: Rob Rosen
Public Relations: Giselle Wetzel
Estimated Sales: Less than $500,000
Number Employees: 1-4
Number of Products: 65
Square Footage: 12000
Type of Packaging: Consumer, Food Service, Private Label, Bulk
Number of Customer Locations: 35
Types of Products Distributed:
  Food Service, Health Food, Produce, Specialty Foods

56774 Great American Seafood Company
1711 W Kirby Ave
Champaigne, IL 61821-55   217-352-0986
          www.greatamericanseafood.com
Seafood
Estimated Sales: $300,000-500,000
Number Employees: 5-9

56775 Great Basin Botanicals
PO Box 12217
Ogden, UT 84412-2217   801-779-9922
                Fax: 801-779-9929
Wholesaler/distributor of herbs including yucca, cedar berries and brigham tea; also, toll processing of health food products available
VP: Farley Quist
VP: Daren Peterson
VP: Dave Nielson
Number Employees: 10-19
Square Footage: 100000
Parent Co: Nutraceutical
Types of Products Distributed:
  Frozen Food, Health Food, Herbs

56776 Great Eastern EquipmentExchange
7 Lee Pl
Clifton, NJ 07011   973-340-9200
       Fax: 973-340-7777 www.greateasterninc.com
Wholesaler/distributor of material handling equipment including forklifts and aerial and man lifts
President: Robert Bogle
Estimated Sales: $2.5-5 Million
Number Employees: 5-9

Private Brands Carried:
  Yale; Clark; Hyster
Types of Products Distributed:
  Frozen Food, General Merchandise, Forklifts, etc.

56777 Great Eastern Mussel Farms
P.O.Box 141
Tenants Harbor, ME 004860-014 207-372-6317
          Fax: 207-372-8256 gem@midcoast.com
Shipper of fresh cultured mussels
President: Endicott Davison
Sales Manager: Terry Gallery
Estimated Sales: $20-50 Million
Number Employees: 50-99

56778 Great Lakes Designs
544 S Green Rd
Cleveland, OH 44121-2843   216-382-6961
          Fax: 216-382-7756 gld@gldesigns.com
Importer and wholesaler/distributor of latex gloves, bread accessories, chrome wire ware and solid wood and high density poly cutting boards; serving the food service market
President: Barry Epstein
Marketing Manager: Jonathon Varble
Estimated Sales: $1-3 Million
Number Employees: 10-19
Square Footage: 40000
Parent Co: Eppco Enterprises
Type of Packaging: Food Service
Types of Products Distributed:
  Food Service, Frozen Food, General Merchandise, Kitchen equipment, latex gloves, etc.

56779 Great Lakes Distributing & Storage
463 E US Highway 30
Valparaiso, IN 46383-9564   219-531-2142
                Fax: 219-462-8121
Wholesaler/distributor of general merchandise
President: Joe Glusak
Quality Control: Theresa Lowe
Contact: Thomas Adams
thomas.adams@glpc.com
Number Employees: 10-19
Types of Products Distributed:
  Frozen Food, General Merchandise

56780 Great Lakes Gelatin
PO Box 917
Grayslake, IL 60030   847-223-8141
        Fax: 847-223-8144 800-232-0328
                  greatlakesgelatin.com
Wholesaler/distributor of unflavored beef gelatin; serving the food service market
President: R K Busscher
Contact: Bob Busscher
bob@greatlakesgelatin.com
Year Founded: 1922
Estimated Sales: $500,000-$1 Million
Number Employees: 6
Type of Packaging: Consumer, Bulk
Private Brands Carried:
  Great Lakes

56781 Great Lakes Gourmet Food Service
24404 Catherne Ind Dr # 308
Novi, MI 48375-2456   248-735-1700
        Fax: 248-735-1800 800-625-4591
Importer of bakery and pastry equipment; wholesaler/distributor and importer of bakery and pastry ingredients; serving the food service market
President: Tom Chaput
Estimated Sales: $1-2 Million
Number Employees: 1
Square Footage: 28000
Type of Packaging: Food Service
Private Brands Carried:
  Patis France; Cocoa Barry; Grand Marnier; Callebut; Schokinag; Guittard; Qzina; Aster
Types of Products Distributed:
  Food Service, Frozen Food, General Line, Bakery & pastry ingredients

56782 Great Lakes Hotel Supply Co
24101 W 9 Mile Rd
Southfield, MI 48033-3972   313-962-9176
          Fax: 313-962-1317 www.glhsco.com
Wholesaler/distributor of commercial kitchen equipment; serving the food service market

President: Mark Israel
marc@glhsco.com
General Manager: Chris Goff
Estimated Sales: $500,000-$1 Million
Number Employees: 20-49
Parent Co: Great Lakes Hotel Supply Company
Private Brands Carried:
  Hobart; Frymaster; Crescor
Types of Products Distributed:
  Food Service, Frozen Food, General Merchandise, Commercial kitchen equipment

56783 Great Lakes Hotel Supply Co
24101 W 9 Mile Rd
Southfield, MI 48033-3972   313-962-9176
          Fax: 313-962-1317 www.glhsco.com
Wholesaler/distributor of food service equipment; serving the food service market
President: Mark Israel
marc@glhsco.com
VP: Dave Israel
Estimated Sales: $2.5-5 Million
Number Employees: 20-49
Private Brands Carried:
  Hobart; South Bend; Groen
Types of Products Distributed:
  Food Service, Frozen Food, General Merchandise, Foodservice equipment

56784 Great Lakes International Trading
858 Business Park Drive
Traverse City, MI 49686   231-947-2141
          Fax: 231-947-0628 glit@glit.com
                    www.glit.com
Importer and exporter of dried fruits, nuts and seeds
President: Verne Powell
Vice President: George Powell
Sales/Marketing Assistant: Emi King
Sales Manager: Denny Malone
Estimated Sales: $5-10 Million
Number Employees: 10-19
Type of Packaging: Private Label, Bulk
Private Brands Carried:
  Golden Palm; Great Lakes
Types of Products Distributed:
  Frozen Food, Produce

56785 Great Midwest Seafood Company
5406 Sheridan St
Davenport, IA 52806-2260   563-388-4770
                Fax: 563-388-4772
Seafood
Owner: Jeff Melchert
kingfish@gmail.com
Estimated Sales: $10-20 Million
Number Employees: 10-19

56786 Great North Foods
170 N Industrial Hwy
Alpena, MI 49707-7729   989-356-2281
        Fax: 989-356-2510 800-968-0117
              www.greatnorthfoods.com
Wholesaler/distributor of frozen foods, general line items, general merchandise, produce, private label items and meats; serving convenience stores
Vice President: Jim Kent
jimkent@greatnorthfoods.com
VP: Ron Baxter
Sales Manager: Ron Baxter
Estimated Sales: $20-50 Million
Number Employees: 100-249
Square Footage: 100000
Private Brands Carried:
  IGA; Red & White; Value Check
Number of Customer Locations: 600
Types of Products Distributed:
  Frozen Food, General Line, General Merchandise, Provisions/Meat, Produce, Equipment, baked goods, etc.

56787 Great Outdoors Spice Company
600 W County Line Road
Highlands Ranch, CO 80129-6512 720-344-8660
        Fax: 770-344-8663 888-844-2816
Wholesaler/distributor of seasoning blends including natural and kosher
Owner: Robert Ritter
Estimated Sales: Less than $500,000
Number Employees: 1-4
Types of Products Distributed:
  Frozen Food, General Line, Blended seasonings

1023

Wholesalers & Distributors / A-Z

56788 Great Plains Beef LLC
PO Box 82545
Lincoln, NE 68501-2545 402-479-2115
Fax: 402-458-4531 info@piedmontese.com
Beef
President: Billy Swain
Number Employees: 1-4

56789 Great Valley Meat Company
Howellville Road
Berwyn, PA 19312 610-644-0561
Wholesaler/distributor of meat products
President: Dominic Medci
Estimated Sales: $2.5-5 Million
Number Employees: 1-4
Square Footage: 12000
Types of Products Distributed:
  Frozen Food, Provisions/Meat

56790 Great West Produce Company
2600 S Eastern Ave
Commerce, CA 90040-1402 323-869-0200
greatwestproduce.com
Wholesale/distributor of produce.
Chief Executive Officer: Paul Villa
Vice President: Daniel Sims
A/R Credit Manager: Paola Arellano
Type of Packaging: Consumer, Private Label, Bulk
Types of Products Distributed:
  Produce

56791 Great Western Beef WHLSCo
4044 S Halsted St
Chicago, IL 60609 773-927-3790
Fax: 773-927-0032 sales@gwbeef.com
www.greatwesternbeef.com
Wholesaler/distributor of portion controlled meats; serving the food service market.
President: John Wilkinson
jwilkinson@gwbeef.com
Year Founded: 1907
Estimated Sales: $10 Million
Number Employees: 20-49
Square Footage: 7000
Types of Products Distributed:
  Food Service, Frozen Food, Provisions/Meat

56792 Great Western Chemical
3595 E Wawona Ave
Fresno, CA 93725-9022 559-485-4150
Fax: 559-485-0605
Wholesaler/distributor of ingredients, additives and cleaning and sanitation chemicals
Manager: James Palmer
Sales/Marketing Executive: Tim Bistolas
Food Processing Business Manager: Thomas Cervenka
Purchasing Manager: Steve Johnson
Estimated Sales: $12 Million
Number Employees: 10-19
Square Footage: 30000
Private Brands Carried:
  Sanichem
Number of Customer Locations: 8000
Types of Products Distributed:
  Frozen Food, General Merchandise, Cleaning products

56793 Great Western Chemical Company
5200 SW Macadam Ave # 200
Portland, OR 97239-3800 503-228-2600
Fax: 503-228-8471 800-547-1400
Manufacturer and wholesaler/distributor of cleaning and sanitation chemicals and food ingredients including acidulants, preservatives, etc
Manager: Jason Keyes
Bus. Mgr.: Tom Cervenka
Bus. Mgr.: Andy Pollard
VP Marketing: Tami Mainero
Estimated Sales: $50-100 Million
Number Employees: 5-9
Private Brands Carried:
  Sanichem
Types of Products Distributed:
  Frozen Food, General Line, General Merchandise, Sanitation chemicals & ingredients

56794 Great Western Foods
550 N Eastern Ave
Idaho Falls, ID 83402-3734 208-524-2444
Fax: 208-522-9815
Wholesaler/distributor of frozen foods; serving the food service market
Manager: Bob Tippetts
Manager: Eugene Tippetts
Head of Purchasing: M Lyon
Estimated Sales: $20-50 Million
Number Employees: 10-19
Number of Customer Locations: 250
Types of Products Distributed:
  Food Service, Frozen Food

56795 Great Western Meats
PO Box 568366
Orlando, FL 32856-8366 407-841-4270
Fax: 407-841-4307
Wholesaler/distributor of meat products; also, poultry and seafood
Sales Manager: Greg Vorhees
Plant Manager: Chuck Farley
Estimated Sales: $10-20 Million
Number Employees: 100-249
Types of Products Distributed:
  Frozen Food, Provisions/Meat, Seafood, Poultry

56796 Greater Knead, The
1690 Winchester Rd
Bensalem, PA 19020 267-522-8523
info@thegreaterknead.com
www.thegreaterknead.com
Gluten free bagels and bagel chips
Founder/CEO: Michelle Carfagno
CFO: Christina Cassetti
Product Investigator: Mengyi Hu
Account Manager: Maxie Walsh
Warehouse Manager: Joe Otto
Year Founded: 2012
Number Employees: 20-49
Types of Products Distributed:
  General Line

56797 Greek Gourmet Limited
38 Miller Avenue PMB 510
Mill Valley, CA 94941-1927 415-480-8050
Fax: 617-833-6056
Greek specialty products
President: George Nassopoulos
Vice President: Diane Nassopoulos
diane@greekgourmet.com
Sales Director: James Contis
Production Manager: P Margaritidis
Estimated Sales: $2.5-5 Million
Number Employees: 5-9
Number of Brands: 4
Number of Products: 35
Square Footage: 20000
Type of Packaging: Consumer, Food Service, Private Label, Bulk
Types of Products Distributed:
  Frozen Food

56798 Green Gold Group LLC
13905 Stettin Dr
Marathon, WI 54448-9476 715-842-8546
Fax: 715-842-4614 888-533-7288
www.greengoldgroup.com
Ginseng, herbs, whole roots and other health products
Owner: Sam Chen
mail@greengoldgroup.com
CEO: Phouangmala Chen
Estimated Sales: $1-3,000,000
Number Employees: 10-19
Square Footage: 7200
Type of Packaging: Consumer, Bulk
Types of Products Distributed:
  Frozen Food, Health Food, Gingseng, herbs, whole roots, etc.

56799 Green Mountain Graphics
P.O.Box 1417
Long Island City, NY 11101 718-472-3377
Fax: 718-472-4040 www.gm-graphics.com
Manufacturer and wholesaler/distributor of signs, awards and promotional products
President: Eric Greenberg
VP Sales: Steve Goldman
Estimated Sales: $1-2,500,000
Number Employees: 10-19
Square Footage: 6000
Parent Co: Eastern Concepts
Number of Customer Locations: 400
Types of Products Distributed:
  Frozen Food, General Merchandise, Promotional products, signs & awards

56800 Green Valley Food Corp
1501 Market Center Blvd
Dallas, TX 75207-3913 214-939-3900
Fax: 214-939-3999 800-853-8399
www.greenvalleyfood.com
Importer and wholesaler/distributor of cheese, meats, pates, cookies, crackers, breads, jams, jellies, preserves, soups, snack foods, pasta and confections; custom packer of domestic and imported cheeses
Owner: George Chang
Estimated Sales: $2,100,000
Number Employees: 20-49
Square Footage: 120000
Types of Products Distributed:
  Frozen Food, General Line, Provisions/Meat, Specialty Foods, Cheese, cookies, jams, pasta, etc.

56801 Greene Poultry Co
370 Broad St NE
Iron City, GA 39859-2115 229-774-2220
Fax: 229-774-2375 800-960-2220
Wholesaler/distributor of frozen foods, seafood, eggs, meats, vegetable oil, poultry and restaurant supplies
President: Ronnie Ingram
greenepoultry@windstream.net
Sales: Brad Ingram
Manager: Ronnie Ingram
Estimated Sales: $10-20 Million
Number Employees: 20-49
Types of Products Distributed:
  General Line, General Merchandise, Provisions/Meat, Seafood, Eggs, restaurant supplies, etc.

56802 Greenebaum Brothers
PO Box 157
Chicago Heights, IL 60412-0157 708-756-1310
Fax: 708-756-3525 800-755-8779
Wholesaler/distributor of bags and boxes
President: James Greenebaum
Estimated Sales: $1-2.5 Million
Number Employees: 5-9
Square Footage: 24000
Types of Products Distributed:
  Frozen Food, General Merchandise, Bags & boxes

56803 Greenfield Noodle & Spec Co
600 Custer St
Detroit, MI 48202-3128 313-873-2212
Fax: 313-873-0515
Noodles
Owner: Kevin Michaels
VP: Mary Michaels
Estimated Sales: $1.3 Million
Number Employees: 10-19
Square Footage: 26000
Type of Packaging: Consumer, Food Service, Private Label, Bulk
Types of Products Distributed:
  Frozen Food, General Line, Specialty Foods, Specialty & kosher foods

56804 Greenfield Packaging
39 Westmoreland Avenue
White Plains, NY 10606-1937 914-993-0233
Fax: 203-934-7172 gpind@aol.com
We sell stock and custom plastic, glass and aluminum bottles, jars and caps; also, print logos, hex-packs and drums available
President: Debra Greenfield
Executive VP: Barbara Greenfield
Estimated Sales: $1-5,000,000
Types of Products Distributed:
  Frozen Food

56805 Greenley Foods Inc
105 Vine St
Hot Springs, AR 71901-4418 501-321-1188
Fax: 501-623-8829 800-872-0406
www.greenleyfoods.com
Wholesaler/distributor of frozen foods and meats; serving the food service market
Owner: Allen Davis
adavis@greenleyfoods.com
Estimated Sales: Less than $500,000
Number Employees: 5-9
Types of Products Distributed:
  Food Service, Frozen Food, Provisions/Meat

Wholesalers & Distributors / A-Z

56806 Greenvale Electric Supply Corp
385 Greenvale Hwy
Greenvale, NY 11548-1020   516-671-1440
Fax: 516-674-4074 www.greenvaleelectric.com
Wholesaler/distributor of electrical supplies and lighting fixtures
President: Norman Fischman
norman@greenvaleelectric.com
Estimated Sales: $3-5 Million
Number Employees: 20-49
Square Footage: 44000
Number of Customer Locations: 300
Types of Products Distributed:
  Frozen Food, General Merchandise, Electrical supplies & lighting fixtures

56807 Greenwood Associates
6280 W Howard St
Niles, IL 60714-3433   847-579-5500
Fax: 847-579-5501
info@greenwoodassociates.com
www.greenwoodassociates.com
Fruit concentrates and purees
President: Ron Kaplan
Estimated Sales: $5-10 Million
Number Employees: 20-49
Square Footage: 1000
Type of Packaging: Bulk
Types of Products Distributed:
  General Line, Juices & concentrates

56808 Greg's Lobster Company
136 Factory Road
Units 1-3
Harwich Port, MA 02645-1675   508-432-8080
Fax: 508-432-2203
Lobster
President: Leslie Sykes
Estimated Sales: $2.75 Million
Number Employees: 20

56809 Gregory's Foods, Inc.
1301 Trapp Rd
St Paul, MN 55121-1247   651-454-0277
Fax: 651-454-2254   800-231-4734
www.gregorysfoods.com
Frozen baked goods, mixes and bases; bakery ingredients and supplies
President: Greg Helland
cburton@gregorysfoods.com
Quality Control: Tom Hoebbel
Sales/Marketing: Randy Clemons
Estimated Sales: $5.7 Million
Number Employees: 50-99
Square Footage: 44000
Type of Packaging: Food Service, Private Label, Bulk
Private Brands Carried:
  Gregory's
Number of Customer Locations: 500
Types of Products Distributed:
  Food Service, Frozen Food, General Line, General Merchandise, Bakery ingredients & supplies

56810 Greis Brothers
551 Gest St
Cincinnati, OH 45203-1716   513-721-6464
Fax: 513-721-6465 www.greisinc.com
Wholesaler/distributor of general line products
Manager: Mark Bresser
graceink@aol.com
Sales Manager: M Bresser
Estimated Sales: $10-20 Million
Number Employees: 10-19
Square Footage: 20000
Number of Customer Locations: 250
Types of Products Distributed:
  Frozen Food, General Line

56811 Grey Eagle Distributors
2340 Millpark Dr
Maryland Heights, MO 63043   314-429-9100
www.greyeagle.com
Distributor of beers and malt beverages.
President & CEO: David Stokes
jpjasiek@greyeagle.com
VP, Sales & Marketing: Scott Drysdale
Chief Operating Officer: Neil Komadoski
Year Founded: 1963
Estimated Sales: $110 Million
Number Employees: 250-499
Types of Products Distributed:
  Alcohol

56812 Grgich Hills Estates
1829 Saint Helena Hwy S
St Helena, CA 94574-2207   707-963-2784
Fax: 707-963-8725   800-532-3057
info@grgich.com www.grgich.com
Wine
President: Miljenko Mike Grgich
VP Sales/Marketing: Violet Grgich
Public Relations: Kristie Nackordo
VP of Production: Ivo Jeramez
Estimated Sales: $5-9.9 Million
Number Employees: 20-49
Number of Brands: 1
Number of Products: 5
Type of Packaging: Consumer
Private Brands Carried:
  Grgich Hills Cellar

56813 Griesedieck Imports
6501 Hall Street
Saint Louis, MO 63147-2910   314-770-1515
Fax: 314-770-0954
Importer and wholesaler/distributor of German beer and wine
President: Alvin Griesedieck
Estimated Sales: $2.5-5 Million
Number Employees: 1-4
Types of Products Distributed:
  Frozen Food, General Line, German beer & wine

56814 Griffin Food Co
111 S Cherokee St
Muskogee, OK 74403-5420   918-687-6311
Fax: 918-687-3579   800-866-6311
www.griffinfoods.com
Contract packager and wholesaler/distributor of sauces, vegetables and condiments including jams and syrups
Owner: John Griffin
johngriffin@griffinfoods.com
Vice President: David Needham
VP Sales/Marketing: Sam Ramos
Director Midwest Sales: D.C. Smith
Director Southeast Region Sales: Wayne Fuller
Estimated Sales: $16,000,000
Number Employees: 50-99
Square Footage: 648297
Type of Packaging: Consumer, Food Service, Private Label, Bulk
Private Brands Carried:
  Delta; Griffin's; Price Taker
Types of Products Distributed:
  Food Service, General Line, Produce, Condiments, sauces, etc.

56815 Griffin's Seafood
24225 Highway 1
Golden Meadow, LA 70357   985-396-2453
Fax: 985-396-2459
Seafood
Owner: Archie Dantin
Estimated Sales: Under $500,000
Number Employees: 1-4

56816 Griffith Laboratories
10 J Keenleyside Street
Winnipeg, NB R2L 2B9
Canada   204-668-7035
Fax: 204-663-4334 www.griffithlaboratories.com
Wholesaler/distributor of spices
Manager: Murray Spark
Parent Co: Griffith Laboratories
Number of Customer Locations: 500
Types of Products Distributed:
  Frozen Food, General Line, Spices

56817 Grigg Box Company
18900 Fitzpatrick Street
Detroit, MI 48228-1428   313-273-9000
Fax: 313-273-9356 rocco@griggbox.com
www.griggbox.com
Packaging equipment
President: Rocco Franco
General Manager: R Gary Turnbull
Packaging Sales: Leon Cote
Contact: Alan Gentinne
alan@griggbox.com
Plant Manager: Ed Schlacht
Estimated Sales: $10-20 Million
Number Employees: 1-4
Types of Products Distributed:
  Frozen Food, Provisions/Meat

56818 Grocers Ice & Cold Storage Company
725 E Market Street
Louisville, KY 40202-1007   502-584-4112
Fax: 502-587-9148
Wholesaler/distributor of ice
President: Ron Turnier
Contact: Monty Crawford
monty.crawford@whatchefswant.com
Estimated Sales: $1-2.5 Million
Number Employees: 10-19
Types of Products Distributed:
  Frozen Food, General Line, Ice

56819 Grocers Supply Co
3131 E Holcombe Blvd
Houston, TX 77021-2199   713-747-5000
www.grocerssupply.com
Wholesaler/distributor of groceries, meats, produce, frozen foods, equipment and fixtures, general merchandise, private label items and specialty foods; serving the retail market.
Vice President, Produce: Tom Henthorn
Year Founded: 1928
Estimated Sales: $3 Billion
Number Employees: 10,000
Square Footage: 747752
Type of Packaging: Consumer
Private Brands Carried:
  TopCare; Parade; Full Circle; Tippy Toes
Number of Customer Locations: 3000
Types of Products Distributed:
  Frozen Food, General Line, Seafood

56820 Groetsch Wholesale Grocer
5615 Jefferson Hwy
Harahan, LA 70123-5110   504-733-9322
Fax: 504-734-8800 www.gogwg.com
Wholesaler/distributor of groceries, meats, produce, dairy products, frozen foods, baked goods, equipment and fixtures, general merchandise, private label items, candy and health and beauty aids; serving the food service market
General Manager: George Groetsch, Jr.
Inside Sales Manager: George Groetsch
Outside Sales Manager: Mike Licciardi
Transportation Manager: Dennis Burke
Day Shift Warehouse Manager: Emile Carter
Purchasing: Bill Lind
Year Founded: 1917
Estimated Sales: $50-100 Million
Number Employees: 20-49
Square Footage: 60000
Parent Co: George W. Groetsch
Private Brands Carried:
  Red & White
Number of Customer Locations: 450
Types of Products Distributed:
  Food Service, Frozen Food, General Line, General Merchandise, Provisions/Meat, Produce

56821 Groff's Meats
33 N Market St
Elizabethtown, PA 17022-2087   717-367-1246
Fax: 717-367-1952 www.groffsmeats.com
Beef, pork, poultry, deli items and specialty foods
Owner: Nancy Groff
nsgroff@aol.com
VP: Virginia Groff
Estimated Sales: $4 Million
Number Employees: 20-49
Square Footage: 9000
Type of Packaging: Consumer, Food Service, Private Label
Types of Products Distributed:
  Frozen Food

56822 Grounds for Change
15773 George Ln NE
Suite 204
Poulsbo, WA 98370
Fax: 360-779-0402   800-796-6820
info@groundsforchange.com
www.groundsforchange.com
Fair trade organic coffee beans
President/Co-Founder: Kelsey Marshall
Co-Founder: Stacy Marshall *Year Founded:* 2003
Types of Products Distributed:
  General Line

Wholesalers & Distributors / A-Z

56823 Groundwork Coffee Co.
5457 Cleon Ave
North Hollywood, CA 91601 818-506-6020
Fax: 818-506-6035 www.groundworkcoffee.com
Organic coffees and teas
Principal: Jeff Chean
Type of Packaging: Consumer

56824 Grower Direct Marketing
5105 W. Nob Hill Blvd
Yakima, WA 98908 509-972-4476
Fax: 209-931-7920 hanson@growerdirect.net
www.growerdirect.net
Distributor of cherries, blueberries and apricots
Owner: Don Walters
Grower Accounting: Tony Huynh
Food & Ssafety Coordinatot: Natalie Rogina
Director of Marketing: Daniel Moznett
Sales: Don Walters
Operations: Chris Carloni
Estimated Sales: $5-10 Million
Number Employees: 10-19

56825 Grumpe's Specialties
140 Market St
Baird, TX 79504-6406 325-854-1106
Fax: 325-854-1107 866-854-1106
artwork@grumpes.com www.grumpes.com
Personalized lollipops
President: Warren Harkins
Number Employees: 10-19

56826 Guans Mushroom Co
37048 Niles Blvd
P.O.Box 2861
Fremont, CA 94536-1648 510-745-8800
Fax: 510-745-8855 www.guansmushroom.com
Importers, wholesaler/distributor of fresh shiitake and oyster mushrooms and other mushroom products
Manager: Juliet Chu
juliet@guansmushroom.com
Vice President: Juliet Zhu
Estimated Sales: $3-5 Million
Number Employees: 10-19
Square Footage: 60000
Private Brands Carried:
  Guan's
Types of Products Distributed:
  Food Service, Specialty Foods, Shiitake & oyster mushrooms, etc.

56827 Guest Products
1110 W Washington St
Paris, TX 75460-6962 866-412-6726
Fax: 903-785-0023 888-820-6515
www.amsan.com
Wholesaler/distributor of general merchandise including chemicals, paper products, plastics, laundry products and office supplies
Manager: Chip Exum
Estimated Sales: $10-20 Million
Number Employees: 10-19
Types of Products Distributed:
  Frozen Food, General Merchandise, Chemicals, office supplies, paper, etc.

56828 Gulf Arizona Packaging
7720 FM 1960 East
Humble, TX 77346 281-582-6700
Fax: 281-852-1590 800-364-3887
Manufacturer and wholesaler/distributor of packaging equipment and materials including bags, containers, closures, conveyors, labels, linings, tapes, ties, etc
Manager: Paul Corley
General Manager: Paul Corley
General Manager: Jay Crabb
Estimated Sales: $5-10 Million
Number Employees: 5-9
Parent Co: Gulf Systems
Types of Products Distributed:
  Frozen Food, General Merchandise

56829 (HQ)Gulf Food Products Co Inc
509 Commerce Pt
New Orleans, LA 70123-3203 504-733-1516
Fax: 504-733-1517 roberthoy@worldnet.att.net
Seafood
Owner: Albert Lin
gulffoodproducts@aol.com
Estimated Sales: Less than $500,000
Number Employees: 1-4
Square Footage: 16000
Private Brands Carried:
  3 Star; Green Dragon; Sun
Types of Products Distributed:
  Food Service, Seafood

56830 Gulf Marine
501 Louisiana St
Westwego, LA 70094-4141 504-436-2682
Fax: 504-436-1585 sales@gulfmarineproducts.com
www.lapack.com
Shrimp, crawfish and other seafood
President: David Lai
Number Employees: 20-49

56831 Gulf Marine & Industrial Supplies Inc
5801 Armour Dr.
Houston, TX 77020 713-514-8010
Fax: 504-525-4761 800-886-6252
service@gulfmarine.net www.gulfmarine.net
Seafood, pork, beef, poultry, canned and frozen foods, fresh vegetables, beer, wine and other general merchandise
President: John Cotsoradis
General Manager: Dimitris Karmoukos
Estimated Sales: $30-50 Million
Number Employees: 50-99
Square Footage: 250000
Type of Packaging: Food Service
Other Locations:
  Houston, TX
  New Orleans, LA
  Tampa, FL
  Long Beach, CA New Orleans
Private Brands Carried:
  Federated
Types of Products Distributed:
  Frozen Food, General Line, General Merchandise, Provisions/Meat, Produce, Seafood, Alcoholic beverages & canned foods

56832 Gulf Packing Company
618 Commerce St
San Benito, TX 78586-4216 956-399-2631
Fax: 956-399-2675
Meat, including heifer calf and packaged meats
CEO: Charlie Booth
VP: Carlos Salinas
Quality Control Manager: Fred Frausto
Manager: Ace Delacerta
Mngr: Frank Esquivel
Estimated Sales: $10-20 Million
Number Employees: 50 to 99
Type of Packaging: Consumer
Types of Products Distributed:
  Frozen Food, Provisions/Meat

56833 Gulf Pecan Company
5456 Highway 90 W
Mobile, AL 36619-4212 251-661-2931
ulfpecanco@yahoo.com
Farm products and raw materials; dried fruits and vegetables
Owner & President: Danny Fritz
Estimated Sales: $5-9.9,000,000
Number Employees: 3
Types of Products Distributed:
  Produce, Specialty Foods, Dried fruits and vegetables

56834 Gulf Stream Crab Company
13871 Shell Belt Rd
Bayou La Batre, AL 36509 251-824-4717
Fax: 251-824-7416
Crabs
President: Bryan Cumbie
Estimated Sales: $.5-1 million
Number Employees: 1-4

56835 Gulf Systems
801 E Fronton St
Brownsville, TX 78520 800-217-4853
Fax: 956-504-9800 www.gulfpackaging.com
Wholesaler/distributor of packaging equipment and materials
Manager: Blanca Puga
bpuga@gulfsys.com
CFO: Debby Malone
Customer Service Representative: Cathy Wyatt
Estimated Sales: Below $5,000,000
Number Employees: 5-9
Parent Co: Gulf Systems
Types of Products Distributed:
  Frozen Food, General Merchandise

56836 Gulf Systems
2109 Exchange Dr
Arlington, TX 76011 817-261-1915
Fax: 817-861-0092
Wholesaler/distributor of packaging equipment and materials
Manager: Denise Stiger
Contact: Todd Williams
todd_esala@lselectric.com
Estimated Sales: $20-50 Million
Number Employees: 20-49
Parent Co: Gulf Systems
Types of Products Distributed:
  Frozen Food, General Merchandise

56837 Gulf Systems
7720 fm 960 e
Humble, TX 77346 405-528-2293
Fax: 281-852-1590 800-364-3887
customerservicehumble@gulfpackaging.com
www.gulfpackaging.com
Wholesaler/distributor of packaging equipment and materials
Customer Service Representative: Cathy Wyatt
Estimated Sales: $2.5-5,000,000
Number Employees: 5-9
Parent Co: Gulf Systems
Types of Products Distributed:
  Frozen Food, General Merchandise

56838 Gulf Systems
7720 fm 960 e
Humble, TX 77346 405-528-2293
Fax: 281-852-1590 800-364-3887
customerservicehumble@gulfpackaging.com
www.gulfpackaging.com
Wholesaler/distributor of packaging equipment and materials
Customer Service Representative: Cathy Wyatt
Estimated Sales: $1-5,000,000
Number Employees: 5-9
Parent Co: Gulf Systems
Types of Products Distributed:
  Frozen Food, General Merchandise

56839 Gulf Systems
3815 N Santa Fe Ave
Oklahoma City, OK 73108 800-364-3887
Fax: 405-557-0903
Wholesaler/distributor of packaging equipment and materials
Customer Service Representative: Cathy Wyatt
Estimated Sales: $5-10,000,000
Number Employees: 5-9
Parent Co: Gulf Systems
Types of Products Distributed:
  Frozen Food, General Merchandise

56840 Gunderland Marine Supply
1221 Cantwell Corpus Cristi
Corpus Christi, TX 98469 361-882-4231
Fax: 361-888-5622
Wholesaler/distributor of groceries, produce, dairy items, baked goods, frozen foods, meats, seafood, equipment and fixtures, etc.; serving the food service market
President: Ken Gunderland
Manager: Bob Beauchamp
Number Employees: 20-49
Square Footage: 216000
Types of Products Distributed:
  Food Service, Frozen Food, General Line, General Merchandise, Provisions/Meat, Produce, Seafood, Groceries, baked goods, etc.

56841 Gunther Salt Co
101 Buchanan St
St Louis, MO 63147-3537 314-241-1725
Fax: 314-241-1725 800-873-7258
info@gunthersalt.com www.gunthersalt.com
Wholesaler/distributor of salt to food manufacturers, distributors and food service companies
Owner: Jerry Gunther
john.gunther@gunthersalt.com
VP Sales/Marketing: John Gunther
Sales Director: David Steidemann
Plant Manager: Jerry Gunther, Jr.
Estimated Sales: $1-2.5 Million
Number Employees: 20-49
Number of Brands: 4
Number of Products: 6
Square Footage: 200000
Type of Packaging: Food Service, Bulk

Wholesalers & Distributors / A-Z

Private Brands Carried:
  Diamond Crystal; Cargill; United; Gunther
Number of Customer Locations: 1
Types of Products Distributed:
  Food Service, General Line, Salt

56842 Gutierrez Brothers
5401 E Tecumseh St
Tulsa, OK 74115-4226   918-584-6179
                    Fax: 918-584-6170
Wholesaler/distributor of bananas
President: Be Gutierrez
Estimated Sales: $1-2.5 Million
Number Employees: 1-4
Square Footage: 36000
Types of Products Distributed:
  General Line, Produce, Bananas

56843 Guy Locicero & Sons
12349 87th Ave
Pleasant Prairie, WI 53158-2403   262-657-7163
         Fax: 262-657-4480 800-851-6888
Wholesaler/distributor of groceries, meat, produce, frozen food, baked goods, paper and cleaning products, seafood and private label items
CEO/President: Ronald Rizzo
Buyer/Manager: Thomas Cardinali
Buyer: Rob Wade
Estimated Sales: $5-10 Million
Number Employees: 10-19
Square Footage: 76000
Private Brands Carried:
  Frosty Acres
Types of Products Distributed:
  General Line, Provisions/Meat, Produce, Seafood, Paper products, baked goods

56844 H & R Coffee Co
2985 Mercury Rd
Jacksonville, FL 32207-7968   904-737-8096
      Fax: 904-737-7946 800-473-7572
sunbelt@coffeeperks.com www.coffeeperks.com
Wholesaler/distributor of coffee, tea, filter and coffee and tea making equipment; serving the food service market
President: Christian Hosking
Manager: Bill Defeo
Manager: Mark Weldon
Estimated Sales: $5-10 Million
Number Employees: 20-49
Private Brands Carried:
  H&R; Maxwell House; Bum-O-Matic
Types of Products Distributed:
  Food Service, Frozen Food, General Line, General Merchandise, Coffee, tea, coffee & tea equipment

56845 H A Phillips & Co
770 Enterprise Ave
Dekalb, IL 60115-7904   630-377-0050
       Fax: 630-377-2706 info@haphillips.com
                    www.haphillips.com
Manufacturer and exporter of float controls, valves and pressure vessels for ammonia refrigeration systems; wholesaler/distributor and importer of pressure regulating and solenoid valves
President/Chief Executive Officer: Michael R. Ryan
Executive Director: John Schroeder
Vice-President of Finance: Janet L. Jones
Vice-President of Engineering: Steve L. . Yagla, P.E
R&D/Quality Control: Mike Ryan
Sales/Marketing: Ed Murziuski
Corporate Sales Manager: Thomas W. Herman
Secretary/Vice President of Human Resour: Mary Wright
Operations Manager: Andrew McCullough
Vice President of Manufacturing: Brian J. Youssi
Plant Manager: David Williams
Purchasing Manager: Rou Coleman
Estimated Sales: $4.2 Million
Number Employees: 20-49
Square Footage: 60000
Private Brands Carried:
  Danfoss
Types of Products Distributed:
  Frozen Food, General Merchandise, Pressure regulating & solenoid valves

56846 H B Day Co
604 W 48th St
New York, NY 10036-1195   212-246-6589
       Fax: 212-586-6349 www.hbday.com
Wholesaler/distributor of groceries and frozen foods; serving the food service market
Manager: Tom Egan Jr
VP: N Egan
Estimated Sales: $20-50 Million
Number Employees: 10-19
Square Footage: 20000
Type of Packaging: Bulk
Types of Products Distributed:
  Food Service, Frozen Food, General Line, Groceries

56847 H Brooks & Co
600 Lakeview Point Dr
St Paul, MN 55112-3494   651-635-0126
       Fax: 651-746-2210 www.hbrooks.com
Wholesaler/distributor of produce and frozen fruits and vegetables
President: Phillip Brooks
phillip.brooks@hbrooks.com
Secretary/Treasurer: Raymond Ralston
Estimated Sales: $20-50 Million
Number Employees: 500-999
Types of Products Distributed:
  Frozen Food, Produce

56848 H Schrier & Co Inc
4901 Glenwood Rd
Brooklyn, NY 11234-1131   718-258-7500
       Fax: 718-258-9586 www.schrierfoodservice.com
Wholesaler/distributor of groceries, frozen foods, produce and general merchandise; serving the food service market.
Estimated Sales: $50-100 Million
Number Employees: 100
Square Footage: 110000
Private Brands Carried:
  Nugget; Rose Leaf
Number of Customer Locations: 3000
Types of Products Distributed:
  Food Service, Frozen Food, General Line, General Merchandise, Produce, Groceries

56849 H Weiss Co LLC
12 Labriola Ct # 1
Armonk, NY 10504-1342   914-273-4400
       Fax: 914-273-4437 Sales@Hweiss.net
Wholesaler/distributor of equipment and supplies; serving the food service market
Owner: Elizabeth Weiss
VP: Joseph Marino
VP: James Weiss
Estimated Sales: $10-20 Million
Number Employees: 20-49
Square Footage: 84000
Types of Products Distributed:
  Food Service, Frozen Food, General Merchandise, Equipment & supplies

56850 H&H Pretzel
P.O.Box 112350
Cleveland, OH 44111   216-251-4490
                    Fax: 216-251-2035
Wholesaler/distributor of snack foods including pretzels, potato chips, cookies and crackers; serving the food service market
President: Carolyn Hufford
Estimated Sales: $10-20 Million
Number Employees: 20-49
Types of Products Distributed:
  Food Service, Frozen Food, Snack foods

56851 (HQ)H&H Wood Products
5600 Camp Rd
Hamburg, NY 14075   716-648-5600
       Fax: 716-648-3246 hhwood1@aol.com
Wooden pallets; heat treating service
President: William Heussler
williamheussler@voestalpine.com
Production Coordinator: Richard Perez
Estimated Sales: $3 Million
Number Employees: 20-49
Square Footage: 52000
Type of Packaging: Bulk
Other Locations:
  H&H Wood Products
  Hamburg, NYH&H Wood Products

56852 H&S Edible Products Corporation
119 Fulton Lane
Mount Vernon, NY 10550-4697   914-664-4041
         Fax: 914-664-8304 800-253-3364
Dry bread crumbs, nuts
President: Mari Rowan
Vice President: Peter Rowan
Estimated Sales: $2,000,000
Number Employees: 20-49
Number of Products: 1
Square Footage: 13000
Type of Packaging: Food Service, Private Label, Bulk
Number of Customer Locations: 37

56853 H.B. Paulk Grocery Company
601 Highway 52 E
Opp, AL 36467   334-493-3255
                    Fax: 334-493-7966
Wholesaler/distributor of groceries, dairy products, frozen foods, equipment and fixtures, general merchandise, private label items, candy and health/beauty aids
President: F Youmans
Executive VP: Jeff Gwinne
VP Sales: Chuck Cates
Estimated Sales: $20-50 Million
Number Employees: 100-249
Square Footage: 70000
Number of Customer Locations: 1250
Types of Products Distributed:
  Frozen Food, General Line, General Merchandise, Groceries, candy, dairy products, etc.

56854 H.C. Williams Peanut Company
123 Westend Avenue
Ashburn, GA 31714-5130   912-567-3315
Wholesaler/distributor of nuts; warehouse providing dry storage of nuts; rail siding services available
President: Tim Brown
Estimated Sales: Less than $500,000
Number Employees: 1-4
Types of Products Distributed:
  General Line, Nuts

56855 H.P. Beale & Sons
PO Box 97
Courtland, VA 23837-0097   757-653-2150
                    Fax: 757-653-0348
Wholesaler/distributor of meats; serving the food service market
President: B Hubert Beale
VP/Manager: Gene Beale
Estimated Sales: $2.5-5 Million
Number Employees: 5-9
Types of Products Distributed:
  Food Service, Frozen Food, Provisions/Meat, Country ham, smoked jowls, etc.

56856 (HQ)H.T. Hackney Company
502 S. Gay St.
PO Box 238
Knoxville, TN 37901   865-546-1291
       Fax: 865-546-1501 www.hthackney.com
Wholesaler/distributor of groceries and frozen foods
President: Bob Hall
CEO: Bill Sanson
CEO: William B Sansom
Contact: Linda Andrews
linda.andrews@hthackney.com
Estimated Sales: $16.6 Million
Number Employees: 3600
Private Brands Carried:
  Del Monte; Kellogg; Campbell's
Types of Products Distributed:
  Frozen Food, General Line, Groceries

56857 H.Y. Louie Company
2821 Production Way
Burnaby, BC V5A 3G7
Canada   604-421-4242
Wholesaler/distributor of frozen foods, groceries and seafood; serving the food service market
President/COO: Brandt Louie
Chairman/CEO: Tong Louie
VP Finance/Management Service: Randy Melynchenko
Private Brands Carried:
  Cavalier; IGA
Number of Customer Locations: 470
Types of Products Distributed:
  Food Service, Frozen Food, General Line, Seafood, Groceries

56858 H20 Technology
885 Arapahoe Avenue
Boulder, CO 80302-6011   303-415-1253
         Fax: 303-447-1392 800-670-7426
Wholesaler/distributor and exporter of bottled water

1027

Wholesalers & Distributors / A-Z

CEO/President: Merlin Yockstick
VP Finances: Hazel Chandler
VP Marketing: Vickie Brown
Number Employees: 1-4
Type of Packaging: Private Label
Private Brands Carried:
  Nordstrom Water; Merlin; Wild Water Plus
Types of Products Distributed:
  Frozen Food, General Line, Bottled water

56859 HAS Packaging System
21500 Blythe St
Canoga Park, CA 91304-4910 818-712-0100
  Fax: 818-712-0470 800-326-5937
Wholesaler/distributor of plastic bags, corrugated and paperboard boxes, blister cards, conveyors, film, cartons, packaging materials and systems and material handling equipment; also, code dating, packaging and wrapping machinery
Owner: Jaz Manak
jazmanak@hsapackaging.com
Estimated Sales: $5-10 Million
Number Employees: 5-9
Types of Products Distributed:
  Frozen Food, General Merchandise, Boxes, bags, film, conveyors, etc.

56860 (HQ)HAVI Group
3500 Lacey Road
Suite 600
Downers Grove, IL 60515 630-353-4200
  Fax: 630-434-0894
Wholesaler/distributor of dry and frozen foods; serving McDonald's
President: Haluk Ilkdemirci
CEO: Russ Smyth
Co-Founder/Chairman: Theodore F Perlman
COO: Dan Musachia
Contact: Wolfgang Urhahn
wurhahn@havigroup.com
Chief Strategy Officer: Howard Katz
Number Employees: 20-49
Other Locations:
  HAVI Group
  Whitewater, WIHAVI Group
Types of Products Distributed:
  Food Service, Frozen Food, General Line, Dry foods

56861 HC Brill Company
1912 Montreal Rd
Tucker, GA 30084 770-938-3823
  Fax: 770-939-2934 800-241-8526
  www.hcbrill.com
Ingredients and mixes
President: Cefo Grteor
CEO: Bret Weaver
Estimated Sales: $5-10 000,000
Number Employees: 50-99

56862 HD Supply Waterworks
5905 Old Rutledge Pike
Knoxville, TN 37924-2242 865-546-3225
  Fax: 865-546-3448 www.hdsupply.com
Wholesaler/distributor of general merchandise including electrical supplies, lamps, switches, air-conditioning and lighting fixtures
Manager: Jeff Smith
Manager: Terry Spencer
Estimated Sales: $1-2.5 Million
Number Employees: 5-9
Parent Co: Hughes Supply
Types of Products Distributed:
  Frozen Food, General Merchandise, Electrical supplies, lamps, etc.

56863 HE Anderson Co
2025 Anderson Dr
Muskogee, OK 74403-2439 918-687-4426
  Fax: 918-682-3342 www.heanderson.com
Wholesaler/distributor of general merchandise, private label items, health/beauty aids and equipment and fixtures; rack jobber services available
President: H E Anderson Jr
deb@heanderson.com
VP: Mark Anderson
Sales Exec: Deb Olinger
Estimated Sales: $20-50 Million
Number Employees: 10-19
Square Footage: 100000
Number of Customer Locations: 2500
Types of Products Distributed:
  Frozen Food, General Merchandise, Rack Jobbers

56864 HERB Enterprises
Pembroke Pines, FL 33025-4313 954-704-1886
  Fax: 954-704-1887 800-498-4076
Wholesaler/distributor of hotel and restaurant equipment; also, construction materials and supplies; serving the food service and hotel market
Owner: Eduardo Flores
CEO: Helene Frankel
Number Employees: 5-9
Types of Products Distributed:
  Food Service, Frozen Food, General Merchandise, Hotel & restaurant equipment, etc.

56865 HFM Foodservice
716 Umi St
Honolulu, HI 96819-2391 808-843-3200
  Fax: 808-843-3211 www.hfmfoodservice.com
Bakery flour and ingredients, frozen and specialty foods, canned goods, meats, etc.
President: Barry O'Connell
boconnell@hfm.com
Executive VP Finance: Michael Fujimoto
Sales Manager: Eric Schwager
Number Employees: 100-249
Parent Co: Kerr Pacific Corporation
Other Locations:
  Maui
  Kahului, HI
  Big Island
  Hilo, HI
  Kauai
  Lihue, HIMauiHilo
Types of Products Distributed:
  Food Service, General Line, General Merchandise, Provisions/Meat, Specialty Foods, Paper products, canned goods, etc.

56866 HIB Foods Inc
3311 Farrington St
Flushing, NY 11354-2820 718-762-1677
  Fax: 718-445-5562
Wholesaler/distributor of frozen food, provisions/meats, cold cuts, dairy products, French cookies and plastic and paper boxes; serving the food service market
President: Frank Roman
Estimated Sales: $10-20 Million
Number Employees: 10-19
Types of Products Distributed:
  Food Service, Frozen Food, General Line, General Merchandise, Provisions/Meat, Cold cuts, dairy products, boxes, etc.

56867 HMG Provisions
PO Box 172
Perkasie, PA 18944-0172 215-257-4606
Wholesaler/distributor of provisions/meats and cheeses; serving the food service market in Southeast Pennsylvania
President: Scott Gulick
VP: Richard Mill
Number Employees: 1-4
Square Footage: 8000
Private Brands Carried:
  Bomberger's Lebanon Bologna
Types of Products Distributed:
  Food Service, Frozen Food, General Line, Provisions/Meat, Cheese

56868 HPC Foodservice
625 Nutmeg Rd N
South Windsor, CT 06074
  Fax: 800-282-5898 800-883-9800
  www.hpcfs.com
Wholesaler/distributor of groceries, dairy products, produce, private label items, chemicals, meat, frozen foods, equipment and fixtures and paper goods; serving the food service market.
President: Barry Pearson
bpearson@hpcfs.com
Controller: Keith Chambers
Chief Information Officer: Kevin Sullivan
Chief Operating Officer: Richard Lotstein
Year Founded: 1908
Estimated Sales: $55 Million
Number Employees: 100-249
Square Footage: 65000
Private Brands Carried:
  Frosty Acre
Types of Products Distributed:
  Food Service, Frozen Food, General Line, General Merchandise, Provisions/Meat, Produce, Dairy products, equipment & groceries

56869 HRS Food Service
P.O.Box 1516
Aberdeen, SD 57402-1516 605-225-1275
  Fax: 605-225-6537 800-888-2617
Wholesaler/distributor of groceries, milk, eggs, frozen foods, produce, baked goods, private label items, equipment and meat; serving the food service market. The company will be merging with Cash-Wa Distributing but will maintaintheir identities for the time being, while operating under the corporate name of Cash-Wa Distributing
President/CEO: Charles Hogg
Estimated Sales: $5-10 Million
Number Employees: 5-9
Square Footage: 368000
Private Brands Carried:
  NIFDA
Number of Customer Locations: 750
Types of Products Distributed:
  Food Service, Frozen Food, General Line, General Merchandise, Provisions/Meat, Produce, Groceries, milk, eggs, etc.

56870 HSN Data Corporation
7828 Carina Court
Lake Worth, FL 33467-7836 561-642-6145
  Fax: 561-642-7738 hsnweb@hsndata.com
Wholesaler/distributor of promotional products; serving the food service market
President: Harvey Newmark
harvey@webtownusa.com
Number Employees: 1-4
Number of Customer Locations: 100
Types of Products Distributed:
  Food Service, Frozen Food, General Merchandise, Promotional products

56871 Hacienda Mexican Foods
6100 Buchanan St
Detroit, MI 48210-2400 313-895-8823
  Fax: 313-894-2439 www.haciendadegutierrez.com
Mexican foods
Owner: Brenda Albores
Sales Director Tim Lee
balbores@detroitmifooddistributor.com
Estimated Sales: $5-10 Million
Number Employees: 50-99

56872 Haddad Supply Company
P.O.Box 329
Enid, OK 73702 580-234-8414
Wholesaler/distributor of frozen foods and provisions/meats; serving the food service market
President: J Haddad
Number Employees: 1-4
Types of Products Distributed:
  Food Service, Frozen Food, Provisions/Meat

56873 (HQ)Haddon House Food Products
250 Old Marlton Pike
Medford, NJ 08055-8760 609-654-7901
  Fax: 609-654-8533
Wholesaler/distributor of specialty foods
President: H Anderson
CEO: David Anderson
danderson@haddonhouse.com
Estimated Sales: $36.7 Million
Number Employees: 200-499
Square Footage: 130000
Other Locations:
  Haddon House Food Products
  Richburg, SCHaddon House Food Products
Private Brands Carried:
  Barondorf; McMurphy's; Medford Farms
Number of Customer Locations: 5000
Types of Products Distributed:
  Frozen Food, Specialty Foods

56874 Hadley Fruit Orchards
48980 Seminole Dr
Cabazon, CA 92230 951-849-5255
  Fax: 951-849-1979 800-854-5655
  www.hadleyfruitorchards.com
Importer, exporter and wholesaler/distributor of dried fruits including apricots, dates, figs and prunes; also, nuts including pecans, cashews and pistachios; gift packs available
Manager: Wayne Dixon
CFO: Fred Bond
Manager: Jay Baczkowski
jbaczkowski@morongo-nsn.gov

Estimated Sales: $2.5-5 Million
Number Employees: 20-49
Square Footage: 200000
Type of Packaging: Consumer
Types of Products Distributed:
  Frozen Food, General Line, Dried fruits & nuts

56875 Hahn Produce Corporation
240 Food Center Drive
Bronx, NY 10474-7030   718-842-1152
Wholesaler/distributor of produce
Manager: Bill McRoberts
Estimated Sales: $1-2.5 Million
Number Employees: 1-4
Parent Co: Nick Penachio Company
Types of Products Distributed:
  Frozen Food, Produce

56876 Haile Resources
2650 Freewood Dr
Dallas, TX 75220-2511   214-357-1471
  Fax: 214-357-9381 debbie@haileresources.com
Broker of flavors, xanthan and other gums, yeast extracts, food grade chemicals and nutraceuticals, frozen produce, fruit juice concentrates and purees, dried fruit and industrial ingredients
President: Chris Beninate
chris@haileresources.com
EVP: Debbie Haile
Sales: Emilea Champion
Operations: Joyce Cokes
Estimated Sales: $40 Million
Number Employees: 5-9
Square Footage: 20000
Type of Packaging: Food Service, Private Label, Bulk

56877 Hain Food Group
255 W Carob Street
Compton, CA 90220-5209   516-237-6200
         Fax: 516-237-7450
Wholesaler/distributor of natural and organic beans, chilis and snack foods including tortilla and potato chips, puffs, corn chips and candy
President: Andrew Jacobson
VP Technical Services: Myron Cooper
General Manager: Steve Schorr
Number Employees: 50-99
Square Footage: 200000
Parent Co: Westbrae Natural
Private Brands Carried:
  Little Bear; Bearitos
Types of Products Distributed:
  Frozen Food, Health Food, Snacks, beans & chilis

56878 Haitai Inc
7227 Telegraph Rd
Montebello, CA 90640   323-724-7337
         www.haitaiusa.com
Wholesaler/distributor of frozen foods, seafood, specialty food items, dairy products, etc.; importer of canned and bottled beverages, dry and frozen fish, grains and pasta; exporter of fresh fruits, orange and pineapple frozenconcentrates and frozen beef.
President & CEO: Warren Jung
Year Founded: 1981
Estimated Sales: $100-500 Million
Number Employees: 50-99
Square Footage: 100000
Number of Customer Locations: 600
Types of Products Distributed:
  Frozen Food, General Line, General Merchandise, Produce, Seafood, Specialty Foods, Grocerices & dairy products

56879 Hal-One Plastics
801 E Highway 56
Olathe, KS 66061-4999   913-782-3535
  Fax: 913-764-7369 800-626-5784
Manufacturer and wholesaler/distributor of reusable plastic tableware and trays
CEO: Joyce Stawarz
1st Executive VP Sales: Galen Soule
Estimated Sales: $10-20 Million
Number Employees: 50-99
Square Footage: 60000
Types of Products Distributed:
  Frozen Food, General Merchandise, Reuseable plastic tableware & trays

56880 Halal Fine Foods
73 Galaxy Blvd
Units 11 & 12
Toronto, ON M9W 5T4
Canada   416-679-8000
  info@halalfinefood.com
  www.halalfinefood.com
Halal foods including mantu, ashak, sauces, ready meals, cookies, and soups
President: Matin Hakimi
CEO, Director: Mohammad Amin
Account Manager: Rita Raji
Office Manager: Iwona Hakimi
Production Manager: Yusif Zafar
Types of Products Distributed:
  General Line

56881 Hale Tea Co
235 Oak Ridge Cir
Richmond Hill, GA 31324-5370   912-727-3993
  Fax: 912-727-3995 888-425-3832
  sales@haletea.com www.haletea.com
Importer and manufacturer of gourmet specialty teas and tea bags
Owner: Lisa Brown
Estimated Sales: Under $500,000
Number Employees: 1-4
Type of Packaging: Food Service, Private Label, Bulk
Private Brands Carried:
  Oglethorpe Tea; Charles Towne Tea; Hale Tea;

56882 (HQ)Hale-Halsell Company
9111 E Pine St
Tulsa, OK 74115   918-835-4484
         Fax: 918-641-5474
Wholesaler/distributor of groceries, meats, dairy products, frozen foods, baked goods and general merchandise
President/COO: J Lewis
Chairman/CEO: R Hawk
VP Marketing: Paul Stephens
Number Employees: 250-499
Square Footage: 1604000
Private Brands Carried:
  High Top
Number of Customer Locations: 387
Types of Products Distributed:
  Frozen Food, General Line, General Merchandise, Provisions/Meat, Baked goods, dairy products, etc.

56883 Hall & Cole Produce
11 New England Produce Center
Chelsea, MA 02150-1720   617-884-2360
  Fax: 617-884-0079 800-225-4486
Wholesaler/distributor of produce
Office Manager: Steve McClusky
Estimated Sales: $5-10 Million
Number Employees: 10-19
Types of Products Distributed:
  Frozen Food, Produce

56884 Hall-Woolford Wood TankCo Inc
5500 N Water St
Philadelphia, PA 19120-3093   215-329-9022
  Fax: 215-329-1177 jackhillman@woodtank.com
         www.woodtank.com
Manufacturer and exporter of noncorrosive wood tanks, vats and tubs; wholesaler/distributor of flexible tank liners; industrial wood products; all products FDA approved. Also industrial wood products
President: Scott Hochhauser
woodtanks@aol.com
Sales Manager: Jack Hillman
Operations Manager: Robert Riepen
Estimated Sales: $1-3 Million
Number Employees: 5-9
Square Footage: 38000
Types of Products Distributed:
  General Merchandise, Flexible tank liners, wood tanks

56885 Halsey Foodservice
401 Lanier Rd.
PO Box 6485
Huntsville, AL 35824-0485   256-772-9691
  Fax: 256-461-8386 800-621-0240
  sales@halseyfoodservice.com
  www.halseyfoodservice.com
Fresh and frozen meats, produce, condiments, canned goods and kitchen supplies
President & CEO: Cecilia Halsey
Estimated Sales: $33 Million
Number Employees: 106
Number of Brands: 9
Square Footage: 157000
Private Brands Carried:
  Code
Types of Products Distributed:
  Food Service, Frozen Food, General Line, General Merchandise, Provisions/Meat, Produce, Dairy & baked goods

56886 Halsey Reid Equipment
395 Sagewood Ter
Buffalo, NY 14221   716-895-7800
         Fax: 716-895-0211
Wholesaler/distributor of forklifts
Manager: James Pettis
VP: James Pettis
Estimated Sales: $2.5-5 Million
Number Employees: 5-9
Private Brands Carried:
  P.C.M.; Prime Mover; Legend
Types of Products Distributed:
  Frozen Food, General Merchandise, Forklifts

56887 Hama Hama Oyster® Company
301 N Webb Rd
Lilliwaup, WA 98555   360-877-6938
  Fax: 360-877-6942 888-877-5844
Seafood
Owner: David Robins
Sales, Wholesale: Adam James
Estimated Sales: $500,000-$1,000,000
Number Employees: 1-4
Type of Packaging: Private Label, Bulk

56888 Hamill Industrial SalesCompany
5800 Monroe St
Sylvania, OH 43560-2263   419-824-5399
         Fax: 419-885-5182
Wholesaler/distributor of material handling equipment including stainless steel conveyors, flow racks and push-back racks
Owner: Skip Agnew
Estimated Sales: $.5-1 million
Number Employees: 1-4
Private Brands Carried:
  J.B. Webb; Buschman; Konstant
Types of Products Distributed:
  Frozen Food, General Merchandise, Material handling equipment

56889 Hamilos Bros Inspected Meat
1117 Greenwood St
Madison, IL 62060-1234   618-876-3710
         Fax: 618-876-3732
Meat and fresh and frozen fish; wholesaler/distributor of canned goods, paper products and pre-packaged meat
Owner: Mike Skinner
Owner: Jeff Skinner
Estimated Sales: $500,000-$1 Million
Number Employees: 5-9
Type of Packaging: Consumer
Types of Products Distributed:
  General Line, General Merchandise, Provisions/Meat, Canned goods, paper products, etc.

56890 Hammill International
PO Box 4968
Orange, CA 92863-4968   714-637-0344
  Fax: 714-637-0469 800-228-2129
Wholesaler/distributor of slip resistant, washable footwear
Operations Manager: Michael Alexander
Estimated Sales: Less than $500,000
Number Employees: 1-4
Types of Products Distributed:
  Food Service, Frozen Food, General Merchandise, Slip resistant, washable footwear

56891 Hamms
213 N Tennessee St
McKinney, TX 75069-3922   972-542-3359
         Fax: 972-562-7511
Wholesaler/distributor of frozen food and provisions/meats; also, rack jobber services available; serving the food service market
Owner: Ken Uselton
VP: E Hamm, Jr.
Estimated Sales: $300,000-500,000
Number Employees: 1-4
Number of Customer Locations: 95

Wholesalers & Distributors / A-Z

Types of Products Distributed:
Food Service, Frozen Food, Provisions/Meat, Rack Jobbers

56892 Hampton Chutney Company
6 Main Street
Amagansett, NY 11930   631-267-3131
      Fax: 631-267-6169   info@hamptonchutney.com
                          www.hamptonchutney.com
Fresh chutneys
Owner: Gary MacGurn
Co-Owner: Isabel MacGurn
Chef: Patty Gentry
Estimated Sales: Less than $500,000
Number Employees: 5-9
Number of Customer Locations: 3

56893 Hampton Roads SeafoodsLtd
PO Box 271
Hampton, VA 23669-0271   757-723-3363
                     Fax: 757-722-5334
Wholesaler/distributor of fresh and frozen seafood; serving the food service market
President: John G Marshall
Plant Manager: Ronald E Saulman
Estimated Sales: $3-5 Million
Number Employees: 5-9
Square Footage: 100000
Type of Packaging: Bulk
Types of Products Distributed:
Food Service, Frozen Food, Seafood

56894 Handi-Rak Service
6139 W US Highway 60
Brookline Station, MO 65619-9441   417-862-2367
                Fax: 417-862-2039 800-221-6773
Wholesaler/distributor of general merchandise
President: R Hudopeth
Secretary: D Webb
Estimated Sales: $20-50 Million
Number Employees: 20-49
Number of Customer Locations: 300
Types of Products Distributed:
Frozen Food, General Merchandise

56895 Handling & Storage Concepts
P.O.Box 4671
Chesterfield, MO 63006   314-776-8146
                     Fax: 314-776-3020
Wholesaler/distributor of material handling equipment
President: Vincent John Nolan
Sales Manager: Tom Nolan
Estimated Sales: $2.5-5 Million
Number Employees: 50-99
Private Brands Carried:
Nissan; Baker; Barrett
Types of Products Distributed:
Frozen Food, General Merchandise, Material handling equipment

56896 Handling Systems Inc
2659 E Magnolia St
Phoenix, AZ 85034-6923   602-275-2228
      Fax: 602-275-2424   800-229-9977
                          catalog@handlingsystems.com
                          www.handlingsystems.com
Wholesaler/distributor of material handling equipment
President: Charles Martiny
Manager: Chris Schmidt
cschmidt@handlingsystems.com
Estimated Sales: F
Number Employees: 100-249
Private Brands Carried:
Nissan; Raymond; Dockstocker
Types of Products Distributed:
Frozen Food, General Merchandise, Material handling equipment

56897 Handling Systems Inc
2659 E Magnolia St
Phoenix, AZ 85034-6923   602-275-2228
      Fax: 602-275-2424   800-229-9977
                          www.handlingsystems.com
Wholesaler/distributor of material handling equipment
President: LeRoy Mohrman
Manager: Chris Schmidt
cschmidt@handlingsystems.com
Estimated Sales: $5-10 Million
Number Employees: 100-249
Private Brands Carried:
Toyota; Prexell; Prime

Types of Products Distributed:
Frozen Food, General Merchandise, Material handling equipment

56898 (HQ)Handy Pax
53 York Ave
Randolph, MA 2368   781-963-8300
Snack foods
President: Jay Sussman
Sales Manager: David Sussman
Number Employees: 10-19
Type of Packaging: Consumer, Private Label
Types of Products Distributed:
Frozen Food, Snack foods

56899 Handy's Milk & Ice Cream
1249 W County Road 125 S
Greencastle, IN 46135-8479   765-653-5181
Wholesaler/distributor of juice and dairy products including milk, cheese and ice cream; serving the food service market
Owner: Norman Handy
Estimated Sales: $5-10 Million
Number Employees: 5-9
Types of Products Distributed:
Food Service, General Line, Dairy products

56900 Hanif's International Foods
563 Ebury Place
Delta, BC V3M 6M8
Canada   604-540-4001
           Fax: 604-540-4002 888-540-4009
                          hanifs@direct.ca
Importer and wholesaler/distributor of spices, beans, lentils and Middle Eastern foods
Owner: Hanif Ratanshi
Co Owner: S Ratanshi
Sales Director: Sheila Ratanshi
Number Employees: 30
Square Footage: 116000
Type of Packaging: Consumer, Food Service, Private Label, Bulk
Types of Products Distributed:
Frozen Food, Health Food, Produce, Specialty Foods, Spices, beans & lentils

56901 Hanmi
5675 Oakbrook Pkwy Ste D
Norcross, GA 30093   770-242-0237
                     Fax: 770-447-6514
Wholesaler/distributor of Oriental foods; serving the food service market
President: Young Kim
Estimated Sales: $2.5-5 Million
Number Employees: 5-9
Types of Products Distributed:
Food Service, Frozen Food, Specialty Foods, Oriental foods

56902 Hannaford Bros Co
145 Pleasant Hill Rd
Scarborough, ME 04074-7118   207-883-2911
      Fax: 207-833-7555   800-213-9040
                          www.hannaford.com
Wholesaler/distributor of general merchandise and groceries
President: Michael Vail
michael_vail@hannaford.com
CEO: Ronald C Hodge
Chairman: J Moody, Jr.
Number Employees: 10000+
Parent Co: Delhaize America
Types of Products Distributed:
Frozen Food, General Line, General Merchandise

56903 Hanover Potato Products Inc
60 Black Rock Rd
Hanover, PA 17331-4106   717-632-0700
                     Fax: 717-632-0756
Potato products
Owner: Kendra Kauffman
office@hanoverchamber.com
Estimated Sales: $250,000
Number Employees: 10-19
Square Footage: 17400
Parent Co: Hanover Foods Corp
Type of Packaging: Food Service
Number of Customer Locations: 426
Types of Products Distributed:
Food Service, Frozen Food, Fresh potatoes: whole, diced & fried

56904 Hanover Uniform Co
3501 Marmenco Ct
Baltimore, MD 21230-3411   410-235-8338
      Fax: 410-235-6071   800-541-9709
                          info@hanoveruniform.com
                          www.hanoveruniform.com
Wholesaler/distributor and exporter of uniforms; serving the food service market
President: John Mintz
jmintz@hanoveruniform.com
Office Manager: John Mintz
Estimated Sales: $2.5-5 Million
Number Employees: 20-49
Type of Packaging: Food Service
Types of Products Distributed:
Food Service, Frozen Food, General Merchandise, Uniforms

56905 Hans Holterbosch Inc
375 Park Ave # 2503
New York, NY 10152-2506   212-421-3800
                     Fax: 212-755-5271
Importer and wholesaler/distributor of beer
Executive Director: Daphne Marcial
Estimated Sales: $1-2.5 Million
Number Employees: 1-4
Type of Packaging: Consumer, Food Service
Private Brands Carried:
Hoffbrau
Types of Products Distributed:
Frozen Food, General Line, Beer

56906 Hansen Beverage Co
1 Monster Way
Corona, CA 92879-7101   951-739-6200
      Fax: 951-739-6210   800-426-7367
                          info@hansens.com www.hansenenergy.com
Wholesaler/distributor and exporter of natural beverages including fruit and apple juices, sodas, lemonade and iced teas; serving the food service market
President & COO: Hilton Schlosberg
CEO: Rodney Sacks
Number Employees: 1-4
Parent Co: HB
Type of Packaging: Consumer, Food Service
Private Brands Carried:
Equator; Hansen's Natural
Types of Products Distributed:
Food Service, Frozen Food, General Line, Natural beverages

56907 Hansen Co
611 4th St
Griswold, IA 51535-8092   712-778-2426
                     Fax: 712-778-2150
Transportation company providing local, long and short haul trucking; warehouse providing dry and refrigerated storage for general commodities
President: Craig Hansen
hanseneg@netins.net
VP: chris Foote
Distribution Operations Manager: Mae Brunk
Sales Manager: Chris Foote
Estimated Sales: $3-5 Million
Number Employees: 20-49
Square Footage: 34000
Private Brands Carried:
Rose Acre Farms; Dutch Farms
Types of Products Distributed:
Frozen Food, General Line, Shelled eggs, juice & cheese

56908 Hansen Distribution Group
96-1282 Waihona St
Pearl City, HI 96782   808-456-3334
           Fax: 808-456-5043   hansenhawaii.com
Importer of seafood including shellfish; wholesaler/distributor of groceries, meats, frozen foods, general merchandise, etc.; serving the food service market.
Director of Special Projects: Diana Allen
Controller: Lorenzo Eagan
Quality Assurance Director: Mike Piccinino
Year Founded: 1957
Estimated Sales: $50-100 Million
Number Employees: 50-99
Number of Products: 8000
Square Footage: 100000
Type of Packaging: Consumer, Food Service
Private Brands Carried:
Hoffy; Hukilau; Jose Diaz
Types of Products Distributed:
Food Service, General Line, General Merchandise, Provisions/Meat, Groceries, etc.

Wholesalers & Distributors / A-Z

56909 (HQ)Hansen Group
1770 Breckinridge Pkwy # 400
Suite 400
Duluth, GA 30096-7567   770-667-1544
Fax: 770-667-1491 sales@thehansengroup.net
www.thehansengroup.net
Manufacturers' representative for food service equipment; serving wholesalers/distributors
Owner: Phil Kenny
tk@thehansengroup.net
Partner: Cris Hansen
Partner: Wayne Jones
Partner: Dave Schwefier
Inside Sales: Ashlee Myhres
Marketing/Inside Sales: Roxana Carjan
Inside/Outside Sales: Dimple Ingalls
tk@thehansengroup.net
Estimated Sales: $3-5 Million
Number Employees: 10-19
Types of Products Distributed:
   Frozen Food

56910 Hanset Brothers Inc Brooms
1105 SE Woodward St
Portland, OR 97202-2592   503-232-5418
Fax: 503-232-6475 800-876-7654
www.hansetbrothersinc.com
Wholesaler/distributor of janitorial supplies including brooms, mops, etc.; serving the food service market
President: David Hanset
Office Manager: Diane Hanset
Purchasing Director: Ron Hanset
Estimated Sales: $2.5-5 Million
Number Employees: 10-19
Square Footage: 80000
Private Brands Carried:
   Brown Beauty
Types of Products Distributed:
   Food Service, Frozen Food, General Merchandise, Brooms, mops, etc.

56911 Hansler Industries
1385 California Avenue
Brockville, ON K6V 5V5
Canada   613-342-4408
Fax: 613-342-9281 800-267-8150
www.hansler.com
Wholesaler/distributor of material handling equipment including forklifts
President: Brian Boucher
Number Employees: 50-99
Types of Products Distributed:
   Frozen Food, General Merchandise

56912 Hanson Brass Rewd Co
7530 San Fernando Rd
Sun Valley, CA 91352-4344   818-767-3501
Fax: 818-767-7891 888-841-3773
info@hansonbrass.com www.hansonhl.com
Sneeze guards, copper carts and brass, chrome and copper lamps; exporter of carving units, food displays; wholesaler/distributor of restaurant equipment and supplies; serving the food service market, alto shaam test kitchen
President: Tom Hanson
VP: Jim Hanson
CFO: Tom Hanson
info@hansonbrass.com
Vice President: Robert Hanson
Plant Manager: Mark Denny
Estimated Sales: $6-7 Million
Number Employees: 10-19
Number of Brands: 2
Square Footage: 32000
Private Brands Carried:
   Alto-Shaam
Types of Products Distributed:
   Food Service

56913 Hanway Restaurant Equipment
31 Melford Drive
#8
Scarborough, ON M1B 2G6
Canada   416-298-2345
Fax: 416-298-6879 sales@hanwaygroup.com
www.hanwaygroup.com
Wholesaler/distributor of restaurant equipment and supplies
Co-Owner: Joe Chan
Co-Owner: Iris Chan
Private Brands Carried:
   Hobart; Vulcan; Garland
Types of Products Distributed:
   Frozen Food, General Merchandise, Restaurant equipment & supplies

56914 Happy Chef Inc
22 Park Pl # 2
Suite 2
Butler, NJ 07405-1377   973-492-2525
Fax: 973-492-0303 800-347-0288
info@happychefuniforms.com
www.happychefuniforms.com
Manufacturer and wholesaler/distributor of uniforms and table linens for kitchen and waiter/waitress personnel. Serving the food service market
Vice President: Howard Curtin
info@happychefuniforms.com
VP: Howard Curtin
VP, Sales/Marketing: Howard Curtin
Estimated Sales: $10 Million
Number Employees: 20-49
Square Footage: 30000
Type of Packaging: Private Label
Private Brands Carried:
   The Happy Chef
Types of Products Distributed:
   Uniforms & textile Products

56915 Happybaby
139 Fulton Street
Suite 907
New York, NY 10038   212-374-2779
Fax: 310-359-0216 bob@happyfamilybrands.com
www.happyfamilybrands.com
Wholesaler of natural and organic baby food
Founder/CEO: Shazi Vizram
Founding Partner/COO: Jessica Rolph
Marketing Director: Helen Bernstein
VP National Sales: Bob Zimmerman
Contact: Clelia Mcvay
clelia@happybabyfood.com
Estimated Sales: $500,000-1 Million
Number Employees: 5-9
Parent Co: Nurture, Inc
Types of Products Distributed:
   Frozen Food

56916 Haram-Christensen Corp
125 Asia Pl
Carlstadt, NJ 07072-2412   201-842-1098
Fax: 201-507-0507 800-937-3474
haramchris@aol.com www.haramchris.com
Importer and wholesaler/distributor of Scandinavian, German and Austrian food specialties
President: Walter Seifert
haramchris@aol.com
Treasurer: Victor Nahum
Assistant to President: Anna Vikki
Estimated Sales: $10-20 Million
Number Employees: 10-19
Square Footage: 63000
Private Brands Carried:
   Landsberg; Muenster-Chris; Chris-Swiss
Types of Products Distributed:
   Specialty Foods

56917 Harbison Wholesale Meats
2115 County Road
Suite 401
Cullman, AL 35057   256-739-5105
Fax: 256-739-8123
Meat
Proprietor: Gary Harbison

56918 Harbor Fish Market
9 Custom House Wharf
Portland, ME 04101-4708   207-775-0251
Fax: 207-879-0611 800-370-1790
info@harborfish.com www.harborfish.com
Seafood
Owner: Benjamin Alfiero
ben@harborfish.com
Owner: Mike Alfiero
Owner/VP: Michael Alfiero
Estimated Sales: $6.2 Million
Number Employees: 20-49
Square Footage: 16058

56919 Harbor Linen LLC
2 Foster Ave
Gibbsboro, NJ 08026-1194   856-545-9149
Fax: 856-346-4598 800-257-7858
sales@harborlinen.com
Wholesaler/distributor of general merchandise including linens, towels, table cloths and wearing apparel
President: Earl Waxman
Executive VP: Gordon Munson
Estimated Sales: $20-50 Million
Number Employees: 5-9
Square Footage: 150000
Types of Products Distributed:
   Frozen Food, General Merchandise, Linens, towels, table clothes, etc.

56920 Harbor Wholesale Foods Inc
3901 Hogum Bay Rd NE
Lacey, WA 98516   360-754-4484
Fax: 360-705-2594 800-624-3614
info@harborwholesale.com
www.harborwholesale.com
Wholesaler/distributor of groceries, meat, frozen food, equipment and fixtures, general merchandise, health and beauty aids and private label items; serving the food service market.
Chairman: Mike Erickson
Chief Executive Officer: Justin Erickson
Chief Financial Officer: Jim Winkle
Chief Operations Officer: Scott Erickson
VP, Sales & Marketing: Ryan Peters
Director of Sales: Bryce Schneider
VP, Operations: Cris Bade
Year Founded: 1923
Estimated Sales: $100-500 Million
Number Employees: 100-249
Square Footage: 55000
Number of Customer Locations: 800
Types of Products Distributed:
   Food Service, Frozen Food, General Line, General Merchandise, Provisions/Meat, Health & beauty aids, etc.

56921 Harco Enterprises
675 the Parkway
Peterborough, ON K9J 7K2
Canada   705-743-5361
Fax: 705-743-4312 800-361-5361
sales@harco.on.ca www.harco.on.ca
Manufacturer, wholesaler/distributor and exporter of promotional items including hot stamping, pad printing, multi-color imprints, glow-in-the-dark custom products, coasters, swizzle sticks, toys, flyers, key tags, spoons, etc; servingthe food service market. Supplier of spare parts to the dairy and food industries
President: Ray Harris
VP Finance: Kathy Perry
VP: Terry Harris
VP Marketing: Kathy Perry
VP Administration: Joan Harris
Number Employees: 10
Square Footage: 64000
Type of Packaging: Food Service
Types of Products Distributed:
   Food Service, General Merchandise, Coasters, spoons, stirrers, etc.

56922 Harders
64 Wiwoole Street
Hilo, HI 96720-5123   808-935-2952
Fax: 808-935-8769
Wholesaler/distributor of extracts, syrups and paper products; serving the food service market
Manager: Karl Hori
Estimated Sales: $5-10 Million
Number Employees: 5-9
Parent Co: CICO Enterprises
Types of Products Distributed:
   Food Service, Frozen Food, General Line, General Merchandise, Syrup, extracts & paper products

56923 Hardscrabble Enterprises
PO Box 1124
Franklin, WV 26807-1124   304-358-2921
Mushrooms
President: Paul Goland
Estimated Sales: Under $500,000
Number Employees: 1-4
Square Footage: 7000
Type of Packaging: Consumer, Food Service, Bulk
Private Brands Carried:
   Hen-of-the-Woods
Types of Products Distributed:
   Frozen Food, General Line, Specialty Foods, Shiitake & maitake

Wholesalers & Distributors / A-Z

56924 Harger's Finest Catch
4475 Cottontown Rd
Scranton, AR 72863 479-938-7773
Fax: 479-938-7023 www.hargers.com
Mullet roe processor, turtle farm
President: Sheila Harger
Estimated Sales: $1 Million
Number Employees: 5-9
Types of Products Distributed:
Frozen Food, Specialty Foods, Mullet Roe, Turtle Meat, Cat Fish

56925 Harker's Distribution
801 6th St SW
Le Mars, IA 51031 712-546-8171
Fax: 712-536-3159 800-798-7700
Frozen foods, including meats, poultry and seafood
President: Ron Geiger
CEO: Jim Harker
Sr. VP Sales/Marketing: Stan Dickman
Contact: Dick Blackwell
dblackwell@harkers.com
Purchasing Agent: Kevin Regan
Number Employees: 100-249
Other Locations:
Harker's Distribution
Denver, COHarker's Distribution
Types of Products Distributed:
Food Service, General Line, Provisions/Meat, Seafood, Center-of-the-plate foods

56926 Harker's Distribution
PO Box 25058
Saint Louis, MO 63125-0058 618-985-9900
Fax: 618-985-9902
Wholesaler/distributor of general merchandise, general line products, equipment and fixtures, meat and seafood; serving the food service market
General Manager: Terry Buschmann
Number Employees: 10-19
Parent Co: Harkers Distribution
Number of Customer Locations: 700
Types of Products Distributed:
Food Service, Frozen Food, General Line, General Merchandise, Provisions/Meat, Seafood

56927 Harlon's LA Fish
606 Short St
Kenner, LA 70062-7157 504-467-3809
Fax: 504-466-1503 www.laseafood.com
Seafood
Owner: Harlon Pearce
nolrah@aol.com
Estimated Sales: $10-20 Million
Number Employees: 10-19

56928 Harold Food Company
11949 Steele Creek Road
Charlotte, NC 28273 704-588-8061
Fax: 704-588-4636
Frozen fruit cobblers, salads, spreads, chili and barbecue products; Dry, paper, frozen, fresh and refrigerated products
Marketing Director: Tom Taylor
General Manager: Butch Summey
Estimated Sales: $20-50 Million
Number Employees: 50-99
Square Footage: 46500
Type of Packaging: Food Service, Private Label, Bulk
Number of Customer Locations: 600
Types of Products Distributed:
Food Service, Frozen Food, General Line, General Merchandise, Dry & paper products, etc.

56929 Harold Leonard & Company
63 Bourbon Street
Wayne, NJ 07470-5473 908-289-1000
Fax: 908-289-3186 888-289-1005
info@halco.com www.halco.com
Wholesaler/distributor of equipment and supplies; serving the food service market
President: Carl Marcus
Director Marketing/Sales: Roger Randall
General Manager: Bruce Paci
Purchasing Manager: Robert Hom
Estimated Sales: $20 Million
Number Employees: 100-249
Types of Products Distributed:
Food Service, Frozen Food, General Merchandise, Equipment & supplies

56930 Harold Leonard Midwest Corporation
4482 S Archer Ave
Chicago, IL 60632-2846 773-927-3300
Fax: 773-927-3304
Wholesaler/distributor of general line products
Manager: Grace Stepin
Estimated Sales: $1-2.5 Million
Number Employees: 5-9
Parent Co: Harold Leonard & Company
Other Locations:
Leonard, Harold, Midwest Corp
Houston, TXLeonard, Harold, Midwest Corp
Types of Products Distributed:
Frozen Food, General Line

56931 Harold Leonard Southwest Corporation
1812 Brittmoore Road
Suite 230
Houston, TX 77043-2216 713-467-8105
Fax: 713-467-0072 800-245-8105
Manufacturer and wholesaler/distrbutor of smallwares
President: Carl Marcus
CEO: Herb Kelleher
Marketing Director: Roger Randall
Sales Representative: Jerry Williams
Estimated Sales: $1-2.5 Million
Number Employees: 6
Square Footage: 100000
Parent Co: Harold Leonard & Company
Types of Products Distributed:
Frozen Food, General Merchandise

56932 Harold Levinson Assoc Inc
19 Banfi Plz N
Farmingdale, NY 11735 631-962-2400
Fax: 631-962-9000 800-325-2512
info@hladistributors.com www.hladistributors.net
Wholesaler/distributor of groceries.
Executive Staff: Kyle Feldman
kfeldman@hladistributors.com
VP, Corporate Development: Michael Berro
VP, Sales: Marty Glick
Director, Human Resources: Susan Farina
Warehouse General Manager: Christopher Hatzfeld
Director, Purchasing: Dennis Williams
Year Founded: 1977
Estimated Sales: $50-100 Million
Number Employees: 600+
Square Footage: 500000
Other Locations:
Albany, NY
Auburn, MA
Waterbury, CT
Ewing, NJ
Jessup, PAAuburn
Private Brands Carried:
Kellogg's; Kraft; Post Cereals
Types of Products Distributed:
Frozen Food, General Line, Groceries

56933 Harpak-Ulma
175 John Quincy Adams Rd
Taunton, MA 02780-1035 508-884-2500
Fax: 508-884-2501 800-813-6644
info@harpak-ULMA.com www.harpak-ulma.com
Supplier of engineered packaging equipment and complete automated systems.
Field Sales Manager: Jerry Rundle
Estimated Sales: $60 Million
Number Employees: 88
Type of Packaging: Food Service, Private Label, Bulk
Types of Products Distributed:
Food Service, Frozen Food, General Merchandise, Health Food, Provisions/Meat, Produce, Rack Jobbers, Seafood, Specialty Foods

56934 Harrill Brothers Wholesale Company
119 Florida Ave
Forest City, NC 28043-3719 828-245-2115
Fax: 828-245-7433
Wholesaler/distributor of candy
Manager: Scott Skipper
Estimated Sales: $5-10 Million
Number Employees: 10-19
Type of Packaging: Bulk
Private Brands Carried:
Hershey; Snickers; Sweet Tarts
Number of Customer Locations: 400

Types of Products Distributed:
Frozen Food, General Line

56935 Harris Equipment Corp
2040 N Hawthorne Ave
Melrose Park, IL 60160-1106 708-343-0866
Fax: 708-343-0995 800-365-0315
customer_service@harrisequipment.com
www.harrisequipment.com
Heat exchangers; wholesaler/distributor of oil free air compressors and compressed air filtration equipment, oil flooded compressor air dryers, stainless steel vavles, filter regulated lubricators
President: Gary Pollack
gpollack@harrisequipment.com
VP: John Pearson
Marketing: Tony Beaman
Purchasing Manager: Humer Lovett
Estimated Sales: $10-20 Million
Number Employees: 20-49
Square Footage: 56000
Types of Products Distributed:
Frozen Food, General Merchandise, Oil free air compressors, etc.

56936 Harrison Oyster Company
6129 Tilghman Island Rd
Tilghman, MD 21671 410-886-2530
Fax: 410-886-2599 cheshse@goeaston.net
Wholesaler/distributor of fresh fish, hard and soft blue crabs and oysters
Owner: Levin F Harrison Iii
General Manager: Levin Harrison
Estimated Sales: $1-2.5 Million
Number Employees: 50-99
Types of Products Distributed:
Frozen Food, Seafood, Oysters, hard & soft blue crabs, etc.

56937 (HQ)Harry Fourtunis
2 Pierpont Ave
Newburgh, NY 12550 845-561-2600
Fax: 845-561-5948
Wholesaler/distributor of frozen foods, general merchandise, groceries, paper supplies and provisions/meats; serving the food service market
President: Harry Fourtunis
Estimated Sales: $20-50 Million
Number Employees: 50-99
Square Footage: 42000
Number of Customer Locations: 1200
Types of Products Distributed:
Food Service, Frozen Food, General Line, General Merchandise, Provisions/Meat, Groceries, paper supplies, etc.

56938 Harry Fourtunis Inc
4 S Plank Rd
Newburgh, NY 12550-3905 845-561-5246
Fax: 845-562-0506
Wholesaler/distributor of frozen foods, groceries, meat, dairy products, baked goods, general merchandise, private label items and specialty food; serving the food service market
President: Harry Fourtunis
VP: Joseph Pucino
Estimated Sales: Less Than $500,000
Number Employees: 1-4
Square Footage: 47000
Parent Co: Fourtunis, Harry
Private Brands Carried:
Rico; H.G.M.; Coppolla; VIP
Number of Customer Locations: 600
Types of Products Distributed:
Food Service, Frozen Food, General Line, General Merchandise, Provisions/Meat, Specialty Foods, Groceries, etc.

56939 Harry Gelb Frozen FoodsInc
8501 Page Ave Ste 5
Overland, MO 63114 314-429-7834
Fax: 314-429-6149
Wholesaler/distributor of frozen foods to grocery stores in the St. Louis metropolitan area
President/Treasurer: L Gelb
VP/Secretary: B Gelb-Zigler
Sales: T Taryle
Public Relations: L Helmick
Office Manager: L Helmick
Purchasing: L Gelb
Estimated Sales: $5 Million
Number Employees: 7
Square Footage: 10000
Type of Packaging: Consumer

Number of Customer Locations: 150
Types of Products Distributed:
  Frozen Food

56940 Harry Nusinov Company
15 Tudor Court
Getzville, NY 14068-1165 716-822-7321
  Fax: 716-822-8528
Wholesaler/distributor of produce including bananas and pineapples
President: Robert Nusinov
Types of Products Distributed:
  Frozen Food, Produce, Bananas & pineapples

56941 Harry Wils & Co Inc
505 Jefferson Ave
Secaucus, NJ 07094-2012 201-770-0857
  Fax: 201-770-1405
Food service distributor
Owner: Harry Wils
Estimated Sales: $5-10 Million
Number Employees: 5-9

56942 Harry's Premium Snacks
50 Charles Lindbergh Blvd
Uniondale, NY 11553-3626 516-794-9360
  Fax: 516-237-6250
Wholesaler/distributor of kettle-cooked potato, tortilla and vegetable chips, sourdough and honey wheat pretzels, salsa, popcorn and fat-free snacks including baked tortilla chips, potato chips, honey mustard, ranch and sourdoughpretzels and bean dips
VP: Adam Levitt
Estimated Sales: $1-2.5 Million
Number Employees: 5-9
Square Footage: 44000
Private Brands Carried:
  Harry's
Types of Products Distributed:
  Frozen Food, General Line, Health Food, Snack foods

56943 Harshfield Brothers
PO Box 202
New Albany, IN 47151-0202 812-948-1847
  Fax: 812-948-1883
Wholesaler/distributor of fresh fruits and vegetables
President: Joseph Robert Winsatt
Estimated Sales: $1-3 Million
Number Employees: 9
Types of Products Distributed:
  Produce, Fruits & vegetables

56944 Hart Lobster
134 Atlantic Ave
West Sayville, NY 11796-1904 631-589-1690
  Fax: 631-589-1698
Wholesaler/distributor of fresh and frozen seafood including live lobsters
Owner: Billy Hart
Manager (Fish): Lou Esposito
Manager: Mike Bennett
Estimated Sales: $1-2.5 Million
Number Employees: 1-4
Square Footage: 32000
Parent Co: Kingston Fish Market
Types of Products Distributed:
  Frozen Food, Seafood, Fresh & frozen seafood

56945 Hartland Distributors
827 Ashmun Street
Sault Sainte Marie, MI 49783-2242 906-632-3389
  Fax: 906-632-6305
Wholesaler/distributor of general line products and general merchandise
Manager: Ron Stevens
Estimated Sales: $20-50 Million
Number Employees: 20-49
Parent Co: Abraham & Sons
Number of Customer Locations: 550
Types of Products Distributed:
  Frozen Food, General Line, General Merchandise

56946 Hartselle Frozen Foods
411 Main Street West
Hartselle, AL 35640-2421 256-773-7261
  Fax: 709-722-1116
Frozen meats
President: Billy Wiley
Secretary/Treasurer: Sam Wiley
Vice President: Danny Wiley

56947 Harvard Seafood Company
PO Box 208
Grand Bay, AL 36541-0208 251-865-0558
  Fax: 251-865-2187
Seafood

56948 Harvest Health Foods
1944 Eastern Ave SE
Grand Rapids, MI 49507-2799 616-245-6268
  Fax: 616-245-8034
www.harvesthealthfoods.tflmag.com
Wholesaler/distributor of herbal teas, supplements, herbs and spices
Manager: Camele Mc Intosh
hhealtheastern@att.net
CEO: Cathy Atsma
Manager: Camele Mc Intosh
hhealtheastern@att.net
Director Purchasing: David Clements
Estimated Sales: $2.5-5 Million
Number Employees: 10-19
Square Footage: 64000
Private Brands Carried:
  Nature's Way; Nature's Herbs; Solgar; Harvest Health Foods
Number of Customer Locations: 2
Types of Products Distributed:
  Frozen Food, Health Food, Herbs

56949 Harvest Time Seafood Inc
208 W Elina St
Abbeville, LA 70510-8239 337-893-9029
  Fax: 337-898-0614
Fresh and frozen crabmeat
Owner: Kevin E Dartez
kevin@hts.glacoxmail.com
Estimated Sales: $5-10 Million
Number Employees: 20-49

56950 Harveys Supermarket
P.O. Box B
Jacksonville, FL 32203-0297
  844-745-0463
www.harveyssupermarkets.com
Wholesaler/distributor of general groceries.
Year Founded: 1924
Number Employees: 4,400
Square Footage: 20000
Parent Co: Southeastern Grocers
Number of Customer Locations: 77
Types of Products Distributed:
  Frozen Food, General Line, General Merchandise, Provisions/Meat, Produce, Seafood

56951 Has Beans Coffee & Tea Co
1078 Humboldt Ave
Chico, CA 95928-5960 530-332-9645
  Fax: 530-926-6503 800-427-2326
info@hasbeans.com www.hasbeans.com
Coffee and tea
President: William Vonk
wv@hasbeans.com
Estimated Sales: $1.62 Million
Number Employees: 1-4
Type of Packaging: Private Label
Types of Products Distributed:
  Coffee, Tea

56952 Hassia
1210 Campus Dr
Morganville, NJ 07751-1262 732-536-8770
  Fax: 732-536-8850 sales@hassiausa.com
www.oystarusa.com
Wholesaler/distributor and importer of high and low acid aseptic packaging and thermoform filling, sealing and pouching equipment for the portion pack market, case and tray packing, palletizing
CEO: Charles Ravalli
Vice President: Juan Rodriguez
Marketing Director: Robert Dono
Sales Director: Don Lander
Estimated Sales: $15 Million
Number Employees: 10-19
Square Footage: 12000
Parent Co: Hassia Verpackungsmaschinen GmbH
Types of Products Distributed:
  General Merchandise, Packaging machinery

56953 Hata Y & Co LTD
285 Sand Island Access Rd
Honolulu, HI 96819 808-447-4321
  www.yhata.com
Broadline food service distributor providing statewide distribution.
Chairman & CEO: Russell Hata
Restaurant Supply Merchandiser: Jackie Cabebe
VP, Finance & Administration: Brian Marting
Senior Director, Business Development: Kelly Wall
Director, Sales: John Smiley
Year Founded: 1922
Estimated Sales: $69 Million
Number Employees: 100-249
Square Footage: 107000
Type of Packaging: Food Service, Private Label, Bulk
Private Brands Carried:
  Pocahontas
Types of Products Distributed:
  Food Service, Frozen Food, General Line, Provisions/Meat, Seafood, Specialty Foods, Paper, Janitorial, Equipment & Supply

56954 Hathaway Coffee Co Inc
6210 S Archer Rd
Summit Argo, IL 60501-1721 708-458-7666
  Fax: 708-458-7668 www.krinos.com
Wholesaler/distributor of coffee and tea; serving the food service market
Owner: Michael Gordon
Estimated Sales: $1-3 Million
Number Employees: 1-4
Parent Co: Ann Hathaway Coffee
Types of Products Distributed:
  Food Service, Frozen Food, Coffee & tea

56955 Hattiesburg Grocery Company
PO Box 350
Hattiesburg, MS 39403-0350 601-584-7544
  Fax: 601-584-7546
Wholesaler/distributor of groceries, frozen foods, general merchandise, equipment and fixtures; serving the food service market; rack jobber services available
President: W Russell, Jr.
VP: Jeannette Russell
Estimated Sales: $20-50 Million
Number Employees: 50-99
Square Footage: 50000
Number of Customer Locations: 587
Types of Products Distributed:
  Food Service, Frozen Food, General Line, General Merchandise, Rack Jobbers, Groceries and equipment & fixtures

56956 Hauser Enterprises
115r Harvard Street
Waltham, MA 02453-4111 781-891-6003
  Fax: 978-443-3438
Wholesaler/distributor of general line and specialty food products including frozen hors d'oeuvres, pestos and baked goods
Owner/President: Grace Hauser
Secretary: Edward Hauser
Estimated Sales: Over $400,000
Number Employees: 3
Square Footage: 8400
Type of Packaging: Food Service
Private Brands Carried:
  Garden Herbs Pesto; David Glass Cakes; Hudson Valley Cakes; Macy's Cheesesticks; Keren's Kitchen Cookies; Frittines
Types of Products Distributed:
  Frozen Food, Specialty Foods, Pestos, baked goods, etc.

56957 Haviland Enterprises Inc
421 Ann St NW
Grand Rapids, MI 49504-2019 616-734-0250
  Fax: 616-361-9772 800-456-1134
Industrial, food grade and U.S.P. specialty cleaners and wastewater treatment chemicals; wholesaler/distributor of various food grade and U.S.P. process chemicals
President: E Bernard Haviland
Cmo: Graham Torr
grahamt@havilandusa.com
CFO: Tom Simmons
Quality Control: Terry Schoew
Sales/Marketing Manager: Eric Earl
Estimated Sales: $20-50 Million
Number Employees: 100-249
Square Footage: 185000
Types of Products Distributed:
  Frozen Food, General Merchandise

Wholesalers & Distributors / A-Z

56958 Hawaii Coffee Company
1555 Kalani St
Honolulu, HI 96817   808-847-3600
Fax: 800-972-0777 800-338-8353
www.hawaiicoffeecompany.com
Coffee
President: Jim Wayman
Chief Marketing Officer: Wenli Lin
National Sales Account Manager: Malia Delapenia
Estimated Sales: $9,000,000
Number Employees: 51-200
Number of Brands: 4
Private Brands Carried:
  Superior Coffee

56959 Hawaii International Seafood
371 Aokea Place
PO Box 30486
Kailua, HI 96819-1828   808-839-5010
Fax: 808-833-0712 info@cryofresh.com
www.cryofresh.com
Fish and seafood
President: Bill Kowalski
Estimated Sales: $2,000,000
Number Employees: 5-9

56960 Hawaiian Coffee Traders
P.O. Box 833
Waimea, HI 96796-833   808-335-3324
Fax: 809-335-3324 800-545-8605
kauaicoffee.com
Wholesaler/distributor of Hawaiian coffee
CEO: Julia Evans
Estimated Sales: $.5-1 million
Number Employees: 1-4
Square Footage: 16000
Parent Co: Kauai Coffee Company
Types of Products Distributed:
  Frozen Food, General Line, Specialty Foods, Hawaiian coffee

56961 (HQ)Hawaiian Grocery Stores
915 Kaihikapu Street
Honolulu, HI 96819   808-839-5121
Fax: 808-839-5707 hgsadm@aloha.net
Wholesaler/distributor of dry groceries, frozen and specialty foods, general merchandise and dairy products
CEO/President: Richard Loeffler
VP Finance: Bruce Barber
Number Employees: 100-249
Square Footage: 292000
Private Brands Carried:
  Springfield
Number of Customer Locations: 450
Types of Products Distributed:
  Frozen Food, General Line, General Merchandise, Specialty Foods

56962 Hawaiian King Candies
550 Paiea St # 501
Honolulu, HI 96819-1837   808-833-0041
Fax: 808-839-7141 800-570-1902
dniiro@lava.net
Macadamia nut snacks
President: David Niiro
Contact: Marvin Sialco
info@hawaiianking.com
Estimated Sales: $10-24,9,000,000
Number Employees: 50-99
Type of Packaging: Consumer, Food Service, Private Label

56963 Hawk Flour Mills
639 Grammes Road
Allentown, PA 18104-9350   610-366-8900
Fax: 610-366-1039
Wholesaler/distributor of bakery supplies and institutional foods; serving the food service market
President: R Hawk
VP: E Hawk
Estimated Sales: $10-20 Million
Number Employees: 20-49
Types of Products Distributed:
  Food Service, Frozen Food, General Merchandise, Bakery supplies

56964 Hawkins Distributing Company
77 Bassett Ave
Madisonville, KY 42431-2144   270-821-2109
Fax: 270-821-7490
Wholesaler/distributor of flour, meal, candies, nuts, grocery items and canned goods; serving the food service market
Owner: Charles Hawkins
Sales Manager: Alvis Pipton
Estimated Sales: $1-3 Million
Number Employees: 10-19
Number of Customer Locations: 50
Types of Products Distributed:
  Food Service, Frozen Food, General Line, Flour, meal, nuts, candies, groceries

56965 Hawthorn Power Systems
10930 Willow Ct
San Diego, CA 92127-2410   858-566-9966
Fax: 858-207-2837 866-266-2244
www.hawthornelift.com
Wholesaler/distributor of material handling equipment
President: Brian Hawthorne
CEO: Tee Ness
Number Employees: 50-99
Parent Co: Naumann/Hobbs Material Handling
Types of Products Distributed:
  Frozen Food, General Merchandise, Material handling equipment

56966 Hawthorne Supply Company
90 Fordham Drive
Matawan, NJ 07747-2146   973-484-5220
Fax: 973-484-1655 800-427-5206
Wholesaler/distributor of food service equipment and supplies, disposables and janitorial supplies; serving the food service market
President: Bill Royal, Jr.
VP Contract Sales: Roger Peterson
General Manager: Bill Heinze
Number Employees: 20-49
Square Footage: 80000
Private Brands Carried:
  Nugget
Types of Products Distributed:
  Food Service, Frozen Food, General Merchandise, Foodservice equipment & supplies, etc.

56967 Haynes Brothers Candy Company
401 W Lytle St
Murfreesboro, TN 37130-3663   615-893-6961
Fax: 615-893-6969
Wholesaler/distributor of general merchandise, general line products and health food
Persident: Fayne Haynes
Estimated Sales: $2.5-5 Million
Number Employees: 5-9
Types of Products Distributed:
  Frozen Food, General Line, General Merchandise, Health Food

56968 Heads & Tails Seafood
2070 Silverside Dr
Baton Rouge, LA 70808-4789   225-767-2525
Fax: 225-767-5894 800-259-4713
fishboy58@aol.com
www.headsandtailsseafood.com
Wholesaler/distributor of shrimp, oysters, crab, catfish, crawfish, speckled trout, flounder, etc. Seafood gumbo voted #1 by the Wall Street Journal
Owner: Michael Cashio
fishboy58@aol.com
Estimated Sales: $1 Million
Number Employees: 5-9
Square Footage: 12000
Type of Packaging: Private Label, Bulk
Number of Customer Locations: 1
Types of Products Distributed:
  Frozen Food, Seafood

56969 Healing Garden
PO Box 576
Maple Valley, WA 98038-0576   888-291-4970
Wholesaler/distributor and exporter of herbs, spices and formulas
Number Employees: 1-4
Types of Products Distributed:
  Frozen Food, General Line, Health Food, Herbal formulas, spices, etc.

56970 Healing Home Foods
73 Westchester Ave
P.O. Box 390
Pound Ridge, NY 10576   914-764-1303
info@healinghomefoods.com
www.healinghomefoods.com
Organic, vegan, gluten-free and GMO-free granolas, crackers, chips, nuts, treats, and other snacks
Founder: Shelley Schulz
Wholesale Inquiries: John Schulz
Types of Products Distributed:
  General Line

56971 Health Flavors
50 Sodom Rd
Brewster, NY 10509-4403   845-940-0190
Fax: 845-278-6277 877-380-3422
Importer and distributer to natural food and gourmet trade
Owner: Josef Rosenfeld
CFO: Christine Zirkelbach
Estimated Sales: $24 Million
Number Employees: 1-4
Number of Products: 700
Square Footage: 5000
Type of Packaging: Consumer, Food Service, Private Label, Bulk
Private Brands Carried:
  Orgran, Candy Tree, Corn Candies
Number of Customer Locations: 600
Types of Products Distributed:
  Health Food, Wheat-free and Gluten-free Foods

56972 Health Food Distributors
1893 Northwood Dr
Troy, MI 48084-5525   248-362-4545
Fax: 248-362-0931 800-482-6188
sales@hfdinc.net www.healthfooddistributors.net
Wholesaler/distributor of health food
President: Norman Bienstock
Vice President: Michael Bienstock
mike@hfdinc.net
Estimated Sales: $1-2.5 Million
Number Employees: 5-9
Types of Products Distributed:
  Frozen Food, Health Food

56973 Health Guardians
PO Box 274
Silver Spring, PA 17575-0274   717-285-4642
Fax: 717-285-4642 800-231-2086
hello@healthguardians.org
Wholesaler/distributor and exporter of shark cartilage capsules, fat burners, stimulants, diet aids, etc
President: Bruce Youm
Founding Partner: Jay Andrew Barcelon
Founding Partner: Graeme Moore
Chief Operating Officer: Brian Kim
Number Employees: 5-9
Square Footage: 4800
Type of Packaging: Private Label, Bulk
Private Brands Carried:
  Health Guardians; Olympic Labs; Predator
Types of Products Distributed:
  Frozen Food, Health Food, Diet aids, fat burners, etc.

56974 Health King Enterprise
238 W 31st St # 1
Chicago, IL 60616-3600   312-567-9978
Fax: 312-567-9986 888-838-8938
service@healthkingenterprise.com
www.healthkingenterprise.com
Importer and exporter of green, medicinal teas and diet and weight loss aids and digestive aids, chinese herb remedies
President: Xingwu Liu
CEO/VP: Joanne Liu
Vice President: Sarah Appleby
sarah.appleby@healthkingenterprise.com
Marketing: Maggie Qiu
Sales: Joaquin Gamino
Operations: Diego Meza
Estimated Sales: $1-3 Million
Number Employees: 1-4
Square Footage: 24000
Type of Packaging: Consumer
Types of Products Distributed:
  Health Food, Dietary Supplement

56975 Health Waters
497 Washington Ave
Carlstadt, NJ 07072-2803   201-896-8000
Fax: 201-896-0111 800-638-2323
www.healthwatersinc.com
Wholesaler/distributor of bottled water
President: Stuart Scott
Contact: Ryan Durant-Bailey
ryandurant-bailey@healthwatersinc.com
Estimated Sales: $1-3 Million
Number Employees: 10-19
Private Brands Carried:
  Mountain Valley

Wholesalers & Distributors / A-Z

Types of Products Distributed:
Frozen Food, General Line, Bottled water

56976 Health Wise Consumer Beverage Products
76 Woodberry Road
Deer Park, IL 60010 800-984-0000
Fax: 847-382-3231 800-408-2664
info@healthwisegc.com
www.healthwisecoffee.com
Wholesalers for roasted healthier gourmet coffee
CEO: Michael Reines
CFO: Marvin Woltov
Marketing Director: Edward Nash
Estimated Sales: Under $500,000
Number Employees: 20-49
Number of Brands: 5
Number of Products: 8
Square Footage: 1500000

56977 Healthmate Products
1510 Old Deerfield Rd Ste 103
Highland Park, IL 60035 847-579-1051
Fax: 847-579-1059 www.healthmateproducts.com
Papaya concentrates
President: Tim Burke
treedburke@gmail.com
CEO/ Manager of Public Relations: Celeste Burke
Estimated Sales: $1 Million
Number Employees: 1-4
Type of Packaging: Consumer, Food Service
Types of Products Distributed:
Health Food, Fruit Juice

56978 Healthwise
13659 Victory Boulevard
Suite 525
Van Nuys, CA 91401-1735 818-982-9966
Fax: 818-982-1471 800-942-3262
Wholesaler/distributor of juicers, yogurt makers, etc.; serving the food service market
Co-Owner: Linda Ellison
Co-Owner: Fran Kalb
General Manager: Robert Gil
Number Employees: 1-4
Square Footage: 10000
Private Brands Carried:
Champion Juicer; Acme Juice; Salton Yogurt Makers
Types of Products Distributed:
Food Service, Frozen Food, General Merchandise, Juicers, yogurt makers, etc.

56979 (HQ)Hearn-Kirkwood
7251 Standard Dr
Hanover, MD 21076 410-712-6000
Fax: 410-712-6058 800-777-9489
bmorrissey@hearnkirkwood.com
www.hearnkirkwood.com
Wholesaler/distributor of frozen foods, produce, provisions/meats, seafood and specialty foods; serving the food service market
President: P Gilbert
Sr VP: C Gilbert
Contact: Helen Anderson
handerson@hearnkirkwood.com
Estimated Sales: $2.5-5 Million
Number Employees: 100-249
Square Footage: 160000
Parent Co: Gilbert Foods
Other Locations:
Hearn-Kirkwood
Baltimore, MDHearn-Kirkwood
Private Brands Carried:
Bonded; Snow Chef; Frosty Acres
Number of Customer Locations: 967
Types of Products Distributed:
Food Service, Frozen Food, Provisions/Meat, Produce, Seafood, Specialty Foods

56980 Hearthy Foods
2043 Imperial St
Los Angeles, CA 90021 213-372-5093
info@hearthyfoods.com
www.hearthyfoods.com
Gluten free desserts & baking flours
President: Riaz Surti *Year Founded:* 2012
Types of Products Distributed:
General Line

56981 Heartland Distributors
PO Box 2648
Grand Rapids, MI 49501-2648 616-776-0500
Fax: 989-732-1045
Wholesaler/distributor of frozen foods, general line items and general merchandise; serving the food service market
Manager: Pete Drzyzga
Estimated Sales: $20-50 Million
Number Employees: 20-49
Square Footage: 19000
Parent Co: Heartland Distributors
Number of Customer Locations: 1000
Types of Products Distributed:
Food Service, Frozen Food, General Line, General Merchandise

56982 Heartland Farms Dairy & Food Products, LLC
3668 South Geyer Road
Suite 205
St. Louis, MO 63127 314-965-1110
Fax: 314-965-1118 888-633-6455
info@heartlandfarmsdairy.com
www.heartlandfarmsdairy.com
Dairy products
President: Tom Jacoby
Marketing Assistant: Pat Hittmeier
Sales of Dry Products: Tim Fann
Contact: Christine Anderson
canderson@heartlandfarmsdairy.com
Weights and Tests: Jenn Jacoby
Type of Packaging: Consumer, Bulk

56983 Heartland Food Products
1900 W 47th Place
Suite 302
Westwood, KS 66205 913-831-4446
Fax: 913-831-4004 866-571-0222
www.heartlandfoodproducts.com
Mashed potatoes
President: Bill Steeb
Founder: Mary Steeb
Contact: Tom Gray
tom.gray@heartlandfpg.com
Estimated Sales: Less than $500,000
Number Employees: 10-19
Type of Packaging: Bulk
Types of Products Distributed:
Frozen Food

56984 Heartland Ingredients LLC
802 West College Street
Troy, MO 63379
Fax: 877-841-2067 800-557-2621
contactus@heartlandingredients.net
www.heartlandingredients.net
Ingredients, food and technical grade chemicals and colors, dairy products, meat products, sugar, artifical sweeteners, close dated finished products.

56985 Heartland Supply Co
1248 E Pump Station Rd
Fayetteville, AR 72701-7273 479-444-0970
Fax: 479-521-5022 877-444-0970
csr@heartlandsupply.com
www.heartlandsupply.com
Wholesaler/distributor of industrial ingredients including acidulants, food phosphates, preservatives, flavor enhancers, starches, milk products, etc.; serving food processors
President: Patricia Pummill
Estimated Sales: $2.5-5 Million
Number Employees: 5-9
Square Footage: 92000
Types of Products Distributed:
Frozen Food, General Line, Industrial ingredients

56986 Heavenly Cheesecakes
1369 Ridgewood Ave
Daytona Beach, FL 32117-2319 386-673-6670
Fax: 386-673-2367 386-673-6670
phyllishut@bellsouth.net
www.heavenlycheesecakes.net
Wholesaler/distributor of rum cakes, straw chocolate, Jamaican butter rum truffle cakes, carrot cakes and frozen cheese cakes; serving the food service market
Owner: Don Rigby
drigby@redp.org
Estimated Sales: Less Than $500,000
Number Employees: 1-4
Types of Products Distributed:
Food Service, Frozen Food, General Line, Cheese cake, etc.

56987 Heerema Co
200 6th Ave
Hawthorne, NJ 07506-1556 973-423-0505
Fax: 973-427-8672 800-346-4729
sales@heeremacompany.com
www.heeremacompany.com
Wholesaler/distributor of industrial refrigeration equipment and sanitary process equipment; installation and service available
Owner: Paul Heerema
heerema@heeremacompany.com
VP: P Heerema
Sales Manager: E Fody
Estimated Sales: $10-20 Million
Number Employees: 20-49
Square Footage: 40000
Types of Products Distributed:
Frozen Food, General Merchandise, Refrigeration & sanitary process equip.

56988 Heeren Brothers Produce
1055 7 Mile Rd NW
Comstock Park, MI 49321-9542 770-713-2435
Fax: 616-243-7070 matt.thiede@heerenbros.com
www.heerenbros.com
Wholesaler/distributor of produce.
President: James Heeren
Chief Operating Officer: Matthew Thiede
Year Founded: 1933
Estimated Sales: $20-50 Million
Number Employees: 150
Square Footage: 180000
Types of Products Distributed:
Frozen Food, Produce

56989 Heinkel's Packing Co
2005 N 22nd St
Decatur, IL 62526 217-428-4401
800-594-2738
sales@heinkelspacking.com
www.heinkelspacking.com
Smoked meats, lunch meats and fresh sausages; boxed beef and pork; venison processing
Owner: Miles Wright
President: Wes Wright
Head of Production: Tom McCarthy
Year Founded: 1912
Estimated Sales: $5-9.9 Million
Number Employees: 20-49
Type of Packaging: Consumer, Food Service, Bulk
Types of Products Distributed:
Food Service, Provisions/Meat, Boxed beef & pork

56990 Helen Ruth's Specialty Foods
PO Box 36902
Charlotte, NC 28236-6902 704-333-9199
Fax: 704-333-9193
Ketchup, grilling sauce, barbecue sauce and seafood sauce
President: Helen Ruth Almond
Estimated Sales: $40,000
Number of Products: 3
Private Brands Carried:
Helen Ruth's Carolina

56991 Helena Wholesale
179 Helendale
Helena, AR 72342-2535 870-753-9251
Fax: 870-338-3424 800-352-0013
Wholesaler/distributor of frozen food and general line products
CEO/President: Gene Ridge
Estimated Sales: $20-50 Million
Number Employees: 20-49
Square Footage: 70000
Number of Customer Locations: 350
Types of Products Distributed:
Frozen Food, General Line

56992 Heller's Food Equipment
2244 E 6th St
Tulsa, OK 74104-3243 918-592-5900
Fax: 918-592-5902
Wholesaler/distributor of cleaning supplies, table top items and equipment; serving the food service market
Partner: J Heller
Estimated Sales: $1-2.5 Million
Number Employees: 1-4
Types of Products Distributed:
Food Service, Frozen Food, General Merchandise, Cleaning supplies, equipment, etc.

Wholesalers & Distributors / A-Z

56993 Helmut's Strudel
45 S Water St
PO Box 607
Stone Ridge, NY 12484   845-687-2833
   Fax: 845-687-2834 info@helmuts-strudel.com
           www.helmuts-strudel.com/
Wholesaler/distributor of frozen fruit strudel and vegetable puffs; serving the food service market
President: Helmut Moelk
Secretary: Anne Moelk
Number Employees: 1-4
Types of Products Distributed:
   Food Service, Frozen Food, General Line, Fruit strudel & vegetable puffs

56994 Hemisphere Group
221 Mt. Pleasant Road
Smithtown, NY 11787   631-382-9850
   Fax: 631-382-9857   800-339-8846
       info@greenfarms.com www.greenfarms.com
Wholesaler/distributor, importer and exporter of sesame, sunflower and pumpkin seeds and nuts: macadamias, brazils, hazelnuts, cashews, pecans, almonds, pinenuts, filberts, walnuts and pistachios; dried fruits: raisins, prunes, applesapricots, peaches, pears and cranberries
President: Adam Green
adam@hemispheredev.com
Estimated Sales: $10-$20 Million
Number Employees: 5-9
Square Footage: 100000
Type of Packaging: Food Service, Bulk
Types of Products Distributed:
   Frozen Food, General Line, Nuts, seeds & dried fruit

56995 Henderson Coffee Corp
3421 S 24th St W
Muskogee, OK 74401-8902   918-682-8751
   Fax: 918-682-4851 www.hendersoncoffee.com
Wholesaler/distributor of grocery products, cleaning supplies, disposables, wraps and table top items; serving the food service market
President: Mark Plaster
Co-Owner: Mark Truitt
Executive: Michael Dayan
mdayan@hendersoncoffee.com
Estimated Sales: $1-2.5 Million
Number Employees: 20-49
Types of Products Distributed:
   Food Service, Frozen Food, General Line, General Merchandise, Groceries, cleaning supplies, etc.

56996 Henderson-Black Wholesale Groc
218 E Academy St
Troy, AL 36081-2016   334-566-0331
                      Fax: 334-566-0332
Wholesaler/distributor of general line products
President: Pete Black
Treasurer: P Black
Estimated Sales: Less Than $500,000
Number Employees: 5-9
Number of Customer Locations: 500
Types of Products Distributed:
   Frozen Food, General Line

56997 Hendrix Hotel & Restaurant Equipment & Supplies
3011 Highway #29 North
Brockville, ON K6V 5V2
Canada
                            613-342-0616
   Fax: 613-342-1921   800-267-8182
                www.hendrixequip.com
Wholesaler/distributor of food service supplies and equipment; serving the food service market
Owner: Larry Vander Baaren
Number Employees: 20-49
Square Footage: 40000
Private Brands Carried:
   Hobart; Garland; Bunn-a-matic
Types of Products Distributed:
   Food Service, Frozen Food, General Merchandise, Foodservice equipment & supplies

56998 Henjes Enterprises
3 Leisure Ln
North Sioux City, SD 57049   605-232-9070
   Fax: 605-232-9108 heinc@pionet.net
Wholesaler/distributor of boxed beef, pre-cut steaks, aged prime and choice Black Angus beef, pork, poultry parts, hot dogs, sausages, sandwich meats, ham, bacon, hamburger, roast beef, cook-in bags and meat casings; serving the foodservice industry
Owner/President: Janice Henjes
VP: Jason Henjes
Estimated Sales: $1-2.5 Million
Number Employees: 1-4
Types of Products Distributed:
   Food Service, Frozen Food, General Merchandise, Provisions/Meat, Boxed beef, sausages, hamburger, etc.

56999 (HQ)Henley Paper Company
4229 Beechwood Dr
Greensboro, NC 27410-8108   336-668-0081
   Fax: 336-605-9366 Atlanta@AtlanticPkg.com
                www.atlanticpkg.com
Manufacturer and wholesaler/distributor of die cutting, hosiery inserts, slitting, rewinding, sheeting, transfer tissue, electrical insulator paper
VP Sales/Marketing: Bill Parks
Estimated Sales: $10-20 Million
Number Employees: 50-99
Types of Products Distributed:
   Frozen Food, General Merchandise

57000 Henry Bresky & Sons Inc
1859 Commerce Dr
Bridgeport, CT 06605-2294   203-335-5114
                      Fax: 203-335-5114
Wholesaler/distributor of industrial and institutional ingredients, bakers' and confectioners' supplies, seafood, specialty foods, general merchandise, groceries, etc.; serving the food service market; rack jobber services available
President: H Bresky
CEO: T Bresky
CFO: D Bresky
Public Relations: Ellen Bresky
Estimated Sales: $3-5 Million
Number Employees: 1-4
Square Footage: 130000
Type of Packaging: Food Service, Private Label, Bulk
Private Brands Carried:
   Bella; Blue Diamond; Briterway; Fleur de Lis
Types of Products Distributed:
   Food Service, General Line, General Merchandise, Provisions/Meat, Rack Jobbers, Seafood, Specialty Foods, Groceries, ingredients, etc.

57001 Henry Davis Company
3405 W 15th Ave
Gary, IN 46404-1964   219-949-8555
                      Fax: 219-949-9764
Seafood
President: Henry Davis
Estimated Sales: $1-3 Million
Number Employees: 20-49

57002 Henry Gonsalves Co
35 Thurber Blvd
Smithfield, RI 02917-1838   401-231-6700
   Fax: 401-231-6707   800-333-2344
                       bompet@yahoo.com
Importer of dry beans, cheese, olives, cod, corn meal, grits, oils, etc.; wholesaler/distributor of general line products and seafood
President: Henry Co
geeco71@gmail.com
Sales Manager: Oliver Furtado
Import Director: Jack Costa
Estimated Sales: $10-20 Million
Number Employees: 20-49
Types of Products Distributed:
   Frozen Food, General Line, Seafood

57003 Henrys Cash & Carry
715 S Lewis Ln
Harlingen, TX 78552-4825   956-428-4202
                      Fax: 956-428-3042
Wholesaler/distributor of general line items; serving the food service market, convenience stores and the general public
President: Enrique Garza
Secretary: Charles Kelsey
Contact: Henry Cash
henry@henryscateringservice.com
henry@henryscateringservice.com
Estimated Sales: $5-10 Million
Number Employees: 10-19
Square Footage: 20000
Types of Products Distributed:
   Food Service, Frozen Food, General Line

57004 Herc-U-Lift Inc
5655 Highway 12 # 69
Maple Plain, MN 55359-9425 763-479-2501
   Fax: 763-479-2296   800-363-3500
       sales@herculift.com www.herculift.com
Wholesaler/distributor of forklifts
President: Les Neilson
CEO: Les Nielsen
lnielsen@herc-u-lift.com
CEO: Les Nielsen
Estimated Sales: $10-20 Million
Number Employees: 100-249
Number of Customer Locations: 20000
Types of Products Distributed:
   Frozen Food, General Merchandise, Forklifts

57005 Herche Warehouse
4735 Leyden Street
Denver, CO 80216-3301   303-371-8186
Manufacturer and wholesaler/distributor of packaging equipment and materials including bags, containers, closures, conveyors, labels, linings, tapes, ties, etc
Customer Service Representative: Cathy Wyatt
Estimated Sales: $1-5,000,000
Parent Co: Gulf Systems
Types of Products Distributed:
   Frozen Food, General Merchandise, Packaging equipment & systems

57006 Hercules Food Equipment
145 Millwick Drive
Weston, ON M9L 1Y7
Canada   416-742-9673
   Fax: 416-742-6486 hercules@interlog.com
Custom stainless steel sinks, counters and exhaust canopies; also, refrigerated and heated display units, barbecue ovens and Chinese cooking equipment; wholesaler/distributor of food service equipment; serving the food servicemarket
President: R Barron
CEO: M Lepage
Number Employees: 20-49
Square Footage: 34000
Types of Products Distributed:
   Food Service, Frozen Food, General Merchandise, Foodservice equipment

57007 Heritage Maintenance Products, LLC
2572 Industry Lane
East-West Norriton Industrial Park
Eagleville, PA 19403   610-539-6960
   Fax: 610-539-6910   800-277-3780
   hmpco@aol.com www.heritagemaintenance.com
Wholesaler/distributor of cleaning products including varnish and brushes for food/dairy processing, floor machines and in-plant power sweeper brushes
Owner: John Munera
VP Sales: Jack Munera
Sales Director: Matthew Munera
Estimated Sales: $1-2.5 Million
Number Employees: 1-4
Square Footage: 7200
Types of Products Distributed:
   General Merchandise, Cleaning supplies

57008 Hermanowski Wholesale
1907 Penn Ave
Pittsburgh, PA 15222-4415   412-566-8121
Wholesaler/distributor of general line and general merchandise products and candy
President: J Hermanowski
Secretary/Treasurer: H Hermanowski
General Manager: E Hermanowski
Estimated Sales: Less than $500,000
Number Employees: 1-4
Square Footage: 32000
Number of Customer Locations: 100
Types of Products Distributed:
   Frozen Food, General Line, General Merchandise, Candy

57009 Herr Foods Inc.
20 Herr Dr.
PO Box 300
Nottingham, PA 19362
                            800-523-5030
                       www.herrfoods.com
Snack foods.

Founder: James Herr
james.herr@herrs.com
Chairman: J.M. Herr
President/CEO: Ed Herr
Year Founded: 1946
Estimated Sales: $100-500 Million
Number Employees: 1000-4999
Type of Packaging: Consumer
Other Locations:
  Herr's
  Seaford, DE
  Herr's
  Elkridge, MD
  Herr's
  Egg Harbor, NJ
  Herr's
  Oakland, NJ
  Herr's
  Somerset, NJ
  Herr's
  Lakewood, NJ
  Herr'sElkridge

57010 Herring Brothers Meats
350 Water St
Guilford, ME 4443   207-876-2631
  Fax: 207-876-2631   herringbros@hotmail.com
                 www.herringbrothersmeats.com
Meats
Owner: Thomas Gilbert
Owner: Trey Gilbert
Owner: Ellie Patterson
Estimated Sales: $5-10 Million
Number Employees: 20-49
Type of Packaging: Consumer, Private Label
Types of Products Distributed:
  Frozen Food, Provisions/Meat

57011 Hershey Co.
19 E Chocolate Dr.
Hershey, PA 17033
                           800-468-1714
            www.thehersheycompany.com
Chocolate, confectionery, snack, refreshment and grocery products.
Chairman/President/CEO: Michele Buck
Senior VP/CFO: Steve Voskuil
Senior VP/General Counsel: Damien Atkins
Year Founded: 1894
Estimated Sales: $7.8 Billion
Number Employees: 15,360
Number of Brands: 31
Type of Packaging: Consumer, Food Service, Private Label

57012 Hialeah Products Co
2207 Hayes St
Hollywood, FL 33020-3437   954-923-3379
     Fax: 954-923-4010   800-923-3379
                          richnuts@aol.com
Nuts, dried fruits, candy and snacks
Owner: Richard Lesser
richard@newurbanfarms.com
CEO: Kathy Lesser
Research & Development: Noah Lesser
Estimated Sales: $10-25 Million
Number Employees: 10-19
Number of Brands: 2
Number of Products: 200+
Square Footage: 120000
Type of Packaging: Consumer, Food Service, Private Label, Bulk
Private Brands Carried:
  Hollywood Nut Co.; Oh Nuts!
Number of Customer Locations: 1500
Types of Products Distributed:
  Food Service, Specialty Foods, Nuts, dried fruits, snack foods, etc.

57013 Hibrett Puratex
7001 Westfield Avenue
Pennsauken, NJ 8110   856-662-1717
     Fax: 856-662-0550   800-260-5124
                   www.hibrettpuratex.com
Manufacturer and wholesaler/distributor of compound cleaning chemicals and water treatment products
CEO: Jerome Ellerbee
Sales: Nelissa Abreu
Contact: Stefanie Geoghegan
sgeoghegan@hibrettpuratex.com
Number Employees: 20
Number of Products: 1000
Square Footage: 42000
Parent Co: Hibrett Puratex

Type of Packaging: Private Label
Types of Products Distributed:
  Frozen Food, General Merchandise, Industrial cleaners, etc.

57014 Hickory Harvest Foods
90 Logan Pkwy
Akron, OH 44319-1177   330-644-6266
     Fax: 330-644-2501   800-448-6887
                   www.hickoryharvest.com
Snack foods
President: Joe Swiatkowski
joe@hickoryharvest.com
VP, Sales: Mike Swiatkowski
Plant Manager: Nicholas Hamilton
Number Employees: 20-49
Type of Packaging: Consumer, Food Service, Private Label, Bulk
Types of Products Distributed:
  Frozen Food, General Line, Specialty Foods, Candy

57015 Higa Food Service
225 N. Nimitz Hwy
Honolulu, HI 96817   808-531-3591
     Fax: 808-521-4951   www.higafoodservice.com
Meats
President/CEO: Sheldon Wright
Vice President, Processing: Jerry Higa
VP of Sales & Marketing: Shane Wright
Contact: Clifford Suwa
clifford@higafoodservice.com
Chief Operations Officer: Shaun Wright
Estimated Sales: $10-19.9 Million
Number Employees: 20-49
Types of Products Distributed:
  Provisions/Meat

57016 High Country Meats
8001 E. 88th Ave.
Suite C
Henderson, CO 80640   303-291-0800
     Fax: 303-291-0668   800-416-1668
                   steve@highcountrymeat.com
                   www.highcountrymeat.com
Meat, particularly beef.
Vice President, Sales & Marketing: Steve Montague
Year Founded: 1994
Parent Co: Greater Omaha Packing Co Inc.
Types of Products Distributed:
  Food Service, Provisions/Meat, Rack Jobbers

57017 High Quality Organics
12101 Moya Blvd.
Reno, NV 89506   775-971-8550
                           hqorganics.com
Offers organic ingredients, including spices & herbs, spice extracts, dried vegetables, baking ingredients, and select grains.
Founder & President: Raju Boligala
Founder: Jerry Tenenberg
Founder: Jay Fishman
CFO: Rick May
VP, Quality & Operations: Chad Flores
Director, Sales: Jonathan Raju
Director, Customer Services: Cynthia Acuna
Director, Supply Chain: Gina Pepple
Year Founded: 1977
Number Employees: 51-200
Type of Packaging: Consumer, Food Service, Private Label, Bulk
Types of Products Distributed:
  Food Service, Ingredients

57018 High Ridge Foods LLC
424 Ridgeway
White Plains, NY 10605-4208 914-761-2900
     Fax: 914-761-2901
Dairy products, sugars and flowers
President: Nestor Alzerez
Sales Manager: Nestor Alzerez, Jr
Estimated Sales: $2.5 000,000
Number Employees: 1-4
Type of Packaging: Private Label, Bulk
Number of Customer Locations: 44
Types of Products Distributed:
  Retail Cheeses, Fruit Drinks

57019 Hill & Sloan
2404 Thelma Ct
Louisville, KY 40220-2938   502-491-0834
Wholesaler/distributor of produce
Owner: Ronald Hall

Estimated Sales: $.5-1 million
Number Employees: 1-4
Types of Products Distributed:
  Frozen Food, Produce

57020 Hill City Wholesale Company
P.O.Box 10246
Lynchburg, VA 24506   434-847-7641
     Fax: 434-847-0807
Wholesaler/distributor of candy, groceries, paper goods, dairy and bakery products, cleaning supplies, etc.; serving the food service market
President: W Thomasson
Sales Manager: M Scott
Estimated Sales: $20-50 Million
Number Employees: 20-49
Square Footage: 30000
Private Brands Carried:
  Hilco
Number of Customer Locations: 400
Types of Products Distributed:
  Food Service, Frozen Food, General Line, General Merchandise, Provisions/Meat, Candy, dairy & bakery products, etc.

57021 Hill Company
8615 Germantown Ave
Philadelphia, PA 19118   215-247-7600
     Fax: 215-247-7603   info@hill-company.com
                   www.hill-company.com
Wholesaler/distributor of outdoor and indoor furniture, umbrellas, benches, picnic tables and cushions
Owner: Linda Moran
Sales Representative (Part Time): Debbie Regan
Contact: Jay Valinis
info@hill-company.com
Estimated Sales: $1-2.5 Million
Number Employees: 5-9
Square Footage: 12000
Types of Products Distributed:
  Frozen Food, General Merchandise, Outdoor & indoor furniture

57022 Hill Specialties
851 Aberdeen Road
Bay Shore, NY 11706   631-853-0139
     Fax: 212-594-1318   800-782-2474
                   tmazzie@hillspecialties.com
                   www.hillspecialties.com
Wholesaler/distributor of general merchandise including advertising specialties, food baskets, fortune cookies with custom messages, premium items and promotional caps, pens, etc
VP/General Manager: Thomas Mazzie
Estimated Sales: $2.5-5 Million
Number Employees: 5-9
Square Footage: 12000
Number of Customer Locations: 2000
Types of Products Distributed:
  Frozen Food, General Merchandise, Advertising specialties

57023 Hill's Pier 19 Restaurant Lighthouse Bar
PO Box 2356
Galveston, TX 77553-2356   409-763-4618
     Fax: 409-763-0090
Wholesaler/distributor of seafood; serving the food service market
Manager: Chico Lowery
Estimated Sales: $1-2.5 Million
Number Employees: 20-49
Types of Products Distributed:
  Food Service, Seafood

57024 Hillcrest Food Svc
2695 E 40th St
Cleveland, OH 44115-3508   216-361-0761
     Fax: 216-361-0764   www.hillcrestfoods.com
Owner: Armin Abraham
aabraham@hillcrestfoods.com
Estimated Sales: $10-20 Million
Number Employees: 100-249

57025 Hillis Farms
4141 Shincke Rd NE
Olympia, WA 98506   360-459-1321
     Fax: 360-459-0090   800-200-1321
Wholesaler/distributor of provisions/meats; serving the food service market
Owner: J Hillis
VP: Jay Hillis
Estimated Sales: $10-20 Million
Number Employees: 10-19

Wholesalers & Distributors / A-Z

Type of Packaging: Bulk
Types of Products Distributed:
  Food Service, Frozen Food, Provisions/Meat

57026 Hilo Fish Company
55 Holomua St
Hilo, HI 96720-5142   808-961-0877
     Fax: 808-935-1603 info@hilofish.com
                         www.hilofish.com
Fresh billfish, bottomfish, tuna, open ocean fish; Frozen tuna, grouper, hamachi, snapper, and other seafood
CEO: Charlie Umamoto
President & COO: Kerry Umamoto
General Manager: Jamiesen Batangan
Marketing: Helene Rousselle
National Sales Manager: Sabrina Vaughn
Operations Manager: Keith Hayashi
Estimated Sales: $20-50 Million
Number Employees: 20-49

57027 Hilts
1738 N Mosley Street
Wichita, KS 67214-1346   800-475-5177
             Fax: 316-262-5582
Wholesaler/distributor of cleaning supplies and disposables; serving the food service market
Parent Co: Hilts
Types of Products Distributed:
  Food Service, Frozen Food, General Merchandise, Cleaning supplies & disposables

57028 Hines Nut Co
990 S Saint Paul St
Dallas, TX 75201-6120   214-939-0253
     Fax: 214-761-0720   800-561-6374
     customerservice@hinesnutcompany.com
Wholesaler/distributor of nuts and dried fruits
President: Chris Hines
Director, Food Safety: Deborah Hines
Marketing: Cullen Hines
National Sales: Peter Ferris
Operations Support: Rod Gutierrez
Estimated Sales: $10-20 Million
Number Employees: 100-249
Type of Packaging: Consumer, Food Service, Private Label, Bulk
Types of Products Distributed:
  General Line, Nuts & dried fruits

57029 Hingham Shellfish
25 Eldridge Ct
Hingham, MA 02043   781-749-1374
             Fax: 405-631-8473
Shellfish
President/Treasure: Myrle Derbyshire
Estimated Sales: $.5-1 million
Number Employees: 1-4

57030 Hinojosa Brothers Wholesale
161 N Efren Ramirez Ave
Roma, TX 78584-8913   956-849-2386
     Fax: 956-849-2386   800-554-4119
Candy and confectionary.
Owner: Antonio Hinojosa
hinojosa_bros@yahoo.com
Estimated Sales: $600,000
Number Employees: 1-4

57031 Hipp Wholesale Foods
8983 E Sharon Dr
Scottsdale, AZ 85260
             Fax: 308-537-7575
Wholesaler/distributor of groceries, meats, produce, dairy products, frozen foods, baked goods, general merchandise, seafood, equipment and fixtures; serving the food service market; also, full service dishwashing, laundry and beverage programs available
President/Manager: Belva Hipp
Sales/Marketing Manager: Dennis Hipp
Operations Manager: Robert Hipp
Estimated Sales: $2.5-5 Million
Number Employees: 20-49
Square Footage: 160000
Private Brands Carried:
  Code
Number of Customer Locations: 1000
Types of Products Distributed:
  Food Service, Frozen Food, General Line, General Merchandise, Provisions/Meat, Produce, Seafood, Groceries, dairy products, etc.

57032 Hiss Stamp Company
100 N Grant Ave
Columbus, OH 43215-5119   614-224-5119
                          Fax: 614-224-0464
Manufacturer and wholesaler/distributor of stamps and FDA approved inks
Manager: Michael Gaborcik
Estimated Sales: Less than $500,000
Number Employees: 4
Square Footage: 7000
Parent Co: Cosco Industries
Types of Products Distributed:
  Frozen Food, General Merchandise, Stamps & inks

57033 Hoban Foods
1599 E Warren Avenue
Detroit, MI 48207-1035   313-833-1500
                          Fax: 313-833-0629
Wholesaler/distributor of frozen foods including pies, cakes, meat, seafood and vegetables; also, dairy products including fresh eggs, butter, cheese, etc
President: Don Van Tiem
Estimated Sales: $20-50 Million
Number Employees: 20-49
Square Footage: 80000
Types of Products Distributed:
  Frozen Food, General Line, Provisions/Meat, Produce, Seafood, Dairy products, pies, cakes, etc.

57034 Hockenbergs Equipment & Supply
7002 F St
Omaha, NE 68117-1013   402-339-8900
     Fax: 402-339-9232   800-228-6102
                          www.hockenbergs.com
Wholesaler/distributor of general merchandise products
CEO: Tom Schrack, Sr.
Estimated Sales: $10-20 Million
Number Employees: 20-49
Square Footage: 140000
Types of Products Distributed:
  Frozen Food, General Merchandise

57035 Hodell International
1750 N University Dr
Coral Springs, FL 33071-8903   954-752-0010
     Fax: 954-752-0080   800-441-4014
                          nosko@aol.com
Wholesaler/distributor and importer of produce cases, freezers, chillers, coolers and dispensers for milk and juice; exporter of refrigeration equipment
Partner: Howard Hoskowicz
Partner: Dell Dahl
Number Employees: 1-4
Square Footage: 80000
Private Brands Carried:
  Hodell; ISA; AHT
Types of Products Distributed:
  Frozen Food, General Merchandise, Produce cases, freezers, dispensers

57036 Hodges & Irvine Inc
1900 Sinclair St
St Clair, MI 48079-5513   810-329-4787
     Fax: 810-329-0151   800-783-4788
             sales@hodgesandirvine.com
             www.hodgesandirvine.com
Reservation books for hotels, restaurants, and all scheduling needs
President: Roger Powers
Sales Director: Lorena Randall
Estimated Sales: Less Than $500,000
Number Employees: 10-19
Types of Products Distributed:
  Frozen Food

57037 Hoffman Miller Advertising
3632 Canal St
New Orleans, LA 70119   504-484-3442
                          www.hmadvertising.com
New-Orleans based marketing, public relations and advertising agency. The company assists manufacturers with their package designs.
President: Nathan Hoffman
Estimated Sales: $.5-1 million
Number Employees: 2-10
Type of Packaging: Consumer, Food Service
Types of Products Distributed:
  Frozen Food, General Merchandise, Advertising specialties

57038 Hoffman's Quality Meats
13225 Cearfoss Pike
Hagerstown, MD 21740   301-739-2332
     Fax: 301-733-5549   800-356-3193
             smoore@hoffmanmeats.com
             www.hoffmanmeats.com
Wholesaler/distributor of fresh beef and pork.
Owner: Jason Trippett
jtrippett@hoffmanmeats.com
Estimated Sales: $20-50 Million
Number Employees: 20-49
Number of Customer Locations: 75
Types of Products Distributed:
  Provisions/Meat, Fresh beef & pork

57039 Hogtowne B-B-Q Sauce Company
1712 W University Avenue
Gainesville, FL 32603   352-375-6969
     Fax: 352-373-6969 www.saltydogsaloon.com
Wholesaler/distributor of hot sauces, BBQ sauces, marinades and other specialty food products
Manager: Keith Singleton
Vice President: Pam Taylor-Kinard
Estimated Sales: $500,000-$1 Million
Number Employees: 20-49
Square Footage: 8000
Parent Co: Original Alan's Cubana
Type of Packaging: Consumer, Food Service, Private Label, Bulk
Types of Products Distributed:
  Specialty Foods

57040 Hoky Central
720 Hanford St # 1
Geneseo, IL 61254   309-944-4592
                          Fax: 309-944-6643
Wholesaler/distributor of nonelectric industrial carpet sweepers
President: Dale Martin
Estimated Sales: $1-2.5 Million
Number Employees: 1-4
Private Brands Carried:
  Hoky
Types of Products Distributed:
  Frozen Food, General Merchandise, Non-electric industrial carper sweepers

57041 Holistic Horizons/Halcyon Pacific Corporation
8154 Belvedere Ave
Sacramento, CA 95826-4724   916-731-4299
     Fax: 916-731-4295   800-852-4261
                          www.holistichorizons.com
Wholesaler/distributor and exporter of herbal supplements including intestinal cleansing formula, intestinal bulking agent and lactobacteria food
President: Caroline Gray
Vice President: Ernest Gray
Contact: Jeffery Lu
service@holistichorizons.com
Office Manager: Ejffrey Lu
Estimated Sales: $500,000-$1 Million
Number Employees: 1-4
Square Footage: 16000
Types of Products Distributed:
  Health Food, Herbal supplements

57042 Holistic Products Corporation
10 W Forest Avenue
Englewood, NJ 07631-4020   201-569-1188
     Fax: 201-569-3224   800-221-0308
Processor, wholesaler/distributor and importer of health food products including propolis lozenges
President: Arnold Gans
a.gans@mdnu.com
VP Sales: Myra Gans
Number Employees: 38
Square Footage: 16000
Parent Co: MNI Group
Types of Products Distributed:
  Frozen Food, Health Food, Propolis lozenges

57043 Holland American International Specialties
10343 Artesia Blvd
Bellflower, CA 90706   562-925-6914
     Fax: 562-925-4507   www.1dutchmall.com
European and domestic specialty gourmet foods.
Manager: Maria Cervantes
Estimated Sales: $.5-1 million
Number Employees: 1-4

Wholesalers & Distributors / A-Z

57044 Holland Beef International Corporation
1084 Queen Anne Rd
Teaneck, NJ 07666   201-833-8100
Fax: 201-833-1920 usfoodproducts.com
Broker, wholesaler and exporter of beef, lamb, veal, dairy products, frozenfruits and vegetables and specialities
President: Edward Holland
CFO: Chona Canillas
Vice President: Philip White
Estimated Sales: $20-50 Million
Number Employees: 20-49
Square Footage: 20000
Type of Packaging: Food Service
Number of Customer Locations: 600
Types of Products Distributed:
 Food Service, Frozen Food, General Line, General Merchandise, Provisions/Meat, Produce, Seafood, Specialty Foods

57045 Holland-American International Specialties
10343 Artesia Blvd
Bellflower, CA 90706   562-925-6914
Fax: 562-925-4507 hais2000@aol.com
Wholesaler/distributor and importer of European gourmet foods
Manager: Maria Cervantes
Sales Director: Karen Spurgeon
Specialty Division Manager: Pauline Bridgeman
Estimated Sales: $10-20 Million
Number Employees: 1-4
Type of Packaging: Consumer
Types of Products Distributed:
 Specialty Foods, Dutch & European gourmet foods

57046 Hollander, Gould & Murray Company
50 Knickerbocker Rd
Moonachie, NJ 07074   212-736-1581
Fax: 201-935-3579
Wholesaler/distributor of frozen food and produce
President: M Laurence
Private Brands Carried:
 Wendy Brand
Types of Products Distributed:
 Frozen Food, Produce

57047 Hollowick Inc
100 Fairgrounds Dr
Manlius, NY 13104-1699   315-682-2163
Fax: 315-682-6948 800-367-3015
info@hollowick.com
Manufacturer and exporter of liquid candle lamps, lamp fuel, wax candles, chafing fuel and silk flowers ceramic vases
President: Alan Menter
info@hollowick.com
CFO: Eugene Duffy
Marketing: Mike Cleveland
Sales: Mike Cleveland
Plant Manager: Tom Palmeter
Estimated Sales: $5-10 Million
Number Employees: 20-49
Types of Products Distributed:
 Food Service

57048 Holly Seafood Company
410 Towne Avenue
Los Angeles, CA 90013   213-625-2513
Fax: 213-620-9653
Wholesaler/distributor of seafood; serving the food service market
President: Rick Merry
VP: Jim Merry
Estimated Sales: $5-10 Million
Number Employees: 1-4
Types of Products Distributed:
 Food Service, Frozen Food, Seafood

57049 Holy Kombucha
Dallas, TX 75220   469-828-1572
855-694-6595
hello@holykombucha.com holykombucha.com
Carbonated probiotic kombucha
President/Owner: Leo Bienati
Number of Brands: 1
Number of Products: 13
Type of Packaging: Consumer

57050 Holyoke Machine Co
514 Main St
Holyoke, MA 01040-5585   413-534-5612
Fax: 413-532-9244 800-994-4326
admin@holyokemachine.com
www.holyokemachine.com
Wholesaler/distributor of food service equipment; serving the food service market
President: James Sagalyn
jsagalyn@holyokemachine.com
Treasurer/VP: Bill Curtis
Executive VP: Peter Curtis
Controller: Robert Leighton
Sales Manager: Thomas E Clark
Plant Superintendent: Jose Cruz
Estimated Sales: $10-20 Million
Number Employees: 50-99
Square Footage: 100000
Types of Products Distributed:
 Frozen Food, General Merchandise, Foodservice equipment

57051 Home Delivery Food Service
1814 Washington St.
PO Box 215
Jefferson, GA 30549   706-367-9551
Fax: 706-367-4646
Frozen foods, meats and chicken
President: William Griffin, Sr.

57052 Home-Like Food Company
422 Jersey Ave
New Brunswick, NJ 8901   732-846-4100
Fax: 732-846-4889
Wholesaler/distributor of specialty ethnic foods; serving diners, restaurants, schools, hotels and health care facilities
President: Jeffrey Greenberg
VP: Bradley Greenberg
Sales Manager: Malcolm Greenberg
Estimated Sales: $10-20 Million
Number Employees: 10-19
Square Footage: 80000
Type of Packaging: Food Service, Private Label, Bulk
Types of Products Distributed:
 Food Service, Frozen Food, General Line, General Merchandise, Health Food, Produce, Seafood, Specialty Foods, Ethnic foods

57053 Homestead Foods
4445 Harvester Road
Burlington, ON L7L 4X1
Canada   905-681-8755
Fax: 905-681-8762
Wholesaler/distributor of seafood, health food, provisions/meats, general line products, frozen food and produce; serving the food service market
Owner/President: John Katsiris
Office Manager: Julie Katsiris
Number Employees: 5-9
Private Brands Carried:
 Cardinal; Maple Leaf; J.D.
Types of Products Distributed:
 Food Service, Frozen Food, General Line, Health Food, Provisions/Meat, Produce, Seafood

57054 Honey Acres
N1557 Hwy 67
Neosho, WI 53059   920-474-4411
info@honeyacres.com
www.honeyacres.com
Honey and honey products, including honey chocolates, honey mustards, andhoney straws.
CEO: John Gabielian
Marketing Manager: Debra Champeau
Director of Inside Sales & Marketing: Tiarra Detert
Plant Manager: Eugene Brueggeman
eugene@honeyacres.com
Year Founded: 1852
Estimated Sales: $5-9.9 Million
Number Employees: 30
Number of Products: 50
Square Footage: 144000
Type of Packaging: Consumer, Food Service, Private Label, Bulk
Types of Products Distributed:
 Frozen Food, General Merchandise, Health Food

57055 (HQ)Honeyville Grain Inc
1080 N Main St
Suite 100
Brigham City, UT 84302   435-494-4200
Fax: 435-734-9482 www.honeyville.com
Bakery mixes and ingredients
Founder: Lowell Sherratt
VP Finance: Robert Anderson
Executive VP: Trevor Christensen
Director Marketing/Sales: Don Mann
Sales Manager: Craig Dunford
Assistant Operations Manager: Garth Rollins
Estimated Sales: $10-20 Million
Number Employees: 10-19
Square Footage: 120000
Type of Packaging: Consumer, Food Service, Private Label, Bulk
Other Locations:
 California Distribution
 Rancho Cucamonga, CA
 Utah Tempsure & Wholesale
 Salt Lake City, UT
 Arizona Wholsale Distribution
 Tempe, AZ
 Honeyville Grain Mill
 Honeyville, UT
 Ohio Distribution Center
 West Chester, OHCalifornia DistributionSalt Lake City
Private Brands Carried:
 ADM; ConAgra
Types of Products Distributed:
 Frozen Food, General Line, Flour, corn meal, soy, edible oils, etc

57056 Honig Vineyard and Winery
850 Rutherford Road
Rutherford, CA 94573   707-963-5618
Fax: 707-963-5639 800-929-2217
www.honigwine.com
Wines
President: Michael Honig
COO: Tony Benedetti
Marketing Director: Regina Weinstein
Estimated Sales: $5-9.9 Million
Number Employees: 5-9
Type of Packaging: Private Label

57057 Hoogwegt, U.S., Inc
100 S Saunders Rd
Suite 200
Lake Forest, IL 60045   847-918-8787
mail@hoogwegtus.com
www.hoogwegtus.com
Wholesaler/distributor of dried dairy and wheat products.
President & CEO: Dalyn Dye
d.dye@hoogwegtus.com
Chief Financial Officer: Arthur Rauch
VP, Transportation & Logistics: David Hedlund
Estimated Sales: $100-500 Million
Parent Co: Hoogwegt Groep B.V.
Private Brands Carried:
 Lactofat; Lactopro
Types of Products Distributed:
 General Line, Dried dairy & wheat products

57058 Horizon Business Svc
1020 Goodlette Rd N
Naples, FL 34102-5449   239-261-5828
Fax: 239-261-0067 800-863-1616
sales@caterease.com www.caterease.com
Wholesaler/distributor of catering and event management software
Owner: Gregory Kopriva
sales@caterease.com
Estimated Sales: $500,000-$1 Million
Number Employees: 20-49
Private Brands Carried:
 Cater-Ease
Types of Products Distributed:
 Frozen Food, General Merchandise, Catering software

57059 Hormel Foods Corp.
1 Hormel Pl.
Austin, MN 55912   507-437-5611
www.hormelfoods.com
Meat and grocery products.
Chairman/President/CEO: Jim Snee
Executive VP/CFO: Jim Sheehan
Senior VP/General Counsel: Lori Marco
Senior VP, R&D: Kevin Myers
Vice President, Quality Management: Richard Carlson
Year Founded: 1891
Estimated Sales: $9 Billion
Number Employees: 20,000
Number of Brands: 52

Wholesalers & Distributors / A-Z

Type of Packaging: Consumer, Food Service, Private Label
Other Locations:
  Manufacturing Facility
  Austin, MN
  Manufacturing Facility
  Algona, IA
  Manufacturing Facility
  Alma, KS
  Manufacturing Facility
  Atlanta, GA
  Manufacturing Facility
  Aurora, IL
  Manufacturing Facility
  Barron, WI
  Manufacturing FacilityAlgona

57060 Hornell Wholesale Grocery Company
11 Collier Street
Hornell, NY 14843-1609   607-324-4710
                Fax: 607-324-4711
Wholesaler/distributor of beverages including beer, soda, juice and water
President: Joe Beckerman
VP/General Manager: John Beckerman
Sales Manager: Joseph Beamer
Number Employees: 10-19
Square Footage: 60000
Types of Products Distributed:
  Frozen Food, General Line, Beverages: beer, soda, juice & water

57061 Horsley Company
1630 S 4800 W
Suite D
Salt Lake City, UT 84104-5337   801-401-5500
      Fax: 801-401-5501 sales@fivestaraa.com
                www.horsleyco.com
Wholesaler/distributor of material handling equipment including conveyors
Manager: Tenielle Whitten
Chairman of the Board: George Horsley
Contact: Randell Crank
rcrank@horsleyco.com
Estimated Sales: $10 Million
Number Employees: 50-99
Square Footage: 22000
Private Brands Carried:
  Rapistan; Roach; Custom Manufacture
Types of Products Distributed:
  Frozen Food, General Merchandise, Material handling equipment

57062 Hosford & Wood Fresh Seafood Providers
2545 E 7th Street
Tucson, AZ 85716-4701   520-795-1920
                Fax: 520-795-1010
Seafood
President: Anita Wood
Secretary: Bruce Hosford

57063 Hoshizaki Northeastern
3502 Borden Ave
Long Island City, NY 11101-2506   718-937-2833
      Fax: 718-937-2967   800-281-5249
Wholesaler/distributor of ice and ice flakers, reach-in refrigerators and water filters; serving the food service market
VP: Dario Stanzini
Estimated Sales: $3-5 Million
Number Employees: 5-9
Parent Co: Hoshizaki America
Private Brands Carried:
  Hoshizaki; Everpure
Types of Products Distributed:
  Food Service, Frozen Food, General Merchandise, Refrigeration equipment, etc.

57064 Hosoda Brothers Inc
1444 Tennessee St
San Francisco, CA 94107-3421   415-648-7144
      Fax: 415-282-6336 www.hosodabros.com
Importer of Oriental food products including rice crackers, soy sauce, pickled vegetables, wholesaler/distributor of specialty foods
President: Lesley Hosoda
lesley@hosodabros.com
Vice President: Carolyn Hosada
Business Development: Jeff Tanabe
Office Manager: Jill & Lesley Hosoda

Estimated Sales: $10-20 Million
Number Employees: 20-49
Square Footage: 40000
Types of Products Distributed:
  Frozen Food, Specialty Foods

57065 Hoss-S
12985 Dunnings Hwy
PO Box 219
Claysburg, PA 16625-8202   814-693-3453
      Fax: 814-239-5922   800-438-7439
                www.hosswares.com
Prepared foods
Owner: Bill Campbell
VP: Mark Spinazzola
Plant Manager: Rocky Rhodes
Estimated Sales: Less Than $500,000
Number Employees: 5-9

57066 Hot Sauce Harry's Inc
1077 Innovation Ave # 109
North Port, FL 34289-9345   941-423-7092
      Fax: 214-956-9885   800-588-8979
                orders@hotlickssauces.com
                www.hotsauceharrys.com
Hot and spicy gourmet foods, licensed gourmet foods for NCAA, MLB, federal dock stamp
Owner: Kevin Harris
VP: Bob Harris
Sales: Lauren Smith
kevin@hotsauceharrys.com
Public Relations: Mari Katz
Estimated Sales: Less Than $500,000
Number Employees: 5-9
Type of Packaging: Consumer, Food Service, Private Label
Private Brands Carried:
  Hot Sauce Harry's, Peach n Pepper, Lime Time, Screaming SP
Types of Products Distributed:
  Food Service, Specialty Foods

57067 House of Spices
12740 Willets Point Blvd
Flushing, NY 11368-1506   718-507-4600
                Fax: 718-507-4798
                customerservice@hosindia.com
                www.hosindia.com
Pickles, condiment pastes, chutney, snack foods, candy, ice cream and frozen foods; importer of Indian-Pakistani basmati rice, lentils, spices, oils and nuts; exporter of pickles, condiments and spices.
President: Candace Kuechler
ckuechler@rich.com
Estimated Sales: $5-10 Millio
Number Employees: 50-99
Number of Brands: 25
Number of Products: 2000
Square Footage: 1200000
Type of Packaging: Consumer, Food Service, Private Label, Bulk
Other Locations:
  Manufacturing Facility
  Stafford, TX
  Manufacturing Facility
  Elk Grove, IL
  Manufacturing Facility
  Forestville, MD
  Manufacturing Facility
  Hayward, CA
  Manufacturing Facility
  Orlando, FL
  Manufacturing Facility
  Norcross, GA
  Manufacturing FacilityElk Grove
Private Brands Carried:
  MAAZA; 817 Elephant; BAS RECE; Nestle; Maggie Noodles; Vicco Natural Herbal Products; Zandu Herbal Products; Parle Biscuits
Types of Products Distributed:
  Food Service, Frozen Food, General Line, General Merchandise, Health Food, Produce, Specialty Foods

57068 House of Webster
1013 N 2nd St
P.O. Box 1988
Rogers, AR 72757   479-636-2974
      Fax: 479-636-2974   800-369-4641
                houseofwebster.com
Jams, jellies, preserves, spreads; relish; salsa; mustard; syrup; BBQ sauce; pickled products; cheese products; crackers; cured meats; nuts; baking mixes; soups; spices and seasonings; tea and coffee.
President: John Griffin

Year Founded: 1934
Estimated Sales: $13 Million
Number Employees: 65
Type of Packaging: Food Service, Private Label

57069 Houston International Packaging Company
Ste 310
4545 Pine Timbers St
Houston, TX 77041-9338   281-298-2259
      Fax: 713-664-0325   800-447-2689
Wholesaler/distributor of semi-bulk bags; serving food manufacturers and processors
President: William Price
Sales: Ron Riddle
Estimated Sales: $.5-1 million
Number Employees: 1-4
Private Brands Carried:
  Jumbo Cel
Types of Products Distributed:
  Frozen Food, General Merchandise, Semi-bulk bags

57070 Houston Poultry & Egg Company
PO Box 16027
Houston, TX 77222-6027   713-699-3585
                Fax: 713-694-3633
Wholesaler/distributor of poultry and eggs; serving the food service market
President: Noel Kennedy
Secretary/Treasurer: Wanda Kennedy
Number Employees: 20-49
Types of Products Distributed:
  Food Service, Frozen Food, General Line, Poultry & eggs

57071 Howard Decorative Packaging
3462 W Touhy Ave
Lincolnwood, IL 60712   847-675-7650
      Fax: 847-675-9042   888-772-9821
                www.howardpkg.com
Wholesaler/distributor of gourmet food packaging including gift basket accessories, candy boxes, candy cake bags, glassine lined and cellophane bags, ribbons, bows, tissue, etc
President: Ronald Watson
Executive VP: Brian Reed
National Sales Director: Julie Sneyfussy
Estimated Sales: $5-10 Million
Number Employees: 50-99
Types of Products Distributed:
  Frozen Food, General Merchandise

57072 Hu Kitchen
78 Fifth Ave
New York, NY 10011   212-510-8919
                hukitchen.com
Organic dark chocolate
CEO: Rita Hudetz
Type of Packaging: Bulk

57073 Hubert Co
9555 Dry Fork Rd
Harrison, OH 45030
      Fax: 800-527-0128   877-276-7773
      customerservice@hubert.com www.hubert.com
Wholesaler/distributor of merchandising products and display fixtures.
Year Founded: 1946
Estimated Sales: $50-100 Million
Number Employees: 50-99
Square Footage: 350000
Parent Co: K&K America
Types of Products Distributed:
  Frozen Food, General Merchandise, Merchandising products & fixtures

57074 Huck's Seafood
508 Cynwood Dr # D
Easton, MD 21601-3892   410-770-9211
                Fax: 410-763-8811
Crabs, oysters and clams; fish
Owner/President: James Ford, Jr
Orders: Amber Ford
Estimated Sales: $.5-1 million
Number Employees: 50
Square Footage: 5000
Type of Packaging: Consumer, Food Service, Bulk
Private Brands Carried:
  Russel Hall; Simmon; York River; Morton
Types of Products Distributed:
  Food Service, Frozen Food, Seafood

Wholesalers & Distributors / A-Z

57075 Hudson Belting & Svc CoInc
85 E Worcester St
Worcester, MA 01604-3649   508-756-0090
Fax: 508-753-6844 www.hudsonbelting.com
Manufacturer and wholesaler/distributor of food grade belting including leather, rubber, conveyor and timing; installation services available
President: Tom Jennette
hudsonbelting@charter.net
Plant Manager: John Whitney
Estimated Sales: Less Than $500,000
Number Employees: 5-9
Square Footage: 15000
Type of Packaging: Consumer, Food Service
Types of Products Distributed:
    Frozen Food, General Merchandise, Belting

57076 Hudson River Foods
P.O. Box 11
Castleton, NY 12033
    888-417-9343
    info@hudsonriverfoods.com
    www.hudsonriverfoods.com
All natural foods including baking mixes, cakes, brownies, cookies, icings, puddings, muffins, hempmilk, hemp tofu, chia greek yogurt, drink mixes, and Kombucha
Co-Founder: Dan Ratner
Co-Founder: Donna Ratner
Manager: Winston Edmonds
Warehouse Manager: Rebecca Sagendorf
Year Founded: 2005
Number Employees: 50-99
Number of Brands: 6
Types of Products Distributed:
    General Line

57077 Hudson River Fruit Distr
65 Old Indian Rd
P.O. Box 246
Milton, NY 12546
    Fax: 845-795-5686 800-640-2774
    info@hudsonriverfruit.com
    www.hudsonriverfruit.com
Wholesaler/distributor of produce including apples.
Founder & President: Harold Albinder
Quality Control: Liz Kovacs
Sales Manager: Pat Ferrara
Chief Operating Officer: Danny Albinder
Operations Manager: Alisha Albinder
General Manager: Rich Farlese
Year Founded: 1963
Estimated Sales: $20-50 Million
Number Employees: 50-99
Parent Co: Allstate Apple Exchange
Types of Products Distributed:
    Frozen Food, Produce, Apples

57078 Hudson Valley Coffee Company
632 Kids Lane
Castleton on Hudson, NY 12033-9687   518-766-9009
    Fax: 518-766-9789 800-637-6550
    bhnelisa@iname.com
Wholesaler/distributor, importer and exporter of specialty coffees and teas; also, infusers and grinders
Director Sales/Marketing: Lisa Goldstein
Service Manager: Diamond Psarianos
VP Purchasing: Jim Topaltzas
Estimated Sales: $2.5-5 Million
Number Employees: 5-9
Square Footage: 80000
Type of Packaging: Consumer, Food Service, Private Label, Bulk
Private Brands Carried:
    Barrie House Buzz; Cool Brew Cafe; Donut Shop Blend; Estate Roast Special; The City Roast Selection
Types of Products Distributed:
    Frozen Food, General Line, General Merchandise, Specialty Foods, Coffee & tea; also, infusers & grinders

57079 Hudson Valley Foie Gras
80 Brooks Rd
Ferndale, NY 12734-5101   845-292-2500
    Fax: 845-292-3009
    www.hudsonvalleyfoiegras.com
Duck foie gras
Operations Manager: Marcus Henley
Vice President: Izzy Yanay
info@hudsonvalleyfoiegras.com
Estimated Sales: $190 Thousand
Number Employees: 100-249

57080 Hudson Valley Malt
320 Co. Rte. 6
Germantown, NY 12526   845-489-3450
    info@hudsonvalleymalt.net
    www.hudsonvalleymalt.net
Artisan craft malt
Co-Owner: Dennis Nesel
Co-Owner: Jeanette Nesel
Number of Brands: 1
Type of Packaging: Consumer, Bulk
Types of Products Distributed:
    Malt

57081 Hue's Seafood
105 S 14th Street
Baton Rouge, LA 70802-4753   225-383-0809
    Fax: 225-383-0809
Seafood
President: Tu Nguyen

57082 Huff Ice Cream
3 Winkler Road
P.O.Box 238
Sidney, NY 13838   607-563-3999
    Fax: 607-563-8303 800-475-6203
    customerservice@huffdelivers.com
    www.huffdelivers.com
Wholesaler/distributor of sorbet; serving the food service market in upstate New York, Northeast Pennsylvania and some areas in Vermont
President, Owner: John H Huff
Owner: Jim Malloy
Secretary: John Huff
Treasurer/Sales/Marketing Manager: Paul Huff
Sales Territory Manager: Steve Frost
Contact: Phyllis Winn
phyllis.hufficecream@citlink.net
Estimated Sales: $500,000-$1 Million
Number Employees: 20-49
Square Footage: 16000
Parent Co: Huff Ice Cream
Private Brands Carried:
    Alexander's Premium Sorbet; Haagen Daas; Ben & Jerry's; Perry Products
Types of Products Distributed:
    Food Service, Frozen Food, General Line, Sorbet

57083 Huger-Davidson-Sale Company
2329 Old Buena Vista Rd
Buena Vista, VA 24416-4627   540-261-7451
    Fax: 540-261-1873
Wholesaler/distributor of candy, canned goods and dairy products
Number Employees: 10-19
Types of Products Distributed:
    Frozen Food, General Line, Candy, canned goods, etc.

57084 Hugg & Hall Equipment
7201 Scott Hamilton Dr
Little Rock, AR 72209   501-562-1262
    Fax: 501-565-8819 www.hugghall.com
Wholesaler/distributor of material handling equipment including forklifts and conveyors.
Owner: Robert Hall
roberth@hugghall.com
Sales Manager: Tim Waychoff
Estimated Sales: $50-100 Million
Number Employees: 100-249
Other Locations:
    Blytheville, AR
    Conway, AR
    El Dorado, AR
    Fort Smith, AR
    Jonesboro, AR
    Springdale, ARConway
Private Brands Carried:
    Crown; Toyota; Clark
Types of Products Distributed:
    Frozen Food, General Merchandise, Material handling equipment

57085 (HQ)Hughes Supply
600 Ferguson Dr
Orlando, FL 32805   407-843-9100
    Fax: 407-839-4613 prf563@hajoca.com
    hughessupply.com
Wholesaler/distributor of plumbing and HVAC products
Year Founded: 1928
Estimated Sales: $50-100 Million
Number Employees: 100-249
Parent Co: Hajoca Corporation
Types of Products Distributed:
    Plumbing & HVAC

57086 Hughes Warehouse Equipment Company
P.O.Box 794
Millersville, MD 21108-0794   410-729-9474
    Fax: 410-729-7994
Wholesaler/distributor of material handling equipment including shelving
President: John Parsons
VP: David Parsons
Estimated Sales: $.5-1 million
Number Employees: 5-9
Private Brands Carried:
    Metro; Penco; Lyon
Types of Products Distributed:
    Frozen Food, General Merchandise, Shelving

57087 Huguenot Sales Corporation
21 West Mall
Plainview, NY 11803-4209   718-417-8947
    Fax: 631-694-4872 800-451-5776
Wholesaler/distributor of food preparation and merchandising supplies
President: Vicki Bergman
Number Employees: 5-9
Square Footage: 14000
Types of Products Distributed:
    Frozen Food, General Merchandise, Food preparation/merchandising supplies

57088 Hull Lift Truck Inc
28747 Old US 33
Elkhart, IN 46516-1699   574-293-9769
    Fax: 574-293-9769 888-284-0364
    www.michianabobcat.com
Wholesaler/distributor of material handling equipment
President: Robert Hull
CEO: Margaret Ashby
margareta@commspecial.com
Estimated Sales: $10-20 Million
Number Employees: 50-99
Private Brands Carried:
    Toyota; Mitsubishi; Crown
Types of Products Distributed:
    Frozen Food, General Merchandise, Material handling equipment

57089 Humboldt Chocolate
PO Box 1206
Eureka, CA 95502   707-630-5355
    Fax: 707-312-8235 info@humboldtchocolate.com
    www.humboldtchocolate.com
All-natural chocolate bars

57090 Hummingbird Wholesale
150 Shelton McMurphey Blvd
Suite 104
Eugene, OR 97401   541-686-0921
    info@hummingbirdwholesale.com
    www.hummingbirdwholesale.com
Organic foods
Quality Control & Compliance Coordinator: Kathryn Collmar
Director Sales & Marketing: Stacy Kraker
Sales Manager: Deirdre Geddes
Human Resources Manager: Ellen Mitchell
Customer Service Manager: Kristen Werner
Purchaser: David Smith
Number Employees: 20-49
Types of Products Distributed:
    General Line, Produce

57091 Hunter Food Inc
3707 La Palma Ave
Anaheim, CA 92806-2122   714-666-1888
    Fax: 714-666-1222 www.hunterfood.com
Fresh, frozen, marinated, and non-marinated poultry
CEO: Huan Hua Le
Year Founded: 1991
Estimated Sales: $20-50 Million
Number Employees: 20-49

57092 Hunter Walton & Co Inc
120 Circle Dr N
Piscataway, NJ 08854-3703   732-805-0808
    Fax: 732-805-0282 hunterwalton@earthlink.com
    www.hunterwalton.com

1041

Wholesalers & Distributors / A-Z

Distributor and manufacturer of dairy products and food oils. Continuous and batch churn butter, domestic natural and processed cheese, dry cheese, milk powders and custom blends, margarine and shortenings (vegetable and animal)
President: Glenn Grimshaw
hunterwalton@earthlink.net
CEO: Peter Love
Sales Director: Gary Behie
Estimated Sales: $18 Million
Number Employees: 10-19
Type of Packaging: Consumer, Food Service, Private Label, Bulk
Types of Products Distributed:
  Food Service, Frozen Food, Specialty Foods, Dairy Products & Food Oils

57093 Huntsville Restaurant Equip
3214 8th Ave SW
Huntsville, AL 35805-3614   256-533-7727
                          Fax: 256-533-0888
Wholesaler/distributor of restaurant equipment
Owner: Jimmy Reed
info@huntsvillerestaurantequiptment.com
Sales Manager: Bill Bolton
Estimated Sales: $1-2.5 Million
Number Employees: 1-4
Types of Products Distributed:
  Food Service, Frozen Food, General Merchandise, Restaurant Equipment

57094 Husky Foods of Anchorage
5901 Old Seward Hwy
Anchorage, AK 99518-1481   907-563-1836
                          Fax: 907-563-5574
Wholesaler/distributor of general line items, health and specialty foods, coffee, meats, snacks, general merchandise, etc.; serving the food service market; rack jobber services available
President: W Wilken
Vice President: S Wilken
Business Operations Manager: J Heathcock
Estimated Sales: $3-5 Million
Number Employees: 10-19
Square Footage: 36000
Private Brands Carried:
  McKee; Snyder's of Hanover; Bon Appetit; Tom's; Superior; Trophy
Types of Products Distributed:
  Food Service, Frozen Food, General Line, General Merchandise, Health Food, Provisions/Meat, Rack Jobbers, Specialty Foods, Groceries, Coffee, etc.

57095 Hutchinson Mayrath Industries
2058 Route 67 North
PO Box 15
Monmouth, IL 61462   309-734-2143
          Fax: 309-734-7755 800-459-4835
              www.hutchinson-mayrath.com
Wholesaler/distributor of grain conveying systems
General Manager: Rick Hanson
VP Finance: Gary Matteson
Estimated Sales: $1-2.5 Million
Number Employees: 1-4
Private Brands Carried:
  Mayrath Augers; NECO Grain Handling
Types of Products Distributed:
  Frozen Food, General Merchandise, Grain conveying systems

57096 Hydra-Flex Inc
32975 Industrial Rd
Livonia, MI 48150-1617   734-522-9090
          Fax: 734-522-9579 800-234-0832
              customerservice@hydra-flex.com
              www.hydra-flex.com
Manufacturer and wholesaler/distributor of hoses, valves, fittings, tubing, etc
President: Charley Blank
cblank@hydra-flex.com
R&D: Jim Poole
VP: Bill Berlin
Sales Manager: Bill Berlin
Warehouse Manager: Jason Pinard
Estimated Sales: $10-20 Million
Number Employees: 10-19
Number of Customer Locations: 2000
Types of Products Distributed:
  Frozen Food, General Merchandise, Components & equipment

57097 Hydrite Chemical Co
300 N Patrick Blvd # 2
Brookfield, WI 53045-5816   262-792-1450
          Fax: 262-792-8721 sales@hydrite.com
              www.hydrite.com
Manufacturer and wholesaler/distributor of industrial cleaning, sanitaring ingredients and water treatment chemicals
CEO: John Honkamp
john.honkamp@hydrite.com
Sales Director: Rob Adams
Sales Director (Special Chemicals): Rich Carmichael
Purchasing Manager: Chuck Krior
Number Employees: 1000-4999
Types of Products Distributed:
  Frozen Food, General Line, General Merchandise, Industrial ingredients & chemicals

57098 Hytrol of California
PO Box 757
San Clemente, CA 92674-0757 626-969-8745
                          Fax: 626-969-7978
Wholesaler/distributor of material handling equipment including conveyors
President: Dereck Worrell
Sales/Marketing Executive: Bill Fish
Purchasing Manager: Marlone DeGuzman
Estimated Sales: $20-50 Million
Number Employees: 20-49
Square Footage: 23000
Types of Products Distributed:
  General Merchandise, Material handling equipment

57099 I Light Ny
13011 90th Ave
Richmond Hill, NY 11418-3310 718-849-3600
                          Fax: 718-441-9056
Distributor of light bulbs, ballast, fixture, LEDS and compact flourescents.
Owner: Toli Pasakiois
toli12@aol.com
Estimated Sales: $5-10 Million
Number Employees: 5-9
Private Brands Carried:
  Sylvania; Phillips; GE; Kicher; NAC
Types of Products Distributed:
  Lighting

57100 I Magid
965 Rue Bergar
Laval, QC H7L 4Z6
Canada   450-629-3737
                          Fax: 450-629-1809
Wholesaler/distributor and importer of canned mackerel, sardines, snails, clams, crab meat, oysters, mussels, shrimp, pineapples, mandarin oranges, olives, tropical fruit cocktail, artichoke hearts, etc
VP/Buyer: Allan Magid
Number Employees: 20-49
Square Footage: 200000
Type of Packaging: Consumer
Private Brands Carried:
  Beaver; Delicium; Alibi; Club Supreme
Types of Products Distributed:
  General Line, Canned fish, fruits, snails, etc.

57101 I Supply Co
1255 Spangler Rd
Fairborn, OH 45324
          Fax: 937-878-9216 800-837-7759
              csr@isupplyco.com www.isupplyco.com
Distributor of paper and plastic disposables and cleaning supplies: serving the food service, grocery, industrial markets, and office building markets. Systems distributor to quick service restaurants serving the lower midwest.
Chairman & CEO: Jerry Parisi
Chief Operating Officer: Victor Ragucci, Jr.
Executive Vice President: Ed Medlock
VP, Systems Sales: Tim Detrick
Year Founded: 1944
Estimated Sales: $50-100 Million
Number Employees: 100-249
Square Footage: 110000
Private Brands Carried:
  Unipro
Number of Customer Locations: 2000
Types of Products Distributed:
  Food Service, Frozen Food, General Line, General Merchandise, Produce, Paper, plastic & cleaning supplies

57102 I Wanna Distributors
480 27th Street
Orlando, FL 32806-4451   407-999-9511
          Fax: 407-999-9512 www.iwannaicecream.com
Wholesaler/distributor, exporter and importer of food service supplies, desserts, cakes, ice cream, cookies and pastries; serving the food service market
President: Susan Sullivan
Vice President: Bill Sullivan
Sales: Bill Sullivan
Estimated Sales: $6 Million
Number Employees: 5-9
Number of Brands: 20
Number of Products: 1000
Square Footage: 36000
Private Brands Carried:
  Symphony; White Toque; Pastry Chef; Wells Dairy; Haagen Daz; Good Humor; Sweet Streets; Hormel; M&M Mars; French Gourmet
Number of Customer Locations: 100
Types of Products Distributed:
  Food Service, Frozen Food, Specialty Foods

57103 I Zakarin & Sons Inc
5296 State Route 42
South Fallsburg, NY 12779-5725 845-434-4430
          Fax: 845-434-4610 800-543-3459
Wholesaler/distributor and exporter of general merchandise including paper, janitorial supplies, kitchen, baking and cooking equipment, etc.; serving the food service market
President: Shirley Zakarin
VP: Judy Averick
Estimated Sales: $5-10 Million
Number Employees: 10-19
Square Footage: 120000
Types of Products Distributed:
  Food Service, Frozen Food, General Merchandise, Paper, janitorial supplies, etc.

57104 I. Grob & Company
PO Box 260026
Bellerose, NY 11426-0026   718-328-4194
                          Fax: 718-991-6972
Importer and wholesaler of sugar, flour and baking products
Types of Products Distributed:
  Frozen Food, Sugar, flour & baking products

57105 I.T. Bauman Company
1641 Manufacturers Dr
Fenton, MO 63026-2838   636-326-9947
                          Fax: 314-771-5031
Wholesaler/distributor of industrial ingredients
CEO: Doug Caldwell
General Manager: Gary Norton
Estimated Sales: $1-2.5 Million
Number Employees: 5-9
Parent Co: Welton Corporation
Types of Products Distributed:
  Frozen Food, General Line, Industrial food ingredients

57106 IBC
2530 N Orange Blossom Trail
Orlando, FL 32804-4807   407-423-7131
Wholesaler/distributor of baked goods; serving the food service market
Manager: Bill Clayton
Parent Co: IBC
Types of Products Distributed:
  Food Service, Frozen Food, General Line, Baked goods

57107 IBF
803 Pressley Road
Suite 101
Charlotte, NC 28217-0771   704-334-6870
                          Fax: 704-335-6861
Importer and wholesaler/distributor of European wine and beer
CEO/President: Ralf Geschke
Estimated Sales: $5-10 Million
Number Employees: 5-9
Number of Customer Locations: 300
Types of Products Distributed:
  Frozen Food, General Line, Specialty Foods, European wine & beer

57108 ICC Industrial Chemical
6333 Sidney St
Houston, TX 77021-2795   713-748-0200
          Fax: 713-748-7408 800-234-1492
              www.iccfoggers.com

Wholesaler/distributor of floor polish; serving the food service market
President: Sharon Hatten
slhat10@aol.com
Secretary: Ruby Grizzell
VP Sales/Marketing: Richard Legg
Estimated Sales: $1-3 Million
Number Employees: 1-4
Type of Packaging: Private Label, Bulk
Private Brands Carried:
  Butchers; Advance; Hoover; Mastercraft; North American; Curtis Dyna Fog; Tornado
Types of Products Distributed:
  Food Service, Frozen Food, General Merchandise, Floor polish

57109 ID Foods Corporation
1800 Autoroute Laval
Laval, QC H7S 2E7
Canada   450-687-2680
Fax: 450-682-4797   800-361-9157
info@idfoods.com   www.IDFoods.com
Importer, exporter and wholesaler/distributor of canned fish, spices, confectionery and specialty food items; serving the food service market
President: Philip Issenman
CFO: Phillip Gattolar
VP Procurement/Compliance: Diana Henault
VP Sales/Marketing: Mario Latendresse
Types of Products Distributed:
  Food Service, Frozen Food, General Merchandise, Health Food, Specialty Foods, Spices, confectionery items, etc.

57110 ILHWA American Corporation
91 Terry St
Belleville, NJ 07109   973-759-1996
Fax: 973-450-0562   800-446-7364
info@ilhwana.com   www.ilhwa-usa.com
Korean ginseng
President: Sang Kil Han
Warehouse Manager: Edner Louis
Estimated Sales: $2.5-5 Million
Number Employees: 1-4
Types of Products Distributed:
  Frozen Food

57111 IMDEC
2061 Freeway Dr Ste E
Woodland, CA 95776   530-661-9091
Wholesaler/distributor of food processing equipment
President: Glen Langstaff
Contact: David Matthews
trgshop@yahoo.com
Estimated Sales: $1-2.5 Million
Number Employees: 5-9
Private Brands Carried:
  Protec; Zilli; Bellini
Number of Customer Locations: 50
Types of Products Distributed:
  Frozen Food, General Merchandise, Food processing equipment

57112 ISI Commercial Refrigeration
1461 S Belt Line Rd # 100
640 W Sixth St
Coppell, TX 75019-4938   214-631-7980
Fax: 713-861-3759   www.isi-texas.com
Wholesaler/distributor of refrigeration equipment; serving the food service market
Manager: Mark Kholshmidt
Vice President: Mark Kohlschmidt
Estimated Sales: $10-20 Million
Number Employees: 100-249
Square Footage: 50000
Parent Co: ISI Commercial Refrigeration
Types of Products Distributed:
  Food Service, Frozen Food, General Merchandise, Refrigeration equipment

57113 ISI Commercial Refrigeration
P.O.Box 569060
Dallas, TX 75356-9060   214-631-7980
Fax: 214-630-5815   800-777-5070
Wholesaler/distributor of ice machines, refrigerators, freezers, microwave ovens, drink systems, walk-in coolers and freezers and ice cream and yogurt machines; serving the food service market
President: Marty Monnat
CEO: Eric Hohn
CFO: Bill Kutnex
VP: Jean McCorkle
Contact: Martin Monnat
m.monnat@isi-texas.com
Estimated Sales: $20-50 Million
Number Employees: 50-99
Square Footage: 40000
Parent Co: ISI Commercial Refrigeration
Types of Products Distributed:
  Food Service, Frozen Food, General Merchandise, Refrigeration equipment, etc.

57114 ISI Commercial Refrigeration
1180 S 4th St
Beaumont, TX 77701   409-835-4904
Fax: 409-835-5421   800-375-4904
www.isi-texas.com
Wholesaler/distributor of refrigeration equipment and fixtures; serving the food service market, ice machines and cooking equipment also
President: Bobby Celli
Contact: Scott Carlton
scarlton@isi-texas.com
Manager: Robert Celli
Estimated Sales: $1-3 Million
Number Employees: 10-19
Square Footage: 40000
Parent Co: ISI Comerical Refrigeration
Types of Products Distributed:
  Food Service, Frozen Food, General Merchandise, Refrigeration equipment & fixtures

57115 ISI North America
175 Route 46 W
Fairfield, NJ 07004-2327   973-227-2426
Fax: 973-227-9140   800-447-2426
customerservice@isinorthamerica.com
www.isinorthamerica.com
Wholesaler/distributor of general merchandise including housewares
President/CEO: Rick Agresta
CFO: Barry Granet
VP: Carol Kentis
Marketing Director: Nancy Hartmann
Sales Director: Carol Kentis
Operations Manager: Tom Lineweaver
Estimated Sales: $5-10 Million
Number Employees: 10-19
Private Brands Carried:
  Kayser
Types of Products Distributed:
  Frozen Food, General Merchandise, Houswares, Cream Whippers, Soda Siphons

57116 Iberia Foods of Florida
7850 NW 80th Street
Medley, FL 33166-2104   305-863-8840
Fax: 305-884-7939
Wholesaler/distributor of canned meat products
Sales Manager: Peter Casais
Number Employees: 100-249
Parent Co: CPC International
Private Brands Carried:
  Iberia
Types of Products Distributed:
  Frozen Food, Provisions/Meat

57117 Icart & Deco Originals
28241 Crown Valley Parkway
Pmb F-612
Laguna Niguel, CA 92677-4441   949-249-1961
Fax: 949-249-9904
Wholesaler/distributor of art deco and nouveau prints and posters from 1900s to 1940s; serving the food service market
Owner: Sandy Verin
Sales/Marketing Executive: Alex Holzman
Types of Products Distributed:
  Vintage Porsters & Prints

57118 Ice & Juice Systems
420 6th St
Daytona Beach, FL 32117   386-254-2734
Fax: 386-254-0818
Wholesaler/distributor of fruit juices, cocktail mixes, ice makers and bar equipment and supplies
Owner: Vincent Cerami
Co-Owner: Dolly Hebert
Estimated Sales: $500,000-$1 Million
Number Employees: 5-9
Private Brands Carried:
  Ice & Juice Systems
Number of Customer Locations: 250
Types of Products Distributed:
  Frozen Food, General Line, General Merchandise, Fruit juices, mixes, ice makers, etc.

57119 Ice Chips Candy
818A 79th Ave SE
Olympia, WA 98501
866-202-6623
www.icechips.com
Sugar-free hard candy
Co-Founder: Charlotte Clary
Co-Founder: Bev Vines-Haines
Number of Brands: 1
Number of Products: 18
Type of Packaging: Consumer

57120 (HQ)Ice Machines
1228 Folsom St
San Francisco, CA 94103-3880   415-864-7200
Fax: 415-864-7709   800-423-8463
Wholesaler/distributor of ice makers, beverage air and continental refrigeration, shelving, cup dispensers, ranges and sinks; serving the food service market
Owner: Royston Lee
roystonl@icominc.com
VP/General Manager: Royston Lee
VP/Operations Manager: David Lee
Estimated Sales: $5-10 Million
Number Employees: 10-19
Square Footage: 68000
Private Brands Carried:
  Crystal Tips; Cari-All; Modular Follett
Types of Products Distributed:
  Food Service, Frozen Food, General Merchandise, Ice makers, shelving, dispensers, inc.

57121 Ice Makers
3606 Ruffin Road
San Diego, CA 92123-1810   858-576-3036
Fax: 858-576-3675   800-541-8590
bud@imice.com
Wholesaler/distributor of groceries, concession equipment and supplies, ice machines and water purification systems; serving the food service market; repair services and rentals available
VP Marketing: B Robinson
Number Employees: 20-49
Square Footage: 32000
Private Brands Carried:
  Slush Puppie; Gold Medal; C. Cretors; Cornelius
Number of Customer Locations: 1500
Types of Products Distributed:
  Food Service, Frozen Food, General Line, General Merchandise, Groceries, concession equipment, etc.

57122 Iceberg Seafood Inc
74 Main St
Sag Harbor, NY 11963-3006   631-725-1100
Fax: 631-725-6048
Import broker and wholesaler/distributor of frozen shellfish and Alaskan/Canadian fish items
President: John Geoffroy
icebergsea@gmail.com
Sales Manager: Charlie Hillen
Purchasing: Eugene Alper
Estimated Sales: $1-2.5 Million
Number Employees: 1-4
Square Footage: 8000
Private Brands Carried:
  49th Star; Arctic Royal
Types of Products Distributed:
  Food Service, Frozen Food, Seafood

57123 Icrest International LLC
1240 E Victoria Street
Carson, CA 90746-1666   310-886-3521
Fax: 310-537-0254
Wholesale food products
Contact: Masamitsn Furuta
masa@fshoten.com

57124 Imex Enterprise
110 Gerstley Rd
Hatboro, PA 19040-1911   215-672-2887
Fax: 215-672-9552   www.imexenterprises.com
Pepper, salt, nutmeg mills and coffee grinders, SS cookware, SS gadgets, SS serving ware, copper molds
President: Norbert Hein
Estimated Sales: $10-20 Million
Number Employees: 10-19

Wholesalers & Distributors / A-Z

57125 Impact Products LLC
2840 Centennial Rd
Toledo, OH 43617-1898   419-841-2891
Fax: 419-841-7861 800-333-1541
custserv@impact-products.com
www.impact-products.com
Wholesaler/distributor of toilet bowl mops, soap dispensers, dust pans, plastic pumps, disposable plastic gloves and washroom accessories
President/Chairman: John Harbal
Founder: James Findlay
Vice President: Cesar Bejar
cbejar69@gmail.com
Quality Assurance Manager: Carolyn Helminiak
Vice President, Marketing: Jeannie McCarthy
Sales & Marketing Executive: Kaiko Laser
Vice President, Operations: Brian Paul
Procurement Manager: James Knechtges
Estimated Sales: $29 Million
Number Employees: 100-249
Square Footage: 155000
Types of Products Distributed:
  Frozen Food, General Merchandise, Mops, dust pans & washroom accessories

57126 Imperial Bag & Paper Company
59 Hook Rd
New jersey, NJ 7002   201-437-7440
Fax: 201-437-7442 www.imperialbag.com
Wholesaler/distributor of disposable products including paper and plastic bags, janitorial supplies, towels, tissue, paper napkins, hot cups, aluminum and food packaging products; serving the food service market
President: Jason Tillis
CEO: Robert Tillis
CFO: Paul Cervino
Senior director: Charles D'Elia
VP Sales: Chris Freeman
Estimated Sales: $10-20 Million
Number Employees: 5-9
Private Brands Carried:
  Diversey; Spartan
Types of Products Distributed:
  Food Service, Frozen Food, General Merchandise, Disposable products

57127 Imperial Dade
255 Route 1 & 9
Jersey City, NJ 07306   201-437-7440
Fax: 201-437-7442 contact@imperialdade.com
www.imperialdade.com
Wholesaler/distributor of paper and plastic products, disposables, janitorial supplies and film for produce and meat.
Chief Executive Officer: Robert Tillis
Office Manager: Ella Raiden
eraiden@dadepaper.com
Sales Director: Richard Beck
General Manager: Chuck Howard
Assistant General Manager: Tere Martin
Operations Manager: Randy Goins
Year Founded: 1935
Estimated Sales: $100+ Million
Number Employees: 2000
Parent Co: Venco
Type of Packaging: Consumer, Food Service, Private Label, Bulk
Number of Customer Locations: 3000
Types of Products Distributed:
  Food Service, Frozen Food, General Merchandise, Paper, plastic & janitorial items

57128 Imperial Food Supply
4800 North St
Baton Rouge, LA 70806-3497   225-924-4222
Fax: 225-924-3362
Grocery Wholesaler
Owner/President: Michael Divincenti, Jr.

57129 Imperial Seafood
500 NE 185th Street
Miami, FL 33179-4541   305-690-0200
Fax: 954-690-9920
Wholesaler/distributor of fresh and frozen seafood
President: Richard Kittay
Estimated Sales: $1-2.5 Million
Number Employees: 10-19
Number of Customer Locations: 150
Types of Products Distributed:
  Frozen Food, Seafood

57130 Imperial Tea Court
8451 Baldwin
Oakland, CA 94621   510-540-8888
Fax: 415-788-6079 800-567-5898
CustomerService@ImperialTea.com
www.imperialtea.com
Retailer of tea
President/CFO: Roy Fong
roy@imperialtea.com
Estimated Sales: $1-2.5 Million
Number Employees: 5-9
Number of Brands: 1
Type of Packaging: Private Label, Bulk

57131 Imperial Trading
9583 Indigo Creek Boulevard
Murrells Inlet, SC 29576-8626   843-215-3835
Fax: 843-215-3836
Wholesaler/distributor of frozen foods, groceries, meats and seafood
Chairman: Ted Petroff
President: Shirley Petroff
VP: Michael Petroff
Estimated Sales: $8 Million
Number Employees: 5-9
Private Brands Carried:
  Armour Swift; Hillshire Farms & Kahn; Jerome Poultry; Bryan Foods; Gwaltney of Smithfield; Food Brand America, Saralee and Tyson
Types of Products Distributed:
  Food Service, Frozen Food, General Line, Provisions/Meat, Seafood

57132 Imported Restaurant Specialties
331 Curie Dr
Alpharetta, GA 30005-2264   404-325-0585
Fax: 404-777-6652 800-875-5551
Importer and wholesaler/distributor of espresso, cappuccino and coffee makers, pasta cookers and machinery, pizza oven and rollers, pastry cases, espresso carts, juice extractors, gelato machines, deli cases, ionia coffee, ice tea loose tea and frozen beverage mixes
President/CEO: Howard Brown
CFO/VP: DiJana DJelicovic
Estimated Sales: $5-10 Million
Number Employees: 1-4
Square Footage: 60000
Private Brands Carried:
  Elite Espresso Machines; Granita Machines; Classico, Ionia Coffee, Southern Bell Ice Tea, Granissimo Frozen Beverage Mixes
Number of Customer Locations: 10000
Types of Products Distributed:
  Food Service, General Merchandise, Coffee & Tea Equipment and Supplies

57133 (HQ)Importex International
PO Box 310
Carboner, NL A1Y 1B7
Canada   709-596-2900
Fax: 709-596-1901
Wholesaler/distributor, importer and exporter of frozen foods, general line products and merchandise, produce, provisions/meats and seafood; serving the retail and food service markets
President: Calvin Powell
Number Employees: 100-249
Square Footage: 340000
Number of Customer Locations: 900
Types of Products Distributed:
  Food Service, Frozen Food, General Line, General Merchandise, Provisions/Meat, Produce, Seafood

57134 In A Bind Inc
8749 Center Rd
Springfield, VA 22152-2234   703-569-0371
Fax: 703-569-2037 800-726-3687
inabindinc@aol.com www.inabindinc.com
Wholesaler/distributor of custom menu covers, wine books, guest checks, guest services, directories, etc.; serving the food service market
Owner: William Gaspelin
william@inabindinc.com
Estimated Sales: $.5-1 million
Number Employees: 1-4
Types of Products Distributed:
  Food Service, Frozen Food, General Merchandise, Custom menu covers, wine books, etc.

57135 In A Nutshell
753 Montague St
San Leandro, CA 94577-4325   510-895-2010
Fax: 510-633-8835 custserv@inanutshell.com
www.inanutshell.com
Wholesaler/distributor of general merchandise, specialty nuts and dried fruit, chocolate, extracts, sweeteners, canned goods, spices, serving the San Francisco Bay area
CEO: Robert Graubr
rob@inanutshell.com
CEO: Tim Wales
Sales Director: Carmen Hernandez
Operations Manager: Monique Wales
Purchasing Agent: Timothy Wales
Estimated Sales: $300,000-500,000
Number Employees: 5-9
Square Footage: 18000
Type of Packaging: Food Service, Bulk
Number of Customer Locations: 300
Types of Products Distributed:
  Food Service, Specialty Foods, Nuts, dried fruit, Spices

57136 Independent Wholesale
10326 107th Street NW
Edmonton, AB T5J 1K2
Canada   780-423-4446
Fax: 780-426-4233
Wholesaler/distributor of confectionery products, seafood and grocery items; serving the food service market; also, rack jobber services available
President: Joel Sapara
Number Employees: 20-49
Square Footage: 120000
Number of Customer Locations: 238
Types of Products Distributed:
  Food Service, Frozen Food, General Line, Rack Jobbers, Seafood, Confectionery

57137 India Emporium
3743 N Rock Rd Ste 200
Wichita, KS 67226   316-687-3266
Fax: 316-687-3266
Wholesaler/distributor of specialty foods including Indian products
Owner: Mohammad Nazir
Manager: Tahira Ali
Estimated Sales: Less than $500,000
Number Employees: 1-4
Square Footage: 10000
Types of Products Distributed:
  Frozen Food, Specialty Foods, Indian products

57138 Indian Springs Water Company
350 Us Highway 46
Rockaway, NJ 07866-3827   973-584-3166
Fax: 973-627-0330
Wholesaler/distributor of spring water
President: Greg Ginsberg
Estimated Sales: $5-10 Million
Number Employees: 50-99
Number of Customer Locations: 3000
Types of Products Distributed:
  Frozen Food, Spring water

57139 Indiana Restaurant Equipment
2653 E US Highway 30
Warsaw, IN 46580-7128   574-267-3288
Fax: 574-267-8299 800-736-3280
www.penguinpoint.com
Wholesaler/distributor of food service equipment and supplies; serving the food service market; also, design and installation services available
President: Randall J Stouder
CEO: W Stouder, Jr.
Sales Director: Noble Carpenter
Purchasing Manager: Sarah Beck
Number Employees: 5-9
Square Footage: 40000
Parent Co: Penguin Point Systems
Types of Products Distributed:
  Food Service, Restaurant equipment & supplies

57140 Indiana Sugars Inc
911 Virginia St
Gary, IN 46401   219-886-9151
Fax: 219-886-5124 john@buysugars.com
www.sugars.com
Wholesaler/distributor of grocery products; serving the food service market.
President & COO: John Yonover
Vice President, Sales & Marketing: Scott Sievers
SVP, Strategic Development: John Tritt

Estimated Sales: $35 Million
Number Employees: 50-99
Square Footage: 400000
Types of Products Distributed:
  Food Service, Frozen Food, General Line, Grocery products

57141 Indianapolis Fruit Company
4501 Massachusetts Ave
Indianapolis, IN 46218 317-546-2425
800-377-2425
www.indyfruit.com
Wholesaler/distributor and importer of produce including peppers, tomatoes, cherry tomatoes, apples, kiwi, etc.
Owner: Joe Corsaro
Vice President: Peter Piazza
Director, Sales & Marketing: Daniel Corsaro
Year Founded: 1947
Estimated Sales: $41 Million
Number Employees: 180
Square Footage: 250000
Types of Products Distributed:
  Produce

57142 Indianapolis Meat Company
1725 Southeastern Avenue
Indianapolis, IN 46201-3956 317-679-5352
Fax: 317-632-9389
Importer of frozen boneless beef, lamb and mutton; wholesaler/distributor of meat
President: Gerald Fivel
Estimated Sales: $1-2 Million
Number Employees: 1-4
Types of Products Distributed:
  Provisions/Meat

57143 Indianhead Foodservice
313 N Hastings Pl
Eau Claire, WI 54703-3440 715-834-2777
Fax: 715-834-3723 800-279-3692
www.callifd.com
Wholesaler/distributor of groceries, meats, produce, dairy items, frozen foods, baked goods, equipment and fixtures, general merchandise, private label items and seafood; serving the food service market
President: Thomas J Gillett
tgillett@callifd.com
Sales Manager: Steve Thompson
Estimated Sales: $20-50 Million
Number Employees: 50-99
Private Brands Carried:
  Nugget
Number of Customer Locations: 2300
Types of Products Distributed:
  Food Service, Frozen Food, General Line, General Merchandise, Provisions/Meat, Produce, Seafood, Baked goods, dairy items, etc.

57144 Indigo Coffee Roasters
660 Riverside Dr # 1
Florence, MA 01062-2763 413-586-4537
Fax: 413-280-0008 800-447-5450
info@indigocoffee.com www.indigocoffee.com
Coffee
President: Lourdes Tallet
Square Footage: 4000
Type of Packaging: Consumer, Food Service, Private Label, Bulk
Types of Products Distributed:
  Coffee & Tea

57145 Indo-European Foods
1000 Air Way
Glendale, CA 91201-3030 818-247-1000
Fax: 818-247-9722 indoeuro1@aol.com
www.indo-euro.com
Wholesaler/distributor and importer of French and Bulgarian foods, feta cheese, lady fingers, Indian basmati, Thailand jasmine rice, couscous, frozen quail, vegetable soup bases and mineral water
President: Albert Bezjian
CEO: Terry Bezjian
CFO: George Callas
Estimated Sales: $20-50 Million
Number Employees: 20-49
Square Footage: 42000
Private Brands Carried:
  Zergut; Al-Wad; Vegeta; Moomtaz; Ploikala; Elephant
Number of Customer Locations: 1310
Types of Products Distributed:
  Frozen Food, General Line, Specialty Foods, Cheese, rice, couscous, quail, etc.

57146 Industrial Commercial Supply
900 Moe Dr
Akron, OH 44310 330-633-0727
Fax: 330-633-0728 800-737-9671
frank@icsponge.com www.icsponge.com
Wholesaler/distributor of cellulose sponges. Converter/fabricator of cellulose sponge
CEO/VP: Larry Rowlands
General Manager: Frank Mushisky
Estimated Sales: $750,000
Number Employees: 10-19
Square Footage: 40000
Parent Co: Distribution Results
Type of Packaging: Consumer, Private Label, Bulk
Private Brands Carried:
  3M; Spontex; VWR
Types of Products Distributed:
  General Merchandise, Cellulose sponges

57147 Industrial Commodities
4134 Innslake Dr
Glen Allen, VA 23060
800-523-7902
inquiries@industrialcommodities.com
www.industrialcommodities.com
Wholesaler/distributor and exporter of sugar, salt, honey, molasses, eggs, dextrose, milk powder, monosodium glutamate, coconut and syrups; serving the food service market.
Vice President: Rick Crowder
Partner Manager: David Hill
dhill@industrialcommodities.com
Year Founded: 1979
Estimated Sales: $20-50 Million
Private Brands Carried:
  Domino; Hubinger
Types of Products Distributed:
  Food Service, Frozen Food, General Line, Produce, Coconut, sugar, salt, molasses, etc.

57148 Industrial Contacts Inc
265 Post Ave # 130
Ste 130
Westbury, NY 11590-2235 516-408-1400
Fax: 212-689-3952 siegel@indcontacts.com
www.indcontacts.com
Wholesaler/distributor of general merchandise including advertising specialties, promotional give-a-ways, jars, packaging, labels and tie-in sales
President: Steve Siegel
siegel@indcontacts.com
VP Sales: Steve Siegel
Estimated Sales: $1-2.5 Million
Number Employees: 5-9
Square Footage: 24000
Types of Products Distributed:
  Frozen Food, General Merchandise, Advertising specialties

57149 Industrial Handling Equipment
846 S Stanford Way
Sparks, NV 89431-6229 775-359-3335
Fax: 775-359-3362 sales@iheofnv.com
www.ihenv.com
Wholesaler/distributor of material handling equipment
President: Tony Fackelmann
tfackelmann@iheofnv.com
Estimated Sales: $2.5-5 Million
Number Employees: 10-19
Private Brands Carried:
  Toyota; Crown; L.M.T.
Types of Products Distributed:
  Frozen Food, General Merchandise, Material handling equipment

57150 Industrial Lift Truck
8264 Brentwood Industrial Dr
Saint Louis, MO 63144 314-644-5100
Fax: 314-644-5371
Wholesaler/distributor of material handling equipment; also, rentals available
Owner: Dennis Gutherz
Estimated Sales: $5-10 Million
Number Employees: 10-19
Private Brands Carried:
  New Prime Mover; Premier
Types of Products Distributed:
  Frozen Food, General Merchandise, Material handling equipment

57151 Industrial Maintenance
1531 Jp Hennessy Dr
La Vergne, TN 37086-3522 615-641-9474
Fax: 615-641-9480 www.ime-corp.com
Wholesaler/distributor of electrical supplies, lighting fixtures, electric lamps, plastic tubing, pneumatic equipment, etc
President: Chris Robinson
crobinson@ime-corp.com
VP: Frank Riddle
Number Employees: 20-49
Types of Products Distributed:
  Frozen Food, General Merchandise, Electrical supplies, lamps, etc.

57152 Industrial Products Supply
9136 E Hampton Dr
Capitol Heights, MD 20743-3809 301-336-0540
Fax: 301-350-9612 800-682-2440
ragdoll@ips-sales.com www.ips-sales.com
Wholesaler/distributor of adhesive tapes and cloths, paper and nonwoven wiping materials, safety and janitorial supplies and material handling equipment
President: Tony Gioia
VP: George Franklin
General Manager: Chele Ennis
Estimated Sales: $5-10 Million
Number Employees: 10-19
Square Footage: 60000
Parent Co: Commercial Wiping Cloth
Types of Products Distributed:
  Frozen Food, General Merchandise, Tape, cloth, janitorial supplies, etc.

57153 Industrial Soap Co
722 S Vandeventer Ave
St Louis, MO 63110-1242 314-241-6363
Fax: 314-533-5556 www.industrialsoap.com
Wholesaler/distributor of janitorial supplies and sanitary chemicals
CEO/President: Robert Shapiro
VP: Mark Shapiro
Estimated Sales: $20-50 Million
Number Employees: 50-99
Square Footage: 100000
Types of Products Distributed:
  Frozen Food, General Merchandise, Janitorial supplies

57154 Industrial Truck Sales & Services
4100 Randleman Road
Greensboro, NC 27406-8119 336-275-9121
Fax: 336-274-7074 800-632-0333
Wholesaler/distributor of material handling equipment; also, sales and service available
President: Denny Boyce
Marketing/Leasing Manager: Chris Webster
Sales Manager: Mike Brown
Estimated Sales: $20-50 Million
Number Employees: 50-99
Square Footage: 250000
Types of Products Distributed:
  Frozen Food, General Merchandise, Material handling equipment

57155 Infinite Peripherals
2312 Touhy Ave
Elk Grove Vlg, IL 60007-5329 224-404-6227
Fax: 847-818-1287 800-278-7860
andy@ipcprint.com www.ipcmobile.com
Importer and wholesaler/distributor of receipt printers
Owner: Andy Graham
andy@ipcprint.com
CEO: Jeff Scott
Estimated Sales: $1-3 Million
Number Employees: 10-19
Private Brands Carried:
  Citizen
Types of Products Distributed:
  Frozen Food, General Merchandise, Receipt printers

57156 Infinite Specialties
8004 Bell Blvd
Jamaica, NY 11427 718-464-9393
Fax: 718-468-6017
Wholesaler/distributor of general merchandise including advertising specialties, executive gifts, premiums, awards programs, calculators, marking and writing pens, T-shirts, aprons, tote bags and food baskets
President: Joanne Misher

Wholesalers & Distributors / A-Z

Estimated Sales: $500,000-$1 Million
Number Employees: 1-4
Number of Customer Locations: 50
Types of Products Distributed:
  Frozen Food, General Merchandise, Advertising specialties

57157 Ingenuities
66 Hoyt St
South Salem, NY 10590-1320   914-763-8100
    Fax: 914-763-2234 www.ingenuities.net
Distributor of upscale health oriented food products
President: Bill Mayer
Vice President: Suzanne Salomon
abc@aol.com
COO: Karen Lehrer
Number Employees: 5-9
Type of Packaging: Private Label
Types of Products Distributed:
  Food Service, Health Food, Specialty Foods, Bakery & snack foods

57158 Ingersoll & Assoc
6n971 Riverside Dr
St Charles, IL 60174-6456   847-742-7960
    Fax: 847-742-9170 888-259-4040
    ingersoll1@prodigy.net
Wholesaler/distributor of stock and custom forms, ticket books, ledgers, journal and inventory control sheets, grain elevator equipment, etc.; importer of promotional items, advertising specialties and health foods including vitamin and lecithin supplements
President: Zoe Ingersoll
zoe@ingersollsales.com
Estimated Sales: $3-5 Million
Number Employees: 1-4
Type of Packaging: Consumer, Food Service, Private Label, Bulk
Private Brands Carried:
  Seedburo; American-Newlong
Types of Products Distributed:
  Health Food, Custom forms, ticket books, etc.

57159 Ingold's HICO Inc
442 Franklin St
Bel Air, MD 21014-2929   410-879-9114
    Fax: 410-879-9393 800-874-6465
    ingolds@bellatlantic.net
Wholesaler/distributor of balers, compactors, industrial trucks and recycling and material handling equipment
President: Glenn Ingold
CEO: Judith Ingold
ingolds@bellatlantic.net
Estimated Sales: $2.5-5 Million
Number Employees: 1-4
Types of Products Distributed:
  General Merchandise, Balers, compactors, trucks, etc.

57160 Ingredient Exchange Co
401 N Lindbergh Blvd # 315
St Louis, MO 63141-7839   314-872-8850
    Fax: 314-872-7550 info@ingexchange.com
    www.ingexchange.com
Importer of cheese, dairy ingredients; buyer of salvage and surplus; jobber of frozen foods, spices, concentrates and sweeteners
President: Jerry Behimer
Manager: Chris Heupel
cheupeo@ingexchange.com
Estimated Sales: $15-20 Million
Number Employees: 1-4
Number of Customer Locations: 1
Types of Products Distributed:
  Specialty Foods

57161 Inland Meats of Spokane
1222 N Regal St
Spokane, WA 99202-3682   509-924-4140
    Fax: 509-924-4704
Wholesaler/distributor of fresh and frozen provisions/meats including beef, pork, lamb and veal; serving the food service market
President: L Mullenix
VP: M Mullenix
Contact: Dan Mullenix
inlandmeatsinc@comcast.net
Estimated Sales: $20-50 Million
Number Employees: 20-49
Types of Products Distributed:
  Food Service, Frozen Food, General Line, Provisions/Meat, Beef, pork, lamb & veal

57162 (HQ)Inland Seafood Inc
1651 Montreal Cir
Atlanta, GA 30084   404-350-5850
    Fax: 404-601-5539 800-883-3474
    marketing@inlandseafood.com
    www.inlandseafood.com
Seafood
President: Chris Rosenberger
Founder, Chief Executive Officer: Joel Knox
Executive Vice President: Robert Novotny
Safety Manager: Patricia Washington
Pomp Agency: Rodney Fund
Vice President of Sales: Stephen Musser
Chief Operating Officer: Bill Demmond
Director of Purchasing: Richard Luff
Estimated Sales: $1-3 Million
Number Employees: 100-249
Other Locations:
  Birmingham, AL
  New Orleans, LA
  Charlotte, NC
  Inland Lobster
  S. Portland, ME New Orleans

57163 Inno-Vite
97 Saramia Crescent
Concord, ON L4K 4P7
Canada   905-761-5121
    Fax: 888-279-3373 800-387-9111
    www.inno-vite.com
Importer and wholesaler/distributor of dietary products, food and nutrition supplements and organic herbs; serving the food service market, supermarkets, pharmacies and health food and specialty stores
President: Cornelius Pasare
VP: Donna Pasare
Number Employees: 10-19
Square Footage: 80000
Types of Products Distributed:
  Food Service, Frozen Food, General Line, Health Food, Organic herbs, dietary products, etc.

57164 Inny's Wholesale
1068 Puuwai St
Honolulu, HI 96819-4330   808-841-3172
    Fax: 808-841-1410
Seafood
President: Stanley Lum
Treasurer: Jane Lum
Estimated Sales: $3-5 Million
Number Employees: 1-4

57165 Inpak Systems Inc
540 Tasman St
Madison, WI 53714-3162   608-221-8180
    Fax: 608-221-4473 sales@inpaksystems.com
    www.inpaksystems.com
Wholesaler/distributor of bagging systems
President: Gerald Hoague
info@inpaksystems.com
Estimated Sales: $5-10 Million
Number Employees: 1-4
Number of Customer Locations: 2000
Types of Products Distributed:
  Frozen Food, General Merchandise, Bagging systems

57166 Insects Limited Inc
16950 Westfield Park Rd
Westfield, IN 46074-9374   317-896-9300
    Fax: 317-867-5757 800-992-1991
    insectsltd@aol.com www.fumigationzone.com
Manufacturer, exporter and wholesaler/distributor of pest control systems including traps, lures, insect monitoring and detection devices, fumigation products, etc.; importer of cigarette beetle pheromone traps; also, pest control audits and seminars available
President: David Mueller
d.mueller@insectslimited.com
CFO: Barbara Bass
VP: John Mueller
General Manager: Patrick Kelley
Estimated Sales: $1 Million
Number Employees: 10-19
Square Footage: 6000
Types of Products Distributed:
  Frozen Food, General Merchandise, Pest control products

57167 Insley-Mc Entee Equipment Co
1112 Emerson St
Rochester, NY 14606-3092   585-458-4660
    Fax: 585-458-4224 888-326-4409
    www.crown.com
Wholesaler/distributor of material handling equipment
Owner: Philip Robinson
insleymc@aol.com
Estimated Sales: $10-20 Million
Number Employees: 20-49
Private Brands Carried:
  Exide; Yale; Crown
Types of Products Distributed:
  Frozen Food, General Merchandise, Material handling equipment

57168 Instantlabs
800 West Baltimore Street
Suite 407
Baltimore, MD 21201   855-800-7085
    info@instantlabs.com
    www.instantlabs.com
Heating and cooling systems
Chief Executive Officer: Steven Guterman
Chief Financial Officer: Sam Wheeler
VP Product Development: Dr. Neil Sharma
Microbiologist: Lauren Bambusch
Contact: Lauren Bambusch
lbambusch@instantlabs.com
Estimated Sales: $15 Million
Number Employees: 35

57169 Institutional Food Service
1903 Selma Ave
Selma, AL 36703-3168   334-872-7438
    Fax: 334-874-7810
Wholesaler/distributor serving the food service market
General Manager: William Plummer
Estimated Sales: $20-50 Million
Number Employees: 20-49
Square Footage: 30000
Parent Co: M.O. Carroll Newton Company
Types of Products Distributed:
  Food Service, Frozen Food

57170 Institutional Wholesale Company
1306 N Washington Ave
Cookeville, TN 38501-1840   931-526-9588
    Fax: 931-537-4016 800-239-9588
Wholesaler/distributor of groceries, meats, produce, dairy products, frozen foods, baked goods, seafood and equipment and fixtures; serving the food service market
Owner: Tina Spisak
Estimated Sales: $20-50 Million
Number Employees: 1-4
Square Footage: 90000
Private Brands Carried:
  Frosty Acres
Number of Customer Locations: 2500
Types of Products Distributed:
  Food Service, Frozen Food, General Line, General Merchandise, Provisions/Meat, Produce, Seafood

57171 Instrumart
35 Green Mountain Dr
South Burlington, VT 05403-7824   802-863-0085
    Fax: 802-863-1193 800-884-4967
    sales@instrumart.com www.instrumart.com
Wholesaler/distributor, importer and exporter of temperature control and recording equipment
President: Bob Berman
bberman@instrumart.com
Engineering Manager: Scott Sabourin
Estimated Sales: $10-20 Million
Number Employees: 20-49
Square Footage: 24000
Types of Products Distributed:
  Frozen Food, General Merchandise, Temperature controls

57172 Insulated Structures/PBGroup
369 Lexington Ave Rm 1201
New York, NY 10017-6527
    Fax: 845-425-2519 800-887-2635
Manufacturers' representative and wholesaler/distributor of food service equipment. Design, installation and service for refrigerated buildings also available
President: Kevin Lewis
VP: Veronica Yacono

Wholesalers & Distributors / A-Z

Number Employees: 5-9
Other Locations:
  Insulated Structures-West
  Novato, CAInsulated Structures-West
Types of Products Distributed:
  Food Service, Frozen Food, General Merchandise, Foodservice equipment

57173 Integrative Flavors
3501 W Dunes Hwy
Michigan City, IN 46360-6717 219-879-8236
  800-837-7687
  www.integrativeflavors.com
Soup bases
President: Georgeann Quealy
VP: Brian Quealy
Director of Research & Development: Peter Hargarten
phargarten@integrativeflavors.com
Director of Regulatory Compliance: John True
Customer Service: Taylor Holm
Estimated Sales: $1,100,000
Number Employees: 10-19
Type of Packaging: Consumer, Food Service, Private Label, Bulk

57174 InterNatural Foods
1455 Broad St
4th Floor
Bloomfield, NJ 07003 973-338-1499
  Fax: 973-338-1485 www.internaturalfoods.com
Importer and distributor of natural and organic food products such as instant coffees, fruit popsicles, stevia sweeteners, cereals, oils and vinegars, crSme filled wafers, red palm oil, coconut oil, sea salts, vegetarian organic soupsno salt spice rubs, organic baby foods, all natural licorice, corn starch, cane sugars, broth bouillon cubes, sunflower oil, yeast, chocolate hazelnut butters, crackers and pastas
Chairwoman: Linda Palame
info@internaturalfoods.com
Type of Packaging: Consumer, Food Service, Bulk
Number of Customer Locations: 1
Types of Products Distributed:
  Health Food, Specialty Foods

57175 Interfood Ingredients
777 Brickell Ave
Suite 210
Miami, FL 33131 786-953-8320
  info@interfood.com
  www.interfood.com
Dairy ingredients and products
Managing Director & VP: Reniers Geoffrey
Year Founded: 1970
Estimated Sales: $235 Million
Number Employees: 200
Parent Co: Interfood Holding
Types of Products Distributed:
  Dairy products

57176 Interior Alaska Fish Processors
2400 Davis Rd
Fairbanks, AK 99701-5700 907-456-3885
  Fax: 907-456-3889 800-478-3885
  order@santassmokehouse.com
Salmon and salmon products
Owner: Janet McCormick
akhunt@ak.net
CEO/President: Virgil Humphenour
Vice President: Marie Mitchell
Marketing Director: Shelbie Umphenour
Estimated Sales: $2.5-5 Million
Number Employees: 10-19
Type of Packaging: Private Label, Bulk

57177 Intermix Beverage
1026 Central Ave NE
Minneapolis, MN 55413-2499 612-746-8880
  Fax: 612-746-8889 800-826-4177
  info@espresso-services.com
  www.espresso-services.com
Importer and wholesaler/distributor of Italian espresso and cappuccino equipment, drip brewers, espresso coffee, syrups, chocolates, etc
Owner: Katie Coughlin
Marketing: Rachel Strand
Sales Director: Curtis Carr
katiec@intermixbev.com
Operations Manager: Jeff Adelman
Estimated Sales: $10-20 Million
Number Employees: 20-49
Square Footage: 8000
Type of Packaging: Consumer, Food Service, Bulk

Private Brands Carried:
  Bunn; American Metalware Drip Brewing
Types of Products Distributed:
  General Line, General Merchandise, Specialty Foods, Coffee machinery, coffee & syrups

57178 Intermountain Specialty Food Group
265 Plymouth Ave
Salt Lake City, UT 84115 801-977-9077
  Fax: 801-977-8202 www.intermountainfood.com
Pasta, sauces, dessert mixes, dip mixes, baking mixes and soup mixes
President: Debbie Chidester
Co-Owner: Jody Chidester
Contact: Jim Hubbard
jimhubbard@intermountainfood.com
Estimated Sales: $700 Thousand
Number Employees: 13
Number of Brands: 4
Type of Packaging: Consumer, Food Service, Bulk
Other Locations:
  Intermountain Foods
  Meridian, IDIntermountain Foods
Private Brands Carried:
  Plentiful Pantry, Pasta Partner, Chidester Farms, Zpasta
Types of Products Distributed:
  General Line

57179 International Beverages
79 N 11th St
#1 Brewers Row
Brooklyn, NY 11249 718-486-7422
  Fax: 718-486-7440 www.brooklynbrewery.com
Importer and wholesaler/distributor of beer
Co-Founder & President: Steve Hindy
Controller: Debra Bascome
Technical Director: Mary Wiles
Marketing Director: Ben Hudson
VP of Sales: Robin Ottaway
Office Manager: Sherwin Chang
Production Manager: Jimmy Valm
Estimated Sales: $5-10 Million
Number Employees: 10-19
Parent Co: Brooklyn Brewery
Type of Packaging: Consumer
Private Brands Carried:
  Youngs; Chimay; Sam Smith; Brooklyn; Mendocino; Duvel
Types of Products Distributed:
  Frozen Food, General Line, Beer

57180 International Business Trading
4833 Fruitland Ave
Vernon, CA 90058-2722 323-277-0000
  Fax: 323-869-8889
Importer and exporter of frozen, fresh and live seafood
President: Albert Leung
Estimated Sales: $10-20 Million
Number Employees: 10-19
Square Footage: 100000
Type of Packaging: Consumer, Food Service, Bulk
Private Brands Carried:
  Supreme
Types of Products Distributed:
  Food Service, Frozen Food, Rack Jobbers, Seafood, Specialty Foods

57181 International Casein Corporation
111 Great Neck Rd
Suite 218
Great Neck, NY 11021-5402 516-466-4363
  Fax: 516-466-4365
Casein
President: Marvin Match
Number Employees: 5-9
Types of Products Distributed:
  Frozen Food, General Line, Casein

57182 International Coconut Corp
225 W Grand St
PO Box 3326
Elizabeth, NJ 07202-1205 908-289-1555
  Fax: 908-289-1556
  sales@internationalcoconut.com
Coconut
Owner: A Kaye
Vice President: Richard Kesselhaut
richard@internationalcoconut.com
Estimated Sales: $2.5-5 Million
Number Employees: 5-9
Square Footage: 46000

Type of Packaging: Consumer, Food Service, Private Label, Bulk
Number of Customer Locations: 2
Types of Products Distributed:
  Food Service

57183 International Commercial Supply Corporation
569 Bantam Road
Litchfield, CT 06759-3203 800-243-1290
  Fax: 800-253-8499 icsc@icscparts.com
  www.icscparts.com
Wholesaler/distributor of replacement parts for food service equipment; serving the food service market
Estimated Sales: $5-10 Million
Number Employees: 20-49
Types of Products Distributed:
  Food Service, Frozen Food, General Merchandise, Replacement parts for equipment

57184 International Culinary
747 Vassar Ave
Lakewood, NJ 08701-6908 732-229-0008
  Fax: 732-886-5885 chefharvey@aol.com
  www.chefharvey.com
Importer and wholesaler/distributor of culinary, stainless steel carving and melon and apple garnishing tools
President: Harvey Rosen
chefharvey@aol.com
Number Employees: 10-19
Number of Customer Locations: 500
Types of Products Distributed:
  General Merchandise, Culinary, garnishing & carving tools

57185 International Dairy Equipment Associates
42 S Broad St
Nazareth, PA 18064-2117 610-759-1228
  Fax: 610-759-3195 ideaincl@aol.com
Wholesaler/distributor of dairy plants and raw materials used in the dairy and food industries; serving food processors; engineering services available
Owner: Greg Prendes
Accountant: Barry Morris
Estimated Sales: $500,000-$1 Million
Number Employees: 5-9
Square Footage: 20000
Types of Products Distributed:
  Frozen Food, General Merchandise, Dairy & food processing equipment

57186 International Distribution
8530 Market Street Rd
Houston, TX 77029-2422 713-672-8000
  Fax: 713-675-5853
Public warehouse of imported foods, groceries and industrial ingredients
President: Doug Walt
VP Sales: Del Heater
Customer Service Manager: Annette Cephus
General Manager: Steve Daugherty
Estimated Sales: $12 Million
Number Employees: 100-249
Types of Products Distributed:
  General Line, General Merchandise, Specialty Foods, Groceries, industrial ingredients, etc.

57187 International Enterprises Unlimited
5628 Mineral Spring Rd
Suffolk, VA 23438-9457 757-986-3800
  Fax: 757-986-3801 877-423-5263
Wholesaler/distributor and importer of all-natural and low-sodium foods including smoked salmon, haddock, caviar, escargot, caviar pate, etc.; also, gourmet specialty items including Icelandic lamb; serving the food service and retailmarkets
President/CEO: L Hayes
COO: Steinunn Hilmarsdottir
Contact: Lloyd Hayes
shawnj@aquik.net
Estimated Sales: $1-2.5 Million
Number Employees: 1-4
Square Footage: 100000
Type of Packaging: Consumer, Food Service, Private Label, Bulk
Private Brands Carried:
  Iceland Gourmet; Artic Delicacies; Triton
Number of Customer Locations: 500
Types of Products Distributed:
  Food Service, Frozen Food, Health Food, Sea-

Wholesalers & Distributors / A-Z

food, Specialty Foods, All-natural & low-sodium seafood, etc.

57188 International Farmers Market
PO Box 81226
Chamblee, GA 30366-1226
770-455-1777
Fax: 770-451-7474
www.internationalfarmersmarket.com
Dairy, meats, seafood, general grocery items, poultry, blue crab, catfish, clams
Contact: Jacqui Chew
jacqui@ifusionmarketing.com

57189 International Marine Products
500 E 7th St
Los Angeles, CA 90014-2410
213-680-0190
Fax: 213-680-0190 www.intmarine.com
Wholesaler/distributor of seafood; serving the food service market
President: Inmp Alfred
alfred@intmarine.com
Estimated Sales: $20-50 Million
Number Employees: 50-99
Parent Co: Eiwashogi
Types of Products Distributed:
Food Service, Frozen Food, Seafood

57190 International Meat Co
7107 W Grand Ave
Chicago, IL 60707
773-622-1400
Fax: 773-622-6829
www.internationalmeatcompany.com
Meat products
Owner: Victor Bomprezzi
Estimated Sales: $5-10 Million
Number Employees: 10-19
Type of Packaging: Consumer, Food Service
Types of Products Distributed:
Provisions/Meat

57191 International Oils & Concentrates
45 US Highway 206 # 104
P.O.Box 185
Augusta, NJ 07822-2044
973-579-0014
Fax: 973-579-2509 info@iocsales.com
iocsales.com
Importer, wholesaler and distributor of fruit juice concentrates, tropical and fruit purees, single strength juices, essential oils and essences; exporter of fruit juice concentrates. Some of their products include Lemon ConcentrateRed Grape Concentrate, Peach Puree, Blueberry Concentrate, Coconut Cream, Apple Essence and more.
President: Don De Stefano
juiceconcentratesioc@yahoo.com
Vice President: Donny De Stefano
Sales: Diane De Stefano
Estimated Sales: $7-8 Million
Number Employees: 4
Square Footage: 6000
Type of Packaging: Bulk
Types of Products Distributed:
Fruit juice concentrates

57192 International Pack & Ship
377b Nassau Road
Roosevelt, NY 11575-1316
516-378-9110
Fax: 516-378-9372 tvlrainbow@aol.com
Wholesaler/distributor, importer and exporter of health food products including vitamins, nutritional supplements, herbal teas, coffees, spices and seasonings
President: Joseph Horton
Number Employees: 1-4
Type of Packaging: Consumer, Bulk
Private Brands Carried:
Vitalabs; New Moon Extracts; Claudio St. James; Prince of Peace; Starwest; Vitamin Power; Strength Systems
Types of Products Distributed:
Frozen Food, General Line, Health Food, Vitamins, coffees, spices, teas, etc.

57193 International Seafoods-Alaska
517 Shelikof St
P.O.Box 2997
Kodiak, AK 99615-6049
907-486-4768
Fax: 907-486-4885 info@isa-ak.com
www.isa-ak.com
Fresh or frozen fish and seafoods
Administrator: Ted Kishimoto
Estimated Sales: $4,200,000
Number Employees: 100-249

Type of Packaging: Consumer, Food Service, Private Label
Types of Products Distributed:
Frozen Food

57194 International Seafoods of Chicago
1133 W Lake St
Chicago, IL 60607-1618
312-243-2330
Fax: 312-243-1923
Seafood
President: Inkie Hong
Estimated Sales: $1,800,000
Number Employees: 5-9

57195 International Sourcing
32 Haviland Street
P.O.Box 90
Norwalk, CT 06854-4906
203-299-3220
Fax: 203-299-1355 800-772-7672
sales@charkit.com
Wholesaler/distributor, importer and exporter of preservatives, mineral supplements, acidulants, vegetable oils, flavorings, firming agents, chelates, antioxidants, buffers, humectants, sweeteners, etc
President: Seymour Friedman
Vice President: Larry Smith
Sales Correspondent: Linda Harth
Technical Division: Laurence Smith
Estimated Sales: $10-20 Million
Number Employees: 20-49
Square Footage: 13200
Types of Products Distributed:
General Line, Industrial ingredients

57196 International Telcom Inc
185 Commerce Ctr
Greenville, SC 29615-5817
864-676-2170
Fax: 864-297-7186 800-433-4043
info@interplas.com www.interplas.com
Manufacturer, importer and wholesaler/distributor of plastic and polyethylene bags, film, boxes, plastic food wrap, ziplock bags, trash bags, etc
President: Steve McClure
CEO: Mark McClure
Quality Control: Lisa Hughes
Marketing Manager: Roger Throckmorton
Sales Director: Chris Davis
Contact: Phillip Malphrus
pmal@intermicro.com
Estimated Sales: $20 Million
Number Employees: 1-4
Square Footage: 56000
Type of Packaging: Consumer, Food Service, Private Label, Bulk
Private Brands Carried:
Clearzip Reusable Bags; Keepcool Insulated Bags; Clearzip Ziplock Bags

57197 (HQ)International Ticket Company
628 State Route 10
Whippany, NJ 07981-1522
973-887-7200
Fax: 973-887-2277 800-635-5468
Wholesaler/distributor of guest and coat checks, parking tickets, pressure sensitive labels, custom forms, etc
President: Roger Manshel
VP: Larry Manshel
Estimated Sales: $500,000-$1 Million
Number Employees: 1-4
Square Footage: 8000
Types of Products Distributed:
Frozen Food, General Merchandise, Paper forms & labels

57198 Intershell Seafood Corp
9 Blackburn Dr
Gloucester, MA 01930-2237
978-281-2523
Fax: 978-283-1303 info@intershell.biz
www.intershell.biz
Shellfish
President: Yibing Gao
yibing@intershell.biz
Chairman: Monte Rome
Accounting: Linda Amaral
Research & Development: Shannon Blakeley
Quality Control: Eric Strong
Sales: Christopher J Blankenbaker
Plant Manager: Eric Strong
Purchasing Manager: Monte Rome
Estimated Sales: $5 Million
Number Employees: 50-99
Type of Packaging: Bulk

57199 Interstate Distributors
425 N Union Street Ext
Canton, MS 39046-3523
601-859-3363
Fax: 601-859-7995
Wholesaler/distributor of food service equipment; serving the food service market
Manager: Pam Noble
Parent Co: Interstate Distributors
Types of Products Distributed:
Food Service, Frozen Food, General Merchandise, Foodservice equipment

57200 Interstate Restaurant Equipment
6517 Ryan Avenue
Minneapolis, MN 55435-1518
612-927-0294
Wholesaler/distributor of new and used restaurant equipment including ice makers, walk-in coolers, hoods, exhaust fans, etc.; serving the food service market
President: Charles Sedgwick
General Manager: David Thayer
Types of Products Distributed:
Food Service, Frozen Food, General Merchandise, New & used equipment

57201 Interthor Inc
1817 Beach St
Broadview, IL 60155-2899
708-345-1270
Fax: 708-345-1290 888-345-1270
Wholesaler/distributor of material handling equipment including ergonomic pallet and container lifts, forklifts, high lifting pallet trucks, stackers, work positioners, container tilters, etc
President: Richard Kopacz
rkopacz@interthor.com
General Manager: Richard Kopacz
Estimated Sales: $2.5-5 Million
Number Employees: 1-4
Square Footage: 40000
Types of Products Distributed:
General Merchandise, Material handling equipment

57202 Ipc Supply Inc
1103 Trammell Rd
1103 Trammell Road
Anderson, SC 29621
864-226-1588
Fax: 864-226-9357 800-922-2165
ipcsupply.com/contact-us/
Wholesaler/distributor of cleaning supplies and equipment including soaps and detergents
President: Lynn Mclay
ipcosupply@earthlink.net
In-House Sales: Billy McAllister
Warehouse Manager: Billy McAlister
Office Manager: Pat Mainous
Estimated Sales: $2.5-5 Million
Number Employees: 5-9
Square Footage: 160000
Types of Products Distributed:
Frozen Food, General Merchandise, Cleaning supplies & equipment

57203 Ipswich Maritime Product Company
43 Avery St
Ipswich, MA 01938
978-356-9866
Fax: 978-356-9894 www.ipswichmaritime.com
Seafood
President: Peter Maistrellis
Contact: George Delaney
gdelaney@ipswichmaritime.com
Estimated Sales: $10-20 Million
Number Employees: 10-19

57204 Ipswich Shellfish Co Inc
8 Hayward St
Ipswich, MA 01938-2012
978-356-4371
Fax: 978-356-9235 800-477-9424
www.ipswichshellfish.com
Seafood
Owner, President: Chrissi Pappas
CEO: Alexis Pappas
Controller: Lou Cellineri
VP: Alexander Pappas
Sales Manager: Michael Gagne
Director of Human Resources: Kathy Waymous
Operations Manager: Bob Butcher
General Manager: Michael Trupiano
Purchasing Director: Vito Finazzo
Estimated Sales: $22.2 Million
Number Employees: 250-499
Square Footage: 35000

Wholesalers & Distributors / A-Z

57205 Ira Higdon Grocery Company
150 IGA Way
Cairo, GA 39828 229-377-1272
jdunn@irahigdongc.com
www.irahigdongc.com
Groceries and meat.
President & CEO: Larry Higdon
Vice President: Katie Higdon
Director of Sales & Marketing: Jim Dunn
Year Founded: 1909
Estimated Sales: $106.3 Million
Number Employees: 100
Square Footage: 170000
Private Brands Carried:
  IGA; Parade
Number of Customer Locations: 200
Types of Products Distributed:
  Frozen Food, General Line

57206 Irish Tea Sales
9216 95th Street
Woodhaven, NY 11421-2707 718-845-4402
Fax: 718-835-5965
Importer and wholesaler/distributor of Irish teas, preserves, biscuits and oatmeal; serving the food service market and retail store
President: Ellen Smith
Sales Director: Eileen Clarke
Estimated Sales: $2.5-5 Million
Number Employees: 1-4
Type of Packaging: Consumer, Food Service
Types of Products Distributed:
  Food Service, General Line, Irish teas, preserves, biscuits, etc.

57207 Irvin
16409 Old Valley Pike
Edinburg, VA 22824 540-984-4114
Fax: 540-984-8719 800-572-5437
Wholesaler/distributor of candy and provisions/meats; also, rack jobber services available; serving the food service market
President: Mark Irvin
General Manager: Mark Irvin
Estimated Sales: $10-20 Million
Number Employees: 20-49
Types of Products Distributed:
  Food Service, General Line, Provisions/Meat, Rack Jobbers, Candy

57208 Irvine Restaurant Supply
90 High Street
Collingwood, ON L9Y 4K2
Canada 800-461-0275
Fax: 705-445-2500
Wholesaler/distributor of food service equipment and supplies; serving the food service market
President: Clark Irvine
Number Employees: 1-4
Private Brands Carried:
  Garland; Volrath; Oneida
Types of Products Distributed:
  Food Service, Frozen Food, General Merchandise, Foodservice equipment & supplies

57209 Irvington Marcus Company
174 Front St
South Plainfield, NJ 07080-3402 908-757-1200
Wholesaler/distributor of spices, seasonings, tenderizers, curing salts, hog, sheep and beef casings and cutlery; serving the food service market
Owner/President: Arnold Marcus
Secretary/Treasurer: Louise Marcus
VP: Greg Marcus
Estimated Sales: $2.5-5 Million
Number Employees: 1-4
Square Footage: 10000
Number of Customer Locations: 450
Types of Products Distributed:
  Food Service, Frozen Food, General Line, General Merchandise, Spices, seasonings, tenderizers, etc.

57210 Isaacson & Stein Fish Company
800 W Fulton Market
Chicago, IL 60607-1375 312-421-2444
Fax: 312-421- 432
Sushi-grade fish
President: Ben Willner
Owner: Sherwin Willner
Estimated Sales: $5-10 Million
Number Employees: 20-49

57211 Ishida Corporation
P.O.Box 272
Rice Lake, WI 54868-0272 715-234-9171
Fax: 715-234-6967 prodinfo@ishidaretail.com
www.ishidaretail.com
Wholesaler/distributor of industrial and retail scales, wrapping machines and private label items
President: Mark Johnson
Business Unit Manager: Sullivan Smith
Product Manager: Grant Sutherland
Estimated Sales: $20-50 Million
Number Employees: 250-499
Types of Products Distributed:
  Frozen Food, General Merchandise, Scales, wrapping machinery, etc.

57212 Island Farms Dairies Cooperative Association
2220 Dowler Place
P.O. Box 38
Victoria, BC V8W 2M1
Canada 250-360-5200
Fax: 250-360-5220 www.islandfarms.com
Dairy products
President: George Aylard
CEO: David McMillan
CFO: Eric Erikson
Quality Control: Sam Arora
Marketing: Jona De Jesus
Sales: Art Paulo
Operations: Greg Martin
Plant Manager: Al Snedden
Purchasing Director: Steve Wainwright
Number Employees: 250-499
Number of Products: 500
Type of Packaging: Consumer, Food Service, Private Label, Bulk
Types of Products Distributed:
  Food Service, Frozen Food, General Line, Dairy products

57213 Island Lobster
PO Box 258
Matinicus, ME 04851-0258 207-366-3937
Fax: 207-366-3380
Lobster
Owner: Marc Ames

57214 Island Refrigeration & Foodservice Equipment
1811 Newbridge Road
North Bellmore, NY 11710-1633 516-785-2424
Fax: 516-826-5048 800-338-3972
islrefrig@aol.com
Wholesaler/distributor of walk-in coolers, refrigerators, stoves, ovens, deep fryers, tables, chairs, ice machines, cup dispensers, freezers, bar equipment, deli show and bakery cases, etc.; serving the food service market
Owner/General Manager: Wayne Puleo
Estimated Sales: $5-10 Million
Number Employees: 10-19
Private Brands Carried:
  Kelvinator; Norlake; Frigidare; Potco; Blodgett; Excellence
Types of Products Distributed:
  Food Service, Frozen Food, General Merchandise, Coolers, freezers, ovens, etc.

57215 Island Seafood
32 Brook Rd
Eliot, ME 03903-1423 207-439-8508
Fax: 207-439-9945 www.islandseafoodlobster.com
Seafood
Owner: Randy Townsend
randyisf@comcast.net
Estimated Sales: $3-5 Million
Number Employees: 20-49

57216 Island Supply
6601 Lyons Rd # B6
Suite B-6
Coconut Creek, FL 33073-3605 954-312-0300
Fax: 954-344-2917 info@IslandSupply.com
www.islandsupply.com
Wholesaler/distributor of food service equipment and supplies including ranges, plates, utensils, etc.; also, grocery items including produce, meat, seafood, canned goods, etc.; serving the food service market
Owner: Ken Cufo
ken@islandsupplyco.com
Manager: Ian Givens
Estimated Sales: $2.5-5 Million
Number Employees: 10-19
Type of Packaging: Food Service
Types of Products Distributed:
  Food Service, Frozen Food, General Line, Provisions/Meat, Produce, Seafood, Canned goods

57217 Islander Import
257 William Street
West Hempstead, NY 11552-1500 516-481-9677
Importer and wholesaler/distributor of German beer
President: Charles Leidner
Number Employees: 1-4
Private Brands Carried:
  Bitburger; Erdinger Weiss
Number of Customer Locations: 100
Types of Products Distributed:
  Frozen Food, General Line, Specialty Foods, German beer

57218 Italfina
635 Westburne Drive
Concord, ON L4K 4T6
Canada 905-879-9656
Fax: 905-879-9484 800-366-0534
Wholesaler/distributor of groceries and specialty foods; serving the food service market
VP: Jack Violante
Number Employees: 20-49
Square Footage: 400000
Private Brands Carried:
  Star; Crodo; Delecco; Lia
Number of Customer Locations: 1000
Types of Products Distributed:
  Food Service, Frozen Food, General Line, Specialty Foods

57219 Italfoods Inc
205 Shaw Rd
S San Francisco, CA 94080-6605 650-877-0724
Fax: 650-871-9437 info@italfoodsinc.com
www.italfoodsinc.com
Wholesaler/distributor and importer of a full line of Italian food products including antipasto, syrups, mineral water, bread, candy, cheese, coffee, tea, dairy products, dry beans, flour, frozen desserts, meat products,etc.; servingthe food service market
Owner: Georgette Guerra
Estimated Sales: $10-20 Million
Number Employees: 100-249
Type of Packaging: Food Service
Private Brands Carried:
  Berni; Torani; San Pellegrino; Bertagni; Schokinag; Vicenzi; Mezzetta
Types of Products Distributed:
  Food Service, Frozen Food, General Line, Provisions/Meat, Produce, Seafood, Specialty Foods, Italian

57220 Italica Imports
411 Theodore Fremd Avenue
Suite 120
Rye, NY 10580
Fax: 914-925-0458 800-431-1529
www.italicaoliveoil.com
Wholesaler/distributor and importer of olive oil, cornichons, capers, olives, pickled vegetables, pepperoncini, jalapeno peppers and wine vinegar
President: Lucy Landesman
Executive Secretary: Emil Cairo
VP of Marketing/Sales: Neil Albert
Estimated Sales: $5-10 Million
Number Employees: 1-4
Parent Co: Cory International Corporation
Type of Packaging: Consumer, Private Label
Types of Products Distributed:
  General Line, Specialty Foods, Olive oil, capers, etc.

57221 Italmade
5601 NW 159th Street
Hialeah, FL 33014-6726 305-573-3335
Fax: 305-573-3511
Wholesaler/distributor of coffee and coffee equipment specializing in fully automatic espresso and cappuccino systems and products; serving the food service market
President: Paolo Cometto
Number Employees: 5-9
Square Footage: 16000
Types of Products Distributed:
  Food Service, Frozen Food, General Line, General Merchandise, Coffee & coffee equipment

1049

Wholesalers & Distributors / A-Z

57222 J & B Seafood
9301 Faith St
Coden, AL 36523-3057   251-824-4512
Fax: 251-824-1260 jbfood1979@aol.com
www.jandbseafood.com
Seafood
Owner: Raymond T. Barbour
Estimated Sales: $7.7 Million
Number Employees: 100-249

57223 J & J Distributing
653 Rice St
St Paul, MN 55103-1849   651-221-0560
Fax: 651-221-0570 800-307-0051
Wholesaler/distributor of fresh produce and nuts
President: James Hannigan
james.hannigan@jjdst.com
Owner: Deborah Hannigan
Estimated Sales: $5-10 Million
Number Employees: 100-249
Types of Products Distributed:
  Frozen Food, General Line, Produce, Nuts

57224 J & M Wholesale Meat Inc
2300 Hoover Ave
Modesto, CA 95354-3908
Canada   209-522-1248
Fax: 209-522-8834 855-522-1248
Fresh and frozen pork
President: J McCullough
Administrator Quality Control: Kevin McCullough
Sales Manager: Nannette McCullough
Number Employees: 20-49
Square Footage: 72000
Type of Packaging: Consumer, Food Service, Bulk
Types of Products Distributed:
  Frozen Food

57225 J & R Distributors
148 Huntington Ave
North Dartmouth, MA 02747-3272   508-993-1758
Fax: 508-993-1758 800-685-9499
jnrcommercial@hotmail.com
www.jr-distributors.us
Wholesaler/distributor of food service equipment and replacement parts; serving the food service market and cruise lines
Owner: Richard Silva
VP: James Dixon
Regional Sales Manager: Richard Silva
International Support Manager: Jan Nillson
Estimated Sales: Less Than $500,000
Number Employees: 1-4
Square Footage: 20000
Private Brands Carried:
  Cecilware; Market Forge; Groen; Lang; Hatco
Types of Products Distributed:
  Food Service, Frozen Food, General Merchandise, Equipment & replacement parts

57226 J Bernard Seafood
1142 Front St
Cottonport, LA 71327   318-876-2716
Fax: 318-876-2925
Wholesaler/distributor of freshwater fish; serving the food service market
Owner: James Bernard
Number Employees: 1-4
Number of Customer Locations: 20
Types of Products Distributed:
  Food Service, Frozen Food, General Line, Freshwater fish

57227 J Bernard Seafood
1142 Front St
Cottonport, LA 71327   318-876-2716
Fax: 318-876-2925 www.crawfish.org
Seafood
President: James Bernard
Estimated Sales: $3.2 Million
Number Employees: 1-4

57228 J H Honeycutt & Sons Inc
215 E Holland St
Chadbourn, NC 28431-2303   910-654-3101
Fax: 910-654-3625 800-426-5505
customerservice@honeycuttproduce.com
www.honeycuttproduce.com
Wholesaler/distributor of produce
President: Johnny Honeycutt
Secretary: Mary Honeycutt
VP: Phil Honeycutt
Number Employees: 20-49
Square Footage: 20000
Types of Products Distributed:
  Produce

57229 J Hoelting Produce Inc
2025 E Olive St
Decatur, IL 62526-5187   217-429-7774
Fax: 217-429-8129 www.hoeltingfoodservice.com
Wholesaler/distributor of frozen food, produce and provisions/meats; serving the food service market
Owner: Robert Pipsword
VP: Debbie Tipsword
Estimated Sales: $10-20 Million
Number Employees: 20-49
Types of Products Distributed:
  Food Service, Frozen Food, Provisions/Meat, Produce

57230 J Kings Food Svc Professionals
700 Furrows Rd
Holtsville, NY 11742-2001   631-289-8401
Fax: 631-758-0187 sales@jkings.com
www.jkings.com
Wholesaler/distributor of produce, groceries, frozen foods, fresh meats, dairy products, etc.; serving the food service market
President: John King
Executive VP: John McElgun
Executive VP: Greg Ferraro
Estimated Sales: $5-10 Million
Number Employees: 250-499
Square Footage: 300000
Number of Customer Locations: 2500
Types of Products Distributed:
  Food Service, Frozen Food, General Line, Provisions/Meat, Produce, Dairy products, etc.

57231 J Moniz Co Inc
91 Wordell St
Fall River, MA 02721-4307   508-674-8451
Fax: 508-673-6464 www.jmoniz.com
Seafood
President/Treasurer/Clerk: John Moniz
joaomoniz@hotmail.com
Estimated Sales: $1,000,000
Number Employees: 5-9

57232 J Moresky & Son
123 W Long Ave
New Castle, PA 16101-4822   724-652-0361
Fax: 724-657-9553
Wholesaler/distributor of confectionery and tobacco products; rack jobber services available
President: Sylvia Moresky
Vice President: Kari Newman
Estimated Sales: $2.5-5 Million
Number Employees: 5-9
Types of Products Distributed:
  Frozen Food, General Line, General Merchandise, Rack Jobbers, Confectionery & tobacco products

57233 J Murray & Co
706 E Broadway St
Mt Pleasant, MI 48858-2730   989-773-7566
Fax: 989-773-7222
Wholesaler/distributor of confectionery products and general merchandise
Owner: Julie Bontrager
jmurray@jmurrayllc.com
Manager: Julie Bontrager
Estimated Sales: $10-20 Million
Number Employees: 10-19
Square Footage: 66000
Number of Customer Locations: 300
Types of Products Distributed:
  General Line, General Merchandise, Confectionery products

57234 J O Spice Co
3721 Old Georgetown Rd
Halethorpe, MD 21227-2534   410-247-5205
Fax: 410-247-5014 800-537-5714
sales@jospices.com www.jospices.com
Wholesaler/distributor of herbs and spices for seafood; serving the food service market; also, custom blending and packaging available
President: Don Ports
CEO: Jane McPhaul
VP: Donald Ports, Jr.
Estimated Sales: $10-20 Million
Number Employees: 10-19
Square Footage: 20000
Types of Products Distributed:
  Food Service, Frozen Food, General Line, Herbs & spices

57235 J P Ice Cream
1305 Macco Dr
Pharr, TX 78577-1906   956-782-0085
Fax: 956-782-4454
Wholesaler/distributor of ice cream and novelties including sandwiches, cups, etc
Owner: Javier Chapa
chapargv@aol.com
Manager: Xavier Chapa
Purchasing Agent: Xavier Chapa, Jr.
Estimated Sales: $5-10 Million
Number Employees: 10-19
Private Brands Carried:
  Good Humor; Blue Bell; Breyers; Holarda
Number of Customer Locations: 300
Types of Products Distributed:
  Frozen Food, General Line, Ice cream cups, novelties, etc.

57236 J P's Shellfish Co
414 Harold L Dow Hwy
Eliot, ME 3903   207-439-6018
Fax: 207-439-7794 jpinfo@jpshellfish.com
www.jpshellfish.com
Seafood
President: John Price
jshellfish@aol.com
Sales Exec: John Price
Estimated Sales: $10-20 Million
Number Employees: 20-49

57237 J Petite & Sons
PO Box 40
English Harbor West, NL A0H 1M0
Canada   709-888-3251
Fax: 709-888-3441
Wholesaler/distributor of lobster
President: Debbie Petite
Number Employees: 250-499
Types of Products Distributed:
  Frozen Food, Seafood, Lobster

57238 J R Kelly Co
703 S Bluff Rd
Collinsville, IL 62234-1339   618-344-2910
Fax: 618-344-2297 888-344-4392
info@jrkelly.com www.jrkelly.com
Export and domestic broker of horseradish roots, spices and produce
President: Dennis Diekemper
dennis.diekemper@jrkelly.com
Estimated Sales: $4 Million
Number Employees: 1-4
Square Footage: 64000
Type of Packaging: Bulk

57239 J T Gibbons Inc
600 Elmwood Park Blvd # 2
New Orleans, LA 70123-3310   504-831-9907
Fax: 504-837-5516
Wholesaler/distributor and export and import broker of frozen foods, groceries, industrial ingredients and private label items
President: Richard Keeney
rkeeney@gibbonsinc.com
CFO: Arthur Schott
Purchasing: Tammy Ducote
Estimated Sales: Less Than $500,000
Number Employees: 1-4
Square Footage: 60000
Type of Packaging: Consumer, Food Service, Private Label

57240 J Turner Seafood
4 Smith St
Gloucester, MA 01930-2710   978-281-8585
Fax: 978-281-1710 www.turners-seafood.com
Seafood
Contact: Peter Stark
pete@turners-seafood.com
Estimated Sales: $2,000,000
Number Employees: 5-9

57241 J W Outfitters
3102 Oakcliff Industrial St
Atlanta, GA 30340-2902   770-457-0447
Fax: 770-457-4157 800-554-7662
CustomerService@JWOutfitters.com
www.jwoutfitters.com

Wholesaler/distributor and exporter of uniforms; serving the food service market
President: Jack Willis
jwoutfitters@mindspring.com
National Sales Manager: Giles Davis
Estimated Sales: $5-10 Million
Number Employees: 50-99
Square Footage: 92000
Type of Packaging: Food Service
Types of Products Distributed:
  Food Service, Frozen Food, General Merchandise, Work apparel & sportswear

57242 J Weil Food Service Co
5907 W Clinton St
Boise, ID 83704-9304   208-377-0590
  Fax: 208-378-1682
Wholesaler/distributor of frozen food
President: Bill Tippetts
btippetts@jweil.com
General Manager: Craig Grow
Estimated Sales: $5-10 Million
Number Employees: 20-49
Number of Customer Locations: 500
Types of Products Distributed:
  Food Service, Frozen Food

57243 J&L Produce Wholesale Company
4101 Massachusetts Avenue
Indianapolis, IN 46218-3175   317-352-1505
  Fax: 317-549-2911
Wholesaler/distributor of produce; serving the food service market
General Manager: Diane Orpurt
Estimated Sales: $2.5-5 Million
Number Employees: 5-9
Square Footage: 32000
Types of Products Distributed:
  Food Service, Frozen Food, Produce

57244 J&M Distribution Company
PO Box 1925
Spartanburg, SC 29304-1925   864-582-4471
  Fax: 864-486-0095
Wholesaler/distributor of meats; serving the food service market
President: Jodie Boiter
VP: Melissa Gunnell
Estimated Sales: $300,000-500,000
Number Employees: 1-4
Types of Products Distributed:
  Food Service, Frozen Food, Provisions/Meat

57245 J&M Food Products Co
P.O. Box 334
Deerfield, IL 60015   847-948-1290
  Fax: 847-948-0468 sales@halalcertified.com
  www.halalcertified.com
Shelf stable halal meals
VP: Mary Anne Jackson   *Year Founded:* 1991
Types of Products Distributed:
  General Line

57246 J&S Food Distributors
4001 Euphrosine Street
New Orleans, LA 70125-1310   504-821-8803
  Fax: 504-821-8874   800-975-2468
  pedster1@bellsouth.net www.jandsfoods.com
Wholesaler/distributor of gourmet and specialty foods
President: Joseph Piediscalzo
Number Employees: 5-9
Square Footage: 40000
Private Brands Carried:
  Cajun Countrey; Oak Grove Smokehouse; River Road Spices
Number of Customer Locations: 50
Types of Products Distributed:
  Frozen Food, Specialty Foods

57247 J. Connor & Sons
355 Main Street
Whitinsville, MA 01588-1860   860-887-9289
  Fax: 860-887-4065
Wholesaler/distributor of candy; also, rack jobber services available
President: Richard Legare
Estimated Sales: $10-20 Million
Number Employees: 10-19
Types of Products Distributed:
  Frozen Food, General Line, Rack Jobbers, Candy

57248 J. Hellman Frozen Foods
1601 E Olympic Blvd
Suite 200
Los Angeles, CA 90021   213-243-9105
  Fax: 213-243-1189 www.jhellmanfrozenfoods.com
Wholesaler/distributor of produce and frozen vegetables, French fries, avocado products, prepared salads, desserts, soups, garlic, spices, groceries, meats, dairy products, seafood, baked goods, etc.; serving the food servicemarket.
General Manager: Chuck Marsh
Year Founded: 1923
Estimated Sales: $20-50 Million
Number Employees: 20-49
Square Footage: 40000
Types of Products Distributed:
  Food Service, General Line, Provisions/Meat, Produce, Seafood, Specialty Foods, Avocado products, garlic, spices, etc.

57249 J. Johnson Fruit & Produce
878 Thompson Drive
Suite A
Florissant, MO 63031-6184   314-231-0415
Wholesaler/distributor of produce; serving the food service market
Owner: Robert Johnson
Bookkeeper: Dolores Johnson
General Manager: Cynthia Hughes
Number Employees: 5-9
Square Footage: 280000
Types of Products Distributed:
  Food Service, Produce

57250 J. Lerner Box Company
1061 W 16th Street
Chicago, IL 60608-2205   312-226-7587
  Fax: 312-226-8194
Wholesaler/distributor of new and used corrugated boxes
President: Michael Lerner
Operations Manager: David Cohen
Number Employees: 10-19
Square Footage: 160000
Types of Products Distributed:
  Frozen Food, General Merchandise, New & used corrugated boxes

57251 J. M. Sealts Company
P.O.Box 300
Lima, OH 45802   419-223-2290
  Fax: 419-224-8095
Wholesaler/distributor of frozen food and general line products; serving the food service market
President: Larry Easterday
Chairman Board: Larry Easterday
Estimated Sales: $10-20 Million
Number Employees: 20-49
Square Footage: 100000
Number of Customer Locations: 300
Types of Products Distributed:
  Food Service, Frozen Food, General Line

57252 J. Quattrocchi & Company
63 Church Street W
P.O.Box 236
Smiths Falls, ON K7A 4T1
Canada   613-283-4980
  Fax: 866-864-4980   800-267-7970
Wholesaler/distributor of groceries; serving the food service market
Director: Joe Quattrocchi
Number Employees: 20-49
Private Brands Carried:
  Kraft; Heinz; Campbell's
Types of Products Distributed:
  Food Service, Frozen Food, General Line

57253 J. Rutigliano & Sons
301 Hollywood Ave
South Plainfield, NJ 07080-4201   908-226-8866
  Fax: 908-226-1534
Importer and wholesaler/distributor of olives, macaroni, tomato products, olive oil, cheese and vinegar
Owner: Joseph Rutigliano
VP: Vincent Rutigliano
Estimated Sales: $5-10 Million
Number Employees: 5-9
Square Footage: 120000
Type of Packaging: Consumer, Food Service
Number of Customer Locations: 100
Types of Products Distributed:
  Frozen Food, General Line, Specialty Foods

57254 J. Sosnick & Sons
258 Littlefield Ave
S San Francisco, CA 94080-6922   650-952-2226
  Fax: 650-952-2439 www.sosnick.com
Wholesaler/distributor of groceries, dairy and private label items, frozen foods, equipment and fixtures, seafood, confectionery and specialty foods
President: Jeffery Sosnick
jsosnick@sosnick.com
CFO: R Sosnick
VP: M Sosnick
General Manager: J Sosnick
Estimated Sales: $20-50 Million
Number Employees: 20-49
Number of Customer Locations: 2500
Types of Products Distributed:
  Frozen Food, General Line, General Merchandise, Seafood, Specialty Foods, Groceries, confectionery, etc.

57255 J. Treffiletti & Sons
4 N Ferry Street
Albany, NY 12207-2405   518-434-3106
  Fax: 518-434-3106
Wholesaler/distributor of frozen foods, general line products, general merchandise and provisions/meats
President: Joe Treffiletti
Secretary: Mary Franchini
Retail Coordinator: Ernie Palmer
Number Employees: 20-49
Square Footage: 240000
Private Brands Carried:
  Red & White
Number of Customer Locations: 100
Types of Products Distributed:
  Frozen Food, General Line, General Merchandise, Provisions/Meat

57256 J.A. King & Company
PO Box 16163
Greensboro, NC 27416-0163   336-674-5007
  Fax: 336-294-1528   800-327-7727
  info@jaking.com www.jaking.com
Wholesaler/distributor of batch control and weighing systems, check weighers, platform and truck scales, precision measurement testing equipment, etc
President: John King
Director Finance/Administration: Joseph Mallory
Director Sales: C Doug Azbell
Estimated Sales: $20-50 Million
Number Employees: 1-4
Square Footage: 20000
Types of Products Distributed:
  General Merchandise, Batch control systems, scales, etc.

57257 J.A. Wendling Foodservice
State Route 47
Pinch, WV 25156   304-965-9565
  Fax: 304-965-9572
Wholesaler/distributor of frozen food, produce and meats; serving the food service market
Chmn./Pres.: John Wendling
Estimated Sales: $20-50 Million
Number Employees: 10-19
Private Brands Carried:
  Pocahontas
Number of Customer Locations: 900
Types of Products Distributed:
  Food Service, Frozen Food, Provisions/Meat, Produce

57258 J.C. Banana & Company
PO Box 2003
Jessup, MD 20794   410-799-1745
  Fax: 410-799-7349
Wholesaler/distributor of bananas
Estimated Sales: $10-20 Million
Number Employees: 20-49
Types of Products Distributed:
  Produce, Bananas

57259 J.C. Produce
1901 Violet St
Los Angeles, CA 90021   213-955-3801
  Fax: 213-236-0623
Wholesaler/distributor of produce and dairy products
VP/Operations Manager: Paul Abess
VP Sales: Barbara Holland
Director Purchasing: Randy Metheny
Number Employees: 20-49
Square Footage: 134000
Parent Co: J.C. Corporation

Wholesalers & Distributors / A-Z

Number of Customer Locations: 300
Types of Products Distributed:
  Frozen Food, General Line, Produce, Dairy products

57260 J.C. Wright Sales Company
7202 S 212th St
Kent, WA 98032   253-395-8799
   Fax: 253-395-8836   800-275-0456
Wholesaler/distributor of groceries and specialty foods; serving the food service market
President: Jack Wright
Estimated Sales: $20-50 Million
Number Employees: 50-99
Number of Customer Locations: 400
Types of Products Distributed:
  Food Service, Frozen Food, General Line, Specialty Foods, Groceries

57261 J.D. Dawson Company
PO Box 219
Belhaven, NC 27810-0219   252-943-2121
   Fax: 252-943-2593
Wholesaler/distributor of groceries, equipment and fixtures, general merchandise, private label items and general line products
President: Melba Smith
VP: Axson Smith, Jr.
Manager: Mark Smith
Number Employees: 20-49
Number of Customer Locations: 200
Types of Products Distributed:
  Frozen Food, General Line, General Merchandise, Groceries, private label items, etc.

57262 J.F. Walker Company
365 E Smithville Road
Bloomington, IN 47401-9359   812-334-1293
   Fax: 502-412-6434
Wholesaler/distributor of candy, frozen foods, etc.; serving convenience stores
General Manager: Ron Lucius
Estimated Sales: $5-10 Million
Number Employees: 5-9
Parent Co: Spartan Grocers
Number of Customer Locations: 300
Types of Products Distributed:
  General Line, Candy, etc.

57263 J.F. Walker Company
3 Audubon Plaza Dr # 450
Louisville, KY 40217-1319   502-636-0800
   Fax: 502-412-6434
Wholesaler/distributor of groceries, candy, etc.; serving the food service market
Manager: Sean Coomer
Estimated Sales: $2.5-5 Million
Number Employees: 1-4
Square Footage: 312000
Parent Co: Spartan Stores
Types of Products Distributed:
  Food Service, General Line, General Merchandise, Groceries, candy, etc.

57264 J.H. Thornton Company
879 N Jan Mar Ct
Olathe, KS 66061   913-764-6550
   Fax: 913-764-1314
Manufacturer, exporter and wholesaler/distributor of conveyor systems; installation services available
President: Douglas Metcalf
Estimated Sales: $3-5 Million
Number Employees: 10
Types of Products Distributed:
  Frozen Food, General Merchandise, Conveyors

57265 J.J. Taylor Distributing
655 N A1A
Jupiter, FL 33477   561-354-2900
   Fax: 561-354-2999 www.jjtaylor.com
Wholesaler/distributor of equipment, general merchandise and nonalcoholic and alcoholic beverages including beer and ale; serving the food service market.
Chairman/President/CEO: John Taylor, III
Vice Chairman: Manuel Portuondo
EVP & Chief Financial Officer: Henri Desplaines
EVP & Chief Operating Officer: Jay Martin
Vice President, Finance: Stuart Shapiro
Vice President, Administration: Jose Rivera
VP, Chief Administrative Officer: Greg Fithian
Vice President, Human Resources: David Miller
Year Founded: 1958
Estimated Sales: $50-100 Million

Number Employees: 100-249
Square Footage: 100000
Private Brands Carried:
  Miller; Presidente; Samuel Adams; St. Pauli Girl; Hatuey
Number of Customer Locations: 5000
Types of Products Distributed:
  Food Service, Frozen Food, General Line, General Merchandise, Alcoholic & non-alcoholic beverages

57266 (HQ)J.L. Henderson & Company
2533 Peralta St
Oakland, CA 94607-1703   510-839-1900
   Fax: 510-839-1944   800-953-1900
   oakland@jlhenderson.com
Wholesaler/distributor of frozen foods, produce, seafood, provisions/meats and general line products; serving the food service market, ship chandlers and rack jobbers
Manager: Marilyn Delacruz
VP: C Kelly
Estimated Sales: $10-20 Million
Number Employees: 10-19
Square Footage: 160000
Other Locations:
  Henderson, J.L., & Co.
  Seattle, WA Henderson, J.L., & Co.
Types of Products Distributed:
  Food Service, Frozen Food, General Line, Provisions/Meat, Produce, Rack Jobbers, Seafood

57267 J.M. Schneider
198 Dawson Road N
Winnipeg, MB R2J 0S7
Canada   204-235-8600
   Fax: 204-235-1613 www.schneiders.ca
Wholesaler/distributor of pork and poultry products
Plant Manager: Scott Auringer
Number Employees: 50-99
Parent Co: J.M. Schneider
Types of Products Distributed:
  Frozen Food, Provisions/Meat, Pork & poultry products

57268 J.O. Demers Beef
PO Box 1079
Woonsocket, RI 02895-0810   401-769-5400
   Fax: 401-769-8096
Wholesaler/distributor of meats; serving the food service market
President: James Demers, Jr.
Types of Products Distributed:
  Food Service, Frozen Food, Provisions/Meat

57269 J.P. Beaudry
9400 Ray Lawson
Anjou, QC H1J 1K9
Canada   514-352-5620
   Fax: 514-352-5739 www.jpbeaudry.com
Wholesaler/distributor of general line products
Director: Cyril Beaudry
Types of Products Distributed:
  Frozen Food, General Line

57270 J.R. Campbell Equipment Company
7461 Worthington Galena Rd
Worthington, OH 43085-6715   614-876-0132
   Fax: 614-876-0779
Wholesaler/distributor of material handling equipment
President: John Campbell
VP Slaes: Chris Campbell
Estimated Sales: $20-50 Million
Number Employees: 50-99
Private Brands Carried:
  Toyota
Types of Products Distributed:
  Frozen Food, General Merchandise, Material handling equipment

57271 J.R. Fish Company
224 Front St
Wrangell, AK 99929   907-874-2399
   Fax: 907-874-2398
Seafood
President: Janell Privett
Secretary/Treasurer: William Privett

57272 J.R. Poultry
2924 Maus Road
Fults, IL 62244-1506   618-458-7194
   Fax: 706-777-8690

Poultry

57273 J.R.'s Seafood
9908 Southwest Highway
Oak Lawn, IL 60453   708-422-4555
   Fax: 914-624-0329
Seafood
President: Frank Cestro
Owner: Carlos Grijalva
Estimated Sales: $1-3 Million
Number Employees: 5-9

57274 J.W. Wood Company
P.O.Box 10246
Lynchburg, VA 24506-0246   434-847-5558
   Fax: 434-528-5601   800-237-6056
Wholesaler/distributor of groceries, meats, dairy products, frozen foods, smallwares, paper/disposable items and equipment and fixtures; serving the food service market
President: Bill Thomasson
Opers.: Carla Smith
Number Employees: 20-49
Square Footage: 60000
Parent Co: Dan Valley Foods
Private Brands Carried:
  Pocahontas
Number of Customer Locations: 300
Types of Products Distributed:
  Food Service, Frozen Food, General Line, General Merchandise, Provisions/Meat, Groceries, dairy products, etc.

57275 JAAMA World Trade
295 Forest Avenue
Suite 127
Portland, ME 04101-2018   207-253-1956
   Fax: 207-878-8455 jaama@gwi.net
   www.gwi.net/~jaama
Wholesaler/distributor, importer and exporter of frozen chicken and meat, dried beans, canned foods, beverages and groceries
President: Brian Cooke
Estimated Sales: $.5-1 million
Number Employees: 10-19
Types of Products Distributed:
  Food Service, Frozen Food, General Line, Dried beans, canned foods & beverages

57276 JBG International
PO Box 6339
Torrance, CA 90504-0339   562-590-9356
   Fax: 562-432-8339
Wholesaler/distributor and importer of olives, olive oil, almonds, honey, rice, artichokes, pimientos, pinenuts, paprika, anchovies, tuna, mandarines, etc
CEO: Juan Garibo
Private Brands Carried:
  Food Agro Products
Types of Products Distributed:
  Frozen Food, General Line, Seafood, Olives, olive oil, almonds, etc.

57277 JBS USA LLC
1770 Promontory Cir.
Greeley, CO 80634   970-506-8000
   www.jbssa.com
Beef, pork and chicken.
CEO: Andre Nogueira
CFO: Denilson Molina
Estimated Sales: $27.8 Billion
Number Employees: 78,000
Number of Brands: 17
Parent Co: JBS S.A.
Type of Packaging: Consumer

57278 JC's Midnite Salsa
PO Box 89451
Tucson, AZ 85752-9451   520-574-3993
   Fax: 520-572-1151   800-817-2572
Salsa
Estimated Sales: $300,000-500,000
Number Employees: 1-4

57279 JC's Sunny Winter
150 N Freeport Drive
Nogales, AZ 85621-2423   520-287-9146
   Fax: 520-287-5068
Wholesaler/distributor of produce including tomatoes
Owner: Jose Cardenas
CEO: Maria Kantor
Private Brands Carried:
  El Milagro; J.C.'s

Wholesalers & Distributors / A-Z

57280 JER Creative Food Concepts, Inc.
5743 Smithway St
Suite 305
Commerce, CA 90040-1549 323-721-1882
Fax: 323-721-4526 800-350-2462
Confectionery products
President: Jonathan Freed
Secretary/Treasurer: Ezekiel Freed
VP: Rose Freed
Purchasing Manager: Kit Phillips
Estimated Sales: $3.5 Million
Number Employees: 5
Square Footage: 12000
Type of Packaging: Bulk
Types of Products Distributed:
Frozen Food

57281 JET Tools
427 New Sanford Rd
La Vergne, TN 37086
800-274-6848
www.jettools.com
Wholesaler/distributor of general merchandise including service carts, scissor lift tables, hydraulic and pallet jacks, hand trucks, hardwood and drum dollies and hoists including electric, chain and manual.
President: Robert Romano
VP, Finance/Controller/CFO: Tony Stratton
VP, Global Supply Chain: Ivan Werhli
SVP, National Sales Account: Bob Varzino
VP, Human Resources: Virginia Schmidt
Year Founded: 1958
Estimated Sales: $50-100 Million
Number Employees: 50-99
Parent Co: Walter Meier Holding
Private Brands Carried:
Jet
Types of Products Distributed:
General Merchandise, Service carts, hand trucks, etc.

57282 JFC International Inc
7101 E Slauson Ave
Commerce, CA 90040 323-721-6100
www.jfc.com
Importer of Japanese foods including mushrooms, chewing gum, mandarin oranges, noodles and fish; exporter of general Japanese groceries.
President: Yoshiyuki Ishigaki
VP, Sales & Marketing: Paul Iiyama
DC Manager: Ian Tennant
Year Founded: 1906
Estimated Sales: $49.4 Million
Number Employees: 100-249
Number of Products: 15
Square Footage: 13075
Type of Packaging: Consumer, Food Service
Other Locations:
Norcross, GA
Los Angeles, CA
Savage, MD
Pompano Beach, FL
Hanover Park, IL
Linden, NJLos Angeles
Types of Products Distributed:
Frozen Food

57283 JK Sucralose
98-A Mayfield Avenue
Edison, NJ 08837 732-512-0889
jkusa@jksucralose.com
www.jksucralose.com
Sweetners, sucralose
General Manager: Hugh Zhang
Quality Control Director: Jianxin An
EVP of Sales & Marketing: Craig Zezima
Contact: Ye Florey
florey@jksucralose.com
Estimated Sales: $25 Million
Number Employees: 219
Number of Brands: 1
Number of Products: 1
Square Footage: 135000
Types of Products Distributed:
Sweetners

Types of Products Distributed:
Frozen Food, Produce, Tomatoes

57284 JM Schneider
4060 78th Avenue SE
Calgary, AB T2C 2I8
Canada 403-720-3860
Fax: 403-236-4255 www.schneiders.ca
Wholesaler/distributor of frozen beef and pork products; importer of frozen entrees
Sales/Marketing Executive: Dan Bradrich
Manager: Doug McFarlane
Number Employees: 50-99
Square Footage: 260000
Parent Co: J.M. Schneider
Types of Products Distributed:
Frozen Food, Provisions/Meat, Beef & pork products

57285 JML Sales Co
2733 Columbia Ave
Lancaster, PA 17603-4115 717-392-5767
Fax: 717-392-0943
Wholesaler/distributor and broker of frozen foods
President: Jeff Lawrence
Estimated Sales: $1-2.5 Million
Number Employees: 1-4
Types of Products Distributed:
Food Service, Frozen Food

57286 JMS
P.O.Box 336
Brookline, MA 02446 617-254-1116
Fax: 617-254-1414
Wholesaler/distributor, importer and exporter of produce and fresh herbs including thyme, basil, oregano, rosemary, mint, chives, sage, cilantro and parsley
President: Joel Shaw
VP: Karen Shaw
Contact: Josephs Leah
jleah@jms-herbs.net
Estimated Sales: $.5-1 million
Number Employees: 1-4
Types of Products Distributed:
Frozen Food, General Line, Produce, Fresh herbs

57287 JNS Foods
3785 Airport Pulling Road N
Suite C
Naples, FL 34105-4518 239-403-9080
Fax: 941-403-9085 jnsfoods@aol.com
Wholesaler/distributor and exporter of dairy/deli products, frozen foods, groceries, meats, seafood, general merchandise, etc.; serving the food service market
President: Jeffrey Siegal
CEO: Nancy Siegal
Estimated Sales: $7 Million
Number Employees: 1-4
Square Footage: 6000
Type of Packaging: Food Service
Number of Customer Locations: 300
Types of Products Distributed:
Food Service, Frozen Food, General Line, Provisions/Meat, Groceries, dairy/deli products, etc.

57288 JUST Inc
2000 Folsom St
San Francisco, CA 94110-1318 415-829-2325
Fax: 415-520-2156 844-423-6637
wecare@justforall.com www.ju.st
Vegan egg substitute, mayonnaise, salad dressing, cookie dough, and lab-grown meat
CEO/Co-Founder: Josh Tetrick
Co-Founder: Josh Balk
COO/CFO: Erez Simha
CTO: Peter Licari
Year Founded: 2011
Estimated Sales: $30 Million
Number Employees: 10-19
Types of Products Distributed:
General Line, Specialty Foods

57289 Jab's Seafood
PO Box 300
Hackberry, LA 70645-0300 337-762-3183
Wholesaler/distributor of seafood
Owner/President: Jab Beard
VP: Sandy Beard
Types of Products Distributed:
Frozen Food, Seafood

57290 Jaccard Corporation
3421 N Benzing Rd
Orchard Park, NY 14127 716-825-3814
Fax: 716-825-5319
Wholesaler/distributor and exporter of food processing equipment including tenderizers, slicers/dicers, cutlet flattening devices, vacuum packagers and pickling injectors; serving the food service market
President: Eric Wangler
Marketing Director: Karen Beamish
Sales Director: Erin Janney
Contact: Paul Eichin
pauleichin@jaccard.com
Operations Manager: Doug Spaetch
Estimated Sales: $2.5-5 Million
Number Employees: 10-19
Type of Packaging: Food Service
Private Brands Carried:
Jaccard
Types of Products Distributed:
Food processing equipment

57291 Jack & Jill Ice Cream
101 Commerce Dr
Moorestown, NJ 08057-4212 856-813-2300
Fax: 856-813-2373 info@jjicc.com
www.jjicc.com
Ice cream and frozen yogurt; cakes and fancy desserts
President: Jay Schwartz
jschwartz@jjicc.com
Founder: Mickey Schwartz
Marketing Director: Shawn Brady
VP Sales: John Corral
General Manager: Ken Schwartz
Number Employees: 500-999
Type of Packaging: Consumer, Food Service
Types of Products Distributed:
Frozen Food, Specialty Foods, Cakes & fancy desserts

57292 Jacks Merchandising & Distribution
4401 SW 23rd Street
Oklahoma City, OK 73108-1750 405-681-9332
Wholesaler/distributor of general merchandise including school supplies, hardware, housewares, mops and brooms
VP Marketing: Jeremie Kubicek
VP Sales: John Loesel
VP Merchandising: Gary Yowell
Number Employees: 250-499
Square Footage: 640000
Parent Co: BMK
Number of Customer Locations: 8000
Types of Products Distributed:
Frozen Food, General Merchandise, School supplies, housewares, etc.

57293 Jackson Newell Paper Co
1212 Grand Ave
Meridian, MS 39301
800-844-8894
meridian.newellpaper.com
Wholesaler/distributor of paper and plastic plates, cutlery, etc.; also, cleaning and warewash chemicals; serving the food service market.
Chairman & CEO: Bill Allen
Year Founded: 1946
Estimated Sales: $50-100 Million
Number Employees: 50-99
Square Footage: 50000
Types of Products Distributed:
Food Service, Frozen Food, General Merchandise, Paper & plastic plates, cutlery, etc.

57294 Jackson Supply Company
4550 Lamar Ave # 500
Paris, TX 75462-5129 903-739-2822
Fax: 903-739-9643
Wholesaler/distributor of cleaning supplies, disposables and wraps; serving the food service market
Owner: Paul T Jackson
Estimated Sales: $5-10 Million
Number Employees: 10-19
Types of Products Distributed:
Food Service, Frozen Food, General Merchandise, Cleaning supplies, disposables & wraps

Wholesalers & Distributors / A-Z

57295 Jackson Wholesale Co
129 Armory Dr
P.O.Box 634
Jackson, KY 41339-9256 606-666-2495
Fax: 606-666-2280 800-874-7964
www.jacksonwholesale.com
Wholesaler/distributor of general merchandise and general line products, produce and provisions/meats; also, rack jobber services available; serving the food service market
President: Alex Mcintyre
alex@jacksonpottery.com
Estimated Sales: $10-20 Million
Number Employees: 20-49
Number of Customer Locations: 800
Types of Products Distributed:
Food Service, Frozen Food, General Line, General Merchandise, Provisions/Meat, Produce, Rack Jobbers, Groceries

57296 Jacob & Sons Wholesale Meats
306 Center St
PO Box 217
Martins Ferry, OH 43935-1793 740-633-3091
Fax: 740-633-3106
www.jacobandsonsqualitymeats.com
Meats and sausages
President: Michael Jacob
Estimated Sales: $1.60 Million
Number Employees: 10-19

57297 Jacob KERN & Sons Inc
60 Nichols St
Lockport, NY 14094-4898 716-434-3577
Fax: 716-434-0821 800-248-8408
Wholesaler/distributor of specialty food products including candy, cookies, general merchandise, etc.; also, rack jobber services available
President: Jacob Kern Iii
kernwholesale@aol.com
Vice President: Paul Kern
Estimated Sales: $10-20 Million
Number Employees: 10-19
Square Footage: 3800
Private Brands Carried:
Lydia
Number of Customer Locations: 250
Types of Products Distributed:
General Line, General Merchandise, Rack Jobbers, Specialty Foods, Candy, cookies, tobacco, etc.

57298 Jacob Licht
765 Westminster St
Providence, RI 02903 401-331-9555
Fax: 401-454-0740 800-695-1098
jlicht@netsense.net
Wholesaler/distributor of food processing machinery, convection ovens, tabletop supplies, fryers, blenders, ice machines, smallwares, etc
President: Gary Licht
Contact: Robert Feinberg
bobm@jacoblicht.com
Operations Manager: Cheryl Johnson
Estimated Sales: $10-20 Million
Number Employees: 20-49
Square Footage: 8000
Types of Products Distributed:
Frozen Food, General Merchandise, Convection ovens, fryers, etc.

57299 Jacobi Lewis Co
622 S Front St
PO Box 1289
Wilmington, NC 28401-5034 910-763-6201
Fax: 910-763-5610 800-763-2433
jl@jacobi-lewis.com www.jacobi-lewis.com
Wholesaler/distributor of equipment, supplies, furniture, etc.; serving the food service market
President: Greg Lewis
Chairman: French Lewis
Vice President: Gloria Ludewic
Marketing/Sales: Chris Gannon
Purchasing Manager: Wilson Horton
Estimated Sales: $7 Million
Number Employees: 10-19
Number of Brands: 700
Square Footage: 45000
Types of Products Distributed:
Food Service, General Merchandise, Equipment, supplies, furniture, etc.

57300 Jacobson & Sons
469 Niagara St
Buffalo, NY 14201-1740 716-854-1150
Wholesaler/distributor of groceries and frozen foods; serving the food service market
General Manager: Paul Jacobson
Estimated Sales: $2.5-5 Million
Number Employees: 1-4
Number of Customer Locations: 320
Types of Products Distributed:
Food Service, Frozen Food, General Line, Groceries

57301 Jade Leaf Matcha
San Francisco, CA 94123
support@jadeleafmatcha.com
www.jadeleafmatcha.com
Organic Japanese matcha
Type of Packaging: Consumer, Bulk

57302 Jake's Variety Wholesale
1101 Charity St
Abbeville, LA 70510-5303 337-893-0342
Fax: 337-898-9188
Wholesaler/distributor of general line products; serving the food service market
Manager: Betty Ister
Estimated Sales: $5-10 Million
Number Employees: 1-4
Number of Customer Locations: 120
Types of Products Distributed:
Food Service, Frozen Food, General Line

57303 Jako Fish
250 Summerlea Road
Brampton, ON L6T 3V6
Canada 905-791-7227
Fax: 905-791-7740
Wholesaler/distributor of fresh and frozen fish and seafood
President: Phil Krant
Number Employees: 5-9
Types of Products Distributed:
Frozen Food, Seafood

57304 Jamac Frozen Foods
570 Grand St
Jersey City, NJ 07302-4115 201-333-6200
Fax: 201-333-2966 www.jamacfrozenfoods.com
Wholesaler/distributor of frozen food, seafood, bakery items and meats; serving the food service market
President/COO: E Marbach
Cmo: Michael Bestine
michael@jamacfrozenfoods.com
Chairman Board: D Marbach
Estimated Sales: $10-20 Million
Number Employees: 100-249
Private Brands Carried:
Big Lou; Fancy Lady
Number of Customer Locations: 475
Types of Products Distributed:
Food Service, Frozen Food, General Line, Provisions/Meat, Seafood, Bakery items

57305 Jamaican Gourmet Coffee Company
250 South 18th Street
Suite 802
Philadelphia, PA 19103
800-261-2859
sales@coffeeforless.com
Coffee, tea
President: Lloyd Parchment
Estimated Sales: Below $5 Million
Number Employees: 20
Square Footage: 55200

57306 Jamaican Teas LimitedC/O Eve Sales Corporation
945 Close Ave
Bronx, NY 10473 718-589-6800
Fax: 718-617-6717 ihopp@evesales.com
www.jamaicanteas.com
Wholesaler/distributor and importer of Caribbean and Mexican foods
Owner: Irving Nadler
Executive VP: Irving Nadler
VP Marketing: Stuart Gale
Sales Manager: Isadore Hoppenfeld
Estimated Sales: $5-10 Million
Number Employees: 10-19
Square Footage: 88000
Types of Products Distributed:
Frozen Food, General Line, Specialty Foods, Caribbean & Mexican foods

57307 James Avery Clark & Sons Inc
720 N East St
Frederick, MD 21701-5239 301-662-2193
Fax: 301-662-2545
Wholesaler/distributor of produce; serving the food service market
President: Jeff Clark
clarkprod@aol.com
Estimated Sales: $5-10 Million
Number Employees: 10-19
Types of Products Distributed:
Produce

57308 James C Thomas & Sons
1 Fulton St
Luzerne, PA 18709-1432 570-288-3681
Fax: 570-288-2266
Wholesaler/distributor of produce
Owner: John C Thomas
Partner/General Manager: John Thomas
Estimated Sales: $2.5-5 Million
Number Employees: 5-9
Types of Products Distributed:
Produce

57309 James D Cofer
1275 Wesley Place NW
Atlanta, GA 30327-1712 404-577-3385
Fax: 404-577-0328
Wholesaler/distributor of groceries, meats, produce, dairy items, frozen foods, general merchandise, snack foods and private label items
President: M Champacde
CFO: F Champacde
General Manager: D Nash
Buyer: T Haney
Estimated Sales: $20-50 Million
Number Employees: 20-49
Square Footage: 40000
Number of Customer Locations: 400
Types of Products Distributed:
Frozen Food, General Line, General Merchandise, Provisions/Meat, Produce, Groceries, dairy items, etc.

57310 James Desiderio Inc
550 Bailey Ave
Buffalo, NY 14206 716-823-2211
www.jamesdesiderio.com
Wholesaler/distributor of produce; serving the food service market; wholesaler of fruits.
Chief Financial Officer: Edward Gibbons
edg@jamesdesiderio.com
Estimated Sales: $20-50 Million
Number Employees: 20-49
Types of Products Distributed:
Food Service, Frozen Food, Produce

57311 James K. Wilson Produce Company
PO Box 850
Nogales, AZ 85628-0850 520-281-0550
Fax: 520-281-4043
Wholesaler/distributor of produce including cantaloupes, cherry tomatoes, bell peppers, vine-ripe tomatoes and hot peppers
Private Brands Carried:
Wilson's
Types of Products Distributed:
Frozen Food, Produce, Tomatoes, peppers, etc.

57312 Janney Marshall Co
401 Princess Anne St
Fredericksburg, VA 22401-6042 540-373-8362
Fax: 540-373-8388
Wholesaler/distributor of frozen foods, general line items, produce, meats and seafood; serving the food service market
Manager: Nancy Russler
Manager: Sue Baxter
General Manager: Carl Anderson
Estimated Sales: $5-10 Million
Number Employees: 1-4
Square Footage: 400000
Private Brands Carried:
Hills Bros; Maxwell House; Kraft Foodservice
Types of Products Distributed:
Food Service, Frozen Food, General Line, Provisions/Meat, Produce, Seafood

Wholesalers & Distributors / A-Z

57313 Janpak
705 Griffith Street
Suite 300
Davidson, NC 28036   704-892-0219
    Fax: 704-731-0978 www.janpak.com
Wholesaler/distributor of paper products and cleaning supplies
Manager: Micheal Brown
Sales Manager: Ray Amerton
General Manager: Gary Drake
Estimated Sales: $5-10 Million
Number Employees: 20-49
Square Footage: 208000
Types of Products Distributed:
    Frozen Food, General Merchandise, Paper Products & Cleaning Supplies

57314 (HQ)Jarosz Produce Farms
PO Box 176
Pine Island, NY 10969-0176   845-258-4071
    Fax: 845-258-0595
Wholesaler/distributor of produce
Co-Owner: Agatha Jarosz
Types of Products Distributed:
    Frozen Food, Produce

57315 Jarrow Formulas Inc
1824 1/2 S Robertson Blvd
Los Angeles, CA 90035-4317   310-204-6936
    Fax: 310-204-2520   800-726-0886
    info@jarrow.com www.jarrow.com
Wholesaler/distributor and exporter of nutritional supplements including antioxidants, vitamins, minerals, herbal formulas, acidophilus capsules and powders
President: Jarrow Rogovin
jarrow@jarrow.com
VP Finance: Benjamin Khowong
R&D VP: Sid Shastro
Sales VP: Clay DuBose
Estimated Sales: $30 Million
Number Employees: 50-99
Square Footage: 8000
Private Brands Carried:
    Bone-Up; Q-Sorb; Joint Sustain; Muscle Optimeal; Jarro-Dophilus EPS; Glycemic Balance; Biosil; Jarro SAM-e; Ala Sustain; Probiotic System; ISO-Rich Soy; Lyco-Sorb
Number of Customer Locations: 5000
Types of Products Distributed:
    Health Food, Vitamins & minerals

57316 Jason Marketing Corporation
10900 NW 97th St Unit 101
Medley, FL 33178   305-882-6716
    Fax: 305-882-6724
Wholesaler/distributor, importer and exporter of dry groceries including canned items, rice, nonalcoholic beverages, paper products, trays, etc.; serving the retail market
President: Norman Welch
Estimated Sales: $5-10 Million
Number Employees: 5-9
Square Footage: 52000
Private Brands Carried:
    Valrico; Valix; Kist
Types of Products Distributed:
    Frozen Food, General Line, Dry groceries

57317 Jasper Glove Company
3530 Newton Street
Suite 189
Jasper, IN 47546-1050   812-482-4473
Wholesaler/distributor of aprons and work gloves including plastic, rubber, leather and cotton
President: Charles Habig
Secretary: Mary Jane Ryder
VP: Donald Habig
Estimated Sales: $500,000-$1 Million
Number Employees: 5-9
Square Footage: 6000
Types of Products Distributed:
    Frozen Food, General Merchandise, Aprons & gloves

57318 Jatex-USA Corporation
777 New Durham Road
Edison, NJ 08817-2859   732-632-4665
    Fax: 732-632-4654
Wholesaler/distributor of nonperishable foods
President: Jack Kogan
VP: Joseph Kogan
Number Employees: 10-19
Types of Products Distributed:
    Frozen Food, General Line, Non-perishable

57319 Java Beans and Joe Coffee
1331 Commerce St.
Petaluma, CA 94549   707-462-6333
    800-624-7031
    sales@javabeansandjoe.com
Coffee, flavored coffee, K-Cups
Owner: Lauren Mountanos
Parent Co: Mountanos Family Coffee & Tea Co.
Types of Products Distributed:
    General Line

57320 Javed & Sons
6711 Hornwood Dr.
Suite 250
Houston, TX 77074   713-835-6850
    javed_sons@hotmail.com
    javednsons.webs.com
Halal chicken
Owner: Iqbal Javed   *Year Founded:* 1999
Types of Products Distributed:
    Provisions/Meat

57321 Jaydon
7800 14th Street W
Rock Island, IL 61201-7402   309-787-4492
    Fax: 309-787-4335
Wholesaler/distributor of general merchandise, private label items and health and beauty aids; also, rack jobber services available
President: J Gellerman
VP: D Gellerman
VP: J Tansey
Number Employees: 250-499
Square Footage: 640000
Number of Customer Locations: 3000
Types of Products Distributed:
    Frozen Food, General Merchandise, Rack Jobbers

57322 Jb Prince
36 E 31st St # 11
New York, NY 10016-6861   212-683-9273
    Fax: 212-683-4488   800-473-0577
    customerservice@jbprince.com www.jbprince.com
Exporter and wholesaler/distributor of food service equipment and supplies including serving and cooking equipment, tableware and chefs' tools; serving the food service market; importer of restaurant kitchen smallware
President: J Prince
VP: L Prince
Manager: John Thompson
jthompson@jbprince.com
Estimated Sales: $5-10 Million
Number Employees: 20-49
Types of Products Distributed:
    Food Service, Frozen Food, General Merchandise, Foodservice equipment & supplies

57323 Jeb Plastics
3519 Silverside Rd Ste 106
Wilmington, DE 19810   302-479-9223
    Fax: 302-479-9227   800-556-2247
    www.jebplastics.com
Wholesaler/distributor/broker of poly bags, vinyl bags, heat sealers and packaging supplies
Owner: Sherri Lindner
Estimated Sales: Below $500,000
Number Employees: 1-4
Square Footage: 4000
Types of Products Distributed:
    Frozen Food, General Merchandise, Poly bags, heat sealers, etc.

57324 Jedwards International Inc
141 Campanelli Dr
Braintree, MA 02184-5206   781-848-1473
    Fax: 617-472-9359 sales@bulknaturaloils.com
    www.bulknaturaloils.com
Organic specialty oils, essential oils, butters, waxes and botanicals
Contact: Jeremy Bamsch
jeremy@bulknaturaloils.com

57325 Jeffer Neely Company
PO Box 609
Hull, GA 30646-0609   706-353-7533
    Fax: 706-549-5537
Wholesaler of general merchandise and private label items; rack jobber services available
Owner/President: James Jeffer
Estimated Sales: $2 Million+
Number Employees: 1-4
Types of Products Distributed:
    Frozen Food, General Merchandise, Rack Jobbers, Private label items

57326 Jefferds Corp
2070 Winfield Rd
St Albans, WV 25177-7802   304-755-8111
    Fax: 304-755-7544 www.jefferds.com
Wholesaler/distributor of forklifts and conveyors
President: K Richard Sinclair
Cio/Cto: Chester Brenan
chesterbrenan@jefferds.com
Estimated Sales: $20-50 Million
Number Employees: 50-99
Private Brands Carried:
    Clark; Hytrol; Interlake
Types of Products Distributed:
    Frozen Food, General Merchandise, Forklifts & conveyors

57327 Jefferson Packing Company
765 Marlene Drive
Gretna, LA 70056-7639   504-366-4451
    Fax: 504-366-9382
Packaging solutions
President: William Marciante

57328 Jeffries Supply Co
49 N 4th St
Newark, OH 43055-5027   740-345-6225
    Fax: 740-345-6225 www.jeffriessupply.com
Wholesaler/distributor of confectionery items
Owner: Rick Gummer
rgummer@jeffriessupply.com
General Manager: Diana Bruckelmyer
Estimated Sales: Less Than $500,000
Number Employees: 1-4
Parent Co: Gummer Wholesale
Types of Products Distributed:
    General Line, Confectionery items

57329 Jeni's Splendid Ice Creams
401 N Front St
Suite 300
Columbus, OH 43215   614-488-3224
    contact@jenis.com
    www.jenis.com
Ice cream
Founder & CCO: Jeni Bauer
CEO: John Lowe
Contact: Steve Boutros
steve.boutros@jenis.com

57330 Jenthon Supply
P.O.Box 65182
San Antonio, TX 78265-5182   210-599-9623
    Fax: 210-599-9646
Wholesaler/distributor of material handling equipment including carts, shelving and mats
President: John Martinez
Owner: Mike Martinez
Estimated Sales: $1-2.5 Million
Number Employees: 1-4
Private Brands Carried:
    Westco; 3M; Logan
Types of Products Distributed:
    Frozen Food, General Merchandise, Carts, shelving, mats, etc.

57331 Jerico
3624 NW 59th St
Miami, FL 33142-2030   305-633-3388
    Fax: 305-633-3388   800-455-1415
    jerico@gate.net www.jericoequip.com
Wholesaler/distributor of baked goods, restaurant supplies and equipment
President: Richard Adelman
jerico@gate.net
VP: Richard Adelman
Sales: Manuel York
Sales Manager: Ian McIntyre
Estimated Sales: $2.5-5 Million
Number Employees: 5-9
Square Footage: 28000
Number of Customer Locations: 150
Types of Products Distributed:
    Food Service, Frozen Food, General Merchandise, Restaurant supplies & equipment

1055

Wholesalers & Distributors / A-Z

57332 Jerilu Fruit Center
101 Ore Dock Rd
Erie, PA 16507-2407 814-452-2492
Fax: 814-480-8832 www.jerilu.com
Wholesaler/distributor of produce
Owner: Mary Eichner
Manager: Joe Rancci
Estimated Sales: $10-20 Million
Number Employees: 20-49
Types of Products Distributed:
Produce

57333 Jeris Health & Nutrition
579 Minnehaha Avenue E
Saint Paul, MN 55130-4150 612-378-4767
Fax: 612-378-4769 800-873-5330
nutrition98@hotmail.com
Wholesaler/distributor of diet, health and digestive food products; also, health and nutritional consulting
CEO: Jeris Morgan
Types of Products Distributed:
Frozen Food, General Line, Health Food, Vitamins, diet & energy products

57334 Jerome Langdon Produce
7756 Nc 50 Hwy N
Angier, NC 27501 919-894-8014
Fax: 919-894-7649
Wholesaler/distributor of sweet potatoes
President: Jerome Langdon
VP: Sue Langdon
Estimated Sales: $1-3 Million
Number Employees: 1-4
Private Brands Carried:
Tasty Brand
Types of Products Distributed:
Frozen Food, Produce, Sweet potatoes

57335 Jerry Brothers Industries Inc
4619 Glasgow St
Richmond, VA 23234 804-271-0689
Fax: 804-271-1258 JBI@MIR-belting.com
www.jerrybrothers.com
Wholesaler/distributor of conveyor belts including smooth, incline, weigh scale and feeder for many parts of the food industry, including bakery, meat processing, salad, tobacco, and boxes for packaging.
Operations Manager: Carras Sayre
Estimated Sales: $2.5-5 Million
Number Employees: 10-19
Type of Packaging: Food Service
Types of Products Distributed:
Frozen Food, General Merchandise, Conveyor belts

57336 Jerry Schulman Produce
P.O.Box 410
Smithtown, NY 11787-0410 631-582-1524
Fax: 631-348-0279 800-645-7776
Wholesaler/distributor of produce including potatoes, lettuce, carrots, spinach, cauliflower, broccoli and cabbage
President: Robert Monzeglio
Sales: Rosie Fardella
VP Sales: Diane Rabin
Sales Manager: David Ludlum
Estimated Sales: $2.5-5 Million
Number Employees: 5-9
Types of Products Distributed:
Frozen Food, Produce, Spinach, cauliflower, broccoli, etc.

57337 Jersey Meat & Provision Company
3336 Fruitland Ave
Vernon, CA 90058 323-583-8921
Fax: 323-585-0756
Wholesaler/distributor of provisions/meats including beef
Owner: Ralph Hackman
Estimated Sales: $3-5 Million
Number Employees: 1-4
Types of Products Distributed:
Frozen Food, Provisions/Meat, Beef

57338 Jess's Market
118 S Main St
Rockland, ME 4841 207-596-6068
Fax: 207-596-7292 877-219-8653
info@jessmarket.com www.jessmarket.com
Products include lobsters, clams, mussels, oysters, crabmeat, shrimp, scallops and a variety of fresh fish.
Owner: Sharon Wiggin
jessmarket@aol.com
Estimated Sales: $1,200,000
Number Employees: 5-9
Number of Customer Locations: 1

57339 Jesse Food Products
1607 N Stevens St
Rhinelander, WI 54501-2126 715-362-4195
Fax: 715-362-2622 800-472-1020
Wholesaler/distributor of produce, frozen foods, general merchandise and meats; serving the food service market
President: David Jesse
Secretary: Mary Jesse
Estimated Sales: $20-50 Million
Number Employees: 20-49
Square Footage: 20000
Types of Products Distributed:
Food Service, Frozen Food, General Merchandise, Provisions/Meat, Produce

57340 Jessom Food Equipment
8 Ralston Avenue
Dartmouth, NS B3B 1H7
Canada 902-468-8778
Fax: 902-468-4597 888-333-9929
Wholesaler/distributor of food service equipment; serving the food service market
President: Don Jessome
VP: Louise Jessome
Number Employees: 10-19
Private Brands Carried:
Vulcan; Hobart; Garland
Types of Products Distributed:
Food Service, Frozen Food, General Merchandise, Foodservice equipment

57341 Jet Set Sam
10918 Phillips Avenue
Burnaby, BC V5A 2V8
Canada 604-283-4362
Fax: 604-444-2661 sales@jetsetsam.com
www.jetsetsam.com/
Wholesaler/distributor, importer and exporter of canned smoked salmon and caviar
Owner: Firoz Jinnah
Number Employees: 1-4
Square Footage: 24000
Parent Co: Jet Set Sam Services
Private Brands Carried:
Jet Set Sam
Types of Products Distributed:
Frozen Food, Seafood, Specialty Foods

57342 Jetro Cash & Carry
566 Hamilton Ave
Brooklyn, NY 11232-1034 718-768-0555
Fax: 718-768-0009 www.restaurantdepot.com
Wholesaler/distributor of general line products and food service equipment; serving the food service market
Manager/Buyer: Freddy Sanchez
Branch Manager: Rocco Delia
Manager: Roy Romano
rromano@jetrord.com
Number Employees: 100-249
Square Footage: 180000
Parent Co: Jetro Cash & Carry Enterprises
Private Brands Carried:
Roland; Red Pack; Kraft
Number of Customer Locations: 6000
Types of Products Distributed:
Food Service, Frozen Food, General Line, General Merchandise, Foodservice equipment

57343 Jetro Cash & Carry Enterprises
1524 132nd St
College Point, NY 11356 718-762-8700
www.jetro.com
Wholesaler/distributor of produce, frozen food, general merchandise and general line products; serving the food service market.
Estimated Sales: $50-100 Million
Number Employees: 50-99
Square Footage: 85000
Private Brands Carried:
Red & White
Number of Customer Locations: 6000
Types of Products Distributed:
Food Service, Frozen Food, General Line, General Merchandise, Produce

57344 (HQ)Jetro Cash & Carry Inc
1524 132nd St
College Point, NY 11356-2440 718-939-6400
Fax: 718-661-9627 www.jetro.com
Wholesaler/distributor of seafood, general merchandise, health and frozen foods, provisions/meats, general line and specialty items and produce; serving the food service market
President: Bryan Emmert
bemmert@jetrord.com
CEO: Stanley Fleishman
Manager: Allen Schwartz
Estimated Sales: $1-3 Million
Number Employees: 1000-4999
Parent Co: Jetro Cash & Carry Enterprises
Other Locations:
Jetro Cash & Carry Enterprise
College Point, NYJetro Cash & Carry Enterprise
Types of Products Distributed:
Food Service, Frozen Food, General Line, General Merchandise, Health Food, Provisions/Meat, Produce, Seafood, Specialty Foods

57345 Jianas Brothers Packaging
2533 Southwest Blvd
Kansas City, MO 64108-2345 816-421-2880
Fax: 816-421-2883
Wholesaler/distributor of confectionery products including candy, chocolates and brittles
Owner: Gus Jianas
Estimated Sales: $2.5-5 Million
Number Employees: 50-99
Types of Products Distributed:
Frozen Food, Specialty Foods, Confectionery

57346 Jilasco Food Exports
1415 2nd Avenue
Unit 2005
Seattle, WA 98101-2072 206-684-9433
Fax: 206-233-9440
Export broker of frozen foods, groceries, meat and meat products, seafood, spices, frying equipment, general merchandise, etc.
President: Eduardo Bicierro
Vice President: Luisa Bicierro
Operations Manager: Bernard Corsles
Number Employees: 1-4
Square Footage: 2200
Parent Co: Jilasco LLC
Type of Packaging: Food Service, Private Label, Bulk
Types of Products Distributed:
Food Service, Frozen Food, Seafood

57347 Jim David Meats
400 T Frank Wathen Rd
Uniontown, KY 42461 270-822-4866
Fax: 270-822-9188
linda.baird@littlekentuckysmokehouse.com
www.littlekentuckysmokehouse.com
Wholesaler/distributor of fresh and frozen provisions/meats; serving the food service market
President: Linda Baird
Owner: Jimmy Baird
jbaird@premiumkentuckyfarms.com
Estimated Sales: $5-10 Million
Number Employees: 20-49
Square Footage: 100000
Parent Co: Union County Live Stock
Types of Products Distributed:
Food Service, Provisions/Meat

57348 Jim's Cheese Pantry
410 Portland Rd
Waterloo, WI 53594-1200 920-478-3571
Fax: 920-478-2320 800-345-3571
Cheese; jams, jellies and crackers
President: James Peschel
CEO: Jim Peschel
VP: Judy Peschel
Estimated Sales: $9.5 Million
Number Employees: 50-99
Square Footage: 100000
Type of Packaging: Consumer, Food Service
Types of Products Distributed:
Food Service, Frozen Food, General Line, Jams, jellies & crackers

57349 Jimmy Durbin Farms
3233 County Road 30
Clanton, AL 35045-7187 205-755-4203
Fax: 205-755-4173 205-755-0203
www.sunshinefarms.com

Wholesaler/distributor of produce including peaches, watermelons, cantaloupes, peppers, cucumbers and tomatoes
Owner: Jimmy Durban
jimdurbanfarms@gmail.com
VP: Tim Minor
Estimated Sales: $.5-1 million
Number Employees: 5-9
Square Footage: 18000
Number of Customer Locations: 40
Types of Products Distributed:
Frozen Food, Produce, Peaches, watermelons, cucumbers, etc.

57350 Jin Han International
2911 Compton Avenue
Los Angeles, CA 90011-2224   213-389-3163
                             Fax: 323-233-0445
Wholesaler/distributor of Korean food
President: J Kim
Estimated Sales: $.5-1 million
Number Employees: 1-4
Types of Products Distributed:
Frozen Food, Korean food

57351 Jo Mar Laboratories
583 Division St # B
Campbell, CA 95008-6915   408-374-5920
         Fax: 408-374-5922   800-538-4545
info@jomarlabs.com www.jomarlabs.com
Health products; contract packaging
President: Joanne Brown
joanne@jomarlabs.com
Estimated Sales: $1-3 Million
Number Employees: 10-19
Square Footage: 14000
Parent Co: Jo Mar Labs
Type of Packaging: Consumer, Private Label
Types of Products Distributed:
Amino acids

57352 Jo Mints
2101 E Coast Highway
Suite 250
Corona Del Mar, CA 92625-1928   310-401-1894
         Fax: 310-388-5647   877-566-4687
tom@jomints.com www.jomints.com
Importers, packers and distributors of food products including canned tomato products, olives, mushrooms, beans, peppers, pickles, giardiniera, artichockes, canned clams, canned shrimp, canned crab meat, canned tuna, and edibleoils.
Marketing: Tom Knutson
Public Relations: Ashley Talbott
Estimated Sales: $5-10 Million
Number Employees: 3
Square Footage: 10000
Type of Packaging: Consumer, Food Service, Private Label
Private Brands Carried:
Scalli, Prima Donna, La Perla
Number of Customer Locations: 300
Types of Products Distributed:
Food Service, General Line, General Merchandise, Rack Jobbers, Specialty Foods

57353 JoDaSa Group International
146 Chelwood Drive
Thornhill, ON L4J 7C4
Canada   905-669-3760
                        Fax: 905-669-4352
Importer and wholesaler/distributor of canned kiwifruit and kiwi syrup, jams, spreads and nectars; also, organic extra virgin olive oil and dried pasta
Managing Director: Sergio Zavarella
Type of Packaging: Consumer, Food Service, Private Label, Bulk
Types of Products Distributed:
Frozen Food, General Line, Health Food, Organic pasta, olive oil, etc.

57354 Jode Company
4834 Vicksburg Street
Dallas, TX 75207-5212   214-637-3720
         Fax: 214-637-6148   800-345-5633
Wholesaler/distributor of general merchandise including valves, fittings, pumps, tubes, pipes, steam accessories and controls
President: Jode Deepree
Marketing Manager: Mike Raglin
Slaes Manager: Forrest Clark
Estimated Sales: $2.5-5 Million
Number Employees: 5-9
Square Footage: 120000
Types of Products Distributed:
Frozen Food, General Merchandise, Steam accessories, pumps, valves, etc.

57355 Jodyana Corporation
18367 NE 4th Ct
Miami, FL 33179-4531   305-651-0110
         Fax: 305-651-4535   888-563-5282
Coffee
President: Corey Colaciello
Chairman: Joe Colaciello
Estimated Sales: $620,000
Number Employees: 5
Number of Brands: 115
Square Footage: 12000
Type of Packaging: Food Service, Private Label, Bulk

57356 Joe Bertman Foods
PO Box 6562
Cleveland, OH 44101-1562   216-431-4460
                           800-749-4460
Wholesaler/distributor of mustard, horseradish and horseradish sauce; serving the food service and retail markets
President: Pat Mazoh
Estimated Sales: $1-3 Million
Number Employees: 1-4
Square Footage: 4000
Private Brands Carried:
Bertamn Original; Ball Park (Spicy brown mustard); Bertman (horseradish sauce)
Types of Products Distributed:
Food Service, General Line, Mustard, horseradish, etc.

57357 Joe Christiana Food Distributing
2055 Sorrel Ave
Baton Rouge, LA 70802-4299   225-387-3297
                        Fax: 225-336-1663
Wholesaler/distributor of groceries, frozen foods, meats, dry goods and paper; serving the food service market; rack jobber services available
Owner: Joe Christiana
Estimated Sales: $20-50 Million
Number Employees: 20-49
Types of Products Distributed:
Food Service, Frozen Food, General Merchandise, Provisions/Meat, Rack Jobbers, Paper & dry goods

57358 Joe Harding Sales & Svc
515 N Range Line Rd
Joplin, MO 64801-1605   417-624-3020
         Fax: 417-624-2855   800-237-3484
www.joeharding.com
Wholesaler/distributor of general merchandise including kitchen and seating area fixtures, equipment and supplies; serving the food service market
President: Robert Harding
Vice President: Bill Harding
Accounting: Richard Webster
Sales/Marketing Executive: Bill Harding
Purchasing Manager: Steve Allen
Estimated Sales: $5-10 Million
Number Employees: 5-9
Square Footage: 240000
Private Brands Carried:
Hobart; Blodgett
Number of Customer Locations: 1500
Types of Products Distributed:
Food Service, Frozen Food, General Merchandise, Kitchen & seating area fixtures

57359 Joe Paulk Company
PO Box 248
Russellville, AR 72811-0248   479-968-8444
                        Fax: 501-968-6882
Wholesaler/distributor of general merchandise, snack foods and candy
President: Martin Jennen
Estimated Sales: $500,000-$1 Million
Number Employees: 10-19
Square Footage: 48000
Number of Customer Locations: 400
Types of Products Distributed:
Frozen Food, General Line, General Merchandise, Snack foods & candy

57360 Joe Pucci & Sons Seafood
678 3rd Street
Oakland, CA 94607-3560   510-444-3769
         Fax: 510-444-3973   800-427-8224
Wholesaler/distributor of seafood and frozen foods; serving the food service market and supermarket chains
President: Chris Lam
Sales Director: Jerry Gibson
Plant Manager: Gary Golden
Purchasing Manager: Steve Pucci
Estimated Sales: $20-50 Million
Number Employees: 50-99
Square Footage: 30000
Parent Co: Blue River Seafood
Type of Packaging: Consumer, Food Service, Private Label, Bulk
Private Brands Carried:
Joe Pucci & Sons
Types of Products Distributed:
Food Service, Frozen Food, Provisions/Meat, Seafood, Specialty Foods

57361 Joey's Fine Foods
135 Manchester Place
Newark, NJ 07104   973-482-1400
         Fax: 973-482-1597 sales@joeysfinefoods.com
                            www.joeysfinefoods.com
Mixes and baked goods
President: Aaron Aihini
Vice President Sales: Anthony Romano
Contact: Joe Aihini
Estimated Sales: $5.5 Million
Number Employees: 40
Square Footage: 168000
Type of Packaging: Consumer, Food Service, Private Label, Bulk
Private Brands Carried:
Joeys; New Englander; Cottage Bake
Number of Customer Locations: 500
Types of Products Distributed:
Food Service, Frozen Food, General Line, General Merchandise, Health Food, Baked goods, mixes & equipment

57362 John B. Wright Fish Company
427 Main St
Gloucester, MA 01930   978-283-4205
                       Fax: 978-281-5944
Seafood
President: Brian Wright
Contact: David Wright
david@johnbwright.com
Estimated Sales: $5-10 Million
Number Employees: 5-9

57363 John Bricks Inc
3900 W Side Ave
North Bergen, NJ 07047-6471   201-601-2201
                        Fax: 973-790-8755
Wholesaler/distributor of confectionery items
Owner: Reshma Shah
johnbricks@yahoo.com
Estimated Sales: $2.5-5 Million
Number Employees: 5-9
Types of Products Distributed:
General Line, Confectionery items

57364 John Cerasuolo Co
38 New England Produce Ctr
Chelsea, MA 02150-1719   617-884-3760
                        Fax: 617-884-8272
Wholesaler/distributor of produce
President: Dominic Cavallaro Jr
Estimated Sales: $1-2.5 Million
Number Employees: 10-19
Types of Products Distributed:
Produce

57365 John D Walsh Co
25 Executive Pkwy
Ringwood, NJ 07456-1429   973-962-1400
         Fax: 973-962-1557 info@johndwalsh.com
                            www.johndwalsh.com
Importer, exporter and wholesaler/distributor of essential oils and aroma chemicals
President: G Lermond
Vice President: L Serafini
Estimated Sales: $5-10 Million
Number Employees: 10-19
Square Footage: 97200
Types of Products Distributed:
General Line, Essential oils & aroma chemicals

57366 John Demartin Company
2080 Jerrold Ave
San Francisco, CA 94124-1605   415-826-7122
                        Fax: 415-826-7120

Wholesalers & Distributors / A-Z

Wholesaler/distributor of fresh fruits and vegetables
Owner: Arnet Lee
Estimated Sales: $3-5 Million
Number Employees: 6
Square Footage: 63360
Number of Customer Locations: 45
Types of Products Distributed:
Frozen Food, Produce

57367 (HQ)John E Koerner & Co Inc
4820 Jefferson Hwy
New Orleans, LA 70121-3127   504-734-1100
Fax: 504-734-0630   800-333-1913
www.koerner-co.com
Wholesaler/distributor of flour and bakery supplies; serving the food service market
President: Tim Koerner
tim.koerner@koerner-co.com
Estimated Sales: $10-20 Million
Number Employees: 20-49
Private Brands Carried:
Allstate; Big Chief; Indian Girl; Perfection
Types of Products Distributed:
Food Service, General Line, Flour & bakery supplies

57368 John Graves Food Service
913 Big Horn Dr
Jefferson City, MO 65109   573-893-3000
gravesfoods.com
Wholesaler/distributor of provisions/meats; serving the food service market.
Owner: Dick Graves
Owner: Tracy Graves
Director, Marketing: Gina Rackers
Transportation: Forrest Graves
Warehouse Production: Piper Graves
Estimated Sales: $27 Million
Number Employees: 50-99
Number of Products: 4000
Square Footage: 21000
Parent Co: John Graves Foodservice
Type of Packaging: Food Service
Types of Products Distributed:
Food Service, Frozen Food, General Line, Provisions/Meat, Seafood, Specialty Foods

57369 John Gross & Company
400 Cheryl Avenue
Mechanicsburg, PA 17055   717-766-2508
800-368-6800
customerservice@jgrossco.com www.jgrossco.com
Wholesaler/distributor of frozen food.
Manager: Brian Gross
Seafood Department Director: Doug Aliff
Chemical Techn Manager: Robert Zimmers
Year Founded: 1950
Estimated Sales: $50-100 Million
Number Employees: 20-49
Types of Products Distributed:
Frozen Food

57370 John Groves Company
3115 Washington Pike
Bridgeville, PA 15017-1434   412-257-1700
Fax: 412-257-5888
Wholesaler/distributor of ice cream products including cones, bases, toppings and coatings; serving the food service market in Pennsylvania, Ohio and West Virginia
President: Bill Virgi
Chairman/CEO: James Crawford
VP of Finance: Frank Kellander
Estimated Sales: $6 Million
Number Employees: 20-49
Square Footage: 300000
Parent Co: Bohrharst & Crowford Limited
Type of Packaging: Food Service
Types of Products Distributed:
Food Service, Frozen Food, Ice cream cones, bases, toppings, etc.

57371 John Hansen & Sons
327 Clay Street
Oakland, CA 94607-3529   510-444-0515
Fax: 510-444-0523
Wholesaler/distributor of coffee, tea and spices
President: Eric Hansen
Estimated Sales: $5-10 Million
Number Employees: 5-9
Types of Products Distributed:
Frozen Food, General Line, Coffee, tea & spices

57372 John J. Moon Produce
47 Produce Row
Saint Louis, MO 63102-1418   314-231-9943
Fax: 314-231-8720
Wholesaler/distributor of produce
President: John Minton
Number Employees: 20-49
Parent Co: J&M Produce
Types of Products Distributed:
Frozen Food, Produce

57373 John Lenore & Company
150 Willow Avenue
City of Industry, CA 91746-2038   619-232-6136
Fax: 619-232-1437
Wholesaler/distributor of soda and beer
Owner: John Lenore
Estimated Sales: $1-2.5 Million
Number Employees: 1-4
Parent Co: Logret Import & Export Company
Private Brands Carried:
Country Springs; Dad's Rootbeer; Big Red
Types of Products Distributed:
Frozen Food, General Line, Soda & beer

57374 John Molinelli Inc
5082 Landis Ave
Vineland, NJ 08360-9340   856-691-4777
Fax: 856-794-8307
Wholesaler/distributor of produce
Owner: John Molinelli
Estimated Sales: $5-10 Million
Number Employees: 10-19
Types of Products Distributed:
Frozen Food, Produce

57375 John Morrell Food Group
PO Box 405020
Cincinnati, OH 45240
800-722-1127
www.johnmorrell.com
Meat products including; ham and turkey, bacon, hot dogs, smoked sausage, lunchmeat, and special reserve hams.
President/CEO, Smithfield Foods: Kenneth Sullivan
Year Founded: 1827
Estimated Sales: Over $1 Billion
Number Employees: 5000-9999
Parent Co: Smithfield Foods
Type of Packaging: Consumer, Food Service, Private Label, Bulk
Types of Products Distributed:
Food Service, Provisions/Meat

57376 John Nagle & Co
306 Northern Ave
Boston, MA 02210   617-542-9418
Fax: 617-423-7830 info@johnnagle.com
www.johnnagle.com
Wholesaler/distributor of fresh and frozen seafood including swordfish and salmon; serving the food service market.
President: Charles Nagle
Chief Financial Officer: Michael Bates
VP, Operations: Robert Nagle
VP, Administration: Vincent Nagle
Year Founded: 1887
Estimated Sales: $50-100 Million
Number Employees: 50-99
Square Footage: 100000
Type of Packaging: Consumer, Food Service, Bulk
Types of Products Distributed:
Frozen Food, Seafood, Swordfish & salmon

57377 John Paton Inc
73 E State St
Doylestown, PA 18901-4359   215-348-7050
Fax: 215-348-8147
questions@goldenblossomhoney.com
www.goldenblossomhoney.com
Wholesaler/distributor of honey
President: Jon Paton
jp@goldenblossomhoney.com
VP: Marie Coreli
Estimated Sales: $1-2.5 Million
Number Employees: 1-4

57378 John S. Dull & Associates
4560 Loma Vista Avenue
Los Angeles, CA 90058-2602   323-581-7166
Fax: 323-583-4012
Wholesaler/distributor of replacement parts and smallwares; serving the food service market

President: James Whitorne
VP: Art Cuadra
Estimated Sales: $5-10 Million
Number Employees: 10-19
Types of Products Distributed:
Food Service, Frozen Food, General Merchandise, Replacement parts & smallwares

57379 John W Williams Inc
48 Little West 12th St
New York, NY 10014-1305   212-243-1293
Wholesaler/distributor of provisions and meats
President: Carmine Maucieri
Estimated Sales: $2.5-5 Million
Number Employees: 1-4
Types of Products Distributed:
Frozen Food, Provisions/Meat

57380 John W. Spaulding Brokerage
2035 W McDowell Rd
Phoenix, AZ 85009-3012   602-254-4777
Fax: 602-258-5623
Wholesaler/distributor of salt products including food grade, water softener, agricultural, etc.; serving the food service market
Owner: John W Spalding Iii
CEO: John Spaulding
Estimated Sales: $500,000-$1 Million
Number Employees: 7
Type of Packaging: Food Service, Private Label, Bulk
Private Brands Carried:
Cargill; Diamond Crystal; Leslie; United Western; MOAB
Types of Products Distributed:
Salt products

57381 John's Dairy
1775 Western Ave # 1
Albany, NY 12203-4672   518-456-7618
Fax: 518-861-0894
Wholesaler/distributor of dairy products, juices, drinks, sodas and soft serve ice cream mix
Owner: Michael John
VP: John Lysiak, Jr.
Purchasing: Steven Lysiak
Estimated Sales: $300,000-500,000
Number Employees: 1-4
Square Footage: 32000
Private Brands Carried:
John's Dairy Orange Juice; Wet Your Whistle; The Good Life
Number of Customer Locations: 500
Types of Products Distributed:
Frozen Food, General Line, Dairy, juices, drinks, soda, etc.

57382 John's Meat Market
225 N 18th St
Bismarck, ND 58501   701-223-7137
Fax: 701-255-4535
Wholesaler/distributor of smoked beef, pork and potato sausage, smoked ham, bacon and bratwurst; serving the food service and retail markets
Owner: Kenneth Selzler
Estimated Sales: $500,000-$1 Million
Number Employees: 1-4
Square Footage: 20000
Types of Products Distributed:
Food Service, Frozen Food, Provisions/Meat, Smoked beef, pork, etc.

57383 John's Wholesale
900-736 Granville Street
Vancouver, B 27863-9488   604-689-4190
Fax: 604-689-4139   888-564-6788
www.johnswholesale.ca
Wholesaler/distributor of industrial gloves and candy
Owner: John Cox
Types of Products Distributed:
Frozen Food, General Line, General Merchandise, Industrial gloves & candy

57384 Johnnie's Restaurant-Hotel Svc
2406 Molly Pitcher Hwy
Chambersburg, PA 17202-9291   717-263-1214
Fax: 717-263-5720   800-262-1214
www.johnniesinc.com
Wholesaler/distributor of general line products and food service equipment; serving the food service market
President: Rod Hocker
rhocker@johnniesinc.com

Wholesalers & Distributors / A-Z

Estimated Sales: $10-20 Million
Number Employees: 50-99
Private Brands Carried:
   Heinz; Pocahontas; Lucky Leaf
Types of Products Distributed:
   Food Service, Frozen Food, General Line, General Merchandise, Foodservice equipment

57385 Johnson Diversified Products
1408 Northland Dr
Suite 406
Mendota Heights, MN 55120-1013   651-688-0014
         Fax: 952-686-7670   800-676-8488
info@jdpinc.com   www.jdpinc.com
Wholesaler/distributor of food service equipment, and HACCP related instruments, tools and systems; serving the food service market
CEO: Thomas Johnson
Vice President: Paul Johnson
Estimated Sales: $5-10 Million
Number Employees: 5-9
Private Brands Carried:
   Randell; Hanna; Chicago Faucets
Types of Products Distributed:
   Food Service, General Merchandise, Foodservice equipment

57386 Johnson Restaurant Supply
4257 James St
East Syracuse, NY 13057-2174   315-463-5268
         Fax: 315-724-4790
Wholesaler/distributor of food service equipment
President: Judith Flihan
Manager: Jeff LA Count
Estimated Sales: $2.5-5 Million
Number Employees: 5-9
Types of Products Distributed:
   Food Service, Frozen Food, Food service equipment

57387 Johnson Sea Products Inc
                                 251-824-2693
Seafood
Manager: Sean Johnson
Estimated Sales: $100+ Million
Number Employees: 50-99

57388 Johnson Wholesale Meat Company
1735 Nicollet Ave
Minneapolis, MN 55403   612-874-1735
Wholesaler/distributor of beef, veal, lamb, pork and poultry; serving the food service market.
Estimated Sales: $2,994,000
Types of Products Distributed:
   Food Service, General Line, Provisions/Meat, Veal, lamb, pork, poultry & beef

57389 Johnston Equipment
#105-581 Chester Road
Annacis Island
Delta, BC V3M 6G7
Canada
                                 604-524-0361
         Fax: 604-524-8961   800-237-5159
couttsd@johnstonequipment.com
         www.johnstonequipment.com
Manufacturer, wholesaler/distributor and exporter of material handling equipment including electric forklifts and pallet racking/shelving systems
President & CEO: Michael Marcotte
Regional Sales Manager: John Binns
Sales Manager: Curt Snigol
Estimated Sales: $1-5 Million
Number Employees: 50-99
Square Footage: 66000
Types of Products Distributed:
   Frozen Food, General Merchandise, Material handling equipment

57390 Johnston Equipment
5990 Avebury Road
Mississauga, ON L5R 3R2
Canada   905-712-6000
         Fax: 905-712-6002   800-668-5586
         www.johnstonequipment.com
Wholesaler/distributor of material handling equipment
President/CEO: Micheal Marcotte
Number Employees: 50-99
Parent Co: Johnston Equipment/Raymond Rebuilt
Private Brands Carried:
   B.T.

Types of Products Distributed:
   Frozen Food, General Merchandise, Material handling equipment

57391 Johnston Farms
13031 Packing House Rd
Bakersfield, CA 93307   661-366-3201
         Fax: 661-366-6534   johnstongiftfruit@gmail.com
Navel oranges, peppers and potatoes
Owner: Dennis Johnston
Co-Prtnr.: Gerald Johnston
Commercial Sales Department: Derek Vaughn
dennisj@johnstonfarms.com
Packinghouse Operations: Steve Staker
Plant Manager: Steve Stacker
Number Employees: 100-249
Private Brands Carried:
   Bluejay; Top J; Victor
Types of Products Distributed:
   Frozen Food, Produce

57392 Joicey Food Services
2780 Coventry Road
Oakville, ON L6H 6R1
Canada   905-825-9665
         Fax: 905-825-0965
Distributor of food service equipment; serving the food service market
President: Jim Witt
CFO: Barbara Furlong
Marketing Director: Fred O'Hearn
National Sales Manager: John Garven
General Manager: Fred O'Hearn
Plant Manager: Glenn Running
Number Employees: 5-9
Square Footage: 60000
Type of Packaging: Food Service
Private Brands Carried:
   Tarrison Shelving; A.P.W.; Crystal Tips; Chef's Special; Waring; Cooktek; Innova
Types of Products Distributed:
   Food Service, Foodservice equipment

57393 Jolar Distributor
11110 Pepper Rd
Hunt Valley, MD 21031-1204   410-329-1892
         Fax: 410-329-1886   800-333-6761
Wholesaler/distributor of fresh and frozen pies; also, fresh cakes, doughnuts, pastries, mini desserts, breads and bagels; fund raising programs available
President: Jim Hopkin
Sales Manager: Jim Moreland
Estimated Sales: $3-5 Million
Number Employees: 5-9
Square Footage: 48000
Types of Products Distributed:
   Frozen Food, General Line, Cakes, pastries, pies, breads, etc.

57394 Jordahl Meats
25585 State Highway 13
Manchester, MN 56007-5020   507-826-3418
Meat products
Owner: Brian Jordahl
Estimated Sales: Less Than $500,000
Number Employees: 1-4
Type of Packaging: Consumer, Food Service, Private Label, Bulk

57395 Jordan Lobster Farms
1 Pettit Pl
Island Park, NY 11558-2218   516-889-3314
         Fax: 516-889-3617
nancy@jordanlobsterfarms.com
         www.jordanlobsterfarms.com
Wholesaler/distributor of fresh fish and lobster
Owner: Amanda Clemens
aclemens@msmc.edu
Estimated Sales: $2.5-5 Million
Number Employees: 20-49
Number of Customer Locations: 400
Types of Products Distributed:
   Frozen Food, Seafood, Lobster & fresh fish

57396 Joseph Antognoli & Co
1800 N Pulaski Rd
Chicago, IL 60639-4916   773-772-1800
         Fax: 773-772-0031
Importer and wholesaler/distributor of groceries, meat, giardiniera, eggplant salad, pepper spread for sandwiches and Italian food including pasta; serving the food service market

Owner: Joseph H Antognoli
info@josephantognoli.com
CEO: Vincent Candice
Estimated Sales: $3-5 Million
Number Employees: 10-19
Square Footage: 120000
Type of Packaging: Consumer, Food Service, Private Label
Private Brands Carried:
   Il Duomo; Pagliacci; Sole
Types of Products Distributed:
   Food Service, Frozen Food, General Line, Provisions/Meat, Italian food

57397 Joseph Apicella & Sons
307 1st Street
Hoboken, NJ 07030-2431   201-659-1665
         Fax: 201-659-8559
Wholesaler/distributor of fresh and frozen fish and seafood
Owner: Wilfredo Fernandez
Estimated Sales: $1-2.5 Million
Number Employees: 5-9
Types of Products Distributed:
   Frozen Food, Seafood, Fish

57398 Joseph J. Sayre & Son Company
1243 Tennessee Ave
Cincinnati, OH 45229   513-641-3661
         Fax: 513-641-4498   800-792-3661
Wholesaler/distributor of labels and packaging, signage, marking and barcoding systems
Sales Consultant: Chris Tucker
Estimated Sales: $500,000-$1 Million
Number Employees: 5-9
Square Footage: 54000
Parent Co: Boehm Stamp & Printing
Types of Products Distributed:
   Frozen Food, General Merchandise, Barcoding systems, labels, etc.

57399 Josheph Gies Import
625 Ridge Ave
Evanston, IL 60202-2632   773-472-4577
         Fax: 773-472-3903
Wines, liqueurs and spirits
Owner: Marianne Gies
Estimated Sales: $500,000-$1 Million
Number Employees: 1-4

57400 Jost Kauffman Import & Export Company
47 Capital Drive
Nepean, ON K2G 0E7
Canada   613-226-3887
         Fax: 613-226-3907
Wholesaler/distributor and exporter of fresh fish
President: Jost Kauffman
Number Employees: 5-9
Types of Products Distributed:
   Frozen Food, Seafood

57401 (HQ)Joyce Brothers Company
P.O.Box 888
Winston Salem, NC 27102   336-765-6927
         Fax: 336-765-0462
Wholesaler/distributor of groceries, frozen foods, equipment and fixtures, general merchandise, produce and private label items; serving the food service market
President: H Joyce
VP: H Joyce, Jr.
Estimated Sales: $10-20 Million
Number Employees: 50-99
Square Footage: 70000
Other Locations:
   Joyce Brothers Co.
   Winston-Salem, NCJoyce Brothers Co.
Number of Customer Locations: 1000
Types of Products Distributed:
   Food Service, Frozen Food, General Line, General Merchandise, Produce, Private label items

57402 Joyce Foods
4787 Kinnamon Rd
Winston Salem, NC 27103   336-766-9900
         Fax: 336-766-9009   www.joycefoods.com
Wholesaler/distributor of all types of poultry; serving the food service market. Manufacturer, processor and wholesaler of premium all natural poultry products, seafood products, and gourmet entrees, for retail grocery and foodservicemarket

1059

Wholesalers & Distributors / A-Z

President: Ron Joyce
VP Finance: Mark Parham
VP: Ron Covel
R&D: Chef Denis Dronne
Quality Control: Jerry Blizard
Public Relations: Lee Miskelly
Production: Derek Thomas
Plant Manager: Moises Flores
Purchasing Director: Jerry Blizard
Estimated Sales: $20-50 Million
Number Employees: 100-249
Square Footage: 36000
Type of Packaging: Consumer, Food Service, Private Label, Bulk
Private Brands Carried:
   Ashleys Farm, Tanglewood Farms, My Personal Chef, Chicken Gourmet
Number of Customer Locations: 500
Types of Products Distributed:
   Food Service, Frozen Food, Health Food, Provisions/Meat, Specialty Foods

57403 Joylin Food Equipment Corporation
51 Chestnut Ln
Woodbury, NY 11797-1918
Fax: 516-742-2123   800-456-9546
joylin1961@aol.com
Manufacturers' representative for food service equipment
President: Rich Kirsner
Marketing Director: Tom Pitts
Sales Director: M Kohn
Operations Manager: Tom DiRusso
Purchasing Manager: Yvette Western
Estimated Sales: $20-50 Million
Number Employees: 21
Number of Brands: 16
Square Footage: 12000
Private Brands Carried:
   Aman
Types of Products Distributed:
   Food Service

57404 Jp Tropical Foods
945 Close Ave
Bronx, NY 10473   718-589-6800
Fax: 718-617-6717 ihopp@evesales.com
www.jptropicalfoods.com
Wholesaler/distributor and importer of Caribbean and Mexican foods
Owner: Irving Nadler
Executive VP: Irving Nadler
VP Marketing: Stuart Gale
Sales Manager: Isadore Hoppenfeld
Estimated Sales: $5-10 Million
Number Employees: 10-19
Square Footage: 44000
Types of Products Distributed:
   Frozen Food, General Line, Specialty Foods, Caribbean & Mexican foods

57405 Judith's Fine Foods International
PO Box 13301
San Juan, PR 00908-3301   787-721-2331
Fax: 787-721-7168
Wholesaler/distributor serving airlines and cruise lines; ship handling services available
VP: John Lohner
Types of Products Distributed:
   Food Service, Frozen Food

57406 Juice Merchandising Corp
9237 Ward Pkwy # 104
Suite 104
Kansas City, MO 64114-3382   816-361-5343
Fax: 816-361-2033   800-950-1998
Plastic juice bottles as well as wholesaler/distributor of juice processing equipment
Owner: Bob Bushman
juice@micro.com
CEO: Helen Bushman
Manager, Operations: Bill Young
Estimated Sales: Below $5 Million
Number Employees: 1-4
Square Footage: 4000
Type of Packaging: Private Label
Private Brands Carried:
   Juice Tree Products

57407 Julian Bakery
624 Garrison St
Oceanside, CA 92054   760-721-5200
customerservice@julianbakery.com
julianbakery.com
Manufacturer of gluten-free, low-carb products
VP, Sales: Barry Octigan
Number of Products: 115

57408 Julius Silvert Company
P.O.Box 46526
231 E Luzerne Street
Philadelphia, PA 19124
Fax: 215-455-1600 www.juliussilvert.com
Wholesaler/distributor of frozen foods, butter, eggs and gourmet cheese
President: Stephen Sorkin
General Manager: Edward Sorkin
Sales Manager: Jim Sorkin
Estimated Sales: $10-20 Million
Number Employees: 20-49
Square Footage: 600000
Private Brands Carried:
   Silvert
Types of Products Distributed:
   Frozen Food, General Line, General Merchandise, Specialty Foods, Butter, eggs & gourmet cheese

57409 Junction City Distributing & Vending Company
217 N Franklin St
Junction City, KS 66441   785-762-2206
Fax: 785-762-5662
Wholesaler/distributor of general merchandise, general line items, produce, meats and seafood; serving the food service market
President: Gale Cynova
VP: Elainea Cynova
Estimated Sales: $2.5-5 Million
Number Employees: 10-19
Types of Products Distributed:
   Food Service, Frozen Food, General Line, General Merchandise, Provisions/Meat, Produce, Seafood

57410 Jungbunzlauer Inc
95 Wells Ave
Suite 150
Newton, MA 02459   617-969-0900
Fax: 617-964-2921 office-bos@jungbunzlauer.com
www.jungbunzlauer.com
Ingredients and additives
President: Michael Alexandrow
Chief Executive Officer: Tom Knutzen
Chief Financial Officer: Michael Klaproth
Vice President, Product Management: Achim Hergel
Estimated Sales: $3.3 Million
Number Employees: 20-49
Parent Co: Jungbunzlauer Suisse AG
Type of Packaging: Bulk
Types of Products Distributed:
   Frozen Food, General Line, Industrial ingredients

57411 K & F Select Fine Coffees
2801 SE 14th Ave
Portland, OR 97202-2203   503-234-7788
Fax: 503-231-9827   800-558-7788
Coffee products, torami syrups and sauces, taza rica cocoas, powdered drink mixes, and liquid fruit smoothie products.
Founder: Don Dominguez
ddominguez@kfcoffee.com
Director Sales/Marketing: Sandy Jumonville
Sales: Steve O Brien
Estimated Sales: $3228000
Number Employees: 10-19
Type of Packaging: Consumer, Food Service, Private Label, Bulk
Private Brands Carried:
   K&F; Torani; Tazo; Guittard; Taza Rica; Ghiradelli; McTaviah; Extreme Foods; SOBE; Cafe D'Amore
Number of Customer Locations: 400

57412 K & G Power Systems
150 Laser Ct
Hauppauge, NY 11788-3912   631-342-1171
Fax: 631-342-1172   800-223-4898
www.kgpowersystems.net
Wholesaler/distributor of air compressors, electric motors, pumps and drives
President: John Gandolfo
VP: Fred Gandolfo
General Manager: John Crispi
Estimated Sales: $20-50 Million
Number Employees: 50-99
Square Footage: 10000
Types of Products Distributed:
   Frozen Food, General Merchandise, Air compressors, electric motors, etc.

57413 K & L Intl
1929 S Campus Ave
Ontario, CA 91761-5410   909-923-9258
Fax: 909-923-9228   888-598-5588
info@knl-international.com
www.knl-international.com
Manufacturer, Importer and Exporter of chopsticks, toothpicks, guest checks, napkins, plastic T-Shirt bags, bamboo skewers, matches, sushi containers, wood sushi plates, wood sushi boats (bridge), swirl bowls, dried seaweed, eel(unagi), wasabi powder and soybean (edamame).
President: David Kao
VP: Susan Lin
Marketing Director: Richard Yeang
Manager: May Lin
Estimated Sales: $5-10 Million
Number Employees: 10-19
Number of Products: 20
Square Footage: 100000
Type of Packaging: Food Service, Private Label
Types of Products Distributed:
   Frozen Food, General Merchandise, Restaurant supplies

57414 K C's Best Wild Rice
1828 Ventura Dr SE
Bemidji, MN 56601-8920   218-751-9750
Fax: 218-751-9750   800-536-9539
www.kcsbestwildrice.com
Wholesaler/distributor of wild rice
Owner: Kent Bahr
Estimated Sales: $1-2.5 Million
Number Employees: 1-4
Types of Products Distributed:
   Frozen Food, General Line, Wild rice

57415 K Doving Co Inc
1171 Folsom St
San Francisco, CA 94103-3930   415-861-6694
Fax: 415-861-7485
Exporter and wholesaler/distributor of restaurant and butcher equipment
Owner: Jim Christensen
Manager: Katie O'Brien
kdoving@att.net
Estimated Sales: $.5-1 million
Number Employees: 5-9
Types of Products Distributed:
   Frozen Food, General Merchandise, Restaurant & butcher equipment

57416 K Heeps Inc
5239 Tilghman St
Allentown, PA 18104
800-322-9504
www.heeps.com
Wholesaler/distributor of provisions/meats.
President: Beau Heeps
Chairman: James Heeps
Vice President: Ted Heeps
Estimated Sales: $20-50 Million
Number Employees: 20-49
Types of Products Distributed:
   Frozen Food, Provisions/Meat

57417 K Horton Specialty Foods
28 Monument Sq
Portland, ME 04101-6447   207-228-2056
Fax: 207-228-2059
Specialty cheeses, olives, dried cured meats and meat pates, smoked seafood.
President: Kris Horton
Number Employees: 1-4

57418 K&C Food Sales
1375 E 6th St Ste 6
Los Angeles, CA 90021   213-689-9566
Fax: 213-689-9716
Wholesaler/distributor of fresh and frozen seafood and private label items; serving all markets
President: Donna Lemoi
Sales Director: Frank Almeida
Plant Manager: Willy Almeida

Wholesalers & Distributors / A-Z

Estimated Sales: $1-2.5 Million
Number Employees: 4
Square Footage: 14000
Private Brands Carried:
  Kings Choice; Royal Court

57419 K&H Equipment Company
2865 Us Highway 92 E
Lakeland, FL 33801   863-665-3144
             Fax: 863-667-0166
Wholesaler/distributor of restaurant equipment; serving the food service market
President: John Hardin
Sales Director: Dave Tebo
Estimated Sales: $500,000-$1 Million
Number Employees: 5-9
Private Brands Carried:
  Electro-Freeze; Smokaroma; Perfect Fry Company
Types of Products Distributed:
  Food Service, General Merchandise, Restaurant equipment

57420 K&K Meat Company
1361 Shallowbend Dr
Midlothian, TX 76065-6972
             Fax: 214-428-6696
Wholesaler/distributor of meats; serving the food service and retail markets
President: Jerry Manak
Estimated Sales: $10-20 Million
Number Employees: 5-9
Square Footage: 8000
Types of Products Distributed:
  Food Service, Frozen Food, Provisions/Meat

57421 K+S Windsor Salt Ltd.
755 boul St. Jean
Pointe Claire, QC H9R 5M9
Canada   514-630-0900
    Fax: 514-694-2451 www.windsorsalt.com
Salt including table, food processing, water conditioning and ice melting.
President/CEO: Wes Clark
Marketing Manager: Michel Prevost
Year Founded: 1893
Estimated Sales: $4.89 Million
Number Employees: 861
Parent Co: K+S
Type of Packaging: Consumer, Food Service, Bulk
Other Locations:
  Canadian Salt Company
  Pugwash, Nova ScotiCanadian Salt
  CompanyMines Seleine, Quebec

57422 K-Lift Material Handling Equipment Company
P.O.Box 455
Richland, MI 49083-0455   269-381-2030
             Fax: 616-381-1302
Wholesaler/distributor of material handling equipment including fork lifts
Owner: Donald Mathews Jr
Sales/Marketing Executive: Rich Kowalski
Estimated Sales: $5-10 Million
Number Employees: 10-19
Square Footage: 96000
Private Brands Carried:
  TCM
Types of Products Distributed:
  Fork Lift Trucks

57423 K-Mama Sauce
4301 Benjamin St NE
Minneapolis, MN 55421   612-460-5156
                           kmamasauce.com
Korean hot sauce
Founder: K.C. Kye

57424 K. Lefkofsky Company
14893 Livernois Avenue
Detroit, MI 48238-2011   313-863-2353
             Fax: 313-345-4720
Wholesaler/distributor of meats/provisions; serving the food service market
President: Danny Lefkofsky
Estimated Sales: $10-20 Million
Number Employees: 10-19
Types of Products Distributed:
  Food Service, Frozen Food, Provisions/Meat

57425 KAST Distributors Inc
541 Harding Hwy
Carneys Point, NJ 08069-3638   856-299-3553
         Fax: 856-299-6226   800-550-9735
         YVournavakis@kastdistributors.com
             www.kastdistributors.com
Wholesaler/distributor of frozen foods, seafood, canned foods, meats and paper products; serving the food service market
CEO: Gus Vournavakis
Sales Manager: Peter Hamilton
Operations Manager: Roland Carlson
Estimated Sales: $5-10 Million
Number Employees: 50-99
Square Footage: 92000
Number of Customer Locations: 300
Types of Products Distributed:
  Food Service, Frozen Food, General Line, General Merchandise, Provisions/Meat, Seafood, Canned foods, paper products, etc.

57426 KHL Engineered Packaging
1640 S Greenwood Ave
Montebello, CA 90640   323-721-5300
             Fax: 323-725-0312
Manufacturer and wholesaler/distributor of flexible packaging equipment and materials including shrink and stretch film, tape, poly and corrugated boxes, chipboard, skin film and poly bags
VP: Jed Wockensuss
General Sales Manager: Bill Browne
Contact: Peter Szymanski
peter.szymanski@khlengpkg.com
Estimated Sales: $5-10 Million
Number Employees: 1,000-4,999
Square Footage: 100000
Types of Products Distributed:
  Frozen Food, General Merchandise, Flexible packaging equipment

57427 KJ's Market
244 Kelley St
P.O. Box 1629
Lake City, SC 29560   843-394-2424
                            www.kjsmarket.com
Wholesaler/distributor of frozen foods, general merchandise, general line products, produce, provisions/meats, ice cream, seafood and specialty foods; serving the grocery and retail markets.
President: Colonel W Henry Johnson
Estimated Sales: $100-500 Million
Number Employees: 250-499
Square Footage: 300000
Types of Products Distributed:
  Frozen Food, General Line, General Merchandise, Provisions/Meat, Produce

57428 KMA Trading Company
10660 S Tryon St
Charlotte, NC 28273-6597   704-588-2727
             Fax: 704-588-2574
Wholesaler/distributor of fresh and frozen meat, frozen vegetables and entrees, dried vegetables, rice and groceries
President: Julie Christman
VP: Robert Christman
Estimated Sales: $1-2.5 Million
Number Employees: 1-4
Parent Co: J&B Sales
Types of Products Distributed:
  Frozen Food, General Line, Provisions/Meat, Groceries, rice, etc.

57429 KOHL Wholesale
130 Jersey St
Quincy, IL 62301-3831   217-222-5000
     Fax: 217-222-5522 www.kohlwholesale.com
Wholesaler/distributor of fresh and frozen meat, seafood, janitorial equipment, smallwares, frozen and canned fruits and vegetables, candy, etc.; serving the food service market
Pres.: R Ehrhart
V.P.: Mark Ehrhart
G.M.: Matt Ehrhart
Estimated Sales: $20-50 Million
Number Employees: 100-249
Square Footage: 125000
Types of Products Distributed:
  Food Service, Frozen Food, General Line, General Merchandise, Provisions/Meat, Produce, Seafood, Janitorial equipment, etc.

57430 KOOL Ice & Seafood Co
110 Washington St
Cambridge, MD 21613-2804   410-228-2300
         Fax: 410-228-1027   800-437-2417
         info@freshmarylandseafood.com
             www.freshmarylandseafood.com
Seafood
Owner: Dave Nickerson
Sales Exec: Tom Collins
tom@freshmarylandseafood.com
Estimated Sales: $5-10 Million
Number Employees: 20-49

57431 KP USA Trading
500 S Anderson Street
Los Angeles, CA 90033-4222   323-881-9871
             Fax: 323-268-3669
Soybean, corn, cottonseed, sesame and other vegetable oils; importer of oriental foods including jasmine, sweet rice, noodles, rice stick and candy
VP: Jerry Wong
Manager: Joe Beatly
Manager: Nancy Wong
Number Employees: 10-19
Square Footage: 100000
Type of Packaging: Consumer, Food Service, Private Label, Bulk
Types of Products Distributed:
  Food Service, Frozen Food, Oriental food

57432 KYD Inc
2949 Koapaka St
Honolulu, HI 96819-1923   808-836-3221
         Fax: 808-833-8995   800-767-4650
                            www.kydinc.com
Wholesaler/distributor of jams, condiments, baked goods, containers, frozen foods and private label gourmet gift foods; serving the food service market
CEO: Gilbert Yamada
gy@kyd-inc.com
CEO: Gilbert Yamada
Manager: Chris Johnson
Estimated Sales: $10-20 Million
Number Employees: 50-99
Square Footage: 90000
Parent Co: KYD
Private Brands Carried:
  Hawaiian Plantations; Old Hawaii Recipes; Hawaiian Passions; Tropics
Number of Customer Locations: 100
Types of Products Distributed:
  Food Service, Frozen Food, General Line, General Merchandise, Health Food, Specialty Foods, Jams, condiments, baked goods, etc.

57433 Kaco Supply Co
2968 Ask Kay Dr SE # C
Smyrna, GA 30082-2304   770-435-8902
         Fax: 770-435-2309   877-275-5226
         sales@kacosupplycompany.com
             www.kacosupplycompany.com
Wholesaler/distributor of institutional food products and paper, plastic and janitorial supplies; serving the food service market
President: Kay Williams
kaco@mindspring.com
Marketing Director: Earl Williams
Estimated Sales: $500,000-$1 Million
Number Employees: 1-4
Square Footage: 7200
Types of Products Distributed:
  Food Service, General Line, General Merchandise, Paper & plastic supplies, etc.

57434 Kadouri International Foods
234 Starr Street
Brooklyn, NY 11237   718-381-6100
             Fax: 718-381-8103
Wholesaler/distributor of dried fruits, nuts, ethnic foods, candy, grains, seeds, beans, peas and spices; serving the food service market
Owner: Ayal Kadouri
rivka.kadouri@gmail.com
VP: Ayal Kadouri
Sales Manager: Danny Kadouri
Estimated Sales: $5-8 Million
Number Employees: 20-49
Square Footage: 40000
Private Brands Carried:
  Melody
Types of Products Distributed:
  Food Service, General Line, Health Food, Produce, Specialty Foods, Dried fruits, nuts, grains, seeds, etc.

Wholesalers & Distributors / A-Z

57435 Kafko International LTD
3555 Howard St
Skokie, IL 60076-4052
847-763-0333
Fax: 847-763-0334 800-528-0334
sales@oileater.com www.kafkointl.com
Manufacturer and supplier of cleaning products
President: Ena Dora
edora@kafkointl.com
Number Employees: 100-249

57436 Kahoka Cheese Shop
166 S Washington St
Kahoka, MO 63445
660-727-3331
Fax: 660-727-3331 800-872-6529
Wholesaler/distributor of natural cheddar and colby cheeses
Owner: Virginia Webster
Estimated Sales: Less than $500,000
Number Employees: 1-4
Types of Products Distributed:
General Line, Natural cheddar & colby cheese

57437 Kaleel Bros Inc
761 Bev Rd
Youngstown, OH 44512
330-758-0861
800-929-3663
info@kaleelbrothers.com www.kaleelbrothers.com
Wholesaler/distributor of frozen foods, grocery products, produce, provisions/meats, seafood and specialty food items; serving the food service market; also, custom distribution programs available for restaurants.
President: Ron Kaleel
rkaleel@kaleelbrothers.com
Vice President: Dennis Kaleel
Secretary/Treasurer: Tom Kaleel
Vice President: Terry Kaleel
Information Technology Manager/Marketing: Jan Paxson
Operations Manager: Jeff Worstell
Estimated Sales: $50-100 Million
Number Employees: 100-249
Square Footage: 150000
Private Brands Carried:
Golbon
Number of Customer Locations: 1000
Types of Products Distributed:
Food Service, Frozen Food, General Line, Produce, Seafood

57438 Kalil Produce Company
3138 Produce Row
Houston, TX 77023-5814
713-923-2721
Fax: 713-923-3168
Wholesaler/distributor of produce including tropical fruit; serving the food service market
Owner: J Kalil
Estimated Sales: $1-2.5 Million
Number Employees: 1-4
Square Footage: 8800
Number of Customer Locations: 50
Types of Products Distributed:
Food Service, Frozen Food, Produce, Tropical fruit

57439 Kallsnick Inc
423 Lawrence St
Batesville, AR 72501-7197
870-793-3924
Fax: 870-793-2090
Wholesaler/distributor of frozen foods, canned goods, produce, chemicals, dairy products, groceries and paper and plastic goods
President: Scott Kallsnick
CEO: Scott Kalsnick
Sales Representative: Mario Merino
Estimated Sales: $20-50 Million
Number Employees: 20-49
Types of Products Distributed:
Frozen Food, General Line, General Merchandise, Produce

57440 Kalot Superfood
Denver, CO
561-757-6541
www.kalotsuperfood.com
Fruit & nut butters
Founder: Jessica Goldstein

57441 Kane's Kandies
2317 Federal Street
21
Camden, NJ 08105-1929
856-963-7911
Wholesaler/distributor of confectionery products
President: Robert Kana
Estimated Sales: $2.5-5 Million
Number Employees: 5-9
Type of Packaging: Bulk
Types of Products Distributed:
Frozen Food, General Line, Specialty Foods, Confectionery

57442 Kanematsu
75 Rockefeller Plaza 22nd FL
New York, NY 10019
212-704-9400
Fax: 213-620-1050
Importer, exporter and wholesaler/distributor of ingredients including potassium sorbate, sorbic acid, riboflavin and whey protein isolate
Manager: James Scott Levy
Number Employees: 20-49
Parent Co: Kanematsu USA
Type of Packaging: Bulk
Types of Products Distributed:
Frozen Food, General Line, Ingredients

57443 Kansas City Sausage
8001 NW 106th St
Kansas City, MO 64153
816-891-9600
www.kcsausageco.com
Wholesaler/distributor of meats; packaging services available.
VP, Sales & Marketing: Paul Forde
Chief Operating Officer: Brady Stewart
Estimated Sales: $50-100 Million
Number Employees: 100-249
Square Footage: 49500
Parent Co: Smithfield Foods
Type of Packaging: Private Label
Types of Products Distributed:
Frozen Food, General Line, General Merchandise, Provisions/Meat

57444 Kansas Marine
5511 NW 163rd St
Hialeah, FL 33014
305-628-5555
Fax: 305-628-5540 marineship@aol.com
Wholesaler/distributor of meats and alcoholic beverages; serving the food service market; also, ship chandler services for cruise ships available
VP: Jim Scott
Manager: Peter Alvino
Estimated Sales: $2.5-5 Million
Number Employees: 1-4
Parent Co: American Fish
Types of Products Distributed:
Food Service, Frozen Food, General Line, Provisions/Meat, Alcoholic beverages

57445 Kappus Co
4755 W 150th St # A
Cleveland, OH 44135-3330
216-367-6677
Fax: 216-367-6699 800-441-8089
www.kappuscompany.com
Wholesaler/distributor of soft serve, shake, slush and cooking equipment and parts; servicing available
President: John Kappus
CEO: Fred Kappus
fredk@kappuscompany.com
Estimated Sales: $5-10 Million
Number Employees: 50-99
Square Footage: 160000
Private Brands Carried:
Taylor
Types of Products Distributed:
Frozen Food, General Merchandise, Equipment, parts & servicing

57446 Kar Wah Trading Company
55 Bellechasse
Montreal, QC H2S 1W2
Canada
514-272-5528
Fax: 514-272-1813
Wholesaler/distributor of groceries and Chinese and Canadian foods; serving restaurants, institutions and hotels
President: Thomas Hum
VP: Allan Hum
Number Employees: 10-19
Square Footage: 60000
Private Brands Carried:
K.W.
Types of Products Distributed:
Frozen Food, General Line, Specialty Foods, Groceries and Chinese & Canadian foods

57447 Karabetian Import & Export
2450 Crystal St
Los Angeles, CA 90039-2813
323-664-8956
Fax: 323-664-8958 karabetian@aol.com
www.karabetian.com
Lebanese foods
Owner: Nabil Karabetian
nabil@karabetian.com
Number Employees: 10-19

57448 Karetas Foods Inc
1012 Tuckerton Ct
Reading, PA 19605-1177
610-926-3663
Fax: 610-926-1002 www.karetasfoods.com
Wholesaler/distributor of frozen foods, fresh fish, produce and canned and dry goods; serving the food service market
President: John Friedmann
johnfriedmann@aol.com
VP: Carl Friedmann
Operations Manager: Brian Bieber
Purchasing Manager: Victoria Friedmann
Estimated Sales: $20-50 Million
Number Employees: 50-99
Square Footage: 42000
Parent Co: Karetas Foods
Private Brands Carried:
Golbon
Types of Products Distributed:
Food Service, Frozen Food, General Line, Provisions/Meat, Produce, Seafood, Specialty Foods, Canned & dry goods, fresh fish, etc.

57449 Karp's Bake Mark
540 S 1st Street
Milwaukee, WI 53204-1605
414-271-7790
Wholesaler/distributor of groceries, baking supplies and equipment
General Manager: Chuck Grote
Estimated Sales: $10-20 Million
Number Employees: 20-49
Parent Co: L. Karp & Son
Number of Customer Locations: 1200
Types of Products Distributed:
Frozen Food, General Line, General Merchandise, Equipment & supplies

57450 Karson Food Services
2109a Heck Avenue
Neptune, NJ 07753-4430
732-922-1900
Fax: 732-869-1472 www.karsonfoods.com
Wholesaler/distributor of general line products including frozen and hot prepared meals; serving the food service market
President: Robert Kardane
Estimated Sales: $5-10 Million
Number Employees: 5-9
Types of Products Distributed:
Food Service, Frozen Food, General Line, Prepared meals: frozen & hot

57451 Kason
8889 Whitney Dr
Lewis Center, OH 43035-7106
740-549-2100
Fax: 740-549-0701 Central@kasonind.com
www.kasonind.com
Food bins, bumper systems for walls and strip doors; wholesaler/distributor of commercial refrigeration hardware and bulk food merchandisers
Manager: Rich Kaiser
central@kasonind.com
Estimated Sales: $1-5 Million
Number Employees: 5-9
Types of Products Distributed:
Frozen Food, General Merchandise, Commercial refrigeration hardware, etc.

57452 Kason Central
7099 Huntley Road
Columbus, OH 43229-1073
614-885-1992
Fax: 614-888-1771
Manufacturer, exporter and wholesaler/distributor of refrigerator latches and hinges, strip curtains, hood lights, grease filters, gaskets, stainless steel food service hardware, thermometers for ovens and refrigerators and plumbing fixtures
Manager: David Katz
Sales Representative: Rich Kaiser
Office Manager: Greg Murray
General Manager: David Katz
Estimated Sales: $1-2.5 Million
Number Employees: 5-9
Square Footage: 8000
Parent Co: Kason Industries

Type of Packaging: Consumer, Food Service, Private Label
Number of Customer Locations: 7
Types of Products Distributed:
Frozen Food, General Merchandise, Equipment parts

57453 Katy's Wholesale Distributing
2700 7th St
Moline, IL 61265-5148   309-764-8662
Wholesaler/distributor of provisions/meats and frozen and specialty foods; serving the food service market
Owner: A Bodenbender
Estimated Sales: $300,000-500,000
Number Employees: 1-4
Private Brands Carried:
Carl Buddig; Sparrer Sausage; Bird Farm Sausage; Renfro Sauces
Types of Products Distributed:
Food Service, Frozen Food, Provisions/Meat, Specialty Foods

57454 Katzin's Uniforms
65 Market St
Newark, NJ 07102   973-623-3457
Fax: 973-623-3522   800-201-0500
Wholesaler/distributor of general merchandise including uniforms, industrial gloves and safety and work shoes
Owner: Bruce Collevechio
CFO: Jeff Grandinetti
Marketing Director: Jeff Grandenetti
Estimated Sales: $2.5-5 Million
Number Employees: 20-49
Types of Products Distributed:
Frozen Food, General Line, Uniforms, work gloves & safety shoes

57455 Kauai Producers
4334 Rice St
Suite 101
Lihue, HI 96766   808-245-4044
Fax: 808-245-9061   800-262-1400
kauai@hvcb.org   www.gohawaii.com
Wholesaler/distributor of produce and dairy, frozen, dry and refrigerated products
President: Scott Nonaka
Vice President: Pearl Nonaka
Marketing Manager: Merle Nonaka
Estimated Sales: $4.5 Million
Number Employees: 23
Types of Products Distributed:
Food Service, Frozen Food, General Line, Produce, Dairy products

57456 Kay's Foods
705 N 7th Ave
Phoenix, AZ 85007   602-252-8911
Fax: 602-252-6515
Wholesaler/distributor and broker of specialty foods including meat, fish, cheese and confectionery products
Owner: Bill Kay
Estimated Sales: $5-10 Million
Number Employees: 10-19
Types of Products Distributed:
Frozen Food, Specialty Foods

57457 Kayem Foods
75 Arlington St.
Chelsea, MA 02150   617-889-1600
800-426-6100
www.kayem.com
Deli products and meats, gourmet chicken, sausage and buns.
President/Chief Executive Officer: Matt Monkiewicz

Year Founded: 1909
Estimated Sales: $129 Million
Number Employees: 500-999
Number of Brands: 8
Square Footage: 160000
Type of Packaging: Consumer, Food Service, Private Label, Bulk
Other Locations:
Genoa Sausage Company
Woburn, MA Genoa Sausage Company
Types of Products Distributed:
Food Service, General Line, General Merchandise, Provisions/Meat, Deli products, packaging & spice

57458 (HQ)KeHE Distributors
1245 E Diehl Rd
Suite 200
Naperville, IL 60563   630-343-0000
800-995-5343
contactus@kehe.com   www.kehe.com
Specialty, fresh, natural & organic foods
President/CEO: Brandon Barnholt
COO: Gene Carter
CFO: Timothy Wiggins
CIO: Brian Wilkinson
Executive Director of Marketing: Ari Goldsmith
EVP Independent Sales & Marketing: Brad Helmer
SVP People Operations: Jennifer Ricks
EVP Warehouse Operations: Larry Hartley
Year Founded: 1953
Estimated Sales: $10-20 Million
Number Employees: 5500
Type of Packaging: Private Label
Private Brands Carried:
Cadia, Made-With, Sage Valley, Harmony Farms, Bonavita
Number of Customer Locations: 30000
Types of Products Distributed:
General Line, General Merchandise, Health Food, Specialty Foods

57459 KeHE Distributors
900 N Schmidt Rd
Romeoville, IL 60446-4056
Specialty, fresh, natural & organic foods
Type of Packaging: Private Label
Types of Products Distributed:
General Line, Specialty Foods

57460 KeHE Distributors
19488 Telegraph Trail
Surrey, BC V4N 4H1
Canada
Specialty, fresh, natural & organic foods
Type of Packaging: Private Label
Types of Products Distributed:
General Line, Specialty Foods

57461 KeHE Distributors
9555 NE Alderwood Rd
Portland, OR 97220
Specialty, fresh, natural & organic foods
Type of Packaging: Private Label
Types of Products Distributed:
General Line, Specialty Foods

57462 KeHE Distributors
4650 Newcastle Rd
Stockton, CA 95215
Specialty, fresh, natural & organic foods
Type of Packaging: Private Label
Types of Products Distributed:
General Line, Specialty Foods

57463 KeHE Distributors
16081 Fern Ave
Chino, CA 91708
Specialty, fresh, natural & organic foods
Type of Packaging: Private Label
Types of Products Distributed:
General Line, Specialty Foods

57464 KeHE Distributors
2600-61 Ave SE
Calgary, AB T2C 4V2
Canada
Specialty, fresh, natural & organic foods
Type of Packaging: Private Label
Types of Products Distributed:
General Line, Specialty Foods

57465 KeHE Distributors
2200 N Himalaya Rd
Aurora, CO 80011
Specialty, fresh, natural & organic foods
Type of Packaging: Private Label
Types of Products Distributed:
General Line, Specialty Foods

57466 KeHE Distributors
101 Enterprise Dr
Flower Mound, TX 75028
Specialty, fresh, natural & organic foods
Type of Packaging: Private Label
Types of Products Distributed:
General Line, Specialty Foods

57467 KeHE Distributors
4024 Rock Quarry Rd
Dallas, TX 75211
Specialty, fresh, natural & organic foods
Type of Packaging: Private Label
Types of Products Distributed:
General Line, Specialty Foods

57468 KeHE Distributors
225 Daniels Way
Bloomington, IN 47404
Specialty, fresh, natural & organic foods
Type of Packaging: Private Label
Types of Products Distributed:
General Line, Specialty Foods

57469 KeHE Distributors
1851 Riverside Pkwy
Douglasville, GA 30135
Specialty, fresh, natural & organic foods
Type of Packaging: Private Label
Types of Products Distributed:
General Line, Specialty Foods

57470 KeHE Distributors
6185 McLaughlin Rd
Mississauga, ON L5R 3W7
Canada
Specialty, fresh, natural & organic foods
Type of Packaging: Private Label
Types of Products Distributed:
General Line, Specialty Foods

57471 KeHE Distributors
4055 Deerpark Blvd
P.O. Box 410
Elkton, FL 32033
Specialty, fresh, natural & organic foods
Type of Packaging: Private Label
Types of Products Distributed:
General Line, Specialty Foods

57472 KeHE Distributors
3225 Meridian Pkwy
Fort Lauderdale, FL 33331
Specialty, fresh, natural & organic foods
Type of Packaging: Private Label
Types of Products Distributed:
General Line, Specialty Foods

57473 KeHE Distributors
860 Nestle Way
Suite 250
Breinigsville, PA 18013
Specialty, fresh, natural & organic foods
Type of Packaging: Private Label
Types of Products Distributed:
General Line, Specialty Foods

57474 Keith Industries
248 Astor Street
Newark, NJ 07114   973-642-3332
Fax: 973-733-9453   sales@keithindustries.com
Wholesaler/distributor of pails, totes, cans and drums
President: Jay Weiss
VP: Caryl Weiss
Sales: Lee Ross
Contact: Sally Towsley
carylee@keithindustries.com
Estimated Sales: $1-2.5 Million
Number Employees: 5-9
Square Footage: 40000
Types of Products Distributed:
Frozen Food, General Merchandise, Pails, cans, totes, drums, etc.

57475 Kelley Bean Co Inc
2407 Circle Dr
Scottsbluff, NE 69361   308-635-6438
Fax: 308-635-7345   info@kelleybean.com
www.kelleybean.com
Dried beans.
President: Kevin Kelley
kkelley@kelleybean.com
Chairman: Robert Kelley, Jr.
EVP & Chief Financial Officer: G. Lee Glenn
Director, Finance: Jim Loveridge
Business Development: Bryce Kelley
Controller: Judy Osborn
Human Resources Manager: Kim Ferguson
Operations/Seed Director: Chris Kelley
Year Founded: 1927
Estimated Sales: $36.1 Million

Number Employees: 20-49
Square Footage: 190000
Types of Products Distributed:
  Frozen Food, General Line, Dried beans

57476 (HQ)Kelley Foods
1697 Lower Curtis Rd
PO Box 708
Elba, AL 36323-8847 334-897-5761
  Fax: 334-897-2712 eddiek@kelleyfoods.com
  www.kelleyfoods.com
Various meats
President: Erik Ennis
eennis@drinkarizona.com
CEO: Eddie Kelley
Controller: Alex Mount
Vice President: J Kelley
VP Marketing: C Kelley
VP Operations: Dwight Kelley
Plant Manager: Max Glisson
Estimated Sales: $10-20 Million
Number Employees: 100-249
Type of Packaging: Food Service
Number of Customer Locations: 1200
Types of Products Distributed:
  Food Service, General Line, General Merchandise, Provisions/Meat, Seafood, Dairy items, paper products, etc.

57477 Kelley-Clarke
PO Box 79019
Seattle, WA 98119-7919 206-622-2581
  Fax: 206-682-0424
Export broker and wholesaler/distributor of frozen salmon, Dungeness crab meat and tiny Pacific shrimp
Manager: Todd Raasch
Estimated Sales: $5-10 Million
Number Employees: 10-19
Parent Co: Kelley-Clarke
Private Brands Carried:
  Black Top; Honey Boy; Pacific Maid; Sea Life
Types of Products Distributed:
  Frozen Food, Seafood

57478 Kellogg Elevator Company
PO Box 628
Carson City, MI 48811 989-584-6543
  Fax: 517-584-3214
Wholesaler/distributor of corn, soybeans and wheat
Co-Owner: Dennis Kellogg
Co-Owner: Harold Kellogg
Estimated Sales: Less than $500,000
Number Employees: 1-4
Square Footage: 3000000
Types of Products Distributed:
  Frozen Food, General Line, Produce, Corn, soybeans & wheat

57479 Kelly's Foods
650 Carter Rd
Winter Garden, FL 34787 407-654-0500
  800-749-2171
  info@kellyfoods.com www.kellysfoods.com
Wholesaler/distributor of poultry, meats and frozen foods.
Owner & CEO: Kenneth Kelly
President: Richard Robertson
VP, Finance: Pat Kenney
p_kenney@kellysfoods.com
VP, Administration: Chris Sharp
VP, Sales: Dale Kelly
VP, Operations: Kenny Kelly, Jr.
Year Founded: 1981
Estimated Sales: $80 Million
Number Employees: 250
Square Footage: 45000
Types of Products Distributed:
  Food Service, Frozen Food, Provisions/Meat, Produce, Poultry

57480 Kemach Food Products
9920 Farragut Rd
Brooklyn, NY 11236-2302 718-272-5655
  Fax: 718-272-6226 info@kemach.com
  www.kemach.net
Drink mixes; soup mixes; crackers; flour; cereals; pasta; baked goods; candy, chocolates, health food, chocolate syrup, juices, pasta sauces, ices, cones, etc.
President: Samuel Salzman
CFO: Aaron Daum
VP: Nik Salzman

Estimated Sales: $2.5-5 Million
Number Employees: 10-19
Square Footage: 15000
Type of Packaging: Consumer, Food Service, Private Label, Bulk
Private Brands Carried:
  Kemach, Mekach, Ta'aman
Number of Customer Locations: 1
Types of Products Distributed:
  Health Food, Specialty Foods, Kosher

57481 Kemps LLC
1270 Energy Ln
St Paul, MN 55108
  www.kemps.com
Frozen yogurt, ice cream, sherbert, milk, juices, cottage cheese, sour cream and dips, and yogurt.
President & CEO: Greg Kurr
CFO: Daniel Jones
SVP, Growth & Innovation: Rachel Kyllo
VP, Operations: Bob Williams
General Manager: Brad Cuthbert
Year Founded: 1914
Estimated Sales: $116.7 Million
Number Employees: 1,125
Square Footage: 40000
Parent Co: Dairy Farmers of America

57482 Ken Ottoboni Mushrooms
21711 NE 10th Ave
Ridgefield, WA 98642 360-887-0902
  Fax: 360-887-0903
Wholesaler/distributor of produce including wild mushrooms and berries
Owner: Steven Hollingsworth
Treas.: Jane Hollingsworth
Secy.: Steve Hollingsworth
Number Employees: 1-4
Square Footage: 6000
Types of Products Distributed:
  Frozen Food, Produce, Wild mushrooms & berries

57483 Ken Young Food Distributors
12842 Western Ave
Blue Island, IL 60406-3861 708-385-4703
  Fax: 708-385-5513
Wholesaler/distributor of deli and specialty foods, spices, sauces and condiments, general merchandise and baked goods; rack jobber services available
President: K Young
CEO: B Young
Manager: Therese Young
kenyoungfooddist@att.net
Estimated Sales: $10-20 Million
Number Employees: 10-19
Number of Products: 1000
Square Footage: 7000
Private Brands Carried:
  Reunion Greens Seasonings
Number of Customer Locations: 450
Types of Products Distributed:
  Specialty Foods

57484 Kendon Candies Inc
460 Perrymont Avenue
San Jose, CA 95125 408-297-6133
  Fax: 408-297-4008 800-332-2639
Lollipops
President: Kate Glass
Contact: Holly Anderson
h.anderson@kendoncandies.com

57485 Kenko International
6984 Bandini Blvd
Los Angeles, CA 90040 323-721-8300
  Fax: 323-721-9600 ronu@kenko-intl.com
  www.kenkoco.com
Sweeteners, food acidulants, antioxidants, preservatives and other food chemicals.
President: Satomi Tsuchibi
Contact: Juliet Cunningham
jcunningham@alere.com
Estimated Sales: $2.7 Million
Number Employees: 15

57486 Kenny Seafood
400 Pontchartrain Dr
Slidell, LA 70458 985-643-2717
  Fax: 985-643-5449 www.kennyseafood.com
Wholesaler/distributor of seafood and value-added seafood products
Co-Ownr.: Brian Cappy

Estimated Sales: $500,000-$1 Million
Number Employees: 5-9
Types of Products Distributed:
  Frozen Food, Seafood, Value-added seafood products

57487 Kenrich Foods Corp
915 Industrial Dr
West Salem, WI 54669-1652 608-786-2310
  Fax: 608-785-7790 800-227-7348
Wholesaler/distributor of sausage
Owner: Carl Colsch
dan1@kenrichfoods.com
Estimated Sales: $10-20 Million
Number Employees: 10-19
Types of Products Distributed:
  Frozen Food, Provisions/Meat, Sausage

57488 Kenshin Trading Corp
22353 S Western Ave # 201
Torrance, CA 90501-4156 310-212-3199
  Fax: 310-212-3299 800-766-1313
  sales@kenshin.com www.kenshin.com
Wholesaler/distributor and importer of Asian health related products; serving food processors, health food stores, etc
Owner: Kunio Suziki
kunio@kenshin.com
Estimated Sales: $500,000-$1 Million
Number Employees: 5-9
Square Footage: 7200
Type of Packaging: Consumer
Types of Products Distributed:
  Health Food, Herbal Supplements

57489 Kenssenich's
131 S Fair Oaks Ave
Madison, WI 53704 608-249-5391
  Fax: 608-249-1628 800-248-0555
  aaugustine@kessenichs.com www.kessenichs.com
Dealer/distributor of food service equipment/supplies
Pres.: Robert Kessenich
Dir. Sls./Mktg.: Chet Gabris
Natl. Sls. Mgr.: Sheila Bookhout
CEO: Cheri Martin
Estimated Sales: $10 Million +
Number Employees: 20-49
Number of Brands: 500
Number of Products: 5000
Square Footage: 100000
Type of Packaging: Food Service
Types of Products Distributed:
  Food Service, Frozen Food, General Merchandise, Foodservice equipment & supplies

57490 Kent's Wharf
31 Steamboat Hl
Swans Island, ME 4685 207-526-4186
  Fax: 207-526-4291
Seafood
Owner: David Niquette
kentswharf@aol.com
Estimated Sales: $300,000-500,000
Number Employees: 1-4

57491 Kentucky Beer Cheese
224 Industry Pkwy
Suite A
Nicholasville, KY 40356-8015 859-887-1645
  Fax: 859-277-6075 info@kentuckybeercheese.com
  www.kentuckybeercheese.com
Processor and wholesaler/distributor of cheese spread and dip including hot, garlic and beer flavored.
Owner, President: Diane Evans
VP, Owner: Chris Evans
Estimated Sales: Less Than $500,000
Number Employees: 1-4
Square Footage: 4000
Parent Co: Evans Gourmet Foods, LLC
Type of Packaging: Consumer, Food Service
Types of Products Distributed:
  Food Service, General Line, Cheese: hot, beer & garlic flavored

57492 Kerekes Bakery & RstrntEquip
6103 15th Ave
Brooklyn, NY 11219-5402 718-232-7044
  Fax: 718-232-4416 800-525-5556
  sales@bakedeco.com
Kerekes is a distributor of quality tools, supplies, and equipment for every food service establishment.

Owner: Tovia Fleischman
pearl@bakedeco.com
CEO: Carlos Rodriguez
CFO: Pearl Fleischman
Estimated Sales: $1-3 Million
Number Employees: 5-9
Square Footage: 80000
Types of Products Distributed:
  Food Service, General Line

57493 Kern Meat Distributing
2711 Wagel Rd
Brooksville, KY 41004   606-756-2255
  Fax: 606-756-2114 webberfarms.com
Meat
President: Ed Kern
Estimated Sales: $10-20 Million
Number Employees: 20-49

57494 Kesten & Associates Restaurant Equipment Sales & Service
1061 Meldon Ave
Donora, PA 15033-1113   724-379-7731
  Fax: 724-379-7732
Wholesaler/distributor of new and used restaurant and cooking equipment including mixers, slicers, dishwashers, custom cooking exhaust hoods and stainless steel fabrication
Owner: R Kesten
Estimated Sales: Under $300,000
Number Employees: 1-4
Square Footage: 60000
Type of Packaging: Food Service

57495 Key Business Systems
250 West Beaver Creek Rd.
Unit 16
Richmond Hill, ON L4B 1C7
Canada
  905-764-0346
  Fax: 905-764-9325 info@keypos.ca
  www.keypos.ca
Wholesaler/distributor of general merchandise including cash registers
Pres.: Harrack Singh
Number Employees: 10-19
Private Brands Carried:
  Sanyo; Uniwell; Sharpe
Types of Products Distributed:
  Frozen Food, General Merchandise, Cash registers

57496 Key Food Stores Cooperative
8925 Avenue D
Brooklyn, NY 11236-1618   718-370-4200
  Fax: 718-251-1851 www.keyfood.com
Wholesaler/distributor of groceries
CEO: Richard Pallitto
Treas.: Sam Kristal
Contllr.: Ron Pillips
Number Employees: 100-249
Private Brands Carried:
  Key Food
Types of Products Distributed:
  Frozen Food, General Line, Groceries

57497 Key Industrial
997 Enterprise Way
Napa, CA 94558-6209   707-252-1205
  Fax: 707-252-9054 800-852-5270
Wholesaler/distributor of dairy, food, wine and beverage processing equipment including stainless steel fittings, pumps, instruments and specialties
Owner: John Boyanich
Outside Sales: John Staats
jboyanich@keyindustrial.com
Estimated Sales: $3-5 Million
Number Employees: 10-19
Square Footage: 100000
Private Brands Carried:
  Tri-Clover; Anderson Instrument; Strahman Valves
Types of Products Distributed:
  Frozen Food, General Merchandise, Processing supplies: food, wine, etc.

57498 Key West Key Lime Pie Co
225 Key Deer Blvd
Big Pine Key, FL 33043   305-872-7400
  Fax: 305-872-7600 877-882-7437
  keywestkeylimepieco.com
Key lime products
President: James Brush
Vice President: Alison Sloat
Estimated Sales: $400,000
Number Employees: 5-9
Number of Brands: 4
Number of Products: 100+
Square Footage: 2400
Type of Packaging: Consumer, Food Service, Private Label

57499 Keyco Distributors Inc
625 New Commerce Blvd
Hanover Twp, PA 18706-1433   570-825-9445
  Fax: 570-825-9891
Wholesaler/distributor serving the food service market
Owner: Frank Kowalski
fkowalski@keycodistributors.com
Estimated Sales: $20-50 Million
Number Employees: 50-99
Types of Products Distributed:
  Food Service, Frozen Food

57500 Keys Fisheries Market & Marina
3502 Gulfview Ave
Marathon, FL 33050-2362   305-743-4353
  Fax: 305-743-3562 866-743-4353
  keys.fisheries@comcast.net
  www.keysfisheries.com
Processor and wholesaler of seafood products.
Owner: Gary Graves
keysfisheries@comcast.net
Vice President: Gary Graves
Estimated Sales: $1-2.5 Million
Number Employees: 20-49
Type of Packaging: Consumer, Food Service
Types of Products Distributed:
  Frozen Food, Seafood

57501 Keystone Cleaning Systems
PO Box 906
798 West 2nd Street
Lansdale, PA 19446   215-362-1133
  Fax: 215-368-5084 www.keyclean.net
Wholesaler/distributor of janitorial equipment and supplies including high pressure washers, steam cleaners, chemicals, portable floor scrubbers, vacuums, carpet extractors, etc.; also, powerwash services for sidewalks and storefrontsavailable
Owner: Peter Marzolf
Svce. Mgr.: Scott Bardsley
Office Mgr.: Tracey Clegg
Estimated Sales: $5-10 Million
Number Employees: 10-19
Square Footage: 20000
Private Brands Carried:
  L&A; Robby; Numatic; Pacific Steamex
Types of Products Distributed:
  Frozen Food, General Merchandise, High pressure washers, chemicals, etc.

57502 Keystone Restaurant Supply
491 W San Carlos St
San Jose, CA 95110-2632   408-288-4000
  Fax: 408-286-2332 800-899-2223
Wholesaler/distributor of restaurant equipment and supplies; serving the food service market
Owner: Henry Down Jr
Estimated Sales: $500,000-$1 Million
Number Employees: 10-19
Parent Co: International Commissary Corporation
Types of Products Distributed:
  Food Service, Frozen Food, General Merchandise, Restaurant equipment & supplies

57503 Kid Zone
4316 N Elston Avenue
Chicago, IL 60641-2144   773-935-0606
  Fax: 773-935-9739
Wholesaler/distributor of bulk vending equipment
Pres.: Neel Clark
Sls. Mgr.: David Rasoff
Estimated Sales: $3-5 Million
Number Employees: 5-9
Private Brands Carried:
  Beaner; Oak; Northwestern
Types of Products Distributed:
  Frozen Food, General Merchandise, Bulk vending equipment

57504 Killer Creamery
Boise, ID 83703
  info@killercreamery.com
  killercreamery.com
Keto-friendly ice cream

Founder: Louis Armstrong
Co-Founder: Liz Armstrong
VP, Marketing: Tate Glasgow

57505 Kimball & Thompson Produce
305 S Lincoln St
Lowell, AR 72745   479-872-0200
  Fax: 479-872-2786 chris@ktproduce.com
  ktproduce.com
Wholesaler/distributor of produce and frozen food.
Owner: Chris Thompson
Chief Financial Officer: Giina Brown
Purchasing: Octavio Galindo
Estimated Sales: $27 Million
Number Employees: 23
Types of Products Distributed:
  Frozen Food, Produce

57506 King Fish Restaurants
7400 New LA Grange Rd
Suite 405
Louisville, KY 40222-8821   502-339-0565
  Fax: 502-339-0230 www.kingfishrestaurants.com
Seafood
Owner: Brown Nolte-Meyer
bnoltemeyer@kingfishrestaurants.com
CEO: Kyle Noltmeyer
Estimated Sales: $10,000,000
Number Employees: 5-9

57507 King Food Service
7810 42nd St W
Rock Island, IL 61201-7319   309-787-4488
  Fax: 309-787-4501 www.kingfoodservice.com
Seafood, poultry & meat
President: Matthew Cutkomp
CEO/CFO: Mike Cutkomp
Director of Sales & Marketing: Kelly McDonald
VP Operations: Chad Gaul
Estimated Sales: $24 Million
Number Employees: 10-19
Number of Products: 1500

57508 King Provision Corporation
220 Ponte Vedra Park Drive
Suite 160
Ponte Vedra Beach, FL 32082-6616   904-725-4211
  Fax: 904-723-3498
Wholesaler/distributor of frozen foods, general merchandise, produce and meats; serving Burger King
Pres.: Ed Hicks
V.P. Fin.: Marc Slater
V.P.: Al Juodvalkis
Number Employees: 10-19
Private Brands Carried:
  Burger King
Number of Customer Locations: 800
Types of Products Distributed:
  Food Service, Frozen Food, General Line, General Merchandise, Provisions/Meat, Produce

57509 Kings Choice Food
2583 N Orange Blossom Trl
Orlando, FL 32804-4808   407-426-9979
  Fax: 407-426-9688 888-426-9979
  netkings@aol.com
Exporter and wholesaler/distributor of vacuum packed steaks, chicken and seafood
President: Ray Reyhani
General Manager: Shawn Kasper
Estimated Sales: $1-2.5 Million
Number Employees: 1-4
Type of Packaging: Consumer, Food Service, Private Label, Bulk
Types of Products Distributed:
  Frozen Food, General Line, Provisions/Meat, Seafood, Black angus steak, pork, seafood, etc.

57510 Kings Seafood Co
3185 Airway Ave
Suite H
Costa Mesa, CA 92626-4601   714-432-0400
  Fax: 714-432-0111 800-269-8425
  samking@kingsseafood.com
  www.kingsseafood.com
Seafood
Owner: Steve Rhee
CEO: Sam King
sking@kingsseafood.com
CFO: Roger Doan
Estimated Sales: $5 Million
Number Employees: 20-49
Square Footage: 60000
Type of Packaging: Food Service

Wholesalers & Distributors / A-Z

Number of Customer Locations: 2000
Types of Products Distributed:
   Frozen Food, Seafood

57511 Kingson Corporation
18 Executive Park Drive
Suite 1804
Atlanta, GA 30329   404-636-4840
Fax: 404-636-5434 kingson@kingsoncorp.com
www.kingsoncorp.com
Wholesaler/distributor of commercial equipment; also, design and installation available; serving the food service market
Pres.: Charles Malikian
Estimated Sales: $500,000-$1 Million
Number Employees: 1-4
Square Footage: 8000
Types of Products Distributed:
   Food Service, Frozen Food, General Merchandise, Commercial equipment

57512 Kingston Candy & Tobacco Co
208 Mac Arthur Ave
New Windsor, NY 12553-7011   845-561-2600
Fax: 845-561-5948 info@kctny.com
www.kctny.com
Wholesaler/distributor of specialty food products, confectionery and tobacco products
President: Jack Raval
kingston@hvc.rr.com
Estimated Sales: $5-10 Million
Number Employees: 50-99
Types of Products Distributed:
   Frozen Food, General Line, General Merchandise, Specialty Foods, Confectionery & tobacco products

57513 Kingston McKnight
419 Avenue Del Ora
Redwood City, CA 94062   650-462-4900
Fax: 650-268-3733 800-900-0463
Manufacturer, importer and exporter of slip-resistant safety shoes serving the hospitality industry
Owner: Jeff Mc Knight
VP: Terry Kingston
Contact: Terry Kingston
tphilipk@yahoo.com
Estimated Sales: $1,000,000
Number Employees: 1-4
Square Footage: 10000
Other Locations:
   Kingston McKnight
   Las Vegas, NVKingston McKnight
Types of Products Distributed:
   Frozen Food, General Merchandise, Chef's cutlery & apparel

57514 Kirby Holloway Provision Co
966 Jackson Ditch Rd
Harrington, DE 19952-2417   302-398-3705
Fax: 302-398-4088 800-995-4729
www.kirbyandhollowayinc.com
Sausage and scrapple; wholesaler/distributor of meat and cheese products
Owner: Russell Kirby
rkirby@kirbyandhollowayinc.com
Owner: Rudy Kirby
General Manager: Bill Moore
Estimated Sales: $7 Million
Number Employees: 20-49
Type of Packaging: Consumer, Food Service, Private Label, Bulk
Types of Products Distributed:
   Frozen Food, General Line, Provisions/Meat, Cheese

57515 Kirby Restaurant & Chemical
809 S Eastman Rd
Longview, TX 75602-2303   903-757-2723
Fax: 903-757-9519 800-877-5472
www.kirbysupply.com
Wholesaler/distributor of equipment and supplies including cleaning supplies and tabletop needs; serving the food service market; also, rack jobber service available
Owner: Mike Bell
mikeb@kirbysupply.com
V.P.: M Bell
Estimated Sales: $10-20 Million
Number Employees: 50-99
Types of Products Distributed:
   Food Service, Frozen Food, Rack Jobbers, Cleaning supplies & tabletop needs

57516 Kirkholder & Rausch
P.O.Box 1742
Buffalo, NY 14240-1742   716-635-9148
Wholesaler/distributor of paper and packaging products and janitorial supplies
President: Henry Chudy, Jr.
Estimated Sales: $250,000
Number Employees: 1-4
Number of Brands: 100
Number of Products: 3000
Square Footage: 20000
Types of Products Distributed:
   Frozen Food, General Merchandise, Paper & packaging products; janitorial

57517 Kissner Milling Company
32 Cherry Blossom Rd.
Cambridge, ON N3H 4R7
Canada   519-279-4860
Fax: 519-650-4222 877-434-8250
www.kissner.com
Wholesaler/distributor of certified kosher salts, food grade ingredients and industrial chemicals
President: Bill Zinger
General Manager: Tim Orleman
Number Employees: 20-49
Square Footage: 140000
Types of Products Distributed:
   Frozen Food, General Line, Specialty Foods, Certified kosher salts & ingredients

57518 Kitchen Maid Foods
3230 Bloomfield Shore Drive
West Bloomfield, MI 48323-3300   248-851-9045
Fax: 248-851-6756 westbloom@aol.com
Wholesaler/distributor of kosher foods including dry, refrigerated and frozen
Pres.: Michael Shanker
V.P.: Myrna Shanker
Number Employees: 1-4
Square Footage: 12000
Parent Co: Kramer Food Company
Private Brands Carried:
   Raskin
Number of Customer Locations: 150
Types of Products Distributed:
   Frozen Food, General Line, Specialty Foods, Kosher foods

57519 Kith Treats
337 Lafayette St
New York, NY 10012   646-648-6285
kith.com
Snackbar, including ice cream and cereal.
Founder: Ronnie Fieg
Year Founded: 2011
Estimated Sales: Less than $500,000
Number Employees: 51-200
Type of Packaging: Consumer, Private Label
Private Brands Carried:
   Apple Jacks; Cap'n Crunch, Cinnamon Toast Crunch; Cheerios; Cocoa Puffs; Cookie Crisp; Corn Flakes; Corn Pops; French Toast Crunch; Fruit Loops; Frosted Flakes; Honey Bunches Of Oats; Lucky Charms; Rice Krispies; Special K
Number of Customer Locations: 6

57520 Kittredge Equipment Co
2155 E Columbus Ave
Springfield, MA 01104-3325   508-581-8877
Fax: 413-781-3352 800-423-7082
www.kittredgeequipment.com
Wholesaler/distributor of food service equipment and supplies
President: Wendy Webber
Purch. Agt.: Mike Harwood
EVP: Arthur Grodd
VP Sales/Operations: Jeff Mackey
Estimated Sales: $10-20 Million
Number Employees: 20-49
Square Footage: 220000
Types of Products Distributed:
   Food Service, Frozen Food, General Merchandise, Foodservice equipment & supplies

57521 Kleen Janitorial SupplyCo.
P.O.Box 2037
Galveston, TX 77553   409-762-0140
Fax: 409-765-7275 800-369-8639
ckleen154@kleensupply.com www.kleensupply.com
Wholesaler/distributor of dry groceries, candy, etc.; serving the food service market
President: Carlo Pena

Estimated Sales: $3-5 Million
Number Employees: 5-9
Number of Customer Locations: 200
Types of Products Distributed:
   Food Service, Frozen Food, General Line, General Merchandise, Dry groceries, candy, etc.

57522 Klein Foods, Inc
1501 E Lyon St
Marshall, MN 56258-3614
507-537-1940 800-657-0174
Fax: 507-537-1945
www.kleinfoods.com
Gourmet honey cremes, sauces, syrups, preserves, and more.
Owner & President: Stephen Klein
kleinfoods@yahoo.com
Estimated Sales: $5-9.9 000,000
Number Employees: 5-9
Other Locations:
   Walnut Grove Mercantile
   Marshall, MNWalnut Grove Mercantile
Types of Products Distributed:
   Specialty Foods, Honey and honey products

57523 Klenke Distributors
94 Greendale Road
Newton, NJ 07860-6054   973-383-0250
Fax: 973-383-5915 888-553-6530
klenke@nac.net
Wholesaler/distributor of sparkling and noncarbonated water and sodas; also, labels, private label, gifts, fundraisers, special ocassion beverages wholesale and retail
Co-Owner/Member: Maryann Klenke
maryannklenke@yahoo.com
Co-Owner/Member: Arthur Klenke, Jr.
Estimated Sales: $3-5 Million
Number Employees: 1-4
Square Footage: 22400
Type of Packaging: Private Label
Types of Products Distributed:
   Soda, water & labels

57524 Klondike Foods
14804-119th Avenue
Edmonton, AB T5L 2P2
Canada   780-451-6677
Fax: 780-451-7733 info@klondikefoods.com
www.klondikefoods.com/
Wholesaler/distributor and import broker of confectionery and dairy/deli products, frozen foods, general merchandise, groceries, private label items, etc. Warehouse providing dry storage for cheese and dry food products alsoavailable
President: Jacob Trach
CEO: Wayne Slosky
CFO: Neville Crawford
Office Manager: Charmaine Slosky
Number Employees: 5
Square Footage: 24000
Parent Co: Klondike Foods Import Export Division
Types of Products Distributed:
   Food Service, Frozen Food, General Line, General Merchandise, Rack Jobbers, Specialty Foods, Candy, groceries, etc.

57525 Kloss Manufacturing Co Inc
7566 Morris Ct
Suite 310
Allentown, PA 18106-9247   610-391-3820
Fax: 610-391-3830 800-445-7100
Processor and exporter of flavoring extracts for Italian ices and slushies; also, concession equipment and supplies, fountain syrups, popcorn, cotton candy, nachos and waffles
Owner: Stephen Lloss
skloss@klossfunfood.com
Estimated Sales: $3-5 Million
Number Employees: 10-19
Square Footage: 120000
Type of Packaging: Food Service, Private Label, Bulk

57526 Knaus Cheese, Inc.
N5722 County Trunk C
Rosendale, WI 54974   920-922-5200
800-236-5200
www.stardairy.com
Wholesaler/distributor of Weyauwega cheese and dairy products
President: Dan Knaus
danielk@riponprinters.com
Parent Co: Weyauwega Star Dairy
Type of Packaging: Consumer, Food Service

Private Brands Carried:
  Weyauwega, Star Dairy
Types of Products Distributed:
  Food Service, Dairy Products

57527 Knotts Fine Foods
125 N Blakemore St
Paris, TN 38242-4197   731-642-1961
Fax: 731-644-1962 joshknott@knottsfoods.com
www.knottsfoods.com
Refrigerated sandwiches and sandwich spreads; wholesaler/distributor of specialty foods
Owner: Josh Knott
joshknott@knottsfoods.com
VP Sales: BJ Knott
Estimated Sales: $5000000
Number Employees: 20-49
Square Footage: 240000
Types of Products Distributed:
  Rack Jobbers, Specialty Foods

57528 Know Brainer
Lafayette, CO 80026   303-475-0456
shari@myknowbrainer.com
www.myknowbrainer.com
Ketogenic coffee creamers, instant coffee, chai tea, matcha tea, and instant hot chocolate
Founder/CEO: Shari Leidich *Year Founded:* 2016
Types of Products Distributed:
  General Line

57529 Knox Cash Jobbers
104 S US Highway 25e
Barbourville, KY 40906-7316   606-546-3440
Wholesaler/distributor of candy; rack jobber services available
Pres.: Wilbert Evans
Estimated Sales: $500,000-$1 Million
Number Employees: 5-9
Types of Products Distributed:
  Frozen Food, General Line, Rack Jobbers, Candy

57530 Knox County Feed & Hatchery
321 N 2nd Street
Vincennes, IN 47591-1304   812-882-5370
Wholesaler/distributor of eggs; serving the food service market
Pres.: Michael Quinett
Estimated Sales: $1-2.5 Million
Number Employees: 1-4
Types of Products Distributed:
  Food Service, General Line, Eggs

57531 Knoxville Poultry & Egg Company
PO Box 3578
Knoxville, TN 37927-3578   865-524-3338
Wholesaler/distributor of poultry and eggs
Pres.: Ben Harrison, Jr.
Private Brands Carried:
  Magnolia Farms
Types of Products Distributed:
  Frozen Food, General Line, Chicken, eggs, etc.

57532 Koalaty Kare
PO Box 2565
Laurel, MD 20709-2565   301-490-9204
Fax: 301-490-5926 800-562-5289
koalatykare@koalaty.com
Wholesaler/distributor of commercial high chairs; serving the food service market
Types of Products Distributed:
  Food Service, Frozen Food, General Merchandise, Commercial high chairs

57533 Koch Bag & Supply Co
999 Bedford Rd
Kansas City, MO 64116-4114   816-221-1883
Fax: 816-221-7070
Wholesaler/distributor and exporter of bags including cotton specialty polyethylene; also, burlap products
President: Diana Byron
d.bryon@kochbag.com
Estimated Sales: $10-20 Million
Number Employees: 10-19
Type of Packaging: Consumer, Bulk
Types of Products Distributed:
  Frozen Food, General Merchandise, Packaging/containerizing products, etc.

57534 Koch Container
797 Old Dutch Rd
Victor, NY 14564-8972   585-924-1600
Fax: 585-924-7040 koch1@frontiernet.net
www.kochcontainer.com
Corrugated boxes and displays; wholesaler/distributor of corner boards, edge protectors, plastic bags and fiber tubes
President: Tom Baumgartner
tomb@kochcontainer.com
Mgr. Cust. Svce.: Cheryl Wessells
Estimated Sales: $20-50 Million
Number Employees: 50-99
Parent Co: Buckeye Corrugated
Types of Products Distributed:
  Frozen Food, General Merchandise, Packaging materials

57535 Koha Food
500 Alakawa St
Suite 104
Honolulu, HI 96817-4576   808-845-4232
Fax: 808-841-5398
Oriental foods
President: Paul Kim
Estimated Sales: $5-10 Million
Number Employees: 20-49

57536 Kohana Coffee
1221 S Mopac Expressway
Suite 100
Austin, TX 78746   512-904-1174
Fax: 512-532-0581 info@kohanacoffee.com
www.kohanacoffee.com
Coffee, decaff and cold brew coffee.
Owner: Victoria Lynden
Sales: Nate Creasey
Contact: Joe Browne
joe@kohanacoffee.com
Operations: Piper Jones
Estimated Sales: Under $500,000
Number Employees: 2

57537 Kohlenberger Inc
12966 Lakeland Rd
Santa Fe Springs, CA 90670-4537 562-903-9220
Fax: 562-903-9222 info@kohlenbergerinc.com
Wholesaler/distributor of industrial refrigeration equipment
Owner: S Thompon
kberger22@aol.com
Estimated Sales: $2.5-5 Million
Number Employees: 1-4
Types of Products Distributed:
  Frozen Food, General Merchandise, Industrial refrigeration equipment

57538 Kolon California Corporation
16700 Valley View Avenue
Suite 130
La Mirada, CA 90638-5844   714-522-0434
Fax: 714-522-0577
Wholesaler/distributor of general merchandise, groceries, frozen foods and meats
Pres.: Y Jeon
G.M.: William Joo
Estimated Sales: $2.5-5 Million
Number Employees: 1-4
Square Footage: 400000
Types of Products Distributed:
  Frozen Food, General Line, General Merchandise, Provisions/Meat

57539 Kols Container
1408 Desoto Rd
Baltimore, MD 21230-1296   410-646-2300
Fax: 410-646-5671 800-457-5657
www.oberk.com
Wholesaler/distributor of glass and plastic containers and plastic and metal closures
President: Marc Gaelei
Sales: Robert Wittlinger
Contact: Larry Blumenauer
lblumenauer@kolscontainers.com
Estimated Sales: $20-50 Million
Number Employees: 20-49
Square Footage: 25000
Parent Co: O'Berk Company
Types of Products Distributed:
  Frozen Food, General Merchandise, Glass & plastic containers, etc.

57540 Kommercial Kitchens
1100 W Freeway Blvd
Vidor, TX 77662   409-769-1199
Fax: 409-769-8800 800-962-1555
info@kommercialkitchens.com
www.kommercialkitchens.com
Wholesaler/distributor of food service equipment; serving the food service market
Owner: Terry Woodard
Estimated Sales: $5-10 Million
Number Employees: 10-19
Private Brands Carried:
  Vollrath; South Bend; Advance
Types of Products Distributed:
  Food Service, Frozen Food, General Merchandise, Foodservice equipment

57541 Kona Cold Lobsters
73-4460 Queen Kaahumanu
Suite 103
Kailua Kona, HI 96740-2637   808-329-4332
Fax: 808-326-2882 info@konacoldlobsters.com
www.konacoldlobsters.com
Lobsters
President: Joseph Wilson
Manager: Philip Wilson
phil@konacoldlobsters.com
Estimated Sales: Less than $300,000
Number Employees: 10-19

57542 Kona Fish Co Inc
73-4776 Kanalani St
Suite 8
Kailua Kona, HI 96740-2625   808-326-7708
Fax: 808-329-3669 www.hilofish.com
Fresh, frozen seafood
Owner: Kerry Umamoto
Estimated Sales: $5-10 Million
Number Employees: 20-49

57543 Kona Pacific Farmers Co-Op
82-5810 Napoopoo Rd
P.O. Box 309
Captain Cook, HI 96704-8210   808-328-2411
Fax: 808-328-2414
Wholesaler/distributor of dry-roasted macadamia nuts
Mgr.: Sotero Agoot
Pres.: Morris Nagata
Manager: Eileen Koyanagi
eileen@kpfc.com
Estimated Sales: $10-20 Million
Number Employees: 10-19
Types of Products Distributed:
  General Line, Dry-roasted macadamia nuts

57544 Koorsen Protection Services
3209 Caprice Ct
Fort Wayne, IN 46808   260-483-7557
Fax: 219-482-8534 888-566-7736
info@koorsen.com www.koorsen.com
Wholesaler/distributor of fire protection systems
President / CEO: Randall R Koorsen
EVP: Jeff Wyatt
Contact: Greg Balewin
gbalewin@koorsen.com
Estimated Sales: $10-20 Million
Number Employees: 20-49
Parent Co: Koorsen Protection Services
Private Brands Carried:
  Ansul; Amerex; Pyrotronics
Types of Products Distributed:
  Frozen Food, General Merchandise, Fire protection systems

57545 Kopcke-Kansas Supply Services
148 Harbor Circle
New Orleans, LA 70126-1102   504-488-7488
Wholesaler/distributor of provisions/meats and paper products; serving the food service market; also, ship chandler service available
G.M.: Jon Klein
Number Employees: 20-49
Parent Co: Kopcke International USA
Types of Products Distributed:
  Food Service, Frozen Food, General Merchandise, Provisions/Meat, Paper products

57546 Kopke, William H
1000 Northern Blvd # 200
Great Neck, NY 11021-5312   516-328-6800
Fax: 516-328-6874
Importer and wholesaler/distributor of produce

Wholesalers & Distributors / A-Z

President: Peter Kopke
Contact: Joe Fox
joefox@kopkefruit.com
Estimated Sales: $20-50 Million
Number Employees: 5-9
Types of Products Distributed:
 Frozen Food, Produce

57547 Kosmos & Associates
445 Lesser St
Oakland, CA 94601-4901   510-261-2080
                         Fax: 510-261-2084
Wholesaler/distributor of food service equipment and supplies; also, consulting, space planning and installation available
Pres.: Chris Kosmos
Estimated Sales: Less than $500,000
Number Employees: 1-4
Types of Products Distributed:
 Food Service, Frozen Food, General Merchandise, Equipment & supplies

57548 Kovacs Group
PO Box 10430
Torrance, CA 90505-1430   310-325-6871
       Fax: 310-325-0571 877-570-8024
                  www.kovacsgroup.com
Wholesaler/distributor of labels and decals; also, die cutting and designing available
Pres.: R Kovacs
V.P.: Don Martin
Contact: Joe Kovacs
joek@kovacsgroup.com
Number of Customer Locations: 40
Types of Products Distributed:
 Frozen Food, General Merchandise, Labels & decals

57549 Kraft Chemical Co
1975 N Hawthorne Ave
Melrose Park, IL 60160-1160   708-345-5200
        Fax: 708-345-0761   800-345-5200
sales@kraftchemical.com www.kraftchemical.com
Wholesaler/distributor of food ingredients and general merchandise
President: Richard Kraft
rkraft@kraftchemical.com
CFO: Sam Ng
Marketing Director: Joyce Segraves
Purchasing Manager: Andy Rock
Estimated Sales: $20-50 Million
Number Employees: 20-49
Square Footage: 60000
Types of Products Distributed:
 General Line, Materials

57550 Kranz Inc
2200 DE Koven Ave
Racine, WI 53403-2442   262-638-2200
        Fax: 262-638-2202 888-638-2201
                   info@kranzinc.com
Wholesaler/distributor of disposable, paper, janitorial and packaging supplies and food processing equipment
Pres.: Jeffrey Neubauer
Dir. Sls./Mktg.: Ed Tutas
Cust. Svce.: Mary Creel
Estimated Sales: $10-20 Million
Number Employees: 50-99
Number of Customer Locations: 2000
Types of Products Distributed:
 Food Service, Frozen Food, General Merchandise, Janitorial & packaging supplies, etc.

57551 (HQ)Krasdale Foods
65 W Red Oak Ln # 3
White Plains, NY 10604-3616   914-694-6400
                       Fax: 914-697-5225
               webmaster@krasdalefoods.com
                    www.krasdalefoods.com
Wholesaler/distributor serving supermarkets and independent grocery stores in the New York Tri-state marketplace. Over 7,000 grocery items in stock, serving more than 3,000 customers
President, CEO: Charles Krasne
Purch. Agt.: Bob Rodesky
Purch. Agt.: Jay Reinstein
Number Employees: 500-999
Type of Packaging: Consumer, Private Label
Other Locations:
 Krasdale Foods
 Bronx, NY Krasdale Foods
Private Brands Carried:
 Krasdale; C-Town; Bravo

Number of Customer Locations: 5000
Types of Products Distributed:
 Frozen Food, General Line, Groceries

57552 Krasdale Foods Distribution
400 Food Center Dr
Bronx, NY 10474-7098   718-378-1100
    Fax: 718-589-0678 www.krasdalefoods.com
Wholesaler/distributor of groceries
CEO/Pres.: Charles Krasne
Supv.: Robert Gewelb
Estimated Sales: $5-10 Million
Number Employees: 250-499
Square Footage: 1400000
Parent Co: Krasdale Foods
Private Brands Carried:
 Krasdale; C-Town; Bravo
Number of Customer Locations: 3300
Types of Products Distributed:
 Frozen Food, General Line, Groceries

57553 Krebs Brothers Restaurant Supl
4310 Landers Rd
N Little Rock, AR 72117-2525   501-664-0117
        Fax: 501-664-0117   800-632-4548
                 www.krebsbrothers.com
Wholesaler/distributor of cleaning supplies, table top needs and equipment; serving the food service market
Pres.: Wally Gieringer
Manager: Jill Clark
jill@krebsbrothers.com
Estimated Sales: $5-10 Million
Number Employees: 5-9
Types of Products Distributed:
 Food Service, Frozen Food, General Merchandise, Cleaning supplies & equipment

57554 Kronos
1 Kronos Dr.
Glendale Heights, IL 60139   224-353-5353
        Fax: 224-353-5400   800-621-0099
              requests@kronosfoodscorp.com
                www.kronosfoodscorp.com
Mediterranean foods including gyro, pita, flatbread, tzatziki sauce, spanakopita, falafel, and tyropita
Chairman: Michael Austin
CEO: Howard Eirinberg
CFO: Herman Brons
Director of Marketing: Karyn Andrew
SVP Sales: Bob Michaels
Year Founded: 1975
Number Employees: 250-499
Types of Products Distributed:
 General Line

57555 Kropf Fruit Company
11930 Fisk Road
Belding, MI 48809-9413   616-794-4220
                        Fax: 616-794-1868
Apple wholesalers
President: Roger Kropf
Marketing Manager: Pom Puerter
Estimated Sales: $10-20 Million
Number Employees: 100-249
Type of Packaging: Bulk

57556 Kuehne Chemical
86 N Hackensack Ave
Kearny, NJ 07032-4673   973-589-0700
         Fax: 973-589-4866 info@kuehnecompany.com
                     www.kuehnecompany.com
Industrial strength bleach including sodium hypochlorite; wholesaler/distributor of caustic soda, caustic potash, chlorine and sulfur
Manager: Emmanuel Cunha
ecunha@kuehnecompany.com
Estimated Sales: $61 Million
Number Employees: 50-99
Square Footage: 10000
Types of Products Distributed:
 Frozen Food, General Merchandise, Caustic soda, caustic potash, etc.

57557 Kuner-Empson Company
PO Box 309
Brighton, CO 80601-0309   303-659-1710
                         Fax: 303-659-7681
Wholesaler/distributor of vegetables and dry beans
G.M.: Bob Seifert
Exec. V.P.: Michael Peroutka
Estimated Sales: $5-10 Million
Number Employees: 5-9
Parent Co: FariBault Foods

Private Brands Carried:
 Kunner; Southwestern
Types of Products Distributed:
 Produce, Vegetables & dry beans

57558 Kusha Inc.
11130 Warland Drive
Cypress, CA 90630   949-930-1400
      Fax: 949-250-1520   800-550-7423
Rice, basmati, jasmine, tea, grape seed oil, cheese
Vice President: Jerry Taylor
Contact: Mukesh Agrawal
mukesh@ltfoodsamericas.com
Estimated Sales: Under $500,000
Number Employees: 30
Type of Packaging: Consumer, Food Service, Private Label, Bulk

57559 Kutter's Cheese Factory
PO Box 345
Heuvelton, NY 13654-0345   315-344-6490
         Fax: 315-344-6416   800-836-8739
                    www.mccadam.com
Wholesaler/distributor of private label items and cheese, sour cream, dips and bread; serving the retail and food service markets
Mgr.: Robert Oh
Co-Mgr.: Joe Ritter
Number Employees: 10-19
Parent Co: McCadam's Cheese
Private Brands Carried:
 Kutter's; McCadam's
Number of Customer Locations: 150
Types of Products Distributed:
 Food Service, Frozen Food, General Line, Cottage cheese, cheddar, dips, etc.

57560 Kwikprint ManufacturingInc
4868 Victor St
Jacksonville, FL 32207-1702   904-737-3755
         Fax: 904-730-0349   800-940-5945
                    www.kwik-print.com
Manufacturer and exporter of foil, gold and hot stamping equipment; also, custom stamping dies and foils; wholesaler/distributor of advertising specialties and promotional items
Owner: Mike Bulger
mbulger@kwik-print.com
V.P.: Lynn Cann
Estimated Sales: Below $5 Million
Number Employees: 5-9
Square Footage: 48000
Type of Packaging: Food Service, Private Label, Bulk
Types of Products Distributed:
 Frozen Food, General Merchandise, Advertising & promotional items

57561 Kyong Hae Kim Company
2330 Kalakaua Ave
Suite 85
Honolulu, HI 96815-5001   808-926-8720
                         Fax: 808-841-2178
Owner: Kyong Kim

57562 L & M Food Svc Inc
885 Airpark Dr
Bullhead City, AZ 86429-5836   928-754-3241
         Fax: 928-754-2241 info@lmfoodservice.com
                    www.lmfoodservice.com
Wholesaler/distributor of equipment and fixtures and general merchandise including paper, janitorial and bar supplies; serving the food service market
President: Ron Laughlin
laughlinrc@lmfoodservice.com
CEO: Andy Roesch
Vice President: Judy Laughlin
Plant Manager: Tom Watkins
Purchasing Manager: Dick Motsinger
Estimated Sales: $14 Million
Number Employees: 20-49
Square Footage: 100000
Private Brands Carried:
 Wolf; True; Advance
Types of Products Distributed:
 Food Service, Frozen Food, General Merchandise, Paper, janitorial & bar supplies, etc.

57563 L ChemCo Distribution
3230 Commerce Center Place
Louisville, KY 40211-1900   502-775-8387
        Fax: 502-775-5981   800-292-1977

Wholesale distributor of commercial and industrial janitorial cleaning supplies and equipment; also including sell of pesticides, weedicides and herbicides
Estimated Sales: $1.5 Million
Number Employees: 9
Square Footage: 28000
Types of Products Distributed:
  Frozen Food, General Merchandise, Floor machines & chemicals

57564 L&C Meat Company
1136 South Vista Avenue
Independence, MO 64056
816-796-6100
Fax: 816-796-6107 sales@lcmeats.com
www.lcmeats.com
Wholesaler/distributor of provisions/meats
President: J Likely
Contact: O Dell Tim
timo@lcmeats.com
Estimated Sales: $10-20 Million
Number Employees: 20-49
Types of Products Distributed:
  Frozen Food, Provisions/Meat

57565 L&M Bakers Supply Company
2501 Steeles Avenue W
Unit # 1
Toronto, ON M3J 2P1
Canada
416-665-3005
Fax: 416-665-8975 800-465-7361
www.lmbakersupply.com
Manufacturer & wholesaler/distributor of cake decorations and baking tools and supplies; serving the food service market
General Manager: Sheba Grinhaus
Number Employees: 20-49
Square Footage: 44000
Types of Products Distributed:
  Food Service, General Line, Cake decorations; Baking equipment

57566 L&M Evans
PO Box 367
Conyers, GA 30012
770-483-9373
Fax: 847-647-1509
Seafood, clams, fish, fillets
President: L W Bill Evans
Owner: Gene Burkett
Estimated Sales: $300,000-500,000
Number Employees: 1-4

57567 L. Cherrick Horseradish Company
2020 N 9th St
Saint Louis, MO 63102
314-421-5431
Fax: 314-421-3277
Wholesaler/distributor and exporter of horseradish
Co-Owner: Vernon Bruns
Co-Owner: Elaine Bruns
Estimated Sales: $2.5-5 Million
Number Employees: 1-4
Type of Packaging: Consumer, Bulk
Types of Products Distributed:
  General Line, Horseradish

57568 L. Craelius & Company
370 N Morgan St
Chicago, IL 60607-1321
312-666-7100
Fax: 312-666-9747
Fresh poultry
President: Lawrence Craelius
Estimated Sales: $20-50 Million
Number Employees: 20-49

57569 L. Dontis Produce Company
Brooklyn Wholesale Market
5600 First Avenue-Bldg A-5
Brooklyn, NY 11220
718-439-9096
Fax: 718-492-0302 jimmy@dontisproduce.com
www.dontisproduce.com
Wholesaler/distributor of frozen food and produce; serving the food service market
Owner: L Dontis
President: Jim Dontis
Estimated Sales: $10-20 Million
Number Employees: 10-19
Types of Products Distributed:
  Food Service, Frozen Food, Produce

57570 L. Holloway & Brother Company
242 Hunters Ridge Rd
Lutherville Timonium, MD 21093-4018
Fax: 410-799-5599
Wholesaler/distributor of produce; serving the food service market
President: Richard Holloway
Estimated Sales: $3-5 Million
Number Employees: 20-49
Types of Products Distributed:
  Food Service, Frozen Food, Produce

57571 L. Lacagnina & Sons
185 Holmes Rd
Rochester, NY 14626
585-453-0238
Wholesaler/distributor of groceries, general merchandise and specialty foods
President: M Lacagnina
Estimated Sales: $5-10 Million
Number Employees: 5-9
Private Brands Carried:
  Clio; Gem
Number of Customer Locations: 200
Types of Products Distributed:
  Frozen Food, General Line, General Merchandise, Specialty Foods, Groceries

57572 L.H. Rodriguez Wholesale Seafood
3541 S 12th Ave
Tucson, AZ 85713-5914
520-623-1931
Fax: 520-623-0737
Seafood
President: Levi Rodriguez
Treasurer: Albert Rodriguez
Vice President: Joe Rodriguez
Estimated Sales: $3-5 Million
Number Employees: 5-9

57573 L.N. Coffman Company
P.O.Box 744
Salem, MO 65560-0744
573-729-6631
Wholesaler/distributor of general line items and general merchandise
Manager: J Kinder
Estimated Sales: $5-10 Million
Number Employees: 5-9
Parent Co: Robert Judson Lumber
Number of Customer Locations: 200
Types of Products Distributed:
  Frozen Food, General Line, General Merchandise

57574 L.P. Shanks Company
P.O.Box 1068
Crossville, TN 38557
931-484-5155
Fax: 931-484-4333
Wholesaler/distributor of frozen foods, general merchandise and general line products; serving the food service market
President: Scott Shanks
Estimated Sales: $20-50 Million
Number Employees: 50-99
Number of Customer Locations: 500
Types of Products Distributed:
  Food Service, Frozen Food, General Line, General Merchandise

57575 LA Bella Ferrara
108 Mulberry St
New York, NY 10013-4641
212-966-7867
www.littleitalynyc.com
Wholesaler/distributor of pastries
Manager: Jean Angileri
Estimated Sales: Less Than $500,000
Number Employees: 5-9
Types of Products Distributed:
  Frozen Food, Specialty Foods

57576 LA Canasta Mexican Foods
3101 W Jackson St
PO Box 6939
Phoenix, AZ 85009-4833
602-269-7721
Fax: 602-269-7725 855-269-7721
www.la-canasta.com
Mexican food products including tortillas, chips, sauces and salsas.
Founder: Carmen Abril
President: Josie Ippolito
jippolito@la-canasta.com
Controller: Roger Kelling
Plant Manager: Ben Garduno
Estimated Sales: $19.9 Million
Number Employees: 100-249
Number of Brands: 2
Square Footage: 72000
Type of Packaging: Food Service, Private Label
Private Brands Carried:
  My Nana's Chips
Types of Products Distributed:
  Food Service, Frozen Food, Specialty Foods

57577 (HQ)LA Cena Fine Foods LTD
4 Rosol Ln
Saddle Brook, NJ 07663-5522
201-797-4600
Fax: 201-797-6988 v.piigjr@lacenafoods.com
Ethnic food distributor (Spanish), Food importer and distributors to supermarket chains.
Owner: Antonio Argueta
VP/Co-Owner: Vincent Puig Jr
Marketing Director: Marcela Carlin
Sales: Jose Badia
a.argueta@lacenafoods.com
Purchasing: Maria Jose Alvarez
Number Employees: 20-49
Private Brands Carried:
  La Cena; Palacio Real; Bajamar; Victorina
Types of Products Distributed:
  Specialty Foods, Olive oil, fruit nectars, etc.

57578 LA Foods
7301 Topanga Canyon Blvd # 200
Canoga Park, CA 91303-1270
818-587-3757
Fax: 818-587-3767 www.la-foods.com
Wholesaler/distributor of canned and frozen vegetables and fruits, condiments, prepared foods and cheese; serving the food service market
Partner: Max Gold
Partner: David Fox
Partner: Mark Davis
Estimated Sales: $20-50 Million
Number Employees: 5-9
Type of Packaging: Food Service, Private Label, Bulk
Private Brands Carried:
  Chef Maxwell; Paseo
Types of Products Distributed:
  Food Service, Frozen Food, General Line, General Merchandise, Provisions/Meat, Condiments, prepared foods & cheese

57579 LA Grange Grocery Co
143 Busch Dr
Lagrange, GA 30241-3699
706-884-7325
Fax: 706-812-8729 www.lagrangegrocery.com
Wholesaler/distributor of beer; serving the food service market
President: James Zachry
james@lagrangegrocery.com
Estimated Sales: $20-50 Million
Number Employees: 50-99
Parent Co: La Grange
Types of Products Distributed:
  Food Service, Frozen Food, General Line, Beer

57580 LA India Packing Co Inc
1520 Marcella Ave
Laredo, TX 78040-7900
956-723-3772
Fax: 956-726-2614
sales@laindiaherbsandspices.com
www.laindiaherbsandspices.com
Wholesaler/distributor of chocolate, herbs, seasonings, spices and chili pods
Owner: Elsa Rodriguez Argu
elsa@laindiaherbsandspices.com
Secretary/Treasurer: E Sanchez
General Manager: Elsa R. Sanchez
Estimated Sales: $1-2.5 Million
Number Employees: 20-49
Types of Products Distributed:
  Specialty Foods, Chocolate, herbs, seasonings & spices

57581 LA Lifestyle Nutritional Products
2230 Cape Cod Way
Santa Ana, CA 92703-3582
714-835-6367
Fax: 714-835-4948 800-387-4786
Processor and wholesaler/distributor of teas and herbal products
Owner: Patricia J Logsdon
Estimated Sales: $10-20 Million
Type of Packaging: Consumer
Types of Products Distributed:
  Frozen Food, General Line, Health Food, Teas & herbal products

57582 LA Rue Distributing
2631 S 156th Cir
Omaha, NE 68130-2514
402-333-9099
Fax: 402-333-6741 800-658-4498
www.laruecoffee.com

Wholesalers & Distributors / A-Z

Wholesaler/distributor of coffees and teas, coffee and tea equipment, paper products, private label and specialty food items, cold beverages, groceries and meat
President: Verlyn L Heureux
verlyn.heureux@laruecoffee.com
Secretary/Treasurer: Susan L'Heureux
VP Operations: Mark Wunderlich
Estimated Sales: $20-50 Million
Number Employees: 50-99
Square Footage: 15000
Type of Packaging: Private Label, Bulk
Private Brands Carried:
  Larue Coffee; China Mist
Types of Products Distributed:
  Frozen Food, General Line, General Merchandise, Specialty Foods, Groceries, cold beverages, etc.

57583 LA Squisita Food Corp
2 South St
Mt Vernon, NY 10550-1708 914-667-8795
  Fax: 718-378-4990 bobbyoil@aol.com
  www.lasquisita.com
Wholesaler/distributor of general line products; serving the food service market
Owner: Robert Debenedictis
Vice President: Joseph DeBenedictis
Sales Manager: Anthony Angarola
bobbyoil@aol.com
Warehouse Manager: John Covais
Purchasing Manager: Nick Domenici
Estimated Sales: $2.5-5 Million
Number Employees: 20-49
Private Brands Carried:
  Chef's Pride; La Gradita; La Squisita; Rosita
Number of Customer Locations: 550
Types of Products Distributed:
  Food Service, Frozen Food, General Line

57584 LA Torilla Factory
3300 Westwind Blvd
Santa Rosa, CA 95403-8273 707-586-4000
  Fax: 707-586-4017 800-446-1516
  info@latortillafactory.com
  www.latortillafactory.com
Corn and flour tortillas and tortilla chips and masa
President: Carlos Tamayo
Owner/President/VP Sales/Marketing: Sam Tamayo
CFO: Stan Mead
R&D Manager: Luz Ana Osbun
Executive Director Sales/Marketing: Jan Remak
Human Resources Manager: Jonna Green
COO/VP/Plant Manager: Sam Tamayo
Estimated Sales: $8000000
Number Employees: 250-499
Square Footage: 18160
Type of Packaging: Consumer, Food Service, Private Label, Bulk
Types of Products Distributed:
  Food Service, Frozen Food, Specialty Foods, Tortilla chips & salsas

57585 LBG Distributors
1190 Sherman Avenue
Hamden, CT 06514-1330 800-648-5611
  Fax: 203-288-5587
Wholesaler/distributor of baked goods, general merchandise, health and beauty aids, equipment and fixtures and general line products
President: B Vitale
VP: L Vitale
Estimated Sales: $20-50 Million
Number Employees: 20-49
Private Brands Carried:
  Lotiss
Number of Customer Locations: 400
Types of Products Distributed:
  Frozen Food, General Line, General Merchandise, Baked goods, equipment & fixtures, etc.

57586 LDC of Lafayette
P.O.Box 3727
Lafayette, LA 70502-3727 337-233-9041
  Fax: 337-232-0738
Wholesaler/distributor of general merchandise including housewares, brooms, mops, etc.; also, specialty food items; rack jobber services available
President/General Manager: J Chachere
VP/Controller: C LeBlanc
Estimated Sales: $2.5-5 Million
Number Employees: 20-49
Number of Customer Locations: 800

Types of Products Distributed:
  Frozen Food, General Line, General Merchandise, Rack Jobbers, Housewares, brooms, mops, etc.

57587 LLJ's Sea Products
PO Box 296
Round Pond, ME 04564-0296 207-529-4224
  Fax: 207-529-4223
Canned and cured fish and seafood.
Owner: Stephen J Brackett
Estimated Sales: $3,000,000
Number Employees: 5-9

57588 LMG Group
792 NW 12th Street
Suite 121
Miami, FL 33136-2351 305-477-9057
  Fax: 305-477-9146
Wholesaler/distributor and exporter of food service equipment including, washers, dryers, ice makers, etc.; serving the food service market
President: Christian Lugo
General Manager: Jenny Gomez
VP: Hector McDougall
Number Employees: 20-49
Parent Co: Grupo Institucional Del Caribe, S.A.
Type of Packaging: Food Service
Types of Products Distributed:
  Food Service, Frozen Food, General Merchandise, Foodservice equipment

57589 LSI Specialty Products
565 Estabrook St
San Leandro, CA 94577-3511 510-357-8637
  Fax: 510-357-8639
Wholesaler/distributor of sweeteners including sugar, corn syrup, molasses, malt syrups and corn derivatives
Owner: John Louis
Vice President: D Terrill
Estimated Sales: $3-5 Million
Number Employees: 10-19
Parent Co: MCP
Private Brands Carried:
  Nulomine; Tricol Syrups; Nulomoline
Types of Products Distributed:
  Frozen Food, General Line, Sugar, corn syrup, molasses, etc.

57590 La Brea Bakery Inc
14490 Catalina St
San Leandro, CA 94577
  855-427-9982
  www.labreabakery.com
Bread and rolls; also, par-baked and frozen available.
President: John Yamin
jyamin@labreabakery.com
Year Founded: 1989
Estimated Sales: $124.4 Million
Number Employees: 100-249
Parent Co: Aryzta AG
Other Locations:
  Direct Store Delivery
  Los Angeles, CA
  Store Baked Delivery Nationwide
  Swedesboro, NJ Direct Store Delivery Swedesboro
Types of Products Distributed:
  Frozen Food

57591 La Grasso Bros Produce
5001 Bellevue St
P.O. Box 2638
Detroit, MI 48202-2638 313-579-1455
  Fax: 313-579-9517 800-538-8823
  info@lagrasso.com www.lagrasso.com
Wholesaler/distributor of produce and dairy products; serving the food service market.
President: Tom LaGrasso, Jr
tom@lagrasso.com
Fleet Manager & Sales: Joseph LaGrasso
Human Resources Manager: Catherine LaGrasso
Chief Operating Officer: Tom LaGrasso III
Warehouse Manager: Steve Rider
Vice President Purchasing: Joseph Henry LaGrasso
Year Founded: 1914
Estimated Sales: $20-50 Million
Number Employees: 100-249
Square Footage: 40000
Types of Products Distributed:
  Food Service, General Line, Produce, Dairy products

57592 La Pine Scientific Company
PO Box 780
Blue Island, IL 60406-0780 708-388-4030
  Fax: 708-388-4084 800-205-6303
Wholesaler/distributor, importer and exporter of laboratory supplies
President/Treasurer: Robert La Pine
Estimated Sales: $970,000
Number Employees: 5-9
Square Footage: 44000
Types of Products Distributed:
  Frozen Food, General Merchandise, Laboratory supplies

57593 La Rinascente Macaroni Company
41 James St
South Hackensack, NJ 07606 201-342-2530
  info@lrmpackaging.com
  www.lrmpackaging.com
Macaroni, flour and packaged food products.
Consultant: John Natali
Estimated Sales: $20-50 Million
Square Footage: 600000
Type of Packaging: Consumer, Food Service, Private Label, Bulk
Types of Products Distributed:
  Frozen Food

57594 La Tang Cuisine Manufacturing
3824 Artdale St
Houston, TX 77063-5245 713-780-4876
  Fax: 713-780-4296
Asian foods including egg rolls, wonton, crab rangoon, spring roll and burritos.
President: Virginia Limbo
CEO: Joey Limbo
Estimated Sales: $250,000-$1 Million
Number Employees: 20-49
Number of Brands: 2
Number of Products: 5
Square Footage: 20000
Type of Packaging: Food Service, Private Label, Bulk
Types of Products Distributed:
  Food Service, Frozen Food, Specialty Foods

57595 La Tortilla Factory
3300 Westwind Blvd
Santa Rosa, CA 95403
  Fax: 707-586-4017 800-446-1516
  info@latortillafactory.com
  www.latortillafactory.com
Tortillas and wraps
President/CEO: Jeff Ahlers
CFO: David Trogdon
EVP: Willie Tamayo
Marketing Project Manager Lori Chellies Friend
Sr. Director, National Sales: Tom Moore *Year Founded:* 1977

57596 LaRocca's Seafood Specialists
489 Midland Ave
Staten Island, NY 10306 718-979-8833
  info@laroccas.com
  www.laroccas.com
Wholesaler/distributor of smoked seafood including Norwegian style and peppered salmon, sturgeon, eel and rainbow trout and albacore, salmon jerky, mussels and beluga
Estimated Sales: $2.5-5 Million
Number Employees: 20-49
Types of Products Distributed:
  Frozen Food, Seafood, Smoked salmon, mussels, trout, etc.

57597 (HQ)Labatt Food Svc
4500 Industry Park
San Antonio, TX 78218 210-661-4216
  Fax: 210-661-0973 www.labattfood.com
Wholesaler/distributor serving the food service market.
President & CEO: Blair Labatt
General Manager & COO: Al Silva
Director of Information Technology: Blair Labatt III
VP of Purchasing & Marketing: Breann Field
VP of Sales & Vendor Lead: Cara Vives
Director, Sales: Matt Silva
Executive Vice President: Tony Canty
Warehouse Manager: Richard Benitez
Transportation Manager: John Heringer

Year Founded: 1910
Estimated Sales: $1.3 Billion
Number Employees: 1,700+
Types of Products Distributed:
  Food Service, Frozen Food

57598 Labatt Food Svc
Office & Warehouse
5824 Elm Ave
Lubbock, TX 79404   806-748-5111
        Fax: 806-748-5115 www.labattfood.com
Wholesaler/distributor serving the food service market.
Types of Products Distributed:
  Food Service, Frozen Food, General Line, General Merchandise

57599 Labatt Food Svc
Office & Warehouse
650 Regal Row
Dallas, TX 75247   214-638-4141
        Fax: 214-688-0418 www.labattfood.com
Wholesaler/distributor serving the food service market.
Square Footage: 500000
Types of Products Distributed:
  Food Service, Frozen Food, General Line, General Merchandise

57600 Labatt Food Svc
Office & Warehouse
6650 Pine Vista Ln
Houston, TX 77092   713-681-3819
        Fax: 713-681-2278 www.labattfood.com
Wholesaler/distributor serving the food service market.
Types of Products Distributed:
  Food Service, Frozen Food

57601 Labatt Food Svc
Office & Warehouse
221 Airport Dr NW
Albuquerque, NM 87121   505-831-1411
        Fax: 505-831-0814 www.labattfood.com
Wholesaler/distributor serving the food service market.
Types of Products Distributed:
  Food Service, Frozen Food

57602 Label House
503 S Raymond Ave
Fullerton, CA 92831-5026   714-449-0632
        Fax: 714-441-0698 800-499-5858
        sales@labelhouse.com www.labelhouse.net
Pressure sensitive labels and tags; wholesaler/distributor of label dispensers and applicators, thermal transfer ribbons, case coders, bar code printers and software
Owner: Al Jiacomin
owner: Karen Freeman
VP Sales: Leone Grant
Estimated Sales: $1-2.5 Million
Number Employees: 10-19
Types of Products Distributed:
  Frozen Food, General Merchandise, Label dispensers, applicators, etc.

57603 Labeltronix LLC
2419 E Winston Rd
Anaheim, CA 92806-5544   714-204-3174
        Fax: 714-516-2323 800-429-4321
        info@labeltronix.com www.labeltronix.com
Wholesaler/distributor of thermal and thermal transfer printers, labels, security tags, ribbons, software and label applicators; also, service available
Owner: Dan Blair
Marketing Supervisor: Megan Golz
Sales Director: Graham Rushall
IT: John Train
jtrail@labeltronix.com
Estimated Sales: $5-10 Million
Number Employees: 50-99
Types of Products Distributed:
  General Merchandise, Labels, security tags, ribbons, etc.

57604 Labov Mechanical, Inc.
6754 W. Washington Avenue
P.O. Box 1547
Pleasantville, NJ 08232   609-383-9600
        Fax: 609-383-9069 www.labovmechanical.com
Wholesaler/distributor of kitchen equipment; also, installation services available
Manager: Jon Rosky
VP Marketing: Eileen Copriotti
Contact: Louis Goodman
louis-goodman@emcorgroup.com
General Manager of Service: John Lare
Number Employees: 20-49
Parent Co: EMCOR Group Company
Types of Products Distributed:
  Frozen Food, General Merchandise, Kitchen equipment

57605 Lacassagne's
495 North 49th Street
Baton Rouge, LA 70806-3453 225-218-0237
Wholesale food distributor
President: Louis Lacassagne
Secretary/Treasurer: Cathy Lacassagne
Estimated Sales: $13 Million
Number Employees: 25
Square Footage: 40000

57606 Ladoga Frozen Food & Retail
237 S Washington St
Ladoga, IN 47954-7019   765-942-2225
Frozen meat including beef and pork; wholesaler/distributor of fruit and vegetables
President: Harold Lowe
Number Employees: 5-9
Type of Packaging: Consumer, Food Service
Types of Products Distributed:
  Frozen Food, Produce

57607 Lady Baltimore of Missouri
PO Box 175001
Kansas City, KS 66117-5001 417-866-0766
        Fax: 417-866-6733
Wholesaler/distributor of cookies, breads, cakes, snack foods, fresh fruit, produce, fresh and frozen meats, frozen foods, dairy products, chemicals, paper goods and restaurant equipment
General Manager: Steve Butts
Director Purchasing: Gary Lindley
Estimated Sales: $5-10 Million
Number Employees: 100-249
Parent Co: Lady Baltimore Foods
Types of Products Distributed:
  Frozen Food, General Line, General Merchandise, Provisions/Meat, Produce, Cookies, breads, cakes, etc.

57608 Laetitia Vineyard & Winery
453 Laetitia Vineyard Dr
Arroyo Grande, CA 93420-9701 805-481-1772
        Fax: 805-481-6920 888-809-8463
        info@laetitiawine.com www.laetitiawine.com
Wine
President & Head Winemaker: Eric Hickey
HR Executive: Jan Wilkinson
jan@laetitiawine.com
Marketing Coordinator: Jackie Ross
Division Sales Manager: Tabitha Alger
Operations: Dave Hickey
President & Head Winemaker: Eric Hickey
Estimated Sales: Below $5 Million
Number Employees: 50-99
Private Brands Carried:
  Barnwood; Laztitia; Avila

57609 Lafayette Restaurant Supply, Inc.
319 Industrial Pkwy
Lafayette, LA 70508   337-235-4534
        Fax: 337-234-1803 sales@lafrest.com
        www.lrsfoodservice.com
Wholesaler/distributor of tabletop supplies and equipment; serving the food service market
Owner: Herman Thibeaux
VP: Herman Thibeaux, Jr.
Contact: Morgan Lejeune
morgan@lafrest.com
Estimated Sales: $1.5 Million
Number Employees: 10
Type of Packaging: Private Label, Bulk
Types of Products Distributed:
  Food Service, Frozen Food, General Merchandise, Tabletop supplies & equipment

57610 Lafitte Seafood Company
5165 Caroline Street
Lafitte, LA 70067   504-689-2041
        Fax: 504-689-4149 info@lffc.net
        www.lafittefrozenfoods.com
Wholesaler/distributor of seafood
Owner: Hai Duong
Manager: Danny Dupont
Estimated Sales: $1-3 Million
Number Employees: 5-9
Types of Products Distributed:
  Frozen Food, Seafood

57611 Lairamore Corp
3304 Hendricks Blvd
Fort Smith, AR 72903-5464   479-646-6895
        Fax: 479-646-1165 lairamore.com
Janitorial supplies including brooms
President: Glynn Shults
Manager: Christi Smith
christi@lairamore.com
Estimated Sales: $1-2.5 Million
Number Employees: 5-9
Types of Products Distributed:
  Frozen Food, General Merchandise, Janitorial supplies

57612 Laird Plastics
700 Industrial Avenue
6 & 7
Ottawa, ON K1G 0Y9
Canada   613-247-9518
        Fax: 613-247-9612 877-227-2296
        www.laird-plastics.com
Wholesaler/distributor of plastic meat-cutting boards, glass boards, acrylic items, etc
General Manager: Mark Yorke
Private Brands Carried:
  Kemlite
Types of Products Distributed:
  Frozen Food, General Merchandise

57613 Laird Plastics Inc
123 Frost St # 1
Unit 2
Westbury, NY 11590-5027   516-334-1124
        Fax: 516-334-6928 800-873-8421
        ny@lairdplastics.com www.lairdplastics.com
Wholesaler/distributor of plastic sheets, rods, tubes, film, foam, panels and adhesives for plastic food containers
Manager: John Demasi
jdemasi@lairdplastics.com
Branch Manager: Mike Grimm
Manager: Mike Grimm
Manager: John Demasi
jdemasi@lairdplastics.com
Estimated Sales: $5-10 Million
Number Employees: 10-19
Types of Products Distributed:
  Frozen Food, General Merchandise

57614 Lake Charles Poultry
2808 Fruge St
Lake Charles, LA 70615-3699 337-433-6818
        Fax: 318-433-7855
Poultry
President: Danny Bellard
Estimated Sales: $5-10 Million
Number Employees: 5-9

57615 Lake Superior Fish Co
1507 N 1st St
Superior, WI 54880-1146   715-392-3101
        Fax: 715-392-5586
Wholesaler/distributor of herring and smelt; serving the food service market
Owner: Richard Martin
rmartin@lakesuperiorfish.com
Estimated Sales: Less Than $500,000
Number Employees: 1-4
Square Footage: 150000
Types of Products Distributed:
  Seafood, Freshwater Fish: Fresh, Frozen, Smoked

57616 Lake Wales Citrus Growers Associates
20205 U.S. 27
Lake Wales, FL 33853   863-676-1411
        Fax: 863-678-1024 www.floridasnatural.com
Wholesaler/distributor of citrus fruit
General Manager: Erroll Fielding
Sales Manager: Jerry Edmonds
Sales: Mark Bryan
Private Brands Carried:
  Prince of Wales; Crown Jewel; Highland Queen
Types of Products Distributed:
  Frozen Food, Produce, Citrus fruit

Wholesalers & Distributors / A-Z

57617 Lakeside Packing Company
657 County Road #50
Harrow, ON N0R 1G0
Canada
519-738-2314
Fax: 519-738-3684 info@lakesidepacking.com
www.lakesidepacking.com
Pickles, peppers, relish, salsa, tomatoes
President/Board Member: Donald Woodbridge
VP/Board Member: Alan Woodbridge
Estimated Sales: $813,000
Number Employees: 20
Type of Packaging: Consumer, Food Service
Number of Customer Locations: 600
Types of Products Distributed:
Frozen Food, General Line, Jams & apple juice

57618 (HQ)Lamb Cooperative Inc
372 Danbury Rd
#207
Wilton, CT 06897-2523
203-529-9100
Fax: 203-529-9101 800-438-5262
www.lambcompany.com
Importer and wholesaler/distributor of frozen and refridgerated lamb, beef, venison, goat and mutton.
President: Tony Ruffo
Vice President of Sales and Marketing: John Dolan
Estimated Sales: $10-20 Million
Number Employees: 10-19
Number of Brands: 2
Type of Packaging: Consumer, Food Service
Other Locations:
The NZ & Aus Lamb Company LTD
Etobicoke, ON, CanadaNew Zealand Lamb Company
Compton, CAThe NZ & Aus Lamb Company LTDRichmond, BC, Canada
Private Brands Carried:
New Zealand Spring Lamb, Opal Valley
Number of Customer Locations: 5
Types of Products Distributed:
Food Service, Frozen Food, Provisions/Meat

57619 Lamm Food Service
3219 NW Evangeline Thruway
Lafayette, LA 70507
337-896-0331
Fax: 337-896-9213 800-223-7752
www.lammfoods.com
Full line food service distributor.
Year Founded: 1972
Estimated Sales: $50-100 Million
Number Employees: 50-99

57620 Lancaster Johnson Company
13031 US Highway 19 N
Clearwater, FL 33764
727-796-5622
Fax: 727-799-1572 800- 4-3 90
www.johnson-lancaster.com
Wholesaler/distributor of food service equipment
President: Gerald Lancaster
Sr. Estimator: Barbara Hacker
Project Manager: Penny Minich
Estimated Sales: $2.5-5 Million
Number Employees: 10-19
Square Footage: 80000
Types of Products Distributed:
Frozen Food, General Merchandise, Equipment

57621 Lancaster Poultry
324 E Wheeling St
Lancaster, OH 43130
740-653-5223
Fax: 740-653-8679
Wholesaler/distributor of provisions/meats; serving the food service market
President: Julia Farmer
Estimated Sales: $5-10 Million
Number Employees: 20-49
Private Brands Carried:
Farmer Brown's
Types of Products Distributed:
Food Service, Frozen Food, Provisions/Meat

57622 Lancer
1150 Emma Oaks Trail
Ste 140
Lake Mary, FL 32746-7120
407-327-8488
Fax: 407-327-1229 800-332-1855
sales@lancer.com www.lancer.com
Wholesaler/distributor and exporter of industrial glassware and instrument washers
Manager: Michael Henley
Technical Sales: Patrick Grady
Contact: Tim Benton
tim.benton@lancer.com
Estimated Sales: $2.5-5 Million
Number Employees: 10-19
Parent Co: Lancer Industries S.A.
Private Brands Carried:
Lancer
Types of Products Distributed:
Frozen Food, General Merchandise, Industrial glassware & washers

57623 (HQ)Land O'Frost Inc.
16850 Chicago Ave.
Lansing, IL 60438
708-474-7100
Fax: 708-474-9329 800-323-3308
www.landofrost.com
Lunch and deli meats such as; beef, chicken, turkey, ham and meat ingredients.
President: Charles Niementowski
Chairman/CEO: Donna Van Eekeren
Chief Financial Officer: George Smolar
Director of Quality Control: Dayna Nicholas
Estimated Sales: $103.6 Million
Number Employees: 500-999
Square Footage: 100000
Type of Packaging: Consumer, Food Service, Private Label
Private Brands Carried:
Land O'Frost
Types of Products Distributed:
Food Service, Provisions/Meat

57624 Land's End Seafood
38 Landing Road
Swanquarter, NC 27885
252-926-2801
Fax: 252-926-2801
Wholesaler/distributor of fresh and frozen soft-shell crabs vacuum packed in foam trays
President: A Sewell
VP: T Sewell
Number Employees: 5-9
Square Footage: 40000
Types of Products Distributed:
Frozen Food, Seafood, Vacuum packed soft-shell crabs

57625 Land-O-Sun Dairies
3939 W Market Street
Greensboro, NC 27407-1303
336-299-0221
Fax: 336-299-0870 www.petdairy.com
Wholesaler/distributor of ice cream
Operations Manager: Will Wright
Number Employees: 10-19
Square Footage: 16000
Parent Co: Land-O-Sun
Private Brands Carried:
Biltmore Brand; Pet
Types of Products Distributed:
General Line, Ice cream

57626 Landmark Coffee
44 Visitacion Ave
#104
Brisbane, CA 94005
415-821-6710
Fax: 415-508-0485 800-821-8184
jim@landmarkcoffee.com
www.landmarkcoffee.com
Wholesaler/distributor of gourmet coffee. High quality, high volume specialits primary outlets: cash and carry and club stores
President/CEO: Jim Landman
CFO: Doris Landman
Estimated Sales: $1-3 Million
Number Employees: 1-4
Type of Packaging: Consumer
Private Brands Carried:
Landmark; Telegraph Hill
Number of Customer Locations: 45
Types of Products Distributed:
Gourmet Coffee Beans

57627 Landphair Meat & Seafood
11145 US Highway 441
Tavares, FL 32778-4647
352-343-5950
Fax: 352-343-5950
Wholesaler/distributor of frozen foods, meat products and seafood; serving the food service market
Owner: Stuart Todd
Estimated Sales: Less Than $500,000
Number Employees: 1-4
Parent Co: Charles Landphair
Types of Products Distributed:
Food Service, Frozen Food, Provisions/Meat, Seafood

57628 Landsberg Kent
1640 S Greenwood Ave
Montebello, CA 90640-6538
323-721-0190
Fax: 323-721-0190 888-526-3723
websupport@landsberg.com www.landsberg.com
Wholesaler/distributor of paper products including bags and boxes
V.P. Sls.: Winston Bowman
Executive: Jed Wockenfuss
Contact: Vivian Alvarez
valvarez@landsberg.com
Number Employees: 5-9
Types of Products Distributed:
Frozen Food, General Merchandise, Paper boxes & bags

57629 Lane Equipment Co
2030 Richmond Ave
Houston, TX 77098-3424
713-529-5761
Fax: 713-529-1249 www.7laneequipment.com
Wholesaler/distributor of equipment; serving the food service market
President: Lin Laney
lin@laneequipment.com
Estimated Sales: $10-20 Million
Number Employees: 50-99
Types of Products Distributed:
Food Service, Frozen Food, General Merchandise

57630 Lane Equipment Co
1507 West Ave
San Antonio, TX 78201-3506
210-736-1616
Fax: 210-736-5487 855-326-9748
Wholesaler/distributor of freezers, ice makers, etc.; serving the food service market
Branch Manager: Jim Raglin
jim@laneequipment.com
Sales Manager: Branden Cummins
Estimated Sales: $10-20 Million
Number Employees: 10-19
Parent Co: Lane Equipment Company
Private Brands Carried:
Taylor; Ice Craft; Beverage-Air
Types of Products Distributed:
Food Service, Frozen Food, General Merchandise, Freezers, ice makers, etc.

57631 Lang's Chocolates
350 Pine St.
Williamsport, PA 17701
570-323-6320
info@langschocolates.com
www.langschocolates.com
Gourmet handcrafted chocolates and confections
Master Chocolatier: William Lang
Types of Products Distributed:
General Line

57632 Langley Corporation
PO Box 3010
Burlington, MA 001803-071
800-225-4499
Fax: 800-343-4291
Wholesaler/distributor material handling equipment including carts, handtrucks, conveyors, etc.; also, bins and shelving, plus stainless items
President: James Cook
Vice President: Steve McLeod
Marketing Specialist: William Mokeler
Number Employees: 50-99
Number of Brands: 1000
Types of Products Distributed:
Frozen Food, General Merchandise, Bins, shelving, carts, handtrucks, etc.

57633 Lantev Distributing Corporation
460 Kent Avenue
Brooklyn, NY 11211-5922
718-599-1900
Fax: 718-599-6307
Wholesaler/distributor of kosher vitamins, minerals, herbs, candy, tea, pasta and rice cakes; serving the retail market
President: Hyman Landau
CEO: Saul Landau
Purchasing Manager: Wolf Landan
Estimated Sales: $2.5-5 Million
Number Employees: 20-49
Number of Products: 100
Square Footage: 120000
Type of Packaging: Consumer, Private Label
Private Brands Carried:
Landau; Taanug; Navitco
Number of Customer Locations: 1000

Wholesalers & Distributors / A-Z

Types of Products Distributed:
Frozen Food, General Line, Kosher vitamins, minerals, etc.

57634 (HQ)Lanzarotta Wholesale Grocers
10 Ronrose Drive
Vaughan, ON L4K 4R3
Canada   905-669-9814
              Fax: 905-669-9570
Wholesaler/distributor of soft drinks, cocktail juices, cookies, peanut butter, coffee, tortilla chips, salsa, frozen foods, dairy products, confectionery, store supplies, sundries, etc.; serving the food service market
President/CEO: Mike Commisso
Chairman: J Gennaro
VP Sales/Marketing/Merchandising: Cosmo Stalteri
Number Employees: 250-499
Square Footage: 900000
Other Locations:
Lanzarotta Wholesale Grocers
Mississauga, ONLanzarotta Wholesale Grocers
Private Brands Carried:
Our Very Own
Number of Customer Locations: 350
Types of Products Distributed:
Food Service, Frozen Food, General Line, General Merchandise, Seafood, Beverages, cookies, chips, salsa, etc.

57635 Laredo Tortilleria & Mexican
1616 Woodside Ave
Fort Wayne, IN 46816-3942   260-447-2576
       Fax: 219-447-2577 800-252-7336
http://www.laredomexicanfoods.com
Processor and wholesaler/distributor of Mexican food products including salsa, tortillas and tortilla chips; serving the food service market
President: Benito Trevino
General Manager: Raul Trevino
VP: Reynol Trevino
Manager: Frank Trevino
Estimated Sales: Less Than $500,000
Number Employees: 1-4
Parent Co: Tregar
Type of Packaging: Consumer, Food Service, Private Label, Bulk
Types of Products Distributed:
Food Service, Frozen Food, General Line, Specialty Foods, Tortillas & tortilla chips

57636 Larick Associates
39 Seaview Ln
Port Washington, NY 11050-1737   516-883-1489
       Fax: 516-883-1682 sales@larick.com
                              www.larick.com
Wholesaler/distributor of advertising specialties, awards, calendars, incentives, premiums and business gifts; also, popcorn
Owner/President: Nancy Larick
sales@larick.com
Estimated Sales: $2.5-5 Million
Number Employees: 1-4
Number of Customer Locations: 500
Types of Products Distributed:
Frozen Food, General Line, General Merchandise, Advertising specialties & popcorn

57637 Larimore Bean Company
PO Box 607
Larimore, ND 58251   701-343-6363
                Fax: 701-343-2842
Wholesaler/distributor of produce
Owner: Ronald Carlson
Estimated Sales: $10-20 Million
Number Employees: 1-4
Types of Products Distributed:
Frozen Food, Produce

57638 Larry J. Williams Company
2686 Savannah Hwy
Jesup, GA 31545-5511   912-427-7729
                Fax: 912-427-0611
Shrimp, crab, oysters, scallps, flounder, etc.
President: Larry Williams
l.williams@larryjwilliams.com
General Manager: Joey Williams
Estimated Sales: $1-3 Million
Number Employees: 20-49

57639 Larry Martindale Company
9724 W 89th Ter
Overland Park, KS 66212-4733   800-771-6205
                Fax: 913-381-7605
Wholesaler/distributor of equipment and supplies; serving the food service market
Owner: Larry Martindale
Private Brands Carried:
First Spice Mixing; Paraclipse
Number of Customer Locations: 200
Types of Products Distributed:
Food Service, Frozen Food, General Merchandise, Equipment & supplies

57640 Larry's Beans
1509 Gavin St
Raleigh, NC 27608-2613   919-828-1234
    Fax: 919-833-4567 www.laryscoffee.com
Wholesale coffee roaster
Owner: Charles Nichols
CFO: Brad Lienhart
VP: Kevin Bobal
Marketing: Kyley Schmidt
Sales: Erik Iverson
charlesnichols@larrysbeans.com
Plant Manager: Neal England
Estimated Sales: $3.0 Million
Number Employees: 10-19

57641 Lartigue Seafood
23043 Perdido Beach Blvd
Orange Beach, AL 36561   251-948-2644
Seafood. Founded in 1979
President: Paul Lartigue Jr
Vice President: Paul Lartigue
Number Employees: 5

57642 Latah Creek Wine Cellar
13030 E Indiana Ave
Spokane Valley, WA 99216-1118   509-926-0164
    Fax: 509-926-0710 www.latahcreek.com
Wines
President: Mike Conway
info@latahcreek.com
VP: Ellena Conway
Estimated Sales: $340,000
Number Employees: 5-9
Type of Packaging: Private Label

57643 Latouraine Coffee Company
9090 Bank Street
Cleveland, OH 44125-3426   800-362-0671
                Fax: 216-267-3912
Wholesaler/distributor of tea, coffee, fruit drinks and hot chocolate; serving the food service market
Branch Manager: Steve Dryer
Number Employees: 10-19
Types of Products Distributed:
Food Service, Frozen Food, General Line, Tea, coffee, fruit drinks, etc.

57644 Laurell Hill Provision Company
Brewery Ln
Greensburg, PA 15601   724-834-1660
                Fax: 724-832-8471
Wholesaler/distributor of frozen foods, general line products and provisions/meats
Owner/President: Jerry Moyer
Estimated Sales: $2.5-5 Million
Number Employees: 5-9
Private Brands Carried:
All-Kitchen
Types of Products Distributed:
General Line, Provisions/Meat

57645 Lavella Brothers
723 W 3rd St
Chester, PA 19013-3807   610-874-6256
                Fax: 610-874-6259
Wholesaler/distributor of produce
Owner: Joseph Lavella
joseph@nightowlprod.com
Estimated Sales: $.5-1 million
Number Employees: 1-4
Types of Products Distributed:
Produce

57646 Lavin Candy Company
PO Box 2863
Plattsburgh, NY 12901-0259   518-563-4630
                Fax: 518-563-4778
Wholesaler/distributor of general merchandise, groceries, meat, bakery goods and health and beauty aids

President: Irvin Reid Jr
Chairman: I Reid, Sr.
VP: P Reid
Estimated Sales: $10-20 Million
Number Employees: 20-49
Square Footage: 46500
Private Brands Carried:
Wise; Snakline
Number of Customer Locations: 800
Types of Products Distributed:
General Line, General Merchandise, Provisions/Meat, Snack foods

57647 Lawrence Lapide
26 Brooklyn Terminal Market
Brooklyn, NY 11236   718-763-3665
       Fax: 718-763-1576 800-722-3665
Wholesaler/distributor of produce including watermelons and grapes
President: John Lapide
Contact: Patty Oesterle
pattyoesterle@gmail.com
Estimated Sales: $10-20 Million
Number Employees: 10-19
Types of Products Distributed:
Frozen Food, Produce, Watermelons & grapes

57648 Layman Candy Company
P.O.Box 1015
Salem, VA 24153   540-986-0123
    Fax: 540-986-0756 www.laymancandy.com
Wholesaler/distributor of general line items
Owner: Juanita Neely
Estimated Sales: $20-50 Million
Number Employees: 20-49
Number of Customer Locations: 500
Types of Products Distributed:
Frozen Food, General Line

57649 Layman Distributing
1630 W Main St
PO Box 1015
Salem, VA 24153   540-389-2000
       Fax: 540-389-2062 800-237-1319
                lcc@laymandistributing.com
                www.laymandistributing.com
Processor and distributor of candy, including brittles, fudge, chocolate, chews, nut clusters and taffy; meat and dairy; and condiments.
Owner: Justin Keen
justin.keen@laymancandy.com
Vice President of Sales: Scott Thomasson
V.P. Customer Relations: Kenny Keen
Estimated Sales: $5-10 Million
Number Employees: 10-19
Number of Brands: 2028
Number of Products: 122
Square Footage: 172000
Number of Customer Locations: 320
Types of Products Distributed:
Candy

57650 Lazzaroni USA
299 Market St
Suite 160
Saddle Brook, NJ 07663-5312   201-368-1240
    Fax: 201-368-1262 www.lazzaroni-ita.com
Manufacturer and distributor of chocolates and cookies
President: Stefano Tombetti
Executive VP: Kathy Ecoffey
Contact: Theresa Strunck
tstrunck@lazzaroniusa.com

57651 Le Cordon Bleu
40 Enterprise Ave N
Secaucus, NJ 07094-2500   070-4 2-17
       Fax: 201-617-1914 800-457-2433
    gourmet@cordonbleu.net www.cordonbleu.net
Importer of gourmet foods, chef's accessories and cutlery
President: Andre Cointreau
Sales Director: Margaret Warren
Contact: Karen Dubois
kdubois@cordonbleu.edu
Estimated Sales: $500,000-$1 Million
Number Employees: 1-4
Type of Packaging: Consumer
Private Brands Carried:
Le Cordon Bleu
Types of Products Distributed:
Specialty Foods

1073

Wholesalers & Distributors / A-Z

57652 Le Smoker
321 Park Avenue
Salisbury, MD 21801-4208   410-677-3233
                Fax: 410-677-3234
Stainless steel smokers, fire place, grills, wood chips, chunks and charcoal; exporter of smokers
President: Richard Isaacs
VP: Dominique Isaacs
Number of Brands: 3
Square Footage: 12000
Type of Packaging: Food Service
Private Brands Carried:
   Robot Coupe
Types of Products Distributed:
   Frozen Food, General Merchandise, Food processing & packaging equipment

57653 Leading Brands of Canada
33 West 8th Avenue
Vancouver, BC V5Y 1M8
Canada   604-685-5200
        Fax: 604-685-5245   866-685-5200
           rmcrae@leadingbrandsinc.com
Packaging, distribution, sales, merchandising and brand management of juices, water, soft drinks, new age beverages, snack food and confectionery items
President/CEO: Ralph McRae
COO: Dave Read
Senior VP: Derek Henrey
Director Marketing: Joanne Saunders
Asst. VP/General Manager: Jody Christopherson
Parent Co: Leading Brands
Private Brands Carried:
   Everfresh; Ocean Spray
Types of Products Distributed:
   Frozen Food, General Line, Juices & bottled water

57654 Leali Brothers Meats
Victor Posner Boulevard
Wheatland, PA 16161   724-342-9501
                Fax: 724-342-1267
Wholesaler/distributor of frozen foods, general line products, provisions/meats and seafood; serving the food service market
Co-Owner: John Leali
Estimated Sales: $5-10 Million
Number Employees: 10-19
Types of Products Distributed:
   Food Service, Frozen Food, General Line, Provisions/Meat, Seafood

57655 (HQ)Lebermuth Company
14000 McKinley Highway
Mishawaka, IN 46545   574-259-7000
        Fax: 574-258-7450   800-648-1213
           info@lebermuth.com www.lebermuth.com
Fragrance and flavor company
President: Rob Brown
CEO: Irvin Brown
Vice President: Alan Brown
Contact: Jodi Aker
jaker@lebermuth.com
Production Manager: Mike Ryan
Plant Manager: Robert Hall
Purchasing Manager: Jim Gates
Estimated Sales: $5-10 Million
Number Employees: 50
Square Footage: 180000
Type of Packaging: Bulk
Types of Products Distributed:
   Spices & Herbs

57656 Leblanc Seafood
PO Box 509
Lafitte, LA 70067-0509   504-689-2631
                Fax: 504-689-4503
Seafood

57657 Lee County Equipment LLC
1104 US Hwy 19 S
Leesburg, GA 31763   229-483-0002
                Fax: 229-483-0005
           henry@leecountyequipmentllc.com
           www.leecountyequipmentllc.com
Wholesaler/distributor of trucking and agriculture equipment.
Estimated Sales: $50-100 Million
Number Employees: 50-99
Square Footage: 135000
Number of Customer Locations: 1200
Types of Products Distributed:
   Food Service

57658 Lee Foods
1948 Kellogg Ave
Carlsbad, CA 92008-6581   760-603-8395
                Fax: 760-603-8396
Wholesaler/distributor of produce and groceries; serving the food service market
President: Rod Mehin
Estimated Sales: $2.5-5 Million
Number Employees: 1-4
Private Brands Carried:
   Pocahontas
Number of Customer Locations: 320
Types of Products Distributed:
   Food Service, Frozen Food, General Line, Produce, Groceries

57659 Lee Grocery Company
4949 SW Meadows Rd
Lake Oswego, OR 97035-4285   503-675-8878
                Fax: 425-349-2578
Wholesaler/distributor of poultry, fish, meats, frozen foods, equipment and general line products; serving the food service market
Owner: James Lee
COO: N Gruel
CFO: Bob Loeffler
Estimated Sales: $300,000-500,000
Number Employees: 5-9
Square Footage: 440000
Number of Customer Locations: 710
Types of Products Distributed:
   Food Service, Frozen Food, General Line, General Merchandise, Provisions/Meat, Seafood, Specialty Foods, Poultry & fish

57660 Lee Packaging Corporation
1133 Old County Rd
San Carlos, CA 94070-4009   650-637-1788
        Fax: 650-637-0185   800-655-3394
Wholesaler/distributor of packaging materials including plastic and polyethylene bags, corrugated boxes and cartons, containers, gummed tapes, pressure sensitive and printed metal labels, interior cushioning and point of purchasedisplays
President: Guy Lee
Secretary/Treasurer: Carol Lee
Customer Service Manager: Betty Anderson
Estimated Sales: $300,000-500,000
Number Employees: 1-4
Square Footage: 4000
Private Brands Carried:
   Jetran; Sus-Rap; Load-Rite Pallets
Types of Products Distributed:
   Frozen Food, General Merchandise, Packaging materials

57661 Leedal Inc
3453 Commercial Ave
Northbrook, IL 60062-1818   847-498-0111
        Fax: 847-498-0198   sink@leedal.com
           www.consolidateddoorintl.com
Manufacturer, importer and exporter of pot and pan washers, disposers, power scrubbers, wire shelving, hot dog cookers, and steam tables
President: Aj Levin
ajlevin@hotmail.com
CFO: Sheldon Levin
Vice President: A Levin
Quality Control: Levin
Sales Director: Josie Negron
Estimated Sales: $5-10 Million
Number Employees: 20-49
Square Footage: 28000
Type of Packaging: Consumer, Food Service, Private Label, Bulk
Types of Products Distributed:
   General Merchandise

57662 Left Hand Brewing Co
1265 Boston Ave
Longmont, CO 80501-5809   303-772-0258
        Fax: 303-772-9572   brewer@lefthandbrewing.com
           www.pourhard.com
Processor and wholesaler/distributor of English style ale, stout and porter; also, German style lager and weiss beer
Owner: John Lindberg
jlindberg@boss-cellular.com
Quality Control: Andy Brown
Marketing/Sales/Public Relations: Chris Lennert
Operations Manager: Joe Schiraldi
Estimated Sales: Below $5 Million
Number Employees: 50-99
Square Footage: 52000
Type of Packaging: Food Service, Bulk
Types of Products Distributed:
   Frozen Food

57663 Legacy Beverage Systems
948 Freeway Drive North
Columbus, OH 43229   877-898-0090
                Fax: 877-503-2018
Wholesaler/distributor of soft drinks, bag-in-box juices, syrups, beer, liquor and coffee systems; also, ice making equipment installation and service available
Office Manager: Sue Wyatt
General Manager: Michael Kennis
Service Manager: Rich Evans
Estimated Sales: $2.5-5 Million
Number Employees: 5-9
Square Footage: 6000
Parent Co: Polar Bear
Types of Products Distributed:
   Food Service, Frozen Food, General Line, General Merchandise, Beverage systems & beverages

57664 Legacy Juice Works
382 Broadway
Saratoga Springs, NY 12866   518-583-1108
           juice@saratogajuicebar.com
           saratogajuicebar.com
Wellness shots, cleanses and cold pressed juices
Co-Owner: Colin MacLean
Type of Packaging: Consumer

57665 Lehmann-Colorado
225 Commercial Avenue
Palisades Park, NJ 07650-1174   201-461-9500
                Fax: 201-461-9506
Wholesaler/distributor of meats, poultry, veal, pork and frozen seafood
Estimated Sales: $20-50 Million
Number Employees: 20-49
Square Footage: 20
Types of Products Distributed:
   Frozen Food, Provisions/Meat, Seafood, Veal, poultry, pork, etc.

57666 Leichtman Ice Cream Company
175 N Vine St Apt 3b
Hazleton, PA 18201   570-454-2428
                Fax: 570-454-2540
Wholesaler/distributor of ice cream
VP: Richard Osepchuk
Estimated Sales: $5-10 Million
Number Employees: 10-19
Types of Products Distributed:
   Frozen Food, Ice cream

57667 Lello Appliances Corp
355 Murray Hill Pkwy # 204
East Rutherford, NJ 07073-2139   201-939-2555
        Fax: 201-939-5074   gbuzzi1063@aol.com
Importer and wholesaler/distributor of food service equipment; serving the food service market
President: G Bucci
lelloappliances@aol.com
Estimated Sales: $5-10 Million
Number Employees: 1-4
Type of Packaging: Food Service
Private Brands Carried:
   Gaggia; Lello
Types of Products Distributed:
   Food Service, Frozen Food, General Merchandise, Foodservice equipment

57668 Lemark Promotional Products
5 Brandywine Dr
Deer Park, NY 11729   631-242-3450
                Fax: 631-242-3499
Wholesaler/distributor of advertising specialties, candies, chocolates, food baskets, popcorn and promotional items; also, custom imprinting available
VP: David Peskin
Estimated Sales: $5-10 Million
Number Employees: 10-19
Square Footage: 12800
Number of Customer Locations: 2000
Types of Products Distributed:
   Frozen Food, General Line, General Merchandise, Advertising specialties

57669 Lemberger Candy Corporation
160 E Midland Ave
Paramus, NJ 07652 201-261-3718
Fax: 201-261-8614 800-977-9921
chocaidlemberger@aol.com
Importer of over 100 unique chocolate novelties
President: David Lemberger
Estimated Sales: $1-3 Million
Number Employees: 1-4
Number of Brands: 2
Number of Products: 100
Type of Packaging: Consumer
Private Brands Carried:
   Choc-Aid; Gumi-Aid; Chocolate Crayons; Chocolate Film
Number of Customer Locations: 3000
Types of Products Distributed:
   Specialty Foods

57670 Lemke Wholesale
1225 N 8th St
Rogers, AR 72756 479-751-4671
Fax: 501-751-4671
Variety of food products.
President: Arnold E Lemke
Secretary: Lorene Lemke
Vice-President: Ronald Lemke

57671 Lems
906 Texas Court
Hutchinson, KS 67502-5136 316-662-4287
Wholesaler/distributor of Oriental foods including sweet and sour, teriyaki, lemon and chili garlic sauce; also, tempura batter mix
Types of Products Distributed:
   Frozen Food, General Line, Specialty Foods, Sauces & tempura batter mix

57672 Lenox-Martell Inc
89 Heath St
Boston, MA 02130-1402 617-442-7777
Fax: 617-522-9455 877-325-2489
www.lenoxmartell.com
Processor of colas and juices; wholesaler/distributor of refrigerators and ice and soda machines; serving the food service market; also, installation and maintenance of draft beer systems available
CEO/Sales Executive: Jim Lerner
jlerner@lenoxmartell.com
Controller: David Nitishin
VP Marketing: John Dixon
Sales/Marketing: Jessica Miller
Operations Director: Rick Freitas
Year Founded: 1950
Estimated Sales: $8 Million
Number Employees: 50-99
Square Footage: 120000
Types of Products Distributed:
   Food Service, Frozen Food, General Merchandise, Refrigerators and ice & soda machines

57673 Lenson Coffee & Tea Company
PO Box 1103
Pleasantville, NJ 08232-6103 609-646-3003
Fax: 609-646-8606
Coffee; wholesaler/distributor of tea; serving the food service market
Owner: Jimmie Anderson
Estimated Sales: $5-10 Million
Number Employees: 20-49
Type of Packaging: Consumer, Food Service, Private Label
Types of Products Distributed:
   Food Service, Frozen Food, General Line, Tea

57674 Leo A Dick & Sons
935 Mckinley Ave NW
Canton, OH 44703-2072 330-452-5010
Fax: 330-452-0527
Wholesaler/distributor of specialty foods
Partner: B Dick
Partner: P Dick
Manager: L Dick
Estimated Sales: $5-10 Million
Number Employees: 10-19
Square Footage: 104000
Number of Customer Locations: 250
Types of Products Distributed:
   Frozen Food, Specialty Foods

57675 Leon Supply Company
34 Mechanic St # 205
Worcester, MA 01608-2424 508-799-4461
Fax: 508-799-6522 www.leonsupply.com
Wholesaler/distributor of groceries, frozen foods, private label items and paper goods; serving the food service market
President: Edward Williams
Administrative VP: Deborah Johnson
Executive VP: Elaine Williams
Estimated Sales: $5-10 Million
Number Employees: 20-49
Square Footage: 108000
Private Brands Carried:
   All Kitchens
Number of Customer Locations: 600
Types of Products Distributed:
   Food Service, Frozen Food, General Line, General Merchandise, Groceries, paper goods, etc.

57676 Leonard & Sons Shrimp Company
902 Anastasia Blvd
St Augustine, FL 32080-4663 904-829-5909
Fax: 904-829-5909
Wholesaler/distributor of seafood
Owner: Kevin Leonardi
Manager: Laverne Ratliff
Estimated Sales: $1-3 Million
Number Employees: 1-4
Types of Products Distributed:
   Frozen Food, Seafood

57677 Leonetti's Frozen Food
5935 Woodland Ave
Philadelphia, PA 19143-5919 215-729-4200
Fax: 215-729-7581 866-551-7168
leonettifrozenfo@aol.com www.beststromboli.com
Frozen stromboli and calzones
President: Beth Di Pietro
leonettifrozenfo@aol.com
Plant Manager: Leroy Douglas
Estimated Sales: $1500000
Number Employees: 20-49
Square Footage: 132000
Type of Packaging: Consumer, Food Service, Private Label, Bulk
Types of Products Distributed:
   Food Service, Frozen Food

57678 Leonidas
485 Madison Ave # 4
New York, NY 10022-5803 212-980-2608
Fax: 212-980-2609 800-900-2462
Importer and wholesaler/distributor of Belgian pralines, solid chocolate wafers and chocolates; serving the food service market
President: Noel Duchateau
General Manager/VP: Jacques Bergier
sales@leonidas-chocolate.com
VP: Jacques Bergier
Estimated Sales: $500,000-$1 Million
Number Employees: 10-19
Square Footage: 3600
Type of Packaging: Consumer, Food Service, Bulk
Types of Products Distributed:
   Food Service, Frozen Food, General Line, Candy: pralines, chocolate wafers, etc.

57679 Les Boulangers AssociesInc
18842 13th Pl S
Seatac, WA 98148-2399 206-241-9343
Fax: 206-433-2844 800-522-1185
www.lba-inc.com
Wholesaler/distributor of frozen baked goods including danishes, croissants, etc
Co-Owner/President: Michel Robert
michel@lba-inc.com
Estimated Sales: $5-10 Million
Number Employees: 20-49
Types of Products Distributed:
   Frozen Food, General Line, Danishes, croissants, etc.

57680 Lesaffre Yeast Corporation
7475 W Main St.
Milwaukee, WI 53214 414-615-4094
800-770-2714
www.lesaffreyeast.com
Yeast
President & CEO: John Riesch
Parent Co: Lesaffre Group
Types of Products Distributed:
   General Line

57681 Lesco Supply Company
14731 S Kedzie Ave
Posen, IL 60469-1433 708-385-0101
Fax: 708-385-3335
Wholesaler/distributor of food service equipment and supplies, frozen foods and general merchandise; serving the food service market
Owner: Russell Nezbit
Secretary/Treasurer: Carolyn Reid
VP/General Manager: Reuben Contreras
Estimated Sales: $1-3 Million
Number Employees: 5-9
Square Footage: 80000
Types of Products Distributed:
   Food Service, Frozen Food, General Line, General Merchandise, Foodservice equipment & supplies, etc.

57682 Levant
3390 Rand Road
S Plainfield, NJ 07080-1307 908-754-1166
Fax: 908-754-9666 www.levantpdx.com
Wholesaler/distributor and importer of spices, dried fruits and nuts
President: Reha Guzelay
Contact: Ray Guzelay
ray@levantinc.com
Estimated Sales: $2.5-5 Million
Number Employees: 1-4
Square Footage: 80000
Private Brands Carried:
   Levant
Types of Products Distributed:
   Frozen Food, Health Food, Specialty Foods, Spices, dried fruits & nuts

57683 Levin Brothers Paper
1325 S Cicero Ave
Cicero, IL 60804 708-652-5600
Fax: 708-780-6975 800-545-6200
clutch@idt.net www.lbpmfg.com
Corrugated boxes, tape and packaging materials; wholesaler/distributor of paper products and restaurant supplies
President: Barry Silverstein
CFO: Mike Schaechter
VP: Matthew Cook
Quality Control: Larry Rosenberg
Contact: Suliman Abdallah
abdallah@lbpmfg.com
Estimated Sales: $10-20 Million
Number Employees: 10-19
Square Footage: 250000
Types of Products Distributed:
   Frozen Food, General Merchandise, Paper products & restaurant supplies

57684 Lew Sander Inc
3401 N 5th St
Philadelphia, PA 19140-4501 215-739-3228
Fax: 215-739-7075 sales@sandersupply.com
www.sandersupply.bizland.com
Wholesaler/distributor of bakery and confectionery equipment and supplies; serving the food service market
Owner: Lew Sander
Estimated Sales: Less Than $500,000
Number Employees: 1-4
Square Footage: 740000
Types of Products Distributed:
   Food Service, Frozen Food, General Merchandise, Bakery/confectionery equipment, etc.

57685 Lewis & McDermott
1294 San Pablo Avenue
Berkeley, CA 94706-2218 510-525-5447
Wholesaler/distributor of meats; serving the food service market
President: Mike McDermott
Manager: Jim McDermott
Estimated Sales: $10-20 Million
Number Employees: 5-9
Number of Customer Locations: 60
Types of Products Distributed:
   Food Service, Frozen Food, Provisions/Meat

57686 Lewis Brothers & Sons
3300 Penn Ave
Pittsburgh, PA 15201 412-683-8500
Fax: 412-683-8550
Wholesaler/distributor of food service equipment; serving the food service market
President: Sam Lewis

Wholesalers & Distributors / A-Z

Estimated Sales: $5-10 Million
Number Employees: 10-19
Private Brands Carried:
  Libby Glass; Lincoln Wearever; Vollrath
Types of Products Distributed:
  Food Service, Frozen Food, General Merchandise, Foodservice equipment

57687 Lewisburg Wholesale Company
PO Box 38
Roncevert, WV 24970-0038 304-645-1500
  Fax: 304-645-1500 800-539-4080
Wholesaler/distributor of groceries, meat, produce, dairy products, frozen foods, equipment and fixtures, etc.; serving the food service market
President: M Moss
Estimated Sales: $1-3 Million
Number Employees: 5-9
Square Footage: 180000
Number of Customer Locations: 500
Types of Products Distributed:
  Food Service, General Line, General Merchandise, Provisions/Meat, Produce

57688 Lexington Foodservice
132 Trade St # A
Lexington, KY 40511-2635 859-254-3444
  Fax: 859-233-9335
Wholesaler/distributor of produce and frozen foods; serving the food service market
President: Donald Sundberg
Estimated Sales: $5-10 Million
Number Employees: 10-19
Types of Products Distributed:
  Food Service, Frozen Food, Produce

57689 Liberto Management Co Inc
621 S Flores St
San Antonio, TX 78204-1220 210-226-4168
  Fax: 210-226-6453 www.ricos.com
Wholesaler/distributor of meats, groceries, cleaning supplies, disposables, wraps and equipment; serving the food service market
President: Keith Belton
kbelton@liberto.org
Estimated Sales: $20-50 Million
Number Employees: 50-99
Types of Products Distributed:
  Food Service, Frozen Food, General Line, General Merchandise, Provisions/Meat, Groceries, cleaning supplies, etc.

57690 Liberto of Harlington
402 S F St # 100
Harlingen, TX 78550-6570 956-423-8771
  Fax: 956-425-2607
Wholesaler/distributor of groceries, frozen foods, table top supplies and equipment; serving the food service market
General Manager: Al Taylor
Estimated Sales: $2.5-5 Million
Number Employees: 5-9
Parent Co: Liberto Management Company
Types of Products Distributed:
  Food Service, Frozen Food, General Line, General Merchandise, Tabletop supplies, equipment, etc.

57691 Liberto of Houston
4321 Old Spanish Trail
Houston, TX 77021-1637 713-747-7757
  Fax: 713-747-4423
Wholesaler/distributor of frozen food, cleaning supplies, disposables, equipment, general line products, etc.; serving the food service market
Customer Service Representative: Lloyd Carmack
Estimated Sales: $10-20 Million
Number Employees: 10-19
Types of Products Distributed:
  Food Service, Frozen Food, General Line, General Merchandise, Groceries, cleaning supplies, etc.

57692 Liberty Bell Wholesale Grocery
400 Rutherford Ave
Charlestown, MA 02129-1646 617-242-2233
  Fax: 617-241-0162
Wholesaler/distributor of general line products; serving the food service market
President: Robert Borzakian
VP: R Borzakian Jr
Estimated Sales: $2.5-5 Million
Number Employees: 1-4
Square Footage: 120000
Private Brands Carried:
  Liberty Bell; Bunkerhill
Number of Customer Locations: 100
Types of Products Distributed:
  Food Service, General Merchandise

57693 Liberty Gold Fruit Co Inc
500 Eccles Ave
S San Francisco, CA 94080-1905 650-583-4700
  Fax: 650-583-4770 timr@libertygold.com
  www.libertygold.com
Wholesaler/distributor and exporter of fruit
Owner: Harry Battatt
harry@libertygold.com
Estimated Sales: $5-10 Million
Number Employees: 10-19
Private Brands Carried:
  Ligo
Types of Products Distributed:
  Frozen Food, Produce, Fruits

57694 Liberty International WHOL
21535 Hoover Rd
Warren, MI 48089-3159 586-755-3629
  Fax: 586-755-3149 libertywholesale.com
Wholesaler/distributor of candy
Owner: Mike Dikhow
mdikhow@aol.com
Estimated Sales: $5-10 Million
Number Employees: 10-19
Private Brands Carried:
  Hershey; Mars; Nestle
Number of Customer Locations: 120
Types of Products Distributed:
  Frozen Food, General Line, Candy

57695 Liberty Marine Products
PO Box 267
Galveston, TX 77553-0267 409-762-8661
  Fax: 409-762-0931
Wholesaler/distributor of frozen food and seafood; serving the food service market
President: Danny Duzich
Estimated Sales: $3-5 Million
Number Employees: 5-9
Types of Products Distributed:
  Food Service, Frozen Food, Seafood

57696 Liberty Natural Products Inc
20949 S Harris Rd
Oregon City, OR 97045-9428 503-631-4488
  Fax: 503-631-2424 800-289-8427
  jim@libertynatural.com www.libertynatural.com
Processor and exporter of gourmet breath fresheners, natural flavors and oils; processor of vitamins; importer of essential oils and botanical extracts; wholesaler/distributor of gourmet breath fresheners
Owner: Jim Derking
Sales Manager: Tabor Helton
jim@libertynatural.com
Operations Manager: Shane Reaney
Purchasing Manager: Michelle Falls
Estimated Sales: $1-2.5 Million
Number Employees: 20-49
Square Footage: 68000
Type of Packaging: Consumer, Bulk
Types of Products Distributed:
  Frozen Food, General Line, Specialty Foods, Gourmet breath fresheners

57697 Liberty Richter
1455 Broad St
Bloomfield, NJ 07003-3047 973-338-0300
  Fax: 973-338-0382 info@worldfiner.com
  www.libertyrichter.com
Wholesaler, distributor and importer of gourmet foods including jam, balsamic vinegar, French sea salt, French olives, olive oil, soups, cookies, pickled vegetables and sugars. Customers they serve include supermarket chains independent grocers, specialty & ethnic stores, convenience stores, drug & mass market stores and foodservice.
Division President: David Billings
Marketing Manager: Killeen Hasan
Director of Sales: Mark Klarich
Contact: Dilenia Chireno
dchireno@worldfiner.com
Estimated Sales: $5-10,000,000
Number Employees: 10-19
Square Footage: 80000
Parent Co: World Finer Foods
Types of Products Distributed:
  General Line, Specialty Foods

57698 Liberty Scale Co Inc
7 Riverside Dr
Mansfield, MA 02048-2726 617-364-4600
  Fax: 508-337-5985
Wholesaler/distributor of scales including industrial and mechanical
Owner: Mel Cass
Estimated Sales: $1-2.5 Million
Number Employees: 1-4
Private Brands Carried:
  Thurman Electronics; Weig-Tronix
Types of Products Distributed:
  Frozen Food, General Merchandise, Scales: industrial & mechanical

57699 Liberty USA Inc
920 Irwin Run Rd.
West Mifflin, PA 15122
  800-289-5872
  www.libertyusa.com
Dairy and deli products, frozen food, groceries, health and beauty aids, candy and paper products.
Year Founded: 1959
Estimated Sales: $100-500 Million
Number Employees: 100-249
Parent Co: Eby-Brown Company, LLC
Number of Customer Locations: 1000
Types of Products Distributed:
  General Line, General Merchandise, Groceries, candy, paper products, etc.

57700 Libido Funk Circus
P.O.Box 2610
Orlando, FL 60462 630-294-7132
  Fax: 708-460-6076 www.lfcentertainment.com
Wholesaler/distributor, importer and exporter of game including antelope, bear, kangaroo, rattlesnake, elk, partridge, alligator, zebra, etc
CEO: Gregory A Landry
Secretary: Carmen Landry
VP Sales/Marketing: Greg Landry
Number Employees: 20-49
Parent Co: LFC
Types of Products Distributed:
  Frozen Food, Provisions/Meat, Specialty Foods, Alligator, zebra, etc.

57701 Lido Chem
20 Village Ct
Hazlet, NJ 07730-1532 732-888-8000
  Fax: 732-264-2751 www.lidochem.com
Wholesaler/distributor of sodium and potassium phosphates, citric acid and chemical additives for the food industry
President: Don Pucillo
Office Manager: Audrey Krane
Vice President: Lisa Pucillo
lpucillo@lidochem.com
VP Sales: Joseph Pucillo
Estimated Sales: $10-20 Million
Number Employees: 5-9
Square Footage: 8000
Types of Products Distributed:
  Frozen Food, Additives, phosphates, citric acid, etc

57702 Lieber Chocolate Food Prod LTD
142 44th St
Brooklyn, NY 11232-3310 718-744-0113
  Fax: 718-499-5636
Wholesaler/distributor of kosher food specialties including jams, jellies, chocolate, cookies, fruit and vegetable juices, nuts, peanut butter, potato chips, pretzels and spices
President: Hersh Beigel
Secretary/Treasurer: Mark Moskowitz
Estimated Sales: $20-50 Million
Number Employees: 5-9
Types of Products Distributed:
  Frozen Food, Specialty Foods, Kosher foods

57703 Lift Atlanta Inc
2425 Park Central Blvd
Decatur, GA 30035-3921 770-987-3200
  Fax: 770-987-5804
Wholesaler/distributor of forklifts
President: Mitchell Milovich
mitchellmilovich@liftatlanta.com
Estimated Sales: $20-50 Million
Number Employees: 50-99
Type of Packaging: Bulk
Private Brands Carried:
  Baker; Mitsubishi

Wholesalers & Distributors / A-Z

Types of Products Distributed:
Frozen Food, General Merchandise, Forklifts

57704 Lift Power
5820 Commonwealth Ave
Jacksonville, FL 32254-2206 904-783-0250
Fax: 904-781-1451 www.liftpower.com
Wholesaler/distributor of forklifts
President: Paul Mohrman
Estimated Sales: $20-50 Million
Number Employees: 50-99
Private Brands Carried:
Crown; Komatsu; Daewoo
Types of Products Distributed:
Frozen Food, General Merchandise, Forklifts

57705 Lift South
P.O.Box 472164
Charlotte, NC 28247-2164 704-442-1635
Fax: 704-522-0604 800-409-7129
sales@liftsouth.com www.liftsouth.com
Wholesaler/distributor of used forklifts
President: Michael Collins
CEO: Marc Knauff
Public Relations: Mike Collins
Estimated Sales: $2.5-5 Million
Number Employees: 1-4
Types of Products Distributed:
Frozen Food, General Merchandise, Used forklifts

57706 Lift Truck Ctr Inc
4000 W 33rd St S
Wichita, KS 67215-1009 316-942-7465
Fax: 316-942-0211
www.ltcenter.com
Wholesaler/distributor of material handling equipment
President: Bill Bolin
bbolin@ltcenter.com
Estimated Sales: $10-20 Million
Number Employees: 20-49
Square Footage: 30000
Private Brands Carried:
Clark; Crown; Toyota
Types of Products Distributed:
Frozen Food, General Merchandise, Material handling equipement

57707 Lift Truck Sales Svc & Rentals
201 Van Huss Ave
Knoxville, TN 37917-5000 865-673-8877
Fax: 865-523-6865 800-968-0885
info@lifttruckinc.com www.lifttruckinc.com
Wholesaler/distributor of forklifts, racking, warehouse, material and handling equipment; also, parts and service and rentals available
President: Owen Guinn
oguinn@lifttruckinc.com
Controller: Karyn Caylor
Service Manager: Daryl Guinn
Parts Manager: Steve Roberson
Purchasing Manager: Michelle Cooper
Estimated Sales: $5-10 Million
Number Employees: 20-49
Square Footage: 40000
Private Brands Carried:
Nissan; Prime Mover; Princeton; Mastercraft
Types of Products Distributed:
General Line, Rack Jobbers, Operator Training

57708 Lift Truck of America
P.O.Box 604
Lincolnshire, IL 60069-604 847-439-9421
Fax: 312-243-4445
Wholesaler/distributor of conveyors, forklifts and ramps
President: Lawrence Salter
Estimated Sales: $5-10 Million
Number Employees: 10-19
Private Brands Carried:
Harker; Magline; B.T. Prime Mover
Types of Products Distributed:
Frozen Food, General Merchandise, Conveyors, forklifts & ramps

57709 Liftech Equipment Co Inc
6847 Ellicott Dr
East Syracuse, NY 13057 315-463-7333
877-543-8324
www.liftech.com
Wholesaler/distributor of forklifts.

President: Joe Verzino
Executive Vice President: Kevin Conley
Chief Financial Officer: Mike Vaughan
General Sales Manager: Bill Rivett
General Operations Manager: Ron LeBlanc
Year Founded: 1988
Estimated Sales: $50-100 Million
Number Employees: 150
Other Locations:
Syracuse, NY
Schenectady, NY
Rochester, NY
Binghamton, NY
Buffalo, NY
Burlington, VTSchenectady
Private Brands Carried:
Hyster
Types of Products Distributed:
Frozen Food, General Merchandise, Forklifts

57710 Liftow
3150 American Drive
Mississauga, ON L4V 1B4
Canada 905-677-3270
Fax: 905-677-1429 www.liftow.com
Wholesaler/distributor of forklifts
Chairman of the Board: Roger Satten
Number Employees: 100-249
Private Brands Carried:
Toyota; EZ-60; Carrier
Types of Products Distributed:
Frozen Food, General Merchandise, Forklifts

57711 Liftruck Service Company
P.O.Box 3336
Davenport, IA 52808-3336 563-322-0983
Fax: 563-322-1603
Wholesaler/distributor of material handling equipment
President: Ed Volquardsen
Estimated Sales: $10-20 Million
Number Employees: 10-19
Private Brands Carried:
Crown; Nissan; Taylor
Types of Products Distributed:
Frozen Food, General Merchandise, Material handling equipment

57712 Light Bulbs Unlimited
2140 Peachtree Rd NW Ste 125b
Atlanta, GA 30360 404-663-7574
Fax: 404-261-6816 888-418-2852
lightingdesigndistrict@gmail.com
Wholesaler/distributor of electrical supplies, lighting fixtures, ballasts, electric lamps, halogen and fluorescent lighting and electric transformers
Manager: P J Sufer
CEO: Stan Civin
Sales/Marketing: Jake Gersosky
Estimated Sales: $1-2.5 Million
Number Employees: 1-4
Types of Products Distributed:
Frozen Food, General Merchandise, Electrical supplies, lamps, etc.

57713 Lilar Corp
1820 S 3rd St
St Louis, MO 63104-4040 314-436-5050
Fax: 314-436-0741 george@lilar.com
www.lilar.com
Wholesaler/distributor of spices and industrial ingredients including ice cream flavor; serving food service operators
President: George Armenta
george@lilar.com
Estimated Sales: $10-20 Million
Number Employees: 10-19
Square Footage: 63000
Private Brands Carried:
Nikken Foods; Rogers Foods; Chiquita; Del Monte; Diamond of California; Universal Flavors
Types of Products Distributed:
Food Service, General Line, Ingredients & spices

57714 Lilly Co Inc
3613 Knight Arnold Rd
Memphis, TN 38118-2729 901-363-6000
Fax: 901-795-7000 800-238-3006
www.lillyforklifts.com

Exporter and wholesaler/distributor of ice processing machinery including breakers and sizers; also, storage systems, fork lift truck parts and material handling equipment
Owner: Frank Clark
fclark@embracesafety.com
CEO: Craig Avery
CFO: Bob Davidson
Estimated Sales: $20-50 Million
Number Employees: 100-249
Square Footage: 40000

57715 Lilly Company
181 Industrial Blvd
La Vergne, TN 37086 615-793-8100
Fax: 615-793-8133 888-564-7978
www.kmhsystems.com
Wholesaler/distributor of material handling equipment including forklifts, storage racks, personal carriers and dock equipment
Manager: Wade Clark
VP: Craig Avery
Sales Manager: Wade Clark
Estimated Sales: $10-20 Million
Number Employees: 20-49
Square Footage: 60000
Parent Co: Lilly Company
Private Brands Carried:
Yale; Taylor Dunn
Types of Products Distributed:
Frozen Food, General Merchandise, Material handling equipment

57716 Lima Grain Cereal Seeds LLC
2040 SE Frontage Rd
Fort Collins, CO 80525-9717 970-498-2200
Fax: 970-223-4302 LCS-info@limagrain.com
www.limagrain.com
Processor and distributor of breakfast cereals in boxes and bags
President: Bernie Blach
Secretary: Cindy Blach
CFO: Kelly Mundorf
Executive VP: Cedric Audebert
cedric.audebert@limagrain.com
Marketing/Technical Manager: Zach Gaines
Number Employees: 5-9
Square Footage: 80000
Type of Packaging: Consumer, Food Service, Private Label, Bulk
Types of Products Distributed:
Popcorn

57717 Limehouse Produce Co
4791 Trade St # G
North Charleston, SC 29418-2824 843-556-3400
Fax: 843-556-3950 info@limehouseproduce.com
www.limehouseproduce.com
Fresh fruits and vegetables
Owner: John F Limehouse
Vice President: Andrea Limehouse
Sales: Ken Strange
limehouseproduce@comcast.net
Number Employees: 20-49

57718 Limitless
1500 W Carroll Ave
Chicago, IL 60607
sales@limitlesscoffee.com
limitlesscoffee.com
Cold brew coffee, coffee beans, green tea and sparkling water
Founder: Matt Matros
Co-Founder: Chris Fanucchi
Co-Founder: Craig Alexander

57719 Limoneira Co
1141 Cummings Rd
Santa Paula, CA 93060-9783 805-525-5541
Fax: 805-525-8761 info@limoneira.com
www.limoneira.com
Packing house for Sunkist Growers, Inc. citrus fruit.
President/CEO: Harold Edwards
VP/Finance & Administration: Don Delmatoff
Senior VP: Alex M Teague
amteague@limoneira.com
Business Development Manager: David McCoy
Marketing Director: John Chamberlain
Director Packing & Sales: Tomas Gonzales
Director Information Systems: Eric Tovias
Agritourism Operations Manager: Ryan Nasalroad
Estimated Sales: $20 Million
Number Employees: 250-499
Type of Packaging: Food Service

Wholesalers & Distributors / A-Z

57720 Linco Caster
10749 Rush St
South El Monte, CA 91733-3433   714-537-5353
Fax: 626-575-7811   866-306-9566
sales@lincocasters.com   www.lincocasters.com
Wholesaler/distributor of casters and storage and handling systems
Owner: Steve Patterson
dpatterson@lincocasters.com
VP: Steve Patterson
Estimated Sales: $1-2.5 Million
Number Employees: 20-49
Types of Products Distributed:
Frozen Food, General Merchandise, Casters & storage and handling systems

57721 Linco Caster
10749 Rush St
South El Monte, CA 91733-3433   714-537-5353
Fax: 626-575-7811   www.lincocasters.com
Wholesaler/distributor of casters, material handling systems and automatic storage and handling systems
Owner: Steve Patterson
Controller: Jeanne Baird
VP Sales: Steven Patterson
dpatterson@lincocasters.com
Mngr.: Barbara Paquette
Estimated Sales: $10-20 Million
Number Employees: 20-49
Type of Packaging: Private Label
Types of Products Distributed:
Frozen Food, General Merchandise, Material handling systems

57722 Lincoln Feed & Supply
5940 Cornhusker Highway
Lincoln, NE 68507-3108   402-580-5625
Wholesaler/distributor of chicken
Manager: Quentin Moore
Estimated Sales: $1-3 Million
Number Employees: 1-4
Private Brands Carried:
Purina Foods
Types of Products Distributed:
Frozen Food, Provisions/Meat, Chicken

57723 Lincoln Shrimp Company
708 Commercial Street
San Francisco, CA 94108-1898   415-982-2398
Wholesaler/distributor of frozen shrimp
VP: Wesley Chan
Estimated Sales: $2.5-5 Million
Number Employees: 5-9
Types of Products Distributed:
Frozen Food, Seafood, Frozen shrimp

57724 (HQ)Lincolnwood Merchandising Company
5359 N Broadway Street
Chicago, IL 60640-2311   773-275-2838
Fax: 773-275-2445   charl@aol.com
Wholesaler/distributor of general merchandise and specialty foods; rack jobber services available
President: Allen Trester
Secretary: C Trester
Sales Manager: B Doss
Estimated Sales: Less than $500,000
Number Employees: 1-4
Square Footage: 30000
Number of Customer Locations: 1500
Types of Products Distributed:
Frozen Food, General Merchandise, Rack Jobbers, Specialty Foods

57725 Lingle Fork Truck Company
3001 W Sawyer Drive
Saginaw, MI 48601   989-754-7801
Fax: 989-754-5810   www.lingle1.com
Wholesaler/distributor of forklifts
President: Randy Lingle
Number Employees: 20-49
Private Brands Carried:
Neissan; Track; Harlow
Types of Products Distributed:
Frozen Food, General Merchandise, Forklifts

57726 Linnea's Cake & Candy Supplies
975 Oak St
San Bernardino, CA 92410-2424   909-885-1446
Fax: 909-383-7201   sales@linneasinc.com
www.linneasinc.com
Cake candy
Manager: Mike Peterson
Manager: Frank Romocean
fromocean@linneasinc.com
Estimated Sales: $1-2.5 Million
Number Employees: 5-9
Type of Packaging: Bulk
Private Brands Carried:
Linnea
Number of Customer Locations: W Cost
Types of Products Distributed:
Cake Candy

57727 Lions Restaurant Equipment & Supplies
225 Merrick Rd
Lynbrook, NY 11563-2621   516-593-5466
Fax: 516-593-5473   www.lionsre.com
Wholesaler/distributor of stoves, refrigerators, fryers, pots, pans, etc.; serving the food service market
President: Steven Gertman
Estimated Sales: $1-2.5 Million
Number Employees: 5-9
Types of Products Distributed:
Food Service, Frozen Food, General Merchandise, Stoves, refrigerators, fryers, etc.

57728 (HQ)Lippert
600 W 172nd St
South Holland, IL 60473   708-333-6900
Fax: 708-333-3888
Wholesaler/distributor of restaurant equipment and supplies; serving the food service market
President: David Wax
VP: Rick Lippert
Estimated Sales: $10-20 Million
Number Employees: 20-49
Other Locations:
Lippert
Peoria, IL Lippert
Number of Customer Locations: 3
Types of Products Distributed:
Food Service, Frozen Food, General Merchandise, Restaurant equipment & supplies

57729 Lippert
7719 N Pioneer Ln
Peoria, IL 61615   309-693-3100
Fax: 309-693-3135
Wholesaler/distributor of food service equipment; serving the food service market
Manager: Robert Easterling
Sales: Bill Riebel
Sales: Gene Vaughn
Estimated Sales: $2.5-5 Million
Number Employees: 5-9
Parent Co: Lippert
Private Brands Carried:
Vulcan Hart; True; Hobart
Types of Products Distributed:
Food Service, Frozen Food, General Merchandise, Foodservice equipment

57730 Lippert
106 Oak Creek Plaza
Bloomington, IL 61704-7595   309-693-3100
Fax: 309-693-3135
Wholesaler/distributor of food service equipment; serving the food service market
Manager: Bob Easterling
Manager: Bob Glendon
Number Employees: 5-9
Parent Co: Lippert
Private Brands Carried:
Dart; Russell; Vollrath
Number of Customer Locations: 85
Types of Products Distributed:
Food Service, Frozen Food, General Merchandise, Foodservice equipment

57731 Lipten & Co
205 National Pl # 123
Longwood, FL 32750-6433   407-425-2651
Fax: 407-425-2670   800-366-3123
bo@liptenandcompany.com   www.lipten.com
Wholesaler/distributor of bakery products, bread flours, specialty and imported foods, chocolates, confectionery products and desserts; serving the food service market
Owner: Michael Kazmerek
liptenandcompany@aol.com
VP: Philip Lipten
Sales: Linda Pogorelskaya
Estimated Sales: $5-10 Million
Number Employees: 5-9
Types of Products Distributed:
Specialty Foods, Imported foods

57732 Lisbon Seafood Co
1428 S Main St
Fall River, MA 02724-2604   508-672-3617
Fax: 508-672-4698
Seafood
Owner: Victor Da Silva
vncc@aol.com
Estimated Sales: $1-3 Million
Number Employees: 10-19

57733 Little Charlie's
115 W College Dr
Marshall, MN 56258-3810   507-532-3274
Fax: 507-537-8226
Wholesaler/distributor of equipment; serving the food service market
Division Manager: John Anderson
Executive VP: John M Beadle
Estimated Sales: $5-10 Million
Number Employees: 10,000
Parent Co: Schwann's Sales
Types of Products Distributed:
Food Service, Frozen Food, General Merchandise, Equipment

57734 Little Produce
202 Palm Street
Hot Springs, AR 71901-4211   501-623-4464
Fax: 501-623-3288
Wholesaler/distributor of frozen food and produce; serving the food service market
President: D Little
Number of Customer Locations: 150
Types of Products Distributed:
Frozen Food, Produce

57735 Little River Lobster Company
PO Box 507
East Boothbay, ME 04544-0507   207-633-2648
Fax: 604-276-8371
Whole fish/seafood
President: Mike Dalton
Estimated Sales: $810,000
Number Employees: 1-4

57736 Littleton Sales Company
P.O.Box 429
Littleton, NC 27850   252-586-3861
Fax: 252-586-3861
Wholesaler/distributor of general merchandise, candy, etc
President: B Hawfield
Estimated Sales: $5-10 Million
Number Employees: 5-9
Square Footage: 40000
Number of Customer Locations: 600
Types of Products Distributed:
Frozen Food, General Line, General Merchandise, Candy

57737 LivBar
249 Liberty St. NE
Suite 232
Salem, OR 97301   971-239-1209
hello@livbar.com
www.livbar.com
Energy bars that are organic, gluten free, dairy free, soy free, corn free, and GMO-free
Co-Founder: Gabe Johansen
Co-Founder: Jan Johansen   *Year Founded:* 2012
Types of Products Distributed:
General Line, Health Food

57738 Livingston DistributionCenters
PO Box 749
Moncton, NB E1C 8M9
Canada   506-857-3026
Fax: 506-383-6550
Wholesaler/distributor of general merchandise and groceries
Types of Products Distributed:
Frozen Food, General Line, General Merchandise, Groceries

57739 Livingston DistributionCenters
137 Horner Avenue
Etobicoke, ON M8Z 4Y1
Canada   416-626-2826
Fax: 416-252-3654
Wholesaler/distributor of general merchandise and groceries

Wholesalers & Distributors / A-Z

Number Employees: 50-99
Square Footage: 1280000
Types of Products Distributed:
 Frozen Food, General Line, General Merchandise, Groceries

57740 Lo Temp Sales
20 W Park Avenue
Suite 303
Long Beach, NY 11561-2019 516-889-0300
 Fax: 516-466-9590 800-645-8086
 lindalotemp@aol.com
Importer, exporter and wholesaler/distributor of commercial equipment including refrigerators, shelving, counters, walk-in freezers and coolers, microwave ovens and popcorn, hot dog and soda machines
Marketing Director: L Conti
Estimated Sales: $2.5-5 Million
Number Employees: 5-9
Square Footage: 80000
Types of Products Distributed:
 Frozen Food, General Merchandise, Refrigerators, freezers, etc.

57741 Lobster Gram
4664 N Lowell Ave
Chicago, IL 60630-4263 773-777-8315
 Fax: 773-777-5546 800-548-3562
 customerservice@lobstergram.com
 www.lobstergram.com
Lobster
President: Michael Robinson
michael@livelob.com
Estimated Sales: $1-3 Million
Number Employees: 10-19

57742 Lobster Warehouse
7514 Jamaica Avenue
Woodhaven, NY 11421-1848 718-296-1991
 Fax: 718-296-1991
Wholesaler/distributor of fresh seafood including live lobsters and shellfish; serving the food service market
Estimated Sales: $500,000-$1 Million
Number Employees: 1-4
Square Footage: 12800
Types of Products Distributed:
 Food Service, Frozen Food, Seafood, Live lobsters & shellfish

57743 Lockwood & Winant
800 Food Center Dr # 99
Bronx, NY 10474-0014 718-620-8400
 Fax: 212-791-2494 www.lockwoodint.com
Wholesaler/distributor of seafood
Owner: Joe Gurrerea
VP: Abe Haymes
Sales: Anthony Bencivnga
Estimated Sales: $10-20 Million
Number Employees: 50-99
Square Footage: 2000
Types of Products Distributed:
 Frozen Food, Seafood

57744 Loeb Equipment
4131 S State St
Chicago, IL 60609-2942 773-496-5720
 Fax: 773-548-2608 Sales@loebequipment.com
 www.loebequipment.com
Wholesaler/distributor of used packaging and processing equipment
President/CEO: Howard Newman
howardn@loebequipment.com
Marketing Director: Sara Bogin
howardn@loebequipment.com
Sales Manager: Tom Larson
Number Employees: 20-49
Square Footage: 600000

57745 Logan
653 Evans City Rd
Butler, PA 16001 724-482-4715
 Fax: 724-482-4498
Wholesaler/distributor of general merchandise, frozen foods, general line items, seafood, etc.; serving the food service market
VP/General Manager: W Allen Ward
Sales Manager: Thomas Kelly
Estimated Sales: $20-50 Million
Number Employees: 20-49
Square Footage: 25000
Private Brands Carried:
 Pocahontas
Types of Products Distributed:
 Food Service, Frozen Food, General Line, General Merchandise, Seafood

57746 Lola Savannah
1701 Commerce St.
Houston, TX 77002-2244 713-222-9800
 Fax: 713-222-9802 888-663-9166
 lola@lolasavannah.com lolacc.com
Roasted coffee and tea
Owner: Duke Furgh
Vice President: Michael Spencer
Contact: Michael Spencer
mcs@lolasavannah.com
Operations Manager: Hank Segelke
Estimated Sales: Less than $500,000
Number Employees: 5-9
Type of Packaging: Consumer, Food Service, Private Label, Bulk
Private Brands Carried:
 Texana; Cafe Organic
Number of Customer Locations: 1

57747 Lollicup
1100 Coiner Ct
City Of Industry, CA 91748-1347 626-965-8882
 Fax: 626-965-8729 tradeshow@lollicup.com
 www.lollicupusa.com
Cocoa/baking chocolate, coffee, hot chocolate, tea, full-line cold non-carbonated beverages, non-alcoholic beverages, foodservice, specialty food packaging i.e. gift wrap/labels/boxes/containers.
Contact: Marvin Cheng
marvin.cheng@lollicup.com
Number Employees: 100-249

57748 Lomar Distributing Inc
2500 Dixon St
Des Moines, IA 50316-1871 515-244-3105
 Fax: 515-244-0515 www.hy-vee.com
Wholesaler/distributor of specialty foods, groceries, meat, dairy products, produce, general merchandise and private label items
President: Monte Weise
VP: Bill Sales
VP: Ken Beckner
Contact: Justin Andersen
justina@lomardistributing.com
Number Employees: 5-9
Square Footage: 220000
Number of Customer Locations: 3500
Types of Products Distributed:
 Frozen Food, General Line, General Merchandise, Provisions/Meat, Produce, Specialty Foods, Groceries, dairy items, etc.

57749 Lombardi Brothers Meat Packers
1926 W Elk Pl
P.O. Box 11277
Denver, CO 80211 303-458-7441
 lombardibrothers.com
Beef, pork, lamb and veal; importer of wild game.
President & Owner: Victoria Phillips
General Manager: Jeff Harvey
Year Founded: 1947
Estimated Sales: $30 Million
Number Employees: 60
Square Footage: 30000
Type of Packaging: Food Service
Other Locations:
 Lombardi Brothers Meat
 Fridley, MN
 Lombardi Brothers Meat
 Le Mars, IALombardi Brothers MeatLe Mars
Private Brands Carried:
 Bella Bella Gourmet Foods; Plume De Veau; Sakura Pork; Durham Ranch; Lower Family Foods; Certified Angus Beef; Boulder Naturals; Grat Range Bison; Mountain States Rosen Company; Heritage Berkshire; Iowa Gold Brand; Colorado Native Foods; King Cole
Types of Products Distributed:
 Food Service, Frozen Food, General Line, Health Food, Provisions/Meat, Seafood, Specialty Foods, Pasta, soups, desserts & smoked fish

57750 Lombardi's Seafood
1152 Harmon Avenue
Winter Park, FL 32789 407-628-3474
 Fax: 407-240-2562 800-879-8411
 quality@lombardis.com www.lombardis.com
Processor, importer and wholesaler/distributor of fresh and frozen seafood; serving the food service market
Owner: Vince Lomabardi
VP: Vince Lombardi
Contact: James Carr
jamescarr@lombardis.com
Supervisor: Mike Lombardi
Estimated Sales: $10-20 Million
Number Employees: 100-249
Type of Packaging: Food Service
Private Brands Carried:
 Farm Fresh
Number of Customer Locations: 1000
Types of Products Distributed:
 Food Service, Frozen Food, Seafood

57751 London Fruit Inc
9010 S Cage Blvd
Pharr, TX 78577-9769 956-781-7799
 800-531-7422
 barry@londonfruit.com www.londonfruit.com
Importer, exporter and wholesaler/distributor of fresh mangos, limes, papaya, coconuts, dry chiles and Mexican peppers.
President: Barry London
barry@londonfruit.com
Purchasing Agent: Jerry Garcia
Year Founded: 1981
Estimated Sales: $20-50 Million
Number Employees: 20-49
Square Footage: 45000
Type of Packaging: Food Service, Bulk
Private Brands Carried:
 London; Bandera
Types of Products Distributed:
 Frozen Food, Produce

57752 Loneoak & Co
3351 E Imperial Hwy
Lynwood, CA 90262-3398 310-638-3350
 Fax: 310-638-6540
Wholesaler/distributor of consumer dishes and olive oil
Owner: Linda Gassoumis
Estimated Sales: Less Than $500,000
Number Employees: 1-4
Types of Products Distributed:
 Frozen Food, General Line, General Merchandise, Consumer dishes & olive oil

57753 Long Company
20 N. Wacker Drive
Suite 1010
Chicago, IL 60606-2901 312-726-4606
 Fax: 312-726-4625 800-400-8615
 info@thelongco.com
President: Bill Zimmerman
CEO: Roger Masa
V.P. Operations-Consulting Services: Gary Swymeler
Director of Quality, R & D: Albert Bachman
Contact: Jo Rustik
jrustik@thelongco.com
Director of Manufacturing Services: Duane Bull
Purchasing Director: Larry Devereux

57754 Long Island Glove & Safety Products
5089 NE 12th Ave
Oakland Park, FL 33334-4916 954-771-2881
 Fax: 954-771-7794 800-645-3256
Wholesaler/distributor of safety supplies and gloves including disposable, vinyl, leather and cotton; serving the food service market
President: Sid Bumberg
Estimated Sales: $500,000-$1 Million
Number Employees: 1-4
Square Footage: 22000
Types of Products Distributed:
 Food Service, Frozen Food, General Merchandise, Gloves & safety supplies

57755 Long Island Promotions
35 Village Way
Smithtown, NY 11787-3720 631-584-4784
 Fax: 631-584-4783 www.lipromotions.com
Wholesaler/distributor of advertising specialties, candy jars, wine, cheeses, cookies and candy
President: William Governale
Vice President: Laura Morgan
Estimated Sales: Less Than $500,000
Number Employees: 1-4

Wholesalers & Distributors / A-Z

Square Footage: 4800
Parent Co: Govy Enterprises
Private Brands Carried:
 Hickory Farms
Number of Customer Locations: 50

57756 (HQ)Long Wholesale Distr Inc
201 N Fulton Dr
Corinth, MS 38834   662-287-2421
                      800-822-5664
customer-service@longwholesale.com
www.longwholesale.com
Wholesaler/distributor of groceries, dairy products, frozen foods, general merchandise, candy, tobacco, beverages and paper products; serving convenience store outlets; also, rack jobber services available.
Vice President: Colby Carmichiel
colby@longwholesale.com
Year Founded: 1922
Estimated Sales: $50-100 Million
Number Employees: 59
Square Footage: 58800
Types of Products Distributed:
 Frozen Food, General Line, General Merchandise, Rack Jobbers, Dairy, beverages, paper products, etc.

57757 Long Wholesale Distributors
5173 Pioneer Rd
Meridian, MS 39301   601-482-3144
                      800-828-5664
customer-service@longwholesale.com
www.longwholesale.com
Wholesaler/distributor of groceries, general merchandise, health and beauty aids, frozen food and produce; serving the food service market.
Estimated Sales: $50-100 Million
Number Employees: 53
Square Footage: 140000
Other Locations:
 Long Wholesale
 Meridian, MSLong Wholesale
Types of Products Distributed:
 Food Service, Frozen Food, General Line, General Merchandise, Produce

57758 Longbottom Coffee & TeaInc
4893 NW 235th Ave # 101
Hillsboro, OR 97124-5835   503-648-1271
 Fax: 503-681-0944 800-288-1271
info@longbottomcoffee.com
www.longbottomcoffee.com
Processor and importer of specialty coffees including certified organics, espresso, flavored, regionals and blends; wholesaler/distributor of espresso machines and fine teas
Owner: Jody Baccelleri
Marketing Director: Lisa Walker
Sales Director: Gabrielle Paeson
jbaccelleri@medicalteams.org
Manufacturing/Operations Director: Tom Brandon
Estimated Sales: $8 Million
Number Employees: 50-99
Square Footage: 112000
Type of Packaging: Consumer, Food Service, Private Label, Bulk
Private Brands Carried:
 La San Marc Espresso Machines; DaVinci; Tollon & Oscars Syrups; Chiardelli Chocolate; Oregon Chai; Big Treat and Jet Tea Blended Drinks
Types of Products Distributed:
 General Merchandise, Specialty Coffee, Teas, Espresso Mach.

57759 Longhorn Liquors
1017 Nederland Ave
Nederland, TX 77627   409-853-1632
nederland@long-hornliquor.com
long-hornliquor.com
Importer and wholesaler/distributor of European wine and beer; wholesaler/distributor of American wine and beer.
Year Founded: 2012
Estimated Sales: $50-100 Million
Number Employees: 50-99
Square Footage: 4000
Other Locations:
 Groves, TX
 Mauriceville, TX
 Lumberton, TX
 Silsbee, TX
 Woodville, TX
 Bookland, TXMauriceville

Types of Products Distributed:
 Frozen Food, General Line, Specialty Foods, European & American wine & beer

57760 Longview Meat & Merchandise Ltd
PO Box 173
Longview, AB T0L 1H0
Canada   403-558-3706
 Fax: 403-558-3708 866-355-3759
Beef jerky, wholesaler of bavarian style sausage and pepperonis
President/Owner: Peter Lawson
Plant Manager: Jacky Lau
Estimated Sales: $1 Million
Number Employees: 12
Square Footage: 26000
Type of Packaging: Consumer, Food Service, Private Label, Bulk
Types of Products Distributed:
 Frozen Food

57761 LonoLife
1722 South Coast Hwy
Suite 4
Oceanside, CA 92054
                      855-843-8566
contact@lonolife.com www.lonolife.com
Bone broth, keto broth, snack broth, collagen, protein coffee, cleanse drink powder, plant based protein
Co-Founder: Jesse Koltes
Co-Founder: Craig Leslie
Types of Products Distributed:
 General Line

57762 Look Lobster Co
32 Old House Point Rd
Jonesport, ME 04649-3385   207-497-2353
 Fax: 207-497-5559 looklobster@myfairpoint.net
www.lookslobster.com
Lobster
President: Bert Sid Look
Vice President, Sales & Logistics: William Look
Estimated Sales: $.5-1 million
Number Employees: 5-9

57763 Lorain Novelty Company
1735 Broadway
Lorain, OH 44052   440-244-3197
 Fax: 440-244-9528
Wholesaler/distributor of general merchandise and specialty foods; serving the food service market
President: Richard Muzilla
Estimated Sales: $1-2.5 Million
Number Employees: 10-19
Types of Products Distributed:
 Food Service, Frozen Food, General Merchandise, Specialty Foods

57764 Lorenz Schneider Co
2000 Plaza Ave
New Hyde Park, NY 11040   516-328-1400
customer_service_mail@nysnacks.com
www.nysnacks.com
Wholesaler/distributor of specialty foods and snacks.
Year Founded: 1936
Estimated Sales: $50-100 Million
Number Employees: 50-99
Number of Customer Locations: 2000
Types of Products Distributed:
 Frozen Food, General Line, Specialty Foods, Snack foods

57765 Lorenz Supply Co
113 S 21st St
P.O. Box 1411
Mattoon, IL 61938-3701   217-234-3677
 Fax: 217-234-8547 800-395-3677
lorenz@lorenzwholesale.com
Wholesaler/distributor of paper goods, party supplies and janitorial equipment
Owner: Brian Titus
cmckillip@lorenzsupply.com
Estimated Sales: $5-10 Million
Number Employees: 20-49
Square Footage: 68000
Types of Products Distributed:
 Frozen Food, General Merchandise, Paper goods, party supplies, etc.

57766 Lorenzo's Wholesale Foods
4278 Fay Rd
Syracuse, NY 13219-3096   315-487-0036
 Fax: 315-487-0336
Wholesaler/distributor of fresh and frozen seafood, groceries, dairy products and meats; serving supermarket chains, delis and food service operators in Central New York
Owner: George Musak
lorenzosgmusak@aol.com
VP: George Musak
Estimated Sales: $20-50 Million
Number Employees: 20-49
Square Footage: 15000
Type of Packaging: Bulk
Types of Products Distributed:
 Food Service, Frozen Food, General Line, Provisions/Meat, Seafood, Groceries & dairy products

57767 Lost Trail Root Beer
PO Box 670
Louisburg, KS 66053-0670   913-837-5202
 Fax: 913-837-5762 800-748-7765
lcmill@micoks.net www.louisburgcidermill.com
Processor, wholesaler/distributor and exporter of apple cider and root beer; also, apple butter
President/Owner: Tom Schierman
Estimated Sales: $500,000-$1 Million
Number Employees: 5-9
Square Footage: 40000
Type of Packaging: Consumer, Private Label
Types of Products Distributed:
 Frozen Food, General Line, Apple cider, apple butter & root beer

57768 Loubat Equipment Company
4141 Bienville St
New Orleans, LA 70119-5149   504-482-2554
 Fax: 504-483-2180 800-878-2554
info@loubat.com www.loubat.com
Wholesaler/distributor of commercial kitchen equipment and supplies; also, layout and design services available
President: Henri Louapre
CFO: Lauren Crutcher
Vice President: Christine Briede
Marketing Director: Christine Briede
Sales Director: Judy Waterman
Contact: Doug Tyler
doug@loubat.com
Operations Manager: Cameron McCall
Plant Manager: Clifford Marine
Estimated Sales: $8 Million
Number Employees: 20-49
Number of Brands: 500
Number of Products: 1350
Square Footage: 44000
Type of Packaging: Food Service
Types of Products Distributed:
 Food Service, Commercial kitchen equipment & supplies

57769 (HQ)Louis Caric & Sons
33398 Cecil Ave
Delano, CA 93215   661-725-9372
 Fax: 661-725-5943
Exporter of table grapes
Owner: Louis Caric
velikel@dslextreme.com
Estimated Sales: $.5-1 million
Number Employees: 100-249
Square Footage: 160000
Type of Packaging: Consumer, Private Label
Private Brands Carried:
 Hi Style (Grapes); Louis IV (Grapes), 3 Bros (Grapes)
Types of Products Distributed:
 Produce, Table grapes

57770 Louis R Polster Co
585 S High St
Columbus, OH 43215-5684   614-221-3295
 Fax: 614-221-5914 888-765-7837
Wholesaler/distributor of food service equipment and supplies, janitorial supplies, bar equipment, furniture and disposables; serving the food service market
President: E Polster
Secretary: M Polster
Treasurer: J Polster
Vice President: L Lowy
Estimated Sales: $3-5 Million
Number Employees: 20-49
Square Footage: 265000

Type of Packaging: Food Service
Types of Products Distributed:
   Food Service

57771 Louisiana Fresh Express
18120 Old Covington Highway
Suite B
Hammond, LA 70403-0652
985-542-1256
Fax: 985-898-5993
Transportation services
President: Mark Malkemus

57772 Louisiana Packaging
4747 Conti Street
New Orleans, LA 70119-4407
504-482-7866
Fax: 504-482-7870
Wholesaler/distributor of glass, plastic and metal containers and closures
Parent Co: Berlin Packaging
Types of Products Distributed:
   Frozen Food, General Merchandise, Containers & closures

57773 Louisiana Pride Seafood
2021 Lakeshore Drive Suite 300
New Orleans, LA 70122
504-286-8736
Fax: 504-286-8738
http://www.louisianaseafood.com
Seafood
President: Anthony Lama

57774 Louisiana Seafood Promotion & Marketing Board
051 North Third Street
3rd Floor
Baton Rouge, LA 70802
225-342-0552
Fax: 504-286-8738 info@louisianaseafood.com
www.louisianaseafood.com
Shrimp
President: Gerard Thomassie
Executive Director: Ewell Smith

57775 Lovecchio & Sons
102 N Wilson Way
Stockton, CA 95205-4927
209-465-9444
Fax: 209-465-5851
Wholesaler/distributor of produce; serving the food service market
President: Don Lovecchio
Secretary/Treasurer: Albert Lovecchio
Estimated Sales: $2.5-5 Million
Number Employees: 5-9
Types of Products Distributed:
   Food Service, Frozen Food, Produce

57776 Lovion International
14 Coachlamp Ln
Stamford, CT 06902
203-327-1405
Fax: 203-325-8636
Wholesaler/distributor and importer of Japanese balanced natural herb mixes; exporter of vitamins and health foods
President: John Tanaka
VP: Kayoko Tanaka
Marketing Director: Kyoko Hirota
Estimated Sales: $2.5-5 Million
Number Employees: 1-4
Types of Products Distributed:
   Frozen Food, Health Food

57777 Lowcountry Shellfish Inc
7195 Bryhawke Circle
Charleston, SC 29418
843-767-9600
Fax: 843-552-6560 800-999-2503
l.brooks@lowcountryshellfish.com
www.ipswichshellfish.com
Seafood
Sales Manager: Paul Filo
Number Employees: 300
Parent Co: Ipswich Shellfish Company, Inc.
Types of Products Distributed:
   Seafood

57778 Lowell Brothers & Bailey
50 Eastern Ave
Chelsea, MA 02150
617-889-1960
Fax: 617-889-5922
Wholesaler/distributor of frozen foods, baked goods, general line products, general merchandise, equipment and specialty produce; serving the food service market
President: G Sexeny
Chairman: W Rogers
VP: A Sexeny

Estimated Sales: $5-10 Million
Number Employees: 20-49
Square Footage: 120000
Number of Customer Locations: 350
Types of Products Distributed:
   Food Service, Frozen Food, General Line, General Merchandise, Produce, Specialty Foods

57779 Lucas Industrial
1445 American Way
PO Box 293
Cedar Hill, TX 75104-8409
972-291-6400
Fax: 972-291-6447 800-877-1720
sales@lucasindustrial.com
www.lucasindustrial.com
Manufacturer, importer and wholesaler/distributor of power transmission products including steel and stainless steel shaft and split collars, linear bearing and shaftings, roller chains and mounted bearing
Owner: Mike Lucas
Sales Manager: Bobby Swann
lucasindustrial@aol.com
Estimated Sales: Below $5 Million
Number Employees: 5-9
Types of Products Distributed:
   Frozen Food, General Merchandise, Power transmission parts

57780 Lucca Packing Company
1137 W Lake Street
Chicago, IL 60607-1618
312-421-4699
Fax: 312-421-2099
Wholesaler/distributor of general line products
President: Fred Nottoli
Types of Products Distributed:
   Frozen Food, General Line

57781 Lucia's Pizza Co
10989 Gravois Industrial Ct
St Louis, MO 63128-2032
314-843-2553
Fax: 314-843-3576
Processor and wholesaler/distributor of frozen pizza
President: Darrell Long
sean@luciaspizza.com
Sales Exec: Sean Lynch
Estimated Sales: $1,600,000
Number Employees: 20-49
Square Footage: 50000
Type of Packaging: Consumer, Private Label
Private Brands Carried:
   Fazio's Ravioli; Gus Frozen Pretzels; Quelle Quiche
Number of Customer Locations: 201
Types of Products Distributed:
   Frozen Food

57782 Ludwig Fish & Produce Company
409 Michigan Ave
La Porte, IN 46350
219-362-2608
Fax: 219-325-8311 800-362-2608
www.ludwigfishproduce.com
Wholesaler/distributor of frozen food, general line products, produce, provisions/meats and seafood; serving the food service market
President: Harold Robinson
Estimated Sales: $3,800,000
Number Employees: 20-49
Types of Products Distributed:
   Food Service, Frozen Food, Provisions/Meat, Produce, Seafood

57783 Luigi Bormioli Corporation
5 Walnut Grove Dr
Horsham, PA 19044
215-672-7111
Fax: 215-757-7115
customerservice@luigibormioli.com
www.luigibormioli.com
Importer and wholesaler/distributor of porcelain dinnerware, barware and glassware; serving the food service market
President: Marcel Trepanier
National Sales Manager: Jay Allie
Contact: Deon Allen
dallen@luigibormioli.com
Project Coordinator: Lora Campbell
Estimated Sales: $2.5-5 Million
Number Employees: 10-19
Parent Co: Luigi Bormioli Spa
Type of Packaging: Food Service
Private Brands Carried:
   Luigi Bormioli; Tognana
Types of Products Distributed:
   Food Service, Frozen Food, General Merchandise, Porcelain dinnerware & glassware

57784 Lumaco Inc
9-11 E Broadway
Hackensack, NJ 07601-6821
201-342-5119
Fax: 201-342-8898 800-735-8258
valvinfo@lumaco.com www.lumaco.com
Stainless steel manual and pneumatic valves
Owner: Anita Buxbaum
Sales Manager: Don Kiefer
Estimated Sales: $2.5-5 Million
Number Employees: 5-9
Square Footage: 10000
Types of Products Distributed:
   Food Service, Frozen Food, Provisions/Meat, Seafood, Valves

57785 Lumar Lobster
297 Burnside Ave
Lawrence, NY 11559
516-371-0083
Live lobster
President: Stanley Jassem
Estimated Sales: Less than $500,000
Number Employees: 1-4
Type of Packaging: Food Service
Types of Products Distributed:
   Frozen Food

57786 Lumber & Things
PO Box 386
Keyser, WV 26726
304-788-5600
Fax: 304-788-7823 800-296-5656
www.lumberandthings.com
We have been in business for over 30 years. Our customers depend on the standards that we build on: Honesty-Quality-Service. We produce: Reconditioned, Remanufactured and New pallets; Reconditioned, Remanufactured and Recycled tier/slipsheets; Reconditioned, Remanufactured and New top frames; Reconditioned and New can and glass bulk pallets. With an attendant standing by our 24 hour hotline we can provide your company with delivery within 24 hours of your phone call.
President: Jack Amoruso
National Accounts Manager: Victor Knight
Customer Service Specialist: Patricia Davis
Plant Manager: Jack Amoruso
Purchasing Director: Ken Winter
Number Employees: 100-249
Square Footage: 150000
Type of Packaging: Consumer, Food Service, Private Label, Bulk
Number of Customer Locations: 250
Types of Products Distributed:
   Pallets

57787 Lumberton Cash & Carry
1601 Godwin Ave
Lumberton, NC 28358-4207
910-738-5390
Fax: 910-738-5764
Wholesaler/distributor of groceries, frozen foods, provisions/meats, ice cream, baked goods, etc
Owner: L Cola Dial
Manager: Ann Duncan
Estimated Sales: $2.5-5 Million
Number Employees: 1-4
Private Brands Carried:
   Del Monte; Tropicana; Gatorade
Types of Products Distributed:
   Frozen Food, General Line, Provisions/Meat, Groceries, ice cream, baked goods, etc.

57788 Lumsden Brothers
6355 Viscount Road
Mississauga, ON L4V 1W2
Canada
Fax: 800-263-5260 800-465-5525
lumsdenwebordering@sobeys.com www.lbl.on.ca
Wholesaler/distributor of groceries
President: Jim Dores
CFO: Tom Johnston
Merchandise VP: Gary Shoeneweiss
Sales VP: George Hampson
Production Manager: Mario Pereira
Number Employees: 200
Square Footage: 600000
Parent Co: Sobey's
Private Brands Carried:
   Smart Choice; Our Compliments
Number of Customer Locations: 1000
Types of Products Distributed:
   Frozen Food, General Line, General Merchandise, Provisions/Meat, Groceries

Wholesalers & Distributors / A-Z

57789 Lusty Lobster
10 Portland Fish Pier
Suite A
Portland, ME 04101-4620   207-773-2829
                        Fax: 207-774-3956
Lobster
President: Doug Douty
Estimated Sales: $10-20 Million
Number Employees: 10-19

57790 Lynard Company
15 Maple Tree Ave
Stamford, CT 06906   203-323-0231
         Fax: 203-323-0231 lynardco@aol.com
Wholesaler/distributor of packaged food and confections
President: Howard Flaster
CEO: Carolyn Goldenberg
Contact: Lilian Flaster
lynardco@aol.com
Estimated Sales: Less than $500,000
Number Employees: 1-4
Type of Packaging: Consumer, Private Label
Types of Products Distributed:
  Frozen Food, General Line, General Merchandise, Packaged food & confections

57791 Lynn Dairy Inc
W1929 US Highway 10
Granton, WI 54436-8899   715-238-7129
         Fax: 715-238-7130 www.lynndairy.com
Wholesaler/distributor of cheese; serving the food service market
President: William L Schwantes
lynndairy@fibernetcc.com
General Manager: Rick Bilky
Sales Manager: N Schwantes
Estimated Sales: $5-10 Million
Number Employees: 100-249
Private Brands Carried:
  Lynn Dairy
Number of Customer Locations: 202
Types of Products Distributed:
  Food Service, Frozen Food, General Line, Cheese

57792 (HQ)Lyons Specialty Company
2800 La Highway 1 N
Port Allen, LA 70767-3417   225-356-1319
         Fax: 225-357-9384 www.lyons-aav.com
Wholesaler/distributor of confectionery products and paper
Owner: Hugh Raetzsch
Contact: Davis D'Aquin
davis@lyons-aav.com
Estimated Sales: $5-10 Million
Number Employees: 50-99
Types of Products Distributed:
  General Line, General Merchandise, Confectionery products & paper

57793 M & G Materials Handling Co
860 Waterman Ave Side
PO Box 14175
East Providence, RI 02914-1334   401-383-7303
         Fax: 401-438-1414 866-445-7491
               www.mandgmaterialshandling.com
Wholesaler/distributor of material handling equipment
Owner: Kenneth Mac Donald
kmacdonald@mandgmaterialshandling.com
Estimated Sales: $10-20 Million
Number Employees: 20-49
Private Brands Carried:
  Yale; Taylor Dunn
Types of Products Distributed:
  Frozen Food, General Merchandise, Material handling equipment

57794 M & V Provisions Co Inc
1827 Flushing Ave
Ridgewood, NY 11385   718-456-7070
         Fax: 718-456-7768 www.mnvprovisions.com
Wholesaler/distributor of dairy products, cold cuts, cheeses, condiments, salads, desserts, frozen foods and fresh meats.
Co-President: Paul Vallario
mrv223@aol.com
Co-President: Tony Ciuffo
Co-EVP & Director, Purchasing: Mike Ciuffo
Co-EVP & General Manager: Joseph Vallario
VP & Plant Manager: Joseph Castrogiovanni
Assistant VP & IT Manager: Joseph Guitian

Year Founded: 1949
Estimated Sales: $20-50 Million
Number Employees: 20-49
Square Footage: 30000
Private Brands Carried:
  Northside
Types of Products Distributed:
  Frozen Food, General Line, Provisions/Meat, Cheeses, condiments, cold cuts, etc.

57795 M & W Beef Packers Inc
2114 Highway 1806 S
Mandan, ND 58554   701-663-2333
         Fax: 701-663-7451 800-489-8589
                         www.mwbeef.com
Wholesaler/distributor of meat products; serving the food service market
President: Steve Moore
CEO: Wes Moore
VP: M Hoffert
Estimated Sales: $2 Million
Number Employees: 10-19
Square Footage: 20000
Type of Packaging: Consumer, Food Service, Private Label, Bulk
Number of Customer Locations: 78
Types of Products Distributed:
  Food Service, Provisions/Meat

57796 M 5 Corp
1619 S Rancho Santa Fe Rd # C
Suite C
San Marcos, CA 92078-5114   760-744-6665
         Fax: 760-744-6065 800-995-6530
                    info@m5corporation.com
Organic and natural gourmet foods, Italian gourmet foods and South American gourmet foods
Owner: Michael Mc Grath
Marketing: Michael McGrath
Estimated Sales: $310,000
Number Employees: 1-4
Type of Packaging: Food Service

57797 M A Sales
280 West Ave
Long Branch, NJ 07740-6139   732-229-7707
                        Fax: 732-229-2964
Wholesaler/distributor of meats and provisions including frankfurters, spiced ham, bologna, liverwurst, cooked salami, kielbasa, assorted cold cuts, etc.; also, packaging available
Owner: Antony Giordano
CFO: Barry Cohen
Sales: Rudy D'Ambrisi
Sales: Chris Haydu
Estimated Sales: $10-20 Million
Number Employees: 5-9
Types of Products Distributed:
  Frozen Food, Provisions/Meat

57798 M Amundson Cigar & Candy Co
9148 Old Cedar Ave S
Bloomington, MN 55425-8604   952-854-2222
         Fax: 952-854-5329 www.mamundsoncigar.com
Wholesaler/distributor of candy
Owner: Ross Amundson
ross@mamundson.com
Estimated Sales: $2.5-5 Million
Number Employees: 10-19
Square Footage: 11600
Number of Customer Locations: 200
Types of Products Distributed:
  Frozen Food, General Line, Candy

57799 M Conley Co
1312 4th St SE
Canton, OH 44707-3200   330-456-8243
         Fax: 330-456-6358 www.mconley.com
Wholesaler/distributor of paper, packaging and sanitary maintenance products; also, bakery items; serving the food service market
President: Robert H Stewart Iii
VP: David Conley
VP: Michael Conley
Estimated Sales: $20-50 Million
Number Employees: 100-249
Square Footage: 150000
Number of Customer Locations: 120
Types of Products Distributed:
  Food Service, Frozen Food, General Line, General Merchandise, Paper, packaging products, etc.

57800 (HQ)M D Stetson Co
92 York Ave
Randolph, MA 02368-1892   781-986-6161
         Fax: 781-961-1764 800-255-8651
              service@mdstetson.com www.mdstetson.com
Cleaning, degreasing and sanitizing chemicals, liquid hand soap and furniture and floor polish; wholesaler/distributor of maintenance equipment and supplies, industrial sweepers and scrubbers
President: Michael Glass
michael.glass@mdstetson.com
Treasurer and R&D and Quality Control: Andrea Adams
Estimated Sales: $15-20 Million
Number Employees: 20-49
Square Footage: 104000
Types of Products Distributed:
  Frozen Food, General Merchandise, Maintenance equipment & supplies

57801 M F & B Restaurant Systems Inc
133 Icmi Rd
Dunbar, PA 15431-2309   724-628-3050
                        Fax: 724-626-0247
Remanufacture conveyor pizza ovens, sell new and used parts
Owner: Mike French
mfrench@edgeoven.com
Vice President: Michael French
Estimated Sales: $400,000
Number Employees: 5-9
Number of Brands: 5
Square Footage: 24000
Types of Products Distributed:
  Remanufactured Pizza Ovens

57802 M Maskas & Sons Inc
142 E 7th Ave
Tarentum, PA 15084-1511   724-224-6009
         Fax: 724-224-7278 RMaskas@Aol.com
Wholesaler/distributor of candy, paper and foods including instant and canned; serving the food service market
President: Randy Maskas
rmaskas@aol.com
Secretary: Larry Maskas
Estimated Sales: $2.5-5 Million
Number Employees: 1-4
Square Footage: 60000
Types of Products Distributed:
  Food Service, Frozen Food, General Line, General Merchandise, Candy, instant foods, paper, etc.

57803 M R Williams Inc
235 Raleigh Rd
Henderson, NC 27536
         Fax: 252-438-2117 800-733-8104
              support@mrwilliams.com www.mrwilliams.com
Wholesaler/distributor of groceries, dairy products, frozen foods, equipment and fixtures, general merchandise, etc.; serving the food service market and convenience stores.
President: Lawson Williams
lawson@mrwilliams.com
VP, Sales: Rohan Rudolph
Year Founded: 1976
Estimated Sales: $100-500 Million
Number Employees: 100-249
Square Footage: 85000
Other Locations:
  Williams, M.R.
  South Boston, VA Williams, M.R.
Number of Customer Locations: 1000
Types of Products Distributed:
  Food Service, Frozen Food, General Line, General Merchandise, Groceries, dairy products, etc.

57804 M Tucker Co Inc
1200 Madison Ave
Paterson, NJ 07503   973-484-1200
              info@mtucker.com www.mtucker.com
Wholesaler/distributor of restaurant equipment and supplies; serving the food service market.
Estimated Sales: $55 Million
Number Employees: 50-99
Number of Products: 7500
Square Footage: 130000
Parent Co: Singer Equipment Co Inc.
Type of Packaging: Food Service
Private Brands Carried:
  Vulcan; Hobart; South Bend

Wholesalers & Distributors / A-Z

Types of Products Distributed:
    Food Service, Frozen Food, General Merchandise, Foodservice equipment

57805 M&F Foods
817 S Orange Ave
East Orange, NJ 07018-2313
        973-674-6700
      Fax: 973-674-3325
Wholesaler/distributor of meats, produce, dairy products, frozen foods, baked goods, equipment and fixtures, general merchandise and seafood; serving the food service market
Owner: Marie Sthilaire
Executive VP: D Barash
VP: A Coehlo
Estimated Sales: $300,000-500,000
Number Employees: 1-4
Private Brands Carried:
    Parade
Types of Products Distributed:
    Food Service, Frozen Food, General Line, General Merchandise, Provisions/Meat, Produce, Seafood, Dairy products, baked goods, etc.

57806 M&L Ventures
1471 W. COMMERCE COURT
Tucson, AZ 85746-6016   520-884-8232
    Fax: 520-770-9649 sales@meritfoods.net
              www.meritfoods.net
Products include produce and groceries, eggs and cheese, deli meats and salad dressings.
President: Matt Sadowsky
Secretary/Treasurer: Lynn Sadowsky
Manager: Bob Richter
Manager: Paul Rosthenhausler

57807 M&N International
P.O.Box 64784
Saint Paul, MN 55164   800-479-2043
    Fax: 800-727-8966 www.mnpartystore.com
Wholesaler/distributor of general line items, general merchandise, paper products, decorations and party supplies
Manager Marketing: Nancy Kewitsch
Types of Products Distributed:
    Frozen Food, General Line, General Merchandise, Paper products, decorations, etc.

57808 M&T Chirico
6599 Slayton Settlement Road
Lockport, NY 14094-1136   716-822-2021
      Fax: 716-822-1202
Wholesaler/distributor of fresh fruits and vegetables
President: Anthony Chirico
Estimated Sales: $5-10 Million
Number Employees: 10-19
Types of Products Distributed:
    Produce, Fresh fruits & vegetables

57809 M. Crews & Company
578 Post Rd E
Westport, CT 06880
      Fax: 203-227-5254
Wholesaler/distributor of general merchandise including advertising specialties, corporate gifts and gift baskets
Owner: Melinda Crews
Number Employees: 1-4
Private Brands Carried:
    Waterford; Cross; Monte Blanc
Number of Customer Locations: 35
Types of Products Distributed:
    Frozen Food, General Merchandise, Advertising specialties

57810 M. Sickles & Sons
913 Twining Rd
Dresher, PA 19025   215-884-7273
    Fax: 215-884-1506 800-523-3636
Wholesaler/distributor of specialty food gift packages
President: M Alan Sickles
Estimated Sales: $1-2.5 Million
Number Employees: 1-4
Square Footage: 4000
Types of Products Distributed:
    Frozen Food, Specialty Foods, Gift packages

57811 M. Zukerman & Company
P.O.Box 1296
Vineland, NJ 08362-1296   856-691-3445
      Fax: 856-692-9472
Wholesaler/distributor of frozen foods, general line products, produce and provisions/meats; serving the food service market
President: R Zukerman
Estimated Sales: $20-50 Million
Number Employees: 20-49
Number of Customer Locations: 1000
Types of Products Distributed:
    Food Service, Frozen Food, General Line, Provisions/Meat, Rack Jobbers

57812 M.E. Carter & Company
P.O.Box 217
Jonesboro, AR 72403   870-932-6668
Wholesaler/distributor of produce, general line items and frozen foods; serving the food service market
President: Warren Gray
Manager: George Kaloghirou
Estimated Sales: $10-20 Million
Number Employees: 20-49
Square Footage: 40000
Number of Customer Locations: 150
Types of Products Distributed:
    Food Service, Frozen Food, General Line, Produce

57813 M.E. Dilanian Company
PO Box 920359
Needham, MA 02492-0004   781-449-4633
      Fax: 781-449-3960
Broker and wholesaler/distributor of dairy/deli and confectionery products, frozen food, groceries and private label items
President: D Dilanian
Chairman: M Dilanian
Estimated Sales: $5-10 Million
Number Employees: 5-9
Types of Products Distributed:
    Food Service, General Line, Provisions/Meat

57814 M.K. Health Food Distributors
12042 Knott St
Garden Grove, CA 92841-2829   714-903-6833
    Fax: 714-379-6501 800-232-3066
              www.natureslife.com
Wholesaler/distributor of dietary supplements and food concentrates
Owner: Minh Vu
COO: Karl Riedel
Marketing Director: Kelly Colwell
Manager: Callista Maclean
Estimated Sales: $5-10 Million
Number Employees: 1-4
Square Footage: 160000
Private Brands Carried:
    Nature's Life; Sports Life; Natural Solutions
Types of Products Distributed:
    Frozen Food, Health Food, Dietary supplements & food concentrates

57815 M.S. Johnston Company
13261 Pennsylvania Ave
Hagerstown, MD 21742   301-733-1066
    Fax: 301-797-9675 www.msjohnston.com
Wholesaler/distributor of food service equipment
President: M Johnston
Controller: Alan Sheeley
VP: M Johnston
Estimated Sales: $5-10 Million
Number Employees: 50-99
Square Footage: 60000
Private Brands Carried:
    Metal Craft Fabrication; ISE; Hill Refrigeration
Types of Products Distributed:
    General Merchandise

57816 MAK Wood Inc
1235 Dakota Dr # E
Unit E
Grafton, WI 53024-9477   262-387-1200
    Fax: 262-387-1400 info@makwood.com
              www.makwood.com
Novelty sugars, cranberry, probiotics, lactobacillus and bifidobacterium. Supplier of L-arabinose, L-fucose, L-rhamnose, lactates, and of other probiotics.
Owner: Mark Brudnak
Secretary/Treasurer: Joseph Brudnak
Sr Executive VP: Mark Brudnak
Manager, Technical Sales Services: Eric Baer
mark@makwood.com
Estimated Sales: $380,000
Number Employees: 5-9
Type of Packaging: Private Label, Bulk

57817 MFS/York/Stormor
2928 E US Highway 30
Grand Island, NE 68801-8318   308-384-9320
    Fax: 308-382-6954 800-247-6621
Manufacturer, exporter and wholesaler/distributor of grain storage, drying, handling and conditioning and conveying equipment; also, seed storage equipment
President: Dan Faltin
dfaltin@mfsyork.com
VP Finance: Charles Stracuzzi
Sales Manager: Randy Van Langen
Executive VP Operations: Wayne Sasges
Production Manager: Dave Forbes
Estimated Sales: $20-50 Million
Number Employees: 50-99
Parent Co: Blount
Types of Products Distributed:
    Frozen Food, General Merchandise, Grain handling equipment

57818 MGH Wholesale Grocery
416 Buffalo Rd
Lawrenceburg, TN 38464   931-762-3615
      Fax: 931-766-2726
Wholesaler/distributor of groceries, meat, frozen food, equipment and fixtures, health and beauty aids, produce and general merchandise; serving the food service market
President: J Hickman
Manager: J Hickman
Estimated Sales: $20-50 Million
Number Employees: 20-49
Square Footage: 30000
Private Brands Carried:
    Stokeley's; Bush; Hunts; Pleezing
Number of Customer Locations: 200
Types of Products Distributed:
    Food Service, Frozen Food, General Line, General Merchandise, Provisions/Meat, Produce, Groceries, etc.

57819 MIA Food Distributing
131 Carlauren Road
Woodbridge, ON L4L 8A8
Canada   905-856-0122
      Fax: 905-856-0526
Wholesaler/distributor of general line items; serving the food service market
President: Paul DiGiammatteo
Private Brands Carried:
    Family Tradition Frozens; Nielsen Dairy; Heinz
Types of Products Distributed:
    Food Service, Frozen Food, General Line

57820 MICROS Retail Systems Inc
1500 Harbor Blvd # 2
Weehawken, NJ 07086-6768   201-866-1000
    Fax: 201-866-8282 www.micros-retail.com
Wholesaler/distributor of point of sale and property management systems; serving the food service market
President: Lubodar Olesnycky
lubodar@microsny.com
Estimated Sales: $300,000-500,000
Number Employees: 50-99
Types of Products Distributed:
    Food Service, Frozen Food, General Merchandise, Point of sale systems, etc.

57821 (HQ)ML Catania Company
575 Orwell Street
Mississauga, ON L5A 2W4
Canada   416-236-9394
    Fax: 416-236-3992 www.cataniaworldwide.com
Wholesaler/distributor and importer of fresh fruits and vegetables
President: Paul Catania, Sr.
Executive VP: Paul Catania, Jr.
Estimated Sales: $8 Million
Number Employees: 10-19
Square Footage: 120000
Parent Co: Catania Worldwide
Other Locations:
    ML Catania Co. Ltd.
    Fresno, CA ML Catania Co. Ltd.
Types of Products Distributed:
    General Line, Produce

57822 MSC Industrial Direct Co Inc
75 Maxess Rd
Melville, NY 11747-3151   516-812-2000
    Fax: 516-349-0265 800-645-7270
              www.mscdirect.com

Wholesalers & Distributors / A-Z

Wholesaler/distributor of material handling equipment
President/CEO: Eric Gershwind
SVP/CIO: Charles Bonomo
CFO/EVP: Jeff Kaczka
SVP/General Counsel & Corp. Secretary: Steve Armstrong
EVP, Sales: Thomas Cox
EVP, Operations: Douglas Jones
Estimated Sales: Over $1 Billion
Number Employees: 5000-9999
Private Brands Carried:
  Chicago Latrobe Drills; Cleveland Twist Drill; Starrett
Types of Products Distributed:
  Frozen Food, General Merchandise, Material handling equipment

57823 MTC Distributing
4900 Stoddard Rd.
Modesto, CA 95356
800-669-6449
info@mtc-dist.com www.mtc-dist.com
General line products, frozen foods, candy, snacks, beverages, health and beauty aids and store supplies.
President: Tom Eakin
Year Founded: 1921
Estimated Sales: $100+ Million
Number Employees: 100-249
Types of Products Distributed:
  Food Service, Frozen Food, General Line, Health Food, Rack Jobbers

57824 MVP Group
5659 Royalmount Ave
Montreal, QC H4P 2P9
Canada
514-737-9701
Fax: 514-342-3854 888-275-4538
sales@mvpgroupcorp.com
www.mvpgroupcorp.com
Wholesaler/distributor of juice extractors and commercial dishwashers.
President: Michael Bromberg
Number Employees: 5-9
Private Brands Carried:
  Jet Tech; Santos; Sharp
Types of Products Distributed:
  Frozen Food, General Merchandise, Juice extractors & dishwashers

57825 MacDonalds Consolidated
1000 King Edward Street
Winnipeg, MB R3H 0R2
Canada
204-631-4470
Fax: 204-631-4472
Wholesaler/distributor of general line products, frozen foods, produce and meats
Branch Manager: Paul Bennett
Types of Products Distributed:
  Frozen Food, General Line, Provisions/Meat, Produce

57826 MacDonalds Consolidated
1020-64th Avenue N.E.
Calgary, AB T2E 5V8
Canada
403-730-3584
Fax: 866-435-7378 800-933-7515
macdonaldsconsolidated.ca
Wholesaler/distributor of general line products, meats, produce and private label items; serving the retail and food service markets
Director Independent Sales: Trent Stuart
Number Employees: 50-99
Parent Co: Canada Safeway
Private Brands Carried:
  Sunny Dawn; Family Foods; Lucerne
Types of Products Distributed:
  Food Service, Frozen Food, General Line, Provisions/Meat, Produce, Groceries & private label items

57827 MacGregors Meat & Seafood
265 Garyray Drive
Toronto, ON M9L 1P2
Canada
416-746-3951
888-383-3663
www.macgregors.com
Poultry, seafood and meat products; importer of beef and seafood
CFO: Ed de Vries
Vice President: John Hercus
VP of Sales, National Accounts: Rob Simpson
Number Employees: 180
Square Footage: 184000

Types of Products Distributed:
  Food Service, Provisions/Meat, Seafood

57828 Macdonald Meat Co
2709 Airport Way S
Seattle, WA 98134-2112
206-623-7993
Fax: 206-623-3835
customerservice@macmeat.com
www.macmeat.com
Wholesaler/distributor and exporter of meats/provisions and general merchandise; serving the food service market
President: Allan Motter
VP: William Jones
Contact: Kris Black
kad@macmeat.com
Estimated Sales: $20-50 Million
Number Employees: 20-49
Number of Customer Locations: 150
Types of Products Distributed:
  Food Service, Frozen Food, General Merchandise, Provisions/Meat

57829 Machias Bay Seafood
503 Kennebec Rd
Machias, ME 04654
207-255-8671
Fax: 207-255-8243
Seafood
Owner: Randy Ramsdell
Estimated Sales: $1-3 Million
Number Employees: 1-4

57830 Machine Ice Co
8915 Sweetwater Ln
Houston, TX 77037-2706
281-448-7823
Fax: 713-868-4424 800-423-8822
www.machineice.com
Wholesaler/distributor and exporter of mobile ice centers, ice plants, ice machines and refrigeration equipment; also, walk-in and reach-in coolers, cold storage facilities, ice cream makers, etc.; serving the food service market
President: Dan Celli
Sales Manager: Walter Felix
Estimated Sales: Less Than $500,000
Number Employees: 1-4
Square Footage: 88000
Private Brands Carried:
  Coldelite; Kold Draft; Vogt Tube Ice
Types of Products Distributed:
  Food Service, Frozen Food, General Merchandise, Ice machines, ice cream makers, etc.

57831 Mack Restaurant Equipment & Supplies
117 Rundle Street
Stellarton, NS B0K 1S0
Canada
902-752-4484
Fax: 902-752-8146 800-556-6225
info@mackfoodequipment.com www.e-mack.com
Wholesaler/distributor of food service supplies and equipment; serving the food service market
President: Ed Ripoll
Number Employees: 10-19
Private Brands Carried:
  Garland; Cheshire; Moyer-Diebel
Types of Products Distributed:
  Food Service, Frozen Food, General Merchandise, Supplies & equipment

57832 Macomb Tobacco & Candy Company
21411 Gratiot Ave
Eastpointe, MI 48021-2833
586-775-6162
Fax: 586-775-7690
Wholesaler/distributor of confectionery products; serving the food service market
Owner: Michael Zanella
VP: Michael Zanella
Estimated Sales: $2.5-5 Million
Number Employees: 5-9
Number of Customer Locations: 150
Types of Products Distributed:
  Food Service, General Line, Confectionery products

57833 Madani Halal
100-15 94th Ave
Ozone Park, NY 11416
718-323-9732
info@madanihalal.com
www.madanihalal.com
Halal goat, lamb, and poultry
President & CEO: Imran Uddin *Year Founded:* 1996

Types of Products Distributed:
  Provisions/Meat

57834 Made In Nature
2500 Pearl St
Suite 315
Boulder, CO 80302
800-906-7426
www.madeinnature.com
Organic dried and fresh fruits and vegetables as well as pizza.
Founder & CEO: Doug Brent
Estimated Sales: $2.6 Million
Number Employees: 16
Square Footage: 2200
Type of Packaging: Consumer

57835 Madison Cash & Carry Wholesale Grocers
5321 Verona Rd
Fitchburg, WI 53711
608-271-2310
Wholesaler/distributor of groceries; serving the food service market
Manager: Jerry Brown
Estimated Sales: $1-2.5 Million
Number Employees: 1-4
Square Footage: 1600
Parent Co: Certco
Types of Products Distributed:
  Food Service, Frozen Food, General Line, Groceries

57836 Madison Food Sales Company
21 Madison St
Paterson, NJ 07501
973-279-0900
Fax: 973-278-1235
Wholesaler/distributor of general merchandise, health foods, produce, provisions; serving the food service market
President: Edward Corditlo
Estimated Sales: $20-50 Million
Number Employees: 20-49
Types of Products Distributed:
  Food Service, Frozen Food, General Merchandise, Health Food, Provisions/Meat, Produce, Seafood

57837 Madison Grocery Company
P.O. Box 580
Richmond, KY 40476-0580
859-623-2416
Fax: 859-623-2446 www.hthackney.com
Wholesaler/distributor of general line products
Finance Executive: Kelvin Roberts
Estimated Sales: $20-50 Million
Number Employees: 20-49
Types of Products Distributed:
  Frozen Food, General Line

57838 Madison Wholesale Co
2214 Hollywood Dr
Jackson, TN 38305-4330
731-664-9567
Fax: 731-664-9605 800-526-3222
Wholesaler/distributor of groceries, candy, frozen food, meat, dairy, produce, etc.; serving the food service market
Partner: Fred Zimmerle
Partner: Chris Zimmerle
Partner: Jeff Zimmerle
Estimated Sales: $5-10 Million
Number Employees: 5-9
Square Footage: 80000
Number of Customer Locations: 300
Types of Products Distributed:
  Food Service, Frozen Food, General Line, General Merchandise, Produce, Candy, groceries & health & beauty aids

57839 Madland Toyota Lift
1258 W Betteravia Rd Ste A
Santa Maria, CA 93455
805-347-7878
Fax: 805-347-7874 800-836-3745
www.madlandtoyota.com
Wholesaler/distributor of material handling equipment
Manager: Leonard Daniels
Contact: Alice Hunter
ahunter@a1fence.com
General Manager: Jeff Eiseman
Estimated Sales: $2.5-5 Million
Number Employees: 5-9
Types of Products Distributed:
  Frozen Food, General Merchandise, Material handling equipment

Wholesalers & Distributors / A-Z

57840 Madys Company
1555 Yosemite Ave
San Francisco, CA 94124-3268
415-822-2227
Fax: 415-822-3673
Herbal, medicinal and regular teas; also, vitamins, ginseng root
Owner: Sandy Su Wing
General Manager: Marian Hong
Number Employees: 10-19
Square Footage: 13600
Parent Co: Azeta Brands
Type of Packaging: Consumer, Food Service, Private Label, Bulk
Types of Products Distributed:
  Frozen Food, Health Food, Herbal, medicinal & regular teas

57841 Maffei Produce Company
2901 Saint James Rd
Belmont, CA 94002-2954
415-824-0927
Fax: 415-695-9398
Wholesaler/distributor of apples, grapes, nectarines and peaches
President: Donald Maffei
VP: Martha Maffei
Estimated Sales: $1-2.5 Million
Number Employees: 1-4
Types of Products Distributed:
  Frozen Food, Produce, Apples, grapes, nectarines & peaches

57842 Maggie Lyon Chocolatiers
6000 Peachtree Industrial Blvd
Norcross, GA 30071
770-446-1299
Fax: 770-446-2191 800-969-3500
sales@maggielyon.com www.maggielyon.com
Products include gourmet chocolates, truffles, toffee, caramels, bark and nut clusters, toffee, special occasion and gift baskets, easter selections, bulk chocolates, and promotional products.
President: Jeffery Pollack
Cfo: Linda Pollack
VP: Michael Pollack
Estimated Sales: $1.8 Million
Number Employees: 15
Type of Packaging: Private Label

57843 Mahoning Swiss Cheese Cooperative
RR 1
Smicksburg, PA 16256-9801
814-257-8884
Wholesaler/distributor of dairy products; serving the food service market
General Manager: Ralph Juart
Types of Products Distributed:
  Food Service, Frozen Food, General Line, Dairy products

57844 Main Street Gourmet
170 Muffin Ln
Cuyahoga Falls, OH 44223
330-929-0000
800-678-6246
www.mainstreetgourmet.com
Gourmet fresh and frozen bakery items including an extensive selection of muffins and muffin batter, cookies, brownies and bars, granola, loaf cakes, cakes and baked goods and toppings.
CEO: Harvey Nelson
Manager, Quality Assurance: Angela Stoughton
Estimated Sales: $69 Million
Number Employees: 100-249
Square Footage: 65000
Parent Co: Clover Capital Partners LLC
Type of Packaging: Consumer, Food Service, Private Label, Bulk

57845 Main Street Wholesale Meat
210 Main St
Farmingdale, NY 11735-2618
516-249-8200
Fax: 516-249-2481 info@mainstreetmeats.com
Wholesaler/distributor of meats
President: Kent Seelig
steaks13@aol.com
Sales Manager: Hal Quinton
Sales/Marketing: Lee Seelig
Estimated Sales: $5-10 Million
Number Employees: 20-49
Types of Products Distributed:
  Frozen Food, Provisions/Meat

57846 Maine Coast Sea Vegetables
3 George's Pond Rd
Franklin, ME 4634
207-565-2907
Fax: 207-565-2144 info@seaveg.com
www.seaveg.com
Edible seaweed products including sea vegetables, seasonings, snack bars, and chips. Wholesaler/distributor of seaweed including whole and ground
President/CEO: Shepard Erhart
President/CEO: Linnette Erhart
Treasurer/CFO: Carl Karush
Contact: Aaron Brown
aaron@seaveg.com
Operations Manager: Mary Ellen Lasell
Production Manager: Hannah Russell
Estimated Sales: $2 Million
Number Employees: 20
Number of Products: 40
Square Footage: 18000
Type of Packaging: Consumer, Bulk
Types of Products Distributed:
  Frozen Food, General Line, Health Food, Whole & ground seaweed

57847 Maine Lobster Outlet
360 US Route 1
York, ME 03909-1631
207-363-4449
Fax: 207-363-0613 info@mainelobsteroutlet.com
Lobster
Owner: Sheila Barnes
sbarnes@mainelobsteroutlet.com
Estimated Sales: $1-3 Million
Number Employees: 10-19

57848 Maine Mahogony Shellfish
8 Johnson Ln
Addison, ME 04606
207-483-2865
Fax: 207-483-4389
Wholesale and retail products include lobster, clams, crab, halibut, mussels, and a wide variety of shellfish.
Manager: Robert Johnson

57849 Maine Shellfish Co Inc
95 Water St
Ellsworth, ME 04605
207-667-5336
Fax: 207-667-6275 800-666-5336
www.ipswichshellfish.com
Wholesaler/distributor of fresh and frozen seafood.
Sales & Marketing: Amy Hopfmann
Credit Manager: Daniel Doyon
dan@meshellfish.com
Year Founded: 1949
Estimated Sales: $20-50 Million
Number Employees: 50-99
Parent Co: Ipswich Shellfish Company, Inc.
Types of Products Distributed:
  Frozen Food, Seafood

57850 (HQ)Maines Paper & Food SvcInc
101 Broome Corporate Pkwy
Conklin, NY 13748-1507
607-779-1200
Fax: 607-723-3245 800-366-3669
www.maines.net
Wholesaler/distributor of groceries, meats, dairy beverages, frozen foods, produce, chicken, baked goods, equipment and fixtures, seafood and paper goods; serving the food service market
President: Christopher Mullin
Executive VP: D Maines
Executive VP: W Maines
IT Executive: William Kimler
william.kimler@maine.net
Estimated Sales: Over $1 Billion
Number Employees: 1000-4999
Square Footage: 700000
Other Locations:
  Maines Paper & Food Service
  Conklin, NYMaines Paper & Food Service
Private Brands Carried:
  Nifda; Parlor City; Maines
Number of Customer Locations: 2000
Types of Products Distributed:
  Food Service, Frozen Food, General Line, General Merchandise, Provisions/Meat, Produce, Seafood, Groceries, baked goods, etc.

57851 Maines Paper & Food SvcInc
199 Oak Leaf Oval
Cleveland, OH 44146-6156
216-643-7500
Fax: 800-726-2776 800-735-7900
www.maines.net
Wholesaler/distributor of frozen foods, paper products, etc.; serving the food service market
President: Jim Erney
erney@maines.net
SVP, CFO: Terri Deane
Operations Manager: Mark Chaloupka
Estimated Sales: $5-10 Million
Number Employees: 100-249
Square Footage: 300000
Parent Co: Maines Paper & Food Services
Number of Customer Locations: 400
Types of Products Distributed:
  Food Service, Frozen Food, General Merchandise, Paper products

57852 Maines Paper & Food SvcInc
101 Broome Corporate Parkway
Conklin, NY 13748
607-779-1200
800-366-3669
www.maines.net
Wholesaler/distributor of frozen food and general line items; serving fast food chains.
VP, Treasury: Terri Deane
VP, Corporate Business Development: Charlie Feldman
Plant Manager: Tom Hoard
Year Founded: 1919
Estimated Sales: $115 Million
Number Employees: 100-249
Square Footage: 360000
Number of Customer Locations: 459
Types of Products Distributed:
  Food Service, Frozen Food, General Line

57853 Maintainco Inc
65 E Leuning St
PO Box 1785
South Hackensack, NJ 07606-1382
201-487-2565
Fax: 201-487-3138 888-714-9647
www.maintainco.com
Wholesaler/distributor of lift trucks, shelving and fork lifts
President: James Picarillo
maintainco@optonline.net
Estimated Sales: $10-20 Million
Number Employees: 20-49
Private Brands Carried:
  Mitsubishi; Toyota; Big Joe
Types of Products Distributed:
  Frozen Food, General Merchandise, Lift trucks, shelving & fork lifts

57854 Maintenance Equipment Company
P.O.Box 385
Tucker, GA 30085
770-939-1970
Fax: 770-938-6302 800-225-6320
www.amsan.com
Wholesaler/distributor of janitorial equipment and supplies
Manager: Fred Adickes
General Manager: Jack Robertson
Sales Manager: Brian Stanley
Purchasing Agent: Leisha Roitan
Estimated Sales: $5-10 Million
Number Employees: 20-49
Square Footage: 128000
Parent Co: Am San
Types of Products Distributed:
  Frozen Food, General Merchandise, Janitorial equipment & supplies

57855 Maison Gourmet
1700 Aimco Boulevard
Mississauga, ON L4W 1V1
Canada
905-624-6310
Fax: 905-624-4033 www.maisongourmet.ca
Maison Gourmet is an importer/distributor of gourmet foods including of cherries, olives and pastry products; serving the food service market
President: Paul Kawaja
Marketing: Eric Landry
Private Brands Carried:
  DGF; PIDV; Swiss Alpine
Types of Products Distributed:
  Food Service, Cherries, olives & pastry products

57856 Majestic Lift Truck Service
1010 W Elizabeth Ave
Linden, NJ 07036
908-820-7965
Fax: 908-474-1098
Wholesaler/distributor of lift trucks and material handling equipment
VP: Matthew Sherman
Estimated Sales: $2.5-5 Million
Number Employees: 10-19

Wholesalers & Distributors / A-Z

57857 Malco Industries
31 King St
Lynn, MA 01902   781-598-4696
Fax: 781-598-9382 800-696-4111
Private Brands Carried:
Nissan; Daewoo; Clark
Types of Products Distributed:
Frozen Food, General Merchandise, Lift trucks & material handling equip.

Wholesaler/distributor of specialty foods and general merchandise; also, rack jobber services available
President: A Goldstein
CEO: M Goldstein
Estimated Sales: $2.5-5 Million
Number Employees: 5-9
Square Footage: 120000
Parent Co: Malden Mop & Brush Company
Types of Products Distributed:
General Merchandise, Rack Jobbers

57858 Malena Produce Inc
947 E Frontage Rd # A
Rio Rico, AZ 85648-6264   520-281-1185
Fax: 520-281-2156 dstoller@malenaproduce.com
Wholesaler/distributor and importer of fruits and vegetables including eggplant, bell and hot peppers, squash and pickles
President: Juanita Avila
javila@malenaproduce.com
Sales Manager: Ana Astrid Celaya
Sales: Oscar Rodriguez
Estimated Sales: $10-20 Million
Number Employees: 10-19
Square Footage: 30000
Type of Packaging: Consumer, Food Service
Private Brands Carried:
Malena; San Isidro; Melisa; Double G; Natalia; Kobys
Types of Products Distributed:
Frozen Food, General Line, Produce, Eggplant, squash, etc.

57859 Maloberti Produce Co
124 Depot St
Greensburg, PA 15601-2108   724-834-2282
Wholesaler/distributor of produce; serving the food service market
Owner: Albert Maloberti
Estimated Sales: $1-2.5 Million
Number Employees: 1-4
Types of Products Distributed:
Food Service, Frozen Food, Produce

57860 Malow Corporation
100 E Progress Rd
Lombard, IL 60148   630-629-9700
Fax: 847-629-9700 800-876-2569
www.khlengpkg.com
Wholesaler/distributor of packaging machinery and materials including shrink, stretch, taping, strapping systems, etc
Manager: David Graney
VP: Neal Malow
Contact: Marshall Gray
marshall@malow.com
Estimated Sales: $10-20 Million
Number Employees: 50-99
Square Footage: 100000
Types of Products Distributed:
Frozen Food, General Merchandise, Packaging machinery & materials

57861 Malt Diastase Co
88 Market St
Saddle Brook, NJ 07663
Fax: 201-845-0028 800-526-0180
www.maltproducts.com
Malt, molasses, natural sweeteners
Owner/President: Amy Targan
VP of Sales: John Johansen
Number Employees: 20-49
Type of Packaging: Bulk
Types of Products Distributed:
Specialty Foods

57862 Manchac Seafood Market
131 Bait Alley
Ponchatoula, LA 70454   985-370-7070
Fax: 985-386-2762
Seafood
President: Duke Robin

57863 Manchester Grocery Company
108 Dickenson Street
Manchester, KY 40962-1221   606-598-2328
Wholesaler/distributor of groceries, produce and provisions/meats
President: J Rice
VP: K Rice
Estimated Sales: $1-2.5 Million
Number Employees: 1-4
Number of Customer Locations: 350
Types of Products Distributed:
Frozen Food, General Line, Provisions/Meat, Produce, Rack Jobbers, Groceries

57864 Manco Distributors
25 Iron Street
Etobicoke, ON M9W 5E3
Canada   416-247-8422
Fax: 416-247-4648 manco@bellnet.com
Wholesaler/distributor of ice making machines, dispensing, ice and beveragesystems and refrigeration products; serving the food service market
President: Murray Gamble
Private Brands Carried:
Manitowoc Ice, Inc.; McCall; Servend; San Jamar

57865 Mancuso Cheese Co
612 Mills Rd # 1
Joliet, IL 60433-2897   815-722-2475
Fax: 815-722-1302 pfalbo@mancusocheese.com
www.mancusocheese.com
Cheese including ricotta, mozzarella, etc.; exporter of pizza supplies; importer of pasta, olive oil, olives and anchovies; wholesaler/distributor of frozen foods, produce, meats, baked goods, general merchandise, etc.
President: Dominic Mancuso
mberta@mancusocheese.com
VP: Philip Falbo
Sales Exec: Mike Berta
Estimated Sales: $6 Million
Number Employees: 20-49
Square Footage: 80000
Type of Packaging: Consumer, Food Service, Bulk
Number of Customer Locations: 300
Types of Products Distributed:
Food Service, Frozen Food, General Merchandise, Provisions/Meat, Produce, Specialty Foods, Institutional food products

57866 Mandeville Company
2800 Washington Ave N
Minneapolis, MN 55411-1683   612-521-3671
Fax: 612-521-3673 800-328-8490
Manufacturer and wholesaler/distributor of equipment for meat processors, delis and restaurants including saws, grinders, mixers, tumblers, marinators, knives, scales, juicers and slicers; also, reconditioned equipment; serving thefood service market
President: Julie Lane
Secretary: Phyllis Stellmaker
Estimated Sales: $2.5-5 Million
Number Employees: 10-19
Square Footage: 40000
Types of Products Distributed:
Food Service, Frozen Food, General Merchandise, Utensils & supplies

57867 (HQ)Mandex Motion Displays
2350 Young Avenue
Thousand Oaks, CA 91360-1840   805-497-8006
Fax: 818-889-4569 800-473-5623
www.ledsignage.com
Wholesaler/distributor of indoor and outdoor programmable electronic menu signs, rentals and sale of equipment
President: Alan Derber
alanderber@gmail.com
Controller: Julie Derber
Estimated Sales: $1-2.5 Million
Number Employees: 10-19
Square Footage: 8000
Types of Products Distributed:
Programmable electronic menu signs

57868 Mando Inc
16 Humphrey St
Englewood, NJ 07631-3445   201-568-9337
Fax: 201-568-9426
Dumplings
President: Kyo Lee
Contact: Kyn Lee
jameschoi21@hotmail.com

Estimated Sales: $2.5-5,000,000
Number Employees: 5-9
Type of Packaging: Consumer, Food Service, Bulk
Types of Products Distributed:
Frozen Food

57869 Manhattan Fire Safety
242 W 30th St # 701
New York, NY 10001-0792   718-322-3959
Fax: 212-563-8641
Wholesaler/distributor of fire extinguishers and first aid kits
Owner: David Tillman
Customer Service Manager: Audrey Layne
Estimated Sales: $20-50 Million
Number Employees: 20-49
Square Footage: 2000
Types of Products Distributed:
Frozen Food, General Merchandise, Fire extinguishers & first aid kits

57870 Manhattan Key Lime Juice Company
4115 46th St
Long Island City, NY 11104-1851   212-696-5378
Fax: 718-829-8834 keylimequeen@hotmail.com
www.manhattankeylime.com
Wholesaler/distributor of key lime juice including with pulp and sweetened; serving the food service market
President: Jeanette Richards
Vice President: Lew Peterla
Estimated Sales: Under $300,000
Number Employees: 5-9
Square Footage: 20000
Type of Packaging: Consumer, Food Service, Bulk
Private Brands Carried:
Key Lime, Lemon Juice and Sweetened Lime Juice
Types of Products Distributed:
Food Service, General Line, Specialty Foods

57871 Manhattan Lights
1941 Coney Island Ave
Brooklyn, NY 11223   718-998-1111
Fax: 718-998-1117 800-922-0045
www.manhattanlights.com
Wholesaler/distributor of lighting fixtures
President: Dale Fishbaum
Estimated Sales: $1-2.5 Million
Number Employees: 10-19
Square Footage: 40000
Private Brands Carried:
Sylvania; GE
Types of Products Distributed:
Frozen Food, General Merchandise, Lighting fixtures

57872 Mani Imports
3601 Parkway Pl
West Sacramento, CA 95691-3420   916-373-1100
Fax: 916-373-1018 info@maniimports.com
www.maniimports.com
Wholesaler/distributor and importer of olive oil, fire-roasted peppers, olives, spices, feta cheese, olive oil soap, tropical fruit pulps and natural sponges
Owner: Peter Cononelos
Corporate Chief: Glenn Weddell
Estimated Sales: $5-10 Million
Number Employees: 10-19
Types of Products Distributed:
Frozen Food, General Line, General Merchandise, Specialty Foods, Olive oil, peppers, olives, etc.

57873 Manning Brothers Food Eqpt Co
210 Sandy Creek Rd
Athens, GA 30607-1149   706-549-7088
Fax: 706-549-8403 www.manningbrothers.com
Wholesaler/distributor of food service equipment
President: Chuck Day
chuck@manningbrothers.com
Estimated Sales: $5-10 Million
Number Employees: 20-49
Private Brands Carried:
Hobart; Vulcan; Vollrath
Types of Products Distributed:
Food Service, Frozen Food, General Merchandise, Foodservice equipment

57874 Manor Electric SuppliesLight
2737 Ocean Ave
Brooklyn, NY 11229-4700   718-648-8003
Fax: 718-648-7351 manorelectric@aol.com

Wholesaler/distributor of electrical supplies and lighting fixtures
Owner: Kenny Rabinowitz
manorelectric@aol.com
VP: Rabin Owitz
Purchasing Agent: Barry Baker
Estimated Sales: $5-10 Million
Number Employees: 10-19
Types of Products Distributed:
  Frozen Food, General Merchandise, Electric supplies & lighting fixtures

57875 Manting Equipment Company
830 Woodlawn Avenue
Grand Haven, MI 49417-2142   616-842-6180
  Fax: 616-842-6189 800-678-1140
Wholesaler/distributor of equipment and supplies; serving the food service market
President: Peter Manting
Sales Director: Sue Chittenden
Estimated Sales: $5-10 Million
Number Employees: 5-9
Square Footage: 80000
Number of Customer Locations: 500
Types of Products Distributed:
  Food Service, General Merchandise, Food Service Equipment

57876 Manuel's Hot Tamales
4709 S Carrollton Avenue
New Orleans, LA 70119-6076   504-482-6616
Wholesaler/distributor of hot tamales; serving the food service market
President: Francis Schneider
Estimated Sales: $2.5-5 Million
Number Employees: 10-19
Types of Products Distributed:
  Food Service, Frozen Food, General Line, Hot tamales

57877 Manuel's Mexican-American Fine Foods
2007 S 300 W
Salt Lake City, UT 84115-1808   801-484-1431
  Fax: 801-484-1440 800-748-5072
Tortilla chips, taco shells, corn tortilla, tostada shells and pre-cut tortillas
President: Orlando Torres
VP: Mike Torres
VP/Sales Exec: Paul Torres
Estimated Sales: Below $5 Million
Number Employees: 40
Type of Packaging: Consumer, Food Service, Private Label, Bulk
Private Brands Carried:
  Manuel's Fine Foods; Don Julio
Types of Products Distributed:
  Food Service, Frozen Food

57878 Maple Hollow
W1887 Robinson Dr
Merrill, WI 54452-9543   715-536-7251
Maple syrup and sugar; wholesaler/distibutor of maple syrup processing machinery
Owner: Joe Polak
Vice President: Barbara Polak
Estimated Sales: $1 Million
Number Employees: 5-9
Number of Brands: 5
Number of Products: 4
Square Footage: 40000
Type of Packaging: Consumer, Private Label
Private Brands Carried:
  Maple Hollow; Heritage; Forest Country
Types of Products Distributed:
  Food Service, Health Food, Specialty Foods, Maple syrup processing machinery

57879 Maple Valley Cooperative
919 Front St
P.O. Box 153
Cashton, WI 54619   608-654-7319
  Fax: 877-579-5073
  customerservice@maplevalley.coop
  www.maplevalleysyrup.coop
Organic maple syrup, maple candy, maple sugar, and maple cream
Founder/President: Cecil Wright
General Manager: Renee Miller *Year Founded:* 2007
Types of Products Distributed:
  General Line

57880 Mar Meat Company
PO Box 470217
St Louis, MO 63147-7217   314-241-3242
  Fax: 314-241-5319
Wholesaler/distributor of fresh pork and beef
President: Edward Oughton
Number Employees: 5-9
Types of Products Distributed:
  Provisions/Meat, Fresh pork & beef

57881 Marci Enterprises
5271 W Jefferson Boulevard
Los Angeles, CA 90016-3841   323-937-5050
  Fax: 323-937-6915
Wholesaler/distributor of food packaging materials including steel drums, tin cans, boxes, plastics, etc
President: Frederick Weiner
Secretary/Treasurer: Marci Weiner
Number Employees: 1-4
Private Brands Carried:
  Marci
Types of Products Distributed:
  Frozen Food, General Merchandise, Packaging materials

57882 Marcus Food Co
P.O. Box 781659
Wichita, KS 67278-1659   316-686-7649
  Fax: 316-684-1266
  information@marcusfoodco.com
  www.marcusfoodco.com
Importer, exporter and wholesaler/distributor of frozen food, seafood and meat products including pork and chicken.
President: Jerry Marcus
Founder & Chairman: Howard Marcus
hmarcus@marcusfoodco.com
Operations Manager: Rick Finney
Year Founded: 1980
Estimated Sales: $140 Million
Number Employees: 10-19
Type of Packaging: Food Service, Private Label, Bulk
Types of Products Distributed:
  Food Service, Frozen Food, Provisions/Meat, Seafood

57883 Marcus Specialty Foods
2700 Avenue D
Birmingham, AL 35218   205-252-0344
  Fax: 205-226-8052 800-277-3354
Wholesaler/distributor of meat, dairy and bakery products, olive oil, salad dressings, desserts, frozen foods and specialty foods; serving the food service market. Has a fleet of 12 trucks delivering to Alabama, Tennessee, Mississippiand the Florida peninsula
President: Nathan Marcus
Secretary: L Marcus
Estimated Sales: $10-20 Million
Number Employees: 10-19
Square Footage: 20000
Number of Customer Locations: 260
Types of Products Distributed:
  Food Service, Frozen Food, General Line, Provisions/Meat, Specialty Foods, Bakery & dairy products

57884 Marek Equipment Trading
2417 Colorado St
Mission, TX 78572-9589   956-584-7777
  Fax: 956-584-2727 877-276-2735
Wholesaler/distributor of meat processing equipment
Manager: Dina Sierra
Estimated Sales: $1-2.5 Million
Number Employees: 1-4
Square Footage: 14400
Types of Products Distributed:
  General Merchandise, Meat processing equipment

57885 Margarita Man
10818 Gulfdale St
San Antonio, TX 78216-3607   210-979-7191
  Fax: 210-979-0718 800-950-8149
  info@margaritamansa.com
  www.margaritamansa.com
Frozen drink mixes; wholesaler/distributor of frozen beverage machines
President: Chris Murphy
ncmargman@nc.rr.com
Plant Manager: Steve Snyder
Estimated Sales: $1 Million
Number Employees: 5-9
Number of Brands: 1
Number of Products: 15
Square Footage: 10000
Types of Products Distributed:
  Frozen Food, General Merchandise, Frozen beverage machines

57886 Margate Wine & Spirit Co
2800 Shore Road
Northfield, NJ 08225   609-404-3000
  Fax: 609-404-4610
Their focus is to work with a select group of producers/owners who will offer their finest wines.
President: Jonathan Shiekman
VP: Richard Shiekman
Director: Morton Shiekman
Estimated Sales: $5-10 Million
Number Employees: 1-4
Private Brands Carried:
  Chantefleur; Leonard de St. Aubin; Robert Michele; McWilliam's Chateau de Maligny; Chateau des Herbeux; Valfieri; Vignamaggio; Saccardi; Delarche; Poggio San Polo; Cecilia Beretta; Casa Donoso; Piduco Creek
Types of Products Distributed:
  Food Service, Frozen Food, General Line, Table wines

57887 MariGold Foods
16693 Coaltown Rd
Willis, TX 77378   936-344-0444
  www.marigoldbars.com
Gluten free, organic, non-GMO protein bars
Co-Owner: Mari Ann Lisenbe
Co-Owner: Steve Lisenbe *Year Founded:* 2012
Types of Products Distributed:
  General Line

57888 Marias Packing Company
PO Box 356
Shelby, MT 59474   406-434-2011
  Fax: 406-434-2012
Wholesaler/distributor of meat products; serving the food service market
Owner: Don Nelson
Estimated Sales: $3-5 Million
Number Employees: 5-9
Types of Products Distributed:
  Food Service, Frozen Food, Provisions/Meat

57889 Marin Hydroponics
55 Frosty Ln
Novato, CA 94949-5601   415-897-2197
  www.marinhydroponics.com
Wholesaler/distributor of frozen and health foods; serving the retail and military markets
Vice President: J Silverstri
Manager: Jason Bedell
jason@lumatekballast.com
Estimated Sales: $1-2.5 Million
Number Employees: 5-9
Square Footage: 44000
Private Brands Carried:
  Frosty Acres
Number of Customer Locations: 200
Types of Products Distributed:
  Food Service, Frozen Food, Health Food

57890 Mariner Neptune Fish & Seafood Company
472 Dufferin Avenue
Winnipeg, NB R2W 2X6
Canada   204-589-5341
  Fax: 204-582-8135 800-668-8862
  www.marinerneptune.com
Distributor of fish, seafood and protein food products
President: John Alexander
VP: Russell Page
Marketing: Evan Page
Sales: Doug Chandler
Plant Manager: Chris Juerson
Estimated Sales: $16 Million
Number Employees: 42
Number of Products: 2000
Type of Packaging: Consumer, Food Service
Types of Products Distributed:
  Food Service, Frozen Food, Seafood, Specialty Foods

Wholesalers & Distributors / A-Z

57891 Mark Pack Inc
3405 Lonergan Dr
Rockford, IL 61109-2622 815-874-5454
Fax: 815-874-1660 888-874-5454
info@markpack.com www.markpack.com
Wholesaler/distributor of packaging equipment including cartoners, case packers, label printers, case erectors and sealers, strapping machines, shrink equipment, stretch wrapper and form/fill/seal equipment
President: Shirley Keller
VP/Sales Manager: Jerry Keller
Manager: Terry Keller
terry@markpack.com
Office Manager: Terry Keller
System Sales Manager: Randy Keller
Estimated Sales: Less Than $500,000
Number Employees: 1-4
Square Footage: 56000
Private Brands Carried:
  S.V. Dice; Orion; Sato; Belcor; Polyair; Sekisui-TA; Bishamon Ind.; PFM H.S. Wrappers
Types of Products Distributed:
  Frozen Food, General Merchandise, Packaging equipment

57892 Mark's International Seafood Brokers
PO Box 602
Fairhaven, MA 02719-0602 508-992-2115
Fax: 508-991-2072
President: Mark Wright
Estimated Sales: $10-20 Million
Number Employees: 20-49

57893 (HQ)Mark-Pack Inc
776 Main St
Coopersville, MI 49404-1363 616-837-5400
Fax: 616-837-5450 dnielsen@markpackinc.com
www.markpackinc.com
Wholesaler/distributor of ink jet printing equipment, case/carton sealing, glue and strapping
President: David Nielsen
dnielsen@markpackinc.com
Vice President: Mike Marine
Purchasing Manager: Donnis Pastor
Estimated Sales: $10-20 Million
Number Employees: 20-49
Number of Brands: 200
Number of Products: 500
Square Footage: 30000
Private Brands Carried:
  Marsh; Label Mill; Signode; ITW Dynatech; Soco; Intertape; Ranpak; Paragon
Types of Products Distributed:
  Frozen Food, General Merchandise, Ink for printing equipment

57894 Market Fisheries
7129 S State St
Chicago, IL 60619-1017 773-483-3233
Fax: 773-483-0724
Seafood
President: Haim Brody
haim@centerstagechicago.com
Estimated Sales: $3-5 Million
Number Employees: 10-19

57895 Market Foods International
730 Kasota Cir SE
Minneapolis, MN 55414 612-378-0455
Fax: 612-378-9542
Wholesaler/distributor of Oriental foods including produce, meats, specialty items and seafood; serving food service markets in Minnesota, North and South Dakota, Iowa, Wisconsin, Nebraska, Montana and Illinois
President: Pete Bergin
Estimated Sales: $2.5-5 Million
Number Employees: 20-49
Square Footage: 200000
Private Brands Carried:
  Market Foods International
Number of Customer Locations: 700
Types of Products Distributed:
  Food Service, Frozen Food, Provisions/Meat, Produce, Seafood, Specialty Foods, Oriental foods

57896 (HQ)Market Grocery Co
16 Forest Pkwy # K1
Forest Park, GA 30297-2099 404-361-8620
Fax: 404-361-3773 www.marketgrocery.com
Wholesaler/distributor of meats, dairy items, frozen foods, equipment and fixtures and general line products
President: Bob Barnette
b.barnette@marketgrocery.com
Estimated Sales: $20-50 Million
Number Employees: 50-99
Other Locations:
  Market Grocery Co.
  Macon, GAMarket Grocery Co.
Types of Products Distributed:
  Frozen Food, General Line, General Merchandise, Provisions/Meat, Dairy items, groceries, etc.

57897 Marko Inc
1310 Southport Rd
Spartanburg, SC 29306-6199 864-585-2259
866-466-2726
rmeehan@markoinc.com www.markoinc.com
Janitorial cleaners, disinfectants and waxes; wholesaler/distributor of paper supplies and janitorial equipment including aerosols and mops
Owner: Anne Meehan
ameehan@markoinc.com
CEO: Ann Meehan
VP Marketing: Richard Meehan, Jr.
Purchasing Manager: Melanie Meehan
Estimated Sales: 800000
Number Employees: 5-9
Number of Brands: 10
Number of Products: 450
Square Footage: 24000
Type of Packaging: Private Label
Private Brands Carried:
  Fort James; Pullman/Holt; Thoromatic; Panasonic; Claire Manufacturing
Types of Products Distributed:
  Frozen Food, General Merchandise, Paper products & janitorial supplies

57898 Markson Lab Sales
5285 NE Elam Young Parkway
Hillsboro, OR 97124-6427 800-528-5114
www.markson.com
Wholesaler/distributor, importer and exporter of laboratory and microbiology equipment
Sales Supervisor: Bob Dickie
General Manager: Steve Ciucci
Production Manager: Jeff Geiger
Number Employees: 20-49
Types of Products Distributed:
  Frozen Food, General Merchandise, Laboratory & microbiology equipment

57899 Markuse Corporation
6c Dunham Road
Billerica, MA 01821-5727 781-275-5777
Fax: 781-275-0036
Wholesaler/distributor of oil and vinegar sets, ice buckets, etc.; serving the food service market
President: Jack Markuse
VP: Vicki Markuse
Sales: Harry Markuse
Purchasing Manager: Gail Berkowitz
Estimated Sales: $2.5-5 Million
Number Employees: 6
Square Footage: 24000
Private Brands Carried:
  Alessi
Number of Customer Locations: 2000
Types of Products Distributed:
  Food Service, General Merchandise, Oil & vinegar sets, ice buckets, etc.

57900 Marky's Caviar
1000 Northwest 159th Drive
Miami, FL 33169-4709 305-758-9288
Fax: 305-758-0008 800-722-8427
info@markys.com www.markys.com
Wholesaler/distributor, importer and exporter of caviar, smoked salmon, foie gras, truffles, mushrooms, saffron, anguila, etc.; wholesaler/distributor of frozen foods and meats
Owner: Mark Gelman
Vice President: Sarah Echevarria
Estimated Sales: $7 Million
Number Employees: 50
Square Footage: 60000
Parent Co: Optimus
Type of Packaging: Consumer, Food Service, Private Label, Bulk
Private Brands Carried:
  Bon Appetit; Marky's; Rougie, Bizac, Malossol, Membrillo Emily, Mimmo's, Pinnacle Of Scotland, Plantin, Redondo USA, Rougie, Russian Osetra Karat Caviar, Serrats White Albacore, Sturgeon AquaFarms, Terroir D'Antan, Vill'Antica, Xquisite Chocolate FigBon
Types of Products Distributed:
  Food Service, Frozen Food, Provisions/Meat, Seafood, Specialty Foods, Caviar, foie gras, truffles, etc.

57901 Marle Company
35 Larkin St
Stamford, CT 06907 203-348-2645
Fax: 203-348-5280 www.needco.com
Wholesaler/distributor of electrical supplies including industrial fans, lighting fixtures and light bulbs
Manager: Scott Brown
scott.brown@needco.com
Manager: Jonathan Levine
Estimated Sales: $10-20 Million
Number Employees: 20-49
Square Footage: 36000
Parent Co: Northeast Electrical Distributor
Number of Customer Locations: 2500
Types of Products Distributed:
  Frozen Food, Electrical supplies

57902 Marlow Candy & Nut Co
65 Honeck St
Englewood, NJ 07631-4125 201-569-3725
Fax: 201-569-9533 800-231-2018
www.marlowcandy.net
Wholesaler of packaged candy and nuts
President: Eric Lowenthal
rickyl@marlowcandy.net
Office Manager: Alden Kirk
Estimated Sales: $10-20 Million
Number Employees: 20-49
Number of Brands: 6
Number of Products: 100+
Type of Packaging: Consumer, Food Service, Private Label
Number of Customer Locations: 4000
Types of Products Distributed:
  Frozen Food, General Line, Rack Jobbers, Packaged candy & nuts

57903 Marriott Distribution Service
601 13th St NW
Washington, DC 20005-3807 202-261-4012
Fax: 202-261-4033
Wholesaler/distributor of frozen, health and specialty foods, produce, seafood and meats; serving the food service market
President/General Manager: Robert Pras
Senior VP Marketing: Gere Lehr
Number Employees: 10-19
Types of Products Distributed:
  Food Service, Frozen Food, Health Food, Provisions/Meat, Produce, Seafood, Specialty Foods

57904 Marrone's Inc
800 E 14th St
Pittsburg, KS 66762 620-231-6610
Wholesaler/distributor of groceries, provisions/meats, seafood, general line products, produce and frozen foods; serving the food service market.
Manager: Ron Marrone
Estimated Sales: $12 Million
Number Employees: 20-49
Private Brands Carried:
  Pleezing
Types of Products Distributed:
  Food Service, Frozen Food, General Line, Provisions/Meat, Produce, Seafood, Groceries

57905 Marroquin Organic Intl.
303 Potero St
Suite 18
Santa Cruz, CA 95060 831-423-3442
Fax: 831-423-3432 info@marroquin-organics.com
www.marroquin-organics.com
Organic and non-GMO ingredients
President: Grace Marroquin
Vice President: Mark Nelson
Organic Ingredient Specialist: Helen Hudson
Contact: Ciaran Cooney
ccooney@paypal.com
Estimated Sales: $4-5 Million
Number Employees: 5-9

Wholesalers & Distributors / A-Z

57906 (HQ)Mars Supermarkets
9627 Philadelphia Rd Ste 100
Rosedale, MD 21237   410-590-0500
www.marsfood.com
Wholesaler/distributor of groceries, meat, produce, dairy products and health and beauty aids; serving the food service market
President: Carmen D'Anna
Estimated Sales: $500,000-$1 Million
Number Employees: 1,000-4,999
Square Footage: 1200000
Number of Customer Locations: 12
Types of Products Distributed:
Food Service, Frozen Food, General Line, Provisions/Meat, Produce, Groceries & dairy items

57907 Marshakk Smoked Fish Company
6980 75th St
Flushing, NY 11379-2531   718-326-2170
Fax: 718-384-6661
Specialty foods
President: Marie Cook
Vice President: Gary Cook
Sales Director: Sean Cook
Estimated Sales: $10-24.9 000,000
Number Employees: 50-99
Type of Packaging: Private Label

57908 Martin Bros Distributing Co
406 Viking Rd
Cedar Falls, IA 50613-6930   319-266-1775
Fax: 319-277-1238 www.martinsnet.com
Wholesaler/distributor of baked goods, dairy items, frozen food, groceries, meat, produce, seafood, janitorial supplies, equipment, etc.; serving the food service market; also, nutritional services, menu consulting, layout and design available
Owner: Ron Guthrie
CFO: Brooks Martin
Manager of Business Development: John Smith
Marketing Manager: Megan Zuniga
VP Sales: Doug Coen
Contact: Tom Banta
tbanta@martinsnet.com
VP of Operations: Doug Karns
VP Purchasing: Diane Chandler
Estimated Sales: $28.6 Million
Number Employees: 100-249
Square Footage: 13209
Private Brands Carried:
Nugget
Number of Customer Locations: 3600
Types of Products Distributed:
Food Service, Frozen Food, General Line, General Merchandise, Provisions/Meat, Produce, Seafood, Baked goods, dairy items, etc.

57909 Martin Brothers Wholesale
15 Lincoln Ave
Selinsgrove, PA 17870   570-743-7117
Fax: 570-743-8281
Wholesaler/distributor of produce and equipment and fixtures
President: Bruce Martin
Shareholder: Alfred Martin
VP: Gregory Martin
Estimated Sales: $1-2.5 Million
Number Employees: 10-19
Square Footage: 40000
Types of Products Distributed:
Frozen Food, General Merchandise, Produce

57910 Martin Food Service Company
690 Success Road
Akron, OH 44310-1627   330-535-3737
Fax: 330-633-1589
Wholesaler/distributor of sandwiches, coffee and concession items; serving the food service market
President: Robert Martin
Estimated Sales: $10-20 Million
Number Employees: 10-19
Type of Packaging: Bulk
Types of Products Distributed:
Food Service, Frozen Food, General Line, Sandwiches, coffee & concessions

57911 Martin Preferred Foods
2011 Silver St
Houston, TX 77007-2801   713-869-6191
800-356-7390
www.martinpreferredfoods.com
Wholesaler/distributor of frozen foods, general line items, cheeses and provisions/meats including chicken, veal, lamb, pork and sausages; serving the food service market
President: M Tapick
Executive VP: Kenneth Goldstein
Estimated Sales: $20-50 Million
Number Employees: 100-249
Number of Customer Locations: 2500
Types of Products Distributed:
Food Service, Frozen Food, General Line, Provisions/Meat, Chicken, veal, lamb, pork, sausage, etc

57912 Martin Produce Co
617 6th St
Greeley, CO 80631-3922   970-352-0015
Fax: 970-352-5687
Wholesaler/distributor of potatoes and onions
President: Buane Zabka
CEO: Dwayne Zabka
Estimated Sales: $20-50 Million
Number Employees: 20-49
Types of Products Distributed:
Frozen Food, Produce, Potatoes & onions

57913 Martin Seafood Company
7901 Oceano Avenue, Units 46, 48, 50 &
P.O.Box 220
Jessup, MD 20794   410-799-5822
Fax: 410-799-3545
Frozen breaded seafood products; wholesaler/distributor of raw frozen seafood products; serving the food service market
Owner: Billy Martin
Secretary: Shawn Isaac
Estimated Sales: $3 Million
Number Employees: 20-49
Square Footage: 100000
Type of Packaging: Consumer, Food Service
Types of Products Distributed:
Food Service, Frozen Food, Seafood

57914 Martin's Potato Chips
5847 Lincoln Hwy W
PO Box 28
Thomasville, PA 17364   717-792-3565
Fax: 717-792-4906   800-272-4477
info2@martinschips.com
Manufacturer of potato chips, popcorn and distributor of pretzels.
President & CEO: Ken Potter
Director of Sales & Marketing: David Potter
Contact: Derek Bennett
derek.bennett@martinschips.com
Year Founded: 1941
Estimated Sales: $34 Million
Number Employees: 200
Square Footage: 75000
Type of Packaging: Consumer, Food Service, Bulk
Types of Products Distributed:
Frozen Food

57915 Martin-Brower Co US
6250 N River Rd
Suite 9000
Rosemont, IL 60018   847-227-6500
Fax: 847-671-4725
USCommunications@martin-brower.com
martinbrower.us
Distribution and supply chain management services
CEO: Bob McGonigle
CFO: Diane Dimberg
Year Founded: 1934
Estimated Sales: $14 Billion
Number Employees: 6,000
Parent Co: Reyes Holdings
Number of Customer Locations: 350
Types of Products Distributed:
Food Service, Frozen Food

57916 Marubeni America Corp.
375 Lexington Ave.
New York, NY 10017   212-450-0100
Fax: 212-450-0700 www.marubeniamerica.com
Marubeni exports grains, meat, sugar and other foodstuffs to Asia.
President/CEO: Fumiya Kokubu
Year Founded: 1951
Estimated Sales: $273,000
Parent Co: Marubeni Corporation

57917 Marwood Sales, Inc
6901 Shawnee Mission Pkwy
Overland Park, KS 66202   913-722-1534
Fax: 913-262-9132   800-745-2881
info@marwoodsales.com www.marwoodsales.com
Producer of dairy products such as natural, processed, and imitation cheese.
President: Mark Woodard
Domestic & International Sales: Larry Johnson
Estimated Sales: $8.2 000,000
Number Employees: 11-50
Types of Products Distributed:
Cheese

57918 Marxana Brand Foods
9166 East Louisiana Place
Denver, CO 80247   303-337-4445
Fax: 303-337-4877   888-560-3562
Pomegranate based sauces

57919 Maryland China
54 Main St
Reisterstown, MD 21136-1210   410-833-5559
Fax: 410-833-1851 info@marylandchina.com
www.marylandchina.com
Porcelain and ceramics
President/Owner: Edward Weiner
VP: Jonathan Weiner
Manager: Jonathan Weiner
jtw@marylandchina.com
Estimated Sales: $5-10 Million
Number Employees: 10-19
Square Footage: 88000
Type of Packaging: Consumer, Private Label, Bulk
Types of Products Distributed:
Food Service, General Merchandise, Dinnerware, serving accessories

57920 Maryland Wholesale Produce Market
7480 Conowingo Ave
Jessup, MD 20794-9430   410-799-5500
Fax: 410-799-7297
Wholesaler/distributor of produce; serving the food service market
President: Frank Fava
Estimated Sales: $.5-1 million
Number Employees: 1-4
Types of Products Distributed:
Food Service, Frozen Food, Produce

57921 Maschari Brothers WHLS Fruits
1111 W Washington St
Sandusky, OH 44870-2294   419-625-7981
Fax: 419-625-8708 mascharibros@yahoo.com
www.mascharibros.com
Wholesaler/distributor of produce
Owner: Paul Maschari
Estimated Sales: $500,000-$1 Million
Number Employees: 5-9
Square Footage: 48000
Number of Customer Locations: 150
Types of Products Distributed:
General Line, Produce, Groceries

57922 Mason Brothers Co
222 4th St NE
Wadena, MN 56482
218-631-1167   800-862-8940
Fax:
contactus@masonbros.com www.masonbros.com
Wholesaler/distributor of groceries, dairy items, equipment, meats, etc.
Sales Manager: Brock Kraft
Year Founded: 1920
Estimated Sales: $58 Million
Number Employees: 50-99
Square Footage: 13494
Number of Customer Locations: 150
Types of Products Distributed:
Frozen Food, General Line, General Merchandise, Provisions/Meat, Groceries, equipment, dairy items, etc.

57923 Masser's Produce
PO Box 48
Leck Kill, PA 17836   570-648-0094
Fax: 570-648-0715
Wholesaler/distributor of produce; serving the food service market
Owner: Timothy Masser
Manager: Michael Masser
Estimated Sales: $1-2.5 Million
Number Employees: 1-4

Wholesalers & Distributors / A-Z

Types of Products Distributed:
 Food Service, Frozen Food, Produce

57924 Master Chemical Products
P.O.Box 1185
Wilkes Barre, PA 18703-1185   570-825-3465
                  Fax: 570-822-1050
Wholesaler/distributor of janitorial supplies
President: Joseph Mitchneck
joem@masterchemicalproducts.com
VP/Treasurer: Walter Volinski
Sales Manager: William Novrocki
Estimated Sales: $5-10 Million
Number Employees: 20-49
Square Footage: 120000
Types of Products Distributed:
 Frozen Food, General Merchandise, Janitorial supplies

57925 Mat Logo Company
PO Box 230
Forest City, IA 50436-0230   641-581-5650
       Fax: 641-581-5647 888-628-5646
       randy@logofloormats.com
       www.logofloormats.com
Wholesaler/distributor and exporter of rubber floor mats with logos
Owner: Randy Bush
randy@logofloormats.com
Types of Products Distributed:
 Frozen Food, General Merchandise, Rubber floor mats with logos

57926 Matanuska Maid Dairy
814 W Northern Lights Blvd
Anchorage, AK 99503-3713   907-561-5223
                  Fax: 907-563-7492
Wholesaler/distributor of orange juice and dairy products including milk, cream, cottage cheese, sour cream and egg nog
President/CEO: Joseph Van Treeck
Comptroller: Linda Bowers
Human Resources Manager: Barb Pinkal
Director Sales/Marketing: Delene Bartel
Plant Manager: Gary Nelson
Estimated Sales: $10-20 Million
Number Employees: 20-49
Types of Products Distributed:
 General Line, Juice & dairy products

57927 (HQ)Matco United
PO Box 973
Monrovia, CA 91017-0973   562-908-5554
       Fax: 562-908-6555 800-218-5554
Wholesaler/distributor of industrial packaging supplies
President/CEO: John Gilmore
Executive VP: Gary Kulper
VP Marketing: Jim Gilmore
Purchasing Manager: Scott Magardichian
Number Employees: 50-99
Square Footage: 480000
Private Brands Carried:
 Network
Number of Customer Locations: 3000
Types of Products Distributed:
 Food Service, General Merchandise, Hobart Meat & Food Films

57928 (HQ)Material Control
P.O.Box 308
North Aurora, IL 60542   630-892-4274
       Fax: 630-892-4931 800-926-0376
       www.materialcontrolinc.com
Conveyor safety stop switches, belt cleaners and hood covers, bin aerators; distributor of plastic bins and totes, shelving, cabinets, mats, matting, fans, measurement and gas monitoring instruments and ventilation equipment
Manager: Jack Pierce
Sales Director: Bob Hutchins
Plant Manager: Jim Pierce
Estimated Sales: $3-5,000,000
Number Employees: 5-9
Other Locations:
 Material Control
 Aurora, IL Material Control
Types of Products Distributed:
 Frozen Food

57929 Material Handling Products
6601 Joy Rd
East Syracuse, NY 13057-1142   315-437-2891
       Fax: 315-437-1218 866-980-4788
       www.mhpcorp.com
Wholesaler/distributor of forklifts
President: Robert Minich
Vice President: John Nelson
jnelson@mhpcorp.com
Number Employees: 50-99
Private Brands Carried:
 Yale; Bendi; Taylor
Types of Products Distributed:
 Frozen Food, General Merchandise, Forklifts

57930 Material Handling Resources
7355 Cockrill Bend Blvd
Nashville, TN 37209-1025   615-350-8900
       Fax: 615-350-5863 800-239-9707
       sales@mhrweb.com
Wholesaler/distributor of conveyors, containers, fork lifts, racks and shelving
Director: Ric Thurston
Sales Manager: Brian Davis
Estimated Sales: $9 Million
Number Employees: 20-49
Square Footage: 40000
Parent Co: Ozburn Hessey Logistics
Private Brands Carried:
 Kamatsu; Rousseau
Types of Products Distributed:
 Frozen Food, General Merchandise, Material handling equipment

57931 Material Handling Services
315 E Fullerton Ave
Carol Stream, IL 60188-1865   630-655-7200
                  Fax: 630-665-4669
Wholesaler/distributor of forklifts and conveyors
President: Gerald Risch
gerry.risch@mhs-inc.com
Estimated Sales: $10-20 Million
Number Employees: 50-99
Private Brands Carried:
 Clark; Mitsubishi; Daewoo; Crown
Types of Products Distributed:
 Frozen Food, General Merchandise, Forklifts & conveyors

57932 Material Handling Specialties Company
2210 Penn Ave
Pittsburgh, PA 15222   412-471-6520
       Fax: 412-471-5833 888-227-9253
       mhs@usaor.net
Wholesaler/distributor of hand trucks, dollies, ramps, pallet jacks, wheels, casters, ratchet straps and load locks
President: Tom Besser
tbesser@handling.com
VP: Jack Vaira
Operations Manager: Lee Brandenberger
Estimated Sales: $2.5-5 Million
Number Employees: 5-9
Square Footage: 8800
Private Brands Carried:
 Bluff; Kinedyne; Lift-Rite; Magline; Wesco
Types of Products Distributed:
 Frozen Food, General Merchandise, Hand trucks, dollies, ramps, etc.

57933 Materials Handling Enterprises
4885 Mcknight Rd # 3 Pmb 290
Office 290
Pittsburgh, PA 15237-3400   412-391-4482
       Fax: 412-391-0120 800-861-4643
       www.mhe-usa.com
Wholesaler/distributor of conveyors, shelving and cranes
President: David Snell
Manager: Mark Weschler
mark@mhe-usa.com
Estimated Sales: $5-10 Million
Number Employees: 1-4
Private Brands Carried:
 Yale; Grisley; Gorbel
Types of Products Distributed:
 Frozen Food, General Merchandise, Conveyors, shelving & cranes

57934 Mathews Packing
950 Ramirez Rd
Marysville, CA 95901-9444   530-743-9000
                  Fax: 530-742-6625
Dried prunes, pitted prunes, rice
Owner: Ed Mathews
VP/Marketing: Mark Mathews
Estimated Sales: $1-$2.5 000,000
Number Employees: 1-4
Type of Packaging: Private Label

57935 Matilija Water Company
1026 Santa Barbara Street
Santa Barbara, CA 93101   805-963-7873
       Fax: 805-966-9811 www.getpurewater.com
Bottled water; also, wholesaler/distributor of water purification systems; serving the food service market
Sales Manager: Eric Berumen
Estimated Sales: $1-3 Million
Number Employees: 10-19
Type of Packaging: Consumer, Food Service
Types of Products Distributed:
 Food Service, General Merchandise, Water purification systems

57936 Matthiesen Equipment
566 N Ww White Rd
San Antonio, TX 78219-2816   210-333-1510
       Fax: 210-333-1563 800-624-8635
       ctorres@matthiesenequipment.com
       www.matthiesenequipment.com
Manufacturer and exporter of material handling processing machinery for ice including bins, baggers, belt and screw conveyors, crushers, bag closers, drying belts, etc.; exporter and wholesaler/distributor of ice machinery
Office Manager: Claudia Torres
Research & Development: Stephen Niestroy
National Sales Manager: Diane Hardekepf
Sales Engineer: Jerry Bosma
Production Manager: Pete Ruiz
Purchasing: John Barratachea
Estimated Sales: $2.5-5 Million
Number Employees: 5-9
Square Footage: 80000
Parent Co: Tour Ice National
Types of Products Distributed:
 Frozen Food, General Merchandise, Ice machines

57937 Mattingly Foods
302 State St
Zanesville, OH 43701-3200   740-454-0136
       Fax: 740-455-6881 800-777-6288
Wholesaler/distributor of groceries, produce, seafood, meats, dairy products, frozen foods and equipment and fixtures; serving the food service market
President: Andrew Hess
CEO: Rick Barnes
rbarnes@centurynationalbank.com
VP, Information Technology: Brandon Hess
SVP Foodservice Operations: Mike Hess
Director, Sales: Mark Blatt
VP, Operations: Michael Callahan
SVP Purchasing: Joe Tyson
Estimated Sales: $40.20 Million
Number Employees: 250-499
Square Footage: 150000
Number of Customer Locations: 750
Types of Products Distributed:
 Food Service, Frozen Food, General Line, General Merchandise, Provisions/Meat, Produce, Seafood, Groceries, etc.

57938 (HQ)Maxim's Import Corporation
2719 NW 24th Street
Miami, FL 33142-7005   915-577-9228
       Fax: 91- 57- 921 800-331-6652
       info@maximsimports.com maximsimports.com
Processor, importer and exporter of shrimp; processor of packaged fish; exporter of frozen chicken, duck, turkey, pork and beef; wholesaler/distributor of shrimp, pork, beef, poultry, fish, produce and frozen, specialty and healthfoods
President: Luis Chi
CEO: Jeo Chi
Contact: Joe Chi
luis.chi@hotmail.com
Estimated Sales: $4.1 Million
Number Employees: 22
Square Footage: 140000
Type of Packaging: Bulk

Wholesalers & Distributors / A-Z

Other Locations:
  Maxim's Import Corp.
  SalvadorMaxim's Import Corp.
Private Brands Carried:
  Maxim's; Fish-House; Alpromar; Colorado Boxed Beef; Cookin' Good; Dial
Number of Customer Locations: 1200
Types of Products Distributed:
  Food Service, Frozen Food, Health Food, Provisions/Meat, Produce, Seafood, Specialty Foods, Poultry, beef, shrimp & pork

57939 Maxin Marketing Corporation
92 Argonaut, Suite #170
Aliso Viejo, CA 92656-5318   949-362-1177
                    Fax: 949-362-0449
Snack foods
President: Terry Kroll
Estimated Sales: Less than $500,000
Number Employees: 1-4
Number of Brands: 2
Number of Products: 10
Type of Packaging: Consumer, Private Label, Bulk
Types of Products Distributed:
  Specialty Foods

57940 Maxwell House & Post
800 Westchester Ave
Rye Brook, NY 10573-1354   914-335-2500
                    Fax: 914-335-2706
Coffee and breakfast foods
President: Ann Fudge
Estimated Sales: Under $500,000
Number Employees: 1-4
Parent Co: Kraft Foods

57941 May Flower
56-72 49th Pl
Maspeth, NY 11378   347-480-4076
           www.shopmayflower.com
Asian sauces and seasonings, snacks, beverages, frozen food, pickled vegetables and cake.
Type of Packaging: Private Label

57942 Maybury Material Handling
90 Denslow Rd
East Longmeadow, MA 01028-3103   413-525-4216
    Fax: 413-525-8231 jmaybury@maybury.com
                    www.maybury.com
Wholesaler/distributor of material handling equipment
President: John Maybury
jmaybury@maybury.com
Sales Director: Brad Albert
Estimated Sales: $20-50 Million
Number Employees: 50-99
Types of Products Distributed:
  General Merchandise, Material handling equipment

57943 Mayer Myers Paper Company
1769 Latham Street
410
Memphis, TN 38106-6205   901-948-5631
    Fax: 901-774-7482 800-766-1466
Wholesaler/distributor of cleaning supplies, disposables, industrial tape and packaging, dunnage supplies, stretch strapping equipment, wraps and plastics; serving the food service market
President: Malcolm Levi, Jr.
Executive VP: Steve Phillips
Estimated Sales: $10-20 Million
Number Employees: 20-49
Square Footage: 200000
Private Brands Carried:
  Network
Types of Products Distributed:
  Food Service, Frozen Food, General Merchandise, Cleaning supplies, disposables, etc.

57944 Mayer-Bass Fromm
PO Box 10824
Yakima, WA 98909-1824   509-248-4084
    Fax: 509-453-6656 800-362-4677
Wholesaler/distributor of hops and hop products; serving the brewing industry
Number Employees: 1-4
Parent Co: Fromm, Mayer-Bass
Types of Products Distributed:
  Frozen Food, General Line, Hops & hop products

57945 Mayfair Provision Company
13 N Michigan Ave
Kenilworth, NJ 7033   908-245-0053
                    Fax: 908-245-1375
Wholesaler/distributor of provisions/meats
President: Pat Venice
Estimated Sales: $10-20 Million
Number Employees: 5-9
Types of Products Distributed:
  Frozen Food, Provisions/Meat

57946 Mayfield Paper Co
702 S 3rd St
Abilene, TX 79602-1697   325-673-5569
    Fax: 325-673-5569 www.mayfieldpaper.com
Wholesaler/distributor of cleaning supplies, disposables, wraps, equipment, etc.; serving the food service market
Manager: Gary Drake
Manager: Mark Blakley
mblakley@mayfieldpaper.com
Chairman: Stanley Mayfield
Estimated Sales: $20-50 Million
Number Employees: 20-49
Types of Products Distributed:
  Food Service, Frozen Food, General Merchandise, Cleaning supplies, disposables, etc.

57947 Mayfield Paper Co
1115 S Hill St
San Angelo, TX 76903-7395   325-653-1444
    Fax: 325-653-7031 800-725-1441
info@mayfieldpaper.com www.mayfieldpaper.com
Wholesaler/distributor of cleaning supplies, disposables, wraps and tabletop supplies; serving the food service market.
President: Stanley Mayfield
smayfield@mayfieldpaper.com
Year Founded: 1949
Estimated Sales: $100-500 Million
Number Employees: 50-99
Types of Products Distributed:
  Food Service, Frozen Food, General Merchandise

57948 Maynard-Fixturcraft
617 Norris Ave
Nashville, TN 37204   615-732-7700
    Fax: 615-255-0637 800-369-0603
Wholesaler/distributor of food service, refrigeration, heating and air conditioning equipment; serving the food service market
President: Bob Maynard
CEO: Pete Zabaski
SVP: Wayne Lowman
Sales: Glenn Hill
Sales: Glenn Harber
Contact: Mark Brooks
mbrooks@mayfix.com
Plant Manager: Frank Osborne
Purchasing Manager: Mark Brooks
Estimated Sales: $10-20 Million
Number Employees: 50-99
Square Footage: 60000
Types of Products Distributed:
  Food Service, Foodservice equipment, etc.

57949 Mayrand Limitee
5650 Metropolitan E Boulevard
St. Leonard, QC H1S 1A7
Canada   514-255-9330
    Fax: 514-255-1647 www.mayrand.ca
Wholesaler/distributor of frozen food, produce and general merchandise; serving the food service market
President: Daniel La Rossognol
Number Employees: 100-249
Number of Customer Locations: 1000
Types of Products Distributed:
  Food Service, Frozen Food, General Line, Produce

57950 Maywood International Sales
PO Box 9292
Sante Fe, NM 87504   505-982-2700
    Fax: 505-982-9780 805-500-5500
Oilseed manufacturer
Sales: Jacques Brazy
Sales: Peter Connick

57951 Mazelle's Cheesecakes Concoctions Creations
9016 Garland Road
Dallas, TX 75218   214-328-9102
    Fax: 214-328-5202 sales@mazelles.com
                    www.mazelles.com
Cheesecakes and cheesecake petit fours vanilla, chocolate decadence, raspberry cassis, chocolate marble, turtle-praline chocolate chip, pumpkin, strawberries nad cream, keylime margarita, amaretto
CEO: Gina Roidopoulos
Estimated Sales: $3-5 Million
Number Employees: 10-19
Type of Packaging: Consumer, Food Service
Types of Products Distributed:
  Frozen Food

57952 Mazo-Lerch Company
2730 Wilmarco Avenue
Baltimore, MD 21223-3306   302-629-4588
Wholesaler/distributor of produce, canned fruits and vegetables, dry goods, fresh and frozen meat, seafood, equipment and supplies, paper and chemicals; serving the food service market
General Manager: Mike McCrea
Purchasing Manager: Vesta Mitchell
Number Employees: 20-49
Square Footage: 160000
Parent Co: Mazo-Lerch Company
Number of Customer Locations: 800
Types of Products Distributed:
  Food Service, Frozen Food, General Line, General Merchandise, Provisions/Meat, Produce, Seafood

57953 Mc Afee Packing Co
102 N Valley St
Wrightsville, GA 31096-2108   478-864-3385
                    Fax: 478-864-8040
Wholesaler/distributor of meats; serving the food service market
Owner: James L Mc Afee Jr
macpac@nlamerica.com
VP: John McAfee
Site Manager: John Mcafee
macpac@nlamerica.com
Estimated Sales: $10-20 Million
Number Employees: 20-49
Number of Customer Locations: 150
Types of Products Distributed:
  Food Service, Frozen Food, Provisions/Meat

57954 Mc Call Co
4013 Tennessee Ave
PO Box 2033
Chattanooga, TN 37409-1322   423-821-4583
    Fax: 423-821-5950 sales@mccallcompany.com
Wholesaler/distributor of packaging materials
Owner: P Henze
Office Manager: Helen Lemacks
Purchasing: Mike Henze
Estimated Sales: $1-2.5 Million
Number Employees: 1-4
Types of Products Distributed:
  General Merchandise, Packaging materials

57955 Mc Lane Foodservice
2444 Tradeport Dr
Orlando, FL 32824-7022   407-816-7600
    Fax: 407-816-7751 800-283-2121
Wholesaler/distributor serving fast food chains
Manager: Calvin Parker
Manager: Marco Guerrero
General Manager: Ron Banks
Estimated Sales: $5-10 Million
Number Employees: 100-249
Parent Co: Ameriserv
Types of Products Distributed:
  Food Service, Frozen Food

57956 McCabe's Quality Foods
17600 NE San Rafael St
Portland, OR 97230-5924   503-256-4770
    Fax: 503-256-1263 www.ssafood.com
Wholesaler/distributor and exporter of meat, fruit, frozen food, general merchandise, general line items, produce and seafood; serving fast food chains
President: Gerald Cobb
Sales Manager: Sandy Thames
Operations Manager: Steve Peil
Estimated Sales: $20-50 Million
Number Employees: 250-499
Square Footage: 100000

1091

Wholesalers & Distributors / A-Z

Number of Customer Locations: 500
Types of Products Distributed:
  Frozen Food, General Line, General Merchandise, Provisions/Meat, Produce, Seafood, Fruit

57957 McCoy's Products
1075 Central Park Ave # 407
Scarsdale, NY 10583-3232
914-472-2737
Fax: 914-472-2738
Wholesaler/distributor and exporter of cod liver oil tablets
President: Richard Sosin
Estimated Sales: $2.5-5 Million
Number Employees: 1-4
Private Brands Carried:
  Pastillas McCoy's; The Real McCoy; McCoy's
Types of Products Distributed:
  Frozen Food, Health Food, Cod liver oil tablets

57958 McDonnell
PO Box 2011
Jessup, MD 20794
410-799-7966
Fax: 410-796-8466
Wholesaler/distributor of produce; serving the food service market
President: James McDonnell
Estimated Sales: $5-10 Million
Number Employees: 10-19
Type of Packaging: Bulk
Types of Products Distributed:
  Food Service, Frozen Food, Produce

57959 McDowell Supply Company
Mercer Street
Welch, WV 24801
304-436-3214
Fax: 304-253-4706
Wholesaler/distributor of general line products and candy
Owner/Manager: D Ramella
Estimated Sales: $500,000-$1 Million
Number Employees: 1-4
Parent Co: McDowell Supply Company
Number of Customer Locations: 275
Types of Products Distributed:
  Frozen Food, General Line, Candy

57960 McGrath Fisheries
1 Elizabeth Pl
Streator, IL 61364-1192
815-672-2654
Fax: 815-672-3474
Wholesaler/distributor of frozen food and seafood; serving the food service market
President: Kevin Gaede
Estimated Sales: Less than $500,000
Number Employees: 1-4
Types of Products Distributed:
  Food Service, Frozen Food, Seafood

57961 McKearnan Packaging
PO Box 7281
Reno, NV 89510-7281
775-356-6111
Fax: 775-356-2181 800-787-7857
surplus@mckernan.com www.mckernan.com
Surplus packaging components
General Manager: Maurice Oschlog
Chief Operating Officer: Frank Maggio

57962 McKeesport Candy Company
PO Box 578
McKeesport, PA 15134-0578
412-678-8851
Fax: 412-673-4406 888-525-7577
support@candyfavorites.com
www.candyfavorites.com
Wholesaler/distributor of nonperishable confectionery products
President: Gerald Prince
Contact: Jon Prince
jonprince@candyfavorites.com
Estimated Sales: $10-20 Million
Number Employees: 10-19
Parent Co: Pennsylvania Corporation
Types of Products Distributed:
  General Line, Non-perishable confectionery

57963 McLane Co Inc
4747 Mclane Pkwy
Temple, TX 76504
254-771-7500
Fax: 254-771-7244 800-299-1401
contact@mclaneco.com www.mclaneco.com
Wholesaler/distributor of groceries, meats, produce, dairy products, frozen foods, baked goods, equipment, general merchandise and private label items; serving the food service and convenience store markets.
Division President: Ken Hardy
Year Founded: 1984
Estimated Sales: $48 Billion
Other Locations:
  McLane Co.
  TaipeiMcLane Co.
Number of Customer Locations: 22000
Types of Products Distributed:
  Food Service, Frozen Food, General Line, General Merchandise, Provisions/Meat, Produce, Groceries, equipment, etc.

57964 McLane Foodservice Inc
2085 Midway Rd
Carrollton, TX 75006-5063
Fax: 972-364-2054 888-792-9300
www.mclaneco.com
Wholesaler/distributor of groceries, meats, produce, dairy products, frozen foods, baked goods, equipment, general merchandise and private label items; serving the food service and convenience store markets.
President: Tom Zatina
VP, Sales & Business Development: Jeff Hayes
EVP & COO: Susan Adzick
Year Founded: 1984
Estimated Sales: $48 Billion
Number Employees: 20,545
Number of Customer Locations: 1000
Types of Products Distributed:
  Frozen Food, General Line, General Merchandise, Produce, Rack Jobbers, Groceries, dairy products & baked goods

57965 McLane Grocery
6201 NW H.K. Dodgen Loop
Temple, TX 76504
254-771-7500
Fax: 254-771-7020 800-299-1401
contact@mclaneco.com www.mclaneco.com
Wholesaler/distributor of groceries, meats, produce, dairy products, frozen foods, baked goods, equipment, general merchandise and private label items; serving the food service and convenience store markets.
Division President: Ken Hardy
Year Founded: 1894
Estimated Sales: $50 Billion
Number Employees: 20,000
Square Footage: 110000
Parent Co: Berkshire Hathaway Inc
Types of Products Distributed:
  Frozen Food, General Line, General Merchandise, Provisions/Meat

57966 McNasby's Seafood Market
723 2nd Street
Annapolis, MD 21403-3323
410-295-9022
Fax: 410-280-3707
Seafood

57967 (HQ)McShane Enterprises
120 Tices Ln
East Brunswick, NJ 08816-2014
732-254-3100
Fax: 732-254-7342 888-946-2761
www.somersetproducts.com
Wholesaler/distributor of sanitary papers, cleaning chemicals, trash bags and floor machines. Plastic products including utensils, plates, napkins, tablecoths, bags, etc. Also grocery, meat, produce and baked goods packaing. Extensiveprivate label program
Owner: David Mc Shane
Controller: Joe McPhadden
Sales/Marketing Executive: Fred Spotts
General Manager: John Marchesi
Purchasing Manager: Chris Blanchet
Estimated Sales: $20-50 Million
Number Employees: 5-9
Number of Brands: 100+
Number of Products: 3500
Square Footage: 80000
Parent Co: Winans-McShane
Type of Packaging: Food Service, Private Label
Other Locations:
  McShane Enterprises
  St. ThomasMcShane Enterprises
Private Brands Carried:
  Somerset janitorial and cleaning supplies
Types of Products Distributed:
  General Merchandise, Provisions/Meat, Produce, Disposable paper & plastic products

57968 McSteven's
5600 NE 88th St
Vancouver, WA 98665
360-816-5259
Fax: 360-944-1302 800-838-1056
mcstevens.com
Cocoa, drink mixes and bulk tea.
Type of Packaging: Private Label, Bulk

57969 Mccadam Cheese Co Inc
39 Mccadam Ln
Chateaugay, NY 12920-4306
518-497-6644
Fax: 518-497-3297 800-639-4031
info@mccadam.com www.mccadam.coop
A variety of cheeses including aged and waxed cheddars; flavored and reduced fat cheddars; muenster cheese; monterey jack cheese, and extra sharp cheddar cheese in addition to smoked cheeses.
Chairman: Carl Peterson
Chief Executive Officer: Paul Johnston
EVP/Finance & Administration: Margaret Bertolino
SVP/Information Services: Ralph Viscomi
SVP/Economics & Legislative Affairs: Robert Wellington
Director International Sales: Peter Gutierrez
Communications Director: Douglas DiMento
EVP/Chief Operating Officer: Richard Wellington
Plant Manager: Ron Davis
Estimated Sales: $10-20 Million
Number Employees: 100-249
Parent Co: Agri-Mark Inc
Types of Products Distributed:
  Frozen Food

57970 Mccomas Sales Co Inc
2315 4th St NW
P.O.Box 25223
Albuquerque, NM 87102-1054
505-243-5263
Fax: 505-243-4880 800-555-555
McComas@aol.com www.mccomassales.com
Wholesaler/distributor of tabletop needs and equipment; serving the food service market
Owner: Jack Mc Comas
VP: Helen McComas
Contract/ Design Division: Mike Martin
IT Executive: Ann Baca
mccomas@aol.com
Estimated Sales: $5-10 Million
Number Employees: 20-49
Square Footage: 92000
Types of Products Distributed:
  Food Service, Frozen Food, General Merchandise, Tabletop needs & equipment

57971 Mccrone Microscopes & Acces
850 Pasquinelli Dr
Westmont, IL 60559-5594
630-288-7087
Fax: 630-887-7764 www.mccrone.com
Consultant providing microscopy and ultramicro-analytical services including materials analysis, characterization and identification; wholesaler/distributor of microscopes and microscopy supplies
CEO/President: Donald Brooks
VP: Richard Bisbing
Manager: David Wiley
mccrone@mccrone.com
VP/Director Operations: Bonnie Betty
Estimated Sales: $5-10 Million
Number Employees: 50-99
Square Footage: 75000
Parent Co: McCrone Group
Types of Products Distributed:
  Frozen Food, General Merchandise, Microscopes & microscopy supplies

57972 (HQ)Mccullagh Coffee Roasters
245 Swan St
Buffalo, NY 14204
800-753-3473
sales@mccullaghcoffee.com
www.mccullaghcoffee.com
Processor, importer and exporter of coffee, tea, non-dairy creamer and hot chocolate
President: Warren Emblidge
VP of Sales and Marketing: Paul Zanghi
Estimated Sales: $9 Million
Number Employees: 50-99
Types of Products Distributed:
  General Line

Wholesalers & Distributors / A-Z

57973 Mcdonald Wholesale Co
2350 W Broadway
Eugene, OR 97402-2790 541-345-8421
 Fax: 541-345-7146 800-637-3071
 www.mcdonaldwhsl.com
Wholesaler/distributor of frozen, refrigerated and dry grocery, nonfoods produce, dairy products, meat; serving the food service market
President: Rod Huey
CFO: Gary Thompson
VP Sales/Marketing: Steve Hayes
Plant Manager: Greg Bettis
Purchasing Manager: Bud Masson
Estimated Sales: $45 Million
Number Employees: 100-249
Private Brands Carried:
 Nabisco, Frito Lay, Steinfield, Nugget, Heinz, Hunts
Types of Products Distributed:
 Food Service, Frozen Food, General Line, Health Food, Provisions/Meat, Produce, Seafood, Dairy products & candy

57974 Mcfarling Foods Inc
333 W 14th St
Indianapolis, IN 46202-2204 317-635-2633
 Fax: 317-687-6844 www.mcfarling.com
Wholesaler/distributor of groceries, provisions/meats, frozen foods, produce and seafood; serving the food service market
President: Len Mcfarling
lmcfarling@mcfarling.com
CFO: Frank Chandler
Vice President: Jeffery Hillis
Quality Control Manager: Christopher Davis
Director of Marketing: Sue Sorley
VP Sales & Marketing: Jerry Ward
Procurement Manager: Len McFarling
Estimated Sales: $48 Million
Number Employees: 100-249
Square Footage: 120000
Types of Products Distributed:
 Food Service, Frozen Food, General Line, Provisions/Meat, Produce, Seafood

57975 Mcgraths Seafood
1 Elizabeth Pl
Streator, IL 61364-1192 815-672-2654
 Fax: 815-672-3474
Frozen food
Owner: Kevin Gaede
Estimated Sales: Less Than $500,000
Number Employees: 1-4

57976 Mckenzie Country Classic's
160 Flynn Ave
Burlington, VT 05401-5400 802-864-4585
 Fax: 802-651-7335 800-426-6100
Meats and cheeses for the food service industry.
Manager: Greg Rouliie
greg.rouliie@mckenziecountryclassics.com
Number Employees: 10-19
Type of Packaging: Consumer, Food Service
Types of Products Distributed:
 Provisions/Meat

57977 Mckinley Equipment Corp
17611 Armstrong Ave
Irvine, CA 92614-5760 949-271-2460
 Fax: 949-955-3875 800-229-7275
 www.mckinleyequipment.com
Wholesaler/distributor of conveyors, racks, shelving, doors, lift tables, dock levelers and storage and handling systems
President: Faruk Abdalah
faruk.abdalah@apsparking.net
Marketing Director: Hal Rothberg
Estimated Sales: $20-50 Million
Number Employees: 100-249
Types of Products Distributed:
 Frozen Food, General Merchandise, Conveyers, racks, shelving, etc.

57978 Mclaughlin Seafood
728 Main St
Bangor, ME 04401-6810 207-942-7811
 Fax: 207-947-9176 800-222-9107
 www.mclaughlinseafood.com
Products include seafood in addition to cookbooks, clothing and kitchenware.
Owner: Reid Mc Laughlin
reid@mclaughlinseafood.com
Estimated Sales: Less Than $500,000
Number Employees: 1-4

57979 Mcnair & Co Inc
730 E Fronton St
Brownsville, TX 78520-5247 956-541-5276
 Fax: 956-541-5279
Wholesaler/distributor of food vending machines
President: H McNair, Sr.
Estimated Sales: Less Than $500,000
Number Employees: 1-4
Types of Products Distributed:
 Frozen Food, General Merchandise, Food vending machines

57980 MeGa Industries
5109 Harvester Road, Unit 3A
Burlington, ON L7L 5Y9
Canada 905-631-6342
 Fax: 905-631-6341 800-665-6342
 sales@megaindustries.com
 www.megaindustries.com
Manufacturer, importer, exporter and wholesaler/distributor of material and bulk handling equipment including vibrating tables, conveyors, bins, feeders, vibrators and bin level controls and indicators
President: Mel Gallagher
Sales: Steve Atkinson
Number Employees: 5-9
Square Footage: 12000
Private Brands Carried:
 Monitor; Dynapac; Oztec; Svedala; Mega
Types of Products Distributed:
 Frozen Food, Material & bulk handling equipment

57981 Meaders Kitchen Equipment
602 SW Evangeline Trwy
Lafayette, LA 70501-8299 337-233-2396
 Fax: 337-235-5746 meaderseqpt@gmail.com
 www.meaderskitchenequip.com
Wholesaler/distributor of food service equipment and supplies including tabletop needs; serving the food service market
President: David Meaders
meaderseqpt@gmail.com
Estimated Sales: $2.5-5 Million
Number Employees: 5-9
Square Footage: 40000
Number of Customer Locations: 300
Types of Products Distributed:
 Food Service, Frozen Food, General Merchandise, Tabletop needs

57982 Meadow Brook Dairy Co
2365 Buffalo Rd
Erie, PA 16510-1459 814-899-3191
 Fax: 814-464-9152 800-352-4010
 www.meadowbrookdairy.com
Wholesaler/distributor of juices, water and dairy products including milk, sour cream, chip dip, half and half, cottage cheese, etc
CAO: Myrna Heise
myrna_heise@deanfoods.com
Administrative Assistant: Charlotte Elwell
VP & General Manager: Jed Davis
Quality Assurance Manager: Jenny Kwitowski
Director of Sales: Leslie Barton
Manager Distribution: Dan Deckman
Plant Manager: Bruce Windeatt
Estimated Sales: $10-20 Million
Number Employees: 100-249
Parent Co: Dean Foods Company
Private Brands Carried:
 Dean Foods; Meadowbrook
Number of Customer Locations: 250
Types of Products Distributed:
 Frozen Food, General Line, Dairy products, water & juice

57983 Meadow Farm Foods
23064 County Highway 1
Fergus Falls, MN 56537-8156 218-739-4585
 Fax: 218-736-0738 800-450-4585
 www.meadowfarmfoods.com
Wholesaler/distributor of groceries, produce, dairy products, frozen foods, bakery products, general merchandise, health foods and health and beauty aids, gourmet foods, and organic foods
Owner: Joan Kohan
joankohan@hotmail.com
Estimated Sales: $500,000-$1 Million
Number Employees: 5-9
Square Footage: 12000
Private Brands Carried:
 Secret Gardens; North Aire; Market; Nature's Gate; Fantastic Foods; Cardinis; Angels; Spectrum; Cuisine; Midwest Northern Nut Company; Browns Best; North Farm; StonyField Farms; Kasni; Army's Kitchen; Nelson Confections; Kiss My Face; Perel
Types of Products Distributed:
 Frozen Food, Health Food, Provisions/Meat, Produce, Seafood

57984 Meadowbrook Farms
1633 Washington Ln
Jenkintown, PA 19046-1132 215-887-5900
 Fax: 215-886-1971 www.meadowbrookfarm.org
Wholesaler/distributor of orange and grapefruit juices, fruit punch, lemonade and dairy products including milk, cream and cottage cheese
Comptroller: Mark Weiss
Sales Exec: Jacqueline Fisher
Estimated Sales: $2.5-5 Million
Number Employees: 10-19
Types of Products Distributed:
 Frozen Food, General Line, Beverages & dairy products

57985 Meat & Fish Fellas
5036 N 54th Ave # 7
Suite 7
Glendale, AZ 85301-7509 623-931-6190
 Fax: 623-931-2960 www.meatandfishfellas.com
Meat and seafood
Owner: J T Tarbell
Partner: Marty Menter
Partner: Inyol Kim
Estimated Sales: $3-5 Million
Number Employees: 20-49

57986 Meatcrafters
3900 Ironwood Pl
Landover, MD 20785 240-764-7653
 Fax: 240-764-7653 info@meatcrafters.com
 www.meatcrafters.com
Sausages and salamis
Marketing: Debra Moser
Sales: Mitchell Berliner
Production: Stanley Feder

57987 Meats Plus Inc
100 E Jefferson St
P.O. Box 155
Loda, IL 60948 217-386-2381
 Fax: 217-386-2672 800-747-3411
 www.meatsplus.com
Wholesaler/distributor of poultry, beef and pork; serving the food service market.
General Manager: Ryan Baumann
President & Owner: Bob Nadarski
Vice President & Owner: Jeff Baumann
jbaumann@meatsplus.com
Operations Manager: Chuck Gooden
Director, Purchasing: Jason Coffey
Year Founded: 1988
Estimated Sales: $20-50 Million
Number Employees: 20-49
Type of Packaging: Food Service
Types of Products Distributed:
 Food Service, Frozen Food, Provisions/Meat

57988 Mecca Coffee Company
1143 E 33rd Place
Tulsa, OK 74105 918-749-3509
 Fax: 918-749-3536 meccacoffee@sbcglobal.net
 www.meccacoffeeco.com
Wholesaler/distributor of gourmet items and spices; serving the food service market
President: Charles Culbreath
Estimated Sales: Less Than $500,000
Number Employees: 5-9
Types of Products Distributed:
 Food Service, Frozen Food, General Line, Specialty Foods, Gourmet items & spices

57989 (HQ)Medina & Medina
PO Box 362200
San Juan, PR 00936-2200 787-782-7575
 Fax: 787-782-7552 www.medinapr.com
Importer and wholesaler/distributor of frozen foods, cheese, fish, meat and poultry
President: Jose Medina
Marketing Manager: Eduardo Medina
Number Employees: 50-99
Number of Customer Locations: 300
Types of Products Distributed:
 Frozen Food, General Line, Provisions/Meat, Seafood, Cheese

Wholesalers & Distributors / A-Z

57990 Mediterranean Gyro Products
1102 38th Ave
Long Island City, NY 11101-6041   718-786-3399
Fax: 718-786-8518 yani@mediterraneanpita.com
www.mediterraneanpita.com
Wholesaler/distributor of Greek specialty items; processor of pita bread
President: Vasilios Memmos
Contact: Sophia Maroulis
smaroulis@corfufoods.com
Purchasing Agent: Sophia Maroulis
Estimated Sales: $24 Million
Number Employees: 20-49
Types of Products Distributed:
Frozen Food, Specialty Foods, Greek

57991 Medley Material Handling Inc
4201 Will Rogers Pkwy
Oklahoma City, OK 73108-2083   405-946-3453
Fax: 405-942-1748 www.medleycompany.com
Wholesaler/distributor of material handling equipment; also, parts and service available
Owner: Mark Medley
mmedley@medleyco.com
General Manager: Scott Davis
Controller: Nita Jones
Estimated Sales: $500,000-$1 Million
Number Employees: 50-99
Types of Products Distributed:
Frozen Food, General Merchandise, Material handling equipment

57992 Medley Restaurant Equipment & Supply Company
425 W Roosevelt Ave
Albany, GA 31701   229-438-1557
Fax: 229-432-6894
Wholesaler/distributor of restaurant equipment and supplies; serving the food service market
President: W David Campbell
VP: S Reed Jackson
Director Purchasing: Marie Moody
Estimated Sales: $10-20 Million
Number Employees: 50-99
Square Footage: 16000
Types of Products Distributed:
Food Service, Frozen Food, General Merchandise, Restaurant equipment & supplies

57993 Medway Creamery Company
295 Waterloo Street
London, ON N6B 2N5
Canada   519-642-1752
Fax: 519-679-2271
Wholesaler/distributor of eggs, butter, margarine, cheese and dressings
President: Richard McKeen
Secretary: James McKeen
Number Employees: 10-19
Private Brands Carried:
Medway; Village Willowgrove
Types of Products Distributed:
Frozen Food, General Line, Eggs, butter, cheese, dressings, etc.

57994 Melba Food Specialties
3720 Skillman Ave
Long Island City, NY 11101   718-786-3142
Fax: 718-786-1026
Wholesaler/distributor of groceries
President/Secretary: M Cook
Estimated Sales: $1-2.5 Million
Number Employees: 10-19
Private Brands Carried:
Melba
Number of Customer Locations: 800
Types of Products Distributed:
Frozen Food, General Line, Groceries

57995 Mello Buttercup Ice Cream Company
P.O.Box 1566
Wilson, NC 27894-1566   252-243-6161
Fax: 252-243-7687
Distributor of ice cream and frozen yogurt; also, frozen novelties and specialty desserts
President: R Barnes
General Manager: Tom Guinan
CFO: Thomas Beaman, CPA
Vice President: Richard Barnes, Jr.
Marketing Director: Len Creech
Estimated Sales: $10-24.9 Million
Number Employees: 10-19
Number of Brands: 3
Type of Packaging: Consumer, Food Service, Private Label, Bulk
Types of Products Distributed:
Frozen Food

57996 Melmart Distributors
6100 Indian Line
Mississauga, ON L4V 1G5
Canada   905-677-7600
Fax: 905-671-8434   800-268-4958
custserv@melmart.com www.melmart.com
Wholesaler/distributor of floor coverings; serving the food service market
Director Marketing: Dean Martin
Number Employees: 50-99
Private Brands Carried:
Kraus Carpets; Manningter Vynal
Types of Products Distributed:
Food Service, Frozen Food, General Merchandise, Floor coverings

57997 Mendez & Company
24 Road 20
Guaynabo, PR 00957   787-793-8888
Fax: 787-783-4085
Wholesaler/distributor of groceries, liquor, wine and beer
VP: J Alvarez
Number Employees: 1-4
Parent Co: Meneco
Types of Products Distributed:
Frozen Food, General Line, Liquor, beer & wine

57998 (HQ)Menu Maker Foods Inc
913 Big Horn Dr
Jefferson City, MO 65109-0336   573-893-3000
Fax: 573-893-2172 www.menumakerfoods.com
Wholesaler/distributor of frozen foods, produce, beverage, chemical, paper, and provisions/meats including steaks, beef patties, and value added beef and pork; serving the food service market
CEO: Dick Graves
Vice President: Creighton Cox
Marketing Director: Ken Goodwin
Sales Director: Brian Upton
Operations Manager: Ed Fairchild
Plant Manager: Phil Magruder
Purchasing Manager: Ron Orr
Estimated Sales: $45 Million
Number Employees: 50-99
Number of Products: 6000
Square Footage: 50000
Parent Co: John Graves Food Service
Private Brands Carried:
Nifda
Number of Customer Locations: 1000
Types of Products Distributed:
Food Service, Frozen Food, General Line, General Merchandise, Provisions/Meat, Produce, Seafood

57999 Mercado Latino
245 Baldwin Park Blvd
City Of Industry, CA 91746-1404   626-333-6862
800-432-7266
www.mercadolatinoinc.com
Manufacturer, importer and distributor of authentic Latin products with nine distribution centers in the western United States.
Estimated Sales: Less Than $500,000
Number Employees: 1-4
Private Brands Carried:
Faraon; Sol-Mex; Milpas; Bebyto; Payaso; Brillasol
Types of Products Distributed:
Frozen Food, General Line, Specialty Foods, Hispanic & Mexican groceries

58000 Merchants Distributors Inc
5005 Alex Lee Blvd
P.O.Box 2148
Hickory, NC 28601-3395   828-725-4100
Fax: 828-323-4527
info@merchantsdistributors.com
www.merchantsdistributors.com
Wholesaler/distributor of groceries, meats, produce, equipment and fixtures and private label items
President: Matt Saunders
matt.saunders@merchantsdistributors.com
VP Sales: D McCoy
Estimated Sales: $1-3 Million
Number Employees: 1000-4999
Parent Co: Alex Lee, Inc.
Number of Customer Locations: 900
Types of Products Distributed:
Frozen Food, General Line, General Merchandise, Provisions/Meat, Produce, Groceries

58001 Merchants Foodservice
1100 Edwards St
Hattiesburg, MS 39401   601-337-9099
800-844-3663
rreed@merchantsfoodservice.com
www.merchantsfoodservice.com
Wholesaler/distributor of produce, dairy products, frozen foods, seafood, groceries, general merchandise, baked goods and meat; serving the food service market.
President & CEO: Andy Mercier
Vice President, Sales & Marketing: Ricky Reed
Vice President, National Sales: Dale Flowers
Vice President, Purchasing: Tom West
Year Founded: 1904
Estimated Sales: $516 Million
Number Employees: 800
Number of Products: 5500
Square Footage: 136000
Parent Co: Tatum Development Company
Type of Packaging: Food Service
Private Brands Carried:
Frosty Acres; Garden Delight; Frosty Fare
Types of Products Distributed:
Food Service, Frozen Food, General Line, General Merchandise, Provisions/Meat, Produce, Seafood, Groceriers, dairy products, etc.

58002 Merchants Grocery Co Inc
800 Maddox Dr
P.O. Box 1268
Culpeper, VA 22701   540-825-0786
Fax: 540-825-9016   877-897-9893
merchants-grocery.com
Wholesaler/distributor of groceries, meat, produce, frozen foods, baked goods, general merchandise and private label items
President: Elvin Smythers
esmythers@merchants-grocery.com
Year Founded: 1917
Estimated Sales: $131.49 Million
Number Employees: 100-249
Square Footage: 120000
Private Brands Carried:
Pleezing
Number of Customer Locations: 1500
Types of Products Distributed:
Frozen Food, General Line, General Merchandise, Provisions/Meat, Produce, Groceries, private label items, etc.

58003 Meridian Supply Rstrnt Depot
9950 Page Ave
St Louis, MO 63132-1431   314-423-5292
Fax: 314-423-7446 www.meridianrs.com
Wholesale/retail outlet store with disposables, equipment, smallwares, janitorial and much more.
President: Tim Miller
timmiller@meridianrs.com
Estimated Sales: $2.5-5 Million
Number Employees: 10-19
Square Footage: 46000
Types of Products Distributed:
Food Service, Frozen Food, General Merchandise, Chemicals, paper goods & equipment

58004 Meridian Trading Co
1136 Pearl Street
Boulder, CO 80302   303-442-8683
Fax: 303-379-5199 info@meridiantrading.com
www.meridiantrading.com
Distribution of herbal products which includes extracts, teas, spices and medicinal herbs
President: David Black
Contact: Jesse Canizio
jesse@meridiantrading.com
Estimated Sales: $5 Million
Number Employees: 1-4

58005 Merlino Foods
4100 4th Ave S
Seattle, WA 98134   206-723-4700
sales@merlino.com
www.merlino.com

Wholesaler/distributor of imported and domestic specialty foods including cheeses, candy, olives, edible oils, pasta, rice, tomato products and mushrooms.
Owner: Todd Biesold
Year Founded: 1900
Estimated Sales: $10 Million
Number Employees: 50-99
Square Footage: 98000
Private Brands Carried:
  Merlino Olive Oil
Types of Products Distributed:
  Frozen Food, General Line, Specialty Foods, Cheeses, candy, olives, etc.

58006 Mermaid Seafoods
Builder Street
Llandudno, GY LL30 1DDR   149-287-8014
Fax: 203-622-9415   800-367-6675
www.mermaidseafoods.co.uk
Importer and wholesaler/distributor of frozen fish including hoki, roughy, pollack, yellowfin sole and cod; wholesaler/distributor of equipment and fixtures and general merchandise
CEO/President: Erna Reingold
CFO: Maria Coro Gorriti
Operations Director: Joel Reingold
Estimated Sales: $3-5 Million
Number Employees: 5-9
Square Footage: 10000
Private Brands Carried:
  Mermaid Seafoods
Types of Products Distributed:
  Frozen Food, General Merchandise, Seafood, Hoki, roughy, pollack, cod, etc.

58007 Merrill Distributing Inc
1301 N Memorial Dr
Merrill, WI 54452   715-536-4551
www.merrilldistributing.com
Wholesaler/distributor of grocery items including chocolate and candy bars, frozen desserts, appetizers and meats; serving the food service market.
President: John Schewe
jschewe@merrilldistributing.com
Customer Service: Terin Rampart
Director, Marketing: Jolene Mann
Director, Sales: Troy Nelson
Warehouse Manager: Kyle Badeau
Year Founded: 1912
Estimated Sales: $19 Million
Number Employees: 50-99
Square Footage: 50000
Number of Customer Locations: 8000
Types of Products Distributed:
  Food Service, Frozen Food, General Line, Provisions/Meat, Grocery items: candy, etc.

58008 Merritt Handling Engineering
22895 Saint George Cir
South Lyon, MI 48178-9446   248-349-8911
Fax: 248-349-5329
Wholesaler/distributor of conveyors, containers, racks and shelving
President: Victor Merritt
Estimated Sales: $2.5-5 Million
Number Employees: 10-19
Square Footage: 48000
Private Brands Carried:
  Interlake; Wildeck; Lyon
Types of Products Distributed:
  Frozen Food, General Merchandise, Conveyors, containers, racks, etc.

58009 Merton Restaurant Equipment Company
207 W Gore Street
Orlando, FL 32806-1034   407-425-4557
Fax: 407-425-4596
Wholesaler/distributor of restaurant equipment; serving the food service market
VP: Hallie Berman
Estimated Sales: $2.5-5 Million
Number Employees: 5-9
Private Brands Carried:
  Libby; Rubbermaid; Lincoln Wearever
Types of Products Distributed:
  Food Service, Frozen Food, General Merchandise, Restaurant equipment

58010 Mesa Bearing
902 W 18th St Ste A
Costa Mesa, CA 92627-6342
Fax: 714-901-9514   800-821-2657

Wholesaler/distributor of food processing equipment, conveyor systems and material handling equipment
President: Keith Faber
Sales Engineer/Order Desk: Randy Faber
Order Desk: Jose Ortega
Estimated Sales: $10-20 Million
Number Employees: 5-9
Types of Products Distributed:
  Frozen Food, General Merchandise, Food processing equipment & machinery

58011 Mesa Cold Storage
9602 W Buckeye Rd
Tolleson, AZ 85353-9101   623-478-9392
dcouryjr@mesacold.com
www.mesacold.com
Warehouse providing coooler, freezer and dry storage; wholesaler/distributor of groceries; transportation firm providing local, long and short haul trucking
Owner: Dan Coury
Number Employees: 50-99
Square Footage: 200000
Number of Customer Locations: 80
Types of Products Distributed:
  Frozen Food, General Line

58012 Messermeister
418 Bryant Circle Suite A
Ojai, CA 93023   805-640-0051
Fax: 805-640-0053   800-426-5134
info@messermeister.com
Wholesaler/distributor and exporter of knives, scissors and cutting boards; importer of cutlery, knife luggage, tools, food torches.
President: Debra Dressler
Contact: Brian Amodio
bamodio@actionac.net
Estimated Sales: $3-5 Million
Number Employees: 10-19
Square Footage: 32000
Private Brands Carried:
  Messermeiser
Types of Products Distributed:
  Frozen Food, General Merchandise, Knives, scissors, cutting boards, etc.

58013 Messina Brothers Manufacturing Company
1065 Shepherd Avenue
Brooklyn, NY 11208-5713   718-345-9800
Fax: 718-345-2441   800-924-6454
Manufacturer, importer and wholesaler/distributor of mops, brooms and brushes
Sales Representative: Robert Messina
General Manager: Lawrence Mirro
Number Employees: 15
Square Footage: 90000
Parent Co: Howard Berger Company
Types of Products Distributed:
  Frozen Food, General Merchandise, Mops, brooms & brushes

58014 Messina Hof Winery & Resort
4545 Old Reliance Rd
Bryan, TX 77808-8995   979-778-9463
Fax: 979-778-1729   marketing@messinahof.com
www.messinahof.com
Wines
President/CEO: Paul Bonarrigo
owners@messinahof.com
CFO: Merrill Bonarrigo
Estimated Sales: $10-20 Million
Number Employees: 20-49
Type of Packaging: Private Label, Bulk

58015 Metompkin Bay Oyster Company
101-105 Eleventh Street
P.O. Box 671
Crisfield, MD 21817   410-968-0662
Fax: 410-968-0670   metbay@verizon.net
www.metompkinseafood.com
Wholesaler/distributor of shellfish including crabmeat, soft crabs and oysters
Owner: Casey Todd
Estimated Sales: $10-20 Million
Number Employees: 100-249
Private Brands Carried:
  Metompkin
Types of Products Distributed:
  Frozen Food, Seafood, Crabmeat, soft crabs & oysters

58016 Metro Food Service Products
3871 Farragut St
Hollywood, FL 33021   954-967-0977
Fax: 800-852-8248   800-852-4637
info@metromaintenancesupplies.com
Wholesaler/distributor of lighting and smallwares and restaurant supplies
President: Jerry Schlanger
Marketing Director: Alex Rock
Sales Manager: Nancy Schwartz
Estimated Sales: $1 Million
Number Employees: 10
Square Footage: 12000
Private Brands Carried:
  Rubbermaid; Prince Castle; Cambro; Lighting-Hard to Find Bulbs
Types of Products Distributed:
  General Merchandise

58017 Metro Touch
2 Executive Dr
Fort Lee, NJ 07024-3308   201-944-3944
Fax: 201-944-8092   888-638-7669
www.metrotouch.com
Wholesaler/distributor of point of sale and reservation systems; serving the food service market
President: Steve Meisels
Estimated Sales: $2.5-5 Million
Number Employees: 10-19
Square Footage: 124000
Private Brands Carried:
  Squirrel; Perfect Host
Number of Customer Locations: 300
Types of Products Distributed:
  Food Service, Frozen Food, General Merchandise, Point of sale & reservation systems

58018 Metro, Inc.
530 Industrial Avenue
Ottawa, ON K1J 0Y9
Canada   613-737-1300
Fax: 613-737-1401   www.metro.ca
Wholesaler/distributor of groceries, dairy products, frozen food, produce, baked goods, general merchandise and private label items; serving the food service market
President, CEO: Eric Richer LaFleche
SVP, CFO and Treasurer: Francois Thibault
Chief Marketing Officer: Marc Giroux
General Manager Operations: Richard Beaubien
Number Employees: 100-249
Parent Co: Metro 2000
Number of Customer Locations: 38
Types of Products Distributed:
  Food Service, Frozen Food, General Line, General Merchandise, Produce, Rack Jobbers, Seafood, Baked goods & dairy products

58019 (HQ)Metro-Richelieu
11011 Maurice Duplessis Boulevard
Montreal, QC H1C 1V6
Canada   514-643-1000
Fax: 514-643-1030   800-561-8429
Wholesaler/distributor of seafood, general merchandise, meats and frozen foods; serving the food service market and supermarkets in Quebec
CEO/President: Pierre Lessard
VP (Groceries): Jean Louis Charpentier
VP (Food): Pierre Paul Bordon
Number Employees: 5,000-9,999
Other Locations:
  Metro-Richelieu 2000
  St. Jean Port Joli, PQ Metro-Richelieu 2000
Private Brands Carried:
  Merite
Types of Products Distributed:
  Food Service, Frozen Food, General Merchandise, Provisions/Meat, Seafood

58020 Metroplex Harriman Corporation
15 Commerce Dr S
Harriman, NY 10926   845-781-5006
Fax: 845-781-5005   800-781-9977
Wholesaler/distributor of frozen foods, general line items, produce and meat
Owner: Peter Grimm
Director Purchasing: Lee Herbert
Estimated Sales: $20-50 Million
Number Employees: 100-249
Square Footage: 73000
Parent Co: Metroplex Holdings
Other Locations:
  Metroplex Harriman Corp.
  Hauppauge, NY Metroplex Harriman Corp.

Wholesalers & Distributors / A-Z

Number of Customer Locations: 580
Types of Products Distributed:
Food Service, Frozen Food, General Line, Provisions/Meat, Produce, Groceries, beverages, etc.

58021 Metropolitan Beer & Soda Dist
2503 3rd Ave
Bronx, NY 10451-6323   718-993-2563
         Fax: 718-665-2273 metrobeers@aol.com
Wholesaler/distributor of beverages including beer and soda
Manager: Paul Eleisch
Number Employees: 1-4
Square Footage: 160000
Types of Products Distributed:
Frozen Food, General Line, Beverages: beer & soda

58022 Mexspice
PO Box 3336
S El Monte, CA 91733-0335   626-579-1276
         Fax: 626-579-1276
Wholesaler/distributor of fava, garbanzo and pinto beans, dry chili pods, paprika, garlic, black pepper, seasoning salt, rice, etc.; importer of Mexican, Indian and Japanese foods including spices and rice
President: Octano Kelly
VP: Marco Kelly
Number Employees: 10-19
Square Footage: 329528
Type of Packaging: Bulk
Types of Products Distributed:
Frozen Food, General Line, Specialty Foods, Paprika, black pepper, fava beans, etc.

58023 Miami Depot Inc
2915 W Okeechobee Rd
Hialeah, FL 33012-4596   305-884-1303
         Fax: 305-887-5038
Exporter of dry foods, cleaning products, paper, etc.; wholesaler/distributor of closeout and salvage groceries
President: Robert Halsey
CFO: John Antiieau
VP Retail: Margaret Halsey
Estimated Sales: Less Than $500,000
Number Employees: 1-4
Square Footage: 81000
Types of Products Distributed:
Frozen Food, General Line, Closeout & salvage

58024 (HQ)Miami Industrial Trucks
2830 E River Rd
Dayton, OH 45439   937-293-4194
         Fax: 937-293-1168 www.mitlift.com
Wholesaler/distributor of industrial trucks.
Chairman: George Malacos
President & CEO: Mark Jones
mjones@mitlift.com
Year Founded: 1956
Estimated Sales: $50-100 Million
Number Employees: 100-249
Private Brands Carried:
Caterpillar; Mitsubishi; B.G. Joe
Types of Products Distributed:
Frozen Food, General Merchandise, Industrial trucks

58025 Miami Industrial Trucks
130 Stanford Pkwy
Findlay, OH 45840   419-424-0042
         Fax: 419-424-0174 www.mitlift.com
Wholesaler/distributor of industrial trucks.
President & CEO: Mark Jones
mjones@mitlift.com
Number Employees: 100-249
Parent Co: Miami Industrial Trucks
Private Brands Carried:
T.C.M.;Mitsubishi; L.P.M. Parts
Types of Products Distributed:
Frozen Food, General Merchandise, Material handling equipment

58026 Miami Plastics & SupplyCorporation
381 NE 69th Street
Miami, FL 33138-5523   305-751-3600
         Fax: 305-751-5240 800-833-1005
Wholesaler/distributor of plastic sneeze guards and cutting boards
President: Bernardo Giraldo
Number Employees: 1-4
Square Footage: 16000

Types of Products Distributed:
Frozen Food, General Merchandise, Cutting boards, sneeze guards, etc.

58027 Miami Wholesale GroceryCompany
1007 N America Way
Suite 407
Miami, FL 33132-2602   305-371-8491
         Fax: 305-374-3931
Wholesaler/distributor of frozen food, general merchandise, general line products, produce and meats; serving the food service market
President: L Pietro
Director Operations: Mike Mairanteregger
Estimated Sales: $5-10 Million
Number Employees: 5-9
Types of Products Distributed:
Food Service, Frozen Food, General Line, General Merchandise, Provisions/Meat, Produce

58028 Michael Distributor Inc
PO Box 8681
Fountain Valley, CA 92728-8681
         Fax: 714-966-1361
Food distributor and related products provider-grocery, cooking oil, meat, sugar, canned foods, produce, dairy, candy & paper goods. Services to Food service and retail industries.
President: Miguel Ortega
Estimated Sales: $8 Million
Type of Packaging: Food Service, Private Label
Types of Products Distributed:
Food Service, General Merchandise, Provisions/Meat, Produce

58029 Michael G. Brown Associates
P.O.Box 352
Yardley, PA 19067   215-497-1060
         Fax: 215-497-8349 mgba@voicenet.com
Wholesaler/distributor of texture analyzers; serving the food service market
President: Michael Brown
Administration: Donna Esposito
Sales Engineer: Karole Tobias
Number Employees: 1-4
Square Footage: 4000
Private Brands Carried:
Stevens; CNS Farnell
Types of Products Distributed:
Food Service, Frozen Food, General Merchandise, Texture analyzers

58030 Michael Raymond Desserts Inc
15986 NW 49th Ave
Hialeah, FL 33014-6309   305-624-9994
         Fax: 305-626-9011
Broker, wholesaler, and distributor of desserts and bakery products including cakes, pies, and cheesecakes
President: Howard Schwartz
drdessert@bellsouth.net
Director Purchasing/Plant Manager: Debbi Cian
Estimated Sales: $5-10 Million
Number Employees: 10-19
Square Footage: 20000
Type of Packaging: Food Service, Private Label
Types of Products Distributed:
Food Service, Specialty Foods

58031 Michael's Cookies
2205 6th Ave. S
Clear Lake, IA 50428   641-454-5577
         Fax: 641-954-5451 800-822-5384
         info@michaelscookies.com
         www.michaelscookies.com
Frozen pre-portioned cookie doughs
COO/CFO: Scott Summeril
Quality Assurance: Myrkantra Dorlean
SVP Sales: Don Smith
Estimated Sales: $20-50 Million
Number Employees: 20-49
Number of Brands: 1
Number of Products: 1
Square Footage: 30000
Type of Packaging: Food Service, Private Label, Bulk
Private Brands Carried:
Bonzers
Types of Products Distributed:
Food Service

58032 Michael's Finer Meats/Seafoods
3775 Zane Trace Dr
Columbus, OH 43228
                              800-282-0518
                              www.michaelsmeats.com
Processor and wholesaler/distributor of meat including beef, pork, lamb, veal and wild game
President: Jonathan Bloch
Vice President of Sales: Jeff Goebel
Number Employees: 100-249
Square Footage: 240000
Type of Packaging: Consumer, Food Service, Bulk
Types of Products Distributed:
Provisions/Meat

58033 Michaelo Espresso
309 S Cloverdale St # D22
Ste D22
Seattle, WA 98108-4572   206-695-4950
         Fax: 206-695-4951 800-545-2883
                              info@michaelo.com
Kiosks, carts and vending equipment; importer and wholesaler/distributor of espresso and granita machinery and panini grills; serving the food service market
President: Michael Myers
info@michaelo.com
General Manager: Russ Myers
National Sales Manager: Douglas Pratt
Estimated Sales: $5-10 Million
Number Employees: 10-19
Square Footage: 40000
Type of Packaging: Food Service
Private Brands Carried:
Elmeco; Aristarco; Cafina
Types of Products Distributed:
Food Service, Frozen Food, General Merchandise, Espresso & granita machinery, etc.

58034 Michele's Bakery
6201 Riverdale Rd
Riverdale, MD 20737-2150   301-985-6050
         Fax: 301-985-6055
Wholesale distribution of bakery products
President: Leonard Banzaca
Estimated Sales: $2.5-5 Million
Number Employees: 1-4
Number of Brands: 1
Number of Products: 30

58035 Michelle's Bakery
6201 Riverdale Rd
Riverdale, MD 20737-2150   301-985-6050
         Fax: 301-985-6055
Wholesaler/distributor of fresh baked goods; serving the food service market
President: Leonard Banzaca
Administrative Assistant: Beth Suit
Number Employees: 5-9
Square Footage: 44000
Types of Products Distributed:
Food Service, Frozen Food, General Line, Fresh baked goods

58036 (HQ)Michigan Agricultural Commdty
445 N Canal Rd
Lansing, MI 48917   517-627-0200
         Fax: 517-627-3510 800-878-8900
                  info@michag.com www.michag.com
Exporter and wholesaler/distributor of sunflower seeds, grains and soybeans.
President: Dave Geers
davegerrs@agcommodites.com
Merchandising Manager: Robert Geers
Estimated Sales: $20-50 Million
Number Employees: 10-19
Types of Products Distributed:
Frozen Food, General Line, Health Food, Grains, seeds & soybeans

58037 Michigan Agricultural Commodities Inc
10894 E US 223
Blissfield, MI 49228   517-486-2171
         Fax: 517-486-2173 800-344-7246
                              www.michag.com
Exporter and wholesaler/distributor of sunflower seeds, grains and soybeans.
Facility Manager: Noel Eisenmann
Number Employees: 10-19

Wholesalers & Distributors / A-Z

58038 Michigan Agriculture Commodities
1601 N Mitchell Rd
Cadillac, MI 49601   989-236-7263
800-344-7263
www.michag.com
Exporter and wholesaler/distributor of sunflower seeds, grains and soybeans.
Northern Michigan Representative: Wes Edington
Number Employees: 10-19
Types of Products Distributed:
General Line, Health Food, Grains, seeds & soybeans

58039 Michigan Agriculture Commodities
216 Eastman St
Breckridge, MI 48615   989-842-3104
Fax: 989-842-3108   800-472-4629
www.michag.com
Exporter and wholesaler/distributor of sunflower seeds, grains and soybeans.
Branch Manager: Adam Geers
Office Manager: Pam Thebo
Number Employees: 10-19
Types of Products Distributed:
General Line, Health Food, Grains, seeds & soybeans

58040 Michigan Agriculture Commodities
7115 Maple Valley Rd
Brown City, MI 48416   810-346-2711
Fax: 810-346-4719   800-851-1448
www.michag.com
Exporter and wholesaler/distributor of sunflower seeds, grains and soybeans.
Branch Manager: Chuck Kunisch
Location Manager: Joe Berry
Number Employees: 10-19
Types of Products Distributed:
General Line, Health Food, Grains, seeds & soybeans

58041 Michigan Agriculture Commodities
1050 Ogden St
Jasper, MI 49248   517-436-3126
Fax: 517-436-3782   www.michag.com
Exporter and wholesaler/distributor of sunflower seeds, grains and soybeans.
Branch Manager: Noel Eisenmann
Facility Manager: Jess Strahan
Number Employees: 10-19
Types of Products Distributed:
General Line, Health Food, Grains, seeds & soybeans

58042 Michigan Agriculture Commodities
3346 Main St
Marlette, MI 48453   989-635-3578
Fax: 989-635-2951   800-647-4628
www.michag.com
Exporter and wholesaler/distributor of sunflower seeds, grains and soybeans.
Branch Manager: Chuck Kunisch
Office Manager: Jenny St. George
Number Employees: 10-19
Types of Products Distributed:
General Line, Health Food, Grains, seeds & soybeans

58043 Michigan Agriculture Commodities
306 N Caroline
Middleton, MI 48856   989-236-7263
Fax: 989-236-7716   800-344-7263
www.michag.com
Exporter and wholesaler/distributor of sunflower seeds, grains and soybeans.
Branch Manager: John Ezinga
Number Employees: 10-19
Types of Products Distributed:
General Line, Health Food, Grains, seeds & soybeans

58044 Michigan Agriculture Commodities
103 Water St
Newaygo, MI 49337   231-652-6017
Fax: 231-652-3811   800-878-5800
www.michag.com
Exporter and wholesaler/distributor of sunflower seeds, grains and soybeans.
Branch Manager: Mitchell Murray
Number Employees: 10-19
Types of Products Distributed:
General Line, Health Food, Grains, seeds & soybeans

58045 Michigan Carbonic Of Saginaw
6273 Dixie Hwy
Bridgeport, MI 48722-9513   989-777-5170
Fax: 989-777-9890
Wholesaler/distributor of ice machines, liquor systems, smokers, freezers and furniture
President: Paul Marshall
datamatic@aol.com
Sales Manager (Wholesale): Dave Morris
Sales Manager (Retail): Steve Ward
Estimated Sales: $10-20 Million
Number Employees: 1-4
Private Brands Carried:
Scotsman (Ice machines); Bery (Liquor systems); Electrofreeze (Freezers); Cook Shack (Smokers); MTS (Furniture)
Types of Products Distributed:
Frozen Food, General Line, Ice machines, liquor systems, etc.

58046 Michigan Industrial Belting
31617 Glendale St
Livonia, MI 48150-1828   734-427-7700
Fax: 734-427-0788   800-778-1650
marty@mibelting.com   www.mibelting.com
Conveyor belts and power transmission conveyor systems; wholesaler/distributor of conveyor belts, bearings, motors and controls
Owner: Bill Kohler
bill@mibelting.com
Estimated Sales: Below $5 Million
Number Employees: 10-19
Square Footage: 240000
Types of Products Distributed:
Frozen Food, General Merchandise, Conveyor belts, bearings, motors, etc.

58047 Michigan Industrial Equipment Company
3707 Roger B Chaffee SE
Grand Rapids, MI 49548   616-243-2443
Fax: 616-243-6648   888-648-8665
www.mit-tool.com
Wholesaler/distributor of material handling equipment
President: George Aye
Estimated Sales: $10-20 Million
Number Employees: 20-49
Private Brands Carried:
Nissan
Types of Products Distributed:
Frozen Food, General Merchandise, Material handling equipment

58048 Michigan Orchard Supply Company
07078 73 1/2 St
South Haven, MI 49090   269-637-1111
Fax: 269-637-7419   800-637-6426
www.michiganorchard.com
Wholesaler/distributor of specialty orchard equipment including irrigation systems, packaging equipment and sprayers
Owner: William De Witt Jr
Sales Director: Dale Overbeek
Purchasing Manager: Jim Lorren
Estimated Sales: $1-2.5 Million
Number Employees: 5-9
Types of Products Distributed:
General Merchandise, Irrigation systems, sprayers, etc.

58049 Michigan Sugar Company
122 Uptown Drive
Suite 300
Bay City, MI 48706   989-686-0161
Fax: 989-671-3719   www.michigansugar.com
Beet sugar
President/CEO: Mark Flegenheimer
CFO: Brian Haraga
Executive Vice President: Jim Ruhlman
VP Sales & Marketing: Pedro Figueroa
Vice President of Operations: Jason Lowry
Number Employees: 10-19
Type of Packaging: Consumer, Food Service, Private Label, Bulk
Other Locations:
Michigan Sugar Factory
Bay City, MI
Michigan Sugar Factory
Caro, MI
Michigan Sugar Factory
Croswell, MI
Michigan Sugar Factory
Sebewaing, MI Michigan Sugar Factory Caro
Types of Products Distributed:
General Line

58050 Mid America Chemical
1801 S Skyline Dr
Oklahoma City, OK 73129-6051   405-670-0101
Fax: 405-670-9270   800-749-6332
robertward5452@att.net
www.midamericachemical.com
Wholesaler/distributor of chemicals (acids, solvents, bleach, etc.)
President: Robert Ward
r.ward@midamericachemical.com
Estimated Sales: $10-20 Million
Number Employees: 1-4
Square Footage: 86000
Private Brands Carried:
MacNem

58051 Mid America Food Sales
4141 Stafford Woods Ct
St Charles, MO 63304-1604   636-447-2201
Fax: 636-447-2201   jcimmarusti@sbcglobal.net
www.midamericafoodsales.com
Wholesaler/distributor of specialty grains, flours and blends, custom granolas, gourmet bread mixes, nuts, fruit juice concentrates, raisins, dry honey and molasses, vegetable proteins and starches, gourmet coffee, natural high fiber ingredients, flavor enhancers, custom blending and packaging, cereals, dairy ingredients, starches, beans and rice, cookie pieces, graham meals, soy ingredients, vegetarian meat substitute, herbs, Extracts Botanicals
Owner: Jeff Cimmarusti
Treasurer: Judy Feinberg
Research & Development: Steven Feinberg
Marketing Director: Brad Feinberg
Sales Director: Steven Feinberg
Purchasing Manager: Amber Feinberg
Estimated Sales: $1-3 Million
Number Employees: 1-4
Type of Packaging: Consumer, Food Service, Private Label, Bulk
Types of Products Distributed:
Food Service, Health Food, Provisions/Meat, Food Ingredients

58052 Mid Atlantic Packaging Co
14 Starlifter Ave
Dover, DE 19901-9200   302-734-8833
Fax: 302-734-8698   800-284-1332
sales@midatlanticpackaging.com
www.midatlanticpackaging.com
Bags, boxes, fill material, labels, ribbons and bows
Owner: Herb Glanden
Marketing: Don Glanden
Sales Director: Donald Glanden
hgmap@dmv.com
Estimated Sales: $3-7 Million
Number Employees: 20-49
Number of Brands: 50
Number of Products: 25
Square Footage: 60000
Number of Customer Locations: 15000
Types of Products Distributed:
Shrink Film, Packaging Materials

58053 Mid States Paper & Notion Co
810 Cherokee Ave
Nashville, TN 37207-5219   615-226-1234
Fax: 615-226-1299
Wholesaler/distributor of general merchandise; serving the food service market
President: Kyle Crecelius
Estimated Sales: Less Than $500,000
Number Employees: 1-4
Number of Customer Locations: 100

Wholesalers & Distributors / A-Z

58054 Mid-America Wholesale
3101 S Van Buren St
Enid, OK 73701 580-237-1040
 800-425-1041
www.mid-america-online.com
Wholesaler/distributor of frozen foods, general merchandise, general line and dairy products, produce and meats.
President: Jeff Dick
jdick@mid-america-online.com
CEO & Buyer: Mark Dick
CFO & Buyer: Roger Beagle
Business Development Director: Michael McCormick
Director of Sales: Chad Buchanan
Buyer: Tim Stephens
Year Founded: 1956
Estimated Sales: $21 Million
Number Employees: 30
Parent Co: Mid-America
Private Brands Carried:
 All-Kitchen
Types of Products Distributed:
 Food Service, Frozen Food, General Line, General Merchandise, Provisions/Meat, Produce, Dairy products, etc.

58055 Mid-Continent Sales
15200 E Girard Avenue
Suite 2075
Aurora, CO 80014-0002 303-695-4275
 Fax: 303-695-0970
Wholesaler/distributor of spices. Broker of dairy/deli products, frozen foods, general merchandise, groceries, industrial ingredients, spices, etc.
President: R Kinn
CEO: J Loyacono
Estimated Sales: Less than $500,000
Number Employees: 1-4
Square Footage: 5600
Types of Products Distributed:
 General Line, Spices

58056 Mid-Michigan Ice Company
1755 Yeager St
Port Huron, MI 48060-2594 989-792-6410
 Fax: 989-792-6408 800-589-6738
Wholesaler/distributor of rock salt and wet and dry ice
President: B Brown
CEO: N Knowlton
CFO: N Knowlton
Estimated Sales: $1-3 Million
Number Employees: 5-9
Square Footage: 28000
Parent Co: Winkler Lucas Ice & Fuel
Private Brands Carried:
 Party Time Ice; Great Lakes Ice Co.; Northern Pure Ice
Number of Customer Locations: 150
Types of Products Distributed:
 Frozen Food, General Line, General Merchandise, Wet & dry ice

58057 Mid-South Fish Company
P.O.Box 185
Aubrey, AR 72311-0185 870-295-5600
 Fax: 870-295-3559
Owner: Algie Jolly
Estimated Sales: $.5-1 million
Number Employees: 1-4

58058 Middendorf Meat
3737 N Broadway
St Louis, MO 63147 314-241-4800
performancefoodservice.com/Middendorf
Wholesaler/distributor of frozen food, general merchandise, general line items, dairy products, baked goods, produce, provisions/meats, seafood and specialty food; serving the food service market.
Estimated Sales: $45 Million
Number Employees: 100-249
Square Footage: 100000
Parent Co: Performance Foodservice
Types of Products Distributed:
 Food Service, Frozen Food, General Line, General Merchandise, Provisions/Meat, Produce, Seafood, Specialty Foods, Wild game

58059 Middle Tennessee Dr Pepper Distributing Center
227 Mountain St
McMinnville, TN 37110 931-473-2108
 Fax: 931-473-4418 800-801-1421
www.mtdrpepper.com
Wholesaler/distributor of beverages including soda
Office Manager: Debbie Morgan
Sales Manager: Sam Woodlee
Estimated Sales: $10-20 Million
Number Employees: 20-49
Square Footage: 60000
Private Brands Carried:
 Diet Dr. Pepper; Diet Sun Drop; Double Cola; Dr. Pepper; Sun Drop; Crush
Types of Products Distributed:
 General Line, Soda & beverages

58060 Midland Grocery of Michigan
PO Box 570
Muskegon, MI 49443-0570 231-722-3151
 Fax: 231-728-4492
Wholesaler/distributor of groceries, meats, dairy and private label items, etc
VP/General Manager: D Miller
VP Sales: Gerry Vossekuil
VP Operations (Perishables): P Raymondo
Number Employees: 100-249
Square Footage: 800000
Parent Co: Roundy's
Private Brands Carried:
 Shurfine; Shurfresh
Number of Customer Locations: 110
Types of Products Distributed:
 Frozen Food, General Line, General Merchandise, Provisions/Meat, Dairy & private label items, etc.

58061 (HQ)Midlantic Sweetener Company
1228 Mays Landing Road
Folsom, NJ 8037 803-548-3877
 Fax: 803-548-3536 800-370-5272
midsweet@aol.com www.atlanticsweetner.com
Wholesaler/distributor of salts, industrial ingredients, dry mustard, fruit products, sweeteners, starches and chemicals; serving food processors and wholesalers/distributors
Owner: Philip Gentlesk Sr
VP/CFO: Philip Gentlesk, Jr.
Sales Manager: Scott Wohlfarth
Estimated Sales: $10-20 Million
Number Employees: 10-19
Square Footage: 30000
Other Locations:
 Midlantic Sweetener Co.
 Raleigh, NCMidlantic Sweetener Co.
Types of Products Distributed:
 Frozen Food, General Line, General Merchandise, Ingredients, sweeteners, starches, etc.

58062 Midori Trading Inc
89-16 126th Street
Richmond Hill, NY 11418 718-461-3835
 Fax: 718-461-3729
Wholesaler/distributor, importer and exporter of produce, specialty and health foods including ginger and green teas
President: Mo Ma
Estimated Sales: $1-2.5 Million
Number Employees: 1-4
Types of Products Distributed:
 Frozen Food, Health Food, Produce, Specialty Foods, Ginseng & green teas

58063 Midtown Electric SupplyCorp
157 W 18th St
New York, NY 10011-4155 212-255-3388
 Fax: 212-255-3177 800-484-7093
www.midtownelectric.com
Wholesaler/distributor of electrical equipment including conduits, energy conservation equipment, lighting fixtures and fluorescent lamps
President: Matthew Gold
mattgold@midtownelectric.com
Office Manager/Bookkeeper: Alex Eckstein
Estimated Sales: $20-50 Million
Number Employees: 50-99
Number of Customer Locations: 400
Types of Products Distributed:
 Frozen Food, General Merchandise, Electrical supplies & lighting fixtures

58064 Midway Container Inc.
2341 Hampden Ave
Saint Paul, MN 55114 651-647-0101
 Fax: 651-647-0106 888-843-4421
info@midwaycontainer.com
www.midwaycontainer.com
Wholesaler/distributor of packaging materials including plastic and metal containers
Owner: Warren W Larson
Sales Manager: Brad Hilbenkamp
Contact: Pat Dingmann
patdingmann@midwaycontainer.com
Estimated Sales: $5-10 Million
Number Employees: 10-19
Square Footage: 120000
Types of Products Distributed:
 Frozen Food, General Merchandise, Packaging materials, etc.

58065 Midwest Badge & NoveltyCo
3337 Republic Ave
Minneapolis, MN 55426-4108 952-927-9901
 Fax: 952-927-9903
Manufacturer, importer and wholesaler/distributor of name badges, buttons and advertising specialties
President: Kevin Saba
kevin.saba@mgincentives.com
Estimated Sales: Less than $500,000
Number Employees: 1-4
Square Footage: 16000
Type of Packaging: Consumer, Private Label, Bulk
Types of Products Distributed:
 General Merchandise, Name badges, buttons, etc.

58066 Midwest Cooperative
101 W 5th Street
Starbuck, MN 56381-2426 320-239-2226
Wholesaler/distributor of grain; serving food processors and manufacturers
Manager: Rod Leien
Types of Products Distributed:
 Frozen Food, Grain

58067 Midwest Distribution Group
103 W 61st St
Westmont, IL 60559 630-769-1330
 Fax: 630-769-1057 800-541-7920
Wholesaler/distributor of ice cream cones and toppings
President: Lorraine Massie
Estimated Sales: $1-3 Million
Number Employees: 1-4
Square Footage: 14400
Type of Packaging: Food Service, Bulk
Private Brands Carried:
 Keebler; M&M/Mars; Henry and Henry Products; Danish Waffle Cone, Sweet Ovations/Novelty Cone, Cr Candies/Cobatco/Proc Foods
Types of Products Distributed:
 Food Service, Specialty Foods

58068 Midwest Fire & Safety Equipment Company
1605 Prospect Street
Indianapolis, IN 46203-2024 317-637-4832
 Fax: 317-637-4832
Wholesaler/distributor of fire safety apparatus; serving the food service market
VP/Marketing: Michael Casse
Estimated Sales: $20-50 Million
Number Employees: 20-49
Types of Products Distributed:
 Food Service, Frozen Food, General Merchandise, Fire safety apparatus

58069 Midwest Food Distributors
2445 Flag Avenue S
Minneapolis, MN 55426-2371 507-625-9301
 Fax: 507-625-9303
Wholesaler/distributor of frozen foods; serving the food service market
Owner: V Kahn
Buyer: James Miller
Types of Products Distributed:
 Food Service, Frozen Food

58070 Midwest Frozen Foods, Inc.
2185 Leeward Ln
Hanover Park, IL 60133-6026 630-784-0123
 Fax: 630-784-0424 866-784-0123

Midwest Frozen Foods provides in house and private label frozen fruits and vegetables to the retail, food services and industrial manufacturing sectors.
President: Zafar Iqbal
VP: Athar Siddiq
Operations: Rob Linchesky
Production: Jose Manjarrez
Estimated Sales: $5 Million
Number Employees: 18
Number of Brands: 2
Number of Products: 100+
Square Footage: 20000
Type of Packaging: Food Service, Private Label, Bulk

58071 Midwest Imports LTD
205 Fencl Ln
Hillside, IL 60162-2001   708-236-1500
    Fax: 708-236-3100 800-621-3372
www.midwestimports.com
Wholesaler/distributor and importer of baking ingredients, chocolate coatings, preserves, Swiss dried sauces and soups
Owner: Todd Ostrowski
info@midwestimports.com
Office Manager/Customer Service: Todd Ostrowski
VP: Frank Jurkowski
Estimated Sales: $10-20 Million
Number Employees: 20-49
Square Footage: 77600
Types of Products Distributed:
    Frozen Food, General Line, Chocolate coatings, preserves, etc.

58072 Midwest Ingredients Inc
103 W Main St
PO Box 186
Princeville, IL 61559-7511   309-385-1035
    Fax: 309-385-1036 www.midwestingredients.com
Midwest Ingredients has purchased excess and close coded food products and ingredients across the continental United States since 1994. The inventory is sold with any restrictions the manufacturer requires. We work with retail orinstitutional packaging and also bulk pack products.
CFO: Ruthi Coats
ruthi@midwestingredients.com
Estimated Sales: Above $5 Million
Number Employees: 5-9
Types of Products Distributed:
    Food Service, Frozen Food, General Line, General Merchandise, Health Food, Provisions/Meat, Rack Jobbers, Seafood, Specialty Foods, Closed Coded Food Items

58073 Midwest Promotional Group
2011 S Frontage Rd
Summit, IL 60527   708-563-0600
    Fax: 708-563-0603 800-305-3388
sales@midwestgrp.com www.midwestgrp.com
Manufacturer and wholesaler/distributor of advertising calendars, embroidered aprons, uniforms, shirts, etc.; also, silk screening available
President: David Lewandowski
CEO: Don Lewandowski
VP: Keith Vacey
Chairman: Don Lewandowski
Sales Director: Rick Dignault
Operations Manager: Roger Wilson
Accounting Executive: Jeff Feichtinger
Estimated Sales: $5-10 Million
Number Employees: 50-99
Square Footage: 33000
Types of Products Distributed:
    Frozen Food, General Merchandise, Uniforms, Rugs, Pop Banners

58074 Midwest Seafood
5500 Emerson Way
Suite A
Indianapolis, IN 46226-1477   317-466-1027
    Fax: 317-466-1033
Estimated Sales: $1-3 Million
Number Employees: 5-9

58075 Mike E. Simon & Company
401 E 9th Street
Douglas, AZ 85607-2123   520-364-3611
    Fax: 520-364-3611
Wholesaler/distributor of general line products; serving the food service market
Estimated Sales: $2.5-5 Million
Number Employees: 1-4

Types of Products Distributed:
    Food Service, Frozen Food, General Line

58076 Mike Kazarian
3440 Huxley Street
Los Angeles, CA 90027-1409   323-662-2216
Wholesaler/distributor of produce
Owner: Mike Kazarian
Number Employees: 5-9
Types of Products Distributed:
    Frozen Food, Produce

58077 Mikey's
    480-696-2483
info@mikeysmuffins.com
www.eatmikeys.com
Gluten-free, dairy-free, soy-free, and paleo English muffins, muffin tops, sliced bread, pizza crusts, tortillas, and pizza pockets
Founder/CEO: Michael Tierney *Year Founded:* 2014
Types of Products Distributed:
    General Line

58078 Mile Hi Frozen Foods Corp.
4770 E. 51st Ave.
Denver, CO 80216   303-399-6066
    800-591-1191
www.milehifoods.com
Frozen foods, general line products, produce, provisions/meats and McDonald's products/stores.
President: Tony Taddonio
Year Founded: 1946
Estimated Sales: $21.2 Million
Number Employees: 100-249
Types of Products Distributed:
    Food Service, General Line, Provisions/Meat, Produce

58079 Milky Whey Inc
910 Brooks St # 203
Suite 203
Missoula, MT 59801-5784   406-542-7373
    Fax: 406-542-7377 800-379-6455
dairy@themilkywhey.com
www.themilkywhey.com
Whey proteins and dry dairy ingredients including nonfat dry milk, whole milk, whey powder, butter, buttermilk powder, caseinates, lactose, nondairy creamers, whey protein concentrates and isolates, and cheese powders
President: Curt Pijanowski
curt@themilkywhey.com
CFO: Steve Schmidt
Vice President: Dan Finch
Operations Manager: Carla Messerly
Reception: Tony Cavanaugh
Estimated Sales: $1.2 Million
Number Employees: 10-19
Type of Packaging: Consumer, Private Label, Bulk
Types of Products Distributed:
    Frozen Food, General Line, Ingredients & dry dairy commodities

58080 Mill Cove Lobster Pound
381 Barters Island Rd
Trevett, ME 4571   207-633-3340
    Fax: 207-633-7206 www.millcovelobster.com
Processor and wholesaler/distributor of seafood including lobster, shrimp, frozen cod, ocean perch, pollack, clams and oysters
President: Jeff Lewis
mclobster@roadrunner.com
Estimated Sales: $4-$5 Million
Number Employees: 10-19
Type of Packaging: Consumer
Types of Products Distributed:
    Frozen Food, Seafood

58081 Millar-Williams Hydronics
4060 Fairview Street
Unit 12
Burlington, ON L7L 4Y8
Canada   905-637-9496
    Fax: 905-333-5446 800-263-6651
Wholesaler/distributor of sani valves, pumps, conveyors, etc
President: Rick Williams
Number Employees: 5-9
Square Footage: 16000
Types of Products Distributed:
    Frozen Food, General Merchandise, Sani valves, pumps, conveyors, etc.

58082 Millbrook Distribution Services
6 Nick Ridge Drive
Washington, MO 63090-4143   636-677-1120
    Fax: 636-677-0793 800-643-8130
Wholesaler/distributor of health and beauty aids, general merchandise and specialty foods
Estimated Sales: $20-50 Million
Number Employees: 20-49
Types of Products Distributed:
    Frozen Food, General Merchandise, Specialty Foods, Health & beauty aids

58083 Millbrook Distribution Service
P.O.Box 790
Harrison, AR 72602   870-741-3425
Wholesale provider of non-food and specialty food products
CEO/President: Robert Sigel
Executive VP/Marketing: William Paul
Senior VP/CFO: Bob Lieberman
Senior VP/Human Resources: Peter Schmidt
Senior VP/Sales & Merchandising: Frank Patrick
Senior VP/CIO: Johnnie Austin
VP: G Epstein
Estimated Sales: $5-10 Million
Number Employees: 5-9
Private Brands Carried:
    Season; Gold Boat; Iceland Waters
Number of Customer Locations: 3000
Types of Products Distributed:
    Frozen Food, Seafood, Specialty Foods

58084 Millbrook Vineyards
26 Wing Rd
Millbrook, NY 12545-5017   845-677-8383
    Fax: 845-677-6186 800-662-9463
millbrookwinery@millwine.com
www.millbrookwine.com
Wine
Owner: John Dyson
millbrookwinery@millwine.com
CFO: Eric Grans
General Manager/Sales Manager: Gary Goddard
Director of Marketing: Stacy Hudson
Director of Sales: Scott Koster
Estimated Sales: $5-10 Million
Number Employees: 10-19
Type of Packaging: Private Label

58085 Millen Fish
PO Box 864
Millen, GA 30442-864   478-982-4988
    Fax: 912-982-1746
Fish and fish products
President: David McMillian
Estimated Sales: $3-5 Million
Number Employees: 10-19

58086 Miller & Hartman
1 Stomel Plaza
West Berlin, NJ 08091-9287   856-767-9830
    Fax: 856-768-9601 800-348-2324
Wholesaler/distributor of general line products, general merchandise, frozen foods, beverages and meats; serving the food service market
General Manager: Bob Shangraw
VP Sales: Ed Gribbon
Purchasing Agent: Mike Ginsberg
Estimated Sales: $2.5-5 Million
Number Employees: 5-9
Number of Customer Locations: 5000
Types of Products Distributed:
    Food Service, Frozen Food, General Line, General Merchandise, Provisions/Meat, Beverages, etc.

58087 Miller Johnson Seafood
4310 Heron Bay Loop Road S
Coden, AL 36523-3714   251-873-4444
    Fax: 252-729-1427
Seafood
Owner: Miller Johnson

58088 Milligan's Island
P.O.Box 3735
Newport, RI 02840-317
    Fax: 203-245-9870
Wholesaler/distributor of root beer and soft drinks
President: Sharon Van Horn
Estimated Sales: $1-3 Million
Number Employees: 1-4
Type of Packaging: Consumer
Private Brands Carried:
    Milligan's Island Awesome Root Beer

Wholesalers & Distributors / A-Z

Types of Products Distributed:
General Line, Root beer, spring water & soft drinks

58089 Mills Brothers Intl
16000 Christensen Rd
Suite 300
Seattle, WA 98188-2967 206-575-3000
Fax: 206-957-1362 mbi@millsbros.com
www.millsbros.com
Specialty and organic grains, dried peas, dried beans, lentils, millet rice and corn products including popcorn kernels, flour, grits, meal and starch
President: Eric Mills
Year Founded: 1982
Estimated Sales: $36306000
Number Employees: 50-99
Square Footage: 26000
Type of Packaging: Consumer, Food Service, Private Label, Bulk
Types of Products Distributed:
Food Service, Frozen Food, General Line, Produce, Beans, peas, lentils, millet, etc.

58090 Millway Frozen Foods
346 Millway Avenue
Unit #11
Concord, ON L4K 3W1
Canada 905-660-9611
Fax: 905-660-0281 www.millwayfoods.com
Wholesaler/distributor of frozen foods; serving the food service market
Owner: Frank Petrolo
Number Employees: 1-4
Private Brands Carried:
Olmstead; Gordon; Atlantic Sugar
Types of Products Distributed:
Food Service, Frozen Food

58091 Milsek Furniture Polish Inc.
5525 E Pine Lake Rd
North Lima, OH 44452 330-542-2700
Fax: 330-542-1059 www.milsek.com
Manufacturer, exporter and wholesaler/distributor of furniture polish and cleaner
President: Jean Hamilton
VP: Susan Bender
Estimated Sales: Under $1 Million
Number Employees: 5-9
Number of Brands: 1
Number of Products: 2
Square Footage: 108000
Private Brands Carried:
Milsek

58092 Milton's Craft Bakers
5875 Avenida Encinas
Carlsbad, CA 92008 858-350-9696
Fax: 858-350-0898 www.miltonscraftbakers.com
Breads, crackers and frozen prepared foods
CFO: Ronald Hendrickson
Marketing: Mike McMurtry
Estimated Sales: $8.4 Million
Number Employees: 28

58093 Minnesota Conway Fire & Safety
575 Minnehaha Ave W
St Paul, MN 55103-1573 651-251-1880
Fax: 650-288-0776 www.summitfire.com
Wholesaler/distributor of general merchandise including fire extinguishers, first aid kits, fire suppression systems, emergency lights, etc.; serving the food service market
President: William C Krebsbach
Division Manager: Loren Albrecht
Sales: Tom Montgomery
Service Manager: Bill Anderson
banderson@mnconway.com
Estimated Sales: $2.5-5 Million
Number Employees: 5-9
Square Footage: 40000
Private Brands Carried:
Amerex; Pyro Chem; Buckeye
Types of Products Distributed:
Food Service, Frozen Food, General Merchandise, Fire extinguishers, etc.

58094 Minuteman Trading
12 Greenway Ave S
Boyce, VA 22620-9735 540-837-1138
Fax: 540-837-2526
Wholesaler/distributor and importer of kitchen utensils; serving the food service market and retail stores
President: Chuck Lockard

Estimated Sales: $3.2 Million
Number Employees: 1-4
Square Footage: 39600
Type of Packaging: Consumer, Food Service
Number of Customer Locations: 1850
Types of Products Distributed:
Food Service, General Merchandise, Kitchen utensils, vegetable slicer

58095 Miracle Exclusives
PO Box 2508
Danbury, CT 06813-2508 203-796-5493
Fax: 203-648-4871 800-645-6360
www.miracleexclusives.com
Wholesaler/distributor and importer of juice extractors, cookware, grain mills, grinders, graters, pasta and yogurt makers, dehydrators, sprouters and wheat grass growers
President: George Drake
VP: John Downey
Estimated Sales: $5-10 Million
Square Footage: 40000
Type of Packaging: Consumer
Private Brands Carried:
Miracle
Number of Customer Locations: 3000
Types of Products Distributed:
Frozen Food, General Merchandise

58096 Mishima Foods USA
2340 Plaza Del Amo
Suite 105
Torrance, CA 90501 310-787-1533
Fax: 310-787-1651 mishima.com
Japanese products
Business Development Manager: Ken Hsu
Contact: Yuho Quintero
yuho@mishima.com
Estimated Sales: $2.5-5 Million
Number Employees: 1-4
Parent Co: Mishima
Type of Packaging: Consumer, Food Service
Private Brands Carried:
Mishima
Types of Products Distributed:
Food Service, Frozen Food, Produce, White & shiitake mushrooms

58097 Miss Grimble Desserts
909 E 135th St
Bronx, NY 10454-3697 718-665-2253
Fax: 718-665-2496
Wholesaler/distributor of gourmet cakes; serving the food service market. bread, cake and related products
Owner: Phillip Goodman
phillip@missgrimble.com
Estimated Sales: $2.5-5 Million
Number Employees: 5-9
Types of Products Distributed:
Food Service, Frozen Food, Specialty Foods

58098 Miss Mary
115 Pacific Ave
Long Beach, WA 98631 360-642-5541
Fax: 360-642-3391
Wholesaler/distributor of frozen pacific ocean spot prawns, albacore tuna
President: Wendy J Murry
CEO: Debra Oakes
CFO: Jared Oakes
Vice President: Tiffany Turner
Estimated Sales: $400,000
Number Employees: 1-4
Number of Brands: 1
Number of Products: 1
Type of Packaging: Private Label
Types of Products Distributed:
Frozen Food, Seafood, Prawns

58099 Mister Fish Inc.
288 Rolling Mill Rd
Baltimore, MD 21224-2033 410-288-2722
Fax: 410-288-4757 ed@misterfishinc.com
www.misterfishinc.com
Seafood
Owner: Frank Petilo
Estimated Sales: $1-3 Million
Number Employees: 20-49

58100 Misty Islands Seafoods
P. O. Box 201 Lepreau
Dipper Harbour, NB E5J 2T1
Canada 506-659-2781
Fax: 506-659-3113
www.mistyharbourseafood.com
Seafood
Manager: Robert Melovidov
Manager: Richard Tremaine
Estimated Sales: $3-5 Million
Number Employees: 1-3
Parent Co: Coastal Enterprises

58101 Mitch Chocolate
300 Spagnoli Rd
Melville, NY 11747-3507 631-777-2400
Fax: 631-777-1449 www.misschocolate.com
Hard candy lollypops; wholesaler/distributor of salt water taffy and fundraising boxed chocolates
President: Lawrence Hirsihheimer
VP Operations: Martin Bloomfield
Estimated Sales: $3-5 Million
Number Employees: 5-9
Square Footage: 16000
Type of Packaging: Consumer, Private Label
Private Brands Carried:
Frolic (Salt water taffy)
Types of Products Distributed:
Frozen Food, General Line, Candy: salt water taffy, etc.

58102 Mitchell Grocery Corp
550 Railroad Ave
Albertville, AL 35950 256-878-4211
www.mitchellgrocery.com
Wholesaler/distributor of general merchandise, seafood, meats, produce, general line items, baked goods, dairy products, frozen foods, etc.; serving supermarkets.
President: David Mitchell
VP of Retail: Jay Mitchell
Year Founded: 1945
Estimated Sales: $100-500 Million
Number Employees: 20-49
Number of Customer Locations: 200
Types of Products Distributed:
Frozen Food, General Line, General Merchandise, Provisions/Meat, Produce, Seafood, Dairy products, baked goods, etc.

58103 Mitchell Handling Systems
24629 Halsted Rd.
Farmington Hills, MI 48335 248-478-3812
Fax: 248-855-2125 800-245-2397
greggs@mitchellsalesinc.com
www.ballcalleliminator.com
Wholesaler/distributor of material handling equipment including conveyors; also, containers available
President: Ronald Mitchell
Estimated Sales: $3-5 Million
Number Employees: 1-4
Private Brands Carried:
White Systems; Emanco; Flexcon
Types of Products Distributed:
Frozen Food, General Merchandise, Material handling equipment

58104 Mivila Foods
226 Getty Ave
Paterson, NJ 07503-2690 973-278-7263
Fax: 973-278-9332 mivila@mivila.com
www.mivila.com
Wholesaler/distributor of fresh, frozen, dry, canned, refrigerated, paper, and equipment
Owner: Soto Apostolopoulos
mivila@hotmail.com
Estimated Sales: $20-50 Million
Number Employees: 100-249
Square Footage: 300000
Type of Packaging: Consumer, Food Service, Private Label, Bulk
Other Locations:
Mivila Foods
Calverian, NYMivila Foods
Private Brands Carried:
Embassy's Lucky Boy, Heinz, Hunt-Wesson, Barilla, Kraft, Dececco, Kelloggs, Domino
Number of Customer Locations: 2
Types of Products Distributed:
Food Service, Frozen Food, General Line, General Merchandise, Health Food, Provisions/Meat, Produce, Seafood, Specialty Foods

Wholesalers & Distributors / A-Z

58105 Mj Kellner Co
5700 International Pkwy
Springfield, IL 62711-4052 217-483-1700
Fax: 217-483-1771 mjk@mjkellner.com
www.mjkellner.com
Wholesaler/distributor of groceries, meats, produce, frozen foods, baked goods, equipment and fixtures, general merchandise and seafood; serving the food service market
Owner: William Kellner
Founder: Maurice Kellner
CFO: Kathy Dierkes
kathyd@mjkellner.com
Sales Manager: Bill Barris
Director of Sales & Marketing: Gary Boston
Number Employees: 50-99
Private Brands Carried:
  Pocahontas
Types of Products Distributed:
  Food Service, Frozen Food, General Line, General Merchandise, Provisions/Meat, Produce, Seafood, Dry foods, baked goods, groceries, etc.

58106 Mobile Bay Seafood
11801 Old Shipyard Rd
Coden, AL 36523 251-973-0410
Fax: 706-538-6850
Seafood
President: Bob Omainsky

58107 Mobjack Bay Seafood
6578 Jarvis Rd
Gloucester, VA 23061-4802 804-693-7597
Fax: 804-693-0581 jvigliotta@ccsinc.com
www.mobjackbayseafood.com
Wholesaler/distributor of shellfish and whole fish
Owner/President: John Vigliotta
johnv@mobjackbayseafood.com
Estimated Sales: $5-10 Million
Number Employees: 10-19
Square Footage: 40000
Private Brands Carried:
  Diamond Shoals
Types of Products Distributed:
  Frozen Food, Seafood, Shellfish & whole fish

58108 Moctezuma Foods
346 Lexington Ave NW
Grand Rapids, MI 49504-5568 616-243-3585
Fax: 616-243-5344 888-802-0412
Wholesaler/distributor of Mexican and frozen foods, general merchandise, groceries, private label items, baked goods, etc
President: Luis Ramirez
Treasurer: William Wissman
VP: Enrique Pena
Estimated Sales: $1-2.5 Million
Number Employees: 20-49
Square Footage: 72000
Number of Customer Locations: 100
Types of Products Distributed:
  Frozen Food, General Line, General Merchandise, Specialty Foods, Mexican foods, baked goods

58109 Model Dairy LLC
500 Gould St
Reno, NV 89502-1466 775-788-7900
Fax: 775-788-7951 800-433-2030
Processor and wholesaler/distributor of a full line of dairy products including ice cream
Cmo: Derrick Alby
derrick_@deanfoods.com
VP/General Manager: Jim Breslin
Controller: Peggy Baker
Manager: Jim Breslin
Number Employees: 100-249
Square Footage: 100000
Parent Co: Suiza Dairy Group
Type of Packaging: Food Service
Types of Products Distributed:
  Food Service, Frozen Food

58110 Modena Fine Foods Inc
158 River Rd
Clifton, NJ 07014-1571 973-470-8499
Fax: 201-842-9001 www.modenafinefoods.com
Balsamic products, including balsamic vinegar, specialty wine vinegars, and balsamic condiments
President: Fred Mortadi
Vice President: Michael Giaimo
michael@modenafinefoods.com
Estimated Sales: $720,000
Number Employees: 10-19

58111 Modern Equipment Co
416 Washington St W
P.O.Box 20474
Charleston, WV 25302-2131 304-343-0101
Fax: 304-343-0115 800-660-1890
www.modernequipmentwv.com
Wholesaler/distributor of restaurant equipment and supplies; serving the food service market
CEO: Gary Werkman
gary@modern-equipment.com
Sales Director: Goerge McWilliam
Estimated Sales: $2.5-5 Million
Number Employees: 5-9
Square Footage: 120000
Types of Products Distributed:
  Food Service, Frozen Food, General Merchandise, Restaurant equipment & supplies

58112 Modern Food Equipment Company
60 Idylwood Dr
Northford, CT 06472-1441 203-484-2901
Fax: 203-772-4621 ajudelson@aol.com
Consultant providing design (CAD) and operation services for users of any type of commercial ffod equipment, even if not being used in food service application. Any size job, any location
President: Alan Judelson
Estimated Sales: Less than $500,000
Number Employees: 1-4

58113 Modern Group
P.O.Box 710
Bristol, PA 19007-0710 215-943-9100
Fax: 215-943-4978 griffithd@moderngroup.com
www.moderngroup.com
Wholesaler/distributor of forklifts; also, parts, service and rental equipment available
Chairman of the Board: Joseph McEwen
President: Dave Griffith
CEO: Dave Griffith
Estimated Sales: $20-50 Million
Number Employees: 100-249
Types of Products Distributed:
  Frozen Food

58114 Modern Macaroni Co LTD
1708 Mary St
Honolulu, HI 96819-3103 808-845-6841
Fax: 808-845-6841 www.modernmacaroni.net
Dry Asian noodles, shrimp flakes and soybean flour
Owner: Darrell Siu
Estimated Sales: $900,000-$1 Million
Number Employees: 10-19
Square Footage: 4800
Type of Packaging: Consumer, Food Service
Types of Products Distributed:
  Food Service, Specialty Foods

58115 Modern Mushroom Farms Inc
1340 Newark Rd
Toughkenamon, PA 19374 610-268-3773
Fax: 610-268-5193 800-330-5711
info@modernmush.com www.modernmush.com
Mushrooms, white, portabella, exotic, stuffed, dried, marinated.
Human Resources Director: Jackie Serrano Lugo
Estimated Sales: $25 Million
Number Employees: 100-249
Square Footage: 375000
Type of Packaging: Consumer, Food Service, Bulk
Types of Products Distributed:
  Frozen Food

58116 Modern Table
Walnut Creek, CA 94597
www.moderntable.com
Plant-based pastas and prepared meals
Marketing: Jennifer Eiseman
National Sales Manager: Jeff Schonhoff
Number Employees: 1,000-4,999
Number of Brands: 1
Number of Products: 12
Type of Packaging: Consumer

58117 Modern Wholesale Company
609 S Main St
Kannapolis, NC 28081 704-933-4161
Fax: 704-933-0666
Wholesaler/distributor of candy, groceries, sugar and specialty foods; serving the food service market
President: Richard Sinclair

Estimated Sales: $10-20 Million
Number Employees: 10-19
Number of Customer Locations: 400
Types of Products Distributed:
  Food Service, Frozen Food, General Line, Specialty Foods, Candy & sugar

58118 Modulightor Inc
246 E 58th St
New York, NY 10022-2011 212-371-0336
Fax: 212-371-0335 www.modulightor.com
Manufacturer, importer and wholesaler/distributor of lighting fixtures
Owner: Ernst Wagner
ernst@modulightor.com
Estimated Sales: $1-2.5 Million
Number Employees: 10-19
Square Footage: 26000
Types of Products Distributed:
  Frozen Food, General Line, Lighting fixtures

58119 Moffett Food Svc
145 W Lakeview Ave
Flint, MI 48503-4199 810-238-7898
Fax: 810-238-7896
Wholesaler/distributor of groceries; serving the food service market
Owner: Jeff Moffett
Estimated Sales: $10-20 Million
Number Employees: 5-9
Number of Customer Locations: 350
Types of Products Distributed:
  Food Service, Frozen Food, General Line, Groceries

58120 Mohn's Fisheries
1144 Great River Rd
Harpers Ferry, IA 52146-7565 563-586-2269
Fax: 563-423-1579
Seafood
Owner: Diane Mohn
Estimated Sales: $300,000-500,000
Number Employees: 1-4

58121 Molinera International
PO Box 557732
Miami, FL 33255-7732 305-883-6060
Fax: 305-887-4997
Wholesaler/distributor of canned fruits, sweet red pimientos, artichokes, asparagus, virgin and pure oil, rice, beans, etc.; importer of olive oil, sweet red pimientos, etc.; exporter of rice, beans and corn and vegetable oils; servingthe food service market
CEO: Fernando Siman
VP: Juan-Carlos Ley
Estimated Sales: $20-50 Million
Number Employees: 20-49
Square Footage: 27000
Types of Products Distributed:
  Food Service, Frozen Food, General Line, Produce, Specialty Foods, Canned fruits, olive oil, beans, etc.

58122 Mom N' Pops Inc
834 Brooks St
New Windsor, NY 12553 845-567-0640
Fax: 845-567-0652
Wholesale manufacturers of candy and lollipops.
President: Barbara Regenbaum
Sales Director: Stacy Zagon
Estimated Sales: $2.5-5 Million
Number Employees: 10-19
Number of Brands: 1
Type of Packaging: Bulk
Private Brands Carried:
  Mom 'N Pops
Types of Products Distributed:
  Specialty Foods

58123 Monarch Seafoods Inc
515 Kalihi St
Honolulu, HI 96819-3268 808-841-7877
Fax: 808-847-3930 www.monarchseafoods.com
Seafood and seafood products
President: Thomas Mukaigawa
Estimated Sales: $.5-1 million
Number Employees: 10-19

58124 Monarch-McLaren
329 Deerhide Crescent
Weston, ON M9M 2Z2
Canada 416-741-9675
Fax: 416-741-2873

1101

Manufacturer, importer and wholesaler/distributor of conveyor and transmission belting, V-belts, timing belts, variable speed belts, hoses, pulleys, chains, sprockets, bearings, speed reducers, casters, motors, couplings, belt lacingleather packings, etc
President: Terence Whitfield
Sales Manager: Brian Flint
Estimated Sales: Below $5 Million
Number Employees: 10
Square Footage: 72400
Types of Products Distributed:
Frozen Food, General Merchandise

58125 Montana Broom & Brush Co
1245 Harrison Ave
Butte, MT 59701-4866   406-723-6860
    Fax: 406-723-6860   800-422-5650
ryanhitchcock@live.com www.mtbroom.com
Wholesaler/distributor of chemicals, janitorial supplies and machines and paper products including plates, napkins, etc
President: Mike Hitchcock
mikeh@mtbroom.com
Sales Manager: Greg Hareland
Estimated Sales: $5-10 Million
Number Employees: 10-19
Square Footage: 80000
Other Locations:
    Montana Broom & Brush Co.
    Helena, MT
    Montana Brush & Broom
    Billings, MT
    Montana Brush & Broom
    Great Falls, MTMontana Broom & Brush Co.Billings
Number of Customer Locations: 600
Types of Products Distributed:
    Frozen Food, General Merchandise, Chemicals, janitorial supplies, etc.

58126 Montana Food Products
PO Box 1000
Florence, MT 59833   406-273-2515
    Fax: 406-248-8575   877-763-2383
Wholesaler/distributor of provisions/meats; serving the food service market
Owner: Steve Buechler
Sales Manager: Steve Buechler
Estimated Sales: $5-10 Million
Number Employees: 5-9
Other Locations:
    Montana Food Products Processing
    Lolo, MT
    Montana Meat Processing Plant
    Laurel, MTMontana Food Products ProcessingLaurel
Number of Customer Locations: 120
Types of Products Distributed:
    Food Service, Frozen Food, Provisions/Meat

58127 Montana Mex
PO Box 11255
Bozeman, MT 59719
    hello@montanamex.com
    www.montanamex.com
BBQ sauces, seasonings and oils
Chef & Co-Founder: Eduardo Garcia
Type of Packaging: Consumer

58128 Montello Inc
6106 E 32nd Pl # 100
Tulsa, OK 74135-5495   918-665-1170
    Fax: 918-665-1480   800-331-4628
    www.montelloinc.com
Importer and distributor of emulsifiers and gums
President: Allen Johnson
allenj@montelloinc.com
VP: Leo Wooldridge
Estimated Sales: $6 Million
Number Employees: 5-9
Types of Products Distributed:
    Frozen Food

58129 Monterrey Provision Co
7850 Waterville Rd
San Diego, CA 92154
    www.monprov.com
Wholesaler/distributor of frozen foods, produce, groceries, dairy products, meats and seafood; serving the retail and food service market.
Year Founded: 1972
Estimated Sales: $14 Million
Number Employees: 50-99
Square Footage: 25000

Private Brands Carried:
    Atalanta; Bay Valley Foods; Capra; Castle Importing; Chuckanut Bay Cheese Cake; Daily's; Deep Blue; English Bay Batter; Flagship Food Group; Flex4Life; FoodMatch Inc.; Foster Farms; Happy Tree; Goosner Foods; Heinz; Pacific Cheese; Oasis Naturals
Number of Customer Locations: 1700
Types of Products Distributed:
    Food Service, Frozen Food, General Line, Provisions/Meat, Produce, Seafood, Groceries & dairy products

58130 Monteverdes
Three Gateway Center
Suite 2300
Pittsburgh, PA 15222-1000   412-391-0419
    Fax: 412-391-0338
    dmartin@monteverdegroup.com
    www.monteverdegroup.com
Wholesaler/distributor of produce
President and Chief Executive Officer: James W. Monteverde
Vice President-Financial Planning: Ryan P. Duchak
SVP, Retirement Plan Services: Wendy W. Astorino
Manager, Business Operations: Terry L. Wargo
Estimated Sales: $3-5 Million
Number Employees: 10-19
Square Footage: 120000
Types of Products Distributed:
    Frozen Food, Produce

58131 Moon's Seafood Company
661 Fern Drive
Merritt Island, FL 32952-3725   321-259-5958
    Fax: 321-610-7143 www.moonseafood.com
Wholesaler/distributor of fresh and frozen seafood including rock shrimp and calico scallops, crabmeat and clams
President: Jay Moon
Sales/Marketing Executive: Rick Madrigul
Estimated Sales: $1-2.5 Million
Number Employees: 1-4
Square Footage: 9600
Types of Products Distributed:
    Frozen Food, Seafood, Rock shrimp & calico scallops

58132 Mooney General Paper Co
1451 Chestnut Ave
Hillside, NJ 07205-1195   973-926-3629
    Fax: 973-926-0425   800-826-7273
    www.mooneygeneral.com
Wholesaler/distributor of janitorial supplies and paper and plastic items including cups, plates, napkins and receptacles; also, baked goods
President: Gary J Riemer
griemer@mooneygeneral.com
VP: Richard Ribakove
Sales Manager: Paul Segal
Plant Manager: Christine Arroyo
Purchasing Manager: Fran Winkler
Estimated Sales: $25 Million
Number Employees: 50-99
Square Footage: 64000
Type of Packaging: Consumer, Food Service
Types of Products Distributed:
    Food Service, Janitorial & disposable supplies

58133 Moonlite Bar-B-Q Inn
2840 W Parrish Ave
Owensboro, KY 42301-2689   270-684-8143
    Fax: 270-684-8105   800-322-8989
    pbosley@moonlite.com www.moonlite.com
Barbecue meats including mutton, pork and beef; also, bean soup, sauces and chili
President: Fred Bosley
fbosley@moonlite.com
VP: Ken Bosley
Marketing Director: Pat Bosley
Estimated Sales: $3 Million
Number Employees: 100-249
Number of Brands: 1
Number of Products: 48
Type of Packaging: Private Label
Private Brands Carried:
    Moonlite
Number of Customer Locations: 1
Types of Products Distributed:
    Food Service, Frozen Food, Barbeque

58134 Moore Equipment
1634 E Main St
Dothan, AL 36301-3014   334-794-4133
    Fax: 334-794-5092   800-741-4134
    sales@moore-warren.com
Wholesaler/distributor of ice machines, refrigerators, etc.; serving the food service market
Owner: Ricky Bond
ricky@moore-warren.com
Estimated Sales: $1-2.5 Million
Number Employees: 10-19
Types of Products Distributed:
    Food Service, Frozen Food, General Merchandise, Ice machines, refrigerators, etc.

58135 Morabito Baking Co Inc
757 Kohn St
Norristown, PA 19401-3739   610-275-5419
    Fax: 610-275-0358   800-525-7747
    www.morabitobaking.com
Sourdough breads and Spoletti rolls
President: Aaron Chanthakoune
aaron@morabito.com
Marketing Manager: Joanna Morabito
Director of Sales: Marc Knox
Director of Human Resources: Cassandra Morabito
Estimated Sales: $10 Million
Number Employees: 100-249
Square Footage: 140000
Type of Packaging: Consumer, Food Service, Private Label, Bulk
Types of Products Distributed:
    Food Service, Frozen Food, General Line, Fresh & frozen bakery products

58136 Moran Foods LLC
100 Corporate Office Dr
Earth City, MO 63045-1511   314-592-9100
    Fax: 314-592-9619 www.save-a-lot.com
Wholesaler/distributor of groceries
President/CEO: Ritchie Casteel
CEO: Eric A Claus
eric.claus@save-a-lot.com
Number Employees: 5000-9999
Parent Co: SUPERVALU
Types of Products Distributed:
    Frozen Food, General Line, Groceries

58137 Moran USA, LLC
25 Jesswig Dr
Hamden, CT 06517-2134   203-288-1757
    Fax: 203-230-8669   800-486-6726
    info@moranusa.com moranusa.com
Retail packaging for wine, beer and spirits. Boxer; wood and corrugated board. Bags; laminated four color, plastic, paper and shrink
President: Jim Moran
Estimated Sales: $3 Million
Number Employees: 1-4
Number of Products: 1200
Square Footage: 8000
Private Brands Carried:
    Moran USA
Types of Products Distributed:
    Support Prolnets for Wine, Beer, Spirit

58138 More For Less Foods
9 Herald Avenue
Corner Brook, NL A2H 4B8
Canada   709-634-1452
    Fax: 709-634-8608   800-565-9066
    mor4less@nfld.net
Wholesaler/distributor of bulk foods including natural and specialty
President: June Alteen
VP/Secretary: Fred Alteen
Number Employees: 5-9
Square Footage: 18000
Number of Customer Locations: 2
Types of Products Distributed:
    Frozen Food, Health Food, Specialty Foods

58139 Morehead Company
187 Elk Mountain Road
Asheville, NC 28804-2045   828-252-3885
Wholesaler/distributor of candy
Warehouse Manager: Jerry Summey
Number Employees: 20-49
Types of Products Distributed:
    Frozen Food, General Line, Candy

Wholesalers & Distributors / A-Z

58140 Morgan Meat Co
1011 Irwin Rd
Barstow, CA 92311-1899   760-256-2221
                Fax: 760-256-3040
Wholesaler/distributor of frozen lamb, beef and pork
General Manager: Judy Zimmerman
Sales Manager: Mark Zimmerman
Estimated Sales: $2.5-5 Million
Number Employees: 10-19
Types of Products Distributed:
   Provisions/Meat, Lamb, beef & pork

58141 Morre-Tec Ind Inc
1 Gary Rd
Union, NJ 07083-5527   908-686-0307
     Fax: 908-688-9005   sales@morretec.com
                www.morretec.com
Manufacturer, importer and exporter of magnesium chloride, food grade and potassium bromate; importer and wholesaler/distributor of low sodium substitutes and licorice, spray, dried and powder
Owner: Rachel Abenilla
rachela@morretec.com
Marketing Director: Michael Fuchs
Operations Manager: Norm Cantoe
Estimated Sales: $10-20 Million
Number Employees: 20-49
Number of Products: 150
Square Footage: 50000
Type of Packaging: Consumer, Bulk
Types of Products Distributed:
   Frozen Food, General Line, Low sodium substitutes, licorice, etc.

58142 Morreale John R Inc
216 N Peoria St
Chicago, IL 60607-1706   312-421-3664
     Fax: 312-421-8928   morrealemeat@aol.com
                www.jrmorreale.com
Distributor of beef and pork products. Provides custom trimmed beef cuts and fresh beef trimmings.
President: Mike Magrini
President: Steve Hurckes
President: Jerry Schomer
Sales: Bob Apato
General Manager: Steve Hurckes
tfrigo@jrmorreale.com
Production Manager: Ramiro Corral
Estimated Sales: $25,000,000
Number Employees: 50-99
Number of Products: 1
Square Footage: 100000
Type of Packaging: Bulk
Types of Products Distributed:
   Provisions/Meat, Beef, pork

58143 Morris A. Elkis & Sons
28 Harrison Street
Woodbury, NJ 08096-5904   856-845-1957
     Fax: 856-384-8972   800-443-5547
Wholesaler/distributor of frozen foods and produce; serving the food service market
President: Dennis Toub
Number Employees: 20-49
Square Footage: 40000
Number of Customer Locations: 300
Types of Products Distributed:
   Food Service, Frozen Food, Produce

58144 Morris Okun
209 Hunts Point Term Mkt
Bronx, NY 10474-7402   718-589-7700
                Fax: 718-328-6148
Importer, exporter and wholesaler/distributor of produce and nuts
President: Tom Cignarella
Chief Executive Officer & Owner: Ronnie Okun
Estimated Sales: $35.3 Million
Number Employees: 150
Square Footage: 30000
Types of Products Distributed:
   Frozen Food, General Line, Produce

58145 Morrison Industrial Equip Co
1825 Monroe Ave NW
Grand Rapids, MI 49505-6291   616-447-3800
     Fax: 616-361-0885   www.morrison-ind.com
Wholesaler/distributor of material handling equipment
CEO: Roger Troost
troost@morrision-ind.com
CEO: Richard Morrison
Estimated Sales: $20-50 Million
Number Employees: 50-99
Private Brands Carried:
   Hyster; Baker; Mitsubishi
Types of Products Distributed:
   Frozen Food, General Merchandise, Material handling equipment

58146 Morrisons Pastry Corp
4901 Maspeth Ave
Flushing, NY 11378-2219   718-326-2200
     Fax: 718-326-0330   sales@morrisonspastry.com
                www.morrisonspastry.com
Wholesaler/distributor of specialty food products including cakes, danish, doughnuts, pies, muffins, cheesecakes, loaves and croissants
President: Wayne Wattenberg
wayne@morrisonpastry.com
Estimated Sales: $1-3 Million
Number Employees: 20-49
Types of Products Distributed:
   Frozen Food, General Line, Specialty Foods, Cakes, danish, doughnuts, pies, etc.

58147 Mortec Industries Inc
29240 County Road R
P.O. Box 977
Brush, CO 80723-9444   970-842-5063
     Fax: 970-842-5061   800-541-9983
joe@mortecscales.com   www.mortecscales.com
Manufacturer and exporter of electronic weighing scales; wholesaler/distributor of computer hardware and software; serving the food service market
Owner: Joe Kral
mortecscales@gmail.com
Estimated Sales: $1-2.5 Million
Number Employees: 1-4
Type of Packaging: Consumer, Food Service
Types of Products Distributed:
   Food Service, Frozen Food, General Merchandise, Computer software & systems

58148 Mortillaro Lobster Company
65 Commercial St
Gloucester, MA 01930-5047   978-282-4621
                Fax: 978-281-0579
Lobster
President: Vincent Mortillaro
Estimated Sales: $5-10 Million
Number Employees: 20-49

58149 Mosby Winery
9496 Santa Rosa Rd
Buellton, CA 93427-9482
                800-706-6729
     info@mosbywines.com   mosbywines.com
Wines, oils and balsamics.
Estimated Sales: $2.5-5 Million
Number Employees: 4
Type of Packaging: Private Label

58150 Moseley & Reece
P.O.Box 1208
Mount Airy, NC 27030   336-786-8366
                Fax: 336-786-6734
Wholesaler/distributor of groceries, meats, dairy products, frozen food, equipment and fixtures, general merchandise and candy
President: John Moseley
VP: Janet Moseley
Sales Manager: Rick Darnell
Estimated Sales: $10-20 Million
Number Employees: 50-99
Square Footage: 136000
Number of Customer Locations: 850
Types of Products Distributed:
   Frozen Food, General Line, General Merchandise, Provisions/Meat

58151 Mosuki
PO Box 671
N Bellmore, NY 11710-0671   631-785-1262
     Fax: 718-345-2958   members.aol.com/mosukiltd
Importer, exporter and wholesaler/distributor of dispensing and food processing equipment for ice cream, yogurt, slushies, frozen cocktails, espresso/cappuccino and granita; also, fresh pasta machinery and wood burning brick pizzaovens
President: Salvatore Favarolo
VP: Anthony Favarolo
Number Employees: 20-49
Square Footage: 160000
Private Brands Carried:
   La Victoria Arduino; Stoelting; Ambrogi
Types of Products Distributed:
   Food Service, Frozen Food, General Merchandise, Pasta machinery, pizza ovens, etc.

58152 Mother Earth Enterprises
15 Irving Place
New York, NY 10003-2316   212-777-1250
     Fax: 212-614-8132   866-436-7688
                denis@hempnut.com
Wholesaler/distributor of hempnuts; hemp oil, meal and flour; and toasted, sterilized and roasted grain hemp (seed). Highly adaptable for baking and cooking needs
President: Denis Cicero
Type of Packaging: Food Service
Types of Products Distributed:
   Frozen Food, General Line, Health Food, Specialty Foods, Hemp oil, meal & flour

58153 Mother's Cake & Cookie Company
12937 NE David Cir
Portland, OR 97230   503-253-1655
Wholesaler/distributor of baked goods including cookies
President/CEO: George Shivari
CFO: Nicola Melillo
Marketing Director: William Klump
Sales Director: Mark O'Toole
Public Relations: Kathy Coggeshall
Operations Manager: Peter Lowes
Estimated Sales: $5-10 Million
Number Employees: 10-19
Parent Co: Parmalat Bakery Group North America
Private Brands Carried:
   Bakery Wagon; Mother's
Number of Customer Locations: 300
Types of Products Distributed:
   General Line, Cookies, etc.

58154 Motion Savers Inc
8573 S Mason Montgomery # 40
Suite #40
Mason, OH 45040-9813   513-742-1000
     Fax: 513-742-6083   877-832-4154
info@motionsavers.com   www.motionsavers.com
Wholesaler/distributor of conveyors, containers, racks, shelving and electric vehicles
Owner: Todd Smith
Estimated Sales: $10-20 Million
Number Employees: 5-9
Private Brands Carried:
   Taylor-Dunn; Blue Giant; United Trailer
Types of Products Distributed:
   Frozen Food, General Merchandise, Material handling equipment

58155 Motivatit Seafoods Inc
412 Palm Ave
Houma, LA 70364-3400   985-868-7191
     Fax: 985-868-7472   www.motivatit.com
Established in 1971. Supplier of fresh oysters and clams.
Owner: Steve Voisin
CEO/VP: Mike Voisin
CFO: Dotty Voisin
Marketing/Purchasing: Kevin Voisin
Sales: Greg Voisin
steven.voisin@motivatit.com
Operations: Wayne DeHart
Estimated Sales: $20-50 Million
Number Employees: 100-249
Square Footage: 100000
Type of Packaging: Consumer, Food Service, Private Label, Bulk
Private Brands Carried:
   Wine Island Oysters
Types of Products Distributed:
   Food Service, Frozen Food, Seafood, Blue crabs, oysters & crawfish

58156 Mountain Dairies-SW IceCream
17 Rock Hill Dr
Rock Hill, NY 12775   845-794-8100
                Fax: 845-791-4397
Wholesaler/distributor of ice cream products, dairy items and produce; serving the food service market
President: Andrew Wahl
Estimated Sales: $20-50 Million
Number Employees: 20-49
Parent Co: Kane-Miller Corporation
Types of Products Distributed:
   Food Service, Frozen Food, General Line, Produce, Dairy & ice cream products

Wholesalers & Distributors / A-Z

58157 Mountain People's Warehouse
4005 6th Avenue S
Seattle, WA 98108-5202   206-767-4269
Fax: 800-210-0104   800-336-8872
Wholesaler/distributor of natural and specialty foods
Estimated Sales: $5-10 Million
Number Employees: 5-9
Square Footage: 400000
Types of Products Distributed:
  Frozen Food, General Line, Health Food, Specialty Foods

58158 Mountain Pride
421 Bell Dr
PO Box 6077
Ketchum, ID 83340   208-725-5600
Fax: 208-725-5601
President: Stuart Siderman
Estimated Sales: $.5-1 million
Number Employees: 1-4

58159 Mountain Sales & Svc Inc
6759 E 50th Ave
Commerce City, CO 80022-4618   303-289-5558
Fax: 303-286-7054   800-847-2557
www.mtnsales.com
Wholesaler/distributor and manufacturers' representative for water filter systems, beer systems and parts, cooking equipment, microwave ovens, soft serve equipment, refrigerators and freezers including walk-in and ice making equipment
General Manager: Rick Muckler
rmuckler@mtnsales.com
Estimated Sales: $10-20 Million
Number Employees: 20-49
Square Footage: 24000
Private Brands Carried:
  Scotsman Ice Systems; Amana; Silver King; True Refrigeration; DCS Cooking Equipment
Types of Products Distributed:
  Frozen Food, General Merchandise, Water filters, beer systems, etc.

58160 Mountain Service Distribution
40 Lake St
S Fallsburg, NY 12779   845-434-5674
Fax: 845-434-0059 saltman@mtnservice.com
www.mtnservice.com
Wholesaler/distributor of frozen foods, general line products, specialty foods and provisions/meats; serving the food service market.
President: Steve Altman
VP, Finance & Human Resources: Michele Elliott
michele@elliotts.com
VP, Purchasing & Marketing: Josh Altman
Sales Manager: Bob Tatz
VP, Operations: Mark Gandulla
Estimated Sales: $27 Million
Number Employees: 50-99
Number of Brands: 4500
Square Footage: 70000
Parent Co: Mountain Candy & Cigar Company
Private Brands Carried:
  Slush Puppie; Best Buy; Jacks; Mountain Run Water
Number of Customer Locations: 2500
Types of Products Distributed:
  Food Service, Frozen Food, General Line, General Merchandise, Health Food, Provisions/Meat, Produce, Tobacco

58161 (HQ)Mountain States Rosen
355 Food Center Dr # C16
C-16
Bronx, NY 10474-7053   718-842-4447
Fax: 718-617-4096   800-872-5262
info@rosenlamb.com
www.mountainstatesrosen.com
Lamb and veal
CEO: Dennis Stiffler
EVP: David Gage
Number Employees: 100-249
Type of Packaging: Food Service
Other Locations:
  Mountain States Rosen, LLC
  Greeley, COMountain States Rosen, LLC
Types of Products Distributed:
  Food Service, Frozen Food, Provisions/Meat, Lamb & veal

58162 Mountain Valley Water
12707 Rives Ave # B
Downey, CA 90242-4161   562-940-4466
Fax: 562-803-5439
www.mountainvalleywaterla.com
Wholesaler/distributor of bottled water
President: Mark Scott
msmountvalley@aol.com
Secretary: Robert Scott
Estimated Sales: $500,000-$1 Million
Number Employees: 5-9
Square Footage: 26000
Private Brands Carried:
  Mountain Valley Spring Water; California Sparkling Water
Types of Products Distributed:
  Frozen Food, Bottled water

58163 Mountain Valley Water Company
PO Box 660070
Miami Springs, FL 33266   305-883-2200
Fax: 305-885-7800
www.mountainvalleyspring.com
Exporter and wholesaler/distributor of bottled spring water
Owner: Lee Holtzman
Number Employees: 5-9
Type of Packaging: Bulk
Private Brands Carried:
  Evian; Mountain Valley; Diamond
Types of Products Distributed:
  Frozen Food, General Line, Health Food, Bottled spring water

58164 Mountain View Supply
2102 2nd Ave N
Billings, MT 59101   406-259-4493
Fax: 406-259-7511   800-736-5295
www.bargreen.com
Wholesaler/distributor of food service equipment and smallwares for restaurants, bars, hospitals, schools, etc
Manager: Joe Zeleniak
Owner: Larry Liptac
Estimated Sales: $5-10 Million
Number Employees: 10-19
Square Footage: 76000
Types of Products Distributed:
  Food Service, Frozen Food, General Merchandise, Equipment & smallwares

58165 Mountain West Distributors Inc
2889 S 900 W
South Salt Lake, UT 84119-2419   801-487-5694
Fax: 801-467-3006 www.mwd1.com
Wholesaler/distributor of general merchandise
Owner: Craig Breinholt
VP: Craig Breinholt
Sales Manager: Garrett Breinholt
cbreinholt@mountainwestdistributors.com
Estimated Sales: $10-20 Million
Number Employees: 20-49
Types of Products Distributed:
  Frozen Food, General Merchandise

58166 Mountanos Family Coffee & Tea Co.
1331 Commerce St.
Petaluma, CA 94549   707-462-6333
800-624-7031
info@mfct.com www.mfct.com
Coffee, tea, and accessories
Director of Operations: Erik Bianchi
Number Employees: 50-99
Types of Products Distributed:
  General Merchandise

58167 Moyer-Mitchell Company
1014 Rural Ave
Voorhees, NJ 8043   856-429-2696
Fax: 856-429-2878   800-936-6937
moyermitchell.com/
Wholesaler/distributor of fresh and frozen chicken and turkey
President: Richard Mitchell III
Estimated Sales: $10-20 Million
Number Employees: 20-49
Square Footage: 54000
Number of Customer Locations: 150
Types of Products Distributed:
  Food Service, Frozen Food, Provisions/Meat, Chicken & turkey

58168 Mr. C's
7021 South 220th St
Kent, WA 98032   253-867-6130
888-929-2378
info@calsonindustries.com
www.calsonindustries.com/mrC
Cocktail mixes
President: Sadru Kabani
Parent Co: Calson Industries
Types of Products Distributed:
  General Line

58169 Mt Pleasant Seafood
1 Seafood Dr
Mt Pleasant, SC 29464-4387   843-884-4122
www.mountpleasantoysterroast.com
Wholesaler/distributor of frozen food and seafood; serving the food service market
Owner: Rial Fitch
Estimated Sales: $500,000-$1 Million
Number Employees: 5-9
Types of Products Distributed:
  Food Service, Frozen Food, Seafood

58170 Mt. Hope Wholesale
853 S Main St
Cottonwood, AZ 86326   928-634-2498
Fax: 928-639-2321
Wholesaler/distributor of specialty nuts and beans, nut mixes, dried fruits and mushrooms, spices, extracts, chiles, rice, grains, seeds and flour
Owner: Herb Trubitz
Marketing: Sara Trubitz
Marketing: Marisa O'Connor
Contact: Michael Millett
mmillett@mounthopewholesale.com
Operations: Patti Marrs
Estimated Sales: $20-50 Million
Number Employees: 20-49
Square Footage: 1200
Type of Packaging: Private Label, Bulk
Number of Customer Locations: 332
Types of Products Distributed:
  Nuts, dried fruits & mushrooms, etc.

58171 Muckenthaler Inc
308 Commercial St
Emporia, KS 66801-4011   620-342-5653
Fax: 620-342-6227   800-279-6825
www.muckenthaler.com
Wholesaler/distributor of equipment; serving the food service market
Owner: Jim Muckenthaler
jimm@muckenthaler.com
Estimated Sales: $500,000-$1 Million
Number Employees: 10-19
Parent Co: Muckenthaler
Private Brands Carried:
  Vulcan Hart; South Bend; Frymaster
Types of Products Distributed:
  Food Service, Frozen Food, General Merchandise, Equipment

58172 Muckenthaler Inc
308 Commercial St
Emporia, KS 66801-4011   620-342-5653
Fax: 620-342-6227   800-279-6825
www.muckenthaler.com
Wholesaler/distributor of food service equipment and supplies; serving the food service market
President/CEO: Jim Muckenthaler
jimm@muckenthaler.com
Vice President: John Muckenthaler
Estimated Sales: $2.5-5 Million
Number Employees: 10-19
Other Locations:
  Munckenthaler
  Topeka, KSMunckenthaler
Types of Products Distributed:
  Equipment & supplies

58173 Mueller Distributing Company
PO Box 6400
Springfield, IL 62708-6400   217-525-1269
Fax: 217-585-9776
Wholesaler/distributor of alcoholic beverages; serving the food service market
President: Daniel Clausner
Estimated Sales: $300,000-500,000
Number Employees: 1-4
Square Footage: 192000
Types of Products Distributed:
  Food Service, General Line, Alcoholic beverages

Wholesalers & Distributors / A-Z

58174 Muir Copper Canyon Farms
951 S 3600 W
Salt Lake City, UT 84104-4587 801-908-6091
  Fax: 801-908-6176 800-564-0949
ldehaan@coppercanyonfarms.com
  www.coppercanyonfarms.com
Packer and exporter of potatoes, onions and frozen ready-to-process cherries; wholesaler/distributor of fresh fruits and vegetables; serving the food service market in the Salt Lake City metropolitan area
President/CEO: Phil Muir
VP/Chief Financial Officer: Chuck Madsen
Controller: Adam Jensen
Sales: John Marsh
Manager: Andy Salmon
asalmon@cooperycanyonfarms.com
Operations Manager: Andy Salmon
Estimated Sales: $16.6 Million
Number Employees: 50-99
Square Footage: 400000
Type of Packaging: Food Service, Private Label, Bulk
Types of Products Distributed:
  Food Service, Produce, Specialty Foods

58175 Muller-Pinehurst Dairy Company
2025 W 1st Street
Dixon, IL 61021-2419 815-284-6971
Wholesaler/distributor of dairy products; serving the food service market
Manager: Rick Powell
Estimated Sales: $1-2.5 Million
Number Employees: 5-9
Parent Co: Muller Pinehurst Dairy
Types of Products Distributed:
  Food Service, Frozen Food, General Line, Dairy products

58176 Multi Marques
4650 Rue Notre-Dame O
Montreal, QC H4C 1S6
Canada 514-934-1866
  Fax: 514-934-1866 www.multimarques.com
Manufacturer and distributor of bread, rolls, fruit cake and sponge cake
Regional Plant Director: Francine Henderson
Number Employees: 2
Square Footage: 14984
Parent Co: Canada Bread
Type of Packaging: Consumer, Food Service
Types of Products Distributed:
  Frozen Food

58177 Multi-Counter Manufacturing Company
100 Park Putn
Guilford, CT 06437 203-457-0557
  Fax: 203-457-0329 800-345-5689
Wholesaler/distributor of portions served counters and coin sorters; serving the food service market
President: John Morgan
Secretary/Treasurer: D Van Deusen
Number Employees: 10-19
Square Footage: 20000
Types of Products Distributed:
  Food Service, Frozen Food, General Merchandise, Counters & coin sorters

58178 Multigrains Bread Co
117 Water St
Lawrence, MA 01841-4720 978-691-6100
  Fax: 978-373-4801 www.multigrainsbakeries.com
Multigrain breads
President: Joseph Faro
joseph@multigrainsbakeries.com
EVP/Director R&D: Chuck Brandano
Director of Quality: Adam Gabour
Director of Purchasing: Darren Gaiero
Number Employees: 100-249

58179 Multiple Organics
200 Linus Pauling Dr
Hercules, CA 94547-1823 415-482-9800
  Fax: 415-482-9801 www.multipleorganics.com
Organic ingredients wholesaler
Marketing Director: Maria Burrow
Type of Packaging: Bulk

58180 Multivac Inc
11021 N Pomona Ave
Kansas City, MO 64153-1146 816-891-0555
  Fax: 816-891-0622 800-800-8552
  muinc@multivac.com
Wholesaler/distributor, importer and exporter of thermoform, fill and seal packaging equipment; also, tray sealers, chamber vacuum packaging and labeling equipment; sales support services available
President: Michel Defenbau
CEO: Werner Britz
werner.britz@multivacsa.com
CEO: Jan Erik Kuhlmann
CFO: Danny Liker
Sales Director: Norm Winkel
Estimated Sales: $50-60Million
Number Employees: 100-249
Square Footage: 60000
Parent Co: Multivac Export AG
Private Brands Carried:
  MR; Multivac
Types of Products Distributed:
  General Merchandise, Packaging equipment

58181 Munchies
1714 Colburn Street
Honolulu, HI 96819-3243 808-841-6641
  Fax: 808-848-8861
Wholesaler/distributor of baked goods, general merchandise, private label items, seafood, dried fruits, nuts, beef jerky, pork jerky, flavored and sweet popcorn, jams, jellies, tea, coffee, chocolates, gummy candies, chips and Hawaiiansnacks
President: Tracy Yokouchi Ng
VP: June Otake
Estimated Sales: $1-3 Million
Number Employees: 10-19
Number of Products: 400
Square Footage: 14000
Parent Co: Ari Group Hawaii USA
Private Brands Carried:
  Munchies
Types of Products Distributed:
  Food Service, Frozen Food, General Line, General Merchandise, Health Food, Rack Jobbers, Seafood, Specialty Foods, Snacks, candy, etc.

58182 Mung Dynasty
2200 Mary St
Pittsburgh, PA 15203-2160 412-381-1350
Asian foods, specialty products
Owner: Chris Wahlberg
Estimated Sales: $1-2.5 Million
Number Employees: 1-4
Square Footage: 20000
Types of Products Distributed:
  Frozen Food, Specialty Foods, Oriental foods

58183 Munroe Material Handling
5211 Northrup Ave
St Louis, MO 63110-2033 314-968-2500
  Fax: 314-968-8831 800-875-8831
  www.munroemh.com
Wholesaler/distributor of conveyors and shelving; also, parts and service available
President: Robert Munroe
bmunroe@munroemh.com
Operations Manager: Barry Gleeson
Estimated Sales: $5-10 Million
Number Employees: 1-4
Private Brands Carried:
  Hytrol; Southwerth; Best
Types of Products Distributed:
  Frozen Food, General Merchandise, Conveyors & shelving

58184 Munsee Meats
1701 W Kilgore Ave
Muncie, IN 47304-4997 765-288-3645
  Fax: 765-282-8076 www.munseemeats.com
Wholesaler/distributor of provisions/meats
President: Steve Henderixson
Estimated Sales: $20-50 Million
Number Employees: 20-49
Types of Products Distributed:
  Frozen Food, Provisions/Meat

58185 Murk Brush Company
P.O.Box 726
New Britain, CT 06050-0726 860-249-2550
  Fax: 860-249-2550
Brushes for the food and beverage industry, FDA approved brush construction; specialist in OEM Brush Design
Sales: Dave Hames
Estimated Sales: 500000
Number Employees: 1-4
Number of Products: 2600
Square Footage: 28000
Type of Packaging: Bulk
Types of Products Distributed:
  General Merchandise, Brushes: bottle, channel, tube, etc.

58186 Murphy/Northstar
1502 S Raccoon Rd # 3
Youngstown, OH 44515-4532 330-793-3400
  Fax: 724-748-4613
Wholesaler/distributor of bakery ingredients
Manager: Steve Murphy
Estimated Sales: $.5-1 million
Number Employees: 10-19
Parent Co: Federal Bakers
Private Brands Carried:
  Dawn; Hormel; Pillsbury
Types of Products Distributed:
  Frozen Food, General Line, Bakery ingredients

58187 Murry's Family of Fine Foods
7852 Walker Dr
Suite 420
Greenbelt, MD 20770
  888-668-7797
customerservice@murrys.com www.murrys.com
Wholesaler/distributor of groceries, meats, dairy products, equipment and fixtures, private label items and frozen and specialty foods.
Square Footage: 162000
Private Brands Carried:
  Murry's Steaks
Number of Customer Locations: 100
Types of Products Distributed:
  Frozen Food, General Line, General Merchandise, Provisions/Meat, Specialty Foods, Groceries, dairy products, etc.

58188 Musco Food Corp
5701 49th St
Flushing, NY 11378-2020 718-628-9710
  Fax: 718-326-1109 www.muscofood.com
Importer and wholesaler/distributor of general line products and specialty foods including cheese, olive oil and canned foods
Owner: Philip Musco
Estimated Sales: $20-50 Million
Number Employees: 20-49
Private Brands Carried:
  Vantia; Merro
Number of Customer Locations: 1000
Types of Products Distributed:
  Frozen Food, General Line, Specialty Foods

58189 Mush & Pinsky
322 Winston Avenue
Dayton, OH 45403-1438 937-252-9961
  Fax: 937-254-6874
Wholesaler/distributor of produce, frozen foods, restaurant supplies and goods; serving the food service market
President: Gary Pavlofsky
VP: Ervin Pavlofsky
Parent Co: Mush & Sons
Types of Products Distributed:
  Food Service, Frozen Food, General Merchandise, Produce, Restaurant supplies & goods

58190 Muskingum Valley Grocery Co
Front St
Malta, OH 43758 740-962-3015
  Fax: 740-962-2795
Wholesaler/distributor of groceries and dairy products; serving the food service market
President: U Allen
Estimated Sales: $10-20 Million
Number Employees: 10-19
Number of Customer Locations: 200
Types of Products Distributed:
  Food Service, Frozen Food, General Line, Groceries & dairy products

58191 Mutual Biscuit
100 Central Avenue
Kearny, NJ 07032-4640 973-466-1020
  Fax: 973-466-1115
Wholesaler/distributor and importer of cookies
General Manager: Eddie Nassour
Types of Products Distributed:
  Frozen Food, General Line, Cookies

58192 Mutual Distributors
2233 Capital Blvd
Raleigh, NC 27604 919-828-3842
  Fax: 919-832-2813 www.mutualdistributing.com

Wholesalers & Distributors / A-Z

Wholesaler/distributor of wine.
Chief Financial Officer: James Burkhardt
Sales Representative: Brett Andersen
Distribution Manager: Michael Enyinnaya
Year Founded: 1946
Estimated Sales: $100-500 Million
Number Employees: 250-499
Other Locations:
   Mutual Distributors
   Pompano Beach, FL Mutual Distributors
Types of Products Distributed:
   Wine

58193 Mutual Fish Co
2335 Rainier Ave S
Seattle, WA 98144   206-322-4368
         Fax: 206-328-5889 www.mutualfish.com
Fresh seafood including salmon, halibut, catfish, cod, sea bass, and oysters
Estimated Sales: $1.5 Million
Number Employees: 20-49
Square Footage: 60000
Types of Products Distributed:
   Seafood

58194 Mutual Trading Co Inc
431 Crocker St
Los Angeles, CA 90013   213-626-9458
         Fax: 213-626-5130 www.lamtc.com
Wholesaler/distributor, importer and exporter of miso, soybean sauce, rice and vinegar.
President: Kosei Yamamoto
Year Founded: 1926
Estimated Sales: $20-50 Million
Number Employees: 100-249
Number of Brands: 2
Types of Products Distributed:
   Frozen Food, General Line, Specialty Foods, Miso, rice, soy sauce & vinegar

58195 Mutual Wholesale Company
2800 N Andrews Avenue Ext
Pompano Beach, FL 33064   954-973-5994
         Fax: 954-974-5461
Wholesaler/distributor of general line items; serving the food service market
Owner/President: Barbara Andrews
General Manager: John Bush
Purchasing Agent: Paul Boerstler
Parent Co: Mutual Distributors
Private Brands Carried:
   Libby; Fine Line; Borden's
Types of Products Distributed:
   Frozen Food, General Line

58196 Mutual Wholesale Liquor
P.O.Box 58829
Los Angeles, CA 90058-0829 323-587-7641
         Fax: 323-587-0820
Importer and wholesaler/distributor of beer and wine
President: Harvey Monterski
Estimated Sales: $20-50 Million
Number Employees: 50-99
Type of Packaging: Consumer, Food Service
Types of Products Distributed:
   Frozen Food, General Line, Beer & wine

58197 My Car Provision Company
20 Westwood Ave
New London, CT 06320   860-442-4401
         Fax: 860-442-4402
Wholesaler/distributor of fresh and frozen beef, lamb, pork, etc.; serving the food service market
Owner: Raymond Capalbo
Estimated Sales: $2.5-5 Million
Number Employees: 1-4
Number of Customer Locations: 110
Types of Products Distributed:
   Food Service, Provisions/Meat, Beef, lamb, pork, etc

58198 My Quality Trading Corp
133 48th St
Brooklyn, NY 11232-4227   718-854-8714
         Fax: 718-854-6816
Wholesaler/distributor, importer and exporter of general line merchandise including nuts, dried fruits, bakery supplies, spices and chocolate candy; serving the food service market
President: Moses Geller
Estimated Sales: $20-50 Million
Number Employees: 20-49
Square Footage: 10000
Number of Customer Locations: 150

Types of Products Distributed:
   Food Service, Frozen Food, General Line, Nuts, dried fruits, spices, candy, etc.

58199 My Style
614 NW Street
Raleigh, NC 27603   919-832-2526
         Fax: 919-832-1546 800-524-8269
Wholesaler/distributor, importer and exporter of teak, cast aluminum, stainless steel and hardwood outdoor furniture; also, wooden and market umbrellas
Director: Ward Usmar
Owner: Klaus Weihe
Owner: Eik Niemann
Marketing Administrator: Ceri Usmar
Number Employees: 1-4
Square Footage: 13500
Private Brands Carried:
   Carribean Shade; Lingot; Siesta Shade
Types of Products Distributed:
   General Merchandise, Umbrellas & outdoor furniture

58200 Myers Equipment Company
7766 Arjons Dr # B
San Diego, CA 92126-4391   858-578-6815
         Fax: 858-587-8594
Wholesaler/distributor of material handling equipment, steel shelving, shipping containers and automatic storage and handling systems
President: John Myers
Estimated Sales: $1-2.5 Million
Number Employees: 1-4
Types of Products Distributed:
   Frozen Food, General Merchandise, Material handling equipment

58201 Myers Restaurant Supply Inc
1599 Cleveland Ave
Santa Rosa, CA 95401-4280   707-570-1200
         Fax: 707-542-0350 800-219-9426
         brett@myersrestaurantsupply.com
         www.myersrestaurantsupply.com
Wholesaler/distributor of restaurant and bar equipment and supplies; serving the food service market
Owner: Rob Myers
CEO: Jon Myers
CFO: Brett Livingstone
Estimated Sales: $2.5-5 Million
Number Employees: 20-49
Square Footage: 44000
Types of Products Distributed:
   Food Service, Frozen Food, General Merchandise, Restaurant & bar equipment & supplies

58202 Myers-Cox Co
8797 Kapp Dr
Peosta, IA 52068
                            800-234-8200
    Dflanagan@myerscox.com www.myerscox.com
Wholesaler/distributor of groceries, equipment and fixtures, paper products, coffee and chemicals; serving the institutional food service market.
President: Mary Carew
Vice President: Christopher Dempsey
Sales Manager: David Flanagan
Warehouse Manager: David May
Year Founded: 1866
Estimated Sales: $20-50 Million
Number Employees: 50-99
Number of Products: 9500
Square Footage: 55000
Number of Customer Locations: 1800
Types of Products Distributed:
   Food Service, Frozen Food, General Merchandise, Paper products, coffee & chemicals

58203 Mylk Labs
City of Industry, CA 91748
                        info@mylklabs.com
                        www.mylklabs.com
Oatmeal cups
Founder: Grace Cheng
Number of Brands: 1
Number of Products: 3
Type of Packaging: Consumer

58204 N.B.J. Enterprises
3950 Demetropolis Rd
Mobile, AL 36693   251-661-2285
         Fax: 251-661-6198
Seafood

Owner: Toni Gulsby
Estimated Sales: $1-3 Million
Number Employees: 10-19

58205 NEBCO Distributing
846 Highway At
Bldg 2
Villa Ridge, MO 63089-2154 636-451-2208
Wholesaler/distributor of snack foods
Owner: Noel Baugh
Estimated Sales: $1-2.5 Million
Number Employees: 1-4
Types of Products Distributed:
   Frozen Food, General Line, Snack foods

58206 NJM Seafood
P.O.Box 302
Murrells Inlet, SC 29576-0302 843-651-5707
         Fax: 843-651-8361
Wholesaler/distributor of fresh and frozen seafood, groceries and general line items; serving the food service market
Owner: Sean English
Manager/Secretary/Treasurer: Catherine Massey
Estimated Sales: $500,000-$1 Million
Number Employees: 1-4
Types of Products Distributed:
   Food Service, Frozen Food, General Line, Seafood, Groceries, etc.

58207 NOW Foods
244 Knollwood Dr.
Bloomingdale, IL 60108
                            888-669-3663
                        www.nowfoods.com
Vitamins, healthy foods, natural personal care and sports nutrition products.
CEO: Jim Emme
CFO: Andy Kotlarz
General Counsel: Beverly Reid
VP, Quality/Regulatory Affairs: Aaron Secrist
VP, Global Sales/Marketing: Dan Richard
Vice President, Human Resources: Michelle Canada
COO: Ernest Shepard
Year Founded: 1968
Estimated Sales: $100 Million
Number Employees: 100-249
Number of Brands: 9
Number of Products: 1500
Square Footage: 203000
Type of Packaging: Consumer, Private Label, Bulk

58208 Nafziger Ice Cream Company
515 Independence Drive
Suite 100
Napoleon, OH 43545-9656   419-592-1112
         Fax: 419-592-4069 800-321-7809
Wholesaler/distributor of ice cream, novelties, frozen yogurt, etc
Manager: Gary Giller
Sales Manager: David Ingall
Estimated Sales: $10-20 Million
Number Employees: 10-19
Square Footage: 120000
Parent Co: Stroh's Ice Cream
Types of Products Distributed:
   Frozen Food, General Line, Ice cream, novelties, etc.

58209 Nagasako Fish
800 Eha St
Suite 12
Wailuku, HI 96793   808-242-4073
         Fax: 808-244-7020
Seafood
Owner: Darryl Flinton
Estimated Sales: $5-10 Million
Number Employees: 10-19

58210 Nagel Paper & Box Company
3286 Industrial Drive
Saginaw, MI 48601   989-753-4405
         Fax: 989-753-2493 800-292-3654
         info@nagelpaper.com www.nagelpaper.com
Fiber tubes, caps and plugs
Contact: James Baker
james@nagelpaper.com
Estimated Sales: $1-3 Million
Number Employees: 18
Square Footage: 80000
Type of Packaging: Food Service
Types of Products Distributed:
   Food Service, Frozen Food, General Merchandise, Packaging supplies, cups, cutlery, etc.

Wholesalers & Distributors / A-Z

58211 Naman Marketing
9870 Pineview Avenue
Theodore, AL 36582-7403
251-438-2617
Fax: 251-433-5032
President: George Naman

58212 Nan Sea Enterprises of Wisconsin
900 Gale St
Waukesha, WI 53186-2515
262-542-8841
Fax: 262-542-4356
Manufacturer and distributor of fresh frozen king, dungeness, golden and snow crab; also, lobster and lobster claws
President: Eric Muehl
VP: Robert Nell
Estimated Sales: $10-20 Million
Number Employees: 5-9
Type of Packaging: Food Service, Private Label
Types of Products Distributed:
Frozen Food

58213 Nancy Q Produce
662 Montreal Street
Kingston, ON K7K 3J4
Canada
613-542-4996
Fax: 613-542-5280
Wholesaler/distributor of fresh vegetables and fruit; serving the food service market
Manager: Joe Quattrocchi
Number Employees: 10-19
Private Brands Carried:
Dole; Chiquita; Foxy
Types of Products Distributed:
Food Service, Frozen Food, Produce

58214 Nancy's Shellfish
91 Falmouth Rd
Falmouth, ME 04105-1841
207-774-3411
Fax: 207-780-0044
Shellfish, seafood
President: Joe Scola
Estimated Sales: $1.4 Million
Number Employees: 5-9

58215 Naples Vending
869 95th Ave N
Naples, FL 34108-2458
239-597-5511
Fax: 239-597-4809 naplesvendingfl@aol.com
www.naplesvendingfl.com
Wholesaler/distributor of snack foods and beverages for vending machines
Owner: Cecilia Diagostino
General Manager: Nick D' Agostino
Estimated Sales: $1-3 Million
Number Employees: 5-9
Private Brands Carried:
Frito-Lay; Coca-Cola; Pepsi-Cola
Types of Products Distributed:
Frozen Food, General Line, Snack foods & beverages

58216 Napoleon Creamery
221 E Washington St
Napoleon, OH 43545
419-592-7831
Fax: 419-592-7831
Wholesaler/distributor of dry and frozen foods, disposables and dairy products including butter; serving the food service market
Owner: Ken Grieser
Estimated Sales: $5-10 Million
Number Employees: 5-9
Types of Products Distributed:
Food Service, Frozen Food, General Line, Dairy products, disposables, etc.

58217 Nappie's Food Svc
8051 Steubenville Pike
Oakdale, PA 15071-9376
724-695-3500
Fax: 724-695-2820
Wholesaler/distributor of frozen foods, cheese, oil, Italian imports, general line items and seafood including shrimp and lobster; serving the food service market
Partner: Edward Napoleone
Partner: Angelo Napoleone
angelo@nappiesfoods.com
Operations Manager: Tim Conso
Estimated Sales: $30 Million
Number Employees: 20-49
Square Footage: 40000
Private Brands Carried:
Cellante; Goliath
Number of Customer Locations: 460

Types of Products Distributed:
Food Service, Frozen Food, General Line, Seafood, Specialty Foods, Shrimp & lobster

58218 Nardelli Brothers
54 Main St
Cedarville, NJ 08311-2320
856-447-4621
Fax: 856-447-3700 www.nardellibrosinc.com
Wholesaler/distributor of produce
Owner: Bill Nardelli
nardellibrosinc@aol.com
Estimated Sales: $2.5-5 Million
Number Employees: 20-49
Types of Products Distributed:
Frozen Food, Produce

58219 Nareg International Inc
3661 San Fernando Rd
Glendale, CA 91204-2939
818-500-8291
Fax: 818-240-8292 888-677-8292
sales@naregint.com
Wholesaler/distributor and importer of table accessories, gift wrapping and disposable tablecloths and napkins
Owner: Adour Aghjayan
sales@naregint.com
Assistant President: Helen Aghjayan
Marketing Director: David Ghoukassian
Estimated Sales: $1.5 Million
Number Employees: 1-4
Square Footage: 20000
Type of Packaging: Consumer, Food Service, Private Label, Bulk
Private Brands Carried:
Tultex Italy; Euronastro; Natural Service
Number of Customer Locations: 6000
Types of Products Distributed:
General Merchandise, Disposable napkins & tablecloths, etc.

58220 Nasco Inc
901 Janesville Ave
P.O. Box 901
Fort Atkinson, WI 53538-0901
800-431-4310
custserv@eNasco.com
Manufacturer and exporter of WHIRL-PAK sample bags; wholesaler/distributor of laboratory supplies.
Regional Sales Director: James Felt
jfelt@enasco.com
Director, Whirl-Pak Sales: Tom Valitchka
Year Founded: 1941
Estimated Sales: $50-100 Million
Number Employees: 50-99
Parent Co: Nasco International
Other Locations:
Nasco
Modesto, CANasco
Types of Products Distributed:
Frozen Food

58221 Nash-DeCamp Company
1612 W Mineral King Ave
Visalia, CA 93291-4438
559-622-1850
Fax: 559-622-1883
Wholesaler/distributor and exporter of produce including plums, grapes, kiwi, lemons and oranges; importer of grapes and kiwi
CEO: Stephen Biswell
Sales/Marketing Executive VP: Tom Whitehouse
Number Employees: 20-49
Square Footage: 56000
Types of Products Distributed:
Frozen Food, Produce, Plums, grapes, etc.

58222 Nass Parts & Svc Inc
9436 Southridge Park Ct # 500
Orlando, FL 32819-8640
407-425-2681
Fax: 407-425-3463 800-432-2795
Wholesaler/distributor of food service equipment and supplies; serving the food service market
President/General Manager: Thomas Walter
Manager: Bart Stamper
bart.stamper@3wire.com
Estimated Sales: $5-10 Million
Number Employees: 20-49
Private Brands Carried:
Market Forge; Wells Manufacturing; Groen
Number of Customer Locations: 2000
Types of Products Distributed:
Food Service, Frozen Food, General Merchandise, Equipment & supplies

58223 (HQ)Nassau Candy Distributors
530 W John St
Hicksville, NY 11801-1039
516-433-7100
Fax: 516-433-9010 sales@nassaucandy.com
www.nassaucandy.com
Manufacturer, importer and distributor of confectionery items and gourmet foods.
President: Barry Rosenbaum
Chairman & CEO: Lesley Stier
Vice President: Carol Baca
carol.baca@nassaucandy.com
Number Employees: 100-249
Other Locations:
Nassau Candy Co.
Deer Park, NYNassau Candy Co.
Types of Products Distributed:
Frozen Food, General Line, Provisions/Meat, Produce, Specialty Foods, Specialty & confectionery items

58224 Nassau Foods
153 Thompson Avenue E
Saint Paul, MN 55118-3261
651-306-9262
Fax: 651-306-9194 800-432-0105
Wholesaler/distributor of spices including garlic powder and allspice; serving the food service market
President: Chuck Sartell
Warehouse Manager: Chris Greenly
Estimated Sales: $1-2.5 Million
Number Employees: 5-9
Private Brands Carried:
Heller's
Types of Products Distributed:
Food Service, Frozen Food, General Line, Spices: allspice & garlic powder

58225 Nassau-Suffolk Frozen Food Company
286 Northern Boulevard
Great Neck, NY 11021-4704
516-466-1820
Fax: 516-466-1820
Wholesaler/distributor of frozen food
Executive VP: V Bahar
VP: S Schwartzreich
Number Employees: 250-499
Private Brands Carried:
Scatturo; Key Food
Number of Customer Locations: 6000
Types of Products Distributed:
Frozen Food

58226 Natchitoches Crawfish Company
1205 Texas Street
Natchitoches, LA 71457
318-352-2194
Fax: 318-379-2816 mcfctr@bellsouth.net
natchitochescrawfish.com
Owner: Jimmy Strickland

58227 Natco Foodservice
321 W 10th St
Reserve, LA 70084-6603
985-479-4200
Fax: 504-525-4499 www.natcofoodservice.com
Wholesaler/distributor serving the food service market
President: Ann Lalle Babvin
ann@natcofoodservice.com
Number Employees: 100-249
Types of Products Distributed:
Food Service

58228 Natco Worldwide Representative
23004 Frisca Dr
Santa Clarita, CA 91354-2225
661-296-8778
Fax: 661-296-8778 npatow@aol.com
www.natcoglobal.com
Importer, Exporter of canned seafood, Broker for frozen seafood
Owner: Natalia Patow
npatow@aol.com
Estimated Sales: $2.5-$5 Million
Number Employees: 5-9
Square Footage: 12000
Type of Packaging: Consumer, Private Label
Private Brands Carried:
Delicias; Grand Duchess
Types of Products Distributed:
Seafood, Canned Seafood

58229 Nathel & Nathel
357 Row C
NYC Terminal Market
Bronx, NY 10474
718-991-6050
Fax: 718-378-1378 www.nnproduce.com
Wholesaler/distributor of produce.

Wholesalers & Distributors / A-Z

President: Ira Nathel
ira@nnproduce.com
Vice President: Sheldon Nathel
Chief Financial Officer: Richard Richer
Controller: Angel Helck Padilla
Operations Manager: Tommy Cifu
Year Founded: 1922
Estimated Sales: $30 Million
Number Employees: 200
Square Footage: 160000
Types of Products Distributed:
Frozen Food, Produce

58230 National Band Saw Co
25322 Avenue Stanford
Santa Clarita, CA 91355-1214 661-294-9552
Fax: 661-294-9554 800-851-5050
harley@nbsparts.com www.nbsparts.com
Manufacturer, exporter and wholesaler/distributor of replacement parts for meat slicing and cutting machinery; importer of slicing knives, tenderizers and bread slicing and patty-making machines; wholesaler/distributor of office and shipping supplies
Owner: Enrique Barbosa
enriqueb@nbarizona.com
VP: Chris Tuttle
R & D: Ron Voytek
Director of IT Computer Services: Jason Jasperson
Production: Ron Voytek
Estimated Sales: Below $5 Million
Number Employees: 10-19
Square Footage: 12200
Type of Packaging: Consumer, Food Service, Private Label, Bulk
Types of Products Distributed:
Frozen Food, General Merchandise, Parts for meat cutters & slicers

58231 National Bulk Food Distributors
7620 Telegraph Road
Taylor, MI 48180-2237 313-292-1550
Fax: 313-292-1822 800-421-6233
Wholesaler/distributor of bulk candy and confections; serving supermarkets and other nationwide retail outlets
President: Avi Brandvain
CEO: William Liberson
CFO: Curt Meehan
Marketing Director: Pete Podolski
Sales Director: Bill Thurner
Operations Manager: Bob Jones
Production Manager: Mike Pavlichek
Plant Manager: Dan Squillets
Purchasing Manager: Barry Berstein
Estimated Sales: $25-30 Million
Number Employees: 75
Number of Brands: 350
Number of Products: 3000
Square Footage: 55000
Type of Packaging: Bulk
Number of Customer Locations: 1750
Types of Products Distributed:
Bulk Candy & Novelty Goods

58232 National Carbonation
PO Box 31007
Charlotte, NC 28231-1007 704-509-0516
Fax: 704-509-0119 866-935-3370
service@airgas.com
www.airgasnationalcarbonation.com
Wholesaler/distributor of liquid carbon dioxide
Manager: Mary Cheek Nicholson
Operations Manager: Michael Turner
Estimated Sales: $5-10 Million
Number Employees: 10-19
Parent Co: National Welders Supply Company
Types of Products Distributed:
Frozen Food, General Line, Liquid carbon dioxide

58233 National Fish & SeafoodInc
11-15 Parker St # 4
Gloucester, MA 01930-3017 978-282-7880
Fax: 978-282-7882 800-229-1750
comments@nationalfish.com
www.nationalfish.com
Seafood
President: Jack Ventola
jventola@nationalfish.com
Number Employees: 20-49

58234 National Food Co LTD
3109 Koapaka St # C
Unit C
Honolulu, HI 96819-1998 808-839-1118
Fax: 808-839-6866
Owner: Teresa Goo
teresa.goo@nfcegypt.com
Estimated Sales: $5-10 Million
Number Employees: 1-4

58235 National Fruit & Essences
11023 Mill Creek Way #703
Ft. Myers, FL 33913 239-225-6111
Fax: 239-225-6112
nationalfruitessences@yahoo.com
Purchases, sells and distributes fruit juice concentrates, essential oils, essences, and natural colors.
President: Kathleen Medore
Sales: Victor Medore & Joleen Medore
Estimated Sales: $2 Million
Number Employees: 3
Other Locations:
Fort Myers, FL

58236 National Grocers
35 Clyde Avenue
Mt. Pearl, NL A1N 4R8
Canada 709-576-1246
Fax: 709-576-1921
Wholesaler/distributor of dairy products, frozen foods, general merchandise, produce, general line items, etc.; serving the food service market
VP Operations: Brad Western
Number Employees: 20-49
Parent Co: Loblaw Companies
Number of Customer Locations: 600
Types of Products Distributed:
Food Service, Frozen Food, General Line, General Merchandise, Produce, Dairy products, etc.

58237 National Grocers Assn
1005 N Glebe Rd # 250
Arlington, VA 22201-5758 703-516-0700
Fax: 703-516-0115 feedback@nationalgrocers.org
www.nationalgrocers.org
Wholesaler/distributor of groceries and produce
President and CEO: Peter J. Larkin
plarkin@nationalgrocers.org
EVP and Chief Operating Officer: Charlie Bray
Director, Communications and Marketing: Laura Strange
Vice President, Public Affairs: Greg Ferrara
Vice President, Operations: Matthew Ott, MS, CAE
Purchasing Agent: Jeff Dollar
Number Employees: 20-49
Private Brands Carried:
President's Choice
Number of Customer Locations: 154
Types of Products Distributed:
Frozen Food, General Line, Produce, Groceries

58238 National Grocers Company
870 Algonquin Boulevard E
Timmins, ON P4N 7N3
Canada 705-264-1359
Fax: 705-268-3118
Wholesaler/distributor of groceries, frozen foods, confectionery products, produce, meats and seafood; serving the food service market
Manager: Drew Clark
Number Employees: 5-9
Parent Co: Loblaw Companies
Number of Customer Locations: 1000
Types of Products Distributed:
Food Service, Frozen Food, General Line, Provisions/Meat, Produce, Seafood, Confectionery products & groceries

58239 National Grocers Company
1070 Webbwood
Sudbury, ON P3C 3B7
Canada 705-673-3606
Fax: 705-673-6897
Wholesaler/distributor of frozen foods, groceries, produce, meats and seafood; serving the food service market
Manager: Tom King
Number Employees: 10-19
Parent Co: Loblaw Companies
Number of Customer Locations: 1200
Types of Products Distributed:
Food Service, Frozen Food, General Line, Provisions/Meat, Produce, Seafood

58240 National Grocers Company
727 Front Street
Pembroke, ON K8A 6J4
Canada 613-732-4012
Fax: 613-732-1228
Wholesaler/distributor of general line items
Manager: Al Wren
Number Employees: 10-19
Square Footage: 76000
Parent Co: Loblaw Companies
Number of Customer Locations: 400
Types of Products Distributed:
Frozen Food, General Line

58241 National Grocers Company
2625 Sheffield Road
Ottawa, ON K1B 1A8
Canada 613-741-4756
Wholesaler/distributor of frozen foods, general line items, produce and seafood; serving the food service market
Distribution Manager: Todd Yates
Number Employees: 250-499
Parent Co: Loblaw Companies
Private Brands Carried:
President's Choice
Number of Customer Locations: 100
Types of Products Distributed:
Food Service, Frozen Food, General Line, Produce, Seafood

58242 National Lecithin
1 Adamson St
Easton, PA 18042 610-252-8350
Fax: 610-252-9901
Wholesaler/distributor of lecithin products
President: Alan Geisler
VP: Patti Bruno
Estimated Sales: $3-5 Million
Number Employees: 5-9
Private Brands Carried:
National Brand
Number of Customer Locations: 100
Types of Products Distributed:
General Line, Lecithin products

58243 National Lighting Source
1724 1st Ave W
Birmingham, AL 35208-5219 205-788-6088
Fax: 205-788-6089 800-273-8497
www.bulbsandballast.com
Wholesaler/distributor of ballasts, lighting fixtures, lamps and light bulbs
Owner: Jeremy Bussey
jeremy@bulbsandballast.com
Office Manager: Jeremy Bussey
Number Employees: 1-4
Number of Customer Locations: 12000
Types of Products Distributed:
Frozen Food, General Merchandise, Ballasts, lighting fixtures, etc.

58244 National Meat & Provision Company
321 W 10th St
Reserve, LA 70084-6603 985-479-4200
Fax: 985-479-4205 www.natcofs.com
Beef, lamb, veal, pork, poultry, sausages, wild game, seafood, and dairy
President: Anne Babin
anne@natcofoodservice.com
Chairman: Leonard Lalla
CEO/Secretary: John Lalla
VP: Earline Lalla
Operations Manager: Joe Schwab
Manager: Sam Najm
Estimated Sales: $39.06 Million
Number Employees: 60
Square Footage: 85000

58245 National Restaurant Company
PO Box 3031
Greenwood, SC 29648-3031 864-374-7356
Fax: 864-374-3180
Wholesaler/distributor of restaurant equipment and supplies
President: A Everett
Estimated Sales: $1-2.5 Million
Number Employees: 1-4
Types of Products Distributed:
Food Service, Frozen Food, General Merchandise, Restaurant equipment & supplies

Wholesalers & Distributors / A-Z

58246 National Restaurant Supply Company
2513 Comanche Rd NE
Albuquerque, NM 87107
877-654-6554
sales@nrsupply.com www.nrsupply.com
Wholesaler/distributor of equipment, supplies, china, silverware, tabletop items, furniture and stainless steel fabrication; serving the food service market.
Types of Products Distributed:
  Food Service, Frozen Food, General Merchandise, Restaurant supplies & equipment

58247 (HQ)National Restaurant Supply Company
7125 Industrial Ave
El Paso, TX 79915
915-544-2121
877-654-6554
sales@nrsupply.com www.nrsupply.com
Wholesaler/distributor of equipment, supplies, china, silverware, tabletop items, furniture and stainless steel fabrication; serving the food service market.
Estimated Sales: $90 Million
Number Employees: 50-99
Other Locations:
  National Restaurant Supply Co
  Albuquerque, NMNational Restaurant Supply Co
Types of Products Distributed:
  Food Service, Frozen Food, China, silverware, furniture, etc.

58248 National Sales Corporation
7250 Oxford Way
Commerce, CA 90040
323-586-0200
Fax: 800-560-4040 800-690-4444
www.e-nsc.com
Exporter and wholesaler/distributor of groceries, general merchandise, health/beauty aids, private label items, sugar, condiments, soups, kitchenware, etc.
Estimated Sales: $50-100 Million
Number Employees: 50-99
Square Footage: 80000
Type of Packaging: Private Label
Private Brands Carried:
  Champs
Number of Customer Locations: 2900
Types of Products Distributed:
  Frozen Food, General Line, General Merchandise, Groceries, health/beauty aids, etc.

58249 National Scale Of New England
710 Berkshire Ave
Springfield, MA 01109-1053
413-733-2053
Fax: 413-827-9387 800-955-9302
natlscale@aol.com www.nationalscaleinc.com
Wholesaler/distributor of counting and weighing machinery including scales
President: Richard Bozenhard
natlscale@aol.com
Sales Manager: Al Bozenhard
Estimated Sales: $500,000-$1 Million
Number Employees: 1-4
Types of Products Distributed:
  Frozen Food, General Merchandise, Scales

58250 National Scoop & Equipment Company
PO Box 325
Spring House, PA 19477-0325
215-646-2040
Manufacturer, wholesaler/distributor and importer of pails, buckets, scales, scoops, skimmers, dippers, disposable paper clothing, sinks and trucks
Manager: Ken Johnson
Types of Products Distributed:
  Frozen Food, General Merchandise, Cleaning supplies, etc.

58251 National Shippng SupplyCo
19950 W 161st St
Olathe, KS 66062-2741
913-764-1551
Fax: 913-764-0779 800-444-8361
Wholesaler/distributor and exporter of labels, tags and cloth bags; also, plastic sampling and reclosable bags
Owner: Rosey Hohendorf
rosey@natshipsupply.com
Customer Service: Rosie Hohendorf
Estimated Sales: $500,000-$1 Million
Number Employees: 1-4
Square Footage: 20000
Parent Co: Victor Enterprises
Private Brands Carried:
  Chaseline; Whirlpak; Nasco; Ennis
Types of Products Distributed:
  Frozen Food, General Merchandise, Labels, tags, cloth bags, etc.

58252 Nationwide Material Handling Equipment
20434 S Susana Rd
Long Beach, CA 90810
310-631-5438
Fax: 310-604-3432 800-367-5543
www.800forklift.com
Wholesaler/distributor of forklifts and parts; also, service available
Manager: Paul Russell
R&D Head: William Laverde
Sales/Marketing Manager: William Laverde
Contact: Mitchell Resnick
onelprods@earthlink.net
Estimated Sales: $20-50 Million
Number Employees: 50-99
Private Brands Carried:
  Komatsu
Types of Products Distributed:
  Frozen Food, General Merchandise, Forklifts & parts

58253 Native State Foods
201 Bicknell Ave
Suite 206
Santa Monica, CA 90405
866-647-2291
nativestatefoods.com
Cereals and snack cups
Co-Founder & Co-CEO: Claudio Ochoa
Co-Founder: Angela Palmieri *Year Founded:* 2014
Type of Packaging: Consumer

58254 Natra US
2535 Camino Dek Rio South
Suite 355
Chula Vista, CA 91910
619-397-4120
Fax: 619-397-4121 800-262-6216
www.natrus.com
Importer and exporter of cocoa powder, butter and extract; also, chocolate, caffeine, theobromine and nutraceuticals
Manager: Maria Dominguez
Vice President: Martin Brabenec
Key Account Manager: Juan Carlos Vinolo
Estimated Sales: $650000
Number Employees: 1-4
Number of Brands: 2
Number of Products: 30
Parent Co: Natra S.A.
Type of Packaging: Consumer, Food Service, Bulk
Types of Products Distributed:
  Frozen Food

58255 (HQ)Natrol Inc
21411 Prairie St
Chatsworth, CA 91311-5829
818-739-6000
Fax: 818-739-6001 800-326-1520
support@natrol.com www.natrol.com
Wholesaler/distributor, exporter and importer of specialty vitamins and dietary supplements
President: Elliott Balbert
CEO: Harun Simbirdi
hsimbirdi@natrol.com
CEO: Craig Cameron
VP Sales: Jon Denis
Number Employees: 250-499
Square Footage: 320000
Type of Packaging: Consumer
Types of Products Distributed:
  Frozen Food, Health Food, Vitamins & dietary supplements

58256 (HQ)Natural Balance
383 Inverness Pkwy # 390
Englewood, CO 80112-5864
303-688-6633
Fax: 303-688-1591 800-624-4260
service@naturalbalance.com
www.naturalbalance.com
Processor and wholesaler/distributor of natural nutrition supplements for energy, weight loss and sports
President: Mark Owens
Executive VP: Tim Hinricks
Sales Coordinator: Scott Smith
Contact: Steven Kahl
skahl@mai-architects.com
Plant Manager: John O'Brien
Purchasing Manager: Stephanie McArthur
Estimated Sales: $11.4 Million
Number Employees: 100-249
Square Footage: 50000
Other Locations:
  Natural Balance
  Castle Rock, CONatural Balance
Types of Products Distributed:
  Frozen Food, Health Food, Nutritional supplements

58257 Natural Casing Co
410 E Railroad St
Peshtigo, WI 54157-1644
715-582-3931
Fax: 715-582-3931 www.naturalcasingco.com
Wholesaler/distributor and importer of sausage casings
President: Stephen Dirtzu
Estimated Sales: $1-2.5 Million
Number Employees: 5-9
Square Footage: 100000
Parent Co: SD Enterprises
Types of Products Distributed:
  General Line, Sausage casings

58258 Natural Choice Distribution
5427 Telegraph Ave Ste U
Oakland, CA 94609
510-653-8212
Fax: 510-653-8163
info@naturalchoicedistribution.com
Salsa and sandwiches, distribution of natural food products
Owner: Steve Cutter
Contact: Douglas Gwosdz
douglasgwosdz@naturalchoicedistribution.com
Estimated Sales: Below $5 000,000
Number Employees: 18
Type of Packaging: Private Label

58259 Natural Dairy Products Corp
316 Markus Ct
Newark, DE 19713-1151
302-455-1261
Fax: 302-455-1262 800-550-6256
www.natural-by-nature.com
Wholesaler/distributor of organic milk, ice cream, pudding, cream cheese, whipped butter, sour cream, ricotta, whipped cream, cottage cheese
General Manager: Dawn Fenstermacher
CEO: Michael Bradley
Vice President: Susan MacArthur
Sales Representative: Jay Totman
Operations Manager: Stephanie Salvato
Customer Service Representative: Amy Hackett
Estimated Sales: $3-5 Million
Number Employees: 1-4
Square Footage: 20000
Type of Packaging: Consumer, Private Label
Private Brands Carried:
  Natural by Nature; Whole Foods; Fresh Fields
Types of Products Distributed:
  Health Food, Specialty Foods

58260 Natural Factors
14224 167th Ave SE
Monroe, WA 98272-2810
360-863-8579
Fax: 425-348-9050 800-322-8704
www.naturalfactors.com
Wholesaler/distributor of vitamins, minerals and herbal supplements
President: John Morley
jemorley@naturalfactors.com
National Sales Manager: Kathy McKnight
Estimated Sales: $1-2.5 Million
Number Employees: 100-249

58261 Natural Food Systems
8301 Torresdale Avenue
Philadelphia, PA 19136-2911
215-624-3559
Fax: 215-624-3559
Wholesaler/distributor of organic, natural and specialty food products including frozen pizza, fat-free snack foods, seafood and nutritional products
National Brands Manager: Jeff Krinsky
Parent Co: Cornucopia Natural Foods
Private Brands Carried:
  Natural Sea; Rudi's Bakery; Oak River Foods; Greenfield Healthy Foods; Cornucopia Pet

Wholesalers & Distributors / A-Z

Food; Muffin-A-Day; Dal Raccolto; Wolfgang Puik Food Co.
Types of Products Distributed:
Frozen Food, Health Food, Specialty Foods

58262 Natural Foods Inc
3040 Hill Ave
Toledo, OH 43607-2983   419-537-1711
Fax: 419-531-6887 vip@bulkfoods.com
www.3qf.com
Wholesaler/distributor, importer and packer of food, candy, nuts, spices, fruit, and chocolates
Owner: Frank Dietrich
Estimated Sales: $5 Million
Number Employees: 20-49
Square Footage: 1800000
Type of Packaging: Food Service, Bulk
Types of Products Distributed:
Frozen Food, General Line, Health Food, Dried fruits, nuts, candies, etc.

58263 Natural Group
909 15th Street
Suite 2
Modesto, CA 95354-1130   209-522-6860
Fax: 209-522-7928 naturalgroup@att.net
Wholesaler/distributor, importer and exporter of sparkling, mineral and natural beverages including water; wholesaler/distributor of groceries
President: Richard Keer
Marketing Manager: Denise Haight
Estimated Sales: $2.5-5 Million
Number Employees: 1-4
Type of Packaging: Consumer, Private Label
Private Brands Carried:
AME; Aqualibra; Purdey's; Avvio Toppings & Sauces; Smoothiepacks; Norfolk Punch; Hildon
Types of Products Distributed:
Health Food, Specialty Foods, Natural & Organic Foods and Beverages

58264 Naturally Nutty
P.O. Box 3151
Traverse City, MI 49685
888-224-9988
customerservice@naturallynutty.com
www.naturallynutty.com
Nut and seed butters
President: Katie Kearney *Year Founded:* 2007
Types of Products Distributed:
General Line

58265 Nature Distributors
16508 E Laser Drive
Suite 104
Fountain Hills, AZ 85268-6512   480-837-8322
Fax: 480-837-8420 800-624-7114
Wholesaler/distributor of vitamins and supplements
President: Mike Minarsich
General Manager: Jeff Martin
VP: Kevin Seifert
Contact: Kevin Seifert
k.seifert@vitameatavegamin.com
Estimated Sales: $5-10 Million
Number Employees: 20-49
Types of Products Distributed:
Frozen Food, General Line, Health Food, Vitamins & supplements

58266 Nature's Best
6 Pointe Dr # 300
Suite 300
Brea, CA 92821-6323   714-255-4600
Fax: 714-255-4691 800-765-3141
www.naturesbest.net
Wholesaler/distributor of health foods and supplements; serving the food service market and supermarkets in Western states; also, direct store delivery available
President: James Beck
VP Marketing/Sales: Tom Echolds
Number Employees: 5-9
Square Footage: 720000
Private Brands Carried:
Nature's Cuisine
Number of Customer Locations: 1200
Types of Products Distributed:
Food Service, Frozen Food, Health Food, Specialty Foods

58267 Nature's Bounty Co.
2100 Smithtown Ave.
Ronkonkoma, NY 11779   631-200-2000
877-774-3361
consumeraffairsmgmt@nbty.com
www.naturesbountyco.com
Nutritional supplements and vitamins.
President/CEO: Paul Sturman
CFO: Ted McCormick
General Counsel/Chief Compliance Officer: Stratis Philipps
Estimated Sales: $3 Billion
Number Employees: 10,000+
Number of Brands: 19
Number of Products: 22K
Parent Co: KKR
Type of Packaging: Consumer, Private Label, Bulk

58268 Nature's Candy
632 Fm 2093
Fredericksburg, TX 78624-7149   830-997-3844
Fax: 830-997-6528 800-729-0085
Processor and wholesaler/distributor of natural and fruit-filled candy, maple-coated nuts and seasoned nuts and seeds
President: Michael Zygmunt
michael@beneficialfoods.com
Office Manager: Karen Gold
Estimated Sales: $482,000
Number Employees: 5-9
Type of Packaging: Consumer, Private Label, Bulk
Types of Products Distributed:
Frozen Food, Specialty Foods, Natural & fruit filled candy

58269 Nature's Fusions
1405 W 820 N
Provo, UT 84601   801-872-9500
www.naturesfusions.com
Essential oils and CBD
CEO: C.J. Peterson
Number of Brands: 1

58270 Nature's Hollow
Probst Farms
3290 West 3500 South
Charleston, UT 84032
Fax: 435-216-9829 www.natureshollow.com
Sugar-free sauces and spreads
Number of Brands: 1

58271 Nature's Provision Company
452 Krumville Rd
Olivebridge, NY 12461-5528   845-657-6020
Powdered health food supplements for circulatory improvement; wholesaler/distributor of pH balanced cleansers and lubricants
President: Clark Jung
Vice President: Ann Jung
Estimated Sales: $130,000
Number Employees: 2
Private Brands Carried:
Dermophin 5.5 (pH balanced cleansers & lubricants)
Types of Products Distributed:
Frozen Food, General Merchandise, pH balanced cleansers & lubricants

58272 Navitas Naturals
15 Pamaron Way
Novato, CA 94949   415-883-8116
Fax: 888-645-4282 888-645-4282
www.navitasorganics.com
Superfood shots, hot drink mixes, superfood ingredients, snack bars, seeds, nuts, and berries
Founder/CEO: Zach Adelman
z.adelman@navitasnaturals.com *Year Founded:* 2003
Types of Products Distributed:
Health Food

58273 Navy Brand
3670 Scarlet Oak Blvd
St Louis, MO 63122-6606   636-861-5500
Fax: 636-861-5509 800-325-3312
navybrand@navybrand.com www.navybrand.com
Manufacturer and wholesaler/distributor of industrial degreasers, cleaners and water treatment systems for boilers and cooling towers
President: Ed Schooling
CEO: Edwin Schooling
Director Sales: Jack Julier
IT: Edwin Schooling
eschooling@navybrand.com
Estimated Sales: $1.5 Million
Number Employees: 10-19
Square Footage: 200000
Types of Products Distributed:
Frozen Food, General Merchandise, Degreasers, cleaners, etc.

58274 Near East Importing Corporation
8000 Cooper Avenue
Suite 6
Glendale, NY 11385-7734   718-894-3600
Fax: 718-326-2832
Importer and wholesaler/distributor of pistachios, pickled olives and vegetables, sesame butter, meat products, beans, raisins, apricots, cherries, mudberries and spices; also, kitchenware items; serving the food service market
Executive Adminstration: A Anasa
Estimated Sales: $2.5-5 Million
Number Employees: 10-19
Private Brands Carried:
Pyramid; Tamek; Melis
Types of Products Distributed:
Food Service, Frozen Food, General Line, General Merchandise, Provisions/Meat, Produce, Pistachios, pickled vegetables, etc.

58275 Nebraska Bean
85824 519th Ave
Clearwater, NE 68726-5239   402-887-5335
Fax: 402-887-4709 800-253-6502
brett@nebraskabean.com www.nebraskabean.com
Experienced grower, processor and packager of quality popcorn. The fully integrated operation offers microwave, bulk, private label and poly bags of popcorn
President: Brett Morrison
brett@nebraskabean.com
VP: Brett Morrison
Sales: Michelle Steskal
Estimated Sales: $10-20 Million
Number Employees: 20-49
Number of Brands: 1
Square Footage: 10000
Type of Packaging: Consumer, Food Service, Private Label, Bulk
Types of Products Distributed:
Frozen Food

58276 Nectar Soda Company
PO Box 9034
Mandeville, LA 70470-9034   985-674-5444
Fax: 985-674-5442 877-463-2827
www.nectarsoda.com
Wholesaler/distributor of carbonated beverage syrup
President: Susan Dunham
Estimated Sales: $.5-1 million
Number Employees: 1-4
Private Brands Carried:
New Orleans Nectar
Types of Products Distributed:
Frozen Food, General Line, Carbonated beverage syrup

58277 Neel's Wholesale Produce Co
2308 Forest Ave
Knoxville, TN 37916-1021   865-524-1402
Fax: 865-522-0147
Wholesaler/distributor of fresh fruits and vegetables
President/CEO: Martha Watkins
Secretary/Treasurer: Karen Gibson
VP: Rick Bagwell
Quality Control: Tim Gibson
Sales Director: Ron Evans
Public Relations: Steve Manuel
Estimated Sales: $2.5-5 Million
Number Employees: 20-49
Square Footage: 140000
Type of Packaging: Food Service, Bulk
Private Brands Carried:
Foxy Lettuce; Bakewell Potatoes; Cowboy Potatoes; Driscoll Strawberries; etc
Types of Products Distributed:
Food Service, Produce, Specialty Foods

58278 Neelands Refrigeration
4131 Palladium Way
Burlington, ON L7M 0V9
Canada
905-332-4555
Fax: 905-332-7090 sales@neelands.com
www.neelands.com
Wholesaler/distributor of commercial refrigeration fixtures and units; serving the food service market
President: Paul Neelands

Wholesalers & Distributors / A-Z

Number Employees: 20-49
Square Footage: 40000
Private Brands Carried:
  Tyler; Barker; Criosbanc
Types of Products Distributed:
  Food Service, Frozen Food, General Merchandise, Commercial refrigeration fixtures, etc.

58279 Neesvig Meats
4350 Duraform Ln
PO Box 288
Windsor, WI 53598-9671   608-846-1150
    Fax: 608-846-1155   800-633-4494
    www.neesvigs.com
Wholesaler/distributor and exporter of portion control meats
President: Lindabob Flanagan
lflanagan@neesvigs.com
President: Marvin Leppert
COO: Paul Greisen
Sales/Marketing Executive: Lee Fritz
Operations Manager: Matt Meyer
Director Operations/Mail Order: Paul Werwinski
Purchasing Manager: Bob Flanagan
Estimated Sales: $1-3 Million
Number Employees: 100-249
Types of Products Distributed:
  Food Service, Frozen Food, Provisions/Meat, Seafood

58280 Neighbors Coffee
3105 E Reno Ave
Oklahoma City, OK 73117   405-552-2100
    Fax: 405-232-3729   800-299-9016
    sales@neighborscoffee.com
    www.neighborscoffee.com
Coffee; wholesaler/distributor of tea, cocoa and cappuccino
President: Steve Neighbors
Sales Manager: Phil Huggard
Contact: Todd Henson
thenson@executivecoffee.com
Estimated Sales: $100,000
Number Employees: 50-99
Type of Packaging: Consumer, Food Service, Private Label, Bulk
Private Brands Carried:
  Neighbors
Types of Products Distributed:
  Food Service, General Line, General Merchandise, Health Food, Specialty Foods, Tea, cocoa & cappuccino

58281 (HQ)Nelipak
3720 W Washington St
Phoenix, AZ 85009-4765   602-269-7648
  Fax: 602-269-7640 drichardson@flexpakcorp.com
    www.nelipak.com
Thermoformed products including shelf organizers, freezer trays, point of purchase displays and shipping and handling trays; also, contract packaging including club packs, assembly, shrink packaging, display packout, bagging andlabeling
President: Donald Bond
qstein@flexpak.net
CFO: Steve Merray
Quality Control: Carlos Pineda
Marketing Director: Don Richardson
Operations Manager: Rick Colton
Purchasing Manager: Jim Boley
Estimated Sales: $20-50 Million
Number Employees: 100-249
Square Footage: 82000
Type of Packaging: Consumer, Food Service, Private Label, Bulk
Types of Products Distributed:
  Food Service, Frozen Food, General Line, General Merchandise, Health Food, Specialty Foods

58282 Nelson Co
4517 North Point Blvd
Sparrows Point, MD 21219-1798   410-477-3000
    Fax: 410-388-0246 info@nelsoncompany.com
    www.nelsoncompany.com
Wooden pallets and skids; wholesaler/distributor of plastic and metal pallets, shrink and stretch wraps, angleboards and void fillers
President: Arthur Caltrider
IT Executive: John Williams
jack.williams@nelsoncompany.com
Estimated Sales: $5-10 Million
Number Employees: 50-99
Parent Co: Nelson Company
Types of Products Distributed:
  Frozen Food, General Merchandise, Pallets, wraps, etc.

58283 Nelson-Jameson Inc
2400 E 5th St
Marshfield, WI 54449-4661   715-387-1151
    Fax: 715-387-8746   800-826-8302
    sales@nelsonjameson.com
    www.nelsonjameson.com
Wholesale distributor serving food and beverage processors. Wide-line distributor of sanitation, maintenance, laboratory, processing and flow control, personnel and safety supplies
President: Jerry Lippert
j.lippert@nelsonjameson.com
CEO: John Nelson
CEO: Bruce Lautenschlager
Estimated Sales: $50-75 Million
Number Employees: 50-99
Number of Brands: 750+
Other Locations:
  Nelson-Jameson
  Twin Falls, ID
  Nelson-Jameson
  Turlock, CANelson-JamesonTurlock

58284 Nema Food Distribution
18 Commerce Rd.
Suite D
Fairfield, NJ 07004   973-256-4415
    Fax: 973-256-4442 www.nemahalal.com
Halal deli meat, beef, poultry, gyro, cheese, bread, heat & serve
President: Beyhan Nakiboglu   *Year Founded:* 2002
Types of Products Distributed:
  Provisions/Meat

58285 Nesbitt Processing
611 NE 7th Ave
Aledo, IL 61231-1061   309-582-5183
Processor and wholesaler/distributor of beef, pork, lamb, goat and deer; slaughtering services available
President/General Manager: Omar Deeds, Jr.
Secretary/Treasurer: Edith Nesbitt
Number Employees: 3
Type of Packaging: Consumer
Types of Products Distributed:
  Frozen Food, Provisions/Meat, Beef, pork, lamb, goat & deer

58286 Neshaminy Valley Natural Foods
5 Louise Dr
Warminster, PA 18974-1542   215-443-5545
    Fax: 215-443-7087 www.nvorganic.com
Wholesaler/distributor of specialty and natural foods, groceries, general merchandise and frozen foods; serving the food service market
Owner: Philip Margolis
info@nvorganic.com
Vice President: Gene Margolis
VP Operations: Gene Mergolis
Estimated Sales: $20-50 Million
Number Employees: 20-49
Square Footage: 31000
Type of Packaging: Consumer, Food Service, Bulk
Types of Products Distributed:
  Food Service, Frozen Food, General Line, Health Food, Specialty Foods, Organic Products

58287 Nesson Meat Sales
PO Box 28010
Richmond, VA 23228-0010   757-622-6625
    Fax: 757-623-2595
Wholesaler/distributor of meats and groceries; serving the food service market
Owner: Robert Goldwasser
Parent Co: Performance Food Group
Types of Products Distributed:
  Food Service, Frozen Food, General Line, Provisions/Meat, Groceries

58288 NeuRoast
45 Wall St Ct
New York, NY 10005
    info@neuroast.com
    www.neuroast.com
Mushroom-enhanced coffee and coffee creamers
Founder: Alex Curtis
Types of Products Distributed:
  General Line, Health Food

58289 Neuman Distributing Company
225 44th Street
Corpus Christi, TX 78405-3303   361-888-8791
    Fax: 361-888-5950
Wholesaler/distributor of frozen foods, canned goods, soft drinks and dairy and specialty food products
Sales Manager: Carl Kiser
Estimated Sales: $5-10 Million
Number Employees: 5-9
Parent Co: Neuman Distributing Company
Types of Products Distributed:
  Frozen Food, General Line, Specialty Foods, Canned goods, dairy products, etc.

58290 Neutec Group
1 Lenox Ave
Farmingdale, NY 11735   516-870-0877
    Fax: 516-977-3774   888-810-5179
    info@neutecgroup.com www.neutecgroup.com
Manufacturer of technologies for the quality control and research and development laboratory.
Founder & CEO: Ronen Neutra
VP: Orna Zohar-Neutra
Private Brands Carried:
  IUL Instruments, Novasina, Biotool, Videometer, Amphasys

58291 Nevada County Wine Guild
11372 Winter Moon Way
Nevada City, CA 95959   530-265-3662
    855-494-7025
    reachus@ourdailyred.com
Wine
Owner: Tony Norskog
Contact: Donn Berdahl
donn@ourdailyred.com
Estimated Sales: Less than $500,000
Number Employees: 1-4

58292 Nevada Seafood Company
1350 E Glendale Avenue
Sparks, NV 89431-6417   775-331-7052
    Fax: 775-331-7499
Wholesaler/distributor of fresh and frozen seafood
President: Jim Crowell
VP: Jan McNeff
Director: Jean Selmi
Estimated Sales: $10-20 Million
Number Employees: 10-19
Square Footage: 11250
Types of Products Distributed:
  Frozen Food, Seafood

58293 New Atlanta Dairies
115 E Felton Rd
Cartersville, GA 30120   770-382-4404
    Fax: 770-387-2489
Wholesaler/distributor of dairy products
Number Employees: 20-49
Parent Co: Parmalat Bakery Group North America
Types of Products Distributed:
  General Line, Dairy products

58294 New Barn Organics
1400 Valley House Dr
Suite 210
Rohnert Park, CA 94928   707-665-6307
    888-635-7102
    admin@newbarnorganics.com
    www.newbarnorganics.com
Organic almond milk, non-dairy creamer, almond creme, almond dip, non-dairy buttery spread, single-serve coffee
Co-Founder: Dan Conrad
Co-Founder/CEO: Ted Robb
COO/CFO: Louis Kanganis
VP Innovation & Marketing: Darleen Scherer
VP Sales: Richard Tidrow
Year Founded: 2015
Number Employees: 20-49
Types of Products Distributed:
  General Line

58295 New Beer Distributors
167 Chrystie St
New York, NY 10002-2809   212-473-8757
    Fax: 212-260-2033 nubeer@aol.com
Wholesaler/distributor of beer, soda, spring and mineral water; serving the food service market
Contact: Beatriz Ruiz
bruiz84910@aol.com
Manager: Lisa Ruiz

Wholesalers & Distributors / A-Z

Estimated Sales: $1-2.5 Million
Number Employees: 1-4
Number of Customer Locations: 500
Types of Products Distributed:
  Food Service, Frozen Food, General Line, Beer, soda, spring & mineral water

58296 New Britain Candy Company
27 Mill Street
Berlin, CT 06037-2351   860-828-4501
  Fax: 860-257-7495 800-382-0515
Wholesaler/distributor of candies, nuts and diet and gourmet products
President: Raymond Hill
Number Employees: 1-4
Types of Products Distributed:
  General Line, Health Food, Specialty Foods, Candies, nuts, etc.

58297 New Brunswick Saw Service
5 Greek Lane
Edison, NJ 08817-2508   732-287-4466
  Fax: 732-287-0148 www.nbssfoodequipment.com
Wholesaler/distributor of restaurant and meat room equipment; serving the food service market
President: Charles Bonapace
Sales Director: Norman Wright
nw@nbssfoodequipment.com
Administration: Robert Bonapace
Estimated Sales: $5-10 Million
Number Employees: 20-49
Types of Products Distributed:
  Food Service, Frozen Food, General Merchandise, Restaurant & meat room equipment

58298 New England Foods
1084 Hartford Tpke
Vernon, CT 06066-4413   860-872-9960
  Fax: 860-871-0546
Wholesaler/distributor of frozen food, provisions and meat, produce, and seafood
Estimated Sales: $5-10 Million
Number Employees: 20-49
Number of Brands: 150
Number of Products: 4500
Square Footage: 160000
Private Brands Carried:
  Pocahontas Foods; Nutmeg Farms; New England Foods
Number of Customer Locations: 750
Types of Products Distributed:
  Food Service, Frozen Food, General Line, General Merchandise, Provisions/Meat, Produce, Rack Jobbers, Seafood

58299 New England Indl Truck Inc
195 Wildwood Ave
Woburn, MA 01801-2024   781-935-9105
  Fax: 781-938-3879 www.neit.com
Wholesaler/distributor of material handling equipment
President: Richard Rossi
VP: James Hall
Estimated Sales: $10-20 Million
Number Employees: 50-99
Square Footage: 110000
Private Brands Carried:
  Nissan; B.T.; Teledyne
Types of Products Distributed:
  Frozen Food, General Merchandise, Material handling equipment

58300 New England Meat Company
60 Walnut Street
Peabody, MA 01960   978-531-0846
  Fax: 978-532-4283 nemeat.com
Wholesaler/distributor of frozen foods, groceries, meats, private label items, seafood and specialty food items
President: Walter Kushner
Contact: Bessie Silva
bsilva@nemeat.com
Estimated Sales: $2.5-5 Million
Number Employees: 1-4
Square Footage: 60000
Type of Packaging: Bulk
Number of Customer Locations: 1000
Types of Products Distributed:
  Frozen Food, General Line, Provisions/Meat, Seafood, Specialty Foods, Groceries & private label items

58301 New Harbor Fisherman's Cooperative
PO Box 125
New Harbor, ME 04554-0125   207-677-2791
  Fax: 207-677-3835 866-883-2922
Lobster, crab and other seafood
Manager: Linda Vannah
Operations Manager: Ken Tonneson
Estimated Sales: $1 million
Number Employees: 1-4
Type of Packaging: Consumer, Bulk
Types of Products Distributed:
  Seafood

58302 New Hope Imports
PO Box 99
Lahaska, PA 18931-0099   215-249-8484
  Fax: 215-249-9910 newhope5@juno.com
Importer and wholesaler/distributor of health supplements including proteins, herbs, dried sea kelp, etc
President: Cheryl Alber
Secretary/Treasurer: Otto Alber
Number Employees: 1-4
Square Footage: 8000
Types of Products Distributed:
  Frozen Food, General Line, Health Food, Herbs, dried sea kelp & proteins

58303 New Jersey Provision Co
350 Indiana St
Union, NJ 07083-4253   908-686-0111
Wholesaler/distributor and packer of meat products and groceries
Owner: David Olivieri
Estimated Sales: $5-10 Million
Number Employees: 1-4
Types of Products Distributed:
  Frozen Food, General Line, Provisions/Meat, Cold cuts & groceries

58304 New Mexico Food Distributors
3041 University Blvd SE
Albuquerque, NM 87106-5040   505-888-0104
  Fax: 505-889-3144 800-637-7084
  www.foodsofnewmexico.com
Processor and wholesaler/distributor of Mexican food products including enchiladas, corn and flour tortillas, green chili, roasted and red chili powders
Plant Manager: Mike Campos
Estimated Sales: $12 Million
Number Employees: 85
Type of Packaging: Consumer, Food Service
Types of Products Distributed:
  Food Service, Frozen Food, General Line, Specialty Foods, Enchiladas, tortillas, etc.

58305 New Nissi Corp.
529 E 39th St
Paterson, NJ 07504   973-278-4400
  info@newnissi.com
  www.nuttycrunchers.com
Natural nut and seed brittles
Founder: Steve Kim
steve.kim@newnissi.com
Year Founded: 1986
Number Employees: 1-4

58306 New Ocean
3077 Mccall Dr # 12
Suite 12
Doraville, GA 30340-2832   770-458-5235
  Fax: 770-485-5235
Seafood, shrimp, scallops, king crab, lobster tails, snow crab
President: Mei Lin
Estimated Sales: Less Than $500,000
Number Employees: 5-9

58307 New Organics
600 Lawnwood Road
Kenwood, CA 95452   734-677-5570
  Fax: 707-833-0105
Organic ingredient supplier-grains, sweetners, oils, soy powders
President: Jethren Phillips
Manager: Mathew Keegan
Estimated Sales: $17.5 Million
Number Employees: 74
Number of Brands: 3
Number of Products: 100
Square Footage: 25000
Type of Packaging: Bulk

Other Locations:
  American Health & Nutrition
  Eaton Rapids, MI American Health & Nutrition
Private Brands Carried:
  Soy N Ergy, Organic Harvest and Organic Garden

58308 New Orleans Gulf Seafood
509 Commerce Pt
New Orleans, LA 70123-3203   504-733-1516
  Fax: 504-733-1517
Seafood
President: Albert Lin

58309 New Vermont Creamery
70 Atwood St
Providence, RI 02909   401-946-6530
  Fax: 401-946-6683
Wholesaler/distributor of cooked meats, dairy products, frozen foods and general merchandise; serving the food service market
Owner: Ken Garber
Estimated Sales: $5-10 Million
Number Employees: 5-9
Number of Customer Locations: 300
Types of Products Distributed:
  Food Service, Frozen Food, General Line, General Merchandise, Provisions/Meat, Dairy products

58310 New York Cash Register Company
2010 Coney Island Ave
Brooklyn, NY 11223   718-375-5551
  Fax: 718-998-8012 800-427-4687
Wholesaler/distributor of cash registers and touch screen point of sale systems; serving the food service market
Manager: Randi Staiti
Estimated Sales: $2.5-5 Million
Number Employees: 10-19
Types of Products Distributed:
  Food Service, Frozen Food, General Merchandise, Cash registers & point of sale systems

58311 New Zealand Lamb Co
19840 S Rancho Way # 101
#101
Compton, CA 90220-6321   310-885-4855
  Fax: 310-885-4966
Importer and wholesaler/distributor of frozen and refrigerated lamb, beef, venison, goat and mutton.
President: Shane O'Hara
Vice President of Operations: Bill Mcmichael
Estimated Sales: $5 Million
Number Employees: 20-49
Number of Brands: 2
Parent Co: The Lamb Co-Operative Inc
Type of Packaging: Consumer, Food Service
Private Brands Carried:
  New Zealand Spring Lamb, Opal Valley
Number of Customer Locations: 5
Types of Products Distributed:
  Food Service, Frozen Food, Provisions/Meat

58312 NewStar Fresh Foods LLC
850 Work St.
Suite 101
Salinas, CA 93901   831-758-7800
  Fax: 831-758-7869 info@newstarfresh.com
  www.newstarfresh.com
Fresh asparagus, iceless green onions, cilantro, spinach, etc.
President/CEO: Anthony Vasquez
Year Founded: 1996
Estimated Sales: $26.1 Million
Number Employees: 250-499
Square Footage: 20000
Type of Packaging: Consumer, Food Service, Private Label, Bulk
Types of Products Distributed:
  Food Service, Produce, Asparagus

58313 Neway Packaging Corporation
19730 Magellan Dr
Torrance, CA 90502   310-771-1400
  Fax: 310-323-4463 mail@newaypkg.com
  newaypackaging.com
Wholesaler/distributor of packaging equipment and supplies including shrink and stretch wrap, straps, tape and vacuum packaging supplies

Wholesalers & Distributors / A-Z

President: Russ Freebury
Vice President: Sarah Bell
Contact: Russell Freebury
russell.freebury@newaypkg.com
General Manager: Kim Guerrero
Estimated Sales: $20-50 Million
Number Employees: 85
Square Footage: 70000
Types of Products Distributed:
  Frozen Food, General Merchandise, Packaging materials

58314 Newman Fixture Co Inc
606 W Gaines St
Monticello, AR 71655-4640   870-367-6218
          Fax: 870-367-3850 800-499-8503
Wholesaler/distributor of food service equipment including grills, fryers, stoves, office furnishings, desks, chairs, etc.; serving the food service market and grocery stores
Owner: Tommy Newman
newman5@ipa.net
VP: Tommy Newman
General Manager: Jim Newman
Estimated Sales: $2.5-5 Million
Number Employees: 5-9
Square Footage: 21600
Private Brands Carried:
  Decker; Star; Terrue; USA Manufacturing; Prince Castle; Penn
Number of Customer Locations: 400
Types of Products Distributed:
  Food Service, Frozen Food, General Merchandise, Grills, fryers, stoves, etc.

58315 Newmeadows Lobster Inc
60 Portland Pier
Portland, ME 04101-4713   207-775-1612
          Fax: 207-874-2456 800-668-1612
Lobster
Owner: Patricia Burch
patriciaburch@newmeadowslobster.com
Estimated Sales: $5-10 Million
Number Employees: 10-19

58316 Newport Marketing
139 E 28th St
Houston, TX 77008-2131   713-880-1591
          Fax: 713-880-1595
Wholesaler/distributor of cooking equipment, catering and restaurant supplies, ice machinery, snack displays and refrigeration equipment
Owner: Edward St Aubyn
Export Sales: Yitza Cosenza
VP Sales: Guy St. Aubyn
General Manager: Ed St. Aubyn
Estimated Sales: $2.5-5 Million
Number Employees: 1-4
Types of Products Distributed:
  Frozen Food, General Merchandise, Cooking equipment, ice machinery, etc.

58317 Newtech Beverage Systems
Suite 205-9485 189th Street
Surrey, BC V4N 5L8
Canada   604-882-6940
          Fax: 604-882-6870 800-459-2882
          www.newtechbeverage.com
Wholesaler/distributor of general merchandise including airpots, thermal coffee dispensers, servers and plastic and wire stands and racks; serving the food service market
President: Ted Chupa
Number Employees: 7
Square Footage: 12000
Private Brands Carried:
  Coffee Karafe
Types of Products Distributed:
  Food Service, Frozen Food, General Merchandise, Airpots, coffee dispensers, etc.

58318 (HQ)Newton Manufacturing Co
1123 1st Ave E
PO Box 927
Newton, IA 50208-3914   641-792-4121
          Fax: 641-792-6261 800-500-7227
Wholesaler/distributor of advertising specialties and gifts
President: Jerome Hoxton
Cio/Cto: David Wexler
dwexler@newtonmfg.com
Treasurer/Secretary: Lee Cochran
VP Sales: Bill Wilder
Number Employees: 100-249

Other Locations:
  Newton Manufacturing Co.
  Owatonna, MNNewton Manufacturing Co.
Types of Products Distributed:
  Frozen Food, General Merchandise, Advertising specialties & gifts

58319 Nhs Labs Inc
11665 W State St
Star, ID 83669-5223   208-939-5100
          Fax: 208-939-5100 888-546-8694
          info@nutritionmanufacturer.com
          www.nutritionmanufacturer.com
Private label sports drinks, supplements, and energy drinks
CEO: Larry Leach
Number Employees: 50-99
Square Footage: 74000

58320 Niagara Restaurant Supply
17 Lloyd Street
St. Catharines, ON L2S 2N7
Canada   905-685-8428
          Fax: 905-685-0200 800-387-9306
Wholesaler/distributor of restaurant supplies including cooking and serving equipment, china, glassware, cutlery, pots, pans and furniture; serving the food service market
President: Tom DeCiccio
Office Manager: Janis Kellestine
Number Employees: 5-9
Square Footage: 24000
Types of Products Distributed:
  Food Service, Frozen Food, General Merchandise, Restaurant supplies

58321 Nicewonger Company
19219 68th Ave S Ste M103
Kent, WA 98032   425-656-0903
          Fax: 425-656-0907 800-732-1236
          www.jgneil.com
Wholesaler/distributor of restaurant equipment including fryers, broilers, espresso, ice cream, etc.; serving the food service market
Owner: Jim Neil
VP: Paul Griff
Sales Manager: Larry Sandusky
Service Manager: Steve Kitley
Estimated Sales: $2.5-5 Million
Number Employees: 10-19
Square Footage: 40000
Private Brands Carried:
  Taylor; Cookshack; Crispy Lite
Types of Products Distributed:
  Food Service, Frozen Food, General Merchandise, Restaurant equipment

58322 Nicholas & Co Inc
5520 W Harold Gatty Dr
Salt Lake City, UT 84116   801-531-1100
          800-873-3663
          custservice@nicholasandco.com
          www.nicholasandco.com
Wholesaler/distributor of seafood, groceries, meats, produce, dairy products, frozen foods, baked goods, equipment and fixtures, general merchandise and private label items.
President & CEO: Peter Mouskondis
peter.mouskkondis@nicholasandco.com
Co-CEO: Nicole Mouskondis
Year Founded: 1939
Estimated Sales: $50-100 Million
Number Employees: 500-999
Square Footage: 175000
Type of Packaging: Consumer, Food Service, Private Label, Bulk
Private Brands Carried:
  Nugget
Number of Customer Locations: 4000
Types of Products Distributed:
  Food Service, Frozen Food, General Line, General Merchandise, Provisions/Meat, Produce, Seafood, Groceries, etc.

58323 Nichols Foodservice
P.O.Box 729
Wallace, NC 28466   910-285-3197
          Fax: 910-285-3596 800-768-3404
Wholesaler/distributor of produce, equipment and fixtures, health and beauty aids and seafood; serving the food service market

President: J Nichols
CEO: Jl Nichols Iii
Contact: Erika Ronco
eronco@nicholsfoodservice.com
VP Purchasing: Joe Brinson
Estimated Sales: $20-50 Million
Number Employees: 50-99
Square Footage: 60000
Private Brands Carried:
  Nifda
Number of Customer Locations: 700
Types of Products Distributed:
  Food Service, Frozen Food, General Merchandise, Produce, Seafood

58324 Nick Sciabica & Sons
2150 Yosemite Blvd
Modesto, CA 95354-3931   209-577-5067
          Fax: 209-524-5367 800-551-9612
          www.baginfusti.com
Extra-virgin olive oil; importer of olive oil, pasta and tomato products; wholesaler/distributor of wine vinegar, olive oil, canned tomatoes, olives and pasta
Partner: Jonathan Sciabica
Controller: Susan Ochoa
VP: Gemma Sciabica
Marketing Manager: Dean Cohan
Production Manager: Daniel Sciabica
Estimated Sales: $2.5 Million
Number Employees: 20-49
Number of Brands: 6
Number of Products: 150
Square Footage: 274912
Type of Packaging: Consumer, Food Service, Private Label, Bulk
Number of Customer Locations: 250
Types of Products Distributed:
  Frozen Food, General Line, Specialty Foods, Wine vinegar, olive oil, olives, etc.

58325 Nicky USA Inc
223 SE 3rd Ave
Portland, OR 97214-1006   503-234-4263
          Fax: 503-234-8268 800-469-4162
          info@nickyusa.com
          www.nickyusa.com
Distributor of natural game birds and meats including pheasant, poussin, quail, venison, buffalo, rabbit, ostrich, alligator, ducks and wild boar; also, sausage, veal, free-range lamb
Owner, President: Geoff Latham
glatham@nickyusa.com
VP: Melody Latham
Sales Office Manager: Ursula McVittie
Production Manager: Jace Hentges
Estimated Sales: $4 Million
Number Employees: 20-49
Square Footage: 20000
Type of Packaging: Consumer, Food Service, Private Label, Bulk
Private Brands Carried:
  Nicky USA
Types of Products Distributed:
  Food Service, Health Food, Provisions/Meat

58326 Nielsen-Massey Vanillas Inc
1550 Shields Dr
Waukegan, IL 60085-8307   847-578-1550
          Fax: 847-578-1570 800-525-7873
          info@nielsenmassey.com www.nielsenmassey.com
Manufacturer of vanilla extracts and pure flavors
CEO: Kirk Trofholz
VP, Global Sales: Brent Allen
Director of Sales: Dan Fox
Year Founded: 1907
Estimated Sales: $20-50 Million
Number Employees: 20-49
Number of Brands: 1
Square Footage: 100500
Type of Packaging: Consumer, Food Service, Bulk
Other Locations:
  Nielsen-Massey Vanillas Inter. B.V.
  Leeuwarden, NetherlandsNielsen-Massey Vanillas Inter. B.V.
Private Brands Carried:
  Nielsen-Massey
Types of Products Distributed:
  Specialty Foods

58327 Night Owls Wholesale Market
723 W 3rd St
Chester, PA 19013-3807   610-874-6256
          Fax: 610-874-6259
Fruit, produce

Wholesalers & Distributors / A-Z

Owner: Joseph Lavella
Co-Owner: Carmen Lavella
Co-Owner: Gabriel Lavella
Estimated Sales: Under $500,000
Number Employees: 1-4

58328 Nikki's Coconut Butter
Hudson, WI
nikki@nikkiscoconutbutter.com
www.nikkiscoconutbutter.com
Coconut butter spreads and chocolate bars
Owner: Andrew Frezza
Owner/CEO: Nikki Frezza
Types of Products Distributed:
   General Line

58329 Nikol Foods
85 Webster St
Pawtucket, RI 02861   401-724-7810
         Fax: 401-725-0891
Wholesaler/distributor and broker of specialty and nonperishable items including pasta, cookies and coffee
Owner: Michael Silva
VP: Bill Gianetti
Estimated Sales: $20-50 Million
Number Employees: 20-49
Number of Customer Locations: 200
Types of Products Distributed:
   Frozen Food, General Line, Specialty Foods, Cookies, coffee & pasta

58330 Nikola's Foods
8301 Grand Ave S
#110
Bloomington, MN 55420   952-229-4183
   Fax: 952-253-5995 888-645-6527
sales@nikolasbakery.com www.nikolasbakery.com
A manufacturing and baking company that offers a full line of bakery products including muffins, cakes, dessert breads, cookies, croissants and macaroons; produces gluten free, organic and kosher products.
Director of Development and Innovation: Michael Itskovich
Contact: Gregory Noah
gnoah@nikolasbakery.com
Estimated Sales: $3.5 Million
Number Employees: 12
Type of Packaging: Consumer, Food Service
Types of Products Distributed:
   General Merchandise

58331 Nisbet Oyster Company
7081 Niawaukum St Hwy 101
P.O. Box 338
Bay Center, WA 98527-0338   360-875-6629
   Fax: 360-875-6684 888-875-6629
sales@goosepoint.com www.goosepoint.com
Processor and exporter of Pacific and farm oysters; Pacific oyster farm operations; retail and food service products fresh and frozen
President, Owner: David Nisbet
Owner: Maureene Nisbet
Sales Manager: Josh Valdiz
Plant Manager: Kathleen Nisbet
Purchasing: Geoff Clarine
Estimated Sales: $10 Million
Number Employees: 75
Number of Brands: 1
Number of Products: 3
Square Footage: 12800
Private Brands Carried:
   Goose Point Oysters

58332 Nissan Lift Of New YorkInc
420 Highland Ave Ext
Middletown, NY 10940-4450   845-343-8615
   Fax: 845-342-3627 800-238-6278
Wholesaler/distributor of forklifts
Vice President: Paul Derderian
pderderian@ihslift.com
VP: Paul Derderian
Estimated Sales: $10-20 Million
Number Employees: 20-49
Private Brands Carried:
   Neissan; Prime Mover
Types of Products Distributed:
   Frozen Food, General Merchandise, Forklifts

58333 Nita Crisp Crackers LLC
454 S. Link Lane
Fort Collins, CO 80524   970-482-9090
   Fax: 970-482-1043 866-493-4609
www.nitacrisp.com
Artisan flatbreads in small batches or in bulk to natural grocers, specialty food stores, and restaurants from coast to coast
Managing Partner: Steve Landry
CEO: Paul Pellegrino
Customer Service / Sales: Michele Hattman
Estimated Sales: $170,000
Number of Products: 1
Square Footage: 5614
Type of Packaging: Consumer, Food Service, Bulk

58334 No Cow
1526 Blake St
Suite 200
Denver, CO 80202
info@nocow.com
nocow.com
Non-dairy bars, butters and cookies
Founder: Daniel Katz
Number of Brands: 1
Number of Products: 3

58335 Noah's Potato Chip Co
2725 Lee St
Alexandria, LA 71301-4316   318-445-0283
Wholesaler/distributor of potato and tortilla chips, pretzels, peanuts and cheese puffs
Owner: Stanley Bohrer
Estimated Sales: $1-2.5 Million
Number Employees: 1-4
Private Brands Carried:
   Guy's; Noah's; Tender Delight Corn Products
Types of Products Distributed:
   Frozen Food, General Line, Potato & tortilla chips, pretzels, etc.

58336 (HQ)Noble Harvest
P.O.Box 612
Edgemont, PA 19028-0612   610-353-5400
   Fax: 610-284-5202 lorimer@voicenet.com
Wholesaler/distributor, importer and exporter of specialty foods, wine, olive oil and beer
Owner: David N Goane
Public Relations: Nicola Gentili
Manager European Operations: Luciano Lambrughi
Estimated Sales: $1-3 Million
Number Employees: 1-4
Square Footage: 20000
Other Locations:
   Noble Harvest Ltd.
   MilanoNoble Harvest Ltd.
Private Brands Carried:
   Villa Foscari; La Cascina; La Filera; Roagna; Trevi; Sommaia
Types of Products Distributed:
   Frozen Food, General Line, Specialty Foods, Wine, olive oil, beer, etc.

58337 Nogales Fruit & Vegetables Dst
2660 N Donna Ave
Nogales, AZ 85621-3568   520-281-0134
   Fax: 520-281-4669
Wholesaler/distributor of produce
President/Sales Manager: Artura Parra
Estimated Sales: $3-5 Million
Number Employees: 5-9
Types of Products Distributed:
   Frozen Food, Produce

58338 Nogg Chemical & Paper Company
6260 Abbott Dr
Omaha, NE 68110-2805   402-453-6644
   Fax: 402-453-5966 800-279-6644
Wholesaler/distributor of janitorial, paper and chemical supplies
President: Rick Faber
COO: Shelley Riha
VP: D Christinson
Contact: Matt Bridges
bridges@nogg.com
Estimated Sales: $20-50 Million
Number Employees: 100-249
Square Footage: 45000
Types of Products Distributed:
   Frozen Food, General Line, Janitorial, paper & chemical supplies

58339 Noh Foods Of Hawaii
2043 S Beretania St # C
Honolulu, HI 96826-1344   808-944-0655
   Fax: 808-944-0830 nohfoods@nohfoods.com
www.nohfoods.com
International seasonings, sauces and drink mixes
President: Raymond Noh
nohfoods@nohfoods.com
CFO: Miriam Noh
Vice President: Howard Noh
Estimated Sales: $3.5 Million
Number Employees: 10-19
Square Footage: 48000
Parent Co: E&M Corp.

58340 Noh Foods of Hawaii
1402 W 178th St
Gardena, CA 90248-3202   808-944-0655
customerservice@nohfoods.com
www.nohfoods.com
International seasonings, sauces and drink mixes
President: Raymond Noh
Number Employees: 4
Square Footage: 35200
Parent Co: E&M Corporation
Type of Packaging: Consumer, Food Service, Bulk
Other Locations:
   NOH Foods of Hawaii
   Honolulu, HINOH Foods of Hawaii

58341 Nona Vegan Foods
Toronto, ON
Canada   416-836-9387
info@nonavegan.com
www.nonavegan.com
Dairy free, gluten free, preservative free creamy pasta sauces including alfredo, cheesy, and carbonara styles
Founder: Kailey Gilchrist   *Year Founded:* 2013
Types of Products Distributed:
   General Line

58342 (HQ)Noon Hour Food ProductsInc
215 N Desplaines St # 1
Floor One
Chicago, IL 60661-1072   312-382-1177
   Fax: 312-382-9420 800-621-6636
Processor and importer of salted, canned and pickled fish, cheese and groceries
President: Paul Buhl
Executive VP: P Scott Buhl
Marketing Manager: Tyler Swanberg
Operations Manager: William Buhl
Estimated Sales: $6.7 Million
Number Employees: 20-49
Square Footage: 620000
Type of Packaging: Food Service
Other Locations:
   Noon Hour Food Products
   Minneapolis, MNNoon Hour Food Products
Types of Products Distributed:
   Food Service, Seafood

58343 Norben Co
38052 Euclid Ave # 209
PO Box 766
Willoughby, OH 44094-6146   440-951-2715
   Fax: 440-951-1366 888-466-7236
sales@norbencompany.com
www.norbencompany.com
Wholesaler/distributor of ingredients including silicone anti-foams, pea protein and fibers, citric acid, potassium sorbate and re-agent and semi acids
President: B J Kresnye
bjkresnye@norbencompany.com
VP Sales: J Kusar
Sales Representative: J Kresnye
Estimated Sales: $1 Million
Number Employees: 5-9
Types of Products Distributed:
   Frozen Food, General Line, Ingredients

58344 Norcal Beverage Co
2150 Stone Blvd
West Sacramento, CA 95691   916-372-0600
   Fax: 916-374-2605 www.ncbev.com
Producer and wholesaler/distributor of beers, hard ciders, and nonalcoholic beverages. Also contract manufacturing and equipment solutions.

Wholesalers & Distributors / A-Z

President & CEO: Shannon Deary-Bell
Chairman: Donald Deary
EVP, Marketing & External Affairs: Roy Grant Deary III
EVP, Transportation & Logistics: Timothy Deary
Year Founded: 1937
Estimated Sales: $36.7 Million
Number Employees: 500-999
Square Footage: 152000
Type of Packaging: Consumer, Food Service, Bulk
Types of Products Distributed:
Food Service, Frozen Food, General Line, Beverages

58345 Norfolk Packing Company
620 E Olney Road
Norfolk, VA 23510-2991   757-622-3216
Fax: 757-624-9115   800-874-7162
Wholesaler/distributor serving the institutional food service market
President: J Cohen
Secretary/Treasurer: R Cohen
Estimated Sales: $10-20 Million
Number Employees: 1-4
Number of Customer Locations: 200
Types of Products Distributed:
Food Service, Frozen Food

58346 Norland Products Inc
2540 US Highway 130 # 100
Cranbury, NJ 08512-3519   609-395-1966
Fax: 609-395-9006   sales@norlandproducts.com
www.norlandproducts.com
Wholesaler/distributor of kosher fish gelatin and hydrolized fish collagen.
President: Eric Norland
enorland@norlandproducts.com
VP: Richard Norland
Estimated Sales: $10-20 Million
Number Employees: 20-49
Square Footage: 30000
Type of Packaging: Bulk
Types of Products Distributed:
Frozen Food, Seafood

58347 Norlift Inc
512 N Fancher Rd
Spokane Valley, WA 99212-1014   509-535-0066
Fax: 509-535-0066   800-666-1774
www.norlift.com
Wholesaler/distributor of material handling equipment
President: Jay Jarvis
jjarvis@norlift.com
Estimated Sales: $10-20 Million
Number Employees: 20-49
Private Brands Carried:
Lyon; Interlake; Toyota; Clark
Types of Products Distributed:
Frozen Food, General Merchandise, Material handling equipment

58348 Norm's Refrigeration
1175 N Knollwood Cir
Anaheim, CA 92801-1332   714-236-4174
Fax: 714-236-0607   800-933-4423
www.normsrefrigeration.com
Wholesaler/distributor of refrigeration equipment; serving the food service market
Owner: Richard Hatfield
Vice President: Tim DE Bine
tim@normsrefrigeration.com
Estimated Sales: $10-20 Million
Number Employees: 20-49
Private Brands Carried:
,Kelvinator, bogt,Iceomatic,
Beverageair,,Remcor,Follet
Types of Products Distributed:
Food Service, Frozen Food, General Merchandise, Refrigeration equipment

58349 Norman Wolff Associates
39 W 19th Street
New York, NY 10011-4225   212-255-4300
Fax: 212-255-4331
Wholesaler/distributor of general merchandise including advertising specialties and food baskets; custom stamping available
Pres.: Stanley Weintraub
Number Employees: 5-9
Parent Co: Advertising Gifts
Types of Products Distributed:
Frozen Food, General Merchandise, Advertising specialties & food baskets

58350 Norman's
86 Division St S
Battle Creek, MI 49017-4197   269-968-6136
Fax: 269-968-6988
Wholesaler/distributor of frozen food, produce and meat products/provisions; serving the food service market
President: W Norman
Contact: Gary Norman
gnorman@normans.com
Estimated Sales: $20-50 Million
Number Employees: 50-99
Number of Customer Locations: 1000
Types of Products Distributed:
Food Service, Frozen Food, Provisions/Meat, Produce

58351 Norman's Wholesale Grocery Company
P.O.Box 67
Bloomingdale, NY 12913   518-891-1890
Wholesaler/distributor of general line products; serving the food service market
President: Arthur Niederbuhl
Estimated Sales: $1-3 Million
Number Employees: 1-4
Number of Customer Locations: 95
Types of Products Distributed:
Food Service, Frozen Food, General Line

58352 Norpaco Inc
80 Bysiewicz Dr
Middletown, CT 06457-7564   860-632-2299
Fax: 860-632-2150   800-252-0222
www.norpaco.com
Manufacturer of Italian-style specialty food products.
Owner: Dean Spilka
dean@norpaco.com
CEO: Donald Spilka
Estimated Sales: F
Number Employees: 1-4
Type of Packaging: Consumer, Private Label, Bulk
Types of Products Distributed:
Frozen Food, General Merchandise, Bar supplies

58353 North American Corp
2101 Claire Ct
Glenview, IL 60025   847-832-4000
Fax: 847-832-4010   800-323-0297
www.na.com
Wholesaler/distributor of paper products and janitorial and packaging equipment; serving the food service market.
President: John Miller
Vice President, Operations: Greg Turrick
Estimated Sales: $100-500 Million
Number Employees: 250-499
Number of Customer Locations: 1500
Types of Products Distributed:
Food Service, Frozen Food, General Merchandise, Paper products

58354 North American Provisioners
5800 Franklin Street
Suite 101
Denver, CO 80216-1249   303-831-1299
Fax: 303-831-1292   888-289-2833
Wholesaler and exporter of buffalo and game meat products
CFO: Rusty Seedig
Sales: Mary Gonsior
Operations: Mike Sobieski
VP Production/Distribution: Jerry Getka
Purchasing: Bruce Klein
Estimated Sales: $2.5-5 Million
Number Employees: 10-19
Number of Products: 300
Square Footage: 120000
Parent Co: New West Foods
Type of Packaging: Consumer, Food Service, Bulk
Private Brands Carried:
New West Foods, Buffalo Nickel, Dales Wild West, Denver Buffalo
Types of Products Distributed:
Food Service, Frozen Food, Health Food, Provisions/Meat, Specialty Foods

58355 North Atlantic Inc
12 Portland Fish Pier # A
Portland, ME 04101-4620   207-774-6025
Fax: 207-774-1614   www.northatlanticseafood.com
President: Jerry Knecht
jerry@northatlanticseafood.com
Estimated Sales: $10-20 Million
Number Employees: 10-19

58356 North Atlantic Lobster
107 Water St
Danvers, MA 01923-3727   978-777-0010
Fax: 978-762-6436   nalc@aol.com
Wholesaler/distributor of live lobsters; international shipping services available
Manager: Hank Rimkewicz
General Manager: H Rimkewicz
Estimated Sales: $1-2.5 Million
Number Employees: 10-19
Square Footage: 56000
Number of Customer Locations: 5000
Types of Products Distributed:
Seafood, Live lobsters

58357 North Atlantic Seafood
12a Portland Fish Pier
PO Box 682
Portland, ME 4101   207-774-6025
800-774-6025
info@northatlanticseafood.com
www.northatlanticseafood.com
Seafood including, bass, flounder, clams, cod, emperor, grouper, haddock, hake, halibut, lobster, mahi mahi, monk, mussels, oysters, perch, pollack, salmon, scallops, seabass, shark, shrimp, snapper, swordfish, tilapia, tuna andsole
Owner and Founder: Gerald Knecht
Chief Executive Officer: Terry Harriman
CFO: Stewart Wooden
VP & General Manager: Michael Norton
Quality Assurance Specialist: Jon Greenberg
Senior Sales Team Leader: Chris Bowker
Shipping/Receiving & Production Lead: Patrick Malia
Director of Procurement: Kevin Bolduc
Number Employees: 10-19

58358 North Bay Seafood
PO Box 832
Agoura Hills, CA 91376-0832   818-889-8316
Fax: 818-889-4860
Owner: Howard Gordon

58359 North Carolina Potato Association
1205 McPherson St
PO Box 2066
Elizabeth City, NC 27909-4664   252-331-4773
Fax: 252-331-4775   tommy.fleetwood@ncagr.gov
www.ncagr.gov/markets/commodit/horticul/potatoes/index.htm
Wholesaler/distributor of white potatoes
Manager: Tommy Fleetwood
tommy.fleetwood@ncagr.gov
Marketing Center Manager (Northeast): William Small
Marketing Specialist: Tommy Fleetwood
Marketing Specialist: John Atdlett
Number Employees: 1-4
Types of Products Distributed:
Frozen Food, Produce, White potatoes

58360 North Central Co
601 Carlson Pkwy
Suite 400
Minnetonka, MN 55305   952-449-0885
www.northcentralco.com
Wholesaler/distributor of meat and dairy products and grains, oils, proteins, seafood.
President: Larry Zilverberg
lzilverbergncc@aol.com
Chief Financial Officer: Jim Reidy
Marketing Director: Dan Zilverberg
Product Development: Zach Siegle
Year Founded: 1984
Estimated Sales: $60 Million
Number Employees: 20-49
Number of Customer Locations: 500
Types of Products Distributed:
Frozen Food, Provisions/Meat, Dairy products-cheeses

58361 North Pacific Seafoods Inc
4 Nickerson St
Suite 400
Seattle, WA 98109   206-726-9900
Fax: 206-352-7421
www.northpacificseafoods.com
Wild Alaska seafood products.

1115

Wholesalers & Distributors / A-Z

President: Hisashi Sugiyama

58362 North Side Banana Co
2554 Airline Dr
Houston, TX 77009 713-869-4325
Fax: 713-869-6620 www.northsidebanana.com
Wholesaler/distributor of produce.
Contact: Randy Henderson
Rhenderson@Northsidebanana.com
Year Founded: 1958
Estimated Sales: $20-50 Million
Number Employees: 50-99
Types of Products Distributed:
Frozen Food, Produce

58363 North West Handling Systems Inc
1100 SW 7th St
Renton, WA 98057 425-255-0500
Fax: 425-228-6946 800-426-3888
www.nwhs.com
Wholesaler/distributor of forklifts, conveyors, shelving and parts.
National Accounts: James Franck
Year Founded: 1971
Estimated Sales: $50-100 Million
Number Employees: 100-249
Other Locations:
Union Gap, WA
Spokane, WA
Anchorage, AK
Portland, OR
Albany, ORSpokane
Private Brands Carried:
Crown; Serco; Rytec
Types of Products Distributed:
Frozen Food, General Merchandise, Forklifts, etc.

58364 Northbay Restaurant Equipment & Design
3600 Standish Avenue
Suite A
Santa Rosa, CA 95407-8143 707-792-2345
Fax: 707-795-0414
Wholesaler/distributor of restaurant equipment and supplies including tables, chairs, espresso machines, etc.; serving the food service market; design services available
Owner: Bill Romaine
Administrative Assistant: Lillian Petker
Estimated Sales: Less than $500,000
Number Employees: 1-4
Square Footage: 16000
Types of Products Distributed:
Food Service, Frozen Food, General Merchandise, Restaurant equipment & supplies

58365 Northern Haserot
21500 Alexander Rd
Cleveland, OH 44146 440-439-0600
Fax: 440-439-1990 800-589-5500
www.northernhaserot.com
Custom cut meats, seafood and produce.
Chief Executive Officer: Douglas Kern
Sales & Marketing: Kate Koren
Inventory Control: Tim Ryan
Year Founded: 1878
Estimated Sales: $100-500 Million
Number Employees: 100-249
Types of Products Distributed:
Provisions/Meat, Produce, Seafood

58366 Northern Keta Caviar
5720 Concrete Way
Juneau, AK 99801-7813 907-586-6095
Fax: 907-586-6094
Salmon caviar
President/CEO: Elisabeth Babich
VP: Sean Fansler
Production Manager: Sean Fansler
Plant Manager: Mark Hiermonymus
Estimated Sales: $1-10 Million
Number Employees: 25

58367 Northern Meats
163 E 54th Ave
Anchorage, AK 99518-1227 907-561-1729
Fax: 907-561-6848
Meats
President: Jerry Urling
Estimated Sales: $10-20 Million
Number Employees: 1-4

58368 Northern Ocean Marine
7 Parker St
Gloucester, MA 01930-3025 978-283-0222
Fax: 978-283-5577
Seafood
Owner: Jim Lebouf
Sales & Marketing: Deke Fyrberg
Estimated Sales: $1.4 Million
Number Employees: 5-9

58369 Northern Orcharad Co Inc
537 Union Rd
Peru, NY 12972-4664 518-643-2367
Fax: 518-643-2751 northernorchard@verizon.net
www.northernorchard.com
Wholesaler/distributor, exporter and packer of macintosh apples and honey
President: Albert Mulbury
Contact: Samson Church
schurch@northernorchard.com
Estimated Sales: $1,950,266
Number Employees: 20-49
Type of Packaging: Consumer
Types of Products Distributed:
Frozen Food, General Line, Macintosh apples & honey

58370 Northern Steel Industrie
16101 South LaSalle St
South Holland, IL 60473 708-333-3400
Fax: 708-333-3455 800-548-4225
Wholesaler/distributor of conveyor systems, racks, shelving, baskets, bins, boxes, containers, fire protection equipment, store fixtures and security equipment
Sales Manager: Bobby MacNider
Conveyor Sales: Dan Frei
Branch Manager: Jim Neidhart
Number Employees: 50-99
Parent Co: American Handing
Types of Products Distributed:
Frozen Food, General Merchandise, Conveyor systems, racks, shelving, etc.

58371 Northern WIS Produce Co
1310 Clark St
Manitowoc, WI 54220-5109 920-684-4461
Fax: 920-684-4471
Wholesaler/distributor of cheese; serving the food service market and retail markets
Owner: Dave Litterman
Vice President: David Lindeman
Estimated Sales: $500,000-$1 Million
Number Employees: 10-19
Number of Customer Locations: 100
Types of Products Distributed:
Food Service, Health Food, Specialty Foods, Cheese

58372 Northland Industrial Truck Company Inc
23 Foss Rd
Lewiston, ME 4240 207-883-5531
Fax: 207-883-5354 866-520-5701
www.nitco-lift.com
Wholesaler/distributor of material handling equipment including fork and personnel lifts
COO: Jeff Lakin
Sales Manager: Peter Haywood
Sales Manager: John Gennette
Contact: Scott Ashton
scott.ashton@nitco-lift.com
Estimated Sales: $10-20 Million
Number Employees: 50-99
Parent Co: Hyster New England
Private Brands Carried:
Hyster; Sky Jack; Rite-Hite
Types of Products Distributed:
Frozen Food, General Merchandise, Fork & personnel lifts

58373 Northland Process Piping
1662 320th Ave
Isle, MN 56342-4303 320-679-2119
Fax: 320-679-2785 mnoffice@nppmn.com
www.nppmn.com
Brine and clean-in place systems, floor plates and drains, platforms, walkways and stairs, pumps, tanks, tubing and valves

Owner: Jennifer Hawk
CFO: Kathy Tramm
Project Sales/Customer Service: Dan Tramm
jennifer.hawk@kellogg.com
Human Resources: Natalie Geist
Foreman: Eirik Andersen
Purchasing/Customer Service: Bruce Richards
Number Employees: 100-249
Other Locations:
Roswell, GA
Lemoore, CA
Horseheads, NYLemoore
Types of Products Distributed:
Frozen Food

58374 Northstar Distributing
7934 Ivory Ave
St Louis, MO 63111 888-631-8501
www.northstarfrozentreats.com
Wholesaler/distributor of ice cream.
Estimated Sales: $20-50 Million
Number Employees: 50-99
Parent Co: Ice Cream Specialty Inc.
Types of Products Distributed:
Frozen Food

58375 Northstate Provision Co
400 Railroad St N
Ahoskie, NC 27910-2620 252-332-2174
Fax: 252-332-8780
Wholesaler/distributor of meat and meat products; serving the food service market
President: Jimmy Cotton
VP: Eddie Drew
Estimated Sales: $5-10 Million
Number Employees: 20-49
Types of Products Distributed:
Food Service, Frozen Food, Provisions/Meat

58376 Northumberland Dairy
256 Lawlor Lane
Miramichi, NB E1V 3M3
Canada 506-627-7720
800-501-1150
info@northumberlanddairy.ca
www.northumberlanddairy.ca
Dairy products including milk and cream; wholesaler/distributor of bottled water, ice cream, ice milk mix, fruit drinks and butter; serving the food service market
Director, Sales & Marketing: Paul Chiasson
Year Founded: 1942
Estimated Sales: $50 Million
Number Employees: 273
Number of Brands: 5
Square Footage: 79416
Parent Co: Agropur Dairy Co-Operative
Type of Packaging: Consumer, Food Service, Private Label
Types of Products Distributed:
Food Service, Frozen Food, Bottled water, ice cream, butter, etc.

58377 (HQ)Northville Winery & Brewing Co
630 Baseline Rd
Northville, MI 48167-1265 248-320-6507
Fax: 248-349-1165 northvillewinery@gmail.com
www.northvillewinery.com
Producer of ciders, wines and beers.
President: Diane Jones
Vice President: Cheryl Nelson
Estimated Sales: $180 Thousand
Number Employees: 1-4
Number of Brands: 1
Parent Co: Parmenter's Northville Cider Mill
Type of Packaging: Consumer, Food Service
Types of Products Distributed:
Food Service, Alcoholic Beverages

58378 Northwest Dairy Association
P.O.Box 34377
Seattle, WA 98124 509-453-4806
Fax: 509-453-4976 877-632-6455
www.nwdairy.coop
Wholesaler/distributor of milk, cottage cheese, yogurt, juice and sour cream; serving the food service market
Contact: Jim Werkhoven
j.werkhoven@nwdairy.coop
Estimated Sales: $5-10 Million
Number Employees: 10-19

Private Brands Carried:
　Rosauers; Good Day; Broadview; Darigold
Types of Products Distributed:
　Food Service, Frozen Food, General Line, Juice & dairy products

58379　Northwest Deli Distribution
79 International Way
Longview, WA 98632-1020　　360-577-6418
　　　　　　　　　　　Fax: 360-577-7950
Wholesaler/distributor of paper products, provisions/meats, general line products, frozen and specialty foods; serving the food service market
President: Scott Alwine
salwine@nwdeli.com
Estimated Sales: $5-10 Million
Number Employees: 10-19
Types of Products Distributed:
　Food Service, Frozen Food, General Line, General Merchandise, Provisions/Meat, Seafood, Specialty Foods, Paper products, etc.

58380　Northwest Forklift
838 Seneca Ave SW
Renton, WA 98057-2903　　800-221-4765
　　　　　　　　　　　Fax: 425-204-6090
Wholesaler/distributor of material handling equipment including forklifts, narrow aisle equipment and container handlers
President: Paul Kennedy
Contact: Johnny Carpenter
johncarpenter@indoor.com
Estimated Sales: $20-50 Million
Number Employees: 10-19
Private Brands Carried:
　Nissan; Kalmar; V-Lift
Types of Products Distributed:
　Frozen Food, General Merchandise, Material handling equipment

58381　Northwest Naturals Company
40 E 78th St # 6f
New York, NY 10075-1830　　212-439-8361
　　　　　　　　　　　Fax: 212-439-8364
Wholesaler/distributor of seafood; exporter of fresh fish and honey; importer of fish, cheese, peanut butter, honey and shellfish
President: Soloman Moussatche
VP: Salomon Moussatche
Estimated Sales: $3-5 Million
Number Employees: 5-9
Square Footage: 5200
Types of Products Distributed:
　Frozen Food, Seafood

58382　Northwest Select Coffee Roasters
14724 184th Street NE
Arlington, WA 98223-7948　　360-435-8577
　　　　　　　　　　　Fax: 360-435-3799
Roast coffee
President: Stedfast Israel
Marketing Director: Sheriah Israel
Estimated Sales: Under $500,000
Number Employees: 1-4
Square Footage: 4000
Parent Co: Stedy's Coffee
Type of Packaging: Consumer, Private Label, Bulk
Private Brands Carried:
　Northwest Select Coffee
Number of Customer Locations: 1

58383　Northwest Wild Products
354 Industry St.
Astoria, OR 97103　　503-791-1907
amanda@northwestwildproducts.com
www.northwestwildproducts.com
Seafood including oysters, Dungeness crab, live lobster, Manila clams, Chinook salmon, coho salmon, wild sturgeon, razor clams, albacore tuna, ling cod, black cod, halibut, crayfish, dover sole, shrimp, scallops, sardines, mackeralanchovies, squid, mussels, and red snapper; Also exotic meats
Co-Owner: Amanda Cordero
Co-Owner: Ron Neva
Number Employees: 1-4
Types of Products Distributed:
　Provisions/Meat, Seafood

58384　Northwestern Foods
1260 Grey Fox Road
Arden Hills, MN 55112　　651-644-8060
　　　　　　Fax: 651-644-8248　800-236-4937
northwestern.n2ocompanies.com
Mixes including cocoa, cake, pancake, cappuccino, iced tea, power drinks and pizza dough
President: Kurt Kiaser
CEO: Bob Schafer
Vice President: Mimie Pollard
Sales Manager: Bob Freemore
Contact: Linda Petersen
lpetersen@n2ocompanies.com
Purchasing Manager: Nadine Vandeventer
Estimated Sales: $10-20 Million
Number Employees: 20-49
Square Footage: 48000
Type of Packaging: Consumer, Food Service, Private Label, Bulk
Types of Products Distributed:
　Frozen Food

58385　Northwestern Fruit Co
616 Pine St
St Paul, MN 55130-4493　　651-224-4373
　　　　　　Fax: 651-224-2351　800-695-9533
www.northwesternfruit.com
Wholesaler/distributor of produce; serving the food service market
President: Robert Meyers
Contact: Mitchell Mulligan
mitch@northwesternfruit.com
General Manager: Charlie Howard
Estimated Sales: $10-20 Million
Number Employees: 20-49
Types of Products Distributed:
　Food Service, Produce

58386　Norvell Fixtures & Equipment Company
PO Box 14838
Augusta, GA 30919-0838　　706-855-7267
　　　　　　Fax: 706-855-7311　800-282-2674
Wholesaler/distributor of food service equipment and supplies; serving the food service market
President: W Sherrill, Jr.
Number Employees: 20-49
Private Brands Carried:
　Hobart; Cambro; Bunn-O-Matic
Types of Products Distributed:
　Food Service, Frozen Food, General Merchandise, Equipment & supplies

58387　Nothing Mundane
5870 Pine Brook Road NE
Atlanta, GA 30328-5226　　404-378-0309
　　　　　　　　　　　Fax: 404-257-5901
www.nothing-mundane.com/index2.html
Wholesaler/distributor of gourmet foods including coffee, chocolate truffles, organic honey, tea, raspberry puree and smoked trout
Owner: Mark Streepy
Private Brands Carried:
　Ashby's (tea); Republic of Tea
Types of Products Distributed:
　Frozen Food, General Line, Specialty Foods, Gourmet foods & beverages

58388　Nott Company
4480 Round Lake Rd W
Arden Hills, MN 55112　　651-415-3400
　　　　　　　　　　　800-634-3301
　　　　　　　　　　　www.nottco.com
Wholesaler/distributor of material handling equipment including forklifts and forklift parts.
Chief Executive Officer: Ed Davis
Year Founded: 1879
Estimated Sales: $50-100 Million
Number Employees: 100-249
Private Brands Carried:
　Hyster; Caterpillar; Blue Giant
Types of Products Distributed:
　Frozen Food, General Merchandise, Material handling equipment

58389　Nourishtea
222 Islington Ave
Suite 6C
Toronto, ON M8V 3W7
Canada
　　　　　　　　　　　416-539-9299
　　　　　　　　　info@nourishtea.ca
　　　　　　　　　www.nourishtea.ca
Herbal tea, black tea, green tea *Year Founded:* 2007
Types of Products Distributed:
　General Merchandise

58390　Nova Seafood
P.O.Box 350
Portland, ME 04112-0350　　207-774-6324
　　　Fax: 207-774-6385　www.novaseafood.com
Canadian seafood: Fresh Whole and Fresh Fillet Products-Cod, Haddock, Hake, Cusk, Catfish, Pollock, Flounder, Dabs, Grey Sole, Yellowtail, Salmon, Monk, Monk Tail, Halibut; Specialty Items: Clams, Maine Shrimp, Swordfish, Scallops(Dry Sea), Tuna Loin, C/K Lobster Meat, Crab Meat
President: Angelo Ciocca
Sales: Ernie Salamone
Estimated Sales: $20-50 Million
Number Employees: 20-49

58391　Novick Brothers Corp
3660 S Lawrence St
Philadelphia, PA 19148　　215-467-1400
　　　　　　　　　　　www.novickbrothers.com
Wholesaler/distributor of groceries, fresh and frozen produce and general merchandise; serving the food service market.
President: Jay Hobby
Senior Advisor: Gary Novick
gary.novick@novickbrothers.com
Senior Vice President: Matt Luchansky
Assistant Controller: Jeff Kaplan
Customer Service: Bill Novick
Year Founded: 1924
Estimated Sales: $20-50 Million
Number Employees: 20-49
Square Footage: 42000000
Private Brands Carried:
　NIFDA; Chef Pak
Types of Products Distributed:
　Food Service, Frozen Food, General Line, General Merchandise, Produce

58392　Nspired Natural Foods
4600 Sleepytime Dr
Boulder, CO 80301
　　　　　　　　　　　800-434-4246
Dried fruits, nuts and trail mixes
Chairman: Charles Lynch
CEO: Gordon Chapple
Number Employees: 5-9
Square Footage: 40000
Other Locations:
　Nspired Natural Foods
　Melville, NYNspired Natural Foods
Private Brands Carried:
　Northwest Delights
Number of Customer Locations: 2000
Types of Products Distributed:
　Frozen Food, General Line, Health Food, Dried fruits, nuts & trail mixes

58393　Nu Concept Food Svc
6909 Cooper Ave
Glendale, NY 11385-7123　　718-416-1222
　　　　　　　　　　　Fax: 718-416-0812
Wholesaler/distributor of general line items; serving schools, hospitals and group homes for private institutions
President: Joseph Saccone
jsaccone@nuconceptfood.com
General Manager: Jay Roth
Estimated Sales: $10-20 Million
Number Employees: 10-19
Square Footage: 13000
Private Brands Carried:
　White Rose; Kraft; Tropicana
Types of Products Distributed:
　Food Service, Frozen Food

58394　Nuco Industries
110 Schmitt Blvd
Farmingdale, NY 11735　　631-752-8600
　　　　　　Fax: 631-752-7848　800-645-9198
　　　　　　　　　　　nuco203@aol.com
　　　　　　　　　www.environmentalsupplies.com
Wholesaler/distributor/manufacturer of environmentally safe merchandise including all purpose cleaners, safety products, lubricants and insecticides
Controller: Joyce Calcagni
CEO: Jeff Berlin
Estimated Sales: $10 Million
Number Employees: 5-9
Square Footage: 40000
Parent Co: Nuco Industries
Types of Products Distributed:
　Frozen Food, General Merchandise

Wholesalers & Distributors / A-Z

58395 Nuherbs Company
3820 Penniman Ave
Oakland, CA 94619   510-534-4372
Fax: 510-534-4384   800-233-4307
herbals@nuherbs.com www.nuherbs.com
Wholesaler/distributor and importer of Chinese herbs, extract powders, ginseng and spices
President: Pat Kwan
Quality Control: Lorenzo Puertas
Sales Director: Maria Yung
Contact: Nuherbs Co
kevinamiles@hotmail.com
Estimated Sales: $1-3 Million
Number Employees: 5-9
Type of Packaging: Consumer, Bulk
Private Brands Carried:
   Herbal Times; Jade Dragon
Types of Products Distributed:
   Health Food, Specialty Foods, Chinese herbs, ginseng & spices

58396 Nui Foods
112 E Orangethorpe Ave
Anaheim, CA 92801
support@eatnui.com
www.eatnui.com
Low carb, low sugar cookies
Co-Founder: Victor Macias
Co-Founder/CEO: Kristoffer Quiaoit
Research & Development Manager: Juan Altamirano
Marketing Manager: Valerie Bui *Year Founded:* 2016
Types of Products Distributed:
   General Line, Health Food

58397 Nutraceutical International
1777 Sun Peak Dr.
Park City, UT 84098   435-655-6000
800-669-8877
info@nutraceutical.com www.nutraceutical.com
Supplements.
CEO: Chad Clawson
Vice President/CFO: Cory McQueen
Cheif Marketing Officer: John D'Alessandro
Senior VP, Sales: David Bunch
COO: Camilla Shumaker
Year Founded: 1993
Estimated Sales: $188.07 Million
Number Employees: 810
Square Footage: 6103
Type of Packaging: Consumer, Food Service, Bulk
Types of Products Distributed:
   Food Service, Health Food

58398 Nutri-Bake Inc
1208 Rue Bergar
Laval, QC H7L 5A2
Canada   450-933-5936
Fax: 888-263-3208 info@nutri-bake.com
www.organic-baked-goods.com
Manufacturer and wholesaler of baked goods
President: Peter Tsatoumas

58399 Nutri-Rich Corp.
Fullerton, CA   855-200-8985
hello@nutri-rich.com www.nutri-rich.com
Wholesaler/distributor of vitamins and nutritional supplements
Manager: Sam Cheng
Sales Manager: Sam Cheng
VP, Operations: Jack Cheng
Estimated Sales: $5-10 Million
Number Employees: 5-9
Private Brands Carried:
   Mega Focus; Mega Beauty; Epadha
Types of Products Distributed:
   Frozen Food, General Line, Health Food, Vitamins & nutritional supplements

58400 NutriCology Allergy Research
30806 Santana Street
Hayward, CA 94544-7060   800-545-9960
Fax: 510-487-8682
Wholesaler/distributor of vitamins and food supplements
Contact: Mark Maiden
markm@nutricology.com
Estimated Sales: Less than $500,000
Number Employees: 1-4
Square Footage: 50000
Number of Customer Locations: 1000
Types of Products Distributed:
   Frozen Food, Health Food, Vitamins & supplements

58401 Nutrinova
1601 Lbj Fwy
Dallas, TX 75234-6034   972-443-4000
Fax: 972-443-4994 800-786-3883
www.nutrinova.com
A global technology and specialty materials company that engineers and manufacturers a wide variety of products essential to everyday living.
President: Graham Hall
cheryl.colline@nutrinova.com
Chairman, Chief Executive Officer: Mark Rohr
Vice President: Jiro Okada
Marketing Manager North America: Patricia Hanley
Contact: Colline Cheryl
cheryl.colline@nutrinova.com
Chief Operating Officer: Doug Madden
Number Employees: 5-9
Parent Co: Nutrinova Nutrition Specialists & Food Ingredients GmbH
Private Brands Carried:
   Hoeschst; Sunett
Types of Products Distributed:
   Frozen Food, General Line, Sweeteners, preservatives, etc.

58402 Nutriscience Laboratories
51 Beverly Hills Drive
Toronto, ON M3L 1A2
Canada   416-240-1234
Fax: 416-249-0341 800-661-2434
Wholesaler/distributor of nutritional supplements
President: Doug Bentley
General Manager: Gail Weismiller
Number Employees: 1-4
Square Footage: 8000
Parent Co: BDR Sports Nutrition Laboratories
Private Brands Carried:
   Hardcore Workouts; Nutriscience
Types of Products Distributed:
   Frozen Food, Health Food, Nutritional supplements

58403 Nutrition Products Company
11112 Decimal Drive
Louisville, KY 40299-2440   270-261-0501
Fax: 270-261-9469
Wholesaler/distributor of marinades and coatings; serving the food service market
President: Alfred Silva
Number Employees: 5-9
Private Brands Carried:
   Poultry & Seafood Solutions
Types of Products Distributed:
   Food Service, Frozen Food, General Line, Marinades & coatings

58404 Nutritional Counselors of America
1267 Archie Rhinehart Pkwy
Spencer, TN 38585-4612   931-946-3600
Fax: 931-946-3602
Vitamins, minerals, herbs, herbal teas, nutritional supplements, and colon cleaners, neutraceuticals and probiotics
President/CEO: June Wiles
Estimated Sales: $3-$5 Million
Number Employees: 5 to 9
Square Footage: 10000
Type of Packaging: Consumer, Private Label
Types of Products Distributed:
   Frozen Food

58405 Nuts & Spice Company
29266 Union City Blvd
Union City, CA 94587   510-489-5836
Fax: 510-489-9307 hathibrand@aol.com
www.hathibrand.com
Wholesaler/distributor of rice, nuts, spices and flour
President: Balwant Birla
VP: Sanjay Birla
Contact: Sanjay Birla
hathibrand@aol.com
Managing Director: Hemant Sherma
Estimated Sales: $10-20 Million
Number Employees: 10-19
Private Brands Carried:
   Hathi; Tata
Number of Customer Locations: 200
Types of Products Distributed:
   Frozen Food, General Line, Rice, nuts, spices & flour

58406 Nuts 'N More
10 Almeida St E
Providence, RI 02914
844-413-2344
questions@nuts-n-more.com www.nuts-n-more.com
Almond and peanut butter spreads and powders
Founder & CEO: Peter Ferreira
Number of Brands: 1
Number of Products: 18

58407 Nuts For Cheese
London, ON
Canada   519-601-5070
info@nutsforcheese.com
www.nutsforcheese.com
Artisan cashew cheeses
Founder: Margaret Coons *Year Founded:* 2015
Types of Products Distributed:
   General Line

58408 Nuttzo
3525 Del Mar Heights Rd
Unit 728
San Diego, CA 92130   888-325-0553
info@nuttzo.com
www.nuttzo.com
Nut and seed butters
Founder and President: Danielle Dietz-LiVolsi

58409 Nylon Net Company
PO Box 592
Memphis, TN 38101   901-526-6500
Fax: 901-526-6538 800-238-7529
Wholesaler/distributor of rope, cord and twine including nylon, polyethylene, polypropylene, manila and cotton
President: Stephen Christides
Sales Contact: Rob Ayres
Purchasing: Helen Beatty
Estimated Sales: $2.5-5 Million
Number Employees: 20-49
Square Footage: 1410240
Types of Products Distributed:
   Frozen Food, General Merchandise, Fishing rope, cord & twine; also, nets

58410 (HQ)O Berk Co LLC
3 Milltown Ct
Union, NJ 07083-8108   908-851-9500
Fax: 908-851-9367 800-631-7392
info@oberk.com www.oberk.com
Wholesaler/distributor of glass, plastic and aluminum containers and closures
President/CEO: Marc Gaelen
Chairman: Norbert Gaelen
CFO: Roy Allan
VP: Joseph Norton
Quality Control: David Gotter
Marketing Director: Steven Nussbaum
Sales Director: Steven Kornbluth
Operations Manager: Joe Norton
Purchasing Manager: Brian Kilduff
Estimated Sales: $40 Million
Number Employees: 50-99
Square Footage: 77000
Type of Packaging: Consumer, Food Service, Private Label, Bulk
Other Locations:
   O. Berk Co.
   New Haven, CTO. Berk Co.
Number of Customer Locations: 4
Types of Products Distributed:
   bottles, jars, cans and closures.

58411 O'Neill Coffee Co
20 Main Street Ext
West Middlesex, PA 16159-3478   724-528-2244
Fax: 724-528-1566 www.oneillcoffee.com
Coffee; wholesaler/distributor of teas and spices
President: Joseph Walsh
jwalsh@oneillcoffee.com
Account Manager: Neil Ostheimer
Estimated Sales: $1-3 Million
Number Employees: 10-19
Types of Products Distributed:
   Frozen Food, General Line, Teas & spices

58412 O-Sesco
559 Selma Road
Springfield, OH 45505-2000   937-324-3251
Fax: 937-324-5011
Wholesaler/distributor of food service equipment and furnishings; serving the food service market

Wholesalers & Distributors / A-Z

President: Gary Wade
CEO: Mike Williams
VP Marketing/Sales: Bruce Smith
Estimated Sales: $500,000-$1 Million
Number Employees: 5-9
Square Footage: 44000
Types of Products Distributed:
  Food Service, Frozen Food, General Merchandise, Equipment & furnishings

58413 O. Lippi & Company
2050 Jerrold Avenue
San Francisco, CA 94124-1605   415-647-6743
                Fax: 415-282-8841
Wholesaler/distributor of fruit; serving the food service market
General Manager: Dennis Martin
Estimated Sales: $2.5-5 Million
Number Employees: 5-9
Types of Products Distributed:
  Food Service, Frozen Food, Produce, Fruits

58414 O.G. Foodservice
PO Box 429
Oneonta, NY 13820-0429   607-432-2450
                Fax: 607-432-8042
Wholesaler/distributor of meat, frozen food and general line products; serving the food service market
President: W Lewis
Estimated Sales: $5-10 Million
Number Employees: 10-19
Number of Customer Locations: 100
Types of Products Distributed:
  Food Service, Frozen Food, General Line, Provisions/Meat

58415 O.W. & B.S. Look Company
8 Western Avenue
Jonesport, ME 04649   207-497-5500
                Fax: 207-497-5559
Wholesaler/distributor of seafood
President: Sid Look
VP: P Look
Estimated Sales: $1-2.5 Million
Number Employees: 5-9
Private Brands Carried:
  Captain Look's
Types of Products Distributed:
  Frozen Food, Seafood

58416 OCS Process Systems
24142 Detroit Rd
Cleveland, OH 44145-1515   440-871-6009
    Fax: 440-871-0855 800-482-6226
    sales@ocsprocess.com www.ocsprocess.com
Wholesaler/distributor and exporter of sanitary process systems for the dairy, beverage and chemical industries; custom design and installation services available
President: Tim Kloos
CEO: Beth Kloos
Vice President: Alan Pleska
Estimated Sales: $5-10 Million
Number Employees: 20-49
Square Footage: 100000
Parent Co: R&J Corporation of Ohio
Private Brands Carried:
  Jensen; Fristman Pumps; Sudmo Valves
Types of Products Distributed:
  General Merchandise, Sanitary process systems

58417 OH Armstrong
PO Box 220
Kingston, NS B0P 1R0
Canada
              902-765-3311
    Fax: 902-765-3856 800-661-6331
    sales@oharmstrong.ca www.oharmstrong.ca
Wholesaler/distributor of frozen foods, provisions/meats and equipment and fixtures; serving the food service market; rack jobber services available
Sales Manager: Thelma Pack
General Manager: John Pierce
Purchsaing Manager: David Book
Number Employees: 50-99
Number of Customer Locations: 300
Types of Products Distributed:
  Food Service, Frozen Food, General Merchandise, Provisions/Meat, Rack Jobbers

58418 OHCO/Oriental Herb Company
P.O. Box 247
Lafayette, CO 80026   303-674-2466
    Fax: 303-674-7346 800-344-2466
    hannah@ohco.com www.ohco.com
Wholesaler/distributor of Chinese herbal remedies
Owner: Hannah Hayes, B. S., M. Ed.
Owner: Donn Hayes, Dipl. Ac., C.H. (N
Research: Donn Hayes
Contact: Joshua Elfers
joshua@ohco.com
Purchasing Manager: Jeremiah Elfer
Number Employees: 5-9
Square Footage: 4000
Private Brands Carried:
  Cold Snap; Stomach Chi; OHCO-Motion
Number of Customer Locations: 600
Types of Products Distributed:
  Health Food, Chinese herbal remedies

58419 OHi Food
750 Wesleyan Bay
Costa Mesa, CA 92626-6919   808-281-7815
                www.ohifoodco.com
Superfood snack bar
Marketing Manager: Kayla Bittner
Number of Brands: 1
Number of Products: 4

58420 OMYA, Inc.
9987 Carver Rd
Suite 300
Cincinnatti, OH 45242   513-387-4600
                800-749-6692
                www.omya.com
Fillers and pigments from calcium carbonate and dolomite, and distributor of chemical products.
President: Anthony Colak
CFO: Michael Phillips
Secretary: Leonard Eisenberg
Asst Sec: Patricia Kirkendall
Manager Technology Services: Michael Roussel
Sales Manager: Maria Burt
Contact: Hilary Allard
hilary.allard@omya.com
Manager: Scott McCalla
Manager Projects Engineering: Scott Schaffner
Director of Engineering: Rob Tikoft
Director Purchasing: Derrell Riley
Estimated Sales: $4.3 Million
Other Locations:
  Proctor, VT
  Cincinnati, OH
  Woodland, WA
  Kingsport, TN
  Lucerne Valley, CA
  Johnsonburg, PACincinnati

58421 Oak Barrel Winecraft
1443 San Pablo Ave
Berkeley, CA 94702-1045   510-849-0400
    Fax: 510-528-6543 info@oakbarrel.com
                www.oakbarrel.com
Oak barrels for wine and beer making, bottles and stoppers for wine, vinegar starter culture and bottling and brewery machinery; importer of wine presses, crushers and barrels; also, wholesaler/distributor of vinegar starter cultureand barrels
President and CFO: Bernard Rooney
info@oakbarrel.com
Vice President: Homer Smith
Estimated Sales: $5-10 Million
Number Employees: 1-4
Square Footage: 12000
Types of Products Distributed:
  Frozen Food, General Merchandise, Vinegar starter culture & barrels

58422 Oak Farms Dairy
2711 N Haskell Ave
Suite 3400
Dallas, TX 75204
              800-303-3400
                www.oakfarmsdairy.com
Wholesaler/distributor/broker of dairy products.
Accounting Manager: Betty Renteria
Sales Director: Eric Eves
Sanitation Lead: Brenda Davis
Year Founded: 1908
Estimated Sales: $100-500 Million
Number Employees: 200-499

58423 Oak Island Seafood Company
PO Box 947
Portland, ME 04104-0947   207-594-9250
                Fax: 207-594-9281
Seafood
President: Jay Trenholm

58424 Oak Ridge Winery LLC
6100 E Victor Rd
Lodi, CA 95240-0804   209-369-4758
    Fax: 209-369-0202 info@oakridgewinery.com
                www.oakridgewinery.com
Produces a wide variety of wines.
President: Rudy Maggio
rmaggi@oakridgewinery.com
Vice President of Marketing and Sales: Stephen Bei
Director of International Sales: Stephen Merritt
Tasting Room Manager: Shelly Maggio-Woltkamp
Director of Winemaking/Production Manage: Chue Her
Estimated Sales: $10-20 Million
Number Employees: 50-99
Number of Brands: 8
Type of Packaging: Consumer, Food Service
Types of Products Distributed:
  Food Service, Alcoholic Beverages

58425 Occidental Foods International, LLC
4 Middlebury Blvd
Suite 3, Aspen Business Park
Randolph, NJ 07869   973-970-9220
    Fax: 973-970-9222 info@occidentalfoods.com
                www.occidentalfoods.com
Representatives and importers of bulk spices and seeds, including paprika; pure mancha saffron; chilies dried, crushed and ground; turmeric; granulated garlic and garlic powder; cardamom; annatto, allspice and sesame seeds
President: Scott Hall
Chief Financial Officer: Denise Hall
Estimated Sales: $4.9 Million
Type of Packaging: Food Service, Bulk
Types of Products Distributed:
  Food Service, Specialty Foods

58426 Ocean Crest Seafoods
P.O. Box 1183
Gloucester, MA 01931   978-281-0232
    Fax: 978-283-3211 800-259-4769
                www.neptunesharvest.com
Seafood
President/CEO: Leonard Parco
Estimated Sales: $1-3 Million
Number Employees: 20-49

58427 Ocean Frost
471 Mulberry St
Newark, NJ 07114-2736   973-622-3200
    Fax: 973-622-4949 ocfrost@optonline.net
Importer and wholesaler/distributor of frozen seafood in the New York metro area; serving restaurants, fish markets, hotels and institutions
Owner: A Joo
jooalavoura@claro.net.co
Estimated Sales: $10-20 Million
Number Employees: 20-49
Square Footage: 11000
Type of Packaging: Food Service
Types of Products Distributed:
  Food Service, Frozen Food, Seafood

58428 Ocean Harvest
PO Box 60
Dennysville, ME 04628-0060   207-726-0609
                Fax: 207-726-9571
Fish and seafood
Owner: Larry Matthews
Estimated Sales: $1-3 Million
Number Employees: 1-4

58429 Ocean Select Seafood
10714 Highway 14
Delcambre, LA 70528   337-685-5315
                Fax: 337-685-6079
Seafood
President: Mitch Polito
Estimated Sales: $5-$10 Million
Number Employees: 1-4

58430 Ocean Union Company
2100 Riverside Pkwy
Suite 129
Lawrenceville, GA 30043-5927   770-995-1957
                Fax: 770-513-8662
Seafood, snapper, grouper, lobster, crab, tuna, eel, mackerel
President: Jackie Tsai

Wholesalers & Distributors / A-Z

58431 Ocean Venture
939 Salem Street
Unit 8
Groveland, MA 01834-1566
978-774-9390
Fax: 978-774-4819
Wholesaler/distributor of frozen seafood
President: Norman Desrouchers
Estimated Sales: $5-10 Million
Number Employees: 5-9
Types of Products Distributed:
Frozen Food, Seafood

58432 Oceanledge Seafoods
138 Rankin Street
Rockland, ME 04841-2318
207-594-4955
Fax: 626-968-0196
Seafood
President: Steve Jonasson
Estimated Sales: $330,000
Number Employees: 2

58433 Oceans Prome Distributing
1413 Waukegan Rd
Glenview, IL 60025
847-998-5813
Fax: 847-729-5228
President: Jeffrey Burhop
Estimated Sales: $5-10 Million
Number Employees: 5-9

58434 (HQ)Odom Corporation
20415 72nd Avenue S
Kent, WA 98032-2392
253-437-0088
800-767-6366
info@odomcorp.com www.odomcorp.com
Wholesaler/distributor of general line items including soft drinks and liquor; serving Alaska
Owner/President: John Odom
Co-Owner: Jim Odom
Co-Owner: Bill Odom
Estimated Sales: $10-20 Million
Number Employees: 10-19
Other Locations:
Odom Corp.
Fairbanks, AKOdom Corp.
Types of Products Distributed:
Frozen Food, General Line, Soft drinks & liquor

58435 Oenophilia
500 Meadowlands Dr
Hillsborough, NC 27278-8504
919-644-0555
Fax: 919-644-1715 www.oenophilia.com
Distribution of wine and accessories
President: Brian Kileff
Vice President: Greg Orlando
greg@oenophilia.com
Number Employees: 10-19

58436 Ohana Seafood, LLC
255 Sand Island Rd
Suite 2C
Honolulu, HI 96819-2292
808-843-1844
Fax: 808-843-1844
Seafood
President: Jeffrey Yee
Vice President: Jeffrey Yee
Estimated Sales: $570,000
Number Employees: 1-4

58437 Ohio Chemical Svc Inc
1066 Kinnear Rd
Columbus, OH 43212-1151
614-486-2488
Fax: 614-486-5580 info@ohiochemical.com
Wholesaler/distributor of organic and inorganic chemicals including sorbic acid, potassium sorbate, cream of tartar and tartaric acid
Owner: Ron Horvath
rhorvath@ohiochemical.com
Estimated Sales: $1-2.5 Million
Number Employees: 5-9
Types of Products Distributed:
Frozen Food, General Line, Organic & inorganic chemicals

58438 Ohio Conveyor & Supply Inc
1310 N Main St
Findlay, OH 45840-3703
419-422-3825
Fax: 419-422-4490
Conveyors and wholesaler/distributor of conveyor belts
President: John R Snyder
jrsnyder@ohioconveyorsupply.com
Estimated Sales: $1-2.5 Million
Number Employees: 5-9
Types of Products Distributed:
Frozen Food, General Merchandise, Conveyor belts

58439 Ohio Farmers
2700 E 55th St
Suite 100
Cleveland, OH 44104-2866
216-391-9733
Fax: 216-391-4023 800-255-3305
Wholesaler/distributor of frozen foods, grocery products, meat products, spices and smallwares; serving the food service market
President: Eliot Gelb
Estimated Sales: $20-50 Million
Number Employees: 50-99
Square Footage: 110000
Private Brands Carried:
Anchor Foods; Cargill Oil; General Foods; Land O' Lakes; Main Street Muffins; Nabisco
Types of Products Distributed:
Food Service, Frozen Food, General Line, Provisions/Meat, Grocery products, spices, etc.

58440 Ohio Materials Handling
7100 Krick Road
Bedford, OH 44146-4484
440-439-5700
Fax: 440-439-5103
Wholesaler/distributor of material handling equipment including forklifts, conveyors, shelving, lifts, etc
President: James Orenga
Contact: Ryan Sanders
ryansanders@ohiomaterialshandling.com
Estimated Sales: $20-50 Million
Number Employees: 50-99
Private Brands Carried:
Yale; Powerboss
Types of Products Distributed:
Frozen Food, General Merchandise, Material handling equipment

58441 Ohio Rack Inc
1405 S Liberty Ave
PO Box 3517
Alliance, OH 44601-4231
330-823-8200
Fax: 330-823-8136 800-344-4164
ohiorack@cannet.com www.ohiorack.com
Wholesaler/distributor of used portable stack racks and pallet rack systems; manufacturer of new portable stack racks
President: George Pilla
ohiorack@cannet.com
Estimated Sales: Below $5,000,000
Number Employees: 5-9
Types of Products Distributed:
Frozen Food, General Merchandise, Portable stack & pallet rack systems

58442 Oklahoma City Meat Co Inc
300 S Klein Ave
Oklahoma City, OK 73108-1495
405-235-3308
Fax: 405-235-9989 www.okcmeat.com
Beef, lamb and pork; wholesaler/distributor of chicken. Founded in 1957.
President: Tommy Saunders
office@okcmeat.com
Estimated Sales: $10-20 Million
Number Employees: 20-49
Type of Packaging: Food Service
Types of Products Distributed:
Food Service, Provisions/Meat, Chicken

58443 Oklahoma Pecan Co
2712 S Commerce St
Ardmore, OK 73401
580-223-5440
Fax: 580-226-8860 800-259-6887
oklahomapecan@yahoo.com
Wholesaler/distributor of health food; serving food service operators
Owner: Jerry Rutledge
Estimated Sales: Less Than $500,000
Number Employees: 1-4
Types of Products Distributed:
Food Service, Frozen Food, Health Food, Pecans

58444 Old Fashion Foods Inc
5521 Collins Blvd
Austell, GA 30106-3693
770-948-1177
Fax: 770-739-3254 www.oldfashfd.com
Wholesaler/distributor of vending machine foods including hamburgers, hot dogs and sandwiches; serving the food service market
President: Sheldon Smith
s.smith@oldfashfd.com
Sr. VP Finance: Joseph Hulsey
Executive VP: Jerry Snecker
Estimated Sales: F
Number Employees: 100-249
Types of Products Distributed:
Food Service, Frozen Food, General Line, Prepared sandwiches for vending machine

58445 Old Point Packing Inc
817 Jefferson Ave
Newport News, VA 23607-6117
757-247-6447
Fax: 757-247-6447
Packing/crating service for wholesale seafood
President: Martin Composano, Jr
Estimated Sales: $11.5 Million
Number Employees: 5-9
Type of Packaging: Consumer, Food Service, Bulk
Types of Products Distributed:
Seafood

58446 Olds Products Co
10700 88th Ave
Pleasant Prairie, WI 53158
262-947-3500
Orders@OldsFitz.com
www.oldsproducts.com
Prepared mustard, specialty mustard blends, and vinegar
Supply Chain Manager: Brian Schnuckel
bschnuckel@oldsfitz.com
Estimated Sales: $6500000
Number Employees: 50-99
Parent Co: Olds Products Company
Type of Packaging: Consumer, Food Service, Private Label, Bulk
Types of Products Distributed:
General Line

58447 Oley Distributing Company
PO Box 4660
Fort Worth, TX 76164-0660
817-625-8251
Fax: 817-626-7269
President: Patricia O'Neal
VP: Phil O'Neal, Jr.
General Manager: Bill Smith
Estimated Sales: $5-10 Million
Square Footage: 225000

58448 Olive Oil Source
1833 Fletcher Way
Santa Ynez, CA 93460-9380
805-688-1014
sales@oliveoilsource.com
www.oliveoilsource.com
Olive oils
President: Shawn Addison
General Manager: Suzette Stahl
Accounting Manager: Joy Jonas
VP Operations: Antoinette Addison
Number Employees: 10-19

58449 Oliver Winery
200 E Winery Rd
Bloomington, IN 47404-2400
812-876-5800
Fax: 812-876-9309 800-258-2783
admin@oliverwinery.com www.oliverwinery.com
Producer of wines, including semi-sweet, semi-dry, dry whites, dry reds, dessert and sparkling.
President: Julie Adams
CEO: Bill Oliver
boliver@oliverwinery.com
Executive Vice President: Kathleen Oliver
Vice President of Wholesale Sales: Chris Hibbert
Human Resources Director: Jessika Hane
VP of Operations, Director of Winemaking: Dennis Dunham
Vineyard Manager: Bernie Parker
Estimated Sales: $18.7 Million
Number Employees: 50-99
Number of Brands: 8
Type of Packaging: Consumer, Food Service, Bulk
Types of Products Distributed:
Food Service, Alcoholic Beverages

58450 Olivina. LLC
4555 Arroyo Road
Livermore, CA 94550
925-455-8710
charles@theolivina.com
www.theolivina.com
Olive oils
President/Owner/CEO: Charles Crohare
charles@theolivina.com
General Manager: Alice Crohare

Estimated Sales: $25 Million
Number Employees: 20

58451 Olomomo Nut Company
4760 Walnut St.
Boulder, CO 80301
877-923-6888
info@olomomo.com www.olomomo.com
Roasted & flavored nuts
Chairman & Founder: Justin Perkins
CEO: Mark Owens
VP Sales & Marketing: Justin Desiderio
Sales & Marketing Coordinator: Sarah Dhanraj
Production: Brian Starkman
Types of Products Distributed:
  General Line

58452 Olsen Fish Co
2115 N 2nd St
Minneapolis, MN 55411-2204   612-287-0838
        Fax: 612-287-8761   800-882-0212
lutefisk@olsenfish.com www.olsenfish.com
Lutfisk and pickled herring
President: Chris Dorff
lutefisk@olsenfish.com
Estimated Sales: $3-5 Million
Number Employees: 10-19
Type of Packaging: Bulk

58453 Olympic Juicer Company
1360 Clifton Avenue
321
Clifton, NJ 07012-1343   973-365-2748
        Fax: 973-365-2285
Wholesaler/distributor of juicers, cutters and mini-sweepers; serving the food service market
President: Joseph Klement
Types of Products Distributed:
  Food Service, Frozen Food, General Merchandise, Juicers, cutters & min-sweepers

58454 Omcan Manufacturing & Distributing Company
3115 Pepper Mill Court
Mississauga, ON L5L 4X5
Canada   905-607-0234
        Fax: 905-828-0897 800-465-0234
sales@omcan.com www.omcan.com
Manufacturer and exporter of butcher knives; personalized knives available; wholesaler/distributor of food service equipment and supplies including cutters, slicers, choppers, bowls, vegetable processors, mixers, etc.; serving the foodservice market
Owner: Tar Nella
General Manager: Tarcisio Nella
Number Employees: 30
Square Footage: 600000
Private Brands Carried:
  Omas Slicer
Types of Products Distributed:
  Food Service, Frozen Food, General Merchandise, Foodservice equipment & supplies

58455 Omega Produce Company
PO Box 277
Nogales, AZ 85628   520-281-0410
        Fax: 520-281-1010
cucumbers and bell peppers
President: George Gotsis
ggomega1@aol.com
Secretary/Treasurer, VP: Toru Fujiwara
Office Manager: Norah Romero
VP Sales: J Nick. Gotsis
Estimated Sales: $10-20 Million
Number Employees: 10-19
Types of Products Distributed:
  Frozen Food, Produce, Cucumbers & bell peppers

58456 Omega-Life
P.O.Box 7
Muskego, WI 53150-0007   262-679-9850
        800-328-3529
Wholesaler/distributor of health and specialty foods
President: David Nelson
Estimated Sales: $.5-1 million
Number Employees: 5-9
Private Brands Carried:
  Fortified Flax; Powerpack Energy Drinkmix, Omega Bar.
Types of Products Distributed:
  Frozen Food, Health Food, Specialty Foods

58457 Omni Food Inc
2001 3rd Ave N
Bessemer, AL 35020-4913   205-426-6650
        www.omnifoodsinc.com
Wholesaler/distributor of general line items; rack jobber services available
President: Arnold Shiland
stuartshiland@bellsouth.net
Estimated Sales: $5-10 Million
Number Employees: 1-4
Square Footage: 220000
Type of Packaging: Consumer, Food Service, Private Label, Bulk
Number of Customer Locations: 75
Types of Products Distributed:
  Frozen Food, General Line, Rack Jobbers

58458 Omni Material Handling Services
11336 Tamarco Drive
Cincinnati, OH 45242-2108   513-469-1500
        Fax: 513-469-1505 www.jungheinrich-us.com
Wholesaler/distributor of fork lifts, conveyors, containers, racks, shelving and parts; also, service and rental available
President: John Sneddon
VP Manager: David Rockett
Estimated Sales: $5-10 Million
Number Employees: 10-19
Square Footage: 40000
Private Brands Carried:
  Nissan; Linde-Baker; Schaeff
Types of Products Distributed:
  Frozen Food, General Merchandise, Material handling equipment

58459 Omni Pacific Company
2499 N Main St Ste 250
Walnut Creek, CA 94597   925-933-0695
        Fax: 925-933-0691
Wholesaler/distributor and exporter of canned fruits, vegetables and fish products; serving government institutions and schools
President: Brett Roberts
Estimated Sales: $5-10 Million
Number Employees: 10-19
Square Footage: 8800
Type of Packaging: Food Service
Private Brands Carried:
  California Cola; Island Sun
Types of Products Distributed:
  Food Service, Frozen Food, General Line, Seafood

58460 One Pie Canning
P.O.Box 400
West Paris, ME 04289   207-674-3920
        Fax: 207-674-2510
Wholesaler/distributor of canned pumpkin and squash pie fillings
President: Richard Penley
Estimated Sales: $300,000-500,000
Number Employees: 1-4
Types of Products Distributed:
  Frozen Food, General Line, Canned pie fillings

58461 One-Shot
901 Norwalk Street
Suite E
Greensboro, NC 27407-2039   336-854-1020
        Fax: 336-854-1577
Importer and wholesaler/distributor of soft serve frozen dessert dispensing equipment; serving the food service market
President: Bill Rhodes
VP Sales: J Cooper
Number Employees: 10-19
Type of Packaging: Food Service
Private Brands Carried:
  One-Shot
Types of Products Distributed:
  Food Service, Frozen Food, General Merchandise, Frozen dessert dispensing equipment

58462 Onnit Labs
4401 Friedrich Ln
Suite 302
Austin, TX 78744
        855-666-4899
help@onnit.com www.onnit.com
Health foods including supplements, protein powders, coffees and teas, and MCT oils, and snacks
Founder & CEO: Aubrey Marcus
Types of Products Distributed:
  Health Food

58463 Ono International
2702 NW 112th Ave
Doral, FL 33172-1805   305-591-1516
        Fax: 305-500-9566 877-387-6273
        onointer@aol.com
Wholesaler/distributor and importer of pre-baked and frozen baguettes, rolls, loaves, croissants, pastries, par-cooked frozen paella 100% natural, brandy (France) and wines (Spain)
Managing Member: Joseph Ayash
Chief of Operation: Rafael Ayash
Estimated Sales: $10 Million
Number Employees: 5-9
Square Footage: 20000
Type of Packaging: Consumer, Food Service, Private Label
Private Brands Carried:
  Fripan; Only Paella; Fresh Bite; Palacio Del Duque; Charles 8; Marnay
Number of Customer Locations: 150
Types of Products Distributed:
  Frozen Food, General Line, General Merchandise, Baguettes, croissants, rolls, etc.

58464 Ontario Glove and Safety Products
5 Washburn Drive
Kitchener, ON N2R 1S1
Canada   519-886-3590
        Fax: 519-886-3597 800-265-4554
sales@ontarioglove.com www.ontarioglove.com
Manufacturer and importer of gloves including PVC, cotton, latex and neoprene; wholesaler/distributor and exporter of leather and synthetic aprons
President: John McCarthy
CFO: Randell Moore
Quality Control: Truedy Henric
Number Employees: 10
Types of Products Distributed:
  Frozen Food, General Merchandise, Aprons

58465 Optimum Nutrition
Dept 75 Meridian Lake Drive
Aurora, IL 60504   630-236-0097
        800-763-3444
        consumer@optimumnutrition.com
        www.optimumnutrition.com
Sports drinks, vitamins and supplements
Founder: Mike Costello
Co-Founder: Tony Costello
Estimated Sales: $1-2.5 Million
Number Employees: 1-4
Types of Products Distributed:
  Frozen Food, Health Food, Vitamins & supplements

58466 Optipure
6984 Bandini Blvd
Commerce, CA 90040-3326   323-726-0700
        Fax: 323-721-8300 800-934-3040
        ronu@optipure.com
Wholesaler/distributor of therapeutic herbal extracts and phytonutrient products
Executive VP: Ron Udell
Contact: Sudha Yadav
sudha@optipure.com
Estimated Sales: $5-10 Million
Number Employees: 5-9
Types of Products Distributed:
  Frozen Food, Health Food, Herbal extracts

58467 (HQ)Orafti Active Food Ingredients
101 Lindenwood Drive
Malvern, PA 19355-1755   610-889-9828
        Fax: 610-889-9821
Wholesaler/distributor and importer of inulin and oligofructose
President: Kathy Niness
CEO: Mark T Izzo
Marketing: Barry Schwartz
Estimated Sales: $5-10 Million
Number Employees: 5-9
Parent Co: Orafti S.A.
Type of Packaging: Bulk
Private Brands Carried:
  Raftiline; Raftilose
Types of Products Distributed:
  General Line, Inulin & oligofructose

Wholesalers & Distributors / A-Z

58468 Oram Material Handling Systems
1034 S 8th St
Kansas City, KS 66105 913-621-4242
Fax: 913-621-5759
Wholesaler/distributor of forklifts
Owner: Fred Oram
VP/General Manager: Frederick Oram
Estimated Sales: $10-20 Million
Number Employees: 50-99
Private Brands Carried:
 Nissan
Types of Products Distributed:
 Frozen Food, General Merchandise, Forklifts

58469 Orange Distributors
3055 Pennington Dr
Orlando, FL 32804-3333 407-295-2217
Fax: 407-291-6455 800-777-6012
www.crownpack.com
Wholesaler/distributor of packaging materials
Manager: Allan Huck
VP/Sales Manager: Robin Cornett
VP/Operations Manager: Mark Moyer
Estimated Sales: $10-20 Million
Number Employees: 10-19
Square Footage: 40000
Types of Products Distributed:
 Frozen Food, General Merchandise, Packaging materials

58470 Orchards Hawaii
PO Box 599
Makawao, HI 96768-599 808-875-4444
Fax: 808-875-7111 888-875-8999
Wholesale tropical juice
President: Russ Burns
Owner: Peter Baldwin
Vice President: Paula Burroughs
Estimated Sales: Less than $500,000
Number Employees: 1-4
Type of Packaging: Consumer, Food Service

58471 Orear Company
2009 NW 10th Street
Oklahoma City, OK 73106-2429 405-528-3397
Wholesaler/distributor of commercial scales and food equipment; serving the food service market
President: Robert Frick
Vice President: Phil Floyd
Estimated Sales: $5-10 Million
Number Employees: 20-49
Private Brands Carried:
 Alto-Shaam; Mettler Toledo; Chesterfield
Types of Products Distributed:
 Food Service, Frozen Food, General Merchandise, Commercial scales & food equipment

58472 Oreck Commercial Sales
1400 Salem Road
Cookeville, TN 38506 800-242-1378
Fax: 877-672-4566 800-219-2044
lagreca@oreck.com www.oreckcommercial.com
Wholesaler/distributor of commercial vacuum cleaners, air machines and floor cleaning products; serving the food service market
President: Tony La Greca
General Manager: Patrick Burke
Estimated Sales: $12 Million
Number Employees: 20-49
Private Brands Carried:
 Oreck Vacuums
Types of Products Distributed:
 Food Service, General Merchandise, Vacuum cleaners, air machines, etc.

58473 Oregon Bark
1400 NE 37th Ave
Portland, OR 97232
mail@oregonbark.com
www.oregonbark.com
Vegan, gluten free candy including peanut butter flake candy and hazelnut rosemary crisp candy
Owner: Anne Smith *Year Founded:* 2012
Types of Products Distributed:
 General Line

58474 Organic Vintages
PO Box 832
Ukiah, CA 95482-0832 707-462-2300
Fax: 707-462-4258 800-877-6655
info@organicvintages.com
www.organicvintages.com
Wholesaler/distributor of organic wine, sake, cider, champagne and beer; serving the food service market; importer of organic wine
President: Steven Frenkel
Estimated Sales: $700,000-800,000
Number Employees: 1-4
Square Footage: 800
Private Brands Carried:
 Fitzpatrick; Frey; Organic Wine Works; Octopus Mountain; Nevada County Wine Guild; Honeyrun Honeywine Co.; Orleans Hill; LaRocca; Badger Mountain
Number of Customer Locations: 1000
Types of Products Distributed:
 Organic wine, sake, champagne, beer etc

58475 Organics Unlimited
8587 Avenida Costa Norte
Suite 2
San Diego, CA 92154 619-710-0658
info@organicsunlimited.com
www.organicsunlimited.com
Organic bananas, plantains, and coconuts
President/CEO: Mayra Velazquez de Leon
Director Operations: Marco Garcia Ojeda
Year Founded: 2000
Number Employees: 10-19
Types of Products Distributed:
 Produce

58476 Original Food
1910 avenue du Sanctuaire
Beauport, QU G1E 3L2 205-424-5199
Fax: 205-425-1270 www.originalfoods.com
Wholesaler/distributor of provisions/meats, seafood, baked goods and Italian specialty food items; serving the food service market
President: Dewaine Carlson
VP: Ginger Carlson
Sales Manager: Wayne Parker
Estimated Sales: $5-10 Million
Number Employees: 10-19
Square Footage: 72000
Number of Customer Locations: 400
Types of Products Distributed:
 Food Service, Frozen Food, General Line, Provisions/Meat, Seafood, Specialty Foods, Italian specialty food items

58477 Original Juan
111 Southwest Blvd
Kansas City, KS 66103 913-432-5228
Fax: 913-432-5880 800-568-8468
Sauces, salsas, dips and snacks.
President & CEO: Joe Polo
VP, Sales: Greg Dennis
VP, Operations: Tom Clark
Year Founded: 1998
Number of Brands: 13
Number of Products: 1700
Square Footage: 60000
Type of Packaging: Consumer, Private Label

58478 Orinoco Coffee & Tea
8265 Patuxent Range Rd
Suite L
Jessup, MD 20794 410-312-5292
Fax: 240-636-5196 info@orinococoffeeandtea.com
www.orinococoffeeandtea.com
Coffe and tea
CEO: Pedro Ramirez
Master Roaster, R&D: Juan Carlos Ramirez

58479 Orioxi International Corporation
1422 Edinger Avenue,
Suite 250
Tustin, CA 92780 71- 99- 899
Fax: 714-824-3386
Importer of walnuts, pine nuts and seeds; exporter of fresh and dried fruits; wholesaler/distributor of nuts, seeds and dried fruits; serving the food service market
President: Ziegfred Young
Number Employees: 5-9
Square Footage: 48000
Types of Products Distributed:
 Food Service, Frozen Food, Produce, Nuts, seeds & fruits

58480 Orlando Fire Equipment Company
4250 L B McLeod Rd
Orlando, FL 32811-5680 407-481-0872
Fax: 407-481-4392
Wholesaler/distributor of fire extinguishers and lighting fixtures
Manager: Jerry Chucko
Estimated Sales: $5-10 Million
Number Employees: 10-19
Private Brands Carried:
 General; Buckeye; Badger; Rangeguard; Pyrochem
Number of Customer Locations: 1500
Types of Products Distributed:
 Frozen Food, General Merchandise, Fire extinguishers & lighting fixtures

58481 Orleans International
30600 Northwestern Hwy
Suite 300
Farmington Hills, MI 48334-3172 248-855-5556
Fax: 248-855-5668 info@orleansintl.com
orleansintl.com
Beef, lamb, pork, poultry, seafood, and wild game.
President: Earl Tushman
Secretary: Larry Tushman
Director of Operations: Reed Tushman
Director of Logistics: Marc Tushman
Senior Vice President: Steve Sanger
Controller: Beth Ehrlich
Estimated Sales: $100-500 Million
Number of Products: 2000
Type of Packaging: Consumer, Food Service
Types of Products Distributed:
 Frozen Food, Provisions/Meat

58482 Orr's Farm Market
Po Box 906
Martinsburg, WV 25402-0906 304-263-1027
Fax: 304-263-1153 dondove@orrsfarmmarket.com
www.orrsfarmmarket.com
Farm market

58483 Ortho-Molecular Products Inc
3017 Business Park Dr
Stevens Point, WI 54482-8835 715-342-9881
Fax: 715-342-9866 800-332-2351
www.discoverourstory.com
Vitamin supplements
President: Gary Powers
g.powers@ompimail.com
VP Sales: Jack Radloff
VP Operations: Dean Kramer
Estimated Sales: $5-10 Million
Number Employees: 50-99
Square Footage: 64000
Parent Co: Ortho Molecular Products
Types of Products Distributed:
 Frozen Food, Health Food, Vitamin supplements

58484 Osage Food Products Inc
120 W Main St # 200
Washington, MO 63090-2121 636-390-9477
Fax: 636-390-9485 sales@osagefood.com
www.osagefood.com
Osage is a multi-dimensional company supplying ingredients and food products. Our ingredients for manufacturing. Our packaged goods division supplies national brands and private label products for food service and retail. Our specialtyproducts division works with manufacturers, marketing residual ingredients and finished goods that are needed to sell
President: William Dickinson
Estimated Sales: $2.5-5,000,000
Number Employees: 5-9
Type of Packaging: Consumer, Food Service, Private Label, Bulk
Types of Products Distributed:
 Food Service, General Line, Produce

58485 Osborn Bros Inc
259 N 5th St
Gadsden, AL 35901-3240 256-547-8601
Fax: 256-546-1634 www.osbornfoodservice.com
Wholesaler/distributor of groceries, meats, produce, dairy products, frozen foods, baked goods, equipment and fixtures, etc.; serving the food service market
President: Joel Osborn
General Manager: Bobby Smith
CFO: J Osborn
VP Sales: B Glass
Operations Manager: David Horsley
Purchasing Manager: Jerry Osborn
Estimated Sales: $20-50 Million
Number Employees: 5-9
Square Footage: 60000

Wholesalers & Distributors / A-Z

Type of Packaging: Food Service
Private Brands Carried:
 Nieda
Types of Products Distributed:
 Food Service, Frozen Food, Provisions/Meat, Produce

58486 Oscar's Wholesale Meats
250 W 31st St
Ogden, UT 84401-3899   801-621-5655
Fax: 801-394-8113 oscarsmeat@live.com
www.oscarsmeat.comcastbiz.net
Steak, beef patties, poultry, bacon and roasts
Owner/President: Darrell Gardner
Estimated Sales: $25.5 Million
Number Employees: 10-19
Type of Packaging: Consumer, Food Service
Types of Products Distributed:
 Frozen Food, Provisions/Meat

58487 Ostrow Jobbing Company
2316 Territorial Road
Saint Paul, MN 55114-1614   651-645-2750
Fax: 651-332-5800
Wholesaler/distributor of groceries, baked goods, general merchandise, private label items, etc.; serving the food service market
President: M Ostrow
Number Employees: 1-4
Private Brands Carried:
 Ostrow's
Number of Customer Locations: 200
Types of Products Distributed:
 Food Service, Frozen Food, General Line, General Merchandise, Baked goods, equipment & fixtures, etc.

58488 Oswalt Restaurant Supply
1015 NW 68th St
Oklahoma City, OK 73116-7201   405-843-9000
Fax: 405-840-4044 www.oswalt.biz
Wholesaler/distributor of restaurant supplies; serving the food service market
President: Rod Baumberger
rod.baumberger@oswalt.biz
Estimated Sales: $10-20 Million
Number Employees: 50-99
Private Brands Carried:
 True; Hobart; Vollrath
Types of Products Distributed:
 Food Service, Frozen Food, General Merchandise, Restaurant supplies

58489 Ottenheimer Equipment Company
PO Box 4395
Lutherville Timonium, MD 21094-4395 410-597-9700
Fax: 410-252-7775
Wholesaler/distributor of food service equipment; serving the food service market; also, consultant for the design of food facilities
Estimated Sales: $.5-1 million
Number Employees: 1-4
Types of Products Distributed:
 Food Service, Frozen Food, General Merchandise

58490 Otto Brehm Inc
75 Tuckahoe Rd
P.O. Box 249
Yonkers, NY 10710   914-968-6100
Fax: 914-968-8926 800-272-6886
www.ottobrehm.com
Wholesaler/distributor of bakery ingredients; serving the food service market.
President: Ernie Brehm, Jr.
VP & Chief Financial Officer: Linda Tritto
Sales Manager: Garett Brehm
Vice President, Operations: Charles Koenig
Warehouse Manager: Frank Rodriguez
Year Founded: 1904
Estimated Sales: $40 Million
Number Employees: 100
Square Footage: 30000
Number of Customer Locations: 2500
Types of Products Distributed:
 Food Service, General Line, Bakery ingredients

58491 Our Lady of Guadalupe Trappist Abbey
9200 NE Abbey Rd
Carlton, OR 97111-9666   503-852-0103
Fax: 503-852-7748 dicklayton@trappistabbey.org
www.trappistabbey.org
Fruitcake, date-nut cake

Business Manager: Richard Laytlon
Estimated Sales: Under $500,000
Number Employees: 20
Types of Products Distributed:
 Specialty Foods

58492 Outback Sales
2555 W Le Moyne St # F-1
Melrose Park, IL 60160-1830   708-345-9000
Fax: 708-345-9005
Owner: Alan Davidson
Estimated Sales: Less Than $500,000
Number Employees: 1-4

58493 Outerbridge Peppers Limited
20 Harry Shupe Blvd
Wharton, NJ 07885   626-296-2400
peppers@logic.bm
www.outerbridge.com
Packaging facility for Outerbridge Peppers LTD, specializing in sherry peppers and a variety of other sauces.
Managing Director: Norma Cross
Number of Brands: 1
Parent Co: Outerbridge Peppers Limited
Type of Packaging: Consumer, Food Service, Bulk
Types of Products Distributed:
 Specialty Foods

58494 Overhead Door Company of Fort Wayne
2501 South State Highway 122 Bus.
Suite 200
Lewisville, TX 75067
Fax: 469-549-7281 800-275-3290
www.overheaddoor.com
Wholesaler/distributor of commercial doors; serving the food service market
General Manager: Bruce Cole
Estimated Sales: $5-10 Million
Number Employees: 50-99
Private Brands Carried:
 Overhead Doors; Allister; Chamberlain
Types of Products Distributed:
 Food Service, Frozen Food, General Merchandise, Commercial doors

58495 Oyang America
1043 S Harvard Boulevard
Los Angeles, CA 90006-2403   323-737-8501
Fax: 213-365-8670
Wholesaler/distributor, importer and exporter of frozen fish, surimi products, frozen seafood, freeze-dried seafood and prepared frozen seafood
President: Kenneth Yoon
Estimated Sales: $2.5-5 Million
Number Employees: 1-4
Parent Co: Oyang Corporation
Private Brands Carried:
 Oyang; Articfresh
Types of Products Distributed:
 Frozen Food, Seafood, Fish & surimi

58496 Oyster Peddler
8139 Tilghman Island Rd
Sherwood, MD 21665-9731   410-745-5971
www.oyster.com
Wholesaler/distributor of seafood including oysters, clams, crabs, soft shell crabs and fish
President: Jacquelyn Scharch
Estimated Sales: Less Than $500,000
Number Employees: 1-4
Square Footage: 4000
Types of Products Distributed:
 Frozen Food, Seafood

58497 Ozark Cooperative Warehouse
PO Box 1528
Fayetteville, AR 72702-1528   479-521-4920
Fax: 501-521-9100
Wholesaler/distributor of natural, health and specialty foods
CEO: Nick Masullo
CFO: Beverly Toll
Sales Director: Richard Davies
Customer Service: Shawn Clark
Operations Manager: Leslie Kroder
Purchasing Manager: Dave Baire
Estimated Sales: $10 Million
Number Employees: 48
Square Footage: 80000
Parent Co: X
Type of Packaging: Consumer, Bulk
Number of Customer Locations: 200

Types of Products Distributed:
 Frozen Food, Health Food, Specialty Foods

58498 Ozarka Drinking Water
4718 Mountain Creek Pkwy
Dallas, TX 75236   817-354-9526
www.ozarkawater.com
Drinking water
Manager: Randy Payne
Estimated Sales: $20-50 Million
Number Employees: 100-249
Parent Co: Ozarka Houston Water Company

58499 PDEQ
PO Box 28511
Fresno, CA 93729   559-490-4412
hello@pdeq.net
pdeq.net
Tapioca-based cheese bread
President/Owner: Flavia Takahashi-Flores

58500 (HQ)P & D Corp
PO Box 11179
Goldsboro, NC 27532-1179   919-778-3000
Fax: 919-778-0604 800-899-3921
Wholesaler/distributor of groceries, meats, produce, dairy products, frozen foods, bakery products, general merchandise and seafood; serving the food service market
President: Mac Sullivan
CEO: Mike Pate
CEO: Malcolm R Sullivan Jr
Estimated Sales: Less than $500,000
Number Employees: 1-4
Square Footage: 248000
Other Locations:
 Pate Dawson Co.
 Fayetteville, NC Pate Dawson Co.
Private Brands Carried:
 Pocahontas; Mt. Stirling; PDC
Types of Products Distributed:
 Food Service, Frozen Food, General Line, General Merchandise, Provisions/Meat, Produce, Seafood, Groceries, baked goods, etc.

58501 P & S Food & Liquor
4910 W Irving Park Rd
Chicago, IL 60641-2619   773-685-0088
Fax: 773-685-0088
Wines
Owner: Edmund Sammando
Estimated Sales: $1 million
Number Employees: 1-4

58502 P A Menard
4373 Michoud Blvd
New Orleans, LA 70129   504-620-2022
Fax: 504-592-2784 800-464-7970
Contract packager of dairy products, frozen and specialty foods and general line products; wholesaler/distributor of groceries, private label items, frozen and specialty foods, etc.; serving the food service market
President: Mike Menard
CEO: Pamela Boyd
CFO: Al Pearson
Purchasing: Joe Abraham
Estimated Sales: $20-50 Million
Number Employees: 20-49
Square Footage: 70000
Private Brands Carried:
 Red & White Label
Number of Customer Locations: 190
Types of Products Distributed:
 Food Service, Frozen Food, General Line, Provisions/Meat, Specialty Foods

58503 P&C Pacific Bakeries
810 81st Ave
Oakland, CA 94621-2510   510-834-3134
Fax: 510-834-4408
Bakery products
Manager: David Shenson
Estimated Sales: $46 Millon
Number Employees: 50-99
Types of Products Distributed:
 Food Service, Frozen Food

58504 P&E Foods
3077 Koapaka St
Suite 202
Honolulu, HI 96819-5105   808-839-9094
Fax: 808-834-8409
Frozen meats

1123

Wholesalers & Distributors / A-Z

President: Stephen S C Lee
Contact: Stephen Leong
sleong@avsupply.com
Manager: Harry Toywooka
Estimated Sales: $5-10 Million
Number Employees: 20-49

58505 P&L Seafood of Venice
401 Whitney Ave # 103
Gretna, LA 70056-2500
504-363-2744
Fax: 504-392-3334 www.chartwellsmenus.com
Seafood
Manager: John Duke

58506 P. Tavilla Company
1245 NW 21st Street
Miami, FL 33142-7725
305-999-6000
Fax: 305-653-5570
Wholesaler/distributor of produce; serving the food service market
President: Walter Vazquez, Sr.
Controller: Eduardo Solana
Director Food Service Operations: Walter Vazquez, Jr.
Estimated Sales: $20-50 Million
Number Employees: 50-99
Square Footage: 60000
Parent Co: Sysco Corporation
Number of Customer Locations: 40
Types of Products Distributed:
  Frozen Food, Produce

58507 P.A. Braunger Institutional Foods
900 Clark St
Sioux City, IA 51101
712-258-4515
Fax: 712-258-1130 www.braungerfoods.com
Frozen meats, general line products
President: Tony Wald
General Manager: J David
Estimated Sales: $10-20 Million
Number Employees: 50-99
Number of Customer Locations: 2000
Types of Products Distributed:
  Food Service, Frozen Food, General Line, Provisions/Meat

58508 P.J. Markos Seafood Company
Eight Topsfield Road
Ipswich, MA 01938-2132
978-356-4347
Fax: 978-356-9380
Seafood
Estimated Sales: $1-3 Million
Number Employees: 5-9

58509 P.J. Merrill Seafood Inc
681 Forest Ave
Portland, ME 04103-4101
207-773-1321
Fax: 207-775-4160 www.pjmerrillseafood.com
Seafood
Owner: Paul Merrill
fpjmerri@maine.rr.com
Estimated Sales: $3-5 Million
Number Employees: 10-19

58510 P.M. Innis Lobster Company
P.O.Box 85
18 Yates Street
Biddeford Pool, ME 04006
207-284-5000
Fax: 207-283-3308 help@poollobster.com
www.poollobster.com
Lobster
Owner: Beth Baskin
Estimated Sales: $3-5 Million
Number Employees: 10-19

58511 P.T. Fish
10b Portland Fish Pier
Portland, ME 04101-4620
207-772-0239
Fax: 907-874-2072
Seafood
Owner: Michael Twiss

58512 P/B Distributors
236 Stephanie Lane
Covington, LA 70435
901-767-1059
Fax: 901-985-9473
Food service equipment
President: Jay El-Kareh

58513 PAFCO Importing Co
15373 Innovation Dr # 105
San Diego, CA 92128-3424
858-487-4844
Fax: 650-692-8950 tsfpafco@aol.com
Focusing on hanlding every aspect of importing your private label.
President: Terence S Fitzgerald
terry@pafcoimporting.com
VP: Barbara Burns
Operations: Myrna Goble
Estimated Sales: $10-20 Million
Number Employees: 1-4
Square Footage: 2800
Type of Packaging: Consumer, Food Service, Private Label, Bulk
Private Brands Carried:
  Terry's
Types of Products Distributed:
  Frozen Food, General Line, Seafood, Pineapple, mango juice, etc.

58514 PAT Vitamins Inc
1751 Curtiss Ct
La Verne, CA 91750-5852
626-810-8886
Fax: 626-821-6601 info@patvitamins.com
www.patvitamins.com
Ingredients distributor to the food, health nutrition, pharma-, cosme- and nutraceutical industries.
Owner: Steve Haung
steve@patvitamins.com
Estimated Sales: $1 Million
Number Employees: 10-19
Type of Packaging: Bulk
Types of Products Distributed:
  Health Food, Vitamins, minerals, health foods, etc.

58515 PAX Spices & Labs Inc
550 N Rimsdale Ave
Covina, CA 91722-3507
626-967-7800
Fax: 626-967-7811 sales@paxspices.com
www.paxspices.com
Importer and distributor of exotic herbs, spices and oils.
President & CEO: Tom Tharayil
providence@paxspices.com
Estimated Sales: Less Than $500,000
Number Employees: 1-4
Other Locations:
  Headquarters
  Covina, CA
  Sales & Distribution
  Schaumburg, ILHeadquartersSchaumburg

58516 PDE Technology Corp
11522 Markon Dr
Garden Grove, CA 92841-1809
714-799-1704
Fax: 714-799-1705 866-547-8090
sales@castertech.com www.pdetechnology.com
Wholesaler/distributor and exporter of zinc and stainless steel finished casters and wheels for all applications; wholesaler/distributor of high temperature and washdown replacement parts for OEM equipment; serving the food servicemarket
President: Chris Merchant
chris@pdetechnology.com
VP Marketing: David Elles
Account Services Manager: Bob Pettingill
Estimated Sales: $5-10 Million
Number Employees: 10-19
Square Footage: 80000
Type of Packaging: Consumer, Food Service, Bulk
Private Brands Carried:
  Javis & Javis; RWM; Darcor
Types of Products Distributed:
  Food Service, General Merchandise, Casters, wheels & replacement parts

58517 PLT Trucking Corporation
1767 S Us Highway 41
Vincennes, IN 47591
812-882-3144
Wholesaler/distributor of frozen food, general line products, produce and meats
Owner: Virgil Lane
Estimated Sales: $300,000-500,000
Number Employees: 1-4
Number of Customer Locations: 40
Types of Products Distributed:
  Frozen Food, General Line, Provisions/Meat, Produce

58518 PMC Specialties Group Inc
501 Murray Rd
Cincinnati, OH 45217-1014
513-242-3300
Fax: 513-482-7373 800-543-2466
davidsc@pmsg.com www.pmcsg.com
Saccharin, BHT, methyl anthranilate and benzonitrile

President: Michael Buchanan
Contact: Antaeus Kelly
antaeusk@pmcsg.com
Estimated Sales: $70 Milion
Number Employees: 250-499
Square Footage: 7500
Parent Co: PMC Global, Inc.
Types of Products Distributed:
  Frozen Food

58519 POP Fishing & Marine
1133 N Nimitz Hwy
Honolulu, HI 96817
808-537-2905
Fax: 808-536-3225 sales@pop-hawaii.com
www.pop-hawaii.com
Seafood
President: Sean Martin
Owner: Jim Cook
Contact: Romeo Caban
romeo@pop-hawaii.com

58520 PYA/Monarch
5425 Williamson Boulevard
Port Orange, FL 32128-7399
904-255-0423
Fax: 904-258-4613 800-866-6368
Wholesaler/distributor of frozen foods, general merchandise, general line products, produce, meat, groceries, dairy products, baked goods, equipment and fixtures, etc.; serving the food service market
Manager: B Baird
Number Employees: 100-249
Parent Co: PYA/Monarch
Number of Customer Locations: 3000
Types of Products Distributed:
  Food Service, Frozen Food, General Line, General Merchandise, Provisions/Meat, Produce, Seafood, Specialty Foods

58521 PYA/Monarch
P.O.Box 6171
Greenville, SC 29606-6171
864-277-6043
Fax: 864-277-6152
Wholesaler/distributor serving the food service market
Owner: Dunk Pye
Estimated Sales: $1-3 Million
Number Employees: 10-19
Parent Co: PYA/Monarch
Types of Products Distributed:
  Food Service, Frozen Food

58522 PYA/Monarch
5205 S Lois Avenue
Tampa, FL 33611-3446
813-831-7260
Fax: 813-832-2301
Wholesaler/distributor serving the food service market
VP/General Manager: Kenneth Hahn
Number Employees: 100-249
Parent Co: PYA/Monarch
Number of Customer Locations: 100
Types of Products Distributed:
  Food Service, Frozen Food

58523 Paar Physica USA
1 Industrial Way W
Eatontown, NJ 07724-2255
804-266-5553
Fax: 804-550-1057 800-688-3569
Wholesaler/distributor, importer and exporter of laboratory instrumentation for measuring viscosity and elasticity of food products; also, rheometers for research and quality assurance
CEO: Sean Race
COO: Abel Gaspar
Number Employees: 10-19
Square Footage: 6000
Types of Products Distributed:
  Frozen Food, General Merchandise

58524 Pacific California FishCompany
512 Stanford Avenue
Los Angeles, CA 90013-2188
213-629-0045
Wholesaler/distributor of seafood; serving the food service market
Types of Products Distributed:
  Food Service, Frozen Food, Seafood

58525 Pacific Choice Seafood Inc
1 Commercial St
Eureka, CA 95501
707-442-2981
info@pacseafood.com
www.pacseafood.com
Wholesaler/distributor of fresh and frozen seafood including shrimp, crab and salmon.

Wholesalers & Distributors / A-Z

Number Employees: 2,500
Square Footage: 50000

58526 Pacific Coast ChemicalsCo
2424 4th St
Berkeley, CA 94710
510-549-3535
Fax: 510-549-0890 info@pcchem.com
www.pcchem.com
Wholesaler/distributor of food ingredients and chemicals.
President: Dominic Stull
Sales Representative: David Orona
Year Founded: 1969
Estimated Sales: $50-100 Million
Number Employees: 20-49
Square Footage: 50000
Types of Products Distributed:
 General Line, Ingredients

58527 Pacific Commerce Company
16320 Bake Parkway
Irvine, CA 92618
949-679-4700
Fax: 949-589-9002
Exporter of maraschino cherries, pie fillings, bakery items, mayonnaise, salad dressings, etc.; wholesaler/distributor of general line products; serving the food service market; warehouse offering dry storage for groceries
President: Bryan McCullough
VP: Mark Roberts
Contact: Mackay Ramsay
mramsay@pacificcommerce.com
Estimated Sales: $2.5-5 Million
Number Employees: 1-4
Square Footage: 73728
Private Brands Carried:
 Oregon; Pennant; Gold N' Soft
Types of Products Distributed:
 Food Service, Frozen Food, General Line

58528 Pacific Compactor Corporation
3901 E Miraloma Avenue
Anaheim, CA 92806
714-993-9194
Fax: 714-993-9202 800-458-8832
www.pacificcompactor.com
Wholesaler/distributor of trash compactors and recycling equipment; serving the food service market
President: Dale Menke
Contact: Cynthia Menke
cmenke@pacificcompactor.com
Estimated Sales: $2.5-5 Million
Number Employees: 10-19
Square Footage: 20000
Parent Co: Harmony Enterprises
Private Brands Carried:
 Power Packer
Types of Products Distributed:
 Food Service, Frozen Food, General Merchandise, Trash compactors & recycling equip.

58529 Pacific Gourmet Seafood
26 Stine Road
Bakersfield, CA 93309-2011
661-533-1260
Fax: 805-831-9740
Seafood
Partner: Kelly Bowman
Partner: Patsy Bowman

58530 Pacific Resources
1021 Mark Ave
Carpinteria, CA 93013-2912
805-684-0624
Fax: 805-684-8624 800-871-8879
www.shoppri.com
Bottled water, honey, sea salt and propolis products
President: David Noll
pri98@earthlink.net
Estimated Sales: $3-5 Million
Number Employees: 1-4
Type of Packaging: Consumer
Types of Products Distributed:
 Frozen Food, General Line, Health Food, Specialty Foods, Propolis products

58531 Pacific Rim Shellfish Corp.
1807 Mast Tower Road
Vancouver, BC V6H 3X7
Canada
604-687-4228
Fax: 604-687-5099
Wholesaler/distributor of shellfish
Partner: Brian Yip
Number Employees: 10-19
Types of Products Distributed:
 Frozen Food, Seafood, Shellfish

58532 Pacific Seafood Co
16797 SE 130th Ave
Clackamas, OR 97015
503-905-4500
info@pacseafood.com
www.pacseafood.com
Wholesaler/distributor of fresh and frozen seafood including shrimp, crab and salmon.
President & CEO: Frank Dominic Dulcich
Year Founded: 1941
Estimated Sales: $50-100 Million
Number Employees: 2,500
Square Footage: 35000
Private Brands Carried:
 Jake's Famous Crawfish & Seafood; Pacific Fresh; Sea Rock; Newport
Types of Products Distributed:
 Frozen Food, Seafood, Fresh & frozen shrimp, crab & salmon

58533 Pacific Shrimp Co
2422 S Canal St
Chicago, IL 60616-2224
312-326-0803
Fax: 312-326-2728
President: Hyman Moy
Estimated Sales: $5-10 Million
Number Employees: 5-9

58534 Pacific Steam Equipment, Inc.
10648 Painter Ave
Santa Fe Springs, CA 90670
562-906-9292
Fax: 562-906-9223 800-321-4114
sales@pacificsteam.com
Manufacturer and exporter of boilers; distributor of food processing machinery
Owner: David Ken
President: William Shanahan
Vice President: Shin King
Marketing Manager: Simon Lee
Sales Manager: Santiago Kuan
Contact: Dave Kang
res@pacificsteam.com
Estimated Sales: $2.9 Million
Number Employees: 25
Square Footage: 90000
Types of Products Distributed:
 Frozen Food, General Merchandise, Food processing machinery

58535 Pacific Tomato Growers
PO Box 159
Westover, MD 21871-0159
941-722-3291
Fax: 941-729-5849
Wholesaler/distributor of fresh tomatoes
Partner/Manager/CEO: Ed English
Estimated Sales: $5-10 Million
Number Employees: 10-19
Parent Co: Pacific Land Company
Number of Customer Locations: 150
Types of Products Distributed:
 Frozen Food, Produce, Fresh tomatoes

58536 Pacific Westcoast Foods
3880 Sw 102nd Ave
Beaverton, OR 97005-3244
503-641-4988
Fax: 755-665-8610 800-874-9333
gourmet@teleport.com
Salad dressings, preserves, fruit syrups and fillings
President: Mark Roth
President: Gloria Sample
Estimated Sales: $280,000
Number Employees: 4
Square Footage: 20000
Type of Packaging: Consumer, Food Service, Private Label, Bulk
Private Brands Carried:
 N.W. Berry Growers; Wild West Foods; Oregon Natural Tea
Number of Customer Locations: 800
Types of Products Distributed:
 Frozen Food, General Line, Rack Jobbers, Specialty Foods, Gift packs & private label items

58537 Pacific World Enterprises
225 Market Street
203
Oakland, CA 94607-2554
510-843-0240
Wholesaler/distributor and exporter of frozen foods, produce, meats and seafood; serving the food service market
President: Edward Chiang
VP/General Manager: Keith Toy
Manager (West Coast): Bill Chiang

Number Employees: 20-49
Square Footage: 72000
Parent Co: Good World Investment Company
Type of Packaging: Food Service
Other Locations:
 Pacific World Enterprises
 Saipan MPPacific World Enterprises
Private Brands Carried:
 Certified Angus Beef; McCain's; Tyson; All Kitchens
Types of Products Distributed:
 Food Service, Frozen Food, Provisions/Meat, Produce, Seafood

58538 Pacific-SEH Hotel SupplyCompany
46 10th Ave
New York, NY 10014-1101
212-243-6700
Fax: 212-929-5772
Wholesaler/distributor of fresh and frozen meat; serving the food service market
President: Christopher Gachot
CEO/Chairman: Charles Gachot
General Manager: H Petrak
Estimated Sales: $10-20 Million
Number Employees: 1-4
Parent Co: Gachot & Gachot
Types of Products Distributed:
 Food Service, Frozen Food, Provisions/Meat

58539 Packaging Equipment Company
P.O.Box 669
Cordele, GA 31010
229-273-3232
Fax: 229-273-3233
Wholesaler/distributor of bag filling and closing equipment
Owner: Dixon Hugins
Estimated Sales: Less than $500,000
Number Employees: 1-4
Types of Products Distributed:
 Frozen Food, General Merchandise, Bag filling & closing equipment

58540 Packaging Services Corp
26100 Pinehurst Dr
Madison Heights, MI 48071-4182
248-548-7770
Fax: 248-548-8947 800-328-7799
sales@pack-serv.com www.pack-serv.com
Wholesaler/distributor of custom packaging and shipping supplies including boxes and bags; serving retail markets
President: Sam Frank
sfrank@pack-serv.com
VP Sales: Mitch Lefton
Estimated Sales: $5-10 Million
Number Employees: 20-49
Types of Products Distributed:
 Frozen Food, General Merchandise, Shipping supplies

58541 Packsource Systems
2158 Union Pl
Simi Valley, CA 93065-1660
818-700-2500
Fax: 805-520-7555 800-463-3100
www.packsourcesys.com
Wholesaler/distributor of general merchandise including boxes, cartons, conveyors, films, labels, weighing systems, packaging and wrapping machinery
President: Steve Ferrato
steve@packsourcesys.com
Sales/Marketing Executive: Sandy Silberstein
Customer Service: Tim Joe
Customer Service: Zuyda Foreman
General Manager: Wendy Gray
Purchasing Agent: Willie Adams
Estimated Sales: $5-10 Million
Number Employees: 5-9
Types of Products Distributed:
 Frozen Food, General Merchandise, Boxes, film, conveyors, packaging, etc.

58542 (HQ)Pacmatic/Ritmica
4140 Tuller Road
Suite 130
Dublin, OH 43017-5013
614-793-0440
Fax: 614-793-0443 800-846-0440
Importer and wholesaler/distributor of packaging machinery including horizontal baggers, overwrappers, shrink bundlers, cartoners, case packers, tray formers and stretch wrapping equipment
President: Andre Pittaluga
Number Employees: 5-9
Square Footage: 24000

Wholesalers & Distributors / A-Z

Types of Products Distributed:
  Frozen Food, General Merchandise, Packaging & stretch wrapping machinery

58543 Pacsea Corporation
PO Box 898
Aiea, HI 96701-0898   808-836-8888
Fax: 808-836-7888
Seafood
President: Michael Li
Treasurer/Bookkeeper: Wendy Puampi
Vice-President: Gladis Li

58544 Pagano M Watermelons
59 Brooklyn Terminal Market
Brooklyn, NY 11236-1511   718-251-7373
Fax: 718-251-7373
Wholesaler/distributor of produce, including watermelons
Owner: Anthony Pagano
anthony@paganomelons.com
Estimated Sales: $1-3 Million
Number Employees: 1-4
Types of Products Distributed:
  Frozen Food, Produce

58545 Painted Cookie
7365 Bluewater Drive
Apt 5
Clarkston, MI 48348-4233   248-620-9730
carol_kurtz@hotmail.com
Wholesaler/distributor of hand painted edible cookies
President: Carol Kurtz
Number Employees: 20-49
Types of Products Distributed:
  Frozen Food, General Line, Hand painted edible cookies

58546 Paisano Distribution Company
7417 Big Bend Drive
El Paso, TX 79904-3542   915-759-7902
Fax: 915-759-7903
Wholesaler/distributor of tabletop supplies and equipment; serving the food service market
President: Candy Aquirre
Types of Products Distributed:
  Food Service, Frozen Food, General Merchandise, Tabletop supplies, equipment, etc.

58547 Palama Meat Co Inc
2029 Lauwiliwili St
Kapolei, HI 96707-1836   808-682-8305
Fax: 808-834-8895 www.hwcny.com
Wholesaler/distributor of provisions/meats and frozen foods; serving the food service market
Owner: Nam Collins
nam@palamameat.com
Number Employees: 100-249
Parent Co: Small Business Contract Bid Intelligence Company
Types of Products Distributed:
  Food Service, Frozen Food, Provisions/Meat

58548 Palamatic Handling USA
901 S Bolmar St Bldg 1c
P.O.Box 2020
West Chester, PA 19380-2020   610-701-6350
Fax: 610-701-6354 info@tnthandling.com
www.tnthandling.com
Wholesaler/distributor and importer of material handling and food processing equipment
President: Tim Carney
Sales Manager: Tom Carney
Estimated Sales: $1-3 Million
Number Employees: 5-9
Square Footage: 11400
Types of Products Distributed:
  Material handling equipment, etc.

58549 Paleewong Trading Corporation
62-04 34th Ave
Woodside, NY 11377   718-507-6520
Fax: 718-507-6528 www.paleewongtrading.com
Importer and wholesaler/distributor of beer
President: Chi Chi Paleewong
Estimated Sales: $.5-1 million
Number Employees: 5-9
Private Brands Carried:
  Thailand Sing Ha Beer
Number of Customer Locations: 200
Types of Products Distributed:
  Frozen Food, General Line, Beer

58550 (HQ)Palm Brothers
1031 Madeira Ave
Minneapolis, MN 55405-2147   612-381-3100
Fax: 612-381-3131 800-328-5133
Wholesaler/distributor of restaurant equipment and supplies; serving the food service market
President: Dave Miller
Operations: Thomas Hoffman
Estimated Sales: $10-20 Million
Number Employees: 50-99
Square Footage: 150000
Other Locations:
  Palm Brothers
  Saint Paul, MNPalm Brothers
Number of Customer Locations: 2
Types of Products Distributed:
  Food Service, Frozen Food, General Merchandise, Restaurant equipment & supplies

58551 (HQ)Palmer Associates
4401 Jackman Rd
Toledo, OH 43612-1529   419-478-7151
Fax: 419-478-3947 www.palmerassoc.com
Wholesaler/distributor of canned, refrigerated and frozen items and disposable nonfood supply items; serving the food service market
Owner: Gerry Ames
games@palmerassoc.com
Estimated Sales: $500,000
Number Employees: 20-49
Square Footage: 40000
Type of Packaging: Food Service
Types of Products Distributed:
  Food Service, Frozen Food, General Merchandise, Disposable non-food supply items, etc.

58552 (HQ)Palmer Candy Co
2600 N US Highway 75
Suite 1
Sioux City, IA 51105-2444   712-258-5543
Fax: 712-258-3224 800-831-0828
vicki@palmercandy.com
www.palmerspecialtyfoods.com
Bagged, multi-pack vending snacks
President: Martin Palmer
Director of Quality Control: Dawn Gorham
VP, Marketing: Bob O'Neill
VP, Operations: Bill Kennedy
Purchasing Manager: Jeff Wilkerson
Estimated Sales: $15.50 Million
Number Employees: 50-99
Square Footage: 420000
Type of Packaging: Consumer, Food Service, Private Label, Bulk
Other Locations:
  Palmer Candy Company
  Kansas City, MOPalmer Candy Company
Types of Products Distributed:
  General Line, Snack foods & confectionery items

58553 Palmer Food Service
900 Jefferson Rd
Rochester, NY 14623   585-424-3210
Fax: 585-424-1035 800-888-3474
www.palmerfoods.com
Wholesaler/distributor of frozen foods, produce, meat products and seafood; serving the food service market.
President: Dwight "Kip" Palmer
Year Founded: 1850
Estimated Sales: $100-500 Million
Number Employees: 100-249
Number of Customer Locations: 800
Types of Products Distributed:
  Food Service, Frozen Food, Provisions/Meat, Produce, Seafood

58554 Palmer Jack M
310 Stanley Blvd
Shelbyville, TN 37160-9163   931-684-7011
Fax: 931-685-9741
robertmartin6357@hotmail.com
www.palmerfoodservice.com
Wholesaler/distributor of groceries, meats, dairy products, produce, chemicals, paper and canned and frozen products; serving the food service market
Owner: Jack M Palmer
Director Sales: Bill Caskey
jpalmer@jackpalmerfoodservice.com
Estimated Sales: $10-20 Million
Number Employees: 50-99
Square Footage: 70000
Private Brands Carried:
  Nugget
Types of Products Distributed:
  Food Service, Frozen Food, General Line, General Merchandise, Provisions/Meat, Produce, Groceries, etc.

58555 Palmer Wholesale Inc
415 S Front St
Murfreesboro, TN 37129-3564   615-893-7672
Fax: 615-849-9753 www.palmerwholesale.com
Wholesaler/distributor of general line products, produce, frozen foods, provisions/meats and general merchandise including cleaning supplies; serving the food service market
President: Paula Atwood
paula@palmerwholesale.com
CFO: Dick Palmer
Sales Director: Jimmy Palmer
Estimated Sales: $10-20 Million
Number Employees: 5-9
Square Footage: 80000
Type of Packaging: Consumer, Food Service, Bulk
Private Brands Carried:
  Federated Foods; Hytop
Number of Customer Locations: 1300
Types of Products Distributed:
  Food Service, Frozen Food, General Line, General Merchandise, Provisions/Meat, Produce

58556 Palmetto Candy & Tobacco Company
1225 Lincoln St
Columbia, SC 29201   803-779-3070
Wholesaler/distributor of general merchandise, general line products and specialty food products
Owner: Thomas M Jackson
Estimated Sales: $2.5-5 Million
Number Employees: 5-9
Types of Products Distributed:
  Frozen Food, General Line, General Merchandise, Specialty Foods

58557 Palsgaard Inc.
101 Gibraltar Dr
Suite 2B
Morris Plains, NJ 07950   973-998-7951
Fax: 973-998-7953 direct@us.palsgaard.com
www.palsgaard.com
Emulsifiers and stabilizers for the food industry.
General Manager: Rosa Regalado
Type of Packaging: Bulk

58558 Pamex Packaging
1550 Rory Lane
Simi Valley, CA 93063-4380   805-584-2897
Fax: 805-584-2897
Wholesaler/distributor of packaging machinery
Owner: David Catourette
Types of Products Distributed:
  Frozen Food, General Merchandise, Packaging machinery

58559 (HQ)Pamida
P.O.Box 3856
Omaha, NE 68103   402-572-6000
Fax: 402-596-7332
Wholesaler/distributor of general merchandise; rack jobber services available
CEO: Paul E Rothamel
Number Employees: 5,000-9,999
Private Brands Carried:
  Pamida
Number of Customer Locations: 220
Types of Products Distributed:
  Frozen Food, General Merchandise, Rack Jobbers

58560 Pan American Papers Inc
5101 NW 37th Ave
Miami, FL 33142-3232   305-635-2534
Fax: 305-635-2538 jvl@panampap.com
www.panampap.com
Distributors of paper
Sr. VP: Jesus Roca
panampap@bellsouth.net
Executive VP: Francisco Valdes
Estimated Sales: $20-50 Million
Number Employees: 10-19
Square Footage: 80000
Types of Products Distributed:
  Frozen Food, General Merchandise, Paper goods

Wholesalers & Distributors / A-Z

58561 Pan's Mushroom Jerky
Vancouver, WA
hello@mushroomjerky.com
www.mushroomjerky.com
Mushroom jerky
President/Owner: Michael Pan
Types of Products Distributed:
Frozen Food

58562 Pantry Shelf Food Corporation
3983 Nashua Drive
Mississauga, ON L4V 1P3
Canada
905-677-7200
info@pantryshelf.com
www.pantryshelf.com
Importer and wholesaler/distributor of canned seafood, fruits, vegetables, pickles, condiments, rice, beans, snack foods, corned beef, concentrates, private label items and confections; serving the food service and retail markets;exporter of beans
President: Kanu Patel
VP: Kantu Patel
Estimated Sales: $8 Million
Number Employees: 25
Square Footage: 45000
Type of Packaging: Consumer, Food Service, Private Label, Bulk
Private Brands Carried:
Ocean King; Pantry Shelf; Everybody's
Types of Products Distributed:
Food Service, Pickles in Jar

58563 Papa Dean's Popcorn
999 East Basse Rd.
Suite 184
San Antonio, TX 78209-3827
877-855-7272
Fax: 210-822-2140 deanneu@aol.com
Flavored popcorn
Owner: Tara Zaglif
Contact: Martha Istueta
papadeans@me.com
Estimated Sales: Less than $500,000
Number Employees: 1-4
Number of Products: 25
Square Footage: 4800
Type of Packaging: Consumer, Food Service, Private Label, Bulk
Types of Products Distributed:
Frozen Food

58564 Paper & Chemical Supply Company
1241 Gnat Pond Rd
Leighton, AL 35646
256-383-3912
Fax: 256-386-7312 800-445-7940
Wholesaler/distributor of food serving trays, janitorial and office supplies, disposable kitchenware, etc
President: David Muhlendorf
Contact: Holt Bayles
hbayles@paperandchemical.com
Estimated Sales: $10-20 Million
Number Employees: 50-99
Types of Products Distributed:
Frozen Food, General Merchandise, Food serving trays, etc.

58565 Papercraft
3710 N Richards Street
Milwaukee, WI 53212-1667
414-332-5092
Fax: 414-332-9714
Wholesaler/distributor of invitations, commercial announcements, cake bags and boxes
President: William Buege
Estimated Sales: $1-2.5 Million
Number Employees: 10-19
Square Footage: 112000
Types of Products Distributed:
General Merchandise, Invitations, cake bags & boxes, etc.

58566 Pappy's Sassafras Tea
10246 Road P
Columbus Grove, OH 45830-9733
419-659-5110
Fax: 419-659-5110 877-659-5110
pappy@q1.net www.sassafrastea.com
Sassafras tea, green tea, raspberry tea and tea concentrate
President: Sandy Nordhaus
pappy@q1.net
VP: Don Nordhaus
Marketing & Sales: Jeff Nordhaus

Estimated Sales: $360,000
Number Employees: 5-9
Number of Brands: 1
Number of Products: 2
Square Footage: 45000
Type of Packaging: Consumer, Food Service, Private Label, Bulk

58567 Papé
550 NE Columbia Blvd
Portland, OR 97211
503-240-6282
www.pape.com
Wholesaler/distributor of forklifts.
Year Founded: 1938
Estimated Sales: $50-100 Million
Number Employees: 50-99
Parent Co: Hyster
Private Brands Carried:
Hyster
Types of Products Distributed:
Frozen Food, General Merchandise, Forklifts

58568 (HQ)Paradise Island Foods
6451 Portsmouth Road
Nanaimo, BC V9V 1A3
Canada
250-390-2644
Fax: 250-390-2117 800-889-3370
lthomson@paradise-foods.com
www.paradise-foods.com
Muffin mixes, cheeses, pasta, yogurt, juice, candy, salad dressings and ethnic foods
President: Len Thomson
Vice President: Kevin Thomson
Estimated Sales: $15 Million
Number Employees: 60
Square Footage: 72000
Type of Packaging: Consumer, Private Label, Bulk
Number of Customer Locations: 250
Types of Products Distributed:
Frozen Food, General Line, Health Food, Specialty Foods, Yogurt, candy, juice, pasta, etc.

58569 Paradise Products
PO Box 568
El Cerrito, CA 94530-0568
510-524-8300
Fax: 510-524-8165 800-227-1092
100 page catalog of theme decorations and party supplies for special events and sales promotions cateterias and clubs
Controller: Alice Rickey
Sales: Shirley Imai
Number Employees: 14
Number of Products: 3000
Square Footage: 80000
Types of Products Distributed:
Frozen Food, General Merchandise, Promotional items: posters, etc.

58570 Paragon Food Equipment
760 E Hastings Street
Vancouver, BC V6A 1R5
Canada
604-255-9991
Fax: 604-251-3372 www.paragondirect.ca
Wholesaler/distributor of food service supplies and equipment
President/Partner: Louis Chang
General Manager/Partner: Angelo Chang
Number Employees: 10-19
Private Brands Carried:
Hobart; Vulcan; Wolf Range
Types of Products Distributed:
Food Service, Frozen Food, General Merchandise

58571 Paramount Coffee
130 N Larch St
Lansing, MI 48912-1244
517-372-5500
Fax: 517-372-2870 800-968-1220
www.paramountcoffee.com
Coffee
President: Jeff Poyer
Chairman and CEO: Angelo Oricchio
VP: Robert Morgan
Manager: Chris King
cking@paramountroasters.com
Estimated Sales: $5-10 Million
Number Employees: 100-249
Parent Co: Interstate Foods
Types of Products Distributed:
Frozen Food

58572 Paramount Confection Company
265 S Pioneer Boulevard
Springboro, OH 45066-1180
800-998-0977
Fax: 888-884-4793
Wholesaler/distributor of confectionery products
Owner: William Powers
Types of Products Distributed:
General Line, Confectionery products

58573 Paramount Produce
74 New England Produce Ctr
Chelsea, MA 02150
617-884-3850
Wholesaler/distributor of frozen food and produce
President: S Leve
VP: M Leve
Number Employees: 1-4
Private Brands Carried:
Paramount
Types of Products Distributed:
Frozen Food, Produce

58574 Paramount Products
PO Box 332
Bedford, TX 76095-0332
800-940-4047
Fax: 800-940-4047
Wholesaler/distributor of cajun-style fish fry batter breadings, black pepper, sausage baking mix, hickory smoke and spices including barbecue, taco and fajita; serving the food service market
President: Benny Sanderlin
Estimated Sales: $1.5-2 Million
Number Employees: 5-9
Square Footage: 4800
Private Brands Carried:
Jaunita's; Scalf's; Butcher Shope; Maria's Best; Ole Podner
Number of Customer Locations: 200
Types of Products Distributed:
Food Service, General Line, General Merchandise, Batter breadings, baking mixes, etc.

58575 Paramount Restaurant Supply Company
10 New Rd
Rumford, RI 2916
401-247-6500
Fax: 401-247-6543 800-776-6640
Wholesaler/distributor of restaurant equipment and fixtures; serving the food service market
CEO/President: Stephen McGarry
General Manager: Sue Pimental
Purchasing Agent: John Crawford
Estimated Sales: $10-20 Million
Number Employees: 100-249
Square Footage: 81548
Parent Co: Monarch Industries
Types of Products Distributed:
Food Service, Frozen Food, General Merchandise, Restaurant equipment & fixtures

58576 Parducci Wine Cellars
501 Parducci Rd
Ukiah, CA 95482-3015
707-463-5357
Fax: 707-462-7260 888-362-9463
info@mendocinowineco.com www.parducci.com
Wines
Manager: Tim Thornhill
timthornhill@mendocinowineco.com
Marketing: David Hance
Winemaker: Robert Swain
Estimated Sales: $2 Million
Number Employees: 20-49
Types of Products Distributed:
Frozen Food, General Line, Wine

58577 Park Avenue Bakery
44 South Park Ave
Helena, MT 59601
406-449-8424
www.parkavenuebakery.net
Breads, pastries, rolls, pizzas

58578 Park Avenue Meats Inc
4047 Park Ave
Bronx, NY 10457-7331
718-731-4996
Fax: 718-731-5144 www.totalfood.com/food8.html
Wholesaler/distributor of frozen foods and meats; serving the food service market
Owner: Ira Kline
Contact: Michael Klein
michael.klein@kimptonhotels.com
Estimated Sales: $20-50 Million
Number Employees: 1-4
Types of Products Distributed:
Food Service, Frozen Food, Provisions/Meat

Wholesalers & Distributors / A-Z

58579 Parker Brothers
209 Patchen Road
South Burlington, VT 05403-5776   802-864-9316
Wholesaler/distributor of snack foods
President: Gary Martin
VP: Grace Martin
Estimated Sales: $5-10 Million
Number Employees: 10-19
Number of Customer Locations: 400
Types of Products Distributed:
   Frozen Food, Snack foods

58580 Parker Fish Company
63 Cross Cedar Rd
PO Box 324
Wrightsville, GA 31096-5300   478-864-3406
   Fax: 478-864-9417
Seafood
President: Jeff Powell
Manager: Dennis Moore
Estimated Sales: $5-10 Million
Number Employees: 10-19

58581 Parker Wholesale Paper Co
9060 Industrial Dr
Bastrop, LA 71220-8710   318-281-4293
   Fax: 318-281-4301 parkerwh@bayou.com
   www.parker-wholesale.com
Wholesaler/distributor of cleaning supplies, disposables and wraps; serving the food service market
President: Britt Hankins
Estimated Sales: $20-50 Million
Number Employees: 20-49
Types of Products Distributed:
   Food Service, Frozen Food, General Merchandise, Cleaning supplies, disposables & wraps

58582 Parker's Wine Brokerage
16101 Maple Park Drive
Suite 4
Maple Heights, OH 44137   216-475-4173
   Fax: 216-472-8990 winebrokaergae@yahoo.com
Import and export food and beverage
President: Michael Parker
Marketing Director: Carolyn Williams
Sales Director: Maud Wilson
Estimated Sales: $500,000
Number Employees: 4
Square Footage: 10000
Type of Packaging: Food Service, Private Label, Bulk

58583 Parkway Systems
5400 N Interstate 35
San Antonio, TX 78218   210-938-0256
   Fax: 210-662-7859 800-477-5438
   parkwaysystems@heb.com
   www.parkwaysystems.com
Wholesaler/distributor of material handling equipment including forklifts and forklift parts.
Year Founded: 1988
Estimated Sales: $50-100 Million
Number Employees: 100-249
Parent Co: H.E. Butt Grocery Company
Private Brands Carried:
   Nissan
Types of Products Distributed:
   Frozen Food, General Merchandise, Material handling equipment

58584 Parr-Mac Sales Company
16547 158th St
Bonner Springs, KS 66012-7243
Wholesaler/distributor of forklifts
Owner: Frank Parra
Estimated Sales: $500,000-$1 Million
Number Employees: 1-4
Private Brands Carried:
   TCM; Cascade; Brudi; Long Reach
Types of Products Distributed:
   Frozen Food, General Merchandise, Forklifts

58585 Parson Food Sales
1180 E Diamond Avenue
Evansville, IN 47711-3997   812-428-5720
   Fax: 812-428-5722
Wholesaler/distributor of general line items, produce, beverages and general merchandise including paper and chemicals
President: Hazel Parson
Estimated Sales: $20-50 Million
Number Employees: 20-49
Types of Products Distributed:
   Frozen Food, General Line, General Merchandise, Produce, Beverages, chemicals, etc.

58586 Parsons Green
P.O.Box 7179
Wilton, CT 06897-7179   203-847-8204
   Fax: 203-834-9806 800-216-5636
   parsonsgreen@hotmail.com
Distributor of Chilly Willee soft ice
President: Philip Sharlach
Number Employees: 2
Square Footage: 8000
Private Brands Carried:
   Parson's Green; Nestle; Chilly Willee
Number of Customer Locations: 100
Types of Products Distributed:
   Food Service, General Line, General Merchandise, Soft ices, hot chocolate & cappuccino

58587 Parts Depot, Inc.
1329 Willoughby Ave
Brooklyn, NY 11237   718-456-6409
   Fax: 718-821-3401 800-738-7750
   partsdepot295inc@aol.com
Wholesaler/distributor of replacement parts for kitchen equipment; serving the food service market
President: R Seeram
Contact: Ram Seeram
ram@parts-depot.com
Number of Customer Locations: 100
Types of Products Distributed:
   Food Service, Frozen Food, General Merchandise, Replacement parts

58588 Partytime Machines Rental
2082 Winchester Blvd
Campbell, CA 95008-3427   408-379-1451
   Fax: 408-379-1128 info@partytimemachines.com
   www.partytimemachines.com
Wholesaler/distributor of frozen yogurt machines; also, margarita machine rentals and upcharge services available
Owner: Ren Calderhead
Office Manager: Mary Jo Bettencourt
Estimated Sales: Less than $500,000
Number Employees: 10-19
Types of Products Distributed:
   Frozen Food, General Merchandise, Frozen yogurt machines

58589 Paskesz Candy Co
4473 1st Ave
Brooklyn, NY 11232-4201   718-215-1752
   Fax: 718-832-3492 customerservice@paskesz.com
   www.paskesz.com
Importer of kosher candy; wholesaler/distributor of kosher candy, cookies and grocery items; serving the food service market
Owner: Henry Schmidt
VP Marketing: Henri Schmidt
VP Sales: David Snyder
Contact: Gavriel Fein
gavriel@paskesz.com
Estimated Sales: Less Than $500,000
Number Employees: 1-4
Square Footage: 130000
Number of Customer Locations: 400
Types of Products Distributed:
   Food Service, Frozen Food, Specialty Foods, Kosher candy, cookies & groceries

58590 Pasolivo Willow Creek Olive Ranch
8530 Vineyard Drive
Paso Robles, CA 93446   805-227-0186
   Fax: 805-226-8809 info@pasolivo.com
   www.pasolivo.com
Olive oils
General Manger: Jillian Pasolivo
Marketing: Joel Pasolivo

58591 Passport Food Group
2539 E Philadelphia St
Ontario, CA 91761   310-463-0954
   customerservice@passportfood.com
   www.passportfood.com
Noodles, appetizers, fortune cookies and tofu, egg roll, wonton and potsticker wrappers
Senior Vice President: Brian Dean
bdean@passportfood.com
VP, Sales & Marketing, Retail: Terry Girch
Broker Sales Manager: Rich Frankey
Territory Sales Manager: Jeffrey Tavares
Year Founded: 1978
Estimated Sales: $50 Million
Number Employees: 200-500
Number of Brands: 4
Type of Packaging: Consumer, Food Service, Private Label, Bulk
Types of Products Distributed:
   Food Service, Frozen Food

58592 Pate-Derby Company
PO Box 53533
Fayetteville, NC 28305-3533   910-483-2131
   Fax: 910-483-2121
Wholesaler/distributor of general line products, general merchandise, frozen foods, meats, seafood and produce; serving the food service market
President: J Pate, Jr.
VP: Dave Runkle
VP: Steve Runkle
Estimated Sales: $10-20 Million
Number Employees: 50-99
Square Footage: 180000
Private Brands Carried:
   PDC; Pocahontas
Types of Products Distributed:
   Food Service, General Line, General Merchandise, Provisions/Meat, Produce, Seafood

58593 Patriot Enterprises
701 Park St
Castle Rock, CO 80109   303-814-1297
   www.patriotpros.com
Wholesaler/distributor of fresh meats, frozen foods, dairy products and produce; serving the food service market
President: Barry Mayer
Executive VP: Gary Mayer
Contact: Javier Hoggard
javi@patriotpros.com
VP Purchasing: Joseph Pavone
Number Employees: 50-99
Square Footage: 88000
Private Brands Carried:
   Golbon; Sea Breeze
Number of Customer Locations: 100
Types of Products Distributed:
   Food Service, Frozen Food, General Line, Provisions/Meat, Produce, Dairy products

58594 Patriot Pickel Inc
20 Edison Dr
Wayne, NJ 07470-4713   973-709-9487
   Fax: 973-709-0995
Pickles
Owner: Mc Bill
billmc@patriotpickle.com
Number Employees: 20-49

58595 Pats Seafood & Cajun Deli
1248 Collins Blvd
Covington, LA 70433-1656   985-892-7287
Wholesaler/distributor of fresh, frozen and vacuum-packed catfish, crawfish and shrimp
Owner: Ralph Patrick Jr
Estimated Sales: $2.5-5 Million
Number Employees: 5-9
Types of Products Distributed:
   Frozen Food, Seafood, Shrimp, crawfish & catfish

58596 Patterson Buckeye
1236 Velma Ct
Youngstown, OH 44512   330-783-1370
   Fax: 330-783-0249
Wholesaler/distributor of coffee, general merchandise, equipment/fixtures and private label items
President: Robert O'Leary
CEO: Alan O'Leary
CFO: J McGinnis
Public Relations: Rhonda Worhatch
Plant Manager: Alan O'Leary
Estimated Sales: $1.5 Million
Number Employees: 5-9
Type of Packaging: Food Service, Private Label
Types of Products Distributed:
   Food Service, General Merchandise, Groceries, coffee, etc.

58597 Patton's Sausage Company
601 Baronne St
New Orleans, LA 70113-1066   504-569-9000
   Fax: 504-569-9002
Wholesaler/distributor of sausage

Owner: J C Patin
VP: Frank De Gardo
Estimated Sales: $5-10 Million
Number Employees: 1-4
Types of Products Distributed:
  Food Service, Frozen Food, Provisions/Meat, Sausage

58598 Paturel International Company
Box 460
Shediac, NB E4P 8Y2
Canada   506-533-1225
                Fax: 506-532-5450
Wholesaler/distributor of canned and frozen seafood
President: James Bateman
Types of Products Distributed:
  Seafood

58599 Paul J. Macrie
189 Weymouth Rd
Hammonton, NJ 08037   609-561-2460
                Fax: 609-561-2966
Wholesaler/distributor of produce
President: Pete Macrie Sr
VP: P Macrie
Estimated Sales: $5-10 Million
Number Employees: 10-19
Number of Customer Locations: 500
Types of Products Distributed:
  Frozen Food, Produce

58600 Paul Perkins Food Distributors
PO Box 347
South Point, OH 45680-0347   740-377-4564
Wholesaler/distributor of specialty foods; direct store delivery available
Owner/Buyer: P Perkins
Buyer/Sales: Brian Perkins
Estimated Sales: $2.5-5 Million
Number Employees: 1-4
Number of Customer Locations: 300
Types of Products Distributed:
  Frozen Food, Specialty Foods

58601 Paul Stevens Lobster
349 Lincoln St
Suite 32
Hingham, MA 02043-1609   781-740-8001
                Fax: 781-749-2240
Fish and seafood; lobsters
Owner: Paul Stevens
Estimated Sales: $870,000
Number Employees: 1-4

58602 Paulie Paul's
7752 Watson St
Philadelphia, PA 19111-3117   215-745-2445
Wholesaler/distributor of deli items
Owner: Edward Poli
Estimated Sales: $300,000-500,000
Number Employees: 1-4
Types of Products Distributed:
  Frozen Food, General Line, Provisions/Meat, Deli items

58603 Paulsen Foods
748 Donald Hollowell Parkway
Atlanta, GA 30318   404-873-1804
                paulsenfoods.com
Wholesale frozen breakfast, apetizers, entrees, and desserts.
Owner: Russell Paulsen
National Sales Manager: Tom Unverferth
Director of Operations: Mayra Vagras
Estimated Sales: $1-2.5 Million
Number Employees: 6
Square Footage: 80000
Type of Packaging: Consumer, Food Service, Private Label
Types of Products Distributed:
  Food Service, Frozen Food

58604 Payless Equipment
5314 N 39th St
Tampa, FL 33610-5154   813-622-7740
       Fax: 813-621-0705 800-226-3620
                sales@paylessequipment.com
                www.paylessequipment.com
Material handling equipment
Estimated Sales: $2.4 Million
Number Employees: 8
Private Brands Carried:
  Durable, Jarvis, Colson, Albion, Blickle, Everest, Heateater, BP Mfg Liberator, Harper, Wesco, Vestil, KMD, Adams Industrial, Brennan Equip, Lakeside Mfg, Nexel Ind, Eagle Mfg, Hallowell, Quantum Storage, Strong Hold
Types of Products Distributed:
  Food Service, Frozen Food, General Merchandise, Cookware

58605 Peace River Trading Company
31 Victoria Road
Woodstock, CT 7925   941-505-8885
       Fax: 941-505-8911 800-996-6306
                www.peaceriver.co.za
Wholesaler/distributor of nuts, seeds, rice, dried and frozen fruits and berry products, etc
President: Denise Henry
Number Employees: 5-9
Parent Co: JRW Marketing Corporation
Types of Products Distributed:
  Frozen Food, General Line, Produce, Rice, nuts, seeds, etc.

58606 Peaceful Fruits
                    330-356-8515
                www.peacefulfruits.com
Organic fruit snacks
Founder/CEO: Evan Delehanty
Types of Products Distributed:
  General Line

58607 Peach State Material Handling
3005 Business Park Drive
Norcross, GA 30071   678-327-2000
       Fax: 678-327-2030 800-998-6517
                www.peachstate.com
Wholesaler/distributor of conveyors, shelving and racks
VP: John Roth
Number Employees: 20-49
Number of Customer Locations: 1500
Types of Products Distributed:
  Frozen Food, General Merchandise, Conveyors, racks & shelving

58608 Peas
PO Box 1310
Castroville, TX 78009-1310   210-218-8063
                Fax: 830-569-6163
Wholesaler/distributor of dried beans, southern peas and general merchandise
Owner: Bob Persyn
Office Manager: Yvonne Irie
Plant Manager: Bob Berwick
Estimated Sales: $5-10 Million
Number Employees: 5-9
Square Footage: 80000
Types of Products Distributed:
  Frozen Food, General Merchandise, Produce, Dried beans & southern peas

58609 Peerless Dust Killer Company
111 Hill St
Orange, NJ 07050-3901   973-676-1868
                Fax: 973-676-4564
Wholesaler/distributor and exporter of maintenance chemicals and janitorialsupplies
Owner: Stan Reichel
Estimated Sales: $.5-1 million
Number Employees: 1-4
Types of Products Distributed:
  Maintenance chemicals

58610 Pelco Equipment
2200 Harlem Rd
Buffalo, NY 14225-4902   716-892-8526
                Fax: 716-892-3880
Wholesaler/distributor of bakery equipment
Manager: Tim Maroney
Manager: Chuck Ziegler
Purchasing Agent: Tim Moroney
Estimated Sales: $1-2.5 Million
Number Employees: 1-4
Square Footage: 40000
Private Brands Carried:
  Blodgett; Pitco; Cutler
Types of Products Distributed:
  Frozen Food, General Merchandise, Bakery equipment

58611 Pelco Refrigeration Sales
1550 Park Ave
Emeryville, CA 94608-3585   415-626-5822
       Fax: 510-653-0338 www.pelco.com
Wholesaler/distributor of refrigeration and restaurant equipment; serving the food service market
Owner: Kevin Bradstock
kbradstock@apexrefrig.com
VP: Terry Pellegrini
Secretary: Penny Barger
Estimated Sales: $2.5-5 Million
Number Employees: 10-19
Square Footage: 60000
Private Brands Carried:
  Scotsman
Types of Products Distributed:
  Food Service, Frozen Food, General Merchandise, Restaurant & refrigeration equipment

58612 Pelican Bay Ltd.
150 Douglas Ave
Dunedin, FL 34698-7908   727-733-3069
       Fax: 727-734-5860 800-826-8982
                sales@pelicanbayltd.com
Baking and drink mixes, spice blends and gifts
Owner: Char Pfaelzer
char@pelicanbayltd.com
CEO: Jim Hubbard
Executive VP: David Pfaelzer
Plant Manager: Justin Pfaelzer
Purchasing: Greg Kathan
Estimated Sales: $4.7 Million
Number Employees: 20-49
Number of Brands: 1
Number of Products: 200
Square Footage: 120000
Type of Packaging: Consumer, Private Label, Bulk
Types of Products Distributed:
  General Merchandise, Baking/drink mixes, spice blends, etc.

58613 Pelican Marine Supply LLC
2911 Engineers Rd
Belle Chasse, LA 70037-3150   504-392-9062
       Fax: 504-394-5528 www.pelicanmarinedist.com
Beef, pork, poultry, fish, seafood and general groceries
President: Peter Bretchel
Manager: James Lutz
jameyl@pelicanmarinedist.com
Estimated Sales: $10-20 Million
Number Employees: 5-9

58614 Pellican Seafood
10635 Old Hammond Highway
Baton Rouge, LA 70816-8238   225-924-1584
Wholesaler/distributor of seafood
Owner: Janet Terrell
Number Employees: 1-4
Number of Customer Locations: 100
Types of Products Distributed:
  Frozen Food, Seafood

58615 Pemaquid Seafood
32 CO OP Rd
Pemaquid, ME 04558-4315   207-677-2801
       Fax: 207-677-2818 866-864-2897
                pemaquidcoop@yahoo.com
Seafood
Manager: Wayne Dighton
Manager: Tom Simmons
Estimated Sales: Less Than $500,000
Number Employees: 1-4

58616 Pemiscot Packing Company
PO Box 4747
Wardell, MO 63879   573-628-3401
                Fax: 573-628-3774
Wholesaler/distributor of produce and provisions/meats; serving the food service market
Estimated Sales: $3-5 Million
Number Employees: 5-9
Types of Products Distributed:
  Food Service, Frozen Food, Provisions/Meat, Produce

58617 Pendergast Safety Equipment Co
8400 Enterprise Ave # 1
Philadelphia, PA 19153-3888   215-937-1900
       Fax: 215-365-7527 800-551-1901
                sales@pendergastsafety.com
                www.pendergastsafety.com
Wholesaler/distributor of industrial personal protective equipment including gloves, safety glasses, disposable clothing, hearing and fall protection and respiratory products
President: William F Grauer
william@pendergastsafety.com
CEO: Bill Grauer
CFO: Bob Webb

Wholesalers & Distributors / A-Z

Estimated Sales: $5-10 Million
Number Employees: 20-49
Number of Brands: 300
Number of Products: 7500
Square Footage: 60000
Type of Packaging: Bulk
Types of Products Distributed:
    Frozen Food, General Merchandise, Industry protection equipment

58618 Penguin Foods
1614 Christina St
Rockford, IL 61104-5190   815-965-8604
    Fax: 815-965-8669 Penguinfoods@comcast.net
    www.penguinfoods.net
Wholesaler/distributor of frozen food and provisions/meats; serving the food service market
Owner: Cathy Ciembronowicz
penguinfoods@comcast.net
Estimated Sales: $2.5-5 Million
Number Employees: 10-19
Types of Products Distributed:
    Food Service, Frozen Food, Provisions/Meat

58619 Penn Herb Co
10601 Decatur Rd
Suite 2
Philadelphia, PA 19154-3212   215-632-4430
    Fax: 215-632-7945 800-523-9971
    www.pennherb.com
Encapsulated herbs ginseng and golden seal root; vitamins and supplements
President: William Betz
wbetz@penton.com
President: Ronald Betz
Estimated Sales: $3500000
Number Employees: 20-49
Square Footage: 92000
Types of Products Distributed:
    Frozen Food, Health Food, Encapsulated herbs including ginseng

58620 Penn Maid
10975 Dutton Rd
Philadelphia, PA 19154   215-824-2800
    www.pennmaid.com
Wholesaler/distributor of dairy products such as cheeses, condiments, cottage cheese, creamers, dips, sour cream, and yogurt.
Year Founded: 1927
Estimated Sales: $100-500 Million
Number Employees: 11-50
Types of Products Distributed:
    Food Service, Frozen Food, Provisions/Meat, Dairy products

58621 Pennsylvania Macaroni Company Inc.
2010 Penn Avenue
Pittsburgh, PA 15222   412-227-1982
    dsunseri@pennmac.com
    www.pennmac.com
Wholesaler/distributor and importer of olive oil, cheese and pasta products; serving the food service market.
President: David Sunseri
Office Manager: Kathy Feinstein
VP, Purchasing: Bill Sunseri
Year Founded: 1902
Estimated Sales: $24 Million
Number Employees: 80
Number of Brands: 300
Number of Products: 5000
Square Footage: 80000
Type of Packaging: Consumer
Private Brands Carried:
    Savoy Quality Italian Foods; Bellisine Food Group
Types of Products Distributed:
    Food Service, Frozen Food, General Line, Provisions/Meat, Produce, Specialty Foods, Olive oil, cheese & pasta products

58622 Pennwell Belting Company
10310 178th St
Jamaica, NY 11433   718-206-3146
    Fax: 718-206-3149
Wholesaler/distributor of installation and vulcanizing food belts
Manager: Kenneth Beckles
Estimated Sales: $1-2.5 Million
Number Employees: 1-4
Square Footage: 24000
Types of Products Distributed:
    Frozen Food, General Merchandise, Installation & vulcanizing food belts

58623 Penny's Meat Products
605 Lombard
Clarence, IA 52216   319-452-3826
Wholesaler/distributor of meats
Owner: Kenneth Richmann
Number Employees: 1-4
Number of Customer Locations: 130
Types of Products Distributed:
    Frozen Food, Provisions/Meat

58624 Penobscot Mccrum LLC
28 Pierce St
PO Box 229
Belfast, ME 04915-6648   207-338-4360
    Fax: 207-338-5742 800-435-4456
    www.penobscotmccrum.com
Potato pancakes, mashers, skins, and wedges.
Managing Partner: Jay McCrum
Managing Partner: David McCrum
Manager, JDR Transport, Inc.: Wade McCrum
Financial Analysis & Marketing: Nick McCrum
Manager, North Maine Farm Operations: Darrell McCrum
Estimated Sales: $33 Million
Number Employees: 100-249
Type of Packaging: Consumer, Food Service
Types of Products Distributed:
    Produce

58625 Pensacola Candy Co Distr
380 Lurton St
Pensacola, FL 32505-5231   850-433-8847
    Fax: 850-438-7187
Wholesaler/distributor of candy
Owner: Jim Moulton
jim@moultonprop.com
Estimated Sales: Less Than $500,000
Number Employees: 1-4
Parent Co: Moulton Properties
Types of Products Distributed:
    Frozen Food, General Line, Candy

58626 Pensacola Restaurant Supply Company
4148 Barrancas Ave
Pensacola, FL 32507   850-456-1633
    Fax: 850-457-1872 800-342-1220
    www.kescoflorida.com
Wholesaler/distributor of nonfood restaurant supplies including paper products, glassware, etc.; serving the food service market
Purchasing Agent: Marcy Friedman
Estimated Sales: $10-20 Million
Number Employees: 20-49
Types of Products Distributed:
    Food Service, Frozen Food, General Merchandise, Paper products, glassware, etc.

58627 Peoples Woods & Charcoal
75 Mill Street
Cumberland, RI 02864-8339   401-725-2700
    Fax: 401-421-5120 800-729-5800
Wholesaler/distributor of general merchandise including grilling, smoking and barbecuing fuels; also, wood charcoal
President/CEO: Don Hysko
Manager: Joyce Fraser
VP Operations: Dennis Hysko
Estimated Sales: $500,000-$1 Million
Number Employees: 5-9
Square Footage: 160000
Private Brands Carried:
    Nature's Own; Treestock; Produits Forrestiers Basques
Types of Products Distributed:
    General Merchandise, Grilling & smoking, fuels, etc.

58628 Peoria Meat Packing
1300 W Lake St
Chicago, IL 60607-1512   312-738-1800
    Fax: 312-738-1180 www.peoriapacking.com
Packaging
Owner: Harry Katsiavlos
Estimated Sales: $10-20 Million
Number Employees: 1-4

58629 Perfection Foods
215 Fitzroy Street
Charlottetown, PE C1A 1S6
Canada   902-566-5515
    Fax: 902-566-2243 perfection@adl.ca
    adl.ca
Wholesaler/distributor of evaporated milk
Branch Manager: David McLellan
Number Employees: 20-49
Parent Co: ADL
Number of Customer Locations: 8
Types of Products Distributed:
    Frozen Food, General Line, Evaporated milk

58630 Perfections by Allan
3 Old Creek Ct
Owings Mills, MD 21117   410-581-8670
    Fax: 410-581-0877 800-581-8670
Dipping cookies and snacks
President: Allan Taylor
ataylor@perfectionsbyallan.com
Estimated Sales: Under $500,000
Number Employees: 1-4
Type of Packaging: Consumer, Private Label
Number of Customer Locations: 120

58631 (HQ)Performance Food Group Co
12500 W Creek Pkwy
Richmond, VA 23238   804-484-7700
    www.pfgc.com
Wholesaler/distributor serving the food service market.
President & CEO: George Holm
EVP, Performance Foodservice: Dave Flitman
EVP & Chief Financial Officer: James Hope
SVP/General Counsel/Secretary: Brent King
Strategic Growth Leader: Tom Ondrof
SVP & Chief Information Officer: Terry West
Manager, Corporate Communications: Joe Vagi
communications@pfgc.com
VP, Investor Relations: Michael Neese
SVP & Chief Human Resources Officer: Carol O'Connell
Year Founded: 1885
Estimated Sales: $2.4 Billion
Number Employees: 14,000
Other Locations:
    Performance Food Group Co.
    Norfolk, VAPerformance Food Group Co.
Types of Products Distributed:
    Food Service, Frozen Food

58632 Performance Food Group Customized Distribution
245 North Castle Heights Ave
Lebanon, TN 37087   615-444-2995
    Fax: 615-444-2276 www.pfgcdc.com
Serves regional and national restaurant chains; specializes in perishable foods
President & CEO: Craig Hoskins
VP: Terry Mayer
General Manager: Farrell Noxdorf
Parent Co: Performance Food Group
Types of Products Distributed:
    Food Service, Provisions/Meat, Produce, Seafood

58633 Performance Food Group Customized Distribution
4041 NE 54th Ave
Gainesville, FL 32609   352-378-8844
    www.pfgcdc.com
Serves regional and national restaurant chains; specializes in perishable foods
General Manager: Rob Krakenberg
Types of Products Distributed:
    Food Service, Provisions/Meat, Produce, Seafood

58634 Performance Food Group Customized Distribution
2930 Performance Dr
Kendallville, IN 46755   260-343-4338
    www.pfgcdc.com
Serves regional and national restaurant chains; specializes in perishable foods
General Manager: Terry Mayer
Types of Products Distributed:
    Food Service, Provisions/Meat, Produce, Seafood

Wholesalers & Distributors / A-Z

58635 Performance Food Group Customized Distribution
500 Highland Dr
Westampton, NJ 08060   609-518-1102
www.pfgcdc.com
Serves regional and national restaurant chains; specializes in perishable foods
General Manager: Bruce Krupa
Types of Products Distributed:
  Food Service, Provisions/Meat, Produce, Seafood

58636 Performance Food Group Customized Distribution
500 Metro Park Dr
McKinney, TX 75071   972-542-4264
www.pfgcdc.com
Serves regional and national restaurant chains; specializes in perishable foods
General Manager: Tom Hoeffel
Types of Products Distributed:
  Food Service, Provisions/Meat, Produce, Seafood

58637 Performance Food Group Customized Distribution
255 North Driver Rd
Shafter, CA 93263   661-391-7200
www.pfgcdc.com
Serves regional and national restaurant chains; specializes in perishable foods
General Manager: Jason Jasso
Types of Products Distributed:
  Food Service, Provisions/Meat, Produce, Seafood

58638 Performance Food Group Customized Distribution
1520 Elkton Rd
Elkton, MD 21921   410-620-2330
www.pfgcdc.com
Serves regional and national restaurant chains; specializes in perishable foods
General Manager: Chris Bibus
Types of Products Distributed:
  Food Service, Provisions/Meat, Produce, Seafood

58639 Performance Food Group Customized Distribution
1441 Firetower Rd
Rock Hill, SC 29730   803-366-6399
www.pfgcdc.com
Serves regional and national restaurant chains; specializes in perishable foods
General Manager: Gil Helms
Types of Products Distributed:
  Food Service, Provisions/Meat, Produce, Seafood

58640 (HQ)Performance Foodservice
12500 W Creek Parkway
Richmond, VA 23238   804-484-7700
www.performancefoodservice.com
General line products specializing in Italian foods; serving the food service market
President & CEO: Craig Hoskins
SVP, Finance: Amy Melton
VP, Procurement: Scott Barnewolt
SVP, Marketing/Brands/Sales Development: Fred Sanelli
SVP, Human Resources: Jane Manion
Year Founded: 1875
Estimated Sales: $17.5 Billion
Number Employees: 5000-9999
Parent Co: Performance Food Group
Private Brands Carried:
  Bay Winds, Ascend, Asian Pride, Assoluti!, Burst Spices, Surety Beef, Allegiance, Braveheart, Contigo, Corazo, Delectable, Dominion, Guest House, Heritage Ovens, Nature's Best Dairy, Northland Star, Entice, FarmSmart, Piancone, Ridgecrest, SilverSource
Number of Customer Locations: 80000
Types of Products Distributed:
  Food Service, Frozen Food, General Line, General Merchandise, Provisions/Meat, Produce, Seafood

58641 Performance Foodservice
5030 Baseline Rd
Montgomery, IL 60538   630-896-1991
          Fax: 630-896-0157
www.performancefoodservice.com/FoxRiver
General line products specializing in Italian foods; serving the food service market
Estimated Sales: $23 Million
Number Employees: 250-499
Square Footage: 120000
Number of Customer Locations: 2400
Types of Products Distributed:
  Food Service, Frozen Food, General Line, General Merchandise, Provisions/Meat, Produce, Seafood, Dairy products, groceries, etc.

58642 Performance Foodservice
543 12th Street Dr NW
P.O. Drawer 2947
Hickory, NC 28601
          800-800-0434
www.performancefoodservice.com/IFHHickory
General line products specializing in Italian foods; serving the food service market
Number of Customer Locations: 3400
Types of Products Distributed:
  Food Service, Frozen Food, General Line, General Merchandise, Provisions/Meat, Produce, Seafood, Groceries, dairy products, etc.

58643 Performance Foodservice
5262 S Air Park Blvd
Morristown, TN 37813   423-318-8700
www.performancefoodservice.com/Hale
General line products specializing in Italian foods; serving the food service market
Types of Products Distributed:
  Food Service, Frozen Food, General Line, General Merchandise, Provisions/Meat, Produce, Seafood, Groceries, dairy products, etc.

58644 Performance Foodservice
3501 Old Oakwood Rd
Oakwood, GA 30566   770-532-7779
www.performancefoodservice.com/Miltons
General line products specializing in Italian foods; serving the food service market
Types of Products Distributed:
  Food Service, Frozen Food, General Line, General Merchandise, Provisions/Meat, Produce, Seafood, Groceries, dairy products, etc.

58645 Performance Foodservice
4141 Lucius McCelvey Dr
Temple, TX 76504   254-778-4519
          800-375-3606
www.performancefoodservice.com/Temple
General line products specializing in Italian foods; serving the food service market
Square Footage: 540000
Number of Customer Locations: 2500
Types of Products Distributed:
  Food Service, Frozen Food, General Line, General Merchandise, Provisions/Meat, Produce, Seafood

58646 Performance Foodservice
301 Heron Dr
Swedesboro, NJ 08085
          800-332-6001
www.performancefoodservice.com/NewJersey
General line products specializing in Italian foods; serving the food service market
Number of Customer Locations: 4500
Types of Products Distributed:
  Frozen Food, General Line, General Merchandise, Provisions/Meat, Produce, Specialty Foods, Groceries, snack foods, etc.

58647 Performance Foodservice
20 Dalton Rd
Augusta, ME 04330   207-623-8451
          877-564-8081
www.performancefoodservice.com/NorthCenter
General line products specializing in Italian foods; serving the food service market
Types of Products Distributed:
  Food Service, General Line, General Merchandise, Provisions/Meat, Produce, Seafood

58648 Performance Foodservice
455 S 75th Ave
Phoenix, AZ 85043   480-405-3000
          Fax: 480-940-8993
www.performancefoodservice.com/Arizona
General line products specializing in Italian foods; serving the food service market
Types of Products Distributed:
  Food Service, General Line, General Merchandise, Provisions/Meat, Produce, Seafood

58649 Performance Foodservice
506 Hwy 35 N
Batesville, MS 38606   662-578-3141
          Fax: 662-578-9276 866-511-3141
www.performancefoodservice.com/Batesville
General line products specializing in Italian foods; serving the food service market
Types of Products Distributed:
  Food Service, General Line, General Merchandise, Provisions/Meat, Produce, Seafood

58650 Performance Foodservice
2324 Bayou Blue Rd
Houma, LA 70364   985-872-1483
          Fax: 985-876-0825 800-395-2276
www.performancefoodservice.com/Caro
General line products specializing in Italian foods; serving the food service market
Types of Products Distributed:
  Food Service, General Line, General Merchandise, Provisions/Meat, Produce, Seafood

58651 Performance Foodservice
5225 Investment Dr
Dallas, TX 75236
          Fax: 972-709-6296 800-433-8148
www.performancefoodservice.com/Dallas
General line products specializing in Italian foods; serving the food service market
Types of Products Distributed:
  Food Service, General Line, General Merchandise, Provisions/Meat, Produce, Seafood

58652 Performance Foodservice
8001 E 88th Ave
Henderson, CO 80640   303-373-9123
www.performancefoodservice.com/Denver
General line products specializing in Italian foods; serving the food service market
Types of Products Distributed:
  Food Service, General Line, General Merchandise, Provisions/Meat, Produce, Seafood

58653 Performance Foodservice
3765 Port Union Rd
Fairfield, OH 45014   513-874-3200
          800-536-1613
www.performancefoodservice.com/Ellenbee
General line products specializing in Italian foods; serving the food service market
Types of Products Distributed:
  Food Service, General Line, General Merchandise, Provisions/Meat, Produce, Seafood

58654 Performance Foodservice
2801 Alex Lee Blvd
Florence, SC 29506
          800-800-6434
www.performancefoodservice.com/IFHFlorence
General line products specializing in Italian foods; serving the food service market
Types of Products Distributed:
  Food Service, General Line, General Merchandise, Provisions/Meat, Produce, Seafood

58655 Performance Foodservice
3150 Gallagher Rd
Dover, FL 33527   813-659-0811
www.performancefoodservice.com/Florida
General line products specializing in Italian foods; serving the food service market
Types of Products Distributed:
  Food Service, General Line, General Merchandise, Provisions/Meat, Produce, Seafood

58656 Performance Foodservice
6855 Business Park Dr
Houston, TX 77041
          800-444-4017
www.performancefoodservice.com/Houston
General line products specializing in Italian foods; serving the food service market

Wholesalers & Distributors / A-Z

58657 Performance Foodservice
1047 17th Ave
Santa Cruz, CA 95062   831-462-4400
www.performancefoodservice.com/Ledyard
General line products specializing in Italian foods; serving the food service market
Types of Products Distributed:
Food Service, General Line, General Merchandise, Provisions/Meat, Produce, Seafood

58658 Performance Foodservice
4901 Asher Ave
Little Rock, AR 72204   501-568-3141
www.performancefoodservice.com/LittleRock
General line products specializing in Italian foods; serving the food service market
Types of Products Distributed:
Food Service, General Line, General Merchandise, Provisions/Meat, Produce, Seafood

58659 Performance Foodservice
1333 Avondale Rd
New Windsor, MD 21776   443-487-5300
                               800-755-4223
www.performancefoodservice.com/CarrollCounty
General line products specializing in Italian foods; serving the food service market
Types of Products Distributed:
Food Service, General Line, General Merchandise, Provisions/Meat, Produce, Seafood

58660 Performance Foodservice
1 Ikea Dr
Elizabeth, NJ 07207
                               800-275-9500
www.performancefoodservice.com/AFI
General line products specializing in Italian foods; serving the food service market
Types of Products Distributed:
Food Service, General Line, General Merchandise, Provisions/Meat, Produce, Seafood

58661 Performance Foodservice
3595 NW 125 St
Miami, FL 33167   305-953-4900
Fax: 305-953-4800 800-222-4030
www.performancefoodservice.com/Miami
General line products specializing in Italian foods; serving the food service market
Types of Products Distributed:
Food Service, General Line, General Merchandise, Provisions/Meat, Produce, Seafood

58662 Performance Foodservice
3737 N Broadway
St. Louis, MO 63147   314-241-4800
www.performancefoodservice.com/Middendorf
General line products specializing in Italian foods; serving the food service market
Types of Products Distributed:
Food Service, General Line, General Merchandise, Provisions/Meat, Produce, Seafood

58663 Performance Foodservice
625 Division St N
Rice, MN 56367
Fax: 320-393-2800 800-328-8514
www.performancefoodservice.com/Minnesota
General line products specializing in Italian foods; serving the food service market
Types of Products Distributed:
Food Service, General Line, General Merchandise, Provisions/Meat, Produce, Seafood

58664 Performance Foodservice
4551 West Junction St
Springfield, MO 65802
Fax: 417-831-3138 800-831-8787
www.performancefoodservice.com/SpringfieldMO
General line products specializing in Italian foods; serving the food service market
Types of Products Distributed:
Food Service, General Line, General Merchandise, Provisions/Meat, Produce, Seafood

58665 Performance Foodservice
401 Maddox-Simpson Pkwy
Lebanon, TN 37090   615-444-2010
www.performancefoodservice.com/Lester
General line products specializing in Italian foods; serving the food service market
Types of Products Distributed:
Food Service, General Line, General Merchandise, Provisions/Meat, Produce, Seafood

58666 Performance Foodservice
6211 Las Positas
Livermore, CA 94551
Fax: 925-449-8927 800-233-6211
www.performancefoodservice.com/NCalifornia
General line products specializing in Italian foods; serving the food service market
Types of Products Distributed:
Food Service, General Line, General Merchandise, Provisions/Meat, Produce, Seafood

58667 Performance Foodservice
2901 Titan Row
Suite 136
Orlando, FL 32809   407-857-2440
Fax: 407-857-1319
www.performancefoodservice.com/Orlando
General line products specializing in Italian foods; serving the food service market
Types of Products Distributed:
Food Service, General Line, General Merchandise, Provisions/Meat, Produce, Seafood

58668 Performance Foodservice
19606 NE San Rafael
Portland, OR 97230
Fax: 503-661-1698 800-666-8998
www.performancefoodservice.com/Portland
General line products specializing in Italian foods; serving the food service market
Types of Products Distributed:
Food Service, General Line, General Merchandise, Provisions/Meat, Produce, Seafood

58669 Performance Foodservice
211 Alton Hall Rd
Cairo, GA 39828   229-378-4444
www.performancefoodservice.com/Powell
General line products specializing in Italian foods; serving the food service market
Types of Products Distributed:
Food Service, General Line, General Merchandise, Provisions/Meat, Produce, Seafood

58670 Performance Foodservice
201 Lawton Ave
Monroe, OH 45050
www.performancefoodservice.com/Presto
General line products specializing in Italian foods; serving the food service market
Types of Products Distributed:
Food Service, General Line, General Merchandise, Provisions/Meat, Produce, Seafood

58671 Performance Foodservice
910 Hwy 461
Somerset, KY 42503   606-274-4858
Fax: 606-274-5141 800-264-2633
www.performancefoodservice.com/Somerset
General line products specializing in Italian foods; serving the food service market
Types of Products Distributed:
Food Service, General Line, General Merchandise, Provisions/Meat, Produce, Seafood

58672 Performance Foodservice
16639 Gale Ave
City of Industry, CA 91745
Fax: 800-929-5558 800-967-7662
www.performancefoodservice.com/SCalifornia
General line products specializing in Italian foods; serving the food service market
Types of Products Distributed:
Food Service, General Line, General Merchandise, Provisions/Meat, Produce, Seafood

58673 Performance Foodservice
1 Performance Blvd
Springfield, MA 01104
                               800-388-0257
www.performancefoodservice.com/Springfield
General line products specializing in Italian foods; serving the food service market
Types of Products Distributed:
Food Service, General Line, General Merchandise, Provisions/Meat, Produce, Seafood

58674 Performance Foodservice
8001 51st St W
P.O. Box 7210
Rock Island, IL 61201   309-787-1234
                               800-475-1234
www.performancefoodservice.com/ThomsProestler
General line products specializing in Italian foods; serving the food service market
Types of Products Distributed:
Food Service, General Line, General Merchandise, Provisions/Meat, Produce, Seafood

58675 Performance Foodservice
204 N Brownson St
Victoria, TX 77901   361-582-7500
Fax: 361-582-7580
www.performancefoodservice.com/Victoria
General line products specializing in Italian foods; serving the food service market
Types of Products Distributed:
Food Service, General Line, General Merchandise, Provisions/Meat, Produce, Seafood

58676 Performance Foodservice
7420 Ranco Rd
Richmond, VA 23228   804-237-1001
                               800-755-6641
www.performancefoodservice.com/Virginia
General line products specializing in Italian foods; serving the food service market
Types of Products Distributed:
Food Service, General Line, General Merchandise, Provisions/Meat, Produce, Seafood

58677 Perino's Inc
6850 Westbank Expy
Marrero, LA 70072-2523   504-347-5410
Fax: 504-341-2504 www.perinosseafood.com
Seafood
Manager: Mark Somme
Manager: Paul Ocrne
Estimated Sales: $3-5 Million
Number Employees: 10-19

58678 Pernod Ricard USA
250 Park Ave.
New York, NY 10177   212-372-5400
Fax: 914-539-4550 www.pernod-ricard-usa.com
Spirits and wines.
Chairman/CEO: Paul Duffy
Chief Financial Officer: Guillaume Thomas
Senior Vice President: James Slack
Chief Marketing Officer: Jonas Tahlin
Chief Commercial Officer: Julien Hemard
Senior VP, Communications/Sustainability: Amandine Robin
Senior VP, New Brand Ventures: Jeff Agdern
Year Founded: 1980
Estimated Sales: $100+ Million
Number Employees: 1000-4999
Number of Brands: 30+
Parent Co: Pernod Ricard SA
Private Brands Carried:
Absolut© Vodka, Aavion Tequila©, Chivas Regal© Scotch Whisky, The Glenlivet© Single Malt Scotch Whisky, Jameson© Irish Whiskey, Malibu©, Kahlua© Liqueur, Aberlour Single Malt Scotch, Altos Tequila, Beefeater© Gin, Lot 40 and Pike Creek Canadian Whiskeys
Types of Products Distributed:
Alcohol

58679 Perry B Duryea & Son Inc
65 Tuthill Rd
Montauk, NY 11954-5460   631-668-2410
Fax: 631-668-2121 800-660-2410
info@duryealobsters.com
www.duryealobsters.com
Wholesaler/distributor of seafood including fresh and frozen lobster and fish; serving the food service market
Owner: Perry B Duryea Iii
Estimated Sales: $5-10 Million
Number Employees: 5-9
Number of Customer Locations: 50
Types of Products Distributed:
Food Service, Frozen Food, Seafood, Fresh & frozen lobster & fish

58680 Perry Videx LLC
25 Mount Laurel Rd
Hainesport, NJ 08036-2711   609-267-1600
Fax: 609-267-4499 info@perryvidex.com
www.perryvidex.com

Wholesaler/distributor, importer and exporter of used food processing equipment; serving the food service market
President/ CEO: Gregg Epstein
gepstein@perryvidex.com
VP-Finance: Bob Bowdoin
VP- Production: Ron Mueller
Sales: Pete D'Angelo
Estimated Sales: $5-10 Million
Number Employees: 20-49
Types of Products Distributed:
  General Merchandise, Used food processing equipment

58681 Pestano Foods
New Rochelle, NY 10801
info@drinktoma.com
www.drinktoma.com
Artisanal Bloody Mary cocktail mix
Founder/Owner: Alejandro Lopez
Number of Brands: 1
Number of Products: 1
Type of Packaging: Consumer, Private Label, Bulk
Private Brands Carried:
  Toma
Types of Products Distributed:
  Cocktail Mix

58682 Pete and Gerry's Organic Eggs
140 Buffum Rd
Monroe, NH 03771
603-638-2827
800-210-6657
familyfarmteam@peteandgerrys.com
www.peteandgerrys.com
Organic free range eggs
Owner/CEO: Jesse Laflamme
CFO: Keith Fortier
COO: Erik Drake
VP Marketing: Paul Turbeville
Number Employees: 50-99
Types of Products Distributed:
  Provisions/Meat

58683 Peter Dudgeon International
740 Kopke St
Honolulu, HI 96819-3315
808-841-8211
Fax: 808-842-5093
Plastic materials
President: Peter Dudgeon
Treasurer: Shawn D Badham
Vice President: Andrew W Dudgeon
Contact: Jorge Delgado
jdelgado@gourmetfoodsinc.com
Estimated Sales: $5-10 Million
Number Employees: 5-9

58684 Peter Johansky Studio
152 W 25th St
New York, NY 10001-7402
212-242-7013
peter@johansky.com
www.johansky.com
Total food ingredient source with technical support. Dry, canned, refrigerated and frozen ingredients
Owner: Peter Johansky
pjohansky@michaelhowardstudios.com
Estimated Sales: Less Than $500,000
Number Employees: 1-4
Square Footage: 202800
Type of Packaging: Bulk

58685 Peter Pan Sales
PO Box 8658
St. John's, NL A1B 3T1
Canada
709-747-1990
Fax: 709-747-1482 800-563-9090
peterpan@nfld.com
Paper and plastic distributor
President: D Spurrell
Vice President: Chris Spurrell
Number Employees: 15
Square Footage: 88000
Number of Customer Locations: 500
Types of Products Distributed:
  Frozen Food, General Line, Confectionery products

58686 Peterson
1102 D St NE
Auburn, WA 98002
800-735-0313
sales@petersoncheese.com
www.petersoncheese.com
Flavorings, cheese, chocolate, meats and bacon.
Chief Executive Officer: Jack Fabulich III
Year Founded: 1947
Estimated Sales: $20-50 Million
Number Employees: 200
Square Footage: 180000
Type of Packaging: Food Service
Number of Customer Locations: 4000
Types of Products Distributed:
  Food Service, General Line, Specialty Foods, Cheese, chocolate, flavorings, etc.

58687 Peterson Sea Food Company
711 N 17th St
Allentown, PA 18104-4103
610-434-6767
Fax: 610-434-3171
Wholesaler/distributor of fresh fish; serving the food service market
Manager: Denise Shultz
Estimated Sales: $500,000-$1 Million
Number Employees: 1-4
Types of Products Distributed:
  Food Service, Frozen Food, Seafood, Fresh fish

58688 Petheriotes Brothers Coffee Company
742 Telephone Road
Houston, TX 77023-3198
713-923-7161
Fax: 713-923-4012
Wholesaler/distributor of coffee, pickles, mayonnaise and ketchup
President: James Petheriotes
Estimated Sales: $1-2.5 Million
Number Employees: 10-19

58689 Petrolab Company
25 Computer Drive East
Albany, NY 12205
518-369-7300
Fax: 918-459-7178 www.petrolab.com
Wholesaler/distributor of viscosity baths, portable FTIR testers and instrumentation for color and load and tensile strength penetration tests; also, vapor pressure and distillation tests
Manager: Michael Palmer
East Coast and Caribbean Region Sales Ma: Richard Palmer
Treasurer: Kathleen Van Pelt
Marketing Director: Angel Schell
Sales Director: Michael Palmer
Public Relations: Angel Schell
General Manager: Michael Palmer
Number Employees: 5-9
Square Footage: 120000
Type of Packaging: Food Service
Private Brands Carried:
  Petrotest; Grabner; Lovibond; Lawler; Bohler
Types of Products Distributed:
  Penetration testing instrumentation

58690 Peyton's
P.O.Box 34250
Louisville, KY 40232-4250
502-429-4800
Fax: 502-429-4834
Wholesaler/distributor of general merchandise
Executive: Charles Mercer
Director Sales/Services: Bob Wilkinson
Number Employees: 1,000-4,999
Parent Co: Kroger Company
Number of Customer Locations: 3500
Types of Products Distributed:
  Frozen Food, General Merchandise

58691 Pharaoh Trading Company
5043 Red Maple Court
Medina, OH 44256-7084
216-749-6070
Fax: 216-749-7327 800-929-4913
Wholesaler/distributor, importer and exporter of groceries, plasticware, industrial equipment and supplies, disposables and cleaning supplies; serving the health care and food service industries
President: Bill Bebawi
Secretary: Mary Bebawi
Exeutive VP: Hany Anis
Estimated Sales: $1-2.5 Million
Number Employees: 5-9
Square Footage: 4800
Private Brands Carried:
  Golden Seal
Number of Customer Locations: 300
Types of Products Distributed:
  Food Service, Frozen Food, General Line, General Merchandise, Groceries, disposables, etc.

58692 Pharmachem Labs
2929 E White Star Ave
Anaheim, CA 92806-2628
714-630-6000
Fax: 714-630-6655 800-717-5770
www.pharmachemlabs.com
Importer, exporter and wholesaler/distributor of bulk vitamins and minerals; also, vegetable powders, fruit powders, botanic powders and nutritional raw materials
President: Howard Simon
Vice President: George Joseph
gjoseph@amer-ing.com
Purchasing: George Joseph
Estimated Sales: $2.5-5 Million
Number Employees: 20-49
Square Footage: 160000
Parent Co: Pharmachem Laboratories
Type of Packaging: Bulk
Types of Products Distributed:
  Frozen Food, Health Food, Vitamins, minerals, etc.

58693 Phat Fudge
578 Washington Blvd
Marina del Rey, CA 90292
www.phatfudge.com
Performance food
Founder/CEO: Mary Shenouda *Year Founded:* 2016
Types of Products Distributed:
  General Line, Health Food

58694 Phil Erb Refrigeration Co
1344 E Sunshine St
Springfield, MO 65804-1199
800-397-1133
Fax: 417-869-5030
Wholesaler/distributor of food service equipment and supplies
Manager: Toby Kiser
Estimated Sales: $1-2.5 Million
Number Employees: 10-19
Types of Products Distributed:
  Food Service, Frozen Food, General Merchandise, Foodservice equipment

58695 Philadelphia Extract CoInc
4124 Blanche Rd
Bensalem, PA 19020-4430
215-548-5225
Fax: 215-424-5225 www.philaextract.com
Wholesaler/distributor of fountain syrups and soda systems
Owner: Burt Katz
Contact: Paul Katz
paul@philaextract.com
Estimated Sales: $2.5-5 Million
Number Employees: 20-49
Private Brands Carried:
  7-Up; Coca-Cola; Elk; Namar; Red Rose Tea
Types of Products Distributed:
  Frozen Food, Fountain syrups & soda systems

58696 Phillips Seafood
1418 Sapelo Ave NE
Townsend, GA 31331-5732
912-832-4423
Fax: 912-832-6228 www.sapeloseafarms.com
Seafood
President: Myron Phillips
Number Employees: 1-4

58697 Phillips Supply Co
1230 Findlay St
Cincinnati, OH 45214-2096
513-579-1762
Fax: 513-579-1903 800-245-8666
store@phillipssupply.com
www.phillipssupply.com
Wholesaler/distributor of warewashing and cleaning supplies including private label items; serving the food service market
President: Donna Ashley
d.ashley@phillipssupply.com
Chairman: Claire Phillips
Vice President: Jerry Wing
Estimated Sales: $10-20 Million
Number Employees: 5-9
Square Footage: 160000
Private Brands Carried:
  SSS; Phillips; ABC
Number of Customer Locations: 8000
Types of Products Distributed:
  Food Service, Frozen Food, General Merchandise, Warewashing & cleaning supplies

Wholesalers & Distributors / A-Z

58698 Phoenix Agro-Industrial Corporation
521 Lowell St
Westbury, NY 11590
516-334-1194
Fax: 516-338-8647
Frozen foods and groceries
President: Tomipor Pasto
Marketing: Julianna Edlyn
Purchasing Director: Neone Din
Estimated Sales: $3-5 Million
Number Employees: 5-9
Square Footage: 40000
Type of Packaging: Consumer, Private Label, Bulk
Types of Products Distributed:
   Frozen Food, General Line

58699 Phoenix Industries Corp
114 N Bedford St
Madison, WI 53703-2610
608-251-2533
Fax: 608-256-2604 888-241-7482
www.negusboxnbag.com
Manufacturer and exporter of corrugated ice cream containers; wholesaler/distributor and exporter of packaging supplies including bags
President: Rod Shaughnessy
contact.nequs@negusboxnbag.com
Sales: Greg Koch
Operations: Al Baler
Estimated Sales: $1-5 Million
Number Employees: 5-9
Square Footage: 40000
Parent Co: Phoenix Industries Corporation
Types of Products Distributed:
   Food Service, Frozen Food, Packaging supplies including bags

58700 Phoenix Wholesale Foodservice
16 Forest Pkwy
Building J
Forest Park, GA 30297-2015
404-363-9800
Fax: 404-363-4562 800-613-1998
sales@coboco.net www.phoenixwfs.com
Fruits, vegetables, dairy, eggs, dressings, prepared meals, oil, tofu and bottled water
Vice President: Carol Peterman
carolp@coboco.net
VP: Richard Monahan
Manager of Sales: David Cowart
Specialty Buyer: Billy Sowers
Estimated Sales: $9.5 Million
Number Employees: 250-499
Square Footage: 320000
Types of Products Distributed:
   Food Service, General Line, Produce

58701 Phyto-Technologies
107 Enterprise Dr
Woodbine, IA 51579
712-647-2755
Fax: 712-647-2885 877-809-3404
extracts@phyto-tech.com www.phyto-tech.com
Nutritional and herbal supplements, extracts and blends
Founder/President: Albert Leung
albert.leung@photo-tech.com
Sales/Marketing: Terry Jinks
Estimated Sales: Below $5 Million
Number Employees: 10-19
Square Footage: 80000
Parent Co: Earth Power
Type of Packaging: Consumer, Private Label
Private Brands Carried:
   Earth Power's Phyto Chi; Earth Power's All American
Number of Customer Locations: 1
Types of Products Distributed:
   Health Food

58702 Piazza's Seafood World LLC
205 James Dr W
St Rose, LA 70087-4036
504-602-5050
Fax: 504-602-1555 info@cajunboy.net
www.cajunboy.net
crawfish, alligator, catfish, shrimp, squid, crabmeat and softshell crabs
Manager: Jennifer Champagne
CFO: Mike Sabolyk
Manager: Jarrod Champagne
jarrod@cajunboy.net
Estimated Sales: $5-10 Million
Number Employees: 10-19
Number of Products: 20
Type of Packaging: Food Service, Private Label

58703 Pickle House
1401 E Van Buren St
Phoenix, AZ 85006-3523
602-257-1915
Fax: 623-257-9224
Wholesaler/distributor of pickles, pasta, oils and vinegar; serving the food service market
Co-Owner/Partner: Philip Arnold Blair
Co-Owner/Partner: Judy Blair
Office Manager: Mardelle Reed
Estimated Sales: $2.5-5 Million
Number Employees: 5-9
Square Footage: 400000
Private Brands Carried:
   Bee-Line; Old Arizona Tradition
Types of Products Distributed:
   Food Service, Frozen Food, General Line, Pickles, pasta, oils, vinegar & coffee

58704 Piedmont Clarklift
P.O.Box 16328
Greenville, SC 29606-7328
864-297-1330
Fax: 864-288-5874
Wholesaler/distributor of forklifts, shelving and personnel lifts
President: Jerry Prince
Sales/Marketing Executive: Steve Johnson
Estimated Sales: $10-20 Million
Number Employees: 5-9
Private Brands Carried:
   Clark; Daewoo
Types of Products Distributed:
   General Merchandise, Forklifts, etc.

58705 (HQ)Piedmont Plastics Inc
5010 W W T Harris Blvd
Charlotte, NC 28269-1861
503-968-8700
Fax: 704-598-7912 800-277-7898
www.piedmontplastics.com
Wholesaler/distributor of standard stock shaped plastics
President: Henry Booth
hbooth@piedmontplastics.com
Vice President: Owen Whitfield
Estimated Sales: $20-50 Million
Number Employees: 50-99
Square Footage: 78000000
Other Locations:
   Piedmont Plastics
   Charlotte, NC Piedmont Plastics
Types of Products Distributed:
   Frozen Food, General Merchandise, Standard stock shaped plastics

58706 Piemonte Bakery Co
1122 Rock St
Rockford, IL 61101-1431
815-962-4833
Bread, dinner rolls and po-boys
Owner: Steve McKebebaer
Secretary: Irene McKeever
Estimated Sales: $2,600,000
Number Employees: 10-19
Type of Packaging: Private Label
Types of Products Distributed:
   Frozen Food, General Line, Bread & rolls

58707 Pierceton Foods Inc
127 N First St
Pierceton, IN 46562-9336
574-594-2344
Fax: 574-594-2344
Porkfritters, cheeseburgers, steaks, beef and tender loins
President: Jerry Wagoner
Plant Manager: Ben Bunyan
Estimated Sales: $1,040,000
Number Employees: 5-9
Number of Brands: 1
Square Footage: 12000
Type of Packaging: Food Service
Private Brands Carried:
   Pauls
Types of Products Distributed:
   Food Service, Frozen Food, General Line, General Merchandise, Provisions/Meat, Produce, Seafood

58708 Pilot Meat & Sea Food Company
405 N Pilot Knob Road
Galena, IL 61036-8803
319-556-0760
Fax: 319-556-4131
Meat and seafood
CEO: Randall Sirk
Accountant: Ted Kipper
Estimated Sales: $1.2 Million
Number Employees: 7

58709 Pine Point Fisherman's Co-Op
96 King St.
Scarborough, ME 04074
207-883-3588
Fax: 207-883-6772 lobster@maine.rr.com
lobsterco-op.com
Lobsters
Estimated Sales: $1-3 Million
Number Employees: 5-9

58710 Pinnacle Foods Inc.
222 W Merchandise Mart Plaza
Chicago, IL 60654
312-549-5000
877-266-2472
www.pinnaclefoods.com
Packaged and frozen foods.
President & CEO, Conagra: Sean Connolly
Year Founded: 1998
Estimated Sales: $3.14 Billion
Number Employees: 4,900
Parent Co: Conagra Brands
Type of Packaging: Consumer
Types of Products Distributed:
   Frozen Food, General Line

58711 Pinto Bros
6700 Essington Ave # G7
Units G7-G9
Philadelphia, PA 19153-3427
215-336-3015
Fax: 215-218-3287 www.pintobrothers.com
Wholesaler/distributor of fruit and produce; serving the food service market
Owner: Louis Penza
lpenza@pintobrothers.com
Estimated Sales: $2.5-5 Million
Number Employees: 20-49
Types of Products Distributed:
   Food Service, Frozen Food, Produce

58712 Pioneer Distributing Co
8900 Maumelle Blvd
N Little Rock, AR 72113-6740
501-812-5030
Fax: 501-812-5031 800-880-0208
sales@pioneerdc.com www.pioneerdc.com
Wholesaler/distributor of food service supplies and equipment; serving the food service market
President: James Crossland
jamie@pioneerdc.com
Number Employees: 5-9
Private Brands Carried:
   Cambro; Polar Ware; Blodgett
Types of Products Distributed:
   Food Service, Frozen Food, General Merchandise, Equipment & supplies

58713 Pioneer Distributing Company
PO Box 2358
Green Bay, WI 54306-2358
920-983-0247
Fax: 920-983-0251
Wholesaler/distributor of confectionery and grocery products, specialty foods and general merchandise
President: J Burke
Number Employees: 20-49
Number of Customer Locations: 500
Types of Products Distributed:
   Frozen Food, General Line, General Merchandise, Specialty Foods, Confectionery & grocery products

58714 Pioneer Lift Truck
2545 S Sarah Street
Fresno, CA 93706-5095
559-268-1994
Fax: 559-486-7587 jpcanales@aol.com
www.pioneerequipment.com
Wholesaler/distributor of forklifts; also, parts and service available
President: James Canales
Estimated Sales: $10-20 Million
Number Employees: 20-49
Private Brands Carried:
   Toyota
Types of Products Distributed:
   Frozen Food, General Merchandise, Forklifts

58715 Pioneer Live Shrimp
2801 Meyers Road
Oak Brook, IL 60523-1623
630-789-1133
Fax: 312-226-7376
Shrimp
President: David Wong
VP: Chun Wah
Secretary: Esther Wong
Estimated Sales: $2.8 Million
Number Employees: 14
Square Footage: 56000

Wholesalers & Distributors / A-Z

58716 Pioneer Marketing
Jefferson Street
Vancouver, WA 98660   360-695-1282
            Fax: 360-695-1284
Wholesaler/distributor of food service equipment including ice systems, drink dispensers, microwaves, etc; serving the food service market
Office Manager: Kelly Roberson
Sales Manager: Joy Sweet
Estimated Sales: $1-2.5 Million
Number Employees: 5-9
Private Brands Carried:
   Amana; Menumaster; Crystal Tips Ice Systems; Booth
Types of Products Distributed:
   Food Service, Frozen Food, General Merchandise, Ice systems, drink dispensers, etc.

58717 Pioneer Sales Co Inc
80 Industrial Way # 6
Wilmington, MA 01887-4614   978-658-1933
            Fax: 978-658-2218 800-221-2596
            sales@pioneersalesco.com
Wholesaler/distributor of commercial equipment including refrigerators, freezers, microwave and convection ovens and gas cooking equipment
President: George Rogers
sales@pioneersalesco.com
Sales Manager: Judy Giglio
Estimated Sales: $2.5-5 Million
Number Employees: 5-9
Square Footage: 52000
Private Brands Carried:
   Caravell; Excellence; Imperial; Kelvinator; Leer; Master Bilt; Nelson; Panasonic; Powers; PureMark; Silver King
Types of Products Distributed:
   Frozen Food, General Merchandise, Refrigerators, ovens & freezers

58718 Pippin Wholesale Co
512 Highway 62 65 N
Harrison, AR 72601-2504   870-741-3421
            Fax: 870-741-4444 www.pippinwholesale.com
Wholesaler/distributor of groceries; serving the food service market
Owner: Ken Milburn
Estimated Sales: $20-50 Million
Number Employees: 20-49
Parent Co: Harrison Grocer Company
Private Brands Carried:
   Pleezing
Number of Customer Locations: 400
Types of Products Distributed:
   Food Service, Frozen Food, General Line, General Merchandise, Groceries

58719 Pittman Brothers Company
4210 127th Trl N
West Palm Beach, FL 33411-8944   561-833-6422
            Fax: 561-833-0097
Wholesaler/distributor of general line products; serving the food service market
President/CEO: David Pittman
Number Employees: 10-19
Types of Products Distributed:
   Food Service, Frozen Food, General Line

58720 Pittsburgh Casing Company
102 33rd St
Pittsburgh, PA 15201   412-281-4327
            Fax: 412-281-0445 800-886-4329
            www.pittsburghspice.com
Importer of natural sewn sausage casing; wholesaler/distributor of spices and seasonings
Owner: Gregory Mancini
Vice President: Gregory Mancini
Estimated Sales: $500,000-$1 Million
Number Employees: 5-9
Square Footage: 100000
Parent Co: Pittsburgh Spice & Seasoning Company
Type of Packaging: Bulk
Types of Products Distributed:
   Frozen Food, General Line, Spices & seasonings

58721 Pizza Products
3131 N Franklin Rd Ste B
Indianapolis, IN 46226   317-897-8865
            Fax: 317-845-0548
Wholesaler/distributor of meat, produce, dairy and bakery products, boxes and pizza products including fresh and pre-baked crusts
President: Micky Heining
Estimated Sales: $10-20 Million
Number Employees: 10-19
Types of Products Distributed:
   Frozen Food, General Line, General Merchandise, Provisions/Meat, Produce, Pizza, dairy & bakery products, etc.

58722 Pk Crown Distributing Inc
1115 W Sunset Blvd
Rocklin, CA 95765-1304   916-645-9124
            Fax: 916-645-9140 www.pkcrown.com
Wholesaler/distributor of general merchandise including paper, cleaners, caterware, kitchenware and glassware; also, janitorial, restroom and tabletop supplies
President: Justin Booth
jbooth@pkcrown.com
Sales Manager: Dave Silveria
Estimated Sales: $5-10 Million
Number Employees: 50-99
Private Brands Carried:
   Colgate-Palmolive
Types of Products Distributed:
   Frozen Food, General Merchandise, Paper, cleaners, kitchenware, etc.

58723 Plaidberry Company
830 Mimosa Ave
Vista, CA 92081   760-727-5403
            dennisdickson@cs.com
Jams, muffins, pie and cake fillings, juices, confections, yogurt bases
President/Owner: Dennis Dickson
plaidberry@yahoo.com
Estimated Sales: Below 5 Million
Number Employees: 4
Number of Products: 6
Square Footage: 74000
Type of Packaging: Consumer, Bulk
Private Brands Carried:
   Plaidberry
Number of Customer Locations: 1
Types of Products Distributed:
   General Merchandise, Berries

58724 Plainfield Winery & Tasting Rm
6291 Cambridge Way
Plainfield, IN 46168-7905   317-837-9463
            Fax: 317-837-8464 888-761-9463
            info@chateauthomas.com
            www.chateauthomas.com
Wines
President: Charles Thomas
Manager: Sheila Cavanaugh
info@chateauthomas.com
Purchasing Manager: Tommy England
Estimated Sales: $5-10 Million
Number Employees: 20-49
Type of Packaging: Private Label

58725 Plasco Safety Products
PO Box 367
Springfield, OH 45501-0367   937-325-1001
Fax: 937-328-6477 www.benchmarkindustrial.com
Wholesaler/distributor of work gloves and personal safety equipment including hearing protectors, eye protectors, aprons, disposable clothing, hand pads and other specialty items
Owner: Mary Walling
Quotation Department: Judy Miller
VP: Claire Williamson
Owner/Sales Manager: Ron Tenkman
tenkman@benchmarkindustrial.com
Estimated Sales: $3-5 Million
Number Employees: 20-49
Square Footage: 600000
Private Brands Carried:
   Ansell/Edmont; Baxter; Best; Charkate; Commodity
Types of Products Distributed:
   Frozen Food, General Merchandise, Personal safety equipment

58726 Platteville Potato Association
PO Box 100
Platteville, CO 80651-0100   970-785-2227
Wholesaler/distributor of potatoes
Manager: John Rupple
Secretary: Kristie Cuykendall
Estimated Sales: $1-2.5 Million
Number Employees: 1-4
Types of Products Distributed:
   Frozen Food, Produce, Potatoes

58727 Plt Health Solutions Inc
119 Headquarters Plz
Morristown, NJ 07960-6834   973-984-0900
            Fax: 973-984-5666 plt@plthomas.com
            www.plthomas.com
Company products includes water soluble gums, hydrocolloids, botanical extracts, mineral gluconates, stabilizers and thickeners. Additional products include agar-agar, carob, fenugreek and fiber, nutraceuticals and spirulina.
President: Paul M Flowerman
Marketing/Public Relations: Paula Nurnberger
Sales Director: Rodger Jonas
Contact: Jenson Chang
jensonchang@hotmail.com
Estimated Sales: $5-10 Million
Number Employees: 50-99
Number of Brands: 15
Number of Products: 200
Other Locations:
   P L Thomas
   Morristown, NJP L Thomas
Private Brands Carried:
   Glisodin, Ecogvar, Ultraguar, Ceamgel 1313, Nutralease, 5-Loxin, Fenupure, Nutricran, Glocal, Mega Natural and Nutra Veggie.

58728 Plum Organics
1485 Park Ave
Emeryville, CA 94608
            877-914-7586
            www.plumorganics.com
Organic baby food, formula, and kids snacks
Founder/CEO: Neil Grimmer
Product Innovation Manager: Meg Verdeyen
SVP Brand Marketing & Innovation: Ben Mand
Year Founded: 2005
Number Employees: 100-249
Types of Products Distributed:
   General Line

58729 Pocono ProFoods
Route 191 and Chipperfield Dr
P.O. Box 669
Stroudsburg, PA 18360   570-421-4990
            Fax: 570-476-5149 800-366-4550
            poconoprofoods.com
Wholesaler/distributor of frozen foods, groceries, produce, provisions/meats, seafood, specialty foods, baked goods, dairy products and private label items; serving the food service market
Year Founded: 1903
Estimated Sales: $29.6 Million
Number Employees: 177
Types of Products Distributed:
   Food Service, Frozen Food, General Line, Provisions/Meat, Produce, Seafood, Specialty Foods, Dairy products, baked goods, etc.

58730 Point Lobster Co
1 St. Louis Ave
Point Pleasant Beach, NJ   732-892-1729
            Fax: 732-892-3928 info@pointlobster.com
            pointlobster.com
Lobster

58731 Poiret International
7866 Exeter Boulevard E
Tamarac, FL 33321-8797   203-926-3700
            Fax: 954-721-0110 800-237-9151
Preserves and organic jams
CEO/Purchasing: Ed Kerzner
CFO: Sheila Kerzner
Marketing Director: Stan Margulese
Plant Manager: Frank Bilisi
Number Employees: 20-49
Square Footage: 100000
Parent Co: Siroper/E. Meurens SA
Type of Packaging: Consumer, Food Service, Private Label, Bulk
Types of Products Distributed:
   Food Service, Frozen Food, Health Food, Specialty Foods

58732 (HQ)Polar Bear
2695 Pine Grove Rd
Cumming, GA 30041   770-292-9222
            Fax: 888-776-5598 888-438-7924
            polarbear@usa.net www.polarbearcoolers.com
Distributor of commercial refrigeration freezers, ice cubers, ice dispensers and ice storage bins

Owner: Michael Kennis
General Manager Sales/Distribution: Vic Lemieux
Contact: Geoff Cole
geoff@polarbearcoolers.com
General Manager Production Plant: Dwayne Whitehill
Estimated Sales: $5-10,000,000
Number Employees: 5-9
Type of Packaging: Private Label
Types of Products Distributed:
  Frozen Food, General Merchandise, Freezers, ice cubers, storage bins, etc

58733 Polean Foods
PO Box 148
Hamsptead, NC 28443 910-319-0850
  Fax: 910-319-0854 866-765-3263
  sales@poleanfoods.com
Wholesaler/distributor, importer and exporter of pork products and ingredients
President: Peter Jazwinski
Sales Director: Steve Eldridge
Estimated Sales: $5-10 Million
Number Employees: 5-9
Square Footage: 4000
Type of Packaging: Consumer, Food Service, Private Label, Bulk
Private Brands Carried:
  Polean; Polean Polska; Deli Ham; Canadian Premium
Types of Products Distributed:
  Food Service, Provisions/Meat, Specialty Foods, Ingredients

58734 Polish Folklore Import Co
2428 Rose St
Franklin Park, IL 60131-3323 847-288-0708
  Fax: 847-288-0816 pfimport@aol.com
  www.polishfolklore.com
Import broker of confectionery products including jams and preserves. Wholesaler/distributor of specialty food products
President: Bogumila Mielski
pfimport@aol.com
Vice President: Christopher Bogacz
Sales Director: Marta Sliwa
Estimated Sales: $2.5-5 Million
Number Employees: 5-9
Number of Customer Locations: 300
Types of Products Distributed:
  Frozen Food, Specialty Foods

58735 Pollak Food Distributors
P.O. Box 17485
1200 Babbitt Road
Euclid, OH 44132 216-851-9911
  Fax: 216-851-9939 800-878-6325
  CustomerService@pollakdist.com
  www.pollakdist.com
Wholesaler/distributor of general line products
President: Arthur Pollak
Contact: Shonda Goldston
shlomo@pollakdist.com
Estimated Sales: $10-12 Million
Number Employees: 20-49
Types of Products Distributed:
  Frozen Food, General Line

58736 Polyplastics
10201 Metropolitan Dr
Austin, TX 78758-4944 512-339-9293
  Fax: 512-339-9317 800-753-7659
  sales@1polyplastics.com www.polyplastics.com
Manufacturer, exporter and wholesaler/distributor of rigid and flexible foamed plastics
President: Dave McArthur
VP: Tim Buckley
Sales Director: Tim Buckley
Manager: Tito Robledo
trobledo@1polyplastics.com
Manufacturing Manager: Harry Stevens
Estimated Sales: $2.5-5 Million
Number Employees: 5-9
Square Footage: 56000
Parent Co: Buckley Industries
Types of Products Distributed:
  Frozen Food, General Line, Rigid & flexible polyurethane foam

58737 Pon Food Corp
101 Industrial Park Blvd
Ponchatoula, LA 70454-8306 985-386-6941
  Fax: 985-386-6755 info@ponfoodcorp.com
  www.ponchatoula-

Groceries, frozen foods, meats, dairy products and seafood
President: Pam Barado
pbarado@ponfoodcorp.com
Co-owner: Michael Berner
Estimated Sales: $7.7 Million
Number Employees: 20-49
Square Footage: 72000
Private Brands Carried:
  Nugget
Number of Customer Locations: 350
Types of Products Distributed:
  Food Service, Frozen Food, General Line, Provisions/Meat, Seafood, Dairy products

58738 Pond Pure Catfish
14429 Market St
Moulton, AL 35650 256-974-6698
  Fax: 403-252-3918
Catfish
Owner: Bobby Norwood
Estimated Sales: $300,000-500,000
Number Employees: 1-4

58739 Pontchartrain Blue Crab
38327 Salt Bayou Rd
Slidell, LA 70461-1103 985-649-6645
  Fax: 504-781-5064
  pbcinfo@pontchartrainbluecrab.com
  www.pontchartrainbluecrab.com
Seafood
President/CEO: Gary Bauer
garyb@pontchartrainbluecrab.com
Estimated Sales: $5,000,000
Number Employees: 5-9

58740 Pontiac Fruit House
103 E Montcalm St
Pontiac, MI 48342-1354 248-332-8388
  Fax: 248-332-0445
Wholesaler/distributor of frozen foods, general line products, produce, meat products, seafood and specialty foods; serving the food service market
Owner: Al Rownski
Estimated Sales: $3-5 Million
Number Employees: 1-4
Number of Customer Locations: 300
Types of Products Distributed:
  Food Service, Frozen Food, General Line, Provisions/Meat, Produce, Seafood, Specialty Foods

58741 Pop's E-Z Popcorn & Supply Company
17151 SE Petrovitsky Road
Renton, WA 98058-9602 425-255-4545
  Fax: 425-255-8181
Wholesaler/distributor of concession equipment and supplies including popcorn, nachos, cotton candy and soft frozen and beverage machinery; serving the food service market
President: David Vreeken
Estimated Sales: $500,000-$1 Million
Number Employees: 5-9
Square Footage: 20000
Private Brands Carried:
  Slush Puppie; Lanikai; Thelma's Lemonade; Weaver's Popcorn; Cretors; Gold Medal; Star; Rico's
Types of Products Distributed:
  Food Service, Frozen Food, General Line, General Merchandise, Concession equipment & supplies

58742 Poppers Supply Company
PO Box 90187
Allentown, PA 18109 503-239-3792
  Fax: 503-235-6221 800-457-9810
  info@poppers.com www.poppers.com
Popcorn and fountain syrup
President: Vernon Ryles Jr
Sales Manager: Jody Riggs
Estimated Sales: $1.4 Million
Number Employees: 10
Type of Packaging: Consumer, Food Service
Types of Products Distributed:
  General Line, General Merchandise, Concession equipment & supplies

58743 Porinos Gourmet Food
280 Rand St
Central Falls, RI 02863-2512 401-273-3000
  Fax: 401-273-3232 800-826-3938
  porinos@aol.com

Pasta and sauces, salad dressings, marinades and pickled pepper
Owner: Michael Dressler
VP Operations: Marshall Righter
Estimated Sales: $1.9 Million
Number Employees: 10-19
Square Footage: 120000
Type of Packaging: Consumer, Food Service, Private Label
Private Brands Carried:
  Primi DiBella; Papa Luigi; Zia Maria
Types of Products Distributed:
  Frozen Food, General Line, Pasta, olive oil & balsamic vinegar

58744 Porky Products
135 Amity Street
Jersey City, NJ 07304-3509 201-333-2333
  Fax: 201-333-3571
Wholesaler/distributor of meat, poultry and seafood
President: Jonathan Ewig
Chairman: M Bernstein
Number Employees: 100-249
Private Brands Carried:
  Western Crown; E.J. Farms
Number of Customer Locations: 1500
Types of Products Distributed:
  Frozen Food, Provisions/Meat, Seafood, Poultry

58745 Port Lobster Co Inc
122 Ocean Ave
Kennebunkport, ME 04046-6302 207-967-2081
  Fax: 207-967-8419 800-486-7029
  www.portlobster.com
Lobster
President: Kenneth Hutchins
portlob@gwi.net
Estimated Sales: $1-3 Million
Number Employees: 5-9
Type of Packaging: Consumer
Types of Products Distributed:
  Seafood

58746 Port Royal Sales LTD
95 Froehlich Farm Blvd # 200
Woodbury, NY 11797-2930 516-921-8483
  Fax: 516-921-8488 www.portroyalsales.com
Importer and wholesaler/distributor of canned peaches, pineapples, pears, tomatoes, mushrooms, olives, tuna and sardines; serving the food service market
President: Steven Zwecker
CEO: Wayne Wellner
wwellner@portroyalsales.com
CEO: Wayne Wellner
VP Marketing: Wayne Wellner
Estimated Sales: $5-10 Million
Number Employees: 10-19
Square Footage: 20000
Type of Packaging: Consumer, Food Service, Private Label
Private Brands Carried:
  Premium
Types of Products Distributed:
  Food Service, Frozen Food, General Line, Canned foods: peaches, tuna, etc.

58747 Port Royal Tapes
1020 SW 10th Avenue
Suite 4
Pompano Beach, FL 33069-4632 954-782-9525
  Fax: 954-782-9611
Wholesaler/distributor of pressure sensitive tapes including masking, duct, foil, packaging, electrical, double coated and carton sealing; also, stretch wrap
CEO/President: Robert Garmella
Estimated Sales: $1-2.5 Million
Number Employees: 5-9
Square Footage: 25200
Private Brands Carried:
  Deerfield Plastic; Bemis; Teesa-Tuck; Central Products
Types of Products Distributed:
  Frozen Food, General Merchandise, Pressure sensitive tapes & stretch wrap

58748 Portage Frosted Foods
344 Day St
Ravenna, OH 44266 330-296-5216
Wholesaler/distributor of frozen foods
President: Tom Veon
Secretary: Linda Jordan
VP: William Jordan

Estimated Sales: Less than $500,000
Number Employees: 1-4
Types of Products Distributed:
 Frozen Food

58749 Porter Wallace Corporation
507 9th Ave
New York, NY 10018-2802   212-244-0088
 Fax: 212-244-0237
Wholesaler/distributor of general merchandise including advertising specialties, marking and writing pens, aprons, T-shirts, caps, hats, labels, baskets, bags and promotional items
Buyer: Sherry Kaufmann
VP: Dan Kessler
Sales Manager: Robert Bixon
Number Employees: 5-9
Private Brands Carried:
 Pfizer; Jim Bean; Seagram Americas
Number of Customer Locations: 70
Types of Products Distributed:
 Frozen Food, General Merchandise, Advertising specialties

58750 Portland Specialty Seafoods
12 Portland Fish Pier
Suite A
Portland, ME 04101-4620   207-775-5765
 Fax: 207-774-1614
Seafood
Manager: Ethan Court
ethan@northlanticseafood.com
Administrator: Jessica Burton
Estimated Sales: $10-20 Million
Number Employees: 20-49

58751 Portugalia Imports
23 Tremont St
Fall River, MA 02720-4821   508-679-9307
 Fax: 508-673-1502 portugaliaimports.com
Seafood, breads, vegetables, and other specialty foods
President/Owner: Fernando Benevides
benevidesf@portugaliaimports.com
Vice President: Michael Benevides *Year Founded:* 1988
Types of Products Distributed:
 General Line, Produce, Seafood

58752 (HQ)Portuguese United Grocer Co-Op
45 Wheeler Point Rd
Newark, NJ 07105-3034   973-344-1561
 Fax: 973-344-8046
Wholesaler/distributor of frozen foods, general line products, meats, fish,specialty foods and candy; serving the food service market; importer of olive oil
President: Joaquim Vieira
CFO: J Jesus Vieira
VP: Alzira Vieira
Estimated Sales: $5 Million
Number Employees: 5-9
Square Footage: 260000
Type of Packaging: Consumer, Food Service
Number of Customer Locations: 400
Types of Products Distributed:
 Food Service, Frozen Food, General Line, General Merchandise, Health Food, Provisions/Meat, Produce, Seafood

58753 Poseidon Enterprises
3516 Green Park Circle
Charlotte, NC 28217-2854   704-944-1164
 Fax: 704-405-0018 800-863-7886
Seafood, salmon, tuna, swordfish, grouper, snapper, live lobster
President: Richard Lavecchia

58754 Positive Impressions
1 Bridge St # 56
Irvington, NY 10533-1558   914-591-4129
 Fax: 914-591-9729 800-895-5505
 sales@positiveimpressions.com
Wholesaler/distributor of advertising specialties, candies, chocolates, etc
Owner: Joan B Landorf
Private Brands Carried:
 Maple Farms
Types of Products Distributed:
 Frozen Food, General Line, General Merchandise, Advertising specialties

58755 Positively 3rd St Bakery
1202 E 3rd St
Duluth, MN 55805-2319   218-724-8619
 Fax: 218-724-4185 3rdstreetbakery@gmail.com
Cookies, bagels, granola and bread
Owner: Paul Steklin
Estimated Sales: Less than $500,000
Number Employees: 10-19
Type of Packaging: Consumer, Food Service, Bulk
Types of Products Distributed:
 Frozen Food

58756 Post & Taback
250 Nyc Term Mkt # A
Bronx, NY 10474-7402   718-589-1000
 Fax: 718-589-7678
Wholesaler/distributor of produce; serving the food service market
Manager: Joseph Fierman
Number Employees: 100-249
Types of Products Distributed:
 Food Service, Frozen Food, Produce

58757 Post Food Service
1230 Aspen Avenue NW
Albuquerque, NM 87104-2210   505-247-4121
Wholesaler/distributor of general merchandise and general line items; serving the food service market
Sales Manager: Ronny Dubos
Number Employees: 20-49
Parent Co: Post Food Service
Types of Products Distributed:
 Food Service, Frozen Food, General Line, General Merchandise

58758 Potato Specialty Company
604 30th Street
Lubbock, TX 79404-1524   806-747-4633
 Fax: 806-747-1607
Wholesaler/distributor of frozen foods, produce, provisions/ meats and seafood; serving the food service market
President: Larry Izell, Jr.
Contact: Chase Ezell
cezell@potatospecialty.com
Estimated Sales: $10-20 Million
Number Employees: 20-49
Types of Products Distributed:
 Food Service, Frozen Food, Provisions/Meat, Produce, Seafood

58759 Poteet Seafood Co
107 Speedy Tostensen Blvd
Brunswick, GA 31520-3149   912-264-5340
 Fax: 912-267-9695
Seafood
Owner: Speedy Tostensen
poteetseafood@bellsouth.net
Estimated Sales: $350,000
Number Employees: 1-4

58760 Potlicker Kitchen
192 Thomas Road
Stowe, VT 05672   802-760-6111
 potlickerkitchen@gmail.com
 potlickerkitchen.com
Beer jelly, wine jelly and artisan jam
Owner: Nancy Warner
Year Founded: 2009
Estimated Sales: $7.4 Million
Number Employees: 38
Types of Products Distributed:
 Beer jelly, wine jelly and jam

58761 Power Creamery
204 S Main St
Crosby, ND 58730   701-965-6382
 Fax: 701-965-6225
Wholesaler/distributor of frozen and specialty foods; also, dairy products including milk, butter, cheese and ice cream
Owner: Charles K Power
Estimated Sales: Less Than $500,000
Number Employees: 1-4
Number of Customer Locations: 50
Types of Products Distributed:
 General Line, Specialty Foods, Dairy products

58762 Power Lift Corporation
8314 E Slauson Ave
Pico Rivera, CA 90660-4323   562-949-1000
 Fax: 562-949-5984
Wholesaler/distributor of new and used forklifts
President: Tim Clearly
Number Employees: 100-249
Private Brands Carried:
 Clark; Nissan
Types of Products Distributed:
 Frozen Food, General Merchandise, Forklifts

58763 Power Pumps
79 N Industrial Park
Sewickley, PA 15143   800-648-6081
 Fax: 412-741-1465 800-441-7305
Wholesaler/distributor of sanitary and ultrahygienic pumps, flow control systems and accessories; serving the food service market
VP: John Matela
Estimated Sales: $2.5-5 Million
Number Employees: 5-9
Types of Products Distributed:
 Food Service, Frozen Food, General Merchandise, Ulrahygienic pumps & pumping systems

58764 Power Source Distributors
1438 Highway 96
Burns, TN 37029-5030   615-441-1521
 Fax: 615-446-3788 800-489-4872
 usalabs@usalabs.com www.usalabs.com
Wholesaler/distributor of vitamins, nutritional supplements, fitness equipment, health foods and beverages
President: Chuck Stokes
International Sales Director: Susan Hazelwood
Operations Manager: Shelby Bethshears
Estimated Sales: $1-2.5 Million
Number Employees: 10-19
Square Footage: 140000
Parent Co: USA Laboratories
Private Brands Carried:
 U.S.A. Sports Labs; Power Source; Future Food
Number of Customer Locations: 5000
Types of Products Distributed:
 Frozen Food, General Line, General Merchandise, Health Food, Specialty Foods, Fitness equipment, vitamins & beverages

58765 Prairie Queen Distributing
1270 Western Ave
Sheldon, IA 51201   712-324-3208
Wholesaler/distributor of baking ingredients including flour and shortening; serving independent bakers
Owner: Marv Meendering
Estimated Sales: $500,000-$1 Million
Number Employees: 1-4
Number of Customer Locations: 35
Types of Products Distributed:
 Frozen Food, General Line, Baking ingredients

58766 Prawn Seafoods Inc
6894 NW 32nd Ave
Miami, FL 33147-6606   305-691-2435
 Fax: 305-693-6348 www.sunset-foods.com
Food service distributor of canned goods, dry goods, frozen foods, frozen vegetables; serving the food service market
President: Jeff Wine
Estimated Sales: $4.5-4.8 Million
Number Employees: 5-9
Square Footage: 80000
Type of Packaging: Food Service
Private Brands Carried:
 Mr Prawn; C.J.
Number of Customer Locations: 85
Types of Products Distributed:
 Food Service, Frozen Food, Produce, Seafood

58767 Precision Pours
12837 Industrial Park Blvd
Minneapolis, MN 55441-3910   763-694-9291
 Fax: 763-694-9343 800-549-4491
 ricksandvik@precisionpours.com
Manufacturer and exporter of pour spouts for liquor, syrups and cooking oils; wholesaler/distributor of pour cleaning systems
President: Rick Sandvik
ricksandvik@precisionpours.com
Accounting: Patrick Sandvik
VP Sales: Duane Nording
Estimated Sales: Below $5,000,000
Number Employees: 10-19
Square Footage: 9600
Types of Products Distributed:
 Frozen Food, General Merchandise, Pour cleaning systems

Wholesalers & Distributors / A-Z

58768 Pregel America
4450 Fortune Ave NW
Concord, NC 28027-7901 704-707-0300
Fax: 646-478-9518 866-977-3435
peeledsnacks@worldpantry.com
www.pregelrecipes.com
Bases, cream flavors, fruit flavors, super sprint line, wellness line, frozen yogurt flavors, fillings and sauces, pastry and confections
President: John Baran
j.baran@pregelcanada.com
Ceo: Marco Casol
Vice President: Vittorio Rebboni
Estimated Sales: $240,000
Number Employees: 1-4

58769 Preiser Scientific Inc
94 Oliver St
St Albans, WV 25177-1796 304-727-2902
Fax: 304-727-2932 800-624-8285
preiser@preiser.com www.preiser.com
Wholesaler/distributor, importer and exporter of laboratory and water testing equipment and supplies. Manufacturer of coal testing equipment
President: A Preiser
CEO: G Preiser
CFO: P Fourney
VP: J Gatens
R&D: K Westfall
Sales: C Cline
Operations: D Meddings
Purchasing: D Martin
Estimated Sales: $5-10 Million
Number Employees: 20-49
Square Footage: 240000
Types of Products Distributed:
　Frozen Food, General Merchandise, Laboratory & water testing supplies

58770 Prejean's Wholesale Meats Inc
112 N Michaud St
Carencro, LA 70520 337-896-6574
Wholesaler/distributor of meats.
Owner: Wayne Prejean
Estimated Sales: $20-50 Million
Number Employees: 20-49
Types of Products Distributed:
　Frozen Food, Provisions/Meat

58771 Premier Foodservice Distributors of America
4226 Coronado Avenue
Stockton, CA 95204-2328 209-948-8122
Fax: 209-461-7403 www.pfds.com
Wholesaler/distributor of general line products, frozen foods and meats; serving the food service market
President: Ted Peralta
COO: Doug Polk
Sr. VP Marketing: Mike Haddix
Sr. VP Procurement: Jerry Scotti
Estimated Sales: $20-50 Million
Number Employees: 50-99
Private Brands Carried:
　Nugget
Types of Products Distributed:
　Food Service, Frozen Food, General Line, General Merchandise, Health Food, Provisions/Meat, Produce, Seafood, Specialty Foods, Imports

58772 Premier Juices
19321 US Highway 19 N
Suite 405
Clearwater, FL 33764-3142 727-533-8200
Fax: 727-533-8500 info@premierjuices.com
www.premierjuices.com
Wholesaler/distributor of juice concentrates; serving food processors
President: Jody Marshburn
jody@premierjuices.com
Partner: Mark Marshburn
Partner: Charles Kern
Estimated Sales: $.5-1 million
Number Employees: 1-4
Parent Co: Premier Juices
Types of Products Distributed:
　Frozen Food, General Line, Juice concentrates

58773 Premier Produce
101000 Franklin Ave
Franklin Park, IL 60131 847-678-0780
Fax: 847-678-6140 premierproduce1.com
Wholesale produce, restaurant supplies, fresh pastas and specialty item for every aspect of the food industry.
President: Lou Minaglia
General Manager: Jack Viverito
Sales Manager: Ray Gutierrez
Warehouse Manager: Armando Gamboa
Estimated Sales: $4 Million
Number Employees: 23
Square Footage: 14416

58774 Premiere Refreshment Svc
3013 Hayneville Rd
Montgomery, AL 36108-3938 334-264-7336
Fax: 334-264-7439
Wholesaler/distributor of vending machines; serving the food service market; also, catering service available
Manager: Ken Miller
kmiller@afsvend.com
Estimated Sales: $10-20 Million
Number Employees: 50-99
Parent Co: Automatic Food Service
Types of Products Distributed:
　Food Service, Frozen Food, General Merchandise, Vending machines

58775 Premiere Seafood
257 Midland Avenue
Lexington, KY 40508-1978 606-259-3474
Fax: 606-389-9390
Seafood
President: Rex Webb

58776 Premium Seafood Co
157 E 57th St # 18a
F.D.R. Station
New York, NY 10022-2115 212-750-5377
Fax: 212-308-0223 premiumsfd@aol.com
www.premiumseafood.com
Broker of seafood
Owner: Patti Sirkus
premiumseafood@premiumseafood.com
VP: Patti Sirkus
Estimated Sales: $1-2.5 Million
Number Employees: 1-4
Types of Products Distributed:
　Frozen Food

58777 Presentations
9 Mahan St Unit C
West Babylon, NY 11704 631-491-6368
Fax: 631-491-6372 www.prezi.com
Wholesaler/distributor of menus, guest checks, matches; serving the food service market
Owner: Tom Vlahakis
Estimated Sales: Less than $500,000
Number Employees: 1-4
Square Footage: 10000
Types of Products Distributed:
　Food Service, Frozen Food, General Merchandise, Menus, guest checks & matches

58778 Pressure King Inc
231 Herbert Ave # 1
Closter, NJ 07624-1332 201-768-1911
Fax: 201-768-4811 800-468-1007
pressurekg@aol.com
Wholesaler/distributor and importer of pressure washers, steam cleaning equipment, carpet extraction systems and detergents for the restaurant industry; exporter of pressure washers, water heaters, steamers, etc
Owner: Harry Mccormick
pressurekg@aol.com
Estimated Sales: $500,000
Number Employees: 1-4
Square Footage: 10000
Private Brands Carried:
　Karcher; Sioux; MiTM; C Tech; Honda; Briggs-Straton
Types of Products Distributed:
　Frozen Food, General Merchandise, Pressure washers & cleaning equipment

58779 Presto Bistro
367 Riverdale Road
Weare, NH 03281-5546 302-777-3786
Wholesaler/distributor of pre-packaged sandwiches, snacks, desserts and beverages
Owner: L Beliveau
Types of Products Distributed:
　Frozen Food, General Line, Pre-packaged sandwiches, snacks, etc.

58780 Presto Foods
201 Lawton Ave
Monroe, OH 45050 937-294-6969
800-589-7004
prestofoods.com
Italian and deli related items.
Director: Robert Weeda
Estimated Sales: $130 Million
Number Employees: 50-99
Square Footage: 80000

58781 Prestolite Electric Inc
46200 Port St
Plymouth, MI 48170 734-582-7200
Fax: 734-453-5032 www.prestolite.com
Wholesaler/distributor of material handling equipment and battery chargers
Manager: Jim Keyser
Contact: James Beirne
j.beirne@prestolite.com
Estimated Sales: $2.5-5 Million
Number Employees: 5-9
Private Brands Carried:
　Deka; Hobart; R.T. Industries
Types of Products Distributed:
　Frozen Food, General Merchandise, Material handling equipment, etc.

58782 Prevor Marketing International
975 Union Ave
Bronx, NY 10459-2926 718-589-5200
Fax: 516-624-3486
Importer, exporter and wholesaler/distributor of produce and poultry
Owner: Barry Prevor
Number Employees: 10-19
Types of Products Distributed:
　Frozen Food, Provisions/Meat, Produce

58783 Price & Co
3530 W Cardinal Dr
Beaumont, TX 77705-2937 409-840-4394
Fax: 409-842-2134 www.priceco.com
Wholesaler/distributor of candy; serving the food service market
Owner: Justen Vogt
CEO/VP: Javed Schawn
CEO: Shawn Javed
Sales Manager: Jerry Diaz
justenv@price-hvac.com
Estimated Sales: $20-50 Million
Number Employees: 20-49
Types of Products Distributed:
　Food Service, Frozen Food, General Line, Candy

58784 Price Harry H & Son
1608 S Harwood St
Dallas, TX 75215-1219 214-421-1593
Fax: 214-421-3292 kylehhp@swbell.net
www.alliedsolutions.net
Wholesaler/distributor of produce
President: John Muennink
mhusemann@alliedsolutions.net
Director, Sales: Brian Ronk
Director of Operations: Calvin Cleary
Production Manager: Hector Daiz
Estimated Sales: $10-20 Million
Number Employees: 20-49
Types of Products Distributed:
　Frozen Food, Produce

58785 Pride Equipment Corp
150 Nassau Ave
Islip, NY 11751-3220 631-224-5000
Fax: 631-224-5152 800-564-7743
www.prideequipment.com
Wholesaler/distributor of forklifts
President: Charles J Noto Sr
cn@prideequipment.com
Estimated Sales: $10-20 Million
Number Employees: 100-249
Private Brands Carried:
　Hyster
Types of Products Distributed:
　Frozen Food, General Merchandise, Forklifts

58786 Pridgen Bros Co
115 E Wall St
Cordele, GA 31015-4254 229-273-2614
Fax: 229-273-1036 hi@pridgenbrothers.com
www.pridgenbrothers.com

Wholesaler/distributor of dry grocery products, janitorial items and paper and container supplies; serving the food service market
President: Ron Cruz
rcruz@pridgenbrothers.com
General Manager: Ron Hobbs
Sales/Marketing Executive: Gene Lavender
Estimated Sales: $10-20 Million
Number Employees: 10-19
Square Footage: 70000
Private Brands Carried:
 Parade
Number of Customer Locations: 600
Types of Products Distributed:
 Food Service, General Line, General Merchandise, Dry groceries, janitorial items, paper

58787 Priester's Pecans
208 Old Fort Rd E
Fort Deposit, AL 36032-4012 334-227-4301
 Fax: 334-227-4294 866-477-4736
 customerservice@priesters.com
 www.priesters.com
Pecan candies, pies, cakes, brownies, chocolates and cheese straws.
President: Thomas Ellis
priesters@aol.com
Owner: Ellen Burkett
CFO: Faye Hood
Plant Manager: Robert Hunter
Year Founded: 1935
Estimated Sales: $20-50 Million
Number Employees: 50-99
Number of Brands: 2
Type of Packaging: Food Service, Private Label, Bulk
Types of Products Distributed:
 Food Service, Specialty Foods

58788 Prime Cut Meat & Seafood Company
2601 N. 31st Ave.
Phoenix, AZ 85009-1522 602-455-8834
  800-277-1054
 www.primecutusa.com
Meat, seafood
President: David Poppen
dpoppen@primemalta.com
VP/Treasurer: Linda Poppen
Estimated Sales: $17 Million
Number Employees: 50-99
Types of Products Distributed:
 Provisions/Meat, Seafood

58789 Prime Machinery Corporation
1031 Snyder Road
Lansdale, PA 19446-4609 215-393-8770
 Fax: 732-960-2380 info@primemachinery.com
Wholesaler/distributor and exporter of used machinery including ribbon, paddle, dispersion, double cone, high intensity, planetary, twinshell and pony mixers; also, mills, kettles, pulverizers, screens, dryers, homogenizers, filtersetc
President: Rick Kronstain
Contact: Richard Kronstain
misc@primemachinery.com
Number Employees: 5-9
Types of Products Distributed:
 Used food processing machinery

58790 Prime Smoked Meats Inc
220 Alice St
Oakland, CA 94607-4394 510-832-7167
 Fax: 510-832-4830
Pork
Owner: Dave Andes
Sales Manager: Tina DeMello
dave.andes@primesmoked.com
Office Manager: Elsie Jorstad
Production Manager: Jose Garcia
Estimated Sales: $5897842
Number Employees: 20-49
Square Footage: 48000
Type of Packaging: Consumer, Food Service, Private Label, Bulk
Types of Products Distributed:
 Frozen Food, Provisions/Meat

58791 Primo Cheese
220 Ellison Street
Paterson, NJ 07505-1602 201-585-2060
 Fax: 973-345-6044
Wholesaler/distributor of gourmet Italian and domestic cheeses and pasta products
Owner: Joe Camilleri
Estimated Sales: Less than $500,000
Number Employees: 1-4
Square Footage: 4000
Private Brands Carried:
 Primo Cheese; Barilla; Lioni Latticini
Number of Customer Locations: 60
Types of Products Distributed:
 Frozen Food, General Line, Specialty Foods, Gourmet Italian cheeses, etc.

58792 Prince of Peace
3536 Arden Rd
Hayward, CA 94545-3908 510-887-1899
 Fax: 510-887-1799 800-732-2328
popsf@popus.com www.princeofpeacecharity.org
Ginseng tea
Vice President: Lolita Lim
lolita@popus.com
VP Finance: Agnes Tsang
National Sales Manager: Mike Jarrett
Purchasing: Maria Wong
Estimated Sales: $11,200,000
Number Employees: 20-49
Square Footage: 145548
Types of Products Distributed:
 Frozen Food, General Line, Health Food, Candy/bakery/dairy/otc health products

58793 Princeton Shelving
873 Center Point Road NE
Cedar Rapids, IA 52402-4664 319-369-0355
 Fax: 319-369-0387
Dealer rep. and distributor of pallet racks, wire decking and containers, POP displays, carts (hand, service), racks, steel and wire shelving. Over 500 different companies
Estimated Sales: $1-5,000,000
Types of Products Distributed:
 Frozen Food

58794 Prissy's of Vidalia
PO Box 1213
Vidalia, GA 30475-1213 570-328-0140
 Fax: 570-287-1663 800-673-7372
 prissys@prissys.com www.prissys.com
Sell specialty foods in quality gourmet shops. Specialize in Georgia Peach and Vidalia Onion products.
President: Priscilla Ruckno
Vice President: Walker Oxley
Contact: Walker Oxley
oxley30@gmail.com
Number of Products: 96
Type of Packaging: Consumer, Food Service, Private Label
Private Brands Carried:
 Prissy's Inc; Walker Oh

58795 Pro Plus Cleaning Products
2010 Sage Ct
Loganville, GA 30052-5510 770-466-3474
 Fax: 770-466-3484 800-786-0607
 primatt@aol.com
Wholesaler/distributor of industrial and institutional cleaning supplies and equipment including chemicals, dishwashers, detergents, bleaches, rinse aids, hand soap, etc.; also, general line and private label products; serving the foodservice market
President: Doshia Ann Reppert
CFO/VP: Matthew Reppert
Marketing Director: Doshia Ann Reppert
Estimated Sales: $300,000-500,000
Number Employees: 1-4
Square Footage: 9600
Parent Co: Pro Plus
Private Brands Carried:
 Proline; Pro Plus; USC; Impact
Number of Customer Locations: 300
Types of Products Distributed:
 Food Service, Frozen Food, General Line, General Merchandise, Cleaning supplies & equipment

58796 ProSource
5598 Lindbergh Lane
Bell, CA 90201-6410 323-263-7152
 Fax: 323-266-6150
Wholesaler/distributor of general merchandise and general line items; serving the food service market
Director Operations: Don Butterfield
Number Employees: 100-249
Types of Products Distributed:
 Food Service, Frozen Food, General Line, General Merchandise

58797 Proacec USA
1158 26th Street
Suite 509
Santa Monica, CA 90403-4621 310-996-7770
 Fax: 310-996-7772 www.proacec.com
Olives and olive oil
President: Paul Short
Estimated Sales: Below $5 Million
Number Employees: 10
Number of Brands: 4
Number of Products: 30
Square Footage: 2000
Type of Packaging: Consumer, Food Service, Bulk
Private Brands Carried:
 Caroliva; Plantio Del Condado; Don Quixate; El Carmen
Types of Products Distributed:
 Food Service, Health Food, Specialty Foods

58798 Probar
190 N Apollo Rd.
Salt Lake City, UT 84116
 Fax: 801-456-8880 800-921-2294
 info@theprobar.com www.theprobar.com
Plant based food products including snack bars, energy bites, and nut butters
President: Jules Lambert
Founder/CEO: Jeff Coleman
Types of Products Distributed:
 General Line

58799 Procacci Bros Sales Corp
3333 S Front St
Philadelphia, PA 19148-5605 215-463-8000
 Fax: 215-467-1144 www.procaccibrothers.com
Wholesaler/distributor of produce
Owner: Joe Procacci
jprocacci@procaccibrothers.com
Sales Director: John Lumblatt
Number Employees: 10-19
Types of Products Distributed:
 Frozen Food, Produce

58800 Process Equipment & Supply Company
PO Box 868
Union City, NJ 07087-0868 201-866-5050
 Fax: 201-866-3170
Wholesaler/distributor of fruit and vegetable juice filters
Sales Manager: Richard Clark
Estimated Sales: $5-10 Million
Number Employees: 10-19
Types of Products Distributed:
 Frozen Food, Fruit & vegetable juice filters

58801 Produce Trading Corp
290 N Grove St
Merritt Island, FL 32953-3444 321-452-7037
 Fax: 321-454-3006 www.gorlin.com
Wholesaler/distributor and exporter of cured pork and beef and dried fruit
President: Richard Champon
Estimated Sales: $.5-1 million
Number Employees: 1-4
Types of Products Distributed:
 Frozen Food, General Line, Provisions/Meat, Cured pork & beef & dried fruit

58802 Production Packaging & Processing Equipment Company
1713 East Victory Drive
Savannah, GA 31404 912-856-4281
 Fax: 912-354-4615 www.kettles.com
Manufacturer, exporter and wholesaler/distributor of new and rebuilt packaging and processing equipment including mixers, fillers, cap tighteners, labeling, cappers, kettles and tanks
President: Louis R Klein
CEO: Jeff Klein
Estimated Sales: $2.5-5 Million
Number Employees: 5-9
Square Footage: 100000
Types of Products Distributed:
 General Merchandise, New & rebuilt packaging equipment, etc.

Wholesalers & Distributors / A-Z

58803 Productos Familia
1511 Calle Loiza
Santurce, PR 00911-1846   787-268-5929
    Fax: 787-268-7717 www.nosotrasonline.com
Supplier of soft paper tissues; wholesaler/distributor, importer and exporter of toilet paper, paper towels and napkins; serving the food service market
President: Fabio Posada
VP: Carlos Upegui
Number Employees: 7
Square Footage: 12000
Parent Co: Productos Familia SA
Type of Packaging: Food Service
Private Brands Carried:
    Petalo; Familia; Blue River; Sunset; Nosotras; Nice Day
Types of Products Distributed:
    Food Service, Frozen Food, General Merchandise, Toilet paper, paper towels, napkins

58804 Professional Food Systems
1707 Broadway Boulevard NE
Albuquerque, NM 87102-1551   505-842-5010
    Fax: 505-842-1424   800-432-5474
Wholesaler/distributor of groceries, frozen food, dairy products and meats; serving the food service market
General Manager: David Elwell
Sales Manager: Gary Smith
Estimated Sales: $10-20 Million
Number Employees: 10-19
Parent Co: Professional Food Systems
Number of Customer Locations: 200
Types of Products Distributed:
    Food Service, Frozen Food, General Line, Provisions/Meat, Dairy products

58805 Professional Food Systems
3710 Lee Street
Alexandria, LA 71302-3931   318-448-3833
    Fax: 318-473-1912
Wholesaler/distributor of meats; serving the food service market
Salesman: Bruce Gremillion
Estimated Sales: $3-5 Million
Number Employees: 5-9
Parent Co: Professional Food Systems
Other Locations:
    Professional Food Systems
    Shreveport, LAProfessional Food Systems
Types of Products Distributed:
    Food Service, Frozen Food, Provisions/Meat

58806 Professional Food Systems
295 Industrial Drive
Jackson, MS 39209-3426   601-352-4426
    Fax: 601-355-8726
Wholesaler/distributor of groceries, frozen foods, seafood, meats and general merchandise; serving the food service market
Manager: Larry Tipton
Estimated Sales: $20-50 Million
Number Employees: 20-49
Parent Co: Professional Food Systems
Types of Products Distributed:
    Food Service, Frozen Food, General Line, General Merchandise, Provisions/Meat, Seafood, Groceries, etc.

58807 Professional Food Systems
422 N Washington Ave
El Dorado, AR 71730   870-863-1773
    Fax: 870-863-1750
Wholesaler/distributor of seafood, meats, frozen foods, produce, etc
President: Rolan Brevard
Estimated Sales: $20-50 Million
Number Employees: 20-49
Parent Co: ConAgra Foods
Number of Customer Locations: 300
Types of Products Distributed:
    Frozen Food, Provisions/Meat, Produce, Seafood

58808 Professional Marketing Group
912 Rainier Avenue S
Seattle, WA 98144-2840   206-322-7303
    Fax: 206-322-4351   800-227-3769
    www.vacuumpackers.com
Importer, exporter and wholesaler/distributor of commercial grade flush and nonflush vacuum packing machinery
Owner: Thom Dolder

Estimated Sales: $2.5-5 Million
Number Employees: 5-9
Types of Products Distributed:
    Frozen Food, General Merchandise, Vacuum packing machinery

58809 Professional Materials Hndlng
4203 North Landmark Dr
Orlando, FL 32817-1210   407-677-0040
    Fax: 407-678-0273   info@pmh-co.com
    www.pmh-co.com
Wholesaler/distributor and importer of turretts and fully automatic lift trucks/alvs. Warehouse management & inventory control software, factoty automation, and material handling planning and integration
President: Charles Nordhorn
    cnordhorn@pmh-co.com
VP: Wolfgang Nordhorn
Estimated Sales: $2.5-5 Million
Number Employees: 10-19
Square Footage: 80000
Private Brands Carried:
    Steinbock; Depotlift; Diaitron
Number of Customer Locations: 350
Types of Products Distributed:
    Frozen Food, General Merchandise, Forklifts

58810 Proficient Food Company
2910 Old Tree Dr
Lancaster, PA 17603-4082   717-293-0081
    Fax: 717-293-0084
Wholesaler/distributor serving the food service market; chain accounts only
Distribution Manager: Brad Bowers
Sales/Marketing Executive: Carolyn Cushwa
Contact: Sino Curreli
    scurreli@mbmfoodservice.com
Administration Manager: Carolyn Cushwa
Estimated Sales: $.5-1 million
Number Employees: 1-4
Square Footage: 360000
Parent Co: MBM Corporation
Number of Customer Locations: 315
Types of Products Distributed:
    Food Service, Frozen Food

58811 Proficient Food Company
PO Box 800
Rocky Mount, NC 27802-0800   847-827-9140
    Fax: 847-827-0959
Wholesaler/distributor of frozen foods, general line items, general merchandise, health foods, meats and seafood; serving the foodservice market; chain accounts only
Distribution Manager: Pat Gebhardt
Number Employees: 50-99
Square Footage: 401600
Parent Co: MBM Corporation
Number of Customer Locations: 265
Types of Products Distributed:
    Food Service, Frozen Food, General Line, General Merchandise, Health Food, Provisions/Meat, Seafood

58812 Progenix Corporation
7566 N 72nd Ave
Wausau, WI 54401   715-675-7566
    Fax: 715-675-4931   800-233-3356
Ginseng, whole root, fiber, prong, powder and extract; capsules, teas and gift packaging
President: Robert Duwe
Number Employees: 20-49
Square Footage: 26000
Type of Packaging: Consumer, Food Service, Bulk
Types of Products Distributed:
    Frozen Food, Health Food, Ginseng products

58813 Progressive Food
600 Providence Highway
Dedham, MA 02026-6804   508-583-2266
Wholesaler/distributor of general line items
Manager: Stan Ross
Parent Co: Pizza Hut
Types of Products Distributed:
    Frozen Food, General Line

58814 Progressive Handling Systems
16 Pocono Rd # 110
Denville, NJ 07834-2905   973-586-3700
    Fax: 973-586-3733   800-526-6001
    www.phsinc.com
Wholesaler/distributor of material handling equipment
President: Jim Santore

Estimated Sales: $10-20 Million
Number Employees: 20-49
Square Footage: 40000
Types of Products Distributed:
    Frozen Food, General Merchandise, Material handling equipment

58815 Proin
142 N Irving Boulevard
Los Angeles, CA 90004-3805   818-241-8869
Wholesaler/distributer of canning and food packing machinery
Co-President: Jim Ruiz
Co-President: Jaime Ruiz
Estimated Sales: $500,000-$1 Million
Number Employees: 1-4
Types of Products Distributed:
    Frozen Food, General Merchandise, Canning & food packing machinery

58816 Prolift Industrial Equipment
P.O.Box 99607
Louisville, KY 40269-0607   502-267-2565
    Fax: 502-267-2576 www.proliftequipment.com
Manufacturer/distributor of material handling equipment including forklifts
President: William Skinner
Contact: Tim Ellis
    tellis@proliftequipment.com
Estimated Sales: $20-50 Million
Number Employees: 100-249
Private Brands Carried:
    Toyota; Prime Mover; Daewoo
Types of Products Distributed:
    Frozen Food, General Merchandise, Material handling equipment

58817 Promotions Ink
11 Goldstein Pl
Norwalk, CT 06855   203-853-2878
Wholesaler/distributor of advertising specialties and promotional items; also, embroidering available
Owner: Bill Belward
Estimated Sales: Less than $500,000
Number Employees: 1-4
Square Footage: 10000
Number of Customer Locations: 15
Types of Products Distributed:
    Frozen Food, General Merchandise, Advertising specialties

58818 Pronatura Inc
1435 E Algonquin Rd
Arlington Hts, IL 60005-4715   847-410-1361
    Fax: 847-545-1008   800-555-7580
Importer, exporter and wholesaler/distributor of herbal remedies including kombucha teas, extracts and capsules, ginseng multi-minerals/vitamins and nutritional, herbal and homeopathic supplements
Manager: Andre Mehrabian
    amehrabian@pronaturainc.com
VP: Andre Mehrabian
Estimated Sales: $500,000
Number Employees: 5-9
Square Footage: 22000
Parent Co: Naturwaren
Types of Products Distributed:
    Frozen Food, Health Food, Herbal & homeopathic supplements, etc.

58819 (HQ)Provigo
1611 Cremezie Boulevard E
Montreal, QC H2M 2P2
Canada   514-383-3000
    Fax: 905-861-2387   800-567-8683
    www.provigo.ca
Wholesaler/distributor of general line items
President: Bernard McDonell
Number Employees: 1,000-4,999
Other Locations:
    Provigo
    Victoriaville, PQProvigo
Number of Customer Locations: 300
Types of Products Distributed:
    Frozen Food, General Line

58820 Provigo Distribution
320 Bd Leclerc O
Granby, QC J2G 1V3
Canada   450-372-8014
    Fax: 514-383-5110   800-361-1168
    www.provigo.ca
Wholesaler/distributor and exporter of meats

Wholesalers & Distributors / A-Z

Maintenance Supervisor: Francis De Roy
Transportation Manager: Mickael Rheaume
Director Operations: Denis Lepine
Number Employees: 100-249
Parent Co: Provigo
Private Brands Carried:
　Provigo; Royal
Types of Products Distributed:
　Frozen Food, Provisions/Meat

58821 Provigo Distribution
550 Avenue Godin Ville
Vanier, QC G1M 2K2
Canada　　　　　　　　　418-688-1830
　　　　　　　　　Fax: 418-687-2185
Wholesaler/distributor of general line items
Director Operations: Daniel Villneuve
Number Employees: 100-249
Parent Co: Provigo
Number of Customer Locations: 450
Types of Products Distributed:
　Frozen Food, General Line

58822 Provigo Distribution
180 Chemin Du Tremblay
Boucherville, QC J4B 7W3
Canada　　　　　　　　　450-449-8000
　　　　　　　　　Fax: 450-449-8052
Wholesaler/distributor of produce
Sr. Director: Andre Theroux
Director Produce: Michel Galli
Director Procurement: Danielle Masson
Number Employees: 20-49
Parent Co: Provigo
Types of Products Distributed:
　Frozen Food, Produce

58823 Provigo Distribution
11625 55th Avenue
Montreal, QC H1E 2K2
Canada　　　　　　　　　514-383-8800
　　　Fax: 514-643-1821 www.provigo.ca
Wholesaler/distributor serving the food service market
President: Bernard McDonell
VP: Yvon Morais
Number Employees: 100-249
Parent Co: Provigo
Private Brands Carried:
　Zel; Dellexo
Types of Products Distributed:
　Food Service, Frozen Food

58824 Pudliner Packing
167 Norton Rd
Johnstown, PA 15906-2906　　814-539-5422
　　　　　　　　　Fax: 814-446-6150
Wholesaler/distributor of provisions/meats; also, slaughtering services available; serving the food service market
Owner: Andrew Pudliner
Estimated Sales: $2.5-5 Million
Number Employees: 5-9
Type of Packaging: Consumer, Private Label
Types of Products Distributed:
　Food Service, Frozen Food, Provisions/Meat, Slaugtering service

58825 Pueblo Trading Co Inc
PO Box 11508
Newport Beach, CA 92658-5032　949-640-6499
　Fax: 949-642-6545 pueblotrading@yahoo.com
　　　　　　　　www.pueblotradingco.com
Wholesaler/distributor and exporter of meat, poultry, cheese, etc
President: Carie Ross
Operations: Gerry Ross
Number Employees: 1-4
Type of Packaging: Consumer, Food Service, Private Label, Bulk
Types of Products Distributed:
　Food Service, Frozen Food, General Merchandise, Provisions/Meat, Produce, Seafood, Poultry & cheese

58826 Pulini Produce
1100 Ferry Ave # A
Camden, NJ 08104-1894　　　856-964-1962
　　　　　　　　　Fax: 856-964-6043
Wholesaler/distributor of produce, meats, frozen foods, canned goods and fish; serving the food service market
Owner: Francis Pulini
Secretary: Joan Davis
Estimated Sales: $10-20 Million
Number Employees: 20-49
Square Footage: 160000
Type of Packaging: Private Label, Bulk
Private Brands Carried:
　Signor Pulini
Types of Products Distributed:
　Food Service, Frozen Food, General Line, Provisions/Meat, Produce, Seafood, Specialty Foods, Frozen food, canned goods, fish, etc.

58827 Pulmuone Foods USA Inc.
2315 Moore Ave.
Fullerton, CA 92833
　　　　　　　　　　　　800-588-7782
　　　　　　　　　inquiry@pulmuone.com
　　　　　　　　www.pulmuonefoodsusa.com
Pastas, sauces, meat, chicken and vegetable patties, soybean products.
CEO: Hyo-Yul Lee
VP, Food Safety & Compliance: Jung Han
Manager, Product Excellence Insights: Faye Lee
Director, Marketing: Sean Kim
Director, Engineering & Technology: Brian Seong-Jun Kim
Year Founded: 1981
Estimated Sales: $1.5 Billion
Number Employees: 110
Number of Brands: 5
Parent Co: Pulmuone Co., Ltd.
Type of Packaging: Consumer, Food Service, Private Label, Bulk
Types of Products Distributed:
　Health Food, Specialty Foods

58828 Pulse Plus
5294 Cobble Creek Road
Apt 141
Salt Lake City, UT 84117-6743　801-573-4000
　　Fax: 801-274-8616 bigbarn@webtv.net
Wholesaler/distributor of health food, nuts, grains and fruits
President: Kenneth Barneycastle
Types of Products Distributed:
　Frozen Food, General Line, Health Food, Produce, Nuts, grains & fruits

58829 Pumodori Brothers Sales
PO Box 24492
San Jose, CA 95154-4492　　408-287-1800
　　　　　　　　　Fax: 408-287-1890
Wholesaler/distributor of canned foods; serving the food service and retail markets
President: Robert Huber
General Manager: Michael Cole
Estimated Sales: $10-20 Million
Number Employees: 10-19
Square Footage: 30000
Types of Products Distributed:
　Food Service, Frozen Food, General Line, Canned foods

58830 Purchase Order Co Of Miami Inc
3724 NW 72nd St
Miami, FL 33147-5820　　　305-696-2190
　Fax: 305-696-2192 poco3724chef@aol.com
Wholesaler/distributor, importer and exporter of caviar, frozen par-baked bagels, truffles, freeze and air-dried vegetables, fruits, spices, herbs, milk, juice, flavors, meats, etc.; serving the food service market
Owner: Jerome Lundy
　jeromelundy@puradyn.com
Secretary: S Tragash
CFO: R Tragash
Estimated Sales: $5-10 Million
Number Employees: 5-9
Square Footage: 20000
Type of Packaging: Food Service
Private Brands Carried:
　E.D. Foods Ltd.; Van Vooren Game Ranch; Gossner Foods; Van Drunen Farms
Types of Products Distributed:
　Food Service, Frozen Food, General Line, Provisions/Meat, Specialty Foods, Truffles, caviar, frozen bagels, etc.

58831 Pure Sealed Dairy
PO Box 642
Huntington, IN 46750-0642　　219-432-3575
　　　　　　　　　Fax: 219-432-7844
Wholesaler/distributor of dairy products including ice cream; serving the food service market
General Manager: Robert Cashdollar
Estimated Sales: $20-50 Million
Number Employees: 20-49
Parent Co: Schenkel Dairy
Types of Products Distributed:
　Food Service, Frozen Food, General Line, Dairy products

58832 Purely Elizabeth
3200 Carbon Pl
Suite 101
Boulder, CO 80301-6135　　　720-242-7525
　Fax: 888-586-9485 support@purelyelizabeth.com
　　　　　　　　　purelyelizabeth.com
Gluten-free baking mixes, granola, oatmeal and superfood bars
Founder & CEO: Elizabeth Stein
　elizabeth@purelyelizabeth.com
Director of Finance: Tracy Baumann
Marketing: Paige Mitchum
Operations: Garrett McBride
Estimated Sales: Less Than $500,000
Number Employees: 10-19

58833 Puritan's Pride Inc
1233 Montauk Highway
P.O.Box 9001
Oakdale, NY 11769-9001　　　623-948-5100
　　　　Fax: 623-948-8150　800-645-1030
　　　　　　　　　www.puritan.com
Wholesaler/distributor of nutritional supplements; serving the retail market
President: Gary Martin
VP Operations: Joe Ned
Number Employees: 50-99
Types of Products Distributed:
　Frozen Food, General Line, Nutritional supplements

58834 Purity Wholesale Grocers, Inc.
5300 Broken Sound Blvd NW
Suite 110
Boca Raton, FL 33487
　　　　　　　　　　　　800-323-6838
　info@pwg-inc.com www.puritywholesale.com
Wholesaler/distributor of groceries.
Chairman: Jeffrey Levitetz
Co-President: David Groomes
Co-President: Alan Rutner
Vice President Supreme: Denise Lawlor
VP, Business Development: Bruce Krichmar
Vice President, Marketing: Dan Davis
Vice President, Human Resources: Karen McGrath
VP, Distribution/Transportation: Jack Carroll
Year Founded: 1982
Estimated Sales: $55 Million
Number Employees: 180
Other Locations: Purity Wholesale Grocers
Number of Customer Locations: 250
Types of Products Distributed:
　Frozen Food, General Line, Groceries

58835 Puro Water Group
40 Marcus Blvd
Hauppauge, NY 11788-3704　　631-864-8800
　　　　　　　　　Fax: 631-864-8510
Wholesaler/distributor of water, water coolers and filters
Manager: William Bjelke
Estimated Sales: Less than $500,000
Number Employees: 20-49
Parent Co: Puro Corporation
Types of Products Distributed:
　Frozen Food, General Line, General Merchandise, Health Food, Water, water coolers & filters

58836 Putnam Candy
60 Woodstock Ave
Putnam, CT 06260-1495　　　860-928-4000
　　　　　　　　　Fax: 860-928-3310
Wholesaler/distributor of specialty confectionery products
General Manager: Tom Beaudry
Estimated Sales: $1-2.5 Million
Number Employees: 1-4
Square Footage: 19200
Number of Customer Locations: 150
Types of Products Distributed:
　General Line, Specialty Foods, Confectionery products

58837 Putnam Group
35 Corporate Dr
Trumbull, CT 06611-6319
　　　　　　　　　　　　203-452-7270
　　　　　　　　　Fax: 203-268-8071

Importer and wholesaler/distributor of promotional items; also, marketing consultant services available
VP: Ann Rerat
Estimated Sales: Less than $500,000
Number Employees: 1-4
Private Brands Carried:
  Zoe Designs
Number of Customer Locations: 100
Types of Products Distributed:
  Frozen Food, General Merchandise, Promotional items

58838 Pylam Products Co Inc
2175 E Cedar St
Tempe, AZ 85281-7415   480-929-0070
          Fax: 480-929-0078 800-645-6096
          safetycoordinator@pylamdyes.com
                    www.pylamdyes.com
Wholesaler/distributor of colors
VP: Robert Reynolds
VP Sales: Robert Reynolds
Manager: Janet Mccarroll
jmccarroll@pylamdyes.com
Estimated Sales: $1-2.5 Million
Number Employees: 10-19
Types of Products Distributed:
  General Line, Colors

58839 Pyramid Juice Company
160 Helman Street
Ashland, OR 97520-1720   541-482-2292
                    Fax: 541-482-1002
Organic fruit and vegetable juices
President/CEO: Judd Pindell
VP: Kim Kemske
Estimated Sales: $5-9.9 Million
Number Employees: 8
Square Footage: 14000
Types of Products Distributed:
  Frozen Food

58840 Pyramid Packaging, Inc
1828 Johns Dr
Glenview, IL 60025   847-901-4300
          Fax: 847-901-4311 800-547-5130
                    info@pyramidpackaging.com
                    www.pyramidpackaging.com
Wholesaler/distributor of packaging equipment and materials
President: Robert Ploen
Controller: Margaret Lord
mlord@pyramidpackaging.com
Estimated Sales: $2.5-5 Million
Number Employees: 5-9
Square Footage: 20000
Types of Products Distributed:
  Frozen Food, General Merchandise, Bagging equipment & materials

58841 QUALITY Frozen Foods
1663 62nd St
Brooklyn, NY 11204-2796   718-256-9100
                    Fax: 718-234-3755
                    orders@qualityfrozenfoods.com
                    www.qualityfrozenfoods.com
Wholesaler/distributor of private label items, groceries, frozen foods and kosher, dairy, refrigerated and specialty products
President: Morris Semel
Secretary/Treasurer: Eli Soffer
VP: Shaya Semel
Manager: Chris Lee
clee@parksidelounge.net
Estimated Sales: $10-20 Million
Number Employees: 50-99
Square Footage: 70000
Private Brands Carried:
  Unger; Chopsie; Noam
Number of Customer Locations: 950
Types of Products Distributed:
  Frozen Food, General Line, Specialty Foods, Groceries, dairy products, etc.

58842 Qchef
20 Harry Shupe Boulevard
Wharton, NJ 07885-1646   800-989-7007
          Fax: 973-366-2769 www.Qchef.com
Wholesaler of fine food

58843 Quadra Foods Company
1177 Branham Lane
319
San Jose, CA 95118-3766   408-268-5460

Wholesaler/distributor of specialty foods including oils, pasta, cheese, spices, vegetables, fruits, etc
Types of Products Distributed:
  Frozen Food, General Line, Produce, Specialty Foods, Oils, pastas, cheeses, spices, etc.

58844 Quail Crest Foods
PO Box 636
Corvallis, OR 97339-0636   541-753-1231
                    Fax: 541-754-6773
Wholesaler/distributor of groceries, meats, produce, dairy products, frozen foods, baked goods, equipment and fixtures, paper products and janitorial supplies; serving institutional and food service markets
President: P Harding
Sales Director: L Barker
Operations Manager: A Plummer
Purchasing Manager: P Harding
Estimated Sales: $1.5 Million
Number Employees: 5-9
Number of Products: 3600
Square Footage: 60000
Type of Packaging: Food Service
Private Brands Carried:
  Golbon
Number of Customer Locations: 390
Types of Products Distributed:
  Food Service, Frozen Food, General Line, General Merchandise, Provisions/Meat, Produce, Janitorials, paper products, etc.

58845 Quaily Storage ProductsInc
8041 186th St # B
Unit B
Tinley Park, IL 60487-9348   708-444-1234
                    Fax: 708-333-3485
                    www.qualitystorageproducts.com
Wholesaler/distributor of material handling equipment including shelving and racks
President: Casey Meehan
casey@qsp.com
Sales Manager: Michael Meehan
Estimated Sales: $2.5-5 Million
Number Employees: 1-4
Private Brands Carried:
  Konstant; Mannis Mann-Demag; Vacu-Hoist
Types of Products Distributed:
  Frozen Food, General Merchandise, Material handling equipment

58846 Quaker Window Products Co
504 N Highway 63
PO Box 128
Freeburg, MO 65035-2539   573-744-5211
          Fax: 573-744-5586 800-347-0438
          sales@quakerwindows.com www.quakerwindows.com
Wholesaler/distributor of health and natural foods including canned vegetarian foods, entrees, analogs and vitamin supplements
President: Mike Knoll
National Sales Manager: Chris Dickneite
General Manager: Kevin Blansett
Plant Manager: Tom Stegeman
Number Employees: 250-499
Types of Products Distributed:
  Health Food

58847 Quality Banana Inc
3196 Produce Row
Houston, TX 77023-5814   713-921-4161
          Fax: 713-921-7859 www.grocerybiz.com
Wholesaler/distributor of banana and pineapple; serving the food service market
Vice President: Paul Zubowski
VP: Paul Zubowski
Estimated Sales: $5-10 Million
Number Employees: 10-19
Types of Products Distributed:
  Food Service, Frozen Food, Produce, Bananas & pineapples

58848 Quality Celery & SproutCompany
10 W South Water Market
Chicago, IL 60608-2210   312-226-1333
Wholesaler/distributor of produce
Estimated Sales: $2.5-5 Million
Number Employees: 5-9
Types of Products Distributed:
  Frozen Food, Produce

58849 Quality Discount Ice Cream
2465 Coral St
Vista, CA 92081   760-598-4978
                    Fax: 760-598-4874

Wholesaler/distributor of ice cream and frozen products to stores, school districts and vending trucks
President: Nasses Palizban
Sales Manager: W Palizban
Estimated Sales: $5-10 Million
Number Employees: 5-9
Square Footage: 20000
Types of Products Distributed:
  Food Service, Frozen Food, Ice cream & frozen products

58850 Quality Distributing Company
708 S Alston St
Nashville, NC 27856   252-459-2918
                    Fax: 252-459-7562
Wholesaler/distributor of general line products
President/General Manager: D Parker
VP/Secretary: P Parker
Estimated Sales: $1-2.5 Million
Number Employees: 5-9
Square Footage: 180000
Number of Customer Locations: 150
Types of Products Distributed:
  Frozen Food, General Line

58851 Quality Eggs & Juices
1950 NW 82nd Ave
Doral, FL 33126   305-591-7480
                    Fax: 305-591-7483
Wholesaler/distributor of fresh eggs and juices; serving the food service and retail markets
Manager: Bob Bagnall
Manager: Vincente Luis
Estimated Sales: $1-2.5 Million
Number Employees: 5-9
Parent Co: Hill & Dale Farms
Types of Products Distributed:
  Food Service, Frozen Food, General Line, Eggs & juices

58852 Quality Equipment Marketing
PO Box 5805
Chesapeake, VA 23324-0936   757-545-7843
          Fax: 757-545-7851 800-357-6551
Wholesaler/distributor of food service equipment; serving food service operators
Service Manager: Dave Kellams
Administrator Assistant: Kim Sawicki
Sales Manager: Jack Tuberty
Number Employees: 5-9
Private Brands Carried:
  Bakbar; Amana; Nieco; Bake-off; CCI; Clear View Door; Add A Griddle; Add A Broiler
Types of Products Distributed:
  Food Service, Frozen Food, General Merchandise, Foodservice equipment

58853 Quality Fisheries
157 Arbor St
Niota, IL 62358-1005   217-448-4241
          Fax: 217-448-4021 qualityfisheries@yahoo.com
                    www.niotafishmarket.com
Seafood
Owner: Kirby Marsden
k.marsden@mchsi.com
Estimated Sales: $1 Million
Number Employees: 5-9
Square Footage: 24000

58854 Quality Food Company
25 Bath Street
Providence, RI 2908   401-421-5668
          Fax: 401-421-8570 877-233-3462
                    info@qualityfoodcompany.com
                    www.qualitybeefcompany.com
Ground beef and seafood
Secretary: William Catauro
billcatauro@qualityfoodcompany.com
Vice President: Vincent Catauro, III
Sales: Gary Flynn
Purchasing: Mark Engelhardt
Year Founded: 1931
Estimated Sales: $10-20 Million
Number Employees: 20-49
Type of Packaging: Food Service
Types of Products Distributed:
  Food Service, Provisions/Meat, Seafood, Ground beef

58855 Quality Food Products Inc
172 N Peoria St
Chicago, IL 60607-2311   312-666-4559
                    Fax: 312-666-7133
Eggs

Wholesalers & Distributors / A-Z

President: George Aralis
Owner: Jim Aralis
qfp@earthlink.net
Estimated Sales: $10-20 Million
Number Employees: 10-19

58856 Quality Foods
P.O.Box 10007
Lynchburg, VA 24506-0007   434-929-6515
                          Fax: 434-929-7924
Wholesaler/distributor of groceries, meats, dairy products, frozen foods, general merchandise and health/beauty aids
President: Ben henderson
Controller: L Vance
Vice Chairman: David Cohen
Contact: Wilton Burgess
wburgess@qfci.com
Director Operations: Robert Capobianco
Plant Manager: David Clark
Estimated Sales: Under $500,000
Number Employees: 100-249
Private Brands Carried:
  Quality Foods
Number of Customer Locations: 800
Types of Products Distributed:
  Frozen Food, General Line, General Merchandise, Provisions/Meat, Groceries, dairy products, etc.

58857 Quality Foods International
6700 Dawson Boulevard
Suite 2a
Norcross, GA 30093-1007   770-416-1611
                           Fax: 770-416-1621
Wholesaler/distributor of frozen and specialty foods, baked goods, general merchandise and private label items
President: Vic Levy
Secretary: Gill Levy
Vice President: Thomas Gallo
Number Employees: 5-9
Square Footage: 72000
Types of Products Distributed:
  Frozen Food, General Line, General Merchandise, Specialty Foods, Baked goods, etc.

58858 Quality Groceries
53 Lunalilo St Ste 4
Wailuku, HI 96793   808-244-9153
       Fax: 808-242-9005 tsamauiq@gte.net
Wholesaler/distributor serving the food service market
President: Hideki Hayashi
Vice President: Alvin Nacua
Estimated Sales: $6 Million
Number Employees: 10-19
Square Footage: 64000
Parent Co: TSA International
Types of Products Distributed:
  Food Service, Frozen Food, General Merchandise, Produce, Seafood

58859 (HQ)Quality Material Handling
900 W Foothill Blvd
Azusa, CA 91702-2842   626-812-9722
       Fax: 626-812-6544 800-429-2729
                      www.qmhinc.com
Wholesaler/distributor of janitorial supplies, racks, shelving, mezzanines, ladders, work benches, bins, boxes, containers, dock equipment, ramps, cabinets, carts, conveyors, cranes, dollies, hand trucks, etc
President: Hector Pinto
hector@qmhinc.com
Estimated Sales: $2 Million
Number Employees: 10-19
Square Footage: 120000
Other Locations:
  Quality Material Handling
  Phoenix, AZQuality Material Handling
Types of Products Distributed:
  Frozen Food, General Merchandise, Material handling equipment

58860 Quality Poultry Co
511 Ann St
Parkersburg, WV 26101-5119   304-422-0471
                          Fax: 304-485-6773
Wholesaler/distributor of poultry
Owner: Charles Liotti
Contact: Beth Liotti
bliotti@qualitypoultryproducts.com
Estimated Sales: $10-20 Million
Number Employees: 10-19

Types of Products Distributed:
  Frozen Food, Provisions/Meat, Poultry

58861 Quality Produce Company
3 Tobias St
Hicksville, NY 11801-5816   516-938-9246
                          Fax: 516-938-9252
Wholesaler/distributor of produce
Owner/President: Tony Alex
Estimated Sales: $.5-1 million
Number Employees: 1-4
Types of Products Distributed:
  Frozen Food, Produce

58862 Quality Wholesale Produce Co
9213 S Baltimore Ave
Chicago, IL 60617-4626   773-768-0072
                          Fax: 773-734-3630
Wholesaler/distributor of fresh, frozen and canned foods, paper goods and janitorial supplies; serving the food service market
Owner: Thomas Procissi
Sales Manager: Joe Reyes
Office Manager: Barb Syler
Estimated Sales: $10-20 Million
Number Employees: 5-9
Types of Products Distributed:
  Food Service, Frozen Food, General Line, General Merchandise, Canned goods, paper items, etc.

58863 Qualy Pak Specialty Foods
640 N Fries Ave
Wilmington, CA 90744   310-518-3624
                          Fax: 310-832-7641
Wholesaler/distributor of seafood
President: Bob Cigliano
Estimated Sales: $10-20 Million
Number Employees: 50-99
Square Footage: 200000
Types of Products Distributed:
  Frozen Food, Seafood

58864 Quandt's Foodservice Distributors
P.O.Box 700
Amsterdam, NY 12010   518-842-1550
       Fax: 518-770-1966 800-666-8443
Wholesaler/distributor of provisions/meats, produce, dairy products, frozen foods, baked goods, equipment and fixtures, seafood, etc.; serving the food service market; warehouse providing dry storage; rail siding available
President: Robert Quandt
Chairman: Thomas Quandt
Secretary/Treasurer: Thomas Quandt, Jr.
Contact: Betsy Niemczyk
bniemczyk@quandts.com
Estimated Sales: $20-50 Million
Number Employees: 100-249
Square Footage: 102001
Private Brands Carried:
  Nugget
Types of Products Distributed:
  Food Service, Frozen Food, General Line, General Merchandise, Provisions/Meat, Produce, Seafood, Dairy products, baked goods, etc.

58865 Quantum Supply Company
2712 Montana Ave
Santa Monica, CA 90403-2241   310-453-1678
                          Fax: 310-453-5298
Wholesaler/distributor of flags, mats and matting
President: Jason Ott
Estimated Sales: $5-10 Million
Number Employees: 5-9
Types of Products Distributed:
  Frozen Food, General Merchandise, Flags, pennants, banners, mats, etc.

58866 Quattrochi Specialty Foods
662 Montreal Street
Kingston, ON K7K 3J4
Canada   613-542-4996
       Fax: 613-542-5280 www.specialtyfood.ca
Wholesaler/distributor of frozen foods, spices, beans, flours, fruit and vegetables
President: Joe Quattrochi
Number Employees: 20-49
Number of Customer Locations: 100
Types of Products Distributed:
  Frozen Food, General Line, Produce, Spices, beans & flours

58867 Quebec Vegetable Distributors
PO Box 838
Champlain, NY 12919-0838   518-298-2090
                          Fax: 450-245-3631
Wholesaler/distributor of produce
President: Ross McNaughton
Parent Co: Hancan Industries
Types of Products Distributed:
  Frozen Food, Produce

58868 Queen City Meats
1720 E Anaheim St
Long Beach, CA 90813   562-591-0113
Wholesaler/distributor of meats

Estimated Sales: $5-10 Million
Number Employees: 1-4
Types of Products Distributed:
  Frozen Food, Provisions/Meat

58869 Queens Tobacco, Grocery & Candy
885 Channel Road
Woodmere, NY 11598-1842   718-657-3500
                          Fax: 718-657-8959
Wholesaler/distributor of candy and confectionery products
Estimated Sales: $20-50 Million
Number Employees: 10-19
Types of Products Distributed:
  Frozen Food, General Line, Candy & confectionery products

58870 (HQ)Queensboro Farm Products
4 Rasbach St
PO Box 227
Canastota, NY 13032-1496   315-687-6133
                          Fax: 315-697-8267
Cottage cheese, ice cream mix, butter and sour cream, milk
President: Steven Miller
General Manager: Don Landry
Estimated Sales: $10-20 Million
Number Employees: 50-99
Square Footage: 27800
Type of Packaging: Consumer
Types of Products Distributed:
  Frozen Food, Health Food, Milk

58871 Queensboro Farm Products
152-02 Liberty Avenue
Jamica, NY 11433   718-658-5000
                          Fax: 718-658-0408
                 www.queensborofarmproducts.com
Dairy
President/CEO: Allen Miller
Controller: Andrew Flitt
Estimated Sales: $33 Million
Number Employees: 80
Number of Products: 80
Type of Packaging: Consumer, Food Service
Types of Products Distributed:
  Frozen Food, Milk

58872 Quick Servant Co
12011 Guilford Rd # 101
Unit 101
Annapolis Jct, MD 20701-1004   301-621-2111
       Fax: 410-796-1248 888-737-8268
                      www.quickservant.com
Wholesaler/distributor of refrigeration, heating and air conditioning equipment
Manager: Jim Peters
Estimated Sales: $5-10 Million
Number Employees: 10-19
Types of Products Distributed:
  Frozen Food, General Merchandise, Refrigeration & heating equipment, etc.

58873 Quick Stamp & Sign Mfg
805 General Mouton Ave
P. O. Box 3272
Lafayette, LA 70501-8509   337-232-2171
       Fax: 337-232-4561 sales@qrstamp.com
                      www.qrstamp.com
Manufacturer and wholesaler/distributor of regular and self-inking rubber stamps, grocery marking ink, price markers for deposit stamps, daters and numberers
President: Patrick Gaubert
sales@qrstamp.com

Wholesalers & Distributors / A-Z

Estimated Sales: Less Than $500,000
Number Employees: 1-4
Square Footage: 7200
Types of Products Distributed:
Frozen Food, General Merchandise, Stamping & marking items

58874 Quinn Co
2200 Pegasus Dr
Bakersfield, CA 93308-6801 661-393-5800
Fax: 661-393-0811 www.quinncompany.com
Wholesaler/distributor of material handling equipment and automatic storage and handling systems
Manager: Ken Dickenson
Manager: Ken Mcmurray
kenmcmurray@quinncompany.com
Estimated Sales: $20-50 Million
Number Employees: 20-49
Parent Co: Catepillar
Other Locations:
Quinn Co.
Corcoran, CAQuinn Co.
Types of Products Distributed:
Frozen Food, General Merchandise, Material handling equipment

58875 Quinn Lift
10273 S Golden State Blvd
Selma, CA 93662-9410 559-896-4040
Fax: 559-891-6700 www.quinngroup.com
Wholesaler/distributor of material handling equipment including forklifts
VP/General Manager: Clay Blanton
Manager: Eric Green
egreen@quinncompany.com
Plant Manager: Bill Padgett
Estimated Sales: $20-50 Million
Number Employees: 50-99
Private Brands Carried:
Caterpillar; Crown
Types of Products Distributed:
Frozen Food, General Merchandise, Material handling equipment

58876 Quinoa Corporation
PO Box 279
Gardena, CA 90248 310-217-8125
Fax: 310-217-8140 quinoacorp@aol.com
Pasta and grains
President: Dave Schnorr
Contact: Tom Spielberger
toms@quinoa.net
Estimated Sales: Below $5 Million
Number Employees: 1-4
Type of Packaging: Bulk

58877 Quip Industries
1 Lakeway Dr
Carlyle, IL 62231 618-594-2437
Fax: 618-594-4707
Wholesaler/distributor of tablecloths, napkins, aprons and skirts; serving the food service market
President: James Bolk
CEO: Tim Bolk
Sales Manager: Mike Bolk
Account Specialty: Millie Lampe
Estimated Sales: $20-50 Million
Number Employees: 100-249
Types of Products Distributed:
Food Service, Tablecloths, napkins, aprons & skirts

58878 Qzina Specialty Foods
1726 W Atlantic Blvd
Pompano Beach, FL 33069-2857 954-590-4000
rex.ciavola@qzina.com
www.qzina.com
Wholesaler distributor of baking ingredients such as; semi sweet chocolate, milk chocolate, white chocolate, pure fountain chocolate, cups and decorations, pastry ingredients, molds and other equipment
President: Rex Ciavola
Founder/CEO: Richard Foley
CFO: Bryan Grobler
VP Sales USA & Canada: Tony Canino
Estimated Sales: $18.3 Million
Number Employees: 100
Square Footage: 25000
Type of Packaging: Food Service
Private Brands Carried:
Callebaut; Dynamic; Fruibel; Segafredo; Cepalor

Types of Products Distributed:
Food Service, Frozen Food, General Line, Chocolate, fruit products, coffee, etc.

58879 R & R Seafood
801 1st Ave
Tybee Island, GA 31328 912-786-5504
Fax: 912-786-5504
Seafood
Owner: Robbie Robertson
Estimated Sales: Less than $100,000
Number Employees: 1-4

58880 R D Smith Co
2703 Bauer St
Eau Claire, WI 54701-4508 715-832-3479
Fax: 715-832-7456 800-826-7336
www.rdsmithco.com
Wholesaler/distributor of equipment and supplies for dairy and food processors
President: Joan Bliesener
joanb@rdsmithco.com
Equipment Sales: Rod Riedel
Purchasing: Bob Kutchera
Estimated Sales: $5-10 Million
Number Employees: 10-19
Square Footage: 40000
Types of Products Distributed:
Frozen Food, General Merchandise, Equipment & supplies

58881 R Equipment
3693 E 6th Rd
Utica, IL 61373-9100 815-539-3666
Fax: 815-539-3664 800-924-9389
www.requipment.com
Wholesaler/distributor of new and used food service equipment; serving the food service market
President: Donald R Barlup
Manager: Kris Murphy
krism@requipment.com
Estimated Sales: $500,000-$1 Million
Number Employees: 20-49
Square Footage: 34000
Types of Products Distributed:
Food Service

58882 R Hirt Jr Co
3000 Chrysler Dr
Detroit, MI 48207-4597 313-831-2020
Fax: 313-831-2024 www.rhirt.com
Wholesaler/distributor of specialty foods including cheeses, sauces, teas, cookies, crackers, pastas, etc
President: Thomas Devries
tomdevries@rhirt.com
Estimated Sales: $2.5-5 Million
Number Employees: 20-49
Types of Products Distributed:
Frozen Food, Specialty Foods

58883 R L Spear Co
5510 Satsuma Ave
North Hollywood, CA 91601-2840 818-735-0822
Fax: 818-487-1763 800-350-5568
www.rlspear.com
Wholesaler/distributor of used material handling equipment, steel shelving and automatic storage and handling systems
Owner: David Spear
Estimated Sales: $5-10 Million
Number Employees: 5-9
Types of Products Distributed:
Frozen Food, General Merchandise, Material handling equipment & shelves

58884 R S Braswell Co Inc
485 S Cannon Blvd
P.O.Box 1197
Kannapolis, NC 28083-5258 704-933-2269
Fax: 704-933-7000 888-628-3550
www.rsbraswell.com
Wholesaler/distributor of new and used forklifts, loaders and attachments
President: Steve Thigpen
bobcat@rsbraswell.com
Service Manager: Bill Wingler
Sales Specialist: Clark Corriher
Parts Manager: David Upright
Buyer: Alton Thigpen
Estimated Sales: $5-10 Million
Number Employees: 20-49
Private Brands Carried:
Bobcat; World

Types of Products Distributed:
Frozen Food, General Merchandise, New & used loaders, forklifts, etc.

58885 R S Porter & Co
611 Palisade Ave
Cliffside Park, NJ 07010-3034 201-943-1822
Fax: 201-941-6285
Wholesaler/distributor of groceries, dried beans and peas
Owner: Robert Jahn
rsporter1902@aol.com
President: Robert Jahn, Jr.
Secretary: Anne-Marie Livoti
Estimated Sales: $2.5-5 Million
Number Employees: 1-4
Private Brands Carried:
Jack Rabbit
Types of Products Distributed:
Frozen Food, General Line, Produce, Groceries, dry beans & peas

58886 R S Stern Inc
1000 S Highland Ave
PO Box 8872
Baltimore, MD 21224-5199 410-342-7676
Fax: 410-243-1650 sales@rsstern.com
www.rsstern.com
Wholesaler/distributor of groceries, meat products, poultry, seafood, dairy products, general merchandise, etc.; supplier for ships; serving the food service market
President: Alan H. Kotz
Manager: Pam Keller
pam@rsstern.com
Operations Manager: Jason Rubenstein
Buyer: H Markowitz
Estimated Sales: $10-20 Million
Number Employees: 10-19
Private Brands Carried:
Big A; Lorko
Number of Customer Locations: 300
Types of Products Distributed:
Food Service, Frozen Food, General Line, General Merchandise, Provisions/Meat, Produce, Seafood, Dairy products

58887 R T Foods Inc
11333 N Scottsdale Rd
Suite 105
Scottsdale, AZ 85254-5186 480-596-1089
Fax: 480-596-3315 888-258-4437
www.rtfoods.com
Tempura and breaded shrimp
Owner: Jeff Krause
jeff@rtfoods.com
Number Employees: 1-4

58888 (HQ)R W Smith & Co
8555 Miralani Dr
San Diego, CA 92126-4352 858-530-1800
Fax: 858-530-0224 800-942-1101
info@rwsmithco.com www.rwsmithco.com
Wholesaler/distributor of restaurant equipment and supplies; serving the food service market
Chairman Board: Ron Woodhill
President: Allan Keck
akeck@rwsmithco.com
Design Director: Art Manni
Sales: Patrice Hagan
Estimated Sales: $10-20 Million
Number Employees: 100-249
Types of Products Distributed:
Food Service, Frozen Food, General Merchandise, Restaurant equipment & supplies

58889 R W Zant Co
1470 E 4th St
Los Angeles, CA 90033 323-980-4950
www.rwzant.com
Wholesaler/distributor of meat, grocery items and dairy products.
President: Will Zant
Year Founded: 1950
Estimated Sales: $50-100 Million
Number Employees: 100-249
Types of Products Distributed:
Frozen Food

58890 R&B Produce
1750 Forest Grove Rd
Vineland, NJ 08360-9173 856-697-7210
Fax: 856-692-1452
Wholesaler/distributor of produce

President: Shirl Densten
Estimated Sales: $.5-1 million
Number Employees: 5-9
Types of Products Distributed:
Frozen Food, Produce

58891 R&F International Corporation
2910 Commerce Park Dr # 2
Boynton Beach, FL 33426-8776   561-533-7900
      Fax: 561-586-1112 rfintl@worldnet.att.net
Wholesaler/distributor of soft serve mixes including yogurt, ice cream, cocktail and nonrefrigerated sorbet; also, concession equipment and supplies for popcorn, cotton candy and snow cones; serving the food service market
President: R Slonim
Estimated Sales: $500,000-$1 Million
Number Employees: 5-9
Types of Products Distributed:
Food Service, Frozen Food, General Line, General Merchandise, Mixes, concession supplies, etc.

58892 R&J Farms
9800 West Pleasant Home Road
West Salem, OH 44287   419-846-3179
      Fax: 419-846-9603 rjfarms@rjfarms.com
            www.rjfarms.com
Soy beans, sesame and sunflower seeds, grains, flour, microwaveable popcorn, chips and pretzels, garbanzo beans
Owner: Todd Driscoll
Number Employees: 5-9
Square Footage: 80000
Type of Packaging: Consumer, Private Label, Bulk
Types of Products Distributed:
Frozen Food

58893 R&J Seafoods
16050 Sterling Hwy
Ninilchik, AK 99639   907-567-3222
      Fax: 907-567-7400 www.rjseafoods.com
Seafood
Plant Manager: Glen Guffey

58894 R&R Equipment Company
1315 S Linden St
Pine Bluff, AR 71603-3346   870-536-8769
                Fax: 870-534-1706
Wholesaler/distributor of groceries, cleaning supplies, disposables, wraps, equipment, etc.; serving the food service market
Owner: Richard Denny
Estimated Sales: $300,000-500,000
Number Employees: 1-4
Types of Products Distributed:
Food Service, Frozen Food, General Line, General Merchandise, Cleaning supplies, etc.

58895 R&R Mill Company
48 W 1st S
Smithfield, UT 84335-1956   435-563-3333
                Fax: 435-563-4093
Exporter of hand wheat mills; importer of corn and grain mills; wholesaler/distributor of hand and electric corn/wheat mills, dehydrators, wheatgrass juicers, kitchen appliances, etc.; serving the food service market
President: Ralph Roylance
Head Shipper: Bart Roylance
Office Manager/Head Shipper: Char Izat
Estimated Sales: Less than $500,000
Number Employees: 1-4
Parent Co: Smithfield Implement Company
Types of Products Distributed:
Food Service, Frozen Food, General Merchandise

58896 R&R Sales Company
2800 NE Loop 410 # 207
San Antonio, TX 78218-1525   210-226-5101
      Fax: 210-225-4415 800-821-1765
Wholesaler/distributor/importer/exporter of jalapeno peppers and private label and general line items; serving supermarket chains and the food service market
President: David Rodriguez
CEO: L Rodriguez
Estimated Sales: $1 Million
Number Employees: 1-4
Number of Brands: 10
Number of Products: 500
Square Footage: 50000
Type of Packaging: Food Service

Private Brands Carried:
Rosita
Number of Customer Locations: 200
Types of Products Distributed:
Food Service, General Merchandise, Groceries, jalapeno peppers, etc.

58897 R-Best Produce
220 Food Center Dr
Bronx, NY 10474   718-617-8300
      Fax: 718-617-8475 800-947-2378
                www.rbest.com
Wholesaler/distributor of produce
President: Philip Delpret
Contact: James Bonaro
jamesbonaro@rbest.com
Estimated Sales: $20-50 Million
Number Employees: 100-249
Types of Products Distributed:
Frozen Food, Produce

58898 R.C. McEntire & Company
P.O.Box 5817
Columbia, SC 29250-5817   803-799-3388
                Fax: 803-254-3540
Tomatoes, peppers, lettuce, onions, cabbage and salads
Owner: Buddy McEntire
Estimated Sales: $10-20 Million
Number Employees: 10-19
Square Footage: 150000
Type of Packaging: Consumer, Food Service, Private Label, Bulk
Types of Products Distributed:
Produce

58899 R.E. Diamond
10 Box Street
Brooklyn, NY 11222   718-389-1700
      Fax: 718-389-7005 www.rediamond.com
Wholesaler/distributor of bakery, restaurant, gourmet and organic ingredients
President: Robert Diamond
Sales/Marketing Executive: Bob Bell
Purchasing Manager: Steven Finklestein
Number Employees: 10-19
Types of Products Distributed:
General Line, Health Food, Specialty Foods, Bakery & organic ingredients, etc.

58900 R.F. Beyers
PO Box 6565
Philadelphia, PA 19138-6565   717-652-4083
      Fax: 717-652-4813 rfbeyes@aol.com
Wholesaler/distributor of dairy/deli products, imported and domestic cheeses, groceries, provisions/meats and gourmet specialty foods
President: Fred Parise
Director Sales/Marketing: Paul Daniels
Estimated Sales: $20-50 Million
Number Employees: 50-99
Square Footage: 43000
Private Brands Carried:
Dari-Ann
Number of Customer Locations: 600
Types of Products Distributed:
Frozen Food, General Line, Provisions/Meat, Specialty Foods, Dairy/deli products, cheeses, etc.

58901 R.H. Forschner
PO Box 1212
Monroe, CT 06468-8212   203-929-6391
      Fax: 203-925-2933 800-243-4032
                www.swissarmy.com
Wholesaler/distributor of imported cutlery
CEO: Rick Taggart
Marketing Director: Donna Girot
Sales Director: Joe Burke
Operations Manager: Jim Cary
Production Manager: Marylynn Karpicki
Purchasing Manager: Mike Smith
Estimated Sales: $20-50 Million
Number Employees: 100-249
Square Footage: 110000
Parent Co: Swiss Army Brands
Type of Packaging: Food Service, Bulk
Private Brands Carried:
Victorinox
Types of Products Distributed:
General Merchandise, Imported cutlery

58902 R.L. Corty & Company
6211 Church Road
Hanover Park, IL 60133   773-736-3510
      Fax: 773-736-4036 800-262-7678
      doncorty@standardus.com www.corty.com
Wholesaler/distributor of steam cleaners, pressure washers, floor sweepers, industrial vacuums and floor scrubbers
VP: Don Corty
Estimated Sales: $2.5-5 Million
Number Employees: 5-9
Square Footage: 48000
Private Brands Carried:
Corty; Tornado; Karcher
Types of Products Distributed:
General Merchandise, Steam cleaners, pressure washers, etc.

58903 R.N. Mason & Son
14437 W Ellsworth Place
Golden, CO 80401-5323   719-384-4465
                Fax: 719-384-4438
Wholesaler/distributor of confectionery items; serving the food service market
President: Jim Rizzuto
Number Employees: 5-9
Types of Products Distributed:
Food Service, Frozen Food, Specialty Foods, Confectionery items

58904 R.S. Hamilton Company
339 Northern Ave
Boston, MA 02210   617-261-1800
                Fax: 617-261-4448
Wholesaler/distributor of fish
Owner: Robert Blaikie
Treasurer: Robert Blaikie Jr
Estimated Sales: $500,000-$1 Million
Number Employees: 1-4
Types of Products Distributed:
Frozen Food, Seafood

58905 R.S. Somers Company
3157 Babashaw Ct
Fairfax, VA 22031-2070   703-204-0033
                Fax: 703-560-0547
Wholesaler/distributor of commercial food service equipment including walk-in coolers; serving the food service market
President: Robert Somers
Secretary/Treasurer: Carolyn Somers
Manager: James Pyle
Estimated Sales: Less than $500,000
Number Employees: 1-4
Square Footage: 4000
Types of Products Distributed:
Food Service, Frozen Food, General Merchandise, Walk-in coolers, etc.

58906 R.T. Greene Company
5949 Bingham Street
Philadelphia, PA 19120-1203   215-925-2750
                Fax: 215-925-3073
Wholesaler/distributor of temperature, pressure, humidity, and waste water instruments
President/CEO: Frank Wagner
CFO: Raymond Greene
Marketing/Sales: David Cohen
Number Employees: 16
Square Footage: 24000
Private Brands Carried:
Weston; Honeywell; Taylor Inst.; Marsn; Trenice
Types of Products Distributed:
Food Service, Specialty Foods

58907 R.W. Davis Oil Company
4383 Lilburn Industrial Way
Lilburn, GA 30047   770-923-4411
                info@davisoil.com
                www.davisoil.com
Wholesaler/distributor of filters and lubricants including grease and oil.
Owner: R. Wendell Davis
Year Founded: 1972
Estimated Sales: $50-100 Million
Number Employees: 10-19
Types of Products Distributed:
Frozen Food, General Merchandise, Filters & lubricants

Wholesalers & Distributors / A-Z

58908 RAPA Scrapple
103 Railroad Ave
Bridgeville, DE 19933
800-338-4727
info@rapascrapple.com   www.rapascrapple.com
Wholesaler/distributor of provisions/meats; serving the food service market.
VP & Manager: Donna Seefried
Year Founded: 1926
Estimated Sales: $30.70 Million
Number Employees: 47
Types of Products Distributed:
  Food Service, Provisions/Meat

58909 RB Packing of California
9255 Customhouse Plz # I
San Diego, CA 92154-7627   619-710-2043
Fax: 619-661-6499
Fruits and vegetables
Contact: Maria Batris
mbatris@masterstouch.com
Number Employees: 5-9

58910 RIPCO
900 Monroe Ave
Ronceverte, WV 24970   304-647-5313
Fax: 304-645-1005
Wholesaler/distributor of frozen food; serving the food service market
Owner: Mike O'Brien
Estimated Sales: $500,000-$1 Million
Number Employees: 5-9
Number of Customer Locations: 10
Types of Products Distributed:
  Food Service, Frozen Food

58911 RM Heagy Foods
227 Granite Run Drive
Suite 200
Lancaster, PA 17601   717-569-1032
Cheese, ice cream and sorbets, butters, dips and sauces, charcuterie meats.
CEO: Chuck Kukic
Chief Financial Officer: Douglas Hilliard
Sales & Marketing Manager: Abigail Heagy
Production Manager: Auston Martzall
Estimated Sales: $20-50 Million
Number Employees: 5-9

58912 RPM Material Handling
P.O.Box 1737
El Centro, CA 92244-1737   760-352-8811
Fax: 760-352-3776
Wholesaler/distributor of automatic storage and handling systems
Manager: Charles Lopez
Sales: Pete Otis
Estimated Sales: $5-10 Million
Number Employees: 10-19
Parent Co: RPM Material Handling
Type of Packaging: Private Label
Types of Products Distributed:
  Frozen Food, General Merchandise, Automatic storage & handling systems

58913 RPM Material Handling Company/Clarklift San Diego
8530 Ave Costa Norte
San Diego, CA 92154-6249   619-661-1575
Fax: 619-661-1574   800-576-1575
rickotis@clarkmhc.com
Wholesaler/distributor of forklifts; also, service and repair, replacement parts and rental/leasing available
President: Harry Otis
VP: Mike Grady
Vice President: Peter Otis
Estimated Sales: $10-20 Million
Number Employees: 5-9
Square Footage: 40000
Private Brands Carried:
  Nissan; Clark; Kalmar; Drexel; Linde
Types of Products Distributed:
  General Merchandise, Forklifts

58914 RPM Total Vitality
18032 Lemon Drive
Suite C
Yorba Linda, CA 92886-3386   714-524-8864
Fax: 714-524-3247   800-234-3092
Antioxidants: pollen and dimethylaminoethanol
Owner: Pat McBride
pat@rpmtv.com
Co-Owner: Roger McBride
Number Employees: 1-4
Square Footage: 4000
Types of Products Distributed:
  Frozen Food, General Line, Health Food, Antioxidants

58915 RTR Packaging
27 W 20th St
New York, NY 10011   212-620-0011
Fax: 212-620-0018   800-972-7489
customerservice@rtrbag.com   www.rtrbag.com
Wholesaler/distributor of general merchandise including advertising specialties, bags, bakery tissue, labels, boxes and biodegradable packaging materials
Owner/Buyer: Ron Raznick
Buyer: Timothy Sullivan
Contact: Cari Brodsky
cari@rtrbag.com
Estimated Sales: $500,000-$1 Million
Number Employees: 5-9
Private Brands Carried:
  Betsy Johnson; Dolce & Gabanna; Eric Stewart
Number of Customer Locations: 1600
Types of Products Distributed:
  General Merchandise, Bags, boxes, bakery tissue, labels

58916 Ra-Bob International
6646 S 143rd St E
Derby, KS 67037   316-776-9556
Wholesaler/distributor of essential, perfume and vitamin E oils
Owner: Lindy Savoy
Estimated Sales: $.5-1 million
Number Employees: 1-4
Types of Products Distributed:
  Frozen Food, General Line, Health Food, Oils: essential, perfume & vitamin E

58917 Rabco Foodservice
880 Milner Ave
Toronto, ON M1B 5N7
Canada   416-321-5823
Fax: 416-321-5826   866-722-2649
sales@rabcofoodservice.com
www.rabcofoodservice.com
Wholesaler/distributor of food service equipment and supplies
President: Steven Rabkin
Sales Manager: Steve Vella
Number Employees: 10-19
Private Brands Carried:
  Carlisle; Edlund; Duraware
Types of Products Distributed:
  Food Service, Frozen Food, General Merchandise, Equipment & supplies

58918 (HQ)Rack Service Company
PO Box 4727
Monroe, LA 71211-4727   318-410-0070
Fax: 318-322-1447   rhchamblis@aol.com
Wholesaler/distributor of specialty foods, general merchandise, equipment and fixtures and groceries; rack jobber services available
President: R Chambliss
VP Finance: P Dalton
Sales Director: J Hodge
Estimated Sales: $2.5-5 Million
Number Employees: 20-49
Square Footage: 320000
Private Brands Carried:
  Lariat
Number of Customer Locations: 1200
Types of Products Distributed:
  General Line, General Merchandise, Rack Jobbers, Specialty Foods, Groceries

58919 Rainbow Foods
1619 W Main St
Albert Lea, MN 56007-1868   507-373-7357
Fax: 507-373-7411
Wholesaler/distributor of seafood, general merchandise, meats, general line items, frozen and specialty foods, produce, etc
President: Chris Nelson
Owner/President: Pat Liska
Estimated Sales: $20-50 Million
Number Employees: 100-249
Parent Co: Fleming Company
Private Brands Carried:
  Best Yet
Types of Products Distributed:
  Frozen Food, General Line, General Merchandise, Provisions/Meat, Produce, Seafood, Specialty Foods

58920 Rainbow Natural Foods
151 West 24 Hwy
Independence, MO 64050   816-836-5757
Wholesaler/distributor of natural, health, specialty, bulk, refrigerated and frozen foods; also, groceries, vitamins, health/beauty aids and organic produce
Estimated Sales: $300,000-500,000
Number Employees: 1-4
Square Footage: 400000
Number of Customer Locations: 700
Types of Products Distributed:
  Frozen Food, General Line, Health Food, Produce, Specialty Foods, Groceries, vitamins, etc.

58921 Rainbow Promotions LLC
3505 Long Beach Blvd # 2g
Suite 2G
Long Beach, CA 90807-3947   562-424-0013
Fax: 562-424-0443   info@rainbowpromotions.com
www.kimbenoit.com
Wholesaler/distributor of imprinted promotional items
President: Steven Goldman
CEO: Kimberly Benoit
Vice President: Marcia Goldman
Estimated Sales: $1-2.5 Million
Number Employees: 1-4
Square Footage: 4800
Private Brands Carried:
  Bic; Garland; Hazel; Thermoserve
Number of Customer Locations: 300
Types of Products Distributed:
  General Merchandise, Imprinted promotional items

58922 Rainbow Seafood Market
4303 Maine Ave
Suite 107
Baldwin Park, CA 91706-2395   626-962-6888
Fax: 626-962-3677
Seafood
Owner: David Tran
Estimated Sales: $800,000
Number Employees: 1-4
Type of Packaging: Consumer

58923 Rainbow Valley Orchards
5115 5th St
Fallbrook, CA 92028-9795   760-723-3911
www.rainbowvalleyorchards.com
Wholesaler/distributor for organic citrus products and avocados; processor of organic juices including orange, grapefruit and raspberry/lemonade; private label packaging available
President: Richard Hart
VP Sales: Patrick Raymond
Contact: Maria Hazen
mhazen@rvorganic.com
Estimated Sales: $6.5 Million
Number Employees: 5-9
Square Footage: 20000
Type of Packaging: Private Label
Types of Products Distributed:
  Frozen Food, Produce

58924 Raisin Administrative Committee
2445 Capitol Street
Suite 200
Fresno, CA 93721-2236   559-225-0520
Fax: 559-225-0652   harry@raisins.org
www.raisins.org
President / Manager: Gary Schulz
Vice President of Accounting & Finance: Ron Degiuli
Statistical Technician/Data Entry: Anna Valdivia
Director of Compliance: Hector Omapas
Sr. Vice President of Marketing: Larry Blagg
International Programs Coordinator: Chris Rosander
SVP, Operations & Human Resources: Debbie Powell
Estimated Sales: $3-5 Million
Number Employees: 20-49

58925 Rakestraw Ice Cream Company
17 E Coover St
Mechanicsburg, PA 17055-4218   717-766-7445
Fax: 717-766-6497   800-800-1903
Wholesaler/distributor of ice cream
General Manager: Paul Heeter
Estimated Sales: $5-10 Million
Number Employees: 5-9

Wholesalers & Distributors / A-Z

Type of Packaging: Private Label
Types of Products Distributed:
   Frozen Food, Ice cream

58926 Ralph Jones Display & Store
2576 E Charleston Blvd
Las Vegas, NV 89104-2323   702-382-4398
   Fax: 702-388-0474   800-208-4398
sales@ralphjones.com   www.ralphjones.com
Wholesaler/distributor of store fixtures
Owner: Hoot Jones Jr
Estimated Sales: $1-2.5 Million
Number Employees: 10-19
Types of Products Distributed:
   Frozen Food, General Merchandise, Store fixtures

58927 Ralph's Packing Co
500 W Freeman Ave
Perkins, OK 74059   405-547-2464
   Fax: 405-547-2364   800-522-3979
comments@ralphspacking.com
www.ralphspacking.com
Fresh and smoked meat products available to consumers and wholesalers.
President: Gary Crane
garycrane@ralphspacking.com
Year Founded: 1959
Estimated Sales: $4 Million
Number Employees: 20-49
Square Footage: 39200
Type of Packaging: Consumer, Food Service, Private Label
Types of Products Distributed:
   Provisions/Meat

58928 Ramarc Foods Inc
14556 John Humphrey Dr
Orland Park, IL 60462-2640   708-403-1700
   Fax: 708-403-2056   800-354-7272
www.ramarcfoods.com
Wholesaler/distributor and exporter of fresh and frozen meats
President: Mark Gehrman
Treasurer: Ray O'Brien
VP: Ray Gehrman
Estimated Sales: $20-50 Million
Number Employees: 10-19
Square Footage: 3000
Types of Products Distributed:
   Frozen Food, Provisions/Meat

58929 Ramco Innovations Inc
1207 Maple St
PO Box 65310
West Des Moines, IA 50265-4497   515-225-6933
   Fax: 515-225-6933   800-328-6286
www.ramcoi.com
Wholesaler/distributor of sensors
President: Hank Norem
hnorem@ramcoinnovations.com
VP Sales: Mike Reelitz
Estimated Sales: $10-20 Million
Number Employees: 20-49
Parent Co: Sunx Sensors
Types of Products Distributed:
   Frozen Food, General Merchandise, Sensors

58930 Ramex Foods
1585 Mabury Road
Suite E
San Jose, CA 95133-1053   510-770-1400
   Fax: 408-254-1846
Wholesaler/distributor of seafood, general merchandise, meats, general line and specialty food products; serving the food service market
CEO/President: Raul Reynoso
CFO/VP: William Harris
Estimated Sales: $2.5-5 Million
Number Employees: 10-19
Square Footage: 30000
Private Brands Carried:
   Ramex; R&M
Number of Customer Locations: 400
Types of Products Distributed:
   Food Service, Frozen Food, General Line, General Merchandise, Provisions/Meat, Seafood, Specialty Foods

58931 Ramsen Inc
17725 Juniper Path
Lakeville, MN 55044-9482   952-431-0400
   Fax: 952-431-8470   dbreuer@ramsendairy.com
www.ramsendairy.com
Dry dairy
Owner: Tim Krieger
Partner: John Baetty
jbaetty@ramsendairy.com
Marketing Director: Kathy Stevens
Sales Manager: Dennis Breuer
Estimated Sales: $10-20 Million
Number Employees: 10-19
Square Footage: 3600
Type of Packaging: Consumer, Food Service
Types of Products Distributed:
   Food Service, Frozen Food, General Line, Food ingredients

58932 Ranch Foods Direct
1228 E Fillmore St
Colorado Springs, CO 80907   719-473-2306
ranchfoodsdirect.com
Wholesaler/distributor of groceries, provisions/meats, produce, dairy products, frozen foods and general merchandise; serving the food service market.
Owner: Mike Callicrate
Year Founded: 2000
Estimated Sales: $50-100 Million
Number Employees: 40
Square Footage: 24000
Parent Co: Federal Fruit & Produce
Other Locations:
   Cattle Ranch
   St. Francis, KS
   Slaughter Facility
   St. Francis, KS
   Cut, Processing & Distribution Ctr
   Colorado Springs, CO Cattle Ranch St. Francis
Private Brands Carried:
   Comsource
Number of Customer Locations: 400
Types of Products Distributed:
   Food Service, Frozen Food, General Line, General Merchandise, Provisions/Meat, Produce

58933 Randall Meat Co
500 Albert Pike Rd # B
Hot Spgs Natl Pk, AR 71913-3814   501-623-5587
   Fax: 501-623-9191   800-464-5587
Wholesaler/distributor of provisions/meats and frozen foods; also beef, pork, catfish, corned beef, bacon and hams serving the food service market
President: Jack Stone
Estimated Sales: $10-20 Million
Number Employees: 5-9
Square Footage: 9600
Number of Customer Locations: 200
Types of Products Distributed:
   Food Service, Frozen Food, Provisions/Meat

58934 Randy's Frozen Meats
1910 5th St NW
Faribault, MN 55021-4606   507-334-7177
   Fax: 507-334-9210   www.randysfoods.com
Pizzas
Co-Owner: Randy Creasman
Number Employees: 20-49
Type of Packaging: Consumer, Food Service, Private Label, Bulk
Private Brands Carried:
   Good Stuff Sandwiches; Good Stuff Pizzas
Types of Products Distributed:
   Food Service, Frozen Food, General Line, General Merchandise, Provisions/Meat, Seafood, Specialty Foods, Baked goods, deli items, etc.

58935 Range Packing Company
2255 Aberdeen St
Kenner, LA 70062   504-469-2333
   Fax: 504-469-3255
Wholesaler/distributor of boxed beef, cold cuts, cheese and fish; serving the food service market
Owner: Scott Scariano
Estimated Sales: $5-10 Million
Number Employees: 10-19
Types of Products Distributed:
   Food Service, Frozen Food, General Line, Provisions/Meat, Seafood, Cheese

58936 Rantec Corp
17 Kukuchka Ln
Ranchester, WY 82839   307-655-9565
   Fax: 307-655-9528   rantec@ranteccorp.com
www.ranteccorp.com
Wholesaler/distributor of industrial grade guar gum
Owner: Lloyd Marsden
Controller: Mary McDowell
Technical Sales: Stephanie Zier
lwm@ranteccorp.com
Production Manager: Echo Mendenhall
Estimated Sales: $5-10 Million
Number Employees: 5-9
Types of Products Distributed:
   Frozen Food, General Line, Industrial grade guar gum

58937 (HQ)Rapid Sales Company
1009 Jonathon Drive
Madison, WI 53713-3228   608-271-2551
Wholesaler/distributor of general merchandise, equipment and fixtures; rack jobber services available, studio operating equipment
President: Marilyn Tarkenton
Number Employees: 50-99
Types of Products Distributed:
   Frozen Food, General Merchandise, Rack Jobbers, Equipment & fixtures

58938 (HQ)Rapids Wholesale Equipment
6201 S Gateway Dr
Marion, IA 52302-9430   319-447-3500
   Fax: 319-447-1680   800-472-7431
Wholesaler/distributor and exporter of restaurant equipment and supplies including refrigeration and draft beer coolers and dispensers; serving the food service market
President: Joe Schmitt
Sales/Marketing Executive: Ross Anderson
Estimated Sales: $10-20 Million
Number Employees: 50-99
Square Footage: 40000
Other Locations:
   Rapids
   Cincinnati, OH Rapids
Types of Products Distributed:
   Food Service, Frozen Food, General Merchandise, Restaurant equipment & supplies

58939 Raw Rev
PO Box 359
Hawthorne, NY 10532   914-326-4095
rawrev.com
Plant-based superfood bars
Founder & President: Alice Benedetto
Types of Products Distributed:
   Frozen Food

58940 Ray & Mascari
324 S New Jersey St
Indianapolis, IN 46204   317-637-0234
   800-428-4221
www.rayandmascari.com
Wholesaler/distributor of produce.
Chief Executive Officer: Michael Ray
Chief Financial Officer: Michael Ray
Vice President, Sales: Rocky Ray
Vice President, Operations: Jason Ray
Chief Operating Officer: Joseph Ray
Year Founded: 1938
Estimated Sales: $20-50 Million
Number Employees: 20-49
Square Footage: 92000
Type of Packaging: Bulk
Types of Products Distributed:
   Frozen Food, Produce

58941 Ray Cosgrove Brokerage Company
PO Box 281
Saddle River, NJ 07458-0281   201-825-0979
   Fax: 201-327-8588
Import and export broker and wholesaler/distributor of seafood, private label items, frozen foods, groceries and health food
President: Ray Cosgrove
Number Employees: 20-49
Type of Packaging: Food Service, Private Label
Types of Products Distributed:
   Seafood

58942 Raymond
1000 Brighton St
Union, NJ 07083   908-624-9570
www.raymond-nj.com
Wholesaler/distributor of material handling equipment including lift trucks.
Rental Manager: Pam Haskell
Estimated Sales: $50-100 Million
Number Employees: 100-249

Wholesalers & Distributors / A-Z

Types of Products Distributed:
  Frozen Food, General Merchandise, Material handling equipment

58943 (HQ)Raymond Handling Concepts Corp
41400 Boyce Rd
Fremont, CA 94538-3113   510-745-7500
    Fax: 510-745-7686 800-675-2500
        info@raymondhandling.com
        www.raymondhandling.com
Wholesaler/distributor of material handling equipment.
President: Stephen Raymond
sraymond@raymondhandling.com
VP, Operations: Al Silar
VP, Finance & CFO: Donald Jones
VP, Human Resources: Heidi Healy
Estimated Sales: $50-100 Million
Number Employees: 100-249
Other Locations:
  Auburn, WA
  Spokane, WA
  Sacramento, CA
  Stockton, CA
  Fresno, CA
  Portland, ORSpokane
Private Brands Carried:
  Raymond; Matthews; Cardex; Anderson Racking; Frazier

58944 Raymond Handling Solutions
9939 Norwalk Blvd
Santa Fe Springs, CA 90670-3321   562-944-8067
    Fax: 562-946-1462 800-982-2444
        info@raymondhs.net
Wholesaler/distributor of material handling equipment
President: James Wilcox
jwilcox@raymondhs.net
Number Employees: 250-499
Private Brands Carried:
  Raymond; B.T. Prime-Mover; Matthews
Types of Products Distributed:
  Frozen Food, General Merchandise, Material handling equipment

58945 Raz Company
2315 E 1st St
Los Angeles, CA 90033-4001   323-264-6928
Wholesaler/distributor of alcoholic beverages
Owner: Robert Rizzo
Estimated Sales: $.5-1 million
Number Employees: 1-4
Types of Products Distributed:
  Frozen Food, General Line, Alcoholic beverages

58946 Rbm Co
2700 Texas Ave
Knoxville, TN 37921   865-524-8621
        www.rbmcompany.com
Wholesaler/distributor of material handling equipment.
Year Founded: 1945
Estimated Sales: $50-100 Million
Number Employees: 20
Square Footage: 25000
Private Brands Carried:
  Lyon; Bink's; OPW
Types of Products Distributed:
  Frozen Food, General Merchandise, Material handling equipment

58947 Ready Food Products
Six Kimball Lane
Lynnfield, MA 1940   617-887-3000
    Fax: 215-824-2820 800-343-6592
        www.hphood.com
Wholesaler/distributor of dairy products; serving the food service market
Chairman, President & CEO: John A. Kaneb
Chief Financial Officer: Gary R. Kaneb
EVP: Jeffery J. Kaneb
SVP, R&D: Mike J. Suever
VP, Marketing: Christopher S. Ross
EVP, Sales: James F. Walsh
SVP, Operations: H. Scott Blake
Plant Manager: Ron Nelson
Estimated Sales: $10-20 Million
Number Employees: 100-249
Parent Co: Crowley Foods
Private Brands Carried:
  Glen Farms PC's; Pure Pack
Number of Customer Locations: 5000

Types of Products Distributed:
  Food Service, Frozen Food, General Line, Dairy products

58948 Ready Portion Meat Co
1546 Choctaw Dr
Baton Rouge, LA 70805-7756   225-355-5641
    Fax: 225-355-8895
Wholesaler/distributor of frozen foods, general line items and meats; serving the food service market
Owner/President/CEO: Kyle Beck
kbeck@realmeatco.sageweb.co.uk
Estimated Sales: $4 Million
Number Employees: 20-49
Square Footage: 28000
Type of Packaging: Bulk
Types of Products Distributed:
  Food Service, Frozen Food, General Line, Provisions/Meat, Groceries & dairy products

58949 Ready Potatoes Inc
2201 NW 25th Ave
Miami, FL 33142-7122   954-527-0111
    Fax: 305-635-9361
Wholesaler/distributor of frozen foods
General Manager/President: Joseph Schriver
Estimated Sales: $10-20 Million
Number Employees: 10-19
Number of Customer Locations: 400
Types of Products Distributed:
  Frozen Food

58950 Real Cajun School Of Cooking
6611 Loreauville Rd
New Iberia, LA 70563-8418   337-229-8455
    Fax: 337-229-8457 800-420-6030
        www.louisianacrawfishman.com
Wholesaler/distributor of Cajun mixes including gumbo, jambalaya, etoufee and seasonings
Owner: Tim Eddler
Estimated Sales: Less Than $500,000
Number Employees: 1-4
Square Footage: 6000
Types of Products Distributed:
  Frozen Food, Specialty Foods, Cajun mixes & seasonings

58951 Real Soda
124 N 35th St
Seattle, WA 98103   206-632-1050
        soda@ginseng.com
        www.ginseng.com
Wholesaler/distributor, exporter and importer of soft drinks, beer and wine
Number Employees: 5-9
Parent Co: Real Soda in Real Bottles
Types of Products Distributed:
  Frozen Food, General Line, Soft drinks, beer & wine

58952 Really Raw Honey Company
3500 Boston St Ste 111
Baltimore, MD 21224   410-675-7233
    Fax: 410-675-7411 800-732-5729
        info@reallyrawhoney.com
        www.reallyrawhoney.com
Wholesaler/distributor of honey including unheated, unstrained and pesticide-free
Owner: Frantz Walker
CEO: Ben Barnett
CFO: Ann Fisher
Estimated Sales: $3-5 Million
Number Employees: 5-9
Square Footage: 10000
Private Brands Carried:
  Really Raw
Types of Products Distributed:
  Health Food

58953 Rebstock Conveyors
810 Fee Fee Rd
Maryland Heights, MO 63043-3228   314-872-9222
    Fax: 314-872-9271 800-872-9223
        www.rebstockconveyors.com
Wholesaler/distributor of conveyors including package, portable, bottle and mesh belt
President: Curt Rebstock
crebstock@rebstockconveyors.com
Number Employees: 10-19
Types of Products Distributed:
  Frozen Food, General Merchandise, Conveyors: package, portable, etc.

58954 Red Chamber Co
1912 E Vernon Ave
Vernon, CA 90058   323-234-9000
    Fax: 323-231-8888 info@redchamber.com
        www.redchamber.com
Seafood
CEO: Ming Bin Kou
CFO: Ming Shin Kou
VP: Andro Chen
VP, Food Innovation and R&D: Wales Yu
Year Founded: 1973
Estimated Sales: $100-500 Million
Number Employees: 100-249
Types of Products Distributed:
  Seafood

58955 Red Diamond Coffee & Tea
400 Park Ave
Moody, AL 35004
    800-292-4651
    qcdept@reddiamond.com www.reddiamond.com
Coffee, tea pods and coffee brewers.
VP, Sales Development: John Padgett
VP, Manufacturing: Joe George
Year Founded: 1906
Estimated Sales: $45.9 Million
Number Employees: 100-249
Square Footage: 195000
Type of Packaging: Consumer, Food Service, Private Label, Bulk

58956 Red Hot Chicago
4649 W Armitage Ave
Chicago, IL 60639   312-829-3434
    Fax: 312-829-2704 800-249-5226
        info@redhotchicago.com www.redhotchicago.com
Wholesaler/distributor of gourmet hot dogs, specialty sausages and processed meats
President: Scott Ladany
Manager: Glenn Olsen
Contact: Billy Ladany
billy@redhotchicago.com
Estimated Sales: $2.5-5 Million
Number Employees: 1-4
Private Brands Carried:
  Red Hot Chicago; Chicago's Choice
Number of Customer Locations: 3000+
Types of Products Distributed:
  Provisions/Meat, Specialty Foods

58957 Red Rose Trading Company
520 N Charlotte St
Lancaster, PA 17603   717-293-7833
Granola, pancake, baking and gluten-free mixes and blends
Owner: J Leichter
Estimated Sales: $3-5 Million
Number Employees: 10-19
Square Footage: 56000
Type of Packaging: Consumer, Food Service, Private Label, Bulk
Private Brands Carried:
  David's Goodbatter; Stark Sisters Granola; Calahari Couscous
Types of Products Distributed:
  Food Service, Frozen Food, General Line, Health Food, Organic & bulk ingredients, etc.

58958 (HQ)Reddy Ice
5720 LBJ Freeway
Suite 200
Dallas, TX 75240   214-526-6740
        800-683-4423
    information@reddyice.com www.reddyice.com
Packaged ice products including cubes, blocks, and dry; Cold storage warehouse
Chairman: Bill Corbin
CEO: Deborah Conklin
CFO: Steven Janusek
COO: Paul Smith
Contact: Karen Apperson
kapperson@reddyice.com
Year Founded: 1927
Estimated Sales: $300 Million
Number Employees: 1000-4999
Types of Products Distributed:
  Frozen Food

58959 Reddy Raw Inc
1 Ethel Blvd # 1
Wood Ridge, NJ 07075-2400   201-804-7633
    Fax: 201-804-7683 www.reddyraw.com
Wholesaler/distributor of frozen foods

Owner: David Rothstein
carla@rcgfoods.com
Estimated Sales: $20-50 Million
Number Employees: 20-49
Types of Products Distributed:
    Frozen Food

58960 Redstone Distributors
PO Box 765
Republic, PA 15475-0765 724-246-9446
        Fax: 724-246-1944 www.redstonecandies.com
Wholesaler/distributor of candy
Co-Owner: David Bashour
Co-Owner: George Bashour
Estimated Sales: $3-5 Million
Number Employees: 5-9
Types of Products Distributed:
    Frozen Food, Candy

58961 Reed Ice
Lincolnton, GA 706-359-3127
        Fax: 706-359-5465 800-927-9612
        reedice@nu-z.net www.reedice.com
Manufacturer, wholesaler and distributor of ice; serving the food service market.
Owner: Talmadge Reed
Estimated Sales: $20-50 Million
Number Employees: 10-19
Type of Packaging: Private Label, Bulk
Types of Products Distributed:
    Food Service, Frozen Food, Ice

58962 Reese & Long Refrigeration
1891 Park Avenue
New York, NY 10035-1128 212-876-7978
        Fax: 212-289-6051 800-246-4440
Wholesaler/distributor of food service equipment including refrigerators and ice machines; serving the food service market
President: Chris Reese
Estimated Sales: $2.5-5 Million
Number Employees: 5-9
Private Brands Carried:
    True; Scotsman; U-Line
Types of Products Distributed:
    Food Service, Frozen Food, General Merchandise, Refrigerators & ice machines

58963 (HQ)Refrigeration & Food Eqpt Inc
1901 W Tudor Rd
Anchorage, AK 99517-3114 907-248-2525
        Fax: 907-243-6709
        www.refrigerationfoodequip.com
Wholesaler/distributor of food service equipment; also, custom stainless steel fabrication, repair and subcontracting services available
Owner: Dona Agosti
President: T Agosti
VP: David Agosti
Estimated Sales: $2.5-5 Million
Number Employees: 5-9
Number of Customer Locations: 300
Types of Products Distributed:
    Food Service, Frozen Food, General Merchandise, Foodservice equipment

58964 Refrigeration Equipment
1118 Clay Street
North Kansas City, MO 64116-4133 816-931-8072
        Fax: 816-756-5760
Wholesaler/distributor of refrigeration, heating and air conditioning equipment and supplies; serving the food service market
President: Terry Tholen
Types of Products Distributed:
    Food Service, Frozen Food, General Merchandise, Refrigeration, etc., supplies & equip.

58965 Regal Distributing Company
9734 Pflumm Rd
Lenexa, KS 66215-1206 913-894-8787
        Fax: 913-894-4005 800-326-2022
        www.getregal.com
Wholesaler/distributor of concession supplies; serving the food service market
President: Lee Kopulos
CEO: Gregory Kopulos
VP/Controller: Dean Kopulas
CEO: Greg Kopeulos
Contact: Daniel Allen
dallen@getregal.com
Estimated Sales: $1-2.5 Million
Number Employees: 20-49
Square Footage: 120000
Types of Products Distributed:
    Food Service, Frozen Food, General Merchandise, Concession supplies

58966 Regal Distributing Company
3950 N 20th Street
Ozark, MO 65721-7433 417-873-9407
        Fax: 913-894-4005
Wholesaler/distributor of concession supplies and equipment including popcorn, cotton candy, funnel cake, hot dogs, nachos, candy, and cones; also, janitorial supplies and equipment and paper, plastic and foam chemicals; serving the food service market
Owner: Greg Kopolus
Branch Manager: Mike Braswell
Number Employees: 1-4
Square Footage: 32000
Parent Co: Regal Distributing Company
Private Brands Carried:
    Lov Ana Oil's; Solo Cups; Gold Medal Products Co.
Types of Products Distributed:
    Food Service, Frozen Food, General Line, General Merchandise, Provisions/Meat, Concession equipment/supplies, etc.

58967 Regal Supply & ChemicalCompany
1335 E Idaho Ave
Las Cruces, NM 88001 575-524-8509
        Fax: 505-524-8721
Wholesaler/distributor of general merchandise including cleaning supplies, disposables and wraps; serving the food service market
Branch Manager: Tom Lucero
Sales Representative: Terry Stevens
Estimated Sales: $1-2.5 Million
Number Employees: 1-4
Parent Co: Regal Supply & Chemical Company
Types of Products Distributed:
    Food Service, Frozen Food, General Merchandise, Equipment & supplies

58968 Regal Supply & ChemicalCompany
6109 Pinehurst Drive
El Paso, TX 79912-2023 915-542-1831
        Fax: 915-542-1839
Wholesaler/distributor of cleaning supplies, disposables and wraps; serving the food service market
President: Sal Maltin
CEO: Harold Ettinger
Estimated Sales: $10-20 Million
Number Employees: 20-49
Types of Products Distributed:
    Food Service, Frozen Food, General Merchandise, Cleaning supplies, disposables, etc.

58969 Regency Coffee & Vending
2022 E Spruce Cir
Olathe, KS 66062-5404 913-829-1994
        Fax: 913-393-0097 Regency@RegencyCoffee.com
        www.regencycoffee.com
Coffees, teas and snacks
Owner: Nancy Robinson
regency@regencycoffee.com
Estimated Sales: $205 Million
Number Employees: 10-19
Number of Brands: 8
Number of Products: 80
Type of Packaging: Consumer, Food Service, Private Label, Bulk
Private Brands Carried:
    Folgers, Lipton, S & D Coffee Inc., Starbucks, Swiss Miss, Nestle, Tazo and Wolfgang Puck
Types of Products Distributed:
    Food Service, Provisions/Meat, Specialty Foods

58970 Regez Cheese Company
PO Box 312
Monroe, WI 53566-0312 608-325-3417
        Fax: 608-325-3499
Wholesaler/distributor of cheese processing and paper supplies
Owner: Mike Einbeck
Estimated Sales: $5-10 Million
Number Employees: 5-9
Types of Products Distributed:
    General Merchandise, Cheese processing & paper supplies

58971 Registry Steak & Seafood
7661 S 78th Ave
Unit B
Bridgeview, IL 60455-1271 708-458-3100
        Fax: 708-458-3103
Meat, seafood
President: Tony Migacz
ynotshrimp@yahoo.com
Senior Vice President: Anthony S Migacz
Estimated Sales: $10 Million
Number Employees: 20-49
Square Footage: 5000
Type of Packaging: Food Service, Private Label, Bulk
Private Brands Carried:
    Campeche Deluxe Shrimp
Number of Customer Locations: 300
Types of Products Distributed:
    Food Service, Frozen Food, Provisions/Meat, Seafood, Specialty Foods, 6 Packs

58972 Reinhart Foodservice LLC
Suite 400N
Chicago, IL 60631
        www.rfsdelivers.com
Wholesaler/distributor of frozen, health and specialty foods, groceries, general merchandise, baked goods, private label items, produce, meats, dairy products, seafood and restaurant equipment; serving the food service market.
President & CEO, PFG Foodservice: Craig Hoskins
Year Founded: 1972
Estimated Sales: $30 Billion
Number Employees: 25,000
Parent Co: Performance Food Group
Private Brands Carried:
    Reinhart
Number of Customer Locations: 3000
Types of Products Distributed:
    Food Service, Frozen Food, General Line, General Merchandise, Health Food, Provisions/Meat, Produce, Seafood, Specialty Foods, Groceries, restaurant equipment, etc.

58973 Reliable Fire Equipment
12845 S Cicero Ave
Alsip, IL 60803-3083 708-444-7339
        Fax: 708-389-1150 fire@reliablefire.com
        www.reliablefire.com
Wholesaler/distributor of restaurant fire suppression and security systems, alarm monitoring, fire alarms, portable, industrial and special hazard fire extinguishers, emergency lights, smoke detectors and first aid equipment, serving the food service market.
President: Debra Horvath
Vice President: Barbara Horvath
VP Sales: Robert Marek
Purchasing Manager: Tim Zurek
Estimated Sales: $22 Million
Number Employees: 50-99
Number of Brands: 30
Number of Products: 200
Square Footage: 40000
Private Brands Carried:
    Ansul; Amerex; Badger; Potter-Roemer; Fike; Notifier; Fenwal
Types of Products Distributed:
    Food Service, Frozen Food, General Merchandise, Fire safety equipment

58974 Reliable Fire Protection
20 Meridian Rd # 1
Eatontown, NJ 07724-2270 732-607-1500
        Fax: 732-643-0076 800-368-0024
        info@reliablefirepro.com
        www.reliablefireprotection.com
Wholesaler/distributor of general merchandise including fire suppression systems, fire extinguishers, first aid cabinets, safety supplies, etc.; serving the food service market
Owner: Doug Coger
doug@reliablefirepro.com
Estimated Sales: $10-20 Million
Number Employees: 10-19
Private Brands Carried:
    Ansul; Pyro Chem; Ranger Guard
Types of Products Distributed:
    Food Service, Frozen Food, General Merchandise, Fire suppression systems, etc.

Wholesalers & Distributors / A-Z

58975 Reliable Mercantile Company
21 Kensett Road
Manhasset, NY 11030-2105   516-365-7808
Fax: 516-365-7808
Importer and wholesaler/distributor of spices
President: M Abrahamian
Types of Products Distributed:
　Frozen Food, Specialty Foods, Spices

58976 Remy Cointreau USA, Inc.
1290 Avenue of the Americas
10th Floor
New York, NY 10104   212-399-4200
www.remyusa.com
Wholesaler/distributor of wines and spirits
President: Guido Corso
VP Finance: Guillaume Penot
General Counsel: Julie Kinch
Estimated Sales: $47.9 Million
Number Employees: 210
Square Footage: 22000
Types of Products Distributed:
　Frozen Food, General Line, Wines & spirits

58977 Ren 500 Food Fair
5 Sunnybrook Road
Bronxville, NY 10708-5425   914-337-5249
Wholesaler/distributor of frozen desserts and pasta
Co-Owner: Frank Costa
Bookkeeper/Sales: Vickie Brenna-Costa
Types of Products Distributed:
　Frozen Food, Frozen desserts & pasta

58978 Renaissance International
PO Box 797792
Dallas, TX 75379-7792   972-713-6373
Fax: 972-713-6372
Wholesaler/distributor of tamale manufacturing extrusion machinery
President: Bernard Geiger
Estimated Sales: $1-3 Million
Number Employees: 1-4
Square Footage: 9600
Types of Products Distributed:
　Frozen Food, General Merchandise, Extrusion machinery

58979 Reno Forklift Inc
171 Coney Island Dr
Sparks, NV 89431-6317   775-329-1384
Fax: 775-329-1266 www.renoforklift.com
Wholesaler/distributor of forklifts, racks and shelving; also, parts, service and rental available
Owner: George Grover
ggrover@hertzequip.com
Corporate Secretary: Pat Pimpl
Estimated Sales: $20-50 Million
Number Employees: 50-99
Types of Products Distributed:
　Frozen Food, General Merchandise, Material handling equipment

58980 Republic National Distributing
8201 Stayton Dr
Jessup, MD 20794-9633   301-725-1551
Fax: 410-724-3350 www.rndc-usa.com
Wholesaler/distributor of spirits, beer and fine wine
President: Patrick Vogel
Senior VP: Gary Maites
Number Employees: 100-249
Types of Products Distributed:
　Frozen Food, General Line, Spirits, beer & fine wine

58981 Resco Restaurant & Store Equip
230 W 700 S
Salt Lake City, UT 84101-2714   801-364-1981
Fax: 801-355-2029 www.rescoslc.com
Wholesaler/distributor of food service equipment and supplies; also, equipment repair and custom fabrication available
President: Legrande Steenblik
leg@recoslc.com
Vice President: Le Grande Steenblik
Sales Director: Norm Gale
Operations Manager: Carter Steenblik
Estimated Sales: $20-50 Million
Number Employees: 50-99
Square Footage: 34000
Type of Packaging: Food Service
Number of Customer Locations: 5000
Types of Products Distributed:
　Food Service, Frozen Food, General Line, General Merchandise, Equipment & supplies

58982 Rescue Earth
1525 Hillsmont Drive
El Cajon, CA 92020-2941   619-588-7700
Fax: 619-593-0633   800-275-0460
Wholesaler/distributor of general merchandise including recycling bins, equipment compactors and bailers and reusable canvas and string bags
President: Simon Kramedjian
Estimated Sales: $1-3 Million
Number Employees: 5-9
Types of Products Distributed:
　Frozen Food, General Merchandise, Recycling bins, compactors, etc.

58983 Reser's Fine Foods Inc
P.O. Box 8
Beaverton, OR 97075   503-643-6431
800-333-6431
www.resers.com
Frozen dinners: cold salads, tortillas, salsas, smoked meats
President & CEO: Mark Reser
CFO & Treasurer: Paul Leavy
EVP, Sales, Marketing and R&D: Peter Sirgy
VP, Supply Chain: Pete Shepard
Year Founded: 1950
Estimated Sales: $310 Million
Number Employees: 3,000
Parent Co: Belletieri Company

58984 Residex
46495 Humboldt Dr
Novi, MI 48377-2446   248-669-7996
Fax: 732-499-0079   855-737-4339
info@residex.com www.residex.com
Wholesaler/distributor of pest control supplies, insecticides and rodenticides
General Manager: Christopher Donaghy
Director Operations: Rich Giglia
IT: Janice Cronin
janice.cronin@turfgrassinc.com
Estimated Sales: $10-20 Million
Number Employees: 20-49
Square Footage: 60000
Parent Co: Western Industries
Types of Products Distributed:
　Frozen Food, General Merchandise, insecticides, etc.

58985 (HQ)ResourceNet International
50 E Rivercenter Boulevard
Suite 700
Covington, KY 41011-1683   859-655-2000
Fax: 859-655-8983
Wholesaler/distributor of paper products and janitorial supplies; serving the food service market
President: Thomas Costello
Estimated Sales: $5-10 Million
Number Employees: 5-9
Types of Products Distributed:
　Food Service, Frozen Food, General Merchandise, Paper products & janitorial supplies

58986 Restaurant Depot
1524 132nd St
College Point, NY 11356   718-765-8700
www.restaurantdepot.com
Wholesaler/distributor of dairy products, groceries, equipment and fixtures, frozen foods and paper goods; serving the food service market.
Manager: Brian Spellman
Estimated Sales: $50-100 Million
Number Employees: 100-249
Parent Co: Jetro Cash & Carry Enterprises
Private Brands Carried:
　Libby's; Del Monte; Drackette
Number of Customer Locations: 1000
Types of Products Distributed:
　Food Service, Frozen Food, General Line, General Merchandise, Groceries, dairy products, etc.

58987 Restaurant Depot
1030 W Division St
Chicago, IL 60642   312-255-9800
www.restaurantdepot.com
Wholesaler/distributor of seafood, general merchandise, health, specialty and frozen foods, produce, specialty foods and general line items; serving the food service market.
Parent Co: Jetro Cash & Carry Enterprises
Private Brands Carried:
　Heinz; Nabisco; Kellogg
Number of Customer Locations: 1000

Types of Products Distributed:
　Food Service, Frozen Food, General Line, General Merchandise, Health Food, Provisions/Meat, Produce, Seafood, Specialty Foods

58988 Restaurant Design & Equip Corp
4 High St
P.O.Box 370
Old Lyme, CT 06371-1529   860-434-9074
Fax: 860-434-3735 www.restaurantdesign.com
Wholesaler/distributor of food service equipment and supplies; serving the food service market; also, facilities planning and installation services available
President: Rick Sevieri
Secretary/Treasurer: Robert Sevieri
COO: John Crim
Operations: John Crim
Purchasing Director: John Crim
Estimated Sales: $5-10 Million
Number Employees: 10-19
Square Footage: 40000
Types of Products Distributed:
　Food Service

58989 Restaurant Designs Development
2885 Aurora Avenue
Suite 7
Boulder, CO 80303-2251   303-449-9331
Fax: 303-449-9333
Wholesaler/distributor of equipment and fixtures; serving the food service market
President: A Acharya
Estimated Sales: $500,000-$1 Million
Number Employees: 1-4
Number of Customer Locations: 35
Types of Products Distributed:
　Food Service, Frozen Food, General Merchandise, Equipment & fixtures

58990 Restaurant Food Supply
2713 Abundance Street
New Orleans, LA 70122-5803   504-948-2234
Wholesaler/distributor of frozen foods, general line and specialty food products; serving the food service market
Owner: LaRue Pope
Estimated Sales: $2.5-5 Million
Number Employees: 5-9
Types of Products Distributed:
　Food Service, Frozen Food, General Line, Specialty Foods, Groceries

58991 Restaurant Supply
633 W Rhapsody Drive
San Antonio, TX 78216-2608   210-733-1001
Wholesaler/distributor of tabletop supplies and equipment; serving the food service market
Manager: R Gernsbacher
Number Employees: 5-9
Number of Customer Locations: 200
Types of Products Distributed:
　Food Service, Frozen Food, General Merchandise, Tabletop supplies & equipment

58992 Retail Data Systems Of Omaha
6515 S 118th St # 200
Omaha, NE 68137-3588   402-597-6477
Fax: 402-597-1954 www.retaildatasystems.com
Wholesaler/distributor of point of sale systems including computers; also, back office inventory control systems
President: Bob Seider
General Manager: Christopher Shaft
Contact: Paul Baumgartner
pbaumgartner@rdspos.com
Estimated Sales: $2.5-5 Million
Number Employees: 10-19
Private Brands Carried:
　Panasonic; NCR; ICL; Digital Dining; Counter Point; Casio; Tec
Types of Products Distributed:
　Frozen Food, General Merchandise, Point of sale systems, etc.

58993 Rex Chemical Corporation
2270 NW 23rd St
Miami, FL 33142   305-634-2471
Fax: 305-634-5546   877-634-5539
rexchem@bellsouth.net www.rexchemical.com
Liquid and powder cleaners; wholesaler/distributor of janitorial supplies
President: Beatriz Granja
Contact: Mary Meier
m.meier@sandc.com

Wholesalers & Distributors / A-Z

Estimated Sales: $10-20 Million
Number Employees: 20-49
Types of Products Distributed:
Frozen Food, General Merchandise, Janitorial supplies

58994 Rex Pacific
409 Littlefield Ave
S San Francisco, CA 94080-6106 650-589-2020
Fax: 510-487-4610
Wholesaler/distributor of diet foods, Southern foods and ethnic foods including Asian and Mexican; serving the food service market
Owner: Al Kolvites
Estimated Sales: $.5-1 million
Number Employees: 5-9
Parent Co: JFC International
Number of Customer Locations: 1000
Types of Products Distributed:
Food Service, Frozen Food, General Line, Health Food, Specialty Foods, Ethnic, diet & Southern foods

58995 Rey Foods
515 Newark Street
Hoboken, NJ 07030-6552 201-902-1955
Fax: 201-902-0236
Wholesaler/distributor of beef, pork and cheese including swiss, american, muenster and cheddar
President: Jose Rey
Number Employees: 10-19
Private Brands Carried:
Casablanca
Types of Products Distributed:
Frozen Food, General Line, Provisions/Meat, Cheese

58996 Rhotens Wholesale Meat Co
3101 Q St
Omaha, NE 68107-2597 402-731-3310
Wholesaler/distributor of meats and provisions, frozen foods and general line items; serving the food service market
Owner: Tim Schleisman
Estimated Sales: $500,000-$1 Million
Number Employees: 1-4
Types of Products Distributed:
Food Service, Frozen Food, General Line, Provisions/Meat

58997 Ricci & Company
162 W Superior St
Chicago, IL 60654 312-787-7660
Fax: 312-787-7609
Wholesaler/distributor of specialty foods and nuts; serving the food service market
Owner: Tino Marselli
VP: Joanne Colatorti
Contact: Joanne Colatorti
riccinut@aol.com
Estimated Sales: $2.5-5 Million
Number Employees: 5-9
Types of Products Distributed:
Food Service, Frozen Food, Specialty Foods, Nuts

58998 Rice Foods
826 Harrington St.
Mount Vernon, IL 62864-3923 618-242-0026
Fax: 618-242-3109
Rice
CEO: Lynn Withworth

58999 Riceland Foods Inc.
PO Box 927
Stuttgart, AR 72160 870-673-5500
855-742-3929
riceland@riceland.com www.riceland.com
Rice and rice bran oils.
CEO: Danny Kennedy
Estimated Sales: $1.3 Billion
Number Employees: 1,500
Type of Packaging: Consumer, Food Service, Private Label, Bulk
Other Locations:
Newport, AR
Weiner, AR
Knobel, AR
Holly Grove, AR
Tuckerman, AR
Corning, AR Weiner

59000 Rich Dairy Products
1020 Plain St # 300
Marshfield, MA 02050-2155 781-834-0090
Fax: 781-834-0109 888-390-0090
www.richdairy.com/default.aspx
Wholesaler/distributor of milk, milk powder and cream
Owner: Mark Armon
mark@richdairy.com
Estimated Sales: $5-10 Million
Number Employees: 5-9
Types of Products Distributed:
Frozen Food, General Line, Milk, milk powder & cream

59001 Richard's Restaurant Supply
235 S Hollywood Rd
P.O.Box 4035
Houma, LA 70360-2716 985-868-9240
Fax: 985-872-9160 800-874-5263
alicia@galley.com www.galley.com
Wholesaler/distributor of restaurant equipment and supplies including serving equipment; serving the food service market
Owner: Henry J Richard
henry@galley.com
Business Development and Design Consulta:
Richard H. Ryan
Estimated Sales: $1-2.5 Million
Number Employees: 10-19
Types of Products Distributed:
Food Service, Frozen Food, General Merchandise, Restaurant equipment & supplies

59002 Richmond Restaurant Svc
201 Haley Rd
Ashland, VA 23005-2451 804-752-7171
Fax: 804-752-2341 www.rrsfoodservice.com
Wholesaler/distributor of groceries, meats, dairy and frozen foods, bakery items, seafood, general merchandise, paper, cleaning supplies, etc.; serving the food service market
Owner: Lynn Townsend
lynnt@rrsfoodservice.com
Estimated Sales: $20-50 Million
Number Employees: 50-99
Square Footage: 100000
Parent Co: J.L. Culpepper
Number of Customer Locations: 2500
Types of Products Distributed:
Food Service, Frozen Food, General Line, General Merchandise, Provisions/Meat, Seafood, Paper, cleaning supplies, etc.

59003 Richmond Supply Company
420 Doughty Blvd
Inwood, NY 11096-1356 516-239-3400
Fax: 516-239-1540 800-698-4774
Wholesaler/distributor of janitorial and food service supplies
President: Robert Golden
General Manager: Elliot Denrich
VP: Tim Harper
Number Employees: 250-499
Square Footage: 216000
Types of Products Distributed:
Food Service, Frozen Food, General Merchandise, Janitorial supplies & equipment

59004 Richter Baking Company
2901 N Arkansas Avenue
Laredo, TX 78043-1848 956-723-9331
Wholesaler/distributor of baked goods including wheat bread, buns, cookies and pies; serving the food service market
Estimated Sales: $5-10 Million
Number Employees: 5-9
Parent Co: Richter Baking Company
Types of Products Distributed:
Food Service, General Line, Bread, buns, cookies & pies

59005 Richter Distributing Company
PO Box 1109
Norfolk, VA 23501-1109 757-622-7339
Wholesaler/distributor of frozen and dry foods, general merchandise, provisions/meats and general line products; serving city, state and federal agencies
President: Sidney Orlins
VP: Scott Orlins
Square Footage: 120000
Private Brands Carried:
Valleybelle; Suresweet; Kernel Brand

Types of Products Distributed:
Food Service, Frozen Food, General Line, General Merchandise, Provisions/Meat

59006 Rider's Ranch Escargot
200 White Spruce Blvd
Rochester, NY 14623-1605 585-427-0270
Fax: 716-271-4422 800-331-8306
Wholesaler/distributor of fresh and frozen escargot
Estimated Sales: $300,000-500,000
Number Employees: 1-4
Types of Products Distributed:
Frozen Food, Seafood, Specialty Foods, Fresh & frozen escargot

59007 Riegel/Mount Vernon Mills
51 Riegel Rd
Johnston, SC 29832
Fax: 864-688-7382 800-845-2232
www.riegellinen.com
Home furnishings and cut-and-sew equipment.
President: Bill Josey
Year Founded: 1838
Estimated Sales: $50-100 Million
Number Employees: 250-499
Type of Packaging: Food Service

59008 Rigel Trading Corporation
P O Box 1994
Grand Cayman, KY 11104 345-949-5037
Fax: 349-949-5038 www.regaltrading.com
Wholesaler/distributor and exporter of poultry equipment
President: Mike Williams
Manager: Craig Blyth
Estimated Sales: $500,000-$1 Million
Number Employees: 1-4
Types of Products Distributed:
Frozen Food, General Merchandise, Poultry equipment

59009 RightWay Foods
3255 Saint Johns Rd
Lima, OH 45804-4022 419-222-7911
Fax: 419-229-1026 800-443-4855
wfs@wcoil.com www.rightwayfoodservice.com
Wholesaler/distributor of groceries, produce, frozen foods, dairy products, baked goods, general merchandise, seafood and meats; serving the food service market
President: Jim Wright
Director Sales: Mike Chartrand
Contact: Steve Stansbery
stevens@rightwayfoodservice.com
Purchasing Agent: Kyle Edwards
Number Employees: 20-49
Private Brands Carried:
Pocohantas
Types of Products Distributed:
Food Service, Frozen Food, General Line, General Merchandise, Provisions/Meat, Produce, Seafood, Dairy products, baked goods, etc.

59010 Rihm Foods
8360 E County Road 950 S
P.O.Box 148
Cambridge City, IN 47327-9608 765-478-3426
Fax: 765-478-4491 800-846-6328
www.rihmfoods.com
Wholesaler/distributor of provisions/meats, seafood and specialty food products; serving the food service market
Owner: Gerald Rihm
Treasurer: Donald Rihm
Secretary: Gerald Rihm
Estimated Sales: $5-10 Million
Number Employees: 5-9
Number of Customer Locations: 100
Types of Products Distributed:
Food Service, Frozen Food, Provisions/Meat, Seafood, Specialty Foods

59011 Rimfire Imports
781 Eha St # A
Wailuku, HI 96793-3403 808-242-6888
Fax: 808-242-9217 800-832-0933
rimfire@maui.com www.stores.rimfireimports.com
Wholesaler/distributor of frozen food, private label items, provisions/meats, seafood and specialty gourmet foods for the institutional and retail market throughout Hawaii
President: Ron Neal
Manager: Douglas Kramp
rimfire@mauii.net

1151

Wholesalers & Distributors / A-Z

Estimated Sales: $6 Million
Number Employees: 5-9
Number of Brands: 500
Number of Products: 1800
Square Footage: 40000
Type of Packaging: Food Service
Private Brands Carried:
  Colavita USA; Golbon; American Roland
Number of Customer Locations: 350
Types of Products Distributed:
  Food Service, Frozen Food, General Merchandise, Provisions/Meat, Seafood, Specialty Foods

59012 Rino Gnesi Company
PO Box 400
Medford, MA 02155-0004   781-395-8821
       Fax: 781-395-9399
Wholesaler/distributor of Italian food; serving the food service market
Owner: Rino Gnesi
Estimated Sales: $10-20 Million
Number Employees: 5-9
Types of Products Distributed:
  Food Service, Frozen Food, Specialty Foods

59013 Rise Bar
16752 Millikan Ave
Irvine, CA 92606
       800-440-6476
cs2@risebar.com www.risebar.com
Protein bars
Founder & CEO: Peter Spenuzza
Year Founded: 2011
Number Employees: 20-49
Types of Products Distributed:
  General Line, Health Food

59014 (HQ)Ritchie Grocer Co
3210 N West Ave
El Dorado, AR 71730-2733   870-863-8191
       Fax: 870-863-8193
Wholesaler/distributor of groceries, candy, janitorial supplies, tabacco, cigarettes, and paper supplies
President: John Benson Jr
VP: William Benson
Estimated Sales: $1-3 Million
Number Employees: 10-19
Square Footage: 260000
Type of Packaging: Consumer, Food Service, Private Label
Private Brands Carried:
  Market Basket
Number of Customer Locations: 150
Types of Products Distributed:
  Frozen Food, General Line, General Merchandise, Candy, janitorial supplies, tobacco

59015 Ritchie's Foods
527 S West St
Piketon, OH 45661-8042   740-289-4393
       Fax: 740-289-4375   800-628-1290
       ritchiefoods.com
Foodservice distributor
CEO: James Ritchie
jritchie@ritchiefoods.com
Estimated Sales: $17.4 Million
Number Employees: 20-49
Square Footage: 30000
Type of Packaging: Consumer, Food Service
Types of Products Distributed:
  Food Service, Frozen Food, General Line, General Merchandise, Produce

59016 Rivard Power Lift
9300 Lee Ct
Leawood, KS 66206-1929   913-262-3090
       Fax: 913-262-3296
Wholesaler/distributor of forklifts
President: Mark Rivard
Estimated Sales: $10-20 Million
Number Employees: 20-49
Types of Products Distributed:
  Frozen Food, General Merchandise, Forklifts

59017 River Valley Foods Inc
5881 Court Street Rd
Syracuse, NY 13206
    888-647-6632   800-288-4828
       Fax: www.rivervalleyfoods.com
Wholesaler/distributor of frozen foods, ice cream, baked goods, groceries and private label items.
Year Founded: 1985
Estimated Sales: $37 Million
Number Employees: 200
Square Footage: 44000
Private Brands Carried:
  River Valley
Number of Customer Locations: 1000
Types of Products Distributed:
  Frozen Food, General Line, Ice cream, baked goods, etc.

59018 Riverside Foods
2520 Wilson St
Two Rivers, WI 54241-2397   920-793-4511
       Fax: 920-794-7332 www.riversidefoods.com
Wholesaler/distributor of frozen food; serving the food service market
President: Mark Kornely
Vice President: Mike Yauger
myauger@riversidefoods.com
Estimated Sales: $5-10 Million
Number Employees: 50-99
Types of Products Distributed:
  Food Service, Frozen Food

59019 Riverside Paper Supply
500 Muller Ln
Newport News, VA 23606-1306   757-249-3312
       Fax: 757-249-3453 www.riversidepaper.net
Wholesaler/distributor of food service packaging paper and chemical supplies; serving the food service market
President: James Hill
jphill@riversidepaper.net
Secretary/Treasurer: JoAnn Hill
VP: James Hill
Estimated Sales: $20-50 Million
Number Employees: 20-49
Types of Products Distributed:
  Food Service, Frozen Food, General Merchandise, Packaging paper & chemical supplies

59020 Riverside RefrigerationAir Conditioning
6210 Harbor Road
Port Orange, FL 32127   386-871-9841
       Fax: 386-788-6969
www.riversideairportorangefl.com
Wholesaler/distributor of freezers, ice-making machinery and air, gas, freeze and vacuum dryers; repair services available
Owner: Darren Lawry
Supervisor (Refrigeration): Keith Bassett
Estimated Sales: $5-10 Million
Number Employees: 10-19
Types of Products Distributed:
  Frozen Food, General Merchandise, Refrigeration equipment

59021 (HQ)Rl Alber T & Son Inc
60 Long Ridge Rd
Suite 300
Stamford, CT 06902-1838   203-622-7465
       Fax: 203-622-7465   800-678-8655
       mainmail@albertscandy.com
       www.albertscandy.com
Importer and wholesaler/distributor of confectionery products including molded chocolates, seasonal candy, lollypops, mints, toffee, etc.
President: Larry Albert
Contact: Ernest Albert
ealbert@albertscandy.com
Number Employees: 5-9
Types of Products Distributed:
  General Line, Confectionery products

59022 Roadrunner Seafood Inc
548 E Crawford St
Colquitt, GA 39837-5200   229-758-6098
       Fax: 229-758-3991 rrsfd@surfsouth.com
Seafood: catfish, conch, croaker, flounder, mullet, oysters and shrimp
President: James Stovall
Finance Executive: Amy Stovall
Number Employees: 20-49

59023 Roanoke Fruit & ProduceCo
1119 4th St SE
Roanoke, VA 24013-2304   540-343-5501
       Fax: 540-342-1643 www.gottrust.org
Wholesaler/distributor of produce; serving the food service market
Owner: Jennifer Najjum
jnajjum@roanokefruitandproduce.com
VP: Bill Najjum

Estimated Sales: $10-20 Million
Number Employees: 20-49
Types of Products Distributed:
  Food Service, Frozen Food, Produce

59024 Robbin's Beef Company
35-37 Foodmart Road
37
S Boston, MA 02127   617-269-1826
Wholesaler/distributor of beef
Estimated Sales: $20-50 Million
Number Employees: 20-49
Types of Products Distributed:
  Frozen Food, Provisions/Meat, Beef

59025 Robby Midwest
15701 Martin Rd
Roseville, MI 48066-2313   586-775-2429
       Fax: 586-778-1218   800-467-6229
       www.vaporlux.com
Wholesaler/distributor of steam cleaners for interior use on all surfaces
Manager: Larry Cavalloro
Owner/President: Jack Mallow
VP Sales: Rick Esdale
Estimated Sales: $2.5-5 Million
Number Employees: 5-9
Square Footage: 11000
Types of Products Distributed:
  Frozen Food, General Merchandise, Steam cleaners

59026 Robert Chermak & Associates
1940 Petra Ln # C
Placentia, CA 92870-6750   714-577-1157
       Fax: 714-577-0470
Wholesaler/distributor of food processing equipment and supplies including insulated clothing, brushes, washdown machinery, safety items, gaskets, O-rings, etc
Owner: Robert Chermak
Office Manager/Sales: Joyce Daniels
Estimated Sales: $1-2.5 Million
Number Employees: 1-4
Private Brands Carried:
  Refrigiwear; Sparta Brush Co.
Types of Products Distributed:
  Frozen Food, General Merchandise, Insulated clothing, brushes, etc.

59027 Robert Cochran & Company
410 Hunts Point Term Mkt # 2
Bronx, NY 10474-7404   718-991-2340
Wholesaler/distributor of produce; serving the food service market
President: Richard Cochran
Estimated Sales: $5-10 Million
Number Employees: 10-19
Number of Customer Locations: 200
Types of Products Distributed:
  Food Service, Frozen Food, Produce

59028 Robert D. Arnold & Associates
35155 Forton Ct
Clinton Township, MI 48035   810-635-8411
       Fax: 810-635-3291
Wholesaler/distributor of groceries, meat, produce, dairy products, bakery items, equipment and fixtures, general merchandise, private label items and specialty foods including imported coffee, diet foods, spices and diet cookies
President: R Arnold
Sales Manager: Don Elmott
Estimated Sales: $10-20 Million
Number Employees: 10-19
Number of Customer Locations: 300
Types of Products Distributed:
  Frozen Food, General Line, General Merchandise, Provisions/Meat, Produce, Specialty Foods, Bakery items, dairy products, etc.

59029 Robert J. Preble & Sons
5 Westvale Road
Kennebunkport, ME 04046-6750   207-967-3477
       Fax: 207-967-8690
Providing trucking services to the food industry.
President: Duane Preble

59030 Robert Ruiz Company
PO Box 1576
Edinburg, TX 78540   956-383-6236
       Fax: 956-383-7361

Wholesaler/distributor of produce including cantaloupe, honeydew, watermelon, cabbage, onions and cherry tomatoes
President: Robert Ruiz
Estimated Sales: Less than $500,000
Number Employees: 1-4
Types of Products Distributed:
 Frozen Food, Produce, Canteloupes, watermelons, etc.

59031 Robert Wholey & Co Inc
1711 Penn Ave
Pittsburgh, PA 15222 412-391-3737
 Fax: 412-391-7247 888-946-5397
customerservice@wholey.com www.wholey.com
Wholesaler/distributor of seafood, poultry and meat including fillets; importer of frozen seafood; serving the food service market.
CEO: James Wholey
Year Founded: 1912
Estimated Sales: $50-100 Million
Number Employees: 100-249
Square Footage: 400000
Type of Packaging: Consumer, Food Service, Private Label, Bulk
Private Brands Carried:
 Wholey
Types of Products Distributed:
 Food Service, Frozen Food, Provisions/Meat, Seafood

59032 Robert's Foods Company
1615 W Jefferson St
Springfield, IL 62702-4772 217-546-3089
 Fax: 217-546-5163 800-922-2633
Wholesaler/distributor of groceries, meats, produce, dairy products, frozen foods, bakery goods, etc
Manager: Brian Aeillo
CFO: Steve Larocca
VP Sales: Gene Dirusso
Contact: Greg Haack
greg.haack@robertsseafoodmarket.com
Estimated Sales: $20-50 Million
Number Employees: 50-99
Square Footage: 50000
Parent Co: Robert's Foods
Number of Customer Locations: 1200
Types of Products Distributed:
 Frozen Food, General Line, General Merchandise, Provisions/Meat, Produce, Seafood, Groceries, dairy & bakery goods, etc.

59033 Roberts Packing Co
1114 W Randolph St
Chicago, IL 60607-1608 312-243-5770
 Fax: 312-243-5821 www.robertspackaging.com
Wholesaler/distributor of meats; serving the food service market
Owner: Michael Monahan
mmp1114@yahoo.com
Plant Manager: Mike Monahan
Estimated Sales: $5-10 Million
Number Employees: 5-9
Number of Customer Locations: 200
Types of Products Distributed:
 Food Service, Frozen Food, Provisions/Meat

59034 Roberts-Boice Paper Company
PO Box 1110
Poughkeepsie, NY 12602-1110 845-454-2600
 Fax: 845-454-2603
Wholesaler/distributor of paper products
President: Charles Spross
Estimated Sales: $10-20 Million
Number Employees: 20-49
Square Footage: 56000
Types of Products Distributed:
 Frozen Food, General Merchandise, Paper products

59035 Robertson Fruit & Produce
101 Horseshoe Lake Rd
Monroe, LA 71203-2001 318-387-5647
 Fax: 318-387-8404 800-235-1822
 www.robertsonproduce.com
Wholesaler/distributor of produce; serving schools, hospitals, nursing homes, restaurants, jails and independent grocery stores
President: Flint Robertson
jc@robertsonproduce.net
VP: Jimmy Robertson
Estimated Sales: $5-10 Million
Number Employees: 20-49
Square Footage: 72000

Private Brands Carried:
 Driscoll; Dole; Del Monte
Number of Customer Locations: 10
Types of Products Distributed:
 Food Service, Frozen Food, Produce

59036 Robin & Cohn Seafood Distributors
3225 Palmisano Boulevard
Chalmette, LA 70043-3633 504-277-1679
 Fax: 504-277-1679
Seafood
President: Fay Cohn

59037 (HQ)Robin's Food Distribution
P.O.Box 617637
Chicago, IL 60661-7637 312-243-8800
 Fax: 312-243-9495
Wholesaler/distributor of re-distribution frozen food items; serving the food service market; rack jobber services available
President: Robin Wold
Redistribution Manager: John Leahy
VP Marketing: Karen Boehning
Estimated Sales: $3-5 Million
Number Employees: 10-19
Square Footage: 100000
Types of Products Distributed:
 Food Service, Frozen Food, Rack Jobbers

59038 Robinson Canning Company
129 E Oakridge Park
Metairie, LA 70005 504-835-1177
 Fax: 504-436-1585
Wholesaler/distributor, importer and exporter of canned shrimp, oysters and crab meat
President: Alan Robinson
CEO: K Robinson
CFO: Leila Robinson
Estimated Sales: $.5-1 million
Number Employees: 1-4
Square Footage: 8800
Types of Products Distributed:
 Seafood, Canned shrimp, oysters & crab meat

59039 Robinson Distributing Co
701 Robinson Rd
London, KY 40741-9018 606-864-2914
 Fax: 606-864-3252 800-230-5131
 www.robinsonmeats50.com
Meats: hog sausage and deli
President: Jimmy Robinson
robinson@mis.net
Estimated Sales: $5,500,000
Number Employees: 20-49
Square Footage: 40000
Type of Packaging: Private Label
Private Brands Carried:
 Robinson's; Robinson's Black Gold; Cathedral
Number of Customer Locations: 950
Types of Products Distributed:
 Frozen Food, General Line, Provisions/Meat, Private label

59040 Robinson Marketing Associates
75 Poningo St
Port Chester, NY 10573-4011 914-934-2067
 Fax: 914-934-0321 www.logomall.com/robinson
Promotional products, premiums, food gifts and custom chocolates
Owner: Ed Robinson
Estimated Sales: $2.5-5 Million
Number Employees: 1-4
Types of Products Distributed:
 Frozen Food, General Merchandise, Advertising specialties

59041 Robinson Steel Company
PO Box 71
Norristown, PA 19404 610-279-6600
 Fax: 610-279-6646 800-275-6702
 sales@rsclockers.com www.rsclockers.com
Wholesaler/distributor of lockers, shelving, lab shop furniture and fixtures and morable walls
VP: Bruce Flint Jr
Estimated Sales: $500,000-$1 Million
Number Employees: 10-19
Square Footage: 40000
Number of Customer Locations: 300
Types of Products Distributed:
 Frozen Food, General Merchandise, Lockers, shelving, etc.

59042 Robinson Tape & Label
32 Park Drive East
Branford, CT 6405 203-481-5581
 Fax: 203-481-6076 800-433-7102
 www.robinsontapeandlabel.com
Pressure sensitive tapes and labels; wholesaler/distributor of tape machines and shipping supplies
President: Edward Pepe
Marketing: Sarah Yale
Sales: Mike Dellavalle
Contact: Timothy Grahm
timothygrahm@robinsontapeandlabel.com
Production: Anthony Martone
Purchasing: Dennis Smith
Estimated Sales: $5-10 Million
Number Employees: 10-19
Square Footage: 22000
Type of Packaging: Consumer, Food Service, Private Label, Bulk

59043 Rochester Midland Corporation
10788 S Monte Vista Ave
Ontario, CA 91762 909-548-4906
 Fax: 909-548-4907 800-688-7624
 www.rochestermidland.com
Wholesaler/distributor of cleaning chemicals and proportioning systems
Manager: Brenda Barr
Sales Representative: Amer Ayoubi
Contact: Darren Dawson
darrendawson@rochestermidland.com
Operations Manager: Mary Swicegood
Number Employees: 20-49
Square Footage: 40000
Parent Co: Rochester Midland Corporation
Types of Products Distributed:
 Frozen Food, General Merchandise, Cleaning chemicals, etc.

59044 Rock Dell Creamery
6832 County Road 3 SW
Byron, MN 55920-6502 507-365-8610
Wholesaler/distributor of butter and cheese
President: David Distad
Estimated Sales: $3-5 Million
Number Employees: 1-4
Types of Products Distributed:
 Frozen Food, General Line, Butter & cheese

59045 Rock Garden South
2950 NW 74th Ave
Miami, FL 33122-1426 305-477-8833
 Fax: 305-477-2594 www.rockgardenherbs.com
Wholesaler/distributor of baby lettuces, mesclun salad mix and fresh herbs including basil, cilantro, marjoram, oregano, mint, rosemary, tarragon and thyme
President: Charlie Coiner
charliec@rockgardenherbs.com
General Manager: Carlos Davis
Production Supervisor: Carlos Alaniz
Estimated Sales: $10-20 Million
Number Employees: 50-99
Types of Products Distributed:
 Frozen Food, General Line, Produce, Fresh herbs, salad mix & baby lettuces

59046 Rock Valley Oil & Chemical Co
1911 Windsor Rd
Loves Park, IL 61111-4293 815-654-2401
 Fax: 815-654-2428 www.rockvalleyoil.com
'Today, Rock Valley has grown to be recognized as an international manufacturer and supplier of superior quality industrial lubricants, metalworking and hydraulic fluids, as well as reference oils and calibrating fluids tailored to the automotive and heavy truck industry'. www.rockvalleyoil.com
President: Roger Schramm
sales@rockvalleyoil.com
Estimated Sales: $12.5 Million
Number Employees: 50-99
Types of Products Distributed:
 Frozen Food, General Merchandise, Lubricants for food processing machy.

59047 Rockford Sausage Co
209 15th Ave
Rockford, IL 61104-5156 815-962-7351
Wholesaler/distributor of frozen foods and provisions/meats; serving the food service market
Owner: James Ciembronowicz
w.mike@alpineassociates.com
Estimated Sales: $1-2.5 Million
Number Employees: 1-4

Number of Customer Locations: 100
Types of Products Distributed:
Food Service, Frozen Food, Provisions/Meat

59048 Rockland Bakery
94 Demarest Mill Rd W
Nanuet, NY 10954-2989   845-623-5800
Fax: 845-623-6921   800-734-4376
contactus@rocklandbakery.com
www.rocklandbakery.com
Bread, rolls, bagels, cakes, pies and challah
President: Sal Battaglai
battaglais@rocklandbakery.com
Director of Sales: Mike Battaglia
COO: Anthony Battaglia
Estimated Sales: $27 Million
Number Employees: 250-499
Type of Packaging: Consumer, Food Service
Types of Products Distributed:
Food Service, Frozen Food, General Line, Hot dog rolls & wrapped danish

59049 Rockland Foodservice
195 Park St
Rockland, ME 04841-2127   207-594-5443
Fax: 207-594-9016
Wholesaler/distributor of meat, dairy products, frozen foods, produce, groceries and general merchandise; serving the food service market
Owner: Jill Perry
jperry@midcoast.com
General Manager: Joe Chasse
Estimated Sales: $5-10 Million
Number Employees: 5-9
Number of Customer Locations: 3
Types of Products Distributed:
Food Service, Frozen Food, General Line, General Merchandise, Provisions/Meat, Produce, Dairy products

59050 Rockport Lobster Co
54 Commercial St
Gloucester, MA 01930-5025   978-281-0225
Fax: 978-281-8578
Lobster
Owner: Craig Babinski
Estimated Sales: Less Than $500,000
Number Employees: 1-4

59051 Rocky Produce Inc
7201 W Fort St
Detroit, MI 48209   313-841-7780
Fax: 313-841-7858 info@rockyproduce.com
www.rockyproduce.com
Wholesaler/distributor of produce and general merchandise; serving the food service market.
Owner: David Holland
dholland@rockyproduce.com
Vice President & Treasurer: Rocky Russo, Jr.
Vice President: Ronald Russo
Year Founded: 1957
Estimated Sales: $20-50 Million
Number Employees: 20-49
Square Footage: 13000
Other Locations:
Rocky Produce
Detroit, MIRocky Produce
Types of Products Distributed:
Food Service, General Merchandise, Produce

59052 Rocky Ridge Maple
1258 Route 249
Middlebury Center, PA 16935   607-742-9566
sales@rockyridgemaple.com
rockyridgemaple.com
Maple syrup
Founder: Joshua C. Bronson
Estimated Sales: Under $500,000
Number Employees: 1-4
Type of Packaging: Private Label, Bulk
Types of Products Distributed:
maple syrup

59053 Roden Electrical SupplyCompany
5101 South Sprinkle Road
Portage, MI 49002   269-978-3838
Fax: 269-381-6390   800-632-5422
www.rodenelectric.com
Wholesaler/distributor of cables, controls, outlets, lighting fixtures, panelboards, plugs and receptacles, switches and electrical supplies
President: Sam McCamy Iii
Estimated Sales: $2.5-5 Million
Number Employees: 50-99

Types of Products Distributed:
Frozen Food, General Merchandise, Lighting fixtures, cables, etc.

59054 Rogers Farms
210 S Main St # 104
Donna, TX 78537-3257   956-464-3346
Fax: 956-464-9287 info@rogersfarms.com
www.rogersfarms.com
Wholesaler/distributor of citrus fruit
Owner: Jerry Rogers
VP: William Rogers
VP: Jerry Rogers
Estimated Sales: Less Than $500,000
Number Employees: 1-4
Square Footage: 160000
Types of Products Distributed:
Frozen Food, Produce, Citrus fruit

59055 Roha USA LTD
5015 Manchester Ave
St Louis, MO 63110-2011   314-289-8300
Fax: 314-531-0461   888-533-7642
roha.usa@rohagroup.com www.roha.com
Distributors of synthetic colors, lake pigments and dye blends. Custom blends. Patent pending, dust free colors
CEO: Rohit Tibrewala
Research & Development: Mike Chin
Estimated Sales: $2.5-5 Million
Number Employees: 50-99
Number of Brands: 3
Parent Co: Roha Dyechem

59056 Rohrer Brothers Inc
200 N 16th St
Sacramento, CA 95811   916-443-5921
Fax: 916-443-6086 sales@rohrerbros.com
www.rohrerbros.com
Wholesaler/distributor of produce; serving the food service market.
President: Gary Chipman
gary.chipman@rohrerbros.com
Estimated Sales: $20-50 Million
Number Employees: 50-99
Types of Products Distributed:
Food Service, Produce

59057 Roland J. Trosclair Canning
PO Box E
Cameron, LA 70631   337-775-5275
Wholesaler/distributor of shrimp
President: Roland Trosclair
Estimated Sales: Less than $500,000
Number Employees: 1-4
Types of Products Distributed:
Frozen Food, Seafood, Shrimp

59058 Roll-O-Sheets Canada
130 Big Bay Point Road
Barrie, ON L4N 9B4
Canada   705-722-5223
Fax: 705-722-7120   888-767-3456
info@roll-o-sheets.com
Manufacturer, importer and exporter of converted PVC film; wholesaler/distributor of vacuum pouches, table covers, Cellophane and plastic sandwich and ovenable containers
General Manager: Bryce Atkinson
Number Employees: 20
Square Footage: 88000
Types of Products Distributed:
Frozen Food, General Merchandise, Vacuum pouches, table covers, etc.

59059 Rollin Dairy Corp
1320 Motor Pkwy
Islandia, NY 11749-5225   631-847-0558
Fax: 631-847-0113 www.rollindairy.com
Wholesaler/distributor of dairy products including milk, sour cream, yogurt, half and half, etc.; also, juices
Owner/President/CEO: Rollin Gianella
rollin@healthplus-ny.org
VP: Juan Monge
Estimated Sales: $1-2.5 Million
Number Employees: 20-49
Types of Products Distributed:
Frozen Food, General Line, Dairy products & juices

59060 Roma Food Svc Of Arizona
9310 S Mckemy St
Tempe, AZ 85284   480-705-3000

Wholesaler/distributor of beverages, dry groceries, frozen and refrigerated foods and paper products; serving the food service market.
Estimated Sales: $50-100 Million
Number Employees: 50-99
Number of Customer Locations: 950
Types of Products Distributed:
Food Service, Frozen Food, General Line, General Merchandise, Beverages, paper products, etc.

59061 Roma of Minnesota
625 Division St N
Rice, MN 56367
Fax: 320-393-2800   800-328-8514
performancefoodservice.com/roma
Wholesaler/distributor of Italian and Mexican general line items, general merchandise, pizza, cheese, frozen foods and meats; serving the food service market.
President & CEO: Dave Flitman
Year Founded: 1951
Estimated Sales: $100-500 Million
Number Employees: 100-249
Parent Co: Performance Foodservice
Number of Customer Locations: 2500
Types of Products Distributed:
Food Service, Frozen Food, General Line, General Merchandise, Provisions/Meat, Specialty Foods, Cheese, pizza, etc.

59062 Ron's Produce
810 E Market St
Taylorville, IL 62568-2340   217-824-2239
Fax: 217-824-2230
Produce wholesalers
Owner: Tyler Nation
tnation21@gmail.com
Estimated Sales: $3-5 Million
Number Employees: 5-9

59063 Ron's Wisconsin Cheese LLC
124 Main St
Luxemburg, WI 54217-1102   920-845-5330
Fax: 920-845-9423 ronscheese@centurytel.net
www.ronscheese.com
Cheese spreads
Co-Owner: Ron Renard
Co-Owner: Terry Renard
ronscheese@centratel.net
Estimated Sales: Less Than $500,000
Number Employees: 10-19
Type of Packaging: Private Label, Bulk
Number of Customer Locations: 30

59064 Rondo Inc
51 Joseph St
Moonachie, NJ 07074-1027   201-229-9700
Fax: 201-229-0018   800-882-0633
info@us.rondo-online.com
Manufacturer, importer and wholesaler/distributor of high volume bakery equipment including mixers and sheeters
President: Jerry Murphy
jerry.murphy@rondo-online.com
VP Sales: Andrea Henderson
Estimated Sales: $2.5-5 Million
Number Employees: 20-49
Types of Products Distributed:
Frozen Food, General Merchandise, Mixers & sheeters

59065 Rosa Food Products
2750 Grays Ferry Ave
Philadelphia, PA 19146-3801   215-467-2214
Fax: 215-467-6850 rosa@rosafoods.com
Manufacturer and wholesaler of pastas, sauces, cooking ingredients, condiments, etc.
President: Jack Foti
CEO: Giacomo Foti
mfoti@rosafoods.com
Chief Financial Officer: Leonardo Foti
Manager: Mary Foti
Estimated Sales: $11 Million
Number Employees: 10-19
Number of Brands: 9
Square Footage: 68000
Type of Packaging: Consumer, Food Service, Private Label, Bulk
Types of Products Distributed:
General Merchandise

Wholesalers & Distributors / A-Z

59066 Rose Hill Distributor
81 Rose Hill Road
Branford, CT 06405-4015 142-283-9456
 Fax: 142-231-6952 www.rosehillrail.com
Wholesaler/distributor of poultry, beef and pork
Treasurer: Dave Shebell
Types of Products Distributed:
 Frozen Food, Provisions/Meat, Beef, poultry & pork

59067 Rose Hill Enterprises
6760 SW Hergert Rd
Cornelius, OR 97113-6024 503-357-7556
 Fax: 503-357-5522 888-410-7556
info@rosehillenter.com www.rosehillenter.com
Importer and distributor of Chinese ginger products
Owner: Elizabeth Rose
elizabeth@rosehillenter.com
CEO: Leonard Rose
Estimated Sales: $5-10 Million
Number Employees: 10-19

59068 Roseland Produce Wholesale
1827 Ironstone Drive
Burlington, ON L7L 5T8
Canada 905-332-4400
 Fax: 905-332-3321 800-914-7348
Wholesaler/distributor of fresh fruits and vegetables; serving the food service market
General Manager: Rick Squires
Office Manager: Debra Wheeler
Number Employees: 10-19
Types of Products Distributed:
 Food Service, Frozen Food, Produce

59069 Rosenthal & Kline
123 NYC Terminal Market
125
Bronx, NY 10474-7303 718-542-1800
 Fax: 718-542-5523
Importer and wholesaler/distributor of produce
President: Burton Kline
Estimated Sales: $10-20 Million
Number Employees: 20-49
Types of Products Distributed:
 Frozen Food, Produce

59070 Rosenthal Foods Corp
1313 11th St # 2
Sioux City, IA 51105-1720 712-255-7943
 Fax: 712-255-9249 www.rosenthalfoods.com
Wholesaler/distributor of produce, frozen foods, meats and groceries; serving the food service market
Owner: Brent Rosenthal
rofoco@aol.com
VP: C Rosenthal
Estimated Sales: $20-50 Million
Number Employees: 5-9
Number of Customer Locations: 250
Types of Products Distributed:
 Food Service, Frozen Food, General Line, Provisions/Meat, Produce

59071 Rosito & Bisani ImportsInc
940 S La Brea Ave
Los Angeles, CA 90036-4808 323-937-1888
 Fax: 323-938-0728 800-848-4444
admin@rosito-bisani.com www.rositobisani.com
Wholesaler/distributor and importer of espresso/cappuccino machines, granita/pasta machines, electric coffee grinders, wood burning pizza ovens, etc.; serving the food service market
President: Rosanna Rosito
rosannar@rosito-bisani.com
CEO: Bosito
Marketing Manager: Michael Teahan
National Sales Manager: Michael Girgis
Estimated Sales: $1-2.5 Million
Number Employees: 20-49
Square Footage: 60000
Private Brands Carried:
 UL; NSF
Types of Products Distributed:
 Food Service, Frozen Food, General Merchandise, Coffee equipment & supplies, etc.

59072 Ross Elevator Supply
1043 Prospect Ave
Carthage, MO 64836 417-358-5942
 Fax: 417-358-0661
Wholesaler/distributor of grain elevators, pallet durability testers, belt conveyors and grinding mills
Owner: Larry Ross
Estimated Sales: Less than $500,000
Number Employees: 1-4
Square Footage: 8000
Types of Products Distributed:
 Frozen Food, General Merchandise, Grain elevators, etc.

59073 Ross Foods
1044 San Fernando Rd
San Fernando, CA 91340-3313 818-361-3645
 Fax: 818-662-9151
Wholesaler/distributor of dairy products including yogurt, cheese and sour cream; also, Mediterranean food items
President/Coordinator: Sahag Arabian
Estimated Sales: $1-2.5 Million
Number Employees: 1-4
Types of Products Distributed:
 Frozen Food, General Line, Specialty Foods, Mediterranean foods, cheese, etc.

59074 Rotelle
1282 Welsh Rd
North Wales, PA 19454-1820 215-699-5300
 Fax: 215-699-2300
Wholesaler/distributor of frozen foods and general line products
Owner: Jim Evans
VP: Christopher Brown
Estimated Sales: $.5-1 million
Number Employees: 1-4
Parent Co: Rich Food Corporation
Number of Customer Locations: 2000
Types of Products Distributed:
 Frozen Food, General Line

59075 Roundy's Inc
875 E Wisconsin Ave
Milwaukee, WI 53202 414-231-5000
 www.roundys.com
Chain supermarket with over 150 locations throughout Wisconsin, the town cities and Chicago.
President: Michael Marx
Year Founded: 1872
Estimated Sales: $3.8 Billion
Number Employees: 20,000
Parent Co: Kroger
Other Locations:
 Ohio Manufacturing Facility
 Lima, OH
 Wisconsin Manufacturing Facility
 Pewaukee, WIOhio Manufacturing FacilityPewaukee
Types of Products Distributed:
 Frozen Food, General Line, General Merchandise

59076 (HQ)Rovira Biscuit Corporation
619 La Ceiba Ave
Ponce, PR 00717-1901 787-844-8585
 Fax: 787-848-7176
customerservice@rovirabiscuits.com
 www.rovirabiscuits.com
Crackers and biscuits; exporter of crackers
President and Director: Rafael Rovira
President, Rovira Foods: Frances Rovira
Executive VP and General Manager: Carlos Rovira
Quality Control: Carla Traverso
Export Sales Manager: Roberto Ponce
Estimated Sales: $50 Million
Number Employees: 300
Square Footage: 180000
Other Locations:
 Rovira Biscuit Corp.
 Pueblo Viejo, PRRovira Biscuit Corp.

59077 Rowland Coffee RoastersInc.
P.O.Box 520845
Miami, FL 33152-0845 305-592-7302
 Fax: 305-592-9471 866-318-0422
 www.javacabana.com
Processor, importer and exporter of coffee; importer and wholesaler/distributor of coffee equipment and supplies including filters
President: Jose Souto
General Manager of Sales: Angeo Soupo
Estimated Sales: $2.5-5 Million
Number Employees: 50-99
Square Footage: 50000
Parent Co: Tetley USA
Type of Packaging: Consumer, Food Service, Private Label
Types of Products Distributed:
 Frozen Food, General Merchandise, Coffee equipment & supplies

59078 Roy Dick Company
152 Harris Street
Griffin, GA 30223-7017 770-227-3916
 Fax: 770-227-3916
Catfish, shrimp, oysters, chicken
Owner: Roy Dick

59079 Royal Accoutrements
172 W Sherwood Road
Okemos, MI 48864-1235 517-347-7983
 Fax: 517-349-0917 888-269-0185
info@royalcoffeemaker.com
 www.royalcoffeemaker.com
Importer and wholesaler/distributor of tabletop coffee brewers; serving the food service market and retail stores
President/CEO: Maria Tindemans
Marketing Director: Katrien Maci
Estimated Sales: $1.2 Million
Number Employees: 5
Square Footage: 7200
Types of Products Distributed:
 Food Service, Frozen Food, General Merchandise, Tabletop coffee brewers

59080 Royal Atlantic Seafood
2 Carrie Lane
Gloucester, MA 01930-2328 978-281-6373
 Fax: 978-283-7185
Seafood
President: Anne Mortillaro

59081 Royal Banana Co
7201 W Fort St # 10
Detroit, MI 48209-4113 313-841-8683
 Fax: 313-841-3330
Wholesaler/distributor of produce
President: Fred Misuraca
Estimated Sales: $5-10 Million
Number Employees: 20-49
Types of Products Distributed:
 Frozen Food, Produce

59082 Royal Broom & Mop Factory Inc
5717 Plauche Ct
New Orleans, LA 70123-4119 504-818-2244
 Fax: 504-818-2266 800-537-6925
sales@royalbroom.com www.royalbroom.com
Brooms and mops; wholesaler/distributor of brushes and paint sundries
Owner: William Staehle III
CEO: Donald Staehle
donald@royalbroom.com
CFO: Donald Staehle
Estimated Sales: $5-10 Million
Number Employees: 5-9
Square Footage: 36000
Type of Packaging: Consumer, Private Label
Types of Products Distributed:
 General Line, General Merchandise, Supermaid Mops

59083 Royal Crown Enterprises
780 Epperson Dr
City of Industry, CA 91748-1336 626-854-8080
 Fax: 626-854-8090
Importer and wholesaler/distributor of canned seafood, general merchandise, Hispanic and Central American grocery products and bulk-packed spices
President/CEO: Juergen Lotter
CFO: Christine Lotter
Vice President: Jerry Lotter
Estimated Sales: $20-50 Million
Number Employees: 50-99
Square Footage: 90000
Type of Packaging: Consumer, Food Service, Bulk
Private Brands Carried:
 Royal Crown; Corona Real; Costa del Sol
Number of Customer Locations: 500
Types of Products Distributed:
 Food Service, Frozen Food, General Line, General Merchandise, Seafood, Specialty Foods, Bulk spices & Hispanic groceries

59084 Royal Cup Coffee
PO Box 170971
Birmingham, AL 35217-0971 800-366-5836
 webjava@royalcupcoffee.com
 www.royalcupcoffee.com
Coffee, tea, and coffee equipment.
CEO: Bill Smith
Chief Financial Officer: William Wann

Wholesalers & Distributors / A-Z

Year Founded: 1896
Estimated Sales: $100-$500 Million
Number Employees: 859
Number of Brands: 4
Square Footage: 260000
Type of Packaging: Food Service
Other Locations:
  Royal Cup
  Birmingham, ALRoyal Cup
Private Brands Carried:
  Royal Cup; Dine-Mor
Types of Products Distributed:
  Food Service, General Merchandise, Coffee & coffee equipment

59085 Royal Doulton Canada
850 Progress Avenue
Scarborough, ON M1H 2X5
Canada   416-431-4202
  Fax: 416-431-0089 800-661-8137
  www.royal-doulton.com/hotel-airlines
Wholesaler/distributor of dinnerware; serving the food service market
National Sales Manager: Wayne Nutfield
Number Employees: 100-249
Parent Co: Royal Doulton
Private Brands Carried:
  Royal Doulton
Types of Products Distributed:
  Food Service, Frozen Food, General Merchandise, Dinnerware

59086 Royal Foods Inc
8098 Excelsior Blvd
Hopkins, MN 55343-3415
                       952-936-0336
                  Fax: 952-936-0498
Wholesaler/distributor of frozen foods, specialty foods and provisions/meats; serving supermarket meat, deli and dairy departments
President: W Ferrell
CEO: William Ferrell
email@royalfoodsinc.com
VP: M Ferrell
Estimated Sales: $20-50 Million
Number Employees: 20-49
Number of Customer Locations: 200
Types of Products Distributed:
  Frozen Food, Provisions/Meat, Specialty Foods

59087 Royal Foods Inc
215 Reindollar Ave
Suite G
Marina, CA 93933-3804   831-582-2495
  Fax: 831-582-2495 800-551-5284
  info@gingerpeople.com www.gingerpeople.com
Wholesaler/distributor and importer of Australian candied ginger and other specialty ginger ingredients
President: B Leeson
General Manager: A Leeson
Sales Director: Frances Krebs
Contact: Abbie Leeson
abbiel@gingerpeople.com
Estimated Sales: $10-20 Million
Number Employees: 10-19
Square Footage: 10000
Type of Packaging: Consumer, Food Service, Private Label, Bulk
Number of Customer Locations: 500
Types of Products Distributed:
  Frozen Food, Specialty Foods, Candied & pickled ginger & fruits

59088 Royal Harvest Foods Inc
90 Avocado St
Springfield, MA 01104-3304   413-737-8392
  Fax: 413-731-9336 sales@royalharv.com
  www.royalharv.com
Poultry processing facility.
President: Jim Vallides
Sales Manager: Frank McNamara
Estimated Sales: Less Than $500,000
Number Employees: 1-4
Number of Brands: 1
Square Footage: 40000
Type of Packaging: Consumer, Food Service, Private Label
Other Locations:
  Royal Harvest Foods
  Marion, ALRoyal Harvest Foods
Types of Products Distributed:
  Food Service, Frozen Food, Provisions/Meat

59089 Royal Industries Inc
4100 W Victoria St
Chicago, IL 60646-6727   773-478-6300
  Fax: 773-478-4948 800-782-1200
  www.royalindustriesinc.com
Wholesaler/distributor of restaurant supplies; serving the food service market
President: Ervin Naiditch
CFO: Joe Lewis
VP: Jay Johnson
Estimated Sales: $10-20 Million
Number Employees: 20-49
Square Footage: 400000
Types of Products Distributed:
  Food Service, Frozen Food, General Merchandise, Restaurant supplies

59090 Royal Lagoon Seafood Inc
5208 Mobile South St
Theodore, AL 36582-1604   251-653-1975
  Fax: 251-653-1972 800-844-6972
  john@royallagoonseafood.com
  www.royallagoonseafood.com
Seafood
Owner: Valmon Hammond
Sales: Tanya Hammond
val@valssfd.com
Estimated Sales: $5,000,000
Number Employees: 5-9

59091 Royal Meats
464 Forest St
Wyandotte, MI 48192   734-285-1410
  Fax: 734-285-0001 888-285-6328
  info@royalmeats.com
Wholesaler/distributor of portion cut meats serving the food service market; rack jobber services available
President: Greg Arnoldy
VP: Cindy Arnoldy
Estimated Sales: $10-20 Million
Number Employees: 1-4
Number of Customer Locations: 25
Types of Products Distributed:
  Frozen Food, Provisions/Meat, Rack Jobbers

59092 Royal Palate Foods
960 E Hyde Park Blvd
Inglewood, CA 90302-1708   310-330-7701
  Fax: 310-330-7710
Processor, exporter and wholesaler/distributor of kosher foods including chicken, beef, soups, sauces, frozen entrees, hors d'oeuvres, etc.; serving the food service market; importer of canned vegetables and fruits
President: William Pinkerson
Estimated Sales: $500,000-$1 Million
Number Employees: 10-19
Square Footage: 32000
Type of Packaging: Food Service, Bulk
Types of Products Distributed:
  Food Service, Frozen Food, General Line, Provisions/Meat, Kosher foods

59093 Rubino's Seafood Company
735 W Lake St
Chicago, IL 60661   312-258-0020
  Fax: 312-258-0028
Seafood
President: James Rubino
Estimated Sales: $1-3 Million
Number Employees: 5-9
Type of Packaging: Food Service

59094 Rudolph Research Analytical
55 Newburgh Rd
Hackettstown, NJ 07840-3903   908-684-2301
  Fax: 973-584-5440
  lverstraete@rudolphresearch.com
  www.rudolphresearch.com
Laboratory equipment and testing supplies.
President & CEO: Richard Spanier
info@rudolphresearch.com
CFO: Joanne Peppe
Technical Sales: Gary Mathurin
Sales Manager: Peter Marriott
Customer Service Manager: Heidi Spanier
Engineering Technician: Joe Grasso
Purchasing: Cathy Macleod
Estimated Sales: $10 Million
Number Employees: 20-49
Number of Products: 2000
Square Footage: 30000

59095 Rumi Spice
1400 W 46th St
Chicago, IL 60609-3212   213-447-6112
  info@rumispice.com
  www.rumispice.com
Saffron and spice blends
Co-Founder: Emily Miller
Director of New Product Development: Laura Willis
Year Founded: 2014
Estimated Sales: $500,000-$1,000,000
Number Employees: 2-10

59096 Russell Food Equipment Limited
70 Coronet Road
Toronto, ON M8Z 2M1
Canada   416-207-9000
  Fax: 416-207-0519 800-207-9210
  www.russellfood.ca
Wholesaler/distributor of food service equipment and supplies
President: Don Russell
Number Employees: 10-19
Parent Co: Russell Food Equipment
Private Brands Carried:
  Garland; Hobart; BunnoMatic
Types of Products Distributed:
  Food Service, Frozen Food, General Merchandise, Equipment & supplies

59097 Russell N. Roy Company
PO Box 183
Holualoa, HI 96725-0183   808-324-1246
  Fax: 808-324-1197 roybye@aloha.net
Wholesaler of frozen seafood
President: Russell Roy
Estimated Sales: $400,000
Types of Products Distributed:
  Food Service, Frozen Food, Provisions/Meat, Seafood

59098 Russo's Seafood
201 E 40th St
Savannah, GA 31401-9120   912-234-5196
  Fax: 912-234-5703 866-234-5196
  www.russoseafood.com
Seafood
Manager: Nolan Mell
Manager: Bryan Gray
bcgray35@aol.com
Estimated Sales: $3-5 Million
Number Employees: 10-19

59099 (HQ)Ruth Hunt Candy Co
550 Maysville Rd
Mt Sterling, KY 40353   859-498-0676
                        800-927-0302
  Info@Ruthhuntcandy.com
  www.ruthhuntcandy.com
Confectionary products including pulled cream candy, bourbon balls, caramels, assorted soft creams, and sugar free chocolates.
President: Larry Kezele
larry@ruthhuntcandy.com
Estimated Sales: $790000
Number Employees: 10-19
Number of Products: 70
Square Footage: 18000
Parent Co: Kezele Corporation
Type of Packaging: Consumer
Types of Products Distributed:
  General Line

59100 Ryan Potato Company
PO Box 388
East Grand Forks, MN 56721   218-773-1155
                        Fax: 218-773-6591
Wholesaler/distributor and exporter of potatoes; serving the food service market
President: Joan Ryan Mangino
Estimated Sales: $20-50 Million
Number Employees: 50-99
Type of Packaging: Consumer, Food Service, Private Label, Bulk
Number of Customer Locations: 100
Types of Products Distributed:
  Food Service, Frozen Food, General Line, Produce, Potatoes

59101 Ryans Wholesale Food Distributors
1629 King Ave W
Billings, MT 59102-6448   406-247-1400
  Fax: 406-247-1406 www.supervalu.com

Wholesalers & Distributors / A-Z

Wholesaler/distributor of dairy products, frozen foods, general merchandise, general line and specialty food items, produce, etc.; serving the food service market
Human Resources: Wes Carahasen
Transportation Director: L Larson
Estimated Sales: $20-50 Million
Number Employees: 100-249
Parent Co: Super Valu Stores
Private Brands Carried:
   IGA; Shoppers Value; Flavorite
Number of Customer Locations: 188
Types of Products Distributed:
   Food Service, Frozen Food, General Line, General Merchandise, Provisions/Meat, Produce, Seafood, Specialty Foods, Dairy products

59102 Rymer Seafood
125 S Wacker Drive
Chicago, IL 60606-4424   312-236-3266
                  Fax: 312-236-4169
Seafood
President: Mark Bailin
Estimated Sales: $.5-1 million
Number Employees: 1-4

59103 S & M Fisheries Inc
1272 Portland Rd US Route 1
Kennebunkport, ME 4046   207-985-3456
   Fax: 207-985-3038 www.thelobsterco.com
Wholesale distributor of shellfish
President: Stephanie Nadeau
dcowan@lobsters.org
Office Manager: Josh Smail
Vice President, Operational VP: Michael Marceau
Estimated Sales: $2.3 Million
Number Employees: 10-19

59104 S & R Products
765 Oak Rd
Bronson, MI 49028-9353   517-369-2351
   Fax: 517-369-2424 800-328-3887
             www.sandrproductsllc.com
Manufacturer and wholesaler/distributor of automatic liquor control pourers
Owner: Scot Kubasiak
scott.kubasiak@srproducts.com
Sales Manager: Rick Sandvik
Estimated Sales: Less Than $500,000
Number Employees: 1-4
Square Footage: 14000
Parent Co: Kazico
Types of Products Distributed:
   Frozen Food, General Merchandise, Automatic liquor control pourer

59105 S & S Indl Maintenance
Main St
Marlton, NJ 8053   856-768-6300
   Fax: 856-768-8979 800-525-4448
Wholesaler/distributor, importer and exporter of general merchandise including fluorescent, halogen and ballast lighting and fixtures, electric hand dryers, rubber maid products, and tuff coated lights for food processing
CEO: Steve Sandro
lights@penn.com
Estimated Sales: $.5-1 million
Number Employees: 1-4
Type of Packaging: Bulk
Number of Customer Locations: 10000
Types of Products Distributed:
   General Merchandise, Fluorescent, ballast & halogen lighting

59106 S L Sanderson & Co
173 Sandy Springs Ln
Berry Creek, CA 95916-9759   530-589-3062
   Fax: 530-589-3062 800-763-7845
Manufacturer and exporter of handheld capsule fillers and tampers; wholesaler/distributor of gelatin capsules
President: Cydney Sanderson
capsulefillers@gmail.com
Estimated Sales: Less Than $500,000
Number Employees: 1-4
Number of Products: 6
Private Brands Carried:
   Cap. M. Quik
Types of Products Distributed:
   Frozen Food, Health Food, Gelatin capsules

59107 S S Lobster LTD
691 River St
Fitchburg, MA 01420-2910   978-342-6135
                  Fax: 978-345-7341
Seafood (lobster, clams, shrimp)
President: Mark Strazdas
Estimated Sales: $10-20 Million
Number Employees: 20-49

59108 S Strock & Co
63 New England Produce Ctr
Chelsea, MA 02150-1703   617-884-0263
   Fax: 617-884-7310 sales@sstrock.com
                  www.sstrock.com
Wholesaler/distributor of produce including fresh fruit.
President: Samuel Strock
sales@sstrock.com
Vice President: Bruce Strock
Year Founded: 1897
Estimated Sales: $20-50 Million
Number Employees: 20-49
Types of Products Distributed:
   Produce

59109 S W Betz Co Inc
7014 Golden Ring Rd
Rosedale, MD 21237-3076   410-574-1414
   Fax: 410-574-8034 800-332-0322
                  www.swbetz.com
Wholesaler/distributor of material handling equipment, scales and weighing equipment, sales rentals, parts and service
President: Linda Hurka
Owner: Randy Farnum
Senior Service Technician: Michael Foltz
Inside Sales/Customer Service: Jackie Cox
Estimated Sales: $5-10 Million
Number Employees: 10-19
Square Footage: 44000
Private Brands Carried:
   Big Joe; Multiton Mic; Wesco; Magline
Types of Products Distributed:
   General Merchandise, Material handling equipment & scales

59110 S&D Bait Company
PO Box 3525
Morgan City, LA 70381-3525   504-252-3500
                  Fax: 504-385-5412
Live bait

59111 S&M Produce Company
PO Box 6718
Chicago, IL 60680-6718   312-829-0155
                  Fax: 312-829-5442
Wholesaler/distributor of fresh fruits and vegetables, soy products and cookies; serving the food service
President: Donald Mided
Estimated Sales: $2.5-5 Million
Number Employees: 5-9
Private Brands Carried:
   Midas's Touch (tofu)
Types of Products Distributed:
   Food Service, Frozen Food, Health Food, Produce, Cookies

59112 S&M Provisions
5925 Woodland Avenue
Philadelphia, PA 19143-5994   215-205-1802
   Fax: 856-423-0025 fastsr@gmail.com
Wholesaler/distributor of pizza supplies including frozen foods, provisions/meats and cheese; serving the food service market
President: F Storniolo
Secretary: L Storniolo Jr
Contact: Leo Storniolo
ljstornio@yahoo.com
Estimated Sales: $5-10 Million
Number Employees: 1-4
Types of Products Distributed:
   Food Service, Frozen Food, Provisions/Meat, Pizza supplies, cheese, etc.

59113 S&S Dayton Supply
1320 Grand Ave # 20
San Marcos, CA 92078-2456   760-744-3783
                  Fax: 760-744-3920
Wholesaler/distributor of casters, material handling systems, motors and storage and handling systems
General Manager: Dale Newell
Estimated Sales: $1-2.5 Million
Number Employees: 1-4
Type of Packaging: Private Label

Number of Customer Locations: 500
Types of Products Distributed:
   Frozen Food, General Line, Casters, material handling equip., etc.

59114 S&S Meat Company
637 Prospect Ave
Kansas City, MO 64124   816-241-4707
   Fax: 816-241-4717 800-800-4707
             admin@steaksanywhere.com
             www.steaksanywhere.com
Wholesaler/distributor of meats
Chairman: Molly Scavuzzo
President: John Scavuzzo
scavuzzo@steaksanywhere.com
Estimated Sales: $3-5 Million
Number Employees: 5-9
Square Footage: 40000
Types of Products Distributed:
   Provisions/Meat

59115 S-A-J Distributors
3017 N Midland Dr
Pine Bluff, AR 71603-4828   870-535-5171
                  Fax: 870-535-5601
Wholesaler/distributor of general merchandise, specialty foods, private label items, etc.; rack jobber services available
President: Steven LaFrance
CEO: Steve Lafrance
Contact: Rodney Boykin
rboykin@sajdistributors.com
Number Employees: 250-499
Private Brands Carried:
   Select Brand
Number of Customer Locations: 1000
Types of Products Distributed:
   Frozen Food, General Merchandise, Rack Jobbers, Specialty Foods

59116 S. Abraham & Son
7500 N 81st St
Milwaukee, WI 53223-3848   414-365-1727
   Fax: 414-365-1770 www.sasinc.com
Wholesaler/distributor of groceries and general merchandise
Manager: Rick Oglevee
Human Resources: Kim Eggleston
Contact: Chris Rosberg
chris.rosberg@sasinc.com
Estimated Sales: $20-50 Million
Number Employees: 100-249
Parent Co: S. Abraham & Son
Private Brands Carried:
   Chemco; Johnson & Johnson; Unilever
Number of Customer Locations: 1000
Types of Products Distributed:
   Frozen Food, General Line, General Merchandise, Groceries

59117 S. Abraham & Sons Inc.
4001 3 Mile Rd. NW
PO Box 1768
Grand Rapids, MI 49534   616-453-6358
   Fax: 616-453-9259 800-477-5455
                  www.sasinc.com
Wholesaler/distributor of groceries, etc.; serving convenience stores.
President/CEO: Alan Abraham
alan.abraham@sasinc.com
Executive Vice President: Jerry Abraham
Year Founded: 1927
Estimated Sales: $500 Million to $1 Billion
Number Employees: 1000-4999
Square Footage: 210000
Parent Co: Imperial Trading Company
Number of Customer Locations: 2000
Types of Products Distributed:
   Frozen Food, General Line, Groceries, etc.

59118 S. Anshin Produce Company
1117 S San Pedro St
Los Angeles, CA 90015   213-749-1418
                  Fax: 213-749-9472
Wholesaler/distributor of produce; serving the food service market
President: Jack Okamoto
Estimated Sales: $5-10 Million
Number Employees: 10-19
Types of Products Distributed:
   Food Service, General Line, Produce, Potatoes, onions, garlic, etc.

Wholesalers & Distributors / A-Z

59119 S. Katzman Produce
Hunts Point Market
Row B, Unit 213
Bronx, NY 10474   718-991-4700
   Fax: 718-589-3655 info@katzmanproduce.com
                       katzmanproduce.com
Fruits and vegetables
President: Stephen Katzman
VP, Finance: Gary Allen
Director of Operations: Andrew Roy
Manager: Mario Andreani
Estimated Sales: $50-100 Million
Number Employees: 5-9
Type of Packaging: Food Service

59120 S.J. Roetzel & Son Produce
301 S Main Street
Munroe Falls, OH 44262-1608   330-630-9801
      Fax: 330-630-9743 800-676-3355
Wholesaler/distributor of produce; serving the food service market
President: Jeffrey Roetzel
Estimated Sales: $2.5-5 Million
Number Employees: 5-9
Square Footage: 20000
Number of Customer Locations: 200
Types of Products Distributed:
   Food Service, Frozen Food, Produce

59121 S.R. Flaks Company
1610 Hill Cir
Colorado Springs, CO 80904-1112
                Fax: 719-471-9810
Wholesaler/distributor of specialty foods including snacks, confectionery products and beverages; serving the food service market
President: Gregory Flaks
VP: Richard Flaks
Estimated Sales: $5-10 Million
Number Employees: 5-9
Types of Products Distributed:
   Food Service, Frozen Food, General Line

59122 S.W. Meat & Provision Company
2019 N 48th St
Phoenix, AZ 85008-3303   602-275-2000
Sausage, ground beef and patties, portion cut steaks and aged beef sides
President: W David Hart
Estimated Sales: $1-2.5 Million
Number Employees: 5-9
Type of Packaging: Food Service
Number of Customer Locations: 100
Types of Products Distributed:
   Food Service, Frozen Food, General Line, General Merchandise, Provisions/Meat

59123 SAPNA Foods
1154 Oakleigh Drive
Atlanta, GA 30344   404-589-0977
   Fax: 404-589-9711 info@sapnafoods.com
                      www.sapnafoods.com
Beans, chocolate, dried chilies and fruits, mushrooms, extracts and flavors, puree, nuts and seeds, teas, ginger, oils, saffron, spices and herbs.
President & CEO: Rishi A. Nagrani
rishi@sapnafoods.com
Vice President, Business Development: Jack Dahlheimer
Sales Representative: Evan Sowers
Director of Operations: William Sowers
Director of Purchasing: Neil Renfroe
Year Founded: 1997
Estimated Sales: $20 Million
Number Employees: 11-50
Type of Packaging: Food Service
Types of Products Distributed:
   Specialty Foods, Ingredients

59124 SC Enterprises
RR 5
Owen Sound, ON N4K 5N7
Canada   519-371-0456
                Fax: 519-371-5944
Fresh and frozen fish and wild game and rainbow trout.
Manager: Winston Jones
Number Employees: 10-19
Square Footage: 36000
Types of Products Distributed:
   Food Service, Frozen Food, Game Meats

59125 SCR Total Bar Control Systems
1541 S Halsted Street
Chicago Heights, IL 60411-3522   708-755-2266
                 Fax: 708-755-2270
Wholesaler/distributor of cash registers and liquor and draft beer control equipment
President: Michael Gella
Vice President: Alex Gella
Purchasing Manager: Joan Kaufmann
Number Employees: 5
Private Brands Carried:
   SCR; CRS; Samsung; Computap; Auper; USC; Metrologir
Types of Products Distributed:
   General Merchandise, Equipment

59126 SGS International Rice Inc
6 Stone Tavern Dr
Millstone Twp, NJ 08510-1733   732-603-5077
   Fax: 732-603-5037 weldonrice@optonline.net
                      www.sgsgroup.us.com
Jasmine rice, basmati rice, coconut milk, coconut juice, canned and dried fruits, beans, spices, fruit juices, nuts and raisins, tuna, cashew, seaseme seeds-packer in put labels
President: Maria Gorfain
mariagorfain@weldonfoods.com
CEO: Surinder Sahni
CFO: Soena Sahni
VP: Gagan Sahni
Research & Development: Avneet Sodhi
Marketing: Harbinder Sahni
Manager: Dee Mirchandani
Production: Manoj Hedge
Purchasing: Harbinder Sahnl
Estimated Sales: $10 Million
Number Employees: 5-9
Square Footage: 1200
Type of Packaging: Consumer, Food Service, Private Label, Bulk
Private Brands Carried:
   Weldon, Mener
Types of Products Distributed:
   Food Service, Specialty Foods

59127 SONOCO
5450 W Main St
Houma, LA 70360-1282   985-851-0727
   Fax: 985-872-2251 800-458-7012
                      www.sontheimeroffshore.com
Provide offshore catering for people on drilling rigs.
President: Kent Sontheimer
Vice President, Finance: Pam Toups
Safety Director: David Soileau
Vice President, Sales: Juan Cosenza
Personnel Manager: Al Robinson
Vice President, Operations: Mark Hepburn
Number Employees: 250-499

59128 SRA Foods
1608 10th Ave N
Birmingham, AL 35203   205-323-7447
                           www.srafoods.com
Wholesale/distributor of meats to restaurants and grocery stores.
President: Anthony Anselmo
anthonya@srafoods.com
Estimated Sales: $50-100 Million
Number Employees: 50-99
Number of Brands: 14

59129 ST Restaurant Supplies
#1-1678 Fosters Way
Delta, BC V3M 6S6
Canada   604-524-0933
   Fax: 604-524-0635 888-448-4244
Manufacturer, importer and wholesaler/distributor of chef hats, hairnets, gloves and aprons; also, woodenware and nylon/metal scrubbers
President: Terry Kuehne
CEO: Sandy Lee
Sales: Sabastien Lachat
Purchasing: Sandy Lee
Number Employees: 21
Number of Products: 220
Square Footage: 160000
Type of Packaging: Food Service, Private Label, Bulk
Other Locations:
   ST Restaurant Supplies
   Dallas, TXST Restaurant Supplies
Number of Customer Locations: 560

Types of Products Distributed:
   Food Service, General Line, General Merchandise, Rack Jobbers

59130 STI International
PO Box 7257
San Carlos, CA 94070-7257   650-592-8320
                 Fax: 650-592-8320
Wholesaler/distributor and exporter of canned meat, fruit, juices and vegetables including tomatoes. Wholesaler/distributor of private label items and health food
President: Todd Stewart
Number Employees: 1-4
Type of Packaging: Consumer, Food Service, Private Label, Bulk
Private Brands Carried:
   Chef's Choice; Nu Crest;; Portofino
Types of Products Distributed:
   Food Service, General Line, Health Food, Provisions/Meat, Produce, Canned fruits & vegetables

59131 STOP Restaurant Supply Ltd
881 Notre Dame Ave
Sudbury, ON P3A 2T2
Canada   705-674-7673
   Fax: 705-674-1655 800-461-4740
   info@shopatstop.com www.shopatstop.com
Wholesaler/distributor of food service supplies and equipment
Owner/President: Boyd Blackwell
Number Employees: 5-9
Private Brands Carried:
   Garland; Rubbermaid; Cambro
Types of Products Distributed:
   Food Service, Frozen Food, General Merchandise

59132 SUPERVALU Distribution
11840 Valley View Road
Eden Prairie, MN 55344
                           www.supervalu.com
Wholesaler/distributor of meat, produce, dairy products, groceries, frozen foods, baked goods, equipment and fixtures, private label and general line items, general merchandise and seafood.
Chairman/CEO, UNFI: Steven Spinner
CEO, SUPERVALU: Sean Griffin
Year Founded: 1926
Estimated Sales: $12.4 Billion
Number Employees: 29,000
Number of Brands: 13
Number of Products: 5000
Square Footage: 185000
Parent Co: United Natural Foods, Inc
Other Locations:
   Supervalu (Eastern Region)
   Baltimore, MDSupervalu (Eastern Region)
Private Brands Carried:
   Richfood; Great Value
Types of Products Distributed:
   Frozen Food, General Line, General Merchandise, Provisions/Meat, Produce, Seafood, Dairy items, baked goods, etc.

59133 SYGMA Network Inc
5550 Blazer Pkwy
Suite 300
Dublin, OH 43017   877-441-1144
                       www.sygmanetwork.com
Wholesaler/distributor of frozen foods, groceries, produce, meats/provisions and specialty foods; serving the food service market.
President/Owner: Greg Keller
Senior Vice President, Operations: David Myers
Chief Financial Officer: Dawn Rezkalla
Vice President, Purchasing: Amy Humenay
Vice President, Human Resources: Ellen Jones
VP, Business Technology & Administration: Mike Bain
Number Employees: 1000-4999
Parent Co: Sysco Corporation
Other Locations:
   Sygma Network
   Columbus, OHSygma Network
Types of Products Distributed:
   Food Service, Frozen Food, General Line, Provisions/Meat, Produce, Specialty Foods, Groceries

59134 Saad Wholesale Meats
2814 Orleans St.
Detroit, MI 48207   313-831-8126
              saadmeats@yahoo.com
              www.saadmeats.com

Halal meats including beef bologna, lunch meats, hot dogs, salami, chicken patties, hamburger patties, chicken nuggets, chicken strips, turkey bacon, beef bacon, hickory smoked bacon, beef snack sticks, and sausage
President: Aref Saad
CEO: Mohamed Saad
Year Founded: 1976
Estimated Sales: $5.8 Million
Number Employees: 48
Number of Brands: 1
Types of Products Distributed:
 Provisions/Meat

59135 Sadler's Smokehouse
1206 N Frisco St
PO Box 1088
Henderson, TX 75652-6924 903-657-5581
 Fax: 903-655-8404 www.sadlerssmokehouse.com
Barbecued beef and pork, smoked poultry and barbecue sauce; wholesaler/distributor of meats/provisions
CFO: Wendy Frey
wendy.frey@sadlersbbq.com
Plant Manager: Saul Quintanilla
Purchasing: Jarrod Ferguson
Estimated Sales: $6.5 Million
Number Employees: 250-499
Square Footage: 720000
Type of Packaging: Consumer, Food Service, Private Label
Types of Products Distributed:
 Food Service, Frozen Food, Provisions/Meat

59136 Saf-T-Gard International Inc
205 Huehl Rd
Northbrook, IL 60062-1972 847-291-1600
 Fax: 847-291-1610 888-548-4273
 webmaster@saftgard.com www.saftgard.com
Wholesaler/distributor of safety equipment and protective clothing including aprons, disposable gloves, hair nets, rubber footwear, etc
President: Richard Rivkin
rrivkin@saftgard.com
Estimated Sales: $5-10 Million
Number Employees: 50-99
Types of Products Distributed:
 Frozen Food, General Merchandise, Safety equipment & protective clothing

59137 Safari Distributing
1630 W 11th Street
Upland, CA 91786-3555 909-982-9821
 Fax: 909-981-6366
Wholesaler/distributor of ice cream
Number Employees: 20-49
Square Footage: 40000
Private Brands Carried:
 Safari
Types of Products Distributed:
 Frozen Food, General Line, Ice cream

59138 (HQ)Safe-Stride Southern
PO Box 3843
Seminole, FL 33775-3843 727-399-8393
 Fax: 727-391-1184 800-566-7547
Wholesaler/distributor and exporter of industrial cleaning chemicals and slip resistant floor treatments
President: Jack O'Connell
Other Locations:
 Safe-Stride Southern
 Springfield, MOSafe-Stride Southern
Types of Products Distributed:
 Frozen Food, General Merchandise, Industrial cleaning chemicals, etc.

59139 Safeco Electric & True Value
201 Toland St
San Francisco, CA 94124-1119 415-206-0368
 Fax: 415-206-9193 safecousa@gmail.com
 www.truevalue.com
Wholesaler/distributor of lamps, bulbs and lighting fixtures
President, CEO: Tony Leong
safecousa@yahoo.com
Inside Sales: Mike Horgan
Estimated Sales: $1-3 Million
Number Employees: 10-19
Square Footage: 160000
Types of Products Distributed:
 Frozen Food, General Merchandise, Lamps, bulbs & lighting fixtures

59140 Safety Wear
1121 E Wallace St
Fort Wayne, IN 46803-2555 260-456-3535
 Fax: 260-744-9231 800-877-3555
 www.safety-wear.com
Wholesaler/distributor of industrial and commercial work gloves and safety equipment including ergonomic products
President: Dan Brough
Controller: Don Bender
Sales Manager: Dan Brough
Sales Director: Joe Fritz
Estimated Sales: $10-20 Million
Number Employees: 20-49
Square Footage: 54000
Parent Co: Sullivan-Brough
Types of Products Distributed:
 Frozen Food, General Merchandise, Work gloves & safety equipment

59141 Safian & Associates
37 E 28th St # 408
New York, NY 10016-7919 212-594-7780
 Fax: 212-643-6279
Wholesaler/distributor of general merchandise
Owner: Ron Liss
Estimated Sales: $500,000-$1 Million
Number Employees: 1-4
Types of Products Distributed:
 Frozen Food, General Merchandise, Advertising specialties

59142 Sagaya Corp
3700 Old Seward Hwy # 4
Anchorage, AK 99503-6037 907-563-0220
 Fax: 907-561-2042 www.newsagaya.com
Offers retail grocery products and services to local customers, as well as wholesale distribution to restaurants and businesses.
Manager: Tom Griffin
Contact: Lorri Peterson
lpeterson@newsagaya.com
Estimated Sales: $30.7 Million
Number Employees: 1-4
Type of Packaging: Consumer, Food Service, Bulk
Types of Products Distributed:
 Food Service, Frozen Food, General Merchandise, Produce, Seafood

59143 Sage V Foods
1470 Walnut St
Suite 202
Boulder, CO 80302 303-449-5626
 sales@sagevfoods.com
 sagevfoods.com
Rice products
Owner: Pete Vegas
Controller: Whilma Aleman
Estimated Sales: $5-10 Million
Number Employees: 50-99
Type of Packaging: Food Service, Private Label, Bulk

59144 Sahadi Fine Foods Inc
4215 1st Ave
Brooklyn, NY 11232-3300 718-369-0100
 Fax: 718-369-0800 800-724-2341
 pwhelan@sahadifinefoods.com
 www.sahadifinefoods.com
Maufacturer of nuts and seeds. Importer of dried fruit, beans, nuts, olives, Mediterranean foods
Owner: Robert Sahadi
VP: Pat Whelan
Sales: Ashraf Bakhoum
rsahadi@sahadifinefoods.com
Operations: Kristin Fernandez
Production: Brian Whelan
Estimated Sales: $11 Million
Number Employees: 20-49
Square Footage: 174000
Types of Products Distributed:
 Food Service, General Line, Health Food, Specialty Foods, Nuts, seeds, candy, citron, etc.

59145 Sahara Date Company
8456A Tyco Road
Vienna, VA 22182 703-745-7463
 info@saharadate.com
 www.saharadate.com
Dates
Co-Founder: Maile Ramzi
Co-Founder: Jean Houpert
Estimated Sales: $6.9 Million
Number Employees: 34
Private Brands Carried:
 Dates

59146 Salad Depot
51 Romeo St
Moonache, NJ 07074 201-507-1980
 Fax: 201-507-9001 888-774-4735
 zsons@carroll.com
Wholesaler/distributor of canned soups, salad dressings, prepared salads, pickles, mayonnaise, mustard, oilve oil, hot sauce, cheese, ham, ribs, etc
President: Dan Zeigler
VP: John Zeigler
Estimated Sales: $2.5-5 Million
Number Employees: 1-4
Types of Products Distributed:
 Frozen Food, General Line, Provisions/Meat, Produce, Seafood, Specialty Foods, Italian salads, ribs, pasta, fish, etc.

59147 Salad Oils Intl Corp
5070 W Harrison St
Chicago, IL 60644-5141 773-261-0500
 Fax: 773-261-7555 saladoiljohn@earthlink.net
 www.saladoils.net
Vegetable and olive oil packager and distributor
President: John Pacente
saladoiljohn@earthlink.net
VP Sales: Aimee Pacente
Estimated Sales: $5-10 Million
Number Employees: 5-9
Square Footage: 45000
Type of Packaging: Food Service, Private Label, Bulk
Types of Products Distributed:
 Food Service

59148 Salem Packing Company
705 Salem Quinton Road
Salem, NJ 8079 856-935-1206
 Fax: 856-935-2481
Wholesaler/distributor of provisions/meats; serving the food service market
President: Josephine Bonaccurso
Estimated Sales: $10-20 Million
Number Employees: 10-19
Types of Products Distributed:
 Food Service, Provisions/Meat

59149 Sales Associates Of Alaska
1900 Phillips Field Rd
Fairbanks, AK 99701-2707 907-452-2201
 Fax: 907-452-2201 800-478-2371
 service@qualitysales.net www.qualitysales.net
Wholesale grocers.
President: Gary Nance
don@qualitysales.net
Secretary/Treasurer: Carl Olson
Estimated Sales: $1 Million
Number Employees: 20-49

59150 Sales King International
782 N Industrial Park Ave
Nogales, AZ 85621-1732 520-761-3000
 Fax: 520-281-4060
Wholesaler/distributor, importer and exporter of garlic, ginger and produce including tomatoes, bell peppers, beans, squash, cantaloupe, honeydew and tropical fruits; serving the food service market
Manager: Hector Muckui
VP Tropical Division: Joe Sandino
Parent Co: Sales King International
Types of Products Distributed:
 Food Service, Frozen Food, Produce, Garlic & ginger

59151 Sally Williams Fine Foods
46 Galaxy Ave
Sandton
Markham, SA 2090
Canada 711-608-3344
 Fax: 905-474-9210 877-969-5400
 info@sallywilliamsusa.com
 www.sallywilliamsfinefoods.com
Chocolate bars

59152 Salmon River Smokehouse
PO Box 40
Gustavus, AK 99826-0040 907-697-2330
 Fax: 907-456-3889
Smoke a variety of fish products.

Wholesalers & Distributors / A-Z

59153 Salt River Lobster Inc
72 Tidewater Dr
Boothbay, ME 04537-4242   207-633-5357
Fax: 207-633-5357 orders@salt-river-lobster.com
www.salt-river-lobster.com
Sells lobster, shrimp, fish, and various other shellfish.
Estimated Sales: Less Than $500,000
Number Employees: 1-4

59154 Salt of the Earth Bakery
630 Flushing Avenue
4th Floor
Brooklyn, NY 11206   646-330-5089
info@saltoftheearthbakery.com
saltoftheearthbakery.com
Sea salt cookies and brownies
President: Haskel Rabbani
Estimated Sales: $1,000,000
Number Employees: 2-10
Types of Products Distributed:
   Baked goods

59155 Salty Girl Seafood
P.O. Box 6557
Santa Barbara, CA 93160   805-699-5025
hello@saltygirlseafood.com
www.saltygirlseafood.com
Sustainable, traceable seafood
Co-Founder: Laura Johnson
Co-Founder: Norah Eddy
Types of Products Distributed:
   Seafood

59156 Salwa Foods
P.O. Box 490579
Lawrenceville, GA 30049   770-263-8207
salwa@salwafoods.com
www.salwafoods.com
Halal chicken and beef products
Owner: Mushtaq "Mike" Mistry *Year Founded:* 2002
Types of Products Distributed:
   Provisions/Meat

59157 Sam Cohen & Sons
1150 E Maiden St
Washington, PA 15301-3789   724-222-0400
Fax: 724-222-4743
Wholesaler/distributor of confectionery products and general merchandise; serving the food service market
Owner: James A Fratto Sr
Manager: Murray Friedman
Estimated Sales: $5-10 Million
Number Employees: 10-19
Parent Co: Frank Prado Wholesale
Types of Products Distributed:
   Food Service, Frozen Food, General Line, General Merchandise, Confectionery

59158 Sam Gordon & Sons Purveyors
73 N Ocean Ave # 1
Patchogue, NY 11772-2011   631-475-0700
Fax: 631-475-0719
Wholesaler/distributor of produce and frozen foods
Manager: James Maone
Estimated Sales: $1-2.5 Million
Number Employees: 1-4
Types of Products Distributed:
   Frozen Food, Produce

59159 Sam Lota & Son Disribution Company
200 N 16th Street
Sacramento, CA 95814-0628   916-443-3975
Wholesaler/distributor of groceries; serving the food service market
Office Manager: John Metheny
Estimated Sales: $5-10 Million
Number Employees: 5-9
Types of Products Distributed:
   Food Service, Frozen Food, General Line, Groceries

59160 Sam Okun Produce Co
33 N Huron St
Toledo, OH 43604-1075   419-241-1501
Fax: 419-242-6586
Wholesaler/distributor of produce; serving the food service market
President: Shelly Okun
VP: M Saltzstein
Estimated Sales: $5-10 Million
Number Employees: 10-19
Number of Customer Locations: 100
Types of Products Distributed:
   Food Service, Frozen Food, Produce

59161 Sam Tell & Son
300 Smith St
Farmingdale, NY 11735-1114   631-501-9700
Fax: 718-497-6513 mtell@samtell.com
www.samtell.com
Wholesaler/distributor of glassware, chinaware, flatware, paper and cleaning supplies, equipment, smallwares, etc.; serving the food service market
CEO: Marc Tell
VP: Dan Saltzman
Purchasing Director: Lily Midina
Estimated Sales: $20-50 Million
Number Employees: 20-49
Square Footage: 67000
Types of Products Distributed:
   Food Service

59162 Sam Wylde Flour Company
5325 N Marine Drive
Portland, OR 97203-6435   503-283-1601
Fax: 503-283-0498
Wholesaler/distributor of bakery ingredients and packaging; serving the food service market
District Ctr. Manager: Stacy Kvam
Sales Manager: Don Alderman
Customer Service: Pat Estes
Estimated Sales: $5-10 Million
Number Employees: 10-19
Parent Co: Sam Wylde Flour Company
Types of Products Distributed:
   Food Service, Frozen Food, General Line, General Merchandise, Bakery ingredients & packaging

59163 Sam's Cakes, Cookies, Candy
Kitsap County
Bremerton, WA 98310   360-373-8587
Fax: 360-373-8587
Wholesaler/distributor of cake, cookies, candy and supplies, chocolate, flavored oils, popcorn, cotton candy, candy molds, etc
President: Sandra Sanders
Number Employees: 1-4
Private Brands Carried:
   Merckens (Chocolate); Lorann (Flavored oils)
Types of Products Distributed:
   Frozen Food, General Line, General Merchandise, Specialty Foods, Candy, cookies, flavored oils, etc.

59164 Sam's Club
2101 SE Simple Savings Dr
Bentonville, AR 72712-4304
   888-781-5763
www.samsclub.com
Wholesaler/distributor of frozen and specialty foods, general merchandise, general line products, produce, meats and seafood.
President & CEO: Kathryn McLay
SVP/Chief Financial Officer: Brandi Joplin
EVP/Chief Merchant: Megan Crozier
SVP/Chief Product Officer: Eddie Garcia
SVP/Chief Member Officer: Tony Rogers
EVP/Chief Operating Officer: Lance de la Rosa
Chief Strategy & Supply Chain Officer: Monique Picou
Year Founded: 1983
Estimated Sales: $57 Billion
Number Employees: 10000+
Parent Co: Wal-Mart Stores
Private Brands Carried:
   Sam's American Choice
Number of Customer Locations: 460
Types of Products Distributed:
   Food Service, Frozen Food, General Line, General Merchandise, Provisions/Meat, Produce, Seafood, Specialty Foods

59165 Sambazon
209 Avenida Fabricante
Suite 200
San Clemente, CA 92672   949-498-8618
877-726-2296
info@sambazon.com www.sambazon.com
Organic açaí products including frozen superfruit packs, frozen desserts, sorbet, fresh juices, and energy drinks
Co-Founder: Jeremy Black
Co-Founder/CEO: Ryan Black
CFO/COO: Ricardo Perdigao
CMO: Renee Junge
Year Founded: 2000
Number Employees: 150
Type of Packaging: Food Service
Types of Products Distributed:
   Frozen Food, General Line, Produce

59166 Sambonet USA
1180 Mclester St # 8
Elizabeth, NJ 07201-2931   908-351-4800
Fax: 908-351-3351 www.sambonet.it
Wholesaler/distributor and importer of general merchandise including cutlery, trays, coffee and tea service equipment, chafing dishes, etc.; serving the food service market
President: Pierre Luigi Coppo
CFO: Harish Patel
VP: Andrea Viannello
Quality Control: Harish Patel
Estimated Sales: $2.5-5 Million
Number Employees: 5-9
Parent Co: Paderno SpA
Private Brands Carried:
   Sambonet
Types of Products Distributed:
   Food Service, Frozen Food, General Merchandise, Cutlery, trays, chafing dishes, etc.

59167 Samir's Imported Food LLC
811 E Genesee St # 1
Syracuse, NY 13210-1574   315-422-1850
Fax: 315-422-1108
Importer of pita bread
Owner: Samir Ashkar
Estimated Sales: Less Than $500,000
Number Employees: 1-4
Types of Products Distributed:
   Frozen Food, Pita bread

59168 Sampac Enterprises
551 Railroad Ave
S San Francisco, CA 94080-3450   650-876-0808
Fax: 650-876-0338 sales@sampacent.com
www.sampacent.com
Teas; wholesaler/distributor of herbs, teas, honey, bee pollen, etc
Owner: Sammy MA
sales@sampacent.com
Estimated Sales: $2.3 Million
Number Employees: 10-19
Square Footage: 80000
Type of Packaging: Private Label, Bulk
Types of Products Distributed:
   Frozen Food, Health Food, Specialty Foods, Herbs, teas, honey, bee pollen, etc.

59169 Sampson Miller Advertising Inc.
1621 East Hennepin Ave
Ste 226
Minneapolis, MN 55414   612-746-0667
Fax: 612-746-0669 www.sampson-miller.com
Wholesaler/distributor of metal and plastic name badges, interior signs and advertising specialties and uniforms
President: Paul Miller
Sales/Marketing Executive: Matt Paine
Estimated Sales: $2.5-5 Million
Number Employees: 5-9
Square Footage: 8000
Types of Products Distributed:
   General Merchandise, Advertising specialties, signs

59170 Samuel Wells & Company
7190 Pondlick Road
Seaman, OH 45679-9798   937-927-5283
Wholesaler/distributor of herbs and dried ginseng
Owner: Paula Wright
Number Employees: 1-4
Square Footage: 30000
Types of Products Distributed:
   Frozen Food, General Line, Health Food, Herbs & dried ginseng

59171 San Diego Products
P.O.Box 2821
Escondido, CA 92033   760-744-9558
Fax: 760-744-9419

Wholesaler/distributor, importer and exporter of snack foods including nuts and dried fruits; also, candy, whole and dried shrimp and spices; serving the American food service market
President: Michael Perez
Vice President: Elias Perez
Sales Director: Josie McKinnon
Contact: James Mckinnon
sdpsnacks@gmail.com
Plant Manager: Lucy Gaices
Purchasing Manager: Michael Perez
Estimated Sales: $1-3 Million
Number Employees: 12
Square Footage: 40000
Type of Packaging: Food Service
Private Brands Carried:
  San Diego Products
Number of Customer Locations: 800
Types of Products Distributed:
  Food Service, Frozen Food, General Line, Seafood, Nuts, spices, snack foods, candy, etc.

59172 San Francisco Herb Co
250 14th St
San Francisco, CA 94103-2495   415-861-7174
Fax: 415-861-4440   800-227-4530
www.sfherb.com
Wholesaler/distributor, importer and exporter of spices, teas, herbs and essential oils; serving the food service market
Owner: Neil Hanscomb
neil@sfherb.com
Quality Control: Greg High
Operations Manager: John Rabiolo
Estimated Sales: $1-2.5 Million
Number Employees: 10-19
Square Footage: 104000
Type of Packaging: Consumer, Food Service
Types of Products Distributed:
  Food Service, Frozen Food, General Line

59173 San Jacinto Frozen Food
314 S Fannin Street
Amarillo, TX 79106-6758   806-374-4202
Wholesaler/distributor of frozen food and provisions/meats; serving the food service market
Owner: H Vogeler
Estimated Sales: $1-2.5 Million
Number Employees: 20-49
Number of Customer Locations: 300
Types of Products Distributed:
  Food Service, Frozen Food, Provisions/Meat

59174 San Jose Imports
2600 W 35th St
Suite 126
Chicago, IL 60632-1602   773-523-8105
Fax: 773-523-8125   877-385-2486
info@dulcelandia.com www.dulcelandia.com
Importer and wholesaler/distributor of candies, pinatas, party favors and confectionery products
Owner: Eduardo Rodrigjuez
sanjoseimports@yahoo.com
CFO: Evelia Rodriguez
VP: Julio Rodriguez
Public Relations: Eve Rodriguez
Estimated Sales: $2.5-5 Million
Number Employees: 10-19
Number of Brands: 125
Number of Products: 400
Square Footage: 152000
Type of Packaging: Private Label

59175 San Rafael DistributingInc
1270 N Industrial Park Ave # C
Suite C
Nogales, AZ 85621-4555   520-281-0566
Fax: 520-281-9282 sara_campa@srppg.com
www.srppg.com
Wholesaler/distributor of produce including cucumbers, bell peppers and tomatoes
Owner: Adolfo Clouthier
Estimated Sales: Less Than $500,000
Number Employees: 1-4
Types of Products Distributed:
  Frozen Food, Produce, Cucumbers, bell peppers & tomatoes

59176 San-Bay Co
161 E Market St
Sandusky, OH 44870-2543   419-621-1941
Fax: 419-621-9763   800-321-3210
www.gergelys.net
Wholesaler/distributor of equipment and fixtures and general merchandise; serving the food service market
Owner: Michael Gergely
President: Maggie Gergely
VP: Mike Gergely
Sales Manager: Jack Pigman
mgergely@gergelys.net
General Manager: Lori Wilson
Purchaser: Ned Lydic
Estimated Sales: $1-2.5 Million
Number Employees: 5-9
Square Footage: 240000
Types of Products Distributed:
  Food Service, Frozen Food, General Merchandise

59177 Sanarak Paper & PopcornSupply
456 Hinman Ave
Buffalo, NY 14216   716-874-5662
Fax: 716-874-4737
Wholesaler/distributor of concession equipment and supplies including candy and popcorn making machinery; also, paper and cleaning products; serving the food service market
President: Jim Rogers
VP: Pat Rogers
Estimated Sales: $500,000-$1 Million
Number Employees: 5-9
Square Footage: 60000
Types of Products Distributed:
  Food Service, General Merchandise, Concession equipment & supplies, etc.

59178 Sanchem Inc
1600 S Canal St
Chicago, IL 60616-1199   312-733-6100
Fax: 312-733-7432   800-621-1603
www.sanchem.com
Wholesaler/distributor of ingredients including botanical flavor extracts, additives, fillers, etc
President: Sanford Flicher
sanchem1600@yahoo.com
VP: Jonothan Flicher
Sales Manager: Barry Flicher
Estimated Sales: $5-10 Million
Number Employees: 10-19
Types of Products Distributed:
  Frozen Food, General Line, Industrial ingredients

59179 Sanders Bros
4131 Whiteside St
Los Angeles, CA 90063-1618   323-269-0494
Fax: 323-268-1112   800-423-0317
Wholesaler/distributor of produce, frozen foods and French fries
President: H Sandler
VP: J Sandler
Sales Representative: M Sandler
Contact: Mori Herscowitz
mh@sandlerbros.com
Estimated Sales: $5-10 Million
Number Employees: 5-9
Types of Products Distributed:
  Frozen Food, General Line, Produce, French fries

59180 Sanders Candy Inc
23770 Hall Rd
Clinton Twp, MI 48036-1275   586-468-4300
Fax: 586-468-9407   800-852-2253
www.sanderscandy.com
Cookies, bread & rolls, danishes, cakes and doughnuts
President/CEO: Judith Brock
CFO: Joseph Talmage
Marketing Specialist: Susan Leso
VP Sales/Marketing: John McGuckin
Plant Manager: Mike Koch
Estimated Sales: $500,000-$1 Million
Number Employees: 100-249
Parent Co: Country Home Bakers
Type of Packaging: Private Label

59181 Sands African Imports
9 Dey St
Newark, NJ 07103-3609   973-824-5500
Fax: 973-824-5502
Wholesaler/distributor and importer of Caribbean sauces and grains; exporter of canned fruits and fruit drinks; serving the food service market
President: Simon Belfer
Customer Service: Bob Montgomery
Warehouse Manager: Michael Sandala
Estimated Sales: $.5-1 million
Number Employees: 1-4
Square Footage: 80000
Parent Co: Sands Brands International Foods
Type of Packaging: Consumer, Food Service, Private Label, Bulk
Types of Products Distributed:
  Food Service, Frozen Food, General Line, Specialty Foods, Caribbean sauces & grains

59182 (HQ)Sands Brands International Food
PO Box 184
Millburn, NJ 07041-0184   973-824-5500
Fax: 973-824-5502   888-407-2637
Wholesaler/distributor, importer and exporter of tropical baking flour, stockfish, coconut products, potato starch, etc; also, gourmet African products available
CEO: Robert Sandala
SE Representative: Josef Sandala
Customer Service: Laauren Sandala
Number Employees: 20-49
Square Footage: 100000
Other Locations:
  Sands Brands International Fo
  Newark, NJSands Brands International Fo
Private Brands Carried:
  Sands Brand; Caribbean Choice; Maggi Cube-Nigeria; Bacchini-Coucous; Nkulenu's
Number of Customer Locations: 250
Types of Products Distributed:
  Frozen Food, General Line, Seafood, Specialty Foods, African foods, starch, coconuts, etc.

59183 Sanmarc Liquidators Inc
13451 Damar Dr # E
Philadelphia, PA 19116-1819   215-969-6955
Fax: 215-969-5079
Liquidator of frozen and dry food products, selling to end users and the retail secondary market and correctional facilities. Meats, seafood, poultry, dairy, canned goods, baked goods, etc.
Vice President: Randy Stark
Estimated Sales: $5 Million
Number Employees: 20-49
Square Footage: 25000
Type of Packaging: Consumer, Food Service, Private Label, Bulk

59184 Sanson Co Inc
3716 Croton Ave
Cleveland, OH 44115-3406   216-431-8560
Fax: 216-431-5619   800-321-9014
www.sansonco.com
Wholesaler/distributor of produce.
President: Salvatore Zingale
Chief Executive Officer: Jeffrey Sanson
Assistant Controller: Michael Gentile
Year Founded: 1914
Estimated Sales: $50-100 Million
Number Employees: 50-99
Square Footage: 210000
Types of Products Distributed:
  Frozen Food, Produce

59185 Sansone Food Products Co
2133 Jericho Tpke
New Hyde Park, NY 11040-4703   516-746-3695
Fax: 516-746-5935 www.sansonefoods.com
Wholesaler/distributor of general line products, provision/meats and Italian foods; serving the food service market
Owner: Rocco Mastrantoni
rocco@sansonefoods.com
VP: R Mastrantoni
Estimated Sales: $10-20 Million
Number Employees: 20-49
Private Brands Carried:
  Sansone
Types of Products Distributed:
  Food Service, Frozen Food, General Line, Provisions/Meat, Specialty Foods, Italian foods

59186 Santa Barbara Bar
233 E Gutierrez Street
Santa Barbara, CA 93101
   855-722-2701
   sbbar.co
Nutritional snack bars
Founder & CEO: Peter Gaum

Wholesalers & Distributors / A-Z

Number Employees: 2-10
Types of Products Distributed:
　Nutritional snack bars

59187　Santa Barbara Merchant Svc Inc
3463 State St # 205
#537
Santa Barbara, CA 93105-2662　　805-259-3211
　　Fax: 805-687-9329　888-472-2664
　　　　　www.sbmerchant.com
Wholesaler/distributor of point of sale and credit card processing systems; serving the retail market
Owner: Chris Nelson
CEO: Craig Saling
info@sbmerchant.com
Estimated Sales: $300,000-500,000
Number Employees: 10-19
Private Brands Carried:
　Santa Barbara
Number of Customer Locations: 1000
Types of Products Distributed:
　Frozen Food, General Merchandise, Point of sale systems, etc.

59188　Santa Claus Industries
5250 Nordic Dr
Cedar Falls, IA 50613-6961　　319-266-7688
　　Fax: 215-752-1965　www.asicomp.com
Wholesaler/distributor of gift baskets and specialty foods
Manager: Julie Thomas
juliet@asicomp.com
Estimated Sales: $20-50 Million
Number Employees: 50-99
Types of Products Distributed:
　Frozen Food, General Merchandise, Specialty Foods, Gift baskets

59189　Santa Cruz Horticultural Supply
P.O.Box 1534
Morro Bay, CA 93443　　805-772-8262
Wholesaler/distributor of insect monitoring and trapping devices; serving stores and warehouses
Owner/Manager: Susan Stewart
Estimated Sales: $.5-1 million
Number Employees: 1-4
Square Footage: 2000
Private Brands Carried:
　Biolure; Scentry; Trece; Advanced Consumer Products
Number of Customer Locations: 250
Types of Products Distributed:
　Frozen Food, General Merchandise, Insect monitoring/trapping devices

59190　Sarasota Restaurant Equipment
2651 Whitfield Ave Ste 101
Sarasota, FL 34243　　941-924-1410
　　Fax: 941-923-1510　800-434-1410
Manufacturer and wholesaler/distributor of restaurant and kitchen equipment
Owner: Marylin Snodell
Project Manager: Thomas Moon
Sales Manager: Joe Todd
Estimated Sales: $2.5-5 Million
Number Employees: 10-19
Square Footage: 20000
Types of Products Distributed:
　Frozen Food

59191　Saratoga Flour
1400 William Street
Buffalo, NY 14206-1813　　518-584-4282
　　Fax: 518-584-4816　800-641-1144
Wholesaler/distributor of flour, refined sugar and bakery ingredients
VP: Bert Grant
Estimated Sales: $10-20 Million
Number Employees: 50-99
Parent Co: Federal Bakers Supply
Private Brands Carried:
　Saratoga
Types of Products Distributed:
　Frozen Food, General Line, Bakery ingredients

59192　Saratoga Peanut Butter Company
P.O. Box 5111
Saratoga Springs, NY 12866
　　　　　888-967-3268
customerservice@saratogapb.com
　　　　www.yopeanut.com
Almond butter, peanut butter, and nut butter blends
Owner: Jessica Arceri
Marketing: Senia Fleming

Types of Products Distributed:
　General Line

59193　Sarver Candy Co
504 College Ave
Bluefield, WV 24701-4645　　304-327-7017
　　　　　Fax: 304-327-8253
Wholesaler/distributor of candy and confectionery products; rack jobber services available
President: Jack Sarver
sarvercandycompany@frontiernet.net
VP: Pete Sarver
Estimated Sales: $5-10 Million
Number Employees: 5-9
Square Footage: 40000
Types of Products Distributed:
　General Merchandise, Rack Jobbers

59194　Sassone Wholesale Groceries Co
1706 Bronxdale Ave
Bronx, NY 10462-3393　　718-792-2828
　　　　　Fax: 718-829-4378
Wholesaler/distributor and importer of general line items, dairy products, frozen foods, general merchandise and private label items; serving Italian-American restaurants and pizzerias
President: Ralph Sassone
Vice President: Joe Carnevalla
Plant Manager: Mike Merc
Purchasing: Joe Carnevalla
Estimated Sales: $10-20 Million
Number Employees: 10-19
Square Footage: 26000
Type of Packaging: Food Service, Private Label, Bulk
Private Brands Carried:
　Susana; Sassone
Number of Customer Locations: 550
Types of Products Distributed:
　Food Service, Frozen Food, Provisions/Meat, Specialty Foods

59195　Satiety Winery & Cafe
1027 Maple Ln
Davis, CA 95616-1720　　530-757-2699
　　　　　Fax: 530-668-9263
Wines, wine vinegars, table grapes, wine grapes
Owner: Sterling Chaykin
Estimated Sales: $270,000
Number Employees: 5-9
Private Brands Carried:
　Satiety
Number of Customer Locations: 2
Types of Products Distributed:
　Wines

59196　Sauder's Eggs
570 Furnace Hills Pike
Lititz, PA 17543-0427　　717-626-2074
　　Fax: 717-626-0493　800-233-0413
info@saudereggs.com　www.saudereggs.com
Eggs
President: Paul Sauder
CEO: Mark Sauder
Customer Sales Manager: Brian Chmiel
Director of Operations: Joe Brussell
Estimated Sales: Under $500,000
Number Employees: 1-4
Type of Packaging: Food Service, Private Label
Types of Products Distributed:
　Produce, Eggs

59197　Saugy Inc.
9 Sachemor Rd
Cranston, RI 02920-4514　　401-640-1879
　　Fax: 401-383-9374　866-467-2849
　　saugy@cox.net　www.saugys.com
Frankfurters
President & CEO: Mary O'Brien
Estimated Sales: $900,000
Number Employees: 3
Type of Packaging: Consumer, Food Service, Private Label, Bulk
Types of Products Distributed:
　Food Service, Provisions/Meat, Rack Jobbers, Specialty Foods

59198　Savage & Company
P.O.Box 540452
Waltham, MA 02454　　781-893-6600
　　　　　Fax: 781-893-6455　800-660-4666
Wholesaler/distributor of baking supplies including flour, sugar, mixes, nuts, seasonings and flavorings

Contact: Charles Savage
charless@savageservices.com
Estimated Sales: $10-20 Million
Number Employees: 20-49
Types of Products Distributed:
　Frozen Food, General Line, Baking supplies: flour, sugar, etc.

59199　Saval Foods Corp
6740 Dorsey Rd
PO Box 8630
Elkridge, MD 21075-6205　　410-379-5100
　　Fax: 410-379-8068　800-527-2825
　　　　　www.savalfoods.com
Meats & poultry, refrigerated products, non-foods, produce, frozen foods, general grocery items, and seafood products available to the commercial restaurant segment of the foodservice industry.
President: Dennis Barry
dennisbarry@savalfoods.com
Vice President: Richard Hatcher
Marketing Manager: Bryan Bernstein
Human Resources Manager: Paul Self
dennisbarry@savalfoods.com
Operations/ Quality Control Manager: Ron Tew
Production Manager: Joe Savage
Number Employees: 100-249
Type of Packaging: Food Service, Private Label, Bulk
Private Brands Carried:
　Nugget
Number of Customer Locations: 1800
Types of Products Distributed:
　Food Service, General Line, General Merchandise, Provisions/Meat, Produce, Seafood, Specialty Foods, Cleaning products, baked goods, etc.

59200　Savannah Distributing
2425 W Gwinnett St
Garden City, GA 31415-9602　　912-233-1167
　　Fax: 912-233-1157　800-551-0777
info@gawine.com　www.savdist.com
Distributor of liquor, craft beers, wines and sparkling wines.
Owner: Henri Gabriel
President: Henry Monsees
Estimated Sales: $10-20 Million
Number Employees: 50-99
Type of Packaging: Food Service
Other Locations:
　Atlanta Warehouse
　Atlanta, GA Atlanta Warehouse
Types of Products Distributed:
　Alcoholic Beverages

59201　Savol Pools
91 Prestige Park Cir # 1
East Hartford, CT 06108-1907　　860-282-0878
　　Fax: 860-291-8195　800-867-0098
lspaulding@savolpools.com　www.savolpools.com
Wholesaler/distributor of household bleach
President: Ken Camello
ken@savolpools.com
Office Manager: Lynn Spaulding
Operations / Distribution Manager: Ron Webb
Estimated Sales: $5-10 Million
Number Employees: 10-19
Square Footage: 42280
Types of Products Distributed:
　Frozen Food, General Merchandise, Bleaches

59202　Saxony Equipment Distributors
500 Fenimore Rd
Mamaroneck, NY 10543-2313　　914-698-8808
　　　　　Fax: 914-381-2383
Wholesaler/distributor of food service equipment including ice cubers, bins, dispensers, ice cream equipment, etc
President: Jeff Hendler
Estimated Sales: $10-20 Million
Number Employees: 1-4
Private Brands Carried:
　True; Sani-Serve; Ice-O-Matic
Types of Products Distributed:
　Frozen Food, General Merchandise, Foodservice equipment

59203　Scandicrafts Inc
740 Pancho Rd
Camarillo, CA 93012-8576　　805-482-0791
　　Fax: 805-484-7971　800-966-5489
sales@scandicrafts.com　www.scandicrafts.com

Wholesaler/distributor, importer and exporter of kitchen tools, bakeware and metal polish
President: Frank Stiernelof
VP: Christa Stiernelof
Marketing: Joi Elliot
Sales: Marilyn Frates
Purchasing: Kathy Bockal
Estimated Sales: $20-50 Million
Number Employees: 20-49
Types of Products Distributed:
  Frozen Food, General Merchandise, Kitchen tools, bakeware, etc.

59204 Scardina Refrigeration Co.
11802 Coursey Blvd
Baton Rouge, LA 70816   225-214-6948
    Fax: 225-926-6317
Wholesaler/distributor of table top needs and equipment; serving the institutional food service market
Owner: Lin Mercil
Estimated Sales: $5-10 Million
Number Employees: 10-19
Number of Customer Locations: 300
Types of Products Distributed:
  Food Service, Frozen Food, General Merchandise, Table top needs & equipment

59205 (HQ)Schaefers
9820 D St
Oakland, CA 94603-2439   510-632-5064
    Fax: 510-632-2754 www.schaefersmeats.com
Warehouse providing freezer storage
President: Otto Schaefer
Manager: Adam Chan
schaefmeats@gmail.com
Estimated Sales: Less Than $500,000
Number Employees: 1-4
Square Footage: 80000
Types of Products Distributed:
  Provisions/Meat

59206 (HQ)Schaper Company
892 County Road 956
Iuka, MS 38852-8523   662-841-2242
    Fax: 662-841-0302 800-647-2537
President: Kenneth Schaper
Secretary/Treasurer: Linda Morgan
Vice President: Phil Vandevander
Estimated Sales: $20-50 Million
Number Employees: 10-19
Type of Packaging: Food Service, Bulk
Types of Products Distributed:
  Frozen Food, Provisions/Meat

59207 Scheidelman
1201 Thorn St
Utica, NY 13502-4930   315-732-6186
    Fax: 315-732-6219
Wholesaler/distributor of groceries, general merchandise and private label items; serving the food service market
President: D Willis
VP: R Willis
Advertising/Promotion: Walt Wadas
Estimated Sales: $20-50 Million
Number Employees: 20-49
Private Brands Carried:
  Nature's Best
Number of Customer Locations: 200
Types of Products Distributed:
  Food Service, Frozen Food, General Line, General Merchandise, Groceries & private label items

59208 Schenck Foods Co
3578 Valley Pike
P.O. Box 2298
Winchester, VA 22604-1498
    Fax: 540-869-9050 844-372-1860
    insidesales@schenckfoods.com
    www.schenckfoods.com
Wholesaler/distributor of frozen foods, produce, meat dealers' provisions, dry groceries and paper products; serving the food service market.
President & CEO: Jason Huntsberry
VP & General Manager: Aaron Gordon
agordon@schenckfoods.Com
Chief Financial Officer: Bill Edmondson
Director, Inside Sales: Gary Hunt
Director, IT Services: Tom Miller
VP & Director, Sales/Purchasing: Carol Abell-Staats
Senior Purchasing Manager: Mike Dehaven
Estimated Sales: $20-50 Million
Number Employees: 100-249
Square Footage: 85000
Private Brands Carried:
  Schencks
Types of Products Distributed:
  Food Service, Frozen Food, General Line, General Merchandise, Provisions/Meat, Produce, Paper products, dry groceries, etc.

59209 Schepps Dairy
3114 S Haskell Ave
Dallas, TX 75223   214-824-8163
    Fax: 214-824-1526 800-395-7004
Dairy products including; fluid milk, buttermilk, cream, half & half, lactose free milk, cottage cheese, sour cream, orange juice, fruit drink, yogurt, creamers, cream cheese, ice cream mix, cream topping, butter, eggs
Director: Debra Bowen
Vice President: Pat Boyle
Sales Director: Steve Schenkel
Contact: Debra Drinane
debra_drinane@deanfoods.com
Parent Co: Dean Foods
Type of Packaging: Consumer, Food Service, Private Label, Bulk
Other Locations:
  Schepps Dairy
  Houston, TX Schepps Dairy
Private Brands Carried:
  Walmart; Albertsons; Tom Thumb
Types of Products Distributed:
  Frozen Food, General Line, Cottage cheese & butter

59210 Schermerhorn Brothers &Co
340 Eisenhower Ln N
Lombard, IL 60148-5470   630-627-9860
    Fax: 630-627-1178 www.schermerhornbrosco.com
Wholesaler/distributor of butchers' twine and rubber bands
President: Douglas Bryant
dbryant@e-sbco.com
Estimated Sales: $10-20 Million
Number Employees: 10-19
Types of Products Distributed:
  Frozen Food, General Merchandise, Butchers' twine & rubber bands

59211 Schisa Brothers
1 Commerce Blvd
Syracuse, NY 13211   315-463-0213
    Fax: 315-463-0248
Processes and manufactures meat and meat products.
President: Bruce Dew
Number Employees: 47
Type of Packaging: Consumer, Food Service
Types of Products Distributed:
  Provisions/Meat

59212 Schischa Brothers
18 Greenpoint Ave
Brooklyn, NY 11222-1515   718-875-0300
    Fax: 718-875-3031
Wholesaler/distributor of groceries
President: Fred Schischa
Estimated Sales: $1-2.5 Million
Number Employees: 1-4
Types of Products Distributed:
  Frozen Food, General Line, Groceries

59213 Schmidt Baking Company Incorporated
601 S Caroline St
Baltimore, MD 21231   410-558-3025
    Fax: 410-558-3096 www.schmidtbaking.com
Wholesaler/distributor of baked goods including bread, rolls and cakes; serving the food service market.
Director, Finance & Budgeting: Rick Koester
VP, Sales & Marketing: John Stewart
District Sales Manager: John Hecker
VP, Operations: Nick Stout
Year Founded: 1886
Estimated Sales: $59 Million
Number Employees: 650
Square Footage: 84000
Types of Products Distributed:
  Food Service, Frozen Food, General Line, Baked goods

59214 Schneck Beverages
5440 Schenck Ave
Rockledge, FL 32955-5803   321-636-7826
    Fax: 321-639-4339
Wholesaler/distributor of beer
President: L Virgil Schenck Iv
Estimated Sales: $20-50 Million
Number Employees: 100-249
Private Brands Carried:
  Red Dog
Number of Customer Locations: 1000
Types of Products Distributed:
  Frozen Food, General Line, Beer

59215 Schneider's Fish & Seafood Co
2150 Old Union Rd
Buffalo, NY 14227-2725   716-668-6165
    Fax: 716-668-6191 www.schneiderseafood.com
Wholesaler/distributor of seafood
President: Steve Perelstein
steve@schneiderseafood.com
VP: B Perelstein
Buyer: S Perelstein
Estimated Sales: $10-20 Million
Number Employees: 20-49
Private Brands Carried:
  Pearl Brand Products
Types of Products Distributed:
  Frozen Food, Seafood

59216 Schneider-Valley Farms Inc
1860 E 3rd St
Williamsport, PA 17701-3923   570-326-2021
    Fax: 570-326-2736
Milk including whole, low-fat, flavored and skim, buttermilk, ice cream products, sherbet, ice cream mixes, sour cream, dips, fruit juices/drinks and iced teas; wholesaler/distributor of whipped topping, cottage cheese, yogurt, butter etc.
President: William Schneider
Director: Clyde Mosteller
Vice President: Ed Schneider
edjr@schneidervfdairy.com
VP Sales: Edward Schneider
Number Employees: 20-49
Parent Co: Schneider's Dairy
Type of Packaging: Food Service
Private Brands Carried:
  Sunny Delight; Healthy Choice
Types of Products Distributed:
  Frozen Food, General Line, Dairy products & fruit drinks

59217 (HQ)Schoenberg Salt Co
381 Sunrise Hwy # 303
Lynbrook, NY 11563-3003   516-256-0369
    Fax: 877-547-8675 800-221-5105
    wintersales@gosalt.com www.gosalt.com
Wholesaler/distributor of salt, charcoal briquettes and calcium chloride for ice melting
President: Irwin Schoenberg
ischoenberg@gosalt.com
VP: Alan Schoenberg
Sales Manager: Mark Schneider
Estimated Sales: $2.5-5 Million
Number Employees: 5-9
Square Footage: 520000
Private Brands Carried:
  White Heat Ice Melter; Halite; Guardian Ice Melter
Types of Products Distributed:
  General Merchandise, Salt for ice melting, etc.

59218 (HQ)Schultz Sav-O-Stores
P.O. Box 419
Sheboygan, WI 53082-0419   920-457-4433
    Fax: 920-457-6295 www.shopthepig.com
Wholesaler/distributor of frozen foods, produce, general line items, meat, dairy and deli products, equipment and fixtures, general merchandise, private label items and baked goods
Chairman/CEO/President: James Dickelman
VP: Thomas J Timler
Sales/Marketing Executive: Michael Houser
Estimated Sales: $300,000-500,000
Number Employees: 1-4
Square Footage: 1600000
Number of Customer Locations: 90
Types of Products Distributed:
  Frozen Food, General Line, General Merchandise, Provisions/Meat, Produce, Groceries, baked goods, etc.

Wholesalers & Distributors / A-Z

59219 (HQ)Schumacher Wholesale Meats
1114 Zane Ave N
Golden Valley, MN 55422-4679 763-546-3291
Fax: 763-546-0053 800-432-7020
Processor and wholesaler/distributor of meat
President: John F Schumacher
Sales/Marketing Manager: Matt Schumacher
Operations Manager: Bob Timm
Purchasing: Bob Timm
Estimated Sales: $6700000
Number Employees: 20-49
Type of Packaging: Consumer, Food Service, Private Label, Bulk
Types of Products Distributed:
Provisions/Meat, Produce, Seafood, Specialty Foods

59220 Schwab Paper Products Co
636 Schwab Cir
Romeoville, IL 60446-1144 815-372-2233
Fax: 815-372-1701 800-837-7225
info@schwabpaper.com www.schwabpaper.com
Manufacturer and exporter of layerboards, wax paper and steak paper for bakery, confectionery, frozen meat, seafood and poultry packaging
President: Kathy Schwab
CEO: Michael Schwab
mike@schwabpaper.com
Estimated Sales: Below $5 Million
Number Employees: 1-4
Square Footage: 120000
Types of Products Distributed:
Frozen Food, General Merchandise, Polyethylene bags

59221 Schwebel Baking Co.
965 E. Midlothian Blvd.
P.O. Box 6018
Youngstown, OH 44502 330-783-2860
Fax: 330-782-1774 800-860-2867
www.schwebels.com
White, wheat, whole and multigrain breads; deli buns, rolls and subs; bagels, light breads, pitas, flat bread and tortillas; cinnamon, italian, sour dough, potato, high fiber and raisin breads.
President/CEO: Steven Cooper
VP Marketing & Corporate Communications: Lee Schwebel
Senior VP, Sales: Alyson Winick
Year Founded: 1906
Estimated Sales: $130 Million
Number Employees: 1000-4999
Number of Brands: 6
Square Footage: 125000
Type of Packaging: Consumer, Food Service, Private Label, Bulk
Other Locations:
Akron, OH
Saybrook, OH
Austintown, OH
Canton, OH
Cleveland, OH
Hilliard, OHSaybrook

59222 Scooter Bay Seafood Sales Company
739 Roosevelt Rd
Glen Ellyn, IL 60137-5877 630-545-2383
Fax: 630-545-9770 www.scooterbay.com
President: Scott Shoub
Estimated Sales: $5-10 Million
Number Employees: 10-19

59223 Scotsburn Ice Cream Co.
4600 Armand-Frappier St.
Saint-Hubert, QC J3Z 1G5
Canada
800-501-1150
www.scotsburn.com
By the scoop ice cream and frozen desserts.
Year Founded: 1900
Estimated Sales: $175 Million
Number Employees: 375
Number of Brands: 1
Number of Products: 5
Square Footage: 52786
Parent Co: Agropur Cooperative
Type of Packaging: Consumer, Food Service, Private Label

59224 Scott & Associates
2454 N McMullen Booth Rd # 205
Clearwater, FL 33759-1300 727-726-1677
Fax: 727-799-2110
Wholesaler/distributor and broker of equipment for the food industry
Manager: Cindy Mollett
Estimated Sales: $.5-1 million
Number Employees: 10-19
Types of Products Distributed:
Frozen Food, General Line, General Merchandise, Health & beauty aids

59225 Scott Lift Truck Corporation
1400 E Higgins Rd
Elk Grove Vlg, IL 60007 847-640-7880
Fax: 847-952-3050
Wholesaler/distributor of lift trucks
General Manager/Controller: Loren Swakow
loren@scottlift.com
Estimated Sales: $20-50 Million
Number Employees: 20-49
Types of Products Distributed:
Frozen Food, General Merchandise, Lift trucks

59226 Scranton Fish Company
417 N Main Avenue
Scranton, PA 18504-1719 570-343-8054
Fax: 570-344-5551
Wholesaler/distributor of fresh and frozen seafood, general line items and general merchandise
Owner: T Kaeb
Estimated Sales: $500,000-$1 Million
Number Employees: 1-4
Number of Customer Locations: 50
Types of Products Distributed:
Frozen Food, General Line, General Merchandise, Seafood

59227 Sea Best Corporation
PO Box 753
Ipswich, MA 01938-0753 978-768-7475
Fax: 314-241-1377
Seafood

59228 Sea Change Seafoods
334 Upper Ganges Road
Salt Spring Island, BC V8K 1R7
Canada
250-537-5641
Fax: 250-537-0778 888-747-5641
mail@seachangeseafoods.com
Wholesaler/distributor of smoked salmon
Sales Coordinator: Susan Lewis
Types of Products Distributed:
Health Food, Seafood, Specialty Foods, Smoked salmon

59229 Sea Fresh USA Inc
45 All American Way
PO Box 398
North Kingstown, RI 02852-2607 401-583-0200
Fax: 401-583-0222 mfox@seafreshusa.com
www.seafreshusa.com
Seafood including Rhode Island calamari, tuna, fluke, monkfish, skate, scup
Owner: James Fox
james@seafreshusa.com
Accounting: Cheryl Anyzaeski
Estimated Sales: $20-50 Million
Number Employees: 20-49

59230 Sea Horse Wharf
245 W Point Rd
Phippsburg, ME 04562-5127 207-389-2312
Fax: 207-389-1005
Seafood
Owner: Douglas Scott
Estimated Sales: $300,000-500,000
Number Employees: 1-4

59231 Sea Lyons
9093 Springway Ct
Spanish Fort, AL 36527-5522 251-626-2841
Fax: 251-626-2841
Seafood.
President: Martha Lyons
Vice President: Wade Lyons

59232 Sea Pearl Seafood
14050 Powell Ave
Bayou La Batre, AL 36509-2216 251-824-4200
Fax: 251-824-2811
Wholesaler/distributor of fresh and frozen seafood
President: David Robicheaux
Estimated Sales: $3-5 Million
Number Employees: 1-4
Types of Products Distributed:
Frozen Food, Seafood

59233 Sea Products West Inc
851 Coho Way # 304
Bellingham, WA 98225-2066 360-733-2992
Fax: 360-733-2991 roger@spwfish.com
www.seaproductswest.com
Wholesaler/distributor of fresh seafood
President: Roger Grummel
roger@spwfish.com
Estimated Sales: $2.5-5 Million
Number Employees: 1-4
Types of Products Distributed:
Frozen Food, Seafood

59234 Sea Salt Superstore
11604 Airport Rd
Suite D300
Everett, WA 98204 425-249-2331
Fax: 425-249-2334
customerservice@seasaltsuperstore.com
www.seasaltsuperstore.com
Flavored sea salt
President: Scott Mackie
Customer Service & Sales: Jenny Mackie
Estimated Sales: $1 Million
Number Employees: 2-10
Types of Products Distributed:
Specialty Foods, Sea salt

59235 Sea-Fresh Seafood Market
1432 Hillcrest Rd
Mobile, AL 36695 251-634-8650
Fax: 714-897-4090
Seafood
President: Patrick Meacham
CFO: Rusty Brennan

59236 Seabreeze Fish
2311 R Street
Bakersfield, CA 93301-2986 661-323-7936
Fax: 805-323-7936
Seafood
Owner: Ben Kim
Estimated Sales: $300,000-500,000
Number Employees: 1-4

59237 Seacore Seafood
81 Aviva Park Drive
Vaughan, ON L4L 9C1
Canada 905-856-6222
Fax: 905-856-9445 800-563-6222
info@seacoreseafood.com
www.seacoreseafood.com
Wholesaler/distributor/importer/custom processor of fresh and frozen seafood, fish, and live lobsters.
Number Employees: 85
Square Footage: 308000
Types of Products Distributed:
Seafood

59238 Seacrest Foods
86 Bennett St
Lynn, MA 01905-3011 781-581-2066
Fax: 781-581-1767 www.seacrestfoods.com
Cheese and dairy, chips, pretzels, snacks, pasta, chocolate, seafood, meat, fruits and nuts, beverages, baked goods and spices.
Owner: Robert Di Tomaso
Sales Manager: Shawn Hockert
bditomaso@seacrestfoods.com
Director, Warehouse Operations: Dominic Garcia
Purchasing: Bob Holmes
Estimated Sales: $2-3 Million
Number Employees: 50-99
Square Footage: 56000
Parent Co: Nautilius Foods
Private Brands Carried:
Sea Sausage; Seacrest Select
Number of Customer Locations: 500
Types of Products Distributed:
Food Service, Frozen Food, Seafood, Smoked seafood products

59239 Seacrest Foods
86 Bennett St
Lynn, MA 01905-3011 781-581-2066
Fax: 781-581-1767 www.seacrestfoods.com

International importer and wholesale distributor of specialty cheeses and fine foods including cheese, specialty meats, pasta, specialty grocery items, chocolates, desserts
Owner: Robert Di Tomaso
bditomaso@seacrestfoods.com
Number Employees: 50-99

59240 Seafare Market Wholesale
PO Box 671
Moody, ME 04054-0671   207-646-5160
                              Fax: 408-294-3948
Seafood
President: John Foye
Estimated Sales: $10-20 Million
Number Employees: 10-19

59241 Seafood & Meat
5681 Highway 90
Theodore, AL 36582-1671   251-653-4600
                              Fax: 251-653-1109
Seafood and meat distributors.
President: Ruth Summerlin

59242 Seafood Connection
841 Pohukaina St # I
Suite I
Honolulu, HI 96813-5332   808-591-8550
Fax: 808-591-8445 sales@seafood-connection.com
www.seafood-connection.com
Seafood and gourmet products
President: Stuart Simmons
Estimated Sales: $10-20 Million
Number Employees: 10-19

59243 Seafood Dimensions Intl
22343 LA Palma Ave # 106
Suite 106
Yorba Linda, CA 92887-3804   714-692-6464
                              Fax: 714-282-8997
Seafood
Owner: Christi Lang
Estimated Sales: $1.4 Million
Number Employees: 5-9
Number of Brands: 20
Number of Products: 50
Type of Packaging: Food Service
Private Brands Carried:
  Lil's Fisherman, Midship, Brooks Street, 20th Century, Harvest Farms, Caltex
Types of Products Distributed:
  Food Service, Frozen Food, Provisions/Meat, Seafood

59244 Seafood Distributors
420 W Bay Street
Savannah, GA 31401-1115   912-233-6048
                              Fax: 612-233-3238
Seafood
President: Walter Bryan

59245 Seafood Express
179 Rossmore Rd
Brunswick, ME 04011   207-729-0887
                              Fax: 207-721-9146
Seafood
Contact: Thida Pov
tpov@seafoodexpress.in

59246 Seafood Merchants LTD
900 Forest Edge Dr
Vernon Hills, IL 60061-3105   847-634-0900
                              Fax: 847-634-1351
                  sales@theseafoodmerchants.com
Seafood
President: Roy Axelson
bonnie@theseafoodmerchants.com
CEO: Bonnie Axelson
bonnie@theseafoodmerchants.com
Sales Exec: Bonnie Axelson
Estimated Sales: $10-20 Million
Number Employees: 20-49
Square Footage: 23000
Type of Packaging: Consumer, Food Service, Bulk

59247 Seafood Packaging Inc
2120 Poydras St
New Orleans, LA 70112-1339   504-522-6677
Fax: 504-522-9008 800-949-9656
                   ksharp@seafoodpackaging.com
                   www.seafoodpackaging.com
Seafood
Owner: Kent Sharp
ksharp@seafoodpackaging.com

Estimated Sales: $5-10 Million
Number Employees: 5-9
Type of Packaging: Consumer

59248 Seafood Plus Corporation
10860 Bear Island Avenue
Orland Park, IL 60467-5397   708-795-4820
                              Fax: 708-795-7719
Seafood
President: Harry A Davros

59249 Seafood Services
49 Bromfield St
Newburyport, MA 01950-3003   508-999-6785
                              Fax: 508-993-4001
Seafood
President: David Horton
Contact: Dan Canavan
dcanavan@foodinno.com
Estimated Sales: $20-50 Million
Number Employees: 20-49

59250 Sealand Lobster Corporation
PO Box 423
Tenants Harbor, ME 04860-0423 207-372-6247
                               Fax: 207-389-1819
Lobster

59251 Sealer Sales Inc
8820 Baird Ave
Northridge, CA 91324-4007   818-718-8818
Fax: 818-718-8857   877-705-0203
contact@sealersales.com   www.sealersales.com
Wholesaler/distributor of heat sealers, packaging machinery and shrink wrap packaging
Owner: Judy Hwang
judy@sealersales.com
Estimated Sales: Less Than $500,000
Number Employees: 1-4
Types of Products Distributed:
  Frozen Food, General Merchandise, Heat sealers & packaging machinery

59252 Seattle Fish Co
6211 E 42nd Ave
Denver, CO 80216   303-329-9595
                              800-766-3787
info@seattlefish.com   www.seattlefish.com
Wholesaler/distributor of seafood; serving the food service and retail market.
Chief Executive Officer: James Iacino
President: Derek Figueroa
Chief Financial Officer: Pete McClure
Chief People Officer: Ann Levine
Chief Operations Officer: Hamish Walker
Year Founded: 1918
Estimated Sales: $34 Million
Number Employees: 135
Square Footage: 62683
Types of Products Distributed:
  Food Service, Frozen Food, Seafood, Specialty Foods

59253 (HQ)Seattle's Best Coffee
PO Box 3717
Seattle, WA 98124-8891
                              800-611-7793
            customercare@seattlesbest.com
                   www.seattlesbest.com
Ground coffee and beans
Manager: James Strasbaugh
Contact: Donald Blankenship
don.blankenship@seattle.gov
Estimated Sales: $10.9 Million
Number Employees: 100-249
Type of Packaging: Consumer, Food Service
Private Brands Carried:
  Seattle's Best
Types of Products Distributed:
  Food Service, Frozen Food, General Line, Ground coffee & beans

59254 Seaview Lobster Co
43 Government St
Kittery, ME 03904-1652   207-439-1599
Fax: 207-439-1476   800-245-4997
              orders@seaviewlobster.com
              www.seaviewlobster.com
Seafood
Owner: Tom Flanagan
seaviewlob@comcast.net
Estimated Sales: $.5-1 million
Number Employees: 10-19

59255 Seaway Company
PO Box 868
Fairhaven, MA 02719-0800   508-992-1221
                              Fax: 508-992-1253
Seafood
Owner: Steve Doonan
Estimated Sales: $1-3 Million
Number Employees: 1-4

59256 Secure Packaging
42 Hunter Ln
Centereach, NY 11720   631-585-2559
Fax: 631-585-3557   800-834-5330
Wholesaler/distributor of plastic bags, film and foam, janitorial supplies, packaging machinery and cartons
Owner: Robert Paolillo
Estimated Sales: $1-2.5 Million
Number Employees: 1-4
Private Brands Carried:
  Secure Wrap

59257 Seder Foods Corporation
P.O.Box 1015
Palmer, MA 01069   413-283-2565
                              Fax: 413-283-9444
Wholesaler/distributor of dairy products, private label items, frozen foods and general line items; serving the food service market; rack jobber services available
President: Ed Greenbaum
VP Sales: B Theodore
Estimated Sales: $20-50 Million
Number Employees: 20-49
Private Brands Carried:
  Grocers Pride; Honey Hill; Thoro Fare
Number of Customer Locations: 130
Types of Products Distributed:
  Food Service, Frozen Food, General Line, Rack Jobbers, Dairy products & private label items

59258 See's Candy Shops
20600 South Alameda Street
Carson, CA 90810   602-266-1727
Fax: 602-265-5115   800-930-7337
           SeesCandiesCustomerCare@sees.com
                       www.sees.com
Wholesaler/distributor of candy and confectionery products
Manager: Debbie Carnahan
Assistant Manager: Cindy Vance
Contact: Kern Derrill
kderrill@sees.com
Estimated Sales: Less than $500,000
Number Employees: 5-9
Types of Products Distributed:
  General Line, Candy & confectionery

59259 Segal's Wholesale
3320 E 41st Street
Minneapolis, MN 55406-3320   612-724-1866
                              Fax: 612-724-1706
Wholesaler/distributor of candy, paper goods and snack foods; serving the food service market
President: R Segal
Secretary/Treasurer: L Segal
VP: S Segal
Estimated Sales: $10-20 Million
Number Employees: 20-49
Types of Products Distributed:
  Food Service, Frozen Food, General Line, General Merchandise, Candy, paper goods & snack foods

59260 Seitz Gift Fruit
P.O.Box 1699
Fredericksburg, TX 78624   888-390-4332
Fax: 830-990-9221   800-423-9764
            info@seitznet.com   www.seitznet.com
Wholesaler/distributor of fruit gift baskets to be used as fundraising items for schools
Manager: Juan Guerrero
Estimated Sales: $300,000-500,000
Number Employees: 1-4
Types of Products Distributed:
  Food Service, Frozen Food, General Merchandise, Fruit gift baskets

59261 Selby Johnson Corporation
779 W 43rd St
Davenport, IA 52806   563-391-8599
Wholesaler/distributor of regular and German-style mustard and horseradish
VP: Ann Johnson

Wholesalers & Distributors / A-Z

Estimated Sales: $1-3 Million
Number Employees: 1-4
Private Brands Carried:
  Max Moeller; Roenfeldt's
Types of Products Distributed:
  General Line, Regular & German mustard & horseradish

59262 Select Meat Company
PO Box 21308
Los Angeles, CA 90021-0308   213-621-0900
                 Fax: 213-621-0909
Wholesaler/distributor, importer and exporter of raw and processed meat, poultry, seafood, coffee, cheese, butter and margarine; serving the food service market
President: Ed Murphy
VP: Gerry Rose
VP (Asian Markets): Nhon Hien
Number Employees: 10-19
Type of Packaging: Food Service
Types of Products Distributed:
  Food Service, Frozen Food, General Line, Provisions/Meat, Seafood, Coffee, cheese, butter, margarine, etc.

59263 Sellers Equipment Inc
1645 S West St
Wichita, KS 67213-1101   316-943-9311
         Fax: 316-943-8116 877-522-4834
Wholesaler/distributor of forklifts, pallet racks and industrial batteries
Vice President: Don Sellers
sellers@sellersequipment.com
VP: Ron Mitchell
Sales Manager: Tom Golden
Estimated Sales: $10-20 Million
Number Employees: 20-49
Private Brands Carried:
  Hyster; Hi-Line; Gnbkhampion
Types of Products Distributed:
  Frozen Food, General Merchandise, Forklifts, pallet racks, etc.

59264 Seltzer Chemicals
5927 Geiger Ct
Carlsbad, CA 92008   760-438-0089
         Fax: 760-438-0336 800-735-8137
Wholesaler/distributor of custom blended bulk fine chemicals, vitamin pre-mixes and colors
Executive VP: Trent Seltzer
Estimated Sales: $50-100 Million
Number Employees: 50-99
Square Footage: 60000
Type of Packaging: Bulk
Types of Products Distributed:
  Frozen Food, Health Food, Raw ingredients, colors, etc.

59265 Serendib Tea Company
4806 W 129th Street
Alsip, IL 60803-3016   708-489-9980
         Fax: 708-489-9973 serendibtea@hotmail.com
Ceylon tea
President: Munira Nomanbhoy
Private Brands Carried:
  Senok; Serendib
Types of Products Distributed:
  Frozen Food, General Line, Ceylon tea

59266 Serendipitea
73 Plandome Rd
Manhasset, NY 11030-2330   516-365-7711
         Fax: 516-365-7733 888-832-5433
tea@serendipitea.com www.serendipitea.com
Tea; premium grade loose leaf
Principal: Linda Villano
tea@serendipitea.com
Estimated Sales: Less than $500,000
Number Employees: 5-9
Number of Brands: 1
Number of Products: 100+
Square Footage: 12000
Type of Packaging: Consumer, Food Service, Private Label, Bulk
Types of Products Distributed:
  Tea, Tisane

59267 Serendipity of the Valley
P O Box 1601
San Benito, TX 78586   956-535-0025
Wholesaler/distributor of jams and jellies
President: Christine Caffey

Estimated Sales: $300,000-500,000
Number Employees: 1-4
Types of Products Distributed:
  Frozen Food, General Line, Jams & jellies

59268 Serv-A-Rack
P.O.Box 310
Lakewood, OH 44107   216-941-6570
                 Fax: 216-941-9919
Wholesaler/distributor of health and beauty aids, lotions, housewares and stationery; also, rack jobber services available
President: W Grimmer
VP: D Grimmer
Estimated Sales: $20-50 Million
Number Employees: 50-99
Square Footage: 80000
Number of Customer Locations: 520
Types of Products Distributed:
  Frozen Food, General Merchandise, Rack Jobbers

59269 Serv-Tek
5235 Timberlea Boulevard
Mississauga, ON L4W 2S3
Canada   905-602-8300
         Fax: 905-602-8303 servtek@idirect.com
Wholesaler/distributor of restaurant equipment; serving the food service market
President: John Green
Secretary/Treasurer: Linda Green
Number Employees: 5-9
Square Footage: 24000
Private Brands Carried:
  Hobart; Vulcan; Garland
Types of Products Distributed:
  Food Service, General Merchandise

59270 Serve Canada Food Equipment
22 Ashwarren Road
Toronto, ON M3J 1Z5
Canada   416-631-0601
         Fax: 416-631-7687 800-263-1455
econstantinou@servecanada.com
www.servecanada.com
Wholesaler/distributor of equipment and supplies; serving the food service market
President: Tom Constantinou
Marketing Director: Tom Constantinou
Number Employees: 20-49
Private Brands Carried:
  Stoelting
Types of Products Distributed:
  Food Service, Frozen Food, General Merchandise, Equipment & supplies

59271 Service Handling Equipment Company
25 W Union St
Suite 202
Ashland, MA 01721-1465   508-429-4542
         Fax: 508-881-6263 800-527-1160
Wholesaler/distributor of general merchandise including material handling equipment
President: Scott Rose
CFO: Beverly Rose
Sales Director: Brad Rose
Estimated Sales: $2.5-5 Million
Number Employees: 1-4
Private Brands Carried:
  Prest; Hamilton; ISC; Intermetro; MetalMasters; Republic
Types of Products Distributed:
  Frozen Food, General Merchandise, Material handling equipment

59272 Service Market
8100 Paradise Rd
Lamont, CA 93241   661-845-0489
Wholesaler/distributor of meats; serving the food service market
Owner: Kuen Lau
Estimated Sales: $1-2.5 Million
Number Employees: 5-9
Types of Products Distributed:
  Food Service, Frozen Food, Provisions/Meat

59273 Service Sales Corporation
390 Richmond St E
South St Paul, MN 55075-5939   651-451-2206
         Fax: 651-451-2710 800-225-6128
Wholesaler/distributor of labels, price marking equipment, bar code printers and thermal supplies
President: Rob Iten

Estimated Sales: $5-10 Million
Number Employees: 10-19
Square Footage: 56000
Types of Products Distributed:
  General Merchandise, Labels, price marking equipment, etc.

59274 Setton International Foods
85 Austin Blvd
Commack, NY 11725   631-543-8090
         Fax: 631-543-8070 800-227-4397
info@settonfarms.com
www.settoninternational.com
Pistachios, cashews, almonds, apricots, candy and snack foods
President: Joshua Setton
VP, Domestic Sales & Marketing: Joseph Setton
Human Resources Coordinator: Kellie Shepard
Logistics Manager: Patrick Braddock
Production Manager: Henry Scott
Plant Manager: Jeffrey Gibbons
Estimated Sales: $64 Million
Number Employees: 250-499
Square Footage: 55000
Type of Packaging: Consumer, Food Service, Private Label, Bulk
Other Locations:
  Processing Facility
  Terra Bella, CA Processing Facility Zutphen, The Netherlands
Types of Products Distributed:
  Nuts & Dried Fruits

59275 Seven K Feather Farm
3155 W 650 N
Taylorsville, IN 47280-7703   812-526-2651
         Fax: 812-526-2723 www.7kfarms.com
Wholesaler/distributor of cheese, produce, canned goods, fresh and frozen foods; serving the food service market
Owner: James Kleinhenz
Estimated Sales: $20-50 Million
Number Employees: 20-49
Types of Products Distributed:
  Food Service, Frozen Food, General Line, Produce

59276 Seven K Feather Farm
3155 W 650 N
Taylorsville, IN 47280-7703   812-526-2651
         Fax: 812-526-2723 www.7kfarms.com
Wholesale/distributor of food
Owner: James Kleinhenz
Estimated Sales: Below $5 Million
Number Employees: 20-49

59277 Seven K Feather Farm
3155 W 650 N
Taylorsville, IN 47280-7703   812-526-2651
         Fax: 812-526-2723 www.7kfarms.com
Owner: James Kleinhenz
Estimated Sales: $20-50 Million
Number Employees: 20-49

59278 Seven Seas Seafoods
901 S Fremont Ave Ste 168
Alhambra, CA 91803   626-570-9129
                 Fax: 626-570-0079
Seafood
President: Christopher Lin
VP: Sean Lin
Estimated Sales: $5-10 Million
Number Employees: 5-9

59279 Sewell's Seafood & Fish Market
1178 Lee St
Rogersville, AL 35652-7816   256-247-1378
                 Fax: 718-617-6851
Seafood
Owner: Tana Springer
tanaspringer@aol.com
Public Relations: Tana Springer
Estimated Sales: $1-3 Million
Number Employees: 1-4

59280 Sfoglini Pasta Shop
630 Flushing Avenue
2nd Floor
Brooklyn, NY 11206   917-338-5955
info@sfoglini.com
www.sfoglini.com
Pasta: durum semolina and grain

Wholesalers & Distributors / A-Z

Co-Founder: Steve Gonzalez
Co-Founder, Marketing & Operations: Scott Ketchum
Estimated Sales: $4 Million
Number Employees: 35
Type of Packaging: Consumer, Private Label
Types of Products Distributed:
  Pasta

59281 Shabazz Fruit Cola Company
P.O. Box 835
Newark, NJ 07101   973-230-4641
  Fax: 973-230-1651 info@shabazzfruitcola.com
Fruit flavored colas
CEO: Frank Shabazz
Types of Products Distributed:
  General Line

59282 Shaheen Bros Inc
95 Haverhill Rd
P.O. Box 897
Amesbury, MA 01913   978-388-6776
  Fax: 978-388-6617 contacts@shaheenbros.com
  www.shaheenbros.com
Wholesaler/distributor of groceries, meats, produce, dairy products, frozen foods, equipment and fixtures and seafood; serving the food service market.
Year Founded: 1940
Estimated Sales: $50-100 Million
Number Employees: 50-99
Square Footage: 70000
Types of Products Distributed:
  Food Service, General Line, General Merchandise, Provisions/Meat, Produce, Seafood, Groceries, dairy products, etc.

59283 Shaklee Distributor
714 Lexington Pl
Gilroy, CA 95020-6008   408-842-4290
  Fax: 408-842-4290
Wholesaler/distributor of food supplements, herbs, cleaning products and water filters and purification systems
Owner: C Haessler
  c.haessler@huismanauctions.com
Partner: Horst Haessler
Estimated Sales: Less Than $500,000
Number Employees: 1-4
Private Brands Carried:
  Shaklee
Types of Products Distributed:
  Frozen Food, General Merchandise, Health Food, Herbs, cleaning products, etc.

59284 Shalhoob Meat Co
220 Gray Ave
Santa Barbara, CA 93101-1871   805-963-7733
  Fax: 805-963-1208 www.shalhoob.com
Wholesaler/distributor of provisions/meats; serving the food service market
Owner: John Shalhoob
Estimated Sales: $20-50 Million
Number Employees: 10-19
Types of Products Distributed:
  Food Service, Frozen Food, Provisions/Meat

59285 Shamrock Farms
1900 W Ruthrauff Rd
Tucson, AZ 85705-1238   520-887-0300
  Fax: 520-888-1059
  www.shamrockfoodservice.com
Wholesaler/distributor of dairy products; serving the food service market.
Accounting Manager: Lupe Gutierrez
Estimated Sales: $20-50 Million
Number Employees: 20-49
Parent Co: Shamrock Foods Company
Types of Products Distributed:
  Food Service, Frozen Food, General Line, Dairy products

59286 (HQ)Shamrock Foods Co
3900 E. Camelback Rd.
Suite 300
Phoenix, AZ 85018   602-233-6400
            800-289-3663
  www.shamrockfoodservice.com
General line items, groceries, meats, produce, dairy products, frozen foods, baked goods, equipment and fixtures, general merchandise and seafood; serving the food service market.
President: Kent McClelland
CFO: Stephen Down
Year Founded: 1922
Estimated Sales: Over $1 Billion
Number Employees: 1000-4999
Number of Brands: 45
Type of Packaging: Food Service
Other Locations:
  Phoenix, AZ
  Commerce City, CO
  Albuquerque, NM
  Eastvale, CACommerce City
Private Brands Carried:
  Bountiful Harvest, Brickfire Bakery, Cobblestreet MKT, Fair Meadow, Intros, Katy's Kitchen, Pier Port, Prarie Greek, ProClean, ProPak, ProSystem, ProWare, Rejuv, Trescerro Premium Teas, Volla Frizzoni, Vista Verde
Types of Products Distributed:
  Food Service, General Line, Provisions/Meat, Produce, Seafood, Dairy products & baked goods

59287 Shamrock Foods Co
Boise Foods Branch
1495 N Hickory Ave
Meridian, ID 83642   208-884-8400
  www.shamrockfoodservice.com
Serves Idaho, Oregon and Utah.
Parent Co: Shamrock Foods Co
Types of Products Distributed:
  Food Service, Frozen Food, General Line, General Merchandise

59288 Shamrock Foods Co
Colorado Foods Branch
5199 Ivy St
Commerce City, CO 80022
              800-289-3595
  coinfo@shamrockfoods.com
  www.shamrockfoods.com
Serves Colorado, Western Kansas, Western Nebraska and Wyoming.
Senior VP: Kent Mullison
  kent_mullison@shamrockfoods.com
Number Employees: 500-999
Parent Co: Shamrock Foods Company
Number of Customer Locations: 3500
Types of Products Distributed:
  Food Service, Frozen Food, General Line, General Merchandise, Provisions/Meat, Produce, Seafood, Groceries, dairy products, etc.

59289 Shamrock Foods Co
Arizona Foods Branch
2540 N 29th Ave
Phoenix, AZ 85009-1682   602-233-6400
  Fax: 928-537-3428   800-289-3663
  azinfo@shamrockfoods.com
  www.shamrockfoodservice.com
Estimated Sales: $100+ Million
Number Employees: 10-19
Parent Co: Shamrock Foods Company

59290 Shamrock Foods Co
Southern California Foods Branch
12400 Riverside Dr
Eastvale, CA 91752
              855-664-5166
  cainfo@shamrockfoods.com
  www.shamrockfoodservice.com
Parent Co: Shamrock Foods Company

59291 Shamrock Foods Co
New Mexico Foods Branch
2 Shamrock Way NW
Albuquerque, NM 87120
              877-577-1155
  nminfo@shamrockfoods.com
  www.shamrockfoodservice.com
Serves New Mexico and West Texas.
Parent Co: Shamrock Foods Company

59292 Shanghai Freemen
2035 Route 27
Suite 08817
Edison, NJ 08817   732-981-1288
  info@shanghaifreemen.com
  shanghaifreemen.com

Dietary supplements and food and beverage ingredients, such as vitamins, stevia, natural beta carotene, energy beverage ingredients, amino acids and joint health products; their collection includes glucosamine, chondroitin, hyaluronicacid, fish gelatin, collagen, ascorbic acid, natural vitamin E, green tea extract, L-Glutamine, L-Valine, melatonin, probiotics, bromelain, vanillin, Sopure Stevia and many more.
President: Hanks Li
Director, Business Development Eastern: Paul Niemann
Director, Business Development Western: Lottie Siann
VP, Sales & Marketing: Christine Balediata
Year Founded: 1995
Estimated Sales: $100 Million
Number Employees: 51-200
Parent Co: Zhucheng Haotian Pharm Co.
Type of Packaging: Bulk
Other Locations:
  Shanghai Freemen Europe B.V.
  The HagueShanghai Freemen Europe B.V.
Types of Products Distributed:
  Food Service, Specialty Foods

59293 Shannon Diversified Inc
1360 E Locust St
Ontario, CA 91761-4567   909-673-1909
  Fax: 909-484-4214 www.shannonco.com
Wholesaler/distributor of material handling equipment including pallet racks and forklifts
President: Robert Buttrill
General Manager: Chris Hanson
CFO: Marcus Scrudder
Estimated Sales: Less Than $500,000
Number Employees: 1-4
Square Footage: 148000
Private Brands Carried:
  Crown; Nissan
Types of Products Distributed:
  Frozen Food, General Merchandise, Material handling equipment

59294 Shari Candies
  info@candyasap.com
  www.sharicandies.com
Wholesaler/distributor of candy, almond bark, baking nuts, glazed fruits, snacks and confectionery products including novelties and seasonal items.
President: Arlen Kitsis
Year Founded: 1944
Estimated Sales: $50-100 Million
Number Employees: 50-99
Square Footage: 90000
Type of Packaging: Private Label
Private Brands Carried:
  Shari
Number of Customer Locations: 1000
Types of Products Distributed:
  Frozen Food, General Line, Candy, nuts, snacks, novelties, etc.

59295 Sharkco's
707 Jump Basin Rd
Venice, LA 70091-4351   504-534-9577
            Fax: 504-534-2217
Seafood
Owner: Tuan Guyn
Estimated Sales: $5-10 Million
Number Employees: 10-19

59296 Sharpe Valves
9517b Almeda Genoa Road
Houston, TX 77075-2407   708-562-9221
  Fax: 708-562-0890 877-774-2773
  info@sharpevalves.com www.sharpevalves.com
Wholesaler/distributor of piping and equipment
Representative (Valve): Troy Richard
Director, Sales: Jeff Robertson
Parent Co: Sharon Piping & Equipment
Private Brands Carried:
  Sharpe Valves
Types of Products Distributed:
  Frozen Food, General Merchandise, Piping & valves

59297 Shaw Equipment Company
115 35th Street S
Birmingham, AL 35222-1714   205-322-1062
            Fax: 205-945-8783
Wholesaler/distributor of forklifts
President: S Gates Shaw

1167

Wholesalers & Distributors / A-Z

Number Employees: 20-49
Private Brands Carried:
   Neisson; Barrett; Baker
Types of Products Distributed:
   Frozen Food, General Merchandise, Forklifts

59298 Shean Equipment Company
3825 Manlius Center Road
East Syracuse, NY 13057   315-437-1410
                  Fax: 315-437-1107
Wholesaler/distributor of material handling equipment
VP: Kenneth Christie
Estimated Sales: $5-10 Million
Number Employees: 10-19
Private Brands Carried:
   Nissan; Blue Giant; Magline
Types of Products Distributed:
   Frozen Food, General Merchandise, Material handling equipment

59299 Sheehan Majestic
6681 Kestrel Dr
Missoula, MT 59808-9643   406-543-5100
                  Fax: 406-549-1902
Wholesaler/distributor of general merchandise
Owner: Stan Feist
sfeist@sheehanmajestic.com
Estimated Sales: $20-50 Million
Number Employees: 20-49
Private Brands Carried:
   NIFDA
Number of Customer Locations: 100
Types of Products Distributed:
   Food Service, Frozen Food, General Merchandise

59300 Sheffield Platers Inc
9850 Waples St
San Diego, CA 92121-2921   858-546-8484
Fax: 858-546-7653 800-227-9242
         mwatkins@sheffieldplaters.com
         www.sheffieldplaters.com
Coffee urns; wholesaler/distributor of punch bowls, chaffing sets, trays, etc.; serving the food service market; repair and replating services available
President: Dale L. Watkins Jr
dwatkins@sheffieldplaters.com
VP: Mark E. Watkins
Director, Business Development: Vincent Noonan
VP, Marketing: Mark Watkins
VP, Sales: Mark Watkins
Estimated Sales: $2.5-5 Million
Number Employees: 20-49
Square Footage: 68000
Types of Products Distributed:
   Food Service, Frozen Food, General Merchandise, Punch bowls, chaffing sets, trays, etc.

59301 Shellman Peanut & Grain
Highway 41 S
Shellman, GA 39886   229-679-5321
                  Fax: 229-679-2192
Wholesaler/distributor of corn, wheat, soybeans, grain sorghum and peanuts
President: Gerald Wilkerson
Manager: Dean Morris
Estimated Sales: $10-20 Million
Number Employees: 1-4
Types of Products Distributed:
   Frozen Food, General Line, Produce, Corn, wheat, soybean, peanuts, etc.

59302 Shelving Rack Systems Inc
4325 Martin Rd
Commerce Twp, MI 48390-4121   248-360-0948
Fax: 248-360-0171   844-589-7225
         sales@srs-i.com www.srs-i.com
Wholesaler/distributor of material handling equipment
Owner: Mike Burskey
mike@shelving.com
Estimated Sales: $300,000-500,000
Number Employees: 20-49
Square Footage: 160000
Private Brands Carried:
   Cole; Space Rack; Tenesco
Types of Products Distributed:
   Frozen Food, General Merchandise, Material handling equipment

59303 Shemen Tov Corporation
150 Oakwood Ave
Orange, NJ 07050   973-673-2350
                  Fax: 973-731-7846
Wholesaler/distributor of essential oils, flavors and fragrances; serving food processors
President: Lee Saal
Sales Manager: Lee Saal
Estimated Sales: $3-5 Million
Number Employees: 1-4
Types of Products Distributed:
   Frozen Food, General Line, Essential oils, flavors & fragrances

59304 Shemper Seafood Co
367 Bayview Ave
Biloxi, MS 39530-2502   228-435-2703
                  Fax: 228-432-2104
Wholesaler/distributor of fresh shrimp
President: Jeffrey Shemper
camelot@datasync.com
Secretary/Treasurer: Gary Shemper
Estimated Sales: Less Than $500,000
Number Employees: 1-4
Types of Products Distributed:
   Seafood, Fresh shrimp

59305 Shenandoah Industrial Rubber
802 Kessler Mill Rd
Salem, VA 24153-3034   540-387-0435
Fax: 540-387-1786   800-523-6127
         admin@sircorubber.com www.sircorubber.com
Wholesaler/distributor of conveyor belting, hoses and couplings; also, belt installation and vulcanizing services available
Owner: Harry Ray
sircorubber@aol.com
Estimated Sales: $10-20 Million
Number Employees: 10-19
Types of Products Distributed:
   Frozen Food, General Merchandise, Conveyor belting, hoses & couplings

59306 Shenandoah Vineyards
12300 Steiner Rd
Plymouth, CA 95669-9503   209-245-4455
         Fax: 209-245-5156 www.sobonwine.com
Wines
President: Leon Sobon
CEO: Shirley Sobon
Estimated Sales: Below $5 Million
Number Employees: 10-19

59307 Shepherdsfield Bakery
777 Shepherdsfield Rd
Fulton, MO 65251-5974   573-642-0009
                  Fax: 573-642-1439
Frozen gourmet waffles, muffins, breads and whole wheat pancake mixes, pies, cookies and flour
Religious Leader: Thomas Mahaney
CEO: Vicki Staudenmyer
Estimated Sales: Less Than $500,000
Number Employees: 1-4
Square Footage: 80000
Type of Packaging: Consumer, Private Label
Types of Products Distributed:
   Frozen Food

59308 Sher Brothers & Company
25 E 1st Street
Duluth, MN 55802-2061   218-722-5563
                  Fax: 218-722-7806
Wholesaler/distributor of provisions/meats; serving the food service market
Owner: Alvin Sher
Manager: David Sher
Comptroller/Buyer: Phillip Sher
Estimated Sales: $2.5-5 Million
Number Employees: 1-4
Number of Customer Locations: 125
Types of Products Distributed:
   Food Service, Provisions/Meat

59309 Sheridan Fruit Co Inc
408 SE 3rd Ave
Portland, OR 97214-1009   503-236-2113
         Fax: 503-235-4105 sales@sheridanfruit.com
                  www.sheridanfruit.com
Wholesaler/distributor of produce, meat, groceries and frozen food; serving the food service market
Owner: Vince Torchia
vince@sheridanfruit.com
Estimated Sales: $10-20 Million
Number Employees: 20-49

59310 (HQ)Sherwood Food Distributors
12499 Evergreen Ave
Detroit, MI 48228-1059   313-659-7300
                  www.sherwoodfoods.com
Wholesaler/distributor of meats, poultry, dairy items, frozen foods, seafood, general line and specialty food products and general merchandise; serving the food service and retail markets.
Co-Founder: Alex Karp
Co-Founder: Earl Ishbia
eishbia@sherwoodfoods.com
Year Founded: 1987
Estimated Sales: $103.5 Million
Number Employees: 250-499
Square Footage: 300000
Number of Customer Locations: 3500
Types of Products Distributed:
   Food Service, Frozen Food, General Line, General Merchandise, Provisions/Meat, Seafood, Specialty Foods, Dairy items, poultry, etc.

59311 Sherwood Food Distributors
5400 Fulton Industrial Blvd
Atlanta, GA 30336   404-348-0001
   Fax: 404-348-0030 www.sherwoodfoods.com
Wholesaler/distributor of meats, poultry, dairy items, frozen foods, seafood, general line and specialty food products and general merchandise; serving the food service and retail markets.
Sales: Jerry Abney
jabney@sherwoodfoods.com
Sales: Danny Bridges
Estimated Sales: $103.5 million
Number Employees: 250-499
Square Footage: 215000
Private Brands Carried:
   Perdue; Thorn Apple Valley
Types of Products Distributed:
   Frozen Food, Provisions/Meat, Poultry items

59312 Sherwood Food Distributors
12345 NW 38th Ave
Opa Locka, FL 33054   305-687-0000
   Fax: 305-769-6539 www.sherwoodfoods.com
Wholesaler/distributor of meats, poultry, dairy items, frozen foods, seafood, general line and specialty food products and general merchandise; serving the food service and retail markets.
Sales: Analia Bonilla
abonilla@sherwoodfoods.com
Sales: Alejandro Chaves
Estimated Sales: $103.5 Million
Number Employees: 250-499
Square Footage: 150000
Parent Co: Sherwood Food Distributors
Types of Products Distributed:
   Food Service, Frozen Food, Provisions/Meat

59313 Sherwood Food Distributors
240 Shorland Dr
Unit 200
Walton, KY 41094-9327   859-795-0100
   Fax: 859-795-2457 www.sherwoodfoods.com
Wholesaler/distributor of meats, poultry, dairy items, frozen foods, seafood, general line and specialty food products and general merchandise; serving the food service and retail markets.
Sales: Keith Bowermeister
Kbowermeister@Sherwoodfoods.Com
Estimated Sales: $103.5 million
Number Employees: 100-249
Square Footage: 100000
Parent Co: Sherwood Food Distributors
Private Brands Carried:
   Amish Valley
Number of Customer Locations: 1500
Types of Products Distributed:
   Food Service, Frozen Food, General Line, Provisions/Meat, Specialty Foods

59314 Sherwood Food Distributors
1025 Osage St
Fort Wayne, IN 46808-3483   260-420-8800
   Fax: 260-420-3300 www.sherwoodfoods.com
Wholesaler/distributor of meats, poultry, dairy items, frozen foods, seafood, general line and specialty food products and general merchandise; serving the food service and retail markets.
Sales: Chuck Greenwood
cgreenwood@sherwoodfoods.com
Estimated Sales: $103.5 million
Number Employees: 100-249
Parent Co: Sherwood Food Distributors

Types of Products Distributed:
  Food Service, Frozen Food, Provisions/Meat

59315 Sherwood Food Distributors
21 Yost Blvd
Suite 203
Pittsburgh, PA 15221   412-829-7430
  Fax: 412-829-7338 www.sherwoodfoods.com
Wholesaler/distributor of meats, poultry, dairy items, frozen foods, seafood, general line and specialty food products and general merchandise; serving the food service and retail markets.
Sales: Robert Swartz
bswartz@sherwoodfoods.com
Estimated Sales: $103.5 million
Number Employees: 100-249
Parent Co: Sherwood Food Distributors
Types of Products Distributed:
  Food Service, Frozen Food, Provisions/Meat

59316 Sherwood Food Distributors
16625 Granite Rd
Maple Heights, OH 44137-4301   216-662-8000
    Fax: 216-662-1591
Wholesaler/distributor of meats, poultry, dairy items, frozen foods, seafood, general line and specialty food products and general merchandise; serving the food service and retail markets.
Sales: Ron Akin
rakin@sherwoodfoods.com
Estimated Sales: $103.5 million
Number Employees: 100-249
Square Footage: 300000
Parent Co: Sherwood Food Distributors
Number of Customer Locations: 150
Types of Products Distributed:
  Food Service, Frozen Food, Provisions/Meat

59317 Sherwood Valley Cold Storage
227 Menasha St
Reedsville, WI 54230-8597   920-754-4325
  Fax: 920-754-4569 800-628-4066
    www.valleycold.com
Cheese, cheese products
Owner: Earl Petersen
Estimated Sales: Less Than $500,000
Number Employees: 1-4
Square Footage: 20000
Type of Packaging: Private Label, Bulk

59318 (HQ)Shetakis Foodservice
3840 A North Civic Center Drive
North Las Vegas, NV 89030   702-940-3663
  Fax: 702-732-0136 info@shetakis.com
    www.shetakis.com
Las Vegas' largest independent distributor of groceries, provisions/meats, dairy products, baked goods, fresh chicken, seafood, frozen foods, and disposables serving the food service market.
Vice President: Charlie Jackson
CFO: Andrew Dannin
Director of Marketing: Angela Silver
Estimated Sales: $80 Million
Number Employees: 50-99
Square Footage: 165000
Other Locations:
  Shetakis Wholesalers
  Reno, NVShetakis Wholesalers
Private Brands Carried:
  Nuggett
Types of Products Distributed:
  Food Service, Frozen Food, General Line, General Merchandise, Provisions/Meat, Seafood, Groceries, disposables, etc.

59319 Shiff & Goldman Foods
3351 Tremley Point Rd # 2
Linden, NJ 07036-3575   732-247-5677
  Fax: 732-545-5502 800-923-7848
Wholesaler/distributor of bakery items, specialty health and frozen foods, general merchandise, groceries, meats/provisions and produce; serving schools and corporate and industrial feeders
President: David Nachman
Marketing Director: David Nachman
Buyer: Brad Nachman
Estimated Sales: $20-50 Million
Number Employees: 20-49
Square Footage: 6500
Types of Products Distributed:
  Food Service, Frozen Food, General Line, General Merchandise, Health Food, Provisions/Meat, Produce, Specialty Foods

59320 Shippers Supply
2815A Cleveland Avenue
Saskatoon, SK S7K 8G1
Canada   306-242-6266
  Fax: 306-933-4333 800-661-5639
    saskatoon@shipperssupply.com
    www.shipperssupply.com
Manufacturer and wholesaler/distributor of printed labels, pressure sensitive tapes, corrugated boxes, material handling equipment, stretch and shrink film and shipping supplies
President: Ron Brown
CFO: Miles Jern
Branch Manager: Neil Nutter
Number Employees: Oover 200
Square Footage: 400000
Types of Products Distributed:
  Frozen Food, General Merchandise, Labels, shipping supplies, etc.

59321 Shippers Supply
2815A Cleveland Avenue
Saskatoon, SK S7K 8G1
Canada   306-242-6266
  Fax: 306-933-4333 800-661-5639
    saskatoon@shipperssupply.com
    www.shipperssupply.com
Manufacturer, wholesaler/distributor and importer of printed labels, pressure sensitive tapes, corrugated boxes, material handling equipment, stretch film and shipping supplies; exporter of labels and printed tape
President: Ron Brown
Branch Manager: Ken Nordyke
Number Employees: Oover 200
Square Footage: 400000
Types of Products Distributed:
  Frozen Food, General Merchandise, Shipping supplies, labels, tapes, etc.

59322 Shippers Supply, Labelgraphic
8-3401 19 Street NE
Calgary, AB T2E 6S8
Canada   403-291-0450
  Fax: 403-291-3641 800-661-5639
    airways@shipperssupply.com
    www.shipperssupply.com
Manufacturer and wholesaler/distributor of printed labels, pressure sensitive tapes, corrugated boxes, material handling equipment, stretch film and shipping supplies
President: Ron Brown
General Manager: Dennis Rhind
Branch Manager: Jerry Pierce
Number Employees: Oover 200
Square Footage: 400000
Parent Co: Shippers Supply
Types of Products Distributed:
  Frozen Food, General Merchandise, Shipping supplies, labels, tapes, etc.

59323 Shire City Herbals
703 W. Housatonic Street
Suite 120
Pittsfield, MA 01201   413-213-6702
    info@firecider.com
    firecider.com
Cider
Co-Owner: Amy Huebner
Co-Founder & CEO: Dana St.Pierre
Sales & Customer Service: Brian Huebner
Wholesale & Customer Service: Bethany Geiger
Number Employees: 11-50
Type of Packaging: Food Service
Types of Products Distributed:
  Cider

59324 Shivji Enterprises
2659 #5 Road
Richmond, BC V5M 1N1
Canada   604-270-3834
  Fax: 604-270-3880 shivjis@hotmail.com
Importer and wholesaler/distributor of rice, spices, beans, frozen yucca and plantano, etc.; serving the food service and retail markets; exporter of flour, beans
Director: Shiraz Shivji
Estimated Sales: $3-5 Million
Number Employees: 5-9
Square Footage: 60000
Type of Packaging: Consumer, Food Service, Private Label, Bulk
Private Brands Carried:
  Golden Pacific; Garden Temple; Golden Elephant
Number of Customer Locations: 200
Types of Products Distributed:
  Food Service, Frozen Food, General Line, General Merchandise, Specialty Foods, Frozen yucca & plantano, rice, beans

59325 Sho-Nuff-Good
1522 Chandlee Avenue
Panama City, FL 32405-4613   850-872-1529
    Fax: 850-872-7455
Wholesaler/distributor of barbecue sauce
CEO: Richard Campbell
Types of Products Distributed:
  Frozen Food, General Line, Barbecue sauce

59326 Shoe Inn, LLC
1482 Linda Way
Sparks, NV 89431   775-356-2778
  Fax: 775-358-0736 877-595-7463
    info@theshoecovers.com
    www.shoeinnshoecovers.com
Automatic shoe covers dispensers, shoe covers, sanitary glove dispensers and gloves, and sticky mats.
Product Manager: Jeff Foster
Year Founded: 1983
Estimated Sales: $50 Million
Number Employees: 125

59327 Shoes for Crews/Mighty Mat
1400 Centrepark Blvd # 31
West Palm Beach, FL 33401-7402   561-683-5090
  Fax: 561-683-3080 800-667-5477
    scotts@shoesforcrews.com
    www.shoesforcrews.com
Shoes for Crews Slip-Resistant Footwear will prevent your slips and falls with over 38 styles to choose from at prices starting at $24.98. We offer the exclusive $5000 Slip & Fall Warranty: If any employee slips and falls wearing SHOESFOR CREWS, we will reimburse your company up to $5000 on the paid workers comp claim. Call us at 1-877-667-5477 for details
Chairman of the Board: Stanley Smith
Contact: Stan Smith
s.smith@shoesforcrews.com
Estimated Sales: $5-10 Million
Number Employees: 1-4
Type of Packaging: Private Label
Private Brands Carried:
  Crewguard, Mighty Mat, Shoes for Crews
Types of Products Distributed:
  Slip Resistant Footwear/Floor Mats

59328 Shoppa's Material Handling
15217 Grand River Rd
Fort Worth, TX 76155   817-359-1100
  Fax: 817-359-1110 866-506-2200
    www.shoppasmaterialhandling.com
Wholesaler/distributor of material handling equipment including forklifts.
President: James Shoppa
Controller: Jeff Little
Vice President, Sales: Scott Carlin
Vice President, Human Resources: Peggy Haynes
Chief Operating Officer: Patrick Collier
Year Founded: 1982
Estimated Sales: $50-100 Million
Number Employees: 100-249
Other Locations:
  Amarillo, TX
  Brownwood, TX
  Lubbock, TX
  Kansas City, MO
  Odessa, TX
  San Angelo, TXBrownwood
Private Brands Carried:
  Toyota
Types of Products Distributed:
  Frozen Food, General Merchandise, Material handling equipment

59329 Shore Distribution Resources
18 Manitoba Way
Marlboro, NJ 07746-1219   732-972-1297
  Fax: 732-972-7669 800-876-9727
    shordist@aol.com
Wholesaler/distributor of packaging materials and equipment including plastic containers, polyester film, cellophane and polypropylene; also, carry out platters, bowls, disposable thermometers and food safety products

Wholesalers & Distributors / A-Z

President: Elaine Shore
CEO: Harvey Shore
shordist@aol.com
Sales: Harvey Shore
Operations: Scott Shore
Estimated Sales: $1-2.5 Million
Number Employees: 5-9
Square Footage: 12000
Type of Packaging: Food Service
Private Brands Carried:
   Trans World Services; Qualitad; Koppol Films; Epsilon-Opti Shrink Films; Anchor; Heat Seal; Ez Pak Systems
Number of Customer Locations: 500
Types of Products Distributed:
   Food Service, General Merchandise, Packaging materials & equipment, etc.

59330 Shryack-Givens Grocery Co.
PO Box 125
Boonville, MO 65233-0125   660-882-6651
   Fax: 660-882-8334
Wholesaler/distributor of groceries and health and beauty aids; serving the food service market
President: Adron Perry
Estimated Sales: $20-50 Million
Number Employees: 20-49
Square Footage: 36000
Number of Customer Locations: 150
Types of Products Distributed:
   Food Service, Frozen Food, General Line

59331 Shryack-Hirst Grocery Company
P.O.Box 178
Jefferson City, MO 65102-0178   573-636-7181
   Fax: 573-636-5133   jerrypowel@sockets.net
Wholesaler/distributor of groceries, general merchandise, janitorial supplies, private label items, candy and paper; serving the food service market
President: J Powell
Secretary/Treasurer: J Jungmeyer
Purchasing Manager: Dennis Toellner
Estimated Sales: $10-20 Million
Number Employees: 10-19
Square Footage: 80000
Private Brands Carried:
   Pleezing
Number of Customer Locations: 150
Types of Products Distributed:
   Food Service, Frozen Food, General Line, General Merchandise, Candy, paper, etc.

59332 Shuckman's Fish Co & Smokery
3001 W Main St
Louisville, KY 40212-1840   502-775-6478
   Fax: 502-775-6373
   shuckmans@kysmokedfish.com
   www.kysmokedfish.com
Smokers of fish & seafood products.
President: Lewis Shuckman
lshuckman@kysmokefish.com
Estimated Sales: $3-5 Million
Number Employees: 10-19

59333 Shullsburg Creamery Inc
208 W Water St
PO Box 398
Shullsburg, WI 53586-9470   608-965-4485
   Fax: 608-965-3778   800-533-9594
   sstocker@shullsburgcreamery.com
   www.shullsburgcreamery.com
Wholesaler/distributor of cheddar, colby, brick, muenster, Monterey Jack, Swiss and farmer cheese
Owner/President/CEO: Scott Stocker
Estimated Sales: $10-20 Million
Number Employees: 20-49
Types of Products Distributed:
   Food Service, General Line, Cheese

59334 Shur-Az Inc
871 High St
Central Falls, RI 02863-2347   401-654-4150
   Fax: 401-723-0148   800-550-0116
   www.shuraz.com
Wholesaler/distributor of detergents, liquid and paste floor polish and other cleaning supplies
President: Thomas Kennedy
shuraz@shuraz.com
VP: Joseph Najjar
Estimated Sales: $1-3 Million
Number Employees: 5-9
Types of Products Distributed:
   Frozen Food, General Merchandise, Cleaning supplies, detergents & polish

59335 Sid Alpers Organic Sales Company
PO Box 242
New Milford, NJ 07646-0242   201-265-3695
   Fax: 201-265-3819
Import and export broker of cereal/breakfast products, grains, flours, kosher foods and syrups
CEO: Sid Alpers
VP: H Alpers
Number Employees: 10
Types of Products Distributed:
   Health Food, Specialty Foods

59336 Sid Goodman Company
7460 Conowingo Ave Ste 6
Jessup, MD 20794   410-799-9077
   Fax: 410-799-2169
Wholesaler/distributor of produce
Owner: Dave Goodman
Vice President: Gede Goodman
Estimated Sales: $10-20 Million
Number Employees: 20-49
Square Footage: 21000
Type of Packaging: Food Service, Bulk
Types of Products Distributed:
   Produce

59337 Sid Green Frozen Foods
7833 N 7th Street
Phoenix, AZ 85020-4132   602-943-4687
   Fax: 602-944-4497
Wholesaler/distributor of seafood and frozen foods
President: Ronald Green
Secretary/Treasurer: Shirley Green
Vice President: Barry Green
Estimated Sales: $3-5 Million
Number Employees: 1-4
Square Footage: 36000
Number of Customer Locations: 100
Types of Products Distributed:
   Food Service, Seafood

59338 Sid Harvey Industries Inc
605 Locust St # A
Garden City, NY 11530-6531   516-745-9200
   Fax: 516-222-9027   info@sidharvey.com
   www.sidharvey.com
Wholesaler/distributor of general merchandise including advertising specialties, T-shirts, labels, caps, jackets and tote and plastic bags
President: Sid Harvey
sharvey@sidharvey.com
Estimated Sales: $1-2.5 Million
Number Employees: 250-499
Square Footage: 4400
Private Brands Carried:
   Sheaffer
Types of Products Distributed:
   Advertising specialties

59339 Sid Wainer & Son Specialty
2301 Purchase St
New Bedford, MA 02746-1686   508-999-6408
   Fax: 508-999-6795   888-743-9246
   sidwainer@sidwainer.com   www.sidwainer.com
Ostrich, Scottish smoked salmon, cheese, vinegars, preserves, olives peppers, oils and produce
Owner: Phil Spadaro
phil.spadaro@staples.com
Estimated Sales: $3-5 Million
Number Employees: 250-499
Types of Products Distributed:
   Frozen Food, General Line, Produce, Specialty Foods, Cheese, vinegars, salmon, olives, etc.

59340 Sid Wainer & Son Specialty
2301 Purchase St
New Bedford, MA 02746-1686   508-999-6408
   Fax: 508-999-6795   800-423-8333
   swgraph@ma.ultranet.com   www.sidwainer.com
Importer and distributor of vegetables, rice, pasta, fruit, chocolate, cheese, and smoked fish
Owner: Phil Spadaro
phil.spadaro@staples.com
Estimated Sales: $3-5 Million
Number Employees: 250-499

59341 Sidehill Farm
PO Box 1558
Brattleboro, VT 05302   802-254-2018
   Fax: 802-254-3381   info@sidehillfarmjam.com
Handmade jams, fruit butters and maple syrup.

Owner: Kelt Naylor
Year Founded: 1976
Estimated Sales: $1 Million
Number Employees: 2-10
Types of Products Distributed:
   Specialty Foods, Jams and toppings

59342 Sidney's
13195 N Wintzell Ave
Bayou La Batre, AL 36509-2131   251-824-2837
   Fax: 251-824-2837   john@sidneys.com
   www.sidneys.com
Wholesaler/distributor of all-purpose batter mixes and breaded shrimp, oysters, clam strips, scallops, etc. serving the food service market
Owner: Donna Hunt
donna@sidneys.com
Estimated Sales: $.5-1 million
Number Employees: 10-19
Private Brands Carried:
   Sidney's
Types of Products Distributed:
   Food Service, Frozen Food, General Line, Seafood, All purpose batter mixes, etc.

59343 Sieb Distributor
412 Seneca Ave
Flushing, NY 11385-1453   718-417-0340
   Fax: 718-821-8120
Importer and wholesaler/distributor of German beer
Manager: Joseph Markovican
Estimated Sales: $2.5-5 Million
Number Employees: 1-4
Type of Packaging: Consumer, Food Service
Private Brands Carried:
   Binkelacker; Spaten; Franzis Kner
Types of Products Distributed:
   Frozen Food, General Line, German beer

59344 Siegmeister Sales & Service
PO Box 767
Hillside, NJ 07205   973-923-6978
   Fax: 973-923-2507
Wholesaler/distributor of supermarket, institutional and restaurant equipment; serving the food service market
President: Carl Tasch
Office Manager: Sheri Staehli
Estimated Sales: $5-10 Million
Number Employees: 50-99
Square Footage: 44000
Types of Products Distributed:
   Food Service, Frozen Food, General Merchandise, Restaurant, supermarket, etc. equipment

59345 Sierra Meat & Seafood Co
1330 Capital Blvd.
Suite A
Reno, NV 89502   775-322-4073
   800-444-5687
   sales@sierrameat.com   sierrameat.com
Meat and seafood.
President/CEO: Chris Flocchini
Executive Vice President: Bernadette Flocchini
Year Founded: 1934
Estimated Sales: $101 Million
Number Employees: 100-249
Square Footage: 25000
Type of Packaging: Food Service
Other Locations:
   Santa Clara, CA
   Monterey, CA
   Reno, NVMonterey

59346 (HQ)Sierra Nut House
3034 E Sierra Ave
Fresno, CA 93710-5999   559-299-3052
   Fax: 559-299-7638   800-397-6887
   www.sierranuthouse.com
Wholesaler/distributor of dried fruit, nuts, candies, soup mixes, coffees, teas, wines, etc
Owner: Joann Sorrenti
sierranuthouse@yahoo.com
VP/Treasurer: Carole Rosenberger
Estimated Sales: $10-20 Million
Number Employees: 20-49
Square Footage: 4000
Number of Customer Locations: 250
Types of Products Distributed:
   Frozen Food, General Line, Specialty Foods, Dried fruit, nuts, candies, etc.

Wholesalers & Distributors / A-Z

59347 Signature Packaging
18 Dockery Dr
West Orange, NJ 7052 973-324-1838
Fax: 973-884-1909 800-376-2299
Plain and printed polyethylene bags for chicken, potatoes, fruits, etc.; also, paper and turkey tags, closures, packaging machinery, paper wrap, etc.; wholesaler/distributor of produce and specialty foods
Estimated Sales: less than $500,000
Number Employees: 1-4
Square Footage: 5000
Types of Products Distributed:
 Frozen Food, Produce, Specialty Foods

59348 Silverado Vineyards Inc
6121 Silverado Trl
Napa, CA 94558-9415 707-257-1770
Fax: 707-257-1538 800-997-1770
neliason@silveradovineyards.com
Processors of wine
Owner: Ron Miller
rmiller@silveradovineyards.com
Owner: Diane Miller
General Manager: Russ Weis
Winemaker: Jon Emmerich
Number Employees: 20-49

59349 Silverstar Foodservice Supply
2204 W Southern Avenue
Tempe, AZ 85282-4346 602-244-1995
Fax: 602-955-1715 888-516-1995
Wholesaler/distributor of food service equipment and general merchandise including smallwares, paper products and parts; serving the food service market
President: Richard Olson
Estimated Sales: $5-10 Million
Number Employees: 10-19
Square Footage: 60000
Types of Products Distributed:
 Food Service, Frozen Food, General Merchandise, Equipment, parts, paper products, etc.

59350 Simco Foods
1180 S Beverly Dr Ste 509
Los Angeles, CA 90035 310-284-8446
Fax: 310-284-8221 info@simco.us
www.simco.us
Tuna, pineapple, mandarins, olives, olive oil, artichokes, mushrooms, peppers, sardines, mackerel, peaches, pears, fruit cocktail, corn and green beans.
President: David Sims
Contact: John Ashworth
john@simco.us
Estimated Sales: $10-20 Million
Number Employees: 12
Number of Brands: 3
Number of Products: 200
Square Footage: 16000
Type of Packaging: Consumer, Food Service, Private Label, Bulk
Private Brands Carried:
 First Harvest; Stella; Sims
Types of Products Distributed:
 Food Service, Seafood, Imported groceries

59351 Simonian Fruit Company
350 N 7th St
Fowler, CA 93625 559-834-5921
Fax: 559-834-2363
Exporter and wholesaler/distributor of fresh fruit including grapes, plums, peaches, pomegranates and apricots; serving the food service market
President: David Simonian
Estimated Sales: $10-20 Million
Number Employees: 100-249
Type of Packaging: Consumer, Food Service, Bulk
Types of Products Distributed:
 Food Service, Frozen Food, Produce

59352 Simply Gum
270 Lafatette St
New York, NY 10012
info@simplygum.com
www.simplygum.com
All-natural chewing gum
Founder/CEO: Caron Proschan
Marketing: Kelsey Jones
Sales/Operations Coordinator: Elise Goree
Sr Operations Manager: Emanuel Storch *Year Founded:* 2014
Types of Products Distributed:
 General Line

59353 SimplyFUEL, LLC
Leawood, KS 913-269-1889
info@simplyfuel.com
simplyfuel.com
Protein balls
Founder: Mitzi Dulan

59354 Simpson & Vail
3 Quarry Rd
Brookfield, CT 06804-1053 203-775-0240
Fax: 203-775-0462 800-282-8327
info@svtea.com www.svtea.com
Processor, exporter and importer of coffee and gourmet tea
President: Jim Harron Jr
CEO: Joan Harron
Estimated Sales: $.5-1 million
Number Employees: 5-9
Square Footage: 32000
Type of Packaging: Food Service
Private Brands Carried:
 Simpson; Vail
Types of Products Distributed:
 Specialty Foods

59355 Simpson Grocery Company
PO Box 271
Rome, GA 30162-0271 706-232-3636
Wholesaler/distributor of beer
President: Gordon Hight
Estimated Sales: $10-20 Million
Number Employees: 50-99
Types of Products Distributed:
 Frozen Food, General Line, Beer

59356 Sims Poultry
PO Box 1489
Bloomington, IN 47402-1489 812-336-5720
Fax: 812-336-4441
Wholesaler/distributor of chicken, turkey and eggs
Owner/Secretary/Treasurer: Richard Dunbar
Estimated Sales: $5-10 Million
Number Employees: 5-9
Types of Products Distributed:
 Provisions/Meat

59357 Sims Wholesale
540 River St
Batesville, AR 72501 870-793-1109
Fax: 870-793-2230
Wholesaler/distributor of general line products; serving the food service market
General Manager: Kenneth Thornton
Manager: Mike Hanson
Types of Products Distributed:
 Food Service, Frozen Food, General Line

59358 Sin-Son Produce
1220 N Hohokam Dr
Nogales, AZ 85621-1365 520-287-2311
Fax: 520-287-4948
Wholesaler/distributor of fire roasted, steam peeled, green chili and dehydrated bell peppers
Manager: Yolanda Contreras
Estimated Sales: $500,000-$1 Million
Number Employees: 1-4
Private Brands Carried:
 Sin-Son
Types of Products Distributed:
 Frozen Food, General Line, Produce, Peppers

59359 Sinclair Trading
1204 E 8th St
Los Angeles, CA 90021-1514 213-627-6063
Fax: 213-627-5340
Wholesaler/distributor and importer of Caribbean and African foods including Jamaican coffee
President: Lloyd Sinclair
CEO: Esperanza Sinclair
CFO: Alton McQueen
Sales Director: Michael Newman
Public Relations: Dave Sinclair
Purchasing Manager: Lloyd Sinclair
Estimated Sales: $5 Million
Number Employees: 10-19
Square Footage: 20000
Type of Packaging: Consumer, Private Label
Private Brands Carried:
 Jamaica Blue Mountain Coffee; Morissas Habanero Hot Pepper Sauce
Types of Products Distributed:
 Frozen Food, Specialty Foods, Caribbean & African foods

59360 Sindoni, Joseph, Wholesale Foods
626 N Salina Street
Syracuse, NY 13208-2509 315-471-5861
Wholesaler/distributor of frozen foods, general line products and produce
President: Daniel Kageafc
CEO: Neo Morohashi
Estimated Sales: $1-5 Million
Number Employees: 10-19
Types of Products Distributed:
 Frozen Food, General Line, Produce, Canned goods

59361 Singer Equipment Co Inc
150 S Twin Valley Rd
Elverson, PA 19520 610-286-8050
Fax: 610-286-8050
info@singerequipment.com
www.singerequipment.com
Wholesaler/distributor of restaurant equipment and supplies; serving the food service market
President & CEO: Frederick Singer
Estimated Sales: $55 Million
Number Employees: 100-249
Square Footage: 105000
Types of Products Distributed:
 Food Service, Frozen Food, General Merchandise, Restaurant equipment & supplies

59362 Singing Dog Vanilla
255 Wallis St
Suite 1
Eugene, OR 97402 541-343-2746
Fax: 541-610-1868 888-343-0002
www.singingdogvanilla.com
Vanilla products

59363 SipDisc
18 East 48th Street
New York, NY 10017 212-319-9700
Fax: 212-319-9778
The SipDisc Straw for the food and beverage industry.
President: Alex Greenberg

59364 Siptop Packaging Inc
2810 Argentia Rd
Mississauga, ON L5N 8L2
Canada 905-814-0531
Fax: 905-814-0531
Siptop Packaging's product line includes beverage packaging technology that utilizes a form, fill and seal machine that produces an innovative stand-up drink pouch that is low cost, environmentally friendly and has a built in strawthat is convenient and eliminates the mess that is created with typical pouch straws.
President: Grant Joyce
Sales Representative: Grant Joyce
Senior Director Operations: Jack Vanderdeen
Type of Packaging: Consumer

59365 Sirca Foodservice
1700 Cliveden Avevue
Delta, BC V3M 6T2
Canada 604-540-3701
Fax: 604-540-3962 800-663-1695
Wholesaler/distributor of groceries, meat, produce, dairy products, frozen foods, baked goods, equipment and fixtures, general merchandise, paper products and seafood; serving the food service market
President: Frank Geier
Sales/Marketing Executive: Dean Noble
Number Employees: 500-999
Parent Co: Sobey's
Private Brands Carried:
 Sirca Food Products
Number of Customer Locations: 1200
Types of Products Distributed:
 Food Service, Frozen Food, General Line, General Merchandise, Provisions/Meat, Produce, Seafood, Paper products

59366 Sisq Distributing Inc
1313 N Foothill Dr
Yreka, CA 96097-9013 530-842-1616
Fax: 530-842-7920
Wholesaler/distributor of frozen food and general line products; serving the food service market
Owner: Ken Barnes
ken@siskiyoudistributing.com
Estimated Sales: $5-10 Million
Number Employees: 10-19

1171

Wholesalers & Distributors / A-Z

Private Brands Carried:
Red & White
Types of Products Distributed:
Food Service, Frozen Food, General Line

59367 Sisters' Gourmet
PO Box 1550
Dacula, GA 30019-0027 216-292-7700
Fax: 216-292-7701 orders@brandcastle.com
www.sistersgourmet.com
Baking mixes: cookie and brownie
R&D Project Manager: Taylor Reagan
Marketing Services: Linda Bina
Number Employees: 11-50
Parent Co: Brand Castle
Type of Packaging: Consumer, Private Label
Types of Products Distributed:
Cookie & brownie mixes

59368 Sisu Group Inc
8252 South Harvard Avenue
Suite 157
Tulsa, OK 74137 918-495-1364
Fax: 918-746-7010 info@sisugrp.com
www.sisugrp.com
Wholesaler/distributor and exporter of condiments and condiment dispensing equipment; serving the food service market
President: Kim Berghall
kberghall@sisugrp.com
CEO: Mike Boudreaux
Advertising Director: Lisa Roth
Type of Packaging: Food Service
Types of Products Distributed:
Food Service, Frozen Food, General Line, General Merchandise, Condiments & dispensing equipment

59369 Skarnes Inc
2100 Niagara Ln N
Minneapolis, MN 55447-4700 763-231-3600
Fax: 763-231-3610 800-752-7637
sales@skarnes.com www.skarnes.com
Wholesaler/distributor of material handling equipment including conveyors, racks and shelving
CEO: T Wanous
IT: Tom Wiygul
twelter@skarnes.com
Estimated Sales: $5-10 Million
Number Employees: 10-19
Private Brands Carried:
Hytrol; Equipto; Interlake
Types of Products Distributed:
Frozen Food, General Merchandise, Material handling equipment

59370 Skelton's Inc
2188 W 4th St
Ontario, OH 44906-1287 419-529-8740
Fax: 419-529-8741 800-522-2027
rex@skeltonsinc.com www.skeltonsinc.com
Wholesaler/distributor of food service equipment and supplies; serving the food service market
President: Rex Skelton
Marketing Director: Beth Peebles
Sales Director: Chad Peebles
Estimated Sales: $2.5-5 Million
Number Employees: 5-9
Square Footage: 28000
Private Brands Carried:
Hobart; Cambro; Green Mts; Rubbermaid; Vollrath; Vulcan;
Types of Products Distributed:
Food Service

59371 (HQ)Skidmore Sales & Distributing Company
9889 Cincinnati Dayton Rd
West Chester, OH 45069-3825 513-755-4200
Fax: 513-759-4270 800-468-7543
stevejackson@skidmore-sales.com
www.skidmore-sales.com
Wholesaler/distributor of industrial ingredients, including fruit powder
President/CEO: Doug Skidmore
Chairman: Gerard Skidmore
CFO: Steppi Frey
Information Technology Manager: Dennis Meyers
VP Sales/Marketing: Steve Jackson
VP Supply Chain: Jack Buecker
Estimated Sales: $8.0 Million
Number Employees: 36
Square Footage: 450000
Other Locations:
Skidmore Sales & Distributing
Hunt Valley, MDSkidmore Sales & Distributing
Private Brands Carried:
A.E. Staley; National Starch; Central Soya; Gilroy Foods; Protein Technologies; French's Ingredients; Kalsec; Rohm Enzyme
Types of Products Distributed:
General Line, Industrial ingredients

59372 Skiles Co Inc
1414 S Main St
Bluffton, IN 46714-3900 260-824-2400
Fax: 260-824-8182 www.skilesrealestate.com
Wholesaler/distributor of groceries and general merchandise items
President: Marland Crabtree
mcrabtree@skilesgroup.com
Chairman: D Skiles
VP: B Skiles
Estimated Sales: $10-20 Million
Number Employees: 10-19
Number of Customer Locations: 250
Types of Products Distributed:
Frozen Food, General Line, General Merchandise

59373 Skone & Conners
112 E Evan Hall
Warden, WA 98857 509-349-2391
Fax: 509-349-2395 www.basingold.com
Wholesaler/distributor of potatoes and onions
Owner: Steve Connors
sconnors@basingold.com
Estimated Sales: $20-50 Million
Number Employees: 20-49
Types of Products Distributed:
Frozen Food, Produce, Potatoes & onions

59374 Skone & Connors Produce
P.O.Box 369
Wapato, WA 98951-0369 509-877-4577
Fax: 509-877-4575 www.basingold.com
Wholesaler/distributor of potatoes and onions
Partner: P Connors
Partner: S Conners
Contact: Richard Betz
betz@basingold.com
Estimated Sales: $20-50 Million
Number Employees: 50-99
Private Brands Carried:
Green Giant Fresh
Types of Products Distributed:
Frozen Food, Produce

59375 Skylark Meats
4430 S 110th St
Omaha, NE 68137-1235 402-592-0300
Fax: 402-592-1414 800-759-5275
skysales@americanfoodsgroup.com
www.skylarkmeats.com
Corned beef and liver.
President: Paul Weiss
Chief Executive Officer: James Leonard
jamesleonard@skylarkmeats.com
Quality Assurance Manager: Jack Warner
Marketing Manager: Steve Giroux
VP Sales: John O'Brien
Human Resources Managers: Shane Keith
Operations Executive: Brayton Howard
Production Manager: Ray Marquez
Purchasing Manager: Barb Bevington
Year Founded: 1970
Estimated Sales: $41.1 Million
Number Employees: 250-499
Square Footage: 175000
Parent Co: Rosen's Diversified
Type of Packaging: Consumer, Food Service
Number of Customer Locations: 700
Types of Products Distributed:
Food Service, Frozen Food, Provisions/Meat

59376 Skyline Provisions
374 E 167th St
Harvey, IL 60426 708-331-1982
Fax: 708-331-1876 skylineprovisions.com
Wholesale/distributor Of beef, lamb, pork, poultry, and veal products.
Vice President: Joe Halper
Estimated Sales: $100+ Million
Number Employees: 10-19

59377 Skymart Enterprises
8725 Naomi Ave
San Gabriel, CA 91775 626-286-3742
Fax: 626-285-6842
Exporter, importer and wholesaler/distributor of food ingredients
Owner: Gene Chen
Types of Products Distributed:
Frozen Food, Food ingredients

59378 Slade Gorton & Co Inc
225 Southampton St
Boston, MA 02118 617-442-5800
Fax: 617-442-9090 800-225-1573
sales@sladegorton.com www.sladegorton.com
Wholesaler/distributor, importer and exporter of fresh and frozen shellfish and salt and smoked fish; serving the food service market and supermarket chains.
Chairman: Mike Gorton, Sr.
President & CEO: Kimberly Gorton
Vice President & National Accounts: Mike Gorton, Jr.
VP, Retail Sales & Product Development: Rachel Fitzgerald
VP, Fresh Business Development: Patrice Flanagan
Chief Operating Officer: Maureen Taylor
Year Founded: 1928
Estimated Sales: $54 Million
Number Employees: 100-249
Square Footage: 35000
Parent Co: Sg Seafood Holdings, Inc.
Type of Packaging: Consumer, Food Service, Bulk
Other Locations:
Slade Gorton & Co.
Maitland, FLSlade Gorton & Co.
Private Brands Carried:
Icybay; Tem Tasty; Sea-Tasty
Types of Products Distributed:
Food Service, Seafood, Shellfish, salt & smoked fish, etc.

59379 SlantShack Jerky
123 Butler St
Brooklyn, NY 11231 201-632-1035
www.slantshack.com
Beef jerky
President/Owner: Joshua Kace
CEO: David Koretz *Year Founded:* 2009

59380 Sleeper Produce Company
1200 3rd Ave # 300
San Diego, CA 92101-4188 619-236-6400
Fax: 619-236-5515 www.sandiego.gov
Wholesaler/distributor of produce; serving the food service market
Manager: Hadi Dehghani
VP: Matt Carmack
Number Employees: 50-99
Types of Products Distributed:
Food Service, Frozen Food, General Line, Produce

59381 Slusser Wholesale Company
P.O.Box 2439
Idaho Falls, ID 83403 208-523-0775
Fax: 208-522-1837
Wholesaler/distributor of health and beauty aids, housewares, snack foods, dry goods, tapes and glassware; rack jobber services available
President: Russ Bradley
Contact: Dean Rotweiler
rotweiler@slusser.net
Estimated Sales: $10-20 Million
Number Employees: 50-99
Parent Co: Slusser Wholesale
Number of Customer Locations: 2500
Types of Products Distributed:
Frozen Food, General Line, General Merchandise, Rack Jobbers, Housewares, tapes, dry goods, etc.

59382 Smart Juice
1139 Lehigh Ave
Suite 300
Whitehall, PA 18052 610-443-1506
Fax: 888-625-0295 smartjuice.us
Organic juices
Contact: Erdem Abdulhay
erdem@smartjuice.us

Wholesalers & Distributors / A-Z

59383 Smile Enterprises
700 S College Ave
Suite A
Bloomington, IN 47403 631-423-0100
Fax: 631-423-1389 800-496-8101
smileservice@smilepromotions.com
www.smilepromotions.com
Wholesaler/distributor of napkins, cups, premium incentives, etc.; also, custom imprinting available
President: Marilyn Knee
Contact: Tracy Bastin
tbastin@smilepromotions.com
Number Employees: 1-4
Square Footage: 4800
Private Brands Carried:
 Bic; Hanes; Libby
Number of Customer Locations: 500
Types of Products Distributed:
 Frozen Food, General Merchandise, Cups, napkins, premium incentives, etc.

59384 Smith & Greene Company
19015 66th Ave S
Kent, WA 98032 425-656-8000
Fax: 425-656-8075 800-232-8050
webinq@smithandgreene.com
www.smithandgreene.com
Wholesaler/distributor of food service equipment and supplies; serving the food service market in Washington, Oregon, Arkansas, Montana, Idaho and Alaska
President: James Smith
CEO: Charles Mullen
Sales Manager: David Leitch
Contact: Christine Allen
christinea@smithandgreene.com
Estimated Sales: $10-20 Million
Number Employees: 50-99
Square Footage: 110000
Types of Products Distributed:
 Food Service, Frozen Food, General Merchandise, Equipment & supplies

59385 Smith & Greene Company
915 W 2nd Ave Ste 2
Spokane, WA 99201 509-483-2330
Fax: 509-483-2332 800-694-6424
www.smithandgreene.com
Wholesaler/distributor of food service equipment and supplies; also, contract design information, shop drawings, consulting and literature services available; serving the food service market
Manager: Jim Lumper
Secretary/Treasurer: Charles Mullen
Sales Manager: David Leitch
Contact: Michelle Molan
michelle@smithandgreene.com
Estimated Sales: Over $1 Billion
Number Employees: 5-9
Square Footage: 24000
Parent Co: Smith & Greene Company
Types of Products Distributed:
 Food Service, Frozen Food, General Merchandise, Foodservice equipment & supplies

59386 Smith & Son Wholesale
1105 NW Atlantic St
PO Box 877
Tullahoma, TN 37388-2354 931-455-2203
Fax: 931-455-2203 800-343-4303
Wholesaler/distributor of general line products; serving the food service market
Owner: Monty Smith
monty@smithandson.net
Estimated Sales: $10-20 Million
Number Employees: 10-19
Types of Products Distributed:
 Food Service, Frozen Food, General Line

59387 (HQ)Smith Restaurant SupplyCo
500 Erie Blvd E
Syracuse, NY 13202-1109 315-474-8731
Fax: 315-478-7004 800-346-2556
www.smithrestaurantsupply.com
Wholesaler/distributor of food service equipment and supplies including coffee, gourmet housewares and cutlery; importer of cutlery and home beer brewery equipment and supplies; serving the food service market
President: John Kuppermann
accounting@smithrestaurantsupply.com
President: Ellison Kuppermann
Sales Manager: Robin Russell
Estimated Sales: $10-20 Million
Number Employees: 5-9
Square Footage: 130000
Type of Packaging: Food Service
Private Brands Carried:
 Hyman Smith Coffee; M.J. Kupper Cutlery; Wholesale 2 U
Types of Products Distributed:
 Food Service, Frozen Food, General Merchandise, Coffee, housewares & cutlery

59388 Smith, Bob, Restaurant Equipment
1890 E Walnut St
Pasadena, CA 91107-3540 626-792-1185
Fax: 626-792-9529
Wholesaler/distributor of food service equipment; also, design and consulting services available
Owner: Greg Golem
Sales Manager: Butch Cummings
Estimated Sales: $500,000-$1 Million
Number Employees: 5-9
Square Footage: 20000
Types of Products Distributed:
 Food Service, Frozen Food, General Merchandise

59389 Smith, S.R.
202 Howerton Avenue
Nashville, TN 37213-1002 615-255-6307
Fax: 615-255-9531
Wholesaler/distributor of provisions/meats including processed and ground products
President: Otis McDaniel
Secretary/Treasurer: Joyce McDaniel
VP: Kenneth Garnand
Estimated Sales: $10-20 Million
Number Employees: 10-19
Types of Products Distributed:
 Provisions/Meat, Processed & ground products

59390 Smiths Sunbeam Bakery
PO Box 17428
Pensacola, FL 32522-7428 850-432-0951
Fax: 850-433-5235
Wholesaler/distributor of bakery products
Director Operations: Vince Windham
Estimated Sales: $5-10 Million
Number Employees: 20-49
Parent Co: Cooper Smith
Types of Products Distributed:
 Specialty Foods, Bakery products

59391 Smitty's Snowballs
29124 Catholic Hall Road
Hammond, LA 70403-8380 225-567-7983
smithwarren@yahoo.com
Wholesaler/distributor and exporter of snow cone syrup, shaved and flavored ice
Types of Products Distributed:
 Frozen Food, General Line, Specialty Foods, Snow cone syrup, shaved & flavored ice

59392 Smoked Turkey Inc
6608 E Marshville Blvd
Marshville, NC 28103-1198 704-624-6628
Fax: 704-624-2510
info@stegallsmokedturkey.com
www.stegallsmokedturkey.com
Frozen hickory-smoked turkey and honey-glazed ham
Estimated Sales: $500,000-$1 Million
Number Employees: 1-4
Square Footage: 440000
Type of Packaging: Private Label
Types of Products Distributed:
 Provisions/Meat

59393 (HQ)Smokey Mountain Grill
960 Clubland Way
Marietta, GA 30068-2569 770-977-7770
Fax: 770-509-7585 800-219-9540
www.gabbq.com
Wholesaler/distributor of barbecue pits, grills, smokers, rotisseries and display cases; also, wood-burning char broilers and catering trailer pits
President: Kevin Livingston
tuffgrill@att.net
VP/Director Operations: Jacquie Livingston
Estimated Sales: Less than $500,000
Number Employees: 1-4
Types of Products Distributed:
 Frozen Food, General Merchandise, Cooking & heating equipment

59394 Smoothie's Frozen Desserts
10 Summer Street
Manchester, MA 01944-1579 860-830-4051
Fax: 978-526-8530 800-237-2381
Wholesaler/distributor of soft ice cream and yogurt equipment; also, frozen yogurt, ice cream, sorbet and frozen beverages
President: Mark Mahoney
Number Employees: 5-9
Square Footage: 40000
Private Brands Carried:
 Mr. Smoothie's
Types of Products Distributed:
 Frozen Food, General Line, General Merchandise, Ice cream & yogurt equipment, etc.

59395 Snack Company
341-105th Street E
Saskatoon, SK S7N 1Z4
Canada 306-373-4967
Fax: 306-955-4659
Wholesaler/distributor of general line products including sandwiches, juices, beef jerky and confectionery items
President: Jack Satterthwaite
Number Employees: 10-19
Square Footage: 32000
Types of Products Distributed:
 Frozen Food, General Line, Sandwiches, juices & beef jerky

59396 Snack King Foods
P.O.Box 16421
Rochester, NY 14616 585-254-3690
Fax: 716-227-7958
Wholesaler/distributor of snack foods; rack jobber services available
Owner: J Lauber
Estimated Sales: $300,000-500,000
Number Employees: 5-9
Number of Customer Locations: 400
Types of Products Distributed:
 Frozen Food, General Line, Rack Jobbers, Snack foods

59397 Snacks Over America Inc
3144 Stage Post Dr # 115
Memphis, TN 38133-4039 901-385-7083
Fax: 901-385-7158
service@snacksoveramerica.com
www.snacksoveramerica.com
Wholesaler/distributor of snack foods, cookies, candy, potato chips, peanuts, cashews, crackers, pretzels, beef jerky and popcorn; also, gift baskets
President: Mitchell Chu-Yang
Estimated Sales: $300,000-500,000
Number Employees: 1-4
Private Brands Carried:
 Nabisco; Keebler; Frito-Lays
Types of Products Distributed:
 Frozen Food, General Line, Cookies, candy, popcorn, peanuts, etc.

59398 Snapple Distributors ofLong Island
120 Adams Boulevard
Farmingdale, NY 11735-6614 516-714-0002
Fax: 516-714-0017
Wholesaler/distributor of iced tea, noncarbonated and sports drinks and juices; serving retail and food service markets in the Long Island area
President: Gil Kaplan
Estimated Sales: $1-2.5 Million
Number Employees: 20-49
Square Footage: 456000
Parent Co: Snapple Beverage Group
Private Brands Carried:
 Snapple (beverages); Stewarts (root beer); Vermont Pure (water)
Number of Customer Locations: 6000
Types of Products Distributed:
 Food Service, Frozen Food, General Line, Sports drinks, iced teas & juices

59399 Snappy Popcorn
610 Main St
Breda, IA 51436-8719 712-673-2347
Fax: 712-673-2347 800-742-0228
jon@snappypopcorn.com
www.snappypopcorn.com
Manufacturer, wholesaler/distributor and exporter of popcorn and supplies

1173

Wholesalers & Distributors / A-Z

President: Alan Tiefenthaler
alan@itien.com
Office Manager: Lori Steinkamp
VP Sales: Jon Tiefenthaler
Estimated Sales: $1-2.5 Million
Number Employees: 20-49
Square Footage: 100000
Type of Packaging: Food Service, Bulk
Types of Products Distributed:
　Food Service, Frozen Food, General Line, General Merchandise, Popcorn & supplies

59400　Snelgrove Ice Cream Company
850 E 2100 S
Salt Lake City, UT 84106-1832　801-486-4456
　Fax: 801-486-3926　800-569-0005
　www.dreyers.com
Processor, exporter and wholesaler/distributor of ice cream and ice cream novelties
President: David Mutzel
Contact: Troy Luckart
troy.luckart@dreyers.com
Estimated Sales: Less than $500,000
Number Employees: 50-99
Parent Co: MKD Distributing
Type of Packaging: Consumer, Food Service, Private Label, Bulk
Types of Products Distributed:
　Frozen Food

59401　Sniderman Brothers
P.O.Box 1252
Youngstown, OH 44501　330-744-4141
　Fax: 330-744-4186
Wholesaler/distributor of general line products; serving the food service market
President: L Sniderman
VP: G Sniderman
Estimated Sales: $10-20 Million
Number Employees: 5-9
Types of Products Distributed:
　Food Service, Frozen Food, General Line

59402　Snow's Ice Cream Co Inc
80 School St
Greenfield, MA 01301-2410　413-774-7438
　Fax: 413-774-5406　www.bartshomemade.com
Ice cream, sorbet and frozen yogurt; wholesaler/distributor of frozen food, candy, snack foods, sauces, mustards and salsa's
Owner: Gary Schaefer
gary@bartshomemade.com
Estimated Sales: Below $5 Million
Number Employees: 5-9
Square Footage: 64000
Parent Co: Another Roadside Attraction
Type of Packaging: Consumer, Food Service, Private Label, Bulk

59403　SnowBird Corporation
379 Broadway
Bayonne, NJ 07002-3631　201-858-8300
　Fax: 201-451-5000　800-576-1616
Bottled filtered, spring, and distilled water, coffee makers and hot foods; wholesaler/distributor of water fountains and bottled water coolers; repair services available
President: Diane Drey
Vice President: Gerald Giannangeli
Estimated Sales: $3-5 Million
Number Employees: 6
Square Footage: 264000
Types of Products Distributed:
　General Merchandise, Water fountains & coolers

59404　(HQ)Snyder Wholesale Inc
1107 David Ln
Blytheville, AR 72315-5456　870-763-7341
　Fax: 870-763-1234
Wholesaler/distributor of groceries, frozens, produce, meats, cleaning supplies, disposables, wraps, supplies and equipment serving the food service market
President: Richard Snyder
rsnyder@snyerwholesale.com
VP: Janeen Snyder
Director Purchasing/Food Service: Gary Karlish
Estimated Sales: $20-50 Million
Number Employees: 20-49
Square Footage: 30000
Private Brands Carried:
　Code

Types of Products Distributed:
　Food Service, Frozen Food, General Line, Provisions/Meat, Produce, Groceries, cleaning supplies, etc.

59405　Snyder's Bakery
31 N 4th Ave
Yakima, WA 98902　509-457-6150
　Fax: 509-249-4102　www.usbakery.com
Importer of snack foods and pastries; wholesaler/distributor of baked goods including bread and sweet goods
Manager: Gene Parke
CEO: Bob Albers
CFO: Jerry Boness
Vice President: Kim Nisbet
Marketing: Todd Cornwell
Contact: Duane Howerton
howertond@usbakery.com
Estimated Sales: $2.5-5 Million
Number Employees: 20-49
Parent Co: United States Bakery
Private Brands Carried:
　Country Hearth; Hillybilly; Roman Meal; Gais; Bimbo; Marinela; Svenhard's; Seattle International
Types of Products Distributed:
　Frozen Food, General Line, Baked goods

59406　So Cal Material Handling
550 S Palm Street
La Habra, CA 90631-5736　714-520-4696
　Fax: 714-520-0351
Wholesaler/distributor of steel shelving, automatic storage and handling systems and pallet racks
Estimated Sales: $1-2.5 Million
Number Employees: 10-19
Number of Customer Locations: 100
Types of Products Distributed:
　Frozen Food, General Merchandise, Steel shelving & storage systems

59407　Sobey's
3337b 8th Street E
Saskatoon, SK S7H 4K1
Canada　306-931-1144
　Fax: 306-933-4266
Wholesaler/distributor of groceries, frozen foods, produce and meats
Owner/President: Bill McEwan
General Manager: Don Ward
Number Employees: 10-19
Square Footage: 6400
Parent Co: Sobey's Capital
Number of Customer Locations: 45
Types of Products Distributed:
　Frozen Food, General Line, Provisions/Meat, Produce, Groceries

59408　Sobey's Ontario
6355 Viscount Road
Mississauga, ON L4V 1W2
Canada　905-672-6633
　Fax: 905-671-5175　www.sobeyscorporate.com
Wholesaler/distributor of dairy products, frozen foods, produce, meats and seafood; serving the food service market
President/CEO: Marc Poulin
CFO: Francois Vimard
Number Employees: 500-999
Parent Co: Sobey's
Private Brands Carried:
　IGA; Price-Chopper; Foodtown; Knechtel
Number of Customer Locations: 3273
Types of Products Distributed:
　Food Service, Frozen Food, General Line, General Merchandise, Provisions/Meat, Produce, Seafood, Dairy products, etc.

59409　Sobey's Quebec Inc
11281 Albert Hudon
North Montreal, QC H1G 3J5
Canada　514-324-1010
　Fax: 514-324-5506　www.sobeyscorporate.com
Wholesaler/distributor of groceries, meats, produce, dairy, frozen and baked foods and private label items
President/CEO: Marc Poulin
CFO: Francois Vimard
Number Employees: 1,000-4,999
Square Footage: 2964692
Parent Co: Sobey's
Private Brands Carried:
　IGA; Our Compliments; Smart Choice
Number of Customer Locations: 1921

Types of Products Distributed:
　Frozen Food, General Line, Provisions/Meat, Produce, Dairy & baked products, etc.

59410　Sobeys Inc.
115 King St
Stellarton, NS B0K 1S0
Canada　902-752-8371
　corporate.sobeys.com
Groceries
President & CEO: Michael Medline
EVP & CFO: Michael Vels
SVP, General Counsel & Corp Secretary: Doug Nathanson
EVP Human Resources: Simon Gagn,
Year Founded: 1907
Estimated Sales: $24 Billion
Number Employees: 125000
Parent Co: Empire Company Ltd.
Types of Products Distributed:
　Frozen Food, General Line, Provisions/Meat, Produce, Seafood

59411　Sobeys Inc.
1020-64 Ave NE
Calgary, AB T2E 7V8
Canada
　800-723-3929
Groceries
Number of Customer Locations: 70
Types of Products Distributed:
　Frozen Food, General Line, General Merchandise, Provisions/Meat, Produce, Seafood

59412　Sobeys Inc.
4980 Tahoe Blvd
Mississauga, ON L4W 0C7
Canada　905-238-7124
Groceries
Private Brands Carried:
　Knechtel
Number of Customer Locations: 350
Types of Products Distributed:
　Frozen Food, General Line, General Merchandise, Provisions/Meat, Produce, Seafood

59413　Sobeys Inc.
11281 Albert-Hudon Blvd
Montreal, QC H1G 3J5
Canada　514-324-1010
Groceries
Number of Customer Locations: 816
Types of Products Distributed:
　Frozen Food, General Line, General Merchandise, Provisions/Meat, Produce, Seafood

59414　Sobeys Inc.
123 Foord St
Stellarton, NS B0K 1S0
Canada　902-752-8371
Groceries
Types of Products Distributed:
　Frozen Food, General Line, General Merchandise, Provisions/Meat, Produce, Seafood

59415　Sobeys Inc.
6649 Butler Cres
Saanichton, BC V8M 1Z7
Canada　250-483-1600
Groceries
Types of Products Distributed:
　Frozen Food, General Line, General Merchandise, Provisions/Meat, Produce, Seafood

59416　Socafe
41 Malvern St
Newark, NJ 07105-1510　973-589-4104
　Fax: 973-589-4429　www.socafe.net
Importer and wholesaler/distributor of espresso equipment; coffee roasting available; serving the food service market
President: Joseph Fernandes
socafe@socafe.com
VP: Isabel Fernandes
Estimated Sales: $10-20 Million
Number Employees: 10-19
Type of Packaging: Consumer, Food Service
Private Brands Carried:
　Fiamma
Types of Products Distributed:
　Food Service, Frozen Food, General Merchandise, Espresso machinery

Wholesalers & Distributors / A-Z

59417 Soda Service
261 Pascone Pl
Newington, CT 06111-4524 860-666-7845
Fax: 860-666-7876 800-423-7632
www.sodaservice.net
Wholesaler/distributor of restaurant equipment; serving the food service market
Owner: Nick Lococo
nlococo@sodaservice.net
Sales Manager: Michael Sullo
Service Manager: Nick Lococo
Number Employees: 10-19
Types of Products Distributed:
Food Service, Frozen Food, General Merchandise, Restaurant equipment

59418 Sofo Foods
253 Waggoner Blvd
Toledo, OH 43612-1952 419-476-4211
Fax: 419-478-6104 800-447-4211
www.sofofoods.com
Appetizers, meat toppings and flour products such as doughs, pasta, cheese blends, and tomatoes.
CEO: Michael Sofo
Chief Operating Officer: Cos Figliomini
Chief Information Officer: Chuck Winters
Director, Corporate Accounting: Roger Bly
Director, Sales: Jeff Peer
VP, Operations: Gary Tolles
Director, Logistics: Jon Steinmetz
Director, Purchasing: Rob Kaufman
Estimated Sales: $20-50 Million
Number Employees: 250-499
Number of Brands: 6
Type of Packaging: Food Service
Other Locations:
New Albany, IN
Suwanee, GA
Houston, TXSuwanee
Number of Customer Locations: 4

59419 (HQ)Sogelco International
Suite 400
Montreal, QC H2Y 2H7
Canada 514-849-2414
Fax: 514-849-0645 sogelco@sogelco.com
Producer and wholesaler/distributor, importer and exporter of seafood, poultry, meats and frozen foods; serving the food service market
President: Gabriel Elbaz
Sales Director: Andre Arseneault
Production/Plant Manager: Carl Desroches
Purchasing: Edmond Elbaz
Estimated Sales: $40 Million
Number Employees: 15
Type of Packaging: Consumer, Food Service, Bulk
Other Locations:
Sogelco International
Baie Ste. Anne, NBSogelco International
Private Brands Carried:
Lobsterine; Crabterine; Shrimperine
Types of Products Distributed:
Food Service, Frozen Food, Provisions/Meat, Seafood, Poultry

59420 Sol Loeb Moving & Storage
5427 Armour Rd
Columbus, GA 31909-4525 706-660-5193
Fax: 706-322-4566 www.solloebmoving.com
Wholesaler/distributor of general line products; serving the food service market
President: Fred Steinhauser
Estimated Sales: Less Than $500,000
Number Employees: 1-4
Square Footage: 40000
Private Brands Carried:
Red & White
Types of Products Distributed:
Food Service, Frozen Food, General Line

59421 Solutions
PO Box 407
Searsport, ME 04974-0407 207-548-2636
Fax: 207-548-2921 800-628-3166
Wholesaler/distributor, exporter and importer of carrageenan, xanthan gum, sodium alginate
President: Donna Ravin
VP: Scott Rangus
R&D: Kevin Johndro
Marketing: Scott Rangus
VP Sales/Marketing: Scott Rangus
Estimated Sales: $15-20 Million
Number Employees: 5-9
Type of Packaging: Bulk

Types of Products Distributed:
Frozen Food, General Line, Carrageenan

59422 Somerset Industries
901 North Bethlehem Pike
Spring House, PA 19477-0927 215-619-0480
Fax: 215-619-0489 800-883-8728
www.somersetindustries.com
Wholesaler/distributor, importer and exporter of closeout items bought and sold. The correctional food specialist. Warehouse and transportation services provided
President: Jay Shrager
CFO: Carole Shrager
VP: Alan Breslow
Marketing Director: Candace Shrager
Sales Manager: Kevin Murray Jr
General Manager: Ben Caldwell
Number Employees: 20-49
Type of Packaging: Food Service, Private Label, Bulk
Private Brands Carried:
Anna Maria, Somerset, 21st Century, Tiny's Treats, Bobbie
Number of Customer Locations: 700
Types of Products Distributed:
Food Service, Frozen Food, Provisions/Meat, Seafood, Kosher, Hallah

59423 Sonoco Products Co
1 N 2nd St
Hartsville, SC 29550-3305 843-383-7000
800-377-2692
corporate.communications@sonoco.com
www.sonoco.com
Global manufacturer of consumer and industrial packing products and provider of packaging services.
President & CEO: R. Howard Coker
VP & CFO: Julie Albrecht
EVP: Rodger Fuller
Corporate VP & CIO: Rick Johnson
VP, Marketing & Innovation: Marcy Thompson
Year Founded: 1899
Estimated Sales: $5 Billion
Number Employees: 21,000

59424 Sonora Foods
7295 Torbram Road
Mississauga, ON L4T 1G8
Canada 905-678-9004
Fax: 905-678-2832 800-815-9115
sonora@sonorafoods.com www.sonorafoods.com
Wholesaler/distributor of specialty Mexican/Southwest foods including tortillas and nachos; serving the food service market
President: Juan Soissa
Number Employees: 10-19
Square Footage: 32000
Types of Products Distributed:
Food Service, Frozen Food, General Line, Specialty Foods, Mexican/Southwest products

59425 Sonstegard Foods Company
5005 S Bur Oak Pl
Sioux Falls, SD 57108
800-533-3184
info@sonstegard.com www.sonstegard.com
Sonstegard Foods Company is a major wholesaler of powdered, liquid, and frozen egg products. We sell egg products to food processors, mix manufacturers, schools, food distributors, and industries including the salad dressing industrycandy industry, pasta industry, and others.
President: Philip Sonstegard
Year Founded: 1972
Estimated Sales: $75-100 Million

59426 Soofer Co
2828 S Alameda St
Vernon, CA 90058-1347 323-234-6666
Fax: 323-234-2447 800-852-4050
info@sadaf.com www.sadaf.com
Wholesaler/distributor and importer of specialty Mid-Eastern and Spanish items including spices, juices, beans, nuts, pickles, jams and syrups; exporter of spices and juices
Owner: Darioush Soofer
Marketing VP: Dariush Soofer
Estimated Sales: $10-20 Million
Number Employees: 20-49
Square Footage: 68000
Type of Packaging: Consumer, Food Service, Bulk

Private Brands Carried:
Sadaf
Types of Products Distributed:
Frozen Food, General Line, Health Food, Specialty Foods, Juices, nuts, pickles, spices, etc.

59427 Soozy's Grain-Free
246 Fifth Ave, 3rd Floor
P.O. Box 20077
New York, NY 10001
hello@soozys.com
www.soozysgrainfree.com
Muffins that are paleo and free from grain, gluten, dairy, peanuts, and soy
President: Mason Sexton
CEO: Susan Chen
Year Founded: 2017
Parent Co: Mindful Foods
Types of Products Distributed:
General Line

59428 (HQ)Sorbee Intl.
9990 Global Rd.
Philadelphia, PA 19115 215-677-5200
Fax: 215-677-7736 800-654-3997
Confectionery items including sugar hard candy, low-fat candy bars and sugar-free items
CEO: Daniel Werther
CFO: Tom Keogh
VP Sales: Barry Sokol
Estimated Sales: $31 Million
Number Employees: 20-49
Other Locations:
Sorbee International Ltd.
Philadelphia, PASorbee International Ltd.
Types of Products Distributed:
Frozen Food

59429 Sorrento Lobster
224 Ocean Ave
Sorrento, ME 04677 207-422-9082
Fax: 207-422-9033
Seafood.
Manager: Rick Freeman
Estimated Sales: $2,100,000
Number Employees: 5-9

59430 Source Naturals
23 Janis Way
Scotts Valley, CA 95066 831-438-1144
800-815-2333
www.sourcenaturals.com
Dietary supplements
President, CEO & Owner: Ira Goldberg
irag@thresholdent.com
Year Founded: 1982
Estimated Sales: $52.9 Million
Number Employees: 500-999
Square Footage: 100000
Parent Co: Threshold Enterprises
Types of Products Distributed:
Frozen Food, General Merchandise, Health Food, Dietary supplements

59431 South Beach Novelties & Confectionery
44 Robin Rd
Staten Island, NY 10305-4799 718-727-4500
Fax: 718-448-4108
Tobacco, tobacco products and confectionary.
Owner: John Lagana
Estimated Sales: $18 Million
Number Employees: 11
Square Footage: 6000
Types of Products Distributed:
Confectionary

59432 South Jersey Paper Products
2400 Industrial Way
Vineland, NJ 08360-1550 856-691-2605
Fax: 856-794-8979 800-232-6927
www.southjerseypaper.com
Wholesaler/distributor of paper supplies, disposables, syrups, toppings and ice cream cones; serving the food service market
President: Bonnie Spector
bspector@southjerseypaper.com
Estimated Sales: $20-50 Million
Number Employees: 20-49
Square Footage: 35000
Types of Products Distributed:
Food Service, Frozen Food, General Line, General Merchandise, Paper supplies, disposables, etc.

Wholesalers & Distributors / A-Z

59433 South Shores Seafood
1822 E Ball Rd
Anaheim, CA 92805-5936
714-956-2722
Fax: 714-956-0277
Seafood
President: Michael Armstrong
Estimated Sales: $2,000,000
Number Employees: 5-9

59434 South Valley Citrus Packers
9600 Road 256
Terra Bella, CA 93270
559-906-1033
Fax: 559-525-4206 vcpg@vcpg.com
Packinghouse and licensed shipper of Sunkist Growers Inc. citrus products.
Manager: Cliff Martin
Grower Service Representative: Maribel Nenna
General Manager Visalia Citrus Packing: Bob Walters
Parent Co: Visalia Citrus Packing Group
Type of Packaging: Food Service

59435 Southeast Cold Storage
18770 NE 6th Ave
Miami, FL 33179
305-652-4622
www.southeastcoldstorage.com
Wholesaler/distributor of groceries, frozen foods, baked goods, meats and dairy products.
President: John Robinson
Estimated Sales: $100-500 Million
Number Employees: 100-249
Square Footage: 165000
Parent Co: Southeast Frozen Foods Company
Number of Customer Locations: 2000
Types of Products Distributed:
Frozen Food, General Line, Provisions/Meat, Baked goods, dairy products, etc.

59436 Southeast Industrial Equipment
P.O.Box 667907
Charlotte, NC 28266-7907
704-588-4522
Fax: 704-393-1714 800-752-6368
Wholesaler/distributor of forklifts and shelving
President: Mark Ahlstrom
Finance Manager: Scot Johnson
VP: Dave James
Head Marketing: Terry Dussell
Accounts Department: Ruth Grissey
Estimated Sales: $20-50 Million
Number Employees: 50-99
Private Brands Carried:
B.T. Prime Mover; Interlake Rack; Toyota
Types of Products Distributed:
Frozen Food, General Merchandise, Forklifts & shelving

59437 Southeastern Grocers
8928 Prominence Parkway
Suite 200
Jacksonville, FL 32256
904-783-5000
800-967-9105
www.segrocers.com
Supermarket portfolio.
President/CEO: Anthony Hucker
Estimated Sales: $1.5 Billion
Number Employees: 45,000
Number of Brands: 4
Type of Packaging: Consumer, Food Service, Private Label

59438 (HQ)Southeastern Grocers
8928 Prominence Pkwy.
Ste. 200
Jacksonville, FL 32256
904-783-5000
800-967-9105
www.segrocers.com
Wholesaler/distrubtor of general groceries, frozen foods, meats, and produce.
CEO: Anthony Hucker
Year Founded: 2013
Number Employees: 47,000
Number of Customer Locations: 550
Types of Products Distributed:
Frozen Food, General Line, General Merchandise, Provisions/Meat, Produce

59439 Southern Culture Foods
6400 Atlantic Blvd
Suite 135
Peachtree Corners, GA 30071
ebarrett@southernculturefoods.com
www.southernculturefoods.com
Pancake and waffle mix in flavors including banana pudding, birthday cake, gingerbread, lemon blueberry, red velvet, strawberry, sweet potato, vanilla, and bourbon salted pecan; Also stone ground grits, cornbread mix, fried chickenmix, and bacon rub
Founder & CEO: Erica Barrett *Year Founded:* 2011
Types of Products Distributed:
General Merchandise

59440 Southern Fish & Oyster Company
1 Eslava St
Mobile, AL 36603
251-438-2408
Fax: 251-432-7773
Seafood, oysters
Owner: Ralph Atkins
Estimated Sales: $1-3 Million
Number Employees: 10-19

59441 Southern Glazer's Wine-Spirits, LLC
2400 SW 145th Ave
Miramar, FL 33027-4228
954-680-4600
866-375-9555
www.southernglazers.com
Beer, wine, equipment and fixtures and general merchandise.
CEO: Wayne Chaplin
waynechaplin@southernwine.com
Chairman: Harvey Chaplin
Executive VP, Finance: Thomas Greenlee
Executive Vice Chairman: Bennett Glazer
Executive VP/COO: Brad Vassar
Year Founded: 1968
Estimated Sales: $16.5 Billion
Number Employees: 22,000
Number of Brands: 5000
Types of Products Distributed:
Food Service, General Line, General Merchandise, Beer & wines

59442 Southern Grocery Company
4050 Middle Avenue
Sarasota, FL 34234-2111
941-355-5151
Fax: 941-355-4255
Wholesaler/distributor of frozen, dry and nonfood items; also, equipment and fixtures; serving the food service market
President/COO: Chuck Donelson
VP Logistics: Charles Puckett
VP Sales: Bud Totten
Contact: Michael Barclaya
michaelb@southernfoodservice.com
Estimated Sales: $10-20 Million
Number Employees: 50-99
Private Brands Carried:
NIFDA; ComSource
Types of Products Distributed:
Food Service, Frozen Food, General Line

59443 Southern Import Distributors
442 W Kennedy Boulevard
Suite 200
Tampa, FL 33606-1464
813-289-7881
Fax: 813-254-7382
Wholesaler/distributor of spring water
President: Todd Walker
Number Employees: 1-4
Private Brands Carried:
Millennium
Types of Products Distributed:
Frozen Food, General Line, Health Food, Spring water

59444 Southern Indiana Butcher's Supply
131 East 10th Street
Lamar, IN 47532
812-998-2277
www.butchersupply.net
Wholesaler/distributor of meat handling and packing supplies including sausage stuffers and makers, meat curers and choppers, smokers, cutlery and butchers' tools; also, sausage casings and seasonings
Owner: Jesse Summers
Number Employees: 1-4
Parent Co: Summers Enterprises
Types of Products Distributed:
Frozen Food, General Line, General Merchandise, Provisions/Meat, Meat handling & packing supplies, etc.

59445 Southern Material Handling Co
8118 E 44th St
Tulsa, OK 74145-4831
918-622-7200
Fax: 918-622-5520 866-296-9034
tulinfo@southernmaterial.com
www.southernmaterial.com
Wholesaler/distributor of material handling equipment
President: Mark Segress
msegress@southernmaterial.com
Estimated Sales: $10-20 Million
Number Employees: 20-49
Private Brands Carried:
Toyota; Clark; Kelly
Types of Products Distributed:
Frozen Food, General Merchandise, Material handling equipment

59446 Southern Produce Distributors
111 NW Center St
Faison, NC 28341-6124
910-267-0011
Fax: 910-267-5041 www.southern-produce.com
Wholesaler/distributor of sweet potatoes
President: Wayne Miller
wayne@southern-produce.com
Sales Manager: Brenda Oglesby
Estimated Sales: $.5-1 million
Number Employees: 100-249
Private Brands Carried:
Danny Boy
Types of Products Distributed:
Frozen Food, Produce, Sweet potatoes

59447 Southern Seafood Distributors
26400 Buford Creel Rd
Franklinton, LA 70438
985-839-6220
Fax: 985-839-6297
Seafood
Owner: Jackie Creel
Estimated Sales: $1-3 Million
Number Employees: 1-4

59448 Southern Shellfish
120 Johnny Mercer Boulevard
Savannah, GA 31410-2142
912-897-3650
Fax: 912-897-6036
Seafood, shellfish

59449 Southern States Toyotalift
115 S 78th St
Tampa, FL 33619-4220
813-626-7535
Fax: 813-626-4713 www.sstlift.com
Wholesaler/distributor of forklifts
President: Michae Baldwin
mbaldwin@sstlift.com
CEO: Jeff Fischer
Estimated Sales: $20-50 Million
Number Employees: 50-99
Private Brands Carried:
Crown; Clark; Daewoo
Types of Products Distributed:
Frozen Food, General Merchandise, Forklifts

59450 Southern Steel ShelvingCompany
601 E 27th St
Baltimore, MD 21218
410-366-4500
Fax: 410-366-4597
Wholesaler/distributor of steel pallet racks and steel shelving
Owner/President: S Jerry Cohn
Contact: Jerry Cohn
jcohn@rackdepot.com
Estimated Sales: $2.5-5 Million
Number Employees: 5-9
Types of Products Distributed:
Frozen Food, General Merchandise, Steel pallet racks & shelving

59451 Southern Stock Foodservice
1 Medical Center Drive
P.O.Box 626
Biddeford, ME 04005
407-328-8121
Fax: 407-328-9180 800-428-8121
info@smhc.org www.smhc.org
Wholesaler/distributor of pizza and baking equipment
President: Jeff Dill
Sales Manager: Sam Wearn
Number Employees: 20-49
Types of Products Distributed:
Pizza & baking equipment

Wholesalers & Distributors / A-Z

59452 Southern Supplies Limited
323 Bloor Street W
Oshawa, ON L1J 6X4
Canada   905-728-6216
Fax: 905-436-7793 info@southernsupplies.ca
Wholesaler/distributor of steel shelving, steel work benches, metal lockers and cold room storage shelving
President: Walter Libby
Sales Manager (Industrial): Bruce Laverty
Number Employees: 20-49
Square Footage: 44000
Parent Co: Southern Supplies
Types of Products Distributed:
  Frozen Food, General Merchandise, Steel shelving, lockers, etc.

59453 Southernfood.com LLC
1025 Johnson Ferry Rd
Suite 136-419
Marietta, GA 30068   770-635-8324
                       800-991-1066
sales@southernfood.com www.southernsupplies.ca
Wholesaler/distributor of British and Irish style bacon and cured pork products
President: William Johnson
Number Employees: 1-4
Types of Products Distributed:
  Frozen Food, General Line, Provisions/Meat, British & Irish style bacon, etc.

59454 Southline Equipment Company
P.O.Box 8867
Houston, TX 77249   713-869-6801
Fax: 713-869-2875 800-444-1173
                      www.eqdepot.com
Wholesaler/distributor of material handling equipment including new and used forklift trucks, parts, service and rental in addition to industrial sweepers/scrubbers.
Manager: Jeff Jones
Finance: F Rigell
Marketing Director: Bob McClelland
Sales Manager: M Zinda
Operations Manager: M Gunter
Estimated Sales: $20 Million
Number Employees: 50-99
Square Footage: 60000
Private Brands Carried:
  Clark; Daewoo; Lindy-Baker
Types of Products Distributed:
  Frozen Food, General Merchandise, Material handling equipment

59455 (HQ)Southside Market & Bbq Inc
1212 Highway 290 E
Elgin, TX 78621-2019   512-281-4650
Fax: 512-285-4433 877-487-8015
Wholesaler/distributor of fresh and frozen meat including sausage, pork, beef and lamb
President: Ernest W Bracewell Sr
Estimated Sales: $2.5-5 Million
Number Employees: 50-99
Types of Products Distributed:
  Provisions/Meat, Sausage, pork, beef & lamb

59456 Southside Seafood Inc
1930 Pittston Ave # 1
Scranton, PA 18505-4497   570-969-9726
Fax: 570-961-5181 www.southsideseafood.net
Seafood
Owner: Carl Pazzaglia
Estimated Sales: $3-5 Million
Number Employees: 5-9

59457 Southwest Distributing Co
5840 Office Blvd NE
Albuquerque, NM 87109-5819   505-344-2861
Fax: 505-345-4494 800-326-5571
Wholesaler/distributor of groceries, cleaning supplies, disposables, wraps, tabletop supplies and equipment; serving the food service market
President: Sheila Snyder
Sales/Marketing: Melissa Hallada
Purchasing Agent: Kevin Burch
Estimated Sales: Less Than $500,000
Number Employees: 1-4
Square Footage: 165960
Parent Co: Distribution Plus
Private Brands Carried:
  Code; Southwest
Number of Customer Locations: 4000
Types of Products Distributed:
  Food Service, Frozen Food, General Line, General Merchandise, Disposables, cleaning supplies, etc.

59458 Southwest Forklift
1906 Johanna Dr # B2
Houston, TX 77055-2470   713-747-8404
Fax: 713-747-7278 www.southwestforklift.com
Wholesaler/distributor of forklifts and personnel lifts
Owner: Jim Wilson
jow2@forkliftsoftexas.com
Estimated Sales: $500,000-$1 Million
Number Employees: 1-4
Private Brands Carried:
  Crown; Yale; Raymond
Types of Products Distributed:
  Frozen Food, General Merchandise, Forklifts & personnel lifts

59459 Southwest Lift
4001 N Panam Expy
San Antonio, TX 78219-2206   210-351-9500
Fax: 210-351-9561 www.tlotx.com
Wholesaler/distributor of material handling equipment
Manager: Ken Townsend
Marketing Manager: Scott Schontos
Estimated Sales: $20-50 Million
Number Employees: 20-49
Private Brands Carried:
  Toyota; Crown; Clark
Types of Products Distributed:
  Frozen Food, General Merchandise, Material handling equipment

59460 Southwest Material Handling
3725 Nobel Ct
Mira Loma, CA 91752-3267   951-727-0477
Fax: 951-727-0407 800-524-8143
                      www.swmhinc.com
Wholesaler/distributor of conveyors, racks, shelving, baskets, bins and metal boxes
President: Gary Little
garyl@swmhinc.com
Engineer: David Mallory
Estimated Sales: $10-20 Million
Number Employees: 100-249
Types of Products Distributed:
  Frozen Food, General Merchandise, Conveyors, racks, shelving, bins, etc.

59461 Southwest Materials Handling
4719 Almond Ave
Dallas, TX 75247-6499   214-630-1375
Fax: 214-638-3609 800-303-6582
swmh1@concentric.net www.usedtaylordunn.com
Wholesaler/distributor of material handling equipment
President: Joe Harper
joeh@swmhc.com
Vice President: Ken Harper
Estimated Sales: $10-20 Million
Number Employees: 20-49
Square Footage: 52000
Private Brands Carried:
  Southworth; Ridg-U-Rak; BT Primo Mover; Taylor Dunn; Big Joe Manufacturing
Types of Products Distributed:
  Material handling equipment

59462 Southwest Thermal Technology
3251 Corte Malpaso
Suite 507
Camarillo, CA 93012   805-499-2726
Fax: 805-376-0659 888-226-8522
sales@southwestthermal.com
www.southwestthermal.com
Wholesaler/distributor of food processing equipment, CIP exchangers, chillers, coolers, air heaters, dairy processing machinery, preheaters and process and refrigerating equipment and supplies
VP: Dennis Linn
VP: Jim Van Arsdals
Estimated Sales: $5-10 Million
Number Employees: 1-4
Square Footage: 4000
Types of Products Distributed:
  General Merchandise, Heat Transfer Equipment/Cip Exchanges

59463 (HQ)Southwest Traders
27565 Diaz Rd
Temecula, CA 92590
                       800-275-7984
                    www.southwesttraders.com
Groceries, meat, produce, frozen yogurt, ice cream, janitorial supplies and equipment and fixtures, etc.
Owner/President: Ken Smith
Chief Financial Officer: Lynne Bredemeier
Sales Director: Nita Smith
Estimated Sales: $50-100 Million
Number Employees: 100-249
Square Footage: 70000
Private Brands Carried:
  Rainbow's End
Number of Customer Locations: 2000
Types of Products Distributed:
  Food Service, Frozen Food, General Line, General Merchandise, Provisions/Meat, Produce, Frozen yogurt, groceries, etc.

59464 Southwest Traders
324 N Fruit Ave
Fresno, CA 93706
                       800-275-7984
                    www.southwesttraders.com
Wholesaler/distributor of groceries, meat, produce, frozen yogurt, ice cream, janitorial supplies and equipment and fixtures, etc.

59465 Southwest Traders
4747 Frontier Way
Stockton, CA 95215
                       800-275-7984
                    www.southwesttraders.com
Wholesaler/distributor of groceries, meat, produce, frozen yogurt, ice cream, janitorial supplies and equipment and fixtures, etc.

59466 Southwest Traders
5115 Peoria
Denver, CO 80239
                       800-275-7984
                    www.southwesttraders.com
Wholesaler/distributor of groceries, meat, produce, frozen yogurt, ice cream, janitorial supplies and equipment and fixtures, etc.

59467 Southwest Traders
2010 Lakeside Pkwy
Flowermound, TX 75237
                       800-275-7984
                    www.southwesttraders.com
Wholesaler/distributor of groceries, meat, produce, frozen yogurt, ice cream, janitorial supplies and equipment and fixtures, etc.

59468 Souza Food Service
1259 Furukawa Way
Santa Maria, CA 93458-4929   805-925-8836
                            Fax: 805-925-1986
Wholesaler/distributor of frozen foods, general merchandise, produce, meats, seafood and specialty food; serving the food service market
Owner/President: Richard Souza
Marketing/Purchasing: Cathy Ramey
Sales/Marketing Executive: Stephine Breault
Contact: Stephanie Brault
steelmorris@fitness19.com
Estimated Sales: $10-20 Million
Number Employees: 20-49
Square Footage: 24000
Private Brands Carried:
  Comsource
Types of Products Distributed:
  Food Service, Frozen Food

59469 Sovrana Trading Corp
14928 S Figueroa St
Gardena, CA 90248-1711   310-323-3357
Fax: 310-217-1832 info@sovrana.com
Wholesaler/distributor and importer of olive oil, whole and ground coffee beans, coffee equipment and coffee mochas and syrups; serving the food service market
Owner: Aldo Bonfante
VP/General Manager/Treasurer: Aldo Bonfante
Estimated Sales: $1-2.5 Million
Number Employees: 10-19
Square Footage: 32000
Parent Co: Espresso World
Type of Packaging: Consumer, Food Service, Private Label

Wholesalers & Distributors / A-Z

Private Brands Carried:
Lavazza; Olivoro; Mocafe
Number of Customer Locations: 1100
Types of Products Distributed:
Food Service, Frozen Food, General Line, General Merchandise, Specialty Foods, Olive oil, coffee & coffee equipment

59470 Soylent
555 Mateo St
Suite 227
Los Angeles, CA 90013
info@soylent.com
www.soylent.com
Meal replacement drinks and powders
CEO: Bryan Crowley
CFO: Demir Vangelov
VP Product Development & Innovation: Julie Daoust
VP Brand Marketing: Andrew Thomas
SVP Sales: Melody Conner
Year Founded: 2013
Number Employees: 50-99
Parent Co: Rosa Foods Inc.
Types of Products Distributed:
General Merchandise, Health Food

59471 (HQ)Space Maker Systems
3310 Childs St
Baltimore, MD 21226   410-355-1000
Fax: 410-355-6048
hsantel@spacemakersystems.com
www.spacemakersystems.com
Wholesaler/distributor of material handling equipment
President: Hobb Santel
VP Sales: Joseph Bakey
VP Operations: Brian Gorman
Estimated Sales: $20-50 Million
Number Employees: 50-99
Square Footage: 33000
Other Locations:
Space Maker Systems
Jessup, MDSpace Maker Systems
Private Brands Carried:
Crown; Clark; Daewoo; Drexel; Unarco; Rousseau
Types of Products Distributed:
General Merchandise, Material handling equipment

59472 Spantec Systems
192 Newtown Rd
Plainview, NY 11803-4304   516-752-7525
Fax: 516-752-7529 info@spantecsystems.com
Wholesaler/distributor of material handling equipment
President: Peter Murphy
petermurphy@spantecsystems.com
Estimated Sales: $.5-1 million
Number Employees: 1-4
Private Brands Carried:
Lift-All; Yale
Types of Products Distributed:
Frozen Food, General Merchandise, Material handling equipment

59473 Spar Mixers
2210 Queen Street E
Toronto, ON M4E 1E7
Canada   416-691-2381
Fax: 416-691-4663 mixersspar@aol.com
www.sparmixers.com
Wholesaler/distributor of spiral and planetary commercial dough mixers
President: Ian Kearns
Quality Control: Roger LaFon
Sales Manager: May Lee
Operations Manager: Joy Guerney
Private Brands Carried:
Spar
Types of Products Distributed:
Frozen Food, General Merchandise, Commercial dough mixers

59474 Sparboe Foods Corp
900 N Linn Ave
New Hampton, IA 50659-1204   641-394-3040
info@sparboe.com
www.sparboe.com
Fresh and frozen eggs
President: Bob Sparboe
Vice President: Beth Fechnell
Manager: Warren Miller

Estimated Sales: $20-50 Million
Number Employees: 100-249
Square Footage: 50000
Type of Packaging: Food Service, Private Label, Bulk
Types of Products Distributed:
Food Service, Frozen Food, General Line, Butter, frozen fruits, cheeses & oils

59475 Sparks Belting Co
3800 Stahl Dr SE
Grand Rapids, MI 49546-6148   616-949-2750
Fax: 616-949-8518 800-451-4537
sbcinfo@sparksbelting.com
www.sparksbelting.com
Wholesaler/distributor of food-approved and package handling conveyor belting; manufacturer of motorized pulleys; importer of thermoplastic belting, motorized pulleys and rollers
President: Steven Swanson
CFO: Martha Vrias
VP: Steven Bayus
Quality Control: Dave Vanderwood
Marketing: Frank Kennedy
Contact: Andy Balog
ajbalog@sparksbelting.com
Operations: Bruce Dielema
Production: Joe Graver
Plant Manager: John Grasmeyer
Purchasing Director: Mark White
Estimated Sales: $20-50 Million
Number Employees: 100-249
Square Footage: 52000

59476 Sparrow Enterprises LTD
98 Condor St
PO Box 13
Boston, MA 02128-1306   617-569-3900
Fax: 617-569-5888 855-532-5552
info@chocolatebysparrow.com
www.chocolatebysparrow.com
Importer and wholesaler/distributor of chocolates and bakery and ice cream ingredients including seeds, milk products, cocoa, sweet and desiccated coconut, chocolate drops and coatings, etc
President: John Baybutt
VP: Henry Baybutt
contact@sparrowenterprises.com
Assistant VP: Sally Baybutt
Estimated Sales: $10-20 Million
Number Employees: 20-49
Square Footage: 45000
Type of Packaging: Food Service, Private Label, Bulk
Types of Products Distributed:
General Line, Chocolates, milk products, etc.

59477 Spartan Foods
1305 Monroe St
Endicott, NY 13760   607-748-7557
Wholesaler/distributor of pita bread, produce and fresh meat
President: George Anastos
Estimated Sales: Less than $500,000
Number Employees: 1-4
Types of Products Distributed:
Frozen Food, General Line, Provisions/Meat, Produce, Pita bread

59478 SpartanNash Co
850 76th St SW
Byron Center, MI 49315-8510   616-878-2000
800-451-8500
contact.us@spartannash.com
www.spartannash.com
Wholesaler/distributor of groceries, meat, produce, dairy products, frozen foods, equipment and fixtures, private label items, seafood and general merchandise; serving the food service market.
Interim President & CEO: Dennis Eidson
EVP/General Manager, Corporate Retail: Tom Swanson
SVP/Chief Information Officer: Arif Dar
President, MDV/Chief Legal Officer: Kathleen Mahoney
EVP/Merchandising & Marketing: Lori Raya
EVP/Chief Financial Officer: Mark Shamber
EVP/Chief Human Resources Officer: Yvonne Trupiano
EVP/President, Food Distribution: Walt Lentz
Year Founded: 1917
Estimated Sales: $7.5 Billion
Number Employees: 11,000
Number of Brands: 11

Other Locations:
Spartan Stores
Flushing, MISpartan Stores
Private Brands Carried:
Spartan
Number of Customer Locations: 550
Types of Products Distributed:
Food Service, Frozen Food, General Line, General Merchandise, Provisions/Meat, Produce, Seafood, Groceries, candy, canned goods, etc.

59479 Specialized Promotions
33 Great Neck Rd # 2
Suite 2
Great Neck, NY 11021-3335   516-466-1067
Fax: 516-466-4048 800-666-7736
sales@specializedpromotions.com
www.specializedpromotions.com
Wholesaler/distributor of advertising specialties; also, custom printing available
President: Ken Sonenberg
sales@specializedpromotions.com
Vice President: Ron Hollander
Purchasing/Office Manager: Claudia Poppe
Estimated Sales: $1-2.5 Million
Number Employees: 1-4
Square Footage: 4000
Private Brands Carried:
Bic; Zippo; Garrity; Cross
Number of Customer Locations: 400
Types of Products Distributed:
Frozen Food, General Merchandise, Advertising specialties

59480 Specialty Box & Packaging
1040 Broadway
Menands, NY 12204-2590   518-465-7344
Fax: 518-465-7347 800-283-2247
www.pennysbags.com
Wholesaler/distributor of packaging materials including boxes, bags, giftware, tissue, bows, ribbons, etc.; customizing available
President: Eric Fialkoff
efialkoff@specialtybox.com
Vice President: Jason Fialkoff
Estimated Sales: $5-10 Million
Number Employees: 5-9
Type of Packaging: Consumer, Food Service, Private Label, Bulk
Types of Products Distributed:
Frozen Food, General Merchandise, Packaging material

59481 (HQ)Specialty Foods Group Inc
6 Dublin Ln
Owensboro, KY 42301   270-926-2324
800-238-0020
www.specialtyfoodsgroup.com
Spices, lunch meats, turkey, and pork products including bacon, ham, and sausage.
Year Founded: 1914
Estimated Sales: $234 Million
Number Employees: 250-499
Number of Brands: 7
Type of Packaging: Consumer, Food Service, Private Label, Bulk
Other Locations:
SFG Production Plant
Owensboro, KY
SFG Production Plant
Humboldt, IA
SFG Production Plant
Chicago, IL
SFG Production Plant
Williamston, NCSFG Production PlantHumboldt

59482 Specialty House of Creation
200 North Walnut Street
P. O. Box 130
Cottonwood Falls, KS 66845   620-273-6900
Fax: 620-273-6910 800-742-9909
ken@shcinc.com www.shcinc.com
Wholesaler/distributor of candy including salt water taffy and fudge
President: Douglas Brookins
Contact: Judi Cassidy
jcassidy@shcinc.com
Estimated Sales: $2.5-5 Million
Number Employees: 5-9
Types of Products Distributed:
Frozen Food, General Line, Candy: salt water taffy & fudge

Wholesalers & Distributors / A-Z

59483 Specialty Merchandise Distributors
3928 Ogeechee Rd
Savannah, GA 31405-1314 912-232-1689
Fax: 912-232-7187 800-841-1102
Wholesaler/distributor of general merchandise; also, rack jobber services available; serving rack jobbers, grocery and convenience store chains
President: Roy Newsome
Secretary: Carol Morris
Estimated Sales: $300,000-500,000
Number Employees: 1-4
Square Footage: 200000
Number of Customer Locations: 1600
Types of Products Distributed:
Frozen Food, General Merchandise, Rack Jobbers

59484 Spener Restaurant Design
726 Hanley Industrial Ct
St Louis, MO 63144-1904 314-781-2225
Fax: 314-781-5874 800-677-8867
Wholesaler/distributor of equipment and furniture; serving the food service market
President: David Brinkley
President: Mark Holder
Estimated Sales: $1-3 Million
Number Employees: 1-4
Square Footage: 48000
Types of Products Distributed:
Food Service, Frozen Food, General Merchandise, Equipment & furniture

59485 Speupak
2212 River Hills Road
Austin, TX 78733 866-766-5199
Fax: 512-263-2415
Exclusive U.S. distributor for Fischer Sohne products
CEO: Deborah Callahan
Sales Director: Bill DeMen
Estimated Sales: $2.5-$5 Million
Number Employees: 5-10
Number of Brands: 1
Number of Products: 100+
Private Brands Carried:
Fischer Sohne

59486 Sphinx Adsorbents Inc
53 Progress Ave
Springfield, MA 01104-3230 413-736-5020
Fax: 413-736-8257 email@sphinxadsorbents.com
Wholesaler/distributor of absorbent materials
President: Douglas C Muth
dmuth@sphinxadsorbents.com
Sales: Doug Muth
Sales: Sandra Peterson
Estimated Sales: Less Than $500,000
Number Employees: 1-4
Square Footage: 104000
Types of Products Distributed:
General Merchandise, Absorbent materials

59487 Spice & Spice
655 Deep Valley Drive
Ste 125
Rolling Hills Estates, CA 90274 310-265-2914
Fax: 310-265-2934 866-729-7742
info@spicenspice.com www.spicenspice.com
Bulk line of whole and ground spice products: black pepper, white pepper, cumin, cinnamon, crush chili, cinnamon stick, chili powder, granulated garlic, dry chili pods
Owner: Anthony Dirocco
CEO: Mukesh Thakker
R & D: Nitul Unekekett
Quality Control: Nina Lukamanje
Contact: Cindy Philips
cindy@calwind.com
Estimated Sales: $5-10 Million
Number Employees: 1-4
Number of Brands: 1
Number of Products: 25
Square Footage: 200000
Type of Packaging: Food Service, Bulk
Private Brands Carried:
Boat Brand
Types of Products Distributed:
General Line, General Merchandise, Specialty Foods, Spice Products

59488 Spice House International Specialties
47 Bloomingdale Road
Hicksville, NY 11801-1512 516-942-7248
Fax: 516-942-7249 www.spicehouseint.com
Spices and blends, specialty foods, hot sauces, dried fruits and nuts; serving the food service market from around the world
President: Anthony Provetto
Estimated Sales: $5-10 Million
Number Employees: 5-9
Square Footage: 18400
Type of Packaging: Consumer, Food Service, Private Label, Bulk
Types of Products Distributed:
Food Service, Frozen Food, General Line, Specialty Foods, Spices, dried fruits, nuts, etc.

59489 Spiral Biotech Inc
2 Technology Way
Norwood, MA 02062-2680 781-320-9000
Fax: 781-320-8181 800-554-1620
mail@aicompanies.com
Manufacturer and exporter of laboratory equipment including fast sample dilutors, spiral platers, automated plate counters and colony counting systems; importer of microbial air samplers and filter bags; wholesaler/distributor of microbial air samplers
President: John Coughlin
VP Operations: P Emond
Estimated Sales: $10-20 Million
Number Employees: 50-99
Square Footage: 6000
Parent Co: Advanced Instruments
Private Brands Carried:
Microbio; Burkard
Types of Products Distributed:
Frozen Food, General Merchandise, Microbial air samplers

59490 Spokane Produce
1996 S Geiger Blvd
Spokane, WA 99224
Fax: 509-444-0516 800-833-8381
www.spokaneproduce.com
Wholesaler/distributor of produce.
President: Craig Higashi
Estimated Sales: $20-50 Million
Number Employees: 250
Square Footage: 100000
Types of Products Distributed:
Frozen Food, Produce

59491 Spoonable
345 Clinton Avenue
#4G
Brooklyn, NY 11238 718-974-0653
info@spoonablellc.com
www.spoonablellc.com
Salty caramel sauce, butterscotch sauce, chewy sesame caramel sauce, spicy chili caramel sauce, flowery lavender caramel sauce, peppered orange caramel sauce
President/Owner: Michelle Lewis
mnlewis@spoonablellc.com
Number Employees: 4
Number of Brands: 1
Number of Products: 7
Type of Packaging: Consumer, Food Service, Private Label, Bulk

59492 Spot Cash Specialty Company
1020 Hickory Ridge Dr
Kosciusko, MS 39090 662-289-7506
Fax: 662-289-1263
Wholesaler/distributor of general line products; serving the food service market
President: Mickey Fowler
Estimated Sales: $300,000-500,000
Number Employees: 1-4
Number of Customer Locations: 340
Types of Products Distributed:
Food Service, Frozen Food, General Line

59493 Springfield Produce Company
PO Box 5023
Springfield, IL 62705-5023 217-544-1715
Fax: 217-544-1719
Wholesaler/distributor of produce
Manager: Henry Enno
Types of Products Distributed:
Frozen Food, Produce

59494 Sprinkman Corporation
PO Box 390
Franksville, WI 53126-0390 262-835-2390
Fax: 262-835-4325 800-816-1610
www.sprnkman.com
Wholesaler/distributor of dairy and food processing equipment and supplies; consultant specializing in the design processing systems; also, installation and reconditioning services available
Chief Operating Officer: Robert Sprinkman
CFO: Dale Metcoff
President: Brian Sprinkman
Vice President: Merlin Winchell
Contact: Jimmi Sukys
j.sukys@sprinkman.com
Estimated Sales: $30 Million
Number Employees: 100
Square Footage: 35000
Parent Co: W.M. Sprinkman Corporation
Types of Products Distributed:
Frozen Food, General Merchandise, Dairy equipment & supplies, etc.

59495 Sprouters
20703 80th Ave S
Kent, WA 98032-1252 253-872-0577
Fax: 253-872-6960
Wholesaler/distributor of alfalfa and bean sprouts
Owner: Theresa Jones
Contact: Bill Jones
bil@sprouter.com
Estimated Sales: $500,000-$1 Million
Number Employees: 5-9
Private Brands Carried:
Sprouters N.W., Inc.
Types of Products Distributed:
Frozen Food

59496 Spuds N' Stuff
33625 Townshipline
Abbotsford, BC V4X 1X9
Canada 604-852-3244
Fax: 604-852-1957 www.spudsnstuff.com
Wholesaler/distributor of potatoes including yukon, pontiac, gold, russett and blue; also, lingonberries, blueberries and corn
Owner: David Anderson
Estimated Sales: $500,000-$1 Million
Number Employees: 1-4
Square Footage: 32000
Types of Products Distributed:
Produce, Potatoes, blueberries, corn, etc.

59497 Square Enterprises Corp
19 Paterson Ave
Wallington, NJ 07057-1115 973-365-1639
Fax: 973-365-0156 square@squareenterprises.com
www.squareenterprises.biz
Polish products
Owner: Adam Szala
adamszala@squareenterprises.com
Number Employees: 20-49

59498 Squid Ink
PO Box 224
New York, NY 10113-0224 212-645-7936
Fax: 212-727-3533
Wholesaler/distributor of squid ink pasta bases, seafood, saffron vegetable powders, lobster meat, mushrooms and mushroom powders
President: Jonathan Lindle
VP Sales: Marty Grossel
Types of Products Distributed:
Frozen Food, General Line, Seafood, Specialty Foods, Vegetable & mushroom powders, etc.

59499 (HQ)St John's Botanicals
7711 Hillmeade Rd
Bowie, MD 20720-4571 301-262-5302
Fax: 301-262-2489 www.stjohnsbotanicals.com
Spice blends, herb teas, essential oils, ginseng products, nutritional supplements
Owner: William Mussenden
Ceo: Sydney Vallentync
CFO: Patti Mussenden
Research/Dev: Diane Tolsen
Quality Control: Diane Tolsen
Marketing: Rayla Cuffey
Sales Manager: Rayla Cuffey
Pub Relations: Maria McCulvey
Operations Manager: Brandy Schwartz
Plant Manager: Diane Tolson
Purchasing: Sydney Vallentyne

Wholesalers & Distributors / A-Z

Estimated Sales: Less Than $500,000
Number Employees: 5-9
Type of Packaging: Private Label, Bulk
Private Brands Carried:
   St. John's Herb Garden; The Perfume Garden; Rose Hill Natural Products
Types of Products Distributed:
   Health Food, Herbal Products/Essential Oils

59500 St. Clair Foods Distributing
5 Colonial Hills
Princeton, WV 24740-9020   304-425-8130
                         Fax: 304-425-5820
Wholesaler/distributor of groceries, re-bagged fresh salad, candy and specialty food items
President: R Repass
VP: E Repass
Estimated Sales: $10-20 Million
Number Employees: 10-19
Square Footage: 51000
Private Brands Carried:
   Kitty's (candies & salads)
Types of Products Distributed:
   General Line, Produce, Specialty Foods, Re-bagged fresh salads & candy

59501 St. Cloud Restaurant Supply
P.O.Box 639
St Cloud, MN 56302-0639   320-654-0200
                  Fax: 320-252-2511 800-892-8501
Wholesaler/distributor of restaurant equipment and supplies; serving the food service market
Owner: Greg Stelten
VP Contract Sales: Jeff Vreeland
VP Sales: Hoobie Eskuri
Estimated Sales: $20-50 Million
Number Employees: 50-99
Number of Customer Locations: 4000
Types of Products Distributed:
   Food Service, Frozen Food, General Merchandise, Restaurant equipment & supplies

59502 St. Helen Seafoods
138 St Helens Avenue
Toronto, ON M6H 4A1
Canada   416-536-5111
Wholesaler/distributor of seafood; serving the food service market
President: Steven Chow
Types of Products Distributed:
   Food Service, Frozen Food, Seafood

59503 St. Ours & Company
1571 Commercial St
East Weymouth, MA 02189-3015   781-331-8520
       Fax: 781-331-8628 email@saintours.com
                          www.saintours.com
Processor of frozen shellfish, including lobster, crab, dehydrated clam and seafood broths; wholesaler and distributor of seafood and specialty foods.
President: Fred St. Ours
Marketing Manager: Sharon St. Ours
Sales: John Christian
Director of Manufacturing: Richard St. Ours
Estimated Sales: $3-5 Million
Number Employees: 5-9
Type of Packaging: Consumer, Food Service, Bulk
Types of Products Distributed:
   Food Service, Frozen Food, General Merchandise, Seafood, Specialty Foods

59504 St. Simons Seafood
130 Paradise Marsh Cir
Brunswick, GA 31525-2143   912-265-5225
                         Fax: 912-264-3181
Seafood and fish
President: Chuck Egeland
Estimated Sales: $1,500,000
Number Employees: 5-9

59505 Stack & Store Systems
2500 N Mayfair Rd
Milwaukee, WI 53226-1409   414-453-2315
                         Fax: 414-453-2354
Wholesaler/distributor of forklifts, conveyors and shelving
Partner: Maria M Steck
Estimated Sales: $10-20 Million
Number Employees: 1-4
Private Brands Carried:
   Nissan; Kalmar; Multiton
Types of Products Distributed:
   Frozen Food, General Merchandise, Forklifts, conveyors & shelving

59506 Stahl
1130 Stuart Dr
Merced, CA 95341-6424
               Fax: 330-264-3319 800-277-8245
                      www.stahltruckbodies.com
Wholesaler/distributor of general line items and general merchandise; serving the food service market
VP Sales: Richard Cromar
Plant Manager: Fred McLane
Buyer: Martie Morgort
Estimated Sales: $3-5 Million
Number Employees: 10-19
Parent Co: The Scott Fetzer Company
Number of Customer Locations: 1085
Types of Products Distributed:
   Food Service, Frozen Food, General Line, General Merchandise

59507 Stainless Equipment & Systems
2145 Barrett Park Drive NW
Kennesaw, GA 30144-3675   770-427-7757
             Fax: 770-423-1270 www.benham.com
Wholesaler/distributor of food and beverage processing equipment; also, design and installation available
President: Kenneth Young
Secretary/Treasurer: Ron Plunkett
VP: Harold Young
Number Employees: 20-49
Parent Co: Benham Companies
Types of Products Distributed:
   Frozen Food, General Merchandise, Food & beverage processing equipment

59508 Stamoolis Brothers Co
2020 Penn Ave
Pittsburgh, PA 15222-4418   412-471-7676
            Fax: 412-471-3621 877-357-0399
       info@stamoolisbros.com www.stamoolis.com
Wholesaler/distributor of general line products and meats; serving the food service market
Owner: Gus Stamoolis
info@stamoolisbros.com
Estimated Sales: $5-10 Million
Number Employees: 5-9
Number of Customer Locations: 300
Types of Products Distributed:
   Food Service, Frozen Food, General Line, Provisions/Meat

59509 Standard Electric Time
3678 Ives Rd
Tecumseh, MI 49286   517-423-8331
                         Fax: 517-423-9486
Wholesaler/distributor of electric clock systems, precision timing and controller instruments, fire alarms, close circuit televisions, security and nurse call stations and communication systems; also, installation services available
Contact: J Harkey
jharkey@setcorp.net
Number Employees: 50-99
Private Brands Carried:
   Faraday; Standard
Types of Products Distributed:
   Frozen Food, General Merchandise, Electric clock systems, etc.

59510 Standard Forms
276 Park Avenue S
New York, NY 10010-6126   212-462-1071
                         Fax: 212-529-4070
Wholesaler/distributor of business and computer forms, office and janitorial equipment and supplies, advertising specialties, etc
VP: Thomas D'Agostino Jr
Sales Manager: Rick Clemente
Number Employees: 50-99
Types of Products Distributed:
   Frozen Food, General Merchandise, Forms, advertising specialties, etc.

59511 Standard Fruit & Vegetable Company
PO Box 225027
Dallas, TX 75222-5027   305-520-8400
             Fax: 305-567-0320 800-428-3600
Importer and wholesaler/distributor of produce including potatoes and tomatoes
Chairman: Marty Rutchik
President: Jay Pack
CFO/VP: Steve Gray
Parent Co: Del Monte
Types of Products Distributed:
   Frozen Food, Produce

59512 Standard Meat Co LP
5105 Investment Dr
Dallas, TX 75236-1420   972-283-8501
             Fax: 214-561-0560 866-859-6313
                      www.standardmeat.com
Sausages and other prepared meats
Partner: Joseph Penshorn
Partner: William Rosenthal
Controller: Garry Custer
Food Safety & Research & Development: Scott Boleman
Quality Assurance: Jonathan Savell
Purchasing Manager: Sam Beede
Estimated Sales: $13.7 Million
Number Employees: 100-249
Square Footage: 195912
Types of Products Distributed:
   General Line, General Merchandise, Provisions/Meat, Seafood

59513 Standard Restaurant Equipment
PO Box 65189
Salt Lake City, UT 84165-0189   801-263-3339
             Fax: 801-261-1952 888-556-7820
Wholesaler/distributor of restaurant equipment and supplies; serving the food service market
President: Ellery Kingston
CFO: Ilona Kingston
VP: Stephen Kingston
Marketing Director: Scot Kingston
Operations: Dale Kingston
Purchasing Director: Edmond Gustafson
Estimated Sales: $20-50 Million
Number Employees: 200-250
Square Footage: 100000
Private Brands Carried:
   Scotsman; Libbey; Hobart
Types of Products Distributed:
   Food Service,

59514 Standard-Rosenbaum
PO Box 40
Buffalo, NY 14213-0040   518-785-0969
                         Fax: 518-785-0273
Wholesaler/distributor of confectionery products, sundries, health and beauty aids, snacks, convenience groceries and fast food items
President: J Naigles
VP/Secretary: E Naigles
Sr. VP: J Beaver
Number Employees: 20-49
Square Footage: 120000
Number of Customer Locations: 700
Types of Products Distributed:
   Frozen Food, General Line, General Merchandise, Sundries, snacks, groceries, etc.

59515 Stanford Trading Company
1004 N Avenue
Suite 100
Plano, TX 75074-8662   972-663-1220
             Fax: 972-633-1977 800-800-4999
Wholesaler/distributor of groceries and general merchandise
President: Allan Birholtz
COO: Darwin Naccarato
Number Employees: 20-49
Square Footage: 120000
Types of Products Distributed:
   Frozen Food, General Line, General Merchandise, Groceries

59516 Stanfos
3908 69th Avenue NW
Edmonton, AB T6B 2V2
Canada   780-468-2165
             Fax: 780-465-4890 800-661-5648
              info@stanfos.com www.stanfos.com
Manufacturer, exporter and wholesaler/distributor of dairy, food and meat processing equipment including pasteurizers
President: Lang Jameson
Sales Manager: Shawna Bungax
Number Employees: 10-19

59517 Stanley's Best Seafood
7475 Patruski Road
Coden, AL 36523-3181   251-824-2801
                         Fax: 919-734-1201
Seafood
Owner: Robert Stanley

Wholesalers & Distributors / A-Z

59518 Stanz Foodservice Inc
1840 Commerce Dr
South Bend, IN 46628-1563   574-232-6666
Fax: 574-236-4169   800-342-5664
www.stanz.com
Family owned food service distributer. Stanz offers services to regions such as Northern Indiana, Southwest Lower Michigan, Eastern and Central Illinois and Nothwest Ohio.
President: Mark Harman
CEO: Shirley Geraghty
Vice President: Wendy Harman
VP, Information Technology: Mark Gaddie
VP, Marketing & Merchandising: Jeff Nicholas
VP, Sales: Todd Stearns
VP, Operations: Dave Dausinas
Estimated Sales: $100+ Million
Number Employees: 100-249
Square Footage: 10000
Types of Products Distributed:
   Food Service

59519 Stapleton Inc
237 S Hemlock Rd
Hemlock, MI 48626-8784   989-642-5211
Fax: 989-642-8201   www.stapletons.com
Wholesaler/distributor serving the food service market
President: Nelson Stapleton
lannydexter@charter.net
Sales Exec: Lanny Dexter
Estimated Sales: $20-50 Million
Number Employees: 20-49
Number of Customer Locations: 500
Types of Products Distributed:
   Food Service, Frozen Food

59520 Star Fisheries
2206 Signal Pl
San Pedro, CA 90731-7227   310-832-8395
Fax: 310-832-7967   www.starfisheries.com
Wholesaler/distributor of groceries, meat, produce, frozen food and seafood including fresh and frozen fish, shrimp, lobster and shellfish; also, breaded and prepared items
Owner: Lou Bozanich
bozanichl@starfisheries.com
General Manager: Rudy Palacios
VP: Louis Bozanich
Estimated Sales: $10-20 Million
Number Employees: 50-99
Types of Products Distributed:
   Frozen Food, General Line, Provisions/Meat, Produce, Seafood, Groceries, etc.

59521 Star Fisheries
2465 S Industrial Park Ave # 7
Tempe, AZ 85282-1822   480-921-0800
Fax: 480-921-3322   www.starfisheries.com
Manager: Mike Riley
Manager: Russell Matthews
rmatthews@starfisheries.com
Estimated Sales: $10-20 Million
Number Employees: 50-99

59522 Star Packaging Corporation
453 Circle 85 Street
Atlanta, GA 30349   404-763-2800
Fax: 404-763-5435   800-252-5414
Specializes in the printing, lamination, and conversion of flexible packaging materials in the form of roll stock, pouches and bags.
President: Michael Wilson
Estimated Sales: $20-50 Million
Number Employees: 100-249
Type of Packaging: Consumer

59523 (HQ)Star Produce
2941 Portage Ave
Saskatoon, SK S7J 3S6
Canada   306-934-3372
   800-667-9292
info@starproduce.com   www.starproduce.com
Wholesales and distributor of produce.
Chief Executive Officer: David Karwacki
President: Greg Kennedy
President, US: Jarrett Little
Marketing Coordinator: Jessica Wells
VP, Sales: Brent Lloyd
SVP, Operations & Human Resources: Scott Wright
Year Founded: 1989
Estimated Sales: $20-50 Million
Number Employees: 250-499
Square Footage: 200000
Type of Packaging: Consumer, Food Service, Private Label, Bulk
Other Locations:
   Calgary Office
   Calgary, AB, Canada Calgary Office Calgary, AB, Canada

59524 Star Produce
3380 Woods Edge Circle
Suite 102
Bonita Springs, FL 34134   239-444-1140
   800-476-1141
lorie@starproduce.com   www.starproduce.com
Wholesaler and distributor of produce.
Year Founded: 1989
Estimated Sales: $20-50 Million
Number Employees: 250-499
Type of Packaging: Consumer, Food Service, Private Label, Bulk
Types of Products Distributed:
   Produce

59525 Star Produce
672 W Frontage Rd
Nogales, AZ 85621   502-281-0011
www.starproduce.com
Wholesaler and distributor of produce.
Year Founded: 1989
Estimated Sales: $20-50 Million
Number Employees: 250-499
Type of Packaging: Consumer, Food Service, Private Label, Bulk
Types of Products Distributed:
   Produce

59526 Star Produce
20415 72nd Ave S
Suite 240
Kent, WA 98032
   253-867-2803
www.starproduce.com
Wholesaler and distributor of produce.
Year Founded: 1989
Estimated Sales: $20-50 Million
Number Employees: 250-499
Type of Packaging: Consumer, Food Service, Private Label, Bulk
Types of Products Distributed:
   Produce

59527 Star Restaurant Equipment & Supply Company
18430 Pacific St
Fountain Valley, CA 92708   714-683-2658
Fax: 818-782-8179   www.chefstoys.com
Wholesaler/distributor of food service equipment and supplies; serving the food service market
President/Owner: Les Birken
Purchasing: Lee Siegel
Estimated Sales: $5-10 Million
Number Employees: 10-19
Square Footage: 30000
Types of Products Distributed:
   Food Service, Frozen Food, General Merchandise, Foodservice equipment & supplies

59528 Star Sales Company
P.O.Box 1503
Knoxville, TN 37901-1503   865-524-0771
Fax: 865-524-4889
Wholesaler/distributor of general merchandise, imported goods and health and beauty care items; also, rack jobber
President: N Foster
VP: Bill Guffey
VP: J Ridenour
Contact: Robin Easterday
reasterday@starsales.com
Estimated Sales: $10-20 Million
Number Employees: 50-99
Square Footage: 350000
Number of Customer Locations: 1000
Types of Products Distributed:
   General Merchandise, Rack Jobbers

59529 Star Sales Company
4751 River Road
Jefferson, LA 70121-4147   504-733-9333
Fax: 504-734-0677   800-444-6646
Wholesaler/distributor of general merchandise; rack jobber services available
President: N Rabin
General Manager: C Rose
Number Employees: 20-49
Square Footage: 140000
Number of Customer Locations: 340
Types of Products Distributed:
   Frozen Food, General Merchandise, Rack Jobbers

59530 Star Seafood
14160 Shell Belt Road
Bayou La Batre, AL 36509   251-824-3110
Fax: 251-824-4199
Seafood

59531 Star Wholesale
16 Getty Ave
Clifton, NJ 07011-2314   973-777-4450
Fax: 973-777-3215
ronaldkrug@starwholesaleinc.com
www.starwholesaleinc.com
Wholesaler/distibutor of salvage groceries including inventory close-outs, odd lots and general commodities
Estimated Sales: $2.5-5 Million
Number Employees: 1-4
Types of Products Distributed:
   General Line, Salvage grocery liquidator

59532 Starbrook Industries Inc
325 S Hyatt St
Tipp City, OH 45371-1241   937-473-8135
Fax: 937-473-0331   www.starbrookind.com/
Product line includes forming and non-forming food packaging films designed for Bi-Vac, Dixie Pak and Multi Vac machines.
Sales Manager: Richard Anderson

59533 Starbruck Foods Corporation
110 Bi County Boulevard
Suite 126
Farmingdale, NY 11735-3987   631-293-9696
Fax: 631-293-9825   starbruck@hotmail.com
Importer and wholesaler/distributor of dried fruits including raisins, papaya, pineapple, banana chips and apricots; also, nuts, seeds and fruit and nut mixes
President: Michael Stern
Number Employees: 1-4
Square Footage: 40000
Types of Products Distributed:
   Frozen Food, General Line, Health Food, Dried fruits, nuts & seeds

59534 Starich
248 Montclair Loop
Daphne, AL 36526-7150   251-626-5037
Seafood

59535 State Fish Distributors
39 S La Salle St.
Suite 1410
Chicago, IL 60603-1706   312-451-0800
Fax: 773-225-4660
Seafood
President: Donald Nathan

59536 State Hotel Supply Company
125 Newark St
Newark, NJ 07103   973-621-7767
Fax: 973-621-1661   800-273-7723
Wholesaler/distributor of fresh and frozen portion controlled Certified Angus beef, veal, pork, poultry and frozen fish
President: Martin Rabinowitz
VP Administration: Louis Louizides
VP Sales: Andy Strasser
Number Employees: 50-99
Square Footage: 100000
Number of Customer Locations: 501
Types of Products Distributed:
   Frozen Food, Provisions/Meat, Seafood, Beef, pork, etc.

59537 State Line Potato Chip Company
PO Box 218
Wilbraham, MA 01095-0218   413-596-8341
Fax: 413-596-8491
Wholesaler/distributor of potato chips
President: Mike Erricolo
Types of Products Distributed:
   Frozen Food, General Line, Potato chips

Wholesalers & Distributors / A-Z

59538 State Restaurant Equipment Co
3163 S Highland Dr
Las Vegas, NV 89109-1070   702-733-1515
    Fax: 702-733-0814 www.staterestaurant.com
Wholesaler/distributor of restaurant supplies including kitchen utensils, serving aids and glass and diningware; serving the food service market
President: Scott Miller
scott.miller@staterestaurant.com
CEO: Eddie Hadad
CFO: Kim Garnett
VP/Sales: Joe Stafford
Account Executive: Ronda Bonar
Purchasing Manager: Kim Garnett
Estimated Sales: $5-10 Million
Number Employees: 20-49
Private Brands Carried:
    Vollrath; Cardinal; Syracuse; Villeroy & Boch; Steelite; Bauscher
Types of Products Distributed:
    Food Service, Frozen Food, General Merchandise, Restaurant equipment

59539 State Wholesale Grocers
2739 Russell Street
Detroit, MI 48207-2614   313-567-7654
    Fax: 313-567-6313
Wholesaler/distributor of groceries and general merchandise; serving the food service market
Owner: R Wohl
Estimated Sales: $10-20 Million
Number Employees: 10-19
Square Footage: 100000
Number of Customer Locations: 1000
Types of Products Distributed:
    Food Service, Frozen Food, General Line, General Merchandise, Groceries

59540 Statewide Meats & Poultry
211 Food Terminal Plz
New Haven, CT 06511   203-777-6669
    Fax: 203-492-4073
Processor and wholesaler/distributor of meat
President: Stephen Falcigno
Estimated Sales: $7900000
Number Employees: 20-49
Types of Products Distributed:
    Frozen Food, Provisions/Meat

59541 Statewide Products Co Inc
4119 Prospect Ave NE
Albuquerque, NM 87110-3898   505-888-4646
    Fax: 505-884-3666
Wholesaler/distributor of specialty foods and groceries
Owner: Joe Smith
joe@statewideproducts.com
Secretary/Treasurer: R Smith
VP: D Bartucci
Estimated Sales: $20-50 Million
Number Employees: 20-49
Square Footage: 6500
Number of Customer Locations: 150
Types of Products Distributed:
    Frozen Food, General Line, Specialty Foods, Groceries

59542 Statex
3947 Street Hubert
Montreal, QC H2L 4A6
Canada   514-527-6039
    Fax: 514-524-0343
Wholesaler/distributor of sensory analysis software; consultant offering training, technical support and quality control services
Vice President: Michel Guillet
Estimated Sales: $1-5,000,000
Types of Products Distributed:
    General Merchandise, Sensory analysis software

59543 Staunton Foods LLC
10 Morris Mill Rd
PO Box 569
Staunton, VA 24401-2901   540-885-1214
    Fax: 540-885-0021 800-932-2228
        www.stauntonfoods.com
Wholesaler/distributor of groceries, provisions/meats, produce, frozen foods and general merchandise; serving the food service market
President: Bob Anders
bobanders@stauntonfoods.com
CEO: James Crawford
Marketing: Ken Coleman
Sales Manager: Cohan Flynn
Office Manager: Terry Robertson
bobanders@stauntonfoods.com
Operations Manager: Gary Bosserman
Purchasing Manager: Ken Coleman
Estimated Sales: $10 Million
Number Employees: 1-4
Square Footage: 64000
Parent Co: Clover Hill Foods
Private Brands Carried:
    Pocahontas
Types of Products Distributed:
    Food Service, Frozen Food, General Line, Provisions/Meat, Produce, Seafood, Groceries

59544 Staunton Fruit & Produce Company
P.O.Box 997
Verona, VA 24482   540-248-4310
    Fax: 540-248-1627
Wholesaler/distributor of produce
Owner: Lucille Rector
Manager: Martin Moskowitz
Estimated Sales: $5-10 Million
Number Employees: 10-19
Types of Products Distributed:
    Frozen Food, Produce

59545 Stavis Seafoods
212 Northern Ave
Suite 305
Boston, MA 02210-2090   617-897-1200
    Fax: 617-897-1291 800-390-5103
        fish@stavis.com www.stavis.com
Fresh and frozen seafood including cod, haddock, pollock, tuna, swordfish, mahi, snapper, grouper and seabass fillets, rockshrimp and baby scallops
President & CEO: Charles Marble
Chief Sustainability Officer: Richard Stavis
CFO: Mary Fleming
Executive Vice President: Stewart Altman
Director of Quality Assurance: Allison Roderick
VP Marketing: Michael Lynch
VP Sales: Stephen Young
VP Operations: Mohamad Fakira
Estimated Sales: $28.9 Million
Number Employees: 100-249
Square Footage: 10000
Type of Packaging: Food Service, Private Label, Bulk
Private Brands Carried:
    Bos'n; Boston Pride; Foods From The Sea; Prince Edward
Types of Products Distributed:
    Seafood

59546 Stay Tuned Industries
8 W Main St
Clinton, NJ 08809-1290   908-730-8455
    Fax: 908-735-8180
Wholesaler/distributor and exporter of steel and aluminum cans and easy-open ends; also, consultant for can manufacturers
Owner: Ray Slocum
Estimated Sales: $500,000-$1 Million
Number Employees: 1-4
Square Footage: 1800
Types of Products Distributed:
    Frozen Food, General Merchandise, Aluminum & steel cans, etc.

59547 Steckel Produce
905 State Highway 16
Jerseyville, IL 62052-2834   618-498-4274
    Fax: 618-498-4780
Fruits and vegetables
Owner: Robert Steckel
rsteckel@sincsurf.net
Estimated Sales: $3 Million
Number Employees: 5-9

59548 Steckel, Isadore
624 Colfax Avenue
Scranton, PA 18510-1942   570-344-3011
Wholesaler/distributor of meats and groceries
Owner/Buyer: I Steckel
Number of Customer Locations: 10
Types of Products Distributed:
    Frozen Food, General Line, Provisions/Meat, Groceries

59549 (HQ)Steel City Corporation
PO Box 1227
Youngstown, OH 44501-1227   330-792-7663
    Fax: 330-792-7951 800-321-0350
        jsmith@scity.com www.scity.com
Manufacturer, wholesaler/distributor, importer and exporter of plastic bags, plastic and wire racks and coin operated vending machines; manufacturer and importer of rubber bands
President: C Kenneth Fibus
CFO: Mike Janak
Quality Control: Steve Speece
National Sales Manager: Jim Smith
VP Sales: Lee Rouse
Sales Department: Erika Flaherty
Estimated Sales: $30-50 Million
Number Employees: 100-249
Square Footage: 150000
Types of Products Distributed:
    Frozen Food, General Merchandise, Racks, plastic bags, etc.

59550 Steinberg Quebec: Aligro
385 Des Chevaliers
Rimouski, QC G5L 1X3
Canada   418-724-4195
Wholesaler/distributor of canned and frozen foods; serving the food service market
Customer Service Manager: M Desbiens
Parent Co: Rodrigue Roussel et Cie Ltee.
Number of Customer Locations: 1500
Types of Products Distributed:
    Food Service, Frozen Food, General Line, Canned goods

59551 Steiner Foods
510 North Ave
New Rochelle, NY 10801   914-235-2300
    Fax: 914-235-2557 www.jalimacoffee.net
Wholesaler/distributor juices including litchi, papaya and pear
Owner: Carmine M Disanto
cdisanto@steinerfoods.com
Estimated Sales: $20-50 Million
Number Employees: 50-99
Private Brands Carried:
    Ceres
Types of Products Distributed:
    Frozen Food, General Line, Fruit Juices

59552 Steinfurth IncElectromechanical Measuring Systems
541 Village Trace
Bldg. 11, Suite 102
Marietta, GA 30067   678-500-9014
    Fax: 678-840-7744 info@steinfurth.de
        www.steinfurth.com
Steinfurth is a producer of specialist measuring devices for the beverage industry, the food industry, pharmaceuticals and mining.
New Technology Development: Martin Falkenstein
Marketing & Sales Manager North America: Yvonne Harper
New Business Development & Technical Sup: Johann Angres
Parent Co: Steinfurth Mess-Systeme GmbH

59553 Steinfurth Instruments
541 Village Trace
Bldg. 11, Suite 102
Marietta, GA 30067   678-500-9014
    Fax: 678-840-7744 info@steinfurth.de
        www.steinfurth.com
Steinfurth Instruments is a producer of specialist measuring devices for the beverage industry, the food industry, pharmaceuticals and mining.
New Technology Development: Martin Falkenstein
Marketing and Sales Manager: Yvonne Harper
New Business Development & Technical Sup: Johann Angres
Parent Co: Steinfurth Mess-Systeme GmbH

59554 Stella Maria's
4401 W Tradewinds Ave
Lauderdl By Sea, FL 33308-4463   954-772-7782
    Fax: 954-493-8968 800-600-2373
Wholesaler/distributor of frozen dietary meals including chicken, fish, pasta, potatoes, enchiladas, etc.; serving the food service market
President: Elizabeth Pettineo
VP: Frank Pettineo
Secretary: Stella Petko

Estimated Sales: $1-2.5 Million
Number Employees: 1-4
Private Brands Carried:
  Stella Maria's, Inc.
Types of Products Distributed:
  Food Service, Frozen Food, General Line, Health Food, Specialty Foods, Dietary meals

59555 Stephan Machinery, Inc.
1385 Armour Blvd
Mundelein, IL 60060 224-360-6206
  Fax: 847-247-0184 800-783-7426
  weirich@stephan-machinery.com
  www.stephan-machinery.com
Designs, engineers and builds the finest food processing equipment available.
CEO: Olaf Pehmoller
CFO: Gunter Dahling
Sales Manager: Eric Weirich
Contact: Rolf Heinze
heinze@stephan-machinery.com
Operations Director: Dirk Kuhnel
Estimated Sales: $7 -10 Million
Number Employees: 5-9
Square Footage: 28000
Types of Products Distributed:
  Frozen Food

59556 Sterling Candy, Inc.
27 Ludy Street
Hicksville, NY 11801 516-932-1104
  Fax: 516-932-8392
Candy manufacturer and wholesaler.
President/CEO: Edward Greenberg

59557 Sterling Promotional Corporation
3010 Westchester Avenue
Purchase, NY 10577 914-694-6500
  Fax: 914-694-2070 office@sterlingpromo.com
Wholesaler/distributor of premium incentives
President: Steven Linder
Estimated Sales: $1-3 Million
Number Employees: 10-19
Number of Products: 12
Type of Packaging: Bulk
Types of Products Distributed:
  Frozen Food, General Merchandise, Premium incentives

59558 (HQ)Sterling Scale Co
20950 Boening Dr
Southfield, MI 48075-5737 248-358-0590
  Fax: 248-358-2275 800-331-9931
  sales@sterlingscale.com www.sterlingscale.com
Manufacturer, importer, exporter and wholesaler/distributor of industrial scales; manufacturer of engineering software for weighing equipment
President: E Donald Dixon
CFO: J Dixon
Vice President: Tom Ulicny
Research & Development: T Klauinger
Quality Control: Jeff Shultz
Marketing Director: Tom Ulicny
Plant Manager: J Holcomb
Purchasing Manager: S Latucca
Estimated Sales: $2-3 Million
Number Employees: 20-49
Number of Brands: 5
Number of Products: 100
Square Footage: 112000
Types of Products Distributed:
  Frozen Food, General Merchandise, Industrial scales

59559 Steve's Fine Food Emporium
PO Box 782
Bala Cynwyd, PA 19004-0782 610-941-0665
  Fax: 610-825-0198 steveklein@hotmail.com
Wholesaler/distributor of specialty foods including Belgium baking chocolate, mushrooms, oils, etc.; serving the food service market
Owner: Steve Klein
Number Employees: 1-4
Square Footage: 12000
Private Brands Carried:
  Callebaut
Number of Customer Locations: 100
Types of Products Distributed:
  Food Service, Frozen Food, General Line, Specialty Foods, Baking chocolate, oils, mushrooms, etc.

59560 Stevenson Co
818 NW Jackson St
Topeka, KS 66608-1331 785-233-0691
  Fax: 785-233-4616
  www.stevensoncompanyinc.com
Wholesaler/distributor of institutional equipment including walk-in freezers, ovens, stoves, etc
Manager: Stephen Clark
stephenclark@stevensoncompanyinc.com
Engineering Department: Joe Pennington
Industrial Plant Work: Howard Brooks
Estimated Sales: $5-10 Million
Number Employees: 5-9
Types of Products Distributed:
  Food Service, Frozen Food, General Merchandise

59561 Stevita Naturals
7650 U.S. 287 Frontage Rd
Arlington, TX 76001 214-556-5933
  800-577-8409
  stevitanaturals.com
Candy, gum and cocoa sweetened with stevia
President/Owner: Oscar Rodes

59562 Stewart & Stevenson LLC
8787 East Fwy
Houston, TX 77029-1799 713-671-6300
  Fax: 713-671-2775 www.stewartandstevenson.com
Wholesaler/distributor of material handling equipment including forklifts
VP/Division Manager: Patrick McPhee
Manager: Bruce Daliege
bdaliege@ssss.com
Estimated Sales: $300,000-500,000
Number Employees: 250-499
Private Brands Carried:
  Hyster; Taylor-Dunn; Maninou
Types of Products Distributed:
  Frozen Food, General Merchandise, Material handling equipment

59563 Stewart Wholesale Hardware Company
1978 Eppinger Bridge Rd
Concord, GA 30206-3150 770-884-5651
  Fax: 706-883-6786
Wholesaler/distributor of grocery and hardware items to independent retail outlets
Owner: James Duty
CEO: C Stewart
Number Employees: 10-19
Square Footage: 120000
Type of Packaging: Bulk
Number of Customer Locations: 799
Types of Products Distributed:
  Frozen Food, General Line, General Merchandise, Grocery & hardware items

59564 (HQ)Stewarts Tristate Svc Co
514 Dellrose Ave
Dayton, OH 45403-1445 937-256-7600
  Fax: 937-256-6444 800-365-7600
  www.stewartstristate.com
Wholesaler/distributor of repair parts for kitchen and restaurant equipment; also, commercial restaurant equipment repair services available
President: Bobby Stewart
Owner: Amy Stewart
Estimated Sales: Less Than $500,000
Number Employees: 5-9
Square Footage: 40000
Other Locations:
  Stewart's Tri-State Service C
  Cincinnati, OHStewart's Tri-State Service C
Types of Products Distributed:
  Frozen Food, General Merchandise, Parts for kitchen/restaurant equipment

59565 Stewarts Tristate Svc Co
514 Dellrose Ave
Dayton, OH 45403-1445 937-256-7600
  Fax: 937-256-6444 800-365-7600
  www.stewartstristate.com
Wholesaler/distributor of parts for kitchen and restaurant equipment; also, commercial restaurant equipment repair services available
Owner: Amy Stewart
Secretary: Tammy Bullock
Estimated Sales: Less Than $500,000
Number Employees: 5-9
Parent Co: Stewart's Tri-State Service Company
Types of Products Distributed:
  Frozen Food, General Merchandise, PArts for kitchen/restaurnt equipment

59566 Stigler Supply Co
11158 Adwood Dr
Cincinnati, OH 45240-3234 513-825-4500
  Fax: 513-825-0549 800-214-7768
  john@stiglersupply.com www.stiglersupply.com
Wholesaler/distributor of janitorial supplies and cleaning equipment for carpets and hard floors; serving the food service market
President: Shaun Clarke
shaun@stiglersupply.com
Secretary/Treasurer: Deb Tenhundfeld
Director, Facility Operations: Drew Curtis
Estimated Sales: $5-10 Million
Number Employees: 10-19
Square Footage: 52000
Types of Products Distributed:
  Food Service, Frozen Food, General Merchandise, Janitorial supplies/cleaning equipment

59567 Stiles Enterprises Inc
114 Beach St # 1w
PO Box 92
Rockaway, NJ 07866-3529 973-625-9660
  Fax: 973-625-9346 800-325-4232
  www.stilesenterprises.com
Packaging machine replacement parts-rubber parts, conveyor belts, drive belts, fabricated belts, resurface rubber rollers, parts for cappers, fillers, labelers, bottle unscramblers, case tapers, form/fill/seal baggers , heattunnels.
Owner: Rich Stiles
CFO: Nancy Stiles
R&D: John Dubowchik
Sales: Ken Stiles
info@stilesenterprises.com
Estimated Sales: $5-10 Million
Number Employees: 10-19
Types of Products Distributed:
  Frozen Food, General Merchandise

59568 (HQ)Stock America Inc
900 Cheyenne Ave # 700
Suite 700
Grafton, WI 53024-1653 262-375-4100
  Fax: 262-375-4101 michaelg@stockamerica.com
  www.stockpackaging.com
Wholesaler/distributor of full-water and steam retorts, temperature and pressure monitoring equipment, fillers, packaging containers and sealing equipment.
President: Michael Galvin
Vice President: Victoria Schlegger
CEO: Michael Galvin
Vice President: Tim Schurr
Marketing: Donette Lambert
Sales Manager: Rick Eleew
Contact: Jay Brunner
jayb@stockamerica.com
Estimated Sales: $5-10 Million
Number Employees: 10-19
Number of Brands: 8
Number of Products: 5
Square Footage: 72000
Type of Packaging: Consumer
Other Locations:
  Stock America
  Montreal, PQ
  Stock America
  Cary, NCStock AmericaCary
Private Brands Carried:
  Stock; Dynopack; Icon 2000
Types of Products Distributed:
  Frozen Food, General Merchandise, Equipment, containers, fillers, etc.

59569 Stock Rack & Shelving Inc
1630 SW 5th Ct # 1500
Pompano Beach, FL 33069-3539 954-971-7225
  Fax: 954-784-2788
Wholesaler/distributor of racks and shelving
President: Mike Comstock
mike@stockrack.com
Estimated Sales: $1-3 Million
Number Employees: 5-9
Types of Products Distributed:
  Frozen Food, General Merchandise, Racks & shelving

Wholesalers & Distributors / A-Z

59570 Stockton Graham & Co
4320 Delta Lake Dr
Suite 199
Raleigh, NC 27612-7000 919-881-0746
Fax: 919-881-0746 800-835-5943
info@stocktongraham.com
www.stocktongraham.com
Wholesale specialty beverages
President: Jeff Vojta
vojta@stocktongraham.com
Estimated Sales: $500,000-$1 Million
Number Employees: 10-19

59571 Stoffel Equipment Co Inc
7764 N 81st St
Milwaukee, WI 53223-3838 414-354-7500
Fax: 414-354-0474 800-354-7502
www.stoffelequip.com
Wholesaler/distributor of general merchandise including forklifts, conveyors and shelving
President: Robert Stoffel Jr
Cmo: Brian Holbrook
bholbrook@stoffelequip.com
Number Employees: 50-99
Private Brands Carried:
  Raymond; Dockstacker; Versa
Types of Products Distributed:
  Frozen Food, General Merchandise, Forklifts, conveyors & shelving

59572 Stone Crabs Inc
11 Washington Ave
Miami Beach, FL 33139-7395 305-534-8788
Fax: 305-532-2704 800-260-2722
Fresh and frozen stone crabs, whole lobsters and lobster tails
President: Stephen Sawitz
alopez@stonecrabsinc.com
CFO: Marc Fine
Marketing Director: Tracie Gordon
Operations Manager: James McClendon
Facilities: Alex Lopez
Plant Manager: Ron Pressley
Estimated Sales: $10-20 Million
Number Employees: 20-49
Type of Packaging: Consumer, Food Service
Number of Customer Locations: 1
Types of Products Distributed:
  Seafood

59573 Stonington Lobster Co-Op
Indian Point Rd
Stonington, ME 4681 207-367-2286
Fax: 207-367-2802
Lobster
Manager: Ronald Trundy
Manager: Steve Robins Iii
Estimated Sales: $5-10 Million
Number Employees: 5-9

59574 Stonyfield Organic
10 Burton Dr
Londonderry, NH 03053-7436 603-437-4040
Fax: 603-437-7594 800-776-2697
www.stonyfield.com
Natural organic yogurt, frozen yogurt, smoothies, snacks, milk, cream, and baby food
Chairman/Co-Founder: Gary Hirshberg
President/CEO: Esteve Torrens
Director Operations/Finance: Rick Burleigh
VP Research & Development: Paul Rosethal
VP Marketing: Christopher Malnar
Senior Director Sales: Mark Murphy
VP Human Resources: Sue Melvin
COO: Diane Carhart
VP Sourcing & Product Development: Rolf Carlson
Year Founded: 1983
Estimated Sales: $370 Million
Number Employees: 400
Types of Products Distributed:
  Frozen Food, General Merchandise

59575 Stop & Shop Manufacturing
104 Meadow Road
Readville, MA 02136-2349 508-977-5132
Processor and wholesaler/distributor of milk, juices and sodas
Marketing Director: William Sress
Estimated Sales: $3-5 Million
Number Employees: 20-49
Parent Co: Stop & Shop Supermarket Company
Type of Packaging: Consumer

Types of Products Distributed:
  Food Service, Frozen Food, Milk, juices & sodas

59576 Storage Equipment
389 Marion Ave
Plantsville, CT 06479 860-426-9000
Fax: 860-426-9080 800-826-5326
www.storage-equipment.com
Wholesaler/distributor of racks and shelving
President: Michael Dubbs
VP: Richard Fox
Estimated Sales: $5-10 Million
Number Employees: 20-49
Private Brands Carried:
  Steel King; Penco; Akro-Mils
Types of Products Distributed:
  Frozen Food, General Merchandise, Racks & shelving

59577 Strasheim Wholesale
9220 Chestnut Ave
Franklin Park, IL 60131-3014 847-288-0300
Wholesaler/distributor of paper and syrup; serving the food service market
President: Nick Flores
Number Employees: 5-9
Types of Products Distributed:
  Food Service, Frozen Food, General Line, General Merchandise, Paper & syrup

59578 Stratecon InternationalConsultants
5215 Mountain View Road
Winston Salem, NC 27104-5117 336-768-6808
Fax: 336-765-5149
weck@foodbusinessresource.com
www.stratecon-intl.com
We combine the experience of twelve seasoned food industry professionals who work together to fulfill client needs. Members have skills in processed foods and ingredients. Specialties: business development, coffee manufacturingdietary fibers, due diligence, food safety, fortification, process and equipment development, product introduction, strategic planning, and training. See website for individual consultant locations
Coordinator: Catherine Side
Estimated Sales: Below $500,000
Number Employees: 2
Types of Products Distributed:
  Frozen Food

59579 Strauss Bakery
5115 13th Ave
Brooklyn, NY 11219-3560 718-851-7728
Fax: 718-437-1882 tzvi@straussbakery.com
www.straussbakery.com
Bakery products
President: Elliot Berman
bakerellyb@aol.com
Sales Manager: John Macley
Estimated Sales: Less Than $500,000
Number Employees: 5-9

59580 Strawhacker's Food Service
11887 E Stirrup High Drive E
Dewey, AZ 86327-6023 641-682-8164
Wholesaler/distributor of frozen foods, produce, provisions/meats and seafood; serving the food service market
Purchasing Director: Skip Lehmkuhl
Number Employees: 20-49
Square Footage: 88000
Parent Co: Lancroft Farms
Private Brands Carried:
  NIFDA
Number of Customer Locations: 50
Types of Products Distributed:
  Food Service, Frozen Food, Provisions/Meat, Produce, Seafood

59581 Streamline Foods
315 University Ave
Belleville, ON K8N 4Z6
Canada 613-961-1265
Fax: 613-961-1075
Blender and co-packer for multinational customers in the retail, foodservice, and private label sectors
President: Don Hill
Estimated Sales: $26.59 Million
Number Employees: 80
Square Footage: 131000

Other Locations:
Sales Office
Oakville, ONSales Office

59582 Streich Equipment Co Inc
833 S 3rd Ave
Wausau, WI 54401-6043 715-842-0531
Fax: 715-842-0534 info@streichequipment.com
www.streichequipment.com
Wholesaler/distributor of food service equipment; serving the food service market
President: Steven Streich
steve@streichequipment.com
Estimated Sales: $5-10 Million
Number Employees: 10-19
Types of Products Distributed:
  Food Service, Frozen Food, General Merchandise, Equipment

59583 Streit Carl & Son Co
703 Atkins Ave
Neptune, NJ 07753-5169 732-775-0803
Fax: 732-775-2274 www.carlstreit.com
Processor and wholesaler/distributor of poultry, Italian sausage and special cuts of beef, lamb, veal and pork
Owner: Jim Robinson Jr
VP: Judith Robinson
Estimated Sales: $10-20 Million
Number Employees: 5-9
Square Footage: 12000
Private Brands Carried:
  IBP; Mopac; National Beef
Types of Products Distributed:
  Frozen Food, Provisions/Meat, Specialty Foods, Beef, lamb, veal, pork, sausage, etc.

59584 Stronach & Sons
165 the Queensway
Toronto, ON M8Y 1H8
Canada 416-259-5000
Fax: 416-252-0110 stronachandsons.com
Wholesaler/distributor of fruits and vegetables
President: Sid Fogle
Director: Barry Fogle
Director: Ted Kurtz
Number Employees: 20-49
Types of Products Distributed:
  Frozen Food, Produce

59585 Strongbow Foods
2405 E US 30
Valparaiso, IN 46383-8362 219-462-5121
Fax: 219-477-4810 800-462-5121
Wholesaler/distributor of frozen turkey pies and cranberry-orange relish
President: Russ Adams
VP: Nancy Adams
Treasurer: Caroline Adams
Estimated Sales: $3-5 Million
Number Employees: 100-249
Parent Co: Strongbow Inn
Private Brands Carried:
  Strongbow Foods
Number of Customer Locations: 20
Types of Products Distributed:
  Frozen Food, General Line, Frozen turkey pies, etc.

59586 Stryka Botanical Co
9142 Owensmouth Ave
Chatsworth, CA 91311-5851 818-227-0555
Fax: 818-227-0560 info@stryka.com
www.stryka.com
Wholesaler/distributor of botanicals, powders and extracts
Manager: Michelle Weeks
Research & Development: John Loftus
Manager: Arthur Negrete
arthurn@stryka.com
Purchasing Manager: Matt Kulick
Estimated Sales: $3-5 Million
Number Employees: 20-49
Type of Packaging: Bulk
Types of Products Distributed:
  Health Food, Botanicals Ingredients

59587 Stryka Botanics
279 Homestead Rd
Hillsborough, NJ 08844-1907 908-281-5577
Fax: 908-281-5392 800-424-3642
info@stryka.com www.stryka.com
Manufacturer and distributor of more than 2,000 herbal extracts, powders and nutritional ingredients.

President: Brian McNally
Number Employees: 10-19
Type of Packaging: Bulk
Types of Products Distributed:
  Health Food, Botanicals Ingredients

59588 Stryka Botanics
369 N 100 W
Suite 3
Cedar City, UT 84720-2590   435-865-5959
    Fax: 435-867-1062 info@stryka.com
    www.stryka.com
Wholesaler/distributor of botanicals, powders and extracts
President: Brian McNally
Research & Development: John Loftus
Purchasing Manager: Matt Kulick
Type of Packaging: Bulk
Types of Products Distributed:
  Health Food, Botanicals Ingredients

59589 Stuart & CO
12 Mcguinness Blvd S
Apt 2B
Brooklyn, NY 11222-4995   347-292-7456
    Fax: 212-202-3868
BBQ sauce, potato chips, spice blends and beef jerky
Founder: Michael Steifman
Type of Packaging: Food Service
Types of Products Distributed:
  BBQ sauces, spice blends, jerky

59590 Sucesores de Pedro Cortes
Manuel Camunas #205, Tres Monjitas
PO BOX 363626
Hato Rey, PR 00918-1485   787-754-7040
    Fax: 787-754-2650 cortesco@tld.net
    www.chocolatecortes.com
Chocolate and cocoa products; private labeling available; importer of chocolate, milk drinks and crackers; wholesaler/distributor of confectionery items, beverages and biscuits
President: Ignacio Cortes Del Valle
VP: Ignacio Cortes Gelpi
Number Employees: 50-99
Number of Brands: 11
Square Footage: 150000
Type of Packaging: Consumer, Private Label, Bulk
Types of Products Distributed:
  General Line, Confectionery, biscuits & beverages

59591 Suffolk Banana Company
19 Old Dock Rd
Yaphank, NY 11980   631-205-2478
Wholesaler/distributor of produce
Owner: John Reina
Estimated Sales: $2.5-5 Million
Number Employees: 5-9
Types of Products Distributed:
  Frozen Food, Produce

59592 Sugarplum Desserts
20381 62nd Avenue
Building 5
Langley, BC V3A SE6
Canada   604-534-2282
    Fax: 604-534-2280 info@sugarplumdesserts.com
    www.sugarplumdesserts.com
Thaw and serve cheesecakes and thaw and bake cookies
President: Leslie Goodman
Number Employees: 15
Square Footage: 32000

59593 Suisan
333 Kilauea Ave
Suite 202
Hilo, HI 96720   808-935-8511
    Fax: 808-935-2737 www.suisan.com
Wholesaler/distributor of fresh produce.
President: Steve Ueda
Past President: Glenn Hashimoto
Year Founded: 1907
Estimated Sales: $20-50 Million
Number Employees: 100-249
Square Footage: 43000
Private Brands Carried:
  Tyson; Swanson; Kraft; Oscar Mayer

59594 Suity Confections Co
8105 NW 77th St.
P.O. Box 558943
Miami, FL 33166   305-639-3300
    Fax: 305-593-7070 info@suity.com
    www.suity.com
Candy, gum, chocolates, and cookies
VP: Jose Garrido Jr
garridojr@waltonpost.com
Quality Control: Luis Perez
Estimated Sales: $20-50 Million
Number Employees: 20-49
Types of Products Distributed:
  Frozen Food, General Line, Candy, chocolate & snack foods

59595 Suki
99 industrial drive
Northampton, MA 1060   305-635-5270
    Fax: 305-633-5618 800-698-5278
    sukiskincare.com/
Wholesaler/distributor of syrups, groceries, fresh and frozen eggs, frozen vegetables, cheese and cola
Owner: Lacodiaz Diac
Controller: Rafael Soto
Contact: Emily Brennan
emily.brennan@sukiskincare.com
Estimated Sales: $10-20 Million
Number Employees: 10-19
Square Footage: 30000
Private Brands Carried:
  Coca-Cola
Types of Products Distributed:
  Frozen Food, General Line, Syrups, groceries, eggs, cola, etc.

59596 Summertime Restaurant Equipment
30 Summertime Drive
St. John, NB E2K 5A5
Canada   506-693-4709
    Fax: 506-658-0601 www.summertime.ca
Wholesaler/distributor of equipment and supplies; serving the food service market
President: Luc Bedard
Number Employees: 5-9
Private Brands Carried:
  Garland; Hobart; Volrath
Types of Products Distributed:
  Food Service, Frozen Food, General Merchandise, Equipment & supplies

59597 Summit Food Service Distributors
100 Legacy Road
Ottawa, ON K1G 5T8
Canada   613-737-7000
    Fax: 613-737-4678 800-267-9610
    headoffice@summit.colabor.com
    summit.colabor.com
Wholesaler/distributor of frozen foods, groceries, meats, general merchandise, dairy products, baked goods and seafood; serving the food service market in Ontario and Quebec
General Manager: Bill Strano
Assistant Branch Manager: Paul Carter
Sales/Marketing Executive: Michael Tierney
Number Employees: 100-249
Square Footage: 420000
Parent Co: Colabor
Types of Products Distributed:
  Food Service, Frozen Food, General Line, General Merchandise, Provisions/Meat, Seafood, Groceries & baked goods

59598 Summit Food Service Distributors
580 Industrial Road
London, ON N5V 1V1
Canada   519-453-3410
    Fax: 519-453-5148 800-265-9267
    headoffice@summit.colabor.com
Wholesaler/distributor of meats, frozen foods and general line items
President: Jack Battersby
Purchasing Agent: Clare Baillie
Parent Co: Cara Operations
Other Locations:
  Summit Food Service Distribut
  Ottawa, ONSummit Food Service Distribut
Private Brands Carried:
  Coca Cola; Kellogg; Kraft
Types of Products Distributed:
  Frozen Food, General Line, Provisions/Meat

59599 Summit Import Corp
100 Summit Pl
Jersey City, NJ 07305-9997   201-985-9800
    Fax: 201-985-8055 800-888-8228
info@summitimport.com www.summitimport.com
President: Whiting Wu
Sales Manager: Tony Tsao
Warehouse Manager: Kent Jia
Year Founded: 1955
Estimated Sales: $20-50 Million
Number Employees: 50-99
Square Footage: 180000
Type of Packaging: Consumer, Food Service, Private Label, Bulk
Private Brands Carried:
  Oriental Mascot; Mount Tai; Gold Key
Number of Customer Locations: 1000
Types of Products Distributed:
  Food Service, Frozen Food, General Merchandise, Seafood, Specialty Foods, Oriental foods

59600 Sun Chlorella USA
3305 Kashiwa Street
Torrance, CA 90505-4022   310-891-0600
    Fax: 310-891-0621 800-829-2828
    www.sunchlorellausa.com
Ginseng and chlorella including tablets, liquid extract and green single cell algae with broken cell walls
President/CEO: Futoshi Nakayama
VP/Chief Financial Officer: Ellen Kubijanto
VP/Chief Operating Officer: Rose Straub
Marketing Manager: Susan Arboua
Public Relations: Janise Zantine
Estimated Sales: $24 Million
Number Employees: 61
Square Footage: 5000
Parent Co: YSK International Corporation
Types of Products Distributed:
  Frozen Food, General Line, Health Food, Ginseng & chlorella

59601 Sun Hing Foods
271 Harbor Way
S San Francisco, CA 94080   650-583-8188
    Fax: 650-583-8187 800-258-6669
    www.sunhingfoods.com
Ethnic food wholesaler and distributor
Exec. VP: Virginia Teng
Sales Director: Takwing Choi
Year Founded: 1981
Estimated Sales: $20-50 Million
Number Employees: 20-49
Number of Brands: 9
Types of Products Distributed:
  Frozen Food

59602 Sun Star Heating Products Inc
306 W Tremont Ave
PO Box 36271
Charlotte, NC 28203-4946   704-372-3486
    Fax: 704-332-5843 888-778-6782
info@sunstarheaters.com www.sunstarheaters.com
Manufacturers of Heavy Duty Patio Heating Products, Mushroom Type Patio Heaters, Tube-Type Infared Gas Heaters, High Intensity Ceramic Infared Natural Gas Heater, Heavy Duty Infared Heater and many more products
President: Frank L Horne Jr
info@sunstarheaters.com
Sales Exec: Bob Genisol
Number Employees: 20-49
Parent Co: Gas-Fired Products, Inc

59603 Sun Valley Fruit Company
P.O.Box 25707
Albuquerque, NM 87125-0707   505-345-2411
    Fax: 505-345-7563 800-432-7903
Wholesaler/distributor of frozen foods and produce; serving the food service market
CEO: Mark Prowell
VP Finances: Jim Hoyt
CEO: Cor Caraffa
VP Operations: Tony Espinoza
Estimated Sales: $20-50 Million
Number Employees: 100-249
Square Footage: 57000
Number of Customer Locations: 3000
Types of Products Distributed:
  Food Service, Frozen Food, Produce

Wholesalers & Distributors / A-Z

59604 Sun Valley Packing
7381 Avenue 432
Reedley, CA 93654-9016 559-591-1515
Fax: 559-591-1616 sunvaly@mobynet.com
Plums, peaches and nectarines
Owner: Walter Jones
wjones@sunvalley.com
Number Employees: 250-499

59605 Sun West Trading
2281 W 205th Street
Suite 107
Torrance, CA 90501-1450 310-320-4000
Fax: 310-320-8444
Importer and wholesaler/distributor of rice gluten, syrups and spray-dried syrup solids
President: Qasim Habib
Administrative Manager: Gafar Habib
Estimated Sales: $2.5-5 Million
Number Employees: 1-4
Parent Co: Habib Arkady
Type of Packaging: Bulk
Types of Products Distributed:
Frozen Food, General Line, Rice gluten, syrups & spray dried syrup

59606 (HQ)SunRidge Farms
423 Salinas Rd
Royal Oaks, CA 95076-5232 831-786-7000
Fax: 831-786-8618 sunridge@cruzio.com
sunridgefarms.com
Natural snacks, trail mixes, candies, nuts and seeds, dried fruits
CEO: Morty Cohen
Year Founded: 1982
Estimated Sales: $10-20 Million
Number Employees: 20-49
Number of Products: 1000
Square Footage: 70000
Other Locations:
Falcon Trading Co.
Petaluma, CAFalcon Trading Co.
Private Brands Carried:
Sun Ridge Farms; Chica Bella
Types of Products Distributed:
Frozen Food, General Merchandise, Health Food, Bulk food dispensing systems

59607 Sunbelt Industrial Trucks
1617 Terre Colony Ct
Dallas, TX 75212 214-819-4150
support@sunbelt-industrial.com
www.sunbelt-industrial.com
Wholesaler/distributor of material handling equipment.
CEO: Warren Cornhil
Year Founded: 1987
Estimated Sales: $50-100 Million
Number Employees: 50-99
Square Footage: 60000
Other Locations:
Arlington, TX
Belton, TX
Dallas, TX
Fort Worth, TX
Irving, TX
McKinney, TXBelton
Private Brands Carried:
Komatsu; Thailift; Nissan
Types of Products Distributed:
Frozen Food, General Merchandise, Material handling equipment

59608 Sunburst Foods
1002 Sunburst Dr
Goldsboro, NC 27534 919-778-2151
Fax: 919-778-9203
Processor and wholesaler/distributor of prepacked sandwiches
President: Ray Lewis
Chairman: B Darden
Vice President: Lori Moss
Maintenance Manager: Bill Sugg
Estimated Sales: $13 Million
Number Employees: 150
Square Footage: 150000
Type of Packaging: Consumer
Types of Products Distributed:
General Line, Prepacked sandwiches

59609 Sunburst Trout Farms
314 Industrial Park Drive
Waynesville, NC 28786 800-673-3051
www.sunbursttrout.com
Trout fillets, caviar and gift baskets
CEO: Sally Eason
Chief Financial Officer: Benjamin Eason
Marketing & HR Director: Anna Eason
Sales & Processing Manager: Wes Eason
Office Manager: Stephanie Strickland
Year Founded: 1948
Number Employees: 11-50
Type of Packaging: Food Service
Types of Products Distributed:
Seafood

59610 Sunchef Farms
4722 Everett Avenue
Vernon, CA 90058-3133 323-588-5800
Fax: 323-588-2285
Portion-controlled chicken including marinated and flavored products
President: Steve Tsatas
Types of Products Distributed:
Frozen Food

59611 Suncrest Farms LLC
97 Minnisink Rd
Totowa, NJ 07512-1945 973-595-0214
Fax: 973-595-0214 www.suncrestmilkman.com
Milk and dairy products
Owner: Ed Seabridge
eseabridge@suncrestfarms.com
Estimated Sales: Less Than $500,000
Number Employees: 1-4
Number of Brands: 5
Type of Packaging: Consumer, Food Service
Types of Products Distributed:
Food Service, General Line, Dairy products

59612 Sunderland Dispensing Service
2120 Pennsylvania Ave N
Minneapolis, MN 55427 763-544-4918
Wholesaler/distributor of beverage dispensing and refrigeration systems; serving the food service market
Owner: R Sunderland
Number Employees: 1-4
Square Footage: 8000
Private Brands Carried:
EDI; Stoelting; Royale; Cornelius; True
Types of Products Distributed:
Food Service, General Merchandise, Beverage dispensing systems, etc.

59613 Sunflower Food Company
14612 W 106 Street
Lenexa, KS 66215 913-894-2233
Fax: 913-894-2244
info@sunflowerfoodcompany.com
www.sunflowerfoodcompany.com
Sunflower seeds, popcorn and nuts
Owner: Casey O'Sullivan
Vice President: Mike Meier
Contact: Barbara Hansen
hansen.barbara@sunflowerfoodcompany.com
Estimated Sales: $5-10 Million
Number Employees: 5-9
Square Footage: 24000
Type of Packaging: Consumer, Food Service, Private Label, Bulk
Types of Products Distributed:
Specialty Foods

59614 Sunflower Restaurant Supply
1647 Sunflower Rd
Salina, KS 67401-1758 785-823-6394
Fax: 785-823-5512
Locally owned and operated offering quality restaurant supplies and equipment.
President/Finance Executive: Leroy Baumberger
leroy@sunflowersrs.com
Estimated Sales: $7.3 Million
Number Employees: 20-49
Square Footage: 144000
Private Brands Carried:
Lyon; Pleezing; Wilsey Food
Number of Customer Locations: 700
Types of Products Distributed:
Food Service, Frozen Food, General Line, General Merchandise, Equipment & fixtures

59615 Sunkist Foodservice Equipment
10509 Business Dr.
Unit B.
Fontana, CA 92337 909-983-5852
Fax: 909-822-2125 800-383-7141
The Sunkist located in Fontana California manufactures commercial foodservice equipment which includes juicers, sectionizers & bar buddy's.
President & CEO: Russell Hanlin
Vice President: Charlie Woltmann
Quality Control/Research & Development: Dennis Pollard
Sales & Marketing Director: Tom Cohn
Public Relations Manager: Michael Wootton
Operations/Production/Plant Manager: Anil Arora
Purchasing: Anil Arora
Parent Co: Sunkist Growers
Types of Products Distributed:
Frozen Food

59616 Sunkist Growers
27770 Entertainment Dr.
Valencia, CA 91355 661-290-8900
www.sunkist.com
Fruit juices, fruit drinks, healthy snacks, baking mixes, carbonated beverages, confections, vitamins, frozen novelties, salad toppings, freshly peeled citrus, chilled jellies and nonfood products.
Chief Executive Officer: Jim Phillips
Chief Operating Officer: Christian Harris
Year Founded: 1893
Estimated Sales: $1 Billion
Number Employees: 6,000
Type of Packaging: Food Service, Private Label
Other Locations:
Sunkist Growers
Toronto Canada, ON
Sunkist Growers
Cary, NC
Sunkist Growers
Pittsburgh, PA
Sunkist Growers
Buffalo, NY
Sunkist Growers
Stafford, TX
Sunkist Growers
Visalia, CA
Sunkist GrowersCary
Types of Products Distributed:
Food Service, Produce

59617 Sunrise Fruit Company
1727 Rhoadmiller Street
Richmond, VA 23220-1108 804-358-6468
Fax: 804-358-6947
Wholesaler/distributor, importer and exporter of tomatoes
Types of Products Distributed:
Frozen Food, Produce, Tomatoes

59618 Sunset Wholesale West
3337 N 35th Ave
Pheonix, AZ 85015 602-354-3870
info@sunsetwholesalewest.com
www.sunsetwholesalewest.com
Smoke shop wholesaler
Estimated Sales: $20-50 Million
Number Employees: 50-99
Types of Products Distributed:
Frozen Food

59619 Sunset of Queens
1878 Victory Boulevard
Staten Island, NY 10314-3514 718-291-3456
Fax: 718-657-0433
Wholesaler/distributor of electrical supplies including lighting fixtures, light bulbs, switches, fuses, etc
Secretary: Jeff Goldberg
Number Employees: 20-49
Square Footage: 48000
Private Brands Carried:
Leviton; Crouse-Hinds; Buss-Fuses
Number of Customer Locations: 500
Types of Products Distributed:
Frozen Food, General Merchandise, Electrical supplies & lighting fixtures

59620 Sunshine Bar Supply Company
90 Thorncliffe Park Drive
Toronto, ON M4H 1M5
Canada 416-422-1261
Fax: 416-421-9654
Wholesaler/distributor of bar supplies including glassware, ash trays, cocktail napkins, mixes, etc.; serving the food service market
Sales Manager: Manuel Mendes
Number Employees: 5-9
Private Brands Carried:
Libby's; Mott's; Obrowne & Co.

Wholesalers & Distributors / A-Z

Types of Products Distributed:
Food Service, Frozen Food, General Line, General Merchandise, Bar supplies

59621 Sunshine Farms
N8873 Currie Rd
Portage, WI 53901-9218   608-742-2016
Fax: 608-742-1577 sunshine@jvlnet.com
www.jvlnet.com
Processor and wholesaler/distributor of cheese and goat milk; wholesaler/distributor of health foods
President: Daniel Considine
sunshine@jvl.net
Estimated Sales: $3-5 Million
Number Employees: 1-4
Type of Packaging: Consumer
Private Brands Carried:
Mt. Sterling (Cheese); Monchevre (Cheese)
Number of Customer Locations: 60
Types of Products Distributed:
Frozen Food, General Line, Health Food, Cheese & goat milk

59622 Sunshine Fresh
4425 Vandenberg Dr
North Las Vegas, NV 89081-2716   702-838-4698
Fax: 702-838-4691   800-832-8081
info@sunshinefresh.com www.majorproducts.com
Pickles; wholesaler/distributor of deli products; serving the food service market, manufactures and packs liquid food products.
President: Michael Rosenblum
Estimated Sales: $8100000
Number Employees: 5-9
Type of Packaging: Consumer, Food Service, Bulk
Types of Products Distributed:
Food Service, Frozen Food, General Line, Deli products

59623 Sunshine Seafood
PO Box 136
Stonington, ME 04681   207-367-2955
Fax: 207-367-6394
Fish, seafood and shellfish.
President: James Eaton
Estimated Sales: $2,600,000
Number Employees: 10-19

59624 Sunspun Foodservice
3225 12 Street NE
Calgary, AB T2E 7S9
Canada   403-291-7884
Fax: 403-291-7740
Wholesaler/distributor of seafood, general line products, meats, frozen foods, specialty foods and produce; serving the food service market in western Canada
Director: David Fedyk
Parent Co: Westfair Foods Ltd
Private Brands Carried:
President's Choice; Sunspun
Types of Products Distributed:
Food Service, Frozen Food, General Line, Provisions/Meat, Produce, Seafood, Specialty Foods

59625 Suntec Power
1910 Bath Ave
Brooklyn, NY 11214-4713   718-333-3636
Fax: 718-333-3639 www.suntecusa.com
Exporter, importer and wholesaler/distributor of health food ingredients, vitamins, herbs, herbal extracts, food additives, spices, amino acids, etc
President: Tommy Liu
suntecpower@gmail.com
Owner: Wei Lin
Estimated Sales: Less Than $500,000
Number Employees: 1-4
Square Footage: 24000
Type of Packaging: Bulk
Types of Products Distributed:
Frozen Food, General Line, Health Food, Ingredients, vitamins, herbs, etc.

59626 Suntreat Packing & Shipping Co
391 Oxford Ave
PO Box 850
Lindsay, CA 93247-2208   559-562-4991
Fax: 559-562-6814 www.suntreat.com
Wholesaler/distributor of oranges, tangelos and lemons
President: Tom Roberts
Cmo: Thomas Roberts
tomr@suntreat.com
Sales: Mike Roberts

Number Employees: 100-249
Types of Products Distributed:
Frozen Food, Produce, Oranges, tangelos & lemons

59627 Super Beta Glucan
5 Holland # 109
Irvine, CA 92618-2570   949-305-2599
Fax: 626-203-0655 service@superbetaglucan.com
www.superbetaglucan.com
Mushroom Beta Glucan (Immulink MBG)
Founder: Dr. S.N. Chen
Vice President: Sherwin Chen
Number Employees: 5-9

59628 Super Natural Distributors
W229n1680 Westwood Dr
Waukesha, WI 53186-1152   262-650-9000
Fax: 262-650-9988   800-888-4008
www.sndonline.com
Wholesaler/distributor of vitamins and health foods
Owner: Trish Calvey
orders@sndonline.com
Estimated Sales: $3-5 Million
Number Employees: 20-49
Types of Products Distributed:
Frozen Food, Health Food, Vitamins

59629 Super Nutrition Distributors
1500 Hempstead Turnpike
Suite 100
East Meadow, NY 11554-1551   516-897-2480
Fax: 888-682-3311   800-777-8844
www.supernut.com
Wholesaler/distributor of national brand health supplements
CEO: Steven Falk
General Manager: Wes Burger
Sales Manager: Bill Britton
Types of Products Distributed:
Frozen Food, Health Food, Health supplements

59630 Super Snooty Sea Food Corporation
7 Fish Pier St E
Boston, MA 02210-2007   617-426-6390
Fax: 617-439-9144
Processor and wholesaler/distributor of frozen seafood including round and filleted flat fish
General Manager: Paul Sousa
Estimated Sales: $1-5 Million
Number Employees: 10-20
Type of Packaging: Consumer
Types of Products Distributed:
Frozen Food, Seafood

59631 Super Store Industries
2800 W March Ln # 210
Stockton, CA 95219-8200   209-473-8100
Fax: 209-473-8930 www.ssica.com
Wholesaler/distributor of frozen foods, general line items and dairy products including milk
President: Jay Simon
jsimon@ssica.com
Estimated Sales: $1-2.5 Million
Number Employees: 5-9
Private Brands Carried:
Sunny Select
Types of Products Distributed:
Frozen Food, General Line, Milk

59632 Superior Beverage Group
871 Michigan Avenue
Columbus, OH 43215   614-294-3555
Fax: 614-299-9210
www.superiorbeveragegroup.com
Wholesaler/distributor of beer
Manager: Chris Merritt
Contact: John Antonucci
j.antonucci@thebevgroup.com
General Manager: Mark Laser
Estimated Sales: $2.5-5 Million
Number Employees: 10-19
Parent Co: Central Beverage Group
Private Brands Carried:
Heineken; Miller; Pabst
Types of Products Distributed:
Frozen Food, General Line, Beer

59633 Superior Foods
275 Westgate Dr
Watsonville, CA 95076-2470   831-728-3691
Fax: 831-722-0926 info@superiorfoods.com
www.superiorfoods.com

Global supplier and manufacturer of frozen fruits, vegetables and grains for the consumer, foodservice, club and industrial markets.
President & CEO: R. Neil Happee
Number Employees: 50-99
Type of Packaging: Consumer, Food Service
Types of Products Distributed:
Frozen Food, Produce

59634 Superior Lamp
866 Kent Ave
Brooklyn, NY 11205   718-388-2066
Fax: 718-388-2077   800-544-4877
sales@superiorlighting-nyc.com
www.superiorlighting-nyc.com
Wholesaler/distributor of electrical supplies including ceiling and exhaust fans, lights and lighting fixtures, electric heaters and intercommunication systems
President: David Brooks
Estimated Sales: $2.5-5 Million
Number Employees: 20-49
Square Footage: 40000
Parent Co: Superiority
Number of Customer Locations: 2000
Types of Products Distributed:
Frozen Food, General Merchandise, Electrical supplies

59635 Superior Ocean Produce
4423 N Elston Ave
Chicago, IL 60630   773-283-8400
Fax: 773-561-0139 bill@fishguy.com
www.fishguy.com
Seafood
Owner: William Dugan
bdugan@fishguy.com
Estimated Sales: $1-3 Million
Number Employees: 10-19

59636 Superior Paper & Plastic Co
1930 E 65th St
Los Angeles, CA 90001-2111   323-235-1228
Fax: 323-581-7777 www.superiorpaper.com
Wholesaler/distributor of disposable paper and plastic products including napkins, cups, plates, cutlery, etc.; serving the food service market
Owner: Mark Penhasian
mark@superiorpaper.com
CEO: John Fong
Vice President: Mourice Penhasian
Sales Director: Joe Diaz
mark@superiorpaper.com
Estimated Sales: $5-10 Million
Number Employees: 20-49
Number of Products: 3500
Square Footage: 128000
Type of Packaging: Food Service
Private Brands Carried:
Reynolds; Solo; Hoffmaster; Pactive; Dart; H.F.A.; Anchor; Genpack
Types of Products Distributed:
Food Service, General Merchandise, Disposable paper & plastic products

59637 Superior Products Company
P.O.Box 64177
Saint Paul, MN 55164   651-636-1110
800-328-9800
comments@superprod.com
Wholesale Distributor of foodservice equipment and supplies
Contact: Charlette Edwards
charlette_edwards@ndgstp.com
Number Employees: 1-4
Type of Packaging: Food Service
Other Locations:
Alexandria, VA
Anaheim, CA
Atlanta, GA
Baltimore, MD
Boston, MA
Charlotte, NCAnaheim

59638 Superior Seafood & MeatCompany
623 S Olive Street
South Bend, IN 46619-3309   574-289-0511
Fax: 574-289-0919
Seafood and meat
President: Joe Neary Sr

Wholesalers & Distributors / A-Z

59639 Superior Seafoods Inc
2625 Causeway Blvd
Tampa, FL 33619-5166   813-248-2749
                Fax: 813-247-4539
Wholesaler/distributor of frozen shrimp
VP: Ernest Donini
edonini@sefsc.noaa.gov
VP: John Donini
Sales: Ernie Donini
Estimated Sales: Less Than $500,000
Number Employees: 1-4
Types of Products Distributed:
  Seafood, Frozen shrimp

59640 Superior Wholesale Distr
435 N Main St
Lima, OH 45801-4314   419-227-2436
  Fax: 419-229-3289 800-472-4150
              www.swdinc.com
Wholesaler/distributor of general line products;
serving the food service market
President: Carl Berger
swdcorp@bright.net
Estimated Sales: $20-50 Million
Number Employees: 50-99
Types of Products Distributed:
  Food Service, Frozen Food, General Line

59641 Supply One
143 Getty Ave
Paterson, NY 07503   718-392-7400
              www.supplyone.com
Wholesaler/distributor of paper and plastic products,
janitorial chemicalsand equipment; serving the food
service market.
President & CEO: Bill Leith
Private Brands Carried:
  Klimax; ViPaco; Criterion
Types of Products Distributed:
  Food Service, Frozen Food, General Merchandise, Packaging materials & machinery

59642 Supply One Inc
11 Campus Blvd
Suite 150
Newtown Square, PA 19073   484-582-5005
  Fax: 484-582-0350 www.supplyone.com
Wholesaler/distributor of paper and plastic products,
janitorial chemicals and equipment; serving the food
service market.
President & CEO: Bill Leith
Year Founded: 1998
Estimated Sales: $50-100 Million
Number Employees: 100-249
Square Footage: 150000
Private Brands Carried:
  Advantage on a Roll
Types of Products Distributed:
  Food Service, Frozen Food, General Merchandise, Paper & plastic products, etc.

59643 Supreme Fixture Company
11900 Vimy Ridge Road
PO Box 193655
Little Rock, AR 72219   501-455-2552
  Fax: 501-455-0802 info@supremefixture.com
            www.supremefixture.com
Wholesaler/distributor of tabletop supplies and
equipment; serving the food service market
President: C Hampel
Contact: Christena Baugh
christena@supremefixture.com
Estimated Sales: $10-20 Million
Number Employees: 20-49
Types of Products Distributed:
  Food Service, Frozen Food, General Merchandise, Tabletop supplies, etc.

59644 Supreme Food
691 14th Street NW
Atlanta, GA 30318-5405   404-872-7372
                Fax: 404-505-8618
Wholesaler/distributor of dairy products and kosher
and specialty food items
President: Alan Kaplan
Manager: Todd Treadwell
Estimated Sales: $1-3 Million
Number Employees: 10-19
Square Footage: 72000
Number of Customer Locations: 450
Types of Products Distributed:
  General Line, Specialty Foods, Kosher food items & dairy products

59645 (HQ)Supreme Foods
8755 Keele Street
Concord, ON L4K2N1
Canada   905-738-4204
Wholesaler/distributor and import broker of kosher
foods, confectionery, frozen foods, general merchandise, natural foods, specialty foods, groceries, meats,
spices, etc.
President: J Simon
Secretary/Treasurer: P Bonder
Vice President: R Simon
Number Employees: 50
Square Footage: 220000
Types of Products Distributed:
  Food Service, Frozen Food, General Line, General Merchandise, Health Food, Provisions/Meat, Specialty Foods, Kosher foods, spices, etc.

59646 Supreme Lobster
220 E North Ave
Villa Park, IL 60181-1207   630-832-6700
  Fax: 630-832-6688 www.supremelobster.com
Wholesaler/distributor of fresh and frozen seafood;
serving the food service and retail markets; transportation firm providing refrigerated trucking
President/CEO: Dominic Stramaglia
Chief Financial Officer: Greg Shuda
VP: Mike Sakshaug
Sales: Tim Stramaglia
Purchasing Manager: Tim Fasshaur
Number Employees: 250-499
Square Footage: 400000
Type of Packaging: Food Service
Number of Customer Locations: 4000
Types of Products Distributed:
  Food Service, Frozen Food, Seafood

59647 Sure Fine Food
P.O.Box 913
Evansville, IN 47706-0913   812-428-0888
                Fax: 812-428-0961
Wholesaler/distributor of frozen food and provisions/meats; serving the food service market
Manager: Jeff Noah
Estimated Sales: $10-20 Million
Number Employees: 10-19
Number of Customer Locations: 290
Types of Products Distributed:
  Food Service, Frozen Food, Provisions/Meat

59648 Sure-Good Food Distributors
6361 Thompson Rd
Syracuse, NY 13206-1448   315-422-1196
                Fax: 315-478-5220
Wholesaler/distributor of poultry
Owner: Jerome Savlov
General Manager: Eric Long
Estimated Sales: $10-20 Million
Number Employees: 10-19
Types of Products Distributed:
  General Line, Poultry

59649 Sustainable Harvest Coffee Company
721 NW 9th Ave Ste 235
Portland, OR 97209   503-235-1119
  Fax: 510-652-2636 info@sustainableharvest.com
            www.sustainableharvest.com
Unroasted green coffee importer, organic and fair
trade coffees
President: David Griswold
Contact: Alfonso Carmona
alfonso@sustainableharvest.com
Estimated Sales: $3 Million
Number Employees: 1-4

59650 Sutherland Produce Sales
1354 Rutherford Rd
Greenville, SC 29609-3145   864-244-5611
                Fax: 864-244-5613
Wholesaler/distributor of produce
Owner: Marion Kirby
Estimated Sales: $5-10 Million
Number Employees: 5-9
Types of Products Distributed:
  Frozen Food, Produce

59651 Swapples

Washington, DC

          info@swapfoods.com
          www.swapfoods.com

Paleo, vegan, and gluten free waffles in both sweet
and savory flavors
Founder/CEO: Rebecca Peress *Year Founded:* 2016
Types of Products Distributed:
  General Line

59652 Sweet Dried Fruit
8105 Breeze Way
Jonestown, TX 78645-9642   512-267-8811
        Fax: 570-745-3362 sweet1888@aol.com
            www.sweetdriedfruit.com
Importer and wholesaler/distributor of raisins, etc.;
exporter of raisins
President: Sidney Sweet
Partner: Scott Fichter
scott@sweetdriedfruit.com
VP: Candace Sweet
Estimated Sales: Less Than $500,000
Number Employees: 1-4
Types of Products Distributed:
  Frozen Food, General Line, Dried fruits & nuts, currants, etc.

59653 Sweet Liberty Candy Company
874 Long Island Avenue
Deer Park, NY 11729-3710   631-243-6100
                Fax: 631-586-8921
Wholesaler/distributor of sugar-free chocolates including milk and dark almond bars, almond butter
crunch, peanut butter truffle, etc
President: Serge Perelmutter
VP: Joan Young
Sales Manager: Elizabeth Newton
Estimated Sales: $1-2.5 Million
Number Employees: 1-4
Types of Products Distributed:
  Frozen Food, General Line, Specialty Foods, Sugar-free chocolates

59654 Sweet Place
4344 21st Street
Long Island City, NY 11101-5002   718-392-7744
        Fax: 718-472-0385   888-433-7737
Wholesaler/distributor of specialty foods and confectionery items
President: Richard Bornstein
Number Employees: 10-19
Types of Products Distributed:
  Frozen Food, General Line, Specialty Foods, Confectionery items

59655 Sweet Sensations
201 Humber Ave
Labrador City, NL A2V 2V3
Canada   709-944-2660
                Fax: 709-944-2656
Chocolate and candies, also nuts and glazed nuts
Owner: Andrea Cormier
Estimated Sales: $1 Million

59656 Sweet Shop USA
1316 Industrial Rd
Mt Pleasant, TX 75455-2614   903-575-0033
        Fax: 817-336-9169   888-957-9338
          customercare@sweetshopusa.com
              www.sweetshopusa.com
Chocolates, truffles, caramels and fudge.
President: Michael Moss
CEO: Jim Webb
jim@sweetshopusa.com
Chief Financial Officer: Matt Kelley
Lead Customer Service Representative: Sherry
Bostick
Manager: Ashlyn Reynolds
Estimated Sales: $4.5 Million
Number Employees: 50-99
Number of Brands: 3
Square Footage: 66000
Type of Packaging: Consumer
Types of Products Distributed:
  Chocolate

59657 Sweet Traders
5362 Oceanus Dr # C
Suite C
Huntington Beach, CA 92649-1000   714-903-6800
        Fax: 714-892-4345 info@sweettraders.com
              www.sweettraders.com
Wine, chocolate, baked goods, and gift baskets; including chocolate wrapped wines and ciders, champagnes and nonalcoholic beverages
Owner: R Louw
rflouw@yahoo.com

Estimated Sales: Less Than $500,000
Number Employees: 1-4
Square Footage: 10000
Type of Packaging: Consumer, Private Label

59658 Sweet Whispers
6031 Crimson Ct
Mclean, VA 22101-0000   954-328-5079
info@sweetwhispers.store
sweetwhispers.store
Meringue filling
Co-Founder: Maria Umana
Co-Founder: Liliana Guerra *Year Founded:* 2016
Types of Products Distributed:
  Meringue filling

59659 Sweetener Products Co
2050 E 38th St
Vernon, CA 90058
Fax: 323-232-3608 800-305-2200
www.sweetenerproducts.com
Wholesaler/distributor of sweeteners, sugar, corn syrups, starch, salt, dextrose, fructose, shortening, lecithin, milk solid, cheese flavors, etc.; serving the food service market.
President & CEO: Joe Tack
joe@spvw.com
Chairman of the Board: Robert Shipp
Vice Chairman: Robert Shipp, Jr.
Controller: Jim Boltinghouse
Director, MIS: Charlie Hengsathorn
Director, Quality Assurance: Lewis Ennist
Vice President, Sales: Tom Rodd
Vice President, Operations: Steve Shanklin
Year Founded: 1923
Estimated Sales: $50-100 Million
Number Employees: 100-249
Square Footage: 90000
Private Brands Carried:
  C&H; Hally; Morton Salt; National Starch
Types of Products Distributed:
  Food Service, Frozen Food, General Line, Sweeteners

59660 Sweety's Candies
8567 Higuera St
Culver City, CA 90232   310-842-8144
Fax: 310-842-8187 888-793-3897
Wholesaler/distributor of candy; also, contracting for promotional candy packaging available
Managing Partner: Will Pastron
President: Marc Arendt
Director Sales: Rosalie Gonzales
Number Employees: 20-49
Private Brands Carried:
  Dorval; Jaret International; Haribo
Types of Products Distributed:
  Frozen Food, General Line, Candy

59661 Swift Chemical & Supplies Inc
11520 Grandview Rd
Kansas City, MO 64137-2823   816-221-1292
Fax: 816-761-7339 www.swiftchemicalsupply.com
Wholesaler/distributor of janitorial supplies
Manager: Juan Swart
Operations Manager/Buyer: Matt Guilfoyle
Estimated Sales: Less Than $500,000
Number Employees: 1-4
Square Footage: 9600
Private Brands Carried:
  Rubbermaid; Procter & Gamble; Drackett Products Co.
Types of Products Distributed:
  Frozen Food, General Merchandise, Janitorial supplies

59662 Swiss American International
1059 E Gartner Rd
Naperville, IL 60540   630-778-7245
Fax: 630-778-7246
Wholesaler/distributor and export broker of natural brewed tea concentrates and industrial ingredients
President: Richard L Hutter
VP: George Kienberger
Estimated Sales: $1-2.5 Million
Number Employees: 1-4
Square Footage: 2400
Type of Packaging: Consumer, Food Service
Types of Products Distributed:
  Food Service, General Line, Tea & industrial ingredients

59663 (HQ)Swiss Chalet Fine Foods
9455 NW 40th Street Rd
Doral, FL 33178-2941   305-592-0008
Fax: 305-592-1651 800-347-9477
info@scff.com www.scff.com
A wide range of quality gourmet products from sweets to savories
CFO: Donna Croup
donna@scff.com
Estimated Sales: $300,000-500,000
Number Employees: 5-9
Private Brands Carried:
  Haco, Hero & Felchlin-Swiss
Types of Products Distributed:
  Food Service, Frozen Food, General Line, Specialty Foods, Sweets, soup mixes, caviar

59664 Swisser Sweet Maple
6242 Swiss Road
Castorland, NY 13620-1244   315-346-1034
Fax: 315-346-1662
Pure NY maple syrup, pure maple cream spread, maple candies, maple lollipops, maple granulated sugar, gift arrangements, wedding party favors and corporate gifts. Retail, wholesale and bulk.
Co-Owner: Barbara Zehr
Co-Owner: Jason Zehr
Number Employees: 6
Type of Packaging: Consumer, Private Label, Bulk
Other Locations:
  Swisser Sweet Maple
  Casta-Land, NY Swisser Sweet Maple

59665 Switchback Group
3778 Timberlake Dr
Richfield, OH 44286-9187   330-523-5200
Fax: 330-523-5212 info@switchbackgroup.com
www.switchbackgroup.com
Compliance packaging machines, vertical appplications of which include condiments; prepared foods; spices; pre-mixes; salad dresings; dessert toppings; and juice.
Manager: Dave Shepherd
dshepherd@switchbackgroup.com
Marketing & Sales Director: David Shepherd
Number Employees: 10-19

59666 Switzer's Inc
209 S Belt E
Belleville, IL 62220   618-234-2225
Fax: 618-271-6339
bellevilleswitzerfoods@gmail.com
Frozen foods, groceries, provisions/meats and general merchandise; serving the food service market
President: Carolyn Hundley
switzerfoods@gmail.com
Estimated Sales: $20-50 Million
Number Employees: 20-49
Number of Customer Locations: 20
Types of Products Distributed:
  Food Service, Frozen Food, General Line, General Merchandise, Provisions/Meat, Groceries

59667 Sycaway Creamery Inc
42 Duncan Ln # 1
Troy, NY 12180-6756   518-273-7761
Fax: 518-273-0047 www.sycawaycreamery.com
Wholesaler/distributor of dairy products including milk and ice cream
Vice President: Mark Duncan
mark@sycawaycreamery.com
VP: Janis Stevens
VP: Mark Duncan
Estimated Sales: $20-50 Million
Number Employees: 10-19
Types of Products Distributed:
  Frozen Food, General Line, Dairy products: milk & ice cream

59668 Sygma Network
8784 Rochester Ave
Rancho Cucamonga, CA 91730   909-980-8998
Fax: 909-980-9539
Wholesaler/distributor of frozen foods, groceries, produce, meats and specialty foods; serving the chain restaurant market
VP/General Manager: Bob Cagle
Contact: Azadeh Nolan
anolan@mappharma.com
Estimated Sales: $5-10 Million
Number Employees: 50-99
Square Footage: 300000
Parent Co: Sysco Corporation
Private Brands Carried:
  Sysco
Types of Products Distributed:
  Food Service, Frozen Food, General Line, Provisions/Meat, Produce, Specialty Foods, Groceries

59669 Sygma Network
11750 S Austin Avenue
Worth, IL 60482   708-371-4107
Fax: 708-371-2460
Wholesaler/distributor of frozen foods, groceries, produce, meats and specialty foods; serving the food service market
VP/General Manager: Dave Myers
Number Employees: 50-99
Parent Co: Sysco Corporation
Private Brands Carried:
  Sysco
Number of Customer Locations: 364
Types of Products Distributed:
  Food Service, Frozen Food, General Line, Provisions/Meat, Produce, Specialty Foods, Groceries

59670 Synergee Foods Corporation
PO Box 3055
Bellevue, WA 98009-3055   425-462-7000
Fax: 425-823-2300
Wholesaler/distributor and exporter of specialty foods including Indian-style popcorn
CEO: Paul Brueggemann
VP: Tracie Brueggeman
VP: Lee White
Marketing: Gretchen Green
Sales: Dawn Swain
Operations: David Longmire
Number Employees: 5-9
Square Footage: 6000
Type of Packaging: Consumer
Private Brands Carried:
  A*maiz*ing; Peristroika Bar; Cookie Bouquet; IQ Bar
Number of Customer Locations: 350
Types of Products Distributed:
  Frozen Food, General Line, Specialty Foods, Indian-style popcorn

59671 (HQ)Sysco Corp
1390 Enclave Pkwy
Houston, TX 77077   281-584-1390
Fax: 281-584-1737 800-337-9726
www.sysco.com
Food products, equipment and supplies for the food service industry
President/CEO: Tom Ben,
Chairman: Jackie Ward
EVP/Chief Financial Officer: Joel Grade
SVP/Chief Accounting Officer: Anita Zielinski
SVP/Merchandising: Brian Todd
SVP/Sysco Labs & Customer Experience: Brian Beach
EVP/Supply Chain: Scott Charlton
SVP/Sales & Marketing: Bill Goetz
EVP/Administration & Corp. Secretary: Russell Libby
SVP/US Foodservice Operations: Greg Bertrand
Year Founded: 1969
Estimated Sales: $59 Billion
Number Employees: 67,000
Type of Packaging: Food Service
Types of Products Distributed:
  Food Service

59672 Sysco Corp
1 Sysco Dr
Lincoln, IL 62656-0620   217-735-6100
Food products, equipment and supplies for the food service industry
Type of Packaging: Food Service
Types of Products Distributed:
  Food Service

59673 Sysco Corp
1 Liebich Ln
Halfmoon, NY 12065-1421   518-877-3200
Food products, equipment and supplies for the food service industry
Type of Packaging: Food Service
Types of Products Distributed:
  Food Service

59674 Sysco Corp
601 Comanche Rd NE
Albuquerque, NM 87107   505-761-1200

Wholesalers & Distributors / A-Z

Food products, equipment and supplies for the food service industry
Type of Packaging: Food Service
Number of Customer Locations: 7800
Types of Products Distributed:
 Food Service

59675 Sysco Corp
4500 Corporate Dr NW
Concord, NC 28027   704-786-4500
Food products, equipment and supplies for the food service industry
Type of Packaging: Food Service
Types of Products Distributed:
 Food Service

59676 Sysco Corp
4000 W 62nd St
Indianapolis, IN 46268-2518   317-291-2020
Food products, equipment and supplies for the food service industry
Type of Packaging: Food Service
Types of Products Distributed:
 Food Service

59677 Sysco Corp
1509 Monad Rd
Billings, MT 59107   406-247-1100
Food products, equipment and supplies for the food service industry
Type of Packaging: Food Service
Types of Products Distributed:
 Food Service

59678 Sysco Corp
7705 National Tpke
Louisville, KY 40214   502-364-4300
Food products, equipment and supplies for the food service industry
Type of Packaging: Food Service
Types of Products Distributed:
 Food Service

59679 Sysco Corp
136 S Mariposa Rd
Modesto, CA 95354   209-527-7700
Food products, equipment and supplies for the food service industry
Type of Packaging: Food Service
Types of Products Distributed:
 Food Service

59680 Sysco Corp
1951 E Kansas City Rd
Olathe, KS 66061   913-829-5555
Food products, equipment and supplies for the food service industry
Type of Packaging: Food Service
Types of Products Distributed:
 Food Service

59681 Sysco Corp
600 Packer Ave
Philadelphia, PA 19148   215-463-8200
Food products, equipment and supplies for the food service industry
Type of Packaging: Food Service
Types of Products Distributed:
 Food Service

59682 Sysco Corp
900 Kingbird Rd
Lincoln, NE 68521   402-423-1031
Food products, equipment and supplies for the food service industry
Type of Packaging: Food Service
Types of Products Distributed:
 Food Service

59683 Sysco Corp
250 Wieboldt Dr
Des Plaines, IL 60016-3192   847-699-5400
Food products, equipment and supplies for the food service industry
Type of Packaging: Food Service
Types of Products Distributed:
 Food Service

59684 Sysco Corp
20 Theodore Conrad Dr
Jersey City, NJ 07305   201-433-2000
Food products, equipment and supplies for the food service industry
Type of Packaging: Food Service

Number of Customer Locations: 3000
Types of Products Distributed:
 Food Service

59685 Sysco Corp
9494 S Prosperity Rd
West Jordan, UT 84081   801-563-6300
Food products, equipment and supplies for the food service industry
Type of Packaging: Food Service
Types of Products Distributed:
 Food Service

59686 Sysco Corp
10710 Greens Crossing Blvd
Houston, TX 77038   713-672-8080
Food products, equipment and supplies for the food service industry
Type of Packaging: Food Service
Types of Products Distributed:
 Food Service

59687 Sysco Corp
10510 Evendale Dr
Cincinnati, OH 45241   513-563-6300
Food products, equipment and supplies for the food service industry
Type of Packaging: Food Service
Types of Products Distributed:
 Food Service

59688 Sysco Corp
714 2nd Pl
Lubbock, TX 79401   806-747-2678
Food products, equipment and supplies for the food service industry
Type of Packaging: Food Service
Number of Customer Locations: 3000
Types of Products Distributed:
 Food Service

59689 Sysco Corp
2400 County Road J
St Paul, MN 55112   763-785-9000
Food products, equipment and supplies for the food service industry
Type of Packaging: Food Service
Types of Products Distributed:
 Food Service

59690 Sysco Corp
6601 Changepoint Dr
Anchorage, AK 99518   907-565-5567
Food products, equipment and supplies for the food service industry
Type of Packaging: Food Service
Types of Products Distributed:
 Food Service

59691 Sysco Corp
3700 Sysco Ct SE
Grand Rapids, MI 49512-2083   616-949-3700
Food products, equipment and supplies for the food service industry
Type of Packaging: Food Service
Types of Products Distributed:
 Food Service

59692 Sysco Corp
5000 Beeler St
Denver, CO 80238   303-585-2000
Food products, equipment and supplies for the food service industry
Type of Packaging: Food Service
Types of Products Distributed:
 Food Service

59693 Sysco Corp
99 Spring St
Plympton, MA 02367   781-422-2300
Food products, equipment and supplies for the food service industry
Type of Packaging: Food Service
Types of Products Distributed:
 Food Service

59694 Sysco Corp
1451 River Oaks Rd W
Harahan, LA 70123   504-731-1015
Food products, equipment and supplies for the food service industry
Type of Packaging: Food Service
Types of Products Distributed:
 Food Service

59695 Sysco Corp
3905 Corey Rd
Harrisburg, PA 17109   717-561-4000
Food products, equipment and supplies for the food service industry
Type of Packaging: Food Service
Number of Customer Locations: 6000
Types of Products Distributed:
 Food Service

59696 Sysco Corp
1000 Sysco Dr
Calera, AL 35040   205-668-0001
Food products, equipment and supplies for the food service industry
Type of Packaging: Food Service
Types of Products Distributed:
 Food Service

59697 Sysco Corp
One Whitney Drive
Harmony, PA 16037   724-452-2100
Food products, equipment and supplies for the food service industry
Type of Packaging: Food Service
Types of Products Distributed:
 Food Service

59698 Sysco Corp
8000 Dorsey Run Rd
Jessup, MD 20794   410-799-7000
Food products, equipment and supplies for the food service industry
Type of Packaging: Food Service
Types of Products Distributed:
 Food Service

59699 Sysco Corp
4400 Milwaukee St
Jackson, MS 39209-2636   601-354-1701
Food products, equipment and supplies for the food service industry
Type of Packaging: Food Service
Types of Products Distributed:
 Food Service

59700 Sysco Corp
4359 B.F. Goodrich Blvd
Memphis, TN 38118-7306   901-795-2300
Food products, equipment and supplies for the food service industry
Type of Packaging: Food Service
Types of Products Distributed:
 Food Service

59701 Sysco Corp
2225 Riverdale Rd
College Park, GA 30337   404-765-9900
Food products, equipment and supplies for the food service industry
Type of Packaging: Food Service
Number of Customer Locations: 7000
Types of Products Distributed:
 Food Service

59702 Sysco Corp
33300 Peach Orchard Rd
Pocomoke, MD 21851   410-677-5555
Food products, equipment and supplies for the food service industry
Type of Packaging: Food Service
Types of Products Distributed:
 Food Service

59703 Sysco Corp
1350 W Tecumseh Rd
Norman, OK 73069-8200   405-717-2700
Food products, equipment and supplies for the food service industry
Type of Packaging: Food Service
Types of Products Distributed:
 Food Service

59704 Sysco Corp
5710 Pan Am Ave
Boise, ID 83716   208-345-9500
Food products, equipment and supplies for the food service industry
Type of Packaging: Food Service
Types of Products Distributed:
 Food Service

Wholesalers & Distributors / A-Z

59705 Sysco Corp
20701 E Currier Rd
Walnut, CA 91789　　　909-595-9595
Food products, equipment and supplies for the food service industry
Type of Packaging: Food Service
Types of Products Distributed:
　Food Service

59706 Sysco Corp
22820 54th Ave S
Kent, WA 98032-4898　　　206-622-2261
Food products, equipment and supplies for the food service industry
Type of Packaging: Food Service
Types of Products Distributed:
　Food Service

59707 Sysco Corp
26250 SW Parkway Center Dr
Wilsonville, OR 97070　　　503-682-8700
Food products, equipment and supplies for the food service industry
Type of Packaging: Food Service
Types of Products Distributed:
　Food Service

59708 Sysco Corp
611 S 80th Ave
Tolleson, AZ 85353　　　623-936-9920
Food products, equipment and supplies for the food service industry
Type of Packaging: Food Service
Types of Products Distributed:
　Food Service

59709 Sysco Corp
131 Sysco Ct
Columbia, SC 29209　　　803-239-4000
Food products, equipment and supplies for the food service industry
Type of Packaging: Food Service
Types of Products Distributed:
　Food Service

59710 Sysco Corp
100 Inwood Rd
Rocky Hill, CT 06067-3422　　　860-571-5600
Food products, equipment and supplies for the food service industry
Type of Packaging: Food Service
Types of Products Distributed:
　Food Service

59711 Sysco Corp
800 Trinity Drive
Lewisville, TX 75056　　　769-384-6000
Food products, equipment and supplies for the food service industry
Type of Packaging: Food Service
Types of Products Distributed:
　Food Service

59712 Sysco Corp
4577 Estes Pkwy
Longview, TX 75603-0900　　　903-252-6100
Food products, equipment and supplies for the food service industry
Type of Packaging: Food Service
Types of Products Distributed:
　Food Service

59713 Sysco Corp
1 Sysco Dr
Jackson, WI 53037　　　262-677-1100
Food products, equipment and supplies for the food service industry
Type of Packaging: Food Service
Types of Products Distributed:
　Food Service

59714 Sysco Corp
2001 W Magnolia Ave
Geneva, AL 36340　　　334-684-4000
Food products, equipment and supplies for the food service industry
Type of Packaging: Food Service
Types of Products Distributed:
　Food Service

59715 Sysco Corp
7000 Harbour View Blvd
Suffolk, VA 23435　　　757-673-4000
Food products, equipment and supplies for the food service industry
Type of Packaging: Food Service
Types of Products Distributed:
　Food Service

59716 Sysco Corp
1501 Lewis Industrial Dr
Jacksonville, FL 32254　　　904-786-2600
Food products, equipment and supplies for the food service industry
Type of Packaging: Food Service
Types of Products Distributed:
　Food Service

59717 Sysco Corp
900 Tennessee Ave
Knoxville, TN 37921-2630　　　865-545-5600
Food products, equipment and supplies for the food service industry
Type of Packaging: Food Service
Types of Products Distributed:
　Food Service

59718 Sysco Corp
1 Hermitage Plz
Nashville, TN 37209　　　615-350-7100
Food products, equipment and supplies for the food service industry
Type of Packaging: Food Service
Types of Products Distributed:
　Food Service

59719 Sysco Corp
3225 12th Ave N
Fargo, ND 58102　　　701-293-8900
Food products, equipment and supplies for the food service industry
Type of Packaging: Food Service
Types of Products Distributed:
　Food Service

59720 Sysco Corp
1032 Baugh Rd
Selma, NC 27576　　　919-755-2455
Food products, equipment and supplies for the food service industry
Type of Packaging: Food Service
Types of Products Distributed:
　Food Service

59721 Sysco Corp
7062 Pacific Ave
Pleasant Grove, CA 95668　　　916-569-7000
Food products, equipment and supplies for the food service industry
Type of Packaging: Food Service
Types of Products Distributed:
　Food Service

59722 Sysco Corp
12180 Kirkham Rd
Poway, CA 92064　　　858-513-7300
Food products, equipment and supplies for the food service industry
Type of Packaging: Food Service
Types of Products Distributed:
　Food Service

59723 Sysco Corp
1999 Dr Martin Luther King Jr Blvd
Riviera Beach, FL 33404　　　561-842-1999
Food products, equipment and supplies for the food service industry
Type of Packaging: Food Service
Types of Products Distributed:
　Food Service

59724 Sysco Corp
300 N Baugh Way
Post Falls, ID 83854　　　208-777-9511
Food products, equipment and supplies for the food service industry
Type of Packaging: Food Service
Types of Products Distributed:
　Food Service

59725 Sysco Corp
3100 Sturgis Rd
Oxnard, CA 93030
　　　877-205-9800
Food products, equipment and supplies for the food service industry
Type of Packaging: Food Service
Types of Products Distributed:
　Food Service

59726 Sysco Corp
5900 Stewart Ave
Fremont, CA 94538　　　510-226-3000
Food products, equipment and supplies for the food service industry
Type of Packaging: Food Service
Types of Products Distributed:
　Food Service

59727 Sysco Corp
910 South Blvd
Baraboo, WI 53913-2793　　　608-356-8711
Food products, equipment and supplies for the food service industry
Type of Packaging: Food Service
Number of Customer Locations: 2000
Types of Products Distributed:
　Food Service

59728 Sysco Corp
4747 Grayton Rd
Cleveland, OH 44135　　　216-201-3000
Food products, equipment and supplies for the food service industry
Type of Packaging: Food Service
Types of Products Distributed:
　Food Service

59729 Sysco Corp
41600 Van Born Rd
Canton, MI 48188-2797　　　734-397-7990
Food products, equipment and supplies for the food service industry
Type of Packaging: Food Service
Types of Products Distributed:
　Food Service

59730 Sysco Corp
5800 Frozen Rd
Little Rock, AR 72209　　　501-562-4111
Food products, equipment and supplies for the food service industry
Type of Packaging: Food Service
Number of Customer Locations: 3500
Types of Products Distributed:
　Food Service

59731 Sysco Corp
1260 Schwab Rd
New Braunfels, TX 78132　　　830-730-1000
Food products, equipment and supplies for the food service industry
Type of Packaging: Food Service
Types of Products Distributed:
　Food Service

59732 Sysco Corp
12500 NW 112th Ave
Medley, FL 33178　　　305-651-5421
Food products, equipment and supplies for the food service industry
Type of Packaging: Food Service
Types of Products Distributed:
　Food Service

59733 Sysco Corp
1 Sysco Pl
Ankeny, IA 50021　　　515-289-5300
Food products, equipment and supplies for the food service industry
Type of Packaging: Food Service
Types of Products Distributed:
　Food Service

59734 Sysco Corp
200 Story Rd
Ocoee, FL 34761　　　407-877-8500
Food products, equipment and supplies for the food service industry
Type of Packaging: Food Service
Types of Products Distributed:
　Food Service

59735 Sysco Corp
2508 Warners Rd
Warners, NY 13164　　　315-672-7000
　　　800-736-6000
Food products, equipment and supplies for the food service industry
Type of Packaging: Food Service

Wholesalers & Distributors / A-Z

59736 Sysco Corp
5081 S Valley Pike
Harrisonburg, VA 22801   540-434-0761
Food products, equipment and supplies for the food service industry
Type of Packaging: Food Service
Types of Products Distributed:
  Food Service

59737 Sysco Corp
36 Thomas Dr
Westbrook, ME 04092   207-871-0700
Food products, equipment and supplies for the food service industry
Type of Packaging: Food Service
Types of Products Distributed:
  Food Service

59738 Sysco Corp
3850 Mueller Rd
St Charles, MO 63301   636-940-9230
Food products, equipment and supplies for the food service industry
Type of Packaging: Food Service
Types of Products Distributed:
  Food Service

59739 Sysco Corp
15750 Meridian Pkwy
Riverside, CA 92518   951-601-5300
Food products, equipment and supplies for the food service industry
Type of Packaging: Food Service
Types of Products Distributed:
  Food Service

59740 Sysco Corp
199 Lowell Ave
Central Islip, NY 11722   631-342-7400
Food products, equipment and supplies for the food service industry
Type of Packaging: Food Service
Types of Products Distributed:
  Food Service

59741 Sysco Corp
900 Hwy 10 S
St Cloud, MN 56304   320-251-3200
Food products, equipment and supplies for the food service industry
Type of Packaging: Food Service
Types of Products Distributed:
  Food Service

59742 Sysco Corp
3000 69th St E
Palmetto, FL 34221   941-721-1450
Food products, equipment and supplies for the food service industry
Type of Packaging: Food Service
Types of Products Distributed:
  Food Service

59743 Sysco Corp
6201 E Centennial Pkwy
Las Vegas, NV 89115   702-632-1800
Food products, equipment and supplies for the food service industry
Type of Packaging: Food Service
Types of Products Distributed:
  Food Service

59744 Systems Online
1001 NW 62nd St
Fort Lauderdale, FL 33309-1900   954-840-3467
  Fax: 954-376-3338 support@sysonline.com
  www.sysonline.com
EZ Trade, the ultimate forms based e-trading solution/distribution management software DiMan for Windows95/98,2000; e-commerce, inventory, sales, purchasing, accounting
Estimated Sales: $1-2.5 Million
Number Employees: 1-4

59745 Systems Services Of America
1025 Montague Expy
Milpitas, CA 95035-6818   408-956-7000
  Fax: 800-637-4447 www.americanprobe.com
Wholesaler/distributor of groceries, meat and dairy, frozen and private label items; serving the food service market

Director Marketing: Lisa Goins
Sales Manager: Gordon Sanderson
Manager: Gary Hull
  garyhull@marriott.com
General Manager: Jim Balding
Estimated Sales: $5-10 Million
Number Employees: 50-99
Square Footage: 452000
Parent Co: Marriot Distribution Services
Private Brands Carried:
  Margate
Types of Products Distributed:
  Food Service, Frozen Food, General Line, Produce, Dairy & private label items

59746 T D Refrigeration Inc
1907 Claiborne Ave
Shreveport, LA 71103-4122   318-747-8844
  Fax: 318-226-1455 td@tdrefrigeration.com
  www.tdrefrigeration.com
Wholesaler/distributor of new and used food service equipment and supplies
Owner: David Buford
  tdrefrigeration@centurytel.net
Estimated Sales: $2.5-5 Million
Number Employees: 10-19
Square Footage: 55600
Types of Products Distributed:
  Food Service, Frozen Food, General Merchandise, New & used foodservice equipment

59747 T O Williams Inc
300 Wythe St
Portsmouth, VA 23704-5208   757-397-0771
  Fax: 757-397-5702 towi@bellatlantic.net
Meat packer
Owner: Pete Chay
  p.chay@towilliamsinc.com
CEO: Diane Chay
VP: Peter J Chay
President: Hyun J Chay
Marketing: Bridgette McClung
Estimated Sales: $1,600,000
Number Employees: 20-49
Square Footage: 39000
Type of Packaging: Food Service

59748 T&T Seafood
14550 Brown Rd
Baker, LA 70714   225-261-5438
     Fax: 225-261-5260
Seafood
President: John Tourere
Estimated Sales: $2 Million
Number Employees: 1-4

59749 T. Baker Restaurant Equipment
168 Neponset Avenue
Dorchester, MA 02122-3338   617-287-1717
Wholesaler/distributor of general merchandise including equipment, paper products, janitorial supplies, smallwares, furniture, etc.; serving the food service market
President: Tim Baker
Estimated Sales: Less than $500,000
Number Employees: 1-4
Square Footage: 6400
Types of Products Distributed:
  Food Service, Frozen Food, General Merchandise, Equipment, paper products, etc.

59750 T.A. Morris & Sons
422 Great East Neck Rd Unit D
West Babylon, NY 11704   631-669-0661
     Fax: 631-669-8595
Wholesaler/distributor of frozen French fries, chicken nuggets, hot dogs and meat balls
Owner: Raymond Morris
Estimated Sales: $20-50 Million
Number Employees: 20-49
Types of Products Distributed:
  Frozen Food, General Line, Provisions/Meat, French fries, hot dogs, etc.

59751 T.B. Seafood
450 Commercial St
Portland, ME 04101-4636   207-871-2420
     Fax: 207-871-0906
Seafood
President: Roderick Wintle Jr

59752 T.B. Venture
7212 W 58th Place
Apt 2n
Summit Argo, IL 60501-1427   773-927-2745
     Fax: 773-581-9343
Importer and wholesaler/distributor of European specialty foods
Owner: Tom Biernat
Types of Products Distributed:
  Frozen Food, General Line, Specialty Foods, European foods

59753 T.C. Food Export/ImportCompany
3169 College Point Boulevard
Flushing, NY 11354-2511   718-461-0375
Importer of canned foods and frozen seafood; exporter of deep sea fish oil and health products; wholesaler/distributor of general merchandise, frozen seafood and health, canned and dried foods; serving the food service market
President: Johnson Tseng
Number Employees: 5-9
Square Footage: 48000
Types of Products Distributed:
  Food Service, Frozen Food, General Line, General Merchandise, Health Food, Produce, Seafood, Canned & dried foods

59754 T.C.P. Restaurant Supply
105 N 2nd St
Philadelphia, PA 19106-2002   215-627-1268
     Fax: 215-627-2830
Wholesaler/distributor of kitchen equipment and supplies; serving the food service market
President: Robert Moshen
Estimated Sales: $5-10 Million
Number Employees: 5-9
Square Footage: 400000
Private Brands Carried:
  T.C.P. Restaurant Supply
Types of Products Distributed:
  Food Service, Frozen Food, General Merchandise, Kitchen equipment & supplies

59755 T.D. Khan
168 Greece Ridge Center Drive
Rochester, NY 14626-2815   716-538-6040
Wholesaler/distributor of provisions/meats; serving the food service market
Owner: T Khan
Estimated Sales: $1-2.5 Million
Number Employees: 1-4
Types of Products Distributed:
  Food Service, Frozen Food, Provisions/Meat

59756 T.J. Kraft
1535 Colburn St
Honolulu, HI 96817-4905   808-842-3474
     Fax: 808-842-3475 tkraft@norpacexport.com
Various types of fresh Hawaiian seafood
President: Thomas Kraft
Estimated Sales: $10-20 Million
Number Employees: 10-19

59757 T.L. Herring & Company
2101 Old Stantonsburg Road
P.O. Box 3186
Wilson, NC 27893   252-291-1141
     Fax: 252-291-1142 TLHERRINGCO@yahoo.com
     www.tlherring.com
Processor and packer of hot dog chili, fresh pork sausage, souse meat, cooked chitterlings, all with Southern flavorings
President: Thomas Mark
CFO: Jean Herring
Vice President: Mike Herring
Estimated Sales: $5-10 Million
Number Employees: 10 to 19
Square Footage: 44700
Private Brands Carried:
  Lundy, Gwaltney, Carolina, Pakers, Wampler, IBP
Types of Products Distributed:
  Food Service, Frozen Food, Provisions/Meat, Seafood

59758 T.M. Patterson Paper Box Company
PO Box 187
Portsmouth, OH 45662-0187   740-354-2871
     Fax: 740-353-3754
Wholesaler/distributor of paper boxes

Wholesalers & Distributors / A-Z

General Manager: Mr. Lutz
Estimated Sales: $1-2.5 Million
Number Employees: 10-19
Types of Products Distributed:
 Frozen Food, General Merchandise, Paper boxes

59759 T.S.A. Distributing
22541 Arctic Ocean
Lake Forest, CA 92630 949-951-6310
 Fax: 949-951-0302
Wholesaler/distributor of general merchandise and health food
President: Ken Teepe
Distribution Manager: Kurt Smith
Estimated Sales: $15 Million
Number Employees: 47
Square Footage: 46000
Private Brands Carried:
 Key Brands; Advanced Research; Power Food; Weider Nutritional; Twin Lab; Hoffmaster
Types of Products Distributed:
 Frozen Food, General Merchandise, Health Food, Health food & health and beauty aids

59760 T.T. Todd Company
2320 Glamis Road
Pensacola, FL 32503-5829 850-433-8311
 Fax: 850-432-5231
Wholesaler/distributor of frozen food and produce; serving the food service market
Chairman: C Todd Sr
Estimated Sales: $5-10 Million
Number Employees: 5-9
Number of Customer Locations: 1200
Types of Products Distributed:
 Food Service, Frozen Food, Produce

59761 TBI Corporation
700 East Industrial Park Dr
Manchester, NH 03109 603-668-6223
 Fax: 603-668-6384
Wholesaler/distributor of frozen foods, general line items and general merchandise; serving the food service market; also, rack jobber services available
President: R Treisman
Estimated Sales: $20-50 Million
Number Employees: 50-99
Number of Customer Locations: 1000
Types of Products Distributed:
 Food Service, Frozen Food, General Line, General Merchandise, Rack Jobbers

59762 TBJ Gourmet
1554 Paoli Pike
Suite 254
West Chester, PA 19380 856-222-2000
 info@tbjgourmet.com
 tbjgourmet.com
Bacon jams
Managing Partner: Michael Oraschewsky
Estimated Sales: $1-2 Million
Type of Packaging: Food Service

59763 TCD Parts
19450 Highway B
Edgerton, MO 64444-9160 816-227-3207
 Fax: 888-823-8233 800-823-8313
 tcdparts@tcdparts.com www.tcdparts.com
Wholesaler/distributor of chemical test papers, tubing, dish machine parts
President: Matt Fisher
Owner/CEO: Mark Fisher
mark@tcdparts.com
CFO: Chris Fisher
Public Relations: Tracy Fisher
Plant Manager: Ellen Shanks
Estimated Sales: Less than $500,000
Number Employees: 5-9
Square Footage: 2000000
Types of Products Distributed:
 Frozen Food, General Merchandise, Chemical test papers

59764 TDR Inc
1819 S Walnut Rd
Turlock, CA 95380-9219 209-667-6455
 Fax: 209-667-6484 www.tdr-inc.com
Wholesaler/distributor of dairy equipment; also, builder of dairy barns
President: Matthew Bruno
mbruno@turlockdairy.com
CFO: Mathew Bruno
Estimated Sales: $5-10 Million
Number Employees: 100-249
Types of Products Distributed:
 Frozen Food, Dairy equipment

59765 TKC Supply
 715-245-5841
 Fax: 877-205-4303 brandonh@tkcsupply.com
 amerisup.com
Wholesaler/distributor of general line products; serving the food service market.
Estimated Sales: $50-100 Million
Number Employees: 50-99
Private Brands Carried:
 Frosty Acres
Types of Products Distributed:
 Food Service, Frozen Food, General Line

59766 Ta-De Distributing Co
144 Old Tucson Rd
Nogales, AZ 85621-9710 520-281-4087
 Fax: 520-281-4087 www.tadeproduce.com
Wholesaler/distributor of cucumbers; serving the food service market
President: Robert Bennen
rlbennen@yahoo.com
Estimated Sales: $2.5-5 Million
Number Employees: 10-19
Types of Products Distributed:
 Food Service, Frozen Food, Produce, Cucumbers

59767 Tablemate Products
851 E State Pkwy
Schaumburg, IL 60173-4528 847-884-0664
 Fax: 847-884-5762 800-837-1532
 www.tablemateusa.com
Wholesaler/distributor of food service supplies; serving the food service market
Owner/President: Tom Berg
Vice President: Raja Aboudaher
raboudaher@tablemateusa.com
Estimated Sales: $5-10 Million
Number Employees: 20-49
Types of Products Distributed:
 Food Service, Frozen Food, General Merchandise, Foodservice supplies

59768 Tabor Grain Company
PO Box 565
Oakland, IL 61943-0565 217-346-3313
 Fax: 217-346-3173
Wholesaler/distributor of food grade whole corn; serving corn chip, tortilla chip and tortilla manufacturers
General Manager: Ron Bodle
Sales Manager: Max Miller
Number Employees: 5-9
Square Footage: 80000
Parent Co: Demeter
Types of Products Distributed:
 Frozen Food, Produce, Food grade whole corn

59769 Takari International Inc
2040 E Locust Ct
Ontario, CA 91761-7617 909-923-9399
 Fax: 909-923-9995 www.takari.com
Snack foods, candy, energy drinks and coffee
Owner: Andy Li
andy@takari.com
Estimated Sales: $1-3 Million
Number Employees: 10-19

59770 Takeda Vitamin & Food
101 Vitamin Drive
Wilmington, NC 28401-2279 800-825-3328
 Fax: 973-426-2837 800-825-3328
Wholesaler/distributor of vitamins and industrial ingredients including microcrystalline cellulose, flavor enhancers, emulsifiers and acidulants
CEO/President: Hideo Yamabe
Executive VP: Marty Slove
VP: Gerry McKiernan
Types of Products Distributed:
 Frozen Food, General Line, Health Food, Vitamins & industrial ingredients

59771 Tallarico Food Products
3305 Lewis Ave
Bethlehem, PA 18020-2847 610-868-9987
 Fax: 610-868-8154 www.tallaricofoods.com
Wholesaler/distributor of specialty foods; serving the food service market
Owner: J Tallarico
Manager: James Tallarico
ctallarico@aol.com
Estimated Sales: $1-2.5 Million
Number Employees: 1-4
Square Footage: 20000
Private Brands Carried:
 Tallarico
Number of Customer Locations: 395
Types of Products Distributed:
 Food Service, Frozen Food, Specialty Foods

59772 Tama Trading Co Inc
1920 E 20th St
Los Angeles, CA 90058 213-748-8242
 www.tamatrading.com
Wholesaler/distributor of paper products, pasta, olive oil, tomato and meat products, mineral water and imported Italian specialties.
President: William Sauro
Sales Representative: Robert Falcone
Year Founded: 1920
Estimated Sales: $50-100 Million
Number Employees: 1000-4999
Types of Products Distributed:
 Frozen Food, General Line, General Merchandise, Provisions/Meat, Produce, Specialty Foods, Pasta, olive oil, mineral water, etc.

59773 Tamashiro Market Inc
802 N King St
Honolulu, HI 96817-4513 808-841-8047
 Fax: 808-845-2722 www.tamashiromarket.com
Japanese foods
President: Cyrus Tamashiro
Estimated Sales: $10-20 Million
Number Employees: 20-49

59774 Tamburo Brothers
7460 Conowingo Ave # 21
Jessup, MD 20794-9361 410-799-7366
 Fax: 410-799-1023
Wholesaler/distributor of produce; serving the food service market
President: Tony Tamburo
Estimated Sales: $10-20 Million
Number Employees: 10-19
Types of Products Distributed:
 Food Service, Frozen Food, Produce

59775 Tanglewood Farm
297 Riverdale Rd
Warsaw, VA 22572-4020 804-394-4505
 Fax: 804-333-0422
Wholesaler/distributor of eggs, produce and fresh and frozen seafood; serving the food service market
President: Earl Lewis Jr
Secretary/Treasurer: John Lewis
Estimated Sales: $500,000-$1 Million
Number Employees: 5-9
Square Footage: 16000
Number of Customer Locations: 75
Types of Products Distributed:
 Food Service, Frozen Food, General Line, Produce, Seafood, Eggs

59776 Tankersley Food Svc
3203 Industrial Park Rd
Van Buren, AR 72956-6109 479-471-6800
 Fax: 479-471-6851 800-726-6182
 www.tankersleyfoods.com
Wholesaler/distributor of frozen foods; serving the food service market. Broadline food service distributor
President: Danny Lloyd
dlloyd@tankersleyfoods.com
CEO: Donald Tankersley
Marketing: Kelly Robertson
Sales: Rick Daugherty
Operations: Jeff Mumme
Purchasing Manager: David Weese
Estimated Sales: Less Than $500,000
Number Employees: 5-9
Types of Products Distributed:
 Food Service, Frozen Food, Broadline foodservice

59777 Tanner Enterprises
P.O.Box 292638
Columbus, OH 43229 614-433-7020
 Fax: 614-433-7533 tannent@cs.com
Wholesaler/distributor of canned and frozen foods, spices, cake mixes, canned fish, condiments, pasta and related products; serving the food service market; rack jobber services available
President: Martha Tanner

1193

Wholesalers & Distributors / A-Z

Estimated Sales: $1-3 Million
Number Employees: 1-4
Types of Products Distributed:
Food Service, Frozen Food, General Line, Rack Jobbers, Seafood, Specialty Foods, Canned fish, condiments, pasta, etc.

59778 Tanzamaji USA
5602 Hummingbird Lane
Fairview, TX 75069
info@tanzamaji.com
tanzamaji.com
Bottled water
Managing Director: Beda Ruefer
Types of Products Distributed:
Bottled water

59779 Taormina Co
1405 E Expressway 83
Weslaco, TX 78599-4520   956-968-4133
                    Fax: 956-968-4304
Wholesaler/distributor of canned jalapeno peppers; serving the food service market
Partner: Randall Ennis
Partner: Frank Taormina
fataormina@hotmail.com
Estimated Sales: $5-10 Million
Number Employees: 20-49
Square Footage: 60000
Private Brands Carried:
Tres Trimos.
Types of Products Distributed:
Food Service, Frozen Food, Specialty Foods, Canned jalapeno peppers

59780 Tape & Label Engineering
2950 47th Avenue N
St Petersburg, FL 33714-3132   727-527-6686
         Fax: 727-526-0163   800-237-8955
Die-cut cloth, foil, mylar, paper and pressure-sensitive labels; wholesaler/distributor of pressure sensitive application equipment
Manager: Bob White
Marketing Director: Chuck Pullich
Sales Director: Charlie Goldson
Production Manager: Tom Bowers
tom.bowers@tle.net
Purchasing Manager: Michael Summers
Estimated Sales: $10-20 Million
Number Employees: 50-100
Square Footage: 168000
Parent Co: Weber Marking Systems
Type of Packaging: Consumer, Private Label
Types of Products Distributed:
General Merchandise, Pressure sensitive application equip.

59781 Tape Tools
3 Horizon Rd
Fort Lee, NJ 07024-6744   201-886-1316
         Fax: 212-489-8548   800-327-2354
Importer and wholesaler/distributor of packaging equipment including bag sealers and tape dispensers
President: Irene Seiden
CEO: Jason Seiden
CFO: Hal Berman
Types of Products Distributed:
Frozen Food, General Merchandise, Packaging equipment

59782 Tapp Label TechnologiesInc
580 Gateway Dr
Napa, CA 94558-7517   707-252-8300
         Fax: 707-251-9852   888-834-8277
info@tapplabel.com   www.tapplabel.com
Wholesaler/distributor of labelers including rotary, jig and vacuum belt; also, foil stamped and embossed labels
President: Niteen Sharma
CEO: John Attayek
jattayek@tapptech.com
Estimated Sales: Less Than $500,000
Number Employees: 1-4
Parent Co: Tapp Technologies
Private Brands Carried:
Impresstik; NEB
Types of Products Distributed:
Frozen Food, General Merchandise, Labelers, foil stamped labels, etc.

59783 Tara Foods LLC
1900 Cowles Ln
Albany, GA 31705-1514   229-431-1330
         Fax: 229-439-1458   www.thekrogerco.com

Sauces, peanut butter, food color
Sales Manager: Marilyne Moore
Plant Manager: Jesse Turner
Estimated Sales: $25-49.9 Million
Number Employees: 100-249
Parent Co: Kroger Company

59784 Taroco Food Corporation
1125 Hudson Street
Hoboken, NJ 07030-5305   201-792-5409
                    Fax: 201-792-0961
Wholesaler/distributor, importer and exporter of frozen fish
General Manager: Jack Sun
Number Employees: 10-19
Type of Packaging: Consumer, Food Service
Private Brands Carried:
Queen's; Taroco
Types of Products Distributed:
Food Service, Frozen Food, Seafood

59785 Tastebuds Popcorn
208 N Main Street
Belmont, NC 28012   704-461-8755
mail@tastebudspopcorn.com
tastebudspopcorn.com
Popcorn
President: Jay Pithwa
General Manager: Jen Colangelo
Estimated Sales: $4 Million
Number Employees: 11-50
Types of Products Distributed:
Popcorn

59786 Tasty Mix Quality Foods
88 Walworth St
Brooklyn, NY 11205-2808   718-855-7680
         Fax: 718-855-7681 tastymx@aol.com
                    www.tastyblend.com
Dough conditioners and stabilizers for the pasta and bakery industries
President: Salvatore Ballarino
Manager: Sal Ballarino Jr
Estimated Sales: $500,000
Number Employees: 5-9
Square Footage: 20000
Type of Packaging: Consumer, Food Service, Private Label, Bulk
Types of Products Distributed:
Frozen Food

59787 Tasty Pure Food Co
841 S Broadway St
Akron, OH 44311-2037   330-434-8141
         Fax: 330-434-3706   800-458-2789
                    www.tastypure.com
Wholesaler/distributor of frozen foods, general line items, dairy products, coffee and assorted beverages, general merchandise and provisions/meats; serving the food service and retail markets in Northeast Ohio
President: Jim Heilmeier
CEO: Greg Heilmeier
CFO: Bill Heilmeier
bheilmeier@tastypure.com
Sales Director: Robert Kress
Purchasing Manager: Dan Heilmeier
Estimated Sales: $20-50 Million
Number Employees: 20-49
Square Footage: 40000
Type of Packaging: Private Label
Private Brands Carried:
National Brands, Broadway Coffee
Number of Customer Locations: 900
Types of Products Distributed:
Private Label

59788 Tatra Sheep Cheese Company
PO Box 190389
Brooklyn, NY 11219-0389   718-782-7975
                    Fax: 718-782-7995
Importer and wholesaler/distributor of regular and grated cheese including romano, sheep, parmesan, frozen fish, kaskaval, feta and kefalotyi; also, giardiniera and pepperoncini
President: Benny Feldman
Vice President: George Frankl
Estimated Sales: $5-10 Million
Number Employees: 5-9
Square Footage: 60000
Types of Products Distributed:
General Line, Specialty Foods, Cheeses, pepperoncini, etc.

59789 Taunton Engineering Company
PO Box 180
Saddle River, NJ 07458-0180   508-823-1776
                    Fax: 508-823-4476
Guest checks menu covers, napkin bands, placemats, paper rolls, table tents guest check accessories
President: Alain Brasseur
Marketing: Sylvie Hertrich
Sales: Ian Levasseur
Number Employees: 5-9
Number of Brands: 1
Number of Products: 10
Parent Co: Sherbrooke OEM Ltd
Type of Packaging: Bulk

59790 Taylor Freezer Equipment Corporation
8012 Fernham Lane
Forestville, MD 20747-4519   301-735-4200
         Fax: 301-736-1907   800-999-2422
Wholesaler/distributor of freezers, ice makers, hand wash systems, etc.; serving the food service market
President: Neil Segal
VP: Noel Segal
Sales Manager: John Bancroft
Number Employees: 20-49
Square Footage: 48000
Private Brands Carried:
Taylor; Flavor Burst; Crystal Tips; Flurry; Instant Burger; Smokaroma
Types of Products Distributed:
Food Service, Frozen Food, General Merchandise, Freezers, ice makers, etc.

59791 Taylor Freezers
52 Armthorpe Road
Brampton, ON L6T 5M4
Canada   905-790-2211
         Fax: 905-790-0063   800-387-2529
                    www.tficanada.com
Wholesaler/distributor of equipment including soft serve ice cream, yogurt, slush, milkshake, cocktail and cooking
Sales Manager: Marty Kagan
Number Employees: 50-99
Parent Co: Taylor Freezers
Private Brands Carried:
Taylor
Types of Products Distributed:
Food Service, Frozen Food, General Merchandise, Equipment: ice cream, yogurt, etc.

59792 Taylor Lobster Co
32 Route 236
Kittery, ME 03904-5525   207-439-1350
         Fax: 207-763-3861 info@taylorlobster.com
                    www.taylorlobster.com
Lobster
Owner: Bret Taylor
Estimated Sales: $1 Million
Number Employees: 10-19

59793 Taylor Utlimate Svc Co
1780 N Commerce Pkwy
Weston, FL 33326-3204   954-217-9100
         Fax: 954-217-0994   800-940-4848
info@taylorus.com www.taylorus.com
Wholesaler/distributor of food service equipment including frozen beverage and soft-serve yogurt and ice cream machines, batch freezers, ovens, broilers, etc.; serving the food service market
President: Raul Piedra
CEO: M Espinoza
Vice President: J Morgan
VP: Tina Smart
Estimated Sales: $10-20 Million
Number Employees: 1-4
Private Brands Carried:
Ser-Vend; Nucol; Taylor; Nieco; Perfect Fry; Flavor Burst; Cimgari
Number of Customer Locations: 1000
Types of Products Distributed:
Food Service, Frozen Food, General Merchandise, Broilers, ovens, batch freezers, etc.

59794 Taylor-Fortune Distributors
4137 Washington Avenue
New Orleans, LA 70125-1941   504-822-7587
                    Fax: 504-822-0174
Wholesaler/distributor of refrigeration equipment; serving the food service market
President: Tony Fortune
Sales Manager: Jimmy Smith

Wholesalers & Distributors / A-Z

Estimated Sales: $10-20 Million
Number Employees: 20-49
Types of Products Distributed:
  Food Service, Frozen Food, General Merchandise, Refrigeration equipment

59795 Tchefa
1100 Albemarle Rd
Brooklyn, NY 11218-2806   718-469-3199
    Fax: 718-462-3370 kcholmes@i-2000.com
Wholesaler/distributor of vegetarian foods, soy flour and meatless flavorings
Publisher: R Amen
National Sales Director: Keith Holmes
Estimated Sales: $1-3 Million
Number Employees: 1-4
Square Footage: 20000
Private Brands Carried:
  SoSoya
Types of Products Distributed:
  Frozen Food, General Line, Vegetarian foods & meatless flavorings

59796 (HQ)Tcheru Enterprises
7500 Liberty Avenue
Saint Louis, MO 63130-1125   314-428-8169
    Fax: 314-428-8231
Wholesaler/distributor of soy-based meat substitute
President: Earl Brown
Other Locations:
  Tcheru Enterprises
  Brooklyn, NYTcheru Enterprises
Private Brands Carried:
  SoSoya
Number of Customer Locations: 20
Types of Products Distributed:
  Frozen Food, Health Food, Soy-based meat substitute

59797 Tec Products Co Inc
100 Middlesex Ave # 3
Carteret, NJ 07008-3499   732-969-8700
    Fax: 732-969-6089 800-922-1998
Wholesaler/distributor of janitorial supplies and paper items including towels, plates, napkins, etc
President: David Holtzman
General Manager: Steve Breitman
Estimated Sales: $5-10 Million
Number Employees: 20-49
Square Footage: 400000
Private Brands Carried:
  Colgate; Dial; Procter & Gamble; SC Johnson Wax; Rubbermaid; GE; DAP; Sherwood Williams; Red Devil; Krylon; Kimberly Clark; Bay West
Number of Customer Locations: 400
Types of Products Distributed:
  Food Service, General Merchandise, Janitorial supplies & paper goods

59798 Tech Pak Solutions
85 Bradley Drive
Westbrook, ME 04092-2013   207-878-6667
    Fax: 425-883-9455
Temperature controlled management for food products.
Vice President: Richard Brown

59799 Tech Sales Inc
4505 Zenith St
Metairie, LA 70001-1235   504-885-8085
    Fax: 504-885-8106 www.tech-sales.net
Exporter of material handling and food processing equipment including conveyor systems, industrial hoses, chain drives, mixers, pumps, valves, fittings and sanitary gaskets; wholesaler/distributor of industrial equipment
President: Carlos Hidalgo
chidalgo@tech-sales.net
Shipping Manager: Alex Pineda
Quality Control: Aurelio Gonzalez
Sales Manager: Ron Barone
General Manager: Jose Mendez
Estimated Sales: $5-10 Million
Number Employees: 10-19
Square Footage: 10800
Types of Products Distributed:
  Frozen Food, General Merchandise, Industrial equipment

59800 Technical Food Sales Inc
1050 Mehring Way
Cincinnati, OH 45203-1832   513-621-0544
    Fax: 513-345-2222 800-622-1050
    service@techfood.com www.techfood.com
Total food ingredients source with technical support. Dry, canned, refrigerated and frozen ingredients
President: Jane Makstell
jmakstell@techfood.com
Regional Sales Manager: Lloyd Makstell
Regional Sales Manager: Nadine Whitsett
Estimated Sales: $25-50 Million
Number Employees: 5-9
Square Footage: 200000
Type of Packaging: Bulk
Types of Products Distributed:
  Frozen Food

59801 Teddy's Tasty Meats
6123 Mackay St
Anchorage, AK 99518-1739   907-562-2320
    Fax: 907-562-1919
Meat
President: Ted Kouris
Secretary/Treasurer: Barbara Kouris
Vice President: Steven Kouris
Number Employees: 20-49

59802 Tee's Plus
90 Knothe Road
Westbrook, CT 06498   800-785-3323
    Fax: 860-581-8289 sales@teesplus.com
    www.teesplus.com
Wholesaler/distributor and exporter of uniforms and aprons; also, silkscreening and embroidering available
VP National Accounts: Ronna Davis
Sales: Christy Kendrick
Contact: Kerri Santana
ksantana@teesplus.com
Number Employees: 50-99
Types of Products Distributed:
  Frozen Food, General Merchandise, Uniforms & aprons

59803 Teitel Brothers
2372 Arthur Ave
Bronx, NY 10458-8107   718-733-9400
    Fax: 718-365-1415 800-850-7055
    www.teitelbros.com
Wholesaler/distributor serving the food service market
Owner: Gill Teitel
Partner: Benjamin Teitel
Estimated Sales: Less Than $500,000
Number Employees: 1-4
Types of Products Distributed:
  Food Service, Frozen Food

59804 Teletec Cash Register Company
2841 Kingston Road
Toronto, ON M1M 1N2
Canada   416-261-4408
    Fax: 416-261-4920 tsi@teletecsystems.com
    www.teletecsystems.com
Wholesaler/distributor of point of sale systems; serving the food service market
President: John Roberts
Director Sales: Andrea Thomas
Number Employees: 10-19
Private Brands Carried:
  IBM; Positouch
Types of Products Distributed:
  Food Service, Frozen Food, General Merchandise, Point of sale systems

59805 Tempest Fisheries LTD
38 Hassey St
New Bedford, MA 02740-7209   508-997-0720
    Fax: 508-990-2117
Fish and seafood
President: Timothy Mello
tempest01@rcn.com
Estimated Sales: $5-10 Million
Number Employees: 5-9

59806 Tenth & M Seafoods
1020 M St
Anchorage, AK 99501-3317   907-272-6013
    Fax: 907-272-1685 800-770-2722
    tenmsea@alaska.net www.10thandmseafoods.com
Processor, exporter and wholesaler/distributor of salmon, halibut, shrimp and king crab and scallops. Also operates under the name Alaska Sea Pack, Inc
President: Skip Winfree
tenmsea@alaska.net
Vice President: Rob Winfree
Sales Manager: Dannon Southall
Estimated Sales: $8 Million
Number Employees: 20-49
Type of Packaging: Consumer, Food Service
Types of Products Distributed:
  Food Service, Frozen Food, Seafood

59807 Tergerson's Fine Foods
3801 Cotton Flat Rd
Midland, TX 79706-6371   432-683-4666
    Fax: 432-683-6015
Wholesaler/distributor of frozen foods, general merchandise, general line and private label items, produce, provisions/meats and seafood; serving the food service market
Owner: Victor Basset
VP: O Jenson
Estimated Sales: $1-3 Million
Number Employees: 20-49
Square Footage: 100000
Number of Customer Locations: 800
Types of Products Distributed:
  Food Service, Frozen Food, General Line, General Merchandise, Provisions/Meat, Produce, Seafood

59808 Terlet USA
520 Sharptown Rd
Swedesboro, NJ 08085   856-241-9970
    Fax: 856-241-9975
Aseptic and sterile process equipment and systems.
Founder: J.W. Terlet
CEO: Philip Stibbe
Contact: Bart Brouwer
b.brouwer@jongia.com
Estimated Sales: $1-2 Million
Parent Co: Stibbe Management Group

59809 Terra Ingredients LLC
Minneapolis, MN
    Fax: 612-486-3954 855-497-3308
    hello@terraingredients.com
    www.terraingredients.com
Whole organic ingredients for feed and consumer products, including flax, beans and lentils, corn, quinoa, millet, buckwheat, oats, rye, barley, wheat, soybeans, chia seeds and complete feed ingredient blends
Year Founded: 2000
Number of Brands: 1
Type of Packaging: Private Label, Bulk
Types of Products Distributed:
  Specialty Foods

59810 Terrafina LLC
204 28th Street
Brooklyn, NY 11232   718-499-5065
    Fax: 718-499-5066 info@terrafinafoods.com
    www.terrafinafoods.com
Natural nuts, dried fruits, trail mixes, candies, natural seeds, snacks, organic, granolas, honey based products, chocolate and yogurt, and nougats
Marketing: Tolga Eyetemir
Contact: James Locke
j.locke@terrafina.us
Estimated Sales: $2.2 Million
Number Employees: 25

59811 (HQ)Terri Lynn Inc
1450 Bowes Rd
Elgin, IL 60123-5539   847-741-1900
    Fax: 847-741-7791 800-323-0775
    sales@terrilynn.com www.terrilynn.com
Manufacturer and wholesaler of nuts, dried fruits and coated nuts.
President: Terri Graziano
Estimated Sales: $5-10 Million
Number Employees: 100-249
Number of Brands: 1
Number of Products: 600
Square Footage: 108000
Type of Packaging: Food Service, Private Label, Bulk
Other Locations:
  Terri Lynn-Pecan Shelling Operation
  Cordele, GATerri Lynn-Pecan Shelling Operation
Types of Products Distributed:
  Nuts

Wholesalers & Distributors / A-Z

59812 Terry Brothers, Inc
5039 Willis Wharf Dr
Willis Wharf, VA 23486   757-442-6251
Fax: 757-824-3461   infoat@terrybrothers.com
www.terrybrothers.com
Clams and oysters
President: N Terry Jr
Estimated Sales: $2.5-5 Million
Number Employees: 5-9
Type of Packaging: Consumer, Food Service
Types of Products Distributed:
    Frozen Food

59813 Terry Foods
Genesis Centre, 18 Innovation Way
North Staffs Business Park
Stoke-on-Trent, ST6 4BF
UK
enquiries@terryfoods.com
www.terryfoods.com
Ingredients wholesaler
CEO: John Gardiner
CFO: Nikolai Terry
Sales Manager: Larry Haws
Estimated Sales: $5-10 Million

59814 Tesdall & Associates
2019 S State College Boulevard
Anaheim, CA 92806-6117   714-939-9926
Fax: 714-939-9926   800-244-3928
Wholesaler/distributor of access control systems, burglar and fire alarms, intercommunication systems and closed circuit televisions
CEO/President: Richard Tesdall
Number Employees: 5-9
Types of Products Distributed:
    Frozen Food, General Merchandise, Fire & burglar alarms, etc.

59815 Tessemae's All Natural
8805 Kelso Dr.
Essex, MD 21221
855-698-3773
customerhappiness@tessemaes.com
www.tessemaes.com
Salad dressings, condiments, and marinades. Keto, vegan, and gluten free options available
Co-Founder: Brian Vetter
Co-Founder/CEO: Greg Vetter
Director Marketing: Keri Nwosu
EVP Sales & Strategy: Shawn McLaughlin
VP National Accounts: Mike Shields
Year Founded: 2009
Number Employees: 50-99
Types of Products Distributed:
    General Line

59816 Tex-Sandia
914 E Produce Rd
Hidalgo, TX 78557   956-843-2216
Fax: 956-843-2492
Wholesaler/distributor of produce
General Office Manager: Darryl Mahan
Estimated Sales: $5-10 Million
Number Employees: 5-9
Types of Products Distributed:
    Frozen Food, Produce

59817 Texas Gunpowder
PO Box 852573
Mesquite, TX 75185-2573   972-686-5688
Fax: 972-552-4443   800-637-9780
Wholesaler/distributor of jalapeno powder, mesquite seasoned salt, blending spices and private label items
President: D Robinson
Owner: Janice Pinnell
Estimated Sales: Less than $500,000
Number Employees: 1-4
Square Footage: 20000
Private Brands Carried:
    Texas Gunpowder; Mesquite's Own
Types of Products Distributed:
    Frozen Food, General Line, Jalapeno powder, salt, spices, etc.

59818 Texas Halal Corporation
P.O. Box 630829
Houston, TX 77263   713-266-4300
Fax: 713-489-0808   ayesha@texashalal.com
www.texashalal.com
Halal beef, lamb, goat and poultry
Operations Manager: Ayesha Abou Taleb *Year Founded:* 2003

Types of Products Distributed:
    Provisions/Meat

59819 Texas Hotel & Restaurant Equipment
2616 White Settlement Rd
Fort Worth, TX 76107   817-921-6146
Fax: 817-924-2518   888-264-9714
Wholesaler/distributor of institutional cleaning supplies, tabletop needs and equipment; serving the food service market
President: Curtis Cargo
VP: T Cargo
Estimated Sales: $5-10 Million
Number Employees: 20-49
Types of Products Distributed:
    Food Service, Frozen Food, General Merchandise, Cleaning supplies, tabletop needs, etc.

59820 Texas Marine II
8050 Harrisburg Boulevard
Houston, TX 77012-1699   713-923-9771
Fax: 713-923-4418
Wholesaler/distributor of groceries, frozen foods, produce, meats, dairy products, cleaning supplies, disposables, etc.; serving the food service market
President: David Jackson
Purchasing Manager: J Curry
Parent Co: Briggs Weaver
Types of Products Distributed:
    Food Service, Frozen Food, General Line, General Merchandise, Provisions/Meat, Produce

59821 Texas Meat Purveyors
4241 Director Dr
San Antonio, TX 78219-3292   210-337-1011
Fax: 210-333-9410   www.freedmanfoods.com
Wholesaler/distributor of meat and seafood products; serving the food service market
Manager: Ken Holland
Plant Manager: Dwayne Padalecki
Estimated Sales: $20-50 Million
Number Employees: 100-249
Square Footage: 17500
Number of Customer Locations: 1000
Types of Products Distributed:
    Food Service, Frozen Food, Provisions/Meat, Seafood

59822 Texas Sausage Co
2915 E 12th St
Austin, TX 78702-2401   512-472-6707
Fax: 512-472-9360   www.texashotsausage.com
Processor and wholesaler/distributor of sausage; serving the food service market
President: Gary Tharp
hotlinks1@yahoo.com
Estimated Sales: $.5-1 million
Number Employees: 5-9
Type of Packaging: Consumer, Food Service
Types of Products Distributed:
    Food Service, Provisions/Meat, Sausage

59823 The Bachman Company
801 Hill Avenue
Wyomissing, PA 19610
bachmancs@utzsnacks.com
www.bachmanco.com
Wholesaler/distributor of specialty and snack foods
Estimated Sales: $500,000-$1 Million
Number Employees: 5-9
Parent Co: UTZ Quality Foods, Inc
Private Brands Carried:
    Bachman
Types of Products Distributed:
    Frozen Food, General Line, Specialty Foods, Snack food

59824 The Chefs' Warehouse
100 E Ridge Rd
Ridgefield, CT 06877   203-897-1345
chefswarehouse.com
Wholesaler/distributor and importer of olives, cheese, olive oil, condiments, pasta, confections, processed meats, specialty foods, etc.
Founder/Chairman/CEO: Christopher Pappas
Founder & Vice Chairman: John Pappas
Chief Financial Officer: James Leddy
Chief Accounting Officer: Timothy McCauley
General Counsel & Corporate Secretary: Alexandros Aldous
Chief Human Resources Officer: Patricia Lecouras

Year Founded: 1956
Estimated Sales: $100-500 Million
Number Employees: 1000-4999
Type of Packaging: Consumer, Food Service, Private Label
Number of Customer Locations: 1200
Types of Products Distributed:
    Food Service, General Line, Provisions/Meat, Specialty Foods, Olives, cheese, olive oil, etc.

59825 The Coconut Cooperative, LLC
234 Fifth Ave. # 406
New York, NY 10001
hello@thecoconutcoop.com
www.thecoconutcoop.com
Organic coconut ingredients (chips, flakes, oil, sugar, flour)
Founder/CEO: Benjamin Weingarten
Number Employees: 2-10
Number of Products: 6
Type of Packaging: Bulk
Types of Products Distributed:
    Health Food, Specialty Foods

59826 The Cookie Dough Cafe
1701 E Empire St
Suite 360
Bloomington, IL 61704-7900   309-539-4585
Fax: 309-539-4585   www.thecookiedoughcafe.com
Cookie dough
Co-Owner: Joan Pacetti
Types of Products Distributed:
    Cookie dough

59827 The Coop
9001 Boul De L'Acadie
Suite 200
Montreal, QC H4N 3H7
Canada   514-384-6450
Fax: 514-384-7176   information@lacoop.coop
www.90.lacoop.coop
Wholesaler/distributor of dairy products, chicken and pork
President: Paul Massicotte
Communications: Martin Berard
Number Employees: 250-499
Types of Products Distributed:
    Frozen Food, General Line, Provisions/Meat, Dairy products, chicken & pork

59828 The Lamb Company
372 Danbury Rd.
Suite 207
Wilton, CT 06897   203-529-9100
Fax: 203-529-9101   800-438-5262
www.thelambcompany.com
Lamb, beef, venison, goat, and mutton from New Zealand and Australia
HR Manager: Brenda Norman
General Manager, Processing & Operation: Philip Fisher
Director of Product Development: Sari Goldenberg
Year Founded: 1964
Number Employees: 50-99
Types of Products Distributed:
    Provisions/Meat

59829 The Matzo Project
575 Union St
3rd Floor
Brooklyn, NY 11215-1024   929-276-2896
hello@matzoproject.com
www.matzoproject.com
Matzo
Co-Owner: Ashley Albert
Co-Owner: Kevin Rodriguez
Types of Products Distributed:
    Matzo

59830 The Piping Gourmets
786-233-8660
info@thepipinggourmets.com
www.thepipinggourmets.com
Gluten free and vegan whoopie pies
Co-Founder: Leslie Kaplan
Co-Founder: Carolyn Shulevitz
Number Employees: 5-9
Types of Products Distributed:
    Frozen Food, General Line

Wholesalers & Distributors / A-Z

59831 The Premium Beer Company
275 Belfield Road
Etobicoke, ON M9W 7H9
Canada   905-855-7743
          Fax: 416-679-1929 800-561-6808
pbctelesales@moosehead.ca www.premiumbeer.ca
Wholesaler/distributor and importer of alcoholic and nonalcoholic beer, ale, lager and cider; serving the food service market
General Manager: Bill Wade
CFO: Gorton Walker
Number Employees: 50-99
Square Footage: 54000
Parent Co: Moosehead Breweries
Type of Packaging: Consumer, Food Service
Types of Products Distributed:
    Food Service, Frozen Food, General Line, Beer, ale, & lager

59832 The Soulfull Project
Camden, NJ
                    megan@thesoulfullproject.com
                    www.thesoulfullproject.com
Vegan hot cereals; gluten free options available
Co-Founder: Megan Shea
Co-Founder: Chip Heim
Types of Products Distributed:
    General Line

59833 The Stroopie
105 Old Dorwart St
Lancaster, PA 17603-3677   717-875-3426
                    sales@stroopies.com
                    www.stroopies.com
Stroopwafel
Co-Founder: Ed McManness
Co-Founder: Dan Perryman
Type of Packaging: Bulk
Types of Products Distributed:
    Stroopwafel

59834 The Tao of Tea
3430 SE Belmont St.
Portland, OR 97214   503-736-0119
     Fax: 503-736-9232 info@taooftea.com
                    taooftea.com
Tea and tea ware
Owner: Veerinder Chawla
Year Founded: 1997
Estimated Sales: $7.3 Million
Number Employees: 11-50
Type of Packaging: Consumer, Food Service, Private Label
Types of Products Distributed:
    Tea

59835 The Toasted Oat Bakehouse
Columbus, OH
                    www.thetoastedoat.com
Gluten- and preservative-free all natural granola blends in various flavors
Founder: Erika Boll
Chief Financial Officer: Tom Kelley
Year Founded: 2013
Number of Brands: 1
Number of Products: 4
Type of Packaging: Consumer, Private Label
Private Brands Carried:
    The Toasted Oat
Types of Products Distributed:
    Granola

59836 The Van Cleve Seafood Company
6910 Fox Ridge Rd.
Spotsylvania, VA 22551   800-628-5202
                    vancleveseafood.com
Crab pie
President & CEO: Monica Van Cleve-Talbert
Chief Financial Officer: Allie Cushing
Estimated Sales: $4-5 Million
Number Employees: 44
Type of Packaging: Food Service
Types of Products Distributed:
    Seafood

59837 Theatre Candy Distributing Company
850 W 2500 S
Salt Lake City, UT 84119-1542   801-973-9939
          Fax: 801-974-0707 800-453-3174
Wholesaler/distributor of frozen foods, general line products, concession supplies and specialty foods; serving the entertainment food service market; also, equipment repair services available
Chairman/CEO: N Chesler
President: L Lockington
VP: S Lockington
Estimated Sales: $10-20 Million
Number Employees: 20-49
Square Footage: 68000
Number of Customer Locations: 1200
Types of Products Distributed:
    Food Service, Frozen Food, General Line, General Merchandise, Specialty Foods, Concession supplies

59838 Third Planet Products
P.O.Box 691231
San Antonio, TX 78269-1231   210-558-7262
          Fax: 210-696-8455 orders3d@flash.net
Wholesaler/distributor of health foods including candy, cookies, snacks, vitamins, proteins, protein bars and soy nut butter; also, general merchandise
Managing Director: Ian Seidler
Estimated Sales: $.5-1 million
Number Employees: 1-4
Number of Customer Locations: 350
Types of Products Distributed:
    Frozen Food, General Line, General Merchandise, Health Food, Specialty Foods, Candy, cookies, snacks, vitamins, etc.

59839 This Bar Saves Lives, LLC
Culver City, CA   310-730-5060
                    hello@thisbarsaveslives.com
                    www.thisbarsaveslives.com
Non-GMO, gluten-free healthy snack bar; with every purchase, the company gives food aid to a child in need from Haiti, the Democratic Republic of the Congo, Guatemala, South Sudan, the Philippines and/or Mexico
Co-Founder: Ryan Devlin
Co-Founder: Todd Grinnell
Co-Founder: Ravi Patel
Year Founded: 2013
Number of Brands: 1
Number of Products: 6
Type of Packaging: Consumer, Private Label
Private Brands Carried:
    This Bar Saves Lives
Types of Products Distributed:
    Health Food

59840 Thomas & Howard Co
812 Post St # A
Greensboro, NC 27405-7268   336-273-5513
Wholesaler/distributor of general merchandise and groceries; serving the food service market
President: Maurice Wentz
President: M Wentz
Estimated Sales: $10-20 Million
Number Employees: 20-49
Number of Customer Locations: 375
Types of Products Distributed:
    Food Service, Frozen Food, General Line, General Merchandise

59841 Thomas & Howard Co Cash & Crry
2112 W Jody Rd
Florence, SC 29501-2032   843-662-5017
Wholesaler/distributor of groceries, frozen foods, meats, seafood, produce, dairy products and general merchandise, etc.; also, rack jobber services available; serving the food service market
Manager: Chuck Walters
Estimated Sales: $2.5-5 Million
Number Employees: 1-4
Parent Co: Thomas & Howard
Private Brands Carried:
    Pocahontas; Parade; Thriftway
Number of Customer Locations: 1000
Types of Products Distributed:
    Food Service, Frozen Food, General Line, General Merchandise, Provisions/Meat, Rack Jobbers, Seafood, Bakery goods, dairy products, etc.

59842 Thomas Brothers CountryHam
1852 Gold Hill Rd
Asheboro, NC 27203-4291   336-672-0337
   Fax: 336-672-1782 www.thomasbrothersham.com
Processor and packer of country hams; wholesaler/distributor of frozen and specialty foods and meats; serving the food service and retail markets in the southeast
President/CFO: Howard M Thomas
frank@thomasbrothersham.com
Quality Control: Don Thomas
Sales/Plant Manager: Don Thomas
Plant Manager: Don Thomas
Estimated Sales: $10-20 Million
Number Employees: 20-49
Number of Brands: 10
Number of Products: 300
Type of Packaging: Consumer, Private Label
Private Brands Carried:
    Thomas Brothers; Farmer Don's
Number of Customer Locations: 850
Types of Products Distributed:
    Food Service, Frozen Food, Provisions/Meat, Seafood

59843 Thomas Colace Company
Oregon & Swanson Street
Philadelphia, PA 19148   215-467-9300
          Fax: 215-467-0414 800-886-1379
Wholesaler/distributor of produce
President: Thomas Colace
Number Employees: 50-99
Number of Customer Locations: 100
Types of Products Distributed:
    Produce

59844 Thomas Ice Cream
1235 Mcdonald Ave
Brooklyn, NY 11230-3322   718-648-2210
       Fax: 718-252-2401 www.thomasicecream.com
Wholesaler/distributor of dry ice, ice cream and freezers; serving the food service market
Owner: Greg Fosdal
greg.fosdal@perrysicecream.com
VP: Abe Zeigerman
Estimated Sales: Less Than $500,000
Number Employees: 10-19
Square Footage: 40000
Type of Packaging: Bulk
Private Brands Carried:
    Bassett's Ice Cream
Number of Customer Locations: 40
Types of Products Distributed:
    Food Service, General Line, General Merchandise, Ice cream, freezers & dry ice

59845 Thomas Lobster Co
45 Bar Rd
Little Cranberry Island
Islesford, ME 4646   207-244-5876
       Fax: 808-244-7020 David@thomaslobster.com
Lobster
President: David Thomas
david@thomaslobster.com
Number Employees: 1-4

59846 Thomas Technical Svc
W4780 US Highway 10
Neillsville, WI 54456-6213   715-743-4666
                    Fax: 715-743-2062
Ultrafiltration and reverse osmosis systems for the dairy industry; wholesaler/distributor of replacement parts
Owner: Randy L Thomas
CEO: Theresa Thomas
CFO: Randy Thomas
Estimated Sales: Below $5 Million
Number Employees: 1-4
Square Footage: 18000
Types of Products Distributed:
    Replacement parts

59847 Thomas W. MacKay & Son
9205 Shaughnessy Street
Vancouver, BC V6P 6R5
Canada   604-324-6561
       Fax: 604-324-6549 www.twmackay.com
Wholesaler/distributor of primary packaging equipment including fillers and palletizers
General Manager: Ritchie Aird
Technical Sales: Mike Fladgate
Number Employees: 10-19
Square Footage: 12000
Private Brands Carried:
    All-Fill, Inc.; Enercon Industries; Goring Kerr Canada, Inc.; General Packaging; Horix Manufacturing; Hi-Speed Checkweigher

Wholesalers & Distributors / A-Z

59848 Thompson & Johnson Equipment
6926 Fly Rd
East Syracuse, NY 13057-9353   315-437-2881
  Fax: 315-437-5034   877-460-9186
Wholesaler/distributor of fork lifts, lift trucks, floor sweepers and scrubbers; leasing and rental services available
President: Sidat Atapattu
atapattu@unu.edu
Sales Manager: Shaun Harrington
VP Customer Service: Chip Gorham
Estimated Sales: $10-20 Million
Number Employees: 50-99
Square Footage: 126000
Private Brands Carried:
  Clark; Toyota; Advance; Daewoo; Cushman; Hawker Powersource
Types of Products Distributed:
  Frozen Food, General Merchandise, Fork lifts & lift trucks

59849 (HQ)Thompson & Little
933 Robeson St
Fayetteville, NC 28305-5613   910-484-1128
  Fax: 910-484-0576   www.thompsonlittle.com
Wholesaler/distributor of food service equipment; serving the food service market
President: Andrew D O'Quinn
andrewo@thompsonlittle.com
Vice President: Andrew O'Quinn
Estimated Sales: $18 Million
Number Employees: 20-49
Other Locations:
  Thompson & Little
  Wilmington, NCThompson & Little
Private Brands Carried:
  Hobart; True; Vulcan
Types of Products Distributed:
  Food Service, Frozen Food, General Merchandise, Equipment

59850 Thompson Dairy
1403 W Jpg Niblo Road
Madison, IN 47250-9733   812-273-1814
  Fax: 812-273-1022
Wholesaler/distributor of dairy products including cottage cheese, yogurt and sour cream; serving the food service market
Manager: Bob Glass
Estimated Sales: $.5-1 million
Number Employees: 1-4
Parent Co: Best Ever Dairy
Private Brands Carried:
  Prairie Farms
Types of Products Distributed:
  Food Service, General Line, Cottage cheese, yogurt & sour cream

59851 Thomson Groceries Ltd.
20 Wagstaff Drive
Toronto, ON M4L 3W9
Canada   416-465-4893
  Fax: 416-461-3552
Wholesaler/distributor of groceries, equipment and fixtures, general merchandise and seafood; serving the food service market, independent grocery outlets, government offices, etc
President: Edith Wallace
General Manager: Bruce Wallace
VP: Craig Wallace
Number Employees: 5-9
Square Footage: 80000
Number of Customer Locations: 325
Types of Products Distributed:
  Food Service, Frozen Food, General Line, General Merchandise, Seafood, Equipment, fixtures, etc.

59852 Three Jerks Jerky
515 Spoleto Dr
Pacific Palisades, CA 90272-4517   424-703-5375
  info@threejerksjerky.com
  www.threejerksjerky.com
Filet Mignon beef jerky
Co-Founder: Jordan Barrocas
Co-Founder: Daniel Fogelson
Estimated Sales: $4.5 Million
Number Employees: 52
Types of Products Distributed:
  Provisions/Meat

59853 Three M Food Service
650 62nd Street
Brooklyn, NY 11220-4113   718-238-0909
  Fax: 718-439-0875
Wholesaler/distributor of general line products
Owner: Vito Mazzarino
Estimated Sales: $10-20 Million
Number Employees: 10-19
Types of Products Distributed:
  Frozen Food, General Line

59854 Three Rivers Fish Company
168 Riverfront Drive
Simmesport, LA 71369-0668   318-941-2467
  Fax: 318-941-2467
Fresh and frozen seafood/fish
Owner: William Arnouville
Estimated Sales: $730,000
Number Employees: 1-4

59855 Ths Foodservice
801 E 12th St
Chattanooga, TN 37403-3208   423-267-3821
  Fax: 423-756-7710   800-829-8472
  wedeliver@thsfs.com   www.thsfs.com
Wholesaler/distributor of groceries, meats, produce, dairy products, frozen foods, baked goods, private label items, equipment and fixtures; serving the food service market
Owner: Henry Poss
Vice President: Henry Poss Jr
Marketing Director: Gene Boulware
Sales Manager: John Gallion
wedeliver@thsfs.com
Estimated Sales: $10 Million
Number Employees: 20-49
Square Footage: 80000
Type of Packaging: Consumer, Food Service, Private Label, Bulk
Private Brands Carried:
  Pocahontas
Types of Products Distributed:
  Food Service, Frozen Food, General Line, General Merchandise, Provisions/Meat, Produce, Groceries, equipment & fixtures, etc.

59856 Thunderbird Food Machinery
P.O. BOX 4768
4602 Brass Way
Blaine, WA 98231   214-331-3000
  Fax: 214-331-3581   866-875-6868
  tbfm@tbfm.com   www.thunderbirdfm.com
Importer and wholesaler/distributor of food processing equipment including mixers, dough sheeters, vegetable and bread slicers, meat grinders, etc
Owner: Ky Lin
Marketing Director: Kara M
Estimated Sales: $1-2.5 Million
Number Employees: 5-9
Types of Products Distributed:
  Frozen Food, General Merchandise, Mixers, dough sheeters, etc.

59857 Thunderbird Real Food Bar
1101-West 34th St. # 229
Austin, TX 78705   512-383-8334
  support@thunderbirdbar.com
  www.thunderbirdbar.com
Gluten-free, non-GMO, vegan, no-sugar-added fruit and nut snack bars in various flavors
Chief Executive Officer: Mike Elhaj
Number of Brands: 1
Number of Products: 14
Type of Packaging: Consumer, Private Label
Private Brands Carried:
  Thunderbird

59858 Thurston Foods Inc
30 Thurston Dr
Wallingford, CT 06492   203-265-1525
  www.thurstonfoods.com
Wholesaler/distributor of frozen foods, general merchandise, general line products, produce and meats; serving the food service market.
Estimated Sales: $100-500 Million
Number Employees: 100-249
Square Footage: 92000
Number of Customer Locations: 2500
Types of Products Distributed:
  Food Service, Frozen Food, General Line, General Merchandise, Provisions/Meat, Produce

59859 Tideland Seafood Company
PO Box 99
Dulac, LA 70353   985-563-4516
  Fax: 985-563-4296
Prepared fresh shrimp; fish & seafood canning and curing.
President: Judith Gibson
Estimated Sales: $5-10 Million
Number Employees: 5-9

59860 (HQ)Tierra Farm
2424 NY-203
Valatie, NY 12184   519-392-8300
  Fax: 518-392-8304   info@tierrafarm.com
  www.tierrafarm.com
Organic and gluten-free nut butters and nuts, raw and roasted seeds, dried fruit mixes, granolas, chocolate snacks and fair-trade coffee beans
Founder/President: Gunther Fishgold
Chief Executive Officer: Todd Kletter
Year Founded: 1999
Number of Brands: 1
Type of Packaging: Consumer, Private Label, Bulk
Private Brands Carried:
  Tierra Farm
Number of Customer Locations: 2
Types of Products Distributed:
  Produce, Coffee

59861 Tiesta Tea
213 West Institute Place # 310
Chicago, IL 60610   312-202-6800
  customerservice@tiestatea.com
  www.tiestatea.com
Loose leaf tea blends in various flavors; cold brew bottled tea
Co-Founder: Patrick Tannous
Co-Founder/Chief Executive Officer: Dan Klein
Year Founded: 2010
Number of Brands: 1
Number of Products: 50
Type of Packaging: Consumer, Private Label
Private Brands Carried:
  Tiesta Tea
Number of Customer Locations: 1
Types of Products Distributed:
  Tea

59862 Tiger Distributors
1603 N Olden Avenue Extension
5028
Trenton, NJ 08638-3205   609-393-5410
Wholesaler/distributor of snack foods; rack jobber services available
Chairman: R Stahl
President: J Hensley
Buyer: J Burr
Estimated Sales: $10-20 Million
Number Employees: 20-49
Square Footage: 60000
Private Brands Carried:
  Wise; Relsman; Quinlan
Number of Customer Locations: 4000
Types of Products Distributed:
  Frozen Food, General Line, Rack Jobbers, Snack foods

59863 Timber Peaks Gourmet
6180 Hollowview Ct
Parker, CO 80134-5808   303-841-8847
  Fax: 303-805-0174   800-982-7687
  www.timberpeaksgourmet.com
Cocoa, bean soups, dessert mixes, bread mixes, trail mixes, and dried salsa
President: Laurie Yankoski
laurie.yankoski@timberpeaksgourmet.com
Estimated Sales: Less Than $500,000
Number Employees: 1-4
Number of Brands: 1
Number of Products: 41
Square Footage: 6000
Type of Packaging: Consumer, Bulk
Private Brands Carried:
  Mountain House Kitchen
Number of Customer Locations: 40
Types of Products Distributed:
  General Line

59864 Time & Alarm Systems
3828 Wacker Dr
Mira Loma, CA 91752-1147   951-685-1761
  Fax: 951-685-1441   www.timeandalarm.com
Wholesaler/distributor of fire alarms and security equipment

Wholesalers & Distributors / A-Z

59865 Timeless Seeds
48 Ulm-Vaughn Rd
P.O. Box 331
Ulm, MT 59485   406-866-3340
Fax: 406-866-3341 orders@timelessfood.com
www.timelessfood.com
Organic lentils, peas, chickpeas, and heirloom grains
Founder/CEO: David Oien
Accounts: Heather Hadley
General Manager: Matthew Leardini
Year Founded: 1987
Number Employees: 10-19
Types of Products Distributed:
General Line

59866 Timely Signs Inc
2135 Linden Blvd
Elmont, NY 11003-3901   516-285-5339
Fax: 516-285-9637   800-457-4467
sales@timelysigns.net
Manufacturer and exporter of labels, marketing signs and banners; wholesaler/distributor of computerized sign making equipment
President: Gene Goldsmith
signs11003@aol.com
Estimated Sales: $1-2.5 Million
Number Employees: 5-9
Square Footage: 4000
Types of Products Distributed:
Frozen Food, General Merchandise, Computerized sign making equipment

59867 Tingfong LLC
19 Anthony Street
Brooklyn, NY 11222-5201   718-387-8880
Fax: 718-387-4800
General Manager: Dat Quan

59868 Tinkels
5608 Decatur Rd
Fort Wayne, IN 46806   800-752-3616
Fax: 260-744-2398   800-752-3616
Wholesaler/distributor of restaurant equipment and supplies; serving the food service market
President: Kenneth Tinkel
Estimated Sales: $1-2.5 Million
Number Employees: 10-19
Private Brands Carried:
Delfield; True; Lincoln
Types of Products Distributed:
Food Service, Frozen Food, General Merchandise, Restaurant equipment & supplies

59869 Tippecanoe Foods
5124 Flowermound Ct
W Lafayette, IN 47906   765-463-3577
Fax: 765-463-3521
Wholesaler/distributor of groceries and meats; serving the food service market
President: R Dexter
Estimated Sales: $10-20 Million
Number Employees: 50-99
Square Footage: 80000
Private Brands Carried:
Nugget
Types of Products Distributed:
Food Service, Frozen Food, General Line, Provisions/Meat, Produce

59870 Tips Uniform
1120 Walnut St
Philadelphia, PA 19107-5513   215-925-1120
Fax: 215-440-9299 info@tipsuniforms.com
www.tipsuniforms.com
Wholesaler/distributor of uniforms
Owner: Bob Smith
blacktiephilly@msn.com
Estimated Sales: $1-2.5 Million
Number Employees: 10-19
Types of Products Distributed:
Frozen Food, General Merchandise, Uniforms

59871 Tirawisu
13705 Ventura Blvd
Sherman Oaks, CA 91423-3023   818-906-2640
Fax: 516-599-6540
Exporter and processor of Italian desserts including chocolate mousse, tiramisu, gelato, tartufo, tortoni and spumoni; importer of Italian cakes and pasta
Owner/President: Aldo Antonoacci
Contact: Peter Kastelan
peter@il-tiramisu.com
Estimated Sales: Less Than $500,000
Number Employees: 5-9
Types of Products Distributed:
Frozen Food

59872 To-Am Equipment Company
1808 Squires Mill Court
Joliet, IL 60431-1605   815-469-2255
Fax: 708-496-1228
Wholesaler/distributor of forklifts, racks and shelving
President: Richard Todd
Number Employees: 10-19
Private Brands Carried:
Clark; Mitsubishi; Raymond
Types of Products Distributed:
Frozen Food, General Merchandise, Material handling equipment

59873 Toastmasters International
23182 Arroyo Vis
Rancho Sta Marg, CA 92688-2699   949-858-8255
Fax: 949-858-1207 www.toastmasters.org
Wholesaler/distributor and importer of ovens, ranges and freezers; serving the food service market
President: Jo Stante
govarea05d@tmdistrict38.org
First Vice President: Jim KoKocki
Number Employees: 50-99
Type of Packaging: Food Service
Private Brands Carried:
Victory; Middleby Marshall; Southbend; Randell; Rationel
Types of Products Distributed:
Food Service, Frozen Food, General Merchandise, Ovens, freezers & ranges

59874 Todd Distributors Inc
269 E Main St
Laurens, SC 29360-2954   864-984-6811
Fax: 864-984-8633
Wholesaler/distributor of frozen foods, general line products, produce, provisions/meats and seafood; serving the food service market
President: T Todd Jr
Estimated Sales: $1-2.5 Million
Number Employees: 20-49
Number of Customer Locations: 350
Types of Products Distributed:
Food Service, Frozen Food, General Line, Provisions/Meat, Produce, Seafood

59875 (HQ)Tom's Evergreen Broom Manufacturing
PO Box 486
Sheboygan, WI 53082-0486   920-452-5220
Fax: 920-452-5220   800-228-1065
Wholesaler/distributor of janitorial supplies; serving the food service market
Owner: Tom Mohar
Estimated Sales: $2.5-5 Million
Number Employees: 1-4
Square Footage: 28800
Other Locations:
Tom's Evergreen Broom Manufac
Sheboygan, WITom's Evergreen Broom Manufac
Types of Products Distributed:
Food Service, Frozen Food, General Merchandise, Janitorial supplies

59876 Tomanetti Food Products
625 Allegheny Ave
Oakmont, PA 15139   412-828-3040
Fax: 412-828-2282 tomanetti@tomanetti.com
Manufacturer and distributor of pizza crusts and flatbreads.
President: Rodney Butcher
Estimated Sales: Under $500,000
Number Employees: 20-49
Parent Co: Hollymead Capital

59877 Tomich Brothers Seafoods
2208 Signal Pl
San Pedro, CA 90731   310-832-5365
Fax: 310-832-9578
Wholesaler/distributor and exporter of seafood
Owner: Frank Tomich
ftomich@tomichbros.com
Sales/Product Inquiries Contact: Julie Heberer
Shipping/Logistics Inquiries Contact: Angela Felix
Estimated Sales: $5-10 Million
Number Employees: 10-19
Types of Products Distributed:
Frozen Food, Seafood

59878 Tomsed Corporation
420 McKinney Pkwy
Lillington, NC 27546   910-814-3800
Fax: 910-814-3899   800-334-5552
Manufacturer and exporter of access control equipment including high security and waist-high turnstiles, handicapped gates, portable posts and sign holders; wholesaler/distributor of portable and fixed crowd railing
President: Robert Sedivy
CEO: Thomas Sedivy
CFO: Karin Sedivy
Sales: Russell Socles
Estimated Sales: $15 Million
Number Employees: 100-249
Number of Brands: 9
Number of Products: 100
Square Footage: 220000
Private Brands Carried:
Lawrence Metal Products
Types of Products Distributed:
General Merchandise, Portable & fixed crowd railing

59879 Tony's Fine Foods
3575 Reed Ave
West Sacramento, CA 95605   916-374-4000
Fax: 916-372-0727   800-464-5429
customerservice@tonysfinefoods.com
www.tonysfinefoods.com
Dairy/deli products, gourmet snack foods, pizza supplies, sausages, groceries, seafood, canned hams, imported cheeses, baked goods.
President: Karl Berger
berger@tonysfinefoods.com
EVP/Chief Financial Officer: Scott Berger
Year Founded: 1934
Estimated Sales: $46 Million
Number Employees: 500-999
Square Footage: 143000
Number of Customer Locations: 1750
Types of Products Distributed:
Food Service, Frozen Food, General Line, Provisions/Meat, Seafood, Specialty Foods, Deli items, groceries, etc.

59880 Tony's Seafood LTD
5215 Plank Rd
Baton Rouge, LA 70805-2730   225-357-9669
Fax: 225-355-3530   800-356-2905
www.tonyseafood.com
Seafood
Owner: Darren Pizzolato
darren.pizzolato@tonyseafood.com
Year Founded: 1959
Estimated Sales: $20-50 Million
Number Employees: 1-4

59881 Too Good Gourmet
2380 Grant Ave
San Lorenzo, CA 94580-1806   510-317-8150
Fax: 510-317-8755   877-850-4663
info@toogoodgourmet.com
www.toogoodgourmet.com
Cookies
President: Jennifer Finley
jennifer@toogoodgourmet.com
Marketing/Sales: Katie Bidstrup
Estimated Sales: $5-10 Million
Number Employees: 50-99
Type of Packaging: Consumer, Food Service, Private Label, Bulk
Private Brands Carried:
Too Good
Number of Customer Locations: 4000+
Types of Products Distributed:
Cookies

59882 Top Distributing Co
1317 Terminal Cres SW
Grand Rapids, MI 49503-4890   616-452-6048
Fax: 616-452-5510   800-446-0001
jwiltjer@topdistco.com
Wholesaler/distributor of bananas, pineapples and coconuts

Wholesalers & Distributors / A-Z

President: John Wiltjer
jwiltjer@topdistco.com
Estimated Sales: $5-10 Million
Number Employees: 20-49
Square Footage: 88000

59883 Top Hat Co Inc
2407 Birchwood Ln
Wilmette, IL 60091-2349   847-256-6565
Fax: 847-256-6579 info@tophatcompany.com
www.tophatcompany.com
Sauces including raspberry, hot, mocha and mint fudges, butterscotch, caramel, double chocolate fondue and bittersweet chocolate
President: Marla Murray
Contact: Brandon Chillingworth
chillingworthbrandon@tophat.com
Estimated Sales: Less than $1,000,000
Number Employees: 5-9
Type of Packaging: Consumer, Food Service, Private Label, Bulk
Types of Products Distributed:
Specialty Foods

59884 (HQ)Top of the Table
2625 Broadway Street
San Antonio, TX 78215-1022   210-271-9021
Fax: 210-271-7321
Wholesaler/distributor of food processing equipment and supplies; serving the food service market
President: Robert Zintgraff
zrobert@strategicequipment.com
Sales Manager: Andy Wuesle
Estimated Sales: $10-20 Million
Number Employees: 20-49
Square Footage: 120000
Types of Products Distributed:
Food Service, Frozen Food, General Merchandise

59885 Topac
231 Cjc Hwy Ste 103
PO Box 660
Cohasset, MA 02025   781-740-8778
Fax: 781-740-8779 877-261-0473
sales@topac.com www.topac.com
Wholesaler/distributor of analytical instruments, data loggers, polarimeters, refractometers, saccharimeters and oxygen and carbon dioxide analyzers for modified atmosphere packaging and leak testing
President: Antoni Drybanski
VP: Julia Perry
Estimated Sales: Less than $500,000
Number Employees: 5-9
Square Footage: 12000
Private Brands Carried:
PBI Dansensor; Schmidt & Haensch
Types of Products Distributed:
Frozen Food, General Merchandise, Data loggers, etc.

59886 Topflight Grain Co-Op
400 E Bodman St
Bement, IL 61813-1299   217-678-2261
Fax: 217-678-8113 www.topflightgrain.com
Stores and distributes corn and grains
Manager: Derrick Bruhn
Manager: Yoshi Hatanaka
hatanaka@us.astellas.com
Estimated Sales: $10-20 000,000
Number Employees: 50-99

59887 Topicz
2121 Section Rd
Cincinnati, OH 45237   513-351-7700
Fax: 800-589-5818 800-589-5809
www.topicz.com
Wholesaler/distributor of groceries, fast food items and candy; serving convenience stores and the food service market; tobacco and cigarettes; rack jobber services available.
Buyer: Darlene Miller
Buyer: Maril Zimmer
Buyer: Angie Streinke
District Sales Manager: Misty Pennington
Year Founded: 1926
Estimated Sales: $309 Million
Number Employees: 100-249
Square Footage: 90000
Parent Co: Novelart Manufacturing Company
Number of Customer Locations: 1000
Types of Products Distributed:
Food Service, General Line, Rack Jobbers, Specialty Foods, Fastfood items, candy, tobacco products

59888 Tor Rey Refrigeration Inc
3741 Yale St
Houston, TX 77018-6563   713-884-1988
Fax: 281-564-3246 888-265-3462
www.tor-rey-refrigeration.com
Wholesaler/distributor of meat grinders and parts, saws, slicers, scales and bandsaw blades
Owner: Jesus Iglecis
gmanager@tor-rey.com
Estimated Sales: $10-20 Million
Number Employees: 5-9
Types of Products Distributed:
Frozen Food, General Merchandise, Meat grinders & parts

59889 Torkelson Brothers
14158 67th St NE
Grafton, ND 58237   701-352-0362
Fax: 701-352-3137
Wholesaler/distributor of red table and white chipping potatoes
President: Tom Torkelson
thudson@rsasecurity.com
Secretary: Deborah Torkelson
VP: Helen Torkelson
Estimated Sales: $2.5-5 Million
Number Employees: 10-19
Square Footage: 240000
Types of Products Distributed:
Frozen Food, Produce, Potatoes

59890 Torkelson Cheese Co
9453 W Louisa Rd
Lena, IL 61048   815-369-4265
info@torkelsoncheese.com
www.torkelsoncheese.com
Manufacturer and wholesaler of cheeses, specifically Muenster, brick, quesadilla and asadero cheeses; lactose manufacturer.
Owner: Lindsey White
Head Cheesemaker: Jamie White
Year Founded: 1985
Estimated Sales: $50-100 Million
Number Employees: 20-49
Number of Brands: 3
Type of Packaging: Consumer, Food Service, Bulk

59891 Torreo Coffee Company
4950 Rhawn St
Philadelphia, PA 19136   215-333-1105
Fax: 215-333-6615 888-286-7736
torreo.com
Premium coffees
President: Eric Patrick
Vice President: H Patrick
Operations Manager: Howard Patrick
Estimated Sales: $500,000-$1 Million
Number Employees: 5-9
Square Footage: 38400
Parent Co: Torreo Coffee & Tea Company
Type of Packaging: Consumer, Private Label, Bulk
Types of Products Distributed:
Coffee

59892 Tortuga Rum Cake Company
14202 SW 142nd Ave
Miami, FL 33186   305-378-6668
Fax: 305-378-0990 877-486-7884
sales@tortugarums.com www.tortugarums.com
Rum cakes, rum treats and fudges, gourmet coffees, jellies, sauces, juices and honey
Contact: Jackie Gil
gilj@tortugaimports.com

59893 Tosi & Company
624 Main Street
Vancouver, BC V6A 2V3
Canada   604-681-5740
Fax: 604-685-5704 tosifoods.com
Wholesaler/distributor and importer of Italian products including vinegar, olive oil, pasta, cheese, salami, almonds, pine nuts, canned tomatoes, rice, beans and stock fish; also, Greek olives; serving the food service market-Rosottoand Balsamic Vinegar
President: Bill Tosi
Sales Manager: J Martin
Plant Manager: R Calabrigo
Purchasing: Angelo Tosi
Estimated Sales: $1.5 Million
Number Employees: 1-4
Square Footage: 36000

Private Brands Carried:
Angelo; Sagra
Number of Customer Locations: 300
Types of Products Distributed:
Food Service, Frozen Food, General Line, Provisions/Meat, Seafood, Specialty Foods, Italian products & Greek olives

59894 Total Beverage Systems
137 Hansen Rd
Norwich, CT 06360-9402   860-822-9667
Fax: 860-822-9667 800-244-1461
info@tbsdraft.com www.tbsdraft.com
Wholesaler/distributor of beer, juice, wine and soda systems
President: Fred Emma
Supervisor (Warehouse): Stephen Thomas Jr
Service Manager: John Sullivan
Estimated Sales: $2.5-5 Million
Number Employees: 1-4
Types of Products Distributed:
Frozen Food, General Merchandise, Beverage systems

59895 Total Lift Equipment Company
2120 W Chestnut Avenue
Santa Ana, CA 92703-4306   310-637-1130
Fax: 714-550-8017 800-499-5438
Wholesaler/distributor of material handling equipment and automatic storage and handling systems; also, industrial and lift trucks
Number Employees: 5-9
Types of Products Distributed:
Frozen Food, General Merchandise, Material handling equipment

59896 Total Liquor Controls
164 Monmouth St
Red Bank, NJ 07701-1164   732-842-3036
Fax: 732-842-3060 888-512-BERG
www.patronpourers.com
Wholesaler/distributor of liquor control systems and equipment
Owner: Albert Dorsey
VP: John Dorsey
Estimated Sales: $2.5-5 Million
Number Employees: 5-9
Types of Products Distributed:
Frozen Food, General Merchandise, Liquor control systems & equipment

59897 Toudouze Market Company
800 Buena Vista St
San Antonio, TX 78207-4405   210-224-1891
Fax: 210-224-5752
Wholesaler/distributor of groceries, frozen foods, general merchandise and provisions/meats; serving the food service market and independent retail chains
President: C Toudouze Jr
Executive VP: J Toudouze
Estimated Sales: $20-50 Million
Number Employees: 20-49
Square Footage: 34000
Number of Customer Locations: 4500
Types of Products Distributed:
Food Service, Frozen Food, General Line, General Merchandise, Provisions/Meat, Groceries

59898 Tourtellot & Co
99 Colorado Ave
Warwick, RI 02888   401-734-4200
Wholesaler/distributor of produce; serving the food service market; also, retail consultation services available.
Vice President: Jamie Manville
Vice President & Part Owner: Steve Sigal
Year Founded: 1898
Estimated Sales: $20-50 Million
Number Employees: 20-49
Square Footage: 65000
Types of Products Distributed:
Food Service, Frozen Food, Produce

59899 Town & Country Fancy Foods
2001 W Main Street
Suite 249
Stamford, CT 06902-4543   203-867-1550
Fax: 203-967-1551
Wholesaler/distributor of gourmet bread, desserts and breakfast items; serving the food service market
Owner: Kathie Pappas
Manager: Keith Roberts
Number Employees: 5-9

Wholesalers & Distributors / A-Z

Types of Products Distributed:
Food Service, Frozen Food, Specialty Foods, Bread, desserts & breakfast items

59900 Town & Country Foods
72 Daggett Hill Rd
Greene, ME 04236-4124   207-946-5489
Fax: 207-946-7370
Meats and wholesale food distributor.
Owner: Janet Lapin
janet@tandcfoods.com
Estimated Sales: $10-20 Million
Number Employees: 20-49

59901 Town & Country Wholesale
1102 12th St
Belle Plaine, IA 52208-1759   319-434-2905
Fax: 319-434-2041   800-373-2905
www.townandcountrywholesale.com
Wholesaler/distributor of frozen foods, candy, paper, janitorial supplies, groceries, baked goods, produce, institutional and refrigerated foods, etc.; serving the food service market
President: William H Palmer
tcwsales@netins.net
Office Manager: Tonja Verdeat
Warehouse Manager: Ken Walton
Estimated Sales: $10-20 Million
Number Employees: 10-19
Square Footage: 60000
Number of Customer Locations: 800
Types of Products Distributed:
Food Service, Frozen Food, General Line, General Merchandise, Produce, Seafood, Candy, paper, baked goods, etc.

59902 Townsend Farms Inc
23400 NE Townsend Way
Fairview, OR 97024-4626   503-666-1780
Fax: 503-618-8257 www.townsendfarms.com
Fresh and frozen blueberries, blackberries and strawberries; fresh black raspberries, mixed fruit, manoes, boysenberries, cherries, marionberries, red raspberries and pineapple; fresh raspberries
President: Tracy Casillas
tracyc@thecanbycenter.org
CEO: Jeff Townsend
CFO: Chris Valenti
Plant Manager: Reyes Pena
Purchasing: Mark Davis
Estimated Sales: $10-20 Million
Number Employees: 1000-4999
Square Footage: 4000
Type of Packaging: Consumer, Food Service, Private Label, Bulk
Private Brands Carried:
Stillwell; Safeway; Albertsons
Types of Products Distributed:
Food Service, Frozen Food, Blackberries, boysenberries, etc.

59903 Toyota Forklifts Of Atlanta
3111 E Ponce DE Leon Ave
Scottdale, GA 30079-1229   404-373-1606
Fax: 404-378-6272 www.hotsyatlanta.com
Wholesaler/distributor of forklifts
President: Lee Smith
leesmith@atlantaforklifts.com
VP: Mike Reynolds
Estimated Sales: $20-50 Million
Number Employees: 20-49
Private Brands Carried:
Toyota
Types of Products Distributed:
Frozen Food, General Merchandise, Forklifts

59904 Toyota Material Handling
5667 E Schaaf Rd
Independence, OH 44131-1305   216-328-0970
Fax: 216-328-0870   800-722-1211
www.tmhoh.com
Wholesaler/distributor of material handling equipment including forklifts and lift trucks
Sales Manager: Kal Auglewicz
Manager: Blaine Bobby
blaine.bobby@istate.com
General Manager: David Graffy
Estimated Sales: $20-50 Million
Number Employees: 20-49
Private Brands Carried:
Toyota
Types of Products Distributed:
Frozen Food, General Merchandise, Material handling equipment

59905 Toyota Material Handling
8310 Airport Hwy
Holland, OH 43528-8637   419-865-8025
Fax: 419-865-3836 www.tmhoh.com
Wholesaler/distributor of material handling equipment including scrubbers and sweepers
President: Phillip Graffy
Contact: Carl Beam
carl@tape-inc.com
General Manager: Robert Navarro
Estimated Sales: $10-20 Million
Number Employees: 20-49
Private Brands Carried:
Toyota; B.T. Prime Mover; Prexell; E-Z Go; Advance
Types of Products Distributed:
Frozen Food, General Merchandise, Scrubbers, sweepers, etc.

59906 Toyota Material Handling
31010 San Antonio St
Hayward, CA 94544-7919   510-675-0500
Fax: 510-675-0400 www.tmhnc.com
Wholesaler/distributor of forklifts, conveyors, containers and racks
Owner: Jerry Lowery
jerry.lowery@toyota-industries.eu
Estimated Sales: $10-20 Million
Number Employees: 50-99
Private Brands Carried:
Toyota; Andersen; Blue Giant
Types of Products Distributed:
Frozen Food, General Merchandise, Forklifts, conveyors, racks, etc.

59907 Toyotalift Inc
1445 N 26th Ave
Phoenix, AZ 85009-3600   602-278-2371
Fax: 602-233-2587 www.toyotaliftinc.com
Wholesaler/distributor of forklifts and shelving
Owner: Garland R Pierce
roy_mohrman@toyotaliftinc.com
Sales Exec: Roy Mohrman
Estimated Sales: $20-50 Million
Number Employees: 50-99
Square Footage: 18000
Private Brands Carried:
Toyota; Daewoo; BT; Blue Giant
Types of Products Distributed:
Frozen Food, General Merchandise, Forklifts & shelving

59908 Trade Diversified
1650 Fremont Court
Ontario, CA 91761-8319   909-923-1208
Fax: 909-923-1212   800-835-8338
brasspeople@msn.com www.tdi4brass.com
Wholesaler/distributor of sneeeze guards, bar and stair rails, glass racks and turnstiles; importer and exporter of brass fittings; also, custom fabrication, bending and finishing services available; serving the food service market
President: King Lu
Marketing Director/Operations Manager: Erica Huang
Sales: Michelle Wong
Contact: Erica Chu
brasspeople@msn.com
Estimated Sales: $1-3 Million
Number Employees: 5
Square Footage: 48000
Types of Products Distributed:
Food Service, Frozen Food, General Merchandise, Sneeze guards, glass racks, etc.

59909 Tradelink
7880 NW 76th Avenue
Medley, FL 33166-7511   305-443-1869
Fax: 305-463-7792
Exporter and wholesaler/distributor of dry groceries, frozen foods, seafood, powdered milk, French cheeses, store equipment, and fresh fruits
President: Jorge Garrido
Vice President: Maria Leon
Estimated Sales: $2.5-5 Million
Number Employees: 1-4
Parent Co: SE Tradelink USA
Types of Products Distributed:
General Line, General Merchandise, Produce, Seafood, Specialty Foods, French cheeses, dry groceries, etc.

59910 Trader Joe's
160 Federal St.
12th Fl.
Boston, MA 02110   857-400-3400
www.traderjoes.com
Wholesaler/distributor of baked goods, beverages, frozen foods, produce, snacks and confections, and general groceries.
CEO: Dan Bane
CFO: Mitch Nadler *Year Founded:* 1967
Number of Customer Locations: 500+
Types of Products Distributed:
Frozen Food, General Line, General Merchandise, Produce, Baked goods

59911 Trans Veyor
364 Parker Ave
Toledo, OH 43605   419-691-2445
Fax: 419-691-0971
Wholesaler/distributor of conveyors and associated components including gear reducers, D.C. controllers, chains, sprockets, belts and sheaves
President: Douglas Moser
Estimated Sales: $2.5-5 Million
Number Employees: 5-9
Square Footage: 32000
Type of Packaging: Food Service, Bulk
Private Brands Carried:
Falk; Eurodrive; Martin; Mag Power
Number of Customer Locations: 1
Types of Products Distributed:
Food Service, Frozen Food, General Line, General Merchandise, Health Food, Provisions/Meat, Seafood, Specialty Foods, Conveyors & associated components

59912 Transnational Foods
1110 Brickell Ave # 808
Suite 808
Miami, FL 33131-3138   305-415-9970
www.transnationalfoods.com
Global manufacturer and distributor of hundreds of consumer products in categories such as beverages, cereals, dressings and soups.
President & CEO: Marcelo Young
myoung@transnationalfoods.com
CFO: Juan Iribarne
COO: Americo Preneste
Number Employees: 20-49
Number of Brands: 5
Number of Products: 500+
Type of Packaging: Consumer, Private Label

59913 Trattore Farms
7878 Dry Creek Road
Geyserville, CA 95441   707-431-7200
info@trattorefarms.com
www.trattorefarms.com
Wines, vinegars, and olive oils
President: Tim Boucher
CEO: Michelle Robson
Vice President: Mary Louise Bucher
Estimated Sales: $20 Million
Number Employees: 18
Other Locations:
Los Angeles, CA
Lodi, CA
South Kearney, NJ
Chicago, IL
Minneapolis, MN
San Francisco, CALodi

59914 Treasure Coast Coffee Company
20 NE Dixie Hwy
Stuart, FL 34958-1511   772-334-3999
Fax: 772-334-5257 info@tc3.org
www.tc3.org
Wholesaler/distributor of espresso machinery, parts and accessories, coffee, espresso, syrups, frothing devices and specialty items
Senior Pastor: Gordon Mularski
Children's Pastor: Andy Brown
Student Pastor: Tom Clark
Worship Arts Pastor: Andy Curtis
Number Employees: 5-9
Types of Products Distributed:
Frozen Food, General Line, General Merchandise, Specialty Foods, Espresso machinery, coffee, etc.

59915 Treasure Foods
2500 S 2300 W # 11
West Valley, UT 84119-7676   801-974-0911
Fax: 801-975-0553 treasurefoods@hotmail.com

Wholesalers & Distributors / A-Z

Processor and exporter of whipped honey butter, flavored fruit honey, scones; wholesaler/distributor of frozen foods and general line items; serving the food service market
Owner: Amin Motilla
CFO: Zarina Motiwala
Vice President: Mohamed Motiwala
Marketing Director: Amin Motiwala
Public Relations: Amin Motiwala
Production Manager: Fawad Motiwala
Plant Manager: Fawad Motiwala
Purchasing Manager: Amin Motiwala
Estimated Sales: $450,000
Number Employees: 5
Number of Brands: 3
Number of Products: 3
Square Footage: 14400
Parent Co: Algilani Food Import & Export
Type of Packaging: Food Service, Private Label, Bulk
Other Locations:
 Treasure Foods
 Salt Lake City, UTTreasure Foods
Private Brands Carried:
 Honeybutter
Types of Products Distributed:
 Food Service, Frozen Food, General Line

59916 Treasury Wine Estates
555 Gateway Dr.
P.O. Box 4500
Napa, CA 94558   707-259-4500
     Fax: 707-259-4542 www.tweglobal.com
Wine
President-Americas: Victoria Snyder
Managing Director & CEO: Michael Clarke
CFO: Matt Young
Chief Marketing Officer: Michelle Terry
Chief People & Legal Officer: Linnsey Caya
COO: Tim Ford
Estimated Sales: $34.6 Million
Number Employees: 3400
Number of Brands: 44

59917 (HQ)Tree of Life Canada
6185 McLaughlin Rd
Mississauga, ON L5R 3W7
Canada   905-507-6161
     Fax: 905-507-2727   800-263-7054
     treeoflife.ca
Natural, ethnic, and specialty foods
President: Bill Ivany
VP Operations/IT/Supply Chain: Barry Sheldrick
VP Finance: Gordon Walker
SVP Customer Development: Chris Powell
VP Human Resources: Helen Morrison
Number Employees: 250-499
Parent Co: KeHE Distributors
Type of Packaging: Food Service
Types of Products Distributed:
 Health Food, Specialty Foods

59918 Tree of Life Canada
19488 Telegraph Trail
Surrey, BC V4N 4H1
Canada   604-991-7100
     Fax: 604-881-7131   800-661-9655
     treeoflife.ca
Natural, ethnic, and specialty foods
Type of Packaging: Food Service
Types of Products Distributed:
 Health Food, Specialty Foods

59919 Tree of Life Canada
6745-76 Ave SE
Calgary, AB T2C 5M1
Canada   403-279-8998
     Fax: 403-279-9224   800-665-1298
     treeoflife.ca
Natural, ethnic, and specialty foods
Type of Packaging: Food Service
Types of Products Distributed:
 Health Food, Specialty Foods

59920 Tree of Life Canada
5626 Boul. Thimens
St. Laurent, QC H4R 2K9
Canada   514-333-3343
     Fax: 514-333-3990   800-363-2606
     treeoflife.ca
Natural, ethnic, and specialty foods
Type of Packaging: Food Service
Types of Products Distributed:
 Health Food, Specialty Foods

59921 Treier Popcorn Farms
16793 County Line Rd
Bloomdale, OH 44817   419-454-2811
     Fax: 419-454-3983 ptreier@wcnet.org
Popcorn including bagged, natural, buttered and microwaveable; wholesaler/distributor of commercial popcorn poppers and other concession supply equipment; serving the food service market
President: Don Treier
Secretary/Treasurer: Peggy Treier
Estimated Sales: $500,000-$1 Million
Number Employees: 15
Number of Brands: 2
Number of Products: 6
Square Footage: 12000
Parent Co: Treier Family Farms
Type of Packaging: Consumer, Food Service, Bulk
Types of Products Distributed:
 Popcorn

59922 (HQ)Trendco Supply
1250 Clough Pike
Batavia, OH 45103   513-752-1871
     Fax: 513-752-2374   888-873-6326
     www.trendcosupply.com
Wholesaler/distributor of racks, shelving, baskets, cutting boards, bar supplies, utensils, carts, cleaning supplies, matting, pans, name badges, etc
VP: Mat Svensson
Contact: Donna Borders
dborders@trendcosupply.com
Estimated Sales: $20-50 Million
Number Employees: 20-49
Types of Products Distributed:
 Frozen Food, General Merchandise, Racks, utensils, carts, cookware, etc.

59923 Trent Valley Distributors Ltd.
300 Bell Boulevard
Belleville, ON K8P 5H7
Canada   613-966-5279
     Fax: 613-966-4547   888-713-9999
Wholesaler/distributor of equipment and supplies; serving the food service market
President: Wayne Fraser
VP: Doug Patriquin
Number Employees: 90
Square Footage: 32000
Type of Packaging: Consumer, Food Service
Private Brands Carried:
 Garland; Wire Diebeo; Arcoroc
Types of Products Distributed:
 Food Service, Frozen Food, General Merchandise, Equipment & supplies

59924 Trenton Bridge Lobster Pound
1237 Bar Harbor Rd
Trenton, ME 04605-6021   207-667-2977
Fax: 207-667-3412 www.trentonbridgelobster.com
Lobster
President: Anthony Pettegrow
info@trentonbridgelobster.com
Estimated Sales: $3-5 Million
Number Employees: 10-19

59925 Tri Car Sales
16 Kipper St
Rio Rico, AZ 85648-6236   520-377-7602
     Fax: 520-281-5888 www.tricarsales.com
Importer and wholesaler/distributor of produce including hydroponic tomatoes, European cucumbers, red, yellow and green bell and jalapeno peppers, green beans and squash, etc.; serving the food service market
President: Juan Cardenas
jcardenas@tricarsales.com
Sales Manager: Frank Calixtro
Sales Director: Richard Morales
Public Relations: Joey Bernal
Operations Manager: Juan Carlos Cardenas
Estimated Sales: $3-5 Million
Number Employees: 10-19
Type of Packaging: Bulk
Private Brands Carried:
 Tricar Rua; Tridan
Types of Products Distributed:
 Produce, Hydroponic tomatoes, cucumbers, etc.

59926 Tri Mark SS Kemp
4587 Willow Pkwy
Cleveland, OH 44125   216-271-7700
     800-729-5367
info@sskemp.com www.trimarkusa.com
Wholesaler/distributor of equipment and supplies; serving the food service market
President: Thomas Wienclaw
tomw@sskemp.com
Executive Vice President: Steve Fishman
Estimated Sales: $30 Million
Number Employees: 100-249
Square Footage: 70000
Private Brands Carried:
 Mantiowoc; Vulcan; Traulsen; Groen; Libbey; Syracuse; Hobart; Oneida; True; Southbend; Vollrath; Homer; Laughlin; Cardinal
Number of Customer Locations: 2000
Types of Products Distributed:
 Equipment & supplies

59927 Tri Mark United East
505 Collins St
South Attleboro, MA 02703   508-399-2400
     Fax: 508-761-3605   888-662-6935
     www.trimarkusa.com
Wholesaler/distributor of food service equipment and supplies; serving the food service market.
Chief Executive Officer: Jerry Hyman
President, TriMark United East: Joe Thibert
President, Marketing: Kim Gill Rimsza
President, Strategy: Marty Monnat
Estimated Sales: $50-100 Million
Number Employees: 250-499
Square Footage: 152000
Parent Co: TriMark
Types of Products Distributed:
 Food Service, Frozen Food, General Merchandise, Foodservice equipment & supplies

59928 Tri-Connect
111 Frank Lloyd Wright Lane
Oak Park, IL 60302-2644   708-660-8190
     Fax: 312-951-6243 triconnect@aol.com
Wholesaler of England Farmhouse Biscuits packaged in gift tins and boxes, d'Orsay Chocolatier featuring imported Belgian chocolate and petit four desserts. Private labeling available
President: Tony Birbeck
CEO: Linda Murphy
CFO: Anthony Cioffi
Estimated Sales: Below $5 Million
Number Employees: 5
Type of Packaging: Private Label, Bulk
Private Brands Carried:
 Farmhouse
Types of Products Distributed:
 Food Service, Biscuits, Cookies, Chocolate

59929 (HQ)Tri-Marine International
10500 NE 8th St
Suite 1888
Bellevue, WA 98004   425-688-1288
     Fax: 425-688-1388 sfarno@trimarinegroup.com
     trimarinegroup.com
Importer and wholesaler/distributor of seafood.
Chief Executive Officer: Renato Curto
Chief Operating Officer: Joe Hamby
Chief Financial Officer: Steve Farno
Director, Enviornmental Policy: Matt Owens
Director, Information Systems: Johnny Yip
Year Founded: 1972
Estimated Sales: $100-500 Million
Number Employees: 20-49
Type of Packaging: Consumer, Food Service
Other Locations:
 Tri-Marine International
 JurongTri-Marine International
Types of Products Distributed:
 Frozen Food, Seafood

59930 Tri-State Wholesale
2801 Cotton St
Mobile, AL 36607-1208   251-478-0070
     Fax: 251-478-8233 tswdllc@aol.com
Wholesaler/distributor of specialty foods
President: D Richards
Marketing Manager: Buck Richards
Contact: Jason Bonnell
jason.bonnell@tristatewholesale.com
Estimated Sales: $1-3 Million
Number Employees: 1-4
Square Footage: 168000
Type of Packaging: Bulk
Number of Customer Locations: 320
Types of Products Distributed:
 Pretzels and Chips

Wholesalers & Distributors / A-Z

59931 Triad Fisheries LTD
514 Hubbard Rd
Lynnwood, WA 98036-7234 425-774-8822
Fax: 425-774-4954 mark@triadfisheries.com
www.triadfisheries.com
Fish
President/Owner: Mark Tupper
info@triadfisheries.com
Marketing: Bruce Gore
Estimated Sales: Less Than $500,000
Number Employees: 1-4

59932 Triangle Seafood
212 Adams Street
Louisville, KY 40206-1862 502-561-0055
Fax: 502-561-0096
Seafood
President: J Shannon Bouchillon

59933 Tribe 9 Foods
2901 Progress Rd
Madison, WI 53716 608-257-7216
www.tribe9foods.com
Fresh pasta, gluten free pasta, bars, cookies, and nut butters
Chairman & CEO: Brian Durst
President & CFO: Richard Ciurczak
Quality Assurance Manager: Margo King
VP Operations: William Ciurczak
Number Employees: 20-49
Types of Products Distributed:
 General Line

59934 Tribest Corp
1143 N Patt St
Anaheim, CA 92801-2568 714-879-7150
Fax: 562-623-7160 888-254-7336
service@tribest.com www.tribest.com
Importer, exporter and wholesaler/distributor of Korean noodle soups, ginseng sodas, tropical juices, cookies and candy; also, juice extractors.
Owner: Brandon Chi
General Manager: John Kim
Sales Manager: Kevin Kim
bran@tribest.com
Estimated Sales: $10-20 Million
Number Employees: 5-9
Square Footage: 20000
Type of Packaging: Food Service
Types of Products Distributed:
 Food Service, Frozen Food, General Line, General Merchandise, Korean noodle soups & juice extractors

59935 Trident Food Svc
10909 Southlake Ct
N Chesterfield, VA 23236-3913 804-379-0666
Fax: 804-379-0776
Wholesaler/distributor of food service equipment; serving the food service market
President: Sean Webb
Office Manager: Becky Viar
Controller: Michelle Davenport
Sales: Julie Cable
IT: Sean Desai
sean.webb@tridentfoodservice.com
Estimated Sales: $500,000-$1 Million
Number Employees: 5-9
Private Brands Carried:
 Hobart; Delfield; Garland
Types of Products Distributed:
 Food Service, Frozen Food, General Merchandise, Equipment

59936 Trident Seafoods Corp
P.O. Box 908
641 Shakes Street
Wrangell, AK 99929 907-874-3346
Fax: 907-874-3035
Processor and exporter of canned, fresh and frozen shrimp, crab, halibut, herring and salmon
Type of Packaging: Food Service, Bulk
Types of Products Distributed:
 Frozen Food

59937 Trifactor Systems LLC
2401 Drane Field Rd
Lakeland, FL 33811-3302 863-577-2239
Fax: 863-644-8329 800-507-4209
contactus@trifactor.com www.trifactor.com
Material handling systems integrator
President: John Phelan
Estimated Sales: $5-10 Million
Number Employees: 20-49

Private Brands Carried:
 HK Systems; Simplimatic; QC Conveyors; Buschman
Types of Products Distributed:
 Frozen Food, General Merchandise, Material handling equipment

59938 Trinity Fruit Sale Co
7571 N Remington Ave # 104
Suite 104
Fresno, CA 93711-5799 559-433-3777
Fax: 559-433-3790 sales@trinityfruit.com
www.trinityfruit.com
Fresh cherries, apricots, peaches, plums, nectarines, kiwi, grapes, apples and pears
President: David White
Marketing Director: John Hein
Sales: Vance Uchiyama
Number Employees: 20-49

59939 Trio Supply Company
3112 North 2nd Street
Minneapolis, MN 55411 612-522-3822
Fax: 612-522-4403 800-910-4607
www.triosupply.com
Wholesaler/distributor of poultry, meat and provisions.
President: Michael P. Ludwig
Contact: Dave Bergdahl
dbergdahl@triosupply.com
Estimated Sales: $10-20 Million
Number Employees: 5-9
Square Footage: 18000
Types of Products Distributed:
 Provisions/Meat, Produce, Poultry

59940 Triple Cities Material Handling
602 Old Front Street
Binghamton, NY 13905-1547 607-772-0766
Fax: 607-772-1083
Wholesaler/distributor of material handling equipment
President: James Wilson
Estimated Sales: $2.5-5 Million
Number Employees: 5-9
Private Brands Carried:
 Nissan; Barrett
Types of Products Distributed:
 Frozen Food, General Merchandise, Material handling equipment

59941 Triple F
98-735 Kuahao Pl
Pearl City, HI 96782 808-842-9133
triplefsupport@fffhawaii.com
www.fffhawaii.com
Wholesaler/distributor of general merchandise and general line products; serving the food service market.
President: Fred Salassa
Year Founded: 1978
Estimated Sales: $50-100 Million
Number Employees: 50-99
Types of Products Distributed:
 Food Service, Frozen Food, General Line, General Merchandise

59942 Triton International
1060 W Florence Ave
Inglewood, CA 90301 310-337-0044
Fax: 310-337-0044 www.tritoninternational.com
Wholesaler/distributor, importer and exporter of fresh and frozen fruits and vegetables including asparagus, baby potatoes, mangos, pineapples, lemons, blackberries, blueberries, papayas, etc.; serving the food service and retail markets
President: Alex Hall
Manager Frozens: Jason Chang
Procurement: Jose Paredes
Estimated Sales: $10-20 Million
Number Employees: 20-49
Square Footage: 20000
Type of Packaging: Consumer, Food Service, Private Label, Bulk
Private Brands Carried:
 Tri Mango
Types of Products Distributed:
 Food Service, Frozen Food, Produce, Baby potatoes & mangos

59943 Trophy Foods
71 Admiral Boulevard
Mississauga, ON L5T 2T1
Canada 905-670-8050
Fax: 905-670-4256
generalinquiries@trophyfoods.com
www.trophyfoods.com
Wholesaler/distributor of nuts and confectionery products; serving the food service market
General Manager: Pat Borg
Purchasing Manager: Sam Di Santo
Number Employees: 50-99
Types of Products Distributed:
 Food Service, Frozen Food, General Line, Nuts & confectionery items

59944 Tropic Fish Hawaii LLC
2312 Kamehameha Hwy E-5
Honolulu, HI 96819 808-591-2936
Fax: 808-591-2934 sales@tropicfishhawaii.com
www.tropicfishhawaii.com
Tuna, billfish, bottomfish, open ocean fish
President & COO: Shawn Tanoue
CEO: Charles Umamoto
General Manager: Daryl Yamaguchi
VP Sales: Toby Arakawa
VP Operations: Shannon Tanoue
Estimated Sales: $20-50 Million
Number Employees: 100-249

59945 Tropic Ice Company
2805 N Commerce Pkwy
Miramar, FL 33025-3956 954-441-9990
Fax: 954-441-9975
Wholesaler/distributor of frozen desserts; serving the food service market
President: Robert Tammara
jtammara@food-marketing-inc.com
Estimated Sales: $10-20 Million
Number Employees: 10-19
Private Brands Carried:
 Good Humor; Breyers
Types of Products Distributed:
 Food Service, Frozen Food, Desserts

59946 Tropical Illusions
1436 Lulu Street
PO Box 338
Trenton, MO 64683-1819 660-359-5422
Fax: 660-359-5347 tropical@tropicalillusions.com
Processor and exporter of frozen drinks mixes including: cocktail, slush and granita, cream base, and smoothies.
President: Vance Cox
Vice President: Carrol Baugher
Estimated Sales: $590,000
Number Employees: 6
Square Footage: 200000
Type of Packaging: Food Service, Private Label
Types of Products Distributed:
 Frozen Food

59947 Tropical Link Canada Ltd.
7668 Winston St.
Burnaby, BC
Canada 778-379-3510
Fax: 778-379-3511 www.tropicallinkcanada.ca
Organic cinnamon powder, cinnamon sticks, turmeric powder, coconut sugar, coconut oil, coconut vinegar, prepared fruit dips, rice blends, bulk dried fruit
Director: Sudhani Perera
Number of Brands: 2
Number of Products: 20
Type of Packaging: Consumer, Private Label, Bulk
Private Brands Carried:
 Snow Farms, Wild Tusker
Types of Products Distributed:
 Specialty Foods

59948 Tropical Paradise
101 Trade Zone Drive
Ronkonkoma, NY 11779-7363 631-585-0986
Fax: 631-585-0988
Wholesaler/distributor of frozen fruit drinks; serving the food service market
President/CEO/Sales Manager: Frank Massobni
Estimated Sales: $5-10 Million
Number Employees: 10-19
Parent Co: Hawaiian Julep Company
Private Brands Carried:
 Hawaiian Julep

Wholesalers & Distributors / A-Z

Types of Products Distributed:
   Food Service, Frozen Food, General Line, Fruit drinks

59949 Tropical Treets
130 Bermondsey Road
North York, ON M4A 1X5
Canada   416-759-8777
   Fax: 416-759-7782 888-424-8229
   www.tropicaltreets.com
Tropical ice cream; wholesaler/distributor of tropical food products, drinks and juices
CEO: Rumi Keshavjee
VP Sales/Marketing: Zahir Keshavjee
Estimated Sales: $471,000
Number Employees: 5
Square Footage: 24000
Private Brands Carried:
   Tropical Treets; Tropikfresh; Jamaica Best
Number of Customer Locations: 1000
Types of Products Distributed:
   Food Service, Frozen Food, General Line, Tropical ice cream, drinks & juices

59950 Troy Foods Inc
404 E US Highway 40
Troy, IL 62294-2205   618-667-6332
   www.troyfoodsinc.us
Meat including home cured ham and bacon, frankfurters, bologna and sausage
President: Don Nihiser
dnihiser@troyfoodsinc.com
Estimated Sales: $2,000,000
Number Employees: 5-9
Type of Packaging: Consumer
Types of Products Distributed:
   Frozen Food

59951 Troyer Foods Inc
17141 State Road 4
PO Box 608
Goshen, IN 46528-6674   574-533-0302
   Fax: 574-533-3851 800-876-9377
   www.troyers.com
Brand Director/President: Paris Ball-Miller
Executive Director: Tony Swihart
CFO & Controller: Neal Yoder
Executive Director: Donald Hixenbaugh
Director of Marketing: Beth Rodick
Director of Sales: Terry Blythe
Operations Manager: Frank Herbes
Production Manager: Steve Gile
Number Employees: 100-249
Other Locations:
   Central Warehouse Troyer Foods
   Bloomington, IN
   South Warehouse Troyer Foods
   Grandview, INCentral Warehouse Troyer FoodsGrandview

59952 TruBrain
Santa Monica, CA   650-241-8372
   team@trubrain.com
   www.trubrain.com
Drinks and bars to improve brain function; ketones
Founder/CEO: Chris Thompson
Finance & Strategy: Gary Epper
Lead Neuroscientist: Dr. Andrew Hill
Product Research & Development: Garrett Ruhland
Marketing: Bill Mackay
Analytics/Operations: Tomas Ferrari
Product Management: Celso Ferrari
Types of Products Distributed:
   Health Food

59953 Trucco, A.J.
343-344 NYC Terminal Market
Bronx, NY 10474-7403   718-893-3060
   Fax: 718-617-9884 866-258-7822
   info@truccodirect.com www.truccodirect.com
Wholesaler/distributor of dried fruits, fresh garlic and chestnuts including fresh, dried and frozen
President: Salvatore Vacca
VP: Diane Vacca
Estimated Sales: $10-20 Million
Number Employees: 10-19
Square Footage: 12000
Type of Packaging: Bulk
Types of Products Distributed:
   Frozen Food, General Line, Produce, Dried fruit, fresh garlic, etc.

59954 Truckee River Winery
11467 Brockway Rd
Truckee, CA 96161-2115   530-587-4626
   Fax: 530-550-8809 russ@truckeeriverwinery.com
   www.truckeeriverwinery.com
Wines
Owner: Russ Jones
russ@truckeeriverwinery.com
Co-Owner: Joan Jones
Sales Manager: Kate Shaw-Outside
russ@truckeeriverwinery.com
Estimated Sales: Under $300,000
Number Employees: 1-4
Type of Packaging: Private Label

59955 True World Foods LLC
24 Link Dr
Rockleigh, NJ 07647-2504   201-750-0024
   Fax: 201-750-0025 info@trueworldfoods.com
   www.trueworldfoods.com
Fresh seafood
President: Jackie Madsuka
CEO: Takeshi Yashiro
yashiro@trueworldfoods.com
Estimated Sales: $20-50 Million
Number Employees: 100-249

59956 Truscello & Sons Wholesalers
7880 NW 62nd Street
Miami, FL 33166-3539   305-592-5070
   Fax: 305-477-9586
Wholesaler/distributor of frozen foods, general line items, meats/provisions and Italian foods; serving the food service market
Owner: Sal Truscello
Estimated Sales: $500,000-$1 Million
Number Employees: 20-49
Number of Customer Locations: 120
Types of Products Distributed:
   Food Service, Frozen Food, General Line, Provisions/Meat, Specialty Foods, Italian foods

59957 Tsar Nicoulai Caviar LLC
60 Dorman Ave
San Francisco, CA 94124-1807   415-543-3007
   Fax: 415-543-5172 800-952-2842
   beluga@tsarnicoulai.com www.tsarnicoulai.com
Caviar, aquaculture operation
President: Mats Engstrom
VP: Dafne Engstrom
Sales/Marketing Manager: A Engstrom
Manager: Marian Mahone
concierge@tsarnicoulai.com
Plant Manager: Dr David Stedhen
Estimated Sales: $5 Million
Number Employees: 20-49
Square Footage: 120000
Type of Packaging: Consumer, Food Service, Private Label, Bulk
Private Brands Carried:
   California Sunshine; Tsar Nicoulai
Number of Customer Locations: 300
Types of Products Distributed:
   Food Service, Seafood, Specialty Foods, Caviar, salmon, trout, sturgeon, etc.

59958 Tuckahoe Manufacturing Co
327 Tuckahoe Rd
Vineland, NJ 08360-9243   856-696-4100
   Fax: 856-691-7312 800-220-3368
Strip doors; wholesaler/distributor of vinyl strip, sheet and panel materials and soft impact doors
President/Owner: John Tombleson
Estimated Sales: Less Than $500,000
Number Employees: 1-4
Square Footage: 3600
Private Brands Carried:
   Fostoria; Ogden; T&S Brass
Types of Products Distributed:
   Frozen Food, General Merchandise, Soft impact doors, etc.

59959 Tucker Pecan Co
350 N Mcdonough St
Montgomery, AL 36104-3652   334-262-4470
   Fax: 334-262-4690 800-239-6540
   sales@tuckerpecan.com www.tuckerpecan.com
Processor and wholesaler/distributor of pecans
President: David Little
sales@tuckerpecan.com
Operations Manager: David Little
Estimated Sales: $450,000
Number Employees: 10-19
Square Footage: 13436

Type of Packaging: Consumer, Food Service, Bulk
Types of Products Distributed:
   Frozen Food, Pecans

59960 Tucson Coop. Warehouse
350 S Toole Avenue
Tucson, AZ 85701-1836   520-884-9951
   Fax: 520-792-3241 800-350-2667
   www.tcwfoodcoop.com/www.shonatural.com
Wholesaler/distributor of health and natural foods
President: Sheila Portillo
General Manager: Regina Smith
Assistant General Manager: Clay Bacon
Marketing Manager: Frank McCormick
Sales Manager: Frank McCormick
Public Relations: Reggie Smith
Operations Manager: Lisa Mainz
Purchasing Manager: Michael Thompson
Estimated Sales: $5-10 Million
Number Employees: 65
Square Footage: 180000
Types of Products Distributed:
   Food Service, Frozen Food, General Line, Health Food, Produce, Specialty Foods, Health & Beaty Aids, Vitamins, Supp.

59961 Tucson Food Svc
810 E 17th St
Tucson, AZ 85719-6609   520-624-8821
   Fax: 520-884-0690
Wholesaler/distributor of produce
President: Thomas M Kusian
Vice President: James Tooley
VP Sales: Alfred Thomas
Number Employees: 50-99
Types of Products Distributed:
   Produce

59962 Tufco International
P.O.Box 456
Gentry, AR 72734-0456   479-736-2201
   Fax: 479-736-2947 800-364-0836
   info@tufcoflooring.com www.tufcoflooring.com
Flooring
President: Brent Mills
VP Sales: Russell Cox
Estimated Sales: Below $5 Million
Number Employees: 50-99

59963 Tufco Technologies Inc
1205 Burris Rd
Newton, NC 28658-1953   828-464-6730
   Fax: 828-464-6732 800-336-6712
   www.tufco.com
Wholesaler/distributor of point of sale displays, place mats and guest checks; serving the food service market
President: John Bonander
CFO: Gene Brittain
gene.brittain@tufco.com
VP Sales/Operations: Judy Joplin
Plant Manager: Charles Sigmon
Estimated Sales: $20-50 Million
Number Employees: 50-99
Square Footage: 125000
Parent Co: Tufco Industries
Types of Products Distributed:
   Food Service, Frozen Food, General Merchandise, Point of sale systems, place mats, etc.

59964 Tully's Coffee
3100 Airport Way S
Seattle, WA 98134   206-233-2070
   Fax: 206-233-2077 www.tullys.com
Retailer, wholesaler, and distributor of coffee and coffee products
President: Carl Pennigton Sr
Contact: Kerry Carlson
kc@tullys.com
Estimated Sales: H
Number Employees: 1,000-4,999

59965 Tuna Fresh
401 Whitney Ave # 103
Gretna, LA 70056-2500   504-363-2744
   Fax: 504-392-3324 www.chartwellsmenus.com
Tuna
Manager: John Duke

59966 Turk Brothers Custom Meats Inc
1903 Orange Rd
Ashland, OH 44805-1399   419-289-1051
   Fax: 419-281-8280 800-789-1051
   www.turkbrothersmeats.com

Wholesalers & Distributors / A-Z

Processor and wholesaler/distributor of beef, pork and lamb; wholesaler/distributor of frozen foods, equipment and fixtures and seafood; serving the food service market; also, slaughtering services available
Owner: Roy M Turk
VP: Kevin Turk
Estimated Sales: $5-10 Million
Number Employees: 10-19
Square Footage: 33684
Type of Packaging: Consumer, Food Service, Bulk
Types of Products Distributed:
 Food Service, Frozen Food, General Merchandise, Provisions/Meat, Seafood, Beef, pork & lamb

59967 Turkana Food
555 N Michigan Avenue
Kenilworth, NJ 07033   908-810-8800
 Fax: 908-810-8820 info@turkanafood.com
 www.turkanafood.com
Ethnic foods: European, Mediterranean and Middle Eastern.
Business Development: Furkan Bugra Er
Admisinstrative Service Manager: Tuncay Yalim
Estimated Sales: $9-11 Million
Number Employees: 11-50
Type of Packaging: Food Service
Types of Products Distributed:
 Specialty Foods

59968 Turner Holdings LLC
2678 S Eason Blvd
Tupelo, MS 38804-5994   662-842-7415
 Fax: 662-842-7418
Wholesaler/distributor of milk, dairy and ice cream products; serving the food service market
Manager: Donny Garner
garyholloway@turnerdairy.com
Sales: William Bryant
Estimated Sales: $3-5 Million
Number Employees: 10-19
Parent Co: Turner Dairies
Types of Products Distributed:
 Food Service, General Line, Dairy & ice cream products

59969 Turtle Island Herbs
4735 Walnut St # F
Boulder, CO 80301-2553   303-546-6362
 Fax: 303-546-0625 800-684-4060
 island@earthnet.net www.earthnet.net
Processor and wholesaler/distributor of organic herbal extracts and syrups
President: Feather Jones
CEO: Bahman Saless
VP Operations: Peter Danielson
Estimated Sales: $300,000-500,000
Number Employees: 1-4
Square Footage: 6000
Types of Products Distributed:
 Frozen Food, General Line, Health Food, Organic herbal extracts & syrups

59970 Tusco Grocers Inc
30 S 4th St
Dennison, OH 44621-1412   740-922-8721
 Fax: 740-922-4443 800-545-4084
 www.laurelgrocery.com
Wholesaler/distributor of frozen, dairy and bakery foods, meats, equipment, etc.; serving the food service market in Ohio, Pennsylvania and West Virginia
Manager: Jennifer Raber
CEO: Gregory Kimble
Estimated Sales: Less Than $500,000
Number Employees: 1-4
Square Footage: 259000
Private Brands Carried:
 Shurfine; Shurfresh; PriceSaver
Number of Customer Locations: 350
Types of Products Distributed:
 Food Service, Frozen Food, General Line, General Merchandise, Dairy & bakery foods, etc.

59971 Tusitala
12400 Creel Rd
PO Box 189
Grand Bay, AL 36541   251-865-4353
 Fax: 251-865-3763
Herbs and herbal supplements
President: George E. Spellmeyer
Secretary: Norma Jean Spellmeyer

59972 Tvc Wholesale Inc
2117 Helton Dr
Florence, AL 35630-1448   256-766-3744
 Fax: 256-766-3448 800-942-3394
Wholesaler/distributor of general merchandise, candy and confectionery products
Manager: Blair White
VP: Dennis Neal
Secretary/Treasurer: Gene Balentine
Manager: Steve Winkle
Estimated Sales: $20-50 Million
Number Employees: 20-49
Square Footage: 27000
Parent Co: Corr-Williams Company
Private Brands Carried:
 Eagle Brand
Number of Customer Locations: 1250
Types of Products Distributed:
 Frozen Food, General Line, General Merchandise, Candy & confectionery products

59973 Twelve Baskets Sales & Market
5200 Phillip Lee Dr SW
Atlanta, GA 30336   404-696-9922
 Fax: 404-696-9099 800-420-8840
Wholesaler/distributor of general line items; also, packer of edible oils
Owner: Ken Mc Millan
ken@twelvebaskets.net
President: Kirk McMillen
Sales: Bob Quinet
Estimated Sales: $20-50 Million
Number Employees: 20-49
Square Footage: 15000
Types of Products Distributed:
 Frozen Food, General Line

59974 Twenty Four Hour Security Services
107 Walker Rd
Byron, GA 31008   478-956-2148
 Fax: 478-956-2148 800-779-2148
Wholesaler/distributor of general merchandise including burglar and fire alarms, intercommunication and security systems and closed circuit TV
Owner: Terry Taylor
Estimated Sales: $1-2.5 Million
Number Employees: 1-4
Types of Products Distributed:
 Frozen Food, General Merchandise, Security services & systems

59975 Twin City Bottle Company
1227 E Hennepin Ave
Minneapolis, MN 55414   612-331-8880
 Fax: 612-379-5118 800-697-0607
Wholesaler/distributor of glass and plastic containers and closures; also, screen printing and labeling for glass and plastic containers available
President: Ken Slater
CEO: Roger Seid
Marketing: Rod Cywinski
Sales: Rod Cywinski
Estimated Sales: $20-50 Million
Number Employees: 50-99
Square Footage: 180000
Types of Products Distributed:
 Packaging Materials

59976 Twin City Wholesale
519 Walker St
Opelika, AL 36801-5999   334-745-4564
 Fax: 334-749-5125 800-344-6935
 johanna@tcwholesale.com
Wholesaler and distributor of products and supplies for convenience stores and grocery chains; offers business floor plan design services.
Owner: Johanna Bottoms
twincity@mindspring.com
Estimated Sales: $76 Million
Number Employees: 50-99
Types of Products Distributed:
 General Merchandise

59977 Two Guys Spice Company
2404 Dennis Street
Jacksonville, FL 32204-1712   949-248-1269
 Fax: 904-791-9330 800-874-5656
 www.twoguysgrilling.net
Broker and wholesaler/distributor of dehydrated onions, garlic and vegetables; also, spices and industrial ingredients
President: Michael Simmons
Vice President: Guy Simmons
Estimated Sales: $2.4 Million
Number Employees: 1-4
Number of Brands: 1
Number of Products: 500
Square Footage: 20800
Type of Packaging: Food Service, Private Label, Bulk
Private Brands Carried:
 Newleywed's Foods; Texas Pete's Hot Sauce & Spice Company; DeFrancesco & Sons; Quick Dry Foods; Harmon Spice
Number of Customer Locations: 50
Types of Products Distributed:
 Food Service, Specialty Foods, Spices, ingredients, etc.

59978 Two Rivers Enterprises
490 River St W
Holdingford, MN 56340-4519   320-746-3156
 Fax: 320-746-3158 joeh@stainlesskings.com
 www.tworiversstainlesskings.com
Restaurant and food service equipment; also provides renovations of processing plants and on-site equipment.
President: Robert Warzecha
bobw@stainlesskings.com
Midwest Regional Sales: Joe Herges
Sales Engineer: Jeff Jones
Midwest Regional Sales: Steve Bairett
Number Employees: 20-49

59979 Tyler Supply Co
3611 E Kilgore Rd
Kalamazoo, MI 49001-5536   269-345-2121
 Fax: 269-345-8337 800-356-7417
 www.tylersupply.com
Wholesaler/distributor of material handling equipment including forklifts, conveyors, etc.; also, parts and service available
Owner: Roy Taylor
Manager: Carl Cacioppo
carl.cacioppo@solocup.com
Estimated Sales: $2.5-5 Million
Number Employees: 5-9
Private Brands Carried:
 Porta; Burroughs; Republic
Types of Products Distributed:
 Frozen Food, General Merchandise, Material handling equipment

59980 Tynan Equipment
5926 Stockberger Pl
Indianapolis, IN 46241-5421   317-247-8474
 Fax: 317-247-6843 www.tynaneq.com
Wholesaler/distributor of forklifts and personnel lifts
Owner: Mike Tynan
mtynan@tynaneq.com
Estimated Sales: $20-50 Million
Number Employees: 50-99
Private Brands Carried:
 Yale; Cushman; Powerboss
Types of Products Distributed:
 Frozen Food, General Merchandise, Forklifts & personnel lifts

59981 (HQ)Tyson Foods Inc.
2200 W. Don Tyson Pkwy.
Springdale, AR 72762   479-290-4000
 www.tysonfoods.com
Chicken, beef and pork products.
CEO: Noel White
President/Director: Dean Banks
Executive VP/CFO: Stewart Glendinning
Executive VP/General Counsel: Amy Tu
Executive VP/Chief Customer Officer: Scott Rouse
Estimated Sales: $40 Billion
Number Employees: 122,000
Number of Brands: 41
Type of Packaging: Consumer, Food Service, Bulk
Types of Products Distributed:
 Frozen Food, Provisions/Meat

59982 U Okada & Co LTD
1000 Queen St
Honolulu, HI 96814-4116   808-597-1102
 Fax: 808-591-6634
Wholesaler/distributor of frozen foods, provisions/meats and seafood; serving the food service market

Wholesalers & Distributors / A-Z

President: Dexter Okada
dexter@uokada.com
President: Saneo Okada
Estimated Sales: $10-20 Million
Number Employees: 20-49
Square Footage: 60000
Types of Products Distributed:
  Food Service, Frozen Food, Provisions/Meat, Seafood

59983 U Roast Em Inc
16778 W US Highway 63
Hayward, WI 54843-7214   715-634-6255
        Fax: 715-934-3221 info@u-roast-em.com
Supplier of green coffee beans, bulk teas, home roasting supplies and coffee flavorings
Manager: Terry Wall
info@u-roast-em.com
Number Employees: 1-4
Type of Packaging: Consumer

59984 (HQ)US Food Products
1084 Queen Anne Rd
Teaneck, NJ 07666-3508   201-833-8100
        Fax: 201-833-1920 edsbeef@aol.com
        www.usfoodproducts.com
Broker, wholesaler and exporter of all categories of frozen-chilled and dry food
President/CEO: Edward W Holland
edsbeef@aol.com
CFO: Chona Canillas
Estimated Sales: $20-50 Million
Number Employees: 20-49
Number of Brands: 50
Number of Products: 5000
Square Footage: 25000
Type of Packaging: Food Service
Types of Products Distributed:
  Food Service, Frozen Food, General Line, Health Food, Provisions/Meat, Produce, Seafood, Specialty Foods

59985 (HQ)US Foods Inc
9399 West Higgings Rd.
Suite 500
Rosemont, IL 60018   847-720-8000
        Fax: 847-720-8099 aem.usfoods.com
Food products, equipment, and logistics for the food service market.
Chairman/CEO: Pietro Satriano
Chief Financial Officer: Dirk Locascio
EVP/General Counsel/CCO: Kristin Coleman
Chief Merchandising Officer: Andrew Iacobucci
Chief Information Officer: Keith Rohland
Year Founded: 1989
Estimated Sales: $24 Billion
Number Employees: 28,000
Number of Brands: 23
Types of Products Distributed:
  Food Service

59986 US Foods Inc
350 S Pacific Hwy
Woodburn, OR 97071   503-980-2500
        aem.usfoods.com
Other Locations:
  Food Services of America
  Spokane, WAFood Services of America
Types of Products Distributed:
  Food Service, Frozen Food

59987 US Foods Inc
10420 Olive Ln
Anchorage, AK 99515   907-344-9400
        aem.usfoods.com
Types of Products Distributed:
  Food Service, Frozen Food, General Line, General Merchandise

59988 US Foods Inc
1001 Shuksan Way
Everett, WA 98203   425-407-6000
        aem.usfoods.com
Number of Customer Locations: 50
Types of Products Distributed:
  Food Service, Frozen Food, General Line, General Merchandise

59989 US Foods Inc
3520 E Francis Ave
Spokane, WA 99217   509-483-4747
        aem.usfoods.com
Types of Products Distributed:
  Food Service, Frozen Food, General Line, General Merchandise, Provisions/Meat, Produce

59990 US Foods Inc
802 Parkway Ln
Billings, MT 59101   406-238-7800
        aem.usfoods.com
Types of Products Distributed:
  Food Service, Frozen Food, General Line, General Merchandise, Provisions/Meat, Produce

59991 US Foods Inc
5820 Piper Dr
Loveland, CO 80538   970-613-4333
        aem.usfoods.com
Types of Products Distributed:
  Food Service, Frozen Food, General Line, General Merchandise, Provisions/Meat, Produce, Seafood, Groceries, baked goods, etc.

59992 US Foods Inc
2204 70th Ave E
Suite 100
Fife, WA 98424   Fax: 253-620-9000 800-572-3810
        aem.usfoods.com
Square Footage: 120000
Types of Products Distributed:
  Food Service, Frozen Food, General Line

59993 US Growers Cold Storage
3141 E 44th St
Vernon, CA 90058-2405   323-583-3163
        Fax: 323-583-2542 800-366-3163
        info@usgrowers.com usgrowers.com
Warehouser providing dry, cooler and freezer storage for frozen foods; rail sides available. Some of the services they offer include computerized inventory control, Pallet Exchange Program, import/export inspection, blast freezingWorldwide distribution and more.
Owner & President: Angelo Antoci
Vice President: Peter Corselli
General Manager: Ralph Newton
Estimated Sales: $20-25 Million
Number Employees: 100 to 249
Types of Products Distributed:
  Food Service, Frozen Food, General Merchandise, Health Food, Provisions/Meat, Produce, Rack Jobbers, Seafood, Specialty Foods

59994 US Marketing Company
2571 Route 212
Woodstock, NY 12498-2115   845-679-7274
        Fax: 845-679-4650 800-948-0739
        usmcompany@hotmail.com
Wholesaler/distributor and exporter of herbal-based vitamins, protein supplements, antioxidants, fitness and exercise equipment as on TV MDSE
President: Alan Altschul
aa@usmarketingcorp.com
CEO: Karen Kingsley
Public Relations: Glenn Taggart
Estimated Sales: $900,000
Number Employees: 5-9
Square Footage: 32000
Type of Packaging: Consumer
Private Brands Carried:
  Herbalife-4000
Types of Products Distributed:
  General Line, General Merchandise, Rack Jobbers

59995 US Materials Handling Corp
6624 Joy Rd
East Syracuse, NY 13057-1187   315-437-2978
        Fax: 315-437-8080 syr@usmaterialshandling.com
        www.usmaterialshandling.com
Wholesaler/distributor of material handling equipment including fork lift trucks, conveyors, pallet racks, loading docks, lockers, cranes, hoists, shelving, etc
Owner: Jon Payne
jpayne@usmaterialshandling.com
VP: Jon Payne
Estimated Sales: $10-20 Million
Number Employees: 20-49
Parent Co: US Material Handling Equipment
Private Brands Carried:
  U.S. Materials Handling Equipment
Types of Products Distributed:
  Frozen Food, General Merchandise, Conveyors, pallet racks, etc.

59996 UTZ Quality Foods Inc.
900 High St.
Hanover, PA 17331   717-637-6644
        Fax: 717-634-5890 800-367-7629
        info@utzsnacks.com
Potato chips, pretzels, popcorn, tortilla chips, cheese curls, pub fries, pork rinds, etc.
President/COO: Tom Flocco
CEO: Dylan Lissette
Executive VP/CFO: Jay Thompson
Executive VP/Chief Customer Officer: Mark Schreiber
Year Founded: 1921
Estimated Sales: $215 Million
Number Employees: 2,500
Number of Brands: 9
Square Footage: 550000
Type of Packaging: Consumer, Food Service, Bulk
Other Locations:
  Utz Distribution Centers
  East Hartford, CT
  Patterson, NY
  Laurel, DE
  Newark, DE
  Auburn, ME
  West Springfield, MA
  Utz Distribution CentersPatterson

59997 UVA Packaging
8111 Virginia Pine Ct
Richmond, VA 23237-2202   804-275-8067
        Fax: 804-271-3096 www.pmb-uvainc.com
Importer and wholesaler/distributor of packaging machinery including vertical form/fill/seal
President: George Van Bergen
Sales/Marketing Manager: Siegfried Gaessner
Estimated Sales: $3-5 Million
Number Employees: 10-19
Square Footage: 44032
Parent Co: PMB-UVA
Private Brands Carried:
  Butler 2; Butler 3; UVA 350A; UVA 600A; Newton.
Types of Products Distributed:
  Frozen Food, General Merchandise, Vertical form/fill/seal machinery, etc.

59998 UW Provision Co.
2315 Pleasant View Rd.
PO Box 620038
Middleton, WI 53562   608-836-7421
        Fax: 608-836-6328 800-832-0517
        www.uwprovision.com
Meat products.
President: Jim Kalscheur
Vice President/Secretary: Ron Krantz
Vice President/Treasurer: Steve Kalscheur
Year Founded: 1958
Estimated Sales: $100-500 Million
Number Employees: 100-249
Types of Products Distributed:
  Provisions/Meat

59999 Uinted Rental
100 Stamford Pl # 1
Suite 700
Stamford, CT 06902-6740   203-316-8599
        800-877-3687
        www.unitedrentals.com
Wholesaler/distributor of material handling equipment
President/CEO: Micheal J Kneeland
COO/EVP: Matthew Flannery
CFO/EVP: William B Plummer
Estimated Sales: $3-5 Million
Number Employees: 1-4
Private Brands Carried:
  Daewoo; Clark; Komatsu
Types of Products Distributed:
  Frozen Food, General Merchandise, Material handling equipment

60000 Ukiah Foods
205 Clara Avenue
Ukiah, CA 95482-7719   707-462-2921
        Fax: 707-462-1068
Wholesaler/distributor of groceries, dairy products, bakery items, frozen food and provisions/meats; serving the food service market
President/Sales Manager: C Pittman
Number Employees: 10-19
Number of Customer Locations: 90

Wholesalers & Distributors / A-Z

Types of Products Distributed:
Food Service, Frozen Food, General Line, Provisions/Meat, Groceries, etc.

60001 Ultimate Foods
P.O. Box 1008
Linden, NJ 07036   908-486-0800
Fax: 908-486-2999 www.ultimatefoodservice.com
Offer a full line of fresh and frozen seafood, produce, meats, oils, pastas, canned tomatoes, and other grocery and specialty items.
General Manager: Scott Greisman
Seafood Buyer/Quality Control: John Parisi
Produce Buyer/Quality Control: Albert Sindoni
Road Sales Manager: Al Ferrentino
Operations Manager: Anthony Stropoli
Dry Goods Buyer: James Boniface
Estimated Sales: $3.6 Million
Number of Brands: 1
Type of Packaging: Food Service, Bulk
Types of Products Distributed:
Frozen Food, General Merchandise, Produce, Seafood, Specialty Foods

60002 Ultrapar Inc.
13 Flintlock Dr
Warren, NJ 07059-5014   908-647-6650
Fax: 908-647-1281 chrisparkinson@ultrapar.com
www.ultrapar.com
Wholesaler/distributor of steam filters, culinary steam filtration systems, air sterilizing filters and liquid sterilizing filtration systems.
President: Chris Parkinson
Vice President: Nancy Siconolfi
Estimated Sales: $1-1.5 Million
Number Employees: 3
Square Footage: 7200
Private Brands Carried:
Parker Domnick Hunter; Parker Zander

60003 Uncle Charlie's Meats
607 Big Hill Ave
Richmond, KY 40475   859-623-1737
davidsparks.ucm@gmail.com
Wholesaler/distributor of provisions/meats; serving the food service market.
President: Ray Parsons
rparjr@aol.com
Estimated Sales: $20-50 Million
Number Employees: 50-99
Types of Products Distributed:
Food Service, Provisions/Meat

60004 Uni Co Supply
5166 W Jefferson Blvd
Los Angeles, CA 90016-3839   323-937-5800
Fax: 323-937-1500   800-959-5587
Wholesaler/distributor of electrical supplies and fire alarms
President: Farhad Noorani
unicomsupply@earthlink.net
Estimated Sales: $3-5 Million
Number Employees: 5-9
Types of Products Distributed:
Frozen Food, General Merchandise, Electrical supplies & fire alarms

60005 UniPro Foodservice, Inc.
2500 Cumberland Pkwy SE
Suite 600
Atlanta, GA 30339   770-952-0871
Fax: 804-261-4394 info@uniprofoodservice.com
Wholesaler/distributor of frozen and canned food, provisions/meats, general merchandise and seafood; serving the food service market
President: David Matthews
CEO: Roger Toomey
CFO: Dan Wolfram
CIO: R.C. Alexander III
Executive VP Marketing: Don Gilligan
EVP Sales, East: Keith Durnell
COO: Bob Stewart
EVP, Supply Chain: John Burke
Number Employees: 100-249
Types of Products Distributed:
Food Service, Frozen Food, General Merchandise, Provisions/Meat, Seafood, Canned foods

60006 Unico
8000 Keele Street
Concord, ON L4K 2A4
Canada   905-669-9637
Fax: 905-669-3585   800-268-1915
consumer.services@unico.ca www.unico.ca
Wholesaler/distributor of Italian food products
President: John Jacobsonc
COO: John Porco
Number Employees: 50-99
Square Footage: 420000
Type of Packaging: Consumer, Food Service, Private Label, Bulk

60007 Unicorn Enterprises
#1-1601 Matheson Blvd
Mississauga, ON L4W 1H9
Canada   905-290-2370
Fax: 905-290-1823   800-355-2538
info@unicorntoys.com www.unicorntoys.com
Wholesaler/distributor of pre-brewed tea concentrate
CEH: Erick Smith
Executive Assistant: Gwendolyn Smith
Number Employees: 1-4
Types of Products Distributed:
Frozen Food, General Line, Pre-brewed tea concentrate

60008 Unilever Canada
160 Bloor St. East
Suite 1400
Toronto, ON M4W 3R2
Canada   416-415-3000
www.unilever.ca
Food products, personal care, and home products.
Director, Customer Development: Bruce Findlay
VP, Brand Strategy & Innovation: Margaret McKellar
Year Founded: 1949
Estimated Sales: $466 Million
Number Employees: 3,400
Square Footage: 80912
Parent Co: Unilever US
Type of Packaging: Consumer, Food Service

60009 Unilever US
800 Sylvan Ave
Englewood Cliffs, NJ 07632
    800-298-5018
www.unileverusa.com
Food products, personal care, and home products.
President, North America: Amanda Sourry
CEO: Alan Jope
CFO: Graeme Pitkethly
Chief R&D Officer: Richard Slater
VP, Human Resources, North America: Mike Clementi
Estimated Sales: $18 Billion
Number Employees: 5000-9999
Parent Co: Unilever N.V. & Unilever plc
Type of Packaging: Consumer, Food Service
Types of Products Distributed:
General Line, General Merchandise

60010 Union Fisheries Corp
6186 N Northwest Hwy
Chicago, IL 60631-2126   773-738-0448
Fax: 773-763-8775
Prepared fresh or frozen fish and seafood
Owner: Jim Gubrow
Estimated Sales: $3-5 Million
Number Employees: 5-9

60011 Union Grocery Company
604 Carter Ave
New Albany, MS 38652   662-534-5089
Fax: 662-534-8085
Wholesaler/distributor of frozen food, general merchandise, provisions/meats and general line products; serving the food service market
President: W T Shannon
Estimated Sales: $10-20 Million
Number Employees: 20-49
Number of Customer Locations: 400
Types of Products Distributed:
Food Service, Frozen Food, General Line, General Merchandise, Provisions/Meat

60012 Union Seafoods
2100 W McDowell Rd
Phoenix, AZ 85009-3011   602-254-4114
Fax: 602-254-4117
Seafood
President: Ernest Linsenmeyer
Estimated Sales: $4,000,000
Number Employees: 1-4

60013 Union Wine Co
19600 SW Cipole Rd
Tualatin, OR 97062
info@unionwinecompany.com
www.unionwinecompany.com
Wine
Founder & Owner: Ryan Harms
Director of Finance/Accounting: Eric Harms
VP Sales: Adam Coremin
Director of Winemaking: JP Caldcleugh
Year Founded: 2005
Number Employees: 20-49
Types of Products Distributed:
Wine

60014 United Bakers & Deli Supply
4600 Blue Pkwy
Kansas City, MO 64130-2815   816-921-7300
Fax: 816-921-8065   800-825-2176
Wholesaler/distributor of general line products, packaging and decorations; also, rack jobber services available; serving the food service market
Owner: Matthew Harre
VP, Warehouse/Delivery Driver: Mike Harre
Account Representative/Business Developm: Doug Hudelston
VP, Marketing: Matthew Harre
VP, Sales: Matthew Harre
harreray@aol.com
Retail Sales Associate: Wanda Roop
Estimated Sales: $5-10 Million
Number Employees: 10-19
Square Footage: 140000
Number of Customer Locations: 2000
Types of Products Distributed:
Food Service, Frozen Food, General Line, General Merchandise, Rack Jobbers, Specialty Foods, Packaging & decorations wholesaler

60015 United Banana Company
27 Griswold St
Binghamton, NY 13904-1543   607-724-0994
Importer and wholesaler/distributor of produce
President: Thomas Burns
VP: Heather Burns
Estimated Sales: $2.5-5 Million
Number Employees: 5-9
Square Footage: 12800
Types of Products Distributed:
Frozen Food, Produce

60016 United Chairs
4600 Steeles Avenue W
Woodbridge, ON L4L 9L5
Canada   905-851-8838
Fax: 905-850-3729
Wholesaler/distributor and importer of chairs; serving the food service market
Types of Products Distributed:
Food Service, Frozen Food, General Merchandise, Chairs

60017 United Dairy Co-Op Svc
12 N Park St # 7
Seneca Falls, NY 13148-1496   315-568-2750
Fax: 315-568-2752 unitedag@flare.net
Wholesaler/distributor of milk
CEO: James Patsos
Manager: Mimma Kisor
Estimated Sales: $3-5 Million
Number Employees: 1-4
Types of Products Distributed:
Frozen Food, General Line, Milk

60018 United Dairy Machinery Corp
301 Meyer Rd
P O Box 257
West Seneca, NY 14224-2091   716-674-0500
Fax: 716-674-0511   800-828-7821
www.udmc.biz
Wholesaler/distributor of sanitary processing equipment including engineering controls, installation pumps, valves, fittings, meters, tanks, etc
Owner: Heather Strupkus
heather@donaldross.com
VP: Steven Sisson
Engineering Manager: Bill Bethune
Estimated Sales: $5-10 Million
Number Employees: 20-49
Parent Co: Weld Tek
Types of Products Distributed:
Frozen Food, General Merchandise, Pumps, valves, fittings, tanks, etc.

Wholesalers & Distributors / A-Z

60019 United Fishing Agency LTD
1131 N Nimitz Hwy # 38
Honolulu, HI 96817-4522   808-536-2148
Fax: 808-526-0137
Seafood
Manager: Frank Goto

Estimated Sales: $20-50 Million
Number Employees: 50-99

60020 United Foods & Fitness
532 N State Road
Briarcliff Manor, NY 10510-1526   914-941-2145
Fax: 914-941-8443   800-638-3800
Importer and wholesaler/distributor of nutritional supplements, energy bars, vitamins, amino acids, protein powders, sports drinks and weight gain supplements
President: Cherie Deglon
Estimated Sales: $2.5-5 Million
Number Employees: 1-4
Type of Packaging: Consumer, Food Service
Private Brands Carried:
   Multipower
Types of Products Distributed:
   Frozen Food, General Line, Health Food, Nutritional supplements

60021 United Forklift Corporation
2160 Blount Rd
Pompano Beach, FL 33069-5111   954-971-9440
Fax: 954-971-9440   www.ringpower.com
Wholesaler/distributor of material handling equipment including forklifts
President: Charles Hathaway
Estimated Sales: $10-20 Million
Number Employees: 5-9
Private Brands Carried:
   Mitsubishi; Pettibone; Teledyne
Types of Products Distributed:
   Frozen Food, General Merchandise, Material handling equipment

60022 United Glassware & China
5005 Washington St
Denver, CO 80216-2092   303-296-1684
Fax: 303-298-7537
Wholesaler/distributor of chinaware and glassware
Owner: Arnold Schatz
Contact: Andrew Archuleta
andrewarchuleta@restaurantsource.com
Estimated Sales: $10-20 Million
Number Employees: 20-49
Private Brands Carried:
   Syracuse; Oneida; Villeroy & Bach; Cardinal International; Libbey; Anchor Hocking; Schott Zwiesel; Judel
Types of Products Distributed:
   Frozen Food, General Merchandise, Chinaware & glassware

60023 United Grain Growers
PO Box 6600
Stn Main
Winnipeg, MB R3C 3A7
Canada   204-944-5406
Fax: 204-947-1779   www.ugg.com
Wholesaler/distributor of mustard seeds
Manager Mustard Operations: Kevin Dick
Number Employees: 1,000-4,999
Square Footage: 40000
Types of Products Distributed:
   Frozen Food, General Line, Mustard seeds

60024 United Lighting & Supply Co
201 Business Park Dr
Lynn Haven, FL 32444-5459   850-271-5405
Fax: 850-271-9525   800-416-5088
www.unitedlighting.com
Wholesaler/distributor of electrical supplies, lighting fixtures, etc
Manager: Paul Spires
paulspires@unitedlynnhaven.com
Estimated Sales: $3-5 Million
Number Employees: 5-9
Parent Co: United Lighting Supply Company
Types of Products Distributed:
   Frozen Food, General Merchandise, Electrical supplies, lighting, etc.

60025 United Machinery & Supply Company
P.O.Box 5900
Springfield, MO 65801-5900   417-862-7411
Fax: 417-862-4922
Wholesaler/distributor of material handling equipment
President: Robert D Reynolds
Estimated Sales: $20-50 Million
Number Employees: 50-99
Private Brands Carried:
   Clark; Crown; Exide
Types of Products Distributed:
   Frozen Food, General Merchandise, Material handling equipment

60026 United Mineral & Chemical Corporation
1100 Valley Brook Ave Ste 203
Lyndhurst, NJ 07071   201-507-3300
Fax: 201-507-1506   800-777-0505
inquiry@umccorp.com   www.umccorp.com
Importer and wholesaler/distributor of magnesium chlorides FCC, sorbic and citric acid, potassium sorbate, and sodium erythorbate
President: A Becidyan
Chemical Department Manager: Sal Morreale
Contact: Michael Sansonetti
msansonetti@umccorp.com
Estimated Sales: $20 Million
Number Employees: 20-49
Type of Packaging: Bulk
Types of Products Distributed:
   Frozen Food, General Line, Sorbic & citric acid, etc.

60027 (HQ)United Natural Foods Inc
313 Iron Horse Way
Providence, RI 02908-5637   401-528-8634
info@unfi.com
www.unfi.com
General line products, frozen foods, natural groceries, supplements.
President/Chairman/CEO: Steve Spinner
Chief Operating Officer: Eric Dorne
Chief Financial Officer: John Howard
Chief Legal Officer/General Counsel: Jill Sutton
President & Chief Marketing Officer: Christopher Testa
Year Founded: 1996
Estimated Sales: $20 Billion
Number Employees: 19,000
Number of Brands: 9
Square Footage: 250000
Other Locations:
   United Natural Foods
   Iowa City, IA
   United Natural Foods
   Mounds View, MN
   United Natural Foods
   New Oxford, PA
   United Natural Foods
   Atlanta, GA
   United Natural Foods
   Auburn, CA
   United Natural Foods
   Auburn, WA
   United Natural FoodsMounds View
Types of Products Distributed:
   Frozen Food, General Line, Health Food, Natural groceries, supplements, etc.

60028 United Noodles
2015 E 24th St
Minneapolis, MN 55404-4195   612-721-6677
Fax: 612-721-4255   www.unitednoodles.com
Wholesaler/distributor of Oriental foods, rice, frozen seafood, fresh vegetables and Chinese herbal products; serving the retail market
President: Teddy Wong
General Manager: Do Nang
Secretary: Ramon Tan
Estimated Sales: $8 Million
Number Employees: 20-49
Square Footage: 80000
Types of Products Distributed:
   Frozen Food, General Line, Health Food, Produce, Seafood, Specialty Foods, Oriental foods, rice, fish & herbs

60029 (HQ)United Pickles
4366 Park Ave
Bronx, NY 10457-2494   718-933-6060
Fax: 718-367-8522   picklebiz@aol.com
www.unitedpickle.com
Pickle, sauerkraut and relish maker.
Owner: Steve Leibowitz
sleibowitz@unitedpickle.com
Number Employees: 1-4
Type of Packaging: Consumer, Food Service, Bulk
Other Locations:
   United Pickle Products Corp.
   Rosenhayn, NJUnited Pickle Products Corp.

60030 United Potato Company
183 W South Water Market
Chicago, IL 60608   312-666-7017
Fax: 312-666-9569
Wholesaler/distributor of onions and potatoes; serving the food service market
Accounting: Sarah Zelkin
Sales: Dan Zelken
Sales: David Zelkin
Estimated Sales: $500,000-$1 Million
Number Employees: 1-4
Types of Products Distributed:
   Food Service, Produce, Onions & potatoes

60031 United Produce
900 Louisville St
Starkville, MS 39759-3857   662-323-8578
Fax: 662-323-9673
Wholesaler/distributor of fresh fruits and vegetables
Manager: John McKissack
Manager: John Mckissack
Buyer: Charles Collier
Estimated Sales: $10-20 Million
Number Employees: 10-19
Types of Products Distributed:
   Produce

60032 United Rentals
811 Post St
Greensboro, NC 27405-7262   336-744-0564
Fax: 336-274-6731   www.unitedrentals.com
Wholesaler/distributor of mobile rentalized kitchens and dining facilities; serving the food service market
President: Ronald Bridges
Sales Manager: Tony Tauer
Manager: Andrew Winney
awinney@ur.com
Estimated Sales: $1-3 Million
Number Employees: 20-49
Types of Products Distributed:
   Food Service, Frozen Food, General Merchandise, Mobile rentalized kitchens

60033 United Restaurant Equipment Co
2654 S Saunders St
2654 S Saunders St
Raleigh, NC 27603-2840   919-832-4546
Fax: 919-821-7050   800-662-7342
ureco@aol.com   www.ureco.com
Wholesaler/distributor of restaurant equipment and supplies; serving the food service market
President: Howard Margulies
seilugram@aol.com
VP: Joann Smith
Sales Manager: Everette Strickland
Estimated Sales: $10-20 Million
Number Employees: 20-49
Square Footage: 60000
Number of Customer Locations: 2500
Types of Products Distributed:
   Food Service, Frozen Food, General Merchandise, Restaurant equipment & supplies

60034 United Seafood Imports
5500 1st Ave N
St Petersburg, FL 33710-8006   727-894-2661
Fax: 727-894-5097
Importer and wholesaler/distributor of frozen shrimp, mahi-mahi, orange roughy and mussels
President: Richard Stowell
CFO: Vincent Arfuso
Vice President: Shane Stowell
Estimated Sales: $20-50 Million
Number Employees: 5-9
Square Footage: 3500
Private Brands Carried:
   Diamonds of the Sea; South Bay; Doble A; Dufer

60035 United Shellfish Co Inc
407 Kent Narrow Way N
Grasonville, MD 21638-1307 410-827-8171
Fax: 410-827-7436 800-368-2565
sales@unitedshellfish.com
www.ipswichshellfish.com
Wholesale seafood processor and distributor of fresh and frozen seafood, scallops, crab meat, live lobsters, lobster meat, shrimp, squid, hard shell clams, soft shell clams, surf clams, oysters, mussels, fresh clam chowder, soups andspecialty restaurant products.
Manager: Dave Messenger
Sales Manager: John Walker
Manager: Howard Brooks
hbrooks@unitedshellfish.com
Estimated Sales: $19,600,000
Number Employees: 50-99
Square Footage: 90000
Parent Co: Ipswich Shellfish Group
Type of Packaging: Food Service
Types of Products Distributed:
Frozen Food, Seafood

60036 United States Beverage LLC
700 Canal St # 4
Stamford, CT 06902-5950 203-961-8215
Fax: 203-961-8217 qq@unitedstatesbeverage.com
www.unitedstatesbeverage.com
President/CEO: Joseph Fisch Jr
CEO: Sergio Acevedo
sergioacevedo@unitedstatesbeverage.com
Estimated Sales: $300,000-500,000
Number Employees: 10-19

60037 United States Sugar Corp
111 Ponce DE Leon Ave
Clewiston, FL 33440-3098 863-983-8121
Fax: 863-983-9827 www.ussugar.com
Wholesaler/distributor of sugar and molasses
Manager: Mike Snow
Vice President: Carl Stringer
carl.stringer@ussugar.com
Number Employees: 1000-4999
Types of Products Distributed:
Frozen Food, General Line, Sugar & molasses

60038 United Sugars Corporation
7803 Glenroy Road
Suite 300
Bloomington, MN 55439 641-423-1214
Fax: 952-896-0400 800-984-3585
www.unitedsugars.com
Wholesaler/distributor of sugar
Manager: John White
Facility Manager: Donna Monson
Contact: Lori Anderson
l_anderson@unitytools.com
Estimated Sales: $5-10 Million
Number Employees: 1-4
Parent Co: American Crystal Sugar
Private Brands Carried:
American Crystal; United Sugars
Types of Products Distributed:
General Line, Sugar

60039 United Universal Enterprises Corporation
7747 N 43rd Ave
Phoenix, AZ 85051 623-842-9691
Fax: 623-842-4605 univenterp@cs.com
Wholesaler/distributor, importer and exporter of general merchandise, frozen seafood, canned fruits, grains, meat, cooking oils and powdered milk; serving the food service market
Manager: Louis Galvac
Vice President: Linda Kirschner
Estimated Sales: $3-5 Million
Number Employees: 10
Square Footage: 28000
Type of Packaging: Food Service, Private Label
Private Brands Carried:
Ocean Gold; Star; Elite; Kraft; Morris; D'Ouro
Types of Products Distributed:
Food Service, Frozen Food, General Line, Provisions/Meat, Seafood, Grains, powdered milk, etc.

60040 United Wholesale Grocery Company
3138 Hill Ave
Toledo, OH 43607 419-531-6084
Fax: 419-531-8845
Wholesaler/distributor of groceries, meat, dairy products, frozen foods, general merchandise, private label items and seafood; serving the food service market
Manager: Matt Kinnee
Manager: Ed Tank
Estimated Sales: $5-10 Million
Number Employees: 1-4
Square Footage: 72000
Parent Co: Spartan Stores
Number of Customer Locations: 1200
Types of Products Distributed:
Food Service, Frozen Food, General Line, General Merchandise, Provisions/Meat, Seafood, Dairy products

60041 United With Earth
2833-7th St.
Berkeley, CA 94710 510-210-4359
Fax: 510-984-0538 www.unitedwithearth.com
Medjool dates, coconut and almond date rolls, pitted dates, California golden figs, Mission figs, Persian cucumbers
Number of Brands: 1
Type of Packaging: Consumer, Private Label, Bulk
Private Brands Carried:
United With Earth
Types of Products Distributed:
Produce

60042 Unity Brands Group
319 W Town Pl
Suite 28
Saint Augustine, FL 32092-3103 904-940-8975
Fax: 866-878-9306 info@unitybrandsgroup.com
unitybrandsgroup.com
Marketing services
President: Praful Mehta
Marketing Executive: William Edwards
Estimated Sales: $1-2.5 Million
Number Employees: 1-10
Type of Packaging: Food Service
Types of Products Distributed:
General Line, Specialty Foods, Teas, rubs and spices

60043 Univar USA
2100 Haffley Ave
National City, CA 91950-6417 619-262-0712
Fax: 619-474-2820 www.univarusa.com
Wholesaler/distributor of industrial chemicals and ammonia
Sales Manager: Rafique Rahimtoola
Estimated Sales: $2.5-5 Million
Number Employees: 10-19
Types of Products Distributed:
Frozen Food, General Merchandise, Industrial chemicals & ammonia

60044 Universal Fish of Boston
31 B St
Burlington, MA 1803 781-273-1144
Fax: 781-273-2033
Wholesaler/distributor of frozen seafood
President: T Katz
Contact: Tom Katz
t.katz@universalfish.com
Estimated Sales: $10-20 Million
Number Employees: 10-19
Types of Products Distributed:
Frozen Food, Seafood

60045 Universal Marketing
1647 Pilgrim Ave
Bronx, NY 10461-4807 914-576-5383
Fax: 914-576-1711 800-225-3114
Wholesaler/distributor, importer and exporter of commercial kitchen equipment including freezers, refrigerators, coolers and fast food cooking equipment; serving the food service market
President: James Deluca
VP: Henry Muench
Estimated Sales: Below $5 Million
Number Employees: 7
Square Footage: 12000
Types of Products Distributed:
Food Service, Frozen Food, General Merchandise, Commercial kitchen equipment

60046 Universal Nutrition
3 Terminal Rd
New Brunswick, NJ 08901 732-545-3130
Fax: 732-509-0458 800-872-0101
info@universalusa.com
Bodybuilding supplements including aminos, bars, fat burners, joint support, proteins, vitamins, and minerals
President: Danny Keller
VP: Robert Gluckin
Chief Sales & Marketing Officer: Tim Tantum
Chief Creative & Strategy Officer: Phil K
Product Director: Jason Budsock
Year Founded: 1977
Number Employees: 250-499
Types of Products Distributed:
Health Food

60047 Universal Preservachem Inc
60 Jiffy Rd
Somerset, NJ 08873-3438 732-568-1266
Fax: 732-568-9040 mravitz@upichem.com
www.upichem.com
Wholesaler/distributor of chemicals and ingredients. Vitamins sweeteners preservatives, antioxidants, acidulants, etc
Chairman of the Board: Herbert Ravitz
President: Dan Ravitz
Vice President: Michael Ravitz
Manager: Daniel Ravitz
dan@upichem.com
Estimated Sales: Less Than $500,000
Number Employees: 10-19
Square Footage: 240000
Type of Packaging: Private Label, Bulk
Types of Products Distributed:
General Line, Health Food, Specialty Foods, Chemical Additives

60048 Universal Restaurant Equipment
1001 N State Line Avenue
200
Texarkana, TX 75501-5231 903-792-8294
Fax: 903-792-7310
Wholesaler/distributor of restaurant equipment and supplies; serving the food service market
Owner/President: Randy Kendrick
Number Employees: 10-19
Types of Products Distributed:
Food Service, Frozen Food, General Merchandise

60049 Universal Sanitizers & Supplies
2491 Stock Creek Blvd
Rockford, TN 37853 865-573-7296
Fax: 865-573-7298 888-634-3196
info@universalsanitizers.com
Consulting services including sanitation testing and analysis, employee training and vendor audits; wholesaler/distributor of industrial cleaners and sanitizers, water treatment products and conveyor lubricant/sanitizer systems
President: Amy Rigo
VP: Emilia Rico
Contact: Emilia Rico
emilia.rico@universalsanitizers.com
Estimated Sales: $5-10 Million
Number Employees: 5-9
Square Footage: 16000
Types of Products Distributed:
Frozen Food, General Merchandise, Industrial cleaners & sanitizers

60050 Universal Sodexho
PO Box 23218
New Orleans, LA 70183-0218 504-733-5761
Fax: 504-731-1679 800-535-1946
Wholesaler/distributor of food supply and gally equipment; serving the institutional food service market
CEO: Kirby McDonald
President: Barry Blackwell
Senior VP: Bob Tallent
Estimated Sales: $20-50 Million
Number Employees: 100-249
Parent Co: Universal Sodexho International
Types of Products Distributed:
Food Service, Frozen Food, General Merchandise, Food supply & gally equipment

60051 Uniwell Systems
3000 Northwoods Pkwy # 115
Norcross, GA 30071-1597 770-246-6011
Fax: 770-448-2571 800-789-0992

Wholesalers & Distributors / A-Z

Wholesaler/distributor of point of sale hardware and software, electronic cash registers
President: Brian Winks
Marketing Director: John Kain
Estimated Sales: $5 Million
Number Employees: 5-9
Types of Products Distributed:
 Frozen Food, General Merchandise, Scales, scanners, etc.

60052 Upcountry Fisheries
85 Kino Pl
Makawao, HI 96768-8891
808-871-8484
Fax: 808-871-6071
Seafood
Owner: Richard Samsing
Estimated Sales: $.5-1 million
Number Employees: 1-4

60053 Upper Lakes Foods Inc
801 Industry Ave
Cloquet, MN 55720
800-879-1265
www.ulfoods.com
Wholesaler/distributor of groceries, meats, produce, dairy products, frozen foods, baked goods, general merchandise, equipment and fixtures; serving the food service market.
President: Sue Ryan
Vice President, Operations: Shawn Sorensen
Bid & Pricing Manager: Renee Parks
EFOOD Administrator: Lori Kobus
Vice President, Sales: Scott Sorensen
Director, Merchandising: Erin Bradshaw
Sales & Commodities: Denise Sorensen
Chief Operating Officer: Jim Bradshaw
Estimated Sales: $175 Million
Number Employees: 250-499
Square Footage: 120000
Types of Products Distributed:
 Food Service, Frozen Food, General Line, General Merchandise, Provisions/Meat, Produce, Groceries, equipment & fixtures, etc.

60054 Upstate Farms
P.O.Box 249
Jamestown, NY 14702-0249
716-892-3156
Fax: 716-484-7142 www.upstatefarms.com
Wholesaler/distributor of milk including homogenized, skim, chocolate and 2%
Manager: Michael Conklin
Sales Manager: Gerald McDonald
Estimated Sales: $10-20 Million
Number Employees: 20-49
Parent Co: Upstate Farms
Types of Products Distributed:
 Frozen Food, General Line, Milk

60055 Uptown Bakers
5335 Kilmer Pl
Hyattsville, MD 20781-1034
301-864-1500
Fax: 301-864-7744 info@uptownbakers.com
www.uptownbakers.com
European pastries and breads including scones, cinnamon bread, muffins, cookies, danish and cakes rolls
Owner: Michael Mc Cloud
orders@uptownbakers.com
CFO: Elliot Person
Estimated Sales: $13.4million
Number Employees: 100-249
Type of Packaging: Consumer, Food Service
Types of Products Distributed:
 Frozen Food

60056 Us Plastics
1390 Neubrecht Rd
Lima, OH 45801-3196
419-228-2242
Fax: 419-228-5034 800-809-4217
usp@usplastics.com www.usplastic.com
Wholesaler/distributor of plastic products including tanks, drums, pipes, cutting boards, conveyor glide bags, trash containers and tubing
President: Wesley Lytle
Owner: R Stanley Tam
Call Center Manager: Eric McRoory
Estimated Sales: $10-20 Million
Number Employees: 100-249
Square Footage: 430000
Types of Products Distributed:
 Frozen Food, General Merchandise, Plastic products

60057 V&B Distributing
4060 Wayne Street
Hilliard, OH 43026-1478
614-777-0630
Fax: 614-777-5647 800-669-0032
Wholesaler/distributor of store supplies, pricing equipment and private label items
Secretary/Treasurer: B Neer
Accounts Manager: B Sugar
Sales Representative: Debbie Pond
Estimated Sales: Less than $500,000
Number Employees: 1-4
Private Brands Carried:
 Meto,Dennison; Pacific Handy Cutter; 3M; Continental
Types of Products Distributed:
 Frozen Food, General Merchandise, Pricing equipment, etc.

60058 V-Suarez Provisions
PO Box 364588
San Juan, PR 00936-4588
787-792-1212
Fax: 787-792-0735
Wholesaler/distributor and importer of canned pastas, teas, soups, juices, sports drinks, paper products, insecticides, cleaning products, evaporated milk, foil, plastic wrap, Mexican foods, prunes, raisins, salad dressings, olive oilseasonings, etc
VP: Javier Arango
Number Employees: 50-99
Square Footage: 600000
Parent Co: V-Suarez & Company
Type of Packaging: Consumer
Private Brands Carried:
 Denia; Kresto
Number of Customer Locations: 900
Types of Products Distributed:
 Food Service, General Line, General Merchandise, Seasonings, teas, soups, etc.

60059 (HQ)V.M. Calderon
4040 Red Rock Ln
Sarasota, FL 34231
941-366-3708
Fax: 941-951-6529 888-654-8365
vmcalderon@aol.com
Wholesaler/distrubutor, import broker and contract packager of brined vegetables, black and green olives, pepperoncini, cherries, capers, onions and pickles
President: Victor Calderon
Estimated Sales: $1-3 Million
Number Employees: 1-4
Square Footage: 7200
Type of Packaging: Consumer, Food Service, Private Label, Bulk

60060 VBS Inc Material Handling
5808 Midlothian Tpke
Richmond, VA 23225-6118
804-232-7816
Fax: 804-232-5149
Wholsaler/distributor of material handling equipment
President: Claud Crosby
ccrosby@vbsmhe.com
Estimated Sales: $10-20 Million
Number Employees: 20-49
Private Brands Carried:
 Hyster Forklifts; Multi Ton; Sellick
Types of Products Distributed:
 Frozen Food, General Merchandise, Material handling equipment

60061 VIP Food Svc
74 Hobron Ave
Kahului, HI 96732-2106
808-877-5055
Fax: 808-877-4960 www.vipfoodservice.com
Foodservice distributor on Hawaiian island of Maui with two stores that are also open to the public.
President: Nelson Okumura
Contact: Brian Tokeshi
btokeshi@vipfoodservice.com
Number Employees: 5-9
Type of Packaging: Consumer, Food Service
Types of Products Distributed:
 Food Service, Frozen Food, General Line, General Merchandise, Provisions/Meat, Produce, Seafood, Dairy products, equip. & fixtures, etc.

60062 VMC Corp
92 Maple St
Weehawken, NJ 07086-5722
201-863-3137
Fax: 201-863-3137 800-863-5606
sales@vmc-health.com
http://www.vmc-health.com/
Wholesaler/distributor and importer of yogurt, cheese, kefir products and processing equipment; exporter of bee pollen, royal jelly and yogurt acidophilus powders
Manager: Alan Cheung
acheung@vmchealth.com
Estimated Sales: $5-10 Million
Number Employees: 10-19
Square Footage: 12000
Type of Packaging: Consumer, Private Label, Bulk
Private Brands Carried:
 Yogurtmet; Hygenia; Malaka Brand; Nature's Own
Number of Customer Locations: 12600
Types of Products Distributed:
 Frozen Food, General Line, Health Food, Yogurt, kefir, cheese cultures, etc.

60063 VWR Funding Inc
100 W Matsonford Rd # 200
Radnor, PA 19087-4558
610-386-1700
Fax: 610-429-5569 www.vwr.com
Wholesaler/distributor of laboratory equipment, apparatus and supplies
President: Paul Pnoak
Senior VP: Stephan W Labonte
stephan_labonte@vwr.com
Number Employees: 250-499
Private Brands Carried:
 Lo Count
Types of Products Distributed:
 Frozen Food, General Merchandise, Laboratory equipment & supplies

60064 VacuWest
1728 Williamsport St
Henderson, NV 89052
702-263-8942
Fax: 702-263-7216 800-776-4513
Wholesaler/distributor of material handling equipment including vacuum hoists, manipulators and overhead rail and bridge systems, chains hoist
President: Buck Buchanan
Estimated Sales: $2.5-5 Million
Number Employees: 1-4
Types of Products Distributed:
 Frozen Food, General Merchandise, Material Handling equipment

60065 Val's Seafood
3437 Winford Drive
Mobile, AL 36619-4309
251-639-2570
Fax: 251-639-1198
Seafood
President: Val Hammond
Estimated Sales: $632,000
Number Employees: 1-4

60066 Vale Enterprises
820 S Monaco Parkway
Pmb 261
Denver, CO 80224-3703
303-338-1111
Fax: 303-695-4341 800-488-8253
www.valeenterprises.com
Wholesaler/distributor of natural foods including herbal teas, nutritional supplements, energy products and detox products
President: Steve Franzmann
General Manager: Neil McCoy
Vice President: Mitch Crossland
Sales/Marketing Executive: Jon Vogt
Contact: Mark Myer
mark@vale-inc.com
Type of Packaging: Consumer
Private Brands Carried:
 Vale's; Rally (Nutritional supplements)
Number of Customer Locations: 1000
Types of Products Distributed:
 General Line, Health Food, Herbal teas, supplements, etc.

60067 Vallero Mercantile Company
3875 Steele St Ste A
Denver, CO 80205
303-383-1606
Fax: 303-383-1686
Wholesaler/distributor of specialty foods
Owner: J Zaremba
Manager/Buyer: T Zaremba
Estimated Sales: $1-3 Million
Number Employees: 1-4
Square Footage: 44000
Number of Customer Locations: 100
Types of Products Distributed:
 Frozen Food, Specialty Foods

Wholesalers & Distributors / A-Z

60068 Vallet Foodservice
472 Badger Rd
Hazel Green, WI 53811-9787
Fax: 563-588-0632 800-553-0516
Wholesaler/distributor of frozen foods, produce, meats and seafood; serving the institutional food service market
Owner: Calvin Buss
Estimated Sales: $5-10 Million
Number Employees: 20-49
Number of Customer Locations: 500
Types of Products Distributed:
   Food Service, Frozen Food, Provisions/Meat, Produce, Seafood, Institutional foods

60069 Valley Distributing Company
1075 E Ramsey Rd
Vincennes, IN 47591   812-882-6066
                      Fax: 812-882-0530
Wholesaler/distributor of frozen food, general line products and produce; serving the food service market
Manager: Dale Barrix
Estimated Sales: $2.5-5 Million
Number Employees: 1-4
Parent Co: E. Bierhaus & Sons
Number of Customer Locations: 10
Types of Products Distributed:
   Food Service, Frozen Food, General Line, Produce

60070 Valley Distributing Company
2819 2nd St NW
Albuquerque, NM 87107   505-344-1623
                      Fax: 505-344-1625
Wholesaler/distributor of general merchandise including paper goods, health and beauty aids, snacks, confectionery products, nuts, carnival goods, etc
President: Frances Garcia
VP: F Charles Garcia
Estimated Sales: $5-10 Million
Number Employees: 10-19
Private Brands Carried:
   Bar X; Big Chief; Frito-Lay Snacks
Number of Customer Locations: 2000
Types of Products Distributed:
   Frozen Food, General Line, General Merchandise, Snacks, confectionery items, nuts, etc.

60071 Valley Distributors
134 Forest Lea Road
Pembroke, ON K8A 7C1
Canada   613-732-9911
           Fax: 613-732-9386 800-267-0195
Wholesaler/distributor of groceries, meat, produce, frozen food, baked goods and general merchandise; serving the food service market
President: R Brash
Sales: Dale Cotnam
Purchasing Director: Robert Lamont
Estimated Sales: $8 Million
Number Employees: 20-49
Square Footage: 76000
Parent Co: Brash's Grocerterias
Type of Packaging: Food Service, Private Label
Private Brands Carried:
   Margarine, Bacon, Cleaning Agents
Number of Customer Locations: 390
Types of Products Distributed:
   Food Service, Frozen Food, General Line, Provisions/Meat, Produce

60072 Valley Foods
1211 E Valley Road
Santa Barbara, CA 93108-2007   805-565-1621
                      Fax: 805-565-1076
Wholesaler/distributor of general line products
General Partner: Donald Sherwin
Military Sales Manager: Susan Hoffer
National Sales Manager: Brian Hofer
Contact: Steve Olesky
solesky@valleyfoods.com
Estimated Sales: $20-50 Million
Number Employees: 5-9
Square Footage: 84000
Types of Products Distributed:
   Frozen Food, General Line

60073 Valley Foods Inc
335 E Boardman St
Youngstown, OH 44503-1845   330-746-4555
           Fax: 330-746-7016 800-228-4053
jeffvalley@valleyfoodsystems.com
www.valleyfoodsystems.com
Full service broadline distributor offering quality deli products, frozen foods and canned goods
Owner: John Valley
CEO: John M. Valley
VP: John M. Valley
VP Sales & Marketing: Jeff Valley
Sales Support: Sara Davis
johnvalley@valleyfoods.com
Customer Support Coordinator: Stefanie Costello
Director of Operations: Chuck Olesky
Director of Purchasing: Steve Olesky
Estimated Sales: $2.6 Million
Number Employees: 50-99
Square Footage: 20000
Type of Packaging: Food Service
Types of Products Distributed:
   Food Service, Frozen Food, Provisions/Meat

60074 Valley Fruit & Produce Company
1601 E. Olympic Blvd.
Bldg.#300 Suites 300-307
Los Angeles, CA 90021   213-627-8736
           Fax: 213-895-6982 www.valleyproduce.com
Wholesaler/distributor of produce and general line products
President: Donald Lalonde
Contact: Jin Ju Wilder
jjw@valleyproduce.com
Estimated Sales: $2.5-5 Million
Number Employees: 50-99
Types of Products Distributed:
   Frozen Food, General Line, Produce

60075 Valley Pride Food Distributor
P.O.Box 2255
McAllen, TX 78502-2255
                      Fax: 956-686-2213
Wholesaler/distributor of groceries, frozen foods and provisions/meats; serving the food service market
President: E Rodriguez
Estimated Sales: $5-10 Million
Number Employees: 5-9
Types of Products Distributed:
   Food Service, Frozen Food, General Line, Provisions/Meat, Groceries

60076 Valu-Line Foods
1830 Como Avenue
Saint Paul, MN 55108-2711   763-571-5353
                      Fax: 763-571-3427
Wholesaler/distributor of specialty foods; serving the food service market
Sales Manager: Paul Roberts
Estimated Sales: Under $500,000
Number Employees: 1-4
Types of Products Distributed:
   Food Service, Frozen Food, Specialty Foods

60077 Van Eerden Foodservice Co Inc
650 Ionia Ave SW
Grand Rapids, MI 49503
           Fax: 616-475-0990 800-833-7374
                      www.vaneerden.com
Wholesaler/distributor of general line food and related items including: meat, poultry, produce, dairy, frozen, bakery products and supplies, etc. serving the food service industry.
Owner: Harold Van Eerden
Chief Executive Officer: Dan Van Eerden
danv@vaneerden.com
Vice President, Purchasing: Andrew Van Eerden
Year Founded: 1920
Number Employees: 100-249
Other Locations:
   Van Eerden DistributionCo.
   Comstock Park, MIVan Eerden DistributionCo.
Private Brands Carried:
   Comsource
Types of Products Distributed:
   Food Service, Frozen Food, General Line, General Merchandise, Provisions/Meat, Produce, Dairy products & groceries

60078 (HQ)Van Solkema Produce Inc
2630 Prescott St SW
Byron Center, MI 49315   616-878-1508
           Fax: 616-878-1557 800-871-1508
                      www.vansolkemaproduce.com
Wholesaler/distributor of fresh vegetables.
President: Jerry Van Solkema
jerryv@vansolkemaproduce.com
Accounting: Scott Dekock
Sales/Purchasing: Todd Van Solkema
Sales/Food Safety: Adam Harnish
Estimated Sales: $20-50 Million
Number Employees: 20-49
Private Brands Carried:
   Red & White; Bunny Bite; Oh Boy
Types of Products Distributed:
   Produce

60079 Van Solkema Produce Inc
120 Hwy 196
Glenville, GA 30427   912-654-0523
Wholesaler/distributor of fresh vegetables.
President: Jerry Van Solkema
jerryv@vansolkemaproduce.com
Estimated Sales: $20-50 Million
Number Employees: 20-49
Types of Products Distributed:
   Produce

60080 Van Waters & Rogers
2145 Skyland Court
Norcross, GA 30071-2960   770-246-7777
                      Fax: 770-368-9651
Wholesaler/distributor of insecticides
Sales Support Services: Julie Fogg
Types of Products Distributed:
   Frozen Food, General Merchandise, Insecticides

60081 Vanilla Corp Of America LLC
2273 N Penn Rd
Hatfield, PA 19440-1952   215-996-1978
                      Fax: 215-996-9867
Grain and field bean merchant wholesalers
President: Doug Daugherty
vanillacorp@aol.com
Estimated Sales: $500,000-1 Million
Number Employees: 5-9
Type of Packaging: Food Service, Bulk

60082 Vantage Performance Materials
3938 Porett Dr
Gurnee, IL 60031   847-244-3410
           Fax: 847-249-6790 800-432-7187
                      www.lambentcorp.com
Manufacture ingredients for the food industry including emulsifiers, release agents, antifoams and waxes. Products available in pail, drum and bulk quantities.
President & CEO: Richard McEvoy
Chief Financial Officer: Craig Yuen
Chief Strategy Officer: Tiffany Kyllmann
Chief Technology Officer: Allison Yake
SVP, Sales & Marketing: Michael Sabatelli
SVP, Sales & Marketing: Germano Coelho
Chief Human Resources Officer: Ben Topercer
Chief Operating Office: Noel Beavis
Estimated Sales: $50-100 Million
Number Employees: 100-249
Number of Brands: 13
Number of Products: 150
Type of Packaging: Bulk

60083 Vantage USA
4740 S Whipple St
Chicago, IL 60632   773-247-1086
           Fax: 708-401-1565 www.VantageUSA.net
Organic/natural & commodity wholesaler consolidator/supplier and logistics provider. Specializing in natural and private label products planning & development.
Owner: Dan Gash
dan@vantageusa.net
Type of Packaging: Food Service, Private Label, Bulk

60084 Vasinee Food Corporation
1247 Grand Street
Brooklyn, NY 11211   718-349-6911
           Fax: 718-349-7002 800-878-5996
info@vasinee.com vasineefoodcorp.com
Thai and Asian food: bamboo, juices, coconut milk, fruits and vegetables, curry and paste, noodles, preserves, rice, beans, sauces and spices.
Director of Business Development: Valaya Dipongam
Logistics & Orders Coordinator: Daniel Lee
Year Founded: 1978
Estimated Sales: $14.3 Million
Number Employees: 15

Wholesalers & Distributors / A-Z

Type of Packaging: Food Service, Private Label, Bulk

60085 Vaughn Packing Company
P.O.Box 568
Greer, SC 29652-0568   864-877-0926
                         Fax: 864-879-3478
Wholesaler/distributor of frozen foods, fresh beef and pork, canned goods, cheese, seafood, produce, dairy, bakery items, condiments and general merchandise including equipment and fixtures
Owner: John Waldrop
VP: M Vaughn
Plant Manager: J Waldrop
Estimated Sales: $10-20 Million
Number Employees: 20-49
Private Brands Carried:
    Vaughn
Number of Customer Locations: 400
Types of Products Distributed:
    Frozen Food, General Line, General Merchandise, Provisions/Meat, Produce, Seafood, Canned goods, cheese, condiments, etc.

60086 Vaughn-Russell Candy Kitchen
401 Augusta Street
Greenville, SC 29601   864-271-7786
    Fax: 704-484-8326 info@vaughnrussell.com
            www.vaughnrussell.com
Confectionary manufacturer; original makers of "Incredible Edibles™" and "Mint Pecans®."
Owner: Chris Beard
Plant Manager: Ashton Beard
Estimated Sales: 500,000
Number Employees: 4
Type of Packaging: Consumer, Food Service, Bulk
Types of Products Distributed:
    Food Service, General Merchandise, Health Food, Specialty Foods

60087 Vegware
Pierside Pavilion
300 Pacific Coast Hwy. # 110
Huntington Beach, CA 92648   949-543-0422
                              844-610-0915
        us.info@vegware.com www.vegwareus.com
Compostable packaging: hot and cold drink cups, food containers, takeout boxes
Founder: Bob Bond
Private Brands Carried:
    Vegware
Types of Products Distributed:
    Packaging

60088 Vend Food Service
1120 Vend Dr
Watkinsville, GA 30677
                              800-241-4170
Wholesaler/distributor of sandwiches and salads; serving the food service market.
General Manager: Tom Hughes
Team Leader: David Savadge
dsavadge@vendfoodservices.com
Estimated Sales: $20-50 Million
Number Employees: 100-249
Parent Co: Restaurant Enterprises
Types of Products Distributed:
    Food Service, Frozen Food, General Line, Sandwiches & salads, coffee

60089 Vending Nut Co
2222 Montgomery St
Fort Worth, TX 76107-4519   817-737-3071
            Fax: 817-377-1316 800-429-9260
                    www.vendingnutco.com
Nuts wholesaler
President: Johnny Minshew
Estimated Sales: $4 Million
Number Employees: 10-19

60090 Vendors Purchasing Council
438 Pellis Rd # 200
Greensburg, PA 15601-7900   724-838-8977
                         Fax: 724-838-9073
Wholesaler/distributor of groceries; serving the food service market
Director Negotiations: Edward Cunningham
Executive Director: Louise Shilobod
Manager: Edward Cunningham
Estimated Sales: Less Than $500,000
Number Employees: 1-4
Square Footage: 4800

Types of Products Distributed:
    Food Service, Frozen Food, General Line, Groceries

60091 Venezia Brothers
715 S East St
Indianapolis, IN 46225-1317   317-632-5544
            Fax: 317-684-9418 www.nkhurst.com
Wholesaler/distributor of produce; serving the food service market
Owner: Frank Venezia
Estimated Sales: $5-10 Million
Number Employees: 10-19
Types of Products Distributed:
    Food Service, Frozen Food, Produce

60092 Ventura Foods LLC
40 Pointe Dr
Brea, CA 92821   714-257-3700
                              800-421-6257
                      www.venturafoods.com
Produces extensive line of branded and private label products, inlcuding: syrups, mayonnaise, salad dressings, oils, shortenings, and sauces. It also provides contract packaging services for a variety of products sold to retail andfoodservice customers.
President/CEO: Christopher Furman
cfurman@venturafoods.com
Executive VP & CFO: Erika Noonburg-Morgan
Executive VP, Sales & Marketing: John Buckles
Chief Administrative Officer: Andy Euser
Parent Co: CHS Inc
Type of Packaging: Consumer, Food Service, Private Label, Bulk
Types of Products Distributed:
    Oils; Sauces; Syrups; Condiments

60093 Venture Packaging & Distribution
One Cityplace Drive
Suite 200
St Louis, MO 63141   314-997-5959
            Fax: 314-997-1405 888-997-5959
                    www.bunzldistribution.com
Wholesaler/distributor of PET and HDPE containers, fiber drums, filling equipment, metal cans and stretchwrap
Manager: Bob Plata
VP: Steve Kopf
Sales: Wes Parks
Estimated Sales: $5-10 Million
Number Employees: 10-19
Types of Products Distributed:
    Frozen Food, General Merchandise, Packaging equipment & materials

60094 Venus Supply Company
47 Rathbone St
Providence, RI 02908   401-751-3680
                         Fax: 401-331-2870
Wholesaler/distributor of cleaning supplies, canned goods, groceries, candy and general line products; serving the food service market
President: Robert Chicoine
VP: Geary Gagne
Estimated Sales: $2.5-5 Million
Number Employees: 1-4
Number of Customer Locations: 150
Types of Products Distributed:
    Food Service, Frozen Food, General Line, General Merchandise, Cleaning supplies, canned goods, etc.

60095 Verde Farms, LLC
300 Trade Center # 3540
Woburn, MA 01801   617-221-8922
            Fax: 617-221-8923 info@verdefarms.com
                       www.verdefarms.com
Organic, free range, hormone-free and grass-fed beef for retail, wholesale, foodservice and ingredient customers
Co-Founder/Chief Executive Officer: Dana Ehrlich
Vice-President, Marketing: Pete Lewis
Co-Founder/Director of Operations: Pablo Garbarino
Year Founded: 2005
Number of Brands: 1
Type of Packaging: Food Service, Bulk
Types of Products Distributed:
    Provisions/Meat

60096 Veritiv Corp
1000 Abernathy Road NE
Suite 1700, Bldg 400
Atlanta, GA 30328
                              844-837-4848
    contactus@veritivcorp.com www.veritivcorp.com
Wholesaler/distributor of packaging items, facility solutions, print and publishing products.
Chairman & CEO: Mary Laschinger
SVP & Chief Financial Officer: Stephen Smith
SVP/General Counsel/Corporate Secretary: Mark Hianik
Group VP, Publishing & Print Management: John Biscanti
SVP, Supply Chain Operations: Tracy Pearson
SVP, Facility Solutions: Barry Nelson
COO: Salvatore Abbate
Year Founded: 2014
Estimated Sales: $8.4 Billion
Number Employees: 8,900
Types of Products Distributed:
    Food Service, Frozen Food, General Line, General Merchandise, Groceries, baked goods, etc.

60097 Vermont Country Naturals
PO Box 238
Charlotte, VT 05445-0238   802-425-5445
            Fax: 866-528-7091 800-528-7021
            sales@vermontcountrynaturals.com
                www.vermontspecialtyfoods.org
Kosher, wildcrafted maple sugar (powder and granules) and maple syrup
President: Joan Savoy
CEO: Jeffrey Madison
Estimated Sales: $300,000-500,000
Number Employees: 3
Square Footage: 14000
Parent Co: Vermont Country Maple Mixes
Types of Products Distributed:
    Specialty Foods

60098 Vermont Wholesale Foods
P.O.Box 9508
South Burlington, VT 05407-9508 802-862-0350
                         Fax: 802-862-2682
Wholesaler/distributor of specialty foods including nonperishable goods and coffee; serving the food service market
Owner: Dennis Campbell
Sales Manager: D Campbell
Estimated Sales: $3-5 Million
Number Employees: 5-9
Square Footage: 32000
Parent Co: Vermont Wholesale Foods
Number of Customer Locations: 1000
Types of Products Distributed:
    Food Service, Frozen Food, Specialty Foods, Non-perishable foods & coffee

60099 Vern's Cheese
312 W Main St
Chilton, WI 53014-1312   920-849-7717
            Fax: 920-849-7883 info@vernscheese.com
                       www.vernscheese.com
Cheeses
President: Vern Knoespel
info@verncheese.com
Estimated Sales: $20-50 Million
Number Employees: 20-49

60100 Vessel Services Inc
1 Portland Fish Pier
Portland, ME 04101-4601   207-772-5718
            Fax: 207-772-2512 atracy@maine.rr.com
                    www.vesselservicesinc.com
President: Guy Torrey
CEO/General Manager: Alan Tracy
atracy@maine.rr.com
Estimated Sales: $3-5 Million
Number Employees: 5-9

60101 Veteran Foods Sales Co
132 Mushroom Blvd
Rochester, NY 14623-3204   585-272-7090
            Fax: 585-272-9454 www.bgiambrone.com
Wholesaler/distributor of frozen foods; serving the food service market
President: Benedict Giambrone
ben@bgiambrone.com
VP: Joseph Giambrone
Estimated Sales: $20-50 Million
Number Employees: 20-49
Parent Co: B. Giambrone & Company

Wholesalers & Distributors / A-Z

Types of Products Distributed:
Food Service, Frozen Food

60102 VetriTech Laboratories
PO Box 2365
Pasco, WA 99302-2365 509-542-0523
Fax: 509-547-8095 800-564-8964
Wholesaler/distributor and importer of food supplements
Estimated Sales: $2.5-5 Million
Number Employees: 1-4
Types of Products Distributed:
Frozen Food, Health Food, Food supplements

60103 Vicky's Artisan Bakery
500 Alden Rd.
Unit 4
Markham, ON L3R 5H5
Canada
905-944-0940
info@artisanbakerycompany.com
artisanbakerycompany.com
Flatbreads
President: Richard Bedford
richard@artisanbakerycompany.com
Co-Founder: Vicky Min
Types of Products Distributed:
Baked goods

60104 Victel Service Co
924 E Main St # 108
Alhambra, CA 91801-4130 626-300-0877
Fax: 626-289-0180
Wholesaler/distributor of burglar and fire alarms; installation available
Manager: Jeffrey Ma
Estimated Sales: $1-2.5 Million
Number Employees: 1-4
Square Footage: 2400
Types of Products Distributed:
Frozen Food, General Merchandise, Burglar & fire alarms

60105 Victorinox Swiss Army Inc
7 Victoria Dr
Monroe, CT 06468-1664 203-929-6391
Fax: 203-925-2933 800-243-4074
www.victorinox.com
Wholesaler/distributor of knives, cleavers, spatulas, sharpening stones, shears, forks, etc
CEO: Rick Taggart
Estimated Sales: $20-50 Million
Number Employees: 100-249
Types of Products Distributed:
Frozen Food, General Merchandise, Knives, spears, cleavers, etc.

60106 Victors Market Co
11735 Prairie Ave
Hawthorne, CA 90250-2698 310-676-0127
Fax: 310-676-2247 victorsmeats@msn.com
www.victorswholesale.com
Wholesaler/distributor of provisions/meats including hamburger patties, steaks and pork chops, fish, poultry, veal and lamb; serving the food service market
Owner: Victor Penso
VP: Victor Penso
Marketing Director: Ronald Banken
Sales Manager: Ed Quigley
victorsmeats@msn.com
Estimated Sales: $4-6 Million
Number Employees: 20-49
Square Footage: 24000
Number of Customer Locations: 3
Types of Products Distributed:
Food Service, Frozen Food, Provisions/Meat, Seafood

60107 Victory Packaging
3061 W Saner Ave
Dallas, TX 75233-1419 214-337-8881
Fax: 214-333-2415 www.victorypackaging.com
Wholesaler/distributor of corrugated boxes
Manager: Jim Tallas
Contact: Rob Mc Auley
rob.mccauley@victory.com
Estimated Sales: $20-50 Million
Number Employees: 50-99
Types of Products Distributed:
Frozen Food, General Merchandise, Corrugated boxes

60108 Victory Spud Service
1601 S Wolcott Ave
Chicago, IL 60608 312-421-1521
Fax: 312-421-3078
Wholesaler/distributor of potatoes and potato products.
President: Steve Nathan
stevenathan@victoryspudservice.com
Year Founded: 1955
Estimated Sales: $20-50 Million
Number Employees: 20-49
Private Brands Carried:
Jiffy Spud
Types of Products Distributed:
Frozen Food, Produce, Potatoes & potato products

60109 (HQ)Vidalia Sweets Brand
818 Ga Highway 56 West
Lyons, GA 30436 912-565-8881
Fax: 912-565-0199
Fresh and pickled onions, onion relish, barbecue sauce, etc.; wholesaler/distributor of vidalia onions and specialty food products; serving the food service market
President: Jim P Cowart
Estimated Sales: $210000
Number Employees: 1-4
Type of Packaging: Consumer, Food Service
Number of Customer Locations: 5
Types of Products Distributed:
Food Service, Frozen Food, Produce, Specialty Foods, Vidalia onions

60110 Vienna Distributing Company
14725 Detroit Ave # 250
Cleveland, OH 44107-4124 216-228-9494
Fax: 216-228-1912
Wholesaler/distributor of provisions/meats; serving the food service market
Manager: James R Vine
Estimated Sales: $1-2.5 Million
Number Employees: 10-19
Types of Products Distributed:
Food Service, Frozen Food, Provisions/Meat

60111 Viking Trading
2375 John Glenn Dr
Suite 106
Atlanta, GA 30341 770-455-8630
Fax: 770-455-9632
Blue crab, caviar, conch, crab, crawfish, kingfish, lobster meat
President: Juan Vales
Principal: Frank Valdez

60112 Villa Park Orchards Assn
960 3rd St
Fillmore, CA 93015-1120 805-524-0411
Fax: 805-524-4286 888-524-4402
frank@vpoa.net www.vpoa.net
Packinghouse for the processing of Sunkist Growers Inc. citrus fruit.
President/General Manager: Brad Leichtfuss
brad@vpoa.net
Field Manager, Grower Relations-Orange: Mike Leichtfuss
Field Superintendent District 1: Hector Moreno
Field Manager, Grower Relations-Distri: Jim Cleland
Field Manager, Grower Relations-Ventur: Bruce Leichtfuss
Sales & Packing Coordinator: Frank Martinez
Grower Relations/Consultant: Don Clift
Number Employees: 100-249
Type of Packaging: Food Service

60113 Vilore Foods Company
3838 Medical Dr
San Antonio, TX 78229 210-509-9496
Fax: 210-616-9934 877-609-9496
www.vilore.com
Wholesaler/distributor, importer and exporter of Hispanic foods including jalapeno peppers, fruit nectars, hot sauce, chicken bouillon, powdered drinks and nopalitos.
President: Marco Mena
Director of Finance: Walter Chapman
National Sales Director: Andrew Boyer
aboyer@vilore.com
Director, Operations & Logistics: Jose Murillo
Year Founded: 1983
Estimated Sales: $219 Million
Number Employees: 103
Square Footage: 470000
Type of Packaging: Consumer, Food Service, Private Label
Other Locations:
Imperial, CA
Santa Fe Springs, CA
Stafford, TX
San Ramon, CA
Glen Ellyn, IL
Laredo, TXSanta Fe Springs
Types of Products Distributed:
Frozen Food, General Line, Produce, Specialty Foods, Mexican: jalapeno peppers, etc.

60114 Vinalhaven Fishermens Co-op
PO Box 366
Camden, ME 04843-0366 207-236-0092
Fax: 207-236-7733 janetvhcoop@hotmail.com
vinalhavencoop.com
Seafood
Owner: John R Long
Estimated Sales: $1-3 Million
Number Employees: 5-9

60115 Vincent Giordano Prosciutto
2600 Washington Ave
Philadelphia, PA 19146-3834 215-467-6629
Fax: 215-467-6339 www.vgiordano.com
Wholesaler/distributor of roast beef, pastrami and corned beef
Owner: Guy Giordano
Estimated Sales: $20-50 Million
Number Employees: 50-99
Types of Products Distributed:
Frozen Food, Provisions/Meat, Roast beef, pastrami & corned beef

60116 Vincent Piazza Jr & Sons
5736 Heebe St
Harahan, LA 70123 504-734-0012
Fax: 504-734-8752 800-259-5016
packages@piazzaseafood.com
www.piazzaseafood.com
Shrimp; wholesaler/distributor of crab, crawfish, alligator, conch, octopus, clams, lobster, frog legs, scallops, turtle, gumbo, etc
Owner: Vincent Piazza Jr
Sales and Inventory Control: Nicholas Piazza
Contact: Bryan Piazza
bryanpiazza@piazzaseafood.com
Computer Systems and Purchasing: Bryan Piazza
Estimated Sales: $2.5-5 Million
Number Employees: 20-49
Square Footage: 24000
Type of Packaging: Food Service
Types of Products Distributed:
Frozen Food, General Line, Seafood, Specialty Foods, Fresh & frozen crab, alligator, etc.

60117 Vineco International Products
27 Scott Street W
St Catharines, ON L2R 1E1
Canada
905-685-9342
Fax: 905-685-9551
Manufacturer and wholesaler/distributor of wine and beer making kits
President: Rob Van Wely
CFO: Jason Hough
R&D: Sandra Sartor
Quality Control: Sandra Sartor
Marketing: Michael Hind
Estimated Sales: $5-10 Million
Number Employees: 45
Parent Co: Andres Wines
Type of Packaging: Consumer

60118 Vineyard Gate
238 Broadway
Millbrae, CA 94030-2508 650-552-9530
Fax: 650-259-0520 800-580-8588
sales@vineyardgate.com
Wholesaler/distributor of California wines including cabernet, chardonnay, zinfandel, merlot, pinot noir, bordeaux, burgundy, rhone and sparkling
Owner: Alex Bernardo
sales@vinyardgate.com
Estimated Sales: $500,000-$1 Million
Number Employees: 1-4
Types of Products Distributed:
Frozen Food, General Line, California wines

1213

Wholesalers & Distributors / A-Z

60119 Viola's Gourmet Goodies
P.O.Box 351075
Los Angeles, CA 90035 323-731-5277
Fax: 323-731-6898 violasgg@pacbell.net
Gourmet relish, jelly, zinger and rim shot
Owner: Nancy Rowland
violasgg@pacbell.net
Estimated Sales: $.5-1 million
Number Employees: 1-4
Type of Packaging: Bulk

60120 Virginia Wholesale Company
P.O.Box 1807
Bristol, VA 24203-1807 276-669-4181
Fax: 276-669-1160
Wholesaler/distributor of frozen foods, produce, groceries, meats, dairy products, equipment and fixtures, health/beauty aids and general merchandise
Chairman: H Moser
President: Edith Moser
VP: Charles White
Estimated Sales: $20-50 Million
Number Employees: 50-99
Square Footage: 50000
Number of Customer Locations: 350
Types of Products Distributed:
  Frozen Food, General Line, General Merchandise, Provisions/Meat, Produce, Groceries, dairy products, etc.

60121 Visalia Fruit Exchange
500 N Santa Fe St
Visalia, CA 93292-5065 559-635-3000
Fax: 559-734-0947 800-366-8238
vcpg@vcpg.com
A packer of citrus fruits including oranges, grapefruits and limes, Visalia Citrus Packing Group (VCPG) is a licensed commercial shipper of Sunkist Growers, Inc.
President: Randy Veeh
randy@vcpg.com
Sales Representative: Greg Romanazzi
Sales Representative: Kathy Dodge
Number Employees: 5-9
Type of Packaging: Consumer

60122 Visalia Produce Sales
201 W Stroud Ave
Kingsburg, CA 93631-9531 559-897-6652
Fax: 559-897-6650 george@visaliaproduce.com
www.visaliaproduce.com
California fruits and vegetables
Owner: Stan Shamoon
Sales Representative: Stan Shamoon
Sales Representative: Aron Gularte
Sales Representative: George Matoian
Estimated Sales: $1-10 Million
Number Employees: 20-49

60123 Vision Seafood Partners
41 Summer Street
Kingston, MA 02364-1418 781-585-2000
Fax: 773-561-0139
Seafood

60124 Vista Food Exchange
1700 W. 40 Hwy
Suite 206
Blue Springs, MO 64015 816-228-7090
Fax: 816-228-9214 vistafood.com
Wholesaler/distributor and exporter of meat, meat products, seafood, poultry, frozen foods and dairy/deli items; importer of lamb, mutton and beef; serving the food service and retail markets
Office Manager: D Martin
Executive Vice President: Phil Stephens
Sales/Transportation: J Dickey
Estimated Sales: $2.5-5 Million
Number Employees: 1-4
Parent Co: Vista Food Exchange
Type of Packaging: Consumer, Food Service, Bulk
Types of Products Distributed:
  Food Service, General Line, Provisions/Meat, Seafood, Dairy products, poultry, etc.

60125 Vista Food Exchange Inc.
B101 Center Arcade
Hunts Point Co-op Market
Bronx, NY 10474 718-542-4401
Fax: 718-542-0042 vlp27@aol.com
www.vistafood.com
Exporter and wholesaler/distributor of fresh and frozen poultry, beef, pork and fish products; serving the food service market
President: Vincent Pacifico
Controller: Alan Butterfass
VP: Phil Stephens
Estimated Sales: $10-20 Million
Number Employees: 10-19
Type of Packaging: Food Service
Number of Customer Locations: 1000
Types of Products Distributed:
  Food Service, Provisions/Meat, Seafood

60126 (HQ)Vistar
12650 E Arapahoe Rd
Centennial, CO 80112
800-880-9900
customercare@pfgc.com www.vistar.com
Distributor of snacks and specialty foods.
President/Performance Food Group: Dave Flitman
President & CEO/Vistar Specialty: Pat Hagerty
phagerty@pfgc.com
Year Founded: 2002
Estimated Sales: $100-500 Million
Number Employees: 1000-4999
Parent Co: Performance Food Group

60127 Vistar Mid-Atlantic
1109 Commerce Blvd
Swedesboro, NJ 08085-1763 856-294-0500
www.vistar.com
Distributor of snacks and specialty foods.

60128 Vistar Northwest
18201 NE Portal Way
Suite 106
Portland, OR 9723053879 503-289-6767
www.vistar.com
Distributor of snacks and specialty foods.
Parent Co: Performance Food Group
Number of Customer Locations: 600
Types of Products Distributed:
  Frozen Food, General Line, General Merchandise, Beverages, paper products, etc.

60129 Vita Coco
38 W 21st St
Suite 404
New York, NY 10010-6922
Fax: 800-407-0439 877-848-2262
info@vitacoco.com www.vitacoco.com
Coconut drink
Co-Founder: Michael Kirban
Co-Founder: Ira Liran
Contact: Dave Agan
dagan@vitacoco.com
Type of Packaging: Food Service

60130 Vitakem Neutraceutical Inc
811 West Jericho Turnpike
Smithtown, NY 11787 855-837-0430
www.vitakem.com
Vitamins and supplements
President/CEO: Bret Hoyt Sr
Contact: Aaron Berkman
aaron@vitakem.com

60131 Vital 18
P.O.Box 1205
Middleburg, FL 32050 904-282-9871
Fax: 904-282-9249 800-633-7692
Wholesaler/distributor of liquefied spirulina concentrate
President: Patricia Brown
CEO: Tracy Brown
CFO: C Brown
Vice President: Tracey Brown
Sales Director: Paula Brittain
Operations Manager: Bonnie Key
Plant Manager: Linda Lane
Estimated Sales: $5-10 Million
Number Employees: 1-4
Square Footage: 32000
Private Brands Carried:
  VITAL-18
Types of Products Distributed:
  Health Food, Spirulina concentrate

60132 Vital Choice
P.O. Box 4121
Bellingham, WA 98227
800-608-4825
www.vitalchoice.com
Wild fish, shellfish, canned fish, meats, omega-3s, supplements, and organic foods
Year Founded: 2001

60133 Vitamin Power
75 Commerce Dr
Hauppauge, NY 11788-3902 631-676-5790
Fax: 516-378-0919 800-645-6567
ContactUs@VitaminPower.com
Wholesaler/distributor of nutritional supplements, vitamins, minerals, herbs, herbal teas and diet aids
Chairman: Ed Friedlander
President: David Friedlander
friedlanderdavid@vitaminpower.com
Estimated Sales: $5-10 Million
Number Employees: 5-9
Square Footage: 80000
Parent Co: Vitamin Power
Types of Products Distributed:
  Frozen Food, Health Food, Vitamins, nutritional supplements, etc.

60134 (HQ)Vitusa Products Inc
343 Snyder Ave # 1
Berkeley Heights, NJ 07922-1527 908-665-2900
Fax: 908-665-2662 www.vitusaproducts.com
Manufacturer of food and industrial grade ingredients such as ammonium bicarbonate, citric acid, glycerine, calcium phosphates, food grade phosphates, potassium sorbate, propylene glycol and others.
Owner: David Grande
dgrande@vitusaproducts.com
Number Employees: 20-49
Other Locations:
  Vitusa Products
  Charlotte, NCVitusa Products
Types of Products Distributed:
  Frozen Food, General Line, Food grade ingredients

60135 Vity Meat & Provisions Company
1418 N 27th Avenue
Phoenix, AZ 85009-3603 602-269-7768
Fax: 602-269-0044
Meats
President: Michael Brown
VP Finance: Gary Rasmussen
Estimated Sales: $.5-1 million
Number Employees: 1-4

60136 Viva Tierra
601 S 2nd St
Mt Vernon, WA 98273 360-855-0560
organic@vivatierra.com
www.vivatierra.com
Organic produce including apples, pears, peaches, and onions
President/CEO: Luis Acuna
EVP/CFO: Steve Mackey
Sales Manager: Matt Roberts
Organic Integrity & Logistics: Addie Pobst
Types of Products Distributed:
  Produce

60137 Vivion Inc
929 Bransten Rd
San Carlos, CA 94070-4073 650-595-3600
Fax: 650-595-2094 800-479-0997
www.vivioninc.com
Broker and distributor of food ingredients.
Founder: Edward Poleselli
President: Michael Poleselli
mpoleselli@vivioninc.com
General Manager: Patrick Rhodes
Estimated Sales: $28 Million
Number Employees: 10-19
Other Locations:
  Branch/Warehouse
  Vernon, CA
  Branch/
  Portland, OR
  Branch
  Ogden, UT
  Branch
  Phoenix/Warehouse, AZ
  Warehouse
  Salt Lake City, UT
  Warehouse
  San Carlos, CA
  Branch/WarehousePortland
Types of Products Distributed:
  Health Food, Ingredients

60138 Vivitar Security Systems
2441 W 205th St Ste C105
Torrance, CA 90501 310-212-7776
Fax: 310-212-0723 800-822-9111

Wholesaler/distributor of burglar and fire alarms and security equipment; also, installation available
Owner: Gary Best
gary.best@comcast.net
VP Sales: William Nichols
Estimated Sales: $500,000-$1 Million
Number Employees: 20-49
Types of Products Distributed:
  Frozen Food, General Merchandise, Fire & burglar alarms; security systems

60139 Vixen Kitchen

Santa Cruz, CA 707-223-5627
info@vixenkitchen.co
www.vixenkitchen.co
Organic, natural, vegan- and paleo-friendly gelato in various flavors
Founder/Chief Executive Officer: Sundara Clark
Number of Brands: 1
Number of Products: 6
Type of Packaging: Consumer, Private Label
Private Brands Carried:
  Vixen Kitchen
Types of Products Distributed:
  Frozen Food

60140 Vogel

Stamford Industrial Park
Stamford, CT 06902 203-973-0740
Fax: 203-973-0068
Wholesaler/distributor and exporter of advertising specialties; hot stamping services available
Owner/President: Peter Blais
Number Employees: 5-9
Square Footage: 4800
Types of Products Distributed:
  Frozen Food, General Merchandise, Decorations & hot stamping fabrications

60141 Vollwerth & Baroni Companies

PO Box 239
Hancock, MI 49930-0239 906-482-1550
Fax: 906-482-0842 800-562-7620
topdog@vollwerth.com www.vollwerth.com
Sausage and meat products; wholesaler/distributor of hotel and restaurant supplies; serving the food service market
President: Robert Vollwerth
Vice President/General Manager: Jim Schaaf
Secretary/Treasurer: Mary Ann Berryman
Sales Representative: Richard Vollwerth
Contact: Mary Berryman
berryman@vollwerth.com
Packaging Manager: Don Hiltunen
Production Manager: Adam Manderfield
Estimated Sales: $3.5 Million
Number Employees: 35
Square Footage: 80000
Types of Products Distributed:
  Food Service, General Merchandise, Hotel & restaurant supplies

60142 Volpe, Son & Kemelhar

4000 Orange Avenue
Cleveland, OH 44115-3566 216-431-3112
Fax: 216-431-9877
Wholesaler/distributor of onions and potatoes; serving the food service market
President: Paul Volpe
Estimated Sales: $2.5-5 Million
Number Employees: 1-4
Private Brands Carried:
  Keegan Idaho
Types of Products Distributed:
  Food Service, Frozen Food, Produce, Onions & potatoes

60143 Volumetric Technologies

401 Cannon Industrial Blvd #1
Cannon Falls, MN 55009 507-263-0034
www.volumetrictechnologies.com
Filling and packaging equipment including conveyors, cup machines, piston fillers/depositors, complete turn key filling lines, dispensing nozzles and net weight filling lines. Applications include meats, soups, dipstaco/burrito/tamale filling, chili, pizzas, bakery items, dairy products, condiments/sauces, precooked dinners, deli products and creamed meats.
President: Timothy Piper
VP: Keith Piper
VP/Secretary: Bruce Piper
Number Employees: 6
Type of Packaging: Bulk

60144 Voorhees Rubber Mfg Co

6846 Basket Switch Rd
Newark, MD 21841-2214 410-632-1582
Fax: 410-632-1522 info@voorheesrubber.com
www.voorheesrubber.com
Manufacturer, exporter and wholesaler/distributor of rubber candy molds
President: Richard Jackson
info@voorheesrubber.com
Vice President: Teresa Jackson
Estimated Sales: Below $5 Million
Number Employees: 5-9
Private Brands Carried:
  Vorhees
Types of Products Distributed:
  Frozen Food, General Merchandise, Rubber candy molds

60145 Voss Equipment Inc

15241 Commercial Ave
Harvey, IL 60426-2396 815-741-0404
Fax: 708-596-6791 866-867-0659
www.vossequipment.com
Wholesaler/distributor of material handling equipment
Owner: Pete Voss Sr
CFO: Tom Mateja
tmateja@vossequipment.com
Estimated Sales: $10-20 Million
Number Employees: 50-99
Private Brands Carried:
  Yale; Cushman; Trackmobile
Types of Products Distributed:
  Frozen Food, General Merchandise, Material handling equipment

60146 Voyageur Trading Division

PO Box 428
Bemidji, MN 56619-0428 763-595-0051
Fax: 763-595-0078
Wholesaler/distributor and exporter of bulk and packaged wild rice
General Manager: Dwight Erickson
Estimated Sales: $10-20 Million
Number Employees: 10-19
Square Footage: 40000
Parent Co: Indian Harvest Specialty Foods
Type of Packaging: Bulk
Private Brands Carried:
  Voyageur; Minnesota Select
Types of Products Distributed:
  Frozen Food, Specialty Foods, Wild rice

60147 Vtopian Artisan Cheeses

Portland, OR
contact@vtopiancheeses.com
www.vtopiancheeses.com
Artisan cashew cheeses including peppercorn brie, port cheddar, aged white cheddar, sharp cheddar, and camembert
Founder, Co-Owner: Imber Lingard
Types of Products Distributed:
  General Line

60148 W & B Distributing Co

219 Lafayette Dr
Syosset, NY 11791-3939 516-921-7070
Fax: 516-921-7358
Wholesaler/distributor of specialty food and snacks
President: Warren Brown
Estimated Sales: $5-10 Million
Number Employees: 10-19
Types of Products Distributed:
  Frozen Food, Specialty Foods, Snack foods

60149 W A DeHart Inc

1130 Old Route 15
New Columbia, PA 17856
Fax: 570-568-1491 800-443-9765
wadehartinc.com
Wholesaler/distributor of confectionery products, paper and vending and institutional food; serving the food service market.
President & Owner: Chris Trate
Customer Relations: Patty Wilver
pattywilver@wadehartinc.com
Estimated Sales: $20-50 Million
Number Employees: 50-99
Types of Products Distributed:
  Food Service, Frozen Food, General Line, General Merchandise, Specialty Foods, Confectionery

60150 W B Stockton & Co Inc

739 Dexter Rd
Roanoke, VA 24019-4332 540-904-6003
Fax: 540-344-0450 800-476-6003
Wholesaler/distributor of bar code printers, product labels and pricing and labeling equipment; serving supermarket chains and industrial markets
Owner: Wayne Owens Sr
wbstocktonco@aol.com
Secretary: Joyce Owens
VP: Lisa Owens
Estimated Sales: Less Than $500,000
Number Employees: 1-4
Types of Products Distributed:
  Frozen Food, General Merchandise, Pricing & labeling equipment

60151 W D Class & Son

7460 Conowingo Ave
Jessup, MD 20794-9361 301-621-1235
Fax: 410-799-7349 www.wdclass.com
Wholesaler/distributor of produce
Sales: Angelo DeAnna
Contact: Edie Mc Greevey
emcgreevey@wdclass.com
Estimated Sales: $10-20 Million
Number Employees: 100-249
Types of Products Distributed:
  Produce

60152 W H Wildman Company

25956 U.S. Route 33
P.O.Box 42
New Hampshire, OH 45870 419-568-7531
Fax: 419-568-7531 scott@wildmanspice.com
www.wildmanspice.com
Wholesale packager; general groceries
Owner: Scott Gray
Estimated Sales: Less than $300,000
Number Employees: 1-4
Type of Packaging: Consumer, Food Service, Private Label, Bulk
Types of Products Distributed:
  Frozen Food

60153 W L Petrey Wholesale CoInc

3150 Tine Ave
Montgomery, AL 36108-2316 334-265-0964
Fax: 334-265-0961 mail@petrey.com
www.petrey.com
Wholesaler of brand named goods
Owner: Bill Jackson
bjackson@petrey.com
Number Employees: 10-19

60154 W. Braun Company

191 N Wacker Dr Ste 3700
Chicago, IL 60606 312-569-1000
Fax: 312-346-6500
Wholesaler/distributor of plastic and glass packaging
VP Sales: Craig Sawicki
Estimated Sales: $2.5-5 Million
Number Employees: 5-9
Private Brands Carried:
  Componetics; Braunlok
Types of Products Distributed:
  Frozen Food, General Merchandise, Plastic & glass packaging

60155 W. Braun Packaging Canada

40 Vogell Road
Unit 15
Richmond Hill, ON L4B 3N4
Canada 416-213-7474
Fax: 416-213-7469
Wholesaler/distributor of plastic and glass containers including pumps and jars
General Manager: Bob Woodger
Number Employees: 10-19
Square Footage: 20000
Parent Co: Kranson Industries
Types of Products Distributed:
  Frozen Food, General Merchandise, Containers

60156 W.A. Beans & Sons

229 Bomarc Road
Bangor, ME 04401 207-947-0364
Fax: 207-990-4211 800-649-1958
sales@beansmeats.com www.beansmeats.com
Processor and wholesaler of meats, including smoked poultry, gourmet sausages, pork chops, bacon, fish, and hams.

Wholesalers & Distributors / A-Z

Estimated Sales: Under $5 Million
Number Employees: 20-49
Square Footage: 16
Type of Packaging: Consumer, Food Service, Private Label, Bulk

60157 W.A. Tayloe Company
PO Box 59226
Dallas, TX 75229-1226   972-484-7260
Fax: 214-357-4576
Wholesaler/distributor of material handling equipment
President: Wilson Tayloe
Estimated Sales: $10-20 Million
Number Employees: 20-49
Private Brands Carried:
  Inca; Rubbermaid; Hamilton
Types of Products Distributed:
  Frozen Food, General Merchandise, Material handling equipment

60158 W.F. Alber Inc.
2571 Filbert Street
San Francisco, CA 94133   415-515-5700
www.alberseafoods.com
Wholesaler/distributor of seafood; specializing in live shellfish
Owner: Don Alber
Estimated Sales: $2.5-5 Million
Number Employees: 1-4
Square Footage: 32000
Parent Co: Alber Seafoods
Number of Customer Locations: 103
Types of Products Distributed:
  Frozen Food, Seafood

60159 W.F. Morgan & Sons
PO Box 42
Weems, VA 22576-0042   804-438-5154
Fax: 804-435-8164
Wholesaler/distributor of seafood
President: Bill Morgan
Estimated Sales: $2.5-5 Million
Number Employees: 5-9
Types of Products Distributed:
  Frozen Food, Seafood

60160 W.F. Ware Company
125 4th Street
P.O. Box 144
Trenton, KY 42286   270-466-5628
Fax: 270-466-5629 bgroves@mchsi.com
866-600-4267
www.wfware.com/
Wholesaler/distributor of popcorn, corn, wheat and soy and soy products
President & General Manager: Barry Groves
Secretary/Treasurer: L Groves
VP: Keith Groves
Estimated Sales: $1-2.5 Million
Number Employees: 10-19
Types of Products Distributed:
  Frozen Food, General Line, Popcorn, corn, wheat, etc.

60161 W.G. White & Company
2131 Us Highway 601 N
Mocksville, NC 27028   336-492-2111
866-600-4267
whiteham@yadtel.net
Wholesaler/distributor of general line items and meat products
President: Doug White
Estimated Sales: $.5-1 million
Number Employees: 1-4
Types of Products Distributed:
  Frozen Food, General Line, Provisions/Meat

60162 W.J. Canaan Inc.
156 Valley St
East Providence, RI 02914-4424   401-435-9222
Fax: 401-435-9555
Wholesaler/distributor of produce
President: Rick Narcessian
Estimated Sales: $5-10 Million
Number Employees: 6
Types of Products Distributed:
  Frozen Food, Produce

60163 W.J. Stearns & Sons/Mountain Dairy
50 Stearns Road
Storrs Mansfield, CT 06268-2701   860-423-9289
Fax: 860-423-3486 www.mountaindairy.com
Processor and wholesaler/distributor of dairy products including cream and milk
President: W Stearns
Vice President: James Stearns
Estimated Sales: $3 Million
Number Employees: 35
Type of Packaging: Consumer, Private Label
Types of Products Distributed:
  Frozen Food, General Line, Dairy products

60164 W.L. Petrey Wholesale Inc.
10345 Petrey Hwy
Luverne, AL 36049   334-230-5674
Fax: 334-335-2422 mail@petrey.com
www.petrey.com
Wholesaler/distributor of frozen food, general merchandise, general line products, provisions/meats and seafood
President: Bill Jackson
CEO: James Jackson
Contact: Kevin Argo
kargo@petrey.com
Number Employees: 500-999
Number of Customer Locations: 1000
Types of Products Distributed:
  Frozen Food, General Line, General Merchandise, Provisions/Meat, Seafood, Groceries

60165 W.O. Sasser
135 Johnny Mercer Blvd
Savannah, GA 31410-2118   912-897-1154
Fax: 912-897-0331
Seafood
Owner: William Sasser
Estimated Sales: $.5-1 million
Number Employees: 5-9

60166 W.R. Hackett
99 North West Road
PO Box 1042
Springfield, OH 45501-1042   937-323-7541
Fax: 937-323-7544   800-922-7541
sales@wrhackett.com www.wrhackett.com
Wholesaler/distributor of produce; serving the food service market
President: W Hackett
VP: S Hackett
VP: W Hackett
Estimated Sales: $10-20 Million
Number Employees: 20-49
Private Brands Carried:
  Simplot; Heinz
Types of Products Distributed:
  Food Service, Produce

60167 W.R. McRae Company Limited
549 Montreal Street
Kingston, ON K7K 3J1
Canada   613-544-6611
Fax: 613-544-6967
Wholesaler/distributor of general line product and confectionary goods; rack jobber services available
President: D Hartnett
General Manager: Gary McLoy
Number Employees: 20-49
Number of Customer Locations: 500
Types of Products Distributed:
  Frozen Food, General Line, Rack Jobbers, Confectionary goods

60168 W.R. Merry Seafood Company
636 Stanford Avenue
Los Angeles, CA 90021-1006   213-623-2306
Wholesaler/distributor of seafood; serving the food service market
President: William Merry
Types of Products Distributed:
  Food Service, Frozen Food, Seafood

60169 W.R. Nykorchuck & Company
PO Box 677
Albany, NY 12201-0677   518-446-9582
Fax: 518-446-0180
Wholesaler/distributor of groceries, canned fruits, juices and dry goods; serving the food service market
President: William Nykorchuck
Sales Director: William Nykorchuck
Operations Manager: Arnold Hoch
Estimated Sales: $10-20 Million
Number Employees: 5
Square Footage: 60000
Private Brands Carried:
  Denice; Labella; Wisconsin Supreme; Iowa Best
Types of Products Distributed:
  Food Service, General Line, Canned fruits, vegetables, juices, etc.

60170 W.R. Pittman & Sons
1043 Bewdley Road
Lancaster, VA 22503-3302   804-462-7955
Wholesaler/distributor of oysters; serving the food service market
President: Ed Pittman
Number Employees: 20-49
Types of Products Distributed:
  Food Service, Frozen Food, Seafood, Oysters

60171 W.R. Whitaker & Company
2339 Pine Hill Rd
Cookeville, TN 38506-7503   931-537-6514
Fax: 931-537-9330
Wholesaler/distributor of beer, soda and water
Owner: Jerri Payne
Estimated Sales: $5-10 Million
Number Employees: 1-4
Types of Products Distributed:
  Frozen Food, General Line, Beer, soda & water

60172 W.S. Lee & Sons
P.O.Box 508
Hollidayburg, PA 16648-508
Fax: 814-696-9350
Wholesaler/distributor of frozen baked goods, general merchandise, general line products, produce, meats, etc.; serving the food service market
President: Robert Donaldson
Sales Manager: J Plummer
VP/Operations Manager: John Bawzuah
Estimated Sales: $20-50 Million
Number Employees: 250-499
Private Brands Carried:
  Lee
Number of Customer Locations: 500
Types of Products Distributed:
  Food Service, Frozen Food, General Line, General Merchandise, Provisions/Meat, Produce, Seafood, Specialty Foods, Frozen baked goods

60173 W.Y. International
2000 S. Garfield Ave.
Los Angeles, CA 90040   323-726-8733
Fax: 323-726-9409 info@wyintl.com
www.wyintl.com
Asian sauces, canned goods, grains, and snacks; European and Californian wine and oils; machinery & tools.
President: David N. Wong
Vice President: Henry P. Wong
Year Founded: 1982
Estimated Sales: $2-5 Million
Number Employees: 2-10
Types of Products Distributed:
  Ethnic

60174 WACO Beef & Pork Processors
523 Precision Dr
Waco, TX 76710-6972   254-772-4669
Fax: 254-772-4579 www.holysmokedsausage.com
Fresh portion controlled beef, chicken and pork including sausage, chorizo and bratwurst; importer of beef skirts; wholesaler/distributor of meat and general merchandise; serving the food service market
Manager: Sara Jones
Estimated Sales: $2.2 Million
Number Employees: 5-9
Square Footage: 28000
Type of Packaging: Food Service
Types of Products Distributed:
  Food Service, General Merchandise, Provisions/Meat

60175 WACO Filtering
11701 NW 100th Rd # 1
Suite 1
Medley, FL 33178-1023   305-887-9257
Fax: 305-751-6465
Wholesaler/distributor of water filters and filters for juice processing
President: Jeff Rose
Sales Manager: Dan Viera
Sales Manager: Bob Sheppard
Sales Manager: Larry Barnes
Number Employees: 10-19
Square Footage: 240000
Private Brands Carried:
  Electro-Flo; Air Care

Wholesalers & Distributors / A-Z

60176 WATTS Equipment Co
17547 Comconex Rd
Manteca, CA 95336-8105   209-825-1700
Fax: 209-825-1511 ckoenig@wattsequipment.com
www.wattsequipment.com
Wholesaler/distributor of forklifts
President: V Brock Watts
Manager: Everett Cardenas
ecardenas@wattsequipment.com
Estimated Sales: $10-20 Million
Number Employees: 50-99
Private Brands Carried:
 Toyota; Crown
Types of Products Distributed:
 Frozen Food, General Merchandise, Forklifts

60177 WESCO
1328 S John B Dennis Hwy
Kingsport, TN 37660   423-247-6195
Fax: 423-247-6215 info@wesco.com
www.wesco.com
Wholesaler/distributor of electrical supplies, lighting fixtures, fluorescent lamps, etc
Manager: Mike Harr
Contact: Garry Carrier
gcarrier@wesco.com
Estimated Sales: $2.5-5 Million
Number Employees: 10-19
Parent Co: WESCO Distribution
Types of Products Distributed:
 Frozen Food, General Merchandise, Electrical supplies, lighting, etc.

60178 WESCO
7643 Alabama 13
Bear Creek, AL 35543   205-486-9511
Fax: 205-486-9514 info@wesco.com
www.wesco.com
Wholesaler/distributor of electrical supplies, lighting fixtures, fluorescent lamps, etc
Branch Administrative Manager: Donna Beasley
Estimated Sales: $1-3 Million
Number Employees: 5-9
Parent Co: WESCO Distribution
Number of Customer Locations: 50
Types of Products Distributed:
 Frozen Food, General Merchandise, Electrical supplies, lighting, etc.

60179 WESCO Distribution Inc
724 Pine Ave
Albany, GA 31701-2423   229-432-1285
Fax: 229-432-0299 800-342-6757
info@wesco.com www.wesco.com
Wholesaler/distributor of electrical supplies, lighting fixtures, fluorescent lamps, etc
Manager: Craig Smith
csmith@wesco.com
Estimated Sales: $5-10 Million
Number Employees: 5-9
Parent Co: WESCO Distribution
Number of Customer Locations: 2000
Types of Products Distributed:
 Frozen Food, General Merchandise, Electrical supplies, lighting, etc.

60180 WESCO Distribution Inc
255 Jordan Rd
Tifton, GA 31794-8329   229-386-8919
Fax: 229-388-8445 info@wesco.com
www.wesco.com
Wholesaler/distributor of electrical supplies, lighting fixtures, fluorescent lamps, etc
Manager: Kurt Fries
kfries@wesco.com
Estimated Sales: $1-3 Million
Number Employees: 10-19
Number of Brands: 1
Number of Products: 100
Parent Co: WESCO Distribution
Number of Customer Locations: 75
Types of Products Distributed:
 Frozen Food, General Merchandise, Electrical supplies, lighting, etc.

60181 WG Thompson & Sons
2 Hyland Dr.
Blenheim, ON N0P 1A0
Canada   519-676-5411
Fax: 519-676-3185 800-265-5225
Agricultural products including soybeans, edible beans, and commercial grains to domestic and export markets.
President: Wes Thompson
Estimated Sales: $100 Million
Number Employees: 350
Type of Packaging: Consumer, Food Service, Private Label, Bulk
Types of Products Distributed:
 Food Service, General Line, General Merchandise, Produce, Beans, grains, etc.

60182 WK Eckerd & Sons
107 Speedy Tostensen Blvd
Brunswick, GA 31520-3149   912-265-0332
Fax: 912-261-8460 eckerd@thebest.net
Seafood
President: William Eckerd
Owner: Bill Eckerd
Estimated Sales: Below $5 Million
Number Employees: 1-4
Types of Products Distributed:
 Seafood

60183 WMF/USA
85 Price Parkway
Farmingdale, NY 11735-1305   704-882-3898
Fax: 631-694-0820 800-999-6347
consumer@WMFAmericas.com
Wholesaler/distributor of flatware, hollowware, cookware, china and crystal
President: Stefan Nisi
VP Sales and Marketing: Peter Braley
National Sales Manager: Emma Popolow
Contact: Markus Glueck
markus.glueck@wmf-usa.com
Parent Co: WMF/AG
Private Brands Carried:
 WMF; Hutschenreuther; Spiegelau; ALFI
Types of Products Distributed:
 Frozen Food, General Merchandise, Flatware, hollowware, cookware, etc.

60184 Wabash Foodservice Inc
1075 E Ramsey Rd
Vincennes, IN 47591   812-882-6066
Fax: 812-882-8371 800-742-9263
info@wabashfoodservice.com
www.wabashfoodservice.com
Wholesaler/distributor of groceries, meats, candy, produce, dairy products, frozen foods and baked goods; serving the food service market.
President/Chief Executive Officer: Jayne Young
General Manager: Joe Gish
Chief Financial Officer: Jeff Mattingly
Customer Service Manager: Susan Peno
Director, Operations: Dave Bauer
Year Founded: 1950
Estimated Sales: $34 Million
Number Employees: 100-249
Square Footage: 130000
Number of Customer Locations: 5000
Types of Products Distributed:
 Food Service, Frozen Food, General Line, Provisions/Meat, Produce, Candy, etc.

60185 Wabash Heritage Mfg LLC
2525 N 6th St
Vincennes, IN 47591-2405   812-886-0147
Fax: 812-895-0064 info@knoxcountyarc.com
www.knoxcountyarc.com
Spices, powders
President: Michael Carney
Vice President: Bobby Harbison
bharbison@knoxcountyarc.com
Research & Development: John TRUE
Quality Control: John TRUE
Plant Manager: Leroy Douffron
Number Employees: 20-49
Number of Brands: 1
Number of Products: 90
Square Footage: 480000
Type of Packaging: Consumer, Food Service, Private Label, Bulk

60186 Wabash Seafood Co
2249 W Hubbard St
Chicago, IL 60612-1613   312-733-5070
Fax: 312-733-2798 john@wabashseafood.net
www.wabashseafood.net
Seafood
President: John Rebello
john@wabashseafood.net
Estimated Sales: $10-20 Million
Number Employees: 20-49

60187 Waco Meat Service
PO Box 7249
Waco, TX 76714-7249   254-772-5644
Fax: 254-772-5151
Wholesaler/distributor of meats and seafood
Owner: Dana Harrell
Sales Manager: Andy Anderson
Estimated Sales: $10-20 Million
Number Employees: 20-49
Number of Customer Locations: 250
Types of Products Distributed:
 Frozen Food, Provisions/Meat, Seafood

60188 Wadden Systems
5674 Sherbrooke Street W
Montreal, QC H4A 1W7
Canada   514-481-1189
Fax: 514-488-2567 800-392-3336
www.wadden.ca
Exporter and wholesaler/distributor of general merchandise including soft serve makers and flavoring systems; serving the food service market
President: Hugh Kane
Number Employees: 20-49
Types of Products Distributed:
 Food Service, Frozen Food, General Merchandise, Soft serve makers & flavoring systems

60189 Wade's Dairy Inc
1316 Barnum Ave
Bridgeport, CT 06610-2825   203-696-0202
Fax: 203-696-6121 800-247-9233
dwade@wadesdairy.com www.wadesdairy.com
Wholesaler/distributor of orange juice, cheese, cream, cakes, pastas, sorbets, ice cream, frozen yogurt, milk, soups, yogurt and eggs; serving the food service market
President: Doug Wade
CEO: Douglas Wade Jr
CFO: Susan Warner
COO: David Wade
Estimated Sales: $9.5 Million
Number Employees: 20-49
Number of Products: 900
Square Footage: 38400
Type of Packaging: Consumer, Food Service
Private Brands Carried:
 Garelick; Crowley; Friendship; Colombo; Dannon; Cabot; Kettle Cuisine; David's Cookies; Country Muffins
Number of Customer Locations: 780
Types of Products Distributed:
 Food Service, Frozen Food, Juice, cheese, cream, cakes, etc.

60190 Wagner Gourmet Foods
10618 Summit St
Lenexa, KS 66215   913-469-5411
Fax: 913-469-1367
customerservice@wagner-gourmet.com
www.hicks-ashby.com
Spices, preserves, jams, ice cream sauces, seasoned rice and gift pack assortments; importer of tea; wholesaler/distributor of snack foods including cookies
President: James T Baldwin
Estimated Sales: $3-5 Million
Number Employees: 5-9
Square Footage: 480000
Parent Co: Wagner Gourmet Foods
Type of Packaging: Consumer, Private Label
Private Brands Carried:
 Callard & Bowser; Walkers; Bahlsen; Demitasse; New York Bagel Chips
Types of Products Distributed:
 General Line, Snack foods: cookies

60191 Wai Sang Meat
944 Avila St
Los Angeles, CA 90012-2905   213-628-3551
Wholesaler/distributor of pork and beef
Owner: Ken Jung
Estimated Sales: $2.5-5 Million
Number Employees: 1-4
Types of Products Distributed:
 Frozen Food, Provisions/Meat

Wholesalers & Distributors / A-Z

60192 Wainani Kai Seafood
2126 Eluwene St
Suite A
Honolulu, HI 96819   808-847-7435
    Fax: 808-841-7536 lpang00@yahoo.com
Seafood
President: Lance Pang
lpang00@yahoo.com
Estimated Sales: $3-5 Million
Number Employees: 5-9

60193 Wakefern Food Corp
5000 Riverside Dr
Keasbey, NJ 08832-1209   908-527-3300
    www2.wakefern.com
Wholesaler/distributor of frozen food, general line items, general merchandise, produce and meats.
President & Chief Operating Officer: Joseph Sheridan
Chairman & Chief Executive Officer: Joseph Colalillo
joseph.colalillo@wakefern.com
Chief Financial Officer: Douglas Wille
Year Founded: 1946
Estimated Sales: $16.3 Billion
Number Employees: 70,000
Private Brands Carried:
    Crown Top; Elizabeth York; Farm Flavor
Number of Customer Locations: 180
Types of Products Distributed:
    Frozen Food, General Line, General Merchandise, Provisions/Meat, Produce, Rack Jobbers

60194 Wakefield Sales Inc
6881 Lock Haven Dr
Lockport, NY 14094-6183   716-478-0555
    Fax: 716-633-1592 800-265-9063
Wholesaler/distributor of material handling equipment including forklifts, conveyors, hoists, etc.; also, parts and service available
VP/Sales Manager: Peter Hey
Estimated Sales: $1-2.5 Million
Number Employees: 5-9
Types of Products Distributed:
    Frozen Food, General Merchandise, Material handling equipment

60195 Waken Meat Co
1015 Boulevard SE
Atlanta, GA 30312-3809   404-627-3537
    Fax: 404-624-3191
Beef, pork, chicken, frozen seafood
President: Charles Waken
Estimated Sales: $300,000-500,000
Number Employees: 5-9

60196 Waleski Produce
3301 S Galloway St Ste 89
Philadelphia, PA 19148   215-336-1570
    Fax: 215-336-2230
Wholesaler/distributor of produce
Owner: John Waleski
Estimated Sales: $1-2.5 Million
Number Employees: 1-4
Types of Products Distributed:
    Frozen Food, Produce

60197 Walker Hatchery
1275 W Main St
Greenwood, IN 46142-1927   317-881-4754
    Fax: 317-881-2113
Wholesaler/distributor of eggs; serving the food service market
Owner: William Walker
b6walker36@aol.com
Estimated Sales: $5-10 Million
Number Employees: 1-4
Types of Products Distributed:
    Food Service, General Line, Eggs

60198 Walker Meats
821 Tyus Carrollton Rd
Carrollton, GA 30117-9609   770-834-8171
    Fax: 770-834-2208 800-741-3601
    info@walkermeats.com www.walkermeats.com
Beef, pork, poultry, produce, seafood
President: Bill Walker
bill@walkermeats.com
Estimated Sales: $10-20 Million
Number Employees: 20-49

60199 Walker's Seafood
312 Southwest Sq
Jonesboro, AR 72401-5984   870-932-0375
    Fax: 870-935-8697
Seafood
President: Darrell Walker
Secretary/Treasurer: Patricia Walker

60200 Wallaby Yogurt Co
12002 Airport Way
Broomfield, CO 80021   707-553-1233
    Fax: 707-553-1293 855-925-4636
info@wallabyyogurt.com www.wallabyyogurt.com
Organic yogurt, kefir, and sour cream
Founder: Jerry Chou
Marketing & Event Manager: Nicole Smith
Operations Manager: Tibi Molnar
Year Founded: 1995
Estimated Sales: $45 Million
Number Employees: 50-99
Parent Co: WhiteWave
Types of Products Distributed:
    General Line

60201 Wallace Fisheries
PO Box 2046
Gulf Shores, AL 36547-2046   251-986-7211
    Fax: 251-987-5127
Seafood

60202 Wallace Foods Inc
2856 Whipple Ave NW
Canton, OH 44708-1532   330-477-6070
    Fax: 330-477-5920 www.wallacefoods.com
Wholesaler/distributor of groceries and frozen foods; serving the food service market
President: Ken Scheurer
kenscheurer@wallacefoods.com
Treasurer: L Wallace
VP: M Wallace
Estimated Sales: $10-20 Million
Number Employees: 10-19
Square Footage: 16000
Private Brands Carried:
    Golbon; E.W.
Number of Customer Locations: 300
Types of Products Distributed:
    Food Service, Frozen Food, General Line, Groceries

60203 Wallace Plant Company
201 High St
Bath, ME 04530-1677   207-443-2640
    Fax: 207-386-0268
Seafood
Owner: Wallace Plant
Estimated Sales: $1 Million
Number Employees: 5-9
Type of Packaging: Consumer

60204 Wallach's Farms
1425 Route 9
Toms River, NJ 08755   732-349-1694
    www.wallachsfarms.com
Wholesaler/distributor of produce, deli meats, pasta, juices and dairy products including butter, cheese and eggs; serving the food service and retail markets.
Owner: Stan Wallach
Year Founded: 1926
Estimated Sales: $20-50 Million
Number Employees: 20-49
Square Footage: 9500
Number of Customer Locations: 200
Types of Products Distributed:
    Food Service, Frozen Food, General Line, Provisions/Meat, Produce, Pasta, juices & dairy products

60205 Walsh Tropical Fruit Sales
721 Walsh Ave
Mission, TX 78572-4955   956-585-4887
    Fax: 956-585-2558
Wholesaler/distributor and importer of mangos, pineapples, seedless limes, coconuts and white onions
Owner: Buddy Walsh
Plant Manager: Noe Elizondo
Estimated Sales: $2.5-5 Million
Number Employees: 100-249
Types of Products Distributed:
    Frozen Food, Produce, Seedless limes, coconuts, etc.

60206 Walsh's Seafood
RR 1
Gouldsboro, ME 04607   207-963-2578
    Fax: 207-963-2578
Seafood
Owner: Craig Walsh

60207 Walter E Jacques & Sons
17 Ewen Road
Hamilton, ON L8S 3C3
Canada   905-318-1543
    Fax: 905-318-1543
Importer and wholesaler/distributor of biscuits and confectionery products
President: Bob Jacques
VP: Bob Baynton
Number Employees: 20-49
Private Brands Carried:
    Anthon Berg; Fox's; Terry's; Callard & Bowser; Wilkinsons; Aguila; Patersons
Types of Products Distributed:
    General Line, Confectionery & biscuits

60208 Waltham Fruit & ProduceCompany
105 2nd St
Chelsea, MA 02150-1803   617-354-1994
    Fax: 617-354-8423 www.baldor.com
Wholesaler/distributor of produce
VP: P Pizzuto Jr
Estimated Sales: $10-20 Million
Number Employees: 20-49
Types of Products Distributed:
    Frozen Food, Produce

60209 Waltkoch Limited
1990 Lakeside Pkwy
Suite 240
Tucker, GA 30084   404-378-3666
    Fax: 404-378-8492 www.waltkoch.com
Poultry frozen foods, meats, seafood.
Owner: Walter Koch
Partner: Sam Stanford
Chief Executive Officer: Keith Steinberg
Year Founded: 1950
Estimated Sales: $43 Million
Number Employees: 54
Type of Packaging: Consumer, Food Service
Types of Products Distributed:
    Frozen Food, General Line, Provisions/Meat, Produce, Seafood, Dairy products

60210 Walton & Post
8105 NW 77th St
Medley, FL 33166   305-591-1111
    Fax: 305-593-7070 mailcenter@waltonpost.com
    www.waltonpost.com
Wholesaler/distributor, importer and exporter of candy, canned fruits and vegetables, cookies, cereals, aluminum foil, plastic cups, film paper, paper napkins, juice, cooking oil, etc
VP: Jose Garrido Jr
VP: Alfredo Cuadrado
CEO: Jose A Garrido Jr
Estimated Sales: $20-50 Million
Number Employees: 20-49
Private Brands Carried:
    Country Best; Suave; Mr. Wapo; Alfredo; Platinum; New York Style
Types of Products Distributed:
    Frozen Food, General Line, General Merchandise, Candy, groceries, etc.

60211 Walton's Inc
3639 N Comotara St
Wichita, KS 67226-1304   316-262-0651
    Fax: 316-262-5136 800-835-2832
    www.waltonsinc.com
Manufacturer and exporter of brine pumps; wholesaler/distributor of meat processing equipment and butchers' supplies including saws, slicers and tenderizers, vacuum machines and bags and smokehouses
Owner: Don Walton
CEO: Brett Walton
brett@waltonsinc.com
Sales Director: Kurt Carter
Sales: Mark Schrag
Operations Manager: Brett Walton
Production Manager: Tim Fox
Purchasing Manager: Brett Walton
Estimated Sales: $1.8 Million
Number Employees: 20-49

Number of Brands: 25
Number of Products: 200
Square Footage: 71000
Type of Packaging: Food Service
Number of Customer Locations: 500
Types of Products Distributed:
  Frozen Food, General Merchandise, Meat processing equipment, etc.

60212 Wards Ice Cream Co Inc
93 Sherwood Ave
Paterson, NJ 07502-1862 973-595-8146
Fax: 973-238-8117
Wholesaler/distributor of ice cream; serving the food service market
Owner: Rod Fernino
wardsic@aol.com
Estimated Sales: $20-50 Million
Number Employees: 20-49
Types of Products Distributed:
  Food Service, Frozen Food, General Line, Ice cream

60213 Warehouse Equipment Inc
1800 Sportsman Ln NW
P.O.Box 11310
Huntsville, AL 35816-1400 256-837-8690
Fax: 256-895-0347 800-239-3435
huntsville@warehouseequipment.com
www.warehouseequipment.com
Wholesaler/distributor of conveyors, racks and shelving
President: David Allen
Estimated Sales: $10-20 Million
Number Employees: 5-9
Private Brands Carried:
  Lyon Metal Products; Frick-Gallager; Master Lock
Types of Products Distributed:
  Frozen Food, General Merchandise, Conveyors, racks & shelving

60214 Warehouse Systems Inc
655 Academy Dr
Northbrook, IL 60062 847-562-9526
Fax: 847-562-9529 info@warehouseSys.com
www.warehousesys.com
Wholesaler/distributor of material handling equipment including conveyors and shelving
President: E Timothy Gorham
Contact: Timothy Gorham
wsi@warehousesys.com
Estimated Sales: $.5-1 million
Number Employees: 5-9
Private Brands Carried:
  Unarco; Automotion; Numerical Control
Types of Products Distributed:
  Frozen Food, General Merchandise, Material handling equipment

60215 Warren E. Conley Corporation
1099 3rd Ave SW
Carmel, IN 46032-2564 317-846-5890
Fax: 317-846-5899 800-367-7875
Manufacturer and wholesaler/distributor of maintenance and cleaning products including brooms, brushes, cleaning polish and concentrates, hand soap, window cleaners, insecticides, kitchen degreasers, lime/rust remover, bowl cleansersdrain openers and squeegees
President: Kevin Conley
Estimated Sales: $1-2.5 Million
Number Employees: 1 to 4
Types of Products Distributed:
  Frozen Food, General Merchandise, Cleaning supplies

60216 Warren Southwest Rfrdgrtn
6423 Cunningham Rd
Houston, TX 77041-4713 713-869-6221
Fax: 713-863-7716
sales@warrenswrefrigeration.com
www.warrensouthwestrefrigeration.com
Wholesaler/distributor of walk-in and reach-in refrigerators, ice machines, beverage cases and warehouse vaults
President: Clem Janak
CEO: Aaron Janak
CFO: Richard Matise
Manager: Richard Matise
richard@warrenswrefrigeration.com
Estimated Sales: Less Than $500,000
Number Employees: 1-4
Square Footage: 16000

Types of Products Distributed:
  Frozen Food, General Merchandise, Walk-in & reach-in refrigerators, etc.

60217 Washington Vegetable Co
2035 Jerrold Ave
San Francisco, CA 94124-1604 415-647-7624
Fax: 415-647-3276
www.washingtonvegetable.com
Wholesaler/distributor of fresh fruits and vegetables; serving the food service market
Owner: John Pizza
IT: Diane Swecker
dianne@washingtonvegetable.com
Estimated Sales: $5-10 Million
Number Employees: 10-19
Types of Products Distributed:
  Food Service, Frozen Food, Produce

60218 Wasserstrom Co
4500 E Broad St
Columbus, OH 43213 614-228-6525
www.wasserstrom.com
Wholesaler/distributor of food service equipment and smallwares; also, complete installation and design services available; serving the food service market.
President & CEO: Rodney Wasserstrom
Year Founded: 1902
Estimated Sales: $110.40 Million
Number Employees: 1,200
Square Footage: 600000
Types of Products Distributed:
  Food Service, Frozen Food, General Merchandise, Equipment & smallwares

60219 Waterfront Market
30555 Us Highway 19 N
Palm Harbor, FL 34684-4415
Fax: 305-296-5849
Wholesaler/distributor of produce
Owner: Russel Pantelis
Estimated Sales: $5-10 Million
Number Employees: 20-49
Types of Products Distributed:
  Frozen Food, Produce

60220 Waterfront Seafood Market
2900 University Ave Ste A4
West Des Moines, IA 50266 515-223-5106
Fax: 515-224-9665 waterfrontseafood@msn.com
www.waterfrontseafoodmarket.com
Seafood
President: Ted Hanke
Estimated Sales: $3-5 Million
Number Employees: 50-99

60221 Watervliet Fruit Exchange
7821 Red Arrow Hwy
Watervliet, MI 49098-9011 269-463-3187
Fax: 269-463-3244
Wholesaler/distributor of fruit including apples, peaches and plums
General Manager: Barbara Parker
Estimated Sales: $20-50 Million
Number Employees: 50-99
Types of Products Distributed:
  Frozen Food, Produce, Apples, peaches & plums

60222 Watkins Distributing Company
3710 State Highway 97a
Wenatchee, WA 98801-9624 509-663-0777
Wholesaler/distributor of beer and wine
President: John Donaghy
Estimated Sales: $20-50 Million
Number Employees: 20-49
Private Brands Carried:
  Coors; Gallo; Inglenook
Number of Customer Locations: 750
Types of Products Distributed:
  Frozen Food, General Line, Beer & wine

60223 Watson Distributing
6244 Deerfield Avenue
San Gabriel, CA 91775-2512 626-286-0952
Fax: 626-286-0769
Wholesaler/distributor of computer peripherals for point of sale equipment; serving the food service market
Estimated Sales: $1-3 Million
Number Employees: 1-4
Types of Products Distributed:
  Food Service, Frozen Food, General Merchandise, Computer peripherals

60224 Watsonville Coast Produce Inc
275 Kearney St
Watsonville, CA 95076 831-722-3851
Fax: 831-768-3755 800-966-8547
wcpi@coastpro.com www.coastpro.com
Wholesaler/distributor of commercial and organic produce; serving the grocery and food service markets.
President: Gary Manfre
gmanfre@coastpro.com
Sales Director: Sandy Karambela
Human Resources: Paul Martinez
Year Founded: 1974
Estimated Sales: $20-50 Million
Number Employees: 100-249
Number of Brands: 200
Number of Products: 400
Square Footage: 44000
Type of Packaging: Consumer, Food Service, Bulk
Types of Products Distributed:
  Food Service, Produce

60225 Waugh Foods Inc
701 Pinecrest Dr
East Peoria, IL 61611-4894 309-427-8000
Fax: 309-694-3115
Wholesaler/distributor of frozen and refrigerated food, fresh dairy and produce.
President: John Waugh
CEO: Joe Waugh
VP Sales: Jim Susin
Operations Manager: Norm Ralph
VP Purchasing: Tim Waugh
Year Founded: 1948
Estimated Sales: $20 Million
Number Employees: 50-99
Square Footage: 51550
Type of Packaging: Food Service
Types of Products Distributed:
  Food Service, Frozen Food, General Line, Produce, Dairy products

60226 Waverly Crabs
3400 Greenmount Ave
Baltimore, MD 21218-2823 410-243-1181
Fax: 410-243-0348
Crab
Owner: Jane Gordon
jgordon@bcps.org
Estimated Sales: $3-5 Million
Number Employees: 10-19

60227 Wayne Estay Shrimp Company
PO Box 946 Oak Street
Grand Isle, LA 70358-0946 504-787-2166
Fax: 504-787-3982 877-787-2166
Fish and seafood
President: Wayne Estay
Sales Manager: Wayne Estay
Estimated Sales: $300,000
Number Employees: 6

60228 We're Full of Promotions
877 Jefferson Ave # E
St Paul, MN 55102-2897 651-642-1282
Fax: 651-642-1314 800-325-8511
Wholesaler/distributor of kid meal premiums, restaurant uniforms and premium apparel programs; serving the food service market
President: Tom Symalla
CEO: Denise Chambers
Estimated Sales: Less than $500,000
Number Employees: 1-4
Square Footage: 12000
Types of Products Distributed:
  Food Service, Frozen Food, General Merchandise, Kid meal premiums, etc.

60229 Weaver Nut Co. Inc.
1925 W Main St
Ephrata, PA 17522-1112 717-738-3781
Fax: 717-733-2226 800-473-2688
info@weavernut.com www.weavergourmet.com
Processor importer and distributor of nuts, dried fruits, candies, confectionery items, snack mixes, gourmet coffees and teas, beans and spices; custom roasting and contract packaging available
President: E Paul Weaver III
Vice President: Michael Reis
Sales Director: Tom Flynn
Manager: Lisa Weaver
retail@weavernut.com
Estimated Sales: $18,000,000
Number Employees: 20-49

Wholesalers & Distributors / A-Z

Number of Products: 3500
Square Footage: 116000
Type of Packaging: Consumer, Private Label, Bulk
Number of Customer Locations: 3000
Types of Products Distributed:
    Candy, Nuts, and Confections

60230 Webeco Foods
PO Box 228764
Miami, FL 33222   305-635-0000
                Fax: 305-639-6052
Wholesaler/distributor, importer and exporter of cheese, cream cheese and butter
Owner: Luis Teijeiro
luis@webecofoods.com
Treasurer: Jose Teijeiro
VP: Luis Teijeiro
Estimated Sales: $10-20 Million
Number Employees: 20-49
Square Footage: 135000
Types of Products Distributed:
    Frozen Food, General Line, Cheese, cream cheese & butter

60231 Webeco Foods, Inc
P.O.Box 228764
8225 NW 80th St
Miami, FL 33166-2160   305-639-2147
        Fax: 305-639-6052   888-635-1188
Import, export broker of cheese. Wholesaler/distributor of dairy products, meats including cheese and private label items
President: Luis Teijeiro
luis@webecofoods.com
VP/Treasurer: Jose Teijeiro
Logistics Manager: Kim Gobie
Marketing Specialist: Filena Hernandez
DSD Sales Manager: Manny Fernandez
Warehouse Manager: Rafael Rodriguez
Buyer: Mercy de la Torre
Estimated Sales: $10-20 Million
Number Employees: 20-49
Square Footage: 62000
Private Brands Carried:
    Gayo Azul; Hollandammer; El Holandes; Crema de Oro
Number of Customer Locations: 200
Types of Products Distributed:
    Frozen Food, General Line, Cheese

60232 Weber Scientific Inc
2732 Kuser Rd
Trenton, NJ 08691-1806   609-584-7677
    Fax: 609-584-8388   800-328-8378
            info@weberscientific.com
            www.weberscientific.com
Products for dairy, food and water testing.
President: Nancy Silvester
nsilvester@weberscientific.com
VP: Joyce Arcarese
Account Manager: MaryBeth Karczynski
National Accounts Manager: Sharon Wilson
Account Manager: Nancy Silvester
Purchasing Manager: John Santillo
Estimated Sales: $1-2.5 Million
Number Employees: 5-9
Square Footage: 100000
Types of Products Distributed:
    General Merchandise, Clothing & uniforms, etc.

60233 Wechsler Coffee Corporation
250 Central Avenue
Teterboro, NJ 07608-1861   201-994-1861
                            800-800-2633
Gourmet coffee, tea and drink bases; importer of green coffee; wholesaler/distributor of general merchandise and groceries including coffee and tea; serving the food service market
President: Mike O'Donnell
VP Finance: Jim Pypen
Estimated Sales: $300,000-500,000
Number Employees: 10-19
Square Footage: 200000
Parent Co: Superior Coffee & Foods
Type of Packaging: Food Service, Private Label
Types of Products Distributed:
    Food Service, Frozen Food, General Line, General Merchandise, Coffee, tea, groceries, equipment, etc.

60234 Weeke Wholesale Company
1600 N 89th St
Fairview Heights, IL 62208   618-397-1900
                Fax: 618-397-7041

Wholesaler/distributor of groceries, meat, frozen foods, equipment and fixtures, general merchandise and confectionery items; serving the food service market
President: Wayne Weeke
VP: Scott Weeke
Estimated Sales: $5-10 Million
Number Employees: 5-9
Square Footage: 120000
Types of Products Distributed:
    Food Service, Frozen Food, General Line, General Merchandise, Provisions/Meat, Confectionery items

60235 Wega USA
524 North York Road
Bensenville, IL 60166-1607   630-350-0066
    Fax: 630-350-0005 info@expressoshoppe.com
                www.expressoshoppe.com
Manufacturer, exporter and importer of coffee grinders and espresso equipment
President: David Dimbert
Estimated Sales: $500,000-$1 Million
Number Employees: 1-4
Square Footage: 20000
Type of Packaging: Food Service
Types of Products Distributed:
    Food Service, General Line, General Merchandise, Specialty Foods, Expresso, Coffee

60236 Welch Equipment Co Inc
5025 Nome St
Denver, CO 80239-2725   303-393-8181
    Fax: 303-371-5878   800-225-1094
            www.welchequipment.com
Wholesaler/distributor of material handling equipment including lift trucks, forklifts, conveyors, shelving, and personnel lifts
President: Steven Rice
CEO: Brittany Andrews
bandrews@welcheq.com
Estimated Sales: G
Number Employees: 100-249
Private Brands Carried:
    Interlake; Raymond; Toyota
Types of Products Distributed:
    Frozen Food, General Merchandise, Material handling equipment

60237 Welton Rubber Co
25615 Dequindre Rd
Madison Heights, MI 48071-3892 248-548-7600
    Fax: 248-548-9419   www.weltonrubber.com
Wholesaler/distributor of conveyor belts, hoses, power transmission items, specialty belts, chains and plastic gaskets for food processing; serving the food service market
President: Dennis Zavis
dennis@weltonrubber.com
Office Manager: Joanne Herzog
Vice President: Karl Norgan Jr
Estimated Sales: $5 Million+
Number Employees: 5-9
Square Footage: 64000
Private Brands Carried:
    3M (Adhesives); Thermoid (Hoses); Gates (Power Transmissions); Weatherhead (Hydraulic hoses & fittings)
Types of Products Distributed:
    Food Service, Frozen Food, General Merchandise, Conveyors, belts, etc.

60238 Werres Corp
807 E South St
Frederick, MD 21701-5737   301-620-4000
        Fax: 301-662-1028 www.werres.com
Wholesaler/distributor of material handling equipment
Owner: Steve Abernethy
sabernethy@werres.com
Estimated Sales: G
Number Employees: 100-249
Private Brands Carried:
    Raymond; Remstar International; Autoquip Corp.
Types of Products Distributed:
    Frozen Food, General Merchandise, Material handling equipment

60239 Wes Design-Supply Company
238 Route 109
Farmingdale, NY 11735-1503   631-249-0298
        Fax: 631-249-5832 www.wesdes.com

Wholesaler/distributor of food service equipment and supplies including tabletop items including glassware and china
Owner: Marc Tell
Owner: Dan Saltzman
CFO: Michael Bitonti
Contact: Dawn Bosak
dbosak@wesdes.com
Estimated Sales: $1-2.5 Million
Number Employees: 20-49
Private Brands Carried:
    Trolsen; Libby; Hobart
Number of Customer Locations: 400
Types of Products Distributed:
    Food Service, Frozen Food, General Merchandise, Glassware, china, etc.

60240 Wes Pak Inc
4572 Avenue 400
Dinuba, CA 93618-9774   559-897-4800
        Fax: 559-897-7500 www.wespak.com
Wholesale marketer of fresh peaches, plums, nectarines, apricots, kiwi, persimmons, pomegranates, plums, and prunes
President: Jim Stewart
jim@wpemail.com
Number Employees: 5-9

60241 Wescotek Inc
700 Tuna St
San Pedro, CA 90731-7340   310-831-3624
    Fax: 310-831-8735 wescotek@wescotek.com
                www.wescotek.com
Wholesaler/distributor, importer and exporter of tuna, seafood and foaming agents, pet food and food ingredients
President: Richard Harpe
dick@wescotek.com
Technical Manager: Mayra Olivera
Marketing Manager: Lee Anderson
Estimated Sales: Less Than $500,000
Number Employees: 1-4
Types of Products Distributed:
    Frozen Food, General Line, Seafood, tuna, foaming agents, etc.

60242 West Bay Fishing
RR 1
Box 752
Gouldsboro, ME 04607-9753   207-963-2392
                Fax: 207-963-7403
Seafood
President: Richard Noble

60243 West Bay Sales
351 Rancho Camino
Fallbrook, CA 92028-8488   760-731-3317
    Fax: 760-731-3221   800-607-0495
            ala@westbaysales.com
Importer of ginger, brewers' yeast spread and glace fruits including apricots, orange slices and peels, pineapple, peaches, pears, figs and kiwifruit. Also diced, dehydrated, and low sugar pineapple, papaya, mango, strawberry, peachpear, and banana, caramel, chocolate ganache, fruit variegates, dried apricots, figs, and tomatoes.
Owner: Alan Sipole
alan@westbaysales.com
Estimated Sales: $2.5-5 Million
Number Employees: 1-4
Square Footage: 8000
Type of Packaging: Consumer, Food Service, Bulk
Types of Products Distributed:
    Food Service, General Line, General Merchandise, Health Food, Produce

60244 West Brothers Lobster
830 Pigeon Hill Rd
Steuben, ME 04680   207-546-3622
                Fax: 207-255-3987
Lobster
Owner: Blair West
Estimated Sales: $300,000-500,000
Number Employees: 1-4

60245 West Central Foodservice
12840 Leyva St
Norwalk, CA 90650   213-629-3600
                            800-464-8349
            westcentral@westcentralla.com
            www.westcentralfoodservice.com
Wholesaler and distributor of produce, including mushrooms.

Wholesalers & Distributors / A-Z

President & CEO: Michael Dodo
Chief Financial Officer: Jamie Purcell
Executive Vice President: Steve Goodman
Controller: Rick Wise
Human Resources: Blanca Gonzalez
Buyer: Russell Tan
Year Founded: 1969
Estimated Sales: $20-50 Million
Number Employees: 250-499
Square Footage: 180000
Type of Packaging: Consumer, Food Service, Bulk

60246 West Coast Ship Chandlers
1611 17th St
Oakland, CA 94607-1641   510-444-7200
        Fax: 510-444-7216 www.wrist.com
Wholesaler/distributor of fresh and frozen food products; serving merchant ships and the food service market
President: Charlie Michelson
sales@westcoastship.com
Estimated Sales: $5-10 Million
Number Employees: 50-99
Types of Products Distributed:
   Food Service, Frozen Food, General Line

60247 West Coast Supplies
2750 Mercantile Dr # 100
Rancho Cordova, CA 95742-7511   916-852-6675
      Fax: 916-852-6676 888-852-6676
            www.westcoastsupplies.com
Wholesaler/distributor of poly, zipper lock and plastic shopping bags; also, foldable canopies, twist ties, berries, three pack strawberry basket
President: Michael Nammour
Contact: Amy Jurgensen
amy@westcoastsupplies.com
Estimated Sales: $500,000
Number Employees: 5-9
Square Footage: 12400
Private Brands Carried:
   Fold-A-Canopy; EZ-Up; CAS (USA) Corp.
Types of Products Distributed:
   Frozen Food, General Merchandise, Bags & canopies

60248 West End Dairy Inc
6055 Route 52
P.O.Box 326
Ellenville, NY 12428-8408   845-647-4600
       Fax: 845-647-4665 www.dusofoods.com
Wholesaler/distributor of general line products; serving the food service market
President: Sandra Richmond
Estimated Sales: $1-3 Million
Number Employees: 20-49
Square Footage: 140000
Parent Co: Duso Company
Types of Products Distributed:
   Food Service, Frozen Food, General Line

60249 West Tenn Dairy Products
119 Paris Pike
Mc Kenzie, TN 38201-1644   731-352-3160
                Fax: 731-352-3285
Wholesaler/distributor of restaurant supplies including ice cream toppings, disposable plastic straws, plates and paper napkins; serving the food service market
Owner: Tom Putman
wtd@westtndairy.com
Estimated Sales: $500,000-$1 Million
Number Employees: 5-9
Types of Products Distributed:
   Food Service, General Line, Specialty Foods, Ice cream toppings, etc.

60250 West Wholesale Grocery
301 S 17th St
Waco, TX 76701-1737   254-756-4251
Wholesaler/distributor of groceries, meats, dairy products, general merchandise, equipment and fixtures
President: John M Langford Sr
Estimated Sales: $3-5 Million
Number Employees: 1-4
Number of Customer Locations: 200
Types of Products Distributed:
   Frozen Food, General Line, General Merchandise, Provisions/Meat

60251 Westco Chemicals Inc
12551 Saticoy St S
North Hollywood, CA 91605-4312   818-255-3655
                Fax: 818-255-3650
ddraney@westcochemicals.com
www.westcochemicals.com
Wholesaler/distributor of aspartame, acidulants, dough conditioners, phosphates, waxes, soy protein concentrates, potassium sorbate and sesame seeds
President: Alan Zwillinger
azwillinger@westcochemicals.com
Sales Manager: Dan Draney PhD
Sales Representative: John Heinze
Sales Representative: Bonnie McKeever Gosline
Estimated Sales: $45 Million
Number Employees: 20-49
Number of Products: 2
Square Footage: 80000
Types of Products Distributed:
   Frozen Food, General Line, Industrial ingredients

60252 Westco Fruit & Nut Company
604 Central Avenue
Suite #4-5
East Orange, NJ 07018   973-673-1937
       Fax: 973-373-7900 email@irvington-nj.com
                www.irvington-nj.com
Vacuum packed canning of dried fruit and nuts
President: Rivka Moradi
CEO: Jacob Moradi
Estimated Sales: $300,000-500,000
Number Employees: 10-19
Square Footage: 30000
Type of Packaging: Food Service, Private Label, Bulk
Types of Products Distributed:
   Nuts, Fruit

60253 Westcoast Engineering Company
390 S Lemon Avenue
Walnut, CA 91789-2736   800-643-0400
                Fax: 909-598-8088
Wholesaler/distributor of insect light traps and air curtains; serving the food service market
Owner: Wallace Brown
Estimated Sales: Less than $500,000
Number Employees: 1-4
Private Brands Carried:
   Gilbert; Berner
Types of Products Distributed:
   Food Service, Frozen Food, General Merchandise, Insect light traps & air curtains

60254 Westerbeke Fishing GearCo Inc
400 Border St
Boston, MA 02128-2402   617-561-9967
       Fax: 617-561-3752 800-536-6387
       westerbekecompany@gmail.com wfg1.com
Wholesaler/distributor of boots, clothing, cutlery, shovels, netting, forks, containers, gloves, etc.; serving the seafood industry; liferaft annual inspections and netting & vinyl products.
Owner: Elaine Halligan
Sales Director: Ed Creamer
westerbekecompany@gmail.com
Purchasing Manager: Ed Creamer
Estimated Sales: $1 Million
Number Employees: 5-9
Square Footage: 24000
Private Brands Carried:
   Grydens, Crosby, Dexter-Russell, ACR, Coleman, Cal-June-Jim, Mercury, Avon, Switlik, Elliot, FEHR
Types of Products Distributed:
   General Merchandise, Aprons, forks, gloves, shovels, etc.

60255 Western Carolina Forklift Inc
6392 Burnt Poplar Rd
Greensboro, NC 27409-9710   336-668-0959
       Fax: 336-668-3833 800-374-1425
Wholesaler/distributor of material handling equipment including forklifts
CEO: David Hayes
dhayes@wcforklift.com
Estimated Sales: $20-50 Million
Number Employees: 20-49
Private Brands Carried:
   Nissan; Cascade; Blue
Types of Products Distributed:
   Frozen Food, General Merchandise, Material handling equipment

60256 Western Family Foods Inc
6700 SW Sandburg St
Tigard, OR 97223-8099   503-639-6300
       Fax: 503-684-3469 www.westernfamily.com
Wholesaler/distributor of private label items including meat, produce, frozen foods, general merchandise, etc.; serving the wholesale grocery distributor
President/CEO: Ron King
CFO: Russ Jones
HR Executive: Martina Nilles
mnilles@westfam.com
VP Sales & Marketing: David Hayden
Estimated Sales: $5-10 Million
Number Employees: 50-99
Square Footage: 144000
Type of Packaging: Private Label
Private Brands Carried:
   Western Family; Shurfine; Shur Saving; Better Buy
Number of Customer Locations: 3000
Types of Products Distributed:
   Food Service, Frozen Food, General Line, General Merchandise, Health Food, Provisions/Meat, Produce, Flour, sugar, butter, spices, etc.

60257 Western Grocers
PO Box 280
Edmonton, AB T5J 2J5
Canada   780-451-7300
Wholesaler/distributor of frozen food, general merchandise, groceries, produce, meats and seafood; serving the food service market; also, rack jobber services available
Manager: G Bryan
Branch Administrator: M Shostak
Parent Co: Loblaw Companies
Private Brands Carried:
   Better Buy; Dutch Oven; Fortune; Home Care; Malkins; Pet Care; Seven Farms; Sunspun; West Care
Number of Customer Locations: 800
Types of Products Distributed:
   Food Service, Frozen Food, General Line, General Merchandise, Provisions/Meat, Produce, Rack Jobbers, Seafood

60258 Western Grocers
101 Weston
Winnipeg, MB R3E 2T4
Canada   204-786-5108
                Fax: 204-786-5189
Wholesaler/distributor of frozen food, general line items, produce, meats, seafood and specialty food; serving the food service market
Branch Manager: Mike Webster
Parent Co: Loblaw Companies
Number of Customer Locations: 170
Types of Products Distributed:
   Food Service, Frozen Food, General Line, Provisions/Meat, Produce, Seafood, Specialty Foods

60259 Western Mandate
6415 64th Street
RR 7
Delta, BC V4K 4E2
Canada   604-952-6035
                Fax: 604-940-8071
Wholesaler/distributor of candy and confectionery products
President: Craig Murray
Private Brands Carried:
   Brach's Candy
Types of Products Distributed:
   General Line, Candy & confectionery products

60260 Western Soap Company
103 E Sprague Avenue
Spokane, WA 99202-1603   509-455-9014
       Fax: 509-455-5237 800-727-7627
Wholesaler/distributor of cleaning supplies including soap
President: Larry Dilley
Estimated Sales: $5-10 Million
Number Employees: 20-49
Private Brands Carried:
   Rubbermaid; 3-M; Butchers
Types of Products Distributed:
   Frozen Food, General Merchandise, Cleaning supplies

Wholesalers & Distributors / A-Z

60261 Western Steel & Wire
1428 Egbert Ave
San Francisco, CA 94124-3222   415-822-5490
                    Fax: 415-822-9674
Wholesaler/distributor of wire bag and bale ties; also, stainless wire
President: Erin Bojarski
bojarskie@westernsteelcs.com
Vice President: Dick Stephens
Estimated Sales: $2.5-5 Million
Number Employees: 1-4
Square Footage: 44000
Types of Products Distributed:
  Frozen Food, General Merchandise, Wire bag & bale ties; also, bare wire

60262 Westland Marketing
P.O.Box 16024
Denver, CO 80216-24   303-296-4544
                    Fax: 303-296-4922
Wholesaler/distributor of espresso equipment and coffee brewing devices and roasters; serving the food service market
President: Charles de Rojo
Contact: Charles Rojo
charlesrojo@msn.com
VP Operations: Linda de Rojo
Types of Products Distributed:
  Food Service, Frozen Food, General Merchandise, Coffee & espresso equipment

60263 Westside Foods
355 Food Center Dr # A23
Bronx, NY 10474-7580   718-842-8500
  Fax: 718-893-8933 www.westsidefoodsinc.com
Wholesaler/distributor of groceries
Manager: Linda Gonzalez
Manager: Dennis Ryan
dpr1799@aol.com
Estimated Sales: $20-50 Million
Number Employees: 100-249
Types of Products Distributed:
  Frozen Food, General Line, Groceries

60264 Westwind Resources
11733 9th Ave NW
Seattle, WA 98177   206-281-9262
  Fax: 206-283-1244 westwindresource@aol.com
Wholesaler/distributor, importer and exporter of fresh and frozen seafood
President: Gail Rowland
Estimated Sales: $5 Million
Number Employees: 1-4
Type of Packaging: Food Service, Bulk
Types of Products Distributed:
  Frozen Food, Seafood

60265 Wetoska Packaging Distributors
1099 Lunt Ave
Elk Grove Vlg, IL 60007-5021   847-437-6100
       Fax: 847-437-8991 www.wetoska.com
Wholesaler/distributor and importer of packaging supplies and vacuum packaging machines; serving the food service market
Owner: John Murray
Controller: S Lombardo
Sales Director: S Wetoska
jmurray@wetoska.com
Purchasing Manager: J Newham
Estimated Sales: $20-50 Million
Number Employees: 10-19
Square Footage: 27000
Type of Packaging: Food Service
Types of Products Distributed:
  Food Service, General Merchandise, Packaging supplies & equipment

60266 Weyauwega Star Dairy
109 N Mill St
P.O. Box 658
Weyauwega, WI 54983   920-867-2870
                    888-813-9720
          www.wegastardairy.com
Cheese manufacturer, specializing in Parmesan, Asiago and Romanao; sting cheeses and curds; meat products; spreadable cheeses. Provide private label, shredding and packing services.
President: James Knaus
Contact: Gerard Knaus
gknaus@wegastardairy.com
Estimated Sales: $12.5 Million
Number Employees: 75
Number of Brands: 7

Type of Packaging: Consumer, Food Service, Private Label, Bulk
Types of Products Distributed:
  Cheese Products

60267 Whaley Pecan Co Inc
1113 S Brundidge Blvd
Troy, AL 36081   334-566-3504
       Fax: 334-566-9336 800-824-6827
    info@whaleypecan.com www.whaleypecan.com
Processors of shelled pecans and some exports
Owner: Bob Whaley
whaleypecan@bellsouth.net
Estimated Sales: $5,000,000
Number Employees: 10-19
Square Footage: 160000
Type of Packaging: Consumer, Food Service, Bulk
Types of Products Distributed:
  Food Service, Health Food

60268 Wham Food & Beverage
1856 Radius Drive
Hollywood, FL 33020   954-920-7857
     Fax: 954-920-9787 Jon@whamfoods.com
                    www.whamfoods.com
Liquidator of food and beverage closeouts by the truckload
President/CEO: Jonathon Auspitz
VP: Adam Busch
Marketing/Sales: Adam Busch
Sales: Mitchell Teger
Contact: Renee Lezcano
renee@whamfoods.com
Operations: Manuel Garrido
Plant Manager: Joann Dellapena
Estimated Sales: $5.4 Million
Number Employees: 12
Number of Brands: 40
Number of Products: 248
Square Footage: 11400
Type of Packaging: Consumer, Food Service, Private Label, Bulk
Types of Products Distributed:
  Frozen Food

60269 Wharton Seafood Sales
43505 Belt Highway
PO Box 440
Paauilo, HI 96776-0440   808-776-1087
       Fax: 877-591-8944 800-352-8507
Seafood
Owner/President: Bailey Wharton
wharton@aloha.net
Estimated Sales: Less than $100,000
Number Employees: 1-4

60270 Wheat Foods Council
51 Red Fox Lane
Unit D
Ridgway, CO 81432   970-626-9828
                wfc@wheatfoods.org
                www.wheatfoods.org
Promotes the category of wheat based foods, including baked goods, cereal, crackers, pretzels, pasta, sweet goods and tortillas.
President: Judi Adams, MS, RD
Vice President: Gayle Veum, RD
Contact: Tim O'Connor
toconnor@wheatfoods.org
Estimated Sales: $300,000-500,000
Number Employees: 1-4

60271 Whipped Pastry Boutique
37 Richards Street
Brooklyn, NY 11231   718-858-8088
           info@whippedpastryboutique.com
           whippedpastryboutique.com
Tarts, pastries, breads, cakes and cookies
President & Founder: Michelle Tampakis
michelle@whippedpastryboutique.com
Estimated Sales: $1-3 Million
Number Employees: 10-20
Type of Packaging: Food Service, Private Label
Types of Products Distributed:
  Baked goods

60272 Whitaker Brothers
12410 Washington Ave
Rockville, MD 20852-1822   301-230-2800
       Fax: 301-770-9217 www.whitakerbrothers.com
Wholesaler/distributor of check, coin/currency, mailroom and time and attendance control supplies

Owner: Joe Mitchell
Sales Manager: Jeff Bishop
Contact: Donald Edsall
donald.r.edsall@lmco.com
Estimated Sales: $20-50 Million
Number Employees: 50-99
Types of Products Distributed:
  Frozen Food, General Merchandise, Money, mailroom & attendance supplies

60273 White Cap Construction Supply
5409 Broadway Ave # 100
Jacksonville, FL 32254-2959   904-388-2926
                    Fax: 904-783-9704
Wholesaler/distributor of general merchandise including electrical supplies, ballasts, fuses, lamps, switches and lighting fixtures
Manager: Matthew Walker
Manager: John Truss
Estimated Sales: $20-50 Million
Number Employees: 10-19
Parent Co: Hughes Supply
Types of Products Distributed:
  Frozen Food, General Merchandise, Electrical supplies, lamps, etc.

60274 White Cliff Minerals
PO Box 213
Tahoe City, NV 96145   202-379-1866
                    tanya@white-cliff.com
Ground calcium carbonate.
Director: Todd Hibberd
Manager: Michael Langoulant
Manager: Brian Thomas
Estimated Sales: $640 Thousand
Parent Co: Kiskeya Minerals, USA

60275 White Feather Farms
404 S Lombard Dr
Muncie, IN 47304   765-288-6636
                    Fax: 765-741-1827
Wholesaler/distributor of groceries, specialty foods, meat, produce, seafood, dairy, frozen and baked goods; serving the food service market
President: Dirk Osterhoff
Administration Manager: L Tucker
Sales Manager: D Osterhoff
Estimated Sales: $10-20 Million
Number Employees: 20-49
Square Footage: 40000
Number of Customer Locations: 350
Types of Products Distributed:
  Food Service, Frozen Food, General Line, Provisions/Meat, Produce, Seafood, Specialty Foods, Dairy & baked goods

60276 White House Chemical Supply
455 Trinity Ave
Trenton, NJ 08619   609-587-6112
                    Fax: 609-587-2502
Wholesaler/distributor of disinfectants, insecticides, cleaners, warewashing and laundry chemicals
President: Richard Prutky
Estimated Sales: $5-10 Million
Number Employees: 10-19
Square Footage: 24000
Parent Co: White House Chemical & Supply
Private Brands Carried:
  Butchers; 3M; Epic; Rubbermaid; Kimberly-Clark
Types of Products Distributed:
  Frozen Food, General Merchandise, Cleaning equipment & supplies

60277 White Plains ElectricalLight
111 E Main St Ste 2
Elmsford, NY 10523   914-592-9555
                    Fax: 914-592-6218
Wholesaler/distributor of electrical supplies including electrical cables, exhaust fans, lighting fixtures, electric and fluorescent lamps and electric transformers
President: Conrad Noble
Consultant: Oliver Noble
Estimated Sales: Less than $500,000
Number Employees: 1-4
Square Footage: 4000
Private Brands Carried:
  Sylvania; Kitchler; Patton
Types of Products Distributed:
  Frozen Food, General Merchandise, Electrical supplies

Wholesalers & Distributors / A-Z

60278 Whitehawk Beef Co
45 Railroad Ave
Eldred, PA 16731-4629   814-225-4755
    Fax: 814-225-4908   800-283-3369
Wholesaler/distributor of beef
President: Steve Slavin
CEO: Jim Slavin
Founder: Cleary Slavin
Estimated Sales: $5-10 Million
Number Employees: 10-19
Square Footage: 60000
Types of Products Distributed:
    Frozen Food, Provisions/Meat, Beef

60279 Whitey Produce Co Inc
46 Brooklyn Terminal Market
Brooklyn, NY 11236-1572   718-251-2345
    Fax: 718-241-5236
Wholesaler/distributor of produce
Owner: Charlie Whitey
whiteyproduce@aol.com
Estimated Sales: $1-2.5 Million
Number Employees: 5-9
Types of Products Distributed:
    Frozen Food, Produce

60280 Whitfield Olive
18 E Goepp Street
Bethlehem, PA 18018-2818   610-865-8245
    Fax: 610-865-8246   800-645-5637
Importer, exporter and wholesaler/distributor of capers, olives, peppercorn, giardiniera, pickles, peppers, olive oil and spices
President: Giel Millner
Number Employees: 10-19
Square Footage: 600000
Type of Packaging: Consumer, Food Service, Private Label, Bulk
Private Brands Carried:
    Amigo; Falcon; Gilyone; Little Elves; Mt. Rose; Perfecto; Ricardo; Socol; Whitfield
Types of Products Distributed:
    Food Service, Specialty Foods

60281 Whitfield Olive
18 W Goepp Street
Bethlehem, PA 18018-2706   610-865-8245
    Fax: 610-865-8246   800-645-5637
Importer, exporter and wholesaler/distributor of capers, olives, pepperoncini, giardiniera, pickles, peppers, olive oil and spices
President: Giel Millner
Sales/Marketing Executive: Danielle George
Estimated Sales: $3-5 Million
Number Employees: 10-19
Square Footage: 400000
Type of Packaging: Consumer, Food Service, Private Label, Bulk
Private Brands Carried:
    Amico; Mount Rose; Country Day; Whitfield; Falcon; Little Elves
Number of Customer Locations: 500
Types of Products Distributed:
    Food Service, Specialty Foods

60282 Whitley Wholesale Grocery
484 W Market St
Smithfield, NC 27577-3321   919-934-2800
    Fax: 919-989-7710
Wholesaler/distributor of tobacco products, candy, vegetables, frozen foods, paper products and janitorial supplies
Owner: J Johnson
whitleygrocery@gmail.com
Secretary/Treasurer: Vicki Johnson
VP: J Anthony Johnson
Estimated Sales: $1-2.5 Million
Number Employees: 5-9
Square Footage: 32000
Types of Products Distributed:
    Frozen Food, General Line, General Merchandise

60283 Whole Life Nutritional Supplements
13340 Saticoy St Ste B
North Hollywood, CA 91605   818-255-5357
    Fax: 818-255-5307   800-748-5841
    wholelife2@aol.com
Wholesaler/distributor and contract packager of vitamins
Manager: Rajen Patel
Director Sales: Irma Arroyo
Contact: Zenit Simmons
wholelife2@aol.com
Estimated Sales: $1-3 Million
Number Employees: 5-9
Square Footage: 10000
Type of Packaging: Private Label
Private Brands Carried:
    Whole Life
Types of Products Distributed:
    Frozen Food, Health Food, Vitamins

60284 Wholesale Cash & Carry Foods
1000 Vine Street
Sacramento, CA 95814-0322   916-441-3005
    Fax: 916-441-4305
Wholesaler/distributor of groceries, meats and frozen foods; serving the food service market
President: G Kassis
CEO: D Lee
Estimated Sales: $5-10 Million
Number Employees: 5-9
Square Footage: 104000
Type of Packaging: Food Service
Private Brands Carried:
    Golbon Label
Types of Products Distributed:
    Food Service, Provisions/Meat, Produce, Seafood

60285 Wholesale Restaurant Equipment
PO Box 860
Pottsville, PA 17901-0860   778-397-7873
    Fax: 778-397-7870   888-997-1560
    wholesalerestaurantequipment.ca
Wholesaler/distributor of food service equipment
President: Mickey Palles
Estimated Sales: $2.5-5 Million
Number Employees: 10-19
Square Footage: 48000
Types of Products Distributed:
    Food Service, Frozen Food, General Merchandise, foodservice equipment

60286 Wholesale Restaurant Supply
3814 Charlotte Ave
Nashville, TN 37209-3737   615-777-1891
    Fax: 615-321-2210   800-869-0056
    sales@wholesalerestaurant.com
Wholesaler/distributor of new and used equipment and supplies; serving food service operators
Owner: Tamay Ozari
tamayozari@yahoo.com
International Sales Manager: Alan Rice
Nashville Sales Manager: Ken Baker
Estimated Sales: $1-2.5 Million
Number Employees: 5-9
Square Footage: 220000
Types of Products Distributed:
    Food Service, Frozen Food, General Merchandise, New & used equipment & supplies

60287 Wholesale Tool Company
P.O.Box 68
Warren, MI 48090-0068   586-754-9270
    Fax: 586-754-8652   888-755-3728
    www.wttool.com
Wholesaler/distributor of material handling, safety and cutting equipment
President: Mark Dowdy
Advertising Director: Matthew Decker
Contact: Larry Cunningham
lcunningham@wttool.com
Estimated Sales: $10-20 Million
Number Employees: 20-49
Square Footage: 194500
Types of Products Distributed:
    Frozen Food, General Merchandise, Material handling equipment

60288 WholesalePortal.com
6135 Seaview Avenue NW
Suite 3a
Seattle, WA 98107-2628   206-782-7040
    Fax: 206-782-9641
Wholesaler

60289 Wholesome Bakery
299 Divisadero St
San Francisco, CA 94117   415-343-5414
    info@wholesomebakery.com
    www.wholesomebakery.com
Gluten-free, dairy free, egg free, soy free, trans fat free & low glycemic baked goods
Founder/CEO: Mandy Harper   *Year Founded:* 2009
Types of Products Distributed:
    General Line

60290 Wholesum Family Farms
2811-3 N Palenque Ave
Nogales, AZ 85621   520-281-9233
    Fax: 520-281-4366   marketing@wh.farm
    www.wh.farm
Organic produce including tomatoes, cucumbers, peppers, eggplants, and squash
Chief Commercial Officer: Ricardo Crisantes
VP Business Development: Steve Lefevre
Quality Assurance: Rebeca Rabago
Marketing Specialist: Joanna Jaramillo
Sales Manager: Kristina Luna
Year Founded: 1928
Number Employees: 50-99
Types of Products Distributed:
    Produce

60291 Wichita Fish Co
1601 W Douglas Ave
Wichita, KS 67213-4022   316-265-3474
    Fax: 316-262-7770   www.wichitafishcompany.com
Owner: Larry Towns
info@360wichita.com
Estimated Sales: Less Than $500,000
Number Employees: 5-9

60292 Wichita Restaurant SuplCo Inc
1122 Scott Ave
Wichita Falls, TX 76301-4650   940-766-4389
    Fax: 940-322-5342   800-533-6983
    www.wichitasupply.com
Wholesaler/distributor of cleaning supplies, tabletop supplies and equipment; serving the food service market
Owner: Lamar Bayer
lamarbaer@wichitasupply.com
CEO: Sandy Hay
VP: Limar Baer
Estimated Sales: $1-3 Million
Number Employees: 5-9
Types of Products Distributed:
    Food Service, Frozen Food, General Merchandise, Tabletop supplies, etc.

60293 Wicked Mix
2321 Cantrell Rd
Little Rock, AR 72202   501-374-2244
    www.wickedmixes.com
Snack mix
President: Stan Roberts
stan@wickedmixes.com
Founder & CEO: Brent Bumpers
Sales Manager: Alex Newberry Robinson
Estimated Sales: $0.5-2 Million
Number Employees: 2-10
Types of Products Distributed:
    Snack mix

60294 Widow's Mite Vinegar Company
1309 P Street NW
Apt 6
Washington, DC 20005-3750   202-462-3669
    Fax: 202-462-3669   877-678-5854
Salad dressing mix and Creole vinegar
President: John Allen Franciscus
Vice President: James Franciscus
Type of Packaging: Consumer, Bulk

60295 Wiese Planning & Engineering
1445 Woodson Rd
Saint Louis, MO 63132   314-997-4000
    Fax: 636-583-9819   www.wieseusa.com
Wholesaler/distributor of material handling equipment
Manager: De Wayne Doyle
Contact: Craig Mccallister
cmccallister@wieseusa.com
Estimated Sales: $20-50 Million
Number Employees: 100-249
Private Brands Carried:
    Caterpillar; Mitsubishi; Trackmobile
Types of Products Distributed:
    Frozen Food, General Merchandise, Material handling equipment

Wholesalers & Distributors / A-Z

60296 Wilcox Frozen Foods
2200 Oakdale Ave
San Francisco, CA 94124-1519   415-282-4116
                                  Fax: 415-282-3044
Wholesaler/distributor of frozen and specialty foods; serving the food service market
President: Rodney Smith
raywilcoxfoods@aol.com
Sales Exec: Ray Shaw
Estimated Sales: $20-50 Million
Number Employees: 20-49
Types of Products Distributed:
   Food Service, Frozen Food, Specialty Foods

60297 Wilcox Paper Co
5916 Court Street Rd
Syracuse, NY 13206-1733   315-437-1496
                              Fax: 315-463-9645   800-466-1496
Wholesaler/distributor of packaging and sanitorial products and tapes including stretch and shrink
President: David Sparks
dsparks@wilcoxusa.com
VP: Brian Sparks
Marketing Manager: Rick Saes
Estimated Sales: $10-20 Million
Number Employees: 5-9
Types of Products Distributed:
   Frozen Food, General Merchandise, Shrink & stretch tapes, etc.

60298 Wild Zora Foods
325 E 4th St.
Loveland, CO 80537   970-541-9672
                         support@wildzora.com
                         www.wildzora.com
Paelo foods including meat & veggie snack bars, soups, teas, and prepared meals
Founder/Owner: Zora Tabin
Content Marketing Manager: Hanna Jensen
Wholesale Manager: Lorenzo Moreno Jr
Project Manager: Michael Arden Conley
Year Founded: 2014
Number Employees: 20-49
Types of Products Distributed:
   General Line, Provisions/Meat

60299 Wilde Brands
2705 Spruce St.
Boulder, CO 80302   720-328-0843
                        hello@wildebrands.com
                        www.wildebrands.com
Chips made from chicken
Founder/CEO: Jason Wright
EVP/CFO: Jerome Metivier
National Marketing Manager: Braden Bingham
Year Founded: 2014
Number Employees: 5-9
Types of Products Distributed:
   General Line, Provisions/Meat

60300 Wilderness Foods
2578 Broadway
Suite 104
New York, NY 10025-5642   914-376-1691
                              Fax: 914-376-1306
Wholesaler/distributor of fresh, frozen and smoked seafood including oysters and wetfish; serving the food service market
President: Peter McNaughton
Number Employees: 1-4
Number of Customer Locations: 50
Types of Products Distributed:
   Food Service, Frozen Food, Seafood, Oysters & wetfish

60301 Wilke International Inc
14321 W 96th Ter
Lenexa, KS 66215-4709   913-438-5544
                           Fax: 913-438-5554   800-779-5545
                           whw@wilkeinternational.com
                           www.wilkeinternational.com
Processor, importer, exporter and wholesaler/distributor of lactic acid, lactates, sports nutrition and dietary supplements
President: Wayne Wilke
wwilke@wilkeinternational.com
Director Administration: John Veazey
General Manager: James France
Estimated Sales: $5-10 Million
Number Employees: 10-19
Type of Packaging: Bulk
Types of Products Distributed:
   Frozen Food, General Line, Health Food, Lactic acid, lactates, supplements, etc

60302 Wilkens-Anderson Co
4525 W Division St
Chicago, IL 60651-1674   773-384-4433
                             Fax: 773-384-6260   800-847-2222
                             waco@wacolab.com   www.wacolab.com
Laboratory and quality control equipment, supplies instruments and chemicals can testing equipment, can seam evaluation equipment
President/CEO: Bruce Wilkens
info@waco-lab-supply.com
Marketing Director: Peter Thomases
Sales Director: Don Hartman
Operations Manager: Eric Jensen
Production Manager: Don Lamonica
Estimated Sales: $6-8 Million
Number Employees: 20-49
Square Footage: 220000
Types of Products Distributed:
   Frozen Food, General Merchandise, Laboratory controls, etc.

60303 Wilkin-Alaska
1851 Fox Ave
Fairbanks, AK 99701-2725   907-456-7088
                               Fax: 907-451-0438
Wholesaler/distributor of snacks foods and bread; serving the food service market; rack jobber services available
Owner: Wayne Carter
wayne@katinc.com
Estimated Sales: $20-50 Million
Number Employees: 20-49
Private Brands Carried:
   Frito-Lay; Wonder Bread; Hostess Cup Cakes; Orowheat Bread
Number of Customer Locations: 110
Types of Products Distributed:
   Food Service, Frozen Food, General Line, Rack Jobbers, Snack foods

60304 Willamette Filbert Growers
14875 NE Tangen Rd
Newberg, OR 97132-6890   503-538-9256
   Fax: 503-538-9256   www.willamettehazelnuts.com
Nuts, hazelnuts, kosher
Owner: Michael Severeid
michael@willamettehazelnuts.com
Estimated Sales: $3 Million
Number Employees: 10-19
Square Footage: 184000
Type of Packaging: Private Label, Bulk

60305 Willamette Valley Pie Co
2994 82nd Ave NE
Salem, OR 97305   503-362-8857
                      info@wvpie.com
                      www.wvpie.com
Pies, cobblers, packaged fruit, jams, and syrups
CEO: Jeff Dunn
CFO/Controller: Michael Schelske
QA Manager: Scott Lemke
Warehouse Manager: Tom Parsons
Year Founded: 1999
Number Employees: 50-99
Types of Products Distributed:
   General Line, Produce

60306 William Consalo & Sons Farms
N Main Rd
Vineland, NJ 08360   856-692-4414
                         Fax: 856-691-0164
Wholesaler/distributor of produce; serving the food service market
Estimated Sales: $5-10 Million
Number Employees: 10-19
Types of Products Distributed:
   Food Service, Frozen Food, Produce

60307 William E. Martin & Sons Company
55 Bryant Avenue
Suite 300
Roslyn, NY 11576   516-605-2444
                       Fax: 516-605-2442   mail@martinspices.com
                       www.martinspices.com
Processor, wholesaler/distributor, exporter and importer of spices, seasonings, salts, herbs and herbal supplements, seeds, powders and raisins. Wholesaler/distributor of dehydrated onion and garlic products, full line of ground spicesand bakery seeds
Owner: William Martin Jr
Contact: Martin Spencer
spencer@martinspices.com
Estimated Sales: $10-20 Million
Number Employees: 22
Number of Brands: 1
Square Footage: 60000
Type of Packaging: Bulk
Types of Products Distributed:
   General Line, Health Food, Spices, seeds, herbs, raisins, etc.

60308 William Rosenstein & Sons
950 N Keyser Ave
P.O. Box 117
Scranton, PA 18504   570-346-5771
                         Fax: 570-969-2620   800-241-0371
                         www.wmrosenstein.com
Wholesaler/distributor of produce; serving the food service market.
President: Philip Rosenstein
Sales Executive Officer: Gregory Lukasik
Estimated Sales: $20-50 Million
Number Employees: 20-49
Types of Products Distributed:
   Food Service, Frozen Food, Produce

60309 Williams Food Equipment Company
2150 Ambassador Drive
Windsor, ON N9C 3R4
Canada   519-969-1919
             Fax: 519-969-2245
Wholesaler/distributor of lay-outs, equipment and smallwares; serving the hospitality industry and food service market
President: Rick Willimas
Office Sales: Judy Markham
Purchasing Manager: Rick Crowley
Number Employees: 10-19
Square Footage: 64000
Types of Products Distributed:
   Food Service, Frozen Food, General Merchandise, Lay-outs, equipment, small wares

60310 Williams Institutional Foods
1325 Bowens Mill Rd SW
Douglas, GA 31533-3933   912-384-5270
                            Fax: 912-384-0533   info@williams-foods.com
                            www.williams-foods.com
Groceries, meat, frozen foods, bakery goods, equipment and general merchandise
President/Sales Manager: Craig McCrary
CEO/Purchasing: Bob Williams
bobwilliams@williams-foods.com
Marketing: Karen Williams
Sales: George Smith
Year Founded: 1951
Estimated Sales: $37000000
Number Employees: 50-99
Types of Products Distributed:
   Food Service, Frozen Food, General Line, General Merchandise, Provisions/Meat, Produce

60311 Williams Resource & Associates
1200 California Street
Suite 255
Redlands, CA 92374   909-748-7671
                         Fax: 909-748-7621
Dairy products for industrial food processors, milk powder, butter, cheese
CEO: H. G. Richard Williams
Operations Manager: Breanna Lucier
Estimated Sales: $2.5-5 Million
Number Employees: 1-4
Type of Packaging: Food Service, Bulk
Private Brands Carried:
   Brewko; Rancho California of Claremont; Classic Roast
Types of Products Distributed:
   Food Service, Dairy, bakery & industrial ingredients

60312 Williams Sausage Co
5132 Old Troy Hickman Rd
Union City, TN 38261-7702   731-885-5841
                                Fax: 731-885-5884   800-844-4242
                                roger@williams-sausage.com
                                www.williams-sausage.com
Wholesaler/distributor of gravy and pork including sausage, bacon and ham; serving the food service market

President: Roger Williams
rwilliams@pcliberty.com
CEO: David Williams
Vice President: David Williams
Quality Control: Jaclyn Coopery
Plant Manager: Tommy Ray
Estimated Sales: $24 Million
Number Employees: 250-499
Number of Brands: 2
Number of Products: 90
Square Footage: 50000
Type of Packaging: Consumer, Food Service, Private Label, Bulk
Private Brands Carried:
Ole South, Williams
Number of Customer Locations: 2000
Types of Products Distributed:
Food Service, Frozen Food, General Line, Provisions/Meat, Gravy & pork

60313 Williamsport Candy Company
PO Box 3366
Williamsport, PA 17701-0366   570-368-1469
Fax: 570-368-1795
Wholesaler/distributor of candy
Partner: Holly Mc Fadden
Partner: Robert Gutherie
Partner: Holly McFadden
Estimated Sales: $5-10 Million
Number Employees: 5-9
Types of Products Distributed:
Frozen Food, General Line, Candy

60314 Willie Laymon
1026 Cumberland Ave
Middlesboro, KY 40965-1052   606-248-3382
Wholesaler/distributor of produce; serving the food service market
President: Dewey England
Estimated Sales: $1-3 Million
Number Employees: 1-4
Types of Products Distributed:
Food Service, Frozen Food, Produce

60315 Willing Group
222 Saint Johns Avenue
Yonkers, NY 10704-2717   914-964-5800
Fax: 914-964-5293 cgctradingintl@aol.com
President: Louis J Goldstein
CEO: Carmela P Goldstein
CFO: Peter L Gallucci
Estimated Sales: $10-20 Million
Number Employees: 20
Square Footage: 15000
Type of Packaging: Consumer, Food Service, Private Label, Bulk
Types of Products Distributed:
Food Service, General Merchandise, Health Food, Specialty Foods

60316 Willow Group LTD
34 Clinton St
Batavia, NY 14020   585-344-2900
Fax: 585-344-0044 800-724-7300
www.willowgroupltd.com
Wicker baskets.
Co-Owner: Bernard Skalny
bernards@willowgroupltd.com
Co-Owner: James Walsh
Year Founded: 1928
Estimated Sales: $20-50 Million
Number Employees: 1-4
Types of Products Distributed:
Food Service, Frozen Food, General Merchandise, Wicker baskets

60317 Willow Run Foods Inc
1006 US Route 11
Kirkwood, NY 13795   607-338-5221
800-234-7500
webmaster@willowrunfoods.com
www.willowrunfoods.com
Wholesaler/distributor of general merchandise and produce; serving the food service market throughout the Northeast.
President & CEO: Terry Wood
terryw@willowrunfoods.com
Vice President, Finance: James Donovan
Vice President, Human Resources: Carol Wallis
Vice President, Operations: Len Basso
Vice President, Purchasing: Richard Koffs
Year Founded: 1989
Estimated Sales: $500 Million
Number Employees: 100-249
Square Footage: 100000
Private Brands Carried:
Code
Types of Products Distributed:
Food Service, Frozen Food, General Merchandise, Produce

60318 Willy Nilly At Home
143 W Main St
Bay Shore, NY 11706-8315   631-665-5510
Fax: 949-240-5117 www.bayshoreelectricinc.com
Wholesaler/distributor of electric and fluorescent lamps, batteries, fuses, etc
President: Marilyn Schulman
bayshorelighting@aol.com
Manager: Lynn Brey
Estimated Sales: $3-5 Million
Number Employees: 10-19
Types of Products Distributed:
Frozen Food, General Merchandise, Lighting

60319 Wilson Ice Machines
13769 Airline Hwy
Baton Rouge, LA 70817-5924   225-753-3955
Fax: 225-751-3060
Wholesaler/distributor of food equipment; rack jobber services available
President: Bart Wilson
terribaker119@yahoo.com
VP: Pat Wilson
Estimated Sales: $1.5 Million
Number Employees: 1-4
Types of Products Distributed:
Food Service, Frozen Food, General Merchandise, Rack Jobbers, Food equipment

60320 Winchester Food
2308 Middle Road
Winchester, VA 22601   540-754-1630
Fax: 540-869-6658 office@visuallink.com
www.visuallink.com
Wholesaler/distributor of groceries, meat, produce, frozen foods and baked goods; serving the food service market
President: Pressley Puller
CFO: John Good
Purchasing Director: James Vardano
Estimated Sales: $5-10 Million
Number Employees: 20-49
Square Footage: 111560
Type of Packaging: Food Service
Private Brands Carried:
CODE
Number of Customer Locations: 400
Types of Products Distributed:
Food Service, Frozen Food, General Line, General Merchandise, Provisions/Meat, Produce, Seafood

60321 Wind & Willow
1430 E Industrial Rd
Mt Vernon, MO 65712-9784   417-466-4646
Fax: 417-466-7140 888-427-3235
customerservice@windandwillow.com
www.windandwillow.com
Cheeseball, mixes, dips, and meat seasonings
Contact: Renee Tettenhorst
r.tettenhorst@windandwillow.com
Number Employees: 10-19

60322 Winder Farms
4400 W 4100 S
West Valley City, UT 84120-5077   801-969-3401
Fax: 801-969-2223 800-946-3371
www.winderfarms.com
Online grocer.
President & CFO: Scott Tanner
CEO: Melanie Robinson
VP, Customer Service: Kent Winder
Estimated Sales: F
Number Employees: 100-249
Types of Products Distributed:
Frozen Food

60323 Windy City Distribution
30 West 315 Calumet Ave.
Warrenville, IL 60555   630-836-9503
webbeerline@reyesholdings.com
www.windycitydistribution.com
Beer.
President/CEO: Bob Collins
Estimated Sales: $840,000
Number Employees: 119
Square Footage: 175000
Parent Co: Reyes Holding Company

60324 Windy City Organics
3320 Commercial Ave.
Northbrook, IL 60062   800-925-0577
info@windycityorganics.com
www.windycityorganics.com
Chocolate, nut butters, snacks and supplements
CEO: Alex Malinsky
Social Marketing & Brand Communications: Anna Speaks
Sales & Account Management: Adam Fohrman
Estimated Sales: $3 Million
Number Employees: 25
Type of Packaging: Consumer, Private Label
Types of Products Distributed:
Specialty Foods

60325 Wine Country Chef LLC
PO Box 1416
Hidden Valley Lake, CA 95461   707-322-0406
Fax: 800-306-2660
Organic spice blends and all natural marinades & sauces
President/Owner: Harold Imbrunetti
chef@winecountrychef.net
Estimated Sales: $250,000
Number Employees: 2
Number of Brands: 4
Number of Products: 4
Type of Packaging: Consumer, Food Service, Bulk
Number of Customer Locations: 13
Types of Products Distributed:
Food Service, Health Food, Specialty Foods, Organic, All Natural

60326 Wing Seafood Company
1133 W Lake St
Chicago, IL 60607-1618   312-421-8686
Fax: 312-942-0391
Seafood
Owner: Wing Ng
Estimated Sales: $1.2 Million
Number Employees: 5-9

60327 (HQ)Wing Sing Chong Company
152 Utah Avenue
Suite 140
S San Francisco, CA 94080-6718   415-552-1234
Fax: 415-552-3812
Manufacturer, importer and wholesaler/distributor of Asian foods
Owner: Roberta Woo
Estimated Sales: $15 Million
Number Employees: 1-4
Square Footage: 150000
Private Brands Carried:
LANTERN
Types of Products Distributed:
Frozen Food, Specialty Foods, Oriental

60328 Wing Sing Seafood Inc
230 Libby St
Honolulu, HI 96819-3960   808-847-2580
Fax: 808-847-2879
Wholesaler/distributor of fresh seafood including shellfish; serving the food service market
Owner: Don Leong
wingsingsfd@aol.com
Estimated Sales: $5-10 Million
Number Employees: 10-19
Types of Products Distributed:
Food Service, Frozen Food, Seafood

60329 Wininger & Assoc
28450 Bradner Rd
Millbury, OH 43447-9721   419-836-5151
Fax: 419-836-5151 boblwin@aol.com
Wholesaler/distributor of software including inventory, production, nutrition labeling, recipe development, nutrition database, costing, order entry, purchasing and accounting
President: Robert Wininger
rwininger@woh.rr.com
Estimated Sales: Less Than $500,000
Number Employees: 1-4
Private Brands Carried:
Batchmaster Software

Wholesalers & Distributors / A-Z

60330 Wink Frozen Desserts
P.O. Box 111375
Stamford, CT 06911   516-323-5283
info@winkfrozendesserts.com
www.winkfrozendesserts.com
Fat free, sugar free ice cream
CEO: Gabriel Wolff
CMO: Jordan Pierson *Year Founded:* 2012
Types of Products Distributed:
    Frozen Food

60331 Winkler Inc
535 E Medcalf St
Dale, IN 47523-9384   812-937-4421
    Fax: 812-937-2044   800-621-3843
winkler@winklerinc.com
Wholesaler/distributor of general line products and groceries
President: L Winkler
CEO: Phil Fischer
p.fischer@winklerinc.com
VP: L Howell
Number Employees: 100-249
Private Brands Carried:
    Plee-Zing; Better Valu; Fine Fare
Number of Customer Locations: 840
Types of Products Distributed:
    Frozen Food, General Line, Groceries

60332 Winkler Meats
733 SW Washington St
Peoria, IL 61602-1657   309-671-1050
    Fax: 309-671-1055
Wholesaler/distributor of meats, frozen foods and seafood; serving the food service market and supermarkets
President: Larry Winkler
lwinkler@fastenal.com
Estimated Sales: $20-50 Million
Number Employees: 5-9
Number of Customer Locations: 150
Types of Products Distributed:
    Food Service, Frozen Food, Provisions/Meat, Seafood

60333 (HQ)Winmix/Natural Care Products
7466 Cape Girardeau Street
Englewood, FL 34224-8004   941-475-7432
    Fax: 941-475-7432
Processor and exporter of soft serve ice cream and sorbets, meat analogs, fruit juice and beverage bases, low-fat replacers and nonfat mixes. Importer of juice and coffee bases.
Board of Directors: Winsor Eveland
Owner: Martha Efird
Estimated Sales: $100000
Number Employees: 2
Number of Products: 350
Square Footage: 8000
Type of Packaging: Consumer, Food Service, Private Label, Bulk
Private Brands Carried:
    Winmix; Natural Care Products; TNO; SoyFlax 5000; CitruSoy 5000; Multygrain Foods
Number of Customer Locations: 75
Types of Products Distributed:
    Food Service, Frozen Food, Health Food, Specialty Foods, Meatless deli items

60334 Winn-Dixie
P.O. Box B
Jacksonville, FL 32203-0297
     844-745-0463
www.winndixie.com
Wholesaler/distributor of general groceries.
EVP: Eddie Garcia
Year Founded: 1925
Number Employees: 41,000
Parent Co: Southeastern Grocers
Number of Customer Locations: 495
Types of Products Distributed:
    Frozen Food, General Line, General Merchandise, Provisions/Meat, Produce, Seafood

60335 Winn-Dixie Stores
5050 Edgewood Ct.
Jacksonville, FL 32254-3699   904-783-5000
     800-967-9105
info@winndixie.com www.winndixie.com
Supermarket chain.
President/CEO, Southeastern Grocers: Anthony Hucker
Year Founded: 1925
Estimated Sales: $10 Billion
Number Employees: 41,000
Parent Co: Southeastern Grocers
Other Locations:
    Manufacturing Facility
    Baldwin, FL
    Manufacturing Facility
    Jacksonville, FL
    Manufacturing Facility
    Orlando, FL
    Manufacturing Facility
    Miami, FL
    Manufacturing Facility
    Hammond, LA
    Manufacturing Facility
    Montgomery, AL
    Manufacturing FacilityJacksonville

60336 Wins Paper Products
321 Murray Road
Springtown, TX 76082-6520   817-281-6550
    Fax: 817-281-0560   800-733-2420
Manufacturer and wholesaler/distributor of paper bags; serving the food service market
President: Douglas Wiley
Chairman: Gordon Wiley
Estimated Sales: Below $5 Million
Number Employees: 10
Square Footage: 156000
Types of Products Distributed:
    Food Service, Frozen Food, General Merchandise, Paper bags

60337 Winter Harbor Co-Op Inc
23 Pendleton Rd
Winter Harbor, ME 04693-3233   207-963-5857
    Fax: 207-963-7275
randy@winterharborlobster.com
www.winterharborlobstercoop.com
Whole fish and seafood
President: Michael Sargeant
Manager: Randy Johnson
Estimated Sales: $600,000
Number Employees: 5-9

60338 Wiper Supply & Chemical
3701 Princeton Dr NE
Albuquerque, NM 87107-4217   505-883-4050
    Fax: 505-883-6115   800-359-2913
Wholesaler/distributor of general merchandise including cleaning supplies, disposables, wraps and table top needs; serving the food service market
Owner: Mark Braddock
markk1230@spinn.net
Estimated Sales: $2.5-5 Million
Number Employees: 5-9
Types of Products Distributed:
    Food Service, Frozen Food, General Merchandise, Equipment & supplies

60339 Wisconsin Allied Products Inc
4170 N 126th St
Brookfield, WI 53005-1881   262-781-2038
    Fax: 262-781-1448
Wholesaler/distributor of ice and juice machines, freezers, refrigerators, water filtration systems, ice cream cabinets, cup dispensers, coffee equipment and wire shelving
Owner: Dick Reinhart
dickr@wiallied.com
VP: Tim McCarthy
Operations Manager: Pat Heagney
Estimated Sales: $5-10 Million
Number Employees: 10-19
Square Footage: 24000
Types of Products Distributed:
    Frozen Food, General Merchandise, Ice machines, refrigerators, etc.

60340 Wisconsin Milk Mktng Board Inc
8418 Excelsior Dr
PO Box 182
Madison, WI 53717-1931   608-836-8820
    Fax: 608-836-5822   800-589-5127
info@eatwisconsincheese.com
www.eatwisconsincheese.com
Cream cheese spreads; shredded mozzarella and cheddar cheeses
President: Jeff Laack
CEO: James Robson
VP: Mark Laack
Estimated Sales: $10-20 Million
Number Employees: 50-99
Square Footage: 50000
Type of Packaging: Consumer, Food Service, Private Label, Bulk
Private Brands Carried:
    Laack's Finest; Laack of Wisconsin
Number of Customer Locations: 50
Types of Products Distributed:
    Food Service, Frozen Food, General Line, Cheeses

60341 Wise Forklift Inc
107 Commercial Ln
Dothan, AL 36303-2345   334-794-8468
    Fax: 334-794-7748   800-239-9040
Wholesaler/distributor of material handling equipment including forklifts and pallet jacks
President: Larry Wise
kjackson@wiseforklift.com
Estimated Sales: $5-10 Million
Number Employees: 5-9
Square Footage: 32000
Private Brands Carried:
    Baker; Komatsu; Blue Giant
Types of Products Distributed:
    Frozen Food, General Merchandise, Material handling equipment

60342 Wise Products Distributors
7902 Belair Rd
Baltimore, MD 21236-3707   410-663-5257
    Fax: 410-342-1445
Wholesaler/distributor of meats, private label products and specialty foods
Owner: Michael Wise
Estimated Sales: $10-20 Million
Number Employees: 20-49
Parent Co: Wise Foods
Types of Products Distributed:
    General Line, Provisions/Meat, Specialty Foods, Private label products

60343 Wishbone Utensil Tableware Line
15 Paramount Pkwy
Wheat Ridge, CO 80215-6615   303-238-8088
    Fax: 253-595-7673   866-266-5928
Forever replaces chopsticks. One piece tong, skewer & ergonomic utensil. Child safe. Dishwasher friendly. Assisted living compatible. Solution for the chopstick challenged. Popular among hotel/resorts, restaurateur and occupationalhealth. Ten motif-friendly colors. FDA approved. Stylish, durable, reusable, fun. Sanitized and individually wrapped. Gourmet quality Feng Shui tableware
CEO: R Farlan Krieger Sr
Estimated Sales: Under $300,000
Number Employees: 9
Number of Brands: 4
Number of Products: 8
Square Footage: 50000
Parent Co: RF Krieger, LLC
Type of Packaging: Consumer, Food Service, Private Label, Bulk
Private Brands Carried:
    Wishbone Utensil
Number of Customer Locations: 2

60344 Wishnev Wine Management
2125 Oak Grove Rd Ste 120
Walnut Creek, CA 94598   925-930-6374
    Fax: 925-930-6388
Wines
Owner: Sanford Wishnev
Estimated Sales: $300,000-500,000
Number Employees: 1-4
Type of Packaging: Private Label
Types of Products Distributed:
    Wine

60345 Wisner Manufacturing Corporation
11 Village Dr
Montville, NJ 07045-9461   973-299-1634
    Fax: 908-233-7331   800-221-0104
Wholesaler/distributor of dairy products, chemical equipment, etc.
President: Jimmy Wisner
Estimated Sales: $300,000-500,000
Number Employees: 1-4
Types of Products Distributed:
    Frozen Food, General Line, General Merchandise, Dairy products & equipment

Wholesalers & Distributors / A-Z

60346 Witmer Foods
P.O.Box 3307
Cumberland, MD 21504-3307
301-724-5950
Fax: 301-724-6935
Wholesaler/distributor of groceries, meats, produce, dairy products, frozen foods, baked goods, general merchandise and seafood; serving the food service market
Owner: Jerri Whitmer
Vice President: Diane Witmer
Sales Director: Jim House
Purchasing Manager: Jerry Witmer
Estimated Sales: $6 Million
Number Employees: 20-49
Number of Products: 3500
Square Footage: 88000
Type of Packaging: Food Service
Private Brands Carried:
  Pocahontas
Number of Customer Locations: 20
Types of Products Distributed:
  Food Service, Frozen Food, General Line, General Merchandise, Provisions/Meat, Produce, Seafood, Groceries, dairy products, etc.

60347 Wohlt Cheese Corp
1005 Orville Dr
P.O. Box 203
New London, WI 54961-9398
920-982-9000
Fax: 920-982-6288
Manufacturer of processed cheeses (including American cheese, cheese food, cheese spread and other cheese products); available in loaves and blocks, flavoured varities, custom blends and various melts. Offer shredding and dicingservices.
President: Marilyn Taylor
Quality Manager: Frederick Ladenburger
Production Manager: Mark Gelhausen
Estimated Sales: $19.6 Million
Number Employees: 50-99
Square Footage: 20000
Type of Packaging: Consumer, Food Service, Private Label, Bulk

60348 Wolverton Seafood
PO Box 1721
Houlton, ME 04730-5721
506-276-4629
Fax: 506-276-1803
Seafood
Owner: Margaret Wolberton

60349 Wood Beverage Company
PO Box 146
Edgemont, PA 19028-0146
610-353-8080
Fax: 610-353-8503
Wholesaler/distributor of beer
Owner: Ernie Grucini
Estimated Sales: $5-10 Million
Number Employees: 10-19
Types of Products Distributed:
  Frozen Food, Beer

60350 Wood Fruitticher Grocery Company
2900 Alton Rd
Birmingham, AL 35210
205-836-9663
www.woodfruitticher.com
Wholesaler/distributor of groceries, paper and restaurant products in Alabama, Georgia, South Carolina, Florida and Mississippi.
President: John Wood
Purchase Manager: Jim Bennett
jbennett@woodfruitticher.com
Year Founded: 1913
Estimated Sales: $300 Million
Number Employees: 100-249
Square Footage: 365000
Types of Products Distributed:
  Frozen Food, General Line, General Merchandise

60351 Wood's Products
2500 Beasley Rd
Benson, NC 27504-6637
919-894-2318
Fax: 919-894-6195
Wholesaler/distributor of sweet potatoes
Co-Owner: J Roland Wood
Co-Owner: Winnefred Wood
Estimated Sales: $10-20 Million
Number Employees: 20-49
Private Brands Carried:
  Suzy's Supreme; Little Mike

Types of Products Distributed:
  Frozen Food, Produce, Sweet potatoes

60352 Woodlake Distributors
179 Avenue of the Cmnnue
Suite 2
Shrewsbury, NJ 07702-4558
732-286-1130
Fax: 732-286-2250
Wholesaler/distributor of eggs, butter and cheese; serving supermarkets and food service operators in New York and New Jersey
President: E Arbeit
VP: S Arbeit
Manager: A Arbeit
Sales Director: M Portskin
Number Employees: 12
Square Footage: 40000
Type of Packaging: Food Service, Bulk
Number of Customer Locations: 600
Types of Products Distributed:
  Food Service, Frozen Food, Eggs, butter & cheese

60353 Woodland Foods
1200 Northwestern Ave
Gurnee, IL 60031-2365
847-625-8600
Fax: 847-625-5050 www.woodlandfoods.com
Dried ingredients: mushrooms, chile pods, pastes and powders, herbs, spices, seasonings and rubs, grains and rices, tomatoes, beans, lentils, couscous and orzo, Asian noodles and flavor bases, flours and meals, corns and polentaspecialty salts, peppercorns and sugars, nuts and seeds, dried fruit, truffle products and snack mixes.
President & CEO: David Moore
davidmoore@woodlandfoods.com
Executive Vice President: Mike Brundidge
Vice President, Operations: Ely Suhre
Number Employees: 50-99
Square Footage: 300000
Type of Packaging: Consumer, Food Service, Private Label, Bulk
Types of Products Distributed:
  Food Service, Health Food, Specialty Foods, Dried Food Ingredients

60354 Woody's Frozen Food Distr
1824 E Independence Ave
Tulare, CA 93274-8011
559-688-8363
Fax: 559-688-8363
Wholesaler/distributor of frozen foods; serving the food service market
Owner: Keith Ruby
Estimated Sales: Less Than $500,000
Number Employees: 1-4
Type of Packaging: Food Service
Types of Products Distributed:
  Frozen Food

60355 Workstead Industries
PO Box 1083
Greenfield, MA 01302-1083
413-772-6816
www.workstead.com
Distributor, packager and exporter of low methoxyl citrus pectin for low and sugar-free jam and jelly processing
Owner: Connie Sumberg
conniesumberg@pomonapectin.com
Estimated Sales: Less Than $500,000
Number Employees: 1-4
Number of Brands: 1
Number of Products: 2
Square Footage: 4000
Type of Packaging: Consumer, Bulk
Private Brands Carried:
  Pomona's Universal Pectin
Number of Customer Locations: 1
Types of Products Distributed:
  Frozen Food, Pectin

60356 World Class Beer Imports
P.O.Box 39588
Fort Lauderdale, FL 33339
954-564-2337
Fax: 954-564-3854 support@worldclassbeer.com
www.worldclassbeer.com
Importer and wholesaler/distributor of beer, wine, cordials and ciders
President: Reubin Share
Estimated Sales: $1-2.5 Million
Number Employees: 5-9
Square Footage: 28800
Parent Co: REU-DOM Investments & Holdings
Number of Customer Locations: 500

60357 (HQ)World Finer Foods Inc
1455 Broad St
4th Floor
Bloomfield, NJ 07003-3039
973-338-0300
Fax: 973-338-0382 800-225-1449
info@worldfiner.com www.worldfiner.com
Importer and wholesaler/distributor of specialty foods including canned vegetables and fish, cooking wines, vinegars, pastas, sauces, seasonings, croutons, soups, olives, olive oils, beans, rice mixes, preserves, cereals, cookiescrispbreads, etc
President: John Affel
affel@worldfiner.com
Chairman: John Beers
CFO: Barry O'Brien
VP & Controller: Neal Kaskel
VP Marketing: Todd Newstadt
VP Sales: Kevin Hubbard
Public Relations Director: Tom Barnes
Manager: Lisa Accunzo-Cheplic
VP Purchasing: Barbara Harloe
Estimated Sales: $13.9 Million
Number Employees: 1-4
Square Footage: 48000
Types of Products Distributed:
  General Line, Health Food, Specialty Foods, Vinegars, pasta, sauces, soups, etc.

60358 World Kitchen
5500 Pearl St Ste 400
Rosemont, IL 60018
847-678-8600
Fax: 847-678-9424
Manufacturer and exporter of plastic containers; wholesaler/distributor and exporter of bakery racks and food trays; serving the food service market
President: Jim Sharman
CEO: Joe Mallof
Contact: Michael Cwiertniakm
cwiertniakm@worldkitchen.com
Estimated Sales: $20-50 Million
Number Employees: 100-249
Parent Co: Borden Inc.
Type of Packaging: Food Service
Types of Products Distributed:
  Food Service, Frozen Food, General Merchandise, Bakery racks & food trays

60359 World Spice
223-235 Highland Parkway
Roselle, NJ 07203
908-245-0600
Fax: 908-245-0696 800-234-1060
sales@wsispice.com www.wsispice.com
Spices, seasonings, herbs and dehydrated vegetables
President: Bela Lowy
Vice President: J Lefbowitz
Estimated Sales: $2 Million
Number Employees: 5-9
Square Footage: 60000
Type of Packaging: Food Service, Bulk
Types of Products Distributed:
  Food Service, General Line, Herbs, spices, seasonings, etc.

60360 World Tableware Inc
300 Madison Ave
Toledo, OH 43604-1561
419-325-2608
Fax: 419-325-2749 800-678-9849
stock@libbey.com www.libbey.com
Importer, exporter and wholesaler/distributor of tabletop supplies including flatware, dinnerware and holloware; serving the food service market
President: John Myer
CEO: Jay Achenbach
achenbachj@libbey.com
Quality Control: Allwyn Cahoun
CEO: John Meier
R & D: Bill Herp
Number Employees: 5-9
Parent Co: Libbey
Type of Packaging: Food Service
Private Brands Carried:
  Bausher; Ultima; World Porcelein
Types of Products Distributed:
  Food Service, Frozen Food, General Merchandise, Flatware, dinnerware, etc.

60361 World Variety Produce
5325 S Soto St
Vernon, CA 90058-3624
323-588-0151
Fax: 323-588-7841 800-468-7111
hotline@melissas.com
Wholesaler/distributor, importer and exporter of produce

1227

Wholesalers & Distributors / A-Z

President: Joe Hernandez
Director Marketing: Bill Schneider
Manager: Luis Sanchez
luiss@melissas.com
Plant Manager: Mike Stephens
Procurement: Jim Hernandez
Estimated Sales: $20-50 Million
Number Employees: 250-499
Square Footage: 125000
Private Brands Carried:
 Melissa's; Jo-San; Don Enrique
Types of Products Distributed:
 Frozen Food, Produce

60362 World Wide Safe Brokers
112 Cromwell Court
Woodbury, NJ 08096 856-863-1225
 Fax: 856-845-2266 800-593-2893
 info@worldwidesafebrokers.com
 www.worldwidesafebrokers.com
Fire safes, electronic safes, gun safes, safe deposit boxes, hotel room safes, insulated files, burglary safe, vaults, vault doors, in-floor safes, depository safes, custom designed and manufactured safes.
President: Edward Dornisch
VP: Mildred Dornisch
Estimated Sales: $.5-1 million
Number Employees: 3
Square Footage: 16000
Types of Products Distributed:
 Security Containers

60363 Wrawp
862 Towne Center Dr.
Suite A
Pomona, CA 91767 909-447-1800
  855-972-9748
 customerservice@wrawp.com www.wrawp.com
Organic, gluten-free veggie wraps, coconut wraps, and pizza crusts
Founder/CEO: Elena Semenova
Co-Founder: Kraig Dooman
Accounting: Iris Medina
Marketing & Brand Partnerships: Daniel Bauer
Operations Manager: Bioncia Martin
Production Manager: Anastasiia Lewis
Engineer: Vadim Kan
Year Founded: 2012
Number Employees: 20-49
Types of Products Distributed:
 General Line

60364 Wrenn Handling
11301 Granite St
Charlotte, NC 28273 704-587-4628
 Fax: 704-588-3892
Wholesaler/distributor of material handling equipment including forklifts
President: Kenneth Brown
Number Employees: 20-49
Private Brands Carried:
 Hyster; Long Reach; Trackmobile; K.D. Manitou
Types of Products Distributed:
 Frozen Food, General Merchandise, Material handling equipment

60365 Wright Brand Oysters
9216 Faith St
Coden, AL 36523-3007 251-824-7880
 Fax: 251-824-7880
Processor and distributor of oysters
President: Stanley Wright
Estimated Sales: $1-3 Million
Number Employees: 10-19

60366 Wustefeld Candy Co Inc
135 Paine St
Green Island, NY 12183 518-272-5600
 Fax: 518-272-5690
Wholesaler/distributor of candy and specialty foods and groceries
President: Bruce Finkle
Estimated Sales: $5-10 Million
Number Employees: 10-19
Number of Customer Locations: 400
Types of Products Distributed:
 Frozen Food, General Line, Specialty Foods, Candy

60367 Wusthoff Trident Cutlery
344 Taft Street NE
Minneapolis, MN 55413 612-379-1300
  866-797-0555
 www.eversharpknives.com
Importer and wholesaler/distributor of kitchen cutlery; serving the food service market
VP Sales: Scott Severinson
Estimated Sales: $5-10 Million
Number Employees: 10-19
Type of Packaging: Food Service
Private Brands Carried:
 Wusthoff Trident
Types of Products Distributed:
 Food Service, Frozen Food, General Merchandise, Kitchen cutlery

60368 X L Energy Drink Corp
521 5th Ave # 2800
32nd Floor
New York, NY 10175-2199 212-594-3080
 Fax: 212-594-3096 usa@xl-energy.com
  www.xl-energy.com
Energy drink/beverage.
Business Development Director: Michael Raunegger
Manager: Jonathan Adler
adler@xl-energy.com
Number Employees: 1-4

60369 Xtreme Beverages, LLC
32565-B Golden Lantern
#282
Dana Point, CA 92629
Canada 949-495-7929
 Fax: 949-495-8015 xtremebeverages@cox.net
Wood and bamboo box; wood and bamboo tea chest; wine box; baskets; tea and coffee accessories; wine accessories; MDF box; cardboard box; wooded tea dispenser; wrought iron tea can rack; wood and bamboo products, candles; candleholders; gourmet gift packaging and food and beverage gift packaging
President: William Quinley
VP: James Moffitt
Estimated Sales: $5 Million
Number Employees: 4
Type of Packaging: Consumer, Food Service, Private Label, Bulk
Types of Products Distributed:
 General Merchandise, Gift Packaging, Giftware, Tableware

60370 YAAX International
3111 Tieton Dr # 300
Yakima, WA 98902-3628 509-249-5555
 Fax: 509-469-2133 info@yaax.com
  www.yaax.com
Wholesaler & distributor of fruit juice concentrates flavors, purees, dehydrated fruit and dairy products, glass and plastic packaged juices. Supplier of processed vegetable products.
President: Bruce Simpson
Marketing: Jennifer Tilley
Number Employees: 2-10
Type of Packaging: Private Label, Bulk
Types of Products Distributed:
 Specialty Foods, Organic and conventional juices

60371 Yai's Thai
3047 Larimer St.
Suite 202
Denver, CO 80205
 info@yaisthai.com
 www.yaisthai.com
Thai curries, almond sauce, ginger lime sauce, garlic hot sauce, relish, and salsa. Products are paleo, vegan, and gluten free
Co-Founder/CEO: Leland Copenhagen
Co-Founder/COO: Sarah Hughes
VP Sales: Aaron Barnholt *Year Founded:* 2016
Types of Products Distributed:
 General Line

60372 Yale Industrial Trucks
2230 N US Highway 301
Tampa, FL 33619-2690 813-621-4671
 Fax: 813-628-0555
Wholesaler/distributor of material handling equipment including forklifts
President: A MacKinnon
Controller: Greg Phrig
Contact: Shawn Bartlett
sbartlett@yaleflorida.com
Estimated Sales: $20-50 Million
Number Employees: 5-9
Private Brands Carried:
 Yale; Huskey; Magliner
Types of Products Distributed:
 Frozen Food, General Merchandise, Material handling equipment

60373 Yale Industrial Trucks:Ontario
340 Hanlan Road
Toronto, ON L4L 3T1
Canada 905-851-6620
 Fax: 905-851-6866 888-781-1042
  www.yaleforklifts.com
Wholesaler/distributor of material handling equipment including forklifts
President/CEO: Alan McFadyen
COO: Mark Barrett
Director General: Serge Tremblay
VP, Sales: John Sedlacek
Number Employees: 100-249
Square Footage: 400000
Private Brands Carried:
 Yale
Types of Products Distributed:
 Frozen Food, General Merchandise, Material handling equipment

60374 Yale Material Handling/Gammon
1960 Concourse Dr
St Louis, MO 63146-4117 314-567-9250
 Fax: 314-567-7280 800-777-9250
  www.yale.com
Wholesaler/distributor of material handling equipment; also, rack jobber services available
Manager: Joe Grana
bwatson@chronline.com
Chairman: W Ronald Gammon
Estimated Sales: $2.5-5 Million
Number Employees: 20-49
Square Footage: 180000
Private Brands Carried:
 Yale; Taylor
Types of Products Distributed:
 Frozen Food, General Merchandise, Rack Jobbers, Material handling equipment

60375 Yamasho Inc
750 Touhy Ave
Elk Grove Village, IL 60007-4916 847-981-9342
 Fax: 847-981-9347 info@yamashoinc.com
  www.yamashoinc.com
Japanese products
President: Kunio Iwadate
Estimated Sales: $20-50 Million
Number Employees: 5-9

60376 Yeager & Associates
79158 Buff Bay Court
Bermuda Dunes, CA 92203-1567 760-345-7404
 Fax: 760-345-8816 pjyeager@gmail.com
Experts in developing new products using chicken, beef and pork for private labels. We have the ability to cook your meat/poultry product to final specification for further processing or packaging for retail sales. We haverepresentation in all major retail markets and food service.
President: Paula Yeager
VP: Robert Carian
Quality Control: Jason Carian
Sales: Paula Yeager
Sales: Lauren Hagadorn
Estimated Sales: $6 Million
Number Employees: 5
Square Footage: 16000
Parent Co: P&R Sales, Inc.
Type of Packaging: Consumer, Food Service, Private Label, Bulk
Types of Products Distributed:
 Frozen Food, Provisions/Meat, Specialty Foods

60377 Yeomen Seafoods Inc
30 Western Ave # 201
Gloucester, MA 01930-3664 978-283-7422
 Fax: 978-283-7522
Whole frozen seafood
Owner: Tim Kennedy
yeomen@gis.net
Estimated Sales: $4.7 Million
Number Employees: 1-4

60378 Yonkers Institutional Food Company
42 Bishop Williams J. Walls Place
Yonkers, NY 10701 914-965-0075
Fax: 914-969-4696 www.institutionalamez.org
Wholesaler/distributor for the food service market
President: B Braun
General Manager: F Braun
Estimated Sales: $10-20 Million
Number Employees: 5-9
Private Brands Carried:
   Albert; Big Ben
Number of Customer Locations: 300
Types of Products Distributed:
   Food Service, Frozen Food

60379 Yorktown Electrical & Lighting
749 Route 109
West Babylon, NY 11704-4113 631-957-9000
Fax: 631-957-1570
Wholesaler/distributor of electrical supplies and lighting fixtures
President: Kevin Norris
info@yorktownelectrical.com
Estimated Sales: $10-20 Million
Number Employees: 5-9
Types of Products Distributed:
   Frozen Food, General Merchandise, Electrical supplies & lighting fixtures

60380 Young & Stout
1684 Andell Rd
Bridgeport, WV 26330 304-624-5411
Fax: 304-624-5411 800-439-5411
www.youngandstout.com
Wholesaler/distributor of meat products including beef and pork; serving the food service market.
President: Abner Stout
Year Founded: 1942
Estimated Sales: $20-50 Million
Number Employees: 10-19
Types of Products Distributed:
   Food Service, Provisions/Meat, Beef & pork

60381 (HQ)Young Pecan, Inc.
2005 Babar Ln
Florence, SC 29501
800-729-6003
www.youngplantations.com
Pecans
President & CEO: James Swink
Executive Vice President: Helen Watts
Estimated Sales: $75-99 Million
Number Employees: 183
Number of Brands: 3
Square Footage: 150000
Parent Co: King Ranch
Type of Packaging: Consumer, Food Service, Bulk
Other Locations:
   Las Cruces, NM
   Los Angeles, CA
   Salem, OR
   Seattle, WA
   Detroit, MI
   Mason, OHLos Angeles
Types of Products Distributed:
   Pecans

60382 Young's Lobster Pound
4 Mitchell Street
Belfast, ME 04915 207-338-1160
Fax: 207-338-3498
Processor, exporter and importer of fresh and frozen seafood including crabs, lobster, live and shucked clams and mussels, scallops and shrimp; wholesaler/distributor of fresh and frozen seafood
Owner: Raymond Young
Co-Owner: Claire Young
Manager; Owner: Raymond Young
Estimated Sales: $3-5 Million
Number Employees: 20-49
Square Footage: 10944
Type of Packaging: Consumer, Food Service
Types of Products Distributed:
   Frozen Food, Seafood

60383 Youngstown Wholesale Grocery
366 Victoria Rd
Youngstown, OH 44515-2092 330-793-8250
Fax: 330-793-4701
www.youngstownwholesale.com
Wholesaler/distributor of groceries, meat and general line products; serving the food service market
President: Michael Fenstemaker
michael@youngstownwholesale.com
Treasurer: J Villano
VP: R Villano
Estimated Sales: $20-50 Million
Number Employees: 20-49
Private Brands Carried:
   Villa Rosa
Number of Customer Locations: 50
Types of Products Distributed:
   Food Service, Frozen Food, General Line, Provisions/Meat, Groceries

60384 Yue's International Company
8665 Kingsbridge Drive
Apt B
Saint Louis, MO 63132-4505 573-983-9352
Fax: 573-983-9352 chinesecooking@hotmail.com
Wholesaler/distributor of Chinese cooking sauces including kung pao, garlic, seafood and sweet and sour
Owner/Manager: Shan Yue
Number Employees: 1-4
Square Footage: 12000
Private Brands Carried:
   Uncle Hsu's
Number of Customer Locations: 4
Types of Products Distributed:
   Frozen Food, General Line, Chinese cooking sauces

60385 Z T Merchandising Inc
8947 Metropolitan Ave
Rego Park, NY 11374-5325 718-896-8420
Fax: 718-275-9053 ziv@ztpackaging.com
www.ztpackaging.com
Wholesaler/distributor of general merchandise including advertising specialties, bags, boxes, labels, packaging, wrapping paper and ribbons
President: Ziv Vinokor
ziv.vv@verizon.net
Estimated Sales: $500,000-$1 Million
Number Employees: 5-9
Square Footage: 12000
Number of Customer Locations: 400
Types of Products Distributed:
   General Merchandise, Packaging, Promotional Products

60386 Z&S Distributing
7090 N. Marks Avenue
Suite 104
Fresno, CA 93711 559-432-1777
Fax: 559-432-2888 800-467-0788
Fruits and vegetables.
President: Martin Zaninovich
Estimated Sales: $7,700,000
Number Employees: 10-19
Type of Packaging: Consumer

60387 ZAK Designs Inc
1604 S Garfield Rd
Airway Heights, WA 99001-9705 509-244-0555
Fax: 509-244-0704 800-331-1089
www.zak.com
Importer, exporter and wholesaler/distributor of children's dinnerware, adult servingware, acrylic drinkware and oven mitts
President: Irv Zakheim
CEO: Thomas Pauley
thewd@st-lukes.org
VP (International): Michelle Jou
National Sales Manager: Ken Long
Estimated Sales: $20-50 Million
Number Employees: 100-249
Square Footage: 100000
Types of Products Distributed:
   Frozen Food, General Merchandise, Dinnerware, servingware, drinkware, etc

60388 ZT Packaging
89-47 Metropolitan Avenue
Rego Park, NY 11374 718-896-8420
Fax: 718-275-9053 800-932-2448
info@ztpackaging.com www.ztpackaging.com
Plastic bags, custom printed bags, paper bags, boxes

60389 Zabiha Halal Meat Processors
1715 Cortland Ct
Addison, IL 60101 630-620-5000
Fax: 630-620-5013 info@fatimabrand.com
www.fatimabrand.com
Meats, poultry, and seafood

Co-Founder: Mohammed Yousuf Khan
Co-Founder: Laila Khan
Team Member: Sajid Khan
Year Founded: 1987
Number of Brands: 1
Types of Products Distributed:
   Provisions/Meat

60390 Zachary Confections Inc
2130 W State Road 28
Frankfort, IN 46041-8771 765-659-4751
Fax: 765-659-1491 800-445-4222
customerservice@zc-inc.com
www.zacharyconfections.com
Wholesaler/distributor of candy
President: Evelyn Aguilar
aevelyn@zc-inc.com
Estimated Sales: $500,000-$1 Million
Number Employees: 250-499
Private Brands Carried:
   Zachary
Types of Products Distributed:
   Frozen Food, General Line, Candy

60391 Zarda King LTD
33 E 35th Pl
Steger, IL 60475-1714 708-755-1007
Fax: 708-755-2445 Sales@zardaking.com
Importer and wholesaler/distributor of saffron incense, candle, spices, dvd, tabacco, henna
President: Bhim Hans
zardakings@aol.com
Estimated Sales: $1-2.5 Million
Number Employees: 1-4
Square Footage: 24000
Number of Customer Locations: 400
Types of Products Distributed:
   Specialty Foods

60392 Zazubean
1529 W 6th Ave
Vancouver, BC V6J 1R1
Canada 604-801-5488
info@zazubean.com
www.zazubean.com
Organic fair trade chocolate
Co-Founder: Tiziana Ienna
Co-Founder: Tara Gilbert
Year Founded: 2007
Number Employees: 2-9
Types of Products Distributed:
   General Line

60393 Zeches Institution Supply
4640 Service Dr
Winona, MN 55987 507-452-4485
Fax: 507-452-4564
Wholesaler/distributor of groceries, health and frozen foods, coffee, tea, canned goods, produce, meats and general merchandise; serving the food service market
CEO: F Zeches
CFO: F Craig Zeches
Estimated Sales: $3-5 Million
Number Employees: 1-4
Square Footage: 110000
Private Brands Carried:
   NIFDA; Comsource; Heinz; Campbell; Trademark Coffee
Number of Customer Locations: 400
Types of Products Distributed:
   Food Service, Frozen Food, General Line, General Merchandise, Health Food, Provisions/Meat, Produce, Coffee, tea, canned foods, etc.

60394 Zego Foods
912 Cole St.
Suite 294
San Francisco, CA 94117 415-706-8094
info@zegofoods.com
www.zegofoods.com
Seed & fruit snack bars, protein, oats, and muesli
Founder/CEO: Colleen Kavanagh
COO: Brian Jansen
Customer Relations: Danielle Schnake *Year Founded:* 2013
Types of Products Distributed:
   General Line

60395 Zel R. Kahn & Sons
2 Fifer Ave Ste 220
Corte Madera, CA 94925 415-924-9600
Fax: 415-924-9690

Wholesalers & Distributors / A-Z

Wholesaler/distributor and exporter of surplus, salvage and closeout merchandise including dried and canned fruits, vegetables, crackers, cereals, etc
President: Scott Kahn
Executive VP: Joel Jutovsky
Estimated Sales: $300,000-500,000
Number Employees: 5-9
Square Footage: 160000
Types of Products Distributed:
    Frozen Food, General Line, Crackers, cereals, etc.

60396 Zellerbach
1059 Vine Street
Suite 102
Sacramento, CA 95814-0339   916-441-6761
                   Fax: 916-563-7900
Wholesaler/distributor of paper, packaging and supplies
Sales Manager (Packaging): Ron Martinelli
Sales Manager (Industrial Products): Mark Howard
Printing Manager: Don Arrington
Parent Co: Zellarbach
Number of Customer Locations: 5000
Types of Products Distributed:
    Frozen Food, General Merchandise, Paper, packaging & supplies

60397 Zetov Inc
4718 18th Ave
Brooklyn, NY 11204-1260   718-972-0808
        Fax: 718-972-0938 Zetov@aol.com
                 www.zetovusa.com
Wholesaler/distributor of snack foods including corn pops, onion rings, flatbreads, party mix, fruit snacks, potato sticks and fat-free bagel chips
Owner: Peter Nadler
VP: J Weinreb
Estimated Sales: $2.5-5 Million
Number Employees: 1-4
Private Brands Carried:
    Kitov; Zetov
Types of Products Distributed:
    Frozen Food, General Line, Snack foods

60398 Ziba Nut Inc
180 Main St
Port Washington, NY 11050-3212   516-944-5112
        Fax: 516-767-1689 info@zibanut.com
                 www.zibanut.com
Wholesaler/distributor, exporter and importer of nuts, organic and natural dried fruits, seeds, cumin seeds, red chilies, ric crackers, and savory snacks, coated peanuts, vegetable chips, plantain chips, and sun dried tomatos
President: Massoud Morshee
CEO: Mehdi Kazemi
mkazemi@zibanut.com
Number Employees: 1-4
Type of Packaging: Bulk
Types of Products Distributed:
    Specialty Foods

60399 Zico Coconut Water
435 Grant Ave
Suite A
Oradell, NJ 07649   201-483-8467
        Fax: 866-620-6783 www.zico.com
Flavored coconut water
Contact: Bill Lange
bill@zico.com

60400 Zink Distributing Co
3150 Shelby St
Indianapolis, IN 46227-3165   317-781-5800
       Fax: 317-781-5810 877-833-2533
               www.zinkdistributing.com
Wholesaler/distributor of beer
Manager: Jim Zink Sr
CFO: Randall Hackworth
randallhackworth@zinkdistributing.com
General Manager: Steve Ward
Estimated Sales: $20-50 Million
Number Employees: 100-249
Private Brands Carried:
    Budweiser; Michelob; Kirin; Red Hook; Scottish Newcastle; Dab; Gosser; Timmermans; Duvel; Belhaven; Youngs; Maisel's
Number of Customer Locations: 450
Types of Products Distributed:
    Frozen Food, General Line, Beer

60401 Zinter Handling Inc
4313 Route 50
Saratoga Springs, NY 12866-2914   518-583-0853
        Fax: 518-583-1063 800-462-1101
              sales@zinterhandling.com
              www.zinterhandling.com
Wholesaler/distributor of cranes and monorails
Owner: Larry Zinter Sr
scott.z@zinterhandling.com
Sales Exec: Scott Zinter
Estimated Sales: $10-20 Million
Number Employees: 20-49
Private Brands Carried:
    Yale; Budget; Harrington
Number of Customer Locations: 70
Types of Products Distributed:
    Frozen Food, General Merchandise, Cranes & monorails

60402 Ziyad Brothers Importing
5400 W 35th St
Cicero, IL 60804-4431   708-222-8330
        Fax: 708-222-1442 info@ziyad.com
               www.ziyad.com
Middle East and Mediterranean food
President: Abraham Ziyad
Manager: Lilian Becker
lbecker@aa.com
Estimated Sales: $5-10 Million
Number Employees: 50-99

60403 Zollman's Dark Canyon Coffee
428 S Main Street
Pendleton, OR 97801-2248   541-276-2242
       Fax: 541-276-2242 888-548-8555
Coffee roasting; wholesale/retail
President: Garry Zollman
CEO/Owner: Kathi Zollman
Vice President: Shaina Zollman
Estimated Sales: Under $500,000
Number Employees: 1-4
Type of Packaging: Private Label

60404 Zuckerman Honickman Inc
191 S Gulph Rd
King of Prussia, PA 19406   610-962-0100
        Fax: 610-962-1080 bromeiser@zh-inc.com
               www.zh-inc.com
Wholesaler/distributor of glass and plastic bottles, jars and closures.
President: Benjamin R Zuckerman
bzuckerman@zh-inc.com
Sales Director: Bob Romeiser
Estimated Sales: $50-100 Million
Number Employees: 20-49
Square Footage: 58000
Types of Products Distributed:
    General Merchandise, Bottles, jars & closures

Wholesale Product Type / Food Service

Food Service

1000 Islands River Rat Cheese, 54501
A & B Distributing Co, 54509
A & W Wholesale Co Inc, 54512
A J Linz Sons, 54517
A J Rinella Co Inc, 54519
A J Silberman & Co, 54520
A La Mode Distributors, 54521
A Tarantino & Sons Poultry, 54523
A&J Produce Corporation, 54531
A&M Enterprises, 54532
A. Berkowitz & Company, 54539
A. Bohrer, 54540
A. De LaChevrotiere, 54541
A. Friscia Seafoods, 54542
A. Simos & Company, 54546
A.B. Wise & Sons, 54548
A.L. Verna Company, 54555
A.M.BRIGGS, 54556
AA Specialty Advertising Products, 54560
Aaburco Inc, 54588
Abatar Institutional Food Company, 54591
Able Sales Company, 54595
AC Paper & Supply, 54566
ACC Distributors Inc, 54567
Ace Chemical, 54601
Ace Fixture Company, 54604
Ace Mart Restaurant Supply, 54605
Acme Food Sales Inc, 54608
Acorn Distributors Inc, 54611
Adams Chapman Co, 54620
Adams Wholesale Co, 54621
ADE Restaurant Service, 54570
Adluh Flour, 54628
Admiral Craft, 54629
Adolf Kusy & Company, 54630
Advanced Chemical, 54634
Adventure Foods, 54638
Adventure Inn Food Trading Company, 54639
Aerolator Systems, 54644
Aetna Plastics Corporation, 54645
Afflink LLC, 54648
Agri-Dairy Products, 54651
Aimonetto and Sons, 54658
Air Savers Inc, 54659
AJC International, 54578
Akron Cotton Products, 54662
Alabama Food Group, 54665, 54666
Alack Refrigeration Co Inc, 54669
Alerta-Mat, 54684
Alex & George, 54685
All Fresh Products, 54696
All Seasons Uniforms & Textile, 54703
All Star Janitorial Supply, 54705
All Star, Ltd., 54706
All State Restaurant Supply, 54707
Allan Chemical Corp, 54712
Allen Brothers Inc, 54716
Allen Rosenthal Company, 54717
Alliance Supply Management, 54719
Allied Food Service, 54723
Allied International Corp, 54725
Allied Provision Company, 54728
Alpha Foods, 54733
Alpine Gloves, 54737
Alsum Farms & Produce, 54741
Alwan & Sons, 54748
AMCON Distributing Co, 54581, 54582
Amenity Services, 54754
American Farms Produce, 54763
American Fish & Seafood Inc, 54764
American Food Equipment, 54766
American Food Traders, 54769
American Frozen Foods, 54771
American Hotel Register Co, 54774
American Legion, 54777
American Metalcraft Inc, 54782
American Produce Company, 54787
American Restaurant Supply, 54790
American Roland Food Corporation, 54792
American Seafood Imports Inc., 54794
American Seaway Foods Inc, 54795
American Specialty Coffee & Culinary, 54799
American Uniforms Sales Inc, 54801
American/Brenner Wholesale, 54804
Amerivap Systems Inc, 54806
Amick Farms LLC, 54807
Ammirati Inc, 54808
AMN Distributors/Premium Blend, 54584
Amos's PA Wonder Products, 54809
Ampak Seafoods Corporation, 54810
Anderson Dubose Company, 54819
Anderson Seafood, 54821
Andre Tea & Coffee Company, 54823
Angel Beltran Corporation, 54826
Angel's Produce, 54827
Angelo M. Formosa Foods, 54828
Angelo Refrigeration & Rstrnt, 54829
Annistion Paper & Supply Company, 54836
Anter Brothers Company, 54837
Anthony's Snack & Vending, 54839
Anthracite Provision Co, 54840
Antone's Import Company, 54842
AP Fish & Produce, 54585
Aramark Uniform Svc, 54854
Arbre Farms Inc, 54855
Arctic Beverages, 54856
Arctic Star Distributing, 54859
Aries Paper & Chemical Company, 54863
Arista Industries Inc, 54864
Arlington Coffee Company, 54870
Armaday Paper, 54871
Arnall Grocery Co, 54874
Aroma Foods, 54878
Arrow Restaurant Equipment, 54882
Asanti Distributors, 54887
Ashley Koffman Foods, 54890
Assemblyonics Inc, 54895
Associated Food Equipment, 54897
Associated Grocers, 54900
Atlanta Fixture & Sales Company, 54910
Atlantic Sea Pride, 54917
Atlantic Store Fixture Company, 54922
Auth Brothers Food Service, 54938
Automation Systems & Services, 54941
Axelrod Foods, 54947
B & B Food Distributors Inc, 54957
B & J Food Svc Inc, 54960
B & M Provision Co, 54962
B & R Quality Meats Inc, 54963
B & W Frozen Foods, 54965
B & W Supply Co, 54966
B Giambrone & Co, 54967
B. Fernandez & Sons, 54975
B/R Sales Company, 54980
Badger Popcorn, 55001
Badger Wholesale Company, 55002
Bagman, 55008
BakeMark Ingredients West Inc, 55015
Baker Bottling & Distributing Company, 55017
Baker Boy Bake Shop Inc, 55018
Bakker Produce, 55028
Baldwin Richardson Foods, 55031
Ballew Distributors, 55035
Balter Meat Co, 55036
Balter Sales Co, 55037
Baltimore Belting Co, 55038
Banana Distributing Company, 55043
Bandwagon Brokerage, 55045
Banner Wholesale Grocers, 55047
Bar Boy Products Inc, 55049
Bar Controls Of Florida, 55050
Bar-Plex, 55053
Bari Italian Foods, 55057
Baring Industries, 55060
Barkett Fruit Company, 55061
Barrel O'Fun of Milwaukee, 55068
Barwell Food Sales, 55072
Basic Food Intl Inc, 55074
Basic Leasing Corporation, 55075
Bassham Institutional Foods, 55078
Bathroom & Towel Systems, 55080
Battistella's Sea Foods, 55082
Baumann Paper Company, 55085
Bay Area Trash Compactor, 55087
Bay Cities Produce Co Inc, 55089
Bay State Restrnt Products Inc, 55092
Bayou Food Distributors, 55097
Bayshore Equipment, 55100
Belair Produce Co Inc, 55117
Belin & Nye, 55120
Bell & Sons, 55121
Belli Produce Company, 55128
Beltram Foodservice Group, 55132
Ben E. Keith, 55133, 55134, 55135, 55136, 55137, 55138, 55139, 55140, 55141, 55142, 55143
Benman Industries Inc, 55165
Benson's Wholesale Fruit, 55168
Bergin Fruit & Nut Co., 55171
Berkel Products Company, 55173
Bertrand's, 55189
Best Buy Uniforms, 55192
Best Friends Cocoa, 55196
Best Restaurant Equip & Design, 55200
Better Beverages Inc, 55202
Better Janitor Supplies, 55204
Better Meat, 55205
Bevistar, 55208
Big Valley Marketing Corporation, 55219
Billingsgate Fish Company, 55222
Birchwood Meats, 55229
Birdseye Dairy-Morning Glory, 55231
Bishop Brothers, 55236
Blachere Group, 55239
Blackburn-Russell Co, 55243
Blanke Bob Sales Inc, 55249
Blondie's, 55251
Blue Buoy Foods, 55255
Blue Delft Supply, 55257
Blue Line Foodservice Distr, 55260
Blue Mountain Meats Inc., 55261
Blue Ribbon Fish Co, 55263
Blue Ribbon Meats, 55264
BMT Commodity Corporation, 54989
Bodean Restaurant & Market, 55272
Bon Ton Food Products, 55279
Boone's Wholesale, 55283
Bosch Industries, 55286
Bosco Food Service, 55287
Boston Showcase Company, 55294
Bottom Line Foods, 55297
Bowlin J P Co LLC, 55303
Boxer-Northwest Company, 55306
Boykin & Southern Wholesale Grocers, 55307
Brace Frozen Foods, 55312
Branton Industries, 55316
Brasco, 55317
Braswell Distributing Co, 55318
Brawner Paper Co Inc, 55321
Brenham Wholesale Groc Inc, 55324
Bresco, 55325
Brevard Restaurant Equipment, 55327
Brewer Meats Inc, 55329
Bridgetown Coffee, 55332
Bringgold Wholesale Meats, 55337
Broadleaf Venison USA Inc, 55344
Broaster Sales & Svc, 55345
Brockman E W Co Inc, 55346
Brody Food Brokerage Corporation, 55348
Bronx Butter & Egg Company, 55349
Brooklyn Boys Pizza & Pasta, 55351
Brooklyn Sugar Company, 55352
Brooks Industries, 55354
Brothers Restaurant Supply, 55357
Brown's Dairy, 55359
Brown's Ice Cream Co, 55360
Browne & Company, 55362
Brucken's, 55365
BS&R Equipment Company, 54993
Buckelew Hardware Co, 55372
Buckelew's Food Svc Equipment, 55373, 55374
Buckhead Beef, 55376
Buffalo Hotel Supply Co Inc, 55381
Buffalo Paper & Detergent Co, 55382
Bunn Capitol Company, 55386
Bunzl Distribution USA, 55387
Bur-Gra Meat & Grocery, 55388
Burlington Equipment Company, 55394
Bush Brothers Provision Co, 55396
Buster Lind Produce Company, 55400
Buz's Crab, 55404
BW Acquisition, 54994
Byczek Enterprises, 55406
Byrne Brothers Foods Inc, 55410
C & R Food Svc Inc, 55412
C & T Design & Equipment Co, 55415
C A Curtze, 55417
C D Hartnett Co, 55418
C M Tanner Grocery Co, 55420
C Pacific Foods Inc, 55421
C. Eberle Sons Company, 55426
C.S. Woods Company, 55432
Cable Meat Center, 55454
Cadco Inc, 55456
Cadillac Meat Company, 55457
Caesar Electric Supply, 55459
Cafe Jumbo, 55461
Calico Industries Inc, 55473
Callahan Grocery Company, 55482
Callif Foods, 55483
Cambridge Packing Company, 55484
Campbell's Food Service, 55487
Campione Resturant Supply, 55488
Canada Cutlery Inc., 55490
Canada Dry Bottling Co, 55491
Canterbury's Crack & Peel, 55499
Canton Foods, 55500
Canty Wiper & Supply Company, 55501
Cape Dairy LLC, 55504
Cape May Fishery Cooperative, 55505
Capitol City Produce, 55509
Capitol Foods, 55510
Cappello Foods, 55512
Captain Morrills Inc, 55519
Carbonella & Desarbo Inc, 55523
Carden Foods Inc, 55525
Cardinal International, 55527
Carlisle Food Systems Inc, 55533
Carole's Cheesecake Company, 55538
Carolina Produce, 55545
Carpenter Snack Food Distribution Company, 55549
Carriage Foods, 55551
Carrot Top Pastries, 55554
Cascade Glacier Ice Cream Company, 55561
Cash Grocery & Sales Company, 55562
Cash Register Sales, 55563
Cash-Wa Distributing, 55564, 55565
Casso Guerra & Company, 55570
Caster Wheels & Indl Handling, 55572
Castino Restaurant Equipment, 55573
Castor Technology Corporation, 55575
Cataract Foods, 55576
Cauble & Field, 55578
Cavazos Candy, Produce & Groceries, 55581
Cavens Meats, 55582
Central Coast Seafood, 55590
Central Distributing Co, 55591
Central Oklahoma Produce Services, 55593
Central Restaurant Supply Inc, 55595
Central Sanitary Supply, 55596
Cerca Foodservice, 55605
CF Imperial Sales, 55441
Challenge Dairy Products, Inc., 55617
Chamberlain Wholesale Grocery, 55618
Chameleon Beverage Co Inc, 55619
Chapman's Food Service, 55621
Chattanooga Restaurant Supl, 55633
Cheese Shop, 55635
Chef John Folse & Co, 55637
Chef's Pride Gifts LLC, 55639
Chef's Supply & Design, 55640
Chellino Cheese Co, 55642
Chem-Mark of Buffalo, 55645

1231

Wholesale Product Type / Food Service

Cheney Brothers Inc, 55648
Chernoff Sales, 55649
Chia I Foods Company, 55654
Chicago Bar & Restaurant Supply, 55655
Chicago Steaks, 55661
Chinese Trading Company, 55665
Choice Restaurant Equipment, 55673
Cirelli Foods, 55689
Ciro Foods, 55690
City Deli Distributing, 55693
City Line Food Distributors, 55696
City Packing Company, 55698
City Produce Co, 55699
City Wholesale Company, 55700
Clarence Mayfield Produce Company, 55703
Clarion Fruit Co, 55704
Clark Food Service Equipment, 55705
Clark Restaurant Svc, 55708
Clayton's Crab Co, 55713
Clearbrook Farms, 55714
Clements Distribution Company, 55717
Clofine Dairy Products Inc, 55724
Clogmaster, 55725
Cloverdale Foods, 55728
Coast to Coast Foods Group, 55729
Coastal Beverage LTD, 55730
Cochran Brothers Company, 55739
Cockrell Banana, 55740
Coffee Break Systems, 55742
Coffee Brothers Inc, 55743
Colorado Chemical Company, 55762
Colorado Restaurant Supply, 55765
Columbia Restaurant & Bar Supply Co., 55768
Comissos Cash & Carry, 55771, 55772, 55773, 55774
Commercial Appliance Svc, 55775
Commissos Cash & Carry, 55776
Commodities Marketing Inc, 55778
Community Coffee Co., 55779
Conagra Brands Canada, 55784
Concession & Restaurant Supply, 55787
Concho Valley Pecan Company, 55789
Connecticut Shellfish Co Inc, 55797
Connellsville Bottling Works, 55799
Conner Produce Co, 55800
Consolidated Poultry & Egg Company, 55804
Consumers Fresh Produce, 55806
Continental Marketing, 55813
Cook's Mate Restaurant Equipment Supply, 55819
Cooker T. Corporation, 55820
Cooseman's D.C., 55825
Coquitlam City Hall, 55827
Corbo Restaurant Supply, 55829
Core-Mark Holding Company, Inc, 55832
Corey Bros Inc WHLS Produce, 55843
Cosgrove Distributors Inc, 55849
Costa Fruit & Produce, 55851
Costco Wholesale Corporation, 55852
Cotati Brand Eggs & Food Svc, 55853
County Supply Co, 55861
Cousin's Uniform, 55863
Crab Connection, 55869
Craver Supply Company, 55873
CRC Products, 55448
Creager Mercantile Cash & Carry, 55875
Crishawn Kitchen Equipment Company, 55883
Cristina Foods Inc, 55885
Crown Restaurant Equipment, 55894
CTS/Bulk Sales, 55451
Culinary Masters Corporation, 55906
Culinary Products Inc, 55907
Culinary Specialties, 55909
Cummings Restaurant Equipment, 55913
Curtis Packing Co, 55915
Curtis Restaurant Equipment, 55916, 55917
Curtis Restaurant Supply, 55918
CW Paper, 55453
D Rosen Co Inc, 55934
D.A. Colongeli & Sons, 55943

D.A. Foodservice, 55944
Dacotah Paper Co, 55961
Daffin Mercantile Company, 55964
Dairy King Milk Farms/Foodservice, 55967
Dairy Source, 55969
Dairyland USA Corp, 55971
Damian's Enterprises Inc, 55976
Dana's Rush Equipment Company, 55977
Danville Paper & Supply, 55980
Datatech Enterprises, 55984
David Puccia & Company, 55987
Davis Coffee Co, 55989
Davis Distributors of Owensboro Company, 55990
Davis-Le Grand Company, 55992
Dayco Distributing, 55993
De Palo & Sons Inc, 55998
Dean & Company, 56002
Dean Supply Co, 56003
Dearborn Cash & Carry Stores, 56005
Dearborn Wholesale Grocers, 56007, 56008, 56009, 56010
Debragga & Spitler, 56012
Deep Foods Inc, 56015
Dees Paper Co, 56019
Delta Bay, 56027
Demak & Company, 56031
Demma Fruit Company, 56032
Deng's, 56034
Denver Restaurant Equipment Company, 56038
Dependable Plastics & Supls, 56040
Designs Furnishings & Eqpt Inc, 56042
Deville Restaurant Equipment & Supply Company, 56046
Dial Industries Inc, 56053
Diamond Chemical & Supply Co, 56054
Dicarlo Distributors Inc, 56059
Dickerson & Quinn, 56061
Dickerson Foods, 56062
Dierks Foods, 56064
DiGregorio Food Products, 56050
Dilgard Frozen Foods, 56068
Dillon Provision Co, 56069
Dinetz Restaurant Equipment, 56072
DiNovo Produce Company, 56052
Discount Equipment Intl, 56080
Dispenser Juice, 56082
Distribution Kowloon, 56084
Distribution Plus, 56085
Diverse Sales, 56086
Divine Ice Cream Company, 56088
Dixie Equipment Co, 56090
Dixie Lily Foods, 56091
Dixie Mart, 56092
Dixie Store Fixtures & Sales, 56093
DMI Distribution, Inc., 55950
Dobert's Dairy, 56095
Doerle Food Svc, 56098
Dolly Madison Ice Cream, 56103
Don Walters Company, 56109
Douglas Brothers Produce Company, 56121
Douglass Produce Company, 56124
Downeast Food Distributors Inc, 56129
DPI Mid Atlantic, 55953
DPI Rocky Mountain, 55955
Dr. Smoothie Brands, 56132
Dr. Willy's Great American Seafood, 56133
Dreyer's Grand Ice Cream Inc., 56140
Dudson USA Inc, 56146
Dunlevy Food Equipment, 56149
Durham Flavor Rich, 56154
Dutch Creek Foods, 56156
Dutch Valley Food Distributors, 56157
Dutchess Restaurant Equipment, 56158
Dutra Distributing, 56159
DWL Industries Company, 55959
Dykes Restaurant Supply Inc, 56163
E A Sweon Co, 56168
E Friedman Assoc, 56170
E G Forrest Co Inc, 56171

E&A Hotel & Restaurant Epment And Supplies, 56174
E. LaRocque & Fils, 56179
E.H. Thompson Company, 56183
Eagle Coffee Co Inc, 56190
Earl Gill Coffee Co, 56194
Earp Distribution, 56195
Earth Grains Baking Co, 56197
Earthgrains, 56200
East Bay International, 56201
East Coast Seafood Inc, 56202
Eastern Bakers Supply Co Inc, 56206
Eastern Refrigeration & Restaurant Equipment, 56209
Eatmore Fruit Company, 56213
Eaton Market, 56215
Eau de Source Boischatel, 56216
Ecological Technologies, 56222
Economy Cash & Carry LP, 56223
Economy Restaurant Fixtures, 56225
Ecoval Dairy Trade, 56227
Edsung, 56236
Edward Don & Co, 56238, 56239, 56240
Edward Don & Company, 56241, 56242
Edward G Rahll & Sons, 56243
Edwards Distributing, 56246
Ehrlich Food Co, 56248
Eklof & Company, 56249
Elco Fine Foods, 56254
Electro Freeze Distrs Inc, 56258
Elegant Desserts, 56260
Elk Provision Co Inc, 56264
Elliot Horowitz & Co, 56267
Elon Products Company, 56274
Emerling International Foods, 56276
Emiliomiti, 56277
Empire Cash Register Systems, 56280
Empire Comfort Systems, 56281
Empire Packing Co, 56283
Empire Tea Svc, 56284
Empress Food Prods Co Inc, 56285
Ener-G Foods, 56289
English Honey Farms, 56293
Enzamar, 56300
Epicurean Foods, 56303
Equipment Distributor Div, 56307
Equipment Picard, 56310
Equipment/Plus, 56313
ERC Parts Inc, 56188
Erman & Son, 56316
Espresso Buy the Cup, 56321
Espresso Coffee Machine Co, 56322
Espresso Machine Experts, 56323
Espresso Magic, 56324
Essbar Equipment Company, 56326
Eternal Marketing Group, 56330
Ettline Foods Corp, 56331
Euclid Fish Co, 56333
Eugene & Company, 56334
Euro Mart/Stolzle Cberg las, 56335
Euro-Bake, 56336
Euro-Excellence, 56337
European Hotel & Restaurant Imports, 56341
Evans BS&R, 56345
Evans Foodservice Inc., 56346
Evco Wholesale Food Corp, 56347
Excellent Food Products, 56353
F & A Food Sales Inc, 56359
F & C Sawaya Wholesale, 56360
F B Mc Fadden Wholesale Co, 56361
F Christiana & Co, 56364
Fab Inc, 56372
Fab-X/Metals, 56373
Fadler Company, 56374
Faema, 56375
Fairview Dairy Inc, 56378
Falls City Mercantile Co Inc, 56381
Family Foods Home Service, 56382
Farmers Seafood Co Wholesale, 56390
Farner-Bocken Co, 56394
Feather Crest Farms, 56397
Federal Supply USA, 56398
Federated Cooperative, 56399
Fein Brothers, 56405

Ferntrade Corporation, 56408
Ferris Coffee & Nut Co, 56409
Fetzers', 56414
Findlay Foods Kingston, 56420
Fireline Corp, 56432
Fisher Mills, 56443
Five Continents, 56448
Flair Beverages, 56453
Flatland Food Distributors, 56458
Flav-O-Rich, 56460
Flavor-Crisp of America, 56463
Flint Provision Inc Zalack's, 56467
Flora Foods Inc, 56468
Florida Beverage Connection, 56469
Florida Carbonic Distributor, 56470
Florida Choice Foods, 56471
Florida Distributing Source, 56472
Florida Fresh Stonecrab, 56473
Florida Smoked Fish Company, 56475
Flowers Foods Inc., 56477
Flynt Wholesale Company, 56480
Follex Distributing Co Inc, 56485
Folmer Fruit & Produce Company, 56486
Food Authority Inc, 56488
Food Buying Service, 56489
Food Equipment Distributors, 56491
Food Equipment Specialist, 56492
Food Supply Inc, 56502
Food Wholesalers Inc, 56503
Food-Products, 56505
Ford Hotel Supply Co, 56510
Foremost Farms USA, 56514
Foremost Foods Company, 56515
Fort Smith Restaurant Supply, 56521
Fort Wayne Door Inc, 56522
Fortville Produce, 56525
Foster Dairy Farms Inc, 56527
Fountain Valley Foods, 56529
Four Oaks Farm, 56530
Foutch's Coffee and Spring Water, 56533
Franco Roma Foods, 56540
Frank G. Schmitt Company, 56543
Franklin Machine Products, 56550
Fred W Albrecht Grocery Co, 56555
Frederick Produce Company, 56556
Fresh Point, 56564
Fresh Point Dallas, 56565
FreshPro Food Distributors, 56567
Freskeeto Frozen Foods Inc, 56568
Friendly Wholesale Co, 56571
Fries Bros Eggs LLC, 56572
Fritzie Fresh Products, 56573
Frontier Bag Co Inc, 56576
Fruit Belt Canning Inc, 56583
Fruit Of The Vine Of De Valley, 56585
Full Harvest, 56591
G & L Import Export Corp, 56596
G&G Distributing, 56600
G&T Terminal Packaging Company, 56602
G.W. Market, 56605
Galli Produce Inc, 56629
Garavaglia Meat Company, 56633
Garden City Supply, 56636
Garden Spot Produce Co, 56638
Gardner & Benoit, 56639
Gatto & Sons, 56645
Gatto Wholesale Produce, 56646
Gaylord's Meat Co, 56647
GCS Service, 56609
General Carriage & Supply Co, 56655
General Cash & Carry, 56656
General Sales, 56657
Genoa Wholesale Foods, 56662
Geoghegan Brothers Company, 56663
George O Pasquel Company, 56670
GET Enterprises LLC, 56610
GFS (Canada) Company, 56611
Giancola Brothers, Inc., 56676
Giant Eagle American Seaway Foods, 56677
Gina Marie Refrigerator Door, 56686
Ginsberg's Institutional Foods, 56687
Giovanni Food Co Inc, 56688
GLAC Seat Inc, 56613

Wholesale Product Type / Food Service

Glandt-Dahlke, 56690
Glazier Packing Co, 56691
Global Harvest, 56693
Globe Equipment Co, 56695
Globe-Monte-Metro Company, 56696
Glosson Food Eqpt-Hobart Svc, 56699
GMT Dairy Products Inc, 56614
GMZ Inc, 56615
Goff's Seafood, 56703
Goldberg & Solovy Foods Inc, 56710
Golden Light Equipment Co, 56717
Golden Moon Tea, 56718
Golden Orchard, 56719
Gone Wild!!!, 56724
Good's Wholesale-Bakery Supls, 56725
Goodwin Brothers Inc, 56728
Gordon Food Service, 56730, 56731, 56732, 56733, 56734, 56735, 56736, 56737, 56738, 56739, 56740, 56741, 56742, 56743, 56744, 56745, 56746, 56747
Gourmet Technologies Inc, 56754
Grainger Industrial Supply, 56761
Gralab Instruments, 56763
Grande Cuisine Systems, 56764
Great American Popcorn Works of Pennsylvania, 56773
Great Lakes Designs, 56778
Great Lakes Gourmet Food Service, 56781
Great Lakes Hotel Supply Co, 56782, 56783
Great Western Beef WHLS Co, 56791
Great Western Foods, 56794
Greenley Foods Inc, 56805
Gregory's Foods, Inc., 56809
Griffin Food Co, 56814
Groetsch Wholesale Grocer, 56820
GSC Enterprises Inc., 56617
Guans Mushroom Co, 56826
Gulf Food Products Co Inc, 56829
Gunderland Marine Supply, 56840
Gunther Salt Co, 56841
GWB Foods Corporation, 56620
H & R Coffee Co, 56844
H B Day Co, 56846
H Schrier & Co Inc, 56848
H Weiss Co LLC, 56849
H&H Pretzel, 56850
H.P. Beale & Sons, 56855
H.Y. Louie Company, 56857
Haddad Supply Company, 56872
Halsey Foodservice, 56885
Hammill International, 56890
Hamms, 56891
Hampton Roads Seafoods Ltd, 56893
Handy's Milk & Ice Cream, 56899
Hanmi, 56901
Hanover Potato Products Inc, 56903
Hanover Uniform Co, 56904
Hansen Beverage Co, 56906
Hansen Distribution Group, 56908
Hanset Brothers Inc Brooms, 56910
Hanson Brass Rewd Co, 56912
Harbor Wholesale Foods Inc, 56920
Harco Enterprises, 56921
Harders, 56922
Harker's Distribution, 56925, 56926
Harold Food Company, 56928
Harold Leonard & Company, 56929
Harpak-Ulma, 56933
Harry Fourtunis, 56937
Harry Fourtunis Inc, 56938
Hata Y & Co LTD, 56953
Hathaway Coffee Co Inc, 56954
Hattiesburg Grocery Company, 56955
HAVI Group, 56860
Hawk Flour Mills, 56963
Hawkins Distributing Company, 56964
Hawthorne Supply Company, 56966
Healthwise, 56978
Hearn-Kirkwood, 56979
Heartland Distributors, 56981
Heavenly Cheesecakes, 56986
Heinkel's Packing Co, 56989
Heller's Food Equipment, 56992
Helmut's Strudel, 56993
Henderson Coffee Corp, 56995
Hendrix Hotel & Restaurant Equipment & Supplies, 56997
Henjes Enterprises, 56998
Henry Bresky & Sons Inc, 57000
Henrys Cash & Carry, 57003
HERB Enterprises, 56864
Hercules Food Equipment, 57006
HFM Foodservice, 56865
Hialeah Products Co, 57012
HIB Foods Inc, 56866
High Country Meats, 57016
High Quality Organics, 57017
Hill City Wholesale Company, 57020
Hill's Pier 19 Restaurant Lighthouse Bar, 57023
Hillis Farms, 57025
Hilts, 57027
Hipp Wholesale Foods, 57031
HMG Provisions, 56867
Holland Beef International Corporation, 57044
Hollowick Inc, 57047
Holly Seafood Company, 57048
Home-Like Food Company, 57052
Homestead Foods, 57053
Hoshizaki Northeastern, 57063
Hot Sauce Harry's Inc, 57066
House of Spices, 57067
Houston Poultry & Egg Company, 57070
HPC Foodservice, 56868
HRS Food Service, 56869
HSN Data Corporation, 56870
Huck's Seafood, 57074
Huff Ice Cream, 57082
Hunter Walton & Co Inc, 57092
Huntsville Restaurant Equip, 57093
Husky Foods of Anchorage, 57094
I Supply Co, 57101
I Wanna Distributors, 57102
I Zakarin & Sons Inc, 57103
IBC, 57106
ICC Industrial Chemical, 57108
Ice Machines, 57120
Ice Makers, 57121
Iceberg Seafood Inc, 57122
ID Foods Corporation, 57109
Imperial Bag & Paper Company, 57126
Imperial Dade, 57127
Imperial Trading, 57131
Imported Restaurant Specialties, 57132
Importex International, 57133
In A Bind Inc, 57134
In A Nutshell, 57135
Independent Wholesale, 57136
Indiana Restaurant Equipment, 57139
Indiana Sugars Inc, 57140
Indianhead Foodservice, 57143
Industrial Commodities, 57147
Ingenuities, 57157
Inland Meats of Spokane, 57161
Inno-Vite, 57163
Institutional Food Service, 57169
Institutional Wholesale Company, 57170
Insulated Structures/PB Group, 57172
International Business Trading, 57180
International Coconut Corp, 57182
International Commercial Supply Corporation, 57183
International Enterprises Unlimited, 57187
International Marine Products, 57189
Interstate Distributors, 57199
Interstate Restaurant Equipment, 57200
Irish Tea Sales, 57206
Irvin, 57207
Irvine Restaurant Supply, 57208
Irvington Marcus Company, 57209
ISI Commercial Refrigeration, 57112, 57113, 57114
Island Farms Dairies Cooperative Association, 57212
Island Refrigeration & Foodservice Equipment, 57214
Island Supply, 57216
Italfina, 57218
Italfoods Inc, 57219
Italmade, 57221
J & R Distributors, 57225
J Bernard Seafood, 57226
J Hoelting Produce Inc, 57229
J Kings Food Svc Professionals, 57230
J O Spice Co, 57234
J W Outfitters, 57241
J Weil Food Service Co, 57242
J&L Produce Wholesale Company, 57243
J&M Distribution Company, 57244
J. Hellman Frozen Foods, 57248
J. Johnson Fruit & Produce, 57249
J. M. Sealts Company, 57251
J. Quattrocchi & Company, 57252
J.A. Wendling Foodservice, 57257
J.C. Wright Sales Company, 57260
J.F. Walker Company, 57263
J.J. Taylor Distributing, 57265
J.L. Henderson & Company, 57266
J.O. Demers Beef, 57268
J.W. Wood Foods, 57274
JAAMA World Trade, 57275
Jackson Newell Paper Co, 57293
Jackson Supply Company, 57294
Jackson Wholesale Co, 57295
Jacobi Lewis Co, 57299
Jacobson & Sons, 57300
Jake's Variety Wholesale, 57302
Jamac Frozen Foods, 57304
James Desiderio Inc, 57310
Janney Marshall Co, 57312
Jb Prince, 57322
Jerico, 57331
Jesse Food Products, 57339
Jessom Food Equipment, 57340
Jetro Cash & Carry, 57342
Jetro Cash & Carry Enterprises, 57343
Jetro Cash & Carry Inc, 57344
Jilasco Food Exports, 57346
Jim David Meats, 57347
Jim's Cheese Pantry, 57348
JML Sales Co, 57285
JNS Foods, 57287
Jo Mints, 57352
Joe Bertman Foods, 57356
Joe Christiana Food Distributing, 57357
Joe Harding Sales & Svc, 57358
Joe Pucci & Sons Seafood, 57360
Joey's Fine Foods, 57361
John E Koerner & Co Inc, 57367
John Graves Food Service, 57368
John Groves Company, 57370
John Morrell Food Group, 57375
John S. Dull & Associates, 57378
John's Meat Market, 57382
Johnnie's Restaurant-Hotel Svc, 57384
Johnson Diversified Products, 57385
Johnson Restaurant Supply, 57386
Johnson Wholesale Meat Company, 57388
Joicey Food Services, 57392
Joseph Antognoli & Co, 57396
Joyce Brothers Company, 57401
Joyce Foods, 57402
Joylin Food Equipment Corporation, 57403
Judith's Fine Foods International, 57405
Junction City Distributing & Vending Company, 57409
K&H Equipment Company, 57419
K&K Meat Company, 57420
K. Lefkofsky Company, 57424
Kaco Supply Co, 57433
Kadouri International Foods, 57434
Kaleel Bros Inc, 57437
Kalil Produce Company, 57438
Kansas Marine, 57444
Karetas Foods Inc, 57448
Karson Food Services, 57450
KAST Distributors Inc, 57425
Katy's Wholesale Distributing, 57453
Kauai Producers, 57455
Kayem Foods, 57457
Kelley Foods, 57476
Kelly's Foods, 57479
Kenssenich's, 57489
Kentucky Beer Cheese, 57491
Kerekes Bakery & Rstmt Equip, 57492
Keyco Distributors Inc, 57499
Keystone Restaurant Supply, 57502
King Provision Corporation, 57508
Kingson Corporation, 57511
Kirby Restaurant & Chemical, 57515
Kittredge Equipment Co, 57520
Kleen Janitorial Supply Co., 57521
Klondike Foods, 57524
Knaus Cheese, Inc., 57526
Knox County Feed & Hatchery, 57530
Koalaty Kare, 57532
KOHL Wholesale, 57429
Kommercial Kitchens, 57540
Kopcke-Kansas Supply Services, 57545
Kosmos & Associates, 57547
KP USA Trading, 57431
Kranz Inc, 57550
Krebs Brothers Restaurant Supl, 57553
Kutter's Cheese Factory, 57559
KYD Inc, 57432
L & M Food Svc Inc, 57562
L&M Bakers Supply Company, 57565
L. Dontis Produce Company, 57569
L. Holloway & Brother Company, 57570
L.P. Shanks Company, 57574
LA Canasta Mexican Foods, 57576
LA Foods, 57578
LA Grange Grocery Co, 57579
La Grasso Bros Produce, 57591
LA Squisita Food Corp, 57583
La Tang Cuisine Manufacturing, 57594
LA Torilla Factory, 57584
Labatt Food Svc, 57597, 57598, 57599, 57600, 57601
Lafayette Restaurant Supply, Inc., 57609
Lamb Cooperative Inc, 57618
Lancaster Poultry, 57621
Land O'Frost Inc., 57623
Landphair Meat & Seafood, 57627
Lane Equipment Co, 57629, 57630
Lanzarotta Wholesale Grocers, 57634
Laredo Tortilleria & Mexican, 57635
Larry Martindale Company, 57639
Latouraine Coffee Company, 57643
Leali Brothers Meats, 57654
Lee County Equipment LLC, 57657
Lee Foods, 57658
Lee Grocery Company, 57659
Legacy Beverage Systems, 57663
Lello Appliances Corp, 57667
Lenox-Martell Inc, 57672
Lenson Coffee & Tea Company, 57673
Leon Supply Company, 57675
Leonetti's Frozen Food, 57677
Leonidas, 57678
Lesco Supply Company, 57681
Lew Sander Inc, 57684
Lewis & McDermott, 57685
Lewis Brothers & Sons, 57686
Lewisburg Wholesale Company, 57687
Lexington Foodservice, 57688
Liberto Management Co Inc, 57689
Liberto of Harlington, 57690
Liberto of Houston, 57691
Liberty Bell Wholesale Grocery, 57692
Liberty Marine Products, 57695
Lilar Corp, 57713
Lions Restaurant Equipment & Supplies, 57727
Lippert, 57728, 57729, 57730
Little Charlie's, 57733
LMG Group, 57588
Lobster Warehouse, 57742
Logan, 57745
Lombardi Brothers Meat Packers, 57749
Lombardi's Seafood, 57750

1233

Wholesale Product Type / Food Service

Long Island Glove & Safety Products, 57754
Long Wholesale Distributors, 57757
Lorain Novelty Company, 57763
Lorenzo's Wholesale Foods, 57766
Loubat Equipment Company, 57768
Louis R Polster Co, 57770
Lovecchio & Sons, 57775
Lowell Brothers & Bailey, 57778
Ludwig Fish & Produce Company, 57782
Luigi Bormioli Corporation, 57783
Lumaco Inc, 57784
Lynn Dairy Inc, 57791
M & W Beef Packers Inc, 57795
M Conley Co, 57799
M Maskas & Sons Inc, 57802
M R Williams Inc, 57803
M Tucker Co Inc, 57804
M&F Foods, 57805
M. Zukerman & Company, 57811
M.E. Carter & Company, 57812
M.E. Dilanian Company, 57813
Macdonald Meat Co, 57828
MacDonalds Consolidated, 57826
MacGregors Meat & Seafood, 57827
Machine Ice Co, 57830
Mack Restaurant Equipment & Supplies, 57831
Macomb Tobacco & Candy Company, 57832
Madison Cash & Carry Wholesale Grocers, 57835
Madison Food Sales Company, 57836
Madison Wholesale Co, 57838
Mahoning Swiss Cheese Cooperative, 57843
Maines Paper & Food Svc Inc, 57850, 57851, 57852
Maison Gourmet, 57855
Maloberti Produce Co, 57859
Mancuso Cheese Co, 57865
Mandeville Company, 57866
Manhattan Key Lime Juice Company, 57870
Manning Brothers Food Eqpt Co, 57873
Manting Equipment Company, 57875
Manuel's Hot Tamales, 57876
Manuel's Mexican-American Fine Foods, 57877
Maple Hollow, 57878
Marcus Food Co, 57882
Marcus Specialty Foods, 57883
Margate Wine & Spirit Co, 57886
Marias Packing Company, 57888
Marin Hydroponics, 57889
Mariner Neptune Fish & Seafood Company, 57890
Market Foods International, 57895
Markuse Corporation, 57899
Marky's Caviar, 57900
Marriott Distribution Service, 57903
Marrone's Inc, 57904
Mars Supermarkets, 57906
Martin Bros Distributing Co, 57908
Martin Food Service Company, 57910
Martin Preferred Foods, 57911
Martin Seafood Company, 57913
Martin-Brower Co US, 57915
Maryland China, 57919
Maryland Wholesale Produce Market, 57920
Masser's Produce, 57923
Matco United, 57927
Matilija Water Company, 57935
Mattingly Foods, 57937
Maxim's Import Corporation, 57938
Mayer Myers Paper Company, 57943
Mayfield Paper Co, 57946, 57947
Maynard-Fixturcraft, 57948
Mayrand Limitee, 57949
Mazo-Lerch Company, 57952
Mc Afee Packing Co, 57953
Mc Lane Foodservice, 57955
Mccomas Sales Co Inc, 57970
Mcdonald Wholesale Co, 57973
McDonnell, 57958
Mcfarling Foods Inc, 57974
McGrath Fisheries, 57960
McLane Co Inc, 57963
Meaders Kitchen Equipment, 57981
Meats Plus Inc, 57987
Mecca Coffee Company, 57988
Medley Restaurant Equipment & Supply Company, 57992
Melmart Distributors, 57996
Menu Maker Foods Inc, 57998
Merchants Foodservice, 58001
Meridian Supply Rstrnt Depot, 58003
Merrill Distributing Inc, 58007
Merton Restaurant Equipment Company, 58009
Metro Touch, 58017
Metro, Inc., 58018
Metro-Richelieu, 58019
Metroplex Harriman Corporation, 58020
MGH Wholesale Grocery, 57818
MIA Food Distributing, 57819
Miami Wholesale Grocery Company, 58027
Michael Distributor Inc, 58028
Michael G. Brown Associates, 58029
Michael Raymond Desserts Inc, 58030
Michael's Cookies, 58031
Michaelo Espresso, 58033
Michelle's Bakery, 58035
MICROS Retail Systems Inc, 57820
Mid America Food Sales, 58051
Mid States Paper & Notion Co, 58053
Mid-America Wholesale, 58054
Middendorf Meat, 58058
Midwest Distribution Group, 58067
Midwest Fire & Safety Equipment Company, 58068
Midwest Food Distributors, 58069
Midwest Ingredients Inc, 58072
Mike E. Simon & Company, 58075
Mile Hi Frozen Foods Corp., 58078
Miller & Hartman, 58086
Mills Brothers Intl, 58089
Millway Frozen Foods, 58090
Minnesota Conway Fire & Safety, 58093
Minuteman Trading, 58094
Mishima Foods USA, 58096
Miss Grimble Desserts, 58097
Mivila Foods, 58104
Mj Kellner Co, 58105
Model Dairy LLC, 58109
Modern Equipment Co, 58111
Modern Macaroni Co LTD, 58114
Modern Wholesale Company, 58117
Moffett Food Svc, 58119
Molinera International, 58121
Montana Food Products, 58126
Monterrey Provision Co, 58129
Mooney General Paper Co, 58132
Moonlite Bar-B-Q Inn, 58133
Moore Equipment, 58134
Morabito Baking Co Inc, 58135
Morris A. Elkis & Sons, 58143
Mortec Industries Inc, 58147
Mosuki, 58151
Motivatit Seafoods Inc, 58155
Mountain Dairies-SW Ice Cream, 58156
Mountain Service Distribution, 58160
Mountain States Rosen, 58161
Mountain View Supply, 58164
Moyer-Mitchell Company, 58167
Mt Pleasant Seafood, 58169
MTC Distributing, 57823
Muckenthaler Inc, 58171
Mueller Distributing Company, 58173
Muir Copper Canyon Farms, 58174
Muller-Pinehurst Dairy Company, 58175
Multi-Counter Manufacturing Company, 58177
Munchies, 58181
Mush & Pinsky, 58189
Muskingum Valley Grocery Co, 58190
My Car Provision Company, 58197
My Quality Trading Corp, 58198
Myers Restaurant Supply Inc, 58201
Myers-Cox Co, 58202
Nagel Paper & Box Company, 58210
Nancy Q Produce, 58213
Napoleon Creamery, 58216
Nappie's Food Svc, 58217
Nass Parts & Svc Inc, 58222
Nassau Foods, 58224
Natco Foodservice, 58227
National Grocers, 58236
National Grocers Company, 58238, 58239, 58241
National Restaurant Company, 58245
National Restaurant Supply Company, 58246, 58247
Nature's Best, 58266
Near East Importing Corporation, 58274
Neel's Wholesale Produce Co, 58277
Neelands Refrigeration, 58278
Neesvig Meats, 58279
Neighbors Coffee, 58280
Nelipak, 58281
Neshaminy Valley Natural Foods, 58286
Nesson Meat Sales, 58287
New Beer Distributors, 58295
New Brunswick Saw Service, 58297
New England Foods, 58298
New Mexico Food Distributors, 58304
New Vermont Creamery, 58309
New York Cash Register Company, 58310
New Zealand Lamb Co, 58311
Newman Fixture Co Inc, 58314
NewStar Fresh Foods LLC, 58312
Newtech Beverage Systems, 58317
Niagara Restaurant Supply, 58320
Nicewonger Company, 58321
Nicholas & Co Inc, 58322
Nichols Foodservice, 58323
Nicky USA Inc, 58325
NJM Seafood, 58206
Noon Hour Food Products Inc, 58342
Norcal Beverage Co, 58344
Norfolk Packing Company, 58345
Norm's Refrigeration, 58348
Norman's, 58350
Norman's Wholesale Grocery Company, 58351
North American Corp, 58353
North American Provisioners, 58354
Northbay Restaurant Equipment & Design, 58364
Northern WIS Produce Co, 58371
Northstate Provision Co, 58375
Northumberland Dairy, 58376
Northville Winery & Brewing Co, 58377
Northwest Dairy Association, 58378
Northwest Deli Distribution, 58379
Northwestern Fruit Co, 58385
Norvell Fixtures & Equipment Company, 58386
Novick Brothers Corp, 58391
Nu Concept Food Svc, 58393
Nutraceutical International, 58397
Nutrition Products Company, 58403
O-Sesco, 58412
O. Lippi & Company, 58413
O.G. Foodservice, 58414
Oak Ridge Winery LLC, 58424
Occidental Foods International, LLC, 58425
Ocean Frost, 58427
OH Armstrong, 58417
Ohio Farmers, 58439
Oklahoma City Meat Co Inc, 58442
Oklahoma Pecan Co, 58443
Old Fashion Foods Inc, 58444
Oliver Winery, 58449
Olympic Juicer Company, 58453
Omcan Manufacturing & Distributing Company, 58454
Omni Pacific Company, 58459
One-Shot, 58461
Orear Company, 58471
Oreck Commercial Sales, 58472
Original Food, 58476
Orioxi International Corporation, 58479
Osage Food Products Inc, 58484
Osborn Bros Inc, 58485
Ostrow Jobbing Company, 58487
Oswalt Restaurant Supply, 58488
Ottenheimer Equipment Company, 58489
Otto Brehm Inc, 58490
Overhead Door Company of Fort Wayne, 58494
P & D Corp, 58500
P A Menard, 58502
P&C Pacific Bakeries, 58503
P.A. Braunger Institutional Foods, 58507
Pacific California Fish Company, 58524
Pacific Commerce Company, 58527
Pacific Compactor Corporation, 58528
Pacific World Enterprises, 58537
Pacific-SEH Hotel Supply Company, 58538
Paisano Distribution Company, 58546
Palama Meat Co Inc, 58547
Palm Brothers, 58550
Palmer Associates, 58551
Palmer Food Service, 58553
Palmer Jack M, 58554
Palmer Wholesale Inc, 58555
Pantry Shelf Food Corporation, 58562
Paragon Food Equipment, 58570
Paramount Products, 58574
Paramount Restaurant Supply Company, 58575
Park Avenue Meats Inc, 58578
Parker Wholesale Paper Co, 58581
Parsons Green, 58586
Parts Depot, Inc., 58587
Paskesz Candy Co, 58589
Passport Food Group, 58591
Pate-Derby Company, 58592
Patriot Enterprises, 58593
Patterson Buckeye, 58596
Patton's Sausage Company, 58597
Paulsen Foods, 58603
Payless Equipment, 58604
PDE Technology Corp, 58516
Pelco Refrigeration Sales, 58611
Pemiscot Packing Company, 58616
Penguin Foods, 58618
Penn Maid, 58620
Pennsylvania Macaroni Company Inc., 58621
Pensacola Restaurant Supply Company, 58626
Performance Food Group Co, 58631
Performance Food Group Customized Distribution, 58632, 58633, 58634, 58635, 58636, 58637, 58638, 58639
Performance Foodservice, 58640, 58641, 58642, 58643, 58644, 58645, 58647, 58648, 58649, 58650, 58651, 58652, 58653, 58654, 58655, 58656, 58657, 58658, 58659, 58660, 58661, 58662, 58663, 58664, 58665, 58666, 58667, 58668, 58669, 58670, 58671, 58672, 58673, 58674, 58675, 58676
Perry B Duryea & Son Inc, 58679
Peterson, 58686
Peterson Sea Food Company, 58687
Pharaoh Trading Company, 58691
Phil Erb Refrigeration Co, 58694
Phillips Supply Co, 58697
Phoenix Industries Corp, 58699
Phoenix Wholesale Foodservice, 58700
Pickle House, 58703
Pierceton Foods Inc, 58707
Pinto Bros, 58711
Pioneer Distributing Co, 58712
Pioneer Marketing, 58716
Pippin Wholesale Co, 58718
Pittman Brothers Company, 58719
Pocono ProFoods, 58729
Poiret International, 58731

Wholesale Product Type / Food Service

Polean Foods, 58733
Pon Food Corp, 58737
Pontiac Fruit House, 58740
Pop's E-Z Popcorn & Supply Company, 58741
Port Royal Sales LTD, 58746
Portuguese United Grocer Co-Op, 58752
Post & Taback, 58756
Post Food Service, 58757
Potato Specialty Company, 58758
Power Pumps, 58763
Prawn Seafoods Inc, 58766
Premier Foodservice Distributors of America, 58771
Premiere Refreshment Svc, 58774
Presentations, 58777
Price & Co, 58783
Pridgen Bros Co, 58786
Priester's Pecans, 58787
Pro Plus Cleaning Products, 58795
Proacec USA, 58797
Productos Familia, 58803
Professional Food Systems, 58804, 58805, 58806
Proficient Food Company, 58810, 58811
ProSource, 58796
Provigo Distribution, 58823
Pudliner Packing, 58824
Pueblo Trading Co Inc, 58825
Pulini Produce, 58826
Pumodori Brothers Sales, 58829
Purchase Order Co Of Miami Inc, 58830
Pure Sealed Dairy, 58831
PYA/Monarch, 58520, 58521, 58522
Quail Crest Foods, 58844
Quality Banana Inc, 58847
Quality Discount Ice Cream, 58849
Quality Eggs & Juices, 58851
Quality Equipment Marketing, 58852
Quality Food Company, 58854
Quality Groceries, 58858
Quality Wholesale Produce Co, 58862
Quandt's Foodservice Distributors, 58864
Quip Industries, 58877
Qzina Specialty Foods, 58878
R Equipment, 58881
R S Stern Inc, 58886
R W Smith & Co, 58888
R&F International Corporation, 58891
R&R Equipment Company, 58894
R&R Mill Company, 58895
R&R Sales Company, 58896
R.N. Mason & Son, 58903
R.S. Somers Company, 58905
R.T. Greene Company, 58906
Rabco Foodservice, 58917
Ramex Foods, 58930
Ramsen Inc, 58931
Ranch Foods Direct, 58932
Randall Meat Co, 58933
Randy's Frozen Meats, 58934
Range Packing Company, 58935
RAPA Scrapple, 58908
Rapids Wholesale Equipment, 58938
Ready Food Products, 58947
Ready Portion Meat Co, 58948
Red Rose Trading Company, 58957
Reed Ice, 58961
Reese & Long Refrigeration, 58962
Refrigeration & Food Eqpt Inc, 58963
Refrigeration Equipment, 58964
Regal Distributing Company, 58965, 58966
Regal Supply & Chemical Company, 58967, 58968
Regency Coffee & Vending, 58969
Registry Steak & Seafood, 58971
Reinhart Foodservice LLC, 58972
Reliable Fire Equipment, 58973
Reliable Fire Protection, 58974
Resco Restaurant & Store Equip, 58981
ResourceNet International, 58985
Restaurant Depot, 58986, 58987
Restaurant Design & Equip Corp, 58988
Restaurant Designs Development, 58989

Restaurant Food Supply, 58990
Restaurant Supply, 58991
Rex Pacific, 58994
Rhotens Wholesale Meat Co, 58996
Ricci & Company, 58997
Richard's Restaurant Supply, 59001
Richmond Restaurant Svc, 59002
Richmond Supply Company, 59003
Richter Baking Company, 59004
Richter Distributing Company, 59005
RightWay Foods, 59009
Rihm Foods, 59010
Rimfire Imports, 59011
Rino Gnesi Company, 59012
RIPCO, 58910
Ritchie's Foods, 59015
Riverside Foods, 59018
Riverside Paper Supply, 59019
Roanoke Fruit & Produce Co, 59023
Robert Cochran & Company, 59027
Robert Wholey & Co Inc, 59031
Roberts Packing Co, 59033
Robertson Fruit & Produce, 59035
Robin's Food Distribution, 59037
Rockford Sausage Co, 59047
Rockland Bakery, 59048
Rockland Foodservice, 59049
Rocky Produce Inc, 59051
Rohrer Brothers, 59056
Roma Food Svc Of Arizona, 59060
Roma of Minnesota, 59061
Roseland Produce Wholesale, 59068
Rosenthal Foods Corp, 59070
Rosito & Bisani Imports Inc, 59071
Royal Accoutrements, 59079
Royal Crown Enterprises, 59083
Royal Cup Coffee, 59084
Royal Doulton Canada, 59085
Royal Harvest Foods Inc, 59088
Royal Industries Inc, 59089
Royal Palate Foods, 59092
Russell Food Equipment Limited, 59096
Russell N. Roy Company, 59097
Ryan Potato Company, 59100
Ryans Wholesale Food Distributors, 59101
S&M Produce Company, 59111
S&M Provisions, 59112
S. Anshin Produce Company, 59118
S.J. Roetzel & Son Produce, 59120
S.R. Flaks Company, 59121
S.W. Meat & Provision Company, 59122
Sadler's Smokehouse, 59135
Sagaya Corp, 59142
Sahadi Fine Foods Inc, 59144
Salad Oils Intl Corp, 59147
Salem Packing Company, 59148
Sales King International, 59150
Sam Cohen & Sons, 59157
Sam Lota & Son Disribution Company, 59159
Sam Okun Produce Co, 59160
Sam Tell & Son, 59161
Sam Wylde Flour Company, 59162
Sam's Club, 59164
Sambonet USA, 59166
San Diego Products, 59171
San Francisco Herb Co, 59172
San Jacinto Frozen Food, 59173
San-Bay Co, 59176
Sanarak Paper & Popcorn Supply, 59177
Sands African Imports, 59181
Sansone Food Products Co, 59185
Sassone Wholesale Groceries Co, 59194
Saugy Inc., 59197
Saval Foods Corp, 59199
SC Enterprises, 59124
Scardina Refrigeration Co., 59204
Scheidelman, 59207
Schenck Foods Co, 59208
Schmidt Baking Company Incorporated, 59213
Seacrest Foods, 59238
Seafood Dimensions Intl, 59243
Seattle Fish Co, 59252

Seattle's Best Coffee, 59253
Seder Foods Corporation, 59257
Segal's Wholesale, 59259
Seitz Gift Fruit, 59260
Select Meat Company, 59262
Serv-Tek, 59269
Serve Canada Food Equipment, 59270
Service Market, 59272
Seven K Feather Farm, 59275
SGS International Rice Inc, 59126
Shaheen Bros Inc, 59282
Shalhoob Meat Co, 59284
Shamrock Farms, 59285
Shamrock Foods Co, 59286, 59287, 59288
Shanghai Freemen, 59292
Sheehan Majestic, 59299
Sheffield Platers Inc, 59300
Sher Brothers & Company, 59308
Sherwood Food Distributors, 59310, 59312, 59313, 59314, 59315, 59316
Shetakis Foodservice, 59318
Shiff & Goldman Foods, 59319
Shivji Enterprises, 59324
Shore Distribution Resources, 59329
Shryack-Givens Grocery Co., 59330
Shryack-Hirst Grocery Company, 59331
Shullsburg Creamery Inc, 59333
Sid Green Frozen Foods, 59337
Sidney's, 59342
Siegmeister Sales & Service, 59344
Silverstar Foodservice Supply, 59349
Simco Foods, 59350
Simonian Fruit Company, 59351
Sims Wholesale, 59357
Singer Equipment Co Inc, 59361
Sirca Foodservice, 59365
Sisq Distributing Inc, 59366
Sisu Group Inc, 59368
Skelton's Inc, 59370
Skylark Meats, 59375
Slade Gorton & Co Inc, 59378
Sleeper Produce Company, 59380
Smith & Greene Company, 59384, 59385
Smith & Son Wholesale, 59386
Smith Restaurant Supply Co, 59387
Smith, Bob, Restaurant Equipment, 59388
Snapple Distributors of Long Island, 59398
Snappy Popcorn, 59399
Sniderman Brothers, 59401
Snyder Wholesale Inc, 59404
Sobey's Ontario, 59408
Socafe, 59416
Soda Service, 59417
Sogelco International, 59419
Sol Loeb Moving & Storage, 59420
Somerset Industries, 59422
Sonora Foods, 59424
South Jersey Paper Products, 59432
Southern Glazer's Wine-Spirits, LLC, 59441
Southern Grocery Company, 59442
Southwest Distributing Co, 59457
Southwest Traders, 59463
Souza Food Service, 59468
Sovrana Trading Corp, 59469
Sparboe Foods Corp, 59474
SpartanNash Co, 59478
Spener Restaurant Design, 59484
Spice House International Specialties, 59488
Spot Cash Specialty Company, 59492
ST Restaurant Supplies, 59129
St. Cloud Restaurant Supply, 59501
St. Helen Seafoods, 59502
St. Ours & Company, 59503
Stahl, 59506
Stamoolis Brothers Co, 59508
Standard Restaurant Equipment, 59513
Stanz Foodservice Inc, 59518
Stapleton Co, 59519
Star Restaurant Equipment & Supply Company, 59527

State Restaurant Equipment Co, 59538
State Wholesale Grocers, 59539
Staunton Foods LLC, 59543
Steinberg Quebec: Aligro, 59550
Stella Maria's, 59554
Steve's Fine Food Emporium, 59559
Stevenson Co, 59560
STI International, 59130
Stigler Supply Co, 59566
Stop & Shop Manufacturing, 59575
STOP Restaurant Supply Ltd, 59131
Strasheim Wholesale, 59577
Strawhacker's Food Service, 59580
Streich Equipment Co Inc, 59582
Summertime Restaurant Equipment, 59596
Summit Food Service Distributors, 59597
Summit Import Corp, 59599
Sun Valley Fruit Company, 59603
Suncrest Farms LLC, 59611
Sunderland Dispensing Service, 59612
Sunflower Restaurant Supply, 59614
Sunkist Growers, 59616
Sunshine Bar Supply Company, 59620
Sunshine Fresh, 59622
Sunspun Foodservice, 59624
Superior Paper & Plastic Co, 59636
Superior Wholesale Distr, 59640
Supply One, 59641
Supply One Inc, 59642
Supreme Fixture Company, 59643
Supreme Foods, 59645
Supreme Lobster, 59646
Sure Fine Food, 59647
Sweetener Products Co, 59659
Swiss American International, 59662
Swiss Chalet Fine Foods, 59663
Switzer's Inc, 59666
Sygma Network, 59668, 59669
SYGMA Network Inc, 59133
Sysco Corp, 59671, 59672, 59673, 59674, 59675, 59676, 59677, 59678, 59679, 59680, 59681, 59682, 59683, 59684, 59685, 59686, 59687, 59688, 59689, 59690, 59691, 59692, 59693, 59694, 59695, 59696, 59697, 59698, 59699, 59700, 59701, 59702, 59703, 59704, 59705, 59706, 59707, 59708, 59709, 59710, 59711, 59712, 59713, 59714, 59715, 59716, 59717, 59718, 59719, 59720, 59721, 59722, 59723, 59724, 59725, 59726, 59727, 59728, 59729, 59730, 59731, 59732, 59733, 59734, 59735, 59736, 59737, 59738, 59739, 59740, 59741, 59742, 59743
Systems Services Of America, 59745
T D Refrigeration Inc, 59746
T. Baker Restaurant Equipment, 59749
T.C. Food Export/Import Company, 59753
T.C.P. Restaurant Supply, 59754
T.D. Khan, 59755
T.L. Herring & Company, 59757
T.T. Todd Company, 59760
Ta-De Distributing Co, 59766
Tablemate Products, 59767
Tallarico Food Products, 59771
Tamburo Brothers, 59774
Tanglewood Farm, 59775
Tankersley Food Svc, 59776
Tanner Enterprises, 59777
Taormina Co, 59779
Taroco Food Corporation, 59784
Taylor Freezer Equipment Corporation, 59790
Taylor Freezers, 59791
Taylor Utlimate Svc Co, 59793
Taylor-Fortune Distributors, 59794
TBI Corporation, 59761

1235

Wholesale Product Type / Frozen Food

Tec Products Co Inc, 59797
Teitel Brothers, 59803
Teletec Cash Register Company, 59804
Tenth & M Seafoods, 59806
Tergerson's Fine Foods, 59807
Texas Hotel & Restaurant Equipment, 59819
Texas Marine II, 59820
Texas Meat Purveyors, 59821
Texas Sausage Co, 59822
The Chefs' Warehouse, 59824
The Premium Beer Company, 59831
Theatre Candy Distributing Company, 59837
Thomas & Howard Co, 59840
Thomas & Howard Co Cash & Crry, 59841
Thomas Brothers Country Ham, 59842
Thomas Ice Cream, 59844
Thompson & Little, 59849
Thompson Dairy, 59850
Thomson Groceries Ltd., 59851
Ths Foodservice, 59855
Thurston Foods Inc, 59858
Tinkels, 59868
Tippecanoe Foods, 59869
TKC Supply, 59765
Toastmasters International, 59873
Todd Distributors Inc, 59874
Tom's Evergreen Broom Manufacturing, 59875
Tony's Fine Foods, 59879
Top of the Table, 59884
Topicz, 59887
Tosi & Company, 59893
Toudouze Market Company, 59897
Tourtellot & Co, 59898
Town & Country Fancy Foods, 59899
Town & Country Wholesale, 59901
Townsend Farms Inc, 59902
Trade Diversified, 59908
Trans Veyor, 59911
Treasure Foods, 59915
Trent Valley Distributors Ltd., 59923
Tri Mark United East, 59927
Tri-Connect, 59928
Tribest Corp, 59934
Trident Food Svc, 59935
Triple F, 59941
Triton International, 59942
Trophy Foods, 59943
Tropic Ice Company, 59945
Tropical Paradise, 59948
Tropical Treets, 59949
Truscello & Sons Wholesalers, 59956
Tsar Nicoulai Caviar LLC, 59957
Tucson Coop. Warehouse, 59960
Tufco Technologies Inc, 59963
Turk Brothers Custom Meats Inc, 59966
Turner Holdings LLC, 59968
Tusco Grocers Inc, 59970
Two Guys Spice Company, 59977
U Okada & Co LTD, 59982
Ukiah Foods, 60000
Uncle Charlie's Meats, 60003
Union Grocery Company, 60011
UniPro Foodservice, Inc., 60005
United Bakers & Deli Supply, 60014
United Chairs, 60016
United Potato Company, 60030
United Rentals, 60032
United Restaurant Equipment Co, 60033
United Universal Enterprises Corporation, 60039
United Wholesale Grocery Company, 60040
Universal Marketing, 60045
Universal Restaurant Equipment, 60048
Universal Sodexho, 60050
Upper Lakes Foods Inc, 60053
US Food Products, 59984
US Foods Inc, 59985, 59986, 59987, 59988, 59989, 59990, 59991, 59992
US Growers Cold Storage, 59993
V-Suarez Provisions, 60058

Vallet Foodservice, 60068
Valley Distributing Company, 60069
Valley Distributors, 60071
Valley Foods Inc, 60073
Valley Pride Food Distributor, 60075
Valu-Line Foods, 60076
Van Eerden Foodservice Co Inc, 60077
Vaughn-Russell Candy Kitchen, 60086
Vend Food Service, 60088
Vendors Purchasing Council, 60090
Venezia Brothers, 60091
Venus Supply Company, 60094
Veritiv Corp, 60096
Vermont Wholesale Foods, 60098
Veteran Foods Sales Co, 60101
Victors Market Co, 60106
Vidalia Sweets Brand, 60109
Vienna Distributing Company, 60110
VIP Food Svc, 60061
Vista Food Exchange, 60124
Vista Food Exchange Inc., 60125
Vollwerth & Baroni Companies, 60141
Volpe, Son & Kemelhar, 60142
W A DeHart Inc, 60149
W.R. Hackett, 60166
W.R. Merry Seafood Company, 60168
W.R. Nykorchuck & Company, 60169
W.R. Pittman & Sons, 60170
W.S. Lee & Sons, 60172
Wabash Foodservice Inc, 60184
WACO Beef & Pork Processors, 60174
Wadden Systems, 60188
Wade's Dairy Inc, 60189
Walker Hatchery, 60197
Wallace Foods Inc, 60202
Wallach's Farms, 60204
Wards Ice Cream Co Inc, 60212
Washington Vegetable Co, 60217
Wasserstrom Co, 60218
Watson Distributing, 60223
Watsonville Coast Produce Inc, 60224
Waugh Foods Inc, 60225
We're Full of Promotions, 60228
Wechsler Coffee Corporation, 60233
Weeke Wholesale Company, 60234
Wega USA, 60235
Welton Rubber Co, 60237
Wes Design - Supply Company, 60239
West Bay Sales, 60243
West Coast Ship Chandlers, 60246
West End Dairy Inc, 60248
West Tenn Dairy Products, 60249
Westcoast Engineering Company, 60253
Western Family Foods Inc, 60256
Western Grocers, 60257, 60258
Westland Marketing, 60262
Wetoska Packaging Distributors, 60265
WG Thompson & Sons, 60181
Whaley Pecan Co Inc, 60267
White Feather Farms, 60275
Whitfield Olive, 60280, 60281
Wholesale Cash & Carry Foods, 60284
Wholesale Restaurant Equipment, 60285
Wholesale Restaurant Supply, 60286
Wichita Restaurant Supl Co Inc, 60292
Wilcox Frozen Foods, 60296
Wilderness Foods, 60300
Wilkin-Alaska, 60303
William Consalo & Sons Farms, 60306
William Rosenstein & Sons, 60308
Williams Food Equipment Company, 60309
Williams Institutional Foods, 60310
Williams Resource & Associates, 60311
Williams Sausage Co, 60312
Willie Laymon, 60314
Willing Group, 60315
Willow Group LTD, 60316
Willow Run Foods Inc, 60317
Wilson Ice Machines, 60319
Winchester Food, 60320
Wine Country Chef LLC, 60325
Wing Sing Seafood Inc, 60328
Winkler Meats, 60332
Winmix/Natural Care Products, 60333

Wins Paper Products, 60336
Wiper Supply & Chemical, 60338
Wisconsin Milk Mktng Board Inc, 60340
Witmer Foods, 60346
Woodlake Distributors, 60352
Woodland Foods, 60353
World Kitchen, 60358
World Spice, 60359
World Tableware Inc, 60360
Wusthoff Trident Cutlery, 60367
Yonkers Institutional Food Company, 60378
Young & Stout, 60380
Youngstown Wholesale Grocery, 60383
Zeches Institution Supply, 60393

Frozen Food

A & B Distributing Co, 54509
A & D Seafood Corp, 54510
A & W Wholesale Co Inc, 54512
A Better Way, 54513
A Dattilo Fruit Co, 54516
A J Linz Sons, 54517
A J Oster Foils LLC, 54518
A J Silberman & Co, 54520
A Plus Marketing, 54522
A Tarantino & Sons Poultry, 54523
A&D Distributors, 54527
A&J Food Wholesalers, Inc., 54529
A&J Forklift & Equipment, 54530
A&J Produce Corporation, 54531
A-1 Seafood Center, 54535
A-A1 Aaction Bag, 54536
A-Line Electric Supply Inc, 54538
A. Bohrer, 54540
A. De LaChevrotiere, 54541
A. Friscia Seafoods, 54542
A. Sargenti Company, 54545
A. Simos & Company, 54546
A. Visconti Company, 54547
A.B. Wise & Sons, 54548
A.C. Covert, 54549
A.J. Jersey, 54553
A/R Packaging Corporation, 54557
A2Z Specialty Advertising, 54559
AA Specialty Advertising Products, 54560
AANTEC, 54561
Abal Material Handling Inc, 54590
Abatar Institutional Food Company, 54591
ABC Country Club Coffee, 54562
ABCO HVACR Supply & Solutions, 54563
Abel IHS, 54594
ABI Limited, 54564
Able Sales Company, 54595
ABM Industries, 54565
Above All Health, 54596
Acatris USA, 54598
ACC Distributors Inc, 54567
Accord International, 54599
Ace Chemical, 54601
Ace Electric Supply, 54602
Ace Endico Corp, 54603
Ace Fixture Company, 54604
Ace Mart Restaurant Supply, 54605
ACK Industrial Electronics, 54568
Ackerman Industrial Equipment, 54606
Acme Food Sales Inc, 54608
ACME Sign Corp, 54569
Acorn Distributors Inc, 54611
Action Advertising, 54612
Action Sales, 54613
Ad Lib Advertising, 54615
Ad Specialty Plus, 54616
Ad-Centive Ideas, 54617
Ad-Craft Products Compay, 54618
Adams & Knickle, 54619
Adams Wholesale Co, 54621
Adams-Burch, 54622
Addison Foods Inc, 54623
ADE Restaurant Service, 54570
Adel Grocery Company, 54624

Adex Medical Inc, 54626
ADI, 54571
Adirondack Direct, 54627
Admiral Craft, 54629
Adolf Kusy & Company, 54630
Adsmith, 54633
ADT Inc, 54573
ADT Security Systems, 54574
Advanced Chemical, 54634
Advanced Equipment Company, 54635
Advanced Handling Systems Inc, 54636
Advantage Gourmet Importers, 54637
Adventure Foods, 54638
Advertising Specialties, 54640
Advertising Specialties Imprinted, 54641
Aerchem Inc, 54642
Aerolator Systems, 54644
Affiliated Resource Inc, 54647
Age International Inc, 54650
Agri-Equipment International, 54652
Agrium Advanced Technologies, 54653
Agro Foods, Inc., 54654
Aidi International Hotels of America, 54655
AIDP Inc, 54575
Aim This Way, 54657
Aimonetto and Sons, 54658
AIN Plastics, 54576
Air Savers Inc, 54659
AJ Trucco, Inc, 54577
Ajax Philadelphia, 54660
AJC International, 54578
Akron Cotton Products, 54662
Al Lehrhoff Sales, 54664
Alabama Food Group, 54665, 54666
Alabama Wholesale Company, 54668
Alack Refrigeration Co Inc, 54669
Alaska Sausage & Seafood, 54670
Albert Guarnieri & Co, 54674
Albert Uster Imports Inc, 54675
Albion Enterprises, 54679
Albion Fisheries, 54680
Alchemie USA Inc., 54681
Alderiso Brothers, 54682
Alerta-Mat, 54684
Alex & George, 54685
Alfa Cappuccino Import LTD, 54686
Alioto Lazio Fish Co, 54691
Aliquippa Fruit Market, 54692
All American Specialty Corporation, 54693
All Caribbean Food Service, 54694
All Fresh Products, 54696
All Lift Equipment, 54697
All Power Inc, 54699
All QA Products, 54700
All Seasons Fisheries, 54701
All Seasons Uniforms & Textile, 54703
All Star Janitorial Supply, 54705
All State Restaurant Supply, 54707
All-Redi Flour & Salt Company, 54709
All-State Industries Inc, 54710
All-Tech Materials Handling, 54711
Allan Chemical Corp, 54712
Allen Brothers Inc, 54716
Allen Rosenthal Company, 54717
Allendale Produce Plant, 54718
Alliance Supply Management, 54719
Allied Blending & Ingredients, 54721
Allied Domecq Spirits USA, 54722
Allied Food Service, 54723
Allied Industrial Equipment, 54724
Allied Premium Company, 54727
Allkind Container Co, 54729
Allstate Insurance Company, 54730
Alnor Oil Co Inc, 54731
Alpha Baking Company, 54732
Alpha Foods, 54733
Alpha Omega Technology, 54734
Alphin Brothers, 54735
Alpine Food Distributing Inc, 54736
Alpine Gloves, 54737
Alpine Industries/Alpine Air Products, 54738
Alson Specialty Company, 54740

Wholesale Product Type / Frozen Food

Alta Equipment Co, 54742
Alternative Health & Herbs, 54745
Altrua Marketing & Design, 54747
Alwan & Sons, 54748
AM-Mac, 54580
Ambassador Fine Foods, 54751
AMCON Distributing Co, 54582
Amenity Services, 54754
American Advertising Specialties Company, 54755
American Bakery Equipment Company, 54758
American Banana Company, 54759
American Classic Ice Cream Company, 54760
American Container Concepts, 54761
American Farms Produce, 54763
American Fish & Seafood Inc, 54764
American Food & Vending Corporation, 54765
American Food Equipment, 54766
American Food Equipment & Supply, 54767
American Food Systems, 54768
American Food Traders, 54769
American Frozen Foods, 54771
American Grocery & Beverage, 54772
American Health & Safety, 54773
American Hotel Register Co, 54774
American International Chemical, 54775
American Legion, 54777
American Lighting & Electric, 54778
American Lighting Supply, 54779
American Material Handling Inc, 54780
American Meat & Seafood, 54781
American Metalcraft Inc, 54782
American Mussel Harvesters Inc, 54783
American Osment, 54784
American Packaging Corporation, 54785
American Produce Company, 54787
American Restaurant Supply, 54790, 54791
American Sales & Marketing, 54793
American Seafood Imports Inc., 54794
American Seaway Foods Inc, 54795
American Select Foods, 54796
American Softshell Crab, 54798
American Specialty Coffee & Culinary, 54799
American Trading Company, 54800
American Uniforms Sales Inc, 54801
American Yeast Sales, 54803
American/Brenner Wholesale, 54804
Amerivap Systems Inc, 54806
Ammirati Inc, 54808
AMN Distributors/Premium Blend, 54584
Amos's PA Wonder Products, 54809
Ampak Seafoods Corporation, 54810
Amster-Kirtz Co, 54812
Amtex Packaging, 54813
Anderson Dubose Company, 54819
Anderson Seafood, 54821
Anderson Studio Inc, 54822
Andre Tea & Coffee Company, 54823
Andrew & Williamson Sales Co, 54824
Angel Beltran Corporation, 54826
Angel's Produce, 54827
Angelo M. Formosa Foods, 54828
Angelo Refrigeration & Rstrnt, 54829
Anixter Inc, 54831
Anniston Paper & Supply Company, 54836
Anter Brothers Company, 54837
Anthony Marano Co Inc, 54838
Anthony's Snack & Vending, 54839
Anton-Argires, 54841
Antone's Import Company, 54842
AP Fish & Produce, 54585
Apache Inc, 54843
Apilico/Cuthbertson Imports, 54844
APM, 54586
Applied Handling Equipment Company, 54846
Applied Handling NW, 54847

Applied Industrial Tech Inc, 54848
Aqua Solutions Inc, 54849
Aqua Source, 54850
Aqua-Tec Co, 54851
Ar Line Promotions Inc, 54852
Aragadz Foods Corporation, 54853
Aramark Uniform Svc, 54854
Arbre Farms Inc, 54855
Arctic Beverages, 54856
Arctic Logistics, 54858
Arctic Star Distributing, 54859
Arctica Showcase Company, 54861
Argus Protective Services, 54862
Aries Paper & Chemical Company, 54863
Arista Industries Inc, 54864
Arizona Storage & Retrieval Systems, 54865
Arkansas Valley Wholesale Grocery Company, 54867
Arla Foods Inc, 54868
Arleen Food Products Company, 54869
Arlington Coffee Company, 54870
Armaday Paper, 54871
Armstrong Jones, 54873
Arnall Grocery Co, 54874
Arnold Machinery Co, 54876
Aroma Foods, 54878
Aron Corporation, 54879
Arrow Chemical Inc, 54880
Arrow Distributing, 54881
Art's Trading, 54883
Artique, 54885
Asanti Distributors, 54887
Asheboro Wholesale Grocery Inc, 54888
Asia Shipping & Trading Corporation, 54891
Aspecialtybox.Com, 54893
Aspen Corporate Identity Group, 54894
Associated Food Equipment, 54897
Associated Food Stores, 54898
Associated Food Stores Inc, 54899
Associated Grocers, 54900
Associated Material Handling, 54901
Associated Wholesale Grocers, 54902
Associates Material Handling, 54903
Atchison Wholesale Grocery, 54907
Atco Marine Service, 54908
Atlanta Fixture & Sales Company, 54910
Atlantic Dominion Distributors, 54911
Atlantic Gem Scallop Co, 54912
Atlantic Industrial & Marine Supplies, 54913
Atlantic Lift Systems, 54914
Atlantic Rentals, 54915
Atlantic Seafood Intl Group, 54920
Atlantic Wholesalers, 54923, 54924
Atlas Equipment Company, 54925
Atlas Lift Truck Rentals & Sales, 54926
Attar Herbs & Spices, 54927
Atwater Foods, 54928
Atwood Lobster Co, 54929
Aust & Hachmann, 54934
Austrade, 54937
Auth Brothers Food Service, 54938
Automation Fastening Company, 54940
Automation Systems & Services, 54941
Avalon Trade Company, 54944
Avatar Corp, 54945
Axelrod Foods, 54947
Aydelotte & Engler Inc, 54950
Aylesworth's Fish & Bait, 54951
Ayush Herbs Inc, 54952
Aztec Secret Health & Beauty, 54953
B & B Beverages, 54955
B & B Distributors Inc, 54956
B & B Food Distributors Inc, 54957
B & G Venegoni Distribution, 54959
B & J Food Svc Inc, 54960
B & K Distributing Inc, 54961
B & M Provision Co, 54962
B & S Wasilko Distr, 54964
B & W Frozen Foods, 54965
B & W Supply Co, 54966
B&B Beer Distributing Company, 54968
B&F Distributing Company, 54969

B&O Beer Distributors, 54972
B&W Distributing Company, 54973
B. Fernandez & Sons, 54975
B.M. Lawrence & Company, 54977
B.M. Sales Company, 54978
B.W. Clifford, 54979
B/R Sales Company, 54980
Babush Conveyor Corporation, 54995
Bachman Foods, 54996
Badger Material Handling, 55000
Badger Popcorn, 55001
Badger Wholesale Company, 55002
Badger Wholesale Meat & Provisions, 55003
Baers Beverage of C.W., 55005
Bailey Co Inc, 55009
Baja Trading Company, 55012
Bake Star, 55013
BakeMark Ingredients West Inc, 55015
Baker Beverage, 55016
Baker Boy Bake Shop Inc, 55018
Baker Distributing Corp, 55019
Baker's Cash & Carry Inc, 55021
Bakery Equipment Sales & Services, 55023
Bakker Produce, 55028
Bakri Trading Inc, 55029
Bald Eagle Beer Store Co, 55030
Balford Farms, 55032
Ballantine Industrial Truck Service, 55033
Ballew Distributors, 55035
Balter Meat Co, 55036
Balter Sales Co, 55037
Baltimore Belting Co, 55038
Bama Budweiser Montgomery, 55039
Bama Budweiser of Anniston, 55040
Bandwagon Brokerage, 55045
Bangkok Market, 55046
Banner Wholesale Grocers, 55047
Bar Boy Products Inc, 55049
Bar Controls Of Florida, 55050
Bar-Plex, 55053
Barber's Poultry Inc, 55056
Bari Italian Foods, 55057
Baring Industries, 55060
Barkett Fruit Company, 55061
Barlean's Fisheries, 55062
Barnett Lighting Corporation, 55064
Baron Spices Inc, 55065
Barr Packing Company, 55066
Barrel O'Fun of Milwaukee, 55068
Barwell Food Sales, 55072
Basic Food Intl Inc, 55074
Basic Leasing Corporation, 55075
Basic Organics, 55076
Bassham Institutional Foods, 55078
Bates Distributing, 55079
Bathroom & Towel Systems, 55080
Battistella's Sea Foods, 55082
Batty & Hoyt, 55083
Baumann Paper Company, 55085
Bay Area Trash Compactor, 55087
Bay State Restrnt Products Inc, 55092
Bayou Food Distributors, 55097
Bayou Land Seafood, 55098
Bayshore Equipment, 55100
BBCA USA, 54981
BBQ Bunch, 54982
BCIS Inc, 54984
Beans & Machines, 55102
Bear Stewart Corp, 55105
Bedessee Imports, 55110
Bedford Enterprises Inc, 55111
Beer Import Co, 55115
Behm's Valley Creamery, 55116
Belair Produce Co Inc, 55117
Belco Packaging Systems, 55118
Belew Sound & Visual, 55119
Bell Fork Lift Inc, 55124
Belleharvest Sales Inc, 55127
Bellin Advertising, 55129
Belting Associates, 55131
Beltram Foodservice Group, 55132

Ben E. Keith, 55133, 55134, 55135, 55136, 55137, 55138, 55139, 55140, 55141, 55142, 55143
Bender Meat, 55163
Benfield Electric Supply Co, 55164
Bennett Material Handling, 55166
Bensinger's, 55167
Bentan Corporation, 55169
Berje, 55172
Berkel Products Company, 55173
Berlin Packaging, 55175, 55176, 55177
Bernard Jensen Intl, 55180
Bernard's Bakery, 55181
Berry Material Handling, 55185
Bertolino Beef Co, 55187
Berton Company, 55188
Bertrand's, 55189
Best Buy Uniforms, 55192
Best Chicago Meat, 55193
Best Friends Cocoa, 55196
Best Industries, 55197
Best Market, 55198
Best Material Handling, 55199
Best Restaurant Equip & Design, 55200
Better Beverages Inc, 55202
Better Health Products, 55203
Better Janitor Supplies, 55204
Better Meat, 55205
Betters International Food Corporation, 55206
Beverage Express, 55207
BFM Equipment Sales, 54985
BI Nutraceuticals, 54986
BI-LO, 54987
Big Al's Seafood, 55212
Big State Vending Company, 55218
Big Valley Marketing Corporation, 55219
Bilas Distributing Company, 55220
Billingsgate Fish Company, 55222
Binghamton Material Handling, 55224
Bintz Restaurant Supply Company, 55225
Bioscience International Inc, 55227
Biostim LLC, 55228
Birchwood Meats, 55229
Birdie Pak Products, 55230
Birdsong Peanuts, 55232
Birmingham Vending Games, 55233
Bisek & Co Inc, 55235
BJ'S Wholesale Club Inc, 54988
Blachere Group, 55239
Blackbur Bros Inc, 55242
Blackburn-Russell Co, 55243
Blackwing Ostrich Meats Inc., 55244
Blake's Creamery Inc, 55246
Blanke Bob Sales Inc, 55249
Blazer Concepts, 55250
Blue Buoy Foods, 55255
Blue Delft Supply, 55257
Blue Line Foodservice Distr, 55260
Blue Mountain Meats Inc., 55261
Blue Rhino Compaction Services, 55262
Blue Ribbon Fish Co, 55263
Blue Ribbon Meats, 55264
Blue Ribbon Wholesale, 55265
Blue Ridge Poultry, 55266
Bmh Equipment Inc, 55269
BNG Enterprises, 54990
Bode-Finn Company, 55271
Bodean Restaurant & Market, 55272
Boelter Companies, 55273
Boeuf Merite, 55274
Bon Appetit International, 55277
Bon Secour Fisheries Inc, 55278
Bon Ton Food Products, 55279
Bono Burns Distributing Inc, 55281
Booker Promotions, 55282
Boone's Wholesale, 55283
Bosch Distributors, 55286
Bosco Food Service, 55287
Bosgraaf Sales Company, 55288
BOSS, 54991
Boston Lobster Co, 55291
Boston Sausage & Provision, 55292
Boston Seafarms, 55293
Boston Showcase Company, 55294

1237

Wholesale Product Type / Frozen Food

Boteilho Hawaii Enterprises, 55296
Bottom Line Foods, 55297
Boulangerie Pelletier, 55298
Bowlin J P Co LLC, 55303
Bowman Produce, 55304
Boxed Meat Revolution, 55305
Boxer-Northwest Company, 55306
Boykin & Southern Wholesale Grocers, 55307
Bozzuto's Inc., 55311
Brace Frozen Foods, 55312
Bradley Kitchen Center, 55313
Bradshaw Home nc, 55314
Branton Industries, 55316
Brasco, 55317
Braswell Distributing Co, 55318
Brauer Material Handling Systs, 55320
Brawner Paper Co, 55321
Brenham Wholesale Groc Co Inc, 55324
Bresco, 55325, 55326
Brevard Restaurant Equipment, 55327
Bridgford Foods Corp, 55333
Briggs Co, 55334
Brilliant Lighting Fixture Corporation, 55335
Bringgold Wholesale Meats, 55337
Brita Foods, 55339
British Aisles, 55340
British Shoppe LLC, 55341
British Wholesale Imports, 55342
Brittain Merchandising, 55343
Broadleaf Venison USA Inc, 55344
Broaster Sales & Svc, 55345
Brockman Forklift, 55347
Bronx Butter & Egg Company, 55349
Brooklyn Sugar Company, 55352
Brooks Barrel Company, 55353
Brooks Industries, 55354
Brooks Tropicals Inc, 55355
Brothers Restaurant Supply, 55357
Brown's Dairy, 55359
Brown's Ice Cream Co, 55360
Brown, R H, 55361
Browns' Ice Cream Company, 55363
Bruce Edmeades Sales, 55364
Brucken's, 55365
Bryant Products Inc, 55368
Bublitz Machinery Company, 55371
Buckelew Hardware Co, 55372
Buckelew's Food Svc Equipment, 55373, 55374
Buckeye Handling Equipment Company, 55375
Buckhead Beef, 55376
Buddy Squirrel LLC, 55379
Buffalo Hotel Supply Co Inc, 55381
Buffalo Paper & Detergent Co, 55382
Bulk Food Marketplace, 55385
Bunn Capitol Company, 55386
Bunzl Distribution USA, 55387
Burch-Lowe, 55389
Burdick Packing Company, 55390
Burgess Mfg. - Oklahoma, 55391
Burkhardt Sales & Svc, 55392
Burklund Distributors Inc, 55393
Burlington Equipment Company, 55394
Burnand & Company, 55395
Business Documents, 55397
Butte Produce Company, 55402
Buz's Crab, 55404
BW Acquisition, 54994
Byczek Enterprises, 55406
Bykowski Equipment, 55407
Bynoe Printers, 55408
Byrne Brothers Foods Inc, 55410
C & R Frozen Svc Inc, 55412
C & S Sales Inc, 55413
C & S Wholesale Grocers Inc, 55414
C & T Design & Equipment Co, 55415
C A Curtze, 55417
C D Hartnett Co, 55418
C H Robinson Worldwide Inc, 55419
C M Tanner Grocery Co, 55420
C Pacific Foods Inc, 55421
C&C Lift Truck, 55422

C&H Store Equipment Company, 55423
C&R Refrigation Inc,, 55424
C&W Frozen Foods, 55425
C. Eberle Sons Company, 55426
C. Lloyd Johnson Company, 55427
C.G. Suarez Distributing Company, 55430
C.H. Robinson Co., 55431
C.S. Woods Company, 55432
C.T. Grasso, 55433
C.W. Shasky & Associates Ltd., 55434
Cable Meat Center, 55454
Cactus Holdings Inc, 55455
Cadillac Meat Company, 55457
Cadillac Packaging Corporation, 55458
Caesar Electric Supply, 55459
Cafe Jumbo, 55461
Cain's Coffee Company, 55465
Cajun Brothers Seafood Company, 55466
Cajun Crawfish Distributors, 55467
Cajun Sugar Company LLC, 55469
Cal Coast Promo-Products, 55470
Cal-West Produce, 55471
Calico Industries Inc, 55473
California Caster & Handtruck, 55475
California Fruit Market, 55476
California Independent Almond Growers, 55477
California Marketing Group Inc, 55478
California Tag & Label, 55480
Callahan Grocery Company, 55482
Cambridge Packing Company, 55484
Campbell's Food Service, 55487
Campione Restaurant Supply, 55488
Canada Pure Water Company Ltd, 55492
Canada Safeway, 55493
Cannon/Tayloe, 55495
Cantab Industries, 55498
Canterbury's Crack & Peel, 55499
Canton Foods, 55500
Canty Wiper & Supply Company, 55501
Cape Dairy LLC, 55504
Cape May Fishery Cooperative, 55505
Capital City Fruit, 55506
Capital Equipment & Handling, 55507
Capitol City Produce, 55509
Capitol Foods, 55510
Cappello Foods, 55512
Cappuccino Express Company, 55513
Captain Morrills Inc, 55519
Captree Clam, 55520
Carbonella & Desarbo Inc, 55523
Carborator Rental Svc, 55524
Carden Foods Inc, 55525
Cardinal Carryor Inc, 55526
Cardinal International, 55527
Carefree Kanopy, 55528
Caribbean Produce Exchange, 55529
Caribbean Restaurants, 55530
Carle & Montanari-O P M, 55532
Carlisle Food Systems Inc, 55533
Carlson Company, 55534
Carlton Company, 55535
Carnival Fruit, 55536
Carole's Cheesecake Company, 55538
Carolina Belting, 55539
Carolina Canners Inc, 55541
Carolina Handling LLC, 55542
Carolina Material Handling, 55543
Carolina Mountain, 55544
Carolina Steel Shelving Company, 55546
Carolina Tractor and Equipment Company, 55547
Carolyn Darden Enterprises, 55548
Carriage Foods, 55551
Carroll Distributing Co, 55552
Carrollton Products Company, 55553
Carrot Top Pastries, 55554
Carter Promotions, 55555
Cascade Glacier Ice Cream Company, 55561
Cash Grocery & Sales Company, 55562
Cash Register Sales, 55563
Cash-Wa Distributing, 55564, 55565
Caspian Trading Company, 55568

Cass Hudson Company, 55569
Casso Guerra & Company, 55570
Caster Wheels & Indl Handling, 55572
Castino Restaurant Equipment, 55573
Castor Technology Corporation, 55575
Cataract Foods, 55576
Cauble & Field, 55578
Cavanna Packaging USA Inc, 55580
Cavazos Candy, Produce & Groceries, 55581
Cavens Meats, 55582
Cb Equipment Co, 55584
CB Mfg. & Sales Co., 55436
CB Pallet, 55437
CBS Food Equipment, 55439
Centerchem, Inc., 55587
Central Carolina Farm & Mower, 55589
Central Coast Seafood, 55590
Central Distributing Co, 55591
Central Illinois Equipment Company, 55592
Central Oklahoma Produce Services, 55593
Central Package & Display, 55594
Central Restaurant Supply Inc, 55595
Central Sanitary Supply, 55596
Central Security Service, 55597
Central Wholesale Grocery Corporation, 55598
Centreside Dairy, 55599
Century 21 Products, 55600
Century Data Systems, 55602
Century Distributors Inc, 55603
Century Fournier Inc, 55604
Cerca Foodservice, 55605
Ceres Solutions, 55607
Certco Inc., 55609
Certified Cleaning Supplies, 55611
Certified Food Service, 55612
Certified Food Services, 55613
Certified Interior Systems, 55615
CF Equipment, 55440
CFE Equipment Corp, 55442
Chamberlain Wholesale Grocery, 55618
Chameleon Beverage Co Inc, 55619
Champaign Plastics Company, 55620
Chapman's Food Service, 55621
Charles C. Parks Company, 55623
Charles Wetgrove Company, 55625
Charlie Beigg's Sauce Company, 55626
Charlton & Hill, 55627
Chatfield Dairy, 55630
Chattanooga Button & Badge Company, 55632
Chattanooga Restaurant Supl, 55633
Cheese Shop, 55635
Chef John Folse & Co, 55637
Chef's Choice Mesquite Charcoal, 55638
Chef's Pride Gifts LLC, 55639
Chef's Supply & Design, 55640
Chellino Cheese Co, 55642
Chem Care, 55644
Chem-Mark of Buffalo, 55645
Chemcraft Industries Inc, 55646
Chemroy Canada, 55647
Cheney Brothers Inc, 55648
Chernoff Sales, 55649
Chia I Foods Company, 55654
Chicago Food Corporation, 55657
Chicago Steaks, 55661
Chipurnoi Inc, 55667
Chocolates by Mark, 55671
Choice Restaurant Equipment, 55673
Christian County Grain Inc, 55677
Christopher Wholesalers, 55678
Church Point Wholesale Grocer, 55682
Cirelli Foods, 55689
Ciro Foods, 55690
Cisco-Eagle, 55691
City Deli Distributing, 55693
City Espresso Roasting Company, 55694
City Fish Sales, 55695
City Line Food Distributors, 55696
City Wholesale Company, 55700
CK Products, 55446

Claremont Herbal Health, 55702
Clark Restaurant Svc, 55708
Clarkson Company, 55710
Clarkson Grain Co Inc, 55711
Class Produce Group LLC, 55712
Clayton's Crab Co, 55713
Clearbrook Farms, 55714
Clements Distribution Company, 55717
Clifford D. Fite, 55719
Clipper Seafood, 55723
Clogmaster, 55725
Clover Leaf Cheese, 55726
Coast to Coast Foods Group, 55729
Coastal Beverage LTD, 55730
Coca-Cola Beverages Northeast, 55735
Coca-Cola Bottling Co. Consolidated, 55736
Cochran Brothers Company, 55739
Cockrell Banana, 55740
Cockrell's Creek Seafood & Deli, 55741
Coffee Break Systems, 55742
Coffee Expresso & Service, 55745
Coffee Heaven, 55746
Cogent Technologies, 55747
Cohen Foods, 55748
Colavita USA, 55750
Cole Brothers & Fox Company, 55753
Collins & Company, 55754
Colorado Boxed Beef Company, 55761
Colorado Chemical Company, 55762
Colorado Potato Growers Exchange, 55764
Colorado Restaurant Supply, 55765
Colors Gourmet Pizza, 55766
Columbia Paper Company, 55767
Columbia Restaurant & Bar Supply Co., 55768
Columbia Scale Company, 55769
Com-Pak International, 55770
Comissos Cash & Carry, 55771, 55772, 55773, 55774
Commissos Cash & Carry, 55776
Comprehensive Lighting Svc, 55782
Computerized Machinery Systs, 55783
Conagra Brands Canada, 55784
Conca D'Oro Importers, 55785
Concept Equipment Corporation, 55786
Concession & Restaurant Supply, 55787
Conchita Foods Inc, 55788
Concho Valley Pecan Company, 55789
Concord Foods Co, 55790
Concord Import, 55792
Confecco, 55794
Conger Industries Inc, 55796
Connecticut Shellfish Co Inc, 55797
Connection Chemical LP, 55798
Conner Produce Co, 55800
Consolidated Beverage Corporation, 55801
Consolidated Bottle Company, 55802
Consolidated Fruit Distributor, 55803
Consolidated Poultry & Egg Company, 55804
Consumers Packing Co, 55807
Container Systems Inc, 55809
Conti Group Company, 55810
Continental Glass & Plastic, 55811
Continental Lift Truck Corp, 55812
Continental Marketing, 55813
Contract & Leisure, 55814
Convenience Food Systems, 55816
Cook Associates Your Co Store, 55817
Cook Flavoring Company, 55818
Cook's Mate Restaurant Equipment Supply, 55819
Cooker T. Corporation, 55820
Cookie Kingdom, 55821
CoolBrands International, 55822
Cooperative Atlantic, 55823
Cooseman's D.C., 55825
Copperwood InternationalInc, 55826
Coquitlam City Hall, 55827
Cora Italian Specialties, 55828

Wholesale Product Type / Frozen Food

Core-Mark Holding Company, Inc, 55830, 55832, 55833, 55834, 55835, 55839, 55840
Corey Bros Inc WHLS Produce, 55843
Coriell Associates, 55845
Corporate Display Specialty, 55847
Cosa Xentaur Corp, 55848
Cosgrove Distributors Inc, 55849
Cost Plus, 55850
Costco Wholesale Corporation, 55852
Cotati Brand Eggs & Food Svc, 55853
Country Cupboard, 55858
Country Springs Hotel, 55860
County Supply Co, 55861
Cousin's Uniform, 55863
Coy's Bakery, 55865
Coyne Chemical Co Inc, 55866
Crab, 55868
Crab Connection, 55869
Cracker Jack Advertising Specialty Corporation, 55871
Craver Supply Company, 55873
CRC Products, 55448
Creager Mercantile Cash & Carry, 55875
Cream of Weeber, 55877
Creative Foods of the Southwest, 55878
Creative Lighting Fixture Company, 55879
Crishawn Kitchen Equipment Company, 55883
Crispy Bagel Co, 55884
Cristina Foods Inc, 55885
Cross Automation, 55888
Crosset Co LLC, 55889
Crown Lift Trucks, 55891
Crown O'Maine Organic Cooperative, 55892
Crown Point, 55893
Crown Sanitary Supply, 55895
CRS Marking Systems, 55449
Crusader Tomato, 55897
Crystal-Vision Packaging Systems, 55899
CSI Material Handling, 55450
Csra Advertising Specialties, 55900
CTS/Bulk Sales, 55451
Cubberley's, 55901
Cudlin's Meat Market, 55902
Culinar Canada, 55904
Culinary Masters Corporation, 55906
Culinary Products Inc, 55907
Culinary Specialties, 55908, 55909
Culture Systems Inc, 55910
Cummings Restaurant Equipment, 55913
CUNICO, 55452
Curley Brothers, 55914
Curtis Restaurant Equipment, 55916, 55917
Curtis Restaurant Supply, 55918
Custom Fabricating & Repair, 55921
Custom Pools Inc, 55925
Cutrufello's Creamery, 55927
Cuyler Food Machinery & Appraisal, 55928
CW Paper, 55453
D A C Labels & Graphic, 55930
D J Enterprises, 55932
D L Systems Inc, 55933
D Rosen Co Inc, 55934
D'Arrigo Brothers Company of New York, Inc, 55938
D'Eon Fisheries, 55939
D. Deodati & Sons, 55941
D. Fillet & Company, 55942
D.A. Foodservice, 55944
D.M. Rothman Company, 55945
Dacotah Paper Co, 55962
Dade Paper Co, 55963
Daffin Mercantile Company, 55964
Dairy King Milk Farms/Foodservice, 55967
Dairy Maid Ravioli Mfg Co, 55968
Dairyland USA Corp, 55971
Dal-Don Produce, 55972
Dale's Meats, 55973
Dalmatian Bay Wine Company, 55974

Dalo Button & Emblem Company, 55975
Damian's Enterprises Inc, 55976
Dana's Rush Equipment Company, 55977
Dana-Lu Imports, 55978
Danish Cones, 55979
Danville Paper & Supply, 55980
Darisil, 55981
Darlington Packing Co, 55982
Dataflow Technologies, 55983
Datatech Enterprises, 55984
David Food Processing Equipment, Inc., 55986
David Puccia & Company, 55987
David's Cookies, 55988
Davis Coffee Co, 55989
Davis Distributors of Owensboro Company, 55990
Davis-Le Grand Company, 55992
Dayco Distributing, 55993
DC Media & Marketing, 55947
De Choix Specialty Foods Company, 55995
De Coty Coffee Co, 55996
De Leone Co, 55997
De Palo & Sons Inc, 55998
De Vara Designs, 55999
Dealers Food Products Co, 56001
Dean & Company, 56002
Dean's Ice Cream Dstrbtn Ctr, 56004
Dearborn Cash & Carry Stores, 56005
Dearborn Wholesale Grocers LP, 56006
Dearborn Wholesale Grocers, 56007, 56008, 56009, 56010
Debbie Wright Sales, 56011
Deep Creek Custom Packing, 56014
Deep Foods Inc, 56015
Deep Sea Products, 56016
Deep South Equipment Co, 56017
Dees Paper Co, 56019
Del Mar Seafood's Inc, 56022
Delisa Pallet Corporation, 56025
Dell Enterprises, 56026
Delta Bay, 56027
Delta Materials Handling Inc, 56029
Demak & Company, 56031
Demma Fruit Company, 56032
Den-Tex Restaurant Supply, 56033
Deng's, 56034
Dent Electrical Supply Company, 56035
Denton Dairy Products Inc, 56037
Denver Restaurant Equipment Company, 56038
Dependable Plastics & Supls, 56040
Designs Furnishings & Eqpt Inc, 56042
Destileria Serralles Inc, 56043
Detroit Popcorn, 56044
Deverell Equipment, 56045
Deville Restaurant Equipment & Supply Company, 56046
DeVries Imports, 56000
Di Mare Fresh Inc, 56049
Dial Industries Inc, 56053
Diamond Nutrition, 56056
Diamond Reef Seafood, 56057
Dicarlo Distributors Inc, 56059
Dick Dunphy Advertising Specialties, 56060
Dickerson & Quinn, 56061
Dickerson Foods, 56062
Dickson Brothers, 56063
Dierks Foods, 56064
Difeo & Sons Poultry Inc, 56065
Diggs Packing Company, 56066
Digital Monitoring Products, 56067
DiGregorio Food Products, 56050
DiLeo Brothers, 56051
Dilgard Frozen Foods, 56068
Dimond Tager Company Products, 56071
Dinetz Restaurant Equipment, 56072
Dino's Sausage & Meat Co Inc, 56073
Dino-Meat Company, 56074
DiNovo Produce Company, 56052
Dipasa USA Inc, 56075
Direct Media, 56076
Direct Promotions, 56077

Direct Seafood, 56078
Dirt Killer Pressure Washer, 56079
Discount Equipment Intl, 56080
Dispenser Juice, 56082
Dispenser Services, 56083
Distribution Kowloon, 56084
Distribution Plus, 56085
Diverse Sales, 56086
Divine Ice Cream Company, 56088
Dixie Advertising Company, 56089
Dixie Equipment Co, 56090
Dixie Lily Foods, 56091
Dixie Mart, 56092
Dixie Store Fixtures & Sales, 56093
DKW International Nutrition Company, 55949
DMI Distribution, Inc., 55950
Dobert's Dairy, 56095
Dockside Seafood & Specs Inc, 56097
Doerle Food Svc, 56098
Doggett Equipment Services Group, 56100
Dol Cice' Gelato Company, 56101
Dolly Madison Ice Cream, 56103
Domestic Casing Co, 56105
Dominion Equipment & Su pply Co., 56106
Don Luis Garcia Fernandez, 56107
Don McDonald & Sons, 56108
Dore Foods, 56113
Dornan Uniforms & Specialty Advertising, 56114
Dorsett & Jackson Inc, 56116
Douglas Brothers Produce Company, 56121
Douglas Freight Salvage, 56122
Douglas Homs Corporation, 56123
Down To Earth Distributors, 56127
Downco Packaging Inc, 56128
Downeast Food Distributors Inc, 56129
DPI Mid Atlantic, 55953
DPI Rocky Mountain, 55955
Dr. Willy's Great American Seafood, 56133
Dragnet Fisheries, 56135
Dragonfly Screen Graphics Inc, 56136
Drake Equipment Co, 56137
Draper's Super Bee, 56138
Draught Services, 56139
Dreyer's Grand Ice Cream Inc, 56140
Droubi's Imports, 56141
Dub Harris Corporation, 56143
Dublin Produce Company, 56144
Dunlevy Food Equipment, 56149
Dura-Flex, 56150
Durham Flavor Rich, 56154
Durham Ranch, 56155
Dutch Creek Foods, 56156
Dutch Valley Food Distributors, 56157
Dutchess Restaurant Equipment, 56158
Dutra Distributing, 56159
Duval Container Co, 56160
Dwan & Company, 56162
DWL Industries Company, 55959
DXP Enterprises Inc, 55960
Dykes Restaurant Supply Inc, 56163
Dyna Tabs LLC, 56164
Dyna-Lift Inc, 56165
E A Sween Co, 56168
E D Farrell Co Inc, 56169
E G Forrest Co Inc, 56171
E Goodwin & Sons, 56172
E M Trisler Sales Co Fd Prods, 56173
E&A Hotel & Restaurant Epment And Supplies, 56174
E&M Fancy Foods, 56175
E&M Packaging, 56176
E. Armata Fruit & Produce, Inc., 56177
E. De la Garza, 56178
E.H. Thompson Company, 56183
Eagle Industrial Distribution, 56191
Eagle Wholesale Drug Company, 56192
Eagle-Concordia Paper Corporation, 56193
Earl Gill Coffee Co, 56194

Earp Distribution, 56195
Earthgrains, 56200
EarthGrains Banking Companies, Inc., 56198
East Bay International, 56201
East Coast Seafood Inc, 56202
East Side Fisheries, 56204
Eastern Bag & Paper Company, 56205
Eastern Bakers Supply Co Inc, 56206
Eastern Energy Lighting Systems, 56207
Eastern Fish Company, 56208
Eastern Refrigeration & Restaurant Equipment, 56209
Eastimpex, 56212
Eatmore Fruit Company, 56213
Eaton Corporation, 56214
Eaton Market, 56215
Eau de Source Boischatel, 56216
Ebonex Corporation, 56217
Eby-Brown Company, 56218
Ecological Formulas, 56221
Economy Restaurant Fixtures, 56225
Economy Wholesale Company, 56226
Ecoval Dairy Trade, 56227
Eden, 56230
Eden Creamery, 56231
Edmer Sanitary Supply Co Inc, 56233
Edner Corporation, 56234
Edom Labs Inc, 56235
Edsung, 56236
Edward Badeaux Company, 56237
Edward Don & Co, 56238, 56239, 56240
Edward Don & Company, 56241, 56242
Edward I. Friedland, 56244
Edwards Distributing, 56246
Ehrlich Food Co, 56248
Eklof & Company, 56249
El Molino Tamales, 56250
El Popular Inc VF Garza, 56251
Elco Fine Foods, 56253, 56254
Electra Supply Co, 56256
Electro Freeze Distrs Inc, 56258
Electroshield Inc, 56259
Elegant Desserts, 56260
Elkhorn Distributing Company, 56265
Elliot Lee, 56268
Elm Electric Supply, 56272
Emco Industrial Plastics, 56275
Emerling International Foods, 56276
EMG Associates, 56186
Emiliomiti, 56277
Emkay Trading Corporation, 56279
Empire Cash Register Systems, 56280
Empire Comfort Systems, 56281
Empire Packing Co, 56283
Empress Food Prods Co Inc, 56285
EMSCO Scientific Enterprises, Inc., 56187
Emulsol Egg Products Corporation, 56287
Encore Sales, 56288
Ener-G Foods, 56289
Engineered Storage Products Company, 56292
English Honey Farms, 56293
Enslin & Son Packing Company, 56295
Enterprise Company, 56296
Enviro-Green Products, 56297
Environmental Packaging Associates, 56299
Enzamar, 56300
Equipco, 56305
Equipment, 56306
Equipment Distributor Div, 56307
Equipment Engineering Company, 56308
Equipment for Industry, 56312
Equipment Inc., 56309
Equipment Picard, 56310
Equipment Specialty Company, 56311
Equipment/Plus, 56313
ERC Parts Inc, 56188
Erickson's Fork Lifts Inc, 56314
Erlab, Inc, 56315
Erman & Son, 56316
Erneston & Sons Produce Inc, 56317

1239

Wholesale Product Type / Frozen Food

Espresso Buy the Cup, 56321
Espresso Coffee Machine Co, 56322
Espresso Magic, 56324
Espresso Roma, 56325
Essbar Equipment Company, 56326
Esteem Products, 56329
Eternal Marketing Group, 56330
Etline Foods Corp, 56331
Euclid Fish Co, 56333
Eugene & Company, 56334
Euro-Bake, 56336
Euro-Excellence, 56337
Eurofood Distributors, 56338
European Foods, 56340
European Hotel & Restaurant Imports, 56341
European Imports, 56342
Eurpac Warehouse Sales, 56343
Evans BS&R, 56345
Evans Foodservice Inc., 56346
Evco Wholesale Food Corp, 56347
Event Equipment Sales, 56348
Evonuk Oregon Hazelnuts, 56350
Excel Food Distribution Company, 56351
Excellence Commercial Products, 56352
Excellent Food Products, 56353
Excello Machine Co Inc, 56354
Excelon, 56355
Express Point Technology Services, 56356
Express Wholesale Grocers, 56357
EZ Foods, 56189
Ezy Trading International, 56358
F & A Food Sales Inc, 56359
F & C Sawaya Wholesale, 56360
F B Mc Fadden Wholesale Co, 56361
F B Wright Co, 56362
F C Bloxom & Co, 56363
F Christiana & Co, 56364
F McConnell & Sons, 56365
F-M Forklift Sales & Svc Inc, 56366
Fab Inc, 56372
Fab-X/Metals, 56373
Fadler Company, 56374
Faema, 56375
Fagerholt Brothers, 56376
Fairs Seafood, 56377
Fairway Foods, 56379
Falcon Trading Intl Corp, 56380
Falls City Mercantile Co Inc, 56381
Family Foods Home Service, 56382
Fancy Delights, 56384
Farm Fish, 56388
Farmers Seafood Co Wholesale, 56390
Farmfresh, 56391
Farmington Foods Inc, 56392
FCM, 56369
Feather Crest Farms, 56397
Federated Cooperative, 56399
Federated Cooperative Lt, 56400, 56401, 56402
Fein Brothers, 56405
Feinkost Ingredients, 56406
Fendall Ice Cream Company, 56407
Ferntrade Corporation, 56408
Ferris Coffee & Nut Co, 56409
Ferris Organic Farms, 56410
Festival Ice Cream, 56412
Fetzers', 56414
Fidelity Container Corporation, 56416
Findlay Foods Kingston, 56420
Fine Distributing, 56422
Finest Foods, 56425
Finger Lakes Organic Growers, 56427
Finke Co, 56428
Fire Device Co, 56429
Fire Master, 56430
Fire Protection Systems Inc, 56431
Fireline Corp, 56432
Firemaster, 56433
Firestone Farms, 56434
First Coast Promotions, 56436
First Fire Systems Company, 56437
Fish Breeders of Idaho, 56440
Fisher Mills, 56443

Fisherman's Seafood Market, 56444
Fitch Co, 56446
Fitness & Nutrition Center, 56447
Five Continents, 56448
Flaghouse, 56451
Flags & Banners Unlimited, 56452
Flair Beverages, 56453
Flamingo Flats, 56454
Flanders, 56455
Flash Foods, 56457
Flatland Food Distributors, 56458
Flavor-Crisp of America, 56463
Fleig Commodities, 56466
Flint Provision Inc Zalack's, 56467
Flora Foods Inc, 56468
Florida Beverage Connection, 56469
Florida Carbonic Distributor, 56470
Florida Choice Foods, 56471
Florida Distributing Source, 56472
Florida Fresh Stonecrab, 56473
Florida Gulf Packaging, 56474
Florida Smoked Fish Company, 56475
Flostor Engineering, 56476
Fluid-O-Tech International Inc, 56478
Flushing Lighting, 56479
Flynt Wholesale Company, 56480
Focus Marketing, 56481
Foley-Belsaw Institute, 56483
Follex Distributing Co Inc, 56485
Foltz Meat Processors, 56487
Food Authority Inc, 56488
Food Buying Service, 56489
Food City, 56490
Food Equipment Distributors, 56491
Food Equipment Specialist, 56492
Food Ingredients, 56496
Food Services Inc, 56501
Food Supply Inc, 56502
Food Wholesalers Inc, 56503
Food-Products, 56505
Foods Etc., 56506
Forbes Frozen Foods, 56509
Ford Hotel Supply Co, 56510
Ford Ice Cream, 56511
Foremost Foods Company, 56515
Forest City Weingart Produce, 56516
Forever Foods, 56517
Forklift Systems Inc-Parts Dpt, 56518
Forklifts, 56519
Fort Smith Restaurant Supply, 56521
Fort Wayne Door Inc, 56522
Forte Industries, 56523
Fortune Equipment Company, 56524
Foster Dairy Farms Inc, 56527
Fought's Mill, 56528
Four Oaks Farm, 56530
Four Today, 56531
Foutch's Coffee and Spring Water, 56533
Fox Brush Company, 56534
Foxtail Foods, 56536
Frabosk Magic Cappuccino, 56537
Frain Industries, 56538
Francis Produce Company, 56539
Franco Roma Foods, 56540
Frank Beer, 56541
Frank G. Schmitt Company, 56543
Frank H Gill Co, 56544
Frank P. Corso, 56546
Franklin Machine Products, 56550
Franklin Produce Company, 56551
Frankstown Fish Co Inc, 56552
Fred Band & Associates, 56553
Fred Hill & Son Co, 56554
Fred W Albrecht Grocery Co, 56555
Frederick Produce Company, 56556
Frederick Wildman & Sons LTD, 56557
Fredon Handling Inc, 56558
Fresco Y Mas, 56561
Fresh Point, 56564
Fresh Point Dallas, 56565
Freskeeto Frozen Foods Inc, 56568
Friedman Bag Company, 56569
Friendly Wholesale Co, 56571
Front Line Safety, 56574
Front Range Snacks Inc, 56575

Frontier Bag Co Inc, 56576
Frontline Inc, 56578
Frosty Products, 56579
Fru-Terra, 56580
Fru-V, 56581
Fruge Aquafarms, 56582
Fruit d'Or, 56587
Fruit Of The Vine Of De Valley, 56585
Fruit Ranch Inc, 56586
Fruitco Corp, 56588
Fullway International, 56591
Futurebiotics LLC, 56592
Futurity Products, 56593
G & L Import Export Corp, 56596
G & W Equipment Inc, 56597
G & W Food Products, 56598
G A B Empacadora Inc, 56599
G&G Distributing, 56600
G&T Commodities, 56601
G&T Terminal Packaging Company, 56602
G.B. Sales & Service, 56603
G.D. Mathews & Sons, 56604
G.W. Market, 56605
GAC Produce Company, 56606
Gachot & Gachot, 56621
Gaggia Espresso Machine Company, 56622
Gaiser's European Style, 56623
Galerie Au Chocolat, 56625
Galilee Splendor, 56626
Galloway's Specialty Foods, 56630
Gandy's Dairies, 56632
Garber Bros Inc, 56634
Garden & Valley Isle Seafood, 56635
Garden City Supply, 56636
Garden Spot Distributors, 56637
Garden Spot Produce Co, 56638
Garuda International, 56641
Garvey Nut & Candy, 56642
Gasketman Inc, 56643
Gatto Wholesale Produce, 56646
Gaylord's Meat Co, 56647
GB Enterprises, 56608
GCS Service, 56609
Gelson's, 56649
Gemsy's Money Handling Systems, 56651
Gen Pac, 56653
General Candy Co, 56654
General Carriage & Supply Co, 56655
General Cash & Carry, 56656
General Sales, 56657
General Sales Associates, 56658
General Sales Co, 56659
General Trading Co, 56660
Generichem Corporation, 56661
Genoa Wholesale Foods, 56662
Geoghegan Brothers Company, 56663
George A Heimos Produce Co, 56664
George D. Spence & Sons, 56665
George Degen & Co, 56666
George Greer Company, 56668
George J Howe Co, 56669
George O Pasquel Company, 56670
GePolymershapes Cadillac, 56648
Gerlau Sales, 56673
Gexpro, 56674
GFS (Canada) Company, 56611
Giambrocco Food Service, 56675
Giancola Brothers, Inc., 56676
Giant Eagle American Seaway Foods, 56677
GIANT Food Stores, 56612
Gibson Wholesale Co Inc, 56678
Gillco Ingredients, 56679
Gillette Creamery, 56680
Gillette Nebraska Dairies, 56681
Gillies Coffee, 56682
Gilster-Mary Lee Corp, 56684
Gimme Sum Mo Cajun Foods Corporation, 56685
Gina Marie Refrigerator Door, 56686
Giumarra Companies, 56689
GLAC Seat Inc, 56613

Glandt-Dahlke, 56690
Glazier Packing Co, 56691
Global Harvest, 56693
Globe Equipment Co, 56695
Globe-Monte-Metro Company, 56696
Glosson Food Eqpt-Hobart Svc, 56699
GMT Dairy Products Inc, 56614
GMZ Inc, 56615
Goetz & Sons Western Meat, 56702
Goff's Seafood, 56703, 56704
Gold Star Foods, 56708
Goldberg & Solovy Foods Inc, 56710
Golden Eye Seafood, 56713
Golden Harvest Pecans, 56715
Golden Lake Electric Supply, 56716
Golden Light Equipment Co, 56717
Golden Orchard, 56719
Golden Valley Popcorn Supply, 56721
Goldy Food Sales Company, 56723
Gone Wild!!!, 56724
Good's Wholesale-Bakery Supls, 56725
Gooding Rubber Company, 56726
Goodwin Brothers Inc, 56728
Gordon Food Service, 56730, 56731, 56732, 56733, 56734, 56735, 56737, 56738, 56739, 56740, 56741, 56742, 56743, 56744, 56745, 56746, 56747
Gosselin Gourmet Beverages, 56748
Gourmet Award Foods, 56749
Gourmet Cafe Wholesale, 56750
Gourmet Foods Intl, 56752
Gourmet Technologies Inc, 56754
Grafco, 56757
Graham Ice & Locker Plant, 56760
Grainger Industrial Supply, 56761, 56762
Gralab Instruments, 56763
Grande Cuisine Systems, 56764
Granite State Fruit, 56766
Gray Lift, 56768
Grayco Products Sales, 56769
Grayon Industrial Products, 56770
Great Age Container, 56771
Great American Health Bar, 56772
Great Basin Botanicals, 56775
Great Eastern Equipment Exchange, 56776
Great Lakes Designs, 56778
Great Lakes Distributing & Storage, 56779
Great Lakes Gourmet Food Service, 56781
Great Lakes Hotel Supply Co, 56782, 56783
Great Lakes International Trading, 56784
Great North Foods, 56786
Great Outdoors Spice Company, 56787
Great Valley Meat Company, 56789
Great Western Beef WHLS Co, 56791
Great Western Chemical, 56792
Great Western Chemical Company, 56793
Great Western Foods, 56794
Great Western Meats, 56795
Greek Gourmet Limited, 56797
Green Gold Group LLC, 56798
Green Mountain Graphics, 56799
Green Valley Food Corp, 56800
Greenebaum Brothers, 56802
Greenfield Noodle & Spec Co, 56803
Greenfield Packaging, 56804
Greenley Foods Inc, 56805
Greenvale Electric Supply Corp, 56806
Gregory's Foods, Inc., 56809
Greis Brothers, 56810
Griesedieck Imports, 56813
Griffith Laboratories, 56816
Grigg Box Company, 56817
Grocers Ice & Cold Storage Company, 56818
Grocers Supply Co, 56819
Groetsch Wholesale Grocer, 56820
Groff's Meats, 56821
GSC Enterprises Inc., 56617
GTM, 56618
Guest Products, 56827

Wholesale Product Type / Frozen Food

Gulf Arizona Packaging, 56828
Gulf Marine & Industrial Supplies Inc, 56831
Gulf Packing Company, 56832
Gulf Systems, 56835, 56836, 56837, 56838, 56839
Gunderland Marine Supply, 56840
GW Supply Company, 56619
GWB Foods Corporation, 56620
H & R Coffee Co, 56844
H A Phillips & Co, 56845
H B Day Co, 56846
H Brooks & Co, 56847
H Schrier & Co Inc, 56848
H Weiss Co LLC, 56849
H&H Pretzel, 56850
H.B. Paulk Grocery Company, 56853
H.P. Beale & Sons, 56855
H.T. Hackney Company, 56856
H.Y. Louie Company, 56857
H20 Technology, 56858
Haddad Supply Company, 56872
Haddon House Food Products, 56873
Hadley Fruit Orchards, 56874
Hahn Produce Corporation, 56875
Hain Food Group, 56877
Haitai Inc, 56878
Hal-One Plastics, 56879
Hale-Halsell Company, 56882
Hall & Cole Produce, 56883
Halsey Foodservice, 56885
Halsey Reid Equipment, 56886
Hamill Industrial Sales Company, 56888
Hammill International, 56890
Hamms, 56891
Hampton Roads Seafoods Ltd, 56893
Handi-Rak Service, 56894
Handling & Storage Concepts, 56895
Handling Systems Inc, 56896, 56897
Handy Pax, 56898
Hanif's International Foods, 56900
Hanmi, 56901
Hannaford Bros Co, 56902
Hanover Potato Products Inc, 56903
Hanover Uniform Co, 56904
Hans Holterbosch Inc, 56905
Hansen Beverage Co, 56906
Hansen Co, 56907
Hansen Group, 56909
Hanset Brothers Inc Brooms, 56910
Hansler Industries, 56911
Hanway Restaurant Equipment, 56913
Happybaby, 56915
Harbor Linen LLC, 56919
Harbor Wholesale Foods Inc, 56920
Harders, 56922
Hardscrabble Enterprises, 56923
Harger's Finest Catch, 56924
Harker's Distribution, 56926
Harold Food Company, 56928
Harold Leonard & Company, 56929
Harold Leonard Midwest Corporation, 56930
Harold Leonard Southwest Corporation, 56931
Harold Levinson Assoc Inc, 56932
Harpak-Ulma, 56933
Harrill Brothers Wholesale Company, 56934
Harris Equipment Corp, 56935
Harrison Oyster Company, 56936
Harry Fourtunis, 56937
Harry Fourtunis Inc, 56938
Harry Gelb Frozen Foods Inc, 56939
Harry Nusinov Company, 56940
Harry's Premium Snacks, 56942
Hart Lobster, 56944
Hartland Distributors, 56945
Harvest Health Foods, 56948
Harveys Supermarket, 56950
HAS Packaging System, 56859
Hata Y & Co LTD, 56953
Hathaway Coffee Co Inc, 56954
Hattiesburg Grocery Company, 56955
Hauser Enterprises, 56956

HAVI Group, 56860
Haviland Enterprises Inc, 56957
Hawaiian Coffee Traders, 56960
Hawaiian Grocery Stores, 56961
Hawk Flour Mills, 56963
Hawkins Distributing Company, 56964
Hawthorn Power Systems, 56965
Hawthorne Supply Company, 56966
Haynes Brothers Candy Company, 56967
HD Supply Waterworks, 56862
HE Anderson Co, 56863
Heads & Tails Seafood, 56968
Healing Garden, 56969
Health Food Distributors, 56972
Health Guardians, 56973
Health Waters, 56975
Healthwise, 56978
Hearn-Kirkwood, 56979
Heartland Distributors, 56981
Heartland Food Products, 56983
Heartland Supply Co, 56985
Heavenly Cheesecakes, 56986
Heerema Co, 56987
Heeren Brothers Produce, 56988
Helena Wholesale, 56991
Heller's Food Equipment, 56992
Helmut's Strudel, 56993
Hemisphere Group, 56994
Henderson Coffee Corp, 56995
Henderson-Black Wholesale Groc, 56996
Hendrix Hotel & Restaurant Equipment & Supplies, 56997
Henjes Enterprises, 56998
Henley Paper Company, 56999
Henry Gonsalves Co, 57002
Henrys Cash & Carry, 57003
HERB Enterprises, 56864
Herc-U-Lift Inc, 57004
Herche Warehouse, 57005
Hercules Food Equipment, 57006
Hermanowski Wholesale, 57008
Herring Brothers Meats, 57010
HIB Foods Inc, 56866
Hibrett Puratex, 57013
Hickory Harvest Foods, 57014
Hill & Sloan, 57019
Hill City Wholesale Company, 57020
Hill Company, 57021
Hill Specialties, 57022
Hillis Farms, 57025
Hilts, 57027
Hipp Wholesale Foods, 57031
Hiss Stamp Company, 57032
HMG Provisions, 56867
Hoban Foods, 57033
Hockenbergs Equipment & Supply, 57034
Hodell International, 57035
Hodges & Irvine Inc, 57036
Hoffman Miller Advertising, 57037
Hoky Central, 57040
Holistic Products Corporation, 57042
Holland Beef International Corporation, 57044
Hollander, Gould & Murray Company, 57046
Holly Seafood Company, 57048
Holyoke Machine Co, 57050
Home-Like Food Company, 57052
Homestead Foods, 57053
Honey Acres, 57054
Honeyville Grain Inc, 57055
Horizon Business Svc, 57058
Hornell Wholesale Grocery Company, 57060
Horsley Company, 57061
Hoshizaki Northeastern, 57063
Hosoda Brothers Inc, 57064
House of Spices, 57067
Houston International Packaging Company, 57069
Houston Poultry & Egg Company, 57070
Howard Decorative Packaging, 57071
HPC Foodservice, 56868
HRS Food Service, 56869

HSN Data Corporation, 56870
Hubert Co, 57073
Huck's Seafood, 57074
Hudson Belting & Svc Co Inc, 57075
Hudson River Fruit Distr, 57077
Hudson Valley Coffee Company, 57078
Huff Ice Cream, 57082
Huger-Davidson-Sale Company, 57083
Hugg & Hall Equipment, 57084
Hughes Warehouse Equipment Company, 57086
Huguenot Sales Corporation, 57087
Hull Lift Truck Inc, 57088
Hunter Walton & Co Inc, 57092
Huntsville Restaurant Equip, 57093
Husky Foods of Anchorage, 57094
Hutchinson Mayrath Industries, 57095
Hydra-Flex Inc, 57096
Hydrite Chemical Co, 57097
I Supply Co, 57101
I Wanna Distributors, 57102
I Zakarin & Sons Inc, 57103
I. Grob & Company, 57104
I.T. Bauman Company, 57105
IBC, 57106
Iberia Foods of Florida, 57116
IBF, 57107
ICC Industrial Chemical, 57108
Ice & Juice Systems, 57118
Ice Machines, 57120
Ice Makers, 57121
Iceberg Seafood Inc, 57122
ID Foods Corporation, 57109
ILHWA American Corporation, 57110
IMDEC, 57111
Impact Products LLC, 57125
Imperial Bag & Paper Company, 57126
Imperial Dade, 57127
Imperial Seafood, 57129
Imperial Trading, 57131
Importex International, 57133
In A Bind Inc, 57134
Independent Wholesale, 57136
India Emporium, 57137
Indian Springs Water Company, 57138
Indiana Sugars Inc, 57140
Indianhead Foodservice, 57143
Indo-European Foods, 57145
Industrial Commodities, 57147
Industrial Contacts Inc, 57148
Industrial Handling Equipment, 57149
Industrial Lift Truck, 57150
Industrial Maintenance, 57151
Industrial Products Supply, 57152
Industrial Soap Co, 57153
Industrial Truck Sales & Services, 57154
Infinite Peripherals, 57155
Infinite Specialties, 57156
Inland Meats of Spokane, 57161
Inno-Vite, 57163
Inpak Systems Inc, 57165
Insects Limited Inc, 57166
Insley-Mc Entee Equipment Co, 57167
Institutional Food Service, 57169
Institutional Wholesale Company, 57170
Instrumart, 57171
Insulated Structures/PB Group, 57172
International Beverages, 57179
International Business Trading, 57180
International Casein Corporation, 57181
International Commercial Supply Corporation, 57183
International Dairy Equipment Associates, 57185
International Enterprises Unlimited, 57187
International Marine Products, 57189
International Pack & Ship, 57192
International Seafoods - Alaska, 57193
International Ticket Company, 57197
Interstate Distributors, 57199
Interstate Restaurant Equipment, 57200
Ipc Supply Inc, 57202
Ira Higdon Grocery Company, 57205
Irvine Restaurant Supply, 57208

Irvington Marcus Company, 57209
Ishida Corporation, 57211
ISI Commercial Refrigeration, 57112, 57113, 57114
ISI North America, 57115
Island Farms Dairies Cooperative Association, 57212
Island Refrigeration & Foodservice Equipment, 57214
Island Supply, 57216
Islander Import, 57217
Italfina, 57218
Italfoods Inc, 57219
Italmade, 57221
J & J Distributing, 57223
J & M Wholesale Meat Inc, 57224
J & R Distributors, 57225
J Bernard Seafood, 57226
J Hoelting Produce Inc, 57229
J Kings Food Svc Professionals, 57230
J Moresky & Son, 57232
J O Spice Co, 57234
J P Ice Cream, 57235
J Petite & Sons, 57237
J W Outfitters, 57241
J Weil Food Service Co, 57242
J&L Produce Wholesale Company, 57243
J&M Distribution Company, 57244
J&S Food Distributors, 57246
J. Connor & Sons, 57247
J. Lerner Box Company, 57250
J. M. Sealts Company, 57251
J. Quattrocchi & Company, 57252
J. Rutigliano & Sons, 57253
J. Sosnick & Sons, 57254
J. Treffiletti & Sons, 57255
J.A. Wendling Foodservice, 57257
J.C. Produce, 57259
J.C. Wright Sales Company, 57260
J.D. Dawson Company, 57261
J.H. Thornton Company, 57264
J.J. Taylor Distributing, 57265
J.L. Henderson & Company, 57266
J.M. Schneider, 57267
J.O. Demers Beef, 57268
J.P. Beaudry, 57269
J.R. Campbell Equipment Company, 57270
J.W. Wood Company, 57274
JAAMA World Trade, 57275
Jab's Seafood, 57289
Jack & Jill Ice Cream, 57291
Jacks Merchandising & Distribution, 57292
Jackson Newell Paper Co, 57293
Jackson Supply Company, 57294
Jackson Wholesale Co, 57295
Jacob Licht, 57298
Jacobson & Sons, 57300
Jake's Variety Wholesale, 57302
Jako Fish, 57303
Jamac Frozen Foods, 57304
Jamaican Teas Limited C/O Eve Sales Corporation, 57306
James D Cofer, 57309
James Desiderio Inc, 57310
James K. Wilson Produce Company, 57311
Janney Marshall Co, 57312
Janpak, 57313
Jarosz Produce Farms, 57314
Jason Marketing Corporation, 57316
Jasper Glove Company, 57317
Jatex-USA Corporation, 57318
Jaydon, 57321
Jb Prince, 57322
JBG International, 57276
JC's Sunny Winter, 57279
Jeb Plastics, 57323
Jeffer Neely Company, 57325
Jefferds Corp, 57326
Jenthon Supply, 57330
JER Creative Food Concepts, Inc., 57280
Jerico, 57331
Jeris Health & Nutrition, 57333

1241

Wholesale Product Type / Frozen Food

Jerome Langdon Produce, 57334
Jerry Brothers Industries Inc, 57335
Jerry Schulman Produce, 57336
Jersey Meat & Provision Company, 57337
Jesse Food Products, 57339
Jessom Food Equipment, 57340
Jet Set Sam, 57341
Jetro Cash & Carry, 57342
Jetro Cash & Carry Enterprises, 57343
Jetro Cash & Carry Inc, 57344
JFC International Inc, 57282
Jianas Brothers Packaging, 57345
Jilasco Food Exports, 57346
Jim's Cheese Pantry, 57348
Jimmy Durbin Farms, 57349
Jin Han International, 57350
JM Schneider, 57284
JML Sales Co, 57285
JMS, 57286
JNS Foods, 57287
JoDaSa Group International, 57353
Jode Company, 57354
Joe Christiana Food Distributing, 57357
Joe Harding Sales & Svc, 57358
Joe Paulk Company, 57359
Joe Pucci & Sons Seafood, 57360
Joey's Fine Foods, 57361
John Demartin Company, 57366
John Graves Food Service, 57368
John Gross & Company, 57369
John Groves Company, 57370
John Hansen & Sons, 57371
John J. Moon Produce, 57372
John Lenore & Company, 57373
John Molinelli Inc, 57374
John Nagle & Co, 57376
John S. Dull & Associates, 57378
John W Williams Inc, 57379
John's Dairy, 57381
John's Meat Market, 57382
John's Wholesale, 57383
Johnnie's Restaurant-Hotel Svc, 57384
Johnson Restaurant Supply, 57386
Johnston Equipment, 57389, 57390
Johnston Farms, 57391
Jolar Distributor, 57393
Jordan Lobster Farms, 57395
Joseph Antognoli & Co, 57396
Joseph Apicella & Sons, 57397
Joseph J. Sayre & Son Company, 57398
Jost Kauffman Import & Export Company, 57400
Joyce Brothers Company, 57401
Joyce Foods, 57402
Jp Tropical Foods, 57404
Judith's Fine Foods International, 57405
Julius Silvert Company, 57408
Junction City Distributing & Vending Company, 57409
Jungbunzlauer Inc, 57410
K & G Power Systems, 57412
K & L Intl, 57413
K C's Best Wild Rice, 57414
K Doving Co Inc, 57415
K Heeps Inc, 57416
K&K Meat Company, 57420
K. Lefkofsky Company, 57424
Kaleel Bros Inc, 57437
Kalil Produce Company, 57438
Kallsnick Inc, 57439
Kane's Kandies, 57441
Kanematsu, 57442
Kansas City Sausage, 57443
Kansas Marine, 57444
Kappus Co, 57445
Kar Wah Trading Company, 57446
Karetas Foods Inc, 57448
Karp's Bake Mark, 57449
Karson Food Services, 57450
Kason, 57451
Kason Central, 57452
KAST Distributors Inc, 57425
Katy's Wholesale Distributing, 57453
Katzin's Uniforms, 57454

Kauai Producers, 57455
Kay's Foods, 57456
Keith Industries, 57474
Kelley Bean Co Inc, 57475
Kelley-Clarke, 57477
Kellogg Elevator Company, 57478
Kelly's Foods, 57479
Ken Ottoboni Mushrooms, 57482
Kenny Seafood, 57486
Kenrich Foods Corp, 57487
Kenssenich's, 57489
Key Business Systems, 57495
Key Food Stores Cooperative, 57496
Key Industrial, 57497
Keyco Distributors Inc, 57499
Keys Fisheries Market & Marina, 57500
Keystone Cleaning Systems, 57501
Keystone Restaurant Supply, 57502
KHL Engineered Packaging, 57426
Kid Zone, 57503
Kimball & Thompson Produce, 57505
King Provision Corporation, 57508
Kings Choice Food, 57509
Kings Seafood Co, 57510
Kingson Corporation, 57511
Kingston Candy & Tobacco Co, 57512
Kingston McKnight, 57513
Kirby Holloway Provision Co, 57514
Kirby Restaurant & Chemical, 57515
Kirkholder & Rausch, 57516
Kissner Milling Company, 57517
Kitchen Maid Foods, 57518
Kittredge Equipment Co, 57520
KJ's Market, 57427
Kleen Janitorial Supply Co., 57521
Klondike Foods, 57524
KMA Trading Company, 57428
Knox Cash Jobbers, 57529
Knoxville Poultry & Egg Company, 57531
Koalaty Kare, 57532
Koch Bag & Supply Co, 57533
Koch Container, 57534
KOHL Wholesale, 57429
Kohlenberger Inc, 57537
Kolon California Corporation, 57538
Kols Container, 57539
Kommercial Kitchens, 57540
Koorsen Protection Services, 57544
Kopcke-Kansas Supply Services, 57545
Kopke, William H, 57546
Kosmos & Associates, 57547
Kovacs Group, 57548
KP USA Trading, 57431
Kranz Inc, 57550
Krasdale Foods, 57551
Krasdale Foods Distribution, 57552
Krebs Brothers Restaurant Supl, 57553
Kuehne Chemical, 57556
Kutter's Cheese Factory, 57559
Kwikprint Manufacturing Inc, 57560
KYD Inc, 57432
L & M Food Svc Inc, 57562
L ChemCo Distribution, 57563
L&C Meat Company, 57564
L. Dontis Produce Company, 57569
L. Holloway & Brother Company, 57570
L. Lacagnina & Sons, 57571
L.N. Coffman Company, 57573
L.P. Shanks Company, 57574
LA Bella Ferrara, 57575
La Brea Bakery Inc, 57590
LA Canasta Mexican Foods, 57576
LA Foods, 57578
LA Grange Grocery Co, 57579
LA Lifestyle Nutritional Products, 57581
La Pine Scientific Company, 57592
La Rinascente Macaroni Company, 57593
LA Rue Distributing, 57582
LA Squisita Food Corp, 57583
La Tang Cuisine Manufacturing, 57594
LA Torilla Factory, 57584
Labatt Food Service, 57597, 57598, 57599, 57600, 57601
Label House, 57602

Labov Mechanical, Inc., 57604
Ladoga Frozen Food & Retail, 57606
Lady Baltimore of Missouri, 57607
Lafayette Restaurant Supply, Inc., 57609
Lafitte Seafood Company, 57610
Lairamore Corp, 57611
Laird Plastics, 57612
Laird Plastics Inc, 57613
Lake Wales Citrus Growers Associates, 57616
Lakeside Packing Company, 57617
Lamb Cooperative Inc, 57618
Lancaster Johnson Company, 57620
Lancaster Poultry, 57621
Lancer, 57622
Land's End Seafood, 57624
Landphair Meat & Seafood, 57627
Landsberg Kent, 57628
Lane Equipment Co, 57629, 57630
Langley Corporation, 57632
Lantev Distributing Corporation, 57633
Lanzarotta Wholesale Grocers, 57634
Laredo Tortilleria & Mexican, 57635
Larick Associates, 57636
Larimore Bean Company, 57637
LaRocca's Seafood Specialists, 57596
Larry Martindale Company, 57639
Latouraine Coffee Company, 57643
Lawrence Lapide, 57647
Layman Candy Company, 57648
LBG Distributors, 57585
LDC of Lafayette, 57586
Le Smoker, 57652
Leading Brands of Canada, 57653
Leali Brothers Meats, 57654
Lee Foods, 57658
Lee Grocery Company, 57659
Lee Packaging Corporation, 57660
Left Hand Brewing Co, 57662
Legacy Beverage Systems, 57663
Lehmann-Colorado, 57665
Leichtman Ice Cream Company, 57666
Lello Appliances Corp, 57667
Lemark Promotional Products, 57668
Lems, 57671
Lenox-Martell Inc, 57672
Lenson Coffee & Tea Company, 57673
Leo A Dick & Sons, 57674
Leon Supply Company, 57675
Leonard & Sons Shrimp Company, 57676
Leonetti's Frozen Food, 57677
Leonidas, 57678
Les Boulangers Associes Inc, 57679
Lesco Supply Company, 57681
Levant, 57682
Levin Brothers Paper, 57683
Lew Sander Inc, 57684
Lewis & McDermott, 57685
Lewis Brothers & Sons, 57686
Lexington Foodservice, 57688
Liberto Management Co Inc, 57689
Liberto of Harlington, 57690
Liberto of Houston, 57691
Liberty Gold Fruit Co Inc, 57693
Liberty International WHOL, 57694
Liberty Marine Products, 57695
Liberty Natural Products Inc, 57696
Liberty Scale Co Inc, 57698
Libido Funk Circus, 57700
Lido Chem, 57701
Lieber Chocolate Food Prod LTD, 57702
Lift Atlanta Inc, 57703
Lift Power, 57704
Lift South, 57705
Lift Truck Ctr Inc, 57706
Lift Truck of America, 57708
Liftech Equipment Co Inc, 57709
Liftow, 57710
Liftruck Service Company, 57711
Light Bulbs Unlimited, 57712
Lilly Company, 57715
Linco Caster, 57720, 57721
Lincoln Feed & Supply, 57722
Lincoln Shrimp Company, 57723

Lincolnwood Merchandising Company, 57724
Lingle Fork Truck Company, 57725
Lions Restaurant Equipment & Supplies, 57727
Lippert, 57728, 57729, 57730
Little Charlie's, 57733
Little Produce, 57734
Littleton Sales Company, 57736
Livingston Distribution Centers, 57738, 57739
LMG Group, 57588
Lo Temp Sales, 57740
Lobster Warehouse, 57742
Lockwood & Winant, 57743
Logan, 57745
Lomar Distributing Inc, 57748
Lombardi Brothers Meat Packers, 57749
Lombardi's Seafood, 57750
London Fruit Inc, 57751
Loneoak & Co, 57752
Long Island Glove & Safety Products, 57754
Long Wholesale Distr Inc, 57756
Long Wholesale Distributors, 57757
Longhorn Liquors, 57759
Longview Meat & Merchandise Ltd, 57760
Lorain Novelty Company, 57763
Lorenz Schneider Co, 57764
Lorenz Supply Co, 57765
Lorenzo's Wholesale Foods, 57766
Lost Trail Root Beer, 57767
Louisiana Packaging, 57772
Lovecchio & Sons, 57775
Lovion International, 57776
Lowell Brothers & Bailey, 57778
LSI Specialty Products, 57589
Lucas Industrial, 57779
Lucca Packing Company, 57780
Lucia's Pizza Co, 57781
Ludwig Fish & Produce Company, 57782
Luigi Bormioli Corporation, 57783
Lumaco Inc, 57784
Lumar Lobster, 57785
Lumberton Cash & Carry, 57787
Lumsden Brothers, 57788
Lynard Company, 57790
Lynn Dairy Inc, 57791
M & G Materials Handling Co, 57793
M & V Provisions Co Inc, 57794
M A Sales, 57797
M Amundson Cigar & Candy Co, 57798
M Conley Co, 57799
M D Stetson Co, 57800
M Maskas & Sons Inc, 57802
M R Williams Inc, 57803
M Tucker Co Inc, 57804
M&F Foods, 57805
M&N International, 57807
M. Crews & Company, 57809
M. Sickles & Sons, 57810
M. Zukerman & Company, 57811
M.E. Carter & Company, 57812
M.K. Health Food Distributors, 57814
Macdonald Meat Co, 57828
MacDonalds Consolidated, 57825, 57826
Machine Ice Co, 57830
Mack Restaurant Equipment & Supplies, 57831
Madison Cash & Carry Wholesale Grocers, 57835
Madison Food Sales Company, 57836
Madison Grocery Company, 57837
Madison Wholesale Co, 57838
Madland Toyota Lift, 57839
Madys Company, 57840
Maffei Produce Company, 57841
Mahoning Swiss Cheese Cooperative, 57843
Main Street Wholesale Meat, 57845
Maine Coast Sea Vegetables, 57846
Maine Shellfish Co Inc, 57849
Maines Paper & Food Svc Inc, 57850, 57851, 57852

Wholesale Product Type / Frozen Food

Maintainco Inc, 57853
Maintenance Equipment Company, 57854
Majestic Lift Truck Service, 57856
Malena Produce Inc, 57858
Maloberti Produce Co, 57859
Malow Corporation, 57860
Manchester Grocery Company, 57863
Mancuso Cheese Co, 57865
Mandeville Company, 57866
Mando Inc, 57868
Manhattan Fire Safety, 57869
Manhattan Lights, 57871
Mani Imports, 57872
Manning Brothers Food Eqpt Co, 57873
Manor Electric Supplies Light, 57874
Manuel's Hot Tamales, 57876
Manuel's Mexican-American Fine Foods, 57877
Marci Enterprises, 57881
Marcus Food Co, 57882
Marcus Specialty Foods, 57883
Margarita Man, 57885
Margate Wine & Spirit Co, 57886
Marias Packing Company, 57888
Marin Hydroponics, 57889
Mariner Neptune Fish & Seafood Company, 57890
Mark Pack Inc, 57891
Mark-Pack Inc, 57893
Market Foods International, 57895
Market Grocery Co, 57896
Marko Inc, 57897
Markson Lab Sales, 57898
Marky's Caviar, 57900
Marle Company, 57901
Marlow Candy & Nut Co, 57902
Marriott Distribution Service, 57903
Marrone's Inc, 57904
Mars Supermarkets, 57906
Martin Bros Distributing Co, 57908
Martin Brothers Wholesale, 57909
Martin Food Service Company, 57910
Martin Preferred Foods, 57911
Martin Produce Co, 57912
Martin Seafood Company, 57913
Martin's Potato Chips, 57914
Martin-Brower Co US, 57915
Maryland Wholesale Produce Market, 57920
Mason Brothers Co, 57922
Masser's Produce, 57923
Master Chemical Products, 57924
Mat Logo Company, 57925
Material Control, 57928
Material Handling Products, 57929
Material Handling Resources, 57930
Material Handling Services, 57931
Material Handling Specialties Company, 57932
Materials Handling Enterprises, 57933
Matthiesen Equipment, 57936
Mattingly Foods, 57937
Maxim's Import Corporation, 57938
Mayer Myers Paper Company, 57943
Mayer-Bass Fromm, 57944
Mayfair Provision Company, 57945
Mayfield Paper Co, 57946, 57947
Mayrand Limitee, 57949
Mazelle's Cheesecakes Concoctions Creations, 57951
Mazo-Lerch Company, 57952
Mc Afee Foodservice Co, 57953
Mc Lane Foodservice, 57955
McCabe's Quality Foods, 57956
Mccadam Cheese Co Inc, 57969
Mccomas Sales Co Inc, 57970
McCoy's Products, 57957
Mccrone Microscopes & Acces, 57971
Mcdonald Wholesale Co, 57973
McDonnell, 57958
McDowell Supply Company, 57959
Mcfarling Foods Inc, 57974
McGrath Fisheries, 57960
Mckinley Equipment Corp, 57977
McLane Co Inc, 57963

McLane Foodservice Inc, 57964
McLane Grocery, 57965
Mcnair & Co Inc, 57979
Meaders Kitchen Equipment, 57981
Meadow Brook Dairy Co, 57982
Meadow Farm Foods, 57983
Meadowbrook Farms, 57984
Meats Plus Inc, 57987
Mecca Coffee Company, 57988
Medina & Medina, 57989
Mediterranean Gyro Products, 57990
Medley Material Handling Inc, 57991
Medley Restaurant Equipment & Supply Company, 57992
Medway Creamery Company, 57993
MeGa Industries, 57980
Melba Food Specialties, 57994
Mello Buttercup Ice Cream Company, 57995
Melmart Distributors, 57996
Mendez & Company, 57997
Menu Maker Foods Inc, 57998
Mercado Latino, 57999
Merchants Distributors Inc, 58000
Merchants Foodservice, 58001
Merchants Grocery Co Inc, 58002
Meridian Supply Rstrnt Depot, 58003
Merlino Foods, 58005
Mermaid Seafoods, 58006
Merrill Distributing Inc, 58007
Merritt Handling Engineering, 58008
Merton Restaurant Equipment Company, 58009
Mesa Bearing, 58010
Mesa Cold Storage, 58011
Messermeister, 58012
Messina Brothers Manufacturing Company, 58013
Metompkin Bay Oyster Company, 58015
Metro Touch, 58017
Metro, Inc., 58018
Metro-Richelieu, 58019
Metroplex Harriman Corporation, 58020
Metropolitan Beer & Soda Dist, 58021
Mexspice, 58022
MFS/York/Stormor, 57817
MGH Wholesale Grocery, 57818
MIA Food Distributing, 57819
Miami Depot Inc, 58023
Miami Industrial Trucks, 58024, 58025
Miami Plastics & Supply Corporation, 58026
Miami Wholesale Grocery Company, 58027
Michael G. Brown Associates, 58029
Michaelo Espresso, 58033
Michelle's Bakery, 58035
Michigan Agricultural Commdty, 58036
Michigan Carbonic Of Saginaw, 58045
Michigan Industrial Belting, 58046
Michigan Industrial Equipment Company, 58047
MICROS Retail Systems Inc, 57820
Mid States Paper & Notion Co, 58053
Mid-America Wholesale, 58054
Mid-Michigan Ice Company, 58056
Middendorf Meat, 58058
Midland Grocery Of Michigan, 58060
Midlantic Sweetener Company, 58061
Midori Trading Inc, 58062
Midtown Electric Supply Corp, 58063
Midway Container Inc., 58064
Midwest Cooperative, 58066
Midwest Fire & Safety Equipment Company, 58068
Midwest Food Distributors, 58069
Midwest Imports LTD, 58071
Midwest Ingredients Inc, 58072
Midwest Promotional Group, 58073
Mike E. Simon & Company, 58075
Mike Kazarian, 58076
Milky Whey Inc, 58079
Mill Cove Lobster Pound, 58080
Millar-Williams Hydronics, 58081
Millbrook Distribution Services, 58082

Millbrook Distribution Service, 58083
Miller & Hartman, 58086
Mills Brothers Intl, 58089
Millway Frozen Foods, 58090
Minnesota Conway Fire & Safety, 58093
Miracle Exclusives, 58095
Mishima Foods USA, 58096
Miss Grimble Desserts, 58097
Miss Mary, 58098
Mitch Chocolate, 58101
Mitchell Grocery Corp, 58102
Mitchell Handling Systems, 58103
Mivila Foods, 58104
Mj Kellner Co, 58105
Mobjack Bay Seafood, 58107
Moctezuma Foods, 58108
Model Dairy LLC, 58109
Modern Equipment Co, 58111
Modern Group, 58113
Modern Mushroom Farms Inc, 58115
Modern Wholesale Company, 58117
Modulightor Inc, 58118
Moffett Food Svc, 58119
Molinera International, 58121
Monarch-McLaren, 58124
Montana Broom & Brush Co, 58125
Montana Food Products, 58126
Montello Inc, 58128
Monterrey Provision Co, 58129
Monteverdes, 58130
Moon's Seafood Company, 58131
Moonlite Bar-B-Q Inn, 58133
Moore Equipment, 58134
Morabito Baking Co Inc, 58135
Moran Foods LLC, 58136
More For Less Foods, 58138
Morehead Company, 58139
Morre-Tec Ind Inc, 58141
Morris A. Elkis & Sons, 58143
Morris Okun, 58144
Morrison Industrial Equip Co, 58145
Morrisons Pastry Corp, 58146
Mortec Industries Inc, 58147
Moseley & Reece, 58150
Mosuki, 58151
Mother Earth Enterprises, 58152
Motion Savers Inc, 58154
Motivatit Seafoods Inc, 58155
Mountain Dairies-SW Ice Cream, 58156
Mountain People's Warehouse, 58157
Mountain Sales & Svc Inc, 58159
Mountain Service Distribution, 58160
Mountain States Rosen, 58161
Mountain Valley Water, 58162
Mountain Valley Water Company, 58163
Mountain View Supply, 58164
Mountain West Distributors Inc, 58165
Moyer-Mitchell Company, 58167
MSC Industrial Direct Co Inc, 57822
Mt Pleasant Seafood, 58169
MTC Distributing, 57823
Muckenthaler Inc, 58171
Muller-Pinehurst Dairy Company, 58175
Multi Marques, 58176
Multi-Counter Manufacturing Company, 58177
Munchies, 58181
Mung Dynasty, 58182
Munroe Material Handling, 58183
Munsee Meats, 58184
Murphy/Northstar, 58186
Murry's Family of Fine Foods, 58187
Musco Food Corp, 58188
Mush & Pinsky, 58189
Muskingum Valley Grocery Co, 58190
Mutual Biscuit, 58191
Mutual Trading Co Inc, 58194
Mutual Wholesale Company, 58195
Mutual Wholesale Liquor, 58196
MVP Group, 57824
My Quality Trading Corp, 58198
Myers Equipment Company, 58200
Myers Restaurant Supply Inc, 58201
Myers-Cox Co, 58202
Nafziger Ice Cream Company, 58208

Nagel Paper & Box Company, 58210
Nan Sea Enterprises of Wisconsin, 58212
Nancy Q Produce, 58213
Naples Vending, 58215
Napoleon Creamery, 58216
Nappie's Food Svc, 58217
Nardelli Brothers, 58218
Nasco Inc, 58220
Nash-DeCamp Company, 58221
Nass Parts & Svc Inc, 58222
Nassau Candy Distributors, 58223
Nassau Foods, 58224
Nassau-Suffolk Frozen Food Company, 58225
Nathel & Nathel, 58229
National Band Saw Co, 58230
National Carbonation, 58232
National Grocers, 58236
National Grocers Assn, 58237
National Grocers Company, 58238, 58239, 58240, 58242
National Lighting Source, 58243
National Restaurant Company, 58245
National Restaurant Supply Company, 58246, 58247
National Sales Corporation, 58248
National Scale Of New England, 58249
National Scoop & Equipment Company, 58250
National Shippng Supply Co, 58251
Nationwide Material Handling Equipment, 58252
Natra US, 58254
Natrol Inc, 58255
Natural Balance, 58256
Natural Food Systems, 58261
Natural Foods Inc, 58262
Nature Distributors, 58265
Nature's Best, 58266
Nature's Candy, 58268
Nature's Provision Company, 58271
Navy Brand, 58273
Near East Importing Corporation, 58274
NEBCO Distributing, 58205
Nebraska Bean, 58275
Nectar Soda Company, 58276
Neelands Refrigeration, 58278
Neesvig Meats, 58279
Nelipak, 58281
Nelson Co, 58282
Nesbitt Processing, 58285
Neshaminy Valley Natural Foods, 58286
Nesson Meat Sales, 58287
Neuman Distributing Company, 58289
Nevada Seafood Company, 58292
New Beer Distributors, 58295
New Brunswick Saw Service, 58297
New England Foods, 58298
New England Indl Truck Inc, 58299
New England Meat Company, 58300
New Hope Imports, 58302
New Jersey Provision Co, 58303
New Mexico Food Distributors, 58304
New Vermont Creamery, 58309
New York Cash Register Company, 58310
New Zealand Lamb Co, 58311
Neway Packaging Corporation, 58313
Newman Fixture Co Inc, 58314
Newport Marketing, 58316
Newtech Beverage Systems, 58317
Newton Manufacturing Co, 58318
Niagara Restaurant Supply, 58320
Nicewonger Company, 58321
Nicholas & Co Inc, 58322
Nichols Foodservice, 58323
Nick Sciabica & Sons, 58324
Nikol Foods, 58329
Nissan Lift Of New York Inc, 58332
NJM Seafood, 58206
Noah's Potato Chip Co, 58335
Noble Harvest, 58336
Nogales Fruit & Vegetables Dst, 58337
Nogg Chemical & Paper Company, 58338

Wholesale Product Type / Frozen Food

Norben Co, 58343
Norcal Beverage Co, 58344
Norfolk Packing Company, 58345
Norland Products Inc, 58346
Norlift Inc, 58347
Norm's Refrigeration, 58348
Norman Wolff Associates, 58349
Norman's, 58350
Norman's Wholesale Grocery Company, 58351
Norpaco Inc, 58352
North American Corp, 58353
North American Provisioners, 58354
North Carolina Potato Association, 58359
North Central Co, 58360
North Side Banana Co, 58362
North West Handling Systems Inc, 58363
Northbay Restaurant Equipment & Design, 58364
Northern Orcharad Co Inc, 58369
Northern Steel Industrie, 58370
Northland Industrial Truck Company Inc, 58372
Northland Process Piping, 58373
Northstar Distributing, 58374
Northstate Provision Co, 58375
Northumberland Dairy, 58376
Northwest Dairy Association, 58378
Northwest Deli Distribution, 58379
Northwest Forklift, 58380
Northwest Naturals Company, 58381
Northwestern Foods, 58384
Norvell Fixtures & Equipment Company, 58386
Nothing Mundane, 58387
Nott Company, 58388
Novick Brothers Corp, 58391
Nspired Natural Foods, 58392
Nu Concept Food Svc, 58393
Nuco Industries, 58394
Nutri-Rich Corp., 58399
NutriCology Allergy Research, 58400
Nutrinova, 58401
Nutriscience Laboratories, 58402
Nutrition Products Company, 58403
Nutritional Counselors of America, 58404
Nuts & Spice Company, 58405
Nylon Net Company, 58409
O'Neill Coffee Co, 58411
O-Sesco, 58412
O. Lippi & Company, 58413
O.G. Foodservice, 58414
O.W. & B.S. Look Company, 58415
Oak Barrel Winecraft, 58421
Ocean Frost, 58427
Ocean Venture, 58431
Odom Corporation, 58434
OH Armstrong, 58417
Ohio Chemical Svc Inc, 58437
Ohio Conveyor & Supply Inc, 58438
Ohio Farmers, 58439
Ohio Materials Handling, 58440
Ohio Rack Inc, 58441
Oklahoma Pecan Co, 58443
Old Fashion Foods Inc, 58444
Olympic Juicer Company, 58453
Omcan Manufacturing & Distributing Company, 58454
Omega Produce Company, 58455
Omega-Life, 58456
Omni Food Inc, 58457
Omni Material Handling Services, 58458
Omni Pacific Company, 58459
One Pie Canning, 58460
One-Shot, 58461
Ono International, 58463
Ontario Glove and Safety Products, 58464
Optimum Nutrition, 58465
Optipure, 58466
Oram Material Handling Systems, 58468
Orange Distributors, 58469
Orear Company, 58471
Original Food, 58476

Orioxi International Corporation, 58479
Orlando Fire Equipment Company, 58480
Orleans International, 58481
Ortho-Molecular Products Inc, 58483
Osborn Bros Inc, 58485
Oscar's Wholesale Meats, 58486
Ostrow Jobbing Company, 58487
Oswalt Restaurant Supply, 58488
Ottenheimer Equipment Company, 58489
Overhead Door Company of Fort Wayne, 58494
Oyang America, 58495
Oyster Peddler, 58496
Ozark Cooperative Warehouse, 58497
P & D Corp, 58500
P A Menard, 58502
P&C Pacific Bakeries, 58503
P. Tavilla Company, 58506
P.A. Braunger Institutional Foods, 58507
Paar Physica USA, 58523
Pacific California Fish Company, 58524
Pacific Commerce Company, 58527
Pacific Compactor Corporation, 58528
Pacific Resources, 58530
Pacific Rim Shellfish Corp., 58531
Pacific Seafood Co, 58532
Pacific Steam Equipment, Inc., 58534
Pacific Tomato Growers, 58535
Pacific Westcoast Foods, 58536
Pacific World Enterprises, 58537
Pacific-SEH Hotel SupplyCompany, 58538
Packaging Equipment Company, 58539
Packaging Services Corp, 58540
Packsource Systems, 58541
Pacmatic/Ritmica, 58542
PAFCO Importing Co, 58513
Pagano M Watermelons, 58544
Painted Cookie, 58545
Paisano Distribution Company, 58546
Palama Meat Co Inc, 58547
Paleewong Trading Corporation, 58549
Palm Brothers, 58550
Palmer Associates, 58551
Palmer Food Service, 58553
Palmer Jack M, 58554
Palmer Wholesale Inc, 58555
Palmetto Candy & Tobacco Company, 58556
Pamex Packaging, 58558
Pamida, 58559
Pan American Papers Inc, 58560
Pan's Mushroom Jerky, 58561
Pap,, 58567
Papa Dean's Popcorn, 58563
Paper & Chemical Supply Company, 58564
Paradise Island Foods, 58568
Paradise Products, 58569
Paragon Food Equipment, 58570
Paramount Coffee, 58571
Paramount Produce, 58573
Paramount Restaurant Supply Company, 58575
Parducci Wine Cellars, 58576
Park Avenue Meats Inc, 58578
Parker Brothers, 58579
Parker Wholesale Paper Co, 58581
Parkway Systems, 58583
Parr-Mac Sales Company, 58584
Parson Food Sales, 58585
Parts Depot, Inc., 58587
Partytime Machines Rental, 58588
Paskesz Candy Co, 58589
Passport Food Group, 58591
Patriot Enterprises, 58593
Pats Seafood & Cajun Deli, 58595
Patton's Sausage Company, 58597
Paul J. Macrie, 58599
Paul Perkins Food Distributors, 58600
Paulie Paul's, 58602
Paulsen Foods, 58603
Payless Equipment, 58604
Peace River Trading Company, 58605
Peach State Material Handling, 58607

Peas, 58608
Pelco Equipment, 58610
Pelco Refrigeration Sales, 58611
Pellican Seafood, 58614
Pemiscot Packing Company, 58616
Pendergast Safety Equipment Co, 58617
Penguin Foods, 58618
Penn Herb Co, 58619
Penn Maid, 58620
Pennsylvania Macaroni Company Inc., 58621
Pennwell Belting Company, 58622
Penny's Meat Products, 58623
Pensacola Candy Co Distr, 58625
Pensacola Restaurant Supply Company, 58626
Perfection Foods, 58629
Performance Food Group Co, 58631
Performance Foodservice, 58640, 58641, 58642, 58643, 58644, 58645, 58646
Perry B Duryea & Son Inc, 58679
Peter Pan Sales, 58685
Peterson Sea Food Company, 58687
Peyton's, 58690
Pharaoh Trading Company, 58691
Pharmachem Labs, 58692
Phil Erb Refrigeration Co, 58694
Philadelphia Extract Co Inc, 58695
Phillips Supply Co, 58697
Phoenix Agro-Industrial Corporation, 58698
Phoenix Industries Corp, 58699
Pickle House, 58703
Piedmont Plastics Inc, 58705
Piemonte Bakery Co, 58706
Pierceton Foods, 58707
Pinnacle Foods Inc., 58710
Pinto Bros, 58711
Pioneer Distributing Co, 58712
Pioneer Distributing Company, 58713
Pioneer Lift Truck, 58714
Pioneer Marketing, 58716
Pioneer Sales Co Inc, 58717
Pippin Wholesale Co, 58718
Pittman Brothers Company, 58719
Pittsburgh Casing Company, 58720
Pizza Products, 58721
Pk Crown Distributing Inc, 58722
Plasco Safety Products, 58725
Platteville Potato Association, 58726
PLT Trucking Corporation, 58517
PMC Specialties Group Inc, 58518
Pocono ProFoods, 58729
Poiret International, 58731
Polar Bear, 58732
Polish Folklore Import Co, 58734
Pollak Food Distributors, 58735
Polyplastics, 58736
Pon Food Corp, 58737
Pontiac Fruit House, 58740
Pop's E-Z Popcorn & Supply Company, 58741
Porinos Gourmet Food, 58743
Porky Products, 58744
Port Royal Sales LTD, 58746
Port Royal Tapes, 58747
Portage Frosted Foods, 58748
Porter Wallace Corporation, 58749
Portuguese United Grocer Co-Op, 58752
Positive Impressions, 58754
Positively 3rd St Bakery, 58755
Post & Taback, 58756
Post Food Service, 58757
Potato Specialty Company, 58758
Power Lift Corporation, 58762
Power Pumps, 58763
Power Source Distributors, 58764
Prairie Queen Distributing, 58765
Prawn Seafoods Inc, 58766
Precision Pours, 58767
Preiser Scientific Inc, 58769
Prejean's Wholesale Meats Inc, 58770
Premier Foodservice Distributors of America, 58771
Premier Juices, 58772

Premiere Refreshment Svc, 58774
Premium Seafood Co, 58776
Presentations, 58777
Pressure King Inc, 58778
Presto Bistro, 58779
Prestolite Electric Inc, 58781
Prevor Marketing International, 58782
Price & Co, 58783
Price Harry H & Son, 58784
Pride Equipment Corp, 58785
Prime Smoked Meats Inc, 58790
Primo Cheese, 58791
Prince of Peace, 58792
Princeton Shelving, 58793
Pro Plus Cleaning Products, 58795
Procacci Bros Sales Corp, 58799
Process Equipment & Supply Company, 58800
Produce Trading Corp, 58801
Productos Familia, 58803
Professional Food Systems, 58804, 58805, 58806, 58807
Professional Marketing Group, 58808
Professional Materials Hndlng, 58809
Proficient Food Company, 58810, 58811
Progenix Corporation, 58812
Progressive Food, 58813
Progressive Handling Systems, 58814
Proin, 58815
Prolift Industrial Equipment, 58816
Promotions Ink, 58817
Pronatura Inc, 58818
ProSource, 58796
Provigo, 58819
Provigo Distribution, 58820, 58821, 58822, 58823
Pudliner Packing, 58824
Pueblo Trading Co Inc, 58825
Pulini Produce, 58826
Pulse Plus, 58827
Pumodori Brothers Sales, 58829
Purchase Order Co Of Miami Inc, 58830
Pure Sealed Dairy, 58831
Puritan's Pride Inc, 58833
Purity Wholesale Grocers, Inc., 58834
Puro Water Group, 58835
Putnam Group, 58837
PYA/Monarch, 58520, 58521, 58522
Pyramid Juice Company, 58839
Pyramid Packaging, Inc, 58840
Quadra Foods Company, 58843
Quail Crest Foods, 58844
Quaily Storage Products Inc, 58845
Quality Banana Inc, 58847
Quality Celery & Sprout Company, 58848
Quality Discount Ice Cream, 58849
Quality Distributing Company, 58850
Quality Eggs & Juices, 58851
Quality Equipment Marketing, 58852
Quality Foods, 58856
Quality Foods International, 58857
QUALITY Frozen Foods, 58841
Quality Groceries, 58858
Quality Material Handling, 58859
Quality Poultry Co, 58860
Quality Produce Company, 58861
Quality Wholesale Produce Co, 58862
Qualy Pak Specialty Foods, 58863
Quandt's Foodservice Distributors, 58864
Quantum Supply Company, 58865
Quattrochi Specialty Foods, 58866
Quebec Vegetable Distributors, 58867
Queen City Meats, 58868
Queens Tobacco, Grocery & Candy, 58869
Queensboro Farm Products, 58870, 58871
Quick Servant Co, 58872
Quick Stamp & Sign Mfg, 58873
Quinn Co, 58874
Quinn Lift, 58875
Qzina Specialty Foods, 58878
R D Smith Co, 58880
R Hirt Jr Co, 58882

Wholesale Product Type / Frozen Food

R L Spear Co, 58883
R S Braswell Co Inc, 58884
R S Porter & Co, 58885
R S Stern Inc, 58886
R W Smith & Co, 58888
R W Zant Co, 58889
R&B Produce, 58890
R&F International Corporation, 58891
R&J Farms, 58892
R&R Equipment Company, 58894
R&R Mill Company, 58895
R-Best Produce, 58897
R.F. Beyers, 58900
R.N. Mason & Son, 58903
R.S. Hamilton Company, 58904
R.S. Somers Company, 58905
R.W. Davis Oil Company, 58907
Ra-Bob International, 58916
Rabco Foodservice, 58917
Rainbow Foods, 58919
Rainbow Natural Foods, 58920
Rainbow Valley Orchards, 58923
Rakestraw Ice Cream Company, 58925
Ralph Jones Display & Store, 58926
Ramarc Foods Inc, 58928
Ramco Innovations Inc, 58929
Ramex Foods, 58930
Ramsen Inc, 58931
Ranch Foods Direct, 58932
Randall Meat Co, 58933
Randy's Frozen Meats, 58934
Range Packing Company, 58935
Rantec Corp, 58936
Rapid Sales Company, 58937
Rapids Wholesale Equipment, 58938
Raw Rev, 58939
Ray & Mascari, 58940
Raymond, 58942
Raymond Handling Solutions, 58944
Raz Company, 58945
Rbm Co, 58946
Ready Food Products, 58947
Ready Portion Meat Co, 58948
Ready Potatoes Inc, 58949
Real Cajun School Of Cooking, 58950
Real Soda, 58951
Rebstock Conveyors, 58953
Red Rose Trading Company, 58957
Reddy Ice, 58958
Reddy Raw Inc, 58959
Redstone Distributors, 58960
Reed Ice, 58961
Reese & Long Refrigeration, 58962
Refrigeration & Food Eqpt Inc, 58963
Refrigeration Equipment, 58964
Regal Distributing Company, 58965, 58966
Regal Supply & Chemical Company, 58967, 58968
Registry Steak & Seafood, 58971
Reinhart Foodservice LLC, 58972
Reliable Fire Equipment, 58973
Reliable Fire Protection, 58974
Reliable Mercantile Company, 58975
Remy Cointreau USA, Inc., 58976
Ren 500 Food Fair, 58977
Renaissance International, 58978
Reno Forklift Inc, 58979
Republic National Distributing, 58980
Resco Restaurant & Store Equip, 58981
Rescue Earth, 58982
Residex, 58984
ResourceNet International, 58985
Restaurant Depot, 58986, 58987
Restaurant Designs Development, 58989
Restaurant Food Supply, 58990
Restaurant Supply, 58991
Retail Data Systems Of Omaha, 58992
Rex Chemical Corporation, 58993
Rex Pacific, 58994
Rey Foods, 58995
Rhotens Wholesale Meat Co, 58996
Ricci & Company, 58997
Rich Dairy Products, 59000
Richard's Restaurant Supply, 59001

Richmond Restaurant Svc, 59002
Richmond Supply Company, 59003
Richter Distributing Company, 59005
Rider's Ranch Escargot, 59006
Rigel Trading Corporation, 59008
RightWay Foods, 59009
Rihm Foods, 59010
Rimfire Imports, 59011
Rino Gnesi Company, 59012
RIPCO, 59013
Ritchie Grocer Co, 59014
Ritchie's Foods, 59015
Rivard Power Lift, 59016
River Valley Foods Inc, 59017
Riverside Foods, 59018
Riverside Paper Supply, 59019
Riverside Refrigeration Air Conditioning, 59020
Roanoke Fruit & Produce Co, 59023
Robbin's Beef Company, 59024
Robby Midwest, 59025
Robert Chermak & Associates, 59026
Robert Cochran & Company, 59027
Robert D. Arnold & Associates, 59028
Robert Ruiz Company, 59030
Robert Wholey & Co Inc, 59031
Robert's Foods Company, 59032
Roberts Packing Co, 59033
Roberts-Boice Paper Company, 59034
Robertson Fruit & Produce, 59035
Robin's Food Distribution, 59037
Robinson Distributing Co, 59039
Robinson Marketing Associates, 59040
Robinson Steel Company, 59041
Rochester Midland Corporation, 59043
Rock Dell Creamery, 59044
Rock Garden South, 59045
Rock Valley Oil & Chemical Co, 59046
Rockford Sausage Co, 59047
Rockland Bakery, 59048
Rockland Foodservice, 59049
Roden Electrical Supply Company, 59053
Rogers Farms, 59054
Roland J. Trosclair Canning, 59057
Roll-O-Sheets Canada, 59058
Rollin Dairy Corp, 59059
Roma Food Svc Of Arizona, 59060
Roma of Minnesota, 59061
Rondo Inc, 59064
Rose Hill Distributor, 59066
Roseland Produce Wholesale, 59068
Rosenthal & Kline, 59069
Rosenthal Foods Corp, 59070
Rosito & Bisani Imports Inc, 59071
Ross Elevator Supply, 59072
Ross Foods, 59073
Rotelle, 59074
Roundy's Inc, 59075
Rowland Coffee Roasters Inc., 59077
Royal Accoutrements, 59079
Royal Banana Co, 59081
Royal Crown Enterprises, 59083
Royal Doulton Canada, 59085
Royal Foods Inc, 59086, 59087
Royal Harvest Foods Inc, 59088
Royal Industries Inc, 59089
Royal Meats, 59091
Royal Palate Foods, 59092
RPM Material Handling, 58912
RPM Total Vitality, 58914
Russell Food Equipment Limited, 59096
Russell N. Roy Company, 59097
Ryan Potato Company, 59100
Ryans Wholesale Food Distributors, 59101
S & R Products, 59104
S L Sanderson & Co, 59106
S&M Produce Company, 59111
S&M Provisions, 59112
S&S Dayton Supply, 59113
S-A-J Distributors, 59115
S. Abraham & Son, 59116
S. Abraham & Sons Inc., 59117
S.J. Roetzel & Son Produce, 59120
S.R. Flaks Company, 59121

S.W. Meat & Provision Company, 59122
Sadler's Smokehouse, 59135
Saf-T-Gard International Inc, 59136
Safari Distributing, 59137
Safe-Stride Southern, 59138
Safeco Electric & True Value, 59139
Safety Wear, 59140
Safian & Associates, 59141
Sagaya Corp, 59142
Salad Depot, 59146
Sales King International, 59150
Sam Cohen & Sons, 59157
Sam Gordon & Sons Purveyors, 59158
Sam Lota & Son Disribution Company, 59159
Sam Okun Produce Co, 59160
Sam Wylde Flour Company, 59162
Sam's Cakes, Cookies, Candy, 59163
Sam's Club, 59164
Sambazon, 59165
Sambonet & Associates, 59166
Samir's Imported Food LLC, 59167
Sampac Enterprises, 59168
Samuel Wells & Company, 59170
San Diego Products, 59171
San Francisco Herb Co, 59172
San Jacinto Frozen Food, 59173
San Rafael Distributing Inc, 59175
San-Bay Co, 59176
Sanchem Inc, 59178
Sanders Bros, 59179
Sands African Imports, 59181
Sands Brands International Food, 59182
Sanson Co Inc, 59184
Sansone Food Products Co, 59185
Santa Barbara Merchant Svc Inc, 59187
Santa Claus Industries, 59188
Santa Cruz Horticultural Supply, 59189
Sarasota Restaurant Equipment, 59190
Saratoga Flour, 59191
Sassone Wholesale Groceries Co, 59194
Savage & Company, 59198
Savol Pools, 59201
Saxony Equipment Distributors, 59202
SC Enterprises, 59124
Scandicrafts Inc, 59203
Scardina Refrigeration Co., 59204
Schaper Company, 59206
Scheidelman, 59207
Schenck Foods Co, 59208
Schepps Dairy, 59209
Schermerhorn Brothers & Co, 59210
Schischa Brothers, 59212
Schmidt Baking Company Incorporated, 59213
Schneck Beverages, 59214
Schneider's Fish & Seafood Co, 59215
Schneider-Valley Farms Inc, 59216
Schultz Sav-O-Stores, 59218
Schwab Paper Products Co, 59220
Scott & Associates, 59224
Scott Lift Truck Corporation, 59225
Scranton Fish Company, 59226
Sea Pearl Seafood, 59232
Sea Products West Inc, 59233
Seacrest Foods, 59238
Seafood Dimensions Intl, 59243
Sealer Sales Inc, 59251
Seattle Fish Co, 59252
Seattle's Best Coffee, 59253
Seder Foods Corporation, 59257
Segal's Wholesale, 59259
Seitz Gift Fruit, 59260
Select Meat Company, 59262
Sellers Equipment Inc, 59263
Seltzer Chemicals, 59264
Serendib Tea Company, 59265
Serendipity of the Valley, 59267
Serv-A-Rack, 59268
Serve Canada Food Equipment, 59270
Service Handling Equipment Company, 59271
Service Market, 59272
Seven K Feather Farm, 59275
Shaklee Distributor, 59283

Shalhoob Meat Co, 59284
Shamrock Farms, 59285
Shamrock Foods Co, 59287, 59288
Shannon Diversified Inc, 59293
Shari Candies, 59294
Sharpe Valves, 59296
Shaw Equipment Company, 59297
Shean Equipment Company, 59298
Sheehan Majestic, 59299
Sheffield Platers Inc, 59300
Shellman Peanut & Grain, 59301
Shelving Rack Systems Inc, 59302
Shemen Tov Corporation, 59303
Shenandoah Industrial Rubber, 59305
Shepherdsfield Bakery, 59307
Sherwood Food Distributors, 59310, 59311, 59312, 59313, 59314, 59315, 59316
Shetakis Foodservice, 59318
Shiff & Goldman Foods, 59319
Shippers Supply, 59320, 59321
Shippers Supply, Labelgraphic, 59322
Shivji Enterprises, 59324
Sho-Nuff-Good, 59325
Shoppa's Material Handling, 59328
Shryack-Givens Grocery Co., 59330
Shryack-Hirst Grocery Company, 59331
Shur-Az Inc, 59334
Sid Wainer & Son Specialty, 59339
Sidney's, 59342
Sieb Distributor, 59343
Siegmeister Sales & Service, 59344
Sierra Nut House, 59346
Signature Packaging, 59347
Silverstar Foodservice Supply, 59349
Simonian Fruit Company, 59351
Simpson Grocery Company, 59355
Sims Wholesale, 59357
Sin-Son Produce, 59358
Sinclair Trading, 59359
Sindoni, Joseph, Wholesale Foods, 59360
Singer Equipment Co Inc, 59361
Sirca Foodservice, 59365
Sisq Distributing Inc, 59366
Sisu Group Inc, 59368
Skarnes Inc, 59369
Skiles Co Inc, 59372
Skone & Conners, 59373
Skone & Connors Produce, 59374
Skylark Meats, 59375
Skymart Enterprises, 59377
Sleeper Produce Company, 59380
Slusser Wholesale Company, 59381
Smile Enterprises, 59383
Smith & Greene Company, 59384, 59385
Smith & Son Wholesale, 59386
Smith Restaurant Supply Co, 59387
Smith, Bob, Restaurant Equipment, 59388
Smitty's Snowballs, 59391
Smokey Mountain Grill, 59393
Smoothie's Frozen Desserts, 59394
Snack Company, 59395
Snack King Foods, 59396
Snacks Over America Inc, 59397
Snapple Distributors of Long Island, 59398
Snappy Popcorn, 59399
Snelgrove Ice Cream Company, 59400
Sniderman Brothers, 59401
Snyder Wholesale Inc, 59404
Snyder's Bakery, 59405
So Cal Material Handling, 59406
Sobey's, 59407
Sobey's Ontario, 59408
Sobey's Quebec Inc, 59409
Sobeys Inc., 59410, 59411, 59412, 59413, 59414, 59415
Socafe, 59416
Soda Service, 59417
Sogelco International, 59419
Sol Loeb Moving & Storage, 59420
Solutions, 59421
Somerset Industries, 59422
Sonora Foods, 59424

1245

Wholesale Product Type / Frozen Food

Soofer Co, 59426
Scrbee Intl., 59428
Source Naturals, 59430
South Jersey Paper Products, 59432
Southeast Cold Storage, 59435
Southeast Industrial Equipment, 59436
Southeastern Grocers, 59438
Southern Grocery Company, 59442
Southern Import Distributors, 59443
Southern Indiana Butcher's Supply, 59444
Southern Material Handling Co, 59445
Southern Produce Distributors, 59446
Southern States Toyotalift, 59449
Southern Steel Shelving Company, 59450
Southern Supplies Limited, 59452
Southernfood.com LLC, 59453
Southline Equipment Company, 59454
Southwest Distributing Co, 59457
Southwest Forklift, 59458
Southwest Lift, 59459
Southwest Material Handling, 59460
Southwest Traders, 59463
Souza Food Service, 59468
Sovrana Trading Corp, 59469
Spantec Systems, 59472
Spar Mixers, 59473
Sparboe Foods Corp, 59474
Spartan Foods, 59477
SpartanNash Co, 59478
Specialized Promotions, 59479
Specialty Box & Packaging, 59480
Specialty House of Creation, 59482
Specialty Merchandise Distributors, 59483
Spener Restaurant Design, 59484
Spice House International Specialties, 59488
Spiral Biotech Inc, 59489
Spokane Produce, 59490
Spot Cash Specialty Company, 59492
Springfield Produce Company, 59493
Sprinkman Corporation, 59494
Sprouters, 59495
Squid Ink, 59498
St. Cloud Restaurant Supply, 59501
St. Helen Seafoods, 59502
St. Ours & Company, 59503
Stack & Store Systems, 59505
Stahl, 59506
Stainless Equipment & Systems, 59507
Stamoolis Brothers Co, 59508
Standard Electric Time, 59509
Standard Forms, 59510
Standard Fruit & Vegetable Company, 59511
Standard-Rosenbaum, 59514
Stanford Trading Company, 59515
Stapleton Inc, 59519
Star Fisheries, 59520
Star Restaurant Equipment & Supply Company, 59527
Star Sales Company, 59529
Starbruck Foods Corporation, 59533
State Hotel Supply Company, 59536
State Line Potato Chip Company, 59537
State Restaurant Equipment Co, 59538
State Wholesale Grocers, 59539
Statewide Meats & Poultry, 59540
Statewide Products Co Inc, 59541
Staunton Foods LLC, 59543
Staunton Fruit & Produce Company, 59544
Stay Tuned Industries, 59546
Steckel, Isadore, 59548
Steel City Corporation, 59549
Steinberg Quebec: Aligro, 59550
Steiner Foods, 59551
Stella Maria's, 59554
Stephan Machinery, Inc., 59555
Sterling Promotional Corporation, 59557
Sterling Scale Co, 59558
Steve's Fine Food Emporium, 59559
Stevenson Co, 59560
Stewart & Stevenson LLC, 59562

Stewart Wholesale Hardware Company, 59563
Stewarts Tristate Svc Co, 59564, 59565
Stigler Supply Co, 59566
Stiles Enterprises Inc, 59567
Stock America Inc, 59568
Stock Rack & Shelving Inc, 59569
Stoffel Equipment Co Inc, 59571
Stonyfield Organic, 59574
Stop & Shop Manufacturing, 59575
STOP Restaurant Supply Ltd, 59131
Storage Equipment, 59576
Strasheim Wholesale, 59577
Stratecon International Consultants, 59578
Strawhacker's Food Service, 59580
Streich Equipment Co Inc, 59582
Streit Carl & Son Co, 59583
Stronach & Sons, 59584
Strongbow Foods, 59585
Suffolk Banana Company, 59591
Suity Confections Co, 59594
Suki, 59595
Summertime Restaurant Equipment, 59596
Summit Food Service Distributors, 59597, 59598
Summit Import Corp, 59599
Sun Chlorella USA, 59600
Sun Hing Foods, 59601
Sun Valley Fruit Company, 59603
Sun West Trading, 59605
Sunbelt Industrial Trucks, 59607
Sunchef Farms, 59610
Sunflower Restaurant Supply, 59614
Sunkist Foodservice Equipment, 59615
SunRidge Farms, 59606
Sunrise Fruit Company, 59617
Sunset of Queens, 59619
Sunset Wholesale West, 59618
Sunshine Bar Supply Company, 59620
Sunshine Farms, 59621
Sunshine Fresh, 59622
Sunspun Foodservice, 59624
Suntec Power, 59625
Suntreat Packing & Shipping Co, 59626
Super Natural Distributors, 59628
Super Nutrition Distributors, 59629
Super Snooty Sea Food Corporation, 59630
Super Store Industries, 59631
Superior Beverage Group, 59632
Superior Foods, 59633
Superior Lamp, 59634
Superior Wholesale Distr, 59640
SUPERVALU Distribution, 59132
Supply One, 59641
Supply One Inc, 59642
Supreme Fixture Company, 59643
Supreme Foods, 59645
Supreme Lobster, 59646
Sure Fine Food, 59647
Sutherland Produce Sales, 59650
Sweet Dried Fruit, 59652
Sweet Liberty Candy Company, 59653
Sweet Place, 59654
Sweetener Products Co, 59659
Sweety's Candies, 59660
Swift Chemical & Supplies Inc, 59661
Swiss Chalet Fine Foods, 59663
Switzer's Inc, 59666
Sycaway Creamery Inc, 59667
Sygma Network, 59668, 59669
SYGMA Network Inc, 59133
Synergee Foods Corporation, 59670
Systems Services Of America, 59745
T D Refrigeration Inc, 59746
T. Baker Restaurant Equipment, 59749
T.A. Morris & Sons, 59750
T.B. Venture, 59752
T.C. Food Export/Import Company, 59753
T.C.P. Restaurant Supply, 59754
T.D. Khan, 59755
T.L. Herring & Company, 59757

T.M. Patterson Paper Box Company, 59758
T.S.A. Distributing, 59759
T.T. Todd Company, 59760
Ta-De Distributing Co, 59766
Tablemate Products, 59767
Tabor Grain Company, 59768
Takeda Vitamin & Food, 59770
Tallarico Food Products, 59771
Tama Trading Co Inc, 59772
Tamburo Brothers, 59774
Tanglewood Farm, 59775
Tankersley Food Svc, 59776
Tanner Enterprises, 59777
Taormina Co, 59779
Tape Tools, 59781
Tapp Label Technologies Inc, 59782
Taroco Food Corporation, 59784
Tasty Mix Quality Foods, 59786
Taylor Freezer Equipment Corporation, 59790
Taylor Freezers, 59791
Taylor Utlimate Svc Co, 59793
Taylor-Fortune Distributors, 59794
TBI Corporation, 59761
TCD Parts, 59763
Tchefa, 59795
Tcheru Enterprises, 59796
TDR Inc, 59764
Tech Sales Inc, 59799
Technical Food Sales Inc, 59800
Tee's Plus, 59802
Teitel Brothers, 59803
Teletec Cash Register Company, 59804
Tenth & M Seafoods, 59806
Tergerson's Fine Foods, 59807
Terry Brothers, Inc, 59812
Tesdall & Associates, 59814
Tex-Sandia, 59816
Texas Gunpowder, 59817
Texas Hotel & Restaurant Equipment, 59819
Texas Marine II, 59820
Texas Meat Purveyors, 59821
The Bachman Company, 59823
The Coop, 59827
The Piping Gourmets, 59830
The Premium Beer Company, 59831
Theatre Candy Distributing Company, 59837
Third Planet Products, 59838
Thomas & Howard Co, 59840
Thomas & Howard Co Cash & Crry, 59841
Thomas Brothers Country Ham, 59842
Thomas W. MacKay & Son, 59847
Thompson & Johnson Equipment, 59848
Thompson & Little, 59849
Thomson Groceries Ltd., 59851
Three M Food Service, 59853
Ths Foodservice, 59855
Thunderbird Food Machinery, 59856
Thurston Foods Inc, 59858
Tiger Distributors, 59862
Time & Alarm Systems, 59864
Timely Signs Inc, 59866
Tinkels, 59868
Tippecanoe Foods, 59869
Tips Uniform, 59870
Tirawisu, 59871
TKC Supply, 59765
To-Am Equipment Company, 59872
Toastmasters International, 59873
Todd Distributors Inc, 59874
Tom's Evergreen Broom Manufacturing, 59875
Tomich Brothers Seafoods, 59877
Tony's Fine Foods, 59879
Top of the Table, 59884
Topac, 59885
Tor Rey Refrigeration Inc, 59888
Torkelson Brothers, 59889
Tosi & Company, 59893
Total Beverage Systems, 59894
Total Lift Equipment Company, 59895

Total Liquor Controls, 59896
Toudouze Market Company, 59897
Tourtellot & Co, 59898
Town & Country Fancy Foods, 59899
Town & Country Wholesale, 59901
Townsend Farms Inc, 59902
Toyota Forklifts Of Atlanta, 59903
Toyota Material Handling, 59904, 59905, 59906
Toyotalift Inc, 59907
Trade Diversified, 59908
Trader Joe's, 59910
Trans Veyor, 59911
Treasure Coast Coffee Company, 59914
Treasure Foods, 59915
Trendco Supply, 59922
Trent Valley Distributors Ltd., 59923
Tri Mark United East, 59927
Tri-Marine International, 59929
Tribest Corp, 59934
Trident Food Svc, 59935
Trident Seafoods Corp, 59936
Trifactor Systems LLC, 59937
Triple Cities Material Handling, 59940
Triple F, 59941
Triton International, 59942
Trophy Foods, 59943
Tropic Ice Company, 59945
Tropical Illusions, 59946
Tropical Paradise, 59948
Tropical Treets, 59949
Troy Foods Inc, 59950
Trucco, A.J., 59953
Truscello & Sons Wholesalers, 59956
Tuckahoe Manufacturing Co, 59958
Tucker Pecan Co, 59959
Tucson Coop. Warehouse, 59960
Tufco Technologies Inc, 59963
Turk Brothers Custom Meats Inc, 59966
Turtle Island Herbs, 59969
Tusco Grocers Inc, 59970
Tvc Wholesale Inc, 59972
Twelve Baskets Sales & Market, 59973
Twenty Four Hour Security Services, 59974
Tyler Supply Co, 59979
Tynan Equipment, 59980
Tyson Foods Inc, 59981
U Okada & Co LTD, 59982
Uinted Rental, 59999
Ukiah Foods, 60000
Ultimate Foods, 60001
Uni Co Supply, 60004
Unicorn Enterprises, 60007
Union Grocery Company, 60011
UniPro Foodservice, Inc., 60005
United Bakers & Deli Supply, 60014
United Banana Company, 60015
United Chairs, 60016
United Dairy Co-Op Svc, 60017
United Dairy Machinery Corp, 60018
United Foods & Fitness, 60020
United Forklift Corporation, 60021
United Glassware & China, 60022
United Grain Growers, 60023
United Lighting & Supply Co, 60024
United Machinery & Supply Company, 60025
United Mineral & Chemical Corporation, 60026
United Natural Foods Inc, 60027
United Noodles, 60028
United Rentals, 60032
United Restaurant Equipment Co, 60033
United Shellfish Co Inc, 60035
United States Sugar Corp, 60037
United Universal Enterprises Corporation, 60039
United Wholesale Grocery Company, 60040
Univar USA, 60043
Universal Fish of Boston, 60044
Universal Marketing, 60045
Universal Restaurant Equipment, 60048
Universal Sanitizers & Supplies, 60049

Wholesale Product Type / General Line

Universal Sodexho, 60050
Uniwell Systems, 60051
Upper Lakes Foods Inc, 60053
Upstate Farms, 60054
Uptown Bakers, 60055
US Food Products, 59984
US Foods Inc, 59986, 59987, 59988, 59989, 59990, 59991, 59992
US Growers Cold Storage, 59993
US Materials Handling Corp, 59995
Us Plastics, 60056
UVA Packaging, 59997
V&B Distributing, 60057
VacuWest, 60064
Vallero Mercantile Company, 60067
Vallet Foodservice, 60068
Valley Distributing Company, 60069, 60070
Valley Distributors, 60071
Valley Foods, 60072
Valley Foods Inc, 60073
Valley Fruit & Produce Company, 60074
Valley Pride Food Distributor, 60075
Valu-Line Foods, 60076
Van Eerden Foodservice Co Inc, 60077
Van Waters & Rogers, 60080
Vaughn Packing Company, 60085
VBS Inc Material Handling, 60060
Vend Food Service, 60088
Vendors Purchasing Council, 60090
Venezia Brothers, 60091
Venture Packaging & Distribution, 60093
Venus Supply Company, 60094
Veritiv Corp, 60096
Vermont Wholesale Foods, 60098
Veteran Foods Sales Co, 60101
VetriTech Laboratories, 60102
Victel Service Co, 60104
Victorinox Swiss Army Inc, 60105
Victors Market Co, 60106
Victory Packaging, 60107
Victory Spud Service, 60108
Vidalia Sweets Brand, 60109
Vienna Distributing Company, 60110
Vilore Foods Company, 60113
Vincent Giordano Prosciutto, 60115
Vincent Piazza Jr & Sons, 60116
Vineyard Gate, 60118
VIP Food Svc, 60061
Virginia Wholesale Company, 60120
Vistar Northwest, 60128
Vitamin Power, 60133
Vitusa Products Inc, 60134
Vivitar Security Systems, 60138
Vixen Kitchen, 60139
VMC Corp, 60062
Vogel, 60140
Volpe, Son & Kemelhar, 60142
Voorhees Rubber Mfg Co, 60144
Voss Equipment Inc, 60145
Voyageur Trading Division, 60146
VWR Funding Inc, 60063
W & B Distributing Co, 60148
W A DeHart Inc, 60149
W B Stockton & Co Inc, 60150
W H Wildman Company, 60152
W. Braun Company, 60154
W. Braun Packaging Canada, 60155
W.A. Tayloe Company, 60157
W.F. Alber Inc., 60158
W.F. Morgan & Sons, 60159
W.F. Ware Company, 60160
W.G. White & Company, 60161
W.J. Canaan Inc., 60162
W.J. Stearns & Sons/Mountain Dairy, 60163
W.L. Petrey Wholesale Inc., 60164
W.R. McRae Company Limited, 60167
W.R. Merry Seafood Company, 60168
W.R. Pittman & Sons, 60170
W.R. Whitaker & Company, 60171
W.S. Lee & Sons, 60172
Wabash Foodservice Inc, 60184
WACO Filtering, 60175
Waco Meat Service, 60187

Wadden Systems, 60188
Wade's Dairy Inc, 60189
Wai Sang Meat, 60191
Wakefern Food Corp, 60193
Wakefield Sales Inc, 60194
Waleski Produce, 60196
Wallace Foods Inc, 60202
Wallach's Farms, 60204
Walsh Tropical Fruit Sales, 60205
Waltham Fruit & Produce Company, 60208
Waltkoch Limited, 60209
Walton & Post, 60210
Walton's Inc, 60211
Wards Ice Cream Co Inc, 60212
Warehouse Equipment Inc, 60213
Warehouse Systems Inc, 60214
Warren E. Conley Corporation, 60215
Warren Southwest Rfrdgrtn, 60216
Washington Vegetable Co, 60217
Wasserstrom Co, 60218
Waterfront Market, 60219
Watervliet Fruit Exchange, 60221
Watkins Distributing Company, 60222
Watson Distributing, 60223
WATTS Equipment Co, 60176
Waugh Foods Inc, 60225
We're Full of Promotions, 60228
Webeco Foods, 60230
Webeco Foods, Inc, 60231
Wechsler Coffee Corporation, 60233
Weeke Wholesale Company, 60234
Welch Equipment Co Inc, 60236
Welton Rubber Co, 60237
Werres Corp, 60238
Wes Design - Supply Company, 60239
WESCO, 60177, 60178
WESCO Distribution Inc, 60179, 60180
Wescotek Inc, 60241
West Coast Ship Chandlers, 60246
West Coast Supplies, 60247
West End Dairy Inc, 60248
West Wholesale Grocery, 60250
Westco Chemicals Inc, 60251
Westcoast Engineering Company, 60253
Western Carolina Forklift Inc, 60255
Western Family Foods Inc, 60256
Western Grocers, 60257, 60258
Western Soap Company, 60260
Western Steel & Wire, 60261
Westland Marketing, 60262
Westside Foods, 60263
Westwind Resources, 60264
Wham Food & Beverage, 60268
Whitaker Brothers, 60272
White Cap Construction Supply, 60273
White Feather Farms, 60275
White House Chemical Supply, 60276
White Plains Electrical Light, 60277
Whitehawk Beef Co, 60278
Whitey Produce Co Inc, 60279
Whitley Wholesale Grocery, 60282
Whole Life Nutritional Supplements, 60283
Wholesale Restaurant Equipment, 60285
Wholesale Restaurant Supply, 60286
Wholesale Tool Company, 60287
Wichita Restaurant Supl Co Inc, 60292
Wiese Planning & Engineering, 60295
Wilcox Frozen Foods, 60296
Wilcox Paper Co, 60297
Wilderness Foods, 60300
Wilke International Inc, 60301
Wilkens-Anderson Co, 60302
Wilkin-Alaska, 60303
William Consalo & Sons Farms, 60306
William Rosenstein & Sons, 60308
Williams Food Equipment Company, 60309
Williams Institutional Foods, 60310
Williams Sausage Co, 60312
Williamsport Candy Company, 60313
Willie Laymon, 60314
Willow Group LTD, 60316
Willow Run Foods Inc, 60317

Willy Nilly At Home, 60318
Wilson Ice Machines, 60319
Winchester Food, 60320
Winder Farms, 60322
Wing Sing Chong Company, 60327
Wing Sing Seafood Inc, 60328
Wink Frozen Desserts, 60330
Winkler Inc, 60331
Winkler Meats, 60332
Winmix/Natural Care Products, 60333
Winn-Dixie, 60334
Wins Paper Products, 60336
Wiper Supply & Chemical, 60338
Wisconsin Allied Products Inc, 60339
Wisconsin Milk Mktng Board Inc, 60340
Wise Forklift Inc, 60341
Wisner Manufacturing Corporation, 60345
Witmer Foods, 60346
WMF/USA, 60183
Wood Beverage Company, 60349
Wood Fruitticher Grocery Company, 60350
Wood's Products, 60351
Woodlake Distributors, 60352
Woody's Frozen Food Distr, 60354
Workstead Industries, 60355
World Kitchen, 60358
World Tableware Inc, 60360
World Variety Produce, 60361
Wrenn Handling, 60364
Wustefeld Candy Co Inc, 60366
Wusthoff Trident Cutlery, 60367
Yale Industrial Trucks, 60372
Yale Industrial Trucks: Ontario, 60373
Yale Material Handling/Gammon, 60374
Yeager & Associates, 60376
Yonkers Institutional Food Company, 60378
Yorktown Electrical & Lighting, 60379
Young's Lobster Pound, 60382
Youngstown Wholesale Grocery, 60383
Yue's International Company, 60384
Zachary Confections Inc, 60390
ZAK Designs Inc, 60387
Zeches Institution Supply, 60393
Zel R. Kahn & Sons, 60395
Zellerbach, 60396
Zetov Inc, 60397
Zink Distributing Co, 60400
Zinter Handling Inc, 60401

General Line

88 Acres, 54507
A & B Distributing Co, 54509
A J Linz Sons, 54517
A J Silberman & Co, 54520
A La Mode Distributors, 54521
A&D Distributors, 54527
A&J Food Wholesalers, Inc., 54529
A-1 Seafood Center, 54535
A. Bohrer, 54540
A. De LaChevrotiere, 54541
A. Sargenti Company, 54545
A. Simos & Company, 54546
A.B. Wise & Sons, 54548
A.C. Kissling Company, 54551
A.M.BRIGGS, 54556
Abatar Institutional Food Company, 54591
ABC Country Club Coffee, 54562
Able Sales Company, 54595
Above All Health, 54596
AC Paper & Supply, 54566
Acatris USA, 54598
ACC Distributors Inc, 54567
Ace Endico Corp, 54603
Acme Steak & Seafood, 54610
Adams Chapman Co, 54620
Adams Wholesale Co, 54621
Adel Grocery Company, 54624
Adluh Flour, 54628
Adventure Foods, 54638
Aerchem Inc, 54642

Afia Foods, 54649
Agro Foods, Inc., 54654
Aidi International Hotels of America, 54655
Aimonetto and Sons, 54658
AJC International, 54578
Al Campisano Fruit Company, 54663
Alabama Food Group, 54665, 54666
Alabama Wholesale Company, 54668
Albert Guarnieri & Co, 54674
Albert Uster Imports Inc, 54675
All Caribbean Food Service, 54694
All Fresh Products, 54696
All-Redi Flour & Salt Company, 54709
Allan Chemical Corp, 54712
Allegro Coffee Co, 54714
Allen Rosenthal Company, 54717
Alliance Supply Management, 54719
Allied Blending & Ingredients, 54721
Allied Food Service, 54723
Alnor Oil Co Inc, 54731
Alpha Baking Company, 54732
Alpine Food Distributing Inc, 54736
Altech Packaging Company, 54743
Alwan & Sons, 54748
Ambassador Fine Foods, 54751
AMCON Distributing Co, 54581, 54582
Amenity Services, 54754
American Banana Company, 54759
American Classic Ice Cream Company, 54760
American Food Systems, 54768
American Food Traders, 54769
American Frozen Foods, 54771
American Grocery & Beverage, 54772
American International Chemical, 54775
American Roland Food Corporation, 54792
American Seaway Foods Inc, 54795
American Select Foods, 54796
American Yeast Sales, 54803
AMN Distributors/Premium Blend, 54584
Amster-Kirtz Co, 54812
Ancient Organics, 54816
Ancora Coffee Roasters, 54817
Anderson Dubose Company, 54819
Andre Tea & Coffee Company, 54823
Angelo M. Formosa Foods, 54828
Anter Brothers Company, 54837
Anthony's Snack & Vending, 54839
Anthracite Provision Co, 54840
Aqua Solutions Inc, 54849
Aragadz Foods Corporation, 54853
Arctic Beverages, 54856
Arctic Star Distributing, 54859
Arkansas Valley Wholesale Grocery Company, 54867
Arla Foods Inc, 54868
Arleen Food Products Company, 54869
Arlington Coffee Company, 54870
Arnall Grocery Co, 54874
Arrow Chemical Inc, 54880
Art's Trading, 54883
Arthur G. Meier Company/Inland Products Company, 54884
Asanti Distributors, 54887
Asheboro Wholesale Grocery Inc, 54888
Ashley Koffman Foods, 54890
Asia Shipping & Trading Corporation, 54891
Associated Food Stores, 54898
Associated Food Stores Inc, 54899
Associated Grocers, 54900
Associated Wholesale Grocers, 54902
Atchison Wholesale Grocery, 54907
Atlantic Dominion Distributors, 54911
Atlantic Wholesalers, 54923, 54924
Attar Herbs & Spices, 54927
Aust & Hachmann, 54934
Austrade, 54937
Auto City Candy Company, 54939
Automation Systems & Services, 54941
Avalon Trade Company, 54944
Axelrod Foods, 54947

1247

Wholesale Product Type / General Line

Aydelotte & Engler Inc, 54950
Ayush Herbs Inc, 54952
Aztec Secret Health & Beauty, 54953
B & B Beverages, 54955
B & B Distributors Inc, 54956
B & G Venegoni Distribution, 54959
B & K Distributing Inc, 54961
B & S Wasilko Distr, 54964
B&B Beer Distributing Company, 54968
B&F Distributing Company, 54969
B&O Beer Distributors, 54972
B&W Distributing Company, 54973
B. Fernandez & Sons, 54975
B.W. Clifford, 54979
B/R Sales Company, 54980
Badger Popcorn, 55001
Badger Wholesale Company, 55002
Baers Beverage of C.W., 55005
Baja Trading Company, 55012
BakeMark Ingredients West Inc, 55015
Baker Beverage, 55016
Baker Bottling & Distributing Company, 55017
Baker Boy Bake Shop Inc, 55018
Baker Distributing Corp, 55019
Baker's Cash & Carry Inc, 55021
Bald Eagle Beer Store Co, 55030
Balford Farms, 55032
Ballew Distributors, 55035
Bama Budweiser Montgomery, 55039
Bama Budweiser of Anniston, 55040
Banner Wholesale Grocers, 55047
Bar Controls Of Florida, 55050
Barber Pure Milk Company(HQ), 55055
Barber's Poultry Inc, 55056
Bari Italian Foods, 55057
Barkett Fruit Company, 55061
Barlean's Fisheries, 55062
Baron Spices Inc, 55065
Bassham Institutional Foods, 55078
Bates Distributing, 55079
Bay Cities Produce Co Inc, 55089
Bay View Food Products, 55093
Bayou Food Distributors, 55097
BBCA USA, 54981
BBQ Bunch, 54982
Bear Creek Operations, 55103
Bear Meadow Gourmet Foods, 55104
Bear Stewart Corp, 55105
Beer Import Co, 55115
Behm's Valley Creamery, 55116
Ben E. Keith, 55133, 55134, 55135, 55136, 55137, 55138, 55139, 55140, 55141, 55142, 55143
Bensinger's, 55167
Bentan Corporation, 55169
Berje, 55172
Berlin Packaging, 55174
Bernard's Bakery, 55181
Best Friends Cocoa, 55196
Best Market, 55198
Better Beverages Inc, 55202
Beverage Express, 55207
BI-LO, 54987
Big Apple Tea Company, 55213
Big Shoulders Coffee, 55216
Big Spoon Roasters, 55217
Birdseye Dairy-Morning Glory, 55231
Bisek & Co Inc, 55235
BJ'S Wholesale Club Inc, 54988
Black's Barbecue, 55241
Blackburn-Russell Co, 55243
Blue Buoy Foods, 55255
Blue Ridge Poultry, 55266
BMT Commodity Corporation, 54989
Bon Ton Food Products, 55279
Bono Burns Distributing Inc, 55281
Boone's Wholesale, 55283
Boricua Empaque, 55285
Bosch Distributors, 55286
Boston Sausage & Provision, 55292
Boteilho Hawaii Enterprises, 55296
Boulangerie Pelletier, 55298
Bowman Produce, 55304

Boykin & Southern Wholesale Grocers, 55307
Bozzuto's Inc., 55311
Bradley Kitchen Center, 55313
Braswell Distributing Co, 55318
Brenham Wholesale Groc Co Inc, 55324
Bridgetown Coffee, 55332
BRINS, 54992
Brita Foods, 55339
British Aisles, 55340
British Shoppe LLC, 55341
British Wholesale Imports, 55342
Brittain Merchandising, 55343
Broaster Sales & Svc, 55345
Brockman E W Co Inc, 55346
Bronx Butter & Egg Company, 55349
Brooklyn Sugar Company, 55352
Brown's Dairy, 55359
Brown's Ice Cream Co, 55360
Bruce Edmeades Sales, 55364
Bulk Food Marketplace, 55385
Bunn Capitol Company, 55386
Bunzl Distribution USA, 55387
Bur-Gra Meat & Grocery, 55388
Burkhardt Sales & Svc, 55392
Burklund Distributors Inc, 55393
Bush Brothers Provision Co, 55396
Butler Foods LLC, 55401
Butte Produce Company, 55402
C & R Food Svc Inc, 55412
C & S Wholesale Grocers Inc, 55414
C A Curtze, 55417
C D Hartnett Co, 55418
C H Robinson Worldwide Inc, 55419
C M Tanner Grocery Co, 55420
C Pacific Foods Inc, 55421
C. Eberle Sons Company, 55426
C.A. Flipse & Sons Company, 55428
Caesar Electric Supply, 55459
Cafe Jumbo, 55461
CAI International, 55435
Cain's Coffee Company, 55465
Cajun Sugar Company LLC, 55469
California Fruit Market, 55476
Callahan Grocery Company, 55482
Campbell's Food Service, 55487
Canada Dry Bottling Co, 55491
Canada Pure Water Company Ltd, 55492
Canada Safeway, 55493
Canadian Gold Seafood, 55494
Canterbury's Crack & Peel, 55499
Canton Foods, 55500
Cape Dairy LLC, 55504
Capitol Foods, 55510
Carbonella & Desarbo Inc, 55523
Carden Foods, Inc, 55525
Caribbean Produce Exchange, 55529
Caribbean Restaurants, 55530
Carolina Canners Inc, 55541
Carpenter Snack Food Distribution Company, 55549
Carriage Foods, 55551
Carroll Distributing Co, 55552
Cash-Wa Distributing, 55564, 55565
Casso Guerra & Company, 55570
Cauble & Field, 55578
Cavazos Candy, Produce & Groceries, 55581
CBS Food Equipment, 55439
Centerchem, Inc., 55587
Central Baking Supplies, 55588
Central Carolina Farm & Mower, 55589
Central Wholesale Grocery Corporation, 55598
Centreside Dairy, 55599
Century Distributors Inc, 55603
Cerca Foodservice, 55605
Ceres Solutions, 55607
Certco Inc., 55609
Certified Food Services, 55613
CF Imperial Sales, 55441
Challenge Dairy Products, Inc., 55617
Chamberlain Wholesale Grocery, 55618
Charles C. Parks Company, 55623
Chatfield Dairy, 55630

Chattanooga Restaurant Supl, 55633
Cheese Shop, 55635
Cheeseland, Inc., 55636
Chelsea Market Baskets, 55643
Chemroy Canada, 55647
Cheney Brothers Inc, 55648
Chia I Foods Company, 55654
Chicago Market Company, 55659
Chile Guy, 55663
Church Point Wholesale Grocer, 55682
Churro Corporation, 55683
Cirelli Foods, 55689
Ciro Foods, 55690
City Espresso Roasting Company, 55694
City Line Food Distributors, 55696
City Produce Co, 55699
City Wholesale Company, 55700
CK Products, 55446
Clarence Mayfield Produce Company, 55703
Clarion Fruit Co, 55704
Clark Restaurant Svc, 55708
Clarkson Grain Co Inc, 55711
Clearbrook Farms, 55714
Clif Bar & Co, 55718
Clifford D. Fite, 55719
Clover Leaf Cheese, 55726
Clover Leaf Seafoods, 55727
Coastal Beverage LTD, 55730
Coca-Cola Bottling Co. Consolidated, 55736
Coca-Cola Bottling Company UNITED, Inc., 55737
Cochran Brothers Company, 55739
Coffee Break Systems, 55742
Coffee Heaven, 55746
Cohen Foods, 55748
Cohokia Bake Mark, 55749
Colavita USA, 55750
Cole Brothers & Fox Company, 55753
Colorado Potato Growers Exchange, 55764
Comissos Cash & Carry, 55771, 55772, 55773, 55774
Commissos Cash & Carry, 55776
Commodities Assistance Corporation, 55777
Commodities Marketing Inc, 55778
Community Coffee Co., 55779
Conca D'Oro Importers, 55785
Conchita Foods Inc, 55788
Concho Valley Pecan Company, 55789
Concord Foods Co, 55790
Concord Import, 55792
Confecco, 55794
Connection Chemical LP, 55798
Connellsville Bottling Works, 55799
Conner Produce Co, 55800
Consolidated Beverage Corporation, 55801
Consolidated Poultry & Egg Company, 55804
Constellation Brands Inc, 55805
Continental Marketing, 55813
COnut Butter, 55447
Cook Flavoring Company, 55818
Copperwood InternationalInc, 55826
Core-Mark Holding Company, Inc, 55830, 55831, 55832, 55833, 55834, 55835, 55839, 55840
Cosgrove Distributors Inc, 55849
Costco Wholesale Corporation, 55852
Cotati Brand Eggs & Food Svc, 55853
Couch's Rich Plan Foods, 55854
Coy's Bakery, 55865
Creager Mercantile Cash & Carry, 55875
Cream of Weeber, 55877
Creative Foods of the Southwest, 55878
Crispy Bagel Co, 55884
Crown Point, 55893
CTS/Bulk Sales, 55451
Cubberley's, 55901
Culinar Canada, 55904
Culinary Specialties, 55908
Culture Systems Inc, 55910

Cutrufello's Creamery, 55927
D.A. Colongeli & Sons, 55943
D.A. Foodservice, 55944
Daffin Mercantile Company, 55964
Dairy Fresh Corporation, 55965, 55966
Dairy King Milk Farms/Foodservice, 55967
Dairyland USA Corp, 55971
Dalmatian Bay Wine Company, 55974
Damian's Enterprises Inc, 55976
Darisil, 55981
Davis Coffee Co, 55989
Davis Distributors of Owensboro Company, 55990
De Choix Specialty Foods Company, 55995
Dealers Food Products Co, 56001
Dean & Company, 56002
Dean Supply Co, 56003
Dean's Ice Cream Dstrbtn Ctr, 56004
Dearborn Cash & Carry Stores, 56005
Dearborn Wholesale Grocers LP, 56006
Dearborn Wholesale Grocers, 56007, 56008, 56009, 56010
Demma Fruit Company, 56032
Deng's, 56034
Denton Dairy Products Inc, 56037
DeVries Imports, 56000
Dharma Bars, 56047
Dial Industries Inc, 56053
Diamond Nutrition, 56056
Dicarlo Distributors Inc, 56059
Dickerson & Quinn, 56061
Dickerson Foods, 56062
Dierks Foods, 56064
Difeo & Sons Poultry Inc, 56065
DiLeo Brothers, 56051
DiNovo Produce Company, 56052
Dipasa USA Inc, 56075
Dispenser Juice, 56082
Distribution Kowloon, 56084
Distribution Plus, 56085
Diverse Sales, 56086
Divine Ice Cream Company, 56088
Dixie Lily Foods, 56091
DMI Distribution, Inc., 55950
Doerle Food Svc, 56098
Dolly Madison Ice Cream, 56103
Don Luis Garcia Fernandez, 56107
Don Walters Company, 56109
Donut Farm, 56111
Dorsel Distribution Company, 56115
Downeast Food Distributors Inc, 56129
DPI Mid Atlantic, 55953
DPI Rocky Mountain, 55955
Dr. John's Candies, 56131
Draper's Super Bee, 56138
Durham Flavor Rich, 56154
Dutch Creek Foods, 56156
Dutch Valley Food Distributors, 56157
Dutra Distributing, 56159
DW Montgomery & Company, 55958
Dwan & Company, 56162
Dyna Tabs LLC, 56164
E G Forrest Co Inc, 56171
E M Trisler Sales Co Fd Prods, 56173
E. De la Garza, 56178
E.A. Robinson & Company, 56181
Eagle Coffee Co Inc, 56190
Earl Gill Coffee Co, 56194
Earp Distribution, 56195
Earth Grains Baking Co, 56197
Earthgrains, 56200
EarthGrains Banking Companies, Inc., 56198
East Bay International, 56201
Eastimpex, 56212
Eau de Source Boischatel, 56216
Ebonex Corporation, 56217
Eby-Brown Company, 56218
Economy Cash & Carry LP, 56223
Economy Wholesale Company, 56226
Ecoval Dairy Trade, 56227
Edsung, 56236
Edward Badeaux Company, 56237

1248

Wholesale Product Type / General Line

Ehrlich Food Co, 56248
Elco Fine Foods, 56253, 56254
Elegant Desserts, 56260
Elkhorn Distributing Company, 56265
Ella's Kitchen, 56266
Empire Packing Co, 56283
Empress Food Prods Co Inc, 56285
Emulsol Egg Products Corporation, 56287
English Honey Farms, 56293
Enzamar, 56300
Epicurean Foods, 56303
Equal Exchange Inc, 56304
Erman & Son, 56316
Espresso Roma, 56325
Eternal Marketing Group, 56330
Ettline Foods Corp, 56331
Euclid Coffee Co, 56332
Euclid Fish Co, 56333
Eugene & Company, 56334
Euro-Excellence, 56337
European Foods, 56340
European Imports, 56342
Evans Foodservice Inc., 56346
Evco Wholesale Food Corp, 56347
Evonuk Oregon Hazelnuts, 56350
Excelon, 56355
Express Wholesale Grocers, 56357
F & C Sawaya Wholesale, 56360
F B Mc Fadden Wholesale Co, 56361
F Christiana & Co, 56364
F McConnell & Sons, 56365
F.A. Davis & Sons, 56368
Fab Inc, 56372
Fairview Dairy Inc, 56378
Fairway Foods, 56379
Falcon Trading Intl Corp, 56380
Falls City Mercantile Co Inc, 56381
Fancy Delights, 56384
Farm Boy Food Svc, 56387
Farmers Seafood Co Wholesale, 56390
Farmfresh, 56391
Farner-Bocken Co, 56394
Feather Crest Farms, 56397
Federated Cooperative, 56399
Federated Cooperative Lt, 56400, 56401, 56402
Feesers, 56404
Feinkost Ingredients, 56406
Fendall Ice Cream Company, 56407
Ferntrade Corporation, 56408
Ferris Coffee & Nut Co, 56409
Ferris Organic Farms, 56410
Ferry-Morse Seed Company, 56411
Festival Ice Cream, 56412
Fidelity Fruit & Produce Co, 56417
Fine Distributing, 56422
Firestone Farms, 56434
Fisher Mills, 56443
Fizz-O Water Co, 56450
Flair Beverages, 56453
Flamingo Flats, 56454
Flash Foods, 56457
Flatland Food Distributors, 56458
Flav-O-Rich, 56460, 56461
Fleig Commodities, 56466
Flora Foods Inc, 56468
Florida Beverage Connection, 56469
Florida Choice Foods, 56471
Florida Smoked Fish Company, 56475
Flynt Wholesale Company, 56480
Food Authority Inc, 56488
Food Buying Service, 56489
Food City, 56490
Food Ingredients, 56496
Food Services Inc, 56501
Food Supply Inc, 56502
Food Wholesalers Inc, 56503
Food-Products, 56505
Foods Etc., 56506
Foremost Farms USA, 56514
Foremost Foods Company, 56515
Forever Foods, 56517
Fort Pitt Candy Co, 56520
Fortville Produce, 56525

Foster Dairy Farms Inc, 56527
Fought's Mill, 56528
Four Oaks Farm, 56530
Foutch's Coffee and Spring Water, 56533
Francis Produce Company, 56539
Franco Roma Foods, 56540
Frank Beer, 56541
Frank G. Schmitt Company, 56543
Frank P. Corso, 56546
Fred W Albrecht Grocery Co, 56555
Fresco Y Mas, 56561
Fresh Point Dallas, 56565
Friendly Wholesale Co, 56571
Fritzie Fresh Products, 56573
Frontier Co-op, 56577
Frosty Products, 56579
Fru-Terra, 56580
Fruit d'Or, 56587
Fruit Of The Vine Of De Valley, 56585
Fullway International, 56591
Futurity Products, 56593
G & W Food Products, 56598
G&T Commodities, 56601
Gachot & Gachot, 56621
GAF Seelig Inc, 56607
Galerie Au Chocolat, 56625
Galilee Splendor, 56626
Gandy's Dairies, 56632
Garavaglia Meat Company, 56633
Garber Bros Inc, 56634
Garden Spot Distributors, 56637
Garuda International, 56641
Garvey Nut & Candy, 56642
Gateway Food Products Co, 56644
Gaylord's Meat Co, 56647
Gelson's, 56649
Gem Berry Products, 56650
General Candy Co, 56654
General Cash & Carry, 56656
General Trading Co, 56660
Genoa Wholesale Foods, 56662
George Greer Company, 56668
George J Howe Co, 56669
George O Pasquel Company, 56670
George Uhe Company, Inc., 56671
GFS (Canada) Company, 56611
Giambrocco Food Service, 56675
Giant Eagle American Seaway Foods, 56677
GIANT Food Stores, 56612
Gillco Ingredients, 56679
Gillette Nebraska Dairies, 56681
Gillies Coffee, 56682
Gilster-Mary Lee Corp, 56684
Gimme Sum Mo Cajun Foods Corporation, 56685
Global Harvest, 56693
GMT Dairy Products Inc, 56614
GMZ Inc, 56615
Go Max Go Foods, 56701
Goldberg & Solovy Foods Inc, 56710
Golden Moon Tea, 56718
Golden Organics, 56720
Golden Valley Popcorn Supply, 56721
Goldy Food Sales Company, 56723
Good's Wholesale-Bakery Supls, 56725
Gordon Food Service, 56730, 56731, 56732, 56733, 56734, 56735, 56736, 56737, 56738, 56739, 56740, 56741, 56742, 56743, 56744, 56745, 56746, 56747
Gosselin Gourmet Beverages, 56748
Gourmet Award Foods, 56749
Gourmet Club Corporation, 56751
Gourmet Foods Intl, 56752
Gralab Instruments, 56763
Great Lakes Gourmet Food Service, 56781
Great North Foods, 56786
Great Outdoors Spice Company, 56787
Great Western Chemical Company, 56793
Greater Knead, The, 56796
Green Valley Food Corp, 56800
Greene Poultry Co, 56801
Greenfield Noodle & Spec Co, 56803

Greenwood Associates, 56807
Gregory's Foods, Inc., 56809
Greis Brothers, 56810
Griesedieck Imports, 56813
Griffin Food Co, 56814
Griffith Laboratories, 56816
Grocers Ice & Cold Storage Company, 56818
Grocers Supply Co, 56819
Groetsch Wholesale Grocer, 56820
Grounds for Change, 56822
GSC Enterprises Inc., 56617
GTM, 56618
Gulf Marine & Industrial Supplies Inc, 56831
Gunderland Marine Supply, 56840
Gunther Salt Co, 56841
Gutierrez Brothers, 56842
Guy Locicero & Sons, 56843
GWB Foods Corporation, 56620
H & R Coffee Co, 56844
H B Day Co, 56846
H Schrier & Co Inc, 56848
H.B. Paulk Grocery Company, 56853
H.C. Williams Peanut Company, 56854
H.T. Hackney Company, 56856
H.Y. Louie Company, 56857
H2O Technology, 56858
Hadley Fruit Orchards, 56874
Haitai Inc, 56878
Halal Fine Foods, 56880
Hale-Halsell Company, 56882
Halsey Foodservice, 56885
Hamilos Bros Inspected Meat, 56889
Handy's Milk & Ice Cream, 56899
Hannaford Bros Co, 56902
Hans Holterbosch Inc, 56905
Hansen Beverage Co, 56906
Hansen Co, 56907
Hansen Distribution Group, 56908
Harbor Wholesale Foods Inc, 56920
Harders, 56922
Hardscrabble Enterprises, 56923
Harker's Distribution, 56925, 56926
Harold Food Company, 56928
Harold Leonard Midwest Corporation, 56930
Harold Levinson Assoc Inc, 56932
Harrill Brothers Wholesale Company, 56934
Harry Fourtunis, 56937
Harry Fourtunis Inc, 56938
Harry's Premium Snacks, 56942
Hartland Distributors, 56945
Harveys Supermarket, 56950
Hata Y & Co LTD, 56953
Hattiesburg Grocery Company, 56955
HAVI Group, 56860
Hawaiian Coffee Traders, 56960
Hawaiian Grocery Stores, 56961
Hawkins Distributing Company, 56964
Haynes Brothers Candy Company, 56967
Healing Garden, 56969
Healing Home Foods, 56970
Health Waters, 56975
Hearthy Foods, 56980
Heartland Distributors, 56981
Heartland Supply Co, 56985
Heavenly Cheesecakes, 56986
Helena Wholesale, 56991
Helmut's Strudel, 56993
Hemisphere Group, 56994
Henderson Coffee Corp, 56995
Henderson-Black Wholesale Groc, 56996
Henry Bresky & Sons Inc, 57000
Henry Gonsalves Co, 57002
Henrys Cash & Carry, 57003
Hermanowski Wholesale, 57008
HFM Foodservice, 56865
HIB Foods Inc, 56866
Hickory Harvest Foods, 57014
Hill City Wholesale Company, 57020
Hines Nut Co, 57028
Hipp Wholesale Foods, 57031
HMG Provisions, 56867

Hoban Foods, 57033
Holland Beef International Corporation, 57044
Home-Like Food Company, 57052
Homestead Foods, 57053
Honeyville Grain Inc, 57055
Hoogwegt, U.S., Inc, 57057
Hornell Wholesale Grocery Company, 57060
House of Spices, 57067
Houston Poultry & Egg Company, 57070
HPC Foodservice, 56868
HRS Food Service, 56869
Hudson River Foods, 57076
Hudson Valley Coffee Company, 57078
Huff Ice Cream, 57082
Huger-Davidson-Sale Company, 57083
Hummingbird Wholesale, 57090
Husky Foods of Anchorage, 57094
Hydrite Chemical Co, 57097
I Magid, 57100
I Supply Co, 57101
I.T. Bauman Company, 57105
IBC, 57106
IBF, 57107
Ice & Juice Systems, 57118
Ice Makers, 57121
Imperial Trading, 57131
Importex International, 57133
Independent Wholesale, 57136
Indiana Sugars Inc, 57140
Indianhead Foodservice, 57143
Indo-European Foods, 57145
Industrial Commodities, 57147
Inland Meats of Spokane, 57161
Inno-Vite, 57163
Institutional Wholesale Company, 57170
Intermix Beverage, 57177
Intermountain Specialty Food Group, 57178
International Beverages, 57179
International Casein Corporation, 57181
International Distribution, 57186
International Pack & Ship, 57192
International Sourcing, 57195
Ira Higdon Grocery Company, 57205
Irish Tea Sales, 57206
Irvin, 57207
Irvington Marcus Company, 57209
Island Farms Dairies Cooperative Association, 57212
Island Supply, 57216
Islander Import, 57217
Italfina, 57218
Italfoods Inc, 57219
Italica Imports, 57220
Italmade, 57221
J & J Distributing, 57223
J Bernard Seafood, 57226
J Kings Food Svc Professionals, 57230
J Moresky & Son, 57232
J Murray & Co, 57233
J O Spice Co, 57234
J P Ice Cream, 57235
J&M Food Products Co, 57245
J. Connor & Sons, 57247
J. Hellman Frozen Foods, 57248
J. M. Sealts Company, 57251
J. Quattrocchi & Company, 57252
J. Rutigliano & Sons, 57253
J. Sosnick & Sons, 57254
J. Treffiletti & Sons, 57255
J.C. Produce, 57259
J.C. Wright Sales Company, 57260
J.D. Dawson Company, 57261
J.F. Walker Company, 57262, 57263
J.J. Taylor Distributing, 57265
J.L. Henderson & Company, 57266
J.P. Beaudry, 57269
J.W. Wood Company, 57274
JAAMA World Trade, 57275
Jackson Wholesale Co, 57295
Jacob KERN & Sons Inc, 57297
Jacobson & Sons, 57300
Jake's Variety Wholesale, 57302

1249

Wholesale Product Type / General Line

Jamac Frozen Foods, 57304
Jamaican Teas Limited C/O Eve Sales Corporation, 57306
James D Cofer, 57309
Janney Marshall Co, 57312
Jason Marketing Corporation, 57316
Jatex-USA Corporation, 57318
Java Beans and Joe Coffee, 57319
JBG International, 57276
Jeffries Supply Co, 57328
Jeris Health & Nutrition, 57333
Jetro Cash & Carry, 57342
Jetro Cash & Carry Enterprises, 57343
Jetro Cash & Carry Inc, 57344
Jim's Cheese Pantry, 57348
JMS, 57286
JNS Foods, 57287
Jo Mints, 57352
JoDaSa Group International, 57353
Joe Bertman Foods, 57356
Joe Paulk Company, 57359
Joey's Fine Foods, 57361
John Bricks Inc, 57363
John D Walsh Co, 57365
John E Koerner & Co Inc, 57367
John Graves Food Service, 57368
John Hansen & Sons, 57371
John Lenore & Company, 57373
John's Dairy, 57381
John's Wholesale, 57383
Johnnie's Restaurant-Hotel Svc, 57384
Johnson Wholesale Meat Company, 57388
Jolar Distributor, 57393
Joseph Antognoli & Co, 57396
Joyce Brothers Company, 57401
Jp Tropical Foods, 57404
Julius Silvert Company, 57408
Junction City Distributing & Vending Company, 57409
Jungbunzlauer Inc, 57410
JUST Inc, 57288
K C's Best Wild Rice, 57414
Kaco Supply Co, 57433
Kadouri International Foods, 57434
Kahoka Cheese Shop, 57436
Kaleel Bros Inc, 57437
Kallsnick Inc, 57439
Kane's Kandies, 57441
Kanematsu, 57442
Kansas City Sausage, 57443
Kansas Marine, 57444
Kar Wah Trading Company, 57446
Karetas Foods Inc, 57448
Karp's Bake Mark, 57449
Karson Food Services, 57450
KAST Distributors Inc, 57425
Katzin's Uniforms, 57454
Kauai Producers, 57455
Kayem Foods, 57457
KeHE Distributors, 57458, 57459, 57460, 57461, 57462, 57463, 57464, 57465, 57466, 57467, 57468, 57469, 57470, 57471, 57472, 57473
Kelley Bean Co Inc, 57475
Kelley Foods, 57476
Kellogg Elevator Company, 57478
Kentucky Beer Cheese, 57491
Kerekes Bakery & Rstrnt Equip, 57492
Key Food Stores Cooperative, 57496
King Provision Corporation, 57508
Kings Choice Food, 57509
Kingston Candy & Tobacco Co, 57512
Kirby Holloway Provision Co, 57514
Kissner Milling Company, 57517
Kitchen Maid Foods, 57518
KJ's Market, 57427
Kleen Janitorial Supply Co., 57521
Klondike Foods, 57524
KMA Trading Company, 57428
Know Brainer, 57528
Knox Cash Jobbers, 57529
Knox County Feed & Hatchery, 57530
Knoxville Poultry & Egg Company, 57531
KOHL Wholesale, 57429
Kolon California Corporation, 57538
Kona Pacific Farmers Co-Op, 57543
Kraft Chemical Co, 57549
Krasdale Foods, 57551
Krasdale Foods Distribution, 57552
Kronos, 57554
Kutter's Cheese Factory, 57559
KYD Inc, 57432
L&M Bakers Supply Company, 57565
L. Cherrick Horseradish Company, 57567
L. Lacagnina & Sons, 57571
L.N. Coffman Company, 57573
L.P. Shanks Company, 57574
LA Foods, 57578
LA Grange Grocery Co, 57579
La Grasso Bros Produce, 57591
LA Lifestyle Nutritional Products, 57581
LA Rue Distributing, 57582
LA Squisita Food Corp, 57583
Labatt Food Svc, 57598, 57599
Lady Baltimore of Missouri, 57607
Lakeside Packing Company, 57617
Land-O-Sun Dairies, 57625
Lang's Chocolates, 57631
Lantev Distributing Corporation, 57633
Lanzarotta Wholesale Grocers, 57634
Laredo Tortilleria & Mexican, 57635
Larick Associates, 57636
Latouraine Coffee Company, 57643
Laurell Hill Provision Company, 57644
Lavin Candy Company, 57646
Layman Candy Company, 57648
LBG Distributors, 57585
LDC of Lafayette, 57586
Leading Brands of Canada, 57653
Leali Brothers Meats, 57654
Lee Foods, 57658
Lee Grocery Company, 57659
Legacy Beverage Systems, 57663
Lemark Promotional Products, 57668
Lems, 57671
Lenson Coffee & Tea Company, 57673
Leon Supply Company, 57675
Leonidas, 57678
Les Boulangers Associes Inc, 57679
Lesaffre Yeast Corporation, 57680
Lesco Supply Company, 57681
Lewisburg Wholesale Company, 57687
Liberto Management Co Inc, 57689
Liberto of Harlington, 57690
Liberto of Houston, 57691
Liberty International WHOL, 57694
Liberty Natural Products Inc, 57696
Liberty Richter, 57697
Liberty USA Inc,, 57699
Lift Truck Sales Svc & Rentals, 57707
Lilar Corp, 57713
Littleton Sales Company, 57736
LivBar, 57737
Livingston Distribution Centers, 57738, 57739
Logan, 57745
Lomar Distributing Inc, 57748
Lombardi Brothers Meat Packers, 57749
Loneoak & Co, 57752
Long Wholesale Distr Inc, 57756
Long Wholesale Distributors, 57757
Longhorn Liquors, 57759
LonoLife, 57761
Lorenz Schneider Company, 57764
Lorenzo's Wholesale Foods, 57766
Lost Trail Root Beer, 57767
Lowell Brothers & Bailey, 57778
LSI Specialty Products, 57589
Lucca Packing Company, 57780
Lumberton Cash & Carry, 57787
Lumsden Brothers, 57788
Lynard Company, 57790
Lynn Dairy Inc, 57791
Lyons Specialty Company, 57792
M & V Provisions Co Inc, 57794
M Amundson Cigar & Candy Co, 57798
M Conley Co, 57799
M Maskas & Sons Inc, 57802
M R Williams Inc, 57803
M&F Foods, 57805
M&N International, 57807
M. Zukerman & Company, 57811
M.E. Carter & Company, 57812
M.E. Dilanian Company, 57813
MacDonalds Consolidated, 57825, 57826
Macomb Tobacco & Candy Company, 57832
Madison Cash & Carry Wholesale Grocers, 57835
Madison Grocery Company, 57837
Madison Wholesale Co, 57838
Mahoning Swiss Cheese Cooperative, 57843
Maine Coast Sea Vegetables, 57846
Maines Paper & Food Svc Inc, 57850, 57852
Malena Produce Inc, 57858
Manchester Grocery Company, 57863
Manhattan Key Lime Juice Company, 57870
Mani Imports, 57872
Manuel's Hot Tamales, 57876
Maple Valley Cooperative, 57879
Marcus Specialty Foods, 57883
Margate Wine & Spirit Co, 57886
MariGold Foods, 57887
Market Grocery Co, 57896
Marlow Candy & Nut Co, 57902
Marrone's Inc, 57904
Mars Supermarkets, 57906
Martin Bros Distributing Co, 57908
Martin Food Service Company, 57910
Martin Preferred Foods, 57911
Maschari Brothers WHLS Fruits, 57921
Mason Brothers Co, 57922
Matanuska Maid Dairy, 57926
Mattingly Foods, 57937
Mayer-Bass Fromm, 57944
Mayrand Limitee, 57949
Mazo-Lerch Company, 57952
McCabe's Quality Foods, 57956
Mccullagh Coffee Roasters, 57972
Mcdonald Wholesale Co, 57973
McDowell Supply Company, 57959
Mcfarling Foods Inc, 57974
McKeesport Candy Company, 57962
McLane Co Inc, 57963
McLane Foodservice Inc, 57964
McLane Grocery, 57965
Meadow Brook Dairy Co, 57982
Meadowbrook Farms, 57984
Mecca Coffee Company, 57988
Medina & Medina, 57989
Medway Creamery Company, 57993
Melba Food Specialties, 57994
Mendez & Company, 57997
Menu Maker Foods Inc, 57998
Mercado Latino, 57999
Merchants Distributors Inc, 58000
Merchants Foodservice, 58001
Merchants Grocery Co Inc, 58002
Merlino Foods, 58005
Merrill Distributing Inc, 58007
Mesa Cold Storage, 58011
Metro, Inc., 58018
Metroplex Harriman Corporation, 58020
Metropolitan Beer & Soda Dist, 58021
Mexspice, 58022
MGH Wholesale Grocery, 57818
MIA Food Distributing, 57819
Miami Depot Inc, 58023
Miami Wholesale Grocery Company, 58027
Michelle's Bakery, 58035
Michigan Agricultural Commdty, 58036
Michigan Agricultural Commodities Inc, 58037
Michigan Agriculture Commodities, 58038, 58039, 58040, 58041, 58042, 58043, 58044
Michigan Carbonic Of Saginaw, 58045
Michigan Sugar Company, 58049
Mid-America Wholesale, 58054
Mid-Continent Sales, 58055
Mid-Michigan Ice Company, 58056
Middendorf Meat, 58058
Middle Tennessee Dr Pepper Distributing Center, 58059
Midland Grocery of Michigan, 58060
Midlantic Sweetener Company, 58061
Midwest Imports LTD, 58071
Midwest Ingredients Inc, 58072
Mike E. Simon & Company, 58075
Mikey's, 58077
Mile Hi Frozen Foods Corp., 58078
Milky Whey Inc, 58079
Miller & Hartman, 58086
Milligan's Island, 58088
Mills Brothers Intl, 58089
Mitch Chocolate, 58101
Mitchell Grocery Corp, 58102
Mivila Foods, 58104
Mj Kellner Co, 58105
ML Catania Company, 57821
Moctezuma Foods, 58108
Modern Wholesale Company, 58117
Modulightor Inc, 58118
Moffett Food Svc, 58119
Molinera International, 58121
Monterrey Provision Co, 58129
Morabito Baking Co Inc, 58135
Moran Foods LLC, 58136
Morehead Company, 58139
Morre-Tec Ind Inc, 58141
Morris Okun, 58144
Morrisons Pastry Corp, 58146
Moseley & Reece, 58150
Mother Earth Enterprises, 58152
Mother's Cake & Cookie Company, 58153
Mountain Dairies-SW Ice Cream, 58156
Mountain People's Warehouse, 58157
Mountain Service Distribution, 58160
Mountain Valley Water Company, 58163
Mr. C's, 58168
MTC Distributing, 57823
Mueller Distributing Company, 58173
Muller-Pinehurst Dairy Company, 58175
Munchies, 58181
Murphy/Northstar, 58186
Murry's Family of Fine Foods, 58187
Musco Food Corp, 58188
Muskingum Valley Grocery Co, 58190
Mutual Biscuit, 58191
Mutual Trading Co Inc, 58194
Mutual Wholesale Company, 58195
Mutual Wholesale Liquor, 58196
My Quality Trading Corp, 58198
Nafziger Ice Cream Company, 58208
Naples Vending, 58215
Napoleon Creamery, 58216
Nappie's Food Svc, 58217
Nassau Candy Distributors, 58223
Nassau Foods, 58224
National Carbonation, 58232
National Grocers, 58236
National Grocers Assn, 58237
National Grocers Company, 58238, 58239, 58240, 58241
National Lecithin, 58242
National Sales Corporation, 58248
Natural Casing Co, 58257
Natural Foods Inc, 58262
Naturally Nutty, 58264
Nature Distributors, 58265
Near East Importing Corporation, 58274
NEBCO Distributing, 58205
Nectar Soda Company, 58276
Neighbors Coffee, 58280
Nelipak, 58281
Neshaminy Valley Natural Foods, 58286
Nesson Meat Sales, 58287
Neuman Distributing Company, 58289
NeuRoast, 58288
New Atlanta Dairies, 58293
New Barn Organics, 58294
New Beer Distributors, 58295

1250

Wholesale Product Type / General Line

New Britain Candy Company, 58296
New England Foods, 58298
New England Meat Company, 58300
New Hope Imports, 58302
New Jersey Provision Co, 58303
New Mexico Food Distributors, 58304
New Vermont Creamery, 58309
Nicholas & Co Inc, 58322
Nick Sciabica & Sons, 58324
Nikki's Coconut Butter, 58328
Nikol Foods, 58329
NJM Seafood, 58206
Noah's Potato Chip Co, 58335
Noble Harvest, 58336
Nogg Chemical & Paper Company, 58338
Nona Vegan Foods, 58341
Norben Co, 58343
Norcal Beverage Co, 58344
Norman's Wholesale Grocery Company, 58351
Northern Orcharad Co Inc, 58369
Northwest Dairy Association, 58378
Northwest Deli Distribution, 58379
Nothing Mundane, 58387
Novick Brothers Corp, 58391
Nspired Natural Foods, 58392
Nui Foods, 58396
Nutri-Rich Corp., 58399
Nutrinova, 58401
Nutrition Products Company, 58403
Nuts & Spice Company, 58405
Nuts For Cheese, 58407
O'Neill Coffee Co, 58411
O.G. Foodservice, 58414
Odom Corporation, 58434
Ohio Chemical Svc Inc, 58437
Ohio Farmers, 58439
Old Fashion Foods Inc, 58444
Olds Products Co, 58446
Olomomo Nut Company, 58451
Omni Food Inc, 58457
Omni Pacific Company, 58459
One Pie Canning, 58460
Ono International, 58463
Orafti Active Food Ingredients, 58467
Oregon Bark, 58473
Original Food, 58476
Osage Food Products Inc, 58484
Ostrow Jobbing Company, 58487
Otto Brehm Inc, 58490
P & D Corp, 58500
P A Menard, 58502
P.A. Braunger Institutional Foods, 58507
Pacific Coast Chemicals Co, 58526
Pacific Commerce Company, 58527
Pacific Resources, 58530
Pacific Westcoast Foods, 58536
PAFCO Importing Co, 58513
Painted Cookie, 58545
Paleewong Trading Corporation, 58549
Palmer Candy Co, 58552
Palmer Jack M, 58554
Palmer Wholesale Inc, 58555
Palmetto Candy & Tobacco Company, 58556
Paradise Island Foods, 58568
Paramount Confection Company, 58572
Paramount Products, 58574
Parducci Wine Cellars, 58576
Parson Food Sales, 58585
Parsons Green, 58586
Pate-Derby Company, 58592
Patriot Enterprises, 58593
Paulie Paul's, 58602
Peace River Trading Company, 58605
Peaceful Fruits, 58606
Pennsylvania Macaroni Company Inc., 58621
Pensacola Candy Co Distr, 58625
Perfection Foods, 58629
Performance Foodservice, 58640, 58641, 58642, 58643, 58644, 58645, 58646, 58647, 58648, 58649, 58650, 58651, 58652, 58653, 58654, 58655, 58656, 58657, 58658, 58659, 58660, 58661, 58662, 58663, 58664, 58665, 58666, 58667, 58668, 58669, 58670, 58671, 58672, 58673, 58674, 58675, 58676
Peter Pan Sales, 58685
Peterson, 58686
Pharaoh Trading Company, 58691
Phat Fudge, 58693
Phoenix Agro-Industrial Corporation, 58698
Phoenix Wholesale Foodservice, 58700
Pickle House, 58703
Piemonte Bakery Co, 58706
Pierceton Foods Inc, 58707
Pinnacle Foods Inc., 58710
Pioneer Distributing Company, 58713
Pippin Wholesale Co, 58718
Pittman Brothers Company, 58719
Pittsburgh Casing Company, 58720
Pizza Products, 58721
PLT Trucking Corporation, 58517
Plum Organics, 58728
Pocono ProFoods, 58729
Pollak Food Distributors, 58735
Polyplastics, 58736
Pon Food Corp, 58737
Pontiac Fruit House, 58740
Pop's E-Z Popcorn & Supply Company, 58741
Poppers Supply Company, 58742
Porinos Gourmet Food, 58743
Port Royal Sales LTD, 58746
Portugalia Imports, 58751
Portuguese United Grocer Co-Op, 58752
Positive Impressions, 58754
Post Food Service, 58757
Power Creamery, 58761
Power Source Distributors, 58764
Prairie Queen Distributing, 58765
Premier Foodservice Distributors of America, 58771
Premier Juices, 58772
Presto Bistro, 58779
Price & Co, 58783
Pridgen Bros Co, 58786
Primo Cheese, 58791
Prince of Peace, 58792
Pro Plus Cleaning Products, 58795
Probar, 58798
Produce Trading Corp, 58801
Professional Food Systems, 58804, 58806
Proficient Food Company, 58811
Progressive Food, 58813
ProSource, 58796
Provigo, 58819
Provigo Distribution, 58821
Pulini Produce, 58826
Pulse Plus, 58828
Pumodori Brothers Sales, 58829
Purchase Order Co Of Miami Inc, 58830
Pure Sealed Dairy, 58831
Puritan's Pride Inc, 58833
Purity Wholesale Grocers, Inc., 58834
Puro Water Group, 58835
Putnam Candy, 58836
PYA/Monarch, 58520
Pylam Products Co Inc, 58838
Quadra Foods Company, 58843
Quail Crest Foods, 58844
Quality Distributing Company, 58850
Quality Eggs & Juices, 58851
Quality Foods, 58856
Quality Foods International, 58857
QUALITY Frozen Foods, 58841
Quality Wholesale Produce Co, 58862
Quandt's Foodservice Distributors, 58864
Quattrochi Specialty Foods, 58866
Queens Tobacco, Grocery & Candy, 58869
Qzina Specialty Foods, 58878
R S Porter & Co, 58885
R S Stern Inc, 58886
R&F International Corporation, 58891
R&R Equipment Company, 58894
R.E. Diamond, 58899
R.F. Beyers, 58900
Ra-Bob International, 58916
Rack Service Company, 58918
Rainbow Foods, 58919
Rainbow Natural Foods, 58920
Ramex Foods, 58930
Ramsen Inc, 58931
Ranch Foods Direct, 58932
Randy's Frozen Meats, 58934
Range Packing Company, 58935
Rantec Corp, 58936
Raz Company, 58945
Ready Food Products, 58947
Ready Portion Meat Co, 58948
Real Soda, 58951
Red Rose Trading Company, 58957
Regal Distributing Company, 58966
Reinhart Foodservice LLC, 58972
Remy Cointreau USA, Inc., 58976
Republic National Distributing, 58980
Resco Restaurant & Store Equip, 58981
Restaurant Depot, 58986, 58987
Restaurant Food Supply, 58990
Rex Pacific, 58994
Rey Foods, 58995
Rhotens Wholesale Meat Co, 58996
Rich Dairy Products, 59000
Richmond Restaurant Svc, 59002
Richter Baking Company, 59004
Richter Distributing Company, 59005
RightWay Foods, 59009
Rise Bar, 59013
Ritchie Grocer Co, 59014
Ritchie's Foods, 59015
River Valley Foods Inc, 59017
Rl Alber T & Son Inc, 59021
Robert D. Arnold & Associates, 59028
Robert's Foods Company, 59032
Robinson Distributing Co, 59039
Rock Dell Creamery, 59044
Rock Garden South, 59045
Rockland Bakery, 59048
Rockland Foodservice, 59049
Rollin Dairy Corp, 59059
Roma Food Svc Of Arizona, 59060
Roma of Minnesota, 59061
Rosenthal Foods Corp, 59070
Ross Foods, 59073
Rotelle, 59074
Roundy's Inc, 59075
Royal Broom & Mop Factory Inc, 59082
Royal Crown Enterprises, 59083
Royal Palate Foods, 59092
RPM Total Vitality, 58914
Ruth Hunt Candy Co, 59099
Ryan Potato Company, 59100
Ryans Wholesale Food Distributors, 59101
S&S Dayton Supply, 59113
S. Abraham & Son, 59116
S. Abraham & Sons Inc., 59117
S. Anshin Produce Company, 59118
S.R. Flaks Company, 59121
S.W. Meat & Provision Company, 59122
Safari Distributing, 59137
Sahadi Fine Foods Inc, 59144
Salad Depot, 59146
Sam Cohen & Sons, 59157
Sam Lota & Son Disribution Company, 59159
Sam Wylde Flour Company, 59162
Sam's Cakes, Cookies, Candy, 59163
Sam's Club, 59164
Sambazon, 59165
Samuel Wells & Company, 59170
San Diego Products, 59171
San Francisco Herb Co, 59172
Sanchem Inc, 59178
Sanders Bros, 59179
Sands African Imports, 59181
Sands Brands International Food, 59182
Sansone Food Products Co, 59185
Saratoga Flour, 59191
Saratoga Peanut Butter Company, 59192
Savage & Company, 59198
Saval Foods Corp, 59199
Scheidelman, 59207
Schenck Foods Co, 59208
Schepps Dairy, 59209
Schischa Brothers, 59212
Schmidt Baking Company Incorporated, 59213
Schneck Beverages, 59214
Schneider-Valley Farms Inc, 59216
Schultz Sav-O-Stores, 59218
Scott & Associates, 59224
Scranton Fish Company, 59226
Seattle's Best Coffee, 59253
Seder Foods Corporation, 59257
See's Candy Shops, 59258
Segal's Wholesale, 59259
Selby Johnson Corporation, 59261
Select Meat Company, 59262
Serendib Tea Company, 59265
Serendipity of the Valley, 59267
Seven K Feather Farm, 59275
Shabazz Fruit Cola Company, 59281
Shaheen Bros Inc, 59282
Shamrock Farms, 59285
Shamrock Foods Co, 59286, 59287, 59288
Shari Candies, 59294
Shellman Peanut & Grain, 59301
Shemen Tov Corporation, 59303
Sherwood Food Distributors, 59310, 59313
Shetakis Foodservice, 59318
Shiff & Goldman Foods, 59319
Shivji Enterprises, 59324
Sho-Nuff-Good, 59325
Shryack-Givens Grocery Co., 59330
Shryack-Hirst Grocery Company, 59331
Shullsburg Creamery Inc, 59333
Sid Wainer & Son Specialty, 59339
Sidney's, 59342
Sieb Distributor, 59343
Sierra Nut House, 59346
Simply Gum, 59352
Simpson Grocery Company, 59355
Sims Wholesale, 59357
Sin-Son Produce, 59358
Sindoni, Joseph, Wholesale Foods, 59360
Sirca Foodservice, 59365
Sisq Distributing Inc, 59366
Sisu Group Inc, 59368
Skidmore Sales & Distributing Company, 59371
Skiles Co Inc, 59372
Sleeper Produce Company, 59380
Slusser Wholesale Company, 59381
Smith & Son Wholesale, 59386
Smitty's Snowballs, 59391
Smoothie's Frozen Desserts, 59394
Snack Company, 59395
Snack King Foods, 59396
Snacks Over America Inc, 59397
Snapple Distributors of Long Island, 59398
Snappy Popcorn, 59399
Sniderman Brothers, 59401
Snyder Wholesale Inc, 59404
Snyder's Bakery, 59405
Sobey's, 59407
Sobey's Ontario, 59408
Sobey's Quebec Inc, 59409
Sobeys Inc., 59410, 59411, 59412, 59413, 59414, 59415
Sol Loeb Moving & Storage, 59420
Solutions, 59421
Sonora Foods, 59424
Soofer Co, 59426
Soozy's Grain-Free, 59427
South Jersey Paper Products, 59432
Southeast Cold Storage, 59435
Southeastern Grocers, 59438

1251

Wholesale Product Type / General Merchandise

Southern Glazer's Wine-Spirits, LLC, 59441
Southern Grocery Company, 59442
Southern Import Distributors, 59443
Southern Indiana Butcher's Supply, 59444
Southernfood.com LLC, 59453
Southwest Distributing Co, 59457
Southwest Traders, 59463
Sovrana Trading Corp, 59469
Sparboe Foods Corp, 59474
Sparrow Enterprises LTD, 59476
Spartan Foods, 59477
SpartanNash Co, 59478
Specialty House of Creation, 59482
Spice & Spice, 59487
Spice House International Specialties, 59488
Spot Cash Specialty Company, 59492
Squid Ink, 59498
ST Restaurant Supplies, 59129
St. Clair Foods Distributing, 59500
Stahl, 59506
Stamoolis Brothers Co, 59508
Standard Meat Co LP, 59512
Standard-Rosenbaum, 59514
Stanford Trading Company, 59515
Star Fisheries, 59520
Star Wholesale, 59531
Starbruck Foods Corporation, 59533
State Line Potato Chip Company, 59537
State Wholesale Grocers, 59539
Statewide Products Co Inc, 59541
Staunton Foods LLC, 59543
Steckel, Isadore, 59548
Steinberg Quebec: Aligro, 59550
Steiner Foods, 59551
Stella Maria's, 59554
Steve's Fine Food Emporium, 59559
Stewart Wholesale Hardware Company, 59563
STI International, 59130
Strasheim Wholesale, 59577
Strongbow Foods, 59585
Sucesores de Pedro Cortes, 59590
Suity Confections Co, 59594
Suki, 59595
Summit Food Service Distributors, 59597, 59598
Sun Chlorella USA, 59600
Sun West Trading, 59605
Sunburst Foods, 59608
Suncrest Farms LLC, 59611
Sunflower Restaurant Supply, 59614
Sunshine Bar Supply Company, 59620
Sunshine Farms, 59621
Sunshine Fresh, 59622
Sunspun Foodservice, 59624
Suntec Power, 59625
Super Store Industries, 59631
Superior Beverage Group, 59632
Superior Wholesale Distr, 59640
SUPERVALU Distribution, 59132
Supreme Food, 59644
Supreme Foods, 59645
Sure-Good Food Distributors, 59648
Swapples, 59651
Sweet Dried Fruit, 59652
Sweet Liberty Candy Company, 59653
Sweet Place, 59654
Sweetener Products Co, 59659
Sweety's Candies, 59660
Swiss American International, 59662
Swiss Chalet Fine Foods, 59663
Switzer's Inc, 59666
Sycaway Creamery Inc, 59667
Sygma Network, 59668, 59669
SYGMA Network Inc, 59133
Synergee Foods Corporation, 59670
Systems Services Of America, 59745
T.A. Morris & Sons, 59750
T.B. Venture, 59752
T.C. Food Export/Import Company, 59753
Takeda Vitamin & Food, 59770

Tama Trading Co Inc, 59772
Tanglewood Farm, 59775
Tanner Enterprises, 59777
Tatra Sheep Cheese Company, 59788
TBI Corporation, 59761
Tchefa, 59795
Tergerson's Fine Foods, 59807
Tessemae's All Natural, 59815
Texas Gunpowder, 59817
Texas Marine II, 59820
The Bachman Company, 59823
The Chefs' Warehouse, 59824
The Coop, 59827
The Piping Gourmets, 59830
The Premium Beer Company, 59831
The Soulfull Project, 59832
Theatre Candy Distributing Company, 59837
Third Planet Products, 59838
Thomas & Howard Co, 59840
Thomas & Howard Co Cash & Crry, 59841
Thomas Ice Cream, 59844
Thompson Dairy, 59850
Thomson Groceries Ltd., 59851
Three M Food Service, 59853
Ths Foodservice, 59855
Thurston Foods Inc, 59858
Tiger Distributors, 59862
Timber Peaks Gourmet, 59863
Timeless Seeds, 59865
Tippecanoe Foods, 59869
TKC Supply, 59765
Todd Distributors Inc, 59874
Tony's Fine Foods, 59879
Topicz, 59887
Tosi & Company, 59893
Toudouze Market Company, 59897
Town & Country Wholesale, 59901
Tradelink, 59909
Trader Joe's, 59910
Trans Veyor, 59911
Treasure Coast Coffee Company, 59914
Treasure Foods, 59915
Tribe 9 Foods, 59933
Tribest Corp, 59934
Triple F, 59941
Trophy Foods, 59943
Tropical Paradise, 59948
Tropical Treets, 59949
Trucco, A.J., 59953
Truscello & Sons Wholesalers, 59956
Tucson Coop. Warehouse, 59960
Turner Holdings LLC, 59968
Turtle Island Herbs, 59969
Tusco Grocers Inc, 59970
Tvc Wholesale Inc, 59972
Twelve Baskets Sales & Market, 59973
Ukiah Foods, 60000
Unicorn Enterprises, 60007
Unilever US, 60009
Union Grocery Company, 60011
United Bakers & Deli Supply, 60014
United Dairy Co-Op Svc, 60017
United Foods & Fitness, 60020
United Grain Growers, 60023
United Mineral & Chemical Corporation, 60026
United Natural Foods Inc, 60027
United Noodles, 60028
United States Sugar Corp, 60037
United Sugars Corporation, 60038
United Universal Enterprises Corporation, 60039
United Wholesale Grocery Company, 60040
Unity Brands Group, 60042
Universal Preservachem Inc, 60047
Upper Lakes Foods Inc, 60053
Upstate Farms, 60054
US Food Products, 59984
US Foods Inc, 59987, 59988, 59989, 59990, 59991, 59992
US Marketing Company, 59994
V-Suarez Provisions, 60058

Vale Enterprises, 60066
Valley Distributing Company, 60069, 60070
Valley Distributors, 60071
Valley Foods, 60072
Valley Fruit & Produce Company, 60074
Valley Pride Food Distributor, 60075
Van Eerden Foodservice Co Inc, 60077
Vaughn Packing Company, 60085
Vend Food Service, 60088
Vendors Purchasing Council, 60090
Venus Supply Company, 60094
Veritiv Corp, 60096
Vilore Foods Company, 60113
Vincent Piazza Jr & Sons, 60116
Vineyard Gate, 60118
VIP Food Svc, 60061
Virginia Wholesale Company, 60120
Vista Food Exchange, 60124
Vistar Northwest, 60128
Vitusa Products Inc, 60134
VMC Corp, 60062
Vtopian Artisan Cheeses, 60147
W A DeHart Inc, 60149
W.F. Ware Company, 60160
W.G. White & Company, 60161
W.J. Stearns & Sons/Mountain Dairy, 60163
W.L. Petrey Wholesale Inc., 60164
W.R. McRae Company Limited, 60167
W.R. Nykorchuck & Company, 60169
W.R. Whitaker & Company, 60171
W.S. Lee & Sons, 60172
Wabash Foodservice Inc, 60184
Wagner Gourmet Foods, 60190
Wakefern Food Corp, 60193
Walker Hatchery, 60197
Wallaby Yogurt Co, 60200
Wallace Foods Inc, 60202
Wallach's Farms, 60204
Walter E Jacques & Sons, 60207
Waltkoch Limited, 60209
Walton & Post, 60210
Wards Ice Cream Co Inc, 60212
Watkins Distributing Company, 60222
Waugh Foods Inc, 60225
Webeco Foods, 60230
Webeco Foods, Inc, 60231
Wechsler Coffee Corporation, 60233
Weeke Wholesale Company, 60234
Wega USA, 60235
Wescotek Inc, 60241
West Bay Sales, 60243
West Coast Ship Chandlers, 60246
West End Dairy Inc, 60248
West Tenn Dairy Products, 60249
West Wholesale Grocery, 60250
Westco Chemicals Inc, 60251
Western Family Foods Inc, 60256
Western Grocers, 60257, 60258
Western Mandate, 60259
Westside Foods, 60263
WG Thompson & Sons, 60181
White Feather Farms, 60275
Whitley Wholesale Grocery, 60282
Wholesome Bakery, 60289
Wild Zora Foods, 60298
Wilde Brands, 60299
Wilke International Inc, 60301
Wilkin-Alaska, 60303
Willamette Valley Pie Co, 60305
William E. Martin & Sons Company, 60307
Williams Institutional Foods, 60310
Williams Sausage Co, 60312
Williamsport Candy Company, 60313
Winchester Food, 60320
Winkler Inc, 60331
Winn-Dixie, 60334
Wisconsin Milk Mktng Board Inc, 60340
Wise Products Distributors, 60342
Wisner Manufacturing Corporation, 60345
Witmer Foods, 60346

Wood Fruitticher Grocery Company, 60350
World Finer Foods Inc, 60357
World Spice, 60359
Wrawp, 60363
Wustefeld Candy Co Inc, 60366
Yai's Thai, 60371
Youngstown Wholesale Grocery, 60383
Yue's International Company, 60384
Zachary Confections Inc, 60390
Zazubean, 60392
Zeches Institution Supply, 60393
Zego Foods, 60394
Zel R. Kahn & Sons, 60395
Zetov Inc, 60397
Zink Distributing Co, 60400

General Merchandise

A & W Wholesale Co Inc, 54512
A J Oster Foils LLC, 54518
A J Silberman & Co, 54520
A&J Food Wholesalers, Inc., 54529
A&J Forklift & Equipment, 54530
A-1 Seafood Center, 54535
A-A1 Aaction Bag, 54536
A-B Products, 54537
A-Line Electric Supply Inc, 54538
A.J. Jersey, 54553
A/R Packaging Corporation, 54557
A2Z Specialty Advertising, 54559
AA Specialty Advertising Products, 54560
AANTEC, 54561
Abal Material Handling Inc, 54590
ABCO HVACR Supply & Solutions, 54563
Abel IHS, 54594
Able Sales Company, 54595
ABM Industries, 54565
ACC Distributors Inc, 54567
Ace Chemical, 54601
Ace Electric Supply, 54602
Ace Endico Corp, 54603
Ace Fixture Company, 54604
Ace Mart Restaurant Supply, 54605
ACK Industrial Electronics, 54568
Ackerman Industrial Equipment, 54606
Acme Scale Co, 54609
Acorn Distributors Inc, 54611
Action Advertising, 54612
Action Sales, 54613
Ad Lib Advertising, 54615
Ad Specialty Plus, 54616
Ad-Centive Ideas, 54617
Ad-Craft Products Compay, 54618
Adams Wholesale Co, 54621
Adams-Burch, 54622
ADE Restaurant Service, 54570
Adel Grocery Company, 54624
Adex Medical Inc, 54626
ADI, 54571
Adirondack Direct, 54627
Admiral Craft, 54629
Adsmith, 54633
ADT Inc, 54573
ADT Security Systems, 54574
Advanced Chemical, 54634
Advanced Equipment Company, 54635
Advanced Handling Systems Inc, 54636
Adventure Foods, 54638
Advertising Specialties, 54640
Advertising Specialties Imprinted, 54641
Aerolator Systems, 54644
Aetna Plastics Corporation, 54645
Affiliated Resource Inc, 54647
Agri-Equipment International, 54652
Agrium Advanced Technologies, 54653
Aidi International Hotels of America, 54655
AIN Plastics, 54576
Air Savers Inc, 54659
Ajax Philadelphia, 54660
Akron Cotton Products, 54662
Al Lehrhoff Sales, 54664

Wholesale Product Type / General Merchandise

Alabama Food Group, 54666
Alack Refrigeration Co Inc, 54669
Albert Uster Imports Inc, 54675
Albion Enterprises, 54679
Alerta-Mat, 54684
Alfa International Corp, 54688
Algen Scale Corp, 54690
Alioto Lazio Fish Co, 54691
All American Specialty Corporation, 54693
All Caribbean Food Service, 54694
All Cinema Sales & Services, 54695
All Lift Equipment, 54697
All Pack Co Inc, 54698
All Power Inc, 54699
All QA Products, 54700
All Seasons Uniforms & Textile, 54703
All Star Janitorial Supply, 54705
All State Restaurant Supply, 54707
All-State Industries Inc, 54710
All-Tech Materials Handling, 54711
Allen Brothers Inc, 54716
Allen Rosenthal Company, 54717
Allied Food Service, 54723
Allied Industrial Equipment, 54724
Allied Premium Company, 54727
Allkind Container Co, 54729
Allstate Insurance Company, 54730
Alpha Omega Technology, 54734
Alpine Gloves, 54737
Alpine Industries/Alpine Air Products, 54738
Alson Specialty Company, 54740
Alta Equipment Co, 54742
Alternative Health & Herbs, 54745
Altrua Marketing & Design, 54747
AM-Mac, 54580
Amenity Services, 54754
American Advertising Specialties Company, 54755
American Bakery Equipment Company, 54758
American Container Concepts, 54761
American European Systems, 54762
American Food & Vending Corporation, 54765
American Food Equipment, 54766
American Food Equipment & Supply, 54767
American Food Systems, 54768
American Forklifter, 54770
American Grocery & Beverage, 54772
American Health & Safety, 54773
American Hotel Register Co, 54774
American Legion, 54777
American Lighting & Electric, 54778
American Lighting Supply, 54779
American Material Handling Inc, 54780
American Metalcraft Inc, 54782
American Osment, 54784
American Packaging Corporation, 54785
American Restaurant Supply, 54790, 54791
American Select Foods, 54796
American Specialty Coffee & Culinary, 54799
American Trading Company, 54800
American Uniforms Sales Inc, 54801
American/Brenner Wholesale, 54804
Amerivap Systems Inc, 54806
Ammirati Inc, 54808
AMN Distributors/Premium Blend, 54584
Amos's PA Wonder Products, 54809
Amster-Kirtz Co, 54812
Amtex Packaging, 54813
Anderson Studio Inc, 54822
Angelo Refrigeration & Rstrnt, 54829
Anixter Inc, 54831
Anniston Paper & Supply Company, 54836
Anthony's Snack & Vending, 54839
Apache Inc, 54843
Apilico/Cuthbertson Imports, 54844
APM, 54586

Applied Handling Equipment Company, 54846
Applied Handling NW, 54847
Applied Industrial Tech Inc, 54848
Aqua-Tec Co, 54851
Ar Line Promotions Inc, 54852
Aramark Uniform Svc, 54854
Arctic Star Distributing, 54859
Argus Protective Services, 54862
Aries Paper & Chemical Company, 54863
Arizona Storage & Retrieval Systems, 54865
Arkansas Valley Wholesale Grocery Company, 54867
Arlington Coffee Company, 54870
Armaday Paper, 54871
Armstrong Jones, 54873
Arnall Grocery Co, 54874
Arnold Machinery Co, 54876
Aroma Foods, 54878
Aron Corporation, 54879
Arrow Restaurant Equipment, 54882
Arthur G. Meier Company/Inland Products Company, 54884
Aspecialtybox.Com, 54893
Aspen Corporate Identity Group, 54894
Assemblyonics Inc, 54895
Associated Bag Co, 54896
Associated Food Equipment, 54897
Associated Food Stores Inc, 54899
Associated Grocers, 54900
Associated Material Handling, 54901
Associates Material Handling, 54903
Atlanta Fixture & Sales Company, 54910
Atlantic Dominion Distributors, 54911
Atlantic Industrial & Marine Supplies, 54913
Atlantic Lift Systems, 54914
Atlantic Rentals, 54915
Atlas Equipment Company, 54925
Atlas Lift Truck Rentals & Sales, 54926
Auromere Inc, 54932
Automation Fastening Company, 54940
Automation Systems & Services, 54941
Avalon Trade Company, 54944
Aylesworth's Fish & Bait, 54951
B & J Food Svc Inc, 54960
B & M Provision Co, 54962
B & W Supply Co, 54966
B. Fernandez & Sons, 54975
B.M. Sales Company, 54978
B/R Sales Company, 54980
Babush Conveyor Corporation, 54995
Baden Baden Food Equipment, 54998
Badger Material Handling, 55000
Badger Popcorn, 55001
Badger Wholesale Company, 55002
Bagel Lites, 55007
Bagman, 55008
Bailey Co Inc, 55009
Bake Star, 55013
BakeMark Ingredients West Inc, 55015
Bakery Equipment Sales & Services, 55023
Bakery Things, 55026
Bakri Trading Inc, 55029
Ballantine Industrial Truck Service, 55033
Balter Sales Co, 55037
Baltimore Belting Co, 55038
Banner Wholesale Grocers, 55047
Bar Boy Products Inc, 55049
Bar Controls Of Florida, 55050
Bar-Plex, 55053
Baring Industries, 55060
Barnett Lighting Corporation, 55064
Basic Leasing Corporation, 55075
Bassham Institutional Foods, 55078
Bates Distributing, 55079
Bathroom & Towel Systems, 55080
Batty & Hoyt, 55083
Baumann Paper Company, 55085
Bay Area Trash Compactor, 55087
Bay Cities Produce Co Inc, 55089
Bay State Restrnt Products Inc, 55092

Bayshore Equipment, 55100
BBQ Bunch, 54982
BCIS Inc, 54984
Beans & Machines, 55102
Bear Stewart Corp, 55105
Bedford Enterprises Inc, 55111
Belco Packaging Systems, 55118
Belew Sound & Visual, 55119
Bell Fork Lift Inc, 55124
Bellin Advertising, 55129
Belting Associates, 55131
Beltram Foodservice Group, 55132
Ben E. Keith, 55133, 55134, 55135, 55136, 55137, 55138, 55139, 55140, 55141, 55142, 55143
Benfield Electric Supply Co, 55164
Benman Industries Inc, 55165
Bennett Material Handling, 55166
Bensinger's, 55167
Bergin Fruit & Nut Co., 55171
Berkel Products Company, 55173
Berlin Packaging, 55174, 55175, 55176, 55177
Berry Material Handling, 55185
Berton Company, 55188
Best Industries, 55197
Best Market, 55198
Best Material Handling, 55199
Best Restaurant Equip & Design, 55200
Better Janitor Supplies, 55204
Beverage Express, 55207
BFM Equipment Sales, 54985
BI-LO, 54987
Big State Vending Company, 55218
Bilas Distributing Company, 55220
Binghamton Material Handling, 55224
Bintz Restaurant Supply Company, 55225
Bioscience International Inc, 55227
Biostim LLC, 55228
Birmingham Vending Games, 55233
Bishop Brothers, 55236
BJ'S Wholesale Club Inc, 54988
Blachere Group, 55239
Blazer Concepts, 55250
Blue Delft Supply, 55257
Blue Line Foodservice Distr, 55260
Blue Rhino Compaction Services, 55262
Bmh Corporation, 55269
Bode-Finn Company, 55271
Boelter Companies, 55273
Bolton & Hay, 55275
Bono Burns Distributing Inc, 55281
Booker Promotions, 55282
Boone's Wholesale, 55283
Boricua Empaque, 55285
Bosch Distributors, 55286
Bosco Food Service, 55287
Boston Showcase Company, 55294
Bowlin J P Co LLC, 55303
Boxer-Northwest Company, 55306
Boykin & Southern Wholesale Grocers, 55307
Bozzuto's Inc., 55311
Bradley Kitchen Center, 55313
Bradshaw Home   nc, 55314
Branton Industries, 55316
Brasco, 55317
Brauer Material Handling Systs, 55320
Brawner Paper Co Inc, 55321
Brenham Wholesale Groc Co Inc, 55324
Bresco, 55325, 55326
Brevard Restaurant Equipment, 55327
Briggs Co, 55334
Brilliant Lighting Fixture Corporation, 55335
Brita Foods, 55339
British Shoppe LLC, 55341
British Wholesale Imports, 55342
Broaster Sales & Svc, 55345
Brockman Forklift, 55347
Brody Food Brokerage Corporation, 55348
Bronx Butter & Egg Company, 55349
Brooklyn Boys Pizza & Pasta, 55351
Brooks Barrel Company, 55353

Brooks Industries, 55354
Brothers Restaurant Supply, 55357
Brown, R H, 55361
Bruce Edmeades Sales, 55364
Brucken's, 55365
Bublitz Machinery Company, 55371
Buckelew Hardware Co, 55372
Buckelew's Food Svc Equipment, 55373, 55374
Buckeye Handling Equipment Company, 55375
Buffalo Hotel Supply Co Inc, 55381
Buffalo Paper & Detergent Co, 55382
Bunzl Distribution USA, 55387
Burch-Lowe, 55389
Burgess Mfg. - Oklahoma, 55391
Burklund Distributors Inc, 55393
Burlington Equipment Company, 55394
Business Documents, 55397
Business Services Alliance, 55398
Butte Produce Company, 55402
Buz's Crab, 55404
BW Acquisition, 54994
Byczek Enterprises, 55406
Bykowski Equipment, 55407
Bynoe Printers, 55408
C & R Food Svc Inc, 55412
C & S Sales Inc, 55413
C & S Wholesale Grocers Inc, 55414
C & T Design & Equipment Co, 55415
C A Curtze, 55417
C D Hartnett Co, 55418
C M Tanner Grocery Co, 55420
C Pacific Foods Inc, 55421
C&C Lift Truck, 55422
C&H Store Equipment Company, 55423
C&R Refrigation Inc,, 55424
C.A. Flipse & Sons Company, 55428
Cadillac Packaging Corporation, 55458
Caesar Electric Supply, 55459
Cal Coast Promo-Products, 55470
Calico Industries Inc, 55473
California Caster & Handtruck, 55475
California Marketing Group Inc, 55478
California Tag & Label, 55480
Campione Resturant Supply, 55488
Canada Cutlery Inc., 55490
Canada Safeway, 55493
Cannon/Tayloe, 55495
Cantab Industries, 55498
Canty Wiper & Supply Company, 55501
Capital Equipment & Handling, 55507
Capitol Foods, 55510
Cappuccino Express Company, 55513
Carbonella & Desarbo Inc, 55523
Carborator Rental Svc, 55524
Cardinal Carryor Inc, 55526
Cardinal International, 55527
Carefree Kanopy, 55528
Carle & Montanari-O P M, 55532
Carlisle Food Systems Inc, 55533
Carlson Company, 55534
Carlton Company, 55535
Carolina Belting, 55539
Carolina Handling LLC, 55542
Carolina Material Handling, 55543
Carolina Steel Shelving Company, 55546
Carolina Tractor and   Equipment Company, 55547
Carolyn Darden Enterprises, 55548
Carrollton Products Company, 55553
Carter Promotions, 55555
Cash Register Sales, 55563
Cash-Wa Distributing, 55564, 55565
Cass Hudson Company, 55569
Casso Guerra & Company, 55570
Caster Wheels & Indl Handling, 55572
Castino Restaurant Equipment, 55573
Castor Technology Corporation, 55575
Cavanna Packaging USA Inc, 55580
Cb Equipment Co, 55584
CB Pallet, 55437
CBS Food Equipment, 55439
Central Distributing Co, 55591

1253

Wholesale Product Type / General Merchandise

Central Illinois Equipment Company, 55592
Central Package & Display, 55594
Central Restaurant Supply Inc, 55595
Central Sanitary Supply, 55596
Central Security Service, 55597
Central Wholesale Grocery Corporation, 55598
Century Data Systems, 55602
Century Distributors Inc, 55603
Century Fournier Inc, 55604
Certified Cleaning Supplies, 55611
Certified Food Service, 55612
Certified Interior Systems, 55615
CF Equipment, 55440
CFE Equipment Corp, 55442
Chamberlain Wholesale Grocery, 55618
Champaign Plastics Company, 55620
Charles C. Parks Company, 55623
Charlton & Hill, 55627
Charmel Enterprises, 55628
Chattanooga Button & Badge Company, 55632
Chattanooga Restaurant Supl, 55633
Chef's Supply & Design, 55640
Chelsea Market Baskets, 55643
Chem Care, 55644
Chem-Mark of Buffalo, 55645
Chemcraft Industries Inc, 55646
Cheney Brothers Inc, 55648
Chernoff Sales, 55649
Chia I Foods Company, 55654
Chicago Bar & Restaurant Supply, 55655
Choice Restaurant Equipment, 55673
Christopher Wholesalers, 55678
Christy Industries Inc, 55680
Cirelli Foods, 55689
Cisco-Eagle, 55691
Clark Restaurant Svc, 55708
Clarkson Company, 55710
Clogmaster, 55725
Coffee Expresso & Service, 55745
Cogent Technologies, 55747
Cohen Foods, 55748
Cole Brothers & Fox Company, 55753
Collins & Company, 55754
Colonial Coffee Roasters Inc, 55755
Colorado Chemical Company, 55762
Colorado Restaurant Supply, 55765
Columbia Paper Company, 55767
Columbia Restaurant & Bar Supply Co., 55768
Columbia Scale Company, 55769
Com-Pak International, 55770
Commercial Appliance Svc, 55775
Commodities Assistance Corporation, 55777
Commodities Marketing Inc, 55778
Composition Materials Co Inc, 55781
Comprehensive Lighting Svc, 55782
Computerized Machinery Systs, 55783
Concept Equipment Corporation, 55786
Concession & Restaurant Supply, 55787
Concord Import, 55792
Conger Industries Inc, 55796
Consolidated Bottle Company, 55802
Consolidated Poultry & Egg Company, 55804
Container Systems Inc, 55809
Continental Glass & Plastic, 55811
Continental Lift Truck Corp, 55812
Contract & Leisure, 55814
Convenience Food Systems, 55816
Cook Associates Your Co Store, 55817
Cook's Mate Restaurant Equipment Supply, 55819
Cooker T. Corporation, 55820
Cooperative Atlantic, 55823
Copperwood InternationalInc, 55826
Core-Mark Holding Company, Inc, 55830, 55833, 55834, 55835, 55839, 55840
Corporate Display Specialty, 55847
Cosa Xentaur Corp, 55848
Cost Plus, 55850

Costco Wholesale Corporation, 55852
County Supply Co, 55861
Cousin's Uniform, 55863
Coyne Chemical Co Inc, 55866
Cracker Jack Advertising Specialty Corporation, 55871
Craver Supply Company, 55873
Creative Lighting Fixture Company, 55879
Crishawn Kitchen Equipment Company, 55883
Cross Automation, 55888
Crown Lift Trucks, 55891
Crown Restaurant Equipment, 55894
Crown Sanitary Supply, 55895
CRS Marking Systems, 55449
Crystal-Vision Packaging Systems, 55899
CSI Material Handling, 55450
Csra Advertising Specialties, 55900
Culinary Depot, 55905
Culinary Masters Corporation, 55906
Culinary Products Inc, 55907
Culinary Specialties, 55908
Cummings Restaurant Equipment, 55913
Curtis Restaurant Equipment, 55916, 55917
Curtis Restaurant Supply, 55918
Custom Fabricating & Repair, 55921
Custom Pools Inc, 55925
Cuyler Food Machinery & Appraisal, 55928
CW Paper, 55453
D A C Labels & Graphic, 55930
D J Enterprises, 55932
D L Systems Inc, 55933
D Rosen Co Inc, 55934
D. Deodati & Sons, 55941
Dacotah Paper Co, 55962
Dade Paper Co, 55963
Daffin Mercantile Company, 55964
Dairy King Milk Farms/Foodservice, 55967
Dalmatian Bay Wine Company, 55974
Dalo Button & Emblem Company, 55975
Dana's Rush Equipment Company, 55977
Dana-Lu Imports, 55978
Danville Paper & Supply, 55980
Dataflow Technologies, 55983
Datatech Enterprises, 55984
David Food Processing Equipment, Inc., 55986
David's Cookies, 55988
Davis-Le Grand Company, 55992
Dayco Distributing, 55993
DC Media & Marketing, 55947
De Leone Corp, 55997
De Palo & Sons Inc, 55998
De Vara Designs, 55999
Dean Supply Co, 56003
Dean's Ice Cream Dstrbtn Ctr, 56004
Dearborn Cash & Carry Stores, 56005
Dearborn Wholesale Grocers LP, 56006
Dearborn Wholesale Grocers, 56007, 56009, 56010
Debbie Wright Sales, 56011
Deep South Equipment Co, 56017
Dees Paper Co, 56019
Delisa Pallet Corporation, 56025
Dell Enterprises, 56026
Delta Bay, 56027
Delta Materials Handling Inc, 56029
Demma Fruit Company, 56032
Den-Tex Restaurant Supply, 56033
Deng's, 56034
Dent Electrical Supply Company, 56035
Denver Restaurant Equipment Company, 56038
Dependable Plastics & Supls, 56040
Designs Furnishings & Eqpt Inc, 56042
Destileria Serralles Inc, 56043
Detroit Popcorn, 56044
Deverell Equipment, 56045
Deville Restaurant Equipment & Supply Company, 56046
DeVries Imports, 56000

Dial Industries Inc, 56053
Dicarlo Distributors Inc, 56059
Dick Dunphy Advertising Specialties, 56060
Dickerson & Quinn, 56061
Dickson Brothers, 56063
Dierks Foods, 56064
Digital Monitoring Products, 56067
DiLeo Brothers, 56051
Dilgard Frozen Foods, 56068
Dinetz Restaurant Equipment, 56072
Direct Media, 56076
Direct Promotions, 56077
Dirt Killer Pressure Washer, 56079
Discount Equipment Intl, 56080
Dishaka Imports, 56081
Distribution Kowloon, 56084
Diverse Sales, 56086
Dixie Advertising Company, 56089
Dixie Equipment Co, 56090
Dixie Mart, 56092
Dixie Store Fixtures & Sales, 56093
Dockmasters Inc, 56096
Doerle Food Svc, 56098
Doggett Equipment Services Group, 56100
Dominion Equipment & Supply Co., 56106
Don McDonald & Sons, 56108
Dornan Uniforms & Specialty Advertising, 56114
Dorsett & Jackson Inc, 56116
Doscher's Candies Co., 56117
Douglas Brothers Produce Company, 56121
Douglas Freight Salvage, 56122
Douglas Homs Corporation, 56123
Down To Earth Distributors, 56127
Downco Packaging Inc, 56128
Dragonfly Screen Graphics Inc, 56136
Drake Equipment Co, 56137
Draught Services, 56139
Dub Harris Corporation, 56143
Dudson USA Inc, 56146
Dunlevy Food Equipment, 56149
Dutch Creek Foods, 56156
Dutchess Restaurant Equipment, 56158
Duval Container Co, 56160
DWL Industries Company, 55959
DXP Enterprises Inc, 55960
Dykes Restaurant Supply Inc, 56163
Dyna Tabs LLC, 56164
Dyna-Lift Inc, 56165
E D Farrell Co Inc, 56169
E Friedman Assoc, 56170
E G Forrest Co Inc, 56171
E&A Hotel & Restaurant Epment And Supplies, 56174
E&M Packaging, 56176
E. De la Garza, 56178
E.A. Robinson & Company, 56181
E.H. Thompson Company, 56183
Eagle Coffee Co Inc, 56190
Eagle Industrial Distribution, 56191
Eagle Wholesale Drug Company, 56192
Eagle-Concordia Paper Corporation, 56193
Earl Gill Coffee Co, 56194
Earp Distribution, 56195
East Bay International, 56201
Eastern Bag & Paper Company, 56205
Eastern Bakers Supply Co Inc, 56206
Eastern Energy Lighting Systems, 56207
Eastern Refrigeration & Restaurant Equipment, 56209
Eastimpex, 56212
Eby-Brown Company, 56218
Ecological Technologies, 56222
Economy Cash & Carry LP, 56223
Economy Restaurant Fixtures, 56225
Economy Wholesale Company, 56226
Edmer Sanitary Supply Co Inc, 56233
Edward Badeaux Company, 56237
Edward Don & Co, 56238, 56239, 56240
Edward Don & Company, 56241, 56242

Ehrlich Food Co, 56248
Eklof & Company, 56249
Elco Fine Foods, 56254
Electra Supply Co, 56256
Electro Freeze Distrs Inc, 56258
Electroshield Inc, 56259
Elkhorn Distributing Company, 56265
Elliot Lee, 56268
Elm Electric Supply, 56272
Emco Industrial Plastics, 56275
EMG Associates, 56186
Emiliomiti, 56277
Emkay Confectionery Machinery Company, 56278
Empire Cash Register Systems, 56280
Empire Comfort Systems, 56281
Empire Forklift Inc, 56282
Empire Tea Svc, 56284
EMSCO Scientific Enterprises, Inc., 56187
Encore Sales, 56288
Engineered Handling Products, 56291
Engineered Storage Products Company, 56292
Enterprise Company, 56296
Enviro-Green Products, 56297
Environmental Packaging Associates, 56299
Epic, 56301
Epicurean Foods, 56303
Equipco, 56305
Equipment, 56306
Equipment Distributor Div, 56307
Equipment Engineering Company, 56308
Equipment for Industry, 56312
Equipment Inc., 56309
Equipment Picard, 56310
Equipment Specialty Company, 56311
Equipment/Plus, 56313
ERC Parts Inc, 56188
Erickson's Fork Lifts Inc, 56314
Erlab, Inc, 56315
Erman & Son, 56316
Espresso Buy the Cup, 56321
Espresso Coffee Machine Co, 56322
Espresso Machine Experts, 56323
Espresso Magic, 56324
Espresso Roma, 56325
Essbar Equipment Company, 56326
Ettline Foods Corp, 56331
Euclid Fish Co, 56333
Euro Mart/Stolzle Cberg las, 56335
European Hotel & Restaurant Imports, 56341
Eurpac Warehouse Sales, 56343
Evans BS&R, 56345
Evans Foodservice Inc., 56346
Evco Wholesale Food Corp, 56347
Event Equipment Sales, 56348
Excellence Commercial Products, 56352
Excello Machine Co Inc, 56354
Express Point Technology Services, 56356
Ezy Trading International, 56358
F & C Sawaya Wholesale, 56360
F B Mc Fadden Wholesale Co, 56361
F B Wright Co, 56362
F McConnell & Sons, 56365
F-M Forklift Sales & Svc Inc, 56366
F.A. Davis & Sons, 56368
Fab Inc, 56372
Fab-X/Metals, 56373
Fairway Foods, 56379
Falls City Mercantile Co Inc, 56381
Farm Boy Food Svc, 56387
Farmfresh, 56391
Farner-Bocken Co, 56394
FCM, 56369
Federal Supply USA, 56398
Federated Cooperative, 56399
Federated Cooperative Lt, 56400
Feesers, 56404
Fein Brothers, 56405
Ferntrade Corporation, 56408
Fetzers', 56414

Wholesale Product Type / General Merchandise

Fidelity Container Corporation, 56416
Filler Paper Company, 56419
Finke Co, 56428
Fire Device Co, 56429
Fire Master, 56430
Fire Protection Systems Inc, 56431
Fireline Corp, 56432
Firemaster, 56433
First Coast Promotions, 56436
First Fire Systems Company, 56437
Fisher Mills, 56443
Fitch Co, 56446
Flaghouse, 56451
Flags & Banners Unlimited, 56452
Flavor-Crisp of America, 56463
Flint Provision Inc Zalack's, 56467
Florida Carbonic Distributor, 56470
Florida Choice Foods, 56471
Florida Distributing Source, 56472
Florida Gulf Packaging, 56474
Flostor Engineering, 56476
Fluid-O-Tech International Inc, 56478
Flushing Lighting, 56479
Focus Marketing, 56481
Foley-Belsaw Institute, 56483
Follex Distributing Co Inc, 56485
Food Authority Inc, 56488
Food Equipment Distributors, 56491
Food Equipment Specialist, 56492
Food Instrument Corp, 56497
Food Services Inc, 56501
Food Supply Inc, 56502
Food-Products, 56505
Ford Hotel Supply Co, 56510
Forklift Systems Inc-Parts Dpt, 56518
Forklifts, 56519
Fort Smith Restaurant Supply, 56521
Fort Wayne Door Inc, 56522
Forte Industries, 56523
Fortune Equipment Company, 56524
Four Oaks Farm, 56530
Fox Brush Company, 56534
Frabosk Magic Cappuccino, 56537
Frain Industries, 56538
Frank G. Schmitt Company, 56543
Frank P. Corso, 56546
Franklin Machine Products, 56550
Fred Band & Associates, 56553
Fred Hill & Son Co, 56554
Fred W Albrecht Grocery Co, 56555
Fredon Handling Inc, 56558
Freiria & Company, 56559
Fresco Y Mas, 56561
Fresh Point Dallas, 56565
Friedman Bag Company, 56569
Friendly Wholesale Co, 56571
Fritzie Fresh Products, 56573
Front Line Safety, 56574
Frontier Bag Co Inc, 56576
Frontline Inc, 56578
Fruit Of The Vine Of De Valley, 56585
G & W Equipment Inc, 56597
G & W Food Products, 56598
G.B. Sales & Service, 56603
Gaggia Espresso Machine Company, 56622
Garavaglia Meat Company, 56633
Garber Bros Inc, 56634
Garden & Valley Isle Seafood, 56635
Garden City Supply, 56636
Gardner & Benoit, 56639
Garland C Norris Co, 56640
Gasketman Inc, 56643
Gatto & Sons, 56645
GCS Service, 56609
Gelson's, 56649
Gemsy's Money Handling Systems, 56651
Gen Pac, 56653
General Candy Co, 56654
General Carriage & Supply Co, 56655
General Cash & Carry, 56656
General Sales, 56657
General Sales Associates, 56658
General Sales Co, 56659

General Trading Co, 56660
George E. Kent Company, 56667
George O Pasquel Company, 56670
George Uhe Company, Inc., 56671
GePolymershapes Cadillac, 56648
Gerlau Sales, 56673
Gexpro, 56674
Giambrocco Food Service, 56675
Giant Eagle American Seaway Foods, 56677
GIANT Food Stores, 56612
Gibson Wholesale Co Inc, 56678
Gillette Nebraska Dairies, 56681
Gilster-Mary Lee Corp, 56684
Gina Marie Refrigerator Door, 56686
Ginsberg's Institutional Foods, 56687
Giovanni Food Co Inc, 56688
GLAC Seat Inc, 56613
Globe Equipment Co, 56695
Globe-Monte-Metro Company, 56696
Glosson Food Eqpt-Hobart Svc, 56699
GMZ Inc, 56615
Goldberg & Solovy Foods Inc, 56710
Golden Lake Electric Supply, 56716
Golden Light Equipment Co, 56717
Golden Valley Popcorn Supply, 56721
Good's Wholesale-Bakery Supls, 56725
Gooding Rubber Company, 56726
Goodwin Brothers Inc, 56728
Gordon Food Service, 56730, 56732, 56733, 56734, 56735, 56736, 56737, 56738, 56739, 56740, 56741, 56742, 56743, 56744, 56745, 56746, 56747
Gosselin Gourmet Beverages, 56748
Gourmet Technologies Inc, 56754
Grace Technologies, 56756
Grafco, 56757
Grainger Industrial Supply, 56761, 56762
Grande Cuisine Systems, 56764
Gray Lift, 56768
Grayco Products Sales, 56769
Grayon Industrial Products, 56770
Great Age Container, 56771
Great American Health Bar, 56772
Great Eastern Equipment Exchange, 56776
Great Lakes Designs, 56778
Great Lakes Distributing & Storage, 56779
Great Lakes Hotel Supply Co, 56782, 56783
Great North Foods, 56786
Great Western Chemical, 56792
Great Western Chemical Company, 56793
Green Mountain Graphics, 56799
Greene Poultry Co, 56801
Greenebaum Brothers, 56802
Greenvale Electric Supply Corp, 56806
Gregory's Foods, Inc., 56809
Groetsch Wholesale Grocer, 56820
GSC Enterprises Inc., 56617
GTM, 56618
Guest Products, 56827
Gulf Arizona Packaging, 56828
Gulf Marine & Industrial Supplies Inc, 56831
Gulf Systems, 56835, 56836, 56837, 56838, 56839
Gunderland Marine Supply, 56840
GW Supply Company, 56619
H & R Coffee Co, 56844
H A Phillips & Co, 56845
H Schrier & Co Inc, 56848
H Weiss Co LLC, 56849
H.B. Paulk Grocery Company, 56853
Haitai Inc, 56878
Hal-One Plastics, 56879
Hale-Halsell Company, 56882
Hall-Woolford Wood Tank Co Inc, 56884
Halsey Foodservice, 56885
Halsey Reid Equipment, 56886
Hamill Industrial Sales Company, 56888
Hamilos Bros Inspected Meat, 56889
Hammill International, 56890
Handi-Rak Service, 56894

Handling & Storage Concepts, 56895
Handling Systems Inc, 56896, 56897
Hannaford Bros Co, 56902
Hanover Uniform Co, 56904
Hansen Distribution Group, 56908
Hanset Brothers Inc Brooms, 56910
Hansler Industries, 56911
Hanway Restaurant Equipment, 56913
Harbor Linen LLC, 56919
Harbor Wholesale Foods Inc, 56920
Harco Enterprises, 56921
Harders, 56922
Harker's Distribution, 56926
Harold Food Company, 56928
Harold Leonard & Company, 56929
Harold Leonard Southwest Corporation, 56931
Harpak-Ulma, 56933
Harris Equipment Corp, 56935
Harry Fourtunis, 56937
Harry Fourtunis Inc, 56938
Hartland Distributors, 56945
Harveys Supermarket, 56950
HAS Packaging System, 56859
Hassia, 56952
Hattiesburg Grocery Company, 56955
Haviland Enterprises Inc, 56957
Hawaiian Grocery Stores, 56961
Hawk Flour Mills, 56963
Hawthorn Power Systems, 56965
Hawthorne Supply Company, 56966
Haynes Brothers Candy Company, 56967
HD Supply Waterworks, 56862
HE Anderson Co, 56863
Healthwise, 56978
Heartland Distributors, 56981
Heerema Co, 56987
Heller's Food Equipment, 56992
Henderson Coffee Corp, 56995
Hendrix Hotel & Restaurant Equipment & Supplies, 56997
Henjes Enterprises, 56998
Henley Paper Company, 56999
Henry Bresky & Sons Inc, 57000
HERB Enterprises, 56864
Herc-U-Lift Inc, 57004
Herche Warehouse, 57005
Hercules Food Equipment, 57006
Heritage Maintenance Products, LLC, 57007
Hermanowski Wholesale, 57008
HFM Foodservice, 56865
HIB Foods Inc, 56866
Hibrett Puratex, 57013
Hill City Wholesale Company, 57020
Hill Company, 57021
Hill Specialties, 57022
Hilts, 57027
Hipp Wholesale Foods, 57031
Hiss Stamp Company, 57032
Hockenbergs Equipment & Supply, 57034
Hodell International, 57035
Hoffman Miller Advertising, 57037
Hoky Central, 57040
Holland Beef International Corporation, 57044
Holyoke Machine Co, 57050
Home-Like Food Company, 57052
Honey Acres, 57054
Horizon Business Svc, 57058
Horsley Company, 57061
Hoshizaki Northeastern, 57063
House of Spices, 57067
Houston International Packaging Company, 57069
Howard Decorative Packaging, 57071
HPC Foodservice, 56868
HRS Food Service, 56869
HSN Data Corporation, 56870
Hubert Co, 57073
Hudson Belting & Svc Co Inc, 57075
Hudson Valley Coffee Company, 57078
Hugg & Hall Equipment, 57084

Hughes Warehouse Equipment Company, 57086
Huguenot Sales Corporation, 57087
Hull Lift Truck Inc, 57088
Huntsville Restaurant Equip, 57093
Husky Foods of Anchorage, 57094
Hutchinson Mayrath Industries, 57095
Hydra-Flex Inc, 57096
Hydrite Chemical Co, 57097
Hytrol of California, 57098
I Supply Co, 57101
I Zakarin & Sons Inc, 57103
ICC Industrial Chemical, 57108
Ice & Juice Systems, 57118
Ice Machines, 57120
Ice Makers, 57121
ID Foods Corporation, 57109
IMDEC, 57111
Impact Products LLC, 57125
Imperial Bag & Paper Company, 57126
Imperial Dade, 57127
Imported Restaurant Specialties, 57132
Importex International, 57133
In A Bind Inc, 57134
Indianhead Foodservice, 57143
Industrial Commercial Supply, 57146
Industrial Contacts Inc, 57148
Industrial Handling Equipment, 57149
Industrial Lift Truck, 57150
Industrial Maintenance, 57151
Industrial Products Supply, 57152
Industrial Soap Co, 57153
Industrial Truck Sales & Services, 57154
Infinite Peripherals, 57155
Infinite Specialties, 57156
Ingold's HICO Inc, 57159
Inpak Systems Inc, 57165
Insects Limited Inc, 57166
Insley-Mc Entee Equipment Co, 57167
Institutional Wholesale Company, 57170
Instrumart, 57171
Insulated Structures/PB Group, 57172
Intermix Beverage, 57177
International Commercial Supply Corporation, 57183
International Culinary, 57184
International Dairy Equipment Associates, 57185
International Distribution, 57186
International Ticket Company, 57197
Interstate Distributors, 57199
Interstate Restaurant Equipment, 57200
Interthor Inc, 57201
Ipc Supply Inc, 57202
Irvine Restaurant Supply, 57208
Irvington Marcus Company, 57209
Ishida Corporation, 57211
ISI Commercial Refrigeration, 57112, 57113, 57114
ISI North America, 57115
Island Refrigeration & Foodservice Equipment, 57214
Italmade, 57221
J & R Distributors, 57225
J Moresky & Son, 57232
J Murray & Co, 57233
J W Outfitters, 57241
J. Lerner Box Company, 57250
J. Sosnick & Sons, 57254
J. Treffiletti & Sons, 57255
J.A. King & Company, 57256
J.D. Dawson Company, 57261
J.F. Walker Company, 57263
J.H. Thornton Company, 57264
J.J. Taylor Distributing, 57265
J.R. Campbell Equipment Company, 57270
J.W. Wood Company, 57274
Jacks Merchandising & Distribution, 57292
Jackson Newell Paper Co, 57293
Jackson Supply Company, 57294
Jackson Wholesale Co, 57295
Jacob KERN & Sons Inc, 57297
Jacob Licht, 57298

1255

Wholesale Product Type / General Merchandise

Jacobi Lewis Co, 57299
James D Cofer, 57309
Janpak, 57313
Jasper Glove Company, 57317
Jaydon, 57321
Jb Prince, 57322
Jeb Plastics, 57323
Jeffer Neely Company, 57325
Jefferds Corp, 57326
Jenthon Supply, 57330
Jerico, 57331
Jerry Brothers Industries Inc, 57335
Jesse Food Products, 57339
Jessom Food Equipment, 57340
JET Tools, 57281
Jetro Cash & Carry, 57342
Jetro Cash & Carry Enterprises, 57343
Jetro Cash & Carry Inc, 57344
Jo Mints, 57352
Jode Company, 57354
Joe Christiana Food Distributing, 57357
Joe Harding Sales & Svc, 57358
Joe Paulk Company, 57359
Joey's Fine Foods, 57361
John S. Dull & Associates, 57378
John's Wholesale, 57383
Johnnie's Restaurant-Hotel Svc, 57384
Johnson Diversified Products, 57385
Johnston Equipment, 57389, 57390
Joseph J. Sayre & Son Company, 57398
Joyce Brothers Company, 57401
Julius Silvert Company, 57408
Junction City Distributing & Vending Company, 57409
K & G Power Systems, 57412
K & L Intl, 57413
K Doving Co Inc, 57415
K&H Equipment Company, 57419
Kaco Supply Co, 57433
Kallsnick Inc, 57439
Kansas City Sausage, 57443
Kappus Co, 57445
Karp's Bake Mark, 57449
Kason, 57451
Kason Central, 57452
KAST Distributors Inc, 57425
Kayem Foods, 57457
KeHE Distributors, 57458
Keith Industries, 57474
Kelley Foods, 57476
Kenssenich's, 57489
Key Business Systems, 57495
Key Industrial, 57497
Keystone Cleaning Systems, 57501
Keystone Restaurant Supply, 57502
KHL Engineered Packaging, 57426
Kid Zone, 57503
King Provision Corporation, 57508
Kingson Corporation, 57511
Kingston Candy & Tobacco Co, 57512
Kingston McKnight, 57513
Kirkholder & Rausch, 57516
Kittredge Equipment Co, 57520
KJ's Market, 57427
Kleen Janitorial Supply Co., 57521
Klondike Foods, 57524
Koalaty Kare, 57532
Koch Bag & Supply Co, 57533
Koch Container, 57534
KOHL Wholesale, 57429
Kohlenberger Inc, 57537
Kolon California Corporation, 57538
Kols Container, 57539
Kommercial Kitchens, 57540
Koorsen Protection Services, 57544
Kopcke-Kansas Supply Services, 57545
Kosmos & Associates, 57547
Kovacs Group, 57548
Kranz Inc, 57550
Krebs Brothers Restaurant Supl, 57553
Kuehne Chemical, 57556
Kwikprint Manufacturing Inc, 57560
KYD Inc, 57432
L & M Food Svc Inc, 57562
L ChemCo Distribution, 57563
L. Lacagnina & Sons, 57571
L.N. Coffman Company, 57573
L.P. Shanks Company, 57574
LA Foods, 57578
La Pine Scientific Company, 57592
LA Rue Distributing, 57582
Labatt Food Svc, 57598, 57599
Label House, 57602
Labeltronix LLC, 57603
Labov Mechanical, Inc., 57604
Lady Baltimore of Missouri, 57607
Lafayette Restaurant Supply, Inc., 57609
Lairamore Corp, 57611
Laird Plastics, 57612
Laird Plastics Inc, 57613
Lancaster Johnson Company, 57620
Lancer, 57622
Landsberg Kent, 57628
Lane Equipment Co, 57629, 57630
Langley Corporation, 57632
Lanzarotta Wholesale Grocers, 57634
Larick Associates, 57636
Larry Martindale Company, 57639
Lavin Candy Company, 57646
LBG Distributors, 57585
LDC of Lafayette, 57586
Le Smoker, 57652
Lee Grocery Company, 57659
Lee Packaging Corporation, 57660
Leedal Inc, 57661
Legacy Beverage Systems, 57663
Lello Appliances Corp, 57667
Lemark Promotional Products, 57668
Lenox-Martell Inc, 57672
Leon Supply Company, 57675
Lesco Supply Company, 57681
Levin Brothers Paper, 57683
Lew Sander Inc, 57684
Lewis Brothers & Sons, 57686
Lewisburg Wholesale Company, 57687
Liberto Management Co Inc, 57689
Liberto of Harlington, 57690
Liberto of Houston, 57691
Liberty Bell Wholesale Grocery, 57692
Liberty Scale Co Inc, 57698
Liberty USA Inc,, 57699
Lift Atlanta Inc, 57703
Lift Power, 57704
Lift South, 57705
Lift Truck Ctr Inc, 57706
Lift Truck of America, 57708
Liftech Equipment Co Inc, 57709
Liftow, 57710
Liftruck Service Company, 57711
Light Bulbs Unlimited, 57712
Lilly Company, 57715
Linco Caster, 57720, 57721
Lincolnwood Merchandising Company, 57724
Lingle Fork Truck Company, 57725
Lions Restaurant Equipment & Supplies, 57727
Lippert, 57728, 57729, 57730
Little Charlie's, 57733
Littleton Sales Company, 57736
Livingston Distribution Centers, 57738, 57739
LMG Group, 57588
Lo Temp Sales, 57740
Logan, 57745
Lomar Distributing Inc, 57748
Loneoak & Co, 57752
Long Island Glove & Safety Products, 57754
Long Wholesale Distr Inc, 57756
Long Wholesale Distributors, 57757
Longbottom Coffee & Tea Inc, 57758
Lorain Novelty Company, 57763
Lorenz Supply Co, 57765
Louisiana Packaging, 57772
Lowell Brothers & Bailey, 57778
Lucas Industrial, 57779
Luigi Bormioli Corporation, 57783
Lumsden Brothers, 57788
Lynard Company, 57790
Lyons Specialty Company, 57792
M & G Materials Handling Co, 57793
M Conley Co, 57799
M D Stetson Co, 57800
M Maskas & Sons Inc, 57802
M R Williams Inc, 57803
M Tucker Co Inc, 57804
M&F Foods, 57805
M&N International, 57807
M. Crews & Company, 57809
M.S. Johnston Company, 57815
Macdonald Meat Co, 57828
Machine Ice Co, 57830
Mack Restaurant Equipment & Supplies, 57831
Madison Food Sales Company, 57836
Madison Wholesale Co, 57838
Madland Toyota Lift, 57839
Maines Paper & Food Svc Inc, 57850, 57851
Maintainco Inc, 57853
Maintenance Equipment Company, 57854
Majestic Lift Truck Service, 57856
Malco Industries, 57857
Malow Corporation, 57860
Mancuso Cheese Co, 57865
Mandeville Company, 57866
Manhattan Fire Safety, 57869
Manhattan Lights, 57871
Mani Imports, 57872
Manning Brothers Food Eqpt Co, 57873
Manor Electric Supplies Light, 57874
Manting Equipment Company, 57875
Marci Enterprises, 57881
Marek Equipment Trading, 57884
Margarita Man, 57885
Mark Pack Inc, 57891
Mark-Pack Inc, 57893
Market Grocery Co, 57896
Marko Inc, 57897
Markson Lab Sales, 57898
Markuse Corporation, 57899
Martin Bros Distributing Co, 57908
Martin Brothers Wholesale, 57909
Maryland China, 57919
Mason Brothers Co, 57922
Master Chemical Products, 57924
Mat Logo Company, 57925
Matco United, 57927
Material Handling Products, 57929
Material Handling Resources, 57930
Material Handling Services, 57931
Material Handling Specialties Company, 57932
Materials Handling Enterprises, 57933
Matilija Water Company, 57935
Matthiesen Equipment, 57936
Mattingly Foods, 57937
Maybury Material Handling, 57942
Mayer Myers Paper Company, 57943
Mayfield Paper Co, 57946, 57947
Mazo-Lerch Company, 57952
Mc Call Co, 57954
McCabe's Quality Foods, 57956
Mccomas Sales Co Inc, 57970
Mccrone Microscopes & Acces, 57971
Mckinley Equipment Corp, 57977
McLane Co Inc, 57963
McLane Foodservice Inc, 57964
McLane Grocery, 57965
Mcnair & Co Inc, 57979
McShane Enterprises, 57967
Meaders Kitchen Equipment, 57981
Medley Material Handling Inc, 57991
Medley Restaurant Equipment & Supply Company, 57992
Melmart Distributors, 57996
Menu Maker Foods Inc, 57998
Merchants Distributors Inc, 58000
Merchants Foodservice, 58001
Merchants Grocery Co Inc, 58002
Meridian Supply Rstrnt Depot, 58003
Mermaid Seafoods, 58006
Merritt Handling Engineering, 58008
Merton Restaurant Equipment Company, 58009
Mesa Bearing, 58010
Messermeister, 58012
Messina Brothers Manufacturing Company, 58013
Metro Food Service Products, 58016
Metro Touch, 58017
Metro, Inc., 58018
Metro-Richelieu, 58019
MFS/York/Stormor, 57817
MGH Wholesale Grocery, 57818
Miami Industrial Trucks, 58024, 58025
Miami Plastics & Supply Corporation, 58026
Miami Wholesale Grocery Company, 58027
Michael Distributor Inc, 58028
Michael G. Brown Associates, 58029
Michaelo Espresso, 58033
Michigan Industrial Belting, 58046
Michigan Industrial Equipment Company, 58047
Michigan Orchard Supply Company, 58048
MICROS Retail Systems Inc, 57820
Mid States Paper & Notion Co, 58053
Mid-America Wholesale, 58054
Mid-Michigan Ice Company, 58056
Middendorf Meat, 58058
Midland Grocery of Michigan, 58060
Midlantic Sweetener Company, 58061
Midtown Electric Supply Corp, 58063
Midway Container Inc., 58064
Midwest Badge & Novelty Co, 58065
Midwest Fire & Safety Equipment Company, 58068
Midwest Ingredients Inc, 58072
Midwest Promotional Group, 58073
Millar-Williams Hydronics, 58081
Millbrook Distribution Services, 58082
Miller & Hartman, 58086
Minnesota Conway Fire & Safety, 58093
Minuteman Trading, 58094
Miracle Exclusives, 58095
Mitchell Grocery Corp, 58102
Mitchell Handling Systems, 58103
Mivila Foods, 58104
Mj Kellner Co, 58105
Moctezuma Foods, 58108
Modern Equipment Co, 58111
Monarch-McLaren, 58124
Montana Broom & Brush Co, 58125
Moore Equipment, 58134
Morrison Industrial Equip Co, 58145
Mortec Industries Inc, 58147
Moseley & Reece, 58150
Mosuki, 58151
Motion Savers Inc, 58154
Mountain Sales & Svc Inc, 58159
Mountain Service Distribution, 58160
Mountain View Supply, 58164
Mountain West Distributors Inc, 58165
Mountanos Family Coffee & Tea Co., 58166
MSC Industrial Direct Co Inc, 57822
Muckenthaler Inc, 58171
Multi-Counter Manufacturing Company, 58177
Multivac Inc, 58180
Munchies, 58181
Munroe Material Handling, 58183
Murk Brush Company, 58185
Murry's Family of Fine Foods, 58187
Mush & Pinsky, 58189
MVP Group, 57824
My Style, 58199
Myers Equipment Company, 58200
Myers Restaurant Supply Inc, 58201
Myers-Cox Co, 58202
Nagel Paper & Box Company, 58210
Nareg International Inc, 58219
Nass Parts & Svc Inc, 58222
National Band Saw Co, 58230
National Grocers, 58236

Wholesale Product Type / General Merchandise

National Lighting Source, 58243
National Restaurant Company, 58245
National Restaurant Supply Company, 58246
National Sales Corporation, 58248
National Scale Of New England, 58249
National Scoop & Equipment Company, 58250
National Shippng Supply Co, 58251
Nationwide Material Handling Equipment, 58252
Nature's Provision Company, 58271
Navy Brand, 58273
Near East Importing Corporation, 58274
Neelands Refrigeration, 58278
Neighbors Coffee, 58280
Nelipak, 58281
Nelson Co, 58282
New Brunswick Saw Service, 58297
New England Foods, 58298
New England Indl Truck Inc, 58299
New Vermont Creamery, 58309
New York Cash Register Company, 58310
Neway Packaging Corporation, 58313
Newman Fixture Co Inc, 58314
Newport Marketing, 58316
Newtech Beverage Systems, 58317
Newton Manufacturing Co, 58318
Niagara Restaurant Supply, 58320
Nicewonger Company, 58321
Nicholas & Co Inc, 58322
Nichols Foodservice, 58323
Nikola's Foods, 58330
Nissan Lift Of New York Inc, 58332
Norlift Inc, 58347
Norm's Refrigeration, 58348
Norman Wolff Associates, 58349
Norpaco Inc, 58352
North American Corp, 58353
North West Handling Systems Inc, 58363
Northbay Restaurant Equipment & Design, 58364
Northern Steel Industrie, 58370
Northland Industrial Truck Company Inc, 58372
Northwest Deli Distribution, 58379
Northwest Forklift, 58380
Norvell Fixtures & Equipment Company, 58386
Nott Company, 58388
Nourishtea, 58389
Novick Brothers Corp, 58391
Nuco Industries, 58394
Nylon Net Company, 58409
O-Sesco, 58412
Oak Barrel Winecraft, 58421
OCS Process Systems, 58416
OH Armstrong, 58417
Ohio Conveyor & Supply Inc, 58438
Ohio Materials Handling, 58440
Ohio Rack Inc, 58441
Olympic Juicer Company, 58453
Omcan Manufacturing & Distributing Company, 58454
Omni Material Handling Services, 58458
One-Shot, 58461
Ono International, 58463
Ontario Glove and Safety Products, 58464
Oram Material Handling Systems, 58468
Orange Distributors, 58469
Orear Company, 58471
Oreck Commercial Sales, 58472
Orlando Fire Equipment Company, 58480
Ostrow Jobbing Company, 58487
Oswalt Restaurant Supply, 58488
Ottenheimer Equipment Company, 58489
Overhead Door Company of Fort Wayne, 58494
P & D Corp, 58500
Paar Physica USA, 58523
Pacific Compactor Corporation, 58528
Pacific Steam Equipment, Inc., 58534
Packaging Equipment Company, 58539
Packaging Services Corp, 58540
Packsource Systems, 58541
Pacmatic/Ritmica, 58542
Paisano Distribution Company, 58546
Palm Brothers, 58550
Palmer Associates, 58551
Palmer Jack M, 58554
Palmer Wholesale Inc, 58555
Palmetto Candy & Tobacco Company, 58556
Pamex Packaging, 58558
Pamida, 58559
Pan American Papers Inc, 58560
Pap,, 58567
Paper & Chemical Supply Company, 58564
Papercraft, 58565
Paradise Products, 58569
Paragon Food Equipment, 58570
Paramount Products, 58574
Paramount Restaurant Supply Company, 58575
Parker Wholesale Paper Co, 58581
Parkway Systems, 58583
Parr-Mac Sales Company, 58584
Parson Food Sales, 58585
Parsons Green, 58586
Parts Depot, Inc., 58587
Partytime Machines Rental, 58588
Pate-Derby Company, 58592
Patterson Buckeye, 58596
Payless Foodservice, 58604
PDE Technology Corp, 58516
Peach State Material Handling, 58607
Peas, 58608
Pelco Equipment, 58610
Pelco Refrigeration Sales, 58611
Pelican Bay Ltd., 58612
Pendergast Safety Equipment Co, 58617
Pennwell Belting Company, 58622
Pensacola Restaurant Supply Company, 58626
Peoples Woods & Charcoal, 58627
Performance Foodservice, 58640, 58641, 58642, 58643, 58644, 58645, 58646, 58647, 58648, 58649, 58650, 58651, 58652, 58653, 58654, 58655, 58656, 58657, 58658, 58659, 58660, 58661, 58662, 58663, 58664, 58665, 58666, 58667, 58668, 58669, 58670, 58671, 58672, 58673, 58674, 58675, 58676
Perry Videx LLC, 58680
Peyton's, 58690
Pharaoh Trading Company, 58691
Phil Erb Refrigeration Inc, 58694
Phillips Supply Co, 58697
Piedmont Clarklift, 58704
Piedmont Plastics Inc, 58705
Pierceton Foods Inc, 58707
Pioneer Distributing Co, 58712
Pioneer Distributing Company, 58713
Pioneer Lift Truck, 58714
Pioneer Marketing, 58716
Pioneer Sales Co Inc, 58717
Pippin Wholesale Co, 58718
Pizza Products, 58721
Pk Crown Distributing Inc, 58722
Plaidberry Company, 58723
Plasco Safety Products, 58725
Polar Bear, 58732
Pop's E-Z Popcorn & Supply Company, 58741
Poppers Supply Company, 58742
Port Royal Tapes, 58747
Porter Wallace Corporation, 58749
Portuguese United Grocer Co-Op, 58752
Positive Impressions, 58754
Post Food Service, 58757
Power Lift Corporation, 58762
Power Pumps, 58763
Power Source Distributors, 58764
Precision Pours, 58767
Preiser Scientific Inc, 58769
Premier Foodservice Distributors of America, 58771
Premiere Refreshment Svc, 58774
Presentations, 58777
Pressure King Inc, 58778
Prestolite Electric Inc, 58781
Pride Equipment Corp, 58785
Pridgen Bros Co, 58786
Pro Plus Cleaning Products, 58795
Production Packaging & Processing Equipment Company, 58802
Productos Familia, 58803
Professional Food Systems, 58806
Professional Marketing Group, 58808
Professional Materials Hndlng, 58809
Proficient Food Company, 58811
Progressive Handling Systems, 58814
Proin, 58815
Prolift Industrial Equipment, 58816
Promotions Ink, 58817
ProSource, 58796
Pueblo Trading Co Inc, 58825
Puro Water Group, 58835
Putnam Group, 58837
PYA/Monarch, 58520
Pyramid Packaging, Inc, 58840
Quail Crest Foods, 58844
Quaily Storage Products Inc, 58845
Quality Equipment Marketing, 58852
Quality Foods, 58856
Quality Foods International, 58857
Quality Groceries, 58858
Quality Material Handling, 58859
Quality Wholesale Produce Co, 58862
Quandt's Foodservice Distributors, 58864
Quantum Supply Company, 58865
Quick Servant Co, 58872
Quick Stamp & Sign Mfg, 58873
Quinn Co, 58874
Quinn Lift, 58875
R D Smith Co, 58880
R L Spear Co, 58883
R S Braswell Co Inc, 58884
R S Stern Inc, 58886
R W Smith & Co, 58888
R&F International Corporation, 58891
R&R Equipment Company, 58894
R&R Mill Company, 58895
R&R Sales Company, 58896
R.H. Forschner, 58901
R.L. Corty & Company, 58902
R.S. Somers Company, 58905
R.W. Davis Oil Company, 58907
Rabco Foodservice, 58917
Rack Service Company, 58918
Rainbow Foods, 58919
Rainbow Promotions LLC, 58921
Ralph Jones Display & Store, 58926
Ramco Innovations Inc, 58929
Ramex Foods, 58930
Ranch Foods Direct, 58932
Randy's Frozen Meats, 58934
Rapid Sales Company, 58937
Rapids Wholesale Equipment, 58938
Raymond, 58942
Raymond Handling Solutions, 58944
Rbm Co, 58946
Rebstock Conveyors, 58953
Reese & Long Refrigeration, 58962
Refrigeration & Food Eqpt Inc, 58963
Refrigeration Equipment, 58964
Regal Distributing Company, 58965, 58966
Regal Supply & Chemical Company, 58967, 58968
Regez Cheese Company, 58970
Reinhart Foodservice LLC, 58972
Reliable Fire Equipment, 58973
Reliable Fire Protection, 58974
Renaissance International, 58978
Reno Forklift Inc, 58979
Resco Restaurant & Store Equip, 58981
Rescue Earth, 58982
Residex, 58984
ResourceNet International, 58985
Restaurant Depot, 58986, 58987
Restaurant Designs Development, 58989
Restaurant Supply, 58991
Retail Data Systems Of Omaha, 58992
Rex Chemical Corporation, 58993
Richard's Restaurant Supply, 59001
Richmond Restaurant Svc, 59002
Richmond Supply Company, 59003
Richter Distributing Company, 59005
Rigel Trading Corporation, 59008
RightWay Foods, 59009
Rimfire Imports, 59011
Ritchie Grocer Co, 59014
Ritchie's Foods, 59015
Rivard Power Lift, 59016
Riverside Paper Supply, 59019
Riverside Refrigeration Air Conditioning, 59020
Robby Midwest, 59025
Robert Chermak & Associates, 59026
Robert D. Arnold & Associates, 59028
Robert's Foods Company, 59032
Roberts-Boice Paper Company, 59034
Robinson Marketing Associates, 59040
Robinson Steel Company, 59041
Rochester Midland Corporation, 59043
Rock Valley Oil & Chemical Co, 59046
Rockland Foodservice, 59049
Rocky Produce Inc, 59051
Roden Electrical Supply Company, 59053
Roll-O-Sheets Canada, 59058
Roma Food Svc Of Arizona, 59060
Roma of Minnesota, 59061
Rondo Inc, 59064
Rosa Food Products, 59065
Rosito & Bisani Imports Inc, 59071
Ross Elevator Supply, 59072
Roundy's Inc, 59075
Rowland Coffee Roasters Inc., 59077
Royal Accoutrements, 59079
Royal Broom & Mop Factory Inc, 59082
Royal Crown Enterprises, 59083
Royal Cup Coffee, 59084
Royal Doulton Canada, 59085
Royal Industries Inc, 59089
RPM Material Handling, 58912
RPM Material Handling Company/Clarklift San Diego, 58913
RTR Packaging, 58915
Russell Food Equipment Limited, 59096
Ryans Wholesale Food Distributors, 59101
S & R Products, 59104
S & S Indl Maintenance, 59105
S W Betz Co Inc, 59109
S-A-J Distributors, 59115
S. Abraham & Son, 59116
S.W. Meat & Provision Company, 59122
Saf-T-Gard International Inc, 59136
Safe-Stride Southern, 59138
Safeco Electric & True Value, 59139
Safety Wear, 59140
Safian & Associates, 59141
Sagaya Corp, 59142
Sam Cohen & Sons, 59157
Sam Wylde Flour Company, 59162
Sam's Cakes, Cookies, Candy, 59163
Sam's Club, 59164
Sambonet USA, 59166
Sampson Miller Advertising Inc., 59169
San-Bay Co, 59176
Sanarak Paper & Popcorn Supply, 59177
Santa Barbara Merchant Svc Inc, 59187
Santa Claus Industries, 59188
Santa Cruz Horticultural Supply, 59189
Sarver Candy Co, 59193
Saval Foods Corp, 59199
Savol Pools, 59201
Saxony Equipment Distributors, 59202
Scandicrafts Inc, 59203
Scardina Refrigeration Co., 59204
Scheidelman, 59207
Schenck Foods Co, 59208

1257

Wholesale Product Type / General Merchandise

Schermerhorn Brothers & Co, 59210
Schoenberg Salt Co, 59217
Schultz Sav-O-Stores, 59218
Schwab Paper Products Co, 59220
Scott & Associates, 59224
Scott Lift Truck Corporation, 59225
SCR Total Bar Control Systems, 59125
Scranton Fish Company, 59226
Sealer Sales Inc, 59251
Segal's Wholesale, 59259
Seitz Gift Fruit, 59260
Sellers Equipment Inc, 59263
Serv-A-Rack, 59268
Serv-Tek, 59269
Serve Canada Food Equipment, 59270
Service Handling Equipment Company, 59271
Service Sales Corporation, 59273
Shaheen Bros Inc, 59282
Shaklee Distributor, 59283
Shamrock Foods Co, 59287, 59288
Shannon Diversified Inc, 59293
Sharpe Valves, 59296
Shaw Equipment Company, 59297
Shean Equipment Company, 59298
Sheehan Majestic, 59299
Sheffield Platers Inc, 59300
Shelving Rack Systems Inc, 59302
Shenandoah Industrial Rubber, 59305
Sherwood Food Distributors, 59310
Shetakis Foodservice, 59318
Shiff & Goldman Foods, 59319
Shippers Supply, 59320, 59321
Shippers Supply, Labelgraphic, 59322
Shivji Enterprises, 59324
Shoppa's Material Handling, 59328
Shore Distribution Resources, 59329
Shryack-Hirst Grocery Company, 59331
Shur-Az Inc, 59334
Siegmeister Sales & Service, 59344
Silverstar Foodservice Supply, 59349
Singer Equipment Co Inc, 59361
Sirca Foodservice, 59365
Sisu Group Inc, 59368
Skarnes Inc, 59369
Skiles Co Inc, 59372
Slusser Wholesale Company, 59381
Smile Enterprises, 59383
Smith & Greene Company, 59384, 59385
Smith Restaurant Supply Co, 59387
Smith, Bob, Restaurant Equipment, 59388
Smokey Mountain Grill, 59393
Smoothie's Frozen Desserts, 59394
Snappy Popcorn, 59399
SnowBird Corporation, 59403
So Cal Material Handling, 59406
Sobey's Ontario, 59408
Sobeys Inc, 59411, 59412, 59413, 59414, 59415
Socafe, 59416
Soda Service, 59417
Source Naturals, 59430
South Jersey Paper Products, 59432
Southeast Industrial Equipment, 59436
Southeastern Grocers, 59438
Southern Culture Foods, 59439
Southern Glazer's Wine-Spirits, LLC, 59441
Southern Indiana Butcher's Supply, 59444
Southern Material Handling Co, 59445
Southern States Toyotalift, 59449
Southern Steel Shelving Company, 59450
Southern Supplies Limited, 59452
Southline Equipment Company, 59454
Southwest Distributing Co, 59457
Southwest Forklift, 59458
Southwest Lift, 59459
Southwest Material Handling, 59460
Southwest Thermal Technology, 59462
Southwest Traders, 59463
Sovrana Trading Corp, 59469
Soylent, 59470
Space Maker Systems, 59471
Spantec Systems, 59472
Spar Mixers, 59473
SpartanNash Co, 59478
Specialized Promotions, 59479
Specialty Box & Packaging, 59480
Specialty Merchandise Distributors, 59483
Spener Restaurant Design, 59484
Sphinx Adsorbents Inc, 59486
Spice & Spice, 59487
Spiral Biotech Inc, 59489
Sprinkman Corporation, 59494
ST Restaurant Supplies, 59129
St. Cloud Restaurant Supply, 59501
St. Ours & Company, 59503
Stack & Store Systems, 59505
Stahl, 59506
Stainless Equipment & Systems, 59507
Standard Electric Time, 59509
Standard Forms, 59510
Standard Meat Co LP, 59512
Standard-Rosenbaum, 59514
Stanford Trading Company, 59515
Star Restaurant Equipment & Supply Company, 59527
Star Sales Company, 59528, 59529
State Restaurant Equipment Co, 59538
State Wholesale Grocers, 59539
Statex, 59542
Stay Tuned Industries, 59546
Steel City Corporation, 59549
Sterling Promotional Corporation, 59557
Sterling Scale Co, 59558
Stevenson Co, 59560
Stewart & Stevenson LLC, 59562
Stewart Wholesale Hardware Company, 59563
Stewarts Tristate Svc Co, 59564, 59565
Stigler Supply Co, 59566
Stiles Enterprises Inc, 59567
Stock America Inc, 59568
Stock Rack & Shelving Inc, 59569
Stoffel Equipment Co Inc, 59571
Stonyfield Organic, 59574
STOP Restaurant Supply Ltd, 59131
Storage Equipment, 59576
Strasheim Wholesale, 59577
Streich Equipment Co Inc, 59582
Summertime Restaurant Equipment, 59596
Summit Food Service Distributors, 59597
Summit Import Corp, 59599
Sunbelt Industrial Trucks, 59607
Sunderland Dispensing Service, 59612
Sunflower Restaurant Supply, 59614
SunRidge Farms, 59606
Sunset of Queens, 59619
Sunshine Bar Supply Company, 59620
Superior Lamp, 59634
Superior Paper & Plastic Co, 59636
SUPERVALU Distribution, 59132
Supply One, 59641
Supply One Inc, 59642
Supreme Fixture Company, 59643
Supreme Foods, 59645
Swift Chemical & Supplies Inc, 59661
Switzer's Inc, 59666
T D Refrigeration Inc, 59746
T. Baker Restaurant Equipment, 59749
T.C. Food Export/Import Company, 59753
T.C.P. Restaurant Supply, 59754
T.M. Patterson Paper Box Company, 59758
T.S.A. Distributing, 59759
Tablemate Products, 59767
Tama Trading Co Inc, 59772
Tape & Label Engineering, 59780
Tape Tools, 59781
Tapp Label Technologies Inc, 59782
Taylor Freezer Equipment Corporation, 59790
Taylor Freezers, 59791
Taylor Ultimate Svc Co, 59793
Taylor-Fortune Distributors, 59794
TBI Corporation, 59761
TCD Parts, 59763
Tec Products Co Inc, 59797
Tech Sales Inc, 59799
Tee's Plus, 59802
Teletec Cash Register Company, 59804
Tergerson's Fine Foods, 59807
Tesdall & Associates, 59814
Texas Hotel & Restaurant Equipment, 59819
Texas Marine II, 59820
Theatre Candy Distributing Company, 59837
Third Planet Products, 59838
Thomas & Howard Co, 59840
Thomas & Howard Co Cash & Crry, 59841
Thomas Ice Cream, 59844
Thomas W. MacKay & Son, 59847
Thompson & Johnson Equipment, 59848
Thompson & Little, 59849
Thomson Groceries Ltd., 59851
Ths Foodservice, 59855
Thunderbird Food Machinery, 59856
Thurston Foods Inc, 59858
Time & Alarm Systems, 59864
Timely Signs Inc, 59866
Tinkels, 59868
Tips Uniform, 59870
To-Am Equipment Company, 59872
Toastmasters International, 59873
Tom's Evergreen Broom Manufacturing, 59875
Tomsed Corporation, 59878
Top of the Table, 59884
Topac, 59885
Tor Rey Refrigeration Inc, 59888
Total Beverage Systems, 59894
Total Lift Equipment Company, 59895
Total Liquor Controls, 59896
Toudouze Market Company, 59897
Town & Country Wholesale, 59901
Toyota Forklifts Of Atlanta, 59903
Toyota Material Handling, 59904, 59905, 59906
Toyotalift Inc, 59907
Trade Diversified, 59908
Tradelink, 59909
Trader Joe's, 59910
Trans Veyor, 59911
Treasure Coast Coffee Company, 59914
Trendco Supply, 59922
Trent Valley Distributors Ltd., 59923
Tri Mark United East, 59927
Tribest Corp, 59934
Trident Food Svc, 59935
Trifactor Systems LLC, 59937
Triple Cities Material Handling, 59940
Triple F, 59941
Tuckahoe Manufacturing Co, 59958
Tufco Technologies Inc, 59963
Turk Brothers Custom Meats Inc, 59966
Tusco Grocers Inc, 59970
Tvc Wholesale Inc, 59972
Twenty Four Hour Security Services, 59974
Twin City Wholesale, 59976
Tyler Supply Co, 59979
Tynan Equipment, 59980
Unted Rental, 59999
Ultimate Foods, 60001
Uni Co Supply, 60004
Unilever US, 60009
Union Grocery Company, 60011
UniPro Foodservice, Inc., 60005
United Bakers & Deli Supply, 60014
United Chairs, 60016
United Dairy Machinery Corp, 60018
United Forklift Corporation, 60021
United Glassware & China, 60022
United Lighting & Supply Co, 60024
United Machinery & Supply Company, 60025
United Rentals, 60032
United Restaurant Equipment Co, 60033
United Wholesale Grocery Company, 60040
Univar USA, 60043
Universal Marketing, 60045
Universal Restaurant Equipment, 60048
Universal Sanitizers & Supplies, 60049
Universal Sodexho, 60050
Uniwell Systems, 60051
Upper Lakes Foods Inc, 60053
US Foods Inc, 59987, 59988, 59989, 59990, 59991
US Growers Cold Storage, 59993
US Marketing Company, 59994
US Materials Handling Corp, 59995
Us Plastics, 60056
UVA Packaging, 59997
V&B Distributing, 60057
V-Suarez Provisions, 60058
VacuWest, 60064
Valley Distributing Company, 60070
Van Eerden Foodservice Co Inc, 60077
Van Waters & Rogers, 60080
Vaughn Packing Company, 60085
Vaughn-Russell Candy Kitchen, 60086
VBS Inc Material Handling, 60060
Venture Packaging & Distribution, 60093
Venus Supply Company, 60094
Veritiv Corp, 60096
Victel Service Co, 60104
Victorinox Swiss Army Inc, 60105
Victory Packaging, 60107
VIP Food Svc, 60061
Virginia Wholesale Company, 60120
Vistar Northwest, 60128
Vivitar Security Systems, 60138
Vogel, 60140
Vollwerth & Baroni Companies, 60141
Voorhees Rubber Mfg Co, 60144
Voss Equipment Inc, 60145
VWR Funding Inc, 60063
W A DeHart Inc, 60148
W B Stockton & Co Inc, 60150
W. Braun Company, 60154
W. Braun Packaging Canada, 60155
W.A. Tayloe Company, 60157
W.L. Petrey Wholesale Inc., 60164
W.S. Lee & Sons, 60172
WACO Beef & Pork Processors, 60174
WACO Filtering, 60175
Wadden Systems, 60188
Wakefern Food Corp, 60193
Wakefield Sales Inc, 60194
Walton & Post, 60210
Walton's Inc, 60211
Warehouse Equipment Inc, 60213
Warehouse Systems Inc, 60214
Warren E. Conley Corporation, 60215
Warren Southwest Rfrdgrtn, 60216
Wasserstrom Co, 60218
Watson Distributing, 60223
WATTS Equipment Co, 60176
We're Full of Promotions, 60228
Weber Scientific Inc, 60232
Wechsler Coffee Corporation, 60233
Weeke Wholesale Company, 60234
Wega USA, 60235
Welch Equipment Co Inc, 60236
Welton Rubber Co, 60237
Werres Corp, 60238
Wes Design - Supply Company, 60239
WESCO, 60177, 60178
WESCO Distribution Inc, 60179, 60180
West Bay Sales, 60243
West Coast Supplies, 60247
West Wholesale Grocery, 60250
Westcoast Engineering Company, 60253
Westerbeke Fishing Gear Co Inc, 60254
Western Carolina Forklift Inc, 60255
Western Family Foods Inc, 60256
Western Grocers, 60257
Western Soap Company, 60260
Western Steel & Wire, 60261
Westland Marketing, 60262
Wetoska Packaging Distributors, 60265
WG Thompson & Sons, 60181

Wholesale Product Type / Health Food

Whitaker Brothers, 60272
White Cap Construction Supply, 60273
White House Chemical Supply, 60276
White Plains Electrical Light, 60277
Whitley Wholesale Grocery, 60282
Wholesale Restaurant Equipment, 60285
Wholesale Restaurant Supply, 60286
Wholesale Tool Company, 60287
Wichita Restaurant Supl Co Inc, 60292
Wiese Planning & Engineering, 60295
Wilcox Paper Co, 60297
Wilkens-Anderson Co, 60302
Williams Food Equipment Company, 60309
Williams Institutional Foods, 60310
Willing Group, 60315
Willow Group LTD, 60316
Willow Run Foods Inc, 60317
Willy Nilly At Home, 60318
Wilson Ice Machines, 60319
Winchester Food, 60320
Winn-Dixie, 60334
Wins Paper Products, 60336
Wiper Supply & Chemical, 60338
Wisconsin Allied Products Inc, 60339
Wise Forklift Inc, 60341
Wisner Manufacturing Corporation, 60345
Witmer Foods, 60346
WMF/USA, 60183
Wood Fruitticher Grocery Company, 60350
World Kitchen, 60358
World Tableware Inc, 60360
Wrenn Handling, 60364
Wusthoff Trident Cutlery, 60367
Xtreme Beverages, LLC, 60369
Yale Industrial Trucks, 60372
Yale Industrial Trucks: Ontario, 60373
Yale Material Handling/Gammon, 60374
Yorktown Electrical & Lighting, 60379
Z T Merchandising Inc, 60385
ZAK Designs Inc, 60387
Zeches Institution Supply, 60393
Zellerbach, 60396
Zinter Handling Inc, 60401
Zuckerman Honickman Inc, 60404

Health Food

A Better Way, 54513
A Plus Marketing, 54522
A&D Distributors, 54527
A&M Enterprises, 54532
A.B. Wise & Sons, 54548
Acatris USA, 54598
Adonis Health Products, 54631
Adventure Foods, 54638
Adventure Inn Food Trading Company, 54639
AIDP Inc, 54575
Aim This Way, 54657
Alchemie USA Inc., 54681
Alfa Chem, 54687
Alternative Health & Herbs, 54745
Amrita Snacks, 54811
Amster-Kirtz Co, 54812
Anthracite Provision Co, 54840
Aragadz Foods Corporation, 54853
Atwater Foods, 54928
Auromere Inc, 54932
Austrade, 54937
Automation Systems & Services, 54941
Ayush Herbs Inc, 54952
Aztec Secret Health & Beauty, 54953
B/R Sales Company, 54980
Bakery Things, 55026
Barlean's Fisheries, 55062
Basic Organics, 55076
Bergin Fruit & Nut Co., 55171
Berlin Packaging, 55174
Bernard Jensen Intl, 55180
Better Health Products, 55203
BI Nutraceuticals, 54986
Bisek & Co Inc, 55235

Bishop Brothers, 55236
BMT Commodity Corporation, 54989
BNG Enterprises, 54990
BOSS, 54991
Bottom Line Foods, 55297
British Aisles, 55340
Caesar Electric Supply, 55459
Canada Pure Water Company Ltd, 55492
Capitol Foods, 55510
CarbRite Diet, 55522
Chameleon Beverage Co Inc, 55619
Chas. Wetterling & Sons, 55629
Christopher's Herb Shop, 55679
Claremont Herbal Health, 55702
Clif Bar & Co, 55718
Commodities Assistance Corporation, 55777
Costco Wholesale Corporation, 55852
Cotati Brand Eggs & Food Svc, 55853
Country Life Foods, 55859
Crown O'Maine Organic Cooperative, 55892
D&E Pharmaceuticals, 55936
D.A. Colongeli & Sons, 55943
Deep Foods Inc, 56015
Diamond Nutrition, 56056
Dipasa USA Inc, 56075
Distribution Kowloon, 56084
Distribution Plus, 56085
DKW International Nutrition Company, 55949
DPI Rocky Mountain, 55955
Dr. John's Candies, 56131
Dr. Smoothie Brands, 56132
Dutra Distributing, 56159
DW Montgomery & Company, 55958
Ecological Formulas, 56221
Ecuadorian Rainforest LLC, 56228
Eden, 56230
Edom Labs Inc, 56235
Ehrlich Food Co, 56248
Elco Fine Foods, 56254
Ener-G Foods, 56290
English Honey Farms, 56293
Esteem Products, 56329
Euclid Fish Co, 56333
F B Mc Fadden Wholesale Co, 56361
Fab Inc, 56372
Fadler Company, 56374
Falcon Trading Intl Corp, 56380
Family Foods Home Service, 56382
Federated Cooperative, 56399
Ferris Organic Farms, 56410
Fitness & Nutrition Center, 56447
Five Continents, 56448
Food City, 56490
Foster Dairy Farms Inc, 56527
Four Today, 56531
Frontier Co-op, 56577
Fruit d'Or, 56587
Fullway International, 56591
Garden Spot Distributors, 56637
Garuda International, 56641
Garvey Nut & Candy, 56642
GB Enterprises, 56608
Generichem Corporation, 56661
Giant Eagle American Seaway Foods, 56677
Gillco Ingredients, 56679
Giovanni Food Co Inc, 56688
Global Botanical, 56692
Global Marketing Assoc, 56694
GMZ Inc, 56615
Golden Moon Tea, 56718
Gopal's Healthfoods, 56729
Govadinas Fitness Foods, 56755
Great American Health Bar, 56772
Great American Popcorn Works of Pennsylvania, 56773
Great Basin Botanicals, 56775
Green Gold Group LLC, 56798
GSC Enterprises Inc., 56617
GWB Foods Corporation, 56620
Hain Food Group, 56877
Hanif's International Foods, 56900

Harpak-Ulma, 56933
Harry's Premium Snacks, 56942
Harvest Health Foods, 56948
Haynes Brothers Candy Company, 56967
Healing Garden, 56969
Health Flavors, 56971
Health Food Distributors, 56972
Health Guardians, 56973
Health King Enterprise, 56974
Healthmate Products, 56977
Holistic Horizons/Halcyon Pacific Corporation, 57041
Holistic Products Corporation, 57042
Home-Like Food Company, 57052
Homestead Foods, 57053
Honey Acres, 57054
House of Spices, 57067
Husky Foods of Anchorage, 57094
ID Foods Corporation, 57109
Ingenuities, 57157
Ingersoll & Assoc, 57158
Inno-Vite, 57163
International Enterprises Unlimited, 57187
International Pack & Ship, 57192
InterNatural Foods, 57174
Jarrow Formulas Inc, 57315
Jeris Health & Nutrition, 57333
Jetro Cash & Carry Inc, 57344
JoDaSa Group International, 57353
Joey's Fine Foods, 57361
Joyce Foods, 57402
Kadouri International Foods, 57434
KeHE Distributors, 57458
Kemach Food Products, 57480
Kenshin Trading Corp, 57488
KYD Inc, 57432
LA Lifestyle Nutritional Products, 57581
Levant, 57682
LivBar, 57737
Lombardi Brothers Meat Packers, 57749
Lovion International, 57776
M.K. Health Food Distributors, 57814
Madison Food Sales Company, 57836
Madys Company, 57840
Maine Coast Sea Vegetables, 57846
Maple Hollow, 57878
Marin Hydroponics, 57889
Marriott Distribution Service, 57903
Maxim's Import Corporation, 57938
McCoy's Products, 57957
Mcdonald Wholesale Co, 57973
Meadow Farm Foods, 57983
Michigan Agricultural Commdty, 58036
Michigan Agricultural Commodities Inc, 58037
Michigan Agriculture Commodities, 58038, 58039, 58040, 58041, 58042, 58043, 58044
Mid America Food Sales, 58051
Midori Trading Inc, 58062
Midwest Ingredients Inc, 58072
Mivila Foods, 58104
More For Less Foods, 58138
Mother Earth Enterprises, 58152
Mountain People's Warehouse, 58157
Mountain Service Distribution, 58160
Mountain Valley Water Company, 58163
MTC Distributing, 57823
Munchies, 58181
Natrol Inc, 58255
Natural Balance, 58256
Natural Dairy Products Corp, 58259
Natural Food Systems, 58261
Natural Foods Inc, 58262
Natural Group, 58263
Nature Distributors, 58265
Nature's Best, 58266
Navitas Naturals, 58272
Neighbors Coffee, 58280
Nelipak, 58281
Neshaminy Valley Natural Foods, 58286
NeuRoast, 58288
New Britain Candy Company, 58296
New Hope Imports, 58302

Nicky USA Inc, 58325
North American Provisioners, 58354
Northern WIS Produce Co, 58371
Nspired Natural Foods, 58392
Nuherbs Company, 58395
Nui Foods, 58396
Nutraceutical International, 58397
Nutri-Rich Corp., 58399
NutriCology Allergy Research, 58400
Nutriscience Laboratories, 58402
OHCO/Oriental Herb Company, 58418
Oklahoma Pecan Co, 58443
Omega-Life, 58456
Onnit Labs, 58462
Optimum Nutrition, 58465
Optipure, 58475
Ortho-Molecular Products Inc, 58483
Ozark Cooperative Warehouse, 58497
Pacific Resources, 58530
Paradise Island Foods, 58568
PAT Vitamins Inc, 58514
Penn Herb Co, 58619
Pharmachem Labs, 58692
Phat Fudge, 58693
Phyto-Technologies, 58701
Poiret International, 58731
Portuguese United Grocer Co-Op, 58752
Power Source Distributors, 58764
Premier Foodservice Distributors of America, 58771
Prince of Peace, 58792
Proacec USA, 58797
Proficient Food Company, 58811
Progenix Corporation, 58812
Pronatura USA, 58818
Pulmuone Foods USA Inc., 58827
Pulse Plus, 58828
Puro Water Group, 58835
Quaker Window Products Co, 58846
Queensboro Farm Products, 58870
R.E. Diamond, 58899
Ra-Bob International, 58916
Rainbow Natural Foods, 58920
Really Raw Honey Company, 58952
Red Rose Trading Company, 58957
Reinhart Foodservice LLC, 58972
Restaurant Depot, 58987
Rex Pacific, 58994
Rise Bar, 59013
RPM Total Vitality, 58914
S L Sanderson Co, 59106
S&M Produce Company, 59111
Sahadi Fine Foods Inc, 59144
Sampac Enterprises, 59168
Samuel Wells & Company, 59170
Sea Change Seafoods, 59228
Seltzer Chemicals, 59264
Shaklee Distributor, 59283
Shiff & Goldman Foods, 59319
Sid Alpers Organic Sales Company, 59335
Soofer Co, 59426
Source Naturals, 59430
Southern Import Distributors, 59443
Soylent, 59470
St John's Botanicals, 59499
Starbruck Foods Corporation, 59533
Stella Maria's, 59554
STI International, 59130
Stryka Botanical Co, 59586
Stryka Botanics, 59587, 59588
Sun Chlorella USA, 59600
SunRidge Farms, 59606
Sunshine Farms, 59621
Suntec Power, 59625
Super Natural Distributors, 59628
Super Nutrition Distributors, 59629
Supreme Foods, 59645
T.C. Food Export/Import Company, 59753
T.S.A. Distributing, 59759
Takeda Vitamin & Food, 59770
Tcheru Enterprises, 59796
The Coconut Cooperative, LLC, 59825
Third Planet Products, 59838

1259

Wholesale Product Type / Produce

This Bar Saves Lives, LLC, 59839
Trans Veyor, 59911
Tree of Life Canada, 59917, 59918, 59919, 59920
TruBrain, 59952
Tucson Coop. Warehouse, 59960
Turtle Island Herbs, 59969
United Foods & Fitness, 60020
United Natural Foods Inc, 60027
United Noodles, 60028
Universal Nutrition, 60046
Universal Preservachem Inc, 60047
US Food Products, 59984
US Growers Cold Storage, 59993
Vale Enterprises, 60066
Vaughn-Russell Candy Kitchen, 60086
VetriTech Laboratories, 60102
Vital 18, 60131
Vitamin Power, 60133
Vivion Inc, 60137
VMC Corp, 60062
West Bay Sales, 60243
Western Family Foods Inc, 60256
Whaley Pecan Co Inc, 60267
Whole Life Nutritional Supplements, 60283
Wilke International Inc, 60301
William E. Martin & Sons Company, 60307
Willing Group, 60315
Wine Country Chef LLC, 60325
Winmix/Natural Care Products, 60333
Woodland Foods, 60353
World Finer Foods Inc, 60357
Zeches Institution Supply, 60393

Produce

5280 Produce, 54505
A Dattilo Fruit Co, 54516
A J Rinella Co Inc, 54519
A&J Produce Corporation, 54531
A. Berkowitz & Company, 54539
A. Bohrer, 54540
A. De LaChevrotiere, 54541
A. Gagliano Co Inc, 54543
A. Simos & Company, 54546
A. Visconti Company, 54547
A.B. Wise & Sons, 54548
A.L. Verna Company, 54555
ACC Distributors Inc, 54567
Ace Endico Corp, 54603
Adams Wholesale Co, 54621
AeroFarms, 54643
AJC International, 54578
Akin & Porter Produce Inc, 54661
Al Campisano Fruit Company, 54663
Alabama Food Group, 54666
Albert Guarnieri & Co, 54674
Alderiso Brothers, 54682
Aliquippa Fruit Market, 54692
Allendale Produce Plant, 54718
Alwan & Sons, 54748
American Banana Company, 54759
American Farms Produce, 54763
American Frozen Foods, 54771
American Produce Company, 54787
Andrew & Williamson Sales Co, 54824
Angel's Produce, 54827
Angelo M. Formosa Foods, 54828
Annapolis Produce & Restaurant, 54834
Anthony Marano Co Inc, 54838
Anthracite Provision Co, 54840
Anton-Argires, 54841
Arctic Star Distributing, 54859
Asanti Distributors, 54887
Associated Food Stores Inc, 54899
Associated Grocers, 54900
Associated Wholesale Grocers, 54902
Atwater Foods, 54928
Auster Company, 54935
Automation Systems & Services, 54941
Awe Sum Organics, 54946
B & M Provision Co, 54962
B Giambrone & Co, 54967

B. Calalani Produce Company, 54974
Badger Wholesale Company, 55002
Bakker Produce, 55028
Banana Distributing Company, 55043
Bandwagon Brokerage, 55045
Barkett Fruit Company, 55061
Barr Packing Company, 55066
Bassham Institutional Foods, 55078
Bay Baby Produce, 55088
Bay Cities Produce Co Inc, 55089
Bayou Food Distributors, 55097
Bear Creek Operations, 55103
Belair Produce Co Inc, 55117
Belleharvest Sales Inc, 55127
Belli Produce Company, 55128
Ben E. Keith, 55133, 55134, 55135, 55136, 55137, 55138, 55139, 55140, 55141, 55142, 55143
Ben H. Roberts Produce, 55162
Bensinger's, 55167
Benson's Wholesale Fruit, 55168
Bergin Fruit & Nut Co., 55171
Best Market, 55198
BI-LO, 54987
Big Horn Co-Op Tire Shop, 55214
Birdsong Peanuts, 55232
Black Diamond Fruit & Produce, 55240
Black's Barbecue, 55241
Blondie's, 55251
Blue Mountain Meats Inc., 55261
Bosco Food Service, 55287
Bosgraaf Sales Company, 55288
Braman Fruit Company, 55315
Brenham Wholesale Groc Co Inc, 55324
Brings Co, 55338
Bronx Butter & Egg Company, 55349
Brooks Tropicals Inc, 55355
Buak Fruit Company, 55369
Burnand & Company, 55395
Buster Lind Produce Company, 55400
Butte Produce Company, 55402
Buz's Crab, 55404
C & R Food Svc Inc, 55412
C A Curtze, 55417
C D Hartnett Co, 55418
C H Robinson Worldwide Inc, 55419
C. Eberle Sons Company, 55426
C.T. Grasso, 55433
Cactus Holdings Inc, 55455
Cal-West Produce, 55471
California Sprout & Celery, 55479
Callif Foods, 55483
Canada Safeway, 55493
Canon Potato Company, 55497
Capital City Fruit, 55506
Capitol City Produce, 55509
Capitol Foods, 55510
Carbonella & Desarbo Inc, 55523
Carden Foods Inc, 55525
Caribbean Produce Exchange, 55529
Carnival Fruit, 55536
Carolina Produce, 55545
Cash-Wa Distributing, 55564, 55565
Casso Guerra & Company, 55570
Cataract Foods, 55576
Cauble & Field, 55578
Cavazos Candy, Produce & Groceries, 55581
Central Oklahoma Produce Services, 55593
Century 21 Products, 55600
Certco Inc., 55609
Chamberlain Wholesale Grocery, 55618
Charles Wetgrove Company, 55625
Chef John Folse & Co, 55637
Chicago Food Corporation, 55657
Christian County Grain Inc, 55677
Cirelli Foods, 55689
City Line Food Distributors, 55696
City Produce Co, 55699
City Wide Produce Distributors, 55701
Clarence Mayfield Produce Company, 55703
Clarion Fruit Co, 55704
Clark Restaurant Svc, 55708

Clarkson Grain Co Inc, 55711
Class Produce Group LLC, 55712
Clifton Fruit & Produce, 55720
Cockrell Banana, 55740
Cold Hollow Cider Mill, 55752
Cole Brothers & Fox Company, 55753
Conner Produce Co, 55800
Consolidated Fruit Distributor, 55803
Consumers Fresh Produce, 55806
Conti Group Company, 55810
Cooperative Atlantic, 55823
Cooseman's D.C., 55825
Corey Bros Inc WHLS Produce, 55843
Costa Fruit & Produce, 55851
Costco Wholesale Corporation, 55852
Cristina Foods Inc, 55885
Crosset Co LLC, 55889
Crown O'Maine Organic Cooperative, 55892
Crusader Tomato, 55897
Culinary Specialties, 55908
Curley Brothers, 55914
D'Arrigo Brothers Company of New York, Inc, 55938
D. Brickman Produce Company, 55940
D.M. Rothman Company, 55945
Daffin Mercantile Company, 55964
Dairy King Milk Farms/Foodservice, 55967
Dairyland USA Corp, 55971
Dal-Don Produce, 55972
Darisil, 55981
David Puccia & Company, 55987
Demak & Company, 56031
Demma Fruit Company, 56032
Dentici Produce, 56036
Dicarlo Distributors Inc, 56059
Dickerson Foods, 56062
Dierks Foods, 56064
Dilgard Frozen Foods, 56068
Dimond Tager Company Products, 56071
DiNovo Produce Company, 56052
Distribution Kowloon, 56084
Distribution Plus, 56085
DNO Inc, 55951
Douglas Brothers Produce Company, 56121
Douglass Produce Company, 56124
DPI Mid Atlantic, 55953
DPI Rocky Mountain, 55955
Dublin Produce Company, 56144
E G Forrest Co Inc, 56171
E. Armata Fruit & Produce, Inc., 56177
E. LaRocque & Fils, 56179
E. Oliver Zellner Company, 56180
Eatmore Fruit Company, 56213
Edinburg Citrus Assn, 56232
Edward G Rahll & Sons, 56243
Edwards Distributing, 56246
Ehrlich Food Co, 56248
Elk Provision Co Inc, 56264
Epicurean Foods, 56303
Erneston & Sons Produce Inc, 56317
Ettline Food Service, 56331
Eugene & Company, 56334
Euro-Excellence, 56337
Evans Foodservice Inc., 56346
Evco Wholesale Food Corp, 56347
F & A Food Sales Inc, 56359
F & C Sawaya Wholesale, 56360
F C Bloxom & Co, 56363
Fab Inc, 56372
Fadler Company, 56374
Fagerholt Brothers, 56376
Fairway Foods, 56379
Falls City Mercantile Co Inc, 56381
Family Foods Home Service, 56382
Farmfresh, 56391
Farner-Bocken Co, 56394
Federated Cooperative, 56399
Federated Cooperative Lt, 56400, 56401
Fidelity Fruit & Produce Co, 56417
Finest Foods, 56425
Finger Lakes Organic Growers, 56427
Five Continents, 56448

Folmer Fruit & Produce Company, 56486
Food Authority Inc, 56488
Food City, 56490
Food Services Inc, 56501
Food-Products, 56505
Forest City Weingart Produce, 56516
Four Oaks Farm, 56530
Francis Produce Company, 56539
Frank's Produce, 56549
Franklin Produce Company, 56551
Fred W Albrecht Grocery Co, 56555
Frederick Produce Company, 56556
Fresco Y Mas, 56561
Fresh Point, 56564
Fresh Point Dallas, 56565
FreshPro Food Distributors, 56567
Fries Bros Eggs LLC, 56572
Fruit Belt Canning Inc, 56583
Fruitco Corp, 56588
Fuji Produce, 56589
Full Harvest, 56590
G & L Import Export Corp, 56596
G A B Empacadora Inc, 56599
G&T Terminal Packaging Company, 56602
G.W. Market, 56605
GAC Produce Company, 56606
GAF Seelig Inc, 56607
Galli Produce Inc, 56629
Gamez Brothers Produce Co, 56631
Garber Bros Inc, 56634
Garden Spot Produce Co, 56638
Gatto & Sons, 56645
Gatto Wholesale Produce, 56646
Gelson's, 56649
General Cash & Carry, 56656
George A Heimos Produce Co, 56664
GFS (Canada) Company, 56611
Giambrocco Food Service, 56675
Giant Eagle American Seaway Foods, 56677
GIANT Food Stores, 56612
Ginsberg's Institutional Foods, 56687
Glandt-Dahlke, 56690
Global Harvest, 56693
Gordon Food Service, 56730, 56731, 56732, 56733, 56734, 56735, 56736, 56737, 56738, 56739, 56740, 56741, 56742, 56743, 56744, 56745, 56746, 56747
Gralab Instruments, 56763
Granite State Fruit, 56766
Grantstone Supermarket, 56767
Great American Popcorn Works of Pennsylvania, 56773
Great Lakes International Trading, 56784
Great North Foods, 56786
Great West Produce Company, 56790
Griffin Food Co, 56814
Groetsch Wholesale Grocer, 56820
GSC Enterprises Inc., 56617
Gulf Marine & Industrial Supplies Inc, 56831
Gulf Pecan Company, 56833
Gunderland Marine Supply, 56840
Gutierrez Brothers, 56842
Guy Locicero & Sons, 56843
H Brooks & Co, 56847
H Schrier & Co Inc, 56848
Hahn Produce Corporation, 56875
Haitai Inc, 56878
Hall & Cole Produce, 56883
Halsey Foodservice, 56885
Hanif's International Foods, 56900
Harpak-Ulma, 56933
Harry Nusinov Company, 56940
Harshfield Brothers, 56943
Harveys Supermarket, 56950
Hearn-Kirkwood, 56979
Heeren Brothers Produce, 56988
Hill & Sloan, 57019
Hipp Wholesale Foods, 57031
Hoban Foods, 57033
Holland Beef International Corporation, 57044

Wholesale Product Type / Produce

Hollander, Gould & Murray Company, 57046
Home-Like Food Company, 57052
Homestead Foods, 57053
House of Spices, 57067
HPC Foodservice, 56868
HRS Food Service, 56869
Hudson River Fruit Distr, 57077
Hummingbird Wholesale, 57090
I Supply Co, 57101
Importex International, 57133
Indianapolis Fruit Company, 57141
Indianhead Foodservice, 57143
Industrial Commodities, 57147
Institutional Wholesale Company, 57170
Island Supply, 57216
Italfoods Inc, 57219
J & J Distributing, 57223
J H Honeycutt & Sons Inc, 57228
J Hoelting Produce Inc, 57229
J Kings Food Svc Professionals, 57230
J&L Produce Wholesale Company, 57243
J. Hellman Frozen Foods, 57248
J. Johnson Fruit & Produce, 57249
J.A. Wendling Foodservice, 57257
J.C. Banana & Company, 57258
J.C. Produce, 57259
J.L. Henderson & Company, 57266
Jackson Wholesale Co, 57295
James Avery Clark & Sons Inc, 57307
James C Thomas & Sons, 57308
James D Cofer, 57309
James Desiderio Inc, 57310
James K. Wilson Produce Company, 57311
Janney Marshall Co, 57312
Jarosz Produce Farms, 57314
JC's Sunny Winter, 57279
Jerilu Fruit Center, 57332
Jerome Langdon Produce, 57334
Jerry Schulman Produce, 57336
Jesse Food Products, 57339
Jetro Cash & Carry Enterprises, 57343
Jetro Cash & Carry Inc, 57344
Jimmy Durbin Farms, 57349
JMS, 57286
John Cerasuolo Co, 57364
John Demartin Company, 57366
John J. Moon Produce, 57372
John Molinelli Inc, 57374
Johnston Farms, 57391
Joyce Brothers Company, 57401
Junction City Distributing & Vending Company, 57409
Kadouri International Foods, 57434
Kaleel Bros Inc, 57437
Kalil Produce Company, 57438
Kallsnick Inc, 57439
Karetas Foods Inc, 57448
Kauai Producers, 57455
Kellogg Elevator Company, 57478
Kelly's Foods, 57479
Ken Ottoboni Mushrooms, 57482
Kimball & Thompson Produce, 57505
King Provision Corporation, 57508
KJ's Market, 57427
KOHL Wholesale, 57429
Kopke, William H, 57546
Kuner-Empson Company, 57557
L. Dontis Produce Company, 57569
L. Holloway & Brother Company, 57570
La Grasso Bros Produce, 57591
Ladoga Frozen Food & Retail, 57606
Lady Baltimore of Missouri, 57607
Lake Wales Citrus Growers Associates, 57616
Larimore Bean Company, 57637
Lavella Brothers, 57645
Lawrence Lapide, 57647
Lee Foods, 57658
Lewisburg Wholesale Company, 57687
Lexington Foodservice, 57688
Liberty Gold Fruit Co Inc, 57693
Little Produce, 57734
Lomar Distributing Inc, 57748

London Fruit Inc, 57751
Long Wholesale Distributors, 57757
Louis Caric & Sons, 57769
Lovecchio & Sons, 57775
Lowell Brothers & Bailey, 57778
Ludwig Fish & Produce Company, 57782
M&F Foods, 57805
M&T Chirico, 57808
M.E. Carter & Company, 57812
MacDonalds Consolidated, 57825, 57826
Madison Food Sales Company, 57836
Madison Wholesale Co, 57838
Maffei Produce Company, 57841
Maines Paper & Food Svc Inc, 57850
Malena Produce Inc, 57858
Maloberti Produce Co, 57859
Manchester Grocery Company, 57863
Mancuso Cheese Co, 57865
Market Foods International, 57895
Marriott Distribution Service, 57903
Marrone's Inc, 57904
Mars Supermarkets, 57906
Martin Bros Distributing Co, 57908
Martin Brothers Wholesale, 57909
Martin Produce Co, 57912
Maryland Wholesale Produce Market, 57920
Maschari Brothers WHLS Fruits, 57921
Masser's Produce, 57923
Mattingly Foods, 57937
Maxim's Import Corporation, 57938
Mayrand Limitee, 57949
Mazo-Lerch Company, 57952
McCabe's Quality Foods, 57956
Mcdonald Wholesale Co, 57973
McDonnell, 57958
Mcfarling Foods Inc, 57974
McLane Co Inc, 57963
McLane Foodservice Inc, 57964
McShane Enterprises, 57967
Meadow Farm Foods, 57983
Menu Maker Foods Inc, 57998
Merchants Distributors Inc, 58000
Merchants Foodservice, 58001
Merchants Grocery Co Inc, 58002
Metro, Inc., 58018
Metroplex Harriman Corporation, 58020
MGH Wholesale Grocery, 57818
Miami Wholesale Grocery Company, 58027
Michael Distributor Inc, 58028
Mid-America Wholesale, 58054
Middendorf Meat, 58058
Midori Trading Inc, 58062
Mike Kazarian, 58076
Mile Hi Frozen Foods Corp., 58078
Mills Brothers Intl, 58089
Mishima Foods USA, 58096
Mitchell Grocery Co, 58102
Mivila Foods, 58104
Mj Kellner Co, 58105
ML Catania Company, 57821
Molinera International, 58121
Monterrey Provision Co, 58129
Monteverdes, 58130
Morris A. Elkis & Sons, 58143
Morris Okun, 58144
Mountain Dairies-SW Ice Cream, 58156
Mountain Service Distribution, 58160
Muir Copper Canyon Farms, 58174
Mush & Pinsky, 58189
Nancy O Produce, 58213
Nardelli Brothers, 58218
Nash-DeCamp Company, 58221
Nassau Candy Distributors, 58223
Nathel & Nathel, 58229
National Grocers, 58236
National Grocers Assn, 58237
National Grocers Company, 58238, 58239, 58241
Near East Importing Corporation, 58274
Neel's Wholesale Produce Co, 58277
New England Foods, 58298
NewStar Fresh Foods LLC, 58312
Nicholas & Co Inc, 58322

Nichols Foodservice, 58323
Nogales Fruit & Vegetables Dst, 58337
Norman's, 58350
North Carolina Potato Association, 58359
North Side Banana Co, 58362
Northern Haserot, 58365
Northwestern Fruit Co, 58385
Novick Brothers Corp, 58391
O. Lippi & Company, 58413
Omega Produce Company, 58455
Organics Unlimited, 58475
Orioxi International Corporation, 58479
Osage Food Products Inc, 58484
Osborn Bros Inc, 58485
P & D Corp, 58500
P. Tavilla Company, 58506
Pacific Tomato Growers, 58535
Pacific World Enterprises, 58537
Pagano M Watermelons, 58544
Palmer Food Service, 58553
Palmer Jack M, 58554
Palmer Wholesale Inc, 58555
Paramount Produce, 58573
Parson Food Sales, 58585
Pate-Derby Company, 58592
Patriot Enterprises, 58593
Paul J. Macrie, 58599
Peace River Trading Company, 58605
Peas, 58608
Pemiscot Packing Company, 58616
Pennsylvania Macaroni Company Inc., 58621
Penobscot Mccrum LLC, 58624
Performance Food Group Customized Distribution, 58632, 58633, 58634, 58635, 58636, 58637, 58638, 58639
Performance Foodservice, 58640, 58641, 58642, 58643, 58644, 58645, 58646, 58647, 58648, 58649, 58650, 58651, 58652, 58653, 58654, 58655, 58656, 58657, 58658, 58659, 58660, 58661, 58662, 58663, 58664, 58665, 58666, 58667, 58668, 58669, 58670, 58671, 58672, 58673, 58674, 58675, 58676
Phoenix Wholesale Foodservice, 58700
Pierceton Foods Inc, 58707
Pinto Bros, 58711
Pizza Products, 58721
Platteville Potato Association, 58726
PLT Trucking Corporation, 58517
Pocono ProFoods, 58729
Pontiac Fruit House, 58740
Portugalia Imports, 58751
Portuguese United Grocer Co-Op, 58752
Post & Taback, 58756
Potato Specialty Company, 58758
Prawn Seafoods Inc, 58766
Premier Foodservice Distributors of America, 58771
Prevor Marketing International, 58782
Price Harry H & Son, 58784
Procacci Bros Sales Corp, 58799
Professional Food Systems, 58807
Provigo Distribution, 58822
Pueblo Trading Co Inc, 58825
Pulini Produce, 58826
Pulse Plus, 58828
PYA/Monarch, 58520
Quadra Foods Company, 58843
Quail Crest Foods, 58844
Quality Banana Inc, 58847
Quality Celery & Sprout Company, 58848
Quality Groceries, 58858
Quality Produce Company, 58861
Quandt's Foodservice Distributors, 58864
Quattrochi Specialty Foods, 58866
Quebec Vegetable Distributors, 58867
R S Porter & Co, 58885
R S Stern Inc, 58886
R&B Produce, 58890

R-Best Produce, 58897
R.C. McEntire & Company, 58898
Rainbow Foods, 58919
Rainbow Natural Foods, 58920
Rainbow Valley Orchards, 58923
Ranch Foods Direct, 58932
Ray & Mascari, 58940
Reinhart Foodservice LLC, 58972
Restaurant Depot, 58987
RightWay Foods, 59009
Ritchie's Foods, 59015
Roanoke Fruit & Produce Co, 59023
Robert Cochran & Company, 59027
Robert D. Arnold & Associates, 59028
Robert Ruiz Company, 59030
Robert's Foods Company, 59032
Robertson Fruit & Produce, 59035
Rock Garden South, 59045
Rockland Foodservice, 59049
Rocky Produce Inc, 59051
Rogers Farms, 59054
Rohrer Brothers Inc, 59056
Roseland Produce Wholesale, 59068
Rosenthal & Kline, 59069
Rosenthal Foods Corp, 59070
Royal Banana Co, 59081
Ryan Potato Company, 59100
Ryans Wholesale Food Distributors, 59101
S Strock & Co, 59108
S&M Produce Company, 59111
S. Anshin Produce Company, 59118
S.J. Roetzel & Son Produce, 59120
Sagaya Corp, 59142
Salad Depot, 59146
Sales King International, 59150
Sam Gordon & Sons Purveyors, 59158
Sam Okun Produce Co, 59160
Sam's Club, 59164
Sambazon, 59165
San Rafael Distributing Inc, 59175
Sanders Bros, 59179
Sanson Co Inc, 59184
Sauder's Eggs, 59196
Saval Foods Corp, 59199
Schenck Foods Co, 59208
Schultz Sav-O-Stores, 59218
Schumacher Wholesale Meats, 59219
Seven K Feather Farm, 59275
Shaheen Bros Inc, 59282
Shamrock Foods Co, 59286, 59288
Shellman Peanut & Grain, 59301
Shiff & Goldman Foods, 59319
Sid Goodman Company, 59336
Sid Wainer & Son Specialty, 59339
Signature Packaging, 59347
Simonian Fruit Company, 59351
Sin-Son Produce, 59358
Sindoni, Joseph, Wholesale Foods, 59360
Sirca Foodservice, 59365
Skone & Conners, 59373
Skone & Connors Produce, 59374
Sleeper Produce Company, 59380
Snyder Wholesale Inc, 59404
Sobey's, 59407
Sobey's Ontario, 59408
Sobey's Quebec Inc, 59409
Sobeys Inc, 59410, 59411, 59412, 59413, 59414, 59415
Southeastern Grocers, 59438
Southern Produce Distributors, 59446
Southwest Traders, 59463
Spartan Foods, 59477
SpartanNash Co, 59478
Spokane Produce, 59490
Springfield Produce Company, 59493
Spuds N' Stuff, 59496
St. Clair Foods Distributing, 59500
Standard Fruit & Vegetable Company, 59511
Star Fisheries, 59520
Star Produce, 59524, 59525, 59526
Staunton Foods LLC, 59543
Staunton Fruit & Produce Company, 59544

Wholesale Product Type / Provisions/Meat

STI International, 59130
Strawhacker's Food Service, 59580
Stronach & Sons, 59584
Suffolk Banana Company, 59591
Sun Valley Fruit Company, 59603
Sunkist Growers, 59616
Sunrise Fruit Company, 59617
Sunspun Foodservice, 59624
Suntreat Packing & Shipping Co, 59626
Superior Foods, 59633
SUPERVALU Distribution, 59132
Sutherland Produce Sales, 59650
Sygma Network, 59668, 59669
SYGMA Network Inc, 59133
Systems Services Of America, 59745
T.C. Food Export/Import Company, 59753
T.T. Todd Company, 59760
Ta-De Distributing Co, 59766
Tabor Grain Company, 59768
Tama Trading Co Inc, 59772
Tamburo Brothers, 59774
Tanglewood Farm, 59775
Tergerson's Fine Foods, 59807
Tex-Sandia, 59816
Texas Marine II, 59820
Thomas Colace Company, 59843
Ths Foodservice, 59855
Thurston Foods Inc, 59858
Tierra Farm, 59860
Tippecanoe Foods, 59869
Todd Distributors Inc, 59874
Torkelson Brothers, 59889
Tourtellot & Co, 59898
Town & Country Wholesale, 59901
Tradelink, 59909
Trader Joe's, 59910
Tri Car Sales, 59925
Trio Supply Company, 59939
Triton International, 59942
Trucco, A.J., 59953
Tucson Coop. Warehouse, 59960
Tucson Food Svc, 59961
Ultimate Foods, 60001
United Banana Company, 60015
United Noodles, 60028
United Potato Company, 60030
United Produce, 60031
United With Earth, 60041
Upper Lakes Foods Inc, 60053
US Food Products, 59984
US Foods Inc, 59989, 59990, 59991
US Growers Cold Storage, 59993
Vallet Foodservice, 60068
Valley Distributing Company, 60069
Valley Distributors, 60071
Valley Fruit & Produce Company, 60074
Van Eerden Foodservice Co Inc, 60077
Van Solkema Produce Inc, 60078, 60079
Vaughn Packing Company, 60085
Venezia Brothers, 60091
Victory Spud Service, 60108
Vidalia Sweets Brand, 60109
Vilore Foods Company, 60113
VIP Food Svc, 60061
Virginia Wholesale Company, 60120
Viva Tierra, 60136
Volpe, Son & Kemelhar, 60142
W D Class & Son, 60151
W.J. Canaan Inc., 60162
W.R. Hackett, 60166
W.S. Lee & Sons, 60172
Wabash Foodservice Inc, 60184
Wakefern Food Corp, 60193
Waleski Produce, 60196
Wallach's Farms, 60204
Walsh Tropical Fruit Sales, 60205
Waltham Fruit & Produce Company, 60208
Waltkoch Limited, 60209
Washington Vegetable Co, 60217
Waterfront Market, 60219
Watervliet Fruit Exchange, 60221
Watsonville Coast Produce Inc, 60224
Waugh Foods Inc, 60225

West Bay Sales, 60243
Western Family Foods Inc, 60256
Western Grocers, 60257, 60258
WG Thompson & Sons, 60181
White Feather Farms, 60275
Whitey Produce Co Inc, 60279
Wholesale Cash & Carry Foods, 60284
Wholesum Family Farms, 60290
Willamette Valley Pie Co, 60305
William Consalo & Sons Farms, 60306
William Rosenstein & Sons, 60308
Williams Institutional Foods, 60310
Willie Laymon, 60314
Willow Run Foods Inc, 60317
Winchester Food, 60320
Winn-Dixie, 60334
Witmer Foods, 60346
Wood's Products, 60351
World Variety Produce, 60361
Zeches Institution Supply, 60393

Provisions/Meat

1000 Islands River Rat Cheese, 54501
A & B Distributing Co, 54509
A Tarantino & Sons Poultry, 54523
A&A Halal Distributors, 54525
A&M Enterprises, 54532
A. Bohrer, 54540
A. De LaChevrotiere, 54541
A.B. Wise & Sons, 54548
A.C. Kissling Company, 54551
A.M.BRIGGS, 54556
Abbot's Butcher, 54592
Academy Packing Co Inc, 54597
ACC Distributors Inc, 54567
Acme Food Sales Inc, 54608
Acme Steak & Seafood, 54610
Adams Chapman Co, 54620
Adams Wholesale Co, 54621
Addison Foods Inc, 54623
Adolf Kusy & Company, 54630
Adventure Foods, 54638
Adventure Inn Food Trading Company, 54639
AJC International, 54578
Alabama Food Group, 54666
Albert Guarnieri & Co, 54674
All Caribbean Food Service, 54694
Allen Brothers Inc, 54716
Allied Food Service, 54723
Allied Provision Company, 54728
Alpine Food Distributing Inc, 54736
Alwan & Sons, 54748
Amana Meat Shop & Smoke House, 54750
AMCON Distributing Co, 54582
American Food Systems, 54768
American Food Traders, 54769
American Frozen Foods, 54771
American Meat & Seafood, 54781
American Seaway Foods Inc, 54795
Amick Farms LLC, 54807
Amster-Kirtz Co, 54812
Andalusia Distributing Co Inc, 54818
Anthracite Provision Co, 54840
Arctic Beverages, 54856
Arctic Star Distributing, 54859
Arrow Distributing, 54881
Asanti Distributors, 54887
Associated Food Stores Inc, 54899
Associated Grocers, 54900
Associated Wholesale Grocers, 54902
Atchison Wholesale Grocery, 54907
Auth Brothers Food Service, 54938
Automation Systems & Services, 54941
B & M Provision Co, 54962
B & R Quality Meats Inc, 54963
B/R Sales Company, 54980
Badger Wholesale Company, 55002
Badger Wholesale Meat & Provisions, 55003
Balter Meat Co, 55036
Barkett Fruit Company, 55061
Basic Food Intl Inc, 55074

Bassham Institutional Foods, 55078
Bayou Food Distributors, 55097
Bear Creek Operations, 55103
Belin & Nye, 55120
Ben E. Keith, 55133, 55134, 55135, 55136, 55137, 55138, 55139, 55140, 55141, 55142, 55143
Bender Meat, 55163
Bensinger's, 55187
Bertolino Beef Co, 55187
Best Market, 55198
Better Meat, 55205
BI-LO, 54987
Billingsgate Fish Company, 55222
Birchwood Meats, 55229
Black's Barbecue, 55241
Blackwing Ostrich Meats Inc., 55244
Blue Buoy Foods, 55255
Blue Mountain Meats Inc., 55261
Blue Ribbon Meats, 55264
Blue Ribbon Wholesale, 55265
Blue Ridge Poultry, 55266
Boeuf Merite, 55274
Bosco Food Service, 55287
Boston Sausage & Provision, 55292
Bottom Line Foods, 55297
Boxed Meat Revolution, 55305
Boyle Meat Company, 55308
Brenham Wholesale Groc Co Inc, 55324
Brewer Meats Inc, 55329
Bridgford Foods Corp, 55333
Bringgold Wholesale Meats, 55337
Brita Foods, 55339
British Wholesale Imports, 55342
Broadleaf Venison USA Inc, 55344
Bronx Butter & Egg Company, 55349
Brooklyn Biltong, 55350
Buckhead Beef, 55376
Buffalo Bills Premium Snacks, 55380
Bunn Capitol Company, 55386
Bur-Gra Meat & Grocery, 55388
Burdick Packing Company, 55390
Butte Produce Company, 55402
Butts Foods, 55403
C & R Food Svc Inc, 55412
C A Curtze, 55417
C D Hartnett Co, 55418
C. Eberle Sons Company, 55426
Cable Meat Center, 55454
Cactus Holdings Inc, 55455
Cadillac Meat Company, 55457
Caesar Electric Supply, 55459
Cambridge Packing Company, 55484
Canada Safeway, 55493
Capitol Foods, 55510
Cappello Foods, 55512
Carriage Foods, 55551
Cartwright's Market, 55556
Cash-Wa Distributing, 55564, 55565
Cataract Foods, 55576
Cauble & Field, 55578
Cavazos Candy, Produce & Groceries, 55581
Cavens Meats, 55582
Cerca Foodservice, 55605
Certco Inc., 55609
Chapman's Food Service, 55621
Charles C. Parks Company, 55623
Chas. Wetterling & Sons, 55629
Chef's Pride Gifts LLC, 55639
Chicago Market Company, 55659
Chicago Steaks, 55661
Church Point Wholesale Grocer, 55682
Circle B Ranch, 55688
Cirelli Foods, 55689
City Deli Distributing, 55693
City Line Food Distributors, 55696
City Packing Company, 55698
Clark Meat Servicing, 55707
Clark Restaurant Svc, 55708
Clark's Wholesale Meats, 55709
Clayton's Crab Co, 55713
Cloverdale Foods, 55728
Coast to Coast Foods Group, 55729
Cole Brothers & Fox Company, 55753

Colorado Boxed Beef Company, 55758, 55759, 55760, 55761
Concord Import, 55792
Consolidated Poultry & Egg Company, 55804
Consumers Packing Co, 55807
Cooperative Atlantic, 55823
Copperwood InternationalInc, 55826
Coquitlam City Hall, 55827
Cost Plus, 55850
Costco Wholesale Corporation, 55852
Couch's Rich Plan Foods, 55854
Country Butcher Shop, 55857
Crescent Foods, 55880
Culinary Specialties, 55908
CUNICO, 55452
Curtis Packing Co, 55915
D.A. Colongeli & Sons, 55943
Daffin Mercantile Company, 55964
Dairy King Milk Farms/Foodservice, 55967
Dale's Meats, 55973
Darisil, 55981
Darlington Packing Co, 55982
De Choix Specialty Foods Company, 55995
Dean & Company, 56002
Dearborn Wholesale Grocers, 56007, 56008, 56009
Debragga & Spitler, 56012
Del Bene Meats, 56021
Demma Fruit Company, 56032
Deng's, 56034
Dicarlo Distributors Inc, 56059
Dickerson & Quinn, 56061
Dickerson Foods, 56062
Dierks Foods, 56064
Difeo & Sons Poultry Inc, 56065
DiGregorio Food Products, 56050
DiLeo Brothers, 56051
Dilgard Frozen Foods, 56068
Dillon Provision Co, 56069
Dino's Sausage & Meat Co Inc, 56073
DiNovo Produce Company, 56052
Distribution Kowloon, 56084
DMI Distribution, Inc., 55950
DNX Foods, 55952
Doerle Food Svc, 56098
Dom's Sausage Co Inc, 56104
Domestic Casing Co, 56105
Downesville Foods, 56130
DPI Mid Atlantic, 55953
DPI Rocky Mountain, 55955
Durham Ranch, 56155
Dutch Creek Foods, 56156
E G Forrest Co Inc, 56171
E&M Fancy Foods, 56175
Earp Distribution, 56195
Eaton Market, 56215
Economy Wholesale Company, 56226
Ehrlich Food Co, 56248
Empire Packing Co, 56283
Enslin & Son Packing Company, 56295
Epicurean Foods, 56303
Ettline Foods Corp, 56331
Euclid Fish Co, 56333
Eugene & Company, 56334
Evans Foodservice Inc., 56346
Evco Wholesale Food Corp, 56347
Excel Food Distribution Company, 56351
F & A Food Sales Inc, 56359
F & C Sawaya Wholesale, 56360
F B Mc Fadden Wholesale Co, 56361
F Christiana & Co, 56364
Fab Inc, 56372
Fadler Company, 56374
Fairs Seafood, 56377
Fairway Foods, 56379
Falls City Mercantile Co Inc, 56381
Family Foods Home Service, 56382
Farm Boy Food Svc, 56387
Farmfresh, 56391
Farmington Foods Inc, 56392
Farner-Bocken Co, 56394
Federated Cooperative Lt, 56400

1262

Wholesale Product Type / Provisions/Meat

Feed The Party, 56403
Ferntrade Corporation, 56408
Flatland Food Distributors, 56458
Flint Provision Inc Zalack's, 56467
Flora Foods Inc, 56468
Florida Smoked Fish Company, 56475
Food City, 56490
Food Services Inc, 56501
Food Supply Inc, 56502
Food-Products, 56505
Foods Etc., 56506
Foremost Foods Company, 56515
Four Oaks Farm, 56530
Fox Deluxe Inc, 56535
Frank Brunckhorst Company, 56542
Frank Wardynski & Sons Inc, 56548
Frankstown Fish Co Inc, 56552
Fred W Albrecht Grocery Co, 56555
Frederick Produce Company, 56556
Freiria & Company, 56559
Fresco Y Mas, 56561
Fresh Point Dallas, 56565
FreshPro Food Distributors, 56567
G & L Davis Meat Co, 56595
G & W Food Products, 56598
Gachot & Gachot, 56621
Gaiser's European Style, 56623
Gamez Brothers Produce Co, 56631
Garavaglia Meat Company, 56633
Garber Bros Inc, 56634
Garden Spot Produce Co, 56638
Gaylord's Meat Co, 56647
Gelson's, 56649
General Trading Co, 56660
Giant Eagle American Seaway Foods, 56677
GIANT Food Stores, 56612
Ginsberg's Institutional Foods, 56687
Glazier Packing Co, 56691
Goetz & Sons Western Meat, 56702
Goldberg & Solovy Foods Inc, 56710
Golden West Food Group, 56722
Gone Wild!!!, 56724
Gordon Food Service, 56730, 56731, 56732, 56733, 56734, 56735, 56736, 56737, 56738, 56739, 56740, 56741, 56742, 56743, 56744, 56745, 56746, 56747
Gourmet Award Foods, 56749
Graham Ice & Locker Plant, 56760
Gralab Instruments, 56763
Great North Foods, 56786
Great Valley Meat Company, 56789
Great Western Beef WHLS Co, 56791
Great Western Meats, 56795
Green Valley Food Corp, 56800
Greene Poultry Co, 56801
Greenley Foods Inc, 56805
Grigg Box Company, 56817
Groetsch Wholesale Grocer, 56820
Gulf Marine & Industrial Supplies Inc, 56831
Gulf Packing Company, 56832
Gunderland Marine Supply, 56840
Guy Locicero & Sons, 56843
H.P. Beale & Sons, 56855
Haddad Supply Company, 56872
Hale-Halsell Company, 56882
Halsey Foodservice, 56885
Hamilos Bros Inspected Meat, 56889
Hamms, 56891
Hansen Distribution Group, 56908
Harbor Wholesale Foods Inc, 56920
Harker's Distribution, 56925, 56926
Harpak-Ulma, 56933
Harry Fourtunis, 56937
Harry Fourtunis Inc, 56938
Harveys Supermarket, 56950
Hata Y & Co LTD, 56953
Hearn-Kirkwood, 56979
Heinkel's Packing Co, 56989
Henjes Enterprises, 56998
Henry Bresky & Sons Inc, 57000
Herring Brothers Meats, 57010
HFM Foodservice, 56865

HIB Foods Inc, 56866
Higa Food Service, 57015
High Country Meats, 57016
Hill City Wholesale Company, 57020
Hillis Farms, 57025
Hipp Wholesale Foods, 57031
Hoban Foods, 57033
Hoffman's Quality Meats, 57038
Holland Beef International Corporation, 57044
Homestead Foods, 57053
HPC Foodservice, 56868
HRS Food Service, 56869
Husky Foods of Anchorage, 57094
Iberia Foods of Florida, 57116
Imperial Trading, 57131
Importex International, 57133
Indianapolis Meat Company, 57142
Indianhead Foodservice, 57143
Inland Meats of Spokane, 57161
Institutional Wholesale Company, 57170
International Meat Co, 57190
Irvin, 57207
Island Supply, 57216
Italfoods Inc, 57219
J Hoelting Produce Inc, 57229
J Kings Food Svc Professionals, 57230
J&M Distribution Company, 57244
J. Hellman Frozen Foods, 57248
J. Treffiletti & Sons, 57255
J.A. Wendling Foodservice, 57257
J.L. Henderson & Company, 57266
J.M. Schneider, 57267
J.O. Demers Beef, 57268
J.W. Wood Company, 57274
Jackson Wholesale Co, 57295
Jamac Frozen Foods, 57304
James D Cofer, 57309
Janney Marshall Co, 57312
Javed & Sons, 57320
Jersey Meat & Provision Company, 57337
Jesse Food Products, 57339
Jetro Cash & Carry Inc, 57344
Jim David Meats, 57347
JM Schneider, 57284
JNS Foods, 57287
Joe Christiana Food Distributing, 57357
Joe Pucci & Sons Seafood, 57360
John Graves Food Service, 57368
John Morrell Food Group, 57375
John W Williams Inc, 57379
John's Meat Market, 57382
Johnson Wholesale Meat Company, 57388
Joseph Antognoli & Co, 57396
Joyce Foods, 57402
Junction City Distributing & Vending Company, 57409
K Heeps Inc, 57416
K&K Meat Company, 57420
K. Lefkofsky Company, 57424
Kansas City Sausage, 57443
Kansas Marine, 57444
Karetas Foods Inc, 57448
KAST Distributors Inc, 57425
Katy's Wholesale Distributing, 57453
Kayem Foods, 57457
Kelley Foods, 57476
Kelly's Foods, 57479
Kenrich Foods Corp, 57487
King Provision Corporation, 57508
Kings Choice Food, 57509
Kirby Holloway Provision Co, 57514
KJ's Market, 57427
KMA Trading Company, 57428
KOHL Wholesale, 57429
Kolon California Corporation, 57538
Kopcke-Kansas Supply Services, 57545
L&C Meat Company, 57564
LA Foods, 57578
Lady Baltimore of Missouri, 57607
Lamb Cooperative Inc, 57618
Lancaster Poultry, 57621

Land O'Frost Inc., 57623
Landphair Meat & Seafood, 57627
Laurell Hill Provision Company, 57644
Lavin Candy Company, 57646
Leali Brothers Meats, 57654
Lee Grocery Company, 57659
Lehmann-Colorado, 57665
Lewis & McDermott, 57685
Lewisburg Wholesale Company, 57687
Liberto Management Co Inc, 57689
Libido Funk Circus, 57700
Lincoln Feed & Supply, 57722
Lomar Distributing Inc, 57748
Lombardi Brothers Meat Packers, 57749
Lorenzo's Wholesale Foods, 57766
Ludwig Fish & Produce Company, 57782
Lumaco Inc, 57784
Lumberton Cash & Carry, 57787
Lumsden Brothers, 57788
M & V Provisions Co Inc, 57794
M & W Beef Packers Inc, 57795
M A Sales, 57797
M&F Foods, 57805
M. Zukerman & Company, 57811
M.E. Dilanian Company, 57813
Macdonald Meat Co, 57828
MacDonalds Consolidated, 57825, 57826
MacGregors Meat & Seafood, 57827
Madani Halal, 57833
Madison Food Sales Company, 57836
Main Street Wholesale Meat, 57845
Maines Paper & Food Svc Inc, 57850
Manchester Grocery Company, 57863
Mancuso Cheese Co, 57865
Mar Meat Company, 57880
Marcus Food Co, 57882
Marcus Specialty Foods, 57883
Marias Packing Company, 57888
Market Foods International, 57895
Market Grocery Co, 57896
Marky's Caviar, 57900
Marriott Distribution Service, 57903
Marrone's Inc, 57904
Mars Supermarkets, 57906
Martin Bros Distributing Co, 57908
Martin Preferred Foods, 57911
Mason Brothers Co, 57922
Mattingly Foods, 57937
Maxim's Import Corporation, 57938
Mayfair Provision Company, 57945
Mazo-Lerch Company, 57952
Mc Afee Packing Co, 57953
McCabe's Quality Foods, 57956
Mcdonald Wholesale Co, 57973
Mcfarling Foods Inc, 57974
Mckenzie Country Classic's, 57976
McLane Co Inc, 57963
McLane Grocery, 57965
McShane Enterprises, 57967
Meadow Farm Foods, 57983
Meats Plus Inc, 57987
Medina & Medina, 57989
Menu Maker Foods Inc, 57998
Merchants Distributors Inc, 58000
Merchants Foodservice, 58001
Merchants Grocery Co Inc, 58002
Merrill Distributing Inc, 58007
Metro-Richelieu, 58019
Metroplex Harriman Corporation, 58020
MGH Wholesale Grocery, 57818
Miami Wholesale Grocery Company, 58027
Michael Distributor Inc, 58028
Michael's Finer Meats/Seafoods, 58032
Mid America Food Sales, 58051
Mid-America Wholesale, 58054
Middendorf Meat, 58058
Midland Grocery of Michigan, 58060
Midwest Ingredients Inc, 58072
Mile Hi Frozen Foods Corp., 58078
Miller & Hartman, 58086
Mitchell Grocery Corp, 58102
Mivila Foods, 58104
Mj Kellner Co, 58105
Montana Food Products, 58126

Monterrey Provision Co, 58129
Morgan Meat Co, 58140
Morreale John R Inc, 58142
Moseley & Reece, 58150
Mountain Service Distribution, 58160
Mountain States Rosen, 58161
Moyer-Mitchell Company, 58167
Munsee Meats, 58184
Murry's Family of Fine Foods, 58187
My Car Provision Company, 58197
Nassau Candy Distributors, 58223
National Grocers Company, 58238, 58239
Near East Importing Corporation, 58274
Neesvig Meats, 58279
Nema Food Distribution, 58284
Nesbitt Processing, 58285
Nesson Meat Sales, 58287
New England Foods, 58298
New England Meat Company, 58300
New Jersey Provision Co, 58303
New Vermont Creamery, 58309
New Zealand Lamb Co, 58311
Nicholas & Co Inc, 58322
Nicky USA Inc, 58325
Norman's, 58350
North American Provisioners, 58354
North Central Co, 58360
Northern Haserot, 58365
Northstate Provision Co, 58375
Northwest Deli Distribution, 58379
Northwest Wild Foods, 58383
O.G. Foodservice, 58414
OH Armstrong, 58417
Ohio Farmers, 58439
Oklahoma City Meat Co Inc, 58442
Original Food, 58476
Orleans International, 58481
Osborn Bros Inc, 58485
Oscar's Wholesale Meats, 58486
P & D Corp, 58500
P A Menard, 58502
P.A. Braunger Institutional Foods, 58507
Pacific World Enterprises, 58537
Pacific-SEH Hotel Supply Company, 58538
Palama Meat Co Inc, 58547
Palmer Food Service, 58553
Palmer Jack M, 58554
Palmer Wholesale Inc, 58555
Park Avenue Meats Inc, 58578
Pate-Derby Company, 58592
Patriot Enterprises, 58593
Patton's Sausage Company, 58597
Paulie Paul's, 58602
Pemiscot Packing Company, 58616
Penguin Foods, 58618
Penn Maid, 58620
Pennsylvania Macaroni Company Inc., 58621
Penny's Meat Products, 58623
Performance Food Group Customized Distribution, 58632, 58633, 58634, 58635, 58636, 58637, 58638, 58639
Performance Foodservice, 58640, 58641, 58642, 58643, 58644, 58645, 58646, 58647, 58648, 58649, 58650, 58651, 58652, 58653, 58654, 58655, 58656, 58657, 58658, 58659, 58660, 58661, 58662, 58663, 58664, 58665, 58666, 58667, 58668, 58669, 58670, 58671, 58672, 58673, 58674, 58675, 58676
Pete and Gerry's Organic Eggs, 58682
Pierceton Foods Inc, 58707
Pizza Products, 58721
PLT Trucking Corporation, 58517
Pocono ProFoods, 58729
Polean Foods, 58733
Pon Food Corp, 58737
Pontiac Fruit House, 58740
Porky Products, 58744

Wholesale Product Type / Rack Jobbers

Portuguese United Grocer Co-Op, 58752
Potato Specialty Company, 58758
Prejean's Wholesale Meats Inc, 58770
Premier Foodservice Distributors of America, 58771
Prevor Marketing International, 58782
Prime Cut Meat & Seafood Company, 58788
Prime Smoked Meats Inc, 58790
Produce Trading Corp, 58801
Professional Food Systems, 58804, 58805, 58806, 58807
Proficient Food Company, 58811
Provigo Distribution, 58820
Pudliner Packing, 58824
Pueblo Trading Co Inc, 58825
Pulini Produce, 58826
Purchase Order Co Of Miami Inc, 58830
PYA/Monarch, 58520
Quail Crest Foods, 58844
Quality Food Company, 58854
Quality Foods, 58856
Quality Poultry Co, 58860
Quandt's Foodservice Distributors, 58864
Queen City Meats, 58868
R S Stern Inc, 58886
R.F. Beyers, 58900
Rainbow Foods, 58919
Ralph's Packing Co, 58927
Ramarc Foods Inc, 58928
Ramex Foods, 58930
Ranch Foods Direct, 58932
Randall Meat Co, 58933
Randy's Frozen Meats, 58934
Range Packing Company, 58935
RAPA Scrapple, 58908
Ready Portion Meat Co, 58948
Red Hot Chicago, 58956
Regal Distributing Company, 58966
Regency Coffee & Vending, 58969
Registry Steak & Seafood, 58971
Reinhart Foodservice LLC, 58972
Restaurant Depot, 58987
Rey Foods, 58995
Rhotens Wholesale Meat Co, 58996
Richmond Restaurant Svc, 59002
Richter Distributing Company, 59005
RightWay Foods, 59009
Rihm Foods, 59010
Rimfire Imports, 59011
Robbin's Beef Company, 59024
Robert D. Arnold & Associates, 59028
Robert Wholey & Co Inc, 59031
Robert's Foods Company, 59032
Roberts Packing Co, 59033
Robinson Distributing Co, 59039
Rockford Sausage Co, 59047
Rockland Foodservice, 59049
Roma of Minnesota, 59061
Rose Hill Distributor, 59066
Rosenthal Foods Corp, 59070
Royal Foods Inc, 59086
Royal Harvest Foods Inc, 59088
Royal Meats, 59091
Royal Palate Foods, 59092
Russell N. Roy Company, 59097
Ryans Wholesale Food Distributors, 59101
S&M Provisions, 59112
S&S Meat Company, 59114
S.W. Meat & Provision Company, 59122
Saad Wholesale Meats, 59134
Sadler's Smokehouse, 59135
Salad Depot, 59146
Salem Packing Company, 59148
Salwa Foods, 59156
Sam's Club, 59164
San Jacinto Frozen Food, 59173
Sansone Food Products Co, 59185
Sassone Wholesale Groceries Co, 59194
Saugy Inc., 59197
Saval Foods Corp, 59199
Schaefers, 59205
Schaper Company, 59206
Schenck Foods Co, 59208

Schisa Brothers, 59211
Schultz Sav-O-Stores, 59218
Schumacher Wholesale Meats, 59219
Seafood Dimensions Intl, 59243
Select Meat Company, 59262
Service Market, 59272
Shaheen Bros Inc, 59282
Shalhoob Meat Co, 59284
Shamrock Foods Co, 59286, 59288
Sher Brothers & Company, 59308
Sherwood Food Distributors, 59310, 59311, 59312, 59313, 59314, 59315, 59316
Shetakis Foodservice, 59318
Shiff & Goldman Foods, 59319
Sims Poultry, 59356
Sirca Foodservice, 59365
Skylark Meats, 59375
Smith, S.R., 59389
Smoked Turkey Inc, 59392
Snyder Wholesale Inc, 59404
Sobey's, 59407
Sobey's Ontario, 59408
Sobey's Quebec Inc, 59409
Sobeys Inc., 59410, 59411, 59412, 59413, 59414, 59415
Sogelco International, 59419
Somerset Industries, 59422
Southeast Cold Storage, 59435
Southeastern Grocers, 59438
Southern Indiana Butcher's Supply, 59444
Southernfood.com LLC, 59453
Southside Market & Bbq Inc, 59455
Southwest Traders, 59463
Spartan Foods, 59477
SpartanNash Co, 59478
Stamoolis Brothers Co, 59508
Standard Meat Co LP, 59512
Star Fisheries, 59520
State Hotel Supply Company, 59536
Statewide Meats & Poultry, 59540
Staunton Foods LLC, 59543
Steckel, Isadore, 59548
STI International, 59130
Strawhacker's Food Service, 59580
Streit Carl & Son Co, 59583
Summit Food Service Distributors, 59597, 59598
Sunspun Foodservice, 59624
SUPERVALU Distribution, 59132
Supreme Foods, 59645
Sure Fine Food, 59647
Switzer's Inc, 59666
Sygma Network, 59668, 59669
SYGMA Network Inc, 59133
T.A. Morris & Sons, 59750
T.D. Khan, 59755
T.L. Herring & Company, 59757
Tama Trading Co Inc, 59772
Tergerson's Fine Foods, 59807
Texas Halal Corporation, 59818
Texas Marine II, 59820
Texas Meat Purveyors, 59821
Texas Sausage Co, 59822
The Chefs' Warehouse, 59824
The Coop, 59827
The Lamb Company, 59828
Thomas & Howard Co Cash & Crry, 59841
Thomas Brothers Country Ham, 59842
Three Jerks Jerky, 59852
Ths Foodservice, 59855
Thurston Foods Inc, 59858
Tippecanoe Foods, 59869
Todd Distributors Inc, 59874
Tony's Fine Foods, 59879
Tosi & Company, 59893
Toudouze Market Company, 59897
Trans Veyor, 59911
Trio Supply Company, 59939
Truscello & Sons Wholesalers, 59956
Turk Brothers Custom Meats Inc, 59966
Tyson Foods Inc., 59981
U Okada & Co LTD, 59982

Ukiah Foods, 60000
Uncle Charlie's Meats, 60003
Union Grocery Company, 60011
UniPro Foodservice, Inc., 60005
United Universal Enterprises Corporation, 60039
United Wholesale Grocery Company, 60040
Upper Lakes Foods Inc, 60053
US Food Products, 59984
US Foods Inc, 59989, 59990, 59991
US Growers Cold Storage, 59993
UW Provision Co., 59998
Vallet Foodservice, 60068
Valley Distributors, 60071
Valley Foods Inc, 60073
Valley Pride Food Distributor, 60075
Van Eerden Foodservice Co Inc, 60077
Vaughn Packing Company, 60085
Verde Farms, LLC, 60095
Victors Market Co, 60106
Vienna Distributing Company, 60110
Vincent Giordano Prosciutto, 60115
VIP Food Svc, 60061
Virginia Wholesale Company, 60120
Vista Food Exchange, 60124
Vista Food Exchange Inc., 60125
W.G. White & Company, 60161
W.L. Petrey Wholesale Inc., 60164
W.S. Lee & Sons, 60172
Wabash Foodservice Inc, 60184
WACO Beef & Pork Processors, 60174
Waco Meat Service, 60187
Wai Sang Meat, 60191
Wakefern Food Corp, 60193
Wallach's Farms, 60204
Waltkoch Limited, 60209
Weeke Wholesale Company, 60234
West Wholesale Grocery, 60250
Western Family Foods Inc, 60256
Western Grocers, 60257, 60258
White Feather Farms, 60275
Whitehawk Beef Co, 60278
Wholesale Cash & Carry Foods, 60284
Wild Zora Foods, 60298
Wilde Brands, 60299
Williams Institutional Foods, 60310
Williams Sausage Co, 60312
Winchester Food, 60320
Winkler Meats, 60332
Winn-Dixie, 60334
Wise Products Distributors, 60342
Witmer Foods, 60346
Yeager & Associates, 60376
Young & Stout, 60380
Youngstown Wholesale Grocery, 60383
Zabiha Halal Meat Processors, 60389
Zeches Institution Supply, 60393

Rack Jobbers

A&M Enterprises, 54532
A. De LaChevrotiere, 54541
Amster-Kirtz Co, 54812
Angers Equipment Company, 54830
Anter Brothers Company, 54837
Anthracite Provision Co, 54840
Applied Handling NW, 54847
Arctic Star Distributing, 54859
Auto City Candy Company, 54939
Automation Systems & Services, 54941
B.M. Sales Company, 54978
Berton Company, 55188
Bon Ton Food Products, 55279
Bozzuto's Inc., 55311
Brittain Merchandising, 55343
Bronx Butter & Egg Company, 55349
Business Systems & Conslnts, 55399
C D Hartnett Co, 55418
Caesar Electric Supply, 55459
Chia I Foods Company, 55654
Colorado Restaurant Supply, 55765
Core-Mark Holding Company, Inc, 55831, 55833, 55834, 55835, 55839, 55840

Costco Wholesale Corporation, 55852
D. Deodati & Sons, 55941
Davis Coffee Co, 55989
Davis-Le Grand Company, 55992
E.A. Robinson & Company, 56181
Eagle Wholesale Drug Company, 56192
Economy Cash & Carry LP, 56223
Ehrlich Food Co, 56248
El Popular Inc VF Garza, 56251
Engineered Handling Products, 56291
Erman & Son, 56316
Eurpac Warehouse Sales, 56343
F & C Sawaya Wholesale, 56360
F.A. Davis & Sons, 56368
Feather Crest Farms, 56397
Finke Co, 56428
Food Services Inc, 56501
Food-Products, 56505
Frank P. Corso, 56546
Fred W Albrecht Grocery Co, 56555
Garber Bros Inc, 56634
George Greer Company, 56668
George J Howe Co, 56669
Glandt-Dahlke, 56690
Hamms, 56891
Harpak-Ulma, 56933
Hattiesburg Grocery Company, 56955
HE Anderson Co, 56863
Henry Bresky & Sons Inc, 57000
High Country Meats, 57016
Husky Foods of Anchorage, 57094
Independent Wholesale, 57136
International Business Trading, 57180
Irvin, 57207
J Moresky & Son, 57232
J. Connor & Sons, 57247
J.L. Henderson & Company, 57266
Jackson Wholesale Co, 57295
Jacob KERN & Sons Inc, 57297
Jaydon, 57321
Jeffer Neely Company, 57325
Jo Mints, 57352
Joe Christiana Food Distributing, 57357
Kirby Restaurant & Chemical, 57515
Klondike Foods, 57524
Knotts Fine Foods, 57527
Knox Cash Jobbers, 57529
LDC of Lafayette, 57586
Lift Truck Sales Svc & Rentals, 57707
Lincolnwood Merchandising Company, 57724
Long Wholesale Distr Inc, 57756
M. Zukerman & Company, 57811
Malco Industries, 57857
Manchester Grocery Company, 57863
Marlow Candy & Nut Co, 57902
McLane Foodservice Inc, 57964
Metro, Inc., 58018
Midwest Ingredients Inc, 58072
MTC Distributing, 57823
Munchies, 58181
New England Foods, 58298
OH Armstrong, 58417
Omni Food Inc, 58457
Pacific Westcoast Foods, 58536
Pamida, 58559
Rack Service Company, 58918
Rapid Sales Company, 58937
Robin's Food Distribution, 59037
Royal Meats, 59091
S-A-J Distributors, 59115
Sarver Candy Co, 59193
Saugy Inc., 59197
Seder Foods Corporation, 59257
Serv-A-Rack, 59268
Slusser Wholesale Company, 59381
Snack King Foods, 59396
Specialty Merchandise Distributors, 59483
ST Restaurant Supplies, 59129
Star Sales Company, 59528, 59529
Tanner Enterprises, 59777
TBI Corporation, 59761
Thomas & Howard Co Cash & Crry, 59841

Wholesale Product Type / Seafood

Tiger Distributors, 59862
Topicz, 59887
United Bakers & Deli Supply, 60014
US Growers Cold Storage, 59993
US Marketing Company, 59994
W.R. McRae Company Limited, 60167
Wakefern Food Corp, 60193
Western Grocers, 60257
Wilkin-Alaska, 60303
Wilson Ice Machines, 60319
Yale Material Handling/Gammon, 60374

Seafood

1000 Islands River Rat Cheese, 54501
A & D Seafood Corp, 54510
A Tarantino & Sons Poultry, 54523
A-1 Seafood Center, 54535
A. Friscia Seafoods, 54542
A.B. Wise & Sons, 54548
A.C. Covert, 54549
A.M.BRIGGS, 54556
ACC Distributors Inc, 54567
Accord International, 54599
Acme Steak & Seafood, 54610
Adams & Knickle, 54619
Addison Foods Inc, 54623
Adventure Inn Food Trading Company, 54639
AJC International, 54578
Alaska Seafood Co, 54671
Albert Guarnieri & Co, 54674
Albion Fisheries, 54680
Alioto Lazio Fish Co, 54691
All Seasons Fisheries, 54701
Allied Provision Company, 54728
Alphin Brothers, 54735
Alpine Food Distributing Inc, 54736
Alwan & Sons, 54748
Amende & Schultz Co, 54753
American Fish & Seafood Inc, 54764
American Mussel Harvesters Inc, 54783
American Roland Food Corporation, 54792
American Seafood Imports Inc., 54794
American Softshell Crab, 54798
Ampak Seafoods Corporation, 54810
Anderson Seafood, 54821
Anthracite Provision Co, 54840
AP Fish & Produce, 54585
Aqua Source, 54850
Arista Industries Inc, 54864
Asanti Distributors, 54887
Atchison Wholesale Grocery, 54907
Atco Marine Service, 54908
Atlantic Gem Scallop Co, 54912
Atlantic Sea Pride, 54917
Atlantic Seafood Intl Group, 54920
Atwood Lobster Co, 54925
Automation Systems & Services, 54941
Aylesworth's Fish & Bait, 54951
B & B Food Distributors Inc, 54957
B & M Provision Co, 54962
B/R Sales Company, 54980
Bama Sea Products Inc, 55042
Basic Food Intl Inc, 55074
Bassham Institutional Foods, 55078
Battistella's Sea Foods, 55082
Bay State Lobster Company, 55091
Bayou Food Distributors, 55097
Bayou Land Seafood, 55098
Bear Creek Operations, 55103
Bender Meat, 55163
Bensinger's, 55167
Best Market, 55198
BI-LO, 54987
Big Al's Seafood, 55212
Billingsgate Fish Company, 55222
Bisek & Co Inc, 55235
Blackbur Bros Inc, 55242
Blue Buoy Foods, 55255
Blue Ribbon Fish Co, 55263
Blue Ribbon Wholesale, 55265
Bodean Restaurant & Market, 55272
Bon Appetit International, 55277

Bon Secour Fisheries Inc, 55278
Boricua Empaque, 55285
Boston Lobster Co, 55291
Boston Sausage & Provision, 55292
Boston Seafarms, 55293
Bottom Line Foods, 55297
Bronx Butter & Egg Company, 55349
Bunn Capitol Company, 55386
Butte Produce Company, 55402
Buz's Crab, 55404
C & R Food Svc Inc, 55412
C & S Wholesale Grocers Inc, 55414
C A Curtze, 55417
C Pacific Foods Inc, 55421
C. Eberle Sons Company, 55426
Caesar Electric Supply, 55459
Cajun Brothers Seafood Company, 55466
Cajun Crawfish Distributors, 55467
Cambridge Packing Company, 55484
Canada Safeway, 55493
Canadian Gold Seafood, 55494
Cape May Fishery Cooperative, 55505
Capitol Foods, 55510
Captain Little Seafood, 55518
Captain Morrills Inc, 55519
Captree Clam, 55520
Carbonella & Desarbo Inc, 55523
Carolina Mountain, 55544
Caspian Trading Company, 55568
Cataract Foods, 55576
Central Coast Seafood, 55590
CF Imperial Sales, 55441
Chef John Folse & Co, 55637
Chicago Food Corporation, 55657
Cirelli Foods, 55689
City Fish Sales, 55695
City Line Food Distributors, 55696
Clayton's Crab Co, 55713
Clover Leaf Seafoods, 55727
Coast to Coast Foods Group, 55729
Cockrell's Creek Seafood & Deli, 55741
Colbourne Seafood, 55751
Connecticut Shellfish Co Inc, 55797
Copperwood InternationalInc, 55826
Cost Plus, 55850
Costco Wholesale Corporation, 55852
Cotati Brand Eggs & Food Svc, 55853
Couch's Rich Plan Foods, 55854
Cozy Harbor Seafood Inc, 55867
Crab, 55868
Crab Connection, 55869
Crocker & Winsor Seafoods, 55887
Culinary Specialties, 55908
D'Eon Fisheries, 55939
D. Fillet & Company, 55942
Daffin Mercantile Company, 55964
Dairy King Milk Farms/Foodservice, 55967
Davis Distributors of Owensboro Company, 55990
De Choix Specialty Foods Company, 55995
Deep Sea Products, 56016
Deiss Sales Co. Inc., 56020
Del Mar Seafood's Inc, 56022
Delta Pride Catfish, 56030
Deng's, 56034
Diamond Reef Seafood, 56057
Dicarlo Distributors Inc, 56059
Dickerson Foods, 56062
Dierks Foods, 56064
Direct Seafood, 56078
Distribution Kowloon, 56084
Distribution Plus, 56085
Dockside Seafood & Specs Inc, 56097
Doerle Food Svc, 56098
Dr. Willy's Great American Seafood, 56133
Dutch Creek Foods, 56156
E G Forrest Co Inc, 56171
E Goodwin & Sons, 56172
East Coast Seafood Inc, 56202
East Side Fisheries, 56204
Eastern Shore Clam Company, 56211
Ehrlich Food Co, 56248

Empire Packing Co, 56283
Epicurean Foods, 56303
Ettline Foods Corp, 56331
Euclid Fish Co, 56333
Eugene & Company, 56334
Evans Foodservice Inc., 56346
F & A Food Sales Inc, 56359
F B Mc Fadden Wholesale Co, 56361
Fab Inc, 56372
Fadler Company, 56374
Fairs Seafood, 56377
Fairway Foods, 56379
Family Foods Home Service, 56382
Farm Fish, 56388
Farmers Seafood Co Wholesale, 56390
Farmfresh, 56391
Farner-Bocken Co, 56394
Federated Cooperative, 56399
Federated Cooperative Lt, 56400
Feesers, 56404
Ferntrade Corporation, 56408
Fish Breeders of Idaho, 56440
Fisherman's Seafood Market, 56444
Five Continents, 56448
Flint Provision Inc Zalack's, 56467
Florida Fresh Stonecrab, 56473
Food Authority Inc, 56488
Food-Products, 56505
Foremost Foods Company, 56515
Fournier R & Sons Seafood, 56532
Frankstown Fish Co Inc, 56552
Fruge Aquafarms, 56582
G & L Import Export Corp, 56596
G.W. Market, 56605
Garavaglia Meat Company, 56633
Garden & Valley Isle Seafood, 56635
Gaylord's Meat Co, 56647
George D. Spence & Sons, 56665
GFS (Canada) Company, 56611
Giant Eagle American Seaway Foods, 56677
GIANT Food Stores, 56612
Ginsberg's Institutional Foods, 56687
Goetz & Sons Western Meat, 56702
Goff's Seafood, 56703, 56704
Goldberg & Solovy Foods Inc, 56710
Golden Eye Seafood, 56713
Gordon Food Service, 56731
Gourmet Club Corporation, 56751
Gourmet Foods Intl, 56752
Great Western Meats, 56795
Greene Poultry Co, 56801
Grocers Supply Co, 56819
Gulf Food Products Co Inc, 56829
Gulf Marine & Industrial Supplies Inc, 56831
Gunderland Marine Supply, 56840
Guy Locicero & Sons, 56843
H.Y. Louie Company, 56857
Haitai Inc, 56878
Hampton Roads Seafoods Ltd, 56893
Harker's Distribution, 56925, 56926
Harpak-Ulma, 56933
Harrison Oyster Company, 56936
Hart Lobster, 56944
Harveys Supermarket, 56950
Hata Y & Co LTD, 56953
Heads & Tails Seafood, 56968
Hearn-Kirkwood, 56979
Henry Bresky & Sons Inc, 57000
Henry Gonsalves Co, 57002
Hill's Pier 19 Restaurant Lighthouse Bar, 57023
Hipp Wholesale Foods, 57031
Hoban Foods, 57033
Holland Beef International Corporation, 57044
Holly Seafood Company, 57048
Home-Like Food Company, 57052
Homestead Foods, 57053
Huck's Seafood, 57074
Iceberg Seafood Inc, 57122
Imperial Seafood, 57129
Imperial Trading, 57131
Importex International, 57133

Independent Wholesale, 57136
Indianhead Foodservice, 57143
Institutional Wholesale Company, 57170
International Business Trading, 57180
International Enterprises Unlimited, 57187
International Marine Products, 57189
Island Supply, 57216
Italfoods Inc, 57219
J Petite & Sons, 57237
J. Hellman Frozen Foods, 57248
J. Sosnick & Sons, 57254
J.L. Henderson & Company, 57266
Jab's Seafood, 57289
Jako Fish, 57303
Jamac Frozen Foods, 57304
Janney Marshall Co, 57312
JBG International, 57276
Jet Set Sam, 57341
Jetro Cash & Carry Inc, 57344
Jilasco Food Exports, 57346
Joe Pucci & Sons Seafood, 57360
John Graves Food Service, 57368
John Nagle & Co, 57376
Jordan Lobster Farms, 57395
Joseph Apicella & Sons, 57397
Jost Kauffman Import & Export Company, 57400
Junction City Distributing & Vending Company, 57409
Kaleel Bros Inc, 57437
Karetas Foods Inc, 57448
KAST Distributors Inc, 57425
Kelley Foods, 57476
Kelley-Clarke, 57477
Kenny Seafood, 57486
Keys Fisheries Market & Marina, 57500
Kings Choice Food, 57509
Kings Seafood Co, 57510
KOHL Wholesale, 57429
Lafitte Seafood Company, 57610
Lake Superior Fish Co, 57615
Land's End Seafood, 57624
Landphair Meat & Seafood, 57627
Lanzarotta Wholesale Grocers, 57634
LaRocca's Seafood Specialists, 57596
Leali Brothers Meats, 57654
Lee Grocery Company, 57659
Lehmann-Colorado, 57665
Leonard & Sons Shrimp Company, 57676
Liberty Marine Products, 57695
Lincoln Shrimp Company, 57723
Lobster Warehouse, 57742
Lockwood & Winant, 57743
Logan, 57745
Lombardi Brothers Meat Packers, 57749
Lombardi's Seafood, 57750
Lorenzo's Wholesale Foods, 57766
Lowcountry Shellfish Inc, 57777
Ludwig Fish & Produce Company, 57782
Lumaco Inc, 57784
M&F Foods, 57805
MacGregors Meat & Seafood, 57827
Madison Food Sales Company, 57836
Maine Shellfish Co Inc, 57849
Maines Paper & Food Svc Inc, 57850
Marcus Food Co, 57882
Mariner Neptune Fish & Seafood Company, 57890
Market Foods International, 57895
Marky's Caviar, 57900
Marriott Distribution Service, 57903
Marrone's Inc, 57904
Martin Bros Distributing Co, 57908
Martin Seafood Company, 57913
Mattingly Foods, 57937
Maxim's Import Corporation, 57938
Mazo-Lerch Company, 57952
McCabe's Quality Foods, 57956
Mcdonald Wholesale Co, 57973
Mcfarling Foods Inc, 57974
McGrath Fisheries, 57960
Meadow Farm Foods, 57983
Medina & Medina, 57989
Menu Maker Foods Inc, 57998

1265

Wholesale Product Type / Specialty Food

Merchants Foodservice, 58001
Mermaid Seafoods, 58006
Metompkin Bay Oyster Company, 58015
Metro, Inc., 58018
Metro-Richelieu, 58019
Middendorf Meat, 58058
Midwest Ingredients Inc, 58072
Mill Cove Lobster Pound, 58080
Millbrook Distribution Service, 58083
Miss Mary, 58098
Mitchell Grocery Corp, 58102
Mivila Foods, 58104
Mj Kellner Co, 58105
Mobjack Bay Seafood, 58107
Monterrey Provision Co, 58129
Moon's Seafood Company, 58131
Motivatit Seafoods Inc, 58155
Mt Pleasant Seafood, 58169
Munchies, 58181
Mutual Fish Co, 58193
Nappie's Food Svc, 58217
Natco Worldwide Representative, 58228
National Grocers Company, 58238, 58239, 58241
Neesvig Meats, 58279
Nevada Seafood Company, 58292
New England Foods, 58298
New England Meat Company, 58300
New Harbor Fisherman's Cooperative, 58301
Nicholas & Co Inc, 58322
Nichols Foodservice, 58323
NJM Seafood, 58206
Noon Hour Food Products Inc, 58342
Norland Products Inc, 58346
North Atlantic Lobster, 58356
Northern Haserot, 58365
Northwest Deli Distribution, 58379
Northwest Naturals Company, 58381
Northwest Wild Products, 58383
O.W. & B.S. Look Company, 58415
Ocean Frost, 58427
Ocean Venture, 58431
Old Point Packing Inc, 58445
Omni Pacific Company, 58459
Original Food, 58476
Oyang America, 58495
Oyster Peddler, 58496
P & D Corp, 58500
Pacific California Fish Company, 58524
Pacific Rim Shellfish Corp., 58531
Pacific Seafood Co, 58532
Pacific World Enterprises, 58537
PAFCO Importing Co, 58513
Palmer Food Service, 58553
Pate-Derby Company, 58592
Pats Seafood & Cajun Deli, 58595
Paturel International Company, 58598
Pellican Seafood, 58614
Performance Food Group Customized Distribution, 58632, 58633, 58634, 58635, 58636, 58637, 58638, 58639
Performance Foodservice, 58640, 58641, 58642, 58643, 58644, 58645, 58647, 58648, 58649, 58650, 58651, 58652, 58653, 58654, 58655, 58656, 58657, 58658, 58659, 58660, 58661, 58662, 58663, 58664, 58665, 58666, 58667, 58668, 58669, 58670, 58671, 58672, 58673, 58674, 58675, 58676
Perry B Duryea & Son Inc, 58679
Peterson Sea Food Company, 58687
Pierceton Foods Inc, 58707
Pocono ProFoods, 58729
Pon Food Corp, 58737
Pontiac Fruit House, 58740
Porky Products, 58744
Port Lobster Co Inc, 58745
Portugalia Imports, 58751
Portuguese United Grocer Co-Op, 58752
Potato Specialty Company, 58758
Prawn Seafoods Inc, 58766
Premier Foodservice Distributors of America, 58771
Prime Cut Meat & Seafood Company, 58788
Professional Food Systems, 58806, 58807
Proficient Food Company, 58811
Pueblo Trading Co Inc, 58825
Pulini Produce, 58826
PYA/Monarch, 58520
Quality Food Company, 58854
Quality Groceries, 58858
Qualy Pak Specialty Foods, 58863
Quandt's Foodservice Distributors, 58864
R S Stern Inc, 58886
R.S. Hamilton Company, 58904
Rainbow Foods, 58919
Ramex Foods, 58930
Randy's Frozen Meats, 58934
Range Packing Company, 58935
Ray Cosgrove Brokerage Company, 58941
Red Chamber Co, 58954
Registry Steak & Seafood, 58971
Reinhart Foodservice LLC, 58972
Restaurant Depot, 58987
Richmond Restaurant Svc, 59002
Rider's Ranch Escargot, 59006
RightWay Foods, 59009
Rihm Foods, 59010
Rimfire Imports, 59011
Robert Wholey & Co Inc, 59031
Robert's Foods Company, 59032
Robinson Canning Company, 59038
Roland J. Trosclair Canning, 59057
Royal Crown Enterprises, 59003
Russell N. Roy Company, 59097
Ryans Wholesale Food Distributors, 59101
Sagaya Corp, 59142
Salad Depot, 59146
Salty Girl Seafood, 59155
Sam's Club, 59164
San Diego Products, 59171
Sands Brands International Food, 59182
Saval Foods Corp, 59199
Schneider's Fish & Seafood Co, 59215
Schumacher Wholesale Meats, 59219
Scranton Fish Company, 59226
Sea Change Seafoods, 59228
Sea Pearl Seafood, 59232
Sea Products West Inc, 59233
Seacore Seafood, 59237
Seacrest Foods, 59238
Seafood Dimensions Intl, 59243
Seattle Fish Co, 59252
Select Meat Company, 59262
Shaheen Bros Inc, 59282
Shamrock Foods Co, 59286, 59288
Shemper Seafood Co, 59304
Sherwood Food Distributors, 59310
Shetakis Foodservice, 59318
Sid Green Frozen Foods, 59337
Sidney's, 59342
Simco Foods, 59350
Sirca Foodservice, 59365
Slade Gorton & Co Inc, 59378
Sobey's Ontario, 59408
Sobeys Inc., 59410, 59411, 59412, 59413, 59414, 59415
Sogelco International, 59419
Somerset Industries, 59422
SpartanNash Co, 59478
Squid Ink, 59498
St. Helen Seafoods, 59502
St. Ours & Company, 59503
Standard Meat Co LP, 59512
Star Fisheries, 59520
State Hotel Supply Company, 59536
Staunton Foods LLC, 59543
Stavis Seafoods, 59545
Stone Crabs Inc, 59572
Strawhacker's Food Service, 59580
Summit Food Service Distributors, 59597
Summit Import Corp, 59599
Sunburst Trout Farms, 59609
Sunspun Foodservice, 59624
Super Snooty Sea Food Corporation, 59630
Superior Seafoods Inc, 59639
SUPERVALU Distribution, 59132
Supreme Lobster, 59646
T.C. Food Export/Import Company, 59753
T.L. Herring & Company, 59757
Tanglewood Farm, 59775
Tanner Enterprises, 59777
Taroco Food Corporation, 59784
Tenth & M Seafoods, 59806
Tergerson's Fine Foods, 59807
Texas Meat Purveyors, 59821
The Van Cleve Seafood Company, 59836
Thomas & Howard Co Cash & Crry, 59841
Thomas Brothers Country Ham, 59842
Thomson Groceries Ltd., 59851
Todd Distributors Inc, 59874
Tomich Brothers Seafoods, 59877
Tony's Fine Foods, 59879
Tosi & Company, 59893
Town & Country Wholesale, 59901
Tradelink, 59909
Trans Veyor, 59911
Tri-Marine International, 59929
Tsar Nicoulai Caviar LLC, 59957
Turk Brothers Custom Meats Inc, 59966
U Okada & Co LTD, 59982
Ultimate Foods, 60001
UniPro Foodservice, Inc., 60005
United Noodles, 60028
United Seafood Imports, 60034
United Shellfish Co Inc, 60035
United Universal Enterprises Corporation, 60039
United Wholesale Grocery Company, 60040
Universal Fish of Boston, 60044
US Food Products, 59984
US Foods Inc, 59991
US Growers Cold Storage, 59993
Vallet Foodservice, 60068
Vaughn Packing Company, 60085
Victors Market Co, 60106
Vincent Piazza Jr & Sons, 60116
VIP Food Svc, 60061
Vista Food Exchange, 60124
Vista Food Exchange Inc., 60125
W.F. Alber Inc., 60158
W.F. Morgan & Sons, 60159
W.L. Petrey Wholesale Inc., 60164
W.R. Merry Seafood Company, 60168
W.R. Pittman & Sons, 60170
W.S. Lee & Sons, 60172
Waco Meat Service, 60187
Waltkoch Limited, 60209
Wescotek Inc, 60241
Western Grocers, 60257, 60258
Westwind Resources, 60264
White Feather Farms, 60275
Wholesale Cash & Carry Foods, 60284
Wilderness Foods, 60300
Winchester Foods, 60320
Wing Sing Seafood Inc, 60328
Winkler Meats, 60332
Winn-Dixie, 60334
Witmer Foods, 60346
WK Eckerd & Sons, 60182
Young's Lobster Pound, 60382

Specialty Food

1000 Islands River Rat Cheese, 54501
A & B Distributing Co, 54509
A La Mode Distributors, 54521
A&D Distributors, 54527
A. Sargenti Company, 54545
A.B. Wise & Sons, 54548
A.L. Verna Company, 54555
A.M.BRIGGS, 54556
Advantage Gourmet Importers, 54637
Adventure Inn Food Trading Company, 54639
Agro Foods, Inc., 54654
Albert Uster Imports Inc, 54675
Alex & George, 54685
Allegro Coffee Co, 54714
Allemagnia Imports Inc, 54715
Allied International Corp, 54725
Altech Packaging Company, 54743
Alternative Health & Herbs, 54745
Alwan & Sons, 54748
American Agrotrading, 54756
American Food Systems, 54768
American Roland Food Corporation, 54792
American Seafood Imports Inc., 54794
Amster-Kirtz Co, 54812
Ancora Coffee Roasters, 54817
Anthracite Provision Co, 54840
Anton-Argires, 54841
Antone's Import Company, 54842
Arctic Beverages, 54856
Aroma Foods, 54878
Art's Trading, 54883
Artique, 54885
Asanti Distributors, 54887
Atchison Wholesale Grocery, 54907
B & M Provision Co, 54962
Bachman Foods, 54996
Baja Trading Company, 55012
Bakery Things, 55026
Bakker Produce, 55028
Baldwin Richardson Foods, 55031
Balford Farms, 55032
Bandwagon Brokerage, 55045
Banner Wholesale Grocers, 55047
Bari Italian Foods, 55057
Barkett Fruit Company, 55061
Bascom Food Products, 55073
Bayou Food Distributors, 55097
Bedessee Imports, 55110
Beer Import Co, 55115
Bell-View Brand Food Products, 55125
Bentan Corporation, 55169
Bergin Fruit & Nut Co., 55171
Berlin Packaging, 55174
Bernard's Bakery, 55181
Bertrand's, 55189
Best Friends Cocoa, 55196
Bewley Irish Imports, 55209
Bisek & Co Inc, 55235
Bishop Brothers, 55236
BMT Commodity Corporation, 54989
Bon Ton Food Products, 55279
Bottom Line Foods, 55297
British Aisles, 55340
British Wholesale Imports, 55342
Bronx Butter & Egg Company, 55349
Butte Produce Company, 55402
C A Curtze, 55417
C Pacific Foods Inc, 55421
C. Eberle Sons Company, 55426
C.G. Suarez Distributing Company, 55430
Caesar Electric Supply, 55459
Canton Foods, 55500
Capalbo's Fruit Baskets, 55503
Capitol Foods, 55510
Capone Foods, 55511
Carrot Top Pastries, 55554
Cataract Foods, 55576
Cauble & Field, 55578
Caudill Seed Co Inc, 55579
Certified Food Services, 55613
Chamberlain Wholesale Grocery, 55618
Chef's Pride Gifts LLC, 55639
Chellino Cheese Co, 55642
Chelsea Market Baskets, 55643
Chia I Foods Company, 55654
Chicago Coffee Roastery, 55656
Chicago Food Corporation, 55657
Chile Guy, 55663
Chipurnoi Inc, 55667
Christopher's Herb Shop, 55679
Cirelli Foods, 55689

1266

Wholesale Product Type / Specialty Food

City Line Food Distributors, 55696
Coffee Express Roasting Co, 55744
Colorado Nut Co, 55763
Commodities Marketing Inc, 55778
Conca D'Oro Importers, 55785
Concord Foods Co, 55790
Consolidated Poultry & Egg Company, 55804
Cooseman's D.C., 55825
Core-Mark Holding Company, Inc, 55832
Coriell Associates, 55845
Costco Wholesale Corporation, 55852
Cotati Brand Eggs & Food Svc, 55853
Country Life Foods, 55859
Creative Foods of the Southwest, 55878
Crispy Bagel Co, 55884
Crown Point, 55893
Culinary Masters Corporation, 55906
Culinary Specialties, 55908, 55909
D.A. Colongeli & Sons, 55943
Dale's Meats, 55973
Dalmatian Bay Wine Company, 55974
Danish Cones, 55979
De Choix Specialty Foods Company, 55995
Deep Foods Inc, 56015
Demma Fruit Company, 56032
Deng's, 56034
Detroit Popcorn, 56044
DeVries Imports, 56000
Dial Industries Inc, 56053
Dickerson Foods, 56062
DiGregorio Food Products, 56050
Dilgard Frozen Foods, 56068
Dipasa USA Inc, 56075
Dishaka Imports, 56081
Distribution Kowloon, 56084
Distribution Plus, 56085
Dolly Madison Ice Cream, 56103
Don Walters Company, 56109
Dore Foods, 56113
Dorsett & Jackson Inc, 56116
Downeast Food Distributors Inc, 56129
DPI Mid Atlantic, 55953
DPI Rocky Mountain, 55955
DPI Specialty Foods Inc., 55956
Dr. John's Candies, 56131
Dr. Smoothie Brands, 56132
Droubi's Imports, 56141
E M Trisler Sales Co Fd Prods, 56173
Economy Paper & Restaurant Inc, 56224
Ecuadorian Rainforest LLC, 56228
EFCO Products Inc, 56185
El Molino Tamales, 56250
El Popular Inc VF Garza, 56251
Elco Fine Foods, 56253, 56254
Elegant Desserts, 56260
Empire Tea Svc, 56284
Engineered Handling Products, 56291
Enzamar, 56300
Euclid Fish Co, 56333
European Foods, 56340
Evan Peters & Company, 56344
EZ Foods, 56189
F & C Sawaya Wholesale, 56360
F B Mc Fadden Wholesale Co, 56361
F McConnell & Sons, 56365
Fab Inc, 56372
Fairs Seafood, 56377
Family Foods Home Service, 56382
Fancy Delights, 56384
Ferntrade Corporation, 56408
Fine Distributing, 56422
Five Continents, 56448
Flamingo Flats, 56454
Flora Foods Inc, 56468
Florida Beverage Connection, 56469
Food Authority Inc, 56488
Food-Products, 56505
Freiria & Company, 56559
FreshPro Food Distributors, 56567
Fruit Of The Vine Of De Valley, 56585
G & L Import Export Corp, 56596
G&G Distributing, 56600
G.D. Mathews & Sons, 56604
Galilee Splendor, 56626
Galli Produce Inc, 56629
Galloway's Specialty Foods, 56630
Garavaglia Meat Company, 56633
Garden Spot Distributors, 56637
George Degen & Co, 56666
Gillco Ingredients, 56679
Gillies Coffee, 56682
Gimme Sum Mo Cajun Foods Corporation, 56685
Giovanni Food Co Inc, 56688
Global Harvest, 56693
Golden Moon Tea, 56718
Golden Orchard, 56719
Golden Valley Popcorn Supply, 56721
Goldy Food Sales Company, 56723
Gone Wild!!!, 56724
Gosselin Gourmet Beverages, 56748
Gourmet Award Foods, 56749
Gourmet Products, 56753
Grantstone Supermarket, 56767
Great American Popcorn Works of Pennsylvania, 56773
Green Valley Food Corp, 56800
Greenfield Noodle & Spec Co, 56803
GSC Enterprises Inc., 56617
GTM, 56618
Guans Mushroom Co, 56826
Gulf Pecan Company, 56833
GWB Foods Corporation, 56620
Haddon House Food Products, 56873
Haitai Inc, 56878
Hanif's International Foods, 56900
Hanmi, 56901
Haram-Christensen Corp, 56916
Hardscrabble Enterprises, 56923
Harger's Finest Catch, 56924
Harpak-Ulma, 56933
Harry Fourtunis Inc, 56938
Hata Y & Co LTD, 56953
Hauser Enterprises, 56956
Hawaiian Coffee Traders, 56960
Hawaiian Grocery Stores, 56961
Hearn-Kirkwood, 56979
Henry Bresky & Sons Inc, 57000
HFM Foodservice, 56865
Hialeah Products Co, 57012
Hickory Harvest Foods, 57014
Hogtowne B-B-Q Sauce Company, 57039
Holland Beef International Corporation, 57044
Holland-American International Specialties, 57045
Home-Like Food Company, 57052
Hosoda Brothers Inc, 57064
Hot Sauce Harry's Inc, 57066
House of Spices, 57067
Hudson Valley Coffee Company, 57078
Hunter Walton & Co Inc, 57092
Husky Foods of Anchorage, 57094
I Wanna Distributors, 57102
IBF, 57107
ID Foods Corporation, 57109
In A Nutshell, 57135
India Emporium, 57137
Indo-European Foods, 57145
Ingenuities, 57157
Ingredient Exchange Co, 57160
Intermix Beverage, 57177
International Business Trading, 57180
International Distribution, 57186
International Enterprises Unlimited, 57187
InterNatural Foods, 57174
Islander Import, 57217
Italfina, 57218
Italfoods Inc, 57219
Italica Imports, 57220
J&S Food Distributors, 57246
J. Hellman Frozen Foods, 57248
J. Rutigliano & Sons, 57253
J. Sosnick & Sons, 57254
J.C. Wright Sales Company, 57260
Jack & Jill Ice Cream, 57291
Jacob KERN & Sons Inc, 57297
Jamaican Teas Limited C/O Eve Sales Corporation, 57306
Jet Set Sam, 57341
Jetro Cash & Carry Inc, 57344
Jianas Brothers Packaging, 57345
Jo Mints, 57352
Joe Pucci & Sons Seafood, 57360
John Graves Food Service, 57368
Joyce Foods, 57402
Jp Tropical Foods, 57404
Julius Silvert Company, 57408
JUST Inc, 57288
Kadouri International Foods, 57434
Kane's Kandies, 57441
Kar Wah Trading Company, 57446
Karetas Foods Inc, 57449
Katy's Wholesale Distributing, 57453
Kay's Foods, 57456
KeHE Distributors, 57458, 57459, 57460, 57461, 57462, 57463, 57464, 57465, 57466, 57467, 57468, 57469, 57470, 57471, 57472, 57473
Kemach Food Products, 57480
Ken Young Food Distributors, 57483
Kingston Candy & Tobacco Co, 57512
Kissner Milling Company, 57517
Kitchen Maid Foods, 57518
Klein Foods, Inc, 57522
Klondike Foods, 57524
Knotts Fine Foods, 57527
KYD Inc, 57432
L. Lacagnina & Sons, 57571
LA Bella Ferrara, 57575
LA Canasta Mexican Foods, 57576
LA Cena Fine Foods LTD, 57577
LA India Packing Co Inc, 57580
LA Rue Distributing, 57582
La Tang Cuisine Manufacturing, 57594
LA Torilla Factory, 57584
Laredo Tortilleria & Mexican, 57635
Le Cordon Bleu, 57651
Lee Grocery Company, 57659
Lemberger Candy Corporation, 57669
Lems, 57671
Leo A Dick & Sons, 57674
Levant, 57682
Liberty Natural Products Inc, 57696
Liberty Richter, 57697
Libido Funk Circus, 57700
Lieber Chocolate Food Prod LTD, 57702
Lincolnwood Merchandising Company, 57724
Lipten & Co, 57731
Lomar Distributing Inc, 57748
Lombardi Brothers Meat Packers, 57749
Longhorn Liquors, 57759
Lorain Novelty Company, 57763
Lorenz Schneider Co, 57764
Lowell Brothers & Bailey, 57778
M. Sickles & Sons, 57810
Malt Diastase Co, 57861
Mancuso Cheese Co, 57865
Manhattan Key Lime Juice Company, 57870
Mani Imports, 57872
Maple Hollow, 57878
Marcus Specialty Foods, 57883
Mariner Neptune Fish & Seafood Company, 57890
Market Foods International, 57895
Marky's Caviar, 57900
Marriott Distribution Service, 57903
Maxim's Import Corporation, 57938
Maxin Marketing Corporation, 57939
Mecca Coffee Company, 57988
Mediterranean Gyro Products, 57990
Mercado Latino, 57999
Merlino Foods, 58005
Mexspice, 58022
Michael Raymond Desserts Inc, 58030
Middendorf Meat, 58058
Midori Trading Inc, 58062
Midwest Distribution Group, 58067
Midwest Ingredients Inc, 58072
Millbrook Distribution Services, 58082
Millbrook Distribution Service, 58083
Miss Grimble Desserts, 58097
Mivila Foods, 58104
Moctezuma Foods, 58108
Modern Macaroni Co LTD, 58114
Modern Wholesale Company, 58117
Molinera International, 58121
Mom N' Pops Inc, 58122
More For Less Foods, 58138
Morrisons Pastry Corp, 58146
Mother Earth Enterprises, 58152
Mountain People's Warehouse, 58157
Muir Copper Canyon Farms, 58174
Munchies, 58181
Mung Dynasty, 58182
Murry's Family of Fine Foods, 58187
Musco Food Corp, 58188
Mutual Trading Co Inc, 58194
Nappie's Food Svc, 58217
Nassau Candy Distributors, 58223
Natural Dairy Products Corp, 58259
Natural Food Systems, 58261
Natural Group, 58263
Nature's Best, 58266
Nature's Candy, 58268
Neel's Wholesale Produce Co, 58277
Neighbors Coffee, 58280
Nelipak, 58281
Neshaminy Valley Natural Foods, 58286
Neuman Distributing Company, 58289
New Britain Candy Company, 58296
New England Meat Company, 58300
New Mexico Food Distributors, 58304
Nick Sciabica & Sons, 58324
Nielsen-Massey Vanillas Inc, 58326
Nikol Foods, 58329
Noble Harvest, 58336
North American Provisioners, 58354
Northern WIS Produce Co, 58371
Northwest Deli Distribution, 58379
Nothing Mundane, 58387
Nuherbs Company, 58395
Occidental Foods International, LLC, 58425
Omega-Life, 58456
Original Food, 58476
Our Lady of Guadalupe Trappist Abbey, 58491
Outerbridge Peppers Limited, 58493
Ozark Cooperative Warehouse, 58497
P A Menard, 58502
Pacific Resources, 58530
Pacific Westcoast Foods, 58536
Palmetto Candy & Tobacco Company, 58556
Paradise Island Foods, 58568
Paskesz Candy Co, 58589
Paul Perkins Food Distributors, 58600
Pennsylvania Macaroni Company Inc., 58621
Performance Foodservice, 58646
Peterson, 58686
Pioneer Distributing Company, 58713
Pocono ProFoods, 58729
Poiret International, 58731
Polean Foods, 58733
Polish Folklore Import Co, 58734
Pontiac Fruit House, 58740
Power Creamery, 58761
Power Source Distributors, 58764
Premier Foodservice Distributors of America, 58771
Priester's Pecans, 58787
Primo Cheese, 58791
Proacec USA, 58797
Pulini Produce, 58826
Pulmuone Foods USA Inc., 58827
Purchase Order Co Of Miami Inc, 58830
Putnam Candy, 58836
PYA/Monarch, 58520
Quadra Foods Company, 58843
Quality Foods International, 58857
QUALITY Frozen Foods, 58841
R Hirt Jr Co, 58882
R.E. Diamond, 58899

1267

Wholesale Product Type / Specialty Food

R.F. Beyers, 58900
R.N. Mason & Son, 58903
R.T. Greene Company, 58906
Rack Service Company, 58918
Rainbow Foods, 58919
Rainbow Natural Foods, 58920
Ramex Foods, 58930
Randy's Frozen Meats, 58934
Real Cajun School Of Cooking, 58950
Red Hot Chicago, 58956
Regency Coffee & Vending, 58969
Registry Steak & Seafood, 58971
Reinhart Foodservice LLC, 58972
Reliable Mercantile Company, 58975
Restaurant Depot, 58987
Restaurant Food Supply, 58990
Rex Pacific, 58994
Ricci & Company, 58997
Rider's Ranch Escargot, 59006
Rihm Foods, 59010
Rimfire Imports, 59011
Rino Gnesi Company, 59012
Robert D. Arnold & Associates, 59028
Roma of Minnesota, 59061
Ross Foods, 59073
Royal Crown Enterprises, 59083
Royal Foods Inc, 59086, 59087
Ryans Wholesale Food Distributors, 59101
S-A-J Distributors, 59115
Sahadi Fine Foods Inc, 59144
Salad Depot, 59146
Sam's Cakes, Cookies, Candy, 59163
Sam's Club, 59164
Sampac Enterprises, 59168
Sands African Imports, 59181
Sands Brands International Food, 59182
Sansone Food Products Co, 59185
Santa Claus Industries, 59188
SAPNA Foods, 59123
Sassone Wholesale Groceries Co, 59194
Saugy Inc., 59197
Saval Foods Corp, 59199
Schumacher Wholesale Meats, 59219
Sea Change Seafoods, 59228
Sea Salt Superstore, 59234
Seattle Fish Co, 59252
SGS International Rice Inc, 59126
Shanghai Freemen, 59292
Sherwood Food Distributors, 59310, 59313
Shiff & Goldman Foods, 59319
Shivji Enterprises, 59324
Sid Alpers Organic Sales Company, 59335
Sid Wainer & Son Specialty, 59339
Sidehill Farm, 59341
Sierra Nut House, 59346
Signature Packaging, 59347
Simpson & Vail, 59354
Sinclair Trading, 59359
Smiths Sunbeam Bakery, 59390
Smitty's Snowballs, 59391
Sonora Foods, 59424
Soofer Co, 59426
Sovrana Trading Corp, 59469
Spice & Spice, 59487
Spice House International Specialties, 59488
Squid Ink, 59498
St. Clair Foods Distributing, 59500
St. Ours & Company, 59503
Statewide Products Co Inc, 59541
Stella Maria's, 59554
Steve's Fine Food Emporium, 59559
Streit Carl & Son Co, 59583
Summit Import Corp, 59599
Sunflower Food Company, 59613
Sunspun Foodservice, 59624
Supreme Food, 59644
Supreme Foods, 59645
Sweet Liberty Candy Company, 59653
Sweet Place, 59654
Swiss Chalet Fine Foods, 59663
Sygma Network, 59668, 59669
SYGMA Network Inc, 59133
Synergee Foods Corporation, 59670
T.B. Venture, 59752
Tallarico Food Products, 59771
Tama Trading Co Inc, 59772
Tanner Enterprises, 59777
Taormina Co, 59779
Tatra Sheep Cheese Company, 59788
Terra Ingredients LLC, 59809
The Bachman Company, 59823
The Chefs' Warehouse, 59824
The Coconut Cooperative, LLC, 59825
Theatre Candy Distributing Company, 59837
Third Planet Products, 59838
Tony's Fine Foods, 59879
Top Hat Co Inc, 59883
Topicz, 59887
Tosi & Company, 59893
Town & Country Fancy Foods, 59899
Tradelink, 59909
Trans Veyor, 59911
Treasure Coast Coffee Company, 59914
Tree of Life Canada, 59917, 59918, 59919, 59920
Tropical Link Canada Ltd., 59947
Truscello & Sons Wholesalers, 59956
Tsar Nicoulai Caviar LLC, 59957
Tucson Coop. Warehouse, 59960
Turkana Food, 59967
Two Guys Spice Company, 59977
Ultimate Foods, 60001
United Bakers & Deli Supply, 60014
United Noodles, 60028
Unity Brands Group, 60042
Universal Preservachem Inc, 60047
US Food Products, 59984
US Growers Cold Storage, 59993
Vallero Mercantile Company, 60067
Valu-Line Foods, 60076
Vaughn-Russell Candy Kitchen, 60086
Vermont Country Naturals, 60097
Vermont Wholesale Foods, 60098
Vidalia Sweets Brand, 60109
Vilore Foods Company, 60113
Vincent Piazza Jr & Sons, 60116
Voyageur Trading Division, 60146
W & B Distributing Co, 60148
W A DeHart Inc, 60149
W.S. Lee & Sons, 60172
Wega USA, 60235
West Tenn Dairy Products, 60249
Western Grocers, 60258
White Feather Farms, 60275
Whitfield Olive, 60280, 60281
Wilcox Frozen Foods, 60296
Willing Group, 60315
Windy City Organics, 60324
Wine Country Chef LLC, 60325
Wing Sing Chong Company, 60327
Winmix/Natural Care Products, 60333
Wise Products Distributors, 60342
Woodland Foods, 60353
World Finer Foods Inc, 60357
Wustefeld Candy Co Inc, 60366
YAAX International, 60370
Yeager & Associates, 60376
Zarda King LTD, 60391
Ziba Nut Inc, 60398

All Brands Index

Numeric

-196 C, 1120
06 Stout, 9688
1-2-3 Gluten Free, 1
10, 2738
10 Barrel Brewing Co., 571
10 Cane, 8452
100 Anos®, 1120
100 Bourbon Whiskey, 10596
100 Calorie Packs, 8729
100 Grandc, 2132
100 Pipers, 9964
100% Flaked Wheat, 6917
100% Purified Non Carbonated Water, 13206
100% Whole Grain, 8844
101, 24499
101 Piterra Place, 10789
10th St. Bakery, 30808
12% Imports, 10666
14'er Esb, 838
1450 Food Pack Analyzer, 29063
150 Bloom, 13498
1710, 5331
1792, 11263
1792 Ridgemont Reserve Bourbon, 11264
18 Rabbits, 5
1848 Winery, 10952
1855®, 6391
1857 Spirits, 1023
1859 Porter, 2911
1883, 10917
19, 3447
19 Crimes, 12937
1911 Originals, 27289
1950 127 Brand, 4591
1st Sneeze Echinacea, 13015
2 Gingers®, 1120
2-Flap, 19913
2-In-1 Time-Saver, 29379
2-In-One Deodorizer, 29826
2-Mix, 783
2000 Plus, 21199
2001, 22348
2001 Estate Cabernet Sauvignon, 13049
20th Century Foods, 11368
21c, 20121
22 K Gold Finish, 20830
225 Bloom, 13498
24 Hour Odor Absorber, 29826
24 Super Amino Acids, 131
24-Hour Royal Jelly, 1914
2404, 18637
25 Imports From France, 8238
2point, 21657
3 George, 4969
3 Girls, 9321
3 Musketeers®, 7952
3 Musketeersc, 2132
3 Springs, 11
3-36, 21051
3-Cup Measurer, 19999
3-D Degreaser, 20830
3-Step, 31185
302 Hawk Labelers, 20107
3100 Sample Concentrator, 30132
34 Degrees, 13
35, 2257
360 Nutrition, 15
360 Vodka, 8062
3m, 18281, 18592, 22208, 23882, 27575
3m Littman, 18003
3pm Bites, 16
3v Classic™, 17
3v Fresh™, 17
3vision, 28834
4 Way Step, 28473
4%, 11664
4-Grain™, 2031
40 Fathoms®, 5844
409, 2766, 20657
44th Street, 7721
450xl, 30854
479 Degrees, 19
4c Beverages, 20
4c Foods, 20
4pure, 21
4th & Heart, 22
4th of July Cola, 6310
5 Fourchettes, 10331
5 Gum®, 7952, 13960
5 Star®, 6391
5-Alive, 2815, 20685
5-Loxin, 9654
51fifty, 25
574 Portable Oxygen Analyzer, 29063
5lung Re-Leaf, 5789
5th Avenue, 2847, 5818, 23750
6-In-1, 4111
6-N-1, 9262
610-D, 13498
67th Street Bbq™, 11363
7 Grain Cereal, 8851
7-Keto, 6236
7/11, 12030
7000 Ht High Temperature Headspace, 30132
710-D, 13498
74-40, 12030
7th Street Pale, 13428
7up®, 3725, 6818, 24802
8 Seconds Canadian Whiskey, 4658
8-Ball Stout, 7554
80-40, 12030
80wheyusa, 25784
815 Mx, 19910
9 Lives, 6380
90 Shilling, 9366
9000 Series, 23958
98% Fat-Free, 4668
99 Brand, 11263
99 Schnapps, 11264
999, 10591
9th Wave, 28919

A

A & M Cookie, 2886
A & S Brewing, 1592
A 3000, 30434
A Brand, 9500
A Dose of Good Fortunes, 5160
A Foot Of, 11083
A Gage, 19429
A Nonini, 57
A Sign of Good Taste, 18087
A Southern Season, 11864
A Taste of China, 551
A Taste of India, 551
A Taste of Thai, 551
A World of Good Fortune, 21059
A Yard Of, 11083
A&B, 18042
A&C, 51
A&D Water Care, 3469
A&J Brand, 849
A&M Cheese, 11777
A&W, 554, 10151
A&W Root Beer®, 3725, 6818, 24802
A'Guania, 6776
A-1, 18058, 24499
A-1 Pickle, 53
A-Frame, 29746
A-Salted, 12178
A-Treat, 54
A. Bauer's, 1086
A. Gagliano, 55
A. Rafanelli, 58
A. Thomas Meats, 4321, 22498
A. Vogel, 67, 10568
A.B. Curry's, 22712
A.C. Calderoni, 60
A.C. Larocco Vegetarian Pizza, 63
A.L. Cook Technology, 20599
A.P. Smith Canning Co., 10035
A/D/F, 4687
A/F Pot, 30654
A2000, 18893
A30, 25215
Aa Brand®, 10777, 28421
Aae Series, 18620
Aaladin, 18244
Aaland, 108
Aangamik Dmg, 4575
Aantek, 18066
Aarsh, 2763
Aasan, 2096
Aastro, 25020
Ab Sealers, 18877
Abacus, 14047
Abanaki Concentrators, 18251
Abanaki Mighty Minn, 18251
Abanaki Oil Grabber, 18251
Abanaki Petro Extractor, 18251
Abanaki Tote-Its, 18251
Abandon Brewing Co., 10666
Abb, 4150
Abba-Zabbac, 583
Abbe, 25579
Abbey Well, 2815, 20685
Abbotsford Farms®, 8225
Abbotsford Growers Co-Op, 112
Abbott's Candy, 115
Abbotts Meat, 116
Abbuland, 118
Abby's Better Nut Butter, 117
Abc, 4804
Abc Tea (A Better Choice), 72
Abc Carrier, 6211, 24226
Abco, 18092, 18262
Abco International, 18261
Abe's, 120
Abel, 18264
Abell-Howe, 20752
Aberlour Single Malt, 9964
Abg, 4827
Abita, 125
Abita Golden, 6797
Abita Purple, 6797
Abita Root Beer, 6797
Abita Seasmals, 6797
Abita Springs®, 3319
Abita Turboday, 6797
Ablex, 18349
Abm, 8649, 18099
Abm's Safemark, 18099
Abn, 4150
Absente, 3165
Absolutc, 9964
Absolute Fruit, 1766, 1767
Absolute Nutrition, 4150
Absolutely Almond, 2604
Absolutenergy, 6310
Absopure, 129
Absorb, 30913
Absorbant Rugs & Pads, 30656
Abu Siouf®, 7952
Abuelita, 130
Abunda Body, 131
Abundant, 18274
Ac Slit & Trim, 18021
Ac'cent Sa-Son®, 864
Ac'cent®, 864
Acacia, 132
Acacia Vineyard, 12937
Acadia Naturals, 13938
Acadian Gourmet, 11349
Acai Roots, 136
Acappella, 10260
Acca, 20808
Acceleron Advantage, 30427
Accent, 18277
Accents Frp, 25773
Acconon®, 126
Accoquat®, 126
Accord® Flavours, 10797, 28438
Accorista, 30957
Accu-Clear, 18295
Accu-Flo, 18295
Accu-Poly, 18295
Accu-Spray, 21044
Accu-Therm, 27352
Accucap, 18300
Accucapper, 18300
Accufitness, 4150
Accuflow, 28876
Accugard, 27499
Acculobe, 30853
Accupour, 21408
Accurol, 22254
Accuseal, 27499
Accusharp, 22784
Accuslitter, 29588
Accutest, 18054
Accuvac, 18300
Accuvue, 20109
Accuweigh, 31391
Ace, 12721, 13691, 18003, 18271, 18308, 30193
Ace & Icore, 30935
Ace Bandito, 5648
Ace-Hi, 7142
Ace-Tuf, 23543
Aces, 6364
Aceto D'Oro, 13812
Acg, 343
Acg Broadcast Gypsum, 343
Acid Free, 27045
Acidoplius Pearls, 4086
Ackerman, 7463
Ackerman's Wild, 6184
Acme, 151, 31007
Acorto, 18331
Acousticair, 30502
Acr Jr., 18112
Acr Powerwatch, 18112
Acrason, 18336
Acrawatt, 18334
Acremax®, 3775
Acri Lok, 18336
Acrison, 18336
Across-The-Line, 22502
Acs Industries, Inc. Scrubble, 18113
Act Ii, 2935
Act Ii®, 2939, 2940, 20821, 20822
Actic Splash, 13145
Action Ade, 5362, 23377
Activate Drinks, 26668
Active Magnetics, 28150
Activia, 3377, 3379
Activin Energy, 6310
Activin™, 11150
Actron, 18352
Acu-Rite, 20433
Acumedia, 24070
Acute Fruit™, 8470
Ad Vantage, 28285
Ad-Lite, 26766
Ad-Touch, 22121
Adagio®, 6818, 24802
Adam Matthews, 161
Adam's Ranch, 167
Adamatic, 27063
Adamation, 18360
Adams, 166, 6380
Adams & Brooks, 163
Adams & Brooks, Inc, 2132
Adams McClure®, 22187
Adapta-Flex, 30102
Adapta-Plus, 30102
Adelsheim Vineyard, 173
Adex, 18369
Adf, 451
Adi-Anmbr, 18124
Adi-Bvf Digester, 18124
Adi-Hybrid, 18124
Adi-Mbr, 18124
Adi-Sbr, 18124
Adironack, 174
Adirondack Amber, 11218
Adirondack Beverages, 10151
Adirondack Cheese, 3
Adirondack Clear N' Natural, 10151
Adirondack Maple Farms, 175
Adjust-A-Fit, 25094
Adkin's, 176
Adkin's Royal Blue, 176
Adluh, 178

1269

All Brands Index

Admar, 31338
Admatch, 18378
Admiral, 23261, 25893
Admiral Nelson's Spiced Rum, 5720
Admire, 19741
Admixer, 18126
Admore®, 22187
Adnaps, 23160
Adolphus®, 10777, 28421
Adr, 22706
Adr®, 24812
Adrenal Cleanse, 5682
Ads Laminaire, 21848
Adsormat, 30633
Advance, 1891, 27546, 31188
Advance 2000, 31025
Advance Aroma System, 18197
Advance Pierre Foods®, 13109
Advance Tabco, 18395
Advanced, 192, 18411
Advanced Digital System, 31200
Advanced Equipment, 18404
Advanced Polybagger, 18420
Advantage, 8191, 18614, 19975
Advantage Rak, 24712
Adventra, 23456
Adventure Foods, 194
Adver-Tie, 27134
Adverteaser, 25421
Aearo/Peltor, 22208
Aef-1, 31085
Aef-25, 31085
Aef-7, 31085
Aegis, 31185
Aep, 81
Aep Institutional Products, 18029
Aerion, 4736
Aero, 21199, 30639
Aero Heat Exchanger, 26630
Aero-Counter, 18515
Aero-Serv, 29055
Aero®, 8945
Aerolator, 18448
Aerolux, 27294
Aeromat, 19677
Aeroplane, 8061
Aeros, 5189
Aeroscout, 29584
Aerospec, 18441
Aerotec, 19677
Aerowhip™, 19108
Aeroxon, 28571
Aesop's Fable, 10214
Aew, 18136
Afc, 22438
Afco, 18553
Affiorato, 3236
Afrique, 11775
Afta, 23436
After Byrne Recovery Drink, 1902
After Dark, 743
After Shock®, 1120
Ag Co-Op, 201
Against the Grain Brewery, 10666
Agalima, 439
Agar, 9833
Agarich, 8534
Agarloid, 8534
Agarmoor, 8534
Agassiz Amber, 4466
Agave Dream, 203
Agave Nectar, 7748
Agavero, 3165
Agavestix, 5073
Agisyn™, 3320
Aglio Di Mirabellac, 170
Agp Grain Ltd, 81
Agp Grain Marketing, 81
Agricap, 26264
Agricare, 23571
Agricom, 5036
Agripac, 216
Agrobotic Technology, 25550
Ags 100, 24940
Agtron, 18480

Aguardiente Caldas, 3545
Aguila, 71
Aguila®, 8460
Agvest, 9032
Ah!Laska®, 1484
Ah-So, 345
Ahlgren Vineyard, 229
Aidell's, 232
Aidells®, 13109
Aie, 21134
Aiello, 9044
Aiellos, 11628
Aim, 2666, 20561
Aimia Foods, 10303, 27797
Air Cush'n, 20651
Air Deck, 21628
Air Flow, 22615, 31142
Air Pro, 18548
Air Repair, 21524
Air Solution, 22015
Air Tech, 21498
Air Therapy, 26055
Air Wick®, 10598
Air-Lec, 18500
Air-Ply, 18221
Air-Savers, 29826
Air-Scent, 18501, 29826
Air-Trax, 25377
Aire Systems, 30382
Aire-02, 18436
Aire-02 Triton, 18436
Airector, 24519
Airex, 8028
Airflex, 18548
Airform, 19919
Airheads, 2132, 9956
Airlie, 235
Airlite, 22348
Airmaster, 18512, 24936
Airmatic Lube, 19654
Airomat, 18513
Airport Network Solutions, 23993
Airsan, 18516
Airserv, 24010
Airship, 4387
Airsource, 11501
Airspeed, 31340
Airswitch, 24010
Airway, 24045
Airx, 20498
Aisle Pro, 19763
Ajax, 20721, 28320
Ajilys®, 239, 18517
Ajinomoto®, 237, 238
Ajipro®-L, 239, 18517
Ak Mak, 241
Aketta, 244
Akra-Pak, 28620
Akro-Bins, 19926
Akro-Mils, 19908, 19927
Akron, 31435
Akron Hawk, 31435
Akron Spartan, 31435
Akta Klor, 30913
Akulon®, 3320
Al Cohen's, 2862
Al Dente, 247, 12030
Al Dente Pasta Selecta, 247
Al Dente Sure Success, 247
Al Gelato, 248
Al Pete, 249
Al Safa Halal, 251
Al's, 252
Al's Best, 2051
Al-Rite, 253
Alabama Rag, 26770
Alacreme, 13700, 31165
Aladdin, 256
Aladdin Products, 23952
Alaga, 13740
Alamo, 259
Alamos®, 3834
Alan Bradley, 27282
Alan's Maniac Hot Sauce, 9481
Alar, 18527

Alarmwork Multimedia, 24050
Alaska Bay, 12365
Alaska Fresh, 9348
Alaska Gold, 11375
Alaska Jack's, 264
Alaska Smoked Salmon, 11864
Alaska Smokehouse, 270
Alaska Tea Traders, 264
Alaska Wild Teas, 263
Alaskan, 268
Alaskan Amber, 271
Alaskan Boreal Bouquet, 263
Alaskan Fireweed, 263
Alaskan Freeride Apa, 271
Alaskan Gold, 263
Alaskan Gourmet, 272
Alaskan Hopothermia, 271
Alaskan Icy Bay Ipa, 271
Alaskan Imperial Red, 271
Alaskan Kicker Session Ipa, 271
Alaskan Leader Fisheries, 273
Alaskan Stout, 271
Alaskan Summer Ale, 271
Alaskan White, 271
Alaskan Winter Ale, 271
Alaskan® Brewing Company, 26668
Alati-Casserta, 275
Alba, 277
Alba Botanica, 5505
Albaglos, 11906
Alban Viognier, 11810
Albany, 21199
Albergo, 4942
Albers, 2971
Alberta Premium®, 1120
Albertson's, 9469, 11260, 12304
Albi, 22599
Albin, 24602
Albino Rhino Ale, 13711
Albion Amber Ale, 7923
Albunate, 4430
Alcalase, 1692
Alcan, 26751
Alcatel, 27729
Alchemist, 13174
Alco, 28967
Alco Tabs, 18542
Alcohol Free Stevia, 9201
Alcohol Prep Pads 100's, 26632
Alcoholado Baluarte, 3545
Alcoholado Superior 70, 3545
Alcojet, 18542
Alcolec, 468
Alcon Plus, 20625
Alconox, 18542
Alcosa, 5555
Alda, 10540
Alden's Ice Cream, 9533
Alden's Organic, 283
Alder Cove, 3394
Alder Ridge, 2909
Alder Springs, 284
Alderfer, 285
Alebrta, 4025
Aleco, 19908
Alegacy, 18026
Ales & Lagers, 1789
Alesco, 24479
Alesia, 209
Alessi, 13404
Alessi Bakery, 289
Alewel's Country Meats, 290, 18551
Alex & Dani's Biscotti, 1397
Alexander Grappa, 27236
Alexander Keith's India Pale Ale, 7123
Alexander Valley, 6375
Alexander Winery, 10952
Alexander's Gourmet Tea, 291
Alexanderwerk, 27362
Alexco, 18554
Alexia®, 2939, 2940, 20821, 20822
Alexis Bailly, 296
Alexis De Portneuf®, 11211
Alfa, 24076, 28832, 30147
Alfa-Kortogleu, 22299

Alfasi, 10952
Alfonso Gourmet Pasta, 298
Alfred & Sam's, 299
Alfred Bakeware, 30490
Alfredo, 303
Alfredobuds, 1880
Algarve, 20964
Algene, 18560
Algonquin Honeybrown, 1702
Algood Blue Label, 305
Algood Jelly, 305
Algood Marmalade, 305
Algood Old Fashioned, 305
Algood Preserves, 305
Algood Red Label, 305
Alhambra, 10303, 27797
Alhambra®, 3220, 3319, 11889
Ali's, 12928
Alicante Bouschet, 2637
Alien Pop, 6158
Alien Poppin' Pops, 6158
Align, 12721, 30193
Alimony Ale, 1837
Aline, 18565
Alive, 9155
Alive & Radiant, 315
Alive & Well, 314
Alive!, 8896
Alkaline, 18572
Alkazone, 18572
Alkazone Alkaline Booster Drops, 18572
Alkazone Antioxidant Water Ionizer, 18572
Alkazone Vitamins & Herbs, 18572
Alkinco, 316
Alkota, 18573
Alkyrol, 11268
All a Cart, 18574
All American, 318, 18578
All American Afternoon Delight, 319
All American Holiday Goose, 11287
All American Precious Stones, 319
All American White Trash, 319
All B-100, 7947
All B-50, 7947
All But Gluten, 13691
All Fresh, 340
All Natural, 4904
All Natural Herbal, 7602
All One, 9258
All Out, 24386
All Packaging Machinery, 18877
All Plastic Belting, 19111
All Round Foods, 322
All Season's Kitchen, 4665
All Soft, 1735
All Sorts, 18585
All Sport®, 3725
All Star, 27240
All Ways, 30878
All-American Sports Pasta, 4794
All-American Squeeze-Salsa, 3957
All-Bottle, 19581
All-Bran, 6766
All-Bran®, 6765
All-In-One, 13184
All-Q™, 3320
Allan, 5818, 23750
Allans, 10186
Alldrin, 328
Alleghanys, 330
Allegheny, 13447
Allegrini, 3834
Allegro, 333, 334, 28493
Allegro Coffee, 332
Allegro Tea, 332
Allen, 10714, 12166, 27709
Allen Bradley, 22482
Allen's, 56, 337, 10659
Allen-Bailey™, 22187
Allen-Bradley, 28472
Allens, 336, 338, 4499
Aller Bee-Gone, 1914
Aller-7, 6236
Aller-Snap Protein Residue Test, 23971

All Brands Index

Allerdophilus® Caps, 13097
Allertonic, 5791
Alley Kat Amber, 339
Alleycat Amber, 7554
Allez, 13280
Alliance, 18613, 18614, 21218
Alliance®, 13595, 31053
Allibert, 28843
Alligator, 22627
Alligator Pepper, 12987
Allirich, 672
Allison Jayne, 8837
Alljuice, 8627, 26351
Allstrong, 18642
Alltec, 20752
Allure, 31188
Allvia®, 9237, 26785
Allwrite, 30434
Alm, 19908
Alma, 338
Almanac Beer Co., 10666
Almark, 352
Almarla Black Lightning, 353
Almarla Soul Train, 353
Almased, 354
Almaviva, 1006
Almond Breeze, 1471, 19742
Almond Chews, 9220
Almond Ingot, 5140
Almond Joy, 2132, 5818, 23750
Almond Toppers, 1471, 12201, 19742
AlmondcrOMe, 8957
Almondina, 13974, 25789
Almondina Biscuits, 13975
Almondmilk, 8957
Almonds, 10984
Alnose, 5474
Alo, 89
Alo®, 11052
Aloe Burst, 359
Aloe Falls, 14000
Aloe Farms, 358
Aloe Gloe, 7036
Aloe Jell Water Less, 23532
Aloe Labs, 359
Aloe'ha, 360
Aloevine, 6400
Aloha, 396, 28342
Aloha Maid, 6327
Alor, 13427
Alouettec, 368
Alox, 23477
Alpaflor®, 3320
Alpaire, 22899
Alpen, 13621
Alpen Cellars, 369
Alpen Dark Chocolate, 13620
Alpen No Added Sugar, 13620
Alpen Original Muesli, 13620
Alpen Sierra, 370
Alpendough, 371
Alpenglow, 11055
Alpenliebe, 9956
Alpenrose, 373
Alpha, 27711, 31200
Alpha Glutamine, 1377
Alpha Gold, 8967
Alpha Laval Flo, 19401
Alpha-Bits, 10213
Alpha-Media, 22257
Alphabet Cookies, 3343
Alphadim, 463
Alpine, 380, 2718, 2971, 19576, 30820
Alpine Coffee, 379
Alpine Lace, 7198
Alpine Start, 382
Alpine Valley, 384, 9332
Alpine Valley Bakery, 4529
Alpine/Xpd, 26337
Alpineaire, 13105
Alpo®, 8945
Alpro, 13734
Alpromar, 8028
Alps Model 7385, 18493
Alps Smart Test Module, 18493
Alps Sx-Flex, 18493
Alps Vision Plus, 18493
Alsum Farms & Produce, 386
Alsum Organics, 386
Alta, 389, 390
Alta Cucina, 12030
Alta Dena, 3442, 21421
Alta Dena Classic, 387
Altanta Dairy, 4290
Altbier, 1507
Alterra Coffee Roasters, 8090
Altima, 7107
Alto Rey, 394
Altoids, 2132
Altoids®, 7952, 13960
Alton, 8806
Altoona Hills, 10952
Altos, 9964
Altria, 541
Alube, 137
Alumaworks, 18685
Alumicube, 18788
Alumiflex, 28488
Alumin-Nu, 18687
Alumitec Elite, 30091
Alumtec, 30091
Alvarado Street Bakery, 397
Alvita, 13097
Alvita Tea, 398
Always, 12721, 30193
Always Can, 29697
Always Discreet, 12721, 30193
Always Sweet, 13192
Amabile Umbro, 8479
Amador Foothill, 403
Amafruits, 4063
Amaizen Crunch, 10235
Amana, 18333
Amana Meats, 409
Amanda Hills, 410
Amano, 414
Amano Jenbrana, 412, 18691
Amano Ocumare, 412, 18691
Amara, 415
Amaretti Virginia, 3381
Amaretto, 9773
Amaretto De Sabroso, 11264
Amark/Simionato, 18693
Amarone Pasta, 9813
Amazake, 5248
Amazin' Raisin, 419
Amazing Herbs, 420
Amazing Meals, 329
Amazingly Tasty, 4668
Amazon, 28154
Amazon Pepper Products, 6015
Amazonas, 2719
Ambake, 416
Amban, 416
Ambassador, 26187
Ambec 10, 22615
Ambec 10r, 22615
Amber, 11585, 11992
Amber Ale, 1097
Amber Brand Deviled Smithfield Ham, 12714
Amber Farms, 6409
Amber Light, 7330
Amber Wheat Beer, 10404
Amberale, 9701
Amberg Wine Cellars, 422
Amberhill, 1543
Ambersweet, 12426, 29855
Ambi Pur, 12721, 30193
Ambootia, 424
Ambretta, 1524
Ambrose, 18699
Ambrosia, 9909, 11235
Ambrosia Honey, 7748
Amburst, 416
Amcel, 18700
Amco, 18692, 18702
Amcoat, 18702
Amcoll, 18702
Ame, 8838
Ame Celebration, 8838
Amelia Bay, 917
Amelia's, 12301
Amelia's Sugar Free Shoppe, 5140
Ameri Color, 494
Ameri-Kart, 19926
America, 5660
America Almond, 438
America's Best, 2389
America's Catch, 436
America's Choice, 6126
America's Classic Foods, 437
America's Fruit, 13181
America's Heartland Beef®, 10893
America's Heartland Organic Beef, 457
America's Northwest, 2905
America's Premium, 10268
American, 2750, 7655, 23809
American Lamb, 2313
American Almond, 438
American Bbq Company, 5141
American Beauty, 648, 6126, 8542
American Beauty™, 10777, 28421
American Body Building, 9510
American Breakfast Blend, 9181, 9182
American Bulk Conveyors, 27314
American Cheesemen, 446
American Chef Larry Forgione's, 485
American Classic Tea, 2437
American Classics, 7446
American Cola®, 8470
American Connoisseur Gourmet, 8666
American Cookie Boy, 11015
American Creamery, 437
American Culinary Gardens, 450
American Dietary, 4063
American Eagle, 18746
American Extrusion International, 18756
American Favorite, 13110
American Food, 455
American Fruit Butters, 485
American Fruit Toppings, 485
American Fruits, 13578
American Grana, 1174
American Greetings, 19611
American Health & Herbs Ministry, 393
American Health®, 8871
American Heritage, 11308, 28903
American Heritage™, 7952
American Ingredients, 30618
American Led-Gible, Inc., 18785
American Licorice Co., 2132
American Metal Ware, 23420
American Metalcraft, 18795
American Micronutrients, 471
American Moir's, 8666
American Mucky Duck, 8666
American Naturals, 393
American Optical, 23974
American Original, 11356
American Pale Ale, 1507, 12153
American Panel, 18805
American Plsener, 11218
American Pride®, 5844
American Queen, 10457
American Range, 18814
American Salad Dazzlers, 485
American Sanders Technology, 20599
American Saucery, 8261
American Savory, 8247, 26074
American Seedc, 10106
American Shiitake, 5583
American Solving, 18821
American Special Edition, 8666
American Spoon Foods, 485
American Spoon Fruits, 485
American Stockyard, 9565
American Terrain, 18743
American Time & Signal, 18831
American Tradition Reserve, 4353
American Tuna, 487
American Vintage Hard Iced Teas, 8279
American Yeast, 7173
American-Lincoln Technology, 20599
Americana, 492
Americandy, 431
Americus Natural Spring Water, 11672
Ameridrives, 18678
Amerigift Sweet Tooth Originals, 434
Ameripure, 495
Ameriqueen Brand, 10457
Ameriseng, 10335
Amerivacs, 18858
Ameriwhite, 23842
Amfec, 18763, 28291
Amgrain, 416
Amhurst Kitchens, 2964
Ami, 2313, 18182
Amicelli™, 7952
Amick Farms Poultry, 500
Amigo, 947, 4891, 10869
Amigos, 501
Aminoplus, 81
Amir, 6255
Amish, 10080
Amish Country, 13822, 13823
Amish Farm, 5420
Amish Gourmet, 8345
Amish Kitchens, 12467
Amish Valley Farms, 1851
Amma's Kitchen, 6026
Ammonia Guard, 4479
Amooza, 6976
Amooza!, 9789
Amore Bianco, 7111
Amorec, 9748
Amoretti, 507
Amoroso's Hearth Baked, 508
Amoy®, 237, 238
Amp Energy Organic®, 9945, 27433
Amphisol®, 3320
Amphora, 509
Amplas Converting Equipment, 23917
Amplexus Advantage, 18881
Amplexus E3/Commerce, 18881
Ampliflave, 9252
Amport Foods, 462
Amrita, 514
Ams, 18028
Amtrax, 18702
Amwell Valley Vineyard, 518
Amy & Brian, 519
Amy's, 498
Amylu, 523
Amys Kitchen, 522
Ana's, 524
Anabol Naturals, 526
AnAi To-Go, 9541
Analette, 27734
Analog Thermostats, 28020
Ananda Hemp, 528
Ancel, 8370
Anchor, 13441, 27575
Anchor Porter, 531
Anchor Small, 531
Anchor Steam, 531
Anchor®, 4552, 8055
Anchorage Brewing Co., 10666
Anchorseal, 25591
Ancient Age, 11263
Ancient Harvest, 534
Ancient Harvest Quinoa, 10467
Ancient Healing Formulas, 14011
Ancient Nutrition, 535
Ancient Secrets, 7562
And Many More, 648, 5489, 12551
And More, 2010, 4353, 10565, 10603
Andechs, 1702
Andersen'sc Soup, 187
Anderson Dairy, 545
Andes Chocolate Mint Chip Cookies, 9399
Andes®, 12880
Andgar, 18931
Andre Prost, Inc., 2132
Andre®, 3834
Andrew & Everettc, 9748
Andrew Alliance, 31041
Andrew's Long Island Iced Tea, 7655
Andrews, 557, 9728

All Brands Index

Andrulis Farmers Cheese, 8248
Andy Boy, 3301
Andy Capp's®, 2939, 2940, 20821, 20822
Andy Roo's, 2019
Andy's Cajun Fish Breading, 560
Andy's Golden Fish Batter, 560
Andy's Hot 'n' Spicy Breading, 560
Andy's Mild Chicken Breading, 560
Andy's Red Fish Breading, 560
Andy's Seasoned Salt, 560
Andy's Shrimp Tempura Batter, 560
Andy's Vegetable Breading, 560
Andy's Yellow Fish Breading, 560
Anejo, 914
Aneri, 27236
Anets', 18940
Angel, 2042
Angel Food, 6912
Angela, 10873
Angelic Bakehouse, 563, 12467
Angelo & Franco, 565
Angels Creek, 6290
Angie's Boomchickapop®, 2939, 2940, 20821, 20822
Angled Pro Picks, 31414
Anglux, 22039
Angostura, 13938
Angostura Bitters, 20020
Angostura®, 8415
Angry Orchard, 569
Angry Orchard®, 1592
Angy's, 570
Anheuser-Busch Inbev®, 26668
Anhydro, 28714
Animal Crackers, 2903, 7940
Animal Friends®, 13097
Animal Pak, 572
Anis Paloma, 3545
Anisi, 5964
Anita's, 573, 10453
Anke Kruse Organics, 5089
Anna Maria, 13266
Anna's, 6255
Anna's Honey, 11390
Anne Taintor, 10229
Anne's Chicken Base, 5634
Anne's Country Gourmet, 11402
Anne's Dumpling Squares, 5634
Anne's Dumpling Strips, 5634
Anne's Flat Dumplings, 5634
Anne's Old Fashioned, 5634
Anne's Pot Pie Squares, 5634
Annie Chun's, 1953
Annie Pie's, 1233
Annie's, 5936, 11645, 18949
Annie's Lane, 12937
Annie's Macaroni & Cheese, 591
Annie's Naturals, 592
Annie's Naturals Magic Sauces, 592
Annie's Naturals Salad Dressings, 592
Annie's Organic Foods, 591
Annie's Supreme, 2964
Annie's®, 4947
Annin, 22650
Anniversary, 21059
Anniversary Bock, 1702
Ansac Cognac, 5720
Anselmi, 27236
Ansul Automan, 30516
Ansulex, 30516
Answer, 2666, 20561
Ant, Roach & Spider, 19364
Antelope Valley, 593
Anthony's, 465
Anthony-Thomas Chocolates, 596
Anthora™, 21362
Anti Oxidant Edge, 1532
Antico, 56
Antimicrobial Sanitizer Scrubs, 24035
Antioxidant, 18572
Antique Blend, 19713
Antique Crown Foods, 12546
Antler Hill, 1358
Antoine's, 46

Antonella, 4028
Antoni Ravioli, 598
Antonia, 7069
Antonio, 2012
Antunes Control, 18023
Anver, 18191
Anysweetplus™, 4837
Anytime, 7150
Anytime Candy, 13845
Ao Vodka, 1120
Ap Checkweigers, 18192
Ap/Ps 1214, 25215
Ap/Ps200 Ii, 25215
Apache, 10815
Apatinsko, 8459
Apc Particle Counters, 19690
Apco, 615
Aperi-Coeur, 10039
Aperiquiche, 10039
Aperoi, 2114
Aperossimo, 5405
Apex, 18971, 21550, 29211
Apg, 741
Aphroteasiac Chai, 7989
Api, 19018, 19021
Api®, 7952
Apiterra, 605
Aplets, 7410
Aplphacel™, 11794
Apollinaris, 2815, 20685
Apollo, 6986
Apollo Peeler, 28181
Apollo®, 750
Apostle Islands Organic Coffee, 9181
Apothic®, 3834
Appeteasers, 183, 18382
Apple & Eve, 56, 608
Apple Blossom, 10478
Apple Brand Juices, 11266
Apple Cinnamon Pecan Cake, 2881
Apple Delight, 5362, 23377
Apple Jack Cheese, 12892
Apple Pears, 6880
Apple Polisher, 19713
Apple Ridge, 6415
Apple Royal, 5362, 23377
Apple Sidra, 3045
Apple Snax, 7282
Apple Strudel Coffee Beans, 7596
Apple Time, 6923
Apple Valley Inn, 10981
Appleblossom, 9833
Applecreek Orchards, 612
Appledore, 2981
Applegate Farms, 614, 30775
Applegate®, 6000, 23861
Applerazzi, 3311
Appletiser, 2815, 20685
Appleton, 615
Applewood Winery, 618
Applied Biosystems, 30217
Applied Stats, 18222
Apr, 23850
Aprenda Haccp, 26666
Apres, 8838, 18007
Apricot Ale, 2911
Apricot Pecan Cake, 2881
Aprikat, 339
Apro™, 4119
Apv, 28714
Apw Wyott, 29580
Aqua, 18328
Aqua Best, 3545
Aqua Blox®, 154
Aqua Br, 19005
Aqua Cb12/24, 19005
Aqua Clara, 620
Aqua Crystal, 21027
Aqua Dm, 19005
Aqua Endura Disc, 19005
Aqua Endura Tube, 19005
Aqua Gf, 19005
Aqua Pro, 28393
Aqua Star, 10603
Aqua Trap, 20725

Aqua-Dyne, 24692
Aqua-Jet Aerator, 19005
Aqua-Vent, 21541
Aquabelt, 18556
Aquabona, 2815, 20685
Aquacare, 24613
Aquacuisine, 622
Aquadisk, 19005
Aquafilm, 19675
Aquafina®, 9945, 27433
Aquafire, 20297
Aquaflakes, 19675
Aquaflex, 27258
Aquafloc, 28731
Aquafruit, 8163
Aqualite, 19008, 23543
Aqualon, 1692
Aqualon Benecel, 1692
Aqualon Klucel, 1692
Aqualon™, 19108
Aqualyzer, 18849
Aquamate, 22203
Aquamax™, 3775
Aquapal, 20093
Aquarian®, 7952
Aquarious, 9155
Aquarius, 2815, 20685
Aquasan, 21321
Aquasnap Water Atp Sample Testing, 23971
Aquasorb™, 19108
Aquastore, 20750
Aquathin, 19008
Aquatral, 24611
Aquatrol, 26276
Aquatrust, 21519
Aquavits, 3165
Aquawipes, 25662
Aqucous Washing Systems, 20885
Aquence, 23726
Aquila D'Ora, 7428
Aquoral®, 8389
Ar Series Rheometers, 29986
Ar200, 25231
Ar600, 25231
Ara Real, 100
Arapahoe, 5304
Arbor Crest, 627
Arbor Hill Wine, 628
Arbuckle, 633
Arbutus Flour, 6917
Arcadia, 635
Archie Moore's, 640
Archimedes, 21203
Archway, 11770
Arco, 101
Arco Coffee, 19024
Arcobaleno, 19025
Arcor, 13610
Arcor Premium Hard Filled Candies, 643
Arcor Value Line Hard Candies, 643
Arctic, 19029
Arctic Air, 19027
Arctic Blast, 6338
Arctic Pride, 10682
Arctica Gardens, 2260
Ardbeg, 8452
Ardmore, 650
Ardmore Farms®, 3083
Ardmore®, 1120
Arena 330 Shipper, 19038
Arena Shipper, 19038
Areo, 28488
Ares, 25785
Argiano®, 3834
Argo Corn Starch, 73
Argomops, 19039
Argonaut, 19039
Argosheen, 19039
Argus Cidery, 10666
Argyle Brut, 659
Aria, 3540, 20256
Arias500, 25231
Ariel, 663, 12721, 30193
Ariel Blanc, 663

Ariel Brut Cuve, 663
Ariel Cabernet, 663
Ariel Chardonnay, 663
Ariel Merlot, 663
Ariel Rouge, 663
Ariel White Zinfandel, 663
Arimex, 18169
Aris, 25094
Arista, 666
Aristo Snacks, 8269
Aristo-Ray, 19882
Aristocrat, 19597, 29654
Arius-Eickert, 21210
Arizona, 670, 4566
Arizona Iced Tea, 4342, 26668
Arizona Ranch Fresh, 5837
Arizona Vineyards, 677
Arjuan Berry Farm, 5036
Arkansas Poly, 19046
Arkansas Rag, 26770
Arkfeld Instant Way Dial Scales, 19048
Arkfeld Security Cabinets, 19048
Arm & Hammer, 2666, 20561
Arm-A-Dor, 28828
Armadillo, 26210
Armanino, 680
Armeno, 683
Armetale, 31241
Armida, 13811
Armistead Citrus Products, 684
Armon, 346
Armorbelt, 24940
Armorlon, 28240
Armour, 11733
Armour Star Canned Foods, 21595
Armour Star®, 2939, 2940, 20821, 20822
Armour®, 27540
Armstrong Forge, 25299
Armstrong®, 11211
Arneg, 19063
Arnite®, 3320
Arnitel®, 3320
Arnold Palmer, 388
Arnold Palmer Spiked Half & Half, 8460
Arnold's Meats, 690
Arnold®, 1359
Arnorld, 892
Arns, 691
Aro, 24220
Aro-Smoke, 10600
Arol, 833
Arom®, 8899
Aroma, 7107
Aroma Cuisiner's Choice, 692
Aroma Mi Amore, 56
Aroma Southern Maison, 692
Aroma Turkish, 692
Aroma Valley, 13551
Aroma Vera, 695
Aroma-Life, 696
Aromahop, 6554
Aromi D'Italia, 700
Arox, 833
Arp, 29452
Arra, 5036
Arracado, 5036
Arrgh! Pale Ale, 7554
Arriba, 10701
Arrid, 2666, 20561
Arrogant Bastard Ale, 12129
Arrow, 703, 7655, 25871
Arrow Clip, 27575
Arrowhead Mills, 5505
Arrowhead Spring Water, 26668
Arrowood, 706
Arroyo Grande, 12513
Art Coco, 707
Art Fidos Cookies, 707
Art Topo, 707
Art's Mexican Products, 708
Art's Tamales, 709
Art-Stik, 26109
Artcraft, 22177
Arte Nova, 56
Artesano, 7908

All Brands Index

Artezin, 5820
Artho Life, 4127
Arthrimin Gs™, 6449, 24506
Articularm, 18498
Artima, 22039
Artisan, 13595, 31053
Artisan Bistro®, 10976
Artisan Blends®, 11228, 28829
Artisan Craft, 13402
Artisan Crafted Series, 11902
Artisan Hearth®, 9736
Artisan Kettle, 715
Artisana, 10249
Artpak, 19056
Artuso, 718
Aruero, 3857
Aryzta, 9590
Arz, 6719
Asahi, 5427
Asante, 8784
Asbach Brandy, 3570
Asbach Uralt, 9035
Ascaso, 19102
Ascend, 5139, 31188
Asg, 22299
Ash, 28557
Ashby's, 11864
Ashby's Iced Teas, 2848
Ashby's Teas of London, 2848
Ashcroft, 19107
Asher, 431
Asher's, 13610
Ashland, 728, 729, 1692
Ashlock, 19110
Ashoka, 6185
Ashwagandha, 11061
Asi Yaupon Tea, 13994
Asiago, 13320
Asian Gourmet®, 1484
Asian Pride, 12334
Asian Star, 13666
Asico, 18054
Ask Foods, 103
Asme, 28967
Asp, 4769, 22896
Aspen, 25725
Aspen Pure, 8955
Aspen Ridge®, 6391
Aspi-Cor, 5683, 23677
Associates, 3765
Assumption Wines, 10789
Astazanthin, 5682
Astica, 4677
Astika, 8459
Astor, 13864
Astoria, 19130
Astra, 2089, 19132
Astral Laser Power, 28915
Astro, 745, 22599, 27058
Astro Pops, 11885
Astro-Pure, 19137
Astro®, 9789
Astrodeck, 30341
Astroflex, 20758
Asym-A-Lyte, 30893
At, 19798
Atago Brand, 21223
Atc, 18221
@Ease®, 12885, 30333
Ateco, 19190
Athena, 10303, 27797
Athena Test, 13120
Athena®, 3220, 3319
Athenian, 5341
Athenos, 2667
Athens, 749, 6986
Athens®, 750
Atkins, 753, 754
Atkins Elegant Desserts, 847
Atkinson's, 757
Atlanta Bread, 758
Atlanta Burning, 759, 19145
Atlanta Sharptech, 19146
Atlantic, 773, 21497
Atlantic Blueberry, 764

Atlantic Capes, 765
Atlantic Coast, 10974
Atlantic Lobster, 27588
Atlantic Meat, 770
Atlantic Queen, 7657
Atlantic Seasonings, 778
Atlas, 13498, 18365, 19164, 31290
Atlas 640 Shipper, 19038
Atlas Peak, 781
Atlas Tag & Label®, 22187
Atmo, 29791
Atmos, 25874
Atomic Fireball, 1417, 2132, 4345
Atripla®, 1721
Attachments, 22890
Attiki, 6986
Attnetion Span, 5883
Attritor, 30612
Attune, 19178
Atwater, 785, 786
Atwater Dried Fruits, 786
Au Pain Dore, 20020
Au Printemps Gourmet, 789
Au Quotidien, 56
Au'some, 2132
Aubrey's Jerky, 11746
Auchentoshan, 1120
Audeocam, 18185
Audisio & Lori, 6255
Auer, 846
Auger Monster, 24649
Augsberger, 9664
August's Fried, 794
Aunt Aggie De's Pralines, 799
Aunt Angies, 9787
Aunt Bertie's, 2250
Aunt Erma's Frugal Foods, 11852
Aunt Flo's Country Fudge, 11051
Aunt Gussie's Cookies & Crackers, 801
Aunt Hattie's, 5917
Aunt Hattie's Quality Breads, 5917
Aunt Jayne's, 890
Aunt Jemima, 811
Aunt Jemima®, 2939, 2940, 9945,
    20821, 20822, 27433, 27540
Aunt Jenny's, 25789
Aunt Kitty's, 805, 5555
Aunt Lizzie's, 806
Aunt Millie's, 807
Aunt Nellie's, 11434
Aunt Patty's, 5073
Aunt Penny's, 12590
Aunt Sally's Creamy Pralines, 808
Aunt Sally's Gourmet, 808
Aunt Sue's®, 11669
Aunt Zelda's, 4854
Auntie Annie's, 6338
Auntie Liu's, 10457
Aura, 9964
Aura Cacia, 4752
Auribella, 1174
Aurity Wrap, 18908
Aurora Angus Beef, 813
Aussie, 4891, 12721, 30193
Aussie Sauce, 4891
Austex Products, 805
Austin, 6766, 24499
Austin Blues Bbq®, 6000, 23861
Austin Company, 10210
Austins, 18029
Austinuts, 819
Austrian Crown, 13401
Authdirect, 23993
Authentic Latino Flavor®, 12996
Authentico®, 1200
Author's Choice, 1610
Authorizer, 30843
Autin's, 823
Auto Abbe, 25231
Auto Fog, 22195
Auto Fry, 18590
Auto Pinch-25, 18300
Auto Pinch-50, 18300
Auto Show, 19053

Auto-Logger, 25766
Auto-Mini, 18300
Auto-Pal, 22850
Auto-Shredder, 25766
Auto-Slicer, 25766
Auto-Slide, 19220
Auto-Vac, 18527
Autobag, 19215
Autobake, 25790
Autobar, 19203
Autobroil, 25790
Autobroil Omni, 25790
Autocapsealer, 25723
Autocrat, 4407, 22564
Autofry, 19206, 26328
Autogard, 28357
Autograph, 24743
Autogrill, 25790
Automa, 24119
Automate, 20633
Automated Boxing Line, 25766
Automated Logic, 20290
Automelt, 25790
Automix, 20633
Automug, 24091
Autoplate 4000, 29499
Autopor, 19203
Autoroast, 25790
Autosearch, 20573
Autotrak, 22039
Autronica, 20290
Autumn Ale, 1687
Autumn Fest, 3746
Autumn Wildflower, 10478
Avagel, 833
Avalanche, 621, 27352
Avalanche Ale, 1687
Avallo, 10161
Avalon, 650
Avalon Organic Coffee, 13381
Avalon Organics, 5505
Avanti, 12350, 25299
Avapol, 833
Avar-E®, 8389
Avar®, 8389
Avatar, 833, 30086
Avatech, 833
Avenacare™ Oat Beta Glucan, 12561
Aventura Gourmet, 9933
Avera Sport, 357
Avert, 31188
Avery, 166, 838
Avery Berkel, 24038
Avery Dennison, 18284
Avi, 25511, 27655
Aviator Ale Micro Brew Mustards, 1034
Avila, 2719, 7133
Avionc, 9964
Avitae, 840
Avitae Xr, 840
Aviva, 2096
Avo, 488
Avo-King, 841
Avolov, 842
Avon, 2260
Avoset, 10714
Avox, 833
Avri Companies, 845
Awake, 9167, 12945
Awaken Foods, 12396
Award Auer/Blaschke, 846
Award Crunchy Dunkers, 846
Awards America, 22129
Awesome, 6882
Awesome Orange, 5362, 23377
Awestruck Ciders, 5286
Awrey's, 20101
Awrey's Maestro, 847
Awt-100, 23275
Axcess, 21329
Axiad Ii, 18453
Axico, 18453
Axiohm, 19274
Axipal, 18453
Axler's, 10526

Ayurveda, 5679
Az-One, 5682
Azactam®, 1721
Azalea, 4969
Azar®, 11504, 29095
Azlon, 21848
Azo, 6107
Aztec Harvest, 12663
Azteca, 7655
Azteca De Oro, 9964
Azteca Trading Co., 9863
Azteca®, 855
Azumaya, 13473

B

B 3 R, 1647
B C Natural, 1647
B&B, 1925
B&B/Benedictine, 914
B&D, 19610
B&D Litho of Arizona®, 22187
B&G Foods, Inc.®, 11504, 29095
B&G®, 864
B&K Coffee, 874, 19305
B&K Manufacturing, 1903
B&M Baked Beans, 1867
B&M®, 864
B'Lure, 13779
B-1, 31085
B-12 Dots™, 13097
B-17, 10534
B. King, 6858
B. Nektar Meadery, 10666
B.Bob's Foods, 7073
B.J. Spot, 28901
B2b, 2060
B5000, 1735
Ba-Tampte, 1079
Baba Foods, 907
Baba Ghannouj, 128
Babara's Vanilla, 13620
Babbco, 19990
Babcock, 25789
Babe, 571
Babe Farms, 910
Babe's, 911
Bablux, 22039
Babo, 22593
Babu's Pocket Sandwiches, 3465
Baby Bola, 22599
Baby Cakes, 2226
Baby Dino Eggs, 6851
Baby Giant, 22080
Baby Ruth, 2132
Baby's Breakfast Roast, 912
Baby's Private Buzz, 912
Baby's Wrelker's Roa, 912
Baby-D™, 6449, 24506
Babycakes®, 7521
Bac Out, 19642
Bac'n Puffs, 9408
Bacala Rico, 2122
Bacardi Breezers, 914
Bacardi Limon, 914
Bacardi Rum, 914
Bacardi Silver™, 26668
Bacardi Spice, 914
Bachelor's Brew, 5217
Bachman, 916, 12631, 13129
Baci, 28305
Bacigalupi Chardonnay, 10963
Back Country Emu Products, 3612
Back Office Assistant, 25988
Back To Basics, 918, 19361
Back To Nature, 864, 919
Backer's, 921
Backsettler Blend, 9182
Backus Vineyard, 6603
Backwoods Smoker, 19363
Bacon 1®, 6000, 23861
Bacount, 19419
Bacross, 19419
Bad Frog Amber Lager, 925
Bad Frog Bad Light, 925

All Brands Index

Bad Frog Micro Malt, 925
Bad Seed, 926
Badger, 928, 26210
Badger Blend, 9182
Badia Canned Vegetables, 930
Badia Hot Sauces, 930
Badia Nuts & Seeds, 930
Badia Seasoning Blends, 930
Badia Spices, 930
Badia Teas, 930
Bafos, 1089
Bagcraft Packaging, 26756
Bagel Biter, 23267, 25144
Bagel Bites, 6976
Bagel Buddy, 24567
Bagel Butler, 25144
Bagel By Bell, 936
Bagel King, 5590
Bagels, 3353
Baggywrinkle, 2691
Bagmaster, 19482
Bags Again, 23143
Bagskets, 26199
Bagstarder, 30596
Bahama, 5539
Bahama BlastÖ, 10714
Bahama Mama®, 5929
Bahl Baby, 2255
Bahlsen, 4592
Bai®, 3725, 6818, 24802
Baier's, 940
Bailey's, 2691
Bailey's Irish Cream, 4986
Baileys™, 11211
Baily, 944
Baja Cafe®, 10681
Bajoz, 3545
Bak-Klene®, 9648
Baka-Snack®, 8804
Bakalars, 948
Bakalon, 21227
Bakbar, 26258
Bake Crafters, 950
Bake Fresh, 28471
Bake King, 21227
Bake Lite All Soy, 2796, 20666
Bake Lite Soy/Cotton, 2796, 20666
Bake Packers, 194
Bake'n Show, 30590
Bake-Rite H & R, 2389
Bake-Soft, 463
Bakeable, 3353
Baked Classics, 2728
Baked Fries Sharing Packs, 11754
Baked Potato Thins, 13815
Bakemark, 954
Baken Joy, 13117
Baken-Ets, 4741
Bakeology, 958
Bakeqwik, 955
Baker, 962, 5105, 11788, 29340
Baker Boy, 959
Baker Boys Baked Goods, 960
Baker Supreme, 965
Baker's, 5105, 6976
Baker's Best, 166, 19499
Baker's Blend, 9182
Baker's Choice, 19384
Baker's Cremes, 12795
Baker's Gold, 4025
Baker's Joy®, 6792, 24785
Baker's Joys®, 864
Baker's Label, 7683
Baker's Rib Inc, 970
Baker's®, 1120
Baker-Eze, 22935
Bakerhaus Veit, 971
Bakers Beauties, 965
Bakers Pride, 19385, 29580
Bakers Secret, 31345
Bakers' Gold, 27263
Bakers®, 8945
Bakery Chef, 20101
Bakery Feeds, 3390
Bakerycorp, 978

Bakesafe 500, 26968
Bakesense, 955
Bakesmart®, 190, 18410
Bakeware Buddy, 24567
Bakon Seasonings, 981
Bakon Yeast, 981
Balagna Winery, 983
Balance, 984
Balance®, 8871
Balanced Breaks®, 11228, 28829
Balanced Coffee, 12601
Balanced Cuisine, 7954
Balanceo Weave, 19111
Balboa Bay, 12866
Balderson, 10834
Balderson®, 9789
Baldinger, 987
Baldwin, 989, 2430, 20445
Bale Tech, 25719
Baler Belt Lacer, 20654
Bali's Best, 4804
Balisto®, 7952
Ball Park, 992
Ball Park®, 1359, 13109
Ballantine, 993
Ballantine Ale, 9137
Ballantine's, 5892, 9964
Ballantine's Finest, 3024
Ballard Bitter, 10629
Ballas, 995
Ballatore®, 3834
Ballatyne, 19413
Ballatyne Smokers, 19413
Ballymore, 19908
Balsamic and Herb Dipping Oil, 869
Balsamic Vinegar of Modena, 869
Balthazar's Blend, 2860
Baltibond, 19419
Baltidrive, 19419
Baltimore Tea, 3893
Balut Sa Puti, 8203
Balvenie, 13811
Bama, 1935
Bama Fruit Spreads, 13635
Bambu Juices, 10568
Ban, 1692
Ban Air, 19127
Ban-O-Dor, 29826
Banana Gold, 12527
Banana Moon Snack Line, 10417
Bananitas, 100
Band-It, 19928
Bandana, 10782
Bandersnatch Milk Stout, 2653
Banderwrapper, 25531
Banditos Salsas, 11873
Banfield®, 7952
Bankers Club, 7146
Banner Guard, 28240
Banquet, 6395
Banquet Better Foods, 7166
Banquet Boats, 19932
Banquet Butter, 7166
Banquet Cheese, 7166
Banquet Series, 22320
Banquet®, 2939, 2940, 20821, 20822
Bansi, 3465
Bantam, 29604
Banza, 1012
Bar B O Boss Sauce Mix, 29301
Bar Boss, 30884
Bar Bq Boss, 29301
Bar Code Creator, 29720
Bar Harbor Ginger Ale, 1015
Bar Harbor Peach Ale, 1015
Bar Keepers Friend, 19434
Bar Maid, 19435
Bar Nun, 19930
Bar S, 5917, 8898
Bar-B-Q Fiesta, 3695
Bar-B-Q Treat, 3695
Bar-B-Que King, 19334
Bar-Maids, 19438
Bar-O-Matic, 24665
Bar-Pak, 7363

Bar-Snitz, 1064
Bar-Tenders, 19837
Baraclude®, 1721
Barbara's, 13621
Barbara's Baked Original, 13620
Barbara's Baked White Cheddar, 13620
Barbara's Bakery, 1020
Barbara's Chocolate Chip, 13620
Barbara's Cinnamon, 13620
Barbara's Cinnamon Crunch, 13620
Barbara's Grainshop, 13620
Barbara's Jalapeno, 13620
Barbara's Oatmeal, 13620
Barbara's Original, 13620
Barbara's Peanut Butter, 13620
Barbara's Vanilla Blast, 13620
Barbara's Weetabix, 13620
Barbary Coast Barley, 9688
Barbecue Bucket, 27670
Barbecue Magic, 7766, 25632
Barber Foods, 1022
Barber Foods®, 184, 13109
Barber's®, 3442, 21421
Barbera, 7238, 9889
Barbera Frantioia, 11864
Barbours, 4820
Barbousville Vineyards, 1026
Barcardi, 913
Barcelona, 1027
Barclay Geneve, 25299
Barclay's, 3024
Barcode Labeler, 30843
Bardo Flex, 19447
Bardo Flex Deburring Wheels, 19447
Bare, 1029
Bare Nature, 13427
Bare®, 9945, 27433
Bare® By Solo®, 21362
Barefoot Bubbly®, 3834
Barefoot®, 3834
Barely Bread, 1031
Barengo®, 8415
Barex, 19342
Bargetto, 1033
Bargreens, 19449
Bari, 11336
Bari®, 11211
Barilla Pasta, 1037
Barilla Pronto™, 1037
Barilla Proteinplus™, 1037
Barista Almondmilk, 8957
Barista Bros®, 6818, 24802
Barista Prima, 6819
Barista Prima Coffeehouse®, 6818, 24802
Baristatude, 2009
Baristella, 507
Baritainer® Jerry Cans, 21848
Barkan Winery, 10952
Barkeater Chocolates, 1038
Barkeep, 30376
Barker Buffs, 19447
Barkthins, 10754
Barley Wine Ale, 1401
Barmen, 8459
Barmen™, 8460
Barnacles Snack Mix, 1470
Barnes, 1045
Barnes Machine Company Bamco, 19458
Barney Flats Oatmeal Stout, 549
Barney's Town & Country, 4244
Barnum's Animals Crackers, 8729
Barnwood, 7133
Baron, 1050, 19460
Baron De Ley, 4677
Baron Edmond De Rothschild, 10952
Baron's, 7655
Baronet Coffees, 1792
Barq's, 2811, 6338
Barquette, 10039
Barrel Head, 252
Barrel O'Fun, 1052
Barricade, 23261
Barrie House, 1053
Barrier, 26662

Barrier-Met, 30730
Barrington Estate, 1054
Barrington Gold, 1054
Barrister, 7146
Barrows, 1055
Barry Blower, 27412
Barry Callebaut, 1056
Bart's Homemade, 11763
Bartelt, 24823
Bartenders Pride, 13686
Bartenura Wines, 10952
Bartlett, 2737
Bartlett Dairy, 1060
Barton, 11264
Bartons, 1638
Barzi, 6210
Barzula, 12896
Base Lock, 21199
Base Pac, 27679
Base Rate, 25407
Baseball Trivia, 21059
Baselock, 18276
Basement Bitters, 13082
Basf, 1692
Basic American Foods, 1069
Basic American Frozen Foods, 4222
Basic Country Goodness, 9699
Basic Promotions, 2132
Basic Research, 4150
Basic Value, 13241
Basics Plus, 7423
Basil Hayden's®, 1120
Basilic Pistou, 4148
Basis, 18946
Basitan's, 4839
Basket Weave, 25665
Baskin Robbins, 1075
Baskin-Robbins®, 3803, 21805
Bass, 7123, 26668
Bass Ale, 5427
Bassett's, 1078
Bassick, 28488
Basso, 5034
Basswood, 10478
Baste & Glaze, 11077
Batch, 19481
Batch Lok, 18336
Batch Pik, 19894
Batch-Con, 22634
Batchmaster, 19482, 19484
Batchpak™, 342
Bates, 21113
Batiste Dry Shampoo, 2666, 20561
Batter Bind™S, 8804
Batter Bites®, 6374, 24434
Batter Blends, 9016, 26612
Batter Boss, 30376
Batter-Moist, 4039
Battistoni, 1084
Battle Creek, 2909
Bau Maniere, 5405
Bauchant, 27236
Bauducco, 1085
Bauer Gear Motor, 18678
Bautam, 28626
Bauza, 5036
Bavarian Brand Sausage, 2162
Baxter, 24038
Baxter®, 11211
Baxters Old Nauvoo, 1093
Bay Beauty, 9344
Bay Shore, 1101, 5608, 13992
Bay State Chowda, 1593
Bay Valley Foods, 12943, 30400
Bay Valley™, 1103
Bayard's, 4645
Bayhawk Ipa, 1097
Bayhawk Stout, 1097
Bayley Fan, 27412
Bayonne Ham, 11894, 29459
Bayou Land Seafood, 1110
Bayou Segnette, 7583
Bayview Farms, 12323
Baywood Cellars, 1112

All Brands Index

Bazelet Ha Golan Winery, 10952
Bazzini, 1114
Bbf, 31085
Bbq Pellets, 25308
Bbq Sauce, 21336
Bbq Shack, 888
Bbq Unribs, 9196
Bbq'n Fools, 889
Bbs Bodacious, 890
Bd-Iii, 19798
Bdi, 23850
Bdii, 23850
Bdiii, 23850
Be Happy 'n Healthy Snacks, 5562
Bea's Best, 2708
Beach, 4668
Beach Blonde, 1097
Beach Bum Blonde Ale™, 26668
Beacon Drive-In Iced Tea, 1118
Beacon Street Cafe™, 11317
Beam, 19506
Beam-Array, 19429
Beam-Tracker, 19429
Beamons, 9284
Bean Brothers, 3177
Bean Coffee, 881
Bean Forge, 1123
Bean Heads, 11320
Beanblossom Hard Cider, 9452
Beanfields, 1124
Beanos's, 2958
Bear Claw, 6796
Bear Country Bavarian, 11846
Bear Creek Brand, 1127
Bear Creek Country Kitchens, 1126, 11536
Bear Creek®, 864
Bear Flag, 13320
Bear Flag®, 3834
Bear Fruit Bar, 8598
Bear Meadow Farm, 1129
Bear Mountain, 10372
Bear River, 1677
Bearitos, 1133, 5505, 13672
Beartooth Kitchens, 6861
Beatrice®, 9789
Beau's All-Natural Brewing, 10666
Beaulieu Vineyard, 12937
Beauty, 23152
Beaver, 1141
Beaver Falls, 5643
Beaver Pop, 7279
Beaverite, 19510
Bebeto, 6810
Because Cookie Dough, 1142
Becel, 13167, 13168
Bech, 6381
Beck 'n Call, 26433
Beck Cafe, 1143
Beck Flavors, 1143
Beck's, 71, 689, 7123, 26668
Beck's Dark, 689
Beck's For Oktoberfest, 689
Beckman's, 1147
Beckmann, 12017
Beckmann's, 1148
Becks Ice Cream, 1144
Beddy By, 1600
Bedell Cellars, 1152
Bee & You, 11036
Bee Gee, 2719
Bee My Honey, 6821
Bee Panacea, 13440
Bee Pollen, 1164
Bee Propolis, 1914
Bee Raw, 1159
Bee Sting, 5304
Bee Supreme, 3411
Bee Sweet, 10323
Beebad, 10454
Beech-Nut, 1161
Beech-Nut Organic, 1161
Beechies, 10724
Beef International, 4244
Beef Master, 3262

Beef Not, 3633
Beefeater, 5892
Beefeater Dry, 3024
Beefeaterc, 9964
Beefmate, 12550
Beefsteak®, 1359
Beefsteakc, 1359
Beehive, 1720, 13643, 31087
Beehive Botanicals, 1164
Beer Clean, 21757
Beer Nutsc, 1168
Beer'n Batter, 12520
Beermaster, 26379
Beermatic, 19203
Beesting, 5516
Beesweet Blueberries, 28090
Beetnik, 1169
Beetroot Delights, 1170
Behlen Big Bin, 19527
Beik's Esb, 549
Beirmeister, 7428
Beit Hashita, 2096
Beka, 19532
Bekal, 4877
Bekaplus®, 898
Bel Arbors, 22525
Bel Line, 31164
Bel Normande - Spritzers, 4148
Belco, 19538
Belcolade, 1175
Belcover, 9802
Belcreme De Lys, 12937
Belgian Ale, 1401
Belgioioso, 1174
Believe It, 20966
Bell, 20000
Bell & Evans the Excellent Chicken, 1178
Bell 'orto, 4111
Bell Bialy, 936
Bell Cellars, 10416
Bell Mini Bagel, 936
Bell' Agio, 1006
Bell's Scotch, 3570
Bella, 10013, 25725, 27494
Bella Crema, 2848, 7511
Bella Famiglia®, 1484
Bella Festa, 4153
Bella Frutta, 9636
Bella Italia, 223
Bella Mercato, 4005
Bella Ravioli, 1189
Bella Rosa, 4111
Bella Sera®, 3834
Bella Sun Luci, 1190
Bella Union, 4258
Bella Vista, 1191
Bellarico's, 541
Bellatoria, 1248
Belle, 27711
Belle + Bella, 8878
Belle Gueule, 7380
Belle Mead, 5566
Belle of Piru, 4387
Belle River, 1195
Belleisle, 13908
Bellentani, 11894, 29459
Bellerose, 1197
Belleweather, 4362
Bellissimo, 11777
Bello Lino®, 23811
Bellocq, 1201
Bellows, 7655
Bellringer, 4658
Bells, 19837
Bellwether, 1205
Belmo, 11664
Belmont Springs, 10303, 27797
Belmont Springs®, 3220, 3319
Belnap, 23160
Belshaw, 25995, 31092
Belt Oranges, 13906
Belt Saver 2000, 18095
Belt-O-Matic, 19339
Belt-Vac, 24550

Beltech, 18873, 18874
Beltrac, 25171
Beltway, 19846
Belvedere, 3024, 8452
Belvita, 8474, 8729
Belvoir Fruit Farms, 1661
Bematek, 19563
Bemistape, 18705
Ben & Jerry, 5137
Ben & Jerry's, 1212, 13169
Ben & Jerry's Frozen Smoothies, 1212
Ben & Jerry's Ice Cream, 1212
Ben Shaws, 10637
Ben's®, 2121
Benbow's, 1217
Bencheley, 4422
Benchmark, 11263
Benco Peak, 12972
Bend-A-Lite, 29816
Bendi, 25128
Benecel™, 19108
Beneflex, 7331
Beneful®, 8945
Benevita, 5819
Beni Di Batasiolo, 1543
Benier, 19567, 19568
Benihana, 14020
Benley's Irish Creme, 5596
Bennett's, 1221
Bennetts, 11458
Bennetts®, 1103
Bennington, 19574
Bensdorp, 1056
Bensons, 10041
Bent Arm Ale®, 6374, 24434
Bent's, 4832
Bentley, 19575
Bentley's, 11263
Benzel's Brand, 1224
Ber Boreale, 7379
Berentzen, 13811
Berg, 19579, 19581, 28357
Bergenbier, 8459
Bergenfield Cocoa, 22560
Berger, 29297
Bergeron, 6395
Berghoff Family, 1231
Berico Dryers, 19527
Beringer Vineyards, 12937
Berk-Cap, 1238
Berkel, 24038
Berkeley Farms, 3442, 21421
Berkley & Jensen, 6126
Berks, 1235
Berkshire Ale, 1237
Berkshire Bark, 1236
Berkshire Ice Cream, 11830
Berkwood Farms, 4321, 22498
Bermuda Dunes, 3565
Bernadette's Biscotti, 1241
Bernadette's Biscotti Soave, 1241
Bernadette's Cookies, 1241
Bernard, 1244
Bernard Fine Foods, 3441
Bernard Pradel Cabernet, 5189
Bernardi®, 237, 238
Bernardo, 1246
Bernardus, 1247
Berne Baby Swiss, 12443
Berne Swiss Lace, 12443
Berner, 19597
Bernheim Original Wheat Whiskey, 5720
Berni, 10565
Bernstein's®, 2939, 2940, 20821, 20822, 27540
Berri Pro, 1253
Berry Cool, 7732
Berry Fine Raspberries, 28090
Berry Good, 8919
Berry Weiss, 7330
Berry White, 6590
Berry-Max, 9997
Berrylicious, 6222
Bert Grant's, 13982
Bertani, 27236

Bertha's, 4362
Berthelet, 10331
Bertil-Ohlsson, 20868
Bertman Raddish Sauce, 6532
Bertoli®, 2939, 2940, 20821, 20822
Bertolli, 13168
Bes Tex, 11888
Bessam-Aire, 19607
Bessie, 1391
Best, 19616
Best & Donovan, 19610
Best Bar Ever, 4150
Best Brown Ale, 10404
Best Buy, 28015
Best China, 23842
Best Choice, 4891, 9621
Best Ever Bar®, 8871
Best Foods, 1267
Best Maid, 1270
Best O' the Wheat, 10846
Best of Health, 416
Best of Luck, 6082
Best of Luck Horseshoe Chocolates, 6082
Best Way, 3811, 13184
Bestdeck, 19518
Bestpack, 22926
Bestread, 19518
Besure, 1659, 13536
Beta Max, 19501
Beta Series, 27217
Beta Stab, 6554
Beta-900, 19501
Beta-Care, 1244
Beta-Kleen, 20966
Betadoor, 19624
Bete Spiral, 19625
Beth's, 1275
Beth's Baking Basics, 1275
Bethune, 7006
Betsy's Best, 1277
Bette's Oceanview Diner, 1280
Better, 7750
Better Bakery™, 184
Better Buy, 2419
Better Health Lab, 18572
Better Made, 1286
Better Oats, 10213
Better Pack, 19634
Better Stevia®, 8725
Better Than, 1288
Better Than Milkc, 9748
Better Way, 13619
Better'n Eggs, 3211
Betterway, 19998
Betterway Pourers, 19999
Betty, 6590
Betty Ann, 8510
Betty Crocker, 11599
Betty Crocker®, 4947
Betty Lou's, 1291
Betty Twist & Match Chocolate Candy, 10898
Between Friends Promotional Candy, 4884
Bev-Con, 22634
Bev-Flex, 18295
Bev-Seal, 18295
Bevcon, 20904, 29035
Bever Marketeer, 19636
Beverage Air, 29466
Beverageware, 23499
Beverly, 4539
Beverly Hills, 6310
Beverly International, 1297
Bevlex, 18295
Bevnaps, 23160
Bevnet, 1294
Beyond Better, 1620
Beyond Meat, 1299
Beyond Vodka, 4658
Bfm, 19327
Bfp, 463
Bfs, 25819
Bhl, 18572
Bhu Fit, 1302

1275

All Brands Index

Bi-Lo, 11838
Bi-O-Kleen, 19642
Bi-Tex, 23160
Bi-Therm, 30084
Bialy, 6970
Bianchi Vineyards, 1306
Biazzo Brand, 1308
Bib Ulmer Spatz, 954
Bibby Turboflex, 18678
Bibigo, 1953
Bible Verse, 21059
Bicerba, 30766
Bick's, 6380
Bickel, 10693
Bickel's, 1309, 5555
Bickford, 1312
Bickle Snacks, 1310
Biclops Installation Tool, 28118
Biena Chickpea Snacks, 1317
Biermann, 8677
Biery, 1320
Bifido Factor, 8816
Bifido Nate, 8816
Big Az®, 184, 13109
Big B, 1324
Big Babol, 9956
Big Baby, 10496
Big Banana, 7702
Big Banana Perfet, 28090
Big Beam, 19649
Big Bear, 9664
Big Beer Series, 11743
Big Ben, 2311, 26875
Big Blue, 54
Big Blue ®, 1339
Big Bol, 10496
Big Boy, 340
Big Boy Blazin Berries, 28090
Big Bruce's Gunpowder Chili, 8291
Big Check, 9212
Big Chief, 1327, 2019, 8251, 21189
Big Chunks Salsa, 4587
Big City Reds, 457, 1328
Big City Reds®, 10893
Big Daddy's, 11316
Big Daddy's™, 11317
Big Dipa, 2763
Big Dipper, 1329, 30205
Big Flipper, 30205
Big Fork, 4321, 22498
Big Green, 21079
Big Horn Premium, 2653
Big House, 11263
Big House Ale, 13428
Big Hunkc, 583
Big Inch, 19634
Big Island Candies, 1333
Big John, 10620
Big League Chew, 2132
Big M, 8668
Big Nasty, 10547
Big Onion, 300
Big Papa, 6353
Big Peach ®, 1339
Big Pineapple ®, 1339
Big Ram, 5409
Big Red, 5294, 13689
Big Red Rhubarb, 28090
Big Red Vanilla Float ®, 1339
Big Red®, 3725, 6818, 7952, 13960, 24802
Big Shot, 8784
Big Sky Ipa, 1344
Big Smiley, 10898
Big Tea, 5612
Big Time, 2172
Big Top Animal Cookies, 9399
Big V, 6354
Big Value, 9226
Big Y, 570
Big Yummy, 2947
Bigelow, 1350, 7124, 8090
Bigger Better, 5590
Bigs®, 2939, 2940, 20821, 20822
Biladi, 3615

Biladi Tohina, 3615
Bilberry Extract, 11268
Bill Bailey's, 11988
Bill Mack's, 7729
Bill's, 4158
Billingsgate, 1355
Billow, 23160
Billy Bee, 8061
Billy Bock, 1837
Bilopage, 2426
Bilsom, 21317
Bilt, 29627
Bilt-Rite, 19659
Biltmore, 1358, 13454
Biltrite, 26020
Bimbo®, 1359
Bin 36, 5499
Bin 49, 30860
Bin Chxn, 1951
Bin-Dicators, 30799
Bind, 24070
Bindi, 1360
Bingham Hill Cheeses, 10834
Binks Industries, Inc., 19664
Binosto®, 8389
Binsert, 24542
Binyamina, 10952
Binyamina Winery, 10952
Bio Cleansing Systems, 26097
Bio Free Trap Clear, 24316
Bio K, 1368
Bio Scan, 28731
Bio-Bin® Waste Disposal, 21848
Bio-Familia, 6279
Bio-Foods, 1366
Bio-Nate, 8816
Bio-Pak, 22682
Bio-Tech Pharmacal, 1370
Bio-Zap, 30391
Bioallers, 13642
Bioallers®, 9237, 26785
Bioastin, 9244
Bioastin Natural Astaxanthin, 3281
Biobed, 19691
Biobest, 745
Biochem, 3080
Biocount, 24212
Bioflora, 13480
Biofree Septic Clear, 24316
Biomega, 783
Bionate®, 3320
Bionova, 5475
Bionutrient, 641
Biopac, 19669
Biopath, 28886
Bioprene, 25775
Biopur, 10366
Biopuric, 19691
Bioscan Ii, 20910
Bioslide, 30913
Biosolo, 21363
Biospan®, 3320
Biosyn, 29030
Biothane, 19691
Biotta Juices, 10568
Biovelop, 1692
Birch Bark, 2108
Birch Logs, 2108
Birchwood Foods, 6790
Bird Brine, 2019
Bird-In-Hand, 1385
Birdie Pak, 1386
Birds Eye C&W, 2939, 2940, 20821, 20822
Birds Eye Voila, 2939, 2940, 20821, 20822
Birds Eye®, 1389, 2939, 2940, 20821, 20822, 27540
Birdseye, 1388
Biringer's Farm Fresh, 11390
Biro, 19697
Birthday, 21059
Bis Train, 2833
Bisca, 6279, 6774
Biscotti Di Lasca, 8927

Biscotti Di Roma, 846
Biscotti Di Suzy™, 1395
Biscotti Toscani, 7111
Bishamon, 19698, 19908
Bison, 2115
Bison®, 13218
Bisquick®, 4947
Bissett's, 1403
Bisto, 2115
Bistro, 11214, 20256
Bistro 36, 6790
Bistro Faire, 3232
Bistro Favorites, 7197
Bistro Soups and Chili®, 13400
Bisurkey, 7443
Bit-O-Honey, 9877
Bitburger, 1208
Bitchin', 12178
Bitchin' Sauce, 1406
Bite Fuel, 1407
Bite-Size Bakery, 1408
Bites, 2580, 20541
Bits O' Butter, 12377
Bits'n'pops, 525
Bittermyx®, 11436, 29018
Bitteroot Extra Special Bitter, 4466
Bittner's, 7876
Bitzels, 7424
Bixby Bar, 1414
Bj Beer, 897
Bke, 19930
Bki Worldwide, 29580
Black, 5323, 19709
Black & Gold, 1977
Black & Tan, 1208
Black & White, 3570
Black + Decker, 29584
Black and Tan, 11218
Black Bear Ale, 13711
Black Beauty, 22935
Black Butte, 3533
Black Canyon® Angus, 8783
Black Canyon® Premium Reserve, 8783
Black Cat, 7006, 28292
Black Cherry Royal, 5362, 23377
Black Cod (Sablefish, 10949
Black Cow, 756
Black Creek®, 11209, 11211
Black Diamond Brewing Company®, 26668
Black Diamond Caviar, 13567
Black Diamond®, 9789
Black Duck, 7655
Black Eagle ®, 13120
Black Forest, 11218, 13110
Black Forest Organic, 1417, 4345
Black Hawk, 8153
Black Hook, 10629
Black Horse, 8459
Black Ice, 8459
Black Jacks, 13997
Black Jewell®, 1420
Black Knight, 13643, 29167
Black Label Bacon®, 6000, 23861
Black Licorice Vines, 469
Black Mesa, 1422
Black Prince, 1423
Black Ranch Gourmet Grains, 1424
Black Roberts, 4515
Black Silk, 4543
Black Swamp, 5402
Black Tea Chai, 11237
Black Tie, 2108
Black Tie Collection, 28934
Black Widow, 12814
Black Wolf Blend, 5794
Blackbird Porter, 4466
Blackburn's, 12469
Blackened Redfish Magic, 7766, 25632
Blackened Steak Magic, 7766, 25632
Blackening Spice, 2499
Blackhawk Stout, 8153
Blackheart Premium Spiced Rum, 5720
Blackjack Pasture Cabernet, 4862
Blackjack Porter, 7310

Blackline, 29520
Blacknight, 18515
Blackout Stout, 5314
Blackwing, 19716
Blackwing Organics, 19716
Bladerunner, 24700
Blair's, 1431
Blake's®, 2939, 2940, 20821, 20822
Blakeslee, 19719
Blanc De Noirs, 3661
Blanc Du Bois, 8513
Blanca, 8335
Blanchard & Blanchard, 6279
Bland Farms, 5132
Blanks ®, 13120
Blanton's, 1438
Blantons, 11263
Blaser's, 1440, 4028
Blasting Powder, 2947
Blazer, 25154
Blazers, 31126
Blazing Star, 180
Blazzin, 1442
Blend Pak, 1443
Blend Tanks, 20875
Blended Breaders, 9016, 26612
Blending Station, 30884
Blends With Benefits, 15
Blendsure™, 4837
Blenheim, 1447
Blenjavas, 5819
Blessing's Mustard, 4587
Bletsoe's Cheese, 1449
Bleu Rock Vineyard Wines, 9334
Blimpy, 29816
Blinky, 27579
Blipack, 26427
Bliss Bar, 5221
Blissfully Better, 1453
Blissmaster, 26257
Blitz Power Mints, 11314
Blizzard Beer Systems, 20633
Blo Apco, 19738
Block Graphics®, 22187
Blodgett, 19733
Blodgett Combi, 19733
Blodis, 19713
Blonde Ale, 13288
Blood Building Broth, 131
Blood Building Powder, 131
Blood Cleanse, 5682
Blood Red, 3746
Bloody Mary Blend, 13222
Bloody Mary Juice Burst, 5460
Bloom, 1457
Bloombuilder, 4374
Bloomfield Farms, 1443
Bloomfield Industries, 29466
Blooming Bags, 26199
Bloomington Brewing, 1460
Bloomsbery & Co., 10229
Blossom Hill, 3815, 12937
Blossom Time, 12826
Blossom Water, 1463
Blouin, 10330
Blount, 1464
Blow Hard Mustard, 6054
Blow Out, 23039
Blubotol, 13697
Blue Angel, 31059
Blue Band, 13168
Blue Barn, 726
Blue Bell Dairy, 1465
Blue Bell Ice Cream, 1465
Blue Bonnet®, 2939, 2940, 20821, 20822
Blue Bottle, 13697
Blue Boy, 2657
Blue Buck, 7733, 25622
Blue Buffalo®, 4947
Blue Bunny®, 13645
Blue Chip Baker, 1506
Blue Chip Group, 1506
Blue Crab Bay, 1470
Blue Curacao, 3545
Blue Diamond, 1471, 12201, 19742

All Brands Index

Blue Diamond Almonds, 1471, 19742
Blue Diamond Hazelnut, 1471, 19742
Blue Diamond Macadamias, 1471, 19742
Blue Evolution, 1473
Blue Fin, 11561
Blue Fish, 27236
Blue Gold, 1474
Blue Goose Minneolas, 13906
Blue Green Organics, 1476
Blue Heron, 8153
Blue Heron Pale Ale, 8153
Blue Hill, 1479
Blue Hill Bay, 151
Blue Jay Orchards, 1481
Blue Light, 7123
Blue Magic, 25470
Blue Monday®, 10998
Blue Moon, 8459
Blue Moon Tea, 1486
Blue Moon®, 8460
Blue Pearl Incense, 7562
Blue Plate, 11865
Blue Plate Mayonnaise, 10657
Blue Plumb Brandy, 2737
Blue Point Brewing Company, 571
Blue Poly Trolleys, 22890
Blue Ribbon, 7163, 8578, 11759, 27346, 28517, 29598
Blue Ribbon Classic, 29598
Blue Ribbon Classics®, 13645
Blue Ribbon Hot Sausage, 12463
Blue Ribbon Orchard Choice, 13254
Blue Ribbon Rice®, 10777, 28421
Blue Ribbon®, 6391
Blue Ridge, 24683
Blue Ridge Farms, 4244
Blue Ridge Teas, 1496
Blue Runner, 1497
Blue Satin, 31010
Blue Seal, 2559
Blue Star, 1500, 7123
Blue Star Farms, 9799
Blue Star Mockiko, 6673
Blue Too, 19741
Blue Valley, 6702
Blue Willow, 1501
Blueberry Ale, 6283
Blueberry Barbeque Sauce, 9116
Blueberry Blossom, 10478
Blueberry King, 1171
Bluebird, 4662
Bluebird Products, 19754
Bluebird Restaurant, 1507
Bluebonnet, 13190
Bluebonnet Coffee, 13191
Bluefield®, 11378, 28946
Bluegiant, 19908
Bluegrass, 5402
Bluegrass Bourbon™ Sauce, 1654
Bluepearl®, 7952
Blueprint Organic, 5505
Bluewater Mfg., Inc., 31214
Blume Honey Water, 1510
Blumer's Root Beer, 1231
Blythedale, 12493
Bnutty, 1513
Boar's Head, 4652
Board-Mate, 24700
Boardwalk, 2172
Boat Brand, 11915
Bob Evans Farms®, 8225
Bob Evans®, 1516
Bob's, 1417, 4345
Bob's Big Boy, 6679
Bob's Red Mill, 1519
Bob's Texas Style, 10173
Bobalu Nuts, 1520
Bobby Flay, 10311
Bobo's, 1523
Boboli, 892
Boboli®, 1359
Boc Edwards, 27729
Boca Bons, 1526
Boca®, 1527
Bocconcino, 1896

Boce Stokes, 27729
Bock, 11846
Boddie, 757
Boddingtons Pub Ale, 7123, 26668
Bodega De San Antonio Sangria, 7740
Bodegas Campillo, 27236
Bodin's, 1531
Bodum, 13112, 30523
Body Fortress®, 8871
Body Fuel, 10708
Body-Fuel, 7947
Bodyguard™, 6449, 24506
Boelube Aerospace, 26968
Boericke & Tafel, 8896
Bogdon's, 10724
Boggiatto, 1538
Bogland, 1540, 2798
Bogland By the Sea, 1540, 2798
Boglandish, 1540
Bohemian, 1542, 8459
Bohemian Maid, 4654
Bohn, 23692
Boisset Classic, 12672
Boisset Mediterranee, 12672
Boissiere, 27236
Boja's, 1545
Boja's Chef's Delight, 1545
Bokobsa Wines, 10952
Bola, 22599
Bola Pop's, 2947
Bold Beans, 3575
Bold Italiano™, 1654
Bomb Pop®, 13645
Bombal, 13273
Bombay, 56, 913, 914, 2922
Bombay Bites, 6026
Bombay Gold 100, 5467
Bombe Glaze, 5399
Bon & Viv Spiked Seltzer, 571
Bon Ca Ca, 2019
Bon Cuisine, 9165
Bon Matin, 8676
Bon Matin®, 2121
Bon Secour, 1550
Bon Terra, 22525
Bon Ton, 1310
Bonafide Provisions, 1552
Bonaqua, 2815, 20685
Bonar, 19788
Bonbon Barnier, 3381
Bond Ost, 9094
Bondalast, 23543
Bonderite, 23726
Bondstar, 24622
Bone Suckin', 1555
Bone Suckin' Sauce, 4587
Bonfaire, 18908
Bongiovi Pasta Sauces, 1558
Bonici®, 13109
Bonk Breaker, 1559
Bonn Dye, 19789
Bonn Trace, 19789
Bonnet, 24038
Bonnet Buff, 20966
Bonnie, 12866
Bonnie Blue, 2235
Bonnie Lee, 13611
Bonnie Maid, 12866
Bonniebrook, 11766
Bonnies, 10900
Bono, 8504
Bonomo, 2132
Bonomo Turkish Taffy®, 13572
Bonterra, 1567
Bonton, 8314
Bonzers, 8228
Bookbinder's, 1569
Booker's®, 1120
Boomchickapop, 567
Boone County Supreme, 11547
Boone Maman, 25789
Boone's Farm®, 3834
Boont Amber, 549
Boord's, 7655
Boordy Vineyards, 1572

Boost, 24672
Boost®, 8945
Boot Scootin', 7364
Borax-Splash, 28242
Borax-Sudz, 28242
Borden, 3862, 6760, 7137, 24672
Borden Dairy, 1576
Borden®, 1103
Borden® Cheese, 3335
Border Springs Farm Lamb, 4321, 22498
Borders, 25773
Boreas, 30576
Borges, 12035
Borgianni, 13811
Borgogno, 1006
Born 3, 5138
Born Free, 10529
Bornstein, 1582
Bornt Family Farms, 1583
Borra, 1584
Borsodi, 8459
Bortilly, 56
Bos'n, 12062
Bosco, 1586, 10229, 11339, 28940
Bosco's Pizza Co.®, 13109
Bosell, 1759
Boskydel, 1589
Bosque Tea Co, 13381
Boss, 29381, 29491
Boss (Boots and Gloves), 19806
Boss Baby, 10229
Bost-Kleen, 19809
Bostitch, 29584
Boston America Corp, 2132
Boston Baked Beans, 1417, 4345
Boston Bakers Exchange, 2683
Boston Beam, 19811
Boston Bumper, 19811
Boston Chowda Co, 10118
Boston Colorguard, 19811
Boston Fruit Slices, 1596
Boston Gear, 18678, 19809
Boston Pride, 12062
Boston Shearpump, 18126
Boston Spices, 1598
Boston Tuffguard, 19811
Boswellin, 11061
Bottega Vinaia, 27236
Bottle Air, 25920
Bottle Caps, 2132
Bottle Duster, 25920
Bottle Green, 1605
Bottle-Buster, 22257
Botto's Genuine Italian Sausage, 1938
Bottom Line, 20788
Bottomup, 29973
Bou, 1607
Bouchard Aine & Fils, 1543
Bouchard Aine Fils, 12672
Bouchard Family Farm, 1609
Boudin, 553
Boudreaux's, 1610
Boueka, 7344
Boulard, 27236
Boulder Canyon, 1613, 10173, 13129
Boulder Cookie, 1614
Boulder Creek, 1615
Boulder Ice Cream, 1617
Boulder Sausage Products, 1619
Bouma, 1622
Bounce, 7870, 12721, 30193
Bountiful Harvest™, 11504, 29095
Bounty, 12721, 30193
Bounty®, 7952
Bourbon Deluxe®, 1120
Bourbon Excelso, 7107
Bourbon Supreme, 7655
Bourbonil, 12085
Boursin, 1172
Bousquette, 9555
Bove's of Vermont, 1629
Bovril, 25789
Bow Valley, 1630
Bowie River, 4078
Bowl & Roll™, 6685

Bowlby's Bits, 525
Bowlpack, 27679
Bowman's, 59, 11263
Bowman's Small Batch, 11263
Bowmore, 1120
Bowmore Islay, 12315
Bowness Baker, 1633
Bowtemp, 19821
Box'fin, 20531
Boxer, 1638, 30413
Boyajian, 1635
Boyd's Coffee, 1636, 19825
Boyds' Kissa Bearhugs, 6291, 24388
Boyer, 1638, 19826
Bp Gourmet, 903
Bpe 2000, 19413
Bpi, 4150
Bpi®, 1163
Bpl 10000, 18095
Bpl 12000, 18095
Bpl 24000, 18095
Bpl 6000, 18095
Bpl 8600, 18095
Br-Lerie Mont Royal®, 6818, 24802
Br-Lerie St. Denis®, 6818, 24802
Brach's, 1417, 4345
Brad's Pretzel Dip, 6918
Bradford Cast Metals, 28809
Bragard, 19839
Bragg, 1652
Braggadocio, 8075
Brahm's Wine Country, 628
Brahma, 71
Brailldots, 28930
Braillplaques, 28930
Brailltac, 21199
Brain Herbs, 9201
Brain Invigoration Powder, 131
Brain Vita, 5682
Brain Well, 9201
Brainstrong, 6107
Brake, 25633
Brakebush®, 1654
Bramble Berry Brew, 1139
Brami Beans, 904
Bran Flakes, 10213
Bran+Luebbe, 28714
Brancaia®, 3834
Brancott Estatec, 9964
Brand Aromatics, 8061
Brander, 1657
Brandguard, 28461
Brandpac, 19069
Brandt, 1662, 1957, 4244
Brandy, 2343
Brandywine, 5028
Branford, 19844
Branik, 8459
Braren Pauli, 1664
Brasal Bock, 1666
Brasal Legere, 1666
Brasal Special Amber, 1666
Brass Ladle, 1665
Brass Master, 19846
Brassica, 1667
Brassica Teas With Sgs, 1667
Brauhaus Pretzel, 6338
Braumeister, 1231
Braumeister Light, 1231
Braumeister Select Ipb, 5193
Braun, 12721, 30193
Brava, 7123, 7157
Bravard, 1672
Bravissimo, 12499
Bravissimo!, 8367
Bravo, 20256, 23571
Bravos Tortilla Chips, 13884
Brazi Bites, 1673
Brazil Celebes, 761
Brazil Serra Negra, 9181
Brazos Legends, 1675, 6787
Bread & Biscuits, 4362
Bread & Chocolate, 1677
Bread Alone, 1678
Bread Glaze, 12795

All Brands Index

Bread, Rice & Pasta Lovers Diet, 7422
Breadeli, 1524
Breading Magic, 7766, 25632
Breads of Venice, 5097, 5098
Breadshop, 25789
Break Up, 13845
Breakfast Choice, 9548
Breakstones, 6760
Breaktime, 3384
Breakwater, 1684
Breathsavers, 2132, 5818, 23750
Breckenridge Brewery, 571
Breckenridge Farm Sparkling Juices, 8135
Breco, 19852
Brecoflex, 19852
Bred-Mate, 6340
Brede Old Fashioned, 11625
Bree, 19636
Breez Proof, 29723
Breeze, 26615
Breezy Hills, 7463
Breidert Air, 28649
Breitenbach, 1688
Brekki, 1689
Bremner, 1690
Bremner Wafers, 1690, 3384
Brenntag, 1692
Brent & Sam's, 5477
Brenton, 19857
Brentwood, 11766
Brer Rabbit®, 864
Breton, 3384
Breton Minis, 3384
Brew Buffers, 12795
Brew Canada, 30860
Brew City, 530
Brew City®, 8055
Brew Dr., 1694
Brew House, 5294
Brew La La Coffee, 12100
Brew La La Tea, 12100
Brew Pub, 1248
Brew Rite, 28471
Brew'n'pour Lid, 29055
Brew-A-Cup: Perfect Potfuls, 2848
Brewer's, 7404
Brewer's Crystals, 6211, 24226
Brewers Clarex®, 3320
Brewers Reserves, 12153
Brewmaster Jack, 10666
Brewmatic, 19863, 22108
Brewski Snack, 1690
Brewster Nutrition, 12638
Breyers, 5137, 13167, 13169, 20946
Breyers Blasts®, 5165
Breyers®, 5165
Brian, 12525
Brianna's, 25789
Brick Premium, 1702
Brick-Pack Clip, 30337
Brickenridge, 8390
Brickfire Bakery®, 11504, 29095
Brico, 19659
Bridalveil Ale, 11448
Bridgetown, 1706
Bridlewood Estate Winery®, 3834
Brie W/Garlic De Luxe, 2409
Briess, 1710
Brifisol®, 898
Brigade, 29520
Brigade +, 29520
Brigham's, 1711
Bright Greens, 1712
Bright Harvest, 1713
Bright Leaf, 2245
Brighton Mills, 5466
Brill, 954
Brill's, 5482
Brill®, 20096
Brillasol, 8161
Brimley Stone, 5245
Brimstone Hill, 1716
Briny Deep, 9094
Brisk, 1718

Brisk®, 9945, 27433
Brisker, 19874
Brisling Sardines, 651
Bristle Ridge, 1719
Brita, 2766, 20657
Brite Bowl, 27045
Brite-Lite, 31217
Britepak, 22548
Britex, 19884
British Class, 13208, 30670
Brittany Acres, 9535
Brittle Duet, 2881
Brittnia, 3336
Brix, 23391
Brix 15hp, 25231
Brix 30, 25231
Brix 35hp, 25231
Brix 50, 25231
Brix 65hp, 25231
Brix 90, 25231
Brix 90hp, 25231
Briz, 12003
Bro Egcellent, 1735
Bro White Sour, 1735
Bro-Tisserie, 19882
Broad Run Vineyards, 1726
Broad St. Brown, 8952
Broadleaf, 1730
Broadleaf Cervena, 1730
Broadway Menu, 30876
Broadway Red, 9182
Broaster, 19882
Broaster Chicken, 19882
Broaster Foods, 19882
Broaster Recipe, 19882
Broccoli Wokly, 7853
Broccosprouts, 1667
Brock, 1732
Brodies, 7995
Broiler Master, 20258
Broken Bow, 1734
Broken Rock Cellars, 5774
Broker's Gin, 8062
Broker's London Dry Gin, 5981
Broker's Whiskey, 5981
Brolio, 13811
Brolite Ia, 1735
Brooklace, 19885
Brooklyn, 1748, 21199, 21866
Brooklyn Baking Pumpernickel Bread, 1744
Brooklyn Baking Rye Bread, 1744
Brooklyn Bean Roastery, 1745
Brooklyn Born Chocolatec, 13056
Brooklyn Bourbon, 12178
Brooklyn Brine, 1749
Brooklyn Cider House, 1750
Brooklyn Java, 5012
Brooklyn Whatever, 1754
Brooks, 19888
Brooks Street Baking, 11368
Brooks®, 2939, 2940, 20821, 20822, 27540
Brookshire's®, 1758, 19889
Brookside, 1759, 5818, 23750
Brookside Reserve, 7655
Brosoft, 1735
Brother Bru Bru's, 1762
Brotherhood, 1764
Brothers Ice Cream, 1766
Broths, 2115
Broughton®, 3442, 21421
Broussard, 27889
Brouwerij St. Bernardus, 10666
Brouwerij Verhaeghe, 10666
Brower, 19894
Brown, 11992, 19899
Brown & Jenkins Fresh Roasted, 1772
Brown 'n' Serve, 833
Brown Ale, 556, 7310, 7315
Brown Bear, 13441
Brown Bear Ale, 13711
Brown Brothers, 27236
Brown Cow, 12145
Brown Cow Farm, 1774

Brown Cow Farm East, 9885
Brown Flax, 10616
Brown Island Bitter, 13711
Brown King, 11832
Brown Kwik, 1531
Brown Paper Goods®, 11504, 29095
Brown's Dairy, 1782
Brown's Dairy®, 3442, 21421
Brown's Ware, 1789
Brownberry®, 1359
Brownie Brittle, 1786, 11534
Brownies & Roses, 2903
Browns Best, 6761
Bru-Mix, 13182
Bruce Baking, 1791
Bruce Cost Ginger Ale, 1793
Bruce Foods, 2019
Bruce Tea, 1795
Bruce's® Mixes, 1794
Bruce's® Yams, 1794
Brucepac, 1796
Bruiser, 11320
Brule Valley, 9127
Bruner, 21145
Bruner-Matic, 21145
Brunkow Cheese, 1800
Bruno, 1802
Bruschetta, 4005
Brush-Rite, 23199
Brussel Bytes, 11415
Brut Classic, 3661
Brutal Bajan, 4895
Brute, 21178
Brute Rack, 19915
Bryan, 6762, 13109
Bryan Products, 805
Bryant Autumn Blush, 1807
Bryant Country White, 1807
Bryant Dixie Blush, 1807
Bryant Festive Red, 1807
Bryant Vineyard, 1807
Bsp901, 26262
Bubba's Bagels, 9736
Bubba's Fine Foods, 1810
Bubba's Yams, 28090
Bubbaganouj Ipa, 4466
Bubbies Homemade Ice Cream, 1812
Bubbilicious, 9995
Bubbilicious Bubble Gum, 1980
Bubble Candy, 7638
Bubble Chocolate, 10229
Bubble Gum, 12211
Bubble King, 9320
Bubble Yum, 5818, 23750
Bubblecraft, 9452
Bubblegum, 1591
Bubblegum Buddies, 6780
Bubbles, 1813
Bubblicious Bubble Gum, 2132
Bubly®, 9945, 27433
Buccaneer, 648, 5861
Bucha, 8955
Buck, 4658, 19923
Buck Ice, 19922
Buckaroo, 13716
Buckeye, 1819, 18281
Buckeye Beans and Herbs, 11390
Buckhead Gourmet, 1821
Buckhoen, 19927
Buckhorn, 11263
Buckingham, 1822
Buckley Farms™, 12885, 30333
Buckley's, 5140
Buckman's Best, 7346
Buckman's Best Snack, 7346
Buckpower™, 9237, 26785
Buckskin Bill, 21808
Buckson, 340
Buckwheat, 10478
Bud Light, 571, 7123
Bud Light Lime, 7123
Bud Lime-A-Ritas, 8279
Buddha Teas, 1826
Buddig Original, 2212
Buddy Fruits, 1827

Buddy Fruits & Veggies, 1827
Buddy Squirrel, 1828
Budget Buy, 12973, 30444
Budget Gourmet®, 1200
Budgetware, 23809
Budgit, 20752
Budibar, 1830
Budweiser, 71, 571, 7123
Budweiser®, 26668
Buena Ventura, 2122
Buena Vida®, 855
Buena Vida™, 864
Buena Vista Winery, 1543
Bueno, 1835
Bueno®, 11504, 29095
Bufalo®, 6000, 23861
Buffalo, 6211, 21769, 24226, 26932
Buffalo Bill's, 12688
Buffalo Bob's Everything Sauce, 4354
Buffalo Brew, 1837
Buffalo Chips, 10417
Buffalo Gold, 7566
Buffalo Grill, 22267
Buffalo Maid, 576
Buffalo Ranchc, 5489
Buffalo Trace, 10596, 11263
Buffalo Trace Distillery Experiment, 11263
Buffaloos®, 13607
Buflovak, 19930
Bug Bites, 4060
Bugles®, 4947
Build-A-Bear, 10229
Built Rite, 20015
Buitoni®, 8945
Bulgarian Style, 1782
Bulk Co2, 7363
Bulkatilt, 28115
Bulkitank, 28115
Bulklift, 19936
Bulkmaster, 29632, 29633
Bulksonics, 26283
Bull and Barrel, 1841
Bull Ice, 9664
Bull's Eye, 6976
Bulldog, 30185
Bullet, 24182
Bullet Guard, 19940
Bullet Lure, 24274
Bullfrog Lavander, 12987
Bulls Eye, 3060
Bumble Bee, 6267, 7331
Bumpy & Jumpy, 11004
Bun Bar, 9877
Bunker Boxes, 19048
Bunker Hill, 805
Bunn, 19292, 19943, 31083
Bunn-O-Matic, 19943
Bunny, 3193
Bunny Bread, 4529
Bunny Pasta, 4794
Bunny®, 7402
Buns & Roses, 1853
Buon Giorno, 7428
Buona Cucina, 12860
Buona Vita, 1854
Buran, 30576
Burg'r Tend'r, 21312
Burgasko, 8459
Burger Buddies, 13630
Burgers N'A Bag, 8698
Burgers Smokehouse, 1858
Burgess, 19952
Burkay, 18074
Burke & Barry, 7655
Burkec, 6000, 23861
Burkec, 1861
Burkle, 21848
Burleson Pure Honey, 1863
Burlle Meats, 1940
Burma, 2966
Burn, 2815, 8485, 20685
Burn Off, 13128
Burnett's London Dry Gin, 5720
Burnett's Vodkas, 5720

All Brands Index

Burnetti's, 1866
Burnguard, 30486
Burning River Pale Ale, 5314
Burnley Vineyards, 1868
Burns, 7875
Burpee, 25545
Burrow, 13193
Burrows Packaging, 26756
Burt's Bees, 2766, 20657
Burtek, 18873
Burtex, 18874
Busboy, 23999
Busch, 571, 7123, 27729
Busch®, 26668
Buschman, 30921
Bush's Best Baked Beans, 1872
Bush's Canned Beans, 1872
Bush's Chili, 1872
Bush's Grilling Beans, 1872
Bushman's Best Mazavaroo, 5765
Bushwhacker's Mustard, 6054
Business Works Accounting, 28342
Busseto, 1875
Busseto Special Reserve, 1875
Busstop, 30498
Buster, 5517
Bustops, 26090
Busy Bee, 1040, 1876
But-R-Creme™, 3412
Butcher Boy, 6881
Butcher Buddy, 25510
Butcher Wagon, 5643
Butcher's Cut, 13402
Butcher's Friend, 12830, 30310
Butcher's Pride, 9187
Butler, 1878, 19977
Butter Better, 31010
Butter Creams, 10596
Butter Flo, 1880
Butter Grahams, 2903
Butter Kernel®, 4267, 22464
Butter Toffee Covered Popcorn, 7845
Butter Up, 31010
Butter-Krust Country, 1881
Butterball, 1882, 1883
Butterbuds, 1880
Butterfield, 338
Butterfinger, 2132
Butterfinger®, 8945
Butterfly, 7758
Buttermist, 1880
Butternut, 10730
Butternut Baked Goods, 10730
Butternut Breads, 4529
Butterscotch, 9773
Butterscotch Bliss, 9019
Butterscotch Krimpetsc, 12551
Buttery Baker, 10981
Button-On, 24519
Buyer Label, 6622
Buzz Bars, 1914
Buzz Buttered Steaks, 1891
Buzzn Bee Farms, 1893
Bvl, 19348
Bx-100, 19878
By Nature By Hand, 13403
Bybee's, 4374
Byblos, 1894
Byington, 1895
Byrd Cookies, 1897
Byrd Missouri Grown, 1899
Byrd's Famous Cookies, 1897
Byrd's Hoot Owl Pecan Ranch Pecans, 1899
Byrne Dairy, 1902
Byron's Barbecue, 10714

C

C & E Sugar, 1908
C Howard Co., 2132
C&D, 7874
C&G, 13513
C&H, 1911, 4517, 12201
C&H Sugar, 3666
C&H®, 12196
C&S, 1928
C&T, 1929
C-Square, 29484
C-Vap, 31273
C-Vat, 31273
C.F. Burger, 1915
C.F. Sauer Company, 1935
C.G. Sargent's Sons, 19935
C.P., 1922, 28967
C.U.E., 30122
C.V.P. Systems, 1968
C/Z, 20710
Ca Bianca, 4677
Ca Donini, 4677
Ca Halibut, 10949
Cab Produkttechnik, 30186
Cab-O-Sil, 20114
Cabana, 1310
Cabaret, 3384
Cabernayzyn, 12746
Cabernet Sauvignon, 4745
Cabernet Vinegar, 869
Cabin Air Filters, 3833, 21863
Cabin Fever Ale, 1237
Cabot, 211, 1972
Cabot Cheeses, 1972
Cacao Barry, 1056
Cachaca 61, 7655
Cache River, 8079
Cache Valley® Cheese, 3335
Cacio De Roma, 11668
Cacio De Roma Cheese, 11668
Cacique, 1977
Cococo, 1978
Cacti-Nea, 9029, 26626
Cactu Life, 1979
Cactus Bills, 13120
Cactus Cooler®, 6818, 24802
Cactus Kid, 20120
Cadbury, 5818, 23750
Cadbury Chocolate, 1981
Cadbury Dairy Milk, 1981
Cadbury Dark, 1981
Cadbury Favourites, 1981
Cadbury Schweppes, 1294, 5975
Cadbury Thins, 1981
Caddy, 18195, 20121
Caddy Cold, 20121
Caddy Connections, 20121
Caddy-All, 26681
Caddy-Flex, 20121
Caddy-Veyor, 20121
Caddymagic, 20121
Cadie, 20122
Cadillac Coffee, 1984
Cadillac Mountain Stout, 1015
Cady, 20752
Cady Creek Farms, 1985
Cae Profile, 18142
Cae Select, 18142
Caesar's, 4244
Caesar's Kitchen, 1986
Caf, Bustelo, 6380
Caf, Classicsc, 187
Caf, Delight Certified Sweeteners, 3574
Caf, Delight Premium Drink Mixes, 3574
Caf, Escapes®, 6818, 24802
Caf, Punta Del Cielo®, 6818, 24802
Cafe, 22959
Cafe Altura, 1987
Cafe Amigo, 947
Cafe Amore, 19449
Cafe Appassionato, 2005
Cafe Bodega, 1053
Cafe Bonjour, 10708
Cafe Bustelo, 10920
Cafe Caracolillo Decafe, 2192
Cafe Caracolillo Expresso, 2192
Cafe Caracolillo Gourmet, 2192
Cafe Caribe, 2847
Cafe Del Mundo, 1991, 20127
Cafe Don Pablo, 1859
Cafe Don Pedro, 13191
Cafe Dontedro, 13190

Cafe Du Monde, 1993
Cafe El Marino, 3420
Cafe Elite, 19737
Cafe Escapes, 6819
Cafe Europa, 2885
Cafe Excellence, 1053
Cafe Extract, 1490
Cafe Fair, 12069
Cafe H®, 6000, 23861
Cafe La Semeuse, 1997
Cafe Latino, 2885
Cafe Orleans, 13190
Cafe Orleans-Coffee, 13191
Cafe Pick, 6497
Cafe Quisqueva, 2192
Cafe Regil, 2192
Cafe Rico Rico, 2192
Cafe Riquisimo, 2192
Cafe Supremo, 2847
Cafe Tequila, 2003
Cafe Tiamo, 6198
Cafe Time, 11940, 12894
Cafe Unico, 13190
Cafe Unico-Espresso, 13191
Cafe-Matic, 24725
Cafe.Com, 23993
Caffarel, 3381
Caffe D'Oro Cappuccino & Cocoa, 2008
Caffe D'Vita, 2009
Caffe La Llave, 4202
Caffe Lolita, 7655
Caffe Trieste Coffee Beans, 2013
Caffreys, 8459
Cafiesa, 22560
Cafix, 6279
Cailler®, 8945
Cain Concept, 2015
Cain Cuv,E, 2015
Cain Five, 2015
Cains, 4928, 11213
Caito, 2016
Cajan Gold, 8772
Cajohns, 2017
Cajun Aujus, 2023
Cajun Bayou, 1279
Cajun Bites, 1531
Cajun Blast, 2019
Cajun Boy, 10029
Cajun Boy's Louisiana, 2018
Cajun Brand Sausage, 2162
Cajun Chef, 2019
Cajun Country, 4232, 9535
Cajun Creole, 2021
Cajun Creole Coffee, 2021
Cajun Creole Coffee & Chicory, 2022
Cajun Creole Hot Nuts, 2021
Cajun Creole Jalapeanuts, 2021
Cajun Flip N Fry, 2019
Cajun Gourmet Magic, 7206
Cajun Hollar, 6334
Cajun House, 11255
Cajun Injector, 2023
Cajun Injector®, 1794
Cajun King®, 1794
Cajun Land, 2019
Cajun Poultry Marinade, 2023
Cajun Smoked Sausage, 2944
Cajunshake, 2023
Cake Comb, 19999
Cake Mate, 11599
Cake-Mate, 6340
Cake-Mix, 27277
Cakebread, 2025
Cakezyme®, 3320
Cal, 20130
Cal Best, 5418
Cal Gold, 11877
Cal Harvest, 5036
Cal India, 2027
Cal Tuf, 19042
Cal Vac, 21134
Cal-Aloe Co., 10587
Cal-Cu-Dri, 21269
Cal-Fruit, 2063
Cal-King, 2026

Cal-Quick®, 13097
Cal-Stat, 30910
Cal-Sun, 8519
Cal-Tex, 2032
Calabro, 2033
Calafia Wines, 2034
Calavo, 2037
Calc-U-Dryer, 21269
Calcitrace, 11269
Calco, 6032
Calcomms, 20130
Caldwell Manufacturing, 20526
Calera, 2044
Calessence, 1692
Calf-Tel, 24984
Calgary Italian, 2045
Calgo, 2040
Calgon®, 10598
Calgrafix, 20130
Calhoun Bend Mill, 2046, 20138
Calibrated®, 22187
Calibration Columns, 24696
Calico Cottage Fudge Mix, 2048, 20140
Calico Jack®, 1120
Calido Chile Traders, 1279
Caliente, 8525
California, 30378
California Almond, 2053
California Champagne, 2637
California Churros, 6338
California Classic, 11149
California Classics, 2059, 2075
California Coast Naturals, 2058
California Collection, 8525
California Connoisseur, 30860
California Crest, 13120
California Crisps, 183, 18382
California Crunchies, 9220
California Cuisine, 5216, 10435
California Farms, 883, 11203
California Finest, 13845
California Gold, 11877
California Golden Pop, 6506, 24551
California Goldminer, 7871, 7875, 7876
California Grown, 7451
California Harvest, 5280, 11864
California Independent Brand, 2068
California Just Chile!, 6015
California Light Blonde, 11846
California Ltd ®, 13120
California Nuggets, 2072
California Nuts, 1471, 19742
California Pale Ale (Cpa), 1097
California Pantry, 6019, 23878
California Rabbit, 1543
California Rag, 26770
California Ranch Fresh, 5837
California Special, 7125
California Specialty Farms, 13950
California Sunshine Dairy Pproducts, 5837
California Trays, 30378
Calio Groves, 2085
Calise, 2086
Calistoga Food, 2087
Calistoga Water, 26668
Calla, 21213
Callaway, 2042
Calle Sabor, 5141
Callebaut®, 1056
Calley Lahvosh, 13256
Calling Card, 21059
Calm Mind, 9201
Calmar Bakery, 2094
Calogix, 20130
Calona Vineyards, 555
Calorie Control, 1244
Calormatic®, 29854
Calp, 26932
Calpro, 2095
Calrose, 1849
Calrose Rice, 4260
Calsaw, 20147
Calvert, 7655
Calypso, 6867

All Brands Index

Calypso Caribbean, 7273
Calypso Gold Rum, 11264
Calypso Light Rum, 11264
Cam, 29584
Cam Frequent Diners, 20806
Cam Spray, 20155
Cam Tron, 20156
Cam-Grid, 20158
Camagsolv, 20188
Camarad, 13425
Camas, 2100
Cambozola, 2409
Cambri-Link, 20158
Cambria, 2101
Cambridge, 20159, 28357
Cambridge Food, 2103
Cambro, 20160
Camellia, 2105, 7027
Camelot, 27090
Camelot Mead, 9452
Cameo, 8729, 19371
Cameron, 2108
Cameron's, 2108
Camilla Pecan, 2110
Camillus Classic Cartridge, 18022
Camino Del Sol, 10333
Camoco, 20279
Camp, 2693
Camp Mixes, 3079
Camp Rite, 7150
Campaniac, 2010
Campari, 2114
Camparron, 3545
Campbells, 2116
Campbells Canada, 2116
Campbells Chunky, 2116
Campbells Foodservice, 2116
Campbells Ready To Enjoy Soups, 2115
Campbells Soup At Hand, 2115
Campeche Bay, 9912
Campesino Jamoneta, 2670
Campfire, 3713, 4891, 6267
Campfire Marshmallows, 6267
Campi Del Sole, 10565
Campino, 12147
Campo Lindoc, 187
Campo Viejo, 9964
Camrose, 2118
Camus Prarie Tea, 13015
Can Jet, 22615
Canada Dry, 252, 1294, 2811
Canada Dry®, 3725, 6818, 24802
Canada Gold, 2693
Canada Goose, 3950
Canada House, 7655
Canadian, 6901
Canadian Bay, 9773
Canadian Blended Whisky Chocolates, 10468
Canadian Club, 56, 3024, 5892, 12315
Canadian Club®, 1120
Canadian Deluxe, 7655
Canadian Gourmet, 2367
Canadian Grand, 13182
Canadian Harvest, 5138
Canadian Host, 11264
Canadian Jumbo Lake, 575
Canadian Ltd, 11264
Canadian Mist, 2124
Canadian Reserve, 7655
Canadian Springs, 7655, 10303, 27797
Canadian Supreme, 11264
Canadian Whiskey, 1784
Canadian Wild Rice, 4508
Canalyzer, 20244
Canandaigua Blend, 4403
Canaplus, 1847
Canard Duchene, 3570
Canco, 18684
Candelari's, 2128
Candelita, 218
Canderel, 8173
Candido, 27236
Candle Cafe Vegan, 5505
Cando, 20175
Cando Pasta, 2129
Candoni De Zan, 652
Candurin®, 2370
Candy Activity, 418
Candy Art, 5160
Candy Ass, 11873
Candy Blox®, 12880
Candy Bracelets, 22917
Candy Carnival®, 12880
Candy Climbers, 6780
Candy Club, 1114
Candy Farm, 3421, 10773
Candy Farms, 12114
Candy Flower Bouquets, 2134
Candy Kaleidoscope, 11552
Candy Stick, 12957
Candy Whistler, 4255
Candy Yams, 1856
Candy Yo-Yo, 790
Candyman Lane, 1027
Candyrific, 2132
Cane Classics, 11885
Canesweet™, 12387
Canguard, 20181
Canine Carry Outs, 6380
Canned Southern Vegetables, 8086
Cannon, 8519, 19611, 23117
Cano Cosecha, 3545
Canoe, 4508, 8305
Canolean, 6395
Canoleo®, 864
Canolla Truffles, 9771
Cantar,, 12348
Cantatti, 3381
Cantech, 20195
Canterbury Naturals, 2950
Cantisano, 7408
Canton, 56, 10333
Canty, 24424
Canvas, 71
Canvasback, 3779
Canyon Bakehouse, 4529
Canyon Oaks, 104
Canyon Oats, 4830
Canyon Road, 4992
Canyon Road®, 3834
Cap 'n Kid, 305
Cap Level Iia, 30799
Cap Snap, 29223
Cap'n Crunch®, 9945, 27433
Cap'n Joe, 12520
Cap'n Poptoy, 11552
Cap'ns Catch, 11356
Cap-O-Mat, 27526
Cap. M. Quik, 28644
Capaciagage, 21103
Capalbo's, 2150
Capamatic, 26482
Capay Canyon Ranch, 2152
Cape Ann, 9291
Cape Cod, 2116, 2156, 2572
Cape Cod Clam Chowder, 2309
Cape Cod Cranberry C, 5477
Cape Cod Cranberry Candy, 2159
Cape Cod Dry, 10151
Cape Cod Lobster Bisque, 2309
Cape Cod Lobster Chowder, 2309
Cape Cod Potato Chips, 11770
Cape Covelle®, 12885, 30333
Cape May, 7054, 24998
Cape May Salt, 765
Cape Mentelle Vineyards, 8452
Cape Royal, 3891
Cape Sandy Vineyards, 3877
Capezzana, 8452
Capital, 13912
Capitan Gold Tequila, 11264
Capitan Tequila & Triple Sec, 11264
Capitan White Tequila, 11264
Capitanelli Fine Foods, 9119
Capitanelli Specialty Foods, 9119
Capitanelli's, 9119
Capitani, 22142
Capitol Foods, 2164
Capitol Hardware, 20214
Capmul®, 126
Capn Clean, 19741
Capo Di Monte, 12444
Capol®, 2370
Capolac®, 19049
Capolla Foods, 2165
Capone Foods, 2166, 20218
Cappo, 2169
Cappuccine, 2171
Cappuccino Supreme, 464
Cappuccio, 1908
Capretta, 10565
Capri, 1080, 13687
Capri-Sun, 2815, 20685
Capric, 2010
Capriccio, 507, 4515
Capricorn, 12437
Caprimo, 1056
Caprisun, 6977
Caprol®, 126
Capstone®, 7786
Capsul®, 8804
Capsul® Ta, 8804
Capsule Works, 2179
Capsulong, 3948
Capsylite, 26990
Capt'n Don's, 2572
Capt'n Eds, 2572
Capt. Fred, 11356
Captain, 24881
Captain Bob's Jet Fuel, 2183
Captain Charlie, 2431
Captain Cook Coffee, 2184
Captain Jac, 6267
Captain Jack's, 6159
Captain Joey, 1357
Captain John's Derst's, 4529
Captain Ken's, 2186
Captain Lawrence Brewing Co., 10666
Captain Mike's, 1019
Captain Morgan, 3545
Captain Neptune, 8938
Captain Pierre, 5438
Captain Space Freeze, 13005
Captain Swain's Extra, 2691
Captain's Call, 9165
Captain's Choice Honey Brine, 2189
Captains, 7146
Captex®, 126
Capture Jet, 23537
Capture Rey, 23537
Capway, 20222
Car Chem, 20682
Car Hartt, 26875
Cara, 25456
Cara Mia, 12035
Cara-Sel, 12668
Caramel Apple Pops®, 12880
Caramel Chews, 9220
Caramel Creams®, 5096
Caramel Milk Roll, 7643
Caramelizer, 20011
Caramels, 6976
Caramilk, 1981
Carando, 11733
Carando Gourmet, 2193
Carapelli, 25789
Caraquet, 2194
Carat, 1175
Caravan, 954
Caravel Gourmet, 11351
Caravella, 11264
Carb Escapes, 11771
Carb Smart®, 5165
Carbernet Sauvignon, 1314
Carbmate, 357
Carbo Mizers, 28872
Carbon Comet, 29592
Carbona Cleanit! Oven Cleaner, 21509
Carbonetor Pumps, 23969
Carbosil®, 3320
Carcos Splutting Saw, 26521
Cardhu, 3570
Cardi C, 2199
Cardiaslim, 6236
Cardinal, 13912, 21576
Cardinal Kettle, 2200
Cardinal Pale Ale, 2653
Cardini's, 7987
Cardinis Salad Dressing, 12467
Cardio Discovery, 7331
Cardio Life, 4127
Cardio Water, 9858
Cardiomax, 9957
Care Bears, 20946
Care Bears Gummi Bears, 12547
Carenero, 2617
Caretree, 7339
Careware, 18328
Carex, 9264
Carey's®, 864
Carfagna, 2275
Carfosel™, 10239
Cargill, 11053, 30775
Cargomaster, 31060
Cariani Italian Dry Salami, 6326
Cariani Italian Specialty Loaves, 6326
Caribbean Chill, 387
Caribbean Condiments, 5516
Caribbean Hot Peppers, 12997
Caribbean Marketplace, 4894
Caribbean Red® Papaya, 1757
Caribbean Shade Market Umbrellas, 26404
Caribe, 8028
Caribou Coffee®, 6818, 24802
Carioca, 31083
Carl Buddig Meats, 2212
Carl Budding, 9431
Carling, 8459
Carlo Rossi®, 3834
Carlos, 7655
Carlsbad Oblaten, 846
Carlson, 6364
Carma®, 1056
Carmel, 209, 7848
Carmel Winery, 10952
Carmela's, 2220
Carmelia, 7842
Carmi Flavors, 2223, 20269
Carmine, 18100
Carminic Acid, 18100
Carnation, 6380
Carnation®, 8945
Carneco Foods, 7538
Carneros, 1834, 2225
Carneros Chardonnay, 869, 13426
Carneros Creek, 2225
Carnival Cajun Classics, 2226
Carnivor®, 3834
Carocare®, 3320
Carol Lee, 2230
Carolan's, 4422
Carolans Irish Cream Liqueur, 5720
Carole's, 2232
Carole's Tops, 2232
Carolina Atlantic Seafood, 2233
Carolina Barbecue, 2416
Carolina Chef, 13912
Carolina Choice, 11844
Carolina Classics, 2237
Carolina Cupboard, 42, 11864
Carolina Gem, 178
Carolina Gold, 2248
Carolina Mountain Spring Water, 8605
Carolina Pride, 2246, 2247
Carolina Rag, 26770
Carolina Treet, 2250
Carolina®, 10777, 28421
Caroline's Sausage, 690
Caroliva, 10319
Carophyll®, 3320
Carousel, 2253, 4586
Carousel Cakes, 2252
Carousel Caser, 28742
Carousel Pop, 6158
Carpet Guard, 23436
Carpet Gun, 22473
Carpet Master, 21352
Carpet Scent, 19741

All Brands Index

Carpet Wizard, 21509
Carpuela, 11894, 29459
Carr Valley, 2256
Carr's, 6766, 25789
Carrabind, 20289
Carrafat, 20289
Carralite, 20289
Carralizer, 20289
Carraloc, 20289
Carravis, 20289
Carrera 1000 M, 24076
Carrera 1000 Pc, 24076
Carrera 2000 Pc, 24076
Carrera 500 M, 24076
Carriage House, 2258
Carrier, 20290, 28967
Carrier Select, 25407
Carriere, 2260
Carrington Tea, 2262
Carroll, 20297
Carroll Chair, 20294
Carroll Shelby Chili Kits, 10657
Carson's, 3847
Cartcelt, 783
Carter, 20305
Carter Hoffmann, 29466
Carter-Hoffmann, 20307
Carthage, 20309
Cartier, 27209
Cartilade, 783
Cartreuse Liqueur, 4677
Cartridge, 18022
Carts, 11755, 19811
Carts of Colorado, 20315
Cartwashable, 21352
Carve Cookie, 2266
Carver Aid, 25299
Carvers Original, 9155
Casa Blanco, 3545
Casa De Carmen, 130
Casa De Corca, 10952
Casa De La Ermita, 3545
Casa Del Norte, 9934
Casa Dibertacchi, 10714
Casa Dilisio, 2269
Casa Europa, 9798
Casa Jorge, 10968
Casa Luca, 2012
Casa Maid, 5555
Casa Nuestra, 2271
Casa Primo, 7069
Casa Tinto, 3545
Casa Verde, 20789
Casa Visco, 2274
Casabe Rainforest Crackers, 4607
Casablanca, 25658
Casafiesta®, 1794
Casale Degli Ulivi, 4386
Casanova, 1638
Casaro, 9780
Casba Ii, 29499
Casba Iv, 29499
Casbah, 5505
Cascade, 8320, 12721, 21934, 30193
Cascade Ale, 3533
Cascade Crest Organics, 2505
Cascade Fresh, 2283
Cascade Glacier, 9533
Cascade Specialties, 2285
Cascades, 18029
Cascades Ifc Disposables, 18029
Cascadia, 13872
Cascadia Only 2 Calories, 8784
Cascadia Sparkling Cider, 8784
Cascadian Farm, 2286, 11711
Cascadian Farm®, 4947
Case Farms Amish Country, 2288
Casella, 20325
Casemate, 25752, 30724
Casestar, 28468
Casettraypackers, 23716
Casey's, 2291
Cash Caddy, 20326
Cash Handler, 25910
Cashew Critters, 7184, 7200

Casing-Net, 24562
Cass, 71
Cass-Clay, 2295
Cassette Feu, 24408
Cassida Fluids and Greasers, 22231
Cassino, 10873
Castelet, 5405
Castellblanch, 4693
Castelletto, 8592
Castellini, 2298
Castello Di Volpaia, 13811
Castello Monachi, 4677
Castered Safety, 25329
Castillo Rums, 914
Castle, 20816
Castle Bag, 20336
Castle Beverages, 2300
Castle Carbonated Beverages, 2300
Castle Cheese, 2301
Castleberry Products, 805
Castor River Farms, 2304
Cat Chow®, 8945
Cat In the Hat Cotton Candy, 12547
Cat In the Hat Sour Gummies, 12547
Cat Pumps, 20339
Catania-Spagna, 20020
Catarcooler, 20256
Catawba Grape Juice, 5731
Catazyme, 1692
Catch of the Day®, 5844
Catelli, 6976
Cater Ease, 28342
Cateraid, 2314
Catered Gourmet, 2314
Caterer's Collection, 10728
Catering, 29271
Catermate, 20028
Catertec, 21989
Caterware, 26020
Caterwrap®, 23811
Cathay Foods, 2317
Catr, 30563
Cats, 30361
Catskill Brewery, 2321
Catskill Distilling Company, 2322
Cattail, 757
Cattaneo Brothers, 2324
Cattle Boyz, 2325
Cattleman's, 2326
Cattlemen's Bbq Sauce, 8061
Cattron, 20348
Catuama, 127
Cavalier, 11859
Cavaliere D'Oro, 12937
Cave Winery, 10952
Cavedoni Balsamic, 10401
Caveman Foods, 4150
Cavendish Farms®, 2332
Cavit, 27236
Cawy Cc, 2338
Cawy Lemon-Lime, 2338
Cawy Watermelon, 2338
Cayenne Kicker™, 1654
Caymus, 2339
Cb's Nuts, 1942
Cbm, 28210
Cbs, 1945
Cbs Baking Band, 19111
Cbs-B, 19798
Cbs-Ch, 19798
Cbw, 1710
Ccbreeze, 26615
Ccc Burners, 25186
Ccff, 2060
Cci, 20043
Ccl, 24805
Ccl Label, 18284
Cd-3 Vendor Cart, 19213
Cdm Coffee & Chicory, 10657
Cdr, 29352
Ce Airestream Hoods, 23722
Ce-15/22, 31058
Cea 266, 20047
Ceamgel 1313, 9654
Cecchetti Sebastiani Napa Valley, 2343

Cecchi, 1006
Cece's Veggie Noodle Co., 2344
Cecor, 20357
Cedar Creek, 2345, 9080
Cedar Crest, 2346
Cedar Farms, 9699
Cedar Grove, 2347, 2351
Cedar Lake, 2350
Cedar Mountain, 2351
Cedar River Farms®, 6391
Cedar Springs Lamb, 8601
Cedar Springs Natural Veal, 8601
Cedar's, 2354
Cedarlane, 2355
Cedarvale, 2357, 7594
Cekol, 1962
Celadrinc, 9997
Celebes, 761
Celebes Kalosi, 10157
Celebrate Line, 24964
Celebration, 20256, 21817
Celebration Libation, 2691
Celebrations®, 7952
Celebri Tea, 2360
Celebrity Cheesecakes, 2359
Celebrity Cups, 30945
Celebrity Stars, 20360
Celentano®, 10899
Celero, 13498
Celeste, 811
Celeste®, 27540
Celeste® Pizza For One, 2939, 2940, 20821, 20822
Celestial, 25789
Celestial Seasonings, 5505, 5506, 6819
Celifibr, 10708
Celio, 223
Cell Charge®, 1377
Cell-O-Core, 20362
Cell-O-Matic, 23305
Cella's Cherries®, 12880
Celler De Capcanes, 10952
Cellmins™, 13097
Cello Foam, 20365
Cello Wrap, 30137
Celloc, 11313
Cellophane, 30528
Celloplus, 30528
Cellotherm, 30528
Cellscale, 25940
Cellu Flo, 23448
Cellu Pore, 23448
Cellu Stacks, 23448
Celluclast, 1692
Cellucor, 4150
Cellulose Gum, 19108
Celographics, 20593
Celsius Heat, 2364
Celsius Live Fit, 2364
Celtic, 12919
Cenprem, 2387, 20397
Centa, 28357
Centanni, 4386
Centennial, 2367
Center Fruit, 9956
Center-Of-The-Plate Specialists, 7721
Centra-Vit, 75
Central Coast, 2044
Central Coast Chardonnay, 2637
Central Market, 5473
Central Valley Creamery, 6719
Central Volky, 26983
Centravac, 30382
Centri-Matic Iii, 18127
Centrie Clutch, 19809
Centrified, 22204
Centrifuges, 24357
Centrimaster, 18321
Centrimil, 22204
Centrisys, 20392
Centrivap, 25041
Centurion, 25320, 25567
Century Harvest Farms, 2385
Century Line, 26826
Ceramicor, 21497

Cereal Match, 3670
Cerelac®, 8945
Cerelose, 6211, 24226
Ceres®, 6869
Ceresota, 13135
Certi-Fresh, 2394
Certicoat®, 7857
Certified Angus Beef, 5141, 5338
Certified Angus Beef®, 6391, 7721, 8783
Certified Hereford Beef®, 8783
Certified Humanec, 13461
Certified Organic Breads, 10965
Certified Organic Buns, 10965
Certified Organic Rolls, 10965
Certified Piedmontese, 5327
Certified Premium Beef, 8783
Certified®, 7857
Certipack, 24881
Certiseal®, 7857
Certo, 6976
Certs, 9995
Certs Breath Mints, 1980
Certs Cool Mint Drops, 1980
Certs Powerful Mints, 1980
Cervera, 9043
Ces, 20752
Cesar®, 7952
Cesco, 20415
Cetus Textile Fabrics, 3833, 21863
Ceylon Classic, 2729
Ceylon Teas, 12272
Cf, 22650
Cf Chefs, 20050
Cfc Dunouy Tensiometer, 20093
Cfc Us Standard, 20093
Cg Supreme, 2964
Cgp, 8191
Ch, 18501
Cha-Cha Chinese Chicken Dressing, 11878
Chachies, 11065, 11187
Chacies®, 11186
Chad's Carolina Corn, 13759
Chaddsford, 2399
Chadwick Bay, 10637
Chafer Shield, 28179
Chafermate, 23245
Chaffee, 20417
Chafing Fuels, 29661
Chai Bites, 6026
Chaidfontaine, 2815, 20685
Chain-Data, 30134
Chain-In-Channel, 24576
Chairman's Reserve®, 13109
Chalet Gourmet, 7998
Chalif, 8539
Chalk Hill Estate Bottled, 2403
Chalk Hill Estate Selection, 2403
Challenge, 2404
Challenge Dairy Products, 2061
Challenge Danish, 2404
Challenger, 18702, 26359, 28816
Cham Cold Brew Tea, 2406, 12719
Chamberlain, 11561
Chambir, 27325
Chambord, 1784, 2407
Chambourcin, 8513
Chameleon Pepper, 12987
Chamisa Gold, 10165
Champ, 2413, 23571
Champ Awards, 20353
Champ's Cola, 2338
Champagne Delight, 5030
Champagne Vinegar, 869
Champale, 9664
Champignon, 2409
Champion, 8802, 18564, 20069, 20084, 20428, 28763
Champions Sports Tile, 24456
Champlain Valley, 9157
Champon, 10359
Champtuf Polyethylene, 20429
Chandler, 23692
Chandler Foods, 2416
Chandon, 8452

1281

All Brands Index

Chanel, 27209
Chaney Instrument, 20433
Chang Food, 2417
Change-O-Matic, 29632, 29633
Channel, 2418
Channel Monster, 24649
Channel Rockfish (Thornyheads, 10949
Channelites, 29242
Chantland, 18877
Chapala, 7655
Chappallet, 2423
Chaqwa, 2815, 20685
Char Crust, 2424
Char Dex, 10600
Char Oil, 10600
Char Sol, 10600
Char Zyme, 10600
Char-Wil, 2425
Chardonayzyn, 12746
Chardonnay, 1314, 3661, 4745
Chardonnay Barrel Select, 5989
Chardonnay Vinegar, 869
Charking®, 12885, 30333
Charles Craft, 20441
Charles De Fere, 12672
Charles Krug, 2432
Charles Shaw, 1738
Charles Spinetta Barbera, 2435
Charles Spinetta Primitivo, 2435
Charles Spinetta Zinfanel, 2435
Charleston Chew, 2102, 2132
Charleston Chew®, 12880
Charlie Flint's Original Lager, 339
Charlie Palmer, 2439
Charlie Robinson's, 10804
Charlie Trotter Foods, 12068
Charlie Trotter's, 13899
Charlie's Salsa, 1141
Charlie's Specialties, 1903, 1904
Charlotte, 20497
Charmin, 12721, 30193
Charming Nancy, 1688
Charms Co., 2132
Charms®, 12880
Charrasc, 9714
Chas. W. Howeth & Bro., 2532
Chase, 20461
Chase & Sanborn, 11212
Chase & Sanborn Coffee, 7995
Chase Brothers, 2450
Chaselock, 20463
Chaser, 3707
Chata, 12823
Chateau, 2457, 5317, 19192, 23349
Chateau Beniot, 2905
Chateau Beychevelle, 12315
Chateau Boswell, 2454
Chateau Boswell Estate, 2454
Chateau Cellars, 1306
Chateau Cheval Blanc, 8452
Chateau Chevalier, 11966
Chateau D'Yquem, 8452
Chateau De Sancerre, 8452
Chateau Diana, 2456
Chateau Frank Champagne Cellars, 3724
Chateau Fuisse, 4677
Chateau Julien, 2459
Chateau La Nerthe, 8452
Chateau Lagrange, 12315
Chateau Montelena, 2461, 11810
Chateau Potelle, 2463
Chateau Rollan De By, 10952
Chateau Souverain, 2465
Chateau St. Jean, 12937
Chateau Thomas, 10097
Chatfield'sc, 9748
Chatham Village, 12467
Chatillon, 18327
Chatsworth, 5735
Chatter Creek, 7286
Chatterbox, 28140
Chatz, 2472
Chaucers, 1033
Chaudier, 27204
Chaya, 932

Che Series, 20256
Cheapshot, 28633
Check Fill, 26944
Check-Temp Ii, 30126
Check-Weigh, 25940
Checker, 20474, 23571
Checker Vision System, 22902
Checkerbites, 3625
Checkers Cookies, 1394
Checkmate, 20981, 30073
Checkmite, 20981
Checktemp, 23571
Cheddar & Bacon Flavored Ranch, 5489
Cheddar Box Cheese, 2479
Cheemo, 5798
Cheer, 12721, 30193
Cheerios®, 4947
Cheerwine, 2234, 13300
Cheerwine Soft Drink, 2234
Cheese Heads®, 11211
Cheese Merchants®, 11504, 29095
Cheese Puffs Sharing Packs, 11754
Cheese Rounds and Bricks, 13823
Cheese Senasations, 530
Cheese Spreads, 13823
Cheese-Mor™, 342
Cheesebuds, 1880
Cheesecake Factory®, 2485
Cheesecake Slicer, 2881
Cheestrings®, 9789
Cheetos, 4741
Cheetos®, 9945, 27433
Cheez Doodles, 13884
Cheez Whiz, 6976
Cheez-It, 6766
Chef, 20479
Chef Alberto Leone, 9752
Chef Antonio, 10728
Chef Apprentice, 22337
Chef Blends®, 11228, 28829
Chef Boyardee, 6267
Chef Boyardee Pastas, 6267
Chef Boyardee®, 2939, 2940, 20821, 20822
Chef Classic, 9680
Chef Creole, 2226
Chef Direct, 24088
Chef Explosion, 22337
Chef Gaston, 6395
Chef Hans, 2489, 6725
Chef Howard's Williecake, 6314
Chef Italia, 7783
Chef Martin, 8390
Chef Master, 207, 26350
Chef Merito, 2490
Chef Michael's®, 8945
Chef Myron's Original #1 Yakitori, 8715
Chef Myron's Ponzu, 8715
Chef Myron's Premium, 8715
Chef Myron's Tsukeya, 8715
Chef One, 13094
Chef Ooh La La Baking Mixes, 12100
Chef Paul Prudhomme's, 2491
Chef Pierre, 11214
Chef Pleaser, 5643
Chef Revival, 20478
Chef Shop, 22996
Chef Stone, 19932
Chef System, 23652
Chef Tang, 7874
Chef Test, 20454
Chef Vito Pasta Meals, 6410
Chef's Choice, 5928, 10399, 19384, 20480, 21120, 22034, 27949
Chef's Companion, 3574
Chef's Craft®, 13607
Chef's Design, 31284
Chef's Exclusive®, 6391
Chef's Favorite, 20122
Chef's Helper, 3989
Chef's Pastry, 2787
Chef's Pride, 2708
Chef's Recipe, 1087, 7927
Chef's Seasoning, 3574
Chef's Select, 30808

Chef's Signature, 3653
Chef-A-Roni, 2503
Chef-Mate®, 8945
Chef-R-Alls, 20481
Chef-Way, 31284
Chef®, 8945
Chefcare, 20478
Chefcutlery, 20478
Chefmaster, 1904
Chefmate, 23236
Chefs Originals, 10712
Chefs-In-A-Bag, 6334
Chefstyle, 5473
Chefsware, 23477
Chefwear, 20481
Cheiljedang, 1953
Chelsea, 51, 18512
Chelsea Market Baskets, 2507
Chelsea Spice, 2499
Chelten House, 2509
Chem Disc, 20491
Chem-Pruf, 20485
Chem-Vac, 20550
Chemex, 20494
Chemgrate, 22528
Chemical Service, 21252
Chemindustrial, 20499
Chemspec, 18281
Chemtek, 30828, 30829
Chemtrol, 20598
Cheolong, 3948
Cher-Make Sausage, 2511
Cheramino®, 13097
Cherchies, 2514
Cheri's Desert Harvest, 2515
Cherith Valley Gardens, 2517
Cherokee Maid, 23409
Cherry & Berry Blast, 11552
Cherry Bomb, 12178
Cherry Central, 2518
Cherry Man, 11434
Cherry Mash, 2449
Cherrybrook Kitchen, 6049
Cherryman, 5288
Cheryl & Co., 2526
Cheryl Lynn, 10399, 27949
Chesapeake Bay Delight, 11571
Chesapeake Bay Ice, 868
Chesapeake Bay's Finest, 2291
Chesapeake Pride, 868, 3097
Cheshire, 30841
Chessters, 10696, 28371
Chester, 20509
Chester Farms, 2530
Chester Farms Popping Corn, 2530
Chester Fried, 23183
Chester Fried Chicken, 2533
Chester Hoist, 20752
Chester's, 4741, 9560
Chesterfield, 2533
Chestertown, 2535
Chestnut Street, 11102
Cheval Des Andes, 8452
Chevalier Chocolates, 2537
Chevrai, 13927
Chevrai™, 11211
Chew-Ets, 5144
Chewels®, 1009
Chewey Kisses, 13845
Chewy Gooey Pretzel Sticks, 1018
Chewy's, 2538
Chex, 13864
Chex®, 4947
Chg 2%, 26000
Chg 4%, 26000
Chi-Chi's Appletini, 11264
Chi-Chi's Caribbean Mudslide, 11264
Chi-Chi's®, 6000, 23861
Chianti Cheese, 6702
Chiappetti, 12162
Chiatai Conti Group, 2970
Chic Jiang, 10457
Chicago 58, 2541
Chicago Cutlery, 31345
Chicago Metallic, 21227

Chicago Mints, 7524
Chicago Steak, 2549
Chicago Style, 5341
Chicama, 2551
Chick Chocolates, 11389
Chick-Fil-A®, 2552
Chick-O-Stick, 756
Chickadee Products, 6768
Chickapea, 2553
Chickapea Pasta, 2553
Chicken Keeper, 22640
Chicken Link, 8620
Chicken Not, 3633
Chicken of the Sea, 2555
Chicken of the Sea Singles, 2555
Chicken of the Sea Tuna Salad Kit, 2555
Chicken-To-Go, 1444, 19726
Chicken-Tuckers, 30305
Chickpea Chipotle, 6522
Chicle Chips, 1158
Chiclets, 9995
Chiclets Gum, 1980
Chicopee Provision, 2559
Chicory Stout, 3644
Chidester Farms, 6246
Chief, 20526
Chief 90, 27045
Chief 900 Series, 29281
Chief Chelan, 2560
Chief Kahai™, 7402
Chief Supreme, 2560
Chief Wenatchee, 2560
Chief's Creations, 3623
Chieftainc, 2561
Chigarid, 10718
Chik'n Giggles®, 1654
Chik'n Gone Wild™, 1654
Chik'n Hoops®, 1654
Chik'n Pretzels™, 1654
Chik'n Stars™, 1654
Chik'n'zips®, 1654
Child's Play®, 12880
Chile, 3393
Chile Chews, 19106
Chili Bowl, 237, 238
Chili Dude, 2565
Chili Supreme, 8724
Chill Master, 26313
Chill Rite, 20530
Chill-Air, 22248
Chill-Vactor, 21091
Chillee Snow Cones, 5333, 23360
Chilliman®, 4267, 22464
Chilly, 8620
Chillycow™, 13645
Chilsonator, 22594
Chiltomaline, 9911
Chimay, 1748
Chimayo, 1835
China Bowl, 5717
China Boy, 4164
China Cola, 10507
China Collection Teas, 5155
China Mist, 2570
China Pack, 6665
China Pride, 345
China Teas, 12272
China White, 5861
China Yunnan Silver Tip Choice, 5228, 23295
China-Brite, 21642
Chinese Chicken Salad Dressing, 5143
Chinese Ginseng, 13531
Chinese Marinade, 11878
Chinese-Lady, 6665
Chinet, 20538
Chino Valley, 2576
Chinoteaque, 2572
Chipico®, 13400
Chipnuts, 10031
Chipper, 13303
Chipper Beef Jerky, 2579
Chips Ahoy!, 8474, 8729
Chips Ahoy!® Cereal, 10213
Chips Deluxe, 6766

All Brands Index

Chipwich, 20946
Chiqui, 9604
Chiquita Banana Cookies, 9399
Chiquita®, 2580, 20541
Chiquititos, 11386
Chitolean, 4575
Chivas Regalc, 9964
Chloroneb, 24840
Chobani, 217
Choc Adillos, 7200
Choc'adillos, 7200
Choc-Adillos, 7184
Choc-Dip, 6340
Choc-O-Lot, 20633
Choc-Quitos, 6787
Chocapic®, 8945
Chocatal, 6497
Chock Full O' Nuts, 7995
Chock Full O'Nuts, 2587, 11212
Choco Berries, 10689
Choco D' Lite, 3670
Choco Milk®, 8103
Choco Pals, 6780
Choco Rocks, 6851
Choco-Matic, 24725
Choco-Starlight, 10428
Chocolat Jean Talon, 2594
Chocolate & Vanilla Nut Spread, 14034
Chocolate By Design, 2598
Chocolate Charlie, 2712
Chocolate Concepts, 20543
Chocolate Cortes, 12185
Chocolate Covered Marshmallows, 2903
Chocolate Covered Graham Crackers, 6525
Chocolate Covered Nuts, 12868
Chocolate Covered Potato Chips, 7845
Chocolate Covered Pretzels, 6787
Chocolate Covered Toffee Popcorn, 7845
Chocolate Delight, 13728
Chocolate Dunkel, 9153
Chocolate Ecstasy, 9019
Chocolate Flavored Coffee Spoons, 6787
Chocolate Fortune Cookies, 6787
Chocolate Jollies, 13845
Chocolate Juniorsc, 12551
Chocolate Kandy Kakesc, 12551
Chocolate Marshmallow, 9753
Chocolate Masters™, 1056
Chocolate Milk Stout, 3746
Chocolate Mint Meltaways, 2604
Chocolate Moose, 9115, 22028
Chocolate Moose Energy, 9115
Chocolate Mousse Hip, 9196
Chocolate Oreos, 4253
Chocolate Pizza, 4253
Chocolate Porter, 1097
Chocolate Products, 5428
Chocolate Slicks, 714
Chocolate Slim, 3753, 21763
Chocolate Stout, 1401
Chocolate Straws, 10104
Chocolate Street of Hartville, 2611
Chocolate Toffee Almonds, 9220
Chocolaterie Bernard Callebaut, 2614
Chocolates a La Carte, 2619
Chocolove, 2623
Chocomite, 3593, 21618
Chocovic, 1056
Choice, 2630, 30459
Choice Foods, 10846
Choice of Vermont, 2631
Choice Organic Teas, 2630
Choki, 12185
Cholesterol Solve, 131
Cholov Yisrael, 2312
Cholula, 12823
Cholula Hot Sauce, 26748
Chomper, 665
Chomps, 2632
Chooljian, 2634
Chop 'n Shake, 28412
Chop Block Breads, 3078
Chop Cut, 29491
Chopin, 3024, 8452

Choppin N Block, 446
Chore-Boy, 20548
Chouinard Red, 2637
Chouinard Rose, 2637
Chowards, 1918
Choxcard, 10229
Choy Sun, 7296
Chr, 1947
Chrisope, 28306
Christian Brothers Brandies, 5720
Christie's Instant-Chef, 2647
Christille Bay, 12999
Christina's Organic, 4111
Christmas, 11992, 21059
Christmas Ale, 531, 1687, 5314
Christoff, 30040
Christophe Cellars, 12672
Christopher Norman Chocolates, 2654
Christopher's, 6375
Christos, 7931
Christy Crops, 2657
Chrom-A-Grav, 20353
Chroma Lamps, 25665
Chromalox, 20555
Chromas, 27258
Chromax, 9259
Chromemate, 6236, 9253
Chromemax, 29596
Chromium, 20118
Chubb, 20290
Chubby 7 Day Cooler, 27597
Chuckles, 1417, 2102, 2132, 4345
Chudleigh's, 2661
Chugwater Chili, 2662
Chummy Chums, 6780
Chun's, 11788, 29340
Chung's, 2665
Chunk a Chew, 4586
Chunk Light Tuna, 12046
Chunks O'Fruit, 8837
Chunky Ready To Go Bowls, 2115
Chunky Ready To Serve Soups/Chili, 2115
Chupa Chups, 9956
Churchills Ports, 4677
Churn Spread®, 13328
Chux, 2766, 20657
Ciao Bella, 2669
Ciao Bella Sorbet, 2669
Cidelite, 20454
Cider Creek Hard Cider, 10666
Cider Drink Mix, 12182
Ciel, 2814
Cielo Azul, 10110
Cien En Boca, 1581
Cii, 20461
Cillit Bang®, 10598
Cimarron Cellars, 2677
Cimfast, 21717
Cimroc, 27083
Cinchona Coffee, 2881
Cincy Style, 6410
Cinderella, 2680
Cinerator Hot Cinnamon Whiskey, 5720
Cini Minis®, 8945
Cinnabar Specialty Foods, 2681
Cinnabon, 10173, 11318
Cinnabon®, 6818, 24802
Cinnamon Bakery, 2683
Cinnamon Mini Donuts, 12551
Cinnamon Ridge, 2899
Cinnamon Toast Crunch®, 4947
Cinnful Coco, 11775
Cintas, 30603
Cinzano, 2114, 3545
Cipriani's Classic Italian, 2684
Cipriani's Premium, 2684
Cirashine, 716, 19094
Circle a Brands Beef Patties, 770
Circle D Lights, 26457
Circle M, 8665
Circle R Gourmet Foods, 2686
Circle Z, 14043
Circle-Air, 20121
Circlea Beef Patties, 770

Circledome, 25224
Circus, 27236
Circus Man, 2689
Circus Sticks, 6780
Circus Wagon Animal Crackers, 3343
Cirrus, 22902
Citadelle, 2693
Citation, 833, 3424
Citizen Foods, 10021
Citra, 27236
Citra Jell, 23532
Citra-Next®, 10797, 28438
Citradelic, 8959
Citranatal®, 8389
Citranox, 18542
Citrasense™, 30438
Citreatt, 12940
Citri-Glow, 26055
Citricidal, 9251
Citrico, 2694
Citrimax, 6310, 9253
Citrimax - French Diet Cola, 6310
Citrin, 11061
Citrin K, 11061
Citrus, 21768
Citrus Pride, 2032
Citrus Punch Sugar-Free, 5460
Citrus Royal, 5362, 23377
Citrus Solvent, 30925
Citrus Sunshine, 9469
Citterio, 2701
City Grillers, 1796
City Lager, 2705
City Light, 2705
City Lites, 24354
City Market, 12516
City Slicker, 2705
City Square, 30820
Cizonin Vineyards, 3179
Cjoy®, 11378, 28946
Ck, 2487
Ck Mondavi, 2432
Clabber Girl®, 2711
Claeys Gourmet Cream Fudge, 2712
Claeys Gourmet Peanut Brittle, 2712
Claeys Old Fashion Hards Candies, 2712
Claiborne & Churchill, 2713
Clair Riley Zinfandel Port, 12227
Clamato, 8586
Clamato®, 3725, 6818, 24802
Clamco, 31362
Clan Macgregor, 13811
Clancy, 10041
Clapier Mill, 11852
Clar-O-Floc, 18527
Clara's Kitchen, 10435
Clardera Brewing, 10666
Clarendon Hills®, 3834
Claret, 11995
Claria® Starches, 12561
Claridge Cork, 20595
Clarified Butter, 5679
Clarisse, 18906
Clarite, 21092
Clark, 31092
Clarke Technology, 20599
Clasen, 2722
Clash Malt, 9664
Class, 19741
Classi-Tray Stand, 28006
Classic, 7643, 7657, 12925, 20256, 26662, 28787, 30073
Classic Apollo, 28154
Classic Banjo, 5819
Classic Blends, 8919
Classic Blue, 13687
Classic Bon Bons, 1767
Classic Caramel, 13574
Classic Caramel®, 13572
Classic Casserole, 1069, 1577
Classic Ceylon, 2729
Classic Choice, 11328
Classic Commissary, 2723
Classic Complements, 4543

Classic Confections, 3541
Classic Country, 3079
Classic Cream, 258
Classic Crystal, 30971
Classic Delight, 2726
Classic Gourmet®, 13328
Classic Home Collection, 28934
Classic Images, 30808
Classic Liquor Cremes, 10596
Classic Malts, 3570
Classic Reserve, 5236
Classic Reserve Ext Sharp Cheddar, 5236
Classic Rotary Lobe Pumps, 30853
Classic Traditions, 3629
Classico, 6976, 6977, 11132
Classico Seating, 20602
Classicware, 30971
Classique, 1997
Classique Fare, 8448
Classy Caps, 24815
Classy Delites, 2730
Classy Kid®, 23811
Claudia Sanders, 7934
Claussen, 6976, 6977
Clausthaler, 1361
Clavies, 19534
Claw Island, 10682
Clawson, 11458
Claxton, 2732
Clayton Coffee & Tea, 2734
Clayton Farms, 5555
Cleaf, 27278
Clean Fit, 26175
Clean Glide, 29175
Clean Kitchen, 11386
Clean N' Natural, 4888
Clean Wheel, 29484
Clean-Pak, 20064
Clean-Roll, 28626
Clean-Sweep, 26529
Cleancycle 12, 23868
Cleanliners, 27240
Cleanmaster, 29706
Cleanroom, 27294
Cleanware, 19534
Clear 'n' Natural, 174
Clear - Go, 22509
Clear Choice, 10637
Clear Coat, 2332
Clear Creek Grappas, 2737
Clear River Farms®, 6391
Clear Sailing, 338
Clear Springs Kitchen®, 2740
Clear Springs®, 2740
Clear Stevia, 9201
Clear Vu, 20355
Clear-Cut, 20802
Clear-Flex Ii, 18547, 18548
ClearùCuts®, 2740
Clearasil®, 10598
Clearblue, 12721, 30193
Clearbrook Frams, 2679
Clearfield, 5400, 11308, 28903
Clearfoil, 28493
Clearfruit, 8784
Cleargard, 28816
Clearjel®, 8804
Clearly Canadian, 2742
Clearly Canadian O+2, 2742
Clearly Invisible Hooks, 28118
Clearly Kombucha, 2743
Clearly Natural, 19509
Clearpac®, 21362
Clearstream, 28361
Clement Pappas, 7236
Clements Pastry Shop, 2749
Clemson Bros., 2752
Clencher, 23261
Clermont, 4968
Cleveland, 20642, 20646, 26476, 31092
Cleveland Tramrail, 29137
Cleveland®, 31093
Cli, 26427
Clif Bar, 2756, 4150
Clif Builder's, 2756

1283

All Brands Index

Clif Crunch, 2756
Clif Kid, 2756
Clif Mojo, 2756
Clif Shot, 2756
Clif's, 8001
Cliffside, 8560
Clifty Farm, 2758
Clima Plus Combi, 28198
Climaplus, 23729
Climaplus Control, 28198
Climate 2000, 19639
Climate Control, 23692
Climate Master, 20649
Cline Cellars, 2759
Clinebell, 25871
Clinton, 13647
Clinton Victory, 2761
Clinton's, 4290
Clio Pomace, 11875
Clio Pure, 11875
Clip Disc, 20491
Clip Go Valve, 22679
Clipmark, 20654
Clipper, 6279, 18035, 20195, 20654, 22627, 24881, 27405
Clipper Foods, 10820
Clipper Precision, 22518
Clipwell, 19743
Clockview, 18354
Clog-Free Slurry Spray Encoater, 29513
Clorets, 9995
Clorets Breath Freshener, 1980
Clorox, 2766, 18592, 20657
Clos Du Val, 2769
Clos Mesorah, 10952
Clos Normand, 4148
Clos Reserve, 4649
Close-Up, 2666, 20561
Clothsaver Paper Tabl-Mats, 25447
Cloud, 20659
Cloud Nine, 2772
Cloud Nine All-Natural Chocolate, 2772
Cloudliner, 26337
Cloudy & Britton, 20660
Cloudy Bay Vineyards, 8452
Clove Valley Farms, 5765
Clover, 10478
Clover Farms, 2778, 2782
Clover Hill, 2784
Clover Hill Cuvee, 2779
Clover Hill Pinot Noir, 2779
Clover Hill Rose, 2779
Clover Leaf, 6267, 13658
Cloverdale, 2783, 2787, 5233
Cloverdale Ranch, 9905
Cloverland, 2786
Cloverland Sweets, 10281
Cloverleaf, 21701
Cloverleaf Farms Peanut Butter, 11029
Club Car, 24220
Club Caribe, 4515
Club Chef, 2298, 2789
Club House, 8061
Club Tahity, 13141
Clubtec, 21989
Cluster Buster, 30038
Clutter Busters, 20256
Clutters Indian Fields, 2790
Clyde's, 2791
Clyde's Soon To Be Famous, 922
Clydeunion Pumps, 28714
Cm, 19908, 20752
Cm - 22, 4827
Cm Packaging, 21227
Cm-L Lifters, 21186
Cm3 Cubers, 28922
Cmbc, 20847
Cmc, 21040
Cmco, 20752
Cmd Converting Solutions, 20070
Cmd Packaging Systems, 20070
Cmp Pasteurizer, 23273
Cms, Inc., 21067
Cns, 1959
Co Yo, 1960

Co-Enzyme Q-10, 21265
Co2 Hard Candy, 1343
Coach Farm, 2793
Coag-U-Loid, 2386
Coast, 4668
Coast Refined Lard, 2796, 20666
Coastal Gourmet, 2798
Coaster Call, 25421
Coasters Plus, 19164
Coastline, 12296
Coastlog, 2805
Cob Dry, 20802
Cobatco, 20678
Cobatco Olde Time, 20678
Cobblestone Bread Co., 4529
Cobblestone Mill, 4662
Cobblestreet Market®, 11504, 29095
Cobit+Care, 20682
Cobra, 8459
Cobra Vanilla, 12987
Coby's Cookies, Inc., 2810
Coca-Cola, 2811, 2814, 2815, 20685
Coca-Cola Light/Diet, 2815, 20685
Coca-Cola Zero, 2814, 2815, 20685
Cochise Farms, 4373
Cocina De Mino, 2816
Cocinaware, 5473
Cock'n Bull, 13300
Cocktail Duet, 9385
Coco, 18040
Coco Libre, 8025, 8955
Coco Lopez, 2820
Coco Lopez, Usa, 4057
Coco Pazzo, 25789
Coco Pops, 6766
Coco Rico, 5177
Coco Solo, 2338
Coco Well, 2202
Coco Wheats, 10213
Cocoa, 12100
Cocoa Amore, 2848
Cocoa Creations, 291
Cocoa Metro, 2822
Cocoa Replacers, 5462
Cocoalaska, 263
Cocoamate, 12550
Cocolalla, 2825
Cocomels, 2826
Coconut Beach, 2828
Coconut Bliss, 2829, 7647
Coconut Code, 20686
Coconut Grove, 7170
Coconut Infusions™, 8725
Coconut Juniorsc, 12551
Coconut Oil, 8896
Coconut Patties, 9877
Coconut Waves, 12027
Coconut Zipper, 11990
Cocoroons, 11415
Cocovia®, 7952
Codaire, 21313
Code, 1891
Code Red Kit, 24700
Code Taper, 19634
Code-A-Can, 25946
Code-A-Plas, 25946
Code-A-Top, 25946
Code®, 30595
Coders, 21398
Coffaro's Baking Company, 11390
Coffee, 362
Coffee Bean, 4276
Coffee Beanery Franchise, 2838
Coffee Blenders, 9211
Coffee Brothers, 2839, 20694
Coffee Clutch, 25005
Coffee Exchange, 2843
Coffee Express, 2844, 4324, 2696
Coffee House Roasters, 1636, 19825
Coffee Masters, 2848
Coffee on the Move, 25005
Coffee People, 3591, 6819
Coffee People®, 6818, 24802
Coffee Rich, 10714
Coffee Rio, 163

Coffee Roasters Ridgeline®, 11504, 29095
Coffee Scapes, 11855
Coffee Time, 6683
Coffee's Choice, 18928
Coffee-Mate®, 8945
Coffee-Pak, 24723
Coffeego, 7769
Coffeehouse Porter, 1237
Coffing, 20752
Cognizin, 7017
Cogruet™, 11211
Cohort, 11759
Col Dorcia, 27236
Colavita, 25789, 30775
Colavita 25-Star Gran Riserva Vin., 2864
Colavita Balsamic Vinegar, 2864
Colavita Classic Hot Sauce, 2864
Colavita Extra Virgin Olive Oil, 2864
Colavita Fat Free Classic Hot Sauce, 2864
Colavita Fat Free Garden Style Sau., 2864
Colavita Fat Free Marinara Sauce, 2864
Colavita Fat Free Mushroom Sauce, 2864
Colavita Garden Style Sauce, 2864
Colavita Healthy Sauce, 2864
Colavita Marinara Sauce, 2864
Colavita Marinated Vegetables, 2864
Colavita Mushroom Sauce, 2864
Colavita Pasta, 2864
Colavita Pasta Plus, 2864
Colavita Puttanesca Sauce, 2864
Colavita Red Clam Sauce, 2864
Colavita White Clam Sauce, 2864
Colbank, 30390
Colby, 19563
Cold Hollow Cider Mill, 2869
Cold Mountain, 8412
Cold River, 6139
Cold Saver, 20710
Cold Space, 23482
Cold Spell, 26698
Cold Stone Creamery, 2132
Cold Tech, 20714
Cold-Cel, 21695
Cold/Hot Pack Tunnel Pasterized, 5027, 23188
Coldelite, 18564, 20288
Coldisc, 26698
Coldmaster, 20256
Coldstream, 20714
Coldstream Hills, 12937
Coldtrak, 21524
Colectivo Keg Company Beers, 2874
Coleman, 9922
Coleman Natural, 2875
Coleman Natural®, 9946
Coleman Organic, 2875
Colflo™ 67, 8804
Colgate, 20721
Colgin, 2876, 10718
Colilert, 24070
Colita, 5861
Collamat, 18284
Collar-Dip, 21639
College Inn®, 3478
Collettramatic, 31273
Collingwood Canadian Whisky, 1784
Collins, 20726
Colloid Mills, 20497
Colloidal Silver, 8009
Coloma, 2883
Colombian Excelso, 10157
Colombian Supremo, 10157
Colombina, 2132
Colombo, 13811
Colon Care™, 13097
Colon Cleanse, 5682
Colonel Lee, 11263
Colonel Lee Bourbon, 11264
Colonial, 13691
Colonial Beef, 7676
Colonial Club, 7655, 9773
Colonial International, 2885

Colonial Jacks, 6222
Colonial Williamsburg, 5285, 11025, 12714
Colonna, 2887, 3439
Colony Meadery, 10666
Color Blaster, 6158
Color Brights, 25299
Color Brush, 26109
Color Cal, 22985
Color Charms, 25299
Color Garden, 2890
Color Graphic, 21769
Color Mark, 30422
Color Run Remover, 21509
Color Scents, 20257
Color-Craft, 26109
Color®, 8899
Colorado Classic, 5945
Colorado Gold, 5409
Colorado Hay Products, 30530
Colorado Kind Ale, 8602
Colorado Native, 8459
Colorado Native™, 8460
Colorado Peanut Butter Nugget, 9836
Colorado Rag, 26770
Colorado Sunshine Honey, 5766
Colorado's Kernels, 7433
Colore, 20288
Colorenhance, 8899
Coloreze, 6261
Colorgems, 25299
Colorpoint, 25456
Colorpure, 10511
Colors Gourmet Pizza, 2901
Colortrend Ht, 23931
Colorwatch, 28834
Colorworx®, 22187
Colossal Crisp®, 7179, 25104
Colosseum, 4411
Colson, 28488
Colt 45, 9664
Colts Bolts, 2903
Columbia, 46, 20747
Columbia Empire Farms, 2905
Columbia Winery®, 3834
Columbian, 761, 12846
Columbus Pale Ale, 2911
Columbus®, 6000, 23861
Colusa Rose®, 10777, 28421
Comark, 20757
Combi, 25785
Combi America, 20761
Combicraft, 20642
Combitherm, 18677
Combo, 24414
Combo Packs™, 23811
Combo-Pack, 23013
Combo/Combo, 29999
Comboliak, 9802
Combos®, 7952
Comeaux's Andouille Sausage, 2918
Comeaux's Crawfish Tails, 2918
Comeaux's Tasso, 2918
Comet, 12721, 21199, 24354, 30193, 30971
Comet Blend, 23261
Comet Rice®, 10777, 28421
Comfiwear, 23974
Comfort Zone, 19151
Comfort-Lume, 25224
Comfortcoat®, 3320
Comfortline, 27799
Comic Animal, 163
Comitrol, 30698
Command, 18003
Commander, 18648
Commander Ii, 23160
Commerical Bagel Biter, 25144
Commodore, 24613
Commodore Perry India Pale Ale, 5314
Common Folk Farm, Inc., 2924
Commonwealth, 4614, 5325
Communication, 21769
Community Bakeries, 2925
Community Bear Works, 10666

All Brands Index

Community Coffee, 2926
Comotion™, 8470
Compac, 31246
Compacker Ii, 20788
Compacker Ii Abf-3, 20788
Compacker Iii, 20788
Compact, 26674
Compact Cube, 25224
Compacta, 24613
Compair, 23032
Companions®, 30595
Compass Forecast System, 24265
Competitor Plus, 30502
Complan, 6977
Compleats®, 6000, 23861
Complimed, 13642
Complimed®, 9237, 26785
Componenter, 18241
Compu-Check, 30914
Computap, 26379
Computer Printers, 30051
Computrac Max, 19041
Computrac Vapor Pro, 19041
Comsource®, 30595
Comstock Wilderness®, 27540
Comtec, 20817
Comtek Supercharger, 20818
Comtrex, 29959
Comus Restaurant Systems, 20819
Con Gusto, 11065
Con Gusto®, 11186
Con Yeager Spices, 2936
Con-Pak, 19629
Con-Tech, 20820
Conaform, 27345
Concannon Vineyard, 2941
Concep2, 26997
Concept Sq, 30853
Concessions, 11755
Concha Y Toro, 1006
Concord Foods, 2943
Concord Grape, 12914
Concord®, 21362
Concorde, 24881
Condado De Almara, 3545
Condensation Gard, 30920
Condex, 2386
Condi Express, 25094
Conditionaire, 23893
Condor, 20065
Conex Clearpro®, 21362
Conex Complements®, 21362
Conex Promotions®, 21362
Coney Island, 3695
Coney Island Classics, 7414
Confection Sunflower Seed, 10616
Confecto, 6261
Congratulations!, 21059
Congusto, 11187
Conidur, 30135
Conmet, 23571
Conn's Bbq Pork Rinds, 2952
Conn's Bean Dip, 2952
Conn's Caramel Popcorn, 2952
Conn's Cheese Corn Popcorn, 2952
Conn's Cheese Curls, 2952
Conn's Cheese Dip, 2952
Conn's Corn Chips, 2952
Conn's Corn Pops Popcorn, 2952
Conn's Green Onion, 2952
Conn's Honey Bbq Jerky, 2952
Conn's Honey Mustard Dip, 2952
Conn's Jalapeno Dip, 2952
Conn's Nacho Tortilla Chips, 2952
Conn's Oat Bran Pretzels, 2952
Conn's Original, 2952
Conn's Original Beef Jerky, 2952
Conn's Party Mix, 2952
Conn's Picante Dip, 2952
Conn's Pork Rinds, 2952
Conn's Pretzel Rods, 2952
Conn's Pretzel Sticks, 2952
Conn's Pretzel Thins, 2952
Conn's Pretzel Twists, 2952
Conn's Restaurant Tortilla Chips, 2952
Conn's Round Tortilla Chips, 2952
Conn's Salsa Supreme Dip, 2952
Conn's Salt & Vinegar, 2952
Conn's Sour Cream, 2952
Conn's Wavy, 2952
Connect-A-Bench, 20192
Connect-A-Veyor, 27159
Connecter, 22917
Connemara®, 1120
Conners Best Bitter, 1702
Connerton, 20844
Connie's Handmade Toffee, 7761
Connie's Pizza, 8367, 9719
Connoisseur, 19192, 21591
Connoisseur Collection, 8724
Connoisseur Master Blend, 5228, 23295
Cono Sur, 1006
Conoco Lubricants, 20753
Conoco/Andero, 20753
Conquest®, 6374, 24434
Conrad-Davis, 2956
Consenso, 781
Consertherm, 19898, 24205
Conservador, 28176
Consolidated Baling Machine Co., 20847
Consorzio, 8764, 25789
Constant Flow, 27516
Consumer Scan, 28344
Consumers, 2966
Contact Marking, 25788
Contadina®, 3478
Container Dri, 30633
Contempo, 20120, 25224, 31092
Contender, 18532, 26359
Conterna, 24074
Conti, 2970
Continental, 20887
Continental Chefc, 8088, 25922
Continental Cuisine, 11402
Continental Refrigerator, 20894
Continu-Weld, 20158
Contiparaguay, 2970
Contrac, 19544
Contrasweet, 13444
Contrax, 29211
Contrec, 20837
Control Ii, 28454
Control Safe, 27760
Controlir, 27325
Conturbex, 30135
Convect a Ray, 21529
Convenience Pac 1000, 31025
Convert-A-Lite, 29866
Convetual Franciscan Friars, 3597
Conveyor Crossovers, 25329
Convotherm®, 31093
Conway's, 7655
Conway's Irish Ale, 5314
Cook Master, 24906
Cook's, 11733
Cook's Pantry Organic, 2979
Cook-Eze, 24700
Cooke, 21199
Cooked Perfect®, 5929
Cookie Art, 5160
Cookie Brittle, 14045
Cookie Craft, 22044
Cookie Crisp®, 8945
Cookie Cupboard, 3399
Cookie Dough Bites, 12547
Cookie Wedgies, 8706
Cookies, 2988
Cookies By Lasca, 8927
Cookietree Bakeries, 2986
Cookin' Cajun, 3147
Cooking Star By Bargard, 19839
Cookquick', 12972
Cookquik Ranch Wagon, 12973, 30444
Cooks Delight, 6234
Cooktek, 20938
Cool, 8459
Cool Beans Coffee, 3217
Cool Blue, 25101
Cool Blues, 24610
Cool Crisp, 5003
Cool Cups, 20309
Cool Mint Drops, 9995
Cool Mountain Gourmet Soda, 2994
Cool Mule, 3180
Cool Natural Sodas, 2992
Cool Off, 20789
Cool Pops, 2136
Cool Quencher Sports, 2992
Cool Runnings, 13208, 30670
Cool Whip, 6976
Cool-E-Pops, 5752
Cool-Kit, 21040
Cool-Pitch, 20945
Cool-Safe, 21040
Coombs Family Farms, 1067
Coon®, 11211
Cooper, 11308, 28903
Cooper's Craft, 1784
Coors, 5975, 8459
Coors®, 8460
Cop, 18594, 31113
Copa, 5499
Copa De Oro Coffee Liqueur, 5720
Copco, 31242
Copeland, 23962, 24919, 28938, 28967
Copes, 6551
Copes-Vulcan, 28714
Copper Brite, 20956
Copper Glo, 19434
Copper Ridge Vineyards®, 3834
Copperhead Pale Ale, 4959
Copperline Amber, 2236
Coppets, 11310
Copyback, 25549
Copytest, 21436
Coqsol, 11778
Coqui Cookies, 4137
Cora®, 6818, 24802
Coral Food, 8649
Corazonas' Heartbar, 6338
Corbett Canyon, 3545
Corby Hall, 20964
Cordon Bleu, 25299
Cordon Bleu Chef Hats, 24815
Core Power, 2811
Core-Chill, 21091
Corelle, 31345
Corenco, 20967
Corex Ii, 20981
Corey Creek, 1152
Corfu, 3028
Corn Appetit, 1683, 10179, 27669
Corn Appetit Ultimate, 10179, 27669
Corn Flakes, 6766
Corn King, 2126
Corn Pops, 6766
Corn Pops®, 6765
Corned Beef, 8783
Cornelius, 20975
Cornell Beverages, 3036
Cornell Pumps and Pumping Systems, 28360
Cornell Versator, 20977
Cornerstone®, 7786
Corning, 20981
Corningware, 31344, 31345
Coromega, 12679
Corona, 71
Corona Extra, 4881, 7123
Corona Light, 4881
Coronado, 7655
Coronet, 21915
Coronet Vsq Brandy, 5720
Corpora Agricola, 5036
Corra-Trough, 27313
Corral Hollow Ranch, 26962
Correctchill, 22112
Corritempo, 25224
Corson, 21000
Corstat, 20831
Cortilite, 13455
Cortland Manor, 5753
Cortona®, 30595
Cosco, 18276, 21003, 21113, 21199, 21201
Cosco Flavors, 3045
Cosmo's, 3048
Cost Guard, 19139
Costa, 3051
Costa Clara, 7702
Costa Coffee, 2814
Costa Deano's, 3050
Costa Pasta, 9813
Costa Rica, 761, 1000
Costa's Pasta, 3053
Costadeanos Gourmet, 3052
Costar, 20981
Costello Banfi, 1006
Cote De Carneros, 2225
Cotlets, 7410
Cott, 20078
Cottage Bake, 6542
Cottage Cuts Potato Chips, 13884
Cottage Delight, 2507
Cottam Gardens, 8782
Cotterman, 19908
Cotton Candy Swirl, 12547
Cotton Queen, 20279
Cottonelle, 24838, 24839
Cottonwood Canyon, 3057
Couch's Original, 2794
Cougar, 24076
Cougar Cloth, 19743
Cougar Gold, 13516
Cougar Mountain, 3059
Coumadin®, 1721
Counterboy, 19634
Country, 10080
Country Archer Beef Jerky, 3063
Country Blend Cereal, 5946
Country Boy, 2045
Country Choice, 3066
Country Christmas, 25299
Country Classic, 6528
Country Club, 7655, 9664
Country Club Malt Liquor, 9137
Country Coffee, 3620
Country Cow, 5777
Country Cow Cocoa, 5777
Country Cream, 5282
Country Cream Butter, 13668
Country Creamery, 9283
Country Delight, 3070
Country Fair, 6352
Country Festival, 4262
Country Flavor Kitchens, 20050
Country Fresh, 3075, 3077
Country Fresh Farms, 3074
Country Fresh Fudge, 3075
Country Fresh™, 3442, 21421
Country Game, 9043
Country Gardens Blush Banquet, 1314
Country Gardens Cuisine, 2919
Country Golden Yolks, 5138
Country Grown, 10488
Country Grown Foods, 5040
Country Harvest, 13691
Country Hearth, 11525
Country Hearth®, 9736
Country Home Bakers, 3078
Country Home Bakery, 6338
Country Home Creations, 3079
Country Hutch, 19008
Country Kitchen Meals, 11979, 29528
Country Krisp®, 1654
Country Life, 3080
Country Maid, 3081
Country Morning, 4078
Country Pasta, 3072
Country Pride®, 10056
Country Road, 6186
Country Save, 21017
Country Select, 2961
Country Spice Tea, 2834
Country Style, 241, 2219
Country Time, 6976
Countryale, 13643
Countrymixes, 6821
Countryside Red, 1672
Courageous Captain's, 2419

1285

All Brands Index

Courtney's, 183, 18382
Courtney's Organic Water Crackers, 183, 18382
Courvoisier, 3024, 5892, 12315
Courvoisier®, 1120
Cousin Rachel Pretzels, 12851
Cousin Willie's, 10551
Covenant Winery, 10952
Covered Bridge Mills, 5331
Coverlak, 9802
Covey Run Winery®, 3834
Covi-Ox, 1692
Covitol, 1692
Cow Belle Creamery's™, 12885, 30333
Cow Lick, 1018
Cow Pie, 1018
Cow Tales®, 5096
Cow-Town and Rancher's, 5477
Cowboy, 10324, 13716
Cowboy Foods, 3099
Cowcium, 4914
Cowgirl Chocolates, 3100
Cowie, 3102
Cowlicks, 12847
Cowpuccino Toppers, 5777
Cowrageous!™, 6676
Cowtown Bbq, 9565
Coyote, 5442, 12814
Coyote Cocina, 3522
Coyote Grill®, 11317
Coyote Star, 5442
Coyote White, 6763
Coyote Wine, 1422
Cozy Cottage, 7866
Cozy-Lite, 29866
Cozzini, 21031
Cplus®, 6818, 24802
Cpt-25, 31058
Cr Food Baskets, 19999
Cr Scoops, 19999
Crab House Nuts, 1470
Crab Teazers, 12520
Cracker Barrel, 6976, 9789
Cracker Barrel®, 11211
Cracker Jack, 4741
Cracker Jack®, 9945, 27433
Cracker Snackers, 9799
Craft Lite, 27294
Craft's, 10280
Craftmaster, 21035
Craftsman, 29584
Crafty, 18375
Crain Ranch, 3110
Craisins, 9355
Cram For Students, 131
Cramarc, 21040
Cramore, 13141
Cran-Maxc, 9997
Cranapple, 9355
Cranberry Blossom, 10478
Cranberry Blush Wine, 13372
Cranberry Gose, 7526
Cranberry Sweets, 3114
Crancherry, 9355
Crane & Crane, 9212
Crane's Aqua Line, 3115
Crane's Blue Line, 3115
Crane's Gray Line, 3115
Crane's Maroon Line, 3115
Crane's Red Line, 3115
Crangrape, 9355
Cranicot, 9355
Cranorange, 9355
Cranrx, 8896
Cransations™, 11654
Crater's Meats, 3117
Crathco, 23420
Crave, 6976
Craven Crab, 3119
Cravin Asian, 11775
Crawfish Monica, 6687
Crayola, 2136, 6810, 20946
Crayon, 24093
Crayon Z-Tra, 24093
Crazy Clean, 29517
Crazy Cow, 387
Crazy Glasses, 22917
Crazy Jerry's, 3123
Cream Ale, 9117
Cream of Peanut, 1151
Cream of the West, 3130
Cream of Vanilla, 7934
Cream of Weber, 4328
Cream of Wheat®, 864
Creamedic, 20830
Creamerie Classique, 13070
Creamette®, 10777, 28421
Creamland, 3131, 3442, 21421
Creamy, 14017
Creamy Head, 13141
Creamy Medley of Popcorn, 10984
Createam, 13802
Creation Nation, 3132
Creation Station, 25094
Creative Bakers, 4244
Creative Carryouts®, 21362
Creative Classics™, 9523
Creative Confections, 3133
Creative Foods, 3136
Creative Gourmet, 11552
Creative Snacks Co., 3139
Creative Spices, 3140
Creekbend, 9452
Creekside, 6290
Creekstone, 5492
Creekstone Farms, 11053
Creemore Springs, 8459
Creemore Springs Premium Lager, 3141
Creemore Springs Urbock, 3141
Crem International®, 31093
Crema De Cacao, 3545
Crema De Coco, 3545
Crema De Many, 1151
Crema Di Miele, 11205
Creme Curls, 3143
Creme D'Lite, 3144
Creme De Cacao, 9773
Creme De Menthe, 9773, 10596
Creme Filled Butterscotch Krimpetsc, 12551
Cremer, 26427
Cremer Cunter, 9978
Cremes, 3145
Cremora®, 1103
Creole Classic, 4886
Creole Classics, 11402
Creole Delicacies, 3147
Creole Delights, 4886
Creole Rose, 4886
Cres Cor, 21077
Crescendo, 20256
Crescent, 3151, 9680
Crescent Confections, 8677
Crescent Ridge Dairy, 3153
Crescentgarniture, 10039
Crest, 12721, 30193
Crestware, 21083
Crete-Lease, 21080
Crete-Trete, 21080
Cretors, 20011
Cribmaster, 29584
Cricklewood Soyfoods, 3163
Crider, 3164
Crimeshield, 18185
Crimson Jewell®, 1420
Crina®, 3320
Cripple Creek, 9561
Crisa®, 25281
Crisco, 6380
Crisp & Delicious, 6451
Crisp 'n Fresh, 12201
Crisp Coat™ Uc, 8804
Crisp Film®, 8804
Crispers®, 9523
Crispin, 8459
Crispin Cider®, 8460
Crispin® Cider, 26668
Crispix®, 6765
Crispy Crowns®, 9523
Crispy Crunchies®, 9523
Crispy Fliers®, 13607
Crispy Keeper, 22640
Crispy Steaks, 14043
Crispy-Lishus®, 1654
Crispycakestm, 12680
Crispycoat Fries, 7179, 25104
Cristal, 9571
Cristal®, 8460
Cristobal, 2122
Critchfield Meats, 3168
Critelli, 3169
Criterion, 3170, 23998, 27377
Cro-Mag, 12023, 29568
Cro-Magnon, 12023, 29568
Cro-Man, 12023, 29568
Croccantinic, 7098
Crock Pot, 28412
Crock Pot®, 864
Crockett's, 3173
Crockpot, 2950
Crofter's, 3176
Crofter's Just Fruit, 3176
Crofter's Superfruit, 3176
Croissant De Paris, 5106
Cronk 2 O, 13697
Crook's, 11864
Crooked River Brewing, 3180
Crooked Stave, 10666
Crosby, 3185
Cross-Flow, 27347
Crosse & Blackwell, 6380
Crosset Company, 2298
Crossweb, 24906
Crotonese, 11668
Croustade 4cm, 10039
Croustade 5cm, 10039
Croustade 7cm, 10039
Crouzet, 21099
Crow Canyon, 104
Crowley, 3188
Crowley Ridge, 1727
Crown, 3195, 11312, 18040, 21109, 30970
Crown Imports®, 26668
Crown Jewel, 9570
Crown Marketing, 31207
Crown Prince Natural, 3194
Crown Prince Seafood, 3194
Crown's Pride, 4650
Crowning Touch, 13894
Crowntonka, 22315
Croyden House, 7848
Cruisin Cool, 10953
Crunch 'n Munch, 6267
Crunch 'n Munch®, 2939, 2940, 20821, 20822
Crunch Pak®, 2505
Crunch'n'munch Glazed Popcorn, 6267
Crunch-A-Mame, 3200
Crunch® Bar, 8945
Cruncha Ma-Mec, 5376
Crunchmaster, 12477
Crunchsters, 3202
Crunchy Nut, 6766
Crunchy Rob's, 11484
Cruse Vineyards, 3204
Crush®, 3725, 6818, 24802
Crustpak, 22548
Crustplus, 18495
Crutchfield, 13803
Cruvinet, 31256, 31263
Cruvinet Collector, 21125
Cruvinet Estate, 21125
Cruzan®, 1120
Cry Baby, 2132
Cry Baby®, 12880
Cryl-A-Chip, 21815
Cryl-A-Flex, 21815
Cryl-A-Floor, 21815
Cryl-A-Quartz, 21815
Cryo Batch, 18495
Cryo Dip, 18495
Cryo Quick, 18495
Cryogel, 12637
Cryogenesis, 31027
Cryojet, 24845
Cryolator, 31209
Cryoscopes, 27734
Crystal, 1087, 3210, 21131
Crystal Bay, 8784, 30820
Crystal Bitter, 9153
Crystal Clean, 31036
Crystal Clear, 7655
Crystal Farms, 3211
Crystal Flex, 30971
Crystal Foods, 1662
Crystal Gum™, 8804
Crystal Lake, 3213, 21132
Crystal Light, 6976
Crystal Palace, 11264
Crystal R-Best, 1662
Crystal Rock Water, 3217
Crystal Shooter Tubes, 19999
Crystal Springs, 3218, 10303, 27797
Crystal Springs®, 3220, 3319
Crystal Tex™ 627m, 8804
Crystal View, 27575
Crystal Vision, 21134
Crystal Wrap, 20178
Crystal-Aire, 30626
Crystal® Springs, 11889
Crystalac®, 7857
Crystalite, 20256
Crystalized, 21131
Cs 750, 24312
Cs Assembled, 28132
Csi, 20940
Cspiust Capsealing System, 25252
Csw, 28454
Cth, 3390
Ctx, 26132
Cubic, 22445
Cubitainer, 23708
Cucamonga, 13511
Cucina & Amore, 3223
Cucina Americana, 24575
Cucina Fresca, 11390
Cucina Sorrenti, 11818
Cucina Viva, 30775
Cuclone Sample Mills, 30530
Cuddy, 11776
Cuetara, 5108
Cuisinart, 31345
Cuisine Nature, 8676
Cuisine Solutions, 3229
Cuisiniers Choice, 692
Cuizina Italia, 3230
Culinaire, 3232
Culinaria, 11303, 28896
Culinary Classic Breast of Turkey N, 14041
Culinary Classic Slices Breast of T, 14041
Culinary Classics, 18908
Culinary Tours®, 12885, 30333
Culligan, 3239, 3469
Culmination, 7526
Cultured Red Neck T-Shirts, 6796
Culturelak, 9802
Culturelle, 6107
Culver City Meat, 5141
Culver Duck, 3244
Cumberland Dairy, 3247
Cumberland Gap, 3248
Cumberland Ridge, 12027
Cumin Gouda, 13840
Cummings & York, 10435
Cup O' Noodles, 9068
Cup-O-Gold, 163
Cupagranols, 3857
Cupful, 11003
Cupid, 4387
Cupkin, 28422
Cupl-Up, 24519
Cupro, 30376
Cure 81®, 6000, 23861
Curlumin C3 Complex, 11061
Curly's, 3258, 11733
Curran Cheese, 3259
Currentc, 3184

All Brands Index

Curry King, 3260
Curt Georgi Flavors & Fragrances, 8891
Curtainaire, 21159
Curtis, 3262, 31200
Curve Flex, 25819
Curve Mesh, 25819
Curvflo, 30724
Curwood, 21134
Cusa Tea, 3263
Cusano's, 3265
Cush-N-Aire, 23543
Cush-N-Flex, 23543
Cush-N-Tuf, 23543
Cushing, 8414
Cushion Ease, 20725
Cushion Walk, 20120
Cusquena®, 8460
Custom, 21178, 21201
Custom Coffee Plan, 4276
Custom Culinary™, 11504, 29095
Custom Fab, 21180
Custom Lable, 6508
Custom Metal Fabricator, 26027
Custom Pac 2000, 31025
Custom Up Cakes, 3541
Customer's Bags, 6506, 24551
Cut-Off, 31010
Cutcher, 8995
Cutie Cupid, 11004
Cutie Pies, 3276
Cutiesc, 12242
Cutrite, 21210
Cutthroat Pale Ale, 9366
Cutty Sark, 3545
Cutty Sarkr Scots Whisky Chocolates, 10468
Cutwater Spirits, 571
Cuvaison, 3280
Cuvee Sauvage, 4649
Cvbreeze, 26615
Cvc 300, 20107
Cvc Specialsties, 1967
Cvf, 5643
Cvi Bulk Wines, 3161
Cvp Fresh Vac, 20108
Cw 250, 24312
Cw 500, 24312
Cwc System, 28368
Cws, 20615
Cybele's Free To Eat, 3282
Cyber Key, 30843
Cyber Lock, 30843
Cyber Point, 30843
Cybernox, 29271
Cyclamen, 21213
Cycle, 4387
Cycle Line, 30481
Cycles, 5499
Cyclesaver, 23868
Cyclojet, 21215
Cyclolift, 21215
Cyclolok, 21215
Cyclonaire, 21215
Cyclone, 13280, 18450, 23702, 24881
Cyclone Xhe, 18074
Cycloseal, 20978
Cyenus Fluids and Greasers, 22231
Cygnet, 3285
Cylactin®, 3320
Cylindicator, 26442
Cyro Rotary, 18495
Cyrolite G-20, 21222
Cytosport, 4150
Czarina, 11264
Czechvar Lager, 26668

D

D Chair, 22599
D Flex, 29167
D&M, 21241
D' Sol, 4687
D'Agostino, 6126
D'Eaubonne Vsop Napoleon, 3024
D'Gari, 12823
D'Gari Gelatin, 26748
D'Haubry, 10188
D'Italiano, 13691
D'Italianoc, 1359
D'Oni Specialty Sauces, 4839
D-Carb 297, 20489
D-Grade, 30391
D-Max, 6629
D-Scale, 20489
D.C. Eye, 30422
D.F.A., 8816
D.J., 26932, 26933
D.J. Jardine, 6456
D.W. Concentrate, 21237
Da 7000, 27457
Da'bomb, 9565
Dab, 1361
Dacam, 21288
Dacopa, 2071
Dad's, 6380
Dad's Old Fashioned®, 6483
Daddy Ray's, 6338
Daddy-Q, 3537
Dadex, 137
Daeab, 8308
Daeco, 21292
Daedol, 137
Daejel, 137
Daelube, 137
Dagoba Organic Chocolate, 3306, 13433
Dahlicious, 3326
Dai Dairy, 345
Dai Juhyo, 1120
Daily Energy, 9201
Daily Foods, 3331, 8130
Daily Green Teas, 10677
Daily Made, 3330
Daily Multiple S/C, 75
Daily Soy, 9201
Daily Sun, 13932
Daily's® Premium Meats, 11363
Dainties, 10104
Dainty Boards, 25079
Dainty Pak, 13365
Dair-E Lite, 10815
Dairfair, 3386
Dairi-San, 25606
Dairi-Sol, 31267
Dairy Fresh, 3336
Dairy Group, 3337
Dairy House Chocolate Dairy Powderc, 6260, 24336
Dairy Housec Milk Flavors, 6260, 24336
Dairy Housec Stabalizers, 6260, 24336
Dairy Housec Vitamins, 6260, 24336
Dairy Maid, 3341
Dairy Maid Dairy, 3340
Dairy Maid Dairy®, 3335
Dairy Mart, 387
Dairy Pure, 7320
Dairy Pure®, 3442, 21421
Dairy Queen, 8109
Dairy Tester Ii, 30530
Dairy's Pride, 7998
Dairyamerica, 2061, 3345
Dairyland, 13875
Dairyland®, 13211
Dairystar®, 11211
Dairytime, 7419
Dairyvision, 22366
Dairyworld, 9469
Daisey Sour Cream, 3350
Daisy Brand Meat Products, 3121
Daisy Cottage Cheese, 3350
Daisy Light Sour Cream, 3350
Daisy Low Fat Cottage Cheese, 3350
Dak®, 10124
Daklinza™, 1721
Dakota, 3353, 29263
Dakota Gourmet, 11802
Dakota Gourmet Heart Smart, 11802
Dakota Gourmet Toasted Korn, 11802
Dakota Growers Pasta, 13475
Dakota Growers Pasta Co®, 8225
Dakota Hearth, 10698
Dakota Maid, 9132
Dakota Seasonings, 423
Dakota Yeast, 8353
Dalla, 3361
Dallis Bros. Coffee, 3362
Dallmayr, 1957, 3714
Dalsorb, 21315
Daltons, 10659
Daminaide, 137
Daminco, 137
Daminet, 137
Damp Rid, 21325
Damron, 3366
Dan Carter, 3367
Dan Tucker, 7655
Dan's Prize®, 6000, 23861
Danactive, 3379
Dancing Bull®, 3834
Dandies Marshmallows, 2550
Dandux, 19997
Dandyc, 3781
Danesi, 3009
Danger Men Cooking, 21336
Daniel Orr, 4487
Daniel Paul, 21561
Danimals, 3377, 3379
Danisa, 7769
Dannon, 3377, 3379
Danzig, 9833
Daphne's Creamery, 3380, 14069
Dapon, 21199
Dapper Actor, 31010
Dapper Duster, 31010
Dar Pro Bioenergy, 3390
Dar Pro Ingredients, 3390
Dar Pro Solutions, 3390
Dar-B-Ques, 21351
Darcia's Organic Crostini, 183, 18382
Dardenella, 1688
Dardimans, 3382
Dare Creme Cookies, 3384
Dare Realfruit Candies, 3384
Dareon, 20143
Dari Pride, 6971
Dari-Cal, 13122
Dari-Dri, 23160
Darjceling Superb 6000, 5228, 23295
Dark & Moody, 12178
Dark Canyon Coffee & Tea, 31459
Dark Dog Organic, 3388
Dark Eyes, 7655
Dark Fruit Chews, 7643
Dark Horse Brewing, 10666
Dark Horse Chocolates, 5578
Dark Horse®, 3834
Dark Lager, 4139
Dark Roast, 1054, 5462
Dark Star, 2860
Dark Star Porter, 1507
Dark Tickle, 3389
Darnell, 20143
Das Ii, 22706
Dasani, 2811, 2814
Dashco, 21363
Dasher Pecan, 11831
Dastony, 13847
Data Loggers, 28020
Data Scale, 21368
Data Visible, 21371
Data-Tabs, 21440
Datacheck, 25024
Dataflex, 21371
Datamax Corporation, 30186
Datapaq Multi-Tracker System, 21373
Datasmith, 25024
Datatrace, 26011
Date Crystals, 11555
Daub, 19567, 19568
Dave, 6590
Dave's Killer Bread, 4529
Daven Island Trade, 12068
David Beards, 5298
David Beards Texas Style, 5298
David Del Curto, 5036
David Nicholson 1843, 7655
David Rio, 2833
David Rio Chai, 3398
David's Cookies, 3399
David's Goodbatter, 21383
David's Gourmet Coffee, 1601, 19813
David's Kosher, 1262
David® Seeds, 2939, 2940, 20821, 20822
Davidson's Inc, 3400
Davidson's®, 8225
Daviess County, 7655
Davinci, 6279
Davinci Gourmet, 2606
Davinci®, 3834
Davinia, 9773
Davis Bread, 3405
Davis Bynum, 3406
Davis Strait Fisheries Ltd, 3408
Davis®, 2711
Davy's Mix, 4521
Dawes Hill, 9485
Dawn, 12721, 30193
Dawn Glo, 5555
Dawn's Foods, 3413
Day By Day, 7505
Day-Lee Foods, 3416
Daybreak, 3417
Daybreak Classics, 1282
Daybreak Foods, 3418
Daydots, 21398
Daygum, 9956
Daymark, 21399
Dayton Nut Specialties, 3421
Dayton's, 10773
Dc Distribution Center, 25277
Dc Uni-Clip, 27575
Dc33 Luxury, 28922
Dca, 25995
Dce Dalamatic, 21705
Dce Siloair, 21705
Dce Sintamatic, 21705
Dce Unicell, 21705
Dce Unimaster, 21705
Dci Cheese®, 11209, 11211
Dde, 21250
Dds, 13130
Dds Acidophilus, 13130
Dds Junior, 13130
Dds Plus, 13130
De Bas Vineyard, 4815
De Beukelaer, 3433
De Caradeuc White, 8513
De Champaque Bakery Snacks, 3615
De Groen's, 999
De Kuyper Geneva, 3024
De L'Ora®, 3479, 21460
De La Marca, 8028
De Lescot, 5405
De Loach, 3509
De Lorimeir, 3510
De Luxe Packaging, 26756
De Mill, 9094
De Rose Vineyards, 2675
De Santa Fe, 11195
De Winkel®, 4552
De-Foamer, 20966
De-Kaffo, 13279
De-Lish-Us, 3501
Dean, 3441, 31092
Dean & Deluca, 3440
Dean's, 3131
Dean's Country, 3443
Dean's™, 3442, 21421
Deans®, 13328
Dear Lady, 11759
Dearborn Sausage, 3446
Dearfoams, 24672
Death and Taxes Black Beer, 8524
Death Valley Habanero, 6015
Deauville, 4515
Deaver Vineyards Wine, 3447
Debba, 21425
Debbie D'S, 3448
Debco, 3424
Debi Lilly™ Design, 11073
Deboles, 5505

1287

All Brands Index

Dec a Cake®, 864
Decacake, 73
Decadent Temptations, 387
Decades, 8869, 8870
Decathlon Series, 22659
Decatur Dairy, 3457
Dececco, 25789
Decel-Air, 24010
Dechiel, 10813
Decker Farms Finest, 3458
Deco-Mate, 30601
Deconna, 3461
Decorail, 31368
Decovery®, 3320
Decoy, 3779
Dedert, 21445
Dee Lite, 12001
Deen, 3463
Deep, 3465
Deep Chi Builder, 5791
Deep Cover, 7310
Deep Cover Brown, 7309
Deep Dairy, 3465
Deep Dish Pecan Pike, 2881
Deep Eddy Vodkas, 5720
Deep Purple, 5539
Deep Rich, 464
Deep River Snacks, 3466
Deep Rock Water, 10303, 11889, 27797
Deep Rock®, 3220, 3319
Deep Sleep, 5791
Deep Valley, 3467
Deepflo, 22173
Deer Creek, 3468
Deer Park, 14055
Deerfield, 3470
Deering, 4369
Deez Nutz, 4299
Defender, 22902
Defrost Controllers, 28020
Degeneve, 8304
Degoede, 954
Dehydrates, 3474
Dei Fratelli, 5893, 5894
Deiorio's, 3427, 21409
Deja Blue®, 3725, 6818, 24802
Dejean, 8995
Dekalb, 11286
Dekuyper®, 1120
Del Campo, 3788
Del Cara, 2375
Del Dia®, 10056
Del Fuerte®, 6000, 23861
Del Grosso, 3494
Del Mar, 3477
Del Mondo, 9808
Del Monte, 56
Del Monte Fresh®, 3479, 21460
Del Monte®, 3478
Del Rio, 3481
Del Sol, 6177
Del Valle, 2814
Del Verde, 25789
Del's, 3482
Del's Italian Ices, 3482
Del's Lemonade, 3482
Delacour, 7655
Delair, 28714
Delallo, 3487
Delancey Dessert, 3488
Delaviuda, 3490
Delco, 21497
Delco Buffalo, 26933
Delco Technology, 20599
Delecto Chocolates, 4884
Deleez, 30590
Delfield®, 31093
Delftree, 3493
Delgrosso, 7635
Deli, 12301
Deli Buddy, 25510
Deli Cuts, 2212
Deli Direct, 11960
Deli Express, 3836
Deli Flavor, 5391

Deli Maid, 13016
Deli Meats, 6000, 23861
Deli Sliced, 5039
Deli Style, 13063
Deli-Best, 11298
Deli-Catessen, 13330
Deli-Dogs, 2541
Deli-Fresh, 3336
Delicare, 2666, 20561
Delicato, 3497
Delice, 10146
Delicia, 10734
Delicioso, 11437
Delicious, 2750, 13728
Delicious™, 12426, 29855
Delico, 6945
Delighted By, 3504
Delights, 3189
Deligraphics, 20593
Delishaved, 7197
Delivers, 20256
Delizia, 13365
Delizza, 10188
Dell Amore's, 25789
Della, 11908
Della Gourmet Rice, 11908
Della Naturac, 12928
Delmonte, 4928
Delnor, 11766
Deloach, 1543
Delouis, 25789
Delphi, 26615
Delphi 7.0, 26615
Delrin®, 21848
Delroyd Worm Gear, 18678
Delta, 12410, 21044, 23409, 24076, 25976
Delta 3000 D-Cam, 24076
Delta 3000 Ld, 24076
Delta 3000 Sb, 24076
Delta Bay, 6290
Delta Dry, 29513
Delta Foods, 3513
Delta Fresh, 3515
Delta Liquid, 29513
Delta Pure, 21519
Delta Rose, 7571
Delta Security Solutions, 20290
Deltamat, 22299
Deltech, 28714
Deluscious, 3438
Deluxe, 3480, 8533, 21529, 31141
Deluxe Fruitcake®, 2881
Delvo®Cheese, 3320
Delvo®Fresh, 3320
Delvotest®, 3320
Delwrap, 26680
Demaria Seafood, 3429
Dematic, 21536
Dement's, 5029
Demi-Glace Veal Gold, 8538
Deming's, 9980
Demitasse After Dinner Tea, 5228, 23295
Demitri's Bloody Mary Seasonings, 3518
Dempster's, 7876
Dempster's®, 2121
Den, 9129
Denali, 26337
Denester, 23716
Denmar, 21541
Denmark: Officer, 5108
Dennis, 11503
Dennison, 6267
Dennison's, 6267
Dennison's®, 2939, 2940, 20821, 20822
Denrado, 648
Densart, 30792
Denta Brite, 21952
Dentyne, 2132, 8474
Dentyne Fire Gum, 1980
Dentyne Ice, 1980, 9995
Dentyne Tango, 1980
Denunzio, 7635
Denver, 2898, 5304
Denver Co, 4079

Depend, 24838
Dependable, 4681
Depiezac, 5791
Depotpac, 27679
Derco, 3530
Derm Ade, 30569
Derma-Pro, 22990
Dermagest, 7422
Dermal, 23152
Dermanex, 783
Des Coteaux, 4748
Descender, 28742
Desco, 20530, 21556
Descote, 9797
Desert Gardens Chile and Spice, 2919
Desert Gold, 9042
Desert Gold Dry, 13299
Desert Pepper, 3537
Desert Pride, 1603
Desert Wonder, 1603
Desi Pak, 30633
Desi View, 30633
Desi-Pak, 26401
Design Master, 24628
Design Series Counters, 18304
Designbags, 21564
Designer Displayer, 20256
Designer Protein, 4150
Designer System, 29441
Designer Whey, 3540
Designer's Choice, 18155
Designerware, 30971
Designs By Anthony, 22612
Desirable, 4387
Desolite® Supercoatings, 3320
Dessert Jewell, 462
Desserts By David Glass, 3544
Dessvilie, 25789
Destab, 9797
Destiny Plastics, 18029
Det-O-Jet, 18542
Det-Tronics, 20290
Detecto, 18327, 21576
Detergent 8, 18542
Detoxwater, 3546
Dettol, 10598
Devil's Fire, 4928
Devil's Lair, 12937
Devils Backbone Brewing Company, 571
Devils Spring, 1423
Devine Nectar, 3550
Devon, 2960
Devondale™, 11211
Devonsheer®, 864
Devro, 3552
Dewalt, 29584
Dewar's Scotch, 914
Dewar's White Label, 3570
Dewater Equipment, 24357
Dewied, 3554, 21588
Dexter Russell, 21591
Dextranase, 1692
Dextrozyme, 1692
Df 5000, 18095
Dft Series, 21640
Dh3, 9240
Dhagold™, 3320
Dhea, 746, 6107, 8009, 11268
Dhea Plus, 9240
Dhidow Enterprise 150x, 3558
Dhidow Enterprise 20x, 3558
Dhidow Enterprise 50x, 3558
Dhidow Enterprise Zero, 3558
Di Amore, 11264
Di Grazia Vineyards, 3597
Di-Mare Gold Label, 3565
Di-Tech, 24870
Diabetiks, 5363
Diablo, 21593, 25190
Diablo Ignited Sours, 1343
Diack, 19042, 30263
Diago, 8387
Diago's®, 8384
Dial Taper, 25788
Dial-A-Fill, 26482

Dialog, 24743
Diamalt, 954, 10247
Diamond, 726, 3572, 5409, 7118, 10421, 12973, 21178, 21600, 21602, 21947, 24517, 30444
Diamond 49 Series, 19032
Diamond 52 Series, 19032
Diamond Bakery, 3571
Diamond Brite, 21952
Diamond Cake, 1061
Diamond Clear, 21968
Diamond D, 7207
Diamond Green Diesel, 3390
Diamond Grip, 21952
Diamond Joe, 13613
Diamond K, 6673
Diamond Spring Water, 8605
Diamond Springs, 3469
Diamond Walnut Shortbread Cookies, 9399
Diamond Wipes, 21608
Diana, 8676, 9873
Diana Sauce, 6976
Diana's, 10086
Diane's Italian Sausage, 12463
Diane's Sweet Heat, 3583
Diane's®, 8384
Dianes, 8387
Dibella, 3566
Dick & Casey's, 4981
Dick Servaes, 5428
Dickies, 13107, 26875, 30603
Dickinson, 25789
Dickinson Frozen Foods, 3588
Dickinson's, 6380
Dickson's Pure Honey, 3589
Diedrich Coffee, 3591
Diedrich Coffee®, 6818, 24802
Dieffenbach's, 3592
Diestel Turkey Ranch, 3594
Diet Big Red ®, 1339
Diet Chaser, 3707
Diet Cheerwine, 2234
Diet Clear Jazz, 5539
Diet Coke, 2814
Diet Dhea, 9240
Diet Double-Cola, 3707
Diet Freeze, 7870
Diet Ice Botanicals, 12510
Diet Lift, 9155
Diet Rite, 4521
Diet Rite3, 10151
Diet Rite®, 3725, 6818, 24802
Diet Ski, 3707
Dieters Tea, 131
Dietz & Watson, 3595
Difiore Pasta, 3563
Digesta-Lac, 8816
Digestive Advantage, 11285
Digestive Care™, 6449, 24506
Digezyme, 11061
Digi, 20520
Digi-Drive, 24664
Digi-Link, 24743
Digi-Stem, 27240
Digibar, 21713
Digiorno, 2667
Digiorno®, 8945
Digiovanni, 13422
Digisort, 23921
Digispense 2000, 24042
Digispense 700, 24042
Digispense 800, 24042
Digistrip, 24743
Digital (Appliance) Thermometers, 28020
Digital Dining, 21624
Digital Moisture Balance, 20093
Digital Thermostats, 28020
Digitronic, 29482
Digivolt, 23489
Dijon Clone, 1128
Dijon Crunch, 8269
Dilberito, 11324
Dilbert Mints&Gummies, 10532

All Brands Index

Dilettante Chocolates, 11390
Dillard's, 3600
Dillman Farm, 3601
Dillman's All Natural, 3601
Dillons, 12516
Dilusso Deli Company®, 6000, 23861
Dimarco, 7927
Dimitri, 7655
Dimo, 9912
Dimple Plate, 28588
Dina, 12301
Dinapoli, 2065
Dinatura, 6806
Dine Aglow, 25190
Dine-A-Wipe, 23160
Dine-A-Wipe Plus, 23160
Dine-Meat Emu Products, 3612
Dinelle, 29336
Diner Mug, 25665
Ding Gua Gua, 1478
Dingdongs®, 6013
Dinkel's, 3609
Dinkel's Famous Stollen, 3609
Dinkel's Sip'n, 3609
Dinkel's Southern Double, 3609
Dinner Check, 20326
Dinner Reddi, 10491
Dinnerware, 23499
Dinny Robb, 5717
Dino's, 3611
Dinosaur Brand, 6880
Dinty Moore®, 6000, 23861
Diosna, 19567, 19568
Dip Indulgence, 13815
Dip N' Joy, 5105
Dip Sticks, 12202
Dip-Idy-Dill, 6528
Dipasa Biladi, 3615
Dipasa De Champagne, 3615
Dipasa Usa, 3615
Dipix Vision Inspection Systems, 21638
Diposables, 27642
Dippin' Candy, 4507
Dippin' Dots, 3616
Dipt'n Dusted, 12520
Dipwell, 21639
Direct Fire Technical, Inc., 21640
Direct It, 21536
Dirt Eraser, 29489
Dirt Killer, 21642
Dirtex, 28852
Dirty, 13129
Discovery, 4575
Discovery Plastics, 19042
Discovery System, 24265
Dishwasher Glisten, 19837
Disintegrator, 19576
Disney, 4659, 20946
Disney Princess, 4507
Dispax Reactor, 24074
Dispensa-Matic, 30186
Dispense Rite, 21647
Dispense-Rite, 21670
Displawall, 25773
Dispomed, 18369
Dispos-A-Way, 19998
Disposable Products Company, 18029
Disposawrapper, 25531
Dispose a Scrub, 24829
Disposer Saver, 24700
Disposertrol, 27760
Disposo-Treet, 23261
Dispoza-Pak, 28428
Dissolve-A-Way, 21399
Distillata, 3621, 21658
Ditka, 1087
Ditrac, 19544
Ditting, 21663
Div-10, 22706
Diver's Hole Dunkelweizen, 7143
Diversified (Dce), 21665
Divian Coffee, 13191
Divine Delights, 3625
Divine Meringues, 9816
Divine Organics, 3627

Diwan Coffee, 13191
Dixie, 3631, 18592, 21677
Dixie Brand, 9763, 27283
Dixie Crystals®, 6164
Dixie Fresh, 10655
Dl Geary Brewing, 3637
Dm Choice, 12550
Dm Ole, 12550
Dme, 21668
Dnx, 3329
DoA Mar¡A™, 6000, 23861
Do Haccp, 26666
Do Sop, 26666
Do-It, 21689
Do-Sys, 28346
Dobake, 3639
Doc's Draft Hard Cider, 13578
Dock Xpress, 25377
Doctor Dread's, 3641
Doctor's, 21059
Doctor's Nutriceuticals, 5698
Doe Mill, 2044
Doering, 21691
Dog Bakery Products, 818
Dog-Gone Chik'n®, 1654
Dog-Gones, 12847
Dogflex, 3753, 21763
Dogsters, 6338, 20946
Dogwood, 3646
Dohlar, 4943
Dolce, 3009, 4258, 6806
Dolcea®, 3834
Dolcia Prima™ Allulose, 12561
Dole, 741, 7213, 12871
Dole Food Products, 20020
Dole Packaged Foods, 30618
Dole® Soft Serve, 6792, 24785
Dolefam, 679
Dolimo®, 7952
Dollarwise, 23809
Dollinger, 28714
Dolly Madison, 28412
Dolores, 3658
Dolphin Natural, 3659
Dom Perignon, 3570, 8452
Dom's, 3660
Domaine Armand Rousseau, 4677
Domaine Breton, 5417
Domaine De Canton, 5720
Domaine De La Vougeraie, 1543
Domaine Du Castel, 10952
Domaine Michel, 8238
Domaine Netofa, 10952
Domaine Noel, 1306
Domaine St. George, 3662
Domaine St. Vincent, 5413
Dominator Wheat, 7844
Dominex, 3664
Dominick's, 6126
Dominion, 26668
Domino, 4517
Domino Sugar, 3666
Domino®, 12196
Don Alfonso, 3667, 10952
Don Bernardo, 7126
Don Enrique, 31350
Don Francisco's, 4202
Don Hilario Estate Coffee, 3669
Don Jose Horchata, 3670
Don Manuel 100% Colombian, 2847
Don Miguel Gascon®, 3834
Don Miguel®, 6000, 23861
Don Pedro, 7219
Don Pedro Jamonada, 2670
Don Pepino, 13437
Don Pepino®, 864
Don Peppe, 223
Don Quixate, 10319
Don's Chuck Wagon, 5898, 11587
Don't Go Nuts, 3675
Donald Duck, 13932
Donatoni, 3679
Doncella Chocolates, 22560
Donettes®, 6013
Dong Dong Joo Rice Wine, 6968

Donita, 100
Donmir Wine Cellars, 13825
Donnelly Chocolates, 3685
Donq Anejo, 3545
Donq Coco, 3545
Donq Cristal, 3545
Donq Gold, 3545
Donq Grand Anejo, 3545
Donq Limon, 3545
Donq Mojito, 3545
Donq Pasion, 3545
Dontil, 5123
Donut House, 6819
Donut House Collection®, 6818, 24802
Donut Shop, 1053, 6819
Doodleberry, 2905
Door County Potato Chips, 3691
Door Spy, 26080
Door-Peninsula, 3692
Doors, 18793
Doorware, 24734
Dopaco, 18029
Dopplerock, 5314
Dor-Blend, 21720
Dor-Mixer, 21720
Dor-Opener, 21720
Dora, 10041
Dorado, 1423
Dorazio, 11481
Dorchest, 2750
Dorden, 26073
Dorell, 21716
Doritos, 4741
Doritos®, 9945, 27433
Dorks, 7643
Drothy, 3697
Dorothy Lynch Home Style, 12557
Dorset Tea, 5612
Dorton, 21720
Dos Gusanos, 7655
Dos Mamacitas, 12162
Dos Trianos, 7655
Dositainer, 18241
Dotmark, 21313
Dots®, 12880
Double Bag, 7526
Double Black, 10629
Double Cut System, 19146
Double D, 7716
Double Decker, 13654
Double Deep Fudge Pecan Pie, 2881
Double Density Miniroller, 22615
Double Dry Gingerale, 3707
Double Fruit, 6380
Double India Pale Ale, 12153
Double J, 31003
Double L, 3463
Double Planetary, 20448
Double Q, 9980
Double R®, 2332
Double Red Provisions, 1658
Double S, 11070
Double Star Espresso, 13160
Double-Cola, 3707
Double-Dry Mixers, 3707
Doublemint®, 7952, 13960
Doublepure Distilled, 4462
Doubletalk, 20593
Douce Provence, 3165
Dough Relaxer, 7540
Dough Stabilizer, 12553
Dough-To-Go, 3709
Doughcart, 27893
Doughpro, 27893
Douglas, 21736
Dove, 8533, 20633
Dove®, 7952
Dove Chocolate, 6483
Dove® Grill Scraper, 31436
Dover Phos Foods, 21740
Dover Sole, 10949
Dow, 18592
Dowd & Rogers™, 9237, 26785
Dowd and Rogers, 3718
Down East, 9291

Downeast, 3719
Downeast Candies, 3720
Downeast Coffee, 3722
Downey's, 5957
Downey'sc, 9748
Downtown After Dark, 6711
Downtown Brown, 7554
Downtown Sumatra, 6547
Downy, 12721, 30193
Dowsport America, 21747
Dox Expander, 18920
Doyen, 22108
Doyle's, 377
Doyon, 21756
Dp, 20064
Dpo, 833
Dr Cookie, 3730
Dr Jerkyll & Mr Hide, 12831
Dr Oetker, 3734
Dr Pepper, 2811
Dr Pepper®, 3725
Dr Praeger's, 3727
Dr Tima, 3740
Dr. Bronner's, 4988
Dr. Konstantin Frank, 3724
Dr. McDougall's, 3733
Dr. McDougall's Right Foods, 11146
Dr. McDougall's Right Foodsc, 8281
Dr. Organic®, 8871
Dr. Pepper, 2815, 9083, 20685
Dr. Pepper®, 6818, 24802
Dr. Pete's, 3726
Dr. Peter's Peppermint Crunch, 6525
Dr. Red Norland, 3216
Dr. Rinse Vita Flo Formula, 8892
Dragnet, 3743
Dragon Cinnamon, 12987
Dragon Eggs, 7562
Dragon's Breath, 8670
Dragone®, 11209, 11211
Drain Out, 24386
Drain Power, 27045
Drain Warden, 31010
Draino, 21757
Drainthru, 24456
Drake's, 8077
Drake's®, 8076
Drakes Amber Ale, 3746
Drakes Blond Ale, 3746
Drakes Fresh, 3747
Drakes Hefe-Weizen, 3746
Drakes Ipa, 3746
Drangle, 3748
Draper Valley Farms®, 9946
Dratco, 21552
Drayman's Porter, 1237
Dre (Direct Reading Echelle Icp), 25215
Dreaco, 21762
Dream, 4025, 5505
Dream Candy, 11817
Dream Greens, 195
Dream Pretzels, 3752
Dreamies, 12551
Dreamies®, 7952
Dreaming Cow, 3755
Dreamworks, 10229
Dreft, 12721, 30193
Dreidoppel, 954
Dreimeister, 3236
Drew's All Natural, 3758
Drewclar, 135
Dreyer Wine, 3759
Dreyer's, 3760
Dreyer's®, 8945
Dri-Sheet, 27260
Drier Meats, 3763
Drinde™, 4119
Drink-Master, 24725
Drip Catchers, 19999
Dripcut, 30376
Driscoll's, 3765
Drive Activated, 1343
Driver's Seat, The, 31171
Driveroll, 24366
Drize, 23160

1289

All Brands Index

Drizzls, 4976
Drogheria & Alimentari, 8061
Dromedary, 8519
Drop-Lok, 29221
Drops O'Gold, 12979
Dropz, 7710
Droste, 25789
Droxia®, 1721
Drsoy, 6279
Drum-Mate, 21776
Drum-Plex, 25224
Drumplex, 25289
Drunken Goat Cheese, 11668
Drusilla, 3770
Dry Creek, 3771
Dry N-3, 1692
Dry Sack, 13320, 13811
Dry-Atlantic Coastal, 13372
Dry-Flo®, 8804
Dry-O-Lite, 30752
Dryden, 3772
Dryden & Palmer, 2132, 10724
Drynites, 24838
Ds Special, 20121
Dsa, 3765
Dsi Escort, 25407
Du Bouchett Liqueurs & Cordials, 5720
Du Crose, 4920
Du Glaze, 4920
Du Sweet, 4920
Du-Good, 21782
Dual Jet, 23693
Dual-Flex, 28556
Dual-Tex, 19878
Duas Rodas Industrial, 9027
Dubbasue and Company, 10219
Dubbel Felix Caspian, 2691
Dubble Bubble, 2132
Dubble Bubble®, 12880
Dubl-Fresh, 19371
Dubl-Tough®, 13595, 31053
Dubl-View, 19371
Dubl-Wax, 19371
Dubleuet, 5405
Dublin's Pub, 56
Dublnature, 13595, 31053
Dublserve®, 13595, 31053
Dublsoft, 13595, 31053
Dubonnet Apperitifs, 5720
Dubreton Natural, 7387
Ducane, 18434
Duchess, 2242
Duchy Originals, 13544
Duck Pond Cellars, 3778
Duck® Brand, 29171
Duckhorn Vineyards, 3779
Ducktrap, 3780
Ducros, 8061
Duct Axial, 23643
Duet, 2761
Duets, 7746
Duff Norton, 20752
Duff's, 5015
Duffy, 3695
Dufour Pastry Kitchens, 3783
Duke's, 3787
Duke's Mayonaise, 1935
Duke's Smoked Shorty, 3787
Duke's®, 2939, 2940, 20821, 20822
Dulany, 10038
Dulux, 26990
Dum Dum Pops, 11885
Dum Dumsc Pops, 2132
Dummbee Gourmet, 3791
Dumor, 20639
Dump Clean, 19212
Dump Trap, 23453
Dun-D, 3796
Dunaweal Vineyard, 2770
Dunbar, 11865
Dunbar Ranch, 8960
Dunbars, 8519
Dunbars Candied Yams, 8519
Dunbars Marinated Roasted Peppers, 8519

Dunbars Roasted Peppers, 8519
Dunbars Sweet Potatoes, 8519
Duncan, 3793
Duncan Hies Wilderness®, 2939, 2940, 20821, 20822
Duncan Hines, 811
Duncan Hines Comstock®, 2939, 2940, 20821, 20822
Duncan Hines®, 2939, 2940, 20821, 20822, 27540
Dundee, 3798
Dundee Brandied, 3794
Dundee Candy Shop, 3795
Dunham-Bush, 28967
Dunhill, 21804
Dunkin Donuts, 2811, 6819
Dunkin' Donuts, 1075, 6380
Dunkin' Donuts®, 3803, 21805
Dunkmaster, 27520
Dunn, 3804
Dunn's, 12170
Dunn's Best, 5094
Dunya Harvest, 11496, 29092
Duo Shield®, 21362
Duo-Stress Place Mats, 25447
Duo-Touch, 19429
Duplin, 3805
Duplux, 22039
Dupont, 18592
Dupont D'Isigny - Candies, 4148
Dur-A-Edge, 27612
Dura, 21814
Dura Klor, 30913
Dura-Base, 23857
Dura-Drive Plus, 29445
Dura-Glide, 29583
Dura-Kote, 20811
Dura-Lite, 30743
Dura-Max, 18074
Dura-Pak, 18693
Dura-Plate, 23990
Dura-San Belt, 20121
Dura-Tool, 18022
Dura-Ware, 21817
Durabit, 22173
Durabrite, 22272
Duracast, 30289
Durachrome, 18142
Duraclamp, 23450
Duracool, 23608
Duracor, 20359
Duracrafic, 28965
Durajet, 19021
Duralast, 23543
Duraliner, 26428
Durallure, 30724
Duralobe, 30853
Duralon, 28357
Duralux, 21566
Duran, 30766
Durango, 3807
Durango Gold, 9672
Durascan, 25549
Durasieve, 28251
Durastrap, 21859
Duratech, 19021
Duratek, 30828, 30829
Duratrax, 22510, 30843
Duratuf, 23112
Duraward, 30843
Durelco, 21814
Durell Vineyard, 6892
Durex®, 10598
Durkee, 73
Durkee®, 864
Duro, 18328
Duro Bag, 26756
Durobor, 24636
Durt Howg, 25806
Durt Tracker, 25806
Durviage, 8676
Dus-Trol, 23261
Dust 'n Clean, 23160
Dust Free Form of Fd&C Colors, 28484
Dust Up, 20591, 29517

Dust-Cat, 30626
Dust-Hog, 30626
Dustalarm, 26283
Duster, 25900
Dusterz, 23999
Dustkop, 18147
Dustmaster, 30503
Dustroyer, 30503
Dusty Miller, 1688
Dutch Ann, 3811
Dutch Boiler, 7767
Dutch Boy, 1537
Dutch Brothers, 10358
Dutch Choux, 1524
Dutch Cocoa Bv, 9027
Dutch Country, 10661
Dutch Delight, 6551
Dutch Farms, 5555
Dutch Garden, 12437
Dutch Garden Super Swiss, 12437
Dutch Girl, 7767
Dutch Gold, 3815, 25789
Dutch Gourmet, 9408
Dutch Henry, 3816
Dutch Kitchen, 3817
Dutch Quality House, 1891
Dutch Waffle, 6338
Dutchess, 21831
Dutchie, 13622, 13623
Duthie, 11416
Dutlettes, 3633
Dutro, 20143, 28488
Dutton Ranch, 6892
Duvel, 1748
Duvillage 1860®, 11211
Dw, 30398
Dyalon, 30255
Dyc Whisky, 1120
Dylan's, 961
Dymo, 21201
Dyna-Link, 25940
Dynablast, 21844
Dynac, 23641
Dynaflex, 26049
Dynagro, 25941
Dynahyde, 30914
Dynalyser, 18235
Dynamaster, 18321
Dynamic Foods, 3830
Dynamic Trio, 1914
Dynamite Energy Shake, 5669
Dynamite Vites, 5669
Dynapac, 25936
Dynaplas, 26428
Dynarap, 20108
Dynaric, 21859
Dynashear, 18126
Dynastrap, 21859
Dynasty, 24495, 30706
Dynatred, 22480
Dynavac, 25840
Dynavac and Watervac Water Systems, 28360
Dyneema Purity®, 3320
Dyneema®, 3320
Dynestene, 18187
Dynoplast, 28750
Dynynstyl, 21864

E

E&S, 344
E(Lm)Inate®, 5665
E-Binder, 23659
E-Gems, 6364
E-P Plus, 27400
E-Z Access, 25777
E-Z Dip, 21882
E-Z Fit Barbecue, 22996
E-Z Keep, 446
E-Z Lift, 21885
E-Z Rak-Clip, 27575
E-Z Seal, 19275
E-Z Serve, 31152
E-Z Tec, 22252

E-Z-Rect, 18620
E-Z-V, 30408
E-Zee Wrap, 24567
E. Waldo Ward, 3838
E.D. Smith, 1103, 3844, 12943, 30400
E.D.G.E., 23832
E.H. Taylor Jr., 11263
E.O.C., 4479
E2 D2, 18185
Eagle, 7173, 19908, 20277, 20639, 20951, 21952, 27391
Eagle Absolute, 21952
Eagle Brand, 3862
Eagle Chair, 21956
Eagle Lager, 71
Eagle Rare, 11263
Eagle River Brand, 6721
Eagle Signal, 28967
Eagle Zephyr, 21199
Eagles-7, 19364
Eagleware, 18026, 18550, 21962, 23616
Earl Grey Superior Mixture, 5228, 23295
Early California, 8692
Early Times, 1784
Earnest Eats, 3866
Earth Balance, 3868
Earth Balance®, 2939, 2940, 20821, 20822, 27540
Earth Power's All American, 10026
Earth Song Whole Food Bars, 3872
Earth Unt Farm, 1548
Earth Wise Tree Free®, 23811
Earth Wise®, 23811
Earth's Best, 3617
Earth's Best Organic, 5505
Earth's Bounty, 8009
Earthbound Farm, 3379
Earthpower's Phytochi, 10026
Earthstone, 21966
Earthwise Systems, 30382
Ease Out, 22999
Easi-63, 22679
Easimount, 24734, 24735
Easisharp, 29049
Easley's, 3877
East Coast, 21970
East Coast Gourmet, 10118
East India Coffee & Tea Co., 11141
East India Coffee and Tea, 4229
East Wind, 3887
East Wind Almond, 3887
East Wind Cashew, 3887
East Wind Organic Peanut Butter, 3887
East Wind Peanut, 3887
East Wind Tahini, 3887
Easten Shore Tea, 1000
Easter, 21059
Easterday, 21974
Eastern, 20646, 21983
Eastern Shore Foods, Llc, 11356
Eastside Deli, 3896
Easy Cheese, 8729
Easy Connect, 19419
Easy Earth, 29592
Easy Florals, 23828
Easy Gluer, 21946
Easy Heat, 23828
Easy Hinge, 23860
Easy Paks, 21757
Easy Pour, 19943
Easy Squeeze Bottle, 5489
Easy Strapper, 21946
Easy Strip, 18387
Easy Sweep, 24829
Easy Swing, 22097
Easy Taper, 21946
Easy Up, 21988
Easy-Lock, 23017
Easy-Rol, 26556
Easybar, 21987
Easylabel, 30186
Easymeal, 9529
Easyprint, 19546
Eat a Bowl, 2497
Eat Clean Organic, 13025

All Brands Index

Eat Natural, 4148
Eat Smart, 4242, 22458
Eat the Bear, 4150
Eat Your Coffee, 3904
Eat Your Vegetables, 11754
Eatec Netx, 21989
Eatec System, 21989
Eatem, 3908, 21990
Eatmor, 178
Eatsmart Snacks, 11770
Eau Galle Cheese, 3910
Ebara, 27729
Eberley, 8898
Eberly, 30775
Ebi-Ultraline, 22366
Ebly®, 7952
Ebonite, 23543
Ebony, 27277
Ebro, 3914, 19107
Ecclestone, 942
Ecco, 4107, 22251
Ecco Domani®, 3834
Ecco One, 28050
Ecco!, 6314
Ech, 7874
Ech20, 18198
Echinacea, 4859
Echinacea Triple Source, 5791
Echinacea/Goldenseal Supreme, 4859
Echo Falls, 9344
Echo Farm Pudding, 3915
Eckrich, 11733
Eclipse, 4407, 19975, 20573, 22348, 22564, 26250
Eclipse®, 7952, 13960
Eco, 18614
Eco Expressions™, 21362
Eco Lamp, 21864
Eco Pure Aqua Straw, 21864
Eco Wrap, 31142
Eco-Bags, 22011
Eco-Dent, 7562
Eco-Serv, 29055
Ecoa, 19698, 29347
Ecocaps®, 1009
Ecofuel, 21864
Ecoguar, 9654
Ecolab®, 11504, 29095
Ecolo, 22015
Ecomega, 11269
Econ-O-Mizer, 30854
Econ-O-Totes, 28872
Econo Pourer, 19999
Econo Pro, 19763
Econo System, 27520
Econo-Beam, 19429
Econo-Board, 28910
Econo-Cover, 22097
Econo-Flash, 22025
Econo-Suds, 22025
Econo-Verter, 18498
Econocold, 28260
Econofil, 26482
Econoflo, 29513
Econofrost, 10344, 22018, 22020
Economarks, 22133
Economaster, 29632, 29633
Economix, 13498
Economy, 2384, 20816, 27238
Economy Pager, 26433
Econoseal, 22019
Econotech, 25597
Econowater, 28039
Ecopaxx®, 3320
Ecoset, 23708
Ecosnax, 498
Ecosoft, 13595, 31053
Ecoson, 3390
Ecoverde Coffee, 8090
Ecrevisse Acadienne, 11349
Ed & Don's Chocolate Macadamias, 3927
Ed & Don's Macadamia Brittles, 3927
Ed & Don's Macadamia Chews, 3927
Ed-Vance, 3948
Eda Sugarfree Hard Candies, 3934

Eda-Zenc, 5376
Edc, 26359
Eddie's, 4919, 6279
Eddie's Spaghetti Organic, 8642
Edelweiss Dressings, 4839
Eden, 3940, 8170, 25789
Eden Farms, 5910
Eden Life, 12486
Eden Organic, 3940
Eden's, 3941
Edenbalance, 3940
Edenblend, 3940
Edensoy, 3940
Edensoy Extra, 3940
Eder, 22650
Ederer, 27083
Edge, 23669
Edge City Ipa, 1720
Edge City Pilsner, 1720
Edge Lite, 20625
Edgeboard, 24032
Edgelite, 29746
Edgemold, 22035
Edgewood Estate, 3946
Edhard Injectors & Depositors, 22037
Edibowl, 3013
Edinburgh Gin, 4677
Editpro, 30361
Edlund, 22041
Edmund Fitzgerald Porter, 5314
Edna Foods, 3953
Edna Valley, 3952
Edna Valley Vineyard®, 3834
Eds, 3471
Edson, 22043
Edward&Sons, 3956
Edwards, 11025, 11316, 20290, 29202
Edwards®, 11317
Edy's, 3760
Eez-Out, 6261
Efa Balanced, 9477
Effen®, 1120
Efferve, 4148
Effervescent, 6449, 24506
Effi, 3851
Efficia, 30596
Efficient Frontiers, 22048
Eficacia, 9029, 26626
Efk, 18352
Efx Sports, 4150
Egg Beaters®, 2939, 2940, 20821, 20822
Egg King, 5062
Egg Low Farms, 3966
Egg Valet, 18127
Egg-Land's Best™, 2031
Egg-O-Lite, 1735
Eggland's Best, 3968
Eggo, 6766
Eggo®, 6765
Eggstreme Bakery Mix 100, 10297
Eggstreme Options, 10297
Eggstreme Yolk, 10297
Eggstreme-We 300, 10297
Egon Muller, 4677
Ehore, 22280
Eid, 22204
Eidelweiss, 773
Eight O'Clock, 3974
Ein Prosit!, 339
Ein Sight, 24212
Eisbock, 3171
Eisenberg, 6767
Eisenberg Beef Hot Dogs, 6773
Eisenberg Corned Bee, 6773
Eisenberg Pastrami, 6773
Eisenberg®, 5929
Eisrebe, 6603
Eiwa, 3852
Ejector, 19419
Ekato, 21908
Ekco, 31345
El Aguilia, 10555
El Almendro, 3490
El Carmen, 10319
El Cerdito, 690

El Charro, 3978
El Condor, 5405
El Conquistador, 4351
El Coto De Rioja, 4677
El Diablo®, 8415
El Dorado Coffee Roasters, 3997
El Ganador Del Premio, 12892
El Guapo, 8061
El Gusto, 4910
El Hombre Hambre, 12543
El Isleno, 4741
El Jimador, 1784, 3545
El Matador Tortilla Chip, 3981
El Mayor, 7655
El Mino, 28
El Monterey®, 10976
El Orgullo De Mi Tierra, 1909
El Panal, 13511
El Paso, 2574, 25789
El Pato, 13541
El Peto, 3987
El Ranchito, 10363
El Rancho, 7064
El Rancho Bean Chips, 7064
El Rancho Salsa Fresca, 7064
El Rancho Tortilla Chips, 7064
El Restaurante®, 27540
El Rey, 2617, 8539
El Sabroso, 11748
El Salvador Finca Las Nubes, 13160
El Sol, 8114
El Taino, 4351
El Tesoro De Don Felipe®, 1120
El Toro Loco, 357
El Toro Tequila, 11264
Elan, 1711, 20256
Elasthane™, 3320
Elastigel™ 1000j, 8804
Elavida™, 3320
Elberta, 22065
Elbicon, 19443
Eldorado, 3998, 31143
Eldorado Miranda, 22067
Eldorado Natural Spring Water, 3996
Eldorado Spring Water, 3996
Eleanor's Best, 3999
Electra, 10415
Electri-Fly, 22211
Electric & Pneumatic Op., 18793
Electric Aire, 31340
Electro Cam, 22482
Electro Freeze, 23458
Electroflo, 21617
Elegance, 26450
Elegant, 20256
Elegant Impressions, 20256
Elegant Sweets, 7756
Element Shrub, 12815
Elephant Brand, 11522, 29116
Elephant Ginger, 12987
Eletone®, 8389
Eleutherogen, 4827
Eleva-Truck, 23543
Elevair, 24720
Elevayor, 25819
Elf, 13454, 21911
Elfin, 23160
Eli's, 4010
Eli's Cheesecake Company, 20020
Eliane™, 8804
Eliason, 22097
Elijah Craig Bourbons, 5720
Eliminator, 25719
Eliot's Adult Nut Butters, 4011
Eliquis®, 1721
Elisir Mp Roux, 3165
Elissa Ipa, 11992
Elite, 4039, 11246, 24109
Elite Bakery, 7358
Elizabeth's, 859
Elk Run, 3837
Ella's Kitchen, 5505
Ella's Oven™, 4024
Ellie's Brown, 838
Ellis Davis, 757

Ellison, 4024
Ellison's, 4025
Ello Raw, 4027
Ellsworth, 4028
Ellsworth Valley, 4028
Ellyndale Foods®, 8725
Elmar, 22116
Elmasu, 11957
Elmeco, 13005
Elmer T. Lee, 11263
Elmhurst Milked, 4034
Elmo Rietschle, 23032
Elopouch, 22122
Elora Esb, 12919
Elora Grand Lager, 12919
Elora Irish Ale, 12919
Elro, 24038
Els, 27258
Elth, 23571
Eltron, 22769
Elvi Winery, 10952
Elwood, 4038
Elyon, 5123, 23203
Elysian Brewing, 571
Elysium, 10415
Elz Super Enzymes, 8967
Embasa®, 6000, 23861
Embassy, 4039, 26187
Embassy Wines, 4104
Ember-Glo, 18696
Emblem, 31127
Emblem & Badge, 22129
Embrace, 2761
Embrazen, 12937
Emdex, 11485
Emer'gen-C, 255
Emerald, 11770, 26450
Emerald Bay Coastak, 2459
Emerald Cove, 5306
Emerald Green, 932
Emerald Nuts, 3575
Emerald Sea, 11559
Emerald Valley Kitchen™, 10365
Emeril's®, 864
Emeril®, 6818, 24802
Emerils, 6819
Emerson, 22482
Emery, 22140
Emflo, 11485
Emflon, 27224
Emgum, 11485
Emile's, 5421
Emily Kestral Cabern, 12227
Emily's, 498
Emily's Gourmet, 3696
Eminence, 196
Emiollomiti, 22142
Emjel, 11485
Emkay, 4046
Emmy's Pickles & Jams, 14069
Emox, 11485
Empact, 4050
Emperor, 21864
Emperor's Kitchen, 5306
Empire, 9179
Empire Kosher, 5505
Empire Kosher Poultry Products, 4052
Empire's Best, 4054
Empliciti™, 1721
Empower, 437
Empress, 21864
Empress Chocolates, 4058
Emsland, 466
Emulsiflex, 19255
Emulso, 22152
Enak, 6340
Encircac, 10078, 27547
Encirclec, 187
Encore, 20800, 21709, 22599
End Smoke, 29826
Endangered Species Chocolate Bars, 4060
Enderma, 9997
Endglow, 29794
Endico, 11108

1291

All Brands Index

Endless Summer Gold, 6711
Endorphin, 4895
Endpacker, 20788
Ends and Curls, 9432
Endurance, 27881, 29520
Endure, 6843
Enduro, 29137
Enduro-Flo, 28936
Enduro-Roll, 28936
Ener Jet, 5682
Ener-G, 4062
Energique®, 4065
Energy Bars, 7419
Energy Brand, 1294
Energy Chews, 1559
Energy Dynamics, 29202
Energy Ice, 10953
Energy Miser, 19419
Energy Mizer, 20662
Energy Powder, 131
Energy Supplements, 5155
Energy-To-Go, 12259
Energyfruits, 6751
Energymaster, 22166
Energysmart®, 190, 18410
Energysource®, 190, 18410
Enerjuice, 7210
Enfagrow®, 8103
Enfakid®, 8103
Enfamil, 24672
Enfamil™, 8103
Enfapro A+®, 8103
Enfield Farms, 4068
Englass, 28396
English Batter, 4070
English Guard ®, 13120
English Pale Ale, 556, 11218
English Toffee, 9055
Engravable Gifts, 20353
Enhance To Go, 3753, 21763
Enhance Vitamin/Waters, 12704
Enhancer, 29513
Enjoying Las Vegas, 5660
Enjoying San Francisco, 5660
Enjoymints, 6926
Ennis®, 22187
Enoferm, 7176
Enrico's, 13326
Enroute, 4258
Enstrom Candies, 4079
Ensuite, 21425
Ensure Quality Check System, 23971
Entech Fog, 22195
Entemanns, 892
Entenmann's®, 1359
Enter Clean, 19151
Entericare®, 1009
Enterprise, 4081
Enting, 22203
Entree, 1006
Entry Gard, 30325
Entry Pro, 19763
Entwine, 13654
Enviro-Board, 25557
Enviro-Clear, 22206
Enviro-Cool, 20710
Enviro-Logs, 26353
Enviro-Therm, 20710
Enviro-Ware, 22210
Enviroclean Gold, 20606
Envirocon, 19666
Enviroflight, 3390
Enviroguard, 23450
Envirokidz Organic, 8889
Envirolert, 30106
Enviromax Enclosures, 23722
Environair, 20297
Environments, 2772
Enviropal/Recy, 25277
Enviroplas, 26428
Envirotex, 30656
Enviro~Chem, 20682
Enviro~Chem Gold, 20682
Enzact, 3548
Enzeco®, 4087

Enzo, 9636
Enzo Organic Balsamic Vinegar, 4085
Enzo Organic Olive Oil, 4085
Enzo's Table, 4085
Enzose, 6211, 24226
Eola, 1202
Eos, 3857
Epi, 7254
Epi De France, 4091
Epi-Guide®, 3320
Epic, 12239, 12437, 20777
Epicure, 6358
Epro, 21044
Epsoakc, 11145
Equacia, 9029, 26626
Equacookor, 21811
Equal, 8173, 9236
Equalizer, 25633, 30502
Equipment Company of America, 29347
Equire, 6586
Era, 12721, 30193, 31041
Eragrainc, 4102
Eramosa Honey Wheat, 12136
Erectomatic, 27405
Erewhon, 13124, 19178
Ergo, 21031, 21213
Ergo-Matic, 25302
Ergo-One, 25094
Ergoscoop, 27863
Eribate, 9656
Eric Condren, 10229
Erica's Rugelach, 4105
Erick Schat, 11279
Erickson, 22248
Erie, 4107, 22251
Erin's Rock Amber and Stout, 2410
Erin's®, 2939, 2940, 20821, 20822, 27540
Erjuv-Powder, 5883
Ermitage, 11894, 29459
Ers Sorter, 22254
Erucical, 716, 19094
Esa, 22204
Esb, 10629
Esband, 19852
Escalera, 26557
Escarcoque, 10039
Escort, 18689
Esd, 21908
Ese, 22902
Eskimo Pie, 20946
Eskimo Pie Coffeepeaks, 11028
Eskimo Pie Miniatures, 11028
Eskimo Pie Snowpeaks, 11028
Esmena, 24317
Espeez, 11051
Esper Deluxe, 4115
Esperto, 8452
Espre, 11816, 29373
Espre-Cart, 11816, 29373
Espre-Matic, 11816, 29373
Espress-Umms, 9185
Espressimo, 23420
Espresso, 1997
Espresso Blend, 6611
Espresso Caruso, 11855
Espresso Gold, 7566
Espresso Maria, 11855
Esprion, 4736
Espuma, 24026
Essaic Formula, 131
Essen Smart Gluten Free, 4208
Essen Smart Single Cookie 2, 4208
Essen Smart Single Cookie 3, 4208
Essen Smart Soy Cookies, 4208
Essence, 23160
Essensia, 10415
Essential, 491, 7173
Essential 10, 3540
Essential Balance, 9477
Essential Elite, 12486
Essential Mints, 13458
Essentials, 8130
Essette Meto, 22271
Essiac (Extract), 4126

Essiac (Powder), 4126
Estancia, 4649
Estate Cabernet Sauvignon, 4980, 7003
Estate Chardonnay, 7003
Estate Grown Olive Oil, 6603
Estate Merlot, 4980, 7003
Estate Syrah, 7003
Estate Viognier, 7003
Estate Zinfandel (Ce, 7003
Estee Lauder, 27209
Esteem Plus, 4127
Ester-C®, 8871
Esterlina, 4128
Estracell, 19053
Estrelitas®, 8945
Estrella, 1738
Estrella Jalisco, 571
Estro Da-Line, 28749
Estro Logic, 13536
Estroven, 6107
Et-2a, 26968
Et-2s, 26968
Etch-A-Sketch, 2136
Ethan's, 4132
Ethel M®, 7952
Ethel's Baking, 4134
Ethical Nutrients, 8193
Ethiopian Moka, 10157
Ethiopian Organic, 13160
Ethnic Delights, 12167
Ethnic Edibles, 4137
Ethos Water, 12042
Etm, 18181
Etmw, 18181
Etna Ale, 4139
Etna Bock, 4139
Etna Doppelbock, 4139
Etna Oktoberfest, 4139
Etna Weizen, 4139
Eton Dumplings, 29396
Etopophos®, 1721
Etr, 26861
Etude, 12937
Eugalan, 1369
Eukanuba, 726
Eukanuba®, 7952
Eureka, 6586, 7160, 22285
Eureka!®, 1359
Euro, 31092
Euro Chocolate, 4145
Euro-Menu, 30713
Eurobubblies, 4148
Eurocode, 26942
Euroflex, 28357
Eurofresh, 7871
European Bakers, 4529
European Gourmet Bakery, 6049
European Monofilaments, 29148
European Select, 30860
Eurostar, 24074
Eurosupreme, 4148
Evactor, 21091
Evan Williams Bourbons, 5720
Evangeline, 2019
Evans, 12972
Eve's Organic Cocoa, 22560
Evelyn Sprague, 6868
Eventmaster, 20344
Ever Clean, 2766, 20657
Evercheck, 23868
Everclear, 7655
Evercrisp®, 1196
Everfilt, 22313
Everfresh, 56, 4163, 8784, 10038, 28957
Everglades, 4165
Everglades Heat, 4165
Everglades Original, 4165
Evergood, 7650, 11728
Evergreen, 7758
Everland, 4170
Everwear, 24503
Every Occasion, 21058
Everybody's Nuts, 13907
Everyday Chef, 12973, 30444
Everything But The..., 2525

Evian, 1661
Evian Connoisseur, 19192
Evian®, 6818, 24802
Evil Twin, 10666
Evo, 2085, 4453
Evo Coffee, 2845
Evo Hemp, 4174
Evol®, 2939, 2940, 20821, 20822, 27540
Evoluna Estate, 12672
Evolution, 11780
Evolution Fresh, 4176, 12042
Evolve™, 6000, 23861
Evon's, 12866
Evonik, 1692
Evotaz®, 1721
Ewa, 9691
Eward Marc Chocolatier, 3958
Ews, 22088
Ex-Cell, 22320
Ex-Seed, 9332
Exact, 10637
Exact Series, 22659
Exact Weight, 22322
Exacta-Flo, 28936
Exacto-Pour, 19998
Exacto-Pour Tester, 19999
Excalibur, 5061, 27799, 30775, 31184
Excel, 6762, 30775, 30841
Exceldor Express, 4183
Excelibur, 20256
Excelle, 6240
Excellency, 18906
Excelon, 25224
Excelpro™, 4119
Excelpro™ Plus, 4119
Except Mix, 11888
Excoriator, 29491
Execuchef Pro, 22337
Executive, 21059
Exhausto, 22342
Exo, 4186
Exocyan, 9029, 26626
Exotica, 12053
Exotico, 7655
Expedition, 3746
Expeller, 18920
Expert Line, 20632
Explore Cuisine, 4187
Expoaire, 22348
Expoframe, 22348
Exporsevilla, 218
Export Lager, 4139
Express, 19634, 24280
Express Delights, 2726
Express Load, 4515
Express Mark, 27805
Expressions, 20256
Expressions®, 21362
Expressnacks, 13923
Expresso, 7655, 24925
Expresspak, 28519
Exquisita, 4189
Exquizita, 4769, 22896
Extend-A-Brush, 26165
Extend®, 13328
Extensograph, 20019
Extinguisher, 469
Extol, 137
Extra Energy, 9201
Extra Gold Lager, 8459
Extra Gold Lager®, 8460
Extra Strength Pickle Juice Shots, 12716
Extra Value, 1658
Extra®, 7952, 13960
Extreme, 3953
Extreme Duty, 25094
Extreme®, 8945
Extremultus, 22755, 26001
Extructor, 19576
Exxtra-C™, 6449, 24506
Ey, 27236
Eye of the Dragon, 11051
Eye of the Hawk, 8153
Eye of the Hawk Select Ale, 8153
Eye-Flex, 31278

All Brands Index

Ez, 9049
Ez Baker, 22935
Ez Bander, 31142
Ez Flo, 24332
Ez Flow, 26214
Ez Loader, 19698
Ez Pack, 18416
Ez Splitter Ii, 26521
Ez Table, 28368
Ez View, 22473
Ez-Beam, 19429
Ez-Bulk, 27265
Ez-Flow, 27265
Ez-Just, 22618
Ez-Lock, 20192
Ez-Lok, 19629
Ez-One, 26458
Ez-Pak, 27265
Ez-Pallet, 27265
Ez-Reach, 20192
Ez-Screen, 19429
Eze-Gloss, 25549
Eze-Therm, 25549
Ezekiel 4:9c, 8831
Ezra Brooks, 7655
Ezy Time, 1444, 19726
Ezy-Way, 19998
Ezy-Way Pourer, 19999

F

F and M Special Draft, 12136
F Domin and Sons, 2559
F&A, 4195
F&V™, 8899
F. Ramond, 22844
F.E.I., Inc., 25918
F.E.S., 28967
F.G. Wilson, 29202
F.R.P., 30388
F1-1 Soy Fibre, 4357
Fa!Rlife, 2814
Fabian International, 30603
Fablene, 22425
Fablon, 22425
Fabreeka, 22425
Fabri-Frame, 18827
Fabri-Kal Corporation, 18029
Fabrianoc, 2010
Fabricork, 20595
Fabsyn, 22425
Fabulene, 22096
Fabuless®, 3320
Fabuloso, 20721, 24414
Fabulous Fiber, 7404
Face Twisters Sour Bubble Gum, 4793
Facets, 25665
Facies, 56
Facino, 10565
Facom, 29584
Factorytalk, 28472
Facts Finder, 26109
Faema, 8619, 19952
Failsafe Guardswitch, 22960
Fair Acres, 9839
Fair Meadow, 11504, 29095
Fairbury, 13689
Fairchild, 22445
Fairfield Farm, 4222
Fairlee, 56
Fairtime, 163
Fairview Swiss Cheese, 6557
Fairway, 1064, 12550
Fairwinds Coffee, 4229
Fairy Food, 1828
Fajita Trivet, 27428
Falafel Dry Mix, 12536
Falco, 22447
Falcon, 4232, 20777
Falcon Business Forms®, 22187
Falcon Orange Soda, 5539
Falcon Pale, 10810
Falcone's, 4233
Falcone's Baked Goods, 4233
Falcone's Cookies, 4233

Falcone's Flatbread, 4233
Falfurrias, 6760
Falk, 28357
Falk Salt, 2879
Fall Creek, 5282
Fall River, 2082, 4235
Fall'n Go, 20256
Fallingwater, 21213
Falstaff, 9664
Family Farmer, 2347
Family Favorite, 386
Family Heritage, 19590
Family Traditions, 1553
Famli, 4537
Famosa, 8457
Famous, 4243
Famous Amos, 6766
Famous Original Formula Staminex, 7404
Fan-C-Fry, 22899
Fan-Sea, 11198
Fancy, 21246
Fancy Brand, 1801
Fancy Dinner Blend, 9182
Fancy Farm, 4245
Fancy Foods, 4244
Fancy Lawnmower, 11992
Fancy Lebanese Bakery, 4246
Fancy Pantry, 12377
Fancy's Finest, 4244
Fanestil, 4249
Fanjet, 26360
Fanny Farmer, 4250
Fanny May Fine Chocolates, 4250
Fanta, 2811, 2814, 2815, 9155, 20685
Fanta Still, 2815, 20685
Fanta Zero, 2815, 20685
Fantaisie, 4544
Fantasia, 721, 4244
Fantastic, 4252
Fantastic Foods, 2286
Fantastic World Foods®, 1484
Fantasy Wrap, 21131
Faqs, 10568
Far Niente, 4258
Far West Meats, 4259
Faraday, 22462
Farallon Foods, 4261
Faraon, 8161
Farberware, 20957, 31345
Farbest, 4263
Farbest Foods, 4262
Farina Mills, 10213, 13124
Farinograph, 20019
Farm Country, 3695
Farm Fed Veal, 779
Farm Fresh, 2789
Farm Pac, 14008
Farm Pantry®, 1654
Farm Rich, 10714
Farman's®, 1103
Farmer Brothers, 340, 4276
Farmer Dons Country Ham, 12761
Farmer Focus, 11467
Farmer Girl, 5555
Farmer Jack, 13871
Farmer John, 2776, 11733
Farmer John Meats, 2776
Farmer King, 13625
Farmer Seed, 10050
Farmer's Almanac, 23087
Farmer's Cheese, 7423
Farmers, 4279, 11625
Farmers Favorite, 13613
Farmers Hen House, 4278
Farmers Ice Cream, 2377
Farmers Market, 4242, 22458
Farmers Pride Natural, 1178
Farmers Way, 4286
Farmhouse, 4386
Farmhouse Biscuits, 30415
Farmhouse Culture, 4288
Farmhouse Originals Ceasar, 5489
Farmhouse Originals®, 6374, 24434
Farmhouse Saison, 1401

Farmhouse™, 2031
Farmland, 1891, 11733
Farmland Dairies, 4290
Farmland Dairies Special Request, 4290
Farmland Dairy, 13647
Farmland Foods, 20020
Farr, 722
Farrell Baking, 4298
Fas-9001, 20048
Fashion Fluorescent, 29242
Fashionglo, 24950
Fashnpoint®, 23811
Fasline, 27799
Fasson, 23882
Fast, 18985
Fast Asleep, 9201
Fast Eddy's, 2991, 20941
Fast Fixin'®, 184, 13109
Fast Kill, 20591
Fast Lane 2000, 23859
Fast'n Easy, 25165
Fast-Fold, 28626
Fast-Seal, 28626
Fast/Bak, 24010
Fastachi, 4301
Faster Freezer, 22112
Fastfilter, 28668
Fastimer, 28668
Fastpak, 28668
Fastraction, 31251
Fastron, 28668
Fastseal, 29081
Fasweet, 4302
Fat Boy, 2294
Fat Dog Stout, 12153
Fat Free®, 5165
Fat Mizer, 29795
Fat Snax, 4303
Fat Tea, 4303
Fat Tire, 8959
Fatal Attraction, 4804
Father & Son, 8781
Father Sam's Pocket Breads, 4306
Father Sam's Tortillas, 4306
Father Sam's Wraps, 4306
Fatima, 14037
Fatina-Murano, 10565
Fattoria Dell'ulivo, 4386
Fattoria Italia, 10565
Fatworks, 4310
Faultless, 19908, 20143
Favorit Swiss Premium, 1957
Favorites, 9722
Favorites of Hawaii, 5660
Fawen, 4312
Fay-Vo-Rite, 22484
Faygo, 8784
Fazio's, 4316, 6535
Fc-950, 19213
Fc-Pack, 20710
Fch, 7874
Fda Steel Container, 20875
Fdc, 20707
Feast of Eden, 20144
Feaster Foods, 13689
Featherweight, 12241
Febreeze, 12721, 30193
Fec, 19935
Federal Industries, 29580
Federal Pretzel, 4318
Federal Pretzel Baking Company, 6338
Fee Brothers, 4320
Felbro, 4324
Felchlin-Swiss, 12438
Feldmeier, 22502
Feline Pine, 2666, 20561
Felix Roma, 4326
Felta Springs, 8301
Fendall's, 4328
Fenestra Winery, 4329
Fenopure, 9654
Fentinel, 9238
Fenton Art Glass, 22512
Fenulife, 137
Feridies, 4335

Ferlac, 7172
Fermaid, 491, 7173, 7176
Fermalife, 4336
Fernandes, 2815, 20685
Fernqvist Prodigy Max, 22516
Ferolito Vultaggio, 4342
Ferolito, Vultaggio & Sons, 670
Ferralet®, 8389
Ferrante, 4343
Ferrara, 4346, 6540
Ferrara Candy Co., 2132
Ferrell-Ross, 18035, 22518
Ferrigno, 4349
Ferris, 4351
Ferrofilt, 23927
Ferroquest, 28731
Ferrosand, 23927
Ferry-Morsec, 10106
Festal, 7161
Festejos, 4483
Festino, 2260
Festival, 1688
Festival Light Ale, 7143
Festival Traus, 20256
Festy, 122
Fetzer, 22525
Fever Sours, 1735
Ff, 4374
Ffc, 29617
Fiamma, 21213
Fib-R-Dor, 22393
Fiber, 7947
Fiber 7, 8719
Fiber Greens, 9516
Fiber One, 5103
Fiber One®, 4947
Fiber Plus, 6766
Fiber Supreme, 8719
Fiber Up®, 9736
Fiber-7, 7947
Fiber-Pul, 22535
Fiberbond, 6211, 24226
Fibercare 5000, 27982
Fibergrate, 22528
Fiberpoptics, 30259
Fiberpro, 22526
Fibersol 2, 18125
Fibersol® Capsules, 13097
Fibrament Baking Stone, 19265
Fibreen Economy, 22780
Fibregum, 9029, 26626
Fibrex, 11794
Fibrim, 3773, 21785
Fibrymid, 3550
Ficks, 4359
Fico, 22535
Fida, 10565
Fiddle Cakes, 4362
Fiddle Faddle, 3430
Fiddle Faddle®, 2939, 2940, 20821, 20822
Fiddlers, 4032
Fiddlers Green Farms, 4362
Fidelio, 26953
Fiebing, 22538
Field, 11902
Field Day®, 1484
Field Roast, 4364
Field Trip, 4366
Field's, 4367
Fieldgate, 4424
Fieldstone Bakery, 8077
Fieldstone™ Bakery, 8076
Fiery Fingers®, 1654
Fiery Rum Cellars, 9334
Fiesta, 1279, 1547, 7746, 8919, 11001, 12241, 23842
Fiesta Del Sol, 4375
Fiesta Del Sole, 4373
Fiesta Juan's, 9565
Fiesta Rice, 12396
Fifth Leg, 12937
Fig & Olive Tapenade, 6522
Fig Food Co., 4378
Figaro, 1087, 4381

1293

All Brands Index

Fighting Cock, 6796
Fighting Cock Bourbon, 5720
Figuerola, 4383
Figure-Maid, 1882
Fiji, 4384
Fiji Water ®, 5884
Filamatic, 26482
Filet of Chicken®, 6025
Filippo Berio, 4386
Filippo Berio Extra Virgin, 4386
Filippo Berio Green, 4386
Filippo Berio 'Olive, 4386
Fillit, 22545
Fillkit, 22545
Fillo Factory, 4388
Film-Gard, 20257
Filt Pro 5000, 22679
Filte-Veyor®, 29854
Filter-Master, 29016
Filter-Max, 31312
Filtration Equipment, 24357
Filtrete, 18003
Filtrine, 22558
Filz-All, 24669
Final, 19544
Final Bite!, 19364
Finalist, 26359
Finast, 570
Finback Brewery, 10666
Finchville Farms, 10801
Finding Home Farms, 4391
Fine, 21246
Fine Coat®, 2332
Fine Mints, 10689
Fine Pak, 21228
Fine Spun, 1061
Fine Vines, 4396
Fine-Mix Dairy, 2764, 20656
Fine-Stik, 26109
Fineline, 26662
Finemix, 13498
Finesse, 19928
Finest Call, 439, 4401
Finest Honey Organic, 300
Finest Honey Selection, 300
Finger Lakes, 5057
Fingerlakes Wine Cellars, 6083
Finish®, 10598
Finlandia, 1784
Finlandia Frost, 1784
Finlandia Lappi, 4405
Finlandia Naturals, 4405
Finlandia Swiss, 4405
Finlay, 9155
Finley, 2815, 20685
Finncrisp, 25789
Finney, 21883
Finocchiona, 9635
Fiori-Bruna, 4410
Fioriware, 22568
Fiorucci, 4411
Fire Braised Meats®, 6000, 23861
Fire Cider, 11563
Fire Jack, 12437
Fire Marshall's Cajun, 8291
Fire Nugget, 3393
Fireball Fat Burner, 5682
Firebreak, 11494
Firefly, 11263
Fireguard, 23116
Firehouse, 13141
Firemixer, 28845
Firenza, 5328
Firenzec, 2010
Firepower, 30768
Fireside, 6267
Fireside Kitchen, 4417
Firestone Walker Brewery™, 26668
Firesystem 2000, 27909
Firetest, 25773
Fireye, 20290
Firm-Tex®, 8804
Firmenich, 9687, 27096
Firmware, 23809
First Choice, 26799

First Colony, 4422
First Crush, 1688
First Line, 20808
First Pick, 13582
First Response, 2666, 20561
First Roasters of Central Florida, 4429
First Tec, 13697
Firstland, 27236
Fis-Chic Wonder Batter, 3769
Fischbein, 22581
Fischbein Bag Closing, 18877
Fischer & Wieser, 4432
Fischer's, 4433, 11902
Fish Brothers, 4436
Fish Crunchies, 2418
Fish House, 8028
Fisher, 6548
Fisher Boy®, 5844
Fisher Honey, 4443
Fisher Scientific, 30217
Fisher Scones, 2950
Fisherman's Pride, 10974
Fisherman's Reef, 4448
Fisherman's Wharf, 9042, 13864
Fishermans Rees, 13993
Fishhawk, 4450
Fishin' Chips, 9197
Fishka, 10039
Fishmarket Seafoods, 4441
Fiske, 18411
Fiske Associates, 18411
Fitmark, 4150
Fitness First, 5483
Fitness®, 8945
Fitpro Go, 4453
Fits All, 26109
Fitz-All, 30337
Fitzmill, 22594
Fitzpatrick, 4455
Fitzpatrick Bros, 9440
Five Farms Irish Cream, 8062
Five Forces of Nature, 5883
Five Leaf, 3229
Five Roses, 6380
Five Star Bars, 7148
Fix, 1702
Fix Dmacs, 24743
Fix Quix, 2212
Fix-A-Form, 26324
Fixodent, 12721, 30193
Fizz Wiz, 2947
Fizzle Flat Farm, 4463
Fjord Fresh, 9106
Fla-Vor-Ice®, 6483
Flagmaster, 28416
Flagship Shiraz, 13701
Flagship Zinfandel, 13701
Flagstone Foods, 12943, 30400
Flakice, 22602
Flam Winery, 10952
Flambe Holiday, 12895
Flamboise, 2737
Flame Gard, 22604
Flame Gard Iii, 22604
Flame Roasted Vegetables, 8724
Flameguard, 27329
Flamigni, 3381
Flamingo, 8219, 9462
Flamingo Pepper, 12987
Flamm's, 4469
Flapjacked, 4473
Flapper, 26264
Flash, 23950, 28952
Flash Link, 21524, 21527
Flashblend, 29239
Flashgril'd, 80
Flaskscrubber, 25041
Flat, 4207
Flat Bed Red, 13049
Flat Oven, 13691
Flat Seat, 25819
Flat Top, 23082
Flat Wire, 19111
Flat Wood Farm, 10283
Flat-Flex, 31278

Flat-Flex El, 31278
Flat-Flex Xt, 31278
Flatboat, 11263
Flathead Lake Monster Gourmet Soda, 22028
Flatlite, 21878
Flatout, 7189, 12467, 25120
Flatout Flatbread, 7987
Flattop, 22140
Flatzza, 563
Flav'r Top, 4008
Flav-A-Brrew, 30337
Flav-R-Fresh, 23652
Flav-R-Grain, 10422
Flav-R-Pac, 8724
Flav-R-Savor, 23652
Flavolin, 4430
Flavor, 5027, 23188
Flavor 86, 4430
Flavor Aid, 6483
Flavor Burst Liquid Citrus Tea, 5460
Flavor Burst Liquid Sweet Tea, 5460
Flavor Burst Liquid Unsweet Tea, 5460
Flavor Charm, 1103
Flavor Classics, 22612
Flavor Crunch, 13742
Flavor Depot, 2223, 20269
Flavor Farmer, 6880
Flavor Fresh, 3574
Flavor House, 13200
Flavor King Blue, 2796, 20666
Flavor King Red, 2796, 20666
Flavor Lock, 26031
Flavor Magic, 7765
Flavor of Central America®, 12996
Flavor of Mexico®, 12996
Flavor of South America®, 12996
Flavor of the Rainforest, 13892
Flavor Originals, 8729
Flavor Pack, 2126
Flavor Roux, 20050
Flavor Safari, 4242, 22458
Flavor Touch, 22612
Flavor Trim, 22612
Flavor Wear, 22612
Flavor Weave, 22612
Flavor-Ettes, 10422
Flavor-Glow, 3441
Flavor-Lites, 10422
Flavor-Mate, 6806
Flavorbank, 4487
Flavorburst, 5460
Flavorganics, 4489
Flavority, 12300
Flavorland, 8999
Flavors of the Heartland, 4494
Flavortight, 8104
Flavour Sensations, 10797, 28438
Flavourcrisp®, 2332
Flavoured Milk, 2377
Flavourzyme, 1692
Flaw Finder, 18768
Flax Country, 11517
Flax N' Honey, 8844
Flb, 4246
Fleet Mark, 28285
Fleetwood, 24623, 28725
Fleischann's, 4499
Fleischer's, 4498
Fleischmann's, 11264
Fleischmann's Baking Powder, 2711
Fleischmann's Yeast, 4500
Fleischmann's®, 2939, 2940, 20821, 20822
Flero Star, 18527
Fletcher's, 4501, 11776
Fletchers, 5391
Fleur De Carneros, 2225
Fleur De Mer®, 3834
Fleurette, 10039
Flex - All, 20256
Flex Able, 6107
Flex Bag, 21186
Flex Net, 26440
Flex Off, 29797

Flex-A-Top, 29119
Flex-Feed, 30118
Flex-Flo, 21932
Flex-Grip, 29283
Flex-Holder, 27575
Flex-Hone, 19913
Flex-Packer, 31435
Flex-Turn, 31278
Flexbarrier, 21133
Flexco, 22627
Flexfilm, 29081
Flexform, 28493
Flexi-1850, 22633
Flexi-Cell, 22633
Flexi-Guide, 21857
Flexidoor, 23860
Flexilinear, 22633
Flexiloader, 22633
Flexipan, 21533
Flexitainer, 18241
Flexlink, 19220
Flexodisc, 21092
Flexoleed, 21092
Flexonite, 23543
Flexprint, 19546
Flexrite, 28763
Flexshape, 22621
Flexspout, 28396
Flexsteel Contract, 21561
Flexstrap, 22503
Flexstyle®, 21362
Flexwrap, 31435
Flexx Flow, 25491
Flexzorber, 22624
Fling Decorating Kits, 27285
Flintrol, 22211
Flip & Grip, 23143
Flip It, 5331
Flip-N-Fresh, 23499
Flip-Pod, 20305
Flipper the Robocook, 18288
Flipsticks, 7643, 13574
Flipsticks®, 13572
Flix, 29520
Flo-Cold, 22643
Flo-Fil, 23857
Flo-Gard, 1692, 30773
Flo-King, 28396
Flo-Pak, 22845
Flo-Pak Bio 8, 22845
Flo-Rite, 28396
Flo-Thru, 20011
Floam ®, 11794
Floating Leaf, 4508
Floclean, 19722
Flodi Pesca, 8028
Flodin, 22646
Flofreeze, 22873
Flomatic, 22648, 29042
Floor Level, 26606
Floor Magic, 30639
Floor Suds, 18387
Floorite, 30639
Floorsaver, 24456
Flor-Essence, 4509
Flora, 4509, 13168
Flora Grow, 665
Flora-Balance, 9287
Florafree, 21425
Floraglo, 6777
Floraglo® Lutein, 3320
Floraglow, 5475
Floralpro, 18375
Florased Valerian, 13015
Florecitas, 1581
Florentine, 18906
Floresta®, 10899
Floria Julep, 6638, 24643
Florida Crystals, 3666, 4517
Florida Food Products, 4518
Florida Key Lime Pie, 2484
Florida Key West, 4520
Florida Old Reserve, 4515
Florida Pik't, 4714
Florida Straits Rum Runner, 4650

1294

All Brands Index

Florida's Gold Cocktail, 4650
Florida's Natural, 4523
Florida's Natural®, 11504, 29095
Florida's Own, 13184
Florida's Pride, 4650
Florigold, 11381
Florina, 6986
Florio, 1006
Flosite, 23672
Flotta, 2065
Floturn, 27924
Flour, 11462
Flour Brands, 955
Flour Fine, 13498
Flow Lite®, 342
Flow Max, 29618
Flow-Flexer, 22634
Floware, 30232
Flowdata, Inc., 20837
Flower Crystals, 4718
Flowery Jasmine-Before the Rain, 5228, 23295
Flowing Gold, 13613
Flowing Wells, 11844
Flowing Wells Natural Water, 11844
Flowpak, 28525
Fluff Out, 25725
Fluffy Stuff, 2132
Fluffy Stuff®, 12880
Fluid, 21908
Fluid Dryer, 26893
Fluidflex, 19654
Fluidized, 27354
Fluidpro, 19262
Fluorodyne, 27224
Fluorophos Test System, 18411
Fluoroshield-Magna, 29046
Flushield™, 6449, 24506
Fly Eaters, 19364
Fly Jinx, 20591
Fly Ribbons, 19364
Flying Saucer, 6880
Flystop, 19597
Fmc, 27709
Fme Flakers, 28922
Fmi, 22664
Fnd-30, 28396
Foam Pac, 27679
Foamatic, 24170
Foamation, 3536
Foamglas, 27557
Foaming Coil, 23039
Foamkill, 21123
Foch, 1672
Focus Foodservice, 4538
Focus Foodservice Bakeware, 4538
Focus Plus, 29185
Fody, 4209
Fog Mountain, 1543, 12672
Fogcutter Double Ipa, 7554
Fogdog, 6603
Fogel, 22677, 24623
Fogg-It, 20121
Foggy Bottom Ale, 9437
Foggy Bottom Lager, 9437
Foggy Bottom Porter, 9437
Foiled Chocolate, 13277
Foiltex, 21564
Fold Flat, 21864
Fold Pak Company, 18029
Folder Express®, 22187
Foley Brothers Brewing, 10666
Folger's Filter Pack, 4543
Folger's Flavor, 4543
Folger's Instant, 4543
Folger's Simply Smooth, 4543
Folgers, 6380, 8090
Folie a Deux, 4544
Folklore, 4545
Folklore Cream Soda, 4545
Folklore Gourmet Syrups, 4545
Folklore Sasaparilla, 4545
Folklore Sparkling Beverages, 4545
Follow Your Heart, 3870
Fomaco, 28291

Fomz™, 12239
Fonda, 23809
Fonda Blanca, 7655
Fontanini®, 6000, 23861
Fonterutoli, 13811
Fontina Cheese, 13700, 31165
Food and Wine, 1034
Food and Wine Mustards, 1034
Food Blends, 2764, 20656
Food Care, 23571
Food Carriers, 30207
Food Chute, 19940
Food Club, 6126, 11331
Food Club®, 12885, 30333
Food Concentrate Corp., 4556
Food For Life, 4570
Food Furniture, 28893
Food Grade, 29690
Food Mill, 4564
Food Pac, 13241
Food Pak, 6971
Food Reserves, 5159
Food Service Management Systems, 20686
Food Should Taste Good, 11711
Food Should Taste Good®, 4947
Food Source®, 9237, 26785
Food System 4 Windows, 30622
Food Tone, 4324
Food Trend, 13241
Food-Trak, 29953
Food4less, 12516
Foodart By Francesco, 22483
Foodbank, 26662
Foodhandler, 24395
Foodies, 4459
Foods From the Sea, 12062
Foodservice Suite, 20028
Foodstirs, 4576
Fool Proof Gourmet, 4577
Fools Gold Ale, 8952
Footguard, 27329
Foothill Farms®, 6792, 24785
Foppiano, 4579, 9500
For Kid's Only, 21059
For Pet's Sake, 12182
Forager Project, 4581
Foray, 30516
Forberg Ii, 27354
Forbidden Fruit, 4253
Forbidden Rice, 7563
Ford Logan Wire, 29437
Ford's Foods, 4587
Fordham, 26668
Foremost®, 388
Forest Center, 10027, 27510
Forest Country, 7869
Forestville, 1738
Foret Noire, 5405
Forge Mountain, 4593
Forklevator, 23559
Forma, 21213
Formflex, 22766
Formica, 25935
Formnumatic, 28904
Formosa Draft, 1702
Formosa Oolong Champagne of Tea, 5228, 23295
Formost Farms Usa, 4591
Forms Manufacturers™, 22187
Formsprag Clutch, 18678
Formul8, 28800
Formula, 22768
Formula 18, 13613
Fornap, 23160
Forster, 24517
Fort Howard, 23160
Fort Pitt, 4732
Forte, 22778, 28493
Fortify, 8896
Fortii®, 3320
Fortitech® Premixes, 3320
Forto, 4608
Forto®, 6818, 24802
Fortress, 5767

Fortress Technology, 18291
Fortune, 6409
Fortune Bubble, 10496
Fortune Macaroni, 8642
Fortune's Catch, 4613
Fortunes, 4614
Forza, 572
Foss, 11294
Fossen Smoked Salmon, 9771
Foster, 24038, 27063
Foster Farms Always Natural, 4621, 22788
Foster Farms Fresh & Natural, 4621, 22788
Foster Farms Naturally Seasoned, 4621, 22788
Foster Farms Organic, 4621, 22788
Foster Farms Saut, Ready, 4621, 22788
Foster Farms Simply Raised, 4621, 22788
Foster's, 2908
Foster's®, 8460
Fosters, 22791
Fountain Court, 4649
Fountain Grove, 7967
Fountain Shake, 4622
Fountainside, 19791
Four Aces, 29671
Four Horsemen, 8374
Four Peaks Brewing Co., 571
Four Roses, 11839
Four Seasons, 20186
Four Sigmatic, 4628
Four Star, 4243
Four Star Beef®, 6391
Fourn,E, 13691
Fox, 5465
Fox Barrell Hard Cider®, 26668
Fox Brook, 10416
Fox Hollow Farm Mustard, 4635
Fox Mountain, 4579, 9500
Fox N Hare, 4639
Fox Run, 4640
Fox's U-Bet, 5465
Fox-More Than a Mustard, 4635
Foxhollow, 1738
Foxjet, 22807
Foxtail, 4644
Foxware Dc Label, 21276
Foxware Dc Manager, 21276
Foxware Edi Manager, 21276
Foxware Rf Manager, 21276
Foxy, 9219
Foxy Lady, 6083
Foxy Salads, 9220
Foy's B.B.Q. Sauce, 3292
Fpc, 27258
Fpec, 22408
Fpi ® Brand, 5844
Frac-Packs, 4152
Fractolak, 9802
Fractured Fortunes, 5160
Fragata, 7931
Fralinger's, 4645
Frameworks, 20593
Fran's Healthy Helpings, 4647
Francesco Rinaldi, 7408, 8898
Francesconi, 4386
Franciscan Oakville Estate, 4649
Franciscan Well, 8459
Francisco's, 11224
Franco's, 280
Franco's Margarita Salt Sombrero, 4650
Frangelico, 4422
Frangelico Liqueur, 13811
Frank & Dean's Cocktail Mixes, 4651
Frank & Teressa's Original Anchor, 13935
Frank & Teressa's Wing Sauce, 13935
Frank's Kraut, 4694
Frank's Redhot, 8061
Frankel's Homestyle, 1251
Frankford, 4659
Frankford Candy, 2132
Frankies, 13183
Franklin Crunch 'n' Munch, 6267

Franklin Street, 2236
Franklinware, 19928
Frankly Natural3, 4668
Frankly Organic, 4668
Franrica, 22833
Franzia, 4670
Franzia Wine, 13851
Franziskaner Hefe-Weisse, 1208
Frapin, 27236
Frappe Creme, 12182
Fratello, 4674
Frazier's Finest, 4675
Fred Imus Southwest, 6170
Fred Imus Turquoise, 6170
Fred Meyer, 3387
Fred Silver, 19908
Fred's®, 237, 238
Freda Deli Meats, 246
Free Flow®, 342
Free Raised, 12162
Free Run, 1864
Free2b, 4679
Freebird, 5505
Freed's, 4681
Freed's Bakery, 7886
Freed, Teller & Fredd, 4681
Freeda, 4682
Freedent®, 7952, 13960
Freedom, 23771
Freelight, 30259
Freemark Abbey, 4688
Freerun, 5138
Freerun Omega 3, 5138
Frees-It, 28910
Freestone, 4689
Freestone Vineyards, 6603
Freeyumm, 4680
Freez-A-Pops, 7279
Freeze Dried Cransations™, 11654
Freeze-Thaw, 4008
Freezefridge®, 6374, 24434
Freezerta, 6971
Freezone, 25041
Freeztand, 30390
Frei Brothers Reserve®, 3834
Freida's Kitchen, 903
Freidel's Finest, 6221
Freightainer, 23543
Freightwrap, 25531
Freihofer's®, 1359
Freihoffer, 892
Freirich Porkette®, 4692
Freixenet Spanish Wines, 4693, 5069
Freixenet Wines, 4693, 5069
French Bull, 10229
French Chew, 3699
French Does, 7377
French Gourmet, 4699
French Market, 4700, 25789
French Market Coffee, 10657
French Paradox, 6310
French Rabbit, 1543
French Square, 28759
French Wines, 10952
French's, 73, 8061
French's Dry Spice Mixes, 73
Frenchie Winery, 1543
Frenchiec, 12267, 29771
Frenzi, 3233
Frenzy Mist, 2570
Frequent Fryer, 27799
Fresca, 2811
Fresca Foods, 10160
Frescados®, 9736
Frescas, 9571
Freschetta, 11316
Freschetta®, 11317
Fresco Y Mas, 11838
Frescobaldi Laudemio, 11864
Fresh 'n Fruity®, 4552
Fresh Aland Beef and Pork, 7001
Fresh As a Baby, 29826
Fresh Beans, 13112, 30523
Fresh Bellies, 4708
Fresh Blendz, 13192

1295

All Brands Index

Fresh Cargo, 2719
Fresh Creations, 7168
Fresh Cut, 13110
Fresh Express, 4709, 22858
Fresh Express®, 2580, 20541
Fresh Facts, 20593
Fresh From the Deli, 3896
Fresh Gourmet, 12201
Fresh Harvest, 2026
Fresh Health, 3315
Fresh Health Kids, 3315
Fresh Ideas, 4712
Fresh Nature, 4717
Fresh Pact, 9839
Fresh Pak, 8860, 28957
Fresh Pik't, 4714
Fresh Pond, 8969
Fresh Samantha, 4722
Fresh Sea Taste, 7583
Fresh Step, 2766, 20657
Fresh Taste Fast!, 6520
Fresh View, 18908
Fresh'n Up, 28471
Fresh-All, 21325
Fresh-Check, 25298
Fresh-O-Matic, 25320
Fresh-Scan, 25298
Freshbakes, 951
Freshbox Farms, 3183
Freshcut, 2332
Freshdry, 3696
Fresher Under Pressure, 22657
Freshman, 5479
Freshmax, 26381
Freshpack Bowls, 28743
Freshpak, 18495
Freshpax, 26381
Freshwrap Cuts, 12437
Freshwrap Slices, 12437
Freze-Cel, 21695
Frialator, 27556
Frick, 28967
Fridgekare, 24700
Friedr. Dick, 22867
Friel's, 11039
Friendly's®, 3442, 21421
Friendlys, 10229
Friends Fun Wine, 9117
Friendship Dairies™, 11211
Friendship Diaries, 2559
Friesinger's, 10773
Friesinger's Fine Chocolates, 3421
Frig-O-Seal, 27602
Frigex® W, 8804
Frigi-Top, 20982
Frigo Cheese®, 11209
Frigo®, 11211
Frigopak, 22873
Frio, 4737
Fris, 9964
Frisches Brot, 1633
Frisk, 9956
Friskem, 22877
Friskem-Af, 22877
Fristam, 22878
Fristch Mills, 23185
Frito Lay, 24672
Frito-Lay2go, 4741
Frito-Lay®, 9945, 27433
Fritos, 4741
Fritos®, 9945, 27433
Fritz, 6372
Fritz Knipschildt, 13433
Frogtape®, 29171
Frolic, 8401
Froma-Dar, 4748
Frontera Foods, 4751
Frontera®, 2939, 2940, 20821, 20822
Frontier, 4752, 4753, 9150, 10076
Frontier Gold, 1324
Frontier Kettle, 30323
Frontier Water, 9170
Frontrunner, 22473
Froot Loops, 6766
Froot Loops®, 6765

Frooties, 2132
Frooties®, 12880
Froozer, 4754
Frost Fire, 1688
Frost Flex, 30971
Frosted Flakes, 6766
Frosted Mini-Wheats, 6766
Frostee Snow Cones, 5333, 23360
Frostline® Frozen Treats, 6792, 24785
Frosty Pak, 7363
Frothee Creamy Head, 12941
Frotious, 27236
Froze-Fresh, 13192
Frozfruit, 4757
Frozfruit All Natural Fruit Bars, 4757
Frozsun, 12297
Frs Company, 4150
Fruehauf, 22894
Frugalume, 30893
Fruice, 3550
Fruigees, 4759
Fruit & Chia™, 3478
Fruit & Nadia, 2815, 20685
Fruit & Oats™, 3478
Fruit 2o, 12281
Fruit 66, 12239
Fruit a Freeze, 20946
Fruit Belt, 4761
Fruit Bliss, 4762
Fruit Breaker, 11320
Fruit By the Foot®, 4947
Fruit Chews®, 12880
Fruit Chocolates, 7410
Fruit Corn Appetit, 10179, 27669
Fruit Crystals, 4718
Fruit Delights, 7410
Fruit Drop, 56
Fruit Festives, 7410
Fruit Fiber, 131
Fruit For Thought, 11605
Fruit Hill White, 1672
Fruit N' Juice, 6159
Fruit of the Sea, 10974
Fruit of the Woods, 12783
Fruit Ole, 427
Fruit Ole Smoothies, 11266
Fruit Parfaits, 7410
Fruit Refreshers®, 3478
Fruit Rush™, 3442, 21421
Fruit Softees, 7410
Fruit Stripe, 1417, 4345
Fruit To The World, 28090
Fruit Topping, 8724
Fruit Tubes, 1827
Fruit Water, 4066
Fruit Wave H2o, 3279
Fruit-To-Go, 12259
Fruitcrown, 4769, 22896
Fruite, 56
Fruitflow®, 3320
Fruitful Juice Products, 3365
Fruitfull, 5562
Fruiticas Lollipops, 12211
Fruitini, 3479, 21460
Fruitland, 5767, 6985
Fruitopia, 2815, 20685
Fruitrim®, 190, 18410
Fruits De Mer, 5325
Fruitsavr®, 190, 18410
Fruitslim, 3753, 21763
Fruitsnax, 9251
Fruitsource®, 190, 18410
Fruitsweet, 13511
Fruittella, 9956
Fruity Ball, 12211
Frumage, 10565
Frutafit, 6163
Frutafit®, 11445
Frutalose®, 11445
Fruti, 8837
Fry Foods, 1891, 4776
Fry Krisp, 4777
Fry Krisp Batter Mixes, 4777
Fry Stix™, 1654
Frye's Measure Mill, 22900

Fryer Pro, 29016
Frymaster, 22901, 31092
Frymaster®, 31093
Frypowder, 26214
Frytech, 18677
Fryz, 14043
Fs1, 22492
Ft-50, 22366
Fuchs Tooth Brushes, 7562
Fudge Gourmet, 14013, 31399
Fudgeroons, 12096
Fudgescotti, 1529
Fudgie Bears, 2604
Fuel Snacks, 4573
Fuji Electric, 22134
Fujy, 18877
Fukusuke Rice, 4260
Ful-Flav-R, 4784, 22906
Ful-Lok, 27199
Ful-Value, 27346
Fulfill Fitness, 12182
Fulflo, 27308
Full Blast Gum, 7560
Full Circle, 11303, 13512, 28896, 30940
Full Circle®, 1758, 12885, 19889, 30333
Full House, 7296
Full Moon Light Ale, 8524
Full Moon Pale Ale, 339
Full Moon Shrimp, 1916
Full Moon®, 9946
Full Power, 648
Full Red, 12030
Full Sail, 4786
Full Service Caterin, 13667
Full Throttle, 8485
Fuller, 28967
Fulton Organic Free Range Chicken, 6770
Fulton Valley Farms, 6770
Fulton's Harvest Cream Liqueur, 5720
Fume Eraser, 29489
Fun Foods, 8269
Fun Fruit, 10496
Fun Fruits Fruit Snacks-Sunkist, 4884
Fun Pops, 258
Fun Stuff, 2947
Fun Whip, 258
Fun-N-Sun, 10760
Functional Teas, 5155
Funda, 29643
Fundae, 10015
Funfoods Holiday Pasta, 4794
Funfoods Premium, 4794
Funfresh Foods®, 9237, 26785
Fungamyl, 1692
Fungusamongus, 11390
Funny Farm, 4093
Funstraws, 22917
Funyun's, 4741
Funyuns®, 9945, 27433
Furama, 11881
Furgale, 22920
Furstenberg, 5427
Fury, 20491
Fuse Burger™, 6000, 23861
Fused, 30481
Fusion Cell, 22850
Fusion Grid, 19111
Fusion®, 21362
Future Bakery, 4806
Futuro, 18003
Fuze, 2811
Fwp - 7000, 30654

G

G, 11093
G & W, 7146
G Blanchet, 6395
G Mommas, 11423
G-Brew, 13444
G-Raff, 19569
G-T 200/100 llt, 18352
G. Cinelli-Esperia Corp., 20571
G.H. Cretors, 3862

G.H. Ford, 4833
G.H. Mumm, 9964
G2 Grease Guard, 22438
Gaba Plus™, 13097
Gabriel & Rose, 21383
Gabriella, 23002
Gabriella's Kitchen, 4854
Gabrielli, 2112
Gabrielli Winery, 2112
Gaby, 4854
Gadoua, 4856
Gadova, 13691
Gadova Multigo, 13691
Gaetano's, 4891
Gage, 23006
Gail's, 8951
Gailuron, 8676
Gain, 12721, 30193
Gaiser's, 4861
Galactic Grape, 5362, 23377
Galante Wines, 4862
Galassi, 4863
Galasso, 4864
Galaware, 31240
Galaxy, 20256, 20258, 23105, 29596
Galaxy Desserts, 4866
Galaxy®, 7952, 21362
Galbani, 7126
Galbani Precious, 7126
Galbani Sorrento, 7126
Galbani®, 9789
Galbusera, 10565
Galena Cellars, 4869
Galigher, 28557
Galilean, 4870
Galileo, 30109
Galleano, 4872
Galley, 23015
Galley Line, 23015
Galliker's, 4873
Gallo Family Vineyards®, 3834
Gallo Salame®, 13109
Galloping Garlic, 6528
Galv, 27921
Gamajet, 23019
Gambelini, 8795
Game Day Snacks, 13445
Gamko, 24038, 29466
Gamla, 10952
Gamma - E, 4827
Gamma 101p, 27377
Gandy's, 3442, 21421
Ganong Chicken Bones, 4884
Ganong Chocolates, 4884
Ganong Fruitfull, 4884
Ganong Sugar Confections, 4884
Garandina, 3545
Garb-El, 23028
Garb-O-Flakes, 29826
Garcia Brand, 3818
Garde, 19713
Gardein, 4889
Gardein®, 2939, 2940, 20821, 20822, 27540
Garden Club, 2750
Garden Fresh, 12334
Garden Goodness, 9129
Garden Harvest, 8806
Garden Hearts, 1538
Garden of Eatin', 5505
Garden Path, 7028
Garden Romance, 19928
Gardenburger, 6766
Gardenburgers, 3773, 21785
Gardennay, 2115
Gardetto's®, 4947
Gardner, 18352
Gardner Denver, 23032
Garelick, 4904
Garelick Farms®, 3442, 21421
Garfield, 10229
Garitech, 28809
Garland, 31092
Garland Ranch, 2459
Garland®, 31093

All Brands Index

Garli Garni, 4907
Garlic Festival, 4907
Garlic Galore, 6528
Garlic Gus, 6353
Garlic Juices, 4908
Garlic Parmesan Crouton Bites, 5489
Garlimax, 9957
Garner Jams & Jellies, 12473
Garro, 23082
Gartenbrau, 2160
Garvey, 21201, 23045
Garvi Gujarat, 6026
Garyline, 23051
Gas Baron, 20047
Gas Baron 2, 20047
Gasil, 21094
Gaslight Pale Ale, 9688
Gastro-Ad, 7172
Gate-Weigh, 19335
Gates, 29052
Gateway - Du Bake, 4920
Gateway Closures, 23064
Gateway Plastics, 23064
Gateway®, 7402
Gatherings®, 6000, 23861
Gatomax, 9571
Gator, 31177
Gatorade, 4150
Gatorade®, 9945, 27433
Gatsby's/Pierre Koenig, 3381
Gaucho, 4922
Gaurmande, 10039
Gavilan, 7655
Gavina, 4202
Gaviscon®, 10598
Gavottes, 7499
Gay 90's, 23810
Gaylord, 23071, 24038
Gbc, 25769
Gbh, 9117
Gd Engineering, 28714
Ge, 22959, 27282
Ge - Oxy 132, 4827
Ge Profile, 22959
Gear Up, 10495
Gebo, 23081
Gedney, 4928
Geefree, 4929
Geevani, 5755
Gehl Gourmet, 4930
Gehl Mainstream Cafe, 4930
Gel B, 8335
Gel N Melt®, 8804
Gelati Celesti, 4933
Gelato, 2669
Gelato Fresco, 4935
Gelita, 4937
Gelite, 6396
Gem, 4829
Gem 100%, 11875
Gem Berry, 4828
Gem Blended, 11875
Gem Extra, 11875
Gem Gem, 1763
Gem System, 20616
Gembond, 7847
Gemini, 21636, 24881, 25224, 25633, 29211, 31200
Gems, 11102
Gemstar, 7847
Gemstone Gourmet Candies, 756
Gemstone Vineyard, 7490
Gemstone®, 7786
Gemwraps, 9010
Genarom, 4943
Gene-Trak, 26551
Generac, 29202
General Financial Supply®, 22187
General Mills, 541, 1891
General Packager, 23121
General Packaging Products, 26756
General Produce, 2298
General Slicing, 23134
Generation Farms, 5782
Generation Ii, 23160

Generic Liquid Dish, 19995
Generic Liquid Laundry, 19995
Genesee Beer, 4950
Genesee Brewing, 9117
Genesee Cream Ale, 4950
Genesee Ice, 4950
Genesee Light, 4950
Genesee N.A., 4950
Genesis, 22140
Genesis 1:29c, 8831
Genesis For Windows, 24050
Genesis Ii, 30421
Genesis R&D, 22266
Genesis Removable Head Press, 21282
Genesis32 Enterprise Edition, 24050
Geneva Freeze, 20789
Genforms®, 22187
Genisis, 30957
Genisoy Soy Products, 4955
Genista, 783
Genivida®, 3320
Genmai Udon, 11773
Genova Tonno, 2555
Genpak, 18029
Gensaco, 23145
Gent-L-Kleen, 21768
Gentle Ben Winter Brau, 4959
Gentle Change, 9201
Gentleman's Cut®, 9338
Genu, 1962
Genu Plus, 1962
Genugel, 1962
Genuine, 11668
Genuine Fulvi Romano Cheese, 11668
Genuine Lager, 7123
Genulacta, 1962
Genutine, 1962
Genuvisco, 1962
George Dickel Whiske, 3570
George Killian's Irish Red®, 8460
George Maid, 12300
George T. Stagg, 11263
George's, 4970
Georgetown Farm Bison, 4973
Georgetown Farm Piedmontese, 4973
Georgia, 2814, 4974
Georgia Fruit Cake, 4974
Georgia Grinders, 4975
Georgia Moon Corn Whiskey, 5720
Georgia Rag, 26770
Georgia Reds, 12300
Georgia Special, 12300
Georgia's, 4976
Georgiana, 1856
Geraldine's Bodacious, 1528
Geraldo's, 4928
Gerard & Dominique, 11358
Gerber 1st Foods, 4982
Gerber 2nd Foods, 4982
Gerber 3rd Fodos, 4982
Gerber Cereal, 4982
Gerber Edge, 30512
Gerber Good Start, 4982
Gerber Graduates, 4982
Gerber®, 8945
Gerbes, 12516
Geri-Med, 9253
Gerimenu, 20028, 20029
Germ-O-Ray, 22979, 24273
German, 5902
German Style Kolsch, 5515
Germany: Wessergold, 5108
Germicidal, 27679
Gerolsteiner, 5108
Gerrit J. Verburg Co., 2132
Gerstel, 23168
Gerstenberg Schroder, 28714
Get Movin Snack Packss, 9799
Get Popped, 12202
Get Well, 21059
Getreide, 7655
Gettelfinger Select, 10268
Gevalia Kaffe, 6976
Geyer, 27158
Geyser Peak, 4992

Gf Harvest, 4830
Gfa, 4831
Gfb: the Gluten Free Bar, 13669
Gg Unique Fiber, 5505
Ghiaccio, 4901
Ghiardelli, 2606
Ghibli, 23172
Ghigi, 10860
Ghiradelli, 6819
Ghiradelli Syrup, 2833
Ghirardelli, 434, 2971, 3009, 4422, 4994
Ghost Pines®, 3834
Ghost Talk, 10764
Gianopac, 24094
Giant, 6126, 29816
Giant Cashews, 8269
Giant Gourmet, 5590
Giants, 3354
Giardino, 6145
Gibbons, 5001, 7150
Gibbs, 5555
Gibson, 22872
Giddy Up & Go, 12779
Giesser, 21883
Gifford's, 5004
Gift Baskets By Carmela, 36
Gift of Bran, 6806
Gigi, 9788
Gigi Baking Company, 11940, 12894
Gila Caf,®, 6818, 24802
Gilbert, 23181
Gilbey's®, 1120
Gild, 27711
Gilda, 4244
Giles, 23183
Gill Netter's Best, 9980
Gillette, 12721, 30193
Gillies, 5012
Gilly's Hot Vanilla, 5013
Gilsonic Autosiever, 23185
Gilt Edge, 5016
Giltron Foilsealer, 23186
Gimme, 5019
Gimme Lean, 7427
Gimme Organic, 5019
Gin Ultimate, 754
Gina Lina's, 10418
Gina Marie Cream Cheese, 5878
Ginbao, 8623
Ginbis, 3852
Ginebra Calvert, 3545
Ginger Ale, 7310
Ginger Kids, 3079
Ginger Shots, 5022
Ginger Snaps, 551, 8729
Gingerbread Ale, 1401
Ginkgold, 8896
Ginnie Lou, 29545
Gino's, 831
Ginsen-Rgy, 7947
Ginseng 4x, 157
Ginseng Extract, 4859
Ginseng Rush, 10495
Ginseng Up, 5027, 23188
Gionelli ®, 13120
Giorgio, 5028
Giotti, 8061
Giovanni, 2012
Giovanni's, 5030
Girard's, 5032, 12467
Girls With Crabs, 12742
Girlwatcher, 13605
Giroux, 13141
Girton King Zeero, 23192
Give Collection, 13403
Give Your Heart a Healthy Start, 9858
Gjetost Ekte, 11968
Gk Communications, 10229
Glac,Au Smart Water, 2814
Glac,Au Vitaminwater, 2814
Glace De Poulet Gold, 8538
Glaceau Smart Water, 2815, 20685
Glaceau Vitamin Water, 2815, 20685
Glaceau Vitaminwater, 4066
Glacier, 24409

Glacier Caviar, 5309
Glacier Freeze, 5041
Glacier Ice, 1966, 8920
Glacier Salmon, 5309
Glacier Valley, 3084
Glacier Valley®, 3083
Glacieruan, 30725
Glad Bags, 2766, 20657
Gladder's Gourmet Cookie, 5043
Glade, 21757
Gladiator, 5499, 28816
Gladstone Candies, 5398
Glalcto, 12795
Glanbia Foods, 5046
Glanz French, 19723
Glare-Eze, 21388
Glaros, 7655
Glaros Ouzo, 9773
Glas-Flo, 26111
Glass & More, 19741
Glass Brite, 19741
Glass Klean, 19197
Glass Maid, 23199
Glass Pac, 27679
Glass Pro, 23199
Glassips, 29498
Glasted, 20256
Gleme, 20591
Glen Ellen, 13851
Glen Garioch, 1120
Glen Grant, 2114
Glen Lake, 12977
Glen Ord Scotch, 3570
Glendale, 4078, 21317
Glendora Quiche Co., 5053
Glendronach, 3024
Glenfiddich, 13811
Glengate, 18778
Glenglassaugh, 1784
Glenlivet, 3545
Glenmark, 1262
Glenmorangie, 8452
Glenmore, 11264
Glenny's, 5055
Glenora, 5057
Glenray, 30323
Glenrothes, 3545
Glenwood, 13912
Glider, 4387
Glier's, 5058
Glisodin, 9654
Glo-Glaze, 26766
Glo-Ice, 22170
Glo-Ons, 26766
Glo-Pro, 30639
Glo-Quartz, 23217
Glo-Ray, 23652
Global, 5062
Global Botanical, 5061
Global Brands, 11817
Global Creations®, 1654
Global Food, 5063
Global Sfa, 26615
Globe, 6211, 20520, 23235, 23236, 24226, 24784
Globe Artichoke, 4315
Globe Plus, 6211, 24226
Glocal, 9654
Glolite, 26766
Gloria Ferrer, 4693
Gloria Jean's Coffees®, 6818, 24802
Gloria Jeans, 3591, 6819
Glorybee, 5073
Glossop's, 5074
Glow, 27328
Glow Pop, 6158
Glow Shots, 27328
Glowmaster, 23245
Gluconal, 5078
Glucophage®, 1721
Glucovance®, 1721
Glutamine, 4736
Gluten-Free Heaven, 5083
Glutino®, 2939, 2940, 20821, 20822, 27540

1297

All Brands Index

Glutiny, 8959
Gluzyme, 1692
Glycomarine, 11269
Glyderm®, 8389
Gma, 28928
Gmi Gelatin, 8891
Go Bananas, 7903
Go Getters, 22328
Go Girl Energy Drink, 26668
Go Lean, 6720
Go Mango, 7903
Go Matcha, 15
Go Raw, 5087
Go Salsa, 3522
Go Texan, 12658
Go Veggie, 4867
Go-Go Drinks, 4066
Go-Jo, 22990
Go-Mex, 573
Goat Island Light, 11561
Goavo, 5088
Gobstopper, 2132
Godiva, 2115, 5092, 11864
Godiva Biscuits, 5092
Godiva Chocolate, 5092
Godiva Ice Cream, 20946
Godshall's, 5093
Godwin, 5094
Godwin Produce, 5094
Godwin's Blue Ribbon, 5094
Goebel, 9664
Goelitz, 6485
Gogo Squeez, 8005
Gold, 362
Gold 'n Soft®, 13328
Gold Award, 7655, 9773
Gold Band Products, 9628
Gold Bond, 178, 23602
Gold Bottle, 30831
Gold Brick, 4032
Gold Buckle Oranges, 13906
Gold Canyon Meat Co.™, 11504, 29095
Gold Circle Farms, 5837
Gold Coast, 2450, 2796, 5098, 20666
Gold Coast Baking Company, 5097
Gold Cow, 9296
Gold Crown Lager, 9137
Gold Cup, 3
Gold Dollar, 5102
Gold Dollar Lemon, 5102
Gold Dollar/Monedade'oro, 5102
Gold Hog Casings, 29572
Gold Kist Farms®, 10056
Gold Label, 3269, 6544, 7874
Gold Label Plus Dairy, 10714
Gold Lion, 19621
Gold Medal, 1891, 1935, 5103, 5233, 10275, 11515
Gold Medal®, 4947
Gold Mine Gum, 11051
Gold N Good, 10846
Gold N. White Bread Flour, 8851
Gold Nectar, 6065
Gold Nugget, 615, 8308
Gold Nugget Butter, 7166
Gold Nugget Cheese, 7166
Gold Peak, 2811
Gold Peak Tea, 2814
Gold Plus, 1718
Gold Premium, 6221
Gold Ribbon, 5643
Gold Rim, 3424
Gold Rush, 12863
Gold Seal, 262
Gold Shield, 21857
Gold Spike Ale, 1237
Gold Standard, 5106
Gold Star, 3768, 5108
Gold Star Coffee, 1601, 19813
Gold'n Plump®, 10056
Gold'n Polenta, 9225
Gold'n Treats, 9225
Gold'n'spice®, 1654
Gold's, 5105
Gold-Tex Flour, 12553

Goldegg, 5138
Golden, 125, 953, 2530, 9744
Golden 100, 5113
Golden Amber, 932
Golden Bake, 2796, 20666
Golden Barclay Geneve, 25299
Golden Barrel, 5157
Golden Beauties, 965
Golden Bird, 9500
Golden Brands, 70
Golden Circle, 6977
Golden Coconut Oil, 13683, 31140
Golden Crest, 4874
Golden Crinkles®, 9523
Golden Crisp, 530, 9833, 10213
Golden Crop, 10425
Golden Crunchies, 10104
Golden Crust, 8649
Golden Dawn, 347
Golden Delicious, 9332
Golden Dragon, 4311, 8754
Golden Dreams, 754
Golden Drip, 19449
Golden Eagle, 5118, 5132, 29189
Golden Eagle Ale, 3519
Golden Farm Candies, 4779
Golden Flake, 5122, 13129
Golden Fluff, 5123
Golden Foods, 70, 13625
Golden Fries™, 9523
Golden Gate, 6451
Golden Glow, 5233
Golden Goodness, 5282
Golden Gourmet, 1310
Golden Gourmet Nuts, 3430
Golden Grain, 465, 7655
Golden Grenadine, 8909
Golden Grill, 1069, 1577
Golden Gripper, 31099
Golden Grower, 754
Golden Harvest, 2026
Golden Hawk, 20277
Golden Island, 5126
Golden Island®, 13109
Golden Joma Palm Oil, 13683, 31140
Golden Kernel, 5127
Golden Kettle, 12866
Golden Kola, 6943
Golden Life, 4127
Golden Loaf, 1950
Golden Magic, 7373
Golden Meal, 10846
Golden Moon Tea, 5129
Golden One, 5132
Golden Oreo's®, 10213
Golden Palm Cake & Icing, 13683, 31140
Golden Palm Margarine, 13683, 31140
Golden Palm Shortening, 13683, 31140
Golden Patties®, 9523
Golden Rich, 2045
Golden Ripe®, 3479, 21460
Golden River, 5132
Golden Road Brewing, 571
Golden Roast, 5462
Golden Rum Cake, 2881
Golden Star, 8028, 23261
Golden State, 13541
Golden State Hops, 4633
Golden Sun, 5132
Golden Temple, 6380, 9245, 14011
Golden Tiger®, 237, 238
Golden Touch, 6267
Golden Treasure, 6119, 24012
Golden Trophy Steaks, 12674
Golden Twirls®, 9523
Golden Valley, 5138
Golden Walnut, 5140
Golden West, 2381, 13070
Golden Wind, 24409
Goldenberg's Peanut Chews®, 6641
Goldenbrook Farms®, 1758, 19889
Goldeneye, 3779
Goldfish, 2116
Goldfish®, 9942
Golding, 5146

Golding Farms, 5146
Golding Gourmand, 5146
Goldrush, 3216, 7915, 20399
Goldtex, 10616
Goldthread, 5148
Goldwater's, 5149
Goldwater's Taste of the Southwest, 5149
Golfer's, 21059
Golfo Mar, 8028
Golia, 9956
Golightly Sugar Free Candy, 5874
Gollath®, 29854
Gollots Brand Shrimp, 1916
Gomacro, 5090
Gonzo's Little Big Meat, 8207
Goo Gone, 25631
Goo Goo Cluster, 12027
Good & Plenty, 5818, 23750
Good Buddies, 5362, 23377
Good Earth, 4537
Good Earth Teas, 5155
Good Food Made Simple, 5158
Good Fortunes, 5160
Good Friends, 6720
Good Health, 13129
Good Humor, 13169
Good Humor®, 5165
Good Karma, 5166
Good Loaf, 11839
Good Lovin' Foods, 5167
Good News Eggs, 3142
Good Planet Foods, 5170
Good Sense®, 13603
Good Simple Food, 12703
Good Spirits, 13184
Good Stuff Cocoa, 6821
Good Taste, 8973
Good Times, 597
Good Year, 21134
Good Zebra, 5175
Goodart's, 5182
Goodbee, 14023
Goodbelly, 5178
Goodbelly Plusshot, 5178
Goodbelly Straightshot, 5178
Goodbites, 5179
Goodbites Cbd, 5179
Goode & Ready, 8688
Goodell, 23270
Goodheart, 5183
Goodie Bags, 26199
Goodlife, 4501
Goodman, 27914
Goodman's, 7848
Goodness Knows, 5185
Goodnessknows®, 7952
Goodniites, 24838
Goodniks®, 13603
Goodseed, 5186
Goodwheat™, 634
Goodwrappers Handwrappers, 23278
Goodwrappers Identi-Wrap, 23278
Goody Shake, 1915
Goodyear, 25029
Gooey Butter Bar, New!, 2903
Gooey Ghouls, 7746
Goof Off, 23436
Goop, 21089
Goose Bay Winery, 10952
Goose Hill, 965
Goose Isalnd, 571
Goose Island Honker's Ale, 26668
Goose Point Oysters, 9066
Goose Watch, 12382
Goosecross, 5189
Gopi, 6719
Gorant & Yum Yum Chocolates, 5192
Gorbel, 19908
Gordo's, 9879
Gordon Biersch, 5193
Gordon's Chesapeake Classics, 8256
Gordon's Gin, 3570
Gordon's Vodka, 3570
Gordos, 21099
Gorilla Bowl, 30080

Gorilla Cloves, 12987
Gorilla Vanilla, 12550
Gorton's Beer Battered Fillets, 5194
Gorton's Fish Sticks, 5194
Gorton's Grilled Tilapia, 5194
Gorton's Natural Catch, 5194
Gorton's Parmesean Crusted Cod, 5194
Gorton's Popcorn Shrimp, 5194
Gorton's Pub Style Cod, 5194
Gorton's Seafood Appetizers, 5194
Gorton's Shrimp Bowl, 5194
Gorton's Simply Bake Salmon, 5194
Gossner Foods, 5195
Gotcha - Sure Snap Sign Holder, 28118
Gotham, 30775
Gotham Dairy, 2669
Gothic, 23842
Gotliebs, 5196
Goubaud, 10346
Gould, 23962
Goundry Fine Wine, 13425
Gourmay, 18928
Gourmet, 3336, 13303, 21246, 27602, 28787
Gourmet Baker, 721
Gourmet Basmati Rice, 11908
Gourmet Brand Blackberries, 28090
Gourmet Brew, 13444
Gourmet Butters & Spreads, 14034
Gourmet Cookie Place, 14013, 31399
Gourmet Deli, 5039
Gourmet Fare, 5280
Gourmet Foods Market, 5208
Gourmet French Chew, 3699
Gourmet Fresh, 5216
Gourmet Garden, 8061
Gourmet Goat, 13927
Gourmet Gold, 4907
Gourmet Grab & Go®, 7599
Gourmet Granola, 9799
Gourmet Grid, 27670
Gourmet Honey Collection, 14034
Gourmet House®, 10777, 28421
Gourmet International, 12543
Gourmet Jose, 5396, 23425
Gourmet Lite, 5213
Gourmet Pepper Sauce, 9745
Gourmet Products, 5211
Gourmet Reserves, 13105
Gourmet Selections, 4543
Gourmet Slim #7, 8961
Gourmet Slim Cuisine, 8961
Gourmet Snack Bags, 3396
Gourmet Specialty Cookies, 5909, 23825
Gourmet Spices, 13665
Gourmet Stuffed Clams, 1464
Gourmet Supreme, 8961
Gourmet To Go, 23499
Gourmet Treats, 5213
Gourmet Valley, 13785
Gourmet Valley Foods, 13785
Gourmet's Choice Tuna Fillets, 12046
Governair, 23292
Governor's Club, 7655
Goya®, 5223
Gp 101, 19668
Gpc, 28928
Gpf-1, 29352
Gpi, 23613
Gpt, 21317
Graber Olives, 1933
Grabmaster, 21753
Grace Rush, 11330
Graceland Fruit, 5229
Graco, Inc., 23297
Graduates® Toddler Foods, 8945
Graeser, 10720
Graffigna & Jacob's Creek, 9964
Grafschafter, 1957
Graft Cider, 5235
Grafton Gold, 5236
Grafton Gold-Ext Aged Cheddar, 5236
Grag Studios, 20325
Graham Dunks, 6787
Graham Sleeving, 18284

All Brands Index

Grain Belt, 796
Grain Millers, 214, 5243
Grain Place, 5244
Grain Trust, 11078
Grain-Pro, 5245
Grainaissance, 5248
Graindance, 12855, 12857
Graines De Vie, 4091
Grainful, 5249
Grainman, 23305
Grainsfirst, 3384
Grainsweet™, 12387
Graintrader Wheat Al, 9688
Gram Dunks, 6787
Grand Archer, 706
Grand Bayou, 12520
Grand Champion, 6438
Grand Chef De Paris, 13401
Grand Cru, 1738
Grand Cru Raclette, 10906
Grand Crue, 10906
Grand Estate Collection, 7746
Grand Isle, 13454
Grand Life Seitan, 12396
Grand Mark, 12489
Grand Marnier, 8452
Grand Muriel, 7655, 9773
Grand Prize, 24906
Grand Slam, 12663
Grand Stands, 24044
Grand Teton, 7166
Grand Teton Brewing, 5255
Grand Teton Cheese, 7166
Grand-MSRe, 1661
Grandaddy's, 13964
Grandco, 23309
Grande, 847, 21500
Grande Bravo Whey Protein, 5259
Grande Chef, 23315
Grande Classics, 8724
Grande Classics Island Blends, 8724
Grande Gusto Natural Flavor, 5259
Grande Italia, 6238
Grande River Vineyards, 5260
Grande River Vineyards Everyday, 5260
Grande River Vineyards Meritage, 5260
Grande Ultra Nutritional Whey Prot., 5259
Grandioso®, 13328
Grandma Brown's, 5263
Grandma Shearer's, 11531
Grandma Shearer's Snacks, 11531
Grandma Sycamore's®, 1359
Grandma Taylor's Gourmet Dip, 9955
Grandma's, 4555, 4741
Grandma's Bake Shoppe, 1134
Grandma's Cookie Mix, 10589
Grandma's Fruit Cake, 1134
Grandma's Molasses, 8586
Grandma's Molasses®, 864
Grandma's Recipe, 9185
Grandma's®, 9945, 27433
Grandpa A'S, 290, 18551
Grandpa John's, 10966
Grandpa Pete's Sunday Sauce, 11457
Grandpa Po's Slightly Spicy, 9234
Grandpa Po's Slightly Sweet, 9234
Grandpa Po's Slightly Unsalted, 9234
Grandpa Vals, 12863
Grandpa's Choice, 3142
Grandpa's Oven, 10907
Grandpa's Secret Omega-3 Muesli, 3872
Grandpops Lollipops, 5269
Grandstand, 24354
Grandview Farms, 5270
Grandyoats, 5271
Granfruttato, 8479
Granny Cheescakes, 5297
Granny Cookies, 818
Granny Goose, 11748
Granny Smith Apple, 2637, 12914
Granny's, 1736, 6070, 28278
Granny's Kitchen, 7886
Granny's Oven, 1394
Granowska's, 5277

Grant County Foods, 2298
Grant's, 13811
Grants Kill Ants, 23319
Granum, 2630
Granville Island Brewing, 8459
Grape Alpho, 9107
Grape Nuts, 10213
Grapefruit, 883
Grapefruit Extract, 9251
Grapeking, 5036
Grapelets, 7410
Grapevine Trading Co., 5280
Graphalloy, 23332
Graphic Revolutions, 29746
Graphilm, 23332
Grass Run Farms®, 6391
Grassland, 5282
Grassland Beef, 13126
Grasso, 28967
Gratifica, 7428
Grav/Tronic, 26852
Graves, 56, 2260
Graves Mountain, 5285
Gravimerik, 25571
Gravy & Gumbo Magic, 7766, 25632
Gravy Master, 5287, 10724
Gravy Train, 6380
Gravymaster, 5287
Greane Bins, 20875
Grease Grabber, 18251
Grease Guard, 22438
Grease Master, 23345
Grease Off, 19670
Great, 3750
Great American, 13689
Great American Barbecue, 5295
Great American Hamburgers, 457
Great American®, 10893
Great Dane, 23346
Great Expectations, 5307
Great Glacier, 8920
Great Golden Ale, 4466
Great Grains, 10213
Great Grub Rubs, 4894
Great Gusto, 9699
Great Hill Blue, 5313
Great Lakes, 5316, 5318
Great Meats, 11312
Great Middwest®, 11211
Great Midwest®, 11209
Great Ocead Road™, 11211
Great Organic Hotdog, 614
Great Pacific, 5326
Great Plains, 5327, 30775
Great Pumpkin, 2763
Great Range Brand Bison, 10823
Great Recipes, 5328
Great San Saba River Pecan, 12687
Great Valley, 13785
Great Valley Mills, 5331
Great Valley Mixes, 5331
Great Western, 10112
Great Western Products Company, 5333, 23360
Great White, 7554, 21425
Great Whites, 4242, 22458
Greater Omaha, 5338
Greaves, 5339
Grebe's, 5340
Greek Yogurt Creamy Ceasar, 5489
Greek Yogurt Lemon Garlic, 5489
Greek Yogurt Ranch, 5489
Greek Yogurt Salad Dressing Mix, 5489
Greek Yogurt Spinach & Feta, 5489
Green & Black's, 8474
Green Bay Puddles, 1018
Green Blaze Ipa, 7526
Green Coffee, 6611
Green Dragon, 3921
Green Earth Orchards, 5348
Green Earth Organics, 12973, 30444
Green Essence, 5349
Green Fingers, 24838
Green Gaint, 1548
Green Giant®, 4947

Green Giant™, 864
Green Gold Wheatgrass, 9951
Green Head, 3301
Green Label, 18155
Green Leaf, 13531
Green Magician, 12228
Green Mountain, 816, 25789
Green Mountain Chocolate Truffle, 5354
Green Mountain Coffee, 6819
Green Mountain Coffee®, 6818, 24802
Green Mountain Creamery, 5356
Green Mountain Farms, 4665
Green Mountain Gringo, 6069, 12473
Green Point, 8452
Green Spot, 54, 5362, 9964, 23377
Green Star, 2570
Green Valley, 4872, 11434
Green Works, 2766, 20657
Green-Freedman, 12328
Green-Go, 5368
Green-T Energy Mints, 1343
Green-Tek, 23379
Greene's, 1482
Greenfield, 5372, 6160
Greenheck, 23387
Greenline, 23990
Greenpod, 11945
Greenpop, 30259
Greens, 9516
Greenwell Farms, 5377
Greenwood, 5379
Greenwood Prairie, 10099, 27564
Greerco, 26490
Greese Gobler, 25008
Greeter's Pale Ale, 7143
Greg Norman Estates, 12937
Gregorio, 2012
Gregory, 22328
Gregory-Adams, 25918
Greig Filters, 23402
Gremlin, 8242
Gremlins, 1290
Grey Goose, 913
Grey Poupon, 6977
Grey Whale, 9673
Grid-Grip, 29283
Grielle, 23789
Griffin, 23409
Griffolyn, 28240
Grifron, 8695
Grifron D-Fraction, 8695
Grifron Mushroom Emperors, 8695
Grifron Prost Mate, 8695
Gril-Classics, 23415
Gril-Del, 23415
Grill Blazin Bbq Sauce, 9332
Grill Greats, 23416
Grill Master, 25308
Grill-In-A-Bottle, 4560
Grilla Gear, 31345
Grillco, Inc., 23417
Grillin', 10600
Grillit 1200, 19439
Grillit 12x12, 19439
Grillmaster, 19130
Grillo's Pickles, 5389
Grills To Go, 23418
Grimaud Farms, 5390
Grimaud Farms Muscovy Ducks, 5390
Grime Grabber, 21768
Grimmway, 5393
Grinch, 1591
Grindmaster, 23420
Gringos, 9934
Grip Clip, 27575
Grip Clips, 21013
Grip Rock, 25865
Grip Top, 19763
Grip-Grate, 29283
Grip-Plate, 29283
Gripper, 25900, 26109, 28115
Grips, 31099
Griptite, 20256
Gritstone, 3171
Grizzlesh, 13797

Grizzly, 26290
Grocer's Garden, 10728
Grocery Grip, 24567
Groeb Farms, 5396, 23425
Groen, 26476
Grolsch Premium Lager®, 8460
Grooner, 4677
Grosfillex, 23429
Grote, 23431
Grote & Weigel, 5400
Grounds For Thought, 5402
Groundwork, 5404
Grouse Hunt Farms, 5406
Grove on the Go, 4840
Grove Sweet, 2699
Grove, Jr, 4840
Grow Gardens, 922
Grow-Pac, 5408
Grower Pete's Certified Organicc, 7480
Grower's Pack, 5663
Growers Company, 8314
Growers Fancy Juice, 7339
Growing Roots, 5411
Growler, 1208
Grown Free, 10529
Gruet Winery, 5413
Gsa, 26235
Gse, 30766
Gsi, 194
Gst, 20290
Gt Uni-Clip, 27575
Gtc, 5473
Gu, 4850
Guacamole Salad, 11883
Guardcraft, 27294
Guardian, 24273, 29044
Guardian Couplings, 18678
Guardmaster, 29706
Guardmax, 9957
Guardsboy, 20882
Guardsmen, 20882
Guardswitch, 22960
Guayabita Best - Pasta De Guayaba, 3545
Guenoc, 5417
Guerlain, 27209
Guerrero, 8387
Guerrero®, 8384
Guflielmo Reserve, 5421
Guggisberg, 5420
Guglielmo, 5421
Guglielmo Vineyard Selection, 5421
Gugulidid, 11061
Guida, 12303
Guida's, 5422
Guida's Dairy, 3335
Guidall, 20305
Guideline, 22624
Guidemaker, 24213
Guido & Sals Old Chicago, 1123
Guido's Serious, 5423
Guidparg Chocolates, 2833
Guildware®, 21362
Guiloriver, 22594
Guiltless Gourmet, 5426, 7848, 25789
Guinness Extra Stout, 7123
Guinness Stout, 5427
Guinness®, 5427
Guittard, 2606, 3009
Gujarati, 3465
Gulden's, 6267
Gulden's®, 2939, 2940, 20821, 20822
Gulf, 3424, 13200
Gulf Belle, 8995
Gulf Central, 5430
Gulf Crown, 5432
Gulf Garden, 8028
Gulf Kist, 11865
Gulf Pride, 5438
Gulf Star, 5430
Gulf-Maid, 102
Gum Time, 10496
Gummi Alien Invaders, 790
Gummy Guy, 12985
Gump, 19930
Gumpert's, 5444

All Brands Index

Gun Powder Pearl Pinhead Green Tea, 5228, 23295
Gurley's, 13827
Gurley's Candy, 5448
Gurley's Golden Recipe Nuts, 5448
Gurley's Natures Harvest, 5448
Guru, 4851
Gurunanda, 5449
Gusano Rojo, 7655
Gustafson's, 2346
Gusto Italia, 12860
Guy's, 5456
Guy's Tea, 4055
Guylian, 6540
Gvp-100, 31119
Gw, 13685
Gwaltney, 11733
Gx Power, 10307
Gyrocompact, 22873
Gyros Usa, 3028
Gyrostack, 22873

H

H&C, 9798
H&G Chum, 11602
H&K Packers, 5470
H&S Bread Crumbs, 5472
H&T, 23927
H-50, 8804
H-E-B, 5473
H-E-B Kitchen & Table, 5473
H-E-B Organics, 5473
H-E-B Select Ingredients, 5473
H-E-Buddy, 5473
H-F 201, 23467
H-F 211, 23467
H-O, 4831
H-S 410, 23467
H.B. Fuller, 23456
H.C. Duke & Son, 23458
H.C. Smoked Sausage, 12463
H.C. Valentine™, 10928, 28576
H.F. Cradle System, 30923
H.K. Anderson®, 2939, 2940, 20821, 20822
H.K. Systems, 18990
H.M. Quackenbush, 25545
H.O.P., 23659
H2o, 5586
H2o To Go, 3469
H2rose, 5480
H3o, 5481
Haagen Dazs, 5137
Haagen-Dazs®, 4947, 8945, 20020
Haake Beck Non-Alcoholic, 689
Habanero Products From Hell, 11873
Habco, 23482
Habero, 7051
Habersham Estates, 5492
Habitant, 2115, 3844
Haccp, 18352
Hacienda, 1738
Hackney, 23515
Hackney Champion, 23515
Hackney Classic, 23515
Hackney Ultimate, 30725
Haco, 12438
Haco Foods, 21246
Haddar, 4104
Haddon House®, 1484
Haddys, 1891
Hadley Date Gardens, 5494
Hafner, 5496
Hag, 10565
Hagafen Winery, 10952
Hagensborg Meltaways Truffles, 5497
Hagerty Foods, 5498, 23518
Haggen, 3387
Hahg, 10027, 27510
Hahn's, 4665
Haier, 22959
Haig, 3570
Haight Vineyard Wines, 5502
Haiku, 5306

Hail Merry, 5503
Hail Queen, 20607
Hain Kidz, 3617
Hain Pure Foods, 5505
Haine Pure Foods, 5506
Haitoglou, 6986
Hakuna Banana, 5511
Hakushu, 12315
Halal Meats, 457
Hale's Celebration Porter, 5515
Hale's Cream, 5515
Hale's Dublin Style Stout, 5515
Hale's Pale American Ale, 5515
Hale's Special Bitter, 5515
Half Moon, 13082
Hallcrest Vineyards, 5524
Hallde, 27362
Hallmark, 5525, 27387
Halloween, 21059
Halls, 8474
Halo, 23489
Halo Heat, 18677
Halo Top, 3939
Haloflex™, 3320
Halos, 4633
Halton, 23538
Ham Sausage, 2162
Hamburger Helper®, 4947
Hamer, 25871
Hamilton, 19908, 28488
Hamilton Beach, 23542
Hamish & Enzo, 10950
Hamm's®, 8460
Hammar, 23547
Hammond's, 5534
Hammons, 5537
Hampshire Laboratories, 13469
Hamptom Farms, 5541
Hampton House, 6394
Han-D, 21080
Hana, 12500
Hana-Nori, 135
Hanco, 23554
Hancock's, 11263
Handgards, 23556
Handi-Foil of America, 18029
Handi-Matic, 30601
Handifold, 23160
Handlair, 20550
Handle Capper, 18300
Handmaster, 29632, 29633
Hands, 21425
Handy, 5547
Handy A&C, 24059
Handy Andy, 31099
Handy Blade, 23563
Handy Fuel Brand, 29661
Handy Wacks, 23564
Handy-Cart, 19608
Handy-Home Helpers, 22579
Hanel Lean-Lift, 23565
Hanel Vertical Carousels, 23565
Hang Ten, 2763
Hangars, 27773
Hank's, 23567
Hankison, 28714
Hanna's, 5553
Hannah's Delight, 7756
Hannegan Seafoods, 444
Hanover, 5555
Hanover Farms, 5555
Hansen, 5558, 5559
Hansen-Norge, 5558
Hanson Brass, 23581
Haolam, 13931
Happiness Sell Sheet, 10229
Happy Cup Tea, 12585
Happy Day Pops, 5752
Happy Drinks, 258
Happy Heart Lollipops, 6158
Happy Herberts, 5569
Happy Hive, 5570
Happy Home, 5245, 11852
Happy Indulgence, 5562
Happy Indulgence Deladent Dips, 5562

Happy Snacks, 7940
Happy Trails Meat Snack Sticks, 12920
Happy Trails T-Shirts, 2903
Happydent, 9956
Harbor, 5579
Harbor Lighthouse Ale, 1015
Harborside, 12703
Harbour Gold, 12919
Hard Bargain, 8075
Hard Cookies, 5909, 23825
Hard-E Foods, 5582
Hard-Edge, 23106
Hard-Tac, 21440
Hardbite, 8855
Hardfast, 572
Hardi-Tainer, 23598
Hardin, 8806
Hardware, 18793
Hardwick, 25893
Harford Duracool, 23607
Hargita, 5108
Hargrave Vineyards, 2299
Hari Om Farms, 5586
Haribo, 2132, 5587
Harida, 8888
Harlan Bakeries, 5590
Harley Activated Pine, 20830
Harlin Fruit, 5591
Harmless Harvest, 5594
Harmonic, 22445
Harmony, 4732
Harmony Bay, 5596
Harmony Cellars, 5597
Harmony Snacks, 3575
Harney & Sons, 5599, 8090
Harold Food Co., 5600
Harp Lager, 5427
Harper Seafood, 5603
Harpic®, 10598
Harpoon, 5606
Harrell Nut, 2110
Harrgate, 4148
Harris, 8995, 25961
Harris Bug Free, 27031
Harris Famous, 27031
Harris Farms, 5609
Harris Fresh, 5609
Harris Ranch, 5609, 5611
Harrisburg Dairies, 5613
Harrison, 5614
Harry & David, 5615
Harry London, 4250
Harry London Chocolates, 5616
Harry's Choice, 3629
Hart, 10404, 23635
Hart Boost, 30010
Hart Treat, 30010
Hart Winery, 5618
Hartford, 5619
Hartford Court, 5619
Hartford Farms®, 7402
Hartley Brandy, 11264
Hartley's, 5460
Hartlift, 30010
Hartness Choice, 11177
Hartstone, 23642
Hartwell Cabernet, 11810
Harvard, 474
Harvest, 7526
Harvest Ale British Esb, 3746
Harvest Bakery, 5628
Harvest Bar, 9116
Harvest Bay®, 1484
Harvest Classic, 10637
Harvest Club®, 12885, 30333
Harvest Delighta, 3366
Harvest Farm, 11368
Harvest Foods, 5630
Harvest Fresh, 7978
Harvest of the Sea®, 9522, 26965
Harvest Pasta, 4794
Harvest Road, 10274
Harvest Selects, 12115
Harvest Splendor®, 8055
Harvest Stone, 12477

Harvest Sweets, 2159
Harvest-Pac, 5637
Harvestland®, 9946
Harvestove, 20750
Harvestvac, 21808
Harveys Supermarket, 11838
Hatc, 26476
Hatchers, 7746
Hatco, 23652
Hatfield, 2559, 5643, 12166
Hatties, 5753
Hatuey Beers, 914
Haug, 23655
Haul-All, 19495
Haus Barhyte Mustard, 1034
Havana Cappuccino, 22028
Havana Cappucino, 9115
Havoc Maker, 5652
Havren, 6460
Hawaii, 4493
Hawaii Coffee Company, 5654
Hawaii Coffee Roasters, 5659
Hawaii's Famous Huli Huli, 9691
Hawaiian Delight, 5660
Hawaiian Festives, 7410
Hawaiian Gold, 8019, 13511
Hawaiian Host, 4592
Hawaiian Hula Dressing, 6736
Hawaiian Island Crisp, 5653
Hawaiian Island Crisp Cookies, 5653
Hawaiian Joys, 5660
Hawaiian King, 5660
Hawaiian Majesty, 5660
Hawaiian Natural Water, 5661
Hawaiian Princess Smoke, 6303
Hawaiian Punch, 8586
Hawaiian Punch®, 3725, 6818, 24802
Hawaiian Snacks®, 2939, 2940, 20821, 20822
Hawaiian Sun, 427, 5662
Hawaiian®, 27540
Hawaiice, 918, 19361
Hawkeye, 7655
Hawkhaven, 5663
Hawthorne Valley Farm, 5666
Hayes Graphics®, 22187
Hayes Ranch, 13654
Haynes, 23667
Hayon Select-A-Spray, 23668
Haystack, 7310
Haz Mat, 20486
Haze-Out, 21315
Hazel Creek, 5670
Hazel's, 8670, 19668
Hazelnut, 10307
Hazle, 5672
Hazlitt, 5673
Hazmax Enclosures, 23722
Hazyme®, 2370
Hb Batters, 6098
Hb Breadings, 6098
Hb Pastis, 3165
Hd Barcode, 23488
Hd Secureid, 23488
Hd Smartcode, 23488
Hd-900, 19798
Hdc Ii, 27224
Hde, 22902
He Man, 10873
Head & Shoulders, 12721, 30193
Head Country, 5675
Head of the Class, 13630
Health Assure, 8891
Health Concerns, 5680
Health Cookie, 6442
Health Creation Caramel Pretzels, 8029
Health Creation Onion Pretzels, 8029
Health Is Wealth, 5687
Health Valley, 3617, 5505, 5684
Health-Fu'd, 12377
Healthbest, 5689
Healthbody, 10314
Healthcare, 23261
Healthcare Naturals, 8882
Healthee, 5691

All Brands Index

Healthline, 2960
Healthnut, 1027
Healthseed, 4702
Healthy Choice®, 2939, 2940, 20821, 20822
Healthy Hemp, 4702
Healthy Himalaya, 11351
Healthy Indulgence, 11856
Healthy Juice, 9734
Healthy Life®, 7402
Healthy Ones, 11733
Healthy Partner Pet Snacks, 5139
Healthy Request Ready To Serve Soup, 2115
Healthy Skoop, 5699
Healthy Sleep™, 6449, 24506
Healthy To Go, 6049
Healthy'n Fit Nutritionals, 5698
Healthy™, 8899
Hearn & Rawlins, 13118
Heart, 3852
Heart Cleanse, 5682
Heart Liteo, 10100
Heart of Tea, 5718
Heart of Wisconsin, 8304
Heart Right ®, 1612
Heart Shape, 11517
Heart Tee, 13779
Heart To Heart, 6720
Hearth, 13767
Hearth & Kettle, 6868
Hearth Club, 2711
Hearthbake, 26290
Heartland, 465, 5707, 11053, 25299
Heartland Brands, 8077
Heartland Chocolates, 5616
Heartland Mill, 5713
Heartland U.S.A., 10268
Heartland®, 1491
Hearts, 13256
Hearttline, 194
Hearty Life®, 1491
Hearty Naturals, 5719
Hearty Originals, 4753
Heat & Eat, 9833
Heat & Serve, 4243
Heat Exhangers, 31049
Heat on Demand, 18525
Heat Prober, 27240
Heat Spy, 27240
Heat-It, 23691
Heat-N-Eat, 12396
Heat-Pro, 25266
Heatcraft, 24919
Heath, 2132, 5818, 23750
Heath & Heather, 4244
Heathy 1, 11559
Heatmaker Uvm, 25298
Heatzone, 23698
Heaven Scent, 3924, 5721
Heaven Scent Butter, 5721
Heaven Scent Butter Cookies, 3924
Heaven Scent Croutons, 3924, 5721
Heaven Scent Fat Free Cookies, 3924
Heaven Scent Natural Foods, 3924
Heaven Scent Windmill Cakes, 5721
Heaven Scent Windmill Cookies, 3924
Heavenly Bees, 9151
Heavenly Cluster, 13180
Heavenly Clusters Collection, 13180
Heavenly Fresh, 24567
Heavenly Hash, 4032
Heavenly Light, 4405
Heavenly Little Cookies, 1275
Heavy Bran, 6917
Heavy Metal, 22480
Heavy Seas Marzen, 2763
Heavyweight Gainer 900, 2411
Hebrew National®, 2939, 2940, 20821, 20822
Hecker Pass, 5726
Heckers, 13135
Hedley's, 10412
Hedliner, 23708
Hedpak, 23708

Heemskerk, 12937
Hef-T-Clean, 26116
Hefe Proper, 1687
Hefe Weizen, 1097, 1139
Hefeweizen, 1237, 7551, 10629
Hefeweizer, 3107
Heidecker, 10782
Heifetz®, 1103
Heine's, 5108
Heineman's, 5731
Heiner's, 1359
Heini's Brand Cheese, 1851
Heinicke, 26481
Heinkel's, 5733
Heinle, 11458
Heins, 10372
Heinz Abc, 6977
Heinz Ketchup, 6976
Heiress, 21425
Heise's, 5738
Heitz, 5739
Hela, 1957, 23747
Helen's Kitchen, 12684
Helena Ranch, 9321
Helena View, 5743
Helical, 26697
Helix, 23587
Hell on the Red, 5744
Hell's Furry Fire Hot Sauce, 7694
Helles Bock, 4950
Hellmann's, 1267, 13167, 13169
Hellmans, 11108
Hello Kitty, 2132, 3852, 4659
Hello Water, 5748
Hells Canyon, 5749
Helms, 5752
Helmut, 3714
Helmuth, 5753
Helshiron, 5754
Heluva Good Cheese, 5757
Helwa, 6279
Hem, 11896
Hemingway's Hair Of, 912
Hemp Bar, 5221
Hemp Cream Ale, 13711
Hemp Fusion, 5758
Hemp Sprout Bag, 11977
Hemp2o, 5761
Hemptails, 9117
Hen-Of-The-Woods, 5583
Hendon, 5765
Hengstenberg, 1957
Heniz, 4111
Hennessy, 8452
Hennessy Cognacs, 3570
Henning's, 5768
Henninger Kaiser Pils, 1702
Henri Abele, 4693
Henri Merchant, 1080
Henri Philipe, 7655
Henri's®, 864
Henry, 28967
Henry & Henry®, 20096
Henry Estate, 5772
Henry Weinhard's, 8459
Henry's Heritage Bread, 11979, 29528
Henry's Kettle, 5479
Hepac, 3390
Hepahop Gold, 6554
Hepavac, 30790
Herb Actives, 5065
Herb Alchemy, 4575
Herb Crystals, 4718
Herb Gouda, 13840
Herb Masters' Original, 8882
Herb Science, 10708
Herb Society of America, 5779
Herb Technology, 14011
Herb's Five Star, 9000
Herbal Essences, 12721, 30193
Herbal Nutrition, 665
Herbal Teas, 5155, 12272
Herbal Teazers, 291
Herbamare Juices, 10568
Herbco, 5782

Herbox®, 6000, 23861
Herbs America, 5790
Herbs For Kids®, 9237, 26785
Herbs Seafood, 5781
Herbs, Etc., 5791
Hercules, 18365, 20258, 28748
Hercules Tables, 19608
Herd King, 20608
Herdez®, 6000, 23861
Hereford Beef, 5338
Heritage, 4891, 5803, 31152
Heritage - the Essence of Tradition, 12906
Heritage Bag, 26756
Heritage By Orbon, 27391
Heritage Chipotle Roasted Salsa, 5795
Heritage Coffee, 5794
Heritage Espresso Pods, 11855
Heritage Fancy Foods, 3629, 5796
Heritage Farms®, 8783
Heritage Fresh Salsa, 5795
Heritage Garlic Mayo, 5795
Heritage Health Foods, 5799
Heritage Hearth, 10846
Heritage Ovens, 2227
Heritage Pride, 4262
Heritage Salmon, 5800
Heritage Select, 11855
Heritage Select Brand, 11046, 28702
Heritage Soups, 3956
Herkimer, 9564
Herlocher's Dipping Mustard, 5805
Herman Joseph's Private Reserve, 8459
Herman Joseph's Private Reserve, 8460
Hermann J. Wiemer, 5808
Hermann Pickle, 5809
Hermann's Dark Lager, 13288
Hermannator Ice Bock, 13288
Hermes, 1120, 6986
Hermitex, 21415
Hernandez, 11958
Hero, 71, 6540, 12438, 25789
Hero Jerky, 5139
Herr's®, 5815
Herradura, 1784
Hershey, 6540
Hershey Chocolate, 13610
Hershey's, 541, 5818, 23750
Hershey's Bliss, 5818, 23750
Hershey's Kisses, 5818, 23750
Hershey's Milkshake, 1782
Hershey'sc, 2132
Hershey®'s Ice Cream, 5819
Herta®, 8945
Herzog Selection, 10952
Herzog Wine Cellars, 10952
Hess Collection, 5820
Hess Estate, 5820
Hess Select, 5820
Hettich, 27835
Hewitt Vineyard, 12937
Hey Nut, 5188
Heyday, 5822
Hf's Outstanding, 1140
Hhp, 22769
Hi - Lo, 20256
Hi Ball Energy, 571
Hi C-Plex, 7947
Hi Flo®, 8804
Hi Praize, 11625
Hi Roller, 23758
Hi Shrink, 26108
Hi West, 9699
Hi-Bak, 6768
Hi-C®, 6483
Hi-Cap, 21269, 26893
Hi-Cap® 100, 8804
Hi-Cone, 24039
Hi-Country, 5826
Hi-Def, 30434
Hi-Drum, 24519
Hi-Heat, 23499
Hi-Line, 21857
Hi-Lites, 20144
Hi-Lo, 20258, 23543

Hi-Maize® 260, 8804
Hi-Maize® Whole Grain Flour, 8804
Hi-Performance, 27405
Hi-Pop, 10661
Hi-Psi-Flex(Water), 21717
Hi-Rise Lls Liquid Separator, 18344
Hi-Set® 322, 8804
Hi-Set® C, 8804
Hi-Speed, 22482
Hi-Speed Cooker, 28845
Hi-Tempir, 27325
Hi-Vi, 22252
Hi0spring, 181
Hiac Royco, 27113
Hiawatha, 4928
Hibernation, 5304
Hibiki, 12315
Hiccuppin' Hot Sauce, 4587
Hickory, 4078, 23763
Hickory Baked, 5832
Hickory Creek Bar-B-Q Cooker, 24487
Hickory Farms, 5833
Hickory Grove, 13499
Hickory Harvest Foods, 5834
Hickory Hills, 3248
Hickory Hollow, 9561
Hickory Smoked Sausage, 2944
Hid-Tuff, 26428
Hidden Valley, 2766, 20657
Hidden Valley®, 13328
Hidden Villa Ranch, 5837
Hide-A-Winner, 29081
Higgins & Burke, 8578
High Brew, 5840
High Brew Coffee®, 6818, 24802
High Country Gourmet, 5842
High Country Kombucha, 6049
High Desert, 1914
High Desert Roasters, 13381
High Impact, 4479
High K, 19419
High Liner Culinary, 5844
High Liner®, 5844
High Meadows, 4244
High Moisture Fresh Jack, 13320
High Mountains, 13686
High Rollers Wheat, 549
High Strength Tenex, 29211
High Tide Seafoods, 5850
High Valley Farm, 5832
Highfield, 28357
Highland, 5852
Highland Estates, 5993
Highland Light, 7655
Highland Mist Scotch, 11264
Highland Piper, 7655
Highland Sugar Vermont, 25789
Highland Sugarworks, 5858, 23769
Highlight Stretch Rappers, 18877
Highwood, 5861
Hilary's, 5864
Hilco, 23776
Hilco Corporation, 2132
Hildon Water, 8838
Hilex 6-40, 23774
Hilex Poly, 26756
Hiline, 8919
Hill & Valley, 6338
Hill Country, 12270
Hill Country Products, 5473
Hill Farms, 5520
Hill of Westchester, 1638
Hill's, 13053
Hill-Tween Farms, 22028
Hillcrest, 5418
Hillcrest Orchard, 5869
Hilliard, 23778
Hillman, 5872
Hills Bros, 7995, 11212
Hills Bros Cappucino, 7995
Hillshire Farm®, 13109
Hillshire Snacking®, 13109
Hillside, 11494
Hillware, 23780
Himac, 30731

1301

All Brands / H

Himalasalt, 5881
Himalayan Chef, 5882, 13510
Himalayan Glow, 13510
Himet, 30731
Hinckley Springs, 10303, 11889, 27797
Hinckley Springs®, 3220, 3319
Hine Cognac, 3570
Hinman Vineyards, 11612
Hinoichi, 6021
Hint Mint, 5886
Hinzerling, 5888
Hip Chick Farms, 5889
Hip Whip, 9196
Hipir Kart, 21857
Hippie Snacks, 5891
Hiram Walkerc, 9964
Hires®, 3725, 6818, 24802
His-470, 28006
Hisaka Works Ltd, 20549
Hivex Expander, 18920
Hmr Merchandiser, 20297
Hms, 23553
Hnery McKenna Single Barrel, 5720
Hnery Weinhard's®, 8460
Ho Hos®, 6013
Ho-Tai, 13625
Hob Nob, 29498
Hobart, 24038, 27063
Hobby, 7160
Hobgoblin - Beer, 4148
Hodag, 716, 19094
Hodgson Mill, 5898, 11587
Hodo, 5899
Hoegaarden, 71, 571, 7123, 26668
Hof Ten Dormaal, 8959
Hoffer, 23805
Hoffer Flow Controls Inc., 20837
Hoffman House®, 1103
Hoffmans, 2667
Hoffmaster, 23809
Hoffy, 11988
Hofmeister, 2409
Hofmeister Haus, 6553
Hog Heaven, 838
Hog Wild Pork Jerky, 10081
Hoge, 23813
Hoghaus, 5903
Hogue, 13425
Hohberger Products, 25017
Hokey Pokey, 8269
Hol Grain, 2956
Hola, 1244
Holac, 28291
Holdit, 27238
Holgrain, 25789
Holidale Barley Wine, 1237
Holiday, 20309
Holiday Bonus, 8860
Holiday Farms, 8560
Holiday Greetings, 21059
Holiday Pasta, 4794
Holiday Royal, 4689
Holiday White, 9069
Holland, 13912
Holland House, 8586
Holland House®, 8415
Holland Mints, 7912
Hollmans, 5910
Hollow Tree, 6747
Holly Hops Spiced Al, 9688
Holly Sugar®, 6164
Hollymatic, 23830
Hollys Coffee®, 6818, 24802
Hollywood, 5505
Holo Flite, 29844
Holopop, 7426
Holsom, 741
Holsum, 1881, 5917, 11525
Holsum Bread, 3056
Holsum®, 9736
Holy Moses White Ale, 5314
Holy Sheet, 2763
Holzofen, 3606
Hom-Pik, 27520
Homaid™, 13614

Homarus, 5924
Home Commercial, 22920
Home Country, 4232
Home Fresh, 7871
Home Game, 2511
Home Health®, 8871
Home Kombucha, 5921
Home of Ramona, 4387
Home Pride, 4529
Home Run Inn, 5931
Home Style, 166, 2873
Home Toter, 27134
Home-Style, 25766
Homecraft® Create, 8804
Homemade Gourmet, 10022
Homemade In Minutes, 4753
Homeopathy For Kids®, 9237, 26785
Homestead, 1759, 5944
Homestead Mills, 5946
Homestyle, 103
Homestyle Italian Pasta Salad, 5489
Hometown Stars, 2216
Hommage Cabernet, 2770
Hommage Chardonnay, 2770
Homs, 18327
Honchos, 3466
Honees, 551
Honest, 2814
Honest John's, 11728
Honest Tea, 2811
Honey, 9761
Honey Acres, 5953
Honey Baked Ham, 5966
Honey Basil Ale, 1401
Honey Bbq Ranchc, 5489
Honey Bear Farms, 7339
Honey Bears, 28759
Honey Blonde, 1097
Honey Brown, 3171
Honey Brown Lager, 9117
Honey Bunches of Oats, 10213
Honey Butter Topping, 12936
Honey Essence, 10450
Honey Fruit Spreads, 14034
Honey Gardens™, 9237, 26785
Honey In the Rough, 3815
Honey In the Straw, 14034
Honey Maid, 8729
Honey Maid® S'Mores, 10213
Honey Silk, 1164
Honey Stinger, 5963
Honey Weiss, 7330
Honey-Touched®, 1654
Honeybake Farms, 2501
Honeycomb, 10213
Honeyman & Wood, 5969
Honeymate, 12550
Honeymoon, 13998
Honeystix, 5073
Honeysuckle, 30775
Honeywood Grande, 5969
Honeywood North American Grape, 5969
Honeywood Premium, 5969
Hongar Farms, 5147
Honig, 6977
Honkers, 5188
Hood®, 5486
Hoodcrest, 8669
Hoodsies®, 5486
Hoodsport, 5984
Hoody's, 5632
Hoopee Doops, 13845
Hoosier Data Forms®, 22187
Hoosier Pride, 9585
Hop Ottin' Ipa, 549
Hop Valley, 8459
Hop Valley®, 8460
Hop-Syn, 23659
Hope, 5990
Hopkins Inn Caesar Dressing, 5992
Hopkins Inn House Dressing, 5992
Hopkins Vineyard, 5993
Hopkins Westwind, 5993
Hoppin' Pops, 6158
Hoppmann, 19220

Hopps Aux Pommes, 1666
Hopps Brau, 1666
Hopsteiner®, 11018
Horio, 6986
Horizon, 11281, 26450
Horizon Orangic, 5837
Horizon Organic, 3379, 13734
Horizon™, 24812
Hormel, 6762
Hormel Chili®, 6000, 23861
Hormel Foods, 1891, 11053
Hormel Foods®, 11504, 29095
Hormel Health Labs, 6000, 23861
Hormel Pepperoni®, 6000, 23861
Hormel Side Dishes, 6000, 23861
Hormel Taco Meats®, 6000, 23861
Hormel®, 6000, 23861
Horne's, 11416
Hornitos Sauza, 3024
Hornitos®, 1120
Horowitz Margareten, 7848
Horseshoe Brand, 6003
Horseshoe Cake, 6082
Horseshoes and Nails, 6082
Horton's, 2981
Hoshizaki America, 23868
Hosmer Mountain Soft Drinks, 6009
Hosokawa, 19576
Hospitality, 5015, 6010
Hospitality Mints, 2132
Hospitality Suite, 20813
Hostaphan®, 26228
Hostess, 6555
Hostess Cupcakes®, 6013
Hostess®, 6483
Hot & Crusty, 7876
Hot 'n' Ready®, 184, 13109
Hot Buffet To Go, 19329
Hot Chocolate Supreme, 464
Hot Chocolate-Fine Chocolate, 12542
Hot Fudge Fantasy, 9019
Hot Mama, 6353
Hot Mix, 3465
Hot N' Tender, 23729
Hot Pockets®, 8945
Hot Pops, 19106
Hot Sauce, 21336
Hot Sauce For Cool Kids, 8433
Hot Shot, 7655
Hot Stuff, 11775
Hot Tamales®, 6641
Hot Tray, 27603
Hot Wachula's Gourmet Dips & Sauces, 6018
Hot Water Extract, 20966
Hot Wok, 3465
Hot! Hot! Hot!, 6015
Hot'n Zesty Links, 6574
Hot-C-Pops, 5752
Hot-N-Coldpops, 5752
Hotel America, 21497
Hotel Bar, 6760
Hothothot, 10435
Hotpack, 26481
Hotpan'zers, 23260
Hotpoint, 22959
Hotslot, 27893
Hound Dog, 7655
House Blend, 3574, 12846
House Foods, 6021
House of Bazzini, 1114
House of Raeford, 6573, 20101
House of Raeford®, 6025
House of Stuart Scotch, 11264
House of Tsang®, 6000, 23861
House of Windsor, 11865
Housewarming, 21059
Howard Johnson, 4369
Howard's, 6034
Howden, 28967
Howe, 20777, 28967
Hoyt's Pure Honey, 6038
Hoyts, 6038
Hp - White Hulled Sesame Seeds, 11462
Hpnotiq, 5720

Hrd, 5981
Hs, 23361
Ht-1001, 26968
Ht-500, 26968
Ht80, 24059
Hub of the Uncompaghre, 10324
Hub Pen, 23906
Hubba Bubba®, 7952, 13960
Hubba Bubbac, 2132
Hubbardson Blue, 13687
Hubbell, 23907
Huber, 1231
Huber Bock, 1231
Hubert's Lemonade, 2811
Hubort, 26476
Hubsch Doppel Bock, 12191
Hubsch Dunkel, 12191
Hubsch Lager, 12191
Hubsch Marzen, 12191
Hubsch Pilsener, 12191
Huck's, 6046
Huckleberry, 3953
Huckleberry's Farm, 12831
Huco, 18678
Hudrage, 7876
Hudson, 11039
Hudson Cream Flour, 12018
Hudson New York, 13082
Hudson Valley, 6050, 6051
Hudson Valley Farms, 1153
Hudson Valley Homestead, 6054
Hudson Valley Malt, 6056
Hudson's Total Control For Windows, 23914
Hudsonville Ice Cream, 6057
Huggies, 24838
Hughes, 23921
Hugo Et Fils, 4677
Huisken, 1659
Hula, 8443
Hulk Candies, 12547
Humane Harvest, 2576
Humble Tea, 4820
Humbly Hemp, 6063
Humitran, 18893
Humitran-C, 18893
Humitran-Dp, 18893
Humitran-T, 18893
Humm, 6071
Hummel Meats, 6072
Hummer, 648
Hummos, 128
Hummus Pod, 8446
Hummustir, 6075
Humpty Dumpty, 9980
Humpty Dumpty Chips, 9191
Humpy Dumpty, 9408
Hung's Noodle House, 6079
Hungerford & Terry, 23927
Hungry Buddha, 1825
Hungry Jack, 1069
Hungry-Man®, 2939, 2940, 20821, 20822
Hunt Country Vineyards, 6083
Hunt's®, 2939, 2940, 20821, 20822
Hunter Filtrator Hf Series, 28050
Hunter Oil Skimmer, 18344
Hunter's Sausage, 6973
Huntingcastle, 4769, 22896
Huntington, 5499
Hunts, 6084
Hurri-Kleen, 23939
Hurricane, 18450
Hurricane Systems, 26129
Hurricane®, 26668
Hurst Family Harvest®, 9074
Hurst's Brand Dry Beans®, 9074
Hurst's Hambeens®, 9074
Huskee, 20882
Huskey, 23943
Huskey Specialty Lubricants, 29469
Husky Master, 18498
Husman's, 6091
Husman's®, 2939, 2940, 20821, 20822, 27540

All Brands Index

Hussong's Tequila, 8062
Hvac, 20894
Hww, 23884
Hy Van, 3945
Hy-Ac Iv, 30924
Hy-D®, 3320
Hy-Drive Systems, 23309
Hy-Tex, 23160
Hy-Trous Plant Foods, 23950
Hybread, 6094
Hybri Flex, 19111
Hybri Grio, 19111
Hybrid, 28396
Hybrute, 20644
Hycom Contact Slides, 19690
Hycor Screening & Dewatering Equip., 27314
Hyde Vineyard, 6892
Hydra Form, 30850
Hydra Mold, 30850
Hydra-Green, 13472
Hydra-Supreme, 23467
Hydrafeed, 23121
Hydrasieve, 18187
Hydrasperse™, 19108
Hydraucuber Super Slicer, 23117
Hydrauflakers, 23117
Hydravax, 8191
Hydrea®, 1721
Hydro-Fil, 23467
Hydro-Kote®, 126
Hydro-Laser, 30028
Hydro-Miser, 18997
Hydroblend, 29397
Hydrocheck, 23571
Hydroclear, 20753
Hydroforce, 21051
Hydroheater, 23964
Hydrohelix, 23964
Hydrologix, 3469
Hydroponic Sweet Basil, 13586
Hydropure Pumps, 23969
Hydroscrubs, 25662
Hydrostatics, 22140
Hydrovane, 23032
Hydrowype, 25662
Hydroxycut, 4150
Hye Delites, 6100
Hye Roller, 6100
Hyfroydol, 22712
Hygeaire, 19152
Hygeia, 6101
Hygeia®, 3442, 21421
Hygenius, 20799
Hygienic Fusedware, 30481
Hygrade, 1478, 7875
Hygrol, 26630
Hyland, 726, 13513
Hylon® Vii, 8804
Hynap, 23160
Hynes, 24015
Hyophen®, 8389
Hypak, 23958
Hyper Clear, 30137
Hypersoft, 20990
Hypo Form, 13179
Hypor, 21425
Hypower, 6769
Hypowr, 13498
Hyskor, 5462
Hyster, 23977
Hytamatic, 23857
Hytrol, 19908
Hytron, 30457
Hytronics, 22140, 30457
Hywave, 6387

I

I Buoonatarula Sini, 11668
I Flex, 6107
I Heart Keenwah, 6102
I Love Pasta, 4794
I Will, 9094
I'Ll Bring the Saladd, 4753
I'M Different, 6106
I-Cool, 6107
I-Rap, 27156
I.M. Good Snacks, 5834
I.P.A., 9688
I.W. Harper Bourbon, 3570
Iac 2000, 31435
Iams®, 7952
Ibarra, 12823
Ibc, 1056, 8586, 11310, 20847, 29663
Ibc Root Beer®, 3725
Ibc®, 6818, 24802
Iberia Malt Liquor, 9137
Ibp, 3262
Ibp Trusted Excellence®, 13109
Ic Light Mango, 10091
Icco Brand, 6126
Ice & Easy, 5334
Ice Beer, 7123
Ice Breakers, 2132, 5818, 23750
Ice Chews, 12390
Ice Chiller, 19419
Ice Chips, 6127, 12390
Ice Chunks, 12390
Ice Cream Joe, 4227
Ice Cubes, 10496
Ice Logic, 19419
Ice Man, 9664
Ice Master, 26313
Ice Road, 9182
Ice Road Blend - Darkest, 9181
Ice Sculptures, 20256
Ice Tea, 12914
Ice Tickles, 2050
Ice-Foe, 21757
Ice-O-Matic, 31092
Ice-O-Matic Ice Machines, 24048
Ice-Stir-Cools, 25665
Iceas, 18097
Iced Fudge Cookies Bars, 12551
Icee, 2132, 6338
Icehouse, 8459
Icehouse®, 8460
Iceland: Armant, 5108
Icelandic, 1057
Icelandic Glacial Water, 26668
Icelandic Provisions, 6132
Icelandic Seafood®, 5844
Icelandic Spring Water, 26668
Iceman, 27764
Ichiban Delight®, 857
Ici, 6252, 29035
Icl Industrial Products, 1692
Ics, 22315
Icy Point, 9344
Id-Alg, 9029, 26626
Ida Mae, 9564
Idaho Lake Wild Rice, 575
Idaho Spud, 6134
Idaho Supreme, 6138
Idaho's Best, 6139
Idaho-Pacific, 6137
Idahoan, 6140
Iddian Hollow, 6186
Ideal, 10399, 18276, 24063, 27949
Ideal Mark, 24059
Idealfold, 21415
Ideco, 24059
Idee, 3714
Identity, 18778
Idf, 6254
Idockusa, 23993
Idol, 7505
Idol Vodka, 1543
Ids, 28306
Iga, 9621
Igloo, 24072
Igloo 2go, 24072
Igloo Stralth, 24072
Iguana, 5516
Iguana Tom's, 13144
Igzu, 6114
Ii Biscotto Della Nonna, 4021
Ii Monello, 8479
Ii Sisters, 6115
Iii, 24130
Ikamag, 24074
Il Caffe, 2839, 20694
Il Hwa, 6116
Il Poggiolo, 8479
Ile, 24178
Illegal Mezcal, 4677
Illinois Prairie, 4753
Illinois Rag, 26770
Illy, 8090, 25789
Illy Chilled Coffee, 26668
Iltaco, 2542
Imag!Ne®, 9945, 27433
Imagex, 24910
Imagine, 5505
Imagine Chocolate, 6150
Imagine Foods, 12017
Imagine Natural Creations, 6151
Imaje 7s, 24093
Imar, 24097
Imeta, 20868
Imlak'esh Organics, 6153
Immaculate Baking®, 4947
Immaculate Consumption, 6155
Immordl, 6156
Immort Ale, 3644
Immumax, 9957
Immune Life, 4127
Immuno Force, 5883
Impacdoors, 18548
Impacdor, 18547
Impact, 23944
Impact Confections, 2132
Impact Island, 29746
Impco, 24119
Imperial, 7309, 9117, 9673, 26718, 29703
Imperial Blent, 11264
Imperial Choice, 13190
Imperial Choice Coff, 13191
Imperial Ipa Black Pilsner, 3746
Imperial Ipa Pilsner, 3746
Imperial Pumpkin, 7526
Imperial Stout, 1237, 3746
Imperial Sugar®, 6164
Impinger, 25320
Impinger a La Carte, 25320
Impress, 6232
Impress™, 21362
Impressions, 30898
Imprintz, 21199
Improved Meat, 6168
Impulse, 24120
Impulse Heat Sealer, 30369
Impulse®, 21362
Impulse™, 24812
Imus Brothers Coffee, 6170
In the Raw, 6172
In-Shear, 24479
In-Sink-Erator, 24124
Ina, 24014
Inc, 24210
Inca Harvest, 12663
Inca Kola, 6943
Incognito, 4815
Incosity, 5246
Incredible Blue, 20966
Indent-A-Mark, 25870
Indenti-Film, 31142
Independant Folders®, 22187
India Beer, 8459
India House, 6653
India Pale Ale, 1139, 1401, 7526, 9366
India Teas, 12272
Indian, 14053
Indian Brown Ale, 3644
Indian Creek, 8204, 14023
Indian Head, 13803
Indian River Pride, 3314
Indian River Select, 6188
Indian Summer, 2518
Indiana Rag, 26770
Indiana Spud®, 7402
Indiana Wire, 24152
Indiana Woven Wire, 19339
Indica India Pale Ale, 7554
Indicoder, 22902
Indigenous, 13082
Indigo, 6197
Indo, 25147
Indramat, 28359
Industravac, 29489
Industri-Sol, 31267
Industrial, 18352, 24198, 24199
Industrial Air, 27412
Industrial Clutch, 18678
Industrial Structures, 31141
Industrial Traffic Mats, 30656
Industrialeveline, 25488
Induveca, 2670
Indy, 24076
Inertia Dynamics, 18678
Infalac, 13122
Inferno, 23600
Inferno Wings®, 1654
Infinity, 19581, 27711, 29189
Infinity Twist, 23261
Infinity®, 6374, 24434
Infit, 26040
Infitec, 24210
Inflation Fighter, 31290
Info Board, 22121
Infogenesis Gsa, 18464
Infogenesis Hospitality, 18464
Infogenesis Iqs, 18464
Infogenesis Its, 18464
Infogenesis Ticketing, 18464
Infraseal, 24037
Infratech, 18434
Ingersoll Rand, 24220
Inglehoffer, 1141
Inglett, 22581
Ingo-Man, 23972
Ingo-Top, 23972
Ingold, 26040
Ingoldby, 12937
Ingot, 5140
Ingredient Integrity, 9743
Ingredionc, 6260, 24336
Inharvest, 6171, 24123
Inhibidor, 21388
Inhibit, 21425
Injectamatic, 24906
Injection Quills, 24696
Ink Stik, 26109
Ink-Koder, 19699
Ink-Stik 'n' Holder, 26109
Inka Chips, 6214
Inka Corn, 6214
Inka Crops Kettle Chips, 6214
Inka Crops Seeds & Nuts, 6214
Inka Crops Veggie Chips, 6214
Inked Organics, 6215
Inksource, 30841
Inline Fill-To-Level Filler, 21033
Inline Piston Filler, 21033
Inn Maid, 12467
Inner Beauty Hot Sauce, 12832
Inner Force, 13998
Innerclean, 746
Innisfree, 6603
Inniskillin, 6223, 13425
Innkeeper's Own, 1134
Innkeepers Choice, 1718
Innovaphase™, 2711
Inpro, 26040
Inquest, 28670
Inscription White, 6763
Insect Inn Iv, 27279
Insect-O-Cutor, 24273
Insight, 20573
Insignia, 6603
Insignia Pops, 24277
Inspecto-Light, 20305
Inspector, 18897
Insta Grains, 1710
Insta Thick, 10297
Insta-Balance, 19430
Insta-Pro, 24280
Insta-Tie, 27134

All Brands Index

Instabowl, 21027
Instacafe, 1490
Instagel, 12637
Instamark, 22018
Instamark Script, 19485
Instamark Signature, 19485
Instamark Stylus, 19485
Instant Burger, 29301
Instant Cappuccino, 12868
Instant Clearjel®, 8804
Instant Dip, 20318
Instant Indulgence, 2525
Instant Pure-Cote, 5246
Instant Pure-Flo® F, 8804
Instant Recovery Fryer, 24744
Instant Roux & Gravy, 12869
Instant Tea, 12868
Instant Textra®, 8804
Instant Whip, 9378
Instant-Ice, 22602
Instantgum, 9029, 26626
Instantwhip, 6233
Instaprep, 27258
Insti-Mash, 24725
Instoematic, 23543
Instore, 23355
Insul-Air, 20922
Insul-Glare, 20922
Insul-Plus, 18525
Insul-Wall, 28176
Insulair, 24287
Insulrock, 18413
Intact, 24906
Intedge, 24290
Integra, 20754
Integra Cm, 20754
Integra T, 20754
Integrale, 3127
Integrated Comfort Systems, 30382
Integrity, 19737
Intelijet, 19546
Intelli Pack, 18339
Intellipack, 30382
Intellorol, 22254
Intense™ Flavored Milks, 13218
Inter Ocean, 8028
Interactive Sales Manager, 24307
Intercept, 26379
Interchange, 27245
Interial Stout, 7310
Interlake, 24317, 24810
Interlogix, 20290
Intermountain Bison, 5139
Internation Seafood of Alaska, 6270
International Baler Corp., 20847
International Brownie, 6248
International Converter, 26756
International Delight, 3379, 13734
International Delight®, 11281
International Delight™, 11211
International Press & Shear, 20847
International Tank & Pipe, 24360
Intimus, 28885
Intrac, 26040
Intralox, Inc., 24375
Intros®, 11504, 29095
Introvigne's, 570
Intrustor, 24984
Invader, 30790
Inver House Scotch, 11264
Invercab, 23927
Invermere, 10426
Invert-A-Bin, 21186
Invertec, 11013
Invertose Hfcs, 6211, 24226
Inview, 18354
Invisi-Bowl, 27277
Invisible Goodness, 463
Invisible Packaging, 27277
Invitrogen, 30217
Involvo, 18082
Iobio, 19419
Ioma, 13565
Iowa Rag, 26770
Iowa State, 1660

Ipa, 4950, 5188
Ipm, 24350
Ips, 20847
Ipswich Ale, 6283
Iq Juice, 6122
Iq120 Minilab, 24022
Iq125 Minilab, 24022
Iq150, 24022
Iq240, 24022
Iqs/3, 21145
Iridescents, 21648
Irilla Extra Virgin O.O., 11096
Iris, 27887
Irish, 21059
Irish Mist, 5892
Irish Mist Liqueur, 5720
Irish Spring, 20721
Irish Stout, 9688
Irish Style Nut Brown Ale, 5515
Iron City, 10091
Iron City Light, 10091
Iron Horse, 9701
Iron Kettle, 6267
Iron Tuff, 28261
Iron Uke, 13643
Iron-Tek, 3080
Irwin, 29584
Isabo Hearts of Palm, 4607
Isahop, 6554
Island Blend, 9182
Island Fruit, 7373
Island Mist Iced Tea, 1636, 19825
Island Prince®, 1140
Island Princess, 6303, 9519
Island Queen®, 1140
Island Spring, 6309
Island Sweetwater, 6310
Island Teriyaki, 11878
Island Trader, 7777
Island Treasures Gourmet, 2296
Islander, 3765
Islander's Choice, 4362
Iso-Flo®, 24812
Iso-Sport, 253
Isobox, 21416
Isolok, 29033
Isomalt, 1219
Isometric, 22615
Isopure, 8870
Isowall, 18413
Issimo Celebrations!, 6314
Issimo's Creme Br-L., 6314
Istara, 7126
It's a Baby!, 21059
It's a Boy, 9753
It's a Girl, 9753
It's It, 6315
It's Soy Delicious, 11771
Italia, 6316, 13365
Italia D'Oro Coffee, 1636, 19825
Italian, 21059
Italian Chef, 9821
Italian Rose, 6322
Italian Village®, 10899
Italico, 1174
Itchy Witchy, 11004
Ithaca Cold-Crafted, 6325
Iti, 24092
Ititropicals, 6276
Itoen, 6327
Itty-Bittie Biscotti, 13216
Itty-Bittie Cookies, 13216
Ivan the Terrible, 10992
Ivanhoe, 6328
Ivanhoe Classics, 6328
Ivanhoe Fresh, 6328
Iveta Gourmet, 6329
Ivex, 24044
Ivis, 20244
Ivory, 12721, 30193
Ivory Almond K'Nuckle, 10984
Iws, 20359
Izze, 6124
Izze®, 9945, 27433

J

J & J, 4035
J Bar B, 6334
J Cup®, 21362
J Moreau Fils, 12672
J Nicole Vineyard Pinot Noir, 12627
J Russian River Vall, 12627
J Sparkling Wine, 12627
J Vineyards & Winery®, 3834
J&J Gourmet, 6451
J&M, 8709
J-Burger Seasoning, 795
J-Press, 30548
J-Series, 19798
J. Berrie Brown Wine Nuts, 4587
J. Crow's, 6371
J. Filippi, 6350
J. Schram, 11307
J.B. Webb Co., 31214
J.C. Ford Co., 24417
J.C. Rivers Gourmet Jerky, 5056
J.F. Braun, 6398
J.M. Schneider, 11768
J.Moreau & Fils, 1543
J.S. McMillan, 6387
J.T.M. Food Group, 6410
Jac-O-Net, 23523
Jack Daniel's, 4422
Jack Daniel's Gentleman Jack, 6416
Jack Daniel's Old No. 7, 6416
Jack Daniel's Single Barrel, 6416
Jack Daniel's Tennessee Fire, 6416
Jack Daniel's Tennessee Honey, 6416
Jack Daniel's Tennessee Rye, 6416
Jack Daniel's®, 6416
Jack Daniels, 1784, 5141, 10468
Jack Link's, 541, 5141, 7449
Jack Links, 4150
Jack Mackerel, 2555
Jack Man, 7310
Jack Miller, 6417
Jack Rabbit, 12972, 12973, 30444
Jack's All American, 10196
Jack's Beans, 2879
Jack's Pumpkin Spice™, 26668
Jackpot, 4232, 5409, 8219
Jackson's Honest, 6423
Jackson-Triggs, 13425
Jacob Best, 9664
Jacobs, 3714
Jacobs Vehicle Systems, 18678
Jacobsen's Toast, 7511
Jacquelynn Cuv'e, 2454
Jacquelynn Syrah, 2454
Jacques Bonet Brandy, 11264
Jade Range, 24495, 30706
Jade Refrigeration, 24495
Jaffa, 10659
Jaffer, 2096
Jagenberg Diana, 24496
Jager, 6433
Jahabow, 19042
Jahbo Showcases, 24003
Jake & Amos, 7193
Jake's Grillin, 6439
Jalapeanuts, 2021, 2022
Jalapeno, 9935
Jalapeno Gouda, 13840
Jalapeno Tnt, 9935
Jalea De Jalapeno, 19106
Jamaica Blue Mountain, 10157
Jamaica Bluemountain, 761
Jamaican Gold, 8988, 10307
James, 10296
James Chocolate Seal Taffy, 6445
James Cream Mints, 6445
James Harbour, 4515
James Remind-O-Timer, 18831
James Salt Water Taffy, 6445
James', 4645
Jamesonc Irish, 9964
Jamieson's Run, 12937
Jamy's Three Dragon, 520, 18891
Jana, 9858

Jane Dough, 3709
Jane Stewart, 11102
Janes, 11776
Janes Family Favourites, 6451
Janus, 26319
Japan Food Canada/Kikkoman, 20020
Japone, 1120
Jar-Lu, 5738
Jardin Savon, 27278
Jaret, 13610
Jarritos, 12823
Jarvis, 24522
Jasmati, 10712
Jasmine, 11908
Jasmine Green, 13746
Jason, 5505, 7848
Jason & Son, 6461
Jason Pharmaceuticals, 6462
Jasper, 7463
Jasvine, 6460
Java Estate, 10157
Java Jacket, 24525
Java Jelly, 5217
Javarama, 10303, 27797
Jaw Busters, 1417, 4345
Jax, 19529
Jax Lubricants, 24526
Jay, 30373
Jay Bee, 24530
Jayhawk Mills, 24532
Jays, 11770
Jayson, 9709
Jazz, 6310, 22599
Jazz Cola, 5539
Jazzie J, 11557
Jazzy Barbecue Sauce, 887
Jazzy Java Custom Flavored Gourmet, 10584
Jb's Extreme, 3279
Jc's Pie Bites, 6393
Jc's Pie Pops, 6393
Jcb By Jean-Charles Boisset, 1543
Jdk & Sons™, 1120
Jean Sweet Potatoes, 10954
Jean-Claude Boisset, 12672
Jecky's Best, 6478
Jeff's Naturals, 6481
Jelen, 8459
Jell-O, 6976
Jello, 6977
Jelly Bean, 5017
Jelly Belly, 6485, 13610
Jelly Belly Candy Company, 4150
Jelly Krimpetsc, 12551
Jemaco, 28714
Jemez Blush, 10165
Jemez Red, 10165
Jemmburger, 1262
Jennair, 25893
Jennfan, 28649
Jennie, 11934
Jennie-O Turkey®, 6000, 23861
Jenny Craig®, 8945
Jenny's, 6491
Jenny's Country Kitchen, 6490
Jensen Foods®, 11504, 29095
Jensen Solos™, 6492
Jensen's Orchard, 11748
Jered, 27083
Jeremiah's Pick, 6497
Jericho Canyon Red, 10845, 10963
Jermann®, 3834
Jerome, 19041
Jerry's, 6500
Jersey Boardwalk, 5400
Jersey Farms, 10664
Jersey Shore®, 2332
Jersey Supreme, 4578
Jesben, 6505
Jesco, 6129
Jess Jones Farms, 6506, 24551
Jessie Lord, Inc., 3078
Jet 2000, 31420
Jet Air, 21756
Jet Cleaner, 23275

All Brands Index

Jet Cut, 25299
Jet Set, 26681
Jet Sifter, 26736
Jet Spray, 20783, 20975
Jet Streamer, 25881
Jet Tea, 3009
Jet White, 27045
Jet-A-Mark, 25870
Jet-A-Mark/Linx, 25870
Jet-Clean, 29489
Jet-O-Mizer, 22662
Jet-Puffed, 6976
Jetaway, 18835
Jetcoat, 11906
Jetflow, 29221
Jetstar, 29596
Jetwrite, 30434
Jetzone, 20085
Jeunesse Wines, 10952
Jewel Laboratories, 13128
Jewel of India, 10435
Jewish, 21059
Jfg Coffee and Tea, 10657
Ji Hao, 734
Jicachipsc, 9574
Jif, 6380
Jif-Pak, 24562
Jif-Y-Clean, 26116
Jiffy Mix, 2508
Jiffy Pop, 6267
Jiffy Pop®, 2939, 2940, 20821, 20822
Jiffy Roll, 21415
Jiffyc, 10106
Jigg-All, 19998, 19999
Jila & Jols, 3381
Jilbert, 3442, 21421
Jim Beam, 3545, 12315, 13454
Jim Beam®, 1120
Jim Candy, 431
Jim's Country Mill Sausage, 14043
Jimmy Dean, 6520
Jimmy Dean®, 13109
Jinglebits, 10104
Jinja, 6523
Jk Sweet, 6402
Jmh Premium, 6405
Jo Citrus, 11549
Jo San, 31350
Jo's Candies, 6525
Jo's Original, 6525
Jo-Lock, 25384
Joan of Arc®, 864, 11209
Job-Built, 23543
Jobhandler, 24395
Jobmaster, 25719
Jodar, 6527
Jody Maroni, 6529
Jody's, 6530
Joe Bertman's Ballpark Mustard, 6532
Joe Clark's Candies, Inc., 6533
Joe Corbi's, 6534
Joe Perry's, 730
Joey's, 6542
Johannisberg Riesling, 7527, 11162
John Foster Green, 20789
John Morrell, 11733, 24583
John Mountain Organic, 12401
John O'S, 1553
John Wm. Macy's Cheesecrips, 6561
John Wm. Macy's Cheesesticks, 6561
John Wm. Macy's Sweetsticks, 6561
John Z'S Big City, 5402
Johnny Boy Vanilla, 13613
Johnny Walker Scotch, 3570
Johnson (Penn), 28967
Johnson Brothers, 31081
Johnson Pump, 28714
Johnson's Alexander Valley, 6569
Johnsondiversey, 18029
Johnsonville Bratwur, 6574
Johnsonville Country, 6574
Johnston County Hams, 11864
Johnston's Winery, 6578
Johr®, 898
Joia All Natural Soda, 6579

Joint Cleanse, 5682
Joint Movement, 8896
Joint Well, 9201
JojÉ, 6580
Joker - Fruit Juice, 4148
Joker's Wild Energy, 3753, 21763
Joki, 24366
Joliesse Vineyards, 12672
Jollie Juan, 13184
Jolly Aid, 7890
Jolly Good, 6985
Jolly Llama, 6581
Jolly Pops, 7890
Jolly Rancher, 2132, 5818, 6483, 23750
Jolly Roger, 13770
Jolly Rogers, 3746
Jolly Time, 478
Jolly Trolley, 30330
Jolt, 13697
Jolt Cola Energy Rush, 12547
Jolt-Cola, 13697
Jomar, 24611
Jomints, 11549
Jon Donaire, 6583, 10714
Jonathan International Foods, 3953
Jonathan T., 13242
Jonathan's Organics, 6585
Jonathan's Sprouts, 6585
Jones, 6589
Jones Sausagest, 6587
Jones Soda Carbonated Candy, 1343
Jones Soda Carbonated Sours, 1343
Jones Soda Energy Boosters, 1343
Jones Sours, 1343
Jones Zylon, 24618
Jonnypops, 6592
Joons Chocolate Popcorn, 10944
Jordan Almonds, 8588
Jordanettes, 11320
Jordon, 22677, 24623
Jordon Scientific, 22677
Jose Cuervo Margarita Salt Sombrero, 4650
Jose Goldstein, 1279
Jose Ole®, 237, 238
Jose Pedro, 5029
Joseph Farms, 8898
Joseph Farms Cheese, 6600
Josh & John's Ice Cream, 6608
Joshua Miguel, 11339, 28940
Josie's Best Blue Tortilla Chips, 11439
Joullian Vineyards, 6612
Journey, 8003
Jow Stiff's Spiked Rootbeer, 13711
Joy, 6614, 6821, 12721, 20165, 30193
Joy Stick, 614
Joy Stiks, 2947
Joy's, 6615
Joy's Gourmet Snacks, 12666
Joyce Farms, 4321, 22498
Joyful Mind, 5883
Joyfuls, 6617
Joyner's, 13237
Joyya™, 11211
Jp's, 12961
Jr Buffalos®, 6374, 24434
Jrs, 21201
Js-1, 28556
Juanita's, 6619
Juarez, 7655
Jubilations, 6621
Jubilee, 6622
Judel, 24636
Juice Bowl, 3279
Juice Bowl Sparkling Juice, 3279
Juice Direct, 3365
Juice Out, 20966
Juice Plus, 6159
Juice Tree, 24639
Juice-It, 23273
Juice-Master, 24725
Juice-Mate, 10314
Juiceburst, 5460
Juicefuls Hard Candy, 10532
Juicemaster, 4521

Juicetyme Delites, 1292
Juicy Fruit®, 7952, 13960
Juicy Juice®, 6483, 8945
Juicy Orange, 6159
Juicy Whip, 6628, 24640
Juju, 7310
Juju Ginger, 7309
Jujyfruits, 1417, 4345
Julian's Recipe, 6630
Juliana, 9766
Julie's Organic, 9533
Julie's Real, 6632
Jumbo Bin, 20606
Jumbo Flavors, 3707
Jumbo Lump, 10429
Jumbo Minisips, 9170
Jumbo Straws, 19999
Jump Start, 2860
Jumping Black Beans, 4252
Juneau, 4748
Jungle Juice, 9251
Jungle Munch, 10542
Junior, 29192
Junior Mints,, 2102
Junior Mints®, 12880
Jupiler, 71
Jupina, 2338
Jura, 31083
Jus-Rol®, 4947
Just, 6649
Just 'n Time, 19434
Just - Ripe, 14035
Just Add Tequila, 7903
Just Bare Chicken®, 10056
Just Born, Inc, 2132
Just Born®, 6641
Just Chips, 6647
Just Crisps, 6647
Just Croutons, 6647
Just Date Syrup, 6643
Just Delicious, 6644
Just Fiber, 11794
Just Flatbread, 6647
Just Great Bakers, Inc., 2810
Just In Time, 10022
Just Juice, 3479, 21460
Just Meringues, 1751, 2599
Just Nuts, 4032
Just Once Natural Herbal Extras, 10537
Just Panela, 6648
Just Pik't, 4714
Just Right®, 6765
Just Snak-It, 12831
Just Whites, 3449
Just-Rite, 18276
Justin, 6651
Justin Vineyard, 3545
Justin's®, 6000, 23861
Justrite, 25698
Juwong, 10331
Jw Dundee's Honey Brown Lager, 4950
Jyoti, 6653

K

K Box, 20866
K Line, 24964
K&F, 6654, 6902
K&S, 6656
K-14, 24721
K-Commander, 24664
K-Cup Packs, 4543
K-Flex Systems, 18455
K-Guard, 30516
K-Link, 24664
K-Mars, 24700
K-Min, 9262
K-Modular, 24664
K-Products, 18778
K-Tron Soder, 24664
K-Way, 24665
K-Wheel, 22480
K10s, 24664
K2-Modular, 24664
K4484, 8804

Ka-Mec, 9748
Kaak, 19567
Kaboom, 2666, 20561
Kady, 24708
Kadyzolvers, 24708
Kaf-Tan, 30337
Kaffe Magnum Opus, 6683
Kaffree Roma, 772
Kagome, 6684
Kahiki, 6685
Kahlua, 5892, 9964
Kahl£A®, 6818, 24802
Kahns, 5792
Kaho Mai, 1849
Kairak, 24038
Kaiseki Select, 2630
Kaktus, 20120
Kakuhunter, 23209
Kal-Tainer, 22427
Kal®, 9237, 26785
Kalamazoo, 6690
Kalena, 6691
Kali Hart Chardonnay, 12506
Kaliber, 5427
Kalin Cellars, 6693
Kalmbach, 726
Kalsec, 6695, 24719
Kam-Lok, 19146
Kambly, 13544
Kamchatka®, 1120
Kamenitza, 8459
Kamis, 8061
Kammerude, 4028
Kamora, 3545
Kamora®, 1120
Kamut®, 6171, 24123
Kan Tong®, 7952
Kana Organics, 6700
Kandy Kookies, 6851
Kane, 22203
Kane-May/Km, 20757
Kanemasa, 8412
Kanga Beans, 1909
Kangaroo®, 2939, 2940, 20821, 20822
Kangavites, 11785
Kanimi-Tem, 11559
Kanonkop, 4677
Kansas City Rag, 26770
Kansas Rag, 26770
Kansas Sun, 2389
Kantner, 6702
Kaori Horoyoi, 1120
Kap-Pak, 24723
Kapit, 22545
Kapiti®, 4552
Kaps-All, 24669
Kaptain's Ketch, 9000
Kara, 6707
Karbach Brewing Company, 571
Karbonaid Xx, 26160
Karen's Fabulous Biscotti, 1397
Karenvolf, 6774
Kargher Chocolate Chips, 6708
Kari-Out, 6665
Karine & Jeff, 6709
Karkov®, 13120
Karl Schnell, 24724
Karl Strauss, 6711
Karlsburger, 6714
Karm'l Dapples, 2050
Karma, 6716
Karoun, 6719
Kars, 4721
Kartell, 21848
Kas, 6666
Kasanofs's, 12328
Kashi Cereals, 6720
Kashi Frozen Foods, 6720
Kashi Snacks, 6720
Kashruth, 6970
Kashu Gold Oranges, 13906
Kasi-Weigh, 18223
Kasilof Fish, 6721
Kasira, 6722
Kasmati, 10712

1305

All Brands Index

Kasomel™, 10239
Kasser, 7146
Kasten/Kamco, 25871
Kastin's, 7279
Katahna, 357
Katchall, 24700
Kate Latters Chocolates, 6725
Kate's, 6726
Katelin, 19150
Katharine Beecher®, 13572
Katherine Beecher, 13574
Kathi, 1957
Kathryn Kennedy, 6729
Kathy's Gourmet Specialties, 6730
Kats, 24906
Katy's Kitchen®, 11504, 29095
Katy's Smokehouse, 6733
Kauai Coffee, 6735, 7995
Kauai Kookie, 6736
Kaukauna, 1172
Kava, 6380
Kava Kava, 1285
Kava King Beverage Mixes, 6740
Kava King Chocolates, 6740
Kavli, 6279
Kay Foods, 6741
Kay Pak, 12250
Kay Toledo Tag™, 22187
Kay's Hot Stuff, 11540
Kayem®, 6744
Kci, 10652
Kcl Cad Foodservice, 24909
Kd Bannerpole, 24675
Kd Jet Streamer, 24092
Kd Majestic, 24675
Kd Party Shade, 24675
Kd Starshade, 24675
Kd Starstage, 24675
Keating's Incredible Frying Machine, 24744
Kec I, 24845
Kedem, 6540, 10952
Kee-Per, 24750
Keebler, 6747, 6766
Keegan Ales, 6748
Keen' Kutter, 24746
Keenan Farms, 6749
Keenedge, 29049
Keenline, 24749
Keenwa Krunch, 3906
Keep, 9238
Keepsake Table Fashions, 24656
Kefir, 7423
Kefir Starter, 7423
Keg Wrap, 24078
Kegmaster, 30573
Kehr's Kandy, 6755
Kek, 24767
Keke, 8062
Kel-Yolk, 6768
Kelapo, 6756
Kelchner's, 6758
Kelcogel, 1962
Kelgum, 1962
Keller's, 6760, 8677, 10873
Keller's® Creamery Butter, 3335
Kelley's, 6762
Kellogg's, 6766
Kellogg's Corn Flakes®, 6765
Kellogg's Frosted Flakes, 6765
Kellogg's®, 11504, 29095
Kelly, 6767, 6769, 6771, 22538
Kelly Corned Beef, 6773
Kelly Duplex, 21810
Kelly's, 6772
Kelson Creek, 6775
Keltrol, 1962
Kelvinator, 22872
Kemach, 6776
Kemps®, 3335
Kenalog®, 1721
Kencraft Classics, 6780
Kendall, 30860
Kendall Brook, 3780
Kenics, 26490

Kenket, 30043
Kenlake Foods, 12699
Kennedy, 23235
Kenny's, 12093
Kenny's Island Style, 12093
Kenny's Key Lime Crunch, 12093
Kent, 27546
Kent Foods, 6791
Kent Quality Foods, 11053
Kent Supermatic, 28632
Kentfield, 30820
Kentuckian Gold, 11902
Kentucky Beer Cheese, 6795
Kentucky Bourbon Chocolates, 10468
Kentucky Bourbonq, 6796
Kentucky Farm, 3443
Kentucky Gentleman, 11263
Kentucky Gentleman Bourbon-A-Blend, 11264
Kentucky Kernel, 5898, 11587
Kentucky Legend, 11902
Kentucky Nip, 13728
Kentucky Nip Cherry Julep, 13728
Kentucky Rag, 26770
Kentucky Tavern, 8700, 11263
Kentucky Tavern Bourbon, 11264
Kentucky's Choice, 7655
Kentucky's Old Reserve, 4515
Kentwood Springs®, 3220, 3319
Kentwood Springs, 10303, 27797
Kentwood® Springs, 11889
Kenwood Vineyards, 6798
Kenwoodc Vineyards, 9964
Kenya Aa, 1123, 10157
Kerian Sizer, 24794
Kerleens, 5909, 23825
Kern Ridge, 6670
Kerri Klean, 19150
Kersen, 6119, 24012
Ketchupepper, 21336
Keto Cups, 3909
Kettle & Fire, 6813
Kettle Brand, 2116, 6814, 11770
Kettle Brand Krinkle Cut, 6814
Kettle Chips, 6918
Kettle Classics, 2728
Kettle Gourmet, 3696
Kettle Uprooted, 6814
Kevita®, 9945, 27433
Kew, 24803
Kew Technology, 20599
Kewanee, 28936
Kewanee K99, 24804
Kewpie, 27959
Key, 23571
Key Farms, 11053
Key Iii, 6823
Key Lime, 11458
Key Lime Cheesecake, 2881
Key Lime Pie Slices Dipped In Choco, 6825
Key Lime Pies Assorted Flavors, 6825
Key-E, 6364
Key-Pak, 24813
Keycall, 25421
Keycel ®, 11794
Keylime Graham Crackers, 4253
Keymaster, 19908
Keyrack, 24810
Keystone, 6829, 8459, 9212, 12631
Keystone®, 7786, 8460
Kg, 19576
Khatsa, 6831
Khg-7, 5683, 23677
Kia Ora, 2815, 20685
Kibbles 'n Bits, 6380
Kibun, 5483
Kick-Off, 20593
Kickapoo Joy Juice®, 8470
Kickapoo of Wisconsin, 8659
Kid Cuisine®, 2939, 2940, 20821, 20822
Kid Wizard, 11051
Kid-Tastic, 13085
Kidalin, 5791
Kidde, 20290

Kiddi Pops, 14021
Kiddie Kakes, 3404
Kidfresh, 6835
Kidney Cleanse, 5682
Kidney Rinse, 13179
Kids Cookie, 6836
Kids Klassics, 2728
Kids Klassics®, 1654
Kidsmania Inc, 2132
Kidz, 5061
Kidzels, 916
Kiev, 7655
Kievit, 9027
Kilbeggan®, 1120
Kilian, 18678
Kill Cliff, 6843
Killawarra, 12937
Killer Joe, 912
Kilwons Foods, 6846
Kim & Scott's Gourmet Pretzels, 6338
Kim Crawford Wines, 13425
Kim's Simple Meals, 5799
Kimac, 24869
Kimball, 6849
Kimco, 6869
Kimes, 6850
Kimtech, 24839
Kind Snacks, 4150
Kinderwood, 7740
Kinetico, 24846
Kinex, 26635
King, 23261
King & Prince, 6855
King Bing, 9722
King Cobra®, 26668
King Cole, 6860
King Cole Tea, 4820
King Conch, 4870
King Core, 5483
King Cove, 5483
King Filters, 24853
King Floyd's, 6864
King Juice, 6867
King Kan, 20882
King Lion, 466
King Neptune, 7929
King Nova, 13521
King O' The-West, 13067
King of All, 24860
King of Fish, 1355
King of Hawaii, 8019
King of Potato Pies, 4853
King of Spice, 11522, 29116
King Oscar, 6871
King Products, 6677
King Salmon, 11602
King Soopers, 12516
King's Arms Tavern, 12714
King's Choice, 4554
King's Delicious®, 6870
King's Hawaiian, 6874
King-Cal, 11985
King-Gage Systems, 24853
Kingchem, 6875
Kingkold, 6868
Kings, 12972
Kings Choice, 5470
Kings Ford, 2766, 20657
Kings Kooker, 26398
Kings Old Fashion, 7163
Kings Ridge, 13174
Kingsey®, 11211
Kingsford, 27670
Kingsgate, 6901
Kingsley's Caramels, 7756
Kingston ®, 13120
Kingston McKnight, 24864
Kinley, 2815, 20685
Kinney, 27729
Kinnikinnick Foods, Inc., 6884
Kinsen Plum, 12500
Kinsley Timing Screw, 24866
Kiona, 6886
Kiosks, 11755
Kip®, 29171

Kirigin Cellars, 6888
Kirin Beer, 6889
Kirin Ichiban, 6889, 26668
Kirin Lager, 6889
Kirk and Glotzer New, 13812
Kirschwasser (Cherry Brandy), 2737
Kisco, 24869
Kisco Bip, 21082
Kiss Me Frog Truffles, 5497
Kiss of Burgundy, 4315
Kissling, 62
Kist, 11844
Kit Kat, 5818, 23750
Kit Katc, 2132
Kitchen Basics, 8061
Kitchen Best, 20889
Kitchen Bouquet, 2766, 20657
Kitchen Buddy, 24567
Kitchen Craft™, 6374, 24434
Kitchen Klenzer, 22593
Kitchen Knight, 27956
Kitchen Pride Farms, 6894
Kitchen Pro, 28272
Kitchen Queen, 26805
Kitchen Table Bakers, 12664
Kitchen Wise, 31346
Kitchens of the Oceans, 10603
Kitchens of the Sea, 13407
Kite Hill, 6898
Kitkat®, 8945
Kiwa, 6903
Kiwa Kids, 6903
Kiwi Kiss, 6904
Kiwi Kola, 6310
Kix®, 4947
Kjeldsens, 6774
Kl Box, 20866
Klampress, 18556
Klara's Gourmet, 6906
Klean Hand, 30925
Klean Scrub, 30790
Kleckner's, 9332
Kleen Aire, 20882
Kleen Bebe, 24838
Kleen Mist, 20882
Kleen Mor, 20639
Kleen-Cup, 24700
Kleen-Flo, 20548
Kleen-Pail, 24700
Kleenex, 24838, 24839
Kleenflo, 21617
Kleenguard, 24839
Kleenitol, 31010
Kleenseal, 23450
Kleenzup, 31010
Kleer-Measure, 21932
Kleergum, 5017
Kleinpeter, 6909
Klement's, 6910
Klene, 9956
Klerzyme®, 2370
Klever Kuvers, 24880
Kling, 30878
Klinger, 25029
Klingshirn Winery, 6911
Klix, 26592
Klondike, 5137, 8533, 13169
Klondike®, 5165
Kloriclean, 25606
Klose, 19314
Kloss, 6914, 24889
Klosterbrot, 3606
Klosterman, 6915
Klucel™, 19108
Kmc Citrus, 6672
Knack & Back®, 4947
Knapp, 6916
Knauss, 3847
Knaust Beans, 5479
Kneadin the Dough, 7639
Knickers Irish Cream Whiskey, 5981
Knife & Steel, 20478
Knight, 6919
Knob Creek®, 1120
Knockout Meats®, 10124

All Brands Index

Knoppers, 12147
Knorr, 13167, 13169, 21246, 25789
Knott's, 6922
Knott's Berry Farm, 6380
Knott's Berry Farms, 1394
Knott's Meat Snacks, 6922
Knott's Novelty Candy, 6922
Knott's Salads, 6922
Knouse Food Service, 6923
Knudsen®, 388
Ko-Sure, 13931
Koak Oddy, 19568
Koala No March Cookie, 7560
Kobra, 24936
Kobricks, 6928
Kobu Beverages, Llc, 6929
Koch, 24906
Koch Filter, 18497
Koch's Golden Anniversary, 4950
Kodiak Cakes, 6932
Kodiak Seafood, 6270
Kodikook, 7549
Koffe King, 19737
Koffee Kake Juniorsc, 12551
Koffee Kup, 6936
Kogee, 4489
Kohinoor, 6939, 8061
Kohler Deli Meats, 246
Koia, 6941
Kojel, 13240
Kokanee, 7123
Kokanee Gold, 7123
Kokanee®, 26668
Koko's Confectionary & Novelty, 2132
Kokopelli's Kitchen, 6942
Kokuho Rose, 6673, 6931
Kokushibori, 1120
Kol-Boy Products, 21387
Kola Champagne, 5177
Kolatin, 23203
Kold Locker, 26662
Kold-Hold, 24921
Kollar, 6946
Kollmorgen, 18678
Kolor Cut, 24700
Kolor Fine, 23448
Kolpak®, 31093
Kolpake, 24925
Komachi Premium Rice, 4260
Kombrewcha, 571
Kombucha Wonder Drink, 6948
Kompact Kitchen, 29795
Kona, 362, 5659
Kona Brewing, 6949
Kona Coast, 5039
Kona Coffee, 6953
Kona Hawaii, 10157
Kona Island, 13716
Kona Pale Ale, 26668
Konared, 6954, 7036
Kondi-Keeper, 30376
Konery, 12698
Konkrete, 31252
Konriko, 2956, 25789
Konto's, 6956
Kook-E-King, 28374
Kookie Kakes, 6780
Kool Pops, 6483
Kool-Aid, 6976, 6977
Kool-Rite, 22248
Kool-Tek, 24700
Koolant Koolers, 24935
Koolgel®, 13648, 31107
Koolit, 20707
Koops' Mustard, 9440
Kopykake, 24936
Kopyrite, 24936
Kor Shots, 6963
Korbel, 1784
Korelock, 25773
Korinek, 4654
Korode-Not, 30893
Korski, 7655, 9773
Kosciusko, 10119
Koshu Plum, 12500

Kosmos Lager, 4881
Koster Keunen, 1692
Kosto, 6971
Kotex, 24838
Kover All Dust Cap, 19999
Kowalski, 6973
Koyo™, 1484
Koziol, 25665
Kozlowski Farms, 6974
Kozy Shack, 6676, 7198
Krackel, 5818, 23750
Kracker Nuts™, 13603
Kraft, 541, 1891
Kraft 100% Parmesan, 6976
Kraft Bbq Sauce, 6976
Kraft Cheese Nips, 8729
Kraft Dinner, 6976
Kraft Handi-Snacks, 8729
Kraft Heinz®, 11504, 29095
Kraft Macaroni & Cheese, 6977
Kraft Mayo, 6976
Kraft Peanut Butter, 6976
Kraft Salad Dressings, 6976
Kraft Singles, 6976
Kraftmark, 24267
Kraissl, 24945
Kramer, 6979
Kramer Shear Press, 22729
Kranzle, 21642
Krave, 6766
Krave®, 6765
Krazy, 12487
Krazy Kloth, 20122
Krazy Koolers, 22917
Krazy Strawston, 22917
Krazy Utensils, 22917
Krema, 6983
Kretschmar, 11733
Kretschmer, 2971
Kringle, 9280
Krispy, 24953
Krispy Kan, 25470
Krispy Kernels, 6987
Krispy Kist, 24953
Krispy Kreme®, 6818, 24802
Kristalene, 21564
Kristall Weizen, 11992
Kristian Regale, 6989
Kristin Hill, 6990
Kroger, 5797, 10170, 13841, 13871
Kroma Jet, 24936
Kroma Kolor, 24936
Kron, 1638
Kronenost, 10906
Krueger, 18497
Krug, 8452
Kruger, 6232
Krunchers!, 11770
Krunchie Wedges®, 6374, 24434
Krupp (Sig Cantech), 20868
Krusovice, 1361
Krusteaz, 2971
Krusteaz Professional, 2971
Kryospray, 21126
Krystal, 2815, 20685
Ksc, 6919
Kt's Kitchens, 6679
Kubla Khan, 6998
Kuchen, 10270
Kudl-Pak, 25966
Kuju Coffee, 7000
Kul, 2705
Kulactic, 13299
Kulana Foods, 7001
Kuli, 2815, 20685
Kulsar, 13299
Kum Chun Brand, 7296
Kumala, 13425
Kuner's®, 4267, 22464
Kuni-Tec, 18295
Kura, 7005
Kurolite, 10680
Kuromaru, 1120
Kusmi Tea, 1661
Kut-Guard, 19621

Kutik's Honey, 7009
Kutztown, 7010
Kw-2001, 19213
Kwai, 127
Kwik Lok, 24704
Kwik Rize, 9570
Kwik Whipper, 20288
Kwik-Dish, 1244
Kwik-Flo, 24700
Kwik-Hook, 19082
Kwik-Hub, 19082
Kwik-Koils, 22133
Kwik-Pak, 30405
Kwikprint, 24972
Ky Poppers, 10268
Kydex®, 21848
Kyger, 7014
Kynar®, 21848
Kyo-Chlorella, 13536
Kyo-Dophilus, 13536
Kyo-Green, 13536
Kyo-Green Harvest Blend, 13536
Kyolic, 13536
Kyrol, 648
Kysor/Warren, 23693

L

L & M Bakery, 7019
L C Germain, 25299
L Gage, 19429
L'Esprit, 7033
L'Il Critters, 2666, 20561
L'Ombrelle, 5405
L'Or Chocolatier, 9299
L'Ortolano, 13832
L-Lysine, 239, 18517
L-Optizinc, 6236
L-Threonine, 239, 18517
L-Tryptophan, 239, 18517
L-Valine, 239, 18517
L.A. Cinnamon, 12381
L.B. Maple Treat, 7037
L.I. Industries, 25107
L.Mawby, 7029
La Baguetterie, 7886
La Boulange, 12042
La Boulangerie, 7040
La Buena Vida Vineyards, 7041
La Caboose, 7080
La Canasta, 7042
La Captive, 1543
La Cascade Del Cielo, 13728
La Chiquita, 7081
La Chiripada, 7044
La Choy, 6084
La Choy®, 2939, 2940, 20821, 20822
La Cocina Mexicana, 10760
La Creme, 3377
La Crosse, 25034
La Donaings De Franc, 13825
La Flor, 7091
La Follette, 7138
La Fortuna, 9833
La Fresh, 21608
La Fruta, 7423
La Granada, 8946
La Grande Folie, 4544
La Herencia®, 6391
La Jolla, 8207
La Joya, 8207
La Laitière®, 8945
La Machine, 28272
La Marca, 947
La Marca®, 3834
La Marne Champ, 25789
La Martinique, 10657
La Merced Organic, 13883
La Mexicana, 7051
La Mexicanita, 6244
La Minita Tarrazu, 10157
La Morella Nuts, 1056
La Napa, 5498, 23518
La Nova, 7097
La Pablanita, 3978

La Panzanellac, 7098
La Patisserie, 3953, 7056
La Paulina®, 11211
La Petite Folie, 4544
La Posada, 25789
La Preferida, 7101, 25789
La Pri Cranberry Apple Drink, 9004
La Pri Grapefruit Dr, 9004
La Pri Orange Drink, 9004
La Prima, 7655, 9773
La Quinta, 7740
La Reina, 573, 7059
La Rinascente Pasta Products, 25039
La Rocca Vineyards, 7060
La Romagnola, 7104
La Ronga Bakery, 7222
La Salle, 7655
La Saltena®, 4947
La San Marco, 6928
La Spiga Doro, 7108
La Superior, 7109
La Tang, 7110
La Tapatia, 7062
La Tonita, 4158
La Torinese, 12895
La Torre, 6244
La Tortilla Factory, 7063
La Vallata, 10565
La Vaquita®, 3335
La Vava Blanca, 11203
La Victoria, 7115, 8898
La Victoria Salsa Su, 7115
La Victoria®, 6000, 23861
La Vida, 7110
La Vigns, 7116
La Vina, 7065
La Yogurt, 6545
Laack's Finest, 13877
Lab M Media, 25682
Lab Master, 30167
Labatt, 9396
Labatt 50, 7123
Labatt Blue, 7123
Labatt Crystal, 7123
Labatt Genuine Honey, 7123
Labatt Ice, 7123
Labatt Lite, 7123
Labatt Sterling, 7123
Labatt Usa, 9117
Label Data-Set, 26497
Label Robotix, 25436
Label-Aire, 30992
Label-Lyte, 22358
Labelette, 25059
Labelflex, 27587
Labelgraphics, 29154
Labellett, 30935
Labelmaster, 28952
Labelmaster Applicator, 18269
Labeloff Wine Label Removers, 27422
Labex, 9103
Labkol, 29669
Labkolax, 29669
Labkolite, 29669
Lablex, 22807
Labmaestro, 25074
Labmaestro Chrom Perfect, 25074
Labmaestro Ensemble, 25074
Laborview, 18354
Labpro Gravimetric, 29499
Labriola, 6338
Labvantage, 25074
Lacas, 7124
Lacey, 7125
Lacey Delite, 2387, 20397
Laco, 10161
Lacprodan®, 19049
Lacroix, 4163, 7117, 8784, 13872
Lacroix Sparkling Water, 5884
Lacrosse Lager, 2705
Lacrosse Light, 2705
Lactaid®, 5486
Lactalins, 5683, 23677
Lactantia®, 9789
Lacteeze, 4279

1307

All Brands Index

Lactiumc, 9997
Lacto, 1369
Lacto Stab, 6554
Lactoperoxidase, 4736
Lactose Pharma, 13881
Lactospore, 11061
Lactoval, 4736
Lactozym Pure, 1692
Lactum®, 8103
Lad's, 7129
Ladder Crossovers, 25329
Lady Aster®, 13109
Lady Bligh, 7655
Lady Dianne, 26830
Lady Genevieve, 1672
Lady In Red, 6796
Lady of the Lake, 8660
Lady Swiss, 23523
Lady Walton's, 7073
Lady's Choice, 2666, 20561
Ladybird®, 13607
Ladybug, 9055
Ladybug White Old Vines, 7514
Laetitia, 7133
Lafave, 953
Lafaza, 7135
Laferia, 11308, 28903
Laffy Taffy, 2132
Lafleur®, 9462
Lafond, 11188
Lagacy, 30860
Lager, 9701
Lagomarcino's, 7141
Laguna Beach Blinde, 7143
Laguna®, 3834
Lahvosh, 13256
Laing's, 11416
Laird Superfood, 7147
Laird's, 7146
Lake Blend, 4403
Lake Cove, 8660
Lake Plains, 12948, 30402
Lake Sonoma Winery, 7154
Lake States, 7155
Lakehouse Lime & Chili, 12178
Lakeland Dairies, 3574
Lakeland®, 9736
Lakeport, 7123
Lakeport Honey Lager, 7157
Lakeport Ice, 7157
Lakeport Light, 7157
Lakeport Pilsener, 7157
Lakeport Strong, 7157
Laker Family of Beers, 1702
Lakeridge, 7158
Lakeshore, 7159
Lakeside, 7160, 25094
Lakeside's, 13700, 31165
Lakeview Farms, 7168
Lakewood, 7170, 18931
Lakewood Vineyards, 7171
Lallemand, 7173
Laloo'sc, 4093
Lalvin, 7176
Lamagna, 7178
Lamanco, 25853
Lamb Weston®, 7179, 11504, 25104, 29095
Lamb's Navy, 3024
Lamb's Palm Breeze, 3024
Lamb's Seasoned®, 7179, 25104
Lamb's Supreme®, 7179, 25104
Lamb's White, 3024
Lambent, 7180
Lambert Bridge Winery, 7181
Lamberti, 4677
Lambeth Band, 25108
Lambeth Groves, 13192
Lambweston®, 4061
Lamchem, 716, 19094
Lamiflex Couplings, 18678
Laminations®, 23355
Laminita, 761
Lamo-Bliss, 26257
Lamo-Tray, 26257

Lamonica, 7054, 24998
Lamont's, 2628
Lamson, 25119
Lamson Sharp, 25119
Lan Elec, 18169
Lancaster, 5818, 23750
Lance, 2116, 11770
Land O Lakes®, 3442, 21421
Land O'Frost, 7197
Land O'Lakes, 7198
Land O'Lakes Half & Half, 13734
Land O'Lakes™, 6792, 24785
Land Shark Lager™, 26668
Landau, 25124
Landmark Damaris Chardonnay, 7203
Landmark Grand Detou, 7203
Landmark Kastania Pi, 7203
Landmark Overlook Ch, 7203
Landry's, 7206
Landscape Series, 22320
Landshark Lager, 571
Landshire, 13016, 13109
Landshire®, 184
Lanes Dairy, 7208
Lange Winery, 7212
Langers Juice, 7213
Langguth, 27819
Langley, 19908
Langlois, 5325
Langnese, 25789
Langser Camp, 18931
Langtry, 5417
Lanico, 20868
Lanimol, 21425
Lanky Franky, 2541
Lantana, 7214
Lantern, 13857
Lanthier, 7215
Lantic, 7216, 10838
Lapas, 11980
Lapham, 9682, 11473
Laphroaig, 3024, 12315
Laphroaig®, 1120
Lapone's Jordan, 9625
Lapostolle, 8452
Lapsang Souchong Smoky #1 Blend, 5228, 23295
Larabar, 11711
Larabar®, 4947
Larceny Bourbon, 5720
Larco, 22558
Laredo, 4232
Larios®, 1120
Larkin, 23692
Larosa's Famous Biscotti, 7224
Larosa's Famous Cannoli, 7224
Larosa's Famous Cookies, 7224
Larry's Vineyards, 7228
Larsen Farms, 7229
Laru, 3390
Las Cruces, 7231
Las Palmas®, 864
Las Palomas Grandes, 7433
Las Rocas®, 3834
Lasalle, 9773
Lasanta Maria, 5034
Lascco, 7549, 9344
Laser, 9664, 19581, 20305
Laser 2000, 20761
Laser Diode, 20305
Laser Malt Liquor, 9137
Laser-Link, 22271
Laserlite Mx, 30843
Laserlite Pro, 30843
Lasernet, 26442
Lashimar, 25091
Lasio, 24274
Last Step, 19364
Lastiglas/Munkadur, 22163
Late Harvest, 2770
Late Harvest Zinfandel, 5989
Late July Snacks, 2116, 11770
Latero-Flora, 9287
Latina®, 4947
Latini Products, 25017

Latta, 7242
Latvia: Unda, 5108
Laudenberg, 27071
Lauder's Scotch, 11264
Laufer Winery, 10952
Laughing Cow, 1172, 1173
Laughing Lab, 1720
Laughing Man®, 6818, 24802
Laundry Detergent Ii, 19197
Laura Chenel's, 7243
Laura Scudder's, 6380
Laura Secord®, 6818, 24802
Laura's, 7245
Laural, 31346
Laure Pristine, 8849
Laurel Hill, 773
Laurentide, 8459
Lavacarica, 11896
Lavazza, 7253, 8090, 11776
Lavazza Coffee, 1000
Lavita, 1033
Lavosh Hawaii, 183, 18382
Lawman's, 13077
Lawrence, 7256, 25177
Lawrence Model 88, 30325
Lawry's, 8061
Lawry's®, 7257
Laxmi, 6026
Lay's, 4741
Lay-Mor, 30982
Layco, 31393
Layflat, 25184
Layman's, 7261
Lazy Boy Stout, 13428
Lazy Creek Vineyards, 7262
Lazy-Man, 25186
Lazzari, 25187
Lba, 7377
Lcp/Dl, 25788
Lcp/Ml8, 25788
Lcs, 20595
Ld Blous, 30800
Ldbxi, 30800
Le Belge Chocolatier, 743
Le Bleu Bottled Water, 7264
Le Cavernet, 21125
Le Cellier, 19358
Le Chatelain, 7126
Le Fiell, 25188
Le Gourmates, 26325
Le Grand Cruvinet, 21125
Le Grand Cruvinet Mobile, 21125
Le Grand Cruvinet Premier, 21125
Le Pain Des Fleurs, 10738
Le Patron, 7104
Le Royal, 1056
Le Saucier, 10331
Le Smoker, 25191
Le Sommelier, 21125
Le Sueur®, 864
Le Younghurt, 387
Lea & Perrins, 3844, 6976
Lea & Perrins®, 7277
Lead Out, 19008
Leader, 7279, 23543
Leader/Fox, 25194
Leadout, 29001
Leaf Cuisine, 7280
Leak-Tec, 18768
Lean Cuisine®, 8945
Lean For Less, 5686
Lean on Me Naturally, 4839
Leaner Wiener, 9160
Learn Haccp, 26666
Least Cost Formulator, 25198
Leather Care, 19713
Leather Magic, 20966
Leaves, 4244
Leaves Pure Tea, 7287
Lebanon Cheese, 7289
Lebistro, 11894, 29459
Lech Premium®, 8460
Lechler, 25203
Lecitase, 1692
Lectro Truck, 24249

Lecturers' Marker, 30878
Lee Kum Kee, 7295, 7296
Lee Kum Kee Premium, 7296
Leech Lake, 7301
Leech Lake Wild Rice, 7302
Leelanau, 7303
Leer, 25216
Leeson, 25013
Leeward, 7306
Leffe, 71, 7123
Leffe Blonde, 26668
Lefrancias, 5917
Lefse House, 7308
Left Field Farms, 3379
Left Hand Black Jack, 7309
Legacy, 6919, 23499
Legacy Juice Works, 7313
Legacy Pork, 10373
Legacy Red Wine, 6375
Legand Brown, 7315
Legand Pilsner, 7315
Legatin, 2666, 20561
Legend, 18074, 26290, 27711
Legend of Kremlin, 10952
Legendary Foods, 7316
Legere, 7123
Legg's Old Plantation, 64, 18067
Legijet, 31077
Legion-Aire, 25224
Legitronic, 31077
Legrow, 19892
Lehi Roller Mills, 7318, 25226
Lehigh, 25227
Lehigh Valley Dairies, 13145
Lehigh Valley®, 3442, 21421
Leibo, 13196
Leibowitz, 13196
Leica, 25231
Leidenfrost Vineyards, 7325
Leidy's, 285, 7327
Leighton's, 7329
Leinenkugel Original, 7330
Leinenkugel's, 8459
Leinenkugel's®, 8460
Leister Heat Guns, 25236
Lejay Lagoute, 1120
Leland, 25238
Leland Southwest, 25237
Lem, 11458
Lem-N-Joy, 12941
Lemon, 11458
Lemon Creek Winery, 7338
Lemon Dew, 1600
Lemon Glo, 24035
Lemon Hart, 3024
Lemon Kleen 32, 27219
Lemon Licious Lemonade, 13728
Lemon Poppy Seed Cake, 2881
Lemon Shortbread, 806
Lemon Splash, 2054
Lemon Tea, 12914
Lemon Twist, 7363
Lemon Velvet, 7581
Lemon-Lime, 883
Lemon-X, 7339
Lemon/Lime Thristaway, 5460
Lemonee-8, 20830
Lemonhead, 1417, 4345
Lemonkind, 7340
Lena Maid, 85
Lender's, 811
Lender's®, 2939, 2940, 20821, 20822, 27540
Lenel-S2, 20290
Lennox, 7349
Lenny's Bee Productions, 7351
Lenora, 1032
Lenox, 29584
Leo Buring, 12937
Leo's, 13521
Leodoro Espresso, 6928
Leon's Sausage, 523
Leon's Texas Cuisine, 7360
Leona's, 7362
Leonard Mountain, 7364

All Brands Index

Leonardo, 2012, 10873
Leone Bianco, 10860
Leonetti Cellar, 7366
Leonetti's, 7367
Leopard Cardamon, 12987
Lepakjr Capsealing System, 25252
Leplus Ultra, 31010
Leroux Creek, 7371
Leroux®, 1120
Leroy Hill, 7372
Les Bourgeois, 7378
Les Domaines Bernard, 12672
Les Moulins D'Haiti, 2970
Les Petites, 10458
Lesley Elizabeth, 7390
Lesley Elizabeth's Crisps, 7390
Lesley Elizabeth's Dipping Oils, 7390
Lesley Elizabeth's Dips, 7390
Lesley Elizabeth's Pesto, 7390
Lesley Elizabeth's Vinegarettes, 7390
Lesley Marinara, 7390
Lesoy, 137
Lesstanol, 4914
Let's Blend, 8505
Let's Do, 3956
Let's Do Organic, 3956
Letan, 10516
Leter Buck Coffee Co., 31459
Letica, 25260
Letter of Marquee 2010, 2763
Letter of Marquee 2011, 2763
Letter-Lites, 25091
Letterbox Fine Tea, 2874
Level Right, 9201
Level Star Ls Level Sensing Fillers, 23678
Levelair, 21657
Levelart, 30792
Levelhead 2, 24235
Levelmatic, 19166
Leveltronic, 30106
Lewa Ecodos, 18783
Lewa Lab, 18783
Lewa Modular, 18783
Lewa Triplex, 18783
Lewis, 28952
Lewis Iqf, 22873
Lewis Labs Rda, 7404
Lewis®, 7402
Lexington, 2327, 20256
Lexington Coffee Tea, 7406
Lexmark Carpet, 21561
Leybold, 27729
Lfc, 21445
Li'l Guy, 7407
Liano Farms, 5036
Libbey®, 25281
Libby's, 6267, 9199, 11434
Libby's Pecan Cookies, 806
Libby's®, 2939, 2940, 20821, 20822
Liberate Your Senses, 6831
Liberte®, 4947
Liberty Ale, 531
Liberty Bell, 13384
Liberty Creek®, 3834
Libertyware, 25289
Libitalia, 22142
Libman, 25290
Library Wines, 10963
Lick My Spoon, 11205
Lick-A-Pig, 1018
Licklers, 14021
Licor 43, 13811
Licorice Ropes, 469
Lid Placers, 23716
Lid Press, 23716
Lid-Off Pail Opener, 19999
Lidd Off, 19998
Liddells™, 11211
Lidpro Lid Dispenser, 30376
Life, 10419, 27983
Life Force, 7413
Life Line Vita Plus, 13455
Life Savers, 7963
Life Savers®, 7952, 13960

Life Savy, 8719
Life Start, 8816
Life Tree Products, 7562
Life Wtr®, 9945, 27433
Life's Dha®, 3320
Life's™Ara, 3320
Life's™Gla, 3320
Life's™Omega, 3320
Life®, 9945, 27433
Lifeline, 773
Lifemount, 22140
Lifesource Foods, 12906
Lifestore, 21951
Lifestyle, 11298, 26450
Lifetime, 7419, 9265, 26302
Lifetime Fat Free Cheese, 7419
Lifetime Lactose/Fat Free Cheese, 7419
Lifetime Low Fat Cheese, 7419
Lifetime Low Fat Rice Cheese, 7419
Lifetree, 29187
Lifewise Ingredients, 7424
Lift, 2815, 20685
Lift Products, 18877
Lift-N-Weigh, 27111
Lift-O-Flex, 28508
Lift-Rite, 19908
Liftabout, 29137
Liftiltruk, 28845
Liftronic Balancer, 28694
Light, 5489, 7330, 11218
Light & Fit, 3379
Light 'n Fluffy®, 10777, 28421
Light and Fit, 3377
Light Burgers, 7427
Light Forms, 25486
Light Hawk, 30876
Light Mountain, 7562
Light Rock, 7425
Lightening Polishers, 31251
Lighthouse, 1123, 25305
Lighthouse Gold, 3180
Lighting, 10344
Lightjet, 24093
Lightjet Vector, 24093
Lightnin, 19401, 28714
Lightning, 7655, 24070
Lightning 101, 9773
Lightning Wrap, 26680
Lightwaves, 25304
Liguria, 7428
Lil Dutch Maid, 122
Lil Kiddies, 14021
Lil Wunder-Miniature Scrub, 24829
Lil' Chicks™, 1654
Lil' Chief, 12124
Lil' Chief Popcorn, 12124
Lil' Devils, 31126
Lil' Fisherman, 11368
Lil' Lollies, 6780
Lil' Momma Nasty, 10547
Lil' Orbits, 25309
Lil' Pepe, 6353
Lil'entrees, 4982
Lil'meals, 4982
Lilletc, 9964
Lilliday Pops, 6158
Lillipos, 11016
Lilly's, 9531
Lilt, 2815, 20685
Lily of the Desert, 7430
Lily's, 7431
Lilycake, 6314
Lilydale, 11776
Lilydale®, 7432
Limbo Ipa, 7526
Lime Lite, 31010
Lime-Elim, 31267
Limited Edition, 1054
Limited Edition Presents, 7435
Limonce, 7655
Limpert Brothers, 7437
Lin Court Vineyards, 7438
Linablue A, 21265
Linbin's, 25337

Linc, 20910
Lincoln, 6923, 8414, 31092
Lincoln Ovens, 25524
Lincoln Road Blend, 11826
Lincoln®, 31093
Linda's Little Lollies, 7440
Linda's Lollies, 7440
Linda-Vista, 8065
Linde, 25323, 27720
Lindeman's, 12937
Linden's, 7442
Lindor Truffles, 7446
Lindsay Farms, 7444
Lindsay Olives, 1185
Lindsay's Tea, 7445
Lindsay's Teas, 8612
Lindt, 2606, 11864, 25789
Lindt Chocolate, 7446
Linear, 18130, 24135
Linear Separator, 26893
Lineir, 27325
Linen-Like, 23809
Linen-Like Natural®, 23811
Linen-Like Supreme®, 23811
Linen-Like®, 23811
Linen-Like® Select™, 23811
Linen-Saver, 24700
Linerter, 28845
Ling Ling®, 237, 238
Lingot Stainless & Hardwood Floors, 26404
Linjector, 30732
Link N Load, 27565
Link-Belt, 28357
Linkerlube, 25332
Linkspot, 23993
Linshelf, 25337
Linumlife, 137
Lion, 7451, 11226
Lion Coffee, 5654
Lionshead Light, 7450
Lionshead Pilsner, 7450
Lipary, 13871
Lipo - Serine, 4827
Lipo Butter, 5462
Lipopan, 1692
Liposofast, 19255
Lipozyme, 1692
Lips of Faith, 8959
Lipton, 8090, 13167, 13169
Lipton®, 9945, 27433
Liquavision, 21657
Liqueur, 362
Liqui-Nox, 18542
Liquid Amber, 10261
Liquid Chalk, 30878
Liquid Freeze, 22602
Liquid Ki, 8389
Liquid Life Essential Day & Night, 5786
Liquid Plumr, 2766, 20657
Liquid Scale, 25349
Liquid Smoke, 2876
Liquidlise, 12483
Liquimax, 7331
Liquimul Black, 5462
Liquiplex, 25429
Liquisoft™, 1009
Liquitote, 23850
Lisanatti, 7458
Lista, 29584
Listo, 25354
Lite, 3540
Lite Lite Tofutti, 12843
Lite Touch, 22615
Lite Writer, 24354
Lite-95, 1244
Lite-N-Tuff, 23543
Litehouse, 4828
Litestrip, 29866
Litewall, 29746
Lithostat®, 8389
Little Bear Organic, 13672
Little David, 25454
Little Debbie, 8077
Little Debbie®, 8076

Little Duck Organics, 7466
Little Giant, 22080
Little Lady, 8367
Little Miss Muffin, 7469
Little Mule, 20752
Little Pig, 2750
Little Red Smokehouse, 24414
Little Rhody Brand, 7473
Little River Seafood, 7475
Little Sizzlers®, 6000, 23861
Little Squirt, 25365, 26941
Little Swan Lake, 7463
Little Swimmers, 24838
Little Vab, 7947
Livabec, 7375
Live a Little Dressings, 7479
Live Brine, 23453
Live Clean, 5505
Live Gourmetc, 7480
Live Link, 23866
Live Love Pop, 7481
Live Plant Juice, 131
Live Soda, 7070
Liver Cleanse, 5682
Liver Detox Formula, 131
Liver Restore, 5786
Liver Rinse, 13179
Livia, 7375
Living Food Concentrates, 7421
Living Hinge, 29318
Living Light, 12776
Living Light Dairy Blend, 12776
Living Now®, 8725
Livingston Cellars®, 3834
Livingston Seed, 10106
Livio Felluga, 8452
Lize Jamaican Style Gourmet Bbq, 1669
Lk Burman, 5555
Llord's, 1423
Lloyd, 25371
Lloyds Barbeque Co®, 6000, 23861
Llsa, 19130
Lmc, 25269
Lo Han, 13511
Lo-Density, 27859
Load Disk Ii, 30800
Load Locker, 25277
Loadbank, 25377
Loadmaster, 26623
Loam Ridge, 7673
Lobana, 30569
Lobster Call, 25421
Lobster Chowder, 2309
Lockhart Fine Foods, 13641
Locktile, 24456
Lockwood Vineyard, 1543
Loco Coco, 11775
Loctite, 23726
Lodgepole Light, 10261
Lodi Estates, 9321
Lodi Zinfandel, 2637
Lodi's, 7505
Loeffler, 23672
Loft 213, 30137
Loftware, 22955
Log Cabin, 811
Log Cabin®, 2939, 2940, 20821, 20822, 27540
Log House, 7511
Log House Candiquik, 7511
Logan Chardonnay, 12506
Logic, 30153
Logix, 24366, 25408
Logo Chocolates, 4253
Logo River, 26553
Logotop, 25485
Logyan's Garden, 1598
Logyn'S Garden Soups, 1598
Loiseau Bleu, 13425
Loison Panetoni, 9119
Lok-A-Box, 28356
Lok-Tight Handle, 24829
Lola, 218
Lola Granola Bar, 7512
Lollipals, 6780

1309

All Brands Index

Lollipop Paint Shop, 6158
Lollipop Tree, 12703
Lolly Lo's, 7279
Loma Linda, 772, 8551
Lombardi's, 7516
Lombardi's Italian Classics, 4665
London Classic Broil, 118
London Herb & Spice, 4614
Lone Creek Cattle Company, 5327
Lone Pine, 3033
Lone Pine Country, 4578
Lone Star, 7520, 7521
Lone Tree Farm, 4623
Long Beach Crude, 1208
Long Boys, 756
Long Grove Confections, 7524
Long Island Iced Tea, 5012
Long Life, 10344
Long Life Beverages, 3080
Long Life Black Teas, 12704
Long Life Green Teas, 12704
Long Life Herbal Teas, 12704
Long Life Iced Teas, 12704
Long Prairie Packing Company®, 10893
Long Reach, 20258
Long Sweet Red, 6763
Long Trail Ale, 7526
Longacre, 7528
Longaniza Cibao, 2670
Longfellow Winter, 11561
Longhorn, 9565
Longhorn Grill, 1244
Longhorns, 7184, 7200
Longleaf Plantation, 7531
Longliner, 11375
Longmorn, 9964
Longreen, 7534
Look!c, 583
Look-O-Look, 9956
Loon, 26520
Loop Plus, 22503
Loose Cannon, 2763
Loose Leaf Session Ale, 9366
Looza, 6255
Lopez Foods, 7538
Lora Brody Bread Dou, 7540
Lord Ansley, 7655
Lord Chesterfield, 8086
Lord's, 7541
Lorina - Lemonade, 4148
Loriva, 7545
Loriva Jazz Roasted Oils, 7545
Loriva Supreme Flavored Oils, 7545
Loriva Supreme Oils, 7545
Lorraine®, 11209, 11211
Lorunita Extra, 4881
Los Arango, 10952
Los Cantores, 1348
Los Gatos Lager, 7551
Los Olivos Vintners, 11199
Los Tios, 12646
Lost Energy®, 26668
Lost Lake, 12866
Lost Mountain Winery, 7556
Lost Sailor India Pale Ale, 1237
Lost Trail, 7557
Lost Trail Root Beer, 7578
Losuds, 19435
Losurdo, 7558
Losweet, 9201
Lot 40 and Pike Creek, 9964
Lotech, 25375
Lotito, 7635
Lotsa Pasta, 7559
Lotta-Pop, 1660
Lotus, 13625
Lotus Bloom, 11203
Lotus Pops, 9194
Lou Pizzo, 7565
Louana®, 13328
Louis Albert & Sons, 9593
Louis Bernard, 1543
Louis Bouillot, 1543
Louis Kemp, 6267
Louis Kemp Crab Delights®, 12968

Louis M. Martini®, 3834
Louis Roederer, 11810
Louis Roederer - Remis, 3545
Louis Trauth, 10664
Louisa Pastas, 7577
Louisburg, 7557
Louisburg Cider, 7578
Louisburg Farms, 7578
Louisiana, 10276
Louisiana Cajun, 10276
Louisiana Fish Fry, 7580
Louisiana Hot Sauce, 1794
Louisiana Mini, 4886
Louisiana Mixes, 2019
Louisiana Premium Seafoods, 7590
Louisiana Rag, 26770
Louisiana® Gold, 1794
Louisiana® Wing Sauce, 1794
Louisianas Best, 11349
Lounsbury, 2357
Lov-It, 11308, 28903
Love & Kisses, 7746
Love Creek Orchards, 7596
Love Mints, 1343
Love My Popper, 23256
Love That, 11775
Love'n Herbs, 7602
Loving Bunny, 10004
Low Boy, 22080
Low Fat Body Mueslix, 4214
Low Profile E-Z Wrap, 18498
Low Sodium Tuna, 12046
Low Temp, 25456
Lowat, 6236
Lowboy, 30342
Lowcoom, 5017
Lowell Farms, 7609
Lowenbrau, 7123
Lowerraters, 18215
Lowery's Coffee, 7613, 25460
Loyal, 25463
Loyola Springs, 9130
Lozier, 19042, 24003
Lozier Reeve, 20004
Lqd, 571
Lr01 Laboratory Refractometer, 25820
Ls-Q50, 28748
Lsc, 833
Lsc Model 614, 25351
Lsc Model 725, 25351
Lsk, 7072
Lube-Gard, 23543
Lubest, 26276
Lubriplate, 22590
Lucarotin, 1692
Lucas, 7620, 7621
Lucerne® Dairy Farms, 11073
Lucia's, 7625
Lucien Georgelin, 1661
Lucienne, 5499
Lucile's, 7627
Lucini Honestete, 11899, 29468
Luck's, 6267
Luck's Beans, 6267
Luck's®, 4267, 22464
Lucky Charms®, 4947
Lucky Dutch, 23409
Lucky Lager, 7123
Lucky Leaf, 6923
Lucky Pasta, 4794
Lucky Seas, 6390
Lucky Star, 13423
Luckybars, 7631
Lucy's Sweets, 12831
Ludford's, 7637
Luetzow, 25479
Luigi Giovanni, 5029
Luigi Vitelli, 6126
Luigi's, 6338
Luis Felipe Edwards, 13811
Luisa's, 7168
Luke's Almond Acres, 25481
Lumaco, 25484
Lumalier, 20779
Lumalux, 26990

Lumen, 194
Luminaire, 29746
Luminaire Ultra, 29746
Luminaire Ultra Ii, 29746
Luminate Ultra, 20625
Lumisolve, 716, 19094
Lumisorb, 716, 19094
Lumistor, 7017
Lumpy Logs, 2947
Lumpy Lous, 2947
Lumulse, 716, 19094
Luna, 2756, 10873
Luna Rossa, 10900
Luna's, 7648
Lunazul Tequilas, 5720
Lunchables, 6977
Lunchmate, 11298
Lundberg, 7650
Lunds, 9094
Lung Tonic, 5791
Lunita®, 25281
Luseaux, 25493
Lush, 3755
Lusterator, 18360
Lustre Rail, 19846
Luv'ya, 5036
Luvo Bowl, 7654
Luvo Flipped Bowl, 7654
Luvo Planted, 7654
Luvo Steam In Pouch, 7654
Luvs, 12721, 30193
Luxury, 465, 7657
Luyties, 7658
Luzianne, 10657
Luzianne Ready-To-Drink, 1782
Lvc, 7484
Lvo, 7411
Lw Private Reserve®, 7179, 25104
Lx®, 21362
Lyco, 25500
Lycomato, 5475
Lycopene, 11268
Lycovit, 1692
Lyeth Estate, 1543, 12672
Lyle's Golden Syrup, 3666
Lyles Golden Syrup®, 12196
Lymphatonic, 5791
Lynden Farms, 9699
Lynfred, 7664
Lynn Dairy, 7665
Lynn Protiens, 7665
Lynnply, 25506
Lynwood Farms, 1547
Lyoferm, 7668
Lyrica, 23842
Lysodren®, 1721
Lysol®, 10598
Lytegress, 25224

M

M & M'S, 2132
M and V, 6460
M B Spices, 8568
M Logic, 19419
M"Zak, 27083
M&Cp Farms, 7673
M&J Valve, 28714
M&M, 1357, 8533
M&M Cookies, 818
M&M Easter Baskets, 8131
M&M's®, 7952
M&R, 24044, 29671
M-8 Slitter, 23117
M-Bond, 8501, 26295
M-Cut, 20902
M-D-G Formula-2, 26165
M-Drive, 20902
M-J, 7889
M-Line™, 21362
M-Purity Ring, 8501, 26295
M-Purity Seal, 8501, 26295
M-Rotary, 20902
M-Shuttle, 20902
M-Track, 20902

M-Traverse, 20902
M-Trim, 20902
M-Ware, 18222
M.Lawrence, 7029
M.O.-Lift, 25530
M074, 24059
M30, 25808
M60 Energy Mints, 11549
M850 Series, 19032
Ma Baensch, 931
Ma Baensch Herring, 931
Maazo, 6026
Maboroshi, 11642
Mac Tools, 29584
Mac's, 7716
Mac's Dumplings, 5634
Mac-Copy, 25549
Mac-Gloss, 25549
Mac-Jet, 25549
Maca Magic, 5790
Macabee, 7724
Macalister, 7655
Macariz, 10708
Macaron Cafe, 7725
Macayo Mexican Foods, 4373
MacDonald's™, 864
Macedonian, 6986
Macewan's, 7720
Macfarms of Hawaii, 7713
Machine Detergent Ii, 19197
Machine Mochers, 26000
Machine-Guard, 19429
Mack's, 6971
Mackay's, 7722
Mackinlay Tea's, 7723
Mackoly Rice Wine, 6968
Macleans Cask Conditioned, 12136
Macleans Pale, 12136
MacMurray Estate®, 3834
MacPhail Pinot, 11810
Macrowave, 28147
Macs, 4158
Mactac, 23882
Mad & Noisy, 8459
Mad Cat, 730
Mad Dog Hot Sauce, 730
Mad Dragon, 4515
Mad Jack, 8459
Mad River Farm, 7735
Mad,Casse, 7745, 11649
Madame Chevre, 13927
Maddalena, 7740
Maddy & Maize, 7741
Made By True, 13032
Made In Nature, 7742
Made In the Shade, 608
Made Rite, 7743
Madegood, 10774
Madeira Farms, 5735
Madelaine, 7746, 10333
Madeleine, 56
Madera, 2074, 13384
Madhouse Munchies, 7749
Madonna Estate Mont St John, 7753
Madre Sicilia, 10565
Madria Sangria®, 3834
Madys, 7758
Maebo Noodle Factory, Inc., 7760
Maestro, 20065
Maestro Giovanni, 12301
Mag Slide, 19945
Mag-Nifique™, 13890
Mag® Melon, 3479, 21460
Magellin Gin, 3165
Maggi Bouillion Cubes®, 8945
Maggi®, 8945
Maggio, 9321
Magic, 25631
Magic Baking Powder, 6976
Magic Buss, 29320
Magic Chef, 25893
Magic Disk, 21325
Magic Gourmet, 9752
Magic Hat Brewing, 9117
Magic Ice, 7765

All Brands Index

Magic Line, 9794, 27318
Magic Master, 24628
Magic Melt, 18375
Magic Mist, 9794, 27318
Magic Mold, 9794, 27318
Magic Mountain, 1600
Magic Munchie, 11645
Magic Pepper Sauce, 7766, 25632
Magic River, 7373
Magic Sauce & Marinades, 7766, 25632
Magic Wall, 18702
Magic Wash, 25008
Magic-Access, 29583
Magic-Flo, 19998
Magic-Mesh, 19998, 19999
Magic-Mix, 7671
Magic-Mounts, 26182
Magic-Swing, 29583
Magical Reindeer Food, 11679
Magically Mexican, 6528
Magicater, 25630
Magictrol, 27760
Magikitch'n, 19733, 25630
Magline, 19908, 20143, 26557
Magliner, 28488
Magna Torq, 29221
Magna-Bar, 20192
Magnaclamp, 27575
Magnamight, 19743
Magnasweet, 7693
Magneflex, 26049
Magneroll, 23082
Magnesol, 21315
Magnet Source, The, 18062
Magnetag, 29055
Magnetek, 20752
Magnetic Menumaster, 24354
Magnetic Scrap Board, 24700
Magnetic Springs, 7771
Magnetically Aligned, 30878
Magnificat, 4649
Magnifico Special, 648
Magnifoodsc, 1861
Magnolia, 784, 7774
Magnolia Bay, 5438
Magnotta, 7776
Magnum, 8459, 13169, 19152, 25645, 29271
Magnum Alert, 26449
Magnum Exotic, 7777
Magnum®, 8460
Magnupeeler, 19169
Magnus, 29211
Magnuwasher, 19169
Magpowr, 25650
Magsys, 25651
Maha Organic Hard Cider, 571
Maharishi, 5679
Mahatma®, 10777, 28421
Mahogany Black, 5462
Mai Green Tea, 8695
Mai Tonic Tea, 8695
Maibock Hefeweizen, 5193
Maid-Rite, 7783
Maier's®, 1359
Mailbock Lager, 1237
Maille, 25789
Maillose, 10600
Main Beach Brown, 7143
Main Street, 28666
Maine Coast Crunch, 7788
Maine Coast Sea Vegetables, 7788
Maine Wild, 7792
Mainland®, 4552
Mainstream, 31089
Mainstreet, 25663
Maisie Jane's, 7793
Maison Cousin, 7876, 8676
Maison De Grand Esprit, 12937
Maison-Cousin, 7875
Maizetos, 5122
Majestic Coffee and Tea, 7795
Major Business Systems™, 22187
Make a Gift Products, 29318
Make Out Mints, 1343

Make Your Own Gummies, 418
Maker Overnight Oats, 6282, 7800
Maker's Mark, 3024, 5892, 12315
Maker's Mark®, 1120
Maker®, 9945, 27433
Makers Mark, 7801
Mako, 5034
Mal-X, 20966
Malabar Gorld Premium, 6611
Malai, 13089
Malaxator, 22594
Mali's, 25674
Malibu, 5892
Malibu Coconut Rum, 3024
Malibuc, 9964
Malk, 7696
Malk Coffee, 7696
Mallomars, 8729
Mallowcreme®, 9648
Malo, 25677
Malpotane, 5683, 23677
Malt Teenies, 4976
Malt-O-Meal, 10213
Malta, 7774
Malta Cawy, 2338
Malta Gran, 10297
Malta Rica, 2338
Malted Peanut, 1151
Maltee, 10330
Maltese Cross, 10686
Maltesers®, 7952
Malthus System V, 25682
Malto Bella, 9151
Maltoferm, 1710
Maltogenase, 1692
Maltopure, 25784
Maltorose, 1710
Maltrin, 5246
Maltrin Qd, 5246
Maltrite®, 7809
Mam Papaul's, 7581
Mama, 6677
Mama Amy's, 7811
Mama Capri, 9565
Mama Del's, 7812
Mama Leone's, 7364
Mama Lina, 6316
Mama Linda, 4111
Mama Lucia's, 10418
Mama Mary's, 7815
Mama Mary's™, 864
Mama Mia, 1854
Mama Mucci, 8664
Mama Nichola's Sago, 9045
Mama Papaul's, 7581
Mama Ranne, 4550
Mama Rosa's, 11316
Mama Rose, 2983
Mama Rose's, 7818
Mama Rosie's, 7819
Mama's, 10252
Mamba, 12148
Mamma Chia, 7823
Mamma Says, 7826
Mammoth®, 4552
Mamor, 23850
Man of War Crab, 9344
Mancakes, 4150
Manchester Farms, 7831
Manchurian Saffron, 9771
Mancini, 7832, 25690
Mancuso, 7833
Manda, 7834
Mandoo, 7838
Mango Mango, 11655
Mango Sunrise Tea, 13746
Manhattan Gourmet, 6489, 11934
Manischewitz, 7848, 7849
Manitoba Harvest, 7850
Manitowoc®, 31093
Mann's International, 12543
Mann's®, 3479, 21460
Manner, 1957
Mannhardt, 25871
Mannhart, 25700

Mannings, 3097
Manny's, 8208
Mansi, 18540
Mansion, 4387
Mansmith's Gourmet, 7856
Manta®, 24812
Mantrocel, 7857
Mantroclear, 7857
Manu Maker, 11639
Manuel's, 7859
Manwich®, 2939, 2940, 20821, 20822
Maola, 7861, 7985
Map, 28981
Map-Fresh, 24550
Map-Seal, 24550
Mapimpianti, 27358
Maple Acres, 7863
Maple Apple Drizzle, 11584
Maple Gardens, 7869
Maple Grove Farms of Vermont, 7866
Maple Grove Farms of Vermont®, 864
Maple Hillc, 7867
Maple Hollow, 7869
Maple Island, 7870
Maple Leaf, 7871, 7872, 7874, 7876, 7877, 11768, 25714
Maple Melts, 5363
Maple Nuts, 10673
Maple Sprinkles, 13347
Mar-Con, 25716
Mar-Jac Brands, 7889
Maramor, 7891
Maranatha, 5505
Marantha, 7892
Marathon, 1208
Marblehead Mints, 5578
Marburger, 7897
Marc Roman, 4677
Marcel Et Henri, 7898
Marcello, 5400
Marchesi, 11205
Marconi, 13422
Marcos, 10085
Mardi Gras King, 7581
Marga-Ezy, 19999
Margao, 8061
Margarita Made Easy, 19998
Margaritaville Paradise Key Teas, 26668
Margaritaville®, 3725
Margherita, 11733
Margin Minder Software, 19442
Margret Holmes, 8086
Margritaville®, 6818, 24802
Mari-Net, 26440
Maria & Son, 7907
Maria and Ricardo's, 5573, 7908
Maria's, 10453
Maria's Premium, 7909
Mariachi, 10435
Mariani, 7910, 7911
Marias, 8387
Marich, 2606, 7912
Marie Brizard, 7913
Marie Callender's®, 2939, 2940, 20821, 20822
Marie McGhee's, 2903
Marie's®, 13328
Mariebellec, 1011
Marimar Torres Estate, 7922
Marin, 7924
Marin Weiss, 7923
Marina, 7927
Marinade Bay, 2509
Marinela®, 1359
Mariner Biscuits, 1472
Mariner Seafoods, 7930
Mariner's Choice, 9165
Mariner-Neptune, 7929
Mario Perelli-Minetti, 13813
Mario's Gelati, 7932
Marioff, 20290
Marion, 25742
Mariquitas Classic, 100
Mark, 23489
Mark Cal, 22985

Mark Ii, 21915, 25231, 30677
Mark Ii Plus, 25231
Mark Iii, 30677
Mark Royal, 27391
Mark V, 21498
Mark-300a, 25758
Mark-Time, 25546
Market Buffet, 30820
Market Forecaster, 25198
Market Master, 24906
Market Place, 9914
Market's Best, 13009
Marking Methods, Inc., 25758
Marko, 25760
Marko Intl., 25761
Markoated, 25761
Markon®, 11504, 29095
Marks & Spencer, 11768
Marksman, 24092
Markwell, 25762
Marla, 3336
Marland Clutch, 18678
Marlate, 24840
Marlboro Village, 1220
Marlen, 25769
Marley Beverage Co., 8955
Marlite, 19042, 25773
Marlite Brand Frp, 25773
Marlite Modules, 25773
Marmalade, 25299
Marmite, 25789
Marnap-Trap, 7948
Marotti Biscotti, 822
Marprene, 25775
Marpro, 10983
Marquerite, 954
Marques De Murrieta, 13811
Marquis, 1517, 7950
Marquis Fountains, 19932
Marquise, 847
Marriott Walker, 25783
Marrone, 13120
Mars, 541, 961, 25785
Mars 5, 20048
Mars, Inc, 2132
Mars-X, 20048
Mars®, 7952
Marsa, 4324
Marsala, 9040
Marshall Blue, 25795
Marshall Pick Under the Sink, 25795
Marshall's, 12467
Marshall's Curry, 12178
Marshallan, 24742
Marshmallow Fluff, 3810
Mart Cart, 19119
Martellc, 9964
Martha's All Natural, 7960
Martha's All Natural Baking Mixes, 7960
Marthedal Berry Farms, 5036
Martin, 7965, 25806
Martin Codax®, 3834
Martin's Virginia Roast, 4239
Martin/Baron, 25811
Martini & Prati, 7967
Martini & Rossi, 913
Martini & Rossi Asti, 914
Martini & Rossi Vermouth, 914
Martini Biscuit, 13180
Martini Party, 2799
Martins, 11461
Marty Griffin Big Red, 5989
Marukan, 7976
Marushka, 5861
Maruyu, 1849
Marva Maid, 7978, 7985
Marvel, 2136, 4659
Marvelous, 8995
Marwood, 7979
Mary B'S, 6338
Mary Jo's Blueberries, 6599
Mary Jo's Fancy, 6599
Mary Kitchen®, 6000, 23861
Mary Phillips, 10229
Mary's, 3603

1311

All Brands Index

Mary's Gone Crackers, 7983
Maryland Chef, 5555
Marzen Lager, 1139
Marzetti, 7189, 7987, 12467, 25120
Marzetti Frozen Pasta, 7987
Marzetti's, 7986
Mas-7000, 20048
Masa Mixta ®, 856
Masala Chai, 7989
Masala Craft, 6026
Masala Roti, 10968
Maseca ®, 856
Mashuga Nuts & Cookies, 11940, 12894
Masienda Bodega, 7990
Maskal Teff, 12605
Maso Canali®, 3834
Mason, 30078
Mason Dixie, 7992
Mason's Ironstone, 31081
Mass Transit, 1720
Massel, 7994
Massetti, 11980
Mastantuono Wines, 7996
Master, 6977, 18878, 24038
Master Baker, 13182
Master Brewer, 13182
Master Chef Ltd., 18594
Master Fit, 18074
Master Jet, 22901
Master Mix, 7998
Master of Mixes, 439, 4401
Master Rigger, 20277
Master Series, 29513
Master Turf, 27881
Master Wrap, 12973, 30444
Master's Mark, 1077
Master's Touch, 3269
Master-Bilt, 29580
Masterbrand, 13183
Mastercraft International, 25841
Mastercut, 2367
Masterfeeds, 81
Masterfoods®, 7952
Mastermark, 25843
Masterpiece, 2766, 20657
Masterson, 8000
Mastertech, 19021, 25828
Mastertech Direct Fired, 25828
Mastro, 11776
Matador, 4741, 8001
Matador®, 9945, 27433
Matangoes, 8002
Matanzas Creek Winery, 8003
Matar By Pelter, 10952
Matassini Seafoods, 6373
Match Pay, 25407
Mate-Lock, 23015
Mateer Burt, 18284
Mateer-Burt, 30935
Materva, 2338
Mati, 7697
Matrix, 18678, 25865
Matrix 916, 25867
Matrix Sneezegaurd, 22180
Matrix1000, 25867
Matt's Cookies, 2985, 8012
Matthew's All Natural, 8640
Matthews 1812 House, 8014
Matthews All Natural, 5942
Matthiesen, 25871
Matua, 12937
Matzo Meal, 6776
Maui Blanc, 8022
Maui Blush, 8022
Maui Brut, 8022
Maui Cup, 25260
Maui Splash, 8022
Maui Style, 4741
Maui Style®, 9945, 27433
Maui Ulupalakua Red, 8022
Maull's Barbecue Sauce, 7574
Mauna La'i, 8586
Maurer, 25874
Maurice French Pastries, 8024
Maurice's, 10051

Maury Island Farm, 11390
Maury's Cookie Dough, 2703
Mavuno Harvest, 8026
Max, 7409
Max Boost Coffee, 6976
Max Cranberry Cocktail, 9170
Max's, 4928
Max's Salsa Sabrosa & Design, 9290
Max-C-Plex, 7947
Max-Sea, 3998
Maxbullet, 18548
Maxchanger, 30390
Maxfield, 8027
Maxi, 28396
Maxi Marketeer, 19636
Maxi-Amo, 19429
Maxi-Beam, 19429
Maxi-Bins, 19926
Maxi-Cap, 26893
Maxi-Con, 20934
Maxi-Duty, 23543
Maxi-Lift, 20923
Maxilact®, 3320
Maxima, 18878, 27602
Maxima Series, 19032
Maximice, 27352
Maximicer, 25882
Maximizer, 23273
Maximo, 4677
Maximount, 24735
Maximum Merchandiser, 25628
Maxine's Heavenly, 8030
Maxinvert®, 2370
Maxipor, 21425
Maxiren®, 3320
Maxispan, 29441
Maxon, 20726
Maxslide, 18548
Maxum, 30841
Maxwell House, 6976, 6977
Maxwell's Extraordinary, 8032
Maya's Tortillas, 9736
Mayacamas Vineyards, 8035
Mayan Farm, 5573
Mayan Harvest, 12663
Mayan Legacy, 12881
Mayberry's Finest, 2628
Mayco, 8042
Mayer Bros., 8037
Mayer Hook N' Loop, 20447
Mayer Magna, 20447
Mayfield Creamery™, 3442, 21421
Mayfield®, 3442, 21421
Mayo Gourmet, 13894
Maypo, 6267
Maytag, 25893
Mazelle's, 8046
Mazza Vineyards, 9926
Mbi, 25811
Mbpxl, 3262
Mbt (Lubeca), 20868
Mc Graw, 8070
Mc2, 25571
Mc3, 25571
McAdams ®, 13120
McArthur Dairy®, 3442, 21421
McCadam, 211
McCaf,, 2811
McCain®, 4061
McCain™, 8055
McCallan, 10468
McCann's, 6279, 25789
McCann's Irish Oatmeal, 12182
McCann's®, 864
McCarthy's Oregon Single Malt, 2737
McClelland's, 1120
McConnell'sc, 1136
McCormick, 8061, 8062
McCrea Vineyard, 6892
McCullagh Coffee Roasters, 8090
McCutcheons, 8091
McDowell, 8066, 13811
McDowell Ovens, 12241
McEvoy Ranch, 11864
McGovern's Best, 9344

McI Group, 21561
McIlhenny Company Tabasco®, 20020
McKay's, 3619
McKenzie, 10106
McKnit, 25906
McLean, 10331
McLure's Maple, 3815
McMillin Wire, 25912
McNarin Packaging, 18029
McP, 24093
McP Barcode, 24093
McP Series, 24093
McT Oil, 8896
McTavish, 8100
Md-16, 20047
Md-Ii, 18336
Md-Ii-200, 18336
Mdc, 30790
Mdgl, 8352
Mdi, 8404
Mdm, 8352
Me and the Bees Lemonade, 8101
Meadow Brook®, 3442, 21421
Meadow Gold, 8105
Meadow Gold®, 3442, 21421
Meadow Valley, 9167
Meadowbrook, 8106, 13070
Meadowbrook Creamery, 10073
Meadows, 25938
Meadows Country Products, 8108
Meadowview, 9909
Meal Mart, 329
Meals-On-Wheels, 31295
Meaning of Lifec, 2010
Measure Fresh, 30337
Measurex, 25941
Meat Magic, 7766, 25632
Meat Marking, 24059
Meat of Wheat, 6331
Meat Pak, 26680
Meat-O-Mat, 81,14
Mec, 27083
Mechanix Orange, 21051
Mechatron Gravimetric Feeders, 28875
Mechatron Volumetric Feeders, 28875
Med Flo, 24332
Med-I-San, 24503
Medaglia D'Oro, 6380
Medalist, 21915
Medallion Naturally, 7876
Medallions, 9176
Medeor® Matrix, 3320
Medetrina, 11780
Medford, 5643
Medford Farms®, 1484
Medicea, 10708
Mediclean, 27847
Medifast, 3773, 21785
Medjool, 10939
Medlee, 8125
Mee Tu, 345
Meese, 20143
Meg-3®, 3320
Mega C-Bio, 7947
Mega Cal™, 6449, 24506
Mega Warheads, 4589, 22756
Mega-Con, 20934
Mega-Mill, 27713
Mega-Slicer, 25766
Mega-Temp, 20121
Mega/Fill, 26852
Megace®, 1721
Megachar, 19008
Megacrunch®, 6374, 24434
Megadophilus, 8816
Megafood, 8130
Meganatural, 9654
Megared, 11285
Megatron, 19152

Meguiar's, 25956
Meguiar's Mirror Glaze, 25956
Meher, 2923
Meica, 1957
Meier's, 8135
Meier's Sparkling Ju, 8135
Meijer, 8137
Meijer Ecowise, 8137
Meijer Elements, 8137
Meijer Gold, 8137
Meijer Natural, 8137
Meijer Organic, 8137
Meinel, 5400
Meistermarken, 954
Mekach, 6776
Mekong, 13208, 30670
Mel's, 2843
Mel-Fry®, 13328
Mel-O Honey, 12401
Mel-O-Cream, 8139
Melatonin, 8009, 11268
Melba, 25789
Melcer, 1064
Melco, 30323
Mele-Koi Hawaiian Coconut Snow, 8143
Melina's, 9937
Melind, 21201
Melinda's, 4382
Meliora Organic, 5139
Melissa, 6986
Melissas, 31350
Melitta, 8146, 13717, 25789, 25963
Meller, 9956
Mellin, 10565
Mello Joy, 2019
Mello Yello, 2811, 2814
Mello-Krisp, 8204
Mellow Corn Whiskey, 5720
Mellowmind, 9201
Melo-Glow, 5517
Melody, 8513
Melster, 13574
Melt Organic, 10347
Melt-N-Mold, 5428
Meluka, 8149
Mem-Pure, 26111
Memco, 25841
Memmert, 27835
Memory, 7774
Menchaca, 11834
Mendes Farms, 11985
Mendocino, 8154
Mendocino Cty. Sauvignon Blanc, 869
Mendoza Ridge, 9540
Menehune Magic, 1123
Menemsha Bites, 8156
Menghini, 8157
Meno-Select, 8009
Mens Bread, 4702
Mental Energy Formula, 9201
Mentor Laser Power, 28915
Mentos, 2132, 9956
Menu, 11308, 28903
Menu a La Carte, 3989
Menu Master, 24354
Menulink, 25988
Menumaster, 18333
Meow Mix, 6380
Mepsco, 25989
Mer, 2815, 20685
Meramec, 8159
Meratrim, 6236
Mercer, 8163
Merchant & Moli-Shields, 26269
Merci, 12147, 12148
Merci Crocant, 12147
Merci Pur, 12147
Mercier Champagnes, 3570
Mercken's, 9031
Mercken's Chocolate, 9031
Merco, 703, 31092
Merco®, 31093
Mercon, 8166
Mercury, 25995, 31092, 31200
Merecol, 4773

All Brands Index

Meredith's, 8167
Meretec, 4773
Merezan, 4773
Meridian, 12937
Meridian Foods, 5479
Merion Park Rye Bread, 508
Merita, 4529
Meritage, 3771
Merix, 26002
Merkts, 1172
Merlayzyn, 12746
Merlin, 27799
Merlin's, 8175
Merlino Baking Co., 11390
Merlino Signature Brands, 8176
Merlot, 1314, 4745
Mermaid Princess, 8938
Mermaid Spice, 8178
Mermaid's Supreme Shrimp, 1916
Merrill's, 8181
Merritt, 8183
Merritt Pecan Co., 8184
Merrychef®, 31093
Merryvale, 8185
Mertz Sausage, 8186
Meso Biomatrix®, 3320
Met-Max, 2411
Met-Rx®, 8871
Meta, 12721, 30193
Meta Boost, 9251
Meta Rest, 9251
Metabolife, 13097
Metabolol, 2411
Metagenics, 8193
Metal Polish Scrubs, 24035
Metala, 12937
Metalarc, 26990
Metalarm, 22252
Metaledge, 27950
Metalife, 31175
Metalix, 18582
Metallic Luster, 29055
Metaloom, 22377
Metalphoto, 27508
Metalwash, 24290
Metaxa, 13811
Meteor, 20256, 20258
Meteorites, 11320
Meter Master, 29513
Meto, 22271
Meto/Primark, 22271
Metrak, 19559
Metromax, 24304, 26031
Metromax Q, 26031
Metropolitan, 8199
Metzger Popcorn Co., 8204
Meukow Cognac, 11264
Meurens, 10146
Mevgal, 6986
Mevon, 28665
Mexamerica, 8206
Mexene® Chili, 1794
Mexi-Frost, 8207
Mexican Accent, 8208
Mexican Bear, 12845
Mexican Original®, 13109
Mexicana, 10869
Meyenberg, 8210
Meyer, 28832
Meyer Natural Angus Beef, 457
Mezzetta, 5039
Mezzo, 13320
Mezzo Mix, 2815, 20685
Mg Vallejo, 13851
Mga, 8693
Mgm, 2350
Mgr, 25871
Mgv, 22018
Mh Press Systems, 20868
Mi Best Soybean Oil, 11096
Mi Casa, 4529, 4662
Mi Mama's, 8214
Mi Ranchito, 8215
Mi-Delc, 9748
Mi-Kee, 7022

Mia, 8217
Mia's Mirror, 5473
Miami Beef, 8218
Mibco, 26073
Mibrush, 26073
Mica Wax, 26680
Mice-A-Fours, 3625
Miceli's, 8222
Michael Angelo's, 8223
Michael David Vineyards, 8224
Michael Foods Inc.®, 11504, 29095
Michael Granese Co., 8226
Michael Merchant Winemaker, 12489
Michael Season's Cheese Curls, 7845
Michael Season's Cheese Puffs, 7845
Michael Season's Kettle Potatoes, 7845
Michael Season's Organically Grown, 7845
Michael Season's Sensations, 7845
Michael Shea's Irish Amber, 4950
Michael's Health Products, 8231
Michaelene's Gourmet, 8233
Michaelene's Gourmet Granola, 8233
Michaelene's Granola, 8233
Michaelok, 12550
Michel De France, 12487
Michel De Francec, 1411
Michel Torino, 4677
Michel's Family Bakery, 8236
Michel-Schlumberger, 8238
Michele's Chocolate Truffles, 8240
Michele's Honey Creme, 8239
Michelina's Grande, 1200
Michelina's Lean Gourmet®, 1200
Michelina's Pizza Snack Rolls, 1200
Michelina's Signature®, 1200
Michelle, 8242
Michelle's, 4919
Michelle's Organic, 8642
Michelle's Rawfoodz, 8243
Michelo Ultra, 7123
Michelob Light®, 26668
Michelob Ultra, 571
Michigan Dessert, 8247, 26074
Michigan Fine Herbs, 5782
Michigan Made, 5951
Michigan Rag, 26770
Michigan Star Thistle, 10478
Michigan Turkey Producers, 11053
Michtex, 12550
Mickelberry's, 11902
Mickey Mouse, 4507
Mickey's, 8459
Mickey's®, 8460
Micorduct, 26108
Micro Basil Nutmeg, 4718
Micro Bmx Bike, 1158
Micro Cucumber, 4718
Micro Fast, 10491
Micro Flex, 26103
Micro Lab, 30216
Micro Mint Lime, 4718
Micro Mustard Dijon, 4718
Micro Phep, 23571
Micro Quad, 30216
Micro Radish Ruby, 4718
Micro Raves, 18908
Micro Scooter, 1158
Micro Tangerine Lace, 4718
Micro Wasabi, 4718
Micro-Amp, 19429
Micro-Brush, 26087
Micro-Con, 20934
Micro-Deck, 22257
Micro-Jet, 22662
Micro-Media, 22257
Micro-Meter Airless, 29513
Micro-Mini, 26109
Micro-Oxymax, 20751
Micro-Petter, 22664
Micro-Precision, 20305
Micro-Pure, 26111
Micro-Recharger, 27435
Micro-Screen, 19429
Microban, 27847

Microbest, Inc., 26097
Microcell, 30800
Microchiller, 31261
Microcoder, 30434
Microcut, 29642
Microduction, 26117
Microfloat, 18436
Microfluidizer Pro.Equipment, 26104
Microfresh, 9839
Microgourmet®, 21362
Microgreen™, 21362
Microgreens, 4718
Microklear, 18527
Microlacer, 20654
Microleak, 21401
Microlene, 29397
Microlog, 19681
Micromask, 9797
Micron One, 31312
Micronair, 22865
Microplate, 19681
Micropower, 23611
Micropower Ac, 23611
Microproof, 23499
Micropub, 26110
Microrollers, 29445
Micros, 26953
Microscan, 26112
Microscrub, 31177
Microsoy Flakes, 8252
Microspense Ap, 24042
Microstar, 21416
Microstat, 26108
Microtouch, 26115
Microtronic, 19798
Microware, 23499
Mid Pacific, 8258
Mid-Atlantic, 8256
Mid-Atlantic Foods, 11356
Mid-Pacific Seafoods, 10603
Mid-Trak, 27575
Middlebe Marshal, 26131
Middleby Marshall, 26132
Middleby Marshall Ovens, 25524
Middlefield, 8263
Midhaven Farm Cafe, 11402
Midheaven Farm, 11402
Midland, 21046
Midleton, 9964
Midori, 5892
Midori Melon, 1120
Midship, 11368
Midtown Caff, 6547
Midwest, 8269, 26144
Midwest Blueberry Farms, 8265
Midwest Marko, 25761
Mieloguard, 20064
Mies, 26160
Mifab, 25577
Migdal, 13931
Mighties, 12242
Mighty Blade, 26861
Mighty Greens, 10067
Mighty Leaf Tea, 8090
Mighty Mini, 18251
Mighty Organic, 1963
Mighty Pine, 19741
Mighty Wild, 11818
Mighty Wipe, 18273
Mighty-Pure, 19152
Mignardise, 10039
Migration, 3779
Miguel's, 8275
Mihel, 2457
Mikaela's Simply Divine, 8276
Mikarla's Best, 9112
Mikawaya, 8277
Mike and Ike®, 6641
Mike's Hard, 8279
Mikesell's, 8282
Miki, 13560
Mikrodyne, 27853
Mikropul, 19576
Mil Lel™, 11211
Mil-E-Qual, 20934

Milano, 1881, 2116
Milano®, 9942
Milat Vineyards, 8290
Milcal, 4914
Milcal-Fg, 4914
Milcal-Tg, 4914
Mild Gouda, 13840
Milea Estate Vineyard, 8292
Milem, 13141
Miles River, 1098
Milford, 23842
Miljoco, 8294, 26171
Milk Bone, 6380
Milk Chugs, 8104
Milk Duds, 5818, 23750
Milk For Life®, 13218
Milk Stout, 7310
Milk-Free, 6340
Milk-Stor, 22850
Milk2go®, 11211
Milkboy, 8296
Milkman, 25784
Milko, 6204, 24221
Milkshake Factory, 3958
Milky Way®, 7952
Milky Wayc, 2132
Mill Creek Vineyards, 8301
Millbrook, 5245, 8303
Mille Lacs, 8304
Millenium Message, 21059
Millennium, 10112
Millennuim, 21004
Miller, 8459
Miller Lite, 24672
Miller's, 3469, 10372, 13931
Miller's Country Ham, 8311
Miller®, 8460
Millflow, 8314
Milliaire Winery, 8315
Millie's, 13688
Millie's Pierogi, 8316
Mills, 2044
Mills Brothers International, 8320
Millstone, 3171, 6819
Millstream, 8323
Milnot, 3862, 8327
Milo's Kitchen, 6380
Milo®, 8945
Milone Brothers, 8328
Milpas, 8161
Milsek, 26191
Milsolv, 8332
Milsorb, 8335
Miltex, 23160
Milwaukee Seltzer Company, 6159
Milwaukee's Best, 8459
Milwaukee's Best®, 8460
Mimi Foods, 20020
Mimi's Muffins, 6291, 24388
Min Tong, 8339
Min-Col, 9262
Mina, 2276, 7747
Minaret™, 13400
Mind's Eye Smart Drinks, 10405
Minerac, 11145
Mineragua, 12823
Minerva, 6986, 8345
Minestrone, 2309
Ming Cha, 1600
Mingo Bay Beverages, 8346
Mingo Bay Beverages, Inc., 10141
Minh, 11316
Minh®, 11317
Mini Babybel, 1172, 1173
Mini Bites®, 12880
Mini Brute, 26697
Mini Dickmann's, 12147
Mini Flower Crystals, 4718
Mini Herb Crystals, 4718
Mini Max Iii, 28050
Mini Me's®, 1484
Mini Moo's, 13734
Mini Rx Hone, 28063
Mini Scents, 19127
Mini Sdx, 21495

All Brands Index

Mini Tubs, 5909, 23825
Mini-6, 18300
Mini-Array, 19429
Mini-Beam, 19429
Mini-Con, 20934
Mini-Croustade, 10039
Mini-Croustade Shell, 10039
Mini-Easre, 10039
Mini-Gas Series, 18620
Mini-Mark, 25788
Mini-Module, 24519
Mini-Mornap, 23160
Mini-Pak, 20710
Mini-Pinch, 18300
Mini-Pro, 22117
Mini-Punch, 18300
Mini-Roulet, 10039
Mini-Screen, 19429
Mini-Sip, 22184
Mini-Sizzlers, 11298
Mini-Vac, 23587
Mini-Wedge Press, 19501
Mini-Wheats®, 6765
Mini-Wheel, 24940
Minigo, 14017
Minikeeper, 22509
Minilab, 24022
Minilab Micro Compouuder, 23503
Minimint, 27470
Minions, 2132
Minipax, 26381
Minipure, 19152
Minispam, 29441
Minit Chef, 7783
Minitree, 24519
Miniveil, 19597
Miniworks, 26337
Minn - Dak, 8352
Minnesaurus Dill Picklodon, 4928
Minnesota Automation, 26206
Minnesota Dehydrated Vegetables, 8355
Minnesota Girl, 648
Minnesota Heartland, 4753
Minnesota Rag, 26770
Minnesota Wild, 8357
Minor's®, 8945
Minowa, 13565
Minski, 4515
Minsley, 8361
Mint, 9995
Mint Balls, 10496
Mint Lumps, 5752
Mint Patties, 9877
Mint Puffs, 5752
Mint Savor, 8362
Mint Shell, 10039
Mint Twists, 756
Minterbrook, 8363
Minute Fudge, 10773
Minute Glow, 25186
Minute Lunch, 13240
Minute Maid, 2811, 2814, 2815, 6338, 8365, 9469, 20685
Minute Maid Juice To Go, 8365
Minute Maid Just 15, 8365
Minute Maid Sparkling, 8365
Minute Menu, 3549
Minute®, 10777, 28421
Mio, 6976
Mione W P-1, 26212
Mipro, 31177
Miprodan®, 19049
Mipueblito, 10363
Mira Mango Nectar, 8366
Mirabel®, 5844
Mirabelle, 11307
Mirabo, 2409
Miracle, 255
Miracle Ade, 9858
Miracle Juice, 9858
Miracle Juice Energy Drink, 9858
Miracle Maize, 7465
Miracle Treec, 1549
Miracle Whip, 6976
Miraclean Griddle, 24744

Miracoli®, 7952
Miracryl, 20256
Mirage, 23523, 28023
Miramar, 8371
Mirassou, 7103
Mirassou®, 3834
Mirch Masala, 3465
Miriam, 13813
Miroil, 26214
Mirro Foley, 26216
Mirror Pond Pale Ale, 3533
Miscela Bar, 6238
Miscela Napoli, 6238
Misfit, 8373
Mishpacha, 7848
Miso Master Organic, 5306
Miss Jones Baking Co., 8379
Miss Kriss, 31010
Miss Leone's, 7364
Miss Meringue, 8380
Miss Sally's, 2261
Miss Scarlett, 8381
Miss Vickie's, 4741
Miss Vickies®, 9945, 27433
Mission, 8387
Mission Foods, 20020
Mission Foodservice®, 11504, 29095
Mission Hill Bistro, 12023, 29568
Mission Mountain, 8388
Mission San Juan Juices, 11266
Mission®, 3479, 8384, 21460
Mississippi Cheese Straws, 8391
Mississippi Delta Fudge, 12546
Mississippi Lime, 1692
Mississippi Mousse, 12546
Mississippi Mud Pupp, 8391
Mississippi Rag, 26770
Missouri Rag, 26770
Missouri's Finest, 7571
Mister Bee, 8393
Mister Fudge, 2048, 20140
Mister Jinx, 20591
Mister Mustard, 13894
Mister Spear, 8398
Mister Tenderizer, 30305
Mistic, 1294
Mistic Iced Tea, 4521
Mistkup, 18147
Misto, 2012
Misto Dark, 2012
Misty Mints, 10104
Mitalena Coffee, 13191
Mitchell Foods, 8403
Mitchell's, 5555
Mitchum Rices, 8404
Mito's, 7859
Mitoku Macrobiotic, 2630
Mitsukan®, 8415
Mitsuko's Vineyard, 2770
Mity-Eye, 30422
Mitydrive, 18945
Mityflex, 18945
Mitzi, 21425
Miwok Weizen Bock, 7923
Mix Master, 24869
Mix'n Machine, 30884
Mix-Mill, 18035
Mix-Ups, 525
Mixer Stix Drink Mix, 12182
Mixers, 8729
Mixograph, 30013
Mixon, 8411
Mixpap, 18541
Miztique™, 9237, 26785
Mjb, 7995, 11212
Mlo Sports Nutrition, 4955
Mm710, 26421
Mo Hotta - Mo Betta, 8433
Mobi-Crane, 28508
Mobile Merchandising Systems, 20315
Mocafe, 3009
Mocha, 10307
Mocha Mix®, 1103
Mocha Mud, 1665
Mocha Mud Cake Mix, 1665

Mochem, 26276
Mochi, 5248
Mochi Ice Cream, 8277
Mod-A-Flex, 18702
Mod-Plex, 25224
Mod-U-Beam, 25224
Mode, 7705
Model #10, 25900
Model Am, 20509
Model Cf, 23105
Model Dairy, 3442, 21421
Model Sam, 27864
Modelo, 71, 7123
Modelo Especial, 4881
Modern Chef, 27391
Modern Mill, 18034
Modern Oats, 8444
Modern Pantry, 10022
Modern Pop, 8447
Moderna Alimentos, 2970
Modicom, 28894
Modleo Especial, 4881
Moducare, 13536
Moduchol, 13536
Modul Print, 31420
Modular Dispensing Systems, 30323
Modular Kt, 26250
Modular Pouch Machine, 20070
Modular Tile, 19151
Modulator, 26254
Moduline, 27980
Moduprost, 13536
Moet & Chandon, 8452
Moffett, 7490
Mogen David, 13851
Moistart, 30792
Moisturlok®, 190, 18410
Mojeska's, 8700
Mojonnier, 28832
Moka-Java, 12846
Moledina, 8456
Molfino®, 11211
Moli-Tron, 26272
Molinaro's, 8457
Moline, 26270
Molinos Champion S.A., 2970
Mollic, 8458
Molly McButter, 864
Molson, 8459
Molson Canadian, 8459
Molson Canadian®, 8460
Molta Roba, 13160
Moly-Xl, 26275
Molyube, 19535
Mom 'n Pops, 8461
Mom's, 4432, 8464
Mom's Choice, 5637
Mom's Famous, 8463
Momarket, 26276
Mommy's Choice, 437
Momokawa, 11093
Mon Ami, 8467
Mon Cheri, 4348
Mona Lisa, 1056
Monadnock Mountain Spring Water, 1480
Monarch, 5981, 22955, 25668, 27655
Monarch Can Crushers, 18034
Monarch-Mclaren, 26280
Monari Federzoni, 6279
Monasterio Sta. Ana Monte, 3545
Mondavi, 10791
Mondelez International, 541, 2132
Mondial, 10041
Mondrian, 28327
Money Candy, 11016
Money Mints, 11051
Money on Honey, 3767
Moneys, 8477
Monfort, 3262
Mongo, 4895
Mongoose, 7157
Monica's, 5140
Monin, 3009

Monini, 8479
Monique's Pasta Sauces, 247
Monitor, 18637
Monkey 47, 9964
Monkey Baking, 8480
Monkey Catering, 8480
Monkey Party, 8480
Monkgold™, 4837
Monksweet™, 4837
Monnini, 25789
Monogram, 22959
Monolyn, 25536
Monorail, 20593
Monospan, 29441
Monsanto, 8452
Monsooned Malabar, 6611
Monster, 2947, 27428
Monster Chews, 2947
Monster Cone, 8486
Monster Cookies, 8635
Monster Energy, 2811, 2815, 8485, 20685
Monster Energy®, 26668
Monsters®, 4947
Mont Blanc Chocolate Syrups, 8487
Mont-Rougr, 10333
Montagnolo, 2409
Montana Big Sky™, 9237, 26785
Montana Mex, 8490
Montchevre®, 11209
Monte Alban Mezcal, 11264
Monte Carlo Bake Shop, 903
Montebello, 2075, 11589, 11980
Montefiore Winery, 10952
Montego Bay, 9842
Montego Bay Rum, 8062
Monterey, 20120
Monterey Cabernet Sauvignon, 2637
Monterey Chardonnay, 2637
Monterey Gourmet Foods, 10365
Monterey Petite Syrah, 2637
Monterrey, 8508
Montesierra, 3545
Montezuma Blue, 11264
Montezuma Tequila, 11264
Montezuma Triple Sec, 11264
Montforte, 11313, 13876
Montpellier, 1738
Montreal Chop Suey, 8514
Monument Dairy Farms, 8516
Moo & Oink, 1262
Moo Chew, 1018
Moo Magic, 12182
Moo-Calcium, 4914
Mooala, 8518
Mood Lite, 31217
Moon, 10275
Moon Lake, 7339
Moon Mountain, 5743
Moon Pads, 8824
Moon's Seafood, 8523
Moonlight, 8525
Moonlight Pale Lager, 8524
Moonlite Bbq Inn, 8528
Moonpie, 2470
Moonshine Madness, 6796
Moonshine Sweet Tea, 8529
Moonshine Trading, 14034
Moonstone, 11093
Moor, 2691
Moore's, 530
Moore's®, 4061, 8055
Moores, 8532
Moose Drool Brown Ale, 1344
Moose Mountain, 1677
Moosehead Lager, 8535
Mop Pac, 27679
Mop Paclite, 27679
Mopac, 8615, 26345
Mor-Fruit, 9763, 27283
Morabito, 8536
Morad Winery, 10952
Moravian Hearth, 11100
More Spice Seasoning, 12869
More-Than-Tofu, 12273

All Brands Index

Morehouse, 8539
Morey's, 8541
Morgro, 18029
Mori-Nu, 3773, 8546, 21785
Mori-Nu Tofu, 8679
Moritz Ice Cubes, 10496
Morn'n Fresh, 6670
Mornap, 23160
Morning Cheer, 5517
Morning Glory, 1388
Morning Moo's, 1506
Morning Spark, 12182
Morning Star, 8549
Morning Star Farms, 6766
Morning Sun, 9182
Morning Tide, 24409
Morningland Dairy, 8550
Morningstar Farms, 8551
Mornington Dairy®, 11211
Morositas, 9956
Morrison Brand, 8563
Morrison Farms, 8915, 26526
Morrison's, 1917
Morse, 26947
Morse's, 8564
Mortein®, 10598
Mortimer Fine Foods, 8567
Morton, 6661
Morton Evaporation Salt, 8569
Morton Kaciff, 20143
Morton Rock Salt, 8569
Morton Salt, 8569
Morton Solar Salt, 8569
Mos-Ness, 11294
Mosaica, 21213
Mosar Design Displayware, 20256
Moshe & Ali's Sprat,, 9863
Mosher Products, 8571
Moss Bay Extra Ale, 5515
Moss Bay Stout, 5515
Moss Creek, 8572
Moss Roxx, 9321
Mossy Bayou, 2019
Mostly Cloudy, 7526
Mother, 8485
Mother Earth, 7028, 8693
Mother Nature's Goodies, 8577
Mother Parkers, 8578
Mother Teresa's Fine Foods, 8581
Mother's, 166, 7848
Mother's Cookies, 6766
Mother's Day, 21059
Mother's Kitchen, 10714
Mother's Prize, 3092
Mother's Pure Preserves, 3092
Mothers ®, 13120
Mothers Free Range, 2576
Mothers Maid, 1866
Motoman, 26330
Mott's, 8585, 8586
Mott's For Tots®, 8585
Mott's Fruit Flavoured Snacks, 8585
Mott's Fruitsations, 8586
Mott's Sensibles™, 8585
Mott's®, 3725, 6818, 24802
Mou Cuisine, 329
Mouli, 26331
Mounds, 5818, 23750
Mount Baker Vineyards & Winery, 8650
Mount Eden Vineyards, 8654
Mount Hagen, 6279
Mount Herman, 1121
Mount Nittany, 8656
Mount Olympus®, 3220, 3319
Mount Olympus™, 11889
Mount Palomar, 8592
Mount Vernon Mantel Company, 24672
Mountain Apple, 1812
Mountain Bar, 1771
Mountain Berry, 11218
Mountain City, 8593
Mountain Country, 2844, 20696
Mountain Dew®, 9945, 27433
Mountain Gold, 12504
Mountain Gold Honey, 7748
Mountain Grown, 4543
Mountain High, 8597
Mountain High®, 4947
Mountain House, 9529
Mountain House Kitchen, 12811
Mountain Mats' Apples, 28090
Mountain Mist, 8920
Mountain Trout, 13447
Mountain Valley, 4143, 4462
Mountain Valley Spring Water, 8605
Mountain Valley Spring Water ™, 5884
Mountain White, 19995
Mountain-Grown Fancy Ceylon, 5228, 23295
Mountainman, 2323
Mountainside Farms, 8609
Mountaire, 8610
Mountaire Fresh Young Chicken, 11053
Mouse Master, 31188
Move Free, 11285
Movenpick®, 8945
Movidrive, 29083
Movidyn, 29083
Movie Trivia, 21059
Movimot, 29083
Movincool, 26343
Moving Pix, 20625
Movingprix, 29746
Movitrac, 29083
Movomech, 28508
Moxie, 2311
Moy Park®, 10056
Moyer Diebel, 18564, 20428
Moyer®, 6391
Moyno, 26346
Mozzaluna, 530
Mozzamia, 530
Mp Series, 19625
Mpi 90, 25591
Mpi-L, 25591
Mr & Mrs T, 8586
Mr Frosty, 11356
Mr Pure, 8784
Mr Snack, 11503
Mr Z, 13421
Mr. & Mrs. T®, 3725
Mr. Boston, 11264
Mr. C'S, 7972
Mr. C'S Pretzels, 12851
Mr. Cheese O'S, 11804
Mr. Clean, 12721, 30193
Mr. Cookie Face, 8394
Mr. Dell's I.Q.F. Country Potatoes, 8618
Mr. Dell's I.Q.F. Hash Browns, 8618
Mr. Dell's I.Q.F. Herb & Garlic, 8618
Mr. Dell's I.Q.F. Santa Fe, 8618
Mr. Doodler, 21769
Mr. Egg Roll, 2040
Mr. Espresso, 8619
Mr. Fancy's, 12178
Mr. Fizz, 25238
Mr. Food, 25545
Mr. G'S, 7972
Mr. Honey & Mrs. Fruit, 10454
Mr. Ice Bucket, 26349
Mr. Induction, 29520
Mr. John, 19741
Mr. Neat, 23143
Mr. P'S, 4756, 22893
Mr. Scrapy, 24613
Mr. Sharp, 12437
Mr. Spice, 7210
Mr. Steam, 31251
Mr. Yam, 8772
Mr.Goodbar, 5818, 23750
Mr.Spinkles, 9748
Mr16, 10344, 22018
Mrs Baird's®, 1359
Mrs Baird'sc, 8626
Mrs Bairds, 892
Mrs Butterworth's, 811
Mrs Dash®, 864
Mrs Difilippo's, 3549
Mrs Fanings, 4831
Mrs Feldman's Desserts, 5322
Mrs Kavanagh's, 5942
Mrs Leeper's, 6279
Mrs Leeper's Wheat/Gluten Free, 8642
Mrs Malibu, 8643
Mrs Paul's, 811
Mrs Renfro's, 10508
Mrs Schlorers, 5157
Mrs Slaby's, 6971
Mrs. Adler's, 7848
Mrs. Asien, 5372
Mrs. Brahms, 628
Mrs. Butterworth's®, 27540
Mrs. Campbells, 5146
Mrs. Crockett's, 3173
Mrs. Dash® Foodservice, 6792, 24785
Mrs. Denson's, 8635
Mrs. Dog's, 8636
Mrs. Filberts, 1935
Mrs. Fisher, 8628
Mrs. Freshley's, 4529
Mrs. Friday's, 6855
Mrs. Grimes®, 4267, 22464
Mrs. Kavanagh's, 8640
Mrs. Klein's, 6908
Mrs. Little's, 14045
Mrs. Paul's®, 27540
Mrs. Powell's Gourmet, 4001
Mrs. Renfro's, 10674
Mrs. Richardson Toppings, 988, 19404
Mrs. Smith's, 11316, 26352
Mrs. Smith's®, 11317
Mrs. Stratton, 8633
Mrs. Sullivan's, 8634
Mrs. T'S, 8648
Mrs. T'S Pierogies, 747
Mrs. Thinsters, 12664
Mrs. Veggies, 8324
Mrs. Weinstein's Toffee, 12414
Mrs. Weiss'®, 10777, 28421
Mrs.Butterworth's®, 2939, 2940, 20821, 20822
Mrs.Paul's®, 2939, 2940, 20821, 20822
Ms-1400, 24550
Ms-25, 24550
Ms-55, 24550
Ms-700, 24550
Ms. Kays, 557
Ms/Rv, 31071
Msi, 8398
Msi-6000, 25940
Msi-9000, 25940
Msr, 26337
Msr Carabiners, 26337
Msrf, 7706
Mt Veeder, 4649
Mt. Betty, 10789
Mt. Harlan, 2044
Mt. Konocti, 8660
Mt. Mama, 10789
Mt. Olive, 8657
Mt. Rainbow Series, 24409
Mt. Shasta, 8784
Mt. Sterling Cheese Co., 8659
Mt. Tom Pale Ale, 7923
Mt. Veeder Blanc De Blancs, 3661
Mt. View Bakery, 8663
Mt. Vikos™, 1484
Mt. Whitney, 11450
Mt20, 18243
Mtj Seating, 21561
Muchmates, 13964
Mucinex®, 10598
Mucky Duck, 8666
Mucon, 24767
Mud, 7707, 12811
Muddy Bears, 12547
Mueller, 10792
Mueller's, 465
Muenchner/Stadtbrot, 3606
Muenster, 4405
Muffin Monster, 24649
Muffin Revolution, 8667
Mug Root Beer®, 9945, 27433
Muginoka, 1120
Mugshots, 11855
Muir Glen, 2286
Muir Glen Organic, 11711
Muir Glen®, 4947
Muirhead, 8670
Muirwood, 104
Mulberry Farms, 10637
Mullen's, 8671
Mulling Cider, 12272
Multi Mixer, 27799
Multi-Beam, 19429
Multi-Con, 20934
Multi-Meter, 28396
Multi-Scale, 24178
Multi-Screen, 19429
Multi-Trix, 31085
Multi-Vessel System, 30800
Multi-Weigh, 30118
Multibulk, 26374
Multichlor, 20489
Multichrome, 10344, 22018
Multifoods®, 20096
Multimix, 28493
Multipack®, 23811
Multiple Media Fixture, 25628
Multiplex, 7421, 24042, 26178
Multiplex®, 31093
Multipurpose, 22039
Multirome®, 3320
Multisac, 31336
Multislicer, 23117
Multispan, 29441
Multispense, 24042
Multitech, 19021
Multivac, 21134
Multy Grain Foods, 13863
Mumm Napac, 9964
Mumsey, 6445
Munchie, 20256
Munchos, 4741
Munchos®, 9945, 27433
Munchrights, 13964
Mung Dynasty, 8679
Munk Pack, 8680
Munkijo, 8681
Munroe Dairy, 32
Munsee Meats, 8682
Munson's, 8683
Muro, 26393
Murphy Goode, 8688
Murphy Oil Soap, 20721
Murray Sugar Free Cookies, 6766
Murray's, 8689
Murrieta's Well, 13654
Murvest, 8691
Muscle Milk®, 6000, 23861
Muscle Nitro, 2411
Musette®, 1484
Musetti, 3009
Museum, 4677
Mushroom Canning Company, 8693
Mushroom Meringue Cookies, 2599
Mushroom Wisdom, 8695
Musillami, 12162
Muslix®, 6765
Mussel King, 12420
Musselman's Apple Sauce Cookies, 9399
Mussleman's, 6923
Mustang, 19798, 26109
Mustang Iv, 19798
Mustard, 6532
Mustard Pretzels, 972
Muth's Kentucky, 8700
Mutual Graphics™, 22187
Muy Frescoc, 187
Mvp, 3397
My Brother Bobby's Salsa, 8703
My Bubby's, 4021
My Country Sweet, 2274
My Daddy's Cheesecake, 8706
My Father's Best, 8781
My Favorite, 4369
My Favorite Jerky, 8707
My Grandma's of New England, 8708, 11864

1315

All Brands Index

My Hero, 6806
My Little Pony, 1591
My M&Ms, 2132
My Mom's Mixes, 3079
My Nana's, 7042
My Selection, 13845
My T Fine®, 6483
My Utapia®, 3319
My-Baby, 13122
My-Dol®, 857
My-T-Lite, 25224
My/Mo Mochi Ice Cream, 8711
Myco Curb, 6777
Myers, 5555
Myers Frozen Food, 8713
Myers Ice Co., 26409
Mylanbox Ibc, 26166
Mylk Labs, 8714
Mynap, 23160
Myntz Breathmints, 11390
Myntz! Breath Mints, 7710
Myntz! Instastripz, 7710
Myntz! Lip Balm, 7710
Myrcenary Double Ipa, 9366
Myron's 20 Gauge, 8715
Myrties, 7524
Myrtle Greens, 13310
Myrtles, 7524
Mystic Lake Dairy, 8717
Mystic Mead, 7171
Mystic River, 7373
Mystic Seaport, 9560
Mystik Spices, 30036
Mythos, 6986
Myti Host Chair, 26229
Myti Lite Tables, 26229
Myti Taff Chair, 26229
Myvacet, 137
Myverol, 137

N

N'Ice Ties, 24700
N-Creamer 46, 8804
N-Dulge™, 8804
N-Lok ® 1930, 8804
N-Oil®, 8804
N-Tack®, 8804
N-Zorbit™, 8804
N.E.M., 26578
N.F. Peeler, 19169
N.M. Riesling, 10165
Na Po'okela O Honaunau, 1908
Nabisco, 13610
Nabisco 12 Packs, 8729
Nabisco Classics, 8729
Nabob, 6976
Nacan, 8730
Naches, 10275
Nacho Grande, 4623
Nadamoo, 8731
Nadamoo Organic, 8731
Nahmias Et Fils, 8734
Nair, 2666, 20561
Najla Gone Chunky, 8736
Nakand, 30618
Nakano®, 8415
Naked Bacon, 8739
Naked Flock, 618
Naked Meats®, 10124
Naked Mountain, 8742
Naked Truth®, 13607
Naked Wild Honey, 1040
Naked®, 9945, 27433
Nalle, 8744
Nalley Lumberjack Table Syrup, 12921
Nalley®, 1103, 2939, 2940, 20821, 20822, 27540
Naltex, 26440
Nalu, 2815, 20685
Nam Power, 19913
Namco, 26442
Namp, 2313
Nana Flakes, 8719
Nana's, 8748

Nana's Cocina, 130
Nana's Cookie Bars, 8748
Nana's No Gluten, 8748
Nana's Own, 1069
Nance's Mustards, 988, 19404
Nanci's, 8749
Nancy's, 8751, 8753, 11971
Nanka Udon, 8754
Nanko, 1120
Nantucker Nectars®, 6818, 24802
Nantucket Nectars®, 3725
Nantucket Tea Trader, 8758
Nantucket Vineyard, 8759
Nantze Springs, 8760
Napa Ridge, 1738
Napa Syrah, 6603
Napa Valley, 1141, 2770, 4649
Napa Valley Barbeque Co., 13849
Napa Valley Harvest, 13849
Napa Valley Homemade, 5039
Napa Valley Mustard Co., 8764
Napa Wine, 8762
Napa Wine Company, 8765
Napkin Deli, 20256
Napolean's Bakery, 14067
Napoleon, 26450
Nara, 10435
Nardone Bros., 8770
Nascar Bottled Water, 7264
Nash's Gold, 8772
Nash's Pride, 8772
Nasim, 7007
Nasoya, 13473
Nasoya®, 10365
Nassco, 26506
Nasty Tricks, 2947
Natalie's Orchid Island, 8777
Natcelt, 783
Natco, 1600
Nate Dog's, 2017
Naterl, 8815
Nathan's, 5105, 12965
Nathan's Famous, 11733, 13196
Nathan's Smoked Salmon, 9344
Nation, 8781
National, 8795, 8804, 24851
National Beef, 11053
National Beef® Prime, 8783
National Drying Wachinery, 19935
National Fisheries, 8787
National Gold, 5132
National Importers/Twinnings, 20020
National Imprint Corporation®, 22187
National Labortory Products, 26481
National One, 5132
National Poultry Company, 3479, 21460
National Steak, 8805
National Tank & Pipe, 24360
Native, 12721, 30193
Native American, 8809
Native Forest, 3956
Native Kjalii, 8811
Native Scents, 8812
Natives Pride, 741
Natra Cacao, 8814
Natra Us, 8814
Natrabio, 13642
Natrabio®, 9237, 26785
Natraceutical, 8814
Natragest, 7422
Natrasorb, 26381
Natrataste, 12201
Natrium, 8817
Natur-Cell®, 10797, 28438
Natura, 100, 9256
Natural Angus Beef, 8783
Natural Balance Pet Foods, 6380
Natural Balance®, 9237, 26785
Natural Blends®, 11228, 28829
Natural Bliss, 8821
Natural Bliss Cold Brew, 8821
Natural Bouncin' Berry, 11785
Natural Brew, 28471
Natural Certified Angus Beef, 3451
Natural Choice, 1766, 1767, 26799

Natural Choice®, 6000, 23861
Natural Country, 3084
Natural Country®, 3083
Natural Exotic Tropicals, 8827
Natural Gourmet Flavor Oil, 7409
Natural Green Leaf Brand, 9634
Natural Harvest, 12826, 13305
Natural Health, 9238
Natural Heaven, 8162
Natural Life, 7331
Natural Light, 571
Natural Light®, 26668
Natural Lite, 18843
Natural Mountain Water, 8606
Natural Ovens Bakery, 374
Natural Personal Care, 3080
Natural Pure, 20846
Natural Sea™, 1484
Natural Sins, 8848
Natural Solutions, 24833
Natural Sport®, 9237, 26785
Natural Sterols, 572
Natural Thompson, 13384
Natural Value, 8850
Natural Vines, 469
Natural's Concept, 13943
Naturalcare®, 9237, 26785
Naturalcrisp®, 6374, 24434
Naturally Aloe, 357
Naturally Clean Eats, 8853
Naturally Delicious, 8854
Naturally Flavored S, 13206
Naturally Healthy, 5146
Naturalmond, 4975, 8858
Naturalvalves, 5061
Naturaselectc, 1861
Nature Actives, 12051
Nature Canada, 10673
Nature Cure, 8859
Nature Kist, 8860
Nature Made, 9998
Nature Nate'sc, 8862
Nature Raised Farms®, 13109
Nature Scent, 18501
Nature Select, 4982
Nature Soothe, 10307
Nature Star, 10120
Nature Valley®, 4947
Nature Works, 127
Nature Zen, 8865
Nature Zone, 9734
Nature's Alchemy, 7562
Nature's Bakery, 8867
Nature's Banditsc, 8868
Nature's Beauty, 4888
Nature's Best, 1864, 6250
Nature's Best Liquid Live, 18710
Nature's Bounty, 11785
Nature's Bounty®, 8871
Nature's Burger Mix, 4252
Nature's Candy, 20144
Nature's Choice, 1020, 8627, 26351
Nature's Dairy, 8873
Nature's Earthly Choice, 8874
Nature's Edge, 3919
Nature's Finest™, 12238
Nature's Fusions, 8877
Nature's Glory, 4888
Nature's Gold, 5987
Nature's Gourmet, 7876
Nature's Guruc, 8879
Nature's Hand, 8881
Nature's Harvest®, 1359
Nature's Herbs, 8882, 13097
Nature's Herbs®, 9237, 26785
Nature's Hollow, 8885
Nature's Kitchen, 8690, 8885
Nature's Legacy, 8886
Nature's Mist, 2190
Nature's Orange, 20498
Nature's Own, 1577, 4529, 4662, 26520
Nature's Own Potato Pearls, 1069
Nature's Path Organic, 8889
Nature's Plus, 5065
Nature's Pride, 1799

Nature's Pride Sweet Potatoes, 8519
Nature's Quest, 4162
Nature's Recipe, 6380
Nature's Resources, 9998
Nature's Select, 8893
Nature's Sungrown Beef, 8898
Nature's Sunshine, 8894
Nature's Touch, 8895
Nature's Twist, 12315
Nature's Wonderland, 9918
Naturebind®, 13648, 31107
Natureflex, 30528
Naturemost Labs, 8861, 26518
Natures Club, 1114
Natures Flavors, 10495
Natures Fountain, 1915
Natures Path, 12017
Natures Plumber, 27238
Naturesafe, 3390
Natureseal®, 7857
Naturessence, 1490
Naturfood, 11144
Naturnes®, 8945
Naturox, 6777
Naturslim, 10314
Natuures Partner®, 5036
Naughty But Nice!, 21059
Naughty Noah's, 8900
Navan, 8452
Navarro, 8902
Naya, 8906
Naylor, 8909
Nbr 2000, 9274, 26796
Nbs Sorter, 22254
Nca, 9262
Ncc, 18179
Ncco®, 11504, 29095
Nci, 19254
Ndex, 29167
Ndex Free, 29167
Ne-Mo's, 8910
Ne-On the Wall, 26554
Neal's, 7083
Near East®, 9945, 27433
Neat, 772, 8914
Neat Seat, 28819
Neatgards, 23556
Nebbiolo, 13375
Nebraska Rag, 26770
Necco, 2132, 8973
Nectarade, 4505
Nedlog 100, 8919
Needlers Jersey English Toffee, 11028
Neem Aura, 7562
Neenah Springs, 8920
Neera's, 2681
Negra Modelo, 4881
Negro Modelo, 4881
Negus Octapak, 27504
Negus Square Pak, 27504
Nehi Cola®, 6818, 24802
Nehi Flavors, 4521
Neige, 1543
Neighbors, 8923
Neilson®, 11211
Nella Bella, 13300
Nelly's Organics, 8931
Nelson, 21213
Nelson Seatreats, 8932
Nelson's, 1550, 8933
Nelson's Dutch Farms, 8933
Nem®, 6449, 24506
Neo Water, 8935
Neo-Image, 26549
Neobee 1053, 12081
Neobee 1095, 12081
Neobee 895, 12081
Neobee M-20, 12081
Neobee M-5, 12081
Neocryl®, 3320
Neokura, 11250
Neon Design-A-Sign, 26553
Neon Lasers, 10496
Neon Light Pegs, 26553
Neon Plus E, 29746

All Brands Index

Neoneon, 21648
Neonetics, 26554
Neopac™, 3320
Neopuntia, 9029, 26626
Neorad™, 3320
Neorez™, 3320
Neosyl, 21094
Nepco, 29223
Neptune, 8937, 8938, 9344, 11368
Neptune Delight, 11347
Neptune Foods, 10603
Neptune's, 12989
Nerds, 2132
Nesbitts ®, 1339
Nescafe, 816
Nescafe®, 8945
Neshaminy Valley Natural, 8940
Nespresso, 8090
Nespresso®, 8945
Nesquik, 1782
Nesquik®, 8945
Nestea, 1661, 2815, 20685
Nestea®, 8945
Nestfresh, 5837, 8942
Nestier, 19926
Nestl,, 2132
Nestl, Professional®, 11504, 29095
Nestle, 541, 19244
Nestle Chocolates, 9191
Nestle Ice Cream, 20020
Nestle Nesquick, 26668
Nestle® Pure Life Water, 8945
Nestle® Toll House, 8945
Nestum®, 8945
Net-All, 30305
Net-Rap, 24135
Net/Mass, 26852
Neto, 8946
Netpac, 24743
Neuhaus, 2592
Neuman, 8950
Neuro®, 6818, 24802
Neurosome™, 6449, 24506
Neutraclean, 20489
Neutral Slush, 5460
Neutrapac, 27679
Neutrase, 1692
Nevada City Winery, 8953
Nevamar, 25935
Never Scale, 20889
Nevlen, 26564
Nevr-Dull Polish, 23150
New Age, 27881
New Classics, 5211
New Day, 6338
New England, 5211
New England Cranberry, 8969
New England Farms Eggs, 2866
New England Naturals, 8971
New England Premium, 5942
New England®, 9736
New Englander, 6542
New Era, 8973
New Generation, 29055
New Glarus Bakery, 8975
New Granola, 6222
New Harmony, 8979
New Harvest Foods, 1947
New Holstein Cheese, 1940
New Image, 12184
New Jamaican Gold Cappuccino, 10307
New Jersey Machine, 26427
New Line Homemade, 4753
New London Eng, 18877
New London Engineering, 25918
New Mexico Rag, 26770
New Mill®, 10777, 28421
New Morning, 13124
New Popc, 10445
New Rinkel, 5371
New Season Foods, 8999
New Southern Tradition Teas, 1296
New World Home Cooking Co., 2323
New York Bakery, 7189, 7987, 25120
New York Bash, 11339, 28940

New York Brand®, 12467
New York Classics, 2587
New York Club, 5660
New York Deli, 13812
New York Flatbread, 25789
New York Flatbreads™, 864
New York Kosher Deli, 329
New York Pizza, 9007
New York Pretzel, 9008
New York Style Cheesecake, 2881
New York Style™, 864
New York, New York, 30898
New-Glass, 26574
Newburgh Brewing Company, 9012
Newby, 9013
Newly Weds, 9016, 26612
Newman, 26614
Newman's Own, 7124, 9018, 9469
Newman's Own Lemonade, 9018
Newman's Own Organic, 5612
Newman's Own Pasta Sauces, 9018
Newman's Own Popcorn, 9018
Newman's Own Salad Dressing, 9018
Newmann's Own Salsa, 9018
Newmann's Own Organics®, 6818, 24802
Newmans Own, 6819
Newport, 9024
Newport Coffee Traders, 4407, 22564
Newton Vineyard, 8452, 9026
Newtons, 8729
Nexcare, 18003
Nexcel, 11910
Nexel, 26623
Nexelite, 26623
Nexelon, 26623
Nexsoy, 11910
Next Day Gourmet, 29810
Next Generation Magic Buss, 29320
Next Organicsc, 13011
Nextwave™, 30438
Niacin-Time, 6364
Niaga®, 3320
Niagara, 3171, 9069
Niagara Chocolates, 13708
Niagra Seed, 5610
Nibble With Gibble's, 7972
Nic-O-Boli, 9045
Nice N Easy, 18687
Nice-N-Clean, 26632
Nichols Farms, 9039
Nicholson's Bestea, 5467
Nicholson's Bottlers, 5467
Nicholson's Chok-Nick, 5467
Nick's Jerky, 9041
Nick's Sticks, 9041
Nickel & Nickel, 4258
Nickelodeon, 4659
Nicky Usa, 9043
Nico-Rx, 13642
Nicola, 6310
Nido®, 8945
Niederegger Lubeck, 1957
Nielsen, 9049
Nielsen-Massey, 9050
Nifda®, 30595
Night Hawk, 9052
Nik-L-Nip®, 12880
Nikki Bars, 985
Nikki's, 9055
Nikola's Biscotti, 3009
Nikos®, 11209
Niksicko, 8459
Nile Spice, 5505
Nilla Wafers, 8729
Nilla® Banana Pudding, 10213
Niman Ranch®, 7721, 9946
Nimble Nectar, 9058
Nimbus Cs, 26648
Nimbus Fs, 26648
Nimbus N, 26648
Nimbus Sierra, 26648
Nimbus Watermaker, 26648
Ninja Sticks, 2947
Nip's Potato Chips, 9063

Nirvana, 7562
Nirwana, 9065
Nishibe, 27071
Nita Crisp, 9070, 26653
Nitri Pro, 29167
Nitro-Flush, 24550
Nitta Gelatin, 9072
Nitty Gritty, 29167
Nk Lawn & Gardenc, 10106
Nme Nugget, 28922
No Bones Wheat-Meat, 9502
No Cow, 9075
No Evil Foods, 9076
No Forks Required, 8324
No Frost, 26630
No Holds Bar, 8869, 8870
No Name, 22920
No Pudge, 9077, 20946
No Pudge! Brownie Mix, 10657
No Survivor, 24274
No Sweat, 31099
No Whey Foods, 9078
No Yolks®, 10777, 28421
No-Cal, 5465
No-Drip, 30323
No-Stick™, 342
No-Tox, 19535
No.5, 12178
Noah's Spring Water, 181
Noah's Treats, 11102
Noah's Water, 13300
Noahs Buddies, 12389
Nob Nob, 31099
Nobadeer Ginger, 2691
Nobella, 5405
Noble, 31346
Noble Popcorn, 9080
Nobles®, 30147
Nobletree, 9081
Nochebuena, 1977
Nodark, 741
Noel, 9083
Nojo, 1373
Nolan Porter, 4959
Nollibel, 9802
Non Diary Toppings, 12201
Non-Dairy Baklava, 9333
Nona Lim, 9089
Noni, 8009
Noni Nonu, 1285
Nonlinear Dynamics, 31041
Nonna D'S, 10435
Nonni's, 9092
Noodle Delights, 2040
Noodle Plus, 13170
Noon Hour, 9094
Noosa, 9095
Noosh, 9096
Nootra, 9097
Nopi, 30160
Noprthern Lites Pancakes, 5946
Nor-Cal, 12253
Nor-Lake, 29580
Nor-Tech, 9100
Norbest, 8553, 9105, 30775
Norchip, 3216
Norden, 2089
Nordic, 2815, 20685
Nordson, 22482
Nordstrom, 27209
Noresco, 20290
Norimoor, 9110
Noritake, 26932
Norivital Vitamins, 9110
Norma Lou, 6564
Norman Bishop, 4839
Norman Machinery, 30989
Norman Rockwell, 13445, 19611
Nornap Jr., 23160
Noroc, 8459
Norpac, 8724, 20020
Norpaco, 9113
Norrbox, 26682
Norris, 29233
Norseman, 20682, 26959

Nortena, 10701
Norteno, 5479
North Aire Simmering Soups, 9114
North Atlantic, 2418, 2419
North Bay, 9126
North Bay Trading Company, 9127
North Breeze, 10540
North Coast, 7860, 9182
North Coast Tea & Sp, 9181
North Country, 9130
North Country Meat & Seafood, 7721
North Country Smokehouse, 9131
North Eastern, 226
North Pacific Seafood, 266
North River Roasters, 9136
North Star, 10495
Northampton, 9141
Northeast Family Farms, 3653
Northeastern, 9144
Northern, 9145
Northern Light Canadian, 11264
Northern Lights, 10682
Northern Pines Gourmet, 5451
Northern Pride, 5508, 23522
Northern Serenitea, 754
Northern Spirit, 754
Northern Vineyards, 9163
Northern Wisconsin Cheese, 9164
Northland, 56, 4928, 9166, 9167, 9535
Northshore Butter, 9170
Northstar®, 22187
Northumberland, 9170
Northville Winery, 9171
Northwest Co, 22920
Northwest Espresso B, 9185
Northwest Gourmet, 2905, 11148
Northwestern, 9183
Northwestern Coffee, 9181
Northwind, 10974
Northwoods, 4928, 7330
Northwoods®, 1103
Norwalk Dairy, 9186
Noryl®, 21848
Nos, 2811, 8485
Nosferatu, 5314
Nosh Organic, 12779
Nossack, 9187
Nostalgic Creations, 6787
Nostimo®, 12885, 30333
Not Dogs, 9160
Not Just Jam, 6821
Not So Sloppy Joe®, 6000, 23861
Note Minder, 22320
Nothing But the Fruit, 9190
Notmilk, 13286
Notta Pasta, 551
Nottingham, 7028
Nouveau, 30073
Nova, 18512, 21213, 23105, 26745, 29466
Nova Ii, 26662
Novamid®, 3320
Novapro®, 13648, 31107
Novation®, 8804
Novella, 3857
Novelty Chocolates, 4253
Novelty Specialties, 2132
Novexx, 18284
Novitool, 22627
Novo Pro D, 1692
Novoshape, 1692
Novozym, 1692
Novozymes, 1692
Novus Plastic, 26757
Now, 19741
Now & Later, 4345
Now and Later, 1417, 4345
Now Real Food®, 8725
Now Real Tea®, 8725
Noyes Precision, 9197
Nozimes, 3471
Npn, 13653
Nr, 27083
Nsc-100, 9261
Nsc-24, 9261

All Brands Index

Ntrinsic™, 8470
Nu, 9202
Nu House, 11759
Nu Life Market, 9200
Nu-Bake, 10703
Nu-Bind, 10703
Nu-Flac, 10703
Nu-Flex, 23543
Nu-Flow, 10703
Nu-Last, 23543
Nu-Mag, 10703
Nu-Nap, 23160
Nu-Pak Performance F-Series, 25766
Nu-Pak Portion, 25766
Nu-Rice, 10703
Nu-Vista, 13943
Nu-Wipes, 18830
Nu-World Amaranth, 9205
Nucita, 122
Nuco2, 26764
Nudges, 13109
Nugget, 3275
Nugget®, 30595
Nugrape ®, 1339
Nuit, 2761
Nulaid, 9216
Nulojix®, 1721
Numanthia, 8452
Numeri-Tech, 18821
Numi Tea, 3009
Numi Teas, 6928
Numic, 9217
Numit, 8549
Numo Broth, 9218
Nunaturals, 9209
Nunes, 9219
Nunez De Prado, 11864
Nuova Simonelli, 26779
Nuparch, 26680
Nupasta, 9210
Nurofen®, 10598
Nuroll, 31442
Nursery ®, 5884
Nursery®, 3220
Nursery® Water, 3319
Nurture, 9222
Nush, 9224
Nusheen, 30550
Nut Barrel, 12992
Nut Brown Ale, 1507, 2911, 7551
Nut Case Collection, 12714
Nut Club, 1114
Nut Goodie, 9877
Nut Harvest®, 9945, 27433
Nut N But Natural, 13574
Nut Thins, 1471, 19742
Nutec, 26781
Nutellac, 2132
Nutfield Auburn Ale, 9228
Nutfield's Classic Root Beer, 9228
Nuthouse, 659, 4969
Nutpods, 9232
Nutra Biogenesis®, 9237, 26785
Nutra Coster, 29857
Nutra Naturally Essentials, 18093
Nutra Nuts, 9234
Nutrafiber, 11794
Nutralease, 9654
Nutralin, 6163
Nutramer, 135
Nutramigen™, 8103
Nutranique Labs, 9242
Nutraplex, 9243
Nutrasense, 13802
Nutrasweet, 9236
Nutravege, 8896
Nutraveggie, 9654
Nutraw Butter, 9227
Nutraw Oil, 9227
Nutraw Snacks, 9227
Nutrawbar, 9227
Nutrceuticals, 13128
Nutren Junior®, 8945
Nutri Source, 918, 19361
Nutri Sperse®, 126

Nutri West, 9260
Nutri-Cell, 9248
Nutri-Fruito, 9246
Nutri-Grain, 6766
Nutri-Grain®, 6765
Nutribio, 9256
Nutribiotic, 9251
Nutricran, 9654
Nutrifaster N-350, 26787
Nutriflax, 9477
Nutriform, 26792
Nutrifresh, 2576
Nutrilac®, 19049
Nutrilait®, 11211
Nutrin Corp, 30618
Nutriose™, 8804
Nutripure, 19152
Nutriquest, 9266
Nutririte, 12262
Nutrisentials™, 6449, 24506
Nutrisoy, 9256
Nutrisoya, 9256
Nutrition Service Suite, 20028
Nutritional Noodle, 4093
Nutritional Therapeutix, 8130
Nutritionist Iv, 22577
Nutritious Living, 9548
Nutrivail, 10078, 27547
Nutrivan, 463
Nutriwest, 9266
Nutriwhip, 7875
Nutro®, 7952
Nuts 'n' Fruit, 4472
Nuts 'n' Things, 4472
Nuts About, 4820
Nuts About You, 9272
Nuts'n'pops, 525
Nutsco, 10683, 28337
Nuttall Gear, 18678
Nutter Butter, 8729, 13816
Nutter Butter® Cereal, 10213
Nuttin' Butter, 7892
Nutty All-Natural Wheat, 8844
Nutty Bavarian, 9274, 26796
Nutty Club, 11331
Nutty Corn®, 13603
Nutty Crunchers, 8991
Nutty Goodness, 9275
Nutty Infusions™, 8725
Nutty Pleasures, 11330
Nuttzo, 9276
Nuturpractic, 10558
Nutworld, 2905
Nuvert®, 7809
Nzmp™, 4552

O

O & C, 5555
O Olive Oil, 9282
O Organics®, 11073
O Vinegar, 9282
O'Bannon's, 1598
O'Boy, 2242
O'Brien Harvest Ale, 5515
O'Canada, 2693
O'Charley's, 2628
O'Doul's, 26668
O'Kane®, 10056
O'Mara's Irish Country Cream, 5720
O-Jay, 1292
O-Ke-Doke, 11770
O-Tex, 26993
O.B., 9297
O.C. Lager, 1097
O.K. Brand, 11352
O.K. Foods, 9389
O.N.E®, 9945, 27433
Oac Gold, 12136
Oak Creek, 9310
Oak Draw, 26834
Oak Farm's, 9311
Oak Farms, 9312, 11281
Oak Farms Dairy, 3442, 21421
Oak Flat, 13067

Oak Grove Smokehouse, 9315
Oak Hill Farms, 13454
Oak Hurst Dairy, 10653
Oak Kleen, 26834
Oak Knoll, 9318, 9319
Oak Kool, 26834
Oak Kote, 26834
Oak Leaf Confections, 13708
Oak Mor, 23448
Oak Protect, 26834
Oak Ridge Winery, 9321
Oak Spring Winery, 9322
Oak State Cookie Jar Delight, 9323
Oak Valley Farms, 3980
Oakhill, 29498
Oakhurst, 9325
Oakland Noodle, 9328
Oakmont Labs®, 9237, 26785
Oakton, 26841
Oakville, 4649
Oakville Estate Red, 10963
Oasis, 56, 2815, 9330, 19669, 20685
Oasis Coffee, 9331
Oasis Wines & Sparkling Wines, 9334
Oat-N-Bran, 4556
Oatbran & Brown Rice, 4362
Oatmeal, 5188
Oatmeal Fruit Squeeze, 8680
Oatmeal Stout, 1687
Oats Overnight, 9336
Oatwell®, 3320
Oatworks, 9337
Obe Sauce, 5967
Obe Sauce Mix, 5967
Oberdorfer, 19348
Oberschulte Syrah, 11810
Oberti, 2074
Oberto®, 9338
Obfs, 25819
Obi Pektin, 11957
Obis One, 9341
Oboy's, 1691
Obsidian Stout, 3533
Obviously Onion, 6528
Oc Guide Bearing, 18010
Ocean 7, 26968
Ocean Beauty Brand, 9344
Ocean Beauty Seafoods, 11380
Ocean Blue, 10276
Ocean Cliff, 9345
Ocean Coffee Roasters, 3722
Ocean Dawn, 703
Ocean Deli, 4613
Ocean Drive Blend, 11826
Ocean Harvest, 2042
Ocean Leader, 1057
Ocean Mist, 9351
Ocean Organics, 1583
Ocean Pac, 8028
Ocean Phoenix, 10250
Ocean Prince Seafood, 3194
Ocean Request, 9165
Ocean Road Blend, 11826
Ocean Spray, 868, 2815, 3314, 9355, 12871, 20685, 22028
Ocean Spray Apple Juice, 9355
Ocean Spray Cranberries, 9355
Ocean Spray Cranberry Cocktail, 9355
Ocean Spray Fruit Punch, 9355
Ocean Spray Fruit Punch Cooler, 9355
Ocean Spray Grapefruit Juice, 9355
Ocean Spray Jellied Cran. Sauce, 9355
Ocean Spray Juice Blends, 9355
Ocean Spray Kiwi Straq. Juice, 9355
Ocean Spray Lemonade, 9355
Ocean Spray Orange Juice, 9355
Ocean Spray Pineapple Grapefruit, 9355
Ocean Spray Pink Grapefruit Juice, 9355
Ocean Spray Ruby Red & Mango, 9355
Ocean Spray Ruby Red Grapefruit, 9355
Ocean Spray Whole Berry Cranberries, 9355
Ocean Tide, 10974
Ocean's Halo, 9359
Oceana, 11269

Oceana Coastal, 12672
Oceanica, 1500
Oceankist, 9668
Oceanway Seafood, 6855
Oceen Fresh, 3336
Octacosanol Gf, 4914
Octaview, 21416
Octopus, 29211
Octron, 26990
Oddy, 19567
Odell's®, 13328
Odense, 551
Odom's Tennessee Pride®, 2939, 2940, 20821, 20822
Odomaster, 29826
Odorid, 19666
Odormute, 28627
Odwalla, 2814, 9369
Odyssey, 10251, 19570, 22348
Oe200, 25231
Oem Products, 26481
Oergon Trail, 9534
Off the Eaten Path®, 9945, 27433
Ogi's, 1736
Oh Canada, 4508
Oh No!, 29826
Oh Nuts, 5828
Oh So Sweet, 8772
Oh Yes!, 9375
Oh's, 10213
Ohana, 8784
Ohaus, 18327, 24178, 26862
Ohganics, 3315
Ohi, 9300
Ohio, 26867
Ohio Rag, 26770
Ohmega, 19936
Ohta's Senbei, 9380
Oikos, 3379
Oil, 11462
Oil Concentrator, 18251
Oil Grabber, 18251
Oil Grabber Multi-Belt, 18251
Oil Miser Oil Recovery Systems, 28360
Oil Rids, 26834
Oil-Dri, 26871
Oilkraft, 30550
Oils of Aloha Macadamia Nut Oil, 9382
Oishii, 2075
Ojai, 9387
Ok, 26801
Okanagan Cider, 8279
Okanagan Spring, 9391
Okf, 10134
Okio, 3107
Oklahoma Rag, 26770
Oktoberfest, 5314, 7330, 7677, 11992
Oktoberfest Lager, 1237
Okzdata, 24911
Ol' Smokey, 3537
Ol' South, 10054
Ol' Spout, 9688
Ola Blanca, 8161
Ola Loa, 9394
Oland, 7123, 9396
Olay, 12721, 30193
Olcott, 23147
Old Abominable Barkey Wine, 12153
Old Bay, 8061
Old Bay®, 13445
Old Brookville, 1006
Old Brown Bag, 11743
Old Brussels, 13330
Old Cape Harbor, 1478
Old Charter, 11263
Old Chester, 5852
Old Chisholm Trail, 4432
Old Comiskey, 8795
Old Country, 9402, 9403
Old Country Cheese, 9401
Old Country Store, 2971
Old Credit, 9404
Old Creek Ranch Winery, 9405
Old Crow®, 1120
Old Dipsea Barley Wine, 7923

All Brands Index

Old Dobbin, 5484
Old Dominion, 9406
Old Dutch, 1327, 9408, 9409, 10657, 22593
Old El Paso®, 4947
Old English®, 8460
Old Faishoned Foods, 9411
Old Faithful, 6134
Old Fashioned, 9226, 9787, 10461, 11625, 13845
Old Fashioned Way®, 6374, 24434
Old Fitzgerald Bourbon, 5720
Old Folks, 4197
Old Forester, 1784
Old Grand-Dad®, 1120
Old Hickory, 12541, 23763
Old Home, 9415
Old Homestead, 25299
Old Kentucky, 3248
Old Kentucky Hams, 9417
Old Kettle, 10782
Old Laredo, 5146
Old London®, 864
Old Mexico, 5861
Old Mill Brand, 7530
Old Milwaukee, 9664
Old Monk, 25789
Old Monmouth, 9421
Old Neighborhood, 9422
Old No.23, 1720
Old North State, 2236
Old Orchard, 56, 9423
Old Overholt®, 1120
Old Pueblo Ranch, 573
Old Red Eye, 11846
Old Rip Van Winkle, 9424
Old Salt Seafood, 11356
Old Santa Fe, 23409
Old Smokehouse®, 6000, 23861
Old Soul, 9321
Old South, 1806
Old South Winery, 9426
Old South Muscadine, 9426
Old Southern, 4891
Old Spice, 12721, 30193
Old Style Pilsner, 8459
Old Tavern Club Cheese, 9427
Old Taylor, 11263
Old Thompson Blend, 11264
Old Thumper Extra Special, 11561
Old Town Roast, 912
Old Tyme, 387, 22900
Old Vienna, 8459
Old Vienna®, 8460
Old Vines, 13741
Old Wessex™, 1484
Old West Bar-B-Q Delight, 3695
Old Wine Cellar, 9430
Old Wisconsin, 2212, 9431
Old Wisconsin Mug, 9432
Old World, 4062, 5105
Old World Creations, 9434
Olde Colony, 9435
Olde Deuteronomy, 339
Olde English 800, 8459
Olde Farm, 23409
Olde Fashioned, 2219
Olde Georgetown Beer, 9437
Olde Heurich, 9437
Olde Philadelphia, 5643
Olde Thompson, 26888
Olde Tyme, 9438
Olde-Fashioned, 11298
Ole, 22599
Ole Hickory Pits, 26889
Ole Salty's, 9441
Ole Style Peanut Butter, 9438
Ole Wye, 11039
Ole' Henry's Nuthouse, 2110
Oled Desiccant, 3833, 21863
Oleocal, 716, 19094
Olf Foghorn, 531
Olfa, 31345
Olinda, 13661
Olio Santo, 2085

Olioro, 9332
Olive Hill Cabernet Sauvignon, 869
Olive Hill Pinot Noir, 869
Olivenos, 530
Oliver, 9452
Oliver Twist, 11663
Olivet Lane, 9905
Olivia's Kitchen, 9454
Olivia's Organics, 12056
Olivier Leflaive, 4677
Olivieri, 7876
Olivir, 4827
Olsen, 9459
Olson Conveyors, 24176
Olymel®, 9462
Olympia, 9664, 28885
Olympia Provisions, 9466, 9470
Olympic Cellars, 9467
Olympic Coffee, 9468
Oma's Own, 7884
Omaha Hereford, 5338
Omaha Natural Angus, 5338
Omaha Steaks International, 9473
Omanhene Cocoa, 9474
Omar Coffee, 9475
Omega, 3028, 25628, 26250, 26911
Omega 48 Series, 19032
Omega 52 Series, 19032
Omega Buffet Series, 19032
Omega Care, 7331
Omega Complete™, 6449, 24506
Omega Foods, 9476
Omega Gold, 8967
Omega Munchies®, 13603
Omega Pro, 1864
Omega Protective Systems, 26909
Omega Suro, 8967
Omega-3 Brain™, 6449, 24506
Omega-3 Calm™, 6449, 24506
Omega-3 Select™, 6449, 24506
Omegaflo, 9477
Omegalift, 27863
Omegaplus Gla, 9477
Omni, 20256
Omni Controls, 26915
Omni Grid, 19111
Omni Spaceguard, 19908
Omni Wand, 30843
Omni-Beam, 19429
Omni-Glh, 26918
Omni-Line, 27087
Omni-Macro, 26918
Omni-Metalcraft, 25918
Omni-Mixer, 26918
Omni-Th, 26918
Omni-Uh, 26918
Omniclip Ii, 28148
Omniflex, 19111, 30342
Omnivision 1200, 22366
Omnivision 900, 22366
On Guard, 27424
On the Borderc, 13029
On-Cor Frozen Entrees, 9482
On-Pak, 20035
Ona, 12964
Once Again Nut Butter, 9485
Oncore®, 24812
Oncovite™, 8389
One, 9306
One Basix, 9306
One Culture Foods, 9487
One Daily Essential With Iron, 75
One Degree Organic Foods, 9488
One Drop, 22473
One Potato Two Potato, 9489
One Row Trac-Pix, 27015
One Spray, 22473
One Step Prep Mix, 29301
One Way Bands, 19146
One World, 5306
One-For-All, 31010
One-Up, 28118
One-Wipe, 23436
Oneida, 26932, 26933
Onity, 20290

Ono Cones, 9496
Ontario Foods, 9498
Ontario Pork, 9499
Onte Verde O.O., 11096
Oodles of Noodles, 9068
Oogly Eyes, 2947
Ooh La La Candy, 12100
Opa's, 9506
Opacarb, 11906
Opal, 26941
Opaque, 7740
Opco, 26969
Opdivo®, 1721
Open Country, 194
Open Nature®, 11073
Open Pit®, 2939, 2940, 20821, 20822, 27540
Open Prairie Natural Angus®, 13109
Opmview, 18354
Oprishear, 18126
Optec, 27271
Optex, 26947
Opti Pure, 26952
Optiberry, 6236
Optic Florentine, 18906
Optichrome, 25549
Optickles, 22526
Opticlear, 25549
Opticrystal, 24636
Optifeed, 18126
Optigrip, 26176
Optima, 9507, 21436
Optimist, 20990
Optimum, 8889, 25606
Optimum Nutrition, 9510
Optimum®, 3775
Optiscan, 25549
Optiserv, 13595, 31053
Optiserv Accent®, 13595, 31053
Optiserv Hybrid®, 13595, 31053
Optisharp® Zeaxanthin, 3320
Optisource Convertible®, 13595, 31053
Optitwist, 30528
Opto Touch, 19429
Optrix®, 3320
Optyx®, 24812
Opus One, 9511
Or Haganuz Winery, 10952
Ora-Plus, 5682
Orajel, 2666, 20561
Oral-B, 12721, 30193
Orange - Go, 22509
Orange Belt, 22508
Orange Blossom, 10478
Orange Blossom Special, 7329
Orange County Distillery, 9514
Orange Glo, 2666, 20561
Orange Honey Cream Ale, 4950
Orange Maison, 56
Orange Mist, 7363
Orange Paradise Cake, 2881
Orange Plus, 12945
Orange Rose, 9182
Orange Thirstaway, 5460
Orangina, 12315
Orangina®, 3725, 6818, 24802
Orangutan Mace, 12987
Orb, 30800
Orbie, 25309
Orbio® Technologies, 30147
Orbit, 11089, 25606, 25900, 25920
Orbit Gum, 2132
Orbit®, 7952, 13960
Orbitz, 2742
Orca Bay, 9518
Orchard, 26962
Orchard Boy, 13720
Orchard Heights, 9519
Orchard Hills, 498
Orchard Mills, 2046, 20138
Orchard Naturals, 2164
Orchard Park, 12334
Orchard Pond, 9520
Orchard Pond Organics, 9520
Orchard Pure™, 3442, 21421

Orchard Stand, 9452
Orchard Valley Harvest, 6548
Orchardpure, 7320
Orchid, 20256
Ore-Ida, 6977
Ore-Ida®, 8055
Oreck, 26966
Oregan Orchard, 5671
Oregon, 575, 6862
Oregon Berries, 3114
Oregon Brewers, 2036
Oregon Chai, 2606, 3009, 9525
Oregon Fruit, 9530
Oregon Hill, 9532
Oregon Natural Sportstonic, 13998
Oregon Spice, 9539
Orelube Industrial, 26968
Orencia®, 1721
Oreo, 8474, 8729, 13816
Oreo Churros, 6338
Oreo O'S, 10213
Orfila Vineyards, 9540
Organic, 5138
Organic Altura, 2282
Organic Bistro, 12684
Organic By Nature, 10380
Organic Coffee, 332
Organic Coffee Co, 4229
Organic Coffee Company, 11140
Organic Country, 3956
Organic Cow, 5996
Organic Creamery®, 11209, 11211
Organic Extra Virgin Olive Oil, 869
Organic Flax Tempeh, 7427
Organic Garden, 8993
Organic Garden Veggie Tempeh, 7427
Organic Germinal, 9543
Organic Gourmet, 9545
Organic Guayaki Yerba Mate, 5416
Organic Harvest, 8993
Organic Lil Buddies, 11771
Organic Matcha™ Powder, 12498
Organic Mexican Altura, 2282
Organic Ocean®, 7721
Organic Pastures, 9552
Organic Planet, 5306, 9553
Organic Prairie, 1963
Organic Pro 30, 3540
Organic Products, 26969
Organic Shell Eggs, 1864
Organic Sierra Madre Blend, 2282
Organic Smoky Tempeh Strips, 7427
Organic Soy Delicious, 11771
Organic Soy Tempeh, 7427
Organic Sunshine, 12302
Organic Sweetleaf Stevia®, 12430
Organic Three Grain Tempeh, 7427
Organic Valley, 1963
Organic Wild Rice Tempeh, 7427
Organic/Fair Trade, 1054
Organicgirl, 9544
Organicville, 11694
Organipure™, 4837
Orient Emporium, 10637
Orient Express®, 6818, 24802
Orientainer, 24669
Oriental Noodle Soup, 11919
Origami Wraps, 9010
Origin Foods, 30036
Original, 6532
Original 1957, 9562
Original Baby, 5420
Original Bagel Guillotine, 25144
Original Bigfoot Bottle Inversion, 25144
Original Chocolates of Vermont, 7148
Original Gourmet, 9563
Original Habanero Pepper Sauce, 4382
Original Heavyweight, 18155
Original Juan, 1279
Original Juan's, 9565
Original Lemon Straw, 8391
Original Maui Kitch'n Cook'd, 8020
Original Philly Cheesesteak Co., 13109
Original Ranch Dips Mix, 5489
Original Ranch Homestyle, 5489

All Brands Index

Original Ranchc Pasta Salad, 5489
Original Sesame Low Fat Crackers, 1472
Original Smoked Sausage, 2944
Orin Swift Cellars®, 3834
Cringer, 2942, 2943
Oriole, 4387
Orion, 26976
Orion®, 8945
Orlando, 9568, 9672
Orleans, 6267, 8995
Oro Glo, 6777
Orobianco-California Nv, 3181
Orogold, 6638, 24643
Oroweat®, 1359
Orowheat, 892
Orr Mountain Winery, 9572
Ortega, 864
Orv's, 1248
Orville Redenbacher, 6084
Orville Redencacher's®, 2939, 2940, 20821, 20822
Orwak, 26982
Orwasher's, 9575
Osage, 8519
Oscar Mayer, 6976, 6977
Oscars Flavoring Syrups, 10584
Osella, 10565
Osem, 9579
Osmette, 27734
Osr, 8899
Osseofit™, 3320
Osteo Bi-Flex®, 8871
Ostravar, 8459
Ostrim #1 Sports Meat Snack, 10353
Ostrim Ostrich Saute, 10353
Otajoy, 9589
Otis Spunkmeyer, 9590, 9591, 20020
Ott Chocolate, 9299
Ott's, 9593
Otter, 26210
Otter Pops®, 6483
Otter Valley, 6230
Ottimo, 6015
Otto's Naturals, 9597
Ou, 30800
Our Best, 9600
Our Counrtry, 11050
Our Daily Red, 8954
Our Famous Texas Chili, 4428
Our Thyme Garden, 12794
Out of a Flower, 9604
Out of Bounds, 838
Outrageoulsy Decadent Cookies, 10981
Ovace®, 8389
Ovacion, 3545
Ovation, 6603, 28667
Ovega-3, 6107
Oven Fresh, 9610
Oven Gem, 26983
Oven Head, 9611
Oven Krisp Coating Mixes, 4777
Oven Lovin' Chik'n™, 1654
Oven Pak, 21133
Oven Poppers, 9612
Oven Ready, 9613, 12520
Oven Spring, 13591
Oven Stone, 19265
Ovenable, 28910
Over the Hill, 21059
Over the Top®, 12885, 30333
Over-The-Top, 21628
Overhill Farms, 9614
Overlake, 9615, 10323
Overlay/Underlay, 30878
Ovn™, 3320
Owen's, 12516
Owl, 13193, 18112
Owl's Brew, 9619
Owl's Nest, 1172
Owner's Blend Premium Congou, 5228, 23295
Owyhee, 6134
Ox/Digifeeder, 24042
Oxford Inn, 11416
Oxi - Gamma, 4827

Oxi - Grape, 4827
Oxi Pro Metabolol, 2411
Oxiclean, 2666, 20561
Oxine, 19666
Oxo, 31345
Oxo Goodgrips, 26831
Oxtran, 26235
Oxy Tower, 30010
Oxy-Caps, 8009
Oxy-Catalytic, 28361
Oxy-Cleanse, 8009
Oxy-Max, 8009
Oxy-Mist, 8009
Oxylite, 10680
Oxymax, 20751
Oxyphyte, 10511
Oxyvac, 9252
Oyler, 24414
Ozark, 8414, 9621
Ozark Hills, 8550
Ozark Mountain Vineyards, 10214
Ozarka, 4143, 4462
Ozujsko, 8459
Ozw, 9321

P

PDeQ, 9627
P&D, 30925
P&S Ravioli, 9632
P'Tit Qu•Bec, 6976
P'Tit Quebec, 9789
P-12 Hydefiner, 28154
P-Bee, 9640
P-Nuff Crunch, 9952
P-Nuttles, 163
P-Nuttles Butter Toffee Peanuts, 163
P-Proplus, 4837
P-R Farms, 9636
P.F. Chang's Home Menu, 2939, 2940, 20821, 20822
P.I.C. Plastics, Inc., 27601
P.L.A.C, 10565
P/D Pot, 30654
P/L, 9199
P0lar Pump, 27630
P3, 27871
Paas, 11599
Pabst Blue Ribbon Beers, 9664
Pac Check, 26235
Pac Crusher I, 20791
Pac Guard, 26235
Pace, 2115, 2116
Pacemaker, 20121, 27089
Pacer, 24881, 27090
Pacha, 10330
Pacheco Ranch, 9667
Pacific, 1057, 9692, 11191, 31141
Pacific Alaska, 11358
Pacific Choice, 9672, 11559
Pacific Coast Brewing Co., 9673
Pacific Coconut, 28090
Pacific Echo, 9677
Pacific Farms, 1141
Pacific Foods, 2116
Pacific Gold, 9683, 9684
Pacific Gold Reserve, 9684
Pacific Gold, 9338
Pacific International, 1849
Pacific Natural Spices, 9695, 27116
Pacific Pilsner, 9701
Pacific Pride, 8028
Pacific Real Draft, 1702
Pacific Surf, 9668
Pacific Treasures, 666
Pacific Valley, 9699
Pacific Westeel, 24607
Pacifica, 10952
Pacificc, 9681
Pacifico, 11437
Pacifico Clara, 4881
Pacifika, 1500
Pack Mule, 31116
Pack of the Roses, 1882
Pack Rite, 27125

Pack Star, 23994
Pack-A-Drum, 27130
Pack-Age, 3320
Pack-Man, 23013
Package, 27137
Package Bulk Key Lime Filling, 6825
Package To Pallet, 27872
Packaging, 23355
Packer, 19634
Packers Blend, 11177
Packers Pride, 7213
Packing House, 26798
Packit, 23914
Pactite, 25819
Paddy's Irish Red, 12919
Paderno, 27204
Padis Vineyards, 10952
Paesana, 7022
Pagoda, 11316
Pahlmeyer, 9709
Pahrump Valley Winery, 9710
Pain 100%, 9565
Pain Is Good, 9565
Painter's Mate, 29171
Paisley Farm, 4694, 9712
Pak It, 21252
Pak Tyer 2000, 22503
Pak-Lap, 24010
Pak-Shaper, 25766
Pakastrip, 29460
Paktronics, 27217
Pakstat, 27217
Pal, 18185
Pal Dek, 27245
Pal Gard, 27245
Pal Labelmaster, 18269
Pal Pac, 24021
Pal-O-Mine Chocolate Bars, 4884
Palace Foods, 9842
Palace Pastry, 1061
Palamatic, 19908
Palasurance, 6777
Palatase, 1692
Palavator, 26606
Pale American, 5515
Pale Crepe Gold, 18614
Pale Wind, 24409
Paleao, 3171
Paleo People, 4150
Paleo Planet, 9237, 26785
Paleo Powder, 9715
Paleo Prime, 9716
Paleothin, 6629
Palermo, 9718
Palermo's, 9719
Pallcell, 27224
Pallenque, 13425
Pallet Mule, 31116
Pallet-Pro, 24176
Palletainer, 29192
Palletflo, 24940
Palletite, 23456
Pallid, 24984
Pallsep, 27224
Palm Bay, 8279
Palm Springs, 22844
Palm Tree Cooler, 24064
Palmalito, 9726, 27241
Palmer, 23160
Palmer Snyder, 27239
Palmetto, 9725
Palmieri, 9728
Palmolive, 20721
Palouse, 13549
Paltier, 27245
Pam, 6267
Pam Cooking Spray, 6267
Pam, 2939, 2940, 20821, 20822
Pama, 28832
Pama Pomegranate Liqueur, 5720
Pamela's, 9730
Pamesello, 7952
Pampac, 12928
Pampers, 12721, 30193
Pampryl, 4148

Pan Am, 10229
Pan Chillers, 24712
Pan De Oro, 11477
Pan Ducale, 6255
Pan Pal, 19741
Pan Pepin, 9734
Pan-O-Gold, 9736
Panache Cocoa and Blender Mix, 2834
Panache Gourmet Coffee, 2834
Panamore, 3320
Panasonic, 27250
Pancheros, 9565
Pancho Villa, 8062
Panco, 21951
Panda, 7295, 10275
Panda Brand, 7296
Pandora's Bock, 1687
Pane Bella, 25132
Pane Relief, 30925
Paneir, 27325
Panel Lite, 18792
Paneleveline, 25488
Panelock, 24734
Panelume, 25224
Panera Bread, 6818, 24802
Panerac, 9740
Paneze, 833
Panforte, 7111
Pangburn's, 10991
Panhandle Milling, 9743
Panhandler Safety-Wall, 27251
Panhandler Twin-Terry, 27251
Panisgood, 1279
Pankote, 833
Pano, 6261
Panola, 9745
Panola & Private Lab, 9745
Panola Pepper Corp, 2019
Panorama, 31092
Panorama Easter Eggs, 8677
Panroast, 3269
Pansaver, 25536
Pantene, 12721, 30193
Pantesin, 7017
Pantethine, 21265
Panther, 13365
Panther Pepper, 12987
Panther Power, 27982
Pantry Bakers, 18526
Paoli One Step, 27254
Papa Dan's World Famous Jerky, 889
Papa Dean's, 9751
Papa Enzo's, 12885, 30333
Papa Joe's, 1547
Papa Joe's Downhome, 3075
Papa Joe's Specialty Food, 12830, 30310
Papa Piazza Brand, 13423
Papa Pita, 9736
Papa Presto, 1282
Papa Scotts, 2019
Papa's Fresh Catch, 13423
Papa's Organic, 9736
Papadina Pasta, 183, 18382
Papadini Hi-Protein, 183, 18382
Papagallo, 7701
Paper City, 9754
Paperlux, 23160
Papermaster, 29632, 29633
Papetti's, 7698, 8225
Pappadums, 12517
Pappardelle's, 9740
Pappy's, 7364, 9758
Pappy's Best Premimum Marinade, 6796
Pappy's Choice, 9757
Pappy's Xxx White Lightnin, 6796
Par, 2750
Par-Kan, 27038
Para-Spec, 29242
Paracube, 18788
Paradigmox, 6777
Paradise, 2065, 9763, 9766, 27283
Paradise Bakery & Cafec, 9740
Paradise Bay, 6806
Paradise Valley Vineyards, 9768
Paraduxx, 3779

1320

All Brands Index

Paragon, 8336, 21512, 27290, 28967
Paraiso, 9770
Paraiso Del Sol, 9768
Parallel-Pak, 20710
Paralume, 25224
Paramount, 6267, 9773, 25041
Paramount Citrus, 13906
Paramount Coffee, 13706
Paramount Farms, 13907
Parampara, 4947
Parasite Annihilation Powder, 131
Paratherm Nf, 27299
Paratherm Or, 27299
Parco-Hesse, 20726
Pares Baltas, 3545
Pari, 7007
Pariolic, 2010
Paris Splendor, 25299
Park 100 Foods, 9778
Park Avenue, 28666
Park Avenue Gourmet, 10944
Park Avenue Ultra, 28666
Park Farm, 7463
Park Star Plus, 23994
Parkay, 2939, 2940, 20821, 20822
Parker, 9783
Parker House, 13717
Parker's Heritage Collection, 5720
Parkson Dynasand Gravity Filters, 27314
Parkson Lamella Plate Settlers, 27314
Parkway, 12103
Parma, 9788
Parmenter's Northville Cider Mill, 9791
Parmesan Low Fat Crackers, 1472
Parmx Cheese, 9792
Parnell's Pride, 9866
Parrot Bay, 3545
Parrot-Beak, 25302
Parrot-Ice, 6338
Parsol, 3320
Partetime, 4689
Partners, 9798, 9799
Party 'tizers, 12664
Party Bags, 30137
Party Chafer, 19329
Party Chef, 22996
Party Creations, 9434
Party Direct, 24964
Party Favors By Astor, 743
Party In a Box, 23811
Party Pak, 9226
Party Plates, 25079
Party Pleaser, 25094
Party Pretzels, 4253
Party Punch, 7671
Party Snacks, 12211
Party Time, 709
Party Yards, 27328
Parve Plain Muffin, 12795
Pasano's Syrups, 7613, 25460
Pascal Coffee, 9800
Pascal Jolivet, 4677
Paselli, 8804
Paslite, 20454
Paso Robles Cabernet Sauvignon, 2637
Paso Robles Orange Muscat, 2637
Pasqualichio, 9804
Passetti's Pride, 9806
Passport, 5660
Pasta Al Dente, 9815
Pasta Campo, 10565
Pasta Della Festa, 4794
Pasta Factory, 9809
Pasta Fiesta, 10331
Pasta International, 9810
Pasta Maltagliati, 5034
Pasta Mami, 9811
Pasta Montana, 9813
Pasta Partners, 6246
Pasta Perfect, 8724
Pasta Pick Ups, 4982
Pasta Plus System, 24744
Pasta Quistini, 9815
Pasta Roni, 9945, 27433
Pasta Salad, 9745

Pasta Sanita, 13475
Pasta Time, 4153
Pasta With Personality, 9816
Pastabilities, 9816
Pastabiz, 22142
Pastamagic, 27488
Pastamatic, 27488
Pastarific Pasta Co., 11141
Pastariso, 5080, 10708
Pastato, 10708
Pastene, 6126, 9819
Pastificio Bacchini, 12358
Pastori, 9822
Pastry Essentials, 743
Pastry Pal, 31010
Pastry Perfect, 11402
Pastry Pride, 10267
Pastry Pro, 10267
Pasture Sini, 11668
Pat O'Brien's, 4650
Pat O'Brien's Cocktail Mixes, 11674
Pat's Best, 10993
Pat's Psyillium Slim, 5682
Pat-Son, 9839
Pata Negra, 3545
Patagonia, 71
Patagonia Cerveza, 571
Patak's, 73, 11522, 20020, 29116
Patchwork, 21213
Path of Life, 9827
Pathfinder, 6869, 25766
Pathline, 30589
Pathlire, 24672
Pathmark, 6126
Pathogel, 20454
Patio, 6338
Patio Squares, 13845
Pationic, 463
Patissa, 1524
Patricia Green Cellars, 826
Patricia Quintana, 9832
Patrick Cudahy, 9833
Patricks Pride, 9833
Patrina's Bake House, 10981
Patriot, 20277
Patriot Plus, 18056
Patriot Series, 18056
Patriotic Pasta, 4794
Patsy's, 9837
Patti's Plum Pudding, 9841
Patty-O-Matic, 27348
Paul Penders, 7562
Paul's, 10046
Paul's Candy, 9846
Paul's Pintos, 1889
Paula, 2260
Paulaner, 1748
Pauline's, 9848
Paulines, 1545
Paulson, 22208
Paumanok Vineyards, 9850
Pavan, 27358
Pavel's Yogurt, 9851
Pavilion, 10873
Pavolami, 2670
Pavone, 9833
Pavoni, 31083
Paws, 13864
Paws Premium, 1758, 19889
Paws, 12885, 30333
Paxrite, 30251
Paxton, 27362
Paxware, 18637
Pay Master, 20805
Pay Master Plus, 20805
Payaso, 8161
Payday, 5818, 23750
Payliner, 23708
Payloader, 19788
Payne Family Farms, 5036
Pazdar Winery, 9856
Pb 8, 2666, 20561
Pb Jamwich, 13109
Pb Jamwich, 184
Pbc-210, 13498

Pc, 13861
Pc-1200, 19798
Pc/Aim, 18946
Pcas, 27790
Pcc, 11906
Pco, 24260
Pcs5000 System, 29959
Pcu-2000, 19629
Pd Plus, 30502
Pdi, 26632, 27237
Pdq Puncher, 233
Pea Poppers, 13603
Peabody Tectank, 20750
Peace Mountain, 9858
Peace Tea, 2811
Peaceful Bend, 9861
Peach, 9773
Peach Ambrosia, 13746
Peach Gal, 2761
Peach Orchard Farms, 5057
Peach Ridge, 6415
Peach Royal, 5362, 23377
Peacock, 5525, 7318, 13067, 25226
Peak, 12973, 30444
Peanut & Tree Nut, 10327
Peanut Butter Bars, 756
Peanut Butter Bing, 9722
Peanut Butter Dream, 4253
Peanut Butter Kandy Kakesc, 12551
Peanut Butter Pretzels, 972
Peanut Chews, 5144
Peanut City, 10359
Peanut Crunchers, 6851
Peanut Kids Company Store, 10327
Peanut Patch, 9868
Peanut Paws, 7184
Peanut Shop of Williamsburg, 9871, 12714
Peanut Wonder, 13905
Pear Blossom, 10777, 28421
Pear Brandy, 2737
Pear's Coffee, 9872
Pearex, 2370
Pearl, 2729, 6187, 7655
Pearl Empress, 4804
Pearl Royal, 10134
Pearl Valley, 9876
Pearl's, 8692
Pearson, 2102
Pearson's Berry Farm, 9878
Pease's, 9881
Pebbles, 10213
Pecan Coffee Cake, 2881
Pecan Duet, 2881
Pecan Halves & Pieces, 2881
Pecan Street Sweets, 4840
Pecanbacks, 11330
Peckam Carts, 20315
Peco, 11053
Peconic Bay, 9884
Pectose-Standard, 6396
Pedia-Vit, 11269
Pedigree, 7952
Pedroncelli, 9890
Peekskill Brewery, 9891
Peel Away, 918, 19361
Peeps, 2136
Peeps Easter Baskets, 8131
Peeps, 6641
Peerless, 27387
Peerless Food Equipment, 24038
Peet's Coffee, 6818, 24802
Peets, 816, 1000
Peg's Saltc, 9897
Peggy Lawton, 9898
Pei Mussel King, 9650
Peju, 9899
Pekarskis, 9901
Pelican Bay, 9903
Pell-Ettes, 10422
Pellegrini, 9905
Peller Estates, 555
Pellman, 9906
Pelton's Hybrid Popcorn, 12948, 30402
Penafiel, 3725, 6818, 24802

Penco, 25474
Pendleton Whisky, 5981
Pendleton1910, 5981
Penelope's, 5954
Penetron, 19634
Penfolds, 12937
Penguin, 6113, 19029, 29522
Penguin Bay, 12382
Penguin Brand, 20234
Penn Dark, 9923
Penn Dutch, 9729
Penn Gold, 9923
Penn Maibok, 9923
Penn Marzen, 9923
Penn Pilsner, 9923
Penn Scale, 27416
Penn Ventilation, 27412
Penn Weizen, 9923
Pennacook Peppers, 9921
Pennant, 5288, 9763, 27283
Pennbarry, 18497
Pennsylvania Dutch, 465, 9924
Pennsylvania Dutch Candies, 13574
Pennsylvania Dutch Candies, 13572
Pennsylvania Dutch Foods, 5406
Pennsylvania Dutchman, 5028
Pennsylvania People, 9914
Pennsylvania Rag, 26770
Penny Fogger, 1208
Penny Lanes, 7746
Penny Lick, 9927
Pennyroyal, 1672
Pennysaver, 11766
Pennysticks Brand, 1224
Penobscot Porridge, 4362
Penrose, 2939, 2940, 20821, 20822
Penta, 1367
Pentafood, 24887
Penthouse, 18155
Pentopan, 1692
Peony Vodka, 12784
Pep Fest, 4928
Pep Talk, 7799
Pepcocide, 20188
Pepe Lopez, 1784
Pepe's, 9933, 10966
Pepe's Sauce, 6015
Peperoncino, 1174
Pepes, 9934
Pepogest, 783
Pepper Chicks, 12542
Pepper Jellies, 11798
Pepperdoux, 2019
Pepperidge Farm, 2115, 2116
Pepperidge Farm, 9942
Pepperjack, 12937
Peppermint, 9773, 27470
Pepperwood Grove, 2343
Pepr, 10422
Pepsi, 9083
Pepsi-Cola, 5975
Pepsi, 9945, 27433
Pepsodent, 2666, 20561
Peptamen Af, 8945
Peptan, 3390
Peptan, 10915
Peptein, 9649
Peptide Fm, 4736
Pepto-Bismol, 12721, 30193
Peptopro, 3320
Perch Creek, 868
Perdinci, 13079
Perdue, 9946, 11504, 29095
Peregrine Golden, 8153
Peregrine Pale Ale, 8153
Perennial Sweets, 5578
Perf, 29604
Perfect, 8870
Perfect 1100, 8869, 8870
Perfect Addition Beef Stock, 9949
Perfect Addition Chi, 9949
Perfect Addition Fis, 9949
Perfect Addition Veg, 9949
Perfect Aminos, 8869
Perfect Animos, 8870

1321

All Brands Index

Perfect Answers, 1654
Perfect Carbs, 8869, 8870
Perfect Choice, 12612
Perfect Croutons, 7479
Perfect Foods Wheatgrass Juice, 9951
Perfect Fry, 27441
Perfect Hanging System, 28118
Perfect Hold Deli Case, 19882
Perfect Image, 20966
Perfect Italiano, 4552
Perfect Pager, 26433
Perfect Pallet, 24534
Perfect Party Mixes, 3079
Perfect Peach, 28090
Perfect Peeler, 30690
Perfect Pitcher, 11501
Perfect Pour, 29558
Perfect Rx, 8869, 8870
Perfect Seal, 29419
Perfect-O-Portion, 7196
Perfecta, 24038
Perfecta Line, 19430
Perfecta Pour, 19430
Perfectagel Mpt, 8804
Perfectamyl, 8804
Perfection, 5334, 23160, 27711
Perfectly Free, 6176
Performance, 25766
Performer, 23261, 26359
Peri Garde, 30569
Perky's Fresh Bakery, 9961
Perma - Sam, 20256
Perma - Sil, 20256
Perma Glo, 27982
Perma Graphic, 21769
Perma Shine, 18387
Perma-Brew, 30337
Perma-Ice, 9794, 27318
Perma-Mark, 26109
Perma/Flo, 21526
Perma/Lok, 21526
Permaclean, 29452
Permafloat, 20365
Permalar, 23114
Permalon, 28240
Permalux, 23291
Permalux Shatter-Kote, 27973
Permanent Press, 23291
Permasan, 30828, 30829
Permaseal, 28816
Permaspan, 20365
Permatank, 23116
Permatran, 26235
Permaware, 24517
Permeator, 29491
Pernodc, 9964
Pero, 6279
Perona Farms, 9965
Peroni, 8460
Perphect, 26976
Perricone Farms, 9966
Perrier Jouet - Epernay, 3545
Perrier-Jouetc, 9964
Perrier, 8945
Perry's, 9969
Perry's Deluxe, 9969
Perry's Free, 9969
Perry's Light, 9969
Perry's Pride, 9969
Personal Edge Supro, 9970
Personnal, 27893
Perthenon Greek Salad Dressing, 9795
Perugina, 6540
Pervidac, 9971
Pesaca, 8028
Pesto Havarti, 10906
Pet, 3862
Pet Air, 26055
Pet Partners, 7952
Pet Stain & Odor Remover, 21509
Pet, 3442, 21421
Petal Mist, 20256
Petaluma Poultry, 9946
Pete's Pride, 249
Pete's Seafood, 9668

Pete's Wicked Ale, 9977
Peter Michael Winery, 9979
Peter Pan, 6084, 9980
Peter Pan, 2939, 2940, 20821, 20822
Peter Vella, 3834
Peter's Beach Sauces, 10388
Peter's Movie Time Products, 5333, 23360
Peterson Farms, 9985
Peterson's, 6870
Petes Pumpkin, 28090
Petit Potc, 9986
Petite Donceur, 8676
Petite Green Mixes, 4718
Petite Sommelier, 21125
Petite Sommelier Cruvinet, 21125
Petite Sorbeteer, 22892
Petoseed, 11427
Petra, 9987
Petran, 13614
Petri, 13120
Petrified Porter, 10261
Petro-Miser, 23900
Petrol, 8049
Petroxtractor, 18251
Pett Spice, 9990
Pewtarex, 26887
Pez, 961, 9991, 27481
Pez Candy, 2132
Pfaff Silberblau, 20752
Pfb (Produits Forresters Baasques), 26520
Pfefferkorn's, 9993
Pfeiffer's, 7986
Pfeil, 9994, 27483
Pgs, 18434
Phamous Phloyd's, 9996
Phandy, 23571
Pharma-Flow, 20522
Pharma-Lok, 29221
Pharmacist Formula, 7331
Pharmaclear, 25549
Pharmalite, 25549
Pharmaseal, 27863
Pharmasoft, 25549
Pharmatose, 4736
Phase 2c, 9997
Phase, 13328
Phasor, 29189
Phep, 23571
Philadelphia, 6976, 6977
Philadelphia Cheese Steak, 10005
Philip Togni, 10008
Philips/Pma, 27958
Phillipino's, 13560
Phillips, 5555, 10012, 10015, 23453
Phillips Candies, 10011
Phillips Level-Edge, 23453
Philly Maid, 11537
Phillyswirl, 6338
Phipps, 10017
Phlauer High Performance Mixers, 18048
Phoenician Herbals, 10020
Phone Pen, 26109
Photo-Mates, 24680
Phytbac, 10511
Phyto Foods, 5475
Phyto-Est, 783
Phytoflow Direct Compression Herbs, 10413
Phytonutriance, 10511
Phytotherapy, 13998
Piako, 4552
Piantedosi, 10028
Piazza Tomasso, 12860
Pica, 5405
Piccadeli, 13235
Piccolo, 23571
Pick, 27516
Pick Director, 21536
Pick O' the Bushel, 1600
Pickard, 27517
Pickle Juice Sport Drink, 12716
Pickle O'Pete, 10752
Picklesmith, 10035

Pickwick, 5606, 27520
Pickwick Catfish, 10036
Picnic Time, 29723
Pico Guard, 19429
Pico Pica, 6619
Picodot, 19429
Pictsweet, 10038
Picture Pops, 11885
Pie Piper, 10040
Pie Rite, 2386
Pieces, 5818, 23750
Pied-Mont, 10041
Piedmont, 10043
Piedra Creek Winery, 10044
Piels, 9664
Piels Light, 9664
Pieman and Montego, 9842
Piemaster, 18243
Piemonte, 10045
Pier Fresh, 1443
Pier Port, 11504, 29095
Pierce Chicken, 10056
Pieropan, 3834
Pierre, 20101
Pierre Santini, 25299
Pierre's, 10049
Pierre, 184
Pigout, 9607
Pike, 10052
Pikeman Gin, 11264
Pikes Peak, 648
Pikes Peak Vineyards, 10053
Pikesville Straight Rye Whiskey, 5720
Piknik, 10054
Pikos Pikosos, 2490
Pilarcitas, 1116
Pilgrim's Pride, 20101
Pilgrim's, 6391, 10056
Pillar Rock, 9344
Piller's Turkey Bites, 10058
Piller's, 10058
Pillsbury, 11768
Pillsbury, 4947
Pilon, 6380
Pilot, 24969
Pilot Divider, 31435
Pilot Project, 9452
Pilsener, 1139, 12153
Pilsner Urquell, 8460
Pin Point, 18768
Pinah's, 7312
Pinch, 10784
Pinch-25, 18300
Pinched Tube, 19056
Pinders, 9728
Pine Ridge Winery, 10063
Pine River, 10065
Pineapple Pecan Cake, 2881
Pines, 10067
Pink Beauty, 9344
Pink Magic, 28635
Pinks, 12078
Pinnacle, 833, 6387
Pinnacle, 1120
Pino's Pasta Veloce, 10068, 27542
Pinocchio, 10069
Pinot Meunier, 3661
Pinot Noir, 3661
Pinot Noir Santa Barbara County, 4353
Pint Size Duds, 20481
Pinto, 26109
Pinty's, 10071
Pintys Delicious Foods, 10072
Pioneer, 1917, 10075, 10079, 10080, 21512
Pioneer Dairy, 10073
Pioneer French Bakery, 5097, 5098
Pioneer Sugar, 8251
Pioneer, 3775, 9237, 26785
Pioneerc, 10078, 27547
Pionite, 25935
Pip Squeaks, 11320
Pipcorn, 10085
Piper, 23874
Piper Industries, 22108

Piper Products, 27554
Piper's Pale Ale, 13288
Pipikaula, 10632
Piping Rock, 7655
Pippin Snack, 10084
Piranha, 30516
Pirate, 5508, 9344, 23522
Pirate's Keg, 13697
Pirates Keg, 13697
Pirel, 18007
Pirineo, 3545
Pirineos, 3545
Pirouette, 24212
Pit Bull, 10090
Pita, 3603
Pita Folds, 5341
Pita Products, 10087
Pitasnax, 10087
Pitch'r Pak, 5735
Pitco, 27556
Pitco Frialator, 19733
Pito, 8735
Pivotmast, 25128
Pixall Big Jack Mark Ii, 27015
Pixall Corn Puller, 27015
Pixall Cornstalker Db18, 27015
Pixall Cornstalker El20, 27015
Pixall One-Row Pull-Pix, 27015
Pixall Super Jack, 27015
Pixall Vst, 27015
Pixeljet, 30434
Pixie Crinkles, 9523
Pixy Stix, 2132
Pizazz, 2387, 20397
Pizootz, 7736
Pizza & Pasta Magic, 7766, 25632
Pizza Corner, 1248
Pizza Pozze, 25965
Pizza Slicer, 19999
Pizzacart, 27893
Pizzaiolo, 12030
Pizzaletto, 12030
Pj's Coffee, 9653
Placido, 1006
Plains Dairy, 10098
Plainville Farms, 5505
Plam Vineyards, 10101
Planet Cola, 8470
Planet Food, 8967
Planet Harmony, 3575
Planet Harvest, 4093
Planetron, 24074
Plank, 25773
Plank 1, 2763
Plant Power, 5786
Plantation, 345
Plantation Pecan, 10105
Planters, 6977, 7963
Plantin Dried Mushro, 9771
Plantio Del Condado, 10319
Plantpower, 9606
Plascolume, 23450
Plasma-Pure, 25215
Plasmon, 6977
Plast-Twist, 29227
Plastawrap, 19965
Plasteel, 18702
Plastex, 23543, 31336
Plasti-Corder, 20019
Plasti-Grit, 20802
Plasti-Guard, 22246
Plasti-Lug, 29221
Plasti-Rivet, 27575
Plastic Fabrication, 30530
Plastic Plus, 18702
Plastichange, 27602
Plastirun Corporation, 18029
Platecoil, 30390
Platform Beer Co., 571
Platinum 90, 19008
Platinum Harvest, 13607
Platinum Hog Casings, 29572
Platte Valley Corn Whiskey, 8062
Plavix, 1721
Playboy, 13605

1322

All Brands Index

Playboy Mints, 1343
Plaza De Espana, 10110
Plaza Sweets, 10109
Pleasant Valley, 10112
Pleasantaire, 20186
Pleasoning Gourmet Seasoning, 10114
Plenish, 3775
Plentiful Pantry, 6246
Plentitud, 24838
Plenty, 28714
Plexus, 29320
Plimouth Lollipop, 10133
Ploccy's Apple Chips, 10120
Plochman's, 10119
Plough Boy, 1355
Ploughman's Pils, 5903
Plow Boy, 13740
Plowshares, 11609
Plue Grass, 5792
Plugra, 6760
Plugra Butter, 3335
Plum Creek, 10122
Plum Organics, 2116
Plume De Veau, 779
Plumpy, 12420
Plumrose, 10124
Plus, 22074
Plus and Moisturlok, 190, 18410
Plus Crusher, 20607
Plus Ii, 20966
Plus-50, 30516
Plush Pippin, 7886
Plusnet, 22074
Ply Skin Cream, 26167
Plyco, 30441
Plyfold, 23160
Plymold, 27612
Plymouth Colony Winery, 10132
Plymouth Pantry, 7511
Plymouthc Gin, 9964
Pneu-Con, 27615
Pneumatic Conveying Systems, 28360
Pneumatic Products, 28714
Pneumix, 22008
Pnut Jumbo, 10496
Poblanos, 4375
Poca's Tacos, 10134
Pocahontas, 3275
Pocas, 10134
Pocasville, 10134
Poche's, 2019
Pocino, 10136
Pocket Genesis, 24050
Pocket Pal, 26616
Pocket Pretzels, 8029
Pocketswab, 20454
Pocono, 1391
Pocono Cheesecake, 10138
Pocono Mountain, 10139
Pocono Spring, 10140
Pocos, 7064
Poe Brands, 2449
Poell, 25789
Poett, 2766, 20657
Poffenberger's Bellville, 1204
Point, 18198
Point Judith, 1464
Point Pleasant, 896
Point Premium, 12101
Point Reyes Porter, 7923
Point Special, 12101
Point St. George, 5525
Pointframe, 20625
Pointsense, 21004
Poiret, 10146
Poise, 24838
Pokanoket Farm, 10149
Pokka, 5662
Pokonobe, 10150
Pol Roger, 4677
Poland Spring, 8945
Poland: Solidarnosc, 5108
Polaner, 864
Polar, 10151, 19788, 27625
Polar Bear, 23260

Polar Bear Ale, 13711
Polar Extruder, 27630
Polar Ice Tassel, 3024
Polar King, 27627
Polar Pack, 26123
Polar Pak, 7363
Polar Pal, 27711
Polar Pitcher, 19999
Polar Sparkling Water, 5884
Polar Ultrashear, 27630
Polar Ware, 27632
Polar-Chill, 24925
Polar-Pak, 24925
Polarica, 10153
Polaris, 24881, 31200
Polarized, 7783
Polaronde, 27711
Polauan, 30725
Poleeko Gold, 549
Poleguards, 21192
Poliback Plastics America, 18029
Polish Sausage, 2162
Polka, 10154
Polka Dot, 3834
Pollenergy, 1914
Polly Orchard, 1596
Polly-O, 2667
Poly - Tuf, 20256
Poly Cal, 22985
Poly Packer, 23771
Poly Perk, 28272
Poly Shield, 20365
Poly-Crete, 21815
Poly-Liner, 26574
Poly-Menu, 30713
Poly-Pole, 19082
Poly-Roll, 24700
Poly-Slice, 24700
Poly-Soleil, 7857
Poly-Tech, 23543
Poly-Tresse, 7857
Poly-Z-Brite, 26623
Polybander, 25531
Polycal, 716, 19094
Polycast, 20889
Polychem, 24135
Polyclad, 19126
Polyclar, 19108
Polyclear Ii, 19502
Polydrain, 18018
Polyduct, 18018
Polyfilm, 25549
Polyflex, 27587, 29148
Polygard, 18702
Polylab, 23503
Polylacton, 7172
Polyliner, 24700
Polymaid, 27643
Polymate, 28731
Polynesian, 345
Polynesian Pleasure, 4521
Polynet, 20932
Polyplast, 26280
Polyquest, 28731
Polystone Cut-Rite, 28478
Polytech, 30127
Polytek, 18873, 18874
Polytex, 23529
Polytwill, 23291
Polywear, 27642
Polyziv, 23379
Pom, 8676, 23160
Pom Poms, 2102
Pom-Etts, 23160
Pom, 2121, 9658
Poma Noni Berry, 13943
Pomarola, 12030
Pometta's, 11806
Pomme De Coeur, 56
Pommeroy, 914
Pommery, 25789
Pompeian Olive Oil, 10161
Pompeii Furniture, 26057
Ponderosa Valley Vineyards, 10165
Ponte Vecckio, 12970

Ponti, 10168
Pontiac Foods, 10170
Pony Boy, 10171
Pony Express, 12663
Pony Malta, 9137
Ponzi's, 10172
Poole's, 8156
Poore Brothers, 10173
Pop, 10176
Pop Candy, 961
Pop Magic, 790
Pop N Go, 27668
Pop Rocks, 2132
Pop Secret, 11770
Pop Strip, 26688
Pop Ups, 11311
Pop Weaver, 13611
Pop'n Snak, 7433
Pop-A-Bear, 6158
Pop-Ice, 6483
Pop-N-Pull, 19998
Pop-Out, 1882
Pop-Tarts, 6766
Pop-Tarts, 6765
Pop-Top, 22634
Pop-Tops, 23499
Poparazzi, 3311
Popart, 7426
Popcorn Dippers, 3034
Popcorn, Indiana, 3862
Poplar Ridge Vineyards, 938
Poppers, 530, 10186
Poppie's, 10187
Poppies, 10188
Poppy Hand-Crafted Popcorn, 10192
Poppy Hill, 7753
Poppy's Pierogies, 2831
Poppycock, 3430
Poppycock, 2939, 2940, 20821, 20822
Popsicle, 13169
Popsicle, 5165
Popstop, 10538
Popt-Rite, 21803
Poptime, 9660
Poptite, 21932
Popular Choice, 26799
Porelon, 24092
Poriloff, 10992
Pork & Veal Magic, 7766, 25632
Pork Clouds, 924
Pork Panko, 924
Porkies, 4158, 10196, 11257
Poromesh, 27950
Poroplate, 27950
Port, 7238
Port Clyde Sardines, 9344
Port Side Amber, 12919
Port-A-Weigh, 25940
Porta-Grills, 19557
Porta-Lamp, 20769
Porta-Weigh-Plus, 25940
Portec Flowmaster, 27676
Portec Pathfinder, 27676
Porter, 7315
Porter & Stout, 11592
Porter House, 3262
Porter-Cable, 29584
Portescap, 18678
Portion Master, 24906
Portion-All, 27799
Portland, 10207
Portland Brewing, 9117
Portland Lighthouse, 10205
Portland Punch, 12921
Porto Cordovero, 10952
Portola Hills, 3179
Portola Packaging, 29223
Portsmouth Chowder Company, 10209
Portsmouth Lager, 11743
Portuguese Baking Company, 10210
Portuguese Sausages, 11224
Pos-A-Trak, 25819
Posada, 237, 238
Posi-Flow, 19597
Posi-Pour, 19998, 25648

Posi-Pour 2000, 19998
Posi-Pour 2000 Pourer, 19999
Posi-Pour Pourer, 19999
Posi-Sync, 23857
Positive Displacement Pumps, 31049
Positively Blueberry, 2232
Positively Pecan, 2604
Positively Pralines, 2232
Positively Strawberry, 2232
Post Familie Vineyards, 10214
Post-It, 18003
Post Hostess Cereal, 10213
Post Shredded Wheat, 10213
Postergrip, 25565
Postmaster, 23802
Postum, 10215
Pot & Pan Pac, 27679
Pot O' Gold, 8256, 13511
Pot-N-Pan Handler, 26116
Potato Mity Red, 741
Potato Pancake Mix, 5946
Potato Pearls, 1069
Potato Pearls Excel, 1069
Potatoe Pearls, 1577
Potel Aviron, 4677
Potentiator Plus, 7424
Potimelt, 23456
Potlatch, 27690
Potlicker, 10217
Potomac Farms, 4873
Potomac River, 6828
Potomac River Brand, 6828
Pott Holdr, 24610
Potty Fresh, 29826
Pouch Pak, 12925, 27914
Pouchmaster Abs System, 18269
Pouchmaster Pac's System, 18269
Pouchmaster Xii, 18269
Poultry Magic, 7766, 25632
Pour & Save, 9839
Pour Mor, 19998, 19999
Pour N' Performance, 10267
Pour N' Whip, 10267
Pour-Eaz, 19998
Pour-O-Matic, 19943
Poura - Clam, 20256
Pow! Pasta, 534
Powder Hound Winter Ale, 1344
Powder Xpress, 29513
Power, 18687
Power Carts, 20315
Power Clean, 19995
Power Crunch, 1377
Power Dishtable, 26467
Power Edge, 12182
Power Fillit, 22545
Power Force, 21717
Power Glide, 30110
Power Herbs, 8882
Power Herbs, 13097
Power Lever, 20986
Power Lube, 21051
Power Mizer, 29489
Power Pack, 22322
Power Pincher, 30854
Power Plumber, 18514
Power Plus, 5786
Power Quota, 31010
Power Rangers Chewable Vitamins, 13128
Power Soak, 26026
Power Wipes Formula Z, 21768
Powerade, 2811, 2814, 2815, 20685
Powerbar, 8945
Powerbarc 10-12g Protein Snack Bar, 10225
Powerbarc 20-30g Proteinplus, 10225
Powerbarc Clean Whey Protein Bar, 10225
Powerbarc Clean Whey Protein Drink, 10225
Powerbarc Energy Blasts, 10225
Powerbarc Energy Gels, 10225
Powerbarc Performance Energy Bar, 10225

All Brands Index

Powerbarc Protein Plus, 10225
Powerbarc Protein Shakes, 10225
Powerbarc Variety Packs, 10225
Powerbite, 30036
Powerbulk, 27706
Powerdry, 28783
Powerful Yogurt, 10226
Powerguard, 20064
Powerline, 18512
Powerliner, 27706
Powermate, 5363
Powermate System, 19146
Powermax, 30768
Powermix, 20448
Powerpac, 30768
Powerpro, 18208
Powerpuff Girls, 1591
Powers, 9964, 13511
Powersaver, 30457
Powersleep, 5363
Powertech, 25597
Powertex Meatstrap, 27706
Powertrac, 19945
Powertree Scrubbers, 31251
Powertwist, 22509
Powervites, 5363
Poznanski, 11625
Ppeppers, 2490
Ppg, 1692
Ppp, 27237
Pr, 27083
Pr/O-Rox, 26379
Prager Winery & Port, 10228
Praim Confections, 10229
Prairie City, 10232
Prairie Farms, 10233
Prairie Fresh, 11363
Prairie Grove, 30775
Prairie Mushrooms, 10236
Prairie Star, 10235
Prairie Sun, 1950, 4039
Prairie Thyme, 10237
Prairieland, 10444
Praline Pack, 5221
Praline Pecan Cheesecake, 2881
Prarie Creek, 11504, 29095
Prarie Grove Farms, 9946
Pravachol, 1721
Prawnto, 27718
Praylev, 10239
Prayphos, 10239
Prc Weight Control Filler, 27740
Pre-Pac, 22322
Pre-Seed, 2666, 20561
Precisa, 8804
Precision, 13509, 19166
Precision Belt Series, 25819
Precision Scientific, 27729
Precision Temp, 27735
Preconditioner Traffic Lane, 20966
Precrushor, 21811
Preda, 28626
Predator, 8485
Predator 1500-3000, 25436
Prego, 2116
Prelude Christmas, 11561
Preludes, 9836
Premier, 12550, 21512, 26109, 27391, 27980
Premier Brass, 27744
Premier Coffee, 1601, 19813
Premier Fields, 1909
Premier Japan, 3956
Premier Nutrition, 10251
Premier One, 9237, 26785
Premier Shots, 10251
Premier/Nugget, 21500
Premiere, 26450
Premiere Pacific, 10250
Premium, 2384, 5323, 7197, 7206, 8729
Premium America, 5333, 23360
Premium Blue, 21768
Premium Brand, 5138
Premium Chicken Breast, 6000, 23861
Premium Cuts, 5141

Premium Rainbow Drops, 10538
Premium Rainbow Pops, 10538
Premium Tea, 427
Premium Trak-Clip, 27575
Premix Technology, 31059
Premoroc, 1861
Premose, 10247
Prenatal Formula, 75
Prentox, 27758
Prenulinc, 9997
Pres-Air-Trol, 27760
Presedente, 571
Presence Plus, 19429
Presentabowls, 21362
Preshipment Planning, 25407
President, 7126
President's Choice, 12276
President, 9789
Presidents Choice, 11410
Presidor, 4852
Presque Isle Wine, 10263, 27767
Pressor, 21811
Pressure Leaf Filter, 23402
Pressure Patch, 20682
Pressware, 30148
Prest Rack, 18990
Prestige, 8649, 13864, 23499, 26450, 29680, 29681
Prestige Proteins, 10265, 10266
Presto, 10657, 10714, 19908
Presto Flex, 23460
Presto Galaxy, 27575
Presto-Tek, 26616
Preston Premium Wines, 10269
Presys1000, 27775
Pretzel Fillers, 6338
Pretzel Pete, 11015
Pretzel Rods, 12551
Pretzel Twisters, 5160
Pretzel Wands, 5160
Pretzeland, 1633
Pretzels, 6918
Preventin Green Tea, 9201
Prevenz, 18532
Price, 1172, 10275
Price Chopper, 6126
Price Marquee, 22271
Price's, 3442, 10277, 21421
Price's Fine Chocolates, 12414
Priceless, 10275
Pricemaster, 28952
Prickly Pecans, 9385
Pricorder, 24155
Pride, 3314, 10267, 10278
Pride New Orleans, 11865
Pride of Alaska, 4440, 6855
Pride of Canada, 7879
Pride of Dixie, 10280
Pride of Idaho, 4435
Pride of Malabar, 11916
Pride of Peace Vegetables, 5764
Pride of Samspon, 13605
Pride of Shandung, 11916
Pride of Spain, 7931
Pride of Szeged, 11916
Pride, 4267, 13328, 22464
Prideland, 10928, 28576
Priester's Pecans, 10281
Prifti Candy, 10282
Prilosec Otc, 12721, 30193
Prim, 23160
Prima, 24093
Prima Brands, 10856
Prima Kase, 10284
Prima Naturals, 10283
Prima Porta, 5643
Prima Quality, 313
Prima, 21362
Primadophilus, 8896
Primal Chocolate, 3909
Primal Kitchen, 10288
Primalthin, 6629
Primasamo Cubes, 530
Prime, 10296
Prime Cap, 10297

Prime Food, 10290
Prime Froz-N, 10038
Prime Label, 25591
Prime Liner, 24416
Prime Naturally, 7876
Prime Pastries, 10294
Prime Plus Irc, 25591
Prime Pro Tex, 6168
Prime Prodata, 27790
Prime Source, 19947
Prime Time, 12602, 24044
Prime Turkey, 7876
Primedge, 21031
Primel, 4148
Primeliner Sacks, 24416
Primeliners, 24416
Primellose, 4736
Primerro, 8367
Primivito Zinfandel, 5989
Primo, 4891
Primo Cappaccino, 31200
Primo Taglio, 11073
Primo, 4552
Primojel, 4736
Primos, 10304
Primrose, 10305
Primrose Oile, 5363
Prince, 23757
Prince Alexis Vodka, 8062
Prince Edward, 12062
Prince Gourmet Foods, 1832
Prince of Orange, 12881
Prince of Peace, 10307
Prince of Peace Hawaiian, 10307
Prince, 10777, 28421
Princess, 6567
Princess Chipper, 20607
Principe, 10308
Pringles, 6766
Print Frame, 29746
Print Graphics, 22187
Print Ons, 27805
Print Protector, 23659
Print-A-Mark, 25870
Printegra, 22187
Printmaster, 26942
Printware, 30992
Printxcel, 22187
Priorato - Mas D' En Gil, 3545
Prismalier, 25224
Pristine, 463, 23842
Pritikin, 6279, 25789
Private Harvest, 10311
Private Harvest Bobby Flay, 10311
Private Harvest Tuscan Hills, 10311
Private Label, 223, 917, 1976, 2060, 3830, 13125, 20119
Private Label Products, 1619
Private Labels, 3931, 8105, 12761
Private Stock, 9664, 12293
Private Stock Malt Liquor, 9137
Privilege, 10331
Prize, 2634
Prize Box, 30134
Prize Taker, 23409
Prl, 10027, 27510
Prm-Ii (Prime Rib Master), 22732
Pro, 27711, 27835
Pro Bowl, 24575
Pro Chef, 24575
Pro Floc, 27902
Pro Mix, 317
Pro Plus, 5786
Pro Seris, 22920
Pro Soap, 26087
Pro Treats, 1785
Pro-Clean Hygiene Surface Test, 23971
Pro-Cut, 27329
Pro-Flo, 26111
Pro-Flo Pourer, 19999
Pro-Flow, 31205
Pro-Icer, 31346
Pro-Life, 2190
Pro-Lims, 25074
Pro-Magic, 20682

Pro-Pal, 27819
Pro-Relight, 9516
Pro-Shake, 15
Pro-Zorb, 27602
Pro/Fill, 26852
Pro/Matic, 26852
Pro/Star, 25299
Proatein, 1692
Proatein, 12561
Probase, 4119
Probio, 833
Probiology, 8878
Probiotic-2000, 7172
Proces-Data, 20837
Prochill, 833
Proclean, 11504, 29095
Procol, 10158, 27656
Procon, 833
Procon Products, 29580
Procount Salt Counter, 24293
Procter Creek, 10201
Proctor, 20085
Proctor Silex, 23542
Prodigy, 27711
Producer, 648
Product Vision, 18424
Produits Marguerite, 955
Profat 2, 20048
Proferm, 6211, 24226
Professional, 21853
Professional Preference, 8210
Profile Ii Plus, 27224
Profiler, 26235
Profire, 18434
Profiserie, 29271
Profit Pals, 31246
Proflavor, 4119
Progold, 31346
Progranola, 6629
Progress, 25606
Progresso, 10337
Progresso, 4947
Progum, 10158, 27656
Prokote, 833
Proline, 21210, 30427, 30743
Prolon Products, 27892
Prolume, 10341
Promaster, 18022
Promech, 30921
Promega, 11269
Promise Pops, 12639
Promitor Dietary Fiber, 12561
Promo Assist, 24265
Promoat, 1692
Promoat Beta Glucan, 12561
Promolux, 10344, 22018
Promotissues, 18378
Pronto, 22206
Prop, 30377
Prop Plus, 30377
Prop Whey, 9252
Propafilm, 30528
Propafiol, 30528
Propak, 31177
Propak, 11504, 29095
Propapeel, 28493
Propaream, 30528
Propaseal, 28493
Propel, 9945, 27433
Proper-Care, 10346
Prophecy, 3834
Prophos, 833
Propmaster, 18321
Proprietor's Reserve, 10001
Proryza P-35, 10709
Proryza Pf-20/50, 10709
Proryza Platinum, 10709
Proscan, 19262
Prosource, 10317
Prosperity, 597
Prosta-Forte, 8009
Prostacare, 783
Prostate Cleanse, 5682
Prostavite, 783
Prostease, 6449, 24506

All Brands Index

Prosur, 13648, 31107
Prosweet, 13444
Prosyn, 833
Prosystem, 11504, 29095
Protake, 10915
Protamex, 1692
Protape, 18614
Protech, 833, 23236
Protecta, 19544
Protecting Wear, 27642
Protecto-Freeze, 24951
Protecto-Temp, 24951
Protector, 13498, 25041, 28816
Protectowire, 27909
Protein Bonk Breaker, 1559
Protein Chef, 11324
Protein Color Meter, 30530
Protein Greens, 9516
Protes, 10318
Protexo, 23911
Protflan, 5629
Protient, 10352
Protizyme, 8191
Proto, 29584
Proto Whey, 1377
Protochill, 23944
Protocol, 23944
Protrolley, 833
Protykin, 6236
Proud Mary, 13141
Provago Wheels, 530
Provatec, 26781
Provecho, 7081
Provell, 31346
Provenance Vineyards, 12937
Proview, 18354
Provimi, 10356
Provitamina, 6449, 24506
Provost Packers, 10358
Proware, 11504, 29095
Prowler, 26210
Prozone, 9251
Pru Lites, 27921
Pruden, 10359
Psagot Winery, 10952
Psgjme, 27071
Psglee, 27071
Psycho Pops, 163
Psycho Psours, 163
Ptl-Condos Systems, 19213
Pub Pies, 8560
Puccinelli, 11957
Puck, 18427
Puckers, 9385
Pudliszki, 6977
Pueblafood, 10363
Puerto Vallarta, 4658
Puff Dough, 10552
Puff Pastry Tartlet, 10039
Puffcorn, 9408
Puffs, 12721, 30193
Pul-A-Nap, 23160
Pull-Ups, 24838
Pullman, 18276
Pullman-Holt Gansow, 31177
Pullulan, 24717
Pulmuone, 10365
Pulsar, 22902, 24093
Pulsarr, 19443
Pulse Point, 30799
Pulse Star, 30843
Pulseprint, 27931
Pulverlaser, 30192
Pumice Jell, 23532
Pumicizied Advantage Plus, 21768
Pumpkin Ale, 1837
Pumpkin Masters, 11599
Pumpsaver, 22624
Punch 'n Fruity, 13728
Pup-Peroni, 6380
Puppet Pals, 6780
Pur, 12722
Pura, 27079
Pura Still, 9117
Purdey's, 8838

Pure & Simple, 18843
Pure 'n Simple, 1040
Pure Alaska Omega, 12968
Pure Assam Irish Breakfast, 5228, 23295
Pure Brand Products, 4870
Pure Chem, 27058
Pure Chocolate Whippet, 3384
Pure Energy, 8493
Pure Flo Water, 10370
Pure Fruit, 5165
Pure Fruite, 2737
Pure Gold, 6869, 10372
Pure Harmony Dakota Clover, 1040
Pure Harmony, 12885, 30333
Pure Leaf, 9945, 27433
Pure Maid, 3336
Pure Nature, 12238
Pure Protein, 4150
Pure Protien, 8871
Pure Rock, 13728
Pure Source, 10382
Pure Via, 8173
Pure Water, 27937
Pure-Bind, 5246
Pure-Cote, 5246
Pure-Dent, 5246
Pure-Flo, 8804
Pure-Gel, 5246
Pure-Li Natural, 5061
Pure-Life, 20372
Pure-Pak, 22122
Pure7, 10385
Pureco, 126
Purecop, 23678
Puree Marsan, 7954
Purefil, 23678
Purefruit Monk Fruit Extract, 12561
Purekick, 6483
Pureliner, 26408
Purely American, 7364, 10388
Purely Elizabeth, 10389
Purely Pinole, 8813
Purepak, 10992
Purestack, 26408
Purestv, 4837
Purevac, 26408
Purex, 30373
Puricit Odor Eliminator, 9648
Purifier, 25041
Purifry, 23402
Purina, 726, 7198
Purina, 8945
Puritan, 1391, 23602, 27945
Puritan's Pride, 8871
Puritron, 18832
Purity, 3442, 10399, 21421, 27949
Purity Candy, 10392
Purity Farms Ghee, 10395
Purity Foods, 8886
Purity Gum, 8804
Purity Pat, 23142
Purity Wrap, 18908
Purity, 8804
Purn Life, 13365
Puroast, 10400
Purogene, 19666
Purple Carrot, 6590
Purple Haze, 125
Pursil, 3320
Purswab, 23602
Push Pop Candy, 2132
Push-Pac, 20550
Push-Pops, 19056
Pushback, 18394
Pushbak Cart, 22173
Put Me Hot, 6536
Put-Ons U.S.A., 27952
Putney Pasta, 10402
Puueo Poi, 10403
Pw 800, 24312
Pw 850, 24312
Py-O-My, 5015
Pyramid Brewing, 9117
Pyramid Juice, 10405
Pyrenees, 10406

Pyrex, 20981, 31344, 31345
Pyrex Plus, 20981
Pyro, 27958
Pyromania, 4895
Pyropure, 27352
Pyrorey, 25281
Pyure Brands, Llc, 1692

Q

Q Cups, 8725
Q Series Thermal Analysis, 29986
Q&Q, 9297
Q&Q Fideo, 9297
Q-50, 29484
Q-Bee, 10450
Q-Ber, 25766
Q-Can, 21536
Q-Matic, 27965
Q-Naturale, 8804
Q-Swab Environmental Collection, 23971
Q.E., 10412
Q31, 27980
Q32, 27980
Qa Products, 30618
Qa-Master, 31372
Qbd, 27967
Qc Assistant, 25198
Qc Database Manager, 25198
Qc Fibers, 3126
Qd-Loop Rapid Dilution Devices, 23971
Qda, 30377
Qda Software, 30377
Qfc, 12516
Qic, 23672
Qlam, 28023
Qmi, 27970
Qmi Safe Septum, 27970
Qpet, 28023
Qslic, 300
Quad-Steer, 27437
Quadnumatic, 28904
Quadra Beam 6600, 30216
Quadro, 27981
Quail Creek, 10416
Quaker, 10419, 10420, 24742, 27983
Quaker Bonnet, 10417
Quaker City, 29722
Quaker Maid, 10418
Quaker, 9945, 27433
Qualcoat, 10266
Qualflo , 11794
Qualheim, 31007
Quali-Tea, 7363
Quali-Carotene, 3320
Qualifreeze, 10425
Qualifresh, 10425
Quality, 226, 9032, 10443, 23261
Quality Bakery, 10426
Quality Candy, 1828
Quality Chef Foods, Inc., 5736
Quality Chekd, 4873, 12304
Quality Chekd Dairy Products, 27993
Quality Hearth, 10427
Quality Minded, 5436
Quality Paper Products, 18029
Quantanium, 31184
Quantum, 20244, 22348, 31184
Quarrymaster, 25840
Quarrymen Pale, 1460
Quartz Collection, 27277
Quartzone, 23698
Quasar, 30515
Quat Clean Sanitizer, 19910
Quat E-2, 26000
Quat F-5, 26000
Quatre Lepages, 9540
Quatro, 2343
Quebon, 8815
Queen Anne, 5288, 10449, 13948, 20256
Queen Helene, 5505
Queen Jasmine, 7723
Queen Mary's, 29094
Queen O Mat, 18040

Queen of America, 10454
Queen of Dixie, 12300
Queen's Pride, 9199
Queens Linen, 30073
Queensboro, 10455
Quelle, 10458
Quencher, 2742
Quero, 6977
Queso Del Valle, 6719
Queso Triangulos, 530
Quest Nutrition, 4150
Questias, 5294
Qugg, 25789
Quibell, 10460
Quic-Cheese, 10436, 28009
Quic-Flavor, 10436, 28009
Quiche, 10039
Quick & Natural Soup, 11919
Quick 'n Easy, 19823
Quick Acid, 300
Quick Chew, 300
Quick Coat, 300
Quick Creations, 13607
Quick Drop, 25910
Quick Dry Foods, 30618
Quick Fibre, 300
Quick Fire Premium Meats, 11363
Quick Glanz, 300
Quick Gum, 300
Quick Lac, 300
Quick Loaf, 12703
Quick Oil, 300
Quick Peanut Porridge, 1151
Quick Pot Pasta, 11919
Quick Shift, 21425
Quick Shine, 300
Quick Start, 1577
Quick Step...The Produce Manager, 25967
Quick Stix, 13316
Quick-Fit, 26529
Quick-Key, 29854
Quick-Start Home Style Chili, 1069
Quick-Step Stair Systems, 26909
Quickcheck, 23489, 29025
Quickchiller, 18677
Quickset, 7150
Quickset, 23811
Quicksilver, 22320
Quickstop, 18995
Quiet Classic, 21362
Quiet Thunder, 23222
Quiet' Slide, 20531
Quik, 21199
Quik 'n Crispy, 27972
Quik - Go, 22509
Quik Flo, 24332
Quik Lock Ii, 20986
Quik Lok, 19823
Quik Pik, 31141
Quik-Change, 23261
Quik-Fence, 22684
Quik-Pik, 21047, 30376
Quik-Space, 30341
Quik-Wipes, 18830
Quikmix, 21776
Quikserv, 27974
Quikstik, 27977
Quiktree, 24519
Quikwater, 28039
Quilceda Creek Vintners, 10462
Quillisascut Cheese, 10464
Quilon Bakeable Paper, 28910
Quinabeer, 2338
Quinine, 13287
Quinn, 10466
Quinn's, 11390
Quinn's Golden Ale, 8602
Quinoa Krunch, 2452
Quinoa Quickies, 12883
Quintessa, 4649
Quintrex, 9264
Quinzani, 10469
Quivira, 10471
Quong Hop, 10472

All Brands Index

Qwik Pack Systems, 28043
Qwik Pak, 19823
Qwip, 10267

R

R&M, 26346
R&R Oatmeal Stout, 1139
R-102, 30516
R-30, 28396
R-Own Cola, 4521
R.H. Phillips, 10494
R.M. Lawton Cranberries, 10483
R.M. Palmer, 10498
R.M.Quiggs, 2956
R.W. Knudsen, 6380
R.W. Zig Zag, 31214
R.W.Knudsen, 12017
Ra, 30398
Raaka, 10520
Rabbit Barn, 10521
Rabbit Creek, 10522
Rabbit Ridge, 10523
Rachel Ray Nutrish, 6380
Rachel's, 12985
Rack & Pour, 27730
Rack & Roll, 20143
Rack-A-Bag, 29266
Rack-Pack, 30228
Rack-The-Knife, 25299
Rackmaster, 30376
Rada, 19059
Radarange, 18333
Radarline, 18333
Radeberger, 1361
Radiant Ray, 18020
Radiant Wrap, 21131
Radio Pack, 21977
Raffaello, 4348
Raffetto, 13141
Raft, 6167
Raga Muffins, 13803
Raggy-O, 10534
Raid, 21757
Rail Head Red Ale, 1139
Railex, 28153
Railtite, 23450
Rain Blo, 1417
Rain Forest, 14011
Rain Sweet, 28090
Rainberry, 7170
Rainblo, 4345
Rainbo-Rich, 12866
Rainbow, 10540
Rainbow Agar, 19681
Rainbow Delight, 21782
Rainbow Hill Vineyards, 10536
Rainbow Light, 10537
Rainbow Light Herbal, 10537
Rainbow of New Colors, 18271
Rainbow Organics, 386
Rainbow Popcorn, 10944
Rainbow Pops, 3415, 10538
Rainbow Springs, 6139
Rainforest, 9245
Rainforest Crunch, 10542
Rainforest Organic, 3956
Rainforest Remedies, 7562
Rainsweet, 10543
Rair 2000, 30379
Rair 7000, 30379
Raisin Bran, 10213
Raisin Bran, 6765
Raisin Royales, 6851
Raisinmate, 12550
Raison D'Etre, 3644
Rak Pak, 29050
Ralph & Paula Adams Scrapple, 6587
Ralph's Italian Ices, 10546
Ralphs, 12516, 28160
Ram Center, 28080
Ram-Jet, 25719
Rama, 23621
Ramon Cardova Winery, 10952
Ramona's, 10548

Ramos Orchards, 10549
Rampro, 25719
Ramsey Medium Rye, 648
Ramun,, 10134
Ranch House, 13200
Ranch Oak Farm, 10553
Ranch Pac, 14008
Ranch Style, 6267
Ranch Style Beans, 2939, 2940, 20821, 20822
Ranch Style Brand Beans, 6267
Ranch Wagon, 12972
Ranchero, 1977
Rancho De Philo, 10554
Rancho Galante Cabernet, 4862
Rancho Palm Springs, 3565
Rancho Sisquoc, 10556
Rancho Zabaco, 3834
Ranco, 28967
Rancraft, 28178
Randall, 10559
Randall Foods, 10560
Randazzo's Honest To Goodness, 10561
Randell, 28178
Ranger Ipa, 8959
Ranieri, 10565
Ranserve, 28178
Ranulio, 31083
Rao's, 10566, 25789
Rap-In-Wax, 20628
Rap-Up 90, 20788
Rapazzini Winery, 10567
Rapes, 12078
Rapi-Kool, 24700
Rapid Assays, 28670
Rapid Brew, 30337
Rapid Fire, 26337
Rapid Flex, 25918
Rapid Freeze, 23893
Rapid Prep, 28670
Rapid Rack, 18990, 24810
Rapid Response, 30790
Rapid Sort, 21536
Rapidase, 2370, 3320
Rapidvap, 25041
Rapiscan, 24910
Rapistan, 21536
Rapplon, 18873, 18874
Rapptex, 18873, 18874
Raps Blue Ribbon, 6294
Rapunzel Pure Organi, 10568
Raquel's, 10472
Rare, 25147
Rare Hawaiian, 10570, 13488
Rare Teas, 3895
Raris, 7952
Rashi Winery, 10952
Raskas, 11308, 28903
Raspberry Barley Wine, 1237
Raspberry Brown, 7554
Raspberry Champagne Vinegar, 869
Raspberry Honey Butter Topping, 12936
Raspberry Rave Wine, 13372
Raspberry Teriyaki, 12497
Raspberry Trail Ale, 7923
Rat Beach Red, 7844
Ratan, 28768
Rather Jolly Tea, 6378
Ratiomatic, 22664
Rational Combi-Steamers, 28198
Ratle Snack, 12814
Ratner's, 11251
Ratofface, 30528
Raven, 20065
Ravenswood, 10573
Ravico, 10574
Ravifruit, 3236
Raw Earth Organics, 167
Raw Live Soda, 7070
Raw Power, 5221
Rawbite, 10576
Rawguru, 13847
Rawmantic Chocolate, 10579
Rawmio, 13847
Rawson's Retreat, 12937

Ray's Headcheese, 10580
Ray's Italian Links, 10580
Ray's Sausage, 10580
Ray's Souse, 10580
Ray-O-Matic, 18020
Raycord, 30251
Raymond Vineyard, 7659
Raymond Vineyards, 1543
Raynal, 3545
Razcal, 3187
Razzaronia, 11654
Razzle Dazzle, 1600
Razzlenuts, 5140
Razzles, 12880
Razzmatazzberry, 7903
Razzykat, 339
Rc, 252
Rc Cola, 1283, 10637
Rc Cola, 3725
Rc Fine Foods, 10477
Rc Q, 10637
Rcci, 10303, 27797
Rcs Air Samplers, 19690
Rdb, 30398
Rdl, 30398
Rdl (Red Deer Lake), 10605
Re-Fresh, 26379
Re-Natured, 5407
Rea-A-Matic, 23275
React-R-Mill, 30530
Reaction Arm, 27685
Read, 7161, 11434
Read Woodfiber Laminate, 28209
Readi-Bake, 6338
Reading Coffee Roast, 10584
Ready Bake, 13691
Ready Cheese, 2387, 20397
Ready Crisp, 7876
Ready Crust, 6747
Ready Grains, 6676
Ready Leaf, 3442, 21421
Ready Made, 24628
Ready Pac, 10586
Ready Roll, 21362
Ready-Cut, 11308, 28903
Readypac, 2789
Reaktor, 8470
Real, 4877
Real Aloe Co., 10587
Real Bacon Toppings, 6000, 23861
Real Cajun, 11255
Real Clean Protein, 1951
Real Cookies, 10589
Real Freshc, 187
Real Hydration, 1559
Real Kosher, 10591
Real Life, 4063
Real Sausage, 10592
Real West, 9500
Realbar, 9554
Realean, 9833
Realemon, 8586
Realemon Lemon Cookies, 9399
Realemon, 3725, 6818, 24802
Realime, 3725
Reallime, 8586
Really Cookin' Chef Gear, 24088
Reames, 12467
Rearn Naturefresh, 8448
Rebecca-Ruth, 10596
Rebel Green, 28217
Rebel Yell, 7655
Rebound, 6310
Rebpure, 4837
Rebsweet, 4837
Record Haccp, 26666
Recotech, 25597
Red, 7330
Red & White Condensed Soups, 2115
Red - Go, 22509
Red Ale, 1401
Red Baron, 1702, 11316
Red Baron, 11317
Red Bird, 204

Red Brick, 10602
Red Bull Malt Liquor, 9664
Red Cap, 1702
Red Cat Amber, 4959
Red Creek, 10604
Red Cross Nurse, 29782
Red Diamond Coffee & Tea, 10606, 28221
Red Dog, 8459
Red Dog, 8460
Red Dragon, 6449, 24506
Red E Made, 2943
Red Eye, 1675
Red Eye Country Picnic, 13237
Red Goat, 24038
Red Gold, 1891
Red Gold, 10608
Red Hot Chicago, 10610
Red Hots, 1417, 11298
Red Jim, 24403
Red Kap, 26875, 28222
Red Label, 5909, 23825
Red Lasoda, 3216
Red Line, 22013
Red Lobster, 2971
Red Mill Farms, 11934
Red Moon, 5141
Red Nectar, 6065
Red Oval Farms Stoned Wheat Thins, 8729
Red Pack, 10608
Red Parrot, 6822
Red Pepper Sauce, 9745
Red Pop, 5177
Red Rain, 10637
Red Ribbon, 11759
Red River, 9664
Red Rock, 10810
Red Rock Deli, 9945, 27433
Red Rock Winery, 3834
Red Rocket, 1720
Red Rooster, 555
Red Rooster Ale, 3519
Red Ropes, 469
Red Rose, 2381, 5612, 13167
Red Rose Hill Cabernet, 4862
Red Rose Ice, 9115
Red Rub, 29301
Red Shoulder Ranch, 11494
Red Sky Ale, 12013
Red Smith, 10620
Red Stag, 1120
Red Star, 10621
Red Tail, 8153
Red Tail Ale, 8153
Red Tea, 10677
Red Trolley Ale, 6711
Red V, 11001
Red Valley, 12157
Red Velvet, 7581
Red Vines, 469, 3204
Red White & Brew, 10624
Red X, 27058
Red-L, 11768
Red.L, 12065
Redbreast Irish, 9964
Redbridge, 26668
Redclay Gourmet, 10506
Redco, 25320
Redcore, 28356
Redd, 10626
Redd's, 8460
Reddi-Wip, 2939, 2940, 20821, 20822
Reddy Glaze, 2942
Redeman, 29154
Redhawk, 10628
Redhook Esb, 26668
Redhots, 4345
Redi Prep Strudel, 4244
Redi Shred, 1577
Redi-Call, 28231
Redi-Flow, 13890
Redi-Grill, 27799
Redi-Prime, 20978
Redi-Shred, 1069

All Brands Index

Redi-Shred Potato Cheese Bake, 1069
Redihop, 6554
Redimix, 10675
Redington, 19985
Redirail, 27979
Redivivo Lycopene, 3320
Redneck, 7364
Redneck Gourmet, 5520
Redondo Iglesias, 10631
Redpath, 4517
Redpath Sugar, 3666
Redpoint, 838
Reducit, 7857
Reducol, 9997
Redwood Ale, 1615
Redwood Creek, 3834
Redwood Empire, 8539
Redwood Hill Farm, 10633
Redwood Vintners, 28236
Reed, 2044, 28239
Reed's, 10507
Reedy Brew Teas, 1296
Reena's, 3465
Reese's, 5818, 23750
Refillo, 23434
Reflections, 1891, 8301, 24044
Reflections, 30595
Refractance Window, 25559
Refractite, 28251
Refrigerated Entre,S, 6000, 23861
Refrigerator Fresh, 9237, 26785
Refrigiwear, 28261
Regal, 3033, 8314, 10640, 20542, 21915, 28265, 28272
Regal Chef, 4692
Regal Crest, 9534
Regal, 21362
Regatta, 3771
Regenie's, 10642
Regent, 3480, 18413
Regent Sheffield, 31345
Reggano, 6126
Regina, 28276
Regina, 864
Regional Delphi, 26615
Regional Recipe, 1577
Rego, 26932, 26933
Reichert, 30775
Reign, 2811, 8485
Reindeer Pies, 12847
Reineveld, 21445
Reinhardt, 3381
Reiter, 10664
Reiter Dairy, 3442, 21421
Rejuv, 11504, 29095
Reko, 9225
Relax & Sleep, 6449, 24506
Relaxmax, 9957
Relentless, 8485
Relentless Energy Drink, 2815, 20685
Reliance, 21362
Relora, 6236
Rema, 26216
Rema Foods Imports, 11504, 29095
Remco, 28303
Remcon, 28304
Remcraft, 28305
Remel, 28306
Remeteas Detoxitea, 398
Remeteas Masculinitea, 398
Remeteas Pms Rescue, 398
Remeteas Visibilitea, 398
Remifemin, 4086, 8896
Remotaire, 30563
Remotecontroller, 20686
Remotemd, 24812
Remtron, 20348
Remy Picot, 9410
Ren,E's, 6976
Renaissance, 4038, 10668
Renaissance Red, 7143
Renato Ratti, 3834
Rencor, 20975
Rendac, 3390
Rene, 10672

Rene Barbier, 4693
Renee's Gourmet, 6240
Renew Life, 2766, 20657
Renn, 22939
Reno, 25769
Renold, 28320
Renovator's Supply, 28321
Renuz-U, 9253
Renwood Wines, 10676
Renwrap, 28317
Repak, 26532
Repellence, 21027
Rephresh, 2666, 20561
Replenish, 12182
Replikale, 22483
Replens, 2666, 20561
Republic, 19908
Republic High Yield, 28324
Republic of Tea, 10677
Rescue Bar, 10229
Reseal, 28816
Reser's American Classics, 10681
Reser's Sensational Sides, 10681
Reserve, 22048
Reserve Brut, 3661
Reserve Brut Rose, 3661
Reserve Cabernet Sauvignon, 11995
Reserve Carneros Chardonnay, 869
Reserve Chardonnay, 13793
Reserve Fume Blanc, 13793
Reserve Merlot, 11995
Reserve Zinfandel, 11995
Resina, 28331
Resinfab, 30828, 30829
Resinol, 29452
Resistat, 20802
Resource, 8945
Respitose, 4736
Rest Ez, 28661
Restaurant Basics, 28766
Restaurant Manager, 18227
Restaurant Quality, 1658
Restaurant Row, 11352
Restaurant Style, 9408
Restore, 6340
Restore Pac, 27679
Resvida, 3320
Retail Basics, 28766
Rethemeyer, 10687
Rethink Beer, 13711
Retriever, 31071
Retsch, 23209
Retzlaff Estate Wines, 10688
Reuben, 13109
Reveal, 31010
Revelstoke, 3024
Revenge, 2411, 28571
Revent, 28346
Revere, 20957, 31345
Revive Kombucha, 10692
Revolution Hall, 1789
Revolution, 13595, 31053
Revolver, 23771
Revolver Brewing, 8459
Revovler, 8460
Revv, 6818, 24802
Rex, 10509, 28099, 28357
Rex Coffee, 2711
Rex Hill, 48
Rexcraft, 28355
Rexfit, 30517
Rexford, 28356
Rexpo, 6395
Rextape, 30517
Reyataz, 1721
Reyes Mares, 13298
Reynolds, 18592
Re_L Cocktail, 439
Rg's, 1659
Rgo Mace O.O., 11096
Rhapsody In Blue, 9069
Rheostress Rs1, 23503
Rheostress Rs150, 23503
Rheostress Rs300, 23503
Rheostress Rv1, 23503

Rhinegeld, 8539
Rhino, 28899
Rhino Nutmeg, 12987
Rhodes, 10698
Rhodes-Stockton Bean, 10697
Rhum Barbancourt, 3165
Rhythm Superfoods, 10699
Rias Baixas, 3545
Rib Chef, 24948
Rib Tred, 27881
Ribera Del Duero, 3545
Ribran, 10709
Ribtype, 18276, 30649
Rica, 1581
Rica Malt Tonic, 2338
Ricardc, 9964
Rice a Roni, 9945, 27433
Rice Complete, 10297
Rice Crunchies, 4668
Rice Krispies, 6766
Rice Krispies Squares, 6765
Rice Krispies, 6765
Rice Master, 30364
Rice Nectar, 12372
Rice Pro 35, 10297
Rice Reality, 10708
Rice Road, 27959
Rice Select, 24672
Rice Select, 10777, 28421
Rice Trin, 10297
Rice's Products, 6105
Riceland, 10710
Ricex, 10713
Rich Cow, 11896
Rich Frosted Mini Donuts, 12551
Rich Ice Creams, 10716
Rich's, 8533
Rich's Eclairs, 10714
Rich's, 11504, 29095
Richard's Gourmet, 10721
Richards' Maple Candy, 10722
Richards' Maple Syrup, 10722
Richardson's Ice Cream, 10727
Riche, 3661
Richgrove King, 13421
Richly Deserved, 5346
Richmond Rye Bread, 508
Richs, 11768
Rick's Chips, 10732
Rickard's, 8459
Rico, 10734
Rico's, 100, 5168
Ricotta Con Latte, 1174
Ricrem, 11211
Rid-A-Gum, 24829
Riddle's, 10736
Ridge Classic, 30860
Ridge Showcase, 30860
Ridge Vineyards, 10737
Ridgeland, 12426, 29855
Ridgeview Farms, 13737
Ridgways, 4614
Riebosam, 27835
Riesen, 12148
Rietz, 19576, 23871
Riffels Gourmet Coffees, 10740
Righetti Specialty, 10741
Righteously Raw Chocolate, 3874
Rigid-Flo, 28936
Rigid-Tex, 28400
Rigidized, 28400
Rigirtex0, 22528
Rigitainer, 29192
Riley's Beef Sausage, 5400
Rimac, 23305
Rindex 3en1, 12721, 30193
Ring Dryer, 21811
Ring Jet, 22615
Ring Lock, 29797
Ring of Fire, 6015
Ringmaster I, 20011
Ringmaster Ii, 20011
Ringolos, 9408
Rinquinquin, 3165
Rinse-O-Latic, 30884

Rinsol, 25606
Rio, 10747, 28404
Rio Caribe, 2617
Rio Grande, 345
Rio Grande Roasters, 13381
Rio Klor, 30913
Rio Mare, 11776
Rio Real, 8208
Rio Trading, 10748
Rio Valley, 10749
Riobli Family Wine Estates, 7740
Rioja, 3545
Riojano, 28
Riosweet, 10746
Rip It, 8784
Ripensa, 10751
Rippin Cherries, 28090
Ripples, 9408
Rips Toll, 4589, 22756
Riser Rims, 23288
Rising Dough, 10758
Rising Moon Organics, 1484
Rising Star Ranch, 11818
Rising Sun, 10759
Ristschic, 27729
Rita, 10188, 10873
Ritas, 571
Ritchey, 10762
Rite, 12965
Ritenap, 23160
Rito, 10764
Rittenhouse Straight Rye Whiskey, 5720
Ritter, 4721
Ritz, 8474, 8729, 8784
Ritz Bits Sandwiches, 8729
Riunite, 1006
River Ale, 1237
River Bank, 10542
River Bend, 3406
River Hills, 10768
River Island, 3274
River of Cream, 23434
River Queen, 7288
River Rat Cheese, 3
River Rice, 10777, 28421
River Road, 1547, 1808
River Road Vineyards, 12726, 30196
River Run, 4242, 10771, 22458
River Town Foods Rib Rub, 10772
River Valley Farms, 3274
River West Stein, 7156
Riverbank, 5924
Riverboat, 12410
Riverside, 4579, 9500, 28415
Riverview Foods Authentic, 10776, 28418
Rivet Rak, 30413
Rivetier, 31141
Riviera, 5317, 10778, 20964, 23349
Rivit Orite, 27405
Rixcaps, 28422
Rizzo's, 7635
Rj Corr, 10495
Rjreynolds, 541
Rmi, 28260
Ro, 2939, 2940, 6267, 20821, 20822, 29221
Roach, 25918
Roach Destroyer, 19364
Roach Prufe, 20956
Road Kill Bbq, 11852
Road Warrior, 23874
Roadhouse, 2200
Roadhouse Red, 1688
Roann's Confections, 11868
Roar, 10928, 28576
Roasted Garlic Ranch, 5489
Roasterie, 10783
Roastworks, 6374, 24434
Rob's Brands, 13308
Robag, 30020
Robby Vapor Systems, 28432
Robert Corr, 10495
Robert De Serbie, 5405
Robert Keenan Winery, 10790

1327

All Brands Index

Robert Pecota, 10793
Robert Rothschild, 10794
Robert Weil, 12315
Roberto Cheese, 10798
Roberts Ferry, 10799
Robin Hood, 6380
Robller Vineyard and Winery, 10805
Robofry, 29561
Robot Coupe, 28456
Robusch, 23032
Robusto, 25530
Roca, 1771, 10510
Roca Beige, 23477
Roccas, 10806
Roche, 6007, 10807
Rocher, 4348
Rock 'n Roll Chews, 2947
Rock N Rye, 9773
Rock Pop Carbonated Beverages, 13728
Rock River Cattle, 457
Rockbridge Vineyard, 10813
Rocket, 23434
Rocket Man, 28465
Rocket Shot, 10251
Rockhill Farms, 11263
Rockin' Rods, 10305
Rocklets, 643
Rocks N' Rolls, 12002
Rockwell Automation, 28472
Rocky Jr, 9974
Rocky Mountain, 4578, 5448, 10822
Rocky Mountain Marshmallows, 11015
Rocky Mountain Popcorn, 4749, 11015
Rocky Mountain Products, 1619
Rocky Ridge Maple, 10826
Rocky Roadc, 583
Rocky the Range, 9974
Rodda Coffee, 10830
Roddenbery's, 1103
Rode Lee, 5297
Rodeo, 9500
Rodgers', 10832
Rodney Strong, 10833
Roe-Lift, 21628
Roederer Estate, 3545
Rofry, 26131
Rofumo, 10906
Rogelio Bueno, 12823
Roger's, 10837
Rogers, 8414, 10838
Rogers Imperials, 10840
Rogue Valley, 1128
Rogue Brewery, 26668
Rokeach, 7848
Rokeach Food, 10845
Roku, 12315
Rol-Brush, 26073
Rol-Lift, 25422
Roland Star, 10847
Roland, 11504, 29095
Rold Gold, 972, 4741
Rold Gold, 9945, 27433
Roldip, 31442
Roll Former/Divider, 21701
Roll Models, 23543
Roll Rite Super Caster, 28488
Roll Tax 200, 30957
Roll-A-Bench, 20919
Roll-A-Matic, 29379
Roll-A-Sign, 28240
Roll-Eze, 24059
Roll-N-Stor, 23543
Roll-Rite Corp., 28488
Roll-Tite, 24866
Roll-Up, 22573
Roller Lacer, 20654
Roller-Brake, 24350
Rollerbites, 5929
Rollerflex, 29796
Rollers, 3931
Rollguard, 23355
Rolling Rock, 7123
Rolling Rock, 26668
Rolo, 5818, 23750
Roma, 1248, 30775

Roma Bakeries, 10853
Roma Gold, 28743
Roma Marble, 28743
Roma Marie, 7769
Roma Silver, 28743
Roman Meal, 5917, 8951
Romance, 2761
Romanoff, 25789
Romanoff, 12467
Romantic, 21059
Romanza, 10161
Rombauer Vineyards, 10858
Romeo, 1866
Romero's, 10859
Romo, 22599
Ron Carlos, 4515
Ron Granado, 3545
Ron Llave, 3545
Ron Palo Viejo, 3545
Ron Rico, 3545
Ron Rio, 8062
Ron Son, 10860
Ronald Reginald's, 11756
Ronco, 465
Rondele, 7126
Ronnie's Ocean, 28515
Ronningen-Petter, 21994
Ronnoco, 10864
Ronozyme, 3320
Ronrico, 1120
Ronzoni, 6126
Ronzoni Garden Delight, 10866
Ronzoni Gluten Free, 10866
Ronzoni Healthy Harvest, 10866
Ronzoni Homestyle, 10866
Ronzoni Organic, 10866
Ronzoni Smart Taste, 10866
Ronzoni Supergreens, 10866
Ronzoni Thick and Hearty, 10866
Ronzoni, 10866
Ronzoni, 10777, 28421
Rookie Spookie, 11004
Roos, 10869
Rooster, 13686
Rooster Run, 431
Root Beer, 11992
Root To Health, 6040
Rooto, 28517
Roovers, 21201
Ropak, 24438
Rope, 30800
Ropiteall, 12672
Ropiteau Freres, 1543
Ropole, 28118
Rosa, 10873
Rosa Canola Oil, 11096
Rosa Corn Oil, 11096
Rosa Peanut Oil, 11096
Rosarita, 6084
Rosarita, 2939, 2940, 20821, 20822
Rose, 4539, 4649
Rose Cottage, 13700, 31165
Rose Forgrove, 24076
Rose Hill, 11997
Rose's, 8586
Rose's, 3725, 6818, 24802
Rosebarb, 1688
Rosebud, 1950
Rosebud Creamery, 10889
Rosecup Mints, 9836
Roseen, 6777
Rosell, 7172
Rosellac, 7172
Rosen's Inc., 10893
Rosenbergers, 10894
Rosenblum, 10895
Rosetti Fine Foods, 10897
Rosie Organic, 9974
Rosie's, 7635, 12078
Rosina Food Products, 20020
Rosina, 10899
Roskamp, 20084
Rosmarino, 10900
Rosport Blue, 2815, 20685
Ross, 20448, 26976, 28291

Ross Fine, 10901
Rostov's Coffee Tea, 10904
Rosy, 3479, 21460
Rota-Blade, 27354
Rota-Chill, 30563
Rota-Cone, 27354
Rota-Sieve, 27713
Rotaball, 20491
Rotajector, 21091
Rotary, 27980
Rotary Dicer, 23117
Rotary Fill-To-Level Filler, 21033
Rotary Piston Filler, 21033
Rotary Recharger, 27435
Rotella Bread, 1940
Rotella's, 10905
Roth Kase, 10906
Rothbury Farms, 10907
Rothsay, 3390
Roti & Chapati, 10968
Rotisserie Keeper, 22640
Roto Gard, 30325
Roto Jet, 28557
Roto Shaker, 18187
Roto-Bin-Dicator, 30799
Roto-Flex Oven, 28556
Roto-Former, 28804
Roto-Jet, 22662
Roto-Sizer, 22662
Roto-Smoker, 28556
Roto-Stak, 26467
Rotocut, 18878
Rotomixx, 18126
Rotopax, 18637
Rotosolver, 18126
Rotostat, 18126
Rototherm, 19093
Rotulos Ferrer, 22519
Roudon Smith Vineyards, 10910
Rouge Et Noir, 7925
Rougemont, 56, 10333
Rougette, 2409
Roughneck, 27428
Rougie, 10911
Roulet, 10039
Roun' Top, 20882
Round Hill Vineyards, 10912
Round Lahvosh, 13256
Round Nose, 30325
Round the Clock, 5555, 29826
Roundpetal, 555
Roundup, 18023
Rounthane, 29148
Roussanne, 14038
Rousselot, 3390
Rousselot, 10915
Route 11 Potato Chips, 10916
Rovimix, 3320
Row L, 28489
Row S, 28489
Rowe, 28565
Rowe Ami, 28565
Rowena's, 10919
Rowena's Gourmet Sauces, 10919
Rowena's Jams & Jellies, 10919
Rowena's Pound Cake, 10919
Rowmark, 21199
Rowoco, 31242
Rox Energy Drink, 12960
Roxi Rimming Supplies, 19999
Roxi Sugar and Salt Spices/Flavors, 19999
Roxo, 28571
Roy, 24438
Roy Rogers Happy Trails, 2903
Royal, 6211, 7007, 8525, 10929, 10939, 24226, 27387
Royal Bavarian, 2409
Royal Blend, 3564
Royal Borinquen Export, 1581
Royal Canadian, 2089
Royal Canin, 7952
Royal City, 12136
Royal Crest, 10927
Royal Crown, 10151

Royal Crown Cola, 6818, 24802
Royal Cup, 10928, 28576
Royal Dansk, 6774
Royal Delights, 6483
Royal Flush, 19741
Royal Garden Tea, 12663
Royal Gem, 8542
Royal Gift, 13845
Royal Gourmet Caviar, 10932
Royal Harvest, 10933, 11517
Royal Icing Decoration, 3460, 21439
Royal Jelly, 1164
Royal Kona Coffee, 5654
Royal Konaccino, 6953
Royal Land, 28584
Royal Leerdam, 25281
Royal Mandalay Chai, 9115
Royal Mark, 28218
Royal Pacific Coffee, 10941
Royal Pacific Tea, 10941
Royal Palate, 10943
Royal Palm, 9098
Royal Pastry, 4025
Royal Pollen Complex, 131
Royal Poultry, 5141
Royal Recipe, 3189
Royal Reef, 6267
Royal Reserve, 3024
Royal Salut, 9964
Royal Seafood, 10200
Royal Sluis, 11427
Royal Touch, 10950
Royal Wrap, 12972
Royal-T, 6211, 24226
Royal, 2711, 6483, 22187
Royale, 7877
Royale Smoothie, 10953
Royalean, 9833
Royce, 28590
Royco, 7952
Rp's Pasta Company, 12964
Rps Pasta, 10515
Rrrogala, 7344
Rse, 22902
Rsv, 10795
Rt, 22480, 23669
Rt 66 Foods, 1129
Rtr 1000, 20754
Ru-Bee, 4374
Rub a Dubs, 26632
Rubatex, 27655
Rubbermaid, 18592, 28600
Rubbermaid, 28599
Ruberg, 18241
Rubicon, 10958, 30820
Rubino & Vero, 6255
Rubschlager, 10960
Ruby Kist, 56, 29404
Rudis, 5505
Rudolph the Red Nosed Reindeer, 4507
Rudolph's, 10966, 10968
Rudy's Tortillas, 10969
Rue's Choice, 1403, 13301
Ruef's Meat Market, 10970
Ruff N Tuff, 27881
Ruffies, 20257
Ruffles, 4741
Ruffles, 9945, 27433
Rug Aroma, 29826
Rugboss, 31177
Ruggles, 11725
Ruinart, 8452
Rule Breaker, 10977
Ruler, 24911
Rum-Ba, 12895
Rumba, 11945
Rumba Energy Juice, 26668
Rumford, 2711
Rumi Spice, 10978
Rumiano, 10979
Rummo Gourmet Imported Pasta, 9119
Runamok, 10982
Running Rabbit, 14045
Rush! Energy, 8470
Rushing Tide, 24409

All Brands Index

Russell, 24919
Russell Cream Ale, 10989
Russell Green River, 21591
Russell Honey Blonde Ale, 10989
Russell International, 21591
Russell Lemon Wheat Ale, 10989
Russell Oager, 10989
Russell Pale Ale, 10989
Russell Stovers, 10991
Russell Winter Ale, 10989
Russell's, 722
Russer, 13109
Russetts, 6882
Russian Caravan Original China, 5228, 23295
Russian Chef's, 10992
Russian Prince, 913
Russo's, 1998
Rust Bust'r, 20966
Rust Gun, 22473
Rustica, 13653
Rustico Cheese, 11668
Rustler Root Beer, 5539
Rutherford, 28620
Rutherford Ranch, 10912
Rutherford Vintners, 1738
Rutter's, 11000
Rw Garcia, 10518
Rwi Logistics, 2298
Rx Extreme Energy Shot, 670
Rxbar, 10519
Ryals Bakery, 11002
Rye, 10629
Ryoto Sugar Ester, 8405
Ryvita, 6279
Ryze, 11078
Rzaca, 11627

S

S & W Beans, 4267, 22464
S!Mply Baked, 23811
S&D Coffee & Tea, 10303, 27797
S&H Uniforms, 28630
S&M, 11011
S&W, 2847
S&W, 3478
S'Forno Winery, 10952
S-Ch, 19798
S-Line, 23266
S. Pellegrino, 8945
S. Rosen's, 374
S. T. Jerrell Nonfat, 11029
S.O.S., 2766, 20657
S.S., 19401
S.S. Ware, 19401
S/M Flaker, 23117
S8 1p65, 24093
S8 Classic, 24093
S8 Contrast, 24093
S8 Master, 24093
Sa Analytical, 28915
Sa Series, 19625
Sa21, 18243
Sabana, 5325
Sabi, 11263
Sabor Del Campo, 12973, 30444
Sabra, 11064
Sabra, 9945, 27433
Sabrett, 7895
Sabritones, 4741
Sabritones, 9945, 27433
Sabroe, 28967, 31401
Sabrosito, 2490
Sabroso Di Cafe Liqueur, 11264
Sac Master Bulk Bag Dischargers, 28875
Sachers, 3714, 13676
Sacramento Baking, 11067
Sacramento, 10608
Sacred Bond, 5720
Sadler, 28748
Sadler's Smokehouse, 11070
Saeco, 31083
Saeco Housewares, 28749
Saf-T-Cote, 30457

Saf-T-Pops, 11885
Saf-T-Rail, 30341
Safari, 3570
Safari Blend Liquid Coffee, 11855
Safe Heat, 20187
Safe T Cut, 28752
Safe-Lode, 19051
Safe-Pack, 25265
Safe-T-Salt, 6661
Safe-T-Seal, 28356
Safe-T-Strip, 21027
Safecatch, 11071
Safeglide, 30388
Safeguard, 12721, 22320, 24734, 30193
Safehold, 22252
Safeline, 26041
Safely Delicious, 11072
Safemaster, 29706
Safepak, 25005
Saferstep, 28006
Safeseal, 21362
Safesec, 30325
Safestep, 30486
Safety Pak, 22712
Safetywrap, 24700
Safeway, 3387, 11260
Saffron Road, 11075
Safgard, 28888
Safpowrbar, 29137
Safrante, 4560
Saftex Flame - Retardant Mitts, 20426
Safti Keeper, 22640
Saga, 12759
Sage, 29968
Sage'n Pepper, 6574
Sagri, 4386
Sahadi, 11082
Sahale Snacks, 6380
Sahara, 6669, 11085
Sahara Date Company, 11086, 28758
Sahara Hot Box, 19569
Sahlen's, 11088
Sai Baba Nag Champa, 7562
Saico, 12241
Sail, 3889
Sailor Plastics, 28759
Sailor's Choice, 11356
Saint Andre Vienna, 12136
Saint Archer, 8459
Saint Archer, 8460
Saint Brendan's, 7655
Saint Brigid's, 5304
Saint Clair Family Estate, 3834
Saint Geron, 1661
Saint Justin, 9370
Saint Louis, 12437
Saint Louis Bread Co.c, 9740
Sainte Genevieve, 11091
Saintsbury, 11092
Salad Crispinsc, 5489
Salad Dazzlers, 485
Salad Depot, 11094
Salad Expressions, 462
Salad Pak, 10491
Salad Pizazz!, 13603
Salad Queen, 10054
Salad Time, 12525
Salad Toppers, 7196
Salada, 5612
Salads of the Sea, 7168
Salamandre Wine Cellars, 11097
Salami Campesino, 2670
Salami Del Pueblo, 2670
Salami Sosua, 2670
Salapeno Salami, 2670
Salazar Farms, 5036
Salem Gibralters, 13997
Salemville, 11209, 11211
Salignac, 1120
Salinas Valley Wax Paper Co., 28768
Salishan, 11106
Salix Sst, 11268
Sall-N-Ann, 7626
Sallie's, 4839
Sally Lane's, 11107

Sally Sherman Foods, 4061
Salmans, 11109
Salmolux, 11608
Salmolux Anti Pasta, 11110
Salmolux Gourmet Smoked Salmon, 11110
Salmolux Saute Butters, 11110
Salmon Bay, 4440
Salmon Magic, 7766, 25632
Salmonberry, 1470
Salometers, 23391
Salpica, 4751
Salsa Criolla, 13969
Salsa Del Rio, 3537
Salsa Del Sol, 5735
Salsa Diablo, 3537
Salsa Divino, 3537
Salsa God, 11113
Salsa Picante, 11883
Salsa Primo, 19106
Salt For Life, 3574
Salt Kriek Cherry Be, 7143
Salt of the Earth, 11116
Salt-Master, 21145
Salted Nut Roll, 9877
Salty Road, 11119
Salty Snacks, 12211
Salute Sante! Grapeseed Oil, 11121
Salutti, 6400
Salvador's, 7655
Salvation, 838
Salvatore's, 11628
Salvo, 12721, 30193
Sam, 27685
Sam & Nick's, 10693
Sam Houston BourbonÖ Chocolates, 10468
Samai, 4607
Samark, 22018
Sambol, 11130
Sambuca Di Amore, 11264
Sambuca Molinari, 3545
Sambucus, 8896
Samco, 28799, 29094
Sammillsc, 11125
Sammy's, 11585
Sammye's Sumptuous, 890
Samos, 10435
Sampco, 11132
Sample Trac, 27377
Sampler, 29320
Sams Clams, 1464
Samsons, 4633
Samuel Adams, 1592
Samuel Smith, 1748
Samuel Wynn & Co., 12937
San Anselmo's, 11134
San Antonio California Champagne, 7740
San Antonio Dessert, 7740
San Antonio Sacramental, 7740
San Antonio Specialty, 7740
San Antonio Winery, 7740
San Benedetto, 11776
San Benito, 9178
San Daniele, 11776
San Diego Salsa, 11065, 11187
San Diego Salsa, 11186
San Diego Soy Dairy, 11138
San Dominique, 11139
San Fab, 28786
San Francisco Bay Traders, 5660
San Francisco Coffee, 11141
San Francisco Fine Bakery, 11142
San Francisco Popcorn, 11144
San Francisco Salt Companyc, 11145
San Franciso Bay, 11140
San Gallio, 10457
San Gennaro, 11148
San Giorgio, 6126, 11154, 28791
San Giorgio, 10777, 28421
San Joaquin Golden Ale, 11448
San Joaquin Supreme, 11149
San Like, 11250
San Marcos, 12823
San Mario, 12640

San Orange, 11250
San Quentin's Breakout Stout, 7923
San Rallo Gourmet Italian, 10899
San Red, 11250
San Simeon, 7740
San Sui, 13473
San Yellow, 11250
San-Ei, 11250
San-J, 11157
Sanborn Sourdough Bakery, 11160
Sand Castle Winery, 11162
Sandbar Trading, 11165
Sandcap, 29318
Sandeman Character Oloroso, 3545
Sandeman Don Fino, 3545
Sanders, 3078
Sanders Brand Candy, 11167
Sanderson Farms, 11169
Sandhill, 555
Sandia Shadows Vineyard & Wine, 11170
Sandiacre, 24076
Sandler Seating, 28801
Sandpiper, 31013
Sandridge Salads Set Free, 11172
Sandstone Winery, 11173
Sandt's, 11174
Sandwhich Bros. of Wisconsin, 2939, 2940, 20821, 20822
Sandwich Naturals, 4405
Sandwich Pals, 13894
Sandwich Shop, 7196
Sanford, 11178
Sangaria, 11032
Sangiovese, 2469, 7527
Sangria Cola, 6310
Sangria Seorial, 12823
Sani - Pail, 20256
Sani Air, 19127
Sani Pac, 27679
Sani-Aire, 29826
Sani-Cloth, 26632
Sani-Flakes, 29826
Sani-Flow, 20522, 24332
Sani-Hands, 26632
Sani-Hanks, 25725
Sani-Link Chain, 22890
Sani-Matic, 28810
Sani-Safe, 21591
Sani-Scent, 29826
Sani-Stack, 26031
Sani-Tech, 19401
Sani-Trolley, 22890
Sani-Wheel, 22890
Sani-Wipe, 26632
Sanifit, 28809
Sanigard, 28816
Saniserv, 28814
Saniset, 19847
Sanitaire, 19152
Sanitary, 27516
Sanitary Split Case Pump, 24042
Sanitech Mark Series Systems, 28817
Sanitron, 19152
Sanogene, 19666
Sanolite, 29862
Sans Sucre, 1244
Sant Andrea, 26933
Sant' Andrea, 26932
Santa Barbara, 11185
Santa Barbara Barc, 11182
Santa Barbara County, 4353
Santa Barbara Pistachio, 11184
Santa Barbara Salsa, 11065, 11187
Santa Barbara Salsa, 11186
Santa Barbara Winery, 11188
Santa Clara, 11189
Santa Cruz, 498, 10500, 11191
Santa Cruz Mountain Vineyard, 11192
Santa Cruz Organic, 6380
Santa Elena, 2970
Santa Elenita, 25281
Santa Fe, 25299
Santa Fe Brewing, 11194
Santa Fe Seasons, 3522, 11195
Santa Fe Vineyards, 11196

All Brands Index

Santa Marta, 5036
Santa Pop, 11004
Santa's Favorite, 11855
Santa's Tipple, 8524
Santa-Claus, 6310
Santa-Elena Coffee, 11193
Santaka Chili Pods, 191
Santana, 27236
Santare, 26736
Santarosa, 10869
Santiago, 1577
Santiago Beans, 1069
Santiam, 8724
Santino Wines, 10676
Santitas, 4741
Santitas, 9945, 27433
Sanyu, 20868
Sap Maple, 11722
Sapna Foods, 11033
Sapore Del Tartufo, 11205
Saporito, 12030
Sapp Birch Water, 11206
Saputo, 11209, 11211
Sara Lee, 541, 5792, 10406, 11214
Sara Lee, 1359, 13109
Sarabeth's, 2669, 11035, 11216
Saragosa Olive Oil, 9648
Sarah's Garden, 10435
Sarah's Vineyard, 11217
Saranac Diet Root Beer, 11218
Saranac Ginger Beer, 11218
Saranac Orange Cream, 11218
Saranac Root Beer, 11218
Sarantis, 6986
Saratoga, 11222, 11223
Saratoga Splash, 11223
Saratoga Vichy, 11223
Sarcmi, 28832
Sardinha's, 11224
Sargento, 11228, 28829
Sarsaparilla, 13728
Sartori, 1006
Sarum Tea, 11232
Sas, 22208
Sas Super 90, 19688
Sasquatch Stout, 4466
Sat-T-Ice, 24700
Sat-T-Mop, 24700
Sateline, 18931
Sathers, 1417, 4345
Satiety, 11235
Satin Doll, 31010
Satin Fan, 31010
Satin Ice, 11236
Satin Oranges, 13906
Satin White Flour, 6917
Satise, 6777
Satman Overseas, 6939
Sato, 18284, 28836
Satori Stocktec, 28837
Satoris, 28837
Sattwa Chai Concentrate, 11237
Sattwa Kovalam Spice Chai, 11237
Sattwa Shanti Herbal Chai, 11237
Sattwa Sun Chai, 11237
Saturn Series, 18620
Sauce Boss, 30376
Sauce Craft, 13328
Sauce For Sissies, 6796
Saucelito Canyon, 11240
Saucy Susan, 345
Sauder's, 11241
Sauer's Everyday Spices, 1935
Sausage a La Carte, 4676
Sausal Wines, 11245
Sausalito, 30820
Sautene, 353
Sauven, 30935
Sauvignon Blanc, 1314, 4745
Sauza, 5892, 13454
Sauza Commemorativo, 3024
Sauza Extra Gold, 3024
Sauza Margarita Salt With Juicer, 4650
Sauza Silver, 3024
Sauza Tequila, 12315

Sauza Triada, 3024
Sauza, 1120
Sava-Klip, 25434
Savage Energy, 2234
Saval, 11246
Savannah, 12284
Savannah Chanelle Vineyards, 11248
Savannah Cinnamon Mix, 11249
Savannah Gold, 6164
Savannah Squares, 11249
Savannah White, 8513
Savarin, 8560
Save - All, 20256
Save-A-Nail, 19998
Save-T, 27875
Savealot, 8404
Savetime, 20910
Savlin, 22258
Savoia, 11253
Savoie's, 2019, 11255
Savorganic, 11258
Savorlok, 4430
Savoro, 10056
Savory, 2750, 11257, 31092
Savory Basics, 11229
Savory Smoke, 11919
Savorymyx, 11436, 29018
Sawtooth, 2909, 7309, 11259
Saxon, 22581
Sayco, 28856
Sayco Tournament, 28856
Sb-3x, 6302, 24394
Sc, 9103
Sc Fibers, 3126
Scalestick, 29397
Scalfani, 864
Scaltrol, 28857
Scan-A-Plate, 19082
Scanmaster, 28834
Scannable Bar Code Hologram, 25591
Scanpro, 4119
Scanvision, 24910
Scapa Single Malt, 3024
Scape Goat Pale Ale, 1344
Scarlet Lady Ale, 12153
Scatter, 29826
Scent Flo, 18501
Scent Sation, 19741
Scent-Flo, 29826
Scent-O-Vac, 11997
Sceptre, 21425
Schabers, 2274
Schaefer, 9664
Schaefer Ms Label, 28865
Schaerer, 28869
Scharffenberger, 9677
Schell's, 796
Schepps Dairy, 11281
Schermer, 14023
Schiff, 11285
Schiff Food, 11284
Schlafly, 11291
Schleicher, 28885
Schlitz, 9664
Schloss Doepken, 11293
Schluckwerder, 13676
Schmerling, 13931
Schmidt, 28893
Schneider, 6379
Schneider Foods, 11300
Schneider's, 11298
Schnitzius, 1064
Schnucks, 11303, 28896
Scho-Ko-Lade, 1957
Schoemaker, 9027
Schoep's, 11305
Scholar, 20981
Scholl, 10598
Schoner, 11368
Schonwald, 26932, 26933
School Chioce, 11308, 28903
School Milk, 13647
School Milk!, 4290
Schooner, 7123
Schott, 26932

Schott Zwiesel, 26933
Schrafft's, 1638
Schramsberg, 11307
Schreiber, 11308, 28903
Schreiber, 11504, 29095
Schug, 11309
Schugi, 19576
Schuil Coffee, 11310
Schumann's, 13676
Schuss, 2815, 20685
Schwab, 11315
Schwan's, 11316
Schwan's Chef Collection, 11316
Schwan's, 11317
Schwarteau, 13676
Schwartz, 8061
Schwebel's, 11318
Schwebel's Organic, 11318
Schwebel's Selects, 11318
Schweppes, 3725, 6818, 24802
Schwepps, 2815, 20685
Sci, 12130
Sciabica's Oil of the Olive, 9040
Science Foods, 9510
Sck, 28668
Sclafani, 13437
Scones, 12936
Sconza, 11320
Scooby Doo, 1591
Scoop Away, 2766, 20657
Scoop It, 22712
Scoop-N-Bake, 20096
Scoopy, 6614
Scope, 12721, 30193
Scora S.A., 1692
Scoralite, 1692
Scoresby Scotch, 3570
Scorned Woman, 5520, 13454
Scorpio, 28919
Scotch, 18003
Scotch Ale, 4950
Scotch Painter's Tape, 18003
Scotch Print, 30512
Scotch-Brite, 18003
Scotcheroons, 12096
Scotian Gold, 11322
Scotsburn, 11211
Scotslants, 28930
Scotsman, 28922
Scott, 24839
Scott & Jon's, 2477
Scott Country, 8542
Scott Pete, 11902
Scott Turbon, 28931
Scott's, 11326, 11328, 11330, 13700, 31165
Scott's Barbeque Sauce, 11329
Scott's of Wisconsin, 11330
Scott-A.D.A.'s Brailleters, 28930
Scott-Elites, 28930
Scott-Thins, 28930
Scott-Trax, 28930
Scottex, 24838
Scottie, 11330
Scottish, 1720
Scotts, 24672
Scottsdale Mustard Co, 4839
Scotty Ii, 19798
Scotty Wotty's, 11332
Scourlite, 19053
Scout 20, 27045
Scramblettes, 3449
Scrapmaster, 28770
Scratch Recipe, 8724
Scratch-Guard, 18548
Scray's Cheese,,11333
Screamer, 11320
Screamin' Sicilian Pizza Co., 9719
Screen-Flo, 23857
Screeners, 28917
Screw-Lift, 28936
Screwballs, 28425
Screwloose, 21051
Scrollware, 23499
Scrub 'n Shine, 18387

Scrub Pac, 27679
Scrub-Vactor, 21091
Scrubbe, 29617
Scrubs In-A-Bucket, 24035
Scully, 9439
Sculptathane, 30914
Sculptured Ice, 29055
Scultahyde, 30914
Sdb, 30398
Sdl, 30398
Sdx, 21495
Sdx Iii, 21495
Sea Bag, 19936
Sea Best, 1140
Sea Breeze, 11339, 28940
Sea Cakes, 7788
Sea Chest, 11102
Sea Chips, 7788
Sea Choice, 9344
Sea Cuisine, 5844
Sea Devils, 666
Sea Dog, 11340
Sea Farer, 11559
Sea Gold, 11343
Sea Maid, 11238
Sea Market, 6390
Sea Mist, 3097, 25165
Sea Pearl, 8785
Sea Pearl Seafood Co., Inc., 11347
Sea Ray, 7583
Sea Salad, 857
Sea Salt Superstore, 11351
Sea Seasonings, 7788
Sea Snack, 11352
Sea Spray, 9165
Sea Valley, 5479
Sea Vegetables, 7788
Sea View, 3565
Sea Watch International, 20020
Sea-View, 24945
Seabear, 11358
Seablends, 9980
Seaboard Farms, 11363
Seabreeze, 11102
Seabrook Farms, 11365
Seabrook, 11378, 28946
Seabulk Powerliner, 27706
Seacure, 27902
Seafest, 6267
Seafood, 13943
Seafood Magic, 7766, 25632
Seafood People, 9731
Seafood Sisters, 12742
Seafreez, 1057
Seaglass, 25665
Seagram's, 2815, 20685
Seagram's Escapades, 9117
Seagram's Extra Dry Ginc, 9964
Seagrams, 10151
Seagull Bay, 11238
Seajoy, 11378, 28946
Seakist, 9980
Seal N' Serve, 23379
Seal the Seasons, 28950
Seal Weld, 20750
Seal-Tite, 28953
Seal-Top, 24855
Sealcup, 23142
Seald Sweet, 6081, 11381
Sealed Air, 27655
Sealgard, 27499
Sealicious, 5325
Sealina Spa, 11351
Sealproof, 29796
Sealstar, 28468
Sealstrip, 28957
Sealtest, 6204, 8815, 24221
Seaman Orchard, 4506
Seapak, 10714
Seaperfect, 11360
Seapoint Edamama, 10229
Seaport, 12650
Seaport Blush, 12142
Seaport White, 12142
Seaport Wines, 12142

All Brands Index

Seapro, 3891
Sear 'n Smoke, 5473
Searchlight, 9344
Seaside, 5479, 6508
Season Brand, 7848
Season Opener, 6880
Season-Ettes, 10422
Seasonc, 11384
Seasoned Cheddar Cheese, 13320
Seasoned Delux, 6486
Seasoned Jack Cheese, 13320
Seasonedcrisp, 6374, 24434
Seasoning Salt, 4148
Seasonings From Hell, 11873
Seasonmaster, 22166
Seaspecialties, 10252
Seassentials, 1500
Seastix, 5483
Seatech, 11386
Seattle Bar, 11388
Seattle Chocolates, 11389
Seattle Series, 30043
Seattle's Best Coffee, 8090, 12042
Seavey Cabernet Sauvignon, 11394
Seavey Chardonnay, 11394
Seavey Marlot, 11394
Seawatch, 11356
Seawater Soaked Potato Chips, 11396
Seawave, 8504
Seaway, 3484
Seca-Pax, 30451
Sechler's, 10545
Second Nature Plus, 28666
Second Nature, 1103
Secret, 12721, 30193
Secret Garden, 11402
Secret Sun, 12234
Securcode Ii, 20910
Secure Panic Hardware, 28828
Secureflo, 342
Securely Yours, 27260
Securi Seal, 31142
Security, 18622
Security Peg Hook, 30259
Securlume, 25224
Sedgefield, 7743
Seditol, 6236
Sedna, 6726
Sedona Baking Company, 10760
See's Candies, 11407
Seeclear, 13498
Seedpak, 25074
Seeds & Suds, 8154
Seeds of Change, 7952
Seely, 4626, 11664
Seepex, 28981
Segafredo Espresso, 11212
Segafredo Zanetti, 7995
Segal, 30603
Segal Winery, 10952
Seghesio, 11413
Segma-Flo, 26111
Segma-Pure, 26111
Segura Viudas, 4693
Sei, 28672
Seitenbacher, 1957
Select, 11416
Select Blend In-Room Coffee, 11855
Select Origins, 6806
Select Recipe, 6374, 24434
Select Wax, 23828
Select-A-Horn/Strobe, 18185
Select-A-Strobe, 18185
Selecta, 856
Selectacom, 30427
Selectech 32 Controls, 30427
Selectrak, 22173
Selectware, 24044
Self Service System, 30376
Selford, 23160
Sell Strip, 22473
Sella & Mosca, 27236
Selleck, 2044
Sellers, 29004
Sello, 13320

Sello Rojo, 10777, 28421
Seltzers, 9729
Semco, 29009
Semdiero, 11557
Semi-Industrialized, 12185
Semiflex, 30732
Seminole, 11428
Sempio, 11429
Senate Beer, 9437
Senators Club, 7146
Seneca, 9167
Seneca Blend, 4403
Seneca Snacks, 11434
Senor Cane, 5755
Senor Felix's, 11437
Senor Paprika, 13648, 31107
Senor Rico, 7168
Senorio De Lazan, 3545
Senorio De Los Llanos, 3545
Sensamatic, 31340
Sensas, 25147
Sensation, 19741
Sensations, 6394, 23809
Sense, 3545
Sensible Carbs, 3836
Sensible Delights, 2726
Sensible Options, 8236
Sensible Portions, 5505
Sensibly Indulgent Cupcakes, 20096
Sensient, 11444
Sensitech, 20290
Sensorvision, 30518
Sentinel, 27655, 29030, 29185
Sentio, 21004
Sentrex, 29583
Sentrol 3l, 27365
Sentrol Em3, 27365
Sentron, 29032
Sentry, 23911, 28816, 30516
Sentry Ii, 23911, 27352
Sentry Seal, 26969
Sentry/Sentry Plus, 29185
Senza, 6806
Separators, 24357
Seppelt, 12937
Sepr, 23209
Sepro Flow, 19739
Sepro Kleen, 19739
Sepro Pure, 19739
Septic Clean, 19364
Sequoia Grove, 11449
Serco, 24607
Sergeant, 19183
Series 9000, 18066
Series S, 26325
Series U, 20047
Series100, 18195
Series4000, 18195
Series6000c, 18195
Serious Foodie, 11455
Serious Kick, 4820
Sermia, 29047
Serrano, 12004
Serranos, 4375
Serranos Salsa, 11456
Serrico, 24274
Sertote, 29050
Serv & Seal, 28957
Serv 'n Express, 25094
Serv 'r Call, 26433
Serv-A-Car, 18419
Serv-Ease, 29299
Servco, 29052
Serve-N-Seal, 21027
Servend, 29042
Server's Choice, 457
Servi-Shelf, 20121
Service First, 30382
Service Manufacturing, 29056
Service Solutions Series, 22320
Serving Stone, 23288
Servo Ii, 23669
Servo-Pak, 27565
Servo/Fill, 26852

Servomatic, 31300
Servotronic, 19798
Sesa-Krunch, 5462
Sesame Birch Sticks, 2108
Sesame Seed, 5462
Sesame Street, 608
Sesamin, 3615
Sesmarkc, 9748
Session, 4786
Session Roasted Coffees, 2874
Set Mark, 29072
Set-N-Serve, 19166
Set-O-Swiv, 23261
Setria, 7017
Setter, 11263
Setterstix, 29074
Setton Farms, 11469
Setton Farms Chewy Bites, 11469
Seven Barrell, 11470
Seven Hills, 11472
Seven Keys, 11473
Seven Seas, 498
Seven-Up, 181, 9083, 10151
Sevigny, 4198
Seville, 23842
Sew 400, 18127
Sew 800, 18127
Sewansecott, 12634
Sexpresso, 912
Seydelmann, 28291
Seyval Blanc, 2761
Seyval Naturel, 2761
Sf-400, 31058
Sfizio Crotonese, 11668
Sg General, 28915
Sgti, 11778
Shabadoo Black and Tan Ale, 1237
Shade Grown Organic, 8612
Shade Tree, 29088
Shadow, 18185
Shadow Mountain Foods, Inc., 2899
Shady Grove Orchards, 11491
Shafer Vineyards, 11494
Shake 'n Bake, 6976
Shaken Country Meadows Sweets, 5874
Shakequik, 7870
Shakers Prepackaged Accessories, 19999
Shaklee Carotomax, 11501
Shaklee Flavomax, 11501
Shal-O-Groove, 29379
Shalina, 11897
Shallon Winery, 11502
Shamiana, 6026
Shamrock, 4143, 12972
Shamrock Farms, 11504, 29095
Shana Spice, 2499
Shandy, 1208
Shang Pin, 734
Shank, 28967
Shape Ups, 6338
Shari Candies, 12547
Shariann's Italian White Beans, 11518
Shariann's Refried Beans, 11518
Shariann's Spicy Vegetable, 11518
Sharifa Halal, 11058
Sharkinator, 7554
Sharp 'n' Easy, 22784
Sharp Cheddar Cheese, 806
Sharp Gouda, 13840
Sharp's, 8459
Sharp's, 8460
Sharples, 18557
Sharpshooter, 18221
Shashi, 11522, 29116
Shasta, 8784, 11524
Shastebury, 9391
Shat-R-Shield, 29117
Shaw, 11525
Shaw's, 570
Shaw-Box, 20752
Shawnee Best, 11529
Shawnee Mills, 11529
Shawnee Springs, 11528
Shear Flow, 26918
Shear Pak, 21069

Shear Sharp, 22784
Shearer, 6928
Sheba, 7952
Sheboygan Sausage Company, 457
Sheboygan Sausage Company, 10893
Sheen Master, 28646
Sheffa, 11533
Shei Brand, 8613
Sheila's Select Gourmet Recipes, 1126, 11536
Sheinman, 11537
Shelby Williams, 20777
Shelf Clean A-1, 26000
Shelf-Aid, 12553
Shelfnet, 21931
Shell Fm Fluids and Greasers, 22231
Shell-Ex, 28834
Shellac, 300
Shelleyglass, 21498
Shelleymatic, 21498
Shelly Williams Seating, 21561
Shelly's Hair Care, 5682
Shelter Pale Ale, 3644
Shelton's, 11542
Shelving By the Inch, 18702
Shemper Seafood, 11543
Shenandoah, 11544, 13720
Shenandoah Vineyards, 11774
Shenk's, 11546
Shephard Ridge, 12099
Shepherd, 11547
Shepherd Supreme, 11547
Shepherd's Pride, 8601
Shephody, 3216
Sherbrooke Oem, 25964
Shercan, 29139
Sherpa Pinkc, 11145
Sherrill, 11551
Shields, 26756
Shiloh Winery, 10952
Shimmer, 26199
Shimp, 25349
Shine-Off, 18387
Shiner Blonde, 11942
Shiner Bock, 4881, 11942
Shiner Dunkelweizen, 11942
Shiner Hefeweizen, 11942
Shiner Kolsch, 11942
Shiner Light, 11942
Shiner Premium, 4881
Shingle Peak, 12937
Shinglgard, 28448
Shinglwrap, 28448
Shining Choice, 11559
Shiny Sinks Plus, 19434
Ship 'n Shop, 20192
Ship Wise, 25407
Shirakabe Gura, 12500
Shire Gate, 4321, 22498
Shirley Foods, 11565
Shirley's, 11023
Shitake Mushroom Soup Mixes (4), 6433
Shmolives, 1754
Shnuts., 1754
Sho Chiku Bai, 6673, 12500
Sho-Bowls, 24044
Sho-Me, 27821
Shock Switch, 29158
Shock Top, 571
Shock Top Belgian White, 26668
Shock Watch, 29158
Shockmaster, 18532
Shoei, 11567
Shoes For Crews, 29159
Shok-Stop, 30228
Shonan, 11568
Shooters Made Easy, 19998
Shop Master, 22920
Shop Rite, 6126
Shopsy's, 7875, 7876
Shoreline Fruit, 786
Short Stop, 23515
Short-Stop, 19082
Shortbread Housf, 2507
Shortening Shuttle, 31334

All Brands Index

Shotball, 4515
Shotskies Gelatin Mixes, 19999
Shove-It Rods, 25819
Show Patrol, 20498
Show-Off, 30393
Showboat, 7571
Showcase, 6391
Shower Patrol Plus, 20498
Showtime, 31010
Shpickles, 1754
Shrimp Butler, 6796
Shrimp Jammers, 12520
Shrimp Magic, 7766, 25632
Shrimp Teazers, 12520
Shrimperfect, 27718
Shrink Bags, 30369
Shrink Bands & Preforms, 30369
Shuckman's Fish Co. & Smokery, Inc., 4321, 22498
Shufflo, 19169
Shur Fine, 12885, 30333
Shur-Grip, 26440
Shur-Wipe, 23160
Shurfine, 10098
Shurtape Brand, 29171
Shurtenda, 14043
Sicao, 1056
Sick Day, 7526
Sicli, 20290
Sico, 29178
Sid and Roxie's, 5364
Side Swipe Spatula, 24700
Sideboard Sweets & Savories, 5140
Sideglow, 29794
Sidehill Farm, 11584
Sidewinders, 6374, 24434
Sidney, 29180
Sidral Mundet, 12823
Sidul, 3666
Sidul, 12196
Siebler, 22299
Sierra, 11589
Sierra Gourmet, 11985
Sierra Madre Brand, 3838
Sierra Madre Honey Co., 13971
Sierra Mist, 9945, 27433
Sierra Nevada, 1748
Sierra Nevada Bigfoo, 11592
Sierra Nevada Celebration, 11592
Sierra Nevada Pale Ale, 11592
Sierra Nevada Stout, 11592
Sierra Nevada Summer, 11592
Sierra Nevada, 26668
Sierra Sausage Co., 6770
Sierra Spring Foods, 10943
Sierra Springs, 10303, 27797
Sierra Springs, 3220, 3319
Sierra Vista, 11593
Sierra Springs, 11889
Siesta, 8161
Siesta Shade Market Umbrellas, 26404
Siete, 11594
Sifers Valomilk Candy Cups, 11595
Siggi's, 9789
Sight Line, 22039
Sightech, 28690
Sigma, 2839, 20694
Sigma Plates, 18197
Sigmark, 30841
Sigmastar, 18197
Sigmatec, 18197
Sigmatherm, 18197
Signal 369, 5363
Signature, 21817, 26450, 27711
Signature Cafe, 11073
Signature Care, 11073
Signature Farms, 11073
Signature Reserve, 11073
Signature Select, 20256
Signature Select, 11073
Signature Series, 23482
Signet, 21915
Signette, 27216
Signorello, 11604
Sil-A-Gran, 11607

Silarom, 11607
Silcard, 29228
Silent Service, 21362
Siler's, 12973, 30444
Silesia, 29219
Silfoam, 1692
Silform, 21533
Silhouette, 22272
Silhouette, 13595, 31053
Siljans, 11608, 13676
Silk, 3379, 11281, 13734
Silk Soy, 8815
Silk Tassel, 3024
Silpat, 21533
Silvan Ridge, 11612
Silvanil, 11607
Silver, 6395
Silver Creek, 4506
Silver Fleece, 5893, 5894
Silver Fox Vineyard, 11618
Silver King, 29233, 29234
Silver Label, 2708
Silver Label Cabernet Sauvigno, 869
Silver Lake, 4244
Silver Mtn Vineyards, 11621, 29235
Silver Palate, 11623
Silver Ridge, 1738
Silver Salmon, 11602
Silver Seyual, 1688
Silver Shield, 20608
Silver Sonic, 23222
Silver Spring, 10151
Silver Spur, 9500
Silver Streak, 11629, 24635
Silver Sword, 18022
Silver Thunder Malt Liquor, 9664
Silver Tray Cookies, 11631
Silver-Grip, 29854
Silver-Span, 29854
Silver-Sweet, 29854
Silver-Weibull, 29238
Silverado Cellars, 2461
Silverbow, 11633
Silverland Desserts, 11634
Silverpak, 18298
Silvers, 4348
Silverson, 29239
Silverstone, 22935
Silvo, 8061
Simarotor, 31113
Simi Ravenswood, 4649
Similac Toddler's Best, 18257
Simmer Kettle, 11919
Simmonds, 5325
Simmons, 11639
Simon, 10461
Simon Fischer, 11788, 29340
Simon's, 3696, 11643
Simonazzi, 28832
Simons, 10461
Simor, 22588
Simpkins, 13676
Simplate, 24070
Simple Beginnings, 12056
Simple Eats, 5141
Simple Elegance, 10981
Simple Mills, 11646
Simple Nevada, 10435
Simple Smart, 5486
Simple Solutions, 19150
Simplesse, 1962
Simplex, 19634, 20121, 21541, 26049, 29251, 29252
Simpli-Clean, 29254
Simpli-Flex, 29254
Simpli-Pak, 29254
Simpli-Pal, 29254
Simpli-Snap, 29254
Simplicity, 31246
Simplot, 1891
Simplot Classic, 6374, 24434
Simplot Daily Pick, 6374, 24434
Simplot Good Grains, 6374, 24434
Simplot Harvest Fresh Avocados, 6374, 24434

Simplot Simple Goodness, 6374, 24434
Simplot Sweets, 6374, 24434
Simplot Thunder Crunch, 6374, 24434
Simplux, 22039
Simply, 4741, 10435
Simply Asia, 8061
Simply Delicious, 13892
Simply Devine, 3550
Simply Divine, 11651
Simply Done, 12885, 30333
Simply Food, 29256
Simply Fresh, 4461
Simply Gold, 6374, 24434
Simply Lite, 5694
Simply Natural, 2509, 3945
Simply Natural-Like, 3945
Simply Natural-Like, 13614
Simply Natural, 13614
Simply Orange, 2814
Simply Organic, 4752
Simply Potatoes, 8225
Simply Ranch Classic Ranch, 5489
Simply Ranch Cucumber Basil, 5489
Simply Rich, 7424
Simply Saline, 2666, 20561
Simply Smart Organics, 9946
Simply Spice, 14024
Simply Supreme Organic, 13894
Simplywell, 6676
Simpson Technology, 20599
Sin Fill, 8247, 26074
Sinai Gourmet, 11662
Sinatra, 5717
Sinbad Sweets, 11663
Sincera Skin Care Products, 11268
Sincerity, 1606, 6869
Sine Pump, 29261
Sinfire Cinnamon Whisky, 5981
Singel Serving Sundae, 3541
Singers Saving Grace, 5791
Single Origin, 1054
Single Serv, 3574
Singleton Seafoods, 10603
Singletree Farms, 6334
Sini Fulvi, 11668
Sinkmaster, 18892
Sintra, 21848
Sioux, 29263
Sioux City, 13728
Sioux City Sarsaparilla, 13728
Sip, 4081
Sip-N-Chew, 469
Sipco Dunking Station, 29266
Siplace, 21536
Sipp, 11670
Sipsmith, 1120
Sir, 31175
Sir Citrus, 13184
Sir Dust-A-Lot, 25668
Sir Flip Flop, 25479
Sir Francis Stout, 3746
Sir George Fudge, 6787
Siracuse, 4148
Sirah, 9889
Sirco, 23357
Sirena, 30462
Sirius Ttr, 3833, 21863
Sirnap, 23160
Sisler's Dairy, 11675
Sister Schubert's, 7189, 12467, 25120
Sister Schuberts, 7987
Sisters Gourmet, 11679
Sisu, 8871
Sitka Gold, 11375
Sivetz Coffee Essence, 11680, 29272
Six Mile Creek, 11681
Six Shooter, 26697
Six Star, 20256
Sjora, 8945
Sk 2000, 29623
Sk 2500, 29623
Sk 3000, 29623
Sk 3400, 29623
Sk 3600 Rock, 29623
Sk-Ii, 12721, 30193

Skat, 23950
Skcs, 27457
Skedaddle, 11683
Skee, 22065
Ski, 3707
Skilcraft, 25305
Skillet Style, 20050
Skim Plus, 4290, 13647
Skin Armor, 21768
Skincredibles, 6374, 24434
Skinner Bakery, 6448
Skinner's, 13124, 19178
Skinner, 10777, 28421
Skinny, 4957
Skinny Dipped Almonds, 13786
Skinny Sticks, 3862
Skinny Truffles, 11389
Skinny Water, 9858
Skinnygirl, 1120
Skinnygirl, 864
Skins, 3320
Skippy, 3574
Skippy, 6000, 23861
Skirt Tie, 27134
Skittles, 6483, 7952, 13960
Skjodt-Barrett, 11691
Skol, 11264
Skor, 5818, 23750
Skull, 961
Skull & Bones, 10435
Sky Master, 18321
Sky Valley, 11694
Sky Vineyards, 11695
Skye, 26235
Skyland, 13720
Skylark, 457
Skylark, 10893
Skylume, 25224
Skyy, 2114
Skyy Vodka, 3545
Sl Laboratory, 28915
Sl Nt, 29030
Sl Test, 20454
Slane Irish Whiskey, 1784
Slap Ya Mama, 2019
Slater's 50/50 Bacon Burger, 6492
Slawsa, 11703
Slc, 11642
Sledgehammer, 12937
Sleeman, 9391
Sleep'n Bag, 20256
Sleepeasy, 9182
Sleepless In Seattle Coffee, 270
Slender, 6310
Slendo, 7978
Slide Pops, 4255
Slide-Rite, 21027
Slim, 5897
Slim 'n' Trim, 4873
Slim Diez, 6811
Slim Jim, 2939, 2940, 20821, 20822
Slim Line Cubers, 28922
Slim Shake, 15
Slim-Fast, 13167
Slimcado Avocado, 1757
Slimdown, 6449, 24506
Slimline, 22074
Slimmilk, 25784
Slimmilk Lf, 25784
Slinky Brand Candy, 2136
Slip, 20192
Slip-Torque, 29175
Slip-Trak, 29175
Slipnot, 29283
Slipstick, 30452
Slo Poke, 756
Slo-Roast Deli, 7876
Sloppy Joe, 4428
Slotkowski, 523
Slow Ride Ipa, 8959
Slush Puppie, 6338
Slush Puppie, 6483
Slushade, 6971
Sm La San Marco, 7995
Smack Cup-A-Ramen, 13170

1332

All Brands Index

Smack Ramen, 13170
Small Batch, 11710
Small Planet Foods, 2286
Small Talk Conversation Hearts, 4032
Smallpics, 29857
Smart, 23866
Smart 300, 18221
Smart Bacon, 7427
Smart Balance, 5837
Smart Balance, 1612, 2939, 2940, 13328, 20821, 20822, 27540
Smart Bbq, 7427
Smart Chart, 21582
Smart Chiken, 12596
Smart Chili, 7427
Smart Choice, 30775
Smart Cookies, 1409
Smart Crackers, 1409
Smart Cup, 29068
Smart Cutlets, 7427
Smart Deli, 7427
Smart Dogs, 7427
Smart Factory, 26818
Smart Flow Meter, 24664
Smart Force Transducer, 24664
Smart Frame, 22121
Smart Gourmet, 4699
Smart Ground, 7427
Smart Hands, 26122
Smart Harvest, 12528
Smart Hood, 25008
Smart Ii, 26262
Smart Kids, 5917
Smart Links, 7427
Smart Lock, 25910
Smart Safe 2000, 25910
Smart Sausage, 7427
Smart Scaling, 19139
Smart Seal, 29068
Smart Shaker, 24812
Smart Single, 26031
Smart System 5, 20048
Smart Tenders, 7427
Smart Track, 26031
Smart Wall, 26031
Smart Water, 4066
Smart Wings, 7427
Smart-Ro, 31031
Smart Flavours, 10797, 28438
Smartbasket, 31177
Smartblade, 23267
Smartbox, 28118
Smartcake, 4957
Smartchocolates, 4795
Smarteye, 30422
Smartfood, 4741
Smartfood, 9945, 27433
Smartfruit, 17
Smartgels, 6676
Smarties, 11716
Smarties, 8945
Smartreader, 18112
Smartreader Plus, 18112
Smartscan, 18995
Smartshapes, 1654
Smartvision, 18112
Smartware, 23809
Smartwater, 2811
Smash Mallow, 11717
Smashpop, 11754
Smc, 29180
Smetco, 29289
Smile Brite, 7562
Smint, 9956
Smith, 11726
Smith & Forge Hard Cider, 8460
Smith & Hook Winery, 5499
Smith & Wesson, 24839
Smith and Forge, 8459
Smith Berger, 29297
Smith Dairy, 13604
Smith Home Cured, 167
Smith's, 11725, 11729, 12516
Smith-Madrone, 11732
Smithfield, 11053, 11733

Smithfield Farmland, 11504, 29095
Smithfield Tavern, 9871, 12714
Smithworks Vodka, 9964
Smitten, 1196
Smog-Hog, 30626
Smoke & Fire, 11735
Smoke It All, 9344
Smoke Right, 29302
Smoke-Master, 24414
Smoked Eggplant Sprat,, 9863
Smoked Habanero Pretzels, 3393
Smoked Porter, 339
Smoked Salmon, 2189
Smoked Spices, 2189
Smokeeter, 30626
Smokehouse, 1471, 19742
Smokehouse 220, 13328
Smokehouse Favorite, 3177
Smokeless Blackened Seasoning, 2022
Smokemaster, 18496
Smokey Mesquite, 2511
Smoking Gun, 22473
Smoky Mountain, 7684
Smoky Mountain Trail Rub, 6796
Smoky Valley, 2511
Smoky's House, 12178
Smooth & Creamy, 437
Smooth & Melty, 13676
Smooth and Melties, 13845
Smooth-N-Melty, 5428
Smoothie Sparkling Choc.Egg Cream, 2410
Smothers/Remick Ridge, 11741
Smucker's, 6380
Smucker's Natural, 6380
Smucker's Toppings, 6380
Smucker's Uncrustables, 6380
Smuttynose Belgian W, 11743
Smuttynose Robust Po, 11743
Snack Bites, 11228, 28829
Snack Factory, 11744
Snack Factory Pretzel Chips, 11770
Snack Factory Pretzel Crisps, 2116
Snack Fu, 12841
Snack Rite, 20238
Snack Zone, 23600
Snack-Mate, 19882
Snackin Fruits, 11311
Snackmasters, 11746
Snacknut, 1027
Snackwell'sD, 864
Snackwells, 8729
Snak King, 11748
Snak N'Go, 9668
Snak Sales, 10196
Snake River, 11749
Snake Shelving, 25023
Snap, 24070
Snap Drape, 19354
Snap'n Clip, 27575
Snap'n Stack, 29318
Snap-Back, 13052
Snap-Ins, 28930
Snap-Lock, 26442
Snap-N-Serve, 29318
Snapoff, 20882
Snappers, 3958
Snapple, 1294, 5975, 20946
Snapple, 3725, 6818, 24802
Snappy, 12957, 18387
Snappy's, 5902
Snaps, 469
Snapshot Universal Atp Sample Test, 23971
Snapshot Wheat, 8959
Snapware, 29318
Snausages, 6380
Sneezeguard, 29320
Snickers, 8533
Snickers, 7952
Sniff-O-Miser, 23900
Snikiddy, 13129
Snips, 11415
Sno Pac, 11758
Sno Van, 23515

Sno-Bal, 12866
Sno-Ball, 8795
Sno-E Tofu, 13286
Sno-Top, 6253, 13183
Sno-White, 23261
Snobanc, 30390
Snocap, 8693
Snoee, 24499
Snokist, 11759
Snolite, 11756
Snoodles, 13170
Snopan, 30390
Snow Ball Ice Shavers, 20607
Snow Cod, 6387
Snow Farms, 13006
Snow Flake, 11177
Snow Goose, 3033
Snow Monkey, 11762
Snow Proof, 22538
Snow White, 833
Snow's Nice Cream, 11763
Snowberry, 12721, 30193
Snowbird, 11764
Snowcrest, 11766
Snowden, 3216
Snowite, 2123
Snowizard, 11756, 11767
Snowlily, 25725
Snowman, 1677
Snowqualmie Falls Lodge, 2971
Snowtime, 7732
Snuggler, 29083
Snugglers, 24838
Snyapa, 10869
Snyder's of Hanover, 2116, 11770
Snyder, 27540
So Clear, 10637
So Delicious, 3379
So Fruitty, 8840
So Good, 9042
So Joao, 10496
So Natural, 12928
So-Dri, 23160
So-Fresh, 29826
So-Good Bar-B-Q Delight, 3695
So-Good Pork Bar-B-Q, 3695
Soap-N-Scrub, 26116
Soauther, 12955
Soba, 11773
Sobe, 11772
Sobe, 9945, 27433
Soberdough, 1167
Sobo, 27157
Sobon Estate, 11774
Soccer Pops, 6158
Sochu Distilled Rice, 6968
Societe, 7126
Society Hill Gourmet Nut Company, 11775
Sockeye Nova, 13521
Soda Fountain, 1966
Soda Pops, 6803
Soda-Lo Salt Microspheres, 12561
Sodex, 3404
Sodia Lite, 19008
Sof-Ette, 28422
Sof-Knit, 23160
Sof-Pac, 20651
Sof-Pak, 24021
Sof-Tac, 21440
Sofgels, 1009
Sofgrain, 7585
Sofgrip, 21591
Soflet Gelcaps, 1009
Soft 'n Fresh, 23160
Soft 'n Gentle, 23160
Soft Bake, 6340
Soft Chews, 5017
Soft Cookies, 5909, 23825
Soft Flight, 29513
Soft Light, 20187
Soft Mac, 12895
Soft N Clean, 19008
Soft Square, 13256
Soft Touch, 21952

Soft White, 833
Soft-Sensor, 28361
Soft-Serve Ice Cream, 22892
Softasilk, 31010
Softform, 29660
Softliner, 26440
Softseal, 27499
Softsoap, 20721
Softstream, 28361
Softtouch, 29783
Softtread, 20120
Softweve McKnit, 25906
Sofwite, 27058
Sogevac, 26858
Soho Natural Lemonades, 11779
Soho Natural Soda &, 11779
Soil Sorb, 23261
Sokoff, 20427
Sokol Blosser, 11780
Sol Cerveza, 8460
Sol De Oro, 7062
Sol-Mex, 8161
Sol-Zol, 21080
Sola, 12730
Solae, 3773, 21785
Solait, 5629
Solana Gold, 11782
Solana Gold Organics, 11782
Solar, 4761
Solar Infrared Heater, 20330
Solar System, 20498
Solaray, 9237, 26785
Soldans, 13676
Soleil-Late Harvest Sauvignon, 3771
Solerac, 11894, 29459
Solero, 6288
Solfresco, 12973, 30444
Solgar, 11785
Solgar, 8871
Solgel, 12637
Solid Elastomer, 21352
Solid Flow Vibratory Feeders, 28875
Solid Protein, 8870
Solid White Albacore Tuna, 12046
Solidome, 28251
Solidsflow, 28876
Solis, 11786
Solkafloc, 11794
Solnuts, 11787
Solo, 4976, 11788, 11789, 18592, 29340
Solo, 21362
Soloman, 11791
Solomon Glatt Kosher, 19716
Soloserve, 21362
Soluble Products, 11793
Soluflex, 3753, 21763
Solugel, 9649
Solutions For a Cleaner World, 30200
Solvaseal, 23529
Solvatrol, 1009
Solvex Expander, 18920
Solving, 18821
Solvit, 29348
Solvo-Miser, 23900
Somacount, 19575
Somaguard, 13746
Somaguard Premium Grape Extract, 13746
Somat, 24038
Somat Classic, 20984
Somat Evergreen, 20984
Somen, 11773
Somerdale, 11365
Somerset, 29352
Somethin' Special, 29101
Something Natural, 11797
Something Special Gourmet Antipasto, 11798
Somewhat Sinful, 11144
Sominus, 13273
Sommer's Food, 11800
Sonac, 3390
Sonargage, 21103
Sonarswitch, 21103
Sonavavitch, 4515

1333

All Brands Index

Song Bird, 12663
Sonic Dried Yeast, 8726
Sonic Eye, 21004
Sonic, 6483
Sonisift, 18187
Sonitrol, 29584
Sonny's Pride, 11325
Sonocell, 30800
Sonolator, 29360
Sonoma, 12809
Sonoma Brewing, 3519
Sonoma Coast, 6892
Sonoma County Classics, 6974
Sonoma County Zinfandel, 5989
Sonoma Creamery, 11804
Sonoma Cuvee, 1543
Sonoma Extra Virgin Olive Oil, 869
Sonoma Foie-Gras, 5390
Sonoma Gourmet, 11806
Sonoma Jack, 11804
Sonoma Organics, 11804
Sonoma Pacific, 4854
Sonoma Syrups, 11899, 29468
Sonoma Valley Merlot, 869
Sonoma Valley Zinfandel, 869
Sonoma Wine, 11809
Sonoma-Cutrer, 1784
Sony Chemicals, 30186
Soo, 6347
Soot-A-Matic, 23275
Soot-Vac, 23275
Sootherbs, 6107
Sootmaster, 25840
Sopakco, 11049, 24672
Sophia, 11814, 29372
Sophia's Authentic, 11815
Sophia's Sauce Works, 11815
Sophie Mae, 756
Sophisticated Chocol, 3396
Sorb Pak, 30633
Sorb-It, 26401, 30633
Sorbee, 11817
Sorbet By Yo Cream, 3378
Sorbeteer, 22892
Sorbicap, 26381
Sorengeti Coffees, 11855
Sorento, 280
Sores, 12196
Sorrell Flavours, 6115
Sorrenti Family Farm, 11818
Sorrento Valley Organics, 2772
Sort Director, 21536
Sortex, 29377
Sos, 23998
Sotac, 6917
Souena, 7051
Sound Sea Vegetables, 2630
Sound Sleep, 7422
Soup Bowl, 13240
Soup For Singles, 11402
Soup Supreme, 8724
Souper 1 Step, 24948
Soupergirl, 11822
Soups For One, 9434
Sour Apple, 9773
Sour Cotton Candy Swirl, 12547
Sour Patch Kids, 6338, 6483
Sour Patch Kids Cereal, 10213
Sour Pops, 6803
Sour Punch, 469
Sour Simon, 12985
Source, 11824, 14017
Source of Life, 5065
Sourdough Bread Enha, 7540
Sourz, 1120
South Beach, 5975
South Bend, 26131
South Bend Chocolate, 11828
South Ceasar Dressing Company, 11829
South Hills, 5728
South Mill Mushroom Sales, 11832
South of the Border Chili, 5946
South Shore, 6537
South Side, 6537
South Texas Spice, 11834

South Valley Manufacturing, 29393
South West, 11872
Southampton, 10482
Southbend, 26132, 26476, 29395
Southeastern Meats, 11053
Southeastern Mills, 11839
Southern, 2019
Southern Biscuit, 10675
Southern Breeze, 11454
Southern Breeze, 5612
Southern Chef, 12300
Southern Comfort, 4422, 11263
Southern Dynamite, 12975
Southern Gold Honey, 11854
Southern Harvest, 5492
Southern Heritage, 11855
Southern Pride, 11862, 29418
Southern Ray's, 1850
Southern Recipe, 10966
Southern Select, 1654
Southern Sensations, 5520
Southern Sin, 12881
Southern Snow, 11867
Southern Special, 12428
Southern Spice, 9745
Southern Style, 6548, 11257
Southern Style Nuts, 11868
Southern Supreme, 6622
Southern Sweetenerc, 8088, 25922
Southern Swirl, 13728
Southern Twist, 11869
Southgate, 13402
Southwest, 25299
Souverain, 3834
Soy Cheese, 7419
Soy Deli, 10472
Soy Delicious Purely Decadent, 11771
Soy Dream, 3009
Soy Flax 5000, 13863
Soy Products, 2764, 20656
Soy Roast, 3548
Soy Supreme, 12294
Soy Treat, 7423
Soy Vay Veri-Veri Teriyaki, 11878
Soy Water, 4066
Soy-Liccous Meals, 8719
Soy-N-Ergy Soy Powders, 8993
Soy-Sation, 7458
Soyboy, 9160
Soydance, 12855, 12857
Soyfine, 2764, 20656
Soygold, 81
Soylife, 137
Soymilk, 2764, 20656
Soynut Crunch Bar, 6442
Soynuts, 6442
Soypreme, 2355
Soypro, 8719
Soypura, 13648, 31107
Soywise, 11881
Sp Precision, 28915
Sp-250 Flattener, 23117
Sp68, 31372
Spa, 13643, 27690
Space Case, 25966
Space Guard 2000, 29437
Space Savers, 22080
Space'saver, 29044
Space-Saver, 23884
Space-Trac, 26623
Spacemaster, 29706
Spacerak, 22283
Spacesaver, 20593, 29625
Spaghettios, 2116
Spam, 6000, 23861
Spangler Candy Canes, 11885
Spangler Chocolates, 11885
Spangler Circus Peanuts, 11885
Spangler Wineyards, 11886
Spanglers, 13803
Spanky's, 7924
Spann Signs, 29443
Spantrack, 30589
Spare-The-Ribs, 12065
Spark Bites, 3062

Sparklaid, 29444
Sparkle, 9183, 18024, 19995
Sparkle 'n' Glo, 31010
Sparkle-Lite, 19153
Sparkleen 310, 20489
Sparkler, 29444
Sparkletts, 10303, 27797
Sparkletts, 3220, 3319
Sparkling Avitae, 840
Sparkling Ice, 5884, 12510
Sparkling Live Drinking Vinegars, 7070
Sparks, 8459
Sparks, 8460
Sparrow Lane, 11864
Sparta, 19401, 20256
Spartan, 30790
Spaten, 11891
Spatter-Cote, 21080
Speas, 8414
Spec-Bar, 29467
Spec-Flex, 29467
Spec-Plus, 29467
Spec-Up, 29467
Spec-Vac, 29467
Spec-Zip, 29467
Special Brew, 9664
Special C-500, 7947
Special K, 6766
Special K, 6765
Special Old, 3024
Special Service Partners, 22187
Specialized Printed Forms, 22187
Specialty, 11895
Specialty Blends, 9743
Specialty Composites Ear, 27655
Specialty Farms, 406
Specialty Flour, 5946
Specialty Food Magazine, 11901
Specialty Grains, 9743
Specialty Minerals, 1692
Speckles, 4976
Speco, 19563, 21883
Specon, 22445
Spectrabiotic, 8967
Spectrum, 5505, 20256, 20642, 26749
Spectrum Nutritional Shake, 9251
Spee-Dee, 29482
Spee-Dee Pop, 10268
Speed Cover, 23770
Speed Energy Drink, 26668
Speed Squeegy, 26196
Speed Sweep, 26196
Speed Trek, 30503
Speed-Flow, 19659
Speed-Lift, 20121
Speed-Rak, 28231
Speedmaster, 22322, 25013
Speedry, 24059
Speedwall, 24021
Speedy Bag Packager, 18583
Speedy Bird, 6025
Speedy Cook'n, 9179
Speedy Mop, 26196
Spendida, 11777
Spendido Nuggets, 14045
Sphere, 24409
Spi-C-Mint, 10428
Spibro, 10651
Spice, 4362
Spice Bouquet, 1600
Spice Choice, 1547
Spice Garden, 8448
Spice Hunter, 8898, 11919, 25789
Spice Hunter Spices & Herbs, 11919
Spice Island, 25789
Spice Islands, 73, 4499
Spice Islands, 864
Spice Products, 4276
Spice Ranch, 1547
Spice So Rite, 12377
Spice Star, 1547
Spice Traderc, 8088, 25922
Spice World, 11926
Spiceland, 11927
Spicely, 473

Spiceman's, 9528
Spicery Shoppe Natural, 4488
Spicetec, 11930
Spicy and Hot Hickory Sausage, 2944
Spicy Olive, 6522
Spicy Wings, 14043
Spider-Man, 1591
Spiderman Cotton Candy, 12547
Spiderman Sour Gummi Mutant Spiders, 12547
Spiedie Sauce, 10784
Spike, 8448
Spin Blend, 4831
Spin-Pik, 27520
Spinbar, 19534
Spinbrush, 2666, 20561
Spindrift, 11102
Spindrift Sparkling Water, 11936
Spingtime, 11844
Spinnin' Spits, 24414
Spir-It, 29498
Spira/Flo, 21526
Spiraflow, 21044
Spiral Flow, 18527
Spiral Grip, 29211
Spiral-Flo, 24812
Spiralfeeder, 19212
Spirithouse, 659
Spiro-Freeze, 23075
Spiromatic, 19567
Spirulina Bee Bar, 7561
Spirulina Hawaiian Spirulina, 3281
Spirulina Pacifica, 9244
Spirulina Trail Bar, 7561
Spirutein, 5065
Spizzico Pepato Aged, 11668
Splash, 2054, 10134, 24409
Splash, 2740
Splenda Sucralose, 12561
Splendar, 8380
Splendid, 1962
Splendid Specialties Chocolate Co, 12894
Splendid Specialties Chocolates, 11940
Splendido, 6126
Splendido Biscotti, 14045
Splinter, 1517
Splitshot, 24064
Spm-45, 29352
Spohrers Bakeries, 11943
Sponge 'n Brush, 30481
Spongebob Squarepants, 4659
Spontaneous Combustion, 11873
Spontex, 29509
Spookyware, 22917
Spoon Fruit, 485
Spoon Toppers, 485
Spoonful of Flavors, 2134
Spoonty, 4148
Spor Tabs, 11947
Sporian, 28967
Sport Kote, 22272
Sport Mate, 29689
Sport Shake, 3335
Sport Stick, 19716
Sport Totoe 'ems, 4255
Sports Cap, 21069
Sports Juice, 9858
Sports Nutrition, 13146
Sports Trivia, 21059
Sportsmate, 24091
Sportsmen's Cannery, 11950
Spot Farms, 9946
Spotcheck Hygiene Surface Test, 23971
Spotcheck Plus Hygiene Surface Test, 23971
Spotir, 27325
Spotlight, 19910
Spoto, 29569
Spraco, 25203
Spray Ball, 20491
Spray Master Technologies, 19119
Spray-Kill With Nylar, 19364
Spraygum, 9029, 26626
Spraymaster, 25798

1334

All Brands Index

Spraymatic, 26411
Spraymist, 30315
Sprayway, 29517
Spread, 23160
Spreadable Fruit, 2679
Spreda, 11957
Spredlite, 22039
Spring Acres, 11958
Spring Blossom, 10478
Spring Bock, 11992
Spring Drops, 9237, 26785
Spring Farm, 9296
Spring Glen, 5555, 11960
Spring Glen Fresh Foods, 5555
Spring Hill Farms, 11973
Spring House, 4462
Spring Kitchen, 11964
Spring Splendor, 10061
Spring Tree, 864
Spring Valley, 8324
Springdale, 8414
Springerlies, 5756
Springfield, 10526
Springhill, 9174, 10383, 11972
Springrip, 27575
Springtide Ale, 8153
Springtime, 9839
Springtime Natural Artesian Water, 11844
Springwater Farms, 11850
Sprint, 26942
Sprinter, 29527
Sprite, 2811, 2814, 2815, 20685
Sprout Creek Farm, 11976
Sprout House & Salad, 11977
Sprouted, 563
Sproutman's Organic, 11977
Sprouts, 11979, 29528
Spruce Point, 3780
Sprycel, 1721
Sps, 22873
Sps 3000, 28683
Spud King, 9042
Spudsters, 6374, 24434
Spun Head, 25819
Spunbond, 23811
Spurgeon Vinyards, 11984
Squalene, 11269
Square, 1120
Square D, 28894
Square One, 743
Squawkers, 1654
Sque'easy, 4592
Squeaks, 2347
Squealing Pig, 12937
Squeezbox, 23273
Squeezers, 5735
Squirrel, 11990, 29535
Squirrel Brand, 6548, 11868
Squirrel Nut Caramel, 11990
Squirrel Nut Chew, 11990
Squirrel Nut Zippers, 11990
Squirt, 9083, 10151, 18835
Squirt, 3725, 6818, 24802
Squozen Frozen, 11654
Sqvalene, 21265
Sqwiggles, 12547
Sqwincher, 6792, 24785
Sqyer, 31010
Sqyntz! Supersourz, 7710
Sriracha Ranchc, 5489
Sro Feeder, 29763
Ssal, 21817
Ssal 2000, 20256
Ssi Robotics, 27083
Ssips, 6545
Sss, 12451
Sst, 25725
Ssw, 30398
St Huberts, 12937
St Peter's, 4148
St. Briogets Strong, 9688
St. Clair Ice Cream, 11994
St. Claire, 3925
St. Croix, 12004
St. Dalfour, 25789

St. Etienne, 5558
St. Hubert, 10331
St. Ides Special Brew, 9664
St. Innocent, 11996
St. James Winery, 12007
St. Joe Pork, 11363
St. Julien Macaroons, 13723
St. Laurent, 9693
St. Martin, 7592
St. Moriz, 20964
St. Nick's, 8784
St. Nicks Poter, 556
St. Ours, 12011
St. Paddy's, 339
St. Stan's Alt Beer, 12013
Sta Fresh, 8956
Sta Series, 28992
Sta-Dri, 18130
Sta-Flat, 23261
Sta-Fresh, 29826, 31433
Sta-Hot, 22712
Sta-Lite Polydextrose, 12561
Sta-Pack, 28992
Sta-Plyer, 25762
Sta-Rite, 29545
Stabak, 26504
Stabil, 8899
Stabilenhance, 8899, 10511
Stabilo, 13498
Stablebond, 6211, 24226
Stacey's, 12014
Stack-N-Roll, 23543
Stack-Sack, 27265
Stackable, 20256
Stackables, 18906
Stackers, 29289
Stacol, 26504
Stacy's, 4741
Stacy's Pita Chips, 9945, 27433
Stadium Mustard, 3407
Stage Coach Sauces, 29551
Stagg Chili, 6000, 23861
Staging Director, 21536
Stags' Leap, 12019
Stags' Leap Winery, 12937
Stahl Cranesystems, 20752
Stahl Meyer, 4244
Stahl-Meyer, 4351
Stain Devils, 21509
Stain Gun, 22473
Stain Stop, 21509
Stain Wizard, 21509
Stain Wizard Wipes, 21509
Stainless, 18594
Stainless One, 29558
Stainless Steel Bearings, 22890
Stainless Steel Trolleys, 22890
Stainless Steel X-Chain, 22890
Stakker, 23734
Stallion, 24575
Stallion X Malt Liquor, 2410
Stam, 2615
Stamere, 4773
Stampede, 6310, 12023, 29568
Stan Barth Farms, 2152
Stan-Pak, 24723
Stan-Ray, 29583
Stancase, 29572
Stand Out, 7526
Standard, 29572
Standard Coffee, 10303, 27797
Standard Coffee, 3319
Standard Econocut Die Cutters, 29574
Standard Excalibur Die Cutters, 29574
Standard Folder Gluers, 29574
Standard Formulation, 7172
Standard Knapp, 30935
Standard Lager, 8459
Standard Systems, 30109
Standard-Keil, 20800
Stanislaus Food Products, 20020
Stanley, 28649, 29584
Stanley's, 7490, 13696
Stapleton, 9182
Staplex, 29588

Star, 4243, 12035, 19803, 25216, 28471, 29592
Star Award Ribbon Co., 22187
Star Blend, 985
Star Brite, 26165
Star Caps, 985
Star Controls, 23952
Star Cross, 5894
Star Dairy, 13700, 31165
Star Guard, 31010
Star Hydrodyne, 29594
Star of David Pasta, 4794
Star Pager, 25421
Star Plus, 20256
Star Ranch Angus, 13109
Star Sucker Sour, 985
Star Suckers, 985
Star Systems, 20048
Star Track, 29866
Star-Van, 12085
Starborne, 23261
Starborough, 3834
Starbound, 10415
Starbucks, 8090
Starbucks Coffee, 12042
Starbucks Frappacino, 9945, 27433
Starbucks Hot Cocoa, 2950
Starburst, 7952, 13960
Starbursts, 6483
Starcross, 5893
Stardrops, 10496
Stargazer, 6711
Starkey, 29604
Starkist Flavor Fresh Pouch, 12046
Starkist Lunch To-Go, 12046
Starkist Select, 12046
Starkist Tuna Creations, 12046
Starline, 20633
Starlite, 23515
Starmax, 29596
Starmist, 30515
Staropramen, 8459
Starr, 19902
Starr Hill Amber Ale, 26668
Starrett, 25216
Starrey's Ion, 7490
Stars, 18849
Stars & Stripes, 6294, 10637
Stars Pride, 11198
Starters, 3696
Startex, 30517
Startwist, 30528
Starvac, 30517
Starvac Ii, 30517
Starvac Iii, 30517
Starview, 29607
Starwest, 12051
Stasero, 12052
Stash, 12053
Stash Premium Organic Teas, 12053
State, 11799
State Fair, 4928, 10784
State Fair, 13109
Static Guard, 864
Static Mixers, 24696
Stauffer's, 12060, 12061
Stawnichy's, 12063
Stay Well, 3919
Staylock, 21362
Staynap, 23160
Staysteady, 9548
Stb Stahlhammer Bommern, 20752
Std Precision Gear & Instrument, 28726
Steady-Mount, 30854
Steak Sauce, 9745, 21336
Steak-Eze, 184
Steak-Umm, 12065
Steak-Umm Sandwich To Go, 12065
Steakeze, 13109
Steakhouse, 13301
Steakhouse Style, 13653
Steakmarkers, 19999
Steakwich, 3549
Steakwich Lite, 3549
Stealth Fries, 7179, 25104

Steam & Serve, 6685
Steam 'n' Hold, 18288
Steam N' Mash, 9523
Steam Pac, 27679
Steam-Flo, 29263
Steamcraft, 20642
Steamflo, 21617
Steamix, 19059
Steamscrubber, 25041
Stearns, 26864, 28357, 29616, 29617
Stearns & Lehman, 6806
Stearns Wharf, 12066
Stearns-Roger, 28206
Steaz, 5693, 12690
Steclite, 20256
Sted Stock Ii, 20256
Steel Creek, 104
Steel It, 29562
Steel It Lite, 29562
Steel Rail Extra Pale Ale, 1237
Steel Reserve, 8459
Steel Reserve, 8460
Steel's Gourmet, 12068
Steelcraft, 21035
Steeler Lager, 7157
Steeline, 20882
Steeltest, 23543
Steeltite, 23450
Steeltree, 24519
Steeluminum, 20256
Steempan, 30390
Steen's Cane Cured Pheasant, 1924
Steens, 2019
Steer Clear, 27346
Stefan Mar, 8028
Stefano's, 12071
Steffens, 21883
Stegall Smoked Turkey, 11737
Stein/Checker, 20474
Steinco Casters, 24564
Steinfeld's, 1103
Stella, 6986, 21213
Stella Artois, 71, 571, 7123, 26668
Stella D'Oro, 11770
Stella Rosa Moscato D'Asti, 7740
Stella, 11209, 11211
Steller Steam, 24065
Stellina Di Notte, 12937
Steltzner, 12079
Stephan, 29642
Steri-Flo, 22558
Sterigenics, 23988, 29645
Sterileware, 19534
Sterilin, 21848
Sterilobe, 30853
Sterisafe, 28731
Sterling, 18614, 23841, 29657, 31346
Sterling Eliminator, 29657
Sterling Old Fashion Flavors, 12085
Sterling Vineyards, 12937
Sterling Vinyards, 3545
Sterno, 24848
Stero, 24038, 27063, 29662
Sterotex, 126
Sterzing's, 12088
Steve & Andy's, 12090
Steve Connolly, 12091
Steve's Mom, 12096
Steven Smith Teamaker Teas, 6928
Stevenot Winery, 12099
Stevia Products, 13883
Steviacane, 6164
Stevison's, 12105
Stewart Sutherland, 18029
Stewart's, 4521, 10054
Stewart's, 6818, 24802
Stewarts, 252, 12110
Stewarts Honey, 4443
Stewarts, 3725
Stews and Sauces, 1598
Stick 'n Stay, 23784
Stickers, 2947
Stickney & Poor, 12115
Stieber, 18678
Stiffel, 25658

1335

All Brands Index

Stillpax, 18637
Stilwell's, 11198
Stilwell, 11317
Stim-O-Stam, 12120
Sting Ray Bloody Mary Mixer, 1470
Stirator, 21269
Stirfresh, 6685
Stirling Gourmet Flavors, 12122
Stirling Syrup, 2833
Stirring Sticks, 6787
Stivers Best, 11839
Stock, 28837
Stock Coster, 29857
Stockmaster, 20923
Stockpop, 30259
Stok, 3379
Stokely, 2260
Stoktin Grahan, 12126
Stolichnaya, 3024, 5892
Stolichnaya Razberi, 3024
Stolichnaya Red, 3024
Stolichnaya Vanil, 3024
Stone Burr Mills, 25938
Stone Cat Ale, 6283
Stone Glo, 30508
Stone Hammer Pilsner, 12136
Stone Haven, 1006
Stone Hill Winery, 12131
Stone Ipa, 12129
Stone Mountain Snacks, 8397
Stone Pale Ale, 12129
Stone Smoked Porter, 12129
Stone Street, 13256
Stone Sublimely, 12129
Stone's, 1006
Stone-Cutter, 30676
Stoned Classics, 2728
Stoneground Mills, 12906
Stonehedge, 1027
Stonemill Kitchens, 10681
Stonemill, 2121
Stonewall Kitchen, 12139
Stoney, 785
Stoney Hill, 1121
Stoney's, 6586
Stoney's Black & Tan, 6586
Stoney's Harvest Gold, 6586
Stoney's Light, 6586
Stoney's Non-Alcoholic Brew, 6586
Stonington, 12142
Stonington Vineyards, 12142
Stony Hill Vineyard, 12143
Stonyfield Farm Frozen Yogurt, 12145
Stonyfield Farm Ice Cream, 12145
Stonyfield Farm Refrig Yogurt, 12145
Stopnot, 9956
Stor-Frame, 29694
Stor-It, 30413
Storage Rack-Steel-Clad, 30655
Storage Wall, 25353
Store'n Pour, 20256
Storehouse Foods, 5159
Storeworks, 25565
Storgard, 24274
Storm King, 13181
Storm Trac, 28261
Storrs, 12150
Story Wine, 12151
Storybook Mountain Winery, 12144
Storypoint, 3834
Storytime, 1677
Stoudt Gold, 12153
Stouffer's, 8945
Stouffers, 19244
Stoutridge, 12154
Stove Top, 6976
Stow Away, 23499
Stowaway, 25034
Strahman, 19401
Straight Coffees, 8612
Straight Up Tea, 3725, 6818, 24802
Strainomatic, 23672
Strand Amber, 7844
Strapping, 20250
Strapslicer System, 18301

Strata, 23936
Stratagraph, 23355
Straub, 12158
Straub Light, 12158
Straubs, 12159
Strauss, 12162
Straw Boss, 30376
Strawberry Blonde, 1208
Strawberry Colada Frozen Batter, 951
Strawberry Shortcake, 1591
Streamlight, 26457
Strebin Farms, 12164
Streblow Vineyards, 12165
Streits, 12167
Strendge Pasta, 3691
Strepsils, 10598
Stress Formula With Zinc, 75
Stressease, 6449, 24506
Stresstech, 18235
Stretch Frame, 20625
Stretch Island, 12169
Stretch-Tite, 31336
Stretch-Vent, 29727
Stretchframe, 29746
Stricklin, 29731
Strico, 29731
Strip Pac, 27679
Stripir, 27325
Striplok, 24704
Stroehmann, 1359
Stroh, 9035
Stroh's, 9664
Strohs Canada, 9391
Strokes, 12127
Stromag, 18678
Strong Bow, 31142
Strong Boy, 11839
Strong Scott, 19576
Strong-Scott, 23871
Stroopies, 12734
Strub's, 12175
Structolene, 20882
Strudelkins, 3603
Stryker Sonoma Winery Vineyards, 12177
Strypel, 27431
Stuart, 21848
Stubb's, 8061, 12180
Stubborn Soda, 9945, 27433
Stubby Clear-Vue, 26323
Stubby Less Crush, 26323
Stubi, 3236
Studio Colors, 23160
Studio Confections, 13142
Sturdi-Frame, 30413
Sturdystyle, 23811
Stutz Olive Oil, 2085
Stylene, 23160
Stylus, 4649, 24277
Styprint, 27431
Styrocups, 31246
Stysorb, 27431
Suarez, 1357
Sublime, 25147
Subsole, 5036
Sucanat, 13751
Success, 10777, 28421
Suckerpunch, 12186
Sudbury, 12189
Suderwerk Doppel, 12191
Suderwerk Dunkel, 12191
Suderwerk Lager, 12191
Suderwerk Mai Bock, 12191
Suderwerk Marzen, 12191
Suderwerk Pilsenser, 12191
Sudlersville, 12190
Suds - Pail, 20256
Sue Bee, 11669
Sugai Kona Coffee Emporium, 12192
Sugai Kona Grove Coffee, 12192
Sugar & Spice, 1856
Sugar Art, 5160
Sugar Babies, 2102
Sugar Babies, 12880
Sugar Bob's Finest Kind, 12194

Sugar Creek, 12197, 29755
Sugar Daddy, 2102
Sugar Daddy, 12880
Sugar Flowers, 12199
Sugar Foods Corporation, 11504, 29095
Sugar Free Cookies, 5909, 23825
Sugar Free Vines, 469
Sugar Grove, 7463
Sugar In the Raw, 12201
Sugar Mama, 2102
Sugar Plum, 25299
Sugar Sticks, 9753
Sugar Tree, 6880
Sugar Twin, 864, 6792, 24785
Sugar Valley, 7853
Sugardale, 4715, 22859
Sugarleaf, 12430
Sugarless Sugar, 8725
Sugarman, 12208
Sugary Wine, 9856
Sugo, 10533
Suja, 12213
Sul-Ray, 746
Sula, 9956
Sullair, 28967
Sullivan Cabernet Sauvignon, 12217
Sullivan Chardonnay, 12217
Sullivan Coeur De Vigne, 12217
Sullivan Merlot, 12217
Sulpice, 12218
Sumatra Mandheling, 10157
Sumbeam, 807
Sumiwataru Umeshu, 1120
Summa-6, 28834
Summer Ale, 7526
Summer Beer, 531
Summer Berry Delight, 13746
Summer Blush, 10061
Summer Fresh, 12219
Summer Golden Ale, 556
Summer Harvest, 6870
Summer Honey Seasonal Ale, 1344
Summer Naturals, 4757
Summer of Lager, 2691
Summer Pils, 11992
Summer Prize, 13598
Summer Sage, 10165
Summer Song, 7170
Summer's Choice, 1190
Summerbright Ale, 1687
Summerfield Farms, 12222
Summerfield's, 12223
Summerlake, 12672
Summerripe, 4242, 22458
Summerset, 7463
Summit, 12225, 22504, 29761
Summit Lake Vinyards, 12227
Summit Lectern, 26229
Sumner, 13582
Sump-Vac, 29489
Sumptuous Ions, 1925
Sun Beauty, 861
Sun Biotics, 13847
Sun Bright, 29101
Sun Chips, 4741
Sun Chips, 9945, 27433
Sun Chlorella, 12228
Sun Crop, 12241
Sun Drop, 3725, 6818, 24802
Sun Garden Sprouts, 12230
Sun Groves, 12233
Sun Leaf, 421
Sun Lovin, 13630
Sun Maid, 1394
Sun Moon Stars, 10673
Sun Oil, 28462
Sun Olive Oil, 12237
Sun Orchard, 12239
Sun Orchards Labels, 12240
Sun Pac, 12241
Sun Ray, 2086
Sun Ridge Farms, 8898
Sun Siberian Ginseng, 12228
Sun Sun, 8161, 12247
Sun Supreme, 12231

Sun Valley, 29056
Sun Valley Mustard, 12249
Sun Valley, 12251
Sun-Bird, 1917
Sun-Dried Tomato Str, 806
Sun-Glo, 12231, 30508
Sun-Maid, 11318, 12256, 13254
Sun-Ripe, 2386
Sun-Ripened, 1490
Sun-Rise Beverages, 12258
Sun-Rype, 12259
Sun-Sugared, 10686
Sunbeam, 2242, 4527, 4662, 27991
Sunbeam Bread, 4529
Sunbelt Bakery, 8077
Sunbelt, 8076
Sunbestc, 12267, 29771
Sunbird Snacks, 8397
Sunblet, 12909
Sunbrand, 25789
Sunburst, 9226, 27982
Sunburst Trout Farms, 12265
Sunbursts, 6851
Suncoc, 12267, 29771
Suncrest Farms, 12268
Suncrisp, 12961
Sundance, 5132
Sunday House, 12270
Sundial Blend Teas, 12272
Sundial Gardens, 12272
Sundown, 11785
Sundown Naturals, 8871
Sunergia Breakfast Style Sausage, 12273
Sunergia More Than Tofu Garlic, 12273
Sunergia More Than Tofu Herbs, 12273
Sunergia More Than Tofu Porcinis, 12273
Sunergia More Than Tofu Savories, 12273
Sunergia More-Than-Tofu, 12273
Sunergia Organic Soy Sausage, 12273
Sunergia Smoked Portabella Sausage, 12273
Sunflo, 3084
Sunflower, 11979, 28808, 29528
Sunfresh, 12275
Sunfresh Freezerves, 12276
Sunfruit, 2059
Sunglo, 5333, 18434, 23360
Sunglow, 13328
Sungold, 11211
Sunkist, 252, 6483, 12871, 13907
Sunkist Citrus, 1343
Sunkist Country Time, 10151
Sunkist Flavour Bursts, 4884
Sunkist Fruit First Fruit Snacks, 4884
Sunkist, 3725, 6818, 24802
Sunland, 676
Sunlike, 56, 12279
Sunlite, 23958
Sunmalt, 24717
Sunmeadow, 4813
Sunmed, 220
Sunnie, 5363
Sunnuts, 12262
Sunny Avocado, 12280
Sunny Boy, 1950
Sunny D, 12281
Sunny D, 6483
Sunny Farm, 2260
Sunny Fresh, 2205, 20246
Sunny Green, 9237, 26785
Sunny Isle, 12103
Sunny Lea, 3084
Sunny Millet, 8844
Sunny Morning, 5334
Sunny Shores, 7853
Sunny Shores Broccoli Wokly, 7853
Sunny South, 12284
Sunnyd, 6818, 24802
Sunnydale Farms, 4290
Sunnydell, 13319
Sunnyland, 12287
Sunnyland Farms, 12286
Sunnyrose Cheese, 12288

All Brands Index

Sunnyside, 5555, 6567
Sunnyside Farms, 12323
Sunpak, 18434
Sunphenon, 12498
Sunrice, 12372
Sunrich, 12294
Sunrich Naturals, 12238
Sunridge Farms, 12295
Sunripe, 9676, 9763, 21447, 27283
Sunrise, 635, 1006, 1808, 11408, 25725
Sunrise Farm Fresh, 500
Sunrise Farms, 13063
Sunset Farm, 12300
Sunset Pink, 6763
Sunshine, 3540, 8519, 12302
Sunshine California, 7451
Sunshine Farms, 12306
Sunshine Pasta Sauce, 12735
Sunshine Snacks, 2960
Sunshine State, 7569
Sunshine Valley, 8833
Sunshine's, 12372
Sunshower, 11609
Sunspire, 5505
Sunsweet, 12313
Suntory Umeshu, 1120
Suntory Whisky, 1120, 12315
Suntree, 9049
Sunup, 12316
Sunvista, 4267, 22464
Sunwest, 12262
Sunwise, 5555
Sup-Ex, 25008
Suparossa, 1305
Super, 3695, 21051, 29790
Super Adjustable, 24304
Super Adjustable Super Erecta, 26031
Super Aged Gouda, 13840
Super Antioxidant Blend, 665
Super B-12 Sublingual, 9253
Super Bar, 22780
Super Blue Green Enzymes, 8967
Super Bowl Cleanse, 131
Super Bubble, 1417, 4345
Super Burgers, 13073
Super C Active, 131
Super Carrot Cutter, 19169
Super Cart, 26681
Super Chef, 18811, 22996, 29795
Super Cutter, 19169
Super Detox, 131
Super Dickmann's, 12147
Super Drive Sifter, 26736
Super Epa, 7947
Super Erecta, 24304, 26031
Super Fabulous Fiber, 7404
Super Fat Burner, 5682
Super Fine, 5555
Super G, 25865
Super Gel B, 8335
Super Good, 6101
Super Green, 131
Super H, 19798
Super Hook, 19082
Super Hot, 18620
Super Iron Out, 24386
Super Iron Out Dignio, 24386
Super Juhyo, 1120
Super Key, 29604
Super Kleaned Wheat, 6869
Super Kmh, 4124
Super Life, 4127
Super Links, 19763
Super Marker, 26109
Super Moderna, 24628
Super Mustang, 19798
Super Oxy-Pure, 12483
Super Pack-Man, 23013
Super Pan Ii, 30898
Super Pik, 19894
Super Power, 20122
Super Q10, 8967
Super Ropes, 469
Super Sack, 19307
Super Salad Oil, 131

Super Scald, 19894
Super Separator, 30854
Super Sheath, 20365
Super Slicer, 19999
Super Smokers Barbecue Sauces, 10772
Super Soynuts, 7297
Super Stress, 7947
Super Strip, 21080
Super Stuffers, 8798
Super Sucker, 790
Super Supreme, 12550
Super Systems, 27554
Super Thins, 2692
Super Tonic, 131
Super Vab, 7947
Super-1-Daily, 6364
Super-Flex, 23543
Super-Flo, 28936
Super-Mix, 7671
Super-Stamp, 29394
Super-Trete, 21080
Super-Trol, 19898
Superba, 243
Superbag, 20886
Superbag Jr., 20886
Superbase, 22272
Superbridge, 25571
Superburgers, 13074
Superc, 6483
Superceptor, 30205
Superchanger, 30390
Supercitrimax, 6236
Superclear, 13498
Supercol, 1692
Supercuts, 10971
Supereats, 12324
Superfex, 13444
Superfine, 5555
Superflex, 29796
Superfly, 26337
Superformer, 18095
Superfreeze, 13444
Supergard, 30957
Supergotcha, 28118
Supergrain, 27387
Supergrain Pasta, 10467
Superguard, 18622
Superior, 7006, 11213, 11909, 12328
Superior Cake, 12331
Superior Chocolatier, 12349
Superior Confections, Inc., 12349
Superior Farms, 12333
Superior Foods, 12334
Superior Monogram, 29810
Superior Nut Company, 12338
Superior Pride, 12334
Superior Rex, 18497
Superior Source, 1967
Superior Spices, 12906
Superior Syrups, 12906
Superior Systems, 23216
Superior's Brand, 4715, 22859
Superla, 13498
Superlast, 23543
Superlevel, 24490, 30043
Supermix, 18181
Supermom's, 12319
Superportable, 20550
Superpretzel, 6338
Superpretzel Bavarian, 6338
Superseedz, 6728
Supershield, 18185
Superskids, 31031
Supersnap High Sensitivity Atp Test, 23971
Supersnax, 12201
Supersocco, 13932
Supersorb, 22554
Superstar Strawberry, 5362, 23377
Superstone, 11233
Superstore, 12323
Supertaut Plus Ii, 29853
Supertex, 13498
Supertilt, 18181
Supertower, 20550

Supervan, 12550
Supervision, 29794
Superwear, 27982
Superwheel, 24940
Superwhip, 13498
Supherb Farms, 12318
Supper Topper, 191
Supr Swivel, 21717
Supr-Safe (Gas), 21717
Supra, 20290
Supraplus, 29001
Suprega, 21425
Supreme, 2796, 7585, 8336, 10330, 11226, 12550, 20256, 20666, 24599, 27412, 28992, 29825
Supreme 7, 5786
Supreme B 150, 7947
Supreme Dairy Farms, 12350
Supreme Dips, 13894
Supreme Stuffers, 6338
Supreme Tender, 13109
Supremes, 12202
Supremo, 3127, 8457
Sur Sweet, 12426, 29855
Suram, 12353
Surco, 29826
Surcota, 29826
Surcotta, 18501
Sure Chef, 23729
Sure Chef Climaplus Combi, 23729
Sure Fresh, 12354
Sure Gard, 31099
Sure Sak, 20257
Sure Shot, 27730
Sure Way, 28734
Sure-Bake, 21227
Sure-Bake & Glaze, 21227
Sure-Grip, 29254
Sure-Kol, 29829
Sure-Stik, 23131
Surebean, 30299
Surebond, 6211, 24226
Suredrain, 23850
Sureflo, 342
Sureflow, 21262
Surefresh Foods, 2393
Sureseal, 27499
Sureshot, 18101
Surety Pwd Hand Soap, 23532
Surf Spray, 9356
Surface Guard, 9252
Surface Systems, 25773
Surge, 2814, 22966, 23080
Surprizers!, 13403
Surry, 11025
Susan Winget, 6291, 24388
Sushi Chef, 1105
Sushi Sonic, 5306
Susie's Smart Cookie, 12360
Suspentec, 8338
Susquehanna Valley, 12362
Sussman, 29839
Sustagen, 8103
Sustained Energy, 3540
Sustamid, 28478
Sustamine, 7017
Sustarin, 28478
Sustatec, 28478
Sustenex, 11285
Sustiva, 1721
Suter, 12365
Sutter Home, 12369
Sutton's, 12370
Suzanna's, 12371
Suzanne's Conserves, 12372
Suzanne's Salad Splash, 14018
Suzi Wan, 7952
Suzie's, 5161
Suzuki Eikodo, 3852
Svendborg Brakes, 18678
Svenhards, 12375
Svk, 28435
Swab 'n' Smile, 31010
Swagger, 12377
Swamp Fire Seafood Boil, 9315

Swan, 9094
Swan Island, 9094
Swan Joseph, 6604
Swan's Touch, 9532
Swans Down Cake Flour, 10657
Swanson, 2116
Swanson Vineyards & Winery, 12378
Swany White, 11402
Swany White Certified Organic, 11402
Swedish Hill, 12382
Sweeping Beauty, 25668
Sweet & Sassy, 11077
Sweet & Saucy Caramel Sauces, 12386
Sweet & Saucy Chocolate Sauces, 12386
Sweet 'n Healthy, 9201
Sweet 'n Low, 12201
Sweet 2 Eat, 10285, 27785
Sweet and Slender Natural Sweetener, 13883
Sweet Baby Ray's, 12388
Sweet Basics, 3114
Sweet Beans, 12294
Sweet Betsy From Pike, 13920
Sweet Blessings, 12389
Sweet Blossoms, 2134
Sweet Breath Xtreme Intense Breath, 12390
Sweet Carolina, 5094
Sweet Cheese, Queso Blanco, 9885
Sweet Cloud, 5306
Sweet Cravings, 2159
Sweet Dessert Wine, 10415
Sweet Drops, 12430
Sweet Earth Natural Foods, 12396
Sweet Home Farm, 14011
Sweet Kiss, 7423
Sweet Leaf, 13883
Sweet Loren's, 12406
Sweet Meadow Farms, 4351
Sweet Moose, 9237, 26785
Sweet Notes, 10764
Sweet Nothings, 903, 11771
Sweet Occasion, 4032
Sweet Onion Low Fat Crackers, 1472
Sweet Organics, 7845
Sweet P'S, 12885, 30333
Sweet Pepper Low Fat Crackers, 1472
Sweet Pleasers Gourmet, 5735
Sweet Portion, 5735
Sweet Savory Cocktai, 13180
Sweet Seduction, 4804
Sweet Shells, 5578
Sweet Shop Usa, 12414
Sweet Singles, 7599
Sweet Sloops, 5578
Sweet Squeeze, 1893
Sweet Stirrings, 2947
Sweet Street, 4244, 12415
Sweet Stripes, 4345
Sweet Stuffers, 6338
Sweet Things, 7179, 25104
Sweet Treasures, 5346
Sweet Whispers, 12421
Sweet Works, 9031
Sweet'n Low, 12422
Sweet-Water, 4269
Sweet-X, 9201
Sweetaly, 12424
Sweetango , 2476
Sweetango Apples, 1196
Sweetcorn, 1882
Sweetdex, 12387
Sweetfire, 2860
Sweetfree Magic, 7766, 25632
Sweetheart Fudge, 14013, 31399
Sweetleaf Stevia, 12430
Sweetmyx, 11436, 29018
Sweetsting, 5516
Sweetwater, 12419
Sweetwater 42, 12419
Sweetwater Blue, 12419
Sweetzyme, 1692
Swell, 11056
Swerve, 12436
Swiffer, 12721, 30193

1337

All Brands Index

Swift Premium, 6391
Swift Set Folding Chairs, 26229
Swift Tooth Bands, 19146
Swift, 6391
Swiftgel, 12637
Swiftwater, 6267
Swifty, 19823
Swing Arm Diverter, 22254
Swing Top, 20882
Swing-A-Way, 4538, 29859
Swingster, 18778
Swirl, 23499
Swirl Freeze, 29860
Swirl Onion, 13653
Swirly Cups, 12551
Swiss, 12440
Swiss 2, 12442
Swiss Air, 29632, 29633
Swiss Alp Mineral Water, 9604
Swiss American Sausage Co., 1861
Swiss Colony Foods, 2888, 20733
Swiss Fudge Sampler Tier, 13277
Swiss Heritage Cheese, 12441
Swiss Kriss, 8448
Swiss Made, 13875
Swiss Miss, 6084
Swiss Party, 831
Swiss Premium, 388, 12442
Swiss Premium Drinks, 8104
Swiss Premium, 3442, 21421
Swiss Valley, 8898
Swiss Valley Farms, 10233
Swiss Whey D'Lite, 1506, 3074
Swissart, 8677
Swissh, 29863
Swivelier, 29866
Sword, 18022
Sycamore, 13067
Sycamore Farms, 12365
Sycoid, 30920
Syfo, 13205
Syfo Brand Original, 13206
Sylvester, 7276
Sylvin Farms, 12450
Symart Systems, 29720
Symbio, 4552
Symbol, 22769
Symbol Jet, 25788
Symetix, 24812
Symmetrix Frp, 25773
Symphony, 5818, 20256, 21817, 23750
Symphony Pastries, 3236
Symtec, 13642, 23611
Synature, 1490
Synchromat, 26482
Syncrospense, 24042
Synedrex, 8191
Synergy, 23771
Synergy Laser Power, 28915
Synergy Systems, 10915
Syr, 28920
Syracuse, 19354, 25282
Syracuse China, 25281
Syrah, 2469, 7490, 14038
Syrah Santa Barbara County, 4353
Syrelec, 21099
Sys-Clean, 30848
Sysco Products, 3387
Syspro, 28739
System 7, 27400
System Iv, 29960
System Master, 22807
System Sensor, 23235
Systemaker, 24213
Systemsure Plus Atp Hygiene, 23971
Sytrinol, 6236

T

T & A, 12525
T&S Brass and Bronze, 29968
T'Gallant, 12937
T'Lish Vinaigrette & Marinade, 12466
T-Line, 23735
T-Rex, 30376
T-Rex, 29171
T.G. Lee, 3442, 21421
T.G. Lee Foods, 12460
T.H. Angermeier, 2386
T.O.P. Chops, 2635
T.S. Smith & Sons, 12472
T2p - Light, 11462
T4p - Medium Toasted Hulled Sesame, 11462
T5p - Dark, 11462
Ta Instruments, 31041
Ta-3, 19262
Ta-Xt2, 30184
Taam Tov, 13931
Tab X-Tra, 2815, 20685
Tabasco, 8072
Tabbee, 28930
Tabernash, 7309
Tabiah Halal, 5141
Tabie Lamps & Stereo Brand, 29661
Table De France, 12487, 21497
Table Joy, 7022
Table Lev'lr, 19998
Table Line, 27980
Table Mate, 29723
Table Talk, 12488, 30041
Table Top, 25766
Table Turner, 26433
Table Two Entree, 6574
Tablecheck, 30042
Tablecraft, 30043
Tablet Press 328, 21282
Tabletote, 28115
Tableware Retrievers, 24700
Tabor Hill, 12489
Tabouli, 12536
Tabouli Salad Mix, 4252
Tabster, 29588
Tackmaster, 25762
Tad, 19698
Tadin, 12490
Taffy Delight, 5017
Taffy Lite, 5017
Tag, 8191
Tahini, 11462, 12536
Tahini Crunch, 1791
Tahiti, 13141
Tahitian Treat, 6818, 24802
Tai Bueno, 9571
Tai Pan, 13241
Tai Pei, 237, 238
Tailgate, 118
Tailgate & Celebrate, 9816
Tait Farm Foods, 12497
Taj, 12499
Taj Mahal, 10968
Tak-A-Number, 23239
Tak-Les, 28081
Takara, 12500
Takara Plum, 12500
Take & Bake Deli Pizza, 12071
Take 10, 18702
Take 5, 5818, 23750
Take a Number, 22271
Take-1, 27575
Takohachi, 857
Taku, 12503
Tal-Furnar, 2960
Talapa Mezcal, 3165
Talbott Chardonnay, 12506
Talbott Diamond T Chardonnay, 12506
Talbott Vineyards, 3834
Talbott's, 12504
Talenti, 13169
Talking Rain, 12510
Talking Rain Biotonical, 12510
Tall-Boy, 1321
Talley Farms, 12513
Talley Vineyards, 12514
Talluto's, 12496
Tally Printer Corporation, 30051
Talmadge Farms, 10497
Tamarind Tree, 591
Tamarindo Bay, 5516
Tambellini, 2312
Tamp-R-Saf, 24855
Tampa Bay Fisheries, 10603
Tampa Maid, 12520
Tampax, 12721, 30193
Tampco, 31435
Tampico, 8105, 12522
Tampico Punches, 12521
Tamxicos, 7076
Tan Cook, 7686
Tanbro, 12525
Tandoor Chef, 3465
Tandoori, 7273
Tang, 6976
Tang Hoi Kee, 10457
Tangerine Wheat Ale, 7554
Tangle Ridge, 1120
Tangle-Trap, 20877
Tanglefoot, 20877
Tango, 947
Tango Shatterproof, 30062
Tangy Bang, 7210
Tank Cleaning Systems, 25203
Tank Master, 19152
Tann-X, 20966
Tanners Select, 18328
Tanqueray Gin, 3570
Tantos, 12527
Tanzanian Peaberry, 1123, 10157
Taorminac, 2010
Taos, 12530
Tap 1, 19581
Tap Juices, 9083
Tap'n Applec, 9748
Tapatio, 12531
Tape Culator, 19634
Tape Shooter, 19634
Tape Squirt, 19634
Taperhex Gold, 24366
Tapi, 10297
Tappers, 1654
Taproom, 1789
Tapt, 12706
Tara Foods, 10435, 12533
Tarantula, 8062
Tarazi, 12535
Tarheel, 11958
Taski, 18281
Tasmanian Devil, 1837
Tasque, 27470
Tasselli, 27063
Tassimo, 6976
Tast-T, 5048
Tast-T Tender, 5048
Taste Adventure, 13805
Taste It, 30775
Taste Maker, 12541
Taste Master, 22558
Taste O'Spring, 4970
Taste of Florida, 2801
Taste of Island Legends, 857
Taste of the Hill, 10772
Taste Pleasers Gourmet, 5735
Taste Republic, 12964
Taste T Pacific Whiting, 9344
Taste the Beauty of North Idaho, 4828
Taste the Beauty of the Rockies, 4828
Taste Waves, 9237, 26785
Taste-T, 11515
Taste, 8899
Tasteboost, 4837
Tastebuds Popcorn, 12548
Tastee, 11013, 12549
Tastemorr Snacks, 1071
Tasteva Stevia Sweetener, 12561
Tasty, 3028, 8795
Tasty Bakery, 1758, 19889
Tasty Bite, 7952
Tastykake, 4529
Tat, 30979
Tata Tea, 12559
Tatangelo, 12560
Tate & Lyle, 20020
Tate & Lyle, 12196
Tate Western, 30080
Tate's Bake Shop, 12562
Tate+Lyle, 3666
Tater Pals, 6374, 24434
Tater Tots, 9523
Tato Skins, 10173
Taurus, 27685
Tavern Traditions, 7179, 25104
Taxco, 2111
Taylor, 30084
Taylor Brothers Farms, 11877
Taylor Company, 29466
Taylor Country Farms, 6858
Taylor Farms, 12567
Taylor Jane's Raspberry Ale, 4959
Taylor Shellfish, 12573
Taylor's Mexican Chili, 12575
Taza Rica Mexican Spiced Cocoa, 6654
Tazarriba, 6902
Tazo, 12042
Tazo Teas, 6928
Tb Wood's, 18678
Tbj Gourmet, 12475
Tchibo, 3714
Tdc, 30451
Tde Dispensers, 28922
Tdm, 8335
Te-Flex, 22624
Tea India, 5612
Tea of Life, 421
Tea Sickles, 6787
Tea Temptations, 4055
Tea Tibet, 6948
Tea Tyme Cookies, 6821
Tea-Master, 24725
Teacher's Highland Cream, 3024
Teacher's, 1120
Teachers, 21059
Teake Furniture, 26404
Teaks, 8362
Teal Lake Winery, 10952
Tealac, 7857
Tealicious Iced Tea, 13728
Team, 10076
Team Realtree, 12920
Teapigs, 12588
Teaports, 5108
Teardrop, 2783
Tearoom, 12586
Teasdale, 12590
Tease, 6821
Teatro, 450
Teavana, 12042
Teavigo, 12498
Teays Valley, 1891
Tebay, 12592
Tec Frames, 30091
Tec Line, 30118
Tec-Loc, 26264
Tech, 18671
Techni-Brew, 1636, 19825
Technichem, 30100
Technicote, 23882
Techniseal, 27294
Technium, 30110
Technomachine, 22142
Technomelt, 23726
Tecneon, 30091
Tectwo, 30091
Tecumseh, 24919, 28967, 30117
Tecweigh, 30118
Teddie, 7288
Teddy Bear, 27743
Teddy Grahams, 8729
Teddy's, 1478, 13196
Tee Lee, 12602
Teeccino Caffeine-Fr, 12601
Teenee Beanee, 6641
Teenies, 4976
Teeny Foods, 12603
Teese Vegan Cheese, 2550
Tefbake, 30046
Teflon, 29046
Teg-U-Lume, 25224
Tegra, 24812
Teixeira, 12606
Tejas Sizzle, 4375

All Brands Index

Tel-Tru, 30126
Telemechanique, 28894
Telescoper, 19919
Telescopic, 28010
Tellem, 22877
Tellerette, 20359
Temo's, 12610
Temp Care, 23571
Temp Check, 23571
Temp Dot, 21524
Temp Guard, 23868
Temp Plate, 27352
Temp-Lock, 20121
Temp-Lock Ii, 20121
Temp-Plate, 27240
Temp-Rite Excel Ii, 18525
Temp-Tech, 29998
Tempeh, 13074
Temperature Sensors, 28020
Tempest, 30059
Templock, 30143
Tempo, 2943
Temprecord, 26282
Tempt Hemp, 6049
Temptale, 29025
Temptale 2, 29025
Temptale 3, 29025
Temptale 4, 29025
Temptation Ice Cream, 2550
Temptations, 7952
Ten High, 11263
Ten High Bourbon, 11264
Ten Ren's Tea, 12614
Tenaro, 8367
Tenax, 29211
Tenayo, 12615
Tenchi, 30144
Tenda Bake, 10675
Tender Crust, 9621
Tender Flake, 7876
Tender Plus, 5643
Tender Quick, 6661
Tenderbird, 9389
Tenderflake, 7875
Tenderit, 23117
Tenderometers, 22729
Tendersweet, 7161
Tendertouch, 19639
Tennant, 30147
Tennessee, 10038
Tennessee Bun, 12616
Tennessee Pride Country Sausage, 9368
Tennessee Rag, 26770
Tenore Measurement Equipment, 22729
Tensabarrier, 25177
Tension, 20625
Tension-Master Ii, 18705
Tenuta Polvaro, 652
Teperberg Winery, 10952
Tequila Rose, 8062
Ter-A-Zip, 27192
Tera's, 13879
Terg-A-Zyme, 18542
Terlato Kitchen, 12619
Termamyl, 1692
Terminator, 31010
Terminix, 30161
Termite Prufe, 20956
Teroson, 23726
Terphane, 30162
Terra, 5505
Terra Alba, 343
Terra Di Seta, 10952
Terra Origin, 12624
Terra Tape, 28240
Terrafood, 4148
Terramoto, 28515
Terraneb, 24840
Terranetti's, 12628
Terrapin, 8459
Terrapin, 8460
Terraza, 10303, 27797
Terrazas De Los Andes, 8452
Terre D'Olivier, 11864
Terry Brothers, 12634

Tesa, 30166
Test-A-Pack, 20254
Testaments Chewing Gum, 12639
Testaments Fruit Flavored Candy, 12639
Testaments Sour Fruit Mints, 12639
Testaments Sugar Free Mints, 12639
Testaments Sugar Mints, 12639
Testlab, 12638
Testoterm, 30001
Teti, 12640
Tetley Teas, 12641
Teton, 5255
Teton Glacier Vodka, 11614
Teton Waters Ranch, 12644
Tetra Ablend, 30171
Tetra Albrix, 30171
Tetra Alcarb Spark, 30171
Tetra Alcip, 30171
Tetra Across, 30171
Tetra Aldose, 30171
Tetra Alvac, 30171
Tetra Alvap, 30171
Tetra Alwin, 30171
Tetra Brik Aseptic, 30169, 30171
Tetra Centri, 30171
Tetra Classic, 30171
Tetra Fino, 30171
Tetra Plantcare, 30171
Tetra Plantmaster, 30171
Tetra Plantopt, 30171
Tetra Plex, 30171
Tetra Prisma, 30171
Tetra Rex, 30169, 30171
Tetra Spiraflo, 30171
Tetra Tebel, 30171
Tetra Therm, 30171
Tetra Top, 30171
Tetra Wedge, 30171
Tetrahop Gold, 6554
Teuscher, 2592
Teva Foods, 5141
Tex-Mex, 11883
Tex-O-Gold, 4428
Tex-Pro, 1244
Texacort, 8389
Texan Wiener, 5400
Texas, 1064
Texas Bay, 9912
Texas Beach, 12648
Texas Best, 8075
Texas Brand, 4201
Texas Chewie, 7200
Texas Chewie Pecan Praline, 7184
Texas Chili, 12649
Texas Crispers, 9523
Texas Gold, 11856
Texas Grown Red Grapefuit, 13906
Texas Hot Salt, 12660
Texas Jack's Tex-Mex, 6410
Texas Lean, 2554
Texas Longhorn, 1279
Texas One Step, 4428
Texas Pepper Works, 10701
Texas Pete, 12473
Texas Red, 12654
Texas Select, 10729
Texas Smokehouse, 6334
Texas Spice, 12656, 30179
Texas Toffee, 12659
Texas Traditions, 12660
Texican, 13085
Texite, 4430
Texjoy, 12650
Texliner, 26440
Texmati, 10712, 25789
Texnap, 23160
Textaid, 8804
Textile Design Collection, 20256
Textra, 8804
Textrion, 4736
Textron, 1692
Textur, 8899
Textura, 13498
Texture Expert For Windows, 30184
Texture Tone, 23288

Tezzatac, 1861
Tform, 26666
Tgf, 13242
Tgi Friday's, 10173
Tgi Fridays Snacks, 13129
Thackrey, 12661
Thai Chef, 12499
Thai Chicken, 7273
Thai Kitchen, 8061
Thai Sauce, 5143
Thank You, 21059
Thank You Pops, 5752
Thanksgiving, 12663
Tharo, 30186
That's Hollywood, 5660
That's Itc, 12665
Thatcher's, 12666
Thatcher's Special Popcorn, 12666
Thaw-N-Sell, 20096
The Aisle-A-Gator, 21267
The Algonquin Tea Co, 304
The Amazing Chickpea, 12667
The Antiquary, 13120
The Aromo Scanner, 19067
The Art of Broth, 12669
The Art of Shaving, 12721, 30193
The Benriach, 1784
The Big O, 8114
The Bitter Housewife, 6167
The Blue, 1120
The Bob-O-Bear, 21136
The Bronx Hot Sauce, 11709
The Brownie Baker, 1785
The Bruss Company, 13109
The Bug Blocker, 28193
The Butler, 25421
The Candy Tree, 1964
The Capsule, 8888
The Carolina Cracker, 2239, 20276
The Chocolate Factory, 12349
The Chute, 23263
The City Bakery, 2703
The Cleaning Solution, 23600
The Cloud, 1658
The Coconut Collaborative, 2830
The Coconut Cult, 7604
The Coffee, 427
The Coffee Mill, 2850
The Coldholder, 20636
The Colorado Spice Co., 2899
The Complete Cookie, 7350
The Cookiec Dough Cafe, 12678
The Crown Restaurant Gourmet, 12546
The Cruvinet, 21125
The Cubby, 31433
The Curious Creamery, 8966
The Daily Crave, 8841
The Dimple, 3570
The Eliminator, 31019
The Epic Seed, 6049
The Epicurean, 779
The Essential Baking Company, 4121
The Famous Pacific Dessert Company, 270
The Farm At Mt. Walden, 13540
The Flylight, 22211
The Funnel Cake Factory, 6338
The Glendronach, 1784
The Glenlivetc Single Malt, 9964
The Good Crisp Company, 12686
The Gotham Collection, 20256
The Greek Gods, 5505
The Grove, 4840
The Honest Stand, 12691
The House of Flavors, 7934
The Informant, 25421
The Inn, 6221
The Jackfruit Company, 6420
The Jersey Tomato Co., 12695
The Jug, 7931
The Kcl Cadalog, 24909
The Keeper, 8824
The Label Dispenser, 29606
The Lancaster Food Company, 12700
The Last Word, 13184

The Lettuce Knife, 24567
The Lid Cutter, 24260
The Lions Head Collection, 20256
The Little Kernel, 12701
The Living Apothecary, 7036
The Lollipop Tree, 12703
The Maple Guild, 12706
The Margarita Man, 7903
The Matzo Project, 12708
The Mediterranean Collection, 20256
The Mensch on a Bench, 10229
The Menu Roll, 23659
The Messenger, 27575
The Mint, 10689
The Muscle Brownie, 7350
The Muscle Muffin, 7350
The Naked Grape, 3834
The New Primal, 12712
The New World Collection, 20256
The Nutra Fig, 11149
The Oceana Collection, 20256
The Ojai Cook, 27959
The Organic Wine Work, 5524
The Original Cookie & Shortbread, 23642
The Original Donut Shop, 6818, 24802
The Original Ranchc, 5489
The Osso Good Co., 9586
The Party Servers, 19645
The Pasta Mill, 9812
The Pastry Chef, 9823
The Peanut Factory, 13742
The Peanut Roaster, 9870
The Perfect Pasta, 6320
The Perfect Pita, 12715
The Pierson Company, 4063
The Prefume Garden, 11997
The Preservatory, 13452
The Pub, 184
The Real Co, 12723
The Real Coconut, 10588
The Real Food Trading Co., 9237, 26785
The Recycler, 25653
The Red Plane, 56
The Resort Collection, 20256
The Reverend, 838
The Ripe Stuff, 8525
The Sadkhin Complexr, 11031
The Salsa Addiction, 7694
The Secret Garden, 11402
The Shed Barbeque & Blues Joint, 12729
The Shed Bbq Sauces & Marinades, 12729
The Shield, 24610
The Shrink, 56
The Sneaky Chef, 11752
The Sopranos, 20946
The Spice Box, 2899
The Spice Co., 2899
The Spice Hunter, 1935
The Store, 7721
The Sunbrite Line, 25978
The Sushi Chef, 1106
The Sweet Life, 12405
The Table Tailors, 24575
The Tape Dispenser, 29606
The Taste of India, 12517
The Tea Spot, 12738
The Tiny Hero, 12818
The Toasted Oat, 12739
The Truffliest, 12740
The Unbeatable Eatable Egg, 3966
The Van Cleve Seafood Co., 12742
The Vine, 12744
The Walking Dead Wine, 12937
The Water Fountain, 3469
The Water Kefir People, 12745
The Whole 9 Yards, 11083
The Whole Earth, 11748
The Wine Tote, 23642
The Wright Pils, 5314
The Yogurt Stand, 3378
Theater Ii, 10180
Thebu Kombucha, 7798
Theimeg, 20348

All Brands Index

Thel-Egg, 6768
Thenatura;, 18328
Ther Cake Loft, 13618
Thera-M Multiple, 75
Theramune Nutritionals, 420
Theraplant, 1797
Therm-L-Bond, 30202
Therm-Tec, 30203
Therma-Kleen, 30204
Thermajet, 21321, 22662
Thermal Bags By Ingrid, 30207
Thermal Cor, 19320
Thermal Flex, 24734, 24735
Thermal Gard, 31433
Thermal Printmaster, 18269
Thermalizer, 26117
Thermalpak, 27185
Thermalrite, 22315
Thermatron, 30214
Thermex, 30214
Thermflo, 8804
Thermo, 30218
Thermo F10, 19005
Thermo Flow, 26662
Thermo Scientific, 30217
Thermo Slim, 5897
Thermo Tropic, 5065
Thermo-Kool, 30224
Thermo-Lock, 20121
Thermo-Plate, 29055
Thermo-Plug, 19417
Thermo-Serv, 29055
Thermo-Serv Sculptured Ice, 29055
Thermo-Tech, 19401
Thermobend, 26476
Thermocode, 26942
Thermoglaze, 21362
Thermoglo, 25790
Thermoguard, 21362
Thermoinsulator, 20256
Thermologic, 31200
Thermomix, 30907
Thermos, 30233
Thermotrace, 21524, 21527
Thermtex, 8804
Thermxchanger, 31195
Theta Sciences, 30235
Thick N' Juicy, 1658
Thiel, 12752, 30236
Thimble, 5140
Thin 'n Trim, 9422
Thin-Pak, 19429
Thinaddictives, 9092
Think Jerkyc, 12753
Thinkideas, 22024
Thinkthin, 12754
Thirs-Tea, 12756
Thirsty Buddha, 1825
Thirty Bench, 555
This Bar Saves Lives, 12757
This Way Jose, 9571
Thistledew Farm's, 12758
Thixogum, 9029, 26626
Thixx, 1244
Thomas, 892, 12763, 12765, 12769, 28357
Thomas Brothers Country Ham, 12761
Thomas Fogarty Winery, 12764
Thomas Fractioner, 30252
Thomas Kemper, 10404
Thomas Kemper Birch Soda, 12766
Thomas Kemper Cola, 12766
Thomas Kemper Cream, 12766
Thomas Kruse Winey, 12767
Thomas', 1359
Thomasson's, 6589
Thomasson's Potato Chips, 6589
Thompson Bagel Machines, 30256
Thompson's Black Tie, 12772
Thomson, 18678
Thomy, 8945
Thonet, 20777
Thor's, 12775
Thornton, 12777
Thoroblender, 27345

Thorogard, 31089
Thorogood, 31089
Thorpe Vineyard, 12778
Thousand Flowers, 5989
Thousand Steps Stout, 7143
Threadconverter, 21776
Threadguard, 21776
Three Bold Brothers, 10976
Three Herb Ranch, 5489
Three Jerks, 12782
Three Star, 9766
Three Trees, 12787
Three-Pin Pale Ale, 4466
Threeworks, 12789
Thrift, 13565
Thrift-T-Pak, 9839
Thrifty Bee, 1040
Thrifty Maid, 13864
Thrifty Pak, 7363
Thrifty Pop, 27289
Thrive, 5090
Throat Control Spray, 9201
Throughbred, 2688
Thru-Put, 20919
Thum-Screw, 27575
Thumann's, 12791
Thunder 101, 9773
Thunder Hole Ale, 1015
Thunder McCloud, 353
Thunderbird, 12792
Thunderhead Stout, 8602
Thyme & Truffles, 12793
Tia Anita, 6619
Tia Rosa, 1359
Tiara, 21131
Tib, 7409
Tic Tac, 4348
Tichon, 12796
Tick Stop, 5683, 23677
Ticolino, 11454
Tidal Marine, 20682
Tide, 12721, 30193
Tidepoint, 13770
Tidynap Jr., 23160
Tie-Net, 30305
Tie-Tie, 23784
Tier-Rack, 30280
Tierra Farm, 12798
Tiesta Tea, 12799
Tietolin, 4430
Tifert Aromatherapy, 7562
Tiffany, 27209
Tiffany Bagged Candy, 4884
Tiger, 12800, 12801
Tiger Balm Analgesic Oitments, 10307
Tiger Brand, 4386
Tiger Pepper, 12987
Tiger Tea, 5654
Tiger Tuff, 20277
Tiger's Milk, 11285
Tiggly Wiggly, 8404
Tigo+, 12802
Tilapia, 13586
Tilda, 5505
Tilenus, 3545
Tilex, 2766, 20657
Tillamook, 12304, 12804
Tillamook Country Smoker, 3896, 12803
Tilt, 26668
Tiltnroll, 20923
Tim's Cascade Snacks, 27540
Timber Crest Farm, 12809
Timber Trails, 12866
Time By Design, 23087
Time Wand I, 30843
Time Wand Ii, 30843
Time-Saver, 30288
Timeclock Plus, 21367
Timely Signs, 30289
Timeware, 20686
Timothy's, 6818, 24802
Timpone's, 25789
Tin Star Foods, 12813
Tina's Las Campanas, 2111
Tiny But Mighty Popcorn, 12817

Tiny Tarts, 12547
Tiny Tim, 24010
Tiny Twists, 9408
Tiny-Eye, 30422
Tinytrol, 27760
Tio Franco, 5987
Tio Gazpacho, 12819
Tio Jorge, 7702
Tio Pepe Winery, 10952
Tio Pepe's Churros, 6338
Tio Tio, 11065, 11187
Tio Tio, 11186
Tip Top, 9291, 12569, 20882, 22593
Tip Top, 4552
Tip Tree, 25789
Tip-On, 27587
Tipper Clippers, 30296
Tippy Toes, 12885, 30333
Tiptrak, 30596
Tisdale Vineyards, 3834
Tita's, 7907
Titan, 19183, 20065, 30790, 30848, 31092
Titan '90, 29044
Titan I, 20301
Titan Ii, 20301
Titanic Esm Mints, 11028
Titebond, 24672
Titora Winery, 10952
Titus, 18497
Titusville Dairy Products, 12826
Tiv Plus, 21425
Tivar, 27979
Tj Toad, 1423
Tk Tomer Kosher, 12861
Tkc Vineyards, 12827
Tleltrack, 19919
Tm1000, 20788
Tm710, 26421
Tmc, 18082
Tmt Transman, 30018
Tnp - Toasted Natural Sesame Seeds, 11462
Tnt Chocolate, 13728
To-Rico's, 10056
Toad Sweat, 9941
Toast King, 23652
Toast Master, 26131
Toast Rite, 23652
Toast'em, 11311
Toast-Qwik, 23652
Toasta Ma-Me, 5376
Toasted Buckwheat, 4362
Toasted Chips, 8729
Toasted Head, 13425
Toastin, 10600
Toastmaster, 26132
Tobacco Sorter 3, 24812
Tobikko, 857
Toblerone, 8474
Today, 1636, 19825
Today's Tamales, 9502
Todd's, 12481
Todd's Salsa, 12832
Todd's Treats, 12831
Toddy, 6484, 12833
Toddy Cappuccino, 12833
Toddy Coffee Crunch, 12833
Toddy Coffee Maker, 12833
Toddy Gourmet Iced Tea Concentrate, 12833
Toddy Mocha, 12833
Toe-Rific Candy, 12836
Toffarassi, 3311
Toffifay, 12148
Toffifee, 12147
Tofu Burger Mix, 4252
Tofu Cream Chie, 13088
Tofu Lin, 9160
Tofu Pudding, 13088
Tofu Pups, 7427
Tofu Scrambler Mix, 4252
Tofu Shop, 12841
Tofurky, 9502, 13073, 13074
Tofutti, 12843

Tofutti Better Than Cheesecake, 12843
Toki, 12315
Toledo, 18327
Toleftar Pilfen, 7310
Tolerant, 7709
Tolibia, 11777
Toll Booth, 23993
Tollok, 28357
Tom Cat Bakery, 12848
Tom Moore, 11263, 11264
Tom Ringhausen, 12850
Tom Sturgis, 10693
Tom Sturgis Pretzels, 12851
Tom's, 11770, 12854
Tom-Tom, 13193
Toma, 9972
Tomales Bay, 10435
Tomasello Winery, 12859
Tomatin, 13120
Tomato Magic, 12030
Tomato Max, 10297
Tombstone, 10435
Tombstone, 8945
Tomintoul, 10952
Tomislav, 8459
Tomlinson, 30323
Tomsed, 30325
Tonalin, 1692
Tone's, 864
Tony Chachere's Orig, 12869
Tony Packo's, 9566
Tony's, 11316
Tony's Chocolonely, 12872
Tony's Seafood, 7580
Tony's, 11317
Tony'sc, 12874
Too Cool Chix, 12877
Toom, 12879
Tooned-In Menus, 28901
Tooterville Express, 30330
Tootsie Roll, 12880
Top, 13052
Top - the Oil Plant, 4854
Top Bakes, 12231
Top Banana, 100
Top Care, 11303, 28896
Top Care, 1758, 12885, 19889, 30333
Top Chews, 13109
Top Dogs, 7876
Top Flo, 30331
Top Hat, 7767, 29489
Top Hat Dessert Sauces, 12881
Top Kut, 8114
Top Loose, 19759
Top N Go, 4741
Top Notch, 340, 20256
Top O' Cup, 28231
Top Ramen, 9068
Top Sail Amber, 1208
Top Sergent, 25008
Top Truck, 26031
Top-Guard, 30508
Top-Squeeze, 26264
Topaz, 1196, 9069
Topcare, 13864
Topiary Toffee, 5578
Topline, 28809
Topliner, 23708
Topo Chico, 12886
Topolos At Russian River Vine, 12887
Toppik, 2666, 20561
Tops, 30337
Topsan, 25606
Toptex, 6340
Torani, 10485
Torani Syrups, 6928
Torbal, 30821
Toresani, 27358
Torgo, 30831
Torgue Seal, 26969
Tork, 28665
Torke, 12891
Torkelson Cheese Co., 12892
Torkgard, 27499
Torklift, 18786

All Brands Index

Tornado, 18450, 26697
Tornado Malt Liquor, 9137
Tornados, 10976
Tornatore, 3834
Toro, 4232
Toro Safron, 12987
Torpac, 30346
Torpedo, 22502
Torq-All, 24669
Torque Tester, 29831
Torquekeeper, 22509
Torquit, 22545
Torrefazione Italia, 12897
Torrefazione Italia Coffee, 12042
Torreo, 12898
Tortiyahs!, 13129
Toscal, 2815, 20685
Toscano Style, 9635
Toshimi, 11339, 28940
Toss 'n' Tote, 31336
Tost, 12482
Tostada, 7553
Tostados, 5122
Tostitos, 4741
Tostitos, 9945, 27433
Total Control, 25421
Total Fit, 8635
Total Man, 4127
Total Touch, 22121
Total Woman, 4127
Total-Stat, 30626
Total, 4947
Totalizer, 22140
Totally Chocolate, 12900
Totally Egg, 3540
Totalsource, 30841
Totani Pouch M/C, 23917
Tote 'ems, 4255
Tote-It, 18251
Toter Worksaver, 30359
Totino's, 4947
Toto's Gourmet Products, 7821
Tott's, 3834
Toucan, 10134
Touch, 25257
Touch Access, 30843
Touch Alert, 30843
Touch and Go Blending Station, 30884
Touch In a Box, 22121
Touch Menus, 30361
Touch of Scent, 28933
Touch Taper, 25788
Touchdown Nuggets, 1654
Touchprobe, 30843
Touchseal, 18810
Tough Guy Totes, 23263
Tough Guy's, 21336
Tough One, 28176
Tour Eiffel, 2426
Tout Fini Cocktail Mixes, 4650
Tova, 12906
Tova's Best, 1802
Tovli, 1251
Tower Dark Ale, 11448
Towie, 5288
Town & Country, 11639
Town House, 6766
Town Tavern, 9403
Townsend, 6352, 29702
Toxic Tommy, 12863
Toy Bus Animal Crackers, 3343
Toy Story, 4507
Toyo Jidoki, 20549
Tpa, 25817
Tpm, 30248
Tpp Tarts Kids Kandy, 2135
Tpro, 26666
Tr, 27083
Tr 1000-2000, 25436
Trace, 25074
Tracer Summit, 30382
Tracey's, 2384
Tracker, 30382
Trackside Cookery, 31171
Tractor Shed Red, 13049

Trade Envelopes, 22187
Trade Winds Coffee, 12915
Trademark Pale Ale, 1687
Trademarx, 30373
Trader Joe's, 9116
Trader Vic's, 12912
Trader Vics, 13120
Tradewinds, 8613
Tradex International, 18029
Tradition, 6395
Traditional, 6374, 24434
Traditional Kentucky, 9417
Traditional Lager, 11218
Traditional Med Ginger Energy, 12918
Traditional Med Gypsy Cold Cure, 12918
Traditional Med Organics, 12918
Traditional Stir Fry Sauce, 5143
Traditionalware, 25320
Traeger, 30375
Trafalgar, 12919
Traffic Graffic, 23114
Trag, 30382
Trail's Best Snacks, 12920
Trailhead, 13643
Trak Clip, 27575
Trak-Air Ii, 30379
Trak-Air V, 30379
Trak-Shield, 26909
Trakstat, 27217
Trampak, 27078
Trancendim, 463
Trane, 30382
Trans Label, 25549
Trans-10, 30385
Trans-100, 30385
Trans-30, 30385
Trans-Zip, 28435
Transaction Drawer, 21870
Transafe, 20982
Transback, 19559
Transchem, 21186
Transilon, 22755, 26001
Transitainer, 21186
Transitions, 25665
Transitray, 19639
Transmart, 20096
Transocean, 12925
Transporter, 20297
Transtex, 22755
Transtore, 21186
Transwheel, 24940
Trantorque, 22509
Traou Mad, 7499
Trap-Zap Plus, 30391
Trapper, 19544, 24734
Trappey's, 12930
Trappey's, 864
Trappist, 12931
Trapr, 30361
Trashpacker, 20523
Trattoria, 12030
Traulsen, 24038, 26476, 30393
Trave Amaretto, 3545
Trave Amaretto - Decanter, 3545
Travel Well, 9201
Travel-Jon, 20395
Traveler, 19051
Traveler, 21362
Traverse Bay Fruit Co, 2518
Tray Star, 19069
Traycon, 30398
Traysaver, 24700
Traytrak, 22173
Trc, 27281
Tre Cafe, 13444
Tre Stelle, 678, 787
Tre Vini Rossi, 229
Tre' Limone, 2742
Treasure, 12769
Treasure Bay, 5430
Treasure Cave, 11209, 11211
Treasure Chest Shrimp, 1916
Treasure Island, 9693
Treasure Pak, 6081
Treat, 916, 12938

Treat-Up, 54
Treattarome, 12940
Trebor, 1982
Tred-Ties Adjustable Railroad Ties, 18344
Tree of Life, 8898
Tree Ripe, 2519, 6545
Tree Saver Bags, 30399
Tree Top, 9469, 12942
Tree-Ripe, 12941
Treehouse Farms, 12944
Treehouse Private Brands, 12943, 30400
Treemont Farms, 3574
Treestock, 26520
Treesweet, 9167
Treesweet Products, 12945
Trefethen Vineyards, 12946
Trega, 12947
Trehalose, 24717
Trench Former System, 18018
Trend, 31198
Trendreader, 18112
Trentadue, 12950
Treo, 12953
Tres Cremas, 10267
Tres Generaciones, 3024
Tres Generaciones, 1120
Tres Riches, 10714
Tres Toffee, 11775
Trescerro, 11504, 29095
Trestle Creek, 5057
Treta Alex, 30171
Treta Alfast, 30171
Treta Almix, 30171
Treta Alrox, 30171
Treta Alsafe, 30171
Treta Alscreen, 30171
Trewax Hardware, 20498
Trewax Industrial, 20498
Trewax Janitorial, 20498
Tri Dragon, 13423
Tri Our, 11759
Tri-Arc Manufacturing, 25329
Tri-C Business Forms, 22187
Tri-Clover, 19401
Tri-Drum, 24519
Tri-Flex, 19621
Tri-Flex Loop, 22624
Tri-Flow, 22850
Tri-Foil, 30418
Tri-Gard, 30418
Tri-Homo, 29360
Tri-Lam, 30418
Tri-Micro, 30854
Tri-Motor, 7209
Tri-Seal, 30418
Tri-Sign, 12957
Tri-Sorb, 30633
Tri-Stacker, 22850
Tri-Star Manufacturing, 29580
Tri-Tray, 22850
Tri-Wall, 26401
Triad, 20625, 29746
Triarc Beverages, 26147
Tribal, 608
Tribali Foods, 12963
Tricam, 28981
Triconfort, 28843
Trident, 8474, 9995
Trident, 12968
Tridyne, 30436
Trifoglio, 10860
Trigal Dorado, 955
Triggi, 11668
Trigo Labs, 8861, 26518
Trigone, 312
Tril-Clear, 30438
Trim & Firm Am/Pm, 4127
Trim Maxx, 1532
Trim-Line, 18620
Trim-Lite, 7671
Trimalta, 2338
Trimino, 7036
Trimlina, 20256
Trimlume, 25224

Trimma, 3753, 21763
Trimspa, 5095
Trine Baffle, 30442
Trine Labeling, 18284
Triner, 30443
Trinkets, 11330
Trio of Cheesecake, 2881
Triola, 20625
Trion Indoor Air Quality, 18497
Trionix, 18532
Triple, 12153
Triple Berry Blast Frozen Batter, 951
Triple Chocolate Cake, 2881
Triple Cream Sherry, 10554
Triple Crown Whiskey, 8062
Triple Erasability System, 30878
Triple H, 12978
Triple Leaf Tea, 12980
Triple Sec, 3545, 5861, 9773
Triple Springs Spring Water, 12982
Triple Xxx, 12984
Triples, 22039
Tripmaster, 29706
Tripper, 12987
Triscuit, 8474, 8729
Tristar, 25299
Trisyl, 30920
Tritab, 27499
Triton Water, 258
Triumph, 11909, 21199, 21883, 30841
Trius Winery, 555
Trivia, 21059
Trix, 20946
Trix, 4947
Trodat, 26302
Trojan, 2666, 20561
Trojan Commercial, 30456
Trokote, 833
Troll, 9106
Trolli, 1417, 4345
Trolls, 10229
Trolly-Freeze, 23075
Tronex, 30459
Trop50, 13012
Trophic, 1467
Trophy, 23602
Trophy Gold Nut Barrel, 12992
Trophy Nut, 12992
Trophy, 21362
Tropi-Kool Smoothies, 5819
Tropic, 9356
Tropic Beach, 11339, 28940
Tropic D'Lite, 3144
Tropic Isle, 12520
Tropic Seafood, 1140
Tropical, 253, 11001, 12996
Tropical AnAi, 12994
Tropical Bee, 25789
Tropical Blends, 8919
Tropical Chile Co, 4894
Tropical Chips, 100
Tropical Coffee, 1601, 19813
Tropical Grove, 56
Tropical Honey Glace, 11775
Tropical Illusions, 13005
Tropical Mist, 7363
Tropical Pepper, 1484
Tropical Pleasure, 4521
Tropical Royal, 5362, 23377
Tropical Source, 2772
Tropical Source Dairy-Free Gourmet, 2772
Tropical Source Organic, 2772
Tropical Wonders, 6926
Tropicana, 7213, 13012, 20946
Tropicana Essentials, 13012
Tropicana Kids, 13012
Tropicana Twister, 13012
Tropicana, 9945, 27433
Tropics, 6159
Troubadour Artisan Breads, 2874
Trouble Shooter, 18692
Troughveyor, 28770
Trout Lake Farm, 13015
Trout Slayer Ale, 1344

1341

All Brands Index

Trout Town, 12725
Troy's, 3956
Troys, 13892
Tru Balance, 23361
Tru Blu, 122
Tru Blue Blueberries, 28090
Tru Brew, 18928
Tru Chocolatec, 13020
Tru Hone, 30468
Tru-Hone, 29049
Tru-Nox, 29517
Tru-Temp, 30084
Tru-Test, 23080
Tru-Trak, 29244
Truchard Vineyards, 13027
Truckee River, 13028
Truckstop, 26090
True, 30471
True Beverages, 13030
True Blue, 1015, 3942
True Chews, 13109
True Citrus, 3574
True Flow, 19212
True Fruit, 4394
True Gold, 10600
True Jerky, 13032
True Lemon, 12201
True Measure, 19348
True Measures Baking Nuts, 12992
True Nopal, 13033
True North, 864
True Organic, 13034
True Pine, 19741
True Recipe, 6374, 24434
True Story Foods, 13035
True Tracker, 22003
True-Sharp, 29379
Truffini, 1733
Truffle Babies, 2903
Trufflecots, 3625
Truffles To Go, 5497
Trufru, 13021
Truitt Bros., 13038, 30475
Truly, 1592
Truly Dutch, 1385
Truly Radient, 2666, 20561
Truman's, 393
Trumoo, 3442, 7320, 21421
Trumoo Chocolate Milk, 388
Truroots, 6380
Trust, 22272
Truth Bar, 13041
Truth In Snacks, 8163
Truvibe, 13025
Try Me Sauces/Seasonings, 10657
Ts Conveyor, 24940
Tsar Nicoulai Caviar, 13042
Tu Me, 13043
Tu-Scrub, 30481
Tu-Way, 23117
Tualatin Estate, 13044
Tubar, 30565
Tubby, 9219
Tube Mastervent, 18321
Tube-Lok, 29118
Tubes, 14017
Tubular Sonics, 26162
Tucel, 30481
Tucher, 1361
Tuck, 30166
Tucker, 13045, 28104
Tucker's Cove, 8256, 11356
Tucson Blonde, 4959
Tucson Tamale, 13048
Tuesday Toffee, 2947
Tuf'n Ega, 21425
Tuf-Flex Volumetric Series Feeders, 28875
Tuf-N-Low, 27111
Tuff Grip (Gloves), 19806
Tuff Guys, 31099
Tuff Stuff, 25606
Tuff-Coder, 22902
Tuff-Cut, 24700
Tuff-Dot, 20277

Tuffgards, 23556
Tufkote, 26826
Tuftboard, 25079
Tugweld, 30038
Tularosa Wines, 13051
Tuldy's, 12646
Tulelake, 1141
Tulip, 2251
Tulip Deli, 20256
Tulip Street Bakery, 1524
Tulip Winery, 10952
Tulkoff, 13052
Tullamore Dew, 3024
Tully's Coffe, 6818, 24802
Tullys, 30492
Tumaro's, 1484
Tumbadorc Chocolate, 13056
Tummytreats, 12928
Tundra, 13059
Tung Hai, 9265
Tuny, 12823
Tuong Ot Sriracha, 10608
Tupperware, 30495
Turano, 13060, 30775
Turbo, 18436, 19975, 23669, 25871
Turbo Sensor, 28361
Turbo-Dryer, 31369
Turbo-Flo, 24812
Turbochef, 30034
Turbodisc, 20491
Turbodog, 125
Turbofan, 26258
Turbula, 23209
Turkey, 7318, 25226
Turkey Creek, 13063
Turkey Hill, 13064, 13065
Turn-O-Matic, 22271
Turning Leaf, 3834
Turris, 13072
Turrisin, 898
Turtlerazzi, 3311
Turveda, 13076
Tuscan, 13145
Tuscan Hills, 10311
Tuscan Traditions Organic, 5029
Tuscan Traditions Premium, 5029
Tuscan, 3442, 21421
Tuscarora Organic, 13080
Tut-50e, 30325
Tut-50r, 30325
Tuthilltown, 13082
Tutti Gourmet, 13083
Tuttle & Bailey, 18497
Tuttorosso, 10608
Tutus, 1812
Tuxedo, 6267
Twang, 13085
Tweety, 11552
Tweety Pops, 11552
Twiflex, 18678
Twin Abs Poucher, 18269
Twin Bing, 9722
Twin Chamber 3002, 31025
Twin Harbors, 11352
Twin Lake, 6537
Twin Marquis, 13094
Twin Pac 2203, 31025
Twin Pac 2204, 31025
Twin Pac 2205, 31025
Twin Taper, 25788
Twin-Pak, 30405
Twin-Shell, 27347
Twin-Stream, 28361
Twin-Tex, 23160
Twinings, 25789
Twinkies, 6013
Twinkle Baker Decor, 30513
Twinlab Bariatric Support, 13097
Twinlab Fuel, 13097
Twinlab Nutrition, 13097
Twintower, 28039
Twis-Tags, 29971
Twist of Fate Bitter Ale, 8524
Twist Pops, 6780
Twist-Ems, 29971

Twist-Off, 29227
Twisted Brand, 10251
Twisted Peaks, 5819
Twisted Tea, 1592
Twistix, 6780
Twisty Punch, 469
Twix, 8533
Twix, 7952
Twizzlers, 5818, 23750
Twm, 30038
Two Chefs on a Roll, 13098
Two Fingers Tequilas, 5720
Two Friends, 13101
Two Sicily's, 1282
Two Stars, 11263
Two-Can, 19788
Twoview, 21657
Ty-Linker, 25332
Ty-Peeler, 25332
Ty-Up, 30278
Tyee, 13106
Tyle Style, 31010
Tyme Chef, 19092
Type 1, 18620
Typhoon, 29360
Tyrconnell, 1120
Tyskie Gronie, 8460
Tysom, 11504, 29095
Tyson, 11053, 19244, 20101
Tyson, 4061, 13109
Tzuba Winery, 10952

U

U-Bake, 4025
U-Don, 13560
U-Fry-It, 22899
U-Noc, 583
U.F.O., 5606
U.N.L.O.C.C., 23705
U.S. Bag, 18522
U.S. Brand, 13119
U.S. Eye, 30422
U.S. Gauge, 18864
U.S. Zinc Votorantim Metals, 1692
Uas Activin Plus, 13130
Uas Coenzyme Q10, 13130
Uas Joint Formula, 13130
Ucii, 6236
Udderly Delightful, 7435
Udf, 13185
Udi's, 27540
Udisco, 20297
Udon, 11773
Udupi, 3465
Uf Feeder, 23082
Ufmt, 30576
Ufo, 24403
Uggly Cake, 12428
Uglies, 3592
Ugly Dog Stout, 3519
Ugly Nut, 12394
Uinta, 13136
Uji, 30672
Ukraine: Chumak, Nektar, 5108
Ukrop, 8404
Ul, 24399
Ullr Nordic Libation, 5981
Ulma, 23619
Ulta Mag, 30289
Ultem, 21848
Ultima, 13137, 23669, 27937, 28743, 30393
Ultimate, 5017, 13140, 13906
Ultimate Apple, 7524
Ultimate Bartender, 2799
Ultimate Biscotti, 13139
Ultimate Comfort, 19151
Ultimate Confections, 13142
Ultimate Food Complex, 665
Ultimate Petite Pretzels, 2133
Ultimate Pretzel, 2133
Ultimate Pretzel Rods, 2133
Ultimate Pretzel Sculptures, 2133
Ultipleat, 27224

Ultipor Gf/Gf Plus, 27224
Ultipor N66, 27224
Ultra, 19741, 23669, 30393, 30725
Ultra Bar, 27845
Ultra Bin, 29618
Ultra Create, 8804
Ultra Cruvinet, 21125
Ultra Dark Rondo Kosher, 8677
Ultra Density, 18702
Ultra Flow, 28810
Ultra Glide, 27764
Ultra Guard, 31185
Ultra Laser Power, 28915
Ultra Lift, 30573
Ultra Pac, 24044
Ultra Pumps, 24761
Ultra Rain Glandulars, 13146
Ultra Siever, 23185
Ultra Slim, 5897
Ultra Taper, 25788
Ultra Thin, 11228, 28829
Ultra Wash, 24899
Ultra Wipe, 23160
Ultra Wrap, 18908
Ultra'cream, 8815
Ultra-Beam, 19429
Ultra-Cool, 18832
Ultra-Crisp, 8804
Ultra-Fil, 23857
Ultra-Gog, 18832
Ultra-Lite, 23543
Ultra-Pure Bestate, 5665
Ultra-Spec, 18832
Ultra-Sperse, 8804
Ultra-Tex, 8804
Ultra-Turrax, 24074
Ultrablister, 20461
Ultrabond, 6211, 24226
Ultracell, 30800
Ultrachef, 26450
Ultraclear, 12426, 29855
Ultrafilter, 30576
Ultrafryer, 29580, 30577
Ultragrain Tortillas, 855
Ultraguar, 9654
Ultrair, 30576
Ultrajet, 30434
Ultralac, 5665
Ultralon, 31184
Ultramax, 30518
Ultramist, 20990
Ultrapac, 30576
Ultraqua, 30576
Ultrascan, 25549
Ultrasealer, 20461
Ultrasep, 30576
Ultrashine, 18387
Ultraslik, 21227
Ultrasnap Atp Test Devices, 23971
Ultrasonic Equipment, 21798
Ultrasonic Sensor, 30800
Ultratensity, 29242
Ultratoc, 30576
Ultravac, 24906
Ultravert, 24094
Ultraware, 30800
Ultrefiner, 28154
Ultrex, 30576
Umc, 13194
Umcka Coldcare, 8896
Umpqua Oats, 13150
Un-Fad Diet Packs, 7947
Un-Soap, 9238
Unarco, 18990
Unbelievable Green, 20966
Unbelievable!, 20966
Unbound Energy, 26668
Uncle Bens, 7952
Uncle Dave's, 5105
Uncle Dougie's, 13154
Uncle Fred's Fine Foods, 13155
Uncle John's Pride, 3177
Uncle Lee's Tea, 13156
Uncle Luke's, 7037
Uncle Matt's Organic, 13157

All Brands Index

Uncle Matt's, 3442, 21421
Uncle Phil's, 13880
Uncle Ralph's, 13158
Uncle Sam, 19178
Uncle Sam Cereal, 13124
Uncle Walter's, 4556
Uncle Waynes Fish Batter, 5946
Unclerays, 13159
Uncommon Threads, 30603
Uncut Before the Butcher, 6492
Underbar, 19203
Underberg Bitters, 9035
Underwood, 13174
Underwood, 864
Unearthed, 7526
Ungar's, 3727
Ungermatic, 30590
Unholey Bagel, 11043
Uni, 1934
Uni-Badge, 27575
Uni-Band, 26467
Uni-Cart, 20919
Uni-Flo, 28748
Uni-Freeze, 23075
Uni-Lift, 20919
Uni-Matic, 25309
Uni-Mod, 21044
Uni-Pac, 21044
Uni-Pak, 20710
Uni-Steel Lockers, 20354
Uni-Strap, 27575
Uni-Tension, 24350
Uni-Vac, 30639
Uni-Versal, 30601
Unibagger, 27089
Unibar, 20654
Unibrew, 13164
Unibroue, 13164
Unibuilt, 31214
Unica, 9980, 13165
Unico, 13191, 30639
Unicorn, 25788
Unicorn Pops, 163
Unicum Zwack, 3165
Unidex, 6211, 24226
Unifab, 30635
Unified Industries, 20752
Unifill, 22122
Unifit, 22554
Uniflo, 18426
Uniflow Fume Hoods, 23722
Uniflow Se, 23722
Unikleen, 27847
Unilast, 23543
Uniline Casework, 23722
Unimark, 26109
Unimax Large Floor Mount Hoods, 23722
Unimix, 21908
Unimove, 30607
Uniplace, 19090
Unipro, 1891, 8193
Unique, 13178
Unique Belgique, 10981
Unique Colonic Rinse, 13179
Unique Ingredients, 13177
Unique Pretzels, 972
Unirack Drive-In Rack, 30621
Unirak Pallet Rack, 30621
Uniroyal Ensolite, 27655
Unisab, 31401
Unisafe, 31401
Unispense, 29513
Unisystem, 18436
Unit Trane, 30382
United, 13196
United Brand, 13196
United Filters, 30636
United Society of Shakers, 11498
United With Earth, 13203
Unitray, 30563
Unitron, 30563
Unity Lab Services, 30217
Universal, 20256, 24517, 27914, 30676, 31049, 31435, 31442

Universal Ph Doser, 18899
Universal Stainless, 30684
Universal-Lift, 18498
Unna, 13212
Unreal, 13151
Unscrambler, 25900
Unsmoke, 27847
Unsteak-Out, 9196
Unturkey, 9196
Unwrap & Roll, 1174
Up Country Naturals, 7866
Up Mountain Switchel, 13213
Up-Right, 29081
Upco, 13196
Upender, 23460
Upper Bay, 865
Upper Crust Biscotti, 13216
Upper Fingers, 1018
Upright, 30695
Upstate Farms, 13218
Uptaste, 29001
Uptime, 13219
Upton's Naturals, 13220
Upzo, 13196
Ur20 Process Refractometer, 25820
Urban Bruce, 1796
Urban Delights, 11818
Urban Foods, 13223
Urban Moonshine, 13224
Urban Nomad Food, 6831
Urban Pie Pizza Co., 9719
Urban Special, 648
Urgasa, 13226
Urge, 2815, 20685
Uribel, 8389
Urnex, 30697
Urockit-K, 8389
Urschalloy, 30698
Urschel, 30698
Us Cola, 883
Us Range, 31092
Us Select, 883
Us Sugars, 13125
Us1, 22492
Usa, 5660
Usa Best, 13128
Usa Beverages, 13127
Usa Laboratories Nutrients, 13128
Usa Mints, 11051
Usa Sports Labs, 13128
Useco, 30563
Usg, 1692
Usil, 30550
Uss In-Tank Filter System, 30654
Ustenborg, 10906
Utc, 3479, 21460
Utec, 20290
Utilimaster, 20726
Utilitier, 24519
Utility, 2389, 30706
Utility Refrigeration, 24495
Utira-C, 8389
Utopia, 12762
Utzy Naturals, 13230
Uvaferm, 7176
Uvvw Decaff, 2854

V

V&V Supremo Cheeses & Meats, 7407
V-Lims, 18396
V-Master, 18498
V-Plus, 30854
V-Ram, 30711
V.G. Blue, 13303
V.I.P. Series, 30860
V.Pearl, 4947
V.W. Joyner Genuine Smithfield, 13237
V8, 2115
V8 Beverages, 2116
V8 Splash, 2115, 3773, 21785
V8 Vgo, 2115
Vac, 30263
Vac Airr, 30727
Vac Trac, 27377

Vac-U-Max, 30728
Vac-U-Pac, 31330
Vac-U-Vator, 20550
Vachon, 2121
Vactank, 30654
Vacu-Lift, 18191
Vacucam, 29011
Vacuhoist, 19963
Vaculet Usa, 18877
Vacumaster, 19183
Vacushear, 18010, 18126
Vacview, 21657
Vahine, 8061
Val Linda, 20144
Val Verde Winery, 13245
Valamont, 8794
Valay, 28717
Valbreso Feta, 7126
Valco, 30935
Valdiguie, 5989
Valdor, 22535
Valentine, 21059
Valentine Sugars, 13248
Valentino, 5405
Valerian, 746
Valerian Extract, 9253
Valhalla Winery, 13250
Valitah 3000, 21282
Vall-Beam, 19429
Valley, 9594, 11312, 30746
Valley Bakery, 13256
Valley Dairy, 4227
Valley Farms, 13218
Valley Forge, 22650
Valley Fresh, 6000, 23861
Valley Gold, 2688
Valley King, 5517
Valley Lahvosh Crackerbread, 13256
Valley Lahvosh Flatbread, 13256
Valley Maid, 916, 10439
Valley of the Moon, 13267
Valley Pokt, 6221
Valley Queen, 13260
Valley Sun Organic Brown Rice, 4260
Valley View, 13266
Valley View Blueberries, 13263
Valley View Cheese, 13264
Valley Wraps, 13256
Vallley View, 29616
Valoroso, 12030
Valpo Velvet, 12741
Valrhona, 13251
Valu Pak, 28015
Valu Time, 1758, 12885, 19889, 30333
Valu-Beam, 19429
Valu-Fil, 343
Value Corner, 11073
Value Glacier, 3218
Value Tough, 23143
Valugards, 23556
Valulacer, 20654
Valutime, 11303, 13864, 28896
Valv-Chek, 27377
Van Asperen Vineyard, 10912
Van De Kamp, 13282
Van De Kamp's, 811
Van De Kamp's, 27540
Van De Walle Farms, 11135
Van Der Heyden, 13269
Van Dierman, 1524
Van Drunen Farms, 13270
Van Holten, 6353
Van Houten Drinks, 1056
Van Houten Professional, 1056
Van Houtte, 6818, 24802
Van Otis Swiss Fudge, 13277
Van Roy, 13279
Van Tone, 13280
Van Waters & Roger, 13281
Van Winkle, 11263
Van's, 13283
Van-Lang, 13284
Vana Life Foods, 13285
Vanaleigh 6b, 12085
Vance's Darifree, 13286

Vancouver Islander Lager, 13288
Vandalex, 25224
Vandalume, 27294
Vande Berg Scales, 30766
Vandon Sea-Pack, 2659
Vangard, 29242
Vangogh, 10906
Vanguard, 21512
Vanilla Imperial, 1581
Vanish, 10598
Vanleer, 1056
Vanmark, 13293, 30769
Vantaggio, 11777
Vantaggio D'Oro, 11777
Vapguard, 21252
Vapor Dragon, 28432
Vapor Lock, 29797
Vapor-Master, 22257
Vaporguard, 30486
Vaporplus, 20990
Vaportron, 25224
Vapure, 27352
Vaqmer, 25500
Var-I-Vol, 23857
Vari-Chain, 22445
Vari-Extenders, 20593
Vari-Pack, 21011
Vari-Pak, 20064
Vari-Temp, 23515
Variable Flow, 27516
Varian, 27729
Varietals, 12534
Varimixer, 31092
Varitrac, 30382
Varitrane, 30382
Vasario, 18195
Vasconia, 30783
Vascustrem, 13179
Vassi Espresso, 6547
Vassilaros, 6547
Vat 69, 3570
Vatore's, 13318
Vaughn Russell, 13302
Vaxa, 13304
Vaxa, 9237, 26785
Vbm, 5036
Vbt-1100, 24550
Vbt-250, 24550
Vbt-550, 24550
Vbz, 13421
Vec Loader, 30790
Vectaire, 26290
Vector, 27083, 31188
Vector Chns/O Analyzer, 30132
Vector Laser Power, 28915
Vector, 6765
Vectran, 20348
Vee Gee, 13498
Veelos, 22509
Veet, 10598
Veethane, 29148
Veg Con Beet, 4518
Veg Con Carrot, 4518
Veg Con Celery, 4518
Veg Fresh, 10491
Veg-A-Fed, 2576
Veg-A-Loid, 2386
Veg-Mix, 24812
Veg-T-Balls, 13315
Vega, 3379
Vega Fina, 10110
Vega Metias, 10110
Vega's Gourmet, 13306
Vegalene, 9648
Vegan Decadence, 4668
Vegan Gourmet, 3870
Vegan Rob's, 11484
Vegapure, 1692
Vegatronic 1000, 24076
Vegatronic 2000, 24076
Vegatronic 3000, 24076
Vege-Coat, 4914
Vegeful, 8448
Vegenaise, 3870
Vegetaballs, 13073

1343

All Brands Index

Vegetable Cocktail, 5555
Vegetable Magic, 7766, 25632
Vegetarian Cornmeal, 13305
Vegetarian Plusc, 13310
Vegetarian Slice of Life, 13316
Vegetarian Tamale, 13305
Vegetrates, 4063
Veggemo, 5064
Veggiballs, 4664
Veggiburger, 4664
Veggidogs, 4664
Veggie Fries, 4295, 5697
Veggie Glace Gold, 8538
Veggie Grownto, 10100
Veggie Ribs, 5629
Veggie Rings, 4295
Veggie Tots, 4295
Veggie-Deli Slices, 5358
Veggie-Deli, 5358
Veggie-DeliQuick Stick, 5358
Veggie-Go's, 12711
Veggie-Jerky, 5358
Veggieland, 13315
Veggimins, 13847
Vegginuggets, 4664
Vegit, 8448
Veglife, 9237, 26785
Vegolin Hvp, 4430
Vegy Vida, 13317
Veko, 13232
Velda, 13319
Vella, 13320
Velletric, 2010
Velure, 27690
Velva-Sheen, 25668
Velvatex, 13498
Velveeta, 6976, 6977
Velvet Creme, 13321
Velvetop, 3412
Velvetx, 13803
Vemag, 28291
Vemon Energy, 3725
Vendor Transport, 19139
Venezia, 4992
Venice Maid Products, 805
Ventana Wines, 13325
Ventilation, 22166
Ventilation & Process Air Systems, 28360
Ventilation Controllers, 28020
Ventomatic, 19898
Ventraflow, 22679
Ventura China, 30372
Venture For the Best, 13329
Venturi 25 Air Conveyor, 30654
Venturi 30, 30654
Venus, 6540, 12721, 20258, 30193
Venus Wafers, 13330
Veo, 24812
Ver-Mex, 2670
Vera Cruz Mexican Foods, 8898
Veramonte, 4649
Verbatim, 28140
Verdaccio, 12437
Verdant Kitchen, 13333
Verday, 13334
Verde, 11883
Verde Farms, 13335
Verdecoat, 7857
Verdegrass, 5663
Verdi Line, 6340
Veri-Fry, 25291
Veri-Fry Pro, 25291
Veribor, 18191
Verifine, 4185
Verilon, 30807
Verisoyc, 13310
Verlasso, 13341
Vermilion, 13342
Vermont, 13343
Vermont Maid, 864
Vermont Meadow Muffins, 12847
Vermont Pasture Patties, 12847
Vermont Pure Water, 3217
Vermont Sprout, 12732

Vermont Sugar Free, 7866
Vermont Tortilla, 13362
Vermont Velvet, 10696, 28371
Vernaccia, 13375
Vernon Bc, 2301
Vernors, 3725, 6818, 24802
Veronique, 9555
Versa Color, 23994
Versa Iii Lub, 19654
Versa Pro, 30080
Versa-Cap, 21033
Versa-Chair, 28006
Versa-Fil, 21033
Versa-Lite, 23489
Versa-Panel, 19051
Versa-Tech, 23543
Versaflow Liquid Filler, 24293
Versaform, 27740
Versajet, 19021
Versaline, 27980
Versamatic, 31251
Versapak, 30133
Versaprint, 30434
Versatech, 19021
Versatilt, 18181
Versatrace, 20951
Versatrol, 1009
Versid, 30059
Versilac, 98
Vertex, 30820
Very Old Barton, 11263
Very Old Barton Bourbon, 11264
Veryfine, 12281, 26147
Veryfine Juices, 13368
Vespron, 28919
Vess, 10637
Vesta, 24038
Vetstar, 18396
Vetter Vineyards, 13371, 30826
Veuve Clicquot, 8452
Veuve Cliquot, 3570
Vex-Cap, 29727
Veza Sur Brewing Co., 571
Vffs Packaging System, 20070
Vg Buck California Foods, 2085
Via Roma, 2847
Viader, 13373
Viaggio Coffee, 1636, 19825
Viaka, 8062
Vial Washer, 25900
Vial Washer-Dryer, 25920
Viano Winery, 13374
Vibe-O-Bin, 23075
Vibe-O-Vey, 23075
Vibra Pad, 21215
Vibra-Ball, 20644
Vibra-Cell, 29362
Vibra-Meter Feeder, 29763
Vibra-Might, 20644
Vibracone, 30654
Vibraflex, 26049
Vibramatic, 26411
Vibro-Block, 19090
Vibro-Energy, 29853
Vic's, 13377
Vicality Albafil, 1692
Vicam, 31041
Vicenzi, 6255
Vichy, 9995
Vichy Springs, 13378
Vichy Springs Mineral Water, 13378
Vickey's Vittles, 13379
Vicki's Rocky Road, 8240
Vicks, 12721, 30193
Vicky's All Natural, 13380
Vicron, 1692
Victor, 13384
Victor's, 6160
Victoria, 71, 13388
Victoria Creams, 10840
Victoria E.S.B., 7143
Victoria Fancy, 13387
Victoria Lager, 13288
Victoria, 864
Victorianox, 21883

Victory, 26476, 30840
Vida, 9964
Vidalia, 13393
Vidalia Sweets, 13394
Vidarome, 13444
Video Munchies, 10179, 27669
Videojet, 30841
Videri Chocolate Factory, 13395
Videx, 1721
Videyards, 3952
Vidmar, 29584
Vie De France, 1891
Vienna, 13398, 13401
Vienna Bageldog, 10040
Vienna Lager, 1139
Vienna, 13400
Vienot, 12672
Vietti, 13402
View-Lok, 20593
Vifan Bt, 30717
Vifan Cl/Cls, 30717
Vifan Cz, 30717
Vigne Regali, 1006
Vigo, 13404
Vigorsol, 9956
Vigorteen, 1151
Viki's Granola, 13409
Viking, 9094, 13407, 13516, 20065, 30743
Viking, 5844
Vilas Del Turbon, 2815, 20685
Viledon, 22865
Villa Cape Winery, 10952
Villa Frizzoni, 11504, 29095
Villa Helena, 13412
Villa Lan Franca, 11205
Villa Mella, 2670
Villa Milan, 13413
Villa Prima, 11317
Villa Prime Pizzeria, 11316
Villa Quenchers, 6867
Villaformosa, 3545
Village, 7463
Village Bakers, 21227
Village Hearth, 9736
Village Roaster, 13415
Village Square, 23772
Villaggio, 2121
Villar Vintners, 13416
Vilter, 30854
Vimco, 10558
Vimo Cave, 31256
Vin Eclipser, 8513
Vin Vault, 3834
Vinatopia, 5524
Vincent, 30858
Vincenza's, 11224
Vincenzo's, 8770
Vincotto, 3236
Vine Series, 9452
Vineco, 555
Vinegar Joe, 10196
Vinitrox, 9029, 26626
Vinmar, 6460
Vino De Pata, 10165
Vino Temp, 31256
Vinoklet, 13429
Vinotheque, 31256
Vinta, 3384
Vintage, 3661, 10637
Vintage Port, 942
Vinter's Choice, 1080
Vintner's Ii, 24636
Vintner's Selection, 24636
Vintnercel, 11794
Vio, 2815, 20685
Vio Bio Limo, 2815, 20685
Viobin, 13435
Viognier, 2044, 6603, 12534
Viognier Santa Barbara County, 4353
Viola's, 13436
Violet, 13437
Violife, 13438
Vip, 13240, 13241, 20120
Vip Lite, 20120

Vip, 237, 238
Viper, 11051, 19975
Viper Blast, 11051
Viper Gum, 11051
Viper Venom, 11051
Viper Vials, 11051
Virgil's, 13439
Virgil's Root Beers, 10507
Virginia, 2075
Virginia Artesianc, 13442, 30863
Virginia Beauty, 5752
Virginia Brand, 13446, 13454
Virginia Diner, 13445
Virginia Gentleman, 59
Virginia Gentlemen, 11263
Virginia Grown, 30864
Virginia Roast, 4239
Virginia Smoked Sausage, 12463
Virginia's Finest, 30864
Virility Plus, 9253
Virture Cider, 571
Visa, 23291, 26187
Visco Lab 400, 20159
Visco Pro 1000, 20159
Visco Pro 2000, 20159
Viscoanalyser, 18235
Viscol, 10158, 27656
Viscolak, 9802
Viscomix, 13498
Viscor, 28462
Viscosity, 28462
Viscozyme L, 1692
Vision, 3948
Visionary Vinegars, 982
Visioneye, 30422
Visions, 22348, 31344, 31345
Visitint, 30878
Vispro, 25530
Vista Classic Line, 26826
Vista D'Oro, 13452
Vista Verde, 1306
Vista Verde, 11504, 29095
Visual Boss, 23859
Visutate, 30878
Visutype, 30878
Vit-A-Boost, 7947
Vit20, 10637
Vita, 4822, 4942, 13454, 13473, 24069
Vita Brand, 13446
Vita Coco, 6818, 24802
Vita Foods, 30618
Vita Lustre, 13816
Vita Plus, 1735
Vita Splash, 12182
Vita-Crunch, 9548
Vita-Curaid, 4430
Vita-Ex, 6340
Vita-Fresh, 2032
Vita-Mix Drink Machine, 30884
Vita-Most, 2032
Vita-Plus, 13455
Vita-Prep, 30884
Vita-Pro, 30884
Vita-Sealed, 8628
Vita-Vista, 13943
Vitaball, 6107
Vitabrownies, 13464
Vitacakes, 13464
Vitafusion, 2666, 20561
Vital Cuisine, 6000, 23861
Vital Farmsc, 13461
Vital K, 4807
Vital Life, 6905
Vital Proteins, 13462
Vitalert, 9957
Vitalfa, 12638
Vitaline Coq10, 4086
Vitality Works, 13466
Vitamin Classics, 4888
Vitamin Water, 2811, 4066
Vitaminder, 30882
Vitaminerals, 13469
Vitamite, 3593, 21618
Vitamixes, 13464
Vitamuffins, 13464

1344

All Brands Index

Vitanat, 7172
Vitaphos, 4430
Vitarich, 13471
Vitaspelt, 8886
Vitatops, 13464
Vito's Bakery, 6410
Vitracite, 20595
Vitter, 28967
Vittles, 14043
Vittleveyor, 21870
Viva, 2815, 8105, 20685, 24838
Viva Lard, 2796, 20666
Viva Manteca Mixta, 2796, 20666
Viva Retail Lard, 2796, 20666
Vivani, 6279
Vivant, 3384
Vive Organic, 13478
Vivident, 9956
Vivienne, 13479
Viviscal, 2666, 20561
Vivolac, 7668, 13480
Vivoo, 13481
Vivrac, 13482
Vivre Dans La Nuit, 56
Vivre Une Double Vie, 56
Vixen Kitchen, 13483
Vlaha, 6986
Vlasic, 27540
Vlier, 20143
Vmc, 30854
Vmc-Nsa, 30720
Vocatura, 13484
Vod, 13243
Vodka Nikolai, 3545
Vogel, 2935
Voget Meats, 13486
Vogt, 25871
Vogt Tube-Ice, 30892
Vogue Beef Base, 13487
Vogue Chicken Base, 13487
Vogue Onion Base, 13487
Vogue Vegebase, 13487
Vogue Vegetarian Chicken Base, 13487
Vol-U-Flex, 28763
Volcano Wings, 3511
Vollrath, 19401
Volpi, 13490
Volpi Foods, 6560
Volta, 18873, 18874
Volufil, 23857
Volvic, 1661
Von Strasser, 13492
Voorhees, 30904
Voortman, 13494
Vortex, 26529, 29489
Vorti-Siv, 30905
Vortron, 18965
Voss Water, 5884
Votatr, 31049
Vox, 1120
Voyager, 21186, 28508
Vpeez, 19743
Vr, 27642
Vratislav, 8459
Vrr, 22706
Vs Bagger, 31085
Vt Tune, 18495
Vt-550, 23503
Vulcalite, 23543
Vulcan, 24038, 27063
Vulcano, 29520
Vulkollan, 30255
Vutec Usa, 31281
Vycor, 20981
Vynecrest Vineyards, 13497

W

W C Insect Finish One, 31010
W&G's, 13499
W-R, 2389
W.A. Brown, 30928
W.E.M., 13810
W.L. Weller, 11263
Wachusett, 13522, 13523

Wack-O-Wax, 12880
Wacker, 1692
Wacky Mac, 10777, 28421
Waco, 31213
Wade Rain, 30972
Wafa, 9863
Wafflewaffle, 13525, 30973
Wagner, 21636
Wagner Brewing Co., 13529
Wagner Vineyards, 13529
Wagshal's, 13530
Wah Maker, 9439
Wahoo! Appetizers, 5294
Wai Lana, 13532
Waiker Conveyor Belt & Equipment, 2436, 20451
Waist Watcher, 174, 10151
Wakasa, 12228
Wakefield, 13120
Wal-Vac, 30977
Walco, 30978
Walden Farms, 13538, 13539
Waldo, 10229
Waldon, 30982
Walker, 30989
Walker's, 13544
Walkers, 13544
Wall Hugger, 20882
Wall Sconce, 18352
Wallabeans, 7912
Wallaby, 13546
Wallaby Organic, 3379
Wallace, 5888
Wallingford, 13551
Walls Berry Farm Organic Preserves, 12921
Walls Berry Farm Preserves, 12921
Wally Biscotti, 13552
Wally Walleye, 1018
Wally's, 10869
Walmart, 11260
Walnut Acres, 5505
Walnut Crest, 1006
Wals Brut, 71
Waltham, 7952
Wampler's Farm, 13559
Wan Ja Shan, 7836, 25691
Wan-Na-Bes, 11552
Wanchai Ferry, 4947
Wanda's, 5711
Wandering Bear Coffee, 13563
Wanderoot, 8459
Wanko, 1120
War Wrap, 26680
Warcon Out, 31010
Warfarers, 3953
Warheads, 6483
Warhol, 10229
Waring, 31007
Warm Grip, 20277
Warme Bakker, 3078
Warner Electric, 18678
Warner Linear, 18678
Warner Vineyards, 13570
Warp Energy Mints, 1343
Warp Micro Hyper Charged Mints, 1343
Warren's Wonderful W, 9688
Warrnambool Cheese and Butter, 11211
Warther Handcrafted Cutlery, 31016
Warwick Distillery, 13578
Warwick Winery, 13578
Wasatch, 11289
Wasbash Heritage, 13517
Wasbash Valley Farm, 10180
Wash & Clean, 19741
Washburn, 4198
Washer Holddown Mats, 19111
Washguard, 25013
Washington, 13803
Washington Natural, 9469
Wasp & Hornet Destroyer, 19364
Wasson, 13584
Waste King, 18892
Wat-A-Mat, 22842
Watch Dog, 19442

Water & Health, 3469
Water Crackers, 3384
Water Drops, 12430
Water Fountain of Edenton, 3469
Water Joe, 13585
Water Maid, 10777, 28421
Water Miser, 21691
Water Pro, 19763
Water Valley Farms, 11639
Water Works, 26337
Waterfall, 11138
Waterfall Hydrochiller, 23042
Waterfield Farms, 13586
Waterford Crystal, 31081
Waterfrontbistro, 11073
Waterloo Dark, 1702
Watermate, 22203
Waterpik, 2666, 20561
Waterpro, 25041, 31031
Watersboten, 11038
Watertyme, 1292
Watson Fine Teas, 1045
Watson-Marlow, 25775
Wattie's, 6977
Watts Island Trading, 1470
Watusee Foods, 13593
Waukesha Cherry-Burrell, 28714
Wave Flavored Vodkas, 11264
Wave'n Dry, 13595, 31053
Waves, 13614
Wawona Frozen Foods, 13598
Wax Orchards, 13599
Wax Tex, 20628
Waxjet, 22807
Way Better Snacks, 13600
Waymar, 31057
Wayne, 9584, 31059
Wayne Farms, 2970, 11053
Wayne Farms, 13607
Wayne Gretzky Estates, 555
Wber Seasonings, 73
Wbm, 13510
We Rub You, 13608
We're Talking Serious Salsa, 4587
Wear-Ever, 25320
Wearever, 23261, 26216
Weat, 7310
Weather-All Bars, 22732
Weatherguard, 28261
Weathershield, 23860
Weaver, 2126, 4387
Weaver Original, 13611
Weaver's, 10486
Weavewear, 20256
Weavewood, 31066
Webb's, 13613
Webblock, 25852
Webcenter, 23993
Weber, 31079
Weber's Horseradish Mustard, 5734
Weber's Hot Garlic M, 5734
Weber's Hot Piocacic, 5734
Weber's Spicy Dill Pickles, 5734
Weber's Sweet Pickle, 5734
Weber-Univers, 23460
Weber, 864
Weco, 24823
Wecobee Fs, 12081
Wecobee M, 12081
Wecobee S, 12081
Wedding, 21059
Wedge Lock, 28327
Wedge Press, 19501
Wedgwood, 31081
Wedron Grills, 19295
Wee Heavy Winter Ale, 5515
Wee Willy, 7157
Weetabix, 1020, 13621
Wega, 31083
Wege, 1310, 13622
Wegmans Gluten Free, 13624
Wegmans Organic, 13624
Wegro Metal Crown, 20868
Wei-Chaun, 13625
Wei-Chuan, 13625

Weigh Down, 7404
Weigh Pack Systems, 31085
Weigh Trac, 30086
Weigh-Master, 23857
Weigh-Tranix, 30766
Weighart, 30792
Weighsquare, 22140
Weight Lifter, 25277
Weight Watchers Smart Ones, 6977
Weight Watchers Baked Goods, 3412
Weihnachtskatze, 339
Weiler, 31087
Weiloss, 7758
Weingut Wittman, 4677
Weinman, 21046
Weinstock, 25658
Weinstock Wine Cellars, 10952
Weir's, 730
Weis, 6126
Weis Five Star, 13512, 30940
Weis Quality, 13512, 30940
Weiser River Whoppers, 13630
Weiss, 7310
Welbilt, 31093
Welch, 27729
Welch's, 5694, 13635
Welch's Chillers, 8797
Welch's Concentrates, 8797
Welch's Essentials, 8797
Welch's Food & Snacks, 8797
Welch's Fruit Fizz, 8797
Welch's Fruit Juices, 8797
Welch's Jams, Jellie & Spreads, 8797
Welch's Light, 8797
Welch's Natural Spreads, 8797
Welch's Refrigerted Juice Cocktails, 8797
Welch's Sparkling, 8797
Welch's, 6483
Welchs, 4659
Welcome, 13637
Welcome Home, 25299
Weldon, 2923
Well Seasoned Traveler, 194
Well Tempered, 21040
Well Yes, 2116
Well's Ace, 10076
Wella Bar, 13641
Weller Bourbon, 3570
Wellesley, 68
Wellesse, 13642
Wellfleet Farms, 9355
Wellfleet Farms Cranberry Sauce, 9355
Wellfleet Farms Specialty Foods, 9355
Wellgate, 2666, 20561
Wellington Foods, 13644
Wellmade Honey, 13114, 30527
Wellness Drops, 9201
Wells Lamont, 31099
Wells Manufacturing, 29466
Welsh Farms, 4290
Welsh Farms - Ice Cream, 13647
Welsite, 30508
Wemco, 28557
Wenatchee Gold, 2560
Wenatchee Valley, 5826
Wendaphos, 13648, 31107
Wendy, 8956
Wenk, 13652
Wenner, 13653
Wensleydale Blueberry, 11968
Wente, 13654
Werner, 20143
Werther's Original, 12147, 12148
Wesco, 28488, 29632, 29633
Wesson, 6084
West Bend, 4538
West Indian Kola, 5177
West Island, 6119, 24012
West Pak, 13666
West Star, 31129
West Weigh, 24045
West's Best, 12758
Westbrae Natural, 5505, 13672
Westco, 955, 13675
Western, 13677, 18022

1345

All Brands Index

Western Beauty, 965
Western Classics, 12276
Western Creamery, 13680
Western Family, 3387, 9469, 12304, 22920
Western Gold, 6267
Western Pacific Storage Systems, 18990
Western Style Soft Drinks, 13728
Western Syrup, 13686
Westfalia, 31153
Westhampton Farms, 9000
Weston, 13691
Weston Gallery, 31242
Westpac, 8724
Westport Farms Sparkling, 13693
Westport Farms Specialty Foods, 13693
Westport Farms White & Rose, 13693
Westport Rivers Vine, 13693
Westsoy, 5505, 13672
Westwood Winery, 13696
Wet-Nap 1000-Pak, 26632
Wetherby, 13698
Wexxar, 31163
Weyauwega, 13700, 31165
Wha Guru Chew, 9245
Whale's Tale, 2691
Whale-Of-A-Pail, 11725
Whaler Vineyard Flag, 13701
Whaley's, 13702
Whaley's Fancy Shelled, 13702
What's For Dinner?, 12467
Whatchamacallit, 5818, 23750
Whatman, 31168
Wheat Nuts, 525
Wheat Thins, 8729
Wheat-Free, 9730
Wheatbrook, 10629
Wheateena, 12269
Wheatena, 6267
Wheaties, 4947
Wheatstone, 13707
Wheatsworth, 8729
Wheel-Ezy, 24784
Wheeler's, 6195
Whetstone Candy, 13708
Whetstone Valley, 11287
Which Ends, 6787
Whidbey's, 10468
While-U-Color, 23152
Whip N Ice, 4483
Whip N Top, 4483
Whip-Master, 24725
Whipped Pastry Boutique, 13709
Whirlaway, 18892
Whirley Pop, 10180
Whisk, 31175
Whiskas, 7952
Whiskey Run, 1123
Whisky Gate Pourer, 19999
Whiskygate, 19998
Whisper Chocolate Bon Bons, 643
Whisper White, 9069
Whisperflow, 19334
Whisperlite, 26337
Whispurr Air, 25785
Whistle, 7952
Whitcraft Winery, 13713
White, 21189
White Board Marker, 26109
White Buffalo, 1837
White Camel, 13714
White Cap, 1464
White Cap, 13328
White Castle, 13551
White Chocolate Moose, 9115
White Dove, 13118
White Hawk, 18622
White Horse, 3570
White House, 13717, 13720
White Label Yerba Mate Soda, 13721
White Lightning, 5861
White Magic, 28635
White Mountain, 9664
White Mule, 31099
White Oak Chardonnay, 13725

White Oak Farm and Tablec, 13722
White Oak Merlot, 13725
White Oak Sauvignon, 13725
White Oak, 11725
White Premium, 7583
White Rabbit, 10457, 31181
White Rascal, 838
White Riesling, 1314
White Rock, 1061, 13728
White Rock Orchards, 13728
White Rock Vineyards, 13729
White Satin, 407
White Stevia, 9201
White Swan, 5288, 9763, 27283, 28808
White Tiger Rice, 7723
White Wave, 3009
White Westinghouse, 22872
White Wings, 1917
Whitecliff, 13735
Whitefish, 5323
Whitehall, 13737
Whitehall Lane, 13736
Whitehaven, 3834
Whitehouse Foods, 8796
Whitewater, 5304
Whitey's, 237, 238
Whitford, 13741
Whiting & Davis, 31185
Whitman's, 10991
Whitney Distributing, 10820
Whitney Yogurt, 13744
Whiz-Lifter, 22837
Whizard Gloves, 24700
Whol-Bean, 13614
Whole Body Cleanse, 4086
Whole Earth, 10488
Whole Spectrum, 4125
Whole Sun, 7569
Wholefruit, 6338, 20946
Wholemec, 13749
Wholesome, 8951
Wholesome Foods, 13751
Wholesome Goat, 11211
Wholly Guacamole, 6000, 23861
Wholly Wholesome, 10981
Whoppers, 5818, 23750
Wichita Clutch, 18678
Wick Fowler Chili Kits, 10657
Wick's, 13758
Wicked Crisps, 13759
Wicked Mixc, 13760
Wicked Weed Brewing, 571
Wicker, 13762
Wide Awake Coffee Co., 12885, 30333
Wide Shoulders Bakin, 7469
Wide Track, 30503
Widman's Country, 10244
Widmer Brothers, 3107
Widmer Hefeweizen, 26668
Widmer's Cheese, 13765
Wiederkehr Wine, 13769
Wiegmann & Rose, 31195
Wigwam, 1061
Wik Stik, 26109
Wilbur, 13772
Wilbur Chocolate, 13610
Wilch, 23420, 31201
Wilcox, 13774
Wild & Ricey, 575
Wild American Herb Co., 13998
Wild and Mild, 1279
Wild Blackberry, 10478
Wild Blend Rice, 7723
Wild Blue, 26668
Wild Crafted Food From the Gulf Of, 7788
Wild Fruitz, 13778
Wild Hibiscus Flowers, 13779
Wild Hog Vineyard, 13780
Wild Horse, 13781
Wild Huckleberry, 5323
Wild Jungle Animal Crackers, 3343
Wild Keta Salmon, 6494
Wild Man, 5520
Wild Olive, 2801

Wild Poppy, 13784
Wild Raspberry, 5304
Wild Red King Salmon, 6494
Wild Rocket, 10815
Wild Roots, 2971
Wild Springs, 1292
Wild Thyme Cottage Products, 13787
Wild Turkey, 2114
Wild Tusker, 13006
Wild Veggie, 9592
Wild Vines, 3834
Wild West, 12688
Wild West Spices, Inc., 13789
Wild White King Salmon, 6494
Wildcat Produce Garden, 13791
Wildcat Strong, 7123
Wildcraft, 4537
Wilder, 31206
Wilderness Family Naturals, 13796
Wildfire, 9935
Wildflower, 10478
Wildfruit Fruit Snacks, 4884
Wildhurst Cabernet F, 13793
Wildhurst Chardonnay, 13793
Wildhurst Merlot, 13793
Wildhurst Zinfandel, 13793
Wildleaf, 13782
Wildman's, 30917
Wildway, 13799
Wildwood, 10365
Wilevco, 31209
Willard, 12003
William Hill, 13814
William Hill Estate, 3834
William Wheeler Winery, 12672
William's Corn, 10274
Williamette Valley Mustard, 1034
Williams, 1917, 13822, 13823, 31231
Williams-Selym Winery, 13821
Williamsburg Winery, 13825
Willie's, 12175
Willoughby's, 13829
Willow, 13830
Willow Farms, 10728
Willow Oak Farms, 13832
Willpak Liquid Systems, 31222
Wilshire, 20975, 20976
Wilson Art, 25935
Wilson Continental D, 13110
Wilson Foods, 13835
Wiltec, 31240
Wilton, 31242
Wiltshire, 2357
Wimberley Valley, 13837
Win Pen, 26109
Win You, 2750
Winchester, 11951, 29510
Wincoat, 31252
Wind & Willow Key Lime Cheeseball, 806
Wind Over Water, 24409
Windansea Wheat, 6711
Windex, 21757
Windguard, 25785
Windham Hearth, 13343
Windmaster, 18321
Windsock, 7209
Windsor, 6661, 30073, 31252
Windsor Nature's Seasons, 6661
Windsor Vineyards, 13434
Windsor Half Salt, 6661
Windstream Windbreak, 7740
Windwalker, 13846
Windy, 25299
Windy Shoal, 8219
Wine Country, 6019, 23878
Wine Country Chef Gourmet Marinade, 13848
Wine Country Chef Lemon Pepper Rub, 13848
Wine Country Chef Spiced Mustard, 13848
Wine Country Chief Spiced Bbq Rub, 13848
Wine Country Kitchens, 13849

Wine Gift Packaging, 5280
Wine Well, 31256, 31261
Winekeeper, 31256, 31263
Winemaker's Choice, 5498, 23518
Winemakers Reserve, 4649
Winematic, 19203
Wines, 2343
Winexpert, 555
Winey Keemun English Breakfast, 5228, 23295
Winfield, 7198
Winfrey's, 13853
Wing Hing Gold Coin, 9807
Wing Hing Panda, 9807
Wing It, 13854
Wing's, 13858, 13861
Wing-Ditties, 1654
Wing-Lok, 29221
Winger, 13860
Winklepress, 18556
Winky Foods, 7168
Winliner, 23708
Winmix, 13863
Winn & Lovett, 13864
Winn-Dixie, 11838, 13864
Winpak, 23708
Winslow, 22140
Winspex, 24005
Winston, 4038
Winsuel, 5095
Winter Block, 5193
Winter Garden, 10038
Winter Gold, 7569
Winter Harbor, 3780
Winter Solstice, 549
Winter Stout, 11992
Winter Warlock, 1720
Winter Warmer, 1401
Winter Wonder, 11846
Winterbraun, 7554
Winterbrook, 13872
Winterfest, 8459
Winterfresh, 7952, 13960
Winterhook, 10629
Winters, 1638
Wintrex, 833
Winworx, 24050
Winworx Open Series, 24050
Wipco, 24549
Wipe Away, 23160, 24499
Wipe Out, 7143
Wire Dek, 29524
Wire Rite, 18419
Wiremaid Usa, 31281
Wiretainer, 29524
Wisco Envelope, 22187
Wiscon, 10335
Wisconsin American Ginseng, 10335
Wisconsin Gold, 10655
Wisconsin Lakeshore, 4753
Wisconsin Pride, 10752
Wisconsin Whey International, 13881
Wisdom & Warter, 1006
Wisdom Nutrition, 13883
Wisdom of the Ancients Herbal Teas, 13883
Wisdom Panel, 7952
Wise Mouth, 13885
Wisecrackers, 9799
Wiser's Deluxe, 3024
Wiser's Special Blend, 3024
Wiser's Very Old, 3024
Wisezone, 23993
Wishbone Utensil Tableware Line, 31293
Wisi Club, 1231
Wisnack, 3501
Wit, 5304
With Our Compliment, 21608
Witness Tree Vineyard, 13889
Witt Printing, 22187
Wittco Foodservice Equipment, 24038
Witte, 31298
Witte Pumps, 24761
Wix-Fresh, 13890
Wiz, 7671

All Brands Index

Wizard, 29360
Wizards, 3956
Wizbanger, 11320
Wm. Wycliff Vineyards, 3834
Wnp - Washed Natural Sesame Seeds, 11462
Wobblers, 27575
Woeber's, 13894
Wok Menu, 3513
Wokvel, 13336
Wolf, 24038, 27063
Wolf Blass, 12937
Wolf Linde, 28967
Wolf Pak, 25277
Wolf's Scottish Cream Ale, 13288
Wolferman's, 13899
Wolffs, 1391
Wollersheim Winery, 13903
Wolverine, 26122
Woman's Select, 8009
Womens Bread, 4702
Wonder, 4529, 6395, 13691
Wonder Bread, 3056, 6555
Wonder Foil, 12973, 30444
Wonder, 10777, 28421
Wonderful Halos, 13906
Wonderful Life, 12486
Wonderful Sweet Scarletts, 13906
Wonka, 4255
Wonka Pixy Stix Mixers, 4255
Wonka, 8945
Wood Care, 19713
Wood Show, 24414
Wood Welded, 26077
Woodbury Vineyards, 13915
Woodchuck Draft Cider, 5355
Woodchuck Pear Cider, 1208
Woodcraft, 18022
Woodee, 31252
Wooden Valley, 13916
Woodfield Farms, 13923
Woodfield Fish & Oyster, 13917
Woodfield Ice, 13917
Woodford Reserve, 1784
Woodford Reserve, 10998
Woodie Pie, 13918
Woodkor, 22065
Woodman, 24881
Woods, 13920
Woodside Vineyards, 13921
Woodstock Wheat, 5903
Woodstock, 1484
Woodwelded, 23826
Woody Stringer, 31331
Woolite, 10598
Woolmaster, 28242
Woolwich Dairy, 11209, 11211
Worcester, 8256
Work Horse, 22322
Work Right, 19151
Work Right Interlock, 19151
Work Station Airlock, 19151
Workmaster, 20923
Workout Energy Drinks, 13728
Worksman Cycles, 31338
World, 31340
World Berries, 9237, 26785
World Classics, 1758, 19889
World Coffee Safari Gourmet, 11855
World Cup, 13934
World Dryer, 29466
World Harbors, 13938
World Harbors, 8415
World Kitchen's, 1796
World of Chia, 13945
World Tableware, 25281
World Wide, 31355
World's Best, 5590
World's Best Griddle, 18288
World's Finest Chocolate, 13948
World-Beam, 19429
Worthington, 5799, 8551
Worthington's, 8459
Worthy Cabernet, 11810
Wos-Wit, 5406

Woven Wire, 19111
Wowie!, 9500
Wp, 31142
Wp Foodfilm, 31142
Wp Handywrap, 31142
Wpc, 20847
Wpc 34, 13881
Wr-25, 31058
Wrap Arounds, 7063
Wrap It, 28489
Wrap King, 19985
Wrap'n Roll, 7252
Wrap-It-Heat, 18334
Wrapitz, 7076
Wrapnet, 31142
Wrappers, 7063
Wrappetizers, 530
Wrappy, 5573
Wright Delicious, 13959
Wright's, 864
Wright-Austin, 23672
Wright, 13109
Wrigley, 541
Wrigley's Spearmint, 13960
Wrigley's Spearminti, 7952
Wrigley's, 7952
Ws-50/Ws-50 Bl, 18352
Wsi, 13944
Wsr, 8899
Wu Wei, 1501
Wuhan Asia-Pacific Condiments, 8061
Wunder Bar, 13834
Wunder Creamery, 13961
Wunder-Bar, 19218
Wunderbar, 10040
Wunderbar, 13109
Wundernuggets, 3109
Wurster & Sanger, 21109
Wurstmeister, 11059
Wussy Hot Sauce, 21336
Wuthrich, 5282
Wwrapps, 10968
Wyandot, 13964
Wyandotte Graystone Winery, 13965
Wyandotte Winery, 13965
Wychwood, 4148
Wyders Cider, 26668
Wye River, 5717
Wyk, 30695
Wyler's, 6483
Wyler's Light, 6483
Wynns Coonawarra Estate, 12937
Wypall, 24839
Wysong, 13967

X

X Stamper, 26302
X-1, 23273
X-Chain, 22890
X-Fine, 13498
X-Gk, 26337
X-Max, 20153
X-Press, 31370
X-Series, 20448
X-Stamper, 18276, 21113, 21199
X-Tra-Touch, 12979
X-Treme Freeze, 4901
Xa Series, 19625
Xactpak, 31044
Xaminer, 29720
Xanadu Exotic Tea, 2834
Xangold, 1692
Xcel, 31175
Xchange, 18995
Xenopressure Xenorol, 22254
Xerolyt, 26040
Xing, 8955
Xip - Salmon Cavier, 9344
Xl, 21315, 27711, 30952
Xl 2000, 13881
Xl 440, 13881
Xl 480, 13881
Xl Airlock, 21526
Xl-1, 20121

Xpresslane, 25377
Xr, 27083
Xspec, 24005
Xt, 21222
Xtc, 13697
Xtra, 2666, 20561
Xtreme Nerds, 4255
Xxx Habanero, 3537
Xylac, 31184
Xylan, 31184
Xylan Eterna, 31184
Xylan Plus, 31184

Y

Ya-Hoo!, 13979
Yago Sant'gria, 7655
Yakima Valley, 13984
Yakisoba, 13560
Yakshi Fragrances, 7562
Yale, 20752
Yamaizumi, 8412
Yamajirushi, 8412
Yamamotoyama 1690, 12053
Yamasa, 13986
Yamato, 31391
Yamato Colony, 7489
Yamazaki, 12315
Yamazaki Aged Umeshu, 1120
Yamhill Wines, 13990
Yamic Yogurt, 792
Yankee Clipperc, 9748
Yanni, 6719
Yardney, 31392
Yardski, 24064
Yata, Pilta, Kapha Teas, 5679
Yatir Winery, 10952
Yaucono, 2004
Yazi Ginger Vodka, 5981
Ye Olde English, 1134
Ye Olde Farm Style, 9585
Year 2000, 21059
Yeats, 26557
Yello-Jacket, 18022
Yellow Emperor, 13998
Yellow Gold Shelf St, 8838
Yellow Jacket, 23222
Yellow Label, 13740
Yellow Out, 24386
Yellow Rose, 11834
Yellowglen, 12937
Yerba Prima, 14000
Yervoy, 1721
Yes, 19008
Yick Lung, 14003
Ying Yang, 10708
Ying's, 14005
Yioryo, 14069
Yiotis, 6986
Yo Baby Yogurt, 12145
Yo Cream, 3378
Yo Cream Smoothies, 3378
Yo Mama's, 14006
Yo-Goat, 2793
Yocream, 3379
Yocrunch, 3379
Yoder Dairies, 3469
Yogi Tea, 14011
Yogourmet, 7667
Yogurt Starter, 8816
Yohimbe, 1532
Yohimbe Bar, 572
Yoki, 4947
Yonique, 1977
Yonkers Brewing Company, 14015
Yoohoo, 3725
Yop, 14017
Yoplait, 20946
Yoplait, 4947
York, 5818, 20526, 23750, 28967
York & Masterrange, 30364
York Mountain, 14018
York Pewter, 26887
Yorkcord, 26280
Yorkedge, 26280

Yorkflex, 26280
Yorkgrip, 26280
Yorklink, 26280
Yorklon, 26280
Yorkmate, 26280
Yorkpack, 26280
Yorktex, 26280
Yorktex Leather, 26280
Yorktown Baking Company, 14019
Yoshida Foods International, 14020
You Win, 14024
You're the Greatest!, 21059
Young's Breading, 3695
Young's Lobster Pound, 14027
Yowser!!, 4586
Yoyummy, 5356
Ypp-Hoo, 8586
Yu-Qui-Tas, 100
Yuccafoam, 1179, 19542
Yuengling, 3310
Yuki Nigori, 12500
Yukon, 27632
Yukon Sourdough Recipe, 10426
Yule Tide, 2763
Yuletide, 10773
Yuletide Porter, 8153
Yum Yum Stix, 6685
Yumbutter, 12964
Yummy Fruit Company, 5036
Yumy Yumy, 6810
Yup!, 2811
Yutaka, 2719
Yves Veggie Cuisine, 3773, 5505, 21785
Yvonne's Gourmet, 14032

Z

Z Gris Dry Rose, 14038
Z Guard, 19846
Z Jet, 31420
Z Patch, 20754
Z-Bird, 14043
Z-Ez, 20761
Z.D. Wines, 14047
Zachary, 14039
Zachlawi, 10952
Zackariah Harris, 11263
Zagnut, 5818, 23750
Zakouski, 10039
Zanae, 6986
Zand Hebs For Kids, 13642
Zand, 9237, 26785
Zany Pretzels, 3396
Zap, 23033
Zap Soakers, 27260
Zap'ems, 1200
Zapatac, 9748
Zapp's Potato Chips, 13129
Zapper, 21768
Zarda, 14042
Zartic, 14043
Zartic Beef Bakeables, 14043
Zartic Chicken Bakeables, 14043
Zartic Chicken Fried Beef Steaks, 14043
Zartic Chicken Fryz Flavorz, 14043
Zartic Chicken Tenderloins, 14043
Zartic Circle Z Beef Burgers, 14043
Zartic Crispy Steaks, 14043
Zartic Homestyle Meatloaf, 14043
Zartic Honey Hugged Chicken, 14043
Zartic Pork Bakeables, 14043
Zartic Pork Sausage Sampler, 14043
Zartic Rockin' Roasted Chicken, 14043
Zartic Veal Entree Legends, 14043
Zartic Veal Specialties, 14043
Zartin, 13273
Zary, 7747
Zatarain's, 8061
Zatec Pilsner, 3746
Zayante, 14044
Zazi Organics, 14045
Zcuvee, 14038
Zebra, 14048, 18284, 22769, 31424
Zebra Value-Line, 14048, 31424
Zebra Xii, 14048, 31424

1347

All Brands Index

Zeelanco, 4081
Zefina, 2909
Zeigler, 10497
Zeigler's, 14050
Zeltex, 31429'
Zeniht, 3753, 21763
Zenipro, 6777
Zenobia, 12293, 14053
Zephyr, 18450, 18500, 19597, 20509, 31436
Zephyrhillis, 14055
Zerit, 1721
Zero, 5818, 23750
Zeroll, 31442
Zerolon, 31442
Zespri, 5036
Zest, 22712

Zesties, 9523
Zia Briosa, 13475
Zico, 2811, 2814, 21883
Ziegenbock, 26668
Zig-Zag, 27347
Zima, 8459
Zinfandel, 4745
Zing, 3666
Zingers, 6013
Zingos Mints, 1771
Zion, 10952
Zip, 3696, 12663
Zipflo, 24940
Zipgards, 23556
Zipkin, 31453
Zipp, 2226
Zippity Doo-Wa Ditties, 1654

Zippy Bagger, 31085
Zippy Pop, 5752
Zippys, 14067
Zito, 2059
Zitos, 14068
Zma, 6236
Zodiac, 8795
Zoe's Meats, 14069
Zoi Greek Yogurt, 792
Zone, 10229, 10487, 23600
Zone Control, 29175
Zontec, 27288
Zoo, 29505
Zoo Crew, 1654
Zoombees, 4374
Zorb-It-All, 29826
Zorro, 8946

Zotz, 551
Zoygs, 11320
Zp, 19544
Zpasta, 6246
Zummo, 14075
Zumo Juices, 11396
Zuni Fire Roasted Salsa, 14076
Zuni Zalsa Verde, 14076
Zwag Nutsche, 29643
Zwanenberg, 13402
Zweigle's, 14078
Zychrome, 6236
Zylicious, 9237, 26785
Zzzquil, 12721, 30193

All Companies Index

Numeric

1-2-3 Gluten Free, 1
10 Strawberry Street, 2
1000 Islands River Rat Cheese, 3, 40000, 54501
1642, 4, 54502
18 Rabbits Inc., 5
21st Century Products, Inc., 6, 41471
21st Century Snack Foods, 7
24 Mantra Organic, 8
24Vegan, 9
3 Gyros Inc, 10
3 Springs Water Co, 11
3 Water, 12
3-D Marketing & Sales, 40001
34-Degrees, 13
350 Cheese Straws, 14
360 Nutrition, 15
3D Instruments LLC, 18000
3DT, LLC, 18001
3Greenmoms LLC, 18002
3M, 18003
3PM Bites, 16
3V Company, 17, 41472
4505 Meats LLC, 18
479 Degrees, 19
4C Foods Corp, 20, 41473
4front Entrematic, 18004
4M Fruit Distribution, 41474, 54503
4Pure, 21
4th & Heart, 22
505 Southwestern, 23
50th State Poultry Processors, 24
51 Fifty Enterprises, 25
518 Corporation, 18005, 54504
5280 Produce, 54505
7 Seas Submarine, 18006, 54506
731 North Beach LLC, 26
80 Acres Farms, 27
814 Americas Inc, 28
88 Acres, 29, 54507
8estiny Plastics, 41475
8th Wonder, 30
9-12 Corporation, 18007
915 Labs, 18008
99 Ranch Market, 31, 18009

A

A & A Global Industries Inc, 54508
A & B Distributing Co, 54509
A & B Process Systems Corp, 18010, 41476
A & D Sales, 18011, 40002
A & D Seafood Corp, 54510
A & E Conveyor Systems Inc, 18012
A & G Foods, 18013, 54511
A & K Development Co, 18014
A & W Wholesale Co Inc, 54512
A A A Awning Co Inc, 18015
A A Label Co, 18016
A Allred Marketing, 18017
A Arnold Logistics, 51501, 52601
A B Co Of Wisconsin, 41477
A B Munroe Dairy Inc, 32
A B T Inc, 18018
A Better Way, 54513
A C Birox, 18019
A C Horn & Co Sheet Metal, 18020, 41478
A C Tool & Machine Co, 18021
A Cajun Life®, LLC, 33
A Couple of Squares, Inc, 34, 54514
A Daigger & Co Inc, 54515
A Dattilo Fruit Co, 54516
A Dozen Cousins, 35
A G Brown & Son, 40003, 41479
A G Russell Knives, 18022, 41480
A Gazerro & Assoc, 40004
A Gift Basket by Carmela, 36, 41481
A Hill of Beans Coffee Roasters, 37
A J Antunes & Co, 18023, 41482
A J Funk & Co, 18024
A J Linz Sons, 54517
A J Oster Foils LLC, 54518
A J Rinella Co Inc, 54519
A J Silberman & Co, 54520
A J's Edible Arts, 38
A la Cart, 47
A La Carte, 39, 18025, 41483
A La Mode Distributors, 54521
A Labar Seafood Co, 40005
A Legacy Food Svc, 18026, 41484
A Line Corporation, 18027
A M S Filling Systems, 18028
A M Source Inc, 18029, 40006
A N Deringer Inc, 51502, 51503
A O A C Intl, 18030
A One Mfg Co, 18031
A Perfect Pear, 40
A Plus Label, 41
A Plus Marketing, 54522
A Snow Craft Co Inc, 18032
A Southern Season, 42
A T C Inc, 18033
A T Ferrell Co Inc, 18034, 18035, 41485, 41486
A T Information Products Inc, 18036
A T Scafati Inc, 18037
A Tarantino & Sons Poultry, 54523
A Taste for Life, 41487, 54524
A Taste of the Kingdom, 43
A Tavola Together, 44
A Tec Technologic, 18038
A Thomas Farris & Son Inc, 40007
A to Z Nutrition International Inc, 52603
A To Z Portion Control Meats, 45
A to Z Wineworks, 48, 51505
A W Sisk & Son, 40008, 51504, 52602
A Zerega's Sons Inc, 46
A&A Halal Distributors, 54525
A&A International, 18039, 41488
A&A Line & Wire Corporation, 18040, 41489
A&A Manufacturing Company, 18041
A&A Marine & Drydock Company, 49, 41490
A&A Spice and Food, 54526
A&B American Style, LLC, 50
A&B Safe Corporation, 18042, 41491
A&C Quinlin Fisheries, 51, 41492
A&D Distributors, 54527
A&D Sales Associates, 40009
A&D Weighing, 18043, 18044, 41493
A&F, 18045
A&F Automation, 18046
A&G Machine Company, 18047
A&H Products, Inc, 52
A&H Seafood Market, 41494, 54528
A&J Food Wholesalers, Inc., 54529
A&J Forklift & Equipment, 54530
A&J Mixing International, 18048, 41495
A&J Produce Corporation, 54531
A&K Automation, 18049
A&L Laboratories, 18050, 41496
A&L Western Ag Lab, 18051
A&M Enterprises, 54532
A&M Industries, 18052, 41497
A&M Process Equipment, 18053, 41498
A&M Seafood Company, 54533
A&M Thermometer Corporation, 18054, 41499
A&M Warehouse & Distribution, 52604
A&R Ceka North America, 18055
A&S Crawfish, 54534
A-1 Booth Manufacturing, 18056, 41500
A-1 Business Supplies Inc, 18057
A-1 Eastern-Homemade Pickle Co, 53
A-1 Refrigeration Co, 18058, 41501
A-1 Seafood Center, 54535
A-A1 Aaction Bag, 18059, 18060, 41502, 54536
A-B Products, 54537
A-B-C Packaging Machine Corp, 18061, 41503
A-L-L Magnetics Inc, 18062, 41504
A-Line Electric Supply Inc, 54538
A-P-A Truck Leasing, 51506
A-Treat Bottling Co, 54
A-Z Factory Supply, 18063, 41505
A. Berkowitz & Company, 54539
A. Bohrer, 54540
A. De LaChevrotiere, 54541
A. Friscia Seafoods, 54542
A. Gagliano Co Inc, 55, 41506, 52605, 54543
A. Klein & Company, 18064
A. Lassonde Inc., 56
A. Nonini Winery, 57, 54544
A. Rafanelli Winery, 58
A. Sargenti Company, 54545
A. Simos & Company, 54546
A. Smith Bowman Distillery, 59, 41507
A. Suarez & Company, 41508
A. Visconti Company, 54547
A.A. Pesce Glass Company, 18065
A.B. Sealer, Inc., 18066, 41509
A.B. Wise & Sons, 54548
A.C. Calderoni, 60
A.C. Covert, 54549
A.C. Inc., 61, 54550
A.C. Kissling Company, 62, 54551
A.C. LaRocco Pizza, 63
A.C. Legg, 64, 18067, 41510
A.D. Cowdrey Company, 18068
A.D. Johnson Engraving Company, 18069
A.D. Joslin Manufacturing Company, 18070, 41511
A.F. Coffee Products, 41512
A.G. Lobster, 54552
A.J. Jersey, 54553
A.J. Seibert Company, 40010
A.J. Trucco, 41513
A.K. Robins, 18071, 41514
A.L. Duck Jr Inc, 65, 41515, 54554
A.L. Verna Company, 54555
A.M. Loveman Lumber & Box Company, 18072
A.M. Manufacturing, 18073, 41516
A.M.BRIGGS, 54556
A.N. Smith & Company, 40011
A.O. Smith Water Products Company, 18074, 41517
A.P.M., 18075
A.R. Pellegrini & Associates, 40012, 41518
A.T. Foote Woodworking Company, 18076
A.T. Gift Company, 66
A.Vogel USA, 67
A.W. Jantzi & Sons, 68
A/R Packaging Corporation, 41519, 54557
A1 Tablecloth Co, 18077, 41520
A2 Milk Company, 69, 54558
A2Z Specialty Advertising, 54559
AA Specialty Advertising Products, 54560
AAA Electrical Signs, 18078
AAA Flag & Banner Manufacturing, 18079
AAA Mill, 18080
Aabbitt Adhesives, 18242, 41596
Aaburco Inc, 18243, 41597, 54588
AADF Warehouse Corporation, 51507, 52606
AAK, 70, 41521
Aak USA Inc, 106, 41598
Aala Meat Market Inc, 107, 54589
Aaladin Industries Inc, 18244, 41599
Aaland Potato Company, 108
Aalint Fluid Measure Solutions, 18245
AAMD, 18081, 41522
AANTEC, 18082, 41523, 54561
Aaron Equipment Co Div Areco, 18246, 41600
Aaron Fink Group, 18247
Aaron Thomas Co Inc, 18248
AB InBev, 71, 41524
AB McLauchlan Company, 18083
AB6, 18084
Abacus Label Applications, 18249
Abal Material Handling Inc, 54590
Abalon Precision Manufacturing Corporation, 18250, 41601
Abanaki Corp, 18251, 41602
Abanda, 18252
Abarbanel Wine Company, 40018, 41603
Abatar Institutional Food Company, 54591
Abatron Inc, 18253
Abattoir A. Trahan Company, 109
Abattoir Aliments Asta Inc., 110
ABB, 18085, 41525
Abb Labels, 18254
Abbeon Cal Inc, 18255, 41604
Abbot's Butcher, 111, 54592
Abbotsford Farms, 18256
Abbotsford Growers Ltd., 112, 41605
Abbott & Cobb Inc, 113, 41606
Abbott Industries, 18257
Abbott Laboratories, 114
Abbott Plastics & Supply Co, 18258
Abbott's Candy Shop, 115, 54593
Abbott's Meat Inc, 116
Abby's Better Nut Butter, 117
Abbyland Foods Inc, 118
ABC Coffee & Pasta, 41526
ABC Country Club Coffee, 54562
ABC Corp, 40013
ABC Enterprises, 40014
ABC Laboratories, 18086
ABC Letter Art, 18087
ABC Research Corp, 18088
ABC Scales, 18089
ABC Stamp Signs & Awards, 18090
ABC Tea House, 72
Abco Automation, 18259
ABCO HVACR Supply & Solutions, 54563
ABCO Industries, 18091
ABCO Industries Limited, 18092, 41527
Abco International, 18260, 18261, 41607
ABCO Laboratories Inc, 18093, 41528
Abco Products, 18262, 41608
Abdallah Candies & Gifts, 119
Abe's Vegan Muffins, 120
Abel & Schafer Inc, 121
Abel IHS, 54594
Abel Manufacturing Co, 18263, 41609
Abel Pumps, 18264
Abell-Howe Crane, 18265
Aberdeen & Rockfish Railroad, 51512
ABG Industries, 18094
ABI Limited, 18095, 41529, 54564
ABIC International Consultants, 18096
Abicor Binzel, 18266
Ability/Tri-Modal Trnsprtn Svc, 51513, 52613
Abimar Foods Inc, 122, 41610
Abimco USA, Inc., 123, 41611
Abingdon Vineyard & Winery, 124
Abita Brewing Co, 125
Abitec Corp, 126
ABJ/Sanitaire Corporation, 18097, 41530
Abkit Camocare Nature Works, 127
Able Brands Inc, 18267
Able Sales Company, 41612, 54595
Abler Transfer, 51514, 52614
ABLOY Security Inc, 18098
ABM Industries, 54565
ABM Marking, 18099, 41531
ABO Industries, 18100, 41532
Abond Plastic Corporation, 18268, 41613
About Packaging Robotics, 18269
Above All Health, 54596
Abraham of North America, 41614
Abraham's Natural Foods, 128
Abramson & Di Benedetto Mktng, 40019
Abresist Kalenborn Corp, 18270
Absolute Custom Extrusions Inc, 18271
Absolute Process Instruments, 18272
Absopure Water Company, 129
Absorbco, 18273, 41615
Abuelita Mexican Foods, 130, 41616
Abunda Life, 131, 41617
Abundant Earth Corporation, 18274
AC Dispensing Equipment, 18101

1349

All Companies Index

AC Label Company, 18102
AC Paper & Supply, 54566
Acacia Vineyard, 132
Academy Awning, 18275
Academy Packing Co Inc, 54597
Acadian Fine Foods, 133
Acadian Ostrich Ranch, 134
Acadian Seaplants, 135, 41618
Acai Roots, 136
Acatris USA, 137, 41619, 54598
ACB, 40015
ACC Distributors Inc, 54567
Accent Mark, 18276
Accent Store Fixtures, 18277
Access Partners, 40020
Access Solutions, 18278, 41620
Accessible Products Co, 18279
Acclaim Marketing & Sales, 40021
ACCO Systems, 18103
Acco Systems, 18280
ACCO Systems, 41533
Accommodation Mollen, 18281
Accommodation Program, 18282
Accord International, 54599
Accra Laboratory, 18283
Accraply/Trine, 18284, 41621
Accro-Seal, 18285
Accu Place, 18286
Accu Seal Corp, 18287
Accu Temp Products Inc, 18288, 41622
Accu-Labs Research, 18289
Accu-Pak, 18290
Accu-Ray Inspection Services, 18291
Accu-Sort Systems, 18292, 41623
Accubar, 18294
Accuflex Industrial Hose LTD, 18295, 41624
Accuform Manufacturing, Inc., 18296
AccuLife, 18293
Accura Tool & Mold, 18297
Accurate Flannel Bag Company, 18298
Accurate Forklift, 54600
Accurate Ingredients Inc, 139, 41625
Accurate Paper Box Co Inc, 18299
Accurex, 140
Accutek Packaging Equipment, 18300, 41626
AccuTemp, 138
Ace Bakery, 141
Ace Chemical, 54601
Ace Co Precision Mfg, 18301, 18302, 41627
Ace Development, 142, 41628
Ace Electric Supply, 54602
Ace Endico Corp, 54603
Ace Engineering Company, 18303, 41629
Ace Fabrication, 18304
Ace Farm USA Inc, 143
Ace Fixture Company, 54604
Ace Manufacturing, 18305
Ace Manufacturing & Parts Co, 18306, 41630
Ace Mart Restaurant Supply, 54605
Ace Signs, 18307
Ace Specialty Mfg Co Inc, 18308, 41631
Ace Stamp & Engraving, 18309
Ace Technical Plastics Inc, 18310, 41632
Ace-Tex Enterprises, 18311
Acebright Inc., 18312
Aceitunas Losada, 144
Acesur North America, 145, 41633
Acetifico Marcello Denigris, 146
Aceto Corporation, 41634
ACH Food Co Inc, 73, 41534
ACH Rice Specialties, 18104
Acharice Specialties, 147, 41635
Achatz Handmade Pie Co, 148
Achem Industry America Inc., 18313
Achilles USA, 18314, 41636
ACI, 18105
ACK Industrial Electronics, 54568
Ackerman Industrial Equipment, 54606
Ackerman Winery, 149
ACLAUSA Inc, 18106, 41535
ACMA/GD, 18107, 41536

Acme, 18315
Acme Awning, 18316
Acme Awning Co Inc, 18317
Acme Bag Co, 18318
Acme Bread Co, 150, 54607
Acme Control Svc Inc, 18319
Acme Display Fixture Company, 18320
Acme Distribution Ctr Inc, 51515, 52615
Acme Engineering & Mfg Corp, 18321, 41637
Acme Equipment Corporation, 18322
Acme Farms + Kitchen, 40022, 51516
Acme Fixture Company, 18323
Acme Food Sales Inc, 54608
Acme Import Co Inc, 41638
Acme International, 18324
Acme International Limited, 18325
Acme Laundry Products Inc, 18326
Acme Pizza & Bakery Equipment, 41639
Acme Scale Co, 18327, 41640, 54609
ACME Sign Corp, 18108, 54569
Acme Smoked Fish Corporation, 151, 41641
Acme Sponge & Chamois Co Inc, 18328, 41642
Acme Steak & Seafood, 152, 41643, 54610
Acme Wire Products Company, 18329
ACME-McClain & Son, 18109
ACO, 18110, 41537
Aco Container Systems, 18330, 41644
ACO Polymer Products, 18111
Acorn Distributors Inc, 54611
Acorn Sales Company, 40023
Acornseekers Inc, 153
Acorsa USA Inc, 41645
Acorto, 18331, 41646
Acosta Sales & Marketing Company, 40024
Acoustical Systems Inc, 18332
Acp Inc, 18333, 41647
ACP, Inc., 74
Acqua Blox LLC, 154
ACR Systems, 18112
Acra Electric Corporation, 18334, 41648
Acraloc Corp, 18335, 41649
Acrison Inc, 18336, 41650
Acro Dishwashing Svc Co, 18337
Acro Plastics, 18338
Acromag Inc., 18339, 41651
Across Foods, LLC, 155
Acrotech, 18340
Acryline, 18341
ACS Industries, Inc., 18113
Acta Health Products, 156, 18342, 41652
Acta Products Corporation, 18343
Action Advertising, 54612
Action Engineering, 18344, 41653
Action Instruments Company, 18345
Action Labs, 157
Action Lighting, 18346, 41654
Action Marketing, 40025
Action Marketing Associates, 40026
Action Marketing Of So Ca, 40027
Action Marketing Services, 40028
Action Packaging Automation, 18347, 41655
Action Sales, 54613
Action Signs By Stubblefield, 18348
Action Technology, 18349, 41656
Actionpac Scales Automation, 18350, 41657
Active Organics, 158
Activon Products, 18351
Actron, 18352, 41658
ACTS, 41538
Acuair, 18353
ACUair/York Refrigeration, 18114
Acumen Data Systems Inc, 18354, 41659
Acushnet Fish Corporation, 159, 54614
Acutemp, 41660
Ad Art Litho., 18355, 41661
Ad Lib Advertising, 54615
Ad Mart Identity Group, 18356
AD Products, 18115

Ad Specialty Plus, 54616
Ad-Centive Ideas, 54617
Ad-Craft Products Compay, 54618
Ad-Pak Systems Co, 18357
Adagio Teas, 41662
Adair Vineyards, 160
Adam Electric Signs, 18358
Adam Matthews Inc, 161
Adam Puchta Winery, 162
Adamatic, 18359, 41663
Adamation, 18360, 41664
Adamba Imports Intl, 41665
Adams & Brooks Inc, 163, 41666
Adams & Knickle, 54619
Adams Chapman Co, 54620
Adams County Winery, 164
Adams Fisheries Ltd, 165, 41667
Adams Foods & Milling, 166
Adams Inc, 18361
Adams Olive Ranch, 167
Adams Precision Screen, 18362
Adams USA Inc., 168
Adams Vegetable Oils Inc, 169, 41668, 51517
Adams Warehouse & Delivery, 51518, 52616
Adams Wholesale Co, 54621
Adams-Burch, 54622
Adapto Storage Products, 18363
Adcapitol, 18364
ADCO, 18116, 18117
ADCO Manufacturing Inc, 18118, 18119, 41539
Adcom Worldwide, 41669, 51519
Adcraft, 18365
ADD Testing & Research, 18120
ADDCHEK Coils, 18121
AddGarlic!, 170
Addison Foods Inc, 54623
ADE Inc, 18122
ADE Restaurant Service, 54570
Adee Honey Farm, 171
Adel Grocery Company, 54624
Adelaida Cellars Inc, 172
Adelman Foods, 54625
Adelsheim Vineyard, 173
Adenna Inc, 18366
Adept Solutions, Inc., 18367
Adept Technology, 18368
Adex Medical Inc, 18369, 41670, 54626
ADH Health Products Inc, 75, 41540
Adheron Coatings Corporation, 18370
Adhesive Applications, 18371, 41671
Adhesive Label, 18372
Adhesive Products Inc, 18373, 18374
Adhesive Technologies Inc, 18375, 41672
Adhesives Research, 18376
Adhesives Research Inc, 18377
ADI, 54571
ADI Systems, 18123, 41541
ADI Systems Inc, 18124
Adirondack Beverages Inc, 174
Adirondack Direct, 54627
Adirondack Maple Farms, 175
ADJR Inc, 76
Adkin & Son Associated Food Products, 176
ADL Group, 54572
Adler Fels Winery, 177
Adluh Flour, 178, 54628
ADM Wild Flavors & Specialty, 77, 41542
ADM/Matsutani LLC, 18125
Admatch Corporation, 18378, 41673
Admiral Beverage Corp, 179
Admiral Craft, 41674, 54629
ADMIX, 18126
Admix Inc., 18379
Adobe Creek Packing Co Inc, 180, 41675
Adobe Springs, 181
Adolf Kusy & Company, 54630
Adolf's Meats & Sausage Kitchen, 182, 41676
Adolph Gottscho, 18380

Adonis Health Products, 41677, 54631
Adprint Specialties, 54632
Adpro, 18381, 41678
Adria Imports, 41679
Adrienne's Gourmet Foods, 183, 18382, 41680
Adro International Inc, 41681
ADSI Inc, 18127, 41543
Adsmith, 54633
Adstick Custom Labels Inc, 18383, 18384
ADT Inc, 18128, 54573
ADT Security Systems, 54574
Adtek Sales, 40029
Advance Adhesives, 18385
Advance Automated Systems Inc, 18386
Advance Cleaning Products, 18387
Advance Distribution Svc, 18388, 52617, 52618
Advance Energy Technologies, 18389, 41682
Advance Engineering Co, 18390
Advance Fittings Corp, 18391, 41683
Advance Grower Solutions, 18392
Advance Lifts Inc, 18393
Advance Marketing, 40030
Advance Pierre Foods, 184, 41684
Advance Sales & Marketing, Inc, 40031
Advance Storage Products, 18394, 41685
Advance Tabco, 18395
Advance Technology Corp, 18396, 41686
Advance Weight Systems Inc, 18397
Advanced Aquaculture Systems, 185
Advanced Bio Development, 186
Advanced Chemical, 54634
Advanced Coating & Converting, 18398, 18399
Advanced Control Technologies, 18400, 41687
Advanced Design Awning & Sign, 18401
Advanced Design Mfg, 18402
Advanced Detection Systems, 18403, 41688
Advanced Equipment, 18404, 41689, 41690
Advanced Equipment Company, 54635
Advanced Ergonomics Inc, 18405
Advanced Food Equipment LLC, 18406
Advanced Food Products LLC, 187
Advanced Food Services, 188
Advanced Food Systems, 189, 18407, 18408, 41691
Advanced Handling Systems Inc, 54636
Advanced Industrial Systems, 18409
Advanced Ingredients, Inc., 190, 18410, 41692
Advanced Instruments Inc, 18411, 18412, 41693
Advanced Insulation Concepts, 18413, 41694
Advanced Labelworx, 18414
Advanced Labelworx Inc, 18415, 41695
Advanced Micro Controls, 18416
Advanced Organics, 18417
Advanced Packaging Techniques Corporation, 18418
Advanced Plastic Coating Svc, 18419
Advanced Poly-Packaging Inc, 18420
Advanced Process Solutions, 18421
Advanced Separation Technologies, 18422
Advanced Separations andProcess Systems, 18423
Advanced Software Designs, 18424
Advanced Spice & Trading, 191, 41696
Advanced Sunflower, 192
Advanced Surfaces Corp, 18425
Advanced Uniflo Technologies, 18426
Advanced Warehouses, 52619
Advantage Gourmet Importers, 40032, 41697, 54637
Advantage Puck Technologies, 18427, 18428, 41698
Advantage Solutions, 40033
Advantage Webco Hawaii, 40034

All Companies Index

Advantec Process Systems, 18429
Advantek, 18430
Advantus Corp., 18431, 41699
Advent Machine Co, 18432
Adventist Book & Food, 193
Adventure Foods, 194, 41700, 54638
Adventure Inn Food Trading Company, 54639
Advertising Concepts, 40035
Advertising Specialties, 54640
Advertising Specialties Imprinted, 54641
Adwest Technologies, 18433
Aei Corp, 18434
AEP Colloids, 78, 41544
AEP Industries, 18129
AEP Industries Inc, 18130, 41545
Aep Industries Inc., 18435
AEP Texas, 18131
Aeration Industries Intl LLC, 18436, 41701
Aeration Technologies Inc, 18437
Aerchem Inc, 54642
AERCO International Inc, 18132
Aercology, 18438
Aero Company, 18439
Aero Housewares, 18440
Aero Manufacturing Co, 18441, 41702
Aero Tec Laboratories/ATL, 18442
Aero-Motive Company, 18443
Aero-Power Unitized Fueler, 18444
Aerocon, 18446
AeroFarms, 195, 54643
Aerofreeze, 18447
AeroFreeze, Inc., 18445, 41703
Aerolator Systems, 18448, 54644
Aeromat Plastics Inc, 18449, 41704
Aeromix Systems, 18450, 41705
Aerotech Enterprise Inc, 18451
Aerotech Laboratories, 18452
Aerovent Co, 18453, 18454, 41706
Aerowerks, 18455, 41707
AERTEC, 18133
Aervoid By Diebel Manufacturing, 41708
Aerzen USA Corp, 18456
AES Corp, 18134
AET Films, 18135
Aetna Plastics Corporation, 54645
AEW Thurne, 18136, 41546
AFA Systems, 18137
Afassco, 18457, 54646
AFCO, 18138
AFCO Manufacturing, 18139
Afec Commodities, 41709
Afeco, 18458
AFF International, 79, 41547
Affiliated Resource Inc, 18459, 41710, 54647
Affiliated Rice Milling, 196, 41711
Affiliated Warehouse Co Inc, 52620, 52621
Afflink LLC, 54648
AFGO Mechanical Svc Inc, 18140
AFI-FlashGril'd Steak, 80
Afia Foods, 197, 54649
Afieneur, 198
Afineur, 199
AFire Inc., 41550
AFL Industries, 18141, 41548
AFS Traffic Consulants, 51508
AFT Advanced Fiber Technologies, 18142, 41549
Aftermarket Specialties Inc, 18460
Afton Mountain Vineyards Inc, 200
AG Beverage, 18143
AG Processing Inc, 81, 41551
Ag-Pak, 18461, 41712
AGA Gas, 18144
Agave Dream, 203
AGC, 18145, 41552
AGC Engineering Portland, 18146
Age International Inc, 41713, 54650
AGET Manufacturing Co, 18147
Agfinity Inc, 204
Agger Fish Corp, 205, 41714
Aggreko Rental, 18463

Agilysys, Inc., 18464
Aglamesis Bros Ice Cream, 206
AGM Container Controls Inc, 18148
Agostoni Chocolate USA, 41715
Agrana Fruit US Inc, 208, 18465, 41717
AgraWest Foods, 207, 41716
Agrexco USA, 209, 41718
Agri-Business Services, 18466
Agri-Dairy Products, 210, 40036, 41719, 54651
Agri-Equipment International, 18467, 54652
Agri-Food Export Group Quebec-Canada, 41720
Agri-Mark Inc, 211, 41721
Agri-Northwest, 18468
Agri-Pack, 212
Agri-Sales Assoc Inc, 18469
Agribuys Incorporated, 18472
Agricor Inc, 214, 41722
Agricore United, 215, 41723
Agricultural Data Systems, 18473
Agricultural Research Service, 18474
Agriculture Consulting Services, 18475
Agriculture Ohio Dept, 41724
AgriFiber Solutions, 18470
AgriNorthwest, 213
Agripac, 216, 18476
AgriTech, 18471
Agrium Advanced Technologies, 54653
Agro Farma Inc., 217
Agro Foods, Inc., 218, 41725, 54654
AGRO Merchants Grp NA, 82
Agrocan, 220, 41727
AgroCepia, 219, 41726
AgroFresh, 18477
Agropur, 221, 222, 41728
Agropur MSI, LLC, 18478
Agrusa, 223, 41729
AgSource Milk Analysis Laboratory, 201
Agspring, 18479
AgStandard Smoked Almonds, 202
AGT Foods USA, 83
AgTracker, 18462
Agtron Inc, 18480, 41730
Agumm, 224
Agusa, 225
Agvest, 226, 41731
Agworld, 18481
Ah Dor Kosher Fish Corporation, 227
Ahara Ghee, 228
AHD International, LLC, 84, 41553
Ahlgren Vineyard, 229
Ahlstrom Filtration LLC, 18482
Ahlstrom Nonwovens LLC, 18483
Ahmad Tea, 230, 41732
Ai Vy Springrolls, Llc, 231
AIB International, 18149
AIB International, Inc., 18150
Aibmr Life Sciences, 18484
AIDCO International, 18151
Aidco International, 18485
Aidells Sausage Co, 232
Aidi International Hotels of America, 18486, 41733, 54655
AIDP Inc, 41554, 54575
Aigner Index, 18487
Aileen Quirk & Sons Inc, 233, 54656
AIM, 18152
Aim Blending Technologies Inc, 18488
Aim This Way, 54657
AIMCAL, 18153
Aimonetto and Sons, 234, 54658
AIN Plastics, 54576
Air Barge Company, 18489
Air Economy Corporation, 18490
Air Land Transport Inc, 51520
Air Liquide USA, LLC, 18491
Air Locke Dock Seal, 18492
Air Logic Power Systems, 18493, 41734
Air New Zealand LTD, 51521
Air Pak Products & Services, 18494
Air Products & Chemicals Inc, 18495
Air Quality Engineering, 18496, 41735
Air Savers Inc, 41736, 54659

Air System Components Inc, 18497
Air Technical Industries, 18498
Air-Knife Systems/PaxtonProducts Corporation, 18499
Air-Lec Industries, Inc, 18500
Air-Scent International, 18501, 41737
Air/Tak Inc, 18502
Airblast, 18503
Aire-Mate, 18504
Airflex, 18505
Airfloat LLC, 18506, 18507, 41738
Airflow Sciences Corp, 18508
Airgas Carbonic, 18509
Airgas Carbonic Inc, 18510
Airlie Winery, 235
Airlite Plastics Co, 18511
Airmaster Fan Co, 18512, 41739
Airomat Corp, 18513, 41740
Airosol Co Inc, 18514, 18515, 41741
Airsan Corp, 18516, 41742
Airschott Inc, 40037, 51522, 52622
Airways Freight Corp, 51523
AIS Container Handling, 18154
Aiya America Inc, 236, 41743
AJ Trucco, 41555, 54577
AJ's Lena Maid Meats Inc, 85
Ajax Philadelphia, 54660
AJC International, 54578
Ajinomoto Foods North America, Inc., 237, 41744
Ajinomoto Frozen Foods USA, Inc., 238, 41745
Ajinomoto Heartland Inc, 239, 18517, 41746
Ajiri Tea Company, 240
AJM Meat Packing, 86
AJM Packaging Corporation, 18155
Ak Mak Bakeries, 241
AK Robbins, 18156
AK Steel Corp, 18157
Akay USA LLC, 242, 41747
AKC Commodities Inc, 41556, 54579
Ake-Sullivan Associates, 40038
Aker BioMarine Antarctic US, LLC., 243
Akers Group, 18518
Aketta, 244
Akicorp, 245, 18519
Akin & Porter Produce Inc, 54661
Akro-Mils, 18520
Akron Cotton Products, 18521, 54662
Akzo Nobel Functional Chemicals, 41748
Al & John's Glen Rock Ham, 246
Al Campisano Fruit Company, 54663
Al Dente Pasta Co, 247
Al Gelato Bornay, 248, 41749
Al Lehrhoff Sales, 54664
Al Pete Meats, 249, 41750
Al Richard's Chocolates, 250
Al Safa Halal, 251, 41751
AL Systems, 18158, 41557
Al's Beverage Company, 252
Al-Rite Fruits & Syrups Co, 253, 41752
Alabama Bag Co Inc, 18522, 41753
Alabama Food Group, 54665, 54666
Alabama Gulf Seafood, 254, 54667
Alabama Power Company, 18523
Alabama Wholesale Company, 54668
Alacer Corp, 255, 41754
Alack Refrigeration Co Inc, 54669
Aladdin Bakers, 256, 41755
Aladdin Label Inc, 18524
Aladdin Temp-Rite, LLC, 18525, 41756
Aladdin Transparent Packaging, 18526
Alakef Coffee Roasters Inc, 257
Alamance Foods, 258
Alamo Tamale Corporation, 259
Alar Engineering Corp, 18527, 41757
Alard Equipment Corp, 18528
Alarm Controls Corp, 18529, 41758
Alaska Aquafarms, 260
Alaska Bounty Seafoods & Smokery, 261
Alaska Direct Transport, 51524
Alaska General Seafoods, 262
Alaska Herb & Tea Co, 263
Alaska Jacks, 264

Alaska Ocean Trading, 265, 41759
Alaska Pacific Seafoods, 266
Alaska Pasta Co, 267
Alaska Railroad Corp, 51525, 52623
Alaska Sausage & Seafood, 268, 41760, 54670
Alaska Seafood Co, 269, 54671
Alaska Smokehouse, 270, 41761
Alaska Traffic Consultants, 51526
Alaskan Brewing Company, 271
Alaskan Gourmet Seafoods, 272, 41762, 54672
Alaskan Leader Fisheries, 273
Alaskan Smoked Salmon & Seafood, 274
Alati-Caserta Desserts, 275, 41763
Alba Foods, Inc, 276
Alba Specialty Seafood Company, 40039, 41764
Alba Vineyard & Winery, 277
Albanese Confectionery Group, 278, 54673
Albany International, 18530
Alberici Constructors Inc, 18531
Albert A Russo Inc, 40040, 41765
Albert Guarnieri & Co, 54674
Albert Uster Imports Inc, 41766, 54675
Albert's Meats, 279
Albert's Organics Inc, 54676
Albert's Organics: South, 54677
Albert's Organics: West, 54678
Alberta Cheese Company, 280
Albion Enterprises, 54679
Albion Fisheries, 54680
Albion Industries Inc, 18532
Albion Machine & Tool Co, 18533, 41767
Alburt Labeling Systems, 18534
Alca Trading Co., 281, 41768
Alcan Foil Products, 18535
Alcan Packaging, 18536
Alchemie USA Inc., 41769, 54681
ALCO Designs, 18159, 18160, 41558
Alcoa - Lake Charles Carbon Plant, 18537
Alcoa - Massena Operations, 18538, 41770
Alcoa - Warrick Operations, 18539
Alcoa Corp, 18540
Alcon Packaging, 18541
Alconox Inc, 18542, 18543, 41771
Alcor Corp, 52624
Alcor PMC, 18544
Alcove Chocolate, 282
Alden's Organic, 283
Alder Springs Smoked Salmon, 284
Alderfer Inc, 285, 41772
Alderiso Brothers, 54682
ALDI, 87
Aldo Locascio, 18545
Aldon Co Inc, 18546
Aleco Food Svc Div, 18547, 18548
Alef Custom Packaging, 18549
Alef Sausage Inc, 287
Alegacy, 18550
Aleias Gluten Free Foods, 288, 54683
Alerta-Mat, 54684
AleSmith Brewing Company, 286
Alessi Bakery, 289
Alewel's Country Meats, 290, 18551
Alex & George, 54685
Alex Delvecchio Enterprises, 18552
Alex E Fergusson Co Inc, 18553
Alexander Gourmet Beverages, 291
Alexander International (USA), 292
Alexander Machinery, 18554, 41773
Alexander, Koetting, Poole & Buehrle Brothers, 40041
Alexandra & Nicolay Chocolate Company, 293
Alexia Foods, 294
Alexian Pfts, 295
Alexis Bailly Vineyard, 296
Alfa Cappuccino Import LTD, 41774, 54686
Alfa Chem, 18555, 41775, 54687

1351

All Companies Index

Alfa International Corp, 41776, 54688
Alfa Laval Ashbrook Simon-Hartley, 18556, 41777
Alfa Laval Inc, 18557, 41778
Alfa Systems Inc, 18558, 41779
Alfacel, 18559
Alfer Laboratories, 297
Alfonso Gourmet Pasta, 298, 41780
Alfred & Sam's Italian Bakery, 299
Alfred L. Wolff, Inc., 300, 41781
Alfred Louie Inc, 301, 54689
Alfred Nickles Bakery Inc, 302
Alfredo Aiello Italian Food, 303
Algen Scale Corp, 54690
Algene Marking Equipment Company, 18560, 41782
Alger Creations, 18561, 41783
Alger Warehouse Company, 52625
Algonquin Tea, 304
Algood Food Co, 305, 41784
Algroup, 18562
Algus Packaging Inc, 18563
Ali Group, 18564, 41785
Alicita-Salsa, 306
Alimentaire Whyte's Inc, 307, 41786
Alimentos Finisterre, 308
Aliments Fontaine Sant, Inc, 309
Aliments Jolibec, Inc, 310
Aliments Prince SEC, 311
Aliments Trigone, 312
Aline Heat Seal Corporation, 18565, 41787
Aline Systems Corporation, 18566
Alioto Lazio Fish Co, 54691
Aliotti Wholesale Fish Company, 313, 41788
Alipack Americas, 18567
Aliquippa Fruit Market, 54692
Aliseo Foods, 41789
Alive & Well Olives, 314
Alive and Radiant, 315
Alkar Rapid Pak, 18568, 18569, 18570, 18571, 41790
Alkazone/Better Health Lab, 18572, 41791
Alkinco, 316
Alkota Cleaning Systems Inc, 18573, 41792
All A Cart Custom Mfg, 18574, 41793
All About Furniture, 18575
All American Container, 18576, 41794
All American Foods Inc, 317
All American Poly, 18577
All American Seasonings, 318, 18578, 41795
All American Snacks, 319
All American Specialty Corporation, 54693
All Bake Technologies, 18579
All Caribbean Food Service, 54694
All Cinema Sales & Services, 54695
All Fill Inc, 18580, 18581, 41796
All Foils Inc, 18582, 41797
All Freight Distribution Co, 52626
All Freight Systems, 52627
All Fresh Products, 54696
All Goode Organics, 320
All Juice Food & Beverage, 321
All Lift Equipment, 54697
All Pack Co Inc, 54698
All Packaging Machinery Corp, 18583, 41798
All Power Inc, 18584, 54699
All QA Products, 41799, 54700
All Round Foods Bakery Prod, 322, 41800
All Seasonings Ingredients Inc, 323, 41801
All Seasons Brokerage Company, 40042
All Seasons Fisheries, 54701
All Seasons International Distributors, 54702
All Seasons Uniforms & Textile, 54703
All Sorts Premium Packaging, 18585
All South Warehouse, 52628

All Southern Fabricators, 18586
All Spun Metal Products, 18587
All Star Carts & Vehicles, 18588, 41802
All Star Dairy Foods, 18589, 54704
All Star Janitorial Supply, 54705
All Star, Ltd., 54706
All State Fabricators Corporation, 18590
All State Restaurant Supply, 54707
All States Caster/F.I.R, 18591
All Valley Packaging, 18592, 54708
All Weather Energy Systems, 18593
All Wrapped Up, 324
All-Clad METALCRAFTERS LLC, 18594, 41803
ALL-CON World Systems, 18161
All-Redi Flour & Salt Company, 54709
All-Right Enterprises, 18595
All-State Food Brokerage, 40043
All-State Industries Inc, 18596, 18597, 54710
All-States Quality Foods, 325
All-Tech Materials Handling, 54711
All-Temp, 52629
Allan Bros. Inc., 326, 41804
Allan Chemical Corp, 54712
Allann Brothers Coffee Roasters, 327, 41805
ALLCAMS Machine Company, 18162
Alldrin Brothers, 328, 41806
Alle Processing Corp, 329
Alleghany Highlands Economic Development Authority, 18599
Allegheny's Fish Farm, 330, 41807
Allegheny Bradford Corp, 18600, 41808
Allegheny Cold Storage Co, 52630
Allegheny Technologies Inc, 18601
Allegheny Valley, 52631, 54713
Allegria Italian Bakers, 331
Allegro Coffee Co, 332, 41809, 54714
Allegro Fine Foods Inc, 333, 41810
Allegro Winery & Vineyards, 334
Allemagnia Imports Inc, 41811, 54715
Allen Brothers Inc, 54716
Allen Coding & Marking Systems, 18602
Allen Flavors Inc, 335
Allen Gauge & Tool Co, 18603, 41812
Allen Harim Foods LLC, 336, 41813
Allen Industries, 41814
Allen Industries Inc, 18604
Allen Rosenthal Company, 54717
Allen Signs Co, 18605, 41815
Allen's Blueberry Freezer Inc, 337
Allen's Pickle Works, 338
Allenair Corp, 18606
Allendale Cork Company, 18607, 41816
Allendale Produce Plant, 54718
Allentown Refrigerated Trmnls, 52632
Allergen Air Filter Corp, 18608
Alley Kat Brewing Co, Ltd, 339
Allflex Packaging Products, 18609
Allfresh Food Products, 340
Alli & Rose, 341
Alliance Bakery Systems, 18610
Alliance Foods, 40044
Alliance Foods Inc, 40045
Alliance Industrial Corp, 18611, 41817
Alliance Knife Inc, 18612
Alliance Products LLC, 18613
Alliance Rubber Co, 18614, 41818
Alliance Shippers Inc, 18615
Alliance Supply Management, 54719
Alliance/PMS, 18616
Allie's GF Goodies, 54720
Allied Adhesive Corporation, 18617
Allied Bakery and Food Service Equipment, 18618
Allied Blending & Ingredients, 342, 54721
Allied Cold Storage Corporation, 51527, 52633
Allied Custom Gypsum Company, 343, 41819
Allied Domecq Spirits USA, 54722
Allied Electric Sign & Awning, 18619
Allied Engineering, 18620, 41820

Allied Food Products, 344
Allied Food Service, 54723
Allied Frozen Storage Inc, 51528, 52634
Allied Gear & Machine Company, 18621
Allied Glove Corporation, 18622, 41821
ALLIED Graphics Inc, 18163
Allied Industrial Equipment, 54724
Allied International Corp, 41822, 41823, 54725
Allied Liquid Coffee Company, 41824
Allied Logistics, 51529, 52635
Allied Marketing Corp, 40046
Allied Metal Spinning, 18623, 41825
Allied Old English Inc, 345, 41826
Allied Packaging, 54726
Allied Premium Company, 54727
Allied Provision Company, 54728
Allied Purchasing Co, 18624
Allied Trades of the Baking Industry, 18625
Allied Uniking Corp Inc, 18626
Allied Wine Corporation, 346, 41827
Allione Agrifood USA, 18627
Allison Systems Inc, 18628
Alliston Creamery, 347
Allkind Container Co, 54729
Allmark Impressions LTD, 18629
Alloy Cast Products Inc, 18630
Alloy Fab, 18631
Alloy Hardfacing & Engineering, 18632, 41828
Alloy Products Corp, 18633
Alloy Wire Belt Company, 18634
Alloyd Brands, 18635, 41829
Allpac, 18636
Allpax Products, 18637
AllPoints Foodservice, 18598
Allsorts Premium Packaging, 18638
Allstate Can Corporation, 18639
Allstate Food & Marketing Inc, 18640
Allstate Insurance Company, 54730
Allstate Manufacturing Company, 18641
Allstrong Restaurant Eqpt Inc, 18642, 41830
Alltech Inc, 348, 18643
Alluserv, 349, 18644
Allylix Inc, 350, 18645
Alma Plantation, 351
Almark Foods, 352
Almarla Vineyards & Winery, 353
Almased USA, 354
Almex USA Inc, 41831
Almond Brothers, 355
Almost Nuts, 356
Alnor Instrument Company, 18646
Alnor Oil Co Inc, 41832, 54731
ALO Drink, 88
ALO Drinks, 89
Aloe Commodities International, 357
Aloe Farms Inc, 358, 41833
Aloe Hi-Tech, 18647
Aloe Laboratories, 359, 41834
Aloe'Ha Drink Products, 360, 41835
Aloecorp, Inc., 361, 41836
ALOHA, 90
Aloha Distillers, 362, 41837
Aloha From Oregon, 363
Aloha Poi Factory Inc, 364
Aloha Shoyu Co LTD, 365
Aloha Tofu Factory Inc, 366
Alois J Binder Bakery, 367
Alouette Cheese USA, 368, 41838
Alouf Plastics, 18648, 41839
ALP Lighting & Ceiling Products, 18164, 41559
Alpack, 18649
Alpen Cellars, 369
Alpen Sierra Coffee Company, 370
Alpendough, 371
Alpenglow Beverage Company, 372
Alpenrose Dairy, 373
Alpert/Siegel & Associates, 18650
Alpha Associates, 18651
Alpha Associates Inc, 18652

Alpha Baking Company, 374, 54732
Alpha Canvas & Awning Co, 18653
Alpha Checkweigher, 18654
Alpha Food Marketing, 40047
Alpha Foods, 54733
Alpha Gear Drives Inc, 18655
Alpha Health, 375
Alpha International, 51531
Alpha MOS America, 18656, 41840
Alpha Omega Technology, 18657, 54734
Alpha Packaging, 18658, 41841
Alpha Productions Inc, 18659
Alpha ProTech, 41842
Alpha Resources Inc, 18660
Alphabet Signs, 18662
AlphaBio Inc, 18661
Alphasonics, 18663
Alphin Brothers, 54735
ALPI Food Preparation Equipment, 18165, 41560
Alpina, 376
Alpine Butcher, 377
Alpine Cheese Company, 378
Alpine Coffee Roasters, 379
Alpine Food Distributing Inc, 54736
Alpine Gloves, 41843, 54737
Alpine Industries/Alpine Air Products, 54738
Alpine Meats, 380, 54739
Alpine Pure USA, 381
Alpine Start Foods, 382
Alpine Store Equipment Corporation, 18664
Alpine Summit Sales Inc, 40048
Alpine Touch Spices, 383
Alpine Valley Water, 384
Alpine Vineyards, 385
Alquima USA Inc, 40049
Alro Plastics, 18665
Alson Specialty Company, 54740
Alstor America, 18666
Alsum Farms & Produce, 386, 41844, 54741
Alta Dena Certified Dairy LLC, 387
Alta Dena Heartland Farms, 388
Alta Equipment Co, 54742
Alta Health Products, 389
Alta Refrigeration Inc, 18667
Alta Vineyard Cellar, 390
Altamura Winery, 391
Alteca Limited, 18668
Altech, 18669
Altech Packaging Company, 18670, 41845, 54743
Altek Co, 18671, 41846
Altek Industries Corporation, 18672
Alter Eco, 392, 54744
Alternative Air & Store Fixtures Company, 18673
Alternative Health & Herbs, 393, 41847, 54745
Althor Products, 18674
Altira Inc, 18675, 41848
Altman Industries, 18676, 41849
Alto Rey Food Corp, 394
Alto Vineyards & Winery, 395
Alto-Hartley, 54746
Alto-Shaam, 18677, 41850
Alton & Southern Railway Co, 51532
Altra Industrial Motion Corp, 18678
Altrafilters, 18679
Altrua Marketing & Design, 18680, 54747
Alturdyne Power Systems LLC, 18681
Alufoil Products Co Inc, 18682
Aluma Shield, 18683, 41851
Alumar, 18684
Alumaworks, 18685, 18686, 41852
Alumin-Nu Corporation, 18687, 41853
Alusett Precision Manufacturing, 18688
Alvalle, 396
Alvan Motor Freight, 51533
Alvarado Manufacturing Co Inc, 18689
Alvarado Street Bakery, 397, 41854
Alvita, 398

All Companies Index

Alwan & Sons, 54748
ALY Group of New York, 18166
Alya Foods, 399
Alyeska Seafoods, 400
AM Graphics, 18167
AM Test Laboratories, 18168
AM Todd Co, 91, 41561
AM-C Warehouses Inc, 52607
AM-Mac, 18169, 41562, 54580
AMAC Plastic Products Corp, 18170
Amador Foothill Winery, 403
Amafruits, 404
Amagic Holographics, 18690
Amalfitano's Italian Bakery, 405
Amalgamated Produce, 406
Amalgamated Sugar Company, 407
Amalthea Cellars Farm Winery, 408
Amana Meat Shop & Smoke House, 409, 54750
Amanda Hills Spring Water, 410
Amanida USA Corp, 411
Amano Artisan Chocolate, 412, 18691
Amano Enzyme USA Company, Ltd, 413, 41855
Amano Fish Cake Factory, 414
Amara Organic Baby Food, 415
Amaranth Resources, 416
Amarillo Mop & Broom Company, 18692, 41856
Amarillo Warehouse Co, 51534, 52636
Amark Packaging Systems, 18693, 41857
Amavi Cellars, 417
Amax Nutrasource Inc, 18694, 51535
Amazing Candy Craft Company, 418
Amazing Fruit Products, 419
Amazing Herbs Nutraceuticals, 420
Amazon Trading, Ltd., 421, 41858
Ambaflex, 18695
Ambassador Fine Foods, 41859, 41860, 54751
Amber Glo, 18696, 41861
Amberg Wine Cellars, 422
Amberland Foods, 423
Ambi-Prestigio Foods Inc, 40050
Ambient Engineering Co, 18697
Ambitech Engineering Corp, 18698
Ambootia Tea Estate, 424
Ambriola Co, 18699
Ambrose CM Co, 18699
Ambrosi Cheese USA, 425
Ambrosial Granola, 426
AmByth Estate, 401
AMC Chemicals, 18171
AMC Industries, 18172
Amcan Beverages Inc, 427
Amcan Industries, 428, 54752
Amcel, 18700
Amco Mechanical, 18701
Amco Metals Indl, 18702, 41863
Amco Products Co, 18703
AMCO Proteins, 92
Amco Warehouse & Transportation, 18704
AMCON Distributing Co, 54581, 54582
Amcor, 18705
Amcor Group Limited, 18706
AME Engineering, 18173
AME Nutrition, 93, 41563, 52608, 54583
AMEC, 18174
Amelia Bay, 429
Amella, 430
Amende & Schultz Co, 41864, 54753
Amenity Services, 54754
Ameranth Inc, 18707
Amerex, 18708
Ameri Candy, 431, 41865
Ameri Quest Transportation Svc, 18709
Ameri-Kal Inc, 432, 41866
Ameri-Khem, 18710
Ameri-Suisse Group, 433
America's Catch, 436
America's Classic Foods, 437, 41867
America's Electric Cooperatives, 18712
America's Service Line, 51537
American & Efird, 18713

American Adhesives, 18714
American Advertising & Shop Cap Company, 18715
American Advertising Specialties Company, 54755
American Agribusiness Assistance, 18716, 40051
American Agrotrading, 41868, 54756
American Air Filter, 18717
American Airlines Inc, 51538
American Almond Products Co, 438
American Apron Inc., 18718
American Art Stamp, 18719
American Association-Meat, 18720
American Auger & Accesories, 18721
American Autoclaves Co, 18722
American Autogard Corporation, 18723
American Bag & Burlap Company, 18724, 41869
American Bag & Linen Co, 18725
American Bakers Association, 54757
American Bakery Equipment Company, 18726, 54758
American Banana Company, 54759
American Beverage Marketers, 439
American Biosciences, 440
American Blanching Company, 441
American Botanicals, 442, 41870
American Bottling & Beverage, 443
American Box Corporation, 18727
American Broom Co, 18728
American Brush Company, 18729, 41871
American Canadian Fisheries, 444
American Cargo Services, 51539
American Cart Company, 18730
American Casting & Mfg Corp, 18731
American Chalkis Intl. Food Corp., 445, 41872
American Cheesemen, 446
American Chocolate Mould Co., 18732
American Classic Ice Cream Company, 447, 54760
American Coaster Company, 18733
American Cold Storage, 51540, 52638, 52639, 52640, 52641
American Commodity & Shipping, 40052, 41873
American Container Concepts, 54761
American Containers Inc, 18734, 41874
American Conveyor Corporation, 18735
American Coolair Corp, 18736, 41875
American Copak Corporation, 448
American Crane & Equip Corp, 18737
American Creative Solutions, 18738
American Crystal Sugar Co., 449
American Culinary Garden, 450, 41876
American Custom Dry Co, 18739
American Cut Edge Inc, 18740
American Cylinder Co, 18741
American Dehydrated Foods, Inc., 451
American Design & Machinery, 18742
American Design Studios, 18743, 41877
American Dish Service, 18744
American Distribution Centers, 51541, 52642
American Dixie Group, 18745
American Eagle Food Machinery, 18746, 41878
American Egg Products Inc, 452
American Electric Power, 18747
American Electronic Components, 18748
American Engineering Corporation, 18749
American Environmental International, 18750
American Equipment Co, 18751
American Equipment Systems Inc, 18752
American European Systems, 18753, 41879, 54762
American Excelsior Co, 18754, 18755, 41880
American Extrusion Intl, 18756, 41881
American Fabric Filter Co Inc, 18757
American Farms Produce, 54763
American Fast Freight, 51542

American Felt & Filter Co, 18758
American Fine Food Corporation, 453, 41882
American Fire Sprinkler Services, Inc, 18759, 41883
American Fish & Seafood Inc, 54764
American Flag & Banner Co Inc, 18760, 41884
American Flatbread, 454
American Foam Corp, 18761
American Food & AG Exporter, 41885
American Food & Vending Corporation, 54765
American Food Equipment, 18762, 41886, 54766
American Food Equipment Company, 18763, 41887
American Food Equipment & Supply, 54767
American Food Ingredients Inc, 455
American Food Products Inc, 456
American Food Systems, 54768
American Food Traders, 41888, 54769
American Foods Group LLC, 457, 41889
American Forklifter, 54770
American Forms & Labels, 18764
American Formula, 18765
American Frozen Foods, 54771
American Fruits & Flavors, 458, 18766
American Fuji Seal, 18767
American Gas & Chemical Co LTD, 18768
American Gas Association, 18769
American Gasket & Rubber Co, 18770
American Glass Research, 18771, 18772, 41890
American Griddle Corp., 18773
American Grocery & Beverage, 54772
American Halal Company, 459
American Hawaiian Soy Company, 460, 18774
American Health, 461
American Health & Safety, 54773
American Holt Corp, 18775
American Hotel Register Co, 41891, 54774
American Housewares, 18776, 41892
American Identification Industries, 18777
American Identity, 18778, 41893
American Importing Co., 462, 41894
American Industrial Supply Company, 18779
American Ingredients Co, 463
American Instants Inc, 464, 41895
American Insulated Panel Co, 18780
American International Chemical, 54775
American International Electric, 18781
American International Tooling, 18782
American Italian Pasta Company, 465, 41896
American Key Food Products Inc, 466, 41897, 54776
American Labelmark Co, 18784, 41899
American Laboratories, 467, 41900
American Lecithin Company, 468, 41901
American Led-Gible, 18785
American Legion, 54777
American LEWA, 18783, 41898
American Licorice, 469
American Lifts, 18786, 41902
American Lighting & Electric, 54778
American Lighting Supply, 54779
American Liquid Pkgng Systs, 18787
American Louver Co, 18788, 41903
American Machinery Corporation, 18789
American Manufacturing-Engrng, 18790, 41904
American Marketing International, 41905
American Material Handling Inc, 18791, 41906, 54780
American Meat & Seafood, 54781
American Menu Displays, 18792
American Mercantile Corp, 470
American Metal Door Company, 18793

American Metal Stamping, 18794
American Metalcraft Inc, 18795, 41907, 54782
American Micronutrients, 471
American Mint, 472
American Municipal Chemical, 18796
American Mussel Harvesters Inc, 54783
American National Rubber, 18797, 41908
American Natural & Organic, 473, 41909
American Nut & Chocolate Co, 474
American Nuts Inc., 475
American Olean Tile Company, 18798
American Osment, 54784
American Packaging Corporation, 18799, 54785
American Packaging Machinery, 18800, 18801, 41910
American Pallet Inc, 18802
American Pallets, 18803
American Palm Oil, 476
American Pan Co, 18804
American Panel Corp, 18805, 41911
American Pasien Co, 477, 18806, 41912
American Patriot Sales Inc, 40053
American Pie Council, 54786
American Pistachio Growers, 18807
American Plant & Equipment, 18808
American Plywood, 18809
American Pop Corn Co, 478, 41913
American Port Services, 51543, 52643
American Printpak Inc, 18810
American Produce Company, 54787
American Production Co Inc, 18811, 41914
American Profol Inc., 18812
American Quality Foods, 479, 54788
American Radionic Co Inc, 18813
American Raisin Packers, 54789
American Range, 18814, 41915
American Renolit Corp LA, 18815, 41916
American Resin Corp, 18816
American Restaurant Supply, 54790, 54791
American Roland Food Corp, 18817
American Roland Food Corporation, 41917, 54792
American Safety Technologies, 18818
American Sales & Marketing, 40054, 41918, 54793
American Seafood Imports Inc, 41919, 54794
American Seafoods, 480, 41920
American Seaway Foods Inc, 54795
American Select Foods, 54796
American Services Group, 18819
American Shipping Co, 51544
American Skin LLC, 481
American Society of Baking, 54797
American Society of Brewing, 18820
American Softshell Crab, 54798
American Solving Inc., 18821, 41921
American Soy Products Inc, 482
American Specialty Coffee & Culinary, 18822, 41922, 54799
American Specialty Confections, 483
American Specialty Foods, 484
American Specialty Machinery, 18823
American Spoon Foods Inc, 485
American Star Cork Company, 18824, 41923
American Store Fixtures, 18825, 41924
American Style Foods, 18826
American Sun Control Awnings, 18827
American Systems Associates, 18828
American Tartaric Products, 486, 41925
American Technical Services Group, 18829
American Textile Mills Inc, 18830
American Time & Signal Co, 18831, 41926
American Trading Company, 40055, 41927, 54800
American Truck Dispatch, 51545
American Tuna, 487

1353

All Companies Index

American Ultraviolet Co, 18832, 41928
American Uniforms Sales Inc, 54801
American Variseal, 18833
American Vegetable Oils, 488
American Ventilation Company, 18834
American Vintage Wine Biscuits, 489
American Warehouse Co, 51546, 52644
American Water Broom, 18835, 41929
American Wax Co Inc, 18836, 41930
American West, 51547
American Whey Company, 18837
American Wholesale Equipment, 18838
American Wholesale Grocery, 490, 54802
American Wire Products, 18839
American Wood Fibers, 18840
American Yeast, 491
American Yeast Sales, 54803
American-Newlong Inc, 18841
American/Brenner Wholesale, 54804
Americana Art China Company, 18842, 41931
Americana Marketing, 18843, 41932
Americana Vineyards & Winery, 492
AmericanLifestyle.Com, 40056
Americasia International, 18844
Americhicken, 493, 54805
Americo, 18845, 41933
Americode LLC, 18846
AmeriCold Logistics LLC, 51536, 52637
Americolor Corp, 494
Americraft Carton Inc, 18847, 18848
Ameridia Innovative Solutions, 18849
AmeriGift, 434
Ameriglobe LLC, 18850, 41934
Amerikooler Inc, 18851
Ameripak Packaging Equipment, 18852, 18853, 41935
Ameripec, 18854
Ameripure Processing Co, 495
AmeriQual Foods, 435, 18711
Ameristamp/Sign-A-Rama, 18855, 41936
Ameritech Laboratories, 18856
Ameritech Signs & Banners, 18857
Amerivacs, 18858, 41937
Amerivap Systems Inc, 18859, 54806
Amerol Chemical Corporation, 496, 41938
Ameron International, 18860
Ames Company, Inc, 497, 40057, 41939
Ames Engineering Corporation, 18861
Ames International Inc, 498, 41940
Amest Food, 499, 41941
Ametco Manufacturing Corp, 18862, 41942
Ametek, 18863, 18864, 41943
AMETEK Brookfield, 18175
Ametek Drexelbrook, 18865
AMETEK Inc, 18176, 18177, 18178, 41564
AMETEK National Controls Corp, 18179, 41565
Ametek Technical & Industrial Products, 18866
Ametek Us Gauge, 18867
AMF Bakery Systems Corp, 18180, 41566
AMF CANADA, 18181, 41567
AMF Pharma, 94
Amfec Inc, 18868
Amherst Milling Co, 18869
Amherst Stainless Fabrication, 18870
AMI, 18182, 41568
AMI/RECPRO, 18183
Amiad Filtration Systems, 18871
Amick Farms LLC, 500, 41944, 54807
Amida Food Corp, 41945
Amigos Canning Company, 501, 41946
Amira Foods, 41947
Amira Nature Foods Ltd., 502
AMISTCO Separation Products, 18184
Amity Packing Co Inc, 503, 41948
Amity Vineyards, 504
Amizetta Vineyards, 505
Ammeraal Beltech, 18872

Ammeraal Beltech Inc, 18873, 18874, 41949
Ammerland America, 506
Ammirati Inc, 41950, 54808
AMN Distributors/Premium Blend, 54584
Amobelge Shipping Corporation, 51548
Amodex Products, 18875
Amoretti, 507, 41951
Amoroso's Baking Co, 508
Amos's PA Wonder Products, 54809
Amot Controls, 18876
Ampac Packaging, LLC, 18877
Ampak, 18878, 41952
Ampak Seafoods Corporation, 41953, 54810
Ampco Pumps Co Inc, 18879, 41954
Amphora International, 509, 41955
Ample Industries, 18880, 41956
Amplexus Corporation, 18881
Amplify Snack Brands, 510
Ampoint Distribution Centers, 52645
Amport Foods, 511
Amrhein's Wine Cellars, 512
Amri Inc, 18882
Amrita Health Foods, 513
Amrita Snacks, 514, 41957, 54811
Amscor Inc, 18883
AMSECO, 18185, 41569
Amsler Equipment Inc, 18884
Amsnack, 515
AMSOIL Inc, 18186, 41570
Amstat Industries, 18885
Amstell Holding, 516
Amster-Kirtz Co, 18886, 54812
Amsterdam Brewing Company, 517
Amsterdam Printing & Litho Inc, 18887, 41958
AMT Labs Inc, 95, 41571
AMT Sales & Marketing, 40016
Amtab Manufacturing Corp, 18888, 41959
AmTech Ingredients, 402, 54749
Amtekco, 18889, 41960
Amtex Packaging, 54813
Amtrade Inc., 41961
Amware Distribution Warehouse, 51549, 52646
Amwell, 18890
Amwell Valley Vineyard, 518
Amy & Brian Naturals, 519
Amy Food Inc, 520, 18891, 54814
Amy's Candy Bar, 521
Amy's Kitchen Inc, 522, 41962
Amylu Foods, 523
Ana's Salsa, 524
Anabol Naturals, 526, 41964
AnaCon Foods Company, 525, 41963
Anadon Logistics, 51550, 52647
Anaheim Manufacturing Company, 18892
Analite, 18893, 41965
Analog Devices Inc, 18894
Analog Technology Corporation, 18895
Analogic Corp., 18896
Analytical Development, 18897, 41966
Analytical Labs, 18898
Analytical Measurements, 18899, 41967
Analytical Technologies Inc, 18900
Analyticon Discovery LLC, 527, 18901
Ananda Hemp, 528, 54815
Anastasia Confections Inc, 529
Anbroco, 18902
Anchor Appetizer Group, 530
Anchor Brewing Company, 531, 41968
Anchor Conveyor Products, 18903
Anchor Crane & Hoist Service Company, 18904, 41969
Anchor Distribution Services, 51551, 52648
Anchor Florida Marketing, 40058
Anchor Frozen Foods, 532
Anchor Glass Container Corporation, 18905

Anchor Hocking Operating Co, 18906, 41970
Anchor Industries, 18907
Anchor Ingredients, 533
Anchor Packaging, 18908, 40059, 41971
Ancient Harvest, 534
Ancient Nutrition, 535
Ancient Organics, 536, 54816
Ancient Peaks Winery, 537
Anco Foods, 538
Anco-Eaglin Inc, 18909
Ancora Coffee Roasters, 539, 54817
Andalucia Nuts, 540
Andalusia Distributing Co Inc, 541, 54818
Andantex USA Inc, 18910
Andco Environmental Processes, 18911, 41972
Andean Naturals LLC, 542, 18912
Andersen 2000, 18913, 41973
Andersen Products Inc, 18914
Andersen Sign Company, 18915
Andersen's Pea Soup, 543
Anderson American Precision, 18916
Anderson Chemical Co, 18917
Anderson Custom Processing, 544
Anderson Dahlen Inc, 18918, 41974
Anderson Dairy Inc, 545
Anderson Daymon Worldwide, 40060
Anderson Dubose Company, 54819
Anderson Erickson Dairy, 546, 547, 41975, 41976
Anderson Instrument Company, 18919
Anderson International Corp, 18920, 41977
Anderson International Foods, 54820
Anderson Machine Sales, 18921, 41978
Anderson Products, 18922
Anderson Seafood, 548, 41979, 54821
Anderson Snow Corp, 18923
Anderson Studio Inc, 54822
Anderson Tool & Engineering Company, 18924, 41980
Anderson Valley Brewing Co, 549
Anderson Wood Products, 18925
Anderson's Conn Valley Vineyards, 550
Anderson-Crane Company, 18926, 41981
Anderson-Negele, 18927, 41982
Andex Corp, 18928, 41983
Andex Industries Inc, 18929
Andfel Corporation, 18930
Andgar Corp, 18931
Andre Prost Inc, 551
Andre Robin And Associates, 18932
Andre Tea & Coffee Company, 54823
Andre's Confiserie Suisse, 552
Andre-Boudin Bakeries, 553
Andrea Basket, 18933
Andrew & Williamson Sales Co, 554, 54824
Andrew H Lawson Co, 18934
Andrew Peller Limited, 555, 41984
Andrew W Nissly Inc, 18935
Andrew's Fixture Co, 18936
Andrews Brewing Co, 556
Andrews Caramel Apples, 557
Andrews Dried Beef Company, 558
ANDRITZ, 18187, 41572
Andritz Separation Inc, 18937
Andros Foods North America, 559, 41985, 54825
Andy J. Egan Co., 18938
Andy Printed Products, 18939
Andy's Seasoning, 560
Anetsberger, 18940, 41986
Anette's Chocolate & Ice Cream, 561
Angel Beltran Corporation, 54826
Angel's Bakeries, 562
Angel's Produce, 54827
Angelic Bakehouse, 563
Angelic Gourmet Inc, 564
Angelina & Neches River Railroad, 51552
Angelo & Franco U.S.A., 565
Angelo M. Formosa Foods, 54828

Angelo Pietro Honolulu, 566
Angelo Refrigeration & Rstrnt, 54829
Angers Equipment Company, 54830
Angie's Artisan Treats LLC, 567
Anglo American Trading, 568, 41987
Angry Orchard Cider Company, LLC, 569, 41988
Anguil Environmental Systems, 18941, 41989
ANGUS Chemical Co, 18188
Angy's Food Products Inc, 570
Anheuser-Busch, 571
Anhydro Inc, 18942, 41990
Animal Pak, 572, 41991
Anita's Mexican Foods Corporation, 573, 41992
Anita's Yogurt, 574
Anixter Inc, 18943, 54831
Anjo's Imports, 41993, 54832
Ankeny Lake Wild Rice, 575, 41994
Ankle Deep Foods, 576
Anko Food Machine USA Co LTD, 18944
Anko Products Inc, 18945
ANKOM Technology, 18189, 18190
Anmar Foods, 577
Anmar Nutrition, 578
Ann Arbor Computer, 18946, 41995
Ann Clark, LTD, 18947, 54833
Ann Hemyng Candy Inc, 579
Ann's House of Nuts, Inc., 580
Anna's Oatcakes, 581
Annabella, 582
Annabelle Candy Co Inc, 583
Annabelle Lee, 584
Annapolis Produce & Restaurant, 585, 54834
Annapolis Winery, 586
Annette Island Packing Company, 587
Annette's Donuts Ltd., 588, 18948, 54835
Annie Chun's, 589
Annie's Frozen Yogurt, 590, 18949, 41996
Annie's Homegrown, 591
Annie's Naturals, 592, 41997
Anniston Paper & Supply Company, 54836
Anova, 18950
Anresco Laboratories, 18951, 18952
Anritsu Industrial Solutions, 18953, 41998
Ansell Healthcare Inc, 18954
Antek Industrial Instruments, 18955
Antelope Valley Winery, 593
Anter Brothers Company, 54837
Anthony & Sons Italian Bakery, 594
Anthony Cea & Associates, 40061
Anthony Marano Co Inc, 54838
Anthony Road Wine Co, 595
Anthony Thomas Candy Co, 596
Anthony's Snack & Vending, 54839
Anthracite Provision Co, 54840
Anton Caratan & Son, 597, 41999
Anton Kimball Design, 18956
Anton Paar USA Inc, 18957
Anton-Argires, 54841
Antone's Import Company, 42000, 54842
Antoni Ravioli Co, 598, 42001
Antonio Mozzarella Factory, 599
Antrim Manufacturing Inc, 18958
Antunes Controls, 18959
ANVER Corporation, 18191
Anver Corporation, 18960
ANVER Corporation, 41573
Anzu Technology, 18961
AOI Matcha, 96
AOI Tea Company, 97, 41574
Aoki Laboratory America, 18962
AP Dataweigh Inc, 18192, 41575
AP Fish & Produce, 54585
APA, 18193
Apa, 18963
Apac Chemical Corporation, 600, 42002
Apache Brokers, 40062

1354

All Companies Index

Apache Inc, 18964, 54843
Apache Stainless Equipment, 18965, 18966, 42003
Apani Southwest, 601
APC Inc, 98, 41576
Apco/Valve & Primer Corporation, 18967
APEC, 18194
Apecka Peppered Pickles, 602
Apex Bakery Equipment, 18968
Apex Fountain Sales Inc, 18969, 42004
Apex Machine Company, 18970, 42005
Apex Marketing Group, 603
Apex Packing & Rubber Co, 18971, 42006
Apex Tool Works Inc, 18972
Apex Welding Inc, 18973
APG Cash Drawer, 18195
Aphrodite Divine Confections, 604
API Foils, 18196
API Heat Transfer Inc, 18197, 41577
API Industries, 18198, 18199
Apigent Solutions, 18974
Apilico/Cuthbertson Imports, 54844
Apiterra, 605
APL Logistics, 51509
Apl Logistics, 51553
APL Logistics, 52609, 52610
Apl Logistics, 52649
Aplen Sierra Coffee Company, 18975
APM, 18200, 18201, 41578, 54586
APM/NNZ Industrial Packaging, 18202
APN Inc, 18203, 41579
Apogee Translite Inc, 18976, 42007
Apollo Acme Lighting Fixture, 18977
Apollo Sheet Metal, 18978
Apotheca Inc, 606, 18979
Appalachian Power, 18980
Apparel Manufacturing Co Inc, 18981
Appennino USA, 42008
Appetizers And, Inc., 607
Apple & Eve LLC, 608, 42009
Apple Acres, 609, 42010
Apple Flavor & Fragrance USA, 610
Apple Food Sales, 40063
Apple Valley Market, 611
Apple-A-Day Nutritional Labeling Service, 18982
Applecreek Speciality Foods, 612
Appledore Cove LLC, 613
Applegate Chemical Company, 18983
Applegate Farms, 614
Appleson Press, 18984
Appleton Produce Company, 615, 42011
Applewood Orchards Inc, 616, 42012
Applewood Seed & Garden Group, 617, 54845
Applewood Winery, 618, 42013
Applexion, 18985
Application Software, 18986
Applied Analytics, 18987
Applied Chemical Technology, 18988, 42014
Applied Fabric Technologies, 18989
Applied Handling Equipment Company, 54846
Applied Handling NW, 18990, 54847
Applied Industrial Tech Inc, 18991, 42015, 54848
Applied Membranes, 18992
Applied Product Sales, 18993
Applied Products Co, 18994
Applied Robotics Inc, 18995, 42016
Applied Technologies, 18996
Applied Thermal Technologies, 18997, 42017
APR Associates Inc, 18204
April Hill Inc, 619
APS BioGroup, 99
APS Packaging Systems, 18205
APS Plastic Systems, 18206
Apt-Li Specialty Brushes, 18998
Aptar Mukwonago, 18999
APV Americas, 18207, 41580
APV Baker, 18208, 41581
Apv Crepaco Inc, 19000

APV Engineered Systems, 18209
APV Fluid Handling, 18210
APV Heat Transfer, 18211
APV Mixing & Blending, 18212
APV Systems, 18213
APV Tanks & Fabricated Products, 18214
APW Wyott Food Service Equipment Company, 18215, 41582
Aqua Blast Corp Mfg, 19001
Aqua Brew, 19002
Aqua Clara Bottling & Distribution, 620
Aqua Foods, 40064, 42018
Aqua Measure, 19003, 42019
Aqua Solutions Inc, 54849
Aqua Source, 54850
Aqua Star, 42020
Aqua Tec Inc, 19004
Aqua Vie Beverage Corporation, 621
Aqua-Aerobic Systems Inc, 19005, 42021
Aqua-Tec Co, 54851
AquaCuisine, 622
Aquafine Corp, 19006
Aquair, 19007
AquaTec Development, 623
Aquatec Seafoods Ltd., 624
Aquatech, 625, 42022
Aquathin Corporation, 19008, 42023
Aquionics Inc, 19009, 42024
Ar Line Promotions Inc, 54852
ARA Food Corp, 100
Aragadz Foods Corporation, 54853
Aralia Olive Oils, 626, 42025
Aramark Uniform Svc, 19010, 54854
Aran USA, 19011
Arbee Transparent Inc, 19012, 42026
ARBO Engineering, 18216
Arbor Crest Wine Cellars, 627
Arbor Hill Grapery & Winery, 628
Arbor Mist Winery, 629
Arbor Springs Water Co, 630
Arboris LLC, 631
Arbre Farms Inc, 632, 52650, 54855
Arbuckle Coffee Roasters, 633
Arc Machines Inc, 19013
ARC Specialties, 18217
Arcadia Biosciences, 634
Arcadia Dairy Farms Inc, 635
Arcadian Estate Winery, 636
Arcar Graphics, 19014
Archer Daniels Midland Company, 637, 638, 19015, 51554, 52651
Archer Wire Intl Corp, 19016
Archibald Frozen Desserts, 639, 19017
Archie Moore's, 640, 42027
Architectural Products, 19018
Architectural Sheet Metals LLC, 19019
Architectural Specialty Products, 19020
Architecture Plus Intl Inc, 19021, 42028
Archon Industries, 19022
Archon Industries Inc, 19023, 42029
Archon Vitamin Corp, 641, 42030
ARCO Coffee, 101
Arco Coffee Co, 19024
Arco Warehouse Co, 51555, 52652
Arcobaleno Pasta Machines, 19025, 42031
Arcoplast Wall & Ceiling Systems, 19026
Arcor USA, 643
Arctic Air, 19027, 42032
Arctic Beverages, 644, 51556, 54856
Arctic Cold Storage, 52653
Arctic Cold Storage Inc, 52654
Arctic Frozen Foods, 52655
Arctic Glacier, 645
Arctic Glacier Premium Ice, 19028, 54857
Arctic Ice Cream Co, 646
Arctic Industries, 19029, 42033
Arctic Logistics, 52656, 54858
Arctic Seal & Gasket, 19030
Arctic Star, 19031
Arctic Star Distributing, 42034, 54859
Arctic Zero, 647, 54860

Arctica Showcase Company, 19032, 54861
Ardagh Group, 19033, 19034
Arde Inc, 19035, 19036, 42035, 42036
Arden Companies, 19037, 42037
Ardent Mills Corp, 648
Ardith Mae Farmstead Goat Cheese, 649
Ardmore Cheese Company, 650
Ardy Fisher, 651
Arel Group Wine & Spirits Inc, 652
Arena & Sons, 653
Arena Products, 19038
Argania Butter, 654
Argee, 655
Argo & Company, 19039, 42038
Argo Century, Inc., 656, 42039
Argo Fine Foods, 657
Argo Tea, 658
Arguimbau & Co, 42040
Argus Protective Services, 54862
Argyle Winery, 659
Ari Industries Inc, 19040, 42041
Ariake USA Inc, 660
Arico Natural Foods, 661
Ariel Natural Foods, 662
Ariel Vineyards, 663, 42042
Aries Paper & Chemical Company, 54863
Aries Prepared Beef, 664
Arise & Shine Herbal Products, 665, 42043
Arista Industries Inc, 666, 42044, 54864
Ariston Specialties, 667
Ariza Cheese Co, 668
Arizmendi Bakery, 669
Arizona Beverage Company, 670
Arizona Cold Storage LLC, 52657
Arizona Cowboy, 671, 42045
Arizona Dairy Ingredient, 42046
Arizona Instrument LLC, 19041, 42047
Arizona Natural Products, 672, 42048
Arizona Nutritional Supplements, 673
Arizona Pepper Products, 674
Arizona Pistachio Company, 675
Arizona Storage & Retrieval Systems, 54865
Arizona Store Equipment, 19042
Arizona Sunland Foods, 676
Arizona Vineyards, 677
Arjo Wiggins, 19043
Arjobex, 19044
Arkansas Glass Container Corp, 19045, 42049
Arkansas Poly, 19046
Arkansas Refrigerated Services, 52658
Arkansas Tomato Shippers, 19047, 54866
Arkansas Valley Wholesale Grocery Company, 54867
Arkfeld Mfg & Distributing Co, 19048, 42050
Arla Foods Inc, 678, 42051, 54868
Arla Foods Ingredients, 19049
Arleen Food Products Company, 54869
Arlen S Gould & Assoc, 679
Arlin Manufacturing Co, 19050
Arlington Coffee Company, 54870
Arlington Display Industries, 19051
Arlyn Johnson & Associates, 19052
Armaday Paper, 54871
Armaly Brands, 19053, 42052
Armand Manufacturing Inc, 19054
Armanino Foods of Distinction, 680, 42053
Armato & Associates, 19055
Armbrust Meats, 681, 54872
Armbrust Paper Tubes Inc, 19056, 42054
Armco, 19057
Armenia Coffee Corporation, 682
Armeno Coffee Roasters LTD, 683, 42055
Armistead Citrus Company, 684
Armstrong Engineering Associates, 19058
Armstrong Hot Water, 19059, 42056
Armstrong International, 19060
Armstrong Jones, 54873

Armstrong Manufacturing, 19061
Armstrong-Hunt, 19062
Arnabal International, Inc., 685, 42057
Arneg LLC, 19063
Arnel's Originals, Inc, 686
Arnett Brokerage Co, 40065, 54875
Arnhalt Transportation Brkrg, 51557
Arnhem Group, 687
Arnold Equipment Co, 19064, 42058
Arnold Farm Sugarhouse, 688
Arnold Foods Company, 689
Arnold Machinery Co, 54876
Arnold's Meat Food Products, 690, 42059
Arns Winery, 691
Arol Closure Systems Spa, 19065
Aroma Coffee Company, 692
Aroma Coffee Roasters Inc, 693, 54877
Aroma Foods, 54878
Aroma Manufacturing Company, 19066
Aroma Ridge, 694
Aroma Vera, 695, 42060
Aroma-Life, 696, 42061
Aromachem, 697, 42062
Aromascan PLC, 19067
Aromatech USA, 698, 19068, 42063
Arome Fleurs & Fruits, 699
Aromi D' Italia, 42064
Aromi d'Italia, 700
Aromor Flavors & Fragrances, 701, 42065
Aron Corporation, 54879
ARPAC Group, 18218
Arpac LP, 19069, 19070, 42066
Arpeco Engineering Ltd, 19071
Arro Corp, 702, 19072, 19073, 52659
Arrow Chemical Inc, 42067, 54880
Arrow Distributing, 54881
Arrow Plastic Mfg Co, 19074, 42068
Arrow Restaurant Equipment, 54882
Arrow Sign & Awning Company, 19075
Arrow Tank Co, 19076, 42069
Arrow-Magnolia Intl Inc, 19077
Arrowac Fisheries, 703, 42070
Arrowhead Beef, 704
Arrowhead Mills, 705
Arrowood Winery, 706
Arroyo Sales Company, 40066
Art CoCo Chocolate Company, 707
Art Craft Lighting, 19078
Art Poly Bag Co, 19079
Art Printing Company, 42071
Art Wire Works Co, 19080, 42072
Art's Mexican Products, 708
Art's Tamales, 709
Art's Trading, 54883
Art's Welding, 19081
Art-Phyl Creations, 19082, 42073
Art-Tech Restaurant Design, 19083
Artco Eq Co, 19084
Artcraft Badge & Sign Company, 19085
Arteasans Beverages LLC, 710
Artek USA, 711
Artel Packaging Systems Limited, 19086
Artemis International, 42074
Artesa Vineyards & Winery, 712
Artesian Honey Producers, 713
Artesian Ice, 52660
Artex International, 19087, 42075
Arthur Corporation, 19088
Arthur D Little Inc., 19089
Arthur G Russell Co Inc, 19090, 42076
Arthur G. Meier Company/Inland Products Company, 40067, 54884
Arthur Products Co, 19091
Artique, 54885
Artisan Confections, 714
Artisan Controls Corp, 19092
Artisan Industries, 19093, 42077
Artisan Kettle, 715
Artisanal Foods, 40068
Artisanal Pantry, 42078
Artist Coffee, 716, 19094, 54886
Artiste Flavor, 19095, 42079

1355

All Companies Index

Artistic Carton, 19096
Artistic Carton Co, 19097
Artistic Packaging Concepts, 19098
Artkraft Strauss LLC, 19099, 42080
Arturo's Spinella's Bakery, 717
Artuso Pastry, 718
Artx Limited, 19100
Arvin Sales Company, 40069
Arway Confections Inc, 719
ARY, 18219
Arylessence Inc, 720
Aryzta, 721
Asael Farr & Sons Co, 722
Asanti Distributors, 54887
Asap Automation, 19101
ASAP Freight Systems, 51510, 52611
Asarasi, 723
ASC Industries Inc, 18220
ASC Seafood Inc, 102
Ascaso, 19102
ASCENT Technics Corporation, 18221, 41583
Aseltine Cider Company, 724
Asepco, 19103
Aseptic Resources, 19104
Asgco Manufacturing Inc, 19105
Ash Enterprises, 19106
Ashcroft Inc, 19107
Asheboro Wholesale Grocery Inc, 54888
Asher's Chocolates, 725
Ashland, 19108
Ashland Cold Storage, 52661
Ashland Equipment, 54889
Ashland Milling, 726
Ashland Nutritional Products, 19109
Ashland Plantation Gourmet, 727
Ashland Sausage Co, 728
Ashland Vineyards & Winery, 729
Ashley Food Co Inc, 730
Ashley Koffman Foods, 54890
Ashlock Co, 19110, 42081
Ashman Manufacturing & Distributing Company, 731
Ashworth Bros Inc, 19111, 42082
ASI Data Myte, 18222, 41584
ASI Electronics Inc, 18223, 41585
Asi Food Safety Consultants, 19112
ASI International, 18224, 41586
ASI MeltPro Systems, 18225
ASI Technologies, 18226
ASI/Restaurant Manager, 18227, 41587
Asia and Middle East Food Traders, 19113
Asia Etc. LLC, 42083
Asia Shipping & Trading Corporation, 54891
Asiago PDO & Speck Alto Adige PGI, 732, 42084
Asiamerica Ingredients, 733, 40070, 42085, 54892
Asian Foods Inc, 734
ASK Foods Inc, 103
Askinosie Chocolate, 735
Aspecialtybox.Com, 54893
Aspect Engineering, 19114
Aspen Corporate Identity Group, 54894
Aspen Distribution, 51558, 52662
Aspen Distribution Inc, 51559, 52663
Aspen Food Marketing, 40071
Aspen Mulling Company Inc., 736, 42086
Aspen Research Corp, 19115
Aspen Research Corporation, 19116
Aspen Systems, 19117
Aspeon, 19118
Aspire, 737
Assembled Products Corp, 19119, 42087
Assembly Technology & Test, 19120, 42088
Assemblyonics Inc, 54895
Asset Design LLC, 19121
Assets Grille & Southwest Brewing Company, 738
Assmann Corp Of America, 19122
Associated Bag Co, 19123, 54896

Associated Food Equipment, 54897
Associated Food Stores, 54898
Associated Food Stores Inc, 54899
Associated Foodservices, 40072
Associated Fruit Company, 739, 42089
Associated Global Systems, 51560, 52664
Associated Grocers, 54900
Associated Industrial Rubber, 19124
Associated Material Handling, 54901
Associated Milk Producers Inc., 740
Associated Packaging Enterprises, 19125
Associated Packaging Equipment Corporation, 19126, 42090
Associated Potato Growers, 741
Associated Products Inc, 19127, 42091
Associated Trucking Co Inc, 51561
Associated Wholesale Grocers, 54902
Associates Material Handling, 54903
Association of Operative Millers, 19128
Association-Nutri, 19129
Astar Inc., 54904
Asti Holdings Ltd, 742
Astor Chocolate Corp, 743, 42092
Astoria General Espresso, 19130, 42093, 54905
Astoria Laminations, 19131
Astra Manufacturing Inc, 19132, 42094
Astral Extracts, 744, 42095, 54906
Astro Arc Polysoude, 19133
Astro Dairy Products, 745
Astro Machine Corp, 19134
Astro Physic Inc, 19135
Astro Plastics, 19136
Astro Pure Water, 19137, 42096
Astro/Polymetron Zellweger, 19138
ASV Wines, 104
ASW Supply Chain Svc, 51511, 52612
At Last Naturals Inc, 746, 42097
At-Your-Svc Software Inc, 19139, 42098
ATAGO USA Inc, 18228
Atalanta Corporation, 42099
Atchison Wholesale Grocery, 54907
Atco Marine Service, 54908
ATD-American Co, 18229, 41588
Ateeco Inc, 747
Athea Laboratories, 19140, 42100
Athena Controls Inc, 19141, 42101
Athena Oil Inc, 748
Athenee Imports Distributors, 42102
Athens Baking Company, 749
Athens Foods Inc, 750
Athletic Brewing Co., 751
ATI, 40017, 41589, 54587
Atir Transportation Services, 51562
ATK, 18230
Atka Pride Seafoods Inc, 752, 54909
Atkins Bob Lin Inc, 51563
Atkins Elegant Desserts, 753, 42103
Atkins Ginseng Farms, 754, 42104
Atkins Jemptec, 19142
Atkins Nutritionals Inc., 755
Atkins Technical, 19143
Atkins Temptec, 42105
Atkinson Candy Co, 756
Atkinson Dynamics, 19144
Atkinson Milling Co., 757
Atkinson Sales Company, 40073
Atkinson-Crawford Sales Co, 40074
ATL-East Tag & Label Inc, 18231
Atlanta Bonded Warehouse Corporation, 51564, 52665
Atlanta Bread Co., 758
Atlanta Burning Bush, 759, 19145
Atlanta Coffee & Tea Co, 760
Atlanta Coffee Roasters, 761
Atlanta Fish Market, 762
Atlanta Fixture & Sales Company, 54910
Atlanta Service Warehouse Inc, 52666
Atlanta SharpTech, 19146, 42106
Atlantic Aqua Farms, 763, 42107
Atlantic Blueberry, 764, 42108
Atlantic Capes Fisheries, 765, 42109
Atlantic Chemicals Trading, 766, 42110

Atlantic Coast Crushers Inc, 19147, 42111
Atlantic Coast Freezers, 52667
Atlantic Container, 51565
Atlantic Dominion Distributors, 54911
Atlantic Fish Specialties, 767, 42112
Atlantic Foam & Packaging Company, 19148
Atlantic Foods, 768
Atlantic Gem Scallop Co, 54912
Atlantic Group Inc, 19149
Atlantic Industrial & Marine Supplies, 54913
Atlantic International Products, 42113
Atlantic Laboratories Inc, 769
Atlantic Lift Systems, 54914
Atlantic Meat Company, 770, 42114
Atlantic Mills, 19150
Atlantic Mussel Growers Corporation, 771, 42115
Atlantic Natural Foods, 772
Atlantic Pork & Provisions, 773
Atlantic Reefer Terminals Inc, 52668
Atlantic Rentals, 54915
Atlantic Rubber Products, 19151, 42116
Atlantic Salmon of Maine, 774, 54916
Atlantic Sea Pride, 775, 54917
Atlantic Seacove Inc, 776, 54918
Atlantic Seafood Direct, 777, 42117, 54919
Atlantic Seafood Intl Group, 54920
Atlantic Seasonings, 778
Atlantic Spice Co, 54921
Atlantic Store Fixture Company, 54922
Atlantic Ultraviolet Corp, 19152, 42118
Atlantic Veal & Lamb Inc, 779, 42119
Atlantic Wholesalers, 54923, 54924
Atlantis Industries Inc, 19153, 42120
Atlantis Pak USA Inc, 780, 19154
Atlantis Plastics Linear Film, 19155, 42121
Atlantis Smoked Foods, 40075, 42122
Atlantix Commodities, 42123
Atlapac Trading Inc, 42124
Atlas Bakery Machinery Company, 19156
Atlas Biscuit Co Inc, 40076
Atlas Body, 19157
Atlas Case Inc, 19158
Atlas Copco Tools & Assembly, 19159
Atlas Corporation, 19160
Atlas Equipment Company, 19161, 54925
Atlas Inspection, 19162
Atlas Labels, 19163
Atlas Lift Truck Rentals & Sales, 54926
Atlas Match Company, 19164, 42125
Atlas Match Corporation, 19165, 42126
Atlas Metal Industries, 19166
Atlas Minerals & Chemicals Inc, 19167, 19168, 42127
Atlas Pacific Engineering, 19169, 42128
Atlas Packaging Inc, 19170, 42129
Atlas Peak Vineyards, 781
Atlas Restaurant Supply, 19171, 40077
Atlas Rubber Stamp & Printing, 19172
Atlas Tag & Label Inc, 19173
Atlas-Stord, 19174
ATM Corporation, 18232, 41590
ATOFINA Chemicals, 18233, 41591
Atoka Cranberries, Inc., 782, 42130
Atomizing Systems Inc, 19175
Atrium Biotech, 783, 42131
ATS, 18234
ATS Rheosystems, 18235, 41592
Attala Development Corporation, 784
Attar Herbs & Spices, 54927
Attias Oven Corp, 19176, 42132
Attracta Sign, 19177
Attune Foods, 19178
ATW Manufacturing Company, 18236
Atwater Block Brewing Company, 785, 42133
Atwater Foods, 786, 42134, 54928
Atwood Cheese Company, 787
Atwood Lobster Co, 54929

ATZ Natural, 18237
Au Bon Climat Winery, 788
Au Printemps Gourmet, 789
Au'some Candies, 790
Auburn Dairy Products Inc, 792
Auburn Label & Tag Company, 19180
Auburn Systems LLC, 19181, 19182
Audion Automation, 19183, 42135
Audrey Signs, 19184
Audsam Printing, 19185
Audubon Sales & Svc, 19186
Aufschnitt Meats, 793
Auger Fab, 19187, 19188, 42136
Auger Manufacturing Spec, 19189
August Foods LTD, 794
August Kitchen, 795
August Schell Brewing Co, 796
August Thomsen Corp, 19190, 42137
Augusta Winery, 797
Augustin's Waffles, 798
Aunt Aggie De's Pralines, 799
Aunt Fannie's Bakery, 800
Aunt Gussie Cookies & Crackers, 801
Aunt Heddy's Bakery, 802, 54930
Aunt Jenny's Sauces/Melba Foods, 803
Aunt Kathy's Homestyle Products, 804
Aunt Kitty's Foods Inc, 805
Aunt Lizzie's Inc, 806
Aunt Millie's Bakeries, 807
Aunt Sally's Praline Shops, 808, 42138, 54931
AuNutra Industries Inc, 791, 19179
Auroma International Inc, 809
Auromere Inc, 42139, 54932
Aurora Air Products Inc, 19191
Aurora Alaska Premium Smoked Salmon & Seafood, 810, 54933
Aurora Design Associates, Inc., 19192, 42140
Aurora Frozen Foods Division, 811
Aurora Organic Dairy, 812
Aurora Packing Co Inc, 813, 42141
Aurora Products, 814
Aurora Storage & Distribution Center, 52669
Aussie Crunch, 815
Aust & Hachmann, 42142, 54934
Auster Company, 54935
Austin Brown Co, 19193
Austin Chase Coffee, 816
Austin Co, 19194
Austin Slow Burn, 817
Austin Special Foods Company, 818, 54936
Austin Transportation, 51566
Austinuts, 819
Austrade, 820, 42143, 54937
Austrian Trade Commission, 821
AUTEC, 41593
Auth Brothers Food Service, 54938
Authentic Biocode Corp, 19195
Authentic Marotti Biscotti, 822
Autin's Cajun Cookery, 823
Autio Co, 19196, 42144
Auto Chlor Systems, 19197
Auto City Candy Company, 54939
Auto Labe, 19198, 42145
Auto Pallets-Boxes, 19199
Auto Quotes, 19200
Auto-Mate Technologies, 19201
Autobar Systems, 19203, 42146
Autobox NA/Jit Box Machines, 19204
Autocon Mixing Systems, 19205, 42147
Autofry, 19206, 42148
Autoline, 19207
Automated Business Products, 19208, 42149
Automated Container Corp, 19209
Automated Control Concepts, 19210
Automated Feeding & Alignment, 19211
Automated Flexible Conveyors, 19212, 42150
Automated Food Systems, 19213, 42151
Automated Machine Technologies, 19214
Automated Packaging Systems, 19215

1356

All Companies Index

Automated Production Systems Corporation, 19216
Automated Retail Systems Inc, 19217
Automatic Bar Controls Inc, 19218, 42152
Automatic Electronic Machines Company, 19219
Automatic Feeder, 19220
Automatic Filters Inc, 19221
Automatic Handling Int, 19222, 42153
Automatic Liquid Packaging Solutions, 19223
Automatic Packaging Systems & Conveyors Company, 40078
Automatic Products, 19224, 42154
Automatic Products/Crane, 19225, 42155
Automatic Rolls Of New Jersey, 824
Automatic Specialties Inc, 19226, 42156
Automatic Timing & Controls, 19227, 42157
Automation Devices Inc, 19228
Automation Equipment, 19229
Automation Fastening Company, 54940
Automation Group, 19230
Automation Ideas Inc, 19231, 42158
Automation Intelligence, 19232
Automation Onspec Software, 19233
Automation Packaging, 19234
Automation Products, 19235
Automation Safety, 19236
Automation Service, 19237
Automation Systems & Services, 54941
Automotion Inc, 19238
AutoPak Engineering Corporation, 19202
Autoprod, 19239, 42159
Autoquip Corp, 19240, 42160
Autosplice Inc, 19241
Autotron, 19242, 42161
Autumn Foods, 40079
Autumn Hill Vineyards/Blue Ridge Wine, 825
Autumn Wind Vineyard, 826
AV Olsson Trading Company, 41594
Avafina Organics, 827
Avalon Canvas & Upholstery Inc, 19243
Avalon Foodservice, 19244
Avalon Gourmet, 828, 54942
Avalon International Breads, 829, 54943
Avalon Manufacturer, 19245, 42162
Avalon Organic Coffees, 830
Avalon Trade Company, 54944
Avantage Group Inc, 19246
Avanti Foods Co, 831
Avanti Polar Lipids, 19247
Avanti Products Inc, 42163
Avary Farms, 832
Avatar Corp, 833, 42164, 54945
Avatar Food Group, 40080
AVC Industries Inc, 18238
Avebe America Inc., 834, 42165
Aveka Inc, 835, 19248
Avena Foods Ltd., 836, 19249
Aventics Corp, 19250
Avenue Gourmet, 837
Avery Brewing Company, 838
Avery Dennison Corporation, 839, 19251, 42166
Avery Filter Company, 19252
Avery Weigh-Tronix, 19253, 42167
Avery Weigh-Tronix LLC, 19254, 42168
Avestin, 19255, 42169
AVG Automation, 18239
Avins Fabricating Co, 19256
Avitae, 840
Avne Packaging Services, 19257
Avo-King Internatl, 841, 42170
Avoca, 843, 42171
AvoLov, 842
Avon Heights Mushrooms, 844
Avon Tape, 19258, 42172
Avondale Mills, 19259
Avri Co Inc, 845
AVRON Resources Inc, 105
Avtec Industries, 19260
Avure Technologies Svc & Sales, 19261

Aw Sheepscot Holding Co Inc, 19262, 42173
Award Baking Intl, 846, 42174
Award's of America's, 19263
Awb Engineers, 19264
Awe Sum Organics, 42175, 54946
Awmco Inc, 19265, 42176
Awning Co Inc, 19266
Awning Enterprises, 19267
Awnings by Dee, 19269
Awnings Plus, 19268
AWP Butcher Block Inc, 18240
Awrey Bakeries, 847
Ax Water, 848
Axces Systems, 19270
Axelrod Foods, 54947
Axelrod, Norman N, 19271, 42177
Axelsson & Johnson Fish Company, 849, 42178
Axia Distribution Corporation, 19272, 54948
Axiflow Technologies, Inc., 19273, 42179
Axiohm USA, 19274, 42180
Axiom Foods, Inc., 850
Axium Foods, 851, 54949
Axon Styrotech, 19275, 19276
Axons Labeling, 19277
Ay Machine Company, 19278
Ayara Products, 852
Aydelotte & Engler Inc, 54950
Ayer Sales Inc, 19279
Aylesworth's Fish & Bait, 54951
Ayoba-Yo, 853
Ayr King Corp, 19280
Ayush Herbs Inc, 42181, 54952
Azar Nut Co, 854
Azbar Plus, 19281
Azbros Inc, 40081, 42182
Azco Corp, 19282
AZO Food, 18241, 41595
Azonix Corporation, 19283
Aztec Grill, 19284, 42183
Aztec Secret Health & Beauty, 54953
Azteca Foods Inc, 855
Azteca Milling, 856
Aztecas Design, 42184
Aztech Systems, 54954
Azuma Foods Intl Inc USA, 857, 42185
Azumex Corp., 42186
Azz/R-A-L, 19285, 42187

B

B & B Beverages, 54955
B & B Distributors Inc, 54956
B & B Food Distributors Inc, 54957
B & B Food Distributors Inc, 858
B & B Pecan Processors, 859
B & B Poultry Co, 860
B & B Produce, 861
B & C Riverside, 862
B & D Foods, 863
B & D Sales & Marketing Inc, 40082
B & G Foods Inc., 864
B & G Products, 19286
B & G Restaurant Supply, 54958
B & G Venegoni Distribution, 54959
B & H Railcorp, 51567
B & J Food Svc Inc, 54960
B & J Seafood, 865
B & K Distributing Inc, 54961
B & M Provision Co, 54962
B & P Process Equipment, 19287, 42188
B & R Classics LLC, 866
B & R Quality Meats Inc, 867, 54963
B & S Wasilko Distr, 54964
B & W Awning Co, 19288
B & W Frozen Foods, 54965
B & W Supply Co, 54966
B C Holland Inc, 19289
B F Nelson Cartons Inc, 19290
B G Smith & Sons Oyster Co, 868, 42189
B Giambrone & Co, 54967

B H Awning & Tent Co, 19291
B H Bunn Co, 19292, 42190
B J Wood Products Inc, 19293
B M T USA LLC, 19294
B R Cohn Winery & Olive Oil Co, 869
B R Machinery, 19295
B S & B Safety Systems LLC, 870, 19296
B S C Signs, 19297
B T Engineering Inc, 19298, 42191
B W Cooney & Associates, 19299, 42192
B&A Bakery, 871
B&B Beer Distributing Company, 54968
B&B Neon Sign Company, 19300
B&D Food Corporation, 872, 42193
B&F Distributing Company, 54969
B&F Sales Corporation, 54970
B&G Machine Company, 19301
B&H Foods, 873, 19302
B&H Labeling Systems, 19303
B&J Machinery, 19304
B&K Agencies, 40083
B&K Coffee, 874, 19305
B&M Enterprises, 875
B&M Fisheries, 876, 54971
B&O Beer Distributors, 54972
B&R Industrial Automation Corp, 19306
B&W Distributing Company, 54973
B-S Foods Company, 877
B-Tea Beverage, LLC, 878
B. Barks & Sons, 52670
B. Calalani Produce Company, 54974
B. Fernandez & Sons, 54975
B. Lloyd's Pecans, 879
B. Nutty, 880
B. Terfloth & Company, 42194, 42195
B.A.G. Corporation, 19307, 42196
B.B. Bean, Coffee, 881
B.C. Fisheries, 882, 54976
B.C. Ritchie Company, 40084
B.C. Tree Fruits Limited, 40085, 42197
B.C.E. Technologies, 19308
B.E. Industries, 19309
B.E.S.T., 19310
B.M. Lawrence & Company, 883, 42198, 54977
B.M. Sales Company, 54978
B.O.S.S. Food Co., 884
B.R. Williams Trucking & Warehouse, 51568, 52671
B.W. Clifford, 54979
B.W. Dyer & Company, 40086
B.W.J.W. Inc., 885
B/R Sales Company, 42199, 54980
Baader-Linco, 19353, 42216
Baba Foods, 907
Babci's Specialty Foods, 908
Babco International, Inc, 19354, 42217
Babcock & Wilcox MEGTEC, 19355
Babcock & Wilcox Power Generation Group, 19356, 42218
Babcock Co, 19357, 42219
Babcock Winery & Vineyards, 909
Babe Farms Inc, 910, 42220
Babe's Honey Farm, 911
Babush Conveyor Corporation, 54995
Baby Mum-Mum, 42221
Baby's Coffee, 912
Bacardi Canada, Inc., 913, 42222
Bacardi USA Inc, 914, 42223
Bacchus Wine Cellars, 19358, 42224
Bacci Chocolate Design, 915
Bacharach Inc, 19359
Bachman Company, 916, 42225
Bachman Foods, 54996
Back Bay Trading, 917
Back Tech, 19360
Back to Basics, 918, 19361
Back to Nature Foods, 919
Back to the Roots, 920, 54997
Backer's Potato Chip Company, 921
Backerhaus Veit Limited, 42226
Backus USA, 19362
Backwoods Smoker Inc, 19363
Backyard Safari Co, 922

Bacon America, 923, 42227
Bacon Products Corp, 19364
Bacon's Heir, 924
Bad Frog Brewery Co, 925
Bad Seed Cider Company, LLC, 926, 42228
Baden Baden Food Equipment, 19365, 54998
Badger Best Pizzas, 927
Badger Gourmet Ham, 928
Badger Island Shell-Fish & Lobster, 929, 54999
Badger Material Handling, 55000
Badger Meter Inc, 19366, 42229
Badger Plug Co, 19367
Badger Popcorn, 55001
Badger Wholesale Company, 55002
Badger Wholesale Meat & Provisions, 55003
Badger Wood Arts, 19368
Badia Spices Inc., 930, 42230
Baensch Food Products Co, 931, 55004
Baers Beverage of C.W., 55005
Bag Company, 19369, 42231
Bag Masters, 19370
Bagai Tea Company, 932
Bagcraft Papercon, 19371, 42232
Bagel Factory, 933, 55006
Bagel Guys, 934
Bagel Lites, 935, 55007
Bagels By Bell, 936
Bagelworks, 937
Bagley's, 938
Bagman, 55008
Bags Go Green, 19372
Bahama Specialty Foods, 939
Bahlsen Gmbh & Co. Kg, 42233
Bahnson Environmental Specs, 19373
Baier's Sausage & Meats, 940
Bailey Co Inc, 55009
Bailey Moore Glazer Schaefer, 19374
Bailey's Basin Seafood, 941, 55010
Baileyana Winery, 942
Bailly Showcase & Fixture Company, 19375
Baily Tea USA Inc, 943, 55011
Baily Vineyard & Winery, 944
Bainbridge Festive Foods, 945
Baird & Bartlett Company, 19376
Baird Dairy LLC, 946
Baja Foods LLC, 947, 40091, 42234
Baja Trading Company, 55012
Bakalars Sausage Co, 948
Bake City, 949
Bake Crafters Food Company, 950
Bake N Joy Foods, 951
Bake Rite Rolls Inc, 952
Bake Star, 19377, 55013
Baked & Wired, 957
BakeMark Canada, 953, 42235
BakeMark Ingredients Canada, 954, 42236, 55014
BakeMark Ingredients West Inc, 55015
BakeMark USA, 955, 956, 42237
Bakeology, 958
Baker & Co, 19378
Baker Beverage, 55016
Baker Bottling & Distributing Company, 55017
Baker Boy Bake Shop Inc, 959, 55018
Baker Boys, 960
Baker Brokerage Company LLC, 40092
Baker Cabinet Co, 19379
Baker Candy Company, 961
Baker Cheese Factory Inc, 962
Baker Commodities Inc, 963
Baker Concrete Construction, 19380
Baker Distributing Corp, 55019
Baker Foodservice Design Inc, 19381
Baker Hughes, 19382, 42238
Baker Maid Products, Inc., 964
Baker Perkins Inc, 19383, 42239
Baker Produce, 965, 42240
Baker Sales, 40093
Baker Transfer & Storage, 51571, 52674

1357

All Companies Index

Baker's Candies Factory Store, 966, 55020
Baker's Cash & Carry Inc, 55021
Baker's Coconut, 967, 42241
Baker's Dozen & Cafe, 968
Baker's Point Fisheries, 969, 42242
Baker's Ribs No 2, 970
Bakerhaus Veit Limited, 971
Bakers Best Snack Food Corp., 972
Bakers Breakfast Cookie, 973
Bakers Choice Products, 19384, 42243
Bakers of Paris, 974
Bakers Pride Oven Company, 19385, 42244
Bakery Associates, 19386
Bakery Barn Inc, 975, 55022
Bakery Crafts, 19387
Bakery Equipment Sales & Services, 55023
Bakery Equipment Svc, 19388
Bakery Essentials Inc, 976
BAKERY Innovative Technology, 19311, 19312
Bakery Machinery & Fabrication, 19389
Bakery Machinery Dealers, 19390
Bakery on Main, 977
Bakery Refrigeration & Services, 19391
Bakery Services, 55024
Bakery Systems, 19392, 42245, 55025
Bakery Things, 42246, 55026
BAKERY.COM, 42200
BakeryCorp, 978
Bakeware Coatings, 19393
Baking Leidenheimer, 979
Baking Machines, 19394
Baking Technology Systems, 19395
Bakipan, 19396
Bakkavor USA, 980, 55027
Bakker Produce, 55028
Bakon Food Equipment, 19397
Bakon Yeast, 981, 42247
Bakri Trading Inc, 55029
Bakto Flavors, 982
BAL Marketing, 40087
Bal Seal Engineering Inc, 19398, 42248
Bal/Foster Glass Container Company, 19399, 42249
Balagna Winery Company, 983
Balance Bar Company, 984
Balanced Health Products, 985
Balboa Dessert Co Inc, 986, 42250
Balchem Corp, 19400
Bald Eagle Beer Store Co, 55030
Baldewein Company, 19401, 42251
Baldinger Baking Co, 987
Baldor Electric Co, 19402, 19403, 42252
Baldor Specialty Foods Inc, 42253
Baldwin & Mattson, 40094
Baldwin Distribution Services, 51572
Baldwin Richardson Foods, 988, 19404, 55031
Baldwin Supply Co, 19405
Baldwin Vineyards, 989
Baldwin-Minkler Farms, 990
Baldwin/Priesmeyer, 19406
Balemaster, 19407
Balford Farms, 55032
Balic Winery, 991
Ball Corp, 19408
Ball Design Group, 19409
Ball Foster Glass, 19410
Ball Foster Glass Container Company, 19411
Ball Glass Container Corporation, 19412
Ball Park Franks, 992
Ballantine Industrial Truck Service, 55033
Ballantine Produce Company, 993, 42254
Ballantyne Food Service Equipment, 19413, 42255
Ballard & Wolfe Company, 19414
Ballard Custom Meats, 994, 55034
Ballas Egg Products Corp, 995, 42256
Ballew Distributors, 55035
Ballreich's Potato Chips, 996

Balluff Inc, 19415
Bally Block Co, 19416, 42257
Bally Refrigerated Boxes Inc, 19417, 42258
Ballymore Company, 19418
Balsu, 997, 42259
Balter Meat Co, 55036
Balter Sales Co, 55037
Baltic Linen Co Inc, 42260
Balticshop.Com LLC, 998
Baltimore Aircoil Co, 19419, 19420, 42261
Baltimore Belting Co, 55038
Baltimore Brewing Company, 999
Baltimore Coffee & Tea Co Inc, 1000
Baltimore International Warehousing, 51573, 52675
Baltimore Sign Company, 19421
Baltimore Spice Inc, 19422
Baltimore Tape Products Inc, 19423
Balzac Brothers & Co Inc, 42262
Bama Budweiser Montgomery, 55039
Bama Budweiser of Anniston, 55040
Bama Fish Atlanta, 1001, 42263, 55041
Bama Foods LTD, 1002, 42264
Bama Frozen Dough, 1003
Bama Sea Products Inc, 42265, 52676, 55042
Bambeck Systems Inc, 19424
Bamco Belting, 19425
Banana Distributing Company, 1004, 55043
Bancroft Bag Inc, 19426
Band Snacks, 55044
Bandon Bay Fisheries, 1005
Bandwagon Brokerage, 55045
Banfi Vintners, 1006, 42266
Bang & Soderlund Inc, 1007
Bangkok Market, 55046
Banner Candy Manufacturing Company, 1008
Banner Chemical Co, 19427, 42267
Banner Day, 19428
Banner Engineering Corp, 19429
Banner Equipment Co, 19430, 42268
Banner Idea, 19431
Banner Pharmacaps, 1009, 42269
Banner Wholesale Grocers, 55047
Bannerland, 19432
Banquet Schusters Bakery, 1010
Bantam Bagels, 1011, 55048
Banza, 1012
Banzos, 1013
Baptista's Bakery, 1014
Bar Boy Products Inc, 55049
Bar Controls Of Florida, 55050
Bar Equipment Corporation of America, 19433
Bar Harbor Brewing Company, 1015
Bar Harbor Foods, 1016, 55051
Bar Keepers Friend Cleanser, 19434, 42270
Bar Maid Corp, 19435, 42271
Bar NA, Inc., 55052
Bar-B-Q Woods, 19437
Bar-Maid Corp, 19438, 42272
Bar-Plex, 55053
Bar-Ron Industries, 19439
Bar-S Foods Co, 1017, 55054
Baraboo Candy Co LLC, 1018
Barataria Spice Company, 1019
Barbara's Bakery, 1020, 42273
Barbeque Wood Flavors Enterprises, 19440, 42274
Barber Dairies, 1021
Barber Foods, 1022, 42275
Barber Pure Milk Company(HQ), 55055
Barber's Farm Distillery LLC, 1023, 42276
Barber's Poultry Inc, 52677, 55056
Barbero Bakery, Inc., 1024
Barbour Threads, 19441
Barboursville Vineyards, 1025
Barca Wine Cellars, 1026
Barcelona Nut Co, 1027

Barclay & Assoc PC, 19442
Barco Inc, 19443, 19444
Barcoding Inc, 19445
Bard Valley Medjool Date Growers, 1028
Bardes Plastics Inc, 19446
Bardo Abrasives, 19447, 42277
Bare Snacks, 1029
Barefoot Contessa Pantry, 1030
Barely Bread, 1031
Baretta Provision, 1032
Bargetto Winery, 1033
Bargreen Ellingson, 19448, 19449
Barhyte Specialty Foods Inc, 1034, 42278
Bari & Gail, 1035
Bari Italian Foods, 42279, 55057
Bari Olive Oil Co, 1036, 55058
Bari Produce, 55059
Barilla USA, 1037, 42280
Baring Industries, 55060
Barkeater Chocolates, 1038
Barker Company, 19450, 42281
Barker System Bakery, 1039
Barker Wire, 19451
Barkett Fruit Company, 55061
Barkley Filing Supplies, 19452
Barkman Honey, 1040
Barksdale Inc, 19453
Barkthins Snacking Chocolate, 1041
Barlean's Fisheries, 1042, 42282, 55062
Barliant & Company, 19454, 40095, 42283
Barlo Signs, 19455
Barn Furniture Mart, 19456, 42284
Barn Stream Natural Foods, 1043
Barnana, 1044, 55063
Barnant Company, 19457
Barnes & Watson Fine Teas, 1045
Barnes Ice Cream Company, 1046
Barnes Machine Company, 19458
Barnett Lighting Corporation, 55064
Barney Butter, 1047
Barney Pork House, 1048
Barnie's Coffee and Tea, 1049
Barnstead/Thermolyne Corporation, 19459
Baron Spices Inc, 19460, 55065
Baron Vineyards, 1050
Barone Foods, 1051
Barr Engineering Co, 19461
Barr Packing Company, 55066
Barr Refrigeration, 19462
Barr Storage, 19463
Barr-Rosin, 19464
Barravox/Metrovox Snacks, 55067
Barrel O' Fun Snack Foods, 1052
Barrel O'Fun of Milwaukee, 55068
Barrett Distribution Ctr, 51574, 52678
Barrett Trucking Co Inc, 51575
Barrette Outdoor Living, 19465, 42285
Barrie House Gourmet Coffee, 1053, 42286
Barrington Coffee Roasting, 1054
Barrington Nutritionals, 19466
Barrington Packaging Systems Group, 19467
Barrow-Agee Laboratories Inc, 19468, 19469
Barrows Tea Company, 1055, 42287
Barry Callebaut USA, 1056
Barry Food Sales, 40096, 42288
Barry Group, 1057, 42289
Barry Wehmiller Design, 19471
Barry Wehmiller Design Group, 19470
Barry-Wehmiller Companies, 19472
Barry-Wehmiller Design Group, 19473
Barsotti Family Juice Co., 1058
Bartek Ingredients, Inc., 1059, 42290
Bartlett & Co, 40097
Bartlett Dairy & Food Service, 1060, 55069
Bartlett Milling Co., 1061
Bartolini Ice Cream, 1062, 55070
Barton Beers, 42291
Bartons Fine Foods, 1063

Bartush Schnitzius Foods Co, 1064
Baruch Box Company, 19474
Baruvi Fresh LLC, 1065, 55071
Barwell Food Sales, 42292, 55072
Basciani Foods Inc, 1066
Bascom Family Farms Inc, 1067, 42293
Bascom Food Products, 42294, 55073
Base Culture, 1068
BASF Corp., 886
Basic Adhesives, 19475
Basic American Foods, 1069, 42295
Basic Concepts, 19476
Basic Food Flavors, 1070, 42296
Basic Food Intl Inc, 42297, 55074
Basic Grain Products, 1071
Basic Leasing Corporation, 19477, 42298, 55075
Basic Organics, 55076
Basic Polymers Industrial Flooring Systems, 19478
Basignani Winery, 1072
Basiloid Products Corp, 19479
Basin Crawfish Processors, 1073, 55077
Basketfull, 1074, 42299
Baskets Extraordinaires, 19480
Baskin-Robbins LLC, 1075
Basque French Bakery, 1076
Bass Lake Cheese Factory, 1077
Bassett's, 1078
Bassett-Carragher Associates, 40098
Bassham Institutional Foods, 55078
Batampte Pickle Prods Inc, 1079
Batavia Wine Cellars, 1080, 42300
Batch, 19481
Batching Systems, 19482, 42301
Batchmaster, 19483
Batchmasters Software, 19484
Batdorf & Bronson, 1081
Bateman Products, 1082
Bates Distributing, 55079
Batesville Cold Storage, 52679
Bathroom & Towel Systems, 55080
Batory Foods, 1083
Battaglia Distributing Corp, 42302, 55081
Battistella's Sea Foods, 55082
Battistoni Italian Spec Meats, 1084
Batty & Hoyt, 55083
Baublys Control Laser, 19485, 42303
Bauducco Foods Inc., 1085, 42304, 55084
Bauer's Mustard, 1086
Bauermeister, 19486
Baumann Paper Company, 55085
Baumer Foods Inc, 1087, 42305
Baumer Limited, 19487
Baumuller LNI, 19488
Baur Tape & Label Co, 19489, 42306
Bauscher Inc, 42307
Bautista Family Organic Date, 1088
Bavaria Corp International, 1089
Bavarian Meat Products, 1090
Bavarian Nut Co, 1091
Bavarian Specialty Foods, LLC, 1092, 55086
BAW Plastics Inc, 19313
Baxter Manufacturing Inc, 19490, 42308, 42309
Baxters Vineyards & Winery, 1093
Bay Area Pallet Company/IFCO Systems, 19491
Bay Area Trash Compactor, 55087
Bay Baby Produce, 1094, 55088
Bay Brokerage Company, 40099
Bay Cities Produce Co Inc, 1095, 55089
Bay Cities Warehouse, 51576, 52680
Bay Haven Lobster Pound, 1096, 55090
Bay Hawk Ales, 1097
Bay Hundred Seafood Inc, 1098
Bay Oceans Sea Foods, 1099
Bay Pac Beverages, 1100
Bay Pacific Marketing, 40100
Bay Shore Chowders & Bisques, 1101
Bay State Lobster Company, 55091
Bay State Milling Co., 1102

All Companies Index

Bay State Restrnt Products Inc, 55092
Bay Valley Foods, 1103, 42310
Bay View Farm, 1104
Bay View Food Products, 55093
Bayard Kurth Company, 19492, 42311
Baycliff Co Inc, 1105, 42312
Baycliff Company, 1106
Bayer Environmental, 19493
Bayer/Wolff Walsrode, 19494
Bayha & Associates, 40101
Bayhead Products Corp., 19495, 42313
Bayley's Lobster Pound, 1107, 55094
Bayou Container & Supply Inc, 19496, 55095
Bayou Crab, 1108, 55096
Bayou Food Distributors, 1109, 42314, 55097
Bayou Land Seafood, 1110, 55098
Bayou Packing, 19497, 55099
Bays English Muffin Corporation, 1111
Bayshore Equipment, 55100
Bayside Motion Group, 19498, 42315
Baywood Cellars, 1112
Bazaar Inc, 1113
Bazzini Holdings LLC, 1114, 42316
Bbc Industries, 19499
BBCA USA, 42201, 54981
BBQ Bunch, 887, 54982
BBQ Pits by Klose, 19314, 42202
BBQ Shack, 888
BBQ'n Fools Catering, LLC, 889
BBS Bodacious BBQ Company, 890
BBS Lobster Co, 891, 54983
BBU Bakeries, 892
Bc Wood Products, 19500
BCFoods, 893
BCGA Concept Corporation, 894
BCIS Inc, 54984
BCN Research Laboratories, 19315
BCS International, 42203
BDP International Inc, 51569, 52672
BDS Natural, 895
Be & Sco, 19501, 42317
BE&K Building Group, 19316
Be-Bop Biscotti, 1115
Bea & B Foods, 1116
Beach Filter Products, 19502, 40102, 42318
Beachaven Vineyards & Winery, 1117
Beacon Distribution Services, 51577, 52681
Beacon Drive Inn, 1118
Beacon Engineering Co, 19503
Beacon Inc, 19504
Beacon Specialties, 19505
Beal's Lobster Pier, 1119, 55101
Beam Industries, 19506, 42319
Beam Suntory, 1120, 42320
Beamon Brothers, 1121
Bean Buddies, 1122
Bean Forge, 1123
Bean Machines, 19507, 42321
Beanfields, 1124
Beanitos, 1125
Beans & Machines, 55102
Bear Creek Country Kitchens, 1126, 42322
Bear Creek Operations, 42323, 55103
Bear Creek Smokehouse Inc, 1127
Bear Creek Winery, 1128
Bear Meadow Farm, 1129
Bear Meadow Gourmet Foods, 55104
Bear Naked, Inc., 1130
Bear Stewart Corp, 1131, 42324, 55105
Bear's Distributing Company, 55106
Bearded Brothers, 1132
Bearitos, 1133
Beatrice Bakery Co, 1134, 42325
Beaucanon Estate Wines, 1135
Beaufurn, 19508, 42326
Beaujolais Panforte, 1136
Beaulieu Vineyard, 1137
Beaumont Products, 19509, 42327, 55107
Beaumont Rice Mills, 1138, 42328

Beaver Dam Cold Storage, 52682
Beaver Enterprises, 55108
Beaver Express Svc LLC, 51578
Beaver Street Brewery, 1139
Beaver Street Fisheries, 1140, 42329
Beaverite Corporation, 19510
Beaverton Foods Inc, 1141, 42330
Beayl Weiner/Pak, 19511, 42331
BEC International, 19317
Because Cookie Dough, 1142
Beck Flavors, 1143, 42332
Beck Western Brokerage, 40103
Beck's Ice Cream, 1144
Beck's Waffles of Oklahoma, 1145
Beckart Environmental Inc, 19512
Becker Brothers Graphite Co, 19513, 42333
Becker Foods, 1146, 19514, 42334, 55109
Beckhoff Automation, 19515
Beckman & Gast Co, 1147
Beckman Coulter Inc., 19516
Beckmann's Old World Bakery, 1148
Beckmen Vineyards, 1149
Becksmith Company, Inc, 40104
Becky's Blissful Bakery, 1150
Becton Dickinson & Co., 19517, 42335
Bede Inc, 1151, 42336
Bedell Northfork LLC, 1152
Bedemco Inc, 1153, 42337
Bedessee Imports, 42338, 55110
Bedford Enterprises Inc, 19518, 42339, 55111
Bedford Industries, 19519, 42340
Bedoukian Research Inc, 1154, 42341
Bedre Fine Chocolate, 1155, 55112
Bedrock Farm Certified Organic Medicinal Herbs, 1156
Bedrosian & Assoc, 19520
Bee Creek Botanicals, 40105
Bee Harmony Honey, 1157
Bee International, 1158, 42342
Bee Jay Sales Of Florida, 40106
Bee Raw Honey, 1159
Bee Seasonal, 1160
Beech Engineering, 19521
Beech-Nut Nutrition Corp, 1161
Beecher's Handmade Cheese, 1162, 55113
Beef Products Inc., 1163
Beehive Botanicals, 1164, 42343
Beehive Cheese, 1165
Beehive- Provisur, 19522
Beehive/Provisur Technologies, 19523, 42344
Beekman 1802, 1166
Beemak-IDL Display, 19524, 42345
Beer Bakers Inc., 1167, 55114
Beer Import Co, 42346, 55115
Beer Magic Devices, 19525, 42347
Beer Nuts Co Store-Plant, 1168
BEERCUP.COM, 19318
Beetnik Foods, LLC, 1169
Beetroot Delights, 1170, 42348
Beford Technology, 19526
Behlen Manufacturing Co., 19527
Behm Blueberry Farms, 1171
Behm's Valley Creamery, 55116
Behn & Bates/Haver Filling Systems, 19528
Behnke Lubricants/JAX, 19529, 42349
Behrens Manufacturing LLC, 19530, 42350
BEI, 19319, 19320, 42204
Beistle Co, 19531
Beka Furniture, 19532
Bekum America Corp, 19533
Bel Brands USA, 1172, 42351
Bel Canto Foods LLC, 42352
Bel Cheese USA, 1173
Bel-Art Products, 19534, 42353
Bel-Ray Co LLC, 19535
Bel-Terr China, 19536
Belair Produce Co Inc, 55117
Belcan Corp, 19537

Belco Packaging Systems, 19538, 55118
Belcolade, 1175
Belcorp, 40107
Belew Sound & Visual, 55119
Belgian Boys, 1176
Belgian Electronic Sorting Technology USA, 19539
BelGioioso Cheese Inc., 1174
Belgium's Chocolate Source, 42354
Belgravia Imports, 1177, 42355
Belin & Nye, 55120
Bell & Evans, 1178, 42356
Bell & Howell Company, 19540
Bell & Sons, 55121
Bell Amore Imports Inc, 42357
Bell Container, 19541
Bell Flavors & Fragrances, 1179, 19542, 42358
Bell Foods, 19543, 55122
Bell Foods International, 1180, 55123
Bell Fork Lift Inc, 55124
Bell Laboratories Inc, 19544
Bell Marketing Inc, 1181
Bell Mountain Vineyards, 1182
Bell Packaging Corporation, 19545
Bell Plantation, 1183
Bell'Amore Imports, 42359
Bell's Brewery Inc, 1184
Bell-Carter Foods Inc, 1185
Bell-Mark Corporation, 19546, 42360
Bell-View Brand Food Products, 55125
Bella Chi-Cha Products, 1186
Bella Coola Fisheries, 1187, 42361
Bella Cucina, 1188
Bella Ravioli, 1189
Bella Sun Luci, 1190, 42362
Bella Vista Farm, 1191
Bella Vita, 19547
Bella Viva Orchards, 1192
Bella-Napoli Italian Bakery, 1193
Belle Isle Awning, 19548
Belle Plaine Cheese Factory, 1194
Belle River Enterprises, 1195, 42363
Belleco Inc, 19549, 55126
Belleharvest Sales Inc, 1196, 42364, 51579, 55127
Bellerose Vineyard, 1197
Belletieri Company, 1198
Belleview, 19550
Belleville Brothers Packing, 1199
Belli Produce Company, 55128
Bellin Advertising, 55129
Bellingham + Stanley, 19551
Bellisio Foods, 1200
Belliss & Morcom, 19552
Bellocq, 1201
Bells Foods International, 1202, 42365
Bellsola-Pan Plus, 19553
Belltown Boxing Company, 19554
Bellucci, 1203
Bellville Meat Market, 1204
Bellwether Farms, 1205
Belly Treats, Inc., 1206, 19555, 42366, 55130
Belmar Spring Water, 1207
Belmont Brewing Co, 1208
Belmont Chemicals, 1209, 42367
Belmont Peanuts-Southampton, 1210
Belshaw Adamatic Bakery Group, 19556, 42368
Belson Outdoors Inc, 19557, 42369
Belt Corporation of America, 19558
Belt Route Warehouse & Storage, 52683
Belt Technologies Inc, 19559, 42370
Belt's Corp, 52684
Beltek Systems Design, 19560
Belting Associates, 55131
Belton Foods Inc, 1211
Beltram Foodservice Group, 19561, 42371, 55132
Belts Logistics Services, 51580, 52685
Belukus Marketing, 42372
Belvac Production Machinery, 19562
Belxport, 42373
BEMA, 19321

Bematek Systems Inc, 19563, 42374
Ben & Jerry's Homemade Inc, 1212
Ben B. Schwartz & Sons, 1213
Ben E. Keith, 55133, 55134, 55135, 55136, 55137, 55138, 55139, 55140, 55141, 55142, 55143, 55144, 55145, 55146, 55147, 55148, 55149, 55150, 55151, 55152, 55153, 55154, 55155, 55156, 55157, 55158, 55159, 55160, 55161
Ben H. Anderson Manufacturers, 19564
Ben H. Roberts Produce, 55162
Ben Heggy's Candy Co, 1214
Ben's Sugar Shack, 1215
Ben-Bud Growers Inc., 1216, 42375
Ben-Lee Motor Service Company, 51581
Benbow's Coffee Roasters, 1217
Benchmark Sales, 40108
Benchmark Thermal, 19565
Bender Meat, 55163
Bender Warehouse Co, 51582, 52686
Bender-Goodman Co Inc, 40109
Bendow, 19566
Beneficial Blends, 1218
Beneo Inc, 1219
Benfield Electric Supply Co, 55164
Benier, 19567
Benier USA, 19568
Benko Products, 19569, 42376
Benlin Freight Forwarding Inc, 51583, 52687
Benman Industries Inc, 55165
Benmarl Wine Co, 1220
Benner China & Glassware Inc, 19570, 42377
Bennett Box & Pallet Company, 19571
Bennett Manufacturing Company, 19572
Bennett Material Handling, 55166
Bennett's Apples & Cider, 1221
Bennett's Auto Inc, 19573
Bennington Furniture Corporation, 19574
Bensinger's, 55167
Benson's Gourmet Seasonings, 1222
Benson's Wholesale Fruit, 55168
Benson-Mitchell, 40110
Bensussen Deutsch & Associates, 52688
Bentan Corporation, 42378, 55169
Bentley Food Marketing, 40111
Bentley Instruments Inc, 19575, 42379
Benton's Seafood Ctr, 1223, 55170
Benzel's Pretzel Bakery, 1224
Benziger Family Winery, 1225
Bepex International LLC, 19576
Bequet Confections, 1226
Berardi's Fresh Roast, 1227
Berberian Nut Company, 1228, 42380
Berco, 19577
Berenz Packaging Corp, 19578
Berg Chilling Systems, 19579, 19580, 42381, 42382
Berg Co, 19581, 42383
Bergen Barrel & Drum Company, 19582
Bergen Marzipan & Chocolate, 1229
Berger Lahr Motion Technology, 19583
Berghausen E Cheml Co, 1230, 19584
Berghoff Brewery, 1231, 42384
Bergin Fruit & Nut Co., 55171
Bergschrond, 19585
Bericap North America, Inc., 19586, 42385
Bering Sea Fisheries, 1232, 42386
Berje, 42387, 55172
Berk Enterprises, 40112
Berke-Blake Fancy Foods, Inc., 1233
Berkel Products Company, 55173
Berkeley Farms, 1234
Berks Packing Company, Inc., 1235
Berkshire Bark Inc, 1236
Berkshire Brewing Co Inc, 1237
Berkshire Dairy, 1238, 42388
Berkshire Mountain Bakery, 1239
Berkshire PPM, 19587
Berkshire Transportation Inc, 52689
Berlekamp Plastics Inc, 19588, 42389

1359

All Companies Index

Berlin Foundry & Mach Co, 19589, 42390
Berlin Fruit Box Company, 19590
Berlin Natural Bakery, 1240
Berlin Packaging, 55174, 55175, 55176, 55177, 55178
Berloc Manufacturing & Sign Company, 19591
Berlon Industries, 19592
Bermar America, 19593, 42391
Bermuda Agencies Inc, 51584
Bernadette Baking Company, 1241
Bernal Technology, 19594, 42392
Bernard & Sons, 1242, 55179
Bernard & Sons Maple Products, 1243
Bernard Food Industries Inc, 1244, 42393
Bernard Jensen Intl, 55180
Bernard Wolnak & Associates, 19595
Bernard's Bakery, 55181
Bernardi Italian Foods Company, 1245
Bernardo Winery, 1246
Bernardus Winery Tasting Rm, 1247
Bernatello's Foods, 1248, 55182
Bernco Specialty Adverti, 55183
Berndorf Belt Technology USA, 19596
Berner Food & Beverage LLC, 1249
Berner International Corp, 19597, 42394
Bernheim Distilling Company, 1250
Bernie's Foods, 1251
Berns Co, 42395, 55184
Berres Brothers Coffee, 1252
Berri Pro, 1253
Berry Global, 19598, 42396
Berry Material Handling, 55185
Berry Processing, 1254
Berry's Arctic Ice, 52690
Berryessa Gap Tasting Room, 1255
Berryhill Signs, 19599
Berrywine Plantations, 55186
Berson Peanuts, 1256
Bert Manufacturing, 19600, 42397
Bertek Systems Inc, 19601, 42398
Bertels Can Company, 19602, 42399
Berthold Technologies, 19603
Berti Produce Co, 42400
Bertie County Peanuts, 1257, 19604
Bertolino Beef Co, 55187
Berton Company, 55188
Bertran Enterprises, 40113
Bertrand's, 55189
Beryl's Cake Decorating & Pastry Supplies, 19605
Besco Grain Ltd, 1258, 19606
Bespoke Provisions, 1259
Bess Eaton, 1260, 55190
Bessamaire Sales Inc, 19607, 42401
Bessco Tube Bending & Pipe Fabricating, 19608
Bessinger Pickle Co, 1261
Best, 19609, 42402
Best & Donovan, 19610, 42403
Best Brands, 40114
Best Brands Home Products, 19611, 42404
Best Brands Incorporated, 55191
Best Buy Uniforms, 19612, 42405, 55192
Best Cheese Corporation, 42406
Best Chicago Meat, 19612, 42407, 55193
Best Chocolate In Town, 1263
Best Cooking Pulses, Inc., 1264, 19613, 42408
Best Diversified Products, 19614, 42409
Best Ever Bakery, 1265
Best Express Foods Inc, 1266, 55194
Best Foods, 1267, 42410, 55195
Best Friends Cocoa, 55196
Best Harvest Bakeries, 1268
Best Industries, 55197
Best Label Co, 19615
Best Maid Cookie Co, 1269
Best Maid Products, Inc., 1270
Best Manufacturers, 19616
Best Manufacturing, 19617
Best Market, 55198
Best Marketing Reps, 40115

Best Material Handling, 55199
Best Pack, 19618
Best Provision Co Inc, 1271, 42411
Best Restaurant Equip & Design, 19619, 55200
Best Sanitizers Inc, 19620
Best Value Textiles, 19621, 42412
BestBins Corporation, 19622
Bestco Inc, 1272
Bestech Inc, 19623, 42413
Beta Pure Foods, 1273, 40116
Beta Screen Corp, 19624, 42414
BetaStatin Nutritional Rsearch, 1274
Bete Fog Nozzle Inc, 19625, 42415
Beth's Fine Desserts, 1275
Bethel Engineering & Equipment Inc, 19626, 42416
Bethel Grain Company, 19627
Bethel Heights Vineyard, 1276
Betsy Ross Manufacturing Company, 19628
Betsy's Best, 1277, 55201
Betsy's Cheese Straws, 1278
Bettag & Associates, 19629
Bettah Buttah, LLC, 1279
Bettcher Industries Inc, 19630, 19631, 42417
Bette's Oceanview Diner, 1280, 42418
Bettendorf Stanford Inc, 19632
Better Bagel Bakery, 1281
Better Baked Foods Inc, 1282
Better Beverages Inc, 1283, 55202
Better Bilt Products, 19633
Better Bites Bakery, 1284
Better Health Products, 55203
Better Janitor Supplies, 55204
Better Living Products, 1285, 42419
Better Made Snack Foods, 1286, 42420
Better Meat, 55205
Better Packages, 19634, 42421
Better Than Coffee, 1287
Better Than Foods USA, 1288
Better Trucking, 51585
BetterBody Foods & Nutrition LLC, 1289
Betters International Food Corporation, 40117, 55206
Betty Jane Homemade Candy, 1290
Betty Lou's, 1291, 42422
Betz Entec, 19635
BEUMER Corp, 19322, 42205
BEVCO, 19323, 42206
Bevco Sales International Inc., 1292
Beverage Air, 19636, 42423
Beverage America, 1293
Beverage Capital Corporation, 1294, 42424
Beverage Express, 42425, 55207
Beverage Flavors Intl, 1295, 19637
Beverage House Inc, 1296
Beverly International, 1297, 42426
Bevinco, 42427
Bevistar, 19638, 55208
Bevles Company, 19639, 42428
Bevsource, 1298, 19640
Bevstar, 19641
Bewley Irish Imports, 42429, 55209
BEX Inc, 19324, 42207
Beyond Meat, 1299
BFB Consultants, 19325
BFD Corp, 19326
BFM Equipment Sales, 19327, 42208, 54985
BFT, 19328
BG Industries, 19329
Bgreen Food, 1300
BGS Jourdan & Sons, 896
Bhakti, 1301
Bhu Foods, 1302
Bhuja Snacks, 1303
Bi Nutraceuticals, 1304
BI Nutraceuticals, 19330, 54986
BI-LO, 54987
Bi-O-Kleen Industries, 19642
Bi-O-Kleen Industry, 55210

Bi-Star Enterprise, 19643
Bia Diagnostics, 19644
Biagio's Banquets, 1305, 42430
Bianchi Winery, 1306, 42431
Bias Vineyards & Winery, 1307
Biazzo Dairy Products Inc, 1308, 42432
Bib Pak, 1645
Bickel's Potato Chip Company, 1309
Bickel's Snack Foods Inc, 1310
Bickford Daniel Lobster Company, 1311, 55211
Bickford Flavors, 1312
Bicknell & Fuller Paperbox Company, 19646
Bidwell Candies, 1313
Bidwell Vineyard, 1314
Biehl & Co, 51586
Bien Cuit, 1315
Bien Padre Foods Inc, 1316, 42433
Biena Foods, 1317
Bieri's Jackson Cheese, 1318
Bierig Brothers Inc, 1319
Biery Cheese Co, 1320
Bifulco Four Seasons, 1321
Big Al's Seafood, 1322, 55212
Big Apple Bagels, 1323
Big Apple Equipment Corporation, 19647
Big Apple Tea Company, 55213
Big B Barbecue, 1324
Big Basket Company, 19648
Big Beam Emergency Systems Inc, 19649
Big Boss Baking Co, 1325
Big Bucks Brewery & Steakhouse, 1326
Big Chief Meat Snacks Inc, 1327
Big City Reds, 1328
Big Dipper Dough Co., 1329
Big Easy Foods, 1330
Big Fatty's Flaming Foods, 1331
Big Fork Brands, 1332
Big Front Uniforms, 19650
Big Horn Co-Op Tire Shop, 55214
Big Island Candies Inc, 1333
Big Island Seafood, LLC, 1334, 55215
Big J Milling Co, 1335
Big John Corp, 19651
Big Mountain Foods, 1336
Big Picture Farm LLC, 1337
Big Poppa Smokers, 1338
Big Red Bottling, 1339
Big Rock Brewery, 1340
Big Russ Beer Cheese, 1341
Big Shoulders Coffee, 1342, 55216
Big Sky Brands, 1343
Big Sky Brewing Co, 1344
Big Spoon Roasters, 1345, 55217
Big State Spring Companyy, 19652
Big State Vending Company, 55218
Big Steer, 1346
Big Train Inc, 1347
Big Tree Farms, 1348
Big Valley Marketing Corporation, 55219
Big Watt Coffee, 1349
Big-D Construction Corp, 19653
Bigelow Tea, 1350
Bijol & Spices Inc, 1351, 42434
Bijur Lubricating Corporation, 19654, 42435
Bilas Distributing Company, 55220
Bilgore's Groves, 1352
Bilinski Sausage Mfg Co, 1353
Bilkays Express/Distribution Warehouse, 51587
Bill Carr Signs, 19655
Bill Clark Truck Line Inc, 51588
Bill Davis Engineering, 19656
Bill's Seafood, 1354, 55221
Billie-Ann Plastics Packaging, 19657
Billingsgate Fish Company, 1355, 55222
Billington Welding & Mfg Inc, 19658
Billy's Seafood Inc, 1356, 55223
Biloxi Freezing Processing Inc., 1357
Bilt-Rite Conveyors, 19659, 42436
Biltmore Estate Wine Company, 1358

Biltmore Trading LLC, 40118
Bimba Manufacturing Co, 19660
Bimbo Bakeries USA Inc., 1359
Bimetalix, 19661
BINDER Inc., 19331
Bindi North America, 1360
Bindi-Dessert Service,Inc, 42437
Binding Brauerei USA, 1361
Bindmax LLC, 19662
Biner Ellison Packaging Systs, 19663, 42438
Binghamton Material Handling, 55224
Bingo Salsa, LLC, 1362
Binkert's Meat Products, 1363
Binks Industries Inc, 19664, 42439
Binner Marketing & Sales, 40119
Binney & Smith, 42440
Binns Vineyards & Winery, 1364
Bintz Restaurant Supply Company, 19665, 55225
Bio Cide Intl Inc, 19666, 42441
Bio Huma Netics, 19667
Bio Industries, 19668
Bio Pac Inc, 19669
Bio Zapp Laboratories, 19670, 42442
Bio-Botanica Inc, 1365
Bio-Foods, 1366, 42443
Bio-Hydration Research Lab, 1367
Bio-K + International Inc., 1368
Bio-Nutritional Products, 1369
Bio-Rad Laboratories Inc., 19671
Bio-Tech Pharmacal Inc, 1370
BioAmber, 1371, 19672, 42444
Bioclimatic Air Systems LLC, 19677, 42446
Biocontrol Systems Inc, 19678, 42447
Bioenergetics Inc, 19679
Bioenergy Life Science, 1376
BioExx Specialty Proteins, 1372, 19673, 42445
Bioionix Inc, 19680
Biolog Inc, 19681, 42448
Biological Services, 19682
Biomed Comm, 19683
Biomerieux Inc, 19684, 19685, 42449
Biomist Inc, 19686
Bionova Produce, 42450
Bionutritional Research Group, 1377
Biopath, 19687
Bioriginal Food and Science Corp, 1378, 55226
Bioscience International Inc, 19688, 55227
Biospringer, 1379
Biostim LLC, 55228
BioSynergy, 1373
BioSys, 19674
Biotec A Z Laboratories, 1380
BioTech Corporation, 1374
BioTech Films, LLC, 19675
Biotek Instruments Inc, 19689
Biotest Diagnostics Corporation, 19690, 42451
Biothane Corporation, 19691, 42452
Biothera, 1381
Biovail Technologies, 19692
BioVittoria USA, 1375, 19676
Birch Benders, 1382
Birch Street Seafoods, 1383, 42453
Birchwood Foods Inc, 1384, 42454
Birchwood Meats, 55229
Bird Marketing, 40120
Bird-In-Hand Farms, 1385
Birdie Pak Products, 1386, 55230
Birdsall Ice Cream Company, 1387
Birdseye Dairy-Morning Glory, 1388, 55231
Birdseye Food, 1389
Birdsong Corp., 1390, 42455
Birdsong Peanuts, 55232
Bireta Company, 40121
Birkett Mills, 1391
Birkholm's Solvang Bakery, 1392, 42456
Birko Corp, 19693
Birko Corporation, 19694, 42457

1360

All Companies Index

Birmingham Controls, 19695
Birmingham Mop Manufacturing Company, 19696
Birmingham Vending Games, 55233
Birnn Chocolates of Vermont, 1393, 55234
Biro Manufacturing Co, 19697, 42458
Biscomerica Corporation, 1394
Biscontini Distribution Centers, 51589, 52691
Biscoti Di Suzy, 1395
Biscottea, 1396
Biscotti & Co., 1397, 42459
Biscotti Goddess, 1398
Bisek & Co Inc, 40122, 55235
Bishamon Industry Corp, 19698, 42460
Bishop Brothers, 1399, 55236
Bishop Farms Winery, 1400
Bishop Machine Shop, 19699
Bismarck Caterers, 19700
Bison Brewing Company, 1401
Bison Foods, 1402
Bison Gear & Engineering Corp., 19701
Bissett Produce Company, 1403, 42461
Bissinger's Handcrafted Chocolatier, 1404
Bissinger's Handcrafted Chocolatier, 1405, 42462
Bitchin' Sauce, 1406
Bite Fuel, 1407
Bite Size Bakery, 1408, 55237
Bitsy's Brainfood, 1409
Bitter Love, 1410
Bittermilk LLC, 1411
Bittersweet Herb Farm, 1412
Bittersweet Pastries, 1413, 42463
Bittinger Sales, 40123
Bivac Enterprise, 19702
Bivans Corporation, 19703
Bixby & Co., LLC, 1414
Bixby Food Sales, 40124
Bizerba USA, 19704, 19705, 55238
BJ's Restaurants Inc., 897
BJ'S Wholesale Club Inc, 54988
Bjm Pumps, 19706
BK Giulini Corporation, 898
BK Graphics, 19332
BK Specialty Foods, 899
BKI, 19333
BKI Worldwide, 19334, 42209
BKW Seasonings, 900
Blachere Group, 42464, 55239
Black Bear Corp, 19707
Black Bear Farm Winery, 1415, 19708
Black Bear Fruits, 1416
Black Brothers, 19709, 42465
Black Diamond Fruit & Produce, 55240
Black Forest Organic, 1417
Black Garlic, 1418
Black Horse Mfg Co, 19710
Black Hound New York, 1419
Black Jewell Popcorn, 1420
Black Market Gelato, 1421
Black Mesa Winery, 1422
Black Prince Distillery Inc, 1423
Black Ranch Organic Grains, 1424
Black River Caviar, 1425, 19711
Black River Pallet Co, 19712
Black Sheep Vintners, 1426
Black Shield, 1427
Black's Barbecue, 1428, 55241
Black's Products of HighPoint, 19713, 42466
Blackbear Coffee Company, 1429
Blackberry Patch, 1430
Blackbur Bros Inc, 55242
Blackburn-Russell Co, 55243
Blackhawk Molding Co Inc, 19714, 42467
Blackmer Co, 19715
Blackwing Ostrich Meats Inc., 19716, 40125, 55244
Blade Runners, 19717
Blair's Sauces & Snacks, 1431, 42468
Blake Corporation, 19718

Blake Hill Preserves, 1432
Blake's All Natural Foods, 1433, 55245
Blake's Creamery Inc, 55246
Blakely Freezer Locker, 1434
Blakeslee, Inc., 19719, 42469
Blako Industries, 19720
Blalock Seafood & Specialty, 1435, 55247
Blanc Industries, 19721, 55248
Blancett, 19722, 42470
Blanche P. Field, LLC, 19723, 42471
Bland Farms INC, 1436
Blanke Bob Sales Inc, 55249
Blansh International, 1437
Blanton's, 1438
Blanver USA, 1439, 42472
Blaser's USA, Inc., 1440
Blast It Clean, 19724, 52692
Blau Oyster Co Inc, 1441, 42473
Blaze Products Corp, 19725, 42474
Blazer Concepts, 19726
Blazzin Pickle Company, 1442
BLC Trucking Inc, 51570, 52673
Blend Pak Inc, 1443, 42475
Blendco Inc, 1444, 19726, 51590, 52693
Blendex Co, 1445, 19727, 52694
Blendtec, 42476
Blendtopia, 1446
Blenheim Bottling Company, 1447
Blentech Corp, 19728
Blessed Herbs, 1448, 42477
Bletsoe's Cheese Inc, 1449
Bleuet Nordic, 1450
BLH Electronics, 19335, 42210
Blickman Supply Company, 19729
Bliss Brothers Dairy, Inc., 1451
Bliss Gourmet Foods, 1452
Blissfield Canning Company, 19730
Blissfully Better, 1453
Blk Enterprises, 1454
Blodgett Co, 19731, 42478
Blodgett Corp, 19732, 42479
Blodgett Oven Co, 19733, 42480
Bloemhof, 19734
Blome International, 19735
Blommer Chocolate Co, 1455, 1456, 19736, 42481
Blondie's, 55251
Bloodworth & Associates, 40126
Bloom Honey, 1457, 55252
Bloomfield Bakers, 1458, 40127
Bloomfield Farms, 1459, 55253
Bloomfield Industries, 19737
Bloomington Brewing Co, 1460
Bloomsbery LLC, 1461
Blossom Farm Products, 1462, 42482
Blossom Water, LLC, 1463
Blount Fine Foods, 1464
Blower Application Co Inc, 19738, 42483
Blue Bell Creameries LP, 1465
Blue Bottle Coffee Co, 19740, 55254
Blue Buoy Foods, 55255
Blue California Co, 1466
Blue Chip Baker, 1467
Blue Chip Cookies, 1468, 55256
Blue Circle Foods, 1469
Blue Crab Bay, 1470, 42485
Blue Cross Laboratories, 19741, 42486
Blue Delft Supply, 55257
Blue Diamond Growers, 1471, 19742, 42487, 55258
Blue Dog Bakery, 1472
Blue Evolution, 1473
Blue Feather Products Inc, 19743, 42488
Blue Giant Equipment Corporation, 19744, 42489
Blue Gold Mussels, 1474
Blue Grass Quality Meat, 1475
Blue Green Organics, 1476
Blue Harbour Cheese, 1477, 55259
Blue Harvest Foods, 1478, 42490
Blue Hill Yogurt, 1479
Blue Hills Spring Water Company, 1480
Blue Jay Orchards, 1481

Blue Lake Products, 19745
Blue Lakes Trout Farm, 1482
Blue Line Cold Storage Chicago, 51591, 52695
Blue Line Foodservice Distr, 19746, 55260
Blue Line Moving & Storage, 51592, 52696
Blue Marble Biomaterials, 1483
Blue Marble Brands, 1484
Blue Monkey, 1485
Blue Moon Foods, 1486
Blue Moose of Boulder, 1487
Blue Mountain Enterprise Inc, 1488, 42491
Blue Mountain Meats Inc., 55261
Blue Mountain Vineyards, 1489
Blue Pacific Flavors & Fragrances, 1490, 42492
Blue Planet Foods, 1491, 42493
Blue Point Brewing Co, 1492
Blue Print Automation, 19747, 19748
Blue Rhino Compaction Services, 55262
Blue Ribbon Farm Dairy Fresh, 1493
Blue Ribbon Fish Co, 42494, 55263
Blue Ribbon Meats, 1494, 55264
Blue Ribbon Packaging Systems, 19749
Blue Ribbon Wholesale, 55265
Blue Ridge Converting, 19750, 42495
Blue Ridge Poultry, 1495, 55266
Blue Ridge Signs, 19751
Blue Ridge Tea & Herb Co, 1496
Blue Runner Foods Inc, 1497
Blue Sky Beverage Company, 1498, 42496
Blue Smoke Salsa, 1499
Blue Star Food Products, 1500, 42497
Blue Tech, 19752
Blue Willow Tea Co, 1501
Blueberry Store, 1503
Bluebird Manufacturing, 19754, 42498
Bluebird Restaurant, 1504
Bluebonnet Meat Company, 1505
Bluechip Group, 1506
Bluefin Seafoods, 55267
Bluegrass Brewing Company, 1507
Bluegrass Dairy & Food, 1508
Bluegrass Packaging Industries, 19755
BlueKey Inc, 19753
Bluepoint Bakery, 1509
Bluewater Environmental, 19756
BlueWater Seafoods, 1502
Bluff Manufacturing Inc, 19757, 42499
Bluffton Motor Works, 19758
Bluffton Slaw Cutter Company, 19759, 42500
Blum & Bergeron, Inc., 55268
Blume Honey Water, 1510
Blumenhof Vineyards-Winery, 1511
Blumer, 19760
BluMetric Environmental Inc., 19739, 42484
Blundell Seafoods, 1512, 42501
BLV Marketing Inc, 40088, 40089
Bma Inc, 19761
BMH, 19336
BMH Chronos Richardson, 19337
Bmh Equipment Inc, 19762, 42502, 55269
BMT Commodity Corporation, 42211, 54989
BN Soda, 901
BNG Enterprises, 54990
BNP Media, 19338
Bnutty, 1513, 55270
BNW Industries, 19339, 42212
Boar's Head, 1514
Boardman Foods Inc, 1515
Boardman Molded Products Inc, 19763, 42503
Bob Evans Farms Inc., 1516
Bob Gedan & Associates, 42504
Bob Gordon & Associates, 1517, 42505
Bob Rowe Sales, 40128
Bob's Custom Cuts, 1518

Bob's Red Mill Natural Foods, 1519
Bob's Seafood, 40129
Bob's Transport & Stge Co Inc, 51593, 52697
Bobalu Nuts, 1520
Bobby D'S, 1521
Bobbysue's Nuts LLC, 1522
Bobo's Oat Bars, 1523
Boboli Intl. Inc., 1524
BOC Gases, 19340
BOC Plastics Inc, 19341
Boca Bagelworks, 1525, 42506
Boca Bons East, 1526, 42507
Boca Foods Company, 1527
Bodacious Foods, 1528
Bode-Finn Company, 55271
Bodean Restaurant & Market, 55272
Bodega Chocolates, 1529
Bodek Kosher Produce Inc, 1530
Bodie-Rickett & Associates, 40130
Bodin Foods, 1531
Bodine Electric Co, 19764
Bodolay Packaging, 19765
Body Breakthrough Inc, 1532, 42508
Bodycote Materials Testing, 19766
Bodyonics Limited, 1533
Boedeker Plastics Inc, 19767
Boeger Winery, 1534
Boehmer Sales Agency, 40131
Boehringer Ingelheim Corp, 1535
Boehringer Mfg. Co. Inc., 19768, 42509
Boekels, 19769
Boelter Companies, 55273
Boelter Industries, 19770
Boesl Packing Co, 1536
Boetje Foods Inc, 1537
Boeuf Merite, 55274
Boggiatto Produce Inc, 1538
Boghosian Raisin Packing Co, 1539
Bogland, 1540
Bogle Vineyards Inc, 1541
Bogner Industries, 19771
Bohemian Brewery, 1542
Bohler Bleche, 19772
Bohn & Dawson, 19773, 42510
Bohnert Construction Company, 19774
Boise Cascade Co, 19775
Boise Cascade Corporation, 19776
Boise Cold Storage Co, 19777, 52698, 52699
Boisset Family Estates, 1543, 42511
Boissons Miami Pomor, 1544
Boja's Foods Inc, 1545
Bold Coast Smokehouse, 1546
BOLD Organics, 902
Boldt Co, 19778
Boldt Technologies Corporation, 19779
Bolling Oven & Machine Company, 19780
Bollore Inc, 19781, 19782
Bolner's Fiesta Spices, 1547, 42512
Bolt House Farms-Shipping Dept, 1548
Bolton & Hay, 55275
Bolzoni Auramo, 19783, 19784, 42513, 42514
Bon Appetit Gourmet Foods, 55276
Bon Appetit International, 42515, 55277
Bon Chef, 1785, 42516
Bon Courage Gourmet, 1549
Bon Secour Fisheries Inc, 1550, 42517, 55278
Bon Ton Food Products, 55279
Bon Ton Products, 1551, 55280
Bonafide Provisions, 1552
Bonar Engineering & Constr Co, 19786
Bonar Plastics, 19787, 19788
Bonded Service Warehouse, 52700
Bonduelle North America, 1553, 42518
Bone Doctors' BBQ, LLC, 1554
Bone Suckin' Sauce, 1555
Bonert's Pies Inc, 1556
Bongard's Creameries, 1557
Bongiovi Brand Pasta Sauces, 1558
Bonk Breaker, 1559
Bonneau Company, 19789, 42519

1361

All Companies Index

Bonnie & Don Flavours Inc., 1560
Bonnie Baking Company, 1561
Bonnie Doon LLC, 1562
Bonnie's Ice Cream, 1563
Bonnie's Jams, 1564
Bonnot Co, 19790, 42520
Bonny Doon Vineyard, 1565
Bono Burns Distributing Inc, 55281
Bono USA, 1566
Bonsai World, 19791
Bonterra Vineyard, 1567
Bonumose LLC, 1568
Bookbinder Specialties LLC, 1569
Booker Promotions, 55282
Boone's Butcher Shop, 1570
Boone's Wholesale, 55283
Booneway Farms, 1571
Boordy Vineyards Inc, 1572
Booth, 19792
Booth, Schwager & Associates, 40132
Boothbay Lobster Wharf, 1573, 55284
Bootz Distribution, 51594, 52701
Boquet's Oyster House, 1574
Borden Canada, 1575
Borden Dairy, 1576
Border Foods, 1577
Borders Sporting Goods, 1578
Bordoni Vineyards, 1579
Borgattis Ravioli, 1580
Borgwaldt KC, 19793
Boricua Empaque, 42521, 55285
Borinquen Biscuit Corporation, 1581
Bormioli Rocco Glass Company, 19794
Bormioli Rocco Hotel Products, 42522
Born Printing Company, 19795
Bornstein Seafoods, 1582
Bornt & Sons Inc, 1583
Borra Vineyards, 1584
Borroughs Corp, 19796, 42523
Borton Brokerage Company, 40133
Bos Smoked Fish Inc, 1585, 42524
Bosch Distributors, 55286
Bosch Packaging Svc, 19797
Bosch Packaging Technology, 19798, 19801, 19802, 42525
Bosch Packaging Technology Inc, 19799, 19800
Bosch Rexroth Corp, 19803
Bosco Food Service, 55287
Bosco Products Inc, 1586
Boscoli Foods Inc, 1587
Bosgraaf Sales Company, 55288
Boska Holland, 19804
Boskovich Farms Inc, 1588, 42526
Boskydel Vineyard, 1589
BOSS, 54991
Boss Linerless Label Company, 19805
Boss Manufacturing Co, 19806, 42527
Bossar, 19807
Bossen, 1590
Bosshart Food Svc, 40134
Bostik Inc, 19808
Boston America Corporation, 1591
Boston Beer Co Inc., 1592, 42528
Boston Chowda, 1593, 42529
Boston Coffee Cake, 1594, 55289
Boston Direct Lobsters, 1595, 55290
Boston Fruit Slice & Confectionery Corporation, 1596
Boston Gear, 19809
Boston Lobster Co, 55291
Boston Rack, 19810
Boston Retail, 19811, 42530
Boston Sausage & Provision, 42531, 55292
Boston Seafarms, 1597, 42532, 55293
Boston Shearpump, 19812
Boston Showcase Company, 55294
Boston Spice & Tea Company, 1598
Boston Stoker, 1599
Boston Tea Company, 1600
Boston's Best Coffee Roasters, 1601, 19813, 42533
Botanical Bakery, LLC, 1602, 55295
Botanical Products, 1603, 42534

Boteilho Hawaii Enterprises, 55296
Botsford Fisheries, 1604, 42535
Bottle Green Drinks Company, 1605
Bottom Line Foods, 1606, 40135, 55297
Bottom Line Processing Technologies, Inc., 19814
Bou Brands, 1607
Bouchaine Vineyards, 1608
Bouchard Family Farm, 1609, 42536
Boudreaux's Foods, 1610
Boulangerie Pelletier, 55298
Boulder Bar, 19815
Boulder Beer, 1611
Boulder Brands, Inc., 1612, 55299
Boulder Canyon Natural Foods, 1613
Boulder Cookie, 1614
Boulder Creek Brewing Company, 1615
Boulder Fruit Express, 55300
Boulder Granola, 1616
Boulder Homemade Inc, 1617
Boulder Organic Foods, 1618
Boulder Sausage Co, 1619, 55301
Boulder Vegans LLC, 1620
Boulevard Brewing, 1621
Bouma Meats, 1622
Boundary Fish Company, 1623, 42537
Bountiful Larder LLC, 1624
Bountiful Pantry, 1625
Bouras Mop Manufacturing Company, 19816, 42538
Bourbon Barrel Foods, 1626
Boutique Seafood Brokers, 1627, 55302
Bouvry Exports Calgary, 1628
Bove's of Vermont, 1629
Bow Valley Brewing Company, 1630
Bower's Awning & Shade, 19817
Bowerman Associates, 40136
Bowers Process Equipment, 19818, 42539
Bowery Farming Inc., 1631
Bowlin J P Co LLC, 55303
Bowlswitch, 19819
Bowman & Landes Turkeys, 1632
Bowman Hollis Mfg Corp, 19820, 42540
Bowman Produce, 55304
Bowness Bakery, 1633
Bowser Meat Processing, 1634
Bowtemp, 19821
Boxco, 19822
Boxed Meat Revolution, 55305
Boxer-Northwest Company, 55306
Boxerbrand, 42541
Boxes.com, 19823, 42542
Boyajian LLC, 1635, 42543
Boyd Lighting Company, 19824, 42544
Boyd's Coffee Co, 1636, 19825, 42545
Boyd's Sausage Co, 1637
Boyer Candy Co Inc, 1638
Boyer Corporation, 19826
Boyer's Coffee, 1639
Boykin & Southern Wholesale Grocers, 55307
Boylan Bottling Company, 1640
Boyle Meat Company, 1641, 19827, 55308
Boyton Shellfish, 1642, 55309
Bozzano Olive Ranch, 1643, 55310
Bozzuto's Inc., 55311
BP, 19342
BP Gourmet, 903
BPH Pump & Equipment, 19343
BPM Inc, 19344
Brace Frozen Foods, 55312
Brad's Organic, 1644
Brad's Raw Foods, 19828
Brad's Taste of New York, 1645
Bradford A Ducon Company, 19829, 42546
Bradford Co, 1646, 19830
Bradford Derustit Corp, 19831
Bradford Soap Works Inc, 19832, 42547
Bradley 3 Ranch, 1647
Bradley Creek Seafood, 1648
Bradley Industries, 19833
Bradley Kitchen Center, 55313

Bradley Lifting, 19834, 42548
Bradley Technologies Canada Inc., 1649
Bradley Ward Systems, 19835
Bradman Lake Inc, 19836, 42549
Bradshaw Home nc, 55314
Bradshaw's Food Products, 1650
Brady Enterprises Inc, 19837, 42550
Brady Worldwide, 19838
Bradye P. Todd & Son, 1651
Bragard Professional Uniforms, 19839, 42551
Bragard Uniforms, 42552
Bragg Live Food Products Inc, 1652
Braham Food Locker Service, 1653
Brakebush Brothers, 1654, 42553
Braman Fruit Company, 55315
BRAMI Snacks, 904
Bran & Luebbe, 19840, 42554
Brand Aromatics Inc, 1655
Brand Castle, 19841
Brand Specialists, 19842
Brandborg Cellars, 1656
Brander Vineyard, 1657
Branding Iron, 1658
Branding Iron Meats, 1659
Brandmeyer Popcorn Co, 1660, 42555
Brands of Britain, 42556
Brands Within Reach, 1661
Brandstedt Controls Corporation, 19843
Brandt Farms Inc, 1662, 42557
Brandt Mills, 1663
Brandywine Frozen Fruit, 40137
Branford Vibrator Company, 19844, 42558
Branson Ultrasonics Corp, 19845, 42559
Branton Industries, 55316
Braren Pauli Winery, 1664
Brasco, 55317
Brass Ladle Products, 1665
Brass Smith, 19846, 42560
Brasserie Brasel Brewery, 1666, 42561
Brassica Protection Products, 1667
Braswell Distributing Co, 55318
Braswell's Winery, 1668, 55319
Brateka Enterprises, 1669
Bratt-Foster-Advantage Sales, 40138, 42562
Brauer Material Handling Systs, 55320
Braum's Inc, 1670
Braun Brush Co, 19847, 19848, 42563, 42564
Braun Seafood Co, 1671
Brauner International Corp, 51595
Bravard Vineyards & Winery, 1672
Bravo Systems International, 42565
Brawner Paper Co Inc, 55321
Brazi Bites, 1673
Brazilian Consulate, 19849
Brazilian Home Collection, 1674
Brazos Legends, 1675, 42566
Brazos Valley Cheese, 1676
Bread & Chocolate Inc, 1677
Bread Alone Bakery, 1678
Bread Box Cafe, 1679
Bread Dip Company, 1680
Breads from Anna, 1681, 55322
Breadworks, 1682
Breaktime Snacks, 1683
Breakwater Fisheries, 1684, 42567
Breakwater Seafoods & Chowder, 1685, 55323
Breaux Vineyards, 1686
Brechbuhler Scales, 19850, 42568
Brechteen, 19851, 42569
Breckenridge Brewery, 1687
Brecoflex Co LLC, 19852, 42570
Breddo Likwifier, 19853, 42571
Breitenbach Wine Cellars, 1688
Brekki, 1689
Bremer Manufacturing Co Inc, 19854
Bremner Biscuit Company, 1690, 42572
Bren Instruments, 19855
Brenham Wholesale Groc Co Inc, 55324
Brennan Food Services, 40139
Brennan Snacks Manufacturing, 1691

Brenner Tank LLC, 19856, 42573
Brenntag North America, 1692
Brenton Engineering Co, 19857, 42574
Brentwood Plastics In, 19858
Bresco, 19859, 55325, 55326
Breslow Deli Products, 1693
Brevard Restaurant Equipment, 19860, 55327
Brew Dr. Kombucha, 1694, 55328
Brewer Meats Inc, 55329
Brewer-Cantelmo Inc, 19861
Brewers Association, 1695
Brewers Outlet-Chestnut Hill, 1696, 19862, 55330
Brewery Ommegang, 1697
Brewla Inc., 1698
Brewmatic Company, 19863, 42575
Brewster Dairy Inc, 1699, 42576
Bri Al, 42577
Briannas Fine Salad Dressings, 1700
Briceland Vineyards, 1701
Brick Brewery, 1702, 42578
Brickerlabs.Com, 1703
Bridenbaugh Orchards, 1704
Bridge Brands Chocolate, 1705
Bridge City Food Marketing, 40140
Bridge Machine Company, 19864, 42579
Bridge Terminal, Inc, 51596, 52702
Bridgeport Wholesale Produce, 55331
Bridgetown Coffee, 1706, 55332
Bridgeview Vineyards Winery, 1707
Bridgewell Resources LLC, 1708, 19865
Bridgford Foods Corp, 1709, 55333
Briel America, 19866
Brierley & King Brokerage Corporation, 40141
Briess Malt & Ingredients Co., 1710
Briggs Co, 55334
Brighams, 1711
Bright Greens, 1712
Bright Harvest Sweet Potato Co, 1713
Bright of America, 19868
Bright Technologies, 19867
BrightFarms, 1714
Bril-Tech, 19869
Brill Manufacturing Co, 19870
Brilliant Lighting Fixture Corporation, 55335
Brimhall Foods, 1715, 55336
Brimrose Corporation of America, 19871
Brimstone Hill Vineyard, 1716
Briney Sea Delicaseas, 1717
Bringgold Wholesale Meats, 55337
Brings Co, 55338
Brinkmann Corporation, 19872, 42580
Brinkmann Instruments, Inc., 19873
BRINS, 905, 54992
Brisk Coffee Co, 1718, 42581
Brisker Dry Food Crisper, 19874, 42582
Bristle Ridge Vineyards, 1719
Bristol Associates Inc, 19875
Bristol Brewing Co, 1720
Bristol Van & Storage Corporation, 52703
Bristol-Myers Squibb Co., 1721
Brita Foods, 55339
British Aisles, 42583, 55340
British Aisles, LTD., 1722
British American Tea & Coffee, 1723
British Confectionery Company, 40142
British Depot, 42584
British Shoppe LLC, 42585, 55341
British Wholesale Imports, 42586, 55342
Britt Food Equipment, 19876
Britt's Barbecue, 19877
Brittain Merchandising, 55343
Brittle Kittle, 1724
Britton Storage Trailers, 51597
Brix Chocolates, 1725
Bro-Tex Inc, 19878
Broad Run Vineyards, 1726
Broadaway Ham Co, 1727
Broadbent B & B Food Products, 1728
Broadcom Inc., 19879
Broadhead Brewing Co, 1729

1362

All Companies Index

Broadleaf Venison USA Inc, 1730, 42587, 55344
Broadley Vineyards, 1731
Broadmoor Baker, 19880
Broadway Companies, 19881
Broaster Co LLC, 19882, 42588
Broaster Sales & Svc, 55345
Brock Awnings LTD, 19883
Brock Seed Company, 1732, 42589
Brockman E W Co Inc, 55346
Brockman Forklift, 55347
Brockmann's Chocolates, 1733
Brody Food Brokerage Corporation, 40143, 55348
Brogdex Company, 19884, 42590
Broken Bow Brewery, 1734
Brokerage Sales Company, 40144
Brokers Logistics LTD, 51598, 52704
Brolite Products Inc, 1735, 42591
Brom Food Group, 1736, 42592
Brome Lake Ducks Ltd, 1737
Broms Brokerage, 40145
Bronco Wine Co, 1738
Bronx Butter & Egg Company, 55349
Brook Locker Plant, 1739
Brook Meadow Meats, 1740
Brookema Company, 1741
Brookfield Farm, 1742, 42593
Brooklace, 19885, 42594
Brooklyn Bagel Company, 1743
Brooklyn Baking Company, 1744
Brooklyn Bean Roastery, 1745
Brooklyn Biltong, 1746, 55350
Brooklyn Boys Pizza & Pasta, 19886, 55351
Brooklyn Brew Shop, 1747
Brooklyn Brewery, 1748
Brooklyn Brine Co LLC, 1749
Brooklyn Cider House, 1750, 42595
Brooklyn Cookie Company, 1751
Brooklyn Cured LLC, 1752
Brooklyn Delhi, 1753
Brooklyn Sugar Company, 42596, 55352
Brooklyn Whatever LLC, 1754
Brookmere Wine & Vineyard, 1755
Brooks Barrel Company, 19887, 55353
Brooks Industries, 55354
Brooks Instrument LLC, 19888, 42597
Brooks Peanut Co, 1756
Brooks Tropicals Inc, 1757, 42598, 55355
Brookshire Grocery Company, 1758, 19889, 51599
Brookside Foods, 1759, 1760, 42599
Brookview Farms, 1761
Brose Chemical Company, 19890
Brother Bru Bru's, 1762
Brother's Trading LLC, 1763
Brotherhood Winery, 1764, 42600, 55356
Brothers All Natural, 1765
Brothers Desserts, 1766
Brothers International Desserts, 1767
Brothers International Food Corporation, 1768, 40146, 42601
Brothers Manufacturing, 19891
Brothers Metal Products, 19892, 42602
Brothers Restaurant Supply, 55357
Brothers Sauces, 1769
Broughton Foods LLC, 1770, 19893
Brower, 19894, 42603
Brower Equipment Co, 19895
Brown & Caldwell, 19896
Brown & Haley, 1771, 42604
Brown & Jenkins Trading Company, 1772
Brown Chemical Co, 19897
Brown County Winery, 1773
Brown Cow Farm, 1774
Brown Dairy Inc, 1775
Brown Dog Fancy, 1776
Brown Family Farm, 1777
Brown Fired Heater, 19898, 42605
Brown Foods, 1778, 55358
Brown International Corp LLC, 19899, 19900, 42606
Brown Machine LLC, 19901, 42607
Brown Manufacturing Company, 19902, 42608
Brown Packing Company, 1779
Brown Paper Goods Co, 19903
Brown Plastics & Equipment, 19904
Brown Produce Company, 1780, 42609
Brown Thompson & Sons, 1781
Brown's Dairy, 1782, 55359
Brown's Ice Cream Co, 1783, 55360
Brown's Sign & Screen Printing, 19905, 42610
Brown, R H, 55361
Brown-Forman Corp, 1784, 42611
Brown/Millunzi & Associates, 19906
Browne & Company, 19907, 55362
Brownie Baker Inc, 1785
Brownie Brittle, LLC, 1786
Brownie Points Inc, 1787
Browniepops LLC, 1788
Browning Brokerage Company, 40147
Browns Brewing Co, 1789
Browns' Ice Cream Company, 1790, 55363
Bruce Baking Company, 1791
Bruce Chaney & Company, 40148
Bruce Coffee Svc Plan USA, 1792, 42612
Bruce Cost Ginger Ale, 1793
Bruce Edmeades Sales, 55364
Bruce Foods Corporation, 1794
Bruce Industrial Co Inc, 19908
Bruce Tea, 1795
Brucepac, 1796
Brucia Plant Extracts, 1797, 42613
Brucken's, 55365
Bruegger's Bagels, 1798, 55366
Bruins Instruments, 19909
Brulin & Company, 19910, 42614
Brum's Dairy, 1799, 42615
Bruni Glass, 19911
Bruni Glass Packaging, 19912
Brunkow Cheese Of Wisconsin, 1800
Brunnett Dairy Co-Op, 1801
Bruno Specialty Foods, 1802
Brush Locker, 1803
Brush Research Mfg Co Inc, 19913, 42616
Bruske Products, 19914
Brute Fabricators, 19915, 42617
Brutocao Cellars, 1804
Bry-Air Inc, 19916, 42618
Bryan Boilers, 19917, 42619
Bryan Foods, 1805, 55367
Bryant Glass, 19918
Bryant Preserving Company, 1806
Bryant Products Inc, 19919, 42620, 55368
Bryant Vineyard, 1807
Bryant's Meat Inc., 1808
Bryce Corp, 19920
BS&R Equipment Company, 54993
BSE Marketing, 40090
BSI Instruments, 19345
Bt. McElrath Chocolatier, 1809
BTS Company/Hail Caesar Dressings, 906
Buak Fruit Company, 55369
Bubba's Fine Foods, 1810, 55370
Bubbies Fine Foods, 1811
Bubbies Homemade Ice Cream, 1812, 42621
Bubbla Inc, 19921
Bubbles Baking Co, 1813
Bubbles of San Francisco, 1814
Bublitz Machinery Company, 55371
Buccia Vineyard, 1815
Buchanan Hollow Nut Co, 1816
BUCHI Corp, 19346, 19347
Buchi Kombucha, 1817
Buck Ice & Coal Co, 19922
Buck Knives, 19923, 42622
Buck's Spumoni Company, 1818
Buckelew Hardware Co, 55372
Buckelew's Food Svc Equipment, 55373, 55374
Buckeye Group, 19924
Buckeye Handling Equipment Company, 55375
Buckeye International, 19925, 42623
Buckeye Pretzel Company, 1819
Buckhead Beef, 1820, 42624, 55376
Buckhead Gourmet, 1821
Buckhorn Canada, 19926, 42625
Buckhorn Inc, 19927, 42626
Buckingham Valley Vineyards, 1822
Buckley, Thorne, Messina & McDermott, 40149
Buckmaster Coffee Co, 1823
Budd Foods, 1824, 55377
Budd Mayer Company of Jackson Inc., 40150
Budd Mayer of Mobile, 40151
Buddha Brands, 1825
Buddha Teas, 1826, 55378
Buddy Fruits, 1827
Buddy Squirrel LLC, 1828, 42627, 55379
Budenheim USA, Inc., 1829
Budget Blinds Inc, 19928, 42628
Budi Products LLC, 1830
Buds Kitchen, 1831
Buedel Food Products, 1832
Buehler Vineyards, 1833
Buena Vista Historic Tstng Rm, 1834, 42629
Bueno Foods, 1835
Buff Bake, 1836
Buffalo Bill Brewing Company, 1837
Buffalo Bills Premium Snacks, 1838, 55380
Buffalo China, 19929
Buffalo Hotel Supply Co Inc, 55381
Buffalo Paper & Detergent Co, 55382
Buffalo Rock Co., 55383
Buffalo Technologies Corporation, 19930, 42630
Buffalo Trace Distillery, 1839, 42631
Buffalo Wild Wings, 1840
Buffalo Wire Works Co Inc, 19931, 42632
Buffet Enhancements Intl, 19932
Buffet Partners, 19933
Buhler Aeroglide Corp, 19934
Buhler Inc., 19935
Buley Patterson Sales Company, 40152
Bulk Bag Express, 55384
Bulk Food Marketplace, 55385
Bulk Lift International, LLC, 19936
Bulk Pack, 19937, 42633
Bulk Sak Intl Inc, 19938, 42634
Bull and Barrel Brewpub, 1841, 42635
Bull's Head, 1842
Bulldog Factory Svc LLC, 19939
Bulldog Hiway Express, 51600
Bullet Guard Corporation, 19940, 42636
Bully Hill Vineyards, 1843
Bulman Products Inc, 19941
Bumble Bee, 1844
Bumbleberry Farms LLC, 1845
Bunge, 1846, 19942
Bunge Canada, 1847, 42637
Bunge Loaders Croklaan, 1848
Bunge North America Inc., 1849, 42638
Bunker Foods Corp., 1850, 42639
Bunker Hill Cheese Co Inc, 1851
Bunn Capitol Company, 55386
Bunn-O-Matic Corp, 19943, 42640
Bunn-O-Matic Corporation, 19944
Bunny Bread, 1852
Buns & Roses Organic Wholegrain Bakery, 1853
Bunting Magnetics Co, 19945
Bunzl Distribution USA, 19946, 55387
Bunzl Processor Distribution LLC, 19947
Buona Vita Inc, 1854
Buonitalia, 1855, 42641
Bur-Gra Meat & Grocery, 55388
Burch Farms, 1856
Burch-Lowe, 55389
Burd & Fletcher, 19948
Burdett Associates, 40153
Burdette Beckmann Inc, 40154
Burdick Packing Company, 55390
Burdock Group, 19949
Burford Corp, 19950
Burger Maker Inc, 1857, 19951
Burgers' Smokehouse, 1858
Burgess Enterprises, Inc, 19952, 42642
Burgess Mfg. - Oklahoma, 19953, 42643, 55391
Burghof Engineering & Mfg Co, 19954
Burke Brands, 1859, 42644
Burke Candy Ingredients Inc, 1860
Burke Corp, 1861, 42645
Burke Industrial Coatings, 19955
Burkert Fluid Control, 19956
Burkhardt Sales & Svc, 55392
Burklund Distributors Inc, 55393
Burleigh Brothers Seafoods, 1862
Burleson Honey, 1863
Burley Brokerage, 40155
Burling Instrument Inc, 19957, 42646
Burlington Equipment Company, 55394
Burlington Northern Santa Fe, LLC, 51601
Burlodge USA Inc, 42647
Burn Brae Farms, 1864
Burnand & Company, 55395
Burnett & Son, 1865
Burnett Bros Engineering, 19958, 42648
Burnette Foods, 1866, 42649
Burnham & Morrill Co, 1867
Burnishine Products, 19959
Burnley Vineyards, 1868
Burns & Mcdonnell Inc, 19960
Burns Chemical Systems, 19961
Burns Engineering Inc, 19962
Burns Industries, 19963
Burrell Cutlery Company, 19964
Burris Logistics, 52705, 52706, 52707, 52708, 52709, 52710, 52711, 52712, 52713, 52714, 52715, 52716, 52717, 52718, 52719
Burrito Kitchens, 1869
Burrows Paper Corp, 19965, 19966, 42650
Burry Foods, 19967
Burt Lewis Ingredients, 1870
Burton Meat Processing, 1871
Busch LLC, 19968
Bush Brothers & Co, 1872
Bush Brothers Provision Co, 1873, 42651, 55396
Bush Refrigeration Inc, 19969, 42652
Bush Tank Fabricators Inc, 19970
Bushman Equipment Inc, 19971, 42653
Bushwick Commission Company, 40156
Business Control Systems, 19972
Business Documents, 55397
Business Facilities, 19973
Business Services Alliance, 55398
Business Systems & Conslnts, 55399
Buske Lines, 51602
Busken Bakery, 1874
Buss America, 19974
Busse/SJI Corp, 19975, 19976, 42654
Busseto Foods, 1875
Buster Lind Produce Company, 55400
Busy Bee Yerba Mate, 1876
Butkevich Associates, 40157
Butler Foods LLC, 1877, 55401
Butler Winery, 1878, 19977
Butte Produce Company, 55402
Butter Baked Goods, 1879
Butter Buds Food Ingredients, 1880, 42655
Butter Krust Baking Company, 1881
Butterball Farms, 1882
Butterball LLC, 1883
Butterfield Foods, 1884
Butterfields, 1885
Butterfly Creek Winery, 1886
Butternut Mountain Farm, 1887
Butterworth Inc, 19978

1363

All Companies Index

Buttonwood Farm Winery & Vineyard, 1888
Butts Foods, 55403
Buxton Foods, 1889
Buyers Laboratory Inc, 19979
Buypass Corporation, 19980
Buywell Coffee, 1890
Buz's Crab, 55404
Buzz Crown Enterprises, 40158
Buzz Food Svc, 1891, 55405
Buzzards Bay Trading Company, 1892, 42656
Buzzn Bee Farms, 1893
BVL Controls, 19348, 42213
BW Acquisition, 54994
BW Container Systems, 19349, 42214
BW Controls, 19350
BWI, Inc., 42215
BWI-PLC, 19351
Byblos Bakery, 1894
Byczek Enterprises, 55406
Byers Transport, 51603, 52720
Byington Vineyard & Winery, 1895
BYK Gardner Inc, 19352
Bykowski Equipment, 55407
Bylada Foods, 1896, 42657
Bynoe Printers, 19981, 55408
Byrd Cookie, 1897
Byrd International, 40159, 42658
Byrd Mill Co, 1898, 55409
Byrd's Pecans, 1899
Byrd's Seafood, 1900
Byrne & Assoc Inc, 40160
Byrne & Carlson, 1901
Byrne Brothers Foods Inc, 55410
Byrne Dairy, Inc., 1902
Byrnes & Kiefer Co, 1903
Byrnes & Kiefer Company, 1904, 42659
Byrnes Packing Shed, 1905
Byron A Carlson Inc, 40161
Byron Vineyard & Winery, 1906
Byrton Dairy Products, 19982

C

C & C Packing Co, 1907
C & D Robotics, 19983
C & D Valve Mfg Co, 19984, 42660
C & E Canners Inc, 1908, 42661
C & F Foods Inc, 1909, 42662
C & G Salsa, 1910
C & H Sugar Co Inc, 1911
C & J Tender Meat Co, 1912, 55411
C & K Machine Co, 19985, 42663
C & L Wood Products Inc, 19986
C & R Food Svc Inc, 55412
C & R Inc, 19987
C & S Sales Inc, 55413
C & S Wholesale Grocers Inc, 55414
C & T Design & Equipment Co, 55415, 55416
C A Curtze, 55417
C C Conway Seafoods, 1913
C C Pollen, 1914, 42664
C D Hartnett Co, 55418
C E Elantech Inc, 42665
C E Rogers Co, 19988, 42666
C E Zuercher, 42667
C F Burger Creamery Co, 1915
C F Gollott & Son Seafood, 1916, 42668
C F Napa Brand Design, 19989
C H Babb Co Inc, 19990, 42669
C H Guenther & Son Inc, 1917
C H Robinson Worldwide Inc, 51604, 55419
C Howard Co, 1918
C J Dannemiller Co, 1919
C J Irwin Co Inc, 40162
C J Vitner Co, 1920
C M Becker Inc, 19991
C M Processing Solutions, 19992
C M Tanner Grocery Co, 55420
C Nelson Mfg Co, 1921, 19993, 19994, 42670
C P Industries, 19995, 42671

C P Vegetable Oil, 1922, 42672
C Pacific Foods Inc, 42673, 55421
C Palmer Mfg Co Inc, 19996
C R Daniels Inc, 19997, 42674
C R England Inc, 51605
C R Mfg, 19998, 19999, 42675
C Roy & Sons Processing, 1923
C S Bell Co, 20000
C S Steen Syrup Mill Inc, 1924
C Summers Inc, 52721
C W Cole & Co, 20001, 42676
C W Resources Inc, 1925
C&C Lift Truck, 55422
C&H Chemical, 20002
C&H Packaging Company, 20003
C&H Store Equipment Company, 20004, 42677, 55423
C&J Trading, 1926
C&M Warehouse, Inc., 52722
C&P Additives, 1927, 42678
C&R Refrigeration Inc,, 20005, 55424
C&R Refrigeration, 20006
C&S Wholesale Meat Company, 1928
C&T Refinery, 1929, 42679
C&W Frozen Foods, 55425
C'est Gourmet, 1930
C-P Flexible Packaging, 20007, 20008, 20009
C-Through Covers, 20010
C. Cretors & Company, 20011, 42680
C. Eberle Sons Company, 55426
C. Gould Seafoods, 1931, 42681
C. Lloyd Johnson Company, 40163, 55427
C. Mascari & Associates, 40164
C.A. Flipse & Sons Company, 55428
C.B. Dombach & Son, 20012
C.B. Powell Limited, 40165, 42682
C.B.S. Lobster Company, 1932, 55429
C.C. Graber Company, 1933
C.E. Fish Company, 1934, 42683
C.F. Sauer Co., 1935
C.F.F. Stainless Steels, 20013
C.G. Suarez Distributing Company, 55430
C.H. Robinson Co., 20014, 40166, 42684, 51606, 55431
C.J. Distributing, 1936
C.J. Figone Cold Storage, 51607, 52723
C.J. Machine, 20015, 20016
C.J. Zone Manufacturing Company, 20017
C.L. Deveau & Son, 1937, 42685
C.M. Goettsche & Company, Inc., 42686
C.M. Lingle Company, 20018
C.P. Rail System, 51608
C.R. Peterson Associates, 40167
C.S. Woods Company, 55432
C.T. Grasso, 55433
C.W. Brabender Instruments, 20019
C.W. Brown Foods, Inc., 1938
C.W. Shasky & Associates Ltd., 20020, 40168, 55434
C2O Pure Coconut Water, 1939
CA Fortune & Company, 1940
CA Griffith International, 20021
Ca Polytechnic State/Alumni, 20112
Cab Technology Inc, 20113
Cable Car Beverage Corporation, 1969
Cable Meat Center, 55454
Cabo Chips, 1970
Cabo Rojo Enterprises, 1971, 42719
Cabot Corp, 20114, 42720
Cabot Creamery Co-Op, 1972, 42721
Cabot/Norit Americas Inc, 20115, 20116
Cacao Prieto, 1973, 20117
Cachafaz US, 1974
Cache Box, 20118, 42722
Cache Cellars, 1975
Cache Creek Foods LLC, 1976, 20119
Cacique, 1977, 42723
Cacoco, 1978
CactuLife, LLC, 1979
Cactus Holdings Inc, 55455

Cactus Mat Manufacturing Company, 20120
Cadbury Adams, 1980
Cadbury Beverages Canada, 1981
Cadbury Trebor Allan, 1982
Cadco Inc, 42724, 55456
Caddo Packing Co, 1983
Caddy Corporation of America, 20121, 42725
Cadie Products Corp, 20122, 42726
Cadillac Coffee Co, 1984
Cadillac Meat Company, 55457
Cadillac Packaging Corporation, 55458
Cadillac Pallets, 20123
Cadillac Plastics, 20124
Cadillac Products Inc, 20125
Cady Bag Co, 20126
Cady Cheese Factory, 1985
CAE Alpheus, 20022
Caesar Electric Supply, 55459
Caesar's Pasta, 1986
Cafe Altura, 1987, 42727
Cafe Bustelo, 1988
Cafe Cartago, 1989
Cafe Chilku, 1990
Cafe Del Mundo, 1991, 20127
Cafe Descafeinado de Chiapas, 1992
Cafe Du Monde Coffee Stand, 1993, 42728
Cafe Fanny, 1994
Cafe Grumpy, 1995, 55460
Cafe Inc, 40173
Cafe Jumbo, 55461
Cafe Kreyol, 1996, 55462
Cafe La Semeuse, 1997
Cafe Moak, 1998, 42729
Cafe Moto, 1999
Cafe Sark's Gourmet Coffee, 2000
Cafe Society Coffee Company, 2001
Cafe Spice, 2002
Cafe Tequila, 2003
Cafe Yaucono/Jimenez & Fernandez, 2004
Cafejo, 42730
Caffe Appassionato Coffee, 2005
Caffe D'Amore, 2006
Caffe D'Amore Gourmet Beverages, 2007
Caffe D'Oro, 2008
Caffe D'Vita, 2009
Caffe Darte, 2010, 55463
Caffe Ibis Gallery Deli, 2011
Caffe Luca Coffee Roaste, 2012, 42731
Caffe Trieste, 2013
Cagles Appliance Center, 55464
Cahoon Farms, 2014
CAI International, 42687, 55435
Cain Awning Co Inc, 20128
Cain Vineyard & Winery, 2015
Cain's Coffee Company, 55465
Caito Fisheries Inc, 2016
Cajohn's Fiery Foods Co, 2017
Cajun Boy's Louisiana Products, 2018, 42732
Cajun Brands, 2019
Cajun Brothers Seafood Company, 55466
Cajun Crawfish Distributors, 2020, 55467
Cajun Creole Products Inc, 2021, 40174, 42733
Cajun Fry Co Inc, 2022
Cajun Original Foods Inc, 2023, 42734
Cajun Seafood Enterprises, 2024, 55468
Cajun Sugar Company LLC, 55469
Cakebread Cellars, 2025
Cal Ben Soap Co, 20129
Cal Coast Promo-Products, 55470
CAL Controls, 20023
Cal Controls, 20130, 42735
Cal Harvest Marketing Inc, 2026, 42736
Cal India Foods Inc, 2027, 42737
Cal Ranch, 2028
Cal Trading Company, 42738
Cal Western Pest Control, 20131
Cal-Coast Manufacturing, 20132

Cal-Grown Nut Company, 2029, 42739
Cal-Java International Inc, 2030
Cal-Maine Foods Inc, 2031, 42740
Cal-Mil Plastic Products Inc, 20133, 42741
Cal-Tex Citrus Juice LP, 2032, 42742
Cal-West Produce, 55471
Calabro Cheese Corp, 2033
Calafia Cellars, 2034
Calamondin Cafe, 2035
Calapooia Brewing Co, 2036
Calavo Growers, 2037, 42743
Calbee America Inc, 2038, 42744
Calcium Chloride Sales Inc, 20134
Calcium Springs Water Company, 2039
Calco of Calgary, 2040
Caldic USA Inc, 2041, 42745, 51616, 52732
Caldwell Group, 20135, 42746
Caldwell Trucking Inc, 51617
Caleb Haley & Co LLC, 2042
Calendar Islands Maine Lobster LLC, 2043
Calera Wine Co, 2044
Calgary Italian Bakery, 2045
Calgene, 20136
Calgon Carbon, 20137
Calgrain Corporation, 42747
Calhoun Bend Mill, 2046, 20138
Cali'flour Foods, 2047
Calia Technical, 20139
Calico Cottage, 2048, 20140, 55472
Calico Industries Inc, 55473
Calidad Foods, 2049
Calif Canning Peach Assn, 20141
Calif Snack Foods, 2050
Calif Watercress Inc, 2051
Califia Farms, 2052
California Agriculture & Foodstuff, 42748, 55474
California Almond Packers, 2053
California Balsamic Inc, 2054
California Blending Co, 2055, 20142
California Cartage Co, 51618, 52733
California Caster & Handtruck, 20143, 55475
California Cereal Products, 2056, 42749
California Citrus Producers, 2057
California Coast Naturals, 2058
California Custom Foods, 2059, 42750
California Custom Fruits, 2060, 42751
California Dairies Inc., 2061, 42752
California Fruit, 2062
California Fruit & Nut, 2063
California Fruit and Tomato Kitchens, 2065
California Fruit Market, 55476
California Fruit Processors, 2064
California Garden Products, 2066
California Garlic Co, 2067
California Hi-Lites, 20144
California Independent Almond Growers, 2068, 42753, 55477
California Juice Co., 2069
California Lavash, 2070
California League of Food Processors, 20145
California Marketing Group Inc, 55478
California Milk Advisory, 20146
California Natural Products, 2071, 42754
California Nuggets Inc, 2072
California Oils Corp, 2073, 42755
California Olive Growers, 2074
California Olive Oil Council, 2075, 42756
California Olive Ranch, 2076
California Packing Company, 2077
California Saw & Knife Works, 20147, 42757
California Shellfish Company, 2078
California Smart Foods, 2079
California Sprout & Celery, 55479
California Tag & Label, 55480
California Toytime Balloons, 20148
California Vibratory Feeders, 20149

All Companies Index

California Walnut Co, 2080
California Wholesale Nut, 2081
California Wild Rice Growers, 2082
California World Trade and Marketing Company, 40175, 42758
California-Antilles Trading, 2083, 55481
Calihan Pork Processors Inc, 2084
Calio Groves, 2085, 42759
Calise & Sons Bakery Inc, 2086
Calistoga Food Company, 2087
Calivirgin Olive Oils, 2088
Caljan America, 20150
Calkins & Burke, 2089, 42760
Callahan Grocery Company, 55482
Callanan Company Alloy Company, 20151
Callaway Packing Inc, 2090
Callaway Vineyards & Winery, 2091
Callie's Charleston Biscuits, 2092
Callif Foods, 55483
Callis Seafood, 2093
Calmar, 20152, 42761
Calmar Bakery, 2094
Caloritech, 20153, 42762
Calpro Ingredients, 2095, 42763
Caltex Foods, 2096
Calumet Diversified Meats Company, 2097
Calvert's, 2098
Calvisius Caviar, 2099
Calzone Case Co, 20154
CAM Campak/Technician, 20024
Cam Spray, 20155, 42764
Cam Tron Systems, 20156
Camas Prairie Winery, 2100
Cambelt International Corporation, 20157
Cambria Winery, 2101
Cambridge Brands Inc, 2102
Cambridge Food, 2103
Cambridge Intl. Inc., 20158, 42765
Cambridge Packing Company, 2104, 55484
Cambridge Viscosity, Inc., 20159, 42766
Cambro Manufacturing Co, 20160, 42767
Camco Chemicals, 20161
Camcorp Inc, 20162
Camel Canvas Shop, 20163
Camellia Beans, 2105, 42768
Camellia General Provision Co, 2106
Cameo China, 42769
Cameo Confections, 2107
Cameo Metal Products Inc, 20164, 55485
Camerican International, 42770
Cameron Birch Syrup & Confections, 2108, 42771
Cameron Intl. Corp., 20165, 42772
Cameron Seafood Processors, 2109, 55486
Camerons Brewing Co., 20166, 42773
Camie Campbell, 20167
Camilla Pecan Company, 2110
Camino Real Foods Inc, 2111
Campagana Winery, 2112, 42774
Campagna Distinct Flavor, 2113
Campak Inc, 20168
Campari, 2114
Campbell Company of Canada, 2115
Campbell Soup Co., 2116, 42775
Campbell Wrapper Corporation, 20169
Campbell's Food Service, 55487
Campbell's Quality Cuts, 2117
Campbell-Hardage, 20170
Campione Resturant Supply, 55488
Campus Collection, Inc., 20171, 42776
Camrose Packers, 2118
Camstar Systems, 20172
Camtech-AMF, 20173
Camtron Systems, 20174
Can & Bottle Systems, Inc., 20175, 42777
Can Am Seafood, 2119, 55489
Can Corp Of America Inc, 20176
Can Creations, 20177, 20178
Can Lines Engineering Inc, 20179, 42778
Can-Am Instruments, 20180

Can-Am LTL, 51619
Canaan Logistics, 51620
Canada Bread Co, Ltd, 2121, 42779
Canada Coaster, 20182
Canada Cutlery Inc., 42780, 55490
Canada Distribution Centres, 51621, 52734
Canada Dry Bottling Co, 55491
Canada Goose Wood Produc, 20183
Canada Maritime Agencies, 51622
Canada Pure Water Company Ltd, 20184, 55492
Canada Safeway, 55493
Canadian Display Systems, 20185, 42781
Canadian Fish Exporters, 2122, 42782
Canadian Food Exporters Association, 42783
Canadian Gold Seafood, 55494
Canadian Harvest-U.S.A., 2123
Canadian Mist Distillers, 2124, 42784
Canadian National Railway, 51623
Canaf Foods International, 2125
Canal Fulton Provision, 2126
CanAmera Foods, 2120
Canarino, 2127
Canarm, Ltd., 20186, 42785
CANBERRA Industries Inc, 20025
Candelari's Specialty Sausage, 2128
Candle Lamp Company, 20187, 42786
Cando Pasta, 2129
Candy & Company/Peck's Products Company, 20188, 42787
Candy Basket Inc, 2130
Candy Bouquet of Elko, 2131
Candy Central, 2132
Candy Cottage Company, 2133
Candy Flowers, 2134, 42788
Candy Manufacturing Co, 20189, 42789
Candy Mountain Sweets & Treats, 2135, 42790
Candy Tech LLC, 42791
CandyMachines.com, 20190
Candyrific, 2136
Caneast Foods, 40176
Canelake's Candy, 2137, 42792
Cangel, 2138, 42793
Cann Brokerage Inc, 40177
Canning & Filling, 20191
Cannoli Factory, 2139, 42794
Cannon Cold Storage, 52735
Cannon Equipment Company, 20192
Cannon's Sweets Hots, 2140
Cannon/Tayloe, 55495
Canoe Lagoon Oyster Company, 2141, 55496
Canoe Ridge Vineyard, 2142
Canon Potato Company, 2143, 20193, 52736, 55497
Canongate Technology, 20194
CanPacific Engineering, 20181
Cantab Industries, 55498
Cantech Industries Inc, 20195, 42795
Canterbury's Crack & Peel, 55499
Cantley-Ellis Manufacturing Company, 20196
Cantol, 20197
Canton Foods, 55500
Canton Noodle Corporation, 2144
Canton Railroad Co, 51624
Canton Sign Co, 20198
Canton Sterilized Wiping Cloth, 20199
Cantrell's Seafood, 2145
Cantwell-Cleary Co Inc, 20200, 20201
Canty Wiper & Supply Company, 55501
Canvas Products, 20202
Canyon Bakehouse LLC, 2146, 55502
Canyon Specialty Foods, 2147
Cap Candy, 2148
Capa Di Roma Inc, 2149
Capaco Plastics, 20204
Capalbo's Fruit Baskets, 2150, 55503
Caparone Winery LLC, 2151
Capay Canyon Ranch, 2152, 42796
Capco Enterprises, 2153
Cape Ann Seafood, 2154

Cape Cod Coffee Roasters, 2155
Cape Cod Potato Chips, 2156, 42797
Cape Cod Provisions, 2157
Cape Cod Specialty Foods, 2158
Cape Cod Sweets, LLC, 2159
Cape Dairy LLC, 55504
Cape May Fishery Cooperative, 55505
Cape Systems, 20205
Capital Brewery & Beer Garden, 2160
Capital City Container Corporation, 20206
Capital City Fruit, 55506
Capital City Processors, 2161
Capital City Signs, 20207
Capital Equipment & Handling, 55507
Capital Industries, 20208
Capital Packaging, 20209
Capital Packers Inc, 2162
Capital Plastics, 20210, 42798
Capital Produce II Inc, 2163, 55508
Capitol Awning Co Inc, 20211
Capitol Carton Company, 20212
Capitol City Container Corp, 20213
Capitol City Produce, 55509
Capitol Foods, 2164, 42799, 55510
Capitol Hardware, Inc.,, 20214, 42800
Capitol Recruiting Group, 20215
Capitol Station 65 Cold Storage, 52737
Capitol Vial, 20216
Capmatic, Ltd., 20217, 42801
Capolla Food Inc, 2165
Capone Foods, 2166, 20218, 55511
Caporale Winery, 2167
Cappello Foods, 55512
Cappello's, 2168
Cappo Drinks, 2169, 42802
Cappola Foods, 2170, 42803
Cappuccine, 2171
Cappuccino Express Company, 42804, 55513
Capresso, 20219
Capri Bagel & Pizza Corporation, 2172, 42805
Capri Sun, 2173
Capriccio, 2174, 42806
Capricorn Coffees Inc, 2175, 20220, 20221
Caprine Estates, 2176
Capriole Inc, 2177, 55514
Caprock Winery Inc, 2178
CapSnap Equipment, 20203
Capsule Works, 2179
Capt Collier Seafood, 2180, 55515
Capt Joe & Sons Inc, 2181, 55516
Captain Alex Seafoods, 2182, 42807, 55517
Captain Bob's Jet Fuel, 2183
Captain Cook Coffee Company, 2184
Captain Foods, Inc., 2185
Captain Ken's Foods Inc, 2186
Captain Lawrence Brewing Co, 2187
Captain Little Seafood, 2188, 55518
Captain Morrills Inc, 55519
Captain's Choice, 2189
Captiva Limited Inc, 2190, 42808
Captree Clam, 55520
Caputo Cheese, 2191
Capway Conveyor Systems Inc, 20222, 42809
Cara Products Company, 20223
Caracolillo Coffee Mills, 2192, 55521
Carando Gourmet Frozen Foods, 2193
Carando Technologies Inc, 20224, 42810
Caraquet Ice Company, 2194
Caraustar, 20225, 20226
Caraustar Industries, Inc., 20227, 42811
Caravan Company, 2195, 20228
Caravan Packaging Inc, 20229, 42812
Caravell, 42813
Carbis Inc, 20230, 42814
Carboline Co, 20231
Carbon Clean Industries Inc, 20232
Carbon's Golden Malted, 2197
Carbonella & Desarbo Inc, 55523
Carbonic Machines Inc, 20233

Carbonic Reserves, 20234
Carborator Rental Svc, 2198, 55524
CarbRite Diet, 2196, 55522
Card Pak Inc, 20235
Cardan Design, 20236
Carden Foods Inc, 55525
Cardi Foods, 2199
Cardinal Brokerage, 40178
Cardinal Carryor Inc, 55526
Cardinal Container Corp, 20237
Cardinal International, 55527
Cardinal Kitchens, 20238
Cardinal Logistics Management, 51625
Cardinal Meat Specialists, 2200, 42815
Cardinal Packaging, 20239
Cardinal Packaging Prod LLC, 20240, 42816
Cardinal Professional Products, 20241
Cardinal Rubber & Seal Inc, 20242, 42817
Cardinal Scale Mfg Co, 20243, 42818
Cardinale Winery, 2201
Care Controls, Inc., 20244, 42819
Care Foods International, 2202
Carefree Kanopy, 55528
Caremoli USA, 2203, 42820
Cargill Inc., 2204, 20245, 42821
Cargill Kitchen Solutions Inc., 2205, 20246, 42822
Cargill Protein, 2206
Cargo, 51626, 52738
Cargo Transporters Inc, 51627
Cargo-Master Inc, 51628
Carhartt, 20247
Carhoff Company, 20248, 42823
Caribbean Coffee Co, 2207
Caribbean Cookie Company, 2208
Caribbean Food Delights Inc, 2209, 42824
Caribbean Produce Exchange, 42825, 55529
Caribbean Products, 2210
Caribbean Restaurants, 55530
Caribou Coffee Co Inc, 2211
Carico Systems, 20249
Caristrap International, 20250, 42827
Carl Brandt, 42828
Carl Buddig & Co., 2212
Carl Rittberger Sr Inc, 2213
Carl Stahl Amer Lifting LLC, 55531
Carl Strutz & Company, 20251
Carl Venezia Fresh Meats, 2214
Carla's Pasta, 2215
Carle & Montanari-O P M, 42829, 55532
Carleton Helical Technologies, 20252, 20253, 42830
Carleton Technologies Inc, 20254, 42831
Carlin Group, 40179
Carlin Manufacturing, 20255, 42832
Carlisle Cereal Company, 2216
Carlisle Food Svc Products Inc, 20256, 42833
Carlisle Food Systems Inc, 55533
Carlisle Plastics, 20257
Carlisle Sanitary Mntnc Prods, 20258, 42834
Carlo Gavazzi Inc, 20259
Carlota Foods International, 42835
Carlson Company, 55534
Carlson Engineering Inc, 20260
Carlson Products, 20261, 42836
Carlson Vineyards Winery, 2217
Carlton Company, 40180, 55535
Carlton Farms, 2218
Carlton Industries, 20262
Carlyle Compressor, 20263
Carmadhy's Foods, 2219
Carman And Company, 20264
Carman Industries Inc, 20265, 20266
Carmel Engineering, 20267, 20268
Carmela's Gourmet, 2220
Carmelita Provisions Company, 2221
Carmenet Winery, 2222

1365

All Companies Index

Carmi Flavor & Fragrance Company, 2223, 20269
Carmichael International Svc, 51629
Carmine's Bakery, 2224
Carmona Designs, 20270
Carmun International, 20271
Carnegie Manufacturing Company, 20272
Carnegie Textile Co, 20273
Carneros Creek Winery, 2225
Carnes Company, 20274, 42837
Carnival Brands Mfg, 2226
Carnival Fruit, 55536
Caro Foods, 2227, 55537
Carob Tree, 2228
Carol Hall's Hot Pepper Jelly, 2229
Carol Lee Donuts, 2230
Carol's Country Cuisine, 2231
Carole's Cheesecake Company, 2232, 55538
Carolina Atlantic Seafood Enterprises, 2233
Carolina Belting, 55539
Carolina Beverage Corp, 2234, 42838, 55540
Carolina Blueberry Co-Op Assn, 2235
Carolina Bonded Storage Co, 51630, 52739
Carolina Brewery, 2236
Carolina Canners Inc, 42839, 55541
Carolina Classics Catfish Inc, 2237
Carolina Cold Storage, 52740
Carolina Container, 20275
Carolina Cookie Co, 2238
Carolina Cracker, 2239, 20276
Carolina Fine Snacks, 2240
Carolina Food Company, 2241
Carolina Foods Inc, 2242
Carolina Glove Co, 20277
Carolina Handling LLC, 55542
Carolina Ingredients Inc, 2243
Carolina Innovative Food Ingredients, Inc., 2244
Carolina Knife, 20278, 42840
Carolina Material Handling, 55543
Carolina Mop, 20279, 42841
Carolina Mountain, 55544
Carolina Packers Inc, 2245
Carolina Pride Foods, 2246, 42842
Carolina Pride Products, 2247
Carolina Produce, 55545
Carolina Products, 2248
Carolina Steel Shelving Company, 55546
Carolina Summit Mountain Spring Water, 2249, 20280
Carolina Tractor and Equipment Company, 55547
Carolina Transfer & Stge Inc, 51631, 52741
Carolina Treet, 2250, 42843
Carolyn Darden Enterprises, 55548
Carolyn's Gourmet, 2251
Carometec Inc, 20281
Caron Products & Svc Inc, 20282
Carotek Inc, 20283
Carothers Olive Oil, 42844
Carousel Cakes, 2252
Carousel Candies, 2253
Carpenter Advanced Ceramics, 20284
Carpenter Associates, 40181
Carpenter Emergency Lighting, 20285, 42845
Carpenter Snack Food Distribution Company, 55549
Carpenter-Hayes Paper Box Company, 20286
Carpet City Paper Box Company, 20287
Carpigiani Corporation of America, 20288, 42846
Carr Cheese Factory/GileCheese Company, 2254
Carr Valley Cheese, 2255
Carr Valley Cheese Company, 2256
Carrabassett Coffee Roasters, 2257, 55550

Carrageenan Company, 20289, 42847
Carriage Foods, 55551
Carriage House Foods, 2258
Carrie's Chocolates, 2259, 42848
Carrier Corp, 20290, 42849
Carrier Rental Systems, 20291
Carrier Transicold, 20292
Carrier Vibrating Equip Inc, 20293, 42850
Carriere Foods Inc, 2260, 42851
Carrington Foods Co Inc, 2261
Carrington Tea Co., 2262
Carroll Chair Company, 20294
Carroll Co, 20295, 20296, 42852
Carroll Distributing Co, 55552
Carroll Manufacturing International, 20297, 42853
Carroll Packaging, 20298
Carrollton Products Company, 55553
Carron Net Co Inc, 20299, 42854
Carrot Top Pastries, 55554
Carrousel Cellars, 2263
Carry-All Canvas Bag Co., 20300, 42855
Carson City Pickle Company, 2264
Carson Industries, 20301
Carson Manufacturing Company, 20302, 42856
Cart Mart, 20303
Carta Blanca, 2265
Carter & Burgess Food and Beverage Division, 20304
Carter & Klaw Foods, 40182
Carter Products, 20305, 42857
Carter Promotions, 55555
Carter-Day International Inc, 20306, 42858
Carter-Hoffmann LLC, 20307, 42859
Carteret Coding Inc, 20308
Carthage Cup Company, 20309
Carton Closing Company, 20310
Carton Service Co, 20311
Cartonplast, 20312
Cartpac Inc, 20313
Carts Food Equipment, 20314, 42860
Carts Of Colorado Inc, 20315, 42861
Cartwright's Market, 55556
Carve Nutrition, 2266
Cary Randall's Sauces & Dressings, 2267
Cary's of Oregon, 2268
Casa Amador, 42862, 55557
Casa di Carfagna, 2275
Casa Di Carfagna, 55558
Casa Di Lisio Products Inc, 2269, 42863
Casa Herrera, 20316, 20317, 42864, 55559
Casa Larga Vineyards, 2270
Casa Nuestra Winery & Vineyard, 2271
Casa Pons USA, 42865
Casa Sanchez Foods, 2272, 55560
Casa Valdez Inc, 2273
Casa Visco, 2274, 42866
Casabar, 20318
Casablanca Foods LLC, 2276
Casablanca Market, 2277
Casados Farms, 2278
Casani Candy Company, 2279
Cascade Cheese Co, 2280
Cascade Clear Water, 2281
Cascade Coffee, 2282
Cascade Corp, 40183
Cascade Earth Sciences, 20319
Cascade Fresh, 2283
Cascade Glacier Ice Cream Company, 55561
Cascade Mountain Winery, 2284, 42867
Cascade Properties, 52742
Cascade Signs & Neon, 20320
Cascade Specialties, Inc., 2285, 52743
Cascade Wood Components, 20321
Cascadian Farm Inc, 2286, 42868
Case Farms, 2287
Case Farms Ohio Division, 2288
Case Lowe & Hart Architects, 20322
Case Manufacturing Company, 20323

Case Side Holdings Company, 2289
Caselites, 20324
Casella Lighting, 20325, 42869
Casey Fisheries, 2290, 42870
Casey's Seafood Inc, 2291, 42871
Cash Caddy, 20326
Cash Grocery & Sales Company, 55562
Cash Register Sales, 42872, 55563
Cash-Wa Distributing, 55564, 55565, 55566
Cashco Inc, 20327
Cashman-Edwards Inc, 40184
Casino Bakery, 2292
Casper Foodservice Company, 2293, 55567
Casper's Ice Cream, 2294
Caspian Trading Company, 42873, 55568
Cass Hudson Company, 55569
Cass Saw & Tool Sharpening, 20328
Cass-Clay Creamery, 2295
Cassandra's Gourmet Classics/Island Treasures Gourmet, 2296
Cassco Refrigerated Services, 52744
Cassel Box & Lumber Co Inc, 20329
Casso Guerra & Company, 42874, 55570
Casso-Solar Corporation, 20330, 42875
Cast Film Technology, 20331
Cast Nylons LTD, 20332
Castell Interlocks Inc, 20333, 51632
Castella Imports Inc, 2297, 20334
Castellini Group, 2298, 51633
Castello di Borghese Vineyard, 2299, 55571
Caster Wheels & Indl Handling, 55572
Castino Restaurant Equipment, 20335, 55573
Castle Bag Co., 20336
Castle Beverages Inc, 2300
Castle Cheese, 2301, 42876
Castle Distribution Svc Inc, 52745
Castle Hill Lobster, 2302, 55574
Castle Rock Meats, 2303
Castor River Farms, 2304
Castor Technology Corporation, 55575
Castrol Industrial, 20337
Casual Gourmet Foods, 2305
Casually Gourmet, 2306
Cat Inc, 20338
Cat Pumps, 20339, 42877
Catalent Pharma Solutions Inc, 20340
Catalina Cylinders, 20341
Catalyst International, 20342, 42878
Catalytic Products Intl Inc, 20343
Catamount Specialties of Vermont, 2307
Catania Bakery, 2308
Catania Hospitality Group, 2309
Catania Oils, 2310
Cataract Foods, 55576
Catawissa Bottling Co, 2311
Catch Up Logistics, 2312, 42879
Catelli Brothers Inc, 2313
Cateraid Inc, 2314
Catering Co, 20345, 55577
CaterMate, 20344
Cates Addis Company, 2315, 42880
Cates Mechanical Corp, 20346
Catfish Wholesale, 2316, 42881
Cathay Foods Corporation, 2317
Catherych, 2318
Catoctin Vineyards, 2319
Catoris Candies Inc, 2320
Catskill Brewery, 2321, 42882
Catskill Craftsmen Inc, 20347, 42883
Catskill Distilling Company, 2322
Catskill Mountain Specialties, 2323, 42884
Cattaneo Brothers Inc, 2324
Cattle Boyz Foods, 2325, 42885
Cattleman Meat & Produce, 2326
Cattron Group International, 20348
Catty Inc, 20349, 42886
Cauble & Field, 55578
Caudill Seed Co Inc, 42887, 55579
Caughman's Meat Plant, 2327

Caulipower, 2328
Cavalla Inc, 20350
Cavallini Coffee & Tea, 42888
Cavanna Packaging USA Inc, 20351, 55580
Cavazos Candy, Produce & Groceries, 55581
Cave Shake, 2329
Caveman Foods, 2330
Cavender Castle Winery, 2331
Cavendish Farms, 2332
Cavens Meats, 2333, 55582
Cavert Wire Co, 20352
Caves Of Faribault/SwissValley, 2334
Caviar & Caviar LLC, 42889
Caviness Beef Packers LTD, 2335, 2336
Cawley Co, 20353, 42890
Cawston Press, 2337
Cawy Bottling Co, 2338, 42891
Cayard's Inc, 55583
Caymus Vineyards, 2339
Cayne Industrial Sales Corp, 20354, 42892
Cayuga Pure Organics, 2340
Cayuga Ridge Estate Winery, 2341
CB Beverage Corporation, 1941
Cb Equipment Co, 55584
CB Mfg. & Sales Co., 20026, 55436
CB Pallet, 55437
CB's Nuts, 1942
CBC Foods, 1943
CBI Freezing Equipment, 20027
CBi Freezing Equipment, 20031
CBN Advertising Sales Company, 55438
CBORD Group Inc, 20028, 20029, 42688
CBP Resources, 1944
CBS Food Equipment, 55439
CBS Food Products Corporation, 1945
CBS International, 20030
CC Custom Technology Corporation, 20032
Cci Industries-Cool Curtain, 20355
CCi Scale Company, 20043, 42691
CCL Container, 20033, 20034, 42689
CCL Label Inc, 20035, 20036
CCL Labeling Equipment, 20037
CCP Industries, Inc., 20038
CCR Data Systems, 20039
CCR USA LLC, 20040
CCS Creative, Inc., 20041
CCS Stone, Inc., 20042, 42690
Ccw Products, 20356, 42893
CDF Corp, 20044
CDI Service & Mfg Inc, 20045, 42692
CE International Trading Corporation, 20046
CEA Instrument Inc, 20047, 42693
Cebro Frozen Food, 2342
Cecchetti Sebastiani Cellar, 2343
Cece's Veggie Co., 2344
Cecor, 20357
Cedar Box Co, 20358
Cedar Creek Winery, 2345
Cedar Crest Specialties, 2346
Cedar Grove Cheese Inc, 2347
Cedar Hill Seasonings, 2348
Cedar Key Aquaculture Farms, 2349
Cedar Lake Foods, 2350, 42894
Cedar Mountain Winery, 2351
Cedar Rapids & Iowa City Railway Company, 51634
Cedar Valley Cheese Store, 2352
Cedar Valley Fish Market, 2353, 55585
Cedar's Mediterranean Foods, 2354
Cedarlane Foods, 2355
Cedarlane Natural Foods Toc, 2356, 55586
Cedarvale Food Products, 2357, 42895
Ceilcote Air Pollution Control, 20359, 42896
Ceilidh Fisherman's Cooperative, 2358, 42897
Celebrity Cheesecake, 2359
Celebrity Promotions, 20360
Celebrity Refrigerated Warehouse, 52746

All Companies Index

Celebrity Tea, LLC, 2360
Celite Corporation, 20361, 42898
Cell-Nique, 2361
Cell-O-Core Company, 20362
Cellier Corporation, 20363
Cello Bag Company, 20364
Cellofoam North America, 20365, 42899
Cellone Bakery Inc, 2362
Cellotape, Inc., 20366
Cellox Corp, 20367, 42900
Cellucap Manufacturing Co, 20368, 42901
Cellucon Inc, 2363
Celplast Metallized Products Limited, 20369
Celright Foods, 40185
Celsis, 20370
Celsis Laboratory Group, 20371
Celsius, 2364
Celtic Sea Salt, 2365
CEM Corporation, 20048, 42694
Centennial Farms, 2366
Centennial Food Corporation, 2367, 42902
Centennial Mills, 2368
Centennial Moldings, 20372
Centennial Transportation Industries, 20373
Centennial Warehousing Corp, 52747
Centent Co, 20374, 42903
Center for Packaging Education, 20375
Center Locker Svc, 2369
Centerchem, 2370, 55587
Centflor Manufacturing Co, 2371, 42904
Centi Mark Corp, 20376
Cento Fine Foods, 2372
Centra Worldwide, 51635, 52748
Central American Warehouse Co, 51636, 52749
Central Bag Co, 20377
Central Bakery, 2373
Central Baking Supplies, 55588
Central Bean Co, 2374
Central California Raisin Packing Co, Inc., 2375
Central Carolina Farm & Mower, 55589
Central Coast Seafood, 2376, 42905, 55590
Central Coated Products Inc, 20378
Central Dairies, 2377
Central Dairy, 2378
Central Decal, 20379, 42906
Central Distributing Co, 55591
Central Electropolishing Company, 20380
Central Fabricators Inc, 20381, 42907
Central Fine Pack Inc, 20382
Central Freight Lines Inc, 51637
Central Global Express, 51638, 52750
Central Ice Machine Co, 20383
Central Illinois Equipment Company, 55592
Central Maine & Quebec Railway, 51639
Central Marketing Assoc, 40186
Central Meat & Provision, 2379
Central Meat Market, 2380
Central Milling Co, 2381
Central Missouri Sheltered Enterprises, 20384
Central Ohio Bag & Burlap, 20385
Central Oklahoma Produce Services, 55593
Central Package & Display, 20386, 42908, 55594
Central Pallet Mills Inc, 20387
Central Paper Box, 20388
Central Restaurant Supply Inc, 55595
Central Sales & Marketing, 40187
Central Sanitary Supply, 55596
Central Seaway Company, Inc., 42909
Central Security Service, 55597
Central Snacks, 2382
Central Solutions Inc, 20389
Central Soyfoods, 2383
Central States Distribution, 51640, 52751

Central States Indl Eqpt & Svc, 20390
Central States Warehouse, 52752
Central Storage & Warehouse Co, 52753
Central Storage & Wrhse Co Inc, 52754
Central Transport Intl, 51641, 52755
Central Transportation System, 51642, 52756
Central Warehouse Operations, Inc., 51643, 52757
Central Wholesale Grocery Corporation, 55598
Central-Cumberland Corp, 51644, 52758
Central/Terminal Distribution Centers, 52759
Centreside Dairy, 2384, 55599
Centrifuge Solutions, 20391
Centrisys, 20392
Century 21 Manufacturing, 20393
Century 21 Products, 55600
Century Agricultural Products LLC, 2385
Century Blends LLC, 2386, 42910
Century Box Company, 20394
Century Chemical Corp, 20395, 42911
Century Conveyor Svc, 55601
Century Crane & Hoist, 20396
Century Data Systems, 55602
Century Distributors Inc, 55603
Century Foods Intl LLC, 2387, 20397, 42912
Century Fournier Inc, 55604
Century Glove Corp, 20398, 42913
Century Industries Inc, 20399, 42914
Century Products, 20400
Century Refrigeration, 20401
Century Rubber Stamp Company, 20402
Century Sign Company, 20403
Cenveo Inc, 20404
Cepco, 20405
Ceramic Color & Chemical Mfg, 20406
Ceramic Decorating Co Inc, 20407
Ceramica De Espana, 20408, 42915
Cerca Foodservice, 55605
Cereal Byproducts, 55606
Cereal Food Processors, 2388
Cereal Food Processors Inc, 2389, 2390, 42916
Cereal Ingredients, Inc., 2391
Ceres Fruit Juices, 2392
Ceres Solutions, 55607
Cericola Farms, 2393
Cermack, 55608
Cermex, 20409
CERT ID LC, 20049
Certco Inc., 55609
Certi Fresh Foods Inc, 2394
Certi-Fresh Foods, Inc, 2395, 55610
Certified Cleaning Supplies, 55611
Certified Food Service, 55612
Certified Food Services, 55613
Certified Grocers Midwest, 20410, 55614
Certified Interior Systems, 55615
Certified Labs, 20411
Certified Labs Of California, 20412
Certified Machinery Inc, 20413
Certified Piedmontese Beef, 2396, 20414
Cervantes Food Products Inc, 2397
Cesco Magnetics, 20415
CF Chef, 20050
CF Equipment, 55440
CF Imperial Sales, 55441
CFC International, Inc., 20051
CFC Logistics, 52724
CFE Equipment Corp, 55442
CFS North America, 20052
CGI Processing Equipment, 20053
CH Imports, 20054
Chacewater Winery and Olive Mill, 2398, 55616
Chad Co Inc, 20416, 42917
Chaddsford Winery, 2399
Chaffee Co, 20417
Chai Diaries, 2400
Chain Restaurant Resolutions, 20418
Chain Store Graphics, 20419
Chaircraft, 20420

Chalet Cheese Co-Op, 2401
Chalet Debonne Vineyards, 2402
Chalk Hill Estate Winery, 2403
Challenge Dairy Products, Inc., 2404, 42918, 55617
Challenger Pallet & Supply Inc, 20421
Chalmur Bag Company, LLC, 20422
Chalone Vineyard, 2405
Cham Cold Brew Tea, 2406
Chamberlain Wholesale Grocery, 55618
Chamberland Engineering, 20423
Chambers Container Company, 20424
Chambersburg Cold Storage Inc, 52760
Chambord, 2407
Chameleon Beverage Co Inc, 55619
Chameleon Cold Brew, 2408
Champaign Plastics Company, 20425, 55620
Champignon North America Inc, 2409
Champion America Inc, 20426
Champion Beverages, 2410
Champion Chemical Co, 20427, 42919
Champion Industries Inc, 20428, 42920
Champion Nutrition Inc, 2411, 42921
Champion Plastics, 20429, 42922
Champion Trading Corporation, 20430, 42923
Champlain Valley Apiaries, 2412
Champlain Valley Milling Corp, 2413
Champlin Co, 20431
Champoeg Wine Cellars Inc, 2414
Champon & Yung Inc, 40188
Champs Chicken, 2415
Chandler Food Sales Co, 40189
Chandler Foods Inc, 2416
Chandre Corporation, 20432
Chaney Instrument Co, 20433, 42924
Chang Food Company, 2417
Change Parts Inc, 20434
Channel Fish Processing, 2419, 42925
Channel Fish Processing Co Inc, 2418
Channing Rudd Cellars, 2420
Chantland Company, The, 20435, 42926
Chaparral Gardens, 2421
Chapman Corp, 20436
Chapman Fruit Co Inc, 40190
Chapman Manufacturing Co Inc, 20437, 42927
Chapman Sign, 20438
Chapman's Food Service, 55621
Chapman-Tait Brokerage, Inc., 40191
Chappaqua Crunch, 2422
Chappellet Winery, 2423
Char Crust, 2424
Char-Wil Canning Company, 2425
Charcuterie LaTour Eiffel, 2426, 42928
Charissa, 2427, 55622
Charles B. Mitchell Vineyards, 2428
Charles Beck Machine Corporation, 20439, 42929
Charles Beseler Company, 20440, 42930
Charles C. Parks Company, 55623
Charles Chocolates, 2429
Charles Craft Inc, 20441
Charles E. Roberts Company, 20442, 42931
Charles Engineering & Service, 20443
Charles Gratz Fire Protection, 20444
Charles H Baldwin & Sons, 2430, 20445, 42932
Charles H. Parks & Company, 2431
Charles Krug Winery, 2432
Charles Lapierre, 20446
Charles M. Schayer & Company, 51645
Charles Mayer Studios, 20447, 42933
Charles Pace & Assoc Inc, 40192
Charles Poultry Company, 2433
Charles R. Bell Limited, 40193
Charles Rockel & Son, 2434, 40194, 55624
Charles Ross & Son Co, 20448, 20449, 42934
Charles Spinetta Winery, 2435
Charles Stube Co Inc, 40195
Charles Tirschman Pallet Co, 20450

Charles Walker North America, 2436, 20451, 52761
Charles Wetgrove Company, 55625
Charleston Tea Plantation, 2437
Charlie Beigg's Sauce Company, 2438, 55626
Charlie Brown Sales Company, 40196
Charlie Palmer Group, 2439
Charlie's Country Sausage, 2440
Charlie's Pride, 2441, 42935
Charlie's Specialties Inc, 2442
Charlito's Cocina, 2443
Charlotte Tent & Awning, 20452
Charlotte's Confections, 2444
Charlton & Hill, 20453, 55627
Charlton Charters, 2445
Charlton Natural Foods, Inc., 2446
Charm Sciences Inc, 20454, 42936
Charmel Enterprises, 42937, 55628
Chart Applied Technologies, 20455
Chart Inc, 20456
Chart Industries Inc, 20457, 42938
Charter House, 20458
Chartrand Imports, 40197
Chartreuse Organic Tea, 2447
Chas Boggini Co., 2448, 42939
Chas. Wetterling & Sons, 55629
Chase & Poe Candy Co, 2449
Chase Brothers Dairy, 2450
Chase Doors, 20459, 20460
Chase Industries Inc, 20461, 42940
Chase Sales Company, 40198
Chase, Leavitt & Company, 51646
Chase-Doors, 20462, 42941
Chase-Goldenberg Associates, 40199
Chase-Logeman Corp, 20463, 42942
Chases Lobster Pound, 2451, 42943
Chaska Chocolate, 20464
Chàsquis Natural Foods, 2452
Chateau Anne Marie, 2453
Chateau Boswell Winery, 2454
Chateau Chevre Winery, 2455
Chateau des Charmes Wines, 2467
Chateau Diana Winery, 2456
Chateau Food Products Inc, 2457
Chateau Grand Traverse Winery, 2458
Chateau Julien Winery, 2459
Chateau LA Fayette Reneau, 2460
Chateau Montelena Winery, 2461
Chateau Morrisette Winery, 2462
Chateau Potelle Winery, 2463
Chateau Ra-Ha, 2464
Chateau Souverain, 2465
Chateau St Jean Winery, 2466
Chatelain Plastics, 20465
Chatfield & Woods Sack Company, 20466
Chatfield Dairy, 55630
Chatila's, 2468, 40200, 55631
Chatillon, 20467
Chatom Vineyards Inc, 2469
Chattanooga Bakery Inc, 2470
Chattanooga Button & Badge Company, 55632
Chattanooga Freight Bureau, 40201, 51647
Chattanooga Labeling Systems, 20468
Chattanooga Restaurant Supl, 55633
Chattanooga Rubber Stamp & Stencil Works, 20469
Chattem Chemicals Inc, 2471
Chattin Awning Company, 20470
Chatz Roasting Co, 2472
Chaucer Consumer Solutions, 2473
Chaucer Foods, Inc. USA, 2474, 42944
Chaucer Press Inc, 20471
Chauvin Coffee Corporation, 2475
Chazy Orchards, 2476
Cheating Gourmet, 2477
Chebe Bread Products, 2478, 55634
Check Savers Inc, 20472
Checker Bag Co, 20473, 42945
Checker Machine, 20474, 42946
Cheddar Box Cheese House, 2479
Cheese & Dairy Products, 40202

1367

All Companies Index

Cheese Factory, 2480
Cheese Merchants of America, 2481, 20475, 42947
Cheese Outlet Fresh Market, 20476
Cheese Shop, 55635
Cheese Straws & More, 2482
Cheesecake Etc Desserts, 2484
Cheesecake Factory Inc., 2485
Cheesecake Momma, 2486
CheeseLand, 2483
Cheeseland, Inc., 42948, 55636
Cheesemakers Inc, 20477
Cheeze Kurls, 2487
Chef America, 2488, 42949
Chef Hans' Gourmet Foods, 2489, 42950
Chef John Folse & Co, 55637
Chef Merito Inc, 2490, 42951
Chef Paul Prudhomme's Magic Seasonings Blends, 2491
Chef Philippe LLC, 2492
Chef Revival, 20478, 42952
Chef Salt, 2493
Chef Shamy Gourmet, 2494
Chef Shells Catering & Roadside Cafe, 2495
Chef Silvio's of Wooster Street, 2496
Chef Soraya, 2497
Chef Specialties, 20479, 42953
Chef Tim Foods, LLC, 2498
Chef Works, 42954
Chef Zachary's Gourmet Blended Spices, 2499
Chef's Choice by EdgeCraft, 42956
Chef's Choice Mesquite Charcoal, 20480, 42955, 55638
Chef's Cut: Real Jerky, 2500
Chef's Pride Gifts LLC, 2501, 55639
Chef's Requested Foods, 2502
Chef's Supply & Design, 55640
Chef-A-Roni Fancy Foods, 2503
Chefwear, 20481, 42957
Chefwise, 2504, 55641
Cheil Jedang Corporation, 20482
Chelan Fresh Marketing, 2505, 42958
Chell Brokerage Co, 40203
Chella's Dutch Delicacies, 2506
Chellino Cheese Co, 55642
Chelsea Flower Market, 2507
Chelsea Market Baskets, 55643
Chelsea Milling Co., 2508
Chelten House Products, 2509, 42959
Chem Care, 55644
Chem Mark International, 20483
Chem Pack Inc, 20484
Chem Pruf Door Co LTD, 20485
Chem-Mark of Buffalo, 55645
Chem-Tainer Industries Inc, 20486, 20487, 42960, 42961
Chemclean Corp, 20489, 42963
Chemco Products Inc, 20490
Chemcraft Industries Inc, 55646
Chemdet Inc, 20491, 42964
Chemetall, 20492
Chemetrics Inc, 20493
Chemex Division/International Housewares Corporation, 20494, 42965
Chemglass Life Sciences, 20495
Chemi-Graphic Inc, 20496
Chemicolloid Laboratories, Inc., 20497, 42966
Chemifax, 20498, 42967
Chemindustrial Systems Inc, 20499, 42968
Chemineer, 20500
Chemir Analytical Svc, 20501
Chempacific Corp, 2510
Chemroy Canada, 55647
ChemtranUSA.com, 20502
Chemtreat, 20503
ChemTreat, Inc., 20488, 42962
Chemtura Corp, 20504
Cheney Brothers Inc, 55648
Chep, 20505
CHEP Palleon Solutions, 20055

Cher-Make Sausage Co, 2511, 42969
Cheraw Packing Plant, 2512
Cherbogue Fisheries, 2513, 42970
Cherchies, 2514
Cheri's Desert Harvest, 2515
Cheribundi, 2516
Cherith Valley Gardens, 2517, 42971
Chernoff Sales, 40204, 55649
Cherokee Trading Co, 42972
Cherry Central Cooperative, Inc., 2518, 42973, 55650
Cherry Hill Orchards, 2519
Cherry Hut, 2520
Cherry Lane Frozen Fruits, 2521
Cherry Moon Farms, 2522, 55651
Cherry's Industrial Eqpt Corp, 20506, 42974
Cherrybrook Kitchen, 2523
Cherryfield Foods, 2524
Cherryvale Farms, 2525
Cheryl's Cookies, 2526, 55652
Chesapeake Bay Crab Cakes & More, 2527
Chesapeake Spice Company, 2528, 42975
Cheshire Signs, 20507
Chesmont Engineering Co Inc, 20508
Chester Dairy Co, 2529
Chester Hoist, 20509, 42976
Chester Inc Information, 2530, 42977
Chester Plastics, 20510, 42978
Chester River Clam Co, 2531, 55653
Chester Transfer, 51648
Chester W. Howeth & Brother, 2532
Chester's International , LLC, 2533, 42979
Chester-Jensen Co., Inc., 2534, 20511, 42980
Chesterfield Awning Co, 20512, 20513
Chestertown Natural Foods, 2535
Chestnut Identity Appare, Inc., 42981
Chestnut Labs, 20514
Chestnut Mountain Winery, 2536
Chevalier Chocolates, 2537
Chevron Global Lubricants, 20515
Chewys Rugulach, 2538
Chex Finer Foods Inc 2539, 42982
Chia Corp USA, 42983
Chia I Foods Company, 42984, 55654
Chic Naturals, 2540
Chicago 58 Food Products, 2541, 42985
Chicago Automated Labeling Inc, 20516
Chicago Avenue Pizza, 2542
Chicago Bar & Restaurant Supply, 55655
Chicago Coffee Roastery, 2543, 55656
Chicago Conveyor Corporation, 20517
Chicago Dowel Co Inc, 20518
Chicago Food Corporation, 42986, 55657
Chicago Food Market, 2544, 55658
Chicago Gourmet Steaks, 2545
Chicago Importing Company, 42987
Chicago Ink & Research Co, 20519
Chicago Market Company, 55659
Chicago Meat Authority Inc, 2546, 42988
Chicago Pastry, 2547
Chicago Premier Meats, 2548, 55660
Chicago Scale & Slicer Company, 20520, 42989
Chicago Show Inc, 20521
Chicago Stainless Eqpt Inc, 20522, 42990
Chicago Steaks, 2549, 55661
Chicago Trashpacker Corporation, 20523
Chicago Vegan Foods, 2550
Chicago Vendor Supply, 55662
Chicagoland Quad Cities Express, 52762
Chicama Vineyards, 2551
Chick-Fil-A Inc., 2552
Chickadee Products, 20524
Chickapea, 2553
Chickasaw Broom Mfg Co Inc, 20525
Chickasaw Trading Company, 2554, 42991
Chicken Of The Sea, 2555, 42992
Chicken Salad Chick, 2556
Chico Nut Company, 2557, 42993
Chico Pops, 2558

Chicopee Provision Co Inc, 2559
Chief Industries, 20526, 42994
Chief Wenatchee, 2560, 42995
Chieftain Wild Rice, 2561
Chihon Biotechnology Co., Ltd., 2562
CHiKPRO, 1951, 55444
Chil-Con Products, 20527, 42996
Chilay Corporation, 40205
Childlife, 2563
Childres Custom Canvas Prods, 20528
Chile Guy, 42997, 55663
Chilean Seafood Exchange, 42998
Chili - Mex, 2564
Chili Dude, 2565
Chili Plastics, 20529
Chill & Moore, 2566, 42999
Chill Pop, 2567
Chill Rite Mfg, 20530
Chilled Solutions LLC, 51649, 52763
Chillers Solutions, 20531, 43000
Chilson's Shops Inc, 20532
Chilton Consulting Group, 20533
Chimayo To Go / Cibolo Junction, 2568
Chimere Winery, 2569
China D Food Service, 20534, 55664
China Food Merchant Corporation, 20535
China Lenox Incorporated, 20536, 43001
China Mist Brands, 2570, 43002
China Pharmaceutical Enterprises, 2571, 43003
China Products, 43004
Chincoteague Seafood Co Inc, 2572, 43005
Chinese Spaghetti Factory, 2573
Chinese Trading Company, 55665
Chinet Company, 20537, 20538
Chino Meat Provision Corporation, 2574
Chino Valley Dairy, 2575
Chino Valley Ranchers, 2576
Chino Works America Inc, 20539
Chip Steak & Provision Co, 2577, 55666
Chip'n Dipped Cookie Co, 2578
Chipmaker Tooling Supply, 20540, 43006
Chipper Snax, 2579
Chipurnoi Inc, 43007, 55667
Chiquita Brands LLC., 2580, 20541, 43008
Chisesi Brothers Meat Packing, 2581
Chisholm Bakery, 2582
CHL Systems, 20056
Chloe's Fruit, 2583
Chlorinators Inc, 20542, 43009
CHLU International, 42695, 55443
Chmura's Bakery, 2584
CHO America, 1946
Chobani, Inc., 2585
ChocAlive, 2586, 55668
Chock Full O'Nuts, 2587, 43010
Choclatique, 2588
Choco Finesse, LLC, 2589
Chocoholics Divine Desserts, 2591
Chocolat, 2592
Chocolat Belge Heyez, 2593, 43011
Chocolat Jean Talon, 2594
Chocolat Michel Cluizel, 2595
Chocolat Moderne, LLC., 2596
Chocolate By Design Inc, 2597, 2598
Chocolate Chix, 2599
Chocolate Chocolate Chocolate, 2600
Chocolate Concepts, 20543, 43012
Chocolate Creations, 2601
Chocolate Delivery Systems Inc, 2602
Chocolate Fantasies, 2603
Chocolate House, 2604, 43013
Chocolate Maven, 2605, 55669
Chocolate Moon, 2606
Chocolate Shoppe Ice Cream Co, 2607
Chocolate Signatures LP, 2608
Chocolate Smith, 2609
Chocolate Soup, 2610
Chocolate Stars USA, 43014
Chocolate Street of Hartville, 2611, 43015
Chocolate Studio, 2612

Chocolate Works, 2613, 55670
Chocolaterie Bernard Callebaut, 2614, 43016
Chocolaterie Stam, 2615
Chocolates a La Carte, 2619, 43017
Chocolates by Mark, 2620, 55671
Chocolates By Mr Roberts, 2616
Chocolates El Rey, Inc, 2617
Chocolates Turin, 2618
Chocolati Handmade Chocolates, 2621
Chocolatier, 2622
Chocolove, 2623
ChocoME US LLC, 2590
Chocomize, 2624
Chocopologie By Knipschildt, 2625
Choctal, 2626
Choctaw Maid Farms, 2627, 43018
Choctaw Transportation Co Inc, 51650
Choctaw-Kaul Distribution Company, 20544
Choice Food Distributors LLC, 2628
Choice Food Group Inc, 2629, 55672
Choice of Vermont, 2631
Choice Organic Teas, 2630, 43019
Choice Reefer Systems, 51651
Choice Restaurant Equipment, 55673
Choklit Molds LTD, 20545, 43020
Chomps, 2632
Chong Imports, 43021
Chong Mei Trading, 2633, 55674
Chooljian Bros Packing Co, 2634, 43022
Chop-Rite Two Inc, 20546
Chops Snacks, 2635
Chord Engineering, 20547
Chore-Boy Corporation, 20548
Chori America, 20549
Chosen Foods, Inc., 2636
Chouinard Vineyards & Winery, 2637
Choyce Produce, 2638, 43023, 55675
Chozen Ice Cream, 2639
CHR Foods, 1947
Chr Hansen Inc, 2640
Chris Candies Inc, 2641
Chris Hansen Seafood, 2642, 55676
Chris' Farm Stand, 2643
Chris's Cookies, 2644
Christensen Ridge Winery, 2645
Christian Brokerage Company/Industrial & Food, 40206
Christian County Grain Inc, 55677
Christianson Systems Inc, 20550, 43024
Christie Cookie, 2646
Christie's, 2647
Christie-Brown, 2648
Christine & Rob's Inc, 2649
Christine Woods Winery, 2650
Christman Screenprint Inc, 20551
Christmas Point Wild Rice Co, 2651
Christopher Creek Winery, 2652
Christopher Joseph Brewing Company, 2653
Christopher Norman Chocolates, 2654
Christopher Ranch LLC, 2655, 43025
Christopher Wholesalers, 55678
Christopher's Herb Shop, 2656, 40207, 55679
Christy Industries Inc, 20552, 43026, 55680
Christy Machine Co, 20553, 43027
Christy Wild Blueberry Farms, 2657, 43028
Chroma Tone, 20554
Chromalox Inc, 20555, 43029
Chronos Richardson, 20556
Chroust Associates International, 20557
Chrysler & Koppin Co, 20558
CHS Inc., 1948, 20057, 42696, 51609
CHS Sunflower, 1949, 42697
CHS Sunprairie, 1950, 42698
Chu's Packaging Supplies, 20559
Chuao Chocolatier, 2658
Chuck Batcheller Company, 40208
Chuck's Seafoods, 2659
Chuckrow Sales LLC, 40209
Chudabeef Jerky Co., 2660

All Companies Index

Chudleigh's, 2661
Chugwater Chili, 2662
Chukar Cherries, 2663
Chunco Foods Inc, 2664
Chungs Gourmet Foods, 2665
Chuppa Knife Manufacturing, 20560, 43030
Church & Dwight Co., Inc., 2666, 20561, 43031, 55681
Church Offset Printing Inc, 20562
Church Point Wholesale Grocer, 55682
Churny Company, 2667, 2668
Churro Corporation, 55683
Ciao Bella Gelato Company, 2669
Ciao Imports, 43032
Cibao Meat Products Inc, 2670, 43033
Cibaria International, 2671, 55684
Cibo Vita, 2672
CIDA, 20058
CideRoad, LLC, 2673
Cielo Foods, 2674, 20564, 55685
Cienega Valley Winery/DeRose, 2675
Cifelli & Sons Inc, 2676
CII Food Svc Design, 20059
Cilurzo Vineyards & Winery, 55686
CIM Bakery Equipment of USA, 20060
CiMa-Pak Corp., 20563
Cimarron Cellars, 2677
Cimino Box & Pallet Co, 20565
Cimpl Meats, 2678
Cin-Made Packaging Group, 20566, 43034
Cincinnati Convertors Inc, 20567
Cincinnati Foam Products, 20568
Cincinnati Freezer Corp, 52764
Cincinnati Industrial Machry, 20569, 20570, 43035
Cincinnati Packaging And Distribution, 51652
Cincinnati Preserving Co, 2679, 43036
Cinderella Cheese Cake Co, 2680
Cinelli Esperia, 20571, 43037
Cinnabar Specialty Foods Inc, 2681, 43038
Cinnabar Winery, 2682
Cinnamon Bakery, 2683
Cintas Corp, 20572
Cintex of America, 20573, 43039
Cipriani, 20574, 43040, 55687
Cipriani's Spaghetti & Sauce Company, 2684, 43041
Ciranda Inc., 20575, 52765
Circle B Ranch, 2685, 55688
Circle Delivery, 51653
Circle Packaging Machinery Inc, 20576
Circle R Ranch, 2686
Circle V Meats, 2687
Circle Valley Produce LLC, 2688, 43042
Circuits & Systems Inc, 20577, 43043
Circus Man Ice Cream Corporation, 2689
Cirelli Foods, 55689
Ciro Foods, 2690, 43044, 55690
Cisco Brewers, 2691, 43045
Cisco Eagle, 20578
Cisco-Eagle, 55691
Cisse Trading Co, 2692
Citadel Computer Corporation, 20579
Citadelle Maple Syrup Producers' Cooperative, 2693, 43046
Citect Inc, 20580
Citra-Tech, 20581, 43047
Citrico, 2694, 43048
Citrin-Pitoscia Company, 40210
Citrobio Inc, 55692
Citromax Flavors Inc, 2695
Citrop Inc, 2696
Citrosuco North America Inc, 2697, 43049
Citrus and Allied Essences, 2700, 20582, 43051
Citrus International, 2698
Citrus Service, 2699, 43050
Citterio USA, 2701, 43052
City Bakery, 2702
City Bakery Cafe, 2703

City Bean, 2704
City Box Company, 20583
City Brewing Company, 2705, 43053, 52766
City Cafe & Bakery, 2706
City Canvas, 20584
City Deli Distributing, 55693
City Espresso Roasting Company, 55694
City Farm/Rocky Peanut Company, 2707
City Fish Sales, 55695
City Foods Inc, 2708, 43054
City Grafx, 20585, 43055
City Line Food Distributors, 55696
City Market, 2709, 55697
City Neon Sign Company, 20586
City Packing Company, 52767, 55698
City Produce Co, 55699
City Saucery, 2710
City Sign Svc Inc, 20587
City Signs LLC, 20588
City Stamp & Seal Co, 20589
City Wholesale Company, 55700
City Wide Produce Distributors, 55701
City-Long Beach Pubc Library, 20590
CJ America, 1952, 42699
CJ Eaton Brokerage, 40169
CJ Foods, 1953
CJ Omni, 1954, 42700
CJ's Seafood, 1955
CJI Group LTD, 42701
CJI Process Systems, 55445
CK Living LLC, 1956
CK Products, 20061, 42702, 55446
CKS Packaging, 20062
CL&D Graphics, 20063, 42703
Clabber Girl Corporation, 2711, 43056
Claeys Candy Inc, 2712
Claiborne & Churchill Vintners, 2713
Claire Manufacturing Company, 20591
Clamco Corporation, 20592, 43057
Clamp Swing Pricing Co Inc, 20593, 43058
Clanton & Company, 20594
Clara Foods, 2714, 2715
CLARCOR Air Filtration Prods, 20064
Clarden Trucking, 51654
Claremont Herbal Health, 55702
Clarence Mayfield Produce Company, 55703
Clarendon Flavor Engineering, 2716, 43059
Clariant, 2717
Claridge Products & Equipment, 20595, 43060
Clarion Fruit Co, 55704
Clark Caster Company, 20596
Clark Food Service Equipment, 55705
Clark Foodservice Equipment, 55706
Clark Meat Servicing, 55707
Clark Restaurant Svc, 55708
Clark Richardson-Biskup, 20597
Clark Spring Water Co, 2718
Clark's Wholesale Meats, 55709
Clark-Cooper Division Magnatrol Valve Corporation, 20598, 43061
Clarke American Sanders, 20599, 43062
Clarke J F Corp, 2719
Clarkson Company, 55710
Clarkson Grain Co Inc, 43063, 55711
Clarkson Scottish Bakery, 2720, 43064
Clarkson Supply, 20600
Clarmil Manufacturing Corp, 2721
Clasen Quality Chocolate, 2722
Class Produce Group LLC, 55712
Classic Commissary, 2723
Classic Confectionery, 2724
Classic Cookings, LLC, 2725
Classic Cuisine Foods, 40211
Classic Delight Inc, 2726
Classic Flavors & Fragrances, 2727, 43065
Classic Foods, 2728
Classic Signs Inc, 20601
Classic Tea, 2729, 43066
Classico Seating, 20602, 43067

Classy Basket, 20603
Classy Delites, 2730
Claude Neon Signs, 20604
Claudia B Chocolates, 2731
Clauson Cold & Cooler, 52768
Clauss Tools, 20605
Clawson Container Company, 20606
Clawson Machine Co Inc, 20607, 43068
Claxton Bakery Inc, 2732, 43069
Claxton Cold Storage, 52769
Clay Center Locker Plant, 2733
Clayton & Lambert Manufacturing, 20608, 43070
Clayton Coffee & Tea, 2734
Clayton Corp., 20609, 43071
Clayton Industries, 20610, 43072
Clayton L. Hagy & Son, 20611
Clayton Manufacturing Company, 20612
Clayton's Crab Co, 2735, 55713
Clean Room Products, 20613
Clean That Pot, 20614
Clean Water Systems, 20615, 43073
Clean Water Technology, 20616, 43074
Clean-All Pool Svc, 20617
Cleanfish Inc, 2736
Cleanfreak, 20618, 52770
Clear Bags, 20619
Clear Creek Distillery, 2737
Clear Lam Packaging, 20620
Clear Mountain Coffee Company, 2738
Clear Products Inc., 2739, 20621
Clear Springs Foods Inc., 2740, 40212, 43075
Clear View Bag Co Inc Of Nc, 20622
Clear View Bag Company, 20623
Clear-Vu Industries, 2741
Clearbrook Farms, 55714
Clearly Canadian Beverage Corporation, 2742, 43076
Clearly Kombucha, 2743
Clearr Corporation, 20625
Cleartec Packaging, 20626
Clearwater Coffee Company, 2744
Clearwater Fine Foods, 2745, 43077
Clearwater Packaging Inc, 20627, 43078
Clearwater Paper Corporation, 20628, 43079
ClearWater Tech LLC, 20624
Cleasby Manufacturing Co, 20629
Cleaver-Brooks Inc, 20630, 43080
CLECO Systems, 20065
Cleco Systems, 20631
Cleland Manufacturing Company, 20632, 43081
Cleland Sales Corp, 20633, 43082
Clem Becker Meats, 2746
Clem's Seafood & Specialties, 2747, 55715
Clemens Family Corporation, 2748
Clement's Pastry Shops Inc, 2749, 55716
Clements Distribution Company, 55717
Clements Foods Co, 2750, 43083
Clements Industries Inc, 20634
Clements Stella Marketing, 40213
Clemmy's, 2751
Clemson Bros. Brewery, 2752
Clerestory, 20635
Cleveland Canvas Goods Mfg Co, 20636
Cleveland Kraut, 2753
Cleveland Menu Printing, 20637, 43084
Cleveland Metal Stamping Company, 20638, 43085
Cleveland Mop Manufacturing Company, 20639
Cleveland Motion Controls, 20640
Cleveland Plastic Films, 20641
Cleveland Range, 20642, 43086
Cleveland Specialties Co, 20643, 43087
Cleveland Syrup Corporation, 2754
Cleveland Vibrator Co, 20644
Cleveland Wire Cloth & Mfg Co, 20645, 43088
Cleveland-Eastern Mixers, 20646, 43089
Clevenger Frable Lavallee, 20647
Clextral USA, 20648, 43090

Clic International Inc, 2755
Clif Bar & Co, 2756, 55718
Cliff Lede Vineyards, 2757
Clifford D. Fite, 55719
Clifton Fruit & Produce, 55720
Clifty Farm Country Meats, 2758
Climate Master Inc, 20649, 43091
Climax Industries, 20650
Climax Packaging Machinery, 20651, 43092
Cline Cellars, 2759
Clinton St Baking Co, 2760, 55721
Clinton Vineyards Inc, 2761
Clio Snacks, 2762
Clipco, 20652
Clippard Instrument Lab Inc, 20653
Clipper Belt Lacer Company, 20654, 43093
Clipper City Brewing, 2763
Clipper Mill, 40214, 55722
Clipper Seafood, 43094, 55723
Clock Associates, 20655
Clofine Dairy Products Inc, 2764, 20656, 40215, 43095, 55724
Clogmaster, 40216, 55725
Cloister Honey LLC, 2765
Clorox Company, 2766, 20657
Clos Du Bois Winery, 2767
Clos Du Lac Cellars, 2768
Clos Du Val Co LTD, 2769, 43096
Clos Pegase Winery, 2770
Clos Saint-Denis, 2771
Closure Systems Intl Inc, 20658
Cloud Inc, 20659, 43097
Cloud Nine, 2772, 43098
Cloud Top, 2773
Cloud's Meat Processing, 2774
Cloudstone Vineyards, 2775
Cloudy & Britton, 20660
Clougherty Packing LLC, 2776
Clover Blossom Honey, 2777
Clover Farms Dairy Co Inc, 2778
Clover Hill Vineyards & Winery, 2779
Clover Leaf Cheese, 2780, 55726
Clover Leaf Seafoods, 55727
Clover Sonoma, 2781
Clover Stornetta Farms Inc, 2782
Cloverdale Foods, 2783, 43099, 55728
Cloverhill Bakery-Vend Corporation, 2784, 43100
Cloverland Dairy, 2785
Cloverland/Green Spring Dairy, 2786
Cloverleaf Cold Storage, 52771, 52772, 52773, 52774, 52775, 52776, 52777, 52778, 52779, 52780, 52781, 52782, 52783, 52784, 52785, 52786, 52787, 52788, 52789, 52790, 52791, 52792, 52793
Clovervale Farms, 2787
Clown Global Brands, 2788, 43101
Club Chef LLC, 2789
Clutter Farms, 2790
CLVMarketing, 40170
Clyde Bergemann Eec, 20661
Clyde's Delicious Donuts, 2791
Clyde's Italian & German Sausage, 2792
CM Ambrose Company, 20066
CM Packaging, 20067
Cma Dishmachines, 20662, 43102
CMA Global Partners/German Foods LLC, 1957
CMA Group, 20068
CMC America Corporation, 20069
CMD Corp, 20070, 20071
CMD Corporation, 20072
CMF Corp, 20073
CMS Fine Foods, 1958, 20074
CMT, 20075, 42704
CMT Packaging & Designs,Inc., 40171, 51610
CNL Beverage Property Group, 20076
CNS Confectionery Products, 1959, 42705
CO YO, 1960
Co-Rect Products Inc, 20663, 43103

1369

All Companies Index

Co-Sales De Credico, 40217
Coach Farm Enterprises, 2793
Coach Sposato's Bar-B-Que, 2794
Coach's Oats, 2795
Coast Controls Inc, 20664
Coast Label Co, 20665
Coast Packing Co, 2796, 20666
Coast Paper Box Company, 20667
Coast Scientific, 20668, 43104
Coast Seafoods Company, 2797, 43105
Coast Signs & Graphics, 20669
Coast to Coast Foods Group, 55729
Coastal Beverage LTD, 55730
Coastal Canvas Products, 20670
Coastal Classics, 2798
Coastal Cocktails, 2799
Coastal Cold Storage Inc, 51655, 52794
Coastal Commodities, 40218
Coastal Goods, 2800
Coastal Mechanical Svc Inc, 20671
Coastal Pallet Corp, 20672
Coastal Pride Co Inc, 40219
Coastal Products Company, 20673
Coastal Promotions, Inc., 2801
Coastal Seafood Partners, 2802, 55731
Coastal Seafood Processors, 2803, 55732
Coastal Seafoods, 2804, 43106
Coastline Equipment Inc, 20674
Coastlog Industries, 2805
Coastside Lobster Company, 2806, 43107, 55733
Coating Place Inc, 43108
Coating Technologies International, 20675
Coats American Industrial, 20676
Coats North America, 20677
Cobatco, 20678, 43109
Cobb & Zimmer, 20679
Cobb Hill Cheese, 2807
Cobb Sign Co Inc, 20680
Cober Electronics, Inc., 20681, 43110
Cobitco Inc, 20682
Coblentz Brothers Inc, 20683
Cobler Food Sales, 40220
Cobraz Brazilian Coffee, 2808
Cobscook Bay Seafood, 2809, 55734
Coburn Company, 20684, 43111
Coby's Cookies, 2810, 43112
Coca-Cola Beverages Northeast, 2811, 55735
Coca-Cola Bottling Co. Consolidated, 2812, 55736
Coca-Cola Bottling Company UNITED, Inc., 2813, 55737
Coca-Cola Co., 2814
Coca-Cola European Partners, 2815, 20685, 43113, 55738
Cochran Brothers Company, 55739
Cocina De Mino, 2816
Cockrell Banana, 55740
Cockrell Distribution System, 51656, 52795
Cockrell's Creek Seafood & Deli, 55741
Cocktail Crate, 2817
Cocktail Kits 2 Go LLC, 2818
Coco International, 2819
Coco Lopez Inc, 2820, 43114
Coco Polo, 2821
Cocoa Metro, 2822
Cocoa Parlor, 2823
CocoaPlanet Inc., 2824
Cocolalla Winery, 2825
Cocomels by JJ's Sweets, 2826
Cocomira Confections, 2827
Coconut Beach, 2828
Coconut Bliss, 2829
Coconut Code, 20686
Coconut Collaborative, 2830
Coddington Lumber Co, 20687
Codeck Manufacturing, 20688
Codema, 20689, 43115
Coding Products, 20690
Codinos Food Inc, 2831
Cody Consulting Services, 20691
Coe & Dru Inc, 20692

Coextruded Packaging Technologies, 20693
Coffee Associates, 2832
Coffee Barrel, 2833
Coffee Bean, 2834
Coffee Bean & Tea Leaf, 2835
Coffee Bean Intl, 2836, 43116
Coffee Bean of Leesburg, 2837
Coffee Beanery LTD, 2838
Coffee Break Systems, 55742
Coffee Brothers Inc, 2839, 20694, 43117, 55743
Coffee Butler Service, 2840
Coffee Culture-A House, 2841
Coffee Enterprises, 2842, 20695
Coffee Exchange, 2843, 43118
Coffee Express Roasting Co, 2844, 20696, 43119, 55744
Coffee Expresso & Service, 55745
Coffee Globe LLC, 2845
Coffee Grounds, 2846
Coffee Heaven, 55746
Coffee Holding Co Inc, 2847
Coffee Inns, 43120
Coffee Masters, 2848
Coffee Mill Roastery, 2849
Coffee Mill Roasting Company, 2850
Coffee Millers & Roasters, 2851
Coffee Millers & Roasting, 2852
Coffee People, 2853
Coffee PER, 20697
Coffee Process, 2854
Coffee Processing Systems, 20698
Coffee Reserve, 2855
Coffee Roasters Inc, 2856
Coffee Roasters Of New Orleans, 2857
Coffee Roasters of New Orleans, 2858
Coffee Sock Company, 20699
Coffee Up, 2859
Coffee Works, 2860
Coffee-Inns of America, 2700
Coffeeco, 43121
Cog-Veyor Systems, Inc., 20701
Cogent Technologies, 55747
Cognis, 2861
Cognitive, 20702
Cohen Foods, 55748
Cohen's Bakery, 2862
Cohen's Coddies Company, 40221
Cohen's Original Tasty Coddie, 2863
Cohokia Bake Mark, 55749
Colavita USA, 2864, 43122, 55750
Colbert Packaging Corp, 20703, 20704, 20705
Colborne Foodbotics, 20706
Colbourne Seafood, 55751
Colchester Bakery, 2865
Colchester Foods, 2866, 43123
Cold Brew EvyTea, 2867
Cold Chain Technologies, 20707, 43124
Cold Fusion Foods, 2868
Cold Hollow Cider Mill, 2869, 43125, 55752
Cold Jet, LLC, 20708, 43126
Cold Spring Bakery Inc, 2870
Cold Storage, 52796
Cold Storage Building Products, 20709
Coldani Olive Ranch LLC, 2871
Colder Products Co, 20711
Coldmatic Building Systems, 20712
Coldmatic Refrigeration, 20713, 43128
ColdStor LLC, 52797
Coldstream Products Corporation, 20714, 43129
Coldwater Fish Farms, 2872
ColdZone, 20710, 43127
Cole Brothers & Fox Company, 55753
Cole's Quality Foods, 2873
Cole-Parmer Instrument Co LLC, 20715
Colecraft Commercial Furnishings, 20716
Colectivo Coffee, 2874
Coleman Manufacturing Co Inc, 20717, 43130
Coleman Natural, 2875, 43131

Coleman Resources, 20718
Coleman Rubber Stamps, 20719
Coley Industries, 20720
Colgate-Palmolive Professional Products Group, 20721, 43132
Colgin Co, 2876
Colibri Pepper Company, 2877
Colin Ingram, 2878, 43133
Collaborative Advantage Marketing, 2879
Collectors Gallery, 20722
College Coffee Roaster, 2880
Collegeville Flag & Manufacturing Company, 20723
Colliers International, 20724
Collin Street Bakery, 2881, 43134
Collins & Aikman, 20725, 43135
Collins & Company, 55754
Collins Associates, 40222
Collins Cavier Co, 2882
Collins International, 43136
Collins Manufacturing Company Ltd, 20726
Collins Technical, 20727
Colmac Coil Mfg Inc, 20728
Colmar Storage Co Warehouse, 20729
Coloma Frozen Foods Inc, 2883, 43137
Colombian Coffee Federation, 43138
Colombina Candy Company, 43139
Colombo Bakery, 2884
Colombo Importing US IncEmma & Casa Italia, 43140
Colombo Services, 51657
Colon Brothers, 40223
Colonial Coffee Roasters Inc, 2885, 43141, 55755
Colonial Cookies, Ltd, 2886
Colonial Freight Systems, 51658
Colonial Marketing Assoc, 20730
Colonial Paper Company, 20731
Colonial Transparent Products Company, 20732
Colonna Brothers Inc, 2887
Colony Brands Inc, 2888, 20733, 52798, 55756
Colony Brokerage Company, 40224
Colony Foods, 2889, 55757
Color Ad Tech Signs, 20734
Color Box, 20735, 43142
Color Carton Corp, 20736
Color Communications Inc, 20737
Color Garden, 2890
Color-Box Inc, 20738
Color-Ons, 43143
Colorado Boxed Beef Company, 55758, 55759, 55760, 55761
Colorado Cellars, 2893
Colorado Chemical Company, 55762
Colorado Cold Storage, 52799
Colorado Hemp Honey, 2894
Colorado Mountain Jams & Jellies, 2895
Colorado Nut Co, 2896, 20739, 43144, 55763
Colorado Popcorn Co, 2897
Colorado Potato Growers Exchange, 55764
Colorado Restaurant Supply, 55765
Colorado Salsa Company, 2898
Colorado Spice Co, 2899
Colorado Sweet Gold, 2900
Colorcon Inc, 20740, 43145
ColorKitchen, 2891
ColorMaker, Inc., 2892
Colors Gourmet Pizza, 2901, 55766
Colortec Associates Inc, 20741
Colson Caster Corp, 20742, 43146
Colter & Peterson, 20743
Colteryahn Dairy, 2902
Colts Chocolates, 2903
Coltsfoot/Golden Eagle Herb, 2904
Columbia Cheese, 52800
Columbia Empire Farms Inc, 2905
Columbia Equipment & Finance, 20744
Columbia Food Laboratories, 43147
Columbia Food Machinery Inc, 40225

Columbia Jet/JPL, 20745
Columbia Labeling Machinery, 20746, 43148
Columbia Lighting, 20747, 43149
Columbia Machine Inc, 20748
Columbia Okura LLC, 20749
Columbia Packing Co Inc, 2906
Columbia Paper Company, 55767
Columbia Phyto Technology, 2907
Columbia Restaurant & Bar Supply Co., 55768
Columbia Scale Company, 55769
Columbia Valley Farms Inc., 2908
Columbia Valley Wine Warehouse, 52801
Columbia Winery, 2909
Columbian Logistics Network, 51659, 52802, 52803
Columbian TecTank, 20750, 43150
Columbine Confections LLC, 2910
Columbus Brewing Co, 2911
Columbus Cold Storage I nc., 52804
Columbus Instruments, 20751, 43151
Columbus McKinnon Corporation, 20752, 43152
Columbus Paperbox Company, 20753
Columbus Salame, 2912
Columbus Vegetable Oils, 2913
Com-Pac International Inc, 20754
Com-Pak International, 20755, 55770
Comalex, 20756
Comanche Tortilla Factory, 2914
Comanzo & Company Specialty Bakers, 2915
Comark Instruments, 20757, 43153
Comasec Safety, Inc., 20758, 43154
Comax Flavors, 2916, 20759
Combake International, 20760
Combi Packaging Systems LLC, 20761, 43155
Combined Computer Resource, 20762
Combustion Systems Sales, 20763
Comco Signs, 20764
Comeau's Seafoods, 2917, 43156
Comeaux's, 2918
Comet Signs, 20765
Comfort Foods, 2919
Comissos Cash & Carry, 55771, 55772, 55773, 55774
Comm-Pak, 20766
Command Belt Cleaning Systems, 20767
Command Communications, 20768, 43157
Command Electronics Inc, 20769, 43158
Command Line Corporation, 20770
Command Packaging, 20771
Commencement Bay Corrugated, 20772, 43159
Commerce Express Inc, 51660
Commercial Appliance Svc, 55775
Commercial Bakeries, 2920
Commercial Cold Storage, 51661, 52805
Commercial Corrugated Co Inc, 20773
Commercial Creamery Co, 2921, 20774, 43160
Commercial Dehydrator Systems, 20775, 43161
Commercial Distribution Ctr, 51662, 52806
Commercial Envelope Manufacturing Company, 20776
Commercial Furniture Group Inc, 20777, 43162
Commercial Kitchen Co, 20778
Commercial Kitchens Reps Inc, 40226
Commercial Lighting Design, 20779, 43163
Commercial Manufacturing, 20780, 43164
Commercial Packaging, 20781
Commercial Printing Company, 20782
Commercial Refrigeration Service, Inc., 20783, 43165
Commercial Seating Specialists, 20784
Commercial Testing Lab Inc, 20785
Commercial Transport Inc, 51663

1370

All Companies Index

Commercial Warehouse Co, 51664, 52807
Commissariat Imports, 2922, 43166
Commissos Cash & Carry, 55776
Commodities Assistance Corporation, 55777
Commodities Marketing Inc, 2923, 40227, 43167, 55778
Commodity Traders International, 20786, 43168
Common Folk Farm, 2924, 43169
Common Sense Natural Soap & Bodycare Products, 20787
Commonwealth Inc, 51665, 52808
Commonwealth Warehouse & Storage, 52809
Community Bakeries, 2925
Community Coffee Co., 2926, 43170, 55779
Community Mill & Bean, 2927
Community Orchards, 2928
Comobar LLC, 43171
Compacker Systems LLC, 20788, 43172
Compact Industries Inc, 20789, 43173
Compact Mold, 20790
Compactors Inc, 20791, 43174
Compania De Comercio, 43175
Company of a Philadelphia Gentleman, 2929
Compass Concepts, 55780
Compass Consolidators, 51666
Compass Forwarding Co Inc, 51667
Compass Group Canada, 20792
Compass Minerals, 2930
Compatible Components Corporation, 20793
Complete Automation, 20794
Complete Packaging & Shipping, 20795, 43176
Complete Packaging Solutions, 20796
Complete Packaging Systems, 20797
Complex Steel & Wire Corp, 20798
Compliance Control Inc, 20799, 43177
Component Hardware Group Inc, 20800, 43178
Composite Can & Tube Institute, 20801
Composition Materials Co Inc, 20802, 43179, 55781
Comprehensive Lighting Svc, 55782
COMPRESSOR Engrg. Corp., 20077
Compris Technologies, 20803, 43180
Compton Dairy, 2931
Compton Transfer Storage Co, 52810
Compusense Inc., 20804
Computer Aid Inc, 20805
Computer Aided Marketing, 20806
Computer Assocs. Intl., 20807
Computer Communications Specialists, 20808
Computer Controlled Machines, 20809, 43181
Computer Group, 20810
Computerized Machinery Syts, 20811, 43182, 55783
Computerway Food Systems, 20812
Computrition, 20813, 43183
Computype Inc, 20814, 43184
Comstar Printing Solutions, 20815
Comstock Castle Stove Co, 20816, 43185
Comte Cheese Association, 2932
Comtec Industries, 20817, 43186
Comtek Systems, 20818
Comus Restaurant Systems, 20819, 43187
Comvita USA, 2933
Con Agra Foods Inc, 2934
Con Agra Snack Foods, 2935, 43188
Con Yeager Spice Co, 2936
Con-tech/Conservation Technology, 20820, 43189
Conagra Brands Canada, 2938, 55784
Conagra Brands Inc, 2939, 20821, 43191
Conagra Foodservice, 2940, 20822, 43192
Conam Inspection, 20823

Conatech Consulting Group, Inc, 20824
Conax Buffalo Technologies, 20825, 43193
Conbraco Industries Inc, 20826
Conca D'Oro Importers, 43194, 55785
Concannon Vineyard, 2941, 43195
Concept Equipment Corporation, 55786
Concept Food Brokers, 40228
Concept Food Sales, 40229
Concept Foods Inc, 20827
Concept Hospitality Group, 20828
Concepts & Design International, Ltd, 20829
Concession & Restaurant Supply, 55787
Conchita Foods Inc, 43196, 55788
Concho Valley Pecan Company, 55789
Concord Chemical Co Inc, 20830
Concord Farms, 2942
Concord Foods Co, 55790
Concord Foods, LLC, 2943, 55791
Concord Import, 52811, 55792
Concord National, 40230, 40231, 40232, 40233, 40234, 40235
Concord Sales-Prairies, 40236
Conductive Containers Inc, 20831, 43197
Conecuh Sausage Co, 2944
Conesco Conveyor Corporation, 20833
Conestoga Cold Storage, 52812, 52813, 52814
ConeTech, 20832
Coney Island Classics, 2945, 55793
Confecco, 55794
Confection Art Inc, 2946, 20834
Confectionately Yours LTD, 2947
Confederation Freezers, 52815, 52816
Conflex Incorporated, 20835
Conflex, Inc., 20836, 43198
Conflow Technologies, Inc., 20837, 43199
Confoco USA, Inc., 2948, 55795
Congdon Orchards Inc., 2949
Congent Technologies, 20838
Conger Industries Inc, 55796
Conifer Foods, 2950
Conifer Paper Products, 20839
Conifer Specialties Inc, 2951
Conimar Corp, 20840, 43200
Conlin Brokerage Company, 40237
Conn Container Corp, 20841
Conn's Potato Chips, 2952
Conneaut Cellars Winery LLC, 2953
Connecticut Culinary Institute, 20842
Connecticut Freezers, 52817
Connecticut Laminating Co Inc, 20843, 43201
Connecticut Shellfish Co Inc, 55797
Connection Chemical LP, 43202, 55798
Connell International Company, 43203
Connellsville Bottling Works, 55799
Conner Produce Co, 55800
Connerton Co, 20844
Connors Aquaculture, 2954
Conoley Citrus Packers Inc, 2955
Conpac, 20845
Conquest International LLC, 20846, 43204
Conrad Rice Mill Inc, 2956
Conrad Sales Company, 40238
Conrotto A. Winery, 2957
Conroy Foods, 2958
Conscious Choice Foods, 2959
Consolidated Baling Machine Company, 20847, 43205
Consolidated Beverage Corporation, 55801
Consolidated Biscuit Company, 2960
Consolidated Bonded Warehouse, 52818
Consolidated Bottle Company, 55802
Consolidated Can Co, 20848, 43206
Consolidated Catfish Co LLC, 2961
Consolidated Commercial Controls, 20849, 43207
Consolidated Commerical Controls, 43208

Consolidated Container Co, 20850, 20852
Consolidated Container Co LLC, 20851, 20853, 43209
Consolidated Display Co Inc, 20854
Consolidated Fruit Distributor, 55803
Consolidated Label Company, 20855, 43210
Consolidated Marketers Inc, 40239
Consolidated Merchandisers, 40240
Consolidated Mills Inc, 2962
Consolidated Plastics Co Inc, 20856
Consolidated Poultry & Egg Company, 55804
Consolidated Rail Corporation, 51668
Consolidated Sea Products, 2963
Consolidated Tea Co Inc, 40241
Consolidated Thread Mills, Inc., 20857, 43211
Consolidated Transfer Co Inc, 51669, 52819
Consorcio, MG SA DE CV, 20858
Constant Sales, 40242
Constantia Colmar, 20859, 20860, 43212
Constar International, 20861, 43213
Constellation Brands Inc, 43214, 55805
Consulting Nutritional Services, 20862
Consumer Brands, 40243
Consumer Cap Corporation, 20863
Consumer Guild Foods Inc, 2964
Consumers Fresh Produce, 55806
Consumers Packing Co, 2965, 55807, 55808
Consumers Packing Company, 20864
Consumers Vinegar & Spice Co, 2966
Consummate Marketing Company, 40244
ConSup North America, 2937, 43190
Contact Industries, 20865
Containair Packaging Corporation, 20866, 43215
Container Handling Systs Corp, 20867
Container Machinery Corporation, 20868, 43216
Container Manufacturing Inc, 20869
Container Services Company, 20870
Container Specialties, 20871
Container Supply Co, 20872, 43217
Container Systems Inc, 55809
Container Testing Lab, 20873
Container-Quinn Testing Lab, 20874
Containment Technology, 20875
Conte's Pasta Co., 2967
Contec, Inc., 20876
Contech Enterprises Inc, 20877, 43218
Contemporary Product Inc, 20878, 43219
Conti Group Company, 55810
Contico Container, 20879, 43220
Continental Carbonic Products, 2968, 20880
Continental Cart by Kullman Industries, 20881, 43221
Continental Coffee Products Company, 2969
Continental Commercial Products, 20882, 43222
Continental Disc Corp, 20883
Continental Envelope, 20884
Continental Equipment Corporation, 20885, 43223
Continental Express Inc, 51670, 52820
Continental Extrusion Corporation, 20886
Continental Food Sales Inc, 40245
Continental Girbau Inc, 20887, 43224
Continental Glass & Plastic, 55811
Continental Grain Company, 2970, 43225
Continental Identification, 20888, 43226
Continental Industrial Supply, 20889
Continental Lift Truck Corp, 55812
Continental Marketing, 20246, 43227, 55813
Continental Mills Inc, 2971, 43228
Continental Packaging Corporation, 20890
Continental Plastic Container, 20891

Continental Products, 20892
Continental Refrigeration, 20893
Continental Refrigerator, 20894, 20895
Continental Sausage, 2972
Continental Seasoning, 2973, 43229
Continental Terminals, 20896
Continental Yogurt, 2974
Continental-Fremont, 20897, 43230
Contour Packaging, 20898, 43231
Contour Products, 20899
Contract & Leisure, 43232, 55814
Contract Chemicals, 20900
Contract Comestibles, 20901
Contrex Inc, 20902, 43233
Control & Metering, 20903, 43234
Control Beverage, 20904, 43235
Control Chief Holdings Inc, 20905, 43236
Control Concepts Inc., 20906, 43237
Control Concepts, Inc., 20907
Control Instrument Service, 20908
Control Instruments Corp, 20909, 43238
Control Module, 20910, 43239
Control Pak Intl, 20911, 43240
Control Products Inc, 20912, 43241
Control Systems Design, 20913
Control Techniques, 20914
Control Technology Corp, 20915
Controls Group International, 55815
COnut Butter, 1961, 55447
Convay Systems, 20916, 43242
Convectronics, 20917, 43243
Convenience Food Systems, 55816
Convenience Marketing Services, 40247
Convergent Label Technology, 20918, 43244
Conveyance Technologies LLC, 20919, 43245
Conveying Industries, 20920
Conveyor Accessories, 20921, 43246
Conveyor Components Co, 20922, 20923, 43247, 43248
Conveyor Dynamics Corp, 20924, 43249
Conveyor Equipment Manufacturers Association, 20925
Conveyor Mart, 20926
Conveyor Supply Inc, 20927
Conveyor Systems & Components, 20928
Conveyor Technologies Intergraded, 20929
Conviron, 20930
Convoy, 20931, 43250
Conway Import Co Inc, 2975, 43251
Conwed Global Netting Sltns, 20932, 43252
Conwed Plastics LLC, 20933
Conxall Corporation, 20934
Cook & Beals Inc, 20935, 43253
Cook Associates, 20936
Cook Associates Your Co Store, 55817
Cook Flavoring Company, 55818
Cook Inlet Processing, 2976
Cook Natural Products, 2977
Cook Neon Signs, 20937
Cook's Gourmet Foods, 2978
Cook's Mate Restaurant Equipment Supply, 55819
Cook's Pantry, 2979
Cook-In-The-Kitchen, 2980
Cooke Aguaculture, 2981
Cooke Marketing Group Inc, 40248, 43255
Cooke Tavern LTD, 2982
Cooker T. Corporation, 55820
Cookie Factory, 2983
Cookie Kingdom, 2984, 20939, 55821
Cookie Specialties Inc, 2985
Cookie Tree Bakeries, 2986, 43256
Cookies By Design Inc, 2987
Cookies Food Products, 2988
Cookies United, 2989, 43257
Cookiezen, LLC, 2990
Cooking Systems International, 20940, 43258
Cookshack, 2991, 20941

1371

All Companies Index

Cookson Plastic Molding, 20942
CookTek, 20938, 43254
Cool, 2992
Cool Brands International, 2993
Cool Care, 20943, 43259
Cool Cargo, 20944, 51671
Cool Mountain Beverages Inc, 2994
Cool-Pitch Co, 20945
CoolBrands International, 20946, 55822
Coolhaus, 2995
Cooling Products Inc, 20947, 43260
Cooling Technology Inc, 20948, 43261
Coombs Family Farm, 2996
Coon Creek Winery, 2997
Cooper Decoration Company, 20949
Cooper Farms Cooked Meats, 2998
Cooper Instrument Corporation, 20950, 43262
Cooper Lake Farm LLC, 2999
Cooper Mountain Vineyards, 3000
Cooper Street Cookies, 3001
Cooper Vineyards, 3002
Cooperative Atlantic, 55823
Cooperative Country, 55824
Cooperative Elevator Co, 3003
Cooperheat/MQS, 20951, 43263
Cooperstown Cookie Company, 3004
Cooseman's D.C., 55825
Copack International, 20952
Copak Solutions, 3005
Cope Plastics Inc, 20953
Coperion Corp, 20954
Copesan, 20955
Copper Brite, 20956, 43264
Copper Clad, 20957
Copper Hills Fruit Sales, 3006, 20958
Copper Moon Coffee LLC, 3007
Copper Tank Brewing Company, 3008
Coppersmith, 51672
Copperwood InternationalInc, 20959, 40249, 55826
Coquitlam City Hall, 55827
Cora Italian Specialties, 3009, 43265, 55828
Cora Texas Mfg Co Inc, 3010
Coral LLC, 3011, 20960
Corazonas Foods, Inc, 3012
Corben Packaging & Display, 20961
Corbett Timber Co, 20962
Corbin Foods-Edibowls, 3013, 43266
Corbion, 3014, 3015, 3016, 3017, 3018, 3019, 3020, 3021, 3022, 3023
Corbo Restaurant Supply, 55829
Corbox-Meyers Inc, 20963
Corby Distilleries, 3024, 43267
Corby Hall, 20964, 43268
Corcoran International Corporation, 51673
Cord Tex, 20965
Cordoba Foods LLC, 3025
Cordon Bleu International, 3026, 43269
Core Group, 40250, 40251
Core Products Co, 20966, 43270
Core-Mark Holding Company, Inc, 55830, 55831, 55832, 55833, 55834, 55835, 55836, 55837, 55838, 55839, 55840
Corea Lobster Cooperative, 3027, 55841
Corenco, 20967, 43271, 55842
Corey Bros Inc WHLS Produce, 55843
Corfab, 20968
Corfu Foods Inc, 3028, 3029, 43272, 55844
Coriell Associates, 43273, 55845
Corim Industries Inc, 3030, 43274, 55846
Corine's Cuisine, 3031
Corinth Products, 20969
Cork Specialties, 20970, 43275
Corky's Ribs & BBQ, 3032
Cormar & Assoc Inc, 20971
Cormier Rice Milling Co Inc, 3033, 43276
Corn Popper, 3034
Corn States Metal Fabricators, 20972
Cornabys, 3035

Cornelia Broom Company, 20973
Cornelius, 20974, 43277
Cornelius Inc., 20975, 43278
Cornelius Wilshire Corporation, 20976
Cornell Beverages Inc, 3036
Cornell Machine Co, 20977, 43279
Cornell Pump Company, 20978, 43280
Cornerstone, 20979
Cornfields Inc, 3037
Corniani, 20980
Corning Life Sciences, 20981
Corning Olive Oil Company, 3038
Cornish Containers, 20982
Cornwall Warehousing, 52821
Corona College Heights, 3039, 43281
Coronet Chandelier Originals, 20983, 43282
Corp Somat, 20984, 43283
Corpak, 20985
Corporate Display Specialty, 55847
Corporate Safe Specialists, 20986
Corpus Christi Stamp Works, 20987
Corr Pak Corp, 20988
Corrections Dept, 20989
Corrigan Corporation of America, 20990
Corrin Produce Sales, 3040, 43284
Corro-Shield International Inc, 20991
Corrobilt Container Company, 20992
Corrugated Inner-Pak Corporation, 20993
Corrugated Packaging, 20994
Corrugated Specialties, 20995
Corrugated Supplies Co., 20996
Corrupad Protective Packaging, 20997
Corsair Display Systems, 20998
Corsair Pepper Sauce, 3041
Corsetti's Pasta Products, 3042
Corso's Cookies, 3043
Corson Manufacturing Company, 20999, 43285
Corson Rubber Products Inc, 21000, 43286
Cortec Aero, 21001, 21002
Corteva Agriscience, 3044
Cosa Xentaur Corp, 43287, 55848
Cosco Home & Office Products, 21003, 43288
Cosco International, 3045
Cosense Inc, 21004
Cosentino Winery, 3046
Cosgrove Distributors Inc, 3047, 55849
Cosgrove Enterprises Inc, 21005, 43289
Cosmic Co, 21006
Cosmo Food Products, 3048, 43290
Cosmo/Kabar, 21007
Cosmopolitan Foods, 3049
Cosmopolitan Wine Agents, 43291
Cosmos International, 21008
Coss Engineering Sales Company, 21009, 43292
Cost Plus, 55850
Costa Broom Works, 21010, 43293
Costa Deano's Gourmet Foods, 3050, 43294
Costa Fruit & Produce, 55851
Costa Macaroni Manufacturing, 3051, 40252
CostaDeano's Enterprises, 3052
Costas Pasta, 3053
Costco Wholesale Corporation, 43295, 55852
Cotati Brand Eggs & Food Svc, 55853
Cotswold Cottage Foods, 3054
COTT Technologies, 20078
Cott Technologies, 21011
Cottage Street Pasta, 3055
Cotter Brothers Corp, 21012
Cotter Merchandise Storage Co, 52822
Cotton Baking Company, 3056
Cotton Goods Mfg Co, 21013, 43296
Cottonwood Canyon Vineyard, 3057
Cottura Commerciale, 43297
Couch & Philippi, 21014, 43298
Couch's Country Style Sausages, 3058
Couch's Rich Plan Foods, 55854

Cougar Mountain Baking Co, 3059, 55855
Cougar Packaging Concepts, Inc., 21015
Cougar Packaging Solutions, 21016
Coulter Giufre & Co Inc, 3060, 43299
Council of International Restaurant Brokers, 43300
Counter Culture Coffee, 3061, 55856
Countertop Productions, 3062
Country Archer Jerky Co., 3063
Country Bob's Inc, 3064
Country Butcher Shop, 3065, 43301, 55857
Country Choice Organic, 3066
Country Club Bakery, 3067
Country Clubs Famous Desserts, 3068
Country Cupboard, 3069, 55858
Country Delite Farms LLC, 3070
Country Estate Pecans, 3071
Country Foods, 3072
Country Fresh, 3073
Country Fresh Farms, 3074
Country Fresh Food & Confections, Inc., 3075
Country Fresh Inc, 3076
Country Fresh Mushroom Co, 3077
Country Home Bakers, 3078
Country Home Creations Inc, 3079, 43302
Country Life, 3080
Country Life Foods, 55859
Country Maid Inc, 3081
Country Oven Bakery, 3082
Country Pure Foods Inc, 3083, 3084, 3085, 3086, 3087, 43303
Country Save Products Corp, 21017, 43304
Country Smoked Meats, 3088, 43305
Country Springs Hotel, 55860
Country Village Meats Inc, 3089
County Gourmet Foods, LLC, 3090
County Neon Sign Corporation, 21018
County Supply Co, 55861
Coupla Guys Foods, 3091
Couprie Fenton, 21019, 43306, 55862
Courtesy Signs, 21020
Courtney Marketing Inc, 40253
Courtright Companies, 21021, 43307
Cousin's Uniform, 55863
Cousins D&N, 43308
Cousins Packaging, 21022
Coutts Specialty Foods Inc, 3092
Couture Farms, 3093, 43309
Couture's Maple Shop/B & B, 3094
Couturier Na Inc, 3095
Covance Inc., 21023
Cove Four, 21024, 43310
Cove Woodworking, 21025
Cover The World, 43311, 55864
Covered Bridge Potato Chip Company, 3096
Covergent Label Technology, 21026
COVERIS, 20079
Coveris, 21027
COVERIS, 42706
Covestro LLC, 21028
COW Industries Inc, 20080
Cowan Costumes, 43312
Cowart Seafood Corp, 3097
Cowboy Caviar, 3098
Cowboy Food & Drink, 3099
Cowgirl Chocolates, 3100
Cowgirl Creamery, 3101
Cowie Wine Cellars & Vineyards, 3102
Cox Food Brokers, 40254
COX Technologies, 20081
COX Transportation Svc Inc, 51611
Coy Laboratory Products Inc, 21029
Coy's Bakery, 55865
Coyne Chemical Co Inc, 55866
Cozy Harbor Seafood Inc, 3103, 55867
Cozzini Inc, 21030
Cozzini LLC, 21031, 21032, 43313
Cozzoli Machine Co, 21033, 43314
CP Kelco, 1962, 42707

CPI Packaging, 20082
CPM Century Extrusion, 20083, 42708
CPM Roskamp Champion, 20084, 42709
CPM Wolverine Proctor LLC, 20085, 20086, 42710
CPT, 20087
Crab, 55868
Crab Connection, 55869
Crab Quarters, 3104, 55870
Craby's Fish Market, 3105
Cracked Candy LLC, 3106
Cracker Jack Advertising Specialty Corporation, 55871
Craft Brew Alliance, 3107
Craft Corrugated Box Inc, 21034
Craft Distillers, 3108, 43315
Craft Industries, 21035
Crafty Counter, 3109
Craig Manufacturing, 21036
Craig Transportation Co, 51674
Crain Ranch, 3110, 43316
Crain Walnut Shelling, Inc., 3111, 21037
Cramer Company, 21038, 43317
Cramer Inc, 21039
Cramer Products, 21040, 43318
Cramer's Bakery, 3112
Cranberry Isles Fisherman's, 3113, 55872
Cranberry Sweets Co, 3114
Crandall Filling Machinery, 21041, 43319
Crane & Crane Inc, 3115, 43320
Crane Carton Corporation, 21042
Crane Composites Inc, 21043, 43321
Crane Environmental, 21044, 43322
Crane National Vendors, 21045
Crane Pumps & Systems, 21046, 43323
Crane Research & Engineering, 21047
Crane Sales Co, 40255
Crane's Pie Pantry Restaurant, 3116
Cranston Air, 51675, 52823
Crate & Fly, 51676, 52824
Crate Ideas by Wilderness House, 21048
Crater Meat Co Inc, 3117
Crave Natural Foods, 3118
Craven Crab Company, 3119
Craver Supply Company, 55873
Craveright, 3120, 55874
Crawford Packaging, 21049
Crawford Sausage Co Inc, 3121
Crayex Corp, 21050
Crazy Go Nuts, 3122
Crazy Jerrys Inc Kahuna-Sauces, 3123
Crazy Mary's, 3124
Crazy Richard's, 3125
CRC Inc, 20088
Crc Industries Inc, 21051, 43324
CRC Products, 55448
Crea Fill Fibers Corp, 3126, 43325
Creager Mercantile Cash & Carry, 55875
Creagri Inc, 3127
Cream Crock Distributors, 3128
Cream Hill Estates, 3129, 55876
Cream of the Valley Plastics, 21052
Cream Of The West, 3130
Cream of Weeber, 55877
Creamery Plastics Products, Ltd, 21053
Creamland Dairies Inc, 3131
Creation Nation, 3132
Creative Automation, 21054, 21055, 43326
Creative Canopy Design, 21056
Creative Coatings Corporation, 21057, 43327
Creative Converting Inc, 21058
Creative Cookie, 21059, 43328
Creative Cotton, 3133
Creative Enterprises, 21060
Creative Essentials, 21061, 43329
Creative Flavors & Specialties LLP, 3134
Creative Flavors Inc, 3135
Creative Foam Corp, 21062, 43330
Creative Food Ingredients, 3136
Creative Foods of the Southwest, 55878
Creative Foodworks Inc, 3137
Creative Forming, 21063, 43331

All Companies Index

Creative Impressions, 21064, 43332
Creative Industries Inc, 21065
Creative Label Designers, 21066
Creative Lighting Fixture Company, 55879
Creative Mobile Systems Inc, 21067
Creative Packaging, 21068
Creative Packaging Corporation, 21069, 43333
Creative Printing Co, 21070
Creative Seasonings, 3138
Creative Signage System,, 21071
Creative Snacks Co LLC, 3139
Creative Spices, 3140
Creative Storage Systems, 21072
Creative Techniques, 21073, 43334
Creative Works, 43335
Creature Comforts Toys, 43336
Creegan Animation Company, 21074, 43337
Creekstone Farms Premium Beef, 21075
Creemore Springs Brewery, 3141
Creighton Brothers, 3142
Creightons, 40256
Creme Curls, 3143
Creme D'Lite, 3144
Creme Unlimited, 3145
Creminelli Fine Meats, 3146
Creole Delicacies Gourmet Shop, 3147
Creole Fermentation Indu, 3148
Crepas & Associates, 21076
Crepini, 3149
Crepini & The Crepe Team, 3150
Cres Cor, 21077, 43338, 43339
Crescent, 52825
Crescent Duck Farm, 3151, 43340
Crescent Foods, 3152, 55880
Crescent Ridge Dairy, 3153
Crescini Wines, 3154
Cresco Food Technologies, 21078, 43341
Cresinco, 55881
Crespac Incorporated, 21079, 43342
Cresset Chemical Company, 21080, 43343
Crest Foods Inc, 3155, 21081
Crest International Corporation, 3156, 55882
Crestar Crusts, 3157
Cresthill Industries, 21082, 43344
Crestmont Enterprises, 3158
Crestware, 21083, 43345
Crete Carrier Corp, 51677
Cretel Food Equipment, 21084
Cretorr, 21085
Creuzebergers Meats, 3159
Crevettes Du Nord, 3160, 43346
CRF Technologies, 20089
Cribari Vineyard Inc, 3161, 40257, 43347
Crickle Company, 3162
Cricklewood Soyfoods, 3163
Crider Brokerage Company, 40258
Criders Poultry, 3164, 43348
Crillon Importers LTD, 3165
Crippen Manufacturing Co, 21086
Crisci Food Equipment Company, 21087
Crishawn Kitchen Equipment Company, 55883
Crispy Bagel Co, 55884
Crispy Green Inc., 3166
Crispy Lite, 21088, 43349
Cristina Foods Inc, 55885
Cristom Vineyards, 3167
Critchfield Meats Inc, 3168
Critelli Olive Oil, 3169, 43350, 55886
Criterion Chocolates Inc, 3170
Critzas Industries Inc, 21089, 43351
Criveller California Corp, 3171
Criveller East, 21090
Crocetti's Oakdale Packing Co, 3172
Crocker & Winsor Seafoods, 55887
Crocker Moving & Storage Co, 52826
Crockett Honey, 3173, 43352
Croda Inc, 3174, 43353
Croft's Crackers, 3175
Crofter's Food, 3176

Crofton & Sons Inc, 3177
Croll Reynolds, 21091, 43354
Croll-Reynolds Engineering Company, 21092
Crompton Corporation, 3178, 21093
Cronin Vineyards, 3179
Crooked River Brewing Company, 3180
Crooked Vine/Stony Ridge Wnry, 3181
Crookston Bean, 3182, 43355
Crop One, 3183
Crop Pharms, LLC, 3184
CROPP Cooperative, 1963, 42711
Crosby Molasses Company, 3185, 43356
Crosfield Company, 21094
Cross Automation, 55888
Crosset Co LLC, 55889
Crossings Fine Foods, 43357
Crossings Winery, 3186
Crossmark, 40259
Crossroads Distribution LTD, 51678, 52827
Crossroads Espresso, 21095
Crosswind Foods, 21096
Crouch Dairy Supply, 21097
Crouse-Hinds, 21098, 43358
Crouzet Corporation, 21099, 43359
Crowley Beverage Corporation, 3187
Crowley Cheese Inc, 3188
Crowley Liner Services, 51679
Crowley Marketing Assoc Park, 40260
Crowley Sales & Export Co, 43360
Crown Battery Mfg, 21100, 43361
Crown Candy Corp, 3189, 43362
Crown Chemical Products, 21101
Crown Closures Machinery, 21102, 43363
Crown Controls Inc., 21103, 43364
Crown Cork & Seal Co Inc, 21104
Crown Custom Metal Spinning, 21105, 43365
Crown Equipment Corp., 21106, 43366, 55890
Crown Foods International, 43367
Crown Holdings, Inc., 3190, 21107, 43368
Crown Industries, 21108
Crown Iron Works Company, 21109, 43369
Crown Jewels Marketing, 21110
Crown Label Company, 21111
Crown Lift Trucks, 55891
Crown Manufacturing Corporation, 21112
Crown Maple Syrup, 3191
Crown Marking, 21113
Crown Metal Manufacturing Company, 21114, 43370
Crown Metal Mfg Co, 21115, 43371
Crown O'Maine Organic Cooperative, 55892
Crown Pacific Fine Foods, 3192
Crown Packaging, 21116
Crown Packing Company, 3193, 43372
Crown Plastics Inc, 21117
Crown Point, 40261, 43373, 55893
Crown Prince Inc, 3194
Crown Processing Company, 3195, 43374
Crown Products, 43375
Crown Regal Wine Cellars, 3196
Crown Restaurant Equipment, 55894
Crown Sanitary Supply, 55895
Crown Steel Mfg, 21118
Crown Tonka Walk-Ins, 21119, 43376
Crown Valley Food Service, 3197, 55896
Crown Verity, 21120, 43377
Crown-Simplimatic, 21121
Crownlite Manufacturing Corporation, 21122, 43378
Crs Inc, 43379
CRS Marking Systems, 20090, 55449
CRST International Inc, 51612
CRT Custom Products Inc, 20091
Crucible Chemical Co, 21123
Cruise Marketing, 40262

Crum Creek Mils, 3198
Crumbs Bake Shop, 3199
Crunch Time Information Systems, 21124
Crunch-A-Mame, 3200
Crunchies Natural Food Company, 3201
Crunchsters, 3202
Crunchy Rollers, 3203
Crusader Tomato, 55897
Cruse Vineyards, 3204
Crush Foods Service, 3205
Crusoe Seafood LLC, 3206
Crustacean Foods, 3207
Crusty Bakery Inc, 3208
Cruvinet Winebar Co LLC, 21125, 43380
Cryochem, 21126, 43381
Cryogenic Systems Equipment, 21127
Cryopak, 21128
Cryovac, 21129
Crystal & Vigor Beverages, 3209
Crystal Chem Inc., 21130
Crystal Cold Storage, 51680, 52828, 52829
Crystal Creamery, 3210, 43382
Crystal Creative Products, 21131, 43383
Crystal Distribution Svc, 52830
Crystal Farms Dairy Company, 3211
Crystal Food Import Corporation, 43384, 43385, 55898
Crystal Geyser Water Co., 3212
Crystal Lake Farms, 3213, 43386
Crystal Lake LLC, 3214
Crystal Lake Mfg Inc, 3215
Crystal Noodle, 3215
Crystal Potato Seed Co, 3216
Crystal Rock LLC, 3217
Crystal Springs, 3218
Crystal Springs Bottled Water, 3219
Crystal Springs Water Company, 3220
Crystal Star Herbal Nutrition, 3221, 43388
Crystal Temptations, 3222
Crystal-Flex Packaging Corporation, 21133, 43389
Crystal-Vision Packaging Systems, 21134, 43390, 55899
CS Brokers, 40172
CS Integrated LLC, 52725
CS Integrated Retail Services, 52727
CS Intergrated Retail Services LLC, 52726
CS Intergrated-Texas Limited Partnership, 52728
CSAT America, 20092
CSC Scientific Co Inc, 20093, 42712
CSC Worldwide, 20094, 42713
CSI Logistics, 51613, 52729
CSI Material Handling, 55450
CSI Tools, 20095
CSM Bakery Solutions, 20096
CSM Worldwide, 20097
CSPI, 20098
Csra Advertising Specialties, 55900
CSRA Bonded Terminal, 52730
CSS Inc, 20099
CSS International Corp, 20100, 42714
CSV Sales, 20101
CSX Transportation, 51614, 52731
CT Logistics, 51615
CTC, 20102
CTC Manufacturing, 1964, 42715
CTI Celtek Electronics, 20103
CTI Foods, 1965
CTK Plastics, 20104, 42716
CTL Foods, 1966
CTS Bulk Sales, 20105
CTS/Bulk Sales, 55451
Cubberley's, 55901
Cube Plastics, 21135, 43391
Cucamonga Sign Shop LLC, 21136
Cucina & Amore, 3223
Cucina Antica Foods Corp, 3224
Cudlin's Meat Market, 3225, 55902
Cuerden Sign Co, 21137
Cugar Machine Co, 21138

Cugino's Gourmet Foods, 3226
Cuisine de France, 43392
Cuisine International, 3227, 55903
Cuisine Perel, 3228
Cuisine Solutions Inc, 3229
Cuizina Food Company, 3230
Culicover & Shapiro, 21139
Culina, 3231
Culinaire, 3232
Culinar, 21140
Culinar Canada, 3233, 55904
Culinart Inc, 21141
Culinary Collective, 21142, 43393
Culinary Depot, 21143, 43394, 55905
Culinary Farms Inc, 3234
Culinary Institute Lenotre, 3235, 43395
Culinary Masters Corporation, 3236, 43396, 55906
Culinary Papers, 21144
Culinary Products Inc, 55907
Culinary Revolution, 3237
Culinary Specialties, 43397, 55908, 55909
Culinary Specialty Produce, 40263
Culligan Company, 21145, 43398
Culligan International Co, 3238, 21146
Culligan International Company, 3239, 43399
Culmac, 21147
Culture, 3240
Culture Republick, 3241
Culture Systems Inc, 3242, 43400, 55910
Cultures for Health, 3243
Culver Duck Farms Inc, 3244, 43401
Culver Fish Farm, 3245, 55911
Cumberland Box & Mill Co, 21148
Cumberland Container Corp, 21149
Cumberland Creamery, 3246
Cumberland Dairy, 3247, 43402
Cumberland Distribution Services, 51681, 52831
Cumberland Farms, 21150, 55912
Cumberland Gap Provision Company, 3248
Cumberland Packing Corp, 43403
Cummings, 21151, 43404
Cummings Restaurant Equipment, 55913
Cummings Studio Chocolates, 3249
Cummins Allison Corp, 43405
Cummins Label Co, 21152
Cummins Power Generation Inc., 21153
Cuneo Cellars, 3250
CUNICO, 55452
Cunningham LP Gas, 21154
Cup 4 Cup LLC, 3251, 3252
Cup Pac Packaging Inc, 21155, 21156, 43406
Cupid Candies, 3253
Cupoladua Oven, 3254
Cupper's Coffee Company, 3255, 43407
Curaleaf, 3256
Curley Brothers, 55914
Curley's Custom Meats, 3257
Curly's Foods Inc, 3258, 43408
Curran's Cheese Plant Inc, 3259
Currie Machinery Co, 21157, 43409
Curry Enterprises, 21158
Curry King Corporation, 3260, 43410
Curtainaire, 21159
Curtice Burns Foods, 3261
Curtis 1000, 21160
Curtis Packaging, 21161, 43411
Curtis Packing Co, 3262, 55915
Curtis Restaurant Equipment, 21162, 55916, 55917
Curtis Restaurant Supply, 55918
Curtis Ward Company, 43412, 55919
Curwood Specialty Films, 21163, 43413
Curzon Promotional Graphics, 21164
Cusa Tea, 3263
Cusack Meats, 3264
Cusano's Baking Company, 3265
Cush-Pak Container Corporation, 21165
Cusham Enterprises, 21166
Cushner Seafoods Inc, 3266, 55920

1373

All Companies Index

Cusick J B Co, 40264
Custom Baking Products, 21167
Custom Bottle of Connecticut, 21168
Custom Brands Unlimited, 21169
Custom Business Interiors, 21170
Custom Business Solutions, 21171
Custom Card & Label Corporation, 21172
Custom Coffee Plan, 3267
Custom Color Corp, 21173
Custom Confections & More, 3268
Custom Control Products, 21174
Custom Conveyor & Supply Corp., 21175
Custom Craft Laminates, 21176
Custom Culinary Inc., 3269, 43414
Custom Diamond International, 21177
Custom Diamond Intl., 21178, 43415
Custom Extrusion Technologies, 21179
Custom Fabricating & Repair, 21180, 55921
Custom Foam Molders, 21181
Custom Food Machinery, 21182, 43416
Custom Food Solutions LLC, 3270
Custom Food Svc Inc, 55922
Custom Foods Inc, 3271, 55923
Custom House Seafoods, 3272, 55924
Custom ID Systems, 21183
Custom Ingredients, 3273
Custom Lights & Iron, 21184
Custom Machining Inc, 21185
Custom Metal Crafts, 21186
Custom Metal Design Inc, 21187, 43417
Custom Metalcraft, Architectural Lighting, 21188
Custom Millers Supply Co, 21189
Custom Mobile Food Equipment, 21190
Custom Molders, 21191
Custom Pack Inc, 21192
Custom Packaging Inc, 21193, 43418
Custom Packaging Systems, 21194
Custom Plastics Inc, 21195
Custom Poly Packaging, 21196, 43419
Custom Pools Inc, 21197, 55925
Custom Produce Sales, 3274, 55926
Custom Quality Products, 21198
Custom Rubber Stamp Co, 21199, 43420
Custom Sales & Svc Inc, 21200, 43421
Custom Source LLC, 43422
Custom Stamp Company, 21201, 43423
Custom Stamping & Manufacturing, 21202
Custom Systems Integration Co, 21203
Custom Table Pads, 21204
Custom Tarpaulin Products Inc, 21205
Custom-Pak Meats, 3275
Customized Equipment SE, 21206, 43424
CUTCO Corp, 20106, 42717
Cutie Pie Corp, 3276, 43425
Cutler Brothers Box & Lumber, 21207
Cutler Industries, 21208, 43426
Cutler-Hammer, 21209
Cutone Specialty Foods, 3277
Cutrale Citrus Juices, 3278
Cutrite Company, 21210, 43427
Cutrufello's Creamery, 55927
Cutter Lumber Products, 21211
Cutting Edge Beverages, 3279
Cuvaison Winery, 3280
Cuyler Food Machinery & Appraisal, 55928
CVC Technologies Inc, 20107
CVC4Health, 1967
CVP Systems Inc, 1968, 20108, 42718
CW Paper, 55453
Cwo Distribution, 52832
CXR Co, 20109, 20110
Cyanotech Corp, 3281, 43428
Cyba-Stevens Management Group, 40265
Cybele's Free To Eat, 3282
CYBER BEARINGS, INC, 20111
Cyborg Equipment Corporation, 21212
Cybros, 3283, 43429
Cyclamen Collection, 21213, 43430
Cycle Computer Consultants, 21214

Cyclonaire Corp, 21215, 43431
Cyclone Enterprises Inc, 3284, 43432
Cygnet Cellars, 3285
Cynter Con Technology Adviser, 21216
Cyntergy Corporation, 21217
Cyplex, 21218
Cypress Grove, 3286
Cypress Point Creamery, 3287
Cypress Systems, 21219
Cyprus Embassy Trade Ctr, 21220
Cyrils Bakery, 3288
Cyrk, 21221, 43433
Cyro Industries/Degussa, 21222, 43434
Cyvex Nutrition, 21223
Czech Stop Grocery & Deli, 3289
Czepiel Millers Dairy, 3290
Czimer's Game & Seafoods, 3291, 55929

D

D & D Distribution Svc, 51682, 52833
D & D Foods Inc, 3292
D & D Sugarwoods Farm, 3293
D & F Equipment, 21224
D & L Manufacturing, 21225, 43435
D & S Mfg, 21226, 43436
D & S Warehouse Inc, 51683, 52834
D & W Fine Pack, 21227, 21228, 43437
D A Berther Inc, 21229
D A C Labels & Graphic, 21230, 55930
D D Bean & Sons Co, 21231, 43438
D D Williamson & Co Inc, 3294, 21232, 43439
D E Shipp Belting Co, 55931
D F Ingredients Inc, 3295, 21233
D I Mfg LLC, 3296, 21234
D J Enterprises, 55932
D L Systems Inc, 55933
D M Sales & Engineering Co, 21235
D R Technology Inc, 21236, 43440
D Rosen Co Inc, 55934
D Seafood, 3297, 55935
D Steengrafe Co Inc, 3298, 43441
D W Air, 51684, 52835
D W Davies & Co, 21237
D Waybret & Sons Fisheries, 3299, 43442
D&D Marketing Group, Inc., 40266
D&D Sign Company, 21238
D&E Pharmaceuticals, 55936
D&H Marketing, Inc, 40267
D&L Manufacturing, 21239
D&M Pallet Company, 21240
D&M Products, 21241
D&M Seafood, 3300, 55937
D&R Food Brokers, 40268
D'Ac Lighting, 21242, 43443
D'Addario Design Associates, 21243
D'Arrigo Brothers Company of California, 3301
D'Arrigo Brothers Company of New York, Inc, 43444, 55938
D'Artagnan, 3302
D'Eon Fisheries, 55939
D'Light Lighting Company, 43445
D'Lights, 21244, 43446
D'Oni Enterprises, 3303
D-Liteful Baking Company, 3304
D. Brickman Produce Company, 55940
D. Deodati & Sons, 55941
D. Fillet & Company, 55942
D. Picking & Company, 21245
D.A. Colongeli & Sons, 21246, 43447, 55943
D.A. Foodservice, 55944
D.D. Jones Transfer & Warehousing, 52836
D.D.& D. Machinery, 21247
D.F. International, 43448
D.J. Powers Company, 51685, 52837
D.M. Rothman Company, 55945
D.R. McClain & Son, 21248
D2 Ingredients, LP., 3305, 21249
Daabon Organic USA, Inc., 3324
DAB-A-DO Delicacies, 43449

Dabrico Inc, 21287
Dabruzzi's Italian Foods, 3325
Dacam Corporation, 21288, 43465
Dacam Machinery, 21289
Dacotah Paper Co, 55961, 55962
Dadant & Company, 40274
Dadant & Sons Inc, 21290
Dade Canvas Products Company, 21291
Dade Engineering, 21292, 43466
Dade Paper Co, 55963
Daesang America Inc, 21293
Daffin Mercantile Company, 55964
Daga Restaurant Ware, 21294
Dagher Printing, 21295
DAGOBA Organic Chocolate, 3306
Dahl-Tech Inc, 21296, 43467
Dahlicious, 3326
Dahmes Stainless, 21297
Daido Corp, 21298
Daily Crave, The, 3327
Daily Greens LLC, 3328
Daily Nutrition, 3329
Daily Printing Inc, 21299, 43468
Daily Soup, 3330
Dailys Premium Meats, 3331
Daimaru New York Corporation, 43469
Dainty Confections, 3332
Dairiconcepts, 3333
DairiConcepts, 21300
Dairiconcepts, 21301
Dairy Connection Inc, 3334
Dairy Conveyor Corp, 21302, 43470
Dairy Farmers Of America, 3335
Dairy Foods, 21303
Dairy Fresh Corporation, 55965, 55966
Dairy Fresh Foods Inc, 3336, 43471
Dairy Group, 3337
Dairy House, 3338
Dairy King Milk Farms/Foodservice, 3339, 55967
Dairy Maid Dairy LLC, 3340
Dairy Maid Ravioli Mfg Co, 3341, 55968
Dairy Management Inc, 3342
Dairy Service & Mfg, 21304
Dairy Services Inc, 21305
Dairy Source, 55969
Dairy Specialties, 21306, 43472, 55970
Dairy State Foods Inc, 3343, 43473
Dairy-Mix Inc, 3344, 43474
DairyAmerica, 3345, 43475
DairyChem Inc., 3346, 43476
Dairyfood USA Inc, 3348
Dairygold, 43477
Dairyland Plastics Company, 21307
Dairyland USA Corp, 43478, 55971
DairyPure, 3347
Dairytown Products Ltd, 3349, 40275
Daisy Brand, 3350, 43479
Daiya Foods, 3351
Dakco International, 40276
Dakota, 3352
Dakota Blenders, 21308
Dakota Brands Intl, 3353
Dakota Corrugated Box, 21309
Dakota Gourmet, 3354
Dakota Marketing Company, 40277
Dakota Specialty Milling, Inc., 3355, 43480
Dakota Style, 3356
Dakota Valley Products, Inc., 3310
Dal-Don Produce, 43481, 55972
Dalare Associates Inc, 21311
Dale & Thomas Popcorn, 3357
Dale T Smith & Sons Inc, 3358
Dale's Meats, 55973
Daleco, 21312
Dalemark Industries, 21313, 43482
Daley Brothers ltd., 3359, 43483
Dalian Xinfeng International Industry & Trade Co., 3360
Dalla Valle Vineyards, 3361
Dallas Container Corp, 21314
Dallas Group of America Inc, 21315, 43484
Dallas Roth Young, 21316

Dallas Transfer & Terminal, 52842
Dallis Brothers, 3362
Dalloz Safety, 21317
Dalls Semiconductor, 21318
Dalmatian Bay Wine Company, 43485, 55974
Dalmec North America, 21319
Dalo Button & Emblem Company, 55975
Dalton Electric Heating Co, 21320
Damafro, Inc, 40278, 43486
Damas Corporation, 21321, 43487
Damascus Bakery, 3363
Damascus Peanut Company, 40279
Damascus/Bishop Tube Company, 21322
Dambeck & Associates, 40280
Damian's Enterprises Inc, 55976
Damiani Wine Cellars LLC, 3364
Damon Industries, 3365, 21323
Damons Graoo, 21324
Damp Rid, 21325, 43488
Damron Corp, 3366
Damrow Company, 21326, 43489
Dan Carter, 3367
Dan Mar Co, 21327
Dan-D Foods Ltd, 3368, 21328, 43490
Dana Labels, 21329
Dana S. Oliver & Associates, 21330
Dana's Rush Equipment Company, 55977
Dana-Lu Imports, 43491, 55978
Danafilms Inc, 21331, 43492
Danbury Plastics, 21332, 43493
Dancing Deer Baking Company, 3369
Dandelion Chocolate, 3370, 21333
Danfoss Drives, 21334, 21335
Dang Foods, 3371
Danger Men Cooking, 21336
Dangold Inc, 43494
Daniel Boone Lumber Industries, 21337
Daniel J. Bloch & Company, 21338
Daniel Le Chocolat Belge, 3372
Daniel Woodhead Company, 21339
Daniel's Bagel & Baguette Corporation, 3373
Daniele Inc, 3374, 43495
Daniele International, 43496
Danieli Awnings, 21340
Daniels Food Equipment, 21341
Danisco-Cultor, 3375
Danish Cones, 55979
Danish Food Equipment, 21342
Danish Maid Butter Co, 3376
Daniso USA, 21343
Danlac Inc, 21344
Danmark Packaging Systems, 21345
Dannon Company, 3377
Dannon Yo Cream, 3378, 43497
Danone North America, 3379
Dansk International Designs, 21346
Danville Economic Development, 21347
Danville Paper & Supply, 55980
DAO Water Company, 55946
Dap Technologies Corporation, 21348
Dapec, 21349
Dapec/Numafa, 21350
Daphne's Creamery, 3380
Daprano & Co, 43498
Daprano & Company, 3381
Dar-B-Ques Barbecue Equipment, 21351
Darcor Casters, 21352, 43499
Darcy Group, 21353
Dardimans California, 3382
Dare Foods, 3383, 43500
Dare Foods Incorporated, 3384
Daregal, 3385
Darfill, 21354
Dari Farms Ice Cream Inc, 21355
Darifair Foods, 3386
Darigold, 3387
Darik Enterprises Inc, 43501
Darisil, 43502, 55981
Dark Dog, 3388
Dark Tickle Company, 3389, 43503
Darling Ingredients Inc., 3390
Darlington Dairy Supply Co Inc, 21356
Darlington Packing Co, 55982

All Companies Index

Darlington Sign Awning & Neon, 21357
Darmex Corporation, 21358
Darnell-Rose Inc, 21359, 43504
Darras Freight, 51691, 52843
Darson Corp, 21360
Dart Canada Inc., 21361
Dart Container Corp., 21362, 43505
Dart Transit Co, 51692
Das Foods, 3391
Dashco, 21363, 43506
Data 2, 21364
Data Consultants, 21365
Data Consulting Associates, 21366
Data Management, 21367
Data Scale, 21368
Data Specialists, 21369, 21370
Data Visible Corporation, 21371
Dataflow Technologies, 55983
Datalogic ADC, 21372
Datapaq, 21373, 43507
Datapax, 21374
Datatech Enterprises, 55984
Date Lady Inc., 3392
Datu Inc, 21375
Daubert Cromwell LLC, 21376
Daubert VCI, 21377
Dauito Produce, 55985
DAV Transportation Services, 51686
Dave Roemer & Associates, 40281
Dave Swain Assoc Inc, 40282
Dave's Gourmet, 3393
Dave's Gourmet Albacore, 3394
Dave's Imports, 21378
Dave's Killer Bread, 3395
Davel Food Brokerage, 40283
Davenport Machine, 21379, 43508
David A Lingle & Son Mfg, 21380
David Bradley Chocolatier, 3396
David Dobbs Enterprise Inc., 21381
David E Grimes Company, 40284
David E. Moley & Associates, 21382
David Food Processing Equipment, Inc., 43509, 55986
David Mosner Meat Products, 3397
David Puccia & Company, 55987
David Rio, 3398
David's Cookies, 3399, 43510
David's Goodbatter, 21383, 43511
Davidson's Organics, 3400, 43512
Davidson's Safest Choice Eggs, 3401, 21384
Davinci Gourmet LTD, 3402
Davis & Assoc Inc, 40285
Davis & Davis Gourmet Foods, 3403
Davis & Small Decor, 21385, 43513
Davis Bakery & Delicatessen, 3404
Davis Bread & Desserts, 3405
Davis Brothers Produce Boxes, 21386
Davis Bynum Winery, 3406
Davis Coffee Co, 55989
Davis Core & Pa, 21387
Davis Distributors of Owensboro Company, 55990
Davis Food Company, 3407
Davis Sales Associates, 40286
Davis Strait Fisheries, 3408, 43514
Davis Street Fish Market, 3409, 55991
Davis Trade & Commodities, 43515
Davis-Le Grand Company, 55992
Davisco Foods International, 3410
Davlynne International, 21388, 43516
Davron Technologies Inc, 21389, 43517
Dawes Hill Honey Company, 3411, 43518
Dawn Food Products, Inc, 3412
Dawn's Foods, 3413
Dawson Sales Co Inc, 40287
Day & Ross Transportation Group, 43519, 51693
Day & Zimmermann Group Inc, 21390
Day & Zimmermann International, 21391
Day Basket Factory, 21392
Day Foods Company, 3414
Day Lumber Company, 21393
Day Manufacturing Company, 21394

Day Nite Neon Signs, 21395
Day Spring Enterprises, 3415, 43520
Day-Lee Foods, Inc., 3416
Day-O-Lite, 21396
Daybreak Coffee Roasters, 3417
Daybreak Foods Inc, 3418
Daybrook Fisheries, 3419
Dayco, 21397
Dayco Distributing, 55993
Daydots, 21398, 43521
Daymar Select Fine Coffees, 3420
Daymark Safety Systems, 21399, 21400, 43522, 43523
Daystar, 21401
Daystar Desserts LLC, 43524
Daytech Limited, 21402
Dayton Bag & Burlap Co, 21403, 43525
Dayton Marking Devices Company, 21404
Dayton Nut Specialties, 3421
Dayton Reliable Tool, 21405
Dayton Wire Products, 21406
Dazbog Coffee Co, 3422
DB Kenney Fisheries, 3307, 43450
DBB Marketing Company, 40269
DBE Inc, 21250, 43451
DC Media & Marketing, 55947
Dc Tech, 21407
DCI Logistics, 51687, 52838
DCI, Inc., 21251
DCL Solutions LLC, 21252, 43452
DCM Tech Corp, 21253
DCS IPAL Consultants, 21254
DCS Sanitation Management, 21255
DCV BioNutritionals, 21256
Dd Reckner Co, 40288
DDW: The Color House, 3308
De Bilio Food Distributors, 55994
De Boer Food Importers, 43526
De Boles Nutritional Foods, 3423
De Bruyn Produce Company, 3424, 43527
De Choix Specialty Foods Company, 43528, 55995
De Coty Coffee Co, 3425, 43529, 55996
De Felsko Corp, 21408
De Fluri's Fine Chocolate, 3426
De Iorio's Foods Inc, 3427, 21409
De Iorios Frozen Dough Co Inc, 3428
De Laval, 21410, 43530
De Leone Corp, 21411, 21412, 21413, 43531, 55997
De Maria's Seafood, 3429
De Medici Imports, 43532
De Met's Candy Co, 3430
De Nigris, 3431
De Palo & Sons Inc, 55998
De Paul Industries, 21414
De Royal Textiles, 21415
De Souza's, 3432
De Ster Corporation, 21416, 43533
De Vara Designs, 55999
De Vere Co Inc, 21417
Deacom, 21418
Deadline Press, 21419
Dealers Choice, 40292
Dealers Food Products Co, 43538, 56001
Dean & Company, 56002
Dean & De Luca Inc, 3440
Dean Custom Awning, 21420
Dean Distributors, Inc., 3441
Dean Foods Co., 3442, 21421
Dean Industries, 21422, 43539
Dean Sausage Co Inc, 3443
Dean Supply Co, 56003
Dean's Ice Cream Dstrbtn Ctr, 56004
Deanna's Gluten Free Baking Co., 3444
Dear North, 3445
Dearborn Cash & Carry Stores, 56005
Dearborn Mid-West Conveyor Co, 21423, 21424, 43540
Dearborn Sausage Co Inc, 3446
Dearborn Wholesale Grocers, 56007, 56008, 56009, 56010

Dearborn Wholesale Grocers LP, 56006
Deaver Vineyards, 3447
Deb Canada, 21425
Debaudringhien Inc., 43541
Debbie D's Jerky & Sausage, 3448
Debbie Wright Sales, 21426, 56011
Debel Food Products, 3449
Debelak Technical Systems, 21427
Debelis Corp, 21428
DeBeukelaer Cookie Co, 3433
DeBeukelaer Corp, 3434
Deboer Food Importers, 43542
Deborah Sales LLC, 21429
Deborah's Kitchen Inc., 3450
Debragga & Spitler, 3451, 56012
Debrand Chocolatier, 3452
Deca & Otto Farms, 3453
Decade Products, 21430
Decadence Cheese Cakes, 3454
Decadent Desserts, 3455
Decagon Devices Inc, 21431
Decal Techniques Inc, 21432
Decartes Systems Group, 21433, 43543
Decas Cranberry Sales Inc, 3456
Decatur Dairy, 3457
Deccofelt Corp, 21434
Decernis, 21435
DECI Corporation, 21257
Decision Analyst Inc, 21436
Decker Farms Inc, 3458
Decker Food Company, 3459
Decker Plastics, 21437
Decker Tape Products Inc, 21438
Decker Truck Line Inc, 51695
Decko Products Inc, 3460, 21439, 43544
Deco Labels & Tags, 21440
Deco Pac Inc, 21441
Decolin, 21442
Deconna Ice Cream, 3461
Decorated Products Company, 21443
Decoren Equipment, 21444
Dedert Corporation, 21445, 43545
DeeBee's Organics, 3462
Deen Meat & Cooked Foods, 3463, 56013
Deep Creek Custom Packing, 3464, 43546, 56014
Deep Foods Inc, 3465, 43547, 56015
Deep River Snacks, 3466, 43548
Deep Sea Fisheries, 43549
Deep Sea Products, 3450, 56016
Deep South Equipment Co, 56017
Deep South Freight, 51696
Deep Valley, 3467
Deer Creek Honey Farms LTD, 3468
Deer Park Spring Water, 56018
Deer Park Spring Water Co, 3469
Deerfield Bakery, 3470
Deerland Probiotics & Enzymes, 3471, 3472, 43551, 43552
Deerwood Rice & Grain Procng, 3473
Dees Paper Co, 56019
DEFCO, 21258
Defontaine of America, 21446
Defranco Co, 21447, 43553
Defreeze Corporation, 21448
Degussa BioActives, 21449
Degussa Flavors, 21450
Dehyco Company, 21451, 43554
Dehydrates Inc, 3474, 43555
Dehydration & Environmental System, 21452
Dei Fratelli, 3475
Deibel Laboratories, 21453, 21454
Deibel Laboratories Inc, 21455, 21456
Deibel Laboratories Of Il, 21457, 21458
Deibert & Associates, 40293
Deiss Sales Co. Inc., 40294, 43556, 56020
Deitz Company, 21459
DeJarnett Sales, 40289, 40290
Deko International Company, 3476, 43557
Del Bene Meats, 56021

Del Corona & Scardigli USA, Inc., 51697
Del Mar Food Products Corp, 3477
Del Mar Seafood's Inc, 56022
Del Monte Foods Inc, 3478, 43558
Del Monte Fresh Produce Inc., 3479, 21460, 21461, 21462, 21463, 21464, 21465, 21466, 21467, 21468, 21469, 21470, 21471, 21472, 21473, 21474, 21475, 21476, 21477, 21478, 21479, 21480, 21481, 21482, 21483, 21484, 21485, 21486, 21487, 21488, 21489, 21490, 21491, 21492, 43559
Del Packaging Inc, 21493
Del Rey Packing, 3480, 43560
Del Rio Nut Company, 3481, 43561
Del Valle Food Products, 56023
Del's Lemonade & Refreshments, 3482
Del's Pastry, 3483
Del's Seaway Shrimp & Oyster Company, 3484
DEL-Tec Packaging Inc, 21259
DeLallo Foods, 3435, 43534
DeLallo Italian Foods, 3436
Delallo's Italian Store, 3487
Delancey Dessert Company, 3488
Delano Growers Grape Products, 3489
Delavan Center, Inc., 52845
Delavan Spray Technologies, 21494, 21495, 43562
Delavan-Delta, 21496, 43563
Delavau LLC, 43564
Delaviuda USA Inc, 3490
Delaware Department of Agriculture, 43565
Delaware Valley Fish Co, 3491
Delbert Craig Food Brokers, 40295
Delco Tableware, 21497
Delectable Gourmet LLC, 3492
Delfield Co, 21498, 43566
Delfin Design & Mfg, 21499, 43567
Delftree Corp, 3493
DelGrosso Foods, 3485, 3486
Delgrosso Foods Inc, 3494, 43568
Deli-Boy Inc, 21500
Delia's Food Co, 3495
Delicae Gourmet, 3496
Delicato Family Vineyards, 3497, 43569
Delice Global Inc, 21501
Delicious Desserts, 3498, 43570
Delicious Frookie, 3499
Delicious Frookie Company, 3500
Delicious Popcorn, 3501, 56024
Delicious Valley Frozen Foods, 3502
Delicious Without Gluten, 3503
Delighted By, 3504
DeLima Coffee, 3437, 43535
Deline Box Co, 21502
Delisa Pallet Corporation, 56025
Delivery Network, 52846
Delizia Olive Oil Company, 43571
Delizza, 3505
Delkor Systems, Inc, 21503
Dell Enterprises, 56026
Dell Marking Systems, 21504
Dell'Amore Enterprises, 3506
Dellaco Classic Confections, 3507
Delmonaco Winery & Vineyards, 3508, 43572
Delmonte Fresh, 21505, 52847
Delmonte Fresh Produce Co, 21506, 52848
Deloach Vineyards, 3509
Delorimier Winery, 3510
Delphi Food Machinery, 21507
Delphos Poultry Products, 3511
Delran Label Corporation, 21508
Delta Bay, 56027
Delta Carbona, 21509
Delta Catfish Products, 3512, 43573, 56028
Delta Chemical Corporation, 21510

1375

All Companies Index

Delta Container Corporation, 21511
Delta Cooling Towers Inc, 21512
Delta Cyklop Orga Pac, 21513
Delta Engineering Corporation, 21514
Delta F Corporation, 21515
Delta Food Products, 3513
Delta Industrial Services, 21516
Delta International, 43574
Delta Machine & Maufacturing, 21517, 43575
Delta Materials Handling Inc, 56029
Delta Pacific Seafoods, 3514
Delta Packing, 3515
Delta Plastics, 21518
Delta Pride Catfish, 3516, 56030
Delta Pure Filtration Corp, 21519, 43576
Delta Signs, 21520
Delta Systems Inc, 21521
Delta T Construction, 21522
Delta Technology Corp, 21523
Delta Trak, 21524
Delta Wire And Mfg., 21525, 43577
Delta/Ducon, 21526
DeltaTrak, 21527, 43578
DeLuscious Cookies, 3438
Delux Manufacturing Co, 21528, 43579
Deluxe Delight, 3517
Deluxe Equipment Company, 21529, 43580
Dema Engineering Co, 21530, 43581
DEMACO, 21260
Demaco, 21531, 43582
Demag Cranes & Components Corp, 21532, 43583
Demak & Company, 56031
Demarle Inc, 21533
Dematic Corp, 21534, 21535
Dematic USA, 21536, 52849
Dembling & Dembling Architects, 21537
DeMedici Imports, 3439, 43536
Demeyere Na, Llc, 21538
Demitri's Bloody Mary Seasonings, 3518
Demma Fruit Company, 56032
DeMoss & Associates, 40291
Dempsey's Restaurant & Brewery, 3519
Dempster Systems, 21539, 43584
Demptos Glass Corporation, 21540
Den Mar Corp, 21541
Den Ray Sign Company, 21542
Den's Hot Dogs, 3520
Den-Tex Restaurant Supply, 56033
Denair Trailer Company, 21543
Denatale Vineyards, 3521
Deneen Foods, 3522
Deng's, 56034
Denice & Filice LLC, 21544
Denman Equipment, 21545
Denning's Point Distillery, LLC, 3523
Dennis Engineering Group, 21546
Dennis Sales, 40296
Dennison Meat Locker, 3524
Dennsi Group, 21547
Denny's 5th Avenue Bakery, 3525
Denomega Pure Health, 3526
Denstor Mobile Storage Systems, 21548
Dent Electrical Supply Company, 56035
DentalOne Partners, 21549
Dentici Produce, 56036
Denton Dairy Products Inc, 56037
Denver Cold Storage, 52850
Denver Instrument Company, 21550
Denver Mixer Company, 21551
Denver Reel & Pallet Company, 21552
Denver Restaurant Equipment Company, 56038
Denzer's Food Products, 3527
Deosen USA, 3528
Dependable Distribution Services, 51698, 52851
Dependable Distributors, 43585, 52852
Dependable Food Corp, 56039
Dependable Machine, Inc., 21553, 43586
Dependable Plastics & Supls, 56040
Deppeler Cheese Factory, 3529
Derco Foods Intl, 3530, 43587

Dere Street, 3531, 56041
Derlea Foods, 3532
Derse Inc, 21554
Des Moines Cold Storage Co, 52853
Des Moines Stamp Mfg Co, 21555
Des Moines Truck Brokers, 51699, 52854
Deschutes Brewery, 3533
Desco Equipment Corporation, 21556
Desco USA, 43588
Descon EDM, 21557, 43589
Deseret Dairy Products, 3534
Desert Box & Supply Corporation, 21558
Desert Farms Inc, 3535
Desert King International, 3536, 43590
Desert Pepper Trading Co, 3537
Desert Valley Date, 3538
Deshazo Crane Company, 21559, 43591
Desiccare, 21560
Design Group, 21561
Design Ideas, 21562
Design Label Manufacturing, 21563
Design Packaging Company, 21564, 43592
Design Plastics Inc, 21565
Design Specialties Inc, 21566
Design Systems Inc, 21567
Design Technology Corporation, 21568, 21569, 43593
Design-Mark Industries, 21570, 43594
Designed Nutritional Products, 3539, 43595
Designer Protein, 3540
Designers Folding Box Corp, 21571
Designers Plastics, 21572
Designpro Engineering, 21573
Designs Furnishings & Eqpt Inc, 56042
Despro Manufacturing, 21574
Dessert Innovations Inc, 3541
Desserts by David Glass, 3544, 43596
Desserts Of Distinction, 3542
Desserts On Us Inc, 3543
Destileria Serralles Inc, 3545, 43597, 56043
Detectamet Inc, 21575
Detecto Scale Co, 21576, 21577, 43598, 43599
Detex Corp, 21578
Detoxwater, 3546
Detroit Chili Co, 3547
Detroit Forming, 21579, 43600
Detroit Marking Products, 21580
Detroit Popcorn, 56044
Detroit Quality Brush Mfg Co, 21581, 43601
Detroit Warehouse Company, 51700, 52855
Devansoy Farms, 3548, 43602
Devar Inc, 21582
Devault Foods, 3549
Developak Corporation, 21583
Development Workshop Inc, 21584
Deverell Equipment, 56045
Deville Restaurant Equipment & Supply Company, 56046
Deville Technologies, 21585
Devine Foods, 3550
Devlin Wine Cellars, 3551
DeVries Imports, 43537, 56000
Devro Inc, 3552
Dewatering Equipment Company, 21586
Dewey & Wilson Displays, 21587
Dewey's Bakery, 3553
Dewied International Inc, 3554, 21588, 43603
Dewig Brothers Packing Company, 3555
Dex-O-Tex Crossfield Products Corporation, 21589
Dexpa, 3556
Dexter Laundry Inc, 21590
Dexter Russell Inc, 21591, 43604
DF Mavens, 3309
DFC Transportation Company, 51688
DFG Foods, LLC, 43453
DFI Organics Inc., 43454, 52839
DFL Laboratories, 21261

DG Yuengling & Son, Inc., 3310
DGZ Chocolate, 3311
DH/Sureflow, 21262, 43455
Dharma Bars, 3557, 56047
Dhidow Enterprises, 3558
DHL Danzas, 51689
DHM Adhesives Inc, 21263
DHP, 21264
Dhx-Dependable Hawaiian Express, 51701, 52856
Di Alfredo Foods, 3559
Di Bruno Bros, 3560
Di Camillo Baking Co, 3561
Di Cola's Seafood, 3562, 56048
Di Engineering, 21592
Di Fiore Pasta Co, 3563
Di Lusso & Be Bop Baskote LLC, 3564, 43605
Di Mare Fresh Inc, 3565, 43606, 56049
Di Meo-Gale Brokerage Company, 40297
Diab International, 43608
Diablo Chemical, 3593, 43609
Diablo Valley Packaging, 21594
Diageo Canada Inc., 3569, 43610
Diageo North America Inc, 3570
Dial Corporation, 21595
Dial Industries Inc, 40298, 56053
Diamond & Lappin, 21596
Diamond Automation, 21597, 43611
Diamond Bakery Co LTD, 3571, 43612
Diamond Blueberry Inc, 3572
Diamond Chain, 21598, 43613
Diamond Chemical & Supply Co, 21599, 40299, 56054
Diamond Chemical Co Inc, 21600, 43614
Diamond Creek Vineyards, 3573
Diamond Crystal Brands Inc, 3574, 43615
Diamond Electronics, 21601
Diamond Foods, 3575, 43616
Diamond Fruit Growers, 3576, 43617
Diamond Herpanacine Assoc, 56055
Diamond Machining Technology, 21602, 43618
Diamond Nutrition, 43619, 56056
Diamond of California, 3579
Diamond Packaging, 21603, 43620
Diamond Pheonix Corporation, 21604
Diamond Reef Seafood, 56057
Diamond Roll-Up Door, 21605
Diamond Seafood, 3577, 56058
Diamond Sign Co, 21606
Diamond Water Bottling Fclty, 3578
Diamond Water Conditioning, 21607
Diamond Wipes Intl Inc, 21608, 43621
Diana Naturals, 3580
Diana's Specialty Foods, 3581
Diane's Signature Products, 3582
Diane's Sweet Heat, 3583
Diaz Foods, 3584
Diaz Sales, 40300
Diazteca Inc, 3585, 21609, 43622
DiBella Baking Company, 3566
Dibpack USA, 21610
DIC International, 21265, 43456
Dicarlo Distributors Inc, 56059
Dick Cold Storage, 52857
Dick Dunphy Advertising Specialties, 56060
Dick Garber Company, 3586, 3587, 40301
Dickerson & Quinn, 43623, 56061
Dickerson Foods, 56062
Dickey Manufacturing Company, 21611, 43624
Dickinson Frozen Foods, 3588
Dicks Packing Plant, 21612
Dickson, 21613
Dickson Brothers, 43625, 56063
Dickson Company, 21614
Dickson's Pure Honey, 3589
Didion Milling Inc, 3590
Die Cut Specialties Inc, 21615, 43626
Diebel Manufacturing Company, 21616
Diebolt & Co, 21617

Diedrich Coffee, 3591
Dieffenbach's Potato Chips, 3592, 43627
Diehl Food Ingredients, 3593, 21618, 43628
Diequa Inc, 21619, 21620
Dierks Foods, 56064
Diestel Family Turkey Ranch, 3594
Dietz & Watson Inc., 3595
Dietzco, 21621, 43629
Difeo & Sons Poultry Inc, 56065
Digatex, 21622
Diggs Packing Company, 3596, 56066
Digital Design, 21623
Digital Dining, 21624
Digital Dynamics Inc, 21625
Digital Image & Sound Corporation, 21626
Digital Monitoring Products, 56067
Digrazia Vineyards, 3597
DiGregorio Food Products, 3567, 56050
DiLeo Brothers, 43607, 56051
Dilettante Chocolates, 3598
Dilgard Frozen Foods, 56068
Dillanos Coffee Roasters, 3599, 43630
Dillard's Bar-B-Q Sauce, 3600
Dilley Manufacturing Co, 21627
Dillin Automation Systems Corp, 21628, 21629
Dillman Farm Inc, 3601
Dillon Candy Co, 3602
Dillon Provision Co, 56069
Dillons Food Stores, 21630, 56070
DiMario Foods, 3568
Dimension Graphics Inc, 21631
Dimensional Insight, 21632
Dimitria Delights Baking Co, 3603
Dimock Dairy Products, 3604
Dimond Tager Company Products, 3605, 56071
Dimpflmeier Bakery, 3606, 43631
Dimplex Thermal Solutions, 21633
Dina's Organic Chocolate, 3607
Dinetz Restaurant Equipment, 56072
Dinex International, 21634
Ding Hau Food Co, Ltd, 3608
Dings Co Magnetic Group, 21635, 43632
Dinkel's Bakery Inc, 3609
Dinner Bell Meat Product, 3610
Dino's Sausage & Meat Co Inc, 3611, 56073
Dino-Meat Company, 3612, 40302, 56074
Dinosaur Plastics, 21636
Dinovo Produce Company, 21637
DiNovo Produce Company, 56052
Dion Herbs & Spices, 3613
Dipal Enterprises, 43633
Dipaolo Baking Co Inc, 3614
Dipasa USA Inc, 3615, 43634, 56075
DIPIX Technologies, 21266
Dipix Technologies, 21638, 43635
Dippin' Dots LLC, 3616
Dippy Foods, 3617
Dipwell Co, 21639, 43636
Direct Fire Technical, 21640, 43637
Direct Media, 56076
Direct Promotions, 56077
Direct Seafood, 56078
Direct South, 21641
Dirt Killer Pressure Washer, 21642, 56079
Discount Equipment Intl, 56080
Discovery Chemical, 21643
Discovery Foods, 3618
Discovery Products Corporation, 21644, 43638
Dishaka Imports, 43639, 56081
Diskey Architectural Signs, 21645
Dismat Corporation, 3619, 43640
Dispensa-Matic Label Dispense, 21646
Dispense Rite, 21647, 43641
Dispenser Juice, 56082
Dispenser Services, 56083
Display Concepts, 21648

1376

All Companies Index

Display Craft Mfg Co, 21649
Display Creations, 21650
Display One, 21651
Display Pack Inc, 21652
Display Studios Inc, 21653, 43642
Display Technologies, 21654
Display Tray, 21655, 43643
Dispoz-O Plastics, 21656
Dist Tech, 51702, 52858
Distant Lands Coffee Roaster, 3620
Distaview Corp, 21657, 43644
Distillata, 3621, 21658
Distinctive Embedments, 21659
Distinguished Products, 43645
Distributed Robotics, 21660
Distribution Kowloon, 56084
Distribution Plus, 56085
Distribution Results, 21661, 43646
Distribution Services-America, 51703, 52859
Distribution Unlimited, 51704, 52860
Distributors Terminal Corp, 52861
Dito Dean Food Prep, 21662, 43647
Ditting USA, 21663, 43648
Divercon Inc, 21664
Diverse Sales, 56086
Diversified Avocado Products, 3622
Diversified Capping Equipment, 21665, 43649
Diversified Foods & Seasonings, 3623
Diversified Foodservice Supply, LLC, 56087
Diversified Label Images, 21666
Diversified Lighting Diffusers Inc, 21667, 43650
Diversified Metal Engineering, 21668, 43651
Diversified Metal Manufacturing, 21669
Diversified Metal Products Inc, 21670
Diversified Panel Systems, 21671
Diversified Plastics Corp, 21672
Diversified Products, 21673
Diversified Transfer & Storage, 51705, 52862, 52863
Diversifood Associates, Inc, 40303
Diversiplast Products, 21674
Dividella, 21675
Divine Chocolate, 3624
Divine Delights, 3625
Divine Foods, 3626
Divine Ice Cream Company, 56088
Divine Organics, 3627
Divis Laboratories, 21676
Divvies, 3628
Dixie Advertising Company, 56089
Dixie Canner Machine Shop, 21677, 43652
Dixie Cullen Interests, 40304
Dixie Dew Prods Co, 3629
Dixie Egg Co, 3630, 43653
Dixie Equipment Co, 56090
Dixie Flag Mfg Co, 21678, 43654
Dixie Graphics, 21679
Dixie Lily Foods, 56091
Dixie Maid Ice Cream Company, 21680
Dixie Mart, 56092
Dixie Neon Company, 21681
Dixie Poly Packaging, 21682
Dixie Printing & Packaging, 21683
Dixie Rice, 3631
Dixie Rubber Stamp & Seal Company, 21684
Dixie Search Associates, 21685
Dixie Signs Inc, 21686
Dixie Store Fixtures & Sales, 56093
Dixie Trail Farms, 3632
Dixie USA, 3633, 43655
Dixie Warehouse Services, 52864
Dixon Lubricants & Specialty Pro Group, 21687
Dixon Marketing Inc, 40305
Dixon's Fisheries, 3634, 56094
Dize Co, 21688
Dizzy Pig BBQ Co, 3635
Djerdan Burek Corp, 3636

DKW International Nutrition Company, 55949
DL Enterprises, 21267
Dl Geary Brewing, 3637
DLX Industries, 21268, 43457
DMC-David Manufacturing Company, 21269, 43458
DMG Financial Inc, 21270
DMH Ingredients Inc, 3313
DMI Distribution, Inc., 55950
DMN Inc, 21271
DNE World Fruit Sales, 3314, 43459
DNO Inc, 3315, 55951
DNX Foods, 3316, 55952
Do Anything Foods, 3638
DO, Cookie Dough Confections, 3317
Do-It Corp, 21689, 43656
Dobake, 3639
Dober Chemical Corporation, 21690
Dobert's Dairy, 56095
Doc's Transfer & Warehouse, 51706, 52865
Dockmasters Inc, 56096
Dockside Market, 3640
Dockside Seafood & Specs Inc, 56097
Doctor Dread's Jerk, 3641
Doctor's Best Inc, 3642
Doering Co, 21691
Doering Machines Inc, 21692, 43657
Doerle Food Svc, 56098
Doerle Food Svc LLC, 3643, 56099
Dogfish Head Craft Brewery, 3644
Doggett Equipment Services Group, 56100
Dogswell LLC, 3645
Dogwood Brewing Company, 3646
Dohar Meats Inc, 3647
Dohler-Milne Aseptics LLC, 3648
Dol Cice' Gelato Company, 3649, 56101
Dolce Nonna, 3650
Dolcera, 3651
Dolci Gelati, 3651
Dolco Packaging Co, 21694, 43658
Dold Foods, 3652
Dole & Bailey Inc, 3653, 56102
Dole Food Company, Inc., 3654, 43659
Dole Pond Maple Products, 3655
Dole Refrigerating Co, 21695, 43660
Dolisos America, 3656
Dollar Food Manufacturing, 3657
Dolliff & Co Inc, 51707
Dolly Madison Ice Cream, 56103
Dolores Canning Co Inc, 3658
Dolphin Natural Chocolates, 3659, 43661
Dom's Sausage Co Inc, 3660, 56104
Domaine Chandon, 3661
Domaine St George Winery, 3662
DomainMarket, 21696, 43662
Domata Living Flour, 3663
Domestic Casing Co, 56105
Dometic Mini Bar, 21697
Dominex, 3664, 43663, 52866
Dominion Equipment & Supply Co., 56106
Dominion Pallet Inc, 21698
Dominion Regala, 21699
Dominion Wine Cellars, 3665
Domino Amjet Inc, 21700
Domino Specialty Ingredients, 3666
Don Alfonso Foods, 3667
Don Bugito, 3668
Don Ford Ltd, 40306
Don Hilario Estate Coffee, 3669
Don Jose Foods, 3670
Don Lee, 21701
Don Lee Farms, 3671
Don Luis Garcia Fernandez, 56107
Don McDonald & Sons, 56108
Don Sebastiani & Sons, 3672
Don Walters Company, 21702, 56109
Don's Dock Seafood Market, 3673, 56110
Don's Food Products, 3674
Don't Go Nuts, 3675
Dona Yiya Foods, 3676, 43664

Donahower & Company, 21703, 43665
Donald E Hunter Meats, 3677
Donald R Conyer Associates, 40307
Donald R Tinsman Co, 40308
Donalds & Associates, 21704
Donaldson Co Inc, 21705, 43666
Donaldson's Finer Chocolates, 3678
Donatoni Winery, 3679
Donells Candies, 3680
Dong Kee Company, 3681
Dong Phuong Oriental Bakery, 3682
Dong Us I, 3683, 21706, 43667
Donna & Company, 3684
Donnelly Fine Chocolates, 3685
Donnelly Industries, Inc, 21707
Donnick Label Systems, 21708
Donoco Industries, 21709, 43668
Donsuemor Madeleines, 3686
Dontech Industries Inc, 21710
Donut Farm, 3687, 56111
Donut Whole, 3688
Doodles Cookies, 3689
Door County Fish Market, 3690, 56112
Door County Potato Chips, 3691
Door Peninsula Winery, 3692
Doosan Industrial Vehicle America Corp, 21711, 43669, 51708
Dopaco, 43670
Dorado Carton Company, 21712
Doral International, 3693
Doran Scales Inc, 21713, 43671
Dorchester Crab Co, 3694
Dordan Manufacturing Co, 21714
Dorden & Co, 21715
Dore Foods, 56113
Dorell Equipment Inc, 21716
Dorina So-Good Inc, 3695, 43672
Dormont Manufacturing Co, 21717
Dornan Uniforms & Specialty Advertising, 56114
Dorner Manufacturing Corp, 21718
Dorothy Dawson Food Products, 3696
Dorothy Timberlake Candies, 3697
Dorpak, 21719
Dorsel Distribution Company, 56115
Dorset Fisheries, 3698, 43673
Dorsett & Jackson Inc, 56116
Dorton Incorporated, 21720, 43674
Dorval Trading Co LTD, 43675
Dosatron International Inc, 21721
Doscher's Candies Co., 3699, 56117
Dot Foods Inc, 51709, 56118
Dot-It Food Safety Products, 21722, 43676
Double B Distributors, 3700, 56119
Double B Foods Inc, 3701
Double Date Packing, 3702
Double E Co LLC, 21723, 21724
Double Envelope Corp, 21725
Double Good, 3703
Double H Plastics, 21726
Double Play Foods, 3704
Double Premium Confections, 3705
Double Rainbow Gourmet Ice Cream, 3706
Double Wrap Cup & Container, 21727, 43677
Double-Cola Company, 3707
Doucette Industries, 21728, 43678
Doug Hardy Company, 3708, 56120
Doug Milne Co, 40309
Dough-To-Go, 3709
Doughmakers, LLC, 21730
Doughpro, 21731
DoughXpress, 21729
Douglas Battery Manufacturing Company, 21732
Douglas Brothers Produce Company, 56121
Douglas Cross Enterprises, 3710
Douglas Freight Salvage, 56122
Douglas Homs Corporation, 43679, 56123
Douglas Machine Inc, 21733, 21734
Douglas Machines Corp, 3711, 21735

Douglas Machines Corp., 21736, 43680
Douglas Products, 21737
Douglas Sales Associates, 40310
Douglas Stephen Plastics Inc, 21738
Douglass Produce Company, 56124
Douknie Winery, 3712
Doumak Inc, 3713, 56125
Douwe Egberts, 3714
Dove Screen Printing Co, 21739, 43681
Dover Chemical Corp, 21740, 43682
Dover Hospitality Consulting, 21741
Dover Industries, 21742
Dover Metals, 21743
Dover Parkersburg, 21744, 43683
Dover Products Company, 21745
Doves and Figs LLC, 3715
Dovex Export Co, 43684
Dow Agro Sciences LLC, 21746
Dow AgroSciences Canada, 3716
Dow Cover Co Inc, 21747
Dow Distribution, 3717, 43685
Dow Industries, 21748, 43686
Dow Packaging, 21749, 43687
Dow Water and Process Solutions, 21750
Dowd & Rogers, 3718
DOWL LLC, 21272
Dowling Signs Inc, 21751
Down East Specialty Products/Cape Bald Packers, 3719, 56126
Down To Earth Distributors, 56127
Downco Packaging Inc, 56128
Downeast Candies, 3720
Downeast Chemical, 21752
Downeast Cider House, 3721
Downeast Coffee Roasters, 3722
Downeast Food Distributors Inc, 56129
Downesville Foods, 56130
Downs Crane & Hoist Co Inc, 21753, 43688
Doyen Medipharm, 21754
Doyle Signs Inc, 21755
Doyon, 3723, 43689
Doyon Equipment, 21756, 43690
DPC, 21273
DPI Mid Atlantic, 55953
DPI Midwest, 43460, 55954
DPI Rocky Mountain, 55955
DPI Specialty Foods Inc., 21274, 55956
Dr Konstantin Frank's Vinifera, 3724, 43691
Dr Mauthe & Assoc, 40311
DR McClain & Son, 21275
Dr Pepper Snapple Group, 3725
Dr Pete's, 3726
Dr Praeger's Sensible Foods, 3727
Dr. B's Beverages, LLC, 3728
Dr. Christopher's Herbal Supplements, 3729, 43692
Dr. Cookie, 3730
Dr. In The Kitchen, 3731
Dr. John's Candies, 43693, 56131
Dr. Lucy's LLC, 3732
Dr. McDougall's Right Foods, 3733
Dr. Oetker Canada Ltd., 3734
Dr. Paul Lohmann Inc., 3735, 43694
Dr. Pete's, 3736
Dr. Pete's/J.C. Specialty Foods, 3737
Dr. Schar USA, 3738
Dr. Smoothie Brands, 3739, 56132
Dr. Tima Natural Products, 3740
Dr. Willy's Great American Seafood, 56133
Drackett Professional, 21757
Draco Natural Products Inc, 3741, 43695, 56134
Drader Manufacturing Industries, 3742
Draeger Safety Inc, 21758
Dragnet Fisheries, 3743, 43696, 56135
Dragonfly Screen Graphics Inc, 56136
Dragunara LLC, 3744
Draiswerke Inc, 21759
Drake Bakeries, 3745
Drake Co, 21760, 43697
Drake Corp, 43698
Drake Equipment Co, 56137

1377

All Companies Index

Drakes Brewing Co, 3746
Drakes Fresh Pasta Co, 3747
Drangle Foods, 3748
Draper Valley Farms, 3749, 43699
Draper's Super Bee, 56138
Drapes 4 Show, 21761, 43700
Draught Services, 56139
DRC Marketing Group, 40270
Dreaco Products, 21762, 43701
Dream Confectioners LTD, 3750, 43702
Dream Foods Intl, 3751
Dream Pretzels, 3752
Dreaming Cow, 3755
DreamPak LLC, 3753, 21763
DreamTime, Inc, 3754
Drehmann Paving & Flooring Company, 21764, 21765, 43703
Dreisbach Enterprises, 52867
Dreisbach Enterprises Inc, 51710, 52868, 52869
Dreisbach-Hilltop, 52870
Drescher Paper Box Inc, 21766
Dresco Belting Co Inc, 21767, 43704
Dresden Stollen Co USA, 3756
Dressel Collins Fish Company, 3757
Dreumex USA, 21768, 43705
Drew's Organics, 3758
Dreyer Marketing, 40312
Dreyer Sonoma, 3759
Dreyer's Grand Ice Cream Inc., 3760, 56140
Dreymiller & KRAY Inc, 3761
Dri Mark Products, 21769, 43706
Dri View Mfg Co, 52871
Driall Inc, 21770, 43707
Driam USA Inc, 21771
Dried Ingredients, LLC., 3762, 21772, 52872
Drier's Meats, 3763
Driftwood Dairy, 3764
Driscoll Label Company, 21773
Driscoll Strawberry Assoc Inc, 3765, 43708
Driscoll's, 3766
Drives Incorporated, 21774
Droga Chocolates, 3767
Droubi's Imports, 3768, 43709, 56141
Drs Designs, 21775
Druid Fire Equipment Company, 56142
Drum Rock Specialty Co Inc, 3769, 43710
Drum-Mates Inc., 21776, 43711
Drusilla Seafood, 3770
Dry Creek Vineyard, 3771, 43712
DRY Soda Co., 3318
Dryden Provision Co Inc, 3772
Drying Technology Inc, 21777
Dryomatic, 21778
DS Services of America, 3319, 55957
DSA Software, 21276
DSC Logistics Inc, 52840
DSI, 21277
DSI Food Brokerage, 40271
DSI Process Systems, 21278
Dsl, 21779
DSM, 3320
DSM Food Specialties, 3321
DSM Fortitech Premixes, 3322, 43461
DSM Nutritional Products LLC, 21279
DSO Fluid Handling Company, 21280
Dsr Enterprises, 21780
DSW Converting Knives, 21281, 43462
DSW Distribution Ctr Inc, 51690, 52841
DT Converting Technologies - Stokes, 21282
DT Industrials, 21283, 43463
DT Packaging Systems, 21284, 21285
Du Bois Chemicals, 21781
Du-Good Chemical Laboratory & Manufacturing Company, 21782
Dual Temp, 21786
Dualite Sales & Svc Inc, 21787, 43714
Dub Harris Corporation, 21788, 56143
Dublin Produce Company, 56144
DuBois Chemicals, 21783

Dubois Seafood, 3777, 56145
Dubor GmbH, 21789
Dubuit Of America Inc, 21790
Dubuque Steel Products Co, 21791
Duck Pond Cellars, 3778
Duck Waok, 21792
Duckhorn Vineyards, 3779
Ducktrap River Of Maine, 3780, 43715
Duct Sox Corp, 21793
Duda Farm Fresh Foods Inc, 3781
Dudson USA Inc, 21794, 43716, 56146
Duerr Packaging Co Inc, 21795
Dufeck Manufacturing Co, 21796
Dufflet Pastries, 3782
Dufour Pastry Kitchens Inc, 3783
Dugdale Beef Company, 3784, 56147
Duguay Fish Packers, 3785
Dugussa Texturant Systems, 21797
Duis Meat Processing, 3786
Dukane Corp, 21798, 21799
Duke Manufacturing Co, 21800, 43717
Duke's, 3787
Dulce de Leche Delcampo Products, 3788
Dulcette Technologies, 3789, 43718
Duluth Sheet Metal, 21801
Duma Meats Inc, 3790
Dumbee Gourmet Foods, 3791
Dunagan Warehouse Corp, 51711, 52873
Dunbar Brokerage DBC Ingredients, 40313
Dunbar Co, 21802, 40314
Dunbar Foods Corp, 3792
Dunbar Manufacturing Co, 21803, 43719
Dunbar Sales Company, Inc, 40315
Duncan Peak Vineyards, 3793
Dundee Brandied Fruit Co, 3794
Dundee Candy Shop, 3795
Dundee Citrus Growers Assn, 3796
Dundee Groves, 3797, 43720
Dundee Wine Company, 3798
Dunford Bakers, 3799
Dungeness Development Associates, 3800, 43721
Dunham & Smith Agencies, 40316
Dunham's Lobster Pot, 3801, 56148
Dunham's Meats, 3802
Dunhill Food Equipment Corporation, 21804, 43722
Dunkin' Brands Inc., 3803, 21805
Dunkley International Inc, 21806, 43723
Dunlevy Food Equipment, 56149
Dunn Vineyards, 3804
Dunn Woodworks, 21807
Dunrite Inc, 21808
Dunsmith International, 51712
Duo-Aire, 21809
Duplex Mill & Mfg Co, 21810, 43724
Duplin Wine Cellars, 3805
DuPont, 21784
Dupont Cheese, 3806
DuPont Nutrition & Biosciences, 3773, 21785, 43713
DuPont Pioneer, 3774, 3775
DuPont Tate & Lyle BioProducts Company, LLC., 3776
Dupps Co, 21811, 43725
Dupuy Storage & Forwarding LLC, 21812
Dur-Able Aluminum Corporation, 21813, 43726
Dura Electric Lamp Company, 21814, 43727
Dura-Flex, 21815, 43728, 56150
Dura-Pack Inc., 21816
Dura-Ware By Carlisle, 43729
Dura-Ware Company of America, 21817, 43730
Durable Corp, 21818
Durable Engravers, 21819, 43731
Durable Packaging, 43732
Durable Packaging Corporation, 21820
Durable Textile Company, 56151
Duralite Inc, 21821, 43733
Duramitt North America, 43734
Durand-Wayland Inc, 21822, 43735

Durango Brewing Co, 3807
Durango-Georgia Paper, 21823, 43736
Durant Box Factory, 21824
Durashield USA, 21825
Durasol Awnings, 21826
Durastill Export Inc, 21827, 43737
Durbin, 56152
Durey-Libby Edible Nuts, 3808, 56153
Durham Ellis Pecan Co, 3809
Durham Flavor Rich, 56154
Durham Manufacturing Co, 21828, 43738
Durham Ranch, 43739, 56155
Durkan Hospitality, 43740
Durkee-Mower, 3810, 43741
Duske Drying Systems, 21829
Dusobox Company, 21830
Dutch Ann Foods Company, 3811
Dutch Cheese Makers Corp, 3812
Dutch Creek Foods, 56156
Dutch Farms Inc, 3813
Dutch Girl Donut Co, 3814
Dutch Gold Honey Inc, 3815, 43742
Dutch Henry Winery, 3816
Dutch Kitchen Bake Shop & Deli, 3817
Dutch Packing Co., Inc., 3818
Dutch Valley Food Distributors, 56157
Dutchess Bakers' Machinery Co, 21831, 43743
Dutchess Bakery, 3819
Dutchess Restaurant Equipment, 56158
Dutchland Frozen Foods, 3820
Dutra Distributing, 56159
Dutro Co, 21832, 43744
Dutter's Food, 21833
Dutterer's Home Food Service, 3821
Duval Bakery Products, 3822
Duval Container Co, 21834, 56160
Duverger, 3823
Duxbury Mussel & Seafood Corporation, 3824, 56161
DVC Brokerage Company, 40272
DW Montgomery & Company, 40273, 55958
Dwan & Company, 56162
Dwayne Keith Brooks Company, 3825
DWC Specialities, 3323
Dwinell's Central Neon, 21835
DWL Industries Company, 21286, 43464, 55959
Dwyer Instruments Inc, 21836, 43745
DXP Enterprises Inc, 55960
Dycem Limited, 21837
Dyco, 21838, 21839, 21840, 43746
Dykes Restaurant Supply Inc, 56163
Dylan's Candy Bar, 3827
Dylog USA Vanens, 21841
Dyna Tabs LLC, 3828, 43747, 56164
Dyna-Lift Inc, 56165
Dyna-Veyor Inc, 21842, 43748
Dynabilt Products, 21843
Dynablast Manufacturing, 21844
Dynaclear Packaging, 21845
Dynaco USA, 21846
Dynalab Corp, 21847
Dynalon Labware, 21848, 56166
Dynamet, 21849
Dynamic Air Inc, 21850, 43749
Dynamic Automation LTD, 21851
Dynamic Coatings Inc, 21852
Dynamic Confections, 3829
Dynamic Cooking Systems, 21853, 43750
Dynamic Foods, 3830
Dynamic Health Laboratories Inc., 3831
Dynamic International, 21854
Dynamic Marketing, 56167
Dynamic Packaging, 21855, 43751
Dynamic Pak LLC, 21856
Dynamic Storage Systems Inc., 21857
Dynapar Corp, 21858
Dynapro International, 3832, 43752
Dynaric Inc, 21859, 43753
Dynasty Transportation, 21860
Dynasys Technologies, 21861

Dynatek Laboratory Inc, 21862
Dynic USA Corp, 3833, 21863
Dynynstyl, 21864, 43754
DyStar Hilton Davis/DyStar Foam Control, 3826
Dzignpak LLC Englander, 21865

E

E & E Process Instrumentation, 21866, 43755
E & J Gallo Winery, 3834, 3835, 43756
E & M Electric & Machinery Inc, 21867
E A Berg & Sons Inc, 40317
E A Bonelli & Assoc, 21868
E A Sween Co, 3836, 56168
E C Shaw Co, 21869
E D Farrell Co Inc, 56169
E F Bavis & Assoc Inc, 21870, 43757
E F Engineering, 21871
E Friedman Assoc, 56170
E G Forrest Co Inc, 56171
E Goodwin & Sons, 56172
E H Wachs Co, 21872
E J Mckernan Co, 21873
E K Bare & Sons Inc, 40318
E K Lay Co, 21874
E L K Run Vineyards, 3837
E M Trisler Sales Co Fd Prods, 56173
E Ruff & Assoc Inc, 40319
E W Carlberg Co, 40320
E Waldo Ward & Son Marmalades, 3838, 43758
E&A Hotel & Restaurant Epment And Supplies, 56174
E&H Packing Company, 3839
E&M Fancy Foods, 56175
E&M Packaging, 56176
E-Control Systems, 21875
E-Cooler, 21876, 43759
E-Fish-Ent Fish Company, 3840, 43760
E-J Industries Inc, 21877, 43761
E-Lite Technologies, 21878, 43762
E-Pak Machinery, 21879
E-Quip Manufacturing, 21880
E-Saeng Company, 21881
E-Z Dip, 21882
E-Z Edge Inc, 21883, 21884, 43763
E-Z Lift Conveyors, 21885, 43764
E-Z Shelving Systems Inc, 21886
E. Armata Fruit & Produce, Inc., 56177
E. Boyd & Associates, 43765
E. De la Garza, 56178
E. Gagnon & Fils, 3841, 43766
E. H. Gourmet, 3842
E. LaRocque & Fils, 56179
E. Oliver Zellner Company, 56180
E.A. Robinson & Company, 56181
E.C. Phillips & Son, 3843, 56182
E.D. Smith Foods Ltd, 3844, 43767
E.F. Lane & Son, 3845, 43768
E.G. Staats & Company, 21887
E.H. Thompson Company, 56183
E.L. Nickell Company, 21888, 43769
E.W. Bowker Company, 3846
E.W. Knauss & Son, 3847, 43770
E2M, 21889
Eagle Associates, 40322
Eagle Bakery Equipment, 21948
Eagle Box Company, 21949
Eagle Brand, 3859
Eagle Coffee Co Inc, 3860, 43793, 56190
Eagle Crest Vineyards LLC, 3861
Eagle Family Foods, 3862
Eagle Foodservice Equipment, 21950, 43794
Eagle Group, 21951, 43795
Eagle Home Products, 21952, 43796
Eagle Ice Cream Company, 3863
Eagle Industrial Distribution, 56191
Eagle Labeling, 21953
Eagle Marketing, 40323
Eagle Packaging Corp, 21954, 21955
Eagle Products Company, 21956, 43797
Eagle Research Inc, 21957

1378

All Companies Index

Eagle Rock Food Co, 3864
Eagle Seafood Producers, 3865
Eagle Wholesale Drug Company, 56192
Eagle Wire Works, 21958
Eagle-Concordia Paper Corporation, 21959, 56193
Eagles Printing & Label, 21960
Eagleware Manufacturing, 21961, 21962, 43798
Eam, 21963
Eam-Mosca Corporation, 21964
Earl Gill Coffee Co, 56194
Earl J Henderson Trucking Company, 51714
Earl Soesbe Company, 21965
Earnest Eats, 3866
Earp Distribution, 56195
Earth & Vine Provisions Inc, 3867
Earth Balance, 3868
Earth Circle Organics, 3869, 56196
Earth Grains Baking Co, 56197
Earth Island, 3870
Earth Saver, 43799
Earth Science, 3871, 43800, 52875
Earth Song Whole Foods, 3872
Earth Source Organics, 3873, 3874
Earthbound Farm, 3875, 56199
Earthgrains, 56200
EarthGrains Banking Companies, Inc., 56198
Earthrise Nutritionals, 3876
Earthstone Oven, 43801
Earthstone Wood-Fire Ovens, 21966, 43802
Earthy Delights, 21967
EAS Consulting Group LLC, 21890
Eash Industries, 21968
Easley Winery, 3877
East Balt Commissary Inc, 3878
East Bay Fixture Co, 21969
East Bay International, 43803, 56201
East Coast Fresh Cuts Inc, 3879
East Coast Group New York, 21970
East Coast Mold Manufacturing, 21971
East Coast Sea Port Corporation, 43804
East Coast Seafood Inc, 43805, 56202
East Coast Warehouse & Distr, 51715, 52876
East Dayton Meat & Poultry, 3880
East Indies Coffee & Tea Co, 3881
East Kentucky Foods, 3882
East Memphis Rubber Stamp Company, 21972
East Point Seafood Company, 3883
East Poultry Co, 3884, 56203
East Shore Specialty Foods, 3885
East Side Fisheries, 56204
East Side Winery/Oak Ridge Vineyards, 3886
East Wind Inc, 3887
Easterday Belting Company, 21973
Easterday Fluid Technologies, 21974, 43806
Eastern Bag & Paper Co, 40324
Eastern Bag & Paper Company, 56205
Eastern Bakers Supply Co Inc, 56206
Eastern Bakery Co, 21975
Eastern Brewing Corporation, 3888
Eastern Cap & Closure Company, 21976
Eastern Container Corporation, 21977
Eastern Design & Development Corporation, 21978
Eastern Distribution Inc, 51716, 52877
Eastern Energy Lighting Systems, 43807, 56207
Eastern Envelope, 21979
Eastern Fish Company, 3889, 43808, 56208
Eastern Food Industries Inc, 3890
Eastern Machine, 21980, 43809
Eastern Overseas Marketing, 43810
Eastern Plastics, 21981
Eastern Poly Packaging Company, 21982
Eastern Refrigerater ExPress, 51717

Eastern Refrigeration & Restaurant Equipment, 56209
Eastern Sales & Marketing, 40325
Eastern Sales and Marketing, 40326
Eastern Sea Products, 3891, 43811
Eastern Seafood Co, 3892, 56210
Eastern Shore Clam Company, 56211
Eastern Shore Railroad, 51718
Eastern Shore Tea, 3893
Eastern Tabletop Mfg, 21983
Eastern Tabletops, 43812
Eastern Tea Corp, 3894, 43813
Eastey Enterprises, 21984
Eastimpex, 43814, 56212
Eastland Food Corp, 43815
Eastman Chemical Co, 43816
Eastport Customs Brokers, 51719
Eastrise Trading Corp., 3895
Eastside Deli Supply, 3896
Eastside Seafood, 3897
Easy Lift Equipment Co Inc, 3898, 21985
Easy-Care Environs, 21986
Easybar Corp, 21987
Easyup Storage Systems, 21988
Eat Dutch Waffles, LLC, 3899
Eat It Corporation, 3900
Eat My Waffles, 3901
Eat Real Snacks USA, 3902
Eat This, 3903
Eat Your Coffee, 3904
Eat Zi's Market & Bakery, 3905
Eatec Corporation, 21989, 43817
Eatem Foods Co, 3908, 21990, 43818
Eating Evolved, 3909
EatKeenwa, Inc., 3906
Eatmore Fruit Company, 56213
Eaton Corporation, 21991, 43819, 56214
Eaton Electrical Sector, 21992
Eaton Equipment, 21993
Eaton Filtration, LLC, 21994, 43820
Eaton Manufacturing Co, 21995, 43821
Eaton Market, 56215
Eaton Quade Plastics & Sign Co, 21996
Eaton Sales & Service, 21997
EatPastry LLC, 3907
Eau de Source Boischatel, 56216
Eau Galle Cheese Factory Shop, 3910
EB Box Company, 21891, 56184
EB Eddy Paper, 21892, 43771
EB Metal Industries, 21893
Ebbert Sales & Marketing, 40327
Ebel Tape & Label, 21998
Ebenezer Flag Company, 21999
Eberbach Corp, 22000
Eberhard Creamery, 3911
Eberle Winery, 3912
Eberly Poultry, Inc., 3913
EBM Technology, 21894
Ebonex Corporation, 43822, 56217
Ebro Foods, 3914
EBS, 21895
Eby-Brown Company, 56218
Ecce Panis Inc, 43823
EcFood.Com, 22001
EcFood.com, 22002
Echo Farms Puddings, 3915
ECHO Inc, 21896
Echo Lake Foods, Inc., 3916
Echo Spring Dairy, 3917
Eckels Bilt, 22003, 43824
Eckert Cold Storage, 3918
Eckert Machines, 56219
Eckhart Corporation, 3919, 43825
Eckhart Seed Company, 3920
Ecklund-Harrison Technologies, 22004, 43826
Eckroat Seed Company, 3921, 43827
Eclat Chocolate, 3922
Eclectic Institute, 3923
Eclipse Electric Manufacturing, 22005
Eclipse Espresso Systems, 22006
Eclipse Innovative Ther mal Solutions, 22007, 43828
Eclipse Systems Inc, 22008, 43829
Eco Fish Inc, 22009

Eco Wine & Spirits, 43830, 56220
Eco-Air Products, 22010, 43831
Eco-Bag Products, 22011, 43832
Eco-Pak Products Engineering, 22012
Eco-Planet Cookies, 3924
Ecodyne Water Treatment, LLC, 22013, 43834
Ecolab Inc, 22014
Ecolo Odor Control Systems Worldwide, 22015, 43835
Ecological Formulas, 56221
Ecological Labs Inc, 22016, 43836
Ecological Technologies, 43837, 56222
ECOM Agroindustrial Corporation Ltd, 3848, 21897
Ecom Manufacturing Corporation, 3926
EcoNatural Solutions, 3925, 43833
Econo Equipment, 22017
Econo Frost Night Covers, 22018, 43838
Econocorp Inc, 22019, 43839
Econofrost Night Covers, 22020, 43840
Economic Sciences Corp, 22021
Economy Cash & Carry LP, 56223
Economy Folding Box Corporation, 22022, 43841
Economy Label Sales Company, 22023, 43842
Economy Novelty & Printing Co, 22024, 43843
Economy Paper & Restaurant Co, 22025, 43844, 56224
Economy Restaurant Fixtures, 56225
Economy Tent Intl, 22026, 43845
Economy Wholesale Company, 56226
Ecoval Dairy Trade, 43846, 56227
Ecover, 22027
Ecs Warehouse, 22028, 43847, 51720, 52878
Ecuadorian Rainforest LLC, 43848, 56228
Ed & Don's Of Hawaii Inc, 3927
Ed Miniat Inc, 3928, 3929
Ed O'Connor Associates, 40328
Ed Oliveira Winery, 3930
Ed Roller Inc, 3931
Ed Smith's Stencil Works LTD, 22029
Ed's Honey Co, 3932
Ed's Kasilof Seafoods, 3933, 56229
EDA International Corp, 43772
Eda's Sugar Free, 3934, 43849
EDCO Food Products Inc, 3849, 43773, 43774
Edco Industries, 22030
Edco Supply Corp, 22031
Eddy's Bakery, 3935
Edelman Meats Inc, 3936
Edelmann Provision Company, 3937
Edelweiss Patisserie, 3938
Eden, 43850, 56230
Eden Creamery, 3939, 56231
Eden Foods Inc, 3940, 43851
Eden Organic Pasta Company, 3941
Eden Processing, 3942
Eden Vineyards Winery, 3943
Eden's Market, 3944
Ederback Corporation, 22032, 43852
Edgar A Weber & Co, 3945, 43853
Edge Manufacturing, 43854
Edge Resources, 22033, 43855
Edgecraft Corp, 22034, 43856
Edgemold Products, 22035
Edgerton Corporation, 22036
Edgewood Estate Winery, 3946
Edhard Corp, 22037, 43857
Edible Software, 22038
Edinburg Citrus Assn, 56232
Edison Grainery, 3947
Edison Price Lighting, 22039, 43858
Edl Packaging Engineers, 22040, 43859
Edlong Corporation, 3948, 43860
Edlund Co, 22041, 43861
Edmer Sanitary Supply Co Inc, 56233
Edmeyer, 22042, 43862
Edmond's Chile Co, 3949
Edmonton Potato Growers, 3950, 43863

Edmunds St. John, 3951
Edna Valley Vineyard, 3952
Edner Corporation, 3953, 56234
Edoko Food Importers, 43864
Edom Labs Inc, 3954, 43865, 56235
Edoughble, 3955
Edson Packaging Machinery, 22043, 43866
Edsung, 56236
EDT Corp, 21898
Educational Institute of the American Hotel & Lodging Assoc., 43867
Educational Products Company, 22044
Edward & Sons Trading Co, 3956, 22045, 43868
Edward Badeaux Company, 56237
Edward Don & Co, 56238, 56239, 56240
Edward Don & Company, 56241, 56242
Edward G Rahll & Sons, 56243
Edward I. Friedland, 56244
Edward Johnson's Salsa, 3957
Edward Marc Brands, 3958, 56245
Edwards Baking Company, 3959
Edwards Distributing, 56246
Edwards Fiberglass, 22046
Edwards Mill, 3960
Edwards Products, 22047
Edy's Grand Ice Cream, 3961
EFA Processing EquipmentCompany, 21899
EFCO Importers, 43775
Efco Importers, 43869
EFCO Products Inc, 3850
Efco Products Inc, 3962
EFCO Products Inc, 21900, 56185
EFD Associate, 40321
EFFi Foods, 3851
Efficient Foodservice Response, 56247
Efficient Frontiers, 22048
Effies Homemade, 3963
EFG Food Solutions, 43776
EFP Corp, 21901
EG&G Instruments, 21902
EGA Products Inc, 21903
Egerstrom Inc, 40329
Egg Cream America Inc, 3964
Egg Innovations, 3965
Egg Low Farms, 3966
Egg Roll Fantasy, 3967
Eggboxes Inc, 22049
Eggland's Best Eggs, 3968
Eggology, 3969
EGS Electrical Group, 21904, 43777
EGW Bradbury Enterprises, 21905, 43778
Egypt Star Bakery Inc, 3970
Ehmke Manufacturing, 22050
Ehresman Packaging Co, 3971
Ehrgott Rubber Stamp Company, 22051
Ehrlich Food Co, 56248
Eichler Wood Products, 22052
Eickman's Processing Co, 3972
Eide Industries Inc, 22053, 43870
Eidon, 3973
Eight O'Clock Coffee Company, 3974
Eilenberger Bakeries, 3975
Eimskip, 51721
Einson Freeman, 22054, 43871
Eirich Machines, 22055, 22056, 43872
Eisai, 22057
Eischen Enterprises, 22058
Eiseman-Gleit Co Inc, 40330
Eisenmann Corp USA, 22059, 43873
Eiserloh Co Inc, 40331
Eiserman Meats, 3976
EIT, 21906, 43779
EIWA America Inc., 3852
EJ Brooks Company, 21907
EJZ Foods, 3853
EKATO Corporation, 21908, 43780
Eklof & Company, 56249
El Brands, 3977
El Cerrito Steel, 22060
El Charro Mexican Food Ind, 3978, 43874

1379

All Companies Index

El Dorado Packaging Inc, 22061, 43875
El Grano De Oro, 3979
El Jay Poultry Corporation, 3980
El Matador Foods, 3981
El Milagro, 3982, 43876
El Molino Tamales, 56250
El Molino Winery, 3983
El Paso Meat Co, 3984
El Paso Winery, 3985
El Perico Charro, 3986
El Peto Products, 3987, 43877
El Popular Inc VF Garza, 56251
El Rancho Tortilla, 3988
El Rey Cooked Meats, 3989, 43878
El Toro Brew Pub, 3990
El Toro Food Products, 3991, 43879
Elaine's Toffee Co., 3992
Elan Vanilla Co, 3993, 22062, 43880
Elanco Food Solutions, 22063
ELAU-Elektronik Automatiions, 21909
ELBA, 21910
Elba Custom Meats, 3994
Elba Pallets Company, 22064
Elberta Crate & Box Company, 22065, 43881
Elco Fine Foods, 3995, 40332, 43882, 43883, 56252, 56253, 56254
Eldetco, 22066
Eldorado Artesian Springs Inc, 3996
Eldorado Coffee Distributors, 3997, 43884
Eldorado Miranda Manufacturing Company, 22067
Eldorado Seafood Inc, 3998
Eleanor's Best LLC, 3999, 43885, 56255
Elecro-Craft/Rockwell Automation, 22068
Electra Supply Co, 56256
Electra-Gear, 22069
Electric City Signs & Neon Inc., 22070
Electric Contract Furniture, 22071, 43886
Electric Forklift Repair, 56257
Electrical Engineering & Equip, 22072
Electro Alarms, 22073
Electro Cam Corp, 22074
Electro Freeze, 22075, 43887
Electro Freeze Distrs Inc, 56258
Electro Lift Inc, 22076, 43888
Electro-Lite Signs, 22077
Electro-Sensors Inc, 22078, 22079
Electro-Steam Generator Corp, 22080
Electrodex, 22081, 43889
Electrol Specialties Co, 22082
Electron Machine Corp, 22083
Electronic Development Labs, 22084
Electronic Filling Systems, 22085
Electronic Liquid Fillers, 22086
Electronic Machine Parts, 22087
Electronic Weighing Systems, 22088, 43890
Electroshield Inc, 56259
Electrostatics Inc, 22089
Electrotechnology Applications Center, 22090
Elegant Awnings, 22091
Elegant Desserts, 4000, 56260
Elegant Edibles, 4001
Elegant Packaging, 22092
Element Snacks, 4002
Elemental Containers, 22093
Elemental Superfood, 4003, 56261
Elementar Americas Inc, 22094
Elements Truffles, 4004
Elena's, 4005, 43891
Elena's Food Specialties, 4006
Eleni's Cookies, 4007
Elettric 80 Inc, 22095
ELF Machinery, 21911, 43781
Elgene, 22096
Elgin Dairy Foods, 4008
Eli's Bread Inc, 4009
Eli's Cheesecake, 4010
Elias Shaker & Co, 40333
Eliason Corp, 22097, 43892
Eliot's Adult Nut Butters, 4011, 56262

ELISA Technologies, Inc., 21912
Elite Forming Design Solutions, 22098, 43893
Elite Naturel USA, 43894
Elite Spice Inc, 4012, 22099, 43895
Elite Storage Solutions Inc, 22100
Elizabeth Town Grain, 56263
Elk Cove Vineyards, 4013
Elk Provision Co Inc, 56264
Elkay Plastics Co Inc, 22101
Elkhorn Distributing Company, 56265
Elki, 43896
Elki Coporation, 4014
Ella's Flats, 4015
Ella's Kitchen, 4016, 56266
Ellab, 22102, 22103
Ellehammer Industries, 22104, 43897
Ellenbee-Leggett Co Inc, 4017
Ellenco, 22105, 43898
Ellenos, 4018
Ellett Industries, 22106, 43899
Ellie's Country Delights, 4019
Ellingers Agatized Wood Inc, 22107, 43900
Ellio's Pizza, 4020
Elliot Horowitz & Co, 22108, 40334, 56267
Elliot Lee, 22109, 43901, 56268
Elliott Bay Baking Co., 4021
Elliott Bay Espresso, 22110
Elliott Manufacturing Co Inc, 22111, 43902
Elliott Seafood Company, 4022, 56269
Elliott-Williams Company, 22112, 43903
Ellis Coffee Co, 4023
Ellis Corp, 22113
Ellis KARR & Co Inc, 51722, 52879
Ellis S. Fine Co., Inc., 40335
Ellison Bakery, Inc., 4024
Ellison Milling Company, 4025, 43904
Elliston Vineyards, 4026
Ello Raw, 4027
Ellsworth Cooperative Creamery, 4028, 56270
Ellsworth Foods, 4029, 56271
Ellsworth Locker, 4030
Elm City Cheese Co Inc, 4031
Elm Electric Supply, 56272
Elm Packaging Company, 22114
Elmar Industries, 22115
Elmar Worldwide, 22116, 43905
Elmark Packaging Inc, 22117
Elmeco SRL, 22118
Elmer Chocolate®, 4032, 43906
Elmer Hansen Produce Inc, 43907
Elmers Fine Foods Inc, 4033
Elmhurst Milked, 4034
Elmira Distributing Company, 56273
Elmo Rietschle - A Gardner Denver Product, 22119, 43908
Elmwood Locker Svc, 4035
Elmwood Pastry Shop, 4036
Elmwood Sensors, 22120, 43909
Elmwood Warehousing Co, 52880
Elo Touch Systems, 22121, 43910
Elon Products Company, 56274
Elopak Americas, 22122, 43911
Elore Enterprises Inc, 4037
ELP Inc, 3854, 21913
Elreha Controls Corporation, 22123
Elrene Home Fashions, 22124
Elro Signs, 22125
Elston Richards Warehouse, 52881
Elwell Parker, 22126, 43912
Elwood International Inc, 4038, 43913
Elwood Safety Company, 22127, 43914
EM Industries, 21914
Embassy Flavours Ltd., 4039, 43915
Embee Sunshade Co, 22128
Emblem & Badge, 22129, 43916
Embria Health Sciences, 4040
Embro Manufacturing Company, 22130
Emc Solutions, 22131, 43917
EMCO, 21915, 43782
Emco Industrial Plastics, 22132, 56275

EMCO Packaging, 21916
EMD Performance Materials, 3855, 21917
EMD Products, 21918
EMD Sales Inc, 3856
Emedco, 22133
Emerald City Closets Inc, 22134, 43918
Emerald Hilton Davis LLC, 4041
Emerald Kalama Chemical, LLC, 4042, 43919
Emerald Packaging Inc, 22135
Emerald Performance Materials, 4043, 43920
Emerling International Foods, 4044, 22136, 40336, 43921, 51723, 52882, 56276
Emerson Industrial Automation, 22137
Emerson Process Management, 22138, 43922
Emery Smith Fisheries Limited, 4045, 43923
Emery Thompson Company, 43924
Emery Thompson Machine &Supply Company, 22139, 43925
Emery Winslow Scale Co, 22140, 43926
EMG Associates, 56186
EMI, 21919
Emico, 22141
Emiliomiti, 22142, 56277
Emjac, 22143
Emkay Confectionery Machinery Company, 56278
Emkay Trading Corporation, 4046, 43927, 56279
Emmeti, 22144
Emmeti USA, 22145
Emmi Roth USA, 4047
Emmy's Candy from Belgium, 4048
Emmy's Organics, 4049, 43928
Emoshun, 22146
Empact Bars, 4050
Empire Bakery Equipment, 22147
Empire Candle Mfg LLC, 22148
Empire Cash Register Systems, 56280
Empire Coffee Company, 4051
Empire Cold Storage, 52883
Empire Comfort Systems, 22149
Empire Forklift Inc, 56282
Empire International, 43929
Empire Kosher Foods, 4052
Empire Mayonnaise Company, LLC., 4053
Empire Packing Co, 56283
Empire Safe Company, 22149
Empire Screen Printing Inc, 22150, 43930
Empire Spice Mills, 4054, 43931
Empire Tea Svc, 4055, 43932, 56284
Emporia Cold Storage Co, 52884
Empresa La Famosa, 4056
Empresas La Famosa, 4057, 43933
Empress Chocolate Company, 4058, 43934
Empress Food Prods Co Inc, 56285
EMSCO Scientific Enterprises, Inc., 56187
Emtrol, 22151, 43935
EMU Americas, LLC, 43783
Emuamericas, 43936, 56286
Emulso, 22152
Emulsol Egg Products Corporation, 56287
En Garde Health Products, Inc., 4059
En-Hanced Products Inc, 22153
Encapsulation Systems, 22155
Encompass Supply, 22156
Encore Fruit Marketing Inc, 40337, 43937
Encore Glass, 22157
Encore Image Inc, 22158
Encore Plastics, 22159, 43938
Encore Sales, 56288
Encore Specialty Foods LLC, 43939
Endangered Species Chocolate, 4060
Endico Potatoes Inc, 4061, 43940

Endress & Hauser, 22160
Endurart Inc, 22161
Ener-G Foods, 4062, 43941, 56289, 56290
Enercon, 22162
Enerfab Inc., 22163
Energen Products Inc, 4063, 43942
Energenetics International, 4064
Energique, 4065
Energy Beverage Company, 43943
Energy Brands/Haute Source, 4066
Energy Foods Intl., 4067
Energy Sciences Inc, 22164, 22165, 43944
Energymaster, 22166, 43945
Enerquip Inc, 22167
Enfield Farms Inc, 4068
Engel's Bakeries, 4069
Engineered Automation, 22168
Engineered Food Systems, 22169
Engineered Handling Products, 56291
Engineered Plastics Inc, 22170, 43946
Engineered Products, 22171, 22172
Engineered Products Corp, 22173, 43947
Engineered Products Group, 22174, 43948
Engineered Security System Inc, 22175, 43949
Engineered Storage Products Company, 56292
Engineered Systems & Designs, 22176
Engineered Textile Products, 22177
Engineering & Mgmt Consultants, 22178
England Logistics, 22179, 51724
English Bay Batter Us Inc, 4070, 43950
English Honey Farms, 56293
English Manufacturing Inc, 22180
English Northwest Marketing, 40338
Englund Equipment Co, 51725, 52885
Engraph Label Group, 22181
Engraving Services Co., 22182, 43951
Engraving Specialists, 22183
Enhance Packaging Technologies, 22184
ENJAY Converters Limited, 21920
Enjay Converters Ltd., 22185
Enjoy Foods International, 4071, 43952
Enjoy Life Foods, 4072
Enlightened, 4073
ENM Co, 21921, 43784
Ennio International, 22186, 43953
Ennis Inc., 22187
Enotech Corporation, 22188
Enpoco, 22189
Enprotech Corp, 56294
Enray, Inc, 4074
Enrick Co, 22190, 43954
Enrico Biscotti Co, 4075
Enrico's/Ventre Packing, 4076
ENSCO Inc, 21922
Ensemble Beverages, 4077, 43955
Ensign Ribbon Burners LLC, 22191, 22192
Ensinger Inc, 22193, 43956
Enslin & Son Packing Company, 4078, 56295
Enstrom Candies, Inc., 4079, 43957
Entech Instruments Inc., 22194
Entech Systems Corp, 22195, 43958
Entenmann's, 4080
Entergy's Teamwork Louisiana, 22196
Enterprise, 22197
Enterprise Box Company, 22198
Enterprise Company, 22199, 43959, 56296
Enterprise Dynamics Corporation, 22200
Enterprise Envelope Inc, 22201
Enterprise Food Brokers, 40339
Enterprise Foods, 4081
Enterprise Products, 22202
Enterprises Pates et Croutes, 4082, 43960
Enting Water Conditioning Inc, 22203, 43961
Entner-Stuart Premium Syrups, 4083
Entoleter LLC, 22204

1380

All Companies Index

Enviro Doors By ASI Technologies, 22205
Enviro-Clear Co, 22206, 43962
Enviro-Green Products, 56297
Enviro-Pak, 22207
Enviro-Safety Products, 22208
Enviro-Test/Perry Laboratories, 22209
Enviro-Ware, 22210
Envirolights Manufacturing, 22211
Enviromental Structures, 22212
Environmental Consultants, 22213
Environmental Express, 22214, 56298
Environmental Packaging Associates, 56299
Environmental Products, 22215
Environmental Products Company, 22217, 43963
Environmental Products Corp, 22216
Environmental Systems, 22218
Environmizer Systems Corporation, 22219
Enviropak Corp, 22220, 22221
EnWave Corporation, 22154
Enz Vineyards, 4084
Enzamar, 43964, 56300
Enzo Olive Oil Co., 4085
Enzymatic Therapy Inc, 4086
Enzyme Development Corporation, 4087, 43965
Enzyme Formulations Inc, 4088
Enzyme Innovation, 4089
Eola Hills Wine Cellars, 4090
EOS Estate Winery, 3857
EP International, 43785
EP Minerals LLC, 21923
EPCO, 21924, 43786
Epcon Industrial Systems, 22222, 43966
EPD Technology Corporation, 21925
Epi De France Bakery, 4091, 43967
EPI Labelers, 21926
EPI World Graphics, 21927
Epic, 43968, 56301
Epic Industries, 22223
Epic Products, 22224
Epic Provisions, 4092, 56302
Epic Source Food, 4093
Epicure Foods Corporation, 43969
Epicurean Butter, 4094
Epicurean Food & Beverages, 43970
Epicurean Foods, 56303
EPL Technologies, 21928
Epogee, 4095
Epsen Hillmer Graphics Co, 22225, 43971
Epsilon Industrial, 22226
Epsilon-Opti Films Corporation, 22227
Epstein, 22228, 22229
EPT Warehouses, 51713, 52874
Equal Exchange Inc, 4096, 4097, 4098, 4099, 4100, 56304
Equator Coffees & Teas, 4101
Equichem International Inc, 22230
Equilon Lubricants, 22231
Equipco, 56305
Equipex Limited, 22232, 43972
Equipment, 56306
Equipment Design & Fabrication, 22233
Equipment Distributing of America, 22234
Equipment Distributor Div, 43973, 56307
Equipment Engineering Company, 56308
Equipment Enterprises, 22235, 22236
Equipment Equities Corporation, 22237
Equipment Exchange Co, 22238
Equipment Express, 22239
Equipment for Coffee, 22243
Equipment for Industry, 56312
Equipment Inc., 56309
Equipment Innovators, 22240
Equipment Outlet, 22241
Equipment Picard, 56310
Equipment Specialists Inc, 22242, 43974
Equipment Specialty Company, 56311
Equipment/Plus, 56313
Equity Cooperative Exchange, 52886

Eragrain, 4102
Erath Vineyards Winery, 4103
Erb International, 22244
Erba Food Products, 4104, 43975
ERBL, 3858
ERC Parts Inc, 21929, 43787, 56188
Erca-Formseal, 22245
Erdner Brothers, 51726, 52887
Erell Manufacturing Co, 22246, 43976
Ergonomic Handling Systems, 22247
Ericas Rugelach & Baking Co, 4105
Erick Schat's Bakery, 4106
Erickson Brothers Brokerage Co, 40340
Erickson Industries, 22248, 43977
Erickson's Fork Lifts Inc, 56314
Erie Container, 22249
Erie Cotton Products, 22250
Erie Foods Intl Inc, 4107, 22251, 43978
Eriez Magnetics, 22252, 43979
Erika Record LLC, 22253
Erivan Dairy, 4108
Erlab, Inc, 43980, 56315
Erlich Foods International, 40341
Erman & Son, 56316
Ermanco, 22254, 43981
Ernest F Mariani Co, 22255
Erneston & Sons Produce Inc, 56317
Ernst Timing Screw Co, 22256
ERO/Goodrich Forest Products, 21930, 43788
Errol's Cajun Foods, 4109
ERS International, 21931
Ertelalsop, 22257, 43982
Erving Industries, 22258
Erwin Food Service Equipment, 22259
Erwyn Products Inc, 22260, 43983
ES Robbins Corp, 21932
Esbelt of North America: Divison of ASGCO, 22261
Escalade Limited, 4110, 43984
Escalon Premier Brand, 4111
Escher Mixers, USA, 22262
Eschete's Seafood, 4112, 56319
Esco Foods Inc, 4113
Esco Manufacturing Inc, 22263, 22264
Esco Products Inc, 22265
ESD Energy Saving Devices, 21933
ESD Waste2water Inc, 21934, 43789
ESE Inc, 21935
ESE, Inc, 21936
Esha Research, 22266, 43985
ESI Group, 21937
ESI Qual Intl, 21938
ESKAY Corporation, 21939
Eskay Metal Fabricating, 22267
Eskimo Candy Inc, 4114, 56320
Esm Ferolie, 40343
Esper Products DeLuxe, 4115
Esposito Brokerage, 40344
Espresso Buy the Cup, 56321
Espresso Carts and Supplies, 22268
Espresso Coffee Machine Co, 43986, 56322
Espresso Machine Experts, 40345, 56323
Espresso Magic, 56324
Espresso Roma, 22269, 56325
Espresso Specialists, 43987
Espresso Vivace, 4116
Espro Manufacturing, 4117, 43988
Esquire Mechanical Corp., 22270, 43989
ESS Technologies, 21940, 43790
Essbar Equipment Company, 56326
Esselte Meto, 22271, 43990
Essen Nutrition Corp, 4118
Essence of India, 56327
Essentia Protein Solutions, 4119
Essentia Water, 4120
Essential Baking Co, The, 4121
Essential Flavors & Fragrances, 4122
Essential Food Marketing, 40346
Essential Industries Inc, 22272, 43991
Essential Living Foods, 4123
Essential Nutrients Inc, 4124

Essential Products of America, 4125, 43992
Essentra Packaging Inc., 22273
Essex Food Ingredients, 56328
Essiac Canada International, 4126, 43993
Esstech, 22274
Esteem Products, 4127, 43994, 56329
Ester International, 22275
Esterle Mold & Machine Co Inc, 22276
Esterlina Vineyard & Winery, 4128
Estes Express Lines Inc, 51727
Esther Price Candies & Gifts, 4129
ESummits, 21941
ET International Technologies, 21942, 43791
Et Oakes Corp, 22277
Etchandy Farms, 4130
Etched Images, 22278
Eternal Marketing Group, 43995, 56330
Eternal Water, 4131
Ethan's, 4132
Ethel M Chocolates, 4133
Ethel's Baking Co., 4134
Ethical Bean Coffee, 4135
Ethical Naturals, 4136
Ethnic Edibles, 4137
Ethnic Gourmet Foods, 4138
Etna Brewing Co, 4139
Etna Sales, 22279
Etobicold, 52888
ETS Laboratories, 21943
Ettinger Rosini & Associates, 40347
Ettline Foods Corp, 56331
Ettlinger Corp, 4140, 43996
Ettore, 22280, 43997
Etube & Wire, 22281
Euchner-USA, 22282
Euclid Coffee Co, 43998, 56332
Euclid Fish Co, 56333
Eugene & Company, 56334
Eugene Freezing & Storage Company, 52889
Eugene Welding Company, 22283
Eunice Locker Plant, 22284
Euphoria Chocolate Company, 4141
Eureka Company, 22285, 43999
Eureka Door, 22286
Eureka Ice & Cold Storage Company, 22287, 52890
Eureka Locker Inc, 4142
Eureka Paper Box Company, 22288
Eureka Water Co, 4143
Eurex International, 44000
Euro American Brands, 44001
Euro Cafe, 4144
Euro Chocolate Fountain, 4145
Euro Mart/Stolzle Cberg las, 44002, 56335
Euro Source Gourmet, 4146, 44003
Euro USA, 44004
Euro USA Inc, 44005
Euro-Bake, 44006, 56336
Euro-Excellence, 44007, 56337
Euro-Pol Bakery Equipment, 22289
Euroam Importers Inc, 4147, 44009
Eurobar Sales Corporation, 22290
EuroBrew Inc., 44008
Eurobubbles, 4148, 44010
Eurocaribe Packing Company, 4149
Eurodib, 22291, 44011
Eurodispenser, 22292
Eurofins DQCI, 22293
Eurofins S-F Analytical Labs, 22294
Eurofins Scientific Inc, 22295
Eurofins Scientific Inc., 22296
Eurofood Distributors, 44012, 56338
Eurogulf Company, 40348
Europa Company, 22297
Europa Sports Products, 4150
Europaeus USA, 40349, 44013
Europe's Finest Imports, 44014, 56339
European Bakers, 4151
European Coffee, 4152
European Egg Noodle Manufacturing, 4153

European Foods, 44015, 56340
European Gift & Houseware, 22298
European Hotel & Restaurant Imports, 44016, 56341
European Imports, 44017, 56342
European Packaging Machinery, 22299
European Roasterie, 4154, 44018
European Style Bakery, 4155
Eurosicma, 22300
Eurotherm, 22301
Eurpac Warehouse Sales, 56343
Eutek Systems, 22302, 44019
Eva Gates Homemade Preserves, 4156
Eval Company of America, 22303
Evan Peters & Company, 56344
Evans & Associates, 40350
Evans Adhesive Corp LTD, 22304
Evans Brokerage Company, 40351
Evans BS&R, 56345
Evans Creole Candy, 4157
Evans Delivery Company, 51728, 52891
Evans Distribution Systems, 52892
Evans Food Group LTD, 4158, 44020
Evans Foodservice Inc., 56346
Evans Properties, 4159
Evanston Awning Co, 22305
Evant, 22306
EVAPCO Inc, 21944, 43792
Evaporator Dryer Technologies, 22307, 44021
Evco Wholesale Food Corp, 56347
Eve Sales Corp, 4160, 44022
Evensen Vineyards, 4161
Event Equipment Sales, 44023, 56348
Ever Extruder Co, 22308
Ever Fresh Fruit Co, 4162, 44024
Everbrite, Inc, 22309, 44025
Everedy Automation, 22310, 44026
Everest Interscience, 22311
Everett Rubber Stamp, 22312
Everfilt Corp, 22313
Everfresh Beverages, 4163, 44027
Everfresh Food Corporation, 4164, 44028
Everglades Foods, 4165
Evergood Fine Foods, 4166
Evergreen International Airlines, 51729
Evergreen Juices Inc., 4167
Evergreen Manufacturing, 44029
Evergreen Packaging, 22314, 44030
Evergreen Sweeteners, Inc, 4168, 51730, 52893
Everidge, 22315
Everland Foods, 4169
Everland Parks, 4170
Everpure, LLC, 22316, 44031
Evers Heilig Inc, 40352
Everson District, 44032, 56349
Everson Spice Co, 4171, 22317
Everspring Farms, 4172
Everything Yogurt, 4173
Evo Hemp, 4174
Evol Foods, 4175
Evolution Fresh, 4176
Evolution Salt Co., 4177
Evolve, 4178
Evonik Corporation North America, 22318, 44033
Evonuk Oregon Hazelnuts, 56350
Evoqua Water Technologies, 22319
Evy Tea, 4179
Eweberry Farms, 4180
Ex Drinks, 4181, 44034
Ex-Cell KAISER LLC, 22320, 44035
Ex-Tech Plastics, 22321
Exact Equipment Corporation, 22322
Exact Mixing Systems Inc, 22323, 22324
Exact Packaging, 22325
Exact Target, 44036
Exaxol Chemical Corp, 22326, 44037
Excalibur Bagel & Bakery Eqpt, 22327
Excalibur Miretti Group LLC, 22328, 44038
Excalibur Seasoning, 4182, 22329, 44039
Excel Chemical Company, 22330
Excel Engineering, 22331

1381

All Companies Index

Excel Food Distribution Company, 56351
Excel-A-Tec Inc, 22332
Exceldor Cooperative, 4183, 44040
Excell Products Inc, 22333
Excellence Commercial Products, 22334, 44041, 56352
Excellent Bakery Equipment Co, 22335
Excellent Food Products, 56353
Excellentia Intl., 4184
Excello Machine Co Inc, 44042, 56354
Excelon, 56355
Excelsior Transparent Bag Manufacturing, 22336
EXE Technologies, 21945
ExecuChef Software, 22337
Executive Line, 22338
Executive Match Inc, 22339
Executive Referral Services, 22340
Exel, 22341, 44043
Exel Inc, 51731, 52894
Exeter Ivanhoe Citrus Assn, 44044
Exeter Produce, 4185, 44045
Exhausto, 22342, 44046
Exhibitron Co, 22343, 44047
Exhibits & More Shopworks, 22344
Eximcan Canada, 44048, 52895
Eximco Manufacturing Company, 22345, 44049
Exo Inc., 4186
Expanko Cork Co, 22346
Expert Customs Brokers, 40353
Expert Industries Inc, 22347
Explore Cuisine, 4187
Expo Displays, 22348, 44050
Expo Instruments, 22349
Export Contract Corporation, 44051
Express Air Cargo, 51732, 52896
Express Card & Label Co Inc, 22350
Express Packaging, 22351
Express Point Technology Services, 56356
Express Wholesale Grocers, 56357
Expresso Shoppe Inc, 22352
Expresso Supply, 44052
Expro Manufacturing, 4188, 22353, 44053
Exquis Confections, 22354
Exquisita Tortillas Inc, 4189
Extech Instruments, 22355
Extracts and Ingredients Ltd, 4190
Extravagonzo Gourmet Foods, 4191
Extreme Creations, 4192
Extrutech Plastics Inc, 22356, 44054
Exxon Mobil, 22357
Exxon Mobil Chemical Company, 22358
Eyrie Vineyards, 4193
Ez Box Machinery Company, 22359
EZ Foods, 56189
EZ-Tek Industries, 21946
EZE-Lap Diamond Products, 21947
Ezy Trading International, 56358
Ezzo Sausage Company, 4194

F

F & A Dairy Products Inc, 4195, 44055
F & A Fabricating Inc, 22360, 44056
F & A Food Sales Inc, 56359
F & C Sawaya Wholesale, 56360
F & F and A. Jacobs & Sons, Inc., 22361
F & S Awning & Sign Co, 22362
F & S Engraving Inc, 22363
F & S Produce Co Inc, 4196
F B Mc Fadden Wholesale Co, 56361
F B Purnell Sausage Co Inc, 4197
F B Washburn Candy Corp, 4198, 44057, 51733
F B Wright Co, 44058, 56362
F C Bloxom & Co, 44059, 56363
F C C, 4199, 44060
F C MEYER Packaging LLC, 22364
F Christiana & Co, 56364
F G Products Inc, 22365
F H Overseas Export Inc, 44061

F I L T E C-Inspection Systems, 22366, 44062
F M Turner Co Inc, 40354
F Mc Lintocks Saloon & Dinin, 40355
F McConnell & Sons, 56365
F N Sheppard & Co, 22367, 44063
F N Smith Corp, 22368, 44064
F P Intl, 22369
F R Drake Co, 22370
F W Bryce Inc, 4200
F&G Packaging, 22371
F&Y Enterprises, 4201, 44065
F-D-S Mfg Co, 22372
F-M Forklift Sales & Svc Inc, 56366
F. Gavina & Sons, 4202, 56367
F. Rothman Enterprises, LLC, 40356
F.A. Davis & Sons, 56368
F.B. Leopold, 22373
F.B. Pease Company, 22374, 44066
F.E. Wood & Sons, 22375
F.G. Publicover & Associates, 40357
F.H. Taussig Company, 44067
F.M. Corporation, 22376, 44068
F.P. Smith Wire Cloth Company, 22377, 44069
Fa Lu Cioli, 4212, 44084
Fab Inc, 56372
Fab-X/Metals, 22420, 56373
Fabbri Sausage Mfg Co, 4213
Fabco, 22421
Faber Foods and Aeronautics, 4214, 44085
Fabick CAT, 22422
Fabio Imports, 4215
Fabohio Inc, 22423, 44086
Fabreeka International, 22424, 22425, 44087
Fabreeka International Inc, 22426
Fabri-Kal Corp, 22427
Fabricated Components Inc, 22428, 44088
Fabricating & Welding Corp, 22429
Fabrication Specialties, 22430
Fabrichem Inc, 22431
Fabricon Products Inc, 22432, 44089
Fabriko, 22433, 44090
Fabrique Delices, 4216
Fabwright Inc, 22434, 44091
Facilitec, 22435
Facilities Design Inc, 22436
Facility Group, 22437
Faciltec Corporation, 22438, 44092
Factory Cat, 22439
FactoryTalk, 22440
Fadler Company, 56374
Faema, 56375
FAGE USA Dairy Ind Inc, 4203, 44070
Fagerholt Brothers, 56376
Faidley Seafood, 4217
Fair Oaks Farms LLC, 4218
Fair Publishing House, 22441, 44093
Fair Scones, 4219
Fairbanks Scales, 22442, 44094
Fairborn USA Inc, 22443, 44095
Fairbury Food Products, 4220
Fairchester Snacks Corp, 4221, 22444
Fairchild Industrial Products, 22445, 44096
Fairco Foods, 44097
Fairfield Farm Kitchens, 4222
Fairfield Line Inc, 22446, 44098
Fairhaven Cooperative Flour Mill, 4223, 44099
Fairley & Co Inc, 40360
Fairlife, 4224
Fairmont Foods Of Minnesota, 4225
Fairmont Snacks Group, 4226
Fairs Seafood, 56377
Fairview Dairy Inc, 4227, 56378
Fairview Swiss Cheese, 4228
Fairway Foods, 56379
Fairwinds Gourmet Coffee, 4229
Fairytale Brownies, 4230
Falafel Republic, 4231
Falco Technologies, 22447, 44100

Falcon Belting, 22448
Falcon Fabricators Inc, 22449
Falcon Rice Mill Inc, 4232, 44101
Falcon Trading Intl Corp, 44102, 56380
Falcone's Cookie Land LTD, 4233
Fall Creek Vineyards, 4234
Fall River Wild Rice, 4235, 44103
Falla Imports, 4236
Fallas Automation Inc., 22450, 44104
Falls Chemical Products, 22451
Falls City Mercantile Co Inc, 56381
Falls Filtration Technologies, 22452
Fallshaw Wheels & Casters, 22453
Fallwood Corp, 4237, 22454, 44105
Fama Sales Co, 4238
Famarco Limited, 4239, 44106
Famco Automatic Sausage Linkers, 22455, 44107
Famco Sausage Linking Machines, 22456
Family Farms Group, 22457
Family Food Company, 4240
Family Foods Home Service, 56382
Family Sweets Candy Company, 4241
Family Tree Farms, 4242, 22458, 44108, 56383
Famous Chili Inc, 4243
Famous Software LLC, 22459
Famous Specialties Co, 4244
Fan Bag Company, 22460
Fancy Delights, 56384
Fancy Farms Popcorn, 4245
Fancy Heat, 44109
Fancy Lebanese Bakery, 4246
Fancy's Candy's, 4247
Fancypants Bakery, 4248
Fanelli's Warehousing-Distrbtn, 52899
Fanestil Packing Company, 4249
Fannie May Fine Chocolate, 4250
Fantapak, 22461
Fantasia, 4251
Fantastic World Foods, 4252, 44110
Fantasy Chocolates, 4253, 44111
Fantasy Cookie Company, 4254
Fantazzmo Fun Stuff, 4255
Fantini Baking Co Inc, 4256
Fantis Foods Inc, 4257, 44112
Far Niente Winery, 4258
Far West Meats, 4259, 44113
Far West Rice Inc, 4260
Faraday, 22462, 44114
Farallon Fisheries Co, 4261, 56385
Farbest Foods Inc, 4262
Farbest-Tallman Foods Corp, 4263, 52900
Fare Foods Corp, 4264, 56386
Farella-Park Vineyards, 4265
Farfelu Vineyards, 4266
Fargo Automation, 22463
Faribault Foods, Inc., 4267, 22464, 52901
Faribault Manufacturing Co, 22465
Farm & Oven Snacks, 4268
Farm 2 Market, 4269, 44115
Farm Boy Food Svc, 4270, 56387
Farm Fish, 56388
Farm Fresh to You, 4271
Farm Pak Products Inc, 4272, 44116
Farm Stores, 56389
Farmdale Creamery Inc, 4275
Farmer Brothers Company, 4276
Farmer Direct Foods, Inc, 44266
Farmer Direct Organic, 4277
Farmer's Co-Op Elevator Co, 22467
Farmer's Hen House, 4278
Farmers Cooperative Dairy, 4279
Farmers Cooperative Grain Co, 4280
Farmers Cooperative-Dorchester, 52902
Farmers Dairies, 4281
Farmers Distributing, 51735
Farmers Meat Market, 4282
Farmers Produce, 4283
Farmers Rice Milling Co, 4284, 44117
Farmers Seafood Co Wholesale, 4285, 56390

Farmers Way, 4286
Farmfresh, 56391
Farmgate Cheese LLC, 4287
FarmGro Organic Foods, 4273
Farmhouse Culture, 4288
Farmington Foods Inc, 4289, 44118, 56392
Farmland Dairies, 4290
Farmland Fresh Dairies, 4291
Farmrail Corp, 51736
Farms For City Kids Foundation, Inc., 4292
FarmSoy Company, 4274
Farmstead At Long Meadow Ranch, 4293, 56393
Farmtrue, 4294
Farmwise LLC, 4295
Farnell Packaging, 22468
Farner-Bocken Co, 56394
Faroh Candies, 4296
Farr Candy Company, 4297
Farrell Baking Company, 4298
Farrell Lines, 51737
Farruggio Express, 51738
Farwest Freight Systems, 51739, 52903
Fas-Co Coders, 22469, 44119
Fashion Industries, 22470
Fashion Snackz, 4299
Fasson Employee FCU, 22471
Fast Bags, 22472
Fast Fixing Foods, 4300, 56395
Fast Industries, 22473, 44120
Fast Pak Trading Inc, 44121
Fast Stuff Packaging, 22474
Fastachi, 4301
Fastcorp, 22475
FASTCORP LLC, 22379
FasTrans, 51740
Fasweet Co, 4302
Fat Snax, 4303
Fat Toad Farm, 4304
Fata Automation, 22476
FatBoy's Cookie Company, 4305
Father Sam's Bakery, 4306
Father's Country Hams, 4307
Father's Table Inc, 4308
Fato Industries, 22477
Fatty Sundays, 4309
Fatworks, 4310
Faubion Central States Tank Company, 22478
Faulk-Collier Bonded Warehouses, 52904
Faulkenberg Inc, 22479
Faultless Caster, 22480
Faure Brothers Inc, 51741, 52905
Favorite Foods, 4311, 44122
Favorite Foods Inc, 22481
Fawema Packaging Machinery, 22482, 44123
Fawen, 4312
Fax Foods, 22483, 44124
Fay Paper Products, 22484, 44125
Fayes Bakery Products, 4313
Faygo Beverages Inc, 4314
Fayter Farms Produce, 4315, 56396
Fazio's Bakery, 4316
FBC Industries, 4204
FBM/Baking Machines Inc, 22380
FCD Tabletops, 22381, 44071
FCF Ginseng, LLC, 22382
FCI Inc, 22383
FCM, 56369
FCN Publishing, 22384
FDC Corporation, 44072
FDI Inc, 4205, 44073, 52897, 56370
FDL/Flair Designs, 22385
Feather Crest Farms, 56397
Feather Duster Corporation, 22485, 44126
Feature Foods, 4317, 44127
FECO/MOCO, 22386, 44074
Fedco Systems, 22486
Federal Business Ctr Inc, 52906
Federal Companies, 51742, 52907
Federal Engineered Systems, 22487

All Companies Index

Federal Heath Sign Co LLC, 22488, 44128
Federal Industries, 22489, 44129
Federal Industries Inc, 22490
Federal Label Systems, 22491
Federal Machine Corp, 22492, 44130
Federal Mfg Co, 22493
Federal Pretzel Baking Company, 4318
Federal Sign, 22494, 22495
Federal Stamp & Seal Manufacturing Company, 22496
Federal Supply USA, 56398
Federal Warehouse Company, 52908
Federated Cooperative, 56399
Federated Cooperative Lt, 56400, 56401, 56402
Federated Group, 40361
Federated Mills, 22497
Federation-Southern Cprtvs, 4319, 44131
Fee Brothers, 4320, 44132
Feed The Party, 4321, 22498, 56403
Feedback Plus, 22499
Feeding the Turkeys, Inc., 4322
Feel Good Foods, 4323
Feenix Brokerage LTD, 40362
Feesers, 56404
Fehlig Brothers Box & Lbr Co, 22500
FEI Co, 22387, 52898
FEI Inc, 22388, 44075
Fein Brothers, 56405
Feinkost Ingredients, 56406
Felbro Food Products, 4324, 44133
Felco Packaging Specialist, 22501, 44134
Feldmeier Equipment Inc, 22502, 44135
Felins USA Inc, 22503, 44136
Felix Custom Smoking, 4325
Felix Roma & Son Inc, 4326
Felix Storch Inc, 22504, 44137
Fell & Co Intl Inc, 22505
Femc, 22506
Fenchem Inc, 4327
Fenco, 22507
Fendall Ice Cream Company, 4328, 56407
Fenestra Winery, 4329
Fenn Valley Vineyards, 4330, 4331
Fenner Drives, 22508, 22509, 44138
Fenner Dunlop Americas Inc, 22510
Fenster Consulting Inc, 22511
Fentimans North America, 4332
Fenton & Lee Chocolatiers, 4333
Fenton Art Glass Company, 22512, 44139
Ferdinand Richards & Son, 40363
Ferguson Containers, 22513
Feridies, 4334, 4335
Ferm-Rite Equipment, 22514
Fermalife, 4336
Ferme Ostreicole Dugas, 4337
Fermenting Fairy, 4338
Fermin Usa, 44140
Fernandez Chili Co, 4339, 44141
Fernando C Pujals & Bros, 4340
Ferncreek Confections LLC, 4341
Fernholtz Engineering, 22515, 44142
Fernqvist Labeling Solutions, 22516, 22517
Ferntrade Corporation, 44143, 56408
Ferolie Esm-Metro New York, 40364
Ferolito Vultaggio & Sons, 4342
Ferrante Winery & Ristorante, 4343
Ferrara Bakery & Cafe, 4344, 44144
Ferrara Candy Co Inc, 4345, 44145
Ferrara Winery, 4346
Ferrari-Carano, 4347
Ferrell-Ross, 22518, 44146
Ferrer Corporation, 22519, 44147
Ferrero USA Inc, 4348
Ferrigno Vineyards & Wine, 4349
Ferris Coffee & Nut Co, 56409
Ferris Organic Farms, 4350, 44148, 56410
Ferris, Stahl-Meyer, 4351
Ferrite Components Inc, 22520
Ferro Corporation, 22521, 44149

Ferroclad Fishery, 4352, 44150
Ferry-Morse Seed Company, 56411
FES West, 22389
Fess Parker Winery, 4353
Festival Ice Cream, 56412
Festive Foods, 4354, 44151
Festo Corp, 22522
Fetco, 22523, 44152
Fettig Laboratories, 22524
Fetzer Vineyards, 4355, 22525, 44153, 56413
Fetzers', 56414
FFE Transportation Services, 22390, 51734
FFI Corporation, 22391, 44076
FFR Merchandising Inc, 22392
FIB-R-DOR, 22393, 44077
Fiber Does, 22526, 44154
Fiber Foods Inc, 56415
Fibercell Packaging LLC, 22527
Fibergrate Composite Strctrs, 22528, 22529
Fiberich Technologies, 22530, 22531
Fiberstar, 4356
Fibertech Inc, 22532, 22533
Fibre Containers Inc, 22534
Fibre Converters Inc, 22535, 44155
Fibre Leather Manufacturing Company, 22536, 44156
Fibred, 4357
Fibreform Containers Inc, 22537
Ficklin Vineyards Winery, 4358
Ficks & Co., 4359
Ficon, 4360
Fidalgo Bay Roasting Co, 4361
Fiddlers Green Farm, 4362
Fidelity Container Corporation, 56416
Fidelity Fruit & Produce Co, 56417
Fiebing Co, 22538, 44157
Fiedler Technology, 22539
Field Coffee, 4363
Field Manufacturing Corporation, 22540
Field Roast, 4364
Field Stone Winery, 4365
Field Trip Jerky, 4366
Field's Pies, 4367
Fieldale Farms, 4368
Fieldbrook Foods Corp., 4369, 44158
Fieldbrook Valley Winery, 4370
Fiera Foods, 4371
Fiesta Candy Company, 4372
Fiesta Canning Co, 4373
Fiesta Farms, 4374, 44159
Fiesta Gourmet of Tejas, 4375, 44160
Fiesta Mexican Foods, 4376
Fiesta Warehousing & Distribution Company, 51743, 52909
Fife Corp, 22541
Fife Vineyards, 4377
FIFO Innovations, 4206
Fig Food Co., 4378
Fig Garden Packing Inc, 4379, 44161
Figamajigs, 4380
Figaro Company, 4381, 44162
Figi's Business Services, 56418
Figueroa Brothers, 4382
Figuerola Laboratories, 4383
Fiji Water Co LLC, 4384
Filet Menu, 22542
Filfil Foods LLC, 4385
Filippo Berio Brand, 4386
Filler Paper Company, 56419
Filler Specialties, 22543, 44163
Filling Equipment Co Inc, 22544, 44164
Fillit, 22545, 44165
Fillmore Piru Citrus, 4387, 44166
Fillo Factory, The, 4388, 44167
Film X, 22546
Film-Pak Inc, 22547
Filmco Inc, 22548, 44168
Filmpack Plastic Corporation, 22549
Filsinger Vineyards & Winery, 4389
Filter Equipment Co, 22550
Filter Products, 22551
Filtercarb LLC/ Filtercorp, 22552

Filtercold Corporation, 22553
Filtercorp, 22554, 44169, 44170
Filtration Solutions, 22555
Filtration Systems, 22556
Filtration Systems Prods Inc, 22557
Filtrine Manufacturing, 22558, 44171
Final Filtration, 22559
Finca La Tacita c/o Falla Imports, 44172
Finch Companies, 51744, 52910
Finchville Farms Country Ham, 4390
Finding Home Farms, 4391, 44173
Findlay Foods Kingston, 56420
Fine & Raw Chocolate, 4392
Fine Chemicals, 44174
Fine Choice Foods, 4393
Fine Cocoa Products, 22560, 44175, 56421
Fine Distributing, 56422
Fine Dried Foods Intl, 4394
Fine Foods Australia, 44176, 56423
Fine Foods Intl, 4395, 22561
Fine Foods Of America Inc, 4396
Fine Foods Trading Company, 4397
Fine Line Seafood, 4398
Fine Woods Manufacturing, 22562
Fineberg Packing Company, 4399
Finer Foods Inc, 4400
Finesaler, 56424
Finest Call, 4401, 44177
Finest Foods, 44178, 56425
Finestkind Fish Market, 4402, 56426
Finger Lakes Coffee Roasters, 4403
Finger Lakes Organic Growers, 56427
Fingerlakes Construction Co, 22563
Finkbiner Transfer & Storage, 52911
Finke Co, 56428
Finkemeier Bakery, 4404
Finlandia Cheese, 4405
Finlay Extracts & Ingredients USA, Inc., 4406, 44179
Finlays, 4407, 22564
Finn & Son's Metal Spinning Specialists, 22565
Finn Industries, 22566
Finn Marketing Group Inc, 40365
Fiore Di Pasta, 4408, 22567
Fiore Winery, 4409
Fiori Bruna Pasta Products, 4410, 44180
Fioriware, 22568
Fiorucci Foods USA Inc, 4411, 44181
Fire & Flavor, 22569
Fire Device Co, 56429
Fire Fruits International, 4412
Fire Master, 56430
Fire Protection Industries, 22570
Fire Protection Systems Inc, 56431
Firebird Artisan Mills, 4413, 22571
Firefly Fandango, 4414
Firehook Bakery & Coffeehouse, 4415
Firelands Winery, 4416
Fireline Corp, 56432
Firemaster, 56433
Firematic Sprinkler Devices, 22572, 44182
Fireside Kitchen, 4417
Firestone Farms, 44183, 56434
Firestone Pacific Foods Co, 4418
Firestone Vineyard, 4419
Firing Industries Ltd, 40366
Firl Industries Inc, 22573, 44184
Firmenich Inc., 4420, 22574
First Bank of Highland P, 22575
First Choice Ingredients, 4421, 56435
First Choice Sales Company, 40367, 44185
First Choice Sign & Lighting, 22576
First Coast Promotions, 56436
First Colony Coffee & Tea Company, 4422, 44186
First Colony Winery, 4423
First DataBank, 22577
First District Association, 4424, 44187
First Fire Systems Company, 56437
First Flight Foods, 40368

First Food Co, 4425
First Food International, 4426
First Midwest of Iowa Corporation, 22578
First Oriental Market, 4427, 56438
First Original Texas Chili Company, 4428
First Plastics Co Inc, 22579
First Roasters of Central Florida, 4429
First Source LLC, 22580, 56439
First Spice Mixing Co, 4430
Firth Maple Products, 4431
Fischbein LLC, 22581, 44188
Fischer & Wieser Spec Foods, 4432
Fischer Group, 40369
Fischer Honey Company, 4433
Fischer Meats, 4434
Fischer Paper Products Inc, 22582
Fish Breeders of Idaho, 4435, 56440
Fish Brothers, 4436
Fish Express, 4437, 56441
Fish Hopper, 4438
Fish King, 4439
Fish King Processors, 4440
Fish Market Inc, 4441, 4442, 56442
Fish Oven & Equipment Co, 22583, 44189
Fisher Honey Co, 4443, 44190
Fisher Manufacturing Company, 22584, 44191
Fisher Mills, 56443
Fisher Ridge Wine Co Inc, 4444
Fisher Scientific Company, 22585, 22586, 44192
Fisher Vineyards, 4445
Fisher's Popcorn, 4446
Fisherman's Market International, 4447
Fisherman's Reef Shrimp Company, 4448
Fisherman's Seafood Market, 56444
Fishermens Net, 4449, 56445
Fishers Investment, 22587, 44193
Fishhawk Fisheries, 4450
Fishland Market, 4451
Fishmore, 22588, 44194
Fishpeople, 4452
Fiskars Brands Inc., 22589
Fiskars Consumer Products, 44195
Fiske Brothers Refining Co, 22590
Fitch Co, 56446
Fitec International Inc, 22591, 44196
Fitness & Nutrition Center, 56447
FitPro USA, 4453
Fittings Inc, 22592
Fitzkee's Candies Inc, 4454
Fitzpatrick Brothers, 22593, 44197
Fitzpatrick Co, 22594, 44198
Fitzpatrick Container Company, 22595
Fitzpatrick Winery & Lodge, 4455
Five Acre Farms, 4456
Five Continents, 22596, 56448
Five Ponds Farm, 4457, 56449
Five Star Food Base Company, 4458
Five Star Foodies, 4459
Five Star Home Foods, Inc., 4460
Five Star Packaging, 40370
Five Star Transport Service, 51745
Five State Brokerage, 40371
Five-M Plastics Company, 22597
FiveStar Gourmet Foods, 4461
Fixtur World, 22598, 44199
Fixtures Furniture, 22599
Fizz-O Water Co, 4462, 56450
Fizzle Flat Farm, L.L.C., 4463, 44200
Fizzy Lizzy, 4464
FJC International, 22394
Flackers, 4465
Flaghouse, 44201, 56451
Flags & Banners Unlimited, 56452
Flagstaff Brewing Co, 4466
Flaherty Inc, 4467
Flair Beverages, 56453
Flair Electronics, 22600
Flair Flexible Packaging Corp, 22601
Flakice Corporation, 22602, 44202
Flambeau Inc, 22603

1383

All Companies Index

Flame Gard, 22604, 44203
FLAMEX Inc, 56371
Flamin' Red's Woodfired, 4468
Flamingo Flats, 44204, 56454
Flamingo Food Service Products, 22605, 44205
Flamm Pickle & Packing, 4469
Flamous Brands, 4470
Flanders, 4471, 56455
Flanders Corp, 22606
Flanigan Farms, 4472, 44206
FlapJacked, 4473, 56456
Flash Foods, 56457
FlashBake Ovens Food Service, 22607
Flashfold Carton Inc, 22608
Flat Cracker Inc., 4474
Flat Plate Inc, 22609, 44207
FLAT Tech Inc., 4207
Flat Tire Bike Shop, 4475
Flathau's Fine Foods, 4476
Flatland Food Distributors, 56458
Flatout Inc, 4477, 56459
Flatten-O-Matic: Universal Concepts, 22610
Flaum Appetizing, 4478
Flav-O-Rich, 56460, 56461
Flavor & Fragrance Specialties, 4479
Flavor Burst, 22611
Flavor Consultants, 40372, 44208
Flavor Dynamics Two, 4480, 44209
Flavor House, Inc., 4481, 44210
Flavor Producers, 4482
Flavor Right Foods Group, 4483
Flavor Savor, 56462
Flavor Sciences Inc, 4484, 44211
Flavor Systems Intl., 4485, 44212
Flavor Wear, 22612, 44213
Flavor-Crisp of America, 44214, 56463
Flavorbank Company, 4487
Flavorchem Corp, 4488, 44215
Flavorganics, 4489, 44216
FlavorHealth, 4486
Flavormatic Industries, 4490, 44217
Flavors and Color, 4491
Flavors from Florida, 4492
Flavors of Hawaii Inc, 4493
Flavors of the Heartland, 4494
Flavorseal, 22613
Flavouressence Products, 4495, 44218
Flavourtech Americas, 22614
Flax Council of Canada, 56464
Flax4Life, 4496
Fleet Fisheries Inc, 4497, 56465
Fleet Wood Goldco Wyard, 22615, 44219
Fleetwood International Paper, 22616
Fleetwood Systems, 22617
FleetwoodGoldcoWyard, 22618, 44220
Fleig Commodities, 44221, 56466
Fleischer's Bagels, 4498, 44222
Fleischmann's Vinegar Co Inc, 4499
Fleischmann's Yeast, 4500, 44223
Fleming Packaging Corporation, 22619
Fletcher's Fine Foods, 4501, 44224
Fleur De Lait Foods Inc, 4502, 44225
Fleurchem Inc, 4503, 44226
Flex Pack USA, 4504, 22620
Flex Products, 22621, 44227
Flex Sol Packaging Corp, 22622, 22623
Flex-Hose Co Inc, 22624, 44228
Flex-O-Glass, 22625
FlexBarrier Products, 22626
Flexco, 22627, 22628, 22629
FLEXcon Company, 22395, 44078
Flexible Foam Products, 22630
Flexible Material Handling, 22631
Flexible Tape & Label Co, 22632
Flexicell Inc, 22633, 44229
Flexicon, 22634, 22635, 44230, 44231
Flexlink Systems Inc, 22636
Flexlume Sign Corp, 22637
Flexo Graphics, 22638
Flexo Printing Equipment Corp, 22639
Flexo Transparent Inc, 22640, 44232
Fliinko, 4505
Flint Boxmakers Inc, 22641

Flint Provision Inc Zalack's, 56467
Flint Rubber Stamp Works, 22642
Flippin-Seaman Inc, 4506, 44233
Flix Candy, 4507
Flo-Cold, 22643
Flo-Matic Corporation, 22644, 44234
Floaire, 22645
Floating Leaf Fine Foods, 4508, 44235
Flodin, 22646
Flojet, 22647, 44236
Flomatic International, 22648, 44237
Floor Master Inc, 22649
Flora Foods Inc, 44238, 56468
Flora Inc, 4509
Flora Springs Winery, 4510
Florart Flock Process, 22650, 44239
Florence Macaroni Manufacturing, 4511
Florence Pasta & Cheese, 4512
Florentyna's Fresh Pasta Factory, 4513
Florida Agents Inc, 40373
Florida Beverage Connection, 56469
Florida Brewery, 4514
Florida Carbonic Distributor, 56470
Florida Caribbean Distillers, 4515
Florida Choice Foods, 44240, 56471
Florida Citrus, 4516
Florida Crystals Corporation, 4517
Florida Distributing Source, 40374, 56472
Florida European Export-Import, 44241
Florida Food Products Inc, 4518, 44242
Florida Freezer LP, 51746, 52912, 52913
Florida Fresh Stonecrab, 56473
Florida Fruit Juices, 4519
Florida Gulf Packaging, 56474
Florida Key West, 4520
Florida Knife Co, 22651, 44243
Florida Natural Flavors, 4521, 44244
Florida Plastics Intl, 22652, 44245
Florida Seating, 22653
Florida Smoked Fish Company, 56475
Florida Veal Processors, 4522
Florida's Natural Growers, 4523, 44246
Florin Box & Lumber Company, 22654
Floron Food Services, 4524
Flostor Engineering, 56476
Flour City Press-Pack Company, 22655
Flow Aerospace, 22656, 44247
Flow International Corp., 22657, 44248
Flow of Solids, 22660
Flow Technology, 22658
Flow Technology Inc, 22659
Flower Essence Svc, 4525
Flowers Baking Co, 4526, 4527, 4528, 44249
Flowers Foods Inc., 4529, 56477
Floyd, 4530
Fluid Air Inc, 22661, 44250
Fluid Energy Processing & Eqpt, 22662, 44251
Fluid Imaging Technologies Inc, 22663
Fluid Metering Inc, 22664, 44252
Fluid Systems, 22665
Fluid-O-Tech International Inc, 44253, 56478
Flurowater, Inc., 4531
Flushing Lighting, 56479
Fluted Partition Inc, 22666
Flux Pumps Corporation, 22667, 44254
Flying Bird Botanicals LLC, 4532
Flying Burrito Co, 4533
Flying Dog Brewery, 4534, 44255
Flying Embers, 4535
Flynn Burner Corporation, 22668
Flynn Sales Associates, Inc., 40375
Flynn Vineyards Winery, 4536
Flynt Wholesale Company, 56480
Flyover International Corporation, 44256
FM Carriere & Son, 40358
Fmali Herb, 4537, 44257
FMB Company, 22396
FMC Corporation, 22397
FMC Fluid Control, 22398
FMI Display, 22399
FMI Fluid Metering, 22400

FMI Food Marketers International Ltd, 40359
FMS, 22401
FMS Company, 22402
FNI Group LLC, 4208
Foam Concepts Inc, 22669, 44258
Foam Fabricator-Corp, 22670
Foam Pack Industries, 22671
Foam Packaging Service Inc, 22672, 44259
Foamex, 22673
Foamold Corporation, 22674
Focke & Co Inc, 22675
Focus, 22676
Focus Foodservice, 4538
Focus Marketing, 56481
FODY Food Co., 4209
Foell Packing Company, 4539, 44260
Fogel Jordon Commercial Refrigeration Company, 22677, 44261
Fogel Rubin & Fogel, 22678
Fogg Filler Co, 22679, 44262
Fogo Island Cooperative Society, 4540, 44263
Foilmark Inc, 22680
Fold-Pak Corporation, 22681, 44264
Fold-Pak LLC, 40376, 44265, 56482
Fold-Pak South, 22682, 44266
Folding Carton/Flexible Packaging, 22683
Folding Guard Co, 22684, 44267
Foley Estates Vineyard, 4541
Foley Sign Co, 22685, 44268
Foley's Chocolates & Candies, 4542
Foley's Famous Aprons, 22686
Foley-Belsaw Institute, 44269, 56483
Folgers Coffee Co, 4543, 44270, 56484
Folie … Deux Winery, 4544
Folklore Foods, 4545, 44271
Follett Corp, 22687, 44272
Follex Distributing Co Inc, 56485
Follmer Development, Inc, 4546
Follow Your Heart, 4547
Folmer Fruit & Produce Company, 56486
Foltz Meat Processors, 4548
Fona International, 4548, 22688, 44273
FOND Bone Broth, 4210
Fonda Group, 22689
Fonseca Coffee, 44274
Fontana Flavors Inc, 4549
Fontanini Italian Meats, 4550
Fontazzi/Metrovox Snacks, 4551
Fonterra Co-operative Group Limited, 4552, 44275
Food & Agrosystems, 22690, 44276
Food & Beverage Consultants, 22691
Food & Vine Inc., 4553
Food Allergy & Anaphylaxis Network, 22692
Food and Dairy Research Associates, 22733
Food Associates of Syracuse, 40377
Food Authority Inc, 56488
Food Business Associates, 22693
Food Buying Service, 56489
Food City, 56490
Food City Pickle Company, 4554
Food City USA, 4555
Food Concentrate Corporation, 4556
Food Consulting Company, 22694
Food Development Centre, 22695
Food Engineering Network, 22696
Food Engineering Unlimited, 22697
Food Equipment BrokerageInc, 22698, 44277
Food Equipment Distributors, 56491
Food Equipment Manufacturing Company, 22699, 44278
Food Equipment Rep Inc, 40378
Food Equipment Specialist, 56492
Food Executives Network, 22700
Food Factory, 4557, 56493
Food First, 4558
Food for Life Baking, 4570, 56504
Food For Thought Inc, 4559, 56494
Food Handling Systems, 22701

Food Industry ConsultingGroup, 22702
Food Industry Equipment, 22703
Food Ingredient Solutions, 4560, 56495
Food Ingredient Specialties, 4561
Food Ingredients, 56496
Food Ingredients Inc, 40379
Food Insights, 22704
Food Institute, 22705
Food Instrument Corp, 22706, 44279, 56497
Food Ireland, Inc., 44280, 56498
Food Link Inc, 52914
Food Machinery of America, 22708
Food Machinery Sales, 22707, 44281
Food Makers Equipment, 22709
Food Management Search, 22710
Food Marketing Servives, 22711
Food Masters, 4562, 44282
Food Matters Again, 4563
Food Mill, 4564
Food of Our Own Design, 4571
Food Pak Corp, 22712, 44283
Food People Inc, 56499
Food Plant Companies, 22713
Food Plant Engineering, 22714, 22715
Food Processing Concepts, 22716
Food Processing Equipment Co, 22717, 44284
Food Processor of New Mexico, 4565
Food Processors Institute, 22718
Food Products Corporation, 4566
Food Products Lab, 22719
Food Resources International, 22720, 44285
Food Safety Net Services Ltd, 22721
Food Sales Systems, 40380
Food Sales West, 40381
Food Sanitation Svc Inc, 22722
Food Scene, 22723
Food Science Associates, 22724
Food Science Consulting, 22725
Food Sciences Corp, 4567
Food Service Associates, 40382
Food Service Connection, 40383
Food Service Design & Furnishings, 56500
Food Service Equipment Corporation, 22726
Food Service Marketing of Pennsylvania, 40384
Food Service Merchandising, 40385
Food Service Specialists, 40386
Food Services Inc, 56501
Food Should Taste Good, 4568
Food Source Company, 4569, 44286
Food Supply Inc, 56502
Food Tech Structures LLC, 22727
Food Technologies, 22728
Food Technology Corporation, 22729, 44287
Food Tools, 22730, 22731, 44288
Food Warming Equipment Co, 22732, 44289
Food Wholesalers Inc, 56503
Food-Products, 56505
Food-Tek, 22734
Food-Trak, 44290
FoodBin Trading, Inc., 40387
Foodchek Systems, 22737
Foodcomm International, 44293
Fooddesign Machinery & Systems, 22738, 22739
FOODesign from tna, 22403
FoodHandler, 22735
Foodie Fuel, 4573
FoodLogiQ, 22736
Foodmark Sales, 40388
Foodmark, Inc., 22740
FoodMatch Inc, 4572
FoodMatch, Inc., 44291
Foodpro International, 22741, 44294
Foods Alive, 4574
Foods Etc., 56506
Foods Research Laboratories, 22742
Foodsales Inc, 40389

All Companies Index

Foodscience Corp, 4575, 44295
Foodservice Center Inc, 52915
Foodservice Consultants Society International, 22743
Foodservice Database Co, 44296
Foodservice Design Associates, 22744
Foodservice East, 22745
Foodservice Equipment & pplie, 22746
Foodservice Equipment Distributors Association, 22747
Foodservice Innovation Network, 22748
Foodservice Innovators, 40390
Foodservice Marketing, 40391
Foodservice Solutions & Ideas, 40392
FoodShowcase.Com, 44292
Foodstirs, 4576
Foodtopia USA, 56507
Foodworks, 22749
Foodworks International, 40393, 44297
Fool Proof Gourmet Products, 4577, 44298
Foote & Jenks, 22750
Foothills Creamery, 4578
Footner & Co Inc, 40394, 44299, 51747
Footprint Retail Svc, 51748
Foppiano Vineyards, 4579, 44300
For Life, 22751
Fora Foods, 4580, 56508
Forager Project, 4581
Foran Spice Inc, 4582, 22752
Forbes Candies, 4583
Forbes Chocolate BP, 4584, 44301
Forbes Co, 4585
Forbes Frozen Foods, 40395, 56509
Forbes Hever & Wallace, Inc., 40396
Forbes Industries, 22753, 44302
Forbes Products Corp, 22754
Forbo Siegling LLC, 22755
Ford Gum & Mach Co Inc, 4586, 44303
Ford Hotel Supply Co, 56510
Ford Ice Cream, 56511
Ford's Gourmet Foods, 4587, 4588
Foreign Candy Company, 4589, 22756, 56512
Foreign Domestic Chemicals, 4590, 56513
Foreman Group, 22757
Foremost Farms USA, 4591, 56514
Foremost Foods Company, 56515
Foremost Machine Builders Inc, 22758, 44304
Forest City Weingart Produce, 56516
Forest Glen Winery, 44305
Forest Manufacturing Co, 22759, 44306
Forever Cheese, 44307
Forever Foods, 44308, 56517
Forever Green Food Inc., 4592
Forge Mountain Foods, 4593
Foris Vineyards, 4594
Fork & Goode, 4595
Forkless Gourmet Inc, 4596
Forklift Systems Inc-Parts Dpt, 56518
Forklifts, 56519
Forma Packaging, Inc., 40397
Forman Group, 40398
Forman Vineyard, 4597
Formaticum, 22760
Formation Systems, 22761
Formel Industries, 22762
Former Tech, 22763
Formers By Ernie, 22764
Formers of Houston, 22765
Formflex, 22766, 44309
Formosa Enterprises Inc, 4598
Formost Friedman Company, 4599
Formost Packaging Machines, 22767, 44310
Formula Espresso, 22768, 44311
Formulator Software, LLC, 22769
Forpack, 22770
Forpak, 22771
Forrest Engraving Company, 22772, 44312
Forseasons Sales, 40399
Forster & Son, 22773

Fort Boise Produce Company, 4600
Fort Dearborn Company, 22774
Fort Garry Brewing Company, 4601
FORT Hill Sign Products Inc, 22404
Fort James Canada, 22775
Fort Lock Corporation, 22776
Fort Pitt Candy Co, 56520
Fort Smith Restaurant Supply, 56521
Fort Transportation & Svc Co, 51749
Fort Wayne Awning, 22777
Fort Wayne Door Inc, 56522
Forte Gelato, 4602
Forte Industries, 56523
Forte Stromboli Company, 4603
Forte Technology, 22778, 44313
Fortella Fortune Cookies, 4604
Fortenberry Mini-Storage, 4605, 22779
Fortifiber Building Systs Grp, 22780
Fortino Winery, 4606
Fortitude Brands LLC, 4607
Forto Coffee, 4608
Fortress Systems LLC, 4609
Fortress Technology, 22781, 22782
Fortuna Cellars, 4610
Fortunate Cookie, 4611
Fortune Cookie Factory, 4612
Fortune Equipment Company, 56524
Fortune Plastics, Inc, 22783, 44314
Fortune Products Inc, 22784, 44315
Fortune Seas, 4613, 44316
Fortunes International Teas, 4614
Fortville Produce, 56525
Forty Second Street Bagel Cafe, 4615
Fort, Products, 4616, 22785
Forum Lighting, 22786, 44317
Foss Nirsystems, 22787, 44318
Foss North America Inc, 22788
Fosselman's Ice Cream Co, 4617
Fossil Farms, 4618
Foster Dairy Farms Inc, 56527
Foster Family Farm, 4619, 44319
Foster Fams, 4620
Foster Farms Inc., 4621, 22788, 44320
Foster Fine Foods, LLC, 44321
Foster Forbes Glass, 22789
Foster Miller Inc, 22790, 44322
Foster Refrigerator Corporation, 22791, 44323
Foster-Forbes Glass Company, 22792
Fotel, 22793
Foth & Van Dyke, 22794
Fought's Mill, 56528
Fountain Shakes/MS Foods, 4622
Fountain Valley Foods, 4623, 44324, 56529
Fountainhead, 22795, 44325
Four Barrel Coffee, 4624
Four Chimneys Farm Winery Trust, 4625
Four Corners Ice, 22796
Four M Manufacturing Group, 22797
Four Oaks Farm, 56530
Four Peaks, Inc., 40400
Four Percent Company, 4626
Four Seasons Produce Inc, 4627, 22798
Four Sigmatic, 4628
Four Sisters Winery, 4629
Four Star Beef, 4630, 22799
Four Today, 56531
Fourinox Inc, 22800, 44326
Fournier R & Sons Seafood, 4631, 56532
Foutch's Coffee and Spring Water, 56533
Fowler Farms, 4632, 44327
Fowler Packing Co, 4633
Fowler Products Co LLC, 22801, 44328
Fox Brush Company, 22802, 56534
Fox Deluxe Inc, 4634, 56535
Fox Hollow, 4635
Fox Iv Technologies, 4636, 22803
Fox Meadow Farm, 4637
Fox Meadow Farm of Vermont, 4638
Fox N Hare Brewing Co., 4639
Fox Run Vineyards, 4640
Fox Stamp Sign & Specialty, 22804
Fox Transportation Inc, 51750, 52916
Fox Valley Wood Products Inc, 22805

Fox Vineyards & Winery, 4641
Fox's Fine Foods, 4642
Fox-Morris Associates, 22806
Foxboro Company, 22808, 44329
Foxcroft Equipment & Svc Co, 22809
Foxen Foxen 7200, 4643
Foxfire Marketing Solutions, 22810
FoxJet, 22807
Foxjet, 22811
Foxon Co, 22812, 44330
Foxtail Foods, 4644, 56536
Fp Development, 22813
FP Packaging Company, 22405
FPC Corp, 22406
FPEC Corp, 22407
FPEC Corporation, 22408, 44079
Frabosk Magic Cappuccino, 56537
Frain Industries, 22814, 56538
Fralinger's, 4645
Framarx Corp, 22815, 44331
Fran's Chocolates, 4646
Fran's Healthy Helpings, 4647
France Delices, 4648, 44332
France Personalized Signs, 22817
Francis & Lusky Company, 22818, 44333
Francis Musto & Co, 40401
Francis Produce Company, 56539
Franciscan Estate, 4649, 44334
Franco Roma Foods, 56540
Franco's Cocktail Mixes, 4650, 44335
Francorp, 22819
Frank & Dean's Cocktail Mixes, 4651
Frank B Ross Co Inc, 22820
Frank Beer, 56541
Frank Brunckhorst Company, 4652, 56542
Frank Family Vineyards, 4653
Frank G. Schmitt Company, 56543
Frank H Gill Co, 56544
Frank Haile & Assoc, 22821
Frank Kinsman Assoc, 40402
Frank Korinek & Co, 4654
Frank M Hartley Inc, 40403, 44336
Frank Mattes & Sons Reliable Seafood, 4655, 56545
Frank O Carlson & Co, 22822
Frank P. Corso, 56546
Frank Pagano Company, 4656, 56547
Frank Torrone & Sons, 22823
Frank Wardynski & Sons Inc, 4657, 56548
Frank's Produce, 56549
Frank-Lin Distributors, 4658
Franke Americas, 22824
Frankford Candy & Chocolate Co, 4659
Frankfort Cheese, 4660
Franklin Automation Inc, 22825
Franklin Baker Company, 4661
Franklin Baking Co., 4662
Franklin Baking Company, 4663
Franklin Crates, 22826
Franklin Equipment, 22827
Franklin Express Co Inc, 51751, 52917
Franklin Farms, 4664
Franklin Foods, 4665
Franklin Hill Vineyards, 4666
Franklin Industries LLC, 44337
Franklin Machine Products, 22828, 44338, 56550
Franklin Produce Company, 56551
Franklin Rubber Stamp Co, 22829
Franklin Storage Inc, 51752, 52918
Franklin Trading Company, 44339
Franklin Uniform Corporation, 22830
Franklin's Cheese, 4667
Frankly Natural Bakers, 4668
Frankston Paper Box Company of Texas, 22831
Frankstown Fish Co Inc, 56552
Franmara, 22832
FranRica Systems, 22816
Franrica Systems, 22833, 44340
Frantz Co Inc, 22834
Franz Bakery Outlet Store, 4669
Franz Haas Machinery-America, 22835

Franzia Winery, 4670
Fraser Stamp & Seal, 22836
Fratelli Beretta USA, 4671
Fratelli Mantova, 4672
Fratelli Perata, 4673
Fratello Coffee Roasters, 4674
Frazier & Son, 22837, 44341
Frazier Industrial Co, 22838
Frazier Nut Farms Inc, 4675, 44342
Frazier Precision Instr Co, 22839, 44343
Frazier Signs, 22840
FRC Environmental, 22409, 44080
FRC Systems International, 22410, 44081
Fred Band & Associates, 56553
Fred Beesley's Booth & Upholstery, 22841
Fred D Pfening Co, 22842, 44344
Fred Hill & Son Co, 56554
Fred Usinger Inc, 4676
Fred W Albrecht Grocery Co, 56555
Fredco Wolf, 40404
Frederick Produce Company, 56556
Frederick Wildman & Sons LTD, 4677, 44345, 56557
Fredericksburg Herb Farm, 4678
Fredman Bag Co, 22843
Fredon Handling Inc, 56558
Fredrick Ramond Company, 22844, 44346
Free Flow Packaging Corporation, 22845
Free2b Foods, 4679
Freed, Teller & Freed, 4681
Freeda Vitamins Inc, 4682, 44347
Freedman's Bakery, 4683
Freedom Food Brokers, 40405
Freedom Foods LLC, 4684
Freedom Packaging, 22846
Freekehlicious, 4685
Freeland Bean & Grain Inc, 4686, 40406, 44348
Freeline Organics USA, 40407
Freely Display, 22847, 44349
Freeman Co, 22848
Freeman Electric Co Inc, 22849
Freeman Fruit Intl, 40408
Freeman Industries, 4687, 44350
Freeman Signature, 40409
Freemark Abbey Winery, 4688, 44351
Freeport Cold Storage Inc, 52919
Freeport Logistics Inc, 52920
FreesTech, 22850, 44352
Freestone Pickle Co, 4689
Freeway Warehouse Corp, 51753, 52921
FreeYumm, 4680
Freeze-Dry Foods Inc, 4690, 44353, 52922
Freeze-Dry Ingredients, 4691
Freiria & Company, 40410, 44354, 56559
Freirich Foods, 4692
Freixenet USA Inc, 4693, 44355
Frelco, 22851, 44356
Frem Corporation, 22852, 44357
Fremont Authentic Brands, 4694, 44358
Fremont Beef Co, 4695
Fremont Die Cut Products, 22853
French & Brawn Marketplace, 4696
French Awning & Screen Co Inc, 22854
French Cheese Club   C/O Solutions Export USA, 44359
French Creek Seafood, 4697, 44360
French Farm, 44361
French Feast Inc, 4698
French Gourmet Inc, 4699
French Market Coffee, 4700
French Market Foods, 4701
French Meadow Bakery & Cafe, 4702
French Oil Mill Machinery Co, 22855, 44362
French Patisserie, 4703
French Quarter Seafood, 4704, 56560
French's Coffee, 4705
French's Flavor Ingredients, 4706
Fres-Co SYSTEM USA Inc, 22856
Fresca Foods Inc., 22857
Fresca Mexican Foods LLC, 4707

1385

All Companies Index

Fresco Y Mas, 56561
Fresh Bellies, 4708
Fresh Express, Inc., 4709, 22858
Fresh Frozen Foods, 4710
Fresh Hemp Foods, 4711
Fresh Ideas, 4712
Fresh Island Fish, 4713, 44363, 56562
Fresh Juice Delivery, 4714, 44364
Fresh Mark Inc., 4715, 22859
Fresh Market Pasta Company, 4716
Fresh Nature Foods, 4717
Fresh Origins, 4718
Fresh Pack Seafood, 4719, 44365, 56563
Fresh Pasta Delights, 4720
Fresh Point, 56564
Fresh Point Dallas, 56565
Fresh Roasted Almond Company, 4721
Fresh Samantha, 4722
Fresh Seafood Distrib, 4723, 56566
Fresh Start Bakeries, 4724
Fresh Tofu Inc, 4725
Fresherized Foods, 44366
Freshloc Technologies, 22860
FreshPro Food Distributors, 56567
Freshwater Farms Of Ohio, 4726
Freshwater Fish Market, 4727
Freshway Distributors, 22861, 51754
Freskeeto Frozen Foods Inc, 56568
Fresno Neon Sign Co Inc, 22862
Fresno Pallet, Inc., 22863
Fresno Tent & Awning, 22864
Freudenberg Nonwovens, 22865, 44367
Frey Vineyards, 4728
Freybe Gourmet Foods Ltd, 4729
FRICK by Johnson Controls, 22411
Frick Winery, 4730
Frick's Quality Meats, 4731
Fried Provisions Company, 4732
Frieda's Inc, 4733
Friedman Bag Company, 22866, 44368, 56569
Friedman Fixtures Co, 56570
Friedr Dick Corp, 22867, 44369
Friedrich Metal Products, 22868, 44370
Friend Box Co, 22869
Friendly City Box Co Inc, 22870
Friendly Wholesale Co, 56571
Friendship Dairies LLC, 4734
Friendship International, 4735, 44371
Fries Bros Eggs LLC, 56572
FrieslandCampina Ingredients North America, Inc., 4736
Frigid Coil, 22871
Frigidaire Co., 22872
Frigoscandia, 22873
Frigoscandia Equipment, 22874, 22875
Frio Foods, 4737
Frisco Baking Co Inc, 4738
Frisinger Cellars, 4739
Frisk Design, 22876
Friskem Infinetics, 22877, 44372
Frisson Normand, 4740
Fristam Pumps USA LLP, 22878, 22879, 44373, 44374
Frito-Lay Inc., 4741, 44375
Fritsch, 22880
Fritsch USA, 22881
Fritzie Fresh Products, 56573
Frobisher Industries, 22882, 44376
Froehlich Alex Packing Co, 4742
Frog City Cheese, 4743
Frog Ranch Foods, 4744
Frog's Leap Winery, 4745
Frohling Sign Co, 22883
From Oregon, 4746
From the Ground Up, 4747
Froma-Dar, 4748
Fromartharie Inc, 40411
Frommelt Safety Products & Ductsox Corporation, 22884
Front Line Safety, 56574
Front Range Snacks Inc, 4749, 44377, 56575
Frontage Enterprises, 22885
Frontenac Point Vineyard, 4750

Frontera Foods, 4751
Frontier Bag, 22886, 44378
Frontier Bag Co Inc, 22887, 56576
Frontier Co-op, 4752, 56577
Frontier Packaging Company, 22888
Frontier Soups, 4753
Frontline Inc, 44379, 56578
Froozer, 4754
Frost ET Inc, 22889, 44380
Frost Food Handling Products, 22890, 44381
Frost Manufacturing Corp, 22891
Frostar Corporation, 52923
Frostproof Sunkist Groves, 4755
Frosty Factory Of America Inc, 22892, 44382
Frosty Products, 56579
Frostyaire for Frozen Foods, 52924, 52925
Frostyaire of Arkansas, Inc., 52926
Frozen Food Associates, 40412
Frozen Specialties Inc, 4756, 22893
Frozen Storage Company, 52927
Frozfruit Corporation, 4757, 44383
FRS Industries, 22412
Fru-Terra, 56580
Fru-V, 4758, 56581
Fruehauf Trailer Services, 22894
Fruge Aquafarms, 56582
Fruigees, 4759
Fruit Acres Farm Market and U-Pick, 4760
Fruit Belt Canning Inc, 4761, 44384, 56583
Fruit Bliss, 4762
Fruit d'Or, 4766, 56587
Fruit Fillings Inc, 4763
Fruit Growers Package Company, 22895, 44385
Fruit Growers Supply Company, 4764, 56584
Fruit of the Boot, 4767
Fruit of the Land Products, 4768
Fruit Of The Vine Of De Valley, 56585
Fruit Ranch Inc, 4765, 56586
Fruitco Corp, 56588
Fruitcrown Products Corp, 4769, 22896, 44386
Fruithill Inc, 4770
Fruition Northwest LLC, 4771, 22897
Frutarom Meer Corporation, 4773, 44387
Frutech International Corp, 4774, 44388
Frutex Group, 44389
FrutStix, 4772
Fruvemex, 4775, 22898
Fry Foods Inc, 4776, 44390
Fry Krisp Food Products, 4777
Fry Tech Corporation, 22899
Frye's Measure Mill, 22900, 44391
Frymaster/Dean, 22901, 44392
FSD International, 44082
FSFG Capital, 22413
Fsi Technologies, 22902
Fst Logistics Inc, 51755, 52928
FTC International Consulting, 22414
FTI International Automation Systems, 22415
FTL/Happold Tensil Structure Design & Engineering, 22416
FTR Processing Equipment, 22417
Fuchs North America, 4778
Fudge Farms, 4779
Fudge Fatale, 4780
Fuji Foods Corp, 4781, 44393
Fuji Health Science/Inc, 4782, 22903
Fuji Labeling Systems, 22904
Fuji Produce, 56589
Fuji Vegetable Oil Inc, 4783
Fujitso Transaction Solutions, 22905
Ful-Flav-R Foods, 4784, 22906
Fulcher's Point Pride Seafood, 4785
Full Harvest, 56590
Full Sail Brewing Co, 4786
Full-View Display Case, 22907
Fullbloom Baking Co, 4787

Fuller Box Co, 22908
Fuller Flag Company, 22909
Fuller Foods, 4788
Fuller Industries LLC, 22910, 44394
Fuller Packaging Inc, 22911, 44395
Fuller Ultra Violet Corp, 22912
Fuller Weighing Systems, 22913, 44396
Fullway International, 44397, 56591
Fulton Boiler Works Inc, 22914
Fulton Fish Market, 4789
Fulton Provision Co, 4790
Fulton-Denver Co, 22915
Fumoir Grizzly, 4791, 44398
Fun City Popcorn, 4792, 22916
Fun Express, 44399
Fun Factory, 4793
Fun Foods, 4794, 44400
Fun-Time International, 22917, 44401
Functional Foods, 4795, 4796
Functional Products LLC, 4797
Fungi Perfecti, 4798
Fungus Among Us, 4799
Funke Filters, 22918
Funkychunky Inc., 4800
Funnibonz LLC, 4801
Funny Apron Co, 22919
Furgale Industries Ltd., 22920, 44402
Furmano's Bakery, 4802
Furnace Belt Company, 22921, 44403
Furniturelab, 22922, 44404
Furukawa Potato Chip Factory, 4803
Fusion Gourmet, 4804
Fusion Jerky, 4805
Fusion Sales Group, 40413
Futura 2000 Corporation, 22923
Futura Coatings, 22924
Futura Equipment Corporation, 22925
Future Bakery & Cafe, 4806
Future Commodities Intl Inc, 22926, 44405
Future Foods, 22927
Futurebiotics LLC, 4807, 56592
Futureceuticals Inc, 4808
Futures, 22928
Futurity Products, 56593
Fuzz East Coast, 4809
Fuzziwig's Candy Factory, 4810
Fuzzy's Wholesale Bar-B-Q, 4811
FW Thurston, 4211
FX Technology & Products, 22418
FX-Lab Company, 22419, 44083
Fygir Logistic Information Systems, 22929
Fyh Bearing Units USA Inc, 22930

G

G & C Packing Co, 22931
G & D Chillers Inc, 22932
G & F Mfg, 22933
G & F Systems Inc, 44406
G & J Awning & Canvas Inc, 22934
G & J Land & Marine Food Distr, 4812, 56594
G & L Davis Meat Co, 56595
G & L Import Export Corp, 44407, 56596
G & S Metal Products Co Inc, 22935
G & W Equipment Inc, 56597
G & W Food Products, 56598
G A B Empacadora Inc, 44408, 56599
G A Food Svc Inc, 4813
G A Systems Inc, 22936
G C Evans Sales & Mfg Co, 22937, 22938
G Cefalu & Brother Inc, 4814
G Debbas Chocolatier, 4815
G K & L Inc, 22939
G K Skaggs Inc, 44409
G L Packaging Products Inc, 22940
G Lighting, 22941
G M Allen & Son Inc, 4816
G M P Laboratories Of Amer Inc, 4817
G Nino Bragelli Inc, 44410
G P 50 New York LTD, 22942
G Scaccianoce & Co, 4818, 44411

G W Berkheimer Co, 22943
G&A Warehouses, 52929
G&G Distributing, 56600
G&H Enterprises, 22944
G&K Vijuk Intern. Corp, 22945
G&R Graphics, 22946, 44412
G&T Commodities, 56601
G&T Terminal Packaging Company, 56602
G-3 Enterprises, 22947
G-M Super Sales Company, 44413
G. Banis Company, 4819
G.A. Davis Food Service, 40414
G.B. Sales & Service, 56603
G.D. Mathews & Sons, 56604
G.E. Barbour, 4820, 44414
G.E.F. Gourmet Foods Inc, 4821
G.F. Frank & Sons, 22948, 44415
G.G. Greene Enterprises, 22949, 44416
G.H. Cretors, 4822
G.P. de Silva Spices Inc, 44417
G.S. Dunn Limited, 4823
G.V. Aikman Company, 22950
G.W. Dahl Company, 22951
G.W. Market, 56605
GA Design Menu Company, 22952
Gabila's Knishes, 4853, 44444
Gabler Trucking Inc, 51759, 52931
Gabriel Container Co, 23001
Gabriella Imports, 23002, 44445
Gabriella's Kitchen, 4854
GAC Produce Company, 56606
Gachot & Gachot, 56621
Gad Cheese Retail Store, 4855
Gadoua Bakery, 4856, 44446
Gadren Machine Company, 23003
Gadsden Cartage Co, 51760, 52932
Gadsden Coffee/Caffe, 4857
Gaea North America LLC, 4858
Gaetano America, 23004, 44447
GAF Seelig Inc, 4824, 22953, 56607
Gafco-Worldwide, 23005
Gage Industries, 23006, 44448
Gaggia Espresso Machine Company, 44449, 56622
Gaia Herbs Inc, 4859
Gail Pittman, 44450
Gainco Inc, 23007, 23008, 44451
Gainesville Neon & Signs, 23009
Gainesville Welding & Mntnc, 23010
Gainey Vineyard, 4860
Gaiser's European Style, 4861, 44452, 56623
Galante Vineyards, 4862
Galassi Foods, 4863
Galasso's Bakery, 4864
Galaxy Chemical Corp, 23011, 44453
Galaxy Dairy Products, 4865
Galaxy Desserts, 4866
Galaxy Nutritional Foods Inc, 4867
Galaxy Tea Company, 56624
Galbraith Laboratories Inc, 23012
Galbreath LLC, 23013, 44454
Galena Canning Co, 4868
Galena Cellars Winery, 4869
Galerie Au Chocolat, 56625
Galil Importing Corp, 44455
Galilean Seafood Inc, 4870
Galilee Splendor, 44456, 56626
Gallagher Sales Corporation, 40418
Galland's Institutional Food, 4871, 56627
Gallard-Schlesinger Industries, 23014
Galleano Winery, 4872
Galleron Signature Wines, 56628
Galley, 23015, 44457
Galli Produce Inc, 56629
Galliker Dairy Co, 4873
Gallimore Industries, 23016, 44458
Gallo, 23017, 44459
Galloway Co, 4874
Galloway's Specialty Foods, 56630
Gallup Sales Company, 4875
Galvinell Meat Co Inc, 4876, 23018
Gama Products, 4877

1386

All Companies Index

Gamajet Cleaning Systems, 23019, 44460
Gamay Flavors, 4878
Gambino's Bakeries Inc, 4879
Gambino's Bakery, 4880
Gambrinus Co, 4881
Gamecock Chemical Co Inc, 23020
Gamewell Corporation, 23021, 44461
Gamez Brothers Produce Co, 56631
GAMPAC Express, 51756
Gamse Lithographing Co Inc, 23022
Ganau America Inc, 23023
Gandy's Dairies, 56632
Gandy's Dairies LLC, 4882
Ganeden, Inc, 4883, 44462
Gann Manufacturing, 23024
Gannett Outdoor of New Jersey, 23025
Ganong Bros Ltd, 4884, 4885, 44463, 44464
Ganz Brothers, 23026, 44465
GAP Food Brokers, 40415, 44418
Gar Products, 23027, 44466
Garavaglia Meat Company, 56633
Garb-El Products Co, 23028, 44467
Garber Bros Inc, 56634
Garber Farms, 4886, 44468
Garber Ice Cream Co Inc, 4887
Garcoa Laboratories Inc, 4888, 44469
Gardein, 4889
Garden & Valley Isle Seafood, 4890, 44470, 56635
Garden City Community College, 23029
Garden City Supply, 56636
Garden Complements Inc, 4891, 44471
Garden Fresh Gourmet, 4892
Garden Gold Foods, Inc, 40419
Garden of Flavor LLC, 4898
Garden of the Gods Gourmet, 4899
Garden Protein International, 4893, 44472
Garden Row Foods, 4894, 4895, 44473
Garden Spot Distributors, 4896, 56637
Garden Spot Produce Co, 56638
Garden Valley Corp, 4897
Gardenville Signs, 23030
Gardiner Paperboard, 23031
Gardner & Benoit, 56639
Gardner Denver Inc., 23032, 44474
Gardner Manufacturing Inc, 23033, 44475
Gardner Pie Co, 4900
Gardner's Gourmet, 4901, 44476
Gardners Candies Inc, 4902
Garelick Farms, 4903, 4904
Garisco Distributing, 40420
Garland C Norris Co, 56640
Garland Commercial Industries, 44477
Garland Commercial Ranges, 23035
Garland Commercial Ranges Ltd., 23034, 44478
Garland Floor Company, 23036
Garland Truffles, Inc., 4905, 23037
Garland Writing Instruments, 23038, 44479
Garlic and Spice, Inc., 44481
Garlic Co, 4906
Garlic Festival Foods, 4907
Garlic Valley Farms Inc, 4908, 44480
Garman Co Inc, 23039
Garman Routing Systems Inc, 4909, 23040, 51761
Garon Foods, 4910
Garrett Popcorn Shops, 4911
Garrison Brewing, 4912
Garrity Equipment Company, 23041
Garroutte, 23042, 44482
Gartner Studios Inc, 4913
Garuda International, 4914, 44483, 56641
Garver Manufacturing Inc, 23043, 44484
Garvey Corp, 23044, 44485
Garvey Nut & Candy, 56642
Garvey Products, 23045, 23046
Garvey Public Warehouse, 52933
Garvin Industries, 23047
Garvis Manufacturing Company, 23048
Gary Farrell Vineyards-Winery, 4915

Gary Manufacturing Company, 23049, 44486
Gary Plastic Packaging Corporation, 23050, 23051, 44487, 44488
Gary Sign Co, 23052
Gary W. Pritchard Engineer, 23053
Gary's Frozen Foods, 4916
Gasketman Inc, 44489, 56643
Gaslamp Co Popcorn, 4917
Gaspar's Linguica Co Inc, 4918, 44490
Gasparini Sales Inc, 40421
Gasser Chair Co Inc, 23054, 44491
Gast Jun-Air, 44492
Gaston County Dyeing Mach Co, 23055
Gaston Dupre, 4919
Gastro-Gnomes, 23056, 44493
Gates, 23057
Gates Corp, 23058
Gates Manufacturing Company, 23059
Gates Mectrol Inc, 23060, 23061, 44494
Gateway Food Products Co, 4920, 44495, 56644
Gateway Food Service, 40422
Gateway Packaging Co, 23062
Gateway Packaging Corp, 23063
Gateway Plastics Inc, 23064
Gateway Printing Company, 23065
Gatewood Products LLC, 23066, 51762, 52934
Gator Hammock Corp, 4921
Gatto & Sons, 56645
Gatto Wholesale Produce, 56646
GATX Corp, 51757
Gaucho Foods, 4922
Gaudet & Ouellette, 4923, 44496
Gavco Plastics Inc, 23067
Gay Truck Line, 51763
Gay's Wild Maine Blueberries, 4924
Gaychrome Division of CSL, 23068
Gayle's Sweet N' Sassy Foods, 4925
Gaylord Container Corporation, 23069, 23070, 44497
Gaylord Industries, 23071, 44498
Gaylord's Meat Co, 56647
Gaynes Labs Inc, 23072
Gaytan Foods Inc, 4926
GB Enterprises, 56608
GB Ratto International Grocery, 4825
Gbn Machine & Engineering, 23073, 44499
Gbs, 23074, 44500
GBS Foodservice Equipment, Inc., 22954
GC Farms, 4826
GCA, 22955
Gch Internatonal, 23075, 44501
GCI Nutrients, 4827, 40416, 44419
GCJ Mattei Company, 22956
GCS Service, 56609
GD Packaging Machinery, 22957
GDM Concepts, 22958
GE Appliances, 22959
GE Interlogix Industrial, 22960, 44420
GE Lighting, 22961
Ge-No's Nursery, 23076
GEA Evaporation Technologies LLC, 22962
GEA FES, Inc., 22963
GEA Filtration, 22964
Gea Intec, Llc, 23077, 44503
GEA Niro Soavi North America, 22965
GEA North America, 22966, 44421
GEA PHE Systems North America, Inc., 22967
Gea Process Engineering Inc, 23078
Gea Processing, 23079
GEA Refrigeration North America, 22968
Gea Us, 23080, 44504
Gearharts Fine Chocolates, 4927
Gebo Conveyors, Consultants & Systems, 23081, 44505
GEBO Corporation, 22969
Gebo Corporation, 23082, 44506
Gecko Electronics, 23083
GED, LLC, 22970, 44422
Gedney Foods Co, 4928, 44507

GEE Manufacturing, 22971
GeeFree, 4929
Geerpres Inc, 23084, 44508
Gehl Foods, Inc., 4930
Gehnrich Oven Sales Company, 23085, 44509
Gehrke Co, 40423
GEI Autowrappers, 22972, 44423
Gei International Inc, 23086
GEI PPM, 22973, 44424
GEI Turbo, 22974, 44425
Geiger Bros, 23087, 44510
Gel Spice Co LLC, 4931
Gelateria Naia, 4932
Gelati Celesti, 4933
Gelato Fiasco, 4934
Gelato Fresco, 4935
Gelato Giuliana, 4936
Gelberg Signs, 23088
Gelita North America, 4937
Gellman Associates, 40424
Gelnex Gelatins, 4938, 44511
Gelsinger Food Products, 4939
Gelson's, 56649
GEM Berry Products, 4828
Gem Berry Products, 4940
GEM Berry Products, 44426
Gem Berry Products, 56650
GEM Cultures, 4829, 44427
Gem Electric Manufacturing Company, 23089
GEM Equipment Of Oregon Inc, 22975, 22976, 44428
Gem Meat Packing Co, 4941
Gem Refrigerator Company, 23090
Gemini Bakery Equipment, 23091, 44512
Gemini Data Loggers Inc, 23092
Gemini Data Systems, 51764
Gemini Plastic Films Corporation, 23093
Gemini Traffic Sales, 51765, 52935
Gems Sensors & Controls, 23094, 23095, 44513
Gemsa Oils, 4942
Gemsy's Money Handling Systems, 56651
Gemtek Products LLC, 23096, 56652
Gen Pac, 56653
Genarom International, 4943, 23097, 44514
Gene & Boots Candies Inc, 4944
Gene Belk Briners, 4945
Gene's Citrus Ranch, 4946
Genecor International, 23098
Genemco Inc, 23099
General Analysis Corporation, 23100
General Bag Corporation, 23101, 44515
General Bonded Warehouses Inc, 51766, 52936
General Cage, 23102, 44516
General Candy Co, 56654
General Carriage & Supply Co, 56655
General Cash & Carry, 56656
General Chemical Corporation, 23103
General Cold Storage, 52937
General Commodities International, 44517
General Conveyor Company, 23104
General Corrugated Machinery Company, 23105, 44518
General Cutlery Co, 23106
General Data Co Inc, 23107
General Electric Company, 23108, 23109
General Equipment & Machinery Company, 23110
General Espresso Equipment, 23111, 44519
General Films Inc, 23112, 44520
General Floor Craft, 23113, 44521
General Formulations, 23114, 44522
General Grinding Inc, 23115
General Industries Inc, 23116
General Machinery Corp, 23117, 44523
General Magnaplate Corp, 23118
General Methods Corporation, 23119, 44524

General Mills, 4947
General Neon Sign Co, 23120
General Packaging Equipment Co, 23121, 44525
General Packaging Products Inc, 23122
General Press Corp, 23123, 44526
General Processing Systems, 23124, 44527
General Resource Corporation, 23125
General Sales, 56657
General Sales Associates, 56658
General Sales Co, 56659
General Shelters Of Texas LTD, 23126
General Sign Co, 23127
General Steel Fabricators, 23128
General Tank, 23129
General Tape & Supply, 23130, 44528
General Trade Mark Labelcraft, 23131, 44529
General Trading Co, 56660
General Truck Body Mfg, 23132
General Warehouse & Transportation Company, 51767, 52938, 52939
General Wax & Candle Co, 23133, 44530
General, Inc, 23134, 44531
Generation Tea, 4948, 44532
Generichem Corporation, 56661
Generous Coffee, 4949
Genesee Brewing Company, 4950, 44533
Genesee Corrugated, 23135, 44534
Genesee Valley Rural Preservation Council, Inc., 52940
Genesis International, 40425
Genesis Machinery Products, 23136
Genesis Marketing, 40426
Genesis Nutritional Labs, 23137
Genesis Today, 4951
Genesis Total Solutions Inc, 23138
GENESTA, 22977
Geneva Awning & Tent Works Inc, 23139
Geneva Food Products, 4952
Geneva Lakes Cold Storage, 23140, 51768, 52941
Genflex Roofing Systems, 23141
Genghis Grill Franchise Concepts, 4953
Genisoy, 4954, 4955
Genius Juice, 4956
Genki USA, 4957
Genoa Wholesale Foods, 56662
Genotec Nutritional, 40427
Genpak, 23142, 44535
Genpak LLC, 23143, 23144, 44536
Gensaco Marketing, 23145, 44537
Gentile Brothers Company, 4958
Gentile Packaging Machinery, 23146
Gentle Ben's Brewing Co, 4959
Gentry's Poultry, 4960
Gentzkow Trucking Svc Inc, 51769
GEO Graphics-Spegram, 22978
Geo. Olcott Company, 23147, 44538
Geoghegan Brothers Company, 56663
Georg Fischer Central Plastics, 23148
Georg Fischer Disa Pipe Tools, 23149
George A Dickel & Company, 4961
George A Heimos Produce Co, 56664
George A Jeffreys & Company, 4962, 44539
George Basch Company, 23150, 44540
George Chiala Farms Inc, 4963, 44541
George D. Spence & Sons, 56665
George Degen & Co, 44542, 56666
George E De Lallo Co Inc, 4964, 44543
George E. Dent Sales, 40428
George E. Kent Company, 56667
George F Brocke & Sons, 4965
George G. Giddings, 23151
George Glove Company, Inc, 23152, 44544
George Gordon Assoc, 23153, 44545
George Greer Company, 56668
George J Howe Co, 56669
George Lapgley Enterpri ses, 23154
George Lauterer Corp, 23155
George Noroian, 4966
George O Pasquel Companies, 56670

1387

All Companies Index

George Perry & Sons Inc, 40429
George Risk Industries Inc, 23156
George Robberecht Seafood, 4967, 44546
George S. Bush & Company, 51770
George Uhe Company, Inc., 56671
George W Saulpaugh & Son, 4968, 44547
George W. Holop Associates, 40430
George's Bakery Svc, 23157
George's Candy Shop Inc, 4969, 44548
George's Inc, 4970
Georgetown Bagelry, 4971
Georgetown Cupcake, 4972
Georgetown Farm, 4973, 44549
Georgia Cold Storage, 23158, 52942
Georgia Cold Storage Inc, 52943
Georgia Duck & Cordage Mill, 23159, 44550
Georgia Fruitcake Co, 4974
Georgia Grinders, 4975
Georgia Nut Co, 4976
Georgia Pacific, 23160
Georgia Seafood Wholesale, 4977, 56672
Georgia Spice Company, 4978, 44551
Georgia Tent & Awning, 23161
Georgia Watermelon Association, 23162
Georgia Wines Inc, 4979
Georgia-Pacific LLC, 23163, 44552
Georis Winery, 4980
GePolymershapes Cadillac, 44502, 56648
Gerard & Dominique Seafoods, 4981
Gerber Agri, 44553
Gerber Cheese Company, 44554
Gerber Innovations, 23164, 44555
Gerber Legendary Blades, 23165, 44556
Gerber Products Co, 4982, 44557
Gerber's Poultry Inc, 4983
Gerhart Coffee Co, 4984
Gerlau Sales, 44558, 56673
GERM-O-RAY, 22979, 44429
Germack Pistachio Co, 4985, 44559
German Bakery at Village Corner, 4986
Germanton Winery, 4987
Germantown Milling Company, 23166
Gerrit J. Verburg Company, 44560
Gerrity Industries, 23167
Gersony Strauss Co, 40431
Gerstel Inc, 23168
Gertrude & Bronner's Magic Alpsnack, 4988
Gertrude Hawk Chocolates, 4989
Gervasi Wood Products, 23169
Gesco ENR, 4990, 44561
Gessner Products, 23170, 44562
GET Enterprises LLC, 22980, 44430, 56610
Getchell Brothers Inc, 4991
Gexpro, 56674
Geyersville Printing Company, 23171
Geyser Peak Winery, 4992, 44563
GF Harvest, 4830
GFA Brands Inc, 4831
GFI Stainless, 22981
GFR Worldwide, 40417
GFS (Canada) Company, 56611
GH Bent Company, 4832
GH Ford Tea Company, 4833, 44431
Gharana Foods, 4993
Ghibli North American, 23172, 44564
Ghirardelli Chocolate Co, 4994
GHM Industries Inc, 22982, 44432
Ghyslain Chocolatier, 4995
Gia Michaels Confections Inc, 4996
Gia Russa, 4997
Giacona Container Co, 44565
Giambri's Quality Sweets Inc, 4998
Giambrocco Food Service, 56675
Giancola Brothers, Inc., 56676
Giant Advertising, 44566
Giant Eagle American Seaway Foods, 56677
Giant Food, 4999
GIANT Food Stores, 56612
Giant Gumball Machine Company, 23173, 44567

Giant Packaging Corporation, 23174
Giant Warehousing Inc, 52944
Gibbon Packing, 5000
Gibbons Bee Farm, 5001
Gibbs & Assoc, 40432
Gibbs Brothers Cooperage, 23175
Gibbs-Mccormick Inc A Ca Corp, 40433
Gibbsville Cheese Company, 5002
Gibraltar Packaging Group Inc, 23176
Gibson Wholesale Co Inc, 56678
Giddings & Lewis, 23177
Gielow Pickles Inc, 5003, 44568
Giesecke & Devrient America, 23178, 44569
Giesser, 44570
Giffin International, 23179
Gifford's Ice Cream, 5004
Gifford's Ice Cream & Candy Co, 5005
Gift Basket Supply World, 5006
Gil's Gourmet Gallery, 5007
Gilbert Foodservice Inc, 40434
Gilbert Industries, Inc, 23180
Gilbert Insect Light Traps, 23181, 44571
Gilbert International, 51771, 52945
Gilchrist Bag Co Inc, 23182, 44572
Gilda Industries Inc, 5008
Gile Cheese Store, 5009
Giles Enterprises Inc, 23183, 44573
Giles Food Service, 44574
Gill's Onions LLC, 5010
Gillco Ingredients, 56679
Gillette Creamery, 40435, 52946, 56680
Gillette Nebraska Dairies, 56681
Gillians Foods, 5011
Gillies Coffee, 5012, 44575, 56682
Gillis Associated Industries, 23184
Gilly Galoo, 44576
Gilly's Hot Vanilla, 5013
Gilmore's Seafoods, 5014, 56683
Gilson Co Inc, 23185, 44577
Gilster-Mary Lee Corp, 5015, 44578, 56684
Gilt Edge Flour Mills, 5016
Giltron Inc, 23186
Gimbals Fine Candies, 5017
Gimme Coffee, 5018
Gimme Health Foods, 5019
Gimme Sum Mo Cajun Foods Corporation, 56685
Gina Marie Refrigerator Door, 56686
Ginco International, 5020, 44579
Ginger People, The, 5021, 44580
Ginger Shots, 5022
Gingerhaus, LLC, 5023
Gingras Vinegar, 5024
Gingro Corp, 5025
Ginkgo International LTD, 44581
Ginnie Nichols Graphic Design, 23187
Ginny Bakes, 5026
Ginsberg's Institutional Foods, 56687
Ginseng Up Corp, 5027, 23188, 44582
Gintzler Graphics Inc, 23189
Giorgio Foods, 5028
Giovanni Food Co Inc, 5029, 44583, 56688
Giovanni's Appetizing Food Co, 5030, 44584
Girard Spring Water, 5031, 23190
Girard Wood Products Inc, 23191
Girard's Food Service Dressings, 5032, 44585
Girardet Wine Cellar, 5033
Girton Manufacturing Co, 23192, 44586
Giulia Speciality Food, 5034
Giuliano's Specialty Foods, 5035
Giumarra Companies, 5036, 40436, 44587, 51772, 56689
Giunta Brothers, 23193
Giusto's Specialty Foods Inc, 5037
Givaudan Fragrances Corp, 5038, 44588
GJ Glass Company, 22983
GKI Foods, 4834, 22984
Gl Mezzetta Inc, 5039, 23194
GLAC Seat Inc, 44433, 56613
Glacial Ridge Foods, 5040

Glacier Cold Storage LTD, 51773, 52947
Glacier Fish Company, 5041, 44589
Glacier Foods, 5042, 44590
Glacier Sales Inc, 40437
Glacier Transit & Storage Inc, 52948
Gladder's Gourmet Cookies, 5043
Gladstone Food Products Company, 5044
Glamorgan Bakery, 5045, 23195
Glanbia Nutritionals, 5046
Glandt-Dahlke, 56690
Glaro Inc, 23196, 44591
Glasko Plastics, 23197
Glass Industries America LLC, 23198, 44592
Glass Pro, 23199, 44593
Glass Tech, 23200
Glass Trucking LLC, 51774
Glassline Corp, 23201
Glastender, 23202, 44594
Glatech Productions LLC, 5047, 23203
Glatfelter P H Co, 23204
Glatt Air Techniques Inc, 23205
Glawe Manufacturing Company, 23206
Glazier Packing Co, 5048, 44595, 56691
GLCC Co, 4835
Glean, LLC, 5049
Gleason Industries, 23207
Glee Gum, 5050
Gleeson Construct & Engineers, 23208, 51775
Glen Mills Inc., 23209
Glen Raven Custom Fabrics LLC, 23210, 44596
Glen Rose Transportation Mgmt, 51776
Glen Summit Springs Water Company, 5051
Glen's Packing Co, 5052
Glendora Quiche Company, 5053
Glenmarc Manufacturing, 23211, 44597
Glenmoor Brokerage, 40438
Glenn Sales Company, 5054, 44598
Glennys, 5055
Glenoaks Food Inc, 5056
Glenora Wine Cellars, 5057
Glenro Inc, 23212
Glenroy Inc, 23213
GLG Life Tech Corporation, 4836, 4837
Glier's Meats Inc, 5058
Glit Microtron, 23214, 44599
Glit/Disco, 23215
GLK Foods, LLC, 4838
Glo Germ Company, 23216
Glo-Quartz Electric Heater, 23217, 44600
Global Bakeries Inc, 5059
Global Beverage Company, 5060
Global Botanical, 5061, 44601, 56692
Global Canvas Products, 23218
Global Carts and Equipment, 23219
Global Citrus Resources, Inc, 40439
Global Egg Corporation, 5062, 44602
Global Environmental Packaging, 23220
Global Equipment Co Inc, 23221, 44603
Global Food Industries, 5063
Global Food Service Publications Group, 44604
Global Food Source, 44605
Global Gardens Group   Inc., 5064
Global Harvest, 56693
Global Health Laboratories, 5065, 44606
Global Impex, 44607
Global Manufacturing, 23222, 44608
Global Marketing Assoc, 44609, 56694
Global Marketing Enterprises, 23223
Global New Products DataBase, 23224
Global Nutrition Research Corporation, 23225
Global Organics, 5066, 23226, 44610
Global Package, 23227, 44611, 51777
Global Packaging Machinery Company, 23228
Global Payment Tech Inc, 23229
Global Preservatives, 5067
Global Product Development Group, 23230
Global Stevedoring, 52949

Global Sticks, Inc., 23231, 44612
Global USA Inc, 23232
Global Water & Energy, 23233
Global Water Group Inc, 23234
Globe Equipment Co, 56695
Globe Fire Sprinkler Corp, 23235, 44613
Globe Food Equipment Co, 23236, 44614
Globe Machine, 23237, 44615
Globe Packaging Co, 23238
Globe Ticket & Label Company, 23239
Globe-Monte-Metro Company, 56696
Globex America, 23240
Globus Coffee LLC, 5068
Glopak, 23241, 44616
Gloria Ferrer Champagne, 5069
Gloria Jean's Gourmet Coffees, 5070
Gloria Kay Uniforms, 56697
Gloria Winery & Vineyard, 5071
Glory Foods, 5072
GloryBee, 5073, 56698
Glosson Food Eqpt-Hobart Svc, 56699
Glossop's Syrup, 5074
Gloucester Engineering, 23242
Glove Cleaners & Safety Products, 44617
Glover Latex, 23243
Glover Rubber Stamp & Crafts, 23244
Glover's Ice Cream Inc, 5075
Glow Gluten Free, 5076
Glowmaster Corporation, 23245, 44618
Gluck Brands, 5077
Glucona America, 5078, 44619
Glue Dots International, 23246
Glue Fast, 23247, 23248
Gluemaster, 23249
Glunz Family Winery & Cellars, 5079
Gluten Free Foods Mfg., 5080
Gluten Free Nation, 5081
Gluten Free Sensations, 5082
Gluten-Free Heaven, 5083
Glutenfreeda Foods Inc, 5084
Glutino, 5085
GM Nameplate, 22985, 44434
GMB Specialty Foods, 4839
GMF, 22986
GMT Dairy Products Inc, 56614
GMW Freight Services Ltd, 51758, 52930
GMZ Inc, 56615
GN Thermoforming Equipment, 22987
GNS Foods, 4840, 56616
GNS Spices, 4841, 44435
GNT USA, 4842
GNTUSA Inc, 22988
Go Cocktails, 56700
Go Max Go Foods, 5086, 56701
Go Raw, 5087
Goat Partners Intl., 5091
GoAvo, 5088
GOBI Library Solutions, 22989
GoBio!, 5089
Godiva Chocolatier, 5092
Godshall Paper Box Company, 23250
Godshall's Quality Meats, 5093
Godwin Produce Co, 5094
Goebel Fixture Co, 23251
Goeman's Wood Products, 23252
Goen Technologies Inc, 5095
Goergen-Mackwirth Co Inc, 23253
Goetz & Sons Western Meat, 56702
Goetze's Candy Co, 5096, 44620
Goex Corporation, 23254, 44621
Goff Distribution, 52950
Goff's Seafood, 56703, 56704
GOJO Industries Inc, 22990, 44436
Golbon, 56705
Gold Band Oysters, 44622
Gold Bond Inc, 23255
Gold Coast Bakeries, 5097
Gold Coast Baking Co Inc, 5098, 56706
Gold Coast Ingredients, 5099, 56707
Gold Crust Baking Co Inc, 5100
Gold Digger Cellars, 5101
Gold Dollar Products, 5102
Gold Medal Bakery Inc, 5103
Gold Medal Products Co, 23256, 44623

All Companies Index

Gold Mine Natural Food Company, 5104
Gold Pure Food Products Co. Inc., 5105, 44624
Gold Standard Baking Inc, 5106
Gold Star Foods, 56708
Gold Star Products, 23257
Gold Star Seafoods, 5107, 56709
Gold Star Smoked Fish Inc, 5108
Gold Sweet Company, 5109
Goldberg & Solovy Foods Inc, 56710
Goldco Industries, 23258, 44625
Goldcoast Salads, 5112
Golden 100, 5113, 44626
Golden Alaska Seafoods LLC, 5114
Golden Beach Inc, 44627
Golden Bridge Enterprises Inc, 44628
Golden Brown Bakery Inc, 5115, 56711
Golden Cannoli, 5116
Golden City Brewery, 5117, 56712
Golden Eagle Extrusions Inc, 23259
Golden Eagle Olive Products, 5118
Golden Eagle Syrup, 5119
Golden Edibles LLC, 5120
Golden Eye Seafood, 5121, 56713
Golden Flake Snack Foods, 5122
Golden Fluff Popcorn Co, 5123, 44629
Golden Fruits, 44630
Golden Gate Co, 44631, 56714
Golden Gulf Coast Packing Co, 5124, 44632
Golden Harvest Pecans, 5125, 44633, 56715
Golden Island Jerky Co., 5126
Golden Kernel Pecan Co, 5127, 44634
Golden Lake Electric Supply, 56716
Golden Light Equipment Co, 56717
Golden Malted, 5128
Golden Moon Tea, 5129, 44635, 56718
Golden Needles Knitting & Glove Company, 23260, 44636
Golden Oldies LTD, 44637
Golden Orchard, 56719
Golden Organics, 56720
Golden Peanut and Tree Nuts, 5130, 44638
Golden Platter Foods, 5131, 44639
Golden River Fruit Company, 5132, 44640
Golden Specialty Foods Inc, 5133, 44641
Golden Star, 5261, 44642
Golden State Foods Corp, 5134, 44643
Golden State Herbs, 5135, 44644
Golden Town Apple Products, 5136, 44645
Golden Valley Dairy Products, 5137
Golden Valley Foods Ltd., 5138, 44646
Golden Valley Industries Inc, 40440
Golden Valley Natural, 5139
Golden Valley Popcorn Supply, 56721
Golden Walnut Specialty Foods, 5140, 44647
Golden West Food Group, 5141, 56722
Golden West Fruit Company, 5142
Golden West Packaging Concept, 23262
Golden West Specialty Foods, 5143
Goldenberg's Peanut Chews, 5144, 44648
Goldenwest Sales, 23263, 44649
GoldFoods, 5110
Goldilocks USA, 5145
Golding Farms Foods, 5146
Goldman Manufacturing Company, 23264
Goldmax Industries, 23265, 44650
GoldRush Mustard, 5111
Goldstar Brands LLC, 5147
Goldthread, 5148
Goldwater's Food's Of Arizona, 5149
Goldy Food Sales Company, 56723
Golick Martins, Inc., 40441
Goll's Bakery, 5150
GoMacro, 5090
Gonard Foods, 5151
Gone Wild!!!, 56724
Gonnella Baking Company, 5152
Gonterman & Associates, 23266, 44651

Good Citizens, 5153
Good Culture, 5154
Good Earth Company, 5155
Good Food For Good, 5156
Good Food Inc, 5157
Good Food Made Simple, 5158
Good For You America, 5159, 44652
Good Fortunes & Edible Art, 5160
Good Groceries, 5161
Good Harbor Fillet Company, 5162
Good Harbor Vineyards & Winery, 5163
Good Health Natural Foods, 5164, 44653
Good Humor-Breyers Ice Cream, 5165, 44654
Good Idea, 23267, 44655
Good Karma Foods, 5166
Good Lovin' Foods, 5167
Good Old Dad Food Products, 5168
Good Old Days Foods, 5169
Good Pack, 23268
Good PLANeT Foods, 5170
Good Rub, 5171
Good Spread, 5172
Good Stuff Cacao, 5173
Good Wives, 5174
Good Zebra, 5175
Good! Snacks, 5176
Good's Wholesale-Bakery Supls, 56725
Good-O-Beverages Inc, 5177, 44656
Goodall Rubber Company, 23269
Goodart Candy Inc, 5182
GoodBelly Probiotics, 5178
GoodBites Snacks, 5179
Goodell Tools, 23270, 44657
Goodheart Brand Specialty Food, 5183, 44658
Goodie Girl, 5184
Gooding Rubber Company, 56726
Goodman & Company, 23271
Goodman Wiper & Paper Co, 23272, 56727
GoodMark Foods, 5180
Goodnature Products, 23273, 44659
Goodness Knows, 5185
Goodpack USA Inc, 51778
GoodPop, 5181
Goodseed Burgers, 5186
Goodson Brothers Coffee, 5187
Goodway Industries Inc, 23274, 44660
Goodway Technologies Corp, 23275, 44661
Goodwin Brothers Inc, 56728
Goodwin Co, 23276, 44662
Goodwin-Cole Co Inc, 23277
Goodwrappers Inc, 23278, 44663
Goodyear Tire & Rubber Company, 23279
Goose Island Beer Co, 5188
Goosecross Cellars Inc, 5189
Gopal's Healthfoods, 5190, 56729
Gopicnic Inc, 5191
Gorant Chocolatier, 5192
Gorbel Inc, 23280, 44664
Gordon Biersch Brewery Restaurant, 5193
Gordon Food Service, 56730, 56731, 56732, 56733, 56734, 56735, 56736, 56737, 56738, 56739, 56740, 56741, 56742, 56743, 56744, 56745, 56746, 56747
Gordon Graphics, 23281
Gorilla Label, 23282
Goring Kerr, 23283
Gormick Food Brokers, 40442
Gorton's Inc, 5194, 44665
Goshen Dairy Company, 23284
Gosselin Gourmet Beverages, 44666, 56748
Gossner Foods Inc, 5195, 44667
Gotham Pen Co Inc, 23285
Gotliebs Guacamole, 5196
Gough-Econ Inc, 23286, 44668
Gould's Maple Sugarhouse, 5197
Gouldsboro Enterprises, 5198
Gourm-E-Company Imports, 44669

Gourmantra Foods, 5199
Gourmedas Inc, 5200
Gourmet Award Foods, 56749
Gourmet Basics, 5201
Gourmet Brokers, 44670
Gourmet Cafe Wholesale, 56750
Gourmet Club Corporation, 44671, 56751
Gourmet COFFEE Roasters, 23287
Gourmet Conveniences Ltd, 5202
Gourmet Croissant, 5203
Gourmet Display, 23288, 44672
Gourmet du Village, 5214
Gourmet Foods Inc, 5204
Gourmet Foods Intl, 23289, 40443, 44673, 56752
Gourmet Gear, 23290, 44674
Gourmet Ghee, 5205
Gourmet House, 5206
Gourmet International Inc, 44675
Gourmet Kitchen, Inc., 5207
Gourmet Market, 5208
Gourmet Mondiale, 5209
Gourmet Nut, 5210
Gourmet Products, 5211, 56753
Gourmet Sorbet Corporation, 5212
Gourmet Table Skirts, 23291, 44676
Gourmet Technologies Inc, 56754
Gourmet Treats, 5213
Gourmet's Finest, 5215, 51779
Gourmet's Fresh Pasta, 5216
Gourmet's Secret, 5217
Gourm, Mist, 5218
Gouvea's & Purity Foods Inc, 5219
Gouw Quality Onions, 5220, 44677
Govadinas Fitness Foods, 5221, 56755
Govatos Chocolates, 5222
Goveco Full Service Food Brokers, 40444
Governair Corp, 23292, 44678
Government Food Service, 23293
Goya Foods Inc., 5223, 44679
GP Plastics Corporation, 22991
GPI USA LLC., 4843, 22992, 44437
Grabbe-Leonard Co, 40445
Grabill Country Meats, 5224
Grace & I, 5225
Grace Baking Company, 5226
Grace Foods International, 5227
Grace Instrument Co, 23294, 44680
Grace Tea Co, 5228, 23295, 44681
Grace Technologies, 56756
Grace-Lee Products, 23296
Graceland Fruit Inc, 5229
Gracious Gourmet, 5230
Graco, 23297, 23298, 44682, 44683
Grady's Cold Brew, 5231
Graeter's Mfg. Co., 5232
Graf Creamery Co, 5233
Grafco, 56757
Graff Tank Erection, 23299
Graffam Brothers, 5234, 56758
Grafoplast Wiremarkers Inc, 23300, 23301
Graft Cider, 5235
Grafton Village Cheese Co LLC, 5236
Graham & Rollins Inc, 5237
Graham Cheese Corporation, 5238
Graham Chemical Corporation, 5239
Graham Engineering Corp, 23302, 44684
Graham Fisheries, 5240, 56759
Graham Ice & Locker Plant, 23303, 56760
Graham Pallet Co Inc, 23304
Graham Transfer & Storage, 51780, 52951
Grain Belt, 5241
Grain Craft, 5242
Grain Machinery Mfg Corp, 23305, 44685
Grain Millers Inc, 5243
Grain Place Foods Inc, 5244
Grain Process Enterprises Ltd., 5245, 44686
Grain Processing Corp, 5246
Grain-Free JK Gourmet, Inc., 5247

Grainaissance, 5248, 44687
Grainful, 5249
Grainger Industrial Supply, 56761, 56762
Grains of Health LLC, 5250
Gralab Instruments, 23306, 56763
Gram Equipment Of America, 23307
Graminex, 5251
Granco Manufacturing Inc, 23309, 44688
Grand Central Bakery, 5252
Grand Cypress, 23310
Grand Metropolitan, 5253
Grand Prix Trading, 44689
Grand Prix Trading Corp, 44690
Grand Rapids Chair Company, 23311
Grand Rapids Label, 23312, 44691
Grand River Cellars, 5254
Grand Silver Company, 23313
Grand Teton Brewing Co, 5255
Grand Valley Labels, 23314
Grand View Winery, 5256
Grandcestors, 5257
Grande Cheese Company, 5258
Grande Chef Company, 23315, 44692
Grande Cuisine Systems, 56764
Grande Custom Ingredients Group, 5259, 44693, 56765
Grande River Vineyards, 5260
Grande Ronde Sign Company, 23316
Grande Tortilla Factory, 5261
Grandma Beth's Cookies, 5262
Grandma Browns Beans Inc, 5263
Grandma Emily, 5264
Grandma Hoerner's Inc, 5265
Grandma Pat's Products, 5266
Grandpa Ittel's Meats Inc, 5267
Grandpa Po's Nutra Nuts, 5268
Grandpops Lollipops, 5269
Grandview Farms, 5270, 44694
GrandyOats, 5271
Grane Warehousing & Distribution, 51781, 52952
Granello Bakery, 5272
Granite Springs Winery, 5273
Granite State Fruit, 56766
Granite State Stamps Inc, 23317
Granny Blossom Specialty Foods, 5274
Granny Roddy's LLC, 5275
Granny's Best Strawberry Products, 5276
Granowska's, 5277
GranPac, 23308
Grant Chemicals, 23318
Grant J. Hunt Company, 40446
Grant Laboratories, 23319
Grant Park Packing, 5278
Grant-Letchworth, 23320
Grantstone Supermarket, 44695, 56767
Granville Gates & Sons, 5279, 44696
Granville Manufacturing Co, 23321
Grapevine Trading Company, 5280
Graphic Apparel, 23322, 44697
Graphic Arts Center, 23323
Graphic Calculator Company, 23324, 44698
Graphic Impressions of Illinois, 23325
Graphic Packaging Corporation, 23326
Graphic Packaging International, 23327
Graphic Packaging Intl, 23328, 44699
Graphic Promotions, 23329
Graphic Technology, 23330, 44700
Graphics Unlimited, 23331
Graphite Metalizing Corp, 23332, 44701
Grass Run Farms, 5281
Grasselli SSI, 23333
Grassland Dairy Products Inc, 5282, 44702
Grasso, 23334
Grasso Foods Inc, 5283
Gratify Gluten Free, 5284
Grating Pacific Inc, 23335
Gratton Warehouse Co, 52953
Graver Technologies LLC, 23336
Graves Mountain Lodge Inc., 5285
Gravity Ciders, Inc., 5286
Gravymaster, Inc., 5287, 44703
Gray & Company, 5288, 44704

1389

All Companies Index

Gray Duck, 5289
Gray Lift, 56768
Gray Transportation, 51782
Gray Woodproducts, 23337
Gray's Brewing Co, 5290
Graybill Machines Inc, 23338
Grayco Products Sales, 23339, 44705, 56769
Graydon Lettercraft, 23340
Grayline Housewares Inc, 23341
Grayling Industries, 23342
Grayon Industrial Products, 56770
Grays Harbor Stamp Works, 23343
Grays Ice Cream, 5291
Graysmarsh Berry Farm, 5292
Grayson Naturla Farms, 5293
Graytech Carbonic, 23344
Grease Master, 23345
Great Age Container, 56771
Great American Appetizers, 5294, 44706
Great American Barbecue Company, 5295
Great American Cookie Company, 5296
Great American Dessert Co, 5297
Great American Foods Commissary, 5298
Great American Health Bar, 56772
Great American Popcorn Works of Pennsylvania, 5299, 56773
Great American Seafood Company, 5300, 56774
Great American Smokehouse & Seafood Company, 5301
Great Atlantic Trading Company, 5302, 40447, 44707
Great Atlantic Trading Inc, 44708
Great Basin Botanicals, 56775
Great Circles, 5303
Great Dane LP, 23346
Great Divide Brewing Co, 5304
Great Earth Chemical, 5305
Great Eastern Equipment Exchange, 56776
Great Eastern Mussel Farms, 56777
Great Eastern Sun Trading Co, 5306, 44709
Great Expectations Confectionery Gourmet Foods, 5307
Great Garlic Foods, 5308
Great Glacier Salmon, 5309, 44710
Great Gourmet Inc, 5310
Great Grains Milling Company, 5311
Great Harvest Bread Co, 5312
Great Hill Dairy Inc, 5313
Great Lakes Brewing Co., 5314
Great Lakes Brush, 23347, 44711
Great Lakes Cheese Company, 5316
Great Lakes Cheese Company, Inc., 5315, 44712
Great Lakes Cold Storage, 23348, 52954, 52955, 52956, 52957
Great Lakes Designs, 44713, 56778
Great Lakes Distributing & Storage, 56779
Great Lakes Foods, 5317, 23349
Great Lakes Gelatin, 56780
Great Lakes Gourmet Food Service, 44714, 56781
Great Lakes Hotel Supply Co, 56782, 56783
Great Lakes International Trading, 44715, 56784
Great Lakes Packing Co, 5318
Great Lakes Scientific, 23350
Great Lakes Software of Michigan, 23351
Great Lakes Tea & Spice, 5319
Great Lakes Warehouse Corp, 52958
Great Lakes Wine & Spirits, 5320
Great Lakes-Triad Package Corporation, 23352
Great Midwest Seafood Company, 5321, 56785
Great North Foods, 56786
Great Northern Baking Company, 5322
Great Northern Brewing Co, 5323

Great Northern Corp, 23353, 23354
Great Northern Corp., 23355, 44716
Great Northern Maple Products, 5324
Great Northern Products Inc, 5325, 44717
Great Outdoors Spice Company, 56787
Great Pacific Seafoods, 5326
Great Plains Beef LLC, 5327, 56788
Great Plains Software, 23356
Great Recipes, 5328
Great River Organic Milling, 5329
Great Southern Corp, 23357, 44718
Great Southern Industries, 23358
Great Southwest Sales Company, 40448
Great Spice Company, 5330, 44719
Great Valley Meat Company, 56789
Great Valley Mills, 5331, 44720
Great West Produce Company, 56790
Great Western Beef WHLS Co, 56791
Great Western Brewing Company, 5332
Great Western Chemical, 56792
Great Western Chemical Company, 23359, 56793
Great Western Co LLC, 5333, 23360, 44721
Great Western Foods, 56794
Great Western Juice Co, 5334, 44722
Great Western Malting Co, 5335, 44723
Great Western Manufacturing Company, 23361, 44724
Great Western Meats, 56795
Great Western Tortilla, 5336
Greater Knead, The, 5337, 56796
Greater Omaha Express, LLC, 51783
Greater Omaha Packing Co Inc., 5338, 44725
Greaves Jams & Marmalades, 5339, 44726
Grebe's Bakery, 5340
Grecian Delight Foods Inc, 5341
Grecon, 23362, 44727
Greek Farms Intl, 44728
Greek Gourmet Limited, 44729, 56797
Greeley Tent & Awning Co, 23363
Green & Black's Organic Chocolate, 5342
Green Bag America Inc., 23364
Green Bay Cheese, 5343
Green Bay Machinery, 23365
Green Bay Packaging Inc., 5344, 23366, 23367, 23368, 44730
Green Beans Coffee Co Inc, 5345
Green Belt Industries Inc, 23369, 44731
Green Brothers, 23370
Green County Foods, 5346, 44732
Green Dirt Farm, 5347
Green Earth Bags, 23371
Green Earth Orchards, 5348
GREEN Energy, 4844
Green Foods Corp., 5349, 44733
Green Garden Food Products, 5350
Green Gold Group LLC, 5351, 44734, 56798
Green Gorilla, 5352
Green Grown Products Inc, 5353, 44735
Green Metal Fabricating, 23372
Green Mountain Awning Inc, 23373
Green Mountain Chocolate Inc, 5354
Green Mountain Cidery, 5355
Green Mountain Creamery, 5356
Green Mountain Graphics, 23374, 56799
Green Mountain Gringo, 5357
Green Options, 5358
Green Pond Development, 23375
Green River Chocolates, 5359
Green Roads CBD, 5360
Green Seams, 23376
Green Source Organics, 5361
Green Spot Packaging, 5362, 23377, 44736
Green Sustainable Solutions, 23378
Green Tek, 23379
Green Turtle Bay Vitamin Company, 5363, 44737
Green Turtle Cannery & Seafood, 5364

Green Valley Food Corp, 5365, 44738, 56800
Green Valley Foods, 5366
Green Valley Packers LLC, 52959
Green Valley Pecan Company, 5367
Green-Go Cactus Water, 5368
Greenberg Cheese Co, 5369
Greenbush Tape & Label Inc, 23380, 44739
Greene Brothers, 23381, 44740
Greene Brothers Specialty Coffee Roaster, 5370
Greene Industries, 23382
Greene Poultry, 56801
Greenebaum Brothers, 56802
Greener Corp, 23383
Greenfield Disston, 23384
Greenfield Mills, 5371
Greenfield Noodle & Spec Co, 5372, 56803
Greenfield Packaging, 23385, 56804
Greenfield Paper Box Co, 23386
Greenfield Wine Company, 5373
Greenheck Fan Corp, 23387, 44741
Greenhills Irish Bakery, 5374
Greenjoy, 5375
Greenley Foods Inc, 56805
Greensburg Manufacturing Company, 23388
Greenstein Trucking Company, 51784
Greenvale Electric Supply Corp, 56806
Greenville Awning Company, 23389
Greenwave Foods, 5376
Greenway Transportation Services, 51785
Greenwell Farms Inc, 5377
Greenwood Associates, 5378, 56807
Greenwood Ice Cream Co, 5379
Greenwood Mop & Broom Inc, 23390
Greenwood Ridge Vineyards, 5380
Greer's Ferry Glass Work, 23391, 44742
Greerco High Shear Mixers, 23392
Grefco, 23393
Greg's Lobster Company, 5381, 56808
Gregg Industries Inc, 23394, 23395
Gregor Jonsson Inc, 23396, 44743
Gregory's Foods, Inc., 5382, 56809
Greif Brothers Corporation, 23397
Greif Inc, 23398, 23399, 23400, 23401
Greig Filters Inc, 23402, 44744
Greis Brothers, 56810
Greitzer, 23403
Gress Enterprises, 5383, 44745, 52960
Gress Public Refrigerated Services, 52961
Gress Refrigerated Services & Logistics, 51786, 52962
Grey Eagle Distributors, 40449, 51787, 52963, 56811
Grey Ghost Bakery, 5384
Grey Owl Foods, 5385, 44746
Greydon Inc, 23404
Greylawn Foods, 51788, 52964
Greyston Bakery Inc, 5386
Grgich Hills Estates, 44747, 56812
Gribble Stamp & Stencil Co, 23405
Gridpath, Inc., 23406, 44748
Griesedieck Imports, 44749, 56813
Griffin Automation, 23407
Griffin Bros Inc, 23408, 44750
Griffin Food Co, 23409, 56814
Griffin Marketing Group, 40450
Griffin Products, 23410
Griffin Rutgers Co Inc, 23411
Griffin's Seafood, 5387, 56815
Griffith Foods Inc., 5388, 23412
Griffith Laboratories, 56816
Grigg Box Company, 23413, 56817
Grigsby Brothers Paper Box Manufacturers, 23414
Gril-Del, 44751
Grill Greats, 23416, 44752
Grillco Inc, 23417
Grillo's Pickles, 5389
Grills to Go, 23418, 44753

Grimaud Farms-California Inc, 5390, 44754
Grimes Co, 23419, 51789, 52965
Grimm's Fine Food, 5391, 44755
Grimm's Locker Service, 5392
Grimmway Farms, 5393
Grindmaster-Cecilware Corp, 23420, 44756
Gringo Jack's, 5394
Grinnell Fire ProtectionSystems Company, 23421, 23422
Grippo Foods, 5395
Grocers Ice & Cold Storage Company, 56818
Grocers Supply Co, 44757, 56819
Grocery Manufacturers Assn, 23423
Grocery Manufacturers of America, 40451
Grocery Products Distribution, 23424
Groeb Farms, 5396, 23425, 44758
Groen Process Equipment, 23426
Groen-A Dover Industries Co, 23427, 23428
Groendyke Transport Inc, 51790
Groetsch Wholesale Grocer, 56820
Groff's Meats, 5397, 56821
Groovy Candies, 5398
Grosfillex Inc, 23429, 44759
Gross & Co Licensed Bus Pro, 23430
Grossingers Home Bakery, 5399
Grote & Weigel Inc, 5400
Grote Co, 23431, 44760
Groth Corp, 23432
Groth Vineyards & Winery, 5401
Grounds for Change, 5403, 56822
Grounds For Thought, 5402
Groundwork Coffee Co., 5404, 56823
Group One Partners, 23433
Group Warehouse, 52966
Groupe Paul Masson, 5405, 44761
Grouse Hunt Farm Inc, 5406
Grow Co, 5407, 44762
Grow-Pac, 5408
Grower Direct Marketing, 56824
Grower Shipper Potato Company, 5409, 44763
Growers Cooperative Juice Co, 5410, 44764
Growing Roots Foods, 5411
Grown-up Soda, 5412
Gruenewald ManufacturingCompany, 23434, 44765
Grueny's Rubber Stamps, 23435
Gruet Winery, 5413
Grumpe's Specialties, 5414, 56825
GS Dunn & Company, 4845, 44438
GS Gelato & Desserts Inc, 4846
GS-AFI, 4847
GSB & Assoc, 4848, 44439
GSC Blending, 22993
GSC Enterprises Inc., 56617
GSC Packaging, 22994
GSMA Division of SWF Co, 22995
GSW Jackes-Evans Manufacturing Company, 22996, 44440
GT International, 22997
GTC Nutrition, 4849
GTCO CalComp, 22998, 44441
GTI, 22999, 44442
GTM, 56618
GU Energy Labs, 4850
Guans Mushroom Co, 44766, 56826
Guapo Spices Company, 5415
Guardsman, 23436
Guayaki, 5416, 44767
Guenoc & Langtry Estate, 5417
Guerra Nut Shelling Co Inc, 5418, 44768
Guers Dairy, 5419
Guest Products, 56827
Guest Supply, 23437
Guggisberg Cheese, 5420
Guglielmo Winery, 5421, 44769
Guida's Dairy, 5422
Guido's International Foods, 5423, 44770
Guidry's Catfish Inc, 5424

1390

All Companies Index

Guilliams Winery, 5425
Guiltless Gourmet, 5426, 44771
Guinness Import Co, 5427, 44772
Guittard Chocolate Co, 5428, 44773
Gulf Arizona Packaging, 23438, 56828
Gulf Atlantic Cold Storage, 52967
Gulf Atlantic Freezers, 5429
Gulf Central Distribution Ctr, 51791, 52968
Gulf Central Seafood, 5430
Gulf City Marine Supply, 5431
Gulf Coast Plastics, 23439, 44774
Gulf Coast Sign Company, 23440
Gulf Cold Storage, 52969
Gulf Crown Seafood Co, 5432, 44775
Gulf Food Products Co Inc, 5433, 44776, 56829
Gulf Marine, 5434, 44777, 56830
Gulf Marine & Industrial Supplies Inc, 5435, 56831
Gulf Packaging Company, 23441
Gulf Packing Company, 5436, 44778, 56832
Gulf Pecan Company, 5437, 56833
Gulf Pride Enterprises, 5438, 44779
Gulf Shrimp, Inc., 5439
Gulf States Canners Inc, 5440
Gulf States Food Service Marketing, 40452
Gulf Stream Crab Company, 5441, 56834
Gulf Systems, 23442, 23443, 23444, 23445, 23446, 56835, 56836, 56837, 56838, 56839
Gum Technology Corporation, 5442, 44780
Gumix International Inc, 5443, 44781
Gumpert's Canada, 5444, 44782
Gunderland Marine Supply, 56840
Gundlach-Bundschu Winery, 5445
Gunnoe Farms Sausage & Salad, 5446
Gunter Wilhelm Cutlery, 23447, 44783
Gunther Salt Co, 56841
Gunther's Gourmet, 5447
Gurley's Foods, 5448
Gurrentz International Corp, 40453
GURU Organic Energy, 4851
GuruNanda, 5449
Gus' Pretzel Shop, 5450
Gusmer Enterprises Inc, 23448, 44784
Gust John Foods & Products, 5451
Gustave A Larson Co, 23449
Gustiamo, 44785
Gustus Vitae Condiments LLC, 5452
Guth Lighting, 23450, 44786
Gutheinz Meats Inc, 5453
Gutierrez Brothers, 56842
Gutsii, 5454
Guttenplan's Frozen Dough, 5455
Guy Locicero & Sons, 56843
Guy's Food, 5456
Guylian USA Inc., 5457
Guyllan USA Inc, 44787
GW Supply Company, 56619
GW&E Global Water & Energy, 23000
GWB Foods Corporation, 4852, 44443, 56620
Gwinn's Foods, 5458

H

H & B Packing Co, 5459
H & G Trading LTD Inc, 40454
H & H Metal Fabrication Inc, 23451
H & H Products Co, 5460, 44788
H & M Bay Inc, 23452, 51792, 52970
H & R Coffee Co, 56844
H & W Foods, 5461
H A Phillips & Co, 23453, 44789, 56845
H A Sparke Co, 23454, 44790
H A Stiles, 23455, 44791
H B Day Co, 56846
H B Fuller Co, 23456
H B Taylor Co, 5462, 44792
H Brooks & Co, 56847
H C Bainbridge Inc, 23457

H C Duke & Son Inc, 23458, 44793
H Cantin, 5463, 44794
H Coturri & Sons Winery, 5464
H F Staples & Co Inc, 23459, 44795
H Fox & Co Inc, 5465, 44796
H G Weber & Co, 23460, 23461, 44797
H H Franz Co, 23462, 23463
H Nagel & Son Co, 5466, 44798
H P Mfg Co, 23464
H R Nicholson Co, 5467, 44799
H S Crocker Co Inc, 23465
H S Inc, 23466
H Schrier & Co Inc, 56848
H T I Filtration, 23467, 44800
H Weiss Co LLC, 56849
H&A Health Products, Inc, 5468
H&H Fisheries Limited, 5469, 44801
H&H Lumber Company, 23468
H&H of the Americas, 23470
H&H Pretzel, 56850
H&H Wood Products, 23469, 56851
H&K Packers Company, 5470, 44802
H&M Warehouse, 52971
H&R Transport, 51793
H&S Bakery, 5471
H&S Edible Products Corporation, 5472, 56852
H&T Food Marketing Company, 40455
H-E-B Grocery Co. LP, 5473
H. Arnold Wood Turning, 23471, 44803
H. Gartenberg & Company, 23472
H. Interdonati, 5474, 44804
H. Reisman Corporation, 5475, 23473, 44805
H. White Sales Company, 40456
H. Yamamoto, 23474
H.B. Dawe, 5476, 44806
H.B. Paulk Grocery Company, 56853
H.B. Trading, 5477
H.B. Wall & Sons, 23475
H.C. Foods Co. Ltd., 23476
H.C. Williams Peanut Company, 56854
H.D. Sheldon & Company, 44807
H.F. Coors China Company, 23477, 44808
H.Gass Seafood, 5478
H.J. Jones & Sons, 23478, 44809
H.K. Canning, 5479, 44810
H.L. Diehl Company, 23479, 44811
H.P. Beale & Sons, 56855
H.P. Neun, 23480, 44812
H.R. Plate & Company, 40457
H.T. Hackney Company, 56856
H.V. Mid State Sales Company, 40458
H.Y. Louie Company, 56857
H20 Technology, 44813, 56858
H2rOse, LLC, 5480
H3O, 5481
HAABTEC Inc, 23481
Haagen-Dazs, 5490
Haake, 23503
Haarslev Inc, 23504
Haas Tailoring Company, 23505
Haban Saw Company, 23506, 44824
Habasit America, 23507, 44825
Habasit America Plastic Div, 23508, 44826
Habasit Belting, 23509
Habasit Canada Limited, 23510
Habby Habanero's Food Products, 5491
Habco, 23511
HABCO Beverage Systems, 23482, 44814
Habersham Vineyards & Winery, 5492
Haby's Alsatian Bakery, 5493
Hach Co, 23512, 23513
Hach Co., 23514, 44827
Hacienda Mexican Foods, 56871
Hackney Brothers, 23515, 44828
Haddad Supply Company, 56872
Haddon House Food Products, 56873
Haden Signs of Texas, 23516
Hadley Fruit Orchards, 44829, 56874
Hadley's Date Gardens, 5494, 44830
Hafner USA, 5495

Hafner Vineyard, 5496
Hagensborg Chocolates LTD., 5497, 44831
Hager Containers Inc, 23517
Hagerty Foods, 5498, 23518
Hahn Family Wines, 5499
Hahn Laboratories, 23519
Hahn Produce Corporation, 56875
Hahn's Old Fashioned Cake Co, 5500, 44832
Haier American Trading, 23520
Haifa Chemicals, 23521
Haig's Delicacies, 5501
Haight Brown Vineyard, 5502
Hail Merry, 5503
Haile Resources, 5504, 40463, 56876
Hain Celestial Group Inc, 5505, 5506, 44833
Hain Food Group, 56877
Haines City Citrus Growers, 5507
Haines Packing Company, 5508, 23522
Hair Of The Dog Brewing, 5509
Hairnet Corporation of America, 23523, 44834
Haitai Inc, 44835, 56878
Hak's, 5510
Hakuna Banana, 5511
Hal Mather & Sons, 23524
Hal-One Plastics, 23525, 56879
Halal Fine Foods, 5512, 56880
Halal Transactions, 40464
HALCO, 44815
Haldin International, 44836
Hale and Hearty Soups, 5514
Hale Indian River Groves, 5513
Hale Tea Co, 44837, 56881
Hale's Brewery, 5515
Hale-Halsell Company, 56882
Half Moon Bay Trading Co, 5516
Half Moon Fruit & Produce Company, 5517
Halfpops Inc, 5518
Haliburton International Inc, 5519
Halifax Group, 5520
Hall & Cole Produce, 56883
Hall Brothers Meats, 5521
Hall China Co, 23526, 44838
Hall Grain Company, 5522
Hall Manufacturing Co, 23527, 44839
Hall Manufacturing Company, 23528
Hall Safety Apparel, 23529, 44840
Hall Street Storage LLC, 52972
Hall's Warehouse Corp, 51794, 52973
Hall-Woolford Wood Tank Co Inc, 23530, 44841, 56884
Halladay's Harvest Barn, 5523
Hallams, 23531
Hallberg Manufacturing Corporation, 23532, 44842
Hallcrest Vineyards, 5524
Halling Company, 40465
Hallmark Equipment Inc, 23533
Hallmark Fisheries, 5525
Hallock Fabricating Corp, 23534
Halmark Systems Inc, 23535
Halmoni's Divine Marinade, 5526
Halpak Plastics, 23536
Halperns' Purveyors of Steak & Seafood, 5527
Halsey Foodservice, 56885
Halsey Reid Equipment, 56886
Halsted Packing House, 5528
Halton Company, 23537, 44843
Halton Packaging Systems, 23538, 44844
Ham I Am, 5529
Hama Hama Oyster® Company, 5530, 56887
HAMBA USA, Inc, 23483
Hamberger Displays, 44845
Hamco Warehouses LTD, 52974
Hamer Inc, 23539
Hamersmith, Inc., 5531, 23540, 44846
Hamill Industrial Sales Company, 56888
Hamilos Bros Inspected Meat, 5532, 56889

Hamilton Awning Co, 23541
Hamilton Beach Brands, 23542, 44847, 44848
Hamilton Caster, 23543, 44849
Hamilton Kettles, 23544, 44850
Hamilton Manufacturing Corp, 23545
Hamilton Marine, 5533
Hamilton Soap & Oil Products, 23546
Hammar & Sons, 23547
Hammer Packaging Inc, 23548
Hammerstahl Cutlery, 23549
Hammill International, 56890
Hammond Pretzel Bakery Inc, 5534
Hammond's Candies, 5535
Hammons Black Walnuts, 5536
Hammons Products Co, 5537, 44851
Hamms, 56891
Hamms Custom Meats, 5538
Hampden Papers Inc, 23550
Hampton Associates & Sons, 5539, 44852
Hampton Chutney Company, 5540, 56892
Hampton Farms, 5541
Hampton Roads Box Company, 23551, 44853
Hampton Roads Seafoods Ltd, 56893
Hampton-Tilley Associates, 23552
Hamrick Manufacturing & Svc, 23553, 44854
Hanan Products Co, 5542, 44855
Hanco Manufacturing Company, 23554
Hancock Gourmet Lobster Co, 5543
Hancock Peanut Company, 5544, 44856
Hand Made Lollies, 5545, 23555
Handgards Inc, 23556, 44857
Handi-Foil Corp, 23557
Handi-Rak Service, 56894
Handicap Sign Inc, 23558
Handley Cellars, 5546
Handling & Storage Concepts, 56895
Handling Specialty, 23559
Handling Systems Inc, 56896, 56897
Handtmann, 23560
Handtmann Inc, 23561, 44858
Handy International Inc, 5547, 44859
Handy Manufacturing Co Inc, 23562, 44860
Handy Pax, 5548, 56898
Handy Roll Company, 23563
Handy Wacks Corp, 23564, 44861
Handy's Milk & Ice Cream, 56899
Hanel Storage Systems, 23565, 44862
Hangzhou Sanhe USA Inc., 5549, 23566
Hanif's International Foods, 44863, 56900
Hanimex Company, 40466, 44864
Hanjin Shipping Company, 51795
Hank Rivera Associates, 23567, 44865
Hankin Specialty Elevators Inc, 23568
Hankison International, 23569, 44866
Hanks Beverage Co, 5550
Hanks Brokerage, 40467
Hanley Sign Company, 23570
Hanley's Foods Inc., 5551
Hanmi, 56901
Hanmi Inc, 5552, 44867
Hanna Instruments, 23571, 44868
Hanna's Honey, 5553
Hannaford Bros Co, 56902
Hannah Max Baking, 5554
Hannan Products, 23572, 44869
Hannay Reels, 23573, 44870
Hannic Freight Forwarders Inc, 23574
Hano Business Forms, 23575
Hanover Cold Storage, 52975
Hanover Foods Corp, 5555, 44871
Hanover Potato Products Inc, 5556, 56903
Hanover Terminal Inc, 51796, 52976
Hanover Uniform Co, 44872, 56904
Hanover Warehouses Inc, 51797, 52977
Hans Holterbosch Inc, 44873, 56905
Hans Kissle Co, 5557
Hansaloy Corp, 23576, 44874

1391

All Companies Index

Hansen Beverage Co, 44875, 56906
Hansen Caviar Company, 5558
Hansen Co, 51798, 52978, 56907
Hansen Distribution Group, 44876, 56908
Hansen Group, 40468, 56909
Hansen Packing Co, 5559
Hansen Storage Co, 51799, 52979
Hansen Technologies Corporation, 23577
Hansen Trucking, 51800
Hansen's Laboratory, 23578
Hanset Brothers Inc Brooms, 56910
Hanset Stainless Inc, 23579
Hansid Company, 40469
Hansler Industries, 56911
Hanson Box & Lumber Company, 23580
Hanson Brass Rewd Co, 23581, 23582, 44877, 44878, 56912
Hanson Lab Furniture Inc, 23583, 44879
Hanson Logistics, 51801, 52980, 52981, 52982, 52983, 52984, 52985, 52986, 52987, 52988
Hanson Thompson Honey Farms, 5560
Hantover Inc, 23584, 44880
Hanwa American Corporation, 44881
Hanway Restaurant Equipment, 56913
Hanzell Vineyards, 5561
Hapag-Lloyd America, 51802
Hapco Inc, 23585, 23586
Hapman Conveyors, 23587, 44882
Happy & Healthy Products Inc, 5562
Happy Acres Packing Company, 5563
Happy Campers, 5564
Happy Chef Inc, 23588, 56914
Happy Cow Creamery, 5565
Happy Egg Dealers, 5566, 44883
Happy Family, 5567
Happy Goat, 5568
Happy Herberts Food Co Inc, 5569
Happy Hive, 5570
Happy Planet Foods, 5571
Happy's Potato Chip Co, 5572, 44884
Happybaby, 56915
Haram-Christensen Corp, 44885, 56916
Harbar LLC, 5573
Harbison Wholesale Meats, 5574, 56917
Harbor Fish Market, 5575, 56918
Harbor Group Inc, 23589
Harbor International, 52989
Harbor Linen LLC, 56919
Harbor Pallet Company, 23590
Harbor Seafood, 5576, 44886
Harbor Spice, 5577
Harbor Sweets, 5578
Harbor Wholesale Foods Inc, 56920
Harbor Winery, 5579
Harborlite Corporation, 23591, 23592, 44887
Harborside Refrigerated Svc, 52990, 52991
Harborside Refrigerator Services, 52992
Harbour House Bar Crafting, 23593, 44888
Harbour House Furniture, 23594
Harbour Lobster Ltd, 5580, 44889
Harbro Packaging Co, 23595
Harco Enterprises, 23596, 44890, 56921
Harcros Chemicals Inc, 23597
Hard Eight Nutrition LLC, 5581
Hard-E Foods, 5582
Harders, 56922
Hardi-Tainer, 23598
Hardin Signs Inc, 23599
Hardscrabble Enterprises, 5583, 56923
Hardt Equipment Manufacturing, 23600, 44891
Hardware Components Inc, 23601, 44892
Hardwood Products Co LP, 23602, 44893
Hardy Diagnostics, 23603
Hardy Farms, 5584
Hardy Process Solutions Inc, 23604
Hardy Systems Corporation, 23605, 44894
Hardy-Graham, 23606
Harford Duracool LLC, 23607

Harford Glen Water, 5585
Harford Systems Inc, 23608, 44895
Harger's Finest Catch, 56924
Hari Om Farms, 5586
Haribo of America, 5587
Haring Catfish, 5588
Harker's Distribution, 5589, 56925, 56926
Harlan Bakeries, 5590, 44896
Harlan Laws Corp, 23609
Harland America, 5610
Harland Simon Control Systems USA, 23611, 44897
Harlin Fruit Co, 5591
Harlon's LA Fish, 5592, 56927
Harlow House Company, 5593
Harman Ice & Cold Storage, 52993
Harmar, 23612
Harmless Harvest, 5594
Harmon's Original Clam Cakes, 5595
Harmony Bay Coffee, 5596
Harmony Cellars, 5597
Harmony Enterprises, 23613, 44898
Harner Farms, 5598
Harney & Sons Tea Co., 5599, 44899
Harold F Haines Manufacturing Inc, 23614
Harold Food Company, 5600, 56928
Harold Import Co Inc, 23615
Harold J. Barrett Company, 40470
Harold L King & Co Inc, 5601, 44900
Harold Leonard & Company, 56929
Harold Leonard Midwest Corporation, 56930
Harold Leonard Southwest Corporation, 23616, 44901, 56931
Harold Levinson Assoc Inc, 56932
Harold M. Lincoln Company, 23617, 40471
Harold Wainess & Assoc, 23618
Harpak-Ulma, 23621, 56933
Harpak-ULMA Packaging LLC, 23619, 23620, 44902
Harper Associates, 23622
Harper Brush Works Inc, 23623, 44903
Harper Trucks Inc, 23624, 44904
Harper's Country Hams, 5602
Harpers Seafood Market, 5603
Harpersfield Vineyard, 5604
Harpo's, 5605
Harpoon Brewery, 5606
Harriet Greenland Enterprises, 40472
Harrill Brothers Wholesale Company, 56934
Harrington Hoists Inc, 23625
Harrington's Equipment Co, 23626
Harrington's of Vermont, 5607
Harris & Company, 23627
Harris Crab House, 5608, 44905
Harris Equipment Corp, 23628, 56935
Harris Farms Inc, 5609
Harris Freeman, 40473, 44906
Harris Moran Seed Co, 5610, 44907
Harris Ranch Beef Co, 5611, 44908
Harris Specialty Chemicals, 23629
Harris Tea Company, 5612
Harrisburg Dairies Inc, 5613
Harrison Electropolishing, 23630, 44909
Harrison Napa Valley, 5614
Harrison of Texas, 23631
Harrison Oyster Company, 56936
Harrisons & Crosfield Teas Inc., 44910
Harro Hofliger Packaging Systems, 23632
Harry & David, 5615
Harry Davis & Co, 23633
Harry E. Hills & Associates, 51803
Harry Fourtunis, 56937
Harry Fourtunis Inc, 56938
Harry Gelb Frozen Foods Inc, 56939
Harry London Candies Inc, 5616
Harry Nusinov Company, 56940
Harry Tinseth Associates, Inc., 40474
Harry Wils & Co Inc, 56941
Harry's Cafe, 5617

Harry's Premium Snacks, 56942
Harsco Industrial IKG, 23634, 44911
Harshfield Brothers, 56943
Hart Design & Mfg, 23635, 44912
Hart Designs LLC, 23636
Hart Lobster, 56944
Hart Winery, 5618
Harten Corporation, 44913
Hartford Containers, 23637
Hartford Despatch Mvg & Stor, 52994
Hartford Family Winery, 5619
Hartford Freezers, 52995
Hartford Plastics, 23638, 44914
Hartford Stamp Works, 23639
Harting Graphics, 23640
Harting's Bakery, 5620
Hartland Distributors, 56945
Hartley S. Johnson & Son, 40475
Hartley's Potato Chip Co, 5621
Hartness International, 23641, 44915
Hartog Rahal Foods, 5622
Hartselle Frozen Foods, 5623, 56946
Hartstone Pottery Inc, 23642, 44916
Hartsville Oil Mill, 5624
Hartville Kitchen, 5625
Hartville Locker Service, 5626
Hartzell Fan Inc, 23643, 44917
Harvard Folding Box Company, 23644, 44918
Harvard Seafood Company, 5627, 56947
Harvest Bakery, 5628
Harvest Direct, 5629
Harvest Food Products Co Inc, 5630, 44919
Harvest Grove Inc, 40476
Harvest Health Foods, 56948
Harvest Innovations, 5631
Harvest Manor Farms, 5632
Harvest Select, 5633
Harvest Song Ventures, 44920
Harvest Time Foods, 5634
Harvest Time Seafood Inc, 5635, 56949
Harvest Valley Bakery Inc, 5636
Harvest-Pac Products, 5637
Harvey W Hottel Inc, 23645
Harvey's Indian River Groves, 23646
Harvey-Winchell Company, 40477
Harveys Supermarket, 56950
Harvin Choice Meats, 5638
Harwil Corp, 23647, 44921
Has Beans Coffee & Tea Co, 5639, 56951
HAS Packaging System, 56859
Hasco Electric Corporation, 23648
Hassia, 44922, 56952
Hassia USA, 23649
Hastings Co-Op Creamery-Dairy, 5640
Hastings Lighting Company, 23650
Hastings Meat Supply, 5641, 44923
Hasty Bake Charcoal Grills, 5651
Hata Y & Co LTD, 56953
Hatch Chile Company, 5642
Hatch-Jennings Inc, 40478
Hatco Corp, 23652, 44924, 44925
Hatfield Quality Meats, 5643, 44926
Hathaway Coffee Co Inc, 5644, 56954
Hathaway Stamps, 23653
Hatteras Packaging Systems, 23654
Hattiesburg Grocery Company, 56955
Haug Quality Equipment, 23655
Haumiller Engineering Co, 23656, 44927
Hausbeck Pickle Co, 5645, 44928
Hauser Chocolates, 5646, 44929
Hauser Enterprises, 56956
Hauser Packaging, 23657
Hausman Foods LLC, 5647, 44930
Hautly Cheese Co, 23658
Havana's Limited, 5648
Havco Services, 44931
Have Our Plastic Inc, 23659, 44932
Haven's Candies, 5649, 23660
Haven's Kitchen Sauces, 5650
Havi Food Services Worldwide, 5651
HAVI Group, 56860
Haviland Enterprises Inc, 23661, 56957
Havoc Maker Products, 5652

Hawaii Candy Inc, 5653, 44933
Hawaii Coffee Company, 5654, 56958
Hawaii International Seafood, 5655, 44934, 56959
Hawaii Papaya Ind Assn, 44935
Hawaii Star Bakery, 5656
Hawaiian Bagel, 5657
Hawaiian Coffee Traders, 56960
Hawaiian Grocery Stores, 56961
Hawaiian Host Inc, 5658
Hawaiian Isles Kona Coffee Co, 5659
Hawaiian King Candies, 5660, 40479, 56962
Hawaiian Natural Water Company, 5661
Hawaiian Sun Products, 5662
Haward Corporation, 23662
Hawk Flour Mills, 56963
Hawkeye Corrugated Box, 23663
Hawkeye Pallet Co, 23664
Hawkhaven Greenhouse International, 5663, 44936
Hawkins Distributing Company, 56964
Hawkins Farm, 5664
Hawkins Inc, 5665
Hawley & Assoc, 40480
Hawthorn Power Systems, 56965
Hawthorne Supply Company, 56966
Hawthorne Valley Farm, 5666
Hayashibara International Inc., 5667
Haydel's Bakery, 5668
Haydenergy Health, 5669
Hayes & Stolz Indl Mfg LTD, 23665, 44937
Hayes Machine Co Inc, 23666
Hayes/Dockside Inc., 52996
Haynes Brothers Candy Company, 56967
Haynes Manufacturing Co, 23667, 44938
Hayon Manufacturing, 23668, 44939
Hayssen Flexible Systems, 23669, 23670, 44940
Hayward Gordon, 23671
Hayward Industries Inc, 23672, 44941
Hazel Creek Orchards, 5670
Hazelnut Growers Of Oregon, 5671, 44942
Hazen Paper Co, 23673
Hazle Park Quality Meats, 5672
Hazlitt 1852 Vineyards, 5673
Hazmat Business Ideas, 23674
Hazy Grove Nuts, 5674
HBD Industries, 23484
HBD Thermoid, Inc., 23485
HC Brill Company, 5482, 56861
HCB Foodservice Sales & Marketing, 40459
HCI Corp, 23486
HCR, 23487
Hcs Enterprises, 23675, 44943
HD Barcode, 23488
HD Electric Co, 23489, 44816
HD Marshall Ltd, 40460
HD Supply Waterworks, 56862
HDT Manufacturing, 23490, 44817
HE Anderson Co, 56863
Head Country, 5675
Heads & Tails Seafood, 56968
Healdsburg Machine Company, 23676, 44944
Healing Garden, 44945, 56969
Healing Home Foods, 5676, 56970
Healing Solutions, 5677
Health & Nutrition Systems International, 5678
Health & Wholeness Store, 5679, 44946
Health Concerns, 5680, 44947
Health Flavors, 44948, 56971
Health Food Distributors, 56972
Health from the Sun, 5686
Health Garden USA, 5681
Health Guardians, 44949, 56973
Health is Wealth Foods, 5687
Health King Enterprise, 44950, 56974
Health Plus, 5682, 44951
Health Products Corp, 5683, 23677, 44952

1392

All Companies Index

Health Star, 23678
Health Valley Company, 5684, 44953
Health Warrior, 5685
Health Waters, 56975
Health Wise Consumer Beverage Products, 56976
Health-Ade LLC, 5688
HealthBest, 5689, 44954
Healthco Canada Enterprises, 5690
Healthee, 5691
HealthFocus, 23679
Healthline Products, 23680
Healthmate Products, 5692, 44955, 56977
Healthstar Inc, 23681
Healthwise, 56978
Healthy Beverage LLC, 5693
Healthy Dining, 23682
Healthy Food Brands LLC, 5694
Healthy Food Ingredients, 5695
Healthy Grain Foods LLC, 5696, 23683
Healthy Habits Delivered, 44956
Healthy Life Brands LLC, 5697
Healthy N Fit International, 5698, 44957
Healthy Skoop, 5699
Healthy Times Baby Food, 5700
Heard Brokerage Company Inc, 40481
Hearn-Kirkwood, 56979
Heart Foods Company, 5701
Heart of Virginia, 23685
Heart Smart International, 23684
Heart to Heart Foods, 5702
Heartbreaking Dawns Artisan Foods, 5703
Hearthside Food Solutions, 5704, 23686, 44958
Hearthstone Whole Grain Bakery, 5705
Heartware Home Products, 44959
Hearty Foods, 5706, 56980
Heartland Brewery, 5707
Heartland Distributors, 56981
Heartland Farms Dairy & Food Products, LLC, 5708, 23687, 56982
Heartland Flax, 5709
Heartland Food Brokers LTD, 40482
Heartland Food Products, 5710, 44960, 56983
Heartland Gourmet LLC, 5711, 44961
Heartland Ingredients LLC, 5712, 23688, 56984
Heartland Mills Shipping, 5713, 44962
Heartland Strawberry Farm, 5714
Heartland Supply Co, 56985
Heartland Sweeteners, 5715
Heartland Vinyards, 5716
Heartline Products, 5717
Hearttea Inc., 5718
Heartwood, 23689
Hearty Naturals, 5719
Heat Seal, 23690
Heat-It Manufacturing, 23691, 44963
Heatcraft Refrigeration Prods, 23692, 44964
Heatcraft Worldwide Refrig, 23693, 44965
Heatec, 23694
Heath & Company, 23695, 23696
Heath Signs, 23697
Heatrex, 23698, 44966
Heatron Inc, 23699
Heaven Hill Distilleries Inc., 5720, 44967
Heavenly Cheesecakes, 56986
Heavenly Hemp Foods, 5721
Heavenly Organics, LLC, 5722
Heavenscent Edibles, 5723
Hebeler Corp, 23700
Hebenstreit GmbH, 23701
Hebert Candies, 5724
Heck Cellars, 5725, 44968
Hecker Pass Winery, 5726
Hector Delorme & Sons, 23702
Hectronic, 23703, 44969
Hedges Neon Sales, 23704
Hedgetree Chemical Manufacturing, 23705

Heding Truck Services, 51804
Hedland Flow Meters, 23706
Hedstrom Corporation, 23707
Hedwin Division, 23708, 44970
Heely-Brown Co Inc, 23709
Heerema Co, 56987
Heeren Brothers Produce, 56988
Hefferman Interactive, 23710
Heffy's BBQ Co., 5727
Hegy's South Hills Vineyard & Winery, 5728
Heico Chemicals Inc, 23711
Heidi's Gourmet Desserts, 5729, 44971
Heidi's Salsa, 5730
Heimann Systems Corporation, 23712
Heineken USA Inc, 44972
Heineman Winery, 5731
Heinke Family Farm, 5732
Heinkel's Packing Co, 5733, 56989
Heinlin Packaging Svc, 23713
Heinrich Envelope Corp, 23714
Heintz & Weber Co, 5734
Heinz Portion Control, 5735, 44973
Heinz Quality Chef Foods Inc, 5736
Heinzen Sales, 23715, 44974
Heirloom Organic Gardens, 5737
Heise Wausau Farms, 5738, 44975
Heisler Machine & Tool Co, 23716
Heiter Truck Line Inc, 51805
Heitz Wine Cellars, 5739, 44976
Hela Spice Company, 5740
Helados Mexico, 5741
Helen Ruth's Specialty Foods, 56990
Helen's Pure Foods, 5742
Helena View/Johnston Vineyard, 5743
Helena Wholesale, 56991
Helken Equipment Co, 23717, 44977
Hell On The Red Inc, 5744
Hella Cocktail, 5745
Hellenic Farms LLC, 44978
Heller Brothers Packing Corp, 5746, 44979
Heller Estates, 5747, 44980
Heller Truck Body Corp, 23718
Heller's Food Equipment, 56992
Hello Water, 5748
Hells Canyon Winery, 5749
Helm New York Chemical Corp, 5750, 44981
Helm Software, 23719
Helman International, 23720
Helmer, 23721
Helms Bakery, 5751
Helms Candy Co., Inc, 5752
Helmut's Strudel, 56993
Helmuth Country Bakery Inc, 5753
Helshiron Fisheries, 5754
Helthe Brands, 5755
Heltzman Bakery, 5756
Heluva Good Cheese, 5757, 44982
Hemco Corp, 23722
Hemisphere Foods, 44983
Hemisphere Group, 44984, 56994
Hemp Fusion, 5758
Hemp Oil Canada, 5759, 44985
Hemp Production Services, 5760
Hemp2o, 5761
HempNut, 5762
Hena Inc, 5763
Hench Control, Inc., 23723
Hendee Enterprises Inc, 23724
Henderson Coffee Corp, 56995
Henderson's Gardens, 5764
Henderson-Black Wholesale Groc, 56996
Hendon & David, 5765
Hendricks Apiaries, 5766
Hendrix Hotel & Restaurant Equipment & Supplies, 56997
Henggeler Packing Company, 5767, 44986
Henjes Enterprises, 56998
Henkel Consumer Adhesive, 23725, 44987
Henkel Corp., 23726
Henley Paper Company, 23727, 56999

Henning Cheese Factory, 5768
Henningsen Cold Storage Co, 51806, 52997, 52998, 52999, 53000, 53001, 53002, 53003, 53004, 53005, 53006, 53007
Henningsen Foods Inc, 5769, 23728
Henny Penny, Inc., 23729, 44988
Henry & Sons Inc, 23730
Henry Bresky & Sons Inc, 57000
Henry Broch & Co, 5770
Henry Davis Company, 5771, 57001
Henry Estate Winery, 5772
Henry Gonsalves Co, 44989, 57002
Henry Group, 23731
Henry H. Misner Ltd., 5773
Henry Hanger & Fixture Corporation of America, 23732, 44990
Henry Hill & Co, 5774
Henry Ira L Co, 23733
Henry J's Meat Specialties, 5775
Henry J. Hips Company, 40483
Henry L Taylor Trucking LLC, 51807, 53008
Henry Lambertz Inc, 44991
Henry Molded Products Inc, 23734
Henry Troemner LLC, 23735, 44992
Henrys Cash & Carry, 57003
Henschel Coating & Laminating, 23736
Herb Barber & Sons Food, 40484
Herb Bee's Products, 5776
HERB Enterprises, 56864
Herb Patch of Vermont, 5777, 44993
Herb Pharm, 5778
Herb Society Of America, 5779
Herb Tea Company, 5780
Herb's Seafood, 5781
Herbal Magic, 5785
Herbal Products & Development, 5786, 44994
Herbal Science LLC, 5787
Herbal Teas International, 44995
Herbal Water, Inc., 5788
Herbalist & Alchemist Inc, 5789
HerbaSway Laboratories, 5784
HerbCo International, 5782
Herbert Miller, 23737
HerbNZest LLC, 5783
Herbs America, 5790
Herbs Etc, 5791, 44996
Herc-U-Lift Inc, 57004
Herche Warehouse, 23738, 57005
Herculean Equipment, 23739
Hercules Food Equipment, 23740, 57006
Herdell Printing Inc, 23741
Heringer Meats Inc, 5792
Heritage Bag Co, 23742
Heritage Books & Gifts, 5793, 44997
Heritage Coffee Co & Cafe, 5794
Heritage Corrugated Box Corporation, 23743
Heritage Equipment Co, 23744
Heritage Family Specialty Foods Inc, 5795
Heritage Fancy Foods Marketing, 5796
Heritage Farms Dairy, 5797
Heritage Food Svc, 44998
Heritage Foods USA, 5798
Heritage Health Food, 5799
Heritage Maintenance Products, LLC, 57007
Heritage Packaging, 23745, 44999
Heritage Salmon, 5800
Heritage Salmon Company, 5801, 45000
Heritage Short Bread, 5802
Heritage Wine Cellars, 5803
Heritage's Dairy Stores, 5804
Herkimer Pallet & Wood Products Company, 23746
Herlocher Foods, 5805
Herman Falter Packing Co, 5806
Herman's Bakery, 5807
Hermann J. Wiemer Vineyard, 5808
Hermann Laue Spice Company, 23747, 45001
Hermann Pickle Co, 5809

Hermann Services Inc, 51808, 53009
Hermann Services Warehouse Corporation, 53010
Hermannhof Vineyards, 5810
Hermanowski Wholesale, 57008
Hernan, 5811
Hero Nutritionals, 5812
Herold's Salads, 5813
Heron Hill Winery, 5814
Herr Foods Inc., 5815, 57009
Herrell's Ice Cream, 5816
Herring Brothers Meats, 5817, 57010
Herrmann Ultrasonics, 23748
Hersey Measurement Company, 23749
Hershey Co., 5818, 23750, 45002, 57011
Hershey Creamery Co, 5819
Herspring, 40485
Herz Meat Company, 45003
Hess Collection, 5820
Hess Machine Intl, 23751, 45004
Hess Trucking Co, 51809
Heterochemical Corp, 5821, 45005
Heuft USA Inc, 23752
Hevi-Haul International LTD, 23753, 45006
Hewitt Manufacturing Co, 23754
Hewitt Soap Company, 23755, 45007
Hewlett-Packard, 23756
Hexion Inc, 23757
Heyday Beverage Co., 5822
Heyerly Bakery, 5823
HFI Foods, 5483, 44818
HFM Foodservice, 56865
HGA Group, 40461
HH Controls Company, 23491
HH Dobbins Inc, 5484, 44819
HHP Inc, 23492, 44820
Hi Country Snack Foods, 5824
Hi Roller Enclosed Belt Conveyors, 23758, 45008
Hi Seas, 5825
Hi-Country Foods Corporation, 5826, 45009
HI-TECH Filter, 23493
Hi-Tech Packaging Inc, 23759
Hi-Temp Inc, 23760
Hialeah Products Co, 5828, 45010, 57012
HIB Foods Inc, 56866
Hiball, Inc., 5829
Hibco Plastics, 23761
Hibiscus Aloha Corporation, 5830
HiBix Corporation, 5827
Hibrett Puratex, 23762, 57013
Hickey Foods, 5831
Hickory Baked Ham Co, 5832
Hickory Farms, 5833
Hickory Harvest Foods, 5834, 45011, 57014
Hickory Industries, 23763, 45012
Hickory Zesti Smoked Specialties, 23764
Hiclay Studios, 23765
HID Global, 23494
Hidden Mountain Ranch Winery, 5835
Hidden Springs Maple, 5836
Hidden Villa Ranch, 5837, 45013
Hiestand USA, 45014
Higa Food Service, 5838, 57015
Higgins & White Inc, 40486
Higgins Seafood, 5839
High Brew Coffee, 5840
High Country Elevators Inc, 5841
High Country Gourmet, 5842
High Country Meats, 57016
High Grade Beverage, 5843
High Ground of Texas, 23766
High Liner Foods Inc., 5844, 45015
High Mowing Organic Seeds, 5845
High Plains Freezer, 53011
High Quality Organics, 5846, 57017
High Ridge Foods LLC, 5847, 57018
High Rise Coffee Roasters, 5848
High Road Craft Ice Cream, Inc., 5849
High Tide Seafoods Inc, 5850
High Valley Farm, 5851
High-Purity Standards, 23767, 45016

1393

All Companies Index

Highland Dairies, 5852
Highland Family Farms, 5853
Highland Farm Foods, 5854
Highland Fisheries, 5855, 45017
Highland Laboratories, 5856
Highland Manor Winery, 5857
Highland Plastics Inc, 23768
Highland Sugarworks, 5858, 23769
Highland Supply Corp, 23770
Highland Transport, 51810
Highlandville Packing, 5859
Highlight Industries, 23771, 45018
Highroad Warehouse, Inc, 51811
Hightower's Packing, 5860
Highwood Distillers, 5861, 45019
Hikari Miso Intl., 5862
Hiland Dairy Foods Co, 5863
Hilary's Eat Well, 5864
Hilden America, 45020
Hilden Halifax, 23772, 45021
Hildreth Wood Products Inc, 23773
Hilex Company, 23774
Hilgenfeld Brokerage Co, 40487
Hill & Sloan, 57019
Hill 'N' Dale Meat, 45022
Hill Brush, Inc., 23775
Hill City Wholesale Company, 57020
Hill Company, 57021
Hill Manufacturing Co Inc, 23776, 45023
Hill Parts, 23777
Hill Specialties, 57022
Hill Top Berry Farm & Winery, 5865
Hill's Pier 19 Restaurant Lighthouse Bar, 57023
Hillandale, 5866
Hillard Bloom Packing Co Inc, 5867
Hillards Chocolate System, 23778
Hillbilly Smokehouse, 5868
Hillcrest Food Svc, 57024
Hillcrest Orchard, 5869
Hillcrest Vineyards, 5870
Hillestad Pharmaceuticals, 5871
Hilliard Corp, 23779
Hillier Storage & Moving, 53012
Hillis Farms, 57025
Hillmans Shrimp & Oyster, 5872
Hillsboro Coffee Company, 5873
Hillsboro Transportation Company, 51812
Hillside Candy Co, 5874, 45024
Hillside Lane Farm, 5875
Hillside Metal Ware Company, 23780, 45025
Hillson Nut Co, 5876
Hilltop Meat Co, 5877
Hilltop Services LLC, 23781
Hillyard Inc, 23782, 45026
Hilmar Cheese Company, 5878, 45027
Hilmar Ingredients, 5879, 45028
Hilo Fish Company, 5880, 45029, 57026
Hilter Stainless, 23783
Hilts, 57027
HimalaSalt, 5881
Himalayan Chef, 5882
Himalayan Heritage, 5883, 45030
Himolene, 23784
Hinchcliff Products Company, 23785, 45031
Hinckley Springs Bottled Water, 5884, 45032
Hinds-Bock Corp, 23786, 45033
Hines III, 23787
Hines Nut Co, 45034, 57028
Hingham Shellfish, 5885, 57029
Hinkle Easter Products, 40488
Hinkle Manufacturing, 23788
Hino Diesel Trucks, 23789
Hinojosa Brothers Wholesale, 57030
Hint Mint, 5886
Hint Water, 5887
Hinzerling Winery, 5888
Hip Chick Farms, 5889
Hipp Wholesale Foods, 57031
Hippeas, 5890
Hippie Snacks, 5891

Hiram Walker & Sons, 5892, 45035
Hirschbach Motor Lines, 51813
Hirzel Canning Co & Farms, 5893, 45036
Hirzel Canning Co., 5894
Hishi Plastics, 23790
Hiss Stamp Company, 23791, 57032
Hitachi Maxco LTD, 23792
Hitec Food Equipment, 23793, 23794, 45037
Hiwin Technologies Corporation, 23795
Hixson Architecture Engrng, 23796, 23797
HK Marketing, 40462
HM Electronics Inc, 44821
HMC Corp, 23495, 44822
HMC Farms, 5485
HMG Provisions, 56867
HMG Worldwide, 23496
HMG Worldwide In-Store Marketing, 23497, 44823
Hnina Gourmet, 5895
Hoarel Sign Co, 23798
Hoban Foods, 57033
Hobarama Corporation, 5896
Hobart, 23799
Hobby Whalen Marketing, 40489
Hobe Laboratories Inc, 5897, 45038
Hockenberg Newburgh, 40490, 40491
Hockenberg-Newburgh Sales, 40492
Hockenbergs Equipment & Supply, 57034
Hodell International, 45039, 57035
Hodge Design Assoc PC, 23800
Hodge Manufacturing Company, 23801
Hodge Transit Warehouse, 53013
Hodges, 23802
Hodges & Irvine Inc, 57036
Hodges Co, 51814, 53014
Hodgson Mill Inc, 5898
Hodo, 5899
Hoegger Alpina, 23803
Hoegger Food Technology, 23804
Hoff's Bakery, 5900
Hoff's United Food, 5901
Hoffer Flow Controls Inc, 23805, 45040
Hoffman & Levy Inc Tasseldepot, 23806, 45041
Hoffman Co, 23807
Hoffman Miller Advertising, 57037
Hoffman's Quality Meats, 57038
Hoffmann LA Roche, 23808
Hoffmaster Group Inc, 23809, 23810, 45042
Hoffmaster Group Inc., 23811
Hoffmeyer Corp, 23812
Hofmann Sausage Co Inc, 5902
Hog Haus Brewing Company, 5903
Hoge Brush Company, 23813
Hogshire Industries, 23814
Hogtown Brewing Company, 5904, 23815
Hogtowne B-B-Q Sauce Company, 5905, 57039
Hohn Manufacturing Company, 23816, 45043
Hohner Corporation, 23817
Hoky Central, 57040
Holcor, 23818
Holden Graphic Services, 23819
Holeman Distribution Ctr, 51815, 53015
Holey Moses Cheesecake, 5906
Holistic Horizons/Halcyon Pacific Corporation, 45044, 57041
Holistic Products Corporation, 5907, 45045, 57042
Holland American Food, 45046
Holland American International Specialties, 5908, 57043
Holland Applied Technologies, 23820
Holland Beef International Corporation, 45047, 57044
Holland Chemicals Company, 23821
Holland Co Inc, 23822, 45048
Holland Manufacturing Co Inc, 23823

Holland-American International Specialties, 45049, 57045
Hollander Horizon International, 23824
Hollander, Gould & Murray Company, 57046
Hollandia Bakeries Limited, 5909, 23825
Hollar & Greene, 40493
Holley Cold Storage Fruit Co, 53016
Hollingsworth Custom Wood Products, 23826, 45050
Hollman Foods, 5910
Hollow Road Farms, 5911
Hollowell Products Corporation, 23827
Hollowick Inc, 23828, 45051, 57047
Holly Camp Springs Inc, 5912
Holly Hill Locker Company, 5913
Holly International, 23829
Holly Seafood Company, 57048
Holly's Oatmeal Inc, 5914
Hollymatic Corp, 23830, 45052
Hollywood Banners, 23831, 45053
Holman Boiler Works, 23832, 45054
Holman Cooking Equipment, 23833
Holman Distribution Center, 51816, 53017
Holmco Container Manufacturing, LTD, 23834, 45055
Holmes Cheese Co, 5915
Holmes Foods, 5916
Holo-Source Corporation, 23835
Holophane, 23836
Holsman Sign Svc, 23837
Holstein Manufacturing, 23838, 45056
Holsum Bakery Inc, 5917
Holt Logistics Corporation, 51817, 53018
Holt's Bakery Inc, 5918
Holton Food Products, 5919
Holton Meat Processing, 5920
Holy Kombucha, 5921, 57049
Holy Smoke LLC, 5922
Holyoke Machine Co, 57050
Hol, Mol,, 5923
Homarus Inc, 5924, 45057
Home Bakery, 5925
Home City Ice Co, 23839
Home Decoration Accessories, 45058
Home Delivery Food Service, 5926, 57051
Home Maid Bakery, 5927
Home Market Food Inc, 5928
Home Market Foods Inc., 5929
Home Plastics Inc, 23840, 45059
Home Roast Coffee, 5930
Home Rubber Co, 23841, 45060
Home Run Inn Frozen Foods, 5931, 45061
Home Style Bakery Of Grand Junction, 5932
Home Style Foods Inc, 5933, 45062
Home-Like Food Company, 57052
Homefree LLC, 5935
Homegrown Naturals, 5936
Homegrown Organic Farms, 5937
Homemade By Dorothy Boise, 5938
Homemade Harvey, 5939
Homeplace Food Group, 40494
HomePlate Peanut Butter, 5934
Homer Laughlin China Co, 23842
Homer's Ice Cream, 5940
Homer's Wharf Seafood Company, 5941
Homestead Baking Co, 5942
Homestead Dairy, 5943
Homestead Fine Foods, 5944
Homestead Foods, 57053
Homestead Meats, 5945
Homestead Mills, 5946, 45063
Homestead Ravioli Company, 5947
Homestyle Bread Bakery, 5948
Hometown Bagel Inc, 5949
Homewood Winery, 5950
Honee Bear Canning, 5951, 45064
Honest Tea Inc, 5952
Honey Acres, 5953, 45065, 57054
Honey Bear Fruit Basket, 5954
Honey Bee Company, 5955

Honey Blossom, 5956
Honey Butter Products Co, 5957
Honey Dew Donuts, 5958
Honey Hut, 5959
Honey Mama's, 5960
Honey Ridge Farms, 5961
Honey Run Winery, 5962
Honey Stinger, 5963
Honey Wafer Baking Co, 5964
Honey World, 5965
Honeybaked Ham, 5966
Honeydrop Beverages, 5967
Honeyville Grain Inc, 5968, 45066, 57055
Honeywell International, 23843, 45067
Honeywell Sensing & Internet of Things, 23844
Honeywell UOP, 23845
Honeywood Winery, 5969, 45068
Hong Kong Noodle Company, 5970
Hong Kong Supermarket, 5971
Hong Tou Noodle Company, 5972
Hongar Farms Gourmet Foods, 5973
HongryHawg of Louisiana, 5974
Honickman Affiliates, 5975
Honig Vineyard and Winery, 5976, 57056
Honiron Corp, 23846, 45069
Honolulu Fish Company, 5977, 45070
Honolulu Freight Svc, 51818
Honso USA, 5978
Hood Home Service, 5979
Hood Packaging, 23847, 23848
Hood River Coffee Co, 5980
Hood River Distillers Inc, 5981, 45071
Hood River Vineyards and Winery, 5982
Hood Sterile Division, 5983
Hoodsport Winery, 5984
Hoogwegt, U.S., Inc, 57057
Hook Line and Savor, 5985
Hooks Cheese Co, 5986
Hoonah Cold Storage, 51819
Hoopeston Foods Inc, 5987
Hoople Country Kitchen Inc, 5988
Hoosier Warehouses Inc, 53019
Hoover Company, 23849, 45072
Hoover Materials Handling Group, 23850, 45073
Hop Growers Of Washington, 23851
Hop Kiln Winery, 5989
Hope Chemical Corporation, 23852
Hope Creamery, 5990
Hope Foods, 5991
Hope Industrial Systems, 23853, 45074
Hope Paper Box Company, 23854
Hopes Country Fresh Cookies, 45075
Hopkins Inn Of Lake Waramaug, 5992
Hopkins Vineyard, 5993
Hopp Co Inc, 23855
Hoppmann Corporation, 23856, 45076
Hops Extract Corporation of America, 5994
Horix Manufacturing Co, 23857, 45077
Horizon Business Svc, 57058
Horizon Cellars Winery, 5995
Horizon Organic Dairy, 5996
Horizon Plastics, 23858
Horizon Poultry, 5997, 45078
Horizon Snack Foods, 5998
Horizon Software International, 23859
Horlacher Meats, 5999
Hormann Flexan Llc, 23860, 45079
Hormel Foods Corp., 6000, 23861, 45080, 57059
Horn & Todak, 23862
Hornell Brewing Company, 6001
Hornell Wholesale Grocery Company, 57060
Horner International, 6002, 23863, 45081
Horseshoe Brand, 6003
Horsley Company, 57061
Horst Seafood, 6004
Horton Fruit Co Inc, 6005, 23864
Horton Vineyards, 6006
Hosch Properties, 23865, 45082
Hose Master Inc, 23866, 45083

All Companies Index

Hosemen & Roche Vitamins & Fine Chemicals, 6007
Hosford & Wood Fresh Seafood Providers, 6008, 45084, 57062
Hoshizaki, 23867
Hoshizaki America Inc, 23868, 45085
Hoshizaki Northeastern, 57063
Hosmer Mountain Bottling Co, 6009
Hosoda Brothers Inc, 45086, 57064
Hosokawa Confectionery &Bakery Technology and Systems, 23869
Hosokawa Micron Powder Systems, 23870
Hosokawa/Bepex Corporation, 23871
Hospitality International, 23872
Hospitality Mints LLC, 6010, 45087
Hoss-S, 6011, 23873, 57065
Host Defense Mushrooms, 6012
Hostess Brands, 6013
Hot Cakes-Molten Chocolate, 6014
Hot Food Boxes, 23874, 45088
Hot Licks, 6015
Hot Mama's Foods, 6016, 23875
Hot Sauce Harry's Inc, 57066
Hot Springs Packing Co Inc, 6017, 45089
Hot Wachula's, 6018
Hotshot Delivery System, 23876
Hotsy Corporation, 23877
Houdini Inc, 6019, 23878, 45090
Houlton Farms Dairy, 6020
House Foods America Corp, 6021, 45091
House of Coffee Beans, 6022
House of Flavors Inc, 6023, 45092
House of Herbs LLC, 6024
House of Raeford Farms Inc, 6025, 45093
House of Spices, 6026, 45094, 57067
House of Thaller Inc, 6027
House of Tsang, 6028
House of Webster, 6029, 57068
House Stamp Works, 23879
House-Autry Mills Inc, 6030
Houser Meats, 6031
Houser Neon Sign Company, 23880
Housewaresdirect Inc, 40495
Houston Atlas, 23881
Houston Calco, Inc, 6032
Houston Central Industries, Ltd., 51820, 53020
Houston International Packaging Company, 57069
Houston Label, 23882, 45095
Houston Poultry & Egg Company, 57070
Houston Stamp & Stencil Company, 23883
Houston Tea & Beverage, 6033, 45096
Houston Wire Works, Inc., 23884, 45097
Hovair Systems Inc, 23885, 45098
Hovus Inc, 23886
Howard Decorative Packaging, 57071
Howard Fabrication, 23887
Howard Foods Inc, 6034
Howard Imprinting Machine Company, 23888, 45099
Howard Overman & Sons, 23889
Howard Turner & Son, 6035, 45100
Howard-Mccray, 23890, 23891, 45101
Howden Group, 23892
Howe Corp, 23893, 45102
Howell Associates, 40496, 45103
Howell Brothers Chemical Laboratories, 23894, 45104
Howell Consulting, 23895
Howell Logistics Services, 53021
Howes S Co Inc, 23896, 23897, 45105
Howjax, 6036
Howlett Farms, 23898
Howson Mills, 6037, 45106
Hoyer, 23899
Hoyt, 40497
Hoyt Corporation, 23900, 45107
Hoyt's Honey Farm, 6038, 45108
HP Hood LLC, 5486
HP Schmid, 5487
HPC Foodservice, 56868

HPI North America/ Plastics, 23498
HPI North America/Plastics, 23499
HRS Food Service, 56869
HSI, 23500
HSI Company, 23501
Hsin Tung Yang Foods Inc, 6039, 45109
HSN Data Corporation, 56870
HSR Associates Inc, 5488
Hsu's Ginseng Enterprises Inc, 6040, 45110
Hu Kitchen, 6041, 57072
Huard Packaging, 23901
Hub City Brush Co, 23902
Hub Electric Company, 23903, 45111
Hub Folding Box Co, 23904
Hub Labels Inc, 23905
Hub Pen Company, 23906, 45112
Hubbard Peanut Co Inc, 6042, 45113
Hubbell Electric Heater Co, 23907, 45114
Hubbell Lenoir City Inc, 23908
Hubbell Lighting Inc, 23909, 45115
Hubber Technology Inc, 23910
Hubble, 6043
Hubco Inc, 23911, 45116
Hubers Orchard Winery-Vineyards, 6044
Hubert Co, 57073
Hubert's Lemonade, 6045
Huck Store Fixture Company, 23912
Huck's Seafood, 6046, 57074
Huckleberry Patch, 6047
Hudson Belting & Svc Co Inc, 23913, 57075
Hudson Commercial Foods, 45117
Hudson Control Group Inc, 23914, 45118
Hudson Henry Baking Co., 6048
Hudson Poly Bag Inc, 23915
Hudson River Foods, 6049, 57076
Hudson River Fruit Distr, 57077
Hudson Valley Brewery, 6050
Hudson Valley Coffee Company, 45119, 57078
Hudson Valley Farmhouse Cider, 6051
Hudson Valley Foie Gras, 6052, 57079
Hudson Valley Fruit Juice, 6053
Hudson Valley Homestead, 6054
Hudson Valley Hops, 6055, 23916, 45120
Hudson Valley Malt, 6056, 45121, 57080
Hudson-Sharp Machine Co, 23917, 45122
Hudson-Sharp Machine Company, 23918, 45123
Hudsonville Ice Cream, 6057
Hue's Seafood, 6058, 57081
Hueck Foils LLC, 23919
Huettinger Electronic Inc, 23920
Huff Ice Cream, 57082
Huger-Davidson-Sale Company, 57083
Hugg & Hall Equipment, 57084
Hugh T. Gilmore Company, 40498
Hughes Co, 23921, 23922, 45124
Hughes Manufacturing Company, 23923, 45125
Hughes Springs Frozen Food Center, 6059
Hughes Supply, 57085
Hughes Warehouse Equipment Company, 57086
Hughson Meat Company, 6060
Hughson Nut Inc, 6061
Huguenot Sales Corporation, 57087
Huhtamaki Food Service Plastics, 23924
Huhtamaki Inc, 23925
Hull Lift Truck Inc, 57088
Hulman & Co, 6062
Huls America, 23926
Humbly Hemp, 6063
Humboldt Bay Coffee Co., 6064
Humboldt Brews LLC, 6065
Humboldt Chocolate, 6066, 57089
Humboldt Creamery, 6067, 45126
Humco Holding Group Inc 6068, 45127
Hume Specialties, 6069
Humeniuk's Meat Cutting, 6070
Humm Kombucha, 6071

Hummel Brothers Inc, 6072
Humming Hemp, 6073
Hummingbird Kitchens, 6074
Hummingbird Wholesale, 57090
Hummustir, 6075
Humphrey Co, 6076
Humphrey's Market, 6077
Humphry Slocombe, 6078
Hundley Brokerage Company, 40499
Hung's Noodle House, 6079
Hungerford & Terry, 23927, 45128
Hungry Sultan, 6080
Hunt Brothers Cooperative, 6081
Hunt Country Foods Inc, 6082
Hunt Country Vineyards, 6083, 45129
Hunt Midwest, 23928
Hunt-Wesson Foods, 6084
Hunter Amenities International, 45130
Hunter Fan Co, 23929
Hunter Farms - High Point Division, 6085
Hunter Food Inc, 6086, 57091
Hunter Graphics, 23930
Hunter Lab, 23931, 45131
Hunter Packaging Corporation, 23932
Hunter Walton & Co Inc, 40500, 45132, 57092
Hunter Woodworks, 23933
Huntington Foam Corp, 23934
Huntington Park Rbr Stamp Co, 23935
Huntsman Packaging, 23936, 45133
Huntsman Packaging Corporation, 23937
Huntsville Restaurant Equip, 57093
Huppen Bakery, 6087
Hurd Orchards, 6088
Hurlingham Company, 23938
Huron Food Sales, 40501
Hurri-Kleen Corporation, 23939
Hurst Corp, 23940
Hurst Labeling Systems, 23941, 45134
Hurt Conveyor Equipment Company, 23942
Husch Vineyards & Winery, 6089
Huse's Country Meats, 6090
Huskey Specialty Lubricants, 23943, 45135
Husky Foods of Anchorage, 57094
Husman Snack Food Company, 6091
Hussmann Corp, 23944, 45136
Hutchinson Group, 45137
Hutchinson Mayrath Industries, 57095
Hutchison-Hayes International, 23945
Huther Brothers, 23946, 45138
Hutz Sign & Awning, 23947
Huy Fong Foods Inc, 6092
HV Food Products Co, 5489
HW Theller Engineering, 23502
Hy-Ko Enviro-MaintenanceProducts, 23948
Hy-Ten Plastics Inc, 23949
Hy-Trous/Flash Sales, 23950
Hyatt Industries Limited, 23951
Hybco USA, 6093
Hybread, 6094
Hybrinetics Inc, 23952, 45139
Hycor Corporation, 23953
Hyde & Hyde Inc, 6095, 23954
Hyde Candy Company, 6096
Hyde Park Brewing Company, 6097
Hyder North America, 23955
Hydra-Flex Inc, 23956, 57096
Hydranautics (A Nitto Denko Company), 23957
Hydrel Corporation, 23958, 45140
Hydrite Chemical Co, 23959, 57097
Hydro Life, 23960
Hydro Seal Coatings Company, 23961
Hydro-Miser, 23962, 45141
Hydro-Tech EnvironmentalSystems, 23963
Hydro-Thermal Corp, 23964
Hydroblend Limited, 6098
HydroCal, 23965
Hydrocal Inc, 23966
Hydromax Inc, 23967, 45142

Hydron, 23968
Hydropure Water Treatment Co, 23969, 45143
Hye Cuisine, 6099, 45144
Hye Quality Bakery, 6100
Hyer Industries, 23970, 45145
Hygeia Dairy Company, 6101, 45146
Hygiena LLC, 23971
Hygiene-Technik, 23972, 45147
Hygienic Fabrics Inc, 23973
Hygrade Gloves, 23974, 45148
Hynes Bond Ellison, 40502, 40503
Hypro, 23975
Hyster Company, 23976, 23977, 45149
Hytrol Conveyor Co Inc, 23978
Hytrol of California, 57098

I

I C Technologies, 23979
I Heart Keenwah, 6102
I Heart Olive Oil, 6103
I J White Corp, 23980
I Light Ny, 57099
I M A North America, 23981
I Magid, 45150, 57100
I P Callison & Sons, 6104, 45151
I Rice & Co Inc, 6105, 45152
I Supply Co, 57101
I Wanna Distributors, 45153, 57102
I Zakarin & Sons Inc, 45154, 57103
I'm Different Snacks, 6106
I-Health Inc, 6107, 45155
I. Deveau Fisheries LTD, 6108, 45156
I. Fm Usa Inc., 23982
I. Grob & Company, 45157, 57104
I.T. Bauman Company, 57105
I.W. Tremont Company, 23983, 45158
IAFIS Dairy Products Evaluation Contest, 23984
Ian's Natural Food, 6125
IASE Co Inc, 23985
IB Concepts, 23986, 45159
IB Roof Systems, 45160
IBA, 23987
IBA Food Safety, 23988
IBC, 57106
IBC Shell Packaging, 23989
Iberia Foods of Florida, 57116
Ibertrade Commercial Corporation, 45189
IBF, 45161, 57107
IBS Trading, 45162
Icart & Deco Originals, 57117
ICatcher Network, 45166
ICB Greenline, 23990, 45163
ICC Industrial Chemical, 57108
Icco Cheese Co, 6126, 45190
Ice & Juice Systems, 57118
Ice Chips Candy, 6127, 57119
Ice Cold Storage, 53022
Ice Cream Bowl, 6128
Ice Cream Club Inc, 6129
Ice Cream Specialties Inc, 6130
Ice King & Cold Storage Inc, 53023
Ice Machines, 57120
Ice Makers, 57121
Ice-Cap, 24046, 45191
Iceberg Seafood Inc, 40509, 57122
Icebox Water, 45192
ICEE, 45164
Icee-USA Corporation, 24047, 45193
Icelandair, 51821
Icelandic Milk and Skyr Corporation, 6131
Icelandic Provisions, 6132
Iceomatic, 24048, 45194
ICI Surfactants, 23991
Icicle Seafoods Inc, 6133
Ickler Co Inc, 24049
ICL Performance Products, 6109, 45165
ICM Controls, 23992
ICOA Inc, 23993
ICONIC Protein, 6110
Iconics Inc, 24050, 45195

1395

All Companies Index

Icrest International LLC, 57123
ID Foods Corporation, 45167, 57109
ID Images, 23994
Id Technology, 24051, 24052
Idaho Beverages Inc, 24053
Idaho Candy Co, 6134
Idaho Frank Association Inc, 6135
Idaho Milk Products, 6136
Idaho Pacific Holdings Inc, 6137, 45196
Idaho Steel Products Inc, 24054, 45197
Idaho Supreme Potatoes Inc, 6138, 45198
Idaho Trout Company, 6139, 45199
Idahoan Foods LLC, 6140
IDC Food Division, 23995
Ideal Dairy Farms, 6141
Ideal Distributing Company, 6142
Ideal of America, 24062
Ideal of America/Valley Rio Enterprise, 24063, 45203
Ideal Office Supply & Rubber Stamp Company, 24055
Ideal Packaging Systems, 24056
Ideal Pak Inc, 24057
Ideal Sleeves, 24058
Ideal Snacks Corp, 6143
Ideal Stencil Machine & Tape Company, 24059, 45200
Ideal Warehouse, 51822, 53024
Ideal Wire Works, 24060, 45201
Ideal Wrapping Machine Company, 24061, 45202
Idealease Inc, 51823
Ideas Etc Inc, 24064, 45204
Ideas in Motion, 24066
Ideas Well Done LLC, 24065
Idec Corp, 24067
IdentaBadge, 24068
Idesco Corp, 24069, 45205
IDEX Corp, 23996
Idexx Laboratories Inc, 24070, 45206
IDL, 23997
Ido, 45207
IEW, 23998, 45168
IFC Disposables Inc, 23999
IFC Solutions, 6111
IFFE/Rainbow Embroidery, 45169
IFive Brands, 6113
IFM, 6112, 45170
Ifm Efector, 24071
iFoodDecisionSciences, 31465
IFS North America, 24000
IGEN, 24001
IGEN International, 24002
Igloo Products Corp, 24072
IGS Store Fixtures, 24003
Igus Inc, 24073
IGZU, 6114
IHS Heath Information, 24004
II Sisters, 6115
Ika-Works Inc, 24074
Il Gelato, 6144
Il Giardino Del Dolce Inc, 6145
Il Valley Container Inc, 24075
Ilapak Inc, 24076, 24077, 45208
Ilc Dover, 24078
ILHWA American Corporation, 6116, 45171, 57110
Illes Seasonings & Flavors, 6146, 45209
Illinois Department of Agriculture, 45210
Illinois Lock Co, 24079
Illinois Range Company, 24080
Illinois Restaurant Association, 24081
Illinois Tool Works, 24082
Illinois Wholesale Cash Rgstr, 24083
Illuma Display, 24084, 45211
Illumination Products Inc, 24085
Illy caffe, 6148
Illy Espresso of the Americas, 6147
Ilsemann Corp, 24086
IMAC, 6117
Imaex Trading Company, 6149
IMAG Organics, 6118
Image Development, 24087
Image Experts Uniforms, 24088, 45212
Image Fillers, 24089

Image National Inc, 24090, 45213
Image Plastics, 24091
Imagine Chocolate, 6150
Imagine Foods, 6151
Imaging Technologies, 24092, 45214
Imaje, 24093, 45215
Iman Pack, 24094, 24095, 45216
Iman Pack Sigma System, 24096
Imani Chimani Chocolate, 6152
Imar, 24097, 45217
Imark of Pennsylvania, 40510
IMAS Corporation, 24005
IMC Instruments, 24006
IMC Teddy Food Service Equipment, 24007
Imdec, 24098
IMDEC, 57111
IMECO Inc, 24008, 45172
Imex Enterprise, 57124
Imex Vinyl Packaging, 24099
IMI Cornelius, 24009, 45173
IMI Precision Engineering, 24010, 24011, 45174
Imlak'esh Organics, 6153
Immaculate Baking Company, 6154
Immaculate Consumption, 6155
Immordl, 6156
Immu Dyne Inc, 6157, 45218
IMO Foods, 6119, 24012, 45175
Impact Awards & Promotions, 24100
Impact Confections, 6158, 45219
Impact Enterprises, 45220
Impact Nutrition, 24101
Impact Products LLC, 24102, 57125
Impaxx Machines, 24103
Imperal Freight Broker, 40511, 51824, 53025
Imperial, 24104, 24105
Imperial Bag & Paper Company, 57126
Imperial Broom Company, 24106
Imperial Cold Storage And Distribution, 53026
Imperial Containers, 24107
Imperial Dade, 40512, 57127
Imperial Flavors Beverage Co, 6159
Imperial Florida Sales, 40513
Imperial Food Supply, 57128
Imperial Foods, Inc, 6160
Imperial Frozen Foods Co, 40514
Imperial House Sales, 40515
Imperial Industries Inc, 24108, 45221
Imperial Manufacturing Co, 24109, 45222
Imperial Nougat Co, 6161
Imperial Packaging Corporation, 24110
Imperial Plastics Inc, 24111, 24112, 45223
Imperial Salmon House, 6162, 45224
Imperial Schrade Corporation, 24113
Imperial Seafood, 57129
Imperial Sensus, 6163, 45225
Imperial Signs & Manufacturing, 24114
Imperial Sugar Company, 6164
Imperial Tea Court, 57130
Imperial Trading, 40516, 57131
Important Wines, 45226
Imported Restaurant Specialties, 45227, 57132
Importers, 51825, 53027
Importers Service Corp, 24115
Importex International, 45228, 57133
Impossible Foods, 6165
Impra USA, 45229
Impress Industries, 24116
Impress USA Inc, 24117
Imprint Plus, 45230
Imprinting Systems Specialty, 24118
Impromtu Gourmet, 6166
Improper Goods, 6167
Improved Blow Molding, 24119, 45231
Improved Nature, 6168
Impulse Signs, 24120, 45232
IMS Food Service™, 24013
Imsco Technology, 24121
Imtec Acculine Inc, 24122

Imuraya USA, 6169
Imus Ranch Foods, 6170
In A Bind Inc, 45233, 57134
In A Nutshell, 57135
In Harvest Inc, 6171, 24123
In Sink Erator, 24124, 45234
In The Raw, 6172
In-Line Corporation, 24125
In-Line Labeling Equipment, 24126
In-Touch Products, 24127
INA Co, 24014, 45176
Inaexpo USA LTD. Co., 45236
Inbalance Health, 6173
Inca Gold Organics, 6174
Incasa Instant Soluble Coffee, 45237
Incinerator International Inc, 24130, 45238
Incinerator Specialty Company, 24131, 45239
Incomec-Cerex Industries, 24132
Incredible Cheesecake, 6175
Incredible Foods, 6176
Incredible Logistics Sol, 24133
Ind-Us Enterprises/Spice'n Flavor, 45240
Indalo USA Corporation, 45241
Indco, 24134
Indeco Products Inc, 24135
INDEECO, 24015, 45177
Indel Food Products Inc, 6177, 45242
Indemax Inc, 24136, 45243
Indena USA Inc, 6178
Independent Bakers Association, 6179
Independent Can Co, 24137, 45244
Independent Can Company: Western Specialty Division, 24138
Independent Dairy Inc, 6180
Independent Dealers Advantage, 24139
Independent Energy, 24140
Independent Ink, 24141, 45245
Independent Meat Co, 6181
Independent Packers Corporation, 6182, 24142
Independent Stave Co, 24143
Independent Wholesale, 57136
Index Instruments Us Inc, 24144
India Emporium, 57137
India Tree, Inc., 45246
India's Rasoi, 6183
Indian Bay Frozen Foods, 6184, 45247
Indian Foods Company, Inc., 6185
Indian Hollow Farms, 6186
Indian Ridge Shrimp Co, 6187, 45248
Indian River Select® LLC, 6188
Indian Rock Vineyards, 6189
Indian Springs Vineyards, 6190
Indian Springs Water Company, 57138
Indian Valley Industries, 24145, 45249
Indian Valley Meats, 6191, 45250
Indiana Botanic Gardens Inc, 6192
Indiana Bottle Co, 24146
Indiana Carton Co Inc, 24147, 45251
Indiana Glass Company, 24148, 45252
Indiana Grain Company, 6193
Indiana Harbor Belt Railroad, 51826
Indiana Michigan Power, 24149
Indiana Restaurant Equipment, 57139
Indiana Sugars, 6194
Indiana Sugars Inc, 57140
Indiana Vac Form Inc, 24150, 45253
Indiana Wiping Cloth, 24151
Indiana Wire Company, 24152
Indianapolis Container Company, 24153
Indianapolis Fruit Company, 45254, 57141
Indianapolis Meat Company, 45255, 57142
Indianhead Foodservice, 57143
Indianola Pecan House Inc, 6195
Indias House, 6196
Indigo Coffee Roasters, 6197, 57144
Indo-European Foods, 45256, 57145
Indulgent Foods, 6198
Industrial Air Conditioning Systems, 24154

Industrial Automation Specs, 24155, 45257
Industrial Automation Systems, 24156
Industrial Brush Corporation, 24157
Industrial Ceramic Products, 24158, 45258
Industrial Chemical, 24159
Industrial Chemicals Inc, 24160
Industrial Commercial Supply, 57146
Industrial Commodities, 45259, 57147
Industrial Consortium, 24161
Industrial Construction Svc, 24162
Industrial Contacts Inc, 57148
Industrial Container Corp, 24163
Industrial Contracting & Rggng, 24164, 45260
Industrial Crating & Packing, 24165
Industrial Custom Products, 24166
Industrial Design Corporation, 24167
Industrial Design Fab, 24168
Industrial Devices Corporation, 24169
Industrial EnvironmentalPollution Control, 24170
Industrial Equipment Company, 24171
Industrial Grinding Inc, 24172
Industrial Handling Equipment, 57149
Industrial Hardwood, 24173
Industrial Hoist Service, 24174
Industrial Information Systems, 24175
Industrial Kinetics, 24176, 45261
Industrial Laboratories Co, 24177
Industrial Laboratory Eqpt Co, 24178, 45262
Industrial Labsales, 24179
Industrial Lift Truck, 57150
Industrial Lumber & Packaging, 24180
Industrial Machine Manufacturing, 24181
Industrial Magnetics, 24182, 45263
Industrial Maintenance, 57151
Industrial Marking Equipment, 24183
Industrial Nameplate Inc, 24184
Industrial Neon Sign Corp, 24185
Industrial Netting Inc, 24186
Industrial Piping Inc, 24187, 45264
Industrial Plastics Company, 24188
Industrial Product Corp, 24189, 45265
Industrial Products Supply, 57152
Industrial Pump Sales & Svc, 24190
Industrial Razorblade, 24191
Industrial Refrigeration Services, 24192
Industrial Screw Conveyors Inc, 24193
Industrial Sign Supply, 24194
Industrial Signs, 24195
Industrial Soap Co, 57153
Industrial Systems Group, 24196
Industrial Test Systems Inc, 24197
Industrial Truck Sales & Services, 57154
Industrial Washing Machine Corporation, 24198, 24199
Industrial Woodfab & Packaging, 24200
Industries For The Blind, 24201, 45266
Industries Inc Kiefer, 24202
Industries of the Blind, 24203
Industrious Software Solutions, 24204
Industronics Service Co, 24205
Indy Lighting, 24206
Ineeka Inc, 6199
Ines Rosales, 45267
Infanti International, 24207, 45268
Inficon, 24208
Infinite Peripherals, 45269, 57155
Infinite Specialties, 57156
Infinity Tapes LLC, 24209
Infitec Inc, 24210, 45270
Inflatable Packaging, 24211
Infometrix, 24212
InFood Corporation, 24128
Infopro Inc, 24213
Infor, 24214
Information Access, 24215
Information Resources, 24216
Informed Beverage Management, 24217
Infra Corp, 24218
InfraReady Products Ltd., 6200
InfraTech Corporation, 24219

1396

All Companies Index

Ingenuities, 57157
Ingenuity Beverages, 6201
Ingersoll & Assoc, 45271, 57158
Ingersoll Rand Inc, 24220, 45272
Ingleby Farms, 6202
Inglenook, 6203
Ingles Markets, 6204, 24221
Ingleside Vineyards, 6205
Inglett & Company, 24222
Ingman Laboratories, 24223
Ingold's HICO Inc, 57159
Ingomar Packing Co, 6206
Ingredia Inc, 6207, 45273
Ingredient Exchange Co, 40517, 45274, 57160
Ingredient Inc, 40518, 45275
Ingredient Innovations, 6208, 40519
Ingredient Masters, 24224
Ingredient Specialties, 6209, 45276
Ingredients Corp Of America, 6210
Ingredients Solutions Inc, 24225, 45277
Ingredion Inc., 6211, 24226, 45278
Ingretec, 6212
InHarvest, 24129, 45235
Initiative Foods, 6213
Inject Star Of The America's, 24227
Inka Crops, 6214
Inked Organics, 6215
Inko's Tea, 6216
Inksolv 30, LLC., 24228, 45279
Inland Cold Storage, 53028
Inland Consumer Packaging, 24229
Inland Empire Distribution, 51827, 53029
Inland Empire Foods, 6217
Inland Label & Marketing Svc, 24230
Inland Meats of Spokane, 57161
Inland Paper Company, 24231
Inland Paperboard & Packaging, 24232
Inland Products, 6218
Inland Seafood Inc, 6219, 57162
Inland Showcase & Fixture Company, 24233
Inland Star Distribution Ctr, 51828, 53030
Inlet Salmon, 6220
Inline Automation, 24234
Inline Filling Systems, 24235, 45280
Inline Plastic Corp, 24236, 24237
Inline Services, 24238
Inman Foodservices Group LLC, 24239
Inmark, Inc, 24240
Inmotion Technologies, 24241
Inn Foods Inc, 6221
Inn Maid Food, 6222
Inn Print, 45281
Innavision Global Marketing Consultants, 24242
Innerspace Design Concepts, 24243
Innio, 24244
Inniskillin Wines, 6223, 45282
Inno-Vite, 45283, 57163
Innocent Chocolate, 6224
Innophos Holdings Inc, 6225, 24245
Innoseal Systems Inc, 24246
Innova Envelopes, 24247, 45284
Innova Flavors, 6226
Innova-Tech, 24248
Innovation Moving Systems, 24249, 45285
Innovations by Design, 24251
Innovations Expressed LLC, 24250
Innovative Beverage Concepts, 6227
Innovative Ceramic Corp, 24252
Innovative Cold Storage Enterprises, 53031
Innovative Components, 24253, 45286
Innovative Controls Corp, 24254
Innovative Energy, 24255
Innovative Fishery Products, 6228, 45287
Innovative Folding Carton Company, 24256
Innovative Food Processors Inc, 24257, 45288
Innovative Food Solutions LLC, 24258

Innovative Foods, Inc., 24259, 45289
Innovative Marketing, 24260, 45290
Innovative Molding, 24261, 45291
Innovative Packaging Solution, 24262
Innovative Plastech, 24263
Innovative Plastics Corp, 24264, 45292
Innovative Rotational Molding, 24265
Innovative Space Management, 24266, 45293
Inny's Wholesale, 6229, 57164
Inovar Packaging Group, 24267
Inovata Foods, 6230
Inovatech, 24268
Inovatech USA, 45294
Inovpack Vector, 24269
Inox Tech, 45295
Inpaco Corporation, 24270
Inpak Systems Inc, 24271, 57165
Inscale, 24272
Insect-O-Cutor Inc, 24273, 45296
Insects Limited Inc, 24274, 45297, 57166
Inshore Fisheries, 6231, 45298
Insight Distribution Systems, 24275
Insight Packaging, 24276
Insignia Systems Inc, 24277, 45299
Insinger Co, 24278, 45300
Insley-Mc Entee Equipment Co, 57167
Inspired Automation Inc, 24279, 45301
Insta-Pro International, 24280, 45302
Instabox, 24281
Instacomm Canada, 24282
Instant Products of America, 6232, 45303
Instantlabs, 57168
Instantwhip Foods Inc, 6233
Institute of Packaging Professionals, 24283
Institutional & Supermarket, 24284
Institutional Equipment Inc, 24285
Institutional Food Service, 57169
Institutional Wholesale Company, 57170
Instrumart, 45304, 57171
Instrumented Sensor Technology, 24286
Insulair, 24287, 45305
Insulated Structures/PB Group, 40520, 57172
InsulTote, 51829
Intec Video Systems, 24288
Intech, 24289
Intedge Manufacturing, 24290, 45306
Integra Marketing Inc, 40521
Integrated Barcode Solutions, 24291
Integrated Distribution, 24292
Integrated Packaging Systems, 24293
Integrated Restaurant Software/RMS Touch, 24294, 45307
Integrated Systems, 24295
Integrative Flavors, 6234, 57173
Integrity Marketing, 40522
Intelligent Controls, 24296, 45308
Intelplex Designers, 24297
Intense Milk, 6235
Intentia Americas, 24298
Inteplast Bags & Films Corporation, 24299
Inteplast Group LTD, 24300
Inter Health Nutraceuticals, 6236
Inter Ocean Seafood Trader, 45309
Inter State Cold Storage, 51830, 53032, 53033
Inter-Access, 24301
Inter-American Products, 6237, 40523
Inter-Cities Cold Storage, 53034
Inter-City Welding & Manufacturing, 24302
Inter-Continental Imports Company, 6238, 45310
Inter-County Bakers Inc, 53035
Inter-Pack Corporation, 24303, 45311
Interactive Sales Solutions, 24307
Interactive Services Group, 24308
Interamerican Coffee, 24309, 45314
Interamerican Quality Foods, 45315
Interbake Foods, 6239
Interbrand Corporation, 24310
Intercard Inc, 24311, 45316

Intercomp, 24312, 45317
Intercontinental Warehouses, 51831, 53036
Intercorp Excelle Foods, 6240
Interep Company, 40524
Interex, 45318
Interfood Ingredients, 6241, 24313, 57175
Interfrost, 6242, 45319
Intergraph Corp, 24314
Interior Alaska Fish Processors, 6243, 57176
Interior Systems Inc, 24315
Interlab, 24316, 45320
Interlake Mecalux, 24317, 45321
Interliance, 24318
Intermec Technologies Corporation, 24319
Intermec/Norand Mobile Systems, 24320
InterMetro Industries, 24304, 45312
Intermex Products USA, 24321
Intermex Products USA LTD, 6244
Intermix Beverage, 45322, 57177
Intermodal Express, 51832
Intermold Corporation, 24322, 45323
Intermountain Canola Cargill, 6245
Intermountain Food Brokerage, 40525
Intermountain Specialty Food Group, 6246, 45324, 57178
International Adhesive Coating, 24323, 45325
International Approval Services, 24324
International Automation, 24325
International Bakers Services, Inc., 6247
International Beverages, 45326, 57179
International Brownie, 6248
International Business Trading, 45327, 57180
International Carbonic, 24326
International Casein Corporation, 6249, 57181
International Casings Group, 6250, 45328
International Cellulose, 45329
International Cheese Company, 6251
International Chemical Corp, 6252, 45330
International Chocolate Company, 45331
International Coatings, 24327
International Coconut Corp, 6253, 45332, 57182
International Coffee Corporation, 40526
International Cold Storage, 24328, 45333
International Commercial Supply, 45334
International Commercial Supply Corporation, 57183
International Container Systems, 24329
International Cooling Systems, 24330, 45335
International Culinary, 45336, 57184
International Dairy Equipment Associates, 57185
International Dehydrated Foods, 6254, 45337
International Delicacies Inc, 6255
International Distribution, 57186
International Enterprises, 6256, 45339
International Enterprises Unlimited, 45338, 57187
International Envelope Company, 24331
International Environmental Solutions, 24332, 45340
International Equipment Trading, 24333
International Farmers Market, 6257, 57188
International Flavors & Fragrances Inc., 6258, 24334
International Food Associates, 45341
International Food Information Service, 24335
International Food Packers Corporation, 6259, 45342
International Food Products, 6260, 24336, 45343

International Foodcraft Corp, 6261, 45344
International Foods & Confections, 45345
International Foodservice Manufacturers' Association, 6262, 24337
International Fresh-Cut Produce Association, 24338
International Fruit Marketing, 6263, 24339
International Glace, 6264, 45346
International Glatt Kosher, 6265
International Gourmet Products, 40527
International Group Inc, 24340
International Harvest, 6266
International Home Foods, 6267, 45347
International Industries Corporation, 45348
International Inflight Food Service Association, 24341
International Ingredients Corporation, 24342
International Knife & Saw, 24343, 45349
International Kosher Supervision, 24344
International Lowell, 45350
International Machinery Xchnge, 24345, 45351
International Marine Products, 57189
International Market Brands, 45352
International Meat Co, 6268, 57190
International Meat Inspection Consultants, 24346
International Media & Cultures, 24347
International Molasses Corp, 45353
International Molded Packaging Corporation, 24348
International Noodle Co, 6269
International Oils & Concentrates, 45354, 57191
International Olive Oil, 45355
International Omni-Pac Corporation, 24349, 45356
International Pacific Sales, 40528
International Pacific Seafood, 40529
International Pack & Ship, 45357, 57192
International Packaging, 53037
International Packaging Machinery, 24350, 45358
International Packaging Network, 24351
International Paper Box Machine Company, 24352, 45359
International Paper Co., 24353
International Paper Food Service Business, 45360
International Patterns, Inc., 24354, 45361
International Polymers Corp, 24355
International Process Plants-IPP, 24356
International Refrigerated, 53038
International Refrigerated Facility, 53039
International Reserve Equipment Corporation, 24357, 45362
International Resources Corporation, 45363
International Roasting Systems, 24358
International Sales & Brokerage Company, 40530
International Seafoods - Alaska, 6270, 57193
International Seafoods of Chicago, 6271, 57194
International Service Group, 6272, 45364
International Silver Company, 45365
International Smoking Systems, 24359
International Sourcing, 45366, 57195
International Specialty Supply, 6273, 45367
International Spice, 6274
International Tank & Pipe Co, 24360, 45368
International Tea Importers, 6275
International Telcom Inc, 45369, 57196
International Thermal Dispensers, 24361
International Ticket Company, 57197
International Trade Impact Inc, 6276

1397

All Companies Index

International Trading Company, 6277, 45370
International Tray Pads, 24362, 45371
International Ventures, 45372
International Vitamin Corporation, 6278, 45373
International Wax Refining Company, 24363
International Wood Industries, 24364, 45374
Internatural Foods, 6279
InterNatural Foods, 45313, 57174
Interocean, 45375
Interpack NW Frozen Food, 40531
Interpex, 40532
Interplast, 24365, 45376
Interport Storage & Distribution Service, 51833, 53040
Interroll Corp, 24366, 24367, 45377
InterSect Business Systems Inc, 24305
Intershell Seafood Corp, 40533, 45378, 57198
Intersouth Foodservice Group, 40534
Interstate Cold Storage, 51835, 53043, 53044
Interstate Cold Storage Co, 53042
Interstate Cold Storage Inc, 51834, 53041
Interstate Distributors, 57199
Interstate Food Brokers, 40535
Interstate Merchandise Warehouse, 53045
Interstate Monroe Machinery, 24368, 45379
Interstate Packaging, 24369, 45380
Interstate Restaurant Equipment, 57200
Interstate Showcase & Fixture Company, 24370
Interstate Underground Wrhse, 53046
Intertape Polymer Group, 24371, 24372, 45381
Intertech Corp, 24373
Intertek USA, 24374
Interthor Inc, 57201
Intervest Trading Company Inc., 6280, 45382
Interwest Ingredient Sales, 40536
InterXchange Market Network, 24306
Intralinks Inc, 40537
Intralox LLC, 24375, 24376, 45383
Intralytix, 24377
Intrex, 24378
Introdel Products, 24379
Invensys APV Products, 24380
Invensys Process Systems, 24381
Inverness Dairy, 6281
Inverso Johnson LLC, 40538
Invictus Systems Corporation, 24382, 45384
Inviting Foods, 6282
IOE Atlanta, 6120
IOM Grain, 6121
Iowa Interstate Railroad LTD, 51836
Iowa Rotocast Plastics Inc, 24383
Ipc Supply Inc, 57202
IPEC, 24016
Ipec, 24384
IPG International Packaging Group, 24017
IPL Inc, 24018
IPL Plastics, 24019, 45178
IPM Coffee Innovations LLC, 24020
IPS International, 24021, 45179
Ipswich Ale Brewery, 6283
Ipswich Maritime Product Company, 6284, 57203
Ipswich Shellfish Co Inc, 6285, 45385, 57204
IQ Juice, 6122
IQ Scientific Instruments, 24022, 45180
IR Systems, 24023
Ira Higdon Grocery Company, 6286, 57205
Irby, 24385
Irene's Bakery & Gourmet, 6287
Iris Brands, 6288
Irish Hospitality/Foodprops, 45386

Irish Tea Sales, 45387, 57206
Iron Horse Vineyards, 6289
Iron Out, 24386
Ironstone Vineyards, 6290
Ironwood Displays, 24387
Irresistible Cookie Jar, 6291, 24388
Irvin, 57207
Irvine Analytical Labs, 24389
Irvine Pharmaceutical Services, 24390
Irvine Restaurant Supply, 57208
Irvington Marcus Company, 57209
Irwin Naturals, 6292
Irwin Research & Development, 24391
Isaacson & Stein Fish Company, 6293, 57210
Isadore A. Rapasadi & Son, 6294, 45388
ISB Sales Company, 40504
Isbre Holding Corporation, 24392
ISC of Indiana, 40505
Ise America Inc, 6295
Isernio Sausage Company, 6296, 45389
ISF Trading, 6123, 45181
Ishida Corporation, 57211
ISI Commercial Refrigeration, 57112, 57113, 57114
ISI North America, 24026
ISi North America, 57115
Isigny Ste Mere, 45390
Island Aseptics, 6297
Island Delights, Inc., 6298, 24393
Island Farms Dairies Cooperative Association, 6299, 57212
Island Lobster, 6300, 57213
Island Marine Products, 6301, 45391
Island Oasis Frozen Cocktail, 6302, 24394, 45392
Island of the Moon Apiaries, 6312
Island Poly, 24395
Island Princess, 6303
Island Refrigeration & Foodservice Equipment, 57214
Island Scallops, 6304, 24396
Island Seafood, 6305, 57215
Island Seafoods, 6306
Island Snacks, 6307
Island Spice, 6308
Island Spring Inc, 6309
Island Supply, 45393, 57216
Island Sweetwater Beverage Company, 6310, 45394
Island Treasures Gourmet, 6311
Islander Import, 45395, 57217
ISM Carton, 24024
Isodiol, 6313
Isola Imports Inc, 45396
Isotherm Inc, 24397
ISS/GEBA/AFOS, 24025
ISSCO, 40506
Issimo Food Group, 6314
It's A Corker, 24398
It's It Ice Cream Co, 6315
ITA Inc, 40507
Itac Label & Tag Corp, 24399, 45397
Italfina, 57218
Italfoods Inc, 45398, 57219
Italgi, 45399
Italgi USA, 24400
Italia Foods, 6316
Italian Bakery of Virginia, 6317
Italian Bottega, 45400
Italian Connection, 6318
Italian Foods Corporation, 6319
Italian Gourmet Foods Canada, 6320
Italian Harvest, Inc., 45401
Italian Peoples Bakery Inc, 6321
Italian Products USA, 45402
Italian Quality Products, 45403
Italian Rose Garlic Products, 6322
Italica Imports, 45404, 57220
Italmade, 57221
Italtech, 24401
Itarca, 6323
ITC Systems, 24027, 24028, 45182, 45183
Itella Foods, 6324

Item Products, 24402, 45405
Ithaca Craft Hummus, 6325
Iti Tropicals Inc, 45406
Ito Cariani Sausage Company, 6326, 45407
Ito En USA Inc, 6327
Ito Packing Company, 24403
ITOCHU International, Inc, 40508
ITS/ETL Testing Laboratories, 24029
ITT Inc, 24030
ITT Jabsco, 24031
ITW Angleboard, 24032, 45184
ITW Auto-Sleeve, 24033
ITW Diagraph, 24034
ITW Dymon, 24035
ITW Dynatec, 24036
ITW Engineered Polymers, 24037, 45185
ITW Food Equipment Group, 24038
ITW Hi-Cone, 24039
ITW Plastic Packaging, 24040
ITW United Silicone, 24041, 45186
Iug Business Solutions, 24404
Ivanhoe Cheese Inc, 6328, 45408
Ivar's Chowders, 45409
Ivarson Inc, 24405, 24406, 45410
IVEK Corp, 24042, 24043
Ives-Way Products, 24407, 45411
Iveta Gourmet Inc, 6329, 45412
IVEX Packaging Corporation, 24044, 45187
Ivy Cottage Scone Mixes, 6330
Ivy Foods, 6331
Iwamoto Natto Factory, 6332
Iwasaki Images Of America Inc, 45413
Iwatani International Corporation of America, 24408, 45414, 45415
IWS Scales, 24045, 45188
Iya Foods LLC, 6333
Izabel Lam International, 24409, 45416
IZZE Beverage, 6124

J

J & B Sausage Co Inc, 6334, 45417
J & B Seafood, 6335, 57222
J & G Poultry & Seafood, 6336
J & J Distributing, 57223
J & J Industries Inc, 24410
J & J Processing, 6337
J & J Snack Foods Corp, 6338, 45418
J & J Trucking, 51837
J & J Wall Bakery Co, 6339
J & J Window Sales Inc, 24411
J & K Ingrediants, 6340, 45419
J & L Grain Processing, 6341
J & L Honing, 24412
J & L Seafood, 6342
J & M Foods Inc, 6343
J & M Industries Inc, 24413
J & M Wholesale Meat Inc, 6344, 45420, 57224
J & R Distributors, 57225
J & R Mfg Inc, 24414, 45421
J A Emilius Sons, 24415
J A Heilferty & Co, 24416, 45422
J B & Son LTD, 6345
J B Hunt Transport Inc, 51838
J Bernard Seafood, 6346, 57226, 57227
J C Ford Co, 24417, 45423
J C Industries Inc, 24418
J C Watson Co, 6347, 45424
J C Whitlam Mfg Co, 24419, 45425
J Carroll & Assoc, 40539
J Cipelli Merchants, 40540
J D Double M Trucking, 51839
J Deluca Fish Co Inc, 6348
J E M Mfg LLC, 24420
J F O'Neill & Packing Co, 6349, 45426
J Filippi Winery, 6350
J G Noble Cheese Company, 6351
J G Townsend Jr & Co, 6352
J G Van Holten & Son Inc, 6353, 45427
J H Honeycutt & Sons Inc, 57228
J H Verbridge & Son Inc, 6354
J Hoelting Produce Inc, 57229

J J Gandy's Pies Inc, 6355
J J Produce, 6356
J Kings Food Svc Professionals, 57230
J L Becker Co, 24421, 45428
J L Clark Corp, 24422, 45429
J Leek Assoc Inc, 24423
J Lohr Vineyards & Wines, 6357
J M Canty Inc E1200 Engineers, 24424, 45430
J M Clayton Co, 6358
J M Packaging Co, 24425, 45431
J M Sales, 40541
J M Swank Co, 6359, 24426, 51840, 53047
J Moniz Co Inc, 6360, 57231
J Moresky & Son, 57232
J Morgan's Confections, 6361
J Murray & Co, 57233
J N Rhodes Co Inc, 40542
J O Spice Co, 57234
J P Green Milling Co, 6362
J P Ice Cream, 57235
J P's Shellfish Co, 6363, 57236
J Petite & Sons, 57237
J R Carlson Laboratories Inc, 6364, 45432
J R Kelly Co, 40543, 57238
J R Short Milling Co, 24427
J Rettenmaier USA LP, 6365, 24428
J T Gibbons Inc, 40544, 45433, 57239
J Turner Seafood, 6366, 57240
J W Hulme Co, 24429
J W Mitchell Investment, 53048
J W Outfitters, 45434, 57241
J W Treuth & Sons, 6367
J Weil Food Service Co, 57242
J&B Cold Storage Inc, 51841, 53049
J&D Transportation, 40545
J&D's Foods, 6368
J&J Brokerage, 40546
J&J Corrugated Box Corporation, 24430
J&J Mid-South Container Corporation, 24431
J&L Produce Wholesale Company, 57243
J&M Distribution Company, 57244
J&M Food Products Co, 6369, 57245
J&M Laboratories, 24432
J&R Fisheries, 6370
J&S Export & Trading Company, 45435
J&S Food Brokerage, 40547
J&S Food Distributors, 57246
J. Connor & Sons, 57247
J. Crocker Exports, 45436
J. Crow Company, 6371
J. Flex International, 45437
J. Fritz Winery, 6372
J. Hellman Frozen Foods, 57248
J. James, 24433
J. Johnson Fruit & Produce, 57249
J. Lerner Box Company, 57250
J. M. Sealts Company, 57251
J. Maganas Sales Company, 40548
J. Matassini & Sons Fish Company, 6373
J. Quattrocchi & Company, 57252
J. R. Simplot Co., 6374, 24434
J. Rutigliano & Sons, 45438, 57253
J. Scott Company, 24435
J. Sosnick & Sons, 57254
J. Stonestreet & Sons Vineyard, 6375
J. Treffiletti & Sons, 57255
J.A. King & Company, 57256
J.A. Thurston Company, 24436, 45439
J.A. Tucker Company, 51842
J.A. Wendling Foodservice, 57257
J.A.M.B. Low Carb Distributor, 6376
J.B. Peel Coffee Roasters, 6377
J.C. Banana & Company, 57258
J.C. Produce, 57259
J.C. Products Inc., 24437
J.C. Wright Sales Company, 57260
J.D. Dawson Company, 57261
J.D. Smith & Sons, 51843, 53050
J.E. Julian & Associates, 40549
J.E. Roy, 24438, 45440
J.F. Benz Company, 40550

All Companies Index

J.F. Braun & Sons, 45441
J.F. Kelly, 40551
J.F. Walker Company, 57262, 57263
J.G. British Imports, 6378
J.G. Machine Works, 24439
J.H. Bridgins & Associates, 40552
J.H. Carr & Sons, 24440
J.H. Thornton Company, 24441, 45442, 57264
J.I. Holcomb Manufacturing, 24442
J.J. Taylor Distributing, 57265
J.K. Harman, Inc., 24443
J.L. DeGraffenreid & Sons, 45443
J.L. Epstein & Son, 40553
J.L. Henderson & Company, 57266
J.M. Rogers & Sons, 24444, 45444
J.M. Schneider, 6379, 57267
J.M. Smucker Co., 6380, 45445
J.M. Swank Company, 24445, 40554
J.N. Bech, 6381
J.O. Demers Beef, 57268
J.P. Beaudry, 57269
J.P. Sunrise Bakery, 6382, 45446
J.R. Campbell Equipment Company, 57270
J.R. Fish Company, 6383, 57271
J.R. Poultry, 6384, 57272
J.R. Ralph Marketing Company, 24446
J.R. Short Canadian Mills, 6385, 45447
J.R.'s Seafood, 6386, 57273
J.S. Ferraro, 24447
J.S. McMillan Fisheries, 6387
J.T. Pappy's Sauce, 6388
J.V. Reed & Company, 24448, 45448
J.W. Harrison & Son, 40555
J.W. Haywood & Sons Dairy, 6389
J.W. Kuehn Company, 40556
J.W. Wood Company, 57274
J/W Design Associates, 24449
Ja-Ca Seafood Products, 6413
JAAMA World Trade, 45449, 57275
Jab's Seafood, 57289
JABEX Associates, LLC, 40557
Jaccard Corporation, 45471, 57290
Jacintoport International LLC, 53051
Jack & Jill Ice Cream, 6414, 45472, 57291
Jack Brown Produce, 6415, 45473
Jack Curren & Associates, 40564
Jack Daniel Distillery, 6416, 45474
Jack Langston Manufacturing Company, 24480
Jack Miller's Food Products, 6417
Jack Stack, 24481, 45475
Jack Stone Lighting & Electrical, 24482
Jack the Ripper Table Skirting, 24483, 45476
Jack's Bean Co LLC, 6418
Jack's Paleo Kitchen, 6419
Jackfruit Company, The, 6420
Jacks Manufacturing Company, 24484, 45477
Jacks Merchandising & Distribution, 57292
Jackson Brothers Food Locker, 6421
Jackson Corrugated Container, 24485
Jackson Meat, 6422
Jackson Msc LLC, 24486
Jackson Newell Paper Co, 57293
Jackson Restaurant Supply, 24487
Jackson Supply Company, 57294
Jackson Wholesale Co, 57295
Jackson's Honest, 6423
Jacksonville Box & Woodwork Co, 24488
Jacmar Foodservice, 51844, 53052
Jaco Equipment Corporation, 24489
Jacob & Sons Wholesale Meats, 6424, 57296
Jacob Holtz Co., 24490, 45478
Jacob KERN & Sons Inc, 57297
Jacob Leinenkugel Brewing Co, 6425
Jacob Licht, 57298
Jacob Tubing LP, 24491
Jacob White Packaging, 24492

Jacob's Meats Inc, 6426
Jacobi Lewis Co, 24493, 57299
Jacobs Engineering Group, 24494
Jacobsen's Salt Co., 6427
Jacobsen-Clahan & Company, 40565
Jacobsmuhlen's Meats, 6428
Jacobson & Sons, 57300
Jacobson Warehouse Company, 51845, 53053
Jacques Pastries, 6429
Jacquet Bakery, 6430
Jada Foods LLC, 6431
Jade Leaf Matcha, 6432, 57301
Jade Products Co, 24495, 45479
Jagenberg, 24496
Jager Foods, 6433
Jagger Cone Co Inc, 6434
Jagla Machinery Company, 24497
Jaguar Yerba Company, 6435
Jagulana Herbal Products, 6436, 24498
Jain Americas Inc, 6437, 45480
Jaindl Farms, 6438
Jake's Grillin, 6439
Jake's Variety Wholesale, 57302
Jakeman's Maple Products, 6440, 45481
Jakes Brothers Country Meats, 6441
Jako Fish, 57303
Jam Group of Company, 40566, 45482
Jamac Frozen Foods, 57304
Jamae Natural Foods, 6442
Jamaica John Inc, 6443
Jamaican Gourmet Coffee Company, 6444, 57305
Jamaican Teas Limited C/O Eve Sales Corporation, 45483, 57306
James Austin Co, 24499
James Avery Clark & Sons Inc, 57307
James C Thomas & Sons, 57308
James Candy Company, 6445
James D Cofer, 57309
James Desiderio Inc, 57310
James Frasinetti & Sons, 6446
James H Clark & Son Inc, 51846
James K. Wilson Produce Company, 57311
James L. Mood Fisheries, 6447, 45484
James P. Smith & Company, 45485
James River Canada, 24500
James Skinner Company, 6448, 45486
James Thompson, 24501, 45487
James V. Hurson Associates, 24502
James Varley & Sons, 24503
James W Valleau & Company, 40567
Jamestown Awning, 24504
Jamestown Container Corporation, 24505
Jamieson Laboratories, 6449, 24506, 45488
Jamison Door Co, 24507, 45489
Jamison Plastic Corporation, 24508
Jammit Jam, 45490
Jana Foods LLC, 45491
JANA Worldwide, 45450
Jane Bakes, 6450
Janedy Sign Company, 24509
Janes Family Foods, 6451
Janney Marshall Co, 57312
Janows Design Associates, 24510
Janowski's Hamburgers Inc, 6452
Janpak, 57313
Jans Enterprises Corp., 45492
Janta International Company, Inc, 45493
Jantec, 24511, 45494
Jantzen International, 51847, 53054
January & Wood Company, 24512
Japan External Trade Organization (JETRO) New York, 24513
Japan Gold USA, 6453
Jaquelina's, 6454
Jarboe Equipment, 24514
Jarchem Industries, 6455, 24515, 45495
Jarden Home Brands, 24516, 24517, 45496
Jardine Foods, 6456
Jardine Ranch, 6457, 45497
Jaret Specialties, 45498

Jarisch Paper Box Company, 24518
Jarke Corporation, 24519
Jarlan Manufacturing, 24520
Jarosz Produce Farms, 57314
Jarrow Formulas Inc, 45499, 57315
Jarrow Industries Inc, 6458
Jarvis Caster Company, 24521, 45500
Jarvis Products Corp, 24522, 45501
Jarvis-Cutter Company, 24523
JAS Manufacturing Company, 24450
Jasmine & Bread, 6459
Jasmine Vineyards, Inc., 6460, 45502
Jason & Son Specialty Foods, 6461
Jason Marketing Corporation, 45503, 57316
Jason Pharmaceuticals, 6462
Jasper Glove Company, 57317
Jasper Products Corp, 6463
Jasper Seating Company, 24524
Jasper Wyman & Son, 6464
Jatex-USA Corporation, 57318
Java Beans and Joe Coffee, 6465, 57319
Java Cabana, 6466
Java Jacket, 24525, 45504
Java Sun Coffee Roasters, 6467
Java-Gourmet/Keuka Lake Coffee Roaster, 6468
Javalution Coffee Company, 6469, 45505
Javed & Sons, 6470, 57320
Javo Beverage Co., Inc., 6471
Jax Inc, 24526, 24527
Jaxon's Ice Cream Parlor, 6472
Jaxport Refrigerated, 53055
Jay Mark Group LTD, 40568
Jay Packaging Group Inc, 24528, 45506
Jay R Smith Mfg Co, 24529
Jay Shah Foods, 6473
Jay-Bee Manufacturing Inc, 24530, 45507
Jaydon, 57321
Jayhawk Boxes, 24531
Jayhawk Manufacturing Co Inc, 24532, 45508
JaynRoss Creations LLC, 6474
Jayone Foods Inc, 6475
Jazz Fine Foods, 6476
Jb Prince, 45509, 57322
JBA International, 24451
JBC Plastics, 24452
JBG International, 45451, 57276
JBS Packing Inc, 6390
JBS USA LLC, 6391, 45452, 57277
JBT Food Tech, 24453
JBT Wolf-Tec Inc, 24454
JC Food, 24455
JC's Midnite Salsa, 6392, 57278
JC's Pie Pops, 6393
JC's Sunny Winter, 57279
JCH International, 24456, 45453
JCS Controls, Inc., 24457
JD Sweid Foods, 6394, 45454
JDG Consulting, 24458
JDO/LNR Lighting, 24459
JDT Corporation, 45455
JE Bergeron & Sons, 6395, 45456
Jean Niel Inc, 6477
Jeb Plastics, 24533, 40569, 57323
Jecky's Best, 6478
Jeco Plastic Products LLC, 24534, 45510
Jed's Maple Products, 6479
Jedwards International Inc, 6480, 24535, 57324
Jeff's Garden, 6481
Jeffcoat Signs, 24536
Jeffer Neely Company, 57325
Jefferds Corp, 57326
Jefferson Packing Company, 24537, 57327
Jefferson Smurfit Corporation, 24538
Jefferson Vineyards, 6482
Jeffries Supply Co, 57328
Jel Sert, 6483, 45511, 53056
Jelks Coffee Roasters, 6484
Jelly Belly Candy Co., 6485, 45512
JEM Wire Products, 24460

Jemm Wholesale Meat Company, 6486
Jemolo Enterprises, 24539, 45513
Jen-Coat, Inc., 24540, 45514
Jenco Fan, 24541
Jeni's Splendid Ice Creams, 6487, 57329
Jenike & Johanson Inc, 24542
Jenkins Sign Co, 24543
Jennie-O Turkey Store, 6488, 45515
Jennies Gluten-Free Bakery, 6489, 45516
Jenny's Country Kitchen, 6490
Jenny's Old Fashioned, 6491
Jensen Fittings Corporation, 24544
Jensen Meat Company, 6492, 45517
Jensen's Bread and Bakeries, 6493
Jensen's Old Fashioned Smokehouse, 6494
Jentek, 24545
Jenthon Supply, 57330
JER Creative Food Concepts, Inc., 6396, 57280
Jer's Chocolates, 6495
Jerabek's New Bohemian Coffee House, 6496
Jeram Associates, 40570
Jeremiah's Pick Coffee Co, 6497
Jergens Inc, 24546
Jerico, 57331
Jerilu Fruit Center, 57332
Jeris Health & Nutrition, 57333
Jerome Langdon Produce, 57334
Jerrell Packaging, 6498
Jerry Brothers Industries Inc, 6499, 57335
Jerry Schulman Produce, 57336
Jerry's Nut House, 6500
Jersey Fruit Co-Op, 6501
Jersey Italian Gravy, 6502
Jersey Meat & Provision Company, 57337
Jersey Shore Steel Co, 24547
Jerusalem House, 6503
Jervis B WEBB Co, 24548, 45518
Jeryl's Jems, 6504
JES Foods, 6397
Jesben, 6505
Jesco Industries, 24549, 45519
Jescorp, 24550, 45520
Jess Jones Vineyard, 6506, 24551, 45521
Jess's Market, 57338
Jesse Food Products, 57339
Jesse Jones Box Corporation, 24552
Jessica's Natural Foods, 6507
Jessie's Ilwaco Fish Company, 6508, 45522
Jessom Food Equipment, 57340
Jessup Paper Box, 24553
Jet Box Co, 24554
Jet Lite Products, 24555
Jet Plastica Industries, 24556, 45523
Jet Set Sam, 45524, 57341
JET Tools, 45457, 57281
Jetnet Corp, 24557
Jetro Cash & Carry, 57342
Jetro Cash & Carry Enterprises, 57343
Jetro Cash & Carry Inc, 57344
Jets Le Frois Corp, 6509
Jetstream Systems, 24558, 45525
Jewel Bakery, 6510
Jewel Case Corp, 24559, 45526
Jewel Date Co, 6511, 45527
Jewell Bag Company, 24560
Jewell/Barksdale Associates, 40571
JF Braun & Sons Inc, 6398
JFC International Inc, 45458, 57282
JFG Coffee, 6399
JGB Enterprises Inc, 24461
JH Display & Fixture, 24462, 45459
Jhrg LLC, 24561
Jiaherb, 6513
Jianas Brothers Packaging, 57345
Jianlibao America, 6514
Jif-Pak Manufacturing, 24562, 45528
Jiffy Mixer Co Inc, 24563
Jilasco Food Exports, 40572, 45529, 57346

1399

All Companies Index

Jillipepper, 6515
Jilson Group, 24564, 45530
Jilz Gluten Free, 6516
Jim David Meats, 57347
Jim Did It Sign Company, 24565, 45531
Jim Foley Company, 6517
Jim Lake Companies, 24566
Jim Palmer Trucking, 51848
Jim Pless & Company, 40573
Jim Scharf Holdings, 24567, 45532
Jim's Cheese Pantry, 6518, 57348
Jimbo's Jumbos Inc, 6519, 24568
Jimmy Dean Foods, 6520
Jimmy Durbin Farms, 57349
JiMMY! Bars, 6512
Jimmys Cookies, 6521
Jimtown Store, 6522
Jin Han International, 57350
Jin+Ja, 6523
JIT Manufacturing & Technology, 24463
JJ Martin Group, 6400
JJ's Tamales & Barbacoa, 6401
JJI Lighting Group, Inc., 24464, 45460
JK Sucralose, 6402, 57283
JI Analytical Svc Inc, 24569
JL Industries Inc, 24465, 45461
JL Stemp Marketing Agents, 40558
JLS Foods International, 45462
JM All Purpose Seasoning, 6403
JM Huber Chemical Corpo ration, 24466
JM Overton Sales & Marketing, 40559
JM Schneider, 45463, 57284
JMA, 24467
JMAC Trading, Inc., 6404
JMC Packaging Equipment, 24468, 45464
JMH International, 6405
JML Sales Co, 40560, 57285
JMS, 45465, 57286
Jms Packaging Consultants Inc, 24570
JMS Specialty Foods, 6406
JNB Foods, LLC, 6407
JNS Foods, 45466, 57287
Jo Mar Laboratories, 6524, 24571, 45533, 57351
Jo Mints, 57352
Jo's Candies, 6525
Jodar Vineyard & Winery, 6527
JoDaSa Group International, 45534, 57353
Jodawnco, 40574
Jode Company, 57354
Jodie's Kitchen, 6528
Jody Maroni's Sausage Kingdom, 6529
Jody's Gourmet Popcorn, 6530, 53057
Jodyana Corporation, 6531, 57355
Joe Bertman Foods, 6532, 57356
Joe Christiana Food Distributing, 57357
Joe Clark Fund Raising Candies, 6533, 45535
Joe Corbis' Wholesale Pizza, 6534
Joe Fazio's Famous Italian, 6535
Joe Harding Sales & Svc, 57358
Joe Hutson Foods, 6536, 45536
Joe Jurgielwicz & Sons, 6537
Joe Patti's Seafood Co, 6538
Joe Paulk Company, 57359
Joe Pucci & Sons Seafood, 57360
Joe Tea and Joe Chips, 6539, 45537
Joel Harvey Distributing, 6540
Joelle's Choice Specialty Foods LLC, 6541
Joey's Fine Foods, 6542, 45538, 57361
Joey's Home Bakery-Gluten Free, 6543
Jogue, 24572
Jogue Inc, 6544
Johanna Foods Inc., 6545, 45539
Johanson Transportation Services, 51850
Johanson Transportation Svc, 24573, 51849
Johlin Century Winery, 6546
John A Vassilaros & Son Inc, 6547
John B. Sanfilippo & Son, 6548
John B. Wright Fish Company, 6549, 57362

John Bean Technologies Corp, 24574
John Boos & Co, 24575, 45540
John Bricks Inc, 57363
John Burton Machine Corporation, 24576, 45541
John Cassidy Intl Inc, 51851, 53058
John Cerasuolo Co, 57364
John Christner Trucking Inc, 51852, 53059
John Conti Coffee Co, 6550
John Copes Food Products, 6551
John Crane Mechanical Sealing Devices, 24577, 45542
John D Walsh Co, 45543, 57365
John Demartin Company, 57366
John E Koerner & Co Inc, 57367
John E. Ruggles & Company, 24578, 45544
John Garner Meats, 6552
John Graves Food Service, 57368
John Gross & Company, 57369
John Groves Company, 57370
John H Thier Co, 40575
John H. Elton, 40576
John Hansen & Sons, 57371
John Henry Packaging, 24579, 45545
John Hofmeister & Son Inc, 6553
John I. Haas, 6554, 45546
John J Wollack Co Inc, 40577
John J. Adams Die Corporation, 24580, 45547
John J. Moon Produce, 57372
John J. Nissen Baking Company, 6555
John Kelly Chocolates, 6556
John Koller & Son Inc, 6557
John L. Denning & Company, 24581
John L. Pieri & Sons, 40578
John Larkin & Co Inc, 24582
John Lenore & Company, 57373
John Mangum Company, 40579
John Molinelli Inc, 57374
John Morrell Food Group, 24583, 57375
John N Wright Jr Inc, 6558
John Nagle & Co, 57376
John Paton Inc, 6559, 57377
John Plant Co, 24584
John R Nalbach Engineering Co, 24585, 45548
John Rock Inc, 24586
John Rohrer Contracting Co, 24587, 45549
John S James Co, 51853, 53060
John S. Dull & Associates, 57378
John Volpi & Co, 6560
John W Keplinger & Sons, 24588
John W Macy's Cheesesticks Inc, 6561
John W Williams Inc, 57379
John W. Spaulding Brokerage, 24589, 57380
John's Dairy, 57381
John's Import Foods, 45550
John's Meat Market, 57382
John's Wholesale, 57383
John-Jeffrey Corporation, 51854, 53061, 53062
Johnnie's Restaurant-Hotel Svc, 57384
Johnny Bee Sales, 40580
Johnny Harris Famous Barbecue Sauce, 6562
Johns Cove Fisheries, 6563, 45551
Johnson & Sbrocco Associates, 45552
Johnson & Sons Manufacturing, 45590
Johnson & Wales University, 24591
Johnson Associates, 24592
Johnson Brothers Manufacturing Company, 24593
Johnson Brothers Produce Company, 6564
Johnson Brothers Sign Co Inc, 24594
Johnson Commercial Agents, 40581
Johnson Controls Inc, 24595
Johnson Corrugated Products Corporation, 24596
Johnson Diversified Products, 24597, 57385

Johnson Estate Winery, 6565
Johnson Food Equipment Inc, 24598
Johnson Foods, Inc., 6566, 45553
Johnson Foods, Inc. - Cannery Plant, 6567
Johnson Holmes & Assoc Inc, 40582
Johnson Industries Intl, 24599, 24600, 45554
Johnson International Materials, 24601, 45555
Johnson O'Hare Co, 40583
Johnson Pump Of America, 24602
Johnson Refrigerated Truck, 24603, 45556
Johnson Restaurant Supply, 57386
Johnson Sea Products Inc, 6568, 57387
Johnson Starch Molding, 24604
Johnson Wholesale Meat Company, 57388
Johnson's Alexander Valley Wines, 6569
Johnson's Food Products, 6570
Johnson's Real Ice Cream, 6571
Johnson's Wholesale Meats, 6572
Johnson, Arlyn & Associates, 40584
Johnson, Nash & Sons Farms, 6573
Johnson-Rose Corporation, 24605, 45557
Johnsonville Sausage LLC, 6574
Johnston Boiler Co Inc, 24606
Johnston County Hams, 6575
Johnston Equipment, 24607, 45558, 57389, 57390
Johnston Farms, 6576, 45559, 57391
Johnston Training Group, Inc., 53063
Johnston's Home Style Products, 6577
Johnston's Winery Inc, 6578
Johnstown Manufacturing, 24608
Joia All Natural Soda, 6579
Joicey Food Services, 57392
JoJo's Chocolate, 6526
Joj, Bar, 6580
Jokamsco Group, 24609
Jolar Distributor, 57393
Jolly Llama, 6581
Jomac Products, 24610, 45560
Jomar Corp, 24611, 45561
Jomar Plastics Industry, 24612
Jomart Chocolates, 6582
Jon Donaire Desserts, 6583
Jon Morris & Company, 40585
Jonathan Lord Cheesecakes, 6584
Jonathan's Sprouts, 6585
Joneca Corp, 24613, 45562
Jones Automation Company, 24614
Jones Brewing Company, 6586, 45563
Jones Dairy Farm, 6587, 45564
Jones Environmental, 24615
Jones Moving & Storage Co, 53064
Jones Neitzel Co, 40586
Jones Packaging Machinery, 24616
Jones Packing Co, 6588
Jones Potato Chip Co, 6589
Jones Soda Company, 6590
Jones-Hamilton Co, 24617, 45565
Jones-McCormick & Associates, 40587
Jones-Zylon Co, 24618, 45566
Jonessco Enterprises, 24619
Jonny Almond Nut Co, 6591
JonnyPops, 6592
Joray Candy, 6593
Jordahl Meats, 6594, 57394
Jordan Box Co, 24620
Jordan Lobster Farms, 57395
Jordan Paper Box Co, 24621, 45567
Jordan Specialty Company, 24622
Jordan's Meats & Deli, 6595
Jordon Commercial Refrigerator, 24623, 45568
Jordon-Fleetwood Commercial Refrigerator Company, 24624
Jos Iorio Company, 40588
Josam Co, 24625
Jose Andres, 45569
Jose M Perez-Pages, 40589
Josef Aaron Syrup Company, 6596
Josef Kihlberg of America, 24626

Joseph Adams Corp, 6597, 45570
Joseph Antognoli & Co, 45571, 57396
Joseph Apicella & Sons, 57397
Joseph Campione Inc, 6598
Joseph Caragol, 40590
Joseph D Teachey Jr Produce Co, 6599
Joseph Farms, 6600
Joseph Gies Import, 45572
Joseph J. Sayre & Son Company, 57398
Joseph J. White, 6601
Joseph Kirschner & Company, 6602
Joseph Manufacturing Company, 24627
Joseph P. Sullivan & Company, 40591
Joseph Phelps Vineyards, 6603, 45573
Joseph Struhl Co Inc, 24628, 45574
Joseph Swan Vineyards, 6604
Joseph Titone & Sons, 24629
Joseph W Ciatti Co, 40592
Joseph W Nath Co, 40593
Joseph's Gourmet Pasta, 6605
Joseph's Lite Cookies, 6606
Josephine's Feast, 6607
Josh & John's Ice Cream, 6608
Josh Early Candies, 6609
Josheph Gies Import, 45575, 57399
Jost Chemical, 6610, 45576
Jost Kauffman Import & Export Company, 45577, 57400
Josuma Coffee Co, 6611
Joullian Vineyards, 6612
Joul, Engineering StaffiSolutions, 24630
Jovial Foods, 6613
Jowat Corp., 24631
Joy Cone Co, 6614
Joy's Specialty Foods, 6615
Joyce Brothers Company, 57401
Joyce Dayton Corp, 24632
Joyce Engraving Co Inc, 24633
Joyce Farms, 6616
Joyce Foods, 57402
Joyfuls, 6617
Joylin Food Equipment Corporation, 24634, 40594, 57403
Joyva Corp, 6618
JP Bissonnette, 40561
JP Carroll Company, 40562
JP Plastics, Inc., 24469
Jp Tropical Foods, 45578, 57404
Jpo/Dow Inc, 40595
JPS Packaging Company, 24470
JR Laboratories, 6408
Jr Mats, 24635, 45579
JS Giles Inc, 24471
JSL Foods, 6409
Jso Associates Inc, 40596, 45580
JTECH Communications Inc, 45467
JTM Food Group, 6410
Juanita's Foods, 6619, 45581
Jubelt Variety Bakeries, 6620
Jubilations, 6621
Jubilee Foods, 6622
Jubilee Gourmet Creations, 6623
Jubilee Sales of Carolina, 40597
Judel Products, 24636, 45582
Judge, 24637
Judge & Sons P Inc, 51855
Judicial Flavors, 6624
Judith's Fine Foods International, 57405
Judy's Cream Caramels, 6625, 45583
Juhl Brokerage, 40598, 40599
Juice Mart, 6626
Juice Merchandising Corp, 24638, 57406
Juice Tree, 24639, 45584
Juice Tyme, Inc., 6627
Juicy Whip Inc, 6628, 24640
Julian Bakery, 6629, 57407
Julian's Recipe, 6630
Julie Anne's, 6631
Julie's Real, 6632
Julito Ramirez Corporation, 40600
Julius Levy Company, 40601
Julius M. Dean Company, 40602
Julius Silvert Company, 57408
Julius Sturgis Pretzel Bakery, 6633
Jumo Process Control, 45585

All Companies Index

JUMO Process Control Inc, 24472, 45468
Juncker Associates, 40603, 45586
Junction City Distributing & Vending Company, 57409
Junction Solutions, 24641
Jungbunzlauer Inc, 6634, 57410
Junior's Cheesecake, 6635
Juno Chef's, 6636
Junuis Food Products, 6637
Jupiter Mills Corporation, 24642, 45587
Jus-Made, 6638, 24643, 45588
Just Bagels, 6639
Just Bare, 6640
Just Born Inc, 6641
Just Cook Foods, 6642
Just Date Syrup, 6643
Just Delicious Gourmet Foods, 6644, 45590
Just Desserts, 6645
JUST Inc, 6411, 57288
Just Jan's Inc., 6646
Just Off Melrose, 6647
Just Panela, 6648
Just Plastics Inc, 24644, 45591
Just Tomatoes, 6649
Just Truffles, 6650
JusTea, 45589
Justin Vineyards & Winery LLC, 6651
Justin's Nut Butter, 6652
Justman Brush Co, 24645, 45592
Justrite Rubber Stamp & Seal, 24646
Jutras Signs & Flags, 24647
Juvenal Direct, 24648
JVC Rubber Stamp Company, 24473
JVM Sales Corp., 6412, 24474
JVNW, 24475
JVR/Sipromac, 24476
JVS Group, 40563
JW Aluminum, 24477, 45469
JW Aluminum Co, 24478
JW Leser Company, 24479, 45470
Jwc Environmental, 24649
Jyoti Cuisine India, 6653, 45593

K

K & F Select Fine Coffees, 6654, 45594, 57411
K & G Power Systems, 57412
K & H Corrugated Corp, 24650
K & I Creative Plastics & Wood, 24651
K & K Gourmet Meats Inc, 6655
K & L Intl, 24652, 45595, 57413
K & M Intl Inc, 24653
K & S Cakes, 6656
K B Systems Inc, 24654
K C Booth Co, 24655, 45596
K C's Best Wild Rice, 57414
K Doving Co Inc, 45597, 57415
K Heeps Inc, 57416
K Horton Specialty Foods, 6657, 57417
K J Plastics Inc, 40604
K Katen & Company, 24656, 45598
K L Keller Imports, 6658, 40605, 45599
K M Davies Co, 53065
K Trader Inc., 24657, 45600
K&C Food Sales, 57418
K&H Container, 24658
K&H Equipment Company, 57419
K&J Logistics, 51856
K&K Express, 51857, 53066
K&K Meat Company, 57420
K&K Truck Brokers, 40606
K&N Fisheries, 6659, 45601
K&R Equipment, 24659
K&S Sales, 40607
K'ul Chocolate, 6660
K+S Windsor Salt Ltd., 6661, 45602, 57421
K-C Products Company, 24660
K-Coe Isom, 24661
K-Lift Material Handling Equipment Company, 57422
K-Mama Sauce, 6662, 57423

K-Patents, 24662
K-Tron, 24663, 45603
K-Tron International, 24664, 45604
K-Way Products, 24665, 45605
K. Lefkofsky Company, 57424
K.B. Hall Ranch, 6663
K.F. Logistics, 24666, 45606
K.R. International, 45607
K.S.M. Seafood Corporation, 6664, 45608
Ka-POP!, 6680
Kaari Foods, 6681
Kabobs, 45633
Kachemak Bay Seafood, 6682, 45634
Kaco Supply Co, 57433
Kadon Corporation, 24707, 45635
Kadouri International Foods, 57434
Kady International, 24708, 45636
Kaeser Compressors Inc, 24709
Kaffe Magnum Opus, 6683
Kafko International LTD, 24710, 57435
Kagetec, 24711
Kagome USA Inc, 6684
Kahiki Foods Inc, 6685
Kahler-Senders Inc, 40612
Kahoka Cheese Shop, 57436
Kaines West Michigan Co, 24713
KaiRak, 24712, 45637
Kairak, 45638
Kaiser Pickles, 6686
Kajun Kettle Foods, 6687
Kak LLC, 51861, 53068
Kakookies, 6688
Kakosi Chocolate, 45639
Kal Pac Corp, 24714, 45640
Kaladi Brothers, 6689
Kalamazoo Creamery, 6690
Kalco Enterprises, 24715
Kaleel Bros Inc, 57437
Kalena, 6691
Kalifornia Keto, 6692
Kalil Produce Company, 57438
Kalin Cellars, 6693
Kalix DT Industries, 24716
Kalle USA Inc, 24717, 45641
Kallsnick Inc, 57439
Kalman Floor Co Inc, 24718
Kalot Superfood, 6694, 57440
Kalsec, 6695, 24719, 45642
Kalustyan, 6696, 45643
Kameda USA Inc., 6697
Kamflex Corp, 24720, 45644
Kamish Food Products, 6698, 45645
Kammann Machine, 24721
Kamran & Co, 24722
Kan-Pak, 6699
Kana Organics, 6700
Kandy King Confections, 40613
KANE Bag Supply Co, 24667
KANE Freight Lines Inc, 51858, 53067
Kane International Corporation, 45646
Kane's Kandies, 57441
Kanematsu, 45647, 57442
Kangaroo Brands, 6701
Kansas City Sausage, 57443
Kansas Marine, 57444
Kantner Group, 6702
Kapaa Bakery, 6703
Kapaa Poi Factory, 6704
Kapak Corporation, 24723
KAPCO, 24668, 45609
Kaplan & Zubrin, 6705
Kapow Now!, 6706
Kappert/Hyzer Company, 40614
Kappus Co, 57445
KAPS All Packaging, 24669, 45610
Kar Wah Trading Company, 57446
Kara Chocolates, 6707
Karabetian Import & Export, 45648, 57447
Karetas Foods Inc, 57448
Kargher Corp, 6708
KARI-Out Co, 6665, 45611
Karine & Jeff, 6709
Karl Ehmer, 6710, 45649

Karl Schnell, 24724
Karl Strauss Brewing Co, 6711, 45650
Karla's Smokehouse, 6712
Karlin Foods, 6713
Karlsburger Foods Inc, 6714
Karma, 24725, 45651
Karma Candy, 6715
Karma Nuts, 6716
Karmalize.Me, 6717
Karn Meats, 6718
Karolina Polymers, 24726
Karoun Dairies Inc, 6719, 40615, 45652
Karp's Bake Mart, 57449
Karson Food Services, 57450
Karyall Telday Inc, 24727
KAS Spirits, 6666, 45612
KASCO Sharp Tech Corp, 24670
KASE Equipment, 24671, 45613
Kasel Engineering, 24728
Kasel Industries Inc, 24729, 24730, 45653
Kashi Company, 6720, 45654
Kashrus Technical Consultants, 24731
Kasilof Fish Company, 6721, 45655
Kasira, 6722
Kason, 24732, 57451
Kason Central, 24733, 45656, 57452
Kason Industries, 24734
Kason Vinyl Products, 24735
Kasseler Food Products Inc., 6723, 45657, 53069
KAST Distributors Inc, 57425
Kastalon, 24736
Kastner's Pastry Shop & Grocery, 6724
Katagiri & Company, 45658
Kate Latter Candy Company, 6725
Kate's Vineyard, 6726
Kateri Foods, 6727
Kathabardehum Idification, 24737
Kathie's Kitchen, 6728
Kathryn Kennedy Winery, 6729
Kathryn's Food Service Brokers, 40616
Kathy's Gourmet Specialties, 6730
Katies Korner Inc, 6731
Katrina's Tartufo, 6732
Katy's Smokehouse, 6733
Katy's Wholesale Distributing, 57453
Katysweet Confectioners Inc., 6734
KATZ Marketing Solutions, 24672
Katzin's Uniforms, 57454
Kauai Coffee Co Inc, 6735
Kauai Kookie, 6736
Kauai Organic Farms, 6737, 45659
Kauai Producers, 6738, 57455
Kaufholz & Company, 40617
Kaufman Engineered Systems, 24738
Kaufman Paper Box Company, 24739
Kauling Wood Products Company, 24740
Kaurina's, LLC, 6739
Kava King, 6740
Kawneer Co Inc, 24741
Kay Foods Co, 6741
Kay Home Products Inc, 24742, 45660
Kay's Foods, 40618, 57456
Kay's Naturals, Inc., 6742
Kayco, 6743, 40619, 45661, 53070
Kaye Instruments, 24743, 45662
Kayem Foods, 6744, 57457
KAYS Processing LLC, 6667
KBR Building Group, 24673
KBRW, 40608
KC Innovations Inc, 6668
KCL Corporation, 24674
KD Canners Inc, 6669
KD Kanopy, 24675, 45614
KDH Sales, 40609
Kdm Foodsales Inc, 40620
Keating Of Chicago Inc, 24744, 45679
Kedco Wine Storage Systems, 24745, 45680
Kedem, 6746, 40621, 45681, 51862
Kedney Warehouse Co Inc, 53071
Keebler Company, 6747
Keegan Ales, 6748, 45682
Keen Kutter, 24746, 45683

Keena Corporation, 24747
Keenan Farms, 6749
Keene Technology Inc, 24748
Keenline Conveyor Systems, 24749, 45684
Keep Healthy, 6750
Keep Moving Inc., 6751
Keeper Thermal Bag Co, 24750, 45685
Keeter's Meat Company, 6752
Keeth & Associates, 40622
Kefiplant, 6753
Kegg's Candies, 6754
KeHE Distributors, 45663, 45664, 45665, 45666, 45667, 45668, 45669, 45670, 45671, 45672, 45673, 45674, 45675, 45676, 45677, 45678, 57458, 57459, 57460, 57461, 57462, 57463, 57464, 57465, 57466, 57467, 57468, 57469, 57470, 57471, 57472, 57473
Kehr's candies, 6755
Kehr-Buffalo Wire Frame Co Inc, 24751, 45686
Keith Industries, 57474
Keith Machinery Corp, 24752, 45687
Kelapo, 6756
Kelble Brothers Inc, 6757
Kelchner's Horseradish, 6758
Keller's Bakery, 6759
Keller's Creamery, 6760
Keller-Charles Of Philadelphia, 24753
Kelley Advisory Services, 24754
Kelley Bean Co Inc, 6761, 57475
Kelley Company, 24755, 45688
Kelley Foods, 6762, 57476
Kelley Supply Inc, 24756
Kelley Wood Products, 24757
Kelley's Island Wine Company, 6763
Kelley's Katch Caviar, 6764
Kelley-Clarke, 40623, 40624, 57477
Kellogg Canada Inc., 6765
Kellogg Co., 6766, 45689
Kellogg Elevator Company, 57478
Kelly Associates/Food Brokers, 40625
Kelly Box & Packaging Corp, 24758
Kelly Corned Beef Co, 6767
Kelly Dock Systems, 24759, 45690
Kelly Flour Company, 6768, 40626
Kelly Foods, 6769, 45691
Kelly Gourmet Foods Inc, 6770, 45692
Kelly Packing Company, 6771
Kelly's Candies, 6772
Kelly's Foods, 57479
Kelly-Eisenberg Gourmet Deli Products, 6773
Kelly/Mincks Northwest Agents, 40627
Kelman Bottles LLC, 24760, 45693
Kelmin Products, 24761
Kelsen, Inc., 6774, 45694
Kelson Creek Winery, 6775
Kem A Trix Inc, 24762
Kemach Food Products, 6776, 45695, 57480
KEMCO, 24676
Kemco Systems Inc, 24763
Kemex Meat Brands, 24764, 45696
Kemin Industries Inc, 6777, 24765, 45697
Kemper Bakery Systems, 24766
Kemper Food Brokers, 40628
Kemps LLC, 6778, 45698, 57481
Kemutec Group Inc, 24767, 45699
Kemwall Distributors LTD, 24768
Ken Coat, 24769, 45700
Ken Ottoboni Mushrooms, 57482
Ken Young Food Distributors, 57483
Ken's Beverage Inc, 24770
Ken's Foods Inc, 6779
Kenco Group Inc, 51863, 53072
Kenco Logistic Svc LLC, 51864, 53073
Kencraft, Inc., 6780
Kendall Frozen Fruits, Inc., 6781, 24771
Kendall Packaging Corporation, 24772
Kendall-Jackson, 6782
Kendel, 24773
Kendon Candies Inc, 6783, 24774, 57484

1401

All Companies Index

Kendrick Gourmet Products, 6784
Kendrick Johnson & Assoc Inc, 24775
Kenko International, 6785, 45701, 57485
Kennebec Fruit Company, 6786
Kennedy Enterprises, 24776
Kennedy Gourmet, 6787
Kennedy Group, 24777, 45702
Kennedy's Specialty Sewing, 24778
Kennesaw Fruit & Juice, 6788
Kennesaw Transportation, 51865
Kennett Roepke Gavilan, 40629
Kenney Sales, 40630
Kenny Seafood, 57486
Kenny's Candy & Confections, 6789, 40631
Kenosha Beef International LTD, 6790
Kenray Associates, 24779
Kenrich Foods Corp, 57487
Kenro, 24780
Kenshin Trading Corp, 45703, 57488
Kensington Lighting Corp, 24781, 45704
Kenssenich's, 57489
Kent Co, 24782
Kent Corp, 24783, 45705
Kent District Library System, 24784
Kent Foods Inc, 6791
Kent Precision Foods Group Inc, 6792, 24785, 45706
Kent Quality Foods Inc, 6793
Kent R Hedman & Assoc, 24786
Kent's Wharf, 6794, 57490
Kentea, 45707
Kentfield's, 24787
Kentmaster Manufacturing Co, 24788, 45708
Kentucky Beer Cheese, 6795, 57491
Kentucky Bourbon, 6796
Kentucky Container Svc, 51866
Kentucky Grocers Assn Inc, 24789
Kentucky Power, 24790
Kentwood Spring Water Company, 24791
Kentwood Springs, 6797
Kenwood Vineyards, 6798, 45709
Kenyon Press, 24792
Kenyon Zero Storage, 53074
Keokuk Junction Railway, 51867
Kepes, 24793
Kerala Curry, 6799
Kerekes Bakery & Rstrnt Equip, 45710, 57492
Kerian Machines Inc, 24794, 45711
Kern Meat Distributing, 6800, 57493
KERN Ridge Growers LLC, 6670, 45615
Kernel Fabyan's Gourmet Popcorn, 6801
Kernel Seasons LLC, 6802
Kerr Brothers, 6803, 45712
KERR Concentrates Inc, 6671
Kerr Jellies, 6804
Kerri Kreations, 6805
Kerrigan Paper Products Inc, 24795
Kerry Foodservice, 6806, 45713
Kerry Sweet Ingredients, 6807
Kerry, Inc, 6808, 24796
Kershenstine Beef Jerky, 6809
Kervan USA, 6810
KES Science & Technology Inc, 24677
Kesry Corporation, 24797
Kess Industries Inc, 24798
Kessenich's Limited, 24799
Kessler Sign Co, 24800
Kesten & Associates Restaurant Equipment Sales & Service, 57494
KETCH, 24678
Ketchup World, 45714
Keto Foods, 6811, 45715
Kett, 24801
Ketters Meat Market & Locker Plant, 6812
Kettle & Fire, 6813
Kettle Brand, 6814
Kettle Cuisine, 6815
Kettle Foods Inc, 6816
Kettle Master, 6817
Keurig Dr Pepper, 6818, 24802
Keurig, Inc, 6819

Kevala, 6820
KeVita, 6745
Kevton Gourmet Tea, 6821
Kew Cleaning Systems, 24803
Kewanee Washer Corporaton, 24804
Key Automation, 24805
Key Business Systems, 57495
Key Carlin O'Brien, LLC, 40632
Key Colony Red Parrot Juice, 6822
Key Container Company, 24806
Key Food Stores Cooperative, 57496
Key III Candies, 6823
Key Impact Sales & Systems Inc, 40633
Key Industrial, 24807, 57497
Key Industries Inc, 24808, 45716
Key International Cranbury, 24809
Key Largo Fisheries, 6824, 45717
Key Material Handling Inc, 24810
Key Packaging Co, 24811, 45718
Key Sales & Marketing, 40634
Key Sales Group, 40635
Key Technology Inc., 24812, 45719
Key West Key Lime Pie Co, 6825, 57498
Key-Bak, 45720
Key-Pak Machines, 24813, 24814, 45721
Keyco Distributors Inc, 57499
KeyImpact Sales & Systems, Inc., 40636
Keynes Brothers Inc, 6826
Keys Fisheries Market & Marina, 6827, 51868, 57500
Keyser Brothers, 6828
Keystone Adjustable Cap Co Inc, 24815, 24816, 45722
Keystone Cleaning Systems, 57501
Keystone Coffee Co, 6829, 45723
Keystone Fruit Marketing Inc, 45724
Keystone Manufacturing Inc, 24817
Keystone Packaging Svc Inc, 24818
Keystone Pretzel Bakery, 6830
Keystone Process Equipment, 24819
Keystone Restaurant Supply, 57502
Keystone Rubber Corporation, 24820, 45725
Keystone Universal Corp, 24821
Keystone Valve, 24822
KH McClure & Company, 40610, 45616
Khatsa & Company, 6831
KHL Engineered Packaging, 24679, 57426
KHL Flavors Inc, 45617
KHM Plastics Inc, 24680, 45618
Khong Guan Corp, 45726
KHS Co, 24681
Khs USA Inc, 24823, 24824, 24825
Kibun Foods, 6833
Kicking Horse Coffee, 6834
Kid Zone, 57503
Kidd Enterprises, 40637
Kidde Residential & Commercial, 24826, 45727
Kidde-Fenwal Inc, 24827
Kidfresh, 6835
Kids Kookie Company, 6836
KidsLuv, 6837
Kidsmania, 6838
Kiefel Technologies, 24828
Kiefer Brushes, Inc, 24829, 45728
Kiefer's, 40638
Kii Naturals Inc, 6839
KiiTO, Inc., 6840
KIK Custom Products, 24682, 24683, 24684
Kiki's Gluten-Free, 6841
Kikkoman Sales USA Inc., 24830
KIKO Foods Inc, 40611
Kilcher Company, 24831
Kildon Manufacturing, 24832
Kilgore Chemical Corporation, 24833
Kilgus Meats, 6842
Kill Cliff, 6843
Kill Sauce, 6844
Killer Creamery, 6845, 57504
Killington Wood ProductsCompany, 24834
Killion Industries Inc, 24835, 45729

Kilwons Foods, 6846
Kim & Scott's Gourmet Pretzels, 6847
Kim and Jake's, 6848
Kim Lighting, 24836, 45730
Kimball & Thompson Produce, 51869, 57505
Kimball Companies, 24837
Kimball Enterprise International, 6849
Kimberly-Clark Corporation, 24838, 45731
Kimberly-Clark Professional, 24839
Kime's Cider Mill, 6850
Kimmie Candy Company, 6851
Kincaid Enterprises, 24840, 45732
Kind Snacks, 6852
Kinder Morgan Inc, 24841
Kinder's BBQ, 6853
Kinder-Smith Company, 40639
Kinematics & Controls Corporation, 24842, 45733
Kinergy Corp, 24843, 45734
Kinetic Co, 24844, 45735
Kinetic Equipment Company, 24845
Kinetico, 24846, 45736
King & Prince Seafood, 6854
King & Prince Seafood Corp, 6855
King 888 Company, 6856, 24847
King Arthur, 24848, 45737
King Arthur Flour, 6857
King B Meat Snacks, 6858, 45738
King Badge & Button Company, 24849
King Bag & Mfg Co, 6850, 45739
King Brewing Company, 6859
King Cole Ducks Limited, 6860, 45740
King Company, 24851, 45741
King Cupboard, 6861
King Electric Sign Co, 24852
King Engineering - King-Gage, 24853, 45742
King Estate Winery, 6862
King Fish Restaurants, 6863, 57506
King Floyd's, 6864
King Food Service, 6865, 40640, 45743, 57507
King Henry's Inc, 6866
King Juice Co, 6867
King Kold Meats, 6868
King Midas Seafood Enterprises, 40641
King Milling Co Inc, 6869
King Nut Co, 6870, 45744
King of All Manufacturing, 24860
King of Pops Inc, 6872
King Oscar, 6871
King Packaging Co, 24854, 45745
King Plastic Corp, 24855, 45746
King Products, 24856, 45747
King Provision Corporation, 57508
King Research Laboratory, 24857
King Sales & Engineering Co, 40642
King Sales & EngineeringCompany, 24858
King Sign Company, 24859
King's Command Foods Inc, 6873
King's Hawaiian Holding Co Inc., 6874
Kingchem, 6875
Kingery & Assoc, 24861, 40643
Kingly Heirs, 6876
Kings Canyon, 6877, 45748
Kings Choice Food, 45749, 57509
Kings Processing, 6878
Kings River Casting, 24862, 45750
Kings Seafood Co, 6879, 40644, 57510
Kingsbrook Foods, 40645
Kingsburg Orchards, 6880
Kingsbury Country Market, 6881
Kingson Corporation, 57511
Kingspan Insulated Panels, Ltd., 24863, 45751
Kingston Candy & Tobacco Co, 57512
Kingston Fresh, 6882, 45752, 51870
Kingston McKnight, 24864, 45753, 57513
Kingsville Fisherman's Company, 6883, 45754
Kinnetic Food Sales, 40646

Kinnikinnick Foods, 6884, 45755
Kinsa Group Inc, 24865
Kinsley Inc, 24866, 24867, 45756
Kiolbassa Provision Co, 6885
KION North America, 24685
Kiona Vineyards Winery, 6886
Kirby Holloway Provision Co, 6887, 57514
Kirby Restaurant & Chemical, 57515
Kirigin Cellars, 6888
Kirin Brewery, 6889
Kirin Brewery Of America LLC, 45757
Kirkbride & Associates, 40647
Kirkco Corp, 24868
Kirkholder & Rausch, 57516
Kirstein Brokerage Company, 40648
Kisco Manufacturing, 24869, 45758
Kiska Farms, 6890
Kiss International/Di-tech Systems, 24870, 45759
Kiss My Keto, 6891
KISS Packaging Systems, 24686, 24687, 45619
Kissner Milling Company, 57517
Kisters Kayat, 24871, 45760
Kistler Vineyards, 6892
Kitchen Cooked Inc, 6893
Kitchen Equipment Fabricating, 24872
Kitchen Maid Foods, 57518
Kitchen Pride Mushrooms Farm, 6894
Kitchen Table, 6895
Kitchener Plastics, 24874, 45761
KitchenRus, 24873
Kitchens Seafood, 6896, 45762
Kitchun Grainfree Food, 6897
Kitcor Corp, 24875
Kite Hill, 6898
Kith Treats, 6899, 57519
Kitt's Meat Processing, 6900
Kittling Ridge Estate Wines & Spirits, 6901, 45763
Kittredge Equipment Co, 57520
Kittridge & Fredrickson LTD, 6902
Kiva Designs, 24876
Kiwa, 6903
Kiwi Coders Corp, 24877
Kiwi Kiss, 6904
KiZE Concepts, 6832
KJ's Market, 57427
KL Products, Ltd., 24688, 45620
Klaire Laboratories, 6905, 45764
Klamath Cold Storage, 53075
Klara's Gourmet Cookies, 6906
Klass Ingredients Inc, 40649
Kleen Janitorial Supply Co., 57521
KLEEN Line Corp, 24689
Kleen Products Inc, 24878, 45765
Kleenpak Systems, 45766
Kleer Pak, 24879
Klein Foods, Inc, 6907, 57522
Klein's Kosher Pickles, 6908
Kleinpeter Farms Dairy LLC, 6909
Klement Sausage Co Inc, 6910
Klenke Distributors, 57523
Klensch Cheese Company, 40650
Klever Kuvers, 24880
Kliklok-Woodman, 24881, 45767
Kline Process Systems Inc, 24882
Kline Transportation, 51871
Klinger & Speros Food Brokers, 40651
Klinger Constructors LLC, 24883
Klingshirn Winery, 6911
Klinke Brothers Ice Cream Co, 6912
Klippenstein Corp, 24884
KLLM Transport Svc LLC, 24690, 51859
Klockner Filter Products, 24885
Klockner Packaging Machinery, 24886
Klockner Pentaplast of America, 24887, 45768
Klomar Ship Supplies Inc, 51872
Klondike Cheese Factory, 6913
Klondike Foods, 40652, 53076, 57524
Kloppenberg & Co, 24888
Kloss Manufacturing Co Inc, 6914, 24889, 45769, 57525

1402

All Companies Index

Klosterman Baking Co., 6915
Klr Machines Inc, 24890
KLT Global, 45621
Kluber Lubrication N America, 24891, 24892
KM International Corp, 24691, 45622
KMA Trading Company, 57428
KMC Citrus Enterprises Inc, 6672
KMJ International, 45623
KMS Inc, 45624
KMT Aqua-Dyne Inc, 24692, 45625
Knall Beverage, 45770
Knapp Container, 24893
Knapp Logistics Automation Inc, 24894
Knapp Manufacturing, 24895
Knapp Shoes, 24896
Knapp Vineyards, 6916
Knappen Milling Co, 6917, 45771
Knaus Cheese, Inc., 57526
Knechtel Laboratories Inc, 24897
Knese Enterprise, 6918
KNF Flexpak Corporation, 24693
Knight Equipment Canada, 24898
Knight Equipment International, 24899, 45772
Knight Ind, 24900
Knight Paper Box Company, 24901
Knight Seed Company, 6919, 45773
Knight's Appleden Fruit LTD, 6920, 45774
Knight's Electric Inc, 24902
Knobs Unlimited, 24903, 45775
Knott Slicers, 24904, 45776
Knott's Berry Farms, 6921
Knotts Fine Foods, 6922, 57527
Knouse Foods Co-Op Inc., 6923, 45777
Know Allergies, 6924
Know Brainer, 6925, 57528
Knox Cash Jobbers, 57529
Knox County Feed & Hatchery, 57530
KNOX Stove Works Inc, 24694
Knoxville Poultry & Egg Company, 57531
Knudsen Candy, 6926
Knutsen Coffees, 40653, 45778
Koala Moa, 6927
Koalaty Kare, 57532
Kobrand Corporation, 45779
Kobricks Coffee Company, 6928
Kobu Beverages, LLC,, 6929
Koch & Assoc, 40654
Koch Bag & Supply Co, 45780, 57533
Koch Container, 24905, 57534
Koch Equipment LLC, 24906, 24907
Koch Foods Inc, 6930
Koch Membrane Systems Inc, 24908
Kochman Consultants LTD, 24909, 45781
Koda Farms, 6931
KODA Farms Inc, 6673
Kodex Inc, 24910, 45782
Kodiak Cakes, 6932
Kodiak Salmon Packers, 6933
KOE Organic Kombucha, 6674
Koegel Meats Inc, 6934
Koehler Borden & Assoc, 40655
Koehler Instrument Co Inc, 24911, 45783
Koehler-Gibson Marking, 24912, 45784
Koeze Company, 6935
KOF-K Kosher Supervision, 24695
Kofab, 24913
Koffee Kup Bakery, 6936
KOFLO Corp, 24696
Koha Food, 6937, 45785, 57535
Kohana Coffee, 6938, 45786, 57536
Kohinoor Foods, 6939
KOHL Wholesale, 57429
Kohlenberger Associates Consulting Engineering, 24914
Kohlenberger Inc, 57537
Kohler Awning Inc, 24915
Kohler Industries Inc, 24916, 24917, 45787
Kohler Original Recipe Chocolates, 6940
Koia, 6941

Koke Inc, 24918
Kokopelli's Kitchen, 6942
Kola, 6943, 45788
Kolatin Real Kosher Gelatin, 6944
Kolb-Lena Bresse Bleu Inc, 6945
Kold Pack, 24919
Kold-Draft, 24920, 45789
Kold-Hold, 24921, 45790
Kole Industries, 24922, 45791
Kolinahr Systems, 24923
Koloa Rum Corp, 6947
Kolon California Corporation, 57538
Kolpak, 24924, 45792
Kolpak Walk-ins, 24925, 45793
Kols Container, 57539
Kollar Cookies, 6946
Kom International, 24926
Komatsu Forklift USA, 24927
Komax Systems Inc, 24928
Kombucha Brooklyn, 24929
Kombucha Wonder Drink, 6948
Komline-Sanderson Engineering, 24930
Kommercial Kitchens, 57540
Kona Brewing, 6949
Kona Coffee Council, 6950
Kona Cold Lobsters, 6951, 45794, 57541
Kona Fish Co Inc, 6952, 57542
Kona Joe Coffee LLC, 45795
Kona Pacific Farmers Co-Op, 57543
Kona Premium Coffee Company, 6953
KonaRed Corp., 6954
Konetzko's Meat Market, 6955
Konica Minolta Corp, 24931, 45796
Konica Minolta Sensing Americas, 24932
Konoike Pacific California, 51873, 53077
Kontane, 24933, 45797
Konto's Foods, 6956
Konz Wood Products Co, 24934
Konzelmann Estate Winery, 6957
Kookaburra, 6958
KOOL Ice & Seafood Co, 6675, 57430
Koolant Koolers, 24935
Koorsen Protection Services, 57544
Kopali Organics, 6959
Kopcke-Kansas Supply Services, 57545
Kopke, William H, 45798, 57546
Kopper's Chocolate, 6960
Koppers Chocolate, 6961, 45799
Koppert Cress USA, 6962
Kopykake, 24936, 45800
Kor Shots, 6963
Korab Engineering Company, 24937, 45801
Korber Medipak Inc, 24938
Korbs Baking Company, 6964
Kord Products Inc., 24939, 45802
Korea Ginseng Corp., 6965
Kornfections, 6966
Kornylak Corp, 24940, 45803
Korte Meat Processors Inc, 6967
Korth Marketing, 40656
Koryo Winery Company, 6968
Kosempel Manufacturing Company, 24941
Koser Iron Works, 24942
Kosher French Baguettes, 6969
Kosmos & Associates, 57547
Kossar's Bagels & Bialys, 6970
Kosto Food Products Co, 6971, 45804
Kotoff & Company, 24943
Koukla Delights, 6972
Kovacs Group, 57548
Kowalski Sausage Co, 6973
Koza's Inc, 24944, 45805
Kozlowski Farms, 6974, 45806
KOZY Shack Enterprises Inc, 6676, 45626
KP Aerofill, 24697
KP USA Trading, 6677, 45627, 57431
Kradjian Importing, 45807
Kraemer Wisconsin Cheese LTD, 6975
Kraft Chemical Co, 57549
Kraft Heinz Canada, 6976, 45808
Kraft Heinz Co., 6977

Kraissl Co Inc, 24945, 45809
Kramarczuk's Sausage Co, 6978
Kramer, 24946
Kramer Brokerage Co, 40657
Kramer Vineyards, 6979
Kranz Inc, 57550
Krasdale Foods, 57551
Krasdale Foods Distribution, 57552
Krass-Joseph, 40658
Kraus & Co, 6980
Kraus & Sons, 24947, 45810
KRAVE Jerky, 6678
Krave Pure Food, 6981
Kreative Koncepts, 24948
Krebs Brothers Restaurant Supl, 57553
Kreher Family Farms, 6982
Kreiner Imports, 45811
Kreissle Forge Ornamental, 24949
Krema Nut Co, 6983
Krenik's Meat Processing, 6984
Krepe-Kraft, 24950
Krewson Enterprises, 24951, 45812
Krier Foods, 6985
Krimstock Enterprises, 24952
Krinos Foods, 6986, 45813
Krispy Kernels, 6987, 45814
Krispy Kist Company, 24953, 45815
Krispy Kreme Doughnuts Inc, 6988
Kristian Regale, 6989, 45816
Kristin Hill Winery, 6990
Kroger Bakery, 6991
Krogh Pump Co, 24954, 45817
KROHNE Inc, 24698
Krones, 24955, 45818
Kronos, 6992, 57554
Kropf Fruit Company, 57555
Krowne Metal Corp, 24956, 45819
Krueger Food Laboratories, 24957
Krueger International Holding, 24958, 45820
Kruger Foods, 6993, 45821
Krupka's Blueberries, 6994
Kruse & Son, 6995
Kruse Meat Products, 6996
Krusoe Sign Co, 24959
Krystal Holographics, 24960
Krystatite Films, 24961
KSW Corp, 24699, 45628
KT's Kitchens, 6679
KTech by Muckler, 24702
KTG, 24700, 45629
KTR Corp, 24701
Kubisch Sausage Mfg Co, 6997
Kubla Khan Food Company, 6998, 45822
Kuecker Equipment Company, 24962
Kuehne & Nagel Inc., 53078
Kuehne Chemical, 24963, 57556
Kuepper Favor Company, Celebrate Line, 24964, 45823
Kuest Enterprise, 24965, 45824
Kuhl Corporation, 24966, 45825
Kuhlmann's Market Gardens & Greenhouses, 6999, 45826
Kuju Coffee, 7000
KUKA Robotics Corp, 24703, 45630
Kulana Foods LTD, 7001
Kuli Kuli, Inc., 7002
Kullman Industries, 45827
Kunde Estate Winery, 7003
Kuner-Empson Company, 57557
Kupris Home Bakery, 7004
Kura Nutrition, 7005
Kuriyama Of America Inc, 24967
Kurtz Food Brokers, 24968, 40659
Kurtz Oil Company, 24969
Kurtz Orchards Farms, 7006, 45828
Kurz Transfer Products LP, 24970
Kusel Equipment Company, 24971, 45829
Kusha Inc., 7007, 45830, 57558
Kusmi Tea, 7008
Kutiks Honey Farm, 7009
Kutter's Cheese Factory, 57559
Kutztown Bologna Company, 7010
KW Transportation Services, 51860

Kwangdong USA, 7011
Kween Foods, 7012
KWIK Lok Corp, 24704, 24705, 45631
Kwikpak Fisheries, 7013
Kwikprint Manufacturing Inc, 24972, 45831, 57560
Kwok Shing Hong, 45832
KWS Manufacturing Co LTD, 24706, 45632
KYD Inc, 57432
Kyger Bakery Products, 7014
Kyler's Catch Seafood Market, 7015
Kyong Hae Kim Company, 7016, 57561
Kyowa Hakko, 7017, 45833
Kyrie Global Inc., 53079
Kysor Panel Systems, 24973, 45834
Kysor/Kalt, 24974
Kyung Il Industrial Company, 24975

L

L & C Plastic Bags, 24976
L & L Packing Co, 7018, 24977
L & L Truck Broker Inc, 51874
L & M Bakery, 7019
L & M Food Svc Inc, 24978, 57562
L & M Lockers, 7020
L & M Slaughterhouse, 7021
L & N Label Co, 24979, 45835
L & S Packing Co, 7022, 7023, 45836
L A Burdick Chocolate, 7024
L A Cabinet & Finishing Co, 24980
L A Hearne Co, 53080
L B Transport Inc, 51875
L C Good Candy Company, 7025
L ChemCo Distribution, 24981, 57563
L Cubed Corp, 24982
L F Lambert Spawn Co, 7026, 45837
L G I Intl Inc, 24983, 45838
L H Gamble Co LTD, 40660
L H Hayward & Co, 7027
L K Bowman, 7028
L Mawby Vineyards, 7029
L T Hampel Corp, 24984, 45839
L&A Engineering and Equipment, 24985
L&A Process Systems, 24986, 45840
L&C Fisheries, 7030, 45841
L&C Meat Company, 57564
L&H Wood Manufacturing Company, 24987
L&L Associates, 24988
L&L Engraving Company, 24989
L&L Reps, 24990
L&M Bakers Supply Company, 7031, 57565
L&M Chemicals, 24991
L&M Evans, 7032, 57566
L&S Pallet Company, 24992
L&S Products, 24993
L&S Sales Company, 40661
L'Esprit De Campagne, 7033
L. A. Smoking & Curing Company, 7034
L. Cherrick Horseradish Company, 45842, 57567
L. Craelius & Company, 7035, 57568
L. Della Cella Company, 45843
L. Dontis Produce Company, 57569
L. Holloway & Brother Company, 57570
L. Lacagnina & Sons, 57571
L.A. Darling Co., LLC, 24994
L.A. Libations, 7036
L.B. Maple Treat, 7037
L.C. Entreposage Storage, 53081
L.C. Thompson Company, 24995, 45844
L.H. Rodriguez Wholesale Seafood, 7038, 57572
L.J. Rench & Company, 45845
L.N. Coffman Company, 57573
L.N. White & Company, 45846
L.P. Shanks Company, 57574
L.T. Overseas, 45847
La Abra Farm & Winery, 7075
LA Bella Ferrara, 57575
La Belle Suisse Corporation, 45870
La Bonita Ole Inc, 7076

1403

All Companies Index

LA Bou Bakery & Cafe, 7039
LA Boulangerie, 7040
La Brasserie McAuslan Brewing, 7077, 45871
La Brea Bakery Inc, 7078, 57590
La Buena Mexican Foods Products, 7079
LA Buena Vida Vineyards, 7041
La Caboose Specialties, 7080
LA Canasta Mexican Foods, 7042, 57576
LA Cena Fine Foods LTD, 45848, 57577
LA Chapalita Inc, 7043
La Chiquita Tortilla Manufacturing, 7081
LA Chiripada Winery, 7044
La Choy, 7082
LA Colonial, 7045
La Cookie, 7083, 7084
LA Costa Coffee Roasting Co, 7046
La Crema Coffee Company, 7085
La Creme Coffee & Tea, 25033
La Crosse, 25034, 45872
La Crosse Milling Company, 7086, 25035
La Crosse Sign Co., 25036
La Cure Gourmande USA, 7087
La Esquina Food Products, 7088
La Ferme Martinette, 7089
La Flor Spices, 7090, 45873
La Flor Spices Company, 7091
LA Foods, 57578
LA Grander Hillside Dairy Inc, 7047
LA Grange Grocery Co, 57579
LA Graphics, 24996
La Grasso Bros Produce, 57591
La Grou Cold Storage, 51879, 53083
La Have Seafoods, 7092, 45874
LA India Packing Co Inc, 57580
LA Jota Vineyard Co, 7048
LA Lifestyle Nutritional Products, 7049, 57581
La Maison Le Grand, 7093
LA Mar's Donuts, 7050
LA Marche Mfg Co, 24997, 45849
La Menuiserie East Angus, 25037
LA Mexicana Tortilla, 7051
LA Mexicana Tortilla Factory, 7052
LA Mexicana Tortilleria, 7053, 45850
La Moderna, 7094
LA Monica Fine Foods, 7054, 24998, 45851
La Morena, 7095
LA Motte Co, 24999
La Newyorkina, 7096
La Nova Wings, 7097
La Panzanella, 7098
LA Pasta Inc, 7055
La Pasta, Inc., 7099
LA Patisserie Bakery, 7056
LA Paz Products Inc, 7057
La Piccolina, 7100, 45875
La Pine Scientific Company, 45876, 57592
La Poblana Food Machines, 25038
La Preferida, Inc., 7101
LA Quercia LLC, 7058
La Regina di San Marzano USA, 7102
LA Reina Inc, 7059
La Rinascente Macaroni Company, 25039, 57593
LA Rocca Vineyards & Winery, 7060
La Rochelle Winery, 7103
La Romagnola, 7104
La Rosa Azzurra, 7105
LA Rosa Refrigeration & Equip, 25000
LA Rue Distributing, 57582
La Rustichella Truffles, 45877
La Segunda Bakery, 7061
La Selva Beach Spice, 7106
La Societe, 7107, 45878
La Spiga D'Oro Fresh Pasta Co, 7108
LA Squisita Food Corp, 57583
La Superior Food Products, 7109
La Tang Cuisine Manufacturing, 7110, 57594
LA Tapatia Tortilleria Inc, 7062
La Tempesta, 7111
LA Teste Services, 40662

LA Torilla Factory, 7063, 45852, 57584
La Tortilla Factory, 7112, 57595
La Tourangelle, 7113
La Vans Coffee Company, 7114
LA Vencedora Products Inc, 7064
La Victoria Foods, 7115
La Vigne Enterprises, 7116
LA Vina Winery, 7065
LA Wholesale Produce Market, 7066, 45853
LAB Equipment, 25001
Labatt Breweries Alberta, 7120
Labatt Breweries Newfoundland, 7121
Labatt Brewery London, 7122
Labatt Brewing Company, 7123, 45881
Labatt Food Svc, 57597, 57598, 57599, 57600, 57601
Labconco Corp, 25041, 45882
Label Art, 25042, 45883
Label Express, 25043
Label House, 25044, 57602
Label Impressions, 25045
Label Makers, 25046, 45884
Label Mill, 25047
Label Products Inc, 25048
Label Solutions, 25049
Label Specialties Inc, 25050, 45885
Label Supply Company, 25051
Label Systems, 25052, 25053, 45886
Label Systems & Solutions, 25054
Label Systems Inc, 25055
Label Technology Inc, 25056
Label World, 25057
Label-Aire Inc, 25058, 45887
Labelette Company, 25059, 45888
Labeling Systems, 25060
Labeling Systems Clearwater, 25061
Labelmart, 25062
Labelmax Inc, 25063
Labelprint America, 25064
Labelquest Inc, 25065, 45889
Labels & Decals International, 25066
Labels By Pulizzi Inc, 25067
Labels Plus, 25068
Labeltronix LLC, 57603
Lablynx Inc, 25069
Laboratory Devices, 25070, 45890
Labov Mechanical, Inc., 57604
Labpride Chemicals, 25071
Labtech Industries, 25072
Labvantage Solutions, 25073
Labvantage Solutions Inc, 25074
Lacas Coffee Co Inc, 7124
Lacassagne's, 57605
Lacey Milling Company, 7125
Laciny Brothers Inc, 25075
Lacollina Toscana Inc, 45891
LaCroix, 7117
Lacroix Packaging, 25076
LaCrosse Milling Company, 7118, 45879
LaCrosse Safety and Industrial, 25040, 45880
Lacrosse-Rainfair SafetyProducts, 25077
Lactalis American Group Inc, 7126, 40669, 45892
Lactalis Ingredients Inc, 7127
Lactalis USA Inc, 7128
LAD Foodservice Sales, 40663
Lad's Smokehouse Catering, 7129
Ladder Works, 25078, 45893
Ladoga Frozen Food & Retail, 7130, 57606
Ladson Homemade Pasta Company, 7131
Lady Baltimore of Missouri, 57607
Lady Gale Seafood, 7132
Lady Mary, 25079
Laetitia Vineyard & Winery, 7133, 40670, 45894, 57608
Lafayette Brewing Co, 7134
Lafayette Restaurant Supply, Inc., 57609
Lafayette Sign Company, 25080
Lafayette Tent & Awning Co, 25081
Lafaza Foods, 7135
Lafitte Cork & Capsule Inc, 25082
Lafitte Frozen Foods Corp, 7136

Lafitte Seafood Company, 57610
Lafleur Dairy Products,, 7137
Lafollette Vineyard & Winery, 7138
Lafourche Sugar LLC, 7139
Laggren's LLC, 25083
Lago Tortillas International, 7140
Lagomarcino's Confectionery, 7141
Lagorio Enterprises, 7142, 45895
Lagrou Distribution Inc, 53084, 53085
Lagrou Warehouse, 53086
Laguna Beach Brewing Company, 7143
Lahaha Tea Co, 7144, 45896
Lahtt Sauce, 7145
Laidig Inc, 25084, 45897
Lail Design Group, 25085
Lairamore Corp, 57611
Laird & Company, 7146, 45898
Laird Plastics, 57612
Laird Plastics Inc, 57613
Laird Superfood, 7147
Laita, 45899
Laitram LLC, 25086
Lake & Lake Inc, 40671
Lake Champlain Chocolates, 7148
Lake Charles Poultry, 7149, 57614
Lake City Foods, 7150, 45900
Lake City Signs, 25087
Lake Country Foods Inc, 7151
Lake Erie Frozen Foods Co, 7152
Lake Erie Warehouse & Distribution Center, 51880, 53087
Lake Eyelet Manufacturing Company, 25088
Lake Michigan Growers, 40672
Lake Michigan Hardwood Company, 25089
Lake Packing Co Inc, 7153
Lake Process Systems Inc, 25090
Lake Shore Industries Inc, 25091, 45901
Lake Sonoma Winery, 7154
Lake States Yeast, 7155, 45902
Lake Superior Fish Co, 57615
Lake Wales Citrus Growers Associates, 57616
Lakefront Brewery Inc, 7156
Lakeland Rubber Stamp Company, 25092
Lakeport Brewing Corporation, 7157, 45903
Lakeridge Winery & Vineyards, 7158
Lakeshore Winery, 7159
Lakeside Container Corp, 25093
Lakeside Food Sales Inc, 40673
Lakeside Foods Inc., 7160, 7161, 7162, 45904, 45905
Lakeside Manufacturing Inc, 25094, 45906
Lakeside Mills, 7163, 45907
Lakeside Packing Company, 7164, 45908, 57617
Lakeside-Aris Manufacturing, 25095, 45909
Lakeview Bakery, 7165
Lakeview Banquit Cheese, 7166
Lakeview Cheese, 7167
Lakeview Farms, 7168
Lakeview Rubber Stamp Co, 25096
Lakewood Engineering & Manufacturing Company, 25097
Lakewood Juice Co., 7169
Lakewood Juice Company, 7170, 45910
Lakewood Processing Machinery, 25098
Lakewood Vineyards Inc, 7171
Lako Tool & Mfg Inc, 25099
Lakos Separators & Filtration, 25100
Lallemand, 7172, 45911
Lallemand American Yeast, 7173
Lallemand Inc, 7174
Lallemand/American Yeast, 7175, 7176
Lam's Food Inc, 7177
Lamagna Cheese Co, 7178
Lamar Advertising Co, 25101, 25102
Lamb Cooperative Inc, 45912, 57618
Lamb Sign, 25103
Lamb Weston Holdings Inc, 7179, 25104
Lambent Technologies, 7180, 45913

Lambert Bridge Winery, 7181
Lambert Company, 25105, 45914
Lambert Material Handling, 25106
Lambertson Industries Inc, 25107, 45915
Lambeth Band Corporation, 25108, 45916
Lamborn & Company, 40674
Lamco Chemical Co Inc, 25109
Lamcor, 25110
Lamcraft Inc, 25111
Lamex Foods Inc., 7182
Laminated Paper Products, 25112
Laminated Papers, 25113
Laminating Technologies Inc, 25114
Laminations, 25115
Lamitech West, 7183, 25116
Lamm Food Service, 57619
Lammes Candies, 7184
Lamonaca Bakery, 7185
LaMonde Wild Flavors, 7119
Lamoreaux Landing Wine Cellars, 7186
Lamports Filter Media, 25117, 45917
Lampost Meats, 7187
Lampson & Tew, 40675
Lampson Tractor Equipment, 25118
Lamson & Goodnow, 25119, 45918
Lanaetex Products Incorporated, 7188, 45919
Lancaster Colony Corporation, 7189, 25120, 45920
Lancaster Company, 53088
Lancaster County Winery LTD, 7190
Lancaster Fine Foods, 7191, 7192
Lancaster Johnson Company, 57620
Lancaster Laboratories, 25121
Lancaster Packing Company, 7193, 40676
Lancaster Poultry, 57621
Lance Agencies, 40677
Lance Private Brands, 7194
Lancer, 45921, 57622
Lancer Corp, 25122, 25123, 45922, 45923
Lanco, 7195
Land O'Frost Inc, 7196, 45924
Land O'Frost Inc., 7197, 45925, 57623
Land O'Lakes Inc, 7198, 45926
Land Span, 51881
Land's End Seafood, 57624
Land-O-Sun Dairies, 57625
Land-O-Sun Dairies Inc, 7199
Landau Uniforms Inc, 25124, 45927
Landen Strapping, 25125
Landers Ag Resources, 40678
Landies Candies Co, 7200
Landis Peanut Butter, 7201
Landis Plastics, 25126, 45928
Landlocked Seafoods, 7202
Landmark Coffee, 57626
Landmark Foods, 40679
Landmark Kitchen Design, 25127
Landmark Vineyards, 7203
Landolfi's Food Products, 7204
Landoll Corp, 25128
Landoo Corporation, 25129, 45929
Landphair Meat & Seafood, 57627
Landreth Wild Rice, 7205, 45930
Landry's Pepper Co, 7206, 45931
Landsberg Kent, 57628
Landsman Foodservice Net, 25130
Landstar System, Inc, 51882, 53089
Lane Award Manufacturing, 25131
Lane Equipment Co, 57629, 57630
Lane Labs, 45932
Lane Marketing Group LLC, 40680
Lane Southern Orchards, 7207
Lane's Dairy, 7208, 45933
Laney & Duke Terminal Wrhse Co, 51883, 53090
Lang Creek Brewery, 7209
Lang Manufacturing Co, 25132, 45934
Lang Pharma Nutrition Inc, 7210
Lang's Chocolates, 7211, 57631
Lange Estate Winery & Vineyard, 7212
Langen Packaging, 25133, 45935

All Companies Index

Langer Juice Co Inc, 7213
Langer Manufacturing Company, 25134, 25135, 45936
Langham Logistics, 51884, 53091
Langley Corporation, 57632
Langsenkamp Manufacturing, 25136, 45937
Langston Co Inc, 25137, 45938
Lanier Cold Storage LLC, 53092
Lanly Co, 25138, 25139, 45939
Lanmar Inc, 25140
Lansing Corrugated Products, 25141
Lansmont Corp, 25142
Lantana Hummus, 7214
LANTECH.COM, 25002
Lanter Distribution LLC, 53093
Lantev Distributing Corporation, 57633
Lanthier Bakery, 7215
Lantic Sugar, 7216
LANXESS Corp., 25003
Lanzarotta Wholesale Grocers, 57634
Lapierre Maple Farms, 7217
Larabar, 7218
Larco, 25143, 45940
Laredo Tortilleria & Mexican, 7219, 57635
Larick Associates, 57636
Larien Products, 25144, 45941
Larimore Bean Company, 57637
Lark Fine Foods, 7220
Larkin Cold Storage, 7221
Larkin Industries, 25145
LaRocca's Seafood Specialists, 57596
Laronga Bakery, 7222
Laros Equipment Co Inc, 25146, 45942
Larosa Bakery Inc, 7223, 7224
Larose & Fils Lte, 25147, 45943
Larry B Newman Printing, 25148
Larry Fox & Co, 40681
Larry J. Williams Company, 7225, 57638
Larry Martindale Company, 57639
Larry's Beans, 7226, 57640
Larry's Sausage Corporation, 7227
Larry's Vineyards & Winery, 7228
Larsen Farms, 7229
Larson Pallet Company, 25149
Lartigue Seafood, 7230, 57641
Las Cruces Brand Products, 7231
Las Cruces Foods, 7232
Las Olas Confections, 7233
Las Vegas Ice & Cold Storage, 53094
Laschober & Sovich Inc, 25150
Lasco Composites, 25151
Lasco Foods Inc, 7234
Lasermation Inc, 25152, 45944
Lasertechnics, 25153
Lasertechnics Marking Corporation, 25154, 45945
Lask Seating Company, 25155
Laska Stuff, 7235
Lassonde Pappas & Company, Inc., 7236, 45946
Latah Creek Wine Cellar, 7237, 57642
Latcham Vineyards, 7238
Late July Snacks, 7239
Latendorf Corporation, 25156, 25157, 45947
Laticrete International, 25158
Latini Products Company, 25159
Latitude, LTD, 7240, 45948
Latonia Bakery, 7241
Latouraine Coffee Company, 57643
Latta USA, 7242
Latter Packaging Equipment, 25160
Laub International, 51885, 53095
Laub-Hunt Packaging Systems, 25161, 45949
Laucks' Testing Laboratories, 25162
Laughlin Sales Corp, 25163, 45950
Lauhoff Corporation, 25164
Laundry Aids, 25165
Laundrylux, 25166
Laura Chenel's Chevre, 7243
Laura Paige Candy Company, 7244
Laura's French Baking Co, 7245

Laurel Awning Co, 25167
Laurel Foods, 7246
Laurel Glen Vineyard, 7247
Laurel Hill Foods, 7248
Laurell Hill Provision Company, 57644
Laurent's Meat Market, 7249
Laurie & Sons, 7250
Lauritzen Makin Inc, 25168
Lava Cap Winery, 7251
Laval Cold Storage Ltd., 53096
Laval Paper Box, 25169, 45951
Lavash Corp, 7252
Lavazza Premium Coffees, 7253, 25170, 45952
Lavella Brothers, 57645
Lavi Industries, 25171, 45953
Lavin Candy Company, 57646
Lavo Company, 25172
Lavoi Corporation, 7254
LAVVA, 7067
Lawler Foods LTD, 7255
Lawless Link, 25173
Lawnelson Corporation, 45954
Lawrence Equipment Inc, 25174, 45955
Lawrence Fabric Structures, 25175
Lawrence Foods Inc, 7256
Lawrence Freezer Corporation, 53097
Lawrence Glaser Associates, 25176
Lawrence Lapide, 57647
Lawrence Metal Products Inc, 25177, 45956
Lawrence Paper Co, 25178
Lawrence Schiff Silk Mills, 25179, 45957
Lawrence Sign, 25180
Lawrence-Allen Group, 25181
Lawry's Foods, 7257
Lawson Industries, 25182
Lax & Mandel Bakery, 7258
Laxson Co, 7259
Lay Packing Company, 7260
Laydon Company, 25183, 45958
Layflat Products, 25184, 45959
Layman Candy Company, 57648
Layman Distributing, 7261, 57649
Lazer Images Instant Signs, 25185
Lazy Creek Vineyards, 7262
Lazy Man Inc, 25186
Lazzari Fuel Co LLC, 25187, 45960
Lazzaroni USA, 7263, 45961, 57650
LB Furniture Industries, 25004, 45854
LBB Imports, 45855
LBG Distributors, 57585
LBM Sales, LLC, 40664
LBP Manufacturing LLC, 25005, 45856
LCI Corporation, 25006
LCL Bulk Transport Inc, 51876
LDC Analytical, 25007
LDC of Lafayette, 57586
LDI Manufacturing Co, 25008, 45857
LDJ Electronics, 25009
LDS Corporation, 25010
Le Bleu Corp, 7264
Le Caramel, 7265
Le Chef Bakery, 7266
Le Chic French Bakery, 7267
Le Cordon Bleu, 45962, 57651
Le Creuset of America, 45963
Le Donne Brothers Bakery, 7268
Le Fiell Co, 25188, 25189, 45964
Le Frois Foods Corporation, 7269
Le Grand, 7270
Le Grand Confectionary, 7271
Le Jo Enterprises, 25190
Le Macaron, 7272
Le Pique-Nique, 7273
Le Roy Ren, 7274
Le Smoker, 25191, 45965, 57652
Le Sueur Cheese Co, 7275, 25192
Le Vigne Winery, 7276
LE VILLAGE.COM, 45858
Lea & Perrins, 7277
Leach Farms Inc, 7278
Leader Candies, 7279, 45966
Leader Corporation, 25193
Leader Engineering-Fab Inc, 25194

Leading Brands of Canada, 57653
Leaf Cuisine, 7280
Leaf Jerky, 7281
Leahy Orchards, 7282
Leal True Form Corporation, 25195
Leali Brothers Meats, 57654
Leaman Container, 25196
Leams, 7283
Leaner Creamer, 7284
Lear Romec, 25197
Least Cost Formulations LTD, 25198, 45967
Leatex Chemical Co, 7285
Leathertone, 25199
Leavenworth Coffee Roast, 7286
Leaves Pure Teas, 7287, 25200
Leavitt & Parris, 25201
Leavitt Corp., The, 7288, 45968
Lebanon Cheese Co, 7289
Lebensmittel Consulting, 25202
Lebermuth Company, 7290, 7291, 45969, 57655
Leblanc Foodservice Marketing, 40683
Leblanc Seafood, 7292, 57656
Lechler Inc, 25203
Leclaire Packaging Corp, 25204
Leclerc Foods USA, 25205
LECO Corp, 25011, 25012
Leco Plastic Inc, 25206
Lecoq Cuisine Corp, 7293
Lee Andersons, 7294
Lee County Equipment LLC, 57657
Lee Engineering Company, 25207
Lee Financial Corporation, 25208, 45970
Lee Foods, 57658
Lee Grocery Company, 57659
Lee Industries, 25209
Lee Kum Kee, 7295, 45971
Lee Kum Kee USA Inc, 7296
Lee Packaging Corporation, 57660
Lee Products Co, 25210
Lee Seed Co, 7297
Lee Soap Company, 25211
Lee Truck Broker Inc, 51886
Lee's Food Products, 7298, 45972
Lee's Ice Cream, 7299
Lee's Sausage Co, 7300
Leech Lake Wild Rice, 7301, 7302
Leedal Inc, 25212, 25213, 45973, 57661
Leeds Conveyor Manufacturer Company, 25214
Leelanau Cellars, 7303
Leelanau Fruit Co, 7304, 45974
Leeman Labs Inc, 25215
Leer Inc, 25216, 45975
LEESON Electric Corp, 25013, 45859
Leeward Resources, 7305
Leeward Winery, 7306, 45976
Lef Bleuges Marinor, 7307, 45977
LEF McLean Brothers International, 7068, 45860
Lefse House, 7308
Left Hand Brewing Co, 7309, 7310, 57662
Lefty Spices, 7311
Legacy Bakehouse, 7312
Legacy Beverage Systems, 57663
Legacy Juice Works, 7313, 57664
Legacy Plastics, 25217
Legal Sea Foods, 25218
Legally Addictive Foods, 7314
Legend Brewing Co, 7315
Legendary Foods, 7316
Legge & Associates, 25219
Leggett & Platt Inc, 25220, 45978
Leggett & Platt Storage, 25221, 45979
Legible Signs, 25222
Legion Export & Import Company, 40684, 45980
Legion Industries Inc, 25223
Legion Lighting Co Inc, 25224, 45981
Legumex Walker, Inc., 7317, 25225
Lehi Mills, 7318, 25226
Lehi Valley Trading Company, 7319
Lehigh Food Sales Inc, 40685, 45982

Lehigh Safety Shoe Co LLC, 25227
Lehigh Valley Dairy Farms, 7320
Lehigh-Pocono Warehouse Inc, 51887, 53098
Lehman Sales Associates, 25228, 45983
Lehmann Brokerage Co, 40686
Lehmann Farms, 7321
Lehmann Mills Inc, 7322, 25229
Lehmann-Colorado, 57665
Lehr Brothers, 7323, 45984
Leibinger-USA, 25230
Leiby's Premium Ice Cream, 7324
Leica Microsystems, 25231
Leichtman Ice Cream Company, 25232, 57666
Leidenfrost Vineyards, 7325
Leidenheimer Baking Co, 7326
Leidos Engineering, 25233
Leidy's, 7327
Leigh Olivers, 7328
Leighton's Honey Inc, 7329
Leinenkugel's, 7330
Leiner Health Products, 7331
Leister/Heely-Brown Company, 25234
Leister/Malcom Company, 25235
Leister/Uneco Systems, 25236
Leisure Craft Inc, 45985
Lejeune's Bakery Inc, 7332
Lekithos, 7333
Leland Limited Inc, 25237, 25238, 45986, 45987
Lello Appliances Corp, 45988, 57667
Lemark Promotional Products, 57668
Lemate Of New England Inc, 7334
Lematic Inc, 25239, 45989
Lemberger Candy Corporation, 45990, 57669
LeMire Sales, 40682
Lemke Wholesale, 7335, 57670
Lemmes Company, 7336
Lemmons Company, 40687
Lemon & Vine, 7337
Lemon Creek Winery, 7338
Lemon-X Corporation, 7339, 45991
Lemoncocco, 7341
LemonKind, 7340
Lems, 57671
Lemur International, 7342
Len Libby Chocolatier-Maine, 7343
Len Miller & Associates, 40688
Lenchner Bakery, 7344, 45992
Lender's Bagels, 7345
Lendy's Cafe Raw Bar, 7346
Lengacher's Cheese House, 7347
Lengerich Meats Inc, 7348
Lengsfield Brothers, 25240, 45993
Lenkay Sani Products Corporation, 25241
Lennox Farm, 7349
Lenny & Larry's, 7350
Lenny's Bee Productions, 7351
Lenox Corp, 25242, 45994
Lenox Locker Company, 25243
Lenox-Martell Inc, 7352, 57672
Lenser Filtration, 25244
Lenson Coffee & Tea Company, 7353, 57673
Lentia Enterprises Ltd., 7354, 25245, 45995
Lentz Milling Co, 25246
Lenweaver Advertising, 25247
Lenze Americas, 25248
Leo A Dick & Sons, 57674
Leo G. Atkinson Fisheries, 7355, 45996
Leo G. Fraboni Sausage Company, 7356
Leo's Bakery, 7357
Leo's Bakery & Deli, 7358
Leon Bush Manufacturer, 25249
Leon C. Osborn Company, 25250
Leon Supply Company, 57675
Leon's Bakery, 7359, 45997
Leon's Texas Cuisine, 7360
Leona Meat Plant, 7361
Leona's Restaurante, 7362
Leonard & Sons Shrimp Company, 57676

1405

All Companies Index

Leonard Fountain Specialties, 7363
Leonard H Sisitzky Sales Inc, 40689
Leonard Mountain Inc, 7364
Leonardo's of Vermont, LLC, 7365
Leonetti Cellar, 7366
Leonetti's Frozen Food, 7367, 57677
Leonidas, 45998, 57678
Leopold & Diner Associates, 40690
Leotta Designers, 25251
Lepage Bakeries, 7368
Lepel Corp, 25252
Leprino Foods Co., 7369, 25253, 45999
Leraysville Cheese Factory, 7370
Lermer Packaging, 25254
Leroux Creek, 7371
Leroy Hill Coffee Co Inc, 7372
Leroy Signs, Inc., 25255
Leroy Smith Inc, 7373, 46000
Leroy's Restaurant Supply, 25256
Lerro Candy Company, 7374
Les Aliments Livabec Foods, 7375, 46001
Les Aliments Ramico Foods, 7376, 46002
Les Boulangers Associes Inc, 7377, 57679
Les Bourgeois Vineyards, 7378
Les Brasseurs Du Nord, 7379
Les Brasseurs GMT, 7380
Les Chocolats Vadeboncoeur Inc., 7381
Les Industries Bernard et Fils, 7382, 46003
Les Industries Touch Inc, 25257, 46004
Les Mouts De P.O.M., 7383
Les Palais Des Thes, 7384
Les Salaisons Brochu, 7385
Les Trois Petits Cochons, 7386
Les Viandes du Breton, 7387, 46005
Les Viandes or Fil, 7388, 46006
Lesaffre Yeast Corporation, 7389, 57680
Lesco Design & Mfg Co, 25258
Lesco Supply Company, 57681
Lesieur Cristal, 46007
Lesley Elizabeth Inc, 7390
Lesley Stowe Fine Foods, 7391
Leslie Leger & Sons, 7392, 46008
Lesserevil Brand Snack Co, 7393, 7394
Lester Box & Mfg Div, 25259
Lester Coggins Trucking, 51888
Let Them Eat Cake, 7395
Letica Corp, 25260, 46009
Letrah International Corp, 25261, 46010
Letraw Manufacturing Company, 25262
Letterman Enterprises Inc., 7396
Lettieri & Co LTD, 46011
Leuze-Lumiflex, 25263
Levain, 7397
Levant, 46012, 57682
Levant Mediterranean Snack Foods LLC, 7398
Levelmatic, 25264
Lever Associates, 40691
Levesque, 7399
Levin Brothers Paper, 25265, 57683
Lew Sander Inc, 57684
Lew-Mark Baking Company, 7400
LEWA Inc, 25014
Lewco Inc, 25266
Lewes Dairy Inc, 7401
Lewin Group, 40692, 46013
Lewis & Clark Company, 25267
Lewis & McDermott, 57685
Lewis Bakeries Inc, 7402
Lewis Brothers & Sons, 57686
Lewis Cellars, 7403
Lewis Label Products Corporation, 25268
Lewis Laboratories International Ltd., 7404
Lewis M Carter Mfg Co Inc, 25269, 46014
Lewis Packing Company, 25270
Lewis Sausage Corporation, 7405
Lewis Steel Works Inc, 25271
Lewis Storage, 51889, 53099
Lewisburg Container Co, 25272

Lewisburg Printing, 25273, 46015
Lewisburg Wholesale Company, 57687
Lewtan Industries Corporation, 25274, 46016
Lexel, 25275
Lexidyne of Pennsylvania, 25276, 46017
Lexington Coffee & Tea, 7406
Lexington Foodservice, 57688
Lexington Logistics LLC, 25277, 25278, 25279, 46018
Leyman Manufacturing Corporation, 25280, 46019
LFI Inc, 7069, 45861
Li'l Guy Foods, 7407
Libbey Inc., 25281, 46020
Libby Canada, 25282
Liberto Management Co Inc, 57689
Liberto of Harlington, 57690
Liberto of Houston, 57691
Liberty Bell Wholesale Grocery, 57692
Liberty Carton Co., 25283
Liberty Distributing Inc, 25284
Liberty Engineering Co, 25285, 46021
Liberty Food Svc, 25286
Liberty Gold Fruit Co Inc, 46022, 57693
Liberty International WHOL, 57694
Liberty Label, 25287
Liberty Machine Company, 25288, 46023
Liberty Marine Products, 57695
Liberty Natural Products Inc, 7409, 46024, 57696
Liberty Orchards Co Inc, 7410, 46025
Liberty Richter, 46026, 57697
Liberty Scale Co Inc, 57698
Liberty USA Inc,, 57699
Liberty Vegetable Oil Co, 7411
Liberty Ware LLC, 25289, 46027
Libido Funk Circus, 46028, 57700
Libman Co, 25290
Libra Technical Center, 25291
Liburdi Group of Companies, 25292
License Ad Plate Co, 25293
Licker Candy Company, 25294
LiDestri Food & Drink, 7408
Lido Chem, 57701
Lido Roasters, 25295
Lieb Cold Storage LLC, 53100
Lieber Chocolate Food Prod LTD, 57702
Life Extension Foundation, 7412, 25296
Life Force Specialty Foods, 7413
Life Plus Style Gourmet, 7414
Life Spice & Ingredients LLC, 7415, 25297
LifeAID, 7416
LifeIce, 7417
Lifeline Food Company, Inc., 7419
Lifeline Technology Inc, 25298
Lifem Spice Ingredients, 7420
Lifestar Millennium, 7421, 46029
Lifestyle Health Guide, 7422, 46030
LifeTime, 7418
Lifetime Brands Inc, 25299, 46031
Lifeway, 7423, 46032
Lifewise Ingredients, 7424, 40693
Lifoam Industries LLC, 25300
Lift Atlanta Inc, 57703
Lift Power, 57704
Lift Rite, 25301, 46033
Lift South, 57705
Lift Truck Ctr Inc, 57706
Lift Truck of America, 57708
Lift Truck Sales Svc & Rentals, 57707
Liftech Equipment Co Inc, 57709
Liftomatic Material Handling, 25302, 46034
Liftow, 57710
Liftruck Service Company, 57711
Light Bulbs Unlimited, 57712
Light Rock Beverage Company, 7425
Light Technology Ind, 25303, 46035
Light Vision Confections, 7426
Light Waves Concept, 25304, 46036
Lighthouse for the Blindin New Orleans, 25305
Lightlife, 7427, 46037

Lightolier, 25306
Lights On, 25307, 46038
Lignetics Inc, 25308
Liguria Foods Inc, 7428, 46039
Lil' Orbits, 25309, 46040
Lilar Corp, 57713
Lilburn Gulf, 40694
Lillie's Q, 7429
Lillsun Manufacturing Co, 25310, 25311, 46041
Lilly Co Inc, 46042, 57714
Lilly Company, 57715
Lily of the Desert, 7430, 46043
Lily's Sweets, 7431
Lilydale Foods, 7432, 46044
Lima Barrel & Drum Company, 25312
Lima Grain Cereal Seeds LLC, 7433, 46045, 57716
Lima Sheet Metal, 25313
Limberis Seafood Processing, 46046
Limehouse Produce Co, 7434, 57717
Limited Edition, 7435
Limitless, 7436, 57718
Limoneira Co, 25314, 57719
Limpert Bros Inc, 7437, 46047
Lin Engineering Inc, 25315
Lin Pac Plastics, 25316, 46048
LIN-PAK, LLC., 40665
Linco Caster, 57720, 57721
Lincoln, 25318
Lincoln Coders Corp, 25319
Lincoln Cold Storage, 51890, 53101
Lincoln Feed & Supply, 57722
Lincoln Food Service, 46050
Lincoln Foodservice, 25320, 46051
Lincoln Shrimp Company, 57723
Lincoln Suppliers, 25321
Lincoln Tent Inc, 25322
Lincolnwood Merchandising Company, 57724
Lincourt Vineyards, 7438
Linda's Gourmet Latkes, 7439
Linda's Lollies Company, 7440, 46052
Linde Material Handling, 25323
Linde North America, 25324
Linden Cheese Factory, 7441
Linden Cookies Inc, 7442
Linden Warehouse & Dstrbtn Co, 51891, 53102
Lindner Bison, 7443
Lindsay Farms, 7444
Lindsay's Teas, 7445
Lindt & Sprungli USA, 7446
Lindy's Homemade Italian Ice, 7447
Line of Snacks Consultants, 25325
Line-Master Products, 25326, 46053
Lineage Logistics, 53103
Linear Lighting Corp, 25328, 46054
LineSource, 25327
Linett Company, 25329
Linette, 25330
Lingle Brothers Coffee, 7448
Lingle Fork Truck Company, 57725
Link Snacks Inc., 7449
Linker Equipment Corporation, 25331
Linker Machines, 25332, 46055
Linnea's Cake & Candy Supplies, 25333, 57726
Linnea's Candy & Cake Supplies, 25334
LinPac, 25317, 46049
Linpac Materials Handling, 25335
Linpac Plastics, 25336
Linvar, 25337, 46056
Linwood-Welch Marketing, 40695
Linx Xymark, 25338
Linzer Products Corp, 25339, 46057
Lion Apparel Inc, 25340
Lion Brewery Inc, 7450
Lion Labels Inc, 25341, 46058
Lion Laboratories, 25342
Lion Raisins Inc, 7451, 46059
Lion/Circle Corp, 25343
Lionel Hitchen Essitional Oils, 7452, 46060
Lioni Latticini Inc, 7453

Lions Restaurant Equipment & Supplies, 57727
Lipid Nutrition, 7454
Lippert, 57728, 57729, 57730
Lipsey Mountain Spring Water, 7455
Lipten & Co, 57731
Liqui-Box, 25344, 46061
Liqui-Box Corp, 25345, 46062
Liquid Assets, 25346
Liquid Controls LLC, 25347
Liquid Sampling Systems, 25348
Liquid Scale, 25349, 25350, 46063
Liquid Solids Control Inc, 25351, 46064
Liquitane, 25352
LIS Warehouse Systems, 25015
Lisa Shively's Kitchen Helpers, LLC, 7456
Lisa's Organics, 7457
Lisanatti Foods, 7458
Lisberg-Voegeli Hanson, 40696
Lisbon Sausage Co Inc, 7459
Lisbon Seafood Co, 7460, 57732
LIST, 25016
Lista International Corp, 25353, 46065
Listo Pencil Corp, 25354, 46066
Litchfield Packaging Machinery, 25355
Litco International Inc, 25356
Lite-Weight Tool & Mfg Co, 25357, 46067
Litecontrol, 25358, 46068
Litehouse Foods, 7461, 7462, 46069
Lithibar Matik, 25359
Lithonia Lighting, 25360, 46070
Little Amana Winery, 7463
Little Bird, 7464
Little Charlie's, 57733
Little Crow Foods, 7465, 46071
Little Duck Organics, 7466
Little Giant Pump Company, 25361, 46072
Little Hills Winery, 7467
Little I, 7468
Little Miss Muffin, 7469
Little Portion Bakery, 7470
Little Produce, 57734
Little Red Dot Kitchen, 7471
Little Red Kitchen, 7472
Little Rhody Brand Frankfurts, 7473
Little River Lobster Company, 7474, 57735
Little River Seafood Inc, 7475
Little Rock Broom Works, 25362
Little Rock Crate & Basket Co, 25363
Little Rock Sign, 25364
Little's Squirt, 25365
Little's Cuisine, 7476
Littleford Day, 25366, 46073
Littler Brokerage Co Inc, 40697
Littleton Sales Company, 57736
Littman & Associates, 40698
Liuzzi Angeloni Cheese, 7477
LivBar, 7478, 57737
Live A Little Gourmet Foods, 7479
Live Floor Systems, 25367
Live Gourmet, 7480
Live Love Pop, 7481
Live Oak Warehouse, 51892, 53104
Live Oaks Winery, 7482
LIVE Soda, 7070
Livermore Falls Baking Company, 7483
Livermore Valley Cellars, 7484
Living Farms, 7485
Living Harvest Foods, 7486
Living Intentions, 7487
Living Raw, 7488
Livingston Distribution Centers, 57738, 57739
Livingston Farmers Assn, 7489, 46074
Livingston Moffett Winery, 7490
Livingston's Bulls Bay Seafood, 7491
Livingston-Wilbor Corporation, 25368, 46075
Lixi Inc, 25369, 46076
Lixi, Inc., 25370, 46077
Liz Lovely Inc, 7492

All Companies Index

Llano Estacado Winery, 7493
LLJ's Sea Products, 7071, 45862, 57587
Lloyd A Gray Co Inc, 40699, 53105
Lloyd Disher Company, 25371, 46078
Lloyd Hollander Company, 40700
Lloyd's, 7494
Lloyd's of Millville, 25373
Lloyd's Register QualityAssurance, 25372
LMC International, 25017, 45863
LMCO, 25018
LMD Integrated Logistic Services, 51877, 53082
LMG Group, 45864, 57588
LMGO International Inc, 40666
LMH, 25019
Lmi Packaging, 25374
LMK Containers, 25020, 45865
LMS Associate, 40667
Lo Temp Sales, 46079, 57740
Loacker USA, 7495
Load King Mfg, 25376, 46081
LoadBank International, 25377, 46082
Loafin' Around, 7496
Loar & Young Inc, 40701
Lobel Food Brokers, 40702
Lobster 4 Dinner, 7497
Lobster Gram, 7498, 57741
Lobster Warehouse, 57742
Lobsters Alive Company, 25378
Lobue's Rubber Stamp Co, 25379
Loc Maria Biscuits, 7499
Local Roots Farms, 7500
Location Georgia, 25380
Lochhead Mfg. Co., 7501, 46083
Lock Inspection Systems, 25381, 25382, 46084
Lockcoffee, 7502
Lockhee Martin Postal Tech Inc, 25383
Locknane, 25384, 46085
Locknetics, 25385, 46086
Lockwood & Winant, 57743
Lockwood Greene Engineers, 25386, 25387, 25388, 25389, 25390, 25391, 25392, 25393, 25394, 25395
Lockwood Greene Technologies, 25396
Lockwood Manufacturing, 25397
Lockwood Packaging, 25398, 46087
Lockwood Vineyards, 7503
Locustdale Meat Packing, 7504
Lodal Inc, 25399, 46088
Lodge Manufacturing Company, 25400, 46089
Lodging By Charter, 25401
Lodi Canning Co, 7505
Lodi Metal Tech, 25402, 46090
Lodi Nut Company, 7506
Loeb Equipment, 25403, 25404, 57744
Loew Vineyards, 7507
Loffredo Produce, 7508
Log 5 Corporation, 7509
Log House Foods, 7510
Logan, 57745
Logemann Brothers Co, 25405, 46091
Loghouse Foods, 7511
Logility, 25406
Logility Transportation Group, 25407
Logisco, 51893, 53106
Logistics Amber Worldwide, 51894, 53107
Logix, 25408
Logo Specialty Advertising Tems, 25409
Logotech Inc, 25410
Lohall Enterprises, 25411
Lola Granola Bar Corporation, 7512
Lola Savannah, 7513, 57746
Lollicup, 57747
Lolonis Winery, 7514
Loma International, 25412, 46092
Loma Systems, 25413
Lomac & May Associates, 40703
Loman Brown, 40704
Lomar Distributing Inc, 57748
Lombardi Brothers Meat Packers, 7515, 46093, 57749

Lombardi's Bakery, 7516
Lombardi's Seafood, 7517, 46094, 57750
Lombardi's Seafood Inc, 7518
Lomont IMT, 25414
London Fruit Inc, 46095, 57751
Lone Elm Sales Inc, 51895
Lone Peak Labeling Systems, 25415
Lone Pine Enterprise Inc, 7519, 46096
Lone Star Bakery, 7520, 46097
Lone Star Consolidated Foods Inc., 7521
Lone Star Container Corp, 25416, 46098
Lone Wolf Farms, 7522
Loneoak & Co, 7752
Lonestar Banners & Flags, 25417, 46099
Long & Littleton, 40705
Long Company, 25418, 57753
Long Food Industries, 7523, 25419
Long Grove Confectionary, 7524
Long Island Cauliflower Assn, 7525
Long Island Glove & Safety Products, 57754
Long Island Promotions, 57755
Long Island Stamp Corporation, 25420
Long Range Systems, 25421
Long Reach ManufacturingCompany, 25422, 46100
Long Trail Brewing Co Inc, 7526
Long Vineyards, 7527
Long Wholesale Distr Inc, 57756
Long Wholesale Distributors, 57757
Longaberger Basket Company, 25423
Longacres Modern Dairy Inc, 7528
Longbottom Coffee & Tea Inc, 7529, 46101, 57758
Longford Equipment International, 25424
Longford Equipment US, 25425
Longford-Hamilton Company, 7530
Longhorn Imports Inc, 25426
Longhorn Liquors, 46102, 57759
Longhorn Packaging Inc, 25427, 46103
Longleaf Plantation, 7531
Longmeadow Building Dept, 7532
Longo's Bakery Inc, 7533
Longreen Corp., 7534
Longview Farms Emu Oil, 46104
Longview Fibre Co, 25428
Longview Fibre Company, 25429, 25430, 46105
Longview Meat & Merchandise Ltd, 7535, 57760
LonoLife, 7536, 57761
Lonza Inc, 25431
Look Lobster Co, 7537, 57762
Loop Cold Storage, 53108
Loos Machine, 25432, 46106
Lopez Foods, 7538
Loprest Co, 25433
Lora Brody Products Inc, 7540
Lorac Union Tool Co, 25434, 46107
Lorain Novelty Company, 57763
LorAnn Oils, 7539
Lord Label Group, 25435, 46108
Lord Label Machine Systems, 25436, 46109
Lord's Sausage & Country Ham, 7541
Loren Cook Co, 25437, 46110
Lorenz Couplings, 25438, 46111
Lorenz Schneider Co, 57764
Lorenz Supply Co, 57765
Lorenzen's Cookie Cutters, 25439
Lorenzo's Wholesale Foods, 57766
Loretta, 40706
Loretta's Authentic Pralines, 7542
Lorey & Lorey, 40707
Loria Awards, 25440
Lorina, Inc., 7543
Lorissa's Kitchen, 7544
Loriva Culinary Oils, 7545, 46112
Lorrich & Associates, 25441
Los Altos Food Products, 7546, 46113
Los Amigo Tortilla Mfg Co, 7547
Los Angeles Chemical Company, 40708
Los Angeles Cold Storage Co, 51896, 53109
Los Angeles Label Company, 25442

Los Angeles Nut House Brands, 7548
Los Angeles Paper Box & Board Mills, 25443
Los Angeles Smoking & Curing Company, 7549, 46114
Los Chileros, 7550
Los Gatos Brewing Company, 7551
Los Gatos Tomato Products, 7552
Los Pericos Food Products, 7553
Lost Coast Brewery, 7554
Lost Coast Roast, 7555
Lost Mountain Winery, 7556
Lost Trail Root Beer, 7557, 46115, 57767
Losurdo Creamery, 7558
LoTech Industries, 25375, 46080
Lotito Foods Inc, 46116
Lotsa Pasta, 7559
Lotte USA Inc, 7560
Lotto International, 40709
Lotus Bakery, 7561
Lotus Brands, 7562, 46117
Lotus Foods, 7563
Lotus Herbs, 46118
Lotus Manufacturing Company, 7564
Lou Pizzo Produce, 7565
Lou-Retta's Custom Chocolates, 7566
Loubat Equipment Company, 57768
Lougheed Fisheries, 7567
Louie's Finer Meats, 7568, 25444
Louis A Roser Company, 7569
Louis Baldinger & Sons, 25446, 46119
Louis Caric & Sons, 46120, 57769
Louis Dreyfus Company Citrus Inc, 7569, 46121
Louis Dreyfus Company LLC, 7570
Louis Dreyfus Corporation, 7571, 46122
Louis F. Leeper Company/Cleveland, 40710
Louis J Rheb Candy Co, 7572
Louis Jacobs & Son, 25447
Louis M Martini Winery, 7573
Louis Maull Co, 7574
Louis R Polster Co, 57770
Louis Roesch Company, 25448
Louis Sherry Premium Chocolate and Tins, 7575
Louis Swiss Pastry, 7576
Louisa Food Products Inc, 7577
Louisburg Cider Mill, 7578
Louise's, 7579
Louisiana Fish Fry Products, 7580
Louisiana Fresh Express, 51897, 57771
Louisiana Gourmet Enterprises, 7581
Louisiana Oyster Processors, 7582
Louisiana Packaging, 57772
Louisiana Packing Company, 7583, 46123
Louisiana Pride Seafood, 7584, 57773
Louisiana Rice Mill, 7585, 46124
Louisiana Seafood Exchange, 7586, 7587, 7588, 46125, 46126, 46127
Louisiana Seafood Promotion & Marketing Board, 7589, 57774
Louisiana Seafoods, 7590
Louisiana Sugar Cane Co-Op Inc, 7591
Louisiana Sugar Cane Cooperative, 7592
Louisville Bedding Co Inc., 25449
Louisville Container Company, 25450
Louisville Dairy, 7593
Louisville Dryer Company, 25451, 46128
Louisville Lamp Co, 25452
Loumidis Foods, 46129
Lounsbury Foods, 7594
Love Beets, 7595
Love Controls Division, 25453, 46130
Love Creek Orchards, 7596
Love Good Fats, 7597
Love Grown Foods, 7598
Love Quiches Desserts, 7599, 46131
Love The Wild, 7600
Love You Foods, 7601
Love'n Herbs, 7602
Love's Bakery, 7603
Lovebiotics LLC, 7604, 46132
Lovecchio & Sons, 57775

Loveshaw Corp, 25454, 46133
Lovin Oven Cakery, 7605
Lovion International, 46134, 57776
Low Country Produce, 7606
Low Humidity Systems, 25455, 46135
Low Temp Industries Inc, 25456, 46136
Lowcountry Produce, 7607
Lowcountry Shellfish Co, 7608, 57777
Lowe & Associates, 40711
Lowe Refrigeration Inc, 25457
Lowell Brothers & Bailey, 57778
Lowell Farms, 7609
Lowell International, 46137
Lowell Paper Box Company, 25458
Lowell-Paul Dairy, 7610
Lowen Color Graphics, 25459
Lower Foods, Inc., 7611
Lowery's Home Made Candies, 7612
Lowery's Premium Roast Gourmet Coffee, 7613, 25460
Lowland Seafood, 7614
Lowry Computer Products Inc, 25461
Loy Lange Box Co, 25462
Loyal Manufacturing, 25463
Lozier Corp, 25464, 46138
LPA Software, 25021
LPACK - Loersch Corporation, 25022
LPI Imports, 25023
LPI Information Systems, 25024, 45866
LPS Industries, 25025
LPS Technology, 25026, 45867
LRM Packaging, 25027
LSI Industries Inc, 25028
LSI Specialty Products, 57589
LSK Smoked Turkey Products, 7072
Lt Blender's Frozen Concoctions, 7615
LT Foods Americas, 25029
LT's Brokerage, 40668, 51878
Ltg Inc, 25465, 46139
LTI Boyd Corp, 25029
LTI Printing Inc, 25030, 45869
Luban International, 7616, 46140
Lubar Chemical, 25466
Lubbers Family Farm, 7617
Lubriplate Lubricants, 25467, 46141
Lubriquip, 25468
Lubrizol Corp, 7618
Lucas Industrial, 25469, 46142, 57779
Lucas Meyer, 7619
Lucas Vineyards & Winery, 7620
Lucas Winery, 7621
Lucca Freezer & Cold Storage, 51898, 53110
Lucca Packing Company, 57780
Luce Corp, 25470
Lucerne Elevator, 53111
Lucerne Foods, 7622
Lucero Olive Oil Mfr, 7623, 7624
Lucia's Pizza Co, 7625, 57781
Luciano Packaging Technologies, 25471
Lucich Santos Farms, 7626, 46143
Lucie Sable Imports, 25472
Lucile's, 7627
Lucille Farms, 25473
Lucille's Own Make Candies, 7628
Lucini Italia Company, 7629
Luckner Steel Shelving, 25474, 46144
Lucks Food Equipment Company, 25475
Lucky Foods, 7630
Lucky Nutrition, 7631
Lucky Seafood Corporation, 7632
Lucky Spoon Bakery LLC, 7633
Lucky You, 7634
Luco Mop Co, 25476
Lucy's Foods, 7635
Lucy's Sweet Surrender, 7636
Ludeca Inc, 25477
Ludell Manufacturing Co, 25478, 46145
Ludfords, 7637, 46146
Ludo LLC, 7638
Ludtke Pacific Trucking Inc, 51899
Ludwick's Frozen Donuts, 7639
Ludwig Dairy Product, 7640
Ludwig Fish & Produce Company, 7641, 57782

1407

All Companies Index

Ludwig Mueller Co Inc, 40712, 46147
Luetzow Industries, 25479, 46148
Lufthansa Cargo, 51900
Luhr Jensen & Sons Inc, 7642, 25480, 46149
Luigi Bormioli Corporation, 46150, 57783
Lukas Confections, 7643, 46151
Luke Soules Southwest, 40713
Luke's Almond Acres, 25481
Luke's Organic, 7644
Luma Sense Technologies Inc, 25482, 46152
Lumaco Inc, 25483, 25484, 57784
Lumacurve Airfield Signs, 25485, 46153
Lumar Lobster, 7645, 57785
Lumax Industries, 25486, 46154
Lumber & Things, 25487, 46155, 51901, 57786
Lumberton Cash & Carry, 57787
Lumen, 7646
Lumenite Control Tech Inc, 25488, 46156
Luminiere Corporation, 25489, 46157
Lumsden Brothers, 57788
Lumsden Corporation, 25490
Lumsden Flexx Flow, 25491, 46158
Luna & Larry's Coconut Bliss, 7647
Luna's Tortillas, 7648
Lund's Fisheries, 7649, 46159
Lund-Iorio Inc, 40714
Lundberg Family Farms, 7650
Lunn Industries, 25492
Lupi-Marchigiano Bakery, 7651
Luseaux Labs Inc, 25493, 46160
Lustrecal, 25494, 46161
Lusty Lobster, 7652, 57789
Luthi Machinery Company, Inc., 25495, 46162
Lutz Pumps Inc, 46163
Luv Yu Bakery, 7653
Luvo Inc., 7654
Luxco Inc, 7655, 40715, 46164
Luxfer Gas Cylinders, 25496
Luxo Corporation, 25497, 46165
Luxor California Exports Corp., 7656, 46166
Luxury Crab, 7657, 46167
Luyties Pharmacal Company, 7658, 46168
Lve & Raymond Vineyards, 7659
LVO Manufacturing Inc, 25031
LWC Brands Inc., 7073
LXE, 25032
Lyco Manufacturing, 25498, 46169
Lyco Manufacturing Inc, 25499
Lyco Wausau, 25500, 46170
Lydall, 25501
Lykes Lines, 51902
Lyman-Morse Fabrication, 25502
Lynard Company, 7660, 57790
Lynch Corp, 25503, 46171
Lynch Foods, 7661
Lynch-Jamentz Company, 25504
Lynchburg Public Warehouse, 53112
Lyndell's Bakery, 7662
Lynden Incorporated, 53113
Lynden Meat Co, 7663, 25505
Lynden Transport Inc, 51903
Lynfred Winery Inc, 7664
Lynn Dairy Inc, 7665, 57791
Lynn Sign Inc, 25506, 46172
Lynn Springs Water LLC, 7666
LYNQ, 7074
Lyo-San, 7667, 46173
Lyoferm & Vivolac Cultures, 7668, 46174
Lyon LLC, 25507, 46175
Lyons Falls Pulp & Paper, 25508
Lyons Magnus, 7669, 7670
Lyons Specialty Company, 57792

M

M & B Fruit Juice Co, 7671
M & B Products Inc, 7672
M & CP FARMS, 7673
M & D Specialties Inc, 25509
M & E Mfg Co Inc, 25510, 46176
M & G Materials Handling Co, 57793
M & G Packaging Corp, 25511
M & H Crate Inc, 25512
M & M Display, 25513
M & M Equipment Corp, 25514
M & M Industries Inc, 25515
M & M Label Co, 7674
M & M Poultry Equipment Inc, 25516
M & O Perry Industries, 25517, 25518
M & Q Packaging Corp, 25519
M & Q Plastic Products, 46177
M & R Sales & Svc Inc, 25520, 46178
M & S Automated Feeding Systs, 25521
M & S Tomato Repacking Co Inc, 7675
M & V Provisions Co Inc, 57794
M & W Beef Packers Inc, 57795
M & W Logistics Group, 51904, 53114
M & W Protective Coating LLC, 25522
M 5 Corp, 46179, 57796
M A Sales, 57797
M Amundson Cigar & Candy Co, 57798
M Arkans & Son, 40716
M Buono Beef Co, 7676
M Conley Co, 57799
M D Stetson Co, 25523, 57800
M F & B Restaurant Systems Inc, 25524, 46180, 57801
M F G Inc, 25525
M Fellinger Co, 40717
M G America Inc, 25526
M G Newell Corp, 25527
M J Barleyhoppers Sports Bar, 7677
M J D Trucking, 25528
M K Food Svc Equipment Inc, 40718
M M Industries Inc, 25529
M Maskas & Sons Inc, 57802
M O Industries Inc, 25530, 46181
M Phil Yen Company, 46182
M R Williams Inc, 57803
M S Plastics & Packaging Inc, 25531, 46183
M S Walker Inc, 7678, 46184
M S Willett Inc, 25532, 25533, 46185
M T C Logistics Corp, 53115, 53116
M Tucker Co Inc, 57804
M&C Sweeteners, 25534
M&F Foods, 57805
M&H Erickson Ranch, 7679
M&L Gourmet Ice Cream, 7680, 46186
M&L Plastics, 25535, 46187
M&L Ventures, 7681, 57806
M&M Food Distributors/Oriental Pride, 7682
M&N International, 57807
M&Q Plastic Products, 25536
M&R Flexible Packaging, 25537, 46188
M&S Manufacturing, 25538
M&S Miltenberg & Samton, 25539
M&T Chirico, 57808
M&W Associates, 40719
M-C McLane International, 46189
M-CAP Technologies, 7683, 46190
M-E-C Co, 25540, 46191
M-One Specialties, 25541
M-Tech & Associates, 25543
M-TEK Inc, 25542
M-Vac Systems Inc, 25544, 46192
M. Crews & Company, 57809
M. Licht & Son, 7684, 46193
M. Marion & Company, 7685
M. Pencar Associates, 40720
M. Sickles & Sons, 57810
M. Soffer Company, 40721
M. Zukerman & Company, 57811
M.A. Hatt & Sons, 7686
M.A. Johnson Frozen Foods, 7687
M.A. Patout & Son LTD, 7688
M.E. Carter & Company, 57812
M.E. Dilanian Company, 40722, 57813
M.E. Franks Inc., 7689
M.E. Heuck Company, 25545, 46194
M.E. Strauss Brokerage Company, 40723
M.E. Swing Company, 7690
M.H. Greenebaum, 7691
M.H. Rhodes Cramer, 25546, 46195
M.J. Borelli & Company, 40724
M.K. Health Food Distributors, 57814
M.S. Johnston Company, 57815
M/S Smears, 7692
Maat Nutritionals, 7711
Maberry & Maberry Berry Associates, 7712
MAC Equipment, 25547, 25548
Mac Farms Of Hawaii Inc, 7713, 46220
Mac Knight Smoke House Inc, 7714, 46221
Mac Papers Inc, 25601
MAC Tac LLC, 25549, 46196
Mac's Donut Shop, 7715
Mac's Farms Sausage Co Inc, 7716
Mac's Meats Inc, 7717
Mac's Oysters, 7718
Mac's Snacks, 7719
Macabee Foods, 7724
Macaron Paris LLC, 7725
Macco Organiques, 7726, 46224
MacCosham Van Lines, 51909, 53121
Macdonald Meat Co, 46225, 57828
Macdonald Signs & Advertising, 25604
MacDonald Steel Ltd, 25602
MacDonalds Consolidated, 57825, 57826
MacEwan's Meats, 7720
Macfarlane Pheasants, 7727
MacGregors Meat & Seafood, 7721, 46222, 57827
Machanix Fabrication Inc, 25605
Machem Industries, 25606, 46226
Machias Bay Seafood, 7728, 57829
Machine Applications Corp, 25607
Machine Brokers, 40728
Machine Builders & Design Inc, 25608, 25609, 46227
Machine Electronics Company, 25610
Machine Ice Co, 25611, 25612, 46228, 46229, 57830
Machinery & Equipment Company, Inc., 25614
Machinery & Equipment Corp, 25613
Machinery Corporation of America, 25615
Machinery Engineering Technology, 25616
Mack Restaurant Equipment & Supplies, 57831
Mack's Bill Ice Cream, 7729
Mack's Homemade Ice Cream, 7730
Mack-Chicago Corporation, 25617
MacKay's Cochrane Ice Cream, 7722
Mackenzie Creamery, 7731, 25618
Mackie International, Inc., 7732
Mackie International. Inc., 25619
MacKinlay Teas, 7723
MacMillan Bloedel Packaging, 25603, 46223
Maco Bag Corp, 25620
Macomb Tobacco & Candy Company, 57832
Macon Awning & Canvas Prod, 25621
Macrie Brothers, 7733, 25622, 46230
Macro Plastics Inc, 25623
Mad Chef Enterprise, 7734
Mad River Farm Kitchen, 7735
Mad Scientist Nuts, 7736
Mad Will's Food Company, 7737
Mada'n Kosher Foods, 7738
Madani Halal, 7739, 57833
Maddalena Restaurant-Sn, 7740, 46231
Maddan & Co Inc, 40729
Madden & Assoc, 40730
Maddox/Adams International, 25624
Maddy & Maize, 7741
Made In Nature, 7742, 57834
Made Rite Foods, 7743
Made-Rite Sandwich Co, 7744
Madecasse, 7745
Madelaine Chocolate Company, 7746, 46232
Madera Enterprises Inc, 7747, 46233
MadgeTech, Inc., 25625, 46234
Madhava Natural Sweeteners, 7748, 46235
Madhouse Munchies, 7749
Madison Cash & Carry Wholesale Grocers, 57835
Madison County Wood Products, 25626
Madison Food Sales Company, 57836
Madison Foods, 7750, 46236
Madison Grocery Company, 57837
Madison Park Foods, 7751
Madison Vineyard, 7752
Madison Warehouse Corporation, 53122
Madison Wholesale Co, 57838
Madix, 25627
Madix Inc, 25628, 46237
Madland Toyota Lift, 57839
Madonna Estate Winery, 7753
Madrange, 7754
Madrinas Coffee, 7755
Madrona Specialty Foods LLC, 7756
Madrona Vineyards, 7757
Madsen Wire Products Inc, 25629, 46238
Madys Company, 7758, 46239, 57840
Madyson's Marshmallows, 7759
Maebo Noodle Factory Inc, 7760
Maersk Sealand, 51910
Maestri d'Italia, 46240
MAF Industries Inc, 25550, 46197
MAFCO Worldwide, 7693, 46198
Maffei Produce Company, 57841
Maggie Lyon Chocolatiers, 7761, 57842
Maggie's Salsa, 7762
Maggiora Baking Co, 7763
Magi Kitch'n, 25630, 46241
Magic American Corporation, 25631, 46243
Magic Gumball Intl, 7764
Magic Ice Products, 7765, 46244
Magic Seasoning Blends, 7766, 25632
Magic Valley Growers, 7767, 46245
Magic Valley Quality Milk, 7768
Magic Valley Truck Brokers Inc, 40731, 51911
MagiKitch'n, 46242
Magline Inc, 25633
Magna Foods Corporation, 7769, 46246
Magna Industries Inc, 25634
Magna Machine Co, 25635, 25636
Magna Power Controls, 25637, 46247
Magnaform Corp, 25638
Magnanini Farm Winery, 7770
Magnatech Corp, 25639, 46248
MagneTek, 25640
Magnetic Products Inc, 25641, 46249
Magnetic Springs, 7771
Magnetic Technologies LTD, 25642
Magnetool Inc, 25643, 46250
Magnificent Muffin, 7772
Magnolia Bakery, 7773
Magnolia Citrus Assn, 7774, 46251
Magnolia Meats, 7775
Magnotta Winery Corporation, 7776, 46252
Magnum Coffee Packaging, 25644
Magnum Coffee Roastery, 7777
Magnum Custom Trailer & BBQ Pits, 25645, 46253
Magnum Systems Inc, 25646
Magnuson, 25647, 46254
Magnuson Industries, 25648, 46255
Magnuson Products, 25649
Magpowr, 25650
Magrabar Chemical Corp, 7778, 46256
Magsys Inc, 25651, 46257
Mah Chena Company, 7779
Mahaffy & Harder Engineering Company, 25652
Mahantongo Game Farm, 7780, 46258
Maher Marketing Services, 7781
Mahoney Environmental, 25653
Mahoning Swiss Cheese Cooperative, 7782, 57843
Maid-Rite Steak Company, 7783, 46259

All Companies Index

Maier Sign Systems, 25654, 46260
Mail-Well Label, 25655, 25656
Main Course Consultants, 25657
Main Lamp Corp, 25658
Main Squeeze, 7784
Main Street Gourmet, 7785, 57844
Main Street Ingredients, 7786
Main Street Marketing, 40732
Main Street Wholesale Meat, 57845
Mainca USA Inc, 25659
Maine Coast Nordic, 7787
Maine Coast Sea Vegetables, 7788, 57846
Maine Industrial Plastics & Rubber Corporation, 25660
Maine Lobster Outlet, 7789, 57847
Maine Mahogony Shellfish, 7790, 57848
Maine Poly Aquisition, 25661
Maine Potato Board, 46261
Maine Sea Harvest, 40733
Maine Sea International, 40734
Maine Seaweed Company, 7791
Maine Shellfish Co Inc, 57849
Maine Wild Blueberry Company, 7792, 46262
Maines Paper & Food Svc Inc, 53123, 57850, 57851, 57852
Mainline Industries Inc, 25662, 46263
Mainstreet Menu Systems, 25663, 46264
Maintainco Inc, 57853
Maintenance Equipment Company, 57854
Maisie Jane's California Sunshine, 7793
Maison Gourmet, 57855
Maison Riviera, 7794
Maison Riviere USA, 46265
Maja Equipment Company, 25664
Majestic, 25665, 46266
Majestic Coffee & Tea, 25666
Majestic Coffee & Tea Inc, 7795
Majestic Flex Pac, 25667
Majestic Foods, 7796
Majestic Industries Inc, 25668, 46267
Majestic Lift Truck Service, 57856
Majesty, 46268
Major Marketing Service, 40735
Majors Transit Inc, 51912
Maju Superfoods, 7797
MAK Enterprises, 7694
MAK Wood Inc, 7695, 25551, 57816
Makana Beverages Inc., 7798, 46269
Makat, 25669
Make It Simple, 7799
Maker Oats, 7800
Maker's Mark Distillery Inc, 7801, 46270
Mako Services, 25670, 40736
Malabar Formulas, 7802
Malaysian Palm Oil Board, 25671
Malco Industries, 57857
Malco Manufacturing Co, 25672
Malcolm Meats Co, 7803
Malcolm Stogo Associates, 25673
Malena Produce Inc, 46271, 57858
Malgor & Company, 46272
Mali's All Natural Barbecue Supply Company, 25674, 46273
Malibu Beach Beverage, 7804
Malie Kai Hawaiian Chocolates, 7805
MALK Organics, 7696
Mall City Containers Inc, 25675
Mallard's Food Products, 7806
Mallory Alexander Intl, 51913, 51914, 53124
Malnove Of Nebraska, 25676, 46274
Malo Inc, 25677, 25678, 46275
Maloberti Produce Co, 57859
Maloney Seafood Corporation, 7807, 46276
Maloney Veitch Associates, 40737
Malow Corporation, 57860
Malpack Polybag, 25679
Malt Diastase Co, 7808, 7809, 46277, 46278, 57861
Maltese Signs, 25680
Malteurop North America, 7810, 25681, 46279, 53125
Malthus Diagnostics, 25682, 46280

Mama Amy's Quality Foods, 7811, 46281
Mama Del's Macaroni, 7812
Mama Lil's Peppers, 7813
Mama Maria's Tortillas, 7814
Mama Mary's, 7815
Mama O's Premium Kimchi, 7816
Mama Rap's & Winery, 7817
Mama Rose's Gourmet Foods, 7818
Mama Rosie's Ravioli, 7819
Mama Tish's Italian Specialties, 7820
Mama Vida's Inc, 7821
Mamie's Pies, 7822
Mamma Chia, 7823
Mamma Lina Ravioli Company, 7824
Mamma Lombardi's All Natural Sauces, 7825
Mamma Says, 7826
Mammoth Creameries, 7827
Man-O Products, 25683, 46282
Man-Tech Associates, 25684
Manabo, 25685
Management Insight, 25686
Management Recruiters, 25687
Management Tech of America, 25688, 46283
Manager's Redbook by Dataworks, 46284
Manassero Farms, 7828
Mancan Wine, 7829
Manchac Seafood Market, 7830, 57862
Manchester Farms, 7831, 46285
Manchester Grocery Company, 57863
Manchester Tool & Die Inc, 25689, 46286
Mancini & Groesbeck, 40738
Mancini Packing Co, 7832, 25690, 40739, 46287
Mancini Sales & Marketing, 40740
Manco Distributors, 57864
Mancuso Cheese Co, 7833, 46288, 57865
Manda Fine Meats Inc, 7834
Mandalay Food Products Corporation, 46289
Mandarin Noodle Manufacturing Company, 7835
Mandarin Soy Sauce Inc, 7836, 25691, 46290
Manderfield's Home Bakery, 7837
Mandeville Company, 25692, 57866
Mandex Motion Displays, 57867
Mando Inc, 7838, 57868
Mane Inc., 7839, 25693, 46291
Manfredi Cold Storage, 53126
Mange, 7840
Manger Packing Corp, 7841, 46292
Mangia Inc., 7842, 46293
Manhattan Bagel Company, 7843
Manhattan Beach Brewing Company, 7844
Manhattan Fire Safety, 57869
Manhattan Food Brands, LLC, 7845
Manhattan Key Lime Juice Company, 57870
Manhattan Lights, 57871
Manhattan Special Bottling, 7846
Manhattan Truck Lines, 25694, 46294
Mani Imports, 46295, 57872
Manicaretti Italian Food Importers, 46296
Manildra Milling Corporation, 7847, 46297
Manischewitz Co, 7848, 46298
Manischewitz Wine Co., 7849
Manitoba Harvest Hemp, 7850
Manitok Food & Gifts, 7851
Manitoulin Group of Companies, 51915, 53127
Manitowoc Foodservice, 25695, 46299
Manitowoc Ice Machine, 25696, 46300
Mankato Tent & Awning Co, 25697
Mankuta Bros Rubber Stamp Co, 25698
Manley Meats Inc, 7852
Mann Packing Co, 7853
Mannhardt Inc, 25699, 57873...

Manning Brothers Food Eqpt Co, 57873
Manning Lighting Inc, 25701, 46301
Manning Systems, 25702
Mannkraft Corporation, 25703
Manns Sausage Company, 7855
Manor Electric Supplies Light, 57874
Mansfield Rubber Stamp, 25704
Mansi, Inc., 46302
Mansmith's Barbeque, 7856
Manta Ray, 25705
Manting Equipment Company, 57875
Mantrose-Haeuser Co Inc, 7857
Manuel's Hot Tamales, 57876
Manuel's Mexican-American Fine Foods, 7858, 40741, 57877
Manuel's Odessa Tortilla, 7859
Manufacturers Agents forthe Foodservice Industry, 25706
Manufacturers Corrugate Box, 25707
Manufacturers Credit Corp, 46303
Manufacturers Railway Company, 25708
Manufacturers Wood Supply Company, 25709, 46304
Manufacturing Business Systems, 25710
Manufacturing Warehouse, 25711, 46305
Manzana Products Co., 7860
Manzo Food Brokers, 40742
Maola Milk & Ice Cream Co, 7862
Maola Milk & Ice Cream Co., 7861
MAP Systems International, 25552
MAP Tech Packaging Inc, 25553, 25554
MapFresh, 25712
Maple Acres Inc, 7863
Maple Donuts, 7864
Maple Donuts Inc, 7865
Maple Grove Farms Of Vermont, 7866
Maple Hill Creamery, 7867
Maple Hill Farms, 7868, 25713
Maple Hollow, 7869, 57878
Maple Island, 7870
Maple Leaf Awning & Canvas Co, 25714
Maple Leaf Bakery, 7871
Maple Leaf Cheesemakers, 7872, 46306
Maple Leaf Consumer Foods, 7873
Maple Leaf Farms, 7874
Maple Leaf Foods, 7875
Maple Leaf Foods International, 7876, 46307
Maple Leaf Meats, 7877
Maple Leaf Pork, 7878, 46308
Maple Products, 7879, 46309
Maple Ridge Farms, 7880
Maple Valley Cooperative, 7881, 57879
Maple's Organics, 7882
Maplebrook Farm, 7883
Maplegrove Foods, 7884
Maplehill Creamery, 7885
Maplehurst Bakeries LLC, 7886, 46310
Maplehurst Farms, 7887
Mapleland Farm, 7888
MAPS Software, 25555
Mar Meat Company, 57880
Mar-Boro Printing & Advertising Specialties, 25715
Mar-Con Wire Belt, 25716, 46311
Mar-Jac Poultry Inc., 7889, 46312
Mar-Key Foods, 7890
Mar-Khem Industries, 25717, 46313
Mar-Len Supply Inc, 25718, 46314
Maramor Chocolates, 7891, 46315
Marantha Natural Foods, 7892, 46316
Marathon Cheese, 7893
Marathon Cheese Corp, 7894
Marathon Enterprises Inc, 7895, 46317
Marathon Equipment Co, 25719, 46318
Marathon Marketing, 40743
Marathon Packing Corp, 7896
Marathon Products Inc, 25720
Marazzi USA, 25721
Marble Manor, 25722
Marbran USA, 40744
Marburg Industries, 25723, 46319
Marburger Farm Dairy, 7897
Marc Refrigeration Mfg Inc, 25724, 46320

Marcal Paper Mills, 25725
Marcel et Henri Charcuterie Francaise, 7898
Marcel S. Garrigues Company, 25726
Marchant Schmidt Inc, 25727, 46321
Marchesini Packaging Machinery, 25728
Marchetti Co, 40745
Marcho Farms Inc, 7899
Marci Enterprises, 57881
Marco Products, 25729
Marconi Italian Specialty Foods, 7900, 46322
Marcus Carton Company, 25730
Marcus Food Co, 46323, 57882
Marcus Specialty Foods, 57883
Mardale Specialty Foods, 7901
Marden Edwards, 25731
Mardi Gras, 7902
Marek Equipment Trading, 57884
Marel Food Systems, Inc., 25732, 46324
Marel Stork Poultry Processing, 25733, 25734, 46325, 46326
Marel Townsend, 25735
Marel USA, 25736
Maren Engineering Corp, 25737, 46327
Marfred Industries, 25738
Margarita Man, 7903, 57885
Margate Wine & Spirit Co, 46328, 57886
Margia Floors, 25739
Marglo Products Corporation, 46329
Mari's Candy, 7904
Mari's New York, 7905
Maria & Son, 7907
Maria and Ricardo's, 7908
Maria's Premium, 7909
Mariani Nut Co, 7910, 46330
Mariani Packing Co., 7911
Marias Packing Company, 57888
Marich Confectionery, 7912
Marie Brizard Wines & Spirits, 7913, 46331
Marie Callender's, 7914
Marie Callender's Gourmet Products/Goldrush Products, 7915
Marie F, 7916, 46332
Marie's Quality Foods, 7917
MarieBelle, 7918
Maries Candies, 7919
Marietta Cellars, 7920
MariGold Foods, 7906, 57887
Marika's Kitchen, 7921
Marimar Torres Estates, 7922
Marin Brewing Co, 7923
Marin Cleaning Systems, 25740
Marin Food Specialties, 7924, 46333
Marin French Cheese Co, 7925
Marin Hydroponics, 57889
Marin Kombucha, 7926
Marina Foods, 7927, 46334
Marine MacHines, 7928
Marineland Commercial Aquariums, 25741, 46335
Mariner Neptune Fish & Seafood Company, 7929, 57890
Mariner Seafood LLC, 7930
Marino Marketing Group, 40746
Mario Camancho Foods, 7931, 46336, 46337
Mario's Gelati, 7932, 46338
Marion Body Works Inc, 25742
Marion Pallet Company, 25743
Marion Paper Box Co, 25744, 46339
Marion's Smart Delights, 7933
Marion-Kay Spice Co, 7934
Maritime International, 53128
Maritime Pacific Brewing Co, 7935
Marjie's Plantain Foods, Inc., 7936
Marjo & Associates, 40747
Marjon Specialty Foods Inc, 7937
Mark Container Corporation, 25745, 46340
Mark NYS, 46341
Mark Pack Inc, 57891
Mark Products Company, 25746, 46342

1409

All Companies Index

Mark Slade ManufacturingCompany, 25747
Mark West Wines, 7938
Mark's International Seafood Brokers, 40748, 46343, 57892
Mark-It Rubber Stamp & Label Company, 25748
Mark-Pack Inc, 57893
Market Fisheries, 7939, 57894
Market Foods International, 57895
Market Forge Industries Inc, 25750, 46344
Market Grocery Co, 57896
Market Pro International, 40749
Market Sales Company, 25751
Market Sign Systems, 25752
Market Smart, 40750
Market Square Food Co., 7940
Market West Company, 40751
MarkeTeam, 25749
Marketing & Technology Group, 25753, 25754
Marketing Agents South, 40752
Marketing Concepts, 25755
Marketing Development Associates, 40753
Marketing Management Inc, 25756, 40754
Markham Vineyards, 7941, 46345
Marking Devices Inc, 25757, 46346
Marking Methods Inc, 25758, 46347
Markko Vineyard, 7942
Marklite Line, 25759
Marko By Carlisle, 46348
Marko Inc, 25760, 25761, 46349, 57897
Marks Meat, 7943
Markson Lab Sales, 46350, 57898
Markuse Corporation, 57899
Markwell Manufacturing Company, 25762, 46351
Marky's Caviar, 46352, 57900
Marland Clutch Products, 25763
Marle Company, 57901
Marlen, 25764, 46353
Marlen International, 25765, 25766, 25767, 46354
Marlen Research, 25768
Marlen Research Corporation, 25769, 25770
Marley Engineered Products LLC, 25771
Marley Orchards Corporation, 7944
Marlin Steel Wire Products, 25772
Marlite, 25773, 46355
Marlo Manufacturing, 25774, 46356
Marlow Candy & Nut Co, 7945, 57902
Marlow Watson Inc, 25775
Marlow Wine Cellars, 7946
Marlyn Nutraceuticals, 7947, 46357
Marmelstein Associates, 40755
Marnap Industries, 7948, 46358
Maro Paper Products Company, 25776
Marpac Industries, 25777
Marq Packaging Systems Inc, 25778, 25779
Marquez Brothers International, 7949
Marquip Ward United, 25780, 25781, 46359
Marquis, 7950
Marquis Products, 25782
Marriott Distribution Service, 57903
Marriott Walker Corporation, 25783, 46360
Marron Foods, 25784
Marrone's Inc, 57904
Marroquin Organic Intl., 7951, 46361, 57905
Mars Air Products, 25785, 46362
Mars Inc., 7952, 46363
Mars Supermarkets, 57906
Mars Systems, 25786
Marsa Specialty Products, 7953
Marsan Foods, 7954, 46364
Marsch Pacific Cork & Foil, 25787
Marsh Company, 25788, 46365

Marshakk Smoked Fish Company, 25789, 57907
Marshall Air Systems Inc, 25790, 46366
Marshall Associates, 40756
Marshall Boxes Inc, 25791
Marshall Cold Storage, 53129
Marshall Durbin Companies, 7955
Marshall Ingredients, 7956, 25792
Marshall Instruments Inc, 25793
Marshall Paper Products, 25794
Marshall Plastic Film Inc, 25795, 46367
Marshall Sales Co, 40757, 46368
Marshall's Biscuit Company, 7957
Marshallville Packing Co, 7958
Marshfield Food Safety, 25796
Marson Food Inc, 46369
Marston Manufacturing, 25797
Mart CART-Smt, 25798, 25799, 46370, 46371
Martco Engravers, 25800
Martech Research, 25801
Marten Transport LTD, 51916
Martens Fresh, 7959
Martha Olson's Great Foo, 7960
Martha's Garden, 7961
Martin & Weyrich Winery, 7962
Martin Bauer Group, 7963
Martin Bros Distributing Co, 57908
Martin Brothers Inc, 25802
Martin Brothers Seafood Co, 7964
Martin Brothers Wholesale, 57909
Martin Cab Div, 25803, 46372
Martin Coffee Co, 7965
Martin Control Systems Inc, 25804
Martin Electric Plants, 25805
Martin Engineering, 25806, 25807, 46373
Martin Farms, 7966
Martin Food Service Company, 57910
Martin Laboratories, 25808, 46374
Martin Preferred Foods, 40758, 57911
Martin Produce Co, 57912
Martin Ray Winery, 7967
Martin Rosols, 7968
Martin Seafood Company, 7969, 57913
Martin Sprocket & Gear Inc, 25809
Martin Vibration Systems, 25810
Martin Warehousing & Distribution, 51917, 53130
Martin's Potato Chips, 7970, 57914
Martin-Brower Co US, 57915
Martin/Baron, 25811, 46375
Martingale Paper Company, 25812
Martini SRL, 25813
Martino's Bakery, 7971
Martins Famous Pastry Shoppe, 7972
Marty Scanlon Brokerage Co, 40759
Marubeni America Corp., 7973, 40760, 46376, 57916
Maruchan Inc, 7974, 46377
Marukai Market, 7975, 46378
Marukan Vinegar USA Inc., 7976
Marukome USA Inc., 7977, 46379
Marv Holland Industries, 25814
Marva Maid Dairy, 7978, 46380
Marvell Packaging Company, 25815
Marwood Sales, Inc, 7979, 57917
Marx Brothers Inc, 7980
Marx Imports, 46381
Marxana Brand Foods, 57918
Mary Ann's Baking Co Inc, 7981
Mary of Puddin Hill, 7982
Mary's Gone Crackers, 7983
Marygrove Awnings-Toledo, 25816
Maryland & Virginia Milk Producers Cooperative, 7985
Maryland China, 46383, 57919
Maryland Packaging Corporation, 25817, 46384
Maryland Plastics Inc, 25818
Maryland Seafood Marketing, 46385
Maryland Wholesale Produce Market, 57920
Maryland Wire Belts, 25819, 46386
MarySue.com, 7984, 46382

Marzetti, 7986
Marzetti Foodservice, 7987
Marzipan Specialties Inc, 7988
Masa Linen, 46387
Masala Chai Company, 7989, 46388
Maschari Brothers WHLS Fruits, 57921
Maselli Measurements Inc, 25820, 25821, 46389, 46390
Masienda, 7990
Mason Brothers Co, 57922
Mason Candlelight Company, 25822, 46391
Mason City Cold Storage, 53131
Mason City Tent & Awning Co, 25823
Mason County Fruit Packers Cooperative, 7991
Mason Dixie Biscuit Co., 7992
Mason Jar Cookie Company, 7993
Mason Transparent Package Company, 25824, 46392
Mason Ways Indestructible, 25825
Massachusetts Central Railroad Corporation, 51918, 53132
Massachusetts Container Corporation, 25826
Massel USA, 7994
Masser's Produce, 57923
Massey-Fair Industrial Southwest, 40761
Massillon Container Co, 25827
Massimo Zanetti Beverage USA, 7995, 46393
Mastantuono Winery, 7996
Master Air, 25828, 46394
Master Brew, 7997
Master Chemical Products, 57924
Master Containers, 25829
Master Disposers, 25830
Master Magnetics, 25831
Master Marketing South, 40762
Master Marketing Sunlow, Inc., 40763
Master Mix, 7998, 46395
Master Package Corporation, 25832
Master Paper Box Co, 25833
Master Printers, 25834
Master Sales & Marketing, 40764
Master Signs-Div Of Masterco, 25835
Master Tape & Label Printers, 25836
Master-Bilt, 25837, 46396
Masterbuilt Manufacturing Inc, 25838
Mastercraft, 25839
Mastercraft Industries Inc, 25840, 46397
Mastercraft International, 25841, 46398
Mastercraft Manufacturing Co, 25842, 46399
Mastermark, 25843
Masternet, Ltd, 25844
Masterpiece Crystal, 25845
Masters Gallery Foods Inc, 7999
Masterson Co Inc, 8000
Mastex Industries, 25846, 46400
Mastio & Co, 25847
Mat Logo Company, 46401, 57925
Matador Processors, 8001, 46402
Matangos Candies, 8002
Matanuska Maid Dairy, 57926
Matanzas Creek Winery, 8003
Match Maker, 51919
MatchaBar, 8004
Matchmaker Transportation Services, 51920
Matco United, 57927
Matcon Americas, 25848
Mateer Burt, 25849, 46403
Material Control, 25850, 57928
Material Handling Products, 57929
Material Handling Resources, 57930
Material Handling Services, 57931
Material Handling Specialties Company, 57932
Material Handling Technology, Inc, 25851
Material Storage Systems, 25852, 25853, 46404, 46405
Material Systems Engineering, 25854
Materials Handling Enterprises, 57933

Materials Handling Equipment Company, 25855
Materials Handling Systems, 25856
Materials Storage Systems, 25857
Materials Transportation Co, 25858, 46406
Materne North America, 8005
Matfer Inc, 25859, 46407, 46408
Mathason Industries, 25860
Mathews Associates, 40765
Mathews Conveyor, 25861
Mathews Packing, 8006, 46409, 57934
MATI Energy, 7697
Matik North America, 25862
Matilija Water Company, 8007, 57935
Matiss, 25863, 46410
Matot - Commercial GradeLift Solutions, 25864, 46411
Matouk International USA Inc, 8008
Matrix Engineering, 25865, 46412
Matrix Group Inc., 25866, 46766
Matrix Health Products, 8009, 46413
Matrix Packaging Machinery, 25867, 46414
Matson Fruit Co, 8010, 46415
Matson LLC, 25868, 46416
Matson Vineyards, 8011
Matt's Cookies, 8012
Mattec Corp, 25869
Matthew's Bakery, 8013
Matthews 1812 House, 8014
Matthews Marking Systems Div, 25870, 46417
Matthiesen Equipment, 25871, 46418, 57936
Matthiesen's Deer & Custom, 8015
Mattingly Foods, 57937
Mattingly Foods Of Louisville, 8016
Matworks Co LLC, 46419
Maui Bagel, 8017
Maui Coffee Roasters Wholesale, 8018
Maui Gold Pineapple Company, 8019, 46420
Maui Potato Chip Factory, 8020
Maui Soda & Ice Works, 8021
Maui Wine, 8022
Maui Wowi Fresh Hawaiin Blends, 25872
Maull-Baker Box Company, 25873, 46421
Maurer North America, 25874, 46422
Maurice Carrie Winery, 8023
Maurice French Pastries, 8024
Mauser Packaging Solutions, 25875, 51921, 53133
Mauser, Schindler & Wagner, 25876
MAV Sales Co, 40725
Maverick Brands, LLC, 8025
Maverick Enterprises Inc, 25877
Maves International Software Corp., 25878
Mavuno Harvest, 8026
Max Landau & Company, 46423
Max Packaging, 25879
Max Pratt Company, 40767
Maxco Supply, 25880
Maxfield Candy, 8027, 46424
Maxi-Vac Inc., 25881, 46425
Maxim's Import Corporation, 8028, 46426, 57938
Maximicer, 25882, 46427
Maximus Systems, 25883
Maxin Marketing Corporation, 8029, 57939
Maxine's Heavenly, 8030
Maxitrol Company, 25884
Maxwell House & Post, 8031, 25885, 57940
Maxwell's Gourmet Food, 8032
May Flower, 46428, 57941
May-Wes Manufacturing Inc, 25886
Maya Kaimal, 8033
Maya Overseas Food Inc, 25887
Mayacamas Fine Foods, 8034, 46429
Mayacamas Vineyards & Winery, 8035, 46430

1410

All Companies Index

Mayakaimal Fine Indian Foods, 8036
Mayberry RFD, 51922
Maybury Material Handling, 57942
Mayco Inc, 25888
Mayekawa USA, Inc., 25889, 46431
Mayer Bros, 8037
Mayer Myers Paper Company, 57943
Mayer's Cider Mill, 8038
Mayer-Bass Fromm, 57944
Mayfair Provision Company, 57945
Mayfield Dairy Farms LLC, 8039
Mayfield Farms and Nursery, 8040
Mayfield Paper Co, 57946, 57947
Maynard-Fixturcraft, 57948
Mayorga Coffee, 8041
Maypak Inc, 25890
Mayr Corporation, 25891
Mayrand Limitee, 57949
Mayrsohn International Inc, 46432
Mays Chemical Co, 25892
Maysville Milling Company, 8042
Maytag Corporation, 25893, 46433
Maytag Dairy Farms Inc, 8043
Mayway Corp, 8044
Maywood Furniture Corp, 25894
Maywood International Sales, 8045, 46434, 57950
Mayworth Showcase Works Inc, 25895
Mazelle's Cheesecakes Concoctions Creations, 8046, 57951
Mazo-Lerch Company, 57952
Mazzetta Company, 8047, 46435
Mazzocco Vineyards, 8048
Mba Suppliers Inc., 25896, 46436
MBC Food Machinery Corp, 25556, 46199
MBH International Corporation, 46200
MBI Heating & Air Conditioning, 46201
MBX Logistics, LLC, 51905
MBX Packaging Specialists, 25557
Mc Afee Packing Co, 57953
Mc Call Co, 25897, 57954
Mc Court Label Co, 25898
Mc Crary & Assoc, 40768
MC Creation, 25558
Mc Glaughlin Oil Co, 8049
Mc Lane Foodservice, 57955
Mc Lean Packaging, 46899
Mc Lure's Honey & Maple Prod, 8050
Mc Namara Assoc Inc, 40769
Mc Steven's Coca Factory Store, 8051, 46437
McAnally Enterprises, 8052, 46438
McArdle, 40770
McArthur Dairy LLC, 8053
Mcbrady Engineering Co, 25920, 46454
McBrady Engineering Inc, 25900
Mcbride Sign Co, 25921
McCabe's Quality Foods, 46439, 57956
Mccadam Cheese Co, inc, 8085, 57969
McCain Foods Ltd., 8054
McCain Foods USA Inc., 8055
McCain Produce Inc., 8056, 25901
Mccall Farms, 8086
McCann's Piggyback Consolidation, 51923
McCarter Corporation, 25902, 46440
Mccartney Produce Co, 8087
McCarty Brokerage Company, 40771
Mcclancy Seasonings Co, 8088, 25922
McClement Sales Company, 40772
McCleskey Mills, 8057, 46441
McClier, 25903
McClure's Pickles LLC, 8058
Mccomas Sales Co Inc, 57970
McConnell's Fine Ice Cream, 8059, 46442
McConnell's Fine Ice Creams, 8060
McCormack Manufacturing Company, 25904, 46443
McCormick & Company, 8061, 46444
McCormick Brokerage Company, 40773
McCormick Distilling Co, 8062
McCormick Enterprises, 25905
Mccourt Manufacturing Co, 46455

McCoy Matt Frontier International, 8063
McCoy's Products, 46445, 57957
Mccracken Motor Freight, 51925, 53135
McCrea's Candies, 8064
Mccreas Candies, 8089
Mccrone Microscopes & Acces, 25923, 57971
Mccullagh Coffee Roasters, 8090, 46456, 57972
Mccullough Industries Inc, 25924, 46457
Mccutcheon Apple Products, 8091
MCD Technologies, 25559, 46202
McDaniel Fruit, 8065, 46446
Mcdonald Wholesale Co, 57973
McDonnell, 57958
McDowell Industries, 25906, 46447
McDowell Supply Company, 57959
McDowell Valley Vineyards & Cellars, 8066
McDuffies Bakery, 8067
McEvoy Ranch, 8068
Mcfadden Farm, 8092, 46458
McFarland Foods, 8069
Mcfarling Foods Inc, 8093, 57974
McGlaughlin Oil Co, 25907
McGovern & Whitten, 40774
McGrath Fisheries, 57960
Mcgraths Seafood, 8094, 57975
McGraw Box Company, 25908
McGraw Hill/London House, 25909
McGraw Seafood, 8070
Mcgregor Vineyard Winery, 8095
Mcguckin & Pyle Inc, 25925
McGunn Safe Company, 25910, 46448
McHenry Vineyard, 8071
McIlhenny Company, 8072
Mcintosh Box & Pallet Co, 25926
McIntosh's Ohio Valley Wines, 8073
Mcintyre Metals Inc, 25927, 46459
McJak Candy Company LLC, 8074
McKaskle Family Farm, 8075
McKearnan Packaging, 25911, 57961
McKee Foods Corp., 8076, 8077, 46449
McKeesport Candy Company, 57962
McKenna Bros., 46450
McKenna Logistic Centres, 53134
Mckenzie Country Classic's, 8096, 57976
Mckey Perforating Co Inc, 25928, 46460
McKinlay Vineyards, 8078
Mckinley Equipment Corp, 57977
McKnight Milling Company, 8079
McLane Co Inc, 57963
McLane Foodservice Inc, 57964
McLane Grocery, 57965
McLane's Meats, 8080
Mclaughlin Gormley King Co, 25929, 46461
Mclaughlin Paper Co Inc, 25930
Mclaughlin Seafood, 8097, 57978
McLean Cargo Specialists, 51924
Mclemores Abattoir Inc, 8098
MCM Fixture Co, 25560
Mcmahon's Farm, 25931
McMillin Manufacturing Corporation, 25912
MCNAB Inc, 25561
Mcnair & Co Inc, 57979
Mcnairn Packaging, 25932
McNasby's Seafood Market, 8081, 57966
McNeil Food Machinery, 25913
McNeil Nutritionals, 8082, 25914, 46451
McNeil Specialty Products Company, 8083, 25915, 46452
Mcneill Signs Inc, 25933
Mcneilly Wood Products Inc, 25934
McNew & Associates, William B., 25916
McNichols Company, 25917
McNichols Conveyor Company, 25918, 46453
McQueen Sign & Lighting, 25919
MCR Technologies Group Inc, 25562
Mcredmond Brothers, 8099
Mcroyal Industries Inc, 25935, 46462
MCS Merchants Cold Storage, 53117
McShane Enterprises, 57967

McSteven's, 8084, 57968
MCT Terminal & Transport Inc., 51906, 53118
Mctavish Shortbread, 8100
MDE Corp, 25563
MDH Packaging Corporation, 25564
MDI Worldwide, 25565
MDR International, 25566
MDS Nordion, 25567, 46203
MDS-Vet Inc, 25568, 46204
MDT, 25569
Me & the Bees Lemonade, 8101
Me At Corral, 8102
Mead & Hunt Inc, 25937
Mead Johnson Nutrition, 8103
Meaders Kitchen Equipment, 57981
Meador Warehousing-Dstrbtn, 53136
Meadow Brook Dairy Co, 8104, 57982
Meadow Farm Foods, 57983
Meadow Gold, 8105
Meadowbrook Farm, 8106
Meadowbrook Farms, 57984
Meadowbrook Meat Company, 8107, 46464
Meadows Brokerage Company, 40775
Meadows Country Products, 8108
Meadows Mills Inc, 25938, 46465
Meadowvale Inc, 8109
Meadwestvaco Corp, 25939, 46466
Meals-In-A-Minute, 8110
Measured Sales & Marketing, 40776
Measurement Systems Intl, 25940
Measurex/S&L Plastics, 25941, 46467
Meat & Fish Fellas, 8111, 57985
Meat & Livestock Australia, 25942, 46468
Meat & Supply Co, 8112
Meat Center, 8113
Meat Marketing & Technology, 25943
Meat Quality, 25944
Meat-O-Mat Corp, 8114
Meatco Sales Ltd., 8115
Meatcrafters, 8116, 57986
Meating Place, 8117
Meatland Packers, 8118
Meatlonn, 25945
Meats Plus Inc, 57987
Mecca Coffee Company, 57988
Mecco Marking & Traceability, 25946, 46469
Mechtronics International, 25947
Mechtronics Paper Corp, 25948
Mectra USA, 25949
Medallion International Inc, 8119, 46470
Medallion Laboratories, 25950, 25951
Medeiros Farms, 8120
Medical Packaging Corporation, 25952
Medina & Medina, 46471, 57989
Medina Cold Storage Co Inc, 53137
Meditalia, 8121
Mediterranean Delight, 46472
Mediterranean Gourmet, 46473
Mediterranean Gyro Products, 8122, 57990
Mediterranean Pita Bakery, 8123
Mediterranean Snack Food Co, 8124, 46474
Medlee Foods, 8125
Medley Material Handling Inc, 57991
Medley Restaurant Equipment & Supply Company, 57992
Mednik Wiping Materials Co, 25953
Medterra CBD, 8126
Meduri Farms, 8127, 46475
Medway Creamery Company, 57993
Mee Industries, 25954
Meech Static Eliminators USA, 25955
Meelunie America, 8128
MeGa Industries, 25936, 46463, 57980
Mega Pro Intl, 8129, 46476
MegaFood, 8130, 46477
Megatoys Inc, 8131
Megpies, 8132
Meguiar's Inc, 25956, 46478
Mehaffies Pies, 8133

Meheen Manufacturing Inc, 25957
Mehu-Liisa Products, 46479
Mei Shun Tofu Products Company, 8134, 46480
Meier's Wine Cellars Inc, 8135, 8136
Meijer Inc, 8137
Meil Electric Fixture Manufacturing Company, 25958
Meilahn Manufacturing Co, 25959
Meister Cheese Company, 8138
Mel-O-Cream Donuts Intl, 8139, 8140
Melba Food Specialties, 57994
Melba's Old School Po Boys, 8141
Melcher Manufacturing Co, 25960, 46481
Melchers Flavors of America, 8142
Melco Steel Inc, 25961, 46482
Mele-Koi Farms, 8143, 46483
Meleddy Cherry Plant, 8144
Meli's Monster Cookies, 8145
Melissa's, 53138
Melitta Canada, 25962
Melitta USA Inc, 8146, 25963, 46484
Mell & Co, 25964
Mellace Family Brands, 8147
Mello Buttercup Ice Cream Company, 57995
Mello Smello LLC, 25965, 46485
Mellos North End Mfr, 8148, 46486
Melmart Distributors, 57996
Melmat Inc, 25966
Melrose Displays, 25967
Melsur Corporation, 25968
Melton Hot Melt Applications, 25969
Meltric Corporation, 25970
Meluka Honey, 8149, 46487
Melville Candy Corp, 8150
Melville Plastics, 25971
Melvin L. Jones Transportation Broker, 51926
Melvina Can Machinery Company, 25972, 46488
Membrane Process & Controls, 25973
Membrane System Specialist Inc, 25974, 46489
Mememe Inc, 8151
Memor/Memtec America Corporation, 25975
Memphis Delta Tent & Awning, 25976
Memphis Meats, 8152
Menasha Corp, 25977
Menasha Packaging Co LLC, 25978
Mendez & Company, 57997
Mendocino Brewing Co Inc, 8153
Mendocino Mustard, 8154
Menehune Mac, 8155
Menemsha Fish Market, 8156
Menghini Winery, 8157
Mengibar Automation, 25979
Menke Marking Devices, 25980, 46490
Menneekes Electrical Products, 25981
Mennel Milling Company, 8158, 25982
Menu Graphics, 25983
Menu Maker Foods Inc, 57998
Menu Men, 25984
Menu Planners, 40777
Menu Promotions, 25985
Menu Solution Inc, 25986, 46491
Menulink, 25988
MenuMark Systems, 25987, 46492
MEPSCO, 25570
Mepsco, 25989, 46493
Meramec Vineyards, 8159
Merb's Candies, 8160
Mercado Latino, 8161, 46494, 57999
Mercantile Refrigerated Warehouses, 53139
Mercantum Corp, 40778
Mercer Foods, 8162
Mercer Processing, 8163
Mercer's Dairy, 8164
Merchandise Multi-Temp Warehouse, 53140
Merchandise Warehouse, 51927, 53141

1411

All Companies Index

Merchandising Frontiers Inc, 25990, 46495
Merchandising Inventives, 25991, 46496
Merchandising Resources, 46497
Merchandising Systems Manufacturing, 25992, 46498
Merchants Distribution Svc, 51928, 53142
Merchants Distributors Inc, 58000
Merchants Export Inc, 46499, 53143
Merchants Foodservice, 58001
Merchants Grocery Co Inc, 58002
Merchants Publishing Company, 25993, 46500
Merchants Transfer Company, 53144
Merci Spring Water, 8165, 46501
Merco/Savory, 25994, 46502
Merco/Savory Equipment, 46503
Mercon Coffee Group.ÿ, 8166
Mercury Equipment Company, 25995, 46504
Mercury Floor Machines Inc, 25996
Mercury Plastic Bag Company, 25997, 46505
Meredith & Meredith, 8167
Meredyth Vineyard, 8168
Meriden Box Company, 25998
Meridian Beverage Company, 8169
Meridian Foods New Inc, 8170
Meridian Nut Growers, 46506
Meridian Products, 40779
Meridian Supply Rstrnt Depot, 58003
Meridian Trading Co, 40780, 46507, 58004
Meridian Trading Co., 8171
Meridian Vineyards, 8172
Merieux Nutrisciences, 25999
Merisant, 8173
Merit Sales Corporation, 40781
Meritech, 26000, 46508
Meritex Logistics, 53145
Meriwether Industries, 26001
Merix Chemical Company, 26002, 46509
Merkley & Sons Packing Co Inc, 8174
Merlin Candies, 8175, 46510
Merlin Development Inc, 26003
Merlin Process Equipment, 26004, 46511
Merlin-Montgomery Imports, 46512
Merlino Foods, 58005
Merlino Italian Baking Company, 8176
Merlinos, 8177
Mermaid Seafoods, 46513, 58006
Mermaid Spice Corporation, 8178, 46514
Merric, 26005
MERRICK Industries Inc, 25571, 46205
Merrill Distributing Inc, 26006, 58007
Merrill Meat Co, 8179
Merrill Seafood Center, 8180
Merrill's Blueberry Farms, 8181, 46515
Merrillville Awning Co, 26007
Merrimack Valley Apiaries, 8182
Merritt Estate Winery Inc, 8183, 46516
Merritt Handling Engineering, 58008
Merritt Pecan Co, 8184, 46517
Merryvale Vineyards, 8185
Merryweather Foam Inc, 26008, 26009
Merton Restaurant Equipment Company, 58009
Mertz L. Carlton Company, 26010
Mertz Sausage Co, 8186
Mesa Bearing, 58010
Mesa Cold Storage, 51929, 53146, 53147, 58011
Mesa Laboratories Inc, 26011
Mesa Salsa, 8187
Mesler Group, 26012
Mesquite Organic Beef LLC, 8188
Messermeister, 46518, 58012
Messina Brothers Manufacturing Company, 26013, 46519, 58013
Messina Hof Winery & Resort, 8189, 58014
Met-Pro Corp, 26014, 26015
MetaBall, 8190
Metabolic Nutrition, 8191, 46520

Metafoods LLC, 8192, 46521
Metagenics, Inc., 8193
Metal, 26016
Metal Container Corporation, 26017
Metal Equipment Company, 26018, 46522
Metal Kitchen Fabricators Inc, 26019
Metal Master Sales Corp, 26020, 46523
Metal Masters Northwest, 26021
Metalcretye Manufacturing Company, 26022
Metaline Products Co Inc, 26023, 46524
Metalloid Corp, 26024, 46525
Metarom Corporation, 8194
Metcalf & Eddy, 26025
Metcraft, 26026
Metko Inc, 26027
Metl-Span I Ltd, 26028
Metlar Us, 26029, 46526
Meto, 26030
Metompkin Bay Oyster Company, 58015
Metompkin Bay Oyster Company, Inc, 8195
Metro Corporation, 26031, 46527
Metro Food Service Products, 58016
Metro Freezer & Storage, 53148
Metro Mint, 8196
Metro Park Warehouses Inc, 51930, 53149
Metro Signs, 26032
Metro Touch, 58017
Metro, Inc., 58018
Metro-Richelieu, 58019
Metrohm USA, 8197
Metron Instruments, Inc, 26033
Metroplex Corporation, 26034
Metroplex Harriman Corporation, 58020
Metropolitan Bakery, 8198
Metropolitan Baking Co, 8199
Metropolitan Beer & Soda Dist, 58021
Metropolitan Flag & Banner Co, 26035
Metropolitan Gourmet, 8200
Metropolitan Lighting Fixture Company, 46528
Metropolitan Sausage Manufacturing Company, 8201
Metropolitan Tea Company, 8202
Metropolitan Trucking Inc, 51931, 53150
Metrovock Snacks, 26036
Metspeed Labels, 26037
Metsys Engineering, 26038
Mettler-Toledo Hi-Speed, 26039
Mettler-Toledo Process Analytics, Inc, 26040, 46529
Mettler-Toledo Safeline Inc, 26041, 46530
Mettler-Toledo, LLC, 26042, 46531
Metz Premiums, 26043, 46532
Metzer Farms, 8203
Metzgar Conveyors, 26044, 46533
Metzger Popcorn Co, 8204, 46534
Metzger Specialty Brands, 8205
Mex America Foods LLC, 8206
Mex-Char, 26045
Mexi-Frost Specialties Company, 8207, 46535
Mexican Accent, 8208, 46536
Mexican Corn Products, 8209
Meximex Texas Corporation, 46537
Mexspice, 46538, 58022
Meyenberg Goat Milk, 8210, 46539
Meyer & Garroutte Systems, 26046
Meyer Brothers Dairy, 8211
Meyer Industries, 26047
Meyer Label Company, 26048, 46540
Meyer Machine & Garroutte Products, 26049, 46541
Meyer Packaging, 26050
Meyer's Bakeries, 8212
Meyers Printing Co, 26051
Meyhen International, 26052
Meyn America LLC, 26053
Mezza, 8213, 26054
MFI Food Canada, 7698, 46206
MFS/York/Stormor, 46207, 57817

MG Fisheries, 7699
MGF.com, 25572
MGH Wholesale Grocery, 57818
MGM Instruments, 25573
MGP Ingredients Inc, 7700, 25574, 46208
MGS Machine Corp, 25575, 25576
Mi Mama's Tortilla Factory Inc, 8214
Mi Ranchito Foods, 8215
Mi Rancho, 8216
MI-AL. Corp, 7701
MIA Food Distributing, 57819
Mia Products, 8217
Mia Rose Products, 26055, 46542
Miami Awning, 26056
Miami Beef Co, 8218, 46543
Miami Coffee Imports, 46544
Miami Crab Corporation, 8219
Miami Depot Inc, 46545, 58023
Miami Foods & Products, 46546
Miami Industrial Trucks, 58024, 58025
Miami Metal, 26057, 46547
Miami Plastics & Supply Corporation, 58026
Miami Purveyors Inc, 8220, 46548
Miami Systems Corporation, 26058
Miami Wholesale Grocery Company, 58027
MIC Foods, 7702, 46209
Mic-Ellen Associates, 26059
Micalizzi Italian Ice, 8221
Miceli Dairy Products Co, 8222
Micelli Chocolate Mold Company, 26060, 46549
Michael Angelo's Inc, 8223
Michael Blackman & Assoc, 26061
Michael David Winery, 8224
Michael Distributor Inc, 26062, 58028
Michael Foods, Inc., 8225, 46550
Michael G. Brown & Associates, 26063
Michael G. Brown Associates, 58029
Michael Granese & Company, 8226
Michael Leson Dinnerware, 26064, 46551
Michael Mootz Candies, 8227
Michael R Fish & Co, 40782
Michael Raymond Desserts Inc, 40783, 58030
Michael's Cookies, 8228, 46552, 58031
Michael's Finer Meats/Seafoods, 8229, 58032
Michael's Gourmet Coffee, 8230
Michael's Naturopathic Prgms, 8231
Michael's Provision Co, 8232
Michaelene's Gourmet Granola, 8233
Michaelo Espresso, 26065, 46553, 58033
Michel de France, 8234
Michel Distribution Service, 53151
Michel et Augustin, 8235
Michel's Bakery, 8236
Michel's Magnifique, 8237
Michel-Schlumberger Wine Est, 8238
Michele Foods, 8239
Michele's Bakery, 58034
Michele's Chocolate Truffles, 8240
Michele's Family Bakery, 8241
Michelle Chocolatiers, 8242, 46554
Michelle's Bakery, 58035
Michelle's RawFoodz, 8243, 8244
Michelman Inc, 26066
Michelson Laboratories Inc, 26067
Michiana Box & Crate, 26068, 46555
Michiana Corrugate Products, 26069
Michigan Agricultural Commdty, 46556, 58036
Michigan Agricultural Commodities Inc, 46557, 58037
Michigan Agricultural Cooperative Marketing Association, 26070
Michigan Agriculture Commodities, 46558, 46559, 46560, 46561, 46562, 46563, 46564, 58038, 58039, 58040, 58041, 58042, 58043, 58044
Michigan Apple Res Committee, 26071
Michigan Box Co, 26072, 46565

Michigan Brush Mfg Co, 26073, 46566
Michigan Carbonic Of Saginaw, 58045
Michigan Celery Cooperative, 8245
Michigan Cold Storage Facilities, 53152
Michigan Dairy LLC, 8246
Michigan Desserts, 8247, 26074, 46567
Michigan Farm Cheese Dairy, 8248
Michigan Food Equipment, 26075
Michigan Freeze Pack, 8249, 46568
Michigan Industrial Belting, 26076, 58046
Michigan Industrial Equipment Company, 58047
Michigan Maple Block Co, 26077, 46569
Michigan Milk Producers Assn, 8250
Michigan Orchard Supply Company, 58048
Michigan Pallet Inc, 26078
Michigan Sugar Company, 8251, 58049
Mickelson & Associates, 40784
Micor Co Inc, 26079
Micosa Inc, 40785, 46570
Micro Affiliates, 26080
Micro Filtration Systems, 26081
Micro Matic, 26082, 46571
Micro Qwik, 26083
Micro Solutions Ent Tech & Dev, 26084
Micro Wire Products Inc, 26085, 46572
Micro-Blend, 26086
Micro-Brush Pro Soap, 26087, 46573
Micro-Chem Laboratory, 26088
Micro-Strain, 26089, 46574
MicroAnalytics, 26090
Microbac Laboratories, 26093, 26094
Microbac Laboratories Inc, 26095
Microbac-Wilson Devision, 26096
Microbest Inc, 26097, 46577
Microbiologics Inc, 26098
Microbiology International, 26099
Microcheck Solutions, 26100
Microcide Inc, 46578
Microcool, 26101
Microdry, 26102, 46579
Microflex Corp, 26103
MicroFlo Company, 26091
Microfluidics International, 26104, 46580
Micromeritics, 26105, 46581
Micron Automation, 26106
Micron Separations, 26107
Microplas Industries, 26108, 46582
Micropoint, 26109, 46583
Micropub Systems International, 26110, 46584
Micropure Filtration Inc, 26111, 46585
MICROS Retail Systems Inc, 57820
Microscan Systems Inc, 26112
MicroSoy Corporation, 8252, 46575
Microtechnologies, 26113, 46586
Microthermics, 26114
MicroThermics, Inc., 26092, 46576
Microtouch Systems Inc, 26115
Microtron Abrasives, 26116
Microwave Research Center, 26117
Microworks Pos Solutions Inc, 26118
Mid America Chemical, 58050
Mid America Food Sales, 58051
Mid Atlantic Packaging Co, 26119, 58052
Mid Atlantic Vegetable Shortening Company, 8253
Mid Cities Paper Box Company, 26120
Mid Columbia Warehouse Inc, 53153
Mid Continent Indl Insultation, 53154
Mid Eastern Cold Storage LLC, 53155
Mid Kansas Co-Op Assn, 8254
Mid South Graphics, 26121
Mid States Express Inc, 51932
Mid States Paper & Notion Co, 58053
Mid Valley Nut Co, 8255, 46587
Mid West Quality Gloves Inc, 26122, 46588
Mid-America Marketing Inc, 40786
Mid-America Wholesale, 58054
Mid-American Brokerage of St. Louis, 40787

All Companies Index

Mid-Atlantic Foods Inc, 8256, 46589
Mid-Continent Sales, 40788, 58055
Mid-Continent Warehouse Company, 53156
Mid-Eastern Molasses Company, 8257
Mid-Florida Freezer Warehouse, 53157
Mid-Lands Chemical Company, 26123, 46590
Mid-Michigan Ice Company, 58056
Mid-Pacific Hawaii Fishery, 8258, 46591
Mid-South Fish Company, 8259, 58057
Mid-Southwest Marketing, 26124
Mid-State Awning & Patio Co, 26125
Mid-State Food Brokers, 40789
Mid-State Metal Casting & Mfg, 26126
Mid-States Mfg & Engr Co Inc, 26127, 46592
Mid-West Associates, 40790
Mid-West Sales Agency, 40791
Mid-West Traffic, 51933
Mid-West Wire Products, 26128, 46593
Mid-Western Enterprises, 46594
Midamar, 8260, 46595
Midas Foods Intl, 8261, 46596
Midbrook Inc, 26129, 46597
Midco Plastics, 26130
Middendorf Meat, 58058
Middle Tennessee Dr Pepper Distributing Center, 58059
Middlebury Cheese Company, 8262
Middleby Corp, 26131, 46598
Middleby Marshall Inc, 26132, 46599
Middlefield Cheese House, 8263
Middleswarth Potato Chips, 8264
Middleton Printing & Label Co, 26133
Middough Inc, 26134
Midland, 46600
Midland Grocery of Michigan, 58060
Midland Manufacturing Co, 26135
Midland Marketing Co-Op Inc, 40792
Midland Research Laboratories, 26136
Midland Terminals, 53158
Midlands Packaging Corp, 26137
Midlantic Sweetener Co, 40793
Midlantic Sweetener Company, 58061
Midmac Systems, 26138
Midnite Express, 51934, 53159
Midori Trading Inc, 46601, 58062
Midstates Marketing Inc, 40794
Midtown Electric Supply Corp, 58063
Midvale Paper Box, 26139
Midway Container Inc., 58064
Midway Games, 46602
Midwest Aircraft Products Co, 26140, 46603
Midwest Assembly Warehouse, 53160
Midwest Badge & Novelty Co, 26141, 46604, 58065
Midwest Blueberry Farms, 8265
Midwest Box Co, 26142
Midwest Coast Logistics LLC, 51935
Midwest Cold Storage & Ice Company, 53161
Midwest Continental Inc, 51936
Midwest Cooperative, 58066
Midwest Distribution Group, 58067
Midwest Distribution Systems, 53162
Midwest Fibre Products Inc, 26143
Midwest Fire & Safety Equipment Company, 58068
Midwest Folding Products, 26144, 46605
Midwest Food, 8266
Midwest Food Distributors, 58069
Midwest Foodservice News, 8267, 26145
Midwest Frozen Foods, Inc., 8268, 40795, 46606, 46607
Midwest Imports LTD, 46607, 58071
Midwest Industrial Packaging, 26146
Midwest Ingredient Sales, 40796
Midwest Ingredients Inc, 40797, 46608, 58072
Midwest Juice, 26147, 40798
Midwest Laboratories, 26148, 26149
Midwest Metalcraft & Equipment, 26150
Midwest Nut Co, 8269

Midwest Paper Products Company, 26151
Midwest Paper Tube & CanCorporation, 26152
Midwest Promotional Group, 26153, 58073
Midwest Rubber Svc & Supply, 26154
Midwest Seafood, 8270, 58074
Midwest Stainless, 26155, 46609
Midwest Wire Products LLC, 26156
Midwest Wire Specialties, 26157
Midwestern Bulk Bag, 26158
Midwestern Industries Inc, 26159
Mies Products, 26160, 46610
Miesse Candies, 8271
MIFAB Inc, 25577, 46210
Migali Industries, 26161, 46611
Migatron Corp, 26162, 46612
Mighty Leaf Tea, 8272, 46613
Mighty Soy Inc, 8273
Mignardise, 8274
Miguel & Valentino - Scout Marketing, 46614
Miguel's Stowe Away, 8275, 46615
Mikaela's Simply Divine, 8276
Mikasa Hotelware, 26163, 46616
Mikawaya LLC, 8277
Mike & Jean's Berry Farm, 8278
Mike E. Simon & Company, 58075
Mike Kazarian, 58076
Mike's Beverage Company, 8279
Mike's Hot Honey, 8280
Mike's Mighty Good, 8281
Miken Cosmpanies, 26164
Mikesell's Potato Chip Company, 8282
Mikey's, 8283, 8284, 58077
Miko Meat, 8285
Mil-Du-Gas Company/Star Brite, 26165, 46617
Milan Box Corporation, 26166, 46618
Milan Provision Co, 8286
Milan Supply Chain Solutions, 51937, 53163
Milani, 8287
Milano Bakery Inc, 8288
Milano's Of New York City, 8289
Milas Foods, LLC, 46619
Milat Vineyards Winery, 8290
Milburn Company, 26167, 46620
Mild Bill's Spices, 8291, 46621
Mile Hi Express, 26168
Mile Hi Frozen Foods Corp., 58078
Milea Estate Vineyard, 8292, 46622
Miles of Chocolate, 8293
Miles Willard Technologies, 26169
Military Club & Hospitality, 26170
Miljoco Corp, 8294, 26171, 46623
Milk Specialties Global, 8295, 46624
Milkadamia, 8297
MilkBoy Swiss Chocolate, 8296
Milky Way Jersey Farm Inc, 8298
Milky Whey Inc, 8299, 40799, 46625, 58079
Mill Cove Lobster Pound, 8300, 58080
Mill Creek Vineyards, 8301
Mill Engineering & Machinery Company, 26172
Mill Equipment Co Inc, 26173
Mill Haven Foods LLC, 8302
Mill Wiping Rags Inc, 26174, 46626
Mill-Rose Co, 26175, 46627
Millar-Williams Hydronics, 58081
Millard Manufacturing Corp, 26176
Millbrook Distribution Service, 58083
Millbrook Distribution Services, 58082
Millbrook Lofts, 53164, 53165
Millbrook Vineyards, 8303, 58084
Mille Lacs Gourmet Foods, 8304
Mille Lacs Wild Rice Corp, 8305, 46628
Millen Fish, 8306, 58085
Millenia Industries Corp, 26177
Miller & Hartman, 58086
Miller & Smith Foods, 40800
Miller & Stryker Assoc Inc, 40801
Miller Baking, 8307
Miller Brothers Packing Company, 8308

Miller Container Corp, 51938, 53166
Miller Group Multiplex, 26178, 46629
Miller Hofft Brands, 26179
Miller Johnson Seafood, 8309, 58087
Miller Manufacturing Co, 26180
Miller Metal Fabrication, 26181
Miller Studio, 26182, 46630
Miller Technical Svc, 26183, 46631
Miller's Cheese Corp, 8310
Miller's Country Hams, 8311
Miller's Market, 40802
Miller's Meat Market, 8312
Miller's Mustard LLC, 8313
Miller, Stabler & Smith, 40803
Millerbernd Systems, 26184, 46632
Millflow Spice Corp., 8314, 46633
Millhiser, 26185
Milliaire Winery, 8315
Millie's Pierogi, 8316
Milligan & Higgins, 8317, 26186, 46634
Milligan's Island, 58088
Milliken & Co, 26187, 46635
Milling Sausage Inc, 8318
MILLIPORE Sigma, 25578
Millrose Restaurant, 8319
Mills Brothers Intl, 8320, 46636, 58089
Mills Coffee Roasting Co, 8321
Mills Seafood Ltd., 8322, 46637
Millstream Brewing Co, 8323
Milltronics, 26188
Millway Frozen Foods, 58090
Millwood Inc, 26189
Milmar Food Group, 8324, 46638
Milne Fruit Products Inc, 8325, 46639
Milnot Company, 8326, 8327
Milone Brothers Coffee Co, 8328
Milos, 8329
Milos Whole World Gourmet, 8330
Milprint, 26190
Milroy Canning Company, 8331
Milsek Furniture Polish Inc., 26191, 46640, 58091
Milsolv Corporation, 8332
Miltenberg & Samton, 26192
Miltenberg & Samton Inc., 40804
Milton A. Klein Company, 8333, 26193, 46641
Milton Can Company, 26194
Milton's Craft Bakers, 58092
Milton's Local, 8334
Milvan Food Equipment Manufacturing, 26195
Milwaukee Dustless Brush Co, 26196, 46642
Milwaukee Sign Company, 26197, 46643
Milwaukee Tool & MachineCompany, 26198, 46644
Milwhite Inc, 8335, 46645
Mimac Glaze, 8336
Mimi et Cie, 26199, 46646
Mimi's Mountain Mixes, 8337
Mims Meat Company, 8338
Min Tong Herbs, 8339, 46647
Minarik Corporation, 26200
Minas Purely Divine, 8340
Mince Master, 26201
Mincing Overseas Spice Company, 8341, 46648
MindFull, Inc., 8342
Mindo Chocolate Makers, 8343
Minerva Cheese Factory, 8344
Minerva Dairy Inc, 8345
Minges Printing & Advg Specs, 26202
Mingo Bay Beverages, 8346, 46649
Mingo River Pecan Company, 8347
Minh Food, 8348
Minh Food Corporation, 8349
Mini Pops Inc, 8350
Mini-Bag Company, 26203
Minipack, 26204
Minn-Dak Farmers Co-Op, 8351
Minn-Dak Growers LTD, 8352, 46650
Minn-Dak Transport Inc, 51939
Minn-Dak Yeast Co Inc, 8353
Minnehaha Spring Water Company, 8354

Minners Designs Inc., 26205
Minnesota Automation, 26206
Minnesota Conway Fire & Safety, 58093
Minnesota Dehydrated Veg Inc, 8355
Minnesota Department-Agrcltr, 46651
Minnesota Freezer Warehouse Co, 53167
Minnesota Hemp Farms, 8356
Minnesota Turkey Research and Promotion, 46652
Minnesota Valley Testing Lab, 26207
Minnestalgia Foods LLC, 8357, 8358
Minnesuing Acres, 26208
Minor Fisheries, 8359
Minsa Corp, 8360
Minsa Southwest Corp, 26209
Minsley, Inc., 8361
Mint Savor, 8362
Minterbrook Oyster Co, 8363, 46653
Minuet Cookies, 46654
Minus the Moo, 8364
Minute Maid Company, 8365
Minuteman Power Boss, 26210, 46655
Minuteman Power Box Inc, 26211
Minuteman Trading, 46656, 58094
Mione Manufacturing Company, 26212
Mira International Foods, 8366
MIRA International Foods, 46211
Miracapo Pizza, 8367, 46658
Miracle Exclusives, 26213, 46659, 58095
Miracle Noodle, 8368
Miracle Tree, 8369
Miramar Cold Storage, 53168
Miramar Fruit Trading Company, 8370
Miramar Pickles & Food Products, 8371
Mirandas' Sales & Merchandising, 40805
Mirasco, 8372, 46660
Mirkovich & Assoc Inc, 40806
Miroil, 26214
MirOil, 46657
Miroil, 46661
Miron Construction Co., 26215
Mirro Company, 26216, 46662
Mirro Products Company, 26217
Mirror Tech Mfg Co Inc, 26218
Mirrotek International, 46663
MISCO Refractometer, 25579, 46212
Misfit Juicery, 8373
Mishawaka Brewing Company, 8374
Mishima Foods USA, 46664, 58096
Mishler Packing Co, 8375
Mishrun, 8376
Miss Ginny's Orginal Vermont Pickle Works, 8377
Miss Grimble Desserts, 58097
Miss Jenny's Pickles, 8378
Miss Jones Baking Co., 8379
Miss Mary, 46665, 58098
Miss Meringue, 8380
Miss Scarlett's Flowers, 8381
Miss Tea Brooklyn Inc, 8382
Mission Foods, 8383
Mission Foods Corp., 8384, 8385, 8386
Mission Foodservice, 8387, 46666
Mission Laboratories, 26219
Mission Mountain Winery, 8388
Mission Pharmacal Company, 8389
Mission Produce Inc, 46667
Mission Valley Foods, 8390
Mississippi Cheese Straw, 8391
Mississippi Cold and Dry Storage, 53169
Missouri Equipment, 26220
Missouri Grocers Assn, 26221
Missouri Wine & Gift, 8392
Mister Bee Potato Chips Co, 8393
Mister Cookie Face, 8394
Mister Fish Inc., 8395, 58099
Mister Label, Inc, 26222, 46668
Mister Pickle's Inc, 8396
Mister Snacks Inc, 8397
Mister Spear, 8398
Misty Islands Seafoods, 8399, 58100
Misty's Restaurant & Lounge, 8400
MIT Poly-Cart Corp, 25580
Mitch Chocolate, 8401, 58101
Mitchel Beck Company, 40807

1413

All Companies Index

Mitchel Dairies, 8402
Mitchell & Co Inc, 40808
Mitchell Agencies, 40809
Mitchell Foods, 8403
Mitchell Grocery Corp, 58102
Mitchell Handling Systems, 58103
Mitchell of Mississippi, 40810
Mitchum Potato Chips, 8404
Mitec, 26223
Mitsubishi Caterpillar Mcfa, 26224
Mitsubishi Chemical Holdings, 8405
Mitsubishi Fuso Truck Of America, 26225
Mitsubishi Gas Chemical America, 26226
Mitsubishi Intl. Corp., 8406, 26227
Mitsubishi Polyester Film, Inc., 26228, 46669
Mitsui & Co Commodity Risk Management Limited, 46670
Mitsui Foods Inc, 46671
Mity Lite Inc, 26229, 46672
Miura Boilers, 26230
Mivila Foods, 58104
MIWE USA, 25581
Mix-A-Lota Stuff LLC, 8407
Mixallogy, 8408
Mixerz All Natural Cocktail Mixers, 8409
Mixes by Danielle, 8410
Mixon Fruit Farms Inc, 8411, 46673
Miyako Oriental Foods Inc, 8412, 46674
Miyoko's Kitchen, 8413
Mizkan Americas Inc, 8414, 8415, 8416, 8417, 8418, 8419, 8420, 8421, 8422, 8423, 8424, 8425, 8426, 8427, 8428, 8429, 8430, 8431
Mj Kellner Co, 8432, 58105
MJ Puehse & Company, 25582
MKE Enterprises LTD, 7703
ML Catania Company, 46213, 57821
MLE Marketing, 40726
MLG Enterprises Ltd., 40727, 46214
Mlp Seating, 26231, 46675
MLP Seating Corporation, 46215
MLS Signs Inc, 25583
Mmi Engineered Soultions Inc, 26232, 46676
MMLC, 25584
MMR Technologies, 25585, 46216
MO Air International, 7704, 51907
Mo Hotta Mo Betta, 8433, 46677
Mo-Ark Truck Services, 51940
Mobern Electric Corporation, 26233
Mobil Composite Products, 26234
Mobile Bay Seafood, 8434, 58106
Mobile Processing, 8435
Mobjack Bay Seafood, 58107
MOCAP Inc, 25586
Moceri South Western, 8436
MOCON Inc, 25587
Mocon Inc, 26235, 46678
Moctezuma Foods, 58108
Mod Squad Martha, 8437
MODAGRAPHICS, 25588, 46217
Modar, 26236, 46679
MODe Sports Nutrition, 7705
Model Dairy LLC, 8438, 58109
Modena Fine Foods Inc, 8439, 58110
Modern Baking Magazine, 26237
Modern Brewing & Design, 26238, 46680
Modern Day Masala, LLC, 8440
Modern Electronics Inc, 26239
Modern Equipment Co, 58111
Modern Food Equipment Company, 58112
Modern Gourmet Foods, 8441
Modern Group, 58113
Modern Italian Bakery of West Babylon, 8442
Modern Macaroni Co LTD, 8443, 46681, 58114
Modern Metalcraft, 26240
Modern Metals Industries, 26241
Modern Mushroom Farms Inc, 58115

Modern Oats, 8444
Modern Packaging, 8445, 26242, 53170
Modern Packaging Inc, 26243
Modern Paper Box Company, 26244
Modern Plastics, 26245
Modern Pod Co., 8446
Modern Pop, 8447
Modern Process Equipment Inc, 26246
Modern Products Inc, 8448, 46682
Modern Stamp Company, 26247
Modern Store Fixtures Company, 26248
Modern Table, 8449, 58116
Modern Tea Packers, 8450
Modern Wholesale Company, 58117
Modesto & Empire Traction Co, 51941
Modesto Tent & Awning, 26249
Modesto WholeSoy, 8451
Modular Packaging, 26250, 26251, 46683
Modular Panel Company, 26252, 46684
Modularm Corporation, 26253
Modulighter Inc, 26254, 46685, 58118
Modutank Inc, 26255
Moeller Electric, 26256
Moen Industries, 26257, 46686
Moet Hennessy USA, 8452, 46687
Moffat, 26258
Moffett Food Svc, 58119
Mogen David Wine Corp, 8453, 46688
Mohawk Northern Plastics, 26259
Mohawk Paper Mills, 26260
Mohawk Western Plastics Inc, 26261
Mohn's Fisheries, 8454, 58120
Moisture Register Products, 26262, 46689
Mokk-a, 8455
Mol Belting Co, 26263
Mold-Rite Plastics LLC, 26264, 46690
Molded Container Corporation, 26265
Molded Fiber Glass Tray Company, 26266
Molded Pulp Products, 26267
Molding Automation Concepts, 26268, 46691
Moledina Commodities, 8456, 46692
Moli-International, 26269, 46693
Molinaro's Fine Italian Foods Ltd., 8457, 46694
Moline Machinery LLC, 26270, 46695
Molinera International, 46696, 58121
Molins/Sandiacre Richmond, 26271, 46697
Moll-Tron, 26272
Mollenberg-Betz Inc, 26273
Mollers North America Inc, 26274
Molli, 8458
Molson Coors Beverage Company, 8459, 46698
Molson Coors North America, 8460
Moly-XL Company, 26275
Mom N' Pops Inc, 8461, 58122
Mom's Bakery, 8462
Mom's Famous, 8463
Mom's Food Company, 8464
Mom's Gourmet, LLC, 8465
Momar, 26276, 46699
Momence Packing Company, 8466
Momence Pallet Corp, 26277
Mon Ami Restaurant, 8467
Mona Lisa Foods, 8468
Monaco Baking Company, 8469
Monadnock Paper Mills Inc, 26278, 46700
Monarc Group, 26279
Monarch Beverage Company, 8470, 46701
Monarch Import Company, 46702
Monarch Seafoods Inc, 8471, 58123
Monarch-McLaren, 26280, 46703, 58124
Monastary Mustard, 8472, 26281
Monastery Fruitcake, 8473
Mondelez International, 8474
Mondial Foods Company, 8475, 46704
Mondiv/Division of Lassonde Inc, 8476
Moneuse Sales Agency, 40811

Money's Mushrooms, 8477, 46705
Monin Inc., 8478, 46706
Monini North America, 8479
Monitor Company, 26282, 46707
Monitor Technologies LLC, 26283, 46708
Monkey Media, 8480
Monks' Specialty Bakery, 8481
Monoflo International Inc, 26285
Monogram Food Solutions, 8482
Monon Process Equipment Co, 26286
MonoSol, 26284
Monroe Environmental Corp, 26287, 46709
Monroe Extinguisher Co Inc, 26288
Monsanto Co, 8483
Monsol, 26289
Monsoon Kitchens, 8484
Monster Beverage Corp., 8485, 46710
Monster Cone, 8486, 46711
Mont Blanc Gourmet, 8487
Montague Co, 26290, 46712
Montalbano Development Inc, 26291, 46713
Montana Broom & Brush Co, 58125
Montana Coffee Traders, 8488
Montana Flour & Grains, 8489
Montana Food Products, 58126
Montana Mex, 8490, 58127
Montana Monster Munchies, 8491
Montana Mountain Smoked Fish, 8492
Montana Naturals, 8493, 46714
Montana Ranch Brand, 8494
Montana Specialty Mills LLC, 8495, 46715
Montana Tea & Spice Trading, 8496, 46716
Montchevre-Betin, Inc, 8497
Monte Cristo Trading, 8498
Monte Glove Company, 26292
Monte Package Co, 26293
Monte Vista Farming Co, 8499, 46717
Montebello Container Corp, 26294
Montebello Kitchens, 8500
Montebello Packaging, 8501, 26295
Montelle Winery, 8502
Montello Inc, 8503, 26296, 46718, 58128
Monterey Bay Food Group, 26297
Monterey Fish Company, 8504
Monterey Food Ingredients, 40812
Monterey Mushrooms Inc, 8505, 46719
Monterey Vineyard, 8506
Monterrey Products, 8507, 8508
Monterrey Provision Co, 58129
Monteverdes, 58130
Montevina Winery, 8509
Monticello Canning Company, 8510
Monticello Vineyards-Corley, 8511
Montione's Biscotti & Baked Goods, 8512
Montmorenci Vineyards, 8513
Montreal Chop Suey Company, 8514
Monument Farms Dairy, 8515, 8516
Monument Industries Inc, 26298, 46720
Moo Chocolate/Organic Children's Chocolate LLC, 8517
Mooala, 8518
Moody Dunbar Inc, 8519, 40813, 51942
Moody's Quick, 51943
Moog Components Group, 26299
Moog Inc, 26300
Moon Dance Baking, 8520
Moon Rabbit Foods, 8521
Moon Shot Energy, 8522
Moon Valley Circuits, 26301
Moon's Seafood Company, 8523, 58131
Mooney General Paper Co, 58132
Mooney International, 40814
Moonlight Brewing Company, 8524
Moonlight, 8525
Moonlight Gourmet, 8526
Moonlight Mixes LLC, 8527
Moonlite Bar-B-Q Inn, 8528, 58133
Moonshine Sweet Tea, 8529
Moonstruck Chocolate Co, 8530

Moore Efficient Communication Aids, 26302
Moore Equipment, 58134
Moore Organics, 8531
Moore Paper Boxes Inc, 26303, 46721
Moore Production Tool Spec Inc, 26304, 46722
Moore Push-Pin Co, 26305
Moore's Candies, 8532
Moorecraft Box & Crate, 26306
Mooresville Ice Cream Co, 8533
Moorhead & Company, 8534, 46723
Moosehead Breweries Ltd., 8535, 46724
Morabito Baking Co Inc, 8536, 58135
Moran Canvas Products Inc, 26307
Moran Distribution Centers, 51944, 53171
Moran Foods LLC, 58136
Moran Logistics, 51945, 53172
Moran USA, LLC, 58137
Moravian Cookies Shop, 8537
Mordhorst Automation, 40815
More For Less Foods, 58138
More Than Gourmet, 8538
Morehead Company, 58139
Morehouse Foods Inc, 8539, 46725
Moretti's Poultry, 8540
Morey's Seafood Intl LLC, 8541, 46726
Morgan & Company, 46727
Morgan Brothers Bag Company, 26308
Morgan Corp, 26309
Morgan Foods Inc, 8542, 46728
Morgan Meat Co, 58140
Morgan Mill, 8543
Morgan Sampson USA, 40816
Morgan Winery, 8544, 46729
Morii Foods, Inc., 8545
Morinaga Nutritional Foods, Inc., 8546
Morley Sales Co, 40817, 46730
Morning Glory Dairy, 8547
Morning Star Coffee, Inc., 26310
Morning Star Foods, 8548, 26311
Morningland Dairy Cheese Company, 8550
MorningStar Coffee Company, 8549
Morningstar Farms, 8551
Morningstar Foods, 8552
Moroni Feed Company, 8553
Morphy Container Company, 26312
Morre-Tec Ind Inc, 8554, 46731, 58141
Morreale John R Inc, 8555, 58142
Morris & Associates, 26313, 46732
Morris A. Elkis & Sons, 58143
Morris Industries, 26314
Morris J Golombeck Inc, 8556, 46733
Morris Kitchen, 8557
Morris National, 8558
Morris Okun, 46734, 58144
Morris Transparent Box Co, 26315
Morrison Farms, 8559
Morrison Industrial Equip Co, 58145
Morrison Lamothe, 8560
Morrison Meat Packers, 8561
Morrison Meat Pies, 8562
Morrison Milling Co, 8563
Morrison Storage & Homes, 53173
Morrison Timing Screw Co, 26316, 46735
Morrison Weighing Systems Inc, 26317
Morrisons Pastry Corp, 58146
Morrissey Displays & Models, 26318, 46736
Morristown & Erie Railway Inc, 51946
Morrow Cold Storage LLC, 53174
Morrow Technologies Corporation, 26319, 46737
Morse Manufacturing Co Inc, 26320, 46738
Morse's Sauerkraut, 8564
Mortec Industries Inc, 26321, 46739, 58147
Mortgage Apple Cake, 8565
Mortillaro Lobster Company, 8566, 58148
Mortimer's Fine Foods, 8567, 46740

1414

All Companies Index

Morton & Associates, 40818
Morton & Bassett Spices, 8568
Morton F Schweitzer Sales, 40819
Morton Salt Inc., 8569, 46741
Mosaic Co, 46742
Mosby Winery, 8570, 58149
Moseley & Reece, 58150
Moseley Realty LLC, 26322
Moser Bag & Paper Company, 26323
Mosher Products Inc, 8571, 40820, 46743
Mosinee Cold Storage, 53175
Moss Creek Winery, 8572
Moss Inc, 26324
Mosshaim Innovations, 26325, 46744
Mossholder's Farm Cheese Factory, 8573
Mosti Mondiale/Gourmet Mondiale, 8574
Mosuki, 26326, 46745, 58151
Moten Company, 40821
Mother Earth Enterprises, 8575, 58152
Mother Murphy's, 8576
Mother Nature's Goodies, 8577
Mother Parker's Tea & Coffee, 8578, 46746
Mother Raw, 8579
Mother Shucker's Original Cocktail Sauce, 8580
Mother Teresa's, 8581
Mother's Cake & Cookie Company, 58153
Mother's Mountain Pantry, 8582
Mother-In-Law's Kimchi, 8583
Motherland International Inc, 8584, 46747
Motion Industries Inc, 26327
Motion Savers Inc, 58154
Motion Technologies, 26328
Motivatit Seafoods Inc, 46748, 58155
Motom Corporation, 26329, 46749
Motoman, 26330
Motry International, 46750
Mott's, 8585
Mott's LLP, 8586
Motto, 8587
Mouli Manufacturing Corporation, 26331, 46751
Mound City Shelled Nut Inc, 8588
Mound Tool Co, 26332
Mount Airy Cold Storage, 53176
Mount Franklin Foods, 8589
Mount Hope Machinery Company, 26333
Mount Mansfield Maple Products, 8590
Mount Olympus Waters, 8591
Mount Palomar Winery, 8592
Mount Vernon Plastics, 26334
Mountain America Shippers, 51947
Mountain City Coffee Roasters, 8593
Mountain Cove Vineyards, 8594
Mountain Creek Marketing, 40822
Mountain Dairies-SW Ice Cream, 58156
Mountain Fire Foods, 8595
Mountain High Organics, 8596
Mountain High Yogurt, 8597
Mountain Organic Foods, 8598
Mountain Pacific Machinery, 26335
Mountain People's Warehouse, 58157
Mountain Pride, 26336, 58158
Mountain Rose Herbs, 8599, 46752
Mountain Safety Research, 26337, 46753
Mountain Sales & Svc Inc, 40823, 58159
Mountain Secure Systems, 26338
Mountain Service Distribution, 58160
Mountain States Pecan, 8600
Mountain States Processing, 26339
Mountain States Rosen, 8601, 58161
Mountain Sun Pubs & Breweries, 8602
Mountain Valley Poultry, 8603
Mountain Valley Products Inc, 8604, 46754
Mountain Valley Spring Company, 8605
Mountain Valley Spring Water, 8606
Mountain Valley Water, 58162
Mountain Valley Water Company, 46755, 58163
Mountain View Fruit Sales, 8607

Mountain View Supply, 58164
Mountain West Distributors Inc, 58165
Mountain-Pacific Machinery, 26340
Mountainbrook of Vermont, 8608
Mountaingate Engineering, 26341
Mountainside Farms Inc, 8609
Mountaire Corporation, 8610
Mountanos Family Coffee & Tea Co., 8611, 58166
Mouron & Co Inc, 26342
Moutanos Brothers Coffee Company, 8612
Movie Breads Food, 8613
MovinCool/DENSO Products and Services Americas, 26343
Moweaqua Packing Plant, 8614
Moyer Diebel, 26344, 46756
Moyer Packing Co., 8615, 26345, 46757
Moyer-Mitchell Company, 58167
Moyno, 26346, 46758
Mozzarella Co, 8616
Mozzicato De Pasquale Bakery, 8617
Mp Equip. Co., 26347
MPBS Industries, 25589
MPE Group, 25590
MPI Label Systems, 25591
MPI Simgraph, 25592
Mpp Inc, 26348
MPS North America, Inc., 25593
Mr Chips For Pickles, 46759
Mr Dell Foods, 8618, 46760
Mr Espresso, 8619
Mr Ice Bucket, 26349, 46761
Mr Jay's Tamales & Chili, 8620
Mr. Bar-B-Q, 26350, 46762
Mr. Broadway Kosher Restaurant, 46763
Mr. C's, 8621, 58168
Mr. Green Tea Ice Cream, 8622
Mr. Mak's, 8623
MRC Bearing Services, 25594, 25595
MRI Upper Westchester, 25596
Mrs Annie's Peanut Patch, 8624
Mrs Auld's Gourmet Foods Inc, 8625, 46764
Mrs Baird's, 8626, 46765
Mrs Clark's Foods, 8627, 26351, 46766
Mrs Fisher's Potato Chips, 8628
Mrs Grissom's Salads Inc, 8629
Mrs Mazzula Food Products Inc, 8630
Mrs Prindables, 8631
Mrs Rios Corn Products, 8632
Mrs Stratton's Salads Inc, 8633
Mrs Sullivan's Pies, 8634
Mrs. Denson's Cookie Company, 8635, 46767
Mrs. Dog's Products, 8636, 46768
Mrs. Field's Hot Cocoas, 8637
Mrs. Fields Original Cookies, 8638
Mrs. Fly's Bakery, 8639
Mrs. Kavanagh's English Muffins, 8640
Mrs. Lauralicious, 8641
Mrs. Leeper's Pasta, 8642, 46769
Mrs. Malibu Foods, 8643
Mrs. May's Naturals, 8644
Mrs. McGarrigle's Fine Foods, 8645
Mrs. Miller's Homemade Noodles, 8646
Mrs. Smith's Bakeries, 26352
Mrs. Smiths Bakeries, 8647
Mrs. Ts Pierogies, 8648
Mrs. Willman's Baking, 8649
MSC Industrial Direct Co Inc, 57822
MSK Covertech, 25597
MSRF, Inc., 7706
MSSH, 25598, 46218
Mt Baker Vineyards, 8650
Mt Bethel Winery, 8651
Mt Capra Products, 8652, 46770
Mt Claire Beverages, 8653
Mt Eden Vineyards, 8654
Mt Franklin Foods, 8655
Mt Nittany Vineyard & Winery, 8656
Mt Olive Pickle Co, 8657
Mt Pleasant Seafood, 58169
Mt Pleasant Winery, 8658
Mt Sterling Co-Op Creamery, 8659

Mt Valley Farms & Lumber Prods, 26353, 46771
Mt Vernon Neon Inc, 26354
Mt Vernon Packaging Inc, 26355
Mt. Hope Wholesale, 58170
Mt. Konocti Growers, 8660, 46772
Mt. Lebanon Awning & Tent Company, 26356
Mt. Olympus Specialty Foods, 8661, 8662, 46773
Mt. View Bakery, 8663
MTC Delaware LLC, 53119
MTC Distributing, 57823
Mtc Food Equipment, 26357
MTE Logistix, 51908, 53120
MTL Etching Industries, 25599, 46219
MTP Custom Machinery Corporation, 25600
Mts Seating, 26358, 46774
Mucci Food Products LTD, 8664
Mucke's Meat Products, 8665
Muckenthaler Inc, 58171, 58172
Muckler Industries, Inc, 26359, 46775
Mucky Duck Mustard Company, 8666
MUD, 7707
Mueller Distributing Company, 58173
Mueller Yurgae, 40824
Muellermist Irrigation Company, 26360, 46776
Muffin Revolution, 8667
Mugnaini Imports, 26361, 46777
Muir Copper Canyon Farms, 8668, 46778, 58174
Muirhead Canning Co, 8669
Muirhead of Ringoes, NJ, Inc., 8670
Mulholland Co, 26362
Mulholland-Harper Company, 26363, 46779
Mullens Dressing, 8671
Muller-Pinehurst Dairy, 8672
Muller-Pinehurst Dairy Company, 58175
Mullica Hill Cold Storage, 53177
Mulligan Associates, 26364, 46780
Mulligan Sales, 8673, 26365
Mullins Cheese Inc, 8674
Mullins Food Products, 8675
Mullnix Packages Inc, 26366
Multi Marques, 8676, 58176
Multi-Color Corp, 26367
Multi-Counter Manufacturing Company, 58177
Multi-Fill Inc, 26368, 46781
Multi-Pak, 26369, 46782
Multi-Panel Display Corporation, 26370, 46783
Multi-Plastics Extrusions Inc, 26371, 46784
Multibulk Systems International, 26374, 46786
MultiFeeder Technology Inc, 26375
Multifilm Packaging Corp, 26376
Multiflex Company, 8677, 46787
Multigrains Bread Co, 8678, 26377, 58178
Multikem Corp, 26378, 46788
MultiMedia Electronic Displays, 26373, 46785
Multiple Organics, 58179
Multiplex Co Inc, 26379, 46789
Multipond America Inc, 26380
Multisorb Technologies Inc, 26381, 26382, 46790
MultiSystems Barcode Solutions, 53178
Multivac, 26383
Multivac Inc, 26384, 46791, 58180
Multy-Grain Foods, 40825
Mumper Machine Corporation, 26385, 46792
Munchies, 40826, 58181
Mundial, 26386, 46793
Mung Dynasty, 8679, 58182
Munk Pack, 8680
Munkijo, 8681
Munn Marketing Group, 40827

Munroe Material Handling, 58183
Munsee Meats, 8682, 58184
Munson Machinery Co, 26387, 46794
Munson's Chocolates, 8683
Munters Corp, 26388, 46795
Muntons Ingredients, 8684, 46796
Muqui Coffee Company, 8685
Murakami Farms, 8686, 46797
Murata Automated Systems, 26389
Murdock Farm Dairy, 8687
Murk Brush Company, 26390, 58185
Murnane Co, 26391
Murnell Wax Company, 26392
Murotech, 26393, 46798
Murphy Bonded Warehouse, 51948, 53179
Murphy Goode Estate Winery, 8688
Murphy Warehouse, 53180
Murphy Warehouse Co, 51949, 53181
Murphy/Northstar, 58186
Murray Cider Co Inc, 8689
Murray Envelope Corporation, 26394, 46799
Murray Industrial Food Sales Inc, 40828
Murray Runin, 26395
Murray's Chickens, 8690
Murray's Transfer Inc, 51950, 53182
Murry's Family of Fine Foods, 58187
Murtech Manufacturing, 26396
Murvest, 8691
Murzan Inc, 26397, 46800
Murzan Inc. Sanitary Sys, 46801
Musco Family Olive Co, 8692, 46802
Musco Food Corp, 46803, 58188
Mush & Pinsky, 58189
MUSH Foods, 7708
Mushroom Co, 8693, 46804
Mushroom Harvest, 8694
Mushroom Wisdom, Inc, 8695, 46805
Music City Metals Inc, 26398, 46806
Music Mountain Water Company, 8696
Musicon Deer Farm, 8697
Muskegon Awning & Fabrication, 26399
Muskingum Valley Grocery Co, 58190
Muskogee Rubber Stamp & Seal Company, 26400
Mustard Seed, 8698
Mutchler's Dakota Gold Mustard, 8699
Muth Associates, 26401, 46807
Muth's Candy Store, 8700
Mutual Biscuit, 46808, 58191
Mutual Distributors, 58192
Mutual Fish Co, 8701, 58193
Mutual Stamping & Mfg Co, 26402
Mutual Trading Co Inc, 46809, 58194
Mutual Wholesale Company, 58195
Mutual Wholesale Liquor, 46810, 58196
MVP Group, 57824
MXO Global, 7709
My Boy's Baking LLC, 8702
My Brother Bobby's Salsa, 8703
My Brother's Salsa, 8704
My Car Provision Company, 58197
My Cup of Cake™, 8705
My Daddy's Cheesecake, 8706, 46811
My Favorite Jerky, 8707
My Grandma's Coffee Cake, 8708, 46812
My Own Meals Inc, 8709
My Quality Trading Corp, 46813, 58198
My Serenity Pond, 26403
My Style, 26404, 46814, 58199
My Sweet, 8710
My/Mo Mochi Ice Cream, 8711
Mycom Group, 26405
Mycom Sales, 26406
Mycom/Mayekawa Manfacturing, 26407
Myers Container, 26408, 46815
Myers Equipment Company, 58200
Myers Frozen Food Provisions, 8713
Myers Ice Company, 26409
Myers Restaurant Supply Inc, 26410, 58201
Myers-Cox Co, 58202
Mylk Labs, 8714, 58203
MYNTZ!, 7710

1415

All Companies Index

Myron's Fine Foods, Inc., 8715
Mystic Coffee Roasters, 8716
Mystic Lake Dairy, 8717
MySuperfoods Company, 8712

N

N & A Mfg, 26411
N A P Engineering, 8718, 26412
N D Labs, 8719
N S I Sweeteners, 46816
N Star Seafood LLC, 40829, 46817
N.A. Krups, 26413
N.B.J. Enterprises, 8720, 58204
N.G. Slater Corporation, 26414, 46818
N.H. Cohen & Associates, 40830
N.Y.K. Line (North America), 8721, 51951
Nabisco, 8729
Nacan Products, 8730
NACCO Materials Handling Group, 26415, 46819
NaceCare Solutions, 46833
NadaMoo, 8731
Nafziger Ice Cream Company, 58208
Nagasako Fish, 8732, 58209
Nagase America Corp., 8733
Nagel Paper & Box Company, 26436, 58210
Nagy Associates, 40832
Nahmias et Fils, 8734, 46834
Naji's Pita Gourmet Restaurant, 8735
Najila's, 8736
Najla's Specialty Foods Inc, 8737
Nakano Foods, 8738
Naked Bacon, 8739
Naked Infusions LLC, 8740
Naked Juice Company, 8741
Naked Mountain Winery Vineyard, 8742
Nalco Water, 26437
Naleway Foods, 8743, 46835
Nalge Process Technologies Group, 26438, 26439, 46836
Nalle Winery, 8744
Naltex, 26440, 46837
Naman Marketing, 26441, 40833, 58211
Namaste Foods, 8745
Namco Controls Corporation, 26442, 46838
Namco Machinery, 26443, 46839
Nameplate, 26444
Nan Sea Enterprises of Wisconsin, 8746, 58212
Nana Mae's Organics, 8747
Nana's Cookie Co., 8748
Nanci's Frozen Yogurt, 8749
Nancy Q Produce, 58213
Nancy's Candy, 8750
Nancy's Probiotic Foods, 8751
Nancy's Shellfish, 8752, 58214
Nancy's Specialty Foods, 8753, 46840
Nanka Seimen Company, 8754
Nanni-Marketal, 40834
Nanocor, 8755
Nanonation Inc, 46841
Nantong Acetic Acid Chemical Co., Ltd., 8756
Nantucket Pasta Company, Inc., 8757
Nantucket Tea Traders, 8758
Nantucket Vineyard, 8759
Nantze Springs Inc, 8760
NAP Industries, 26416, 46820
Napa Barrel Care, 8761, 53186
Napa Cellars, 8762
NAPA Distribution Ctr, 53183
Napa Fermentation Supplies, 26445
Napa Hills, 8763
Napa Valley Bung Works, 26446
Napa Valley Kitchens, 8764, 46842
Napa Wine Company, 8765
Napa Wooden Box Co, 26447
Napco Graphics Corporation, 26448
Napco Marketing Corp, 46843
Napco Security Systems Inc, 26449, 46844

Naples Vending, 58215
Napoleon Appliance Corporation, 26450, 46845
Napoleon Co., 40835, 46846
Napoleon Creamery, 58216
Napoleon Locker, 8766
Napoli Pasta Manufacturers, 8767
Nappie's Food Svc, 58217
NAR, 8722
NAR Gourmet, 46821
Naraghi Group, 8768, 46848
NaraKom, 26451, 46847
Nardelli Brothers, 58218
Nardi Breads, 8769
Nardone Brothers, 8770
Nareg International Inc, 46849, 58219
Naron Mary Sue Candies, 8771
Nasco Inc, 46850, 58220
Nash Produce, 8772
Nash Wright Brokerage, 40836
Nash-DeCamp Company, 46851, 58221
Nashoba Valley Winery, 8773
Nashua Corporation, 26452, 26453, 46852, 46853
Nashua Motor Express, 51954
Nashville Display Manufacturing Company, 26454, 46854
Nashville Wire Products, 26455
Nashville Wraps LLC, 26456
Nasonville Dairy, 8774
Nasoya Foods, 8775
Nass Parts & Svc Inc, 58222
Nassau Candy Distributors, 8776, 46855, 58223
Nassau Foods, 58224
Nassau-Suffolk Frozen Food Company, 58225
Nat-Trop, 46856
Natale Machine & Tool Co Inc, 26457, 46857
Natalie's Orchid Island Juice Co., 8777, 46858
Natchez Pecan Shelling Company, 8778
Natchitoches Crawfish Company, 8779, 58226
Natco Foodservice, 58227
Natco Worldwide Representative, 40837, 46859, 58228
Nathel & Nathel, 58229
Natierra, 8780
Nation Pizza & Foods, 8781
Nation Wide Canning Ltd., 8782
Nation/Ruskin, 26458
National Air Cargo Inc, 51955, 53187
National Ammonia Co, 26459
National Association-Pediatric, 46860
National Band Saw Co, 26460, 46861, 58230
National Bar Systems, 26461, 46862
National Beef Packing Co LLC, 8783, 51956
National Beverage Corporation, 8784
National Brokerage Network, 40838
National Bulk Food Distributors, 58231
National Carbonation, 58232
National Carriers Inc, 40839, 51957
National Cart Co, 26462, 46863
National Chemicals Inc, 26463
National Cold Storage Inc, 53188
National Commodity Sales, 40840
National Computer Corporation, 26464, 46864
National Construction Services, 26465
National Construction Technologies Group, 26466
National Conveyor Corp, 26467, 46865
National Datacomputer, 26468
National Discount Textile, 26469
National Distribution Centers, 51958, 53189, 53190
National Distributor Services, 26470, 46866
National Drying Machry Co Inc, 26471, 46867
National Emblem, 26472

National Embroidery Svc Inc, 26473
National Energy Consultants, 26474
National Equipment Corporation, 26475, 46868
National FABCO Manufacturing, 26476
National Fish & Oyster, 8785, 46869
National Fish & Seafood Inc, 8787
National Fish & Seafood Inc, 8786, 58233
National Flavors, 8788
National Foam, 26477, 46870
National Food Co LTD, 8789, 58234
National Food Corporation, 8790, 46871
National Food Group, 40841
National Food Laboratories Inc, 26478
National Food Product Research Corporation, 26479
National Food Sales, 40842, 40843
National Food Trading Co, 46872
National Foods, 8791, 8792, 8793, 46873
National Foodservice Marketing, 40844
National Frozen Foods Corp, 8794, 46874
National Fruit & Essences, 40845, 58235
National Fruit Flavor Co Inc, 8795, 46875
National Fruit Product Co Inc, 8796
National Grape Co-Op, 8797
National Grocers, 58236
National Grocers Assn, 58237
National Grocers Company, 58238, 58239, 58240, 58241
National Harvest, 8798
National Heritage Sales Company, 40846
National Honey Board, 26480
National Hotpack, 26481, 46876
National Importers, 8799, 46877
National Instruments, 26482, 46878
National Interchem Corporation, 26483, 46879
National Label Co, 26484, 46880
National Lecithin, 58242
National Lighting Source, 58243
National Marker Co Inc, 26485
National Marking Products Inc, 26486
National Meat & Provision Company, 8800, 58244
National Menuboard, 26487, 46881
National Metal Industries, 26488, 46882
National Novelty Brush Co, 26489, 46883
National Oilwell Varco, 26490
National Package Sealing Company, 26491, 46884
National Packaging, 26492, 46885
National Pen Co, 26493
National Plastics Co, 26494, 46886
National Poly Bag Manufacturing Corporation, 26495
National Polymers, 26496
National Pretzel Company, 8801
National Printing Converters, 26497, 46887
National Provisioner, 26498
National Purity LLC, 26499
National Raisin Co., 8802, 46888
National Restaurant Company, 58245
National Restaurant Supply Company, 26500, 58246, 58247
National Retail Marketing Network Inc., 40847
National Sales Corporation, 46889, 58248
National Scale Of New England, 58249
National Scoop & Equipment Company, 26501, 46890, 58250
National Shippng Supply Co, 46891, 58251
National Sign Corporation, 8803, 26502, 40848
National Sign Systems, 26503
National Stabilizers, 26504, 46892
National Starch Food Innovation, 8804
National Steak & Poultry, 8805
National Steel Corporation, 26505

National Stock Sign Co, 26506
National Sunflower Assn, 26507
National Tape Corporation, 26508, 46893
National Time Recording Eqpt, 26509, 46894
National Towelette, 26510
National Velour Corp, 26511, 46895
National Vinegar Co, 8806
National Warehouse Corporation, 53191
National Wine & Spirits, 8807
National Wooden Pallet & Container Association, 8808, 26512
Nationwide Boiler Inc, 26513
Nationwide Material Handling Equipment, 58252
Nationwide Pennant & Flag Mfg, 26514, 46896
Nationwide Wire & Brush Manufacturing, 26515
Native American Herbal Tea, 8809
Native American Natural Foods, 8810
Native Kjalii Foods, 8811
Native Lumber Company, 26516
Native Scents, 8812, 46897
Native State Foods, 8813, 58253
Natra US, 8814, 46898, 58254
Natrel, 8815
Natren Inc, 8816
Natrium Products Inc, 8817, 46899
Natrol Inc, 46900, 58255
Natur Sweeteners, Inc., 8818, 46901
Naturade Inc, 8819
Natural Alpha Omega, 46902
Natural Balance, 8820, 58256
Natural Bliss, 8821
Natural By Nature, 8822
Natural Casing Co, 46903, 58257
Natural Choice Distribution, 8823, 58258
Natural Company, 8824
Natural Dairy Products Corp, 58259
Natural Earth Products, 8825
Natural Enrichment Industries, 8826
Natural Exotic Tropicals, 8827
Natural Factors, 58260
Natural Feast Corporation, 8828
Natural Flavors, 8829, 46904
Natural Food Holdings, 8830, 46905
Natural Food Mill, 8831
Natural Food Source, 8832, 46906
Natural Food Supplements Inc, 8833
Natural Food Systems, 58261
Natural Food World, 8834
Natural Foods Inc, 8835, 46907, 58262
Natural Formulas, 8836
Natural Fruit Corp, 8837, 46908
Natural Group, 8838, 46909, 58263
Natural Habitats USA, 8839
Natural Ice Fruits, 8840
Natural Intentions, Inc., 8841
Natural Marketing Institute, 26517
Natural Nectar, 8842
Natural Oils International, 8843, 46910
Natural Ovens Bakery Inc, 8844
Natural Products Inc, 8845
Natural Quick Foods, 8846
Natural Rush, 8847, 46911
Natural Sins, 8848
Natural Spring Water Company, 8849
Natural Value, 8850, 46912
Natural Way Mills Inc, 8851, 46913
Naturalife Laboratories, 8852
Naturally Clean Eats, 8853
Naturally Delicious Inc, 8854
Naturally Homegrown, 8855
Naturally Nutty, 8856, 58264
Naturally Scientific, 8857
Naturalmond Almond Butter, 8858
Nature Cure Northwest, 8859
Nature Distributors, 58265
Nature Kist Snacks, 8860
Nature Most Laboratories, 8861, 26518, 46914
Nature Nate's, 8862
Nature Quality, 8863, 46915
Nature Soy Inc, 8864, 26519

1416

All Companies Index

Nature Zen USA, 8865
Nature's Apothecary, 8866, 46916
Nature's Bakery, 8867
Nature's Bandits, 8868
Nature's Best, 58266
Nature's Best Inc, 8869, 8870, 46917
Nature's Bounty Co., 8871, 46918, 58267
Nature's Candy, 8872, 58268
Nature's Dairy, 8873
Nature's Earthly Choice, 8874
Nature's Finest Products, 8875
Nature's First Inc, 8876
Nature's Fusions, 8877, 58269
Nature's Godfather, 8878
Nature's Guru, 8879, 46919
Nature's Habit Brand. Inc., 8880
Nature's Hand Inc, 8881
Nature's Herbs, 8882, 46920
Nature's Hilights, 8883
Nature's Hollow, 8884, 58270
Nature's Kitchen, 8885
Nature's Legacy Inc., 8886, 46921
Nature's Love, 8887
Nature's Nutrition, 8888
Nature's Own, 26520, 46922
Nature's Path Foods, 8889, 46923
Nature's Plus, 8890, 46924
Nature's Products Inc, 8891, 40849, 46925, 51959
Nature's Provision Company, 8892, 58271
Nature's Select Inc, 8893
Nature's Sunshine Products Company, 8894, 46926
Nature's Touch, 8895
Nature's Way, 8896
Naturel, 8897
Natures Sungrown Foods Inc, 8898, 46927
Naturex Inc, 8899, 46928
Naughton Equipment Sales, 26521
Naughty Noah's, 8900
Naumes, Inc., 8901
Navarro Pecan Co, 8902, 46929
Navarro Vineyards, 8903
Navas Instruments, 8904
Navco, 26522, 46930
Navitas Naturals, 8905, 58272
Navy Brand, 26523, 58273
Naya, 8906, 46931
Naylor Association Solutions, 8907, 26524
Naylor Candies Inc, 8908, 46932
Naylor Wine Cellars Inc, 8909
NB Corporation of America, 26417
Nbi Fresh Juices Distribution, 46933
NCC, 26418, 46822
NCR Corp, 26419
NCR Counterpoint, 26420
NDC Infrared EngineeringInc, 26421, 46823
Ne-Mo's Bakery Inc, 8910, 46934
Neal Walters Poster Corporation, 26525, 46935
Neal's Chocolates, 8911
Nealanders Food Ingredients, 8912
Near East Food Products, 8913
Near East Importing Corporation, 46936, 58274
Neat Foods, 8914
NEBCO Distributing, 58205
Nebraska Bean, 8915, 26526, 46937, 58275
Nebraska Beef Council, 8916
Nebraska Corn-Fed Beef, 46938
Nebraska Department of Agriculture, 46939
Nebraska Neon Sign Co, 26527
Nebraska Warehouse Co, 51960, 53192
Necco, 8917
Necedah Pallet Co Inc, 26528
NECO/Nebraska Engineering, 26422, 46824
Nectar Island, 8918
Nectar Soda Company, 58276

Nederman, 26529, 26530, 46940
Nedlog Company, 8919
Needham Inc, 53193
Neel's Wholesale Produce Co, 58277
Neelands Refrigeration, 58278
Neenah Springs, 8920
Neese Country Sausage Inc, 8921
Neesvig Meats, 46941, 58279
Nefab, 26531
Nefab Packaging Inc, 26532, 26533
Nefab Packaging Inc., 26534
Nefab Packaging, Inc., 26535, 46942
Neff Packaging, 26536
Nehalem Bay Winery, 8922
Neighbors Coffee, 8923, 58280
Neil Jones Food Company, 8924, 46943
Neilly's Foods, 8925
Neilson Canvas Company, 26537
Nekta, 8926
Nelipak, 26538, 58281
Nell Baking Company, 8927
Nelles Automation, 26539, 46944
Nello's Sauce, 8928
Nellson Candies Inc, 8929, 46945
Nellson Nutraceutical LLC, 8930
Nelly's Organics, 8931
Nelson & Associates Recruiting, 26540
Nelson Cheese Factory, 40850, 46946
Nelson Co, 26541, 58282
Nelson Container Corp, 26542
Nelson Crab Inc, 8932, 46947
Nelson Custom Signs, 26543
Nelson Ice Cream, 8933
Nelson, Gene, 26544
Nelson-Jameson Inc, 26545, 58283
NEMA Associates, 40831
Nema Food Distribution, 8934, 58284
Nemco Electric Company, 26546
Nemco Food Equipment, 26547, 46948, 46949
Nemeth Engineering Assoc, 26548
Neo North America Inc., 8935
Neo-Image Candle Light, 26549
Neo-Ray Products, 26550, 46950
Neogen Corp, 26551, 46951
Neokraft Signs Inc, 26552
Neon Design-a-Sign, 26553, 46952
Neonetics Inc, 26554, 46953
Neos, 26555, 46954
NEPA Pallet & Container Co, 26423, 46825
Nepco Egg Of Ga, 8936, 46955
Neptune Fisheries, 8937, 46956
Neptune Foods, 8938, 46957
Nercon Engineering & Manufacturing, 26556, 46958
Nesbitt Processing, 8939, 58285
Nesco Brokerage Company, 40851
Neshaminy Valley Natural Foods, 8940, 58286
Nesson Meat Sales, 58287
Nest Eggs, 8941
Nestelle's, Inc., 8943
NestFresh, 8942
Nestle USA, 8944, 46959
Nestle USA Inc, 8945
Nestor Imports Inc, 46960
Net Material Handling, 26557
Net Pack Systems, 26558
Neto's Market & Grill, 8946
Network FOB, 51961
Network Food Brokers, 8947
Network Sales, Inc, 40852
Netzsch Pumps North America, 26559, 46961
Neuchatel Chocolatier, 8949
Neugart, 26560
Neuhaus, 46962
Neuman Bakery Specialties, 8950
Neuman Distributing Company, 58289
Neupak, 26561, 26562
NeuRoast, 8948, 58288
Neutec Group, 26563, 58290
Nevada Baking Company, 8951
Nevada City Brewing, 8952

Nevada City Winery, 8953
Nevada Cold Storage, 53194
Nevada County Wine Guild, 8954, 58291
Nevada Seafood Company, 58292
Nevlen Co. 2, Inc., 26564, 46963
Nevo Corporation, 26565, 46964
New Age Beverages, 8955
New Age Industrial, 26566, 46965
New Atlanta Dairies, 58293
New Attitude Beverage Corporation, 26567, 46966
New Bakery Company of Ohio, 8956
New Barn, 8957
New Barn Organics, 8958, 58294
New Beer Distributors, 58295
New Belgium Brewing Co, 8959
New Braunfels Smokehouse, 8960
New Britain Candy Company, 58296
New Brunswick Intl Inc, 26568
New Brunswick Saw Service, 58297
New Brunswick Scientific Co, 26569
New Business Corp, 8961
New Canaan Farms, 8962
New Carbon Company, 26570
New Castle Industries Inc, 26571
New Centennial, 26572
New Century Snacks, 8963
New Chapter, 8964
New Chief Fashion, 26573, 46967, 46968
New City Packing Company, 8965, 46969
New Court, 26574
New Data Systems Inc, 26575
New Direction Foods, 8966
New Earth, 8967, 46970
New England Cheese Making Supply Company, 26576
New England Country Bakers, 8968
New England Cranberry, 8969, 46971
New England Foods, 58298
New England Herbal Foods, 46972
New England Indl Truck Inc, 58299
New England Label, 26577
New England Machinery Inc, 26578, 46973
New England Meat Company, 58300
New England Muffin Co Inc, 8970
New England Natural Bakers, 8971, 46974
New England Overshoe Company, 26579
New England Pallets & Skids, 26580, 46975
New England Tea & Coffee Co, 8972
New England Wooden Ware, 26581, 46976
New Era Canning Company, 8973, 46977
New Era Label Corporation, 26582
New Federal Cold Storage, 53195
New Generation Foods, 8974
New Generation Software Inc, 26583
New Glarus Bakery & Tea Room, 8975
New Glarus Brewing CompaNy, 8976
New Grass Bison, 8977
New Hampton Transfer & Storage, 51962, 53196
New Harbor Fisherman's Cooperative, 8978, 58301
New Harmony Coffee & Tea Co., 8979
New Harvest Foods, 8980
New Hatchwear Company, 26584
New Haven Awnings, 26585
New High Glass, 26586
New Holland Brewing Co, 8981
New Hope Imports, 46978, 58302
New Hope Mills Mfg Inc, 8982
New Hope Natural Media, 8983, 26587
New Hope Winery, 8984
New Horizon Farms, 8985
New Horizon Foods, 8986, 26588, 46979
New Horizon Technologies, 26589
New Horizons, 40853
New Horizons Baking Co, 8987
New Jamaican Gold, 8988
New Jersey Department OfAgriculture, 26590

New Jersey Provision Co, 58303
New Jersey Wire Stitching Machine Company, 26591
New Klix Corporation, 26592, 46980
New Land Vineyard, 8989
New Lisbon Wood ProductsManufacturing Company, 26593
New London Engineering, 26594
New Mexico Food Distributors, 58304
New Mexico Green Chile Company, 8990
New Mexico Products Inc, 26595
New Nissi Corp., 8991, 58305
New Ocean, 8992, 58306
New Organics, 8993, 40854, 46981, 58307
New Orleans Cold Storage& Warehouse, 53198
New Orleans Cold Storage-Wrhse, 51963, 53197, 53199
New Orleans Fish House II LLC, 8994
New Orleans Food Co-op, 8995, 46982
New Orleans Gulf Seafood, 8996, 58308
New Packing Company, 8997
New Pig Corp, 26596
New Resina Corporation, 26597
New Salem Tea-Bread Company, 8998
New Season Foods Inc, 8999, 46983
New South Co Inc, 26598
New Tiger International, 26599
New Vermont Creamery, 58309
New Wave Cuisine, 9000
New Way Packaging Machinery, 26600, 46984
New World Pasta Co, 9001
New York, 51964
New York Apple Assn Inc, 46985
New York Apple Sales Inc, 9002, 46986
New York Bakeries Inc, 9003, 46987
New York Bottling Co Inc, 9004
New York Cash Register Company, 58310
New York Corugated Box Co, 26601
New York Department of Agriculture & Markets, 46988
New York Export Co, 46989
New York Folding Box Co Inc, 26602
New York Frozen Foods Inc, 9005
New York Intl Bread Co, 9006
New York Izabel Lam, 46990
New York Pizza, 9007
New York Pretzel, 9008, 46991
New York Ravioli, 9009
New York State Electric & Gas, 26603
New Zealand Lamb Co, 46992, 58311
New-Ma Co. Llc, 26604
Newark Refrigerated Warehouse, 53200
Newark Wire Cloth Co, 26605, 46994
Neway Packaging Corporation, 58313
Newburg Corners Cheese Factory, 9011
Newburgh Brewing Company, 9012
Newby Teas, 9013
Newcastle Co Inc, 26606, 46995
Newco Enterprises Inc, 26607, 46996
Newco Inc, 26608
Newcourt, Inc., 26609
Newell Brands, 26610, 46997
Newell Lobsters, 9014, 46998
Newfound Resources, 9015, 46999
NewGem Products, 9010
Newlands Systems, 26611, 47000
Newly Weds Foods Inc, 9016, 9017, 26612, 47001
Newman Fixture Co Inc, 58314
Newman Labeling Systems, 26613
Newman Sanitary Gasket Co, 26614, 47002
Newman's Own, 9018, 47003
Newmarket Corp, 26615
Newmarket Foods, 9019
Newmeadows Lobster Inc, 9020, 58315
Newport Electronics Inc, 26616, 47004
Newport Flavours & Fragrances, 9021
Newport Ingredients, 9022
Newport Marketing, 58316

1417

All Companies Index

Newport Meat Co North, 9023
Newport St Paul Cold Storage, 51965, 53201
Newport Vineyards & Winery, 9024
Newstamp Lighting Factory, 26617, 26618, 47005
NewStar Fresh Foods LLC, 46993, 58312
Newtech Beverage Systems, 58317
Newtech Inc, 26619
Newton Broom Co, 26620
Newton Candy Company, 9025
Newton Manufacturing Co, 58318
Newton OA & Son Co, 26621, 47006
Newton Vineyard, 9026
Newtown Foods, 47007
Newtown Foods USA Inc, 9027
Newtree America, 47008
Newwaveenviro, 26622
Nexcel Natural Ingredients, 9028
Nexel Industries Inc, 26623, 47009
Nexen Group, 26624
Nexeo Solutions, 26625
Nexira, 9029, 26626, 47010
Next Phase Enterprises, 40855
Nexthermal, 26627
NFI Industries Inc, 51952, 53184
Nhs Labs Inc, 9030, 26628, 58319
Ni Source Inc, 26629
Niagara Blower Company, 26630, 47011
Niagara Chocolates, 9031
Niagara Foods, 9032, 47012
Niagara Restaurant Supply, 58320
Niantic Awning Company, 26631
NibMor, 9033
Nicasio Vineyards, 9034
Nice-Pak Products Inc, 26632, 47013
Nicewonger Company, 58321
Niche Gourmet, 47014
Niche Import Co, 9035
Niche W&S, 9036
Nichelini Family Winery Inc, 9037
Nichem Co, 9038, 47015
Nichimen America, 47016
Nicholas & Co Inc, 40856, 58322
Nicholas Machine and Grinding, 26633
Nicholas Marketing Associates, 26634
Nichols Farms, 9039
Nichols Foodservice, 58323
Nichols Specialty Products, 26635, 47017
Nichols Wire, 26636
Nick Sciabica & Sons, 9040, 47018, 58324
Nick's Sticks, 9041
Nickabood's Inc, 9042
Nicky USA Inc, 9043, 47019, 58325
Nicol Scales & Measurement LP, 26637, 47020
Nicola International, 9044, 47021
Nicola Pizza, 9045
Nicola Valley Apiaries, 9046
Nicole's Divine Crackers, 9047, 47022
Nicomac Inc, 26638
Nicosia Creative Expresso, 26639
Nidec Minster Corp., 26640
Niebaum-Coppola Estate Winery, 9048
Nieco Corporation, 26641, 47023
Nielsen Citrus Products Inc, 9049, 47024
Nielsen-Massey Vanillas Inc, 9050, 47025, 58326
Niemuth's Steak & Chop Shop, 9051
Nifty Packaging, 26642
Night Hawk Frozen Foods Inc, 9052
Night Owls Wholesale Market, 58327
Nigrelli Systems Purchasing, 26643, 47026
Nijal USA, 26644
Nijhuis Water Technology, 26645
Nikka Densok, 26646
Nikken Foods, 9053, 47027
Nikki's Coconut Butter, 9054, 58328
Nikki's Cookies, 9055, 47028
Nikko Ceramics, 47029
Nikol Foods, 40857, 58329
Nikola's Foods, 9056, 40858, 58330
Nilfisk, Inc., 26647

Niman Ranch, 9057
Nimble Nectar, 9058
Nimbus Water Systems, 26648, 47030
NIMCO Corp, 26424
Nimeks Organics, 9059
Nina Mauritz Design Service, 26649
Nina's Gourmet Dip, 9060
Ninety Six Canning Company, 9061
Ninth Avenue Foods, 9062
Nippon Cargo Airlines Co LTD, 51966, 53202
Nippon Food Company, 40859
Nips Potato Chips, 9063
Niro, 26650, 47031
Niroflex, USA, 26652, 47032
Nirvana Natural Spring Water, 9064
Nirwana Foods, 9065, 47033
Nisbet Oyster Company, 9066, 47034, 58331
Nissan Lift Of New York Inc, 58332
Nissho Iwai American Corporation, 47035
Nisshodo Candy Store, 9067
Nissin Foods USA Co Inc, 9068
Nissley Vineyards & Winery, 9069
Nita Crisp Crackers LLC, 9070, 26653, 58333
Nitech, 26654, 47036
Nitsch Tool Co Inc, 26655, 47037
Nitta Casings Inc, 9071
Nitta Corp Of America, 26656
Nitta Gelatin NA, 9072
Niutang Chemical, Inc., 9073, 47038
NJM Packaging, 26425, 26426
NJM Seafood, 58206
NJM/CLI, 26427, 46826
Nk Hurst Co Inc, 9074
No Cow, 9075, 58334
No Evil Foods, 9076
No Pudge! Foods, 9077
No Whey Foods, 9078
Noah's Potato Chip Co, 58335
Nobert Marketing, 40860
Noble Chocolates NV, 9079
Noble Foods, 40861
Noble Harvest, 47039, 58336
Noble House Trading Company, 40862
Noble Popcorn, 9080
Nobletree Coffee, 9081
Nocs South Atlantic, 53203, 53204
NOCS West Gulf, 53185
Nocus West Gulf, 53205
Nodine's Smokehouse Inc, 9082
Noel Corp, 9083, 47040
Nog Incorporated, 9084
Nogales Fruit & Vegetables Dst, 58337
Nogg Chemical & Paper Company, 58338
Noh Foods Of Hawaii, 9085
Noh Foods of Hawaii, 47041
Noh Foods Of Hawaii, 58339
Noh Foods of Hawaii, 58340
NOKA, 8723
Nolechek Meats Inc, 9086
Nolon Industries, 26657, 47042
Nolu Plastics, 26658
Nomaco, 26659
Nomafa, 26660
Nomi Snacks, 9087
Nomolas Corp, 9088
Nomura & Co, 40863
Nona Lim, 9089
Nona Vegan Foods, 9090, 58341
Nonna Pia's Gourmet Sauces, 9091
Nonni's Foods LLC, 9092, 47043
Nonpareil Farms, 9093, 47044
Nook Industries, 26661
Noon Hour Food Products Inc, 9094, 47045, 58342
Noon International, 40864, 47046
Noosa Yoghurt, 9095
Noosh Brands, 9096
Nootra Life, 9097
Noour Inc., 9098

Nor-AM Cold Storage, 53206
Nor-Am Cold Storage, 53207
Nor-Cliff Farms, 9099, 47047
Nor-Lake, 26662, 47048
Nor-Tech Dairy Advisors, 9100
Nora Snacks, 9101
Nora's Candy Shop, 9102
Norac Technologies, 9103, 47049
Noral, 26664, 47050
Norandal, 26665, 47051
Norback Ley & Assoc, 26666, 26667, 47052
Norben Co, 9104, 58343
Norbest, LLC, 9105, 47053
Norcal Beverage Co, 26668, 58344
NorCrest Consulting, 26663
Norden Inc, 26669
Nordic Doors, 26670
Nordic Group Inc, 9106, 47054
Nordic Logistics and Warehousing, LLC, 53208, 53209
Nordic Printing & Packaging, 26671
Nordic Ware Food Service, 47055
Nordica Warehouses Inc, 53210
Nordman Of California, 9107
Nordson Corp, 26672, 47056
Nordson Sealant Equipment, 26673, 47057
Noren Products Inc, 26674, 47058
Norfolk Hatchery, 9108, 47059
Norfolk Packing Company, 58345
Norfolk Southern Corp, 51967
Norfolk Warehouse Distribution Centers, 53211
Norfood Cherry Growers, 9109
Norgren Inc., 26675
Norgus Silk Screen Co Inc, 26676
Norimoor Company, 47060
Norimoor Lic, 9110
Norjo Distribution Services, 51968
Norland International, 26677
Norland Products Inc, 58346
Norlift Inc, 58347
Norm's Farms, 9111
Norm's Refrigeration, 58348
Norman Brokerage Co, 40865
Norman G. Jensen, 51969, 53212
Norman Hecht, 40866
Norman International, 26678
Norman Wolff Associates, 58349
Norman's, 58350
Norman's Wholesale Grocery Company, 58351
Normandie Metal Fabricators, 26679
Norpac Fisheries Inc, 9112
NORPAC Foods Inc, 8724, 46827
Norpaco Inc, 9113, 58352
Norpak Corp, 26680, 47061
Norris Products Corp oration, 26681
Norristown Box Company, 26682, 26683
Norse Dairy Systems, 26684
Norseland Foods Inc, 47062
North Aire Market, Inc., 9114
North American Beverage Co, 9115
North American Blueberry Council, 9116
North American Breweries Inc., 9117
North American Coffees, 9118
North American Container Corp, 26685
North American Corp, 58353
North American Deer Farmers Association, 26686
North American Enterprises, 9119, 47063
North American Packaging Corp, 26687, 47064
North American Plastic Manufacturing Company, 26688
North American Provisioners, 47065, 58354
North American Reishi/Nammex, 9120, 47066
North American Roller Prod Inc, 26689
North American Signs, 26690
North American Warehousing, 53213
North American Water Group, 9121
North Atlantic Equipment Sales, 26691

North Atlantic Inc, 9122, 58355
North Atlantic Lobster, 58356
North Atlantic Products, 9123, 47067
North Atlantic Seafood, 9124, 58357
North Bay Fisherman's Cooperative, 9125, 47068
North Bay Produce Inc, 9126, 47069, 53214
North Bay Seafood, 40867, 58358
North Bay Trading Co, 9127, 40868, 47070
North Carolina Potato Association, 58359
North Carolina State Ports Authority: Port of Wilmington, 53215
North Carolina's Southeast, 26692
North Central Co, 58360
North Coast Farms, 9128
North Coast Processing, 9129, 47071
North Company, 26693
North Country Natural Spring Water, 9130, 47072
North Country Smokehouse, 9131
North Dakota Mill & Elevator Assn., 9132
North Eastern Sales Solutions, 40869
North Fork Weld & Steel Supl, 26694
North Lake Fish Cooperative, 9133, 47073
North of the Border, 9140
North Pacific Seafoods Inc, 9134, 47074, 58361
North Park Transportation Co, 51970
North Peace Apiaries, 9135, 47075
North River Roasters, 9136, 47076
North Shore Bottling Co, 9137
North Side Banana Co, 58362
North Side Packing Co, 26695
North Star, 26696
North Star Agency, 40870
North Star Engineered Products, 26697, 47077
North Star Ice EquipmentCorporation, 26698, 47078
North Star World Trade Svc, 51971
North Taste Flavourings, 9138, 47079
North West Handling Systems Inc, 58363
North West Pharmanaturals Inc, 9139
North Western Warehouse Co, 53216
Northampton Brewing Company, 9141
Northbay Restaurant Equipment & Design, 58364
Northbrook Laboratories, 26700
Northcoast Woodworks, 26701
Northeast Box Co, 26702
Northeast Calamari Inc, 40871, 47080
Northeast Container Corporation, 26703
Northeast Distributors Inc, 26704
Northeast Foods Inc, 9142
Northeast Fresh Foods Alliance, 26705
Northeast Group Exporters Inc, 47081
Northeast Kingdom Mustard Company, 9143
Northeast Laboratory Svc, 26706
Northeast Packaging Co, 26707, 47082
Northeast Packaging Materials, 26708, 47083
Northeast Refrigerated, 51972, 53217
Northeast Retail Services, 40872
Northeastern Enterprises, 40873
Northeastern Products Company, 9144
Northeastern Products Corp, 26709, 47084
Northern Air Cargo, 51973
Northern Berkshire Tourist, 26710
Northern Box Co Inc, 26711
Northern Breweries, 9145
Northern Dairy, 9146
Northern Discovery Seafoods, 9147
Northern Falls, 9148
Northern Farmhouse Pasta LLC, 9149
Northern Feed & Bean Company, 9150, 47085
Northern Flair Foods, 9151
Northern Haserot, 58365
Northern Keta Caviar, 9152, 58366

All Companies Index

Northern Lights Brewing Company, 9153
Northern Meats, 9154, 58367
Northern Metal Products, 26712
Northern Metals & Supply, 26713
Northern Neck, 9155
Northern Ocean Marine, 9156, 58368
Northern Orchard Co Inc, 9157, 47086, 58369
Northern Package Corporation, 26714
Northern Packing Company, 9158
Northern Products Corporation, 9159, 47087
Northern Soy Inc, 9160
Northern Stainless Fabricating, 26715, 47088
Northern Steel Industrie, 58370
Northern Utah Manufacturing, 9161
Northern Valley Baking Co, 9162
Northern Vineyards Winery, 9163
Northern Wind Inc, 9165, 47089
Northern WIS Produce Co, 9164, 58371
Northfield Freezing Systems, 26716, 47090
Northland Cold Storage Inc, 51974, 53218
Northland Consultants, 26717
Northland Corp, 26718, 26719, 47091
Northland Cranberries, 9166
Northland Express Transport, 40874, 51975
Northland Industrial Truck Company Inc, 58372
Northland Juices, 9167
Northland Labs, 26720
Northland Organic Foods Corporation, 40875, 47092
Northland Process Piping, 26721, 58373
Northridge Laboratories, 9168, 47093
Northside Bakery, 9169
Northstar Distributing, 58374
NorthStar Print Group, 26699
Northstate Provision Co, 58375
Northtech Workholding, 47094
Northumberland Dairy, 9170, 40876, 58376
Northview Laboratories, 26722, 26723
Northview Pacific Laboratories, 26724
Northville Laboratories Inc, 26725
Northville Winery & Brewing Co, 9171, 58377
Northwest Analytical Inc, 26726, 47095
Northwest Art Glass, 26727, 47096
Northwest Cherry Growers, 26728
Northwest Chocolate Factory, 9172, 47097
Northwest Dairy Association, 58378
Northwest Deli Distribution, 58379
Northwest Fisheries, 9173, 47098
Northwest Food Processors Assn, 26729
Northwest Forklift, 58380
Northwest Hazelnut Company, 9174
Northwest Laboratories, 26730
Northwest Meat Company, 9175
Northwest Molded Products Classic Line, 26731
Northwest Natural Foods, 9176
Northwest Naturals Company, 47099, 58381
Northwest Naturals LLC, 9177, 47100
Northwest Packing Co, 9178
Northwest Pea & Bean Co, 9179
Northwest Products, 26732
Northwest Select Coffee Roasters, 58382
Northwest Wild Products, 9180, 58383
Northwestern, 26733
Northwestern Coffee Mills, 9181, 9182, 47101
Northwestern Corp, 26734, 47102
Northwestern Extract, 9183, 47103
Northwestern Foods, 9184, 40877, 58384
Northwestern Fruit Co, 58385
Northwestern Ice & Cold Storage, 53219
Northwind Inc, 26735
Northwoods Candy Emporium, 9185

Norvell Co Inc, 26736, 47104
Norvell Fixtures & Equipment Company, 58386
Norwalk Dairy, 9186
Norwalt Design Inc, 26737
Norwood Marking Systems, 26738, 47105
Norwood Paper Inc, 26739
Nosaj Disposables, 26740
Nosco, 26741
Nossack Fine Meats, 9187, 47106
Nostalgic Specialty Foods, 9188
Noteworthy Company, 26742
Nothin' But Foods, 9189
Nothing But The Fruit, 9190
Nothing Mundane, 58387
Nothum Food Processing Systems, 26743, 47107
Notre Dame Bakery, 9191
Notre Dame Seafoods Inc., 9192, 47108
Nott Company, 58388
Nottingham Spirk, 26744
Nourishtea, 9193, 58389
Nouveau Foods, 9194
Nova Hand Dryers, 26745, 47109
Nova Industries, 26746, 47110
Nova Seafood, 40878, 47111, 58390
Nova Transportation Inc, 51976
Novacart Inc, 26747
Novamex, 26748, 47112
Novar, 26749
Novax Group/Point of Sales, 26750
Novel Ingredient Services, LLC, 47113
Novelis Foil Products, 26751
Novelty Advertising, 26752, 47114
Novelty Baskets, 26753
Novelty Crystal, 26754, 47115
Noveon Inc, 26755
Novick Brothers Corp, 58391
NOVOLEX, 26428
Novolex, 26756
Novozymes North America Inc, 9195, 47116
Novus, 26757, 47117
Now & Zen, 9196
Now Designs, 47118
NOW Foods, 8725, 46828, 58207
Now Plastics Inc, 26758, 47119
Nowakowski, 26759
Noyes, P J, 9197, 47120
Nozzle Nolen Inc, 26760
NPC Dehydrators, 8726, 8727
NPC Display Group, 26429
Nrd LLC, 26761, 26762, 26763, 47121
NS International, 26430
NSF International, 26431
NSG Transport Inc, 8728, 46829
Nspired Natural Foods, 9198, 58392
NST Metals, 26432, 46830
Ntc Marketing, 9199, 47122
NTN Wireless, 26433, 46831
NTS, 26434
Nu CO2 LLC, 26764
Nu Concept Food Svc, 58393
Nu Life Market, 9200
Nu Naturals Inc, 9201
Nu Products Co Inc, 9202
Nu-Con Equipment, 26765
Nu-Dell Manufacturing, 26766
Nu-Lane Cargo Services, 40879, 51977, 53220
Nu-Meat Technology, 26767
Nu-Star Inc, 26768, 47123
Nu-Tek Food Science, 9203
Nu-Tex Styles, Inc., 26769, 47124
Nu-Towel Co, 26770
Nu-Trend Plastics Thermoformer, 26771, 47125
Nu-Vu Food Service Systems, 26772
Nu-Way Potato Products, 9204
Nu-World Amaranth Inc, 9205, 47126
Nu-World Foods, 9206
Nuance Solutions, 26773, 47128
Nuchief Sales Inc, 9212, 47129
Nuco Industries, 58394

Nucon Corporation, 26775, 47130
Nueces Canyon Range, 9213
Nueske's Applewood Smoked Meat, 9214
NuGo Nutrition, 9207
Nuherbs Company, 47131, 58395
Nui Foods, 9215, 58396
Nulaid Foods Inc, 9216, 47132
Nulco Lighting, 26776
NuLeaf Naturals, 9208
Numatics Inc, 26777
Numeric Computer Systems Inc, 26778
Numi Organic Tea, 9217
Numo Broth, 9218
NuNaturals, 9209
Nunes Co Inc, 9219, 47133
Nunes Farms Marketing, 9220, 47134
Nuova Distribution Centre, 26779, 47135
Nuova Simonelli, 47136
Nuova Simonelli USA, 26780
Nuovo Pasta Productions LTD, 9221
NuPasta, 9210
Nurture, 9222
Nurture Ranch, 9223
Nush Foods, 9224
Nustef Foods, 9225, 47137
Nut Factory, 9226, 47138
Nutec Manufacturing Inc, 26781, 26782, 26783, 47139
Nutfield Brewing Company, 9228
Nutiva, 9229
Nutmeg Vineyard, 9230
NuTone, 26773, 47127
Nutorious LLC, 9231
Nutpods, 9232
Nutra Food Ingredients, LLC, 9233, 26784, 47140, 53221
Nutra Nuts, 9234
Nutraceutical International, 9237, 9238, 9239, 26785, 47142, 58397
Nutraceutics Corp, 9240, 47143
Nutralliance, 9241
Nutranique Labs, 9242, 47144
Nutraplex, 9243
NutraSpa Soap, 47141
NutraSun, 9235
NutraSweet Company, 9236
NutRaw Foods, 9227
Nutrex Hawaii Inc, 9244, 47145
Nutri Base, 9245
Nutri Fruit, 9246
Nutri-Bake Inc, 9247, 26786, 58398
Nutri-Cell, 9248, 47146
Nutri-Nation, 9249
Nutri-Rich Corp., 58399
Nutribiotic, 9251, 47147
Nutricepts, 9252, 47148
NutriCology Allergy Research, 58400
Nutrifaster Inc, 26787, 47149
NutriFusion, 9250
Nutrilabs, 9253, 47150
Nutrilicious Natural Bakery, 9254
Nutrin Distribution Company, 26788
Nutrinfo Corporation, 26789
Nutrinova, 26790, 58401
Nutriscience Laboratories, 58402
Nutrisciences Labs, 9255, 26791
Nutrisoya Foods, 9256, 47151
Nutrisport Pharmacal, 9257
Nutritech Corporation, 9258, 47152
Nutrition & Food Associates, 26792, 47153
Nutrition 21 Inc, 9259
Nutrition Center Inc, 9260
Nutrition Network, 26793
Nutrition Products Company, 58403
Nutrition Research, 26794
Nutrition Supply Corp, 9261, 47154
Nutritional Counselors of America, 9262, 47155, 58404
Nutritional Labs Intl, 9263, 47156
Nutritional Research Associates, 9264, 47157
Nutritional Specialties, 9265, 47158
Nutriwest, 9266, 47159

Nutro Laboratories, 9267
Nuts & Spice Company, 58405
Nuts & Stems, 9268
Nuts 'N More, 9269, 58406
Nuts + Nuts, 9270
Nuts About Granola, 9271
Nuts About You, 9272
Nuts For Cheese, 9273, 58407
Nutsco Inc, 26795
Nutty Bavarian, 9274, 26796
Nutty Goodness, 9275
Nuttzo, 9276, 58408
Nuun Active Hydration, 9277
NuZee, Inc., 9211
Nyco Products Co, 26797
Nydree Flooring, 26798, 47160
NYK Line North America Inc, 51953
Nylon Net Company, 58409
Nyman Manufacturing Company, 26799, 47161
NYP, 26435, 46832
Nysco Products Inc, 9278
Nyssa-Nampa Beet Growers, 9279

O

O & H Danish Bakery Inc, 9280
O A Newton & Son Co, 26800
O Berk Co LLC, 58410
O C Schulz & Sons, 9281
O K Mfg, 26801
O Olive Oil, 9282
O'Boyle's Ice Cream Company, 9283
O'Brian Brothers Food, 9284
O'Brian Tarping Systems Inc, 26802
O'Brien & Associates Brokerage Company, 40880
O'Brien Bros Inc, 26803
O'Brien Installations, 26804, 47162
O'Brines Pickling, 9285
O'Byrne Distribution Ctr Inc, 51978, 53222
O'Danny Boy Ice Cream, 9286
O'Dell Corp, 26805, 47163
O'Donnell Formulas Inc, 9287
O'Donnell-Usen, 9288
O'Doughs, 9289
O'Garvey Sauces, 9290
O'Hanlon Group, 40881
O'Hara Corp, 9291, 47164
O'Neal's Fresh Frozen Pizza Crust, 9292
O'Neil's Distributors, 9293
O'Neill Coffee Co, 9294, 58411
O'Neill Marketing Agents, 40882
O'Sole Mio, 9295
O-At-Ka Milk Prods Co-Op Inc, 9296, 47165
O-Cedar, 26806, 26807, 47166
O-G Packing & Cold Storage Co, 53223
O-Sesco, 58412
O. Lippi & Company, 58413
O.B.S. Trading, 26808
O.C. Adhesives Corporation, 26809
O.D. Kurtz Associates, 26810
O.G. Foodservice, 58414
O.K. Marking Devices, 26811
O.R. Elder, 40883
O.W. & B.S. Look Company, 58415
O/K International Corporation, 26812
Oak Barrel Winecraft, 26832, 47174, 58421
Oak Creek Brewing Company, 9310
Oak Creek Pallet Company, 26833
Oak Farm's Dairy, 9311
Oak Farms, 9312
Oak Farms Dairy, 40884, 58422
Oak Grove Dairy, 9313
Oak Grove Orchards Winery, 9314
Oak Grove Smoke House Inc, 9315
Oak Harbor Freight Lines, 51980
Oak Hill Farm, 9316
Oak International, 26834, 47175
Oak Island Seafood Company, 9317, 58423
Oak Knoll Dairy, Inc., 9318

1419

All Companies Index

Oak Knoll Winery, 9319
Oak Leaf Confections, 9320, 47176
Oak Leaf Sales Co, 40885
Oak Ridge Winery LLC, 9321, 58424
Oak Spring Winery, 9322
Oak State Products Inc, 9323
Oak Street Manufacturing, 9324, 26835
Oakes & Burger, 26836
Oakes Carton Co, 26837
Oakhurst Dairy, 9325
Oakhurst Industries, 9326
Oakite Products, 26838
Oakland Bean Cleaning & Storage, 9327
Oakland Noodle Co, 9328
Oaklee International, 26839, 26840
Oakrun Farm Bakery, 9329, 47177
Oakton Instruments, 26841
Oasis Breads, 9330
Oasis Coffee Co Inc, 9331
Oasis Food Co, 9332
Oasis Mediterranean Cuisine, 9333
Oasis Winery, 9334
Oates Flag Co Inc, 26842
Oatly, 9335
Oats Overnight, 9336
Oatworks, 9337
OB Macaroni Company, 9297
Oberburg Engineering, 26843
Oberto Brands, 9338
Oberweis Dairy Inc, 9339
Obester Winery, 9340
Obis One, 9341
Oborn Transfer & Stge Co Inc, 51981, 53225
Oc Lugo Co Inc, 9342, 26844
Occidental Chemical Corporation, 26845, 26846
Occidental Foods International, LLC, 40886, 47178, 53226, 58425
Ocean Approved, 9343
Ocean Beauty Seafoods Inc, 9344, 47179
Ocean Cliff Corp, 9345, 47180
Ocean Crest Seafoods, 9346, 58426
Ocean Food Co. Ltd., 9347
Ocean Fresh Seafoods, 9348
Ocean Frost, 47181, 58427
Ocean Garden Products Inc, 47182
Ocean Harvest, 9349, 58428
Ocean King International, 9350, 47183
Ocean Mist Farms, 9351
Ocean Pride Fisheries, 9352, 47184
Ocean Pride Seafood, 9353
Ocean Select Seafood, 9354, 58429
Ocean Spray International, 9355, 47185
Ocean Springs Seafood, 9356
Ocean Union Company, 9357, 47186, 58430
Ocean Venture, 58431
Ocean World Lines, 51982, 53227
Ocean's Balance, 9358
Ocean's Halo, 9359
Oceana County Freezer Storage, 53228
Oceanfood Sales, 9360, 47187
Oceanledge Seafoods, 9361, 58432
Oceanpower America, 26847
Oceans Prome Distributing, 9362, 58433
Oceanside Knish Factory, 9363
Ocena Wineary & Vineyards, 9364
OCG Cacao, 9298
Ockerlund Industries, 26848
Ocme America Corporation, 26849
OCS Checkweighers Inc, 26813
Ocs Checkweighers, Inc., 26850
OCS Process Systems, 47167, 58416
Octavia Tea LLC, 9365
Odell Brewing Co, 9366
Odell's, 9367, 26851
Oden Machinery, 26852
Odenberg Engineering, 26853, 47188
Odessa Packaging Services, 26854
Odom Corporation, 58434
Odom's Tennessee Pride Sausage Company, 9368
Odor Management, 26855
ODW Logistics Inc, 51979, 53224

Odwalla, 9369
Oekerman Sales, 40887
Oenophilia, 26856, 58435
Oerlikon Balzers Coating USA, 26857
Oerlikon Leybold Vacuum, 26858, 26859, 47189
Oess Foods Inc, 47190
Oetiker Inc, 26860
Office General des Eaux Minerales, 9370, 47191
Offshore Seafood Co, 9371
Offshore Systems Inc, 9372, 51983
OFI Markesa Intl, 47168
Ogden Manufacturing Company, 26861, 47192
Ogeki Sake USA Inc, 9373
OH Armstrong, 58417
Oh Baby Foods, Inc., 9374
OH Chocolate, 9299
Oh Yes! Foods, 9375
Oh, Sugar! LLC, 9376
Ohana Seafood, LLC, 9377, 58436
Ohaus Corp, 26862, 47193
OHCO/Oriental Herb Company, 58418
OHi Food, 9300, 58419
Ohio Association Of Meat, 9378
Ohio Chemical Svc Inc, 58437
Ohio Commerce Center, 51984, 53229
Ohio Conveyor & Supply Inc, 26863, 58438
Ohio Farmers, 58439
Ohio Magnetics Inc, 26864, 47194
Ohio Materials Handling, 58440
Ohio Medical Corp, 26865
Ohio Mushroom Company, 9379
Ohio Rack Inc, 26866, 58441
Ohio Soap Products Company, 26867
Ohio Valley Shippers Assn, 51985, 53230
Ohlson Packaging, 26868, 47195
Ohly Americas, 26869
Ohm Design, 40888
Ohta Wafer Factory, 9380
OI Analytical, 26814
Oil & Olives Company, 9381
Oil Skimmers Inc, 26870
Oil-Dri Corporation of America, 26871
Oils Of Aloha, 9382
Oilseeds International LTD, 9383, 9384
Ojai Cook, 9385
Ojai Cook LLC, 9386
Ojai Vineyard, 9387
Ojeda USA, 9388, 26872
Ok Industries, 9389, 47196
OK International Group, 9301
Ok Kosher Certification, 26873, 26874
OK Stamp & Seal Company, 26815
Ok Uniform Co Inc, 26875, 47197
Okahara Saimin Factory LTD, 9390
Okanagan Spring Brewery, 9391
Oklabs, 26876
Oklahoma City Meat Co Inc, 9392, 58442
Oklahoma Neon, 26877
Oklahoma Pecan Co, 58443
Okuhara Foods Inc, 9393
Okura USA Inc, 26878, 47198
Ola Loa, 9394
Olam Spices, 9395, 26879
Oland Breweries, 9396
Olcott Plastics, 26880, 47199
Old Cavendish Products, 9397
Old Chatham Sheepherding Co, 9398
Old Colony Baking Co Inc, 9399
Old Country Bakery, 9400
Old Country Cheese, 9401
Old Country Meat & Sausage Company, 9402
Old Country Packers, 9403
Old Credit Brewing Co. Ltd., 9404
Old Creek Ranch Winery, 9405
Old Dominion Box, 26881
Old Dominion Box Co Inc, 26882
Old Dominion Box Company, 26883, 47200
Old Dominion Peanut Corp, 9406

Old Dominion Spice Company, 9407
Old Dominion Wood Products, 26884, 47201
Old Dutch Foods LTD, 9408
Old Dutch Mustard Company, 9409
Old English Printing & Label Company, 26885
Old Europe Cheese Inc, 9410
Old Fashion Foods Inc, 58444
Old Fashioned Foods, 9411
Old Fashioned Kitchen Inc, 9412
Old Fashioned Natural Products, 9413
Old Firehouse Winery, 9414
Old Home Foods Inc, 9415
Old House Vineyards, 9416
Old Kentucky Hams, 9417
Old London Foods, 9418
Old Mansion Inc, 9419, 26886, 47202
Old Mill Winery, 9420
Old Monmouth Candies, 9421
Old Neighborhood, 9422
Old Orchard Brands, LLC, 9423
Old Point Packing Inc, 58445
Old Rip Van Winkle Distillery, 9424
Old Sacramento Popcorn Company, 9425, 47203
Old South Winery, 9426
Old Tavern Food Products Inc, 9427
Old Time Candy Co, 9428
Old Tyme Mill Company, 9429
Old Wine Cellar, 9430
Old Wisconsin Food Products, 9431
Old Wisconsin Sausage Inc, 9432
Old World Bakery, 9433
Old World Spices Inc, 9434
Olde Colony Bakery, 9435
Olde Country Reproductions Inc, 26887, 47204
Olde Estate, 9436
Olde Heurich Brewing Company, 9437
Olde Thompson Inc, 26888
Olde Tyme Food Corporation, 9438, 47205
Olde Tyme Mercantile, 9439
Olds Products Co, 9440, 58446
Ole Hickory Pits, 26889, 47206
Ole Salty's Potato Chips, 9441
Ole Smoky Candy Kitchen, 9442
Oles De Puerto Rico Inc, 26890
Oley Distributing Company, 9443, 40889, 58447
Oliva Verde USA, 9444
Olive & Sinclair Chocolate Co, 9445
Olive Can Company, 26891, 47207
Olive Growers Council, 9446
Olive Oil Factor, 9447
Olive Oil Source, 9448, 58448
Oliveo LLC, 9449
Oliver Bentleys, 26892
Oliver Egg Products, 9450
Oliver Manufacturing Company, 26893
Oliver Packaging & Equipment Co., 9451, 26894
Oliver Products Company, 26895, 47208
Oliver Winery, 9452, 58449
Olivia's Croutons, 9453
Olivia's Kitchen, 9454
Olivier's Candies, 9455, 47209
Olivina. LLC, 9456, 26896, 58450
Olivio Premium Products, 9457
OLLI Salumeria Americana, 9302
Olmarc Packaging Company, 26897
Olney Machinery, 26898, 47210
Olomomo Nut Company, 9458, 58451
Olsen Fish Co, 9459, 58452
Olson Co, 51986, 53231
Olson Commercial Cold Storage, 53232
Olson Livestock & Seed, 9460
Olson Locker, 9461
Olson Wire Products Co, 26899
Olymel, 9462, 47211, 51987
Olympia Candies, 9463
Olympia International, 9464, 26900, 47212
Olympia Oyster Co, 9465

Olympia Provisions, 9466
Olympic Cellars, 9467
Olympic Coffee & Roasting, 9468
Olympic Foods, 9469, 47213
Olympic Juicer Company, 58453
Olympic Provisions Northwest, 9470
Olympus America Inc, 26901
Olympus Dairy, 47214
Om Mushrooms, 9471
Omaha Fixture Mfg, 26902
Omaha Meat Processors, 9472, 47215
Omaha Neon Sign Co, 26903
Omaha Steaks Inc, 9473, 47216
Omanhene Cocoa Bean Co, 9474
Omar Awnings & Signs, 26904
Omar Coffee Co, 9475
Omcan Inc., 26905, 47217
Omcan Manufacturing & Distributing Company, 26906, 47218, 58454
Omega Company, 26907
Omega Design Corp, 26908, 47219
Omega Foods, 9476
Omega Industrial Products Inc, 26909, 47220
Omega Industries, 26910
Omega Nutrition, 9477, 47221
Omega Produce Company, 9478, 47222, 58455
Omega Products Inc, 26911, 47223
Omega Protein, 9479, 47224
Omega Pure, 9480
Omega Thermo Products, 26912
Omega-Life, 58456
OMG! Superfoods, 9303
OMGhee, 9304
Omicron Steel Products Company, 26913, 47225
Omni Apparel, 26914
Omni Controls Inc, 26915, 47226
Omni Craft Inc, 26916, 47227
Omni Facility Resources, 26917
Omni Food Inc, 40890, 58457
Omni International, 26918, 47228
Omni Lift Inc, 26919
Omni Material Handling Services, 58458
Omni Metalcraft Corporation, 26920, 47229
Omni North America, 51988
Omni Pacific Company, 47230, 58459
Omni Technologies Inc, 26921
Omnicor, 47231
Omnimark Instrument Corporation, 26922
Omnion, 26923, 47232
Omnipak Import Enterprises Inc, 26924
Omnitech International, 26925, 47233
Omnitemp Refrigeration, 26926, 47234
OMNOVA Solutions, 26816
Omnova Solutions Inc., 47235
OMRON Systems LLC, 26817, 26818
OMYA, Inc., 9305, 26819, 58420
On Assignment Inc, 26927
On Site Gas Systems Inc, 26928
On The Verandah, 9481
On-Campus Hospitality, 26929
On-Cor Frozen Foods, 9482
On-Cor Frozen Foods Redi-Serve, 9483
On-Hand Adhesives, 26930
Onalaska Brewing, 9484
Once Again Nut Butter, 9485, 47237
Once Upon a Farm, 9486
ONE Brands, 9306
One Culture Foods, 9487
One Degree Organic Foods, 9488
One Pie Canning, 58460
One Potato Two Potato, 9489
One Source, 9490
One Vineyard and Winery, 9491
One World Enterprises, 9492
One-Shot, 47238, 58461
Oneida Food Service, 26932, 47239
Oneida LTD Silversmiths, 26933
Oneonta Starr Ranch Growers, 9493, 9494
Onevision Corp, 26934, 47240

All Companies Index

Onguard Industries LLC, 26935, 26936, 47241
Onieda Cold Storage And Warehouse, 53233, 53234
Onieta Cold Storage And Warehouse, 53235
Onnit Labs, 9495, 58462
Ono Cones of Hawaii LLC, 9496
Ono International, 47242, 58463
Onoway Custom Packers, 9497
Onset Computer Corp, 26937
Onsite Sycom Energy Corporation, 26938
Ontario Foods, 9498
Ontario Glove and Safety Products, 26939, 47243, 58464
Ontario International, 47244
Ontario Pork, 9499
Ontario Produce Company, 9500, 47245, 53236
OnTrack Automation Inc, 26931, 47236
Oogie's Snack LLC, 9501
Oogolow Enterprises, 9502, 47246
Ooh La La Candy, 9503
Oorganik, 9504
Op Sec Security, 26940
Opa! Originals, 9505
Opa's Smoked Meats, 9506
Opal Manufacturing Ltd, 26941, 47247
Open Date Systems, 26942, 47248
Opie Brush Company, 26943, 47249
Optek Inc, 26944, 47250
Optek-Danulat, 26945
Optel Vision, 26946
Optex, 26947, 47251
Optical Security Group, 26948
Optima Corp, 26949
Optima Foods, 47252
Optima International, 26950
Optima Wine Cellars, 9507
Optimal Automatics, 9508, 26951
Optimal Nutrients, 9509, 47253
Optimum Nutrition, 9510, 58465
Optipure, 26952, 58466
Opus One, 9511
Oracle Hospitality, 26953, 47254
Oracle Packaging, 26954
Orafti Active Food Ingredients, 47255, 58467
Oram Material Handling Systems, 58468
Orange Bakery, 9512, 47256
Orange Bang Inc, 9513
Orange County Cold Storage, 51989, 53237
Orange County Distillery, 9514
Orange Cove-Sanger Citrus, 9515, 47257
Orange Distributors, 58469
Orange Peel Enterprises, 9516, 47258
Orange Plastics, 26955
Orangeburg Pecan Co, 9517, 47259
Orangex, 26956
Oration Rubber Stamp Company, 26957
ORB Weaver Farm, 9307, 26820
Orber Manufacturing Co, 26958
ORBIS, 26821, 26822, 26823, 26824
Orbis Corp., 26959
ORBIS RPM, 26825
Orbisphere Laboratories, 26960
Orca Bay Foods, 9518, 47260
Orca Foods, 40891
Orca Inc, 26961, 47261
Orchard Gold, 26962
Orchard Heights Winery, 9519
Orchard Paper, 40892
Orchard Pond, 9520
Orchards Hawaii, 58470
Orchem Corporation, 26963
Orchid Island Juice Co, 9521
Order-Matic Corporation, 26964
Ore-Cal Corp, 9522, 26965, 47262
Ore-Ida Foods, 9523, 47263
Orear Company, 58471
Oreck Commercial Sales, 58472
Oreck Manufacturing Co, 26966
Orefield Cold Stge & Dstrbtng, 53238
Oregon Bark, 9524, 58473

Oregon Chai, 9525, 47264
Oregon Cherry Growers Inc, 9526, 9527, 47265, 47266
Oregon Coffee Roaster, 47267
Oregon Flavor Rack, 9528
Oregon Freeze Dry, Inc., 9529, 47268
Oregon Fruit Products Co, 9530, 47269
Oregon Harvest, 9531
Oregon Hill Farms, 9532, 47270
Oregon Ice Cream Co., 9533
Oregon Pacific Bottling, 26967
Oregon Potato Co, 9534, 9535, 47271
Oregon Pride, 9536
Oregon Raspberry & Blackberry Commission, 9537
Oregon Seafoods, 9538
Oregon Spice Co Inc, 9539
Oregon Transfer Co, 51990, 53239
Orelube Corp, 26968, 47272
Orfila Vineyards, 9540
Organic Amazon, 9541
Organic Gemini, 9542
Organic Germinal, 9543
Organic Girl Produce, 9544
Organic Gourmet, 9545, 47273
Organic India USA, 9546
Organic Juice USA, 47274
Organic Liaison, LLC, 9547
Organic Milling, 9548, 47275
Organic Nectars LLC, 9549
Organic Olive Juice, 9550
Organic Partners Intl., 9551
Organic Pastures, 9552
Organic Planet, 9553
Organic Products Co, 26969
Organic Products Trading Co, 47276
Organic RealBar, 9554
Organic Vintages, 47277, 58474
Organic Wine Co Inc, 9555
Organically Grown Co, 9556, 47278
Organics Unlimited, 9557, 47279, 58475
Orics Industries, 26970, 47280
Oriental Foods, 9558, 47281
Oriental Motor USA Corporation, 26971
Orientex Foods, 9559
Original American Beverage Company, 9560
Original Chili Bowl, 9561
Original Food, 58476
Original Foods, 9562
Original Gourmet Food Co, 9563
Original Herkimer Cheese, 9564
Original Juan, 9565, 58477
Original Lincoln Logs, 26972
Original Packaging & Display Company, 26973
Original Swiss Aromatics, 47282
Original Tony Packo's, 9566
Original Wood Seating, 26974
Orinoco Coffee & Tea, 9567, 47283, 58478
Orion Packaging Systems Inc, 26975
Orion Research, 26976, 47284
Orion Trading Corp, 47285
Orioxi International Corporation, 47286, 58479
Orkin LLC, 26977
Orlando Baking Co, 9568
Orlando Fire Equipment Company, 58480
Orlando Food Corp, 47287
Orleans International, 47288, 58481
Orleans Packing Co, 9569, 47289
Orlinda Milling Company, 9570
Ormand Peugeog Corporation, 9571
Orr Mountain Winery, 9572
Orr's Farm Market, 26978, 58482
Ortemp, 26979
Ortho-Molecular Products Inc, 9573, 58483
Orthodox Union, 26980
Ortmayer Materials Handling, 26981
Orto Foods, 9574
Orwak, 26982, 47290
Orwasher's Bakery, 9575

Osage Food Products Inc, 26983, 40893, 58484
Osage Pecan Co, 9576
Osborn Bros Inc, 58485
Osborn Food Sales Company, 40894
Osborne USA Inc, 47291
Oscar's Wholesale Meats, 9577, 58486
Oscartek, 26984, 47292
Oscartielle Equipment Company, 26985
Osceola Farms Sugar Warehouse, 9578
Osem USA Inc, 9579
OSF, 26826, 47169
OSF Flavors Inc, 9308
Osgood Industries, 26986, 26987
Oshikiri Corp Of America, 26988
Oshkosh Cold Storage, 9580
Oskaloosa Food Products, 9581, 47293
Oskar Blues Brewery, 9582
Oskri Corporation, 9583, 47294
Osowski Farms, 9584
OSRAM SYLVANIA, 26827
Osram Sylvania, 26989, 26990
Oss Food Plant Sanitation Services, 26991
Ossian Smoked Meats, 9585
Ossid Corp, 26992
Osso Good, LLC, 9586, 47295
Osterneck Company, 26993, 47296
Ostrem Chemical Co. Ltd, 26994
Ostrom Mushrooms, 9587
Ostrow Jobbing Company, 58487
Oswalt Restaurant Supply, 58488
Ota Tofu, 9588
Otafuku Foods, 9589
OTD Corporation, 26828, 47170
Otis McAllister Inc., 47297
Otis Spunkmeyer, 9590, 9591
OTP Industrial Solutions, 26829, 47171
Otsuka America Foods Inc, 9592
Ott Food Products Co, 9593
Ott Packagings, 26995
Ottawa Valley Grain Products, 9594
Ottenberg's Bakers, 9595
Ottenheimer Equipment Company, 26996, 58489
Ottens Flavors, 9596, 47298
Otterbine Barebo Inc, 26997
Otto Braun Bakery Equipment, 26998
Otto Brehm Inc, 58490
Otto Material Handling, 26999
Otto's Naturals, 9597
Ottumwa Tent & Awning Co, 27000
Ouachita Lumber Co, 9598
Ouachita Machine Works, 27001, 47299
Ouellette Machinery Systems, 27002
Ouhlala Gourmet, 9599
Our Best Foods, 9600
Our Cookie, 9601
Our Farms To You, LLC, 9602
Our Lady of Guadalupe Trappist Abbey, 9603, 58491
Our Name is Mud, 27003
Out of a Flower, 9604
Outback Kitchens LLC, 9605
Outback Sales, 40895, 58492
Outer Aisle, 9606
Outerbridge Peppers Limited, 47300, 51991, 58493
Outlook Packaging, 27004, 47301
Outotec USA Inc, 27005, 47302
Outside the Lines, Inc, 27006
Outstanding Foods, 9607
Outta the Park Eats, 9608
Outterson, LLC, 27007
Ovalstrapping Inc, 27008
Oven Arts, 9609
Oven Deck Shop, 27009
Oven Fresh Baking Company, 9610
Oven Head Salmon Smokers, 9611, 47303
Oven Poppers, 9612
Oven Ready Products, 9613
Ovention, 27010
Ovenworks, 27011
Overflo, 51992, 53240

Overhead Conveyor Co, 27012
Overhead Door Company of Fort Wayne, 58494
Overhill Farms Inc, 9614
Overlake Foods, 9615, 47304
Overnight Labels Inc, 27013
Oversea Casing Co, 9616
Oversea Fishery & Investment, 9617, 47305
Overseas Food Trading, 47306
Overseas Service Corp, 40896
OWD, 26830, 47172
Owens-Illinois Inc, 27014, 47307
Owensboro Grain Co, 9618
Owl's Brew, 9619
OWYN, 9309
Oxbo International Corp, 27015, 47308
Oxford Frozen Foods, 9620, 47309
Oxidyn, 27016
OXO International, 26831, 47173
Oxoid, 27017
Oxygen Import LLC, 47310
Oyang America, 47311, 58495
Oystar North America, 27018
Oyster Bay Pump Works Inc, 27019, 47312
Oyster Peddler, 58496
Ozark Cooperative Warehouse, 58497
Ozark Empire, 9621
Ozark Tape & Label Co, 27020
Ozark Truck Brokers, 51993
Ozark Trucking, 51994
Ozarka Drinking Water, 9622, 27021, 58498
Ozburn-Hessey Logistics LLC, 51995, 53241
Ozery Bakery, 9623
Ozery Bakery Inc, 9624
Ozone Confectioners & Bakers Supplies, 9625, 47313
Ozotech Inc, 27022
Ozuna Food Products Corporation, 9626

P

PDEQ, 9627, 58499
P & A Food Ind Recruiters, 27023
P & D Corp, 58500
P & F Machine, 27024, 47314
P & H Crystalite, LLC, 47315
P & J Oyster Co, 9628
P & L Poultry, 9629
P & L Specialties, 27025
P & L System, 27026
P & M Staiger Vineyard, 9630
P & S Food & Liquor, 9631, 58501
P & S Ravioli Co, 9632
P & T Flannery Seafood Inc, 9633
P A Menard, 58502
P C Teas Co, 9634
P G Molinari & Sons, 9635
P J Rhodes Corporation, 47316
P M Plastics, 27027
P R Farms Inc, 9636, 27028, 47317
P&C Pacific Bakeries, 58503
P&E, 27029
P&E Foods, 9637, 58504
P&H Milling Group, 9638, 27030
P&L Seafood of Venice, 9639, 47318, 58505
P-Bee Products, 9640
P. Janes & Sons, 9641, 47319
P. Tavilla Company, 58506
P.A. Braunger Institutional Foods, 9642, 58507
P.D.I Cone-Dutch Treat, 9643
P.F. Harris Manufacturing Company, 27031, 47320
P.J. Markos Seafood Company, 9644, 58508
P.J. Merrill Seafood Inc, 9645, 58509
P.L. Thomas & Company, 27032, 47321
P.M. Innis Lobster Company, 9646, 58510
P.T. Fish, 9647, 58511

1421

All Companies Index

P/B Distributors, 58512
Pa R Systems Inc, 27082, 27083, 47348
Paar Physica USA, 47349, 58523
Pabst Brewing Company, 9664, 47350
PAC Equipment Company, 27033
Pac Strapping Products, 27084
Paca Foods Inc, 9665
Pacari Organic Chocolate, 9666
Pace Labels Inc, 27086
Pace Packaging Corp, 27087, 47351
Pace Products, 27088
Pace Target Brokerage, 40899
Pacemaker Packaging Corp, 27089
Pacer Pumps, 27090, 47352
Pacheco Ranch Winery, 9667
Pacific American Fish Co Inc, 9668, 47353
Pacific Bag, 27091
Pacific Beach Peanut Butter, 9669
Pacific Bearing Company, 27092
Pacific California Fish Company, 58524
Pacific Cartage & Warehousing, 52000, 53245
Pacific Chai, 9670
Pacific Cheese Co, 9671
Pacific Choice Brands, 9672, 47354
Pacific Choice Seafood Inc, 58525
Pacific Coast Brewing, 9673
Pacific Coast Chemicals Co, 58526
Pacific Coast Container, 27093
Pacific Coast Fruit Co, 9674, 47355
Pacific Coast Producers, 9675
Pacific Coast Warehouse Co, 52001, 53246
Pacific Cold Storage, 53247
Pacific Collier Fresh Company, 9676
Pacific Commerce Company, 47356, 53248, 58527
Pacific Compactor Corporation, 58528
Pacific Echo Cellars, 9677
Pacific Ethanol Inc., 9678
Pacific Expresso, 27094
Pacific Farms, 9679
Pacific Foods, 9680, 47357
Pacific Foods of Oregon, 9681
Pacific Fruit Processors, 9682, 47358
Pacific Gold Marketing, 9683
Pacific Gold Snacks, 9684
Pacific Gourmet Seafood, 9685, 58529
Pacific Grain & Foods, 9686
Pacific Handy Cutter Inc, 27095
Pacific Harvest Products, 9687, 27096, 53249
Pacific Hop Exchange Brewing Company, 9688
Pacific Ingredient Exchange, 40900
Pacific Isles Trading, 27097
Pacific Merchants, 27098
Pacific Northwest Canned Pear, 27099
Pacific Northwest Wire Works, 27100
Pacific Nutritional, 9689, 47359
Pacific Oasis Enterprise Inc, 27101, 47360
Pacific Ocean Produce, 9690
Pacific Ozone Technology, 27102
Pacific Packaging Machinery, 27103
Pacific Packaging Systems, 27104
Pacific Paper Box Co, 27105
Pacific Plaza Imports, 47361
Pacific Pneumatics, 27106
Pacific Poultry Company, 9691
Pacific Press Company, 27107
Pacific Process Machinery, 27108
Pacific Process Technology, 27109
Pacific Refrigerator Company, 27110, 47362
Pacific Resources, 47363, 58530
Pacific Rim Shellfish Corp., 58531
Pacific Salmon Company, 9692, 40901, 47364
Pacific Scale Company, 27111
Pacific Scientific, 27112
Pacific Scientific Instrument, 27113, 47365
Pacific Seafood Co, 58532

Pacific Seafoods International, 9693, 47366
Pacific Shrimp Co, 40902, 58533
Pacific Sign Construction, 27114
Pacific Southwest Container, 27115
Pacific Soybean & Grain, 9694
Pacific Spice Co, 9695, 27116, 47367
Pacific Standard Distributors, 9696, 47368
Pacific Steam Equipment, Inc., 27117, 47369, 58534
Pacific Store Designs Inc, 27118, 47370
Pacific Sun Olive Oil, 9697
Pacific Tank, 27119
Pacific Tomato Growers, 58535
Pacific Trading Company International, 40903
Pacific Transload Systems, 53250
Pacific Trellis, 9698, 47371
Pacific Valley Foods, 9699, 47372
Pacific Westcoast Foods, 9700, 58536
Pacific Western Brewing Company, 9701
Pacific World Enterprises, 47373, 58537
Pacific-SEH Hotel Supply Company, 58538
Pacifica Culinaria, 9702
Paciugo Distribution, 9703
Pack & Process, 27120
Pack Air Inc, 27121
Pack All, 27122
Pack Line Corporation, 27123, 47374
Pack Process Equipment, 27124
Pack Rite Machine Mettler, 27125, 27126, 47375
Pack Star, 27127
Pack West Machinery, 27128, 47376
Pack'R North America, 27129
Pack-A-Drum, 27130, 47377
Pack-Rite, 27131
Package Automation Corporation, 27132
Package Concepts & Materials Inc, 27133, 47378
Package Containers Inc, 27134
Package Converting Corp, 27135
Package Conveyor Co, 27136, 47379
Package Machinery Co Inc, 27137, 47380
Package Nakazawa, 27138
Package Products, 27139
Package Service Company of Colorado, 27140
Package Supply Equipment, 27141
Package Systems Corporation, 27142, 47381
Packaged Ice, 53251, 53252
Packaged Products Division, 9704
Packagemasters, 27143
Packaging & Processing Equipment, 27144, 47382
Packaging Aids Corporation, 27145, 47383
Packaging and Converting Hotline, 27183
Packaging Associates, 27146
Packaging By Design Of Il, 27147
Packaging Concept Company, 27148
Packaging Consultants Associated Inc, 27149
Packaging Corporation of America, 27150
Packaging Design Corp, 27151
Packaging Distribution Svc, 27152
Packaging Dynamics, 27153, 27154, 47384
Packaging Dynamics Corp, 27155, 47385
Packaging Dynamics International, 27156, 47386
Packaging Enterprises, 27157, 27158, 47387, 47388
Packaging Equipment & Conveyors, Inc, 27159, 47389
Packaging Equipment Company, 58539
Packaging Graphics LLC, 27160
Packaging Group, 27161
Packaging Machine Service Company, 27162

Packaging Machinery, 27163, 47390
Packaging Machinery & Equipment, 27164, 47391
Packaging Machinery International, 27165, 47392
Packaging Machinery Svc, 27166
Packaging Machines International, 27167
Packaging Materials Co, 27168
Packaging Materials Inc, 27169
Packaging Partners, Ltd., 27170
Packaging Parts & Systems, 27171
Packaging Products Corp, 27172, 47393
Packaging Progressions, 27173
Packaging Service Co Inc, 27174, 47394
Packaging Services Corp, 58540
Packaging Solutions, 27175
Packaging Specialties Inc, 27176
Packaging Store, 27177
Packaging Systems Automation, 27178
Packaging Systems Intl, 27179, 47395
Packaging Technologies, 27180, 27181, 27182
Packexpo.Com, 27184
Packing Material Company, 27185
Packing Specialities, 27186
PacknWood, 27187
Packotronics, 27188
Packrite Packaging, 27189
Packsource Systems, 58541
Packworld USA, 27190, 27191
Pacmac Inc, 27192, 47396
Pacmaster by Schleicher, 27193
Pacmatic Corporation, 27194
Pacmatic/Ritmica, 47397, 58542
Pacmoore Products, 27195
PacNorth Group, 40898
Paco Label Systems Inc, 27196
Paco Manufacturing, 27197
Pacosy, 27198
Pacquet Oneida, 27199
Pacsea Corporation, 9705, 58543
PacTech Engineering, 27085
Pactiv, 27200
Pactiv LLC, 27201, 47398
Pacur, 27202, 47399
Paddack Enterprises, 9706
Paddington Corporation, 27203
Paderno, 47400
Padinox, 27204, 47401
Paesana Products, 9707
PAFCO Importing Co, 47322, 58513
Pafra/Veritec, 27205
Pagano M Watermelons, 58544
Pagatech, 47402
Page & Jones Inc, 52002
Page Mill Winery, 9708
Page Slotting Saw Co Inc, 27206
Paget Equipment Co, 27207, 47403
Pagoda Industries Inc, 27208
Pahlmeyer Winery, 9709
Pahrump Valley Winery, 9710
Painted Cookie, 58545
Paisano Distribution Company, 58546
Paisano Food Products, 9711
Paisley Farms Inc, 9712
Pak 2000 Inc, 27209
Pak Technologies, 27210, 52003
Pak-Rapid, 27211
Pak-Sak Industries I, 27212
Pak-Sher, 27213
Paket Corporation, 27214
Paket Corporation/UniquePack, 27215
Paklab Products, 9713, 47404
Pakmark, 27216, 47405
Paktronics Controls, 27217, 47406
PAL Marking Products, 27034
Palace Packaging Machines Inc, 27218
Palacios & Sons, 9714
Palama Meat Co Inc, 58547
Palamatic Handling USA, 47407, 58548
Paleewong Trading Corporation, 47408, 58549
Paleo Powder Seasoning, 9715
Paleo Prime Foods, 9716
Paleo Ranch, 9717

Palermo Bakery, 9718
Palermo's Pizza, 9719
Paley-Lloyd-Donohue, 27219
Palintest USA, 27220
Pall Corp, 27221, 27222, 27223
Pall Filtron, 27224, 47409
Pallet Management Systems, 27225
Pallet Masters, 27226
Pallet One Inc, 27227, 27228, 27229, 47410
Pallet Pro, 27230
Pallet Reefer International LLC, 27231
Pallet Service Corp, 27232
Pallets Inc, 27233
Pallister Pallet, 27234
Pallox Incorporated, 27235, 47411
Palm Bay Imports, 27236
Palm Beach Foods, 9720
Palm Brothers, 58550
Palme d'Or, 9721, 47412
Palmer Associates, 58551
Palmer Candy Co, 9722, 47413, 58552
Palmer Distributors, 27237, 47414
Palmer Fixture Company, 27238, 47415
Palmer Food Service, 58553
Palmer Jack M, 58554
Palmer Logistics, 52004, 53253
Palmer Meat Packing Co, 9723
Palmer Snyder, 27239, 47416
Palmer Vineyards Inc, 9724
Palmer Wahl, 27240
Palmer Wholesale Inc, 58555
Palmetto Brewing Co, 9725
Palmetto Candy & Tobacco Company, 58556
Palmetto Canning, 9726, 27241, 47417
Palmetto Packaging, 27242
Palmetto Pigeon Plant, 9727
Palmieri Food Products, 9728
Palmland Paper Company, 27243
Palms & Co, 40904, 47418
Palmyra Bologna Co Inc, 9729
Palo Alto Awning, 27244
Palsgaard Inc., 58557
Paltier, 27245, 47419
PAM Fastening Technology Inc, 27035
Pamco Label Co Inc, 27246
Pamela's Products, 9730, 47420
Pamex Packaging, 58558
Pamida, 58559
Pamlico Packing Company, 9731
Pan American Coffee Co, 9732
Pan American Papers Inc, 27247, 47421, 58560
Pan De Oro Tortilla Chip Co, 9733
Pan Pacific Plastics Inc, 27248, 47422
Pan Pepin, 9734
Pan's Mushroom Jerky, 9735, 58561
Pan-O-Gold Baking Co., 9736
Panalpina Inc., 53254
Panamerican Logistics, 27249, 53255
Panapesca USA LLC, 47423
Panasonic Commercial Food Service, 27250, 47424
Pandol Brothers Inc, 9737, 9738, 9739, 47425, 47426, 47427
Panera Bread, 9740
Pangaea Sciences, 47428
Pangburn Candy Company, 9741
Panhandle Food Sales, 9742
Panhandle Milling, 9743
Panhandler, Inc., 27251, 47429
Pankow Associates Inc, 40905
Panoche Creek Packing, 9744, 47430
Panola Pepper Co, 9745
Panorama Foods Inc., 9746
Panorama Meats, 9747
Panoramic Inc, 27252
Panos Brands, 9748
Panther Creek Cellars, 9749
Panther Industries Inc, 27253
Pantry Shelf Food Corporation, 47431, 58562
Pantry Shelf/Mixxm, 9750
Paoli Properties, 27254, 47432

All Companies Index

Papa Dean's Popcorn, 9751, 58563
Papa Leone Food Enterprises, 9752
Papas Chris A & Son Co, 9753
Papelera Puertorriquena, 27255
Paper & Chemical Supply Company, 58564
Paper Box & Specialty Co, 27256, 47433
Paper City Brewery, 9754
Paper Converting Machine Company, 27258, 47435
Paper Converting MachineCompany, 27257, 47434
Paper Machinery Corp, 27259
Paper Pak Industries, 27260, 27261
Paper Product Specialties, 27262
Paper Products Company, 27263
Paper Service, 27264, 47436
Paper Systems Inc, 27265, 47437
Paper Tubes Inc, 27266, 27267
Paper Works Industries Inc, 27268
Paper-Pak Products, 27269
Paperbag Manufacturers Inc, 27270
Papercraft, 58565
Papertech, 27271, 47438
Paperweights Plus, 27272, 47439
Papes Pecan House, 9755
Papillon Ribbon & Bow, 27273
Pappardelle's Inc, 9756
Pappas Inc., 27274
Pappy Meat Company, 9757
Pappy's Sassafras Tea, 9758, 47440, 58566
Papy's Foods Inc, 9759
Pap,, 58567
Paques ADI, 27275
PAR Tech Inc, 27036, 47323
PAR Visions Systems Corporation, 27037
PAR-Kan, 27038, 47324
Par-Pak, 27276, 27277, 47441
PAR-Way Tryson Co, 9648, 47325
Parachem Corporation, 27278, 47442
Paraclipse, 27279, 47443
Parade Packaging, 27280
Paradigm Foodworks Inc, 9760
Paradigm Packaging Inc, 27281
Paradigm Technologies, 27282
Paradis Honey, 9761
Paradise Food Brokers, 40906
Paradise Fruits NA, 9762
Paradise Inc, 9763, 27283, 47444
Paradise Island Foods, 9764, 47445, 58568
Paradise Locker Inc., 9765
Paradise Plastics, 27284
Paradise Products, 27285, 47446, 58569
Paradise Products Corporation, 9766, 47447
Paradise Tomato Kitchens, 9767
Paradise Valley Vineyards, 9768
Paragon Coffee Trading Co, 47448
Paragon Electric Company, 27286
Paragon Films Inc, 27287, 47449
Paragon Food Equipment, 58570
Paragon Fruits, 9769
Paragon Group USA, 27288, 47450
Paragon International, 27289, 47451
Paragon Labeling, 27290, 27291, 47452
Paragon Packaging, 27292
Paraiso Vineyards, 9770
Parallel Products Inc, 27293
Paramount Caviar, 9771
Paramount Coffee, 9772, 58571
Paramount Confection Company, 58572
Paramount Distillers, 9773
Paramount Export Co., 47453
Paramount Industries, 27294, 47454
Paramount Manufacturing Company, 27295
Paramount Packaging Corp, 27296
Paramount Packing & Rubber Inc, 27297
Paramount Produce, 58573
Paramount Products, 58574
Paramount Restaurant Supply Company, 58575
Parasol Awnings, 27298

Paratherm Corporation, 27299, 47455
Parducci Wine Cellars, 9774, 47456, 58576
Paris Foods Corporation, 9775
Paris Gourmet, 47457
Paris Paper Box Company, 40907
Paris Pastry, 9776
Parish Chemical Company, 9777, 47458
Parish Manufacturing Inc, 27300, 47459
Parisi Inc, 27301, 47460
Parisian Novelty Company, 27302
Parity Corp, 27303, 27304, 47461
Park 100 Foods Inc, 9778
Park Avenue Bakery, 9779, 58577
Park Avenue Meats Inc, 58578
Park Cheese Company Inc, 9780, 47462
Park Custom Molding, 27305
Parker Brothers, 58579
Parker Farm, 9781
Parker Fish Company, 9782, 58580
Parker Flavors Inc, 9783
Parker House Sausage Co, 9784
Parker Products, 9785
Parker Sales & Svc, 27306
Parker Wholesale Paper Co, 58581
Parker's Wine Brokerage, 40908, 47463, 58582
Parker-Hannifin Corp, 27307, 27308, 27309, 27310, 27311
Parkers Farm, 9786
Parkland, 27312, 47464
Parks Brokerage Company, 40909
Parkside Candy Co, 9787
Parkside Warehouse Inc, 53256
Parkson Corp, 27313, 27314, 47465, 47466
Parkson Corporation, 27315
Parkway Plastic Inc, 27316, 47467
Parkway Systems, 58583
Parlor City Paper Box Co Inc, 27317, 47468
Parma Sausage Products, 9788
Parmalat Canada, 9789, 47469
Parmela Creamery, 9790
Parmenter's Northville Cider Mill, 9791
Parmx, 9792
Parny Gourmet, 9793
Parr-Mac Sales Company, 58584
Parrish's Cake Decorating, 9794, 27318, 47470
Parson Food Sales, 58585
Parsons Green, 58586
Parsons Manufacturing Corp., 27319, 47471
Parta, 27320
Partex Corporation, 27321
Parthenon Food Products, 9795
Particle Control, 9796
Particle Dynamics, 9797, 47472
Particle Sizing Systems, 27322
Partner Pak, 27323
Partners Alliance Cold Storage, 53257
Partners Coffee LLC, 9798
Partners in Hospitality, 47473
Partners International, 27324
Partners: A Tasteful Choice, 9799
Partnership Resources, 27325, 47474
Parts Depot, Inc., 58587
Party Linens, 27326, 47475
Party Perfect Catering, 27327
Party Yards, 27328, 47476
Partytime Machines Rental, 58588
Parvin Manufacturing Company, 27329, 47477
Pascal Coffee, 9800
Pascha Chocolate, 9801
Paschall Truck Lines Inc, 52005
PASCO, 27039, 47326
Pasco Poly Inc, 27330
Pascobel Inc, 9802
Paskesz Candy Co, 47478, 58589
Pasolivo Willow Creek Olive Ranch, 9803, 58590
Pasquale Trucking Co, 52006
Pasqualichio Brothers Inc, 9804

Pasquini Espresso Co, 27331, 47479
Passage Foods LLC, 9805
Passetti's Pride, 9806
Passport Food Group, 9807, 47480, 58591
Pasta Del Mondo, 9808, 47481
Pasta Factory, 9809, 47482
Pasta Filata International, 27332
Pasta International, 9810
Pasta Mami, 9811
Pasta Mill, 9812
Pasta Montana, 9813
Pasta Prima, 9814
Pasta Quistini, 9815, 47483
Pasta Shoppe, 9816, 47484
Pasta Sonoma, 9817
Pasta Valente, 9818
Pastabiz Pasta Machines, 27333
Pastene Co LTD, 9819, 47485
Pastor Chuck Orchards, 9820
Pastorelli Food Products, 9821, 47486
Pastori Winery, 9822
Pastry Art & Design, 27334
Pastry Chef, 9823, 47487
Pat LaFrieda Meat Purveyors, 9824
PAT Vitamins Inc, 58514
Pat's Meat Discounter, 9825
Patagonia Provisions, 9826
Patane Brothers Freezer Wrhses, 53258
Patchogue - Medford Lib rary, 27335
Pate International, 27336
Pate-Derby Company, 58592
Pater & Associates, 27337
Paterno Imports LTD, 47488
Path of Life, 9827
Pati-Petite Cookies Inc, 9828
Patience Fruit & Co., 9829
Patio Center Inc, 27338
Patio King, 27339
Patisserie Wawel, 9830
Patlite Corp, 27340
Patman Foods Inc, 40910
Patman Meat Group, 40911
Patric Chocolate, 9831
Patricia Quintana, 9832
Patrick & Co, 27341
Patrick Cudahy LLC, 9833, 47489
Patrick E. Panzarello Consulting Services, 27342
Patrick Signs, 27343
Patriot Enterprises, 58593
Patriot Pickel Inc, 9834, 58594
Pats Seafood & Cajun Deli, 58595
Patsy's Brands, 9835
Patsy's Candy, 9836
Patsy's Italian Restaurant, 9837
PatsyPie, 9838
Patterson Buckeye, 58596
Patterson Co Inc, 40912
Patterson Fan Co Inc, 27344
Patterson Frozen Foods, 9839, 47490
Patterson Industries, 27345, 47491
Patterson Laboratories, 27346
Patterson Vegetable Company, 9840
Patterson-Kelley Hars Company, 27347
Patti's Plum Puddings, 9841
Patton's Sausage Company, 58597
Patty O Matic Machinery, 27348
Patty Palace Foods, 9842, 47492
Patty Paper Inc, 27349, 47493
Paturel International Company, 58598
Paul Esposito Inc, 40913
Paul G Nester & Son Co Inc, 40914
Paul G. Gallin Company, 27350, 47494
Paul Hawkins Lumber Company, 27351
Paul Inman Associates, 40915
Paul J. Macrie, 58599
Paul L. Broussard & Associate, 52007
Paul Mueller Co Inc, 27352
Paul N. Gardner Company, 27353, 47495
Paul O. Abbe, 27354, 27355, 47496
Paul Perkins Food Distributors, 58600
Paul Piazza & Son Inc, 9843
Paul Schafer Meat Products, 9844

Paul Stevens Lobster, 9845, 58601
Paul T. Freund Corporation, 27356
Paul's Candy Factory, 9846
Paulaur Corp, 9847
Paulie Paul's, 58602
Pauline's Pastries, 9848
Paulsen Foods, 9849, 58603
Paumanok Vineyards, 9850
Pavailler Distribution Company, 27357, 47497
Pavan USA Inc, 27358, 47498
Pavel's Yogurt, 9851
Pavero Cold Storage, 9852
Paw Paw Grape Juice Company, 9853
Pawelski Farm, 9854
PAX Spices & Labs Inc, 47327, 58515
Paxall, 27359
Paxar, 27360
Paxon Polymer Company, 27361
Paxton Corp, 27362, 47499
Paxton North America, 27363
Paxton Products Inc, 27364, 47500
Payless Equipment, 58604
Payne Controls Co, 27365, 47501
Payne Packing Co, 9855
Pazdar Winery, 9856
PB Leiner USA, 9649, 47328
PBB Global Logistics, 51996, 53242
PBC, 27040, 47329
PBC Manufacturing, 27041
PBI Dansensor America, 27042
PBM Inc, 27043
PC/Poll Systems, 27044, 47330
PCI Inc, 27045
Pci Membrane Systems Inc, 27366
PCM Delasco Inc, 27046
PDC International, 27047, 47331
PDE Technology Corp, 47332, 58516
PDMP, 27048
PDQ Plastics Inc, 27049
Peaberry's Coffee & Tea, 9857
Peace Industries, 27367, 47502
Peace Mountain Natural Beverages, 9858, 47503
Peace River Citrus Products, 9859, 47504
Peace River Trading Company, 58605
Peace Village Organic Foods, 9860, 47505
Peaceful Bend Winery, 9861
Peaceful Fruits, 9862, 58606
Peaceworks, 9863
Peach State Material Handling, 58607
Peacock Crate Factory, 27368, 47506
Peak Corporation, 40916
Peak Foods, 9864
PEAK Technologies, Inc., 27050
Peanut Butter & Co., 9865
Peanut Corporation of America, 9866
Peanut Patch, 9867
Peanut Patch Gift Shop, 9868, 47507
Peanut Processors Inc, 9869
Peanut Roaster, 9870
Peanut Shop, 9871
Pear's Coffee, 9872
Pearl Coffee Co, 9873, 47508
Pearl Crop, 9874
Pearl River Pastry & Chocolate, 9875
Pearl Valley Cheese Inc, 9876
Pearson Candy Co, 9877
Pearson Packaging Systems, 27369, 27370, 47509
Pearson Research Assoc, 27371
Pearson Signs Service, 27372
Pearson's Berry Farm, 9878, 47510
Pearson's Homestyle, 9879
Peas, 58608
Peas of Mind, 9880
Pease Awning & Sunroom Co, 27373
Pease's Candy, 9881
Peasley Transfer & Storage, 52008, 53259
Pecan Deluxe Candy Co, 9882, 27374, 47511
Pechiney Plastic Packaging, 27375, 27376

1423

All Companies Index

Peco Controls Corporation, 27377, 47512
Peco Foods Inc., 9883, 47513
Peconic Bay Winery, 9884
Pecoraro Dairy Products, 9885, 47514
Pecos Valley Spice Company, 9886
Pede Brothers Italian Food, 9887
Pederson's Natural Farms, 9888
Pedrizzetti Winery, 9889
Pedroncelli J Winery, 9890
Peekskill Brewery, 9891
Peekskill Hair Net, 27378
Peeled Snacks, 9892
Peeler's Jersey Farms, 9893
Peer Foods Group Inc, 9894
Peerless Cartons, 27379
Peerless Coffee & Tea, 9895
Peerless Conveyor & Mfg Corp, 27380
Peerless Dough Mixing and Make-Up, 27381
Peerless Dust Killer Company, 47515, 58609
Peerless Food Equipment, 27382, 27383, 47516, 47517
Peerless Gouet LLC, 27384
Peerless Lighting Corporation, 27385, 47518
Peerless Machine & Tool Corp, 27386
Peerless Machinery Corporation, 27387, 47519
Peerless of America, 27390, 47521
Peerless Ovens, 27388, 47520
Peerless Packages, 27389
Peerless Trucking Company, 52009, 53260
Peerless-Premier Appliance Co, 27391, 47522
Peerless-Winsmith Inc, 27392, 47523
Peet's Coffee, 9896
Peg's Salt, 9897
Peggy Lawton Kitchens, 9898
PEI Mussel King, 9650
Peju Province Winery, 9899
Pekarna Meat Market, 9900
Pekarski Sausage, 9901
Peking Noodle Co Inc, 9902, 47524
Pel-Pak Container, 27393
Pelco Equipment, 58610
Pelco Packaging Corporation, 27394
Pelco Refrigeration Sales, 58611
Pelican Bay Ltd., 9903, 47525, 58612
Pelican Displays, 27395
Pelican Marine Supply LLC, 27396, 58613
Pelican Products Inc, 27397, 47526
Pelican Seafoods, 9904
Pell Paper Box Company, 27398
Pellegrini Wine Co, 9905
Pellenc America, 27399
Pellerin Milnor Corporation, 27400, 47527
Pellican Seafood, 58614
Pellman Foods Inc, 9906
Pelouze Scale Company, 27401, 47528
Pemaquid Seafood, 9907, 58615
Pemberton & Associates, 27402, 27403, 47529
Pemberton's Foods Inc, 9908
Pemiscot Packing Company, 58616
Penasack Co Inc, 27404
Penauta Products, 9909, 47530
Penco Products, 27405, 47531
Penda Form Corp, 27406, 47532
Pender Packing Co Inc, 9910
Pendergast Safety Equipment Co, 58617
Pendery's, 9911, 47533
Pengo Attachments Inc, 27407
Penguin Cold Storage, 53261
Penguin Foods, 58618
Penguin Frozen Foods Inc, 9912, 47534
Penguin Natural Food Inc, 9913, 27408
Peninsula Airways Inc, 52010
Peninsula Plastics, 27409
Penley Corporation, 27410, 47535
Penn Barry, 27411, 27412
Penn Bottle & Supply Company, 27413

Penn Cheese, 9914
Penn Dutch Meat & Seafood Market, 9915, 9916, 9917
Penn Herb Co, 9918, 47536, 58619
Penn Maid, 58620
Penn Products, 27414
Penn Refrigeration Service Corporation, 27415, 47537
Penn Scale Manufacturing Company, 27416
Penn Shore Winery Vineyards, 9919
Penn Street Bakery, 9920
Pennacook Peppers, 9921
Pennfield Farms, 9922
Pennickers Food Distribution, 40917
PennPac International, 27417
Pennsylvania Apple Mktng Prgm, 47538
Pennsylvania Brewing Company, 9923
Pennsylvania Dutch: Birch Beer, 9924
Pennsylvania Food Merchants Association, 27418
Pennsylvania Macaroni Company, 9925
Pennsylvania Macaroni Company Inc., 47539, 58621
Pennsylvania Renaissance Faire, 9926
Pennwell Belting Company, 58622
Penny Lick Ice Cream Company, 9927
Penny Plate, 27419
Penny's Meat Products, 58623
Penobscot Mccrum LLC, 9928, 47540, 58624
Penotti USA, 9929
Pensacola Candy Co Distr, 58625
Pensacola Restaurant Supply Company, 58626
Pensacola Rope Company, 27420
Penser SC, 52011, 53262
Penske Logistics, 52012, 53263
Penske Truck Leasing Corp, 27421
Penta Manufacturing Company, 9930, 47541
Penta Water, 9931
Pentad Group Inc, 27422
Pentair Valves & Controls, 27423
Pentwater Wire Products Inc, 27424
People's Sausage Co, 9932
Peoples Cartage Inc, 52013, 53264
Peoples Woods & Charcoal, 58627
Peoria Meat Packing, 27425, 58628
Peoria Tent & Awning, 27426
Pepe's Inc, 9933, 47542
Pepe's Mexican Restaurant, 9934, 47543
Pepetti's Hygrade Egg Product, 27427
Pepper Creek Farms, 9935, 47544
Pepper Island Beach, 9936
Pepper Mill, 27428
Pepper Mill Imports, 9937
Pepper Source Inc, 9938, 27429
Pepper Source LTD, 9939
Pepper Source, Rogers, 9940
Pepperama, 47545
Peppered Palette, 9941
Pepperell Paper Company, 27431, 47546
Pepperidge Farm Inc., 9942
Pepperl & Fuchs Inc, 27432
Pepperland Farms, 9943
Peppers, 9944
PepperWorks, 27430
PepsiCo., 9945, 27433
Per Pak/Orlandi, 27434
Per-Fil Industries Inc, 27435, 47547
Perception, 27436
Perdue Farms Inc., 9946, 47548
Pereg Gourmet Spices, 9947
Peregrine Inc, 27437, 47549
Perez Food Products, 9948
Perfecseal, 27438
Perfect Addition, 9949
Perfect Bite Co, 9950
Perfect Equipment Inc, 27439, 47550
Perfect Fit Glove Company, 27440
Perfect Foods Inc, 9951
Perfect Fry Company, 27441, 47551
Perfect Life Nutrition, 9952
Perfect Plank Co, 27442

Perfect Puree of Napa Valley, 9953
Perfect Score Company, 27443
Perfect Snacks, 9954
Perfection Foods, 58629
Perfections by Allan, 9955, 58630
Perfetti Van Melle USA Inc, 9956
Perfex Corporation, 27444, 47552
Performance Contracting, 27445
Performance Food Group Co, 58631
Performance Food Group Customized Distribution, 58632, 58633, 58634, 58635, 58636, 58637, 58638, 58639
Performance Foodservice, 58640, 58641, 58642, 58643, 58644, 58645, 58646, 58647, 58648, 58649, 58650, 58651, 58652, 58653, 58654, 58655, 58656, 58657, 58658, 58659, 58660, 58661, 58662, 58663, 58664, 58665, 58666, 58667, 58668, 58669, 58670, 58671, 58672, 58673, 58674, 58675, 58676
Performance Imaging Corp, 27446
Performance Labs, 9957, 47553
Performance Packaging, 27447, 27448
Peri & Sons Farms, 9958
Perino's Inc, 9959, 58677
Perky Jerky, 9960
Perky's Pizza, 9961, 47554
Perl Packaging Systems, 27449, 47555
Perlarom Technology, 9962
Perley-Halladay Assoc, 27450, 47556
Perlick Corp, 27451, 47557
Perma-Vault Safe Co Inc, 47558
Permacold Engineering Inc, 27452
Permaloc Security Devices, 27453
Perna USA, 27454
Pernicious Pickling, 9963
Pernod Ricard USA, 9964, 58678
Perona Farms, 9965
Perplas, 27455
Perricone Juices, 9966
Perrigo Nutritionals LLC, 9967
Perry B Duryea & Son Inc, 58679
Perry Creek Winery, 9968
Perry Videx LLC, 27456, 47559, 58680
Perry's Ice Cream Co Inc, 9969
Perry's Mustards, 9982
Persistination, 47560
Personal Edge Nutrition, 9970
Perten Instruments, 27457, 27458, 27459, 47561
Pervida, 9971
Peryam & Kroll Research, 27460
Peskin Sign Co, 27461
Pestano Foods, 9972, 47562, 58681
Pestcon Systems Inc, 27462
Pester-USA, 27463
Pestos with Panache, 9973
PET Dairy, 9651
Petal, 27464
Petaluma Poultry, 9974
Pete & Joy's Bakery, 9975
Pete and Gerry's Organic Eggs, 9976, 58682
Pete's Brewing Company, 9977, 47563
Peter Blease Sales, 40918
Peter Cremer North America, 9978
Peter Drive Components, 27465
Peter Dudgeon International, 27466, 58683
Peter Gray Corporation, 27467
Peter Johansky Studio, 40919, 53265, 58684
Peter Kalustian Associates, 27468
Peter Michael Winery, 9979
Peter Pan Sales, 27469, 58685
Peter Pan Seafoods Inc., 9980, 47564
Peter Pepper Products Inc, 27470
Peter Rabbit Farms, 9981, 47565
Peter's Mustards, 9982
Peterboro Basket Co, 27471
Peters & Fair, 40920

Peters & Peters Manufacturer's Agents, 40921
Peters Imports Inc., 47566
Petersen Ice Cream Company, 9983
Peterson, 47567, 58686
Peterson & Sons Winery, 9984
Peterson Farms Inc, 9985, 52014
Peterson Fiberglass Laminates, 27472
Peterson Manufacturing Company, 27473, 47568
Peterson Sea Food Company, 58687
Peterson Sign Co, 27474
Petheriotes Brothers Coffee Company, 58688
Petit Pot, 9986
Petoskey Plastics, 27475
Petra International, 9987, 47569
Petrini Foods International, DBA Foodworld Sales, 47570
Petro Moore Manufacturing Corporation, 27476, 47571
Petro-Canada Lubricants, 27477
Petrochem Insulation, 27478
Petrofsky's Bakery Products, 9988, 47572
Petrolab Company, 58689
Petroleum Analyzer Co LP, 27479, 47573
Petschl's Quality Meats, 9989, 47574
Pett Spice Products Inc, 9990
Pexco Packaging Corporation, 27480
Peyton's, 58690
Pez Candy Inc, 9991, 27481, 47575
Pfankuch Machinery Corporation, 27482, 47576
Pfanstiehl Inc, 9992, 47577
Pfefferkorn's Coffee Inc, 9993
Pfeil & Holding Inc, 9994, 27483, 47578
PFI Displays Inc, 27051, 47333
Pfizer, 9995
PFM Packaging Machinery Corporation, 27052
PFS Transportation, 51997
PGP International, 9652
Phamous Phloyd's Barbecue, 9996
Pharaoh Trading Company, 47579, 58691
Pharmaceutic Litho & Label Co., 27485
Pharmaceutical & Food Special, 27486, 47580
Pharmachem Laboratories, 9997, 47581
Pharmachem Labs, 47582, 58692
Pharmavite LLC, 9998, 47583
Pharmco Aaper, 9999
Phase Fire Systems, 27487
Phase II Pasta Machine Inc, 27488, 47584
Phat Fudge, 10000, 58693
PHD Inc, 27053
Pheasant Ridge Winery, 10001
Phelps Industries, 27489, 47585
Phenix Label Co, 27490, 47586
Phenomenal Fudge Inc, 10002
PhF Specialist, 27484
PHF Specialists, 27054
PHI Enterprises, 27055
Phil Erb Refrigeration Co, 58694
Philadelphia Baking Company, 10003
Philadelphia Candies Inc, 10004
Philadelphia Cheese Steak, 10005, 47587
Philadelphia Extract Co Inc, 58695
Philadelphia Glass Bending Company, 27491
Philadelphia Macaroni Co, 10006, 47588
Philadelphia Warehousing & Cold Storage Company, 53266
Phildesco, 47589
Philip P Massad Movers, 52015
Philip R's Frozen Desserts, 10007
Philip Togni Vineyard, 10008
Philipp Lithographing Co, 27492, 47590
Philips Lighting Company, 27493, 47591
Phillip's Candy House, 10009
Phillips Beverage Company, 10010
Phillips Candies, 10011
Phillips Foods, 10012
Phillips Gourmet Inc, 10013, 27494

# All Companies Index

Phillips Plastics and Chemical, 27495
Phillips Refrigeration Consultants, 27496
Phillips Sales Co, 40922
Phillips Seafood, 10014, 58696
Phillips Supply Co, 58697
Phillips Syrup Corp, 10015
Philmont Manufacturing Co., 27497
Phin & Phebes, 10016
Phipps Desserts, 10017
Phivida Organics, 10018
Phoenicia Patisserie, 10019
Phoenician Herbals, 10020, 47592
Phoenix & Eclectic Network, 27498
Phoenix Agro-Industrial Corporation, 10021, 47593, 58698
Phoenix Closures Inc, 27499, 47594
Phoenix Coatings, 27500
Phoenix Contact Inc, 27501
Phoenix Engineering, 27502, 27503
Phoenix Food Sales, 40923
Phoenix Foods, 10022
Phoenix Foods Inc, 40924
Phoenix Industries Corp, 27504, 47595, 58699
Phoenix Industries LLC, 52016, 53267, 53268
Phoenix Laboratories, 10023
Phoenix Process Equipment, 27505
Phoenix Sign Company, 27506
Phoenix Wholesale Foodservice, 27507, 58700
Photo Graphics Co, 27508
Phranil Foods, 10024
Physical Distribution, 53269
Phyter Foods, 10025
Phyto-Technologies, 10026, 58701
Phytopia Inc, 27509
Phytotherapy Research Laboratory, 10027, 27510, 47596
Piab USA Inc, 27511, 27512
PIAB Vacuum Conveyors, 27056
Piab Vacuum Products, 27513
Piacere International, 27514
Piantedosi Baking Co Inc, 10028
Piazza's Seafood World LLC, 10029, 47597, 58702
Pica Trade Company, 47598
Picaflor, 10030
Picard Bakery Equipment, 27515
Picard Peanuts, 10031
Pick Heaters, 27516, 47599
Pickard China, 27517, 47600
Pickle Cottage, 10032
Pickle House, 58703
Pickle Packers International Inc., 27518
Pickled Pink, 10033
Pickled Planet, 10034
Pickles Olives Etc, 47601
Picklesmith Inc, 10035
Pickney Molded Plastics, 27519
Pickwick Catfish Farm, 10036
Pickwick Manufacturing Svc, 27520, 47602
Picnic Time Inc, 27521
Picnik, 10037
Pictsweet Co, 10038, 47603
Pidy Gourmet Pastry Shells, 10039
Pie Piper Products, 10040, 47604
Pieco, 27522, 27523
Pied-Mont/Dora, 10041, 47605
Piedmont Candy Co, 10042
Piedmont Clarklift, 58704
Piedmont Distribution Centers, 52017, 53270
Piedmont Distribution Services, 53271
Piedmont Plastics Inc, 58705
Piedmont Vineyards & Winery, 10043
Piedra Creek Winery, 10044
Piemonte Bakery Co, 10045, 58706
Piepenbrock Enterprises, 27524
Pieper Automation, 27525
Pier 1 Imports, 27526, 47606
Pierce Cartwright Company, 40925
Pierce Laminated Products Inc, 27527
Pierceton Foods Inc, 10046, 58707

Pierino Frozen Foods, 10047
Pierre's French Bakery, 10048
Pierre's French Ice Cream Inc, 10049
Pierrepont Visual Graphics Inc, 27528
Pierz Cooperative Association, 10050
Piggie Park Enterprises, 10051
Pike Awning Co, 27529
Pike Brewing Co, 10052
Pikes Peak Vineyards, 10053
Piknik Products Company, 10054, 47607
Pilant Corp, 27530, 47608
Pilgrim Foods, 10055
Pilgrim Plastics, 27531, 47609
Pilgrim's Pride Corp., 10056, 47610
Pillar Technologies, 27532
Piller Sausages & Delicatessens, 10057, 47611
Piller's Fine Foods, 10058, 47612
Pillsbury, 10059
Pilot Brands, 27533
Pilot Freight Svc, 52018, 53272
Pilot Meat & Sea Food Company, 10060, 58708
Pilz Automation Safety LP, 27534
Pinckney Molded Plastics, 27535
Pindar Vineyards, 10061
Pine Bluff Crating & Pallet, 27536
Pine Point Fisherman's Co-Op, 27537, 58709
Pine Point Seafood, 10062
Pine Point Wood Products Inc, 27538
Pine Ridge Vineyards, 10063
Pine River Cheese & Butter Company, 10064
Pine River Pre-Pack Inc, 10065
Pineland Farms, 10066
Pines International, 10067, 47613
Pinn Pack Packaging LLC, 27539
Pinnacle Foods Inc., 27540, 58710
Pinnacle Furnishing, 27541, 47614
Pino's Pasta Veloce, 10068, 27542
Pinocchio Italian Ice Cream Company, 10069
Pinquist Tool & Die Company, 27543
Pinski Portugal & Associate, 40926
Pinter's Packing Plant, 10070
Pinto Bros, 58711
Pinty's Premium Foods, 10071
Pintys Delicious Foods, 10072, 47615
Pioneer Chemical Co, 27544
Pioneer Cold Logistics, 53273
Pioneer Dairy, 10073
Pioneer Distributing Co, 58712
Pioneer Distributing Company, 58713
Pioneer Food Brokers, 40927
Pioneer Food Service, 40928
Pioneer Foods Industries, 10074
Pioneer Freight Systems Inc, 52019
Pioneer Frozen Foods, 10075
Pioneer Growers, 10076, 47616
Pioneer Labels Inc, 27545
Pioneer Lift Truck, 58714
Pioneer Live Shrimp, 10077, 58715
Pioneer Manufacturing Co Inc, 27546
Pioneer Marketing, 58716
Pioneer Marketing International, 10078, 27547, 40929
Pioneer Mat Company, 47617
Pioneer Nutritional Formula, 10079
Pioneer Packaging, 27548
Pioneer Packaging & Printing, 27549
Pioneer Packaging Machinery, 27550
Pioneer Packing Co, 10080, 47618
Pioneer Plastics Inc, 27551, 47619
Pioneer Sales Co Inc, 58717
Pioneer Sign Company, 27552
Pioneer Snacks, 10081
Pioneer Valley Refrigerated Warehouse, 52020, 53274
Pioneer Warehouse Corporation, 53275
Piper & Leaf, 10082
Piper Meat Processing, 10083
Piper Products Inc, 27553, 27554, 47620, 47621
Pippin Snack Pecans, 10084, 47622

Pippin Wholesale Co, 58718
Pipsnacks, 10085
Piqua Paper Box Co, 27555
Piqua Pizza Supply Co Inc, 10086
Pita King Bakery, 10087
Pita Pal, 10088
Pita Products, 10089
Pitbull Energy Products, 10090
Pitco Frialator Inc, 27556, 47623
Pitt Ohio, 52021
Pittman Brothers Company, 58719
Pittsburgh Brewing Co, 10091, 47624
Pittsburgh Casing Company, 47625, 58720
Pittsburgh Corning Corp, 27557, 47626
Pittsburgh Tank Corp, 27558
Pittsfield Rye Bakery, 10092
Pittsfield Weaving Company, 27559
Pitzer Transfer & Storage Corp., 52022, 53276
Piveg, Inc., 10093
Pizza Products, 10094, 58721
Pizzamatic USA, 27560
Pizzey's Milling & Baking Company, 10095, 47627
PJ's Coffee & Tea, 9653
Pk Crown Distributing Inc, 58722
Placemat Printers, 27561
Placon Corp, 27562, 27563
Plaidberry Company, 10096, 58723
Plainfield Winery & Tasting Rm, 10097, 58724
Plains Dairy Products, 10098
Plainview Milk Products, 10099, 27564
Plainville Farms, 10100
Plam Vineyards & Winery, 10101
Planet Oat, 10102
Planet Products Corp, 27565, 47628
Plant Based Foods, 10103
Plantation Candies, 10104, 47629
Plantation Pecan & Gift Company, 10105
Plantation Products Inc, 10106
Planters Cooperative, 53277
Plas-Ties Co, 27566
Plascal Corp, 27567, 47630
Plasco Safety Products, 58725
Plaskid Company, 27568
Plassein International, 27569
Plasseint International, 27570
Plast-O-Matic Valves Inc, 27571
Plastech, 27572, 47631
Plastech Corp, 27573
Plasti Print Inc, 27574
Plasti-Clip Corp, 27575, 47632
Plasti-Line, 27576, 47633
Plasti-Mach Corporation, 27577, 47634
Plastic Art Signs, 27578
Plastic Assembly Corporation, 27579
Plastic Container Corp, 27580
Plastic Craft Products Corp, 27581
Plastic Equipment, 27582
Plastic Fantastics/Buck Signs, 27583
Plastic Industrial Products, 40930
Plastic Ingenuity, 27584
Plastic Packaging Technologies, 27585
Plastic Printing LLC, 27586
Plastic Suppliers Inc, 27587, 47635
Plastic Supply Inc, 27588, 47636
Plastic Systems Inc, 27589
Plastic Tagtrade Check, 27590
Plastic Turning Company, 27591
Plastican Corporation, 27592
Plasticard-Locktech Intl, 27593
Plastics Color Corp, 27594
Plastics Inc, 27595
Plastics Industries, 27596
Plastilite Corporation, 27597
Plastimatic Arts Corporation, 27598
Plastipak Industries, 27599
Plastipak Packaging, 27600, 47637
Plastipro, 27601
Plastiques Cascades Group, 27602
Plastocon, 27603
Plate-Mate Inc USA, 47638
Platte Valley Creamery, 10107

Platteville Potato Association, 58726
Plaxall Inc, 27604
Playtex Products, LLC, 27605
Plaza de Espana Gourmet, 10110, 47640
Plaza House Coffee, 10108
Plaza Sweets Bakery, 10109, 47639
Plaze Inc, 27606
Pleasant Grove Farms, 10111, 47641
Pleasant Valley Wine Co, 10112
Pleasant View Dairy, 10113
Pleasoning Gourmet Seasonings, 10114
Plehn's Bakery Inc, 10115
Plentiful Pantry, 10116
Plenty, 10117
Plenus Group Inc, 10118
PlexPack Corp, 27607, 47642
Plicon Corporation, 27608
Plitek LLC, 27609
PLM Trailer Leasing, 27057
Plochman Inc, 10119
Plocky's Fine Snacks, 10120
PLT Health Solutions Inc, 9654, 40897, 47334
Plt Health Solutions Inc, 47643, 58727
PLT Trucking Corporation, 58517
Pluester Quality Meat Co, 10121
Plum & Assoc Inc, 40931
Plum Creek Winery, 10122
Plum Organics, 10123, 58728
Plumrose USA, 10124
Plus CBD Oil, 10125
Plus Pharma, 10126, 27610
Plush Puffs Marshmallows, 10127
Pluto Corporation, 27611, 47644
Plyley's Candy, 10128
Plymold, 27612, 47645
Plymouth Artisan Cheese, 10129
Plymouth Beef Co., 10130, 47646
Plymouth Cheese Counter, 10131
Plymouth Colony Winery, 10132
Plymouth Lollipop Company, 10133
Plymouth Rock Transportation, 52023
Plymouth Tube Company, 27613
PM Chemical Company, 27058, 47335
PM Plastics, 27059
PM&O Line, 51998
PMC Global Inc., 27060
PMC Specialties Group Inc, 9655, 47336, 58518
PME Equipment, 27061
PMI Cartoning Inc, 27062
PMI Food Equipment Group, 27063
PMMI Bookstore, 27064
PMP Fermentation Products, 9656, 47337
PMS, 47338
Pneucon, 27614
Pneumatic Conveying Inc, 27615, 47647
Pneumatic Scale Angelus, 27616, 47648
Poblocki Sign Co, 27617
Pocantico Resources Inc, 27618
Pocas International, 10134
Poche's Smokehouse, 10135
Pocino Foods, 10136, 47649
Poco Dolce, 10137
Pocono Cheesecake Factory, 10138
Pocono Mountain Bottling Company, 10139
Pocono ProFoods, 58729
Pocono Spring Company, 10140
Podnar Plastics Inc, 27619, 47650
POG, 9657
Pohlig Brothers, 27620
Point Group, 10141, 47651
Point Judith Fisherman's Company, 10142
Point Lobster Co, 10143, 58730
Point Reyes Farmstead Cheese Co., 10144
Point Saint George Fisheries, 10145
Pointing Color, 27621
Poiret International, 10146, 47652, 58731
Poison Pepper Company, 10147
Pok Pok Som, 10148
Pokanoket Ostrich Farm, 10149, 47653
Pokonobe Industries, 10150, 47654

1425

All Companies Index

Polanis Plastic of America, 27622
Polar Bear, 27623, 58732
Polar Beer Systems, 27624, 47655
Polar Beverages Inc., 10151
Polar Cold Storage, 53278
Polar Hospitality Products, 27625, 47656
Polar Ice, 27626
Polar King Transportation, 27627, 47657
Polar Peaks, 27628
Polar Plastics, 27629, 47658
Polar Process, 27630
Polar Tech Industries Inc, 27631
Polar Ware Company, 27632, 47659
Polar Water Company, 10152
Polarica USA, Inc., 10153
Polarville, 53279
Polean Foods, 47660, 58733
Polibak Plastics America Inc, 27633
Poliplastic, 27634
Polish Folklore Import Co, 40932, 58734
Polka Home Style Sausage, 10154
Pollak Food Distributors, 58735
Pollard Brothers, 27635
Pollinger Company, 27636
Pollio Dairy Products, 10155
Pollman's Bake Shop, 10156
Polly's Gourmet Coffee, 10157
Poly One Corp, 27637
Poly Plastic Products Inc, 27638
Poly Processing Co, 27639, 47661
Poly Shapes Corporation, 27640
Poly-Clip System Corp, 27641
Polyair, 27644
Polyair Packaging, 27645
Polybottle Group, 27646
Polychem Corp, 27647
Polyclutch, 27648
Polycon Industries, 27649, 47664
PolyConversions, Inc., 27642, 47662
Polyfoam Corp, 27650
PolyMaid Company, 27643, 47663
Polymer Solutions International, 27651
Polymercia, 27652
Polypack Inc, 27653, 47665
Polyplastic Forms Inc, 27654
Polyplastics, 27655, 47666, 58736
Polypro International Inc, 10158, 27656, 47667
Polyscience, 27657, 47668
Polysource Inc, 27658
Polyspec, 27659
Polytainers, 27660, 47669
Polytarp Products, 27661
Polytemp Corp, 27662
Polytop Corporation, 27663
Polytype America Corporation, 27664
POM Wonderful LLC, 9658, 47339
Pomi USA, 47670
Pommeraie Winery, 10159
Pomodoro Fresca Foods, 10160
Pomona Service & Pkgng Co LA, 27665, 47671
Pompeian Inc, 10161, 47672
Pon Food Corp, 10162, 58737
Ponce Carribian Distributors, 27666
Pond Brothers Peanut Company, 10163
Pond Pure Catfish, 10164, 58738
Ponderosa Valley Vineyard, 10165
Pondini Imports, 10166
Pontchartrain Blue Crab, 10167, 58739
Ponti USA, 10168
Pontiac Coffee Break, 10169
Pontiac Foods, 10170
Pontiac Fruit House, 58740
Pony Boy Ice Cream, 10171
Ponzi Vineyards, 10172
Poore Brothers, 10173
Pop & Bottle Inc., 10174
Pop Art Snacks, 10175
POP Fishing & Marine, 9659, 58519
Pop Gourmet LLC, 10176
Pop n Go, 27668
Pop Tops Co Inc, 27667
Pop Zero, 10177

Pop's E-Z Popcorn & Supply Company, 58741
Popchips, 10178
Popcorn Connection, 10179, 27669, 47673
Popcorn Popper, 10180, 47674
Popcorn World, 10181
Popcorner, 10182
Popcornopolis LLC, 10183
Popkoff's, 10184
Poppa's Granola, 10185
Poppers Supply Company, 10186, 47675, 58742
Poppie's Dough, 10187, 47676
Poppies International, 10188
Poppilu, 10189
Poppin Popcorn, 10190
Poppingfun Inc, 10191
Poppy Hand-Crafted Popcorn, 10192
Popsalot, 10193
POPTime, 9660
Porcelain Metals Corporation, 27670, 47677
Porinos Gourmet Food, 10194, 47678, 58743
Pork Shop of Vermont, 10195
Porkie Company of Wisconsin, 10196
Porky Products, 58744
Porky's Gourmet Foods, 10197
Port Canaveral Authority, 27671, 52024
Port City Pretzels, 10198
Port Elizabeth Terminal Corp, 52025, 53280
Port Erie Plastics Inc, 27672
Port Jersey Logistics, 52026, 53281
Port Lobster Co Inc, 10199, 58745
Port Of Corpus Christi, 53282
Port Of Miami Cold Storage Inc, 53283
Port of Palm Beach Cold, 53284
Port Of Pasco, 27673
Port of Virgina, 53285
Port Royal Sales LTD, 47679, 58746
Port Royal Seafood, 10200
Port Royal Tapes, 58747
Port Terminal Railroad, 52027
Portable Cold Storage, 27674
Portage Frosted Foods, 58748
Portco Corporation, 27675
Portec Flowmaster, 27676
Porter & Porter Lumber, 27677
Porter Bowers Signs, 27678, 47680
Porter Creek Vineyards, 10201
Porter Wallace Corporation, 58749
Porter's Pick-A-Dilly, 10202
Portier Fine Foods, 10203, 47681
Portion-Pac Chemical Corp., 27679, 47682
Portland Creamery, 10204
Portland Paper Box Company, 27680
Portland Shellfish Company, 10205, 47683
Portland Specialty Seafoods, 10206, 58750
Portlandia Foods, 10207
Porto Rico Importing, 10208
Portola Allied, 27681
Portsmouth Chowder Co, 10209
Portugalia Imports, 27682, 47684, 58751
Portuguese Baking Company, 10210
Portuguese United Grocer Co-Op, 47685, 58752
POS Pilot Plant Corporation, 27065
Poseidon Enterprises, 10211, 58753
Poser Envelope, 27683
Posimat S A, 27684
Positech Corp, 27685
Positive Employment Practice, 27686
Positive Impressions, 58754
Positively 3rd St Bakery, 10212, 58755
POSitively Unique, 27066
Poss USA, 27687
Post & Taback, 58756
Post Consumer Brands, 10213, 53286
Post Familie Vineyards, 10214
Post Food Service, 58757

Posterloid Corporation, 27688, 47686
Posternak Bauer Associates, 40933
Postum, 10215
POSWarehouse.com, 47340
Potato Specialty Company, 58758
Potdevin Machine Co, 27689
Poteet Seafood Co, 10216, 40934, 58759
Potlatch Corp, 27690, 47687
Potlicker Kitchen, 10217, 58760
Potomac Farms Dairy Inc, 10218
Potter Siding Creamery Company, 10220
Powder Pure, 10221
Powdersize Inc, 27691
Powell & Mahoney Ltd., 10222
Powell May International, 40935
Powell Systems, 27692
Power Brushes, 27693, 47688
Power Creamery, 58761
Power Crunch, 10223
Power Electronics Intl Inc, 27694, 47689
Power Flame Inc, 27695
Power Group, 27696
Power Industrial Supply, 27697
Power Industries Inc, 27698
Power Lift Corporation, 58762
Power Logistics, 27699, 53287, 53288
Power Machine Company, 27700
Power of 3, 10224
Power Packaging Inc, 27701, 27702, 53289
Power Pumps, 58763
Power Soak by Metcraft, 27703
Power Source Distributors, 58764
Power-Pack Conveyor Co, 27704
Poweramp, 27705, 47690
PowerBar, 10225
Powerful Foods, 10226
Powers Baking Company, 10227
Powertex Inc, 27706, 27707, 47691
Poynette Distribution Center, 27708
PPC Perfect Packaging Co, 27067, 47341, 53243
PPG Industries Inc, 27068
PPI, 27069
PPI Printing Press, 27070
PPI Technologies Group, 27071, 47342
Ppm Technologies LLC, 27709, 27710
PQ Corp, 27072
PR Bar, 9661
Practical Promotions, 47692
Praga Food Products, 27693
Prager Winery & Port Works, 10228
Praim Co, 10229, 47694
Prairie Berries Inc., 10230
Prairie Cajun Wholesale, 10231, 47695
Prairie City Bakery, 10232
Prairie Farms Dairy Inc., 10233
Prairie Malt, 10234, 47696
Prairie Mills Products LLC, 10235
Prairie Mushrooms, 10236, 47697
Prairie Packaging Inc, 27711
Prairie Queen Distributing, 58765
Prairie Thyme LTD, 10237
Prairie View Industries, 27712
Prana, 10238
Prater Industries, 27713
Pratt Industries, 27714, 27715, 27716
Pratt Poster Company, 27717
Prawn Seafoods Inc, 47698, 58766
Prawnto Systems, 27718, 27719, 47699, 47700
Praxair Inc, 27720, 47701
Prayon Inc., 10239, 47702
Precise Food Ingredients, 10240
Precision, 27721
Precision Automation Co, 27723
Precision Automation Co Inc, 27722, 27724
Precision Blends, 10241
Precision Brush, 27725, 47703
Precision Component Industries, 27726, 47704
Precision Micro Control, 27727
Precision Plastics Inc, 27728

Precision Plus, 27729
Precision Pours, 27730, 47705, 58767
Precision Printing & Packaging, 27731
Precision Solutions Inc, 27732
Precision Stainless Inc, 27733
Precision Systems Inc, 27734
Precision Temp Inc, 27735, 47706
Precision Wood of Hawaii, 27737
Precision Wood Products, 27736, 47707
Precit, 27738, 47708
Preco Inc, 27739
Preferred Brands Inc, 10242
Preferred Brokerage Company, 40936
Preferred Freezer Services, 52028, 53290, 53291, 53292, 53293, 53294, 53295, 53296, 53297, 53298, 53299, 53300, 53301, 53302, 53303, 53304, 53305, 53306, 53307, 53308, 53309, 53310, 53311, 53312, 53313, 53314, 53315, 53316, 53317, 53318, 53319, 53320, 53321, 53322, 53323, 53324, 53325, 53326, 53327, 53328, 53329
Preferred Machining Corporation, 27740, 47709
Preferred Meal Systems Inc, 10243, 47710
Preferred Packaging, 27741
Preferred Packaging Systems, 27742, 47711
Preferred Popcorn, 10244, 47712
Preferred Produce & Food Service, 47713
Pregel America, 58768
Preisco Jentash, 40937
Preiser Scientific Inc, 47714, 58769
Prejean's Wholesale Meats Inc, 58770
Premier, 27743, 40938, 47715
Premier Beverages, 10245
Premier Brand Imports, 47716
Premier Brass, 27744, 47717
Premier Food Marketing, 40939
Premier Food Service Sales, 40940
Premier Foods, 27745
Premier Foodservice Distributors of America, 58771
Premier Glass & Package Company, 27746
Premier Juices, 10246, 58772
Premier Malt Products Inc, 10247
Premier Marketing, 40941
Premier Meat Co, 10248, 47718
Premier Organics, 10249
Premier Pacific Seafoods Inc, 10250, 47719
Premier Packages, 27747
Premier Plastics Inc, 27748
Premier Produce, 58773
Premier Protein, 10251
Premier Restaurant Equipment, 27749
Premier Skirting Products, 27750, 47720
Premier Smoked Fish Company, 10252
Premier Southern Ticket Co, 27751
Premiere Packing Company, 10253
Premiere Refreshment Svc, 58774
Premiere Seafood, 10254, 58775
Premium Air Systems Inc, 27752
Premium Brands, 10255
Premium Chocolatiers LLC, 10256
Premium Foil Products Company, 27753, 47721
Premium Gold Flax Products & Processing, 10257
Premium Ingredients International US, LLC, 10258, 27754
Premium Meat Co, 10259
Premium Pallet, 27755
Premium Seafood Co, 40942, 58776
Premium Water, 10260, 47722
Prengler Products, 27756
Prent Corp, 27757
Prentiss, 27758, 47723

All Companies Index

Prepared Foods Magazine & Food Engineering Magazine, 27759
Pres-Air-Trol Corporation, 27760, 47724
Pres-On Products, 27761, 47725
Pres-On Tape & Gasket Corp, 27762
Prescolite, 27763, 47726
Prescott Brewing Co, 10261
Presence From Innovation LLC, 27764, 47727
Presentations, 58777
Presentations South, 27765, 47728
President Container Inc, 27766
President's Choice, 10262
Presque Isle Wine Cellars, 10263, 27767
Pressed Paperboard Technologies LLC, 27768
Pressery, 10264
Pressure King Inc, 47729, 58778
Pressure Pack, 27769
Prestige Label Company, 27770
Prestige Marketing, 40943
Prestige Metal Products Inc, 27771
Prestige Plastics Corporation, 27772, 47730
Prestige Proteins, 10265, 47731
Prestige Sales, 40944
Prestige Sales & Marketing, 40945
Prestige Skirting & Tablecloths, 27773, 47732
Prestige Technology, 10266, 47733
Presto Avoset Group, 10267
Presto Bistro, 58779
Presto Foods, 58780
Prestolabels.Com, 27774
Prestolite Electric Inc, 58781
Preston Farms Popcorn, 10268, 47734
Preston Premium Wines, 10269
Preston Scientific, 27775, 47735
Preston Vineyards & Winery, 10270
Pretium Packaging, 27776, 27777, 27778, 47736
Pretium Packaging, LLC., 27779, 47737
Pretty Products, 27780
Pretzel Perfection, 10271
Pretzel Pete, 10272
Pretzelmaker, 10273
Pretzels Inc, 10274, 47738
Prevor Marketing International, 47739, 58782
Pri-Pak Inc, 27781
Price & Co, 58783
Price Co, 10275
Price Harry H & Son, 58784
Price Seafood, 10276
Price Truck Lines Inc, 52029
Price's Creameries, 10277, 52030
Pride Container Corporation, 27782
Pride Dairies, 10278
Pride Enterprises Glades, 10279
Pride Equipment Corp, 58785
Pride Neon Inc, 27783
Pride of Dixie Syrup Company, 10280
Pride Polymers LLC, 27784
Pridgen Bros Co, 58786
Priester's Pecans, 10281, 58787
Prifti Candy Company, 10282
Prima Foods, 47740
Prima Foods International, 10283, 47741
Prima Kase, 10284
Prima® Wawona, 10285, 27785
Primal Essence, 10286
Primal Kitchen, 10287
Primal Nutrition, 10288
Primarily Seating Inc, 47742
Primarque Products Inc, 47743
Primary Liquidation, 27786
Prime Cut Meat & Seafood Company, 10289, 58788
Prime Equipment, 27787
Prime Food Processing Corp, 10290
Prime Inc., 27788
Prime Ingredients Inc, 10291, 47744
Prime Label Consultants Inc, 27789
Prime Machinery Corporation, 47745, 58789

Prime Ostrich International, 10292, 47746
Prime Pak Foods Inc, 10293
Prime Pastries, 10294
Prime Play, 47747
Prime ProData, 27790
Prime Produce, 10295
Prime Smoked Meats Inc, 10296, 47748, 58790
Prime Tag & Label, 27791
Primera Meat Service, 10298
Primera Technology, 27793
PrimeSource Equipment, 27792
Primex International Trading, 10299, 47749
Primex Plastics Corp, 27794
Primitive Feast, 10300
Primlite Manufacturing Corporation, 27795, 47750
Primo Cheese, 58791
Primo Foods, 10301, 10302
Primo Roasting Equipment, 27796
Primo Water Corporation, 10303, 27797, 47751
Primos Northgate, 10304
Primrose Candy Co, 10305, 47752
Primus Laboratories, 27798
Prince Castle Inc, 27799, 47753
Prince Industries Inc, 27800, 47754
Prince Michel, 10306
Prince of Peace, 10307, 47756, 58792
Prince Seating Corp, 27801
Prince Waffles, 47755
Princeton Shelving, 27802, 58793
Principe Foods USA, 10308
Prinova, 10309, 27803
Print & Peel, 27804
Print Ons/Express Mark, 27805
Print-O-Tape Inc, 27806
Print-Tech, 27807
Printape Corporation of America, 27808
Printcraft Marking Devices Inc, 27809
Printex Packaging, 27810
Printpack Inc, 27811
Printpack Inc., 10310, 27812, 47757
Printpak, 27813, 27814
Printsafe Inc, 27815
Printsource Group, 27816
Priority Air Express, 52031, 53330
Priority Food Processing, 27817
Priority One America, 27818, 47758
Priority One Packaging, 27819, 47759
Priority One Packaging Machinery, 27820
Priority Plastics Inc, 27821, 47760
Prism, 27822, 27823
PRISM Team Services, 51999, 53244
Prism Team Services, Inc, 52032, 53331
Prism Visual Software Inc, 27824, 27825
Prissy's of Vidalia, 58794
Private Harvest, 10311
Private Label Foods, 10312
Private Spring Water, 10313
Pro Active Sltns Chaska, 27826
Pro Active Solutions USA LLC, 27827
Pro Bake Inc, 27828
Pro Controls Inc, 27829
Pro Form Labs, 10314, 47761
Pro Line Co, 27830, 47762
Pro Line Marketing Inc, 40946
Pro Media Inc, 27831
Pro Pac Labs, 10315
Pro Pacific Agents, 40947
Pro Pack Systems Inc, 27832
Pro Plus Cleaning Products, 58795
Pro Portion Food, 10316
Pro Refrigeration, 27833
Pro Reps W, 40948
Pro Scientific, 27834
Pro Scientific Inc, 27835, 47763
Pro Sheet Cutter, 27836
Pro-Ad-Co Inc, 27837
Pro-Com Security Systems, 27838
Pro-Dex Inc, 27839

Pro-Flo Products, 27840, 47764
Pro-Gram Plastics Inc, 27841
Pro-Quip Corporation, 40949
Pro-Source Performance Prods, 10317
Pro-Tex-All Co, 27842
Pro-Western Plastics, 27843
Proacec USA, 10319, 47769, 58797
Proact Inc, 27850
Proactive Sales & Marketing, 40950
ProAmpac, 27844, 47765
Probar, 10320, 58798
ProBar Systems Inc., 27845, 47766
Probat Inc, 27851
Probiotic Solutions, 27852
Procacci Bros Sales Corp, 58799
Procedyne Corp, 27853, 47770
Procell Polymers, 10321, 27854
Procesamiento De Carne, 27855
Process Automation, 27856
Process Displays, 27857, 47771
Process Engineering & Fabrication, 27858, 47772
Process Equipment & Supply Company, 58800
Process Heating Co, 27859, 47773
Process Heating Corp, 27860, 47774
Process Plus, 27861
Process Sensors Corp, 27862, 47775
Process Solutions, 27863, 47776
Process Systems, 27864
Processors Co-Op, 27865, 40951
Procold Refrigerated Svc, 53332
PROCON Products, 27073, 47343
Prodo-Pak Corp, 27866, 47777
Produce Buyers Company, 10322
Produce Trading Corp, 47778, 58801
Producer Marketing Overlake, 10323
Producers Cooperative, 10324, 47779
Producers Cooperative Oil Mill, 10325, 47780
Producers Dairy Foods Inc, 10326
Producers Peanut Company, 10327, 47781
Producers Rice Mill Inc., 10328, 47782
Product Dynamics, 27867
Product Saver, 27868
Product Solutions, 27869
Production Equipment Co, 27870, 47783
Production Packaging & Processing Equipment Company, 27871, 47784, 58802
Production Systems, 27872, 47785
Production Techniques Limited, 27873
Productos Del Plata, 10329
Productos Familia, 27874, 47786, 58803
Products A Curtron Div, 27875, 47787
Products Distribution, 53333
Produits Alimentaire, 10330, 10331, 47788, 47789
Produits Belle Baie, 10332, 47790
Produits Ronald, 10333, 47791
Profamo Inc, 27876
Professional Bakeware Company, 27877, 47792
Professional Engineering Assoc, 27878
Professional Food Service, 40952
Professional Food Systems, 58804, 58805, 58806, 58807
Professional Home Kitchens, 47793
Professional Image, 27879
Professional Manufacturers' Representatives, 40953
Professional Marketing Group, 27880, 47794, 58808
Professional Materials Hndlng, 47795, 58809
Professional Reps of Arizona, 40954
Professional Transportation Brokers, 52033
Proffitt Manufacturing Company, 27881, 47796
Proficient Food Company, 58810, 58811
Profire Stainless Steel Barbecue, 27882, 47797

Profood International, 10334, 47798, 53334
ProFormance Foods, 10318
Progenix Corporation, 10335, 47799, 58812
Progress Lighting, 27883, 47800
Progressive Brokerage Co Inc, 40955
Progressive Flavors, 10336
Progressive Flexpak, 27884
Progressive Food, 58813
Progressive Food Service Broker, 40956
Progressive Handling Systems, 58814
Progressive International/Mr. Dudley, 47801
Progressive Marketing Systems, 40957
Progressive Packaging Inc, 27885
Progressive Plastics, 27886
Progressive Sales & Marketing, 40958
Progressive Software, 27887
Progressive Specialty Glass, 47802
Progressive Technology International, 27888
Progressive Tractor & Implement Co., 27889
Progresso Quality Foods, 10337
Proheatco Manufacturing, 27890, 47803
Prohibition Distillery, LLC, 10338
Proin, 58815
Project 7, 10339
Prolamina, 27891
Prolift Industrial Equipment, 58816
Prolimer Foods, 10340
Prolon, 27892
Prolume, 10341
Proluxe, 27893, 47804
PROMA Technologies, 27074
Promac, 27894
ProMach, 27846
Promarks, 27895, 47805
Promega, 27896
Promens, 27897, 47806
Promesa, 40959
Prominent Fluid Controls Inc, 27898, 27899
Promised Land Dairy, 10342
Prommus Brands, 10343
Promo Bar/Howw, 47807
Promo Edge, 27900
Promofood International, 47808
Promolux Lighting, 10344
Promotion in Motion Companies, 10345, 27901, 47809
Promotional Resources, 47810
Promotions Ink, 58817
Pronatura Inc, 47811, 58818
Pronova Biopolymer, 27902, 27903, 47812
Pronto Products Company, 27904, 47813
Propac Marketing Inc, 27905
Propak, 27906
Proper-Chem, 10346, 47814
ProRestore Products, 27847, 47767
ProSource, 58796
Prosperity Organic Foods, 10347
Prospero Equipment Corp, 27907
Prosys Innovative Packaging Equipment, 27908
Protano's Bakery, 10348
ProTeam, 27848, 47768
Protectowire Co Inc, 27909, 47815
Protein Research, 10349, 27910, 47816
Protex International Corp., 27911
Protexall, 27912, 47817
Protica Inc, 27913, 47818
Protient, 10351, 10352
Protos Inc, 10353
Prototype Equipment Corporation, 27913, 27914, 47819
Prova, 10354
Provender International, 47820
Providence & Worcester RR Company, 52034
Providence Bay Fish Co, 40960
Providence Brokerage, 40961
Providence Cheese, 10355

1427

All Companies Index

Providence Packaging, 27915
Provigo, 58819
Provigo Distribution, 47821, 58820, 58821, 58822, 58823
Provimi Foods, 10356, 47822
Provincial, 40962
Provisioner Data Systems, 27916
ProVisions Software, 27849
Provisur Technologies, 27917, 27918, 27919, 47823
Provisur Technologies, Inc., 27920
Provitas LLC, 10357
Provost Packers, 10358
Pruden Packing Company, 10359, 47824
Prudential Lighting, 27921
Pruitt's Packaging Services, 27922
Prystup Packaging Products, 27923
PS Seasoning & Spices, 9662
Psc Floturn Inc, 27924, 47825
PSI, 27075
PSI Preferred Solutions, 27076
Psion Teklogix, 27925
Psycho Donuts, 10360
Psyllium Labs, 10361, 27926, 47826, 53335
PTC International, 47344
PTI Packaging, 27077, 47345
PTR Baler & Compactor Co, 27078, 47346
Public Service Company of Oklahoma, 27927
Publix Super Market, 10362, 27928
Pucel Enterprises Inc, 27929, 47827
Pudgies Famous Chicken, 47828
Pudliner Packing, 58824
Puebla Foods Inc, 10363, 47829
Pueblo Trading Co Inc, 47830, 58825
Puerto Rico Cold Storage, 53336
Puget Sound Inline, 27930
Pulakos 926 Chocolate, 10364
Pulini Produce, 58826
Pulmuone Foods USA Inc., 10365, 58827
Pulse Plus, 58828
Pulse Systems, 27931, 47831
Pulsetech Products Corp, 27932
Pulva Corp, 27933, 47832
Pumodori Brothers Sales, 58829
Pump Solutions Group, 27934
PURA, 27079, 47347
PURAC America, 27080
Purac America, 27935, 47834
Puratos Canada, 10366, 47835
Puratos Corp, 27936
Purcell & Madden Associates, 40963
Purcell International, 47836
Purchase Order Co Of Miami Inc, 47837, 58830
Pure & Secure LLC-Cust Svc, 27937, 47838
Pure Batch, 10367
Pure Dark, 10368
Pure Extracts Inc, 10369
Pure Fit Nutrition Bars, 27938, 47839
Pure Flo Water Co, 10370, 52035
Pure Food Ingredients, 10371, 47840
Pure Foods, 10372, 47841
Pure Foods Meat, 10373
Pure Gourmet, 10374
Pure Ground Ingredients, 10375
Pure Indian, 10376
Pure Inventions LLC, 10377
Pure Life Organic Foods, 10378, 27939, 47842, 53337
Pure Milk & Ice Cream Company, 10379
Pure Planet, 10380
Pure Process Systems, 27940
Pure Sales, 10381, 40964, 47843
Pure Sealed Dairy, 58831
Pure Source LLC, 10382, 47844
Pure Sweet Honey Farms Inc, 10383, 47845
Pure's Food Specialties, 10384
Pure-1 Systems, 27941
Pure-Chem Products Company, 27942
Pure7 Chocolate, 10385

PureCircle USA, 10386, 27943, 47846
Purefect Ice, 53338
PureForm CBD, 10387
Purely American, 10388
Purely Elizabeth, 10389, 58832
Purely Pecans, 10390
Purico USA, 27944
Puritan Manufacturing Inc, 27945, 47847
Puritan's Pride Inc, 58833
Puritan/ATZ Ice Cream, 10391
Puritan/Churchill Chemical Company, 27946, 47848
Purity Candy Co, 10392
Purity Dairies LLC, 10393
Purity Factories, 10394, 47849
Purity Farms, 10395
Purity Foods Inc, 10396, 27947
Purity Ice Cream Co, 10397
Purity Laboratories, 27948
Purity Organic, 10398
Purity Products, 10399, 27949, 47850
Purity Wholesale Grocers, Inc., 58834
PurJava, 47833
Puro Water Group, 58835
Puroast Coffee Co Inc, 10400
Purolator Facet Inc, 27950, 47851
Puronics Water Systems Inc, 27951
Purse Valet, 47852
Put-Ons USA, 27952
Putnam Candy, 58836
Putnam Group, 27953, 47853, 58837
Putney House Trading LLC, 10401
Putney Pasta, 10402
Putsch & Co Inc, 27954
Puueo Poi Shop, 10403
PVI Industries LLC, 27081
PYA/Monarch, 58520, 58521, 58522
PYCO Industries Inc, 9663
Pylam Products Co Inc, 58838
Pyramid Alehouse-Seattle, 10404
Pyramid Flexible Packaging, 27955
Pyramid Juice Company, 10405, 58839
Pyramid Packaging, Inc, 58840
Pyrenees French Bakery, 10406
Pyro-Chem, 27956, 47854
Pyromation Inc, 27957, 47855
Pyrometer Instrument Co Inc, 27958, 47856
Pyure Brands, 10407

Q

Q & B Foods, 27959, 47857
Q A Supplies LLC, 27960, 47858
Q Bell Foods, 10408
Q C Industries, 27961
Q Drinks, 10409
Q Laboratories, 27962
Q Mixers, 10410
Q Pak Inc, 27963
Q Vac, 27964
Q's Nuts, 10411
Q-Matic Technologies, 27965, 47859
Q-Sales & Leasing, 47860
Q.E. Tea, 10412, 47861
QAD Inc, 27966
QBD Modular Systems, 27967, 47862
QBI, 10413, 47863
QC, 27968
Qchef, 58842
QDC Plastic Container Co, 27969
QMI, 27970, 47864
QMS International, Inc., 27971, 47865
QNC Inc, 27972
Qosina Corporation, 27975, 47867
QSR Industrial Supply, 27973
Qst Industries Inc, 27976
QST Ingredients, 10414
Qsx Labels, 27977, 47868
Quadra Foods Company, 58843
Quadra-Tech, 27978
Quadrant Epp USA Inc, 27979
Quadrel Labeling Systems, 27980, 47869
Quadro Engineering, 27981
Quady Winery, 10415

Quail Crest Foods, 58844
Quail Ridge Cellars & Vineyards, 10416
Quaily Storage Products Inc, 58845
Quaker Bonnet, 10417
Quaker Chemical Company, 27982, 47870
Quaker Maid Meats, 10418
Quaker Oats Company, 10419, 10420, 27983, 47871
Quaker Sugar Company, 10421
Quaker Window Products Co, 58846
Quali Tech Inc, 10422
Quali-Tech Tape & Label, 27984
Qualicaps Inc, 10424, 47873
Qualicon, 27985
Qualiform, Inc, 27986, 47874
Qualifresh Michel St. Arneault, 10425, 47875
QualiGourmet, 10423, 47872
Qualita Paper Products, 27987
Quality Aluminum & Hm Imprvmt, 27988
Quality Assured Label Inc, 27989
Quality Assured Packing, 27990
Quality Bakers of America, 27991
Quality Bakery, 10426
Quality Bakery Products, 10427
Quality Banana Inc, 58847
Quality Brokerage Company, 40965
Quality Cabinet & Fixture Co, 27992, 47876
Quality Candy Company, 10428
Quality Celery & Sprout Company, 58848
Quality Chekd Dairies Inc, 27993
Quality Container Company, 27994, 47877
Quality Containers, 27995, 47878
Quality Containers of New England, 27996
Quality Control Equipment Co, 27997, 47879
Quality Controlled Services, 27998
Quality Corporation, 27999, 47880
Quality Crab Co Inc, 10429
Quality Croutons, 10430, 28000
Quality Cup Packaging Machinery Corporation, 28001
Quality Dairy Co, 10431
Quality Discount Ice Cream, 58849
Quality Distributing Company, 58850
Quality Eggs & Juices, 58851
Quality Equipment Marketing, 58852
Quality Fabrication & Design, 28002, 47881
Quality Films, 28003
Quality Fisheries, 10432, 58853
Quality Food Company, 10433, 40966, 58854
Quality Food Equipment, 28004
Quality Food Products Inc, 10434, 28005, 58855
Quality Foods, 10435, 58856
Quality Foods International, 58857
QUALITY Frozen Foods, 58841
Quality Groceries, 58858
Quality Highchairs, 28006
Quality Industries, 28007
Quality Industries Inc, 28008, 47882
Quality Ingredients, 10436, 28009
Quality Instant Teas, 10437
Quality Kitchen Corporation, 10438, 47883
Quality Logistics Systems, 52036, 53339
Quality Material Handling, 58859
Quality Meats & Seafood, 10439
Quality Mop & Brush Manufacturers, 28010
Quality Natural Casing, 28011
Quality Naturally Foods, 10440, 47884
Quality Nut Co, 10441
Quality Packaging Inc, 28012
Quality Plastic Bag Corporation, 28013
Quality Poultry Co, 58860
Quality Produce Company, 58861

Quality Rep Source, 40967
Quality Sales & Marketing, 40969
Quality Sales & Marketing, Inc., 40968
Quality Sausage Company, 10442, 47885
Quality Seafood, 10443
Quality Seating Co, 28014, 47886
Quality Snack Foods Inc, 10444
Quality Snacks, 10445
Quality Transparent Bag Co, 28015
Quality Wholesale Produce Co, 58862
Qualtech, 28016
Qualtrax, 28017
Qualy Pak Specialty Foods, 58863
Quandt's Foodservice Distributors, 53340, 58864
Quanex Building Products Corp, 28018
Quantek Instruments, 28019
Quantem Corp, 28020
Quantis Secure Systems, 28021
Quantum Energy Squares, 10446
Quantum Net, 28022
Quantum Performance Films, 28023, 47887
Quantum Storage Systems Inc, 28024, 47888
Quantum Supply Company, 58865
Quantum Topping Systems Quantum Technical Services Inc, 28025
Quasar Industries, 28026
Quast & Company, 52037
Quattrochi Specialty Foods, 58866
Quebec Ministry of Agriculture, 10447
Quebec Vegetable Distributors, 58867
Queen Ann Ravioli & Macaroni, 10448
Queen Anne Coffee Roaster, 10449
Queen Bee Gardens, 10450, 47889
Queen City Awning, 28027
Queen City Coffee Company, 10451
Queen City Meats, 58868
Queen City Sausage & Provision, 10452
Queen City Warehouse Corporation, 52038, 53341
Queen International Foods, 10453
Queen of America, 10454
Queens Tobacco, Grocery & Candy, 58869
Queensboro Farm Products, 10455, 10456, 58870, 58871
Queensway Foods Company, 10457, 47890
Queensway Foods Inc., 47891
Quelle Quiche, 10458, 47892
Quest, 28028
Quest Corp, 28029, 47893
Quetzal Foods International Company, 28030
Quetzal Internet Cafe, 10459
Quibell Spring Water Beverage, 10460
Quick Delivery, 52039, 53342
Quick Judith & Assoc, 28031
Quick Label Systems, 28032, 28033
Quick Point Inc, 28034, 47894
Quick Servant Co, 58872
Quick Stamp & Sign Mfg, 28035, 58873
Quickdraft, 28037, 47895
Quickie Manufacturing Corp, 28038
QuickLabel, 28036
Quigley Industries Inc, 10461, 47896
QUIKSERV Corp, 27974, 47866
Quikwater Inc, 28039
Quilceda Creek Vintners, 10462
Quillin Produce Co, 10463
Quillisascut Cheese Co, 10464
Quinault Pride, 10465, 47897
Quinn Co, 58874
Quinn Lift, 58875
Quinn Snacks, 10466
Quinoa Corporation, 10467, 47898, 58876
Quintessential Chocolates, 10468
Quintex Corp, 28040, 28041
Quinzani Bakery, 10469
Quip Industries, 47899, 58877
Quipco Products Inc, 28042, 47900
Quirch Foods, 10470

1428

All Companies Index

Quivira Vineyards & Winery, 10471
Quong Hop & Company, 10472
Quorn Foods, 10473
Qwik Pack Systems, 28043
Qyk Syn Industries, 28044
Qzina Specialty Foods, 47901, 58878

R

R & D Brass, 28045
R & D Sausage Co, 10474
R & R Seafood, 10475, 58879
R & S Mexican Food, 10476
R A Jones & Co Inc, 28046, 47902
R C Fine Foods Inc, 10477
R C Molding Inc, 28047
R C Musson Rubber Co, 28048
R C Smith Co, 28049
R D Laney Family Honey Co, 10478
R D Smith Co, 58880
R Equipment, 58881
R F Hunter Co Inc, 28050, 47903
R F Mac Donald Co, 28051
R F Schiffmann Assoc., 28052
R F Technologies Inc, 28053
R Four Meats, 10479
R G Sellers Co, 40970
R H Moulton Company, 40971
R H Saw Corp, 28054, 47904
R Hirt Jr Co, 58882
R I Provision Co, 10480
R J Bickert & Associates, 40972
R J Mc Cullough Co, 28055
R K Electric Co Inc, 28056, 47905
R L Schreiber Inc, 10481
R L Spear Co, 58883
R L Swearer Co Inc, 52040
R M Felts' Packing Co, 10482, 47906
R M Lawton Cranberries Inc, 10483
R Murphy Co Inc, 28057
R P Adams, 28058
R R Donnelley, 28059
R R Street & Co, 28060, 47907
R S Braswell Co Inc, 58884
R S Porter & Co, 58885
R S Stern Inc, 58886
R T C, 28061, 47908
R T Foods Inc, 10484, 47909, 58887
R Torre & Co, 10485, 47910
R W Bozel Transfer Inc, 52041, 53343
R W Smith & Co, 58888
R W Zant Co, 58889
R Weaver Apiaries, 10486
R Wireworks Inc, 28062
R X Honing Machine Corp, 28063, 47911
R&A Imports, 10487, 47912, 53344
R&B Produce, 58890
R&C Pro Brands, 28064
R&D Glass Products, 28065
R&F Cocoa Services, 40973
R&F International Corporation, 58891
R&G Machinery, 28066
R&J Farms, 10488, 47913, 58892
R&J Seafoods, 10489, 58893
R&R Corrugated Container, 28067
R&R Equipment Company, 58894
R&R Homestead Kitchen, 10490
R&R Industries, 28068
R&R Mill Company, 47914, 58895
R&R Sales Company, 47915, 58896
R-Best Produce, 58897
R-Biopharm Inc, 28069
R. Becker Marketing & Sales, 40974
R. Markey & Sons, 28070
R.A.V. Colombia, 47916
R.B. Morriss Company, 47917
R.C. Keller & Associates, 28071
R.C. McEntire & Company, 10491, 58898
R.D. Offutt Farms, 10492
R.E. Diamond, 58899
R.E. Meyer Company, 10493, 47918
R.F. Beyers, 58900
R.F. Cannon Company, 40975
R.F.K. Transportation Service, 52042

R.G. Stephens Engineering, 28072
R.H. Chandler Company, 28073, 47919
R.H. Forschner, 58901
R.H. Phillips, 10494
R.I. Enterprises, 28074
R.J. Corr Naturals, 10495
R.J.K. Sales, 40976
R.L. Albert & Son, 10496
R.L. Corty & Company, 58902
R.L. Instruments, 28075
R.L. Zeigler Company, 10497, 47920
R.M. Palmer Co., 10498, 47921
R.N. Mason & Son, 58903
R.N.C. Industries, 28076
R.P. Childs Stamp Company, 28077
R.R. Scheibe Company, 28078
R.S. Hamilton Company, 58904
R.S. Somers Company, 58905
R.T. Greene Company, 58906
R.W. Berkeley & Associates, 40977
R.W. Davis Oil Company, 58907
R.W. Frookies, 10499
R.W. Garcia, 10500, 47922
RA Jones & Company, 28079
Ra-Bob International, 58916
Raaka Chocolate, 10520
RAB Food Group, 10501
Rabbeco, 28133
Rabbit Barn, 10521
Rabbit Creek, 10522
Rabbit Ridge Winery, 10523
Rabco Foodservice, 58917
Rabe Sales Corp, 40981
Raber Packing Co, 10524
Rabin Worldwide, 28134
Raburn, 28135
Raceland Raw Sugar Corporation, 10525
Rachael's Smoked Fish, 10526, 47939
Racine County Court Cmmssnr, 28136
Racine Danish, 10527
Racine Paper Box Manufacturing, 28137, 47940
Rack Service Company, 58918
Racket Group, 28138
Racks, 28139
Raco Mfg & Engineering Co, 28140
Radanovich Vineyards & Winery, 10528
Radcliffe System, 28141
Radding Signs, 28142
Rademaker USA, 28143
Rader Company, 47941
Radiant Industrial Solutions, 28144
Radiation Processing Division, 28145, 47942
Radio Cap Company, 28146
Radio Frequency Co Inc, 28147, 47943
Radius Display Products, 28148, 47944
Radlo Foods, 10529, 47945
Rafael Soler, 28149
Raffield Fisheries Inc, 10530, 47946
Ragersville Swiss Cheese, 10531
Ragold, 47947
Ragold Confections, 10532
Ragozzino Foods Inc, 10533, 47948
Ragsdale-Overton Food Traditions, 10534
Ragtime, 28150, 47949
Rahco International, 47950
Rahmann Belting & Industrial Rubber Products, 28151, 47951
Rahr Malting Co, 10535, 28152
Railex Corp, 28153, 47952
Rainbow, 40982
Rainbow Foods, 58919
Rainbow Hills Vineyards, 10536
Rainbow Industrial Products, 28155
Rainbow Light Nutritional Systems, 10537
Rainbow Natural Foods, 58920
Rainbow Neon Sign Company, 28156
Rainbow Pops, 10538, 47954
Rainbow Promotions LLC, 58921
Rainbow Sales & Marketing, 40983
Rainbow Seafood Market, 10539, 58922
Rainbow Seafoods, 10540, 47955

Rainbow Sign Co, 28157
Rainbow Valley Frozen Yogurt, 10541, 47956
Rainbow Valley Orchards, 58923
Rainforest Company, 10542, 47957
Rainier Cold Terminal, 53350
Rainier Cold-Storage & Ice, 53351, 53352
RainSoft Water Treatment System, 28154, 47953
Rainsweet Inc, 10543, 47958
Rairdon Dodge Chrysler Jeep, 28158, 47959
Raisin Administrative Committee, 58924
RAJB Hog Foods Inc, 10502
Rakestraw Ice Cream Company, 58925
Raleigh W. Johnson & Company, 40984
Rallis Whole Foods, 10544
Ralph Jones Display & Store, 58926
Ralph L. Mason,, 28159
Ralph Moyle Inc, 52045, 53353
Ralph Sechler & Son Inc, 10545
Ralph's Famous Italian Ices, 10546
Ralph's Grocery Company, 28160
Ralph's Packing Co, 10547, 52046, 58927
Ralphs Pugh Conveyor Rollers, 28161, 47960
RAM Center, 28080, 47923
RAM Center: Automated Equipment Group (AEG), 47924
Ram Equipment Co, 28162, 47961
Ram Industries, 28163
Ram Machinery Corp, 28164
Ramarc Foods Inc, 47962, 58928
Ramco Innovations Inc, 28165, 58929
Ramco Systems Corp, 28166
Ramex Foods, 58930
Ramona's Mexican Foods, 10548, 47963
Ramondin USA Inc, 28167
Ramoneda Bros Stave Mill, 28168, 47964
Ramos Orchards, 10549, 47965
Ramsay Signs Inc, 28169
Ramsen Inc, 10550, 58931
Ramsey Popcorn Co Inc, 10551, 47966
Ramsey Winch Co, 28170
Ranaldi Bros. Frozen Food Products, 10552
Ranch Foods Direct, 58932
Ranch Oak Farm, 10553
Rancho Cold Storage, 53354
Rancho De Philo Winery, 10554
Rancho Sales & Marketing, 40985
Rancho Sierra, 10555
Rancho Sisquoc Winery, 10556
Rancho's, 10557
Rancolio North America, 28171
Rand-Whitney Group LLC, 28172, 28173, 28174
Rand-Whitney Packaging Corp, 28175
Randag & Assoc Inc, 40986
Randal Optimal Nutrients, 10558
Randall Food Products, 10559
Randall Foods Inc, 10560
Randall Manufacturing Inc, 28176, 47967
Randall Meat Co, 58933
Randall Printing, 28177
Randazzo's Honest To Goodness Sauces, 10561
Randell Manufacturing Unified Brands, 28178, 47968
Randolph Packing Co, 10562
Randware Industries, 28179
Randy's Donuts, 10563
Randy's Frozen Meats, 10564, 58934
Range Packing Company, 58935
Ranger Blade Manufacturing Company, 28180
Ranger Tool Co Inc, 28181, 47969
Ranieri Fine Foods, 10565
Rankin Delux, 28182
Ranpak Corp, 28183
Ransco Industries, 28184
Rantec Corp, 58936
RAO Contract Sales Inc, 28081, 47925

RAO Design Intl, 28082
Rao's Specialty Foods Inc, 10566
Rapa Products (USA), 28185
RAPA Scrapple, 58908
RAPAC Inc, 28083
Rapak, 28186
Rapat Corp, 28187, 47970
Rapazzini Winery, 10567
Rapid Displays Inc, 28188
Rapid Industries Inc, 28189, 47971
Rapid Pallet, 28190, 47972
Rapid Rack Industries, 28191, 47973
Rapid Sales Company, 58937
Rapids Wholesale Equipment, 47974, 58938
Rapunzel Pure Organics, 10568
Raque Food Systems, 28192
Raquelitas Tortillas, 10569
Rare Hawaiian Honey Company, 10570
RAS Process Equipment Inc, 28084, 47926
Rasco Industries, 28193
Rast Produce Co, 40987
Ratcliff Food Brokers, 40988
Ratcliff Hoist Company, 28194
Rath Manufacturing Company, 28195, 47975
Rathe Productions, 28196
Ratioflo Technologies, 28197
Rational Cooking Systems, 28198, 47976
Ratners Retail Foods, 10571
Raven Creamery Company, 10572
Ravenswood Winery, 10573
Ravico USA, 10574
Ravioli Store, 10575
Raw Bite, 10576
Raw Rev, 10577, 58939
RawFusion, 10578
Rawlings Sporting Goods Co Inc, 47977
Rawmantic Chocolate, 10579
Ray & Mascari, 58940
Ray C. Sprosty Bag Company, 28199
Ray Cosgrove Brokerage Company, 40989, 47978, 58941
Ray West Warehouses/Transport, 52047, 53355
Ray's Pride Brokerage Company, 40990
Ray's Sausage Co, 10580
Ray-Craft, 28200, 47979
Raye's Mustard, 10581
Raye's Old Fashioned Gourmet Mustard, 10582
Raymond, 58942
Raymond Corp, 28201, 47980
Raymond Handling Concepts Corp, 58943
Raymond Handling Solutions, 58944
Raymond-Hadley Corporation, 10583, 47981
Rayne Sign Co, 28202
Raypak Inc, 28203, 47982
Raypress Corp, 28204
Raytek Corporation, 28205
Raytheon Co, 28206, 47983
Raz Company, 58945
Razor Edge Systems, 28207
RB Packing of California, 58909
RBA-Retailer's Bakers Association, 28085
Rbm Co, 58946
RBM Manufacturing Co, 28086
RBS Fab Inc, 28087
RBW Logistics, 53345
RC Bottling Company, 10503
RCS Limited, 28088
RCW International, 47927
RDA Container Corp, 28089
RDM International, 28090, 47928
RDM Technologies, 28091
RDM-Sesco, 28092
RDS of Florida, 28093
RE Botanicals, 10504
REA Elektronik, 28094
Rea UltraVapor, 28208
Read Products Inc, 28209, 47984

1429

All Companies Index

Readco Kurimoto LLC, 28210, 47985
Reading Bakery Systems Inc, 28211, 47986
Reading Box Co Inc, 28212
Reading Coffee Roasters, 10584, 47987
Reading Plastic Fabricators, 28213
Reading Technologies Inc, 28214
Ready Access, 28215, 47988
Ready Food Products, 58947
Ready Foods Inc, 10585
Ready Pac Foods Inc, 10586
Ready Portion Meat Co, 58948
Ready Potatoes Inc, 58949
Ready White, 28216
Real Aloe Company, 10587, 47989
Real Cajun School Of Cooking, 58950
Real Coconut Co. Inc., The, 10588, 47990
Real Cookies, 10589, 47991
Real Food Marketing, 10590, 40991
Real Kosher Sausage Company, 10591, 47992
Real Sausage Co, 10592
Real Soda, 47993, 58951
Real Torino, 10593
Really Raw Honey Company, 58952
Realsalt, 10594
REBBL, 10505
Rebec Vineyards, 10595
Rebecca-Ruth Candy Factory, 10596
Rebel Green, 28217
Rebel Stamp & Sign Co, 28218
Rebound, 10597
Rebstock Conveyors, 58953
Recco International, 28219, 47994
Rechner Electronics Industries, 28220
Reckitt Benckiser LLC, 10598
Rector Foods, 10599, 47995
Red Arrow Products Co LLC, 10600
Red Baron, 10601
Red Brick Brewing Company, 10602
Red Chamber Co, 10603, 47996, 58954
Red Creek Marinade Company, 10604
Red Deer Lake Meat Processing, 10605
Red Diamond Coffee & Tea, 10606, 28221, 47997, 58955
Red Duck Foods, 10607
Red Gold Inc., 10608
Red Hat Cooperative, 10609, 47998
Red Hot Chicago, 10610, 47999, 58956
Red Hot Foods, 10611
Red Kap Image Apparel, 48000
Red Kap Industries, 28222
Red Lion Controls Inc, 28223
Red Lion Spicy Foods Company, 10612
Red Monkey Foods, 10613
Red Pelican Food Products, 10614, 48001
Red Plate Foods, 10615
Red River Commodities Inc, 10616, 48002
Red River Foods Inc, 10617, 48003
Red River Lumber Company, 28224, 48004
Red Rocker Candy, 10618
Red Rose Trading Company, 10619, 48005, 58957
Red Smith Foods Inc, 10620, 48006
Red Star BioProducts, 28225
Red Star Yeast, 10621
Red Steer Meats, 10622
Red V Foods, 10623
Red Valve Co Inc, 28226
Red White & Brew, 10624
Red's All Natural, 10625
Red-Ray Manufacturing Co Inc, 28227
REDCLAY Gourmet, 10506
Redd Superfood Energy Bars, 10626
Reddi-Pac, 28228
Redding Pallet Inc, 28229, 48007
Reddy Ice, 10627, 53356, 53357, 58958
Reddy Raw Inc, 58959
Redex Packaging Corporation, 28230
Redhawk Vineyard & Winery, 10628
Redhook Brewery, 10629

Redi-Call Inc, 28231, 48008
Redi-Print, 28232, 48009
Redicon Corporation, 28233
Redlake Imaging Corporation, 28234
Redlake MASD, 28235
Redmond Minerals Inc, 10630, 48010
Redondo Iglesias USA, 10631
Redondo's LLC, 10632
Redstone Distributors, 58960
Redwood Hill Farm, 10633
Redwood Vintners, 28236
Reed & Barton Food Service, 28237, 48011
Reed Ice, 28238, 58961
Reed Lang Farms, 10634
Reed Oven Co, 28239, 48012
Reed Trucking Co, 52048
REED'S Inc, 10507
Reed's, Inc., 10635
Reede International Seafood Corporation, 40992, 48013
Reef Industries Inc, 28240
Reefco Logistics, 52049
Reelcraft Industries Inc, 28241, 48014
Reeno Detergent & Soap Company, 28242, 48015
Rees Inc, 28243, 48016
Reese & Long Refrigeration, 58962
Reese Brokerage Co, 40993
Reese Enterprises Inc, 28244, 48017
Reeve Store Equipment Co, 28245, 48018
Reeve Wines, 10636
Reeves Enterprises, 28246
Refcon, 28247, 48019
Refinishing Touch, 28248
Reflectronics, 28249
Reflex International, 28250
Refractron Technologies Corp, 28251, 48020
Refresco Beverages US Inc., 10637, 48021
Refrigerated Design Tech, 28252
Refrigerated Food Distributors, 53358
Refrigerated Warehouse Marketing Group, 28253, 53359
Refrigerated Warehousing, 28254
Refrigeration & Food Eqpt Inc, 58963
Refrigeration Design & Svc, 28255
Refrigeration Engineering, 28256
Refrigeration Equipment, 58964
Refrigeration Research, 28257, 48022
Refrigeration Systems Company, 28258
Refrigeration Technology, 28259
Refrigerator Manufacturers LLC, 28260, 48023, 58973
Refrigiwear Inc, 28261, 28262, 48024, 48025
Refrigue USA, 28263
Regal Box Corp, 28264
Regal Crown Foods Inc, 10638, 48026
Regal Custom Fixture Company, 28265, 48027
Regal Distributing Company, 58965, 58966
Regal Equipment Inc, 28266
Regal Food Service, 10639
Regal Health Food, 10640, 48028
Regal Manufacturing Company, 28267
Regal Pinnacle Integrations, 28268
Regal Plastic Company, 28269
Regal Plastic Supply Co, 28270
Regal Power Transmission Solutions, 28271
Regal Springs Trading Company, 48029
Regal Supply & Chemical Company, 58967, 58968
Regal Ware Inc, 28272, 48030
Regatta Craft Mixers, 10641
Regco, 10642
Regency Coffee & Vending, 28273, 58969
Regency Hearts of Palm, 48031
Regency Label Corporation, 28274
Regency Service Carts, 48032

Regenie's Crunchy Pi, 10643
Regennas Candy Shop, 10644
Regez Cheese & Paper Supply, 10645
Regez Cheese Company, 58970
Reggie Balls Cajun Foods, 10646, 28275
Reggie's Roast, 10647
Regina USA, 28276, 48033
Regina-Emerson, 28277
Reginald's Homemade LLC, 10648
Regional Produce, 28278
Register Meat Co, 10649
Registry Steak & Seafood, 10650, 58971
Rego China Corporation, 28279, 48034
Rego Smoked Fish Company, 10651, 48035
Reheis Co, 10652, 28280, 48036
Rehemond Farm Inc, 10653
Rehrig Pacific Co, 28281
REI Systems Inc, 28095
Reichenbach & Associates, 40994
Reichert Analytical Instruments, 28282, 48037
Reid Boiler Works, 28283
Reid Foods, 10654
Reid Graphics Inc, 28284
Reidler Decal Corporation, 28285, 48038
Reilly Dairy & Food Company, 10655, 48039
Reilly Foam Corporation, 28286
Reilly's Sea Products, 10656, 48040
Reily Foods Company, 10657
Reimann Food Classics, 10658
Reiner Products, 28287, 48041
Reinhart Foods, 10659, 48042
Reinhart Foodservice LLC, 58972
Reinhold Ice Cream Company, 10660
Reinhold Sign Svc Inc, 28288
Reinke & Schomann, 28289, 48043
Reis Robotics, 28290, 48044
Reiser, 28291
Reist Popcorn Co, 10661, 48045
Reit-Price Manufacturing Company, 28292
Reiter Affiliated Companies, 10662
Reiter Dairy, 10663
Reiter Dairy LLC, 10664
Rejuvila, 10665
Relco Unisystems Corp, 28293, 48046
Reliable Container Corporation, 28294, 48047
Reliable Fire Equipment, 28295, 58973
Reliable Fire Protection, 58974
Reliable Food Service Equipment, 28296
Reliable Label, 28297
Reliable Mercantile Company, 40995, 48048, 58975
Reliable Tent & Awning Co, 28298
Reliance Product, 28299
Reliance-Paragon, 28300
REM Ohio Inc, 28096
Rema Foods Inc, 48049
Remarkable Liquids, 10666
Rembrandt Foods, 10667
Remco Industries International, 28301, 48050
Remco Products Corp, 28302, 28303, 48051
Remco Specialty Products, 48052
Remcon Plastics Inc, 28304
Remcraft Lighting Products, 28305, 48053
Remel, 28306, 48054
Reminox International Corporation, 28307
Remmele Engineering, 28308
Remmey Wood Products, 28309
Remote Equipment Systems, 28310
Rempak Industries, 28311
Remstar International, 28312, 48055
Remy Cointreau USA, Inc., 58976
Ren 500 Food Fair, 58977
Renaissance International, 58978
Renaissance Vineyard & Winery, 10668
Renard Machine Company, 28313, 48056
Renard's Cheese, 10669

Renato Specialty Product, 28314, 48057
Renau Electronic Lab, 28315
Renault Winery, 10670
Render, 28316
Rendulic Meat Packing Corp, 10671
Rene Produce Dist, 10672, 48058
Rene Rey Chocolates Ltd, 10673
Rene Rivet, 40996
Renfro Foods, 10674
RENFRO Foods Inc, 10508, 47929
Rennco LLC, 28317, 48059
Rennoc Corporation, 48060
Reno Forklift Inc, 58979
Reno Technology, 28318
Renold Ajax, 28319
Renold Products, 28320, 48061
Renovator's Supply, 28321, 48062
Renwood Mills, 10675
Renwood Winery, 10676
Reotemp Instrument Corp, 28322, 48063
Rep Source, 40997
Replacements LTD, 28323, 48064
Republic Del Cacao, 48065
Republic Foil, 28324, 48066
Republic National Distributing, 58980
Republic of Tea, 10677
Republic Refrigeration Inc, 28325
Republic Sales, 28326
Republic Storage Systems LLC, 28327
Republica Del Cacao LLC, 10678
Request Foods Inc, 10679
Rer Services, 28328, 48067
RES & Associates, 28097
Res-Q Network, 40998
Resco Restaurant & Store Equip, 58981
Rescue Earth, 58982
Research & Development Packaging Corporation, 28329
Research Products Co, 10680, 28330, 48068
Reser's Fine Foods Inc, 10681, 58983
Residex, 58984
Resina, 28331, 48069
Resource Alliance, 53360
Resource Equipment, 28332
Resource One, 40999
Resource One/Resource Two, 28333
Resource Optimization, 28334
Resource Trading Company, 10682, 48070
ResourceNet International, 58985
Resources in Food & FoodTeam, 28335
Respirometry Plus, LLC, 28336, 48071
Restaurant Data, 10683, 28337
Restaurant Depot, 58986, 58987
Restaurant Design & Equip Corp, 58988
Restaurant Designs Development, 58989
Restaurant Development Svc, 28338
Restaurant Equipment Professionals, 41000
Restaurant Food Supply, 58990
Restaurant Lulu Gourmet Products, 10684
Restaurant Partners, 28339
Restaurant Supply, 58991
Restaurant Systems International, 10685
Restaurant Technologies Inc, 28340
Restaurant Workshop, 28341
Resturantorows.com, 48072
Retail Automations Products, 28342
Retail Data Systems Of Omaha, 58992
Retail Decor, 28343
Retalix, 28344, 48073
Reter Fruit, 10686, 48074
Rethemeyer Coffee Company, 10687
Retrotec, 28345
RETROTECH, Inc, 28098
Retzlaff Vineyards, 10688
Reutter Candy & Chocolates, 10689
Reuven International, 41001
Reva Foods, 10690
Revel, Gelato, 10691
Revent Inc, 28346, 48075, 48076
Revere Group, 28347, 28348
Revere Packaging, 28349

All Companies Index

Reviss Service, 28350
Revive Kombucha, 10692
Revonah Pretzel LLC, 10693
Rex & Company, 53361
Rex Art Manufacturing Corp., 28351
Rex Carton Co Inc, 28352
Rex Chemical Corporation, 28353, 58993
Rex Pacific, 58994
REX Pure Foods, 10509, 28099
Rexam Containers, 28354
Rexcraft Fine Chafers, 28355, 48077
Rexford Paper Company, 28356, 48078
Rexnord Corporation, 28357, 28358, 48079
Rexroth Corporation, 28359, 48080
Rey Foods, 58995
Reyco Systems Inc, 28360, 48081, 48082
Reynold Water Conditioning, 28361
Reynolds Foodservice Packaging, 28362
Reynolds Sugar Bush, 10694
Reynolds Transfer & Storage, 52050, 53362
Rez-Tech Corp, 28363
Rezolex LLC, 10695
RFC Wire Forms Inc, 28100
RFDI, 53346
RFi Ingredients, 10511, 47930
RFS Limited, 10510
RGF Environmental Group Inc, 28101
RGL Headquarters, 52043, 53347
RGN Developers, 28102
RH Forschner, 28103
RH Sulker Sales, 40978
Rhee Brothers, 28364, 48083
Rheo-Tech, 28365
Rheometric Scientific, 28366
Rheon, 28367
Rheon USA, 28368, 48084
Rheon, U.S.A., 28369, 48085
Rheuark/F.S.I. Sales, 41002
RHG Products Company, 28104
Rhineland Cutlery, 28370
Rhino Foods Inc, 10696, 28371
Rhoades Paper Box Corporation, 28372
Rhode Island Label Work Inc, 28373
Rhodes Bakery Equipment, 28374, 48086
Rhodes Bean & Supply Co-Op, 10697
Rhodes International Inc, 10698
Rhodes Machinery International, 28375, 48087
Rhotens Wholesale Meat Co, 58996
Rhythm Superfoods, 10699
Rib Rack, 10700
Riba Foods, 10701
Ribble Production, 10702, 28376
Ribus Inc., 10703, 48088
RIC, Inc, 40979
Ricca Chemical Co, 28377
Ricci & Company, 58997
Rice Company, 10704, 48089
Rice Foods, 10705, 58998
Rice Fruit Co, 10706, 48090
Rice Hull Specialty Products, 10707
Rice Innovations, 10708, 48091
Rice Lake Weighing Systems, 28378, 48092
Rice Packaging Inc, 28379
Rice Paper Box Company, 28380
RiceBran Technologies, 10709
Riceland Foods Inc., 10710, 48093, 53363, 58999
Rices Potato Chips, 10711
Ricetec, 10712, 48094
Ricex Company, 10713
Rich Audette Associates, 41003
Rich Dairy Products, 59000
Rich Products Corp, 10714, 10715, 48095
Rich Xiberta USA Inc, 28381
Rich's Ice Cream Co Inc, 10716
Richard Bagdasarian Inc, 10717
Richard E. Colgin Company, 10718
Richard Green Company, 10719
Richard L. Graeser Winery, 10720

Richard Read Construction Company, 28382
Richard's Gourmet Coffee, 10721
Richard's Restaurant Supply, 59001
Richards Industries Systems, 28383
Richards Maple Products, 10722
Richards Natural Foods, 10723
Richards Packaging, 28384, 48096
Richardson Brands Co, 10724, 48097
Richardson International, 10725, 28385, 48098
Richardson Petkovsek & Associates, 41004
Richardson Researches, 28386
Richardson Seating Corp, 28387
Richardson Vineyards, 10726
Richardson's Ice Cream, 10727
Richardson's Stamp Works, 28388
Richelieu Foods Inc, 10728
Richland Beverage Association, 10729, 48099
Richmond Baking Co, 10730, 10731
Richmond Cold Storage Smithfield, 53364
Richmond Corrugated Box Company, 28389
Richmond Printed Tape & Label, 28390
Richmond Restaurant Svc, 59002
Richmond Supply Company, 59003
Richport International Inc, 48100
Richs Sales Company, 41005
Richter Baking Company, 59004
Richter Distributing Company, 59005
Richway Industries, 28391
Richwill Enterprises, 52051, 53365
Richwood Imports Inc, 48101
Rick's Chips, 10732
Rick's Picks, 10733
Rico Foods Inc, 10734
Rico Packaging Company, 28392, 48102
Ricoh Technologies, 28393
Ricos Candy Snack & Bakery, 10735
Riddles' Sweet Impressions, 10736
Rider's Ranch Escargot, 59006
Ridg-U-Rak, 28394
Ridge Vineyards Inc, 10737
RidgeView Products LLC, 28395
Ridout Plastics, 48103
Riega, 10738
Riegel/Mount Vernon Mills, 59007
Rieke Packaging Systems, 28396, 48104
Rier Smoked Salmon, 10739
Rietschle, 28397
Riffel's Coffee Company, 10740
Rig-A-Lite Inc, 28398
Rigel Trading Corporation, 48105, 59008
Righetti Specialties Inc, 10741
RightWay Foods, 59009
Rigid Plastics Packaging Institute, 28399
Rigidized Metal Corp, 28400, 48106
Rigoni Di Asiago, 10742
Rihm Foods, 59010
Riley & Geehr, 28401
Riley Cole Professional Recruitment, 28402
Rill Specialty Foods, 10743
Rimex Metals Inc, 28403
Rimfire Imports, 59011
Rinehart Meat Processing, 10744
Ringland Associates, 41006
Rino Gnesi Company, 59012
Rio Grande Valley Sugar Growers, 10745
Rio Naturals, 10746
Rio Syrup Co, 10747, 28404, 48107
Rio Trading Company, 10748
Rio Valley Canning Co, 10749
Rios, J J, 28405
Rip Van, 10750
Rip-N-Ready Foods, 48108
RIPCO, 58910
Ripensa A/S, 10751
Ripon Manufacturing Co Inc, 28406, 48109
Ripon Pickle Co Inc, 10752, 48110
Ripple, 10753

Ripple Brand Collective, 10754
Rippons Seafood, 10755
Risco USA Corp, 28407
Rise Bar, 10756, 59013
RISE Brewing Co., 10512
Rishi Tea, 10757
Rising Dough Bakery, 10758
Rising Sun Farms, 10759, 48111
Risvold's Inc., 10760
Rita's Italian Ice, 10761
Ritchey's Dairy, 10762
Ritchie Creek Vineyard, 10763
Ritchie Grocer Co, 59014
Ritchie's Foods, 28408, 59015
Rite-Hite, 28409
Riteway Co, 41007
Rito Mints, 10764, 48112
Ritrovo, 48113
Ritt-Beyer Inc, 41008
Ritt-Ritt & Associates, 28410
Ritual Coffee Roasters, 10765
Ritz Packaging Company, 28411
Rival Manufacturing Company, 28412, 48114
Rivard Popcorn Products, 10766
Rivard Power Lift, 59016
Rivella USA, 10767
River City Sales & Marketing, 28413, 41009
River Hills Harvest, 10768
River Market Brewing Company, 10769
River Road Coffee, 10770
River Run Vintners, 10771
River Terminal Distribution & Warehouse, 52052, 53366
River Town Foods Corp, 10772
River Valley Foods Inc, 59017
Riverdale Fine Foods, 10773
Riverport Warehouse Company, 53367
Rivers Transportation, 52053
Riverside Foods, 59018
Riverside Industries, 28414
Riverside Manufacturing Company, 28415, 28416, 48115, 48116
Riverside Natural Foods, 10774
Riverside Paper Supply, 59019
Riverside Refrigeration Air Conditioning, 59020
Riverside Wire & Metal Co., 28417, 48117
Riverton Packing, 10775
Riverview Foods, 10776, 28418
Riverwood International, 28419, 28420
Riviana Foods Inc., 10777, 28421, 48118
Riviera Ravioli Company, 10778
Rixie Paper Products Inc, 28422, 48119
Rizwitsch Sales, 41010, 41011
RJ Balson and Sons Inc, 10513
RJ Jansen Company, 28105
RJ Jansen Confectionery, 28106
RJ Wetrz Products Company, 28107
Rjo Associates, 28423
RJO Produce Distr Inc, 28108
RJR Executive Search, 28109
Rjr Technologies, 28424, 48120
Rjs Carter Co Inc, 28425, 48121
Rl Alber T & Son Inc, 48122, 59021
RL Instruments, 28110
RLS Equipment Company, 28111
RLS Logistics, 28112, 52044, 53348, 53349
RM Heagy Foods, 10514, 58911
RM Waite Inc, 28113
RMCI Foodservice, 40980
RMF Companies, 28114, 47931
RMI-C/Rotonics Manaufacturing, 28115, 47932
RMS-Touch/Web4Pos, 47933
RMX Global Logistics, 28116
Ro-An Industries Corporation, 28426
Road's End Organics, 10780
Roadrunner Seafood Inc, 10781, 59022
Roads West Transportation, 52054
Roanoke Apple Products, 10782
Roanoke Fruit & Produce Co, 59023

Roaring Brook Dairy, 28427
Roasterie Inc, 10783
Rob Salamida Co Inc, 10784, 48123
Robar International Inc, 28428, 48124
Robatech USA Inc, 28429, 28430
Robbie Manufacturing Inc, 28431
Robbie's Natural Products, 10785
Robbin's Beef Company, 59024
Robbins Packing Company, 10786
Robbins Sales Co, 41012
Robby Midwest, 59025
Robby Vapor Systems, 28432, 48125
Robecco, 28433
Robelan Displays Inc, 28434, 48126
Roberian Vineyards, 10787
Robert & James Brands, 10788
Robert A. Haines Companies, 41013
Robert Bosch LLC, 28435
Robert C Vncek Design Assoc, 28436
Robert Chapter Company, 41014
Robert Chermak & Associates, 59026
Robert Cochran & Company, 59027
Robert D. Arnold & Associates, 59028
Robert Emig & Associates, 41015
Robert F Pliska & Company Winery, 10789
Robert J. Preble & Sons, 52055, 59029
Robert Keenan Winery, 10790
Robert Mondavi Winery, 10791, 48127
Robert Mueller Cellars, 10792
Robert Pecota Winery, 10793
Robert Rothschild Farm, 10794
Robert Ruiz Company, 59030
Robert Sinskey Vineyards Inc, 10795
Robert W. Hayman Inc, 41016
Robert Wholey & Co Inc, 48128, 59031
Robert's Bakery, 10796
Robert's Foods Company, 59032
Robert-James Sales, 28437, 48129
Robertet Flavors, 10797, 28438, 48130
Roberto A Cheese Factory, 10798
Roberts Ferry Nut Co, 10799, 48131
Roberts Packaging Equipment, 28439
Roberts Packing Co, 59033
Roberts Pallet Co, 28440
Roberts Poly Pro Inc, 28441, 48132
Roberts Seed, 10800, 48133
Roberts Systems, 28442
Roberts Technology Group, 28443
Roberts-Boice Paper Company, 59034
Roberts-Gordon LLC, 28444
Robertson Fruit & Produce, 59035
Robertson Furniture Co Inc, 28445, 48134
Robertson's Country Meat Hams, 10801
Robertson-Johnson Warehouses, 52056, 53368
Robin & Cohn Seafood Distributors, 10802, 59036
Robin Shepherd Group, 28446, 48135
Robin's Food Distribution, 59037
Robinett & Assoc, 28447
Robinette Co, 28448
Robinson & Co, 53369
Robinson Canning Company, 48136, 59038
Robinson Cold Storage, 28449, 53370
Robinson Distributing Inc, 10803, 59039
Robinson Industries, 28450, 48137
Robinson Marketing Associates, 59040
Robinson Steel Company, 59041
Robinson Tape & Label, 28451, 59042
Robinson's No 1 Ribs, 10804, 48138
Robinson/Kirshbaum Industries, 28452, 28453
Robller Vineyard Winery, 10805
Robocom Systems Intl, 28454, 28455
Robot Coupe, 28456, 48139
Robot Factory, 48140
Robotic Vision Systems, 28457
Rocca's Italian Foods Inc, 10806
Roche Caneros Estate Winery, 10807
Roche Fruit LLC, 10808
Rocheleau Blow Molding Systems, 28458

1431

All Companies Index

Rochester Cheese, 10809
Rochester Midland Corp, 28459, 28460, 28461, 48141
Rochester Midland Corporation, 59043
Rochester Refrigerating Corporation, 53371
Rock Bottom Restaurant & Brewery, 10810
Rock Dell Creamery, 59044
Rock Garden South, 59045
Rock Point Oyster Company, 10811
Rock Valley Oil & Chemical Co, 28462, 48142, 59046
Rock-N-Roll Gourmet, 10812
Rock-Ola Manufacturing Corp, 48143
Rock-Tenn Company, 28463, 48144
Rockaway Baking, 28464
Rockbridge Vineyard, 10813
Rocket Fizz, 10814
Rocket Man, 28465, 48145
Rocket Products Company, 10815
Rockford Chemical Co, 28466
Rockford Sanitary Systems, 28467
Rockford Sausage Co, 59047
Rockford-Midland Corporation, 28468, 48146
Rockland Bakery, 10816, 59048
Rockland Foods, 28469
Rockland Foodservice, 59049
Rockland Technology, 28470
Rockline Industries, 28471, 48147
Rockport Lobster Co, 10817, 59050
Rockview Farms, 10818
Rockwell Automation Inc, 28472
Rockwell Truck Line, 52057
Rocky Mountain Chocolate Factory, 10819
Rocky Mountain Coffee Roasters, 10820
Rocky Mountain Honey Company, 10821
Rocky Mountain Meats, 10822
Rocky Mountain Motel, 41017
Rocky Mountain Natural Meats, 10823
Rocky Mountain Packing Company, 10824
Rocky Point Shrimp Association, 10825, 48148
Rocky Produce Inc, 59051
Rocky Ridge Maple, 10826, 59052
Rocky Shoes & Boots Inc, 28473
Rocky Top Country Store, 10827
Rocky Top Farms, 10828, 48149
Rod Golden Hatchery Inc, 10829, 48150
Rodda Coffee Company, 10830
Roddy Products Pkgng Co Inc, 28474, 48151
Rodelle Inc, 10831
Rodem Inc, 28475
Roden Electrical Supply Company, 59053
Rodes Professional Apparel, 28476
Rodgers' Puddings, 10832
Rodney Strong Vineyards, 10833
Rodo Industries, 28477
Rodon Foods, 41018
Rodsan, 48152
Roechling Engineered Plastics, 28478, 48153
Roechling Machined Plastics, 28479
Roederer Transfer & Storage, 53372
Roehl Corp, 41019
Roelli Cheese Co, 10834
Roesch Inc, 28480
Roeslein & Assoc Inc, 28481
Rofin-Baasel Inc, 28482
Roflan Associates, 28483
Roger J. Wood Company, 41020
Roger Wood Foods Inc, 10835
Roger's Recipe, 10836
Rogers Collection, 48154
Rogers Farms, 59054
Rogers International Inc, 48155, 48156
Rogers Sugar Inc., 10837, 10838, 10839
Rogers' Chocolates Ltd, 10840, 48157
Rogue Ales Brewery, 10841, 48158
Rogue Creamery, 10842
Roha USA LTD, 10843, 28484, 59055

Rohm America Inc., 28485
Rohrbach Brewing Co, 10844
Rohrer Brothers Inc, 59056
Rohrer Corp., 28486, 48159
ROI Software, LLC, 28117
Rokeach Food Corp, 10845
Roland Foods, 48160
Roland Foods, LLC, 48161
Roland J. Trosclair Canning, 59057
Roland Machinery, 10846, 48162
Roland Seafood Co, 10847
Rolet Food Products Company, 10848
Rolfs @ Boone, 28487, 48163
Roll Rite Corp, 28488
Roll-O-Sheets Canada, 28489, 48164, 59058
Rolland Machining & Fabricating, 28490
Roller & Associates, 41021
Rollhaus Seating Products Inc, 28491
Rollin Dairy Corp, 59059
Rolling Pin Bakery, 10849, 10850
Rollingstone Chevre, 10851
Rollon Corp, 28492
Rollprint Packaging Prods Inc, 28493, 48165
Rollstock Inc, 28494, 28495
Roma & Ray's Italian Bakery, 10852
Roma Bakeries, 10853
Roma Food Svc Of Arizona, 59060
Roma of Minnesota, 59061
Roma Packing Company, 10854
Romaco Inc, 28496
Roman Packing Company, 10855
Roman Sausage Company, 10856, 48166
Romanian Kosher Sausage Co, 10857
Romanow Container, 28497, 28498, 48167
Romatic Manufacturing Co, 28499
Rombauer Vineyards, 10858
Rome LTD, 28500
Rome Machine & Foundry Co, 28501, 48168
Romero's Food Products Inc, 10859
Romicon, 28502
Romme Lag USA Inc, 28503
Ron Son Foods Inc, 10860, 48169
Ron Teed & Assoc, 28504
Ron Ungar Engineering Inc, 28505
Ron Vallort & Associates, 28506
Ron Vallort and Associates, Ltd, 28507
Ron's Home Style Foods, 10861
Ron's Produce, 59062
Ron's Wisconsin Cheese LLC, 10862, 59063
Ron-Son Mushroom Products, 48170
Ronchi America, 28509
Rondo Inc, 28510, 48171, 59064
Rondo of America, 28511, 48172
Rondo Specialty Foods LTD, 10863
Ronell Industries, 28512
RonI, 28508
Roni LLC, 28513
Ronnie Dowdy, 28514, 52058
Ronnie's Ceramic Company, 28515, 48173
Ronnoco Coffee Co, 10864
Ronny Brook Farm Dairy, 10865
Ronzoni, 10866, 48174
Roode Packing Company, 10867
Roofian, 28516
Rooibee Red Tea, 10868
Roos Foods, 10869
Roos-Mohan, 41022
Roosevelt Dairy Trade, Inc, 41023, 48175
Root Cellar Preserves, 10870
Rooto Corp, 28517, 48176
Ropak, 28518, 48177
Ropak Manufacturing Co Inc, 28519, 48178
Roplast Industries Inc, 28520
Roquette America Inc., 10871, 48179
RoRo's Baking Company, 10779
Rosa Brothers Milk Co Inc, 10872

Rosa Food Products, 10873, 53373, 59065
Rosa Mexicano, 10874
Rosa's Horchata, LLC, 10875
Rosalind Candy Castle Inc, 10876
Rosanna Imports Warehouse, 10877
Rosati Italian Water Ice, 10878
Rosco Inc, 28521, 48180
Rose Acre Farms, 10879
Rose Acre Farms Inc, 10880
Rose City Awning Co, 28522
Rose City Label, 28523
Rose City Pepperheads, 10881
Rose City Printing & Packaging, 28524
Rose Creek Vineyards, 10882
Rose Forgrove, 28525, 28526, 48181
Rose Frozen Shrimp, 10883
Rose Hill Distributor, 59066
Rose Hill Distributors, 10884
Rose Hill Enterprises, 48182, 59067
Rose Hill Seafood, 10885
Rose Packing Co Inc, 10886, 48183
Rose Plastic, 28527
Rose Randolph Cookies, LLC, 10887
Rosebrand Corp, 10888
Rosebud Creamery, 10889
Roseland Manufacturing, 10890
Roseland Produce Wholesale, 59068
Roselani Tropics Ice Cream, 10891
Rosemark Bakery, 10892
Rosemount Analytical Inc, 28528
Rosen's Diversified Inc., 10893, 52059
Rosenberger Cold Storage Company, 53374
Rosenberger's Dairies, 10894
Rosenblum Cellars, 10895
Rosenfeld & Gigante, 41024
Rosenthal & Kline, 48184, 59069
Rosenthal Foods Corp, 59070
Rosenthal Manufacturing Co Inc, 28529
Rosenwach Tank Co LLC, 28530
Roses Ravioli, 10896
Rosett Brokerage Company, 41025
Rosetti's Fine Foods Biscotti, 10897
Roseville Charcoal & Mfg Co, 28531, 48185
Roseville Corporation, 10898
Rosina Food Holdings Inc, 10899, 48186
Rosito & Bisani Imports Inc, 48187, 59071
Rosmarino Foods/R.Z. Humbert Company, 10900
Ross & Wallace Inc, 28532, 48188
Ross Computer Systems, 28533, 28534, 48189
Ross Cook, 28535
Ross Elevator Supply, 59072
Ross Empire State Brokers, 41026
Ross Engineering Inc, 28536, 48190
Ross Express Inc, 52060
Ross Fine Candies, 10901
Ross Foods, 59073
Ross Industries Inc, 28537, 28538, 48191
Ross Systems, 28539
Ross Systems & Controls Inc, 28540
Ross Technology Corp, 28541, 48192
Ross-Smith Pecan Company, 10902, 48193
Rossi Pasta LTD, 10903
Rosson Sign Co, 28542
Rostov's Coffee & Tea Co, 10904
Rotella's Italian Bakery Inc., 10905
Rotelle, 59074
Roth & Associates PC, 28543
Roth Cheese USA, 10906
Roth KASE USA, 48194
Roth Sign Systems, 28544, 48195
Roth Young Bellevue, 28545
Roth Young Chicago, 28546
Roth Young Farmington Hills, 28547
Roth Young Hicksville, 28548
Roth Young Minneapolis, 28549
Roth Young Murrysville, 28550
Roth Young New York, 28551
Roth Young of Tampa Bay, 28553

Roth Young Washougal, 28552
Rothbury Farms, 10907
Rothchild Printing Company, 28554
Rothfos Corp, 48196
Rothman's Food Inc, 10908
Rotisol France Inc, 28555, 48197
Roto-Flex Oven Co, 28556, 48198
Roto-Jet Pump, 28557
Rotonics Manufacturing, 28558
Rotronic Instrument Corp Inc, 28559
Rotronics Manufacturing, 28560
Rotteveel Orchards, 10909, 48199
Roudon-Smith Vineyards, 10910
Roughstock Distillery, 41027
Rougie Foie Gras, 10911
Round Hill Vineyards, 10912
Round Noon Software, 28561
Round Paper Packages Inc, 28562
Round Rock Honey Co, LLC, 10913
Roundup Food Equip, 28563, 48200
Roundy's Inc, 59075
Rousseau Farming Co, 10914
Rousselot Inc, 10915
Route 11 Potato Chips, 10916
Routin America, 10917, 48201
Rovema, 28564
Rovira Biscuit Corporation, 10918, 48202, 59076
Rowe International, 28565, 48203
Rowena, 10919, 48204
Rowland Coffee Roasters Inc., 10920, 48205, 59077
Rowland Technologies, 28566, 48206
Rowlands Sales Company, 28567
Rownd & Son, 28568
Rox America, 28569
Roxanne Signs Inc, 28570
Roxide International, 28571, 48207
Roxy Trading Inc, 41028, 48208
Roy Dick Company, 10921, 59078
Roy's Folding Box, 28572
Royal Accoutrements, 48209, 59079
Royal ACME, 28573
Royal Atlantic Seafood, 10922, 59080
Royal Baltic LTD, 10923, 48210, 52061
Royal Banana Co, 59081
Royal Banquet, 48211
Royal Broom & Mop Factory Inc, 28574, 59082
Royal Caribbean Bakery, 10924, 48212
Royal Caviar Inc, 10925
Royal Center Locker Plant, 10926
Royal Chemical Co Inc, 28575
Royal Coffee Inc, 48213
Royal Crest Dairy, 10927
Royal Crown Enterprises, 48214, 59083
Royal Cup Coffee, 10928, 28576, 59084
Royal Display Corporation, 28577
Royal Doulton, 48215
Royal Doulton Canada, 59085
Royal Ecoproducts, 28578, 48216
Royal Food Products, 10929
Royal Foods & Flavor, 10930
Royal Foods Inc, 10931, 48217, 59086, 59087
Royal Gourmet Caviar, 10932, 48218
Royal Group, 28579
Royal Harvest Foods Inc, 10933, 59088
Royal Hawaiian Orchards LP, 10934
Royal Home Bakery, 10935
Royal Ice Cream Co, 10936
Royal Industries Inc, 28580, 48219, 59089
Royal Jordanian, 52062, 53375
Royal Label Co, 28581, 48220
Royal Lagoon Seafood Inc, 10937, 59090
Royal Madera Vineyards, 10938
Royal Meats, 59091
Royal Medjool Date Gardens, 10939, 48221
Royal Oak Enterprises, 28582, 48222
Royal Oak Peanuts, 10940
Royal Pacific Coffee Co, 10941
Royal Pacific Fisheries, 10942
Royal Palate Foods, 10943, 48223, 59092

1432

All Companies Index

Royal Palm Popcorn Company, 10944
Royal Paper Box Co, 28583
Royal Paper Products, 28584, 48224
Royal Prestige Health Moguls, 28585
Royal Products, 10945
Royal Range Industries, 28586
Royal Resources, 10946
Royal Ridge Fruits, 10947
Royal Rose Syrups, LLC, 10948
Royal Seafood Inc, 10949
Royal Silver Mfg Co Inc, 28587
Royal Touch Foods, 10950
Royal Vista Marketing Inc, 10951, 48225
Royal Welding & Fabricating, 28588, 48226
Royal Wine Corp, 10952, 41029, 48227
Royale Brands, 10953, 48228
Royalton Foodservice Equip Co, 28589
Royce C. Bone Farms, 10954
Royce Corp, 28590, 48229
Royce Rolls Ringer Co, 28591, 48230
Royer Corporation, 48231
RP's Pasta Company, 10515
RPA Process Technologies, 28118, 47934
Rpac LLC, 10955, 48232
RPE Inc, 47935
RPM Material Handling, 58912
RPM Material Handling Company/Clarklift San Diego, 58913
RPM Total Vitality, 10516, 47936, 58914
Rqa Product Dynamics, 28592
RSI ID Technologies, 28119
Rtech Laboratories, 28593, 28594
RTG Films, 28120
RTI Inc, 28121
RTI Laboratories, 28122
RTI Shelving Systems, 28123, 47937
RTR Packaging, 58915
RTS Packaging, 28124, 28125, 28126, 28127
Ruark & Ashton, 10956
Rubashkin, 10957
RubaTex Polymer, 28595, 48233
Rubbair Door, 28596
Rubber Fab Molding & Gasket, 28597
Rubber Stamp Shop, 28598
Rubbermaid, 28599, 48234
Rubbermaid Canada, 28600
Rubbermaid Commercial Products, 28601, 28602, 48235, 48236
Rubenstein Seafood Sales, 41030
Rubicon Food Products, 10958
Rubicon Industries, 28603
Rubino's Seafood Company, 10959, 59093
Rubschlager Baking Corp, 10960, 48237
Ruby Manufacturing & Sales, 28604, 48238
Ruby Rockets, 10961
Rubys Apiaries, 10962
Rudd Container Corp, 28605
Rudd Winery, 10963
Rude Custom Butchering, 10964
Rudi's Organic Bakery, 10965
Rudolph Brady, Inc, 41031
Rudolph Foods Co, 10966, 48239
Rudolph Industries, 28606, 48240
Rudolph Research Analytical, 59094
Rudolph's Market & Sausage, 10967
Rudolph's Specialty Bakery, 10968, 48241
Rudy's L&R, 28607
Rudy's Tortillas, 10969
Ruef's Meat Market, 10970
Rueff Sign Co Inc, 28608
Ruffino Paper Box Co, 28609
Ruffner's, 10971
Rufus Teague, 10972
Ruger LLC, 10973
Ruggiero Seafood, 10974, 48242
Ruggles Sign Company, 28610
Ruiz Flour Tortillas, 10975, 28611
Ruiz Food Products Inc., 10976, 48243
Ruland Manufacturing Co Inc, 28612
Rule Breaker, 10977

Rumi Spice, 10978, 48244, 59095
Rumiano Cheese Co., 10979, 48245
Rumiano Cheese Factory, 10980
Run-A-Ton Group Inc, 10981
Runamok Maple, 10982
Runk Candy Company, 10983
Rural Route 1 Popcorn Co, 10984
Rus Dun Farms Inc, 10985
Rusken Packaging, 28613
Ruskin Redneck Trading Company, 10986
Russ & Daughters, 10987
Russel T. Bundy Associates, Inc., 28614
Russell, 28615
Russell & Kohne Inc, 10988
Russell Breweries, Inc., 10989
Russell E. Womack, Inc., 10990, 48246
Russell Finex Inc, 28616
Russell Food Equipment Limited, 59096
Russell N. Roy Company, 59097
Russell Stover Candies Inc., 10991
Russell-William, 28617
Russian Chef, 10992, 48247
Russo Farms, 10993
Russo's Seafood, 10994, 59098
Rust-Oleum Corp, 28618
Rustic Bakery Inc., 10995
Rustic Crust Inc, 10996
Rutan Poly Industries Inc, 28619
Ruth Ashbrook Bakery, 10997
Ruth Hunt Candy Co, 10998, 59099
Rutherford Engineering, 28620, 48248
Rutherford Hill Winery, 10999
Rutler Screen Printing, 28621
Rutter's Dairy, 11000
Rv Industries, 11001, 48249
RVS, 28128
RW Delights, 10517
RW Garcia, 10518
RW Products, 28129
RWH Packaging, 28130
RWI Resources, 28131
RXBAR, 10519
RXI Silgan Specialty Plastics, 28132, 47938
Ryals Bakery, 11002
Ryan Potato Company, 48250, 59100
Ryan Technology Inc., 28622
Ryans Wholesale Food Distributors, 59101
Ryder, 52063
Ryder Integrated Logistics, 52064, 53376
Ryder System, Inc, 28623, 52065
Rye Fresh, 11003
Rygmyr Foods, 11004
Ryke's Bakery, 11005
Rymer Foods, 11006
Rymer Seafood, 11007, 48251, 59102
Ryowa Company America, 28624
Ryson International, 28625
Rytec Corporation, 28626, 48252
Ryter Corporation, 28627
Ryther-Purdy, 28628

S

S & D Coffee Inc, 11008, 48253
S & E Organic Farms Inc, 11009
S & G Resources Inc, 28629
S & H Uniform Corp, 28630
S & H Uniform Corporation, 48254
S & J Laboratories Inc, 28631
S & L Produce Inc, 11010
S & L Store Fixture, 28632, 48255
S & M Communion Bread Co, 11011
S & M Fisheries Inc, 11012, 59103
S & R Products, 28633, 59104
S & S Indl Maintenance, 48256, 59105
S & S Metal & Plastics Inc, 28634
S & S Soap Co, 28635
S & S Svc Parts, 28636
S & W Pallet Co, 28637
S A Carlson Inc, 11013
S A L T Sisters, 11014
S B Davis Co, 41032

S B Global Foods Inc, 11015
S E & M, 28638
S Hochman Company, 28639
S I Jacobson Mfg Co, 28640
S J Controls Inc, 28641, 48257
S Kamberg & Co LTD, 28642, 41033
S L D Commodities Inc, 48258
S L Doery & Son Inc, 28643
S L Sanderson & Co, 28644, 48259, 59106
S P Enterprises, 11016
S S Lobster LTD, 11017, 59107
S S Steiner Inc, 11018, 48260
S Strock & Co, 59108
S T Specialty Foods Inc, 11019
S W Betz Co Inc, 59109
S Walter Packaging Corp, 28645
S Zitner Co, 11020
S&B International Corporation, 11021
S&D Bait Company, 11022, 59110
S&K Sales Company, 41034
S&M Manufacturing Company, 28646
S&M Produce Company, 59111
S&M Provisions, 59112
S&N Food Company, 11023
S&O Corporation, 28647
S&P Marketing, Inc., 11024, 28648, 48261
S&P USA Ventilation Systems, LLC, 28649, 48262
S&R Imports, 48263
S&R Machinery, 28650
S&S Dayton Supply, 59113
S&S Meat Company, 59114
S-A-J Distributors, 59115
S-H-S International of Wilkes, 28651
S-W Mills Inc, 48264
S. Abraham & Son, 59116
S. Abraham & Sons Inc., 59117
S. Anshin Produce Company, 59118
S. B. C. Coffee, 28652, 48265
S. Ferens & Company, 48266
S. Kamberg & Company, 41035
S. Katzman Produce, 28653, 59119
S. Wallace Edward & Sons, 11025
S.A.K.S. Foods International, 41036
S.A.S. Foods, 11026, 48267
S.D. Mushrooms, 11027, 48268
S.J. Roetzel & Son Produce, 59120
S.L. Canada Packaging Machine, 28654
S.L. Kaye Company, 11028, 48269
S.R. Flaks Company, 59121
S.S.I. Schaefer System International Limited, 28655
S.T. Jerrell Company, 11029
S.V. Dice Designers, 28656, 48270
S.W. Meat & Provision Company, 11030, 59122
SA Wald Reconditioners, 28657
Saad Wholesale Meats, 11058, 59134
Saag's Products LLC, 11059
Saatitech, 28740
Sabal Marketing, 41045
Sabate Co, 28741
Sabatino North America, 48306
Sabatino Truffles USA, 11060
Sabbers & Assoc Inc, 41046
Sabel Engineering Corporation, 28742, 48307
Sabert Corp, 28743, 28744, 48308
Sabinsa Corp, 11061
Sable & Rosenfeld Foods, 11062
Sable Technology Solution, 28745, 48309
Sabor Mexicano, 11063
Sabra Blue & White Food Products, 11064
Sabra Dipping Company,LL, 11065, 48310
Sabra-Go Mediterranean, 11066
Sachem Co, 41047
Sack Storage Corporation, 52071, 53384
Sackett Systems, 28746
Sacramento Bag Manufacturing, 28747
Sacramento Baking Co, 11067
Sacramento Cookie Factory, 11068

Saddle Creek Corp, 53385
Saddle Creek Logistics Svc, 52072, 52073, 53386, 53387, 53388
Saddleback Cellars, 11069
SADKHIN Complex, 11031
Sadler Conveyor Systems, 28748, 48311
Sadler's Smokehouse, 11070, 59135
Saeco, 28749, 48312
Saeplast Canada, 28750, 48313
SAF Products, 28658
Saf-T-Gard International Inc, 28751, 59136
Safari Distributing, 59137
Safe Catch, 11071
Safe-Stride Southern, 48314, 59138
Safe-T-Cut Inc, 28752, 48315
Safeco Electric & True Value, 59139
Safely Delicious, 11072
Safesteril/Belt-O-Matic, 48316
Safety Fumigant Co, 28753
Safety Light Corporation, 28754
Safety Seal Industries, 28755
Safety Wear, 59140
Safeway Freezer Storage Inc, 52074, 53389
Safeway Inc., 11073, 53390
Safeway Milk Plant, 11074
Safeway Solutions, 28756
Saffron Road, 11075
Safian & Associates, 59141
Safie Specialty Foods, 11076
Sagawa's Savory Sauces, 11077, 48317
Sagaya Corp, 48318, 59142
Sage Automation Inc, 28757
Sage V Foods, 11078, 48319, 59143
Sagely Naturals, 11079
Saggese Brothers, 41048
Saguaro Food Products, 11080
Sahadi Fine Foods Inc, 11081, 48320, 59144
Sahadi Importing Company, 11082, 48321
Sahagian & Associates, 11083, 48322
Sahalee of Alaska, 11084, 48323
Sahara Coffee, 11085
Sahara Date Company, 11086, 28758, 59145
Sahara Natural Foods, 11087
Sahlen's, 11088
Saia, Inc., 52075
Sailor Plastics, 28759
Sainsbury & Company, 48324
Saint Albans Cooperative Creamery, 11089
Saint Armands Baking Company, 11090
Saint-Gobain Corporation, 28760, 48325
Saint-Gobain Performance Plastics, 28761
Sainte Genevieve Winery, 11091
Saintsbury, 11092
Sakeone Corp, 11093
Salad Depot, 11094, 59146
Salad Girl Inc, 11095
Salad Oils Intl Corp, 11096, 41049, 48326, 59147
Salamandre Wine Cellars, 11097
Salamatof Seafoods, 11098, 48327
Salba Smart Natural Prod LLC, 11099, 48328
Salem Baking Company, 11100
Salem China Company, 28762, 48329
Salem Oil & Grease Company, 11101, 48330
Salem Old Fashioned Candies, 11102
Salem Packing Company, 59148
Salem-Republic Rubber Co, 28763, 48331
Salemville Cheese, 11103
Sales, 41050
Sales & Marketing Dev, 41051, 48332
Sales Associates Of Alaska, 11104, 59149
Sales Building Systems, 28764
Sales Corporation of Alaska, 41052
Sales King International, 48333, 59150

1433

All Companies Index

Sales Marketing Svc LLC, 41053
Sales Partner System, 28765
Sales Results, 41054
Sales Specialties, 41055
Sales USA, 11105, 48334
SalesData Software, 28766
Salient Corp, 28767
Salinas Valley Wax Paper Co, 28768, 48335
Salishan Vineyards, 11106
Sally Lane's Candy Farm, 11107
Sally Sherman, 11108
Sally Williams Fine Foods, 59151
Salmans & Assoc, 11109, 41056
Salmolux, 11110, 48336
Salmon Creek Cellars, 48337
Salmon River Smokehouse, 11111, 59152
Salonika Imports Inc, 11112, 28769
Salsa God, 11113
Salt Lake Macaroni & Noodle Company, 11114
Salt of the Earth Bakery, 11116, 59154
Salt River Lobster Inc, 11115, 59153
SaltWorks, 11117
Saltworks, Inc., 48338
Salty Girl Seafood, 11118, 59155
Salty Road, 11119
Salty Wahine Gourmet Hawaiian Sea Salt, 11120
Salute Sante! Food & Wine, 11121
Salvajor Co, 28770, 48339
Salvy Sousa Dealer Locator, 11122
Salwa Foods, 11123, 59156
Sam Cohen & Sons, 59157
Sam Gordon & Sons Purveyors, 59158
Sam KANE Beef Processors Inc, 11124, 48340
Sam Lota & Son Disribution Company, 59159
Sam Mills USA, 11125
Sam Okun Produce Co, 59160
Sam Pievac Company, 28771
Sam Tell & Son, 59161
Sam Wylde Flour Company, 59162
Sam's Cakes, Cookies, Candy, 59163
Sam's Club, 59164
Sam's Leon Mexican Food, 11126
Samadi Sweets Cafe, 11127
Sambazon, 11128, 59165
Sambets Cajun Deli, 11129
Sambol Meat Company, 11130
Sambonet USA, 28772, 48342, 59166
Samco Freezerwear, 28773
Samir's Imported Food LLC, 48343, 59167
SamMills USA, 48341
Sampac Enterprises, 11131, 48344, 59168
Sampco, 11132, 48345
Sampson Miller Advertising Inc., 59169
Samsill Corp, 28774
Samson Controls, 28775, 48346
Samsung Electronics America, Inc., 28776
Samuel P. Harris, 28777
Samuel Pressure Vessel Group, 28778, 48347
Samuel Shapiro & Company, 52076
Samuel Strapping Systems, 28780
Samuel Strapping Systems Inc, 28779, 48348
Samuel Underberg Food Store, 28781
Samuel Wells & Company, 59170
Samuels Products Inc, 28782
San Aire Industries, 28783, 48349
San Angelo Packing, 11133
San Anselmo's Cookies & Biscotti, 11134
San Antonio Cold Storage, 53391
San Antonio Farms, 11135
San Antonio Packing Co, 11136
San Bernardo Ice Cream, 11137
San Diego & Imperial Valley Rr, 52077
San Diego Cold Storage Inspctn, 53392, 53393
San Diego Health & Nutrition, 28784

San Diego Paper Box Company, 28785
San Diego Products, 48350, 59171
San Diego Soy Dairy, 11138
San Dominique Winery, 11139
San Fab Conveyor, 28786, 48351
San Francisco Bay Coffee, 11140
San Francisco Bay Coffee Company, 11141
San Francisco Fine Bakery, 11142
San Francisco French Bread, 11143, 48352
San Francisco Herb Co, 48353, 59172
San Francisco Popcorn Works, 11144
San Francisco Reps, 41057
San Francisco Salt, 11145, 48354
San Francisco Spice Co., 11146
San Francisco Wine Exchange, 41058
San Franola Granola, 11147
San Gennaro Foods Inc, 11148
San Jacinto Frozen Food, 59173
San Jamar, 28787, 48355
San Joaquin Figs Inc, 11149
San Joaquin Pool Svc & Supply, 28788
San Joaquin Vly Concentrates, 11150, 48356
San Jose Apartments, 11151
San Jose Awnings, 28789
San Jose Distribution Service, 52078, 53394
San Jose Imports, 48357, 59174
San Juan Coffee Roasting Co, 11152
San Juan Signs Inc, 28790
San Luis Valley Hemp Co., 11153
San Marco Coffee, Inc., 11154, 28791
San Marzano Imports, 11155, 48358
San Miguel Label Manufacturing, 28792
San Rafael Distributing Inc, 59175
San-Bay Co, 59176
San-Ei Gen FFI, 11156, 48359
San-J International Inc, 11157, 11158, 48360
San-Rec-Pak, 28793, 48361
Sana Foods, 41059
Sanarak Paper & Popcorn Supplies, 11159
Sanarak Paper & Popcorn Supply, 59177
Sanborn Sourdough Bakery, 11160
Sanchelima International, 28795, 48362
Sanchem Inc, 59178
Sanchez Distributors, 11161
Sanco Food Brokerage, 41060
Sanco Products Co Inc, 28796
Sancoa International, 28797, 48363
Sand Castle Winery, 11162
Sand Hill Berries, 11163
Sand Springs, 11164
Sandbar Trading Corp, 11165
Sandco International, 11166, 48364
Sanden Vendo America Inc, 28798, 48365
Sanders Bros, 59179
Sanders Candy Inc, 11167, 59180
Sanders Manufacturing Co, 28799
Sanders Meat Packing Inc, 11168
Sanderson Computers, 28800
Sanderson Farms, 11169, 48366
Sandia Shadows Vineyard & Winery, 11170
Sandler Seating, 28801, 48367
Sandors Bakeries, 11171
Sandridge Food Corp, 11172
Sands African Imports, 48368, 59181
Sands Brands International Food, 48369, 59182
Sandstone Winery, 11173
Sandt's Honey Co, 11174
Sandusky Filling & Brittle, 11175
Sandusky Plastics, 28802
Sandvik Process Systems, 28804, 48370
Sandvik Process Systems Inc, 28803
Sandy Butler Group, 28805
Sandy Candy, 11176
Sanford Milling Co Inc, 11177
Sanford Redmond, 28806

Sanford Redmond Company, 28807, 48371
Sanford Winery, 11178
Sangamon Mills, 28808
SANGARIA USA, 11032, 48271
Sangudo Custom Meat Packers, 11179
Sani-Fit, 28809, 48372
Sani-Matic, 28810, 48373
Sani-Pure Food Laboratories, 28811
Sani-Tech Group, 28812
Sani-Top Products, 28813
Sanicrete, 28815
SaniServ, 28814, 48374
Sanitary Bakery, 11180
Sanitary Couplers, 28816, 48375
Sanitary Tortilla Manufacturing Company, 11181
Sanitech Inc, 28817, 48376
Sanitek Products Inc, 28818, 48377
Sanitor Manufacturing Co, 28819
Sanmarc Liquidators Inc, 53395, 59183
SanSai North America Franchising, LLC, 28794
Sanson Co Inc, 59184
Sansone Food Products Co, 59185
Santa Barbara Bar, 11182, 59186
Santa Barbara Merchant Svc Inc, 59187
Santa Barbara Olive Company, 11183, 48378
Santa Barbara Pistachio Co, 11184
Santa Barbara Roasting Co, 11185
Santa Barbara Salsa, 11186
Santa Barbara Salsa/California Creative, 11187
Santa Barbara Winery, 11188
Santa Clara Nut Co, 11189, 48379
Santa Claus Industries, 59188
Santa Cruz Chili & Spice, 11190
Santa Cruz Horticultural Supply, 59189
Santa Cruz Mountain Brewing, 11191
Santa Cruz Mountain Vineyard, 11192
Santa Elena Coffee Company, 11193
Santa Fe Bag Company, 28820
Santa Fe Brewing Co, 11194
Santa Fe Seasons, 11195
Santa Fe Vineyards, 11196
Santa Maria Foods, 11197
Santa Monica Seafood Co., 11198, 48380
Santa Ynex Trading Company, 28821
Santa Ynez Wine Corp, 11199
Santa's Smokehouse, 11200
Santana Products, 28822
Santanna Banana Company, 11201
Sante Specialty Foods, 11202
Santemp Co, 53396
Santini Foods, 11203, 11204, 48381
Santucci Associates, 41061
Sanyo Corporation of America, 41062, 48382
Sapac International, 28823, 48383
Sapat Packaging Industry, 28824
SAPNA Foods, 11033, 59123
Sapore della Vita, 11205, 48384
Sapp Birch Water, 11206
Sappore Coffee Co Of Alaska, 11207
Sapporo USA, Inc., 11208, 48385
Saputo Cheese USA Inc., 11209, 48386
Saputo Dairy Division (Canada), 11210
Saputo Inc., 11211
Saquella U.S.A., 48387
Sara Lee Coffee & Tea, 11212
Sara Lee Foodservice, 11213
Sara Lee Frozen Bakery, 11214
Sara Snacker Cookie Company, 11215
Sarabeth's Office, 11216
Sarah's Vineyard, 11217
Saranac Brewery, 11218, 48388
Sarant International Cmmdts, 11219, 48389
Sarasota Restaurant Equipment, 28825, 59190
Saratoga Flour, 59191
Saratoga Food Safety, 41063
Saratoga Food Specialties, 11220, 48390

Saratoga Peanut Butter Company, 11221, 59192
Saratoga Salad Dressing, 11222
Saratoga Spring Water Co, 11223
Sardee Industries Inc, 28826, 28827, 48391
Sardinha's Sausage, 11224
Sardinia Cheese, 11225
Sargent & Greenleaf, 28828
Sargent and Greenleaf, 11226
Sargent's Bear Necessities, 11227
Sargent's Trucking, 41064
Sargento Foods Inc, 11228, 28829, 48392
Sarliz LLC, 11229
Saroni Co, 53397
Sarris Candies Inc, 11230
Sartori Co, 11231
Sartorius Corp, 28830, 28831
Sarum Tea Company, 11232
Sarver Candy Co, 59193
SAS Cargo, 52066, 53377
SASA Demarle, 28659
Sasib Beverage & Food North America, 28832, 48393
SASIB Biscuits and Snacks Division, 11034
SASOL North America, 28660
Sassafras Enterprises Inc, 11233
Sasser Signs, 28833
Sassone Wholesale Groceries Co, 48394, 59194
Satake USA, 28834, 48395
Saticoy Foods Corp, 11234
Saticoy Lemon Association, 28835
Satiety Winery & Cafe, 11235, 59195
Satin Fine Foods, 11236, 48396
Sato America, 28836, 48397
Satoris America, 28837
Sattwa Chai, 11237
Saturn Freight Systems, 52079, 53398
Saturn Overhead Equipment, 28838
Sau-Sea Foods, 11238
Sauce Crafters, 53399
Sauces N' Love, 11239
Saucilito Canyon Vineyard, 11240
Sauder's Eggs, 11241, 59196
Saudi Arabian Airlines, 52080
Sauereisen, 28839
Saugy Inc., 11242, 41065, 59197
Saunder Brothers, 28840, 48398
Saunders Manufacturing Co., 28841, 48399
Saunders West, 28842
Sausage Kitchen, 11243
Sausages by Amy, 11244
Sausal Winery, 11245
Sauvagnat Inc, 28843
Sauve Company Limited, 28844
Sav Enterprises, 52081
Savage & Company, 59198
Savage Brothers Company, 28845
Saval Foods Corp, 11246, 59199
Savanna Pallets, 28846, 48847
Savannah Bee Co., 11247
Savannah Chanelle Vineyards, 11248
Savannah Cinnamon & Cookie Company, 11249
Savannah Distributing, 52082, 53400, 59200
Savannah Food Co, 11250, 48400
Savasort Inc, 28848
Save-A-Tree, 28849
Save-O-Seal Corporation, 28850, 48401
Savello USA, 48402
Saver Glass Inc, 28851
Saverino & Assoc, 41066
Saveur Food Group, 11251
Savino's Italian Ices, 11252
Savogran Co, 28852
Savoia Foods, 11253, 48403
Savoie Industries, 11254
Savoie's Sausage and Food Products, 11255
Savol Pools, 59201
Savor California, 48404

All Companies Index

Savor Street, 11256
Savory Foods, 11257, 48405
Savoury Systems Inc, 11258, 48406
Savoye Packaging, 28853
Sawtooth Winery, 11259
Saxby Foods, 11260, 48407
Saxco International LLC, 28854, 28855
Saxon Chocolates, 11261
Saxon Creamery, 11262
Saxony Equipment Distributors, 59202
Sayco Yo-Yo Molding Company, 28856, 48408
Sazerac Co Inc, 11263
Sazerac Company, Inc., 11264, 48409
SBA Software, 28661
SBB & Associates, 28662
SBK Preserves, 11035, 48272
SBN Associates, 28663
SBS Americas, 11036
SBS of Financial Industries, 28664
SC Enterprises, 11037, 59124
SCA Hygiene Paper, 28665
SCA Tissue, 28666
SCA Tissue North America, 28667
Scala-Wisell International Inc., 11265
Scally's Imperial Importing Company Inc, 11266
Scaltrol Inc, 28857, 48410
Scan American Food Company, 48411
Scan Coin, 28858, 48412
Scan Corporation, 28859, 48413
Scan Group, 28860
Scandia Packaging Machinery Co, 28862, 48414
Scandia Seafood Company, 11267
Scandic Food Inc, 48415
Scandicrafts Inc, 48416, 59203
Scandinavian Formulas Inc, 11268, 48417
Scandinavian Laboratories, 11269, 48418
Scanning Devices Inc, 28863
ScanTech Sciences, 28861
Scardina Refrigeration Co., 59204
Scattaglia Farm LLC, 28864
Scavuzzo Sales & Marketing, 41067
Scenic Fruit Co, 11270
Scenic Valley Winery, 11271
Schadel's Bakery, 11272
Schaefer Machine Co Inc, 28865, 48419
Schaefer Technologies Inc, 28866
Schaefers, 48420, 53401, 59205
Schaefers Market, 11273, 11274
Schaeff, 28867
Schaeffler Group USA Inc, 28868
Schaerer USA Corp, 28869
Schafer Fisheries Inc, 11275
Schaffer Poidometer Company, 28870
Schaller & Weber Inc, 11276
Schaller's Bakery Inc, 11277
Schanno Transportation, 28871
Schaper Company, 41068, 59206
Schare & Associates, 41069
Scharffen Berger Chocolate Maker, 11278
Schat's Dutch Bakeries, 11279
Scheb International, 28872, 48421
Schebler Co, 28873
Scheidegger, 28874, 48422
Scheidegger Trading Co Inc, 41070
Scheidelman, 59207
Schenck Foods Co, 59208
Schenck Process, 28875, 28876, 28877, 48423
Schenk Packing Co Inc, 11280, 48424
Schenker International, 52083
Schenker Logistics Inc, 53402
Schepps Dairy, 11281, 59209
Schermer Pecan Co, 11282
Schermerhorn Brothers & Co, 59210
Schermerhorn Inc, 28878
Scherping Systems, 28879
Schiavone's Casa Mia, 11283
Schiefer Packaging Corporation, 28880
Schiff & Co, 28881

Schiff Food Products Co Inc, 11284, 41071, 48425
Schiff Nutrition International, 11285
Schiffenhaus Industries, 28882
Schiffmayer Plastics Corp., 28883
Schilli Transportation Services, 52084, 53403
Schillinger Genetics Inc, 11286, 48426
Schiltz Foods Inc, 11287, 48427
Schimpffs Confectionery LLC, 11288
Schirf Brewing Company, 11289
Schisa Brothers, 11290, 59211
Schischa Brothers, 59212
Schlafly Tap Room, 11291
Schlagel Inc, 28884, 48428
Schleicher & Company of America, 28885
Schleicher & Schuell MicroSience, 28886
Schleswig Specialty Meats, 11292
Schloss Doepken Winery, 11293
Schloss Engineered Equipment, 28887
Schlotterbeck & Foss Company, 11294
Schlotzsky's, 11295
Schlueter Company, 28888, 28889, 28890, 48429
Schmalz, 28891
Schmersal, 28892
Schmidt Baking Company Incorporated, 59213
Schmidt Bros Inc, 11296
Schmidt Progressive, 28893, 48430
Schneck Beverages, 59214
Schneider Cheese, 11297
Schneider Electric, 28894, 48431
Schneider Foods, 11298, 11299, 11300, 48432
Schneider National Inc, 52085
Schneider Packaging Eqpt Co, 28895, 48433
Schneider's Dairy Inc, 11301
Schneider's Fish & Seafood Co, 59215
Schneider-Valley Farms Inc, 11302, 59216
Schnuck Markets, Inc., 11303, 28896
Schober USA Inc, 28897
Schobert's Cottage Cheese Corporation, 11304
Schoenberg Salt Co, 59217
Schoeneck Containers Inc, 28898
Schoep's Ice Cream, 11305
Scholle IPN, 28899, 48434
Schoneman Inc, 28900
School Marketing Partners, 28901
Schoppaul Hill Winery atIvanhoe, 11306
Schraad & Associates, 41072
Schramsberg Vineyards, 11307
Schreck Software, 28902
Schreiber Foods Inc., 11308, 28903, 41073, 48435
Schroeder Machine, 28904, 48436
Schroter, USA, 28905
Schubert Packaging Systems, 28906
Schug Carneros Estate Winery, 11309
Schugel J & R Trucking Inc, 52086
Schuil Coffee Co, 11310
Schultz Sav-O-Stores, 59218
Schulze & Burch Biscuit Co, 11311
Schumacher Wholesale Meats, 11312, 59219
Schuman Cheese, 11313, 48437
Schurman's Wisconsin Cheese Country, 28907, 41074
Schuster Marketing Corporation, 11314
Schutte Buffalo Hammermill, 28908
Schwaab, Inc, 28909
Schwab Meat Co, 11315
Schwab Paper Products Co, 28910, 48438, 59220
Schwan's Company, 11316
Schwan's Food Service Inc., 11317
Schwartz Manufacturing Co, 28911
Schwarz Supply Source, 28912
Schwebel Baking Co., 11318, 52087, 59221
Schwerdtel Corporation, 28913

Scialo Brothers Bakery, 11319
Scienco Systems, 28914, 48439
Scientech, Inc, 28915, 48440
Scientific Fire Prevention, 28916
Scientific Process & Research, 28917, 48441
SCK Direct Inc, 28668, 28669, 48273
Sconza Candy Co, 11320, 48442
Scooter Bay Seafood Sales Company, 41075, 59222
Scooty's Wholesome Foods, 11321
Scope Packaging, 28918, 48443
Scorpio Apparel, 28919, 48444
Scot Young Research LTD, 28920, 48445
Scotian Gold, 11322
Scotsburn Ice Cream Co., 11323, 59223
Scotsman Beverage System, 28921, 48446
Scotsman Ice Systems, 28922, 48447
Scott & Associates, 41076, 59224
Scott & Daniells, 28923
Scott Adams Foods, 11324
Scott Equipment Co, 28924
Scott Farms Inc, 11325
Scott Group, 28925
Scott Hams, 11326, 48448
Scott Laboratories Inc, 28926
Scott Lift Truck Corporation, 59225
Scott Packaging Corporation, 28927
Scott Pallets Inc, 28928
Scott Process Equipment & Controls, 28929
Scott Sign Systems, 28930, 48449
Scott Turbon Mixer, 28931, 28932, 48450
Scott's Auburn Mills, 11327
Scott's Candy, 11328, 48451
Scott's Liquid Gold-Inc, 28933
Scott's of Wisconsin, 11330
Scott's Sauce Co Inc, 11329
Scott-Bathgate, 11331, 48452
Scotty Wotty's Creamy Cheesecake, 11332
SCR Total Bar Control Systems, 59125
Scranton Fish Company, 59226
Scranton Lace Company, 28934
Scray's Cheese, 11333
Screamin' Onionz, 11334, 48453
Screen Print Etc, 28935, 48454
Screenflex Portable Partition, 48455
Screw Conveyor Corp, 28936
Scripture Candy, 11335
Scrivner Equipment Co Inc, 28937
Scroll Compressors LLC, 28938, 48456
SCS Sales Company, 41037
SCS Supply Chain Solutions LLC, 53378, 53379
Sculli Brothers, 11336
SD Watersboten, 11038
SDIX, 28670, 48274
SDS Global Logistics, Inc., 52067, 53380
Se Kure Controls Inc, 28939, 48457
Sea Bear Smokehouse, 11337, 48458
Sea Best Corporation, 11338, 59227
Sea Breeze Fruit Flavors, 11339, 28940, 48459
Sea Change Seafoods, 59228
Sea Dog Brewing Company, 11340
Sea Farm & Farm Fresh Importing Company, 11341, 48460
Sea Fresh USA Inc, 11342, 59229
Sea Gold Seafood Products Inc, 11343
Sea Gull Lighting Products, LLC, 28941
Sea Horse Wharf, 11344, 59230
Sea Lyons, 11345, 59231
Sea Pac Of Idaho Inc, 11346
Sea Pearl Seafood, 11347, 59232
Sea Products West Inc, 59233
Sea Ridge Winery, 11348
Sea Safari, 11349, 48461
Sea Salt Superstore, 11350, 11351, 59234
Sea Snack Cold Storage, 53404
Sea Snack Foods Inc, 11352, 48462
Sea Stars Goat Cheese, 11353
Sea Veggies, 11354

Sea View Fillet Company, 11355
Sea Watch Intl, 11356, 48463
Sea-Fresh Seafood Market, 11357, 59235
SeaBear Wild Salmon, 11358
Seaberghs Frozen Foods, 11362
Seaboard Bag Corporation, 28942
Seaboard Carton Company, 28943
Seaboard Cold Storage, 53405, 53406
Seaboard Cold Storage Inc, 53407, 53408
Seaboard Folding Box Corp, 28944, 48465
Seaboard Foods, 11363, 41077, 48466, 53409
Seaboard Warehouse Terminals, 52088, 53410
Seaborard Marine, 53411
Seabreeze Fish, 11364, 59236
Seabrook Brothers & Sons, 11365
Seachase Foods, 41078, 48467
Seacore Seafood, 48468, 59237
Seacrest Foods, 48469, 59238, 59239
Seafare Market Wholesale, 11366, 59240
Seafood & Meat, 59241
Seafood Connection, 11367, 48470, 53412, 59242
Seafood Dimensions Brokerage, 41079
Seafood Dimensions Intl, 11368, 59243
Seafood Distributors, 59244
Seafood Express, 11369, 59245
Seafood Hawaii Inc, 11370, 41080, 48471
Seafood International, 11371, 41081, 48472
Seafood Merchants LTD, 11372, 48473, 59246
Seafood Packaging Inc, 11373, 59247
Seafood Plus Corporation, 11374, 59248
Seafood Producers Co-Op, 11375, 48474
Seafood Sales, 41082
Seafood Services, 11376, 59249
Seafood Specialties, 11377
Seaga Manufacturing Inc, 28945
Seagate Transportation, 52089
Seajoy, 11378, 28946
Seal King North America, 28947
Seal Pac USA, 28948
Seal Science Inc, 28949
Seal the Seasons, 28950
Seal-A-Tron Corp, 28951
Seal-O-Matic Corp, 28952, 48475
Seal-Tite Bag Company, 28953
Sealand Lobster Corporation, 11379, 59250
Sealaska Corp, 11380
Seald Sweet, 11381, 48476
Sealed Air Corp, 28954
Sealer Sales Inc, 59251
Sealeze Inc, 28955
Sealstrip Corp, 28956
Sealstrip Corporation, 28957, 48477
Seamark Corporation, 41083, 48478
SeamTech, 28958
Seaonus, 52090, 53413
SeaPak Shrimp, 11359
SeaPerfect Atlantic Farms, 11360, 48464
Seapoint Farms, 11382, 48479
Search West, 28959
Seaschott, 52091, 53414
Seaside Ice Cream, 11383
Seasnax, 48480
Season Brand, 11384
Season Harvest Foods, 11385, 28960
Seasons 4 Inc, 28961, 48481
SeaSpecialties, 11361
Seatech Corporation, 11386, 48482
Seatex Ltd, 28962, 48483
Seating Concepts Inc, 28963, 48484
Seatrade Corporation, 11387
Seattle Bar Company, 11388
Seattle Boiler Works Inc, 28964, 48485
Seattle Chocolates, 11389
Seattle Fish Co, 59252
Seattle Gourmet Foods, 11390
Seattle Menu Specialists, 28965, 48486
Seattle Plastics, 28966

1435

All Companies Index

Seattle Refrigeration & Manufacturing, 28967, 48487
Seattle Seasonings, 11391
Seattle's Best Coffee, 11392, 28968, 59253
Seattle-Tacoma Box Co, 28969, 28970, 48488
Seaver's Bakery, 11393
Seavey Vineyard, 11394
Seaview Lobster Co, 11395, 48489, 59254
Seawater Food & Beverage, 11396
Seaway Company, 11397, 59255
Seawind Foods, 48490
Sebastiani Vineyards, 11398
Sebastiano's, 11399
Sebesta Blomberg & Assoc, 28971
Sebring Container Corporation, 28972
SEC, 28671
Sechler's Fine Pickles, 11400
Sechrist Brothers, 11401
Seco Industries, 28973, 28974
Seco Systems, 48491
Secret Garden, 11402
Secret Tea Garden, 11403
Secure Packaging, 59256
Security Bonded Warehouse, 53415
Security Link, 28975
Security Packaging, 28976
Sedalia Cold Storage Company, 53416
Sedalia Janitorial & Paper Supplies, 28977
Seder Foods Corporation, 59257
Sedex Kinkos, 28978
Sediment Testing Equipment, 28979
Sedlock Farm, 11404
Sedona Baking Company, 11405
See Smell Taste, 11406
See's Candies, 11407, 48492
See's Candy Shops, 59258
Seed Enterprises Inc, 11408, 48493
Seeds of Change, 11409, 28980
Seenergy Foods, 11410, 48494
Seepex Inc, 28981, 48495
Sefar, 28982
Sefi Fabricators Inc, 28983
Segal's Wholesale, 59259
Segall Nathan Co Inc, 11411
Seger Egg Corporation, 11412
Seghesio Family Vineyards, 11413
SEI Consultants, 28672
Seiberling Associates Inc, 28984
Seidenader Equipment, 28985
Seidman Brothers, 28986
Seiler Plastics, 28987
Seitenbacher America LLC, 11414
Seitz Gift Fruit, 59260
Seitz Memtec America Corporation, 28988
Seitz Schenk Filter Systems, 28989
Seitz Stainless Inc, 28990
Seiz Sign Co Inc, 28991
Sejoyia Foods, 11415
Sekisui TA Industries, 28992, 48496
SEKO Worldwide Inc, 52068, 53381
Selby Johnson Corporation, 59261
Selby Sign Co Inc, 28993
Selby/Ucrete Industrial Flooring, 28994
Selco Products Company, 28995
Select Appliance Sales, Inc., 28996
Select Food Products, 11416, 48497
Select Harvest USA, 11417
Select Meat Company, 48498, 59262
Select Origins, 11418
Select Sales & Marketing Inc, 41084
Select Stainless, 28997
Select Supplements Inc, 11419
Select Technologies Inc, 28998
Selectdrinkware.com, 48499
Selective Foods, 28999
Selecto, 29000
Selecto Sausage Co, 11420
Selecto Scientific, 29001, 48500, 48501
Selig Chemical Industries, 29002
Selina Naturally, 11421

Sell Group, 41085
Sellers Cleaning Systems, 29003
Sellers Engineering Division, 29004, 48502
Sellers Equipment Inc, 59263
Sells Best, 11422
Selma Good Company, 11423
Selma Wire Products Company, 29005
Selma's Cookies, 11424
Selo, 29006
Seltzer Chemicals, 29007, 59264
Selwoods Farm Hunting Preserve, 11425
Semanco International, 29008
SEMCO, 28673, 48275
Semco Manufacturing Company, 29009, 48503
Semco Plastic Co, 29010, 48504
SEMCO Systems, 28674
Semi-Bulk Systems Inc, 29011, 48505
Semifreddi's Bakery, 11426
Seminis Vegetable Seeds Inc, 11427
Seminole Foods, 11428
Sempio Foods, 11429
Senape's Bakery Inc, 11430
Senba USA, 11431, 48506
Sencha Naturals, 11432
Sencon Inc, 29012
Sencorp White, 29013
Seneca Environmental Products, 29014, 48507
Seneca Foods Corp, 11433, 11434, 48508, 48509
Seneca Juice, 11435
Seneca Tape & Label, 29015
Senior Flexonics, 29016
Senior Housing Options Inc, 29017
Senomyx Inc, 11436, 29018, 48510
Senor Felix's Gourmet Mexican, 11437
Senor Murphy Candymaker, 11438
Senor Pinos de Santa Fe, 11439
Sensaphone, 29019
Sensational Sweets, 11440
Sensible Foods LLC, 11441
Sensible Portions, 11442
Sensidyne, 29020, 48511
Sensient Colors Inc, 29021, 48512
Sensient Flavors and Fragrances, 11443, 29022, 48513
Sensient Technologies Corp, 11444
Sensitech, 29023
Sensitech Inc, 29024, 29025, 48514
Sensor Systems, 29026
Sensors Quality Management, 29027
Sensory Computer Systems, 29028
Sensory Spectrum, 29029
Sensus America Inc, 11445, 48515
Sentinel Lubricants Inc, 29030, 48516
Sentinel Polyolefins, 29031
Sentron, 29032
Sentry Equipment Corp, 29033, 48517
Sentry Equipment/Erectors Inc, 29034
Sentry Seasonings, 11446, 48518
Sentry/Bevcon North America, 29035, 48519
Separators Inc, 29036, 48520
Seppic Inc, 11447
Sepragen Corp, 29037, 48521
Septimatech Group, 29038
Septipack, 29039
Sequa Can Machinery, 29040
Sequoia Brewing Co, 11448
Sequoia Grove, 11449
Sequoia Pacific, 29041
Sequoia Specialty Cheese Company, 11450
Serac Inc, 29043
SERCO Laboratories, 28675
Serenade Foods, 11451, 48523
Serendib Tea Company, 48524, 59265
Serendipitea, 11452, 48525, 59266
Serendipity Cellars, 11453
Serendipity of the Valley, 59267
Serengeti Tea Co, 11454
Serfilco, 29044, 48526
Sergeant E M Pulp & Chem Co, 29045

Serious Foodie, 11455
Sermatech ISPA, 29046
Sermia International, 29047, 48527
Serpa Packaging Solutions, 29048, 48528
Serr-Edge Machine Company, 29049, 48529
Serranos Salsa, 11456
Serro Foods LLC, 11457
Sertapak Packaging Corporation, 29050, 48530
Serti Information Solution, 29051
Sertodo Copper, 48531
Serv-A-Rack, 29268
Serv-Agen Corporation, 11458
Serv-Rite Meat Co Inc, 11459
Serv-Tek, 59269
Serval Foods, 48532
Servco Equipment Co, 29052, 48533
Serve Canada Food Equipment, 59270
SerVend International, 29042, 48522
Servend International, 48534
Server Products Inc, 29053, 48535
Service Brass & AluminumFittings, 29054
Service By Air Inc, 52092
Service Cold Storage Inc, 53417, 53418
Service Craft Distribution Systems, 52093, 53419
Service Foods, 11460
Service Group, 41086
Service Handling Equipment Company, 59271
Service Ideas, 29055, 48536
Service Manufacturing, 29056, 48537
Service Market, 59272
Service Master Co LLC, 29057
Service Neon Signs, 29058
Service Packing Company, 11461, 48538
Service Sales Corporation, 29059, 59273
Service Stamp Works, 29060
Service Tool International, 29061
Service Warehouse & Distribution, 53420
Servin Company, 29062
Serviplast, 53421
Servitrade, 48539
Servomex, 29063
Servomex Inc, 29064
Servpak Corp, 29065, 48540
Sesaco Corp, 11462, 48541
Sesame King Foods, 41087
Sesame Label System, 29066
Sesinco Foods, 11463, 48542
Sessions & Associates, 41088
Sessions Co Inc, 11464, 29067, 48543
Set Point Paper Company, 29068
Setaram/SFIM, 29069
Setco, 29070, 29071, 48544
Seth Ellis Chocolatier, 11465
Sethness Caramel Color, 11466, 48545
Seton Indentification Products, 29072
Settables Inc, 41089
Setter, Leach & Lindstrom, 29073
Setterstix Corp, 29074, 48546
Setton Farms, 11467
Setton International Foods, 11468, 48547, 59274
Setton Pistachio, 11469, 48548
Seven B Plus, 29075
Seven Barrel Brewery, 11470
Seven Hills Coffee Co, 11471
Seven Hills Winery, 11472
Seven K Feather Farm, 59275, 59276, 59277
Seven Keys Co Of Florida, 11473, 48549
Seven Lakes Vineyard & Winery, 11474
Seven Mile Creek Corp, 29076
Seven Seas Seafoods, 11475, 48550, 59278
Seven Sundays, LLC, 11476
Severance Foods Inc, 11477
Severino Pasta Mfg Co Inc, 11478
Severn Newtrent, 29077
Severn Peanut Co, 11479
Severn Trent Svc, 29078, 29079, 48551
Seville Display Door, 29080

Seville Flexpack Corp, 29081, 29082, 48552
Seville Olive Company, 11480
Sevilo Inc, 48553
Seviroli Foods, 11481, 48554
Seviroli Foods Inc, 11482
SEW Friel, 11039, 48276
Sew-Eurodrive Inc, 29083, 48555
Sewell's Seafood & Fish Market, 11483, 59279
Sexton Sign, 29084
Sexy Pop LLC, 11484
Seydel Co, 11485, 48556
Seymour & Sons Seafoods Inc, 11486
Seymour Housewares, 29085
Seymour Woodenware Company, 29086
SFB Plastics, 28676
Sfb Plastics Inc, 29087, 48557
SFBC, LLC dba Seaboard Folding Box, 28677
SFK Danfotech, Inc., 28678
Sfoglia Fine Pastas & Gourmet, 11487
Sfoglini Pasta Shop, 11488, 59280
SFP Food Products, 11040, 48277
SFS intec, 28679
SFS Marketing, 41038
SG Frantz Company, 28680
SGS International, 28681
SGS International Rice Inc, 41039, 48278, 59126
SHA Services, 41040
Shaanxi Jiahe Phytochem Co., Ltd., 11489
Shabazz Fruit Cola Company, 11490, 59281
Shadetree Canopies, 29088, 48558
Shady Grove Orchards, 11491
Shady Maple Farm, 11492, 48559
Shae Industries, 29089
Shafer Commercial Seating, 29090, 48560
Shafer Lake Fruit Inc, 11493
Shafer Vineyards, 11494
Shafer-Haggart, 11495, 48561
Shaffer Sports & Events, 29091
Shaffer Trucking, 52094
Shah Trading Company, 11496, 29092, 48562
Shaheen Bros Inc, 59282
Shaker Country Meadowsweets, 11497
Shaker Museum, 11498
Shaker Valley Foods, 11499
Shakespeare's, 11500
Shaklee Corp, 11501, 48563
Shaklee Distributor, 59283
Shalhoob Meat Co, 59284
Shallon Winery, 11502
Shallowford Farms Popcorn, Inc., 11503
Shambaugh & Son, 29093
Shammi Industries, 29094, 48564
Shamrock Farms, 59285
Shamrock Foods Co, 11504, 11505, 11506, 11507, 11508, 11509, 29095, 29096, 29097, 29098, 29099, 29100, 59286, 59287, 59288, 59289, 59290, 59291
Shamrock Paper Company, 29101
Shamrock Plastics, 29102
Shamrock Seafood, 41090
Shamrock Slaughter Plant, 11510
Shamrock Technologies Newark, 29103, 48565
Shamrock Warehouse, 53422
Shane Candy Co, 11511
Shaner's Family Restaurant, 11512
Shanghai Co, 11513
Shanghai Freemen, 11514, 29104, 59292
Shank's Extracts Inc, 11515, 48566
Shanker Industries, 29105, 48567
Shanley Farms, 11516
Shannon Diversified Inc, 59293
Shanzer Grain Dryer, 29106, 48568
Shape Foods, 11517
Shaped Wire, 29107
Shared Data Systems, 29108

All Companies Index

Shari Candies, 59294
Shariann's Organics, 11518
Sharkco's, 11519, 59295
Sharon Manufacturing Inc, 29109, 48569
Sharon Mill Winery, 11520
Sharp Brothers, 29110, 48570
Sharp Electronics Corporation, 29111, 48571
Sharp Packaging Systems Inc, 29112
Sharp Rock Farm B & B, 11521
Sharpe Measurement Technology, 29113
Sharpe Valves, 59296
Sharpsville Container Corp, 29114, 29115
Shashi Foods, 11522, 29116
Shashy's Bakery & Fine Foods, 11523
Shasta Beverages Inc, 11524
Shat R Shield Inc, 29117, 48572
Shaw & Slavsky Inc, 29118
Shaw Baking Company, 11525
Shaw Equipment Company, 59297
Shaw Montgomery Warehouse Company, 52095, 53423
Shaw Warehouse Company, 53424
Shaw's Southern Belle Frozen, 53425
Shaw's Southern Belle Frozen, Inc., 11526
Shaw-Clayton Corporation, 29119, 48573
Shawano Specialty Papers, 29120, 48574
Shawmut Fishing Company, 11527
Shawnee Canning Co, 11528
Shawnee Milling Co, 11529, 11530, 48575
Shawnee Trucking Co Inc, 53426
Sheahan Sanitation Consulting, 29121
Shean Equipment Company, 59298
Shear/Kershman Laboratories, 29122
Shearer's Foods Inc, 11531
Sheboygan Paper Box Co, 29123
Shedd Food Products, 11532
Sheehan Majestic, 59299
Sheffa Foods, 11533
Sheffield Platers Inc, 29124, 59300
Sheila G Brands LLC, 11534
Sheila Gs Brownie Brittle Co, 11535
Sheila's Select Gourmet Recipe, 11536
Sheinman Provision Co, 11537
Shekou Chemicals, 11538, 48576
Shelburne Falls Coffee Roaster, 11539
Shelby Co, 29125
Shelby Pallet & Box Company, 29126
Shelby Williams Industries Inc, 29127, 29128, 48577, 48578
Shelcon Inc, 29129
Shelden, Dickson, & Steven Company, 29130, 48579
Sheldon Wood Products, 29131
Shell Oil Company, 29132
Shell Ridge Jalapeno Project, 11540
Shelley Cabinet Company, 29133
Shelley's, 11541
Shellman Peanut & Grain, 59301
Shelton's Poultry Inc, 11542
Shelving Rack Systems Inc, 59302
Sheman Tov Corporation, 29134
Shemen Tov Corporation, 59303
Shemper Seafood Co, 11543, 59304
Shen Manufacturing Co Inc, 29135, 48580
Shenandoah Industrial Rubber, 59305
Shenandoah Mills, 11544
Shenandoah Vineyards, 11545, 48581, 59306
Shenk's Foods, 11546
Shepard Brothers Co, 29136, 48582
Shepard Niles Parts, 29137, 48583
Shepard's Moving & Storage, 52096, 53427
Shepherd Farms Inc, 11547, 48584
Shepherdsfield Bakery, 11548, 59307
Sher Brothers & Company, 59308
Sherbrooke OEM Ltd, 11549
Sheridan Fruit Co Inc, 59309
Sheridan Sign Company, 29138
Sherm Edwards Candies, 11550

Sherman Specialty Toy Company, 48585
Sherrill Orchards, 11551
Sherwood Brands, 11552, 48586
Sherwood Brands of Rhode Island Inc, 11553
Sherwood Food Distributors, 59310, 59311, 59312, 59313, 59314, 59315, 59316
Sherwood Tool, 29139, 48587
Sherwood Valley Cold Storage, 59317
Sheryl's Chocolate Creations, 11554
Shetakis Foodservice, 59318
Shibuya International, 29140, 48588
Shick Esteve, 29141, 48589
Shields Bag & Printing Co, 29142, 48590
Shields Brokerage, 41091
Shields Date Garden, 11555
Shields Products Inc, 29143
Shiff & Goldman Foods, 59319
Shiffer Industries, 29144, 48591
Shilad Overseas Enterprises, 48592
Shild Company, 29145
Shillington Box Co LLC, 29146
Shiloh Farms, 11556
Shimadzu Scientific Instrs, 29147
Shine Companies, 11557, 48593
Shine Foods Inc, 11558
Shingle Belting, 29148, 48594
Shining Ocean Inc, 11559
Ship Rite Packaging, 29149
Shipley Basket Mfg Co, 29150, 48595
Shipley Do-Nut Franchise Co, 11560
Shipley Sales, 48596
Shipmaster Containers Ltd., 29151
Shippers Paper Products Co, 29152, 48597
Shippers Supply, 29153, 29154, 29155, 48598, 59320, 59321
Shippers Supply, Labelgraphic, 29156, 59322
Shippers Warehouse, 53428
Shipyard Brewing Co, 11561, 11562, 48599
Shire City Herbals, 11563, 59323
Shirer Brothers Meats, 11564
Shirley Foods, 11565
Shirley J Ventures, LLC, 11566
Shivji Enterprises, 48600, 59324
Shivvers, 29157, 48601
Sho-Nuff-Good, 59325
ShockWatch, 29158
Shoe Inn, LLC, 59326
Shoei Foods USA Inc, 11567, 48602
Shoes for Crews/Mighty Mat, 29159, 48603, 59327
Shonan USA Inc, 11568
Shonna's Gourmet Goodies, 11569, 48604
Shook Kelley Design Group, 29160
Shooting Star Farms, 11570
Shoppa's Material Handling, 59328
Shoppers Plaza USA, 29161
Shore Distribution Resources, 29162, 41092, 59329
Shore Paper Box Co, 29163
Shore Seafood Distr, 11571
Shore Trading Co, 11572, 48605
Shoreham Cooperative Apple Producer, 53429
Shoreland Inc, 53430
Shoreline Chocolates, 11573
Shoreline Freezers, 52097, 53431, 53432
Shoreline Fruit, 11574, 48606, 53433
Shorewood Engineering Inc, 29164
Shorewood Packaging, 29165
Short Freight Lines Inc, 52098
Short's Brewing Co, 11575
Shouldice Brothers SheetMetal, 29166
Showa-Best Glove, 29167, 48607
Showeray Corporation, 29168, 48608
Shreve Meats Processing, 11576
Shrimp Tex Distributors, 41093
Shrinkfast Marketing, 29169, 48609
Shrums Sausage & Meats, 11577
Shryack-Givens Grocery Co., 59330

Shryack-Hirst Grocery Company, 59331
Shuckman's Fish Co & Smokery, 11578, 59332
Shuff's Meat Market, 11579
Shullsburg Creamery Inc, 59333
Shur-Az Inc, 59334
Shur-Good Biscuit Co., 11580
Shure-Glue Systems, 29170
SHURflo, 28682, 48279
Shurtape Technologies LLC, 29171
Shuster Corporation, 29172
Shuster Laboratories, 29173, 29174
Shuttleworth North America, 29175, 48610
SI Systems Inc, 28683
Si-Lodec, 29176, 48611
Sibu Sura Chocolates, LLC, 11581
Sicht-Pack Hagner, 29177
SICK Inc, 28684
Sico Inc, 29178, 48612, 48613
SICOM Systems, 28685
Sid Alpers Organic Sales Company, 41094, 59335
Sid Goodman Company, 59336
Sid Green Frozen Foods, 41095, 59337
Sid Harvey Industries Inc, 59338
Sid Wainer & Son Specialty, 48614, 48615, 59339, 59340
Sidari's Italian Foods, 11582
Side Hill Farm, 11583
Sidehill Farm, 11584, 59341
Sidel Inc, 29179
Sidney Manufacturing Co, 29180, 48616
Sidney's, 59342
Sieb Distributor, 48617, 59343
Sieberts Engineers, 29181
Sieco USA Corporation, 11585, 48618
Siegel Egg Co, 11586
Siegerr, Ken, 41096
Siegmeister Sales & Service, 59344
Sielt Stone, 29182
Siemens Dematic, 29183
Siemens Industry Inc, 29184
Siemens Measurement Systems, 29185
Siemer Milling Co, 11587
Siena Foods, 11588, 48619
Sierra Cheese Mfg Co, 11589
Sierra Converting Corporation, 29186
Sierra Dawn Products, 29187, 48620
Sierra Madre Coffee, 11590
Sierra Madre Mushrooms, 52099
Sierra Meat & Seafood Co, 52100, 53434, 59345
Sierra Nevada Cheese Co., 11591
Sierra Nevada Taproom & Rstrnt, 11592
Sierra Nut House, 59346
Sierra Pacific Distribution, 53435, 53436
Sierra Pacific Refrigerated, 53437
Sierra Vista Winery, 11593
Siete Farms, 11594
Sifers Valomilk Candy Co, 11595
Sifter Parts & Svc, 29188
SIG Combibloc, 28686
SIG Combibloc USA, Inc., 28687, 48280
Sig Pack, 29189, 48621
SIG Pack Services, 28688
SIG Packaging Technologies, 28689
SIGCO Sun Products, 11041
Siggi's Dairy, 11596, 11597
SIGHTech Vision Systems, 28690, 48281
Sigma Engineering Corporation, 29190, 48622
Sigma Industrial Automation, 29191
Sigma Industries, 29192, 48623
Sign Art, 29193
Sign Classics, 29194, 48624
Sign Expert, 29195, 48625
Sign Factory, 29196
Sign Graphics, 29197
Sign Products, 29198
Sign Systems, Inc., 29199, 48626
Sign Warehouse, 29200
Signal Equipment, 29202
SignArt Advertising, 29201
Signature Beverage, 11598

Signature Brands LLC, 11599, 48627
Signature Foods, 11600, 29203
Signature Fruit, 11601
Signature Packaging, 29204, 59347
Signature Seafoods Inc, 11602
Signco Inc, 29205
Signco Stylecraft, 29206
Signet Graphic Products, 29207
Signet Marking Devices, 29208, 48628
Signets/Menu-Quik, 29209
Signmasters, 29210
Signode Industrial Group LLC, 29211, 29212, 48629
Signore Winery, 11603
Signorello Vineyards, 11604
Signs & Designs, 29213
Signs & Shapes Intl, 29214, 48630
Signs O' Life, 29215
Signtech Electrical Advg Inc, 29216
Sigona's, 11605
Siko Products Inc, 29217
Silani Sweet Cheese, 11606, 48631
Silent Watchman Security Services LLC, 29218, 48632
Silesia Flavors, 11607
Silesia Grill Machines Inc, 29219, 29220, 48633, 48634
Silgan Containers LLC, 29221, 48635
Silgan Plastic Closure Sltns, 29222, 29223, 29224, 48636, 48637
Silgan Plastics Canada, 29225, 48638
Silgan Plastics LLC, 29226
Silgan White Cap LLC, 29227, 48639
Siljans Crispy Cup Company, 11608, 48640
Silk Road Teas, 48641
Sill Farm Market, 11609
Sillcocks Plastics International, 29228, 48642
Silliker Canada Company, 29229
Silliker Laboratories Of Ga, 29230
Silliker Laboratories-Pa Inc, 29231
Silliker, Inc, 29232
Silva Farms, 11610
Silva International, 11611
Silva Regal Spanish, 48643
Silvan Ridge Winery, 11612
Silvateam USA, 11613
Silver Creek Distillers, 11614
Silver Creek Farms, 11615
Silver Creek Specialty Meats, 11616
Silver Fern Chemical Inc, 11617, 48644
Silver Fox Vineyards, 11618
Silver King Refrigeration Inc, 29233, 29234, 48645
Silver Lake Sausage Shop, 11619
Silver Lining Seafood, 11620, 48646
Silver Mountain Vineyards, 11621, 29235
Silver Oak, 11622
Silver Palate Kitchens, 11623, 48647
Silver Spoon, 11624
Silver Spring Foods, 11625, 48648
Silver Springs Citrus Inc, 11626, 48649
Silver Spur Corp, 29236
Silver Star Meats Inc, 11627
Silver State Foods Inc, 11628
Silver State Plastics Inc, 29237
Silver Streak Bass Co, 11629
Silver Sweet Candies, 11630
Silver Tray Cookies, 11631
Silver Weibull, 29238, 48650
Silverado Vineyards, 11632, 59348
Silverbow Honey Company, 11633
Silverfern Specialties, 48651
Silverland Bakery, 11634, 48652
Silverleaf International Corp, 11635
Silverson Machines Inc, 29239, 48653
Silverstar Foodservice Supply, 59349
Silverston Fisheries, 11636
Simard Warehouses, 52101, 53438
SIMBA USA, 28691
Simco, 29240, 29241
Simco Foods, 48654, 59350
Simi Winery, 11637
Simit + Smith, 11638

1437

All Companies Index

Simkar Corp, 29242, 48655
Simkins Industries Inc, 29243
Simmons Engineering Corporation, 29244, 48656
Simmons Foods Inc, 11639, 48657
Simmons Hot Gourmet Products Corp., 11640
Simolex Rubber Corp, 29245, 48658
Simon Hubig Company, 11641
Simon Levi Cellars, 11642
Simon S. Jackel Plymouth, 29246
Simon's Specialty Cheese, 11643
Simonds International, 29247, 29248, 48659, 48660
Simonian Fruit Company, 48661, 59351
Simoniz USA Inc, 29249, 48662
Simonson Group, 29250
Simpatica, 11644
Simple Foods, 11645
Simple Mills, 11646
Simplex Filler Co, 29251, 48663
Simplex Time Recorder Company, 29252, 29253, 48664, 48665
Simplimatic Automation, 29254, 48666
Simplot Food Group, 11647
Simply 7 Snacks, 11648
Simply Auri, 11649
Simply Delicious, 11650
Simply Divine, 11651
Simply Gourmet Confections, 11652
Simply Gum, 11653, 59352
Simply Incredible Foods, 11654
Simply Manufacturing, 29255
Simply Panache, 11655
Simply Products, 29256
Simply Scruptious Confections, 11656
Simply Shari's Gluten Free, 11657
SimplyFUEL, LLC, 11658, 59353
Simpson & Vail, 11659, 48667, 59354
Simpson Electric, 29257
Simpson Grocery Company, 59355
Simpson Imports, 48668
Simpson Spring Co, 11660
Sims Machinery Co Inc, 29258, 48669
SIMS Manufacturing Co Inc, 28692
Sims Poultry, 59356
Sims Superior Seating, 29259
Sims Wholesale, 11661, 59357
Sin-Son Produce, 59358
Sinai Gourmet, 11662
Sinbad Sweets, 11663, 48670
Sinclair Trading, 48671, 59359
Sinco, 29260, 41097, 48672
Sindoni, Joseph, Wholesale Foods, 59360
Sine Pump, 29261, 48673
Singer Equipment Co Inc, 59361
Singer Extract Laboratory, 11664
Singer Lee & Associates, 41098
Singing Dog Vanilla, 11665, 59362
Singleton Seafood, 11666, 48674
Singleton Seafood Company, 11667
Sini Fulvi U.S.A., 11668, 48675
Sinicrope & Sons Inc, 29262
Sioux Corp, 29263, 48676
Sioux Falls Rbr Stamp Works, 29264
Sioux Honey Assn., 11669, 48677
Sipco, 29265
Sipco Products, 29266, 48678
SipDisc, 59363
Sipp, 11670
SIPROMAC Inc., 28693
Siptop Packaging Inc, 59364
Sir Kensington's, 11671
Sir Real Foods, 11672
Sirca Foodservice, 59365
Sirco Systems, 29267, 48679
Siren Snacks, 11673
Sirman Spa/IFM USA, 29268
Sirocco Enterprises Inc, 11674, 48680
Sisler's Ice & Ice Cream, 11675
Sisq Distributing Inc, 59366
Sisson Imports, 48681
Sister River Foods, 11676
Sister's Gourmet, 11677, 11678
Sisters' Gourmet, 11679, 59367

Sisu Group Inc, 48682, 59368
SIT Indeva Inc, 28694, 28695, 48282
Sitka Store Fixtures, 29269
Sitma USA, 29270, 48683
Sitram/Global Marketing, 29271
Sivetz Coffee, 11680, 29272
Six Hardy Brush Manufacturing, 29273
Six Mile Creek Vineyard, 11681
SJ Industries, 28696
Sjaak's Organic Chocolates, 11682
SJE Marketing Corporation, 41041
SJH Enterprises, 11042, 41042
SJR Foods, 11043
SK Food International, 28697, 48283
Skalar Inc, 29274
Skarnes Inc, 59369
Skc Inc, 29275
Skd Distribution Corp, 29276, 48684
SKE Midwestern, 48284
Skedaddle Maple, 11683
Skelton's Inc, 59370
SKF Motion Technologies, 28698
Skidmore Sales & Distributing Company, 41099, 59371
Skiles Co Inc, 59372
Skillet Street Food, 11684
Skim Delux Mendenhall Laboratories, 11685, 48685
Skimpy Cocktails LLC, 11686
Skinetta Pac-Systems, 29277
Skinner Sheet, 29278
Skinners' Dairy, 11687
Skinny Mixes LLC, 11688
Skinny Souping, 11689
Skipping Stone Productions, 11690
Skjodt-Barrett Foods, 11691
Skone & Conners, 59373
Skone & Connors Produce, 59374
Skratch Labs, 11692
Skrmetta Machinery Corporation, 29279, 48686
SKW Biosystems, 28699
SKW Gelatin & Specialties, 28700, 48285
SKW Industrial Flooring, 28701
SKW Nature Products, 11044, 11045, 48286
Sky Haven Farm, 11693
Sky Valley Foods, 11694
Sky Vineyards, 11695
Sky West Airlines Inc, 52102
Skylark Meats, 11696, 48687, 59375
Skyline Chili Inc, 11697
Skyline Provisions, 59376
Skymart Enterprises, 48688, 59377
Slade Gorton & Co Inc, 48689, 59378
Slagle & Associates, 41100
SlantShack Jerky, 11698, 59379
Slap Ya Mama Cajun Seasoning, 11699
Slate Quarry Winery, 11700
Slathars Smokehouse, 11701
Slather Brand Foods LLC, 11702
Slattery Marketing Corporation, 41101
Slautterback Corporation, 29280, 48690
Slawsa, 11703
Slaybaugh & Associates, 41102
Sleeman Breweries, Ltd., 11704, 48691
Sleeper Produce Company, 59380
Slicechief Co, 29281, 48692
Slide Ridge LLC, 11705
Slidell, 29282
Slim Jim, 11706
Slingshot Foods, 11707
Slip Not, 29283, 48693
Slip-Not Belting Corporation, 29284, 48694
Slm Manufacturing Corp, 29285
Slo Roasted Coffee, 11708
Sloan Sales Inc, 41103
SLT Group, 11046, 28702, 48287
Slusser Wholesale Company, 59381
SLX International, 28703
Small Axe Peppers, 11709
Small Batch Organics, 11710
Small Planet Foods, 11711

Smalley Manufacturing Co Inc, 29286
Smalley Package Company, 29287
Smart Baking Co., 11712
Smart Cycling, Inc., 41104
Smart Flour Foods, LLC, 11713
Smart Juice, 11714, 59382
Smarties, 11716, 48695
Smartscan, Inc, 29288
SmartSweets, 11715
Smashmallow, 11717
SMC Corp Of America, 28704, 28705
Smedley Company, 53439
Smeltzer Orchard Co, 11718, 48696
Smetco, 29289, 48697
Smg Summit Cold Storage, 53440
SMI USA, 28706
Smico Manufacturing Co Inc, 29290, 48698
Smigiel Marketing & Sales Ltd., 41105
Smile Enterprises, 59383
Smiling Fox Pepper Company, 11719
Smiling Hill Farm, 11720
Smirk's, 11721, 48699
Smith & Greene Company, 59384, 59385
Smith & Loveless Inc, 29291
Smith & Salmon, 11722
Smith & Son Wholesale, 59386
Smith & Sons Seafood, 11723
Smith & Taylor, 29292
Smith & Truslow, 11724
Smith Cartage, 52103
Smith Dairy, 11725
Smith Design Associates, 29293
Smith Frozen Foods Inc, 11726, 48700
Smith Meat Packing, 11727
Smith Packaging, 29294, 48701
Smith Packing Regional Meat, 11728, 48702
Smith Pallet Co Inc, 29295
Smith Provision Co Inc, 11729
Smith Restaurant Supply Co, 48703, 59387
Smith Terminal Distribution, 52104, 53441
Smith Vineyard & Winery, 11730
Smith's Bakery, 11731
Smith, Bob, Restaurant Equipment, 59388
Smith, RD, Company, 29296
Smith, S.R., 59389
Smith-Berger Marine, 29297
Smith-Emery Co, 29298
Smith-Lee Company, 29299, 48704
Smith-Lustig Paper Box Manufacturing, 29300, 48705
Smith-Madrone Vineyards & Winery, 11732
Smithfield Foods Inc., 11733, 48706
Smiths Sunbeam Bakery, 59390
Smitty's Snowballs, 48707, 59391
Smoak's Bakery & Catering Service, 11734
Smokaroma, 29301, 48708
Smoke & Fire Natural Food, 11735
Smoke House, 11736
Smoke Right, 29302
Smoked Turkey Inc, 11737, 59392
Smokehouse Limited, 29303
Smokehouse Winery, 11738
Smokey Denmark Sausage Co, 11739
Smokey Mountain Grill, 59393
Smolich Bros. Home Made Sausage, 11740
Smoot Co, 29304
Smoothie's Frozen Desserts, 59394
Smothers Brothers Tasting Room, 11741
SMP Display & Design Group, 28707
Smuggler's Kitchen, 11742
Smurfit Kappa, 29305
Smurfit Stone, 29306, 29307
Smurfit Stone Container, 29308, 29309, 48709
Smurfit-Stone Container Corp, 29310
Smurfit-Stone Container Corporation, 29311

Smuttynose Brewing Co, 11743
Smyrna Container Co, 29312
Smyth Co, 29313
Smyth Co LLC, 29314, 48710
Snack Company, 59395
Snack Factory, 11744, 48711
Snack Food Assn, 29315
Snack King Foods, 59396
Snack Works/Metrovox Snacks, 11745
Snackerz, 11747
SnackMasters, LLC, 11746
Snacks Over America Inc, 59397
Snak King Corp, 11748, 48712
Snake River Brewing Company, 11749
Snap Drape Inc, 29316, 48713
Snap Drape International, 29317, 48714
Snapdragon Foods, 11750, 48715
Snapple Distributors of Long Island, 59398
Snappy Popcorn, 11751, 48716, 59399
Snapware, 29318
Snax Sales Company, 41106
Sneaky Chef Foods, The, 11752, 48717
Snee Chemical Co, 29319
Sneezeguard Solutions, 29320, 48718
Snelgrove Ice Cream Company, 11753, 48719, 59400
Snhook.com/P.K. Torten Ent, 48720
Sniderman Brothers, 59401
Snikiddy, LLC, 11754
Sno Shack Inc, 11755, 48721
Sno Temp Cold Storage, 53442
Sno Wizard Inc, 11756, 48722
Sno-Co Berry Pak, 11757
Sno-Pac Foods Inc, 11758, 48723
Snokist Growers, 11759
Snow Beverages, 11760
Snow Dairy Inc, 11761
Snow Monkey, 11762
Snow's Ice Cream Co Inc, 11763, 59402
Snowbear Frozen Custard, 11765
SnowBird Corporation, 11764, 59403
Snowcrest Packer, 11766, 48724
Snowden Enterprises Inc, 29321
Snowizard Extracts, 11767
Snyder Crown, 29322, 48725
Snyder Foods, 11768, 48726
Snyder Industries Inc, 29323
Snyder Industries Inc., 29324
Snyder Wholesale Inc, 59404
Snyder's Bakery, 48727, 59405
Snyder's of Hanover, 11769, 48728
Snyder's-Lance Inc., 11770, 48729
So Cal Material Handling, 59406
So Delicious Dairy Free, 11771, 48730
Sobaya, 11773, 48731
SoBe Beverages, 11772
Sobel Corrugated Containers, 29326
Sobey's, 59407
Sobey's Ontario, 59408
Sobey's Quebec Inc, 59409
Sobeys Inc., 59410, 59411, 59412, 59413, 59414, 59415
Sobon Estate, 11774
Socafe, 48732, 59416
Society Hill Snacks, 11775
Soco System USA, 29327, 29328
Soda Service, 59417
Sodexo Inc, 29329
Sodus Cold Storage Co, 53443
Sofina Foods Inc, 11776
Sofo Foods, 11777, 59418
Soft Cell Technology, 11778
Sogelco International, 48733, 59419
Sohn Manufacturing, 29330
Soho Beverages, 11779
Sokol Blosser Winery, 11780
Sol Loeb Moving & Storage, 59420
Solana Beach Baking Company, 11781
Solana Gold Organics, 11782
Solapak, 29331
Solarflo Corp, 29332
Solazyme Inc, 11783, 29333
Solbern Corp, 29334, 48734
Sole Grano LLC, 11784, 48735

1438

All Companies Index

Solganik & Associates, 29335
Solgar Vitamin & Herbal, 11785
Solid Surface Acrylics, 29336
Solis Winery, 11786
Solka-Floc, 29337
Sollas Films & PackagingSystems, 29338
Solnuts, 11787
Solo Cup Company, 29339, 41107
Solo Foods, 11788, 29340, 48736
Solo Worldwide Enterprises, 11789
Soloman Baking Company, 11790, 11791
Solon Manufacturing Company, 29341, 48737
Soluble Products Company, 11793
SoluBlend Technologies LLC, 11792
Solus Industrial Innovations, 29342
Solutions, 48738, 59421
Solutions By Design, 29343
Solutions Plus, 29344
Solvaira Specialties, 11794, 48739
Solvay, 48740
Solvay Specialty Polymers LLC, 29345, 29346
Solve Needs International, 29347, 48741
Solvit, 29348
Solvox Manufacturing Company, 29349
Somat Company, 29350
Somebody's Mother's Chocolate, 11795
Somerset Food Service, 29351
Somerset Industries, 29352, 48742, 48743, 52105, 53444, 59422
Somerset Syrup & Concessions, 11796
Somerville Packaging, 29353, 29354
Something Different Linen, 29355, 48744
Something Natural LLC, 11797
Something Special Deli-Foods, 11798
Sommer Awning Company, 29356
Sommer Maid Creamery Inc, 11799
Sommer's Food Products, 11800
Sommers Organic, 11801, 48745
Sommers Plastic Product Co Inc, 29357, 48746
Sonderen Packaging, 29358
Sonic Air Systems Inc, 29359
Sonic Corp, 29360, 48747
Sonicor, 29361
Sonics & Materials Inc, 29362, 48748
Sonne, 11802
SONOCO, 11047, 59127
Sonoco Alloyd, 29363
Sonoco Paperboard Specialties, 29364, 48749
Sonoco Products Co, 29365, 59423
Sonoco ThermoSafe, 29366, 48750
Sonofresco, 29367
Sonoita Vineyards, 11803
Sonoma Creamery, 11804
Sonoma Flatbreads, 11805
Sonoma Gourmet, 11806
Sonoma Pacific Company, 29368
Sonoma Seafoods, 11807
Sonoma Signatures, 29369
Sonoma Syrup Co. Inc., 11808
Sonoma Wine Services, 11809
Sonoma-Cutrer Vineyards, 11810
Sonora Foods, 59424
Sonora Seafood Company, 48751
Sonstegard Foods Company, 59425
Sonwil Distribution Center, 52106, 53445
Soodhalter Plastics, 29370, 48752
Soofer Co, 48753, 59426
Sooner Scientific, 29371
SoOPAK, 29325
Soozy's Grain-Free, 11811, 59427
Sopak Co Inc, 52107, 53446
SOPAKCO Foods, 11048
Sopakco Foods, 11812
SOPAKCO Foods, 28708, 53382
SOPAKCO Packaging, 11049
Sopako Foods, 11813
Sophia Foods, 11814, 29372
Sophia's Sauce Works, 11815
Sopralco, 11816, 29373, 48754
Sorbee Intl., 11817, 48755, 59428
Sorensen Associates, 29374

Sorenson, 29375
Sorg Paper Company, 29376
Sorrenti Family Farms, 11818
Sorrento Lobster, 11819, 59429
Sortex, 29377, 48756
Sortie/Kohlhaas, 29378
SOS Global Express Inc, 52069, 53383
Sossner Steel Stamps, 29379, 48757
Soten, 29380
Soteria, 11820
Soudal Accumetric, 29381
Soudronic Limited, 41108
Sould Manufacturing, 29382
Souperb LLC, 11821
Soupergirl, 11822
SOUPerior Bean & Spice Company, 11050
Source Atlantique Inc, 48758
Source Distribution Logistics, 29383
Source Food Technology, 11823, 48759
Source for Packaging, 29386, 48760
Source Marketing, 29384
Source Naturals, 11824, 59430
Source Packaging Inc, 29385
Souris Valley Processors, 11825
South Akron Awning Co, 29387
South Atlantic Warehouse Corporation, 52108, 53447
South Beach Coffee Company, 11826
South Beach Novelties & Confectionery, 11827, 59431
South Bend Chocolate Co, 11828
South Bend Warehousing & Distribution, 52109, 53448
South Cape Seafood, 41109
South Carolina Beef Board, 48761
South Ceasar Dressing Company, 11829
South County Creamery, 11830
South East Sales, 41110
South Georgia Pecan Co, 11831, 48762
South Group Marketing, 41111
South Jersey Awning, 29388
South Jersey Paper Products, 59432
South Jersey Store Fixtures Co, 29389
South Mill, 11832, 48763, 52110, 53449
South River Machine, 29390
South Shore Controls Inc, 29391, 48764
South Shores Seafood, 11833, 59433
South Texas Freezer Company, 53450
South Texas Spice Co LTD, 11834
South Valley Citrus Packers, 29392, 59434
South Valley Farms, 11835, 48765
South Valley Mfg Inc, 29393
South Well Co, 29394
Southbend, 29395, 48766
Southeast Asia Market, 29396
Southeast Cold Storage, 59435
Southeast Dairy Processors Inc, 11836
Southeast Food Distribution, 53451
Southeast Foods, 48767
Southeast Industrial Equipment, 59436
Southeastern Filtration Systs, 29397
Southeastern Fisheries Assn, 11837, 29398
Southeastern Freezer, 53452
Southeastern Grocers, 11838, 59437, 59438
Southeastern Manufacturer's, 41112
Southeastern Mills Inc, 11839
Southeastern Paper Group Inc, 41113
Southend Janitorial Supply, 29399
Southern Ag Co Inc, 29400, 48768
Southern Aluminum, 48769
Southern Art Company, LLC, 11840
Southern Atlantic Label Co, 29401
Southern Automatics, 29402, 48770
Southern Awning & Sign Company, 29403
Southern Baking, 11841
Southern Bar-B-Que, 11842
Southern Belle Refrigerated, 53453
Southern Belle Sandwich Company, 11843
Southern Beverage Packers Inc, 11844

Southern Brown Rice, 11845
Southern California Brewing Company, 11846
Southern California Packaging, 29404
Southern Champion Tray LP, 29405, 48771
Southern Cold Storage Co, 53454
Southern Colorado Court Svc, 53455
Southern Commodities Inc, 41114
Southern Container Corporation, 29406
Southern Cotton Oil Co, 11847
Southern Culture Foods, 11848, 59439
Southern Delight Gourmet Foods, 11849
Southern Express, 29407
Southern Farms Fish Processors, 11850
Southern Film Extruders, 29408, 48772
Southern Fish & Oyster Company, 11851, 59440
Southern Flavoring Co, 11852
Southern Gardens Citrus, 11853, 29409, 48773
Southern Glazer's Wine-Spirits, LLC, 59441
Southern Gold Honey Co, 11854, 48774
Southern Grocery Company, 59442
Southern Heritage Coffee Company, 11855, 48775
Southern Ice Cream Specialties, 11856
Southern Imperial Inc, 29410, 48776
Southern Import Distributors, 59443
Southern Indiana Butcher's Supply, 59444
Southern Material Handling Co, 59445
Southern Metal Fabricators Inc, 29411, 48777
Southern Minnesota Beet Sugar Cooperative, 11857
Southern Missouri Containers, 29412
Southern Okie, 11858
Southern Packaging & Distribution, 53456
Southern Packaging Machinery, 29413, 29414, 29415
Southern Packing Corp, 11859
Southern Pallet, 29416
Southern Peanut Co Inc, 11860
Southern Perfection Fab, 29417
Southern Popcorn Company, 11861
Southern Pride Catfish Company, 11862, 48778
Southern Pride Distributing, 29418, 48779
Southern Produce Distributors, 59446
Southern Roasted Nuts, 11863
Southern Rubber Stamp, 29419, 48780
Southern Seafood Connection, 41115
Southern Seafood Distributors, 59447
Southern Season, 11864
Southern Shell Fish Company, 11865, 48781
Southern Shellfish, 11866, 59448
Southern Snow, 11867, 48782
Southern States Toyotalift, 59449
Southern Steel Shelving Company, 59450
Southern Stock Foodservice, 59451
Southern Store Fixtures Inc, 29420, 48783
Southern Style Nuts, 11868
Southern Supplies Limited, 59452
Southern Tailors Flag & Banner, 29421
Southern Tool, 29422, 48784
Southern Twist Cocktail, 11869
Southern United States Trade Association, 29423
Southern Warehousing & Distribution, 53457
Southern Warehousing-Dstrbtn, 53458
Southernfood.com LLC, 59453
Southland Packaging, 29424
Southline Equipment Company, 29425, 59454
Southpack LLC, 29426
Southshore Enterprises, 52111, 53459
Southside Market & Bbq Inc, 59455
Southside Seafood Inc, 11870, 59456

Southwest Cheese Company, 11871
Southwest Distributing Co, 59457
Southwest Endseals, 29427
Southwest Fixture, 29428
Southwest Foods, 11872
Southwest Forklift, 59458
Southwest Indiana and American Cold Storage, 29429
Southwest Lift, 59459
Southwest Logistics, 53460
Southwest Material Handling, 59460
Southwest Materials Handling, 59461
Southwest Neon Signs, 29430
Southwest Specialty Food, 11873
Southwest Spirit, 11874
Southwest Thermal Technology, 59462
Southwest Traders, 59463, 59464, 59465, 59466, 59467
Southwest Truck Service, 52112
Southwest Vault Builders, 29431
Southwestern Electric Power Company, 29432
Southwestern Motor Transport, 52113
Southwestern Porcelain Steel, 29433, 48785
Southworth Products Corp, 29434
Souza Food Service, 59468
Sovena USA Inc, 11875, 48786
Sovrana Trading Corp, 48787, 59469
Sow's Ear Winery, 11876
Sowden Brothers Farm, 11877, 48788
Soy Vay Enterprises, 11878
Soyatech Inc, 29435
Soyfoods of America, 11881
Soylent, 11882, 59470
Soylent Brand, 11883
SoyLife Division, 11879
Soynut Butter Co, 11884, 29436
SoyTex, 11880
SP Enterprises, Inc., 11051
SP Graphics, 28709
SP Industries, 28710, 48288
SP Industries Inc, 28711, 48289
Spa Natural Spring Water, 48789
Space Center Inc, 52114, 53461
Space Maker Systems, 59471
Spaceguard Products, 29437
Spacekraft Packaging, 29438, 29439
Spacesaver Corp, 29440, 48790
Span Tech LLC, 29441
Spanco Crane & Monorail Systems, 29442, 48791
Spangler Candy Co, 11885, 48792
Spangler Vineyards, 11886
Spanish Gardens Food Manufacturing, 11887
Spann Sign Company, 29443
Spantec Systems, 59472
Spar Mixers, 59473
Sparboe Foods Corp, 11888, 48793, 59474
Sparkler Filters Inc, 29444, 48794
Sparkletts, 11889
Sparks Belting Co, 29445, 48795, 59475
Sparks Companies, 29446
Sparrow Enterprises LTD, 48796, 59476
Sparrow Lane, 11890
Spartan Flag Co, 29447
Spartan Foods, 59477
Spartan Logistics, 52115, 53462
Spartan Showcase, 29448, 48797
Spartan Tool LLC, 29449
Spartanburg Steel Products Inc, 29450
Spartanics, 29451
SpartanNash Co, 59478
Spartec Plastics, 29452, 48798
Spartech Plastics, 29453, 29454, 48799, 48800
Spartech Poly Com, 29455, 48801
Spaten North America Inc, 11891
Spaten West, Inc, 48802, 53463
Spaulding & Assoc, 11892
SPC Transport Co, 52070
Spear Packing, 29456
Special Events Supply Company, 29457

1439

All Companies Index

Special Products, 29458
Specialities Importers & Distributers, 11894, 29459, 48803
Specialized Packaging London, 29460
Specialized Promotions, 59479
SpecialTeas, 11893
Specialty Bakers, 11895, 48804
Specialty Blades, 29461, 48805
Specialty Box & Packaging, 29462, 59480
Specialty Cheese Co Inc, 11896
Specialty Cheese Group Limited, 29463
Specialty Coffee Roasters, 11897, 48806
Specialty Commodities Inc, 11898, 29464, 48807
Specialty Equipment Company, 29465, 29466, 48808, 48809
Specialty Equipment Sales Co, 41116
Specialty Films & Associates, 29467
Specialty Food America Inc, 11899, 29468
Specialty Food Association, 11900
Specialty Food Magazine, 11901
Specialty Foods Group Inc, 11902, 48810, 59481
Specialty Foods South LLC, 11903
Specialty House of Creation, 59482
Specialty Ingredients, 11904
Specialty Lubricants, 29469
Specialty Meats & Gourmet, 11905, 48811
Specialty Merchandise Distributors, 59483
Specialty Minerals Inc, 11906, 48812
Specialty Packaging Inc, 29470, 48813
Specialty Paper Bag Company, 29471
Specialty Partners, 41117
Specialty Products, 11907, 48814
Specialty Rice Inc, 11908, 48815
Specialty Sales & Marketing, 41118
Specialty Saw Inc, 29472
Specialty Wood Products, 29473, 48816
Specific Mechanical Systems, 29474, 48817
Speco Inc, 11909, 48818
Spectape Inc, 29475
Spectratek Technologies Inc, 29476
Spectro, 29477, 48819
Spectronics Corp, 29478
Spectrum Ascona, 29479
Spectrum Enterprises, 29480
Spectrum Foods Inc, 11910, 48820
Spectrum Foodservice Associates, 41119
Spectrum Foodservices, 41120
Spectrum Plastics, 29481
Spee-Dee Packaging Machinery, 29482, 48821
Speed Queen, 48822
Speedrack Products Group LTD, 29483
Speedways Conveyors, 29484, 48823
Spelt Right Foods, LLC, 11911
Spence & Company, 11912, 48824
Spence Wells Assoc, 41121
Spencer & Assoc, 41122
Spencer Business Form Company, 29485
Spencer Packing Company, 11913, 29486
Spencer Research Inc, 29487
Spencer Strainer Systems, 29488
Spencer Turbine Co, 29489, 48825
Spener Restaurant Design, 59484
Sperling Boss, 29490
Sperling Industries, 29491, 29492, 29493, 48826, 48827
Sperry Apiaries, 11914
Speupak, 59485
SPG International, 28712, 48290
Sphinx Adsorbents Inc, 59486
SPI West Port, Inc, 11052
SPI's Film and Bag Federation, 28713
Spice & Spice, 11915, 48828, 59487
Spice Chain, 11916
Spice Galleon, 11917
Spice House International Specialties, 11918, 48829, 59488
Spice Hunter Inc, 11919

Spice King Corporation, 11920, 48830
Spice Lab, 11921
Spice O' Life, 11922
Spice Of Life Co, 11923
Spice Rack Chocolates, 11924
Spice Rack Extracts, 41123
Spice Time Foods, 11925
Spice World Inc, 11926, 48831
Spiceland, 11927
Spicely, 11928
Spices of Life Gourmet Coffee, 11929
Spicetec Flavors & Seasonings, 11930, 29494
Spicy Sense, 11931
Spiech Farms Fruit & Floral, 11932
Spike Seasoning Magic, 11933
Spilke's Baking Company, 11934
Spin-Tech Corporation, 29495, 48832
Spinato's Fine Foods, 11935
Spinco Metal Products Inc, 29496, 48833
Spindrift Beverage, 11936
Spinelli Coffee Company, 11937
Spinney Creek Shellfish, 11938
Spinzer, 29497
Spir-It/Zoo Piks, 29498, 48834
Spiral Biotech Inc, 29499, 48835, 59489
Spiral Manufacturing Co Inc, 29500, 48836
Spiral Slices Ham Market, 29501
Spiral Systems, 29502
Spiral-Matic Corp, 29503
Spirax Sarco Inc, 29504
Spirit Foodservice, Inc., 29505, 48837
Spiro-Cut Equipment Co, 29506
Spiroflow Systems Inc, 29507
Spitz USA, 11939
Splendid Specialties, 11940
Splendid Spreads, 11941
Spoetzl Brewery, 11942
Spohrers Bakeries, 11943
Spokandy, 11944
Spokane House of Hose Inc, 29508
Spokane Produce, 59490
Spokane Seed Co, 11945, 48838
Spontex, 29509
Spoonable, 11946, 48839, 59491
Sportabs International, 11947, 48840
Sporting Colors LLC, 11948
Sportsman's Paradise Whites Ranch, 11949
Sportsmen's Cannery, 11950
Sportsmen's Cannery & Smokehouse, 11951, 29510
Sportsmens Seafoods, 11952
Spot Cash Specialty Com pany, 59492
Spot Wire Works Company, 29511
Spotted Tavern Winery & Dodd's Cider Mill, 11953
Spottswoode, 11954
Sprague Foods, 11955
Spray Drying, 29512, 48841
Spray Dynamics LTD, 29513, 48842
Spray Tek Inc, 29514
Spraying Systems Company, 29515, 48843
Spraymation Inc, 29516
Sprayway Inc, 29517, 48844
Sprecher Brewing Co, 11956
Spreda Group, 11957, 48845
Spring Acres Sales Company, 11958
Spring Air Systems, 29518
Spring Cove Container Div, 29519
Spring Creek Natural Foods, 11959
Spring Glen Fresh Foods, 11960
Spring Grove Foods, 11961
Spring Hill Meat Market, 11962
Spring Hill Pure Water, 11963
Spring Kitchen, 11964
Spring Ledge Farm Stand, 11965
Spring Mountain Vineyard, 11966
Spring Street Bake Shop, 11967
Spring USA Corp, 11968, 48846
Spring Wood Products, 29521
Springbank Cheese Company, 11968
Springdale Cheese Factory, 11969

Springdale Ice Cream & Bev, 11970
Springer-Penguin, 29522, 48847
Springfield Creamery Inc, 11971, 48848
Springfield Metal Products Co, 29523
Springfield Produce Company, 59493
Springfield Underground, 53464
Springhill Cellars, 11972
Springhill Farms, 11973
Springport Steel Wire Products, 29524, 48849
Springprint Medallion, 29525
Springville Meat & Cold Storage, 11974
Sprinkles Cupcakes, 11975
Sprinkman Corporation, 29526, 59494
Sprinter Marking Inc, 29527
Sprout Creek Farm, 11976, 48850
Sprout House, 11977
Sprout Nutrition, 11978
Sprouters, 59495
Sprouts Farmers Market Inc., 11979, 29528
Spruce Foods, 11980, 48851
Spruce Lane Investments, 11981
Spruce Mountain Blueberries, 11982
Sprucewood Handmade Cookie Company, 11983
Spudnik Equipment Co, 29529, 48852
Spuds N' Stuff, 59496
Spurgeon Co, 29530, 48853
Spurgeon Vineyards & Winery, 11984
Spurrier Chemical Companies, 29531
Spurry & Associates, 41124
SPX Corporation, 28714
SPX Flow Inc, 28715, 28716, 48291, 48292
SQP, 28717, 48293
Squab Producers of California, 11985, 48854
Squair Food Company, 11986
Squar-Buff, 29532, 48855
Square Enterprises Corp, 48856, 59497
Square One Organics, 11987
Square-H Brands Inc, 11988
Squid Ink, 59498
Squid Ink Mfg Inc, 29533
Squier Associates, 41125
Squire Boone Village, 11989
Squire Corrugated Container Company, 29534
Squirrel Brand Company, 11990
Squirrel Systems, 29535, 48857
SRA Foods, 11053, 59128
SRC Vision, 28718
SRI, 28719
SSE Software Corporation, 28720
SSOE Group, 28721
SSW Holding Co Inc, 28722, 48294
St Armands Baking Co, 11991
St Arnold Brewing Co, 11992
St Charles Trading Inc, 11993, 41126, 41127, 48858, 52116
St Clair Ice Cream Co, 11994
St Francis Winery & Vineyards, 11995
St Innocent Winery, 11996
St John's Botanicals, 11997, 48859, 59499
St Joseph Packaging Inc, 29536, 48860
St Julian Winery, 11998, 48861
St Laurent Brothers, 11999
St Mary Sugar Co-Op, 12000
St Onge Ruff & Associates, 29537, 52117
ST Restaurant Supplies, 28723, 48295, 59129
St-Germain Bakery, 12001
St. Amour Inc/French Cookies, 12002
St. Clair Foods Distributing, 59500
St. Clair Industries, 12003, 48862
St. Clair Pakwell, 29538, 48863
St. Cloud Restaurant Supply, 59501
St. Croix Beer Company, 12004
St. Elizabeth Street Display Corporation, 29539
St. George Crystal, 29540
St. Helen Seafoods, 59502
St. Jacobs Candy Co., 12005

St. James Sugar Cooperative, 12006
St. James Winery, 12007
St. John Brothers, 52118
St. Julien Macaroons, 12008
St. Killian Importing, 48864
St. Lawrence Starch, 12009
St. Louis Carton Company, 29541
St. Louis Stainless Service, 29542
St. Maurice Laurent, 12010
St. Ours & Company, 12011, 41128, 59503
St. Pierre Box & Lumber Company, 29543
St. Simons Seafood, 12012, 59504
St. Simons Trading, 29544
St. Stan's Brewing Company, 12013
STA Packaging Tapes, 28724
Sta-Rite Ginnie Lou Inc, 29545, 48865
Staban Engineering Corp, 29546
Stablized Products, 29547
Stacey's Famous Foods, 12014
Stack & Store Systems, 59505
Stackbin Corp, 29548
Stacy's Pita Chip Co, 12015
Stadelman Fruit LLC, 12016, 48866
Stadia Corporation, 29549
Staff Of Life Natural Foods, 12017
Stafford County Flour Mills Company, 12018
Stafford-Smith Inc, 29550
Stage Coach Sauces, 29551
Stage One Coldstorage, 53465
Stags' Leap Winery, 12019
Stahl, 59506
Stahlbush Island Farms Inc, 12020, 48867
Stahmann Farms, 12021
Stainless, 29552, 48868
Stainless Equipment & Systems, 59507
Stainless Equipment Manufacturing, 29553
Stainless Fabricating Company, 29554
Stainless Fabrication Inc, 29555
Stainless International, 29556
Stainless Motors Inc, 29557
Stainless One DispensingSystem, 29558, 48869
Stainless Products, 29559, 48870
Stainless Specialists Inc, 29560, 48871
Stainless Steel, 29561
Stainless Steel Coatings, 29562, 48872
Stainless Steel Fabricator Inc, 29563, 29565
Stainless Steel Fabricators, 29564
StainlessDrains.com, 29566
Stallings Head Cheese Co, 12022
Stamfag Cutting Dies, 29567
Stamoolis Brothers Co, 59508
Stampede Meat, Inc., 12023, 29568
Stampendous, 29569, 48873
Stan-Mark Food Products Inc, 12024, 48874
Stancase Equipment Company, 29570
Stanchfield Farms, 12025
Stand Fast Pkgng Prods Inc, 29571
Standard Bakery Inc, 12026
Standard Casing Company, 29572, 48875
Standard Electric Time, 59509
Standard Folding Cartons Inc, 29573, 48876
Standard Forms, 59510
Standard Fruit & Vegetable Company, 48877, 59511
Standard Functional Foods Grp, 12027, 48878
Standard Meat Co LP, 12028, 48879, 59512
Standard Paper Box Mach Co Inc, 29574, 48880
Standard Pump, 29575
Standard Rate Review, 29576
Standard Refrigeration Co, 29577, 48881
Standard Restaurant Equipment, 59513
Standard Terry Mills, 29578, 48882

All Companies Index

Standard Transportation Svc, 52119, 53466
Standard Warehouse, 52120, 53467
Standard-Knapp Inc, 29579
Standard-Rosenbaum, 59514
Standex International Corp., 29580
Stanford Chemicals, 29581
Stanford Refrigerated Warehouse, 53469
Stanford Refrigerated Warehouses, 53468
Stanford Trading Company, 59515
Stanfos, 29582, 48883, 59516
Stangl's Bakery, 12029
Stanislaus Food Prod, 12030
Stanley Access Technologies, 29583, 48884
Stanley Black & Decker Inc, 29584
Stanley Orchards Sales, Inc., 12031, 48885, 52121, 53470
Stanley Provision Company, 12032
Stanley Roberts, 29585
Stanley's Best Seafood, 12033, 59517
Stanly Fixtures Co Inc, 29586
Stanpac, Inc., 29587, 48886
Stanz Foodservice Inc, 53471, 59518
Stapleton Inc, 59519
Stapleton Spence Packing Co, 48887
Staplex Co Inc, 29588, 48888
Stapling Machines Co, 29589, 48889
Star Anise Foods, 12034
Star Container Company, 29590
Star Container Corporation, 29591
Star Distribution Systems, 52122, 53472
Star Filters, 29592, 48890
Star Fine Foods, 12035
Star Fisheries, 59520, 59521
Star Glove Company, 29593
Star Industries, Inc., 29594, 48891
Star Kay White Inc, 12036, 48892
Star Label Products Inc, 29595
Star Manufacturing Intl Inc, 29596, 48893
Star Micronics, 29597
Star of the West Milling Co., 12041
Star Pacific Inc, 29598, 48894
Star Packaging Corporation, 59522
Star Poly Bag Inc, 29599, 48895
Star Produce, 59523, 59524, 59525, 59526
Star Ravioli Mfg Co, 12037
Star Restaurant Equipment & Supply Company, 29600, 59527
Star Route Farms, 12038
Star Sales Company, 59528, 59529
Star Seafood, 12039, 59530
Star Shipping, 52123
Star Snacks, 12040
Star Wholesale, 59531
Star-K Kosher Certification, 29601
Starbrook Industries Inc, 29602, 59532
Starbruck Foods Corporation, 48896, 59533
Starbucks, 12042, 48897
Starflex Corporation, 29603
Starich, 12043, 59534
Stark Candy Company, 12044, 48898
Starkel Poultry, 12045, 48899
Starkey Chemical Process Company, 29604, 48900
Starkist Co, 12046
Starliper & Associates, 41129
Starlite Food Service Equipment, 29605
Starlite Manufacturing/Sugar Daddy's, 48901
STARMIX srl, 28725
Starport Foods, 12047
Starr & Brown, 12048
Starr Distribution Services Company, 52124, 53473
Starr Hill Winery & Vineyard, 12049
Start International, 29606
Startupcandy Co, 12050
Starview Packaging Machinery, 29607, 48902
Starwest Botanicals Inc, 12051, 48903
Stasero International, 12052
Stash Tea Co, 12053
Stassen North America, 12054
Statco Engineering, 29608
State Center Warehouse & Cold Storage, 53474
State Container Corp, 29609
State Fish Distributors, 12055, 59535
State Garden Inc., 12056
State Hotel Supply Company, 59536
State Industrial Products Corp, 29610
State Line Potato Chip Company, 59537
State Of Maine Cheese Co, 12057
State Products, 29611, 48904
State Restaurant Equipment Co, 59538
State Wholesale Grocers, 59539
Statewide Brokerage Company, 41130
Statewide Meats & Poultry, 12058, 59540
Statewide Products Co Inc, 59541
Statex, 29612, 59542
Stauber Performance Ingrdients, 12059, 48905
Stauffer Biscuit Co, 12060, 48906
Stauffer's, 12061
Staunton Foods LLC, 59543
Staunton Fruit & Produce Company, 59544
Stavin Inc, 29613
Stavis Seafoods, 12062, 48907, 59545
Stawnichy Holdings, 12063
Stay Tuned Industries, 29614, 48908, 59546
STD Precision Gear, 28726, 48296
Ste Chapelle Winery, 12064
STE Michelle Wine Estates, 11054, 48297
Steak-Umm Company, 12065, 48909
Steamway Corporation, 29615
Stearns Packaging Corp, 29616
Stearns Technical Textiles Company, 29617, 48910
Stearns Wharf Vintners, 12066
Stearnswood Inc, 29618, 48911
Steckel Produce, 12067, 59547
Steckel, Isadore, 59548
Steel Art Co, 29619, 48912
Steel Art Signs, 29620
Steel City Corporation, 29621, 48913, 59549
Steel Craft Fluorescent Company, 29622, 48914
Steel King Industries, 29623, 48915
Steel Products, 29624, 48916
Steel Storage Systems Inc, 29625, 48917
Steel's Gourmet Foods, Ltd., 12068, 48918
Steelite International USA, 29626, 48919
Steelmaster Material Handling, 29627, 48920
Steep & Brew, 12069, 29628
Stefani Premium Foods, 12070
Stefanich & Company, 29629
Stefano Foods, 12071
Stegall Mechanical INC, 29630, 48921
Stehlin & Sons Company, 12072
Stein-DSI, 29631
Steinberg Quebec: Aligro, 59550
Steiner Cheese, 12073
Steiner Company, 29632, 48922
Steiner Foods, 59551
Steiner Industries Inc, 29633, 48923
Steinfurth Inc Electromechanical Measuring Systems, 59552
Steinfurth Instruments, 59553
Steingart Associates Inc, 29634
Steinmetz Machine Works Inc, 29635
Stella D'oro, 12074, 48924
Stella Foods, 12075
Stella Maria's, 59554
Stella Reedsburg, 12076
Stellar Group, 29636
Stellar Pasta Company, 12077
Stellar Steam, 29637
Stello Foods Inc, 12078
Stello Products Inc, 29638
Stelray Plastic Products Inc, 29639
Steltzner Vineyards, 12079
Stemm Transfer & Storage, 52125, 53475
Stengel Seed & Grain Co, 12080, 48925, 53476
Step Products, 29640
Stepan Co., 12081, 48926
Stephan Machinery GmbH, 29641, 48927
Stephan Machinery, Inc., 29642, 48928, 59555
Steri Technologies Inc, 29643, 29644, 48929
Sterigenics International, 29645
Steril-Sil Company, 29646, 48930
STERIS Corp, 28727
Steritech Food Safety & Environmental Hygiene, 29647
Sterling Ball & Jewel, 29648, 48931
Sterling Bay Companies, 53477
Sterling Candy, Inc., 12082, 59556
Sterling Caviar LLC, 12083, 12084
Sterling China Company, 29649
Sterling Corp, 29650, 48932
Sterling Electric Inc, 29651
Sterling Extract Co Inc, 12085
Sterling Foods LLC, 12086
Sterling Net & Twine Company, 29652, 48933
Sterling Novelty Products, 29653, 48934
Sterling Paper Company, 29654, 48935
Sterling Process Engineering, 29655
Sterling Promotional Corporation, 59557
Sterling Rubber, 29656, 48936
Sterling Scale Co, 29657, 48937, 59558
Sterling Systems & Controls, 29658, 48938
Sterling Transportation, 52126
Sterling Truck Corporation, 29659
Sterling Vineyards, 12087
Stern Ingredients, 41131
Stern International Consultants, 41132, 48939
Sterner Lighting Systems, 29660, 48940
Sterno, 29661, 48941
Stero Co, 29662, 48942
Stertil Alm Corp, 29663, 48943
Sterzing Food Co, 12088
Steuk's Country Market & Winery, 12089
Steve & Andy's Organics, 12090
Steve Connolly Seafood Co Inc, 12091
Steve Mendez, 12092
Steve's Authentic Key Lime Pies, 12093, 48944
Steve's Doughnut Shop, 12094
Steve's Fine Food Emporium, 59559
Steve's Ice Cream, Craft Collective, 12095
Steve's Mom, 12096
Steve's PaleoGoods, 12097
Steven Label Corp, 29664
Steven Roberts Originals, 12098
Stevenot Winery, 12099
Stevens & Associates, 41133
Stevens Creative Enterprises, Inc., 12100
Stevens Linen Association, 29665, 48945
Stevens Point Brewery, 12101, 48946
Stevens Sausage Co, 12102
Stevens Transport, 29666, 52127
Stevens Tropical Plantation, 12103, 48947
Stevenson Co, 59560
Stevenson-Cooper Inc, 12104, 29667, 48948
Stevison Ham Co, 12105
Stevita Naturals, 12106, 59561
Steviva Ingredients, 12107
Stewart & Stevenson LLC, 59562
Stewart Assembly & Machining, 29668, 48949
Stewart Candies, 12108
Stewart Laboratories, 29669
Stewart Marketing Services, 29670
Stewart Mechanical Seals, 29671
Stewart Sutherland Inc, 29672
Stewart Systems Baking LLC, 29673, 29674, 48950
Stewart Wholesale Hardware Company, 59563
Stewart's Beverages, 12109
Stewart's Private Blend Foods, 12110, 48951
Stewart's Shops Corp, 12111
Stewarts Market, 12112
Stewarts Seafood, 12113
Stewarts Tristate Svc Co, 59564, 59565
STI Certified Products Inc, 48298
STI International, 41043, 48299, 59130
Stichler Products Inc, 12114, 48952
Stick Pack USA, 48953
StickerYou, 29675
Stickney & Poor Company, 12115, 48954
Stickney Hill Dairy Inc, 12116, 29676
Sticky Fingers Bakeries, 12117
Sticky Toffee Pudding Company, 12118
Stiebs, 12119
Stiefel Associates, 41134
Stigler Supply Co, 59566
Stiles Enterprises Inc, 29677, 59567
Stimo-O-Stam, Ltd., 12120, 48955
Stinking Rose, The, 12121
Stirling Foods, 12122, 48956
Stirrings, 12123
STM Mortgage Co, 28728
STOBER Drives Inc, 28729
Stock America Inc, 29678, 59568
Stock Popcorn Ind Inc, 12124, 48957
Stock Rack & Shelving Inc, 59569
Stock Yards Packing Company, 12125, 48958
Stockdale & Reagan, 41135
Stocker & Son Inc, 29679
Stockett Associates, 41136
Stockton Cold Storage, 53478
Stockton Graham & Co, 12126, 59570
Stoffel Equipment Co Inc, 59571
Stoffel Seals Corp, 29680, 29681, 48959, 48960
Stogsdill Tile Co, 29682, 48961
Stokes, 29683
Stokes Canning Company, 12127
Stokes Material Handling Systs, 29684
Stolle Machinery Co LLC, 29685
Stoller Fisheries, 12128, 48962
Stone Brewing, 12129
Stone Container, 29686, 29687, 48963
Stone Crabs Inc, 12130, 41137, 59572
Stone Enterprises Inc., 29688, 48964
Stone Forwarding Company, 52128
Stone Hill Winery, 12131
Stone Meat Processor, 12132
Stone Mountain Pecan Co, 12133
Stone Mountain Vineyards, 12134
Stone Soap Co Inc, 29689, 48965
Stone's Home Made Candy Shop, 12135
Stonegate, 12137
Stonegrill America, 48967
StoneHammer Brewing, 12136, 48966
Stonepath Logistics, 52129, 53479
Stoner, 29690
Stoneridge Winery, 12138
Stonewall Kitchen, 12139, 48968
Stoneway Carton Company, 29691, 48969
Stonhard, 29692
Stonhard, Inc., 29693
Stonie's Sausage Shop, 12140
Stonington Lobster Co-Op, 12141, 59573
Stonington Vineyards, 12142
Stony Hill Vineyard, 12143
Stonybrook Mountain Winery, 12144
Stonyfield Organic, 12145, 59574
Stop & Shop Manufacturing, 12146, 59575
STOP Restaurant Supply Ltd, 59131
Stor-Loc, 29694
Stor-Rite Freezer Storage, 29695
Storad Tape Company, 29696
Storage Equipment, 59576
Storage Unlimited, 29697, 48970
Storax, 29698
Storck Canada, 12147

1441

All Companies Index

Storck U.S.A., 12148
StoreHouse Foods, 12149
Stork Fabricators Inc, 29699
Stork Food Dairy Systems, 29700
Stork Food Machinery, 29701
Stork Townsend Inc., 29702, 48971
Storm Industrial, 29703, 48972
Stormax International, 29704, 48973
Storopack Packaging Systs USA, 29705
Storrs Winery, 12150
Storsack Inc, 29706
Story Winery, 12151
Story's Popcorn Company, 12152
Stoudt Brewing Co, 12153
Stout Sign Company, 29707, 48974
Stoutridge Vineyard, 12154
Strahl & Pitsch Inc, 29708
Strahman Valves Inc, 29709, 48975
Straight Line Filters, 29710
Straits Steel & Wire Co, 29711
Strand Lighting, 29712, 48976
Strapack, 29713
STRAPEX Corporation, 28730
Strapex Corporation, 29714
Strasburg Provision, 12155
Strasburger & Siegel, 29715
Strasheim Wholesale, 59577
Strassburger Steaks, 12156
Stratecon, 29716
Stratecon International Consultants, 29717, 59578
Strategic Development Concepts, 53480
Strategic Equipment & Supply, 29718
Strathroy Foods, 12157, 48977
Stratis Plastic Pallets, 29719
Stratix Corp, 29720
Straub Brewery Inc, 12158
Straub Designs Co, 29721, 29722, 48978, 48979
Straub's, 12159
Straubel Company, 29723
Straus Family Creamery, 12160
Strauss Bakery, 12161, 59579
Strauss Brands International, 12162
Strawberry Commission, 48980
Strawberry Hill Grand Delights, 12163
Strawhacker's Food Service, 59580
Streamfeeder, 29724
Streamline Foods, 59581
Streamline Shippers-Affiliates, 52130, 53481
Streater Inc, 29725
Streator Dependable Mfg, 29726, 48981
Strebin Farms, 12164
Streblow Vineyards, 12165
Streich Equipment Co Inc, 59582
Streit Carl & Son Co, 12166, 59583
Streit's, 12167
Stremick's Heritage Foods, 12168, 48982
Stretch Island Fruit, 12169, 48983
Stretch-Vent Packaging System, 29727, 48984
Stretchtape, 29728
Stribbons, 29729
Stricker & Co, 29730
Stricklin Co, 29731, 48985
Stripling's General Store, 12170
Stripper Bags, 29732, 48986
Stroh Brewery, 12171
Stroh's Beer, 12172
Strohmeyer & Arpe Co Inc, 29733, 48987
Stronach & Sons, 59584
Strong & Associates, 41138
Strong Hold Products, 29734
Strong Roots, 12173
Strongarm, 29735
Strongbow Foods, 59585
Stronghaven Containers Co, 29736, 48988
Strossner's Bakery & Cafe, 12174
Stroter Inc, 29737
Stroup Ingredients Resources, 41139
Strub Pickles, 12175, 48989
Strube Celery & Vegetable Co, 12176

Structural Transport, 29738
Structure, 29739
Structure Probe, 29740
Stryco Wire Products, 29741
Stryka Botanical Co, 59586
Stryka Botanics, 59587, 59588
Stryker Sonoma, 12177
Stuart & CO, 12178, 59589
Stuart Hale Co, 12179
Stuart W Johnson & Co, 29742
Stubb's Legendary BBQ, 12180
Studd & Whipple Company, 29743
Stumptown Coffee Roasters Inc, 12181
Sturdi-Bilt Restaurant Equipment, 29744
Sturdivant Company, 41140
Sturgill Food Brokerage, 41141
Sturm Foods Inc, 12182, 48990
Stutz Candy Company, 12183
Stutz Products Corp, 29745
Stylmark Inc, 29746, 48991
Suan Farma, 29747
Subco Foods Inc, 12184
Suburban Corrugated Box Company, 29748
Suburban Laboratories Inc, 29749
Suburban Sign Company, 29750
Suburban Signs, 29751
Success Systems, 29752
Sucesores de Pedro Cortes, 12185, 48992, 59590
SuckerPunch Gourmet, 12186
Sucre, 12187, 12188
Sudbury Soups and Salads, 12189
Sudlersville Frozen Food Locker, 12190
Sudmo North America, Inc, 29753
Sudwerk Privatbrauerei Hubsch, 12191
SUEZ Water Technologies & Solutions, 28731, 48300
Suffolk Banana Company, 59591
Suffolk Cold Storage, 53482
Suffolk Iron Works Inc, 29754, 48993
Sugai Kona Coffee, 12192
Sugar & Plumm, 12193
Sugar Bob's Smoked Maple Syrup, 12194
Sugar Bowl Bakery, 12195
Sugar Cane Growers Co-Op of Florida, 12196
Sugar Creek, 12197, 29755, 48994
Sugar Creek Winery, 12198
Sugar Flowers Plus, 12199
Sugar Foods Corp, 12200, 12201, 48995
Sugar Plum, 12202
Sugar Plum LLC, 12203, 29756
Sugar Stix, 48996
Sugar Sugar, 12204
Sugarbush Farm, 12206
SugarCreek, 12205
Sugardale Foods Inc, 12207
Sugarman of Vermont, 12208, 48997
Sugarplum Desserts, 12209, 29757, 59592
Sugarright, 12210
Suhner Manufacturing, 29758
Suisan, 59593
Suity Confections Co, 12211, 48998, 59594
Suiza Dairy Corporation, 12212
Suja Juice, 12213
Suji's Korean Cuisine, 12214
Sukhi's Gourmet Indian Food, 12215
Suki, 59595
Sullivan & Fitzgerald Food Brokers, 41142, 48999
Sullivan Harbor Farm, 12216
Sullivan Transportation Inc, 53483
Sullivan Vineyards, 12217
Sulpice Chocolate, 12218
Sultan Linen Service, 29759, 49000
Sumitomo Machinery Corp, 29760
Summer Fresh, 12219
Summer Garden Food Manufacturing, 12220
Summer In Vermont Jams, 12221
Summerfield Farm Products, 12222

Summerfield Foods, 12223, 49001
Summerland Sweets, 12224
Summertime Restaurant Equipment, 59596
Summit Brewing Company, 12225
Summit Brokerage, 41143
Summit Commercial, 29761, 49002, 49003
Summit Food Service Distributors, 59597, 59598
Summit FS LTD, 41144
Summit Hill Flavors, 12226, 49004
Summit Import Corp, 49005, 59599
Summit Industrial Equipment, 29762
Summit Lake Vineyards, 12227
Summit Machine Builders Corporation, 29763, 49006
Summit Premium Tree Nuts, 29764
Summitville Tiles Inc, 29765
Sun Chlorella USA, 12228, 49007, 59600
Sun Empire Foods, 12229
Sun Food Service Brokerage, 41145
Sun Garden Sprouts, 12230
Sun Glo Of Idaho, 12231, 49008
Sun Grove Foods Inc, 12232, 49009
Sun Groves Inc, 12233
Sun Harvest Foods Inc, 12234, 49010
Sun Harvest Salt, LLC, 49011
Sun Hing Foods, 59601
Sun Industries, 29766
Sun Marketing Agents Inc, 41146
Sun Noodle, 12235
Sun Noodle New Jersey, 12236, 49012
Sun Olive Oil Company, 12237
Sun Opta Inc., 12238
Sun Orchard INC, 12239
Sun Orchard Inc, 12240
Sun Pac Foods, 12241, 49013
Sun Pacific, 12242
Sun Paints & Coatings, 29767, 49014
Sun Plastics, 29768
Sun Ray International, 12243
Sun Ray Sign Group Inc, 29769
Sun Rich Fresh Foods USA Inc, 12244, 41147
Sun Star Heating Products Inc, 59602
Sun State Beverage, 12245
Sun States, 12246
Sun Sun Food Products, 12247
Sun Tropics Inc, 12248
Sun Valley Fruit Company, 59603
Sun Valley Mustard, 12249
Sun Valley Packing, 12250, 59604
Sun Valley Raisins Inc, 12251
Sun West, 12252
Sun West Foods, 12253, 49015
Sun West Trading, 49016, 59605
Sun World Intl LLC, 12254
Sun-Brite Canning, 12255, 49017
Sun-Maid Growers of California, 12256, 49018
Sun-Re Cheese Co, 12257
Sun-Rise, 12258
Sun-Rype Products, 12259
Sunbeam Products Co LLC, 29770
Sunbelt Industrial Trucks, 59607
Sunburst Foods, 12264, 59608
Sunburst Trout Farms, 12265, 59609
SunButter, 12260
Sunchef Farms, 12266, 59610
Sunco & Frenchie, 12267, 29771, 49020
Suncrest Farms, 12268
Suncrest Farms LLC, 59611
Sundance Architectural Prod, 29772
Sundance Industries, 12269
Sunday House Foods, 12270
Sunderland Dispensing Service, 59612
Sundia Corp, 12271
Sundial Herb Garden, 12272, 49021
Sundown Foods USA, Inc., 41148
Sundyne Corp, 29773
Sunergia Soyfoods, 12273
SunFed Ranch, 12261
Sunflower Food Company, 59613
Sunflower Packaging, 29774

Sunflower Restaurant Supply, 49022, 59614
Sunfood, 12274, 49023
Sunfresh Beverages Inc., 12275
Sunfresh Foods, 12276
Sungjae Corporation, 29775, 29776
Sunja's Oriental Foods, 12277
Sunkist Foodservice Equipment, 59615
Sunkist Growers, 29777, 49024, 59616
Sunland Distribution, 53484
Sunland Inc/Peanut Better, 12278
Sunland Manufacturing Company, 29778
Sunlike Juice, 12279, 49025
Sunmark Special Markets, 29779
Sunmaster Of Naples Inc, 29780
Sunny Avocado, 12280, 49026
Sunny Cove Citrus LLC, 29781
Sunny Delight Beverage Company, 12281
Sunny Dell Foods Inc, 12282
Sunny Fresh Foods, 12283
Sunny South Pecan Company, 12284
Sunnydale Meats Inc, 12285
Sunnyland Farms, 12286, 49027
Sunnyland Mills, 12287
Sunnyrose Cheese, 12288
Sunnyside Farms, 12289
Sunnyside Farms LLC, 12290
Sunnyside Organics Seedlings, 12291
Sunnyside Vegetable Packing, 12292
Sunpoint Products, 29782
Sunray Food Products Corporation, 12293
Sunrich LLC, 12294, 49028
Sunridge Farms, 12295, 49029
SunRidge Farms, 59606
Sunridge Farms Inc, 12296
Sunrise Commodities, 49030
Sunrise Fruit Company, 49031, 59617
Sunrise Growers, 12297, 49032
Sunrise Markets, 12298
Sunrise Winery, 12299
Sunroc Corporation, 29783, 49033
Sunset Farm Foods Inc, 12300, 49034
Sunset of Queens, 59619
Sunset Paper Products, 29784
Sunset Sales, 29785
Sunset Specialty Foods, 12301, 49035
Sunset Wholesale West, 59618
Sunshine Bar Supply Company, 59620
Sunshine Burger & Spec Food Co, 12302
Sunshine Dairy, 12303
Sunshine Dairy Foods Inc, 12304
Sunshine Farm & Garden, 12305, 49036
Sunshine Farms, 12306, 59621
Sunshine Food Sales, 12307, 49037
Sunshine Fresh, 12308, 59622
Sunshine International Foods, 12309
Sunshine Nut Company, 12310, 49038
Sunshine Seafood, 12311, 59623
Sunspun Foodservice, 59624
Sunstone Vineyards & Winery, 12312
Sunsweet Growers Inc., 12313, 49039
Suntec Power, 49040, 59625
Sunterra Meats, 12314, 49041
Suntory International, 12315
Suntreat Packing & Shipping Co, 59626
Sunup Green Coffee, 12316
SunWest Foods, Inc., 12262, 49019
SunWest Organics, 12263
Sunwest Sales Co, 41149
Sup Herb Farms, 12317, 29786
Supelco Inc, 29787, 49043
Super Beta Glucan, 29788, 59627
Super Cooker, 29789, 49044
Super Mom's LLC, 12319
Super Natural Distributors, 59628
Super Nutrition Distributors, 59629
Super Nutrition Life Extension, 12320
Super Radiator Coils, 29790, 49045
Super Sale Brokerage Company, 41150
Super Seal Manufacturing Limited, 29791, 49046
Super Smokers Bar-B-Que, 12321

All Companies Index

Super Snooty Sea Food Corporation, 12322, 59630
Super Steel, 29792
Super Store Industries, 59631
Super Stores Industries, 12323
Super Sturdy, 29793
Super Vision International, 29794, 49047
Super-Chef Manufacturing Company, 29795, 49048
Superbrand Dairies, 12326, 12327
SuperEats, 12324
SuperFat, 12325
Superflex Limited, 29796, 49049
Superfos Packaging Inc, 29797
Superior Bakery Inc, 12328
Superior Baking Co, 12329
Superior Bean & Spice Company, 12330
Superior Belting, 29798
Superior Beverage Group, 59632
Superior Brush Company, 29799, 49050
Superior Cake Products, 12331
Superior Dairy, 12332
Superior Distributing Co, 29800, 49051
Superior Farms, 12333
Superior Food Brokers, 41151
Superior Food Machinery Inc, 29801, 49052
Superior Foods, 12334, 49053, 59633
Superior Imaging Group Inc, 29802
Superior Industries, 29803, 49054
Superior Label Company, 29804
Superior Lamp, 59634
Superior Linen & Work Wear, 29805
Superior Manufacturing Division, 49055
Superior Meat Co, 12335
Superior Menus, 29806
Superior Mushroom Farms, 12336
Superior Neon Signs Inc, 29807
Superior Nut & Candy, 12337
Superior Nut Company, 12338
Superior Nutrition Corporation, 12339
Superior Ocean Produce, 12340, 59635
Superior Pack Group, 53485
Superior Packaging Equipment Corporation, 29808, 49056
Superior Paper & Plastic Co, 49057, 59636
Superior Pasta Co, 12341
Superior Pecans, 12342
Superior Product Pickup Services, 29809
Superior Products Company, 29810, 59637
Superior Quality Foods, 12343, 49058
Superior Seafood, 12344
Superior Seafood & Meat Company, 12345, 59638
Superior Seafoods Inc, 59639
Superior Tank, 29811
Superior Uniform Group, 29812, 49059
Superior Wholesale Distr, 59640
Superior-Studio Specialties, 29813
Superklean Washdown Products, 29814
Supermarket Associates, 29815
Supermarket Representatives, 41152
Superseedz, 12346
SUPERVALU Distribution, 59132
SupHerb Farms, 12318, 49042
SuppliesForLess, 29816
Supply Corp, 29817
Supply One, 59641
Supply One Inc, 29818, 59642
Supramatic, 29819, 49060
Suprema Specialties, 12347
Supreme Artisan Foods, 12348
Supreme Chocolatier, 12349, 49061
Supreme Corporation, 29820, 29821, 49062
Supreme Dairy Farms Co, 12350, 49063
Supreme Fabricators, 29822
Supreme Fixture Company, 59643
Supreme Food, 59644
Supreme Foods, 41153, 59645
Supreme Foodservice Sales, 41154
Supreme Frozen Products, 12351, 12352
Supreme Lobster, 52131, 59646

Supreme Manufacturing Co Inc, 49064
Supreme Metal, 29823, 49065
Supreme Murphy Truck Bodies, 29824
Supreme Products, 29825
Suram Trading Corporation, 12353, 49066
Surco Products, 29826, 49067
Sure Beam Corporation, 29827
Sure Clean Corporation, 29828
Sure Fine Food, 59647
Sure Kol Refrigerator, 29829
Sure Shot Dispensing Systems, 29830, 49068
Sure Torque, 29831, 49069
Sure-Feed Engineering, 29832
Sure-Fresh Produce Inc, 12354, 49070
Sure-Good Food Distributors, 12355, 59648
Surekap Inc, 29833, 49071
Surface Banana Company, 12356, 49072
Surface Measurement Systems, 29834
Surface Skil Corporation, 29835
Surfine Central Corporation, 29836
Surfing Goat Dairy, 12357
Surgital America, 12358
Surlean Foods, 12359
Surtec Inc, 29837, 49073
Sus-Rap Protective Packaging, 29838
Susie's Smart Cookie, 12360
Susie's South Forty Confection, 12361
Susquehanna Valley Winery, 12362
Suss Sweets, 12363
Sussman Electric Boilers, 29839, 49074
Sustainable Harvest Coffee Company, 59649
Sustainable Sourcing, 12364
Suter Co Inc, 12365
Sutherland Produce Sales, 59650
Sutherland Stamp Company, 29840
Sutherland's Foodservice, 12366
Sutter Basin Growers Cooperative, 53486
Sutter Buttes Olive Oil, 12367
Sutter Foods LLC, 12368
Sutter Home Winery, 12369, 49075
Sutter Process Equipment, 29841
Sutton Designs, 29842
Sutton Honey Farms, 12370
Sutton International, 41155
Suzanna's Kitchen, 12371
Suzanne's Specialties, 12372, 49076
Suzanne's Sweets, 12373
Suzhou-Chem Inc, 12374, 29843, 49077
SV Dice Designers, 28732
SV Research, 28733
SVB Food & Beverage Company, 11055, 48301
Svedala Industries, 29844, 29845, 49078, 49079
Svenhard's Swedish Bakery Inc, 12375
Sverdrup Facilities, 29846, 29847
Svresearch, 29848
Svzusa Inc, 12376
Swagger Foods Corp, 12377, 49080
Swan Label & Tag Co, 29849, 49081
Swan Transportation, 52132
Swancock Designworks, 29850
Swander Pace & Company, 29851
Swanson Vineyards & Winery, 12378
Swanson Wire Works Industries, Inc., 29852
Swany White Flour Mills LTD, 12379
Swapples, 12380, 59651
Swatt Baking Co, 12381
Sweco Inc, 29853, 49082
Swedish Hill Vineyard & Winery, 12382
Sweeney's Gourmet Coffee Roast, 12383
Sweenors Chocolates, 12384
Sweet & Sara, 12385
Sweet & Saucy Inc, 12386
Sweet Additions, 12387
Sweet Baby Ray's, 12388
Sweet Blessings, 12389
Sweet Breath, 12390
Sweet Candy Company, 12391
Sweet Christine's Bakery, 12392

Sweet City Supply, 12393
Sweet Corn Products Co, 12394, 49083
Sweet Designs Chocolatier Inc, 12395
Sweet Dried Fruit, 49084, 59652
Sweet Earth Foods, 12396
Sweet Endings Inc, 12397, 49085
Sweet Fortunes of America, 12398
Sweet Gallery Exclusive Pastry, 12399
Sweet Grass Dairy, 12400
Sweet Harvest Foods, 12401, 49086
Sweet Jubilee Gourmet, 12402
Sweet Lady Jane, 12403
Sweet Leaf Tea Company, 12404
Sweet Liberty Candy Company, 59653
Sweet Life Enterprises, 12405, 49087
Sweet Loren's, 12406
Sweet Manufacturing Co, 29854
Sweet Mavens, LLC, 12407
Sweet Megan Baking Company, 12408
Sweet Mountain Magic, 12409
Sweet Peas Floral Design, 12410
Sweet Pillar, 12411
Sweet Place, 59654
Sweet Sams Baking Corp, 12412
Sweet Sensations, 12413, 59655
Sweet Shop USA, 12414, 59656
Sweet Street Desserts, 12415, 49088
Sweet Sue Kitchens, 12416, 49089
Sweet Swiss Confections Inc, 12417
Sweet Traders, 12418, 59657
Sweet Water Brewing Co, 12419
Sweet Water Seafood, 12420
Sweet Whispers, 12421, 59658
Sweet'N Low, 12422
Sweetaly, 12424
Sweetcraft Candies, 12425
Sweetener Products Co, 59659
Sweetener Supply Corp, 12426, 29855
Sweeteners Plus Inc, 12427, 29856, 52133
Sweetery, 12428
Sweetleaf Co, 12429, 12430
Sweetstacks LLC, 12431
Sweetware, 29857, 49090
Sweetwater Spice Company, 12432
Sweetwood Cattle Co, 12433
SweetWorks Inc, 12423
Sweety Novelty, 12434
Sweety's Candies, 59660
SWELL Philadelphia Chewing Gum Corporation, 11056, 48302
Swerseys Chocolate, 12435
Swerve Sweetener, 12436
SWF Co, 28734, 28735, 28736, 28737, 48303
SWF McDowell, 28738, 48304
Swift Chemical & Supplies Inc, 59661
Swift Creek Forest Products, 29858
Swing-A-Way Manufacturing Company, 29859, 49091
Swirl Freeze Corp, 29860, 29861, 49092
Swisher Hygiene, 29862, 49093
Swiss American Inc, 12437, 49094
Swiss American International, 41156, 59662
Swiss Chalet Fine Foods, 12438, 59663
Swiss Dairy, 12439
Swiss Food Products, 12440, 49095
Swiss Heritage Cheese Inc, 12441
Swiss Premium Dairy Inc, 12442
Swiss Way Cheese, 12443
Swiss-American Sausage Company, 12444, 49096
Swisscorp, 49097
Swisser Sweet Maple, 12445, 59664
Swissh Commercial Equipment, 29863, 49098
Swissland Milk, 12446
Swisslog Logistics Inc, 29864, 29865, 49099
Switch Beverage, 12447
Switchback Group, 59665
Switzer's Inc, 12448, 59666
Swivelier Co Inc, 29866, 49100
SWMCO Multi Products, 41044, 48305

Sybo Composites LLC, 29867
Sycamore Containers, 29868
Sycamore Vineyards, 12449
Sycaway Creamery Inc, 59667
Syfan USA Corporation, 29869
SYFO Beverage Company of Florida, 11057
Sygma Network, 59668, 59669
SYGMA Network Inc, 59133
Sylvin Farms Winery, 12450
Symmetry Products Group, 29870, 49101
Symms Fruit Ranch Inc, 12451, 49102
Symons Frozen Foods, 12452, 49103
Symons-Bodtker Associates, 41157
Sympak, Inc., 29871, 49104
Symphony Foods, 12453
Symrise Inc., 12454, 49105
Symtech,Inc, 29872
Synchro-Systems Technology, 29873
Synergee Foods Corporation, 49106, 59670
Synergy, 12455
Synergy Flavors Inc, 12456, 49107
Synergy Plus, 12457
Syngenta, 29874
Synthite USA Inc., 12458, 49108
Synthron Inc., 29875, 49109
Syracuse Casing Co, 12459
Syracuse China Company, 29876
Syracuse Label Co, 29877
Sysco Corp, 29878, 29879, 29880, 29881, 29882, 29883, 29884, 29885, 29886, 29887, 29888, 29889, 29890, 29891, 29892, 29893, 29894, 29895, 29896, 29897, 29898, 29899, 29900, 29901, 29902, 29903, 29904, 29905, 29906, 29907, 29908, 29909, 29910, 29911, 29912, 29913, 29914, 29915, 29916, 29917, 29918, 29919, 29920, 29921, 29922, 29923, 29924, 29925, 29926, 29927, 29928, 29929, 29930, 29931, 29932, 29933, 29934, 29935, 29936, 29937, 29938, 29939, 29940, 29941, 29942, 29943, 29944, 29945, 29946, 29947, 29948, 29949, 29950, 59671, 59672, 59673, 59674, 59675, 59676, 59677, 59678, 59679, 59680, 59681, 59682, 59683, 59684, 59685, 59686, 59687, 59688, 59689, 59690, 59691, 59692, 59693, 59694, 59695, 59696, 59697, 59698, 59699, 59700, 59701, 59702, 59703, 59704, 59705, 59706, 59707, 59708, 59709, 59710, 59711, 59712, 59713, 59714, 59715, 59716, 59717, 59718, 59719, 59720, 59721, 59722, 59723, 59724, 59725, 59726, 59727, 59728, 59729, 59730, 59731, 59732, 59733, 59734, 59735, 59736, 59737, 59738, 59739, 59740, 59741, 59742, 59743
SYSPRO USA, 28739
Systech Illinois, 29951
Systech International, 29952
System Concepts Inc, 29953
System Graphics Inc, 29954
System Packaging, 29955
System Plast, 29956
System-Plast, 29957
Systemate Numafa, 29958
Systems Comtrex, 29959, 49110
Systems IV, 29960, 49111
Systems Modeling Corporation, 29961

All Companies Index

Systems Online, 29962, 53487, 59744
Systems Services Of America, 59745
Systems Technology Inc, 29963, 29964, 49112

T

T & A Metal Products Inc, 29965
T & C Stainless, 29966
T & M Distributing Co, 29967
T & S Brass & Bronze Work, 29968, 29969, 49113, 49114
T & S Perfection Chain Prods, 29970, 49115
T & T Industries Inc, 29971
T & T Valve & Instrument Inc, 29972
T C Jacoby & Co, 41158
T D Refrigeration Inc, 59746
T D Sawvel Co, 29973, 49116
T E Ibberson Co, 29974, 29975
T G Lee Dairy, 12460
T Hasegawa USA Inc, 12461, 49117
T J Smith Box Co, 29976
T M Duche Nut Co, 12462, 49118
T O Williams Inc, 12463, 59747
T P Freight Lines Inc, 52134
T Q Constructors, 29977
T Sterling Assoc, 12464
T&G Machinery, 29978
T&S Blow Molding, 29979, 49119
T&T Seafood, 12465, 59748
T'Lish Dressings and Marinades, 12466
T-Drill Industries Inc, 29980
T. Baker Restaurant Equipment, 59749
T. Marzetti Company, 12467
T. McConnell Sales & Marketing, 41159
T.A. Morris & Sons, 59750
T.B. Seafood, 12468, 59751
T.B. Venture, 49120, 59752
T.C. Food Export/Import Company, 49121, 59753
T.C.P. Restaurant Supply, 59754
T.D. Khan, 59755
T.D. Rowe Company, 29981
T.F.S. & Associates, 41160
T.J. Blackburn Syrup Works, 12469
T.J. Hines & Company, 41161
T.J. Kraft, 12470, 49122, 59756
T.J. Topper Company, 29982
T.K. Designs, 29983
T.K. Products, 29984, 49123
T.L. Herring & Company, 12471, 59757
T.M. Patterson Paper Box Company, 59758
T.O. Plastics, 29985, 49124
T.S. Smith & Sons, 12472, 49125
T.S.A. Distributing, 59759
T.T. Todd Company, 59760
T.W. Garner Food Company, 12473, 12474
T.W. Wilson & Son, 41162
TA Instruments Inc, 29986
Ta-De Distributing Co, 59766
Tabard Farm Potato Chips, 12484
Tabatchinick Fine Foods, 12485
Tabco Enterprises, 12486, 49147
Table De France, 12487
Table De France: North America, 30040
Table Decor International, 49148
Table Shox, 49149
Table Talk Pies Inc, 12488, 30041
Tablecheck Technologies, Inc, 30042, 49151
Tablecloth Co Inc, 49152
Tablecraft Products Co Inc, 30043, 49153
Tablemate Products, 59767
Tables Cubed, 30044
Tablet & Ticket Co, 30045, 49154
TableToyz, 49150
Tabor Grain Company, 59768
Tabor Hill Winery & Restaurant, 12489
TAC-PAD, 29987
Taconic, 30046, 49155
Tadin Herb & Tea Co, 12490
Tafco Inc, 30047

Taffy Town Inc, 12491
Taft Street Winery, 12492
Taftsville Country Store, 12493
Tag-Trade Associated Group, 30048
Tahana Confections LLC, 12494
Tahitian Gold, 12495
Tai Foong USA Inc, 49156
Taif Inc, 12496
Taiko Enterprise Corp, 49157
Tait Farm Foods, 12497
Taiyo International Inc., 12498
Taj Gourmet Foods, 12499, 49158
Takara Sake USA Inc, 12500
Takari International Inc, 49159, 59769
Takasago International Corp, 12501
Takeda Vitamin & Food, 59770
Takeiya USA, 12502
Taku Smokehouse, 12503, 49160
Talbert Display, 30049
Talbot Industries, 30050
Talbott Farms, 12504, 49161
Talbott Teas, 12505
Talbott Vineyards, 12506
Talenti Gelato e Sorbetto, 12507
Talisman Foods, 12508
Talk O'Texas Brands Inc, 12509
Talking Rain Beverage Co, 12510
Tall Grass Toffee Co, 12511
Tall Talk Dairy, 12512
Tallarico Food Products, 59771
Talley Farms, 12513, 49162
Talley Vineyards, 12514
Tallgrass Beef Company, 12515
Tallygenicom, 30051, 49163
Tama Trading Co Inc, 59772
Tamanet (USA) Inc, 30052
Tamarack Farms Dairy, 12516
Tamarack Products Inc, 30053, 49164
Tamarind Tree, 12517, 49165
Tamashiro Market Inc, 12518, 59773
Tamburo Brothers, 59774
Tampa Bay Copack, 30054
Tampa Bay Fisheries Inc, 12519, 49166
Tampa Corrugated Carton Company, 30055, 49167
Tampa Maid Foods Inc, 12520, 49168
Tampa Pallet Co, 30056, 49169
Tampa Sheet Metal Co, 30057
Tampico Beverages Inc, 12521, 49170
Tampico Spice Co, 12522
Tamuzza Vineyards, 12523
Tanaco Products, 30058
Tangent Systems, 30059, 49171
Tangerine Promotion, 30060
Tangible Vision, 30061
Tanglewood Farm, 59775
Tanglewood Farms, 12524
Tango Shatterproof Drinkware, 30062, 49172
Tangra Trading, 49173
Tanimura Antle Inc, 12525, 49174
Tanita Corp Of America, 49175
Tank Temp Control, 30063
Tank's Meats Inc, 12526
Tankersley Food Svc, 59776
Tanner Enterprises, 59777
Tantec, 30064
Tantos Foods International, 12527, 49176
Tanzamaji USA, 12528, 49177, 59778
Taormina Co, 59779
Taormina Sales Company, 41166, 49178
Taos Brewing Supply, 12529
Taos Mesa Brewing Co, 12530
Tap Packaging Solutions, 30065
Tapatio Hot Sauce, 12531, 49179
Tape & Label Converters, 30066, 49180
Tape & Label Engineering, 30067, 59780
Tape Tools, 49181, 59781
Tapesolutions, 30068
Tapp Label Technologies Inc, 59782
Tapp Technologies, 49182
Taprite-Fassco Mfg Inc, 30069
Taqueria El Milagro, 12532
Tar-Hong MELAMINE USA, 30070
Tara Communications, 30071

Tara Foods, 12533
Tara Foods LLC, 30072, 59783
Tara Linens, 30073, 49183
Tara Tape, 30074
Tarara Winery, 12534
Tarason Packaging, LLC., 30075
Tarazi Specialty Foods, 12535, 12536, 49184
Target Flavors Inc, 12537, 49185
Target Industries, 30076, 49186
Taroco Food Corporation, 49187, 59784
Tarrison Products, 49188
Tartaric Chemicals, 49189
Tartaric Chemicals Corporation, 30077
Tartine Bakery, 12538
Tase-Rite Co, 12539
Task Footwear, 30078
Tasler Inc, 30079
Taste It Presents Inc, 12540, 49190
Taste Maker Foods, 12541
Taste of Gourmet, 12546, 49193
Taste of Nature Inc., 12547
Taste Teasers, 12542, 49191
Taste Traditions Inc, 12543, 49192
Taste Weavers, 12544
Taste Wine Co, 12545
Tastebuds Popcorn, 12548, 59785
Tastee Apple, 12549
Tastepoint, 12550, 49194
Tasty Baking Company, 12551
Tasty Brand Inc, 12552
Tasty Mix Quality Foods, 12553, 59786
Tasty Pure Food Co, 59787
Tasty Seeds Ltd, 12554
Tasty Selections, 12555
Tasty Tomato, 12556
Tasty Toppings Inc, 12557
Tastybaby, 12558
Tata Tea, 12559, 49195
Tatangelo's Wholesale Fruit & Vegetables, 12560
Tate & Lyle PLC, 12561
Tate Western, 30080, 49196
Tate's Bake Shop, 12562
Tatra Herb Co, 12563
Tatra Sheep Cheese Company, 49197, 59788
Taunton Engineering Company, 59789
Taurus Spice, 49198
Tavalon Tea, 12564
TAWI-USA Inc, 29988
Taylor Box Co, 30081, 49199
Taylor Cheese Corp, 12565
Taylor Farms, 12566
Taylor Farms Pacific, 12567
Taylor Freezer Equipment Corporation, 59790
Taylor Freezers, 59791
Taylor Lobster Co, 12568, 59792
Taylor Made Custom Products, 30082
Taylor Manufacturing Co, 30083, 49200
Taylor Meat Co, 12569
Taylor Orchards, 12570, 49201
Taylor Precision Products, 12571, 30084, 30085, 49202
Taylor Products Co, 30086, 49203
Taylor Provisions Company, 12572
Taylor Shellfish Farms, 12573
Taylor Utlimate Svc Co, 59793
Taylor Warehouse, 53490
Taylor Wine Company, 12574
Taylor's Mexican Chili Co Inc, 12575
Taylor's Poultry Place, 12576
Taylor's Sausage Co, 12577
Taylor-Fortune Distributors, 59794
Taylor-Made Labels Inc, 30087
Taylor-Wharton-Cryogenics, 49204
Taymar Industries, 30088
Tayse Meats, 12578
Taza Chocolate, 12579
Taziki's Cafe, 12580
Tazmanian Freight Forwarding, 52137, 53491
Tazo Tea, 12581
TBI Corporation, 59761

TBJ Gourmet, 12475, 59762
TC/American Monorail, 29989, 49126
TCC Enterprises, 29990
TCD Parts, 59763
TCG Technologies, 29991
Tchefa, 59795
Tcheru Enterprises, 59796
TCHO Ventures, 12476
TCT Logistics, 53488
TCT&A Industries, 29992
TDF Automation, 29993, 49127
TDH, 29994, 49128
TDR Inc, 59764
Tea Aura, 12582
Tea Beyond, 12583
Tea Forte, 12584
Tea Importers Inc, 49205
Tea Needs Inc, 12585
Tea Room, 12586
Tea To Go, 49206
Tea-n-Crumpets, 12587
Teaco, 30089
Teal's Express Inc, 52138
Team Hardinger, 52139, 53492
Team Northwest, 41167, 41168
Teamwork Technology, 30090
Teapigs, 12588
Tearrific Ice Cream, 12589
Teasdale Quality Foods Inc, 12590
Teasley & Assoc, 41169
Teawolf LLC, 12591
Tebay Dairy Company, 12592
TEC, 29995
TEC America, 29996
Tec Art Industries Inc, 30091
Tec Products Co Inc, 59797
Tec-Era Engineering Corporation, 30092
Tec5USA, 30093
TecArt Signs, 49207
Tech Development, 30094
Tech Lighting LLC, 30095, 49208
Tech Pak Solutions, 30096, 59798
Tech Sales Inc, 49209, 59799
Tech-Roll Inc, 30097, 49210
Techform, 30098
Technetics Industries, 30099
Techni-Chem, 30100
Technibilt/Cari-All, 30102, 49211
Technical Food Sales Inc, 41170, 53493, 59800
Technical Inc, 30103
Technical Instrument SanFrancisco, 30104
Technical Sales Associates, 41171
Technical Tool Solutions Inc., 30105
Technipac, 30107
TechnipFMC, 30106, 49212
Techniquip, 30108
TechniStar Corporation, 30101
Technistar Corporation, 30109, 49213
Technium, 30110, 49214
Techno Food Ingredients Co., Ltd, 12593
Techno USA, 12594, 49215
Techno-Design, 30111
Technology Flavors & Fragrances, 12595, 49216
Technomic Inc, 30112
Technoquip Co, 30113
Tecnicam Inc, 49217
Tecnocap, 30114
Tecogen Inc, 30115
Tectonics, 30116
Tecumseh Poultry, LLC, 12596
Tecumseh Products Co., 30117, 49218
Tecweigh, 30118, 49219
Ted Drewes Frozen Custard, 12597
Ted L. Rausch Company, 52140
Ted Shear Assoc Inc, 12598, 49220
Teddy's Tasty Meats, 12599, 59801
Tedea-Huntliegh, 30119
Tee Pee Olives, Inc., 12600, 49221
Tee's Plus, 49222, 59802
Tee-Jay Corporation, 30120, 49223
Teeccino, 12601
Teelee Popcorn, 12602, 49224

All Companies Index

Teeny Foods Inc, 12603
Teeny Tiny Spice Company of Vermont LLC, 12604
Teepak LLC, 30121
Tees & Persse Brokerage, 41173
Tees & Persse Brokerage Acosta Sales And Marketing Company, Inc, 41172
Teff Co, 12605
TEI Analytical Svc Inc, 29997
Teilhaber Manufacturing Corp, 30122, 49225
Teitel Brothers, 59803
Teixeira Farms, Inc., 12606
Tejas Logistics System, 52141, 53494
Tejon Ranch Co, 12607, 49226
Tek Visions, 30123, 49227
Tekita House Foods, 12608
Teknor Apex Co, 30124
Teksem LLC, 30125, 49228
Tel-Tru Manufacturing Co, 30126, 49229
Telechem Corp, 30128
Teledyne Benthos Inc, 30129, 30130, 49231
Teledyne ISCO, 30131
Teledyne TEKMAR, 30132, 49232
Telesonic Packaging, 30133, 49233
Teletec Cash Register Company, 59804
TeleTech Label Company, 30127, 49230
Televend, 30134, 49234
Tell City Pretzel Company, 12609
Telman Incorporated, 49235
Telwar International Inc, 49236
Tema Systems Inc, 30135, 49237
Temco, 30136, 49238
Temkin International, 30137
Temo Candy, 12610
Temp Air Inc, 30138, 30139
TEMP-TECH Company, 29998, 49129
Tempco Electric Heater Corporation, 30140, 49239
Tempera/Sol, 30141
Tempest Fisheries LTD, 12611, 59805
Templar Food Products, 12612, 49240
Temple-Inland, 30142
Templock Corporation, 30143, 49241
Temptee Specialty Foods, 12613
Ten Ren Tea & Ginseng Co Inc, 12614
Tenayo, 12615
Tenchy Machinery Corporation, 30144
Tenent Laboratories, 30145
Tenka Flexible Packaging, 30146
Tennant Co, 30147, 49242
Tenneco Inc, 30148, 49243
Tenneco Packaging, 30149
Tenneco Specialty Packaging, 30150, 49244
Tennessee Bun Company, 12616
Tennessee Cold & Dry Storage, 53495
Tennessee Commercial Wrhse Inc, 53496
Tennessee Mills, 30151
Tennessee Packaging, 30152
Tennessee Valley Packing Co, 12617
Tennsco Corp, 30153, 49245
Tenor Controls Company, 30154
Tente Casters Inc, 30155, 30156, 30157, 49246
Tenth & M Seafoods, 12618, 49247, 59806
Tepper & Assoc, 41174
Tepromark International, 30158
TEQ, 29999
Tergerson's Fine Foods, 59807
Terkelsen Machine Company, 30159, 49248
Terlato Kitchen, 12619
Terlet USA, 30160, 59808
Terminal Cold Storage Co Inc, 53497
Terminix, 30161, 49249
Terphane Inc, 30162, 49250
Terra Botanica Products, 12620
Terra Flavors & Fragrances, 12621
Terra Ingredients, 12622
Terra Ingredients LLC, 12623, 49251, 59809
Terra Nova Brokers, 41175

Terra Origin, Inc., 12624, 49252
Terra Sol Chile Company, 12625
Terra's, 12626
Terrace At J Vineyards, 12627
Terracon Corp, 30163
Terrafina LLC, 59810
Terranettis Italian Bakery, 12628
Terrapin Ridge, 12629
Terrell Meats, 12630
Terrell's Potato Chip Co, 12631
Terressentia Corp., 12632
Terri Lynn Inc, 12633, 59811
Terriss Consolidate, 30164, 49253
Terry Brothers, Inc, 12634, 59812
Terry Foods, 12635, 59813
Terry Manufacturing Company, 30165, 49254
TES-Clean Air Systems, 30000
Tesa Tape Inc, 30166, 49255
Tesdall & Associates, 59814
Tesoro USA, LLC, 49256
Tessemae's All Natural, 12636, 59815
Tessenderlo Kerley Inc, 12637, 49257
Test Laboratories Inc, 12638, 49258
Testaints Sales-Distribution, 12639
Testing Machines Inc, 30167, 49259
TESTO, 30001
Testo, 30168
TESTO, 49130
Teti Bakery, 12640, 49260
Tetley Tea, 12641
Tetley USA, 12642, 12643, 49261
Teton Waters Ranch LLC, 12644, 49262
Tetra Pak, 30169, 30170, 30171, 30172
Tew Manufacturing Corp, 30173, 49263
Tex-Mex Cold Storage, 12645, 53498
Tex-Mex Gourmet, 12646
Tex-Sandia, 59816
TexaFrance, 12647
Texas Baket Company, 30174
Texas Beach, 12648
Texas Cartage Warehouse Inc, 52142, 53499
Texas Chili Co, 12649
Texas Coffee Co, 12650, 49264
Texas Coffee Traders Inc, 12651
Texas Corn Roasters, 30175
Texas Crumb & Cookie Food Products, 12652
Texas Food Research, 49265
Texas Foods, 41176
Texas Gunpowder, 59817
Texas Halal Corporation, 49266, 59818
Texas Heat, 12653
Texas Hill Country Barbacue, 30176
Texas Hotel & Restaurant Equipment, 59819
Texas Marine II, 59820
Texas Meat Purveyors, 59821
Texas N Western Railway Company, 52143
Texas Neon Advertising Inc, 30177
Texas Reds Steak House, 12654
Texas Refinery Corp, 30178, 49267
Texas Sausage Co, 12655, 59822
Texas Spice Co, 12656, 30179
Texas Tamale Co, 12657
Texas Tito's, 12658
Texas Toffee, 12659, 49268
Texas Traditions Gourmet, 12660, 49269
Texican Specialty Products, 30180
Texpak Inc, 30181
Textile Buff & Wheel, 30182, 49270
Textile Products Company, 30183, 49271
Texture Technologies Corporation, 30184, 49272
TGI Texas, 30002
TGR Container Sales, 30003
TGW International, 30004
TH Foods, Inc., 12477
Thackrey & Co, 12661
Thaigrocer.com, 49273
Thamesville Metal Products Ltd, 30185
Thanasi Foods LLC, 12662
Thanksgiving Coffee Co, 12663
THARCO, 30005, 30006, 49131

Tharo Systems Inc, 30186, 49274
That's How We Roll, LLC, 12664, 49275
That's It Nutrition, 12665
Thatcher's Gourmet Specialties, 12666
The Amazing Chickpea, 12667, 49276
The Ardent Homesteader, 12668, 49277
The Art of Broth, LLC, 12669, 49278
The Bachman Company, 59823
The Bauman Family, 12670
The Bites Company, 12671
The Boisset Collection, 12672
The Brand Passport, 49279
The Brooklyn Salsa Co LLC, 12673
The Bruss Company, 12674, 49280
The Canvas Exchange Inc, 30187
The Carriage Works, 30188, 49281
The Chalet Market, 12675
The Chefs' Warehouse, 49282, 59824
The Cherry Company Ltd., 41177, 49283
The Chili Lab, 12676
The Coconut Cooperative, LLC, 49284, 59825
The Coffee Bean & Tea Leaf, 12677
The Commercial Exchange, Inc., 53500
The Consumer Goods Forum, 30189
The Cookie Dough Cafe, 12678, 59826
The Coop, 59827
The Coromega Company, 12679, 49285
THE Corporation, 30007, 49132
The Crispery, 12680
The Daphne Baking Company, LLC, 12681
The Dow Chemical Company, 12682
The Eli's Cheesecake Company, 12683
The Food Collective, 12684
The Frank Pesce International Group, L.L.C.
The Good Bean, 12685
The Good Crisp Company, 12686, 49287
The Good Food Institute, 30190
The Great San Saba River Pecan Company, 12687
The Great Western Tortilla Co., 12688
The Hampton Popcorn Company, 12689
The Healthy Beverage Company, 12690
The Honest Stand, 12691, 49288
The Humphrey Co, 12692
The Invisible Chef, 12693
The Irish Dairy Board Holdings, 49289
The Jackson Kearney Group, 53501
The Jam Stand, 12694
The Jersey Tomato Company, 12695
The Junket Folks, 12696
The King's Kitchen, 12697
The Konery, 12698
The Kroger Co., 12699
The Lamb Company, 49290, 59828
The Lancaster Food Company, 12700, 49291
The Little Kernel, 12701, 49292
The Lobster Place, 12702, 30191
The Lollipop Tree, Inc, 12703
The Long Life Beverage Company, 12704, 49293
The Lovely Candy Company LLC, 12705
The Maple Guild, 12706
The Mapled Nut Co., 12707
The Matzo Project, 12708, 59829
The Meeker Vineyard, 12709
The Murphs Famous Inc., 12710
The N Beverage Group, 49294
The Naked Edge, LLC, 12711, 49295
The National Provisioner, 30192, 49296
The New Primal, 12712
The Pantry Club, 12713
The Peanut Butter Shop of Williamsburg, 12714
The Perfect Pita, 12715
The Pickle Juice Company, 12716
The Pillsbury Company, 12717
The Piping Gourmets, 12718, 59830
The Poseidon Group, 12719
The Power of Fruit, 12720
The Premium Beer Company, 49297, 59831

The Procter & Gamble Company, 12721, 30193, 49298
The Pub Brewing Company, 30194, 30195
The Pur Company, 12722
The Real Co, 12723, 49299
The Really Great Food Company, 12724
The Roscoe NY Beer Company, Inc., 12725
The Rubin Family of Wines, 12726, 30196
The Safe + Fair Food Company, 12727
The Saucey Sauce CompanyInc., 12728
The Scoular Company/TSC Container Freight, 49300, 52144
The Shed Saucery, 12729
The Sola Company, 12730, 49301
The Soulfull Project, 12731, 59832
The Sprout House, 12732
The Stephan Company, 12733
The Stroopie, 12734, 59833
The Sunshine Tomato Company, 12735
The Swiss Bakery, 12736
The Tao of Tea, 12737, 59834
The Tea Spot, Inc., 12738, 49302
The Terminal Corporation, 52145, 53502
The Thurber Company, 41178
The Toasted Oat Bakehouse, 12739, 49303, 59835
The Tombras Group, 30197
The Truffleist, 12740
The Valpo Velvet Shoppe, 12741
The Van Cleve Seafood Company, 12742, 59836
The Veri Soda Company, 12743
The Vine, 12744
The Water Kefir People, 12745
The Wine RayZyn Company, 12746
The Worlds Best Cheese, 12747
Theatre Candy Distributing Company, 59837
Theimeg, 30198
Theingredienthouse, 30199
Theo Chocolate, 12748
Theochem Laboratories Inc, 30200, 49304
Theos Foods, 30201
Theriault's Abattoir Inc, 12749
Therm L Tec Building Systems, 30202, 49305
Therm-Tec Inc, 30203, 49306
Therma Kleen, 30204, 49307
Thermaco Inc, 30205, 49308
Thermafreeze, 30206
Thermal Bags By Ingrid Inc, 30207, 49309
Thermal Engineering Corp, 30208
Thermal Package Testing Laboratory, 30209
Thermal Technologies, 30210
Thermaline Inc, 30211
Thermalogic Corp, 30212
Thermedics Detection, 30213
Thermex Thermatron, 30214
Thermice Company, 12750
Thermo BLH, 30215
Thermo Detection, 30216, 49310
Thermo Fisher Scientific, 30217
Thermo Instruments, 30218
Thermo Jarrell Ash Corporation, 30219
Thermo King Corp, 30220
Thermo Pac LLC, 12751, 30221
Thermo Service, 30222
Thermo Wisconsin, 30223
Thermo-KOOL/Mid-South Ind Inc, 30224, 49311
Thermodynamics, 30226, 49313
Thermodyne Foodservice Prods, 30227, 49314
Thermodyne International LTD, 30228, 49315
Thermoil Corporation, 30229, 49316
Thermolok Packaging Systems, 30230
Thermomass, 30231
Thermoquest, 30232, 49317

1445

All Companies Index

Thermos Company, 30233
Thermoseal, 30234
ThermoWorks, 30225, 49312
Theta Sciences, 30235, 49318
Thiel Cheese & Ingredients, 12752, 30236, 49319
Thiele Engineering Company, 30237, 49320
Thiele Technologies Inc, 30238, 30239
Thiele Technologies-Reedley, 30240, 49321
Thielmann Container Systems, 30241
Think Jerky, 12753
Thinkthin, LLC, 12754
Thinque Systems Corporation, 30242
Third Planet Products, 59838
Third Street Inc, 12755
Thirs-Tea Corp, 12756, 49322
Thirstenders International, 30243
Thirty Two North Corporation, 30244
This Bar Saves Lives, LLC, 12757, 49323, 59839
Thistledew Farm, 12758
Tholstrup Cheese, 12759
Thoma Vineyards, 12760
Thomas & Howard Co, 59840
Thomas & Howard Co Cash & Crry, 59841
Thomas Brothers Country Ham, 12761, 59842
Thomas Canning/Maidstone, 12762
Thomas Colace Company, 59843
Thomas Dairy, 12763
Thomas Fogarty Winery, 12764
Thomas Food Brokers, 41179
Thomas Gourmet Foods, 12765
Thomas Ice Cream, 59844
Thomas J Payne Market Devmnt, 30245
Thomas Kemper Soda Company, 12766
Thomas Kruse Winery, 12767
Thomas L. Green & Company, 30246, 49325
Thomas Lighting Residential, 30247, 49325
Thomas Lobster Co, 12768, 59845
Thomas Packing Company, 12769
Thomas Precision, Inc., 30248, 49326
Thomas Pump & Machinery, 30249, 30250
Thomas Tape & Supply Co Inc, 30251, 49327
Thomas Technical Svc, 30252, 30253, 59846
Thomas Vaccaro Inc, 41180
Thomas W. MacKay & Son, 59847
Thomas, Large & Singer, 41181
Thomasen, 30254
Thombert, 30255
Thompson & Johnson Equipment, 59848
Thompson & Little, 59849
Thompson Bagel Machine Mfg, 30256, 49328
Thompson Dairy, 59850
Thompson Packers, 12770, 49329
Thompson Scale Co, 30257
Thompson Seafood, 12771
Thompson's Fine Foods, 12772
Thomsen Group LLC, 30258
Thomson Groceries Ltd., 59851
Thomson Meats, 12773
Thomson-Leeds Company, 30259, 41182, 49330
Thor Inc, 12774, 30260
Thor-Shackel Horseradish Company, 12775
Thorco Industries LLC, 30261, 49331
Thoreson Mc Cosh Inc, 30262, 49332
Thormann Associates, 41183
Thorn Smith Laboratories, 30263, 49333
Thornton Foods Company, 12776
Thornton Plastics, 30264
Thornton Winery, 12777
Thorpe & Associates, 30265, 49334
Thorpe Rolling Pin Co, 30266
Thorpe Vineyard, 12778

Thoughtful Food, 12779, 49335
Three Acre Kitchen, 12780
Three Bakers Gluten Free Bakery, 12781
Three D Brokers, 52146, 53503
Three Jerks Jerky, 12782, 59852
Three Lakes Winery, 12783
Three M Food Service, 59853
Three Meadows Spirits LLC, 12784
Three P, 30267, 49336
Three Rivers Fish Company, 12785, 59854
Three Springs Farm, 12786
Three Trees Almondmilk, 12787, 49337
Three Twins Ice Cream, 12788
Three-A Sanitary Standards Symbol, 30268
ThreeWorks Snacks, 12789, 49338
Threshold Rehabilitation Svc, 30269
Thrive Farmers, 12790
Ths Foodservice, 59855
Thumann Inc., 12791
Thunder Group, 49339
Thunder Pallet Inc, 30270
Thunderbird Food Machinery, 30271, 49340, 59856
Thunderbird Label Corportion, 30272
Thunderbird Real Food Bar, 12792, 49341, 59857
Thurman Scale, 30273
Thurston Foods Inc, 59858
Thwing-Albert Instrument Co, 30274
Thyme & Truffles Hors d'Oeuvres, 12793
Thyme and Truffles, 49342
Thyme Garden Herb Co, 12794
Thymly Products Inc, 12795
Tiax LLC, 30275
Tibersoft, 30276
TIC Gums, 12478
Tichon Sea Food Corp, 12796
Tideland Seafood Company, 12797, 59859
Tidland Corp, 30277
Tieco-Unadilla Corporation, 30278, 49343
Tiefenthaler Machinery Co, Inc, 30279
Tier-Rack Corp, 30280, 49344
Tierra Farm, 12798, 49345, 59860
Tiesta Tea, 12799, 49346, 59861
Tifa (CI), 30281
Tiffin Metal Products Co, 30282
Tiger Botanicals 1, 49347
Tiger Corporation/I-Ward, 49348
Tiger Distributors, 59862
Tiger Meat & Provisions, 12800
Tiger Mushroom Farm, 12801
Tiger-Vac, 30283
Tighe Warehousing-Distribution, 52147, 53504
Tigo+, 12802, 49349
Tilkin & Cagen Inc, 41184
Tillamook Country Smoker, 12803, 49350
Tillamook County Creamery Association, 12804, 49351
Tillamook Meat Inc, 12805
Tiller Foods Company, 12806
Tillie's Gourmet, 12807
Tilly Industries, 30284, 49352
Tim's Cascade Snacks, 12808, 49353
Timber Crest Farms, 12809
Timber Lake Cheese Company, 12810
Timber Peaks Gourmet, 12811, 59863
Timberline Cold Storage Inc, 53505
Timberline Consulting, 30285
Timbertech Company, 30286
Timco Inc, 30287
Time & Alarm Systems, 59864
Time Products, 30288
Timeless Seeds, 12812, 59865
Timely Signs Inc, 30289, 49354, 59866
Timemed Labeling Systems, 30290, 49355
Tin Box Co Of America Inc, 30291
Tin Star Foods, 12813, 49356

Tin Whistle Brewing Co, 12814
Tinadre Inc, 30292
Tincture Distillers, 12815
Tindall Packaging, 30293, 49357
Tingfong LLC, 59867
Tinkels, 59868
Tinkyada, 12816
Tinwerks Packaging Co, 30294
Tiny But Mighty Popcorn, 12817
Tiny Drumsticks, 30295
Tiny Hero Foods, 12818, 49358
Tio Gazpacho, 12819
Tip Top Canning Co, 12820
Tip Top Poultry Inc, 12821, 49359
Tipiak Inc, 12822, 49360
Tipp Distributors Inc, 12823
Tippecanoe Foods, 59869
Tipper Tie Inc, 30296, 49361
Tippmann Group, 30297, 53506, 53507, 53508
Tips Uniform, 59870
Tirawisu, 12824, 49362, 59871
Tisdale Food Ingredients, 41185
Tisma Machinery Corporation, 30298, 49363
Titan Corporation, 30299
Titan Farms, 12825
Titan Industries Inc, 30300, 49364
Titan Plastics, 30301
Titan Ventures International, Inc, 30302
Titusville Dairy Products Co, 12826
TKC Supply, 59765
Tkc Vineyards, 12827
TKF Inc, 30008, 49133
TKO Doors, 30009
TLB Corporation, 30010, 49134
TLC & Associates, 30011
Tlf Graphics Inc, 30303
TMB Baking Equipment, 30012
TMC Foods, 41163
TMCo Inc.ÿ, 30013, 30014, 49135
TMF Corporation, 30015
TMI Trading Co, 12479
TMI-USA, 30016
TMS, 30017
TMT Software Company, 30018
TMT Vacuum Filters, 30019
TNA Packaging Solutions, 30020, 49136
Tnemec Co Inc, 30304
Tni Packaging Inc, 30305, 49365
Tnn-Jeros Inc, 30306
TNN-Jeros, Inc., 30021
TNT Container Logistics, 30022, 30023
TNT Crust, 12480, 49137
To Market To Market, 12828
To Your Health Sprouted Flour Co., Inc., 12829
To-Am Equipment Company, 59872
Toastmaster, 30307, 49367
Toastmaster A Middleby Company, 49366
Toastmasters International, 49368, 59873
Tobiason Potato Co Inc, 41186
Todd Brokerage Company, 41187
Todd Construction Services, 30308
Todd Distributors Inc, 59874
Todd Uniform, 30309
Todd's, 12830, 12831, 30310, 49369, 49370
Todd's Salsa, 12832
TODDS Enterprises Inc, 12481, 49138
Toddy Products Inc, 12833, 49371
Todhunter Foods, 12834, 12835, 49372, 49373
Toe-Food Chocolates and Candy, 12836
Toffee Boutique, 12837
Toffee Co, 12838
Tofield Packers Ltd, 12839
Toft Dairy Inc, 12840
Tofu Shop Specialty Foods Inc, 12841
Tofurky, 12842
Tofutti Brands Inc, 12843, 49374
Toho America Corporation, 41188
Token Factory, 30311, 49375
Tokheim Co, 30312, 49376

Tokunaga Farms, 12844
Tolan Machinery Company, 30313, 49377
Tolas Health Care Packaging, 30314, 49378
Tolco Corp, 30315
Toledo Sign Co Inc, 30316
Toledo Ticket Co, 30317, 49379
Toledo Wire Products, 30318
Tolteca Foodservice, 12845, 52148, 53509
Tom & Dave's Coffee, 12846
Tom & Sally's Handmade Chocolates, 12847
Tom Cat Bakery Inc, 12848
Tom Farms, 12849
Tom Lockerbie, 30319
Tom McCall & Associates, 30320
Tom Quinn & Associates, 41189
Tom Ringhausen Orchards, 12850
Tom Sturgis Pretzels Inc, 12851
Tom Tom Tamale & Bakery Co, 12852
Tom's Evergreen Broom Manufacturing, 59875
Tom's Foods, 12853
Tom's Snacks Company, 12854, 49380
Tomac Packaging, 30321
Tomahawk Warehousing Services, 53510
Tomanetti Food Products, 12856, 12857, 59876
Tomanetti Food Products Inc, 12855
Tomaro's Bakery, 12858
Tomasello Winery, 12859
Tomasso Corporation, 12860
Tomco2 Systems, 30322
Tomer Kosher Foods, 12861
Tomich Brothers Seafoods, 49381, 59877
Tomlinson Industries, 30323, 49382
Tommy Tang's Thai Seasonings, 12862
Tommy's Jerky Outlet, 12863, 49383
Tomorrow Enterprise, 12864
Tomric Systems Inc, 30324
Toms Moms Foods, LLC, 12865
Tomsed Corporation, 30325, 49384, 59878
Tone Products Inc, 12866, 49385
Tonewood Maple, 12867
Tonex, 12868, 49386
Tonnellerie Mercier, 30326
Tonnellerie Montross, 30327
Tonnellerie Radoux USA Inc, 30328
Tonnellerie Remond, 30329
Tonnino, 49387
Tony Chachere's Creole Foods, 12869
Tony Downs Foods, 12870, 49388
Tony Vitrano Company, 12871
Tony's Chocolonely, 12872
Tony's Fine Foods, 59879
Tony's Ice Cream Co, 12873
Tony's Pizza, 12874
Tony's Seafood LTD, 12875, 59880
Tonya's Gluten-Free Kitchen, 12876
Too Cool Chix, 12877
Too Good Gourmet, 12878, 59881
Toom Dips, 12879, 49389
Tooterville Trolley Company, 30330, 49390
Tootsi Impex, 49391
Tootsie Roll Industries Inc., 12880, 49392
Top Distributing Co, 59882
Top Hat Co Inc, 12881, 59883
Top Line Process Equipment Company, 30331, 49393
Top O' The Table, 41190
Top of the Table, 59884
Top Pot Doughnuts, 12882
Top Source Industries, 30332
Top Tier Foods Inc., 12883, 49394
Topac, 59885
Topaz Farm, 12884
Topco Associates LLC, 12885, 30333
Topflight Grain Co-Op, 30334, 53511, 59886
Topicz, 59887

1446

All Companies Index

Topo Chico Mineral Water, 12886, 49395
Topolos at Russian River Vine, 12887
Topor's Pickle & Food Svc Inc, 12888
Topos Mondial Corp, 30335
Toppo by Carlisle, 49396
Tops Business Forms, 30336
Tops Manufacturing Co, 30337, 49397
TOPS Markets, 41164
TOPS Software Corpora tion, 30024
Tor Rey Refrigeration Inc, 30338, 59888
Tor Rey USA, 30339
TOR-REY USA, 49139
Torani, 12889
Toray Plastics America Inc, 30340
Torbeck Industries, 30341, 49398
Torbit Dry Products Group, 53512
Torie & Howard LLC, 12890
Torke Coffee Co, 12891
Torkelson Brothers, 59889
Torkelson Cheese Co, 12892, 59890
Torn & Glasser, 12893
Torn Ranch, 12894
Toroid Corp, 30342, 49399
Toromont Process Systems, 30343, 49400
Toronto Fabricating & Manufacturing, 30344, 49401
Toronto Kitchen Equipment, 30345
Torpac Capsules, 30346, 49402
Torre Products Co Inc, 12895, 49403
Torrefazione Barzula & Import, 12896, 49404
Torrefazione Italia, 12897
Torreo Coffee Company, 12898, 59891
Torter Corporation, 41191, 49405
Tortilla Industry Associ, 30347
Tortillas Inc, 12899
Tortuga Rum Cake Company, 59892
Tosca Ltd, 30348
Toscarora, 30349, 49406
Toshoku America, 49407
Tosi & Company, 49408, 59893
Tosi Trading Company, 49409
Toska Foodservice Systems, 30350
Toss Machine Components, 30351
TOST Beverages LLC, 12482
Total Beverage Systems, 59894
Total Control Products, 30352
Total Foods Corporation, 30353
Total Identity Group, 30354
Total Lift Equipment Company, 59895
Total Liquor Controls, 59896
Total Logistic Control, 53513
Total Logistics Control, 53514
Total Lubricants, 30355
Total Quality Corp, 30356
Total Quality Corporation, 30357
Total Scale Systems, 30358
Totally Chocolate, 12900
Tote Vision, 49410
Toteco Packaging Co, 41192
Totem Ocean Trailer Express, 52149
Toter Inc, 30359, 49411
Totino's, 12901
Toucan Chocolates, 12902
Touch Controls, 30360
Touch Menus, 30361, 49412
Touche Bakery, 12903, 12904
Touchtunes Music Corporation, 49413
Toudouze Market Company, 59897
Toufayan Bakeries, 12905, 49414
Tourtellot & Co, 30362, 59898
Tova Industries LLC, 12906
Tower Intercontinental Group, 41193
Tower Pallet Co Inc, 30363
Town & Country Fancy Foods, 59899
Town & Country Foods, 59900
Town & Country Wholesale, 59901
Town Dock, 49415
Townfood Equipment Corp, 30364, 49416
Townsend Farms Inc, 12907, 49417, 59902
Townsend Research Laboratories, Inc, 30365
Townsend-Piller Packing, 30366

Toyo Seikan Kaisha, 30367
Toyota Forklifts Of Atlanta, 59903
Toyota Material Handling, 59904, 59905, 59906
Toyota Tsusho America Inc., 30368
Toyotalift Inc, 59907
TPS International, 30025
Tr International Trading Co, 41194
Trace Minerals Research, 12908
Traco Manufacturing Inc, 30369
Tracy Cold Storage, 53515
Tracy Luckey Pecans, 12909
Trade Diversified, 49418, 59908
Trade Farm, 49419
Trade Fixtures, 30370, 49420
Trade Marcs Group, 12910
Trade Winds Pizza, 12911
Trade Wings, 30371
Tradeco International Corp, 30372, 49421
Tradelink, 49422, 59909
Trademark Transportation, 52150
Trademarx Inc, 30373
Tradepaq Corporation, 30374
Trader Joe's, 59910
Trader Vic's Food Products, 12912, 49423
Tradeshare Corporation, 12913
Tradewinds, 12914
Tradewinds Coffee Company, 12915
Tradin Organics USA, 12916
Trading Corporation of America, 41195
Traditional Baking Inc, 12917
Traditional Medicinals Inc, 12918
Traeger Industries, 30375, 49424
Traex, 30376, 49425
Trafalgar Brewing Company, 12919
Tragon Corp, 30377
Trail's Best Snacks, 12920
Trailblazer Foods, 12921
Trailwood Warehouse LLC, 52151, 53516
Traina Foods Inc, 12922
Traitech Industries, 30378, 49426
Trak-Air/Rair, 30379, 49427
Traker Systems, 30380
Tram Bar LLC, 12923
Tramontina USA, 30381
Trane Inc, 30382, 49428
Trans Act Technologies Inc, 49429
Trans Flex Packagers Inc, 30383
Trans Pecos Foods, 12924, 49430
Trans Veyor, 59911
Trans World Services, 30384, 49431
Trans-Chemco Inc, 30385, 49432
Trans-Ocean Products Inc, 12925
Trans-Packers Svc Corp, 12926
Transamerica Wine Corporation, 12927
Transatlantic Foods, 41196, 49433
Transbotics Corp, 30386, 49434
Transcor, 53517
Transit Trading Corporation, 41197, 49435
Transition Equipment Company, 30387
Transmundo Company, 49436
Transnational Foods, 12928, 59912
Transnorm System Inc, 30388, 49437
Transpacific Foods Inc, 12929, 49438
Transparent Container Co, 30389
Tranter INC, 30390, 49439
Trap-Zap Environmental, 30391
Trappey's Fine Foods Inc, 12930
Trappist Preserves, 12931
Trappistine Quality Candy, 12932
Trattore Farms, 12933, 59913
Traub Container Corporation, 30392
Traulsen & Co, 30393, 49440
Travaini Pumps USA, 30394
Travel Chocolate, 12934
Travelon, 30395, 49441
Travis Manufacturing Corp, 30396
Travis Meats Inc, 12935
Tray-Pak Corp, 30397
Traycon Manufacturing Co, 30398, 49442

TRC, 30026, 49140
TRC Corp, 12483
Treasure Coast Coffee Company, 59914
Treasure Foods, 12936, 49443, 59915
Treasury Wine Estates, 12937, 59916
Treat Ice Cream Co, 12938
Treats Island Fisheries, 12939
Treatt USA Inc, 12940
Tree of Life Canada, 59917, 59918, 59919, 59920
Tree Ripe Products, 12941, 49444
Tree Saver, 30399
Tree Top Inc, 12942
Treehouse Farms, 12944, 49445
TreeHouse Foods, Inc., 12943, 30400
Treen Box & Pallet Inc, 30401
Treesweet Products, 12945
Trefethen Family Vineyards, 12946, 49446
Trega Foods, 12947
Treier Popcorn Farms, 12948, 30402, 59921
Treif USA, 30403, 49447
Treif USA Inc, 30404
Tremblay's Sweet Shop, 12949
Trend Marketing Services, 41198
Trendco Supply, 59922
Trent Corp, 30405
Trent Valley Distributors Ltd., 59923
Trentadue Winery, 12950
Trenton Bridge Lobster Pound, 12951, 59924
Trenton Cold Storage, 53518
Trenton Mills Inc, 30406
Trenton Processing Ctr, 12952
Treo Brands, 12953
Treofan America LLC, 30407
Trepte's Wire & Metal Works, 30408
TresOmega, 12954
Trevor Industries, 30409, 49448
Trevor Owen Limited, 30410, 49449
TREX Corp Inc., 49141
TRFG Inc, 30027, 41165
Tri Car Sales, 49450, 59925
Tri County Citrus Packers, 30411, 52152
Tri Mark SS Kemp, 59926
Tri Mark United East, 59927
Tri State Beef Co, 12955
Tri Tool Inc, 30412
Tri-Boro Fruit Co, 12956
Tri-Boro Shelving & Partition, 30413
Tri-Clover, 30414
Tri-Connect, 30415, 59928
Tri-Counties Packing Company, 12957
Tri-K Industries Inc, 30416
Tri-Marine International, 49451, 59929
Tri-Pak Machinery Inc, 30417, 49452
Tri-Seal, 30418, 49453
Tri-State Farms, 12958
Tri-State Ingredients, 12959
Tri-State Logistics Inc, 12960, 41199, 49454
Tri-State Plastics, 30419, 30420, 49455, 49456
Tri-State Wholesale, 59930
Tri-Sterling, 30421, 49457
Tri-Sum Potato Chip Company, 12961
Tri-Temp Distribution, 53519
Tri-Tronics, 30422, 49458
Tri-Waters Warehouse, 53520
Triad Brokers Inc, 41200
Triad Fisheries LTD, 59931
Triad Pallet Co Inc, 30423
Triad Products Company, 30424
Triad Scientific, 30425, 30426, 49459
Triangle Package Machinery Co, 30427, 49460
Triangle Sales, 41201
Triangle Seafood, 12962, 59932
Triangle Sign & Svc, 30428
Tribali Foods, 12963, 49461
Tribe 9 Foods, 12964, 59933
Tribe Mediterranean, 12965, 49462
Tribeca Oven, 12966
Tribest Corp, 49463, 59934

Tribology Tech Lube, 30429, 49464
Trickling Springs Creamery, 12967
Trico Converting Inc, 30430, 49465
Tricor Systems Inc, 30431, 30432
Tricore AEA, 30433
Trident, 30434
Trident Food Svc, 59935
Trident Plastics, 30435, 49466
Trident Seafoods Corp, 12968, 12969, 49467, 49468, 59936
Tridyne Process Systems, 30436, 49469
Trifactor Systems LLC, 59937
Trigo Corporation, 12970
Triland Foods Inc, 12971
Trilla Steel Drum Corporation, 30437
Trilogy Essential Ingredients, 30438, 49470
Trimble Agriculture, 30439
Trimen Foodservice Equipment, 30440, 49471
Trimline Corp, 30441
Trine Rolled Moulding Corp, 30442, 49472
Triner Scale & Mfg Co, 30443, 49473
Trinidad Benham Company, 12972
Trinidad Benham Corporation, 12973, 30444, 49474
Trinity Fruit Sale Co, 12974, 49475, 59938
Trinity Packaging, 30445, 49476
Trinity Spice, 12975
Trinity Transport & Distribution Services, 52153
Trinkle Sign & Display, 30446, 49477
Trio Packaging Corp, 30447, 49478
Trio Products, 30448, 49479
Trio Supply Company, 59939
Trio's Original Italian Pasta Co., 12976
Triple A Containers, 30449
Triple A Neon Company, 30450
Triple Cities Material Handling, 59940
Triple D Orchards Inc, 12977, 49480
Triple Dot Corp, 30451, 49481
Triple F, 59941
Triple H Food Processors Inc, 12978
Triple K Manufacturing Company, Inc., 12979
Triple Leaf Tea Inc, 12980, 49482
Triple Rock Brewing Co Brkly, 12981
Triple S Dynamics Inc, 30452, 49483
Triple Springs Spring Water Co, 12982
Triple U Enterprises, 12983
Triple XXX Root Beer Co., 12984
Triple-A Manufacturing Company, 30453, 49484
Triple-C, 12985
Tripoli Bakery Inc, 12986
Tripper Inc, 12987, 49485
Trisep Corporation, 30454
Tristao Trading, 12988
TRITEN Corporation, 30028, 49142
Triton International, 49486, 59942
Triton Seafood Co, 12989
Triton System Of Delaware LLC, 49487
Triumph Brewing Co, 12990
Triumph Foods, LLC, 12991
Triune Enterprises, 30455
Trojan Commercial Furni ture Inc, 30456, 49488
Trojan Inc, 30457, 49489
Trola Industries Inc, 30458
Tronex Industries, 30459
Tronics America, 30460
Trophy Foods, 59943
Trophy Nut Co, 12992
Tropic Fish Hawaii LLC, 12993, 59944
Tropic Ice Company, 59945
Tropic KOOL, 30461
Tropical Acai LLC, 12994, 49490
Tropical Blossom Honey Co, 12995
Tropical Cheese, 12996, 49491
Tropical Commodities, 12997, 49492
Tropical Foods, 12998, 12999, 13000, 13001, 13002, 13003, 13004, 49493
Tropical Illusions, 13005, 49494, 59946

1447

All Companies Index

Tropical Link Canada Ltd., 13006, 49495, 59947
Tropical Nut & Fruit Co, 13007
Tropical Nut Fruit & Bulk Cndy, 13008
Tropical Paradise, 59948
Tropical Preserving Co Inc, 13009, 49496
Tropical Soap Company, 30462
Tropical Treets, 13010, 59949
Tropical Valley Foods, 13011
Tropicana Products Inc., 13012, 49497
Troppers, 13013
Trotter Soft Pretzels, 13014
Trotters Importers, 49498
Trout Lake Farm, 13015, 49499
Trout Lake Farm Company, 30463
Troverco, 13016
Trowelon, 30464
Troxler Electronic Lab Inc, 30465
Troy Foods Inc, 13017, 59950
Troy Lighting, 30466, 49500
Troy Pork Store, 13018
Troyer Foods Inc, 13019, 59951
Tru Chocolate, 13020
Tru Form Plastics, 30467
Tru Fru, LLC, 13021, 49501
Tru Hone Corp, 30468, 30469, 49502, 49503
Tru-Blu Cooperative Associates, 13022
Truan's Candies, 13026
TruBrain, 13023, 59952
Trucco, A.J., 59953
Truchard Vineyards, 13027
Truckee River Winery, 13028, 59954
Truco Enterprises, 13029
True Beverages, 13030
True Blue Farms, 13031, 49506
True Food Service Equipment, Inc., 30471, 49507
True Jerky, 13032, 49508
True Manufacturing, 30472
True Nopal Cactus Water, 13033, 49509
True Organic Product Inc, 13034, 49510
True Pac, 30473, 49511
True Story Foods, 13035, 49512
True World Foods LLC, 13036, 49513, 59955
Truesdail Laboratories, 30474
Truffle Treasures, 13037
TruHeat Corporation, 30470, 49504
Truitt Bros Inc, 13038, 30475
Truly Nolen Pest Control, 30476
Trumark, 13039, 49514
Trumbull Nameplates, 30477
TruMoo, 13024
Trumps Food Interest, 13040
Truscello & Sons Wholesalers, 59956
Truth Bar LLC, 13041, 49515
TruVibe Organics, 13025, 49505
Try Coffee Group, 30478
Try The World, 49516
Try-Angle Food Brokers Inc, 41202
Tryco Coffee Service Annex Warehouse, 30479
TSA Griddle Systems, 30029, 49143
Tsar Nicoulai Caviar LLC, 13042, 49517, 49518, 59957
TSE Industries Inc, 30030
TSG Merchandising, 30031
TTS Technologies, 30032
Tu Me Beverage Company, 13043, 49519
Tualatin Estate Vineyards, 13044, 49520
Tubesales QRT, 30480
Tucel Industries, Inc., 30481, 49521
Tuchenhagen, 30482, 49522
Tuchenhagen North America, 30483
Tuchenhagen-Zajac, 30484
Tuckahoe Manufacturing Co, 30485, 59958
Tucker Cellars, 13045
Tucker Industries, 30486, 49523
Tucker Packing Co, 13046
Tucker Pecan Co, 13047, 59959
Tucker Sales, 41203
Tucson Container Corp, 30487, 49524
Tucson Coop. Warehouse, 59960

Tucson Food Svc, 59961
Tucson Frozen Storage, 53521
Tucson Tamale Company, 13048, 49525
Tudal Winery, 13049
Tudor Pulp & Paper Corporation, 30488, 49526
Tufco International, 30489, 59962
Tufco Technologies Inc, 49527, 59963
Tufts Ranch, 13050, 41204
Tufty Ceramics Inc, 30490, 49528
Tularosa Vineyards, 13051
Tulip Group Inc, 41205
Tulip Molded Plastics Corp, 30491
Tulkoff's Food Products Inc, 13052
Tull Hill Farms Inc, 13053
Tully's Coffee, 30492, 59964
Tulocay Cemetery, 13054
Tulox Plastics Corporation, 30493
Tulsa Plastics Co, 30494
TULSACK, 30033
Tumai Water, 13055
Tumbador Chocolate, 13056
Tumericalive Healing Enterprise, 13057
Tuna Fresh, 13058, 59965
Tundra Wild Rice, 13059, 49529
Tupperware Brands Corporation, 30495
Turano Baking, 13060, 13061
Turbana Corp., 49530
Turbo Refrigerating Company, 30496, 49531
Turbo Systems, 30497
TURBOCHEF Technologies, 30034, 49144
Turck, 30498, 30499
Turk Brothers Custom Meats Inc, 13062, 59966
Turkana Food, 30500, 49532, 59967
Turkey Creeks Snacks Inc, 13063
Turkey Hill Dairy Inc, 13064
Turkey Hill Sugarbush, 13065, 49533
Turkey Store, 13066
Turlock Cold Storage, 53522
Turlock Fruit Co, 13067, 49534
Turnbull Bakeries, 13068
Turnbull Cone Baking Company, 13069
Turner & Pease Company, 13070
Turner Dairy Farms Inc, 13071
Turner Holdings LLC, 59968
Turri's Italian Foods, 13072
Turtle Island Foods, 13073, 13074, 49535
Turtle Island Herbs, 13075, 59969
Turtle Wax, 30501, 49536
Turveda, 13076, 49537
Tuscan Bakery, 13077
Tuscan Dairy Farms, 13078
Tuscan Eat/Perdinci, 13079, 49538
Tuscarora Organic Growers Cooperative, 13080
Tusco Grocers Inc, 59970
Tusitala, 13081, 59971
Tusla Cold Storage, 53523
Tuthill Vacuum & Blower Systems, 30502, 49539
Tuthilltown Spirits, 13082
Tutt Global Industries, 49540
Tutti Gourmet, 13083
Tuv-Taam Corp, 13084
Tuway American Group, 30503, 49541
Tuxton China, 30504, 49542
TVC Systems, 30035
Tvc Wholesale Inc, 59972
TVT Trade Brands, 30036, 49145
TW Metals Inc, 30037
TW Transport Inc, 52135
Twang Partners LTD, 13085, 49543
Twelve Baskets Sales & Market, 30505, 59973
Twenty First Century Design, 30506
Twenty First Century Snacks, 13086
Twenty Four Hour Security Services, 59974
Twenty Rows, 13087
Twenty-First Century Foods, 13088, 49544
Twenty-Two Desserts, 13089

Twenty/Twenty Graphics, 30507
Twi Laq, 30508, 49545
Twin Cities Dry Storage Ltd., 53524
Twin City Bagels, 13090
Twin City Bottle, 30509
Twin City Bottle Company, 59975
Twin City Food Brokers, 41206
Twin City Foods Inc., 13091
Twin City Pricing & Label, 30510
Twin City Wholesale, 30511, 52154, 59976
Twin County Dairy, 13092
Twin Hens, 13093
Twin Marquis, 13094, 49546
Twin Modal, 52155
Twin Oaks Community, 13095
Twin State Signs, 30512
Twin Valley Developmental Services, 13096
Twinings North America Inc, 49547
Twinkle Baker Decor USA, 13055
Twinlab Corporation, 13097, 49548
TWL Corporation, 52136, 53489
TWM Manufacturing, 30038, 49146
Two Chefs on a Roll, 13098, 13099
Two Chicks and a Ladle, 13100
Two Friends Chocolates, 13101
Two Guys Spice Company, 13102, 41207, 59977
Two Leaves & A Bud Inc, 13103
Two Moms In The Raw, 13104
Two Rivers Enterprises, 30514, 59978
TXS, 30039
Tyco Fire Protection Products, 30515, 30516, 49550, 49551
Tyco Plastics, 30517, 49552
Tyco Retail Solutions, 30518, 49553
Tycodalves & Controls, 30519
Tyee Wine Cellars, 13106
Tyler Candy Co LLC, 13107
Tyler Packing Co, 13108
Tyler Supply Co, 59979
Tynan Equipment, 59980
Typecraft Wood & Jones, 30520
TyRy Inc, 13105, 49549
Tyson Foods Inc., 13109, 13110, 49554, 59981

U

U B KLEM Furniture Co Inc, 30521
U L Wholesale Lighting Fixture, 30522, 49555
U Okada & Co LTD, 13111, 59982
U Roast Em Inc, 13112, 30523, 59983
U-Line Corporation, 30524, 49556
U.C. Import & Company, 49557
U.S. Range, 13113, 30525, 49558
UAA, 30526
Uas Laboratories, 13130, 49578
UBC Food Distributors, 13114, 30527, 49559
UBC Marketing, 41208
UBF Food Solutions, 13115
Ubons Sauce LLC, 13131
UCB Inc, 30528
Ucc Ueshima Coffee Co Inc, 49579
UDEC Corp, 30529, 49560
Udi's Food, 30564
Udi's Gluten-Free Foods, 13132
Udi's Granola, 13133
UDY Corp, 30530
UFE, 30531
UFE Incorporated, 30532
UFL Foods, 13116, 49561
UFP Technologies, 30533
Ugo Di Lullo & Son, 13134
Uhlmann Co, 13135
Uhrden, 30565
Uhtamaki Foods Services, 30566
Uinta Brewing Co, 13136
Uinted Rental, 59999
Ukiah Foods, 60000
Ulcra Dynamics, 30567, 49580
ULDO USA, 13117

Ullman, Shapiro & Ullman LLP, 30568, 49581
Ulmer Pharmacal, 30569
Ultima Health Products Inc., 13137, 49582
Ultimate Bagel, 13138
Ultimate Biscotti, 13139
Ultimate Foods, 13140, 52159, 53530, 60001
Ultimate Gourmet, 13141
Ultimate International, 49583
Ultimate Nut & Candy Company, 13142
Ultimate Nutrition, 13143, 49584
Ultimate Salsa, 13144
Ultimate Textile, 30570
Ultra Cool International, 30571
Ultra Dairy, 13145
Ultra Enterprises, 13146, 49585
Ultra Industries Inc, 30572
Ultra Lift Corp, 30573
Ultra Packaging Inc, 30574
Ultra Process Systems, 30575
Ultra Seal, 13147, 49586
Ultrafilter, 30576, 49587
Ultrafryer Systems Inc, 30577, 49588
Ultrak, 30578
Ultralight Plastic, 30579
Ultrapak, 30580
Ultrapar Inc., 30581, 60002
Ultratainer, 30582
Umanoff & Parsons, 13148
Umec Solar Inc, 30583
Umpqua Dairy, 13149, 49589
Umpqua Oats, 13150
Unarco Industries LLC, 30584, 49591
Unarco Material Handling Inc, 30585, 49592
Uncle Andy's Cafe, 13152
Uncle Charley's Sausage, 13153
Uncle Charlie's Meats, 60003
Uncle Dougie's, 13154, 49593
Uncle Fred's Fine Foods, 13155, 49594
Uncle Lee's Tea Inc, 13156, 49595
Uncle Matt's Organic, 13157, 49596
Uncle Ralph's Cookies, 13158
Uncle Ray's Potato Chips, 13159
Uncommon Grounds Coffee, 13160
Underground Warehouses, 53531
Underwriters Laboratories Inc, 30586
Une-Viandi, 13161, 49597
Uneco Systems, 30587
Unette Corp, 30588
UNEX Manufacturing, 30534
Unex Manufacturing Inc, 30589
Ungars Food, 13162
Unger Co, 30590, 49598
Ungerer & Co, 13163, 49599
Uni Carriers Americas Corp, 30591
Uni Co Supply, 60004
Uni First Corp, 30592
Uni-Chains Manufacturing, 30593
Unibloc-Pump Inc, 30597, 30598
Unibroue/Unibrew, 13164, 49601
Unica, 13165
UniChem Enterprises, 30594
Unichema North America, 30599
Unico, 60006
Unicold Corp, 52160, 53532, 53533, 53534
Unicorn Enterprises, 60007
Unidex, 30600
Unified Food Ingredients, 13166, 49602
Unifiller Systems, 30601
Unifoil Corp, 30602, 49603
Uniforms To You, 30603, 49604
Uniforms To You & Co, 30604
Unilever Canada, 13167, 49605, 60008
Unilever Food Solutions, 13168
Unilever US, 13169, 49606, 60009
Uniloy Milacron, 30605
Unimar Inc, 30606
Unimove LLC, 30607, 49607
Union, 13170, 49608
Union Camp Corporation, 30608
Union Confectionery Machinery, 49609

All Companies Index

Union Cord Products Company, 30609, 49610
Union Fish Co, 49611
Union Fisheries Corp, 13171, 60010
Union Grocery Company, 60011
Union Ice Co, 53535
Union Industries, 30610, 49612
Union Pacific Railroad Co, 52161
Union Plastics Co, 30611
Union Process, 30612, 49613
Union Seafoods, 13172, 60012
Union Square Wines & Spirits, 13173
Union Standard Equipment Company, 41211
Union Storage & Transfer Co, 52162, 53536
Union Wine Co, 13174, 60013
Unipac Shipping, 30613
Unipak Inc, 30614
Uniplast Films, 30615, 49614
UniPro Foodservice, Inc., 30595, 60005
Unique Beverage Company, 13175, 49615
Unique Boxes, 30616
Unique Foods, 13176
Unique Ingredients LLC, 13177, 49616
Unique Manufacturing, 30617, 49617
Unique Manufacturing Company, 30618, 49618
Unique Plastics, 30619
Unique Pretzel Bakery, Inc., 13178, 49619
Unique Solutions, 30620, 49620
Unique Vitality Products, 13179, 49621
Uniquely Together, 13180
Unirak Storage Systems, 30621, 49622
Unisoft Systems Associates, 30622
Unisource Manufacturing Inc, 30623
Unitech Scientific, 30624
United Ad Label, 30625, 49623
United Air Specialists Inc, 30626, 49624
United Apple Sales, 13181, 49625
United Bags Inc, 30627, 49626
United Bakers & Deli Supply, 60014
United Bakery Equipment, 30628
United Bakery Equipment Company, 30629, 49627
United Banana Company, 49628, 60015
United Barrels, 30630
United Basket Co Inc, 30631
United Brands, 41212
United Brokers Company, 41213
United Canadian Malt, 13182, 49629
United Canning Corporation, 13183
United Chairs, 49630, 60016
United Citrus, 13184, 49631
United Cold Storage, 53537
United Commercial Corporation, 30632
United Dairy Co-Op Svc, 60017
United Dairy Farmers Inc., 13185
United Dairy Inc., 13186
United Dairy Machinery Corp, 60018
United Dairymen of Arizona, 13187
United Desiccants, 30633, 49632
United Electric Controls Co, 30634, 49633
United Express, 52163
United Fabricators, 30635
United Facilities, 53538
United Filters Intl, 30636, 49634
United Fire & Safety Service, 30637
United Fishing Agency LTD, 13188, 60019
United Flexible, 30638, 49635
United Floor Machine Co, 30639, 49636
United Foods & Fitness, 49637, 60020
United Foods USA, 13189
United Foodservice Sales, 41214
United Forklift Corporation, 60021
United Glassware & China, 60022
United Grain Growers, 60023
United Industries Group Inc, 30640, 49638
United Industries Inc, 30641
United Insulated Structures, 30642

United International Indstrs, 41215, 49639
United Intertrade Corporation, 13190
United Intratrade, 13191
United Juice Companies of America, 13192
United Label Corp, 30643
United Lighting & Supply Co, 60024
United Machinery & Supply Company, 60025
United Marketing Exchange, 13193, 49640
United Mc Gill Corp, 30644
United Meat Company, 13194, 49641
United Mineral & Chemical Corporation, 49642, 60026
United Natural Foods Inc, 60027
United Noodle Manufacturing Company, 13195
United Noodles, 60028
United Olive Oil Import, 30645, 49643
United Pentek, 30646
United Performance Metals, 30647, 49644
United Pickles, 13196, 49645, 60029
United Pies Of Elkhart Inc, 13197
United Potato Company, 60030
United Produce, 60031
United Products & Instr Inc, 30648
United Provision Meat Company, 13198
United Pulse Trading Inc, 13199
United Refrigerations Svc, 53539
United Rentals, 60032
United Restaurant Equipment Co, 60033
United Restaurant Specialties, 41216
United Ribtype Co, 30649, 49646
United Salt Corp, 13200, 49647
United Seafood Imports, 49648, 60034
United Seal & Tag Corporation, 30650, 49649
United Shellfish Co Inc, 60035
United Showcase Company, 30651, 49650
United Sign Corp, 30652
United Specialty Flavors, 30653
United States Beverage LLC, 49651, 60036
United States Cold Storage, 53540, 53541, 53542, 53543, 53544, 53545, 53546, 53547, 53548, 53549, 53550, 53551, 53552, 53553, 53554, 53555, 53556, 53557, 53558, 53559, 53560, 53561, 53562, 53563, 53564, 53565, 53566, 53567, 53568, 53569, 53570, 53571, 53572, 53573, 53574, 53575, 53576, 53577, 53578, 53579, 53580
United States Sugar Corp, 60037
United States Systems Inc, 30654, 49652
United Steel Products Company, 30655, 49653
United Sugars Corporation, 60038
United Supermarkets, 13201
United Supply, 49654
United Textile Distribution, 30656, 49655
United Universal Enterprises Corporation, 49656, 60039
United Valley Bell Dairy, 13202, 49657
United Warehouse Co, 53581
United Wholesale Grocery Company, 60040
United With Earth, 13203, 49658, 60041
Unitherm Food System, 30657, 30658, 49659
UniTrak Corporation, 30596, 49600
Unity Brands Group, 30659, 49660, 60042
Univar USA, 30660, 41217, 49661, 53582, 60043
Universal Aqua Technologies, 30661
Universal Beef Products, 13204
Universal Beverage Equipment, 30662

Universal Beverages Inc, 13205, 13206, 49662
Universal Coatings, 30663
Universal Commodities Tea, 49663
Universal Container Corporation, 30664
Universal Die & Stampings, 30665, 49664
Universal Dynamics Technologies, 30666, 49665
Universal Fish of Boston, 60044
Universal Folding Box, 30667
Universal Folding Box Company, 30668
Universal Formulas, 13207
Universal Handling Equipment, 30669, 49666
Universal Impex Corporation, 13208, 30670
Universal Industries Inc, 30671, 49667
Universal Jet Industries, 30672, 49668
Universal Labeling Systems Inc, 30673
Universal Machine Co, 30674
Universal Marketing, 30675, 41218, 49669, 60045
Universal Nutrition, 13209, 60046
Universal Overall, 30676
Universal Packaging Inc, 30677, 49670
Universal Packaging Mchry Corp, 30678
Universal Paper Box, 30679, 49671
Universal Plastics, 30680
Universal Poultry Company, 13210
Universal Preservachem Inc, 13211, 60047
Universal Restaurant Equipment, 60048
Universal Sanitizers & Supplies, 30681, 60049
Universal Security Instrs Inc, 49672
Universal Sign Company and Manufacturing Company, 30682, 30683
Universal Sodexho, 60050
Universal Stainless, 30684
Universal Stainless & Alloy, 30685
Universal Strapping, 30686
Universal Tag Inc, 30687
University Products, 30688
University-Brink, 30689
Univex Corp, 30690, 49673
Uniweb Inc, 30691
Uniwell Systems, 60051
Unlimited Exports & Imports, 49674
Unna Bakery, 13212
UNOI Grainmill, 13118
UnReal Brands, 13151, 49590
Up Mountain Switchel, 13213
UPACO Adhesives, 30555
Upcountry Fisheries, 13214, 60052
Update International, 30692, 49675
Upham & Walsh Lumber, 30693, 49676
UPM Raflatac, 30536
UPN Pallet Company, 30537
Upper Crust Bakery USA, 13215
Upper Crust Biscotti, 13216
Upper Lakes Foods Inc, 60053
Upper Limits EngineeringCompany, 30694
Upright, 30695, 49677
UPS Freight, 52156
UPS Logistics Technologies, 30538
Upstate Farms, 13217, 60054
Upstate Niagara Co-Op Inc., 13218
Uptime Energy, Inc., 13219, 49678
Upton's Naturals, 13220, 49679
Uptown Bakers, 13221, 60055
Urania Engineering Co Inc, 30696
Urban Accents, 13222
Urban Foods LLC, 13223
Urban Moonshine, 13224
Urban Oven, 13225
Urbani Truffles, 49680
Urgasa, 13226
Urnex Brands Inc, 30697, 49681
URS Logistics, 53525, 53526
Ursel Laboratories, 30698, 49682
Ursini Plastics, 30699
Ursula's Island Farms Company, 13227

US Apple Assn, 30539
Us Bottlers Machinery Co Inc, 30700, 49683
US Can Company, 30540, 49562
US Cap Systems Corporation, 30541
US Chemical, 30542, 49563
US Chocolate Corp, 13119, 49564
US Coexcell Inc, 30543
US Cooler Company, 30544
US Distilled Products Co, 13120, 41209, 49565
US Durum Products LTD, 13121
US Filter, 30545, 30546
US Filter Corporation, 30547
US Filter Dewatering Systems, 30548, 49566
US Filter/Continental Water, 30549
Us Flag & Signal, 30701
US Food Products, 41210, 49567, 59984
US Foods & Pharmaceuticals Inc, 13122
US Foods Inc, 59985, 59986, 59987, 59988, 59989, 59990, 59991, 59992
US Growers Cold Storage, 53527, 59993
US Industrial Lubricants, 30550, 49568
US Ingredients, 13123
US Jet Logistical Warehouses, 53528
US Label Corporation, 30551, 49569
US Line Company, 30552, 49570
US Magnetix, 30553
US Marketing Company, 49571, 59994
US Materials Handling Corp, 59995
US Mills, 13124, 49572
US Plastic Corporation, 30554
Us Plastics, 60056
US Product, 30555
Us Rubber, 30702, 49684
US Seating Products, 30556, 49573
US Standard Sign, 30557
US Sugar Company, 13125
US Tag & Label, 30558
US Tsubaki Holdings Inc, 30559
US Wellness Meats, 13126
USA Beverage, 13127
USA Canvas Shoppe, 30560
USA Laboratories Inc, 13128, 49574
USAir, 52157
USC Consulting Group, 30561
USDA-NASS, 30562, 49575
USECO, 30563, 49576
Useco/Epco Products, 30703
Utah Coffee Roasters, 13229
Utah PaperBox Company, 30704
Utica Cutlery Co, 30705, 49686
Utility Refrigerator Company, 30706, 49687
UTZ Quality Foods Inc, 52158, 53529
UTZ Quality Foods Inc., 13129, 59996
Utzy, Inc., 13230
UVA Packaging, 49577, 59997
Uvalde Meat Processing, 13231
UW Provision Co., 59998

V

V & E Kohnstamm Inc, 13232, 49688
V & V Supremo, 13233
V C 999 Packaging Systems, 30707, 30708, 49689
V Chocolates, 13234
V L Foods, 13235
V R Food Equipment Inc, 30709
V Sattui Winery, 13236
V&B Distributing, 60057
V&R Metal Enterprises, 30710
V-Ram Solids, 30711, 30712, 49690
V-Suarez Provisions, 49691, 60058
V-Tech Ingredients, 41219
V.M. Calderon, 41220, 49692, 60059
V.W. Joyner & Company, 13237, 49693
Vac Air Inc, 30727
Vac-U-Max, 30728, 49705
Vacaville Fruit Co, 13244, 49706
Vacuform Inc., 30729, 49707
Vacumet Corp, 30730, 49708

1449

All Companies Index

Vacumet Corporation, 30731
Vacuum Barrier Corp, 30732, 49709
Vacuum Depositing Inc, 30733
VacuWest, 60064
Vader & Landgraf, 41222
Vaisala Inc, 30734
Val Verde Winery, 13245
Val's Seafood, 13246, 60065
Val-Pak Direct Market Systems, 30735, 49710
Valad Electric Heating Corporation, 30736, 49711
Valco Melton, 30737, 49712
Valdez Food Inc, 13247
Vale Enterprises, 60066
Valentine Chemicals, 13248
Valentine Enterprises Inc, 13249, 49713
Valentino USA, 49714
Valeo, 30738, 49715
Valesco Trading, 30739, 49716
Valhalla Winery, 13250
Valhrona, 13251
Vallero Mercantile Company, 60067
Vallet Foodservice, 60068
Valley Bakery, 13252
Valley City Sign Co, 30740
Valley Container Corporation, 30741
Valley Container Inc, 30742, 49717
Valley Craft Inc, 30743, 49718
Valley Distributing Company, 60069, 60070
Valley Distributors, 60071
Valley Distributors & Storage Company, 52164, 53583
Valley Farms LLC, 13253
Valley Fig Growers, 13254, 49719
Valley Fixtures, 30744, 49720
Valley Foods, 60072
Valley Foods Inc, 60073
Valley Fruit & Produce Company, 60074
Valley Grain Products, 13255
Valley International Cold Storage, Inc., 53584
Valley Lahvosh, 13256
Valley Lea Laboratories Inc, 30745
Valley Meat Company, 13257
Valley Meats, 13258
Valley Milk Products, 13259
Valley of the Moon Winery, 13267
Valley Packaging Supply Co, 30746, 49721
Valley Pride Food Distributor, 60075
Valley Queen Cheese Factory, 13260
Valley Seafoods, 49722
Valley Storage Company, 53585
Valley Sun Products Inc, 13261
Valley Tea & Coffee, 13262
Valley View Blueberries, 13263
Valley View Cheese Co Inc, 13264
Valley View Packing Co, 13265, 49723
Valley View Winery, 13266
Vallos Baking Co, 13268
Valmont Composite Structures, 30747
Valrhona, 49724
Valspar Corp, 30748
Valspar Paint, 30749
Valu Guide & Engineering, 30750
Valu-Line Foods, 60076
Valvinox, 30751, 49725
Van Air Systems, 30752, 49726
Van Blarcom Closures Inc, 30753, 49727
Van Brunt Port Jersey Warehouse, 52165, 53586
Van Dam Machine Corp, 30754
Van Damme Confectionery, 49728
Van de Kamps, 13282, 49733
Van Der Graaf Corporation, 30755, 49729
Van Der Heyden Vineyards, 13269
Van der Pol Muller International, 30761
Van Dereems Mfg Co, 30756
Van Drunen Farms, 13270, 49730
Van Dyke Ice Cream, 13271
Van Eeghen International Inc, 13272
Van Eerden Foodservice Co Inc, 60077

Van Hees Gmbh, 13273
Van Kam, G Trading Company, 41223
Van Leer Chocolate Corporation, 13274
Van Leer Flexibles, 30757
Van Leeuwen, 13275
Van Lock Co, 30758
Van Nuys Awning Co, 30759
Van Oriental Food Inc, 13276, 49731
Van Otis Chocolates, 13277
Van Pak Corporation, 30760
Van Peenans Dairy, 13278
Van Reed Sales Company, 41224
Van Rex Gourmet Foods, 41225
Van Roy Coffee Co, 13279
Van Solkema Produce Inc, 60078, 60079
Van Tone Creative, 13280
Van Vooren Game Ranch, 49732
Van Waters & Roger, 13281
Van Waters & Rogers, 60080
Van Wyk Freight Lines, 52166
Van's International Foods, 13283
Van-Lang Food Products, 13284
Vana Life Foods, 13285, 49734
Vance Metal Fabricators Inc, 30763
Vance's Foods, 13286, 49735
Vanco Products Company, 30764
Vanco Trading Inc, 13287
Vancouver Island Brewing Company, 13288
Vancouver Manufacturing, 30765
Vande Berg SCALES/Vbs Inc, 30766
Vande Walle's Candies Inc, 13289
Vanderburgh & Company, 49736
Vanee Foods Co, 13290
Vanguard Packaging Film, 30767
Vanguard Technology Inc, 30768, 49737
Vanilla Corp Of America LLC, 13291, 49738, 53587, 60081
Vanilla Saffron Imports, 49739
Vanlab Corporation, 13292
Vanmark Equipment, 13293, 30769, 49740
Vanmark Equipment LLC, 30770, 49741
Vanns Spices LTD, 13294
VanSan Corporation, 30762
Vansco Products, 30771
Vantage Foods, 13295
Vantage Pak International, 30772
Vantage Performance Materials, 30773, 30774, 49742, 60082
Vantage USA, 30775, 52167, 60083
Vapor Power Intl LLC, 30776, 49743
Varco Brothers, 13296
Varco Products, 30777
Varda Chocolatier, 13297
Varet Street Market, 13298
Variant, 30778, 49744
Varick Enterprises, 30779
Varied Industries Corp, 13299, 49745
Variety Glass Inc, 30780, 49746
Varimixer North America, 30781, 49747
Varitronic Systems, 30782, 49748
Varni Brothers/7-Up Bottling, 13300, 49749
Vasconia Housewares, 30783
Vasinee Food Corporation, 30784, 49750, 60084
Vaughan Co Inc, 30785
Vaughan-Chopper Pumps, 30786
Vaughn Belting Co-Main Acct, 30787
Vaughn Packing Company, 60085
Vaughn Rue Produce, 13301
Vaughn-Russell Candy Kitchen, 13302, 49751, 53588, 60086
Vauxhall Foods, 13303, 49752
Vaxa International, 13304
VBS Inc Material Handling, 60060
VC Menus, 30713, 49694
VCF Films Inc, 30714
VCG Uniform, 30715
VCI Beverage Center, 49695
VCPB Transportation, 13238, 49696
Vector Corp, 30788, 49753
Vector Packaging, 30789
Vector Technologies, 30790, 49754

Vee Gee Scientific Inc, 30791
Vega Americas Inc, 30792, 49755
Vega Food Industries Inc, 13306
Vega Mfg Ltd., 30793
Vega Trading Company, 49756
Vegan Metal Fabricators Co, 13307
Vegan Rob's, 13308
Vegan Treats, 13309
Vege USA, 13310
Vege-Cool, 13311
Vegetable Juices Inc, 13312
Vegetarian Resource Group, 49757
Vegetarian Traveler, 13313
Veggie Grill, 13314
Veggie Land, 13315, 49758, 49759
VegGuide.org, 13305
Vegi-Deli, 13316, 49760
Vegware, 30794, 60087
Vegy Vida, 13317
Velatis, 13318
Velcro USA, 30795
Velda Farms, 13319
Vella Cheese Co, 13320
Velvet Creme Popcorn Co, 13321
Velvet Ice Cream Co Inc, 13322
Vend Food Service, 60088
Vending Nut Co, 13323, 49761, 60089
Vendome Copper & Brass Works, 30796, 49762
Vendors Purchasing Council, 60090
Venetian Productions, 49763
Venezia Brothers, 60091
Venice Baking Co, 13324
Venner International Products, 49764
Vent Master, 30797, 49765
Vent-A-Hood Co, 30798, 49766
Ventana Vineyards Winery, 13325
Ventre Packing Company, 13326, 49767
Ventura Coastal LLC, 13327, 49768
Ventura Foods LLC, 13328, 60092
Venture Measurement Co LLC, 30799, 30800, 49769, 49770
Venture Packaging & Distribution, 60093
Venture Packaging Inc, 30801
Venture Vineyards, 13329, 49771
Venturetech Corporation, 30802
Venus Corp, 30803
Venus Supply Company, 60094
Venus Wafers Inc, 13330, 49772
Veramar Vineyard, 13332
Verax Chemical Co, 30804, 49773
Verdant Kitchen, 13333
Verday, 13334, 49774
Verde Farms, LLC, 13335, 49775, 60095
Verdure Sciences, 13336
Verhoff Alfalfa Mill Inc, 13337
Veri Fone Inc, 30805
Verifine Dairy, 13338
Verify Brand Inc, 30806
Verilon Products Co, 30807
Veritas Chocolatier, 13339
Veritas Vineyard, 13340
Veritiv Corp, 60096
Verlasso, 13341, 49776
Vermilion Packers Ltd, 13342
Vermillion Flooring, 30808, 49777
VerMints Inc., 13331
Vermont Bag & Film, 30809
Vermont Bread Co, 13343
Vermont Chocolatiers, 13344
Vermont Coffee Co, 13345
Vermont Commercial Warehouse, 53589
Vermont Confectionery, 13346
Vermont Container Corp, 30810
Vermont Country Naturals, 13347, 60097
Vermont Creamery, 13348, 13349
Vermont Food Experience, 13350
Vermont Harvest Spec Food LLC, 13351
Vermont Liberty Tea, 13352
Vermont Made Richard's Sauces, 13353
Vermont Natural Co, 13354
Vermont Nut Free Chocolates, 13355
Vermont Pretzel & Cookie Co., 13356
Vermont Railway Inc, 52168
Vermont Signature Sauces, 13357

Vermont Smoke and Cure, 13358
Vermont Specialty Food Association, 13359
Vermont Sweetwater Bottling Co, 13360
Vermont Tea & Trading Co Inc, 13361, 49778
Vermont Tent Co, 30811
Vermont Tissue Paper Company, 30812
Vermont Tortilla Company, 13362
Vermont Village, 13363
Vermont Wholesale Foods, 60098
Vern's Cheese, 13364, 30813, 60099
Vernon Plastics, 30814
Veroni USA, 49779
Veronica Foods Inc, 13365, 49780
Veronica's Treats, 13366, 30815
Versa Cold, 53590
Versa Conveyor, 30816, 49781
Versa-Matic Pump Company, 30817
Versacold Logistics Services, 52169, 53591
Versailles Lighting, 30818, 49782
Versatile Mobile Systems, 30819
Verst Group Logistics Inc, 52170, 53592
Vertex China, 30820, 49783
Vertex Interactive, 30821, 49784
Vertical Systems Intl, 30822, 49785
Vertique Inc, 30823
Verve Coffee Roasters, 13367
Veryfine Products Inc, 13368
Vescom America, 30824, 49786
Vessel Services Inc, 60100
Vessey & Co Inc, 13369, 49787
Vestergaard Farms, 13370
Vesture Corp, 49788
Veteran Foods Sales Co, 60101
Vetrerie Bruni, 30825
Vetrerie Bruni USA, 49789
VetriTech Laboratories, 49790, 60102
Vetter Vineyards Winery, 13371, 30826
Via Della Chiesa Vineyards, 13372
Viacam, 30827
Viader Vineyards & Winery, 13373
Viano Vineyards, 13374
Viansa Winery, 13375
Viatec, 30828, 49791
Viatec Process Storage System, 30829, 49792
Viatran Corporation, 30830
Viau Foods, 13376
Vibrac LLC-Fax, 30831
VibroFloors World, 30832
Vic's Corn Popper, 13377
VICAM, 30716
Vichy Springs Mineral Water, 13378, 49793
Vickey's Vittles, 13379
Vicksburg Chemical Company, 30833, 49794
Vicky's Artisan Bakery, 13380, 60103
Vicmore Manufacturing Company, 30834, 49795
Victel Service Co, 60104
Victone Manufacturing Company, 30835
Victor Allen Coffee Company, 13381
Victor Allen's Coffee and Tea, 13382
Victor Associates, 30836
Victor International, 49796
Victor Joseph Son Inc, 49797
Victor Ostrowski & Son, 13383
Victor Packing, 13384, 49798
Victor Preserving Company, 13385
Victoria Amory & Co LLC, 13386
Victoria Fancy Sausage, 13387
Victoria Fine Foods, 13388, 49799
Victoria Gourmet Inc, 13389
Victoria Porcelain, 30837, 49800
Victoria's Catered Traditions, 13390
Victorinox Swiss Army Inc, 60105
Victors Market Co, 60106
Victory Box Corp, 30838
Victory Packaging, 60107
Victory Packaging, Inc., 30839
Victory Refrigeration, 30840
Victory Spud Service, 60108

1450

All Companies Index

Victrola Coffee Roasters, 13391
Vida Blend, 13392
Vidalia Brands Inc, 13393
Vidalia Sweets Brand, 13394, 60109
Videojet Technologies Inc, 30841, 30842, 49801
Videri Chocolate Factory, 13395
Videx Inc, 30843
Vie De France Yamazaki Inc, 13396
Vie-Del Co, 13397, 49802
Vienna Bakery, 13398
Vienna Beef LTD, 13399, 13400, 49803
Vienna Distributing Company, 60110
Vienna Meat Products, 13401, 49804
Vietti Foods Co Inc, 13402
View-Rite Manufacturing, 30844, 49805
VIFAN Canada, 30717, 49697
Vifan USA, 30845
Vigneri Chocolate Inc., 13403, 49806
Vigo Importing Co, 13404, 49807
Viki's Montana Classics, 13405
Viking Corp, 30846, 49808
Viking Distillery, 13406
Viking Identification Product, 30847
Viking Industries, 30848, 49809
Viking Label Inc, 30849
Viking Machine & Design Inc, 30850
Viking Packaging & Display, 30851
Viking Pallet Corp, 30852
Viking Pump Inc, 30853
Viking Seafoods Inc, 13407
Viking Trading, 13408, 60111
Vikis Foods, 13409
Viktoria's Gourmet Foods, LLC, 13410
Villa Barone, 13411
Villa Helena/Arger-Martucci Winery, 13412
Villa Milan Vineyard, 13413
Villa Mt. Eden Winery, 13414, 49810
Villa Park Orchards Assn, 60112
Village Roaster, 13415
Villar Vintners of Valdese, 13416
Vilore Foods Co Inc, 13417, 49811
Vilore Foods Company, 49812, 60113
Vilter Manufacturing Corporation, 30854, 49813
Vimco, 30855
Vin-Tex, 30856
Vinalhaven Fishermens Co-op, 13418, 60114
Vince's Seafoods, 13419, 49814
Vincent Arroyo Winery, 13420
Vincent B Zaninovich & Sons, 13421, 49815
Vincent Commodities Corporation, 30857
Vincent Corp, 30858, 49816
Vincent Formusa Company, 13422, 49817
Vincent Giordano Prosciutto, 60115
Vincent Piazza Jr & Sons, 13423, 60116
Vincent's Food Corporation, 13424
Vincor Canada, 13425, 49818
Vine Solutions, 30859
Vine Village Day, 13426
Vineco International Products, 30860, 49819, 60117
Vineland Ice & Storage, 53593
Vineyard Gate, 60118
Vingcard/Elsafe, 49820
Vinh Hoan USA, Inc., 49821
VINITECH, 30718
Vink & Beri, 13427
Vino's Brew Pub, 13428
Vinoklet Winery, 13429
Vinos USA, 49822
Vinquiry Wine Analysis, 13430
Vintage, 30861
Vintage Bee Inc., 13431
Vintage Food Corp, 49823
Vintage Italia, 13432
Vintage Plantations Cho colates, 13433
Vintage Wine Estates, 13434
Viobin USA, 13435, 49824
Viola's Gourmet Goodies, 13436, 60119
Violet Packing Holdings LLC, 13437

Violife, 13438, 49825
VIP Food Svc, 13239, 60061
VIP Foods, 13240, 49698
VIP Real Estate LTD, 30719, 49699
VIP Sales Company, 13241, 49700
Virgil's Root Beer, 13439
Virgin Cola USA, 30862
Virgin Raw Foods LLC, 13440, 49826
Virginia & Spanish Peanut Co, 13441
Virginia Artesian Bottling Company, 13442, 30863
Virginia Chutney Company, 13443
Virginia Dare Extract Co, 13444, 49827
Virginia Department of Agriculture & Consumer Services, 30864
Virginia Diner Inc, 13445
Virginia Fruit Sales Service, 41226
Virginia Honey Company, 13446
Virginia Industrial Services, 30865, 49828
Virginia Plastics Co, 30866, 49829
Virginia Trout Co, 13447
Virginia Wholesale Company, 60120
Virtual Packaging, 30867
Visalia Citrus Packing Group, 13448, 30868
Visalia Fruit Exchange, 49830, 60121
Visalia Produce Sales, 13449, 60122
Viscofan USA Inc, 30869
Vision Pack Brands, 13450
Vision Seafood Partners, 13451, 60123
Visionary Design, 30870
Visions Espresso Svc, 30871
Visipak, 30872
Visiplex, 49831
Viskase Co Inc, 30873, 49832
Vista D'Oro Farms, 13452
Vista Food Exchange, 49833, 60124
Vista Food Exchange Inc, 49834, 60125
Vista Internatlonal Packaging, 30874, 30875
Vistar, 60126
Vistar Mid-Atlantic, 60127
Vistar Northwest, 60128
Visual Graphics Systems, 49835
Visual Marketing Assoc, 30876
Visual Packaging Corp, 30877
Visual Planning Corp, 30878, 49836
Vit-Best Nutrition, 13453
Vita Coco, 60129
Vita Craft Corp, 30879, 49837
Vita Food Products Inc, 13454, 49838
Vita Juice Corporation, 30880
Vita Key Packaging, 30881
Vita Plus Corp, 13455
Vita-Pakt Citrus Products Co, 13456, 49839
Vita-Pure Inc, 13457
Vitakem Neutraceutical Inc, 13459, 30883, 60130
Vital 18, 60131
Vital Choice, 13460, 60132
Vital Farms, 13461
Vital Proteins LLC, 13462, 49841
Vitale Poultry Company, 13463
Vitalicious, 13464
Vitality Life Choice, 13465
Vitality Works, 13466, 49842
Vitamer Laboratories, 13467
Vitamilk Dairy, 13468
Vitamin Power, 60133
VitaMinder Company, 30882, 49840
Vitaminerals, 13469, 49843
Vitamins, 13470
Vitamix, 30884, 49844
Vitarich Ice Cream, 13471, 49845
Vitarich Laboratories, 13472, 49846
Vitasoy USA, 13473, 49847
Vitatech Nutritional Sciences, 13474, 30885
VitaThinQ Inc., 13458
Viterra, Inc, 13475, 49848, 52171
Vitex Packaging Group, 30886
Vitro Packaging, 30887, 30888
Vitro Seating Products, 30889, 49849

Vitusa Products Inc, 60134
Vity Meat & Provisions Company, 13476, 60135
Viva Tierra, 13477, 60136
Vive Organic, 13478
Vivienne Dressings, 13479
Vivion Inc, 41227, 53594, 60137
Vivitar Security Systems, 60138
Vivolac Cultures Corp, 30890
Vivolac Cultures Corporation, 13480, 49850
Vivoo, 13481, 49851
Vivra Chocolate, 13482
Vixen Kitchen, 13483, 60139
VLR Food Corporation, 13242
VMC Corp, 49701, 60062
VMC Signs, 30720
Vocatura Bakery Inc, 13484
VOD Gourmet, 13243
Vogel, 49852, 60140
Vogel Lubrication Systems, 30891
Vogel Popcorn, 13485
Voget Meats Inc, 13486
Vogt Tube Ice, 30892, 49853, 49854
Vogue Cuisine Foods, 13487
Voigt Lighting Industries Inc., 30893
Volcano Island Honey Company, 13488
Volckening Inc, 30894, 49855
Volk Corp, 30895, 49856
Volk Enterprises Inc, 30896
Volk Packaging Corp, 30897, 49857
Vollrath Co LLC, 30898, 49858
Vollwerth & Baroni Companies, 13489, 60141
Volpe, Son & Kemelhar, 60142
Volpi Foods, 13490
Volta Belting Technology, Inc., 30899, 49859
Volumetric Technologies, 30900, 60143
Volunteer Express, 52172, 52173
Vomela/Harbor Graphics, 30901
Von Gal Corp, 30902
Von Stiehl Winery, 13491
Von Strasser, 13492
Vonco Products LLC, 30903
Voodoo Doughnut, 13493
Voorhees Rubber Mfg Co, 30904, 49860, 60144
Voortman Bakery, 13494
Vorti-Siv, 30905, 49861
Vortron Smokehouse/Ovens, 30906, 49862
Vorwerk, 30907
Vosges Haut-Chocolat, 13495
Voss Belting & Specialty Co, 30908
Voss Equipment Inc, 60145
Voyageur Trading Division, 49863, 60146
VP Northeast, 41221
VPC Gordon Sign, 30721
VPI, 30722
VPI Manufacturing, 30723, 49702
Vresso International Corporation, 49864
Vrymeer Commodities, 30909
VT Industries Inc, 30724, 49703
VT Kidron, 30725, 49704
Vtopian Artisan Cheeses, 13496, 60147
Vulcan Electric Co, 30910, 49865
Vulcan Food Equipment Group, 30911, 49866
Vulcan Industries, 30912, 49867
Vulcan Materials Co, 30913
VWR Funding Inc, 60063
VWR Scientific, 30726
Vynatex, 30914
Vynecrest Winery, 13497
Vyse Gelatin Co, 13498, 49868

W

W & B Distributing Co, 60148
W & G Marketing Company, 13499, 49869
W A DeHart Inc, 60149
W A Powers Co, 30915

W B Stockton & Co Inc, 60150
W D Class & Son, 60151
W H Cooke & Co Inc, 30916
W H Laboratories, 49870
W H Wildman Company, 30917, 60152
W J Beitler Co & Beitler Truck, 52174, 53595
W J Byrnes & Co, 52175, 53596
W J Egli & Co, 30918, 49871
W L Jenkins Co, 30919, 49872
W L Petrey Wholesale Co Inc, 60153
W N Daul Transfer Lines, 52176
W R Grace & Co, 30920, 49873
W T Young Storage Co, 52177, 53597
W&H Systems, 30921
W. Braun Company, 60154
W. Braun Packaging Canada, 60155
W. Forrest Haywood Seafood Company, 13500
W. M. Stone & Company, 52178
W.A. Beans & Sons, 13501, 60156
W.A. Golomski & Associates, 30922
W.A. Schmidt Company, 30923, 49874
W.A. Tayloe Company, 60157
W.B. Marketing Group, 41228
W.F. Alber Inc., 60158
W.F. Morgan & Sons, 60159
W.F. Ware Company, 60160
W.G. Durant Corporation, 30924, 49875
W.G. White & Company, 60161
W.H. Escott Company, 41229
W.H. Moseley Co., 41230, 49876
W.H. Schilbe Citrus Brokerage / Citriservices, 41231
W.H. Sullivan & Associates, 41232
W.J. Canaan Inc., 60162
W.J. Stearns & Sons/Mountain Dairy, 13502, 60163
W.L. Petrey Wholesale Inc., 13503, 60164
W.M. Barr & Co Inc., 30925
W.M. Sprinkman Corporation, 30926
W.O. Sasser, 13504, 60165
W.R. Delozier Sausage Company, 13505
W.R. Hackett, 60166
W.R. McRae Company Limited, 60167
W.R. Merry Seafood Company, 60168
W.R. Nykorchuck & Company, 60169
W.R. Pittman & Sons, 60170
W.R. Whitaker & Company, 60171
W.S. Lee & Sons, 60172
W.S. Wells & Sons, 13506
W.T. Ruark & Company, 13507
W.T.I., 13508
W.Y. International, 30927, 49877, 60173
WA Brown & Son, 30928, 49878
WA Imports, 49879
Wabash Foodservice Inc, 60184
Wabash Heritage Mfg LLC, 13517, 53599, 60185
Wabash Power Equipment Co, 30969
Wabash Seafood Co, 13518, 60186
Wabash Valley Farms, 13519
Wabash Valley Mfg Inc, 49910
Wabash Valley Produce Inc, 13520
Wabi Fishing Company, 13521
Wachusett Brewing Co, 13522
Wachusset Potato Chip Co Inc, 13523
Wackym's Kitchen, 13524
WACO Beef & Pork Processors, 13509, 49880, 60174
Waco Broom & Mop Factory, 30970
WACO Filtering, 60175
Waco Meat Service, 60187
Wadden Systems, 49911, 60188
Waddington North America, 30971, 49912
Wade Manufacturing Company, 30972, 49913
Wade's Dairy Inc, 60189
WaffleWaffle, 13525, 30973
Wag Industries, 30974, 49914
Wagner Brothers Containers, 30975
Wagner Excello Food Products, 13526

1451

All Companies Index

Wagner Gourmet Foods, 13527, 49915, 60190
Wagner Seafood, 13528
Wagner Vineyards, 13529, 49916
Wagshal's Imports, 13530, 49917
Wah Yet Group, 13531, 49918
Wahlstrom Manufacturing, 30976
Wai Lana Snacks, 13532
Wai Sang Meat, 60191
Wainani Kai Seafood, 13533, 49919, 60192
Wainwright Dairy, 13534
Wakefern Food Corp, 60193
Wakefield Sales Inc, 60194
Waken Meat Co, 13535, 60195
WAKO Chemicals USA Inc, 30929
Wakunaga Of America Co LTD, 13536, 49920
Wal-Vac, 30977, 49921
Walcan Seafood, 13537
Walco, 30978, 49922
Walco-Linck Company, 30979, 49923
Wald Imports, 30980
Wald Wire & Mfg Co, 30981
Walden Farms, 13538, 13539, 49924
Walden Foods, 13540
Waldon Manufacturing LLC, 30982
Waleski Produce, 60196
Walker Bag Mfg Co, 30983, 49925
Walker Brush Inc, 30984
Walker Co, 30985
Walker Engineering Inc, 30986
Walker Foods, 13541, 49926
Walker Hatchery, 60197
Walker Magnetics Group Inc, 30987, 30988, 49927
Walker Meats, 13542, 60198
Walker Stainless Equipment Co, 30989, 49928
Walker's Seafood, 13543, 60199
Walkers Shortbread, 13544, 49929
Wall Conveyor & Manufacturing, 30990
Wall Meat Processing, 13545
Wallaby Yogurt Co, 13546, 60200
Wallace & Hinz, 30991, 49930
Wallace Computer Services, 30992, 30993
Wallace Edwards & Sons, 13547
Wallace Fisheries, 13548, 49931, 60201
Wallace Foods Inc, 60202
Wallace Grain & Pea Company, 13549, 49932
Wallace Plant Company, 13550, 60203
Wallach's Farms, 60204
Walle Corp, 30994, 49933
Wallin Group Inc, 41237
Wallingford Coffee Inc, 13551
Wallis & Barcinski, 41238
Wally Biscotti, 13552
Walnut Acres, 13553
Walnut Packaging Inc, 30995, 49934
Walong Marketing, 30996, 49935
Walsh & Simmons Seating, 30997, 49936
Walsh Transportation Group, 52181, 53600
Walsh Tropical Fruit Sales, 49937, 60205
Walsh's Coffee Roasters, 13554
Walsh's Seafood, 13555, 60206
Walsroder Packaging, 30998
Waltco Truck Equipment Company, 30999
Walter E Jacques & Sons, 49938, 60207
Walter Molzahn & Company, 31000
Walter P Rawl & Sons Inc, 13556
Walters Brothers, 31001
Waltham Beef Company, 13557
Waltham Fruit & Produce Company, 60208
Waltham Fruit Company, 31002
Waltkoch Limited, 13558, 49939, 60209
Walton & Post, 49940, 60210
Walton's Inc, 31003, 49941, 60211
Wampler's Farm Sausage Company, 13559, 49942
Wan Hua Foods, 13560

Wanchese Fish Co Inc, 13561, 49943
Wanda's Nature Farm, 13562, 49944
Wandering Bear Coffee, 13563
Wang Cheong Corporation USA, 31004
Wapsie Creamery, 13564, 49945
Wapsie Produce, 13565, 49946
War Eagle Mill, 13566
Warbac Sales Co, 49947
Warbucks Seafood, 13567
Ward Hughes Co, 41239
Ward Ironworks, 31005, 49948
Ward Trucking Corporation, 53601
Wardcraft Conveyor & Quick Die, 31006, 49949
Warden Peanut Company, 13568
Wards Ice Cream Co Inc, 60212
Warehouse Associates LP, 52182, 53602
Warehouse Equipment Inc, 60213
Warehouse Service Inc, 52183, 53603
Warehouse Specialists Inc, 52184, 53604, 53605
Warehouse Systems Inc, 60214
Warehousing of Wisconsin, 53606
Waring Products, 31007, 49950
Warner Candy, 13569
Warner Electric Inc, 31008
Warner Vineyards, 13570
Warner-Lambert Confections, 13571
Warrell Corp, 13572, 13573, 13574, 49951
Warren & Son Meat Processing, 13575
Warren Analytical Laboratory, 31009
Warren E. Conley Corporation, 31010, 60215
Warren Laboratories LLC, 13576
Warren Packaging, 31011
Warren Pallet Co Inc, 31012
Warren Rupp Inc, 31013
Warren Southwest Rfrdgrtn, 60216
Warrenton Products, 31014
Warsaw Chemical Co Inc, 31015, 49952
Warsteiner Importers Agency, 49953
Warther Museum, 31016
Warwick Ice Cream, 13577
Warwick Manufacturing & Equip, 31017, 49954
Warwick Products, 31018
Warwick Valley Winery & Distillery, 13578, 49955
Wasatch Meats Inc, 13579
Washing Systems, 31019
Washington Cold Storage, 53607
Washington Frontier, 31020, 49956
Washington Fruit & Produce Company, 13580, 49957, 53608
Washington Group International, 31021, 31022
Washington Potato Company, 13581, 49958
Washington Rhubarb Grower Assn, 13582
Washington State Juice, 13583, 31023
Washington State Potato Cmsn, 49959
Washington Vegetable Co, 60217
Wasserman Bag Company, 31024
Wasserstrom Co, 60218
Wasson Brothers Winery, 13584
Waste Away Systems, 31025
Waste King Commercial, 31026, 49960
Waste Minimization/Containment, 31027, 49961
Wastequip Inc, 31028, 49962
Wastequip Teem, 31029, 49963
Water & Oil Technologies Inc, 31030
Water & Power Technologies, 31031, 49964
Water Concepts, 13585
Water Equipment Svc, 31032
Water Furnace Renewable Energy, 31033, 49965
Water Management Resources, 31034
Water Savers Worldwide, 31035
Water Sciences Services, Inc., 31036, 49966
Water System Group, 31037

Waterfield Farms, 13586
Waterfront Market, 60219
Waterfront Seafood, 13587
Waterfront Seafood Market, 13588, 60220
Waterlink Technologies, 31038
Waterlink/Sanborn Technologies, 31039, 49967
Waterloo Container, 31040
Watermark Innovation, 13589
Waters Corp, 31041
Watershed Foods, 13590, 31042
Watervliet Fruit Exchange, 60221
Waterway Foods Intl, 41240
Watkins Distributing Company, 60222
Watlow Electric, 31043, 31044, 31045, 49968, 49969
Watson & Associates, 41241
Watson Distributing, 60223
Watson Inc, 13591, 13592, 49970
Watsonville Coast Produce Inc, 60224
WATTS Equipment Co, 60176
Watts Premier Inc, 31046, 49971
Watts Radiant Inc, 31047
Watts Regulator Co, 31048
Watusee Foods, 13593
Waugh Foods Inc, 13594, 60225
Waukesha Cherry-Burrell, 31049, 31050, 49972
Waukesha Foundry Inc, 31051
Waukesha Specialty Company, 31052, 49973
Wausau Paper Corp., 13595, 31053
Wausau Tile/Textura Designs, 31054
Wave Chemical Company, 31055
Waverly Crabs, 13596, 60226
Wawa Inc, 13597
Wawona Frozen Foods Inc, 13598, 49974
Wax Orchards, 13599
Waxine, 31056
Way Better Snacks, 13600
Wayco Ham Co, 13601
Wayfield Foods, 13602
Waymar Industries, 31057, 49975
Waymouth Farms Inc, 13603
Wayne Automation Corp, 31058, 49976
Wayne Combustion Systems, 31059, 49977
Wayne Dairy Products Inc, 13604
Wayne E Bailey Produce Co Inc, 13605
Wayne Engineering, 31060, 49978
Wayne Estay Shrimp Company, 13606, 60227
Wayne Farms LLC., 13607, 49979
Wayne Group LTD, 31061
Wayne Industries, 31062
Waypoint, 41242
Waypoint Analytical Inc, 31063
WBM International, 31510
WCB Ice Cream, 30930, 30931, 49881
WCB Ice Cream USA, 30932
WCC Honey Marketing, 13511, 49882
WCR, 30933
WCS Corp, 30934
WE Killam Enterprises, 30935, 49883
WE Lyons Contruction, 30936
We Pack Logistics, 53609
We Rub You, 13608
We're Full of Promotions, 60228
Wearwell/Tennessee Mat Company, 31065
Weaver Brothers, 13609
Weaver Nut Co. Inc., 13610, 49980, 60229
Weaver Popcorn Co Inc, 13611, 49981
Weavewood, Inc., 31066, 49982
Web Industries, 31067
Web Industries Inc, 31068
Web Label, 31069, 49983
Webb's Candy, 13612
Webb's Machine Design, 31070
WEBB-Stiles Co, 30937, 49884
Webb-Triax Company, 31071, 49984
Webber Smith Assoc, 31072, 31073
Webbpak Inc, 13613

Webco General Partnership, 41243
Webeco Foods, 49985, 60230
Webeco Foods, Inc, 41244, 60231
Weber Display & Packaging Inc, 31074
Weber Distribution, 53610
Weber Flavors, 13614
Weber Inc, 31075, 31076
Weber Logistics, 52185, 53611, 53612, 53613, 53614, 53615, 53616, 53617, 53618, 53619, 53620, 53621
Weber Packaging Solutions Inc, 31077, 49986
Weber Scientific Inc, 31078, 60232
Weber-Stephen Products Company, 31079
Webster City Custom Meats Inc, 13615
Webster Farms, 13616
Webster Packaging Corporation, 31080
Wechsler Coffee Corporation, 13617, 49987, 60233
Wedding Cake Studio, 13618
Wedemeyer's Bakery, 13619
Wedgwood USA, 31081, 49988
Wedlock Paper ConvertersLtd., 31082, 49989
Weeke Wholesale Company, 60234
Weetabix Canada, 13620, 49990
Weetabix Food Co., 13621
Wega USA, 31083, 49991, 60235
Wege of Hanover, 13623
Wege Pretzel Company, 13622
Wegmans Food Markets Inc., 13624, 53622
Wehrfritz & Associates, 41245, 49992
WEI Equipment, 30938, 30939
Wei-Chuan USA Inc, 13625, 49993
Weibel Vineyards, 13626
Weigh Right Automatic Scale Co, 31084
Weighpack Systems, 31086
WeighPack Systems/Paxiom Group, 31085, 49994
Weil's Food Processing, 13627, 49995
Weiler & Company, 31087, 49996
Weiler Equipment, 31088
Weinberg Foods, 13628, 49997
Weinbrenner Shoe Co, 31089, 49998
Weinstein International, 49999
WEIS Markets Inc., 13512, 30940
Weisenberger Mills, 13629, 50000
Weiser River Packing, 13630, 50001
Weiss Brothers Smoke House, 13631
Weiss Homemade Kosher Bakery, 13632
Weiss Instruments, Inc, 31090, 50002
Weiss Noodle Company, 13633
Weiss Sheet Metal Inc, 31091
Welbilt Corporation, 31092, 50003
Welbilt Inc., 31093, 50004
Welch Brothers, 31094
Welch Equipment Co Inc, 60236
Welch Foods Inc, 13634, 50005
Welch Foods Inc., 13635
Welch Holme & Clark Co, 41246, 50006
Welch Packaging Group Inc, 31095
Welch Stencil Company, 31096
Welch's Global Ingredients Group, 13636
Welcome Dairy Inc, 13637
Weldon Ice Cream Co, 13638
Well Dressed Food Company, 13639
Well Luck, 50007
Well-Pict Inc, 13640, 50008
Wella Bar, 13641
Wellesse, 13642, 50010
Welling Company, 52186, 53623
Wellington Brewery, 13643
Wellington Foods, 13644
Welliver Metal Products Corporation, 31098, 50011
Wells Enterprises Inc., 13645, 50012
Wells Lamont, 31099, 31100, 31101
Wells Manufacturing Company, 31102, 31103, 50013
WellSet Tableware Manufacturing Company, 31097, 50009
Welltep International Inc, 31104, 41247
Welsh Farms, 13646, 13647

All Companies Index

Welton Rubber Co, 60237
Wemas Metal Products, 31105, 50014
Wemco Pumps, 31106
Wenda America Inc, 13648, 31107
Wendell August Forge, 31108
Wendlandt Brokerage Company, 41248
Wendysue & Tobey's, 13649
Wenger Spring Brook Cheese Inc, 13650
Wenger's Bakery, 13651
Wenglor, 31109
Wenix International Corporation, 50015
Wenk Foods Inc, 13652, 50016
Wenner Bakery, 13653
WENS Brokerage, 41233
Wente Family Estates, 13654
Wenzel's Bakery, 13655
Wepackit, 31110, 50017
WePackItAll, 31064
Werling & Sons Slaughterhouse, 13656
Wermuth Winery, 13657
Werner Enterprises Inc, 52187
Werres Corp, 60238
Werthan Packaging, 31111
Wes Design - Supply Company, 60239
Wes Inc, 31112
Wes Pak Inc, 60240
WES Plastics, 30941
Wes Tech Engineering Inc, 31113
WESCO, 60177, 60178
WESCO Distribution Inc, 60179, 60180
Wesco Food Brokerage, 41249
Wesco Industrial Products, 31114
Wescor, 31115, 50018
Wescotek Inc, 50019, 60241
Wesley International Corp, 31116, 50020
Wesley-Kind Associates, 31117
Wesnic Services Inc, 41250
Wessanan, 13658
West Agro, 31118, 50021
West Bay Fishing, 13659, 60242
West Bay Sales, 50022, 60243
West Brothers Lobster, 13660, 60244
West Brothers Trailer Rental, 52188, 53624
West Carrollton Parchment Company, 31119, 50023
West Central Foodservice, 60245
West Chemical Products, 31120, 50024
West Coast Industries Inc, 31121
West Coast Products, 13661, 50025
West Coast Seafood Processors Association, 13662, 50026
West Coast Ship Chandlers, 60246
West Coast Specialty Coffee, 13663, 31122, 50027
West Coast Supplies, 60247
West End Dairy Inc, 60248
West Hawk Industries, 31123, 50028
West India Trading Company, 50029
West Liberty Foods LLC, 13664, 50030
West Logistics, 52189, 53625
West Louisiana Ice Svc, 31124
West Metals, 31125
West Oregon Wood Products Inc, 31126, 50031
West Pac, 13665
West Pak Avocado Inc, 13666, 50032
West Park Wine Cellars, 13667
West Penn Oil Co Inc, 31127
West Point Dairy Products, 13668
West Rock, 31128, 50033
West Star Industries, 31129
West Tenn Dairy Products, 60249
West Texas Warehouse Company, 53626
West Thomas Partners, LLC, 13669, 50034
West Wholesale Grocery, 60250
West-Pak, 31130
Westar Nutrition Corporation, 13670
Westbend Vinyards, 13671
Westbrae Natural Foods, 13672, 13673, 50035
Westbrook Trading Company, 13674, 50036
Westco Chemicals Inc, 60251

Westco Fruit & Nut Company, 60252
Westco-BakeMark, 13675, 50037
Westcoast Engineering Company, 60253
Westcon Foods, 41251
Westdale Foods Company, 13676
Westec Tank & Equipment, 31131
Westeel, 31132
Westerbeke Fishing Gear Co Inc, 31133, 60254
Western Ag Enterprises Inc, 52190
Western Bagel Baking Corp, 13677, 50038
Western Beef Jerky, 13678
Western Buffalo Company, 13679
Western Carolina Forklift Inc, 60255
Western Carriers, 31134, 53627
Western Combustion Engineering, 31135, 50039
Western Container Company, 31136, 50040
Western Creamery, 13680
Western Exterminator Co, 31137
Western Family Foods Inc, 60256
Western Gateway Storage Co, 53628
Western Grocers, 60257, 60258
Western Laminates, 31138
Western Lighting Inc, 31139
Western Mandate, 60259
Western Manufacturers Agents, 41252
Western Meat Co, 13681
Western New York Syrup Corporation, 13682
Western Overseas Corp, 52191
Western Pacific Oils, Inc., 13683, 31140
Western Pacific Produce, 13684, 50041
Western Pacific Stge Solutions, 31141, 50042
Western Plastics, 31142, 31143, 31144, 50043, 50044
Western Polymer Corp, 31145, 50045
Western Precooling, 31146
Western Pulp Products Co, 31147
Western Refrigerated Freight Systems, 31148, 52192
Western Soap Company, 60260
Western Square Industries, 31149
Western Steel & Wire, 60261
Western Stoneware, 31150, 50046
Western Sugar Cooperative, 13685
Western Syrup Company, 13686, 50047
Western Textile & Manufacturing Inc., 31151, 50048
Westervelt Co Inc, 31152
Westex, 41253
Westfalia Separator, 31153, 50049
Westfield Farm, 13687
Westfield Foods, 13688
Westfield Sheet Metal Works, 31154
Westin Foods, 13689, 50050
Westland Marketing, 60262
Westnut, 13690
Weston Emergency Light Co, 31155, 50051
Weston Foods, 13691
Weston Solutions Inc, 31156
Westport Locker LLC, 13692
Westport Rivers Vineyard, 13693
Westra Construction, 31157
Westrick Paper Co, 31158
Westside Foods, 60263
Westtown Brew Works, 13694
Westvaco Corporation, 31159, 31160, 50052
Westway Trading Corporation, 13695, 50053
Westwind Resources, 50054, 60264
Westwood International, 50055, 50056
Westwood Winery, 13696
Wet Planet Beverage, 13697
Wet Towel International, 50057
Wetherby Cranberry Company, 13698
Wetoska Packaging Distributors, 50058, 60265
Wetterau Wood Products, 31161
Wexler Packaging Products, 31162

Wexxar Corporation, 31163, 50059
Wexxar Packaging Inc, 31164
Weyand's Fishery, 13699
Weyauwega Star Dairy, 13700, 31165, 60266
Weyerhaeuser Co, 31166
WG Thompson & Sons, 13513, 49885, 60181
WGN Flag & Decorating Co, 30942
Whaler Vineyard, 13701
Whaley Pecan Co Inc, 13702, 50060, 60267
Whallon Machinery Inc, 31167, 50061
Wham Food & Beverage, 60268
Wharton Seafood Sales, 13703, 50062, 60269
What's Brewing, 13704
Whatman, 31168, 31169, 50063
Wheat Foods Council, 60270
Wheat Montana Farms Inc, 13705
Wheaton Plastic Containers, 31170
Wheel Tough Company, 31171, 50064
Wheeling Coffee & Spice Co, 13706
Whetstone Candy Company, 13707
Whetstone Chocolates, 13708
Whey Systems, 31172
Whipped Pastry Boutique, 13709, 60271
Whirl Air Flow, 31173
Whirley Drink Works, 50065
Whirley Industries Inc, 31174, 50066
Whisk Products Inc, 31175, 50067
Whistler Brewing Company, 13710, 13711, 50068
Whit-Log Trailers Inc, 31176, 50069
Whitaker & Assoc Architects, 13712
Whitaker Brothers, 60272
Whitby Co, 41254
Whitcraft Winery, 13713
White Camel Foods Group, 13714
White Cap Construction Supply, 60273
White Cap Fish Market, 13715
White Cliff Minerals, 60274
White Cloud Coffee, 13716
White Coffee Corporation, 13717, 50070
White Feather Farms, 60275
White Fence Farm, 13718
White Hall Vineyards, 13719
White House Chemical Supply, 60276
White House Foods, 13720, 50071
White Label Yerba Mate Soda, 13721
White Mop Wringer Company, 31177, 50072
White Mountain Freezer, 31178, 50073
White Mountain Lumber Co, 31179
White Oak Farm and Table, 13722
White Oak Farms Inc, 13723
White Oak Pastures, 13724
White Oak Vineyards & Winery, 13725
White Oaks Frozen Foods, 13726, 31180, 50074
White Packing Company, 13727
White Plains Electrical Light, 60277
White Rabbit Dye Inc, 31181, 50075
White Rock Products Corp, 13728, 50076
White Rock Vineyards, 13729
White Stokes International, 13730, 31182
White Toque, 13731, 50077
White Way Sign & Maintenance, 31183, 50078
White's Meat Processing, 13732
White-Stokes Company, 13733
Whitecliff Vineyard & Winery, 13735, 50079
Whitehall Lane Winery, 13736
Whitehall Specialties Inc, 13737
Whitehawk Beef Co, 60278
WhiteWave Foods, 13734
Whitewave Foods Company, 13738, 50080
Whitey Produce Co Inc, 60279
Whitey's Ice Cream Inc, 13739
Whitfield Foods Inc, 13740
Whitfield Olive, 50081, 50082, 60280, 60281
Whitford Cellars, 13741

Whitford Corporation, 31184, 50083
Whiting & Davis, 31185, 50084
Whiting Distribution Services, 52193, 53629
Whitley Manufacturing Company, 31186, 50085
Whitley Peanut Factory Inc, 13742, 50086
Whitley Wholesale Grocery, 60282
Whitlock Packaging Corp, 31187
Whitmire Microgen Research Lab, 31188
Whitney & Sons Seafood, 13743
Whitney Foods Inc, 13744
Whittle & Mutch Inc, 31189
Whole Earth Bakery, 13745
Whole Herb Co, 13746, 50087
Whole in the Wall, 13748
Whole Life Nutritional Supplements, 13747, 60283
WholeMe, 13749
Wholesale Cash & Carry Foods, 60284
Wholesale Restaurant Equipment, 60285
Wholesale Restaurant Supply, 60286
Wholesale Tool Company, 60287
WholesalePortal.com, 31190, 60288
Wholesome Bakery, 13750, 60289
Wholesome!, 13751, 50088
Wholesum Family Farms, 13752, 60290
Wholly Wholesome, 13753
Wiards Orchards Inc, 13754
Wiberg Corporation, 13755
Wichita Fish Co, 13756, 60291
Wichita Packing Co Inc, 13757
Wichita Restaurant Supl Co Inc, 60292
Wichita Stamp & Seal Inc, 31191
Wick's Packaging Service, 31192, 31193, 50089
Wick's Pies Inc, 13758, 41255
Wicked Crisps, 13759
Wicked Mix, 13760, 60293
Wicked Whoopies, 13761
Wickers Food Products Inc, 13762
Wicklund Farms, 13763, 50090
Wico Corporation, 31194
Widman's Candy Shop, 13764
Widmer's Cheese Cellars Inc, 13765
Widmers Wine Cellars, 13766
Widoffs Modern Bakery, 13767
Widow's Mite Vinegar Company, 13768, 60294
Wieber-McLain Company, 41256
Wiederkehr Wine Cellars Inc, 13769
Wiegardt Brothers, 13770, 50091
Wiegmann & Rose Thermxchanger, 31195
Wiese Planning & Engineering, 60295
Wifag Group Polytype America Corp, 31196
Wiginton Corp, 31197
Wika Instrument LP, 31198, 31199, 50092
Wikel Bulk Express, 52194
Wilbur Chocolate Candy, 13771, 13772
Wilbur Curtis Co, 31200, 50093
Wilbur Packing Company, 13773
Wilch Manufacturing, 31201, 50094
Wilco Distributors Inc, 31202
Wilco Precision Testers, 31203
Wilco, USA, 31204
Wilcox Farms, 13774
Wilcox Frozen Foods, 60296
Wilcox Paper Co, 60297
Wild Aseptics, LLC, 13775
Wild Bill's Foods, 13776, 50095
Wild Blueberries, 13777
WILD Flavors (Canada), 13514, 49886
Wild Fruitz Beverages, 13778
Wild Hibiscus Flower Company, 13779
Wild Hog Vineyard, 13780
Wild Horse Winery & Vineyards, 13781
Wild Leaf Active Tea, 13782
Wild Planet Foods, 13783
Wild Poppy, 13784
Wild Rice Exchange, 13785, 50096
Wild Things Snacks, 13786

1453

All Companies Index

Wild Thyme Cottage Products, 13787, 50097
Wild Thymes Farm Inc, 13788
Wild West Spices, 13789
Wild Zora Foods, 13790, 60298
Wildcat Produce, 13791
Wilde Brands, 13792, 60299
Wilden Pump & Engineering LLC, 31205
Wilder Manufacturing Company, 31206, 50098
Wilderness Foods, 60300
Wildes Printing Co Inc, 31207
Wildhurst Vineyards, 13793
Wildlife Cookies Co, 13794
Wildly Delicious, 13795
Wildly Organic, 13796
Wildtime Foods, 13797
Wildtree, 13798
Wildway, 13799
Wileman Brothers & Elliott Inc, 13800, 50099
Wilen Professional Cleaning Products, 31208, 50100
Wilevco Inc, 31209, 50101
Wilheit Packaging LLC, 31210
Wilhelm Foods, 13801
Wilhelm Machinery Movers, 52195
Wilhelmsen Consulting, 31211
Wilhite Sign Company, 31212
Wilke International Inc, 13802, 50102, 60301
Wilkens-Anderson Co, 31213, 50103, 60302
Wilkie Brothers Conveyor Inc, 31214, 50104
Wilkin-Alaska, 60303
Wilkins Rogers Inc, 13803, 50105
Wilkinson Manufacturing Company, 31215, 50106
Wilkinson-Spitz, 13804
Wilks Precision Instr Co Inc, 31216
Will & Baumer, 31217
Will-Pak Foods, 13805, 50107
Will-Pemco Inc, 31218
Willamette Filbert Growers, 60304
Willamette Industries, 31219, 31220, 31221, 31222, 50108, 50109
Willamette Valley Pie Co, 13806, 60305
Willamette Valley Walnuts, 13807, 50110
Willard Packaging Co, 31223
Willcox Meat Packing House, 13808
Willett America, 31224
William B Meyer Inc, 52196, 53630
William B. Steedman & Sons, 41257
William Bernstein Company, 41258, 50111
William Bounds, 13809
William Brown Co Inc, 31225
William Consalo & Sons Farms, 60306
William E. Martin & Sons Company, 13810, 50112, 60307
William Grant & Sons, 13811
William Harrison Winery LLC, 13812, 13813
William Hecht, 31226
William Hill Estate Winery, 13814
William Hyman Jr Associates, 41259
William J. Mills & Company, 31227
William M. Dunne & Associates Ltd, 41260
William Poll Inc, 13815
William R. Hill & Company, 53631
William Rosenstein & Sons, 60308
William Willis Worldwide, 31228
Williams & Bennett, 13816
Williams & Mettle Company, 31229
Williams Brokerage Company, 41261
Williams Candy Co, 13817
Williams Candy Company, 13818
Williams Food Equipment Company, 60309
Williams Institutional Foods, 13819, 60310
Williams Pallet, 31230
Williams Pork, 13820

Williams Refrigeration, 31231, 50113
Williams Resource & Associates, 41262, 50114, 60311
Williams Sausage Co, 60312
Williams Selyem Winery, 13821
Williams Shade & Awning Company, 31232
Williams-R J, 13822, 13823
Williamsburg Chocolatier, 13824
Williamsburg Metal Spinning, 31233
Williamsburg Millwork, 31234
Williamsburg Winery LTD, 13825
Williamson & Co, 31235, 50115
Williamson Cold Storage Inc, 53632
Williamsport Candy Company, 60313
Willie Laymon, 60314
Willie's Smoke House LLC, 13826
Willing Group, 41263, 50116, 60315
Willis Day Storage, 52197, 53633
Willmar Cookie & Nut Company, 13827
Willmark Sales Company, 13828, 50117
Willoughby's Coffee & Tea, 13829
Willow Foods, 13830
Willow Group LTD, 50118, 60316
Willow Run Foods Inc, 60317
Willow Specialties, 31236
Willow Tree Poultry Farm Inc, 13831
Willowcroft Farm Vineyards, 13833
WillowOak Farms, 13832
Willson Industries, 31237
Willy Nilly At Home, 60318
Wilmington Bonded Warehouse, 53634
Wilmington Cold Storage, 53635
Wilson AL Chemical Co, 31238, 50119
Wilson Candy Co, 13834
Wilson Food Brokers, 41264
Wilson Ice Machines, 60319
Wilson Steel Products Company, 31239
Wilson Trucking Corp, 52198
Wilson's Fantastic Candy, 13835
Wilsons Oysters, 13836
Wiltec, 31240
Wilton Armetale, 31241, 50120
Wilton Brands LLC, 31242, 50121
Wilton Industries CanadaLtd., 31243
Wiltsie & Company, 41265
Wimberley Valley Winery, 13837
Win-Holt Equipment Group, 31244, 50122
Winans Chocolates & Coffees, 13838
Winchell's Donut House, 13839
Winchester Carton, 31245
Winchester Cheese Company, 13840
Winchester Cold Storage, 53636
Winchester Farms Dairy, 13841
Winchester Food, 60320
Wincup Holdings, 31246
Wind & Willow, 60321
Wind River Environmental, 31247
Windcrest Meat Packers, 13842
Winder Farms, 60322
Windhorst Blowmold, 31248
Windmill Candies, 13843
Windmill Electrastatic Sprayers, 31249
Windmill Water Inc, 13844
Windmoeller & Hoelscher Corporation, 31250
Windsor Confections, 13845
Windsor Industries Inc, 31251, 50123
Windsor Wax Co Inc, 31252, 50124
Windwalker Vineyards & Winery, 13846
Windy City Distribution, 60323
Windy City Organics, 13847, 60324
Wine Analyst, 31253
Wine Appreciation Guild, 31254
Wine Cap Company, 31255
Wine Chillers of California, 31256, 50125
Wine Concepts, 31257
Wine Country Cases, 31258
Wine Country Chef LLC, 13848, 60325
Wine Country Kitchens, 13849
Wine Country Pasta, 13850
Wine Group, 13851
Wine Things Unlimited, 31259

Wine Thingsÿ, 31260
Wine Well Chiller Co, 31261, 50126
Wine World Wide, 50127
Wine-A-Rita, 13852
WineAndHospitalityJobs.com, 31262
Winekeeper, 31263, 50128
Wineracks by Marcus, 31264, 50129
Winfrey Fudge & Candy, 13853
Wing It Inc, 13854
Wing Nien Food, 13855, 50130
Wing Seafood Company, 13856, 60326
Wing Sing Chong Company, 13857, 50131, 60327
Wing Sing Seafood Inc, 60328
Wing's Food Products, 13858
Wing-Time, 13859
Winger Cheese, 13860
Wings Foods of Alberta Ltd, 13861
Wininger & Assoc, 60329
Wink Frozen Desserts, 13862, 60330
Winkler Inc, 60331
Winkler Meats, 60332
Winkler USA LLC, 31265
Winmark Stamp & Sign, 31266
Winmix/Natural Care Products, 13863, 41266, 50132, 60333
Winn-Dixie, 60334
Winn-Dixie Stores, 13864, 60335
Winn-Sol Products, 31267
Winnebago Sign Company, 31268
Winning Solutions Inc, 13865, 50133
Winona Foods, 13866
Winona Packing Company, 13867
Winpac, 41267
Winpak Lane Inc, 31269
Winpak Portion Packaging, 31270, 50134
Winpak Technologies, 31271, 50135, 52199
Wins Paper Products, 31272, 60336
Winsor SB Dairy, 13868
Winston Industries, 31273, 50136
Winston Laboratories Inc, 31274
Winter Harbor Co-Op Inc, 13869, 60337
Winter Park Farm, 13870
Winter Sausage Manufacturing Company, 13871
Winterbrook Beverage Group, 13872
Wintergreen Winery, 13873
Winzen Film, 31275, 50137
Wipe-Tex International Corp, 31276
Wipeco Inc, 31277
Wiper Supply & Chemical, 60338
Wire Belt Co Of America, 31278, 50138
Wire Products Mfg, 31279, 50139
Wirefab Inc, 31280, 50140
Wiremaid Products Div, 31281, 50141
Wireway Husky Corp, 31282
Wisco Industries Assembly, 31283, 50142
Wisconsin & Southern Railroad, 52200
Wisconsin Allied Products Inc, 60339
Wisconsin Aluminum Foundry Co, 31284, 50143
Wisconsin Bakers Assn Inc, 31285
Wisconsin Bench Mfg, 31286
Wisconsin Box Co, 31287, 31288, 50144, 50145
Wisconsin Cheese Group, 41268
Wisconsin Cheeseman, 13874, 50146
Wisconsin Converting Inc, 31289
Wisconsin Dairyland Fudge Company, 13875
Wisconsin Farmers Union, 13876
Wisconsin Film & Bag Inc, 31290
Wisconsin Milk Mktng Board Inc, 13877, 60340
Wisconsin Packaging Corp, 13878
Wisconsin Precision Casting, 31291
Wisconsin Specialty Protein, 13879, 50147
Wisconsin Spice Inc, 13880, 50148
Wisconsin Whey International, 13881, 50149
Wisconsin Wilderness Food Products, 13882

Wisdom Adhesives Worldwide, 31292
Wisdom Natural Brands-Uani, 13883
Wise Foods Inc, 13884
Wise Forklift Inc, 60341
Wise Mouth, 13885
Wise Products Distributors, 60342
Wish Farms, 13886
Wishbone Utensil Tableware Line, 31293, 41269, 50150, 60343
Wishnev Wine Management, 13887, 60344
Wisner Manufacturing Corporation, 60345
Wisteria Candy Cottage, 13888
Witmer Foods, 60346
Witness Tree Vineyard LTD, 13889
WITT Industries, 30943, 49887
Witt Plastics, 31294
Wittco Foodservice Equipment, 31295, 31296, 50151, 50152
Witte Brothers Exchange Inc, 31297, 52201
Witte Co Inc, 31298, 50153
Wittemann Company, 31299, 50154
Wittern Group, 31300, 50155
Wixon Inc., 13890
Wixson Honey Inc, 13891, 50156
Wizards Cauldron, LTD, 13892, 50157
WJ Pence Company, 41234
WK Eckerd & Sons, 13515, 60182
WMF/USA, 30944, 60183
WMK Marketing, 41235
WNA, 30945, 30946, 30947, 49888, 49889
Wna Comet West Inc, 31301
WNA Hopple Plastics, 30948
Wnc Pallet & Forest Pdts Co, 31302
Wockenfuss Candy Co, 13893
Woeber Mustard Mfg Co, 13894
Woerner Wire Works, 31303
Wohl Associates Inc, 31304, 31305
Wohlt Cheese Corp, 13895, 31306, 60347
Wohrles Foods, 13896
Wolens Company, 31307, 50158
Wolf Canyon Foods, 13897, 50159
Wolf Company, 31308, 50160
Wolf Creek Winery, 13898
Wolf Packaging Machines, 31309
Wolf Works, 31310
Wolferman's, 13899
Wolfgang Puck Food Company, 13900
Wolfies Roasted Nut Co, 13901
Wolfkiny, 31311
Wolfson Casing Corp, 13902, 50161
Wollersheim Winery, 13903
Wolverton Seafood, 13904, 60348
Womack International Inc, 31312, 50162
Wonder Natural Foods Corp, 13905
Wonderful Citrus, 13906
Wonderful Pistachios & Almonds, 13907, 50163
Wonderware Corp, 31313
Wong Wing, 13908
Wonton Food, 13909, 13910, 13911, 50164, 50165, 50166
Wood & Laminates, 31314
Wood Beverage Company, 60349
Wood Brothers Inc, 13912
Wood Fruitticher Grocery Company, 60350
Wood Goods Industries, 31315
Wood Stone Corp, 31316, 31317, 50167
Wood Sugarbush, 13913
Wood's Products, 60351
Woodard, 31318
Woodbine, 13914
Woodbury Vineyards, 13915
Wooden Valley Winery, 13916
Woodfield Fish & Oyster Company, 13917
Woodfold-Marco Manufacturing, 31319, 50168
Woodhead, 31320
Woodie Pie Company, 13918
Woodlake Distributors, 60352

1454

All Companies Index

Woodlake Ranch, 13919
Woodland Foods, 50169, 60353
Woods Fabrication, 31321
Woods Smoked Meats Inc, 13920
Woodside Vineyards, 13921
Woodsmoke Provisions, 13922
Woodson, 31322
Woodson Pallet Co, 31323
Woodson-Tenent Laboratories, 31324, 31325, 31326, 31327
Woodstock Farms Manufacturing, 13923, 50170
Woodstock Line Co, 31328, 50171
Woodstock Plastics Co Inc, 31329, 50172
Woodward Canyon, 13924
Woodward Manufacturing, 31330
Woodworth Honey & Bee Co, 13925
Woody Associates Inc, 31331, 50173
Woody's Bar-B-Q Sauce Company, 13926
Woody's Frozen Food Distr, 60354
Woollard Company, 41270
Woolsey & Assoc Inc, 41271
Woolwich Dairy, 13927, 50174
Wooster Novelty Company, 31332
Wootton Transportation Services, 52202, 53637
WORC Slitting & Mfg Co, 30949, 49890
Worcester Envelope Co, 31333
Worcester Industrial Products, 31334
Worden, 13928, 50175
Work Well Company, 31335, 50176
Workman Packaging Inc., 31336, 50177
Worksafe Industries, 31337, 50178
Worksman 800 Buy Cart, 31338, 50179
Workstead Industries, 50180, 60355
World Art Foods, 13929
World Casing Corp, 13930
World Cheese Inc, 13931, 50181
World Citrus West, 13932
World Class Beer Imports, 50182, 60356
World Confections Inc, 13933, 50183
World Cup Coffee & Tea, 13934, 50184
World Division, 31339, 50185
World Dryer Corp, 31340, 50186
World Famous Buffalo Wing Sauce, 13935
World Finer Foods, 31341
World Finer Foods Inc, 50187, 60357
World Flavors Inc, 13936
World Food Processing LLC, 31342
World Food Tech Services, 31343
World Ginseng Ctr Inc, 13937, 50188
World Harbors, 13938
World Herbs Gourmet, 13939
World Kitchen, 31344, 31345, 50189, 50190, 60358
World Nutrition, Inc., 13940, 50191
World Of Chantilly, 13941
World of Chia, 13945
World Of Coffee, 13942
World of Spices, 13946
World Organics Corporation, 13943
World Pride, 31346
World Spice, 13944, 50192, 60359
World Tableware Inc, 31347, 50193, 60360
World Technitrade, 31348
World Trade Center Harrisburg, 31349
World Trade Distribution, 53638
World Variety Produce, 31350, 50194, 60361
World Water Works, 31351, 31352, 50195
World Wide Beverage, 31353
World Wide Fitting Corp, 31354
World Wide Hospitality Furn, 31355, 50196
World Wide Safe Brokers, 31356, 41272, 50197, 60362
World's Best Cheeses, 50198
World's Best Donuts, 13947
World's Finest Chocolate Inc, 13948, 50199
World's Greatest Ice Cream, 13949

Worldwide Dispensers, 31357
Worldwide Express Inc, 41273, 52203
Worldwide Food Imports, 50200
Worldwide Specialties In, 13950, 50201
Worley Warehousing Inc, 53639
Wornick Company, 13951, 31358, 50202
Worthen Industries Inc, 31359, 50203
Worthington Foods, 13952
Worthmore Food Products Co, 13953
WOW Logistics, 52179, 53598
Wow! Factor Desserts, 13954
WOW! Nutrition, 49891
WP Bakery Group, 30950
WR Key, 30951, 49892
WR Zanes & Company of Louisiana, 52180
Wrap Pack, 31360
Wrap-It Packaging, 41274
Wrapade Packaging Systems, 31361, 50204
Wraps, 31362, 50205
Wrawp, 13955, 60363
Wrench Mints, 13956
Wrenn Handling, 60364
Wright Brand Oysters, 13957, 60365
Wright Brothers Paper Box Company, 31363
Wright Enrichment Inc, 13958, 50206
Wright Global Graphic Solutions, 31364
Wright Metal Products Crates, 31365, 50207
Wright Plastics Company, 31366
Wright's Ice Cream Co, 13959
Wrigley, 13960
WS Packaging Group Inc, 30952, 30953, 30954, 30955, 30956, 30957, 30958, 30959, 30960, 30961, 30962, 30963, 30964, 30965, 30966, 30967, 30968, 49893, 49894, 49895, 49896, 49897, 49898, 49899, 49900, 49901, 49902, 49903, 49904, 49905, 49906, 49907, 49908, 49909
WSU Creamery, 13516
Wt Nickell Co, 31367
WTD Associates, 41236
Wunder Creamery, 13961
Wunder-Bar, 50208
Wuollet Bakery, 13962
Wurth Dairy, 13963
Wustefeld Candy Co Inc, 60366
Wusthoff Trident Cutlery, 50209, 60367
Wyandot Inc, 13964, 50210
Wyandotte Winery LLC, 13965
Wylie Systems, 31368, 50211
Wyman Foorman, 41275
Wynnewood Pecan Company, 13966
Wysong Corp, 13967
Wyssmont Co Inc, 31369, 50212

X

X L Energy Drink Corp, 60368
X-Press Manufacturing, 31370, 50213
X-R-I Testing Inc, 31371, 50214
X-Rite Inc, 31372
Xango LLC, 31374, 50216
Xcel Tower Controls, 31375, 50217
Xcell International, 31376
XDX Innovative Refrigeration, 50215
Xela Pack Inc, 31377
Xena International, 13968, 50218
Xiaoping Design, 31378
Ximena's Latin Flavors, 13969
XL Corporate & Research Services, 31373
Xochitl, 13970
Xooz Gear, 13971
Xpander Pak, 31379
XPO Logistics, 52204, 53640
Xpresso, 50219
Xtreme Beverages, LLC, 31380, 50220, 60369

Xylem Inc, 31381

Y

Y & T Packing Co, 13972
Y Not Foods, 13973
Y Z Enterprises Inc, 13974, 13975, 50221
Y&W Shellfish, 13976
Y-Pers Inc, 31382, 50222
Y-Z Sponge & Foam Products, 31383
Y.M.C. Corp., 13977
Ya-Hoo Baking Co, 13979, 50224
YAAX International, 31384, 60370
Yai's Thai, 13980, 60371
Yakima Chief-Hopunion LLC, 13981, 50225
Yakima Craft Brewing Company, 13982, 50226
Yakima Fresh, 13983, 50227
Yakima River Winery, 13984
Yakima Wire Works, 31389, 50228
Yale Industrial Trucks, 60372
Yale Industrial Trucks: Ontario, 60373
Yale Material Handling/Gammon, 60374
Yamada International, 31390
Yamamotoyama of America, 13985
Yamasa Corp USA, 13986
Yamasa Fish Cake Co, 13987
Yamasho Inc, 13988, 50229, 60375
Yamate Chocolatier, 13989
Yamato Corporation, 31391, 50230
Yamhill Valley Vineyards, 13990
Yancey's Fancy, 13991
Yang Ming Line Holding Co, 52206
Yankee Marketers, 41276
Yankee Specialty Foods, 13992, 50231
Yardney Water Management Syst, 31392, 50232
Yargus Manufacturing Inc, 31393, 50233
Yarmer Boys Catfish International, 13993
Yarnall Warehouse Inc, 53641
Yates Industries Inc, 31394
Yates Sales Associates, 41277
Yaupon Tea, 13994
Yaya Imports, 50234
Yaya's, 13995
Yayin Corporation, 13996
YB Meats of Wichita, 13978
YCU Air/York International, 31385
Ye Olde Pepper Co, 13997
Yeager & Associates, 41278, 50235, 60376
Yeager Wire Works, 31395
Yellow Emperor Inc, 13998
Yemat Foods, 50236
Yeomen Seafoods Inc, 13999, 60377
Yerba Prima, 14000, 50237
Yerba Santa Goat Dairy, 14001
Yerecic Label Co, 31396
Yergat Packing Co, 14002, 50238
Yerger Wood Products, 31397
YESCO, 31386, 50223
Yeuell Name Plate & Label, 31398
Yick Lung Company, 14003
Ying Leong Look Funn Factory, 14004
Ying's Kitchen, 14005
Yo Mama's Foods, 14006
Yoakum Packing Co, 14008
Yoder Dairies, 14009
YoFiit, 14007, 50239
Yogavive, 14010
Yogi® Tea, 14011, 50240
Yogurtland Franchising Inc, 14012
Yohay Baking Co, 14013, 31399, 50241
Yokohl Packing Co, 14014
Yonkers Brewing Company LLC, 14015
Yonkers Institutional Food Company, 60378
Yoo-Hoo Chocolate Beverage Company, 14016
Yoplait, 14017
York Cheese, 41279
York Cold Storage LLC, 53642
York Container Co, 31400
York Hospitality & Gaming, 41280

York Mountain Winery, 14018
York Rail Logistics, 52207, 53643
York Refrigeration Marine US, 31401
York River Pallet Corporation, 31402
York Saw & Knife, 31403, 50242
York Sutch & Assoc, 41281
York Tape & Label Company, 31404
York Tent & Awning, 31405
Yorkraft, 31406, 50243
Yorktown Baking Company, 14019
Yorktown Electrical & Lighting, 60379
Yoshida Food Products Co, 14020, 50244
Yost Candy Co Inc, 14021, 50245
YottaMark, 31407
Young & Associates, 31408
Young & Stout, 60380
Young & Swartz, 31409
Young Industries Inc, 31410
Young Pecan, 14022
Young Pecan, Inc., 14023, 60381
Young Winfield, 14024, 50246
Young's Bakery, 14025
Young's Jersey Dairy, 14026
Young's Lobster Pound, 14027, 50247, 60382
Young's Lobster Shore Pound, 31411
Young's Noodle Factory Inc, 14028
Young-Block Associates, 41282
Youngstown Wholesale Grocery, 60383
Your Bar Factory, 14029
Your Place Menu Systems, 31412, 50248
Yowell Transportation, 52208
YRC Worldwide Inc, 52205
YSI Inc, 31387
Yuan Fa Can-Making, 31413
Yuba City Refrigerating Company, 53644
Yue's International Company, 60384
Yum Yum Donut Shops Inc, 14030
Yum Yum Potato Chips, 14031, 50249
Yvonne's Gourmet Sensations, 14032

Z

Z 2000 The Pick of the Millenium, 31414, 50250
Z Foods Inc., 14033
Z Specialty Food, LLC, 14034, 50251
Z T Merchandising Inc, 60385
Z&A Vending, 41283
Z&S Distributing, 14035, 60386
Z-Loda Systems Engineering Inc, 31415, 50252
Z-Trim Holdings, Inc, 14036, 31416
Zabiha Halal Meat Processors, 14037, 60389
Zaca Mesa Winery, 14038
Zachary Confections Inc, 14039, 50254, 60390
Zachys Wine, 14040
Zacky Farms, 14041
Zacmi USA, 31417
Zafari Art & Decor Design, 50255
Zahm & Nagel Co, 31418
ZAK Designs Inc, 50253, 60387
Zaloom Marketing Corp, 31419, 50256
Zambito Produce Sales, 41284
Zamilco International, 50257
Zanasi USA, 31420
Zander Insurance Group, 31421
Zanichelli & Associates, 41285
Zapata Industries, 31422
Zarda Bar-B-Q & Catering Company, 14042
Zarda King LTD, 50258, 60391
Zartic Inc, 14043
Zayante Vineyards, 14044
Zazi Baking Company, 14045
Zazubean, 14046, 60392
Zd Wines, 14047, 50259
Zealco Industries, 31423, 50260
Zebra Technologies Corporation, 14048, 31424, 50261
Zeches Institution Supply, 60393
Zed Industries, 31425, 50262

1455

All Companies Index

Zeeco Inc, 31426, 50263
Zego Foods, 14049, 60394
Zeier Plastic & Mfg Inc, 31427, 50264
Zeigler's, 14050
Zel R. Kahn & Sons, 50265, 60395
Zelco Industries, 31428
Zelda's Sweet Shoppe, 14051
Zellerbach, 60396
Zeltex, 31429, 31430, 50266
Zemas Madhouse Foods Inc., 14052
Zenar Corp, 31431, 50267
Zener America, 50268
Zengine, 50269
Zenith Cutter, 31432, 50270
Zenith Specialty Bag Co, 31433, 50271
Zenobia Co, 14053, 50272
Zentis Sweet Ovations, 14054, 50273
Zep Superior Solutions, 31434
Zepa Trade, 50274
Zepf Technologies, 31435, 50275
Zephyr Hills, 14055
Zephyr Manufacturing Co, 31436, 50276
Zephyrhills Bottled Water Company, 14056, 31437

Zerand Corp, 31438, 50277
Zerna Packing, 14057
Zero Manufacturing Inc, 31439
Zero Mountain, Inc., 53645
Zero Temp, 31440, 50278
Zero-Max Inc, 31441
Zeroll Company, 31442, 50279
Zeroloc, 31443
Zeroodle, 14058
Zest Tea LLC, 14059
Zesto Food Equipment Manufacturing, 31444, 50280
Zesty Z: The Za'atar Company, 14060
Zetov Inc, 60397
Zevia, 14061
Zhena's Gypsy Tea, 14062
Ziba Nut Inc, 50281, 60398
Zico Coconut Water, 60399
Ziegenfelder Ice Cream Co, 14063
Zimmer Custom-Made Packaging, 31445, 50282
Zimmerman Cheese Inc, 14064
Zimmerman Handling Systems, 31446, 50283

Zinda Products, 14065
Ziniz, 31447, 50284
Zink & Triest Company, 14066
Zink Distributing Co, 60400
Zink Marketing, 41286
Zinter Handling Inc, 60401
Zip-Net Inc, 31448
Zip-Pak, 31449, 31450, 31451, 31452
Zippy's Inc, 14067
Zipskin, 31453
Zitos Specialty Foods, 14068
Zitropack Limited, 31454
Ziyad Brothers Importing, 60402
Zmd International, 31455
Zoe's Meats, 14069
Zoelsmann's Bakery & Deli, 14070
Zoia Banquetier Co, 31456, 50285
Zojirushi America Corporation, 31457
Zol-Mark Industries, 31458
Zollman's Dark Canyon Coffee, 31459, 60403
Zone Perfect Nutrition Company, 14071
Zonner, 41287
Zoom Communications, 50286

Zotter Chocolates, 14072
Zoup! Fresh Soup Co LLC, 14073
ZT Packaging, 60388
Zuccaro Produce, 14074
Zuckerman Honickman Inc, 60404
Zumbiel Packaging, 31460
Zume, 31461
Zume Manufacturing, 31462
Zummo Meat Co, 14075
Zumtobel Staff Lighting, 31463, 50287
Zuni Foods, 14076
Zurheide Ice Cream Company, 14077
Zurn Industries LLC, 31464
Zweigle's Inc, 14078
Zwilling J.A. Henckels, 50288

2020 Title List

Visit www.GreyHouse.com for Product Information, Table of Contents, and Sample Pages.

Opinions Throughout History
Opinions Throughout History: Drug Use & Abuse
Opinions Throughout History: Gender: Roles & Rights
Opinions Throughout History: Globalization
Opinions Throughout History: Guns in America
Opinions Throughout History: Immigration
Opinions Throughout History: National Security vs. Civil & Privacy Rights
Opinions Throughout History: Presidential Authority
Opinions Throughout History: Robotics & Artificial Intelligence
Opinions Throughout History: Social Media Issues
Opinions Throughout History: The Death Penalty
Opinions Throughout History: The Environment
Opinions Throughout History: Voters' Rights

This is Who We Were
This is Who We Were: Colonial America (1492-1775)
This is Who We Were: 1880-1899
This is Who We Were: In the 1900s
This is Who We Were: In the 1910s
This is Who We Were: In the 1920s
This is Who We Were: A Companion to the 1940 Census
This is Who We Were: In the 1940s (1940-1949)
This is Who We Were: In the 1950s
This is Who We Were: In the 1960s
This is Who We Were: In the 1970s
This is Who We Were: In the 1980s
This is Who We Were: In the 1990s
This is Who We Were: In the 2000s
This is Who We Were: In the 2010s

Working Americans
Working Americans, 1880-2011 - Vol. 1 The Working Class
Working Americans, 1880-1999 - Vol. 2: The Middle Class
Working Americans, 1880-1999 - Vol. 3: The Upper Class
Working Americans, 1880-1999 - Vol. 4: Children
Working Americans, 1880-2015 - Vol. 5: At War
Working Americans, 1880-2015 - Vol. 6: Working Women
Working Americans, 1880-2016 - Vol. 7: Social Movements
Working Americans, 1880-2017 - Vol. 8: Immigrants
Working Americans, 1770-1869 - Vol. 9: From the Revolutionary War to the Civil War
Working Americans, 1880-2009 - Vol. 10: Sports & Recreation
Working Americans, 1880-2009 - Vol. 11: Inventors & Entrepreneurs
Working Americans, 1880-2011 - Vol. 12: Our History Through Music
Working Americans, 1880-2011 - Vol. 13: Education & Educators
Working Americans, 1880-2016 - Vol. 14: African Americans
Working Americans, 1880-2018: Vol. 15: Politics & Politicians
Working Americans, 1880-2020: Vol. 16: Farming & Ranching

Education
Complete Learning Disabilities Resource Guide
Educators Resource Guide
The Comparative Guide to Elem. & Secondary Schools
Charter School Movement
Special Education: A Reference Book for Policy & Curriculum Development

General Reference
African Biographical Dictionary
American Environmental Leaders
America's College Museums
Constitutional Amendments
Encyclopedia of African-American Writing
Encyclopedia of Historical Warrior Peoples & Modern Fighting Groups
Encyclopedia of Invasions & Conquests
Encyclopedia of Prisoners of War & Internment
Encyclopedia of Religion & the Law in America
Encyclopedia of Rural America
Encyclopedia of the Continental Congresses
Encyclopedia of the United States Cabinet
Encyclopedia of War Journalism
The Environmental Debate
The Evolution Wars: A Guide to the Debates
Financial Literacy Starter Kit
From Suffrage to the Senate
The Gun Debate: An Encyclopedia of Gun Rights & Gun Control in the US
History of Canada
Human Rights and the United States
Political Corruption in America
Privacy Rights in the Digital Age
Religious Right and American Politics
Speakers of the House of Representatives
The Value of a Dollar 1600-1865 Colonial to Civil War
The Value of a Dollar 1860-2019
US Land & Natural Resources Policy
World Cultural Leaders of the 20th Century

Business Information
Business Information Resources
The Complete Broadcasting Industry Guide: Television, Radio, Cable & Streaming
Directory of Mail Order Catalogs
Environmental Resource Handbook
Food & Beverage Market Place
The Grey House Homeland Security Resources
The Grey House Performing Arts Industry Guide
Guide to Healthcare Group Purchasing Organizations
Guide to U.S. HMOs and PPOs
Guide to Venture Capital & Private Equity Firms
Hudson's Washington News Media Contacts Guide
New York State Directory
Sports Market Place

Consumer Health
Comparative Guide to American Hospitals
Complete Mental Health Resource Guide
Complete Resource Guide for Pediatric Disorders
Complete Resource Guide for People with Chronic Illness
Complete Resource Guide for People with Disabilities
Dementia Handbook & Resource Guide
Older Americans Information Resource

Grey House Publishing | Salem Press | H.W. Wilson | 4919 Route, 22 PO Box 56, Amenia NY 12501-0056

2020 Title List

Visit www.GreyHouse.com for Product Information, Table of Contents, and Sample Pages.

Statistics & Demographics
America's Top-Rated Cities
America's Top-Rated Smaller Cities
Ancestry & Ethnicity in America
The Comparative Guide to American Suburbs
The Hispanic Databook
Profiles of America
Profiles of California
Profiles of Connecticut & Rhode Island
Profiles of Florida
Profiles of Illinois
Profiles of Indiana
Profiles of Massachusetts
Profiles of Michigan
Profiles of New Jersey
Profiles of New York
Profiles of North Carolina & South Carolina
Profiles of Ohio
Profiles of Pennsylvania
Profiles of Texas
Profiles of Virginia
Profiles of Wisconsin
Weather America

Canadian Resources
Canadian Almanac & Directory
Canadian Environmental Update
Associations Canada
Financial Services Canada
Libraries Canada
Canadian Parliamentary Guide
Canadian Venture Capital & Private Equity Firms
Health Guide Canada
Major Canadian Cities: Compared & Ranked, First Edition
Canadian Who's Who
Cannabis Canada
Financial Post Directory of Directors
FP Survey: Industrials
FP Survey: Mines & Energy
FP Survey: Predecessor & Defunct
FP Bonds: Corporate
FP Bonds: Government
FP Equities: Preferreds & Derivatives
Careers & Employment Canada

Weiss Financial Ratings
Financial Literacy Basics
Financial Literacy: How to Become an Investor
Financial Literacy: Planning for the Future
Weiss Ratings Consumer Guides
Weiss Ratings Guide to Banks
Weiss Ratings Guide to Credit Unions
Weiss Ratings Guide to Health Insurers
Weiss Ratings Guide to Life & Annuity Insurers
Weiss Ratings Guide to Property & Casualty Insurers
Weiss Ratings Investment Research Guide to Bond & Money Market Mutual Funds
Weiss Ratings Investment Research Guide to Exchange-Traded Funds
Weiss Ratings Investment Research Guide to Stock Mutual Funds
Weiss Ratings Investment Research Guide to Stocks

Books in Print Series
American Book Publishing Record® Annual
American Book Publishing Record® Monthly
Books In Print®
Books In Print® Supplement
Books Out Loud™
Bowker's Complete Video Directory™
Children's Books In Print®
El-Hi Textbooks & Serials In Print®
Forthcoming Books®
Law Books & Serials In Print™
Medical & Health Care Books In Print™
Publishers, Distributors & Wholesalers of the US™
Subject Guide to Books In Print®
Subject Guide to Children's Books In Print®

Grey House Publishing | Salem Press | H.W. Wilson | 4919 Route, 22 PO Box 56, Amenia NY 12501-0056

2020 Title List

Visit www.SalemPress.com for Product Information, Table of Contents, and Sample Pages.

Critical Insights

- Critical Insights: A Midsummer Night's Dream
- Critical Insights: A Portrait of the Artist as a Young Man
- Critical Insights: A Streetcar Named Desire
- Critical Insights: Abraham Lincoln
- Critical Insights: Absalom, Absalom!
- Critical Insights: Adventures of Huckleberry Finn
- Critical Insights: Aeneid
- Critical Insights: Albert Camus
- Critical Insights: Alice Munro
- Critical Insights: Alice Walker
- Critical Insights: All Quiet on the Western Front
- Critical Insights: American Creative Non-Fiction
- Critical Insights: American Multicultural Identity
- Critical Insights: American Road Literature
- Critical Insights: American Short Story
- Critical Insights: American Sports Fiction
- Critical Insights: American Writers in Exile
- Critical Insights: Ancient Greek Literature
- Critical Insights: Animal Farm
- Critical Insights: Arthur Miller
- Critical Insights: Barbara Kingsolver
- Critical Insights: Beloved
- Critical Insights: Benjamin Franklin
- Critical Insights: Billy Budd, Sailor
- Critical Insights: Brave New World
- Critical Insights: Censored & Banned Literature
- Critical Insights: Charles Dickens
- Critical Insights: Civil Rights Literature, Past & Present
- Critical Insights: Coming of Age
- Critical Insights: Conspiracies
- Critical Insights: Contemporary Canadian Fiction
- Critical Insights: Contemporary Immigrant Short Fiction
- Critical Insights: Contemporary Latin American Fiction
- Critical Insights: Contemporary Speculative Fiction
- Critical Insights: Cormac McCarthy
- Critical Insights: Crime and Detective Fiction
- Critical Insights: Crisis of Faith
- Critical Insights: Cultural Encounters
- Critical Insights: David Foster Wallace
- Critical Insights: Death of a Salesman
- Critical Insights: Dracula
- Critical Insights: Dystopia
- Critical Insights: Edith Wharton
- Critical Insights: Emily Dickinson
- Critical Insights: Ernest Hemingway
- Critical Insights: Eugene O'Neill
- Critical Insights: F. Scott Fitzgerald
- Critical Insights: Fahrenheit 451
- Critical Insights: Family
- Critical Insights: Feminism
- Critical Insights: Flannery O'Connor
- Critical Insights: Flash Fiction
- Critical Insights: Frederick Douglass
- Critical Insights: Gabriel Garcia Marquez
- Critical Insights: Gender, Sex and Sexuality
- Critical Insights: Geoffrey Chaucer
- Critical Insights: George Eliot
- Critical Insights: George Orwell
- Critical Insights: Good & Evil
- Critical Insights: Great Expectations
- Critical Insights: Greed
- Critical Insights: Gustave Flaubert
- Critical Insights: Gwendolyn Brooks
- Critical Insights: Hamlet
- Critical Insights: Harlan Ellison
- Critical Insights: Harlem Renaissance
- Critical Insights: Harry Potter Series
- Critical Insights: Heart of Darkness
- Critical Insights: Henry James
- Critical Insights: Herman Melville
- Critical Insights: Historical Fiction
- Critical Insights: Holocaust Literature
- Critical Insights: Horton Foote
- Critical Insights: I Know Why the Caged Bird Sings
- Critical Insights: In Cold Blood
- Critical Insights: Inequality
- Critical Insights: Invisible Man
- Critical Insights: Isaac Asimov
- Critical Insights: Isabel Allende
- Critical Insights: Jack London
- Critical Insights: James Baldwin
- Critical Insights: James Joyce
- Critical Insights: James McBride
- Critical Insights: Jane Austen
- Critical Insights: Jane Eyre
- Critical Insights: John Cheever
- Critical Insights: John Steinbeck
- Critical Insights: John Updike
- Critical Insights: Joseph Conrad
- Critical Insights: King Lear
- Critical Insights: Kurt Vonnegut
- Critical Insights: Langston Hughes
- Critical Insights: Leo Tolstoy
- Critical Insights: LGBTQ Literature
- Critical Insights: Life of Pi
- Critical Insights: Lillian Hellman
- Critical Insights: Literature of Protest
- Critical Insights: Little Women
- Critical Insights: Lolita
- Critical Insights: Lord of the Flies
- Critical Insights: Louisa May Alcott
- Critical Insights: Louise Erdrich
- Critical Insights: Macbeth
- Critical Insights: Magical Realism
- Critical Insights: Malcolm X
- Critical Insights: Margaret Atwood
- Critical Insights: Mario Vargas Llosa
- Critical Insights: Mark Twain
- Critical Insights: Martin Luther King, Jr.
- Critical Insights: Mary Shelley
- Critical Insights: Maya Angelou
- Critical Insights: Midnight's Children
- Critical Insights: Midwestern Literature
- Critical Insights: Moby-Dick
- Critical Insights: Modern Japanese Literature
- Critical Insights: Mrs. Dalloway
- Critical Insights: Nathaniel Hawthorne
- Critical Insights: Nature & the Environment
- Critical Insights: Neil Gaiman
- Critical Insights: Nineteen Eighty-Four
- Critical Insights: Of Mice and Men
- Critical Insights: One Flew Over the Cuckoo's Nest
- Critical Insights: One Hundred Years of Solitude
- Critical Insights: Oscar Wilde
- Critical Insights: Paradise Lost
- Critical Insights: Paranoia, Fear & Alienation
- Critical Insights: Philip Roth
- Critical Insights: Political Fiction
- Critical Insights: Post-Colonial Literature
- Critical Insights: Pride and Prejudice
- Critical Insights: Pulp Fiction of the '20s and '30s
- Critical Insights: Ray Bradbury
- Critical Insights: Raymond Carver
- Critical Insights: Rebellion
- Critical Insights: Richard Wright
- Critical Insights: Robert A. Heinlein
- Critical Insights: Robert Frost
- Critical Insights: Roberto Bolano
- Critical Insights: Romeo and Juliet
- Critical Insights: Russia's Golden Age
- Critical Insights: Salman Rushdie
- Critical Insights: Satire
- Critical Insights: Saul Bellow
- Critical Insights: Sherman Alexie
- Critical Insights: Short Fiction of Flannery O'Connor
- Critical Insights: Slaughterhouse-Five
- Critical Insights: Social Justice and American Literature
- Critical Insights: Southern Gothic Literature
- Critical Insights: Southwestern Literature
- Critical Insights: Stephen King
- Critical Insights: Survival
- Critical Insights: Sylvia Plath
- Critical Insights: T. S. Eliot

SALEM PRESS
2020 Title List

Visit www.SalemPress.com for Product Information, Table of Contents, and Sample Pages.

Critical Insights (continued)
- Critical Insights: Technology & Humanity
- Critical Insights: Tennessee Williams
- Critical Insights: The American Comic Book
- Critical Insights: The American Dream
- Critical Insights: The American Thriller
- Critical Insights: The Awakening
- Critical Insights: The Bell Jar
- Critical Insights: The Canterbury Tales
- Critical Insights: The Catcher in the Rye
- Critical Insights: The Crucible
- Critical Insights: The Diary of a Young Girl
- Critical Insights: The Fantastic
- Critical Insights: The Grapes of Wrath
- Critical Insights: The Graphic Novel
- Critical Insights: The Great Gatsby
- Critical Insights: The Handmaid's Tale
- Critical Insights: The Hero's Quest
- Critical Insights: The Hobbit
- Critical Insights: The House on Mango Street
- Critical Insights: The Hunger Games Trilogy
- Critical Insights: The Immigrant Experience
- Critical Insights: The Inferno
- Critical Insights: The Joy Luck Club
- Critical Insights: The Kite Runner
- Critical Insights: The Metamorphosis
- Critical insights: The Odyssey
- Critical Insights: The Outsiders
- Critical Insights: The Pearl
- Critical Insights: The Poetry of Baudelaire
- Critical Insights: The Poetry of Edgar Allan Poe
- Critical Insights: The Red Badge of Courage
- Critical Insights: The Scarlet Letter
- Critical Insights: The Slave Narrative
- Critical Insights: The Sound and the Fury
- Critical Insights: The Sun Also Rises
- Critical Insights: The Tales of Edgar Allan Poe
- Critical Insights: The Woman Warrior
- Critical Insights: Things Fall Apart
- Critical Insights: Thomas Jefferson
- Critical Insights: Tim O'Brien
- Critical Insights: To Kill a Mockingbird
- Critical Insights: Toni Morrison
- Critical Insights: Violence in Literature
- Critical Insights: Virginia Woolf & 20th Century Women Writers
- Critical Insights: Walt Whitman
- Critical Insights: War
- Critical Insights: War and Peace
- Critical Insights: Willa Cather
- Critical Insights: William Faulkner
- Critical Insights: Zora Neale Hurston
- Critical Insights: Film - Alfred Hitchcock
- Critical Insights: Film - Bonnie & Clyde
- Critical Insights: Film - Casablanca
- Critical Insights: Film - Stanley Kubrick

Literature
- Critical Approaches to Literature: Feminist
- Critical Approaches to Literature: Moral
- Critical Approaches to Literature: Multicultural
- Critical Approaches to Literature: Psychological
- Critical Survey of American Literature
- Critical Survey of Drama
- Critical Survey of Graphic Novels: Heroes & Superheroes
- Critical Survey of Graphic Novels: History, Theme, and Technique
- Critical Survey of Graphic Novels: Independents and Underground Classics
- Critical Survey of Graphic Novels: Manga
- Critical Survey of Long Fiction
- Critical Survey of Mystery and Detective Fiction
- Critical Survey of Mythology & Folklore: Gods & Goddesses
- Critical Survey of Mythology & Folklore: Heroes and Heroines
- Critical Survey of Mythology & Folklore: Love, Sexuality, and Desire
- Critical Survey of Mythology & Folklore: World Mythology
- Critical Survey of Poetry
- Critical Survey of Science Fiction & Fantasy Literature
- Critical Survey of Shakespeare's Plays
- Critical Survey of Shakespeare's Sonnets
- Critical Survey of Short Fiction
- Critical Survey of World Literature
- Critical Survey of Young Adult Literature
- Cyclopedia of Literary Characters
- Cyclopedia of Literary Places
- Introduction to Literary Context: American Poetry of the 20th Century
- Introduction to Literary Context: American Post-Modernist Novels
- Introduction to Literary Context: American Short Fiction
- Introduction to Literary Context: English Literature
- Introduction to Literary Context: Plays
- Introduction to Literary Context: World Literature
- Magill's Literary Annual
- Masterplots
- Masterplots, 2010-2018 Supplement
- Notable African American Writers
- Notable American Women Writers
- Novels into Film: Adaptations & Interpretation
- Recommended Reading: 600 Classics Reviewed

The Decades
- The Sixties in America
- The Fifties in America
- The Seventies in America
- The Eighties in America
- The Nineties in America
- The Forties in America
- The Thirties in America
- The Twenties in America
- The 2000s in America
- The 1910s in America

Grey House Publishing | Salem Press | H.W. Wilson | 4919 Route, 22 PO Box 56, Amenia NY 12501-0056

2020 Title List

Visit www.SalemPress.com for Product Information, Table of Contents, and Sample Pages.

Defining Documents in American History
Defining Documents: American West
Defining Documents: Business Ethics
Defining Documents: Capital Punishment
Defining Documents: Civil Rights
Defining Documents: Civil War
Defining Documents: Dissent & Protest
Defining Documents: Drug Policy
Defining Documents: Environment & Conservation
Defining Documents: Espionage & Intrigue
Defining Documents: Exploration and Colonial America
Defining Documents: Immigration & Immigrant Communities
Defining Documents: LGBTQ+
Defining Documents: Manifest Destiny and the New Nation
Defining Documents: Mental Health
Defining Documents: Native Americans
Defining Documents: Political Campaigns, Candidates & Discourse
Defining Documents: Postwar 1940s
Defining Documents: Prison Reform
Defining Documents: Secrets, Leaks & Scandals
Defining Documents: Slavery
Defining Documents: Supreme Court Decisions
Defining Documents: The 1900s
Defining Documents: The 1910s
Defining Documents: The 1920s
Defining Documents: The 1930s
Defining Documents: The 1950s
Defining Documents: The 1960s
Defining Documents: The 1970s
Defining Documents: The American Revolution
Defining Documents: The Cold War
Defining Documents: The Emergence of Modern America
Defining Documents: The Free Press
Defining Documents: The Gun Debate
Defining Documents: The Legacy of 9/11
Defining Documents: Reconstruction Era
Defining Documents: Vietnam War
Defining Documents: U.S. Involvement in the Middle East
Defining Documents: World War I
Defining Documents: World War II

Defining Documents in World History
Defining Documents: Asia
Defining Documents: Nationalism & Populism
Defining Documents: Renaissance & Early Modern Era
Defining Documents: The 17th Century
Defining Documents: The 18th Century
Defining Documents: The 19th Century
Defining Documents: The 20th Century (1900-1950)
Defining Documents: The Ancient World
Defining Documents: The Middle Ages
Defining Documents: The Middle East
Defining Documents: Women's Rights

Great Events from History
Great Events from History: The Ancient World
Great Events from History: The Middle Ages
Great Events from History: The Renaissance & Early Modern Era
Great Events from History: The 17th Century
Great Events from History: The 18th Century
Great Events from History: The 19th Century
Great Events from History: The 20th Century, 1901-1940
Great Events from History: The 20th Century, 1941-1970
Great Events from History: The 20th Century, 1971-2000
Great Events from History: Modern Scandals
Great Events from History: African American History
Great Events from History: The 21st Century, 2000-2016
Great Events from History: LGBTQ Events
Great Events from History: Human Rights

Great Lives from History
Computer Technology Innovators
Fashion Innovators
Great Athletes
Great Athletes of the Twenty-First Century
Great Lives from History: African Americans
Great Lives from History: American Heroes
Great Lives from History: American Women
Great Lives from History: Asian and Pacific Islander Americans
Great Lives from History: Inventors & Inventions
Great Lives from History: Jewish Americans
Great Lives from History: Latinos
Great Lives from History: Scientists and Science
Great Lives from History: The 17th Century
Great Lives from History: The 18th Century
Great Lives from History: The 19th Century
Great Lives from History: The 20th Century
Great Lives from History: The 21st Century, 2000-2017
Great Lives from History: The Ancient World
Great Lives from History: The Incredibly Wealthy
Great Lives from History: The Middle Ages
Great Lives from History: The Renaissance & Early Modern Era
Human Rights Innovators
Internet Innovators
Music Innovators
Musicians and Composers of the 20th Century
World Political Innovators

History & Government
American First Ladies
American Presidents
Civil Rights Movements: Past & Present
The 50 States
The Ancient World: Extraordinary People in Extraordinary Societies
The Bill of Rights
The Criminal Justice System
The U.S. Supreme Court

Grey House Publishing | Salem Press | H.W. Wilson | 4919 Route, 22 PO Box 56, Amenia NY 12501-0056

SALEM PRESS
2020 Title List

Visit www.SalemPress.com for Product Information, Table of Contents, and Sample Pages.

Social Sciences
Countries, Peoples and Cultures
Countries: Their Wars & Conflicts: A World Survey
Education Today: Issues, Policies & Practices
Encyclopedia of American Immigration
Ethics: Questions & Morality of Human Actions
Issues in U.S. Immigration
Principles of Sociology: Group Relationships & Behavior
Principles of Sociology: Personal Relationships & Behavior
Principles of Sociology: Societal Issues & Behavior
Racial & Ethnic Relations in America
World Geography

Science
Ancient Creatures
Applied Science
Applied Science: Engineering & Mathematics
Applied Science: Science & Medicine
Applied Science: Technology
Biomes and Ecosystems
Earth Science: Earth Materials and Resources
Earth Science: Earth's Surface and History
Earth Science: Earth's Weather, Water and Atmosphere
Earth Science: Physics and Chemistry of the Earth
Encyclopedia of Climate Change
Encyclopedia of Energy
Encyclopedia of Environmental Issues
Encyclopedia of Global Resources
Encyclopedia of Mathematics and Society
Forensic Science
Notable Natural Disasters
The Solar System
USA in Space

Principles of Science
Principles of Anatomy
Principles of Astronomy
Principles of Biology
Principles of Biotechnology
Principles of Botany
Principles of Chemistry
Principles of Climatology
Principles of Communications Technology
Principles of Computer Science
Principles of Ecology
Principles of Mathematics
Principles of Modern Agriculture
Principles of Pharmacology
Principles of Physical Science
Principles of Physics
Principles of Programming & Coding
Principles of Robotics & Artificial Intelligence
Principles of Scientific Research
Principles of Sustainability
Principles of Zoology

Health
Addictions, Substance Abuse & Alcoholism
Adolescent Health & Wellness
Aging
Cancer
Community & Family Health Issues
Complementary & Alternative Medicine
Genetics and Inherited Conditions
Infectious Diseases and Conditions
Magill's Medical Guide
Nutrition
Principles of Health: Anxiety & Stress
Principles of Health: Diabetes
Principles of Health: Obesity
Principles of Health: Pain Management
Psychology & Behavioral Health
Women's Health

Careers
Careers in Building Construction
Careers in Business
Careers in Chemistry
Careers in Communications & Media
Careers in Education & Training
Careers in Environment & Conservation
Careers in Financial Services
Careers in Gaming
Careers in Green Energy
Careers in Healthcare
Careers in Hospitality & Tourism
Careers in Human Services
Careers in Information Technology
Careers in Law, Criminal Justice & Emergency Services
Careers in Manufacturing & Production
Careers in Nursing
Careers in Physics
Careers in Protective Services
Careers in Psychology & Behavioral Health
Careers in Public Administration
Careers in Sales, Insurance & Real Estate
Careers in Science & Engineering
Careers in Social Media
Careers in Sports & Fitness
Careers in Sports Medicine & Training
Careers in Technical Services & Equipment Repair
Careers in the Arts: Fine, Performing & Visual
Careers in Transportation
Careers in Writing & Editing
Careers Outdoors
Careers Overseas
Careers Working with Infants & Children

Business
Principles of Business: Accounting
Principles of Business: Economics
Principles of Business: Entrepreneurship
Principles of Business: Finance
Principles of Business: Globalization
Principles of Business: Leadership
Principles of Business: Management
Principles of Business: Marketing

Grey House Publishing | Salem Press | H.W. Wilson | 4919 Route, 22 PO Box 56, Amenia NY 12501-0056

2020 Title List

Visit www.HWWilsonInPrint.com for Product Information, Table of Contents, and Sample Pages.

The Reference Shelf
Affordable Housing
Aging in America
Alternative Facts, Post-Truth and the Information War
American Military Presence Overseas
Arab Spring
Artificial Intelligence
Business of Food, The
Campaign Trends & Election Law
Conspiracy Theories
Democracy Evolving
Dinosaurs
Embracing New Paradigms in Education
Faith & Science
Families - Traditional & New Structures
Future of U.S. Economic Relations: Mexico, Cuba, & Venezuela
Global Climate Change
Graphic Novels and Comic Books
Guns in America
Hate Crimes
Immigration
Immigration in the United States
Internet Abuses & Privacy Rights
Internet Law
Internet Safety
LGBTQ in the 21st Century
Marijuana Reform
National Debate Topic 2014/2015: The Ocean
National Debate Topic 2015/2016: Surveillance
National Debate Topic 2016/2017: US/China Relations
National Debate Topic 2017/2018: Education Reform
National Debate Topic 2018/2019: Immigration
National Debate Topic 2019/2020: Arms Sales
National Debate Topic 2020/2021: Criminal Justice Reform
New Frontiers in Space
The News and its Future
Paranormal, The
Politics of the Oceans
Pollution
Prescription Drug Abuse
Propaganda and Misinformation
Racial Tension in a Postracial Age
Reality Television
Representative American Speeches, Annual Edition
Rethinking Work
Revisiting Gender
Robotics
Russia
Social Networking
Social Services for the Poor
Space Exploration and Development
Sports in America
The American Dream
The Brain
The Digital Age
The South China Sea Conflict
The Supreme Court
The Transformation of American Cities
The Two Koreas
U.S. Infrastructure
Whistleblowers

Core Collections
Children's Core Collection
Fiction Core Collection
Graphic Novels Core Collection
Middle & Junior High School Core
Public Library Core Collection: Nonfiction
Senior High Core Collection
Young Adult Fiction Core Collection

Current Biography
Current Biography Cumulative Index 1946-2017
Current Biography Monthly Magazine
Current Biography Yearbook

Readers' Guide to Periodical Literature
Abridged Readers' Guide to Periodical Literature
Readers' Guide to Periodical Literature

Indexes
Index to Legal Periodicals & Books
Short Story Index
Book Review Digest

Sears List
Sears List of Subject Headings
Sears: Lista de Encabezamientos de Materia

History
Speeches of the American Presidents
American Reformers
American Game Changers: Invention, Innovation & Transformation

Facts About Series
Facts About American Immigration
Facts About China
Facts About the 20th Century
Facts About the Presidents
Facts About the World's Languages

Nobel Prize Winners
Nobel Prize Winners: 1901-1986
Nobel Prize Winners: 1987-1991
Nobel Prize Winners: 1992-1996
Nobel Prize Winners: 1997-2001
Nobel Prize Winners: 2002-2018

Famous First Facts
Famous First Facts
Famous First Facts About American Politics
Famous First Facts About Sports
Famous First Facts About the Environment
Famous First Facts: International Edition

American Book of Days
The American Book of Days
The International Book of Days

Grey House Publishing | Salem Press | H.W. Wilson | 4919 Route, 22 PO Box 56, Amenia NY 12501-0056